BLACK'S
LAW DICTIONARY

Definitions of the Terms and Phrases of
American and English Jurisprudence,
Ancient and Modern

By

HENRY CAMPBELL BLACK, M. A.

Author of Treatises on Judgments, Tax Titles, Intoxicating Liquors,
Bankruptcy, Mortgages, Constitutional Law, Interpretation
of Laws, Rescission and Cancellation of Contracts, Etc.

FIFTH EDITION

BY

THE PUBLISHER'S EDITORIAL STAFF

Contributing Authors

JOSEPH R. NOLAN
Associate Justice, Massachusetts Superior Court
and
M. J. CONNOLLY
Associate Professor of Linguistics
and Eastern Languages, Boston College

ST. PAUL MINN.
WEST PUBLISHING CO.
1979

COPYRIGHT © 1891, 1910, 1933, 1951, 1957, 1968 By WEST PUBLISHING COMPANY

COPYRIGHT © 1979 By WEST PUBLISHING CO.

Library of Congress Cataloging in Publication Data

Black, Henry Campbell, 1860–1927.
  Black's Law dictionary.

  First ed., 1891, has title: A dictionary of law.
  1. Law—Dictionaries. I. Nolan, Joseph R.
II. Connolly, Michael J. III. West Publishing Company,
St. Paul. IV. Title. V. Title: Law dictionary.
KF156.B53 1979   340'.03   79–12547
ISBN 0–8299–2041–2
ISBN 0–8299–2045–5 deluxe

PREFACE

In the period since the Fourth Edition of Black's Law Dictionary, most all areas of the law have undergone substantial change and development. The vocabulary of the law has shown corresponding change and growth, particularly in the areas of commercial and constitutional law, civil and criminal procedure, taxes, finance, uniform laws, and federal legislation. In addition, many common law doctrines and concepts have been replaced or modified with new statutory rights and remedies. These major developments have occasioned the need to not only greatly expand the legal words and terms included in Black's Law Dictionary, but also to reexamine all existing entries for currentness of legal usage. This thorough review has resulted in the inclusion of over 10,000 new or revised entries, as well as numerous new usage examples, in this Fifth Edition. It should also be mentioned however, that, while this new edition reflects the very latest changes and developments in law and practice, old English, European and feudal law words and terms have been retained in that such continue to form the foundation for much of our modern jurisprudence.

A considerable effort has been made in this Fifth Edition to provide more than basic definitions of legal words and terms. In those instances where traditional legal concepts and doctrines have over the years been either superseded, modified or supplemented by court decisions or legislation, such developments and changes are fully reflected. Additionally, because so many areas of law and practice are now governed by uniform or model acts and rules, such major sources of law as the Uniform Commercial Code, Restatements of the Law, and Federal Rules (Civil, Criminal, Appellate, and Evidence) are fully reflected. Similarly, the growth and importance of federal legislation and agencies, with their impact on matters that were traditionally state or local in nature, is evidenced with a considerable number of new entries covering federal acts, agencies, departments and officials. Likewise, the ever expanding importance of financial terminology has necessitated the inclusion of numerous new tax and accounting terms.

Because of the inter-relationship of so many legal words and terms, the number of internal cross-references has been greatly increased. The number of abbreviation entries has also been substantially expanded, as has the Table of Abbreviations. The following new Appendices have also been added: Constitution of the United States; Listing of Justices and Terms of U.S. Supreme Court; and U.S. Government Organizational Chart.

A major new feature in this Fifth Edition is the inclusion of pronunciation guides after all entries which pose pronunciation difficulties. A comprehensive explanation of these guides is set forth on pages VII–XIV with a shorter pronunciation Key appearing on the inside front cover.

PREFACE

New and revised words and terms for this Fifth Edition were contributed by Joseph R. Nolan, Associate Justice, Massachusetts Superior Court. The pronunciation transcription system and guides were prepared by M. J. Connolly, Associate Professor of Linguistics and Eastern Languages, Boston College.

For additional definitions of legal words, terms and phrases, reference should be made to "Words and Phrases."

THE PUBLISHER

St. Paul, Minn.
July, 1979

CONTENTS

*

THE PRONUNCIATION OF LATIN

A majority of the Latin terms in this revised edition of *Black's Law Dictionary* and also occasional English and foreign terms have been provided with pronunciation entries. The pronunciations follow a *descriptive* scheme and are based on actual usage rather than on any attempt to *prescribe* a uniform pronunciation. Where alternate pronunciations exist the philologically more 'appropriate' pronunciation generally receives first listing, however. The entries provide an acceptable pronunciation in a transcription system compatible with the major varieties of North American English and extendable to other pronunciations.

Despite its continuing decline as a working language of scholarship and jurisprudence, Latin still supplies a formidable stock of legal terms and phrases. The ability to use a Latin phrase correctly and pronounce it with authority and consistency belongs to the equipment of a well-rounded jurist. Those who actually study Latin today, however, will in all probability learn a pronunciation (either the reformed philological or the Italianate) at variance with the Anglo-Latin system which prevails in legal and medical spheres. Injection of the 'newer' school pronunciations actually serves to increase confusion and uncertainty: Where masculine plural *alumni* and feminine plural *alumnae* were once differentiated in speech as /ələ́mnay/ and /ələ́mniy/ respectively, one widespread variant of the philological pronunciation actually *reverses* the opposition with masculine /ələ́mniy/ and feminine /ələ́mnay/. The status of *amicus curiae*, traditionally pronounced /əmáykəs kyúriyiy/, now has variants /əmíykəs kúriyày/ (adapted philological), /amíykus kúriyèy/ (Italianate), and numerous hybrids. A parliamentarian of the old school, perhaps even well versed in Latin, adjourns a meeting *sine die* /sáyniy dáyiy/ only to have a junior colleague suggest that the 'correct' pronunciation is /síyney díyey/.

Strictly speaking, of course, any attempt at 'correct' pronunciations of foreign terms can at best be only weak approximations. The linguistic contortions of a purist attempting to weave foreign sounds and intonations into the texture of an English sentence usually strike us as pedantic or affected. Although Julius Caesar may have pronounced his name something like /yúwliyus káysar/ and later Romans may have called him /chéyzar/, few speakers of English have place for anything other than the Anglo-Latin /júwl(i)yəs síyzər/.

Three major systems of Latin pronunciation, outlined below, coexist in the English-speaking world. Each has its proper cultural and scholarly context. The *reformed* (or *new*, or *philological*, or *Roman*) pronunciation represents a modification to English speech habits of the reconstructed sounds of Latin as it must have been in the classical period. Philologists, classical historians, and most teachers of Latin employ this pronunciation in their professional activity. *Anglo-Latin* (or English) pronunciation, the form most commonly encountered in law, medicine, the natural sciences, and in general usage, reflects the centuries of sound change that English has undergone. Although it may not possess the authenticity of linguistic reconstruction, the Anglo-Latin system enjoys the authority of a persevering and distinct cultural tradition. The *Italianate* pronunciation is derived from the pronunciation of Later Latin and is viewed as the standard in Roman Catholicism (including canon law), in music, in art history, and in medieval studies. Thus, a school master may leave the classroom, where he has just taught his pupils Latin imperatives including *venite* 'come' /weníyte/, go to chapel to rehearse with the choir the *Venite* /vənáydiy/ (Psalm 95 in Anglican morning prayer), and then sing the text in a Latin setting as /veyníytey èksultéymus . . ./. Each pronunciation is correct in its own context.

OUTLINE OF LATIN PRONUNCIATIONS

Letter	Reformed Philological	Italianate	Anglo-Latin
a	/a/		/a, æ, ə, o/
b	/b/		
c	/k/	/ch/ before /i, e/ /k/ elsewhere	/s, sh, z, k/
d	/d/		
e	/ey, e/		/e, ey, ə, i, iy/
f	/f/		
g	/ŋ/ before *n* /g/ elsewhere	/j/ before /i, e/ /g/ elsewhere /gn/ pronounced /ny/	/j, g/
h	/h/	/h/ or silent /k/ in *nihil, mihi*	/h/ or silent
i	/i, iy/		/i, iy, ay, ə/
j	/y/		/j/
k	/k/		
l	/l/		
m	/m/		
n	/n, ŋ/		
o	/o, ow/		/o, a, ə, ow/
p	/p/		
qu	/kw/		
r	/r/		
s	/s/	/z/ between vowels /s/ elsewhere	/s, z, sh, zh/
t(h)	/t/	/ts/ before *i* plus vowels except after *s, t, x* /t/ elsewhere	/t, d, sh, ch/ *th* as /θ/
u	/u, uw, w/	/w/ after *q* or *ng* /uw/ elsewhere	/yuw, uw, u, yə, ə, i, w/

IX

Letter	Reformed Philological	Italianate	Anglo-Latin
v	/w/	/v/	
x	/ks/ x + /ch/ = /ksh/		/ks, gz, z, s/
y	/i, iy/	/iy/ or Gmn *ü*	/ay, iy, i, y/
z	/z/	/z, dz/	/z/

Attested forms in Anglo-Latin pronunciation sometimes fail to correspond in qualitative or accentual details with the forms we might expect on an etymological or systematic basis. Thus,

> *bona fide* appears as /bównə fáydiy/ instead of */bónə fídiy/
>
> *industry* appears as /índəstriy/ instead of */ində́striy/
>
> *minor* appears as /máynər/ instead of */mínər/, etc.

Numerous developments in the sound system of English have tended to override the expected forms. Analogies with sibling or quasi-sibling forms often keep doublets flourishing side by side:

> *licet* 'it is permitted' as /láysət/ (cf. *license*) or /lísət/ (cf. *licit*)
>
> *debet* 'one must' as /díybət/ or /débət/ (cf. *debit and credit*)
>
> *capias* 'thou shouldst seize' as /kéypiyəs/ (cf. *cape*) or /kǽpiyəs/ (cf. *capture*)

Language traditions usually resolve such conflicts in good time, favoring 'usage' over 'correctness', and then promptly create new conflicts.

TRANSCRIPTION

The transcription system employed for these listings is derived from one of the traditional phonemic analyses of American English (Trager-Smith). The values of the symbols vary with context, i.e., their specific pronunciations depend on the nature of the surrounding sounds. The pronunciation habits of a normal speaker of English will, however, in practically all cases supply the accustomed variants for that speaker's usage if the elements presented in the key are substituted in accordance with the sample indications. This system enables the speakers of a range of dialects to use one and the same transcription and yet produce a pronunciation natural to their speech. For this reason, in addition to the considerations given above concerning the treatment of foreign terms in English, sounds foreign to English have been represented by the customary English substitutes. Thus, for example, the voiceless velar fricative of German *Bach* would be rendered with a simple stop /k/ and French front rounded *eu* with /yuw/. Readers who wish to affect the foreign sounds will find guidance in their own linguistic experience or in the appropriate grammars and dictionaries. Similarly, readers who prefer pronunciations closer to the spelling than those presented here should feel free to substitute their preferences, e.g., /t/ for intervocalic, post-tonic *t*, various changes for unaccented /ə/, even to restoring the *t* in *often*. Finally, readers who already feel secure (or even superior) in their own renderings of words and phrases should retain these. The editors will always appreciate information on local variants and will welcome suggestions for improving the transcriptions.

The rubrics (sets of examples) under any given major symbol should always be applied *in order*. The earlier, more specific contexts take preference over the later, 'elsewhere' variant.

The special symbols

/æ/ (ash) /ð/ (edh) /ə/ (schwa) /ŋ/ (angma) /θ/ (theta)

appear respectively after

/a/   /d/   /e/   /n/   /t/

The reader will, of course, be aware that the transcription symbols do not necessarily have the same alphabetic values as in English. Rather, the symbols must be viewed as arbitrary signs, although in many cases their forms will aid the user in remembering and associating the key sounds and symbols.

GUIDE TO PRONUNCIATION SYMBOLS

a

/ay/   as in the bold portions of **aye**, **eye**, **I** /áy/   **lie** /láy/
buy, **by**, **bye** /báy/   **high** /háy/   **aisle**, **isle**, **I'll** /áyl/
idea /aydíyə/
/aw/   as in **out** /áwt/   **how** /háw/
/ar/   as in **bark** /bárk/   **car** /kár/
/a/   elsewhere as in **father** /fáðər/.   In many dialects identical with /o/.

æ

/æ/   as in **cat** /kǽt/

b

/b/   as in **bill** /bíl/

ch

/ch/   as in **chill** /chíl/   **church** /chə́rch/   **nature** /néychər/
question /kwés(h)chən/

d

/d/   as in **dill** /díl/   **odor** /ówdər/.   In many dialects *better*, *bed-der* may both appear as /bédər/.

ð

/ð/   as in **this** /ðís/   **smooth** /smúwð/   **thou** /ðáw/   not to be con-fused with /θ/

e

/ey/   as in **they** /ðéy/   **make** /méyk/   **sail**, **sale** /séyl/   **neigh**, **nay** /néy/
/ehr/   as in **error** /éhrər/   **merry** /méhriy/.   In dialects where /ehr/
is not distinct from /er/ the diacritic /h/ may be ignored.
/er/   as in **there**, **their** /ðer/   **air**, **e'er** /ér/
/e/   elsewhere as in **dell** /dél/   **bet** /bét/

ə

/əhr/   as in **current** /kə́hrənt/.   In dialects where /əhr/ is not distinct
from /ər/ the diacritic /h/ may be ignored.
/ər/   as in **murder** /mə́rdər/   **were** /wə́r/   **mother** /máðər/
world /wə́rld/   **whirr** /(h)wə́r/
/ə́/   /ə̀/   (with either primary or secondary stress) as in **but**, **butt** /bə́t/
blood /blə́d/   **above** /əbə́v/
/ə/   elsewhere (unstressed) as in **sofa** /sówfə/   **another** /ənáðər/

f

/f/   as in **fill**, **Phil** /fíl/   **rough** /rə́f/

g

/g/ always 'hard' as in **g**all /gól/ **G**aul /góe/ la**g** /lǽg/

h

/h/ as silent diacritic in combinations /ehr, əhr, ihr, ohr/ and /ch, sh, zh/ otherwise as in **h**ill /híl/ mouse**h**ole /máws-hòwl/

i

/iy/ as in ma**ch**ine /məshíyn/ b**e**, b**ee**, B**ea** /bíy/ **ea**ch /íych/
/ihr/ as in **i**rrigate /íhrəgeyt/ sp**i**rit /spíhrət/. In dialects where /ihr/ is not distinct from /ir/ the diacritic /h/ may be ignored.
/ir/ as in p**ier**, p**eer** /pír/ h**ear**, h**ere** /hír/
/i/ elsewhere as in s**i**t /sít/ pr**e**tty /prídiy/ (or /pə́rdiy/)

j

/j/ as in **J**ill /jíl/ **g**eneral /jén(ə)rəl/ ed**g**e /éj/ sol**di**er /sówljər/ carria**g**e /kǽrəj/

k

/k/ as in **k**ill /kíl/ **c**ool /kúwl/

l

/l/ as in **L**ill /líl/

m

/m/ as in **m**ill /míl/

n

/n/ as in **n**il /níl/
/ŋ/ as in thi**ng** /θíŋ/ si**ng**er /síŋər/ fi**ng**er /fíŋgər/

o

/oy/ as in b**oy** /bóy/ n**oi**se /nóyz/
/ow/ as in kn**ow** /nów/ s**ew**, s**o**, s**ow** (seed) /sów/
/ohr/ as in f**or**eign /fóhrən/ b**or**row /bóhrow/. In dialects where /ohr/ is not distinct from /or/ the diacritic /h/ may be ignored.
/or/ as in b**or**e, b**oar** /bór/ c**our**se, c**oar**se /kórs/
/o/ elsewhere as in r**o**t, wr**ough**t /rót/ w**a**ll /wól/ **ough**t, **augh**t /ót/ l**aw** /ló/. Some dialects merge /o/ and /a/ while others treat diphthongal spellings as /o/ but others as /a/.

p

/p/ as in **p**ill /píl/ li**p** /líp/

r

/r/ as in **r**ill /ríl/. See also the coloring function of /r/ in diphthongs /ar, e(h)r, ə(h)r, i(h)r, o(h)r, ur/.

s

/sh/   as in **sh**ill /shíl/   **s**ugar /shúgər/   i**ss**ue /íshyuw/
/s/   as in **s**ill /síl/   **c**ity /sídiy/

t

/t/   as in **t**ill /tíl/   hi**t** /hít/

θ

/θ/   as in **th**in /θín/   **th**ought /θót/ not to be confused with /ð/:
      ether /íyθər/
      either /íyðər/

u

/uw/   as in **too, two** /túw/   th**rough**, th**rew** /θrúw/   c**ru**de /krúwd/
/ur/   as in j**u**ry /júriy/   **poor** /púr/
/u/   elsewhere as in p**u**t /pút/   g**oo**d /gúd/   c**ou**ld /kúd/

w

/w/   as in **w**ill /wíl/   **w**eather /wéðər/.   See also the function of /w/
      in diphthongs /aw, ow, uw/.

y

/y/   as in **y**es /yés/   **u**nion /yúwnyən/.   See also the function of /y/
      in diphthongs /ay, ey, iy, oy/.

z

/zh/   as in Doctor **Zh**ivago /dókdər zhəvágow/   plea**s**ure /plézhər/
       ga**r**age /gərázh/ (in some dialects /°áj/)
/z/   as in **z**oo /zúw/   ro**s**e, row**s** (lines) /rówz/   **X**enophon /zénəfòn/

⟋ primary (strong) stress   ⟍ secondary (weaker) stress
         telegraphic /tèləgrǽfək/
         telegram /téləgræm/

( ) 'may include or exclude'; optional elements
        e.g. *new* /n(y)úw/ pronounced either /nyúw/ or /núw/
             ratio /réysh(iy)ow/ pronounced /réyshiyow/ or /réyshow/

° 'and the rest that precedes/follows'; replaces identical parts of variant
        pronunciations
        e.g. *alumni* /ələ́mnay/°niy/ = /ələ́mnay/ or /ələ́mniy/
             inter alios /íntər éyl(i)yows/°ǽl°/
                 = /íntər éyl(i)yows/ or /íntər ǽl(i)yows/
             habeas corpus /héybiyəs kórpəs/heybiyz°/
                 = /héybiyəs kórpəs/ or /héybiyz kórpəs/.

BLACK'S
DICTIONARY OF LAW
FIFTH EDITION

A

A. The first letter in the English and most other alphabets derived from the Roman or Latin alphabet, which was one of several ancient Italian alphabets derived from the Greek, which was an adaptation of the Phoenician. The first letter in the Phoenician alphabet was called *aleph*, meaning "ox", which is also the meaning of the first letter in the Greek alphabet, *alpha*. *Alpha* and the second letter of the Greek alphabet, *beta*, were combined to form "alphabet," which is largely the same in different languages.

A in Latin and law Latin. Anglo-American law abounds in Latin and French words and phrases, and the use of A in these languages is important to the English-speaking lawyer. In Latin "A" was used both as an abbreviation and as a symbol. For example "A" was an abbreviation for "Aulus," a praenomen, or the first of the usual three names of a person by which he was distinguished from others of the same family; also for "ante" in "a.d.," *ante diem* (before the day), and for "anno" (year) in a.u.c., *anno urbis conditae* (the year of the building of the city) and in *anno ab urbe condita* (from the year of the building of the city). As a preposition, the form was either A, AB or ABS. A was used before consonants; ab was usually used before vowels, but sometimes before consonants, whereas abs was used before "c" or "t." The meaning was "from," "away from," "on the side of," "at," "after," "since," "by," "by means of," "out of," "with reference to," "in regard of," "near by," and "along." For example, *A fronte* in front; *ab tergo*, from behind; *a puertitia*, from youth; *ab sole orbe*, from or at sunrise; *ab intestato*, without a will, intestate. In law Latin, "a" means "by," "with," "from," "in," "of," and "on," and AB means "by," "from," and "in".

A in French and law French. In French A is a preposition, the meaning of which largely depends on context. It is usually translated as "into," "at," "to," "in," "by," "of," "with," "on," "from," "for," "under," "till," "within," "between," etc. It also changes into *au* and *aux* when combined with "the." A is also the third person, singular number, present tense, indicative mood of the verb *avoir*, (to have): *Il a* (he has). In law French "a" is used as a preposition meaning "at," "for," "in," "of," "on," "to," and "with."

The word "a" has varying meanings and uses. "A" means "one" or "any," but less emphatically than either. It may mean one where only one is intended, or it may mean any one of a great number. It is placed before nouns of the singular number, denoting an individual object or quality individualized.

The article "a" is not necessarily a singular term; it is often used in the sense of "any" and is then applied to more than one individual object. Lewis v. Spies, 43 A.D.2d 714, 350 N.Y.S.2d 14, 17. So under a statute providing that the issuance of "a" certificate to one carrier should not bar a certificate to another over the same route, a certificate could be granted to more than two carriers over the same route. State ex rel. Crown Coach Co. v. Public Service Commission, 238 Mo.App. 287, 179 S.W.2d 123, 127. But the meaning depends on context. For example, in Workmen's Compensation Act, on, or in or about "a" railway, factory, etc., was held not to mean any railway, factory, etc., but *the* railway, factory, etc., of the employer. Where the law required the delivery of a copy of a notice to husband and a copy to wife, the sheriff's return that he had delivered "a copy" to husband and wife was insufficient. State v. Davis, Tex.Civ.App., 139 S.W.2d 638, 640.

AAA. Agricultural Adjustment Act; American Accounting Association; American Arbitration Association.

A.A.C. *Anno ante Christum,* the year before Christ.

A.A.C.N. *Anno ante Christum natum,* the year before the birth of Christ.

AALS. Association of American Law Schools.

A aver et tener /èy éyvər et ténər/. L. Fr. (L. Lat. *habendum et tenendum.*) To have and to hold. *A aver et tener a luy et a ses heires, a touts jours,*—to have and to hold to him and his heirs forever.

Ab. The eleventh month of the Jewish civil year, and the fifth of the sacred year. It answers to the moon that begins in July, and consists of thirty days. On the 24th is observed a feast in memory of the abolishment of the Sadducean law, which required sons and daughters to be equal heirs and heiresses of their parents' estates.

Ab, at the beginning of English-Saxon names of places, is generally a contraction of abbot or abbey; whence it is inferred that those places once had an abbey there, or belonged to one elsewhere, as Abingdon in Berkshire.

A.B. Able-bodied seaman. In English law a seaman is entitled to be rated A. B. when he has served at sea three years before the mast. In the United States the term "Able Seaman" is used. For the requirements of able seaman, see 46 U.S.C.A. § 672. Also *artium baccalaureus,* bachelor of arts. In England, generally written B. A.

A.B.A. American Bar Association.

Ab; Abr. Abridgment.

Ab abusu ad usum non valet consequentia /æb əbyúwz(y)uw æd yúwzəm non vælət konsəkwénsh(iy)ə/. A conclusion as to the use of a thing from its abuse is invalid.

Abacist or **abacista** /æbəsístə/. A caster of accounts, an arithmetician.

Abaction /əbǽkshən/. A carrying away by violence.

Ab actis /æb ǽktəs/. Lat. An officer having charge of *acta,* public records, registers, journals, or minutes. An officer who entered on record the *acta* or proceedings of a court; a clerk of court; a notary or actuary. See "*Acta.*" This, and the similarly formed epithets *à cancellis, à secretis, à libellis,* were also anciently the titles of a chancellor *(cancellarius)* in the early history of that office.

Abactor /æbǽktər/. A stealer and driver away of cattle or beasts by herds or in great numbers at once, as distinguished from a person who steals a single animal or beast. Also called *abigeus, q.v.*

Ab agendo /æb eyjéndow/. Disabled from acting; unable to act; incapacitated for business or transactions of any kind.

A.B.A.J. American Bar Association Journal.

Abalienate /əbéyliyəneyt/. To transfer interest or title.

Abalienatio /əbèyliyənéysh(iy)ow/. In Roman law, the perfect conveyance or transfer of property from one Roman citizen to another. This term gave place to the simple *alienatio,* which is used in the Digest and Institutes, as well as in the feudal law, and from which the English "alienation" has been formed.

Abalienation /æbèyliyənéyshən/. In the civil law, a making over of realty, or chattels to another by due course of law.

Abamita /əbǽmədə/. In the civil law, a great-great-grandfather's sister *(abavi soror).* Called *amita maxima.*

Abandon. To desert, surrender, forsake, or cede. To relinquish or give up with intent of never again resuming one's right or interest. To give up or to cease to use. To give up absolutely; to forsake entirely; to renounce utterly; to relinquish all connection with or concern in; to desert. It includes the intention, and also the external act by which it is carried into effect.

Abandonee. A party to whom a right or property is abandoned or relinquished by another. Applied to the insurers of vessels and cargoes.

Abandonment. The surrender, relinquishment, disclaimer, or cession of property or of rights. Voluntary relinquishment of all right, title, claim and possession, with the intention of not reclaiming it. State v. Bailey, 97 N.J.Super. 396, 235 A.2d 214, 216. The giving up of a thing absolutely, without reference to any particular person or purpose, as vacating property with the intention of not returning, so that it may be appropriated by the next comer or finder. Intention to forsake or relinquish the thing is an essential element, to be proved by visible acts. The voluntary relinquishment of possession of thing by owner with intention of terminating his ownership, but without vesting it in any other person. Dober v. Ukase Inv. Co., 139 Or. 626, 10 P.2d 356, 357. The relinquishing of all title, possession, or claim, or a virtual, intentional throwing away of property.

"Abandonment" includes both the intention to abandon and the external act by which the intention is carried into effect. In determining whether one has abandoned his property or rights, the intention is the first and paramount object of inquiry, for there can be no abandonment without the intention to abandon. Roebuck v. Mecosta County Road Commission, 59 Mich.App. 128, 229 N.W.2d 343, 345. Generally, "abandonment" can arise from a single act or from a series of acts. Holly Hill Lumber Co. v. Grooms, 198 S.C. 118, 16 S.E.2d 816, 821.

Time is not an essential element of "abandonment", although the lapse of time may be evidence of an intention to abandon, and where it is accompanied by acts manifesting such an intention, it may be considered in determining whether there has been an abandonment. Ullman ex rel. Eramo v. Payne, 127 Conn. 239, 16 A.2d 286, 287.

"Abandonment" differs from surrender in that surrender requires an agreement, and from forfeiture, in that forfeiture may be against the intention of the party alleged to have forfeited.

See also **Desertion; Discharge; Release; Waiver.**

Actions, in general. Failure to prosecute or bring action within statutorily prescribed period (see **Statute of limitations**); failure to object to or submit jury instructions (Fed.R. Civil P. 51); failure to demand jury trial (Fed.R. Civil P. 38).

Adverse possession. To destroy continuity of adverse claimant's possession, there must be an intent to relinquish claim of ownership as well as an act of relinquishment of possession and mere temporary absence is not sufficient. Bruch v. Benedict, 62 Wyo. 213, 165 P.2d 561.

Assignment of error. Failure to object at trial. Meyer v. Hendrix, 311 Ill.App. 605, 37 N.E.2d 445, 446. Error not presented in brief. Roubay v. United States, C.C.A.Cal., 115 F.2d 49, 50. Error not supported by point, argument or authority. Cone v. Ariss, 13 Wash.2d 650, 126 P.2d 591, 593.

Children. Desertion or willful forsaking. Foregoing parental duties. Wright v. Fitzgibbons, 198 Miss. 471, 21 So.2d 709, 710. See also **Desertion**.

Contracts. To constitute "abandonment" by conduct, action relied on must be positive, unequivocal, and inconsistent with the existence of the contract. Abandonment is a matter of intent, Lohn v. Fletcher Oil Co., 38 Cal.App.2d 26, 100 P.2d 505, 507, and implies not only nonperformance, but an intent not to perform which may be inferred from acts which necessarily point to actual abandonment.

Copyright. "Abandonment" of a copyright turns on state of mind of copyright proprietor and occurs whenever he engages in some overt action which manifests his purpose to surrender his rights in the work and to allow the public to enjoy it. Rexnord, Inc. v. Modern Handling Systems, Inc., D.C.Del., 379 F.Supp. 1190, 1199.

Easements. To establish "abandonment" of an easement created by deed, there must be some conduct on part of owner of servient estate adverse to and inconsistent with existence of easement and continuing for statutory period, or nonuser must be accompanied by unequivocal and decisive acts clearly indicating an intent on part of owner of easement to abandon use of it. Permanent cessation of use or enjoyment with no intention to resume or reclaim. Intention and completed act are both essential. A mere temporary or occasional obstruction or use of an easement by the servient owner is not an "abandonment". Gerber v. Appel, Mo.App., 164 S.W.2d 225, 228.

Ground for divorce. Abandonment as cause for divorce must be willful and intentional without intention of returning, and without consent of spouse abandoned. This ground is commonly termed "desertion" in state divorce statutes. See also **Desertion**.

Inventions. The giving up of rights by inventor, as where he surrenders his idea or discovery or relinquishes the intention of perfecting his invention, and so throws it open to the public, or where he negligently postpones the assertion of his claims or fails to apply for a patent, and allows the public to use his invention. Electric Storage Battery Co. v. Shimadzu, Pa., 307 U.S. 5, 613, 616, 59 S.Ct. 675, 681, 83 L.Ed. 1071.

Leases in general. To constitute an "abandonment" of leased premises, there must be an absolute relinquishment of premises by tenant consisting of act and intention.

Mineral leases. "Abandonment" consists of an actual act of relinquishment, accompanied with the intent and purpose permanently to give up a claim and right of property. A distinction exists between "abandonment" and "surrender" which is the relinquishment of a thing or a property right thereto to another, which is not an essential element of abandonment. Distinction also exists between elements of "abandonment" and those of estoppel. Neither formal surrender of oil and gas lease nor release is necessary to effectuate "abandonment"; for example, failing to start work under the lease for more than 40 years, Chapman v. Continental Oil Co., 149 Kan. 822, 89 P.2d 833, 834; breach of implied obligation to proceed with search and development of land with reasonable diligence, Wood v. Arkansas Fuel Oil Co., D.C.Ark., 40 F.Supp. 42, 45; no drilling on leased land for more than two years, and failure to pay rentals, Rehart v. Klossner, 48 Cal.App.2d 40, 119 P.2d 145, 147; drawing of casing from well with no intention of replacing it, have all been held to constitute "abandonment". But there must be an intention by lessee to relinquish leased premises, Carter Oil Co. v. Mitchell, C.C.A.Okl., 100 F.2d 945, 950, 951; or an intention not to drill, Carter Oil Co. v. Mitchell, C.C. A.Okl., 100 F.2d 945, 950, 951. And ceasing of operations is not alone sufficient. Fisher v. Dixon, 188 Okl. 7, 105 P.2d 776, 777.

Office. Abandonment of a public office is a species of resignation, but differs from resignation in that resignation is a formal relinquishment, while abandonment is a voluntary relinquishment through nonuser. It is not wholly a matter of intention, but may result from the complete abandonment of duties of such a continuance that the law will infer a relinquishment. It must be total, and under such circumstances as clearly to indicate an absolute relinquishment; and whether an officer has abandoned an office depends on his overt acts rather than his declared intention. It implies nonuser, but nonuser does not, of itself constitute abandonment. The failure to perform the duties pertaining to the office must be with actual or imputed intention on the part of the officer to abandon and relinquish the office. The intention may be inferred from the acts and conduct of the party, and is a question of fact. Abandonment may result from an acquiescence by the officer in his wrongful removal or discharge, but, as in other cases of abandonment, the question of intention is involved. McCall v. Cull, 51 Ariz. 237, 75 P.2d 696, 698.

Patents. There may be an abandonment of a patent, where the inventor dedicates it to the public use; and this may be shown by his failure to sue infringers, sell licenses, or otherwise make efforts to realize a personal advantage from his patent. Sandlin v. Johnson, C.C.A.Mo., 141 F.2d 660.

Property. "Abandoned property" in a legal sense is that to which owner has relinquished all right, title, claim, and possession, with intention of not reclaiming it or resuming its ownership, possession or enjoyment. Jackson v. Steinberg, 186 Or. 129, 200 P.2d 376, 377, 378. There must be concurrence of act and intent, that is, the act of leaving the premises or property vacant, so that it may be appropriated by the next comer, and the intention of not returning. Relinquishment of all title, possession, or claim; a virtual intentional throwing away of property. Ex parte Szczygiel, Sup., 51 N.Y.S.2d 699, 702.

Rights in general. The relinquishment of a right. It implies some act of relinquishment done by the owner without regard to any future possession by himself, or by any other person, but with an intention to abandon. See **Waiver.**

Trade-marks and trade names. There must be not only nonuser, but also an intent to abandon and to give up use of trade-marks permanently. Neva-Wet Corporation of America v. Never Wet Processing Corporation, 277 N.Y. 163, 13 N.E.2d 755, 761.

Water rights. "Abandonment," as applied to water rights may be defined to be an intentional relinquishment of a known right. It is not based on a time element, and mere nonuser will not establish "abandonment" for any less time, at least, than statutory period, controlling element in "abandonment" being matter of intent. Hammond v. Johnson, 94 Utah 20, 66 P.2d 894, 899. To desert or forsake right. The intent and an actual relinquishment must concur. Concurrence of relinquishment of possession, and intent not to resume it for beneficial use. Neither alone is sufficient. Osnes Livestock Co. v. Warren, 103 Mont. 284, 62 P.2d 206, 211.

Abandun, abandum, or **abandonum** /əbǽndən(əm)/. Anything sequestered, proscribed, or abandoned. *Abandon, i. e., in bannum res missa,* a thing banned or denounced as forfeited or lost, whence to *abandon, desert,* or *forsake,* as lost and gone.

Ab ante /ǽb ǽntiy/. Lat. Before; in advance. Thus, a legislature cannot agree *ab ante* to any modification or amendment to a law which a third person may make.

Ab antecedente /ǽb ǽntəsiydéntiy/. Lat. Beforehand; in advance.

Ab antiquo /ǽb æntáykwow/. From old times; from ancient time; of old; of an ancient date. 3 Bl.Comm. 95.

Abarnare /ǽbarnériy/. Lat. To discover and disclose to a magistrate any secret crime.

Ab assuetis non fit injuria /ǽb əswíydəs non fid injúriyə/. From things to which one is accustomed (or in which there has been long acquiescence) no legal injury or wrong arises. If a person neglects to insist on his right, he is deemed to have abandoned it.

Abatable nuisance. A nuisance which is practically susceptible of being suppressed, or extinguished, or rendered harmless, and whose continued existence is not authorized under the law. Fort Worth & Denver City Ry. Co. v. Muncy, Tex.Civ.App., 31 S.W.2d 491, 494.

Abatamentum /əbèydəméntəm/. L. Lat. In old English law, an abatement of freehold; an entry upon lands by way of interposition between the death of the ancestor and the entry of the heir.

Abatare /ǽbətériy/. To abate.

Abate. To throw down, to beat down, destroy, quash. To do away with or nullify or lessen or diminish. In re Stevens' Estate, Cal.App., 150 P.2d 530, 534. To bring entirely down or demolish, to put an end to, to do away with, to nullify, to make void, Sparks Milling Co. v. Powell, 283 Ky. 669, 143 S.W.2d 75, 77. See also **Abatement; Abatement of action.**

Abatement. A reduction, a decrease, or a diminution. The suspension or cessation, in whole or in part, of a continuing charge, such as rent.

Legacies. A proportional diminution or reduction of the pecuniary legacies, when the funds or assets out of which such legacies are payable are not sufficient to pay them in full. Model Probate Code, § 184. See **Ademption,** infra, as to specific legacies and devises.

Nuisance. See **Nuisance.**

Plea in abatement. See **Plea.**

Taxes. Diminution or decrease in the amount of tax imposed. Abatement of taxes relieves property of its share of the burdens of taxation after the assessment has been made and the tax levied. Sheppard v. Hidalgo County, 126 Tex. 550, 83 S.W.2d 649, 657.

Abatement of action. Abatement is an entire overthrow or destruction of the suit so that it is quashed and ended. Carver v. State, 217 Tenn. 482, 398 S.W.2d 719. By local court rule in certain U.S. district courts a civil action may be abated (dismissed) if service of process is not made within a specified period after filing of the complaint.

Pleas in abatement have been abolished by Fed.R. Civil P. 7(c); such being replaced by a motion to dismiss under Rule 41. In certain states however this plea still exists to attack jurisdiction, or service of process, or to allege that a prior action between the same parties concerning the same subject matter is pending.

Abator /əbéydər/. In real property law, a stranger who, having no right of entry, contrives to get possession of an estate of freehold, to the prejudice of the heir or devisee, before the latter can enter, after the ancestor's death. In the law of torts, one who abates, prostrates, or destroys a nuisance.

Abatuda /ǽbətyúwdə/. Anything diminished. *Moneta abatuda* is money clipped or diminished in value.

Abavia /əbǽviyə/. Lat. In the civil law, a great-great-grandmother.

Abavita /əbǽmədə/. A great-great-grandfather's sister. This is a misspelling for *abamita (q.v.).*

Abavunculus /ǽbəvǽŋkyələs/. Lat. In the civil law, a great-great-grandmother's brother *(avavioe frater).* Called *avunculus maximus.*

Abavus /ǽbəvəs/. Lat. In the civil law, a great-great-grandfather.

Abbacinare /ǽbəsənériy/. To blind by placing a burning basin or red-hot irons before the eyes. A form of punishment in the Middle Ages. Also spelled "abacinare." The modern Italian is spelled with two b's, and means to blind. Abbacination. Blinding by placing burning basin or red-hot irons before the eyes.

Abbacy /ǽbəsiy/. The government of a religious house, and the revenues thereof, subject to an abbot, as a bishopric is to a bishop. The rights and privileges of an abbot.

Abbey. A monastery or nunnery for the use of an association of religious persons, having an abbot or abbess to preside over them.

Abbot. A prelate in the 13th century who had had an immemorial right to sit in the national assembly.

Abbot, abbat. The spiritual superior or governor of an abbey. Feminine, *Abbess.*

Abbreviatio placitorum /əbrìyviyéysh(iy)ow plæ-sətórəm/. An abstract of ancient judicial records, prior to the Year Books.

Abbreviators /əbríyviyeydərz/. In ecclesiastical law, officers whose duty it is to assist in drawing up the Pope's briefs, and reducing petitions into proper form to be converted into papal bulls.

Abbrochment, or **abbroachment** /əbrówchmənt/. The act of forestalling a market, by buying up at wholesale the merchandise intended to be sold there, for the purpose of selling it at retail. See **Forestalling the market**.

Abbuttals. See **Abuttals.**

ABC test. Unemployment compensation law exclusion tests providing that employer is not covered if individuals he employs are free from his control, the services are performed outside employer's places of business, and employees are customarily engaged in independently established trades or professions are known as the "ABC tests". Employment Sec. Commission v. Wilson, Alaska, 461 P.2d 425, 427.

ABC transaction. In mining and oil drilling operations, a transfer by which A, the operator, conveys the working interest to B for cash consideration, reserving a production payment usually larger than the cash consideration paid by B. Later, A sells the reserved production payment to C for cash. The tax advantages of this type of transaction were eliminated by the Tax Reform Act of 1969.

Abdication /æbdəkéyshən/. Renunciation of the privileges and prerogatives of an office. The act of a sovereign in renouncing and relinquishing his government or throne, so that either the throne is left entirely vacant, or is filled by a successor appointed or elected beforehand. Also, where a magistrate or person in office voluntarily renounces or gives it up before the time of service has expired. It differs from resignation, in that resignation is made by one who has received his office from another and restores it into his hands, as an inferior into the hands of a superior; abdication is the relinquishment of an office which has devolved by act of law. It is said to be a renunciation, quitting, and relinquishing, so as to have nothing further to do with a thing, or the doing of such actions as are inconsistent with the holding of it.

Abditorium /æbdətóriyəm/. An abditory or hiding place, to hide and preserve goods, plate or money.

Abduction. The offense of taking away a wife, child, or ward, by fraud and persuasion, or open violence. Model Penal Code, § 212.4.

To take away surreptitiously by force in kidnapping. The unlawful taking or detention of any female for purposes of marriage, concubinage, or prostitution. In many states this offense is created by statute and in most cases applies to females under a given age. By statute in some states, abduction includes the withdrawal of a husband from his wife, as where another woman alienates his affection and entices him away and causes him to abandon his wife.

See also **Alienation of affections; Kidnapping.**

Abearance /əbérəns/. Behavior; as a recognizance to be of good abearance signifies to be of good behavior.

Ab epistolis /æb iypístələs/. Lat. An officer having charge of the correspondence (*epistolæ*) of his superior or sovereign; a secretary.

Aberemurder /æbərmə́rdər/. (From Sax. *abere*, apparent, notorious; and *mord*, murder.) Plain or downright murder, as distinguished from the less heinous crime of manslaughter, or chance medley.

Abesse /æbésiy/. Lat. In the civil law, to be absent; to be away from a place. Said of a person who was *extra continentia urbis*, (beyond the suburbs of the city.)

Abet. To encourage, incite, or set another on to commit a crime. This word is usually applied to aiding the commission of a crime. To abet another to commit a murder is to command, procure, counsel, encourage, induce, or assist. Short v. Commonwealth, 240 Ky. 477, 42 S.W.2d 696, 697; Wyatt v. U. S., 388 F.2d 395, 400 (10 Cir.). To facilitate the commission of a crime, promote its accomplishment, or help in advancing or bringing it about. State v. Lord, 42 N.M. 638, 84 P.2d 80, 86. It includes knowledge of the wrongful purpose of the perpetrator and counsel and encouragement in the crime. People v. Terman, 4 Cal.App.2d 345, 40 P.2d 915, 916.

A French word combined of two words "a" and "beter"—to bait or excite an animal.

See also **Abettor; Accomplice; Aid and abet.**

Abetment. Act of encouraging, inciting or aiding another.

Abettator /æbətéydər/. L. Lat. In old English law, an abettor. See **Abettor.**

Abettor /əbédər/. An instigator, or setter on; one who promotes or procures a crime to be committed. Handy v. State, 326 A.2d 189. One who commands, advises, instigates, or encourages another to commit a crime. A person who, being present or in the neighborhood, incites another to commit a crime, and thus becomes a principal. To be an "abettor" accused must have instigated or advised commission of crime or been present for purpose of assisting in its commission; he must share criminal intent with which crime was committed. People v. Francis, 71 C.2d 66, 75 Cal.Rptr. 199, 203, 450 P.2d 591.

Ab extra /æb ékstrə/. Lat. *Extra*, beyond, without. From without.

Abeyance /əbéyən(t)s/. Lapse in succession during which there is no person in whom title is vested. In the law of estates, the condition of a freehold when there is no person in being in whom it is vested. In such cases the freehold has been said to be *in nubibus* (in the clouds), *in pendenti* (in suspension); and *in gremio legis* (in the bosom of the law). Where there is a tenant of the freehold, the remainder or reversion in fee may exist for a time without any particular owner, in which case it is said to be in abeyance. A condition of being undetermined or in state of suspension or inactivity. Sales to third parties, of property acquired by county at tax sale, being held in "abeyance", means that certain rights or conditions are in expectancy. Willard v. Ward County, 72 N.D. 291, 6 N.W.2d 566, 568.

Abiaticus, or **aviaticus** /æ̀viyéydəkəs/. L. Lat. In feudal law, a son's son; a grandson in the male line.

Abide. To accept the consequences of; to rest satisfied with; to wait for. With reference to an order, judgment, or decree of a court, to perform, to execute.

Abide by. To adhere to, to obey, to accept the consequences of. Detroit Fidelity & Surety Co. v. U. S., C.C.A.Ohio, 36 F.2d 682, 683.

Abiding conviction. A definite conviction of guilt derived from a thorough examination of the whole case. Used commonly to instruct juries on the frame of mind required for guilt proved beyond a reasonable doubt. Hopt v. Utah, 120 U.S. 439, 7 S.Ct. 614, 30 L.Ed. 708. A settled or fixed conviction. People v. Castro, 68 Cal.App.2d 491, 157 P.2d 25, 30.

Abigeatores /əbìjiyətóriyz/. See **Abigeus**.

Abigeatus /əbìjiyéydəs/. Lat. In the civil law, the offense of stealing or driving away cattle. See **Abigeus**.

Abigei /əbíjiyay/. See **Abigeus**.

Abigere /əbíjiriy/. Lat. In the civil law, to drive away. Applied to those who drove away animals with the intention of stealing them. Applied, also, formerly to the similar offense of cattle stealing on the borders between England and Scotland. See **Abigeus**.

To drive out; to expel by force; to produce abortion.

Abigeus /əbíjiyəs/. Lat. (Pl., *abigei*, or more rarely *abigeatores*.) In the civil law, a stealer of cattle; one who drove or drew away (*subtraxit*) cattle from their pastures, as horses or oxen from the herds, and made booty of them, and who followed this as a business or trade. The term was applied also to those who drove away the smaller animals, as swine, sheep, and goats. In the latter case, it depended on the number taken, whether the offender was *fur* (a common thief) or *abigeus*. But the taking of a single horse or ox seems to have constituted the crime of *abigeatus*. And those who frequently did this were clearly *abigei*, though they took but an animal or two at a time. 4 Bl.Comm. 239.

Ability. Capacity to perform an act or service; e. g. to support spouse and family. Financial ability is usually construed as referring to pecuniary ability. See also **Capacity; Incapacity.**

Ab inconvenienti /æb ìnkənvìyniyéntay/. From hardship, or inconvenience. An argument founded upon the hardship of the case, and the inconvenience or disastrous consequences to which a different course of reasoning would lead.

Ab initio /æb inísh(iy)ow/. Lat. From the beginning; from the first act; from the inception. A party may be said to be a trespasser, an estate said to be good, an agreement or deed said to be void, or a marriage or act said to be unlawful, *ab initio*. Contrasted in this sense with *ex post facto*, or with *postea*.

Ab initio mundi /æb inísh(iy)ow mə́nday/. Lat. From the beginning of the world. *Ab initio mundi usque ad hodiernum diem*, from the beginning of the world to this day.

Ab intestat. Intestate.

Ab intestato /æb ìntestéydow/. Lat. In the civil law, from an intestate; from the intestate; in case of intestacy. *Hœreditas ab intestato*, an inheritance derived from an intestate. *Successio ab intestato*, succession to an intestate, or in case of intestacy. This answers to the descent or inheritance of real estate at common law. 2 Bl.Comm. 490, 516. "Heir *ab intestato*." The phrase "*ab intestato*" is generally used as the opposite or alternative of *ex testamento*, (from, by, or under a will.) *Vel ex testamento, vel ab intestato [hœreditates] pertinent,*—inheritances are derived either from a will or from an intestate (one who dies without a will).

Ab invito /æb inváydow/. Unwillingly. Against one's will. By or from an unwilling party. A transfer ab invito is a compulsory transfer. See **In invitum; Invito.**

Ab irato /æb ayréydow/. Lat. By one who is angry. A devise or gift made by a man adversely to the interest of his heirs, on account of anger or hatred against them, is said to be made ab irato. A suit to set aside such a will is called an action *ab irato*.

Abishering, or **abishersing** /əbíshər(s)iŋ/. Quit of amercements. It originally signified a forfeiture or amercement, and is more properly called *mishering, mishersing*, or *miskering*, according to certain writers. It has since been termed a liberty of freedom, because, wherever this word is used in a grant, the persons to whom the grant is made have the forfeitures and amercements of all others, and are themselves free from the control of any within their fee.

Abjudicatio /æ̀bjuwdəkéysh(iy)ow/. In old English law, the depriving of a thing by the judgment of a court; a putting out of court; the same as *forisjudicatio*, forjudgment, forjudger. A removal from court.

Used to indicate an adverse decision in a writ of right: Thus, the land is said to be *abjudged* from one of the parties and his heirs.

Abjuration /æ̀bjəréyshən/. A renunciation or abandonment by or upon oath. The renunciation under oath of one's citizenship or some other right or privilege. See also **Abjure.**

Abjuration of the realm /æ̀bjəréyshən əv ðə rélm/. In ancient English law, a renunciation of one's country, a species of self-imposed banishment, under an oath never to return to the kingdom unless by permission.

Abjure. To renounce, or abandon, by or upon oath. See **Abjuration**.

Able. See **Ability**.

Able-bodied. As used in a statute relating to service in the militia, this term does not imply an absolute freedom from all physical ailment. It imports an absence of those palpable and visible defects which evidently incapacitate the person from performing the ordinary duties of a soldier.

Ablegati /æbləgéyday/. Papal ambassadors of the second rank, who are sent to a country where there is not a nuncio, with a less extensive commission than that of a nuncio. This title is equivalent to *envoy*.

Able seaman. A grade of merchant seamen. 46 U.S. C.A. § 672.

Able to earn. The phrase in Workers' Compensation Act in reference to wages does not mean the maximum sum earned in any one pay period, but a fair average of the weekly or monthly wages which an employee is able to earn covering a sufficient period of time to determine his earning capacity. Amount one is capable of earning if employed. Ferrara v. Clifton Wright Hat Co., 125 Conn. 140, 3 A.2d 842, 843.

Ability to obtain and hold employment means that the person referred to is either able or unable to perform the usual duties of whatever employment may be under consideration, in the manner that such duties are customarily performed by the average person engaged in such employment. Kinyon v. Kinyon, 230 Mo.App. 623, 71 S.W.2d 78, 82.

Able to purchase. "Ability" in sales contracts, dependent on ability to purchase, usually means financial ability. Anderson v. Craig, 111 Mont. 182, 108 P.2d 205, 206; House v. Hornburg, Sup., 39 N.Y.S.2d 20, 22. Purchaser must have financial ability and legal capacity to acquire land. Campbell v. Hood, Tex. Com.App., 35 S.W.2d 93, 95. Purchaser is able to purchase, as respects broker's right to commission, if he is financially able to command the necessary funds to close the deal within the time required. Hersh v. Garau, 218 Cal. 460, 23 P.2d 1022. See **Financially able**.

Ablocatio /æblowkéysh(iy)ow/. A letting out to hire, or leasing for money. Sometimes used in the English form "ablocation."

Abmatertera /æbmətárdərə/. Lat. In the civil law, a great-great-grandmother's sister (*abaviæ soror*). Called *matertera maxima*.

Abnepos /æbnépo(w)s/. Lat. A great-great-grandson. The grandson of a grandson or granddaughter.

Abneptis /æbnéptəs/. Lat. A great-great-granddaughter. The granddaughter of a grandson or granddaughter.

Abode. One's home; habitation; place of dwelling; or residence. Ordinarily means "domicile." Living place impermanent in character. Fowler v. Fowler, 156 Fla. 316, 22 So.2d 817, 818. The place where a person dwells. In re Erickson, 18 N.J.Misc. 5, 10 A.2d 142, 146. Residence of a legal voter. Pope v.

Board of Election Com'rs, 370 Ill. 196, 18 N.E.2d 214, 216. Fixed place of residence for the time being. Augustus Co., for Use of Bourgeois v. Manzella, 19 N.J.Misc. 29, 17 A.2d 68, 70. For service of process, one's fixed place of residence for the time being; his "usual place of abode." Fed.R. Civil P. 4. Kurilla v. Roth, 132 N.J.L. 213, 38 A.2d 862, 864. See **Domicile; Residence**.

Abogado /àvowgáðow/. Sp. An advocate. See **Bozero**.

Ab olim /æb ówləm/. Of old.

Abolish. To do away with wholly; to annul; to repeal; to rescind; to abrogate; to dispense with. Put an end to. Stretch v. Murphy, 166 Or. 439, 112 P.2d 1018, 1021. Imports absolute destruction having its root in the Latin word "abolere," meaning to destroy utterly. Applies particularly to things of a permanent nature, such as institutions, usages, customs, as the abolition of slavery.

Abolition. The destruction, annihilation, abrogation, or extinguishment of anything. See **Abolish**.

In the Civil, French and German law, abolition is used nearly synonymously with pardon, remission, grace.

A bon droit /éy bòn dróyt/. With good reason; justly; rightfully.

Aboriginal title /æbəríjənəl táydəl/. Type of title of Indians based on continuous occupancy and use to exclusion of others. Bennett County, S. D. v. U. S., C.A.S.D., 394 F.2d 8, 11.

Abortee /əbórtìy/. The woman upon whom an abortion is performed.

Abortifacient /əbòrdəfeysh(iy)ənt/. Drug or medicine capable of, or used for, producing abortion.

Abortion. The knowing destruction of the life of an unborn child or the intentional expulsion or removal of an unborn child from the womb other than for the principal purpose of producing a live birth or removing a dead fetus. However, prior to approximately the end of the first trimester of pregnancy the attending physician in consultation with his patient is free to determine, without regulation by state, that in his medical judgment the patient's pregnancy should be terminated, and if that decision is reached such judgment may be effectuated by an abortion without interference by the state. Roe v. Wade, 410 U.S. 113, 93 S.Ct. 705, 35 L.Ed.2d 147. See also **Viability; Viable child**.

Abortionist. One who criminally produces abortions, or one who follows business or practices of crime of producing abortions.

Abortus /əbórdəs/. Lat. The fruit of an abortion; the child born before its time, incapable of life.

About. Near in time, quantity, number, quality, or degree. Substantially, approximately, almost, or nearly. Odom v. Langston, 351 Mo. 609, 173 S.W.2d 826, 829.

When used with reference to time, the term is of flexible significance, varying with the circumstances and the connection in which it is employed. But its use does not necessarily render time immaterial, nor make a contract one terminable at will. In a charter party, "about to sail" means just ready to sail. With relation to quantity, the term suggests only an estimate of probable amount. Its import is that the actual quantity is a near approximation to that mentioned, and it has the effect of providing against accidental variations. Norrington v. Wright, 115 U.S. 188, 6 S.Ct. 12, 29 L.Ed. 366. It may be given practically the same effect as the phrase more or less. Synonymous with "on" or "upon," as in offense of carrying concealed weapons. Near by, close at hand, convenient of access. Brown v. U. S., 30 F.2d 474, 475, 58 App.D.C. 311. As to number, it merely implies an estimate of a particular lot or class and not a warranty. In connection with distance or locality, the term is of relative significance, varying with the circumstances.

Aboutissement /abùwtismón/. Fr. An abuttal or abutment.

Above. Higher; superior. As, court above; plaintiff or defendant above. *Above all incumbrances* means in excess thereof. Principal, as distinguished from what is auxiliary or instrumental.

Abpatruus /æbpǽtruwəs/. Lat. A great-great-uncle; or, a great-great-grandfather's brother (*abavi frater*). It sometimes means uncle, and sometimes great-uncle.

Abridge. To reduce or contract; usually spoken of written language. See **Abridgment**.

Copyright law. To epitomize; to reduce; to contract. It implies preserving the substance, the essence, of a work, in language suited to such a purpose. In making extracts there is no condensation of the author's language, and hence no abridgment. To abridge requires the exercise of the mind; it is not copying. Between a compilation and an abridgment there is a clear distinction. A compilation consists of selected extracts from different authors; an abridgment is a condensation of the views of one author.

Abridgment. Condensation; contraction. An epitome or compendium of another and larger work, wherein the principal ideas of the larger work are summarily contained. Abridgments of the law are brief digests of the law, arranged alphabetically. In this context, the term "digest" (*q.v.*) has generally supplanted that of "abridgment." See also **Abstract; Headnote; Syllabus**.

Abridgment of damages. The right of the court to reduce the damages in certain cases. See **Remittitur**.

Abroad. In English chancery law, beyond the seas.

Abrogate /ǽbrəgeyt/. To annul, cancel, repeal, or destroy. To annul or repeal an order or rule issued by a subordinate authority; to repeal a former law by legislative act, or by usage.

Abrogation /æbrəgéyshən/. The destruction or annulling of a former law, by an act of the legislative power, by constitutional authority, or by usage. It stands opposed to *rogation*; and is distinguished from *derogation*, which implies the taking away only some part of a law; from *subrogation*, which denotes

the substitution of a clause; from *dispensation*, which only sets it aside in a particular instance; and from *antiquation*, which is the refusing to pass a law. Implied abrogation takes place when the new law contains provisions which are positively contrary to former laws, without expressly abrogating such laws; and also when the order of things for which the law has been made no longer exists. Ex parte Lum Poy, D.C.Wash., 23 F.2d 690.

For "Express abrogation," see that title. See also **Annul; Repeal**.

Abscond /əbskónd/. To go in a clandestine manner out of the jurisdiction of the courts, or to lie concealed, in order to avoid their process. To hide, conceal, or absent oneself clandestinely, with the intent to avoid legal process. Postponing limitations. Keck v. Pickens, 207 Ark. 757, 182 S.W.2d 873, 875. Fleeing from arresting or prosecuting officers of the state. See **Fugitive**.

Absconding debtor. One who absconds from his creditors. An absconding debtor is one who lives without the state, or who has intentionally concealed himself from his creditors, or withdrawn himself from the reach of their suits, with intent to frustrate their just demands. Such act was formerly an "Act of bankruptcy" (*q.v.*). Thus, if a person departs from his usual residence, or remains absent therefrom, or conceals himself in his house, so that he cannot be served with process, with intent unlawfully to delay or defraud his creditors, he is an absconding debtor; but if he departs from the state or from his usual abode, with the intention of again returning, and without any fraudulent design, he has not absconded, nor absented himself, within the intendment of the law. Doughnut Corporation of America v. Tsakirides, 121 N.J.L. 136, 1 A.2d 467, 469.

Absence. The state of being absent, removed, or away from one's domicile, or usual place of residence. Not present at particular time; opposite of appearance at a specified time.

Absent. Being away from; at a distance from; not in company with.

Absente /æbséntiy/. Lat. Being absent; often used in the old reports of one of the judges not present at the hearing of a cause.

Absente reo /æbséntiy ríyow/. The defendant being absent.

Absentee. One who is absent from his usual place of residence or domicile.

Absentee landlord. Lessor of real property (normally the owner) who does not live on the premises.

Absentee voting. Participation (usually by mail) in elections by qualified voters who, because of serious illness, military service, or absence from home for business or other reasons, are unable to appear at the polls in person on election day.

Absentem accipere debemus eum qui non est eo loci in quo petitur /æbséntəm əksípəriy dəbíyməs íyəm kwày nón est íyow lówsay in kwów pédədər/. We ought to consider him absent who is not in the place where he is demanded (or sought).

Absentia ejus qui reipublicæ causa abest, neque ei neque alii damnosa esse debet /æbsénsh(iy)ə íyjəs kwày ríyaypə́bləsiy kózə ǽbest, níykwiy íyay níykwiy ǽliyay dæmnówsə ésiy díybət/. The absence of him who is away in behalf of the republic (on business of the state) ought not to be prejudicial either to him or to another.

Absoile, assoil, assoile. To pardon; to deliver from excommunication.

Absoluta sententia expositore non indiget /ǽbsəl(y)úwdə sənténsh(iy)ə ekspozətóriy non índəjet/. An absolute sentence or proposition (one that is plain without any scruple, or absolute without any saving) needs not an expositor.

Absolute. Complete; perfect; final; without any condition or incumbrance; as an absolute bond *(simplex obligatio)* in distinction from a conditional bond. Unconditional; complete and perfect in itself; without relation to or dependence on other things or persons.

As to absolute Conveyance; Covenant; Delivery; Divorce; Estate; Gift; Guaranty; Interest; Legacy; Nuisance; Nullity; Obligation; Property; Rights; Rule; Sale; Title, see those titles.

Absolute deed. A document of conveyance without restriction or defeasance; generally used in contradistinction to mortgage deed.

Absolute law. The true and proper law of nature, immutable in the abstract or in principle, in theory, but not in application; for very often the object, the reason, situation, and other circumstances, may vary its exercise and obligation. See also **Natural law**.

Absolute liability. Responsibility without fault or negligence. Rylands v. Fletcher, 3 H.L. 330; Clark-Aiken Co. v. Cromwell-Wright Co., Inc. (Mass.), 323 N.E.2d 876. See **Strict liability**.

Absolutely. Completely; wholly; without qualification; without reference or relation to, or dependence upon, any other person, thing, or event. Thus, *absolutely void* means utterly void. *Absolutely necessary* may be used to make the idea of necessity more emphatic. Independently or unconditionally, wholly or positively. Collins v. Hartford Accident & Indemnity Co., 178 Va. 501, 17 S.E.2d 413, 418.

"Absolutely void" is that which the law or nature of things forbids to be enforced at all, and that is "relatively void" which the law condemns as a wrong to individuals and refuses to enforce against them. Kyle v. Chaves, 42 N.M. 21, 74 P.2d 1030; Scudder v. Hart, 45 N.M. 76, 110 P.2d 536, 541.

Absolution. In *Canon Law*, a juridical act whereby the clergy declare that the sins of such as are penitent are remitted. Among Protestants it is chiefly used for a sentence by which a person who stands excommunicated is released or freed from that punishment.

In the *Civil Law*, a sentence whereby a party accused is declared innocent of the crime laid to his charge.

In *French Law*, the dismissal of an accusation.

Absolutism /ǽbsəl(y)uwtìzəm/. In politics, a system of government in which public power is vested in some person or persons, unchecked and uncontrolled by any law, institution, constitutional device, or coordinate body. Currently refers to any government which is run by a dictator whose power is without restriction and without any checks or balances.

Absolve. To set free, or release, as from obligation, debt, or responsibility. State ex rel. St. Louis Car Co. v. Hughes, 348 Mo. 125, 152 S.W.2d 193, 194. See also **Amnesty; Pardon.**

Absorption /əbzórpshən/. Term used in collective bargaining agreements to provide seniority for union members if employer's business is merged with another. Humphrey v. Moore, Ky., 375 U.S. 335, 84 S.Ct. 363, 369. Partial or complete payment of freight charges by seller or freight carrier.

Absque /ǽbskwiy/. Without. Occurs in phrases taken from the Latin; such as those immediately following.

Absque aliquo inde redendo /ǽbskwiy ǽləkwow índiy rədéndow/. Lat. Without reserving any rent therefrom; without rendering anything therefrom. A term used of a free grant by the crown.

Absque consideratione curiæ /ǽbskwiy kənsidəreyshiyówniy kyúriyiy/. In old practice, without the consideration of the court; without judgment.

Absque hoc /ǽbskwiy hók/. Without this. These are technical words of denial, used in pleading at common law by way of special traverse, to introduce the negative part of the plea, following the affirmative part or inducement. See also **Traverse**.

Absque impetitione vasti /ǽbskwiy ìmpətishiyówniy véystay/. Without impeachment of waste; without accountability for waste; without liability to suit for waste. A clause anciently often inserted in leases (as the equivalent English phrase sometimes is) signifying that the tenant or lessee shall not be liable to suit *(impetitio)* or challenged, or called to account, for committing waste. See **Waste**.

Absque tali causa /ǽbskwiy téylay kózə/. Lat. Without such cause. A form of replication, now obsolete, in an action *ex delicto* which works a general denial of the whole matter of the defendant's plea of *de injuria*.

Abstention doctrine. Doctrine of "abstention" permits a federal court, in the exercise of its discretion, to relinquish jurisdiction where necessary to avoid needless conflict with the administration by a state of its own affairs. Surowitz v. New York City Emp. Retirement System, D.C.N.Y., 376 F.Supp. 369, 376; Railroad Commission of Texas v. Pullman Co., 312 U.S. 496, 61 S.Ct. 643, 85 L.Ed. 971. See also **Equitable abstention doctrine.**

Abstinence. Refraining completely from indulgence in some act such as eating or drinking, unlike temperance which presupposes moderate indulgence. Mayfield v. Fidelity & Casualty Co. of N. Y., 16 C.A.2d 611, 61 P.2d 83.

Abstract /ǽbstrækt/, *n.* A less quantity containing the virtue and force of a greater quantity; an abridgment. A transcript is generally defined as a copy, and is more comprehensive than an abstract. Summary or epitome, or that which comprises or concentrates in itself the essential qualities of a larger thing or of several things. Robbins Inv. Co. v. Robbins, 49 Cal. App.2d 446, 122 P.2d 91, 92. See **Abridge; Abridgment; Digest; Headnote; Syllabus.**

Abstract /ǝbstrǽkt/, v. To take or withdraw from; as, to abstract the funds of a bank. To remove or separate. To summarize or abridge.

Abstraction. Taking from with intent to injure or defraud. "Wrongful abstraction" is "unauthorized and illegal taking or withdrawing of funds, etc., and appropriation thereof to taker's benefit." Pacific Coast Adjustment Bureau v. Indemnity Ins. Co. of North America, 115 Cal.App. 583, 2 P.2d 218, 219.

Abstract of a fine. In old English conveyancing, one of the parts of a fine, being an abstract of the writ of covenant, and the concord, naming the parties, the parcels of land, and the agreement. 2 Bl.Comm. 351. More commonly called the "note" of the fine. See **Fine; Concord.**

Abstract of record. A complete history in short, abbreviated form of the case as found in the record, complete enough to show that the questions presented for review have been properly reserved. Synopsis or summary of facts, rather than table of contents of transcript. Abbreviated accurate and authentic history of proceedings. Brown v. Reichmann, 237 Mo. App. 136, 164 S.W.2d 201, 207.

Abstract of title. A condensed history of the title to land, consisting of a synopsis or summary of the material or operative portion of all the conveyances, of whatever kind or nature, which in any manner affect said land, or any estate or interest therein, together with a statement of all liens, charges, or liabilities to which the same may be subject, and of which it is in any way material for purchasers to be apprised. An epitome of the record evidence of title, including maps, plats, and other aids. Commissioners' Court of Madison County v. Wallace, 118 Tex. 279, 15 S.W.2d 535, 536. An epitome of the conveyances, transfers, and other facts relied on as evidence of title, together with all such facts appearing of record as may impair the title. State ex rel. Freeman v. Abstracters Board of Examiners, 99 Mont. 564, 45 P.2d 668, 670. Memorandum or concise statement in orderly form of the substance of documents or facts appearing on public records which affect title to real property. State ex rel. Doria v. Ferguson, 145 Ohio St. 12, 60 N.E.2d 476, 478. See also **Torrens title system.**

Abstract question. One which does not rest upon existing facts or rights. Morris Plan Bank of Fort Worth v. Ogden, Tex.Civ.App., 144 S.W.2d 998, 1004. Hypothetical question.

Absurdity. Anything which is so irrational, unnatural, or inconvenient that it cannot be supposed to have been within the intention of men of ordinary intelligence and discretion. Obviously and flatly opposed to the manifest truth; inconsistent with the plain dictates of common sense; logically contradictory; nonsensical; ridiculous.

Abundans cautela non nocet /ǝbǽndǝnz kotíylǝ non nósǝt/. Abundant or extreme caution does no harm. This principle is generally applied to the construction of instruments in which superfluous words have been inserted more clearly to express the intention.

Ab urbe condita /ǽb ə́rbiy kóndidǝ/. From the founding of the city. See A.U.C.

Abus de confiance /ǝbyúw dǝ kònfiyón(t)s/. Fraudulently misusing or spending to anybody's prejudice goods, cash, bills, documents, or contracts handed over for a special object.

Abuse /ǝbyúws/, n. Everything which is contrary to good order established by usage. Departure from reasonable use; immoderate or improper use. Physical or mental maltreatment. Misuse. Deception.

"Abuse" means to wrong in speech, reproach coarsely, disparage, revile, and malign. State v. Neubauer, 2 Conn.Cir. 169, 197 A.2d 93, 96. See **Defamation.**

Child abuse. See **Child abuse.**

Civil law. The destruction of the substance of a thing in using it. See **Abuse,** v.

Corporate franchise or entity. The abuse or misuse of its franchises by a corporation signifies any positive act in violation of the charter and in derogation of public right, willfully done or caused to be done. The use of rights or franchises as a pretext for wrongs and injuries to the public.

Discretion. "Abuse of discretion" is synonymous with a failure to exercise a sound, reasonable, and legal discretion. It is a strict legal term indicating that appellate court is of opinion that there was commission of an error of law by the trial court. It does not imply intentional wrong or bad faith, or misconduct, nor any reflection on the judge but means the clearly erroneous conclusion and judgment—one is that clearly against logic and effect of such facts as are presented in support of the application or against the reasonable and probable deductions to be drawn from the facts disclosed upon the hearing; an improvident exercise of discretion; an error of law. State v. Draper, 83 Utah 115, 27 P.2d 39; Ex parte Jones, 246 Ala. 433, 20 So.2d 859, 862. A discretion exercised to an end or purpose not justified by and clearly against reason and evidence. Unreasonable departure from considered precedents and settled judicial custom, constituting error of law. Beck v. Wings Field, Inc., C.C.A.Pa., 122 F.2d 114, 116, 117. "Abuse of discretion" by trial court is any unreasonable, unconscionable and arbitrary action taken without proper consideration of facts and law pertaining to matter submitted. Harvey v. State, Okl.Cr., 458 P.2d 336, 338.

Drug abuse. See that title.

Female child. An injury to the genital organs in an attempt at carnal knowledge, falling short of actual penetration. Lee v. State, 246 Ala. 69, 18 So.2d 706, 707. But, according to other authorities, "abuse" is here equivalent to ravishment or rape. Any injury to private parts of girl constitutes "abuse" within meaning of criminal statute proscribing abuse of girl under age of 12 years in attempt to have carnal knowledge of her; mere hurting of private parts of girl, even though they are not bruised, cut, lacerated or torn, is sufficient. Ard v. State, 57 Ala.App. 250, 327 So.2d 745, 747. See also **Carnal abuse; Child abuse.**

Police officer. As used in statute prohibiting one from obstructing, resisting, or abusing an officer, word "abuses" means to wrong in speech, reproach coarsely, disparage, revile, or malign an officer who is performing his duty. State v. Neubauer, 2 Conn.Cir. 169, 197 A.2d 93.

Power. Use of one who possesses it in a manner contrary to law. Improper use of power, distinguished from usurpation of power which presupposes exercise of power not vested in the offender. Swenson v. Cahoon, 111 Fla. 788, 152 So. 203, 204.

Process. The gist of an action for "abuse of process" is improper use or perversion of process after it has been issued. Publix Drug Co. v. Breyer Ice Cream Co., 347 Pa. 346, 32 A.2d 413, 415. A malicious abuse of legal process occurs where the party employs it for some unlawful object, not the purpose which it is intended by the law to effect; in other words, a perversion of it. 500 West 174 St. v. Vasquez, 67 Misc.2d 993, 325 N.Y.S.2d 256, 258. Thus, where the purpose of a prosecution for issuance of a check without funds was to collect a debt, the prosecution is an abuse of criminal process. Regular and legitimate use of process, although with a bad intention, is not a malicious "abuse of process." Priest v. Union Agency, 174 Tenn. 304, 125 S.W.2d 142, 143. Action for "abuse of process" is distinguished from action for "malicious prosecution," in that action for abuse of process rests upon improper use of regularly issued process, while "malicious prosecution" has reference to wrong in issuance of process. McInnis v. Atlantic Inv. Corporation, 137 Or. 648, 4 P.2d 314, 315; Lobel v. Trade Bank of New York, 132 Misc. 643, 229 N.Y.S. 778, 781. See also **Malicious abuse of legal process; Malicious use of process.**

Abuse /əbyúwz/, *v.* To make excessive or improper use of a thing, or to employ it in a manner contrary to the natural or legal rules for its use. To make an extravagant or excessive use, as to abuse one's authority.

Abused and neglected children. Those who are suffering serious physical or emotional injury inflicted on them, including malnutrition. See **Abuse** *(Female child);* **Child abuse.**

Abusive. Tending to deceive; practicing abuse; prone to ill-treat by coarse, insulting words or harmful acts. Using ill treatment; injurious, improper, hurtful, offensive, reproachful.

Abut. To reach; to touch. To touch at the end; be contiguous; join at a border or boundary; terminate on; end at; border on; reach or touch with an end. The term "abutting" implies a closer proximity than the term "adjacent." No intervening land.

Abuttals /əbə́dəlz/. The buttings or boundings of lands, showing to what other lands, highways, or places they belong or are abutting. It has been used to express the end boundary lines as distinguished from those on the sides, as "buttals and sidings".

Abutter. One whose property abuts, is contiguous, or joins at a border or boundary, as where no other land, road, or street intervenes.

Abutting owner. An owner of land which abuts or adjoins. The term usually implies that the relative parts actually adjoin, but is sometimes loosely used without implying more than close proximity. See **Abut.**

A.C. *Anno Christi,* the year of Christ.

A/C means account and is much used by bookkeepers. As used in a check, it has been held not a direction to the bank to credit the amount of the check to the person named, but rather a memorandum to identify the transaction in which the check was issued.

Academic. Pertaining to college, university, or preparatory school. Sisters of Mercy v. Town of Hooksett, 93 N.H. 301, 42 A.2d 222, 225. A question or issue which is not relevant to case or is premature or hypothetical. In re Battell's Will, 286 N.Y. 97, 35 N.E.2d 913. See **Academic question.**

Academic freedom. Right to teach as one sees fit, but not necessarily the right to teach evil. Kay v. Bd. of Higher Education of City of N. Y., 173 Misc. 943, 18 N.Y.S.2d 821, 829.

Academic question. An issue which does not require answer or adjudication by court because it is not necessary to case; hypothetical or moot question. In re Electrolux Corp., 288 N.Y. 440, 43 N.E.2d 480. See **Hypothetical question.**

Academy. An institution of higher learning. An association of experts in some particular branch of art, literature, or science. In its original meaning, an association formed for mutual improvement, or for the advancement of science or art; in later use, a species of educational institution, of a level between the elementary school and the college. U. S. ex rel. Jacovides v. Day, C.C.A.N.Y., 32 F.2d 542, 544; Sisters of Mercy v. Town of Hooksett, 93 N.H. 301, 42 A.2d 222, 225. In current usage, term commonly refers to private high school or one of the service academies (e. g. Air Force Academy). See **School.**

A cancellando /èy kænsəlǽndow/. From cancelling. 3 Bl.Comm. 46.

A cancellis /èy kænséləs/. The Chancellor.

A cancellis curiæ explodi /èy kænséləs kyúriyiy èksplówday/. To be expelled from the bar of the court.

Acapte. In French feudal law, a species of relief; a seignorial right due on every change of a tenant. A feudal right which formerly prevailed in Languedoc and Guyenne, being attached to that species of heritable estates which were granted on the contract of *emphyteusis.*

A causa de cy /ey kózə də síy/. For this reason.

Accedas ad curiam /æksíydəs æd kyúriyəm/. (Lat. That you go to court.) An original writ out of chancery directed to the sheriff, for the purpose of removing a replevin suit from a Court Baron or a hundred court to one of the superior courts of law. It directs the sheriff *to go to the lower court,* and enroll the proceedings and send up the record. 3 Bl.Comm. 34.

Accedas ad vice comitem /æksíydəs ǽd váysiy kómidəm/. L. Lat. (You go to the sheriff.) A writ formerly directed to the coroners of a county in England, commanding them to go to the sheriff, where the latter had suppressed and neglected to return a writ of *pone,* and to deliver a writ to him requiring him to return it. See **Pone.**

Accede. To consent; agree.

Accelerated depreciation. Various methods of depreciation that yield larger deductions in the earlier years of the life of an asset than the straight-line method. Examples include the double declining-balance and the sum of the years' digits methods of depreciation. See **Depreciation.**

Acceleration. The shortening of the time for the vesting in possession of an expectant interest. Hastening of the enjoyment of an estate which was otherwise postponed to a later period. Blackwell v. Virginia Trust Co., 177 Va. 299, 14 S.E.2d 301, 304. If the life estate fails for any reason the remainder is "accelerated". Elliott v. Brintlinger, 376 Ill. 147, 33 N.E.2d 199, 201.

Doctrine of "acceleration", as applied to law of property, refers to hastening of owner of future interests toward status of present possession or enjoyment by reason of failure of preceding estate. Aberg v. First Nat. Bank in Dallas, Tex.Civ.App., 450 S.W.2d 403, 408. A remedy used where there has been an anticipatory repudiation or a possibility of a future breach. Rose City Transit Co. v. City of Portland, 18 Or.App. 369, 525 P.2d 1325, 1353.

Acceleration clause. A provision or clause in a mortgage, note, bond, deed of trust, or other credit agreement, which allows a lender the opportunity to call monies due under the instrument. Such clause operates when there has been a default such as nonpayment of principal, interest, or failure to pay insurance premiums. General Motors Acceptance Corp. v. Shuey, 243 Ky. 74, 47 S.W.2d 968. U.C.C. § 1–208 provides that if the provision for acceleration is "at will" such demand must be made only under a "good faith" belief that the prospect of payment is impaired.

Acceleration of remainders. Hastening of owner of remainder interest in property toward status of present possession or enjoyment by reason of failure preceding estate. Aberg v. First Nat'l Bank in Dallas, Tex.Civ.App., 450 S.W.2d 403, 408.

Acceleration premium. Increased rate of pay for increased production.

Accept. To receive with approval or satisfaction; to receive with intent to retain. Morris v. State, 102 Ark. 513, 145 S.W. 213, 214. Also, in the capacity of drawee of a bill, to recognize the draft, and engage to pay it when due (see **Acceptance,** infra). Admit and agree to; accede to or consent to; receive with approval; adopt; agree to. Rocha v. Hulen, 6 Cal. App.2d 245, 44 P.2d 478, 482, 483. Means something more than to receive, meaning to adopt, to agree to carry out provisions, to keep and retain.

Acceptance. The taking and receiving of anything in good part, and as it were a tacit agreement to a preceding act, which might have been defeated or avoided if such acceptance had not been made. The act of a person to whom a thing is offered or tendered by another, whereby he receives the thing with the intention of retaining it, such intention being evidenced by a sufficient act. Aetna Inv. Corporation v. Chandler Landscape & Floral Co., 227 Mo.App. 17, 50 S.W.2d 195, 197. The exercise of power conferred by an offer by performance of some act. In re Larney's Estate, 148 Misc. 871, 266 N.Y.S. 564.

Commercial paper. Acceptance is the drawee's signed engagement to honor the draft as presented. It must be written on the draft, and may consist of his signature alone. It becomes operative when completed by delivery or notification. U.C.C. § 3–410. Certification of a check is acceptance. U.C.C. § 3–411. A draft may be accepted although it has not been signed by the drawer or is otherwise incomplete or is overdue or has been dishonored. U.C.C. § 3–410(2). See also **Acceptor; Banker's acceptance; Honor.**

Contracts. Compliance by offeree with terms and conditions of offer constitute an "acceptance". Davis & Clanton v. C. I. T. Corporation, 190 S.C. 151, 2 S.E.2d 382, 383. See also **Confirmation; Offer and acceptance.**

Deed. Act by which vendee vests himself with title to the property. Hardin v. Kazee, 238 Ky. 526, 38 S.W.2d 438.

Insurance. In a contract of insurance, the "acceptance" occurs when insurer agrees to accept application and to issue policy. Acacia Mut. Life Ass'n v. Berry, 54 Ariz. 208, 94 P.2d 770, 772. Delay or inaction on the part of an insurer cannot constitute an "acceptance". French American Banking Corporation v. Fireman's Fund Ins. Co., D.C.N.Y., 43 F.Supp. 494, 498. More than mere mental resolution or determination on part of insurer to accept application is required; such must be communicated to applicant. Limbaugh v. Monarch Life Ins. Co., Springfield, Mass., Mo.App., 84 S.W.2d 208, 212. Term as applied to policy means assent, acquiescence or agreement to terms and conditions of policy. Baker v. St. Paul Fire & Marine Ins. Co., Mo.App., 427 S.W.2d 281, 291.

Sale of goods. U.C.C. § 2–606 provides three ways a buyer can accept goods: (1) by signifying to the seller that the goods are conforming or that he will accept them in spite of their nonconformity, (2) by failing to make an effective rejection, and (3) by doing an act inconsistent with the seller's ownership. Acceptance of a part of any commercial unit is acceptance of that entire unit.

Types of acceptance.

Conditional. An engagement to pay the draft or accept the offer on the happening of a condition. A "conditional acceptance" is in effect a statement that the offeree is willing to enter into a bargain differing in some respects from that proposed in the original offer. The conditional acceptance is, therefore, itself a counter offer.

Express. An undertaking in direct and express terms to pay the bill, draft, etc.; an absolute acceptance.

Implied. An undertaking to pay the draft inferred from acts of the drawee of a character which fairly warrant such an inference. In case of a bilateral contract, "acceptance" of an offer need not be expressed, but may be shown by any words or acts indicating the offeree's assent to the proposed bargain.

Qualified. One either conditional or partial, and which introduces a variation in the sum, mode, or place of payment. In contract law, an acceptance based on a variation of the terms of the offer and hence a counteroffer. In negotiable instruments, a variation in the terms of the instrument by the acceptor.

Acceptance au besoin /àkseptóns òw bəzwǽn/. Fr. Acceptance in case of need. An acceptance by one whom a bill is drawn *au besoin*, that is, in case of refusal or failure of the drawee to accept.

Acceptare /ǽkseptériy/. Lat. To accept; to assent; to assent to a promise made by another.

Accepteur par intervention. In French law, acceptor of a bill of honor.

Acceptilation /æksèptəléyshən/. In the civil and Scotch law, release made by a creditor to his debtor of his debt, without receiving any consideration. It is a species of donation, but not subject to the forms of the latter, and is valid unless in fraud of creditors. The verbal extinction of a verbal contract, with a declaration that the debt has been paid when it has not; or the acceptance of something merely imaginary in satisfaction of a verbal contract.

Acceptor. One who engages that he will pay the draft according to its tenor at the time of his engagement or as completed pursuant to authority on incomplete instruments. U.C.C. § 3–413.

Acceptor supra protest /əkséptar s(y)úwprə prówtèst/. One who accepts a bill which has been protested, for the honor of the drawer or any one of the indorsers.

Access. Freedom of approach or communication; or the means, power, or opportunity of approaching, communicating, or passing to and from. Sometimes importing the occurrence of sexual intercourse, Jackson v. Jackson, 182 Okl. 74, 76 P.2d 1062, 1066; otherwise as importing opportunity of communication for that purpose as between husband and wife.

In real property law, the term "access" denotes the right vested in the owner of land which adjoins a road or other highway to go and return from his own land to the highway without obstruction. See **Access, easement of.** "Access" to property does not necessarily carry with it possession. People v. Brenneauer, 101 Misc. 156, 166 N.Y.S. 801, 806.

Multiple access. The defense of several lovers in paternity actions. Yarmark v. Strickland, 193 So.2d 212.

Public records. The right of access to public records includes not only a legal right of access but a reasonable opportunity to avail oneself of the same. See **Freedom of Information Act.**

Accessary. See **Accessory.**

Access, easement of /íyzmənt əv ǽkses/. An easement of access is the right which an abutting owner has of ingress to and egress from his premises, in addition to the public easement in the street.

Accessio /ǽksésh(iy)ow/. In Roman law, an increase or addition; that which lies next to a thing, and is supplementary and necessary to the principal thing; that which arises or is produced from the principal thing; an "accessory obligation" *(q.v.)*. One of the modes of acquiring property, being the extension of ownership over that which grows from, or is united to, an article which one already possesses.

Accessio includes both accession and accretion as used in the common law. See **Adjunction.**

Accession. Coming into possession of a right or office; increase; augmentation; addition.

The right to all which one's own property produces, whether that property be movable or immovable; and the right to that which is united to it by accession, either naturally or artificially. The right to own things that become a part of something already owned; *e.g.* riparian owners' right to abandoned river beds and rights of alluvion by accretion and reliction. Manry v. Robison, 122 Tex. 213, 56 S.W.2d 438, 443, 444. See **Accretion.**

A principle derived from the civil law, by which the owner of property becomes entitled to all which it produces, and to all that is added or united to it, either naturally or artificially, (that is, by the labor or skill of another) even where such addition extends to a change of form or materials; and by which, on the other hand, the possessor of property becomes entitled to it, as against the original owner, where the addition made to it by his skill and labor is of greater value than the property itself, or where the change effected in its form is so great as to render it impossible to restore it to its original shape.

The commencement or inauguration of a sovereign's reign.

International law. The absolute or conditional acceptance by one or several nations of a treaty already concluded between other sovereignties. It may be of two kinds: *First,* the formal entrance of a third state into a treaty so that such nation becomes a party to it; and this can only be with the consent of the original parties. *Second,* a nation may accede to a treaty between other nations solely for the purpose of guarantee, in which case, though a party, it is affected by the treaty only as a guarantor. See **Adhesion.**

Accessions. Goods which are installed in or affixed to other goods. U.C.C. § 9–314(1).

Accessorium non ducit, sed sequitur suum principale /æksesóriyəm non dyúwsət sed sékwədər syúwəm prinsəpéyliy/. That which is the accessory or incident does not lead, but follows, its principal.

Accessorius sequitur naturam sui principalis /æksesóriyəs sékwədər neychúrəm syúway prìnsəpéyləs/. An accessary follows the nature of his principal. One who is accessary to a crime cannot be guilty of a higher degree of crime than his principal.

Accessory. Anything which is joined to another thing as an ornament, or to render it more perfect, or which accompanies it, or is connected with it as an incident, or as subordinate to it, or which belongs to or with it.

Adjunct or accompaniment. Louis Werner Saw Mill Co. v. White, 205 La. 242, 17 So.2d 264, 270. A thing of subordinate importance. Aiding or contributing in secondary way or assisting in or contributing to as a subordinate. Gilfoil v. Greenspon, La.App., 216 So.2d 829, 831.

Accessory after the fact. A person who, knowing a felony to have been committed by another, receives, relieves, comforts or assists the felon, in order to enable him to escape from punishment, or the like. Robinson v. State, 5 Md.App. 723, 249 A.2d 504, 507; 18 U.S.C.A. § 3. See also **Harbor; Obstructing justice.**

Accessory before the fact. One who orders, counsels, encourages, or otherwise aids and abets another to commit a felony and who is not present at the commission of the offense. Com. v. Leach, 455 Pa. 448, 317 A.2d 293, 294. The primary distinction between the accessory before the fact and the principal in the second degree is presence. Virtually all states have now expressly abrogated the distinction between principals and accessories before the fact; the latter now being classified as principals.

Accessory during the fact. One who stands by without interfering or giving such help as may be in his power to prevent the commission of a criminal offense.

Criminal law. Contributing to or aiding in the commission of a crime. One who, without being present at the commission of a felonious offense, becomes guilty of such offense, not as a chief actor, but as a participator, as by command, advice, instigation, or concealment; either before or after the fact or commission; a *particeps criminis.* Model Penal Code, § 2.06.

One who is not the chief actor in the offense, nor present at its performance, but in some way concerned therein, either *before or after* the act committed. One who aids, abets, commands, or counsels another in the commission of a crime. See also **Abettor; Aid and abet; Accomplice.**

Accessory building. Structures used for benefit of main building; *e.g.* tool shed. Out-buildings.

Accessory contract. An accessory contract is made for assuring the performance of a prior contract, either by the same parties or by others; such as suretyship, mortgage, and pledge.

Accessory obligation. An obligation which is incidental to another or principal obligation; *e.g.* the obligation of a surety.

Accessory use. With reference to zoning law, an "accessory use" in its ordinary signification is a use which is dependent on or pertains to principal or main use. Town of Foxborough v. Bay State Harness Horse Racing & Breeding Ass'n, Inc., Mass.App., 366 N.E.2d 773, 777. Accessory use is one which is subordinate to, clearly incidental to, customary in connection with, and ordinarily located on same lot with, principal use. Board of County Com'rs of Boulder County v. Thompson, 177 Colo. 277, 493 P.2d 1358, 1360.

Access to counsel. Right of one to consult with his attorney guaranteed by the 6th Amendment. U.S. Const. Geders v. U. S., 425 U.S. 80, 96 S.Ct. 1330, 47 L.Ed.2d 592. See also **Counsel, right to.**

Access to courts. Right of person to require fair hearing from judiciary. Gilmore v. Lynch, D.C.Cal., 319 F.Supp. 105, 110.

Accident. The word "accident" is derived from the Latin verb "accidere" signifying "fall upon, befall, happen, chance." In an etymological sense anything that happens may be said to be an accident and in this sense, the word has been defined as befalling a change; a happening; an incident; an occurrence or event. In its most commonly accepted meaning, or in its ordinary or popular sense, the word may be defined as meaning: a fortuitous circumstance, event, or happening; an event happening without any human agency, or if happening wholly or partly through human agency, an event which under the circumstances is unusual and unexpected by the person to whom it happens; an unusual, fortuitous, unexpected, unforeseen or unlooked for event, happening or occurrence; an unusual or unexpected result attending the operation or performance of a usual or necessary act or event; chance or contingency; fortune; mishap; some sudden and unexpected event taking place without expectation, upon the instant, rather than something which continues, progresses or develops; something happening by chance; something unforeseen, unexpected, unusual, extraordinary or phenomenal, taking place not according to the usual course of things or events, out of the range of ordinary calculations; that which exists or occurs abnormally, or an uncommon occurrence. The word may be employed as denoting a calamity, casualty, catastrophe, disaster, an undesirable or unfortunate happening; any unexpected personal injury resulting from any unlooked for mishap or occurrence; any unpleasant or unfortunate occurrence, that causes injury, loss, suffering or death; some untoward occurrence aside from the usual course of events. An event that takes place without one's foresight or expectation; an undesigned, sudden, and unexpected event. Kochring Co. v. American Auto. Ins. Co., C.A.Wis., 353 F.2d 993, 996. See also **Act of God; Casualty; Inevitable accident.**

Automobiles. The word "accident" as used in automobile liability policy requiring notice of any "accident" to be given to the insurer as a condition precedent to liability means an untoward and unforeseen occurrence in the operation of the automobile which results in injury to the person or property of another. Ohio Casualty Ins. Co. v. Marr, C.C.A.Okl., 98 F.2d 973, 975. The word "accident", requiring operator of vehicle to stop immediately in case of accident, contemplates any situation occurring on the highway wherein he so operates his automobile as to cause injury to the property or person of another using the same highway. See also **Hit and run accident.**

Insurance contract. An accident within accident insurance policies is an event happening without any human agency, or, if happening through such agency, an event which, under circumstances, is unusual and not expected by the person to whom it happens. A more comprehensive term than "negligence," and in its common signification the word means an unexpected happening without intention or design.

Maritime law. "Accidents of navigation" or "accidents of the sea" are such as are peculiar to the sea or to usual navigation or the action of the elements, which do not happen by the intervention of man, and are not to be avoided by the exercise of proper prudence, foresight, and skill. The G. R. Booth, 171 U.S. 450, 19 S.Ct. 9, 43 L.Ed. 234. See also **Perils of the sea.**

Unavoidable accident. One which is not occasioned in any degree, either directly or remotely, by the want of such care and prudence as the law holds every man bound to exercise. Vincent v. Johnson, Tex.Civ. App., 117 S.W.2d 135. One which could not have been prevented by exercise of due care by both parties under circumstances prevailing. Woodiwiss v. Rise, 3 Wash.App. 5, 471 P.2d 124, 126. One which occurs while all persons concerned are exercising ordinary care, which is not caused by fault of any of persons and which could not have been prevented by any means suggested by common prudence. Cavanaugh v. Jepson, Iowa, 167 N.W.2d 616, 623. See also Restatement, Second, Torts § 8.

Workers' compensation acts. A befalling; an event that takes place without one's foresight or expectation; an undesigned, sudden, and unexpected event; chance; contingency; often, an undesigned and unforeseen occurrence of an afflictive or unfortunate character; casualty; mishap; as, to die by an accident. Its synonyms are chance, contingency, mishap, mischance, misfortune, disaster, calamity, catastrophe.

Accidental. Happening by chance, or unexpectedly; taking place not according to usual course of things; casual; fortuitous. Norris v. New York Life Ins. Co., C.C.A.Md., 49 F.2d 62, 63; Murphy v. Travelers Ins. Co., 141 Neb. 41, 2 N.W.2d 576, 578, 579. See also **Accident.**

Accidental cause. That which produces result which is not foreseen; producing an unexpected effect. Fernandez v. Flint Bd. of Ed., C.A.Mich., 283 F.2d 906, 908.

Accidental death. One caused by unexpected or unintended means. Sanders v. Metropolitan Life Ins. Co., 104 Utah 75, 138 P.2d 239.

Accidental death benefit. Provision in insurance policy encompassing death caused by sudden, unexpected, external force. Maneval v. Lutheran Bros., Del.Super., 281 A.2d 502, 506.

Accidental killing. One resulting from an act which is lawful and lawfully done under a reasonable belief that no harm is possible; distinguished from "involuntary manslaughter," which is the result of an unlawful act, or of a lawful act done in an unlawful way.

Accidental vein. See **Vein.**

Accident proneness. Tendency towards being involved in or contributing to accidents.

Accidere /æksídəriy/. Lat. To fall; fall in; come to hand; happen. Judgment is sometimes given against an executor or administrator to be satisfied out of assets *quando acciderint; i.e.,* when they shall come to hand.

Accion /àksiyówn/. In Spanish law, a right of action; also the method of judicial procedure for the recovery of property or a debt.

Accipere quid ut justitiam facias, non est tam accipere quam extorquere /æksípərə kwíd àt jàstíshiyəm féyshiyəs, nòn est tǽm æksípərə kwǽm ekstórkwəriy/. To accept anything as a reward for doing justice is rather extorting than accepting.

Accipitare /æksìpətériy/. To pay relief to lords of manors. *Capitali domino accipitare, i.e.,* to pay a relief, homage, or obedience to the chief lord on becoming his vassal.

Accola /ǽkələ/. *Civil law.* One who inhabits or occupies land near a place, as one who dwells by a river, or on the bank of a river.

Feudal law. A husbandman; an agricultural tenant; a tenant of a manor. A name given to a class of villeins in Italy.

Accomenda /ǽkəméndə/. In maritime law, a contract between the owner of goods and the master of a ship, by which the former intrusts the property to the latter to be sold by him on their joint account. In such case, two contracts take place: First, the contract called *mandatum*, by which the owner of the property gives the master power to dispose of it; and the contract of partnership, in virtue of which the profits are to be divided between them. One party runs the risk of losing his capital; the other, his labor. If the sale produces no more than first cost, the owner takes all the proceeds. It is only the profits which are to be divided.

Accommodated party. One to whom the credit of the accommodation party is loaned, and is not necessarily the payee, since the inquiry always is as to whom did the maker of the paper loan his credit as a matter of fact; not third person who may receive advantage. See also **Accommodation party.**

Accommodation /əkòmədéyshən/. An arrangement or engagement made as a favor to another, not upon a consideration received. Something done to oblige, usually spoken of a loan of money or commercial paper; also a friendly agreement or composition of differences. The word implies no consideration. While a party's intent may be to aid a maker of note by lending his credit, if he seeks to accomplish thereby legitimate objects of his own, and not simply to aid maker, the act is not for accommodation.

Accommodation bill or **note.** See **Accommodation paper.**

Accommodation indorsement. See **Indorsement.**

Accommodation indorser. A party who places his name to a note without consideration for purpose of benefiting or accommodating some other party. U.C.C. § 3–415.

Accommodation lands. Land bought by a builder or speculator, who erects houses thereon, and then leases portions thereof upon an improved ground-rent.

Accommodation line. Insurance policies accepted by insurer because agent or brokers account in general is satisfactory, even though specific policy would otherwise likely not be acceptable.

Accommodation loan. Loan furnished as an act of friendship or assistance without tangible consideration; money or credit extended for such reasons.

Accommodation maker. One who puts his name to a note without any consideration with the intention of lending his credit to the accommodated party. In re Chamberlain's Estate, Cal.App., 109 P.2d 449, 454. U.C.C. § 3–415. See also **Accommodation party**.

Accommodation note. One to which accommodating party has put his name, without consideration, to accommodate some other party, who is to issue it and is expected to pay it. U.C.C. § 3–415.

Accommodation paper. An accommodation bill or note is one to which the accommodating party, be he acceptor, drawer, or indorser, has put his name, without consideration, for the purpose of benefiting or accommodating some other party who desires to raise money on it, and is to provide for the bill when due. Hickox v. Hickox, Tex.Civ.App., 151 S.W.2d 913, 917. Such must be executed for the purpose of loaning credit, and incidental benefit to party is insufficient. Morrison v. Painter, Mo.App., 170 S.W.2d 965, 970.

Accommodation party. One who signs commercial paper in any capacity for purpose of lending his name to another party to instrument. U.C.C. § 3–415. Such party is a surety.

Accommodation road. A road opened for benefit of certain individuals to go from and to their homes, for service of their lands, and for use of some estates exclusively. See also **Easement**.

Accommodatum /əkòmədéydəm/. The same as **Commodatum** *(q.v.)*.

Accompany. To go along with. To go with or attend as a companion or associate; to occur in association with. United States v. Lee, C.C.A.Wis., 131 F.2d 464, 466. The word has been defined judicially in cases involving varied facts; thus, an automobile driver under sixteen is not accompanied by an adult person unless the latter exercises supervision over the driver; an unlicensed driver is not accompanied by a licensed driver unless the latter is near enough to render advice and assistance.

Accomplice /əkómpləs/. One who knowingly, voluntarily and with common intent unites with the principal offender in the commission of a crime. Smith v. State, Tenn.Cr.App., 525 S.W.2d 674, 676; Model Penal Code, § 2.06(3). One who is in some way concerned or associated in commission of crime; partaker of guilt; one who aids or assists, or is an accessory. McLendon v. U. S., C.C.A.Mo., 19 F.2d 465, 466. Equally concerned in the commission of crime. Fryman v. Commonwealth, 289 Ky. 540, 159 S.W.2d 426, 429. An "accomplice" is one who is guilty of complicity in crime charged, either by being present and aiding and abetting in it, or having advised and encouraged it, though absent from place when it was committed, though mere presence, acquiescence, or silence, in the absence of a duty to act, is not enough, no matter how reprehensible it may be, to constitute one an accomplice. One is liable as an accomplice to the crime of another if he gave assistance or encouragement or failed to perform a legal duty to prevent it with the intent thereby to promote or facilitate commission of the crime. See also **Abet; Aid and abet; Accessory**.

Accomplice liability. Criminal responsibility of one who acts with another before, during or after the perpetration of a crime. Model Penal Code, § 2.06.

Accomplice witness. A person who either as principal, accomplice, or accessory, was connected with crime by unlawful act or omission on his part, transpiring either before, at time of, or after commission of offense, and whether or not he was present and participated in crime. Johnson v. State, Tex.Cr.App., 502 S.W.2d 761, 763.

Accord, *n.* A satisfaction agreed upon between the party injuring and the party injured which, when performed, is a bar to all actions upon this account. An accord being a contract, the requirements of mutual assent and consideration must be met. Buob v. Feenaughty Machinery Co., 191 Wash. 477, 71 P.2d 559, 564. An agreement to accept, in extinction of an obligation, something different from or less than that to which the person agreeing to accept is entitled. Whepley Oil Co. v. Associated Oil Co., 6 Cal.App.2d 94, 44 P.2d 670, 677. It may arise both where the demand itself is unliquidated or in dispute, and where the amount and nature of the demand is undisputed, and it is agreed to give and take less than the demand. See **Accord and satisfaction; Compromise and settlement; Executory accord**.

Accord, *v.* In practice, to agree or concur, as one judge with another. In agreement with.

Accordance. Agreement; harmony; concord; conformity. City and County of San Francisco v. Boyd, 22 Cal.2d 685, 140 P.2d 666, 668.

Accord and satisfaction. A method of discharging a claim whereby the parties agree to give and accept something in settlement of the claim and perform the agreement, the "accord" being the agreement and the "satisfaction" its execution or performance, and it is a new contract substituted for an old contract which is thereby discharged, or for an obligation or cause of action which is settled, and must have all of the elements of a valid contract. Holm v. Hansen, Iowa, 248 N.W.2d 503, 506. An executory bilateral contract of "accord" is an agreement embodying a promise, express or implied, to accept at some future time a stipulated performance in satisfaction or discharge in whole or in part of any present claim, cause of action or obligation, and a promise express or implied to render such performance. An "accord and satisfaction arises" where parties, by a subsequent agreement, have satisfied the former one, and the latter agreement has been executed. The execution of a new agreement may itself amount to a satisfaction, where it is so expressly agreed by the parties; and without such agreement, if the new promise is founded on a new consideration, in which case the taking of the new consideration amounts to the satisfaction of the former contract.

In some jurisdictions, novation is a species of accord and satisfaction.

See **Composition; Compromise and settlement; Novation; Settlement.**

Affirmative defense. A defense which must be pleaded affirmatively in the defendant's answer. Fed.R. Civ.P. 8(c).

Accordant /əkórdənt/. Fr. and Eng. Agreeing; concurring.

Accord executory. A bilateral agreement of settlement which has not yet been performed (satisfied). Restatement of Contracts, § 417.

Accouchement /akùwshmón/. The act of a woman in giving birth to a child. The fact of the accouchement, which may be proved by the direct testimony of one who was present, as a physician or midwife, is often important evidence in proving parentage.

Account. A detailed statement of the mutual demands in the nature of debit and credit between parties, arising out of contracts or some fiduciary relation. A statement in writing, of debts and credits, or of receipts and payments; a list of items of debts and credits, with their respective dates. A statement of pecuniary transactions; a record or course of business dealings between parties; a list or statement of monetary transactions, such as payments, losses, sales, debits, credits, etc., in most cases showing a balance or result of comparison between items of an opposite nature.

Any account with a bank; including a checking, time, interest or savings account. U.C.C. § 4–194.

Account means any right to payment for goods sold or leased or for services rendered which is not evidenced by an instrument or chattel paper, whether or not it has been earned by performance. This covers the ordinary account receivable. Rights arising under a ship charter are also accounts. See U.C.C. § 9–106.

See also Aging of accounts; Blocked account; Charge account; Common account; Community account; Custody account; Contra accounts; Escrow account; Impond account; Intermediate account; Liquidated account; Ledger; Long account; Margin account; Nominal account; Stated account; Statement of account. For Open account, see **Open.**

Account annexed. Form of simplified statement used in pleading a common count (*e.g.* money had and received) impliedly authorized for use under Fed.R. Civil P. 8(a)(2).

Account balance. Difference between debit and credit sides of an account.

Account debtor. Person who is obligated on an account, chattel paper or general intangible. U.C.C. § 9–105(1)(a).

Account payable. A debt, owed by an enterprise, that arises in the normal course of business dealings and has not been replaced by a note payable of a debtor. For example, bills for materials received but not yet paid. Contract obligations owing by a person

on open account. State Tax Commission v. Shattuck, 44 Ariz. 379, 38 P.2d 631, 639. A liability representing an amount owed to a creditor, usually arising from purchase of merchandise or materials and supplies; not necessarily due or past due.

Account receivable. A debt, owed to an enterprise, that arises in the normal course of business dealings and is not supported by negotiable paper. For example, the charge accounts of a department store. But income due from investments (unless investments are the business itself) is not usually shown in accounts receivable. A claim against a debtor usually arising from sales or services rendered; not necessarily due or past due. For accounts receivable insurance, see **Insurance.**

Account rendered. An account made out by the creditor, and presented to the debtor for his examination and acceptance. When accepted, it becomes an account stated.

Account settled. One in which the balance has been in fact paid, thereby differing from an account stated.

Account stated. An "account stated" arises where there have been transactions between debtor and creditor resulting in the creation of matured debts and the parties by agreement compute a balance which the debtor promises to pay and the creditor promises to accept in full payment for the items of account.

Adjunct account. An account that accumulates additions to another account.

Bank account. See **Bank.**

Book account. See **Book.**

Closed account. An account to which no further additions can be made on either side, but which remains still open for adjustment and set-off, which distinguishes it from an account stated.

Contra account. An account, such as accumulated depreciation, that accumulates subtractions from another account, such as machinery. Contrast with *adjunct account*, supra.

Current account. An open or running or unsettled account between two parties; the antithesis of an account stated.

Mutual accounts. Accounts comprising mutual credits between the parties; or an existing credit on one side which constitutes a ground for credit on the other, or where there is an understanding that mutual debts shall be a satisfaction or set-off *pro tanto* between the parties.

Open account. An account which has not been finally settled or closed, but is still running or open to future adjustment or liquidation. Open account, in legal as well as in ordinary language, means an indebtedness subject to future adjustment, and which may be reduced or modified by proof.

Account, or **account render.** "Account," sometimes called "account render," was a form of action at common law against a person who by reason of some fiduciary relation (as guardian, bailiff, receiver, etc.) was bound to render an account to another, but refused to do so. Peoples Finance & Thrift Co. of Visalia v. Bowman, 58 Cal.App.2d 729, 137 P.2d 729, 731.

Accountability. State of being responsible or answerable. See also **Liability.**

Accountable. Subject to pay; responsible; liable.

Accountable receipt. An instrument acknowledging the receipt of money or personal property, coupled with an obligation.

Accountant. Person skilled in keeping books or accounts; in designing and controlling systems of account; in giving tax advice and preparing tax returns.

"Accountant" means accountant authorized under applicable law to practice public accounting, and includes professional accounting association, corporation, or partnership, if so authorized. Bankruptcy Act, § 101(1).

Certified Public Accountant (CPA). An accountant who has satisfied the statutory and administrative requirements of his or her jurisdiction to be registered or licensed as a public accountant. In addition to passing the Uniform CPA Examination administered by the AICPA, the CPA must meet certain business experience, educational and moral requirements that differ from jurisdiction to jurisdiction.

Accountant privilege. Protection afforded to client from disclosure by accountant of materials submitted to or prepared by accountant.

Accountants, chartered. Persons skilled in the keeping and examination of accounts, who are employed for the purpose of examining and certifying to the correctness of accounts of corporations and others. British Commonwealth equivalent of Certified Public Accountant.

Accountant's lien. Possessory right of accountant to papers prepared by him and held until payment is made for his services.

Account book. A book kept by a merchant, trader, mechanic, or other person, in which are entered from time to time the transactions of his trade or business. Entries made therein are admissible in evidence as exception to hearsay rule under certain conditions. Fed.Evid.R. 803.

Account computatio. The primary idea of "account computatio", whether in proceedings of courts of law or equity, is some matter of debt and credit, or demand in nature thereof. Coleman v. Kansas City, 351 Mo. 254, 173 S.W.2d 572, 576.

Account for. To pay over the money to the person entitled thereto. U. S. v. Rehwald, D.C.Cal., 44 F.2d 663.

Accounting. An act or system of making up or settling accounts; a statement of account, or a debit and credit in financial transactions. Kansas City v. Burns, 137 Kan. 905, 22 P.2d 444. Rendition of an account, either voluntarily or by order of a court. In the latter case, it imports a rendition of a judgment for the balance ascertained to be due. The term may include payment of the amount due.

The methods under which income and expenses are determined for tax purposes. Major accounting methods are the cash basis and the accrual basis.

Special methods are available for the reporting of gain on installment sales, recognition of income on construction projects (*i.e.*, the completed-contract and percentage-of-completion methods), and the valuation of inventories (*i.e.* last-in first-out and first-in first-out). The various types of accounting methods appear below:

Accrual method. A method of keeping accounts which shows expenses incurred and income earned for a given period, although such expenses and income may not have been actually paid or received. Right to receive and not the actual receipt determines inclusion of amount in gross income. When right to receive an amount becomes fixed, right accrues. H. Liebes & Co. v. Commissioner of Internal Revenue, C.C.A.9, 90 F.2d 932, 937. Obligations payable to or by taxpayer are treated as if discharged when incurred. H. Liebes & Co. v. Commissioner of Internal Revenue, C.C.A.9, 90 F.2d 932, 936. Entries are made of credits and debits when liability arises, whether received or disbursed. Insurance Finance Corporation v. Commissioner of Internal Revenue, C.C.A.3, 84 F.2d 382. See also **Accrual basis; Accrue** (*Taxation*).

Cash method. The practice of recording income and expense only when received or paid out; used in contradistinction to accrual method. See **Cash basis accounting.**

Completed contract method. A method of reporting gain or loss on certain long-term contracts. Under this method of accounting, gross income and expenses are recognized in the tax year in which the contract is completed.

Cost method. The practice of recording the value of assets in terms of their cost.

Fair value method. Refers to present value as used in valuation of assets; means same as actual value, market value. Kerr v. Klinchfield Coal Corp., 169 Va. 149, 192 S.E. 741, 744.

Flow through method. Type of calculation of depreciation used by regulated utilities for income tax purposes. Federal Power Commission v. Memphis Light, Gas, & Water Division, 411 U.S. 458, 93 S.Ct. 1723, 36 L.Ed.2d 426.

Installment method. Procedure applied in reflecting collection of sales price in installments.

Price level accounting. Modern method of valuing assets in a financial statement which requires use of gross national product to reflect current values. See also **Change of accounting method.**

See also Generally accepted accounting principles; Installment method; Interim statements; Percentage of completion method; Purchase method of accounting; T-Account; Trial balance.

Accounting for profits. Action for equitable relief against one in a fiduciary relation to recover profits taken in breach of relation.

Accounting period. The period of time, usually a year, used by a taxpayer for the determination of tax liability. Unless a fiscal year is chosen, taxpayers must determine and pay their income tax liability by using the calendar year (*i.e.*, January 1 through December 31) as the period of measurement. An example of a fiscal year is July 1 through June 30. A change in accounting periods (*e.g.*, from a calendar year to a fiscal year) generally requires the consent of the Internal Revenue Service. New taxpayers, such as a newly formed corporation or an estate created upon the death of an individual taxpayer, are free to select either a calendar or a fiscal year without the consent of the Internal Revenue Service. See **Annual accounting period.**

Account in trust. Account established by an individual to be held in trust for the benefit of another.

Account payable. See **Account.**

Account receivable. See **Account.**

Account stated. See **Account.**

Accouple. To unite; to marry. *Ne unques accouple*, never married.

Accredit /əkrédət/. To give official authorization or status. To recognize as having sufficient academic standards to qualify graduates for higher education or for professional practice. In international law: (1) To acknowledge; to receive as an envoy in his public character, and give him credit and rank accordingly. (2) To send with credentials as an envoy. This latter use is now the accepted one.

Accredited law school. Law school which has been approved by the state and the Association of American Law Schools and/or the American Bar Association. In certain states (*e.g.* Calif.) a law school might be accredited by the state, but not by either the AALS or ABA. In most states only graduates of AALS or ABA accredited law schools are permitted to take the state bar exam.

Accredited representative. As respects service of process, representative having general authority to act.

Accredulitare /əkrèdyələtériy/. Lat. To purge an offense by oath.

Accretion /əkríyshən/. The act of growing to a thing; usually applied to the gradual and imperceptible accumulation of land by natural causes, as out of the sea or a river.

Civil law. The right of heirs or legatees to unite or aggregate with their shares or portions of the estate the portion of any co-heir or legatee who refuses to accept it, fails to comply with a condition, becomes incapacitated to inherit, or dies before, the testator.

Land. Addition of portions of soil, by gradual deposition through the operation of natural causes, to that already in possession of owner. Willett v. Miller, 176 Okl. 278, 55 P.2d 90, 92. Accretion of land is of two kinds: By *alluvion*, *i.e.*, by the washing up of sand or soil, so as to form firm ground; or by *dereliction*, as when the sea shrinks below the usual water-mark. The term "alluvion" is applied to deposit itself, while "accretion" denotes the act. However, the terms are frequently used synonymously. Land uncovered by gradual subsidence of water is not an "accretion" but a "reliction".

Trust property. Receipts other than those ordinarily considered as income.

See **Accrue; Alluvion; Avulsion; Reliction.**

Accroach. To encroach; to exercise power without authority.

Accrocher /əkrowshéy/. Fr. To delay; retard; put off. *Accrocher un proces*, to stay the proceedings in a suit.

Accrual basis. A method of accounting that reflects expenses incurred and income earned for any one tax year. In contrast to the cash basis of accounting, expenses do not have to be paid to be deductible nor does income have to be received to be taxable. Unearned income (*e. g.*, prepaid interest and rent) generally is taxed in the year of receipt regardless of the method of accounting used by the taxpayer. See **Accounting.**

Accrual, clause of. See **Accruer, clause of.**

Accrual method of accounting. See **Accounting.**

Accrue /əkrúw/. Derived from the Latin, "ad" and "creso," to grow to. In past tense, in sense of due and payable; vested. It means to increase; to augment; to come to by way of increase; to be added as an increase, profit, or damage. Acquired; falling due; made or executed; matured; occurred; received; vested; was created; was incurred. H. Liebes & Co. v. Commissioner of Internal Revenue, C.C.A.9, 90 F.2d 932, 936. To attach itself to, as a subordinate or accessory claim or demand arises out of, and is joined to, its principal. Lifson v. Commissioner of Internal Revenue, C.C.A.8, 98 F.2d 508.

The term is also used of independent or original demands, meaning to arise, to happen, to come into force or existence; to vest; as in the phrase, "The right of action did not *accrue* within six years." Amy v. Dubuque, 98 U.S. 470, 476, 25 L.Ed. 228. To become a present right or demand; to come to pass. H. Liebes & Co. v. Commissioner of Internal Revenue, C.C.A.9, 90 F.2d 932, 936. See also **Vested.**

Cause of action. A cause of action "accrues" when a suit may be maintained thereon. Dillon v. Board of Pension Com'rs of City of Los Angeles, 18 Cal.2d 427, 116 P.2d 37, 39. Cause of action "accrues," on date that damage is sustained and not date when causes are set in motion which ultimately produce injury. City of Philadelphia v. Lieberman, C.C.A.Pa., 112 F.2d 424, 428. Date of injury. Fredericks v. Town of Dover, 125 N.J.L. 288, 15 A.2d 784, 787. When actual damage has resulted. National Lead Co. v. City of New York, C.C.A.N.Y., 43 F.2d 914, 916. As soon as contract is breached. Wichita Nat. Bank v. United States Fidelity & Guaranty Co., Tex.Civ.App., 147 S.W.2d 295, 297. An action for malpractice against an attorney does not accrue until the client knows or should know of the attorney's error. Hendrickson v. Sears, 365. Mass. 83, 310 N.E.2d 131. The point in time at which a cause of action "accrues" is important for purposes of running of statute of limitations.

Taxation. Income "accrues" to taxpayer when there arises to him a fixed or unconditional right to receive it. Franklin County Distilling Co. v. Commissioner of Internal Revenue, C.C.A.6, 125 F.2d 800, 804, 805. But not unless there is a reasonable expectancy that the right will be converted into money or its equivalent. Swastika Oil & Gas Co. v. Commissioner of Internal Revenue, C.C.A.6, 123 F.2d 382, 384. Where taxpayer makes returns on accrual basis, item "accrues" when all events occur which fix amount payable and determine liability of taxpayer. Hudson Motor Car Co. v. U. S., Ct.Cl., 3 F.Supp. 834, 847. Tax "accrues" for deduction when all events have occurred which fix amount of tax and determine liability of taxpayer for it, although there has not yet been assessment or maturity. Elmhirst v. Duggan, D.C.N.Y., 14 F.Supp. 782, 784.

Accrued alimony. Alimony which is due but not yet paid.

Accrued compensation. Awarded compensation, due and payable, but not yet paid.

Accrued depreciation. Amount reserved each year in the accounting system for replacement of asset. Portion of useful service life which has expired. State ex rel. City of St. Louis v. Public Service Commission, 341 Mo. 920, 110 S.W.2d 749, 768. A loss which is not restored by current maintenance, and which is due to all factors involved causing ultimate retirement of the property, including wear, tear, decay, and inadequacy. Iowa-Illinois Gas & Elec. Co. v. Iowa City, 255 Iowa 1341, 124 N.W.2d 840, 845.

Accrued dividend. A share of net earnings declared but not yet paid as a dividend.

Accrued expense. Expense incurred but not yet paid.

Accrued income. Income which is earned but not yet due and payable. In re Schlinger's Will, 48 Misc.2d 345, 438, 265 N.Y.S.2d 32, 35.

Accrued interest. Interest that has been earned but is not yet paid or payable.

Accrued liability. An obligation or debt which is properly chargeable in a given accounting period but which is not yet payable.

Accrued right. A matured cause of action, as legal authority to demand redress.

Accrued salary. Compensation to employee which is chargeable to employer but not yet payable.

Accrued taxes. Taxes which are properly chargeable in a given accounting period but not yet payable.

Accruer (or accrual), clause of. An express clause, frequently occurring in the case of gifts by deed or will to persons as tenants in common, providing that upon the death of one or more of the beneficiaries his or their shares shall go to the survivor or survivors. The share of the decedent is then said to *accrue* to the others.

Accruing /əkrúwiŋ/. Inchoate; in process of maturing. That which will or may, at a future time, ripen into a vested right, an available demand, or an existing cause of action. Arising by way of increase or augmentation. Globe Indemnity Co. v. Bruce, C.C.A. Okl., 81 F.2d 143, 153.

Accounting. Allocation of income and expense, which has been earned or incurred but not yet collected or paid out, to the accounting period in which the income is earned or expense incurred.

Accruing costs. Costs and expenses incurred after judgment.

Accruing interest. Running or accumulating interest, as distinguished from accrued or matured interest. Interest daily accumulating on the principal debt but not yet due and payable.

Accruing right. One that is increasing, enlarging, or augmenting.

Acct. Abbreviation for "account", of such universal and immemorial use that the courts will take judicial notice of its meaning.

Accumulated dividend. Dividend due shareholder which has not been paid. See **Accumulative dividends; Dividend** (*Cumulative*).

Accumulated earnings credit. A deduction allowed in arriving at accumulated taxable income for purposes of determining the accumulated earnings tax. See **Accumulated earnings tax; Accumulated taxable income**.

Accumulated earnings tax. A special tax imposed on corporations that accumulate (rather than distribute via dividends) their earnings beyond the reasonable needs of the business. The accumulated earnings tax is imposed on accumulated taxable income in addition to the corporate income tax. See also **Excess profits tax**.

Accumulated legacy. Portion of distributable estate not yet paid to legatees or donees.

Accumulated profits. Earned surplus or undivided profits. Flint v. Commissioner of Corporations and Taxation, 312 Mass. 204, 43 N.E.2d 789, 791, 792. Such include profits earned and invested. Commissioner of Corporations and Taxation v. Filoon, 310 Mass. 374, 38 N.E.2d 693, 698, 700.

Accumulated surplus. In statutes relative to the taxation of corporations, this term refers to the fund which the company has in excess of its capital and liabilities.

Accumulated taxable income. The income upon which the accumulated earnings tax is imposed. Basically, it is the taxable income of the corporation as adjusted for certain items (*e.g.*, the Federal income tax, excess charitable contributions, the 85% dividends received deduction) less the dividends paid deduction and the accumulated earnings credit.

Accumulations /əkyùmyəléyshənz/. Increase by continuous or repeated additions, or, if taken literally, means either profit accruing on sale of principal assets, or increase derived from their investment, or both. Adding of interest or income of a fund to principal pursuant to provisions of a will or deed, preventing its being expended. When an executor or other trustee masses the rents, dividends, and other income which he receives, treats it as a capital, invests it, makes a new capital of the income derived therefrom, invests that, and so on, he is said to accumulate the fund, and the capital and accrued income thus procured constitute *accumulations*.

Accumulations, rule against. A rule rendering an accumulation of income beyond the period of perpetuities void.

Accumulation trust. A trust in which the trustee is directed to accumulate income for a period of time before distribution.

Accumulative. That which accumulates, or is heaped up; additional. Said of several things heaped together, or of one thing added to another.

Accumulative dividends. Same as cumulative dividends; characteristic of preferred stockholders' agreement by which they receive their agreed dividends before common stockholders. Dividends which accumulate from year to year when not paid. See **Dividend** (*Cumulative*).

Accumulative judgment. Where a person has already been convicted and sentenced, and a second or additional judgment is passed against him, the execution of which is postponed until the completion of the first sentence, such second judgment is said to be *accumulative*. See also **Accumulative sentence.**

Accumulative legacy. A second, double or additional legacy; a legacy given in addition to another given by the same instrument, or by another instrument. See also **Legacy.**

Accumulative sentence. A sentence, additional to others, imposed on a defendant who has been convicted upon an indictment containing several counts, each of such counts charging a distinct offense, or who is under conviction at the same time for several distinct offenses; one of such sentences to begin at the expiration of another. Consecutive sentences. See **Sentence.**

Accusation /æ̀kyəzéyshən/. A formal charge against a person, to the effect that he is guilty of a punishable offense, laid before a court or magistrate having jurisdiction to inquire into the alleged crime. See **Accuse; Indictment; Information.**

Accusatory body. Body such as grand jury whose duty is to hear evidence to determine whether a person should be accused (charged) of a crime; to be distinguished from a traverse or petit jury which is charged with duty of determining guilt or innocence.

Accusatory instrument. A document in which an accusation of crime is set forth like an indictment, information or complaint.

Accusatory part. The "accusatory part" of an indictment is that part where the offense is named.

Accusatory pleading. An indictment or complaint in which a person is accused of crime and on which the government tries such person. Fed.R.Crim.P. 3.

Accusatory procedure. System of American jurisprudence in which the government accuses and bears the burden of proving the guilt of a person for a crime; to be distinguished from inquisitorial system. Rogers v. Richmond, 365 U.S. 534, 81 S.Ct. 735, 5 L.Ed.2d 760.

Accuse. To bring a formal charge against a person, to the effect that he is guilty of a crime or punishable offense, before a court or magistrate having jurisdiction to inquire into the alleged crime. See also **Indictment; Information.**

Accused. The generic name for the defendant in a criminal case. Person becomes "accused" within meaning of guarantee of speedy trial only at point at which either formal indictment or information has been returned against him, or when he becomes subject to actual restraints on his liberty imposed by arrest, whichever first occurs. State v. Almeida, 54 Haw. 443, 509 P.2d 549, 551.

Accuser. The person by whom an accusation is made.

Accustomed. Habitual; often used; synonymous with usual or customary.

A ce. For this purpose.

A cel jour /ə sél zhúr/. At this day.

Acequia /əsíykwiyə/. A ditch, channel, or canal, through which water, diverted from its natural course, is conducted, for use in irrigation or other purposes; public ditches.

Ac etiam /æ̀k éshiyəm/. (Lat. And also.) The introduction of the statement of the real cause of action, used formerly in those cases where it was necessary to allege a fictitious cause of action to give the court jurisdiction, and also the real cause in compliance with the statutes. It is sometimes written *acetiam*. See Bill of Middlesex under Bill, definition 2.

Achieve subject matter. The English equivalent for patentability. Mesta Mach. Co. v. Federal Machine & Welder Co., C.C.A.Pa., 110 F.2d 479, 480.

Acid test. Method of financial analysis; ratio of cash and receivables to current liabilities. Sum of cash, marketable securities, and receivables divided by current liabilities. Also called the "quick ratio."

Acknowledge. To own, avow, or admit; to confess; to recognize one's acts, and assume the responsibility therefor.

Acknowledgment. To "acknowledge" is to admit, affirm, declare, testify, avow, confess, or own as genuine. Favello v. Bank of America Nat. Trust & Savings Ass'n, 24 Cal.App.2d 342, 74 P.2d 1057, 1058. Implying obligation or incurring responsibility. Weyerhaeuser Timber Co. v. Marshall, C.C.A.Wash., 102 F.2d 78, 81. Most states have adopted the Uniform Acknowledgment Act. See also **Receipt.**

Debt. Part payment of obligation which tolls statute of limitations is a form of "acknowledgment of debt". In re Badger's Estate, 156 Kan. 734, 137 P.2d 198, 205.

Instruments. Formal declaration before authorized official, by person who executed instrument, that it is his free act and deed. The certificate of the officer on such instrument that it has been so acknowledged. See also **Attestation clause; Jurat; Notary public; Verification.**

Paternity. An avowal or admission that the child is one's own. Recognition of a parental relation, either by a written agreement, verbal declarations or statements, by the life, acts, and conduct of the parties, or any other satisfactory evidence that the relation was recognized and admitted.

A.C.L.U. American Civil Liberties Union.

A cœlo usque ad centrum /èy síylow ə́skwiy æd séntrəm/. From the heavens to the center of the earth. Or more fully, *Cujus est solum ejus est usque ad cœlum et ad inferos.* The owner of the soil owns to the heavens and also to the lowest depths. Or, *Cujus est solum est usque ad cœlum,*—the owner of the soil owns to the heavens. This doctrine has, however, been abrogated; the flight of airplanes and oil and gas regulations have qualified the owner's dominion not only in the heavens but in the lowest depths. See **Air rights.**

A communi observantia non est recedendum /èy kəmyúwnay obzərvǽnsh(iy)ə nón est rìysədéndəm/. From common observance there should be no departure; there must be no departure from common usage. A maxim formerly applied to the practice of the courts, to the ancient and established forms of pleading and conveyancing, and to professional usage generally. Lord Coke applies it to common professional opinion.

A confectione /éy kənfèkshiyówniy/. From the making.

A confectione præsentium /éy kənfèkshiyówniy prəzénsh(iy)əm/. From the making of the indentures.

A consiliis /éy kənsíliyəs/. (Lat. *consilium,* advice.) Of counsel; a counsellor. The term is used in the civil law by some writers instead of *a responsis.*

A contrario sensu /èy kəntrériyow sénsyuw/. On the other hand; in the opposite sense.

Acquainted. Having personal, familiar, knowledge of a person, event, or thing. "Acquaintance" expresses less than familiarity; familiarity less than intimacy. Acquaintance springs from occasional intercourse, familiarity from daily intercourse, intimacy from unreserved intercourse. Atkins Corporation v. Tourny, 6 Cal.2d 206, 57 P.2d 480, 483. To be "personally acquainted with," and to "know personally," are equivalent terms; Kelly v. Calhoun, 95 U.S. 710, 24 L.Ed. 544. When used with reference to a paper to which a certificate or affidavit is attached, it indicates a substantial knowledge of the subject-matter thereof.

Acquereur /ǽkərár/. In French and Canadian law, one who acquires title, particularly to immovable property, by purchase.

Acquest /əkwést/. An estate acquired newly, or by purchase.

Acquêts /àkéy/. In the civil law, property which has been acquired by purchase, gift, or otherwise than by succession. Immovable property which has been acquired otherwise than by succession. Profits or gains of property, as between husband and wife. Civil Code La. art. 2402. The profits of all the effects of which the husband has the administration and enjoyment, either of right or in fact, of the produce of the joint industry of both husband and wife, and of the estates which they may acquire during the marriage, either by donations made jointly to them both, or by purchase, or in any other similar way, even though the purchase be only in the name of one of the two, and not of both. See **Community; Conquêts.**

Acquiesce /ǽkwiyés/. To give an implied consent to a transaction, to the accrual of a right, or to any act, by one's mere silence, or without express assent or acknowledgment.

Acquiescence /ǽkwiyésəns/. Conduct recognizing the existence of a transaction, and intended, in some extent at least, to carry the transaction, or permit it to be carried, into effect. It is some act, not deliberately intended to ratify a former transaction known to be voidable, but recognizing the transaction as existing, and intended, in some extent at least, to carry it into effect, and to obtain or claim the benefits resulting from it, and thus differs from "confirmation," which implies a deliberate act, intended to renew and ratify a transaction known to be voidable. De Boe v. Prentice Packing & Storage Co., 172 Wash. 514, 20 P.2d 1107, 1110. Passive compliance or satisfaction; distinguished from avowed consent on the one hand, and, on the other, from opposition or open discontent. Paul v. Western Distributing Co., 142 Kan. 816, 52 P.2d 379, 387. Acquiescence from which assent may be reasonably inferred. Frank v. Wilson & Co., 24 Del.Ch. 237, 9 A.2d 82, 86. Equivalent to assent inferred from silence with knowledge or from encouragement and presupposes knowledge and assent. Imports tacit consent, concurrence, acceptance or assent. Natural Soda Products Co. v. City of Los Angeles, Cal.App., 132 P.2d 553, 563. A silent appearance of consent. Failure to make any objections. Submission to an act of which one had knowledge.

It is to be distinguished from avowed consent, on the one hand, and from open discontent or opposition, on the other.

It arises where a person who knows that he is entitled to impeach a transaction or enforce a right neglects to do so for such a length of time that, under the circumstances of the case, the other party may fairly infer that he has waived or abandoned his right. A form of equitable estoppel. Schmitt v. Wright, 317 Ill.App. 384, 46 N.E.2d 184, 192.

Acquiescence and *laches* are cognate but not equivalent terms. The former is a submission to, or resting satisfied with, an existing state of things, while laches implies a neglect to do that which the party ought to do for his own benefit or protection. Hence laches may be evidence of acquiescence. Laches imports a merely passive assent, while acquiescence implies active assent. In re Wilbur's Estate, 334 Pa. 45, 5 A.2d 325, 331. "Acquiescence" relates to inaction during performance of an act while "laches" relates to delay after act is done.

See also **Admission; Confession; Estoppel; Ratification.**

Internal Revenue Service. In agreement with the result reached. The I.R.S. follows a policy of either acquiescing (*i.e.,* A, Acq.) or non-acquiescing (*i.e.,* NA, Non-Acq.) in the results reached in the regular decisions of the U.S. Tax Court.

Acquiescence, estoppel by. Acquiescence is a species of estoppel. An estoppel arises where party aware of his rights sees other party acting upon mistaken notion of his rights. Injury accruing from one's acquiescence in another's action to his prejudice creates "estoppel". Lebold v. Inland Steel Co., C.C.A.Ill., 125

F.2d 369, 375. Passive conduct on the part of one who has knowledge of the facts may be basis of estoppel. Winslow v. Burns, 47 N.M. 29, 132 P.2d 1048, 1050. It must appear that party to be estopped was bound in equity and good conscience to speak and that party claiming estoppel relied upon acquiescence and was misled thereby to change his position to his prejudice. Sherlock v. Greaves, 106 Mont. 206, 76 P.2d 87, 91. See also **Estoppel.**

Acquietandis plegiis /əkwàyətǽndəs plíyjiyəs/. A writ of justices, formerly lying for the surety against a creditor who refuses to acquit him after the debt has been satisfied.

Acquire. To gain by any means, usually by one's own exertions; to get as one's own; to obtain by search, endeavor, investment, practice, or purchase; receive or gain in whatever manner; come to have. In law of contracts and of descents, to become owner of property; to make property one's own. To gain ownership of. Commissioner of Insurance v. Broad Street Mut. Casualty Ins. Co., 312 Mass. 261, 44 N.E.2d 683, 684. The act of getting or obtaining something which may be already in existence, or may be brought into existence through means employed to acquire it. Ronnow v. City of Las Vegas, 57 Nev. 332, 65 P.2d 133, 140. Sometimes used in the sense of "procure." It does not necessarily mean that title has passed. Includes taking by devise. U. S. v. Merriam, 263 U.S. 179, 44 S.Ct. 69, 70, 68 L.Ed. 240. See also **Accession; Acquisition; Purchase.**

Acquired. To get, procure, secure, acquire. Jones v. State, 126 Tex.Cr.R. 469, 72 S.W.2d 260, 263.

Acquired rights. Those which one does not naturally enjoy, but which are owing to his or her own procurement, as sovereignty, or the right of commanding, or the right of property.

Acquired surplus. Surplus arising from changes of the capital structure of one or more businesses; *e.g.* from the purchase of one business by another business.

Acquisition /ǽkwəzíshən/. The act of becoming the owner of certain property; the act by which one acquires or procures the property in anything. State ex rel. Fisher v. Sherman, 135 Ohio St. 458, 21 N.E.2d 467, 470. Used also of the thing acquired. Taking with, or against, consent. Scribner v. Wikstrom, 93 N.H. 17, 34 A.2d 658, 660. Term refers especially to a material possession obtained by any means. Jones v. State, 126 Tex.Cr.R. 469, 72 S.W.2d 260, 263.

See **Accession; Acquire; Purchase; Tender offer.**

Derivative acquisitions are those which are procured from others. Goods and chattels may change owners by act of law in the cases of forfeiture, succession, marriage, judgment, insolvency, and intestacy, or by act of the parties, as by gift or sale.

Original acquisition is that by which a man secures a property in a thing which is not at the time he acquires it, and in its then existing condition, the property of any other individual. It may result from occupancy; accession; intellectual labor—namely, for inventions, which are secured by patent rights; and for the authorship of books, maps, and charts, which is protected by copyrights.

An acquisition may result from the act of the party himself, or those who are in his power acting for him, as his children while minors.

Acquisitive offenses. A generic term to describe all forms of larceny and offenses against the title or possession of property.

Acquit /əkwít/. To set free, release or discharge as from an obligation, burden or accusation. To absolve one from an obligation or a liability; or to legally certify the innocence of one charged with crime. See also **Acquittal.**

Acquitment. See **Absolution.**

Acquittal /əkwídəl/. *Contracts.* A release, absolution, or discharge from an obligation, liability, or engagement.

Criminal law. The legal and formal certification of the innocence of a person who has been charged with crime; a deliverance or setting free a person from a charge of guilt; finding of not guilty. Also, one legally acquitted by a judgment rendered otherwise than in pursuance of a verdict, as where he is discharged by a magistrate because of the insufficiency of the evidence, or the indictment is dismissed by the court or a *nol. pros.* entered. Or, it may occur even though the question of guilt or innocence has never been submitted to a jury, as where a defendant, having been held under an indictment or information, is discharged because not brought to trial within the time provided by statute.

Acquittals in fact are those which take place when the jury, upon trial, finds a verdict of not guilty.

Acquittals in law are those which take place by mere operation of law; as where a man has been charged merely as an accessory, and the principal has been acquitted.

See **Autrefois acquit; Jeopardy; Nolle prosequi; Verdict.**

Feudal law. The obligation on the part of a mesne lord to protect his tenant from any claims, entries or molestations by lords paramount arising out of the services due to them by the mesne lord.

Acquittance /əkwídəns/. A written discharge, whereby one is freed from an obligation to pay money or perform a duty. This word, though perhaps not strictly speaking synonymous with "receipt," includes it. A receipt is one form of an acquittance; a discharge is another. A receipt in full is an acquittance, and a receipt for a part of a demand or obligation is an acquittance *pro tanto.*

Acquitted /əkwídəd/. Released; absolved; purged of an accusation. Judicially discharged from accusation; released from debt, etc. Includes both civil and criminal prosecutions. See **Acquittal.**

Acre. A quantity of land containing 160 square rods, 4,840 square yards, or 43,560 square feet of land, in whatever shape. See **Land measure.**

Acre foot. 325,850 gallons, or the amount of water which will cover one acre one foot in depth.

Acre right. Formerly the share of a citizen of a New England town in the common lands. The value of the acre right was a fixed quantity in each town, but varied in different towns. A 10-acre lot or right in a certain town was equivalent to 113 acres of upland and 12 acres of meadow, and a certain exact proportion was maintained between the acre right and salable lands.

Across. From side to side. Transverse to the length of. It may mean "over," or "upon and along," or "upon," or "within".

Act, n. Denotes external manifestation of actor's will. Restatement, Second, Torts § 2. Expression of will or purpose; carries idea of performance; primarily that which is done or doing; exercise of power, or effect of which power exerted is cause; a performance; a deed. In its most general sense, this noun signifies something done voluntarily by a person; the exercise of an individual's power; an effect produced in the external world by an exercise of the power of a person objectively, prompted by intention, and proximately caused by a motion of the will. In a more technical sense, it means something done voluntarily by a person, and of such a nature that certain legal consequences attach to it. Thus a grantor acknowledges the conveyance to be his "act and deed," the terms being synonymous. It may denote something done by an individual, as a private citizen, or as an officer; or by a body of men, as a legislature, a council, or a court of justice; including not merely physical acts, but also decrees, edicts, laws, judgments, resolves, awards, and determinations. Some general laws made by the Congress of the United States are styled joint resolutions, and these have the same force and effect as those styled acts.

Acts under private signature are those which have been made by private individuals under their hands.

Criminal act. External manifestation of one's will which is prerequisite to criminal responsibility. There can be no crime without some act, affirmative or negative. An omission or failure to act may constitute an act for purpose of criminal law.

Legislative act. An alternative name for statutory law. When introduced into the first house of the legislature, a piece of proposed legislation is known as a bill. When passed to the next house, it may then be referred to as an act. After enactment the terms "law" and "act" may be used interchangeably. An act has the same legislative force as a joint resolution but is technically distinguishable, being of a different form and introduced with the words "Be it enacted" instead of "Be it resolved."

Acts are either public or private. Public acts (also called general acts, or general statutes, or statutes at large) are those which relate to the community generally, or establish a universal rule for the governance of the whole body politic. Private acts (formerly called special), are those which relate either to particular persons (personal acts) or to particular places (local acts), or which operate only upon specified individuals or their private concerns. Unity v. Burrage, 103 U.S. 447, 454, 26 L.Ed. 465. Public acts are those which concern the whole community and of which courts of law are bound to take judicial notice.

A "special" or "private" act is one operating only on particular persons and private concerns. A "local act" is one applicable only to a particular part of the legislative jurisdiction.

See also **Governmental act; Legislation; Legislative act; Statute**.

Private acts are those made by private persons as registers in relation to their receipts and expenditures, schedules, acquittances, and the like.

Public acts are those which have a public authority, and which have been made before public officers, are authorized by a public seal, have been made public by the authority of a magistrate, or which have been extracted and been properly authenticated from public records.

Acta diurna /ǽktə dayə́rnə/. Lat. In the Roman law, daily acts or chronicles; the public registers or journals of the daily proceedings of the senate, assemblies of the people, courts of justice, etc. Supposed to have resembled a modern newspaper.

Acta exteriora indicant interiora secreta /ǽktə ekstìriyórə índəkænt intìriyórə səkríydə/. External acts indicate undisclosed thoughts.

Acta in uno judicio non probant in alio nisi inter easdem personas /ǽktə in yúwnow juwdíshiyow non prówbænt in éyliyow náysay íntər iyéysdəm pərsównəs/. Things done in one action cannot be taken as evidence in another, unless it be between the same parties.

Acta publica /ǽktə pə́wbləkə/. Lat. Things of general knowledge and concern; matters transacted before certain public officers.

Acte /ǽkt/ákt/. In French law, denotes a document, or formal, solemn writing, embodying a legal attestation that something has been done, corresponding to one sense or use of the English word "act."

Actes de naissance are the certificates of birth, and must contain the day, hour, and place of birth, together with the sex and intended christian name of the child, and the names of the parents and of the witnesses. *Actes de mariage* are the marriage certificates, and contain names, professions, ages, and places of birth and of domicile of the two persons marrying, and of their parents; also the consent of these latter, and the mutual agreements of the intended husband and wife to take each other for better and worse, together with the usual attestations. *Actes de décès* are the certificates of death, which are required to be drawn up before any one may be buried. *Les actes de l'état civil* are public documents.

Acte authentique /ákt òtontíyk/. A deed executed with certain prescribed formalities, in the presence of a notary, mayor, *greffier, huissier,* or other functionary qualified to act in the place in which it is drawn up.

Acte de francisation /ákt də fránkəzasyówn/. The certificate of registration of a ship, by virtue of which its French nationality is established.

Acte d'héritier /ákt dèyrətyéy/. Act of inheritance. Any action or fact on the part of an heir which manifests his intention to accept the succession; the acceptance may be express or tacit.

Acte extrajudiciaire /ǽkt ètrəjuwdisksiyér/. A document served by a *huissier,* at the demand of one party upon another party, without legal proceedings.

Acting. Doing duty for another; officiating or holding a temporary rank or position or performing services temporarily; as, an acting captain, manager, president. Pellecchia v. Mattia, 121 N.J.L. 21, 1 A.2d 28. Performing; operating.

Acting executor. One who assumes to act as executor for a decedent, not being the executor legally appointed or the executor in fact.

Acting officer. Term is used to designate, not an appointed incumbent, but merely a locum tenens, who is performing the duties of an office to which he himself does not claim title.

Acting within scope of employment. See **Scope of employment**.

Act in pais /ǽkt in péy(s)/. An act done out of court, and not a matter of record. A deed or an assurance transacted between two or more private persons in the country, that is, according to the old common law, upon the very spot to be transferred, is matter *in pais.*

Actio /ǽkshiyow/. Lat. In the civil law, an action or suit; a right or cause of action. Term means both the proceeding to enforce a right in a court and the right itself which is sought to be enforced.

Actio ad exhibendum /ǽkshiyow æd ègzibéndəm/. An action for the purpose of compelling a defendant to exhibit a thing or title in his power. It was preparatory to another action, which was always a real action in the sense of the Roman law; that is, for the recovery of a thing, whether it was movable or immovable.

Actio æstimatoria; actio quanti minoris /ǽkshiyow ìystəmətóriyə ǽkshiyow kwóntay mənórəs/. In the criminal law, two names of an action which lay in behalf of a buyer to reduce the contract price proportionately to the defects of the object, not to cancel the sale; the *judex* had power, however, to cancel the sale.

Actio arbitraria /ǽkshiyow àrbətrériyə/. Action depending on the discretion of the judge. In this, unless defendant would make amends to plaintiff as dictated by the judge in his discretion, he was liable to be condemned.

Actio bonæ fidei /ǽkshiyow bówniy fáydiyay/. An action of good faith. A class of actions in which the judge might at the trial *ex officio*, take into account any equitable circumstances that were presented to him affecting either of the parties to the action.

Actio calumniæ /ǽkshiyow kəlámniyiy/. An action to restrain defendant from prosecuting a groundless proceeding or trumped-up charge against plaintiff. An action for malicious prosecution.

Actio civilis /ǽkshiyow sívələs/. In the common law, a civil action, as distinguished from a criminal action.

Actio commodati /ǽkshiyow kòmədéyday/. Included several actions appropriate to enforce the obligations of a borrower or a lender.

Actio commodati contraria /ǽkshiyow kòmədéyday kəntrériyə/. An action by the borrower against the lender, to compel the execution of the contract.

Actio commodati directa /ǽkshiyow kòmədéyday dəréktə/. An action by a lender against a borrower, the principal object of which is to obtain a restitution of the thing lent.

Actio communi dividundo /ǽkshiyow kəmyúwnay dìvədándow/. An action to procure a judicial division of joint property. It was analogous in its object to proceedings for partition in modern law.

Actio condictio indebitati /ǽkshiyow kəndí(k)shiyow indèbətéyday/. An action by which the plaintiff recovers the amount of a sum of money or other thing he paid by mistake.

Actio confessoria /ǽkshiyow kònfəsóriyə/. An affirmative petitory action for the recognition and enforcement of a servitude. So called because based on plaintiff's affirmative allegation of a right in defendant's land. Distinguished from an *actio negatoria,* which was brought to repel a claim of defendant to a servitude in plaintiff's land.

Actio contrario /ǽkshiyow kəntrériyow/. Counter action or cross action.

Actio criminalis /ǽkshiyow krìmənéyləs/. Criminal action.

Actio damni injuria /ǽkshiyow dǽmnay injúriyə/. The name of a general class of actions for damages, including many species of suits for losses caused by wrongful or negligent acts. The term is about equivalent to our "action for damages."

Actio de dolo malo /ǽkshiyow dìy dówlow mǽlow/. An action of fraud; an action which lay for a defrauded person against the defrauder and his heirs, who had been enriched by the fraud, to obtain the restitution of the thing of which he had been fraudulently deprived, with all its accessions *(cum omni causa;)* or, where this was not practicable, for compensation in damages.

Actio de peculio /ǽkshiyow dìy pəkyúwliyow/. An action concerning or against the *peculium,* or separate property of a party.

Actio de pecunia constituta /ǽkshiyow dìy pəkyúwniyə kònstətyúwdə/. An action for money engaged to be paid; an action which lay against any person who had engaged to pay money for himself, or for another without any formal stipulation.

Actio depositi contraria /ǽkshiyow dəpózəday kəntrériyə/. An action which the depositary has against the depositor, to compel him to fulfil his engagement towards him.

Actio depositi directa /ǽkshiyow dəpózəday dəréktə/. An action which is brought by the depositor against the depositary, in order to get back the thing deposited.

Actio de tigno juncto /ǽkshiyow dìy tígnow jə́ŋktow/. An action by the owner of material built by another into his building.

Actio directa /ǽkshiyow dəréktə/. A direct action; an action founded on strict law, and conducted according to fixed forms; an action founded on certain legal obligations which from their origin were accurately defined and recognized as actionable. See **Actio utilis**.

Actio empti /ǽkshiyow ém(p)tay/. An action employed in behalf of a buyer to compel a seller to perform his obligations or pay compensation; also to enforce any special agreements by him, embodied in a contract of sale.

Actio ex conducto /ǽkshiyow èks kəndáktow/. An action which the bailor of a thing for hire may bring against the bailee, in order to compel him to redeliver the thing hired.

Actio ex contractu /ǽkshiyow èks kəntrǽktyuw/. In the civil and common law, an action of contract; an action arising out of, or founded on, contract. 3 Bl.Comm. 117.

Actio ex delicto /ǽkshiyow èks dəlíktow/. In the civil and common law, an action of tort; an action arising out of fault, misconduct, or malfeasance. 3 Bl. Comm. 117. *Ex maleficio* is the more common expression of the civil law; which is adopted by Bracton.

Actio exercitoria /ǽkshiyow egzàrsətóriyə/. An action against the *exercitor* or employer of a vessel.

Actio ex locato /ǽkshiyow èks lowkéydow/. An action upon letting; an action which the person who let a thing for hire to another might have against the hirer.

Actio ex stipulatu /ǽkshiyow eks stìpyəléytyuw/. An action brought to enforce a stipulation.

Actio familiæ erciscundæ /ǽkshiyow fəmíliyiy àrsiskándiy/. An action for the partition of an inheritance.

Actio furti /ǽkshiyow fárday/. An action of theft; an action founded upon theft. This could be brought only for the penalty attached to the offense, and not to recover the thing stolen, for which other actions were provided. An appeal of larceny. The old process by which a thief can be pursued and the goods vindicated.

Actio honoraria /ǽkshiyow (h)onərériyə/. An honorary, or prætorian action. *Actiones honorariæ* are those forms of remedies which were gradually introduced by the prætors and ædiles, by virtue of their equitable powers, in order to prevent the failure of justice which too often resulted from the employment of the *actiones civiles*. These were found so beneficial in practice that they eventually supplanted the old remedies, of which in the time of Justinian hardly a trace remained.

Actio in factum /ǽkshiyow in fǽktəm/. In action adapted to the particular case, having an analogy to some *actio in jus*, the latter being founded on some subsisting acknowledged law. The origin of these actions is similar to that of actions on the case at common law.

Actio in personam /ǽkshiyow in pərsównəm/. In the civil law, an action against the person, founded on a personal liability; an action seeking redress for the violation of a *jus in personam* or right available against a particular individual. See **In personam**.

Actio in rem /ǽkshiyow in rém/. In the civil and common law, an action *for a thing;* an action for the recovery of a thing possessed by another. An action for the enforcement of a right (or for redress for its invasion) which was originally available against all the world, and not in any special sense against the individual sued, until he violated it. See **In rem**.

Actio judicati /ǽkshiyow jùwdəkéyday/. In the civil law, an action instituted after four months had elapsed after the rendition of judgment, in which the judge issued his warrant to seize, first, the movables, which were sold within eight days afterwards; and then the immovables, which were delivered in pledge to the creditors, or put under the care of a curator, and if, at the end of two months, the debt was not paid, the land was sold.

Actio legis aquiliæ /ǽkshiyow líyjəs əkwíliyiy/. An action under the Aquilian law; an action to recover damages for maliciously or injuriously killing or wounding the slave or beast of another, or injuring in any way a thing belonging to another. Otherwise called *damni injuriœ actio*.

Actio mandati /ǽkshiyow mændéyday/. In the civil law, term included actions to enforce contracts of mandate or obligations arising out of them.

Actio mixta /ǽkshiyow míkstə/. A mixed action, an action brought for the recovery of a thing, or compensation for damages, and also for the payment of a penalty; partaking of the nature both of an *actio in rem* and *in personam*.

Action. Conduct; behavior; something done; the condition of acting; an act or series of acts.

Term in its usual legal sense means a suit brought in a court; a formal complaint within the jurisdiction of a court of law. Pathman Const. Co. v. Knox County Hospital Ass'n, Ind.App., 326 N.E.2d 844, 853. The legal and formal demand of one's right from another person or party made and insisted on in a court of justice. An ordinary proceeding in a court of justice by which one party prosecutes another for the enforcement or protection of a right, the redress or prevention of a wrong, or the punishment of a public offense. It includes all the formal proceedings in a court of justice attendant upon the demand of a right made by one person of another in such court, including an adjudication upon the right and its enforcement or denial by the court.

See also Case (*Cases and controversies*); Cause of action; Civil action; Collusive action; Counterclaim; Cross claim; Direct action; Forms of action; Penal action; Petitory action; Plenary action; Proceeding; Suit; Transitory action.

Merger of law and equity. In the federal courts, and most state courts, there is only one form of action—civil action—which embraces all actions formerly denominated suits in equity and actions at law. While there has been a merger of law and equity for procedural purposes, substantive principles of equity still govern. Fed.R.Civ.P. 2.

Types of action. Such phrase is used to describe action for damages as distinguished from suit in equity for equitable relief. This distinction however has been abolished under Fed. Rules of Civil Procedure and in those states which have adopted Rules tracking the Federal Rules. Fed.R.Civ.P. 2.

Action for death. See **Wrongful death action**.

Action in equity. Action in which person seeks equitable relief as distinguished from damages; *e.g.* injunction or specific performance of real estate agreement. Term has been abolished by Fed. Rules of Civil Procedure (Rule 2) in favor of single form of action—civil action—which embraces both law and equity actions.

Action in personam. See **In personam**.

Action in rem. See **In rem**.

Action quasi in rem. See **In rem**.

Civil actions are such as lie in behalf of persons to enforce their rights or obtain redress of wrongs in their relation to individuals. Fed.R.Civ.P. 2.

Class actions. See **Class or representative action; Derivative action**.

Common law actions are such as will lie, on the particular facts, at common law, without the aid of a statute. Actions are called, in common-law practice, *ex contractu* when they arise out of a contract, and *ex delicto* when they arise out of a tort. If a cause of action arises from a breach of promise, the action is "ex contractu", and, if it arises from breach of duty growing out of contract, it is "ex delicto".

Criminal actions are such as are instituted by the sovereign power (*i.e.* government), for the purpose of punishing or preventing offenses against the public.

Local action. See **Local action**.

Mixed actions partake of twofold nature of real and personal actions, having for their object the demand and restitution of real property and also personal damages for a wrong sustained. In the civil law, an action in which some specific thing was demanded, and also some personal obligation claimed to be performed; or, in other words, an action which proceeded both *in rem* and *in personam*.

Penal actions are such as are brought, either by the state or by an individual under permission of a statute, to enforce a penalty imposed by law for the commission of a prohibited act.

Personal action. In civil law, an action *in personam* seeks to enforce an obligation imposed on the defendant by his contract or delict; that is, it is the contention that he is bound to transfer some dominion or to perform some service or to repair some loss. In common law, an action brought for the recovery of some debt or for damages for some personal injury, in contradistinction to the old real actions, which related to real property only. An action which can be brought only by the person himself who is injured, and not by his representatives. See **In personam**.

Popular actions, in English usage, were those actions which were given upon the breach of a penal statute, and which any man that will may sue on account of the king and himself, as the statute allowed and the case required. Because the action was not given to one especially, but generally to any that would prosecute, it was called "action popular;" and, from the words used in the process (*qui tam pro domino rege sequitur quam pro se ipso*, who sues as well for the king as for himself) it was called a *qui tam* action.

Real actions. At common law, one brought for the specific recovery of lands, tenements, or hereditaments. They are *droitural* when they are based upon the right of property, and *possessory* when based upon the right of possession. They are either writs of right; writs of entry upon disseisin (which lie in the per, the per et cui, or the post), intrusion, or alienation; writs ancestral possessory, as mort d'ancestor, aiel, besaiel, cossinage, or nuper obiit. The former class was divided into *droitural*, founded upon demandant's own seisin, and *ancestral droitural* upon the demandant's claim in respect of a mere right descended to him from an ancestor. Possessory actions were divided in the same way—as to the demandant's own seisin and as to that of his ancestor. Among the civilians, real actions, otherwise called "vindications," were those in which a man demanded something that was his own. They were founded on dominion, or *jus in re*. The real actions of the Roman law were not, like the real actions of the common law, confined to real estate, but they included personal, as well as real, property. See **In rem**.

Statutory actions are such as can only be based upon the particular statutes creating them. Contrast *Common law* actions, supra.

Transitory actions are those founded upon a cause of action not necessarily referring to or arising in any particular locality. Their characteristic feature is that the right of action follows the person of the defendant. Actions are "transitory" when the transactions relied on might have taken place anywhere, and are "local" when they could not occur except in some particular place; the distinction being in the nature of the subject of the injury, and not in the means used or the place at which the cause of action arises. The test of whether an action is local or transitory is whether the injury is done to a subject-matter which, in its nature, could not arise beyond the locality of its situation, in contradistinction to the subject causing the injury. Actions triable where defendant resides are termed "transitory" and those triable where the subject-matter is situated are termed "local."

Actionable. That for which an action will lie, furnishing legal ground for an action. (See **Cause of action; Justiciable controversy**.)

Actionable fraud. Deception practiced in order to induce another to part with property or surrender some legal right. A false representation made with an intention to deceive; may be committed by stating what is known to be false or by professing knowledge of the truth of a statement which is false, but in either case, the essential ingredient is a falsehood uttered with intent to deceive. To constitute "actionable fraud," it must appear that defendant made a material representation; that it was false; that when he made it he knew it was false, or made it recklessly without any knowledge of its truth and as a positive assertion; that he made it with intention that it should be acted on by plaintiff; that plaintiff acted in reliance on it; and that plaintiff thereby suffered injury. Vertes v. GAC Properties, Inc., D.C.Fla., 337 F.Supp. 256, 266. Essential elements are representation, falsity, scienter, deception, and injury. See **Fraud**.

Actionable misrepresentation. A false statement respecting a fact material to the contract and which is influential in procuring it. See **Fraud; Misrepresentation.**

Actionable negligence. The breach or nonperformance of a legal duty, through neglect or carelessness, resulting in damage or injury to another. It is failure of duty, omission of something which ought to have been done, or doing of something which ought not to have been done, or which reasonable man, guided by considerations which ordinarily regulate conduct of human affairs, would or would not do. Essential elements are failure to exercise due care, injury, or damage, and proximate cause. See **Negligence.**

Actionable nuisance. Anything wrongfully done or permitted which injures or annoys another in the enjoyment of his legal rights. Miller v. City of Dayton, 70 Ohio App. 173, 41 N.E.2d 728, 730. Anything injurious to health, or indecent, or offensive to the senses, or an obstruction to the free use of property so as to interfere with the comfortable enjoyment of life or property. See **Nuisance.**

Actionable per quod. Words actionable only on allegation and proof of special damage. Knapp v. Post Printing & Publishing Co., 111 Colo. 492, 144 P.2d 981, 984. Words not actionable *per se* upon their face, but only in consequence of extrinsic facts showing circumstances under which they were said or the damages resulting to slandered party therefrom. Not injurious on their face in their usual and natural signification, but only so in consequence of extrinsic facts and requiring innuendo. See **Libelous per quod.**

Actionable per se. Words in themselves libelous or slanderous. Knapp v. Post Printing & Publishing Co., 111 Colo. 492, 144 P.2d 981, 984. Words which law presumes must actually, proximately and necessarily damage defendant for which general damages are recoverable and whose injurious character is a fact of common notoriety, established by the general consent of men, necessarily importing damage. Actions based on such words require no proof of damages. Words actionable per se include imputation of crime, a loathsome disease, unchastity, or words affecting plaintiff's business, trade, profession, office or calling. See **Libelous per se.**

Actionable tort. To constitute an "actionable tort," there must be a legal duty, imposed by statute or otherwise, owing by defendant to the one injured, and in the absence of such duty damage caused is "injury without wrong" or "damnum absque injuria." Coleman v. California Yearly Meeting of Friends Church, 27 Cal.App.2d 579, 81 P.2d 469, 470. See **Tort.**

Actionable words. In law of libel and slander, such words as naturally imply damage. See **Libel; Slander.**

Actionable wrong. Committed when a responsible person has neglected to use a reasonable degree of care for protection of another person from such injury as under existing circumstances should reasonably have been foreseen as a proximate consequence of that negligence.

Actionare /ǽksh(iy)ənériy/. L. Lat. (From *actio*, an action.) To bring an action; to prosecute; or sue.

Actionary /ǽkshən(ə)riy/. A foreign commercial term for the proprietor of an *action* or share of a public company's stock; a stockholder.

Actio negatoria (or negativa) /ǽkshiyow nègətóriyə /°nègətáyvə/. An action brought to repel a claim of the defendant to a servitude in the plaintiff's land. See **Actio confessoria.**

Actio negotiorum gestorum /ǽkshiyow nəgòwshiyórəm jestórəm/. Included actions between principal and agent and other parties to an engagement, whereby one person undertook the transaction of business for another.

Actiones legis /ǽkshiyówniyz líyjəs/. In the Roman law, legal or lawful action; actions of or at law (*legitmæ actiones*).

Actiones nominatae /ǽkshiyówniyz nòmənéydiy/. (Lat. named actions). In the English chancery, writs for which there were precedents. The statute of Westminster, 2, c. 24, gave chancery authority to form new writs *in consimili casu;* hence the action on the case.

Action ex contractu /ǽkshən èks kəntrǽktyuw/. An action for breach of promise set forth in a contract, express or implied. McCullough v. The American Workmen, 200 S.C. 84, 20 S.E.2d 640.

Action ex delicto /ǽkshən èks dəlíktow/. An action arising from a breach of duty growing out of contract.

Action for accounting. Action in equity based on inadequacy of legal remedy and particularly applicable to mutual and complicated accounts and where confidential or fiduciary relationship exists. Action to adjust mutual accounts and to strike a balance.

Action for money had and received. Action in assumpsit based upon promise to repay implied by law, and in respect of limitation is a stated or liquidated account. Action brought where one person has received money or its equivalent under such circumstances that in equity and good conscience he ought not to retain it and in justice it belongs to another. Interstate Life & Accident Co. v. Cook, 19 Tenn.App. 290, 86 S.W.2d 887, 891.

Action for poinding /ǽkshən for píndiŋ/. An action by a creditor to obtain a sequestration of the rents of land and the goods of his debtor for the satisfaction of his debt, or to enforce a distress.

Action in personam. See **In personam.**

Action in rem. See **In rem.**

Action of assize /ǽkshən əv əsáyz/. A real action at common law which proved the title of the demandant, merely by showing his ancestor's possession. See **Assumpsit.**

Action of assumpsit. See **Assumpsit.**

Action of book debt. A form of common law action for the recovery of claims, such as are usually evidenced by a book-account.

Action of contract. An action brought to enforce rights whereof the contract is the evidence, and usually the sufficient evidence.

Action of writ. A phrase in common law pleading used when a defendant pleads some matter by which he shows that the plaintiff had no cause to have the writ sued upon, although it may be that he is entitled to another writ or action for the same matter.

Actio non /ǽkshiyow nón/. In the common law pleading, the Latin name of that part of a special plea which follows next after the statement of appearance and defense, and declares that the plaintiff "ought not to have or maintain his aforesaid action thereof against" the defendant (in Latin, *actionem non habere debet*).

Actio non accrevit infra sex annos /ǽkshiyow nòn əkríyvət ínfrə séks ǽnows/. The name of the plea of the statute of limitations, when the defendant alleges that the plaintiff's action has not accrued within six years.

Actio non datur non damnificato /ǽkshiyow nòn déydər nòn dæmnəfəkéydow/. An action is not given to one who is not injured.

Actio non facit reum, nisi mens sit rea /ǽkshiyow nòn féysət ríyəm, náysay ménz sìt ríyə/. An act does not make one guilty, unless the intention be bad.

Action on the case. A common law species of personal action of formerly extensive application, otherwise called "trespass on the case," or simply "case," from the circumstance of the plaintiff's whole *case or cause of complaint* being set forth at length in the original writ by which formerly it was always commenced. In its most comprehensive signification it includes *assumpsit* as well as an action in form *ex delicto*; though when it is mentioned it is usually understood to mean an action in form *ex delicto*. It is founded on the common law or upon acts of Parliament, and lies generally to recover damages for torts not committed with force, actual or implied; or having been occasioned by force where the matter affected was not tangible, or the injury was not immediate but consequential; or where the interest in the property was only in reversion, in all of which cases trespass is not sustainable. In the progress of judicial contestation it was discovered that there was a mass of tortious wrongs unattended by direct and immediate force, or where the force, though direct, was not expended on an existing right of present enjoyment, for which the then known forms of action furnished no redress. The action on the case was instituted to meet this want. And wrongs which will maintain an action on the case are frequently committed in the nonobservance of duties, which are but the implication of contract obligation, duties of requisite skill, fidelity, diligence, and a proper regard for the rights of others, implied in every obligation to serve another. If the cause of action arises from a breach of promise, the action is "ex contractu"; but if the cause of action arises from a breach of duty growing out of the contract, it is in form ex delicto and case. When there is a contract, either express or implied, from which a common-law duty results, an action on the case lies for the breach of that duty. Such form of action no longer exists under Code and Rule pleading. See **Assumpsit.**

Actio non ulterius /ǽkshiyow nòn əltíriyəs/. In English pleading, a name given to the distinctive clause in the plea to the *further maintenance* of the action, introduced in place of the plea *puis darrein continuance*; the averment being that the plaintiff ought not *further (ulterius)* to have or maintain his action.

Actio noxalis /ǽkshiyow nokséyləs/. In civil law, a noxal action; an action which lay against a master for a crime committed or injury done by his slave; and in which the master had the alternative either to pay for the damage done or to deliver up the slave to the complaining party. So called from *noxa*, the offense or injury committed.

Action quasi in rem /ǽkshən kwéysay in rém/. An action brought against persons which only seeks to subject certain property of those persons to discharge of claims asserted and judgment therein is only conclusive between parties and their privies. Tobin v. McClellan, 225 Ind. 335, 75 N.E.2d 149, 151. See **In rem.**

Action redhibitory /ǽkshən rəd(h)íbit(ə)riy/. See **Redhibitory action.**

Action to quiet title. One in which plaintiff asserts his own estate and declares generally that defendant claims some estate in the land, without defining it, and avers that the claim is without foundation, and calls on defendant to set forth the nature of his claim, so that it may be determined by decree. It differs from a "suit to remove a cloud," in that plaintiff therein declares on his own title, and also avers the source and nature of defendant's claim, points out its defect, and prays that it may be declared void as a cloud on plaintiff's estate. It embraces every sort of a claim whereby the plaintiff might be deprived of his property or his title clouded or its value depreciated, or whereby the plaintiff might be incommoded or damnified by assertion of an outstanding title already held or to grow out of the adverse pretension. Bank of American Nat. Trust & Savings Ass'n v. Town of Atherton, 60 Cal.App.2d 268, 140 P.2d 678, 680.

Actionum genera maxime sunt servanda /ǽkshiyównəm jénərə mǽksəmiy sànt sərvǽndə/. The kinds of actions are especially to be preserved.

Actio perpetua /ǽkshiyow pərpéchuwə/. An action without limitation period.

Actio personalis /ǽkshiyow pərsənéyləs/. In the civil and common law, a personal action. See **In personam.**

Actio personalis moritur cum persona /ǽkshiyow pərsənéyləs mórədər kəm pərsówney/. A personal right of action dies with the person. The maxim was originally applied to almost every form of action, whether arising out of contract or tort, but the common law was modified by the Statute of 4 Edward the III. Momand v. Twentieth-Century Fox Film Corporation, D.C.Okl., 37 F.Supp. 649, 652.

Actio pignoratitia /ǽkshiyow pìgnəreytíshiyə/. An action of pledge; an action founded on the contract of pledge (*pignus*).

Actio pœnalis /ǽkshiyow piynéyləs/. Called also *actio ex delicto*. An action in which a penalty was recovered of the delinquent.

Actiones pœnales and *actiones mixtæ* comprehended cases of injuries, for which the civil law permitted redress by private action, but which modern civilization universally regards as crimes; that is, offenses against society at large, and punished by proceedings in the name of the state alone. Thus, theft, receiving stolen goods, robbery, malicious mischief, and the murder or negligent homicide of a slave (in which case an injury to property was involved), gave rise to private actions for damages against the delinquent.

Actio pœnalis in hæredem non datur, nisi forte ex damno lòkyəplíyshər híriyz fǽktəs sìt/. A penal action is not həríydəm nòn déydər náysay fórdiy èks dǽmnow lòkyəplíyshər híriyz fǽktəs sìt/. A penal action is not given against an heir, unless, indeed, such heir is benefited by the wrong.

Actio præjudicialis /ǽkshiyow prìyjuwdìshiyéyləs/. A preliminary or preparatory action. An action instituted for the determination of some preliminary matter on which other litigated matters depend, or for the determination of some point or question arising in another or principal action; and so called from its being *determined before* (*prius*, or *præ judicari*).

Actio præscriptis verbis /ǽkshiyow prəskríptəs várbəs/. A form of action which derived its force from continued usage or the *responsa prudentium*, and was founded on the unwritten law. The distinction between this action and an *actio in factum* is said to be, that the latter was founded not on usage or the unwritten law, but by analogy to or on the equity of some subsisting law.

Actio prætoria /ǽkshiyow prətóriyə/. A prætorian action; one introduced by the prætor, as distinguished from the more ancient *actio civilis* (*q.v.*).

Actio pro socio /ǽkshiyow pròw sówshiyow/. An action of partnership. An action brought by one partner against his associates to compel them to carry out the terms of the partnership agreement.

Actio publiciana /ǽkshiyow pəblìshiyéynə/. An action which lay for one who had lost a thing of which he had *bona fide* obtained possession, before he had gained a property in it, in order to have it restored, under color that he had obtained a property in it by prescription. It was an honorary action, and derived its name from the prætor Publicius, by whose edict it was first given.

Actio quælibet in sua via /ǽkshiyow kwíyləbèt in s(y)úwə váyə/. Every action proceeds in its own way.

Actio quod jussu /ǽkshiyow kwòd jásyuw/. An action given against a master, founded on some business done by his slave, acting under his *order* (*jussu*).

Actio quod metus causa /ǽkshiyow kwòd médəs kózə/. An action granted to one who had been compelled by unlawful force, or fear (*metus causa*) that was not groundless (*metus probabilis* or *justus*) to deliver, sell, or promise a thing to another.

Actio realis /ǽkshiyow riyéyləs/. A real action. The proper term in the civil law was *rei vindicatio*.

Actio redhibitoria /ǽkshiyow rəd(h)ìbətóriyə/. An action to cancel a sale in consequence of defects in the thing sold. It was prosecuted to compel complete restitution to the seller of the thing sold, with its produce and accessories, and to give the buyer back the price, with interest, as an equivalent for the restitution of the produce. See **Redhibitory action**.

Actio rerum amotarum /ǽkshiyow rírəm èymowtérəm/. An action for things removed; an action which, in cases of divorce, lay for a husband against a wife, to recover things carried away by the latter, in contemplation of such divorce. It also lay for the wife against the husband in such cases.

Actio rescissoria /ǽkshiyow rèsəsóriyə/. An action for restoring plaintiff to a right or title which he has lost by prescription, in a case where the equities are such that he should be relieved from the operation of the prescription. An action to rescind a prescriptive title by one who was entitled to exemption from the prescription law, as a minor, etc.

Actio serviana /ǽkshiyow sàrviyéynə/. An action which lay for the lessor of a farm, or rural estate, to recover the goods of the lessee or farmer, which were pledged or bound for the rent.

Actio stricti juris /ǽkshiyow stríktay jurəs/. An action of strict right. The class of civil law personal actions, which were adjudged only by the strict law, and in which the judge was limited to the precise language of the formula, and had no discretionary power to regard the *bona fides* of the transaction.

Actio tèmporalis /ǽkshiyow tèmpəréyləs/. An action which must be brought within a limited time. See **Limitation**.

Actio tutelæ /ǽkshiyow t(y)uwtíyliy/. Action founded on the duties or obligations arising on the relation analogous to that of guardian and ward.

Actio utilis /ǽkshiyow yúwdələs/. In the civil law, a beneficial action or equitable action. An action founded on equity instead of strict law, and available for those who had equitable rights or the beneficial ownership of property. Actions are divided into *actiones directæ* or *utiles*. The former are founded on certain legal obligations which from their origin were accurately defined and recognized as actionable. The latter were formed analogically in imitation of the former. They were permitted in legal obligations for which the *actiones directæ* were not originally intended, but which resembled the legal obligations which formed the basis of the direct action.

Actio venditi /ǽkshiyow véndəday/. An action employed in behalf of a seller, to compel a buyer to pay the price, or perform any special obligations embodied in a contract of sale.

Actio vi bonorum raptorum /ǽkshiyow váy bownórəm ræptórəm/. An action for goods taken by force; a species of mixed action, which lay for a party whose goods or movables (*bona*) had been taken from him by force (*vi*), to recover the things so taken, together with a penalty of triple the value. Bracton describes it as lying *de rebus mobilibus vi ablatis sive robbatis* (for movable things taken away by force, or robbed).

Actio vulgaris /ǽkshiyow vɔlgérəs/. A legal action; a common action. Sometimes used for *actio directa*.

Active. That is in action; that demands action; actually subsisting; the opposite of passive. An active debt is one which draws interest. An active trust is a confidence connected with a duty. An active use is a present legal estate.

Active concealment. Term implies a purpose or design accomplished by words or acts, while passive concealment consists in mere silence where there is a duty to speak. Vendt v. Duenke, Mo.App., 210 S.W.2d 692, 699. Concealment becomes a fraud where it is effected by misleading and deceptive talk, acts, or conduct, where it is accompanied by misrepresentations, or where, in addition to a party's silence, there is any statement, word, or act on his part which tends affirmatively to a suppression of the truth. Such conduct is designated active concealment. Equitable Life Ins. Co. of Iowa v. Halsey, Stuart & Co., C.C.A.Ill., 112 F.2d 302, 309.

Active negligence. A term of extensive meaning embracing many occurrences that would fall short of willful wrongdoing, or of crass negligence, for example, all inadvertent acts causing injury to others, resulting from failure to exercise ordinary care; likewise, all acts the effects of which are misjudged or unforeseen, through want of proper attention, or reflection, and hence the term covers the acts of willful wrongdoing and also those which are not of that character. Cohen v. Noel, Tenn.App., 104 S.W.2d 1001, 1005.

Active negligence denotes some positive act or some failure in duty of operation which is equivalent of a positive act and is omission of due care and affirmative action by person in control, or negligence occurring in connection with activities conducted on the premises. Pachowitz v. Milwaukee & Suburban Transport Corp., 56 Wis.2d 383, 202 N.W.2d 268, 275. Difference between "active" and "passive" negligence is that one is only passively negligent if he merely fails to act in fulfillment of duty of care which law imposes upon him, while one is actively negligent if he participates in some manner in conduct or omission which caused injury. King v. Timber Structures, Inc. of Cal., 240 C.A.2d 178, 49 Cal.Rptr. 414, 417.

See also **Negligence**.

Active trust. See **Trust**.

Act malum in se. See **Malum in se**.

Act malum prohibitum. See **Malum prohibitum**.

Act of attainder. A legislative act, attainting a person. See **Attainder**.

Act of bankruptcy. Any act which renders a person liable to be proceeded against involuntarily as a bankrupt, or for which he may be adjudged bankrupt.

The Bankruptcy Act, § 3 (11 U.S.C.A. § 21 (1952)) lists the following as acts of bankruptcy: Acts of bankruptcy by a person shall consist of his having (1) conveyed, transferred, concealed, removed, or permitted to be concealed or removed any part of his property, with intent to hinder, delay, or defraud his creditors or any of them; or (2) transferred, while insolvent, any portion of his property to one or more

of his creditors with intent to prefer such creditors over his other creditors; or (3) suffered or permitted, while insolvent, any creditor to obtain a lien upon any of his property through legal proceedings and not having vacated or discharged such lien within thirty days from the date thereof or at least five days before the date set for any sale or other disposition of such property; or (4) made a general assignment for the benefit of his creditors; or (5) while insolvent or unable to pay his debts as they mature, procured, permitted, or suffered voluntarily or involuntarily the appointment of a receiver or trustee to take charge of his property; or (6) admitted in writing his inability to pay his debts and his willingness to be adjudged a bankrupt. The new Bankruptcy Act (effective Oct. 1, 1979) no longer provides for specific acts of bankruptcy but rather provides for involuntary bankruptcy when the debtor, in general, is not paying his debts as they become due. Bankruptcy Act, § 303.

Act of Elizabeth. See **Act of supremacy**.

Act of God. An act occasioned exclusively by violence of nature without the interference of any human agency. It means a natural necessity proceeding from physical causes alone without the intervention of man. It is an act, event, happening, or occurrence, due to natural causes and inevitable accident, or disaster; a natural and inevitable necessity which implies entire exclusion of all human agency which operates without interference or aid from man and which results from natural causes and is in no sense attributable to human agency. It is an accident which could not have been occasioned by human agency but proceeded from physical causes alone. Watts v. Smith, D.C.App., 226 A.2d 160, 162; Middaugh v. U. S., D.C.Wyo., 293 F.Supp. 977, 980. See **Inevitable accident; Perils of the sea; Vis major**.

Act of grace. The term is often used to designate a general act of parliament, originating with the crown, such as has often been passed at the commencement of a new reign, or the coming of age or marriage of a sovereign, or at the close of a period of civil troubles, declaring pardon or amnesty to numerous offenders. See also **Days of grace; Grace period**.

Act of insolvency. Within the meaning of the national currency act, an act which shows a bank to be insolvent, such as nonpayment of its circulating notes, bills of exchange, or certificates of deposit; failure to make good the impairment of capital, or to keep good its surplus or reserve; in fact, any act which shows that the bank is unable to meet its liabilities as they mature, or to perform those duties which the law imposes for the purpose of sustaining its credit. Kullman & Co. v. Woolley, C.C.A.Miss., 83 F.2d 129, 132; Garvin v. Chadwick Realty Corporation, 212 Ind. 499, 9 N.E.2d 268, 271.

Act of law. The operation of fixed legal rules upon given facts or occurrences, producing consequences independent of the design or will of the parties concerned; as distinguished from "act of parties." Also an act performed by judicial authority which prevents or precludes a party from fulfilling a contract or other engagement. See **Act in pais**.

Act of parliament. A statute; a law made by the British sovereign, with the advice and consent of the lords and the commons, in parliament assembled. Acts of parliament form the *leges scriptæ, i.e.,* the written laws of the kingdom. Such acts are of three kinds: public, local or special, private or personal.

Act of providence. An accident against which ordinary skill and foresight could not guard. Equivalent to "act of God" (*q.v.*).

Act of sale. An official record of a sale of property, made by a notary who writes down the agreement of the parties as stated by them, and which is then signed by the parties and attested by witnesses.

Act of settlement. The English statute (12 & 13 Wm. III, c. 2) limiting the crown to the Princess Sophia of Hanover, and to the heirs of her body being Protestants. 1 Bl.Comm. 128. One clause of it made the tenure of judges' office for life or good behavior independent of the crown.

Act of state. An act done by the sovereign power of a country, or by its delegate, within the limits of the power vested in him. An act of state cannot be questioned or made the subject of legal proceedings in a court of law. See **Act of state doctrine.**

Act of state doctrine. The act of state doctrine precludes the courts of this country from inquiring into the validity of governmental acts of a recognized foreign sovereign committed within its own territory. Banco Nacional de Cuba v. Sabbatino, 376 U.S. 398, 84 S.Ct. 923, 11 L.Ed.2d 804; Ricaud v. American Metal Co., 246 U.S. 304, 38 S.Ct. 312, 62 L.Ed. 733; Oetjen v. Central Leather Co., 246 U.S. 297, 38 S.Ct. 309, 62 L.Ed. 726; F. Palicio y Compania, S. A. v. Brush, 256 F.Supp. 481 aff'd, 375 F.2d 1011 (2d Cir.), cert. denied, 389 U.S. 830, 88 S.Ct. 95, 19 L.Ed.2d 88.

Act of supremacy. An act of 26 Hen. VIII, c. 1, and also 1 Eliz., c. 1, which recognized the king as the only supreme head on earth of the Church of England having full power to correct all errors, heresies, abuses, offenses, contempts and enormities. The oath, taken under the act, denies to the Pope any other authority than that of the Bishop of Rome.

Act of uniformity. The English statute of 13 & 14 Car. II, c. 4, enacting that the book of common prayer, as then recently revised, should be used in every parish church and other place of public worship, and otherwise ordaining a uniformity in religious services, etc.

Acton Burnel, statute of. In English law, a statute, otherwise called *Statutum Mercatorum* or *de Mercatoribus*, the statute of the merchants, made at a parliament held at the castle or village of Acton Burnel in Shropshire, in the 11th year of the reign of Edward I. It was a statute for the collection of debts, the earliest of its class, being enacted in 1283. A further statute for the same object, and known as De Mercatoribus, was enacted 13 Edw. I, (c. 3). See **Statute merchant.**

Act on petition. A form of summary proceeding formerly in use in the high court of admiralty, in England, in which the parties stated their respective cases briefly, and supported their statements by affidavit.

Actor. One who acts. The term is used in the Restatement of Torts, Second, to designate either the person whose conduct is in question as subjecting him to liability toward another, or as precluding him from recovering against another whose tortious conduct is a legal cause of the actor's injury. Sec. 2.

Old European law. A patron, proctor, advocate, or pleader; one who acted for another in legal matters; one who represented a party and managed his cause. An attorney, bailiff, or steward; one who managed or acted for another. The Scotch "doer" is the literal translation.

Roman law. One who acted for another; one who attended to another's business; a manager or agent. A slave who attended to, transacted, or superintended his master's business or affairs, received and paid out moneys, and kept accounts. The word has a variety of closely-related meanings, very nearly corresponding with manager. Thus, *actor dominæ,* manager of his master's farm; *actor ecclesiæ,* manager of church property; *actores provinciarum,* tax-gatherers, treasurers, and managers of the public debt.

> *Actor ecclesiæ.*—An advocate for a church; one who protects the temporal interests of a church. *Actor villæ* was the steward or head-bailiff of a town or village.

Plaintiff or complainant. In a civil or private action the plaintiff was often called by the Romans "*petitor;*" in a public action (*causa publica*) he was called "*accusator.*" The defendant was called "*reus,*" both in private and public causes. This term, however, might signify either party, as might be concluded from the word itself. In a private action, the defendant was often called "*adversarius,*" but either party might be called so.

Also, the term is used of a party who, for the time being, sustains the burden of proof, or has the initiative in the suit.

Actore non probante reus absolvitur /æktóriy non prowbǽntey ríyǝs æbzólvǝdǝr/. When the plaintiff does not prove his case the defendant is acquitted (or absolved).

Actori incumbit onus probandi /æktóray iŋkǽmbǝd ównǝs prǝbǽnday/. The burden of proof rests on the plaintiff (or on the party who advances a proposition affirmatively.)

Actor qui contra regulam quid adduxit, non est audiendus /æktòr kwày kóntrǝ régyǝlǝm kwíd ǝdǝ́ksǝt, nón èst òdiyéndǝs/. A plaintiff (or pleader) is not to be heard who has advanced anything against authority (or against the rule).

Actor sequitur forum rei /æktòr sékwǝdǝr fórǝm ríyay/. According as *rei* is intended as the genitive of *res,* a thing, or *reus,* a defendant, this phrase means: The plaintiff follows the forum of the property in suit, or the forum of the defendant's residence.

Actrix /ǽktriks/. Lat. A female actor; a female plaintiff.

Acts of court. Legal memoranda made in the admiralty courts in England, in the nature of pleas.

Acts of possession. To constitute adverse possession, acts of possession must be: (1) hostile or adverse, (2) actual, (3) visible, notorious, and exclusive, (4) continuous, and (5) under claim of ownership. Bilyeu v. Plant, 75 Ill.App.2d 109, 220 N.E.2d 513. See **Adverse possession**.

Actual. Real; substantial; existing presently in act; having a valid objective existence as opposed to that which is merely theoretical or possible. Opposed to potential, possible, virtual, theoretical, hypothetical, or nominal. Something real, in opposition to constructive or speculative; something existing in act. It is used as a legal term in contradistinction to virtual or constructive as of possession or occupation. *Actually* is opposed to seemingly, pretendedly, or feignedly, as *actually engaged in farming* means really, truly in fact. As to actual Bias; Damages; Delivery; Fraud; Malice; Notice; Occupation; Ouster; Possession; Residence; Seisin; Total loss, see those titles.

Actual authority. In the law of agency, such authority as a principal intentionally confers on the agent, or intentionally or by want of ordinary care allows the agent to believe himself to possess. National Cash Register Co. v. Wichita Frozen Food Lockers, Tex. Civ.App., 172 S.W.2d 781, 787. Includes both express and implied authority.

Actual bias. See **Bias**.

Actual cash value. The fair or reasonable cash price for which the property could be sold in the market in the ordinary course of business, and not at forced sale. The price it will bring in a fair market after reasonable efforts to find a purchaser who will give the highest price. What property is worth in money, allowing for depreciation. Ordinarily, "actual cash value", "fair market value", and "market value" are synonymous terms. See **Actual value; Fair market value; Fair value**.

Actual change of possession. In statutes of frauds, an open, visible and unequivocal change of possession, manifested by the usual outward signs, as distinguished from a merely formal or constructive change.

Actual controversy. See **Case** (*Cases and controversies*).

Actual cost. The actual price paid for goods by a party, in the case of a real *bona fide* purchase, which may not necessarily be the market value of the goods. It is a general or descriptive term which may have varying meanings according to the circumstances in which it is used. It imports the exact sum expended or loss sustained rather than the average or proportional part of the cost. Its meaning may be restricted to materials, labor, and overhead or extended to other items.

Actual damages. Compensation for actual injuries or loss. Chappell v. City of Springfield, Mo., 423 S.W.2d 810, 814. Term used to denote the type of damage award as well as the nature of injury for which recovery is allowed; thus, actual damages flowing from injury in fact are to be distinguished from damages which are nominal, exemplary or punitive. Rasor v. Retail Credit Co., 87 Wash.2d 516, 554 P.2d 1041, 1049.

Actual delivery. See **Delivery**.

Actual eviction. An actual expulsion of the tenant out of all or some part of the demised premises. A physical ouster or dispossession from the very thing granted or some substantial part thereof. Cauley v. Northern Trust Co., 315 Ill.App. 307, 43 N.E.2d 147, 155, 315. See **Constructive eviction; Eviction; Forcible entry and detainer; Summary process**.

Actual fraud. See **Fraud**.

Actual loss. One resulting from the real and substantial destruction of the property insured.

Actual malice. See **Malice**.

Actual market value. In custom laws, the price at which merchandise is freely offered for sale to all purchasers; the price which the manufacturer or owner would have received for merchandise, sold in the ordinary course of trade in the usual wholesale quantities.

Actual notice. See **Notice**.

Actual possession. See **Possession**.

Actual practice. Active, open and notorious engagement in business, vocation or profession as opposed to casual or clandestine practice. State ex rel. Laughlin v. Washington State Bar Ass'n, 26 Wash.2d 914, 176 P.2d 301, 309.

Actual residence. The abode, where one actually lives, not mere naked legal residence. In re McGrath, 243 App.Div. 803, 278 N.Y.S. 135. See **Domicile; Residence**.

Actual use. Term "actual use" in automobile liability policy providing coverage for nonowned automobile if the actual operation or actual use of automobile by relative of insured is with permission of owner means present or active use or a use existing in fact or reality as distinguished from an imputed or constructive use. United Services Auto. Ass'n v. United States Fire Ins. Co., 36 C.A.3d 765, 111 Cal.Rptr. 595, 598.

Actual value. Actual value to be awarded in condemnation proceeding is price that would probably result from negotiations between willing seller and willing buyer. "Actual value," "market value," "fair market value," "just compensation" and the like may be used as convertible terms. "Saleable value," "actual value," "cash value," and other like terms used in directions to tax assessing officers, all mean generally the same thing. In re Lang Body Co., C.C.A. Ohio, 92 F.2d 338, 340.

Actual violence. An assault with actual violence is an assault with physical force put in action, exerted upon the person assailed. The term violence is synonymous with physical force, and the two are used interchangeably in relation to assaults.

Actuarial table /æ̀kchuwériyəl téybəl/. A form of organized statistical data which indicates the life expectancy of a person and which is admissible in evidence through an expert witness. Leave v. Boston Elevated Railway, 306 Mass. 391, 397, 28 N.E.2d 483. Such tables are used by insurance companies in determining premiums. See also **American experience table of mortality; Life tables; Mortality tables**.

Actuarius /æ̀kchuwériyəs/. In Roman law, a notary or clerk. One who drew the acts or statutes, or who wrote in brief the public acts. An officer who had charge of the public baths; an officer who received the money for the soldiers, and distributed it among them; a notary. See also **Actor**.

Actuary /ǽkchuweriy/. A statistician who computes insurance and pension rates and premiums on the basis of experience tables.

Actum /ǽktəm/. Lat. A deed; something done.

Actus /ǽktəs/. In the civil law, an act or action. *Non tantum verbis, sed etiam actu;* not only by words, but also by act.

A species of right of way, consisting in the right of driving cattle, or a carriage, over the land subject to the servitude. It is sometimes translated a "road," and included the kind of way termed *"iter,"* or path.

In old English law, an act of parliament; a statute. A distinction, however, was sometimes made between *actus* and *statutum*. *Actus parliamenti* was an act made by the lords and commons; and it became *statutum*, when it received the king's consent.

Actus curiæ neminem gravabit /ǽktəs kyúriyiy némənəm grəvéybət/. An act of the court shall prejudice no man. Where a delay in an action is the act of the court, neither party shall suffer for it.

Actus Dei nemini est damnosus /ǽktəs díyay némənəy èst dæmnówsəs/. The act of God is hurtful to no one. That is, a person cannot be prejudiced or held responsible for an accident occurring without his fault and attributable to the "act of God." See **Act of God**.

Actus Dei nemini facit injuriam /ǽktəs díyay némənəy féysəd ənjúriyəm/. The act of God does injury to no one. 2 Bl.Comm. 122. A thing which is inevitable by the act of God, which no industry can avoid, nor policy prevent, will not be construed to the prejudice of any person in whom there was no laches.

Actus inceptus, cujus perfectio pendet ex voluntate partium, revocari potest; si autem pendet ex voluntate tertiæ personæ, vel ex contingenti, revocari non potest /ǽktəs inséptəs, kyúwjəs pərféksh(iy)ow péndəd èks vòləntéydiy tə́rshiyiy pərsówniy, vél èks kòntinjéntay, rèvəkéray nòn pówdəst/. An act already begun, the completion of which depends on the will of the parties, may be revoked; but if it depend on the will of a third person, or on a contingency, it cannot be revoked.

Actus judiciarius coram non judice irritus habetur, de ministeriali autem a quocunque provenit ratum esto /ǽktəs jədìshiyériyəs kórəm nòn júwdəsiy íhrədəs həbíydər, dìy mìnəstìriyéylay ódəm èy kwowkə́ŋkwiy prəvíynət réydəm èstow/. A judicial act by a judge without jurisdiction is void; but a ministerial act, from whomsoever proceeding, may be ratified.

Actus legis nemini est damnosus /ǽktəs líyjəs némənəy èst dæmnówsəs/. The act of the law is hurtful to no one. An act in law shall prejudice no man.

Actus legis nemini facit injuriam /ǽktəs líyjəs némənəy féysəd ənjúriyəm/. The act of the law does injury to no one.

Actus legitimi non recipiunt modum /ǽktəs ləjídəmay nòn rəsípiyənt mówdəm/. Acts required to be done by law do not admit of qualification.

Actus me invito factus non est meus actus /ǽktəs mìy ənváydow fǽktəs nón èst míyəs ǽktəs/. An act done by me, against my will, is not my act.

Actus non facit reum, nisi mens sit rea /ǽktəs non féysət ríyəm, náysay ménz sìt ríyə/. An act does not make [the doer of it] guilty, unless the mind be guilty; that is, unless the intention be criminal. The intent and the act must both concur to constitute the crime.

Actus repugnus non potest in esse produci /ǽktəs rəpáwgnəs nòn pówdest in ésiy prəwd(y)úsay/. A repugnant act cannot be brought into being, *i.e.*, cannot be made effectual.

Actus reus /ǽktəs ríyəs/. A wrongful deed which renders the actor criminally liable if combined with mens rea; a guilty mind.

Actus servi in iis quibus opera ejus communiter adhibita est, actus domini habetur /ǽktəs sə́rvay in áyəs kwíbəs ówpərə íyjəs kəmyúwnədər ədhíbədə èst ǽktəs dómənəy həbíydər/. The act of a servant in those things in which he is usually employed, is considered the act of his master.

A cueillette /à kəyét/. In French law, in relation to the contract of affreightment, signifies when the cargo is taken on condition that the master succeeds in completing his cargo from other sources.

Ad /æd/. Lat. At; by; for; near; on account of; to; until; upon; with relation to or concerning.

A.D. An abbreviation of Anno Domini meaning in the year of our Lord.

Ad abundantiorem cautelam /æ̀d əbəndǽnshiyórəm kòtíyləm/. Lat. For more abundant caution. Otherwise expressed, *ad cautelam ex superabundanti*.

Ad admittendum clericum /æd æ̀dmiténdəm klérəkəm/. For the admitting of the clerk. A writ in the nature of an execution, commanding the bishop to admit his clerk, upon the success of the latter in a *quare impedit*.

Ad aliud examen /æd éyliyəd əgzéymən/. To another tribunal; belonging to another court, cognizance, or jurisdiction.

Ad alium diem /æd éyliyəm dáyəm/. At another day. A common phrase in the old reports.

Adamson Act. Act of Congress (1916) establishing the 8 hour workday. 45 U.S.C.A. § 45.

Adapted. Capable of use. Indicates that the object referred to has been made suitable; has been made to conform to; has been made fit by alteration. Raynor v. United States, C.C.A.Ind., 89 F.2d 469, 471.

Ad assisas capiendas /æd əsáyzəs kæpiyéndeys/. To take assises; to take or hold the assises. 3 Bl.Comm. 185, 352. *Ad assisam capiendam;* to take an assise.

A dato /èy déydow/. From the date. See **A datu.**

A datu /èy déyduw/. Law Latin. From the date. See **A dato.**

Ad audiendam considerationem curiæ /æd òdiyéndəm kənsìdəreyshiyównəm kyúriyiy/. To hear the judgment of the court.

Ad audiendum et determinandum /æd òdiyéndəm et dətàrmənéndəm/. To hear and determine. 4 Bl. Comm. 278.

Ad barram /æd bárəm/. To the bar; at the bar.

Ad barram evocatus /æd bárəm ìyvowkéydəs/. Called to the bar.

Ad campi partem /æd kæmpay párdəm/. For a share of the field or land, for champert.

Ad captum vulgi /æd kæptem váljay/. Adapted to the common understanding.

Ad coelum doctrine /æd síyləm dóktrən/. A person owns the space above his real estate to the extent that no one may acquire a right to such air space that will limit the owner's enjoyment of it. This doctrine has been rejected by most courts. U. S. v. Causby, 328 U.S. 256, 66 S.Ct. 1062, 90 L.Ed. 1206. Literally, to heaven. See **Air rights**.

Ad colligendum /æd kòləjéndəm/. For collecting; as an administrator or trustee *ad colligendum.*

Ad colligendum bona defuncti /æd kòləjéndəm bównə dəfáŋktay/. For collecting the goods of the deceased. See **Administration of estates**.

Ad communem legem /æd kəmyúwnəm líyjəm/. At common law, the name of a writ of entry (now obsolete) brought by the reversioners after the death of the life tenant, for the recovery of lands wrongfully alienated by him.

Ad commune nocumentum /æd kəmyúwniy nòkyəméntəm/. To the common nuisance.

Ad comparendum /æd kòmpəréndəm/. To appear. *Ad comparendum, et ad standum juri,* to appear and to stand to the law, or abide the judgment of the court.

Ad computum reddendum /æd kəmpyúwdəm rədéndəm/. To render an account.

Adcordabilis denarii /æ(d)kordéybələs dəníriyay/. Money paid by a vassal to his lord upon the selling or exchanging of a feud.

Ad culpam /æd kálpəm/. Until misbehavior.

Ad curiam /æd kyúriyəm/. At a court. To court.

Ad curiam vocare /æd kyúriyəm vowkériy/. To summon to court.

Ad custagia /æd kəstéyj(iy)ə/. At the costs.

Ad custum /æd kástəm/. At the cost. 1 Bl.Comm. 314.

Add. To unite; attach; annex; join. See also **Addition; Additional**.

Ad damnum /æ(d) dæmnəm/. In pleading, "To the damage." The technical name of that clause of the writ, declaration, or, more commonly, the complaint, which contains a statement of the plaintiff's money loss, or the damages which he claims. Fed.R.Civil P. 8(a).

Such clause informs an adversary of the maximum amount of the claim asserted without being proof of injury or of liability. Natale v. Great Atlantic & Pacific Tea Co., 8 App.Div. 781, 186 N.Y.S.2d 795, 796.

Ad defendendum /æ(d) dəfendéndəm/. To defend. 1 Bl.Comm. 227.

Addendum /ædéndəm/. A thing that is added or to be added; a list or section consisting of added material.

Addicere /ædísəriy/. Lat. In the civil law, to adjudge or condemn; to assign, allot, or deliver; to sell. In the Roman law, *addico* was one of the three words used to express the extent of the civil jurisdiction of the prætors.

Addict. Any individual who habitually uses any narcotic drug so as to endanger the public morals, health, safety, or welfare, or who is or has been so far addicted to the use of such narcotic drugs as to have lost the power of self-control with reference to his addiction. 18 U.S.C.A. § 4251. People v. McKibben, 24 Ill.App.3d 692, 321 N.E.2d 362, 364.

Addictio /ædíkshiyow/. In the Roman law, the giving up to a creditor of his debtor's person by a magistrate; also the transfer of the (deceased) debtor's goods to one who assumes his liabilities.

Addictive drugs. Any drug, natural or synthetic, which causes periodic or chronic intoxication by its repeated consumption.

Ad diem /æ(d) dáyəm/. At a day; at the day. *Ad alium diem,* at another day. *Ad certum diem,* at a certain day. *Solvit ad diem,* he paid at or on the day.

Addition. Implies physical contact, something added to another. Structure physically attached to or connected with building itself. Mack v. Eyssell, 332 Mo. 671, 59 S.W.2d 1049. Extension; increase; augmentation. Meyering v. Miller, 330 Mo. 885, 51 S.W.2d 65, 66. That which has become united with or a part of. See **Fixture.**

In insurance law, the word "addition", as applied to buildings usually means a part added or joined to a main building; though the term has also been held to apply to buildings appurtenant to some other building though not actually in physical contact therewith.

At common law, whatever was added to a man's name by way of title or description. In English law, there were four kinds of *additions,*—additions of *estate,* such as yeoman, gentleman, esquire; additions of *degree,* or names of dignity, as knight, earl, marquis, duke; additions of *trade,* mystery, or occupation, as scrivener, painter, mason, carpenter; and additions of *place* of residence as London, Chester, etc.

Additional. This term embraces the idea of joining or uniting one thing to another, so as thereby to form one aggregate. Ex parte Boddie, 200 S.C. 379, 21 S.E.2d 4, 8.

Additional burden. See **Eminent domain**.

Additionales /ædìsh(iy)ənéyliyz/. In the law of contracts, additional terms or propositions to be added to a former agreement.

Additional extended coverage. Insurance policy indorsement covering dwellings; covering water damage from plumbing and heating systems, vandalism and malicious mischief, glass breakage, falling trees, ice, snow, etc.

Additional instructions. Charge by judge to jury beyond the original instructions. Frequently required when the jury returns from deliberations with a question concerning the evidence, point of law, or some portion of the original charge.

Additional insured. Person(s) covered by policy in addition to the named insured; *e.g.* a person using another's automobile, which is covered by liability policy containing statutory omnibus clause, only when insured's permission is expressly or impliedly given for particular use. Stewart v. City of Rio Vista, 72 Cal.App.2d 279, 164 P.2d 274, 275.

Additional legacy. See **Legacy**.

Additional servitude. The imposition of a new and additional easement or servitude on land originally taken by eminent domain proceedings. A use of a different character, for which owner of property is entitled to compensation.

Additional work. Of nature involved in modifications and changes, not independent project. Maryland Casualty Co. v. City of South Norfolk, C.C.A.Va., 54 F.2d 1032, 1037. Work which results from a change or alteration in plans concerning work which has to be done under a contract, while "extra work" relates to work which is not included within the contract itself. De Martini v. Elade Realty Corp., Co.Ct., 52 N.Y.S.2d 487, 489.

Additio probat minoritatem /ədísh(iy)ow prówbət mənòrətéydəm/. An addition [to a name] proves or shows minority or inferiority. That is, if it be said that a man has a fee tail, it is less than if he has the fee.

Additur /ǽdətər/. The power of trial court to assess damages or increase amount of an inadequate award made by jury verdict, as condition of denial of motion for new trial, with consent of defendant whether or not plaintiff consents to such action. Dorsey et al. v. Barba et al., Cal.App., 226 P.2d 677. This is not allowed in the Federal system. Dimick v. Schiedt, 293 U.S. 474, 55 S.Ct. 296, 79 L.Ed. 603.

Add on clause. A clause in an installment contract that makes earlier purchases with that firm security for new purchases.

Addone, addonne /ǽdówniy/. L. Fr. Given to.

Address. Place where mail or other communications will reach person. Munson v. Bay State Dredging & Contracting Co., 314 Mass. 485, 50 N.E.2d 633, 636. Generally a place of business or residence.

Equity pleading. Part of a bill wherein is given the appropriate and technical description of the court in which the bill is filed. See **Caption**.

Address to the crown. In England when the royal speech has been read in Parliament, an address in answer thereto is moved in both houses. Two members are selected in each house by the administration for moving and seconding the address. Since the commencement of the session 1890–1891, it has been a single resolution expressing their thanks to the sovereign for his gracious speech.

Adduce. To present, bring forward, offer, introduce. Used particularly with reference to evidence.

Ad ea quæ frequentius accidunt jura adaptantur /ǽd íyə kwìy frəkwénsh(iy)əs ǽksədənt júrə ədǽptǽntər/. Laws are adapted to those cases which most frequently occur.

Adeem. To take away, recall, or revoke. To satisfy a legacy by some gift or substituted disposition, made by the testator, in advance. Woodburn Lodge No. 102, I. O. O. F. v. Wilson, 148 Or. 150, 34 P.2d 611, 614. See **Ademption**.

Ad effectum /ǽd əféktəm/. To the effect, or end. *Ad effectum sequentem*, to the effect following.

Adeling, or **atheling** /ǽd(ə)liŋ/. Noble; excellent. A title of honor among the Anglo-Saxons, properly belonging to the king's children.

Ademptio /ædém(p)sh(iy)ow/. Lat. In the civil law, a revocation of a legacy; an ademption. Where it was expressly transferred from one person to another, it was called *translatio*.

Ademption /ədém(p)shən/. Extinction or withdrawal of legacy by testator's act equivalent to revocation or indicating intention to revoke. Tagnon's Adm'x v. Tagnon, 253 Ky. 374, 69 S.W.2d 714.

  Removal. Lewis v. Hill, 387 Ill. 542, 56 N.E.2d 619, 621. Testator's giving to a legatee that which he has provided in his will, or his disposing of that part of his estate so bequeathed in such manner as to make it impossible to carry out the will. Hurley v. Schuler, 296 Ky. 118, 176 S.W.2d 275, 276. Revocation, recalling, or cancellation of a legacy, according to the apparent intention of the testator, implied by the law from acts done by him in his life, though such acts do not amount to an express revocation of it.

  To take away, recall, revoke, or to satisfy legacy by some gift or substituted disposition, made by testator, in advance. In re Burnett's Estate, 49 N.J.Super. 439, 140 A.2d 242, 244.

  The act by which the testator pays to his legatee, in his life-time, a general legacy which by his will he had proposed to give him at his death; and the act by which a specific legacy has become inoperative on account of the testator having parted with the subject. Dillender v. Wilson, 228 Ky. 758, 16 S.W.2d 173, 174.

  See **Advancement**.

Adeo /ǽdiyow/. Lat. So, as. *Adeo plene et integre*, as fully and entirely.

Adequate. Sufficient; commensurate; equally efficient; equal to what is required; suitable to the case or occasion; satisfactory. Equal to some given occasion or work. Nissen v. Miller, 44 N.M. 487, 105 P.2d 324, 326.

Adequate care. Such care as a man of ordinary prudence would himself take under similar circumstances to avoid accident; care proportionate to the risk to be incurred. See also **Care**.

Adequate cause. Sufficient cause for a particular purpose.

In criminal law, adequate cause for the passion which reduces a homicide committed under its influence from the grade of murder to manslaughter, means such cause as would commonly produce a degree of anger, rage, resentment, or terror, in a person of ordinary temper, sufficient to render the mind incapable of cool reflection. Insulting words or gestures, or an assault and battery so slight as to show no intention to inflict pain or injury, or an injury to property unaccompanied by violence are not adequate causes. Berry v. State, 143 Tex.Cr.R. 67, 157 S.W.2d 650, 652. See **Adequate provocation; Cause; Probable cause**.

Adequate compensation. Just value of property taken under power of eminent domain, payable in money, as guaranteed by 5th Amendment. Market value of property when taken. It may include interest and may include the cost or value of the property to the owner for the purposes for which he designed it. Such only as puts injured party in as good a condition as he would have been in if injury had not been inflicted. Town of Winchester v. Cox, 129 Conn. 106, 26 A.2d 592, 597. See also **Fair market value; Just compensation**.

Adequate consideration. One which is equal, or reasonably proportioned, to the value of that for which it is given. One which is not so disproportionate as to shock our sense of that morality and fair dealing which should always characterize transactions between man and man. Fair and reasonable under circumstances. Reasonably just and equitable. See **Fair market value; Fair value; Just compensation**.

Adequate notice. Notice reasonably calculated to apprise a person of an action, proceeding, or motion. Notice sufficient to permit an objection or defense. U. S. v. San Juan Lumber Co., D.C.Colo., 313 F.Supp. 703, 709. See **Notice**.

Adequate or reasonable facilities. Such railroad facilities as might be fairly demanded, with regard to size of place, extent of demand for transportation, cost of furnishing additional accommodation asked for, and to all other facts which would have bearing upon question of convenience and cost. Kurn v. State, 175 Okl. 379, 52 P.2d 841, 843.

Adequate preparation. Embraces full consultation with accused, interviews with witnesses, study of facts and law, and determination of character of defense to be made and policy to be followed during trial. Nelson v. Commonwealth, 295 Ky. 641, 175 S.W.2d 132, 133.

Adequate provocation. An adequate provocation to cause a sudden transport of passion that may suspend the exercise of judgment and exclude premeditation and a previously formed design is one that is calculated to excite such anger as might obscure the reason or dominate the volition of an ordinary reasonable man. See **Adequate cause**.

Adequate remedy. An "adequate remedy at law," for purposes of rule that a litigant who fails to avail himself of a remedy provided by law and who is subsequently barred from pursuing that remedy because of his own lack of diligence cannot rely on the absence of a remedy at law as a basis for equitable jurisdiction, is one which is as complete, practical and as efficient to the ends of justice and its prompt administration as a remedy in equity, and which is obtainable as of right. In re Wife, K., Del.Ch., 297 A.2d 424, 426.

An "adequate remedy at law", preventing relief by injunction, means a remedy which is plain and complete and as practical and efficient to ends of justice and its prompt administration as a remedy in equity, and although an injunction will issue when legal remedy is inadequate, injunction should not be granted where complainant has an adequate remedy at law. Hancock v. Bradshaw, Tex.Civ.App., 350 S.W.2d 955, 957.

A remedy that affords complete relief with reference to the particular matter in controversy, and is appropriate to the circumstances of the case. Must reach end intended, and actually compel performance of duty in question. Must be plain, accurate, certain, speedy, specific, and appropriate to the particular circumstances, and must also be equally as convenient, beneficial, and effective as the remedy by mandamus. Simpson v. Williams Rural High School Dist., Tex.Civ.App., 153 S.W.2d 852, 856.

Adessee /ædésiy/. In the civil law, to be present; the opposite of *abesse*.

Adeu /ədyúw/. Without day, as when a matter is finally dismissed by the court. *Alez adeu*, go without day. See **Adieu**.

Ad eversionem juris nostri /æd əvə̀rz(h)iyównəm júrəs nóstray/. To the overthrow of our right.

Ad excambium /æd ekskǽmbiyəm/. For exchange; for compensation.

Ad exhæredationem /æd eks-hìrədeyshiyównəm/. To the disherison, or disinheriting; to the injury of the inheritance. 3 Bl.Comm. 288. Formal words in the old writ of waste, which calls upon the tenant to appear and show cause why he hath committed waste and destruction in the place named, *ad exhæredationem*, etc.

Ad exitum /æd égzədəm/. At issue; at the end (of the pleadings).

Ad faciendum /æd feyshiyéndəm/. To do. *Ad faciendum, subjiciendum et recipiendum;* to do, submit to, and receive. *Ad faciendam juratam illam;* to make up that jury.

Ad feodi firmam /æd fyúwday fə́rməm/. To fee farm.

Ad fidem /æd fáydəm/. In allegiance. Subjects born *ad fidem* are those born in allegiance.

Ad filum aquæ /æd fáyləm ǽkwiy/. To the thread of the water; to the central line, or middle of the stream. *Usque ad filum aquæ*, as far as the thread of the stream. A phrase of which *ad medium filum aquæ (q.v.)* is another form, and etymologically more exact.

Ad filum viæ /æd fáyləm váyiy/. To the middle of the way; to the central line of the road.

Ad finem /æd fáynəm/. Abbreviated *ad fin.* To the end. It is used in citations to books, as a direction to read from the place designated to the end of the chapter, section, etc. *Ad finem litis,* at the end of the suit.

Ad firmam /æd fərməm/. To farm. Derived from an old Saxon word denoting rent. *Ad firmam noctis* was a fine or penalty equal in amount to the estimated cost of entertaining the king for one night. *Ad feodi firmam,* to fee farm.

Ad fundandam jurisdictionem /æd fəndǽndəm jùrəsdìk-shiyównəm/. To make the basis of jurisdiction.

Ad gaolas deliberandas /æd jeyləs dəlìbərǽndəs/. To deliver the gaols; to empty the gaols. *Ad gaolam deliberandam;* to deliver the gaol; to make gaol de-livery.

Ad gravamen /æd grævéymən/. To the grievance, inju-ry, or oppression.

Adhering. Joining, leagued with, cleaving to; as, "ad-hering to the enemies of the United States." "Adher-ing" consists in giving to the United States the loyalty due from a citizen. United States v. Stephan, D.C. Mich., 50 F.Supp. 738, 741. Any intentional act fur-thering hostile designs of enemies of the United States, or an act which intentionally strengthens or tends to strengthen enemies of the United States, or which weakens or tends to weaken power of the United States to resist and attack such enemies, con-stitutes "adhering" to such enemies. United States v. Haupt, D.C.Ill., 47 F.Supp. 836, 839.

Adhesion. Agreement to join; adherence. The en-trance of another nation into an existing treaty with respect only to a part of the principles laid down or the stipulations agreed to. Properly speaking, by adhesion the third nation becomes a party only to such parts as are specifically agreed to, and by acces-sion it accepts and is bound by the whole treaty. See **Accession.**

Adhesion contract. Standardized contract form offered to consumers of goods and services on essentially "take it or leave it" basis without affording consumer realistic opportunity to bargain and under such condi-tions that consumer cannot obtain desired product or services except by acquiescing in form contract. Dis-tinctive feature of adhesion contract is that weaker party has no realistic choice as to its terms. Wheeler v. St. Joseph Hospital, Cal.App., 63 Cal.App.3d 345, 133 Cal.Rptr. 775, 783; Standard Oil Co. of Calif. v. Perkins, C.A.Or., 347 F.2d 379, 383. Not every such contract is unconscionable. Lechmere Tire and Sales Co. v. Burwick, 360 Mass. 713, 720, 721, 277 N.E.2d 503.

Adhibere /ædhəbériy/. In the civil law, to apply; to employ; to exercise; to use. *Adhibere diligentiam,* to use care. *Adhibere vim,* to employ force.

Ad hoc /æd hó(w)k/. For this; for this special pur-pose. An attorney ad hoc, or a guardian or curator ad hoc, is one appointed for a special purpose, gener-ally to represent the client or infant in the particular action in which the appointment is made.

Ad hoc arbitration. Submission of a particular issue to arbitration.

Ad hominem /æd (h)ómənəm/. To the person. A term used in logic with reference to a personal argument.

Ad hunc diem /æd (h)əŋk dáyəm/. At this day.

Ad idem /æd áydəm/. To the same point, or effect. *Ad idem facit,* it makes to or goes to establish the same point.

A die confectionis /èy dáyiy kənfèkshiyównəs/. From the day of the making.

A die datus /èy dáyiy déydəs/. From the day of the date. Used in leases to determine the time or running of the estate, and when so used includes the day of the date.

Adieu /ədyúw/. L. Fr. Without day. A common term in the Year Books, implying final dismissal from court.

A digniori fieri debet denominatio /èy digniyóray fáyəray débət dənòmənéysh(iy)ow/. Denomination ought to be from the more worthy. The description (of a place) should be taken from the more worthy subject (as from a will).

A digniori fieri debet denominatio et resolutio /èy dig-niyóray fáyəray débət dənòmənéysh(iy)ow et rèzəl(y)-uwsh(iy)ow/. The title and exposition of a thing ought to be derived from, or given, or made with reference to, the more worthy degree, quality, or species of it.

Ad inde /æd índiy/. Thereunto. *Ad inde requisitus,* thereunto required.

Ad infinitum /æd ìnfináydəm/. Without limit; to an infinite extent; indefinitely.

Ad inquirendum /æd iŋkwəréndəm/. To inquire; a writ of inquiry; a judicial writ, commanding inquiry to be made of anything relating to a cause pending in court.

Ad instantiam /æd instǽnsh(iy)əm/. At the instance. *Ad instantiam partis,* at the instance of a party.

Ad interim /æd íntərəm/. In the meantime. An officer *ad interim* is one appointed to fill a temporary vacan-cy, or to discharge the duties of the office during the absence or temporary incapacity of its regular incum-bent.

Adiratus /ædəréydəs/. Lost; strayed; a price or value set upon things stolen or lost, as a recompense to the owner.

Adjacent. Lying near or close to; sometimes, contigu-ous; neighboring. *Adjacent* implies that the two objects are not widely separated, though they may not actually touch, Harrison v. Guilford County, 218 N.C. 718, 12 S.E.2d 269, while *adjoining* imports that they are so joined or united to each other that no third object intervenes. Wolfe v. Hurley, D.C.La., 46 F.2d 515, 521. See **Adjoining.**

Adjective law. The aggregate of rules of procedure or practice. As opposed to that body of law which the courts are established to administer (called "substan-tive law"), it means the rules according to which the substantive law is administered; *e.g.* Rules of Civil Procedure. That part of the law which provides a method for enforcing or maintaining rights, or obtaining redress for their invasion. Maurizi v. Western Coal & Mining Co., 321 Mo. 378, 11 S.W.2d 268, 272. Pertains to and prescribes practice, method, procedure or legal machinery by which substantive law is enforced or made effective. Ambrose v. State Dept. of Public Health and Welfare, Mo.App., 319 S.W.2d 271, 274.

Adjoining. The word in its etymological sense means touching or contiguous, as distinguished from lying near to or adjacent. To be in contact with; to abut upon. State ex rel. Boynton v. Bunton, 141 Kan. 103, 40 P.2d 326, 328. And the same meaning has been given to it when used in statutes. See **Adjacent**.

Adjoining owners. Those persons who own land touching the subject land and who, as a result, have right to notice of proceedings concerning the subject real estate as, for example, in zoning and licensing matters. Bayport Civic Ass'n v. Koehler, Sup., 138 N.Y. S.2d 524, 530.

Adjourn /əjə́rn/. To put off; defer; recess; postpone. To postpone action of a convened court or legislative body until another time specified, or indefinitely; the latter being usually called to adjourn *sine die*. To suspend or recess during a meeting, legislature or assembly, which continues in session. Suspending business for a time, delaying. See **Adjournment**.

Adjournamentum est ad diem dicere seu diem dare /əjə̀rnəméntəm èst æ̀(d) dáyəm dísərey syuw dáyəm dérey/. An adjournment is to appoint a day or give a day. Hence the formula "*eat sine die.*"

Adjournatur /æ̀jərnéydər/. L. Lat. It is adjourned. A word with which the old reports very frequently concluded a case.

A continuation of the same meeting, and at such adjourned meeting the governing body can do any act which might have been done if no adjournment had taken place, and limitations imposed on governing body as regards action at original meeting obtain at adjourned meeting. One ordered by board at regular meeting, and which is to convene after termination of such regular meeting and prior to next regular meeting. Byrd v. Byrd, 193 Miss. 249, 8 So.2d 510, 513.

Adjourned summons. A summons taken out in the chambers of a judge, and afterwards taken into court to be argued by counsel.

Adjourned term. In practice, a continuance, by adjournment, of a regular term. Distinguished from an "additional term," which is a distinct term. A continuation of a previous or regular term. The same term prolonged, wherein power of court over business which has been done, and the entries made at the regular term, continues.

Adjournment. A putting off or postponing of business or of a session until another time or place. The act of a court, legislative body, public meeting, or officer, by which the session or assembly is dissolved, either temporarily or finally, and the business in hand dismissed from consideration, either definitely or for an interval. If the adjournment is final, it is said to be *sine die*. See also **Recess**.

Adjournment day. A further day appointed by the judges at the regular sittings at *nisi prius* to try issue of fact not then ready for trial.

Adjournment day in error. In English practice, a day appointed some days before the end of the term at which matters left undone on the affirmance day are finished.

Adjournment in eyre /əjə́rnmənt in ér/. In English law, the appointment of a day when the justices in eyre mean to sit again.

Adjournment sine die /əjə́rnmənt sáyniy dáy(iy)/°síyney díyey/. An adjournment without setting a time for another meeting or session. See **Sine die**.

Adjudge /əjə́j/. To pass on judicially, to decide, settle, or decree, or to sentence or condemn. People v. Rave, 364 Ill. 72, 3 N.E.2d 972, 975. Judgment of a court of competent jurisdiction; equivalent of convicted and sentenced. Implies a judicial determination of a fact, and the entry of a judgment. See also **Judgment**.

Adjudicate /əjúwdəkèyt/. To settle in the exercise of judicial authority. To determine finally. Synonymous with *adjudge* in its strictest sense. United States v. Irwin, 127 U.S. 125, 8 S.Ct. 1033, 32 L.Ed. 99.

Adjudicated rights. Rights which have been recognized in a judicial or administrative proceeding.

Adjudicatee /əjùwdəkeytíy/. In French and civil law, the purchaser at a judicial sale.

Adjudicatio /əjùwdəkéysh(iy)ow/. In the civil law, an adjudication. The judgment of the court that the subject matter is the property of one of the litigants; confirmation of title by judgment.

Adjudication /əjùwdəkéyshən/. The formal giving or pronouncing a judgment or decree in a cause; also the judgment given. The entry of a decree by a court in respect to the parties in a case. Samuel Goldwyn, Inc., v. United Artists Corporation, C.C.A.Del., 113 F.2d 703, 706. It implies a hearing by a court, after notice, of legal evidence on the factual issue(s) involved. Genzer v. Fillip, Tex.Civ.App., 134 S.W.2d 730, 732. The equivalent of a "determination." Campbell v. Wyoming Development Co., 55 Wyo. 347, 100 P.2d 124, 132. And contemplates that the claims of all the parties thereto have been considered and set at rest. Miller v. Scobie, 152 Fla. 328, 11 So.2d 892, 894. See **Administrative adjudication; Judgment**.

Adjudicative claims arbitration. Concerned primarily with tort and other claims involving small amounts as distinguished from the traditional categories of arbitration in the fields of labor, commerce and international trade. Designed to relieve courts of burden of handling such cases.

Adjudicative facts. Factual matters concerning the parties to an administrative proceeding as contrasted with legislative facts which are general and usually do not touch individual questions of particular parties to a proceeding. Facts which concern a person's motives and intent, as contrasted with general policy issues. U. S. v. Bishop Processing Co., D.C.Md., 287 F.Supp. 624, 633.

Adjudicatory hearing. A proceeding before an administrative agency in which the rights and duties of particular persons are adjudicated after notice and opportunity to be heard.

Adjudicatory process. Method of adjudicating factual disputes; used generally in reference to administrative proceedings in contrast to judicial proceedings.

Adjudicature /əjúwdəkəchər/. In Canadian law, a purchaser at a sheriff's sale.

Ad judicium /æ̀(d) juwdísh(iy)əm/. To judgment; to court. *Ad judicium provocare;* to summon to court; to commence an action; a term of the Roman law.

Adjunct /ǽjəŋkt/. Something added to another, but in a subordinate, auxiliary, or dependent position. See also **Appurtenance**.

One associated with another in a subordinate or an auxiliary manner; an associate.

Adjunction /əjə́ŋ(k)shən/. Adding, affixing or attaching to another. Act of adjoining. In civil law, the attachment or union permanently of a thing belonging to one person to that belonging to another. The common law implicitly adopts the civil law doctrines. See **Accession**.

Adjunctum accessorium /əjə́ŋktəm æ̀ksəsóriyəm/. An accessory or appurtenance.

Ad jungendum auxilium /æ̀(d) jə̀njéndəm ogzíl(i)yəm/. To join in aid. See **Aid prayer**.

Ad jura regis /æ̀(d) júra ríyjəs/. To the rights of the king; a writ which was brought by the king's clerk, presented to a living against those who endeavored to eject him, to the prejudice of the king's title.

Adjuration /æ̀jəréyshən/. A swearing or binding upon oath.

Adjust. To settle or arrange; to free from differences or discrepancies. To bring to satisfactory state so that parties are agreed, as to adjust amount of loss by fire or controversy regarding property or estate. To bring to proper relations; to settle. To determine and apportion an amount due. Accounts are adjusted when they are settled and a balance is struck. Term is sometimes used in the sense of pay, when used in reference to a liquidated claim. Combination Oil & Gas Co. v. Brady, Tex.Civ.App., 96 S.W.2d 415, 416. Determination of amount to be paid to insured by insurer to cover loss or damage sustained. See **Adjuster; Adjustment; Settlement**.

Adjusted basis. The cost or other basis of property reduced by depreciation allowed or allowable and increased by capital improvements. See **Basis**.

Adjusted cost basis. For income tax purposes, original cost plus additions to capital less depreciation results in the "adjusted cost basis." Herder v. Helvering, 70 U.S.App.D.C. 287, 106 F.2d 153, 162.

Adjusted gross estate. The gross estate less I.R.C. §§ 2053 and 2054 expenses equals the adjusted gross estate. Generally, I.R.C. §§ 2053 and 2054 expenses include administration expenses, debts of the decedent, and losses incurred by the estate. Fifty percent of the adjusted gross estate measures the maximum amount of the marital deduction allowed for death tax purposes. See **Administration expense; Gross estate; Marital deduction**.

Adjusted gross income. Term used in individual taxation to describe gross income less certain allowable deductions. I.R.C. § 62.

Adjuster. One appointed to adjust a matter; to ascertain or arrange or settle. One who makes any adjustment or settlement, or who determines the amount of a claim, as a claim against an insurance company. A representative of the insurer who seeks to determine the extent of the firm's liability for loss when a claim is submitted. A person who acts for the insurance company or the insured in the determination and settlement of claims. "Public adjusters" represent claimants only. See **Claim adjuster; Claimant adjuster; Independent adjuster**.

Adjustment. An arrangement; a settlement. In the law of insurance, the adjustment of a loss is the ascertainment of its amount and the ratable distribution of it among those liable to pay it. The settling and ascertaining the amount of the indemnity which the assured, after all allowances and deductions made, is entitled to receive under the policy, and fixing the proportion which each underwriter is liable to pay.

Adjustment board. See **Board of adjustment**.

Adjustment bond. See **Bond**.

Adjustment securities. Stocks and bonds which are issued during a corporate reorganization.

Adjutant general /ǽjədən(t) jén(ə)rəl/. An officer in charge of the National Guard of one of the States. The administrative head of a military unit having a general staff.

Adjuvari quippe nos, non decipi, beneficio oportet /æ̀juwvéray kwípiy nóws, non désəpay, bènəfísh(iy)ow əpórdət/. We ought to be favored, not injured by that which is intended for our benefit. (The species of bailment called "loan" must be to the advantage of the borrower, not to his detriment.)

Ad largum /æ̀d lárgəm/. At large; as, title at large; assize at large. Also at liberty; free, or unconfined. *Ire ad largum,* to go at large. A special verdict was formerly called a verdict at large.

Adlegiare /ædliyjiyériy/. To purge one's self of a crime by oath.

Ad libitum /æ̀d líbidəm/. At pleasure. 3 Bl.Comm. 292.

Ad litem /æ̀d láydəm/. For the suit; for the purposes of the suit; pending the suit. A guardian *ad litem* is a guardian appointed to prosecute or defend a suit on behalf of a party incapacitated by infancy or otherwise.

Ad lucrandum vel perdendum /æ̀d l(y)uwkrǽndəm vèl pərdéndəm/. For gain or loss. Emphatic words in the old warrants of attorney. Sometimes expressed in English, "to lose and gain."

Ad majorem cautelam /æ̀d məjórəm kotíyləm/. For greater security.

Admanuensis /ædmæ̀nyuwénsəs/. A person who swore by laying his hands on the book.

Ad manum /æd méynəm/. At hand; ready for use. *Et querens sectam habeat ad manum;* and the plaintiff immediately have his suit ready.

Admeasurement /ædmézhərmənt/. Ascertainment by measure; measuring out; assignment or apportionment by measure, that is, by fixed quantity or value, by certain limits, or in definite and fixed proportions.

Admeasurement of dower. A common law remedy which lay for the heir on reaching his majority to rectify an assignment of dower made during his minority, by which the doweress had received more than she was legally entitled to.

Admeasurement of pasture. In English law, a writ which lay between those that had common of pasture appendant, or by vicinage, in cases where any one or more of them surcharged the common with more cattle than they ought. This remedy has long been abolished in England and in the United States.

Admeasurement, writ of. A common law remedy which lay against persons who usurped more than their share, in the two following cases: Admeasurement of dower, and admeasurement of pasture.

Ad medium filum aquæ /æd míydiyəm fáyləm ǽkwiy/. To the middle thread of the stream. See **Ad filum aquæ.**

Ad medium filum viæ /æd míydiyəm fáyləm váyiy/. To the middle thread of the way.

Ad melius inquirendum /æd míyliyəs ìnkwəréndəm/. A writ directed to a coroner commanding him to hold a second inquest.

Admensuratio /ædmènsyəréysh(iy)ow/. In old English law, admeasurement.

Adminicle /ædmínəkəl/. Used as an English word in the statute of 1 Edw. IV, c. 1, in the sense of aid, or support. In civil law, imperfect proof. See **Adminiculum.**

Adminicular /ædməníkyələr/. Auxiliary or subordinate to. "The murder would be *adminicular* to the robbery" (*i. e.,* committed to accomplish it).

Adminicular evidence /ædməníkyələr évidən(t)s/. Auxiliary or supplementary evidence; such as is presented for the purpose of explaining and completing other evidence. (Chiefly used in ecclesiastical law.)

Adminiculate /ædməníkyəleyt/. To give adminicular evidence.

Adminiculator /ædməníkyəleydər/. An officer in the Roman Catholic Church who administered to the wants of widows, orphans, and afflicted persons.

Adminiculum /ædməníkyələm/. Lat. An adminicle; a prop or support; an accessory thing. An aid or support to something else, whether a right or the evidence of one. It is principally used to designate evidence adduced in aid or support of other evidence, which without it is imperfect.

Administer. To manage or conduct. Glocksen v. Holmes, 299 Ky. 626, 186 S.W.2d 634, 637. To discharge the duties of an office; to take charge of business; to manage affairs; to serve in the conduct of affairs, in the application of things to their uses; to settle and distribute the estate of a decedent. Also, to give, as an oath; to direct or cause to be taken.

To "administer" a decree is to execute it, to enforce its provisions, to resolve conflicts as to its meaning, to construe and to interpret its language. U. S. v. Hennen, D.C.Nev., 300 F.Supp. 256, 263.

To apply, as medicine or a remedy; to give, as a dose of something beneficial or suitable. Barfield v. State, 71 Okl.Cr. 195, 110 P.2d 316, 317. To cause or procure a person to take some drug or other substance into his or her system; to direct and cause a medicine, poison, or drug to be taken into the system.

Administration. Management or conduct of an office or employment; the performance of the executive duties of an institution, business, or the like. In public law, the administration of government means the practical management and direction of the executive department, or of the public machinery or functions, or of the operations of the various organs or agencies. Direction or oversight of any office, service, or employment. Greene v. Wheeler, C.C.A.Wis., 29 F.2d 468, 469. The term "administration" is also conventionally applied to the whole class of public functionaries, or those in charge of the management of the executive department.

Administration expense. Administrative expenses imply disbursements incidental to the management of the estate which are deductible in computing estate taxes. Such deductions are allowed for such expenses or claims only to the extent that they "are allowable by the laws of the jurisdiction" under which the estate is being administered. I.R.C. § 2053.

Administration letters. The instrument by which an administrator or administratrix is authorized by the probate court, surrogate, or other proper officer, to have the charge and administration of the goods and property of an intestate. See **Administrator.**

Administration of estates. The management and settlement of the estate of an intestate, or of a testator who has no executor, performed under the supervision of a court, by a person duly qualified and legally appointed, and usually involving: (1) the collection of the decedent's assets; (2) payment of debts and claims against the estate; (3) payment of estate taxes; (4) distribution of the remainder of the estate among those entitled thereto. See **Administrator; Letters of administration.**

Administration of estates is principally of the following kinds:

Ad colligendum bona defuneti. To collect the goods of the deceased. Special letters of administration granted to one or more persons, authorizing them to collect and preserve the goods of the deceased.

Ad prosequendum. An administrator appointed to prosecute or defend a certain action (*e.g.* wrongful death) or actions in which the estate is concerned.

Ancillary administration is auxiliary and subordinate to the administration at the place of the decedent's domicile; it may be taken out in any foreign state or country where assets are locally situated, and is merely for the purpose of collecting such assets and paying debts there.

Cum testamento annexo (CTA). Administration with the will annexed. Administration granted in cases where a testator makes a will without naming any executors; or where the executors who are named in the will are incompetent to act, are deceased, or refuse to act.

De bonis non (DBN). Administration granted for the purpose of administering such of the goods of a deceased person as were not administered by the former executor or administrator.

De bonis non cum testamento annexo (DBNCTA). That which is granted when an executor dies leaving a part of the estate unadministered.

Durante absentia. That which is granted during the absence of the executor and until he has proved the will.

Durante minori ætate. Exists where an infant is made executor, in which case administration with will annexed is granted to another during the minority of such executor, and until he shall attain his lawful age to act.

Foreign administration. That which is exercised by virtue of authority properly conferred by a foreign power.

General administration. The grant of authority to administer upon the entire estate of a decedent, without restriction or limitation, whether under the intestate laws or with the will annexed.

Pendente lite. Administration granted during the pendency of a suit touching the validity of a will.

Public administration is such as is conducted (in some jurisdictions) by an officer called the public administrator, who is appointed to administer in cases where the intestate has left no person entitled to apply for letters.

Special administration. Authority to administer upon some few particular effects of a decedent, as opposed to authority to administer his whole estate.

Administrative. Connotes of or pertains to administration, especially management, as by managing or conducting, directing, or superintending, the execution, application or conduct of persons or things. Fluet v. McCabe, 299 Mass. 173, 12 N.E.2d 89, 93. Particularly, having the character of executive or ministerial action. Mauritz v. Schwind, Tex.Civ.App., 101 S.W.2d 1085, 1090. In this sense, administrative functions or acts are distinguished from such as are judicial. People ex rel. Van Sickle v. Austin, 20 App.Div. 1, 46 N.Y.S. 526.

Administrative acts. Those acts which are necessary to be done to carry our legislative policies and purposes already declared by the legislative body or such as are devolved upon it by the organic law of its existence. Ex parte McDonough, 27 Cal.App.2d 155, 80 P.2d 485, 487.

Administrative adjudication. The process by which an administrative agency issues an order, such order being affirmative, negative, injunctive or declaratory in form. Adm. Procedure Act, § 551.

Administrative agency. A governmental body charged with administering and implementing particular legislation. Examples are worker's compensation commissions, Joseph H. Weiderhoff, Inc., v. Neal, D.C. Mo., 6 F.Supp. 798, 799; Federal Trade Commission, Hastings Mfg. Co. v. Federal Trade Commission, C.C. A.6th, 153 F.2d 253, certiorari denied 328 U.S. 853, 66 S.Ct. 1344, 90 L.Ed. 1626; tax commissions, First State Bank of Mountainair v. State Tax Commission, 40 N.M. 319, 59 P.2d 667; public service commissions, New York Cent. R. Co. v. Public Service Commission, 212 Ind. 329, 7 N.E.2d 957; and the like. In addition to "agency", such governmental bodies may be called commissions, corporations (*e.g.* F.D.I.C.), boards, departments, or divisions.

The term "agency" includes any department, independent establishment, commission, administration, authority, board or bureau of the United States or any corporation in which the United States has a proprietary interest, unless the context shows that such term was intended to be used in a more limited sense. 18 U.S.C.A. § 1.

Administrative authority. The power of an agency or its head to carry out the terms of the law creating the agency as well as to make regulations for the conduct of business before the agency; distinguishable from legislative authority to make laws.

Administrative board. This term is very broad and includes bodies exercising varied functions, some of which involve orders made or other acts done ex parte or without full hearing as to the operative facts, while others are done only after such a notice and hearing, and the functions of the former kind are plainly "administrative" and those of the latter are "quasi judicial." Beaverdale Memorial Park v. Danaher, 127 Conn. 175, 15 A.2d 17, 21. Administrative boards differ from "courts" in that boards frequently represent public interests entrusted to boards, whereas courts are concerned with litigating rights of parties with adverse interests. Rommell v. Walsh, 127 Conn. 16, 15 A.2d 6, 9.

Administrative crime. An offense consisting of a violation of an administrative rule or regulation and carrying with it a criminal sanction.

Administrative determination. See **Administrative adjudication.**

Administrative deviation. Departure from the administrative provisions of a trust by the trustee acting alone or with prior approval of the court. Anderson v. Ryland, 232 Ark. 335, 336 S.W.2d 52.

Administrative discretion. Term means that the doing of acts or things required to be done may rest, in part at least, upon considerations not entirely susceptible of proof or disproof and at times which considering the circumstances and subject-matter cannot be supplied by the Legislature, and a statute confers such discretion when it refers a commission or office to beliefs, expectations, or tendencies instead of facts for the exercise of the powers conferred. Culver v. Smith, Tex.Civ.App., 74 S.W.2d 754, 757.

Administrative hearing. An oral proceeding before an administrative agency consisting of argument or trial or both. Procedural rules are more relaxed at such hearings as contrasted with civil or criminal trials; *e.g.* rules governing admissibility of evidence are usually quite liberal. See also **Hearing.**

Administrative interpretation. Meaning given to a law or regulation by an administrative agency.

Administrative law. Body of law created by administrative agencies in the form of rules, regulations, orders, and decisions.

Administrative law judge. One who presides at an administrative hearing, with power to administer oaths, take testimony, rule on questions of evidence and make agency determinations of fact. Formerly called "hearing officer" or "hearing examiner". Adm. Procedure Act, § 556.

Administrative officer. Politically, and as used in constitutional law, an officer of the executive department of government, and generally one of inferior rank; legally, a ministerial or executive officer, as distinguished from a judicial officer.

Administrative order. The final disposition of a matter before an administrative agency; product of an administrative adjudication. Such order may be declaratory or it may contain an affirmative or negative command. Adm. Procedure Act, § 554.

A regulation issued by an administrative agency interpreting or applying the provisions of a statute. Administrative acts having force of law, designed to clarify or implement a law or policy.

Administrative procedure. Methods and processes before administrative agencies as distinguished from judicial procedure which applies to courts. Procedural rules and regulations of most federal agencies are set forth in the Code of Federal Regulations. See also **Administrative Procedure Act**.

Administrative Procedure Act. *Federal.* Law enacted in 1946 (60 Stat. 237, 5 U.S.C.A.) governing practice and proceedings before federal administrative agencies.

State. Individual states have enacted variations of the federal Act, *e.g.* M.G.L.A. (Mass.) c. 30A. Such acts govern proceedings for state administrative agencies.

Administrative process. In general, the procedure used before administrative agencies; in particular, the means of summoning witnesses before such agencies, *e.g.* subpoena.

Administrative remedy. Non-judicial remedy provided by agency, board, commission, or the like. In most instances, all administrative remedies must have been exhausted before a court will take jurisdiction of a case; *e.g.* U.S. District Courts will not consider a social security case unless all hearing, appeal, etc. remedies before the Social Security Administration have been exhausted.

Administrative review. Generally refers to judicial review of administrative proceedings; may also embrace appellate review within the administrative agency itself. Adm. Procedure Act, § 557.

Administrative rule-making. Power of an administrative agency to make rules and regulations for proceedings before it. Adm. Procedure Act, § 553.

Administrative tribunal. A particular administrative agency before which a matter may be heard or tried as distinguished from a judicial forum.

Administrator. A person appointed by the court to administer (*i.e.,* manage or take charge of) the assets and liabilities of a decedent (*i.e.,* the deceased). Such person may be a male (*i.e.,* administrator) or a female (*i.e.,* administratrix). If the person performing these services is named by the decedent's will, he is designated as the executor, or she the executrix, of the estate.

An instrumentality established by law for performing the acts necessary for transfer of effects left by deceased to those who succeed to their ownership. Behnke v. Geib, D.C.Md., 169 F.Supp. 647, 650.

Domestic. One appointed at the place of the domicile of the decedent; distinguished from a foreign or an ancillary administrator.

Foreign. One appointed or qualified under the laws of a foreign state or country, where the decedent was domiciled.

Public. An official provided for by statute in some states to administer upon the property of intestates in certain cases.

Administrator ad litem /ædmìnəstréydər æd láydəm/. A special administrator appointed by court to supply a necessary party to an action in which deceased or his estate is interested.

Administrator cum testamento annexo (C.T.A.) /ædmìnəstréydər kəm testəméndow ənéksow/. See **Cum testamento annexo**.

Administrator de bonis non (D.B.N.) /ædmìnəstréydər dìy bównəs nòn/. "Administrators de bonis non administratis" are, as the term signifies, persons appointed by the court of probate to administer on the effects of a decedent which have not been included in a former administration.

Administrator pendente lite /ædmìnəstréydər pèndéntey láydiy/. A temporary administrator appointed before an adjudication of intestacy has been made for purpose of preserving assets of the estate.

Administrator with will annexed. One appointed administrator of deceased's estate after executors named in will have refused or are unable to act.

Administratrix /ədmìnəstréytrəks/. A woman who administers, or to whom letters of administration have been granted.

Admiralitas /ædmərǽlətæs/. L. Lat. Admiralty; the admiralty, or court of admiralty. In European law, an association of private armed vessels for mutual protection and defense against pirates and enemies.

Admiralty. See **Maritime**.

Admiralty court. A court exercising jurisdiction over all maritime contracts, torts, injuries, or offenses. Federal district courts have jurisdiction over admiralty and maritime actions. 28 U.S.C.A. § 1333. Procedure in such actions is governed by the Fed.R. Civil P. and Supp. Admiralty Rules. See also **Saving to suitors clause**.

Admiralty, First Lord of the. In England, formerly the normal head of the executive department of state which presided over the naval forces of the kingdom was the lord high admiral, but in practice the functions of the great office were discharged by several Lords Commissioners, of whom one, being the chief, was called the "First Lord," and was a member of the Cabinet. He was assisted by other lords, called Sea Lords, and by various secretaries.

Admiralty law. The terms "admiralty" and "maritime" law are virtually synonymous. See **Maritime law**.

Admissible. Pertinent and proper to be considered in reaching a decision. Used with reference to the issues to be decided in any judicial proceeding.

Admissible evidence. As applied to evidence, the term means that the evidence introduced is of such a character that the court or judge is bound to receive it; that is, allow it to be introduced at trial. Admissibility of evidence in federal courts is governed by Federal Rules of Evidence. See **Evidence; Limited admissibility; Relevant evidence**.

Admission. *Admission temporaire.* Admission of goods into country duty-free for processing and eventual export.

Bail. The order of a competent court or magistrate that a person accused of crime be discharged from actual custody upon the taking of bail.

Evidence. Ruling by trial judge that trier of fact, judge or jury, may consider testimony or document or other thing (real evidence) in determining ultimate question. See **Evidence**.

Admissions. Confessions, concessions or voluntary acknowledgments made by a party of the existence of certain facts. More accurately regarded, they are statements by a party, or some one identified with him in legal interest, of the existence of a fact which is relevant to the cause of his adversary.

A voluntary acknowledgement made by a party of the existence of the truth of certain facts which are inconsistent with his claims in an action. Vockie v. General Motors Corp., Chevrolet Division, D.C.Pa., 66 F.R.D. 57, 60. An admission is not limited to words, but may also include the demeanor, conduct and acts of the person charged with a crime. People v. Baldi, 80 Misc.2d 118, 362 N.Y.S.2d 927, 933.

Admissions against interest. A statement made by one of the parties to an action which amounts to a prior acknowledgment by him that one of the material facts relevant to the issues is not as he now claims. Nagel v. Hopingardner, Tex.Civ.App., 464 S.W.2d 472, 476. Any statements made by or attributable to a party to an action, which constitute admissions against his interest and tend to establish or disprove any material fact in the case. Kellner v. Whaley, 148 Neb. 259, 27 N.W.2d 183, 189.

Admissions by party-opponent. A statement is not hearsay if the statement is offered against a party and is (A) his own statement, in either his individual or a representative capacity, or (B) a statement of which he has manifested his adoption or belief in its truth, or (C) a statement by a person authorized by him to make a statement concerning the subject, or (D) a statement by his agent or servant concerning a matter within the scope of his agency or employment, made during the existence of the relationship, or (E) a statement by a coconspirator of a party during the course and in furtherance of the conspiracy. Fed. Evid.R. 801(d)(2).

Admissions by silence. If a statement is made by another person in the presence of a party to the action, containing assertions of facts which, if untrue, the party would under all the circumstances naturally be expected to deny, his failure to speak has traditionally been receivable against him as an admission. Failure of one not under arrest to respond by denial to accusation of crime, or element of crime, may be construed as admission of guilt if such person understood accusation and could have responded. See also **Estoppel; Silence**.

Adoptive admission. Action by a party in which he approves statement of one for whom he is responsible thereby accepting truth of statement. Silence, actions, or statements which manifest assent to the statements of another person. Such may be received into evidence as admissions of the defendant if it can be shown that the defendant adopted the statements as his own. See Fed.Evid.R. 801(d)(2)(B).

Criminal admissions. A statement by accused, direct or implied, of facts pertinent to issue, and tending, in connection with proof of other facts, to prove his guilt. State v. Johnson, 277 Minn. 368, 152 N.W.2d 768, 773. The avowal of a fact or of circumstances from which guilt may be inferred, but only tending to prove the offense charged, and not amounting to a confession of guilt. A statement by defendant of fact or facts pertinent to issues tending, in connection with proof of other facts or circumstances, to prove guilt, but which is, of itself, insufficient to authorize conviction. Does not include statements which are part of the res gestae. State v. Clark, 102 Mont. 432, 58 P.2d 276, 278.

Discovery practice. Requests for admissions in civil actions are governed by Fed.R. Civil P. 36. Any matter admitted under Rule 36 is conclusively established unless the court on motion permits withdrawal or amendment of the admission. See **Request** (*Request for admission*); **Stipulation**.

Distinguished from confession. A confession is a statement admitting or acknowledging all facts necessary for conviction of the crime. An admission, on the other hand, is an acknowledgment of a fact or facts tending to prove guilt which falls short of an acknowledgment of all essential elements of the crime. Gladden v. Unsworth, 9th Cir., 396 F.2d 373, 375 n. 2; People v. Fitzgerald, 56 Cal.2d 855, 861, 17 Cal.Rptr. 129, 132, 366 P.2d 481, 484. The term "admission" is usually applied to civil transactions and to those matters of fact in criminal cases which do not involve criminal intent, while the term "confession" is generally restricted to acknowledgments of guilt. People v. Sourisseau, 62 Cal.App.2d 917, 145 P.2d 916, 923.

Implied admissions are those which result from some act or failure to act of the party; *e.g.* part payment of a debt is an admission of liability to pay debt.

Incidental admissions are those made in some other connection, or involved in the admission of some other fact.

Judicial admissions are those made in court by a person's attorney for the purpose of being used as a substitute for the regular legal evidence of the facts at the trial. Such as are made voluntarily by a party, which appear of record in the proceedings of the court. Formal acts done by a party or his attorney in court on the trial of a cause for the purpose of dispensing with proof by the opposing party of some fact claimed by the latter to be true. Hofer v. Bituminous Gas. Corp., 260 Iowa 81, 148 N.W.2d 485, 486.

Pleading. The acknowledgment or recognition by one party of the truth of some matter alleged by the opposite party, made in a pleading, the effect of which is to narrow the area of facts or allegations required to be proved by evidence. Averments in a pleading to which a responsive pleading is required are admitted when not denied in the responsive pleading. Fed.R. Civil P. 8(d).

Quasi admission. See that title.

Request for admission. See **Request.**

Tacit admissions. See **Tacit admissions.**

Admissions tax. Form of tax imposed as part of price of being admitted to a particular function or event.

Admit. See **Admission; Admissions.**

Admittance. In English law, the act of giving possession of a copyhold estate. It is of three kinds: (1) Upon a voluntary grant by the lord, where the land has escheated or reverted to him. (2) Upon surrender by the former tenant. (3) Upon descent, where the heir is tenant on his ancestor's death. Copyholds were abolished by Part V of Law of Property Act 1922.

Admittendo clerico /ædmətĕndow klέrəkow/. An old English writ issuing to the bishop to establish the right of the Crown to make a presentation to a benefice. A writ of execution upon a right of presentation to a benefice being recovered in *quare impedit,* addressed to the bishop or his metropolitan, requiring him to admit and institute the clerk or presentee of the plaintiff.

Admittendo in socium /ædmətĕndow in sówshiyəm/. An old English writ for associating certain persons, as knights and other gentlemen of the county, to justices of assize on the circuit.

Admixture /ædmíks(h)chər/. A substance formed by mixing; state of being mixed; act of mixing.

Admonish /ædmónəsh/. To caution or advise. To counsel against wrong practices, or to warn against danger of an offense. See **Admonition.**

Admonition /ædməníshən/. Any authoritative oral communication or statement by way of advice or caution by the court to the jury respecting their duty or conduct as jurors, the admissibility or nonadmissibility of evidence, or the purpose for which any evidence admitted may be considered by them. Reprimand or cautionary statement addressed to counsel by judge.

In English law, a reprimand from a judge to a person accused, on being discharged, warning him of the consequences of his conduct, and intimating to him that, should he be guilty of the same fault for which he has been admonished, he will be punished with greater severity. The admonition was authorized as a species of punishment for slight misdemeanors. In ecclesiastical law, this is the lightest form of punishment.

Admonitio trina /ædmənĭshiyow tráynə/. The threefold warning given to a prisoner who stood mute, before he was subjected to *peine forte et dure (q.v.).* 4 Bl.Comm. 325.

Ad mordendum assuetus /æd mordĕndəm əswíydəs/. Accustomed to bite. A material averment in declarations for damage done by a dog to persons or animals.

Admortization /ædmòrdəzéyshən/. In feudal customs, the reduction of property of lands or tenements to mortmain.

Adnepos /ædnəpows/. The son of a great-great-grandson.

Adneptis /ædnéptəs/. The daughter of a great-great-granddaughter.

Adnichiled /ædníkəld/. Annulled, canceled, made void.

Adnihilare /ædnày(h)əlériy/. In old English law, to annul; to make void; to reduce to nothing; to treat as nothing; to hold as or for nought.

Ad nocumentum /æd nòkyəméntəm/. To the nuisance, or annoyance; to the hurt or injury. *Ad nocumentum liberi tenementi sui,* to the nuisance of his freehold. Formal words in the old assise of nuisance. 3 Bl.Comm. 221.

Adnotatio /ædnowtéysh(iy)ow/. In the civil law, the subscription of a name or signature to an instrument. A rescript *(q.v.)* of the prince or emperor, signed with his own hand, or sign-manual. In the imperial law, casual homicide was excused by the indulgence of the emperor, signed with his own sign-manual, *annotatione principis.* 4 Bl.Comm. 187.

Ad officium justiciariorum spectat, unicuique coram eis placitanti justitiam exhibere /æd əfísh(iy)əm jəstìshiyèriyórəm spéktət yùwnək(yuw)áykwiy kórəm íyəs plæsətæntay jəstísh(iy)əm eksəbíriy/. It is the duty of justices to administer justice to every one pleading before them.

Adolescence. That age which follows puberty and precedes the age of majority.

Ad omissa vel male appretiata /æd əmísə vel mæliy əprìysh(iy)éydə/. With relation to omissions or wrong interpretations.

Adopt. To accept, appropriate, choose, or select. To make that one's own (property or act) which was not so originally. To accept, consent to, and put into effective operation; as in the case of a constitution, constitutional amendment, ordinance, court rule, or by-law.

Adoption. Legal process pursuant to state statute in which a child's legal rights and duties toward his natural parents are terminated and similar rights and duties toward his adoptive parents are substituted. To take into one's family the child of another and give him or her the rights, privileges, and duties of a child and heir. The procedure is entirely statutory and has no historical basis in common law. Most adoptions are through agency placements. See **Adoption by estoppel; De facto adoption; Equitable adoption; Placement; Private placement** (*Adoption*).

Adoption by estoppel. Equitable adoption of a child by promises and acts which preclude such person and his estate from denying adopted status to child. Heien v. Crabtree, Tex., 369 S.W.2d 28, 30. See also **Equitable adoption.**

Adoption by reference. Statement in writing by which another statement in a separate writing is incorporated by reference. Statement in pleading may be adopted by reference in a different part of same pleading or in another pleading or motion. Fed.R. Civil P. 10(c).

Adoptive act. An act of legislation which comes into operation within a limited area upon being adopted, in manner prescribed therein, by the inhabitants of that area.

Ad opus /æd ówpəs/. To the work.

Ad ostendendum /æd òstəndéndəm/. To show. Formal words in old writs.

Ad ostium ecclesiæ /æd óstiyəm əklíyziyiy/. At the door of the church. One of the five species of dower formerly recognized by the English law. 2 Bl.Comm. 132.

Ad pios usus /æd páyows yúwzəs/. Lat. For pious (religious or charitable) uses or purposes. Used with reference to gifts and bequests.

Ad prosequendam /æd pròsəkwéndəm/. To prosecute.

Ad proximum antecedens fiat relatio nisi impediatur sententia /æd próksəməm æntəsíydenz fáyæt rəléysh(iy)ow náysay impìydiyéydər sènténsh(iy)ə/. Relative words refer to the nearest antecedent, unless it be prevented by the context. Brown v. Brown, Del., 3 Terry 157, 29 A.2d 149, 153.

Ad punctum temporis /æd páŋktəm témpərəs/. At the point of time.

Ad quærimoniam /æd kwìrəmówniyəm/. On complaint of.

Ad quæstionem facti non respondent judices; ad quæstionem juris non respondent juratores /æd kwès(h)chiyównəm fǽktay nón rəspóndənt júwdəsiyz; æd kwès(h)chiyównəm júrəs nón rəspóndənt jùrətóriyz/. Means that juries must answer to questions of fact and judges to questions of law. Ex parte United States, C.C.A.Wis., 101 F.2d 870, 874.

Ad quæstiones legis judices, et non juratores, respondent /æd kwes(h)chiyówniyz líyjəs júwdəsìyz, et nòn jurətóriyz, rəspóndənt/. Judges, and not jurors, decide questions of law.

Ad quem /æd kwém/. To which. A term used in the computation of time or distance, as correlative to *a quo;* denotes the end or terminal point. See **A quo.**

The *terminus a quo* is the point of beginning or departure; the *terminus ad quem,* the end of the period or point of arrival.

Ad questiones facti non respondent judices; ad questiones legis non respondent juratores /æd kwès(h)chiyówniyz fǽktay nón rəspóndənt júwdəsiyz; æd kwès(h)chiyówniyz líyjəs nón rəspóndənt jùrətóriyz/. Judges do not answer questions of fact; juries do not answer questions of law.

Adquieto /ædkwayíydow/. Payment.

Ad quod curia concordavit /æd kwòd kyúriyə kòŋkərdéyvət/. To which the court agreed.

Ad quod damnum /æd kwò(d) dámnəm/. The name of a writ formerly issuing from the English chancery, commanding the sheriff to make inquiry "to what damage" a specified act, if done, will tend.

It is a writ which ought to be sued before the king grants certain liberties, as a fair, market or such like, which may be prejudicial to others, and thereby it should be inquired whether it will be a prejudice to grant them, and to whom it will be prejudicial, and what prejudice will come thereby.

There is also another writ of *ad quod damnum,* if any one will turn a common highway and lay out another way as beneficial.

A "writ of ad quod damnum" is of ancient origin, and could be issued as a writ of right when landowner was dissatisfied with assessment of damages by condemnation commission. Lewis v. Du Pont, Del. Super., 2 Terry 347, 22 A.2d 832, 834.

Ad quod non fuit responsum /æd kwód nòn fyúwət rəspónsəm/. To which there was no answer. A phrase used in old reports, where a point advanced in argument by one party was not denied by the other; or where a point or argument of counsel was not met or noticed by the court; or where an objection was met by the court, and not replied to by the counsel who raised it.

A.D.R. Asset Depreciation Range.

Ad rationem ponere /æd rèyshiyównəm pównəríy/. To cite a person to appear. A technical expression in the old records of the Exchequer, signifying, to put to the bar and interrogate as to a charge made; to arraign on a trial.

Ad recognoscendum /æd rìykognəséndəm/. To recognize. Formal words in old writs.

Adrectare /ædrektériy/. To set right, satisfy, or make amends.

Ad recte docendum oportet, primum inquirere nomina, quia rerum cognitio a nominibus rerum dependet /æd réktey dowséndəm owpórdət, práyməm ìnkwáyrəriy nómənə, kwáyə rírəm kògníshiyow èy nəmínəbəs rírəm dəpéndət/. In order rightly to comprehend a thing, inquire first into the names, for a right knowledge of things depends upon their names.

Ad rectum /æd réktəm/. To right. To do right. To meet an accusation. To answer the demands of the law. *Habeant eos ad rectum.* They shall render themselves to answer the law, or to make satisfaction.

Ad reparationem et sustentationem /æd rèpərèyshiyównəm et səstentèyshiyównəm/. For repairing and keeping in suitable condition.

Ad respondendum /æd rəspondéndəm/. For answering; to make answer. Words used in certain writs employed for bringing a person before the court to make answer in defense in a proceeding, as in *habeas corpus ad respondendum* and *capias ad respondendum, q.v.*

Adrhamire /æ̀drəmáyriy/. In old European law, to undertake, declare, or promise solemnly; to pledge; to pledge one's self to make oath.

Adrogation /æ̀drowgéyshən/. In the civil law, the adoption of one who was *impubes;* that is, if a male, under fourteen years of age; if a female, under twelve.

Ads. An abbreviation for *ad sectam (q.v.),* meaning "at the suit of."

Ad satisfaciendum /æ̀d sæ̀dəsfèyshiyéndəm/. To satisfy. The emphatic words of the writ of *capias ad satisfaciendum,* which requires the sheriff to *take* the person of the defendant *to satisfy* the plaintiff's claim.

Adscendentes /æ̀dsendéntiyz/. Lat. In the civil law, ascendants.

Adscripti /ædskríptay/. See **Adscriptus.**

Adscripti glebæ /ædskríptay glíybiy/. Slaves who served the master of the soil, who were annexed to the land, and passed with it when it was conveyed.

Adscriptitii /æ̀dskriptíshiyay/. Lat. A species of serfs or slaves. Those persons who were enrolled and liable to be drafted as legionary soldiers.

Adscriptus /ædskríptəs/. In the civil law, added, annexed, or bound by or in writing; enrolled, registered; united, joined, annexed, bound to, generally. *Servus colonœ adscriptus,* a slave annexed to an estate as a cultivator. *Fundus adscriptus,* an estate bound to, or burdened with a duty.

Ad sectam /æ̀d séktəm/. At the suit of. Commonly abbreviated to *ads.* Used in entering and indexing the names of cases, where it is desired that the name of the defendant should come first. Thus, "B. *ads.* A." indicates that B. is defendant in an action brought by A., and the title so written would be an inversion of the more usual form "A. *v.* B."

Adsessores /æ̀dsəsóriyz/. Side judges. Assistants or advisers of the regular magistrates, or appointed as their substitutes in certain cases. See **Assessor.**

Adstipulator /æ̀dstìpyəléydər/. In Roman law, an accessory party to a promise, who received the same promise as his principal did, and could equally receive and exact payment; or he only stipulated for a part of that for which the principal stipulated, and then his rights were coextensive with the amount of his own stipulation. One who supplied the place of a procurator at a time when the law refused to allow stipulations to be made by procuration.

Ad terminum annorum /æ̀d tə́rmənəm ənórəm/. For a term of years.

Ad terminum qui præterit /æ̀d tə́rmənəm kwày prédərət/. For a term which has passed. Words in the Latin form of the writ of entry employed at common law to recover, on behalf of a landlord, possession of premises from a tenant holding over after the expiration of the term for which they were demised.

Ad testificandum /æ̀d tèstəfəkǽndəm/. To testify. Type of writ of habeas corpus used to bring prisoner to court to testify. See **Habeas corpus.**

Ad tristem partem strenua est suspicio /æ̀d trístəm párdəm strényuwə èst səspísh(iy)ow/. Suspicion lies heavy on the unfortunate side.

Ad tunc et ibidem /æ̀d tə́nk əd əbáydəm/°íbədəm/. In pleading, the Latin name of that clause of an indictment containing the statement of the subject-matter "then and there being found."

Adult. One who has attained the legal age of majority; generally 18 years. At civil law, a male who had attained the age of 14; a female who had attained the age of 12. See **Legal age; Majority.**

Adulter /ədə́ltər/. One who corrupts; one who seduces another man's wife. *Adulter solidorum.* A corruptor of metals; a counterfeiter.

Adultera /ədə́ltərə/. In the civil law, an adulteress; a woman guilty of adultery.

Adulteration. The act of corrupting or debasing. The act of mixing something impure or spurious with something pure or genuine, or an inferior article with a superior one of the same kind. The term is generally applied to the act of mixing up with food or drink intended to be sold other matters of an inferior quality, and usually of a more or less deleterious quality. The act, process or omission to act by which food becomes impure and unfit for consumption. Such is prohibited and regulated by federal and state statutes and agencies. See **Food and Drug Administration; Food, Drug and Cosmetic Act.**

Adulterator /ədə́ltəreydər/. A corrupter. In the civil law, a forger; a counterfeiter.

Adulteratores monetæ /ədə̀ltərətóriyz məníydiy/. Counterfeiters of money.

Adulterine /ədə́ltərən/. Begotten in an adulterous intercourse. Those are not deemed adulterine who are begotten of a woman openly married through ignorance of a former wife being alive. In the Roman and canon law, adulterine bastards were distinguished from such as were the issue of two unmarried persons, and the former were treated with more severity, not being allowed the *status* of natural children, and being ineligible to holy orders.

Adulterine guilds. Traders acting as a corporation without a charter, and paying a fine annually for permission to exercise their usurped privileges.

Adulterium /æ̀dəltíriyəm/. A fine anciently imposed for the commission of adultery.

Adulterous bastards. Those produced by an unlawful connection between two persons, who at the time when the child was conceived, were, either of them or both, connected by marriage with some other person. Civil Code La. art. 182.

Adultery /ədə́ltəriy/. Voluntary sexual intercourse of a married person with a person other than the offender's husband or wife. Franzetti v. Franzetti, Tex.Civ. App., 120 S.W.2d 123, 127. In some states, however, as was also true under the Roman and Jewish law, this crime is committed only when the *woman* is married to a third person; the unlawful commerce of a married man with an unmarried woman not being of the grade of adultery. In other jurisdictions, both parties are guilty of adultery, even though only one of them is married. In some jurisdictions, also, a distinction is made between double and single adultery, the former being committed where both parties are married to other persons, the latter where one only is so married. See also **Illicit cohabitation**.

Open and notorious adultery. To constitute living in open and notorious adultery, the parties must reside together publicly in the face of society, as if conjugal relations existed between them, and their so living and the fact that they are not husband and wife must be known in the community.

Ad ultiman vim terminorum /æd ə́ltəmən vím tərmənórəm/. To the most extended import of the terms; in a sense as universal as the terms will reach.

Ad usum et commodum /æd yúsəm et kómədəm/. To the use and benefit.

Ad valentiam /æd vəlénsh(iy)əm/. To the value. See **Ad valorem**.

Ad valorem /æd vəlórəm/. According to value. A tax imposed on the value of property. The more common ad valorem tax is that imposed by states, counties, and cities on real estate. Ad valorem taxes, can, however, be imposed upon personal property; *e.g.,* a motor vehicle tax may be imposed upon the value of an automobile and is therefore deductible as a tax. A tax levied on property or an article of commerce in proportion to its value, as determined by assessment or appraisal. Callaway v. City of Overland Park, 211 Kan. 646, 508 P.2d 902, 907.

Duties are either *ad valorem* or *specific;* the former when the duty is laid in the form of a percentage on the value of the property; the latter where it is imposed as a fixed sum on each article of a class without regard to its value.

Advance. To move something forward in position, time or place. To pay money or render other value before it is due; to furnish something before an equivalent is received; to loan; to furnish capital in aid of a projected enterprise, in expectation of return from it. To supply beforehand; to furnish on credit or before goods are delivered or work done; to furnish as a part of a stock or fund; to pay money before it is due; to furnish money for a specific purpose understood between the parties, the money or sum equivalent to be returned; furnishing money or goods for others in expectation of reimbursement; money or commodities furnished on credit. A loan, or gift or money advanced to be repaid conditionally; may be equivalent to "pay." See also **Advances.**

Advance bill. Bill of exchange drawn before shipment of goods.

Advancement. Money or property given by a parent to his child or, sometimes, presumptive heir, or expended by the former for the latter's benefit, by way of anticipation of the share which the child will' inherit in the parent's estate and intended to be deducted therefrom. It is the latter circumstance which differentiates an advancement from a gift or a loan.

Advance payment. Payments made in anticipation of a contingent or fixed future liability.

Advances. Moneys paid before or in advance of the proper time of payment; money or commodities furnished on credit; a loan or gift, or money advanced to be repaid conditionally. Payments advanced to the owner of property by a factor or broker on the price of goods which the latter has in his hands, or is to receive, for sale. See also **Advance.**

Advance sheets. Pamphlets (published weekly for National Reporter System) containing the most recently reported opinions of specific courts (*e.g.* Federal Reporter) or the courts of several jurisdictions (*e.g.* Pacific Reporter). The volume and page numbers usually are the same as in the subsequently bound volumes of the series, which cover several numbers of the advance sheets.

Advantagium. In old pleading, an advantage.

Advena /ǽdvənə/. In Roman law, one of foreign birth, who has left his own country and settled elsewhere, and who has not acquired citizenship in his new locality; often called *albanus.*

Advent. A period of time recognized by the English common and ecclesiastical law, beginning on the Sunday that falls either upon St. Andrew's day, being the 30th of November, or the next to it, and continuing to Christmas day.

Adventitious /ædvəntíshəs/. That which comes incidentally, fortuitously, or out of the regular course.

Adventitius /ædvəntísh(iy)əs/. Lat. Fortuitous; incidental; coming from an unusual source. *Adventitia bona* are goods which fall to a man otherwise than by inheritance. *Adventitia dos* is a dowry or portion given by some friend other than the parent.

Ad ventrem inspiciendum /æd véntrəm inspishiyéndəm/. To inspect the womb. A writ for the summoning of a jury of matrons (*q.v.*) to determine the question of pregnancy.

Adventura /ædvənchúrə/. An adventure. Flotsam, jetsam, and lagon are styled *adventuræ maris* (adventures of the sea).

Adventure. A hazardous and striking enterprise. A bold undertaking accompanied by possible hazards, risks and unforeseen events.

A common word in marine insurance policies, used as synonymous, or nearly so, with "perils." A shipment of goods in charge of an agent to be disposed of for the best price obtainable.

Adventure, bill of. In commercial law, a writing signed by a merchant, stating that the property in goods shipped in his name belongs to another, to the adventure or chance of which the person so named is to stand, with a covenant from the merchant to account to him for the produce.

Gross adventure. In maritime law, a loan on bottomry. So named because the lender, in case of a loss, or expense incurred for the common safety, must contribute to the *gross* or general average.

Joint adventure. A commercial or maritime enterprise undertaken by several persons jointly; a limited partnership,—not limited in the statutory sense as to the liability of the partners, but as to its scope and duration. An association of two or more persons to carry out a single business enterprise for profit, for which purpose they combine their property, money, effects, skill, and knowledge. A special combination of two or more persons, where, in some specific adventure, a profit is jointly sought, without any actual partnership or corporate designation. See also **Joint venture**.

Adventurer. One who undertakes uncertain or hazardous actions or enterprises. It is also used to denote one who seeks to advance his own interests by unscrupulous designs on the credulity of others.

Adversary proceeding. One having opposing parties; contested, as distinguished from an ex parte hearing or proceeding. One of which the party seeking relief has given legal notice to the other party, and afforded the latter an opportunity to contest it.

Adversary system. The jurisprudential network of laws, rules and procedures characterized by opposing parties who contend against each other for a result favorable to themselves. In such system, the judge acts as an independent magistrate rather than prosecutor; distinguished from inquisitorial system.

Adverse. Opposed; contrary; in resistance or opposition to a claim, application, or proceeding. Having opposing interests; having interests for the preservation of which opposition is essential.

Use of land is "adverse", as against owner, if it is not made in subordination to him, is open and notorious and is not wrongful as to him; "adverse" means that one making use shall not recognize in those as against whom it is claimed to be adverse an authority either to prevent or to permit its continuance, and refers to nonrecognition of such authority at time use is made. Benson v. Fekete, Mo., 424 S.W.2d 729, 738.

As to adverse Enjoyment; User; Verdict; Witness, see those titles.

Adverse claim. An alleged right of one person asserted against the interest of another person. U.C.C. § 8–301.

Adverse enjoyment. See **Adverse possession**.

Adverse interest. The "adverse interest" of a witness, so as to permit cross-examination by the party calling him, must be so involved in the event of the suit that a legal right or liability will be acquired, lost, or materially affected by the judgment, and must be such as would be promoted by the success of the adversary of the party calling him. See also **Adverse witness**.

Adverse party. A party to an action whose interests are opposed to or opposite the interests of another party to the action.

Appeal. An "adverse party" entitled to notice of appeal is every party whose interest in relation to the judgment or decree appealed from is in conflict with the modification or reversal sought by the appeal. Such term includes the following: Every party interested in sustaining the judgment or decree. All parties appearing against losing party unless reversal of case will not be to party's detriment. Any party who would be prejudicially affected by a modification or reversal of the judgment appealed from. One who

has interest in opposing object sought to be accomplished by appeal. Party to record, whose interest in subject-matter of appeal is adverse to reversal or modification of judgment or order appealed from.

Discovery. When the parties exchange pleadings, one asserting a claim for relief against the other, the parties are "adverse," within rule allowing written interrogatories to be served upon any adverse party. Carey v. Schuldt, D.C.La., 42 F.R.D. 390, 393, 394, 395.

Adverse possession. A method of acquisition of title to real property by possession for a statutory period under certain conditions. Lowery v. Garfield County, 122 Mont. 571, 208 P.2d 478, 486. It has been described as the statutory method of acquiring title to land by limitation. Field v. Sosby, Tex.Civ.App., 226 S.W.2d 484, 486.

Because of the statute of limitations on the bringing of actions for the recovery of land, title can be acquired to real property by adverse possession. In order to establish title in this manner, there must be proof of nonpermissive use which is actual, open, notorious, exclusive and adverse for the statutorily prescribed period. Ryan v. Stavros, 348 Mass. 251, 203 N.E.2d 85. State statutes differ with respect to the required length of possession from an upper limit of 20 years to a lower one of 5 years, with even more extreme time periods covering certain special cases. There may be different periods of time even within a single state, depending on whether or not the adverse possessor has color of title and/or whether or not taxes have been paid. In some cases a longer possession is required against public entities than against individuals.

Adverse possession depends on intent of occupant to claim and hold real property in opposition to all the world, Sertic v. Roberts, 171 Or. 121, 136 P.2d 248; and also embodies the idea that owner of or persons interested in property have knowledge of the assertion of ownership by the occupant, Field v. Sosby, Tex.Civ.App., 226 S.W.2d 484, 486.

Adverse possession consists of actual possession with intent to hold solely for possessor to exclusion of others and is denoted by exercise of acts of dominion over land including making of ordinary use and taking of ordinary profits of which land is susceptible in its present state. U. S. v. Chatham, D.C.N.C., 208 F.Supp. 220, 226.

See also **Constructive adverse possession; Prescription; Tacking**.

Adverse use. Use without license or permission; an element necessary to acquire title or easement by prescription. Shuggars v. Brake, 248 Md. 38, 234 A.2d 752.

Adverse witness. A witness who gives evidence prejudicial to the party then examining him. Commonly used to describe a witness whose testimony is prejudicial to the party who called him and as a result, such witness may be impeached. Foremost Dairies Inc. of South v. Cutler, Fla.App., 212 So.2d 37, 40, 41. See also **Adverse interest; Hostile or adverse witness**.

Adversus /ædvə́rsəs/. In the civil law, against (*contra*). *Adversus bonos mores*, against good morals.

Adversus extraneos vitiosa possessio prodesse solet /ædvársəs ekstréyniyows vishiyówzə pəzesh(iy)ow prowdésiy sówlət/. Prior possession is a good title of ownership against all who cannot show a better.

Advertise. To advise, announce, apprise, command, give notice of, inform, make known, publish. On call to the public attention by any means whatsoever. Any oral, written, or graphic statement made by the seller in any manner in connection with the solicitation of business and includes, without limitation because of enumeration, statements and representations made in a newspaper or other publication or on radio or television or contained in any notice, handbill, sign, catalog, or letter, or printed on or contained in any tag or label attached to or accompanying any merchandise. See also **Printers Ink Statute.**

Comparative advertising. Advertising that specifically compares the advertised brand with other brands of the same product.

Competitive advertising. Advertising that contains basically little information and is used only to allow a producer to maintain a share of the market for that product.

Informative advertising. Advertising that gives information about the suitability and quality of products. To be contrasted with competitive advertising.

Advertisement. Notice given in a manner designed to attract public attention. Edwards v. Lubbock County, Tex.Civ.App., 33 S.W.2d 482, 484. Information communicated to the public, or to an individual concerned, as by handbills, newspaper, television, billboards, radio. First Nat. Corporation v. Perrine, 99 Mont. 454, 43 P.2d 1073, 1077.

Advice. View; opinion; information; the counsel given by lawyers to their clients; an opinion expressed as to wisdom of future conduct. Hughes v. Van Bruggen, 44 N.M. 534, 105 P.2d 494, 496.

The instruction usually given by one merchant or banker to another by letter, informing him of shipments made to him, or of bills or drafts drawn on him, with particulars of date, or sight, the sum, and the payee. Bills presented for acceptance or payment are frequently dishonored for *want of advice.*

Advice of counsel. A defense used in actions for malicious prosecution which requires a finding that defendant presented all facts to his counsel and that he honestly followed counsel's advice. Boylen v. Tracy, 254 Mass. 105, 108, 149 N.E. 674.

Ad vim majorem vel ad casus fortuitus non tenetur quis, nisi sua culpa intervenerit /æd vím majórəm vèl æd kéysəs fərt(y)úwədəs nòn təníydər kwís, náysay s(y)úwə kə́lpə intərvənírət/. No one is held to answer for the effects of a superior force, or of accidents, unless his own fault has contributed.

Advisare /ædvəzériy/ or **advisari** /ædvəzéray/. Lat. To consult, deliberate, consider, advise; to be advised. Occurring in the phrase *curia advisari vult* (*q.v.*), (usually abbreviated *cur. adv. vult,* or *C.A.V.*), the court wishes to be advised, or to consider the matter.

Advise. To give an opinion or counsel, or recommend a plan or course of action; also to give notice. To encourage, inform, or acquaint. It is different in meaning from "instruct" or "persuade." Hughes v. Van Bruggen, 44 N.M. 534, 105 P.2d 494, 497. Where a statute authorizes the trial court to *advise* the jury to acquit, the court has no power to *instruct* the jury to acquit. The court can only counsel, and the jury are not bound by the advice. "Advise" imports that it is discretionary or optional with the person addressed whether he will act on such advice or not.

Advised. Prepared to give judgment, after examination and deliberation. "The court took time to be advised."

Advisedly. With deliberation; intentionally.

Advisement. Consideration; deliberation; consultation. The consultation of a court, after the argument of a cause by counsel, and before delivering their opinion. In re Hohorst, 150 U.S. 653, 14 S.Ct. 221, 37 L.Ed. 1211.

Advisory. Counselling, suggesting, or advising, but not imperative or conclusive. A verdict on an issue out of chancery is advisory.

Advisory counsel. Attorney retained to give advice as contrasted with trial counsel.

Advisory jury. In actions in Federal Court in which there is no jury trial as of right, court may try case with an advisory jury and its verdict is not binding on court. Fed.R.Civ.P. 39(c). See also **Jury.**

Advisory opinion. Such may be rendered by a court at the request of the government or an interested party indicating how the court would rule on a matter should adversary litigation develop. An advisory opinion is thus an interpretation of the law without binding effect. While the International Court of Justice and some state courts will render advisory opinions the federal courts will not; their jurisdiction being restricted to cases or controversies. See, however, **Declaratory judgment.**

Advisory trial. See **Advisory jury.**

Advisory verdict. See **Advisory jury.**

Ad vitam /æd váydəm/. For life. *In feodo, vel ad vitam;* in fee, or for life.

Ad vitam aut culpam /æd váydəm òt kə́lpəm/. For life or until fault. Words descriptive of a tenure of office "for life or good behavior," equivalent to *quamdiu bene se gesserit.*

Advocacy /ædvəkəsiy/. The act of pleading for, supporting, or recommending active espousal. Gitlow v. People of State of New York, 268 U.S. 652, 45 S.Ct. 625, 626, 69 L.Ed. 1138.

Advocare /ædvəkériy/. Lat. To defend; to call to one's aid; to vouch; to warrant.

Advocassie /ædvəkəsiy/. L. Fr. The office of an advocate; advocacy.

Advocata /ædvəkéydə/. In old English law, a patroness; a woman who had the right of presenting to a church.

Advocate /ǽdvəķèyt/, *v.* To speak in favor of or defend by argument. To support, vindicate, or recommend publicly.

Advocate /ǽdvəkət/, *n.* One who assists, defends, or pleads for another. One who renders legal advice and aid and pleads the cause of another before a court or a tribunal, a counselor. A person learned in the law, and duly admitted to practice, who assists his client with advice, and pleads for him in open court. An assistant; adviser; a pleader of causes.

Advocati /ǽdvəkéyday/. Lat. In Roman law, patrons; pleaders; speakers.

Advocatia /ǽdvəkéysh(iy)ə/. In the civil law, the quality, function, privilege, or territorial jurisdiction of an advocate. The functions, duty, or privilege of an advocate.

Advocati ecclesiæ /ǽdvəkéyday əklíyziyiy/. Advocates of the church. A term used in the ecclesiastical law to denote the patrons of churches who presented to the living on an avoidance. This term was also applied to those who were retained to argue the cases of the church. These were of two sorts: those retained as pleaders to argue the cases of the church and attend to its law-matters; and advocates, or patrons of the advowson.

Advocati fisci /ǽdvəkéyday físay/. In civil law, those chosen by the emperor to argue his cause whenever a question arose affecting his revenues. 3 Bl.Comm. 27. Advocates of the fisc, or revenue; fiscal advocates *(qui causam fisci egissent)*. Answering, in some measure, to the king's counsel in English law.

Advocating overthrow of government. Such conduct is a federal crime. 18 U.S.C.A. §§ 2384, 2385.

Advocatione decimarum /ǽdvowkèyshiyówniy dèsəmérəm/. A writ which lay for tithes, demanding the fourth part or upwards, that belonged to any church.

Advocator /ǽdvowkéydər/. In old practice, one who called on or vouched another to warrant a title; a voucher. *Advocatus;* the person called on; or vouched; a vouchee.

Advocatus /ǽdvowkéydəs/. A pleader; a narrator. In the civil law, an advocate; one who managed or assisted in managing another's cause before a judicial tribunal. Called also *"patronus."* But distinguished from *causidicus.*

Advocatus diaboli /ǽdvowkéydəs dayǽbəlay/. In ecclesiastical law, the devil's advocate; the advocate who argues against the canonization of a saint.

Advocatus est, ad quem pertinet jus advocationis alicujus ecclesiæ, ut ad ecclesiam, nomine proprio, non alieno, possit præsentare /ǽdvowkéydəs ést, ǽd kwém párdənət jós ǽdvowkèyshiyównəs ǽliykyúwjəs əklíyziyiy, ə́ əd əktlíyziyəm, nóməniy prówpriyow, non ǽliyíynow, pósət preyzəntériy/. A patron is he to whom appertains the right of presentation to a church, in such a manner that he may present to such a church in his own name, and not in the name of another.

Ad voluntatem /ǽd vòləntéydəm/. At will. *Ad voluntatem domini,* at the will of the lord.

Advoutrer /ǽdváwtrər/. In old English law, an adulterer.

Advoutry /ǽdváwtriy/. In old English law, adultery between parties both of whom were married. Or the offense by an adulteress of continuing to live with the man with whom she committed the adultery. Sometimes spelled "advowtry." See **Advoutrer.**

Advowee, or **avowee** /ǽ(d)vawíy/. The person or patron who has a right to present to a benefice.

Advowee paramount. The sovereign, or highest patron.

Advowson /ǽdváwzən/. In English ecclesiastical law, the right of presentation to a church or ecclesiastical benefice; the right of presenting a fit person to the bishop, to be by him admitted and instituted to a certain benefice within the diocese, which has become vacant. The person enjoying this right is called the "patron" *(patronus)* of the church, and was formerly termed *"advocatus,"* the advocate or defender, or in English, *"advowee."* When there is no patron, or he neglects to exercise his right within six months, it is called a *lapse,* and a title is given to the ordinary to collate to a church: when a presentation is made by one who has no right, it is called a *usurpation.*

Advowsons are of different kinds:

Advowson appendant is an advowson annexed to a manor, and passing with it, as incident or appendant to it, by a grant of the manor only, without adding any other words. 2 Bl.Comm. 22.

Advowson collative. Where the bishop happens himself to be the patron, in which case (presentation being impossible, or unnecessary) he does by one act, which is termed *"collation,"* or conferring the benefice, all that is usually done by the separate acts of presentation and institution. 2 Bl.Comm. 22, 23.

Advowson donative exists where the patron has the right to put his clerk in possession by his mere gift, or deed of donation, without any presentation to the bishop, or institution by him. Donative benefices were converted into *presentative* by the Benefices Act of 1898.

Advowson in gross is an advowson separated from the manor, and annexed to the person. 2 Bl.Comm. 22.

Advowson presentative is the usual kind of advowson, where the patron has the right of *presentation* to the bishop, or ordinary, and moreover to demand of him to institute his clerk, if he finds him canonically qualified. 2 Bl.Comm. 22.

Advowtry /ǽdváwtriy/. See **Advoutry.**

Ad waractum /ǽd wəréktəm/. To follow.

Ædes /íydiyz/. Lat. In the civil law, a house, dwelling, temple, place of habitation, whether in the city or country. In the country everything upon the surface of the soil passed under the term *"œdes."*

Ædificare /ìydəfəkériy/. Lat. In civil and old English law, to make or build a house; to erect a building.

Ædificare in tuo proprio solo non licet quod alteri noceat /ìydəfəkériy in t(y)úwow prówpriow sówlow nòn láysət kwòd ǽltəray nósiyət/. To build upon your own land what may injure another is not lawful. A proprietor of land has no right to erect an edifice on his own ground, interfering with the due enjoyment of adjoining premises, as by overhanging them, or by throwing water from the roof and eaves upon them, or by obstructing ancient lights and windows.

Ædificatum solo solo cedit /ìydəfəkéydəm sówlow sólow síydət/. What is built upon land belongs to or goes with land.

Ædificia solo cedunt /ìydəfísh(iy)ə sówlow síydənt/. Buildings belong to [go with] the soil.

Ædilitum edictum /ìydílədəm ìydíktəm/. In the Roman law, the Ædilitian Edict. An edict providing remedies for frauds in sales, the execution of which belonged to the curule ædiles. That provision by which the buyer of a diseased or imperfect slave, horse, or other animal was relieved at the expense of the vendor who had sold him as sound knowing him to be imperfect.

Æfesn. In old English law, the remuneration to the proprietor of a domain for the privilege of feeding swine under the oaks and beeches of his woods.

Ægroto /iygrówdow/. Lat. Being sick or indisposed. A term used in some of the older reports.

Ægylde. Uncompensated, unpaid for, unavenged. From the participle of exclusion, *a, œ,* or *ex,* (Goth.) and *gild,* payment, requital.

Æl /éyl/. A Norman French term signifying "grandfather." It is also spelled *"aieul"* and *"ayle."*

Æquior est dispositio legis quam hominis /íykwiyor èst dispəzísh(iy)ow líyjəs kwǽm hómənəs/. The disposition of the law is more equitable than that of man.

Æquitas /íykwətǽs/. In the civil law, equity, as opposed to *strictum* or *summum jus (q.v.).* Otherwise called *œquum, œquum bonum, œquum et bonum, œquum et justum.* See **Æquum et bonum est lex legum.**

Æquitas agit in personam /íykwətǽs éyjət ìn pərsównəm/. Equity acts upon the person.

Æquitas est correctio legis generaliter latæ, qua parte deficit /íykwətǽs èst kəréksh(iy)ow líyjəs jenəréylədər léydiy, kwéy párdiy défəsət/. Equity is the correction of that wherein the law, by reason of its generality, is deficient.

Æquitas est correctio quædam legi adhibita, quia ab eâ abest aliquid propter generalem sine exceptione comprehensionem /íykwətǽs èst kəréksh(iy)ow kwíydəm líyjay æd(h)íbədə kwáyə æb íyəy ǽbèst ǽləkwəd próptər jènəréyləm sáyniy eksèpshiyówniy kòmprəhènshiyównəm/. Equity is a certain correction applied to law, because on account of its general comprehensiveness, without an exception, something is absent from it.

Æquitas est perfecta quædam ratio quæ jus scriptum interpretatur et emendat; nulla scriptura comprehensa, sed solum in verâ ratione consistens /íykwətǽs èst pərféktə kwíydəm réyshiyow kwíy jás skríptəm intàrprətéydər ed əméndət; nálə skripchúrə kòmprəhénsə, sed sówləm in vírə rèyshiyówniy kənsístènz/. Equity is a certain perfect reason, which interprets and amends the written law, comprehended in no writing, but consisting in right reason alone.

Æquitas est quasi æqualitas /íykwətǽs èst kwéysay iykwólətǽs/. Equity is as it were equality; equity is a species of equality or equalization.

Æquitas ignorantiæ opitulatur, oscitantiæ non item /íykwətǽs ìgnərǽnshiyiy owpìchəléydər, òsətǽnshiyiy non áydəm/. Equity assists ignorance, but not carelessness.

Æquitas non facit jus, sed juri auxiliatur /íykwətǽs non féysət jás, sèd júrày ogzìliyéydər/. Equity does not make law, but assists law.

Æquitas nunquam contravenit legis /íykwətǽs nə́ŋkwəm kòntrəvíynət líyjəs/. Equity never counteracts the laws.

Æquitas sequitur legem /íykwətǽs sékwədər líyjəm/. Equity follows the law.

Æquitas supervacua odit /íykwətǽs sùwpərvǽkyuwə ówdət/. Equity abhors superfluous things.

Æquitas uxoribus, liberis, creditoribus maxime favet /íykwətǽs əxóriybəs, líbərəs, kredətóriybəs mǽksəmiy féyvət/. Equity favors wives and children, creditors most of all.

Æquum et bonum est lex legum /íykwəm ət bównəm èst léks líygəm/. What is equitable and good is the law of laws.

Æquus /íykwəs/. Lat. Equal; even. A provision in a will for the division of the residuary estate *ex œquus* among the legatees means equally or evenly.

Æra, or era /írə/. A fixed point of chronological time, whence any number of years is counted; thus, the Christian era began at the birth of Christ, and the Mohammedan era at the flight of Mohammed from Mecca to Medina. The derivation of the word has been much contested.

Ærarium /ìrériyəm/. Lat. In the Roman law, the treasury *(fiscus).*

Æs /íyz/. Lat. In the Roman law, money (literally, brass); metallic money in general, including gold.

Aes alienum /íyz æliyíynəm/. A civil law term signifying a debt. Literally translated, the money of another. The civil law considered borrowed money as the property of another, as distinguished from *œs suum,* one's own money.

Æsnecia /iysníysh(iy)ə/. In old English law, Esnecy; the right or privilege of the eldest born.

Æsnecius /ìysníyshiyəs/. See **Anecius; Aesnecia.**

Æs suum /íys s(y)úwəm/. One's own money. In the Roman law, debt; a debt; that which others owe to us *(quod alii nobis debent).*

Æsthetic /əsθédik/. Relating to that which is beautiful or in good taste.

Æsthetic value. The artistic worth of something as contrasted with its practical value.

Æstimatio capitis /èstəméysh(iy)ow kǽpədəs/. Lat. The value of a head. In Saxon law, the estimation or valuation of the head; the price or value of a man. The price to be paid for taking the life of a human being. By the laws of Athelstan, the life of every man not excepting that of the king himself was estimated at a certain price, which was called the *were*, or *œstimatio capitis*.

Æstimatio præteriti delicti ex postremo facto nunquam crescit /èstəméysh(iy)ow prətérəday dəlíktay èks powstríymow fǽktow nə́ŋkwəm krésət/. The weight of a past offense is never increased by a subsequent fact.

Ætas /íytæs/. Lat. In the civil law, age.

Ætas infantiæ (also written **infantili**) **proxima** /íytæs infǽnshiyiy próksəmə/. The age next to infancy; the first half of the period of childhood (*pueritia*), extending from seven years to ten and a half. 4 Bl.Comm. 22. See **Age**.

Ætas legitima /íytæs ləjídəmə/. Lawful age. See **Legal age; Majority**.

Ætas perfecta /íytæs pərféktə/. Complete age; full age.

Ætas prima /íytæs práymə/. The first age; infancy (*infantia*).

Ætas pubertati proxima /íytæs pyùwbərtéyday próksəmə/. The age next to puberty; the last half of the period of childhood (*pueritia*), extending from ten and a half years to fourteen, in which there might or might not be criminal responsibility according to natural capacity or incapacity. 4 Bl.Comm. 22. See **Age**.

Ætate probanda /ìytéydiy prowbǽndə/. A writ (now obsolete) which inquired whether the king's tenant holding in chief by chivalry was of full age to receive his lands. It was directed to the escheater of the county.

Ætheling /íyðəliŋ/. In Saxon law, a noble; generally a prince of the blood.

A.F.D.C. Aid to Families with Dependent Children.

Affair. (Fr.) A law suit.

Affairs. An inclusive term, bringing within its scope and meaning anything that a person may do. Walker v. United States, C.C.A.Mo., 93 F.2d 383, 391. A person's concerns in trade or property; business. That which is done or to be done. General operations carried on by an employer. Gocs v. Thomas E. Coale Coal Co., 142 Pa.Super. 479, 16 A.2d 720, 723. See also **Statement of affairs**.

Affect. To act upon; influence; change; enlarge or abridge; often used in the sense of acting injuriously upon persons and things. To lay hold of or attack (as a disease does); to act, or produce an effect upon; to impress or influence (the mind or feelings); to touch.

Affected with a public interest. Affirmatively, phrase means that a business or property must be such or be so employed as to justify the conclusion that it has been devoted to a public use, and its use thereby in effect granted to the public. Negatively, it does not mean that a business is affected with a public interest merely because it is large or because the public are warranted in having a feeling of concern in respect of its maintenance. H. Earl Clack Co. v. Public Service Commission of State of Montana, 94 Mont. 488, 22 P.2d 1056. Business affecting the community at large.

Affecting commerce. Any activity which touches or concerns business or industry, favorably or burdensomely; commonly used within context of Labor Management Relations Act regarding a labor dispute which burdens commerce. U. S. v. Ricciardi, C.A. N.Y., 357 F.2d 91, 95.

The term "affecting commerce" means in commerce, or burdening or obstructing commerce or the free flow of commerce, or having led or tending to lead to a labor dispute burdening or obstructing commerce or the free flow of commerce. National Labor Relations Act, § 2(7).

The term "industry affecting commerce" means any industry or activity in commerce or in which a labor dispute would burden or obstruct commerce or tend to burden or obstruct commerce or the free flow of commerce. Labor Management Relations Act, § 501(1).

Affection. The making over, pawning, or mortgaging of a thing to assure the payment of a sum of money, or the discharge of some other duty or service. In a medical sense, an abnormal bodily condition.

Affectio tua nomen imponit operi tuo /əféksh(iy)ow t(y)úwə nówmən ìmpównət ówpəray t(y)úwow/. Your disposition (or motive, intention) gives name (or character) to your work or act.

Affectus /əféktəs/. Disposition; intention, impulse or affection of the mind. One of the causes for a challenge of a juror is *propter affectum*, on account of a suspicion of *bias* or favor. 3 Bl.Comm. 363.

Affectus punitur licet non sequatur effectus /əféktəs pyuwnáydər láysət nòn səkwéydər əféktəs/. The intention is punished although the intended result does not follow.

Affeer /əfír/. To assess, liquidate, appraise, fix in amount.

Affeerors /əfírərz/. In common law, persons who, in court-leets, upon oath, settled and moderated the fines and amercements imposed on those who had committed offenses arbitrarily punishable, or that had no express penalty appointed by statute. They were also appointed to moderate fines, etc., in courts-baron.

Affermer /æfərméy/. L. Fr. To let to farm. Also to make sure, to establish or confirm.

Affiance. To assure by pledge. An agreement by which a man and woman promise that they will marry each other.

Affiant /əfáyənt/. The person who makes and subscribes an affidavit. The word is used, in this sense, interchangeably with "deponent." But the latter term should be reserved as the designation of one who makes a deposition.

Affidare /æ̀fədériy/. At common law, to swear faith to; to pledge one's faith or do fealty by making oath. Used of the mutual relation arising between landlord and tenant. 1 Bl.Comm. 367. Affidavit is of kindred meaning.

Affidari /æ̀fədəray/. To be mustered and enrolled for soldiers upon an oath of fidelity.

Affidatio /æ̀fədéysh(iy)ow/. At common law, a swearing of the oath of fidelity or of fealty to one's lord, under whose protection the quasi-vassal has voluntarily come.

Affidatio dominorum /æ̀fədéysh(iy)ow dòmənórəm/. An oath taken by the lords in parliament.

Affidatus /æ̀fədéydəs/. At common law one who was not a vassal, but who for the sake of protection had connected himself with one more powerful.

Affidavit /æ̀fədéyvət/. A written or printed declaration or statement of facts, made voluntarily, and confirmed by the oath or affirmation of the party making it, taken before a person having authority to administer such oath or affirmation. State v. Knight, 219 Kan. 863, 549 P.2d 1397, 1401. See also **Certification; Jurat; Verification.**

Affidavit of defense. An affidavit stating that the defendant has a good defense to the plaintiff's action on the merits; *e.g.* affidavit filed with motion for summary judgment. Fed.R. Civil P. 56(e).

Affidavit of merits. One setting forth that the defendant has a meritorious defense (substantial and not technical) and stating the facts constituting the same. See **Affidavit of defense.**

Affidavit of notice. A sworn statement that affiant has given proper notice of hearing to other parties to action.

Affidavit of service. An affidavit intended to certify the service of a writ, notice, summons, or other document or process. In federal courts, if service is made by a person other than a United States Marshall or his deputy, he shall make affidavit thereof. Fed.R. Civil P. 4(g).

Affidavit to hold to bail. An affidavit required in many cases before the defendant in a civil action may be arrested. Such an affidavit must contain a statement, clearly and certainly expressed, by someone acquainted with the fact, of an indebtedness from the defendant to the plaintiff, and must show a distinct cause of action.

Affilare /əfiliyériy/. L. Lat. To put on record; to file or affile. *Affiletur,* let it be filed. *De recordo affilatum,* affiled of record.

Affile /əfáyl/. A term employed in old practice, signifying to put on file. In modern usage it is contracted to *file.*

Affiliate /əfíliyeyt/. Signifies a condition of being united; being in close connection, allied, associated, or attached as a member or branch.

Affiliate company. Company effectively controlled by another company. Under Investment Company Act (15 U.S.C.A. § 80a–2), company in which there is

ownership (direct or indirect) of 5 percent or more of the voting stock.

Corporations which are related as parent and subsidiary, characterized by identity of ownership of capital stock. Northeastern Consol. Co. C. v. U. S., C.A.Ill., 406 F.2d 76, 79. See also **Holding company.**

Affiliation. Act or condition of being affiliated, allied, or associated with another person, body, or organization. Imports less than membership in an organization, but more than sympathy, and a working alliance to bring to fruition the proscribed program of a proscribed organization, as distinguished from mere cooperation with a proscribed organization in lawful activities, is essential. Bridges v. Wixon, Cal., 326 U.S. 135, 65 S.Ct. 1443, 1447, 89 L.Ed. 2103. It includes an element of dependability upon which the organization can rely which, though not equivalent to membership duty, rests upon course of conduct that could not be abruptly ended without giving at least reasonable cause for charge of breach of good faith. U. S. ex rel. Kettunen v. Reimer, C.C.A.N.Y., 79 F.2d 315, 317. See also **Association.**

The act of imputing or determining the paternity of a bastard child, and the obligation to maintain it.

Affines /əfáyniyz/. In the civil law, connections by marriage, whether of the persons or their relatives. Neighbors, who own or occupy adjoining lands. From this word is derived affinity, denoting relationship by marriage. The singular, *affinis,* is used in a variety of related significations—a boundary; a partaker or sharer, *affinis culpæ* (an aider or one who has knowledge of a crime).

Affinis mei affinis non est mihi affinis /əfáynəs míyay əfáynəs non est máhay əfáynəs/. One who is related by marriage to a person related to me by marriage has no affinity to me.

Affinitas /əfínətæs/. Lat. In the civil law, affinity; relationship by marriage.

Affinitas affinitatis /əfinətæs əfinətéydəs/. Remote relationship by marriage. That connection between parties arising from marriage which is neither consanguinity nor affinity. This term signifies the connection between the kinsmen of the two persons married, as, for example, the husband's brother and the wife's sister.

Affinity /əfínədiy/. A close agreement; relation; spiritual relation or attraction held to exist between certain persons. State ex inf. Norman v. Ellis, 325 Mo. 154, 28 S.W.2d 363, 367. Relation which one spouse because of marriage has to blood relatives of the other. State v. Hooper, 140 Kan. 481, 37 P.2d 52.

The connection existing, in consequence of marriage, between each of the married persons and the kindred of the other. Kest v. Lewis, 169 Ohio St. 317, 159 N.E.2d 449, 450.

Degrees of relationship by affinity are computed as are degrees of relationship by consanguinity. The doctrine of affinity grew out of the canonical maxim that marriage makes husband and wife one. The husband has the same relation, by affinity, to his wife's blood relatives as she has to them by consanguinity and vice versa. State v. Hooper, 140 Kan. 481, 37 P.2d 52.

Affinity is distinguished into three kinds: (1) *Direct*, or that subsisting between the husband and his wife's relations by blood, or between the wife and the husband's relations by blood; (2) *secondary*, or that which subsists between the husband and his wife's relations by marriage; (3) *collateral*, or that which subsists between the husband and the relations of his wife's relations.

In a larger sense, consanguinity or kindred.

Quasi affinity. In the civil law, the affinity which exists between two persons, one of whom has been betrothed to a kinsman of the other, but who have never been married.

Affirm. To ratify, make firm, confirm, establish, reassert. To make affirmation; to make a solemn and formal declaration or asseveration that an affidavit is true, that the witness will tell the truth, etc., this being substituted for an oath in certain cases. Also, to give testimony on affirmation. See **Affidavit; Jurat; Verification**.

Judgment. In the practice of appellate courts, to *affirm* a judgment, decree, or order, is to declare that it is valid and right and must stand as rendered below; to ratify and reassert it; to concur in its correctness and confirm its efficacy. If the appellate court *remanded* the case, it would be sending it back to the lower court with instructions to correct the irregularities specified in the appellate opinion. If the appellate court *reversed* the court below, it would have changed the result reached below.

Pleading. To allege or aver a matter of fact; to state it affirmatively. The opposite of deny or traverse.

Affirmance. The confirming, or ratifying of a former law, or judgment. The confirmation and ratification by an appellate court of a judgment, order, or decree of a lower court brought before it for review. See **Affirm**.

The ratification or confirmation of a voidable contract or act by the party who is to be bound thereby. The term is in accuracy to be distinguished from *ratification*, which is a recognition of the validity or binding force as against the party ratifying, of some act performed by another person; and from *confirmation*, which would seem to apply more properly to cases where a doubtful authority has been exercised by another in behalf of the person ratifying; but these distinctions are not generally observed.

Affirmance day general. In the English court of exchequer, a day appointed by the judges of the common pleas, and barons of the exchequer, to be held a few days after the beginning of every term for the general affirmance or reversal of judgments.

Affirmant /əfɚ́rmənt/. A person who testifies on affirmation, or who affirms instead of taking an oath. Used in affidavits and depositions which are *affirmed*, instead of sworn to in place of the word "deponent." See also **Affirmation; Jurat; Verification**.

Affirmanti, non neganti incumbit probatio /ǽfərmǽntay, nón nəgǽntay inkǽmbət prowbéysh(iy)ow/. The [burden of] proof lies upon him who affirms, not upon one who denies.

Affirmantis est probare /ǽfərmǽntəs èst prowbériy/. He who affirms must prove.

Affirmation. A solemn and formal declaration or asseveration that an affidavit is true, that the witness will tell the truth, etc.; this being substituted for an oath in certain cases. A solemn religious asseveration in the nature of an oath. See also **Confirmation; Jurat; Oath; Verification**.

Affirmation of fact. A statement concerning a subject-matter of a transaction which might otherwise be only an expression of opinion but which is affirmed as an existing fact material to the transaction, and reasonably induces the other party to consider and rely upon it, as a fact.

Affirmatio unius exclusio est alterius /ǽfərméysh(iy)ow yuwnáyəs èksklúwzhiyow èst oltíriyəs/. The affirmance of one thing is the exclusion of the other.

Affirmative. That which declares positively; that which avers a fact to be true; that which establishes; the opposite of negative.

As to affirmative Plea; Proof; Warranty, see those titles.

Affirmative action programs. Employment programs required by federal statutes and regulations designed to remedy discriminatory practices in hiring minority group members; *i.e.* designed to eliminate existing and continuing discrimination, to remedy lingering effects of past discrimination, and to create systems and procedures to prevent future discrimination; commonly based on population percentages of minority groups in a particular area. Factors considered are race, color, sex, creed and age. National Labor Relations Board v. Fansteel Metallurgical Corporation, 306 U.S. 240, 59 S.Ct. 490, 497, 83 L.Ed. 627; National Labor Relations Board v. Leviton Mfg. Co., C.C.A.2, 111 F.2d 619, 621. The "affirmative action" which the National Labor Relations Board is authorized to take to effectuate the policies of the National Labor Relations Act is action to make effective the redress of rights conferred upon employees by the act. National Labor Relations Board v. National Casket Co., C.C.A.2, 107 F.2d 992, 998.

Affirmative charge. The general "affirmative charge" is an instruction to the jury that, whatever the evidence may be, defendant cannot be convicted under the count in the indictment to which the charge is directed.

Affirmative defense. In pleading, matter constituting a defense; new matter which, assuming the complaint to be true, constitutes a defense to it. Under the Fed. Rules of Civil Procedure, and also under most state Rules, all affirmative defenses must be raised in the responsive pleading (answer); such defenses include accord and satisfaction, assumption of risk, contributory negligence, duress, estoppel, etc. See Fed.R. Civil P. 8(c).

Affirmative defenses in criminal cases include insanity, intoxication, self-defense, automatism, coercion, alibi, and duress.

Affirmative easement. An easement which gives to the owner of the dominant tenement the right to use the servient tenement, or to do some act thereon which would otherwise be unlawful. Clements v. Taylor, Tex.Civ.App., 184 S.W.2d 485, 487.

Affirmative pregnant. In common law pleading, an affirmative allegation implying some negative in favor of the adverse party.

Affirmative proof. Such evidence of the truth of matters asserted as tends to establish them, regardless of character of evidence offered.

Affirmative relief. Relief, benefit, or compensation which may be due and granted to defendant. Relief for which defendant might maintain an action independently of plaintiff's claim and on which he might proceed to recovery, although plaintiff abandoned his cause of action or failed to establish it. Specific performance (q.v.) is a type of affirmative relief that may be granted to plaintiff.

Affirmative statute. A statute couched in affirmative or mandatory terms. One which directs the doing of an act, or declares what shall be done; as a *negative* statute is one which prohibits a thing from being done, or declares what shall not be done.

Affirmative warranty. Affirms existence of a fact at time insurance policy is entered into, while promissory warranty requires that something be done or not done after policy has taken effect. Sentinel Life Ins. Co. v. Blackmer, C.C.A.Colo., 77 F.2d 347, 350. See also **Warranty.**

Affix. Fix or fasten in any way; to attach physically. To attach to, inscribe, or impress upon, as a signature, a seal, a trade-mark. To attach, add to, or fasten upon, permanently, as in the case of fixtures annexed to real estate. A thing is deemed to be affixed to land when it is attached to it by the roots, as in the case of trees, vines, or shrubs; or imbedded in it, as in the case of walls; or permanently resting upon it, as in the case of buildings; or permanently attached to what is thus permanent, as by means of cement, plaster, nails, bolts, or screws. See **Fixture.**

Affixing. Securely attached.

Affixus /əfíksəs/. In the civil law, affixed, fixed, or fastened to.

Affliction. A distress of mind or body; that which causes continuing anguish or suffering.

Afforare /æfərériy/. To set a price or value on a thing.

Afforatus /æfəréydəs/. Appraised or valued, as things vendible in a market.

Afforce /əfórs/. To add to; to increase; to strengthen; to add force to.

Afforce the assize /əfórs ðiy əsáyz/. In old English practice, a method of securing a verdict, where the jury disagreed, either by confining them without meat and drink, or, more anciently, by adding other jurors to the panel, to a limited extent, until twelve could be found who were unanimous.

Afforciamentum /əfòrshəméntəm/. In old English law, a fortress or stronghold, or other fortification. The calling of a court upon a solemn or extraordinary occasion.

Afforest /əfórəst/. To convert land into a forest in the legal sense of the word.

Afforestation /əfòrəstéyshən/. The turning of a part of a country into forest or woodland or subjecting it to forest law, q.v.

Affouage /àfuwázh/. In French law, the right of the inhabitants of a commune or section of a commune to take from the forest the fire-wood which is necessary for their use.

Affranchir /àfronshír/. L. Fr. To set free.

Affranchise /əfrǽnchayz/. To liberate; to make free.

Affray. The fighting of two or more persons in some public place to the disturbance of the people, e.g. where two or more persons voluntarily or by agreement engage in any fight, or use any blows or violence towards each other in an angry or quarrelsome manner, in any public place to the disturbance of others. See also **Disorderly conduct; Riot.**

Affrectamentum /əfrèktəmentəm/. Affreightment; a contract for the hire of a vessel.

Affreightment /əfreytmənt/. A contract of affreightment is a contract with a ship-owner to hire his ship, or part of it, for the carriage of goods. The Fred Smartley, Jr., C.C.A.Va., 100 F.2d 971, 973. Such a contract generally takes the form either of a charterparty or of a bill of lading.

Affretement /əfrètmón/. Fr. In French law, the hiring of a vessel; affreightment (q.v.). Called also *nolissement.*

Affri /ǽfray/. In old English law, plow cattle, bullocks or plow horses. *Affri,* or *afri carucœ;* beasts of the plow.

Affront /əfrǽnt/. An insult or indignity; assault, insolence.

A fine force. Of pure necessity.

A.F.L. American Federation of Labor. Merged with CIO (Congress of Industrial Organizations) in 1955.

A force /ey fórs/. Of necessity.

A force et armis /ey fórs ed árməs/. With force and arms.

Aforesaid. Before, or already said, mentioned, or recited; premised. Preceding; opposite of following.

Aforethought. In criminal law, deliberate; planned; premeditated; prepense. As used in the definition of murder in the first degree, means thought of beforehand and for any length of time, however short, before the doing of the act, and is synonymous with premeditation. See **Malice aforethought; Premeditation.**

A forfait et sans garantie /à forféy èy són gàrontíy/. In French law, a formula used in indorsing commercial paper, and equivalent to "without recourse."

A fortiori /èy forshiyóray/. With stronger reason; much more. A term used in logic to denote an argument to the effect that because one ascertained fact exists, therefore another, which is included in it, or analogous to it, and which is less improbable, unusual, or surprising, must also exist.

After. Later, succeeding, subsequent to, inferior in point of time or of priority or preference. Subsequent in time to. Cheney v. National Surety Corporation, 256 A.D. 1041, 10 N.Y.S.2d 706. On and after. New York Trust Co. v. Portland Ry. Co., 197 A.D. 422, 189 N.Y.S. 346, 348.

After-acquired. Acquired after a particular date or event. Thus, a judgment is a lien on after-acquired realty, *i.e.*, land acquired by the debtor after entry of the judgment.

After acquired property. Property of debtor which is acquired after security transaction is perfected. U.C.C. § 9–204. May also refer to property acquired by testator after execution of will.

    After acquired property clause. A clause in a mortgage providing that any property acquired by the borrower after the date of the loan and mortgage will automatically become additional security for the loan.

After acquired title. Doctrine under which title acquired by grantor who previously attempted to convey title to land which he did not in fact own, inures automatically to benefit of prior grantees. Perkins v. White, 208 Miss. 157, 43 So.2d 897, 899; Morris v. Futischa, 194 Okl. 224, 148 P.2d 986, 987. See **Estoppel** (*Estoppel by deed*).

After born child. Refers to child born after execution of will or to child born after time in which class gift closes. Generally, birth of child after father has executed his will does not revoke will. See **En ventre sa mere**; **Heirs**; **Posthumous child**.

After born heirs. A person entitled to property born after the death of the ancestor intestate. See **Descent**; **Heirs**.

After-discovered. Discovered or made known after a particular date or event.

After-discovered evidence. See **Evidence**.

After-market. The term describing the market for a security after it has been initially sold by the issuer through underwriters.

Afternoon. May mean the whole time from noon to midnight (*e.g.* U.C.C. § 4–104(1)(b)), or it may mean the earlier part of that time as distinguished from evening, or may mean that part of day between noon and evening.

After sight. This term as used in a bill payable so many days after sight, means after legal sight; that is, after legal presentment for acceptance. The mere fact of having seen the bill or known of its existence does not constitute legal "sight."

After the fact. Subsequent to an event from which time is reckoned, *e.g.* accessory after fact is one who harbors, conceals or aids in concealment of the principal felon after the felony has been committed.

Afterthought. A thought composed after the event and with deliberation.

Afterward, afterwards. Subsequent in point of time; synonymous with "thereafter."

Against. Adverse to; contrary. Cram v. Meagher, 113 Vt. 463, 35 A.2d 855; In re Dean's Estate, 350 Mo. 494, 166 S.W.2d 529, 533. Signifies discord or conflict; opposed to; without the consent of; in conflict with. Sometimes meaning "upon," which is almost, if not altogether, synonymous with word "on." Northern Pac. Ry. Co. v. Gas Development Co., 103 Mont. 214, 62 P.2d 204, 205.

Against interest. Commonly used to describe a declaration or admission by one, the content of which is adverse to his position, interest or title; *e.g.*, an exception to hearsay rule is a declaration by one against his pecuniary or proprietary interest at the time when it was made. Fed.Evid.Rule 804. See also **Admission**; **Declaration** (*Declaration against interest*).

Against public interest. An agreement or act which is or has been declared to be adverse to the general good or public welfare; such that a judge may on his own declare void.

Against the evidence. Means "against the weight of the evidence." Cram v. Meagher, 113 Vt. 463, 35 A.2d 855.

Against the form of the statute. Technical words which must be used in framing an indictment for a breach of the statute prohibiting the act complained of. The Latin phrase is *contra forman statuti, q.v.*

Against the peace. A technical phrase used in alleging a breach of the peace.

Against the weight of the evidence. Contrary to the evidence. Russell v. Pilger, 113 Vt. 537, 37 A.2d 403, 411.

Against the will. Technical words used in framing an indictment for robbery from the person, rape and some other offenses. See also **Coercion**; **Duress**; **Force**.

Agalma /əgǽlmə/. An impression or image of anything on a seal.

Agard /əgárd/. L. Fr. An award. *Nul fait agard* /nə̂l féyd agárd/; no award made.

Agarder /àgardéy/. L. Fr. To award, adjudge, or determine; to sentence, or condemn.

Age. The length of time during which a person has lived. The time at which one attains full personal rights and capacities. In law the term signifies those periods in the lives of persons of both sexes which enable them to do certain acts which, before they had arrived at those periods, they were prohibited from doing. See *e.g.* **Age of consent**; **Age of majority**; **Legal age**; **Majority**.

    As used in particular statutes, the term implies disability and, by definition, has been applied to all minors under a certain age and to others disabled by old age. Hampton v. Ewert, C.C.A.Okl., 22 F.2d 81, 87.

Aged person. One advanced in years; refers to his or her chronological, not mental age.

Agency. Relation in which one person acts for or represents another by latter's authority, either in the relationship of principal and agent, master and servant, or employer or proprietor and independent contractor. Gorton v. Doty, 57 Idaho 792, 69 P.2d 136, 139. It also designates a place at which business of company or individual is transacted by an agent. Johnson Freight Lines v. Davis, 170 Tenn. 177, 93 S.W.2d 637, 639. The relation created by express or implied contract or by law, whereby one party delegates the transaction of some lawful business with more or less discretionary power to another, who undertakes to manage the affair and render to him an account thereof. State ex rel. Cities Service Gas Co. v. Public Service Commission, 337 Mo. 809, 85 S.W.2d 890, 894. Or relationship where one person confides the management of some affair, to be transacted on his account, to other party. Or where one party is authorized to do certain acts for, or in relation to the rights or property of the other. But means more than tacit permission, and involves request, instruction, or command. Klee v. U. S., C.C.A.Wash., 53 F.2d 58, 61. The consensual relation existing between two persons, by virtue of which one is subject to other's control. Tarver, Steele & Co. v. Pendleton Gin Co., Tex.Civ.App., 25 S.W.2d 156, 159.

Agency is the fiduciary relation which results from the manifestation of consent by one person to another that the other shall act on his behalf and subject to his control, and consent by the other so to act. Restatement, Second, Agency § 1.

See also **Agent; Authority.**

Actual agency. Exists where the agent is really employed by the principal.

Administrative agency. See **Administrative agency.**

Agency by estoppel. One created by operation of law and established by proof of such acts of the principal as reasonably lead to the conclusion of its existence. Arises where principal, by negligence in failing to supervise agent's affairs, allows agent to exercise powers not granted to him, thus justifying others in believing agent possesses requisite authority.

Deed of agency. A revocable and voluntary trust for payment of debts.

Del credere. Type of agency in which agent is entrusted with goods, documents or securities and in which he is given broad authority to collect from the buyer and in some cases has been held responsible for the buyer's solvency.

Exclusive agency. An agreement by owner that during life of contract he will not sell property to a purchaser procured by another agent, which agreement does not preclude owner himself from selling to a purchaser of his own procuring, while a contract giving a broker "exclusive sale" is more than such exclusive agency, and is an agreement by the owner that he will not sell the property during the life of the contract to any purchaser not procured by the broker in question. See also **Exclusive agency.**

Executive agency. See that title.

General agency. That which exists when there is a delegation to do all acts connected with a particular trade, business or employment. It implies authority on the part of the agent to act without restriction or qualification in all matters relating to the business of his principal.

Implied agency. One created by act of parties and deduced from proof of other facts. It is an actual agency, proved by deductions or inferences from other facts, and third party need have no knowledge of the principal's acts, nor have relied on them.

Intervening agency. See that title.

Ostensible agency. One which exists where the principal intentionally or by want of ordinary care causes a third person to believe another to be his agent who is not really employed by him. See also *Agency by estoppel, supra.*

Special agency. One in which the agent is authorized to conduct a single transaction or a series of transactions not involving a continuity of service.

Universal agency. One in which agent is empowered to conduct every transaction lawfully delegable by principal to agent.

Agency by operation of law. See *Agency by estoppel* under **Agency,** *supra.*

Agency coupled with an interest. A relationship known to the law of agency wherein the agent has an interest in the property or subject matter in which he is dealing. This special type of agency relationship will not terminate automatically upon the death of the principal.

Interest in continued existence of power or authority to act with reference to business, where secured by contract and based on consideration moving from agent to principal looking to exercise of power as means of reimbursement, creates agency coupled with an interest. Agent must have an interest or estate in the thing to be disposed of or managed under the power.

Agency in fact. An agency relationship established by agreement of principal and agent as distinguished from one imposed by law; *e.g.* agency by estoppel.

Agency of the United States. A department, division, or administration within the federal government.

Agency relationship. An employment for purpose of representation in establishing legal relations between principal and third persons. See **Agency; Agent.**

Agency shop. A union-security device whereby, in order to continue employment, any nonunion member employee is required to pay to the Union sums equivalent to those paid by union members, either in an amount equal to both union dues and initiation fees, or in an amount equal to dues alone. Ficek v. International Broth. of Boilermakers, Iron Ship Builders, Blacksmiths, Forgers and Helpers, Local # 647, N.D., 219 N.W.2d 860, 862. See also **Open shop.**

Agenda. Memoranda of things to be done, as items of business or discussion to be brought up at a meeting; a program consisting of such items.

Agenesia /èyjəníyz(i)yə/. Impotentia generandi; sexual impotence; incapacity for reproduction, existing in either sex, whether arising from structural or other causes.

Agenfrida. In Saxon law, the true master or owner of a thing.

Agenhina. In Saxon law, a guest at an inn, who, having stayed there for three nights, was then accounted one of the family.

Agens /éyjənz/. Lat. An agent, a conductor, or manager of affairs. Distinguished from *factor*, a workman. A plaintiff.

Agent. A person authorized by another to act for him, one intrusted with another's business. Humphries v. Going, D.C.N.C., 59 F.R.D. 583, 587. One who represents and acts for another under the contract or relation of agency (*q.v.*). A business representative, whose function is to bring about, modify, affect, accept performance of, or terminate contractual obligations between principal and third persons. One who undertakes to transact some business, or to manage some affair, for another, by the authority and on account of the latter, and to render an account of it. One who acts for or in place of another by authority from him; a substitute, a deputy, appointed by principal with power to do the things which principal may do. One who deals not only with things, as does a servant, but with persons, using his own discretion as to means, and frequently establishing contractual relations between his principal and third persons.

One authorized to transact all business of principal, or all of principal's business of some particular kind, or all business at some particular place. Farm Bureau Mut. Ins. Co. v. Coffin, 136 Ind.App. 12, 186 N.E.2d 180, 182.

See also Agency; Bargaining agent; Corporate agent; Foreign agent; Forwarding agent; Innocent agent; Servant; Subagent; Transfer agent.

Apparent agent or ostensible agent. One whom the principal, either intentionally or by want of ordinary care, induces third persons to believe to be his agent, though he has not, either expressly or by implication, conferred authority on him. A person who, whether or not authorized, reasonably appears to third person, because of manifestations of another, to be authorized to act as agent for such other. Restatement, Second, Agency § 8.

Bargaining agent. See **Bargaining agent**.

Co-agent. One who shares authority to act for the principal with another agent and who is so authorized by the principal.

Diplomatic agent. One representing government in dealings with foreign government.

Dual agent. See *Co-agent*, above.

Exclusive agent. The only agent permitted to act for principal in a particular territory or matter, though the principal may act for himself; *i.e.* exclusive sales territory given to agent does not bar principal from selling in this territory. Stahlman v. Nat'l Lead Co., C.A.Miss., 318 F.2d 388, 393.

Foreign agent. See **Foreign agent**.

General agency business. One not engaged as agent for single firm or person, but holding himself out to public as being engaged in business of being agent. Comer v. State Tax Commission of New Mexico, 41 N.M. 403, 69 P.2d 936.

General agent. One who is authorized to act for his principal in all matters concerning particular business or employment of particular nature. Morpul Research Corp. v. Westover Hardware, Inc., 263 N.C. 718, 140 S.E.2d 416, 418.

High managerial agent. An officer of a corporation or any other agent in a position of comparable authority with respect to formulation of corporate policy or the supervision in a managerial capacity of subordinate employees.

Independent agent. One who is an independent contractor exercising his own judgment and subject to the one who hired him only for the result of the work performed. Donroy, Limited v. U. S., C.A.Cal., 301 F.2d 200, 206.

Insurance agent. See **Insurance**.

Local agent. One appointed to act as the representative of a corporation and transact its business generally (or business of a particular character) at a given place or within a defined district.

Managing agent. A person who is invested with general power, involving the exercise of judgment and discretion, as distinguished from an ordinary agent or employee, who acts in an inferior capacity, and under the direction and control of superior authority, both in regard to the extent of the work and the manner of executing the same. One who has exclusive supervision and control of some department of a corporation's business, the management of which requires of such person the exercise of independent judgment and discretion, and the exercise of such authority that it may be fairly said that service of summons upon him will result in notice to the corporation.

Mercantile agents. Agents employed for the sale of goods or merchandise are called "mercantile agents," and are of two principal classes,—brokers and factors (*q. v.*); a factor is sometimes called a "commission agent," or "commission merchant."

Private agent. An agent acting for an individual in his private affairs; as distinguished from a *public* agent, who represents the government in some administrative capacity.

Public agent. An agent of the public, the state, or the government; a person appointed to act for the public in some matter pertaining to the administration of government or the public business. Whiteside v. United States, 93 U.S. 247, 23 L.Ed. 882.

Real-estate agent. Person whose business it is to sell, or offer for sale, real estate for others, or to rent houses, stores, or other buildings, or real estate, or to collect rent for others.

Special agent. One employed to conduct a particular transaction or piece of business for his principal or authorized to perform a specified act. An agent authorized to conduct a single transaction or a series of transactions not involving continuity of service. Rowen & Blair Electric Co. v. Flushing Operating Corp., 66 Mich.App. 480, 239 N.W.2d 633, 638.

Subagent. One authorized by agent to help perform functions for principal. Generally, absent express or implied authority, an agent has no authority to appoint a subagent. The subagent is subject to control by both agent and principal. Restatement, Second, Agency § 5.

Superior agent. See *High managerial agent, supra.*

Transfer agent. Any person who engages on behalf of an issuer of securities or on behalf of itself as an issuer of securities in (A) countersigning such securities upon issuance; (B) monitoring the issuance of such securities with a view to preventing unauthorized issuance, a function commonly performed by a person called a registrar; (C) registering the transfer of such securities; (D) exchanging or converting such securities; or (E) transferring record ownership of securities by bookkeeping entry without physical issuance of securities certificates. Securities Exchange Act of 1934, § 3.

Undercover agent. See that title.

Universal agent. See *Universal agency* under topic **Agency**.

Agentes et consentientes pari pœna plectentur /əjéntiyz ət kənsènshiyéntiyz péray piynə plekténtər/. Acting and consenting parties are liable to the same punishment.

Agent provocateur /éyjənt prəvòkət(y)úr/. A spy; a secret agent hired to penetrate an organization to gather evidence against its members or to incite trouble.

Age of consent. Age at which persons may marry without parental approval. Age at which a female is legally capable of agreeing to sexual intercourse and below which age the male commits statutory rape if he has sexual intercourse with her. See also **Legal age; Majority.**

Age of majority. Age at which a person may contract *sui juris*; now 18 in most jurisdictions. Sometimes referred to as full age; legal age; majority; adulthood. Age at which one may execute a valid will or vote; age at which payments for support by parents may generally be terminated. See also **Legal age; Majority.**

Age of reason. Age at which a child is deemed to be capable of acting responsibly; commonly the age of 7. In general, one between the ages of 7 and 14 is rebuttably presumed to be incapable of committing a crime. Below the age of 7 a child is conclusively presumed to be incapable of committing crime. See **Infancy.**

Ager /éyjər/. Lat. A field; land generally. A portion of land enclosed by definite boundaries.

Aggravated assault. A person is guilty of aggravated assault if he: attempts to cause serious bodily injury to another, or causes such injury purposely, knowingly or recklessly under circumstances manifesting extreme indifference to the value of human life; or, attempts to cause or purposely or knowingly causes bodily injury to another with a deadly weapon. Model Penal Code, § 211.1(2). In all jurisdictions statutes punish such aggravated assaults as assault with intent to murder (or rob or kill or rape) and assault with a dangerous (or deadly) weapon more severely than "simple" assaults. See also **Assault.**

Aggravated battery. Unlawful application of force to another characterized by unusual or serious consequences or attending circumstances such as a danger-

ous weapon. This offense was unknown at common law. See **Aggravated assault.**

Aggravation. Any circumstance attending the commission of a crime or tort which increases its guilt or enormity or adds to its injurious consequences, but which is above and beyond the essential constituents of the crime or tort itself. See *e.g.* **Aggravated assault.**

Aggravation of the disability. Refers to the course or progress of the workman's condition resulting from the specific injury for which an award or arrangement of compensation has been made. Keefer v. State Industrial Accident Commission, 171 Or. 405, 135 P.2d 806, 809.

Aggregate. Entire number, sum, mass, or quantity of something; total amount; complete whole. One provision under will may be the aggregate if there are no more units to fall into that class. Composed of several; consisting of many persons united together; a combined whole.

Aggregate corporation. See **Corporation.**

Aggregate income. Total income of husband and wife who file a joint tax return.

Aggregate theory of partnership. A partnership is the totality of persons engaged in a business and not an entity in itself as in the case of a corporation.

Aggregatio mentium /ægrəgéysh(iy)ow ménsh(iy)əm/. The meeting of minds. The moment when a contract is complete. A supposed derivation of the word "agreement," *(q.v.).*

Aggregation /ægrəgéyshən/. The combination of two or more elements in patent claims, each of which is unrelated, and each of which performs separately and without cooperation, where combination does not define a composite integrated mechanism. Bowser, Inc. v. U. S., 388 F.2d 346, 351, 181 Ct.Cl. 834. Term means that the elements of a claimed combination are incapable of co-operation to produce a unitary result, and in its true sense does not need prior art patents to support it.

Aggregation doctrine. Rule which precludes totalling of claims for Federal jurisdictional amount purposes. Georgia Ass'n of Independent Ins. Agents v. Travelers Indem. Co., D.C.Ga., 313 F.Supp. 841, 842.

Aggressor. One who first employs hostile force. Penn v. Henderson, 174 Or. 1, 146 P.2d 760, 766. The party who first offers violence or offense. He who begins a quarrel or dispute, either by threatening or striking another.

Aggrieved. Having suffered loss or injury; damnified; injured.

Aggrieved party. One whose legal right is invaded by an act complained of, or whose pecuniary interest is directly affected by a decree or judgment. One whose right of property may be established or divested. The word "aggrieved" refers to a substantial grievance, a denial of some personal or property right, or the imposition upon a party of a burden or obligation. See **Party; Standing.**

Aggrieved person. See **Aggrieved party**.

Agiler /əjáylər/. In Saxon law, an observer or informer.

Agillarius /æjəlériyəs/. L. Lat. In old English law, a hayward, herdward, or keeper of the herd of cattle in a common field.

Aging of accounts. Arranging the accounts (such as receivables or payables) in chronological order and grouping the accounts by intervals, such as accounts less than 30 days old, 30 to 60 days old, and so on. The process of classifying accounts receivable by the time elapsed since the claim came into existence for the purpose of estimating the amount of uncollectible accounts receivable as of a given date.

Agio /əjíyow/. In commercial law, a term used to express the difference in point of value between metallic and paper money, or between one sort of metallic money and another.

Agiotage /àzh(i)yotázh/. A speculation on the rise and fall of the public debt, or the public funds. The speculator is called "*agioteur.*"

Agist /əjíst/. An ancient law term meant to take in and give feed to the cattle of strangers in the king's forest, and to collect the money due for the same to the king's use.

Agister /əjístər/. A person engaged in the business of pasturing of cattle as a bailee in consideration of an agreed price to be paid by owner of cattle. Walker v. Nelson, 137 Colo. 519, 327 P.2d 285, 287.

Agistment /əjístmənt/. A contract whereby a person, called an agister, has control of animals and retains possession of land. Cox v. Pithoud, 221 C.A.2d 571, 34 Cal.Rptr. 582, 583. The taking in and feeding or pasturing of horses, cattle, or similar animals for a reward and is a species of bailment. Marcus v. Eastern Agr. Ass'n, Inc., 58 N.J.Super. 584, 157 A.2d 3, 8.

There is also agistment of *sea-banks*, where lands are charged with a tribute to keep out the sea; and *terræ agistatæ* are lands whose owners must keep up the sea-banks.

In canon law, a composition or mean rate at which some right or due might be reckoned.

Tithe of agistment was a small tithe paid to the rector or vicar on cattle or other produce of grass lands. It was paid by the occupier of the land and not by the person who put in his cattle to graze.

Agistor /əjístər/. See **Agister; Agistment**.

Agitator /æjəteydər/. One who stirs up; excites; ruffles; perturbs. One who incessantly advocates a social change.

Agnates /ægneyts/ægnéydiyz/. In the law of descents, relations by the father, or on the father's side. This word is used in the Scotch law, and by some writers as an English word, corresponding with the Latin *agnati (q.v.)*.

Agnati /ægnéyday/. In Roman law, the term included all the cognates who trace their connection exclusively through males. A table of *cognates* is formed by taking each lineal ancestor in turn and including all his descendants of both sexes in the tabular view. If, then, in tracing the various branches of such a genealogical table or tree, we stop whenever we come to the name of a female, and pursue that particular branch or ramification no further, all who remain after the descendants of women have been excluded are *agnates*, and their connection together is agnatic relationship. All persons are agnatically connected together who are under the same *patria potestas*, or who have been under it, or who might have been under it if their lineal ancestor had lived long enough to exercise his empire.

The *agnate family* consisted of all persons living at the same time, who would have been subject to the *patris potestas* of a common ancestor, if his life had been continued to their time.

Cognates were all persons who could trace their blood to a single ancestor or ancestress, and agnates were those cognates who traced their connection exclusively through males. Between *agnati* and *cognati* there is this difference: that, under the name of agnati, *cognati* are included, but not è *converso;* for instance, a father's brother, that is, a paternal uncle, is both *agnatus* and *cognatus*, but a mother's brother, that is, a maternal uncle, is a *cognatus* but not *agnatus*.

Agnatic /ægnǽdək/. [From *agnati, q.v.*] Derived from or through males. 2 Bl.Comm. 236.

Agnatio /ægnéysh(iy)ow/. In the civil law, relationship on the fathers' side; the relationship of *agnati;* agnation. *Agnatio a patre est*.

Agnation /ægnéyshən/. Kinship by the father's side. See **Agnates; Agnati**.

Agnomen /ægnówmən/. Lat. An additional name or title; a nickname. A name or title which a man gets by some action or peculiarity; the last of the four names sometimes given a Roman. Thus, Scipio *Africanus* (the African) from his African victories. See **Nomen**.

Agnomination /ægnòmənéyshən/. A surname; an additional name or title; agnomen.

Agony. Extreme physical pain or mental distress.

Agraphia. See **Aphasia**.

Agrarian /əgréríyən/. Relating to land, or to a division or distribution of land; as an agrarian law.

Agrarian laws. In Roman law, laws for the distribution among the people, by public authority, of the lands constituting the public domain, usually territory conquered from an enemy. In common parlance the term is frequently applied to laws which have for their object the more equal division or distribution of landed property; laws for subdividing large properties and increasing the number of landholders.

Agrarium. A tax upon or tribute payable out of land.

A gratia /èy gréysh(iy)ə/. By grace; not of right.

Agreamentum /əgrìyəméntəm/. In old English law, agreement; an agreement.

Agree. To concur; come into harmony; give mutual assent; unite in mental action; exchange promises; make an agreement; arrange; to settle. Concur or acquiesce in; approve or adopt. *Agreed or agreed to*, are frequently used (like *accord*), to show the concurrence or harmony of cases; *e.g. Agreed per curiam.* Usually implies some contractual undertaking. To grant or covenant, as when a grantor agrees that no building shall be erected on an adjoining lot; or a mortgagor agrees to cause all taxes to be paid. See **Agreement; Contract.**

Agreed. Settled or established by agreement. Commonly synonymous with "contracted."

Agreed amount clause. Provision in insurance policy that the insured will carry a stated amount of insurance coverage.

Agreed case. See *Case agreed on* under **Case.**

Agreed judgment. See **Judgment.**

Agreed price. The consideration for sale of goods arrived at by mutual agreement as contrasted with "open price". U.C.C. § 2–305.

Agreed statement of facts. A statement of facts, agreed on by the parties as true and correct, to be submitted to a court for a ruling on the law of the case. United States Trust Co. v. New Mexico, 183 U.S. 535, 22 S.Ct. 172, 46 L.Ed. 315. See *Case agreed on* under **Case.** See also **Stipulation.**

Agreed statement on appeal. Narrative statement of facts in case which may be filed on appeal in lieu of report of proceedings below. It is required that all parties agree to content of narrative.

Agreed value. The worth or value of property upon which persons agree beforehand as in a partnership contract in which the parties agree on the value of a partner's interest in a specified amount. Walraven v. Ramsay, 335 Mich. 331, 55 N.W.2d 853, 856.

Agreement. A coming together of minds; a coming together in opinion or determination; the coming together in accord of two minds on a given proposition. In law, a concord of understanding and intention between two or more parties with respect to the effect upon their relative rights and duties, of certain past or future facts or performances. The consent of two or more persons concurring respecting the transmission of some property, right, or benefits, with the view of contracting an obligation, a mutual obligation.

The act of two or more persons, who unite in expressing a mutual and common purpose, with the view of altering their rights and obligations. The union of two or more minds in a thing done or to be done; a mutual assent to do a thing. A compact between parties who are thereby subjected to the obligation or to whom the contemplated right is thereby secured.

Although often used as synonymous with "contract", agreement is a broader term; *e.g.* an agreement might lack an essential element of a contract. The bargain of the parties in fact as found in their language or by implication from other circumstances including course of dealing or usage of trade or course of performance. U.C.C. § 1–201(c); Uniform Consumer Credit Code, § 1.301(3).

The writing or instrument which is evidence of an agreement.

See also Binding agreement; Compact; Consent; Contract; Covenant; International agreements; Meeting of minds.

Classification

Conditional agreements. The operation and effect of such depend upon the existence of a supposed state of facts, or the performance of a condition, or the happening of a contingency.

Executed agreements. Such have reference to past events, or which are at once closed and where nothing further remains to be done by the parties.

Executory agreements. Such agreements as are to be performed in the future. They are commonly preliminary to other more formal or important contracts or deeds, and are usually evidenced by memoranda, parol promises, etc.

Express agreements. Those in which the terms and stipulations are specifically declared and avowed by the parties at the time of making the agreement.

Implied agreement. (1) Implied in fact. One inferred from the acts or conduct of the parties, instead of being expressed by them in written or spoken words. Baltimore Mail S. S. Co. v. U. S., C.C.A.Md., 76 F.2d 582, 585. (2) Implied in law; more aptly termed a constructive or quasi contract. One where, by fiction of law, a promise is imputed to perform a legal duty, as to repay money obtained by fraud or duress. Baltimore Mail S. S. Co. v. U. S., C.C.A.Md., 76 F.2d 582, 585. One inferred by the law where the conduct of the parties with reference to the subject-matter is such as to induce the belief that they intended to do that which their acts indicate they have done. Baltimore & O. R. Co. v. U. S., 261 U.S. 592, 43 S.Ct. 425, 67 L.Ed. 816.

Parol agreements. At common law, such as are either by word of mouth or are committed to writing, but are not under seal. The common law draws only one great line, between things under seal and not under seal.

Agreement for insurance. An agreement often made in short terms preliminary to the filling out and delivery of a policy with specific stipulations. See also **Binder.**

Agreement not to be performed within a year. An agreement that necessarily must require more than year for performance. Incapable of performance within one year. Street v. Maddux, Marshall, Moss & Mallory, 58 App.D.C. 42, 24 F.2d 617, 619.

Agreement of sale; agreement to sell. An agreement of sale may imply not merely an obligation to sell, but an obligation on the part of the other party to purchase, while an agreement to sell is simply an obligation on the part of the vendor or promisor to complete his promise of sale. Treat v. White, 181 U.S. 264, 21 S.Ct. 611, 45 L.Ed. 853. It is a contract to be performed in future, and, if fulfilled, results in a sale; it is preliminary to sale and is not the sale.

Agreement to sell land. A contract to be performed in future which if fulfilled results in sale. In re Frayser's Estate, 401 Ill. 364, 82 N.E.2d 633, 638.

Agreer /æ̀greyéy/. Fr. In French marine law, to rig or equip a vessel.

Agrez /əgréy/. Fr. In French marine law, the rigging or tackle of a vessel.

Agri /ǽgrày/. Arable lands in common fields.

Agricultural. Pertaining to, or dealing with, agriculture; also, characterized by or engaged in farming as the leading pursuit. Oak Woods Cemetery Ass'n v. Murphy, 383 Ill. 301, 50 N.E.2d 582, 587. See **Farming operation; Farming products; Farming purposes; Husbandry.**

Agricultural commodities. Generally synonymous with agricultural or farm products, and not including agricultural implements. Bowles v. Rock, D.C.Neb., 55 F.Supp. 865, 868. See **Commodities.**

Agricultural employment. Synonymous with farm labor, including all farm work and work incidental thereto.

Agricultural labor. Services performed on farm, for owner or tenant. California Employment Commission v. Butte Candy Rice Growers Ass'n, 25 Cal.2d 624, 154 P.2d 892, 894. Broader in meaning than farming or farm labor and includes one engaged in horticulture, St. Louis Rose Co. v. Unemployment Compensation Commission, 348 Mo. 1153, 159 S.W.2d 249, 250, crop dusting, Florek v. Sparks Flying Service, Inc., 83 Idaho 160, 359 P.2d 511, 514, and similar services. Latimer v. United States, D.C.Cal., 52 F.Supp. 228, 234, 235, 236, 237. "Agricultural labor" which is excepted from the Unemployment Compensation Law, is a broad term and includes farming in all of its incidents, such as gardening, horticulture, viticulture, dairying, poultry, bee raising, and ranching, and refers to the field or farm with all its wants, appointments and products. Pioneer Potato Co. v. Division of Employment Sec. Dept. of Labor and Industry, 31 N.J.Super. 553, 107 A.2d 519, 520, 521.

Agricultural lien. A statutory lien to secure money or supplies advanced to an agriculturist to be expended or employed in the making of a crop and attaching to that crop only.

Agricultural Marketing Agreement Act. Federal law passed in 1937 to establish and maintain orderly marketing conditions for farm commodities; to protect purchasing power of farmers. 7 U.S.C.A. § 601 et seq. See **Parity.**

Agricultural product. Things which have a situs of their production upon the farm and which are brought into condition for uses of society by labor of those engaged in agricultural pursuits as contradistinguished from manufacturing or other industrial pursuits. That which is the direct result of husbandry and the cultivation of the soil. The product in its natural unmanufactured condition.

Agri limitati /ǽgrày lìmətéyday/. In civil law, lands whose boundaries are strictly limited by the lines of government surveys.

In Roman law, lands belonging to the state by right of conquest, and granted or sold in plots.

AICPA. American Institute of Certified Public Accountants.

Aid. To support, help, assist or strengthen. Act in cooperation with; supplement the efforts of others. State v. Upton, Iowa, 167 N.W.2d 625, 628.

Distinguished from abet. "Aid" within aider and abettor statute means to help, to assist, or to strengthen while "abet" means to counsel, to encourage, to incite or to assist in commission of criminal act. State v. Trocodaro, 36 Ohio App.2d 1, 301 N.E.2d 898, 902.

Aid and abet. Help, assist, or facilitate the commission of a crime, promote the accomplishment thereof, help in advancing or bringing it about, or encourage, counsel, or incite as to its commission. State v. Fetters, Iowa, 202 N.W.2d 84, 90. It comprehends all assistance rendered by words, acts, encouragement, support, or presence, actual or constructive, to render assistance if necessary. See **Abet; Abettor; Accessory; Accomplice; Aider and abettor.**

Aid and comfort. Help; support; assistance; counsel; encouragement. As an element in the crime of treason (Constitution of the United States, Art. III, § 3), the giving of "aid and comfort" to the enemy may consist in a mere attempt. It is not essential to constitute the giving of aid and comfort that the enterprise commenced should be successful and actually render assistance. An act which intentionally strengthens or tends to strengthen enemies of the United States, or which weakens or tends to weaken power of the United States to resist and attack such enemies. United States v. Haupt, D.C.Ill., 47 F.Supp. 836, 839. Any intentional act furthering hostile designs of enemies of the United States. United States v. Haupt, D.C.Ill., 47 F.Supp. 836, 839.

Aid bond. See **Bond.**

Aider and abettor. One who assists another in the accomplishment of a common design or purpose; he must be aware of, and consent, to such design or purpose. Peats v. State, 213 Ind. 560, 12 N.E.2d 270, 277. One who advises, counsels, procures, or encourages another to commit a crime, himself being guilty of some overt act or advocacy or encouragement of his principal, actually or constructively present when crime is committed, and participating in commission thereof by some act, deed, word, or gesture, Turner v. Commonwealth, 268 Ky. 311, 104 S.W.2d 1085, and sharing the criminal intent of the principal. One who assists another to commit a crime; may be a principal, if present, or an accessory before or after fact of crime. The crime must usually be a felony because all parties to misdemeanor are generally principals.

Aider by verdict. The healing or remission, by a verdict rendered, of a defect or error in pleading which might have been objected to before verdict. The presumption of the proof of all facts necessary to the verdict as it stands, coming to the aid of a record in which such facts are not distinctly alleged. Amendment of pleadings to conform to the evidence is provided for by Fed.R.Civil P. 15.

Aiding an escape. Any overt act, intended and useful to assist attempted or completed departure of prisoner from lawful custody before his discharge by due process of law. See **Accessory** (*Accessory after the fact*); **Obstructing justice.**

Aid of the king. In old English law, the king's tenant prayed this, when rent was demanded of him by others.

Aid prayer. In English practice, a proceeding formerly made use of, by way of petition in court, praying in aid of the tenant for life, etc., from the reversioner or remainderman, when the title to the inheritance was in question. It was a plea in suspension of the action. 3 Bl.Comm. 300.

Aids. In feudal law, originally mere benevolences granted by a tenant to his lord, in times of distress; but at length the lords claimed them as of right. They were principally three: (1) To ransom the lord's person, if taken prisoner; (2) to make the lord's eldest son and heir apparent a knight; (3) to give a suitable portion to the lord's eldest daughter on her. A *reasonable aid* was a duty claimed by the lord of the fee of his tenants, holding by knight service, to marry his daughter, etc. Abolished by Tenures Abolition Act of 1660.

Also, extraordinary grants to the Crown by the house of commons, which were the origin of the modern system of taxation. 2 Bl.Comm. 63, 64.

Aid societies. See **Benefit societies.**

Aiel (spelled also Ayel, Aile, Ayle, and Aieul) /íy(ə)l/. L. Fr. A grandfather.

A writ which lay where the grandfather was seized in his demesne as of fee of any lands or tenements in fee simple the day that he died, and a stranger abated or entered the same day and dispossessed the heir. 3 Bl.Comm. 186.

Aielesse /ìy(ə)lés/. A Norman French term signifying "grandmother".

Aile /íyl/. A corruption of the French work aieul, grandfather. See **Aiel.**

Ailment. Commonly means indisposition of body or mind; a slight illness. Mutual Life Ins. Co. of New York v. Burton, 167 Tenn. 606, 72 S.W. 778, 781. In life insurance application does not include mere temporary indisposition, which though requiring medical treatment is readily remediable, Zogg v. Bankers' Life Co. of Des Moines, Iowa, C.C.A.W.Va., 62 F.2d 575, 578; nor passing disorders which could not properly be called diseases.

Aim a weapon. To point it intentionally. "Aim" denotes direction toward some minute point in an object, while "point" implies direction toward the whole object.

Ainesse /èynés/. In French feudal law, the right or privilege of the eldest born; primogeniture; esnecy.

Airbill. A document serving for air transportation as a bill of lading does for marine or rail transportation, and includes an air consignment note or air waybill. U.C.C. § 1–201(6).

Air piracy. Any seizure or exercise of control, by force or violence or threat of force or violence and with wrongful intent, of any aircraft in flight in air commerce. 49 U.S.C.A. § 1472(i).

Air rights. The right to use all or a portion of the air space above real estate. Such right is vested by grant; *e.g.* fee simple, lease, or other conveyance. While commercial airlines have a right to fly over one's land, if such "flight paths" interfere with the owners use of such land, the owner is entitled to recover the extent of actual damage suffered by him. United States v. Causby, 328 U.S. 256, 66 S.Ct. 1062, 90 L.Ed. 1206. On the other hand, the owner of the land is precluded by state and federal laws from polluting the air.

Aisiamentum (spelled also *Esamentum, Aismentum*) /èyshiyəméntəm/. In old English law, an easement.

Aisne or eigne /éyn/. In old English law, the eldest or first born.

A issue. At issue.

Ajournment /àzhurnmón/. In French law, the document pursuant to which an action or suit is commenced, equivalent to the writ of summons in England. Actions, however, are in some cases commenced by *requête* or petition.

A jure suo cadunt /èy júriy s(y)úwow kǽdənt/. They (for example, persons abandoning chattels) lose their right.

A justitia (quasi a quodam fonte) omnia jura emanant /èy jəstísh(iy)ə (kwéyzay ey kwóndəm fóntiy) ómniyə júrə émənǽnt/. From justice, as a fountain, all rights flow.

Akin /əkín/. In old English law. Of kin. "Next-a-kin."

Al. L. Fr. At the; to the. *Al barre;* at the bar. *Al huis d'esglise;* at the church door.

A la grande grevaunce /à lə grónd grəvón(t)s/. To the great grievance.

A large /à lárzh/. Free; at large.

Alarm list. The list of persons liable to military watches, who were at the same time exempt from trainings and musters. Const.Mass. c. 11, § 1, art. 10; Pub.St.Mass.1882, p. 1287.

A latere /èy lǽdəriy/. Lat. Collateral. Used in this sense in speaking of the succession to property. From, on, or at the side; collaterally. *A latere ascendit (jus).* The right ascends collaterally. Justices of the *Curia Regis* are described as *a latere regis residentes*, sitting at the side of the King.

In the Civil Law, a synonym for *e transverso*, across.

Applied also to a process or proceeding, meaning out of the regular or lawful course; incidentally or casually.

From the side of; denoting closeness of intimacy or connection, as a court held before auditors *specialiter a latere regis destinatis*.

Apostolic; having full powers to represent the Pope as if he were present.

Albacea /àlbəséyə/. In Spanish law, an executor or administrator; one who is charged with fulfilling and executing that which is directed by the testator in his testament or other last disposition.

Alba firma /ǽlbə fə́rmə/. In old English law, white rent; rent payable in silver or white money, as distinguished from that which was anciently paid in corn or provisions, called black mail, or black rent; *reditus nigri.*

Albanagium /ælbənéyjiyəm/. In old French law, the state of alienage; of being a foreigner or alien.

Albanus /ælbéynəs/. In old French law, a stranger, alien, or foreigner.

Albinatus /àlbənéydəs/. In old French law, the state or condition of an alien or foreigner.

Albinatus jus /ælbənéydəs jə́s/. In old French law, the *droit d'aubaine* in France, whereby the king, at an alien's death, was entitled to all his property, unless he had peculiar exemption. Repealed in 1791.

Album breve /ǽlbəm bríyviy/. A blank writ; a writ with a blank or omission in it.

Albus liber /ǽlbəs láybər/. The white book; an ancient book containing a compilation of the law and customs of the city of London.

Alcaide /àlkayíydey/. Jailer, warden, governor of a fortress.

Alcoholic liquors. "Alcoholic, spirituous and malt liquors" mean intoxicating liquors which can be used as a beverage, and which, when drunk to excess, will produce intoxication. F. W. Woolworth Co. v. State, 72 Okl.Cr. 125, 113 P.2d 399, 403.

Alcoholism. The pathological effect (as distinguished from physiological effect) of excessive indulgence in intoxicating liquors. See also **Chronic alcoholism; Intoxication.**

Alderman. Municipal officer; member of the legislative body of a municipality. Often called a councilman.

Aldermannus /æ̀ldərmǽnəs/òl°/. L. Lat. An alderman.

Aldermannus civitatis vel burgi /æ̀ldərmǽnəs sìvətéydəs vèl bə́rjày/. In old English law, alderman of a city or borough, from which the modern office of alderman has been derived.

Aldermannus hundredi seu wapentachii /æ̀ldərmǽnəs hə́ndrədày syúw wòpəntéykiyay/. Alderman of a hundred or wapentake.

Aldermannus regis /æ̀ldərmǽnəs ríyjəs/. Alderman of the king. So called, either because he received his appointment from the king or because he gave the judgment of the king in the premises allotted to him.

Aldermannus totius angliæ /æ̀ldərmǽnəs towshíyəs ǽ̀ngliyiy/. Alderman of all England. An officer among the Anglo-Saxons; similar to the chief justiciary of England in later times.

Alea /éyliyə/. Lat. In the civil law, a game of chance or hazard. The chance of gain or loss in a contract.

Aleator /èyliyéydər/. Lat. (From *alea, q.v.,* meaning dice). In the civil law, a gamester; one who plays at games of hazard.

Aleatory contract /éyliyətòriy kóntrækt/. A mutual agreement, of which the effects, with respect both to the advantages and losses, whether to all the parties or to some of them, depend on an uncertain event. Restatement of Contracts, § 291.

Contracts in which promise by one party is conditioned on fortuitous event. Southern Surety Co. v. MacMillan Co., C.C.A.Okl., 58 F.2d 541, 549. A contract, the obligation and performance of which depend upon an uncertain event, such as insurance, engagements to pay annuities, and the like. A contract is aleatory or hazardous when the performance of that which is one of its objects depends on an uncertain event. It is certain when the thing to be done is supposed to depend on the will of the party, or when in the usual course of events it must happen in the manner stipulated.

Aleatory promise. A promise, the performance of which is by its own terms subject to happening of uncertain and fortuitous event or upon some fact existence or past occurrence of which is also uncertain and undetermined. Tyree v. Stone, 62 Wash.2d 694, 384 P.2d 626, 629.

Aleatory transaction. An event dependent on a fortuitous or uncertain happening. See **Aleatory contract.**

Aler a dieu /əléy ədyúw/. L. Fr. In old practice, to be dismissed from court; to go quit. Literally, "to go to God."

Aler sans jour /əléy sæ̀n júr/. In old practice, a phrase used to indicate the final dismissal of a case from court without continuance. "To go without day."

Ale silver. A rent or tribute paid annually to the lord mayor of London, by those who sell ale within the liberty of the city.

Aleu /əl(y)úw/. Fr. In French feudal law, an allodial estate, as distinguished from a feudal estate or benefice.

Alfet /ǽlfət/. A cauldron into which boiling water was poured, in which a criminal plunged his arm up to the elbow, and there held it for some time, as an ordeal.

Alfred's code /ǽlfrədz kówd/. See **Dombec, Domboc.**

Algarum maris /ælgérəm mǽrəs/. Probably a corruption of *Laganum maris, lagan* being a right, in the middle ages, like *jetsam* and *flotsam,* by which goods thrown from a vessel in distress became the property of the king, or the lord on whose shores they were stranded.

A.L.I. American Law Institute.

Alia /ǽliyə/éyl(i)yə/. Lat. Other things.

Alia enormia /ǽliyə ənórmiyə/. Other wrongs. The name given to a general allegation of injuries caused by the defendant with which the plaintiff in an action of trespass under the common-law practice concluded his declaration.

Aliamenta /æl(i)yəméntə/. In old English law, a liberty of passage, open way, water-course, etc., for the tenant's accommodation.

Alias /éyliyəs/. Term used to indicate another name by which a person is known. Short for "alias dictus"; otherwise known as (a. k. a.). When used in connection with a description of a person, it indicates that he has used or been known by another name. John v. Tribune Co., 24 Ill.2d 437, 181 N.E.2d 105, 107. See also **Fictitious name**; **Name.**

Alias dictus /éyliyəs díktəs/. "Otherwise called." Antone v. State, 49 Ariz. 168, 65 P.2d 646, 649, (shorter and more usual form, *alias*). Known by both those names, and is called one or the other. People v. Mellon, 171 Misc. 171, 11 N.Y.S.2d 786, 790. A fictitious name assumed by a person is colloquially termed an "alias". State v. Neal, 231 La. 1048, 93 So.2d 554, 556. See also **Alias.**

Alias execution. One issued after first has been returned without having accomplished its purpose. Richards-Conover Hardware Co. v. Sharp, 150 Kan. 506, 95 P.2d 360, 364. See **Alias process.**

Alias process. A second or further writ, summons, execution or subpoena, used when the first or earlier process has for any reason failed to accomplish its purpose.

Alias subpoena /éyliyəs səpíynə/. One issued after the first has been returned without having accomplished its purpose. Richards-Conover Hardware Co. v. Sharp, 150 Kan. 506, 95 P.2d 360, 364.

Alias summons. A summons issued when original has not produced its effect because defective in form or manner of service, and when issued, supersedes the first writ.

Alias tax warrant. One issued after the first has been returned without having accomplished its purpose. Richards-Conover Hardware Co. v. Sharp, 150 Kan. 506, 95 P.2d 360, 364.

Alias writ. A second or further writ. Ditmar v. Beckham, Tex.Civ.App., 77 S.W.2d 893, 894.

Alias writ of execution. One issued after the first has been returned without having accomplished its purpose. Richards-Conover Hardware Co. v. Sharp, 150 Kan. 506, 95 P.2d 360, 364.

A libellis /éy ləbélas/. L. Lat. An officer who had charge of the *libelli* or petitions addressed to the sovereign. A name sometimes given to a chancellor (*cancellarius*) in the early history of that office.

Alibi /ǽləbày/. A defense that places the defendant at the relevant time in a different place than the scene involved and so removed therefrom as to render it impossible for him to be the guilty party. Com. v. Warrington, 230 Pa.Super. 332, 326 A.2d 427, 429. Notice of intention to offer a defense of alibi is governed in federal courts by Fed.R.Crim.P. 12.1.

Alien, *n.* /éyl(i)yən/. A foreign born person who has not qualified as a citizen of the country; but an alien is a person within the meaning of the due process clause of the U.S. Constitution to same extent as a citizen. Galvan v. Press, 347 U.S. 522, 74 S.Ct. 737, 742, 98 L.Ed. 911.

Alien or **aliene**, *v.* To transfer or make over to another; to convey or transfer the property of a thing from one person to another; to alienate. Usually applied to the transfer of lands and tenements. See **Alienation.**

Alienability. The quality or attribute of being transferrable; *e.g.*, interest in property.

Alienability of future interests. The right of an owner of an interest which vests in possession or enjoyment in the future to transfer such interest beforehand.

Alienable /éyl(i)yənəbəl/. Proper to be the subject of alienation or transfer.

Alienage /éyl(i)yənəj/. The condition or state of an alien.

Alien amy. In international law, alien friend. An alien who is the subject or citizen of a foreign government at peace with our own.

Alien and sedition laws. Acts of Congress of July 6 and July 14, 1978, which made it a criminal offense to utter or publish any false, scandalous and malicious writings against the federal government with intent to defame it, or bring it into contempt or disrepute or to excite hatred of people or stir up sedition against it. These short-lived acts tightened residency requirements for citizenships, granted presidential powers to deport and jail aliens, and provided penalties for seditious writings or speech critical of the government. See also **Sedition.**

Aliena negotia exacto officio geruntur /ǽliyíynə nəgówshiyə egzǽktow əfísh(iy)ow jəréntər/. The business of another is to be conducted with particular attention.

Alienate /éyl(i)yənèyt/. To convey; to transfer the title to property. *Alien* is very commonly used in the same sense. See **Alienation.**

Alienation /èyl(i)yənéyshən/. In real property law, the transfer of the property and possession of lands, tenements, or other things, from one person to another. The term is particularly applied to absolute conveyances of real property. The voluntary and complete transfer from one person to another. Disposition by will. Every mode of passing realty by the act of the party, as distinguished from passing it by the operation of law. See also **Restraint on alienation.**

Alienation clause. A provision in a document giving a person the right to transfer or forbidding him from transferring the property which is the subject of the document. Provision in fire insurance policy voiding such policy upon transfer of ownership by insured.

Alienation in mortmain. See **Amortization**; **Mortmain.**

Alienation of affections. Action of "alienation of affections" is a tort based upon willful and malicious interference with marriage relation by third party, without justification or excuse. Donnell v. Donnell, 220 Tenn. 169, 415 S.W.2d 127, 132. The elements constituting the cause of action are wrongful conduct of defendant, plaintiff's loss of affection or consortium of spouse and causal connection between such conduct and such loss. Kundert v. Johnson, 268 Wis. 484, 68 N.W.2d 42. Certain states have abolished the right to bring an alienation of affections action. See **Consortium**; **Heart-balm statutes.**

Alienation office. In English practice, an office for the recovery of fines levied upon writs of covenant and entries.

Alienatio rei præfertur juri accrescendi /èyliyənéyshiyow ríyay priyfə́rdər júray ǽkrəsénday/. Alienation is favored by the law rather than accumulation.

Alien corporation. A corporation organized under the laws of a foreign power.

Alienee /èyl(i)yəníy/. One to whom an alienation, conveyance, or transfer of property is made. See **Alienor.**

Alien enemy. In international law, an alien who is the subject or citizen of some hostile nation or power. A person who, by reason of owing a permanent or temporary allegiance to a hostile power, becomes, in time of war, impressed with the character of an enemy. Subjects of a foreign nation at war with United States. Caparell v. Goodbody, 132 N.J.Eq. 559, 29 A.2d 563, 569.

Alien friend. Subjects of a foreign state at peace with the United States. Caparell v. Goodbody, 132 N.J.Eq. 559, 29 A.2d 563, 569, 570.

Alienigena /èyliyənáyjənə/. One of foreign birth; an alien.

Alieni generis /èyliyíynay jénərəs/. Lat. Of another kind.

Alieni juris /èyliyíynay júrəs/. Lat. Under the control, or subject to the authority, of another person; *e.g.,* an infant who is under the authority of his father or guardian. The term is contrasted with Sui Juris *(q.v.).*

Alien immigrant. One who has come into the country from a foreign country and has not yet been naturalized.

Alienism /éyl(i)yənìzəm/. The state, condition, or character of an alien.

Alienist /éyl(i)yənist/. A seldom used term meaning one who has specialized in the study of mental diseases. Persons qualified by experience, knowledge, and previous opportunities to express opinion as to defendant's mental condition at a particular time. People v. Norton, 138 Cal.App. 70, 31 P.2d 809, 810.

Alien nee. An alien born, *i.e.,* a person who has been born an alien.

Alienor /éyl(i)yənər/. He who makes a grant, transfer of title, conveyance, or alienation. Correlative of *alienee.*

Alien Registration Act. Act of Congress (1940) which requires annual registration of all aliens over the age of 13, and the fingerprinting of all such registrants.

Alienus /ǽliyíynəs/. Lat. Another's; belonging to another; the property of another. *Alienus homo,* another's man, or slave. *Aliena res,* another's property.

Alignment. The act of laying out or adjusting a line. The state of being so laid out or adjusted. The ground plan of a railway or other road or work as distinguished from its profile or gradients. An adjustment to a line.

Alike. Similar to another. The term is not synonymous with "identical," which means "exactly the same."

Alimenta /ǽləméntə/. Lat. In the civil law, aliments; things necessary to sustain life; means of support, including food (*cibaria*), clothing (*vestitus*) and habitation (*habitatio*).

Alimony /ǽləməniy/. Comes from Latin "alimonia" meaning sustenance, and means, therefore, the sustenance or support of the wife by her divorced husband and stems from the common-law right of the wife to support by her husband. Allowances which husband or wife by court order pays other spouse for maintenance while they are separated, or after they are divorced (permanent alimony), or temporarily, pending a suit for divorce (pendente lite). Generally, it is restricted to money unless otherwise authorized by statute. But it may be an allowance out of the spouse's estate. LaChance v. LaChance, Md.App., 346 A.2d 676, 679, 680. State statutes which provide for payment of alimony only to the wife have been held to be unconstitutional. Orr v. Orr, 99 S.Ct. 1102. See also **Gross alimony; Lump-sum alimony; Palimony; Periodic alimony; Permanent alimony; Trust** (*Alimony trust*).

Alimony in gross, or in a lump sum, is in the nature of a final property settlement, and hence in some jurisdictions is not included in the term "alimony," which in its strict or technical sense contemplates money payments at regular intervals. Refers to those alimony arrangements where entire award is a vested and determined amount and not subject to change. Imbrie v. Imbrie, 94 Ill.App.2d 60, 236 N.E.2d 381, 383.

Alimony pendente lite (temporary alimony). An allowance made pending a suit for divorce or separate maintenance including a reasonable allowance for preparation of the suit as well as for support. Davis v. Davis, 15 Wash.2d 297, 130 P.2d 355, 359. See also **Allowance pendente lite.**

Permanent alimony. A provision for the support and maintenance of a wife during her lifetime.

Tax treatment. Alimony and separate maintenance payments are includible in the gross income of the recipient and are deductible by the payor. The payments must be periodic and made in discharge of a legal obligation arising from a marital or family relationship. Child support and voluntary payments are not treated as alimony. I.R.C. § 71.

Alimony trust. See **Trust.**

A l'impossible nul n'est tenu /à lǽmposíyblə núl néy tenyúw/. No one is bound to do the impossible.

Alio intuitu /ǽliyow int(y)úwəduw/. Lat. In a different view; under a different aspect. With another view or object; with respect to another case or condition.

Aliquid conceditur ne injuria remaneat impunita, quod alias non concederetur /ǽləkwəd kənsíydədər nìy injúriyə rəmǽniyət impyúwnədə, kwòd ǽliyəs nòn kənsìydəríydər/. Something is (will be) conceded, to prevent a wrong remaining unredressed, which otherwise would not be conceded.

Aliquid possessionis et nihil juris /ǽləkwəd pəzèshiyównəs èt náyəl júrəs/. Somewhat of possession, and nothing of right (but no right).

Aliquis non debet esse judex in propria causa, quia non potest esse judex et pars /ǽləkwəs nòn débəd ésiy júwdeks in prówpriyə kózə, kwáyə nòn pòwdəst ésiy júwdeks èt párz/. A person ought not to be judge in his own cause, because he cannot act as judge and party.

Aliquot /ǽləkwòt/. Strictly speaking, means contained in something else an exact number of times. But as applied to resulting trusts, "aliquot" is treated as meaning fractional, and means any definite interest.

Aliquot part rule. A rule which requires that a person intend to acquire a fractional part of the ownership of property before the court can declare a resulting trust in his favor.

Aliter /ǽlədər/. Otherwise; as otherwise held or decided.

Aliud est celare, aliud tacere /ǽliyəd èst səlériy, ǽliyəd təsériy/. To conceal is one thing; to be silent is another.

Aliud est possidere, aliud esse in possessione /ǽliyəd èst pòsədíriy, ǽliyəd ésiy in pəzèshiyówniy/. It is one thing to possess; it is another to be in possession.

Aliud est vendere, aliud vendenti consentire /ǽliyəd èst véndəriy, ǽliyəd vendéntay kònsəntáyriy/. To sell is one thing; to consent to a sale (seller) is another thing.

Aliud examen /ǽliyəd əgzéymən/. A different or foreign mode of trial.

Aliunde /èyliyándiy/. Lat. From another source; from elsewhere; from outside.

Evidence aliunde. Evidence from outside, from another source. In certain cases a written instrument may be explained by evidence *aliunde*, that is, by evidence drawn from sources exterior to the instrument itself, *e.g.*, the testimony of a witness to conversations, admissions, or preliminary negotiations. Evidence aliunde (*i.e.*, from outside the will) may be received to explain an ambiguity in a will. See **Parol evidence.**

Aliunde rule /èyliyándiy rúwl/. A verdict may not be impeached by evidence of juror unless foundation for introduction thereof is first made by competent evidence aliunde, or from some other source. State v. Adams, 141 Ohio St. 423, 48 N.E.2d 861, 863.

Alius /ǽliyəs/. Lat. Other. The neuter form is *aliud*, something else; another thing.

Alive. As respects birth, it means that child shall have an independent life of its own for some period, even momentarily, after birth; evidenced by respiration or other indications of life, such as beating of heart and pulsation of arteries (Hydrostatic test); or heart tones in response to artificial respiration, or pulsation of umbilical cord after being severed. See also **Born alive; Child; Life; Live; Viable child.**

In respect of estate matters, a child *en ventre sa mere* is "born" and "alive" for all purposes for his benefit. In re Holthausen's Will, 175 Misc. 1022, 26 N.Y.S.2d 140, 143.

All. Means the whole of—used with a singular noun or pronoun, and referring to amount, quantity, extent, duration, quality, or degree. The whole number or sum of—used collectively, with a plural noun or pronoun expressing an aggregate. Every member of individual component of; each one of—used with a plural noun. In this sense, all is used generically and distributively. "All" refers rather to the aggregate under which the individuals are subsumed than to the individuals themselves. State v. Hallenberg-Wagner Motor Co., 341 Mo. 771, 108 S.W.2d 398, 401. See **Both.**

All and singular. All without exception. A comprehensive term often employed in conveyances, wills, and the like, which includes the aggregate or whole and also each of the separate items or components.

All cases at law. Within constitutional guaranty of jury trial, refers to common law actions as distinguished from causes in equity and certain other proceedings. Breimhorst v. Beckman, 239 Minn. 409, 35 N.W.2d 719, 734.

Allegans contraria non est audiendus /ǽləgænz kəntrériyə nòn est òdiyéndəs/. On alleging contrary or contradictory things (whose statements contradict each other) is not to be heard. Applied to the statements of a witness.

Allegans suam turpitudinem non est audiendus /ǽləgænz s(y)úwəm tərpətyúwdənəm nón est òdiyéndəs/. One who alleges his own infamy is not to be heard.

Allegari non debuit quod probatum non relevat /ǽləgéray non déb(y)uwət kwòd prəbéydəm nòn réləvæt/. That ought not to be alleged which, if proved, is not relevant.

Allegata /ǽləgéydə/. In Roman law, a word which the emperors formerly signed at the bottom of their rescripts and constitutions; under other instruments they usually wrote *signata* or *testata*.

Allegata et probata /ǽləgéydə èt prowbéydə/. Lat. Things alleged and proved. The allegations made by a party to a suit, and the proof adduced in their support.

Allegatio contra factum non est admittenda /ǽləgéysh(iy)ow kóntrə fǽktəm nòn est ædmətƏndə/. An allegation contrary to the deed (or fact) is not admissible.

Allegation. The assertion, claim, declaration, or statement of a party to an action, made in a pleading, setting out what he expects to prove. See *e.g.* Fed.R. Civil P. 8. See also **Charge; Claim; Complaint.**

A material allegation in a pleading is one essential to the claim or defense.

In ecclesiastical law, the statement of the facts intended to be relied on in support of the contested suit.

Allegation of fact. Generally, narration of transaction by stating details according to their legal effect, and statement of right or liability flowing from certain facts is conclusion of law.

Allegation of faculties. A statement made by the wife of the property of her husband, in order to obtain alimony. See **Faculties.**

Allege /əléj/. To state, recite, assert, or charge; to make an allegation.

Alleged. Stated; recited; claimed; asserted; charged.

Allegiance /əlíyjəns/. Obligation of fidelity and obedience to government in consideration for protection that government gives. U. S. v. Kuhn, D.C.N.Y., 49 F.Supp. 407, 414. See also **Oath of allegiance.**

Acquired allegiance, is that binding a naturalized citizen.

Local or actual allegiance, is that measure of obedience due from a subject of one government to another government, within whose territory he is temporarily resident. From this are excepted foreign sovereigns and their representatives, naval and armed forces when permitted to remain in or pass through the country or its waters.

Natural allegiance. In English law, that kind of allegiance which is due from all men born within the king's dominions, immediately upon their birth, which is intrinsic and perpetual, and cannot be divested by any act of their own. In American law, the allegiance due from citizens of the United States to their native country, and also from naturalized citizens, and which cannot be renounced without the permission of government, to be declared by law.

Allegiare /əlìyjiyériy/. To defend and clear one's self; to wage one's own law. An archaic word which simply means to define or justify by due course of law.

Alleging diminution /əléjiŋ dìmən(y)úwshən/. The allegation in an appellate court, of some error in a subordinate part of the *nisi prius* record. See **Diminution.**

Allen charge. An instruction advising jurors to have deference for each other's views, that they should listen, with a disposition to be convinced, to each other's argument; deriving its name from the case of Allen v. United States, 164 U.S. 492, 17 S.Ct. 154, 41 L.Ed. 528, wherein the instruction was approved. Coupe v. United States, 72 App.D.C. 86, 113 F.2d 145, 149; Green v. U. S., C.A.Fla., 309 F.2d 852. Variously called dynamite charge, shotgun instruction, third degree instruction. The Allen charge is prohibited in certain states; *e.g.* California, People v. Gainer, 19 Cal.3d 835, 566 P.2d 997, 139 Cal.Rptr. 861.

Allergy. A susceptibility to disease. Vogt v. Ford Motor Co., Mo.App., 138 S.W.2d 684, 688. The condition of being hypersensitive to something.

All events test. For accrual method taxpayers, income is earned when: (1) all the events have occurred which fix the right to receive the income and (2) the amount can be determined with reasonable accuracy. Accrual of income cannot be postponed simply because a portion of the income may have to be returned in a subsequent period.

Alleviare /əlìyviyériy/. L. Lat. In old records, to levy or pay an accustomed fine or composition; to redeem by such payment.

All faults. A sale of goods with "all faults" covers, in the absence of fraud on the part of the vendor, all such faults and defects as are not inconsistent with the identity of the goods as the goods described. U.C.C. § 2–316. See **As is.**

All fours. Two cases or decisions which are alike in all material respects, and precisely similar in all the circumstances affecting their determination, are said to be or to run on "all fours."

Alliance. The relation or union between persons or families contracted by intermarriage; affinity. State of being allied.

In international law, a union, association or confederation of two or more states or nations, formed by league or treaty, for the joint prosecution of a war (offensive alliance), or for their mutual assistance and protection in repelling hostile attacks (defensive alliance). The league or treaty by which the association is formed. The act of confederating, by league or treaty, for the purposes mentioned.

The term is also used in a wider sense, embracing unions for objects of common interest to the contracting parties, as the "Holy Alliance" entered into in 1815 by Prussia, Austria and Russia for the purpose of counteracting the revolutionary movement in the interest of political liberalism.

Allision. The running of one vessel into or against another, as distinguished from a collision, *i. e.,* the running of two vessels against each other. But this distinction is not very carefully observed.

Allocable /ǽləkəbəl/. Synonymous with "distributable". In analyzing accounts, the breaking down of a lump sum charged or credited to one account into several parts to be charged or credited to other accounts.

Allocation. Assignment or allotment. Jacobson v. Bowles, D.C.Tex., 53 F.Supp. 532, 534.

Allocatione facienda /ǽləkèyshiyówniy fæshiyénda/. In old English practice, a writ for allowing to an accountant such sums of money as he hath lawfully expended in his office; directed to the lord treasurer and barons of the exchequer upon application made.

Allocation of dividends. In trust accounting, cash dividends are credited or allocated to income; whereas, generally, stock dividends are credited to principal and the basis of the stock on which the dividend has been paid is changed in the portfolio. If the cash dividend is a liquidating dividend, it is commonly allocated to principal.

Allocation of income. When two or more businesses are controlled by the same interests, the Commissioner of Internal Revenue may allocate or distribute income to prevent tax evasion. I.R.C. § 482. In trust accounting, the process by which income is distributed as between principal and income.

Allocation of principal and income. See **Allocation of dividends; Allocation of income.**

Allocatur /ǽləkéydər/. Lat. It is allowed. A word formerly used to denote that a writ or order was allowed. A word denoting the allowance by a master or prothonotary of a bill referred for his consideration, whether touching costs, damages, or matter of account. *A special allocatur* is the special allowance of a writ (particularly a writ of error) which is required in some particular cases.

Allocatur exigent /æləkéydər égzəjənt/. A species of writ anciently issued in outlawry proceedings, on the return of the original writ of exigent. See **Exigent**.

Allocution /æləkyúwshən/. Formality of court's inquiry of prisoner as to whether he has any legal cause to show why judgment should not be pronounced against him on verdict of conviction. State v. Pruitt, Mo., 169 S.W.2d 399, 400.

Allocutus /æləkyúwdəs/. See **Allocution**.

Allodarii /ælədériyay/. Owners of allodial lands. Owners of estates as large as a subject may have.

Allodial /əlówdiyəl/. Free; not holden of any lord or superior; owned without obligation of vassalage or fealty; the opposite of feudal.

Allodium /əlówdiyəm/. Land held absolutely in one's own right, and not of any lord or superior; land not subject to feudal duties or burdens. An estate held by absolute ownership, without recognizing any superior to whom any duty is due on account thereof.

Allograph /æləgræf/. A writing or signature made for a person by another; opposed to autograph.

Allonge /əlónj/. A piece of paper annexed to a bill of exchange or promissory note, on which to write endorsements for which there is no room on the instrument itself. Such must be so firmly affixed thereto as to become a part thereof. U.C.C. § 3-202(2).

Allot /əlót/. To apportion, distribute; to divide property held in common among those entitled, assigning to each his ratable portion, to be held in severalty. To set apart specific property, a share of a fund, etc., to a distinct party. In the law of corporations, to allot shares, debentures, etc., is to appropriate them to the applicants or persons who have applied for them.

Allotment. A share or portion; that which is allotted; apportionment, division; the distribution of shares in a public undertaking or corporation. Partition; the distribution of land under an inclosure act. The term ordinarily and commonly used to describe land held by Indians after allotment, and before the issuance of the patent in fee that deprives the land of its character as Indian country. See **Allottee**.

Allotment certificate. A document issued to an applicant for shares in a company or public loan announcing the number of shares allotted or assigned and the amounts and due dates of the calls or different payments to be made on the same.

Allotment note. In English law, a writing by a seaman, made on an approved form, whereby he makes an assignment of part of his wages in favor of his wife, father or mother, grandfather or grandmother, brother or sister.

Allotment system. Designates the practice in England of dividing land in small portions for cultivation by agricultural laborers, gardeners and others.

Allotment warden. By the English general inclosure act, 1845, § 108, when an allotment for the laboring poor of a district had been made on an inclosure under the act, the land so allotted was to be under the management of the incumbent and church warden of the parish, and two other persons elected by the parish, and they were to be styled "the allotment wardens" of the parish.

Allottee. One to whom an allotment is made; who receives a ratable share under an allotment. A person to whom land under an inclosure act or shares in a corporation or public undertaking are allotted.

Allow. The word has no rigid or precise meaning, its import varying according to circumstances or context in connection with which it is used. It may mean to bestow or assign to any one as his right or due. To approve of, accept as true, admit, concede, adopt, or fix. To grant something as a deduction or an addition; to abate or deduct; as, to allow a sum for leakage. Pittsburgh Brewing Co. v. Commissioner of Internal Revenue, C.C.A.3, 107 F.2d 155, 156. To sanction, either directly or indirectly, as opposed to merely suffering a thing to be done; to acquiesce in; to suffer; to tolerate. See also **Acquiescence; Consent**.

Allowance. A deduction, an average payment, a portion assigned or allowed; the act of allowing. For "Family," see that title.

Allowance pendente lite /əláwəns pendéntiy láydiy/. The court ordered provision for a spouse and children during the pendency of a divorce or separate support proceeding. See also **Alimony**.

Allowed claim. Against an estate it is a debt or charge which is valid in law and entitled to enforcement. Commissioner of Internal Revenue v. Lyne, C.C.A.1, 90 F.2d 745, 747.

Alloynour /əlóynər/. L. Fr. One who conceals, steals, or carries off a thing privately. See **Eloigne**.

All the estate. The name given in England to the short clause in a conveyance or other assurance which purports to convey "all the estate, right, title, interest, claim, and demand" of the grantor, lessor, etc., in the property dealt with.

Alluvio maris /əl(y)úwviyow mǽrəs/. Lat. In the civil and old English law, the washing up of the sea; the soil thus formed; formation of soil or land from the sea; maritime increase.

Alluvion /əl(y)úwviyən/. That increase of the earth on a shore or bank of a stream or the sea, by the force of the water, as by a current or by waves, which is so gradual that no one can judge how much is added at each moment of time. Garrett v. State, 118 N.J.Super. 594, 289 A.2d 542, 545. "Accretion" denotes the act. However, the terms are frequently used synonymously. Avulsion is sudden and perceptible. See **Accretion; Avulsion**.

All Writs Act. See **Writ**.

Ally. A nation which has entered into an alliance with another nation. A citizen or subject of one of two or more allied nations.

Almaria /ælmériyə/. The archives, or, as they are sometimes styled, muniments of a church or library.

Almesfeoh /á(l)mzfiy/. In Saxon law, alms-fee; alms-money. Otherwise called "Peter-pence."

Almoin /ǽlmóyn/. Alms; a tenure of lands by divine service. See **Frank-almoigne.**

Almoner /ǽlmənər/. One charged with the distribution of alms. The office was first instituted in religious houses and although formerly one of importance is now in England almost a sinecure.

Alms. Charitable donations. Any species of relief bestowed upon the poor. That which is given by public authority for the relief of the poor.

Alms fee. Peter-pence (or Peter's pence), which see.

Almshouse. A house for the publicly or privately supported paupers of a city or county; may also be termed a "mission". In England an almshouse is not synonymous with a workhouse or poorhouse, being supported by private endowment.

Alnager /ǽlnəjər/ or **ulnager** /álnəjər/. A sworn officer of the king whose duty it was to look to the assise of woolen cloth made throughout the land, and to the putting on the seals for that purpose ordained, for which he collected a duty called "alnage."

Alod, alode, alodes, alodis /ǽləd/. L. Lat. In feudal law, old forms of *alodium* or *allodium* (*q.v.*). A term used in opposition to *feodum* or *fief*, which means property, the use of which was bestowed upon another by the proprietor, on condition that the grantee should perform certain services for the grantor, and upon the failure of which the property should revert to the original possessor.

Alodiarii. See **Allodarii.**

Alone. Apart from others; singly; sole.

Along. Lengthwise of, implying motion or at or near, distinguished from across. By, on, up to, or over, according to the subject-matter and context. The term does not necessarily mean touching at all points; nor does it necessarily imply contact.

A lour foy /ə lár fwá/. In their allegiance.

Also. Besides; as well; in addition; likewise; in like manner; similarly; too; withal. Some other thing; including; further; furthermore; in the same manner; moreover; nearly the same as the word "and" or "likewise."

A.L.T.A. American Land Title Association.

Alta proditio /ǽltə prowdíshiyow/. L. Lat. In old English law, high treason. 4 Bl.Comm. 75. See **Treason.**

Altarage /ólt(ə)rəj/. In ecclesiastical law, offerings made on the altar; all profits which accrue to the priest by means of the altar.

Alta via /ǽltə váyə/. L. Lat. In old English law, a highway; the highway. *Alta via regia;* the king's highway; "the king's high street."

Alter. To make a change in; to modify; to vary in some degree; to change some of the elements or ingredients or details without substituting an entirely new thing or destroying the identity of the thing affected. To change partially. To change in one or more respects, but without destruction of existence or identity of the thing changed; to increase or diminish. See **Alteration; Amend; Change.**

Alteration. Variation; changing; making different. A change of a thing from one form or state to another; making a thing different from what it was without destroying its identity. See **Alter.**

An act done upon an instrument by which its meaning or language is changed. Language different in legal effect, or change in rights, interests, or obligations of parties. It introduces some change into instrument's terms, meaning, language, or details. The term is not properly applied to any change which involves the substitution of a practically new document. An alteration is said to be *material* when it affects, or may possibly affect, the rights of the persons interested in the document. U.C.C. § 3–407. See **Material alteration; Mutilation; Spoliation.**

Alteration of contract. A change in the provisions of a contract. If alteration is material, it extinguishes the right of the party who alters it and discharges the other party. The test of whether it is material is whether the rights of the obligee would be varied as to the party making the alteration or to a third party. Restatement of Contracts, § 434.

Alteration of trust. An act by settlor of trust changing the terms of the trust, generally pursuant to a power to alter and amend within the original trust instrument.

Altercation. Warm contentions in words. Dispute or controversy carried on with heat or anger. Ivory v. State, 128 Tex.Cr.R. 408, 81 S.W.2d 696, 698.

Alter ego /ólter íygow/. Second self. Under doctrine of "alter ego", court merely disregards corporate entity and holds individual responsible for acts knowingly and intentionally done in the name of corporation. Ivy v. Plyler, 246 Cal.App.2d 678, 54 Cal.Rptr. 894, 897. To establish the "alter ego" doctrine, it must be shown that the stockholders disregarded the entity of the corporation, made corporation a mere conduit for the transaction of their own private business, and that the separate individualities of the corporation and its stockholders in fact ceased to exist. Sefton v. San Diego Trust & Savings Bank, Cal.App., 106 P.2d 974, 984. The doctrine of "alter ego" does not create assets for or in corporation, but it simply fastens liability on the individual who uses the corporation merely as an instrumentality in conducting his own personal business, and that liability springs from fraud perpetrated not on the corporation, but on third persons dealing with corporation. Garvin v. Matthews, 193 Wash. 152, 74 P.2d 990, 992. See also **Instrumentality rule.**

Alterius circumventio alii non præbet actionem /æltíriyəs sàrkəmvénsh(iy)ow ǽliyay nòn príybəd ækshiyównəm/. The deceiving of one person does not afford an action to another.

Alternat /óltərnət/. A usage among diplomatists by which the rank and places of different powers, who have the same right and pretensions to precedence, are changed from time to time, either in a certain regular order or one determined by lot. In drawing up treaties and conventions, for example, it is the usage of certain powers to alternate, both in the preamble and the signatures, so that each power occupies, in the copy intended to be delivered to it, the first place.

Alternate legacy. See **Legacy**.

Alternate valuation date. Property passing from a person by death may be valued for death tax purposes as of the date of death or the alternate valuation date. The alternate valuation date is six months from the date of death or the date the property is disposed of by the estate, whichever comes first. The use of the alternate valuation date requires an affirmative election on the part of the executor or administrator of the estate.

Alternatim /òltərnéydəm/. Lat. Interchangeably.

Alternativa petitio non est audienda /oltàrnətáyvə pətísh(i)yow nón est òdiyéndə/. An alternative petition or demand is not to be heard.

Alternative. One or the other of two things; giving an option or choice; allowing a choice between two or more things or acts to be done.

Alternative contract. A contract whose terms allow of performance by the doing of either one of several acts at the election of the party from whom performance is due.

Alternative judgment. See **Judgment**.

Alternative obligation. An obligation allowing the obligor to choose which of two things he will do, the performance of either of which will satisfy the instrument. A promise to deliver a certain thing or to pay a specified sum of money is an example of this kind of obligation.

Alternative pleading. A form of pleading which was formerly prohibited but now recognized under Federal and state Rules of Civ.Proc. by which the pleader sets forth two or more statements by way of claim or defense which are not necessarily consistent with each other. When two or more statements are made in the alternative and one of them if made independently would be sufficient, the pleading is not made insufficient by the insufficiency of one or more of the alternative statements. See Fed.R.Civil P. 8(e)(2).

Alternative relief. Under Fed.Rules Civ.Proc. 8(a) the party seeking a judgment may demand it in the alternative, or in various forms, *e.g.* demand for a money judgment and for equitable relief.

Alternative remainders. Remainders in which disposition of property is made in alternative, one to take effect only in case the other does not, and in substitution of it.

Alternative remedies. See **Alternative relief**.

Alternative tax. An option allowed taxpayers in computing the tax on net long-term capital gains.

Alternative writ. A common law writ commanding the person against whom it is issued to do a specified thing, or show cause to the court why he should not be compelled to do it. Under the common-law practice, the first *mandamus* is an alternative writ; but in modern practice this writ is often dispensed with and

its place is taken by an order to show cause. See **Mandamus**.

Alterum non lædere /óltərəm nòn líydəriy/. Not to injure another. This maxim, and two others, *honeste vivere*, and *suum cuique tribuere*, *(q.v.)* are considered by Justinian as fundamental principles upon which all the rules of law are based.

Alteruter /òltəryúwdər/. Lat. One of two; either.

Altius non tollendi /ǽlsh(i)yəs nòn təléndày/. In the civil law, a servitude due by the owner of a house, by which he is restrained from building beyond a certain height.

Altius tollendi /ǽlsh(i)yəs təléndày/. In the civil law, a servitude which consists in the right, to him who is entitled to it, to build his house as high as he may think proper. In general, however, every one enjoys this privilege, unless he is restrained by some contrary title.

Alto et basso /ǽltow ət bǽsow/. High and low. This phrase is applied to an agreement made between two contending parties to submit all matters in dispute, *alto et basso*, to arbitration.

Altum mare /ǽltəm mǽriy/. L. Lat. In old English law, the high sea, or seas. The deep sea. *Super altum mare*, on the high seas.

A lui et a ses heritiers pour toujours. To him and to his heirs forever.

Alveus /ǽlviyəs/. The bed or channel through which the stream flows when it runs within its ordinary channel. *Alveus derelictus*, a deserted channel.

A.M. *Ante meridiem*, before noon. Only the abbreviation is ordinarily used. Also *artium magister*, master of arts. Also *annus mirabilis*, the wonderful year— 1666, the year of the defeat of the Dutch fleet and of the great London fire. Also *anno mundi*, in the year of the world; that is, when the creation of the world is said to have taken place, 4004 B. C.

A.M.A. American Medical Association.

A ma intent. On my action.

Amalgamation /əmælgəméyshən/. Union of different races, or diverse elements, societies, unions, associations, or corporations, so as to form a homogeneous whole or new body; interfusion; intermarriage; consolidation; merger; coalescence; as, the amalgamation of stock.

Amalphitan code or **table** /əmǽlfədən kowd/°téybəl/. A collection of sea-laws, compiled about the end of the eleventh century, by the people of Amalphi. It consists of the laws on maritime subjects, which were or had been in force in countries bordering on the Mediterranean; and was for a long time received as authority in those countries. It became a part of the law of the sea. See **Code**.

A manibus /èy mǽnibəs/. Lat. Royal scribe. See **Amanuensis**.

Amanuensis /əmǽnyuwénsəs/. One who writes on behalf of another that which he dictates.

A manu servus /èy mǽnuw sɔ́rvəs/. Lat. A handservant; a scribe; a secretary.

Ambactus /æmbǽktəs/. A messenger; a servant sent about; one whose services his master hired out.

Ambasciator /æmbæ̀shiyéydər/. A person sent about in the service of another; a person sent on a service. A word of frequent occurrence in the writers of the middle ages.

Ambassador. A public officer clothed with high diplomatic powers, commissioned by a government to transact the international business of his government with a foreign government.

An Ambassador of the United States is the personal representative of the President and reports to the President through the Secretary of State. Ambassadors have full responsibility for implementing the U.S. foreign policy by any and all U.S. Government personnel within their country of assignment, except those under military commands. Their responsibilities include negotiating agreements between the United States and the host country, explaining and disseminating official U.S. policy, and maintaining cordial relations with that country's government and people.

A distinction was formerly made between Ambassadors *Extraordinary,* who were sent to conduct special business or to remain for an indeterminate period, and Ambassadors *Ordinary,* who were sent on permanent missions; but this distinction is no longer observed.

See also **Diplomatic agent.**

Ambidexter /æ̀mbədékstər/. Skillful with both hands; one who plays on both sides. Applied anciently to an attorney who took pay from both sides, and subsequently to a juror guilty of the same offense.

Ambigua responsio contra proferentem est accipienda /æmbígyuwə rəspónsh(iy)ow kóntrə pròfəréntəm ést əksipiyéndə/. An ambiguous answer is to be taken against (is not to be construed in favor of) him who offers it.

Ambiguis casibus semper præsumitur pro rege /æmbígyuwəs kéyzəbəs sémpər priyz(y)úwmədər pròw ríyjiy/. In doubtful cases, the presumption always is in behalf of the crown.

Ambiguitas /æ̀mbəgyúwətæs/. Lat. From *ambiguus,* doubtful, uncertain, obscure. Ambiguity; uncertainty of meaning.

Ambiguitas latens, a latent ambiguity; *ambiguitas patens,* a patent ambiguity. See **Ambiguity.**

Ambiguitas contra stipulatorem est /æ̀mbəgyúwətæs kóntrə stìpyəleytórəm ést/. Doubtful words will be construed most strongly against the party using them.

Ambiguitas verborum latens verificatione suppletur; nam quod ex facto oritur ambiguum verificatione facti tollitur /æ̀mbəgyúwətæs vərbórəm lèydənz vèhrəfəkèyshiyówniy səplíydər, næm kwód èks fǽkt(y)uw óhrədər æmbígyuwəm vèhrəfəkèyshiyówniy fǽktay tólədər/. A latent ambiguity in the language may be removed by evidence; for whatever ambiguity arises from an extrinsic fact may be explained by extrinsic evidence. Said to be "an unprofitable subtlety; inadequate and uninstructive."

Ambiguitas verborum patens nulla verificatione excluditur /æ̀mbəgyúwətæs vərbórəm péytènz nə́lə vèhrəfəkèyshiyówniy ekslúwdədər/. A patent ambiguity cannot be cleared up by extrinsic evidence (or is never holpen by averment).

Ambiguity /æ̀mbəgyúwədiy/. Doubtfulness; doubleness of meaning. Duplicity, indistinctness, or uncertainty of meaning of an expression used in a written instrument. Want of clearness or definiteness; difficult to comprehend or distinguish; of doubtful import. For "Extrinsic Ambiguity," see that title.

Language in contract is "ambiguous" when it is reasonably capable of being understood in more than one sense. City of Sioux Falls v. Henry Carlson Co., Inc., S.D., 258 N.W.2d 676, 679. Test for determining whether a contract is "ambiguous" is whether reasonable persons would find the contract subject to more than one interpretation. Tastee-Freez Leasing Corp. v. Milwid, Ind.App., 365 N.E.2d 1388, 1390.

Ambiguity of language is to be distinguished from unintelligibility and inaccuracy, for words cannot be said to be ambiguous unless their signification seems doubtful and uncertain to persons of competent skill and knowledge to understand them. It does not include uncertainty arising from the use of peculiar words, or of common words in a peculiar sense. It is *latent* where the language employed is clear and intelligible and suggests but a single meaning, but some extrinsic fact or extraneous evidence creates a necessity for interpretation or a choice among two or more possible meanings, as where a description apparently plain and unambiguous is shown to fit different pieces of property. Logue v. Von Almen, 379 Ill. 208, 40 N.E.2d 73, 82. A *patent* ambiguity is that which appears on the face of the instrument, and arises from the defective, obscure, or insensible language used.

Ambiguity upon the factum. An ambiguity in relation to the very foundation of the instrument itself, as distinguished from an ambiguity in regard to the construction of its terms. The term is applied, for instance, to a doubt as to whether a testator meant a particular clause to be a part of the will, or whether it was introduced with his knowledge, or whether a codicil was meant to republish a former will, or whether the residuary clause was accidentally omitted.

Ambiguum pactum contra venditorem interpretandum est /æmbígyuwəm pǽktəm kóntrə vèndətórəm intàrprətǽndəm ést/. An ambiguous contract is to be interpreted against the seller.

Ambiguum placitum interpretari debet contra proferentem /æmbígyuwəm plǽsədəm intàrprətéray débət kóntrə pròfəréntəm/. An ambiguous plea ought to be interpreted against the party pleading it.

Ambit. A boundary line, as going around a place; an exterior or inclosing line or limit. The limits or circumference of a power or jurisdiction; the line circumscribing any subject-matter.

Ambitus /ǽmbədəs/. The procuring of a public office by money or gifts; the unlawful buying and selling of a public office.

Amblotic /æmblódək/. Having the power to cause abortion; anything used to produce abortion.

Ambulance chaser. A popular name for one who solicits negligence cases for an attorney. One seeking out persons and directing them to an attorney in consideration of a percentage of the recovery. A term descriptive of the practice of some attorneys, on hearing of a personal injury which may have been caused by the negligence or wrongful act of another, of at once seeking out the injured person with a view to securing authority to bring action on account of the injury. Laymen's acquainting themselves with occurrence of accidents and approaching injured persons or their representatives with a view toward soliciting employment for an attorney in the litigation arising from the accident. See also **Runner**.

Ambulatoria est voluntas defuncti usque ad vitæ supremum exitum /æmbyələtóriyə èst volántæs dəfáŋktay ə́skwiy æ̀d váydiy s(y)əpríyməm égzídəm/. The will of a deceased person is ambulatory until the latest moment of life.

Ambulatory. Lat. *ambulare*, to walk about. Movable; revocable; subject to change; capable of alteration.

Ambulatoria voluntas (a changeable will) denotes the power which a testator possesses of altering his will during his life-time.

Courts. The court of king's bench in England was formerly called an ambulatory court, because it followed the king's person, and was held sometimes in one place and sometimes in another. So, in France, the supreme court or parliament was originally ambulatory. 3 Bl.Comm. 38, 39, 41.

Ambulatory disposition. A judgment, decree, or sentence which is subject to change, amendment or revocation.

Ambush. To lie in wait, to surprise, to place in ambush.

A me /èy míy/. Lat. *ego,* I. A term in feudal grants denoting direct tenure of the superior lord. Unjustly detaining from me. He is said to withhold *a me* (from me) who has obtained possession of my property unjustly. To pay *a me,* is to pay from my money.

Ameliorating waste /əmíyl(i)yəreydiŋ wéyst/. An act of lessee, though technically constituting waste, yet in fact resulting in improving instead of doing injury to land. Generally, equity will not enjoin such waste.

Ameliorations /əmìyl(i)yəréyshənz/. Betterments; improvements.

Amenable /əmíynəbəl/°mén°/. Subject to answer to the law; accountable; responsible; liable to punishment.

Also means tractable, that may be easily led or governed; formerly applied to a wife who is governable by her husband.

Amend. To improve. To change for the better by removing defects or faults. To change, correct, revise. Texas Co. v. Fort, 168 Tenn. 679, 80 S.W.2d 658, 660. See **Amendment**.

Amende honorable /əmónd onərábəl/. An apology. In old English law, it was a penalty imposed upon a person by way of disgrace or infamy, as a punishment for any offense, or for the purpose of making reparation for any injury done to another, as the walking into church in a white sheet, with a rope about the neck and a torch in the hand, and begging the pardon of God, or the king, or any private individual, for some delinquency. A punishment somewhat similar to this, which bore the same name, was common in France for offenses against public decency or morality. It was abolished by the law of the 25th of September, 1791. In 1826 it was re-introduced in cases of sacrilege and was finally abolished in 1830.

Amendment. To change or modify for the better. To alter by modification, deletion, or addition.

Practice and pleading. The correction of an error committed in any process, pleading, or proceeding at law, or in equity, and which is done either as of course, or by the consent of parties, or upon motion to the court in which the proceeding is pending. Under Fed.R.Civil P., any change in pleadings, though not necessarily a correction, which a party may accomplish once as a matter of course at any time before a responsive pleading has been served. Such amendment may be necessary to cause pleadings to conform to evidence. Rule 15(a), (b). The amendment relates back to the original pleading if the subject of it arose out of the transaction set forth or attempted to be set forth in the original pleading. Fed.R.Civil P. 15(c). *Compare* **Supplemental pleadings.**

Amendment of judgment. Under Fed.R.Civil P., Rule 59(e), a judgment may be altered or amended by motion served not later than 10 days after entry of judgment.

Amendment of trust. An addition which alters the original terms of a trust, the power to accomplish which may be reserved by the settlor in the original trust instrument.

Amendment on court's own motion. A change or addition to a pleading or other document accomplished by the judge without a prior motion of a party.

Amends. A satisfaction given by a wrongdoer to the party injured, for a wrong committed.

Amenity /əménidiy/. In real property law, such circumstances, in regard to situation, view, location, access to a water course, or the like, as enhance the pleasantness or desirability of the property for purposes of residence, or contribute to the pleasure and enjoyment of the occupants, rather than to their indispensable needs. Extras or intangible items often associated with property. They may be tangible. Often amenities in a condominium include swimming pools, landscaping, and tennis courts.

In the law of *easements*, an "amenity" consists in restraining the owner from doing that on his property which, but for the grant or covenant, he might otherwise lawfully have done. Sometimes called a "negative easement" as distinguished from that class of easements which compel the owner to suffer something to be done on his property by another. Equitable Life Assur. Soc. v. Brennan, 30 Abb.N.C. 260, 24

N.Y.S. 784, 788. A restrictive covenant. South Buffalo Stores v. W. T. Grant Co., 153 Misc. 76, 274 N.Y.S. 549, 555.

Amens /éymenz/. See **Demens**.

A mensa et thoro /èy ménsə et θórow/. Lat. From table and bed, but more commonly translated, from bed and board. A kind of divorce, which is rather a separation of the parties by law, than a dissolution of the marriage.

Amentia. Insanity; idiocy. See **Insanity**.

Amerce /əmə́rs/. To impose an amercement or fine; to publish by a fine or penalty.

Amercement /əmə́rsmənt/. A money penalty in the nature of a fine imposed upon an officer for some misconduct or neglect of duty. Sherman v. Upton, Inc., S.D., 242 N.W.2d 666, 667. At common law, it was assessed by the peers of the delinquent, or the affeerors, or imposed arbitrarily at the discretion of the court or the lord.

American. Of or pertaining to the United States.

American Arbitration Association. National organization of arbitrators from whose panel arbitrators are selected for labor and civil disputes. The Association has produced a Code of Ethics and Procedural Standards for use and guidance of arbitrators.

American Bar Association. A National association of lawyers, a primary purpose of which is the improvement of lawyers and the administration of justice. Membership in the ABA is open to any lawyer who is in good standing in his or her state.

American Bar Foundation. An outgrowth of the American Bar Association given to sponsoring and funding projects in legal research, education and social studies.

American clause. In marine insurance, a proviso in a policy to the effect that, in case of any subsequent insurance, the insurer shall nevertheless be answerable for the full extent of the sum subscribed by him, without right to claim contribution from subsequent underwriters.

American experience table of mortality. A series of tables dealing with life insurance, costs and values, varying according to the age of the insured, the period during which the policy has been in force, and the term of the particular policy.

American Federation of Labor. An affiliation of labor unions.

American Law Institute. Group of American legal scholars who are responsible for the Restatements in the various disciplines of the law and who, jointly with the National Conference of Commissioners on Uniform State Laws, prepare some of the Uniform State Laws, e.g. Uniform Commercial Code. See **Restatement of Law.**

American rule. The traditional "American Rule" is that attorney fees are not awardable to the winning party unless statutorily or contractually authorized; however exceptions exist in that an award may be made to successful party if the opponent has acted in bad faith, vexatiously, wantonly or for oppressive reasons or if the litigation confers a substantial benefit on the members of an ascertainable class and the court's subject matter jurisdiction makes possible an award that will operate to spread the costs proportionately among them. Huecker v. Milburn, C.A.Ky., 538 F.2d 1241, 1245. In addition a court may in its discretion award attorney fees in civil rights actions to the prevailing defendant if the action was frivolous, unreasonable or without foundation. Christiansburg Garment Co. v. EEOC, 434 U.S. 412, 98 S.Ct. 694.

Ameublissement /əmyùwbləsmón/. In French law, a species of agreement which by a fiction gives to immovable goods the quality of movable.

Ami; amy. A friend; as *alien ami*, an alien belonging to a nation at peace with us; *prochein ami*, a next friend suing or defending for an infant, married woman, etc.

Amiables compositeurs. See **Amicable compounders**.

Amicable. Friendly; mutually forbearing. Agreed or assented to by parties having conflicting interests or a dispute; as opposed to hostile or adversary.

Amicable action. An action brought and carried on by the mutual consent and arrangement of the parties, to obtain judgment of court on a doubtful question of law, the facts being usually settled by agreement. See **Case** (*Case agreed on*).

Amicable compounders. In Louisiana law and practice, amicable compounders are arbitrators authorized to abate something of the strictness of the law in favor of natural equity.

Amicable scire facias to revive a judgment /æməkéybliy sáyriy féyshiyəs/. A written agreement, signed by the person to be bound by the revival, in the nature of a writ of scire facias with a confession of judgment thereon, which must be duly docketed, but which requires no judicial action on the part of the court, and which has the force and effect of a judgment rendered upon an adverse or contested writ of scire facias.

Amicus curiæ /əmáykəs kyúriyiy/əmíykəs kyúriyay/. Means, literally, friend of the court. A person with strong interest in or views on the subject matter of an action may petition the court for permission to file a brief, ostensibly on behalf of a party but actually to suggest a rationale consistent with its own views. Such amicus curiae briefs are commonly filed in appeals concerning matters of a broad public interest; *e.g.* civil rights cases. Such may be filed by private persons or the government. In appeals to the U.S. courts of appeals, such brief may be filed only if accompanied by written consent of all parties, or by leave of court granted on motion or at the request of the court, except that consent or leave shall not be required when the brief is presented by the United States or an officer or agency thereof. Fed.R.App.P. 29.

Amita /ǽmədə/. Lat. An aunt on the father's side. *Amita magna.* A great-aunt on the father's side. *Amita major.* A great-great-aunt on the father's side. *Amita maxima.* A great-great-great-aunt, or a great-great-grandfather's sister.

Amitinus /æmətáynəs/. The child of a brother or sister; a cousin; one who has the same grandfather, but different father and mother.

Amittere /əmídəriy/. Lat. In the civil and old English law, to lose. Hence the old Scotch "amitt."

Amittere curiam /əmídəriy kyúriyəm/. To lose the court; to be deprived of the privilege of attending the court.

Amittere legem terræ /əmídəriy líyjəm tériy/. To lose the protection afforded by the law of the land.

Amittere liberam legem /əmídəriy líbərəm líyjəm/. In old English law, to lose one's frank-law. A term having the same meaning as *amittere legem terræ, (q.v.)*. He who lost his law lost the protection extended by the law to a free man, and became subject to the same law as thralls or serfs attached to the land. To lose the privilege of giving evidence under oath in any court; to become infamous, and incapable of giving evidence. If either party in a wager of battle cried "craven" he was condemned *amittere liberam legem;* 3 Bl.Comm. 340.

Amnesia. Loss of memory as a result of organic trauma, delirium lesions of the diencephalon area of the brain, hysteria or epilepsy. Functionally, identity loss can represent a means of coping with neurotic conflict. Three types of amnesia are: anterograde (inability to retain new impressions; may be a feature of senility); retrograde (failure to recall prior experiences); lacunar (loss of memory for certain periods of life). Such condition is not generally sufficient for lack of competency to stand trial. U. S. ex rel. Parsons v. Anderson, 354 F.Supp. 1060, 1071–1072, aff'd 481 F.2d 94.

Amnesty /ǽmnəstiy/. A sovereign act of oblivion for past acts, granted by a government to all persons (or to certain persons) who have been guilty of crime or delict, generally political offenses,—treason, sedition, rebellion,—and often conditioned upon their return to obedience and duty within a prescribed time.

A general pardon or proclamation of such pardon from subjects' offenses against the government; while usually exerted in behalf of certain classes of persons, subject to trial, but not convicted, it is not confined to such cases.

A declaration of the person or persons who have newly acquired or recovered the sovereign power in a nation, by which they pardon all persons who composed, supported, or obeyed the government which has been overthrown.

Amnesty is the abolition and forgetfulness of the offense; pardon is forgiveness. Knote v. U. S., 95 U.S. 149, 152, 24 L.Ed. 442. The first is usually addressed to crimes against the sovereignty of the nation, to political offenses; the second condones infractions of the peace of the nation. Burdick v. United States, 236 U.S. 79, 35 S.Ct. 267, 271, 59 L.Ed. 476.

Compare **Pardon; Parole.**

Express amnesty is one granted in direct terms.

Implied amnesty is one which results when a treaty of peace is made between contending parties.

Amobarbital /èymowbárbətòl/. Nonproprietary name for isoamyl-ethylbarbituric acid.

Among. Mingled with or in the same group or class. Intermingled with. In company or association with. In shares to each of, *e.g.* divided "among" the heirs. In or through the midst of.

Amortization /əmòrdəzéyshən/. The allocation (and charge to expense) of the cost or other basis of an intangible asset over its estimated useful life. Intangible assets which have an indefinite life (*e.g.*, goodwill) are not amortizable. Examples of amortizable intangibles include patents, copyrights and leasehold interests. A reduction in a debt or fund by periodic payments covering interest and part of principal, distinguished from: (1) depreciation, which is an allocation of the original cost of an asset computed from physical wear and tear as well as the passage of time, and (2) depletion, which is a reduction in the book value of a resource (such as minerals) resulting from conversion into a salable product. The operation of paying off bonds, stock, a mortgage, or other indebtedness, commonly of a state or corporation, by installments, or by a sinking fund. An "amortization plan" for the payment of an indebtedness is one where there are partial payments of the principal, and accrued interest, at stated periods for a definite time, at the expiration of which the entire indebtedness will be extinguished.

Amortization reserve. An account created for bookkeeping purposes to extinguish an obligation gradually over a period of time.

Amortized mortgage. Repayment of a mortgage over regular specified time intervals, with equal payments. This would reduce the principal, after any monies owing for interest are applied.

Amotio /əmówsh(iy)ow/. In the civil law, a moving or taking away. "The slightest *amotio* is sufficient to constitute theft, if the *animus furandi* be clearly established." See **Amotion.**

Amotion /əmówshən/. A putting or turning out, as the eviction of a tenant or a removal from office. Dispossession of lands. Ouster is an *amotion* of possession. A moving or carrying away; the wrongful taking of personal chattels.

In *corporation law*, the act of removing an officer, or official representative, of a corporation from his office or official station, before the end of the term for which he was elected or appointed, but without depriving him of membership in the body corporate. In this last respect the term differs from "disfranchisement," or expulsion.

Amount. The whole effect, substance, import, result, or significance. The sum of principal and interest. See also **Sum certain.**

Amount covered. In insurance, the amount that is insured, and for which underwriters are liable for loss under a policy of insurance.

Amount in controversy. The damages claimed or relief demanded; the amount claimed or sued for. Glenwood Light & Water Co. v. Mutual Light, Heat & Power Co., 239 U.S. 121, 36 S.Ct. 30, 60 L.Ed. 174; Wabash Ry. Co. v. Vanlandingham, C.C.A.Mo., 53

F.2d 51. Amount of alleged damages required for diversity jurisdiction in Federal courts. 28 U.S.C.A. § 1332. See **Jurisdictional amount.**

Amount of loss. In insurance, the diminution, destruction, or defeat of the value of, or of the charge upon, the insured subject to the assured, by the direct consequence of the operation of the risk insured against, according to its value in the policy, or in contribution for loss, so far as its value is covered by the insurance.

Amount realized. The amount received by a taxpayer upon the sale or exchange of property. The measure of the amount received is the sum of the cash and the fair market value of any property or services received. Determining the amount realized is the starting point for arriving at realized gain or loss. I.R.C. § 1001(b). See **Realized gain or loss; Recognized gain or loss.**

Amount to. To reach in the aggregate, to rise to or reach by accumulation of particular sums or quantities.

Amove. To remove from a post or station.

Amoveas manus /èymówviyəs mǽnəs/. Lat. That you remove your hands. In old English law, after office found, the king was entitled to the things forfeited, either lands or personal property; the remedy for a person aggrieved was by "petition," or *"monstrans de droit,"* or *"traverses,"* to establish his superior right. Thereupon a writ issued, *quod manus domini regis amoveantur.*

Amparo /æmpárow/. In Spanish-American law, a document issued to a claimant of land as a protection to him, until a survey can be ordered, and the title of possession issued by an authorized commissioner.

Amphetamine /æmfédəmiyn/æmfédəmən/. A drug which stimulates the central nervous system. Com. v. Crockett, 229 Pa.Super. 80, 323 A.2d 257, 259. "Methedrine" is its trade name. Colorless, volatile, mobile liquid, inhalation of which vapor causes shrinking of nasal mucosa in head colds, sinusitis and hay fever.

Ampliation /æmpliyéyshən/. In *civil law,* a deferring of judgment until a cause be further examined. An order for the rehearing of a cause on a day appointed, for the sake of more ample information.

In *French law,* a duplicate of an acquittance or other instrument. A notary's copy of acts passed before him, delivered to the parties.

Amplius /æmpliyəs/. In the Roman law, more; further; more time. A word which the prætor pronounced in cases where there was any obscurity in a cause, and the *judices* were uncertain whether to condemn or acquit; by which the case was deferred to a day named.

Amputation of right hand. An ancient punishment for a blow given in a superior court; or for assaulting a judge sitting in the court.

Amtrack. National Railroad Passenger Corporation.

A multo fortiori /èy máltow forshiyóray/. By far the stronger reason.

Amusement. Pastime; diversion; enjoyment. A pleasurable occupation of the senses, or that which furnishes it. Young v. Board of Trustees of Broadwater County High School, 90 Mont. 576, 4 P.2d 725, 726.

Amusement tax. A government levy imposed on tickets sold to places of amusement, sporting events, etc.; expressed as a percentage of the price of the ticket. See also **Luxury tax.**

Amy. See **Ami; Prochein ami.**

An. The English indefinite article, equivalent to "one" or "any"; seldom used to denote plurality.

Anacrisis /ænəkráyzəs/. In the civil law, an investigation of truth, interrogation of witnesses, and inquiry made into any fact, especially by torture.

Analogous /ənǽləgəs/. Derived from the Greek ana, up, and logos, ratio. Means bearing some resemblance or likeness that permits one to draw an analogy.

Analogy. Identity or similarity of proportion, where there is no precedent in point. In cases on the same subject, lawyers have recourse to cases on a different subject-matter, but governed by the same general principle. This is reasoning by analogy. The similitude of relations which exist between things compared.

Analytical jurisprudence. A theory and system of jurisprudence wrought out neither by inquiring for ethical principles or the dictates of the sentiments of justice nor by the rules which may be actually in force, but by analyzing, classifying and comparing various legal conceptions. See **Jurisprudence.**

Anaphrodisia /ænæfrədíz(h)iyə/. Impotentia cœundi; frigidity; incapacity for sexual intercourse existing in either man or woman, and in the latter case sometimes called "dyspareunia."

Anarchist. One who professes and advocates the doctrines of anarchy, *q.v.* In the immigration statutes, it includes, not only persons who advocate the overthrow of organized government by force, but also those who believe in the absence of government as a political ideal, and seek the same end through propaganda.

Anarchy. Absence of government; state of society where there is no law or supreme power; lawlessness or political disorder; destructive of and confusion in government. At its best it pertains to a society made orderly by good manners rather than law, in which each person produces according to his powers and receives according to his needs, and at its worst, the word pertains to a terroristic resistance of all present government and social order. For "criminal anarchy," see **Criminal.**

Anathema /ənǽθəmə/. An ecclesiastical punishment by which a person is separated from the body of the church, and forbidden all intercourse with the members of the same. It differs from excommunication, which simply forbids the person excommunicated from going into the church and taking the communion with the faithful.

Anathematize /ənǽθəmətayz/. To pronounce anathema upon; to pronounce accursed by ecclesiastical authority; to excommunicate. See **Anathema.**

Anatocism /anǽdəsizəm/. In the civil law, repeated or doubled interest; compound interest; usury.

Anatomical gift. Testamentary donation of a vital organ, generally for purpose of medical research. Most states have adopted the Uniform Anatomical Gift Act which authorizes the gift of all or part of a human body after death for specified purposes.

Ancestor. One from whom a person lineally descended or may be descended; a progenitor. A former possessor; the person last seised. A deceased person from whom another has inherited land. Embraces both collaterals and lineals. Correlative of "heir."

Ancestral /ænséstrəl/. Relating to ancestors, or to what has been done by them; as *homage ancestral (q.v.)*. Derived from ancestors.

Ancestral estates are such as are transmitted by descent, and not by purchase; or such as are acquired either by descent or by operation of law. Realty which came to the intestate by descent or devise from a dead ancestor or by deed of actual gift from a living one, there being no other consideration than that of blood. Real estate coming to distributee by descent, gift, or devise from any kinsman. Allotments to members of Indian tribes or their heirs have been treated as an ancestral estate. McDougal v. McKay, 237 U.S. 372, 35 S.Ct. 605, 607, 59 L.Ed. 1001.

Ancestry. Line of descent; persons comprising such. Term which embraces the study of the antecedents of humans and animals; pedigree. May be proved by general reputation.

Anchorage. In English law, a duty paid by the owners of ships for the use of the port or harbor where they cast anchor.

Ancient. Old; that which has existed from an indefinitely early period, or which by age alone has acquired certain rights or privileges accorded in view of long continuance.

Ancient deed. A deed 30 [or 20] years old and shown to come from a proper custody and having nothing suspicious about it. See **Ancient writings**.

Ancient demesne. Manors which in the time of William the Conqueror were in the hands of the crown, and are so recorded in the Domesday Book. Also, in old English law, a species of copyhold, which differs, however, from common copyholds in certain privileges, but yet must be conveyed by surrender, according to the custom of the manor. There are three sorts: (1) Where the lands are held freely by the king's grant; (2) customary freeholds, which are held of a manor in ancient demesne, but not at the lord's will, although they are conveyed by surrender, or deed and admittance; (3) lands held by copy of court-roll at the lord's will, denominated copyholds of base tenure.

Ancient documents. See **Ancient writings**.

Ancient readings. Readings or lectures upon the ancient English statutes, formerly regarded as of great authority in law.

Ancient records. See **Ancient writings**.

Ancient rent. The rent reserved at the time the lease was made, if the building was not then under lease.

Ancients /éynshənts/. In English law, gentlemen of the inns of court and chancery. In Gray's Inn the society consists of benchers, ancients, barristers, and students under the bar; and here the ancients are of the oldest barristers. In the Middle Temple, those who had passed their readings used to be termed "ancients." The Inns of Chancery consist of ancients and students or clerks; from the ancients a principal or treasurer is chosen yearly.

Ancient serjeant. In English law, the eldest of the queen's serjeants.

Ancient street. The doctrine is not based upon fact that streets have existed for a long time, but is invoked when it appears that common grantor owning land comprising street in question as well as property in question and other lots has given deeds to lots bounding them by street, thereby not only dedicating the street to public use but at same time creating private easements in the street, which cannot be taken without compensation. Dwornick v. State, 251 A.D. 675, 297 N.Y.S. 409, 411.

Ancient wall. A wall built to be used, and in fact used, as a party-wall, for more than twenty years, by the express permission and continuous acquiescence of the owners of the land on which it stands. Schneider v. 44–84 Realty Corporation, 169 Misc. 249, 7 N.Y. S.2d 305, 309.

Ancient water course. A water course is "ancient" if the channel through which it naturally runs has existed from time immemorial independent of the quantity of water which it discharges. Earl v. De Hart, 12 N.J.Eq. 280.

Ancient writings. Documents bearing on their face every evidence of age and authenticity, of age of 30 [or 20] years, and coming from a natural and reasonable official custody. Hartzell v. U. S., C.C.A.Iowa, 72 F.2d 569, 579. These are presumed to be genuine without express proof, when coming from the proper custody.

Under Federal Rules of Evidence, a document is admissible if it is in such condition as to create no suspicion as to its authenticity, was in a place where it, if authentic, would likely be, and has been in existence 20 years or more at the time it is offered. Fed.Evid.R. 901(b)(8).

Anciently /éynshəntiy/. Eldership; seniority. Used in the statute of Ireland, 14 Hen. VIII.

Ancilla /ænsílə/. Lat. A handmaid, an auxiliary, a subordinate.

Ancillary /ænsəlèriy/. Aiding; attendant upon; describing a proceeding attendant upon or which aids another proceeding considered as principal. Auxiliary or subordinate.

Ancillary administration. Administration in state where decedent has property and which is other than where decedent was domiciled. First Nat. Bank v. Blessing, 231 Mo.App. 288, 98 S.W.2d 149, 151. Administration or probate taken out in a second or subsequent jurisdiction to collect assets or to commence litigation on behalf of the estate in that jurisdiction.

Ancillary attachment. One sued out in aid of an action already brought; its only office being to hold the property attached under it for the satisfaction of the plaintiff's demand.

Ancillary bill or **suit.** One growing out of and auxiliary to another action or suit, either at law or in equity, such as a bill for discovery, or a proceeding for the enforcement of a judgment, or to set aside fraudulent transfers of property. One growing out of a prior suit in the same court, dependent upon and instituted for the purpose either of impeaching or enforcing the judgment or decree in a prior suit. Caspers v. Watson, C.C.A.Ill., 132 F.2d 614, 615.

Ancillary claim. Term "ancillary" denotes any claim that reasonably may be said to be collateral to, dependent upon, or otherwise auxiliary to a claim asserted within federal jurisdiction in action. Hartley Pen Co. v. Lindy Pen Co., D.C.Cal., 16 F.R.D. 141, 154. Claim is "ancillary" when it bears a logical relationship to the aggregate core of operative facts which constitutes main claim over which court had independent basis of federal jurisdiction. Nishimatsu Const. Co., Ltd. v. Houston Nat. Bank, C.A.Tex., 515 F.2d 1200, 1205.

Ancillary jurisdiction. Power of court to adjudicate and determine matters incidental to the exercise of its primary jurisdiction of an action.

Under "ancillary jurisdiction doctrine" federal district court acquires jurisdiction of case or controversy as an entirety and may, as incident to disposition of matter properly before it, possess jurisdiction to decide other matters raised by case, though district court could not have taken cognizance of them if they had been independently presented. Ortman v. Stanray Corp., C.A.Ill., 371 F.2d 154, 157. "Ancillary jurisdiction" of federal court generally involves either proceedings which are concerned with pleadings, processes, records or judgments of court in principal case or proceedings which affect property already in court's custody. Cooperative Transit Co. v. West Penn. Electric Co., C.C.A.W.Va., 132 F.2d 720, 723.

Ancillary legislation. Legislative enactment which is auxiliary to or in aid of other and principal legislation.

Ancillary proceeding. One growing out of or auxiliary to another action or suit, or which is subordinate to or in aid of a primary action, either at law or in equity. Register v. Stone's Independent Oil Distributors, 122 Ga.App. 335, 177 S.E.2d 92, 94. In state courts, a procedural undertaking in aid of the principal action; for example, a bill for discovery in aid of a lawsuit or a garnishment proceeding.

Ancillary process. Any process which is in aid of or incidental to the principal suit or action; *e.g.* attachment. See **Ancillary proceeding.**

Ancillary receiver. One appointed in aid of, and in subordination to, a foreign receiver for purpose of collecting and taking charge of assets, as of insolvent corporation, in the jurisdiction where he is appointed.

Ancipitis usus /ænsípədəs yuwzəs/. Lat. In international law, of doubtful use; the use of which is doubtful; that may be used for a civil or peaceful, as well as military or warlike, purpose.

And. A conjunction connecting words or phrases expressing the idea that the latter is to be added to or taken along with the first. Added to; together with; joined with; as well as; including. Sometimes construed as "or." Land & Lake Ass'n v. Conklin, 182 A.D. 546, 170 N.Y.S. 427, 428.

It expresses a general relation or connection, a participation or accompaniment in sequence, having no inherent meaning standing alone but deriving force from what comes before and after. In its conjunctive sense the word is used to conjoin words, clauses, or sentences, expressing the relation of addition or connection, and signifying that something is to follow in addition to that which proceeds and its use implies that the connected elements must be grammatically co-ordinate, as where the elements preceding and succeeding the use of the words refer to the same subject matter. While it is said that there is no exact synonym of the word in English, it has been defined to mean "along with", "also", "and also", "as well as", "besides", "together with". Oliver v. Oliver, 286 Ky. 6, 149 S.W.2d 540, 542.

When expression "and/or" is used, that word may be taken as will best effect the purpose of the parties as gathered from the contract taken as a whole, or, in other words, as will best accord with the equity of the situation. Bobrow v. U. S. Casualty Co., 231 A.D. 91, 246 N.Y.S. 363, 367.

Androgynus /ændrójənəs/. A hermaphrodite.

Androlepsy /ǽndrowlépsiy/. The taking by one nation of the citizens or subjects of another, in order to compel the latter to do justice to the former.

Andromania /æ̀ndrowméyniyə/. Nymphomania.

Androphonomania /æ̀ndrowfònəméyniyə/. Homicidal insanity.

Anecius /əníysh(iy)əs/. Lat. Spelled also *œsnecius, enitius, œneas, eneyus,* Fr. *aisne.* The eldest-born; the first-born; senior, as contrasted with the *puis-né* (younger).

An et jour /ón ey zhúr/. Fr. Year and day; a year and a day.

Aneurism, or **aneurysm.** A sac formed by the dilatation of the weakened walls of an artery, usually resulting in a soft pulsating tumor.

Anew. To try a case or issue "anew" or "de novo" implies that the case or issue has been heard before. See **De novo.**

Angaria /æŋgériyə/. A term used in the Roman law to denote a forced or compulsory service exacted by the government for public purposes; as a forced rendition of labor or goods for the public service; in particular, the right of a public officer to require the service of vehicles or ships.

In *feudal law,* any troublesome or vexatious personal service paid by the tenant or villein to his lord.

In *maritime law,* a forced service (*onus*) imposed on a vessel for public purposes; an impressment of a vessel. See **Angary, right of.**

Angary, right of. In international law, formerly the right (*jus angariæ*) claimed by a belligerent to seize merchant vessels in the harbors of the belligerent and to compel them, on payment of freight, to transport troops and supplies to a designated port.

The right of a belligerent to appropriate, either for use, or for destruction in case of necessity, neutral property temporarily located in his own territory or in that of the other belligerent. The property may be of any description whatever, provided the appropriation of it be for military or naval purposes.

Angel. An ancient English coin, of the value of ten shillings sterling.

Angild /ǽngìld/. In Saxon law, the single value of a man or other thing; a single weregild (q.v.); the compensation of a thing according to its single value or estimation. The double gild or compensation was called "twigild," the triple, "trigild," etc. See **Angylde**.

When a crime was committed, before the Conquest, the angild was the money compensation that the person who had been wronged was entitled to receive.

Anglescheria /æ̀ngləshíriyə/. In old English law, Englishery; the fact of being an Englishman.

Angliæ jura in omni casu libertatis dant favorem /ǽngliyiy júrə in ómniy kéyzyuw lìbərtéydəs dǽnt fəvórəm/. The laws of England in every case of liberty are favorable (favor liberty in all cases).

Anglice /ǽnglǝsiy/. In English, a term formerly used in pleading when a thing is described both in Latin and English, inserted immediately after the Latin and as an introduction of the English translation.

Anglo-Indian. An Englishman domiciled in the Indian territory of the British crown.

Anglo-Saxon law. English law derived from those people who conquered Britain in the 5th and 6th centuries and who dominated England until the Norman Conquest.

Anguish. Extreme pain of body or mind; excruciating distress. Carson v. Thompson, Mo.App., 161 S.W.2d 995, 1000. Agony, but, as used in law, particularly mental suffering or distress of great intensity. It is not synonymous with inconvenience, annoyance, or harassment.

Angylde. In Saxon law, the rate fixed by law at which certain injuries to person or property were to be paid for; in injuries to the person, it seems to be equivalent to the "were," i.e., the price at which every man was valued. It seems also to have been the fixed price at which cattle and other goods were received as currency, and to have been much higher than the market price, or ceapgild. See **Angild**.

Anhlote. In old English law, a single tribute or tax, paid according to the custom of the country as scot and lot.

Aniens, or **anient.** Null, void, of no force or effect. See **Anniented**.

Animal. Non-human, animate being which is endowed with the power of voluntary motion. Animal life other than man. Bernardine v. City of New York, 182 Misc. 609, 44 N.Y.S.2d 881, 883.

Domestic animals are tame as distinguished from wild; living in or near the habitations of man or by habit or special training in association with man.

Domitæ are those which have been tamed by man; domestic.

Fera naturæ are those which still retain their wild nature.

Mansuetæ naturæ are those gentle or tame by nature, such as sheep and cows.

Wild animals are those whose habitat is generally the woods; undomesticated; untamed.

Animals of a base nature. Animals in which a right of property may be acquired by reclaiming them from wildness, but which, at common law, by reason of their base nature, are not regarded as possible subjects of a larceny. Some animals which are now usually tamed come within this class, as dogs and cats; and others which, though wild by nature and often reclaimed by art and industry, clearly fall within the same rule, as bears, foxes, apes, monkeys, ferrets, and the like.

Animo /ǽnǝmow/. Lat. With intention, disposition, design, will. *Quo animo*, with what intention. *Animo cancellandi*, with intention to cancel. *Furandi*, with intention to steal. 4 Bl.Comm. 230. *Lucrandi*, with intention to gain or profit. *Manendi*, with intention to remain. *Morandi*, with intention to stay, or delay. *Republicandi*, with intention to republish. *Revertendi*, with intention to return. 2 Bl.Comm. 392. *Revocandi*, with intention to revoke. *Testandi*, with intention to make a will. See **Animus** and the titles which follow it.

Animo et corpore /ǽnǝmow et kórpǝriy/. By the mind, and by the body; by the intention and by the physical act.

Animo felonico /ǽnǝmow fǝlónǝkow/. With felonious intent.

Animus /ǽnǝmǝs/. Lat. Mind; soul; intention; disposition; design; will; that which informs the body. *Animo* (q.v.), with the intention or design. These terms are derived from the civil law.

Animus ad se omne jus ducit /ǽnǝmǝs ǽd síy ómniy jǝs d(y)úwsǝt/. It is to the intention that all law applies. Law always regards the intention.

Animus cancellandi /ǽnǝmǝs kæ̀nsǝlǽnday/. The intention of destroying or canceling (applied to wills).

Animus capiendi /ǽnǝmǝs kæpiyénday/. The intention to take or capture.

Animus dedicandi /ǽnǝmǝs dedǝkǽnday/. The intention of donating or dedicating.

Animus defamandi /ǽnǝmǝs dèfǝmǽnday/. The intention of defaming.

Animus derelinquendi /ǽnǝmǝs dìyrelǝŋkwénday/. The intention of abandoning.

Animus differendi /ǽnǝmǝs difǝrénday/. The intention of obtaining delay.

Animus donandi /ǽnəməs downǽnday/. The intention of giving. Expressive of the intent to give which is necessary to constitute a gift.

Animus et factum /ǽnəməs et fǽktəm/. To constitute a change of domicile, there must be an "animus et factum"; the "factum" being a transfer of the bodily presence, and the "animus" the intention of residing permanently or for indefinite period. See **Animus manendi.**

Animus et factus /ǽnəməs et fǽktəs/. Intention and act; will and deed. Used to denote those acts which become effective only when accompanied by a particular intention.

Animus furandi /ǽnəməs fyərǽnday/. Intent to steal, or feloniously to deprive the owner permanently of his property. State v. Hudson, W.Va., 206 S.E.2d 415, 419.

Animus hominis est anima scripti /ǽnəməs hómənəs èst ǽnəmə skríptay/. The intention of the party is the soul of the instrument. In order to give life or effect to an instrument, it is essential to look to the intention of the individual who executed it.

Animus lucrandi /ǽnəməs l(y)uwkrǽnday/. The intention to make a gain or profit.

Animus manendi /ǽnəməs mənénday/. The intention of remaining; intention to establish a permanent residence. This is the point to be settled in determining the domicile or residence of a party. See **Animus et factum.**

Animus morandi /ǽnəməs mərǽnday/. The intention to remain, or to delay.

Animus possidendi /ǽnəməs pòwzəsénday/. The intention of possessing.

Animus quo /ǽnəməs kwów/. The intent with which.

Animus recipiendi /ǽnəməs rəsìpiyénday/. The intention of receiving.

Animus recuperandi /ǽnəməs rək(y)uwpərǽnday/. The intention of recovering.

Animus republicandi /ǽnəməs rəpèbləkǽnday/. The intention to republish.

Animus restituendi /ǽnəməs rəstìtyuwénday/. The intention of restoring.

Animus revertendi /ǽnəməs rìyvərténday/. The intention of returning.

Animus revocandi /ǽnəməs rèvowkǽnday/. The intention to revoke.

Animus signandi /ǽnəməs signǽnday/°saynǽnday/. Intention to sign instrument as and for a will. Hamlet v. Hamlet, 183 Va. 453, 32 S.E.2d 729, 732.

Animus testandi /ǽnəməs tèstǽnday/. Intention or purpose to make will. Also expressed as *animo testandi.*

An, jour, et waste. In feudal law, year, day, and waste. A forfeiture of the lands to the crown incurred by the felony of the tenant, after which time the land escheats to the lord. See **Year** (*Year, day, and waste*).

Annates /ǽneyts/ǽnəts/. In ecclesiastical law, first-fruits paid out of spiritual benefices to the Pope, so called because the value of one year's profit was taken as their rate.

Annex /ənéks/. Derived from the Latin "annectere," meaning to tie or bind to. To attach, and often, specifically, to subjoin. To add to; to unite. The word expresses the idea of joining a smaller or subordinate thing with another, larger, or of higher importance. To consolidate, as school districts. To make an integral part of something larger.

It implies physical connection or physically joined to, yet physical connection may be dispensed with, and things may be annexed without being in actual contact, when reasonably practicable. Elliott Common School Dist. No. 48 v. County Board of School Trustees, Tex.Civ.App., 76 S.W.2d 786, 789. Something appended to, as a supplementary structure or wing. See also **Appendant.**

Annexation. The act of attaching, adding, joining, or uniting one thing to another; generally spoken of the connection of a smaller or subordinate thing with a larger or principal thing. Term is usually applied with respect to land or fixtures, as: the acquisition of territory or land by a nation, state or municipality; the legal incorporation of a town or city into another town or city.

The attaching an illustrative or auxiliary document to a deposition, pleading, deed, etc., may be called "annexing" it.

In the law relating to fixtures, *actual annexation* includes every movement by which a chattel is joined or united to the property; *constructive annexation* is the union of such things as have been holden parcel of the realty, but which are not actually annexed, fixed, or fastened to the property.

See also **Fixture.**

Anniented /ǽniyèntəd/. Made null, abrogated, frustrated, or brought to nothing.

Anniversary. An annual day, recurring each year on the same date; commonly to commemorate an important event. In old-ecclesiastical law, a day set apart in memory of a deceased person. Also called "year day" or "mind day."

Anniversary date. As applied to insurance policy, means yearly recurring date of the initial issuance date.

Anno domini /ǽnow dómənay/. In the year of the Lord. Commonly abbreviated A.D. The computation of time, according to the Christian era, dates from the birth of Christ.

Annonæ civiles /ənównay sívəliyz/. A species of yearly rents issuing out of certain lands, and payable to certain monasteries.

Annotatio /ǽnowtéysh(iy)ow/. In the civil law, the sign-manual of the emperor; a rescript of the emperor, signed with his own hand. It is distinguished both from a rescript and pragmatic sanction.

Annotation /ǽnətéyshən/. A remark, note, case summary, or commentary on some passage of a book, statutory provision, or the like, intended to illustrate or explain its meaning. See also **Digest; Headnote.**

Civil law. An imperial rescript (see **Rescript**) signed by the emperor. The answers of the prince to questions put to him by private persons respecting some doubtful point of law. Also summoning an absentee, and, as well the designation of a place of deportation.

Statutory. Brief summaries of the law and facts of cases interpreting or applying statutes passed by Congress or state legislatures which are included (normally following text of statute) in annotated statutes or codes.

Announced. A decision is "announced," preventing nonsuit, when court's conclusion on issue tried is made known from bench or by any publication, oral or written, even if judgment has not been rendered.

Annoyance. Discomfort; vexation. Not generally synonymous with anguish, inconvenience, or harassment. Such may result from either physical or mental conditions. It includes feeling of imposition and oppression. See also **Harassment; Nuisance.**

Annual /ǽnyuwəl/. Of or pertaining to year; returning every year; coming or happening yearly. Occurring or recurring once in each year; continuing for the period of a year; accruing within the space of a year; relating to or covering the events or affairs of a year. Once a year, without signifying what time in year. See **Annually**.

Annual accounting period. In determining a taxpayer's income tax liability, only those transactions taking place during a particular tax year are taken into consideration. For reporting and payment purposes, therefore, the tax life of taxpayers is divided into equal annual accounting periods. See **Accounting period**.

Annual assay. An annual trial of the gold and silver coins of the United States, to ascertain whether the standard fineness and weight of the coinage is maintained. 31 U.S.C.A. § 363.

Annual average earnings. Term used in worker's compensation law to describe a claimant's income both from seasonal and nonseasonal employment, but for inclusion the nonseasonal income is limited to employment of the same class as the seasonal.

Annual depreciation. The annual loss, not restored by current maintenance, which is due to all the factors causing the ultimate retirement of the property. These factors embrace wear and tear, decay, inadequacy, and obsolescence. The annual loss in service value not restored by current maintenance and incurred in connection with the consumption or prospective retirement of property in the course of service from causes known to be in current operation, and whose effect can be forecast with a reasonable approach to accuracy. State v. Hampton Water Works Co., 91 N.H. 278, 18 A.2d 765, 770. See **Depreciation**.

Annual exclusion. The amount each year which can be excluded in computing the gift tax on the donor without using the lifetime exemption.

Annually. In annual order or succession; yearly, every year, year by year. At end of each and every year during a period of time. Imposed once a year, computed by the year. Yearly or once a year but does not in itself signify what time in year. Phillips Petroleum Co. v. Harnly, Tex.Civ.App., 348 S.W.2d 856, 860.

Annual percentage rate. The actual cost of borrowing money, expressed in form of annual rate to make it easy for one to compare cost of borrowing money among several lenders or sellers on credit. Full disclosure of such is required by the Truth-in-Lending Act *(q.v.).* Commonly abbreviated APR.

Annual permit. Yearly requirement in certain states for domestic corporations to do business in state. The fee is set according to the capitalization of the corporation.

Annual report. A report for stockholders and other interested parties prepared once a year; includes a balance sheet, an income statement, a statement of changes in financial position, a reconciliation of changes in owners' equity accounts, a summary of significant accounting principles, other explanatory notes, the auditor's report, and often comments from management about the year's business and prospects for the next year. By law, any public corporation that holds an annual stockholders meeting is required to issue an annual report.

Annual statement. See **Annual report**.

Annual value. The net yearly income derivable from a given piece of property. Its fair rental value for one year, deducting costs and expenses; the value of its use for a year.

Annua nec debitum judex non separat ipsum /ǽnyuwə nèk débədəm júwdeks nòn sépərəd ípsəm/. A judge (or court) does not divide annuities nor debt. Debt and annuity cannot be divided or apportioned by a court.

Annua pensione /ǽnyuwə pènshiyówniy/. An ancient writ to provide the king's chaplain, if he had no preferment, with a pension.

Annuity /ən(y)úwədiy/. A right to receive fixed, periodic payments, either for life or for a term of years. Moore v. O'Cheskey, App., 87 N.M. 66, 529 P.2d 292, 293. A fixed sum payable to a person at specified intervals for a specific period of time or for life. Payments represent a partial return of capital and a return (interest) on the capital investment. Therefore, an exclusion ratio must generally be used to compute the amount of taxable income. Special rules apply to employee retirement plan annuities.

Annuity bond. A bond without a maturity date, that is, perpetually paying interest.

Annuity certain. Payable for specified period; no matter the time of death of the annuitant.

Annuity trust. See that title.

Cash refund annuity. Policy which provides for the lump sum payment at the death of the annuitant of the difference between the total received and the price paid.

Contingent annuity. Funded annuity with payments to commence on the happening of an uncertain event; *e.g.* death of named person other than annuitant. An annuity whose number of payments depends upon the outcome of an event whose timing is uncertain at the time the annuity is set up.

Deferred annuity. Payments begin at some specified future date provided the beneficiary is alive at such date.

Group annuity contract. A contract to make periodic payments to a member of a group covered by such contract. The usual type is a pension plan providing annuities upon retirement for individual employees under a master contract.

Joint and survivorship annuity. An annuity which is payable to the named annuitants during the period of their joint lives, with the annuity to continue to the survivor when the first annuitant dies.

Joint annuity. An annuity which is paid to the two named persons until the first one dies, at which time the annuity ceases.

Life annuity. Provides for payment of income to annuitant only during his lifetime; even though death is premature.

Private annuity. A contract for periodic payments to the annuitant from private as distinguished from public or life insurance company.

Refund annuity. Annuitant is assured a specified annual sum during his life, with the further assurance that in the event of his premature death there will be paid to his estate an additional amount which represents the difference between the purchase price and the amount paid out during annuitant's life. See also **Refund annuity contract.**

Retirement annuity. Policy in which payments to annuitant commence at some future date; *e.g.* after retirement. If annuitant dies in interval or surrender is desired, an agreed upon amount is refunded to annuitant's estate.

Straight annuity. A contract usually by an insurance company to make periodic payments at monthly or yearly intervals; distinguishable from life insurance contract which looks to longevity, while annuity looks to transiency. Helvering v. LeGierse, 312 U.S. 531, 541, 61 S.Ct. 646, 85 L.Ed. 996. Straight annuity contract calls for a fixed amount of payment as distinguished from the variable annuity.

Straight life annuity. See *Life annuity; Straight annuity, supra.*

Survivorship annuity. See *Joint and survivorship annuity, supra.*

Variable annuity. A contract calling for payments to the annuitant in varying amounts depending on the success of the investment policy of the insurance company; unlike a straight annuity which requires the payment of a fixed amount. Purpose of this type of annuity is to offset deflated value of dollar caused by inflation.

Annuity policy. An insurance policy providing for monthly payments to insured to begin at fixed date and continue through insured's life. Hamilton v. Penn Mut. Life Ins. Co., 196 Miss. 345, 17 So.2d 278, 280.

Annuity trust. A form of trust calling for payment of a fixed amount of income regardless of the amount of principal. In re McQueen's Will, 65 N.Y.S.2d 201, 205.

Annul /ənə́l/. To reduce to nothing; annihilate; obliterate; to make void or of no effect; to nullify; to abolish; to do away with. To cancel; destroy; abrogate. To annul a judgment or judicial proceeding is to deprive it of all force and operation, either *ab initio* or prospectively as to future transactions.

Annulment. To nullify, to abolish, to make void by competent authority. Honegger v. Reclamation Dist. No. 1619, 190 C.A.2d 684, 12 Cal.Rptr. 76, 80. An "annulment" differs conceptually from a divorce in that a divorce terminates a legal status, whereas an annulment establishes that a marital status never existed. Whealton v. Whealton, 67 Cal.2d 656, 63 Cal.Rptr. 291, 294, 432 P.2d 979.

Annum, diem, et vastum /ǽnəm, dáyəm, ət véystəm/. See **Year, day, and waste.**

Annus /ǽnəs/. Lat. In civil and old English law, a year; the period of three hundred and sixty-five days. See **Annual.**

Annus, dies, et vastum /ǽnəs, dáyiyz, ət véystəm/. In old English law, year, day, and waste. See **Year, day, and waste.**

Annus est mora motus quo suum planeta pervolvat circulum /ǽnəs èst mórə mówdəs kwòw s(y)úwəm plənéydə pərvólvət sə́rk(y)ələm/. A year is the duration of the motion by which a planet revolves through its orbit.

Annus et dies /ǽnəs ət dáyiyz/. A year and a day.

Annus inceptus pro completo habetur /ǽnəs ənséptəs pròw kəmplíydow həbíydər/. A year begun is held as completed.

Annus luctus /ǽnəs lə́wktəs/. The year of mourning. It was a rule among the Romans, and also the Danes and Saxons, that widows should not marry *infra annum luctûs* (within the year of mourning).

Annus utilis /ǽnəs yúwdələs/. A year made up of available or serviceable days. In the plural, *anni utiles* signifies the years during which a right can be exercised or a prescription grow. In prescription, the period of incapacity of a minor, etc., was not counted; it was no part of the *anni utiles.*

Annuus reditus /ǽnəs rédədəs/. A yearly rent; annuity. 2 Bl.Comm. 41.

Anomalous /ənómələs/. Deviating from common rule, method, or type. Irregular; exceptional; abnormal; unusual.

Anomalous Indorser /ənómələs əndórsər/. A stranger to a note, who indorses it after its execution and delivery but before maturity, and before it has been indorsed by the payee.

Anomalous plea /ənómələs plíy/. One which is partly affirmative and partly negative.

Anon., An., A /ənón/. Abbreviations for anonymous.

A non posse ad non esse sequitur argumentum necessarie negative, licet non affirmative /éy nòn pósiy æd nón ésiy sékwədər àrgyəméntəm nèsəsériyiy nègatáyviy, láysət nòn əfərmətáyviy/. A literal translation—From impossibility to non-existence the inference follows necessarily in the negative, though not in the affirmative—is as ambiguous as the original. It could be translated thus: The negative inference of non-existence necessarily follows from impossibility of existence, but the affirmative inference of existence cannot be drawn from mere possibility.

Anonymous. Nameless; lacking a name or names; *e.g.* a publication, article, or the like, without any designation of authorship; an unsigned letter; a tip from an unknown service.

Another. Additional. Distinct or different.

Another action pending. See **Autre action pendant.**

Anoysance /ənóyzəns/. Annoyance; nuisance.

Ansel, ansul, or **auncel** /ónsəl/. In old English law, an ancient mode of weighing by hanging scales or hooks at either end of a beam or staff, which, being lifted with one's finger or hand by the middle, showed the equality or difference between the weight at one end and the thing weighed at the other.

Answer. As a verb, the word denotes an assumption of liability, as to "answer" for the debt or default of another. See also **Affirmative defense; Defense; Denial; Supplemental answer.**

Discovery. A person who fails to answer, or answers evasively or incompletely, deposition or interrogatory questions, may be compelled to do so under Fed.R. Civil P. 37.

Frivolous answer. See *Sham answer,* infra.

Irrelevant answer. One that has no substantial relation to the controversy; distinguishable from a sham answer. Such may be ordered stricken under Fed.R. Civil P. 12(f).

Pleading. A pleading by which defendant endeavors to resist the plaintiff's demand by an allegation of facts, either denying allegations of plaintiff's complaint or confessing them and alleging new matter in avoidance, which defendant alleges should prevent recovery on facts alleged by plaintiff. In pleading, under the Codes and Rules of Civil Procedure, the answer is the formal written statement made by a defendant setting forth the grounds of his defense; corresponding to what in actions under the common-law practice is called the "plea." See Fed.R. Civil P. 8 and 12.

Under Fed.R.Civil P. 12, a person may use an answer to set up all defenses, but he also has the option to use a motion to assert certain defenses.

In chancery pleading, the term denotes a defense in writing, made by a defendant to the allegations contained in a bill or information filed by the plaintiff against him.

Sham answer. One sufficient on its face but so clearly false that it presents no real issue to be tried. One good in form, but false in fact and not pleaded in good faith. A frivolous answer, on the other hand, is one which on its face sets up no defense, although it may be true in fact.

Antapocha /æntǽpəkə/. In the Roman law, a transcript or counterpart of the instrument called *"apocha"* (*q.v.*), signed by the debtor and delivered to the creditor.

Ante. Lat. Before. Usually employed in old pleadings as expressive of time, as *præ* (before) was of place, and *coram* (before) of person.

Occurring in a report or a text-book, it is used to refer the reader to a previous part of the book. Synonymous to *"supra"*; opposite of *"post"* or *"infra."*

Antea /æntíyə/. Lat. Formerly; heretofore.

Antecedent /æntəsíydənt/. Prior in point of time.

Antecedent claim. In law of negotiable instruments, a holder takes for value if he takes the instrument for an antecedent claim against any person whether or not the claim is due. U.C.C. § 3–303(b).

Antecedent creditors. Those whose debts are created before the debtor makes a transfer not lodged for record.

Antecedent debt. In contract law, that which may or may not furnish consideration for a new contract to pay. A negotiable instrument given for an antecedent debt is supported by adequate consideration. U.C.C. § 3–408.

In bankruptcy law, a debt which is incurred before four months prior to filing of bankruptcy petition and hence is not a preference. Bankruptcy Act (1898), § 60a.

Antecessor /æntəsésər/. An ancestor (*q.v.*).

Antedate. To affix an earlier date; to date an instrument as of a time before the time it was written. Such does not affect the negotiability of the instrument. U.C.C. § 3–114.

Ante exhibitionem billæ /ǽntiy eksəbishiyównəm bíliy/. Before the exhibition of the bill. Before suit begun.

Ante-factum /ǽntiy-fǽktəm/ or **ante-gestum** /ǽntiy-jéstəm/. Done before. A Roman law term for a previous act, or thing done before.

Antejuramentum /ǽntiyjurəméntəm/. In Saxon law, a preliminary or preparatory oath (called also *"præjuramentum,"* and *"juramentum calumniæ,"* (*q.v.*), which both the accuser and accused were required to make before any trial or purgation; the accuser swearing that he would prosecute the criminal, and the accused making oath on the very day that he was to undergo the ordeal that he was innocent of the crime with which he was charged.

Ante litem motam /ǽntiy láydəm mówdəm/. At time when declarant had no motive to distort truth. Before suit brought, before controversy instituted. Also, before the controversy arose.

Ante mortem interest /ǽntiy mòrdəm ínt(ə)rəst/. Interests existing only prior to, and not after, transferor's death.

Antenati /æntiynéyday/. See **Ante natus.**

Ante natus /ǽntiy néydəs/. Born before. A person born before another person or before a particular event. The term is particularly applied to one born in a country before a revolution, change of government or dynasty, or other political event, such that the question of his rights, *status*, or allegiance will depend upon the date of his birth with reference to such event. In England, the term commonly denotes one born before the act of union with Scotland; in America, one born before the declaration of independence. Its opposite is *post natus*, one born after the event.

Antenuptial /æntiynǽpshəl/. Made or done before a marriage.

Antenuptial agreement. A contract between spouses made in contemplation of marriage. Antenuptial agreements are generally entered into by people about to enter marriage in an attempt to resolve issues of support, distribution of wealth and division of property in the event of the death of either or the failure of the proposed marriage resulting in either separation or divorce. Commonly, within the statute of frauds which requires a writing and signing to be enforceable, the consideration must be adequate. Kosik v. George, 253 Or. 15, 452 P.2d 560. See also **Antenuptial settlements.**

Antenuptial gift. A transfer of property from one party to the marriage to the other before the marriage without consideration.

Antenuptial settlements. Contracts or agreements between a man and woman before marriage, but in contemplation and generally in consideration of marriage, whereby the property rights and interests of either the prospective husband or wife, or both of them, are determined, or where property is secured to either or both of them, or to their children. In re Carnevale's Will, 248 A.D. 62, 289 N.Y.S. 185, 188. See **Antenuptial agreement; Palimony.**

Antenuptial will. A will executed by a person prior to his marriage. Such will is generally deemed revoked unless it appears on the face of the will that it is in contemplation of marriage.

Anthropometry /ænθrəpómətriy/. In criminal law and medical jurisprudence, the measurement of the human body. A system of measuring the dimensions of the human body, both absolutely and in their proportion to each other, the facial, cranial, and other angles, the shape and size of the skull, etc., for purposes of comparison with corresponding measurements of other individuals, and serving for the identification of the subject in cases of doubtful or disputed identity. It was largely adopted after its introduction in France in 1883, but fell into disfavor as being costly and as liable to error. It has given place to the "finger print" system devised by Francis Galton. See **Bertillon System.**

Antichresis /æntəkríyzəs/. In the civil law, a species of mortgage, or pledge of immovables. An agreement by which the debtor gives to the creditor the income from the property which he has pledged, in lieu of the interest on his debt. In the French law, if the income was more than the interest, the debtor was entitled to demand an account of the income, and might claim any excess.

By the law of Louisiana, there are two kinds of pledges,—the pawn and the antichresis. A pawn relates to movables, and the antichresis to immovables. The antichresis must be reduced to writing; and the creditor thereby acquires the right to the fruits, etc., of the immovables, deducting yearly their proceeds from the interest, in the first place, and afterwards from the principal of his debt. He is bound to pay taxes on the property, and keep it in repair, unless the contrary is agreed. The creditor does not become the proprietor of the property by failure to pay at the agreed time, and any clause to that effect is void. He can only sue the debtor, and obtain sentence for sale of the property. The possession of the property is, however, by the contract, transferred to the creditor. La.Civil Code Arts. 3176–3181. The "antichresis" is an antiquated contract, and has been resorted to in Louisiana in but a few instances.

Anticipation. Act of doing or taking a thing before its proper time. To do, take up, or deal with, before another; to preclude or prevent by prior action; to be before in doing.

In conveyancing, the act of assigning, charging, or otherwise dealing with income before it becomes due.

In patent law, a person is said to have been anticipated when he patents a contrivance already known within the limits of the country granting the patent. Topliff v. Topliff, 145 U.S. 156, 12 S.Ct. 825, 36 L.Ed. 658. Defense of "anticipation" in suit for patent infringement is made out when, except for insubstantial differences, the prior patent contains all of the same elements operating in the same fashion to perform an identical function. Ropat Corp. v. West Bend Co., D.C.Ill., 382 F.Supp. 1030, 1036. Unless all of same elements are found in exactly same situation and are united in same way to perform identical function in a single prior art reference, there is no "anticipation" which will invalidate that patent. Ceramic Tilers Supply, Inc. v. Tile Council of America, Inc., C.A.Cal., 378 F.2d 283, 284.

In law of negligence, "anticipation" is not confined to expectation. It means probability, not possibility, as applied to duty to anticipate consequences of conduct attacked as negligent. Empire Dist. Electric Co. v. Harris, C.C.A.Mo., 82 F.2d 48, 52.

Anticipation note. Discount or rebate for prepayment.

Anticipatory breach of contract. Such occurs when the promisor without justification and before he has committed a breach makes a positive statement to promisee indicating he will not or cannot perform his contractual duties. Daun v. Superior Court, Sutter County, 228 C.A.2d 283, 39 Cal.Rptr. 443, 446.

The right of one party to a contract to sue for breach before the date set for performance when the other party conveys his intention not to perform (U.C.C. § 2–610), though the repudiating party may retract his repudiation prior to date for performance if the other party has not acted on the repudiation (U.C.C. § 2–611). Some jurisdictions require the aggrieved party to wait for the date for performance before commencing suit.

Anticipatory nuisance. The right in equity to prevent a condition from becoming a nuisance by injunction or other order of the court.

Anticipatory offense. A crime which has as its object a further crime, such as an attempt, a conspiracy, a solicitation, all of which are crimes in themselves.

Anticipatory repudiation. See **Anticipatory breach of contract.**

Anti-deficiency legislation. Statutes which are enacted to provide revenue when a budget deficiency is created.

Anti-Dumping Act. See **Dumping Act.**

Anti-dumping duty. Tariff, purpose of which is to prevent imports of goods for sale at a lower price than that charged in the country of origin. See **Dumping Act.**

Antigraphus /æntígrəfəs/. In Roman law, an officer whose duty it was to take care of tax money. A comptroller.

Antigraphy. A copy or counterpart of a deed.

Anti-lapse statute. Legislation enacted in most jurisdictions to provide for the testamentary passing of property to heirs and next of kin of the designated legatee or devisee if he dies before the testator, thus preventing a lapse of the legacy and the passing of such property through intestacy to the heirs and next of kin of the testator.

Anti manifesto. A term used in international law to denote a proclamation or manifesto published by one of two belligerent powers, alleging reasons why the war is defensive on its part.

Antinomia /æntənówmiyə/. In Roman law, a real or apparent contradiction or inconsistency in the laws. Conflicting laws or provisions of law; inconsistent or conflicting decisions or cases.

Antinomy /æntínəmiy/. A term used in logic and law to denote a real or apparent inconsistency or conflict between two authorities or propositions; same as *antinomia (q.v.).*

Antiqua custuma /æntáykwə kǽst(y)əmə/. In old English law, an export duty on wool, woolfells, and leather, imposed during the reign of Edw. I. It was so called by way of distinction from an increased duty on the same articles, payable by foreign merchants, which was imposed at a later period of the same reign and was called *"custuma nova."*

Antiquare /æntəkwériy/. In Roman law, to restore a former law or practice; to reject or vote against a new law; to prefer the old law. Those who voted against a proposed law wrote on their ballots the letter "A," the initial of *antiquo,* I am for the old law.

Antiqua statuta /æntáykwə stətyúwdə/. Also called *"Vetera Statuta."* English statutes from the time of Richard I to Edward III. See **Nova statuta.**

Antiquum dominicum /æntáykwəm dəmínəkəm/. In old English law, ancient demesne.

Anti-Racketeering Act. Federal act prohibiting robbery, extortion, or other unlawful interference with interstate commerce. See **Hobbs Act.**

Antithetarius /æntəθətériyəs/. In old English law, a man who endeavors to discharge himself of the crime of which he is accused, by retorting the charge on the accuser. He differs from an approver in this: that the latter does not charge the accuser, but others.

Antitrust acts. Federal and state statutes to protect trade and commerce from unlawful restraints, price discriminations, price fixing, and monopolies. Most states have mini-antitrust acts patterned on the federal acts. The principal federal antitrust acts are: Sherman Act (1890); Clayton Act (1914); Federal Trade Commission Act (1914); Robinson-Patman Act (1936). See **Boycott; Combination in restraint of trade; Price fixing; Restraint of trade; Rule** (*Rule of reason*).

Antitrust Civil Process Act. Federal statute permitting antitrust action by way of a petition in U.S. District Court for an order for enforcement of law. 15 U.S. C.A. § 1314.

Anxiety. An unpleasant affective state with the expectation but not the certainty of something happening; sometimes manifested as a sense of fear, poorly understood by the subject, which arises without justifiable cause; anxious state may have overtones of "impending" danger rather than present danger. See **Phobia.**

Any. Some; one out of many; an indefinite number. One indiscriminately of whatever kind or quantity. Federal Deposit Ins. Corporation v. Winton, C.C.A. Tenn., 131 F.2d 780, 782. One or some (indefinitely). Slegel v. Slegel, 135 N.J.Eq. 5, 37 A.2d 57, 58. "Any" does not necessarily mean only one person, but may have reference to more than one or to many. Doherty v. King, Tex.Civ.App., 183 S.W.2d 1004, 1007.

Word "any" has a diversity of meaning and may be employed to indicate "all" or "every" as well as "some" or "one" and its meaning in a given statute depends upon the context and the subject matter of the statute. Donohue v. Zoning Bd. of Appeals of Town of Norwalk, 155 Conn. 550, 235 A.2d 643, 646, 647.

It is often synonymous with "either", "every", or "all". Its generality may be restricted by the context; thus, the giving of a right to do some act "at any time" is commonly construed as meaning within a reasonable time; and the words "any other" following the enumeration of particular classes are to be read as "other such like," and include only others of like kind or character.

A.O.C. *Anno orbis conditi,* the year of the creation of the world.

A.P.A. Administrative Procedure Act.

A pais. To the country; at issue.

Apanage /ǽpənáj/. In old French law, a provision of lands or feudal superiorities assigned by the kings of France for the maintenance of their younger sons. An allowance assigned to a prince of the reigning house for his proper maintenance out of the public treasury.

Apartment house. A building arranged in several suites of connecting rooms, each suite designed for independent housekeeping, but with certain mechanical conveniences, such as heat, light, or elevator services, in common to all families occupying the building. Sometimes called a flat or flat house.

Apatisatio /əpæ̀dəzéysh(iy)ow/. An agreement or compact.

A.P.C. Alien Property Custodian.

A.P.C.N. *Anno post Christum natum*, the year after the birth of Christ.

Aperta brevia /əpə́rdə bríyviyə/. Open, unsealed writs.

Apertum factum /əpə́rdəm fǽktəm/. An overt act.

Apertura testamenti /æ̀pərtyúrə tèstəméntay/. In the civil law, a form of proving a will, by the witnesses acknowledging before a magistrate their having sealed it.

Apex. The summit or highest point of anything; the top; *e.g.*, in mining law, "apex of a vein." See Larkin v. Upton, 144 U.S. 19, 12 S.Ct. 614, 36 L.Ed. 330. An "apex" is all that portion of a terminal edge of a mineral vein from which the vein has extension downward in the direction of the dip. Stewart Mining Co. v. Ontario Mining Co., 237 U.S. 350, 35 S.Ct. 610, 614, 59 L.Ed. 989. Or it is the juncture of two dipping limbs of a fissure vein. Jim Butler Tonopah Mining Co. v. West End Consol. Mining Co., 247 U.S. 450, 38 S.Ct. 574, 576, 62 L.Ed. 1207.

Apex juris /éypèks júrəs/. The summit of the law; a legal subtlety; a nice or cunning point of law; close technicality; a rule of law carried to an extreme point, either of severity or refinement. A term used to denote a stricter application of the rules of law than is indicated by the phrase *summum jus (q.v.)*.

Apex rule. In mining law, the mineral laws of the United States give to the locator of a mining claim on the public domain the whole of every vein the apex of which lies within his surface exterior boundaries, or within perpendicular planes drawn downward indefinitely on the planes of those boundaries; and he may follow a vein which thus apexes within his boundaries, on its dip, although it may so far depart from the perpendicular in its course downward as to extend outside the vertical side-lines of his location; but he may not go beyond his end-lines or vertical planes drawn downward therefrom. This is called the apex rule. 30 U.S.C.A. § 26.

Aphasia /əféyzh(iy)ə/. Loss of the faculty or power of articulate speech; a condition in which the patient, while retaining intelligence and understanding and with the organs of speech unimpaired, is unable (in "motor aphasia") to utter articulate words, or unable to vocalize the particular word which is in his mind and which he wishes to use, or utters words different from those he believes himself to be speaking, or (in "sensory aphasia" or apraxia) is unable to understand spoken or written language. *Sensory aphasia* includes *word blindness* and *word deafness*, visual and auditory aphasia. *Motor aphasia* often includes *agraphia*, or the inability to write words of the desired meaning. The seat of the disease is in the brain, but it is not a form of insanity.

Aphonia /əfówniyə/. Loss of the power of articulate speech in consequence of defective conditions of some of the vocal organs. It may be incomplete, in which case the patient can whisper. It is to be distinguished from congenital inability to speak, and from temporary loss of voice through extreme hoarseness or minor affections of the vocal cords, as also from aphasia, the latter being a disease of the brain without impairment of the organs of speech.

Apices juris non sunt jura [jus] /éypəsiyz júrəs nón sə̀nt júrə (°jə́s)/. Extremities, or mere subtleties of law are not rules of law [are not law]. Legal principles must not be carried to their extreme consequences, without regard for equity and good sense. See **Apex juris**.

Apices litigandi /éypəsiyz lidəgǽnday/. Extremely fine points, or subtleties of litigation. Nearly equivalent to the modern phrase "sharp practice." "It is unconscionable to take advantage of the *apices litigandi*, to turn a plaintiff around and make him pay costs when his demand is just." Per Lord Mansfield, in 3 Burr. 1243.

A piratis aut latronibus capti liberi permanent /éy pəréydəs ót lətrównəbəs kǽptay líbəray pérmənənt/. Persons taken by pirates or robbers remain free.

A piratis et latronibus capta dominum non mutant /éy pəréydəs èt lətrównəbəs kǽptə dəmíniyəm nòn myúwtænt/. Capture by pirates and robbers does not change title. No right to booty vests in piratical captors; no right can be derived from them by recaptors to the prejudice of the original owners.

Apnœa /æpníyə/. Want of breath; difficulty in breathing; partial or temporary suspension of respiration; specifically, such difficulty of respiration resulting from over-oxygenation of the blood, and in this distinguished from "asphyxia" *(q.v.)*, which is a condition resulting from a deficiency of oxygen in the blood due to suffocation or any serious interference with normal respiration. The two terms were formerly (but improperly) used synonymously.

Apocha (also *Apoca*) /ǽpəkə/. Lat. In the civil law, a writing acknowledging payments; acquittance. It differs from acceptilation in this: that acceptilation imports a complete discharge of the former obligation whether payment be made or not; apocha, discharge only upon payment being made. See **Antapocha**.

Apochæ oneratoriæ /ǽpəkiy ònəreytóriyiy/. In old commercial law, bills of lading.

Apocrisarius /æ̀pəkrisériyəs/. In civil law, a messenger; an ambassador.

In ecclesiastical law, one who answers for another. An officer whose duty was to carry to the emperor messages relating to ecclesiastical matters, and to take back his answer to the petitioners. An officer who gave advice on questions of ecclesiastical law. An ambassador or legate of a pope or bishop. A messenger sent to transact ecclesiastical business and report to his superior; an officer who had charge of the treasury of a monastic edifice; an officer who took charge of opening and closing the doors.

Apocrisarius cancellarius /æ̀pəkrisériyəs kæ̀nsəlériyəs/. In the civil law, an officer who took charge of the royal seal and signed royal dispatches. Called, also, *secretarius, consiliarius* (from his giving advice); *referendarius; a consiliis* (from his acting as counsellor); *a responsis*, or *responsalis.*

Apographia /æpəgrǽfiyə/. In civil law, an examination and enumeration of things possessed; an inventory.

Apoplexy /ǽpəplèksiy/. The failure of consciousness and suspension of voluntary motion from suspension of the functions of the cerebrum. The group of symptoms arising from rupture of a minute artery and consequent hemorrhage into the substance of the brain or from the lodgment of a minute clot in one of the cerebral arteries.

Apostacy (also spelled *Apostasy*). The total renunciation of Christianity, by embracing either a false religion or no religion at all. In old English law, this offense could take place only in such as had once professed the Christian religion. 4 Bl.Comm. 43.

Apostata /æpəstéydə/. In civil and old English law, an apostate; a deserter from the faith; one who has renounced the Christian faith.

Apostata capiendo /æpəstéydə kæpiyéndow/. An obsolete English writ which issued against an apostate, or one who had violated the rules of his religious order. It was addressed to the sheriff, and commanded him to deliver the defendant into the custody of the abbot or prior.

A posteriori /èy postìriyóray/. Lat. From the effect to the cause; from what comes after. A term used in logic to denote an argument founded on experiment or observation, or one which, taking ascertained facts as an effect, proceeds by synthesis and induction to demonstrate their cause.

Apostille, or **appostille** /əpóstəl/. L. Fr. An addition; a marginal note or observation.

Apostles. In English admiralty practice, a term borrowed from the civil law, denoting brief dismissory letters granted to a party who appeals from an inferior to a superior court, embodying a statement of the case and a declaration that the record will be transmitted.

Apostoli /əpóstəlày/. In civil law, certificates of the inferior judge from whom a cause is removed, directed to the superior. See **Apostles.**

Apostolus /əpóstələs/. A messenger; an ambassador, legate, or nuncio.

Apotheca /æpəθíykə/. In the civil law, a repository; a place of deposit, as of wine, oil, books, etc.

Apparator /æpəréydər/. A furnisher or provider. Formerly the sheriff, in England, had charge of certain county affairs and disbursements, in which capacity he was called *"apparator comitatus"* (apparator for the county), and received therefor a considerable emolument.

Apparent. That which is obvious, evident, or manifest; what appears, or has been made manifest. That which appears to the eye or mind; open to view; plain; patent. In respect to facts involved in an appeal or writ of error, that which is stated in the record. See also **Appear on face.**

Apparent agency. See **Agency.**

Apparent authority. In the law of agency, such authority as the principal knowingly or negligently permits the agent to assume, or which he holds the agent out as possessing. Such authority as he appears to have by reason of the actual authority which he has. Such authority as a reasonably prudent man, using diligence and discretion, in view of the principal's conduct, would naturally suppose the agent to possess. Finnegan Constr. Co. v. Robino-Ladd Co., 354 A.2d 142, 144. Such authority as a principal intentionally or by want of ordinary care causes or allows third person to believe that agent possesses. Lewis v. Michigan Milers Mut. Ins. Co., 154 Conn. 660, 228 A.2d 803, 806. It includes the power to do whatever is usually done and necessary to be done in order to carry into effect the principal power conferred.

The power to affect the legal relations of another person by transactions with third persons, professedly as agent for the other, arising from and in accordance with the other's manifestations to such third persons. Restatement, Second, Agency § 8.

Apparent danger. As used with reference to the doctrine of self-defense in homicide, means such overt actual demonstration, by conduct and acts, of a design to take life or do some great personal injury, as would make the killing apparently necessary to self-preservation.

Apparent defects. Those defects in goods which can be discovered by simple inspection; see U.C.C. § 2–605. Also, may refer to title defects which appear on the record. See **Patent** (*Patent defect*).

Apparent easement. See **Easement.**

Apparent heir. One whose right of inheritance is indefeasible, provided he outlives the ancestor. To be contrasted with presumptive heir whose claim to inheritance is defeated on the birth of an heir closer in relationship to the ancestor, though at a given point in time the heir presumptive is entitled to the inheritance.

Apparent necessity. See **Apparent danger.**

Apparitor /əpǽrədər/. In old English law, an officer or messenger employed to serve the process of the spiritual courts and summon offenders.

In the civil law, an officer who waited upon a magistrate or superior officer, and executed his commands.

Apparlement /əpárl(ə)mənt/. In old English law, resemblance; likelihood; as apparlement of war.

Apparura /æpərúrə/. In old English law, the apparura were furniture, implements, tackle, or apparel.

App. Ct. Appellate Court.

Appeal. Resort to a superior (*i.e.* appellate) court to review the decision of an inferior (*i.e.* trial) court or administrative agency. There are two stages of appeal in the federal and many state court systems; to wit, appeal from trial court to intermediate appellate court and then to Supreme Court. There may also be several levels of appeal within an administrative agency; *e.g.* appeal from decision of Administrative

Law Judge to Appeals Council in social security case. In addition, an appeal may be taken from an administrative agency to a trial court (*e.g.* from Appeals Council in social security case to U.S. district court). Also, an appeal may be as of right (*e.g.* from trial court to intermediate appellate court) or only at the discretion of the appellate court (*e.g.* by writ of certiorari to U.S. Supreme Court). Provision may also exist for joint or consolidated appeals (*e.g.* Fed.R. App.P. 3) and for cross appeals (where both parties to a judgment appeal therefrom).

Appeal was also the name formerly given to the proceeding in English law where a person, indicted of treason or felony, and arraigned for the same, confessed the fact before plea pleaded, and *appealed,* or accused others, his accomplices in the same crime, in order to obtain his pardon. In this case he was called an "approver" or "prover," and the party appealed or accused, the "appellee."

See also Consolidated appeal; Courts of Appeals, U.S.; Cross appeal; Interlocutory appeal; Interlocutory Appeals Act; Limited appeal.

Appealable order. A decree or order which is sufficiently final to be entitled to appellate review, as contrasted with an interlocutory order which generally is not appealable until the case has been tried and judgment entered, *e.g.* a denial of motion for summary judgment is not appealable but the allowance of such motion is a final judgment and hence appealable. Fed.R. Civil P. 56.

Appeal bond. The bond given on taking an appeal, by which the appellant and his sureties are bound to pay costs if he fails to prosecute the appeal with effect. See *e.g.* Fed.R.App.P. 7.

Appeal in forma pauperis /əpíyl in fórmə pópərəs/. A privilege given indigent person to prosecute an appeal, otherwise and independently allowable, without payment of fees and costs incident to such prosecution. See *e.g.* Fed.R.App.P. 24.

Appeal record. See **Record** (*Record on appeal*).

Appeals council. Body to which appeal is taken from finding and ruling of administrative law judge in social security matters. 42 U.S.C.A. § 405(b).

Appeals courts. See **Appellate court; Court of Appeals, U.S.; Court of Customs and Patent Appeals; Court of Military Appeals; Supreme Court**

Appear. To be properly before a court; as a fact or matter of which it can take notice. To be in evidence; to be proved. Coming into court by a party to a suit, whether plaintiff or defendant. See **Appearance**.

Appearance. A coming into court as party to a suit, either in person or by attorney, whether as plaintiff or defendant. The formal proceeding by which a defendant submits himself to the jurisdiction of the court. The voluntary submission to a court's jurisdiction.

In civil actions the parties do not normally actually appear in *person*, but rather through their attorneys. Also, at many stages of criminal proceedings, particularly involving minor offenses, the defendant's attorney appears on his behalf. See *e.g.* Fed.R.Crim.P. 43.

An appearance may be either *general* or *special*; the former is a simple and unqualified or unrestricted submission to the jurisdiction of the court, the latter a submission to the jurisdiction for some specific purpose only, not for all the purposes of the suit. A special appearance is for the purpose of testing the sufficiency of service or the jurisdiction of the court; a general appearance is made where the defendant waives defects of service and submits to the jurisdiction. Insurance Co. of North America v. Kunin, 175 Neb. 260, 121 N.W.2d 372, 375, 376.

See also **General appearance; Notice to appear.**

Appearance by attorney. An act of an attorney in prosecuting an action on behalf of his client. Document filed in court in which attorney sets forth fact that he is representing a party to the action.

Appearance docket. A docket kept by the clerk of the court in which appearances are entered, containing also a brief abstract of all the proceedings in the cause.

Common law classifications. At common law an appearance could be either *compulsory* or *voluntary*, the former where it was compelled by process served on the party, the latter where it was entered by his own will or consent, without the service of process, though process may be outstanding. Also, *optional* when entered by a person who intervened in the action to protect his own interests, though not joined as a party; *conditional*, when coupled with conditions as to its becoming or being taken as a general appearance; *gratis*, when made by a party to the action, but before the service of any process or legal notice to appear; *de bene esse*, when made provisionally or to remain good only upon a future contingency; or when designed to permit a party to a proceeding to refuse to submit his person to the jurisdiction of the court unless it was finally determined that he had forever waived that right; *subsequent*, when made by a defendant after an appearance had already been entered for him by the plaintiff; *corporal*, when the person was physically present in court.

Initial appearance. A court proceeding for a defendant charged with a felony, during which the judge advises the defendant of the charges against him and of his rights, decides upon bail and/or other conditions of release, and sets the date for a preliminary hearing. See *e.g.* Fed.R.Crim.P. 5.

Notice of appearance. A notice given by defendant to a plaintiff that he appears in the action in person or by attorney.

Appear on face. That which is clear and apparent from a reading of the document. A defect in process or venue which can be gleaned from examining the pleadings and which does not require going outside the record. See also **Apparent.**

Appellant. The party who takes an appeal from one court or jurisdiction to another. Used broadly or nontechnically, the term includes one who sues out a writ of error.

Appellate. Pertaining to or having cognizance of appeals and other proceedings for the judicial review of adjudications. Word "appellate" has a general meaning, and it has a specific meaning indicating the distinction between original jurisdiction and appellate jurisdiction. Woodruff v. Bell, 143 Kan. 110, 53 P.2d 498, 499.

Appellate court. A court having jurisdiction of appeal and review; a court to which causes are removable by appeal, certiorari, error or report. A reviewing court, and, except in special cases where original jurisdiction is conferred, not a "trial court" or court of first instance. See *e.g.* **Court of Appeals; Court of Customs and Patent Appeals; Court of Military Appeals; Supreme Court.**

Appellate jurisdiction. The power vested in an appellate court to review and revise the judicial action of an inferior court, evidenced by an appealable order or an appealable judgment rendered by such court. Trengen v. Mongeon, N.D., 200 N.W.2d 50, 53. The power and authority to take cognizance of a cause and proceed to its determination, not in its initial stages (*i.e.* original jurisdiction) but only after it has been finally decided by an inferior court, *i.e.*, the power of review and determination on appeal, writ of error, certiorari, or other similar process. Jurisdiction on appeal; jurisdiction to revise or correct the proceedings in a cause already instituted and acted upon by an inferior court, or by a tribunal having the attributes of a court. Limits of appellate jurisdiction are governed by statutes (*e.g.* 28 U.S.C.A. § 1291 et seq.) or constitutions.

Appellate review. Examination of lower court proceeding by an appellate court brought about by appeal, bill of exceptions, report or certiorari. Such may also embrace review of administrative board's decision by an inferior court; *e.g.* review by federal district court of social security administration decision.

Appellate rules. Rules governing procedure in taking appeals and in practicing before appellate courts; *e.g.* Federal Rules of Appellate Procedure; Massachusetts Rules of Appellate Procedure. See **Federal Rules of Appellate Procedure.**

Appellatio /æpəléysh(iy)ow/. Lat. An appeal.

Appellator /æpəléydər/. An old law term having the same meaning as "appellant" (*q.v.*).

In the civil law, the term was applied to the judge ad quem, or to whom an appeal was taken.

Appellee. The party in a cause against whom an appeal is taken; that is, the party who has an interest adverse to setting aside or reversing the judgment. Sometimes also called the "respondent." It should be noted that a party's status as appellant or appellee does not necessarily bear any relation to his status as plaintiff or defendant in the lower court.

Appello /æpélow/. Lat. In the civil law, "I appeal." The form of making an appeal *apud acta.*

Appellor /æpélər/. In old English law, a criminal who accused his accomplices, or who challenged a jury. See **Approver.**

Append. To add or attach.

Appendage. Something added as an accessory to or the subordinate part of another thing. See **Appendant; Appendix.**

Appendant. A thing annexed to or belonging to another thing and passing with it. Something added or attached.

At common law, a thing of inheritance belonging to another inheritance which is more worthy; as an advowson, common, etc., which may be appendant to a manor, common of fishing to a freehold, a seat in a church to a house, etc. It differs from appurtenance, in that appendant must ever be by prescription, *i.e.*, a personal usage for a considerable time, while an appurtenance may be created at this day; for if a grant be made to a man and his heirs, of common in such a moor for his beasts levant or couchant upon his manor, the commons are appurtenant to the manor, and the grant will pass them.

See also **Appendix; Appurtenance; Appurtenant.**

Appenditia /æpəndísh(iy)ə/. The appendages or appurtenances of an estate or house, dwelling, etc.; thus, *penthouses* are the *appenditia domus.*

Appendix. Supplementary materials added to appellate brief; *i.e.* record on appeal. In federal appellate procedure, the appellant is required to file an appendix to the briefs which shall contain the following: (1) the relevant portions of the pleadings, charge, findings or opinion; (2) the judgment, order or decision in question; and (3) any other parts of the record to which the parties wish to direct the particular attention of the court. Fed.R.App.P. 30.

Appensura /æpens(y)úrə/. Payment of money by weight instead of by count.

Appertain. To belong to; to have relation to; to be appurtenant to. See **Appurtenance; Appurtenant.**

Appertaining. Connected with in use or occupancy.

Applicable. Fit, suitable, pertinent, or appropriate.

Applicable local law. Term used to determine the persons who come within the term heirs and is the law which would be used to ascertain the heirs of the designated ancestor if he had owned the property and had died intestate. Restatement of Law of Property, § 305, Comment e.

Applicant. An applicant, as for letters of administration, is one who is entitled thereto, and who files a petition asking that letters be granted.

Applicare /æpləkériy/. Lat. In old English law, to fasten to; to moor (a vessel). Anciently rendered, "to apply."

Applicatio est vita regulæ /æpləkéysh(iy)ow èst váydə régyəliy/. Application is the life of a rule.

Application. A putting to, placing before, preferring a request or petition to or before a person. The act of making a request for something. A petition. The use or disposition made of a thing. A bringing together, in order to ascertain some relation or establish some connection; as the *application* of a rule or principle to a case or fact. See also **Apply; Petition.**

Insurance. The preliminary request, declaration, or statement made by a party applying for an insurance policy, such as one on his life, or against fire.

Payments. Appropriation of a payment to some particular debt; or the determination to which of several demands a general payment made by a debtor to his creditor shall be applied.

Purchase money. The disposition made of the funds received by a trustee on a sale of real estate held under the trust.

Application of rules. Refers to area of practice governed by rules of procedure and not left to common law or statutory law.

Apply. To make a formal request or petition, usually in writing, to a court, officer, board, or company, for the granting of some favor, or of some rule or order, which is within his or their power or discretion. For example, to apply for an injunction, for a pardon, for a policy of insurance, or for a receiver. See **Application; Petition.**

To use or employ for a particular purpose; to appropriate and devote to a particular use, object, demand, or subject-matter. Thus, to apply payments to the reduction of interest. See **Appropriate.**

To put, use, or refer, as suitable or relative; to co-ordinate language with a particular subject-matter; as to apply the words of a statute to a particular state of facts.

The word "apply" is used in connection with statutes in two senses. When construing a statute, in describing the class of persons, things, or functions which are within its scope; as that the statute does not "apply" to transactions in interstate commerce. When discussing the use made of a statute, in referring to the process by which the statute is made operative; as where the jury is told to "apply" the statute of limitation if they find that the cause of action arose before a given date.

Appoint. To designate, ordain, prescribe, constitute, or nominate. To allot or set apart. To assign authority to a particular use, task, position, or office.

Term is used where exclusive power and authority is given to one person, officer, or body to name persons to hold certain offices. It is usually distinguished from "elect," meaning to choose by a vote of the qualified voters of the city; though this distinction is not invariably observed.

See also **Appointment.**

Appointee. A person who is appointed or selected for a particular purpose; as the appointee under a power of appointment is the person who is to receive the benefit of the power.

Appointment. The designation of a person, by the person or persons having authority therefor, to discharge the duties of some office or trust. In re Nicholson's Estate, 104 Colo. 561, 93 P.2d 880, 884. See **Illusory appointment; Power of appointment.**

The exercise of a right to designate the person or persons who are to take the use of real estate. The act of a person in directing the disposition of property, by limiting a use, or by substituting a new use for a former one, in pursuance of a power granted to him for that purpose by a preceding deed, called a "power of appointment"; also the deed or other instrument by which he so conveys. Where the power embraces several permitted objects, and the appointment is

made to one or more of them, excluding others, it is called "exclusive."

Appointment may signify an appropriation of money to a specific purpose. It may also mean the arranging of a meeting.

Office or public function. The selection or designation of a person, by the person or persons having authority therefor, to fill an office or public function and discharge the duties of the same. The term "appointment" is to be distinguished from "election." "Election" to office usually refers to vote of people, whereas "appointment" relates to designation by some individual or group. Board of Education of Boyle County v. McChesney, 235 Ky. 692, 32 S.W.2d 26, 27.

Appointment, power of. See **Power of appointment.**

Appointor. The person who appoints, or executes a power of appointment; as *appointee* is the person to whom or in whose favor an appointment is made. One authorized by the donor, under the statute of uses, to execute a power.

Apport. L. Fr. In old English law, tax; tallage; tribute; imposition; payment; charge; expenses.

Apportion. To divide and distribute proportionally.

Apportionment /əpórshənmənt/. Determination of the number of representatives which a State, county, or other subdivision may send to a legislative body. The U.S. Constitution provides for a census every ten years, on the basis of which Congress apportions representatives according to population; but each State must have at least one representative. "Districting" is the establishment of the precise geographical boundaries of each such unit or constituency. Seaman v. Fedourich, 16 N.Y.2d 94, 262 N.Y.S.2d 444, 209 N.E.2d 778, 779. Apportionment by state statute which denies the rule of one-man, one-vote is violative of equal protection of laws. Baker v. Carr, 369 U.S. 186, 82 S.Ct. 691, 7 L.Ed.2d 663. See also **Legislative apportionment; Reapportionment.**

The allocation of a charge or cost such as real estate taxes between two parties, often in the same ratio as the respective times that the parties are in possession or ownership of property during the fiscal period for which the charge is made or assessed.

Contracts. The allowance, in case of a severable contract, partially performed, of a part of the entire consideration proportioned to the degree in which the contract was carried out.

Corporate shares. The *pro tanto* division among the subscribers of the shares allowed to be issued by the charter, where more than the limited number have been subscribed for.

Estate taxes. Unless the will otherwise provides, taxes shall be apportioned among all persons interested in the estate. The apportionment is to be made in the proportion that the value of the interest of each person interested in the estate bears to the total value of the interests of all persons interested in the estate. The values used in determining the tax are to be used for that purpose. If the decedent's will directs a method of apportionment of tax different from the method described in the Probate Code, the method described in the will controls. Uniform Probate Code, § 3–916(b).

Incumbrances. Where several persons are interested in an estate, apportionment, as between them, is the determination of the respective amounts which they shall contribute towards the removal of the incumbrance.

Liability. Legal responsibility of parties to a transaction or tort may be distributed or apportioned among them by statute or by agreement. See **Comparative negligence; Contribution**.

Rent. The allotment of shares in a rent to each of several parties owning it. The determination of the amount of rent to be paid when the tenancy is terminated at some period other than one of the regular intervals for the payment of rent.

Representatives. The determination upon each decennial census of the number of representatives in congress which each state shall elect, the calculation being based upon the population. See U.S.Const., Art. 1, § 2; Amend. 14, § 2.

Taxes. The apportionment of a tax consists in a selection of the subjects to be taxed, and in laying down the rule by which to measure the contribution which each of these subjects shall make to the tax.

Apportionment clause. Insurance policy clause which distributes insurance in proportion to the total coverage.

Apports en nature /əpórts òn nətyúr/. In French law, that which a partner brings into the partnership other than cash; for instance, securities, realty or personalty, cattle, stock, or even his personal ability and knowledge.

Apportum /əpórdəm/. In old English law, the revenue, profit, or emolument which a thing brings to the owner. Commonly applied to a corody or pension.

Apposer /əpówzər/. In old English law, an officer in the exchequer, clothed with the duty of examining the sheriffs in respect of their accounts. Usually called the "foreign apposer." The office is now abolished.

Appostille, or **apostille** /əpóstəl/. In French law, an addition or annotation made in the margin of a writing.

Appraisal. A valuation or an estimation of value of property by disinterested persons of suitable qualifications. The process of ascertaining a value of an asset or liability that involves expert opinion rather than explicit market transactions. See also **Appraise.**

Appraisal clause. Clause in insurance policy providing that the insurer has the right to demand an appraisal of the loss or damage.

Appraisal remedy. The dissenting shareholder's appraisal remedy is essentially a statutory creation to enable shareholders who object to certain extraordinary matters to dissent and to require the corporation to buy their shares at the value immediately prior to the approval of such matter and thus to withdraw from the corporation. In different jurisdictions, the appraisal remedy often applies to sales of substantially all corporate assets other than in the regular course of business, mergers, and consolidations, more rarely to certain amendments of the articles of incorporation or miscellaneous matters, but usually not to dissolution. The appraisal remedy is often limited to shareholders of record entitled to vote on the matter.

Appraisal rights. See **Appraisal remedy**.

Appraise. To fix or set a price or value upon; to fix and state the true value of a thing, and, usually, in writing. To value property at what it is worth. To "appraise" money means to count. See also **Appraisal.**

Appraisement. A just and true valuation of property. A valuation set upon property under judicial or legislative authority. A valuation or estimation of the value of property. See also **Appraisal.**

Appraiser. A person selected or appointed by competent authority or interested party to make an appraisement; to ascertain and state the true value of goods or real estate. Frequently appointed in probate and condemnation proceedings; also used by condemnation authorities, banks and real estate companies to ascertain market value of real property.

Appreciable. Capable of being estimated, weighed, judged of, or recognized by the mind. Capable of being perceived or recognized by the senses. Perceptible but not a synonym of substantial.

Appreciate. To estimate justly; to set a price or value on. When used with reference to the nature and effect of an act, "appreciate" may be synonymous with "know" or "understand" or "realize."

Appreciation in value. Increase in the market value of an asset over its value at some earlier time. May be due from inflation and/or increased demand for asset.

Apprehend. To take hold of, whether with the mind (as to conceive, believe, fear, dread, understand, be conscious or sensible of), or actually and bodily (as to seize or arrest a person).

Apprehensio /æprəhénsh(iy)ow/. Lat. In the civil and old English law, a taking hold of a person or thing; apprehension; the seizure or capture of a person.

One of the varieties or subordinate forms of *occupatio*, or the mode of acquiring title to things not belonging to any one.

Apprehension. The seizure, taking, or arrest of a person on a criminal charge.

Civil law. A physical or corporal act (*corpus*), on the part of one who intends to acquire possession of a thing, by which he brings himself into such a relation to the thing that he may subject it to his exclusive control; or by which he obtains the physical ability to exercise his power over the thing whenever he pleases. One of the requisites to the acquisition of judicial possession, and by which, when accompanied by intention, (*animus*) possession is acquired.

Apprendre. A fee or profit taken or received.

Apprentice en la ley /əpréntəs òn lə léy/. An ancient name for students at law, and afterwards applied to counsellors, *apprentici ad barras*, from which comes the more modern word "barrister." In some of the ancient law-writers the terms apprentice and barrister are synonymous.

Apprenticeship. An apprentice is a person who agrees to work for an employer for a specified time for the purpose of learning the craft, trade or profession in which the employer agrees to instruct him. In a more popular sense the term is used to convey the idea of a learner in any field of employment or business. The requirements of an apprenticeship contract both as to contents and manner of execution are prescribed by statute in a number of states. See also **Articles of apprenticeship.**

The term during which an apprentice is to serve; the *status* of an apprentice; the relation subsisting between an apprentice and his master.

Apprenticius ad legem /æprentíshiyəs æd líyjəm/. An apprentice to the law; a law student; a counsellor below the degree of serjeant. See **Apprentice en la ley.**

Approach. To come nearer in place or time.

Approaches. A way, passage, street, or avenue by which a place or building can be approached; an access.

Approach, right of. In international maritime law, the right of a ship of war, upon the high sea, to draw near to another vessel for the purpose of ascertaining the nationality of the latter. The Marianna Flora, 24 U.S. 1, 11 Wheat. 1, 6 L.Ed. 405. At present the right of approach has no existence apart from the right of visit.

Approbation /æprəbéyshən/. Denotes approval and generally includes commendation. Application of N. Y. Soul Clinic, 208 Misc. 612, 144 N.Y.S.2d 543, 545.

Appropriate. To make a thing one's own; to make a thing the subject of property; to exercise dominion over an object to the extent, and for the purpose, of making it subserve one's own proper use or pleasure. To prescribe a particular use for particular moneys; to designate or destine a fund or property for a distinct use, or for the payment of a particular demand. Also used in the sense of distribute. In this sense it may denote the act of an executor or administrator who distributes the estate of his decedent among the legatees, heirs, or others entitled, in pursuance of his duties and according to their respective rights. See **Appropriation; Expropriation.**

Appropriated surplus. In accounting, portion of surplus set aside for specific purpose other than for existing liability.

Appropriation. The act of appropriating or setting apart; prescribing the destination of a thing; designating the use or application of a fund. McKenzie Const. Co. v. City of San Antonio, Tex.Civ.App., 50 S.W.2d 349, 352.

In governmental accounting, an expenditure authorized for a specified amount, purpose, and time.

See also **Appropriate; Misappropriation.**

Appropriation of land. The act of selecting, devoting, or setting apart land for a particular use or purpose, as where land is appropriated for public buildings, military reservations, or other public uses. Taking of private property for public use in the exercise of the power of eminent domain. In this sense it may refer merely to physical occupation and contemplate payment prior thereto, in contra-distinction to "taking," referring to a legal taking and presupposing payment after damages are due. See **Condemnation; Eminent domain; Expropriation.**

Appropriation of payments. The application of a payment to the discharge of a particular debt. Thus, if a creditor has two distinct debts due to him from his debtor, and the latter makes a general payment on account, without specifying at the time to which debt he intends the payment to apply, it is optional for the creditor to *appropriate* (apply) the payment to either of the two debts he pleases.

Appropriation of water. An appropriation of water flowing on the public domain consists in the capture, impounding, or diversion of it from its natural course or channel and its actual application to some beneficial use private or personal to the appropriator, to the entire exclusion (or exclusion to the extent of the water appropriated) of all other persons. To constitute a valid appropriation, there must be an intent to apply the water to some beneficial use existing at the time or contemplated in the future, a diversion from the natural channel by means of a ditch or canal, or some other open physical act of taking possession of the water, and an actual application of it within a reasonable time to some useful or beneficial purpose. In re Manse Spring and Its Tributaries, Nye County, 60 Nev. 262, 108 P.2d 311, 314; State of Neb. v. State of Wyo., 325 U.S. 589, 65 S.Ct. 1332, 1349, 89 L.Ed. 1815. It follows water to its original source whether through surface or subterranean streams or through percolation, Justesen v. Olsen, 86 Utah 158, 40 P.2d 802, 809; and entitles appropriator to continuing right to use water to extent of appropriation, but not beyond that reasonably required and actually used. State of Arizona v. State of California, Ariz. & Cal., 298 U.S. 558, 56 S.Ct. 848, 852, 80 L.Ed. 1331.

Public law. The act by which the legislative department of government designates a particular fund, or sets apart a specified portion of the public revenue or of the money in the public treasury, to be applied to some general object of governmental expenditure, or to some individual purchase or expense. Authority given by legislature to proper officers to apply distinctly specified sum from designated fund out of treasury in given year for specified object or demand against state. State ex rel. Murray v. Carter, 167 Okl. 473, 30 P.2d 700, 702.

A *specific* appropriation is an act of the legislature by which a named sum of money has been set apart in the treasury, and devoted to the payment of a particular demand.

Appropriation bill. A measure before a legislative body authorizing the expenditure of public moneys and stipulating the amount, manner, and purpose of the various items of expenditure. Appropriation bills in Congress must originate in the House. U.S.Const. Art. I, Sec. 7. See also **Appropriation** (*Public law*).

Appropriator. One who makes an appropriation; as, an appropriator of water.

Approval. The act of confirming, ratifying, assenting, sanctioning, or consenting to some act or thing done by another. "Approval" implies knowledge and exercise of discretion after knowledge. McCarten v. Sanderson, 111 Mont. 407, 109 P.2d 1108, 1112. The act of a judge or magistrate in sanctioning and accepting as satisfactory a bond, security, or other instrument which is required by law to pass his inspection and receive his approbation before it becomes operative. See Affirm; Approve; Assent; Condonation; Confirmation; Connivance; Consent; Ratification. For "sale on approval", see **Sale.**

Approval sales. A buyer may, by agreement, accept goods on approval, and title does not pass until he has indicated his approval. Approval is a condition precedent to passing of title and risk. U.C.C. § 2–326.

Approve. To be satisfied with; to confirm, ratify, sanction, or consent to some act or thing done by another. To sanction officially; to ratify; to confirm; to pronounce good; think or judge well of; admit the propriety or excellence of; be pleased with. Distinguishable from "authorize," meaning to permit a thing to be done in future. To take to one's proper and separate use. To improve; to enhance the value or profits of anything. To inclose and cultivate common or waste land. See also **Approval; Confirmation; Ratification.**

Approved indorsed notes. Notes indorsed by another person than the maker, for additional security, the indorser being satisfactory to the payee. See **Accommodation paper; Accommodation party.**

Approvement. In English law, the improvement or partial inclosure of a common. The profits arising from the improvement of land approved.

In old English law, a practice of criminal prosecutions by which a person accused of treason or felony was permitted to exonerate himself by accusing others and escaping prosecution himself. The custom existed only in capital cases, and consisted in the accused, called "approver", being arraigned and permitted to confess before plea and appeal or accuse another as his accomplice of the same crime in order to obtain his pardon. See **Approver.**

Approver. L. Fr. To approve or prove; to vouch.

In old English law, an accomplice in crime who accused others of the same offense, and was admitted as a witness at the discretion of the court to give evidence against his companions in guilt. He was vulgarly called "King's Evidence." One who confessed himself guilty of felony and accused others of the same crime to save himself from punishment. If he failed to convict those he accused he was at once hung. See also **Antithetarius.**

In old English law, certain men sent into the several counties to increase the farms (rents) of hundreds and wapentakes, which formerly were let at a certain value to the sheriff.

Approximate. Used in the sense of an estimate merely, meaning more or less, but about and near the amount, quantity, or distance specified. Near to; about; a little more or less; close. "Approximately" is very nearly synonymous with "proximately", meaning very nearly, but not absolutely.

Approximation. Equitable doctrine by which precise terms of charitable trust can be varied under certain circumstances. Applicable to charitable trusts and employed only where on failure of trust the court finds a general charitable intent. Under this doctrine, the general intent of the donor is carried out as nearly as may be even if the particular method pointed out by him cannot be followed. Harris v. Attorney General, 31 Conn.Sup. 93, 324 A.2d 279, 283. See **Cy-Pres.**

Appruare /æpruwériy/. To take to one's use or profit.

Appurtenance /əpə́rdənəns/. That which belongs to something else; an adjunct; an appendage. Something annexed to another thing more worthy as principal, and which passes as incident to it, as a right of way or other easement to land; an outhouse, barn, garden, or orchard, to a house or messuage. Joplin Waterworks Co. v. Jasper County, 327 Mo. 964, 38 S.W.2d 1068, 1076. An article adapted to the use of the property to which it is connected, and which was intended to be a permanent accession to the freehold. A thing is deemed to be incidental or appurtenant to land when it is by right used with the land for its benefit, as in the case of a way, or watercourse, or of a passage for light, air, or heat from or across the land of another. See also **Appendant.**

Appurtenant. Belonging to; accessory or incident to; adjunct, appended, or annexed to; answering to *accessorium* in the civil law. Employed in leases for the purpose of including any easements or servitudes used or enjoyed with the demised premises. A thing is "appurtenant" to something else when it stands in relation of an incident to a principal and is necessarily connected with the use and enjoyment of the latter. A thing is deemed to be incidental or *appurtenant* to land when it is by right used with the land for its benefit, as in the case of a way, or water-course, or of a passage for light, air, or heat from or across the land of another.

APR. See **Annual percentage rate.**

A.P.R.C. *Anno post Roman conditam,* year after the foundation of Rome.

A prendre /à próndər/. L. Fr. To take; to seize. *Bref à prendre la terre,* a writ to take the land. A right to take something out of the soil of another is a profit *à prendre,* or a right coupled with a profit. Distinguished from an easement. Sometimes written as one word, *apprendre, apprender.* See **Profit à prendre.**

A priori /èy prayóray/. Lat. From the cause to the effect; from what goes before. A term used in logic to denote an argument founded on analogy, or abstract considerations, or one which, positing a general principle or admitted truth as a cause, proceeds to deduce from it the effects which must necessarily follow.

A provisione viri /èy prəvìzhiyówniy víhray/. By the provision of man.

Apt. Fit; suitable; appropriate.

Apta viro /æptə vírow/. Fit for a husband; marriageable; a woman who has reached marriageable years.

Apt words. Words proper to produce the legal effect for which they are intended; sound technical phrases.

Apud acta /ǽpəd ǽktə/. Among the acts; among the recorded proceedings. In the civil law, this phrase is applied to appeals taken orally, in the presence of the judge, at the time of judgment or sentence. Credit Co., Ltd., v. Arkansas Cent. Ry. Co., 128 U.S. 258, 9 S.Ct. 107, 108, 32 L.Ed. 448.

Aqua /ǽkwə/. In the civil and old English law, water; sometimes a stream or water-course.

Aqua æstiva /ǽkwə íystivə/. In Roman law, summer water; water that was used in summer only.

Aqua cedit solo /ǽkwə síydət sówlow/. Water follows the land. A sale of land will pass the water which covers it. 2 Bl.Comm. 18.

Aqua currens /ǽkwə kə́hrenz/. Running water.

Aqua currit et debet currere, ut currere solebat /ǽkwə kə́hrət èt débət kə́hrəriy, ət kə́hrəriy sowlíybət/. Water runs, and ought to run, as it has used to run. A running stream should be left to flow in its natural channel, without alteration or diversion; that water is the common and equal property of every one through whose domain it flows.

Aqua dulcis, or **frisca** /ǽkwə də́lsəs/°frískə/. Fresh water.

Aquæ ductus /ǽkwiy dǽktəs/. In the civil law, a servitude which consists in the right to carry water by means of pipes or conduits over or through the estate of another.

Aquæ haustus /ǽkwiy hóstəs/. In the civil law, a servitude which consists in the right to draw water from the fountain, pool, or spring of another.

Aquæ immittendæ /ǽkwiy ìməténdiy/. A civil law easement or servitude, consisting in the right of one whose house is surrounded with other buildings to cast waste water upon the adjacent roofs or yards. Similar to the common law easement of drip.

Aqua fontanea /ǽkwə fontéyniyə/. Spring water.

Aquagium /əkwéyjiyəm/. A canal, ditch, or water course running through marshy grounds. A mark or gauge placed in or on the banks of a running stream, to indicate the height of the water, was called "aquagaugium."

Aqua profluens /ǽkwə prófluwenz/. Flowing or running water.

Aqua quotidiana /ǽkwə kwowtìdiyéynə/. In Roman law, daily water; water that might be drawn at all times of the year (qua quis quotidie possit uti, si vellet).

Aqua salsa /ǽkwə sǽlsə/. Salt water.

Aquatic rights. Rights which individuals have to the use of the sea and rivers, for the purpose of fishing and navigation, and also to the soil in the sea and rivers. See **Riparian rights; Water** (Water rights).

Aquilian law. See **Lex aquilia.**

A quo /èy kwów/. Lat. From which. A court a quo (also written "a qua") is a court from which a cause has been removed. The judge a quo is the judge in such court. A term used, with the correlative ad quem (to which), in expressing the computation of time, and also of distance in space. Thus, dies a quo, the day from which and dies ad quem, the day to which, a period of time is computed. So, terminus a quo, the point or limit from which, and terminus ad quem, the point or limit to which, a distance or passage in space is reckoned.

A quo invito aliquid exigi potest /èy kwów inváydow ǽləkwəd égzəjay pówdəst/. From whom something may be exacted against his will.

A.R. Anno Regni. In the year of the reign; as A. R. V. R. 22, (Anno Regni Victoriae Reginae vicesimo secundo) in the twenty-second year of the reign of Queen Victoria.

Arabant /əréybənt/. They plowed. A term of feudal law, applied to those who held by the tenure of plowing and tilling the lord's lands within the manor.

Arable land /ǽrəbəl lǽnd/. That which is fit for plowing or tillage, and thus is distinguishable from swamp land, which is land that is too wet for cultivation.

Araho. In feudal law, to make oath in the church or some other holy place. All oaths were made in the church upon the relics of saints, according to the Ripuarian laws.

Aralia /əréyliyə/. Plowlands. Land fit for the plow. Denoting the character of land, rather than its condition.

Arator. A plowman; a farmer of arable land.

Aratrum terræ /əréytrəm tériy/. In old English law, a plow of land; a plowland; as much land as could be tilled with one plow (or by a single "arator" or plowman).

Aratura terræ /ærətyúrə tériy/. The plowing of land by the tenant, or vassal, in the service of his lord.

Araturia /ærət(y)úriyə/. Land suitable for the plow; arable land.

Arbiter /árbədər/. A person chosen to decide a controversy; an arbitrator, referee. A person bound to decide according to the rules of law and equity, as distinguished from an arbitrator, who may proceed wholly at his own discretion, so that it be according to the judgment of a sound man.

In the Roman law, a judge invested with a discretionary power. A person appointed by the prætor to examine and decide that class of causes or actions termed bonæ fidei," and who had the power of judging according to the principles of equity, (ex æquo et bono) distinguished from the judex, (q.v.) who was bound to decide according to strict law.

Arbitrage /árbətrəj/. The simultaneous purchase in one market and sale in another of a security or commodity in hope of making a profit on price differences in the different markets. See **Arbitration of exchange.** For "arbitrage bond", see **Bond.**

Arbitrament /àrbítrəmənt/. The award or decision of arbitrators upon a matter of dispute, which has been submitted to them.

Arbitrament and award /àrbítrəmənt ænd əwórd/. A plea to an action brought for the same cause which had been submitted to arbitration and on which an award had been made.

Arbitramentum æquum tribuit cuique suum /arbìtrəméntəm íykwəm tríbyuwət káykwiy s(y)úwəm/. A just arbitration renders to every one his own.

Arbitrarily. See **Arbitrary**.

Arbitrariness. Conduct or acts based alone upon one's will, and not upon any course of reasoning and exercise of judgment. Garman v. Myers, 183 Okl. 141, 80 P.2d 624, 626.

Arbitrary. Means in an "arbitrary" manner, as fixed or done capriciously or at pleasure. Without adequate determining principle; not founded in the nature of things; nonrational; not done or acting according to reason or judgment; depending on the will alone; absolutely in power; capriciously; tyrannical; despotic; Corneil v. Swisher County, Tex.Civ.App., 78 S.W.2d 1072, 1074. Without fair, solid, and substantial cause; that is, without cause based upon the law, U. S. v. Lotempio, D.C.N.Y., 58 F.2d 358, 359; not governed by any fixed rules or standard. Ordinarily, "arbitrary" is synonymous with bad faith or failure to exercise honest judgment and an arbitrary act would be one performed without adequate determination of principle and one not founded in nature of things. Huey v. Davis, Tex.Civ.App., 556 S.W.2d 860, 865.

Arbitrary and capricious. Characterization of a decision or action taken by an administrative agency or inferior court meaning willful and unreasonable action without consideration or in disregard of facts or without determining principle. Elwood Investors Co. v. Behme, 79 Misc.2d 910, 361 N.Y.S.2d 488, 492.

Arbitrary power. Power to act according to one's own will; especially applicable to power conferred on an administrative officer, who is not furnished any adequate determining principle. Fox Film Corporation v. Trumbull, D.C.Conn., 7 F.2d 715, 727.

Arbitrary punishment. That punishment which is left to the decision of the judge, in distinction from those defined by statute. See **Sentence**.

Arbitration /àrbətréyshən/. The reference of a dispute to an impartial (third) person chosen by the parties to the dispute who agree in advance to abide by the arbitrator's award issued after a hearing at which both parties have an opportunity to be heard.

An arrangement for taking and abiding by the judgment of selected persons in some disputed matter, instead of carrying it to established tribunals of justice, and is intended to avoid the formalities, the delay, the expense and vexation of ordinary litigation. Wauregan Mills Inc. v. Textile Workers Union of America, A.F.L.–C.I.O., 21 Conn.Sup. 134, 146 A.2d 592, 595. Such arbitration provisions are common in union collective bargaining agreements.

The majority of the states have adopted the Uniform Arbitration Act.

A major body offering arbitration services is the American Arbitration Association (q.v.).

See also **Conciliation; Mediation; Reference**.

Compulsory arbitration is that which occurs when the consent of one of the parties is enforced by statutory provisions. Examples of such are state statutes requiring compulsory arbitration of labor disputes involving public employees.

Interest and grievance arbitration distinguished. Interest arbitration involves settlement of terms of a contract between the parties as contrasted with grievance arbitration which concerns the violation or interpretation of an existing contract. School Committee of Boston et al. v. Boston Teachers Union etc., 363 N.E.2d 485.

Voluntary arbitration is by mutual and free consent of the parties.

Arbitration Acts. Federal and state laws which provide for submission of disputes to process of arbitration, including labor grievances and disputes of public employees. An example of a federal Act is Title 9, U.S.C.A. § 1 *et seq.* which governs settlement of disputes involved in maritime transactions and commerce under federal statutes. Most states have arbitration acts, many of which are patterned on the Uniform Arbitration Act. The purpose of such acts, in general, is to validate arbitration agreements, make the arbitration process effective, provide necessary safeguards, and provide an efficient procedure when judicial assistance is necessary.

Arbitration and award. An affirmative defense to the effect that the subject matter of the action has been settled by a prior arbitration. Fed.R. Civil P. 8(c).

Arbitration board. A panel of arbitrators appointed to hear and decide a dispute according to rules of arbitration. Such services are offered by the American Arbitration Association.

Arbitration clause. A clause inserted in a contract providing for compulsory arbitration in case of dispute as to rights or liabilities under such contract; *e.g.* disputes arising under union collective bargaining agreement, or disputes between consumer and retailer or manufacturer.

Arbitration of exchange. This takes place where a merchant pays his debts in one country by a bill of exchange upon another. The business of buying and selling exchange (bills of exchange) between two or more countries or markets, and particularly where the profits of such business are to be derived from a calculation of the relative value of exchange in the two countries or markets, and by taking advantage of the fact that the rate of exchange may be higher in the one place than in the other at the same time. See **Arbitrage**.

Arbitrator. A private, disinterested person, chosen by the parties to a disputed question, for the purpose of hearing their contention, and giving judgment between them; to whose decision (award) the litigants submit themselves either voluntarily, or, in some cases, compulsorily. See **Referee; Umpire**.

Arbitrium /arbítriyəm/. The decision of an arbiter, or arbitrator; an award; a judgment.

Arbitrium est judicium /arbítriyəm èst juwdíshiyəm/. An award is a judgment.

Arbitrium est judicium boni viri, secundum æquum et bonum /arbítriyəm èst juwdíshiyəm bówniy víray, səkǽndəm íykwəm ət bównəm/. An award is the judgment of a good man, according to justice.

Arbor civilis /árbər sívələs/. A genealogical tree.

Arbor consanguinitatis /árbər kònsæŋgwìniytéydəs/. A table, formed in the shape of a tree, showing the genealogy of a family; *e.g.* the *arbor civilis* of the civilians and canonists.

Arbor finalis /árbər fənéyləs/. In old English law, a boundary tree; a tree used for making a boundary line.

Arcana imperii /arkéynə impíriyày/. State secrets. 1 Bl.Comm. 337.

Arcarius /arkériyəs/. In civil and old English law, a treasurer; a keeper of public money.

Archaionomia /àrkeyənówmiyə/. A collection of Saxon laws, published during the reign of Queen Elizabeth, in the Saxon language, with a Latin version by Lambard.

Archdeaconry /archdíykənriy/. A division of a diocese, and the circuit of an archdeacon's jurisdiction.

Archdeacon's court. In English ecclesiastical law, a court held before a judge appointed by the archdeacon, and called his official. Its jurisdiction comprised the granting of probates and administrations, and ecclesiastical causes in general, arising within the archdeaconry. It was the most inferior court in the whole ecclesiastical polity of England.

Archery. In feudal law, a service of keeping a bow for the lord's use in the defense of his castle.

Arches Court /árchəz kórt/. In English ecclesiastical law, a court of appeal belonging to the Archbishop of Canterbury, the judge of which is called the "Dean of the Arches", because his court was anciently held in the church of Saint Mary-le-Bow (*Sancta Maria de Arcubus*), so named from the steeple, which is raised upon pillars built archwise. The court was afterwards held in the hall belonging to the College of Civilians, commonly called "Doctors' Commons". It is now held in Westminster Hall. Its proper jurisdiction is only over the thirteen peculiar parishes belonging to the archbishop in London, but, the office of Dean of the Arches having been for a long time united with that of the archbishop's principal official, the Judge of the Arches, in right of such added office, it receives and determines appeals from the sentences of all inferior ecclesiastical courts within the province. Many original suits are also brought before him from which the inferior judge has waived jurisdiction. From the Court of Arches an appeal lies to the Judicial Committee of the Privy Council.

Archetype /árkətàyp/. The original from which a copy is made.

Archicapellanus /àrkiykæpəléynəs/. L. Lat. In old European law, a chief or high chancellor (*summus cancellarius*).

Architect. One who makes plans and specifications for a building and superintends its construction. Stephens County v. J. N. McCammon, Inc., 122 Tex. 148, 52 S.W.2d 53. Also one who plans and constructs landscape work. State v. McIlhenny, 201 La. 78, 9 So.2d 467, 470.

Architect's lien. A lien on real estate created by statute in favor of the architect who drew the plans and supervised the construction of the real estate for purpose of insuring payment of his fee.

Archives. Place where old books, manuscripts, records, etc. are kept.

Archivist /árkəvist/. Custodian of archives.

Arcifinious /àrsəfíniyəs/. (Lat. *arcifinius* or *arcifinalis*; Fr. *arcifinie*). Pertaining to landed estates having natural boundaries, such as woods, mountains, or rivers. The owners of such estates, unlike the owners of "agri limitati" (*q.v.*), have the right of alluvion. Also, having a frontier forming a natural defense.

Arcta et salva custodia /árktə èt sǽlvə kəstówdiyə/. Lat. In strict (or close) and safe custody or keeping. When a defendant is arrested on a *capias ad satisfaciendum* (ca.sq.), he is to be kept *arcta et salva custodi.* 3 Bl.Comm. 415.

Ardent spirits. Synonymous with distilled or spirituous liquors and, sometimes, with intoxicating liquors generally, though the term is properly applied only to liquors obtained by distillation, such as rum, whiskey, brandy, and gin. Sarlls v. U. S., 152 U.S. 570, 572, 14 S.Ct. 720, 38 L.Ed. 556.

Ardour /árdər/. In old English law, an incendiary; a house burner. An arsonist.

Area. A surface, a territory, a region. Fleming v. Farmers Peanut Co., C.C.A.Ga., 128 F.2d 404, 406. Any plane surface, also the inclosed space on which a building stands. A particular extent of space or surface or one serving a special purpose. In the civil law, a vacant space in a city; a place not built upon. For "common area", see **Common**.

Area bargaining. Negotiation of collective bargaining agreement between a union and more than one employer within a given geographical area.

Area variance. Such variance authorizes deviations from restrictions upon construction and placement of buildings and structures which are employed to serve permitted statutory use. Bienz v. City of Dayton, 29 Or.App. 761, 566 P.2d 904, 919.

A remenaunt /à rəméynənt/. Forever.

A rendre /à róndər/. Fr. To render, to yield. That which is to be rendered, yielded, or paid. *Profits à rendre* comprehend rents and services.

Arentare /æ̀rəntériy/. Lat. To rent; to let out at a certain rent. *Arentatio.* A renting.

Areopagite /æ̀riyópəgayt/. In ancient Greek law, a lawyer or chief judge of the Areopagus in capital matters in Athens; a tribunal so called after a hill or slight eminence, in a street of that city dedicated to Mars, where the court was held in which those judges were wont to sit.

Arere /ərír/. L. Fr. Behind; in arrear; back; again.

A rescriptis valet argumentum /èy rəskríptəs vǽləd argyuwméntəm/. An argument from rescripts [*i.e.* original writs in the register] is valid.

A responsis /èy rəspónsəs/. L. Lat. In ecclesiastical law, one whose office it was to give or convey answers; otherwise termed *responsalis*, and *apocrisiarius*. One who, being consulted on ecclesiastical matters, gave answers, counsel, or advice; otherwise termed *a consiliis*.

Aretro /èyríytrow/. In arrear; behind. Also written *a retro*.

Arg. An abbreviation of *arguendo*.

Argent. In heraldry.

Argentarius /àrjəntériyəs/ (*pl.*, **argentarii** /àrjəntériyày/). In the Roman law, a money lender or broker; a dealer in money; a banker. *Argentarium*, the instrument of the loan, similar to the modern word "bond" or "note."

Argentarius miles /àrjəntériyəs máyliyz/. A money porter in the English exchequer, who carried the money from the lower to the upper exchequer to be examined and tested.

Argenteus /arjéntiyəs/. An old French coin, similar to the English shilling.

Argentum /arjéntəm/. Silver; money.

Argentum album /arjéntəm ǽlbəm/. Bullion; uncoined silver; common silver coin; silver coin worn smooth.

Argentum dei /arjéntəm díyay/. God's money; God's penny; money given as earnest in making a bargain.

Arguendo /àrgyuwéndow/. In arguing; in the course of the argument. A statement or observation made by a judge as a matter of argument or hypothetical illustration, is said to be made *arguendo*, or in the abbreviated form, *arg*.

Argument. An effort to establish belief by a course of reasoning. In rhetoric and logic, an inference drawn from premises, the truth of which is indisputable, or at least highly probable. See also **Oral argument**.

Argument by counsel. Remarks addressed by attorney to judge or jury on the merits of case or on points of law. Oral presentation to appellate court in which attorney's brief is argued; generally limited in time, order, and content by court rule (see *e.g.* Fed.R. App.P. 34). See **Opening statement**.

Argument to jury. Closing remarks of attorney to jury in which he strives to persuade jury of merits of case; generally limited in time by rules of court. The argument is not evidence. See also **Closing argument**.

Argumentative. Characterized by argument; controversial; given to debate or dispute. A pleading is so called in which the statement on which the pleader relies is implied instead of being expressed, or where it contains, in addition to proper statements of facts, reasoning or arguments upon those facts and their relation to the matter in dispute, such as should be reserved for presentation at the trial.

Argumentative instruction. A jury instruction which singles out or unduly emphasizes a particular issue, theory, or defense, or one which tends to invade the province of the jury with regard to the weight, probative effect, or sufficiency of the evidence or the inferences to be drawn therefrom.

Argumentative question. A faulty form of examination of witness by propounding a question which suggests answer in a manner favorable to party who advances the question or which contains a statement in place of a question. See **Leading question**.

Argumentum ab auctoritate est fortissimum in lege /àrgyəméntəm æb oktòrətéydiy èst fortísəməm in líyjiy/. An argument from authority is the strongest in the law. "The book cases are the best proof of what the law is."

Argumentum ab impossibili valet in lege /àrgyəméntəm æb imposíbəlay vǽləd in líyjiy/. An argument drawn from an impossibility is forcible in law.

Argumentum ab inconvenienti /àrgyəméntəm æb iŋkənvìyniyéntay/. An argument arising from the inconvenience which the proposed construction of the law would create.

Where the constitutionality of a statute is concerned, it is only when the question is close and doubtful that this doctrine will be applied and consideration taken of the consequences of declaring the statute unconstitutional. Calhoun County v. Early County, 205 Ga. 169, 52 S.E.2d 854; Smith v. City Council of Augusta, 203 Ga. 511, 47 S.E.2d 582, 587.

Argumentum ab inconvenienti est validum in lege; quia lex non permittit aliquod inconveniens /àrgyəméntəm æb iŋkənvìyniyéntay èst vǽlədəm in líyjiy; kwáyə léks non pərmídəd ǽləkwəd iŋkənvíyniyenz/. An argument drawn from what is inconvenient is good in law, because the law will not permit any inconvenience.

Argumentum ab inconvenienti plurimum valet [est validum] in lege /àrgyəméntəm æb iŋkənvìyniyéntay pl(y)úrəməm vǽləd in líyjiy/°èst vǽlədəm°/. An argument drawn from inconvenience is of the greatest weight [is forcible] in law. If there be in any deed or instrument equivocal expressions, and great inconvenience must necessarily follow from one construction, it is strong to show that such construction is not according to the true intention of the grantor; but where there is no equivocal expression in the instrument, and the words used admit only of one meaning, arguments of inconvenience prove only want of foresight in the grantor.

Argumentum a communiter accidentibus in jure frequens est /àrgyəméntəm èy kəmyúwnədər æksədéntəbəs in júriy fríykwenz èst/. An argument drawn from things commonly happening is frequent in law.

Argumentum a divisione est fortissimum in jure /àrgyəméntəm ey divìzhiyówniy èst fortísəməm in júriy/. An argument from division [of the subject] is of the greatest force in law.

Argumentum a majori ad minus negative non valet; valet e converso /àrgyəméntəm èy məjóray æd máynəs negətáyviy nòn vǽlət; vǽləd iy kənvérsow/. An argument from the greater to the less is of no force negatively; affirmatively (or conversely) it is.

Argumentum a simili valet in lege /àrgyuwméntəm èy síməlay væləd in líyjiy/. An argument from a like case (from analogy) is good in law.

Aribannum /ærəbǽnəm/. In feudal law, a fine for not setting out to join the army in obedience to the summons of the king.

Arierban, or **arriere-ban** /ær(i)yéy bæn/. An edict of the ancient kings of France and Germany, commanding all their vassals, the noblesse, and the vassals' vassals, to enter the army, or forfeit their estates on refusal. See **Arrier ban**.

Arimanni /ærəmǽnay/. A mediæval term for a class of agricultural owners of small allodial farms, which they cultivated in connection with larger farms belonging to their lords, paying rent and service for the latter, and being under the protection of their superiors. Military tenants holding lands from the emperor.

Arise. To spring up, originate, to come into being or notice; to become operative, sensible, visible, or audible; to present itself. Bergin v. Temple, 111 Mont. 539, 111 P.2d 286, 289, 290.

A case "arises" under the Constitution or a law of the United States, so as to be within the jurisdiction of a federal court, whenever its correct decision depends on the construction of either. Blease v. Safety Transit Co., C.C.A.S.C., 50 F.2d 852, 854.

A cause of action or suit "arises", so as to start running of limitation, when party has a right to apply to proper tribunal for relief, Washington Security Co. v. State, 9 Wash.2d 197, 114 P.2d 965, 967; and it arises at time when and place where act is unlawfully omitted or committed. State ex rel. Birnamwood Oil Co. v. Shaughnessy, 243 Wis. 306, 10 N.W.2d 292, 295. See **Limitation** *(Statute of limitation)*.

Arising out of and in the course of own employment. Workmen's Compensation Acts provide for compensating an employee whose injury is one "arising out of and in the course of the employment." These words describe an injury directly and naturally resulting in a risk reasonably incident to the employment. Thomas v. Proctor & Gamble Mfg. Co., 104 Kan. 432, 179 P. 372, 374; Trudenich v. Marshall, D.C.Wash., 34 F.Supp. 486, 488. They mean that there must be some causal connection between the conditions under which the employee worked and the injury which he received.

The words "arising out of employment" refer to the origin of the cause of the injury, while "course of employment" refers to the time, place, and circumstances under which the injury occurred. An injury arises "out of" employment if it arises out of nature, conditions, obligations and incidents of the employment. Newman v. Bennett, 212 Kan. 562, 512 P.2d 497, 501.

Aristocracy. A government in which a class of men, believed to be superior, rules supreme. A form of government which is lodged in a minority consisting of those believed to be best qualified; a privileged class of the people; nobles, dignitaries, people of wealth and station.

Aristo-democracy. A form of government where the power is divided between the nobles (or the more powerful) and the people.

Arma /árma/. Lat. Arms; weapons, offensive and defensive; armor; arms or cognizances of families.

Arma dare /árma dériy/. To dub or make a knight.

Arma in armatos sumere jura sinunt /árma in arméydos s(y)úwmariy júra sáynant/. The laws permit the taking up of arms against armed persons.

Arma moluta /árma məl(y)úwdə/. Sharp weapons that cut, in contradistinction to such as are blunt, which only break or bruise.

Arma reversata /árma rəvàrséydə/. Reversed arms, a punishment for a traitor or felon.

Armata vis /arméydə vís/. In the civil law, armed force.

Armed. Furnished or equipped with weapons of offense or defense. People ex rel. Griffin v. Hunt, 150 Misc. 163, 270 N.Y.S. 248, 254.

Armed neutrality. An attitude of neutrality between belligerents which the neutral state is prepared to maintain by armed force if necessary.

Armed peace. A situation in which two or more nations, while actually at peace with each other, are armed for possible or probable hostilities.

Armed robbery. An aggravated form of robbery in which the defendant is armed with a dangerous weapon, though it is not necessary to prove that he used the weapon to effectuate the robbery. The taking of property from person or presence of another by use of force or by threatening use of force while armed with a dangerous weapon. People v. Redding, 43 Ill.App. 1024, 2 Ill.Dec. 784, 357 N.E.2d 1227, 1230.

Armiger /ármajər/. An armor-bearer; an esquire. A title in old English law of dignity belonging to gentlemen authorized to bear arms. In its earlier meaning, a servant who carried the arms of a knight. A tenant by scutage; a servant or valet; applied, also, to the higher servants in convents.

Arming one's self. Equipping one's self with a weapon or weapons.

Armiscara /àrməskérə/. An ancient mode of punishment, which was to carry a saddle at the back as a token of subjection.

Armistice. A suspending or cessation of hostilities between belligerent nations or forces for a considerable time. An armistice differs from a mere "suspension of arms" *(q.v.)* in that the latter is concluded for very brief periods and for local military purposes only, whereas an armistice not only covers a longer period, but is agreed upon for political purposes. It is said to be *general* if it relates to the whole area of the war, and *partial* if it relates to only a portion of that area. Partial armistices are sometimes called truces *(q.v.)* but there is no hard and fast distinction.

Arm of the sea. A portion of the sea projecting inland, in which the tide ebbs and flows. It is considered as extending as far into the interior of a country as the water of fresh rivers is propelled backwards by the ingress of the tide. See **Fauces terræ**.

Armorial bearings /armóriyəl bériŋz/. In English law, a device depicted on the (now imaginary) shield of one of the nobility, of which gentry is the lowest degree. The criterion of nobility is the bearing of arms, or armorial bearings, received from ancestry.

Armorum appellatione, non solum scuta et gladii et galeæ, sed et fustes et lapides continentur /armórəm æpəlèyshiyówniy, nòn sówləm sk(y)úwdə èt glǽdiyay et gǽliyiy, sèd et fə́stiyz et lǽpədiyz kontənéntər/. Under the name of arms are included, not only shields and swords and helmets, but also clubs and stones.

Armory. A building where arms, ammunition, and instruments of war are stored.

Arms. Anything that a man wears for his defense, or takes in his hands as a weapon. See also **Bear arms**.

Arms, law of. Agreements (as established *e.g.* by Geneva Convention) which give precepts and rules concerning conditions of war; *e.g.* treatment of prisoners, wounded, etc.

Arm's length transaction. Said of a transaction negotiated by unrelated parties, each acting in his or her own self interest; the basis for a fair market value determination. Commonly applied in areas of taxation when there are dealings between related corporations, *e.g.* parent and subsidiary. Inecto, Inc. v. Higgins, D.C.N.Y., 21 F.Supp. 418. The standard under which unrelated parties, each acting in his or her own best interest, would carry out a particular transaction. For example, if a corporation sells property to its sole shareholder for $10,000, in testing whether $10,000 is an "arm's length" price it must be ascertained for how much the corporation could have sold the property to a disinterested third party in a bargained transaction.

Arms, right to. Right guaranteed by Second Amendment, U.S. Constitution; does not however permit a person to carry gun in violation of state or federal gun law. Com. v. Jackson, Mass., 344 N.E.2d 166.

Army. Armed forces of a nation intended for military service on land.

Regular army. The permanent military establishment, which is maintained both in peace and war according to law. Compare **Militia**.

Around. In the vicinity of; near or close-by.

Arpen, arpent, arpennus. A civil and French measure of land equal to about an acre.

Arpentator /àrpəntéydər/. A measurer or surveyor of land.

Arra /ǽrə/. In the civil law, earnest; earnest-money; evidence of a completed bargain. Used of a contract of marriage, as well as any other. Spelled, also, *Arrha, Arrhœ, Arrœ. Cf.* Arles.

Arraign /əhréyn/. In old English law, to order; or set in order; to conduct in an orderly manner; to prepare for trial. *To arraign an assise* was to cause the tenant to be called to make the plaint, and to set the

cause in such order as the tenant might be enforced to answer thereunto. See **Arraignment**.

Arraignment /əhréynmənt/. Procedure whereby the accused is brought before the court to plead to the criminal charge in the indictment or information. The charge is read to him and he is asked to plead "guilty" or "not guilty" or, where permitted, "nolo contendere." State v. McCotter, 288 N.C. 227, 217 S.E.2d 525, 529.

Arraignment shall be conducted in open court and shall consist of reading the indictment or information to the defendant or stating to him the substance of the charge and calling on him to plead thereto. He shall be given a copy of the indictment or information before he is called upon to plead. Fed.R.Crim.P. 10.

See also **Information**.

Arraignment, deed of. In England, arrangements between debtors and creditors outside of bankruptcy. Deeds of Arraignment Act of 1914.

Arraigns, clerk of. In old English law, an assistant to the clerk of assise.

Arrangement with creditors. A plan of a debtor for the settlement, satisfaction, or extension of the time of payment of his debts. Chapter XI of the federal Bankruptcy Act provides for a device whereby, under the protection and supervision of the court, a financially troubled business may work out a composition or extension agreement with its creditors permitting it to stay in business, rather than going bankrupt. Arrangements of individual debtors with their creditors are provided for under Chapter XIII of the Act. See also **Composition with creditors; Wage earner's plan**.

Array /əhréy/. The whole body of persons summoned to serve as jurors, from which the final trial jury is selected. Also, the list of jurors impaneled. See **Jury panel**.

Arrears, arrearages. Money which is overdue and unpaid; *e.g. overdue mortgage or rent payments.*

Term used to describe cumulative preferred stock dividends that have not been declared on time.

Arrent /əhrént/. In old English law, to let or demise at a fixed rent. Particularly used with reference to the public domain or crown lands; as where a license was granted to inclose land in a forest with a low hedge and a ditch, under a yearly rent, or where an encroachment, originally a purpresture, was allowed to remain on the fixing and payment of a suitable compensation to the public for its maintenance.

Arrest. To deprive a person of his liberty by legal authority. Taking, under real or assumed authority, custody of another for the purpose of holding or detaining him to answer a criminal charge or civil demand. State v. Ferraro, 81 N.J.Super. 213, 195 A.2d 227; People v. Wipfler, 37 Ill.App.3d 400, 346 N.E.2d 41, 44.

Arrest involves the authority to arrest, the assertion of that authority with the intent to effect an arrest, and the restraint of the person to be arrested. Village of Hoffman Estates v. Union Oil Co. of California, 13 Ill.Dec. 277, 370 N.E.2d 1304, 1308. All that is required for an "arrest" is some act by officer indicating his intention to detain or take person into custody and therby subject that person to the actual control and will of the officer; no formal declaration of arrest is required. Com. v. Brown, 230 Pa.Super. 214, 326 A.2d 906, 907.

See also Booking; Citizen's arrest; Custodial arrest; False arrest; Lawful arrest; Probable cause; Reasonable grounds; Warrantless arrest.

Citizen's arrest. See **Citizen's arrest**.

Civil arrest. The apprehension of a person by virtue of a lawful authority to answer the demand against him in a civil action. Also includes arrest of a ship or cargo in maritime in rem actions. Fed.R. Civil P., Supp.Admir.R. C(3), D.

Parol arrest. One ordered by a judge or magistrate from the bench, without written complaint or other proceedings, of a person who is present before him, and which is executed on the spot; as in case of breach of the peace in open court.

Privilege from arrest. See **Privilege.**

Rearrest. Right of officer to take without warrant one who has escaped after arrest, or violated parole, or failed to respond to bond for appearance.

Warrantless arrest. Seizure of a person without warrant but based on probable cause that he has committed felony. May also be made for commission of misdemeanor amounting to breach of peace in presence of officer. Wong Sun v. U. S., 371 U.S. 471, 83 S.Ct. 407, 9 L.Ed.2d 441.

Warrant of arrest. See **Warrant.**

Arrestandis bonis ne dissipentur /æ̀rəstǽndəs bównəs níy dəsəpéntər/. In old English law, a writ which lay for a person whose cattle or goods were taken by another, who during a contest was likely to make away with them, and who had not the ability to render satisfaction.

Arrestando ipsum qui pecuniam recepit /æ̀rəstǽndow ípsow kwày pəkyúwniyəm rəsíypət/. In old English law, a writ which issued for apprehending a person who had taken the ken's prest money to serve in the wars, and then hid himself in order to avoid going.

Arrestatio /æ̀rəstéysh(iy)ow/. In old English law, an arrest *(q.v.).*

Arresto facto super bonis mercatorum alienigenorum /əhrèstow fǽktow s(y)úwpər bównəs mə̀rkətórəm æ̀liyìynəjənórəm/. In old English law, a writ against the goods of aliens found within this kingdom, in recompense of goods taken from a denizen in a foreign country, after denial of restitution. The ancient civilians called it *"clarigatio,"* but by the moderns it is termed *"reprisalia."*

Arrest of inquest. Pleading in arrest of taking the inquest upon a former issue, and showing cause why an inquest should not be taken.

Arrest of judgment. The act of staying a judgment, or refusing to render judgment in an action at law and in criminal cases, after verdict, for some matter intrinsic appearing on the face of the record, which would render the judgment, if given, erroneous or reversible. The court on motion of a defendant shall arrest judg-

ment if the indictment or information does not charge an offense or if the court was without jurisdiction of the offense charged. Fed.R.Crim.P. 34.

Arrest record. Official form completed by police department when a person is arrested. Also, cumulative record of instances in which a person has been arrested, commonly maintained by probation office and useful to judge in setting sentences for second, third, etc. offenders.

Arrest warrant. See **Warrant.**

Arret /arét/aréy/. Fr. A judgment, sentence, or decree of a court of competent jurisdiction. The term is derived from the French law, and is used in Canada and Louisiana.

Saisie arrêt is an attachment of property in the hands of a third person.

Arretted /əhrédəd/. Convened before a judge and charged with a crime.

Arrhabo /əhréybow/. In the civil law; earnest money given to bind a bargain.

Arrhæ /ǽriy/. In the civil law, money or other valuable things given by the buyer to the seller, for the purpose of evidencing the contract; earnest money. See **Arra; Pot-de-vin.**

Arrhæ sponsalitiæ were the earnest or present given by one betrothed to the other at the betrothal.

Arriage and carriage /ǽrəj ən kǽrəj/. In English and Scotch law, indefinite services formerly demandable from tenants, but prohibited by statute.

Arrier ban /ərí(y)ər bǽn/. In feudal law, a second summons to join the lord, addressed to those who had neglected the first. A summons of the inferiors or vassals of the lord. See **Arier ban.**

Arriere fief, or **fee** /ərí(y)ər fíy(f)/. In feudal law, a fief or fee dependent on a superior one; an inferior fief granted by a vassal of the king, out of the fief held by him.

Arriere vassal /ərí(y)ər vǽsəl/. In feudal law, the vassal of a vassal.

Arrival. To come to, or reach, a particular place. The attainment of an end or state. The act of arriving.

In marine insurance, arrival of a vessel means an arrival for purposes of business, requiring an entry and clearance and stay at the port so long as to require some of the acts connected with business, and not merely touching at a port for advices, or to ascertain the state of the market, or being driven in by an adverse wind and sailing again as soon as it changes. F. S. Royster Guano Co. v. U. S., C.C.A.Va., 18 F.2d 469, 470.

Arrogation. In the civil law, the adoption of a person who was of full age or *sui juris.*

Arsæ et pensatæ /ársiy èt pənséydiy/. Burnt and weighed. A term formerly applied to money tested or assayed by fire and by weighing.

Arsenals /ársənəlz/. Store-houses for arms; dockyards, magazines, and other military stores.

Arser in le main /arséy òn lə mǽn/. Fr. Burning in the hand. The punishment by burning or branding the left thumb of lay offenders who claimed and were allowed the benefit of clergy, so as to distinguish them in case they made a second claim of clergy.

Arson. At common law, the malicious burning of the house of another. This definition, however, has been broadened by state statutes and criminal codes. For example, the Model Penal Code, § 220.1(1), provides that a person is guilty of arson, a felony of the second degree, if he starts a fire or causes an explosion with the purpose of: (a) destroying a building or occupied structure of another; or (b) destroying or damaging any property, whether his own or another's, to collect insurance for such loss.

In several states, this crime is divided into arson in the first, second, and third degrees, the first degree including the burning of an inhabited dwelling-house in the nighttime; the second degree, the burning (at night) of a building other than a dwelling-house, but so situated with reference to a dwelling-house as to endanger it; the third degree, the burning of any building or structure not the subject of arson in the first or second degree, or the burning of property, his own or another's with intent to defraud or prejudice an insurer thereof.

Arson clause. Clause in insurance policy voiding coverage if fire is set under direction or by insured.

Arsura /ars(y)úrə/. The trial of money by heating it after it was coined. The loss of weight occasioned by this process. A pound was said to *burn* so many pence *(tot ardere denarios)* as it lost by the fire. The term is now obsolete.

Art. Systematic application of knowledge or skill in effecting a desired result; also an employment, occupation or business requiring such knowledge or skill; a craft; as industrial arts.

In the law of patents, this term means a useful art or manufacture which is beneficial and which is described with exactness in its mode of operation. Such an art can be protected only in the mode and to the extent thus described. It is synonymous with process or method when used to produce a useful result, and may be either a force applied, a mode of application, or the specific treatment of a specific object, and must produce physical effects. Emmett v. Metals Processing Corporation, C.C.A.Ariz., 118 F.2d 796, 798.

In seduction cases, "art" means the skillful and systematic arrangement of means for the attainment of a desired end.

Arteriosclerosis. Abnormal thickening and hardening of the arteries.

Artesian basin. A body of water more or less compact, moving through soils with more or less resistance.

Arthel, ardhel, or **arddelio.** In old English law, to avouch; as if a man were taken with stolen goods in his possession he was allowed a lawful *arthel, i.e.,* vouchee, to clear him of the felony.

Article. A separate and distinct part of an instrument or writing; one of several things presented as connected or forming a whole. A particular object or substance, a material thing or a class of things. Material or tangible object. See **Articles**.

In English ecclesiastical law, a complaint exhibited in the ecclesiastical court by way of libel. The different parts of a libel, responsive allegation, or counter allegation in the ecclesiastical courts.

Articled clerk. In English law, a clerk bound to serve in the office of a solicitor in consideration of being instructed in the profession. This is the general acceptation of the term; but it is said to be equally applicable to other trades and professions.

Articles. A connected series of propositions; a system of rules. The subdivisions of a document, code, book, etc. A specification of distinct matters agreed upon or established by authority or requiring judicial action.

A statute; as having its provisions articulately expressed under distinct heads.

A system of rules established by legal authority; as *articles* of war, *articles* of the navy, *articles* of faith. (See *infra.*)

A contractual document executed between parties, containing stipulations or terms of agreement; as *articles* of agreement, *articles* of partnership.

A naval term meaning employment contract. South Chicago Coal & Dock Co. v. Bassett, C.C.A.Ill., 104 F.2d 522, 526.

In chancery practice, a formal written statement of objections filed by a party, after depositions have been taken, showing ground for discrediting the witnesses.

In ecclesiastical law, a complaint in the form of a libel exhibited to an ecclesiastical court. See **Article**.

Articles of agreement. A written memorandum of the terms of an agreement.

Articles of amendment. Terms and conditions of corporate management enacted subsequent to articles of incorporation. See **Articles of incorporation**.

Articles of apprenticeship. Written agreement between master and minor under which minor agrees to work for master for stated period of time in return for instruction in a trade by the master.

Articles of association. Basic instrument filed with the appropriate governmental agency (*e.g.* Sec. of State) on the incorporation of a business. It sets forth the purposes of the corporation, its duration, the rights and liabilities of shareholders and directors, etc., Model Bus. Corp. Act, § 48. Certificate (similar to one of incorporation) used by non-stock companies such as charitable and mutual corporations. Articles of association are to be distinguished from a charter, in that the latter is a grant of power from the sovereign or the legislature. See **Articles of incorporation**; **Certificate of incorporation**.

Articles of Confederation. The name of the instrument embodying the compact made between the thirteen original states of the Union, operative from March 1, 1781 to March 4, 1789, before the adoption of the present Constitution.

Articles of consolidation. Document filed with Secretary of State setting forth terms and conditions of merger or consolidation. Model Bus. Corp. Act, §§ 68, 69.

Articles of dissolution. Document to be filed in duplicate with Secretary of State after corporation has provided for all its debts and the distribution of all its net assets, prior to dissolution. Model Bus. Corp. Act, §§ 85, 86.

Articles of faith. In English law, the system of faith of the Church of England, more commonly known as the "Thirty-Nine Articles."

Articles of impeachment. A formal written allegation of the causes for impeachment; answering the same office as an indictment in an ordinary criminal proceeding. See **Impeachment**.

Articles of incorporation. The basic instrument filed with the appropriate governmental agency (*e.g.* Sec. of State) on the incorporation of a business; sometimes also called "certificate of incorporation". The contents thereof are prescribed in the general incorporation statutes. In many jurisdictions official forms are also prescribed. In most jurisdictions, corporate existence begins with the filing, usually with the secretary of state, of the articles or certificate of incorporation. In some jurisdictions, duplicate articles of incorporation are filed, and corporate existence begins with the issue of a formal certificate appended thereto called a "certificate of incorporation". Various conditions precedent to doing business might also be imposed. See **Articles of association; Certificate of incorporation**.

Articles of partnership. A written agreement by which the parties enter into a co-partnership upon the terms and conditions therein stipulated.

Articles of the clergy. The title of a statute passed in the ninth year of Edward II for the purpose of adjusting and settling the great questions of cognizance then existing between the ecclesiastical and temporal courts.

Articles of the Navy. Articles (statutes) for the government of the Navy.

Articles of the peace. In English law, a complaint made or exhibited to a court by a person who makes oath that he is in fear of death or bodily harm from some one who has threatened or attempted to do him injury. The court may thereupon order the person complained of to find sureties for the peace, and, in default, may commit him to prison. Such articles were formerly issued in the High Court; but since 1938 the procedure has only been available in courts of summary jurisdiction.

Articles of union. In English law, articles agreed to, A.D. 1707, by the parliaments of England and Scotland, for the union of the two kingdoms. They were twenty-five in number.

Articles of war. Codes framed for the government of a nation's army or navy; *e.g.* Code of Military Justice.

Articulated pleading. The stating in separate paragraphs, separately numbered, of each material fact of the petition, complaint, answer, etc. See *e.g.* Fed.R. Civil P. 10(b).

Articulately /artíkyələtliy/. Article by article; by distinct clauses or articles; by separate propositions.

Articuli /artíkyəlay/. Lat. Articles; items or heads. A term applied to some old English statutes, and occasionally to treatises.

Articuli cleri /artíkyəlay klíray/. "Articles of the clergy" (*q.v.*). See **Circumspecte agatis**.

Articuli de moneta /artíkyəlay díy məníydə/. Articles concerning money, or the currency. The title of a statute passed in the twentieth year of Edward I.

Articuli magnæ chartæ /artíkyəlay mǽgniy kárdiy/. The preliminary articles, forty-nine in number, upon which the *Magna Charta* was founded.

Articuli super chartas /artíkyəlay s(y)úwpər kárdəs/. Articles upon the charters. The title of a statute passed in the twenty-eighth year of Edward I, st. 3, confirming or enlarging many particulars in *Magna Charta*, and the *Charta de Foresta*, and appointing a method for enforcing the observance of them, and for the punishment of offenders.

Articulo mortis /artíkyəlow mórdəs/. (Or more commonly *in articulo mortis*.) At the point of death; in the article of death, which means at the moment of death; in the last struggle or agony.

Artifice /árdəfəs/. An ingenius contrivance or device of some kind, and, when used in a bad sense, it corresponds with trick or fraud. It implies craftiness and deceit, and imports some element of moral obliquity. See also **Sham**.

Artificer /artífəsər/. One who buys goods in order to reduce them, by his own art or industry, into other forms, and then to sell them.

One who is actually and personally engaged or employed to do work of a mechanical or physical character, not including one who takes contracts for labor to be performed by others, *i.e.* a mechanic or workman as contrasted from the employer of such. One who is master of his art, and whose employment consists chiefly in manual labor. A craftsman; an artisan.

Artificial. As opposed to "natural", means created or produced by man. California Casualty Indemnity Exchange v. Industrial Accident Commission of California, 13 Cal.2d 529, 90 P.2d 289. Created by art, or by law; existing only by force of or in contemplation of law. Humanly contrived. A will or contract is described as "artificially" drawn if it is couched in apt and technical phrases and exhibits a scientific arrangement.

Artificial force. In patent law, a natural force so transformed in character or energies by human power as to possess new capabilities of action; this transformation of a natural force into a force practically new involves a true inventive act.

Artificial insemination. Method by which a female is impregnated through injection of semen from a donor other than her husband; and other than through sexual intercourse.

Artificially developed water. Artifically developed water, to which one may acquire right superior to adjudicated rights of earlier appropriators of natural waters of stream into which he turns it, is water produced and contributed by him, which would not have reached stream if left to flow in accordance with natural laws. In re Nix, 96 Colo. 540, 45 P.2d 176, 178.

Artificial persons. Persons created and devised by human laws for the purposes of society and government, as distinguished from natural persons. Corporations are examples of artificial persons.

Artificial presumptions. Also called "legal presumptions;" those which derive their force and effect from the law, rather than their natural tendency to produce belief. See **Presumption**.

Artificial succession. The succession between predecessors and successors in a corporation aggregate or sole.

Artificial water course. See **Water course**.

Artisan. One skilled in some kind of trade, craft, or art requiring manual dexterity; *e.g.* a carpenter, plumber, tailor, mechanic.

Artisan's lien. The statutory right of an artisan to keep possession of the object that he has worked on until he has been paid for such labor.

Art, words of. Words used in a technical sense; words scientifically fit to carry the sense assigned them.

A rubro ad nigrum /èy rúwbrow æd náygrəm/. Lat. From the red to the black; from the rubric or title of a statute (which, anciently, was in *red* letters), to its body, which was in the ordinary *black*.

Arura /ərúrə/. An old English law term, signifying a day's work in plowing.

AS or A/S or A/s. Account sales; also after sight, at sight.

As. Lat. In the Roman and civil law, a pound weight; and a coin originally weighing a pound, (called also *"libra"*) divided into twelve parts, called *"unciæ"*. The parts were reckoned as follows: *uncia*, 1 ounce; *sextans*, 2 ounces; *triens*, 3 ounces; *quadrans*, 4 ounces; *quincunx*, 5 ounces; *semis*, 6 ounces; *septunx*, 7 ounces; *bes*, 8 ounces; *dodrans*, 9 ounces; *dextans*, 10 ounces; *deunx*, 11 ounces. Frequently applied in the civil law to inheritances; the whole inheritance being termed "as", and its several proportionate parts *"sextans"*, *"quadrans"*, etc. The term "as", and the multiples of its *unciæ*, were also used to denote the rates of interest. 2 Bl.Comm. 462, note *m*.

Any integral sum, subject to division in certain proportions.

As. Used as an adverb, etc., means like, similar to, of the same kind, in the same manner, in the manner in which. It may also have the meaning of because, since, or it being the case that; in the character or under the name of with significance of in degree; to that extent; so far.

As against; as between. These words contrast the relative position of two persons, with a tacit reference to a different relationship between one of them and a third person. For instance, the temporary bailee of a chattel is entitled to it *as between* himself and a stranger, or *as against* a stranger; reference being made by this form of words to the rights of the bailor.

A savoir. To wit.

Ascend. To go up; to pass up or upwards; to go or pass in the ascending line.

Ascendants. Persons with whom one is related in the ascending line; one's parents, grandparents, great-grandparents, etc.

Ascent. Passage upward; the transmission of an estate from the ancestor to the heir in the ascending line.

Ascertain. To fix; to render certain or definite; to estimate and determine; to clear of doubt or obscurity. To insure as a certainty. To find out by investigation, U. S. v. Carver, 260 U.S. 482, 43 S.Ct. 181, 182, 67 L.Ed. 361. Sometimes it means to "assess"; or to "hear, try, and determine".

Ascertained as aforesaid. Manner theretofore prescribed.

Ascriptitius (or ascripticius) /æskriptíshiyəs/. In Roman law, a foreigner who had been registered and naturalized in the colony in which he resided.

Asexualization. See **Vasectomy**.

Aside. On one side; apart. *To set aside*; to annul; to make void.

As is. A sale of goods by sample "as is" requires that the goods be of the kind and quality represented, even though they be in a damaged condition. U.C.C. § 2–313. Use of expression in sales agreement that goods are sold "as is" implies that buyer takes the entire risk as to the quality of the goods involved and he must trust to his own inspection. Implied and express warranties are excluded in sales of goods "as is". U.C.C. § 2–316.

Ask. Demand, request, solicit, petition, appeal, apply for, move for, pray for.

Asking price. The price at which a seller lists his property for sale. Generally connotes a willingness to sell for less than the listed or asking price. May be applied to both real and personal property for sale though more commonly used in sales of real estate.

As per. A term which is not susceptible of literal translation, but which is commonly understood to mean, "in accordance with", or "in accordance with the terms of", or "as by the contract authorized".

Aspersions /əspárzhənz/. Term may mean the making of calumnious report or may mean nothing more than criticism or censure.

Asphyxia /æsfíksiyə/. Apparent death, suspended animation, in living organism due to deficiency of oxygen and excess of carbon dioxide in the blood.

Asphyxia carbonica /æsfíksiyə karbónəkə/. A suffocation from inhalation of coal gas, water gas, or carbon monoxide.

Asphyxiation /əsfiksiyéyshən/. A state of asphyxia.

Asportation /æspərtéyshən/. The removal of things from one place to another. The carrying away of goods; one of the circumstances requisite to constitute the offense of larceny. The distance away which the property must be moved to constitute the crime need not be substantial; a slight distance will do. Smith v. United States, C.A.Nev., 291 F.2d 220. But the entire property must be moved.

Asportation was an essential element of common-law kidnapping.

Asportavit /æspərtéyvət/. He carried away. Sometimes used as a noun to denote a carrying away. An "asportavit of personal chattels".

ASPR. Armed Services Procurement Regulations.

Assart /əsárt/. In English law, the offense committed in the forest, by pulling up the trees by the roots that are thickets and coverts for deer, and making the ground plain as arable land. It differs from waste, in that waste is the cutting down of coverts which may grow again, whereas assart is the plucking them up by the roots and utterly destroying them, so that they can never afterward grow. This is not an offense if done with license to convert forest into tillage ground.

Assart rents. Rents paid to the Crown for assorted lands.

Assassination /əsæsənéyshən/. Murder committed, usually, though not necessarily, for hire, without direct provocation or cause of resentment given to the murderer by the person upon whom the crime is committed; though an assassination of a public figure might be done by one acting alone for personal, social or political reasons. It is a federal crime, punishable as a homicide, to assassinate the President, President-elect, Vice President, or if there is no Vice President, the officer next in order of succession to the office of President, the Vice-President-elect, or any individual who is acting as President under the Constitution. 18 U.S.C.A. § 1751. In addition, advocating the overthrow of the government by assassination of any officer of such government is a crime under 18 U.S.C.A. § 2385.

Assault. Any willful attempt or threat to inflict injury upon the person of another, when coupled with an apparent present ability so to do, and any intentional display of force such as would give the victim reason to fear or expect immediate bodily harm, constitutes an assault. An assault may be committed without actually touching, or striking, or doing bodily harm, to the person of another. State v. Murphy, 7 Wash. App. 505, 500 P.2d 1276, 1281.

Frequently used to describe illegal force which is technically a battery. For crime of assault victim need not be apprehensive of fear if the outward gesture is menacing and defendant intends to harm, though for tort of assault, element of victim's apprehension is required. Com. v. Slaney, 345 Mass. 135, 185 N.E.2d 919. It is unlawful attempt to commit a battery. People v. Lopez, 271 C.A.2d 754, 77 Cal. Rptr. 59, 63.

In some jurisdictions degrees of the offense are established as first, second and even third degree assault.

See also Aggravated assault; Aggravated battery; Battery; Conditional assault; Felonious assault; Fresh complaint rule; Malicious assault with deadly weapon.

Aggravated assault. One committed with the intention of committing some additional crime; or one attended with circumstances of peculiar outrage or atrocity. This class includes assault with a dangerous or deadly weapon (*q.v.*).

A person is guilty of aggravated assault if he: (a) attempts to cause serious bodily injury to another, or causes such injury purposely, knowingly or recklessly under circumstances manifesting extreme indifference to the value of human life; or (b) attempts to cause or purposely or knowingly causes bodily injury to another with a deadly weapon. Model Penal Code, § 211.1.

Simple assault. An assault unaccompanied by any circumstances of aggravation. A person is guilty of simple assault if he (a) attempts to cause or purposely, knowingly or recklessly causes bodily injury to another; or (b) negligently causes bodily injury to another with a deadly weapon; or (c) attempts by physical menace to put another in fear of imminent serious bodily injury. Model Penal Code, § 211.1.

Assault and battery. Any unlawful touching of another which is without justification or excuse. It is both a tort, Trogun v. Fruchtman, 58 Wis.2d 569, 207 N.W.2d 297, as well as a crime, Scruggs v. State, Ind.App., 317 N.E.2d 807, 809. The two crimes differ from each other in that battery requires physical contact of some sort (bodily injury or offensive touching), whereas assault is committed without physical contact. In most jurisdictions, statutes have created aggravated assaults and batteries, punishable as felonies, and worded in various ways. See **Battery**.

Assault with dangerous or deadly weapon. An unlawful attempt or offer to do bodily harm without justification or excuse by use of any instrument calculated to do harm or cause death. An aggravated form of assault as distinguished from a simple assault; *e.g.* pointing loaded gun at one is an assault with dangerous weapon. State v. Gregory, 108 Ariz. 445, 501 P.2d 387, 390.

Assault with intent to commit manslaughter. An unlawful assault committed in such manner and with such means as would have resulted in commission of crime of manslaughter if person assaulted had died from effects of assault.

Assault with intent to commit murder. To constitute this assault, specific intent to kill, actuated by malice aforethought, must concur. Perez v. State, 114 Tex. Cr.R. 473, 22 S.W.2d 309, 310.

Assault with intent to commit rape. Crime is constituted by the existence of the facts which bring the offense within the definition of an assault, coupled with an intention to commit the crime of rape. Steptoe v. State, 134 Tex.Cr.R. 320, 115 S.W.2d 916, 917.

Assay /əséy/æsey/. The proof or trial, by chemical experiments, of the purity or fineness of metals; particularly of the precious metals, gold and silver. West v. State, 140 Tex.Cr.R. 493, 145 S.W.2d 580, 584. Examination and determination as to characteristics (as weight, measure, or quality).

Assayer. One whose business it is to make assays of the precious metals. West v. State, 140 Tex.Cr.R. 493, 145 S.W.2d 580, 584.

Assayer of the king. An officer of the royal mint, appointed by St. 2 Hen. VI, c. 12, who received and tested the bullion taken in for coining; also called *"assayator regis."*

Assay office. The U.S. Assay Office, under the Bureau of the Mint, is responsible for the process of assaying gold and silver, required by government, incidental to maintaining the coinage.

Assecurare /əsèkyərériy/. To assure, or make secure by pledges, or any solemn interposition of faith.

Assecuration /əsèkyəréyshən/. In European law, assurance; insurance of a vessel, freight, or cargo.

Assecurator /əsèkyəréydər/. In maritime law, an insurer.

Assemblage. A collection of persons. Also the act of coming together. Public address upon public grounds. In re Whitney, 57 Cal.App.2d 167, 134 P.2d 516, 521. Combining of adjoining lots into single large lot.

Assembly. The concourse or meeting together of a considerable number of persons at the same place. Also the persons so gathered.

Political assemblies are those required by the constitution and laws: for example, the general assembly.

The lower or more numerous branch of the legislature in many of the states (*e.g.* N.Y.) is also called the "Assembly" or "House of Assembly." See also **House of Representatives.**

Popular assemblies are those where the people meet to deliberate upon their rights; these are guaranteed by the Constitution. See **Assembly, right of.**

Assemblyman. Member of state Assembly (*q.v.*).

Assembly, right of. Right guaranteed by First Amendment, U.S. Constitution, allowing people to meet for any purpose connected with government; it encompasses meeting to protest governmental policies and actions and the promotion of ideas. See **Unlawful assembly.**

Assembly, unlawful. The congregating of people which results in antisocial behavior of the group, *e.g.* blocking a sidewalk, obstructing traffic, littering streets; but, a law which makes such congregating a crime because people may be annoyed is violative of the right of free assembly. Coates v. City of Cincinnati, 402 U.S. 611, 91 S.Ct. 1686, 29 L.Ed.2d 214. See **Unlawful assembly.**

Assent. Compliance; approval of something done; a declaration of willingness to do something in compliance with a request; acquiescence; agreement. To approve, ratify and confirm. It implies a conscious approval of facts actually known, as distinguished from mere neglect to ascertain facts. Sometimes it is equivalent to "authorize". See **Approval; Approve; Consent.**

Express assent. That which is openly declared.

Implied assent. That which is presumed by law, and proved by conduct of the parties. See **Consent** (*Implied consent*).

Mutual assent. The meeting of the minds of both or all the parties to a contract; the fact that each agrees to all the terms and conditions, in the same sense and with the same meaning as the others.

Assert. To state as true; declare; maintain.

Assertory covenant /əsɔ́rdəriy kǽvənənt/. One which affirms that a particular state of facts exists; an affirming promise under seal. See **Affirmation; Jurat.**

Assertory oath /əsɔ́rdəriy ówθ/. See **Oath.**

Assess /əsés/. To ascertain; fix the value of. To fix the amount of the damages or the value of the thing to be ascertained. To impose a pecuniary payment upon persons or property. To ascertain, adjust, and settle the respective shares to be contributed by several persons toward an object beneficial to them all, in proportion to the benefit received. To tax.

In connection with taxation of property, means to make a valuation and appraisal of property, usually in connection with listing of property liable to taxation, and implies the exercise of discretion on the part of officials charged with duty of assessing, including the listing or inventory of property involved, determination of extent of physical property, and placing of a value thereon. To adjust or fix the proportion of a tax which each person, of several liable to it, has to pay; to apportion a tax among several; to distribute taxation in a proportion founded on the proportion of burden and benefit. To calculate the rate and amount of taxes. To levy a charge on the owner of property for improvements thereto, such as for sewers or sidewalks.

"Access" is sometimes used as synonymous with "levy".

See also **Assessment.**

Assessable insurance. Insurance policy under which insured is liable for additional premium if losses are unusually large.

Assessable stock. Stock where the stockholder may have to pay more than his original investment if corporate affairs so require.

Assessed. Term is equivalent to "imposed." To value or appraise. Abrams v. City and County of San Francisco, 48 Cal.App.2d 1, 119 P.2d 197, 199.

Assessed valuation. Value on each unit of which a prescribed amount must be paid as property taxes. The worth or value of property established by taxing authorities on the basis of which the tax rate is applied. Commonly, however, it does not represent the true or market value of the property.

Assessment. In a general sense, the process of ascertaining and adjusting the shares respectively to be contributed by several persons towards a common beneficial object according to the benefit received. A valuation or a determination as to value of property. It is often used in connection with assessing property taxes or levying of property taxes. Also the amount assessed. See also **Assess; Equalization.**

Corporations. Installments of the money subscribed for shares of stock, called for from the subscribers by the directors, from time to time as the company requires money, are called "assessments," or, in England, "calls." While the terms "call" and "assessment" are generally used synonymously, the latter term applies with peculiar aptness to contributions above the par value of stock or the subscription liability of the stockholders; whereas "call" or "installments" means action of the board of directors demanding payment of all or portion of unpaid subscriptions.

Damages. Fixing the amount of damages to which the successful party in a suit is entitled after judgment has been taken; also the name given to the determination of the sum which a corporation proposing to take lands for a public use must pay in satisfaction of the demand proved or the value taken.

Insurance. An apportionment made in general average upon the various articles and interests at risk, according to their value at the time and place of being in safety, for contribution for damage and sacrifices purposely made, and expenses incurred for escape from impending common peril.

A sum specially levied in mutual benefit insurance upon a fixed and definite plan within the limit of the company's or society's fundamental law of organization to pay losses, or losses and expenses incurred, being to a certain degree substantially the equivalent of premiums. The periodical demands made by a mutual insurance company, under its charter and by-laws, upon the makers of premium notes, are also denominated "assessments." Meaning "premiums," Ancient Order of United Workmen of Kansas v. Hobbs, 136 Kan. 708, 18 P.2d 561, 562; and being the consideration for the insurance contracts.

Special assessment. A "special assessment" is in the nature of a tax levied upon property according to benefits conferred on the property. Davies v. City of Lawrence, 218 Kan. 551, 545 P.2d 1115, 1120. A levy upon the owners of property adjacent to a public improvement (*e.g.* sidewalks) to defray the capital cost thereof. It differs from a tax in that it is levied for a specific purpose and in an amount proportioned to the direct benefit of the property assessed.

Taxation. The listing and valuation of property for the purpose of apportioning a tax upon it, either according to value alone or in proportion to benefit received. Moore v. Johnson Service Co., W.Va., 219 S.E.2d 315, 319. Also determining the share of a tax to be paid by each of many persons; or apportioning the entire tax to be levied among the different taxable persons, establishing the proportion due from each. Northwestern Imp. Co. v. Henneford, 184 Wash. 502, 51 P.2d 1083, 1085. It fixes the liability of the taxpayer and ascertains the facts and furnishes the data for the proper preparation of the tax rolls. Dallas Joint Stock Land Bank of Dallas v. State, Tex.Civ. App., 118 S.W.2d 941, 942.

The process whereby the Internal Revenue Service imposes an additional tax liability. If, for example, the IRS audits a taxpayer's income tax return and finds gross income understated or deductions overstated, it will assess a deficiency in the amount of the tax that should have been paid in light of the adjustments made.

See also **Deficiency assessment; Jeopardy assessment.**

Assessment base. Total assessed value of all property in an assessment district.

Assessment company. In life insurance, a company in which a death loss is met by levying an assessment on the surviving members of the association.

Assessment contract. One wherein the payment of the benefit is in any manner or degree dependent on the collection of an assessment levied on persons holding similar contracts. See also **Assessment insurance.**

Assessment district. In taxation, any subdivision of territory, whether the whole or part of any municipality, in which by law a separate assessment of taxable property is made by the officers elected or appointed therefor.

Assessment for benefits. A burden levied under the power of taxation. Jackson v. City of Lake Worth, 156 Fla. 452, 23 So.2d 526, 528. See **Assessment.**

Assessment fund. The assessment fund of a mutual benefit association is the balance of the assessments, less expenses, out of which beneficiaries are paid.

Assessment insurance. Exists when benefit to be paid is dependent upon collection of such assessments as may be necessary for paying the amounts to insured. Keen v. Bankers Mut. Life Co., 230 Mo.App. 1072, 93 S.W.2d 85, 90. Type of mutual insurance where the policyholders are assessed whenever there is a loss.

Assessment list. The list furnished by the assessor to the board of equalization or board of assessment. See **Assessment roll.**

Assessment period. Means taxable period. Johnson City v. Clinchfield R. Co., 163 Tenn. 332, 43 S.W.2d 386, 387.

Assessment ratio. For purposes of taxation of property is the ratio of assessed value to fair market value. Campbell Chain Co. of Cal. v. Alameda County, 12 C.A.3d 248, 90 Cal.Rptr. 501, 504.

Assessment roll. In taxation, the list or roll of taxable persons and property, completed, verified, and deposited by the assessors.

Assessment work. Under the mining laws of the United States, the holder of an unpatented mining claim on the public domain is required, in order to hold his claim, to do labor or make improvements upon it to the extent of at least one hundred dollars in each year. 30 U.S.C.A. § 28. This is commonly called by miners "doing assessment work."

Assessor. An officer chosen or appointed to appraise, value, or assess property. A person learned in some particular science or industry, who sits with the judge on the trial of a cause requiring such special knowledge and gives his advice.

Asset Depreciation Range (ADR). The range of depreciable lives allowed by the Internal Revenue Service for a specific depreciable asset.

Asset dividend. See **Dividend.**

Assets /ǽsets/. Property of all kinds, real and personal, tangible and intangible, including, *inter alia*, for certain purposes, patents and causes of action which belong to any person including a corporation and the estate of a decedent. The entire property of a person, association, corporation, or estate that is applicable or subject to the payment of his or her or its debts.

See also **Dead asset; Marshalling assets.**

Accrued assets. Assets arising from revenues earned but not yet due.

Assets entre mains. L. Fr. Assets in hand; assets in the hands of executors or administrators, applicable for the payment of debts.

Assets per descent. That portion of the ancestor's estate which descends to the heir, and which is sufficient to charge him, as far as it goes, with the specialty debts of his ancestors.

Bankruptcy. The property or effects of a bankrupt or insolvent, applicable to the payment of his debts.

Capital assets. For income tax purposes, a capital asset is defined as all property held by a taxpayer (*e.g.* house, car, stocks, bonds), except for certain assets listed in I.R.C. § 1221. Under the tax laws however, a given asset may be treated as a capital asset for one purpose, and as an ordinary asset for another.

Broadly speaking, all assets are capital except those specifically excluded. Major categories of non-capital assets include: property held for resale in the normal course of business (*i.e.* inventory), trade accounts and notes receivable, depreciable property and real estate used in a trade or business (*i.e.* I.R.C. "§ 1231 assets"). I.R.C. § 1221.

Commercial assets. The aggregate of available property, stock in trade, cash, etc., belonging to a merchant or mercantile company.

Current assets. Assets readily convertible into cash, *e.g.* securities, notes, accounts receivable. See also *Quick assets*, infra.

Equitable assets. All assets which are chargeable with the payment of debts or legacies in equity, and which do not fall under the description of legal assets. Those portions of the property which by the ordinary rules of law are exempt from debts, but which the testator has voluntarily charged as assets, or which, being non-existent at law, have been created in equity. They are so called because they can be reached only by the aid and instrumentality of a court of equity, and because their distribution is governed by a different rule from that which governs the distribution of legal assets.

Fixed assets. Assets of a permanent or long-term nature used in operation of business and not intended for sale.

Frozen assets. Assets which are difficult to convert into cash (*e.g.* real estate for which there is no market); also, assets which cannot be used because of legal restriction.

Intangible assets. Assets to which an arbitrary dollar value is attached; *e.g.* patents, trademarks, goodwill.

Legal assets. See **Legal assets.**

Liquid assets. See *Current assets*, supra.

Net assets. Excess of assets over liabilities.

Net operating assets. The excess of cash and other assets which will be converted into cash in near future through normal operation over current liabilities.

Nominal assets. Assets whose value is difficult to determine, *e.g.* a judgment or claim; also, book value of asset in contrast to actual value.

Personal assets. Chattels, money, and other personal property belonging to a bankrupt, insolvent, or decedent estate, which go to the assignee or executor. See also **Personal effects.**

Probate assets. Property of a decedent available for the payment of debts and legacies; the estate coming to the heir or personal representative which is chargeable, in law or equity, with the obligations which such heir or representative is required, in his representative capacity, to discharge.

Quick assets. Accounting term used to describe cash and receivables, including notes and sometimes marketable investments, which will be converted into cash as part of normal operations. See also *Current assets*, supra.

Real assets. Land and real estate.

Wasting assets. Assets exhausted through use or loss of value; *e.g.* patents, oil wells, coal deposits.

Asseveration /əsèvəréyshən/. An affirmation; a positive assertion; a solemn declaration. This word is seldom, if ever, used for a declaration made under oath, but denotes a declaration accompanied with solemnity or an appeal to conscience, whereas by an oath one appeals to God as a witness of the truth of what one says.

Assign. To transfer, make over, or set over to another. To appoint, allot, select, or designate for a particular purpose, or duty. To point at, or point out; to set forth, or specify; to mark out or designate; to particularize, as to *assign errors* on a writ of error; to *assign breaches* of a covenant. See also **Assignment.**

Assignability. Quality or legal attribute which permits a thing to be transferred or negotiated.

Assignable. See **Assignability.**

Assignable lease. A lease which contains a provision permitting its transfer by lessee or one which is silent as to lessee's right to transfer his interest and hence a lease which may be transferred. Assignment of lease is distinguishable from sublease to extent, inter alia, that in assigning, lessee transfers his entire estate in the demised premises, whereas in sublease the sublessee acquires something less than the lessee's entire interest. Spears v. Canon de Carnue Land Grant, 80 N.M. 766, 461 P.2d 415, 417.

Assignation house. A bawdy house; a house of prostitution.

Assignatus utitur jure auctoris /æsəgnéydəs yúwdədər júriy októrəs/. An assignee uses the right of his principal; an assignee is clothed with the rights of his principal.

Assigned account. Pledge of account receivable to bank or factor as security for loan.

Assigned counsel. An attorney appointed by court to represent an indigent person; most commonly in criminal cases. See U.S. Constitution, Sixth Amendment (right to counsel); Fed.R.Crim.P. 44. See also **Counsel, right to.**

Assigned risk. A risk which is not ordinarily acceptable to insurers but for which coverage is required by state statute and which is, therefore, assigned to insurers participating in an assigned risk pool. See **Assigned risk plan.**

Assigned risk plan. In those states having compulsory motor vehicle insurance, statutes provide that persons who are unable to buy coverage may secure insurance through a statutory plan under which insurers are compelled to write coverage for such persons. The insurance is handled through a pool of insurers.

Assignee /æsə(g)níy/. A person to whom an assignment is made; grantee.

Under U.C.C., assignee is subject to all defenses which may be asserted against assignor by account debtor. U.C.C. § 9–318.

Assignee in fact is one to whom an assignment has been made in fact by the party having the right.

Assignee in law is one in whom the law vests the right; as an executor or administrator.

Assignee clause. A provision in Judiciary Act of 1789 preventing one who could not show diversity of citizenship to bring suit in Federal Court from assigning his claim to one who had the required diversity; modified in 28 U.S.C.A. § 1359 to prevent only assignment made collusively to invoke diversity jurisdiction. See Caribbean Mills, Inc. v. Kramer, C.A.5th, 392 F.2d 387.

Assignment. A transfer or making over to another of the whole of any property, real or personal, in possession or in action, or of any estate or right therein. It includes transfers of all kinds of property (Higgins v. Monckton, 28 Cal.App.2d 723, 83 P.2d 516, 519), including negotiable instruments. The transfer by a party of all of its rights to some kind of property, usually intangible property such as rights in a lease, mortgage, agreement of sale or a partnership. Tangible property is more often transferred by possession and by instruments conveying title such as a deed or a bill of sale.

Assignment for benefit of creditors. A general assignment for benefit of creditors is transfer of all or substantially all of debtor's property to another person in trust to collect any money owing to debtor, to sell property, to distribute the proceeds to his creditors and to return the surplus, if any, to debtor. Under Bankruptcy Act of 1898, such assignment was an "act of bankruptcy" if made within 4 months of bankruptcy. Bankruptcy Act (1898) § 3a(4). See also **Preferential assignment.**

Assignment of account. Transfer to assignee giving him a right to have moneys when collected applied to payment of his debt. Nanny v. H. E. Pogue Distillery Co., 56 Cal.App.2d 817, 133 P.2d 686, 688.

Assignment of counsel. See **Assigned counsel; Assistance of counsel; Counsel, right to.**

Assignment of dower. The act by which the share of a widow in her deceased husband's real estate is ascertained and set apart to her.

Assignment of error. See **Error.**

Assignment of income. A procedure whereby a taxpayer attempts to avoid the recognition of income by assigning the property that generates the income to another. Such a procedure will not avoid the recognition of income by the taxpayer making the assignment if it can be said that the income was earned at the point of the transfer. In this case, usually referred to as an anticipatory assignment of income, the income will be taxed to the person who earns it.

Assignment of wages. Transfer of right to collect wages from wage earner to creditor; generally, statutes govern the extent to which such assignment may be made.

Assignment pro tanto. Where an order is drawn upon a third party and made payable out of a particular fund then due or to become due to the drawer, the delivery of the order to the payee operates as an assignment pro tanto of the fund. Doyle v. East New York Sav. Bank, 44 N.Y.S.2d 318, 323.

Assignment with preferences. An assignment for the benefit of creditors, with directions to the assignee to prefer a specified creditor or class of creditors, by paying their claims in full before the others receive any dividend, or in some other manner. More usually termed a "preferential assignment." Such assignments may constitute an "act of bankruptcy" *(q.v.).*

Foreign assignment. An assignment made in a foreign country, or in another state.

General assignment. An assignment made for the benefit of *all* the assignor's creditors, instead of a few only; or one which transfers the *whole* of his estate to the assignee, instead of a part only.

Voluntary assignment. An assignment for the benefit of his creditors made by a debtor voluntarily, as distinguished from a compulsory assignment which takes place by operation of law in proceedings in bankruptcy. Such constitutes an assignment of a debtor's property in trust to pay his debts generally, in distinction from a transfer of property to a particular creditor in payment of his demand, or to a conveyance by way of collateral security or mortgage.

Assignor /əsáynər/. A person who assigns or transfers property to another. See **Grantor.**

Assigns. Assignees; those to whom property is, will, or may be assigned. Used *e.g.* in the phrase, in deeds, "heirs, administrators, and assigns to denote the assignable nature of the interest or right created." It generally comprehends all those who take either immediately or remotely from or under the assignor, whether by conveyance, devise, descent, or act of law.

Assisa /əsáyzə/. In old English and Scotch law, an assise; a kind of jury or inquest; a writ; a sitting of a court; an ordinance or statute; a fixed or specific time, number, quantity, quality, price, or weight; a tribute, fine, or tax; a real action; the name of a writ. See **Assise.**

Assisa armorum /əsáyzə armórəm/. Assise of arms. A statute or ordinance requiring the keeping of arms for the common defense.

Assisa cadere /əsáyzə kǽdəriy/. To fail in the assise; *i.e.*, to be nonsuited. 3 Bl.Comm. 402.

Assisa cadit in juratum /əsáyzə kǽdəd ən jəréydəm/. The assise falls (turns) into a jury; hence to submit a controversy to trial by jury.

Assisa continuanda /əsáyzə kəntìnyuwǽndə/. An ancient writ addressed to the justices of assise for the continuation of a cause, when certain facts put in issue could not have been proved in time by the party alleging them.

Assisa de Clarendon /əsáyzə dìy klǽrəndən/. The assise of Clarendon. A statute or ordinance passed in the tenth year of Henry II, by which those that were accused of any heinous crime, and not able to purge themselves, but must abjure the realm, had liberty of forty days to stay and try what succor they could get of their friends towards their sustenance in exile.

Assisa de foresta /əsáyzə dìy fóréstə/. Assise of the forest; a statute concerning orders to be observed in the royal forests.

Assisa de mensuris /əsáyzə dìy mens(y)úrəs/. Assise of measures. A common rule for weights and measures, established throughout England by Richard I, in the eighth year of his reign.

Assisa de nocumento /əsáyzə dìy nòkyəméntowə/. An assise of nuisance; a writ to abate or redress a nuisance.

Assisa de utrum /əsáyzə dìy yúwtrəm/. An obsolete writ, which lay for the parson of a church whose predecessor had alienated the land and rents of it.

Assisa friscæ fortiæ /əsáyzə frískiy fórshiyiy/. Assise of fresh force, which see.

Assisa mortis d'ancestoris /əsáyzə mórdəs dǽnsestórəs/. Assise of mort d'ancestor, which see.

Assisa novæ disseysinæ /əsáyzə nówviy dəsíyzəniy/. Assise of novel disseisin, which see.

Assisa panis et cerevisiæ /əsáyzə pǽnəs èt sərəvíshiyiy/. Assise of bread and ale, or beer. The name of a statute passed in the fifty-first year of Henry III, containing regulations for the sale of bread and ale; sometimes called the "statute of bread and ale."

Assisa proroganda /əsáyzə pròwrowgǽndə/. An obsolete writ, which was directed to the judges assigned to take assises, to stay proceedings, by reason of a party to them being employed in the king's business.

Assisa ultimæ præsentationis /əsáyzə ə́ltəmiy prèzəntèyshiyównəs/. Assise of darrein presentment *(q.v.)*.

Assisa venalium /əsáyzə vənéyliyəm/. The assise of salable commodities, or of things exposed for sale.

Assise, or **assize** /əsáyz/. An ancient species of court, consisting of a certain number of men, usually twelve, who were summoned together to try a disputed cause, performing the functions of a jury, except that they gave a verdict from their own investigation and knowledge and not upon evidence adduced. From the fact that they sat together *(assideo)*, they were called the "assise." A court composed of an assembly of knights and other substantial men, with the baron or justice, in a certain place, at an appointed time. The verdict or judgment of the jurors or recognitors of assise. 3 Bl.Comm. 57, 59.

In later English law, the name "assises" or "assizes" was given to the court, time, or place where the judges of assise and *nisi prius*, who were sent by special commission from the crown on circuits through the kingdom, proceeded to take indictments, and to try such disputed causes issuing out of the courts at Westminster as were then ready for trial, with the assistance of a jury from the particular county. These judges of assise were the successors of the ancient "justices in eyre." They sat by virtue of four separate authorities: (1) Commission of Oyer and Terminter, (2) of goal delivery, (3) of nisi prius, and (4) Commission of Peace. In 1971 the Crown Court was established which superseded the criminal jurisdiction of courts of assise and all the jurisdiction of quarter sessions. The assise courts were accordingly abolished.

Anything reduced to a certainty in respect to time, number, quantity, quality, weight, measure, etc.

A species of writ, or real action, said to have been invented by Glanville, chief justice to Henry II, and having for its object to determine the right of possession of lands, and to recover the possession. 3 Bl. Comm. 184, 185.

The whole proceedings in court upon a writ of assise. The verdict or finding of the jury upon such a writ. 3 Bl.Comm. 57.

See also **Certificate of assize.**

Assise of Clarendon. See **Assisa.**

Assise of darrein presentment. A writ of assise which formerly lay when a man or his ancestors under whom he claimed presented a clerk to a benefice, who was instituted, and afterwards, upon the next avoidance, a stranger presented a clerk and thereby disturbed the real patron. 3 Bl.Comm. 245. It has given way to the remedy by *quare impedit.*

Assise of fresh force. In old English practice, a writ which lay by the usage and custom of a city or borough, where a man was disseised of his lands and tenements in such city or borough. It was called "fresh force," because it was to be sued within forty days after the party's title accrued to him.

Assise of mort d'ancestor. A real action which lay to recover land of which a person had been deprived on the death of his ancestor by the abatement or intrusion of a stranger. 3 Bl.Comm. 185. It was abolished by St. 3 & 4 Wm. IV, c. 27.

Assise of Northhampton. A re-enactment and enlargement (1176) of the Assise of Clarendon.

Assise of novel disseisin. A writ of assise which lay for the recovery of lands or tenements, where the claimant had been lately disseised.

Assise of nuisance. A writ of assise which lay where a nuisance had been committed to the complainant's freehold; either for abatement of the nuisance or for damages.

Assise of the forest. A statute touching orders to be observed in the king's forests.

Assise of utrum. A writ of assise which lay for a parson to recover lands which his predecessor had improperly allowed the church to be deprived of. 3 Bl.Comm. 257.

An assise for the trial of the question of whether land is a lay fee, or held in frankalmoigne.

Assise rents. The certain established rents of the freeholders and ancient copyholders of a manor; so called because they are *assised*, or made precise and certain.

Grand assize. A peculiar species of trial by jury, introduced in the time of Henry II, giving the tenant or defendant in a writ of right the alternative of a trial by battel, or by his peers. Abolished by 3 & 4 Wm. IV, c. 42, § 13. 3 Bl.Comm. 341. See **Battel**.

Assiser /əsáyzər/. An assessor; juror; an officer who has the care and oversight of weights and measures.

Assisors /əsáyzərz/. In Scotch law, jurors; the persons who formed that kind of court which in Scotland was called an "assise," for the purpose of inquiring into and judging divers civil causes, such as perambulations, cognitions, molestations, purprestures, and other matters; like jurors in England.

Assist. To help; aid; succor; lend countenance or encouragement to; participate in as an auxiliary. To contribute effort in the complete accomplishment of an ultimate purpose intended to be effected by those engaged.

Assistance, or (assistants) court of. See **Court of assistants**.

Assistance of counsel. Sixth Amendment to Federal Constitution, guaranteeing accused in criminal prosecution "assistance of counsel" for his defense, means effective assistance, as distinguished from bad faith, sham, mere pretense or want of opportunity for conferences and preparation. Fed.R.Crim.P. 44; Gideon v. Wainwright, 372 U.S. 335, 83 S.Ct. 792, 9 L.Ed.2d 799; Geders v. U. S., 425 U.S. 80, 96 S.Ct. 1330, 47 L.Ed.2d 592. See **Assigned counsel; Counsel, right to**.

Assistance, writ of. See **Writ of assistance**.

Assistant. A deputy, aide, or subordinate; as an assistant assessor. One who stands by and aids or helps another. Ordinarily refers to employee whose duties are to help his superior, to whom he must look for authority to act. State ex rel. Dunn v. Ayers, 112 Mont. 120, 113 P.2d 785, 788.

Assisus /əsáyzəs/. Rented or farmed out for a specified assise; that is, a payment of a certain assessed rent in money or provisions.

Assize /əsáyz/. See **Assise**.

Assizes de Jerusalem /əsáyzəz də jərúwzələm/. A code of feudal jurisprudence prepared by an assembly of barons and lords A.D. 1099, after the conquest of Jerusalem. It was compiled principally from the laws and customs of France.

Associate. Signifies confederacy or union for a particular purpose, good or ill. To join together, as *e.g.* partners. See **Association**.

Having subordinate status; *e.g.* associate professor.

An officer in each of the English courts of common law, appointed by the chief judge of the court, and holding his office during good behavior, whose duties were to superintend the entry of causes, to attend the sittings of *nisi prius*, and there receive and enter verdicts, and to draw up the posteas and any orders of *nisi prius*. The associates were later officers of the Supreme Court of Judicature, and are styled "Masters of the Supreme Court". Duties of associates are now carried out by clerks in the Crown Office and Associates Department of the Central Office of the Supreme Court.

Associate justices. Judges of courts, other than the presiding or chief justice.

Associates in office. Those who are united in action; who have a common purpose; who share the responsibility or authority and among whom is reasonable equality. Those who are authorized by law to perform the duties jointly or as a body.

Association. The act of a number of persons in uniting together for some special purpose or business. It is a term of vague meaning used to indicate a collection or organization of persons who have joined together for a certain or common object. Also, the persons so joining; the state of being associated.

An unincorporated society; a body of persons united and acting together without a charter, but upon the methods and forms used by incorporated bodies for the prosecution of some common enterprise. Clark v. Grand Lodge of Brotherhood of Railroad Trainmen, 328 Mo. 1084, 43 S.W.2d 404, 408. It is not a legal entity separate from the persons who compose it. See also **Affiliation**.

An organization treated as a corporation for Federal tax purposes even though it may not qualify as such under applicable state law. What is designated as a trust or a partnership, for example, may be classified as an association if it clearly possesses corporate attributes. Corporate attributes include: centralized management, continuity of existence, free transferability of interests, and limited liability. I.R.C. § 7701(a)(3).

A "business trust" is an "association" when it has a continuing entity throughout trust period, centralized management, continuity of trust uninterrupted by death among beneficial owners, means for transfer of beneficial interests, and limitation of personal liabilities of participants to property embarked in undertaking. Fletcher v. Clark, D.C.Wyo., 57 F.Supp. 479, 480.

See also Articles of association; Confederacy; Joint stock association; Non-profit association; Professional association; Unincorporated association.

Partnership association. See **Partnership**.

Professional corporation. See **Corporation** (*Professional corporation*).

Unincorporated association. A confederation of individuals organized for a specific purpose which may or may not be profit making but which is not chartered as a corporation.

Association, freedom of. See **Assembly, right of**.

Association of American Law Schools, The. AALS is literally an association of law schools. After a school has graduated at least three annual classes it is eligible to apply for membership. Compliance with the rules of membership are determined through a three or four person inspection team. Recommendations for admission to membership are made by the Executive Committee, upon advice of the Accreditation Committee. Membership is attained by action of the House of Representatives.

Assoil /əsóyl/. (Spelled also *assoile, absoile, assoilyie*.) To absolve; acquit; to set free; to deliver from excommunication.

As soon as. This term has a relative meaning according to the thing which is to be done. It may denote merely a reasonable time; or may be equivalent to "whenever", or may mean "immediately".

As soon as may be. Promptly and with due diligence; as soon as was reasonably possible; within a reasonable time; as soon as possible; forthwith; as soon as they conveniently can. George A. Fuller Co. v. Jersey City, 21 N.J.Misc. 38, 29 A.2d 720, 722.

As soon as practicable. Means reasonable time. These words are not synonymous with "as soon as possible"; they mean ordinarily as soon as reasonably can be expected; or "in due time". But the words have also been construed as practically synonymous with speedily.

The words "as soon as practicable" within liability policy requirement the insured will notify the insurer of an occurrence as soon as practicable means within reasonable time in view of all the facts and circumstances of each particular case. Greenway v. Selected Risks Ins. Co., D.C.App., 307 A.2d 753, 755.

As speedily as possible. Means within reasonable time or without unreasonable delay having regard to all the circumstances of the case and the things to be done. Tatum v. Levi, 117 Cal.App. 83, 3 P.2d 963, 967.

Assume. To pretend. To undertake; engage; promise. To take to or upon one's self. Also taking up, receiving, adopting, taking to oneself, or to put on deceitfully, take appearance of, affect, or outwardly seem. To take on, become bound as another is bound, or put oneself in place of another as to an obligation or liability. Texas Employers' Ins. Ass'n v. Texas & P. Ry. Co., Tex.Civ.App., 129 S.W.2d 746, 749. See also **Assumption**.

Assumed facts. Facts concerning which no evidence has been introduced at trial and hence no rulings of law or jury instructions are required. In argument, a hypothetical set of facts used to illustrate a point of law.

Assumed name. See **Alias**.

Assumed risk. See **Assumption of risk**.

A summo remedio ad inferiorem actionem non habetur regressus, neque auxilium /èy sə́mow rəmíyd(i)yow æd infiriyórəm ǽkshiyównəm nòn həbíydər rəgrésəs, nékwiy ogzíl(i)yəm/. From (after using) the highest remedy, there can be no recourse (going back) to an inferior action, nor assistance (derived from it). A maxim in the old law of real actions, when there were grades in the remedies given; the rule being that a party who brought a writ of right, which was the highest writ in the law, could not afterwards resort or descend to an inferior remedy. 3 Bl.Comm. 193, 194.

Assumpsit /əsə́m(p)sət/. Lat. He undertook; he promised.

A promise or engagement by which one person assumes or undertakes to do some act or pay something to another. It may be either oral or in writing, but is not under seal. It is *express* if the promisor puts his engagement in distinct and definite language; it is *implied* where the law infers a promise (though no formal one has passed) from the conduct of the party or the circumstances of the case. Dukes v. Rogers, 67 Ga.App. 661, 21 S.E.2d 295, 297.

A common law form of action which lies for the recovery of damages for the non-performance of a parol or simple contract; or a contract that is neither of record nor under seal. A liberal and equitable action, applicable to almost every case where money has been received which in equity and good conscience ought to be refunded; express promise is not necessary to sustain action, but it may be maintained whenever anything is received or done from the circumstances of which the law implies a promise of compensation. The action of *assumpsit* differs from *trespass* and *trover*, which are founded on a tort, not upon a contract; from *covenant* and *debt*, which are appropriate where the ground of recovery is a sealed instrument, or special obligation to pay a fixed sum; and from *replevin*, which seeks the recovery of specific property, if attainable, rather than of damages.

Express assumpsit. See **Express assumpsit**.

General (common or indebitatus) assumpsit is an action of assumpsit brought upon the promise or contract implied by law in certain cases. It is founded upon what the law terms an implied promise on the part of defendant to pay what, in good conscience, he is bound to pay to plaintiff.

Special assumpsit is an action of assumpsit brought upon an express contract or promise.

Assumpsit for money had and received. Is of equitable character and lies, in general, whenever defendant has received money which in equity and good conscience he ought to pay to plaintiff.

Assumpsit on quantum meruit /əsə́m(p)sət òn kwóntəm méruwət/. When a person employs another to do work for him, without any agreement as to his compensation, the law implies a promise from the employer to the workman that he will pay him for his services as much as he may deserve or merit. In such case, the plaintiff may suggest in his declaration that the defendant promised to pay him as much as he reasonably deserved, and then aver that his trouble was worth such a sum of money, which the defendant has omitted to pay. This is called an "assumpsit on quantum meruit". Travis v. Kennedy, Tex.Civ.App., 66 S.W.2d 444, 446. See also **Quantum meruit**.

Assumption. The act of conceding or taking for granted. Laying claim to or taking possession of.

The act or agreement of assuming or taking upon one's self. The undertaking or adoption of a debt or obligation primarily resting upon another, as where the purchaser of real estate "assumes" a mortgage resting upon it, in which case he adopts the mortgage debt as his own and becomes personally liable for its payment. The difference between the purchaser of land assuming a mortgage on it and simply buying subject to the mortgage, is that in the former case he makes himself personally liable for the payment of the mortgage debt, while in the latter case he does not. When he takes the conveyance subject to the mortgage, he is bound only to the extent of the property. Where one "assumes" a lease, he takes to himself the obligations, contracts, agreements, and benefits to which the other contracting party was entitled under the terms of the lease. See **Assumption of mortgage**.

Assumption clause. In mortgages, a provision that the mortgage may not be assumed without written consent of mortgagee. See **Assumption of mortgage**. Also a provision in an instrument of transfer in which the transferee agrees to assume an obligation of the transferor.

Assumption fee. Lender's charge for processing records for new buyer assuming an existing loan (mortgage).

Assumption of care. See **Good Samaritan doctrine**.

Assumption of indebtedness. Means for one person to bind himself to pay debt incurred by another. Pawnee County Excise Board v. Kurn, 187 Okl. 110, 101 P.2d 614, 618.

Assumption of mortgage. To take or acquire a mortgage or deed of trust from some prior holder. Thus, a purchaser may assume or take over the mortgage of the seller. Often this requires permission of the mortgagee. This is distinguishable from taking equity of redemption subject to mortgage because in latter case grantee is not contractually bound to pay mortgage, whereas if he assumes the mortgage, he binds himself to mortgagor to pay the mortgage and to fulfill all other terms and conditions of mortgage. See also **Assumption**.

Assumption of risk. The doctrine of assumption of risk, also known as volenti non fit injuria, means legally that a plaintiff may not recover for an injury to which he assents, i.e., that a person may not recover for an injury received when he voluntarily exposes himself to a known and appreciated danger. The requirements for the defense of volenti non fit injuria are that: (1) the plaintiff has knowledge of facts constituting a dangerous condition, (2) he knows the condition is dangerous, (3) he appreciates the nature or extent of the danger, and (4) he voluntarily exposes himself to the danger. An exception may be applicable even though the above factors have entered into a plaintiff's conduct if his actions come within the rescue or humanitarian doctrine. Clarke v. Brockway Motor Trucks, D.C.Pa., 372 F.Supp. 1342, 1347.

A defense to action of negligence which consists of showing that the plaintiff, knowing the dangers and risk involved, chose to act as he did. An affirmative defense which the defendant in a negligence action must plead and prove. Fed.R.Civil P. 8(c). It is not a defense under state workers' compensation laws or in FELA actions. Many states have abolished the defense of assumption of risk in automobile cases with the enactment of no-fault insurance acts or comparative negligence acts.

Assurance. The act or action of assuring; e.g. a pledge, guaranty, or surety. A declaration tending to inspire full confidence.

The deed or instrument by which real property is conveyed; also, the act of conveying such.

Same as "Insurance"; term used in Canada and England.

In England, the legal evidences of the transfer of property are called the "common assurances" of the kingdom, whereby every man's estate is assured to him, and all controversies, doubts, and difficulties are either prevented or removed.

Assurance, further, covenant for. See **Covenant** (Covenant for further assurance).

Assure. To make certain and put beyond doubt. To declare, aver, avouch, assert, or ensure positively. To declare solemnly; to assure to any one with design of inspiring belief or confidence. Used interchangeably with "insure" in insurance law. In real property documents it means a warranty; and in business documents, generally, it means a pledge or security. Utilities Engineering Institute v. Kofod, 185 Misc. 1035, 58 N.Y.S.2d 743, 745.

Assured. A person who has been insured by some insurance company, or underwriter, against losses or perils mentioned in the policy of insurance. Ordinarily synonymous with "insured".

Assured clear distance ahead. Requires driver to keep automobile under such control that he can stop in distance that he can clearly see; the distance varying with circumstances. Lauerman v. Strickler, 141 Pa. Super. 240, 14 A.2d 608, 610; Smiley v. Arrow Spring Bed Co., 138 Ohio St. 81, 33 N.E.2d 3, 5, 6, 7, 9.

Assurer. An insurer against certain perils and dangers; an underwriter; an indemnifier.

Astipulation /əstìpyəléyshən/. A mutual agreement, assent, and consent between parties; also a witness or record.

Astitrarius hæres /æstrətériyəs híriyz/. An heir apparent who has been placed, by conveyance, in possession of his ancestor's estate during such ancestor's lifetime.

Astitution /æstət(y)úwshən/. An arraignment (q.v.).

Astrarius /æstrériyəs/. In old English law, a householder; belonging to the house; a person in actual possession of a house.

Astrarius hæres /æstrériyəs híriyz/. Where the ancestor by conveyance hath set his heir apparent and his family in a house in his lifetime.

Astrer /ǽstrər/. In old English law, a householder, or occupant of a house or hearth.

Astrihiltet. In Saxon law, a penalty for a wrong done by one in the king's peace. The offender was to replace the damage twofold.

Astrum /ǽstrəm/. A house, or place of habitation.

Asylum /əsáyləm/. A sanctuary, or place of refuge and protection, where criminals and debtors found shelter, and from which they could not be taken without sacrilege. Shelter; refuge; protection from the hand of justice. The word includes not only place, but also shelter, security, protection. While a foreign country has the right to offer an asylum to fugitives from other countries, there is no corresponding right on the part of the alien to claim asylum. This right of asylum has been voluntarily limited by most countries by treaties providing for the extradition (q.v.) of fugitive criminals (international extradition).

In time of war, a place of refuge in neutral territory for belligerent warships.

An institution for the protection and relief of unfortunates, as asylums for the poor, or for the insane; though this term is no longer generally used for such institutions.

At. A term of considerable elasticity of meaning, and somewhat indefinite. A function word to describe or indicate presence or occurrence in, on, or near; or to indicate the means, cause, or manner; or to indicate that with which one is occupied or employed. As used to fix a time, it does not necessarily mean *eo instante* or the identical time named, or even a fixed definite moment. Often expresses simply nearness and proximity, and consequently may denote a reasonable time.

Atamita /ətǽmədə/. In the civil law, a great-great-great-grandfather's sister.

At any time. Grant of time without limit. Haworth v. Hubbard, 220 Ind. 611, 44 N.E.2d 967, 970. Period of time limited by circumstances. Imes v. Globe Oil & Refining Co., 184 Okl. 79, 84 P.2d 1106, 1107, 1108. Within a reasonable time. Haworth v. Hubbard, 220 Ind. 611, 44 N.E.2d 967, 970.

At any time prior to. Synonymous with "not later than". Hughes v. United States, C.C.A.Tenn., 114 F.2d 285, 287.

At arm's length. Beyond the reach of personal influence or control. Parties are said to deal "at arm's length" when each stands upon the strict letter of his rights, and conducts the business in a formal manner, without trusting to the other's fairness or integrity, and without being subject to the other's control or overmastering influence. See **Arm's length transaction.**

Atavia /ətéyviyə/. In the civil law, a great-grandmother's grandmother.

Atavunculus /æ̀dəváŋkyələs/. The brother of a great-grandfather's grandmother, or a great-great-great-grandfather's brother.

Atavus /ǽdəvəs/. The male ascendant in the fifth degree. The great-grandfather's or great-grandmother's grandfather; a fourth grandfather.

Ataxia. Condition involving impaired coordinative control over the extremities; power present in the extremities, but control is lacking.

At bar. Before the court. "The case at bar," etc.

A tempore cujus contrarii memoria non existet /èy témpəriy kyúwjəs kəntrériyay memóriyə non egzístət/. From a time of which there is no memory to the contrary.

A teneris annis /èy ténərəs ǽnəs/. By reason of youth.

A terme. For a or the term.

A terme de sa vie. For the term of his life.

A terme que n'est mye encore passe. For a term that has not yet passed.

A terme que passe est. For a term that has passed.

Atha /áθə/. (Spelled also *Atta, Athe, Atte.*) In Saxon law, an oath; the power or privilege of exacting and administering an oath.

Atheist. One who does not believe in the existence of a God.

Atia /éysh(iy)ə/. Hatred or ill-will. See **De odio et atia.**

Atilian law. See **Lex atilia.**

Atinian law. See **Lex atinia.**

At issue. Whenever the parties come to a point in the pleadings which is affirmed on one side and denied on the other, they are said to be at an issue.

ATLA. American Trial Lawyers Association.

At large. Not limited to any particular place, district, person, matter, or question; open to discussion or controversy; not precluded. Free; unrestrained; not under corporal control, as a ferocious animal so free from restraint as to be liable to do mischief. Fully; in detail; in an extended form.

Elected officials chosen by the voters of the State as a whole rather than from separate Congressional or legislative districts.

At law. According to law; by, for, or in law. Particularly in distinction from that which is done in or according to equity; or in titles such as sergeant at law, barrister at law, attorney or counsellor at law.

At least. In deed of trust covenant specifying amount of fire insurance, means at lowest estimate, at smallest concession or claim, in smallest or lowest degree, at smallest number. Browne v. Franklin Fire Ins. Co., 225 Mo.App. 665, 37 S.W.2d 977, 979.

Atmatertera /æ̀tmeytárdərə/. A great-grandfather's grandmother's sister (*ataviæ soror*), called by Bracton "*atmatertera magna.*"

Atomize. To reduce to atoms or atom-like particles; pulverize; spray. Stearns-Roger Mfg. Co. v. Greenawalt, C.C.A.Colo., 62 F.2d 1033, 1039.

At once. In contracts of various kinds the phrase is construed as synonymous with "immediately" and "forthwith," where the subject-matter is the giving of notice. The use of such term does not ordinarily call for instantaneous action, but rather that notice shall be given within such time as is reasonable in view of the circumstances. Likewise, contracts or statutes requiring the performance of a particular act "at once" are usually held to mean simply within a reasonable time. An order to "ship at once" is synonymous with "as soon as possible". Myers v. Hardin, 208 Ark. 505, 186 S.W.2d 925, 928.

A tort. Without reason; unjustly; wrongfully.

A tort et a travers. Without consideration or discernment.

A tort ou a droit. Right or wrong.

At par. Said of a bond or preferred stock issued or selling at its face value.

Atpatruus /ætpǽtruwəs/. The brother of a great-grandfather's grandfather.

Atrocious assault and battery. An assault by maiming and wounding. Aggravated assault.

Atrocity. A word implying conduct that is outrageously or wantonly wicked, criminal, vile, cruel; extremely horrible and shocking.

Atrophy /ǽtrəfiy/. Degeneration or wasting away of tissues, organs or parts due to lack of use; disease or interference with nerve supply.

ATS. At suit of.

At sea. Out of the limits of any port or harbor on the sea-coast. U. S. v. Symonds, 120 U.S. 46, 7 S.Ct. 411, 30 L.Ed. 557.

Attach. Seizure of property under a writ of attachment. See **Attachment**.

To bind, fasten, tie, or connect, to make fast or join; its antonyms are separate, detach, remove.

Attaché /ædəshéy/ətǽshèy/. A person attached to an embassy, to the office of an ambassador, or to a foreign legation. One connected with an office, *e.g.*, a public office.

Attached. A term describing the physical union of two otherwise independent structures or objects, or the relation between two parts of a single structure, each having its own function. As applied to buildings, the term is often synonymous with "annexed." See, also **Fixture.**

Attached account. Account against which court order has been issued; payments can only be made with consent of court.

Attachiamenta /ətæch(iy)əméntə/. L. Lat. **Attachment**.

Attachiamenta bonorum /ətæch(iy)əmentə bownórəm/. A distress formerly taken upon goods and chattels, by the legal *attachiators* or bailiffs, as security to answer an action for personal estate or debt.

Attachiamenta de placitus coronæ /ətæch(iy)əméntə diy plǽsədəs kərówniy/. Attachment of pleas of the crown.

Attachiamenta de spinis et boscis /ətæch(iy)əméntə dìy spáynəs èt bóskəs/. A privilege granted to the officers of a forest to take to their own use thorns, brush, and windfalls, within their precincts.

Attachiamentum /ətæch(iy)əméntəm/. L. Lat. An attachment.

Attaching creditor. See **Creditor**.

Attachment. The act or process of taking, apprehending, or seizing persons or property, by virtue of a writ, summons, or other judicial order, and bringing the same into the custody of the court for the purpose of securing satisfaction of the judgment ultimately to be entered in the action. While formerly the main objective of attachment was to coerce the defendant debtor to appear in court by seizer of his property, today the writ of attachment is used primarily to seize the debtor's property in order to secure the debt or claim of the creditor in the event that a judgment is rendered. The remedy of attachment is governed strictly by state statutes, with such differing considerably as to when attachment is available (the majority of states providing that such is available at or after the commencement of the main action until entry of judgment). Federal courts follow the local rules or statutes relating to attachment. Fed.R.Civil P. 64.

A remedy ancillary to an action by which plaintiff is enabled to acquire a lien upon property or effects of defendant for satisfaction of judgment which plaintiff may obtain. Lipscomb v. Rankin, C.C.A.Tex., 139 S.W.2d 367, 369.

See also **Garnishment; Levy.**

Distinguished from execution. See **Execution.**

Domestic and foreign. In some jurisdictions it is common to give the name "domestic attachment" to one issuing against a resident debtor (upon the special ground of fraud, intention to abscond, etc.), and to designate an attachment against a non-resident, or his property, as "foreign."

Where the defendant is a non-resident, or beyond the territorial jurisdiction of the court, his goods or land within the territory may be seized upon process of attachment; whereby he will be compelled to enter an appearance, or the court acquires jurisdiction so far as to dispose of the property attached. This is sometimes called "foreign attachment." In such a case, the proceeding becomes in substance one in rem against the attached property.

Persons. A writ issued by a court of record, commanding the sheriff to bring before it a person who has been guilty of contempt of court, either in neglect or abuse of its process or of subordinate powers. A capias (*q.v.*).

Property. A species of mesne process, by which a writ is issued at the institution or during the progress of an action, commanding the sheriff to seize the property, rights, credits, or effects of the defendant to be held as security for the satisfaction of such judgment as the plaintiff may recover. It is principally used against absconding, concealed, or fraudulent debtors. Mass.R. Civil P. 4.1.

Attachment bond. A bond used to dissolve an attachment so as to free the property subject to the attachment for sale or other disposition; may be surety company bond or personal bond with sureties. Plaintiff then looks to bond for satisfaction of his judgment.

Attachment execution. A name given in some states to a process of garnishment for the satisfaction of a judgment. As to the judgment debtor it is an execution; but as to the garnishee it is an original process—a summons commanding him to appear and show cause, if any he has, why the judgment should not be levied on the goods and effects of the defendant in his hands.

Attachment of privilege. In old English law, a process by which a man, by virtue of his privilege, calls another to litigate in that court to which he himself belongs, and who has the privilege to answer there. A writ issued to apprehend a person in a privileged place.

Attachment of risk. Used to describe point in time, generally when title passes, when risk of loss for destruction of property which is subject of sale passes to buyer from seller. U.C.C. § 2–509.

Attachment of the forest. In old English law, one of the three courts formerly held in forests. The highest court was called "justice in eyre's seat;" the middle, the "swainmote;" and the lowest, the "attachment."

Attain. To reach or come to by progression or motion; to arrive at; as, to attain a ripe old age. Watkins v. Metropolitan Life Ins. Co., 156 Kan. 27, 131 P.2d 722, 723.

Attainder /ətéyndər/. At common law, that extinction of civil rights and capacities which took place whenever a person who had committed treason or felony received sentence of death for his crime.

The effect of "attainder" upon such felon was, in general terms, that all his estate, real and personal, was forfeited. At the common law, attainder resulted in three ways, viz.: *by confession, by verdict,* and *by process* or *outlawry.* The first case was where the prisoner pleaded guilty at the bar, or having fled to sanctuary, confessed his guilt and abjured the realm to save his life. The second was where the prisoner pleaded not guilty at the bar, and the jury brought in a verdict against him. The third, when the person accused made his escape and was outlawed.

In England, by statute 33 & 34 Vict. c. 23, attainder upon conviction, with consequent corruption of blood, forfeiture, or escheat, was abolished. In the United States, the doctrine of attainder is now scarcely known, although during and shortly after the Revolution acts of attainder were passed by several of the states. The passage of such bills is expressly forbidden by the Constitution (Art. I, Sec. 9).

Bills of attainder. Such special acts of the legislature as inflict capital punishments upon persons supposed to be guilty of high offenses, such as treason and felony, without any conviction in the ordinary course of judicial proceedings. If an act inflicts a milder degree of punishment than death, it is called a "bill of pains and penalties," but both are included in the prohibition in the Constitution (Art. I, Sec. 9). Losier v. Sherman, 157 Kan. 153, 138 P.2d 272, 273; State v. Graves, 352 Mo. 1102, 182 S.W.2d 46, 54. See also **Bill.**

Attaint /ətéynt/. Attainted, stained, or blackened.

In old English practice, a writ which lay to inquire whether a jury of twelve men had given a false verdict, in order that the judgment might be reversed. 3 Bl.Comm. 402. This inquiry was made by a grand assise or jury of twenty-four persons, usually knights, and, if they found the verdict a false one, the judgment was that the jurors should become infamous, should forfeit their goods and the profits of their lands, should themselves be imprisoned, and their wives and children thrust out of doors, should have their houses razed, their trees extirpated, and their meadows plowed up, and that the plaintiff should be restored to all that he lost by reason of the unjust verdict. 3 Bl.Comm. 404.

Attaint d'une cause /ətéyn d(y)ùwn kówz/. In French law, the gain of a suit.

Attempt. In statutes and in cases other than criminal prosecutions an "attempt" ordinarily means an intent combined with an act falling short of the thing intended. It may be described as an endeavor to do an act, carried beyond mere preparation, but short of execution.

Criminal law. An effort or endeavor to accomplish a crime, amounting to more than mere preparation or planning for it, which, if not prevented, would have resulted in the full consummation of the act attempted, but which, in fact, does not bring to pass the party's ultimate design. The requisite elements of an "attempt" to commit a crime are: (1) an intent to commit it, (2) an overt act toward its commission, (3) failure of consummation, and (4) the apparent possibility of commission. State v. Stewart, Mo.App., 537 S.W.2d 579, 581.

A person is guilty of an attempt to commit a crime if, acting with the kind of culpability otherwise required for commission of the crime, he: (a) purposely engages in conduct which would constitute the crime if the attendant circumstances were as he believes them to be; or (b) when causing a particular result is an element of the crime, does or omits to do anything with the purpose of causing or with the belief that it will cause such result without further conduct on his part; or (c) purposely does or omits to do anything which, under the circumstances as he believes them to be, is an act or omission constituting a substantial step in a course of conduct planned to culminate in his commission of the crime. Model Penal Code, § 5.01.

Attendant, *n.* One who owes a duty or service to another, or in some sort depends upon him. One who follows and waits upon another.

Attendant, *adj.* Accompanying, or connected with.

Attendant circumstances. Facts surrounding an event, such as the time, place and declarations of a testator prior to and immediately following execution of his will.

Attendant terms. In English law, terms (usually mortgages), for a long period of years, which are created or kept outstanding for the purpose of *attending* or waiting upon and protecting the inheritance. A phrase used in conveyancing to denote estates which are kept alive, after the objects for which they were originally created have ceased, so that they might be deemed merged or satisfied, for the purpose of protecting or strengthening the title of the owner. By the Satisfied Terms Act of 1845, any attendant term becoming satisfied after the Act immediately ceased. But the Act did not apply to leaseholds. That Act was repealed and replaced by Sec. 5 of the Law of Property Act of 1925, which applies to terms created out of leaseholds as well as terms created out of freeholds.

Attentat /əténtət/. Lat. He attempts.

In the civil and canon law, anything wrongfully innovated or *attempted* in a suit by an inferior judge (or judge *a quo*) pending an appeal.

Attention. Consideration with a view to action; notice; attentiveness; the act or state of attending.

Atterminare /ətàrmənériy/. In old English law, to put off to a succeeding term; to prolong the time of payment of a debt.

Attermining /ətə́rməniŋ/. In old English law, a putting off; the granting of a time or term, as for the payment of a debt.

Attermoiement. In canon law, a making terms; a composition, as with creditors.

Attest. To bear witness to; to bear witness to a fact; to affirm to be true or genuine; to act as a witness to; to certify; to certify to the verity of a copy of a public document formally by signature; to make solemn declaration in words or writing to support a fact; to signify by subscription of his name that the signer has witnessed the execution of the particular instrument. Lindsey v. Realty Trust Co., Tex.Civ.App., 75 S.W.2d 322, 324; City Lumber Co. of Bridgeport v. Borsuk, 131 Conn. 640, 41 A.2d 775, 778. Also the technical word by which, in the practice in many of the states, a certifying officer gives assurance of the genuineness and correctness of a copy. Thus, an "attested" copy of a document is one which has been examined and compared with the original, with a certificate or memorandum of its correctness, signed by the persons who have examined it. See **Affirmation; Jurat; Oath; Verification.**

Attestation. The act of witnessing an instrument in writing, at the request of the party making the same, and subscribing it as a witness. The act of witnessing the execution of a paper and subscribing the name of the witness in testimony of such fact. In re Carlson's Estate, 156 Or. 597, 68 P.2d 119, 121. See **Affirmation; Jurat; Oath; Verification.**

Attestation clause. That clause (*e.g.* at the end of a will) wherein the witnesses certify that the instrument has been executed before them, and the manner of the execution of the same. A certificate certifying as to facts and circumstances attending execution of will. In re Bragg's Estate, 106 Mont. 132, 76 P.2d 57, 62. See Uniform Probate Code, § 2–502.

Attestation of will. Act of witnessing performance of statutory requirements to valid execution. Zaruba v. Schumaker, Tex.Civ.App., 178 S.W.2d 542, 543. See **Attestation clause.**

Attested copy. See **Attest.**

Attesting witness. One who signs his name to an instrument, at the request of the party or parties, for the purpose of proving and identifying it.

Attestor. One who attests or vouches for.

At the courthouse door. In proximity of courthouse door. At place provided for posting of legal notices in courthouse. Matson v. Federal Farm Mortg. Corporation, Tex.Civ.App., 151 S.W.2d 636, 640, 641.

At the end of the will. The words "at the end of the will" within statute providing that every will shall be subscribed by testator at the end of the will mean the end of the language and not paper on which it is written. In re Hildreth's Will, 36 N.Y.S.2d 938, 939, 940.

At the market. Order to broker to buy or sell a stock at the current market price, rather than at a specified price.

At time cause of action accrues. Term is sometimes applied to present enforcible demand, but more often simply means to arise or come into existence. Stone v. Phillips, 142 Tex. 216, 176 S.W.2d 932, 933.

Attincta /ətíŋktə/. L. Lat. An attaint, stain, or blackening; a conviction or finding of guilty of some offense.

Attorn /ətə́rn/. To turn over; to transfer to another money or goods; to assign to some particular use or service. To consent to the transfer of a rent or reversion. To agree to become tenant to one as owner or landlord of an estate previously held of another, or to agree to recognize a new owner of a property or estate and promise payment of rent to him.

Attornare /ætərnériy/. Lat. To attorn; to transfer or turn over; to appoint an attorney or substitute.

Attornare rem /ætərnériy rém/. To turn over money or goods, *i.e.*, to assign or appropriate them to some particular use or service.

Attornato faciendo vel recipiendo /ætərnéydow fæshiyéndow vèl rəsìpiyéndow/. An obsolete writ, which commanded a sheriff or steward of a county court or hundred court to receive and admit an attorney to appear for the person that owed suit of court.

Attornatus /ætərnéydəs/. One who is attorned, or put in the place of another; a substitute; hence, an attorney.

Attornatus fere in omnibus personam domini representat /ætərnéydəs fíriy in ómnəbəs pərsównəm dómənay rèprəzéntət/. An attorney represents the person of his master in almost all respects.

Attorne /ətórn/. L. Fr. In old English law, an attorney.

Attorney. In the most general sense this term denotes an agent or substitute, or one who is appointed and authorized to act in the place or stead of another. Nardi v. Poinsatte, D.C.Ind., 46 F.2d 347, 348. An agent, or one acting on behalf of another. Sherts v. Fulton Nat. Bank of Lancaster, 342 Pa. 337, 21 A.2d 18. In its most common usage, however, unless a contrary meaning is clearly intended, this term means "attorney at law", "lawyer" or "counselor at law".

"Attorney" means attorney, professional law association, corporation, or "partnership," authorized under applicable law to practice law. Bankruptcy Act, § 101(3).

The word "attorney" includes a party prosecuting or defending an action in person. New York C.P.L.R. § 105.

See also Attorney for government; Attorney General; Barrister; District (*District Attorney*); House counsel; Lawyer; Prosecuting attorney; States' Attorney; United States Attorney.

Attorney ad hoc. See **Ad hoc.**

Attorney at large. In old practice, an attorney who practiced in all the courts.

Attorney at law. Person admitted to practice law in his respective state and authorized to perform both civil and criminal legal functions for clients, including drafting of legal documents, giving of legal advice, and representing such before courts, administrative agencies, boards, etc.

In English law, a public officer belonging to the superior courts of common law at Westminster, who conducted legal proceedings on behalf of others, called his clients, by whom he was retained; he answered to the solicitor in the courts of chancery, and the proctor of the admiralty, ecclesiastical, probate, and divorce courts. An attorney was almost invariably also a solicitor. It was provided by the judicature act, 1873, § 87, that solicitors, attorneys, or proctors of, or by law empowered to practice in, any court the jurisdiction of which is by that act transferred to the high court of justice or the court of appeal, shall be called "solicitors of the supreme court."

Attorney ethics. See **Code of Professional Responsibility.**

Attorney fees. See **American rule; Fee; Minimum fee schedules; Retainer**.

Attorney in fact. A private attorney authorized by another to act in his place and stead, either for some particular purpose, as to do a particular act, or for the transaction of business in general, not of a legal character. This authority is conferred by an instrument in writing, called a "letter of attorney," or more commonly a "power of attorney."

Attorney of record. Attorney whose name must appear somewhere in permanent records or files of case, or on the pleadings or some instrument filed in the case, or on appearance docket. Person whom the client has named as his agent upon whom service of papers may be made. Reynolds v. Reynolds, 21 Cal.2d 580, 134 P.2d 251, 254.

An attorney who has filed a notice of appearance (*e.g.,* through a praecipe) and who hence is formally mentioned in court records as the official attorney of the party. Once an attorney becomes an attorney of record, he often cannot withdraw from the case without court permission.

Every pleading of a party represented by an attorney shall be signed by at least one attorney of record in his individual name, whose address shall be stated. Fed.R. Civil P. 11.

Attorney's license. A formal document issued by a state supreme court, normally after passage of a bar examination, which permits one to practice law in that jurisdiction. Also, a similar document issued by federal courts to attorneys admitted to practice in state courts. Such licenses may be revoked because of disbarment or suspended for attorney misconduct.

Attorney's lien. See **Attorney's lien**.

Letter of attorney. A power of attorney; a written instrument by which one person constitutes another his true and lawful attorney, in order that the latter may do for the former, and in his place and stead, some lawful act. An instrument of writing, appointing an attorney in fact for an avowed purpose and setting forth his powers and duties. It is, in effect, a mere contract of agency. A *general* power authorizes the agent to act generally in behalf of the principal. A *special* power is one limited to particular acts.

Power of attorney. The instrument by which authority of one person to act in place and stead of another as attorney in fact is set forth.

Practice of law. See **Practice.**

Public attorney. A name sometimes given to an attorney at law, as distinguished from a *private* attorney, or attorney in fact.

Right to attorney. See **Counsel, right to.**

Attorney-client privilege. In law of evidence, client's privilege to refuse to disclose and to prevent any other person from disclosing confidential communications between he and his attorney. That privilege which permits an attorney to refuse to testify as to communications from client to him though it belongs to client, not to attorney, and hence client may waive it. See also **Client's privilege**.

Attorney for government. Includes the Attorney General, an authorized assistant of the Attorney General, a United States Attorney, an authorized assistant of a United States Attorney and when applicable to cases arising under the laws of Guam means the Attorney General of Guam or such other person or persons as may be authorized by the laws of Guam to act therein. Fed.R.Crim.P. 54(c).

Attorney General. The Attorney General, as head of the Department of Justice and chief law officer of the Federal Government, represents the United States in legal matters generally and gives advice and opinions to the President and to the heads of the executive departments of the Government when so requested. The Attorney General appears in person to represent the Government in the U.S. Supreme Court in cases of exceptional gravity or importance. See also **Solicitor General**.

In each state there is also an attorney general, who is the chief law officer of the state. He gives advice and opinions to the governor and to executive and administrative departments or agencies.

In England, the principal law officer of the Crown, and head of the bar of England.

Attorney general's bill. An indictment presented to grand jury by leave of court without prior complaint before magistrate and holding for court. Commonwealth v. Wilson, 134 Pa.Super. 222, 4 A.2d 324, 327.

Attorney general's opinion. An opinion furnished by U.S. Attorney General to President, members of executive department or governmental agencies on request concerning question of law. Also, opinion rendered by state attorney general to Governor or state agencies on request concerning an interpretation of law.

Attorney, right to. See **Counsel, right to.**

Attorneyship. The office of an agent or attorney.

Attorney's lien. The right of an attorney at law to hold or retain in his possession the money or property of a client until his proper charges have been adjusted and paid. It requires no equitable proceeding for its establishment. Also a lien on funds in court payable to the client, or on a judgment or decree or award in his favor, recovered through the exertions of the attorney, and for the enforcement of which he must invoke the equitable aid of the court.

Charging lien. An attorney's lien, for his proper compensation, on the fund or judgment which his client has recovered by means of his professional aid and services. It is a specific lien covering only the services rendered by an attorney in the action in which the judgment was obtained, whereas a retaining lien is a general lien for the balance of the account between the attorney and his client, and applies to the property of the client which may come into the attorney's possession in the course of his employment.

Retaining lien. The lien which an attorney has upon all his client's papers, deeds, vouchers, etc., which remain in his possession, entitling him to retain them until satisfaction of his claims for professional services. It is a general lien.

Attornment /ətə́rnmənt/. In feudal and old English law, a turning over or transfer by a lord of the services of his tenant to the grantee of his seigniory.

Attornment is the act of a person who holds a leasehold interest in land, or estate for life or years, by which he agrees to become the tenant of a stranger who has acquired the fee in the land, or the remainder or reversion, or the right to the rent or services by which the tenant holds. It is an act by which a tenant acknowledges his obligation to a new landlord.

The agreement of a person to recognize a third party as a permissible successor party to a contract; most often, the agreement of a tenant to pay rent to a new landlord, especially a mortgagee who has foreclosed.

Attractive agencies doctrine. See **Attractive nuisance doctrine.**

Attractive instrumentalities doctrine. See **Attractive nuisance doctrine.**

Attractive nuisance doctrine. The doctrine is that person who has an instrumentality, agency, or condition upon his own premises, or who creates such condition on the premises of another, or in a public place, which may reasonably be apprehended to be a source of danger to children, is under a duty to take such precautions as a reasonably prudent man would take to prevent injury to children of tender years whom he knows to be accustomed to resort there, or who may,

by reason of something there which may be expected to attract them, come there to play. See Restatement, Second, Torts § 339.

Attribution. Under certain circumstances, the tax law applies attribution rules to assign to one taxpayer the ownership interest of another taxpayer. If, for example, the stock of X Corporation is held 60% by M and 40% by S, M may be deemed to own 100% of X Corporation if M and S are mother and son. In such a case, the stock owned by S is attributed to M. Stated differently, M has a 60% "direct" and a 40% "indirect" interest in X Corporation. It can also be said that M is the "constructive" owner of S's interest.

Aubaine /òwbéyn/. See **Droit d'aubaine.**

A.U.C. Ab urbe condita. From the founding of the city.

Auction /ókshən/. An auction is a public sale of property to the highest bidder by one licensed and authorized for that purpose. The auctioneer is employed by the seller and is primarily his agent. However, when the property is struck off he is also the agent of the buyer to the extent of binding the parties by his memorandum of sale, thus satisfying the statute of frauds. Hawaii Jewelers Ass'n v. Fine Arts Gallery, Inc., 51 Hawaii 502, 463 P.2d 914, 916.

A sale by auction is complete when the auctioneer so announces by the fall of the hammer or in other customary manner. Such a sale is with reserve unless the goods are in explicit terms put up without reserve. U.C.C. § 2–328.

Dutch auction. A method of sale by auction which consists in the public offer of the property at a price beyond its value, and then gradually lowering the price until some one becomes the purchaser.

Auctionariæ /òksh(iy)ənériyiy/. Catalogues of goods for public sale or auction.

Auctionarius /òksh(iy)ənériyəs/. A seller; a regrator; a retailer; one who bought and sold; an auctioneer, in the modern sense. One who buys poor, old, worn-out things to sell again at a greater price.

Auctioneer. A person authorized or licensed by law to sell lands or goods of other persons at public auction. One who sells goods at public auction for another on commission, or for a recompense.

Auctioneers differ from *brokers*, in that the latter may both buy and sell, whereas auctioneers can only sell; also brokers may sell by private contract only, and auctioneers by public auction only.

Auctor /óktər/. In the Roman law, an auctioneer. In the civil law, a grantor or vendor of any kind. In old French law, a plaintiff.

Auctoritas /òktórətæs/. In the civil law, authority. In old European law, a diploma, or royal charter.

Auctoritates philosophorum, medicorum, et poetarum, sunt in causis allegandæ et tenendæ /oktòrətéydiyz fəlosəfórəm mèdəkórəm èt pòwətérəm sánt in kózəs ǽləgǽndiy èt tənéndiy/. The opinions of philosophers, physicians, and poets are to be alleged and received in causes.

Aucupia verborum sunt judice indigna /òkyúwpiyǝ vǝrbórǝm sǝ̀nt júwdǝsiy indígnǝ/. Catching at words is unworthy of a judge. Applied in State v. Flemming, 66 Me. 142, 151.

Audi alteram partem /ódày ǽltǝrǝm párdǝm/. Hear the other side; hear both sides. No man should be condemned unheard. Lowry v. Inman, 46 N.Y. 119; Shaw v. Stone, 55 Mass. (1 Cush.) 228.

Audience. In international law, a hearing; interview with the sovereign. The king or other chief executive of a country grants an audience to a foreign minister who comes to him duly accredited; and, after the recall of a minister, an "audience of leave" ordinarily is accorded to him.

Audience court. In English law, a court belonging to the Archbishop of Canterbury, having jurisdiction of matters of form only, as the confirmation of bishops, and the like. This court has the same authority with the Court of Arches, but is of inferior dignity and antiquity. The Dean of the Arches is the official auditor of the Audience court. The Archbishop of York has also his Audience court. These courts, as separate courts, have long since been disused.

Audiendo et terminando /òdiyéndow èt tòrmǝnǽndow/. A writ or commission to certain persons to appease and punish any insurrection or great riot.

Audit /ódǝt/. Inspection and verification by I.R.S. of a taxpayer's return or other transactions possessing tax consequences.

Systematic inspection of accounting records involving analyses, tests, and confirmations.

The hearing and investigation had before an auditor. An audience; a hearing; an examination in general. A formal or official examination and authentication of accounts, with witnesses, vouchers, etc. Green-Boots Const. Co. v. State Highway Commission, 165 Okl. 288, 25 P.2d 783.

See also **Auditor; Generally Accepted Auditing Principles.**

Correspondence audit. See **Correspondence audit.**

Desk audit. Review of civil service positions to determine if duties and responsibilities of position fit job classification and pay grade.

Field audit. An audit by the Internal Revenue Service conducted on the business premises of the taxpayer or in the office of the tax practitioner representing the taxpayer. To be distinguished from a correspondence audit or an office audit (*q.v.*).

Independent audit. One conducted by an outside person or firm not connected in any way with the company being audited.

Internal audit. One conducted by company personnel.

Office audit. See **Office** (*Office audit*).

Tax audit. An examination of books, vouchers and records of a taxpayer conducted by agents of the I.R.S. See **Correspondence audit; Office** (*Office audit*); **RAR.**

Audita querela /òdáydǝ kwǝríylǝ/. The name of a common law writ constituting the initial process in an action brought by a judgment defendant to obtain relief against the consequences of the judgment on account of some matter of defense or discharge arising since its rendition and which could not be taken advantage of otherwise. Barnett v. Gitlitz, 290 Ill. App. 212, 8 N.E.2d 517, 520. May also lie for matters arising before judgment where defendant had no opportunity to raise such matters in defense. Louis E. Bower, Inc. v. Silverstein, 298 Ill.App. 145, 18 N.E.2d 385, 387.

This writ has been abolished in most states that have adopted Rules of Civil Procedure, being supplanted by motion for relief from judgment. Rule of Civil Procedure 60(b).

Audit committee. A committee of the board of directors of a corporation usually consisting of outside directors who nominate the independent auditors and discuss their work with them. If the auditors believe certain matters should be brought to the attention of stockholders, the auditors first bring these matters to the attention of the audit committee.

Auditor. One who checks the accuracy, fairness, and general acceptability of accounting records and statements and then attests to them; *e.g.* a Certified Public Accountant.

A State official whose duty is to examine the accounts of state agencies to determine if expenditures were made in accordance with authorizations by the legislature. See also **General Accounting Office.**

An officer of a business who examines and verifies accounts for accuracy.

An officer (or officers) of the court, assigned to state the items of debit and credit between the parties in a suit where accounts are in question, and exhibit the balance. Under the Rules of Civil Procedure in many states, the term "master" is used to describe those persons formerly known as auditors; *e.g.* Mass.R. Civil P. 53. See **Master; Reference.**

Auditor of the imprest. Any of several officers in the English exchequer, who formerly had the charge of auditing the accounts of the customs, naval and military expenses, etc., now performed by the commissioners for auditing public accounts.

Auditor of the receipts. An officer of the English exchequer.

Public auditor. Examines account records of private businesses for a fee.

State auditor. See first general definition above.

Augmentation /ògmǝntéyshǝn/. The increase of the crown's revenues from the suppression of religious houses and the appropriation of their lands and revenues. Also the name of a court (now abolished) erected 27 Hen. VIII, to determine suits and controversies relating to monasteries and abbey-lands. The court was dissolved in the reign of Mary, but the office of augmentations remained long after.

A share of the great tithes temporarily granted to the vicars by the appropriators, and made perpetual by statute 29 Car. II, c. 8. The word is used in a similar sense in the Canadian law.

Augmented estate. Estate reduced by funeral and administration expenses, homestead allowance, family allowances, exemptions, and enforceable claims to which is added value of property transferred to anyone other than bona fide purchaser and value of property owned by surviving spouse at decedent's death. Uniform Probate Code, § 2–202.

Augusta legibus soluta non est /əgə́stə líyjəbəs səl(y)úwdə nòn ést/. The empress or queen is not privileged or exempted from subjection to the laws. 1 Bl.Comm. 219.

Aula /ólə/. In old English law, a hall, or court; the court of a baron, or manor; a court baron. This word was employed in mediæval England along with *curia;* it was used of the meetings of the lord's men held there in the same way that the word *court* was used.

Aula ecclesiæ /ólə əklíyziyiy/. A nave or body of a church where temporal courts were anciently held.

Aula regis /ólə ríyjəs/. (Called also *Aula Regia.*) The king's hall or palace. The chief court of England in early Norman times. It was established by William the Conqueror in his own hall. It was composed of the great officers of state, resident in the palace, and followed the king's household in all his expeditions. See, also, **Curia regis.**

Aulic /ólək/. Pertaining to a royal court.

Aulnage. See **Alnager.**

Aulnager. See **Alnager.**

Aumone, service in. Where lands are given in alms to some church or religious house, upon condition that a service or prayers shall be offered at certain times for the repose of the donor's soul.

Aunt. The sister of one's father or mother, and a relation in the third degree, correlative to niece or nephew.

Aures /óhriyz/. A Saxon punishment by cutting off the ears, inflicted on those who robbed churches, or were guilty of any other theft.

Aurum reginæ /óhrəm rəjáyniy/. Queen's gold. A royal revenue belonging to every queen consort during her marriage with the king.

Australian ballot. An official ballot on which the names of all the candidates are printed. Its use is accompanied by safeguards designed to maintain secrecy in voting. The so-called Australian ballot laws, widely adopted in various forms in the United States, have generally been sustained by the courts.

Auter /ówtər/, **autre** /°trə/. L. Fr. Another; other. See **Autre.**

Authentic /oθéntik/. Genuine; true; real; pure; reliable; trustworthy; having the character and authority of an original; duly vested with all necessary formalities and legally attested. Competent, credible, and reliable as evidence.

Authentic act. In the civil law, an act which has been executed before a notary or public officer authorized to execute such functions, or which is testified by a public seal, or has been rendered public by the authority of a competent magistrate, or which is certified as being a copy of a public register.

Authentication /əθèntəkéyshən/. In the law of evidence, the act or mode of giving authority or legal authenticity to a statute, record, or other written instrument, or a certified copy thereof, so as to render it legally admissible in evidence. Verifications of judgments. An attestation made by a proper officer by which he certifies that a record is in due form of law, and that the person who certifies it is the officer appointed so to do. Acts done with a view of causing an instrument to be known and identified. See also **Verification**.

Authentication of a writing means (a) the introduction of evidence sufficient to sustain a finding that it is the writing that the proponent of the evidence claims it is or (b) the establishment of such facts by any other means provided by law. Calif.Evid.Code.

The requirement of authentication as a condition precedent to admissibility of evidence is satisfied by evidence sufficient to support a finding that the matter in question is what its proponent claims. Fed. Evid.Rule 901.

Self authentication. Statutes frequently provide that certain classes of writings shall be received in evidence "without further proof." The following fall into this category: (1) deeds, conveyances or other instruments, which have been acknowledged by the signers before a notary public, (2) certified copies of public records, and (3) books of statutes which purport to be printed by public authority. See Fed.Evid. Rule 902.

Authenticum /oθéntəkəm/. In the civil law, an original instrument or writing; the original of a will or other instrument, as distinguished from a copy.

Author. One who produces, by his own intellectual labor applied to the materials of his composition, an arrangement or compilation new in itself. A beginner or mover of anything; hence efficient cause of a thing; creator; originator; a composer, as distinguished from an editor, translator or compiler.

Authorities. Citations to statutes, precedents, judicial decisions, and text-books of the law, made on the argument of questions of law or the trial of causes before a court, in support of the legal positions contended for, or adduced to fortify the opinion of a court or of a text writer upon any question. Authorities may be either primary (*e.g.* statutes, court decisions, regulations), or secondary (*e.g.* Restatements, treatises).

Authority. Permission. Right to exercise powers; to implement and enforce laws; to exact obedience; to command; to judge. Control over; jurisdiction. Often synonymous with power. The power delegated by a principal to his agent. The lawful delegation of power by one person to another. Power of agent to affect legal relations of principal by acts done in accordance with principal's manifestations of consent to agent. See Restatement, Second, Agency § 7.

Refers to the precedential value to be accorded an opinion of a judicial or administrative body. A court's opinion is binding authority on other courts directly below it in the judicial hierarchy. Opinions of lower courts or of courts outside the hierarchy are governed by the degree to which it adheres to the doctrine of stare decisis. See **Stare decisis**.

Legal power; a right to command or to act; the right and power of public officers to require obedience to their orders lawfully issued in the scope of their public duties.

See also Actual authority; Apparent authority; Binding authority; Commission; Competent authority; Control; Credentials; Implied authority; Power; Precedent; Scope of authority.

Apparent authority. That which, though not actually granted, the principal knowingly permits the agent to exercise, or which he holds him out as possessing. The power to affect the legal relations of another person by transactions with third persons, professedly as agent for the other, arising from and in accordance with the other's manifestations to such third persons. Restatement, Second, Agency, § 8. See *Authority by estoppel.*

Authority by estoppel. Not actual, but apparent only, being imposed on the principal because his conduct has been such as to mislead, so that it would be unjust to let him deny it. See *Apparent authority.*

Authority coupled with an interest. Authority given to an agent for a valuable consideration, or which forms part of a security.

Express authority. That given explicitly, either in writing or orally. See **Express authority**.

General authority. That which authorizes the agent to do everything connected with a particular business. It empowers him to bind his principal by all acts within the scope of his employment; and it cannot be limited by any private direction not known to the party dealing with him.

Implied authority. Actual authority circumstantially proved. That which the principal intends his agent to possess, and which is implied from the principal's conduct. It includes only such acts as are incident and necessary to the exercise of the authority expressly granted.

Incidental authority. Such authority as is necessary to carry out authority which is actually or apparently given, *e.g.* authority to borrow money carries with it as an incidental authority the power to sign commercial paper to effectuate the borrowing.

Inferred authority. See *Incidental authority*, above.

Inherent authority. Such power as reposes in an agent by virtue of the agency itself.

Limited authority. Such authority as the agent has when he is bound by precise instructions.

Naked authority. That arising where the principal delegates the power to the agent wholly for the benefit of the former.

Ostensible authority. See *Apparent authority*, supra.

Presumptive authority. See *Implied authority*, supra.

Special authority. That which is confined to an individual transaction. Such an authority does not bind the principal, unless it is strictly pursued.

Unlimited authority. That possessed by an agent when he is left to pursue his own discretion.

Authorize. To empower; to give a right or authority to act. To endow with authority or effective legal power, warrant, or right. People v. Young, 100 Ill.App.2d 20, 241 N.E.2d 587, 589. To permit a thing to be done in the future. It has a mandatory effect or meaning, implying a direction to act.

"Authorized" is sometimes construed as equivalent to "permitted"; or "directed", or to similar mandatory language. Possessed of authority; that is, possessed of legal or rightful power, the synonym of which is "competency." Doherty v. Kansas City Star Co., 143 Kan. 802, 57 P.2d 43, 45.

Authorized capital. See **Authorized issue**.

Authorized issue. Total number of shares of capital stock which charter or articles of incorporation permits corporation to sell.

Autocracy /òtókrəsiy/. The name of an unlimited monarchical government. A government at the will of one man (called an "autocrat"), unchecked by constitutional restrictions or limitations.

Autograph. One's handwriting; written with one's own hand.

Automatism /ətómətìzəm/. Behavior performed in a state of mental unconsciousness or dissociation without full awareness, *i.e.*, somnambulism, fugues. Term is applied to actions or conduct of an individual apparently occurring without will, purpose, or reasoned intention on his part; a condition sometimes observed in persons who, without being actually insane, suffer from an obscuration of the mental faculties, loss of volition or of memory, or kindred affections. "Ambulatory automatism" describes the pathological impulse to purposeless and irresponsible wanderings from place to place often characteristic of patients suffering from loss of memory with dissociation of personality. Automatism may be asserted as a criminal defense to negate the requisite mental state of voluntariness for commission of a crime. See *e.g.* Model Penal Code, § 2.01.

Automobile guest. See **Family automobile doctrine; Family purpose doctrine; Guest; Guest statute**.

Automobile insurance. A comprehensive term which embraces insurance coverage for all risks involved in owning and operating an automobile, such as personal injury protection, property damage to another and to the insured, fire, theft and vandalism. See **Insurance**.

Autonomy. The political independence of a nation; the right (and condition) of power of self-government. The negation of a state of political influence from without or from foreign powers. Green v. Obergfell, 73 App.D.C. 298, 121 F.2d 46, 57.

Autoptic evidence. An exhibit of a thing offered before jury as evidence to be seen through jury's own eyes. Johnson v. State, 139 Tex.Cr.R. 279, 139 S.W.2d 579, 581. See **Autoptic proference; Demonstrative evidence.**

Autopsy /ótopsiy/. The dissection of a dead body for the purpose of inquiring into the cause of death. A post mortem examination to determine the cause, seat, or nature of a disease. Such is normally required by statute for deaths by violent or unnatural means.

Autoptic proference. Proffering or presenting in open court of articles for observation or inspection of the tribunal. See **Auto-optic evidence; Demonstrative evidence.**

Auto theft. A form of larceny, the subject matter of which is a motor vehicle. The taking and carrying away of a motor vehicle from the owner or possessor with intent to deprive him permanently of it. The intent distinguishes larceny from a lesser offense of use without authority. See also **Joy riding.**

Autre action pendant /ówtrə àksiyówn pòndón/. In common law pleading, another action pending. A species of plea in abatement.

Autre droit /ówtrə dr(w)ó/. In right of another, *e.g.,* a trustee holds trust property in right of his *cestui que trust.* A *prochein amy* sues in right of an infant. 2 Bl.Comm. 176.

Autrefois /òwtrəfwó/. L. Fr. At another time; formerly; before; heretofore.

Autrefois acquit /òwtrəfwó əkíy/°əkwít/. Fr. Formerly acquitted. The name of a plea in bar to a criminal action, stating that the defendant has been once already indicted and tried for the same alleged offense and has been acquitted.

Autrefois attaint /òwtrəfwó ətǽn/°əteynt/. In criminal law, formerly attainted. An old English plea (now obsolete) that the defendant has already been attainted for one felony, and therefore cannot be criminally prosecuted for another.

Autrefois convict /òwtrəfwó kənvíkt/. Fr. Formerly convicted. A plea by a criminal in bar to an indictment that he has been formerly convicted of the same crime. 4 Bl.Comm. 336.

Autre vie /ówtrə viy/. Another's life. A person holding an estate for or during the life of another is called a tenant *"pur autre vie,"* or *"pur terme d'autre vie."* See **Estate pur autre vie.**

Auxiliary /ogzíl(iy)əriy/. Aiding; attendant on; ancillary *(q.v.);* as, an auxiliary bill in equity, an auxiliary receiver. Synonymous with "subsidiary." Baker v. Fenley, 233 Mo.App. 998, 128 S.W.2d 295, 298.

Auxiliator /ogzìliyéydər/. Lat. Helper or assistant; the word is closely related to the English word auxiliary.

Auxilium /ogzíliyəm/. In feudal and old English law, aid; compulsory aid, hence a tax or tribute; a kind of tribute paid by the vassal to his lord, being one of the incidents of the tenure by knight's service.

Auxilium ad filium militem faciendum et filiam maritandam /ogzíliyəm ǽd fíliyəm mílətəm fǽshiyéndəm èt fíliyæm mǽrətǽndəm/. An ancient writ which was addressed to the sheriff to levy compulsorily an aid towards the knighting of a son and the marrying of a daughter of the tenants *in capite* of the crown.

Auxilium curiæ /ògzíliyəm kyúriyiy/. In old English law, a precept or order of court citing and convening a party, at the suit and request of another, to warrant something.

Auxilium regis /ògzíliyəm ríyjəs/. In old English law, the king's aid or money levied for the royal use and the public service, as taxes granted by parliament. A subsidy paid to the king.

Auxilium vice comiti /ògzíliyəm váysiy kómǝday/. An ancient duty paid to sheriffs.

Available. Suitable; useable; accessible; obtainable; present or ready for immediate use. Having sufficient force or efficacy; effectual; valid.

Avail of marriage. In feudal law, the right of marriage, which the lord or guardian in chivalry had of disposing of his infant ward in matrimony. A guardian in socage had also the same right, but not attended with the same advantage. 2 Bl.Comm. 88.

Aval /əvál/. In French law, the guaranty of a bill of exchange; so called because usually placed at the foot or bottom *(aval)* of the bill.

In Canadian law, the act of subscribing one's signature at the bottom of a promissory note or of a bill of exchange; properly an act of suretyship, by the party signing, in favor of the party to whom the note or bill is given.

Avanture /əvònt(y)úr/. L. Fr. Chance; hazard; mischance.

Avaria, avarie /əvériyə/. Average; the loss and damage suffered in the course of a navigation. See **Average.**

Avarice. Excessive greed or desire for wealth or gain.

Avenage. A certain quantity of oats paid by a tenant to his landlord as rent, or in lieu of some other duties.

Aventure, or **adventure** /ə(d)vénchər/. A mischance causing the death of a man, as where a person is suddenly drowned or killed by any accident, without felony.

Aver /əvár/, *v.* In pleading, to declare or assert; to set out distinctly and formally; to allege. See also **Averment.**

In old pleading, to avouch or verify; to make or prove true; to make good or justify a plea.

Aver /éyvər/, *n.* In old English and French, property; substance, estate and particularly live stock or cattle; hence a working beast, a horse or bullock.

Aver corn. A rent reserved to religious houses, to be paid in corn. Corn drawn by the tenant's cattle.

Aver land. In feudal law, land plowed by the tenant for the proper use of the lord of the soil.

Aver penny. Money paid towards the king's averages or carriages, and so to be freed thereof.

Aver silver. A custom or rent formerly so called.

Avera /əvírə/. A day's work of a ploughman, formerly valued at eight pence.

Average. A mean proportion, medial sum or quantity, made out of unequal sums or quantities. Brisendine v. Skousen Bros., 48 Ariz. 416, 62 P.2d 326, 329. In ordinary usage the term signifies the mean between two or more quantities, measures, or numbers. If applied to something which is incapable of expression in terms of measure or amount, it signifies that the thing or person referred to is of the ordinary or usual type.

In maritime law, loss or damage accidentally happening to a vessel or to its cargo during a voyage. Also a small duty paid to masters of ships, when goods are sent in another man's ship, for their care of the goods, over and above the freight. See subdefinitions below.

In old English law, a service by horse or carriage, anciently due by a tenant to his lord. A labor or service performed with working cattle, horses, or oxen, or with wagons and carriages.

General average. A contribution by the several interests engaged in a maritime venture to make good the loss of one of them for the voluntary sacrifice of a part of the ship or cargo to save the residue of the property and the lives of those on board, or for extraordinary expenses necessarily incurred for the common benefit and safety of all. The law of general average is part of the maritime law, and not of the municipal law, and applies to maritime adventures only. Ralli v. Troop, 157 U.S. 386, 15 S.Ct. 657, 39 L.Ed. 742.

Gross average. More commonly called "general average" *(q.v.)*. Where loss or damage occurs to a vessel or its cargo at sea, *average* is the adjustment and apportionment of such loss between the owner, the freight, and the cargo, in proportion to their respective interests and losses, in order that one may not suffer the whole loss, but each contribute ratably.

Particular average is a loss happening to the ship, freight, or cargo which is not to be shared by contribution among all those interested, but must be borne by the owner of the subject to which it occurs. It is thus called in contradistinction to *general* average.

Petty average denotes such charges and disbursements as, according to occurrences and the custom of every place, the master necessarily furnishes for the benefit of the ship and cargo, either at the place of loading or unloading, or on the voyage; such as the hire of a pilot for conducting a vessel from one place to another, towage, light money, beaconage, anchorage, bridge toll, quarantine and such like.

Simple average is the same as "particular average" *(q.v.)*.

Average clause. A clause providing that similar items in one location or at several locations which are covered by one insurance policy shall each be covered in the proportion that the value in each bears to the value in all.

Average daily balance. Average amount of money that a depositor keeps on deposit in a bank on any given day.

Average man test. Used to determine bias of prospective juror who asserts that he is without prejudice but who is so connected with case that ordinary man under circumstances would be biased without recognition of his prejudice. U. S. v. Haynes, C.A.Conn., 398 F.2d 980, 984.

Averaging up or **down.** Practice of purchasing the same security at different price levels, thus realizing a higher or lower average cost than the first purchase.

A verbis legis non est recendendum /ey várbis líyjis nón est rəsèndéndəm/. The words of a statute must not be departed from. A court is not at liberty to disregard the letter of a statute, in favor of a supposed intention.

Averiis captis in withernam /əvíriyəs kæptəs ìn wíðərnəm/. In old English pleading, a writ granted to one whose cattle were unlawfully distrained by another and driven out of the county in which they were taken, so that they could not be replevied by the sheriff.

Averium /əvíriyəm/. Lat. Goods; property. A beast of burden.

Averment /əvármənt/. In pleading, to allege or assert positively. All averments in pleadings are required to be simple, concise, and direct. Fed.R. Civil P. 8(e).

In old pleading, an offer to prove a plea, or pleading. The concluding part of a plea, replication, or other pleading, containing new affirmative matter, by which the party offers or declares himself "ready to *verify.*"

Averrare /ævərériy/. In feudal law, a duty required from some customary tenants, to carry goods in a wagon or upon loaded horses.

Aversio /əvárz(h)(iy)ow/. In the civil law, an averting or turning away. A term applied to a species of sale in gross or bulk.

Letting a house altogether, instead of in chambers.

Averum /əvírəm/. Goods, property, substance; a beast of burden.

Avia /éyviyə/. In the civil law, a grandmother.

Aviaticus /éyviyǽdəkəs/. In the civil law, a grandson.

Aviation Act. Federal law that created Federal Aviation Agency (FAA) which is responsible for regulation of aviation including aircraft safety, aircraft marking, etc. and which continues Civil Aeronautics Board (CAB) as an arm of the federal government.

A vinculo matrimonii /ey víŋkyəlow mætrəmówniyay/. Lat. From the bond of matrimony. A term descriptive of a kind of divorce, which effects a complete dissolution of the marriage contract. See **Divorce.**

Avocat. Fr. An advocate; a barrister.

Avocation /ævəkéyshən/. A calling away, a diversion; suggesting idea of smaller affairs of life, or subordinate or occasional employments, or hobbies, as distinguished from one's ordinary or principal occupation.

Avoid. To annul; cancel; make void; to destroy the efficacy of anything. To evade; escape.

Avoidable consequences, doctrine of. Doctrine imposes duty on person injured to minimize damages. Baglio v. N. Y. Central R. Co., 344 Mass. 14, 180 N.E.2d 798. The general rule relating to duty of party who has been wronged by breach of contract to mitigate damages; *i.e.* to not sit idly by and allow damages to accumulate. Restatement of Contracts, § 336(i). See also **Mitigation of damages.**

Avoidance. A making void, useless, empty, or of no effect; annulling, cancelling; escaping or evading. See also **Evasion.**

In pleading, the allegation or statement of new matter, in opposition to a former pleading, which, admitting the facts alleged in such former pleading, shows cause why they should not have their ordinary legal effect. Fed.R. Civil P. 8(c). See also **Affirmative defense; Confession and avoidance.**

Avoirdupois /ǽvərd(y)uwpóyz/. The name of a system of weights (sixteen ounces to the pound) used in weighing articles other than medicines, metals, and precious stones; so named in distinction from the Troy weight.

Avoucher /əváwchər/. The calling upon a warrantor of lands to fulfill his undertaking. See **Voucher.**

Avoué /àvuwéy/. In French and Canadian law, a barrister, advocate, solicitor, or attorney. An officer charged with representing and defending parties before the tribunal to which he is attached.

Avow /əváw/. In pleading, to acknowledge and justify an act done. To make an avowry. See **Avowal; Avowry; Justification.**

Avowal /əváwəl/. An open declaration. Purpose is to enable the court to know what the witness would have stated in answer to the question propounded, and to inform the court what the interrogator would prove contrary to the testimony given at the trial. See **Offer of proof.**

Avowant. One who makes an avowry.

Avowry /əváwry/. A common law pleading in the action of replevin, by which the defendant *avows*, that is, acknowledges and justifies the taking of the distress or property complained of, where he took it in his own right, and sets forth the reason of it; as for rent in arrear, damage done, etc.

Avowterer /əváwdərər/. In English law, an adulterer with whom a married woman continues in adultery.

Avowtry. In old English law, adultery.

Avulsion /əválshən/. A sudden and perceptible loss or addition to land by the action of water, or a sudden change in the bed or course of a stream. Valder v. Wallis, 196 Neb. 222, 242 N.W.2d 112, 114. The removal of a considerable quantity of soil from the land of one man, and its deposit upon or annexation to the land of another, suddenly and by the perceptible action of water.

Where running streams are the boundaries between states, the same rule applies as between private proprietors, and, if the stream from any cause, natural or artificial, suddenly leaves its old bed and forms a new one by the process known as "avulsion," the resulting change of channel works no change of boundary, which remains in the middle of the old channel though no water may be flowing in it and irrespective of subsequent changes in the new channel. State of Arkansas v. State of Tennessee, 246 U.S. 158, 38 S.Ct. 301, 304, 62 L.Ed. 638; Stull v. U. S., C.C.A.Neb., 61 F.2d 826, 830.

To constitute "avulsion," rather than "accretion," so as to preclude change in boundary between riparian owners, it is not necessary that soil washed away be identifiable; it being sufficient that change is so sudden that owner of land washed away is able to point out approximately as much land added to opposite bank as he had washed away. Goins v. Merryman, 183 Okl. 155, 80 P.2d 268.

See **Accretion; Alluvion; Reliction.**

Avunculus /ævángkyələs/. In the civil law, a mother's brother. 2 Bl.Comm. 230. *Avunculus magnus,* a great-uncle. *Avunculus major,* a great-grandmother's brother. *Avunculus maximus,* a great-great-grandmother's brother.

Avus /ǽvəs/eyvəs/. In the civil law, a grandfather.

Await. Used in old statutes to signify a lying in wait, or waylaying.

Award, *v.* To grant, concede, or adjudge to. To give or assign by sentence or judicial determination or after careful weighing of evidence. Thus, a jury *awards* damages; the court *awards* an injunction; one *awards* a contract to a bidder. To confer as being deserved or merited.

Award, *n.* The decision or determination rendered by arbitrators or commissioners, or other private or extrajudicial deciders, upon a controversy submitted to them; also the writing or document embodying such decision. See also **Final award; Prize.**

Away-going crop. A crop sown before the expiration of a tenancy, which cannot ripen until after its expiration to which, however, the tenant is entitled. Broom, Max. 412; Miller v. Gray, Tex.Civ.App., 108 S.W.2d 265, 267, 268.

A.W.W. Abbreviation for "average weekly wage". Term used in worker's compensation computations.

Ayant cause. In French law, and also in Louisiana, this term signifies one to whom a right has been assigned, either by will, gift, sale, exchange, or the like; an assignee. An *ayant cause* differs from an heir who acquires the right by inheritance.

B

Baby Act. A plea of infancy, interposed for the purpose of defeating an action upon a contract made while the person was a minor, is vulgarly called "pleading the baby act". By extension, the term is applied to a plea of the statute of limitations.

Bachelor. One who has taken the first undergraduate degree (baccalaureate) in a college or university.

An unmarried man. A kind of inferior knight; an esquire.

Back, *v.* To indorse; to sign on the back; to sign generally by way of acceptance or approval; to substantiate; to countersign; to assume financial responsibility for. In old English law where a warrant issued in one county was presented to a magistrate of another county and he signed it for the purpose of making it executory in his county, he was said to "back" it.

Back, *adv.* To the rear; backward; in a reverse direction. Also, in arrear.

Backadation. See **Backwardation.**

Backberend (also Backberende) /bǽkberənd/. Sax. Bearing upon the back or about the person. Applied to a thief taken with the stolen property in his immediate possession. Used with *handhabend*, having in the hand.

Backbond. A bond of indemnification given to a surety.

Back carry. In forest law, the crime of having, on the back, game unlawfully killed. See **Backberend.**

Backdating. Predating a document prior to the date it was actually drawn. The negotiability of an instrument is not affected by the fact that it is backdated. U.C.C. § 3–114.

Backhaul. In freight transportation, to carry a shipment back over a segment of a route already covered.

Backing. Indorsement.

Backing a warrant. See **Back.**

Back lands. A term of no very definite import, but generally signifying lands lying back from (not contiguous to) a highway or a water course.

Backlog. Accumulation of unfilled orders.

Back pay award. Difference between wages already paid an employee and higher wages granted retroactively. A determination by a judicial or quasi judicial body that an employee is entitled to accrued but uncollected salary or wages. Such may be awarded in employment discrimination cases.

Back-seat driver. A highly nervous passenger whether sitting in rear or by driver, who by unwarranted advice and warnings interferes in careful operation of automobile.

Backside. In English law, a term formerly used in conveyances and also in pleading; it imports a yard at the back part of or behind a house, and belonging thereto.

Backspread. Less than normal price difference in arbitrage.

Back taxes. Those assessed for a previous year or years and remaining due and unpaid from the original tax debtor.

Back to work agreement. Agreement between union and employer covering terms and conditions upon which employees will return to work following settlement of strike.

Backwardation (also called **Backadation**) /bǽkwərdéyshən/. In the language of the stock exchange, this term signifies a consideration paid for delay in the delivery of stock contracted for, when the price is lower for time than for cash.

Backwards. In a policy of marine insurance, the phrase "forwards and backwards at sea" means from port to port in the course of the voyage, and not merely from one terminus to the other and back.

Backwater. Water in a stream which, in consequence of some dam or obstruction below, is detained or checked in its course, or flows back.

Bacon-Davis Act. Federal law (1931) granting Secretary of Labor power to set wage rates on public construction work to meet wages in private sector.

Baculus /bǽk(y)ələs/. A rod, staff, or wand, used in old English practice in making livery of seisin where no building stood on the land. A stick or wand, by the erection of which on the land involved in a real action the defendant was summoned to put in his appearance; this was called *"baculus nuntiatorius."* 3 Bl. Comm. 279.

Bad. Vicious, evil, wanting in good qualities; the opposite of good. Defective, faulty, inferior, or imperfect. Kniffley v. Reid, 287 Ky. 212, 152 S.W.2d 615, 616.

Bad character. Absence of moral virtue; the predominance of evil habits in a person. In law of evidence, such character may be shown to affect credibility of witness by introduction of record of convictions for crimes or by reputation. Fed.Evid.R. 608, 609.

Bad check. A check which is dishonored on presentation for payment because of no, or insufficient, funds or closed bank account. Writing or passing of bad checks is a misdemeanor in most states. Model Penal Code § 224.5. See also **Check kiting.**

Bad debt. A debt which is uncollectible; a permissible deduction for tax purposes in arriving at taxable income. I.R.C. § 166. Different tax treatment is afforded business and non-business bad debts. A business debt is defined by the Internal Revenue Code as a debt created or acquired in connection with a trade or business of the taxpayer, or a debt which becomes worthless in the taxpayer's trade or business.

A deduction is permitted if a business account receivable subsequently becomes worthless providing the income arising from the debt was previously included in income. The deduction is allowed only in the year of worthlessness. If a reserve method is used, partial or totally worthless accounts are charged to the reserve.

Non-business bad debt. A bad debt loss not incurred in connection with a taxpayer's trade or business. Such loss is deductible as a short-term capital loss and will only be allowed in the year the debt becomes entirely worthless. In addition to family loans, many investor losses fall into the classification of nonbusiness bad debts. I.R.C. § 166.

Bad debt reserve. An account used in bookkeeping to reflect the true worth of receivables in the balance sheet by predicting those debts which may not be collected and which ultimately will be written off as bad debts and claimed as a deduction for tax purposes. See also **Reserve.**

Bad faith. The opposite of "good faith," generally implying or involving actual or constructive fraud, or a design to mislead or deceive another, or a neglect or refusal to fulfill some duty or some contractual obligation, not prompted by an honest mistake as to one's rights or duties, but by some interested or sinister motive. Term "bad faith" is not simply bad judgment or negligence, but rather it implies the conscious doing of a wrong because of dishonest purpose or moral obliquity; it is different from the negative idea of negligence in that it contemplates a state of mind affirmatively operating with furtive design or ill will. Stath v. Williams, Ind.App., 367 N.E.2d 1120, 1124.

Badge. A mark or cognizance worn to show the relation of the wearer to any person or thing; the token of anything; a distinctive mark of office or service.

Badger. In old English law, one who made a practice of buying corn or victuals in one place, and carrying them to another to sell and make profit by them.

Badges of fraud. A term used relatively to the law of fraudulent conveyances made to hinder and defraud creditors. It is defined as a fact tending to throw suspicion upon a transaction, and calling for an explanation. It is a suspicious circumstance that overhangs a transaction, or appears on the face of the papers. A circumstance which does not alone prove fraud, but which warrants inference of fraud, especially where there is a concurrence of many such badges. Brennecke v. Riemann, Mo., 102 S.W.2d 874, 877. Recognized "badges of fraud" include fictitious consideration, false statements as to consideration, transactions different from usual course of doing business, transfer of all of a debtor's property, insolvency, confidential relationship of parties, and transfers in anticipation of suit or execution. Hendrix v. Goldman, Mo., 92 S.W.2d 733, 736.

Badges of servitude. Congressional power to eliminate all vestiges of involuntary servitude pursuant to Thirteenth Amendment to U.S.Const.; Civil Rights Act of 1866. Jones v. Alfred H. Mayer Co., 392 U.S. 409, 88 S.Ct. 2186, 20 L.Ed.2d 1189.

Bad motive. Intentionally doing a wrongful act knowing at the time that it is wrongful. Luhmann v. Schaefer, Mo.App., 142 S.W.2d 1088, 1090; Davis v. Nash Central Motors, Mo.App., 332 S.W.2d 475, 480.

Bad title. One which conveys no property to the purchaser of the estate. One which is so radically defective that it is not marketable, and hence such that a purchaser cannot be legally compelled to accept it.

Baga /bǽgə/. In old English law, a bag or purse. Thus there was the petty-bag-office in the common-law jurisdiction of the court of chancery, because all original writs relating to the business of the crown were formerly kept in a little sack or bag, *in parvâ bagâ.*

Bagavel. In old English law, the citizens of Exeter had granted to them by charter from Edward I the collection of a certain tribute or toll upon all manner of wares brought to that city to be sold, toward the paving of the streets, repairing of the walls, and maintenance of the city, which was commonly called bagavel, bethugavel and chippinggavel.

Bail, *v.* To procure release of one charged with an offense by insuring his future attendance in court and compelling him to remain within jurisdiction of court. Manning v. State ex rel. Williams, 190 Okl. 65, 120 P.2d 980, 981. To deliver the defendant to persons who, in the manner prescribed by law, become security for his appearance in court. To set at liberty a person arrested or imprisoned, on security being taken for his appearance on a day and a place certain, which security is called "bail," because the party arrested or imprisoned is delivered into the hands of those who bind themselves for his forthcoming. See also **Release on own recognizance.**

The object of "bail" in civil cases is either directly or indirectly to secure payment of a debt or performance of other civil duties, while in criminal cases object is to secure appearance of principal before the court when his presence is needed. Johnson v. Shaffer, 64 Ohio App. 236, 28 N.E.2d 765, 767. In its more ancient signification, the word includes the delivery of property, real or personal, by one person to another. See also **Civil bail.**

Bail, *n.* The surety or sureties who procure the release of a person under arrest, by becoming responsible for his appearance at the time and place designated. Those persons who become sureties for the appearance of the defendant in court.

Bail absolute. Sureties whose liability is conditioned upon the failure of the principal to duly account for money coming to his hands as administrator, guardian, etc.

Bail bond. A written undertaking, executed by the defendant or one or more sureties, that the defendant designated in such instrument will, while at liberty as a result of an order fixing bail and of the execution of a bail bond in satisfaction thereof, appear in a designated criminal action or proceeding when his attendance is required and otherwise render himself amenable to the orders and processes of the court, and that in the event he fails to do so, the signers of the bond will pay to the court the amount of money specified in the order fixing bail. Fed.R.Crim.P. 46; 18 U.S. C.A. § 3141 et seq. See also **Personal recognizance.**

Cash bail bond. A sum of money, in the amount designated in an order fixing bail, posted by a defendant or by another person on his behalf with a court or other authorized public officer upon condition that such money will be forfeited if the defendant does not comply with the directions of a court requiring his attendance at the criminal action or proceeding involved and does not otherwise render himself amenable to the orders and processes of the court.

Unsecured bail bond. A bail bond for which the defendant is fully liable upon failure to appear in court when ordered to do so or upon breach of a material condition of release, but which is not secured by any deposit of or lien upon property.

Bail common. At common law a fictitious proceeding, intended only to express the appearance of a defendant, in cases where special bail is not required. It is put in in the same form as special bail, but the sureties are merely nominal or imaginary persons, as John Doe and Richard Roe. 3 Bl.Comm. 287.

Bail court. In old English law and practice, an auxiliary court of the court of queen's bench at Westminster, wherein points connected more particularly with pleading and practice are argued and determined. It has been abolished.

Bail dock. Formerly at the Old Bailey, in London, a small room taken from one of the corners of the court, and left open at the top, in which certain malefactors were placed during trial.

Bail in error. That given by a defendant who intends to bring a writ of error on the judgment and desires a stay of execution in the meantime.

Bail piece. A formal entry or memorandum of the recognizance or undertaking of special bail in civil actions, which, after being signed and acknowledged by the bail before the proper officer, is filed in the court in which the action is pending. 3 Bl.Comm. 291.

Bail point scale. System whereby a predetermined number of points are given for all positive aspects of the defendant's background. The total number of points determine whether the defendant will be released on his own recognizance or the amount of bail to be set for his release.

Bail to the action of bail above. See *Special bail,* infra.

Bail to the sheriff or bail below. Persons who undertake that a defendant arrested upon mesne process in a civil action shall duly appear to answer the plaintiff; such undertaking being in the form of a bond given to the sheriff, termed a "bail bond" *(q.v.).* 3 Bl.Comm. 290. Sureties who bind themselves to the sheriff to secure the defendant's appearance, or his putting in bail to the action on the return-day of the writ.

Civil bail. See that title.

Common bail. Fictitious sureties formally entered in the proper office of the court. See *Bail common,* supra.

Special bail. Responsible sureties who undertake as bail above. Persons who undertake jointly and severally in behalf of a defendant arrested on mesne process in a civil action that, if he be condemned in the action, he shall pay the costs and condemnation (that is, the amount which may be recovered against him), or render himself a prisoner, or that they will pay it for him. 3 Bl.Comm. 291. See *Bail to the sheriff or bail below,* supra.

Straw bail. Nominal or worthless bail. In English law, irresponsible persons, or men of no property, who make a practice of posting bail for any one who will pay them a fee therefor, and who originally, as a mark of their purpose, wore straw in their shoes.

Bailable. Capable of being bailed; admitting of bail; authorizing or requiring bail.

Bailable action. One in which the defendant is entitled to be discharged from arrest only upon giving bond to answer.

Bailable offense. One for which the prisoner may be admitted to bail.

Bailable process. Such as requires the officer to take bail, after arresting the defendant. That under which the sheriff is directed to arrest the defendant and is required by law to discharge him upon his tendering suitable bail as security for his appearance.

Bailee. In the law of contracts, one to whom goods are bailed; the party to whom personal property is delivered under a contract of bailment. A species of agent to whom something movable is committed in trust for another. Smith v. State, 78 Okl.Cr. 343, 148 P.2d 206, 208. Under U.C.C., a person who by warehouse receipt, bill of lading or other document of title acknowledges possession of goods and contracts to deliver them. U.C.C. § 7–102. See **Gratuitous bailee.**

Bailee for hire. A person to whom possession of personal property is transferred and who is compensated for caring for such property; *e.g.* a mechanic to whom an automobile is entrusted for repairs is a bailee for hire. See also **Bailment** *(Bailment for mutual benefit).*

Bailee policies. Floating insurance policies which cover goods while in possession of bailee without particular description in the policy. Gillespie v. Federal Compress & Warehouse Co., 37 Tenn.App. 476, 265 S.W.2d 21, 27.

Bailee's lien. Bailee's right (usually statutory) to retain bailed goods for payment of services.

Bailiff. A court officer or attendant who has charge of a court session in the matter of keeping order, custody of the jury, and custody of prisoners while in the court. One to whom some authority, care, guardianship, or jurisdiction is delivered, committed, or intrusted. One who is deputed or appointed to take charge of another's affairs; an overseer or superintendent; a keeper, protector, or guardian; a steward.

A person acting in a ministerial capacity who has by delivery the custody and administration of lands or goods for the benefit of the owner or bailor, and is liable to render an account thereof.

Bailiff-errant. A bailiff's deputy.

Bailiffs of franchises. In old English law, officers who performed the duties of sheriffs within liberties or privileged jurisdictions, in which formerly the king's writ could not be executed by the sheriff.

Bailiffs of hundreds. In old English law, officers appointed over hundreds, by the sheriffs, to collect fines therein, and summon juries; to attend the judges and justices at the assises and quarter sessions; and also to execute writs and process in the several hundreds. 1 Bl.Comm. 345.

Bailiffs of manors. In old English law, stewards or agents appointed by the lord (generally by an authority under seal) to superintend the manor, collect fines, and quit rents, inspect the buildings, order repairs, cut down trees, impound cattle trespassing, take an account of wastes, spoils, and misdemeanors in the woods and demesne lands, and do other acts for the lord's interest.

High bailiff. An officer formerly attached to an English county court. His duties were to attend the court when sitting; to serve summonses; and to execute orders, warrants, writs, etc. He also had similar duties under the bankruptcy jurisdiction of the county courts.

Special bailiff. A deputy sheriff, appointed at the request of a party to a suit, for the special purpose of serving or executing some writ or process in such suit.

Bailivia /beylíviyə/. In old law, a bailiff's jurisdiction, a bailiwick; the same as *bailium*. See **Bailiwick**.

In old English law, a liberty, or exclusive jurisdiction, which was exempted from the sheriff of the county, and over which the lord of the liberty appointed a bailiff with such powers within his precinct as an under-sheriff exercised under the sheriff of the county.

Bailiwick /béyləwìk/. A territorial segment over which a bailiff or sheriff has jurisdiction; not unlike a county in today's governmental divisions.

Bailment. A delivery of goods or personal property, by one person to another, in trust for the execution of a special object upon or in relation to such goods, beneficial either to the bailor or bailee or both, and upon a contract, express or implied, to perform the trust and carry out such object, and thereupon either to redeliver the goods to the bailor or otherwise dispose of the same in conformity with the purpose of the trust.

Delivery of personalty for some particular use, or on mere deposit, upon a contract, express or implied, that after purpose has been fulfilled it shall be redelivered to the person who delivered it, or otherwise dealt with according to his directions, or kept until he reclaims it, as the case may be. Simpkins v. Ritter, 189 Neb. 644, 204 N.W.2d 383, 385.

Generally, no fiduciary relationship is created by a bailment and hence it is not accurate to refer to the transfer as "in trust", because no trustee-beneficiary relationship is created.

See also **Pledge**.

Actual bailment. One which exists where there is either: (a) an "actual delivery," consisting in giving to the bailee or his agent the real possession of the chattel, or (b) a "constructive delivery," consisting of any of those acts which, although not truly comprising real possession of the goods transferred, have been held by legal construction equivalent to acts of real delivery.

Bailment for hire. A contract in which the bailor agrees to compensate the bailee. See also **Bailee for hire**, *supra; Bailment for mutual benefit,* below.

Bailment for mutual benefit. One in which the parties contemplate some price or compensation in return for benefits flowing from the bailment, necessarily involving an express or implied agreement or undertaking to that effect. For example, delivery of automobile to one who, for a consideration, undertakes to repair it.

Bailment lease. A legal method by which one desiring to purchase an article but unable to pay therefor at the time, may secure possession thereof with the right to use and enjoy it as long as he pays stipulated rentals and becomes absolute owner after completing such installment payments, on payment of an additional sum which may be nominal. This right or option is common in auto lease agreements.

Constructive bailment. One arising where the person having possession of a chattel holds it under such circumstances that the law imposes upon him the obligation to deliver it to another. Wentworth v. Riggs, 159 App.Div. 899, 143 N.Y.S. 955, 956. See, also, *Involuntary bailment, infra.*

Gratuitous bailment. Another name for a depositum or naked bailment, which is made only for the benefit of the bailor and is not a source of profit to the bailee.

Involuntary bailment. One arising by the accidental leaving of personal property in the possession of any person without negligence on the part of its owner. See *Constructive bailment,* above.

Lucrative bailment. One which is undertaken upon a consideration and for which a payment or recompense is to be made to the bailee, or from which he is to derive some advantage. See *Bailment for hire, supra.*

Bailor. The party who *bails* or delivers goods to another in the contract of bailment.

Bailout. Various procedures whereby the owners of an entity can obtain its profits with favorable tax consequences. With corporations, for example, the bailout of corporate profits at capital gain rates might well be the desired objective. The alternative of distributing the profits to the shareholders as dividends generally is less attractive since dividend income is taxed as ordinary income. See **Preferred stock** (*Preferred stock bail-out*).

Acquisition of a corporation for the principal purpose of favorable tax consequences by securing benefits of deduction, credit or other allowance which the acquiring corporation would not otherwise enjoy. I.R.C. § 269.

Bailout stock. When preferred stock is issued as a stock dividend and is non-taxable, it is called bailout stock. I.R.C. § 305.

Bait and switch. A deceptive sales practice. Such tactic usually involves advertising a low-priced product to lure customers to a store, then inducing them to buy higher-priced models by failing to stock sufficient quantities of the lower-priced item to satisfy demand, or by disparaging the less-expensive product. Tashof v. F. T. C., 437 F.2d 707, 709.

Balance. An equality between the sums total of the two sides of an account, or the excess on either side. The difference between the sum of debit entries minus the sum of credit entries in an account. If positive, the difference is called a debit balance; if negative, a credit balance.

Often used in the sense of residue or remainder, and, in a general sense, may be defined as what remains or is left over.

See also **Average daily balance**.

Balance of payments. The difference between all payments made by one nation to all other nations in the world and the payments made to that nation by all other nations.

Balance of power. In international law, a distribution and an opposition of forces, forming one system, so that no nation or country shall be in a position, either alone or united with others, to impose its will on any other nation or country or interfere with its independence. See also **Separation of powers**.

Balance of trade. Part of the balance of payments. It shows the net figure for the value of all the goods imported and exported by one nation. An excess of imports over exports constitutes a trade deficit.

Balance sheet. A statement of financial position of any economic unit, disclosing as at a given moment of time, its assets, at cost, depreciated cost, or other indicated value, its liabilities, and the equity of the owners in conformity with generally accepted accounting principles. See also **Profit and loss statement**.

Consolidated balance sheet. Covers combined operations of affiliated companies, divisions, or subsidiaries.

Net balance. In commercial usage, the balance of the proceeds, as from a sale of stock, after deducting the expenses incident to the sale.

Balancing of interests. Constitutional doctrine invoked when court is examining interplay between state action involving intrastate commerce and federal laws regarding interstate commerce. If there is legitimate state interest and if there is no clear congressional intent to preempt the field, state action will be upheld. Southern Pacific Co. v. State of Arizona ex rel., 325 U.S. 761, 65 S.Ct. 1515, 89 L.Ed. 1915.

Balancing test. A constitutional doctrine in which the court weighs the right of an individual to certain rights guaranteed by the Constitution with the rights of a state to protect its citizens from the invasion of their rights; used in cases involving freedom of speech and equal protection.

Balancing the equities. Doctrine commonly invoked in cases involving, for example, encroachment of building on another's land in which court will deny equitable relief to offended party in favor of money damages if the encroachment was made innocently and by mistake (not intentionally) and if encroachment is slight as compared with injury to offending party if he is required to remove. Adamec v. McCray, 63 Wash.2d 217, 386 P.2d 427, 428.

Baliva /bəláyvə/. (Spelled also *Balliva;* equivalent to *Balivatús, Balivia*). L. Lat. In old English law, a bailiwick; the jurisdiction of a sheriff; the whole district within which the trust of the sheriff was to be executed. 3 Bl.Comm. 283.

Balivo amovendo. See **Ballivo amovendo**.

Ballastage. A toll paid for the privilege of taking up ballast from the bottom of a port or harbor. This arises from the property in the soil.

Ballistics /bəlístəks/. The science of gun examination frequently used in criminal cases, especially cases of homicide, to determine the firing capacity of a weapon, its fireability, and whether a given bullet was fired from a particular gun.

Ballium /béyl(i)yəm/. A fortress or bulwark; also bail.

Ballivo amovendo /bəláyvow èymowvéndow/. An ancient writ to remove a bailiff from his office for want of sufficient land in the bailiwick.

Balloon mortgage. A mortgage providing for specific payments at stated regular intervals, with the final payment considerably more than any of the periodic payments.

Balloon note. A form of promissory note which commonly calls for minimum payments of principal, if any, and the payment of interest at regular intervals, but which requires a substantial payment of principal at the end of the term; the final payment frequently representing essentially all the principal.

Balloon payment. The final payment of principal under a balloon note; commonly represents essentially the entire principal. See **Balloon mortgage; Balloon note**.

Ballot. Derived from ballotta, a round bullet, used for casting a vote. Process or means of voting, usually in secret, by written or printed tickets or slips of paper, or voting machine. Piece of paper or levers on voting machine on which the voter gives expression to his choice. Sawyer Stores v. Mitchell, 103 Mont.

148, 62 P.2d 342, 348. A means, or instrumentality, by which a voter secretly indicates his will or choice so that it may be recorded as being in favor of a certain candidate or for or against a certain proposition or measure. Porter v. Oklahoma City, Okl., 446 P.2d 384, 391.

The whole amount of votes cast. Also, list of candidates running for office.

Australian ballot. See **Australian ballot**.

Joint ballot. In parliamentary practice, an election or vote by ballot participated in by the members of both houses of a legislative assembly sitting together as one body, the result being determined by a majority of the votes cast by the joint assembly thus constituted, instead of by concurrent majorities of the two houses.

Massachusetts ballot. See that title.

Mutilated ballot. One from which the name of the candidate is cut out. One which is destitute or deprived of some essential or valuable part; greatly shortened.

Office block ballot. A ballot form on which the names of all candidates for a particular office are listed under the office title. Listings are made under various titles regardless of the various party affiliations of the candidates.

Official ballot. Depending on its use in local statutes, this term has a varied meaning. It may refer to a ballot which has been furnished by the clerk; or it may contemplate that a ballot must have been printed under the supervision of a designated member of the electoral board, sealed by the board, and by resolution declared to be one of the official ballots for the election to be held.

Party column ballot. Ballot form on which the names of all candidates of each political party are placed in separate columns under party names and symbols, regardless of the offices sought by the candidates.

Secret ballot. The expression by ballot, voting machine, or otherwise, but in no event by proxy, of a choice with respect to any election or vote taken upon any matter, which is cast in such a manner that the person expressing such choice cannot be identified with the choice expressed.

Ballot-box. A locked box wherein ballots are deposited.

Balnearii /bælniyériyay/. In the Roman law, those who stole the clothes of bathers in the public baths. 4 Bl.Comm. 239.

Ban. In old English and civil law, a proclamation; a public notice; the announcement of an intended marriage. An excommunication; a curse, publicly pronounced. A proclamation of silence made by a crier in court before the meeting of champions in combat. A statute, edict, or command; a fine, or penalty. An expanse; an extent of space or territory; a space inclosed within certain limits; the limits or bounds themselves. An open field; the outskirts of a village. A privileged space or territory around a town, monastery, or other place.

Banc /bǽŋk/báŋk/. Bench; the place where a court permanently or regularly sits; the seat of judgment; as, *banc le roy*, the king's bench; *banc le common pleas*, the bench of common pleas.

The full bench, full court. A "sitting *en banc*" is a meeting of all the judges of a court as distinguished from the sitting of a single judge or panel of judges.

Banci narratores /bænsay næ̀rətóriyz/. In old English law, advocates; countors; serjeants. Applied to advocates in the common pleas courts. 1 Bl.Comm. 24.

Banco /bǽŋkow/. Ital. A seat or bench of justice; also, in commerce, a word of Italian origin signifying a bank. Also a small tract of land on opposite side of river from country to which it belongs, and so existing by virtue of an avulsive change in the river. San Lorenzo Title & Improvement Co. v. City Mortgage Co., Tex.Civ.App., 48 S.W.2d 310, 314. See, also, **Banc**.

Bancus /bǽŋkəs/. A high seat, or seat of distinction; a seat of judgment, or tribunal for the administration of justice. Often used for the court itself; thus, the English court of common pleas was formerly called *Bancus*.

Bancus reginæ /bǽŋkəs rəjáyniy/. The queen's bench. See **Queen's bench**.

Bancus regis /bǽŋkəs ríyjəs/. The king's bench; the supreme tribunal of the king after parliament. 3 Bl.Comm. 41.

Bancus superior /bǽŋkəs səpíriyər/. The upper bench. The king's bench was so called during the Protectorate.

Bandit. An outlaw; a man *banned*, or put under a ban; a brigand or robber. *Banditti*, a band of robbers.

Banditry. Organized robbery; brigandage; form of crime practiced by outlaws and plunderers.

Bane. A malefactor. Also a public denunciation of a malefactor; the same with what was called "*hutesium*," hue and cry.

Baneret, or **banneret** /bǽnərət/. In old English law, a knight made in the field, by the ceremony of cutting off the point of his standard, and making it, as it were, a banner. Knights so made were accounted so honorable that they were allowed to display their arms in the royal army, as barons did, and could bear arms with supporters. They were sometimes called "*vexillarii*."

A degree of honor next after a baron's, when conferred by the king; otherwise, it ranks after a baronet. 1 Bl.Comm. 403.

Bani /béynay/. Deodands (*q.v.*).

Banishment. A punishment inflicted upon criminals, by compelling them to leave a country for a specified period of time, or for life. Synonymous with exilement or deportation, importing a compulsory loss of one's country. See also **Deportation**.

Bank. A bank is an institution, usually incorporated, whose business it is to receive money on deposit, cash checks or drafts, discount commercial paper, make loans, and issue promissory notes payable to bearer, known as bank notes. U.C.C. § 1–201(4). American commercial banks fall into two main categories: state chartered banks and federally chartered national banks. See also **Banking.**

A bench or seat; the bench of justice; the bench or tribunal occupied by the judges; the seat of judgment; a court. The full bench, or full court; the assembly of all the judges of a court. See **Banc.**

An acclivity; an elevation or mound of earth, especially that which borders the sides of a water course. The land adjacent to a river. That part of a stream which retains the water. The elevation of land which confines the waters of a stream in their natural channel when they rise the highest and do not overflow the banks. A water-washed and relatively permanent elevation or acclivity at the outer line of a river bed which separates the bed from the adjacent upland, and serves to confine the waters within the bed and to preserve the course of the river. The land lying between the edge of the water of a stream at its ordinary low stage and the line which the edge of the water reaches in its ordinary high stage. An elevation of land which confines the waters of a stream when they rise out of the bed. Neither the line of ordinary high-water mark, nor of ordinary low-water mark, nor of a middle stage of water can be assumed as the line dividing the bed from the banks. Banks are fast land, on which vegetation appropriate to such land in the particular locality grows wherever the bank is not too steep to permit such growth, and bed is soil of a different character, and having no vegetation, or only such as exists, when commonly submerged in water. On the borders of navigable streams, where there are levees established according to law, the levees form the "banks of the river."

Advising bank. A bank which gives notification of the issuance of a credit by another bank. U.C.C. § 5–103(e).

Bank acceptance. Draft drawn on and accepted by bank.

Bank-account. A sum of money placed with a bank or banker, on deposit, by a customer, and subject to be drawn out on the latter's check. The statement or computation of the several sums deposited and those drawn out by the customer on checks, entered on the books of the bank and the depositor's passbook. Any account with a bank, including a checking, time, interest or savings account. U.C.C. § 4–104(a). See also **Joint bank account.**

Bank bill. See *Bank note, infra.*

Bank book. A book kept by a customer of a bank, showing the state of his account with it. See **Passbook.**

Bank call. Demand made on bank by state or federal supervisory personnel for examination of balance sheets.

Bank charter. Document issued by appropriate federal or state authority which permits corporation to commence business as a bank.

Bank credit. A credit with a bank by which, on proper credit rating or proper security given to the bank, a person receives liberty to draw to a certain extent agreed upon.

Bank debit. Total of checks and other commercial paper charged to deposit accounts.

Bank deposit. Placement of money in bank thereby creating contract between bank and depositor. U.C.C. § 4–103.

   Demand deposit. Right to withdraw deposit at any time.

   Time deposit. Deposit which is subject to notice (*e.g.* thirty days) before withdrawal.

Bank depositor. One who delivers to or leaves with a bank a sum of money subject to his order. Wharton v. Poughkeepsie Sav. Bank, 262 App.Div. 598, 31 N.Y.S.2d 311, 313.

Bank draft. A check, draft, or other order for payment of money, drawn by an authorized officer of a bank upon either his own bank or some other bank in which funds of his bank are deposited. Perry v. West, 110 N.H. 351, 266 A.2d 849, 852.

Bank note. A promissory note issued by a bank or banker authorized to do so, payable to bearer on demand, and intended to circulate as money. See **Federal reserve notes.**

Bank of circulation. One which issues bank notes payable to bearer. See *Bank of issue, infra.*

Bank of deposit. A savings bank or any other bank which receives money on deposit.

Bank of discount. One which lends money on collateral or by means of discounts of commercial paper.

Bank of issue. Bank with authority to issue notes intended to circulate as currency.

Bank rate. Interest rate charged customers on loans. See **Interest**; **Legal interest**.

Bank statement. Financial statement showing financial condition of bank at a given time. Federal (national banks) and state laws require that such statements be published several times a year.

Bank stock. Shares in the capital of a bank; shares in the property of a bank.

Bank teller. See **Teller.**

Branch banking. See **Branch bank.**

Central banks. Federal Reserve banks.

Collecting bank. Any bank handling the item for collection except the payor bank. U.C.C. § 4–105(d). See also **Collecting bank.**

Commercial bank. See **Commercial bank.**

Confirming bank. A bank which engages either that it will itself honor a credit already issued by another bank or that such a credit will be honored by the issuer or a third bank. U.C.C. § 5–103(f). See also **Confirming bank.**

Correspondent bank. Bank which acts as agent for another bank, or engages in an exchange of services with that bank, in a geographical area to which the other does not have direct access.

Custodian bank. Any bank or trust company which is supervised and examined by state or federal authority having supervision over banks and which is acting as custodian for a clearing corporation. U.C.C. § 8–102(4).

Depository bank. The first bank to which an item is transferred for collection even though it is also the payor bank. U.C.C. § 4–105(a).

Export-import bank. See **Export-Import Bank**.

Federal land bank. See **Federal Land Banks.**

Federal reserve bank. See **Federal Reserve System**.

Intermediary bank. Any bank to which an item is transferred in course of collection except the depositary or payor bank. U.C.C. § 4–105(c). See also **Intermediary bank**.

Land bank. See **Land bank.**

Member bank. See **Member bank.**

Mutual savings bank. See **Mutual savings bank**.

National bank. See **National bank.**

Payor bank. A bank by which an item is payable as drawn or accepted. U.C.C. § 4–105(b).

Presenting bank. Any bank presenting an item except a payor bank. U.C.C. § 4–105(e).

Remitting bank. Any payor or intermediary bank remitting for an item. U.C.C. § 4–105(f).

Savings and loan bank. See **Mutual savings bank; Savings and loan association.**

Savings bank. Type of bank that receives deposits, and pays interest thereon, and makes certain types of loans (*e.g.* home financing loans), but does not provide checking services. See **Mutual savings bank; Savings and loan association.** *Compare* **Commercial bank.**

Bankable paper. Notes, checks, bank bills, drafts and other securities for money, received as cash by banks.

Bank clearings. See **Clearinghouse**.

Banker. In general sense, person that engages in business of banking. In narrower meaning, a private person who keeps a bank; one who is engaged in the business of banking without being incorporated. One who carries on the business of banking by receiving money on deposit with or without interest, by buying and selling bills of exchange, promissory notes, bonds or stock, or other securities, and by loaning money without being incorporated.

Under some statutes, an individual banker, as distinguished from a "private banker" (*q.v.*), is a person who, having complied with the statutory requirements, has received authority from the state to engage in the business of banking, while a private banker is a person engaged in banking without having any special privileges or authority from the state.

See also **Investment banker**.

Person who holds stake in gambling game or wager.

Bankerout. Eng. Bankrupt; insolvent; indebted beyond the means of payment.

Banker's acceptance. A bill of exchange draft payable at maturity that is drawn by a creditor against his or her debtor. Banker's acceptances are short-term credit instruments most commonly used by persons or firms engaged in international trade. They are comparable to short-term government securities (for example, Treasury Bills) and may be sold on the open market at a discount.

Banker's lien. A lien which a banker has by virtue of which he can appropriate any money or property in his possession belonging to a customer to the extinguishment of any matured debt of such customer to the bank, provided such property or money has not been charged, with the knowledge of the bank, with the subservience of a special burden or purpose, or does not constitute a trust fund of which the banker has notice.

Banker's note. A commercial instrument resembling a bank note in every particular except that it is given by a private banker or unincorporated banking institution.

Bank Holding Company Act. Federal law which governs any company which directly or indirectly owns or controls, with power to vote, more than 5% of voting shares of each of two or more banks. Independent Bankers Ass'n of Ga. v. Dunn, 230 Ga. 345, 197 S.E.2d 129, 139.

Bank holiday of 1933. Presidential Proclamations No. 2039, issued March 6, 1933, and No. 2040, issued March 9, 1933, temporarily suspended banking transactions by member banks of the Federal Reserve System. Normal banking functions were resumed on March 13, subject to certain restrictions. The first proclamation, it was held, had no authority in law until the passage on March 9, 1933, of a ratifying act (12 U.S.C.A. § 95b). The present law forbids member banks of the Federal Reserve System to transact banking business, except under regulations of the Secretary of the Treasury, during an emergency proclaimed by the President. 12 U.S.C.A. § 95.

Banking. The business of banking, as defined by law and custom, consists in the issue of notes payable on demand intended to circulate as money when the banks are banks of issue; in receiving deposits payable on demand; in discounting commercial paper; making loans of money on collateral security; buying and selling bills of exchange; negotiating loans, and dealing in negotiable securities issued by the government, state and national, and municipal and other corporations. Mercantile Bank v. New York, 121 U.S. 138, 156, 7 S.Ct. 826, 30 L.Ed. 895; In re Prudence Co., D.C.N.Y., 10 F.Supp. 33, 36.

Investment banking. Business of underwriting or distributing bond, stock or other securities issues.

Banking a deal. Means making to one who wishes to consummate a deal a loan of money on collateral for a consideration which may consist of interest, a fee, or a part of the securities or property involved in the deal. Cray, McFawn & Co. v. Hegarty, Conroy & Co., D.C.N.Y., 27 F.Supp. 93, 99.

Banking commission. State regulatory body charged with supervision of banking institutions. See also **Federal Reserve Board of Governors** with respect to regulation of national banks.

Banking day. That part of any day on which a bank is open to the public for carrying on substantially all of its banking functions. U.C.C. § 4–104(c).

Banking game. Gambling game at which money is bet or hazarded.

Banking hours. A term which, in addition to the regular hours, includes time to allow presentment, after closing, to the bank returning a check, if such presentment is necessary in fact. Columbia-Knickerbocker Trust Co. v. Miller, 156 A.D. 810, 142 N.Y.S. 440, 445.

Bank night. A device by which a theater provides a registration book which any person over eighteen years of age, whether a patron of the theater or not, may sign. The book is placed in the lobby or outside the doors of the theater and no charge is made for registration nor need one who does so buy a ticket to the theater. A number is given to each name. On stated occasions, the numbers representing all the names registered are placed in a container on the stage of the theater and one number is drawn. The name of the person having that registration number is announced both inside and outside the theater and on coming forward within a certain time, he receives a sum of money which the theater provides from its own funds. If the person whose number is drawn is outside the theater, he is permitted to enter and claim the award without paying the admission. If he does not come forward within the time set, the money is added to the sum to be awarded on the next bank night. Under the plan, various safeguards are imposed on the operation to insure fairness in the allotment of the money. If not a *lottery*, a bank night is at least a *gift enterprise*. But it is generally considered to be a *lottery*. Furst v. A. & G. Amusement Co., 128 N.J.L. 311, 25 A.2d 892, 893; Commonwealth v. Lund, 142 Pa.Super. 208, 15 A.2d 839, 846.

Bankrupt. The state or condition of one who is unable to pay his debts as they are, or become, due. Amenability to the bankruptcy laws. The condition of one who (under the Bankruptcy Act of 1898) has committed an "act of bankruptcy" (*q.v.*), and is liable to be proceeded against by his creditors therefor, or of one whose circumstances are such that he is entitled, on his voluntary application, to take the benefit of the bankruptcy laws. The term includes a person against whom an involuntary petition has been filed, or who has filed a voluntary petition, or who has been adjudged a bankrupt. Person or municipality referred to as a "debtor" under Bankruptcy Act, § 101(12). See Act of bankruptcy; Arrangement with creditors; Bankruptcy Act; Bankruptcy proceedings; Composition in bankruptcy; Composition with creditors; Contemplation of bankruptcy; Insolvency; Wage earner's plan.

Bankruptcy Act. A federal law (11 U.S.C.A.) for the benefit and relief of creditors and their debtors in cases in which the latter are unable or unwilling to pay their debts. The Act was substantially revised in 1978, effective October 1, 1979. Straight bankruptcy is in the nature of a liquidation proceeding and involves the collection and distribution to creditors of all the bankrupt's non-exempt property by the trustee in the manner provided by the Act. The debtor rehabilitation provisions of the Act (Chapters 11 and 13) differ however from straight bankruptcy in that the debtor looks to rehabilitation and reorganization, rather than liquidation, and the creditor looks to future earnings of the bankrupt, rather than property held by the bankrupt to satisfy their claims (see *e.g.* Wage earner's plan). See **Act of bankruptcy; Bankruptcy proceedings.**

Bankruptcy proceedings. The taking of possession by the trustee of the property of the bankrupt actually or constructively in his possession at time of filing of petition in bankruptcy, the distribution of the proceeds received from such property, ratably, among bankrupt's creditors whose claims have been filed and allowed, and the discharge of bankrupt from liability for the unpaid balance of such claims. In re Public Leasing Corp., C.A.Okl., 488 F.2d 1369. Bankruptcy (in the sense of proceedings taken under the bankruptcy law) is either voluntary or involuntary; the former where the proceeding is initiated by the debtor's own petition to be adjudged a bankrupt and have the benefit of the law, the latter where he is forced into bankruptcy on the petition of a sufficient number of his creditors. See **Bankruptcy Act,** *supra.*

Bankruptcy proceedings are governed by the federal Bankruptcy Act (11 U.S.C.A.) and Official Rules and Forms.

Adjudication of bankruptcy. The judgment or decree of the bankruptcy court that a person against whom a petition in bankruptcy has been filed, or who has filed his voluntary petition, be ordered and adjudged to be a bankrupt.

Bankruptcy courts. Federal courts, as adjuncts to U.S. District Courts, which are concerned exclusively with the administration of Bankruptcy Act and presided over by a bankruptcy judge. 28 U.S.C.A. § 151. Bankruptcy courts exercise jurisdiction as generally provided in 28 U.S.C.A. § 1471.

Bankruptcy discharge. Order of Bankruptcy Court which discharges bankrupt from all dischargeable obligations and debts. For effect of, and exceptions to, discharge, see Bankruptcy Act §§ 523, 524, 727.

Bankruptcy distribution. After payment of administration, priority and other debts and expenses of bankrupt estate, trustee in bankruptcy makes pro rata distribution to creditors. See 11 U.S.C.A. § 726.

Bankruptcy forms. Official forms used in Bankruptcy Court for most matters (*e.g.* petitions, schedules).

Bankruptcy rules. Rules governing proceedings in bankruptcy courts; a great many of which make the Federal Rules of Civil Procedure applicable.

Bankruptcy schedules. Official forms for listing of bankrupt's assets, liabilities, and all unsecured creditors.

Bankruptcy trustee. One appointed by Bankruptcy Court to take charge of bankrupt estate, to collect assets, to bring suit on bankrupt's claims, and to defend actions against it; he has power to examine bankrupt, to initiate actions to set aside preferences, etc. 11 U.S.C.A. § 321 et seq. United States Trustees are provided for under Chapter 15 of the Bankruptcy Act (11 U.S.C.A. § 1501 et seq.).

Bank Secrecy Act. Federal Act (1970), officially titled the "Currency and Foreign Transactions Reporting Act," which requires banks and other financial institutions to report to the Internal Revenue Service detailed information on each unusual cash transaction over $10,000. The Act also requires anyone who transports, physically or through the mails, more than $5,000 in cash into or out of the United States to file a report with the United States Custom Service. Its final provision requires United States taxpayers who have foreign bank accounts to file a report with the Treasury Department. The act provides for both criminal and civil penalties for failure to comply fully with these reporting requirements. 31 U.S.C.A. § 1051 et seq.

Banleuca /bænl(y)úwkə/. (Same as the French *ban-lieue*). An old law term, signifying a space or tract of country around a city, town, or monastery, distinguished and protected by peculiar privileges.

Banni /bǽnay/, or **bannitus** /bǽnədəs/. In old law, one under a ban *(q.v.);* an outlaw or banished man.

Banni nuptiarum /bǽnay nəpshiyérəm/. L. Lat. In old English law, the banns of matrimony.

Bannitio /bænísh(iy)ow/. Banishment; expulsion by a ban or public proclamation.

Bannitus /bǽnədəs/. See **Banni.**

Banns of matrimony. Public notice or proclamation of a matrimonial contract, and the intended celebration of the marriage of the parties in pursuance of such contract. Such announcement is required by certain religions to be made in a church or chapel, during service, on three consecutive Sundays before the marriage is celebrated. The object is to afford an opportunity for any person to interpose an objection if he knows of any impediment or other just cause why the marriage should not take place.

Bar. The court, in its strictest sense, sitting in full term. The presence, actual or constructive, of the court. Thus a trial *at bar* is one had before the full court, distinguished from a trial had before a single judge at *nisi prius*. So the "case at bar" is the case now before the court and under its consideration; the case being tried or argued.

In another sense, the whole body of attorneys and counsellors, or the members of the legal profession, collectively, who are figuratively called the "bar". They are thus distinguished from the "bench," which term denotes the whole body of judges. See **Bar association.**

In the practice of legislative bodies, the outer boundary of the house; therefore, all persons, not being members, who wish to address the house, or are summoned to it, appear *at the bar* for that purpose.

In the law of contracts, an impediment, obstacle, or preventive barrier. Thus, relationship within the prohibited degrees is a *bar* to marriage. In this sense also we speak of the "bar of the statute of limitations."

That which defeats, annuls, cuts off, or puts an end to. Thus, a provision "in bar of dower" is one which has the effect of defeating or cutting off the dower-rights which the wife would otherwise become entitled to in the particular land.

In pleading, a special plea, constituting a sufficient answer to an action at law; so called because it *barred, i.e.,* prevented, the plaintiff from further pros-

ecuting it with effect, and, if established by proof, defeated and destroyed the action altogether. Called a special "plea in bar." It may be further described as a plea or peremptory exception of a defendant to destroy the plaintiff's action. Under Fed.Rules Civ. Proc., pleas in bar are abolished in favor of affirmative pleading of defenses in answer. Rule 8(c). See **Plea** *(Plea in bar).*

With respect to claim preclusion, a valid and final personal judgment on the merits against a claimant precludes (bars) a later suit on the same claim or cause of action.

A judgment rendered in a case is a bar to further action in the state in which it was rendered and in all other jurisdictions if the court which rendered it had required jurisdiction and if the subsequent action is brought by a party to first action or his privy. See **Res** *(Res judicata).*

A particular part of the court-room; for example, the place where prisoners stand at their trial, hence the expression "prisoner at the bar."

In England, a partition or railing running across a court-room, intended to separate the general public from the space occupied by the judges, counsel, jury, and others concerned in the trial of a cause. In the English courts it is the partition behind which all outer-barristers and every member of the public must stand. Solicitors being officers of the court, are admitted within it; as are also queen's counsel, barristers with patents of precedence, and serjeants, in virtue of their ranks. Parties who appear in person also are placed within the bar on the floor of the court.

Bar admission. Act by which one is licensed to practice before courts of a particular state or jurisdiction after satisfying requirements such as bar examination, period of residency or admission on grounds of reciprocity after period of years as member of bar of another jurisdiction.

Baragaria. Span. A concubine, whom a man keeps alone in his house, unconnected with any other woman.

Bar association. An association of members of the legal profession. Such associations have been organized in most states and also on the national level (American Bar Association; Federal Bar Association), and even on the city level (*e.g.* New York City Bar Ass'n). The first was established in Mississippi in 1825, but it is not known to have had a continued existence. An association of Grafton and Coos counties in New Hampshire had an existence before 1800, and probably a more or less continuous life since then, having finally merged into a state association.

Bar integration. See **Integrated bar.**

Barat. See **Berat.**

Baratriam committit qui propter pecuniam justitiam baractat /bəréytriyəm kəmídət kwáy próptər pək(y)úwniyəm jəstíshiyəm bərǽktət/. He is guilty of barratry who for money sells justice. (This maxim, however, is one pertaining more to the meaning of "barratry" as used in Scotch law than to its common-law meaning.) See **Barratry.**

Barbiturate /barbíchərət/. A general term denoting a derivative of barbituric acid formed by the substitution of an aliphatic or aromatic group on a carbon or nitrogen atom in the acid; used in medicine as hypnotic and sedative drugs.

Bareboat charter. A document under which one who charters or leases a boat becomes for the period of the charter the owner for all practical purposes. Reed v. The Yaka, 373 U.S. 410, 83 S.Ct. 1349, 10 L.Ed.2d 448. Lease of vessel without a crew. Gillentine v. McKeand, C.A.Mass., 426 F.2d 717, 719.

Bare or **mere licensee.** One whose presence on premises is merely tolerated; while a "licensee" or "invitee" is one who is on the premises by invitation, express or implied. Chicago, R. I. & P. Ry. Co. v. McCleary, 175 Okl. 347, 53 P.2d 555, 557.

Bare patent license. A grant of authority to make, use or vend patented product throughout the United States or in a given part thereof, with no right of exclusion.

Baret. L. Fr. A wrangling suit.

Bare trustee. One whose trust is to convey, and the time has arrived for a conveyance by him. Trustee of a dry trust; or a trustee to whose office no duties were originally attached, or who, although such duties were originally attached to his office, would, on the requisition of his *cestuis que trust*, be compellable in equity to convey the estate to them or by their direction.

Bar fee. In old English law, a fee taken by the sheriff, time out of mind, for every prisoner who is acquitted. "Extortion." Abolished by St. 14 Geo. III, c. 26; 55 Geo. III, c. 50; 8 & 9 Vict., c. 114.

Bargain. A mutual undertaking, contract, or agreement. A contract or agreement between two parties, the one to sell goods or lands, and the other to buy them. To negotiate over the terms of a purchase or contract. To come to terms.

Bargain money. These words in a contract for the sale of land have much the same significance as earnest money.

Catching bargain. A bargain by which money is loaned, at an extortionate or extravagant rate, to an heir or any one who has an estate in reversion or expectancy, to be repaid on the vesting of his interest; or a similar unconscionable bargain with such person for the purchase outright of his expectancy. That kind of fraud often perpetrated upon young, inexperienced, or ignorant people. See **Unconscionable bargain.**

Bargain and sale. In conveyancing, the transferring of the property of a thing from one to another, upon valuable consideration, by way of sale. A contract or bargain by the owner of land, in consideration of money or its equivalent paid, to sell land to another person, called the "bargainee," whereupon a use arises in favor of the latter, to whom the seisin is transferred by force of the statute of uses. The expression "bargain and sale" is also applied to transfers of personalty, in cases where there is first an executory agreement for the sale (the bargain), and then an actual and completed sale.

Bargain and sale deed. A deed that has a recitation of consideration coupled with words of conveyance of real property.

Bargainee. The grantee of an estate in a deed of a bargain and sale. The party to a bargain to whom the subject-matter of the bargain or thing bargained for is to go.

Bargaining agent. Union recognized and certified as such by NLRB as the exclusive representative of employees in a bargaining unit.

Bargaining for plea. Commonly referred to as plea bargaining in which defendant seeks a lesser sentence in return for plea of guilty; or an attempt to plead guilty to lesser included offense which carries a less severe penalty. See **Plea bargaining.**

Bargaining unit. Labor union or group of jobs authorized to carry on collective bargaining in behalf of employees. A particular group of employees with a similar community of interest appropriate for bargaining.

Bargain money. See **Earnest money**.

Bargainor. The person who makes a bargain. The party to a bargain who is to receive the consideration and perform the contract by delivery of the subject-matter.

Bargain or **contract in restraint of trade.** Any bargain or contract which purports to limit in any way right of either party to work or to do business.

Bargain sale or **purchase.** A sale of property for less than the fair market value of such property. The difference between the sale or purchase price and the fair market value of the property will have to be accounted for in terms of its tax consequences.

Bark. Term is sometimes figuratively used to denote the mere words or letter of an instrument, or outer covering of the ideas sought to be expressed, as distinguished from its inner substance or essential meaning.

Barnard's inn. An inn of chancery. See **Inns of Chancery.**

Baro /bǽrow/. In old law, a man, whether slave or free. In later usage, a freeman or freedman; a strong man; a good soldier; a hired soldier; a vassal; a baron; a feudal tenant or client. A man of dignity and rank; a knight. A magnate in the church. A judge in the exchequer (*baro scaccarii*). The first-born child. A husband.

Baron /bǽrən/. A lord or nobleman; the most general title of nobility in England. 1 Bl.Comm. 398, 399. A particular degree or title of nobility, next to a viscount. The lowest title in Great Britain. A judge of the court of exchequer. 3 Bl.Comm. 44. A freeman. Also a vassal holding directly from the king. A husband; occurring in this sense in the phrase *"baron et feme,"* husband and wife. The term has essentially the same meanings as *baro (q.v.).*

Baronage. In English law, the collective body of the barons, or of the nobility at large.

Baron court. See **Court-baron**.

Barones scaccarii. See **Barons of the exchequer**.

Baronet. An English name or hereditary title of dignity or rank (but not a title of nobility, being next below that of baron), established in 1611 by James I. It is created by letters patent, and descends to the male heir.

Baron et feme /bǽrən ey fém/. Man and woman; husband and wife. A wife being under the protection and influence of her *baron*, lord, or husband, is styled a *"feme-covert" (fœmina viro cooperta)*, and her state of marriage is called her "coverture."

Barons of the exchequer. The six judges of the court of exchequer in England, of whom one is styled the "chief baron;" answering to the justices and chief justice of other courts.

Barony. The dignity of a baron; a species of tenure; the territory or lands held by a baron.

Barony of land. In England, a quantity of land amounting to 15 acres. In Ireland, a subdivision of a county.

Barra, or **barre.** In old practice, a plea in bar. The bar of the court. A barrister.

Barrator /bǽrədər/. One who commits barratry. See **Barretor**.

Barratrous /bǽrətrəs/. Fraudulent; having the character of barratry.

Barratry /bǽrətriy/. Also spelled "Barretry." The offense of frequently exciting and stirring up quarrels and suits, either at law or otherwise. State v. Batson, 220 N.C. 411, 17 S.E.2d 511, 512, 513.

In maritime law, an act committed by master or mariners of a vessel for some fraudulent or unlawful purpose contrary to their duty to owner and resulting in injury to owner. Isbell Enterprises, Inc. v. Citizens Cas. Co. of New York, D.C.Tex., 303 F.Supp. 549, 552.

See also **Barretor; Champerty**.

Barred. Obstructed by a bar. Subject to hindrance or obstruction by a bar or barrier which, if interposed, will prevent legal redress or recovery; as, when it is said that a claim or cause of action is "barred by the statute of limitations."

Barrel. A measure of capacity, equal (in England) to 36 imperial gallons. The standard United States measure, except as to barrels of petroleum, equals 31½ gallons.

In agricultural and mercantile parlance, as also in the inspection laws, the term means, *prima facie*, not merely a certain quantity, but, further, a certain state of the article; namely, that it is in a cask.

Barren money. In the civil law, a debt which bears no interest.

Barrenness. Sterility; the incapacity to bear children.

Barretor /bǽrədər/. A common mover, exciter, or maintainer of suits and quarrels either in courts or elsewhere in the country; a disturber of the peace who spreads false rumors and calumnies, whereby discord and disquiet may grow among neighbors.

One who frequently excites and stirs up groundless suits and quarrels, either at law or otherwise. State v. Batson, 220 N.C. 411, 17 S.E.2d 511, 512, 513.

Barrister. In England, an advocate; a counsellor learned in the law who has been admitted to plead at the bar, and who is engaged in conducting the trial or argument of causes. A person called to the bar by the benches of Inns of Court, giving exclusive right of audience in the Supreme Court.

Barter. To exchange goods or services without using money. Rosenberg v. State, 12 Md.App. 20, 276 A.2d 708, 711. See also **Exchange**.

Bas. Fr. Low; inferior; subordinate.

Basal fracture. A fracture of the skull beginning at the base of the skull to the rear and left extending to the top of the skull.

Bas chevaliers /béys shevəlírz/bá shəvalyéy/. In old English law, low, or inferior knights, by tenure of a base military fee, as distinguished from *barons* and *bannerets*, who were the chief or superior knights.

Base, *adj*. Low in place or position; inferior; servile; of subordinate degree; impure, adulterated, or alloyed.

Base animal. See **Animal**.

Base bullion. Base silver bullion is silver in bars mixed to a greater or less extent with alloys or base materials.

Base coin. Debased, adulterated, or alloyed coin (*e.g.* copper, nickel) as distinguished from silver or gold.

Base court. In old English law, an inferior court, that is, not of record, as the court baron.

Base estate. The estate which "base tenants" (*q.v.*) have in their land.

Base fee. One that may last forever if the contingency does not happen, but debased because its duration depends upon collateral circumstances which qualify it; sometimes called a conditional, determinable, or qualified fee.

In old English law, an estate or fee which has a qualification subjoined thereto, and which must be determined whenever the qualification annexed to it is at an end. Scobey v. Beckman, 111 Ind.App. 574, 41 N.E.2d 847, 850.

Base services. In feudal law, such services as were unworthy to be performed by the nobler men, and were performed by the peasants and those of servile rank. 2 Bl.Comm. 62.

Base tenants. Tenants who performed to their lords services in villenage; tenants who held at the will of the lord, as distinguished from *frank* tenants, or freeholders.

Base tenure. A tenure by villenage, or other customary service, as distinguished from tenure by military service; or from tenure by free service.

Base, *n*. Bottom, foundation, groundwork, that on which a thing rests. The locality on which a military or naval force relies for supplies or from which it initiates operations; *e.g.* air base; military base; marine base; naval base; submarine base.

Base line. Survey line used in the government survey to establish township lines. Horizontal elevation line used as centerline in a highway survey.

Base pay. Wages, exclusive of overtime, bonuses, etc.

Basic or **pioneer patent.** One discovered in new field and recognized by scientific world or industry as startling, unexpected, and unprophesied. Northwest Engineering Corporation v. Keystone Driller Co., C.C. A.Wis., 70 F.2d 13, 16.

Basileus /bæsəlyúws/. A Greek word, meaning "king." A title assumed by the emperors of the Eastern Roman Empire. It is used by Justinian in some of the Novels; and is said to have been applied to the English kings before the Conquest. 1 Bl.Comm. 242.

Basilica /bəsíləkə/. The name given to a compilation of Roman and Greek law, prepared about A.D. 880 by the Emperor Basilius, and published by his successor, Leo the Philosopher. It was written in Greek, was mainly an abridgment of Justinian's *Corpus Juris*, and comprised sixty books, only a portion of which are extant. It remained the law of the Eastern Empire until the fall of Constantinople, in 1453.

Basils. In old English law, a kind of money or coin abolished by Henry II.

Basin. When speaking of a large river, ordinarily means or includes the entire area drained by the main stream and its tributaries. City of Tulsa v. Peacock, 181 Okl. 383, 74 P.2d 359, 360.

In admiralty law and marine insurance, a part of the sea inclosed in rocks.

Basis. Fundamental principle; groundwork; support; the foundation or groundwork of anything; that upon which anything may rest or the principal component parts of a thing.

Accounting. Term used in accounting, especially in tax accounting, to describe the value of an asset for purpose of determining gain (or loss) on its sale or transfer or in determining value in the hands of a donee of a gift.

Acquisition cost, or some substitute therefor, of an asset used in computing gain or loss on disposition or retirement. The amount assigned to an asset for income tax purposes. For assets acquired by purchase, the basis would be cost [I.R.C. § 1012]. Special rules govern the basis of property received by virtue of another's death [I.R.C. §§ 1014, 1023] or by gift [§ 1015], the basis of stock received on a transfer of property to a controlled corporation [§ 358], the basis of the property transferred to the corporation [§ 362], and the basis of property received upon the liquidation of a corporation [§ 334].

Adjusted basis. In tax accounting, the value of property placed on it after its acquisition and after reflecting increases and decreases to the dollar amount of the original basis. The cost or other basis of property reduced by depreciation allowed or allowable and increased by capital improvements.

Stepped-up basis. In tax accounting, value placed on property which is acquired in a taxable transaction or purchase. I.R.C. § 1012.

Substituted basis. In tax accounting, value placed on property acquired in a transaction in which gain or loss is not recognized. I.R.C. § 1014. See also **Substituted basis.**

See also **Accrual basis.**

Basis of bargain. That on which any affirmation of fact or promise relating to goods sold is predicated, creating an express warranty. U.C.C. § 2–313(1)(a). See **Essence of the contract.**

Bastard. An illegitimate child; a child born before the lawful marriage of its parents; *i.e.* born out of lawful wedlock.

A child born after marriage, but under circumstances which render it impossible that the husband of his mother can be his father. State v. Coliton, 73 N.D. 582, 17 N.W.2d 546, 548, 549.

Bastard eigné. In old English law, bastard elder. If a child was born of an illicit connection, and afterwards the parents intermarried and had another son, the elder was called bastard eigné, or, as it is now spelled, ainé, and the second son was called puisné, or since born, or sometimes he was called mulier puisné. 2 Bl.Comm. 248.

Bastardize. To declare one a bastard, as a court does. To give evidence to prove one a bastard. A mother (married) cannot bastardize her child.

Bastardus non potest habere hæredem nisi de corpore suo legitime procreatum /bæstárdəs nòn pówdəst həbíriy həríydiy náysay diy kórpəriy s(y)úwow ləjídəmiy pròwkriyéydəm/. A bastard can have no heir unless it be one lawfully begotten of his own body.

Bastardus nullius est filius, aut filius populi /bæstárdəs nəláyəs èst fíliyəs òt fíliyəs pòpyəlay/. A bastard is nobody's son, or the son of the people.

Bastardy proceedings. Court proceeding in which the paternity of a child is determined. The method provided by statute of proceeding against the putative father to secure a proper maintenance for the bastard.

Bastille /bæstíyl/. A prison, citadel, fortress. Prison constructed in Paris in 1369 and destroyed in 1789.

Baston /bǽstən/bətón/. In old English law, a baton, club, or staff. A term applied to officers of the wardens of the prison called the "Fleet," because of the staff carried by them. See **Trail-baston.**

Bas ville /bà víyl/. In French law, the suburbs of a town.

Batable-ground. Land that is in controversy, or about the possession of which there is a dispute, as the lands which were situated between England and Scotland before the Union.

Bataille /bætáy/. In old English law, battel; the trial by combat or *duellum.*

Batiment /bætəmón/. In French marine law, a vessel or ship.

Batonnier /bæ̀tonyéy/. The chief of the French bar in its various centres, who presides in the council of discipline.

Battel /bǽdəl/. Trial by combat; wager of battel. See **Wager of battel**.

Battered child. A child who is suffering serious physical or emotional injury resulting from abuse inflicted upon him including sexual abuse, or from neglect, including malnutrition, or who is determined to be physically dependent upon an addictive drug at birth. See also **Child abuse.**

Battery. Criminal battery, defined as the unlawful application of force to the person of another, may be divided into its three basic elements: (1) the defendant's conduct (act or omission); (2) his "mental state," which may be an intent to kill or injure, or criminal negligence, or perhaps the doing of an unlawful act; and (3) the harmful result to the victim, which may be either a bodily injury or an offensive touching. What might otherwise be a battery may be justified; and the consent of the victim may under some circumstances constitute a defense. Com. v. Hill, 237 Pa.Super. 543, 353 A.2d 870. The consummation of an unlawful assault.

The actual offer to use force to the injury of another person is *assault;* the use of it is *battery,* which always includes an assault; hence the two terms are commonly combined in the term "assault and battery."

See also **Assault and battery.**

Aggravated battery. An unlawful act of violent injury to the person of another, accompanied by circumstances of aggravation, such as the use of deadly weapon, great disparity between the ages and physical conditions of the parties, or the purposeful infliction of shame and disgrace.

Simple battery. One not accompanied by circumstances of aggravation, or not resulting in grievous bodily injury.

Technical battery. A technical battery occurs when a physician or dentist, in the course of treatment, exceeds the consent given by a patient. Although no wrongful intent is present, and in fact there may be a sincere purpose to aid the patient, recovery is permitted unless there is an emergency. However, if the patient benefits from the battery only nominal damages may be recovered.

Battle of the forms. Term used to describe effect of multitude of forms used by buyers and sellers to accept and to confirm terms expressed in other forms. U.C.C. § 2–207.

Batture /bətyúr/. A marine term, used to denote a bottom of sand, stone, or rock, mixed together, and rising towards the surface of the water; as a technical word and also in common parlance, an elevation of the bed of a river, under the surface of the water. The term is, however, sometimes used to denote the same elevation of the bank, when it has risen above the surface of the water, or is as high as the land on the outside of the bank. Conkey v. Knudsen, 143 Neb. 5, 8 N.W.2d 538, 541. In this latter sense it is synonymous with "alluvion." It means, in common-law language, land formed by accretion. The term is used in Louisiana, and is applied principally to certain portions of the bed of the Mississippi river which are uncovered at time of low water but are covered annually at time of ordinary high water.

Bawd /bód/. One who procures opportunities for persons of opposite sexes to cohabit in an illicit manner; who may be, while exercising the trade of a bawd, perfectly innocent of committing in his or her own proper person the crime either of adultery or of fornication. A madam.

Bawdy-house. A house of ill fame; a house of prostitution; a brothel. A house or dwelling maintained for the convenience and resort of persons desiring unlawful sexual connection. A place for convenience of people of both sexes in resorting to lewdness, a place many may frequent for immoral purposes or a house where one may go for immoral purposes without invitation. Riley v. U. S., D.C.App., 298 A.2d 228, 231.

Bay. A pond-head made of a great height to keep in water for the supply of a mill, etc., so that the wheel of the mill may be turned by the water rushing thence, through a passage or flood-gate. (This is generally called a forebay.)

A bending or curving of the shore of the sea or of a lake, so as to form a more or less inclosed body of water. An opening into the land, or an arm of the sea, where the water is shut in on all sides except at the entrance.

Baygall. A low-lying wet land matter with vegetable fibres and often with gallberry and other thick-growing bushes.

Bayley /béyliy/. In old English law, bailiff. This term was used in the laws of the colony of New Plymouth, Mass., A.D. 1670, 1671.

Bayou /báyuw/báyow/. A species of creek or stream common in Louisiana and Texas. An outlet from a swamp, pond, or lagoon, to a river, or the sea.

B.C. An abbreviation for "before Christ," "bail court," "bankruptcy cases," and "British Columbia."

B.E. An abbreviation for "Baron of the Court of Exchequer."

Beach. This term, in its ordinary signification, when applied to a place on tide waters means the space between ordinary high and low water mark; or the space over which the tide usually ebbs and flows. It is a term not more significant of a sea margin than "shore." In common parlance designates that portion of shore consisting generally of sand and pebbles, resulting usually from the action of water, as distinct from the upland, to which it often extends above normal high-water mark. Beach is synonymous with "shore," "strand," or "flats." The term may also include the sandy shore above mean high water which is washed by storms and exceptionally high tides.

To "beach" a ship is to run it upon the beach or shore; this is frequently found necessary in case of a fire, leak, etc.

See **Foreshore; Seashore.**

Public beach. Beach dedicated by governmental body to the common use of the public, which the unorganized public and each of its members have a right to use while it remains such.

Beacon. A light-house, or sea-mark, formerly used to alarm the country, in case of the approach of an enemy, but now used for the guidance of ships at sea, by night, as well as by day.

Beaconage. Money paid for the maintenance of a beacon or signal-light.

Beadle. In English ecclesiastical law, an inferior parish officer, who is chosen by the vestry, and whose business is to attend the vestry, to give notice of its meetings, to execute its orders, to attend upon inquests, and to assist the constables. See **Bedel**.

Beams and balance. Instruments for weighing goods and merchandise.

Bear. To support, sustain, or carry. To give rise to, or to produce, something else as an incident or auxiliary. To render, to manage, or direct, or to conduct; to carry on, or maintain. To produce as yield; *e.g.* "bear" interest. One who believes stock prices will decline; opposite of a "bull."

Bear arms. The Second Amendment, U.S. Constitution, provides that the "right of the people to bear arms, shall not be infringed." This right has been restricted however by state and federal laws regulating the transportation, sale, use, and possession of weapons.

Bearer. The person in possession of an instrument, document of title, or security payable to bearer or indorsed in blank. U.C.C. § 1–201(5). When a check, note, draft, etc., is payable to "bearer," it imports that such shall be payable to any person who may present the instrument for payment. See also **Payable to bearer**.

Bearer bond. Bonds payable to the person having possession of them. Such bonds do not require endorsement to transfer ownership but only the transfer of possession.

Bearer instrument. An instrument is payable to bearer when by its terms it is payable to (a) bearer or the order of bearer; or (b) a specified person or bearer; or (c) "cash" or the order of "cash", or any other indication which does not purport to designate a specific payee. U.C.C. § 3–111.

Bearer paper. Commercial paper payable to bearer; *i.e.* to the person having possession of such. See **Bearer instrument**.

Bearing date. Disclosing a date on its face; having a certain date. Words frequently used in pleading and conveyancing to introduce the date which has been put upon an instrument.

Bear interest. To yield, generate, or produce interest on the principal.

Bear market. A market in which prices are falling or are expected to fall.

Beat, v. To strike or hit repeatedly, as with blows. In the criminal law and the law of torts, with reference to assault and battery, the term includes any unlawful physical violence offered to another. See **Battery**.

Beat, n. In some of the southern states (as Alabama, Mississippi, South Carolina) the principal legal subdivision of a county, corresponding to towns or townships in other states; or a voting precinct.

Beating. The infliction of extreme force to another. See **Battery**.

Beating of the bounds. An ancient custom in England by which, once a year, the minister, etc., of a parish walked about its boundaries to preserve a recollection of them.

Beaupleader /bòwplíydər/. (L. Fr. fair pleading). A writ of prohibition directed to the sheriff or another, directing him not to take a fine for beaupleader. There was anciently a fine imposed called a fine for beaupleader, which is explained by Coke to have been originally imposed for bad pleading.

Bed. The hollow or channel of a water course; the depression between the banks worn by the regular and usual flow of the water. The land that is covered by the water in its ordinary low stage. Area extending between the opposing banks measured from the foot of the banks from the top of the water at its ordinary stage, including sand bars which may exist between the foot of said banks as thus defined. Town of Refugio v. Heard, Tex.Civ.App., 95 S.W.2d 1008, 1010. It includes the lands below ordinary high water mark. United States v. Chicago, M., St. P. & P. R. Co., 312 U.S. 592, 313 U.S. 543, 61 S.Ct. 772, 775, 85 L.Ed. 1064.

Also, the right of cohabitation or marital intercourse; as in the phrase "divorce from bed and board," or *a mensa et thoro*.

Bed and board. Divorce a mensa et thoro. See **Divorce**.

Bedel /bíydəl/. In English law, a crier or messenger of court, who summons men to appear and answer therein. A herald to make public proclamation. An inferior officer of a parish or liberty, to give notice of vestry meetings, etc.

An officer of the forest, similar to a sheriff's special bailiff. A collector of rents for the king.

Bedelary /bíydəlèriy/. The jurisdiction of a bedel, as a bailiwick is the jurisdiction of a bailiff.

Bederepe /bíydriyp/. A service which certain tenants were anciently bound to perform, as to reap their landlord's corn at harvest.

Before. Prior to; preceding; in front of; at the disposal of; in a higher position. In the presence of; under the official purview of; as in a magistrate's jurat, "*before* me personally appeared," etc.

When used as a preposition, does not indicate a period of time as do the prepositions "for," "during," and "throughout," but merely an event or act preceding in time, or earlier than, or previously to, the time mentioned. First Nat. Corp. v. Perrine, 99 Mont. 454, 43 P.2d 1073, 1077.

Beg. To solicit alms or charitable aid.

Beget. To procreate as the father.

Beggar. One who lives by begging charity, or who has no other means of support than solicited alms.

Begin. To originate; to come into existence; to start; to institute; to initiate; to commence. People ex rel. Northchester Corporation v. Miller, 263 App.Div. 83, 31 N.Y.S.2d 586, 587.

Behalf. Benefit, support, defence, or advantage.

Behavior. Manner of having, holding, or keeping one's self; manner of behaving, whether good or bad; conduct; manners; carriage of one's self, with respect to propriety and morals; deportment. State v. Roll, 1 Ohio Dec. 284; Schneiderman v. United States, 320 U.S. 118, 63 S.Ct. 1333, 1340, 87 L.Ed. 1796. See also **Character; Reputation.**

Behetria /bèyeytríyə/. In Spanish law, lands situated in districts and manors in which the inhabitants had the right to select their own lords.

Behoof. Use; benefit; profit; service; advantage. It occurs in conveyances, *e.g.*, "to his and their use and behoof."

Being struck. Collision, or striking together of two objects, one of which may be stationary. Condition of a person who has been traumatized. Business closed or affected by labor strike. See also **Strike.**

Belief. A conviction of the truth of a proposition, existing subjectively in the mind, and induced by argument, persuasion, or proof addressed to the judgment. Latrobe v. J. H. Cross Co., D.C.Pa., 29 F.2d 210, 212. A conclusion arrived at from external sources after weighing probability. Conviction of the mind, arising not from actual perception or knowledge, but by way of inference, or from evidence received or information derived from others.

Knowledge is an assurance of a fact or proposition founded on perception by the senses, or intuition; while "belief" is an assurance gained by evidence, and from other persons. "Suspicion" is weaker than "belief," since suspicion requires no real foundation for its existence, while "belief" is necessarily based on at least assumed facts. Cook v. Singer Sewing Mach. Co., 138 Cal.App. 418, 32 P.2d 430, 431.

Belief-action distinction. The distinction noted in analysis of cases under First Amendment, U.S. Constitution—freedom of speech and religion—to the effect that one is guaranteed the right to any belief he chooses, but when that belief is translated into action, the state also has rights under its police power to protect others from such actions. Reynolds v. U. S., 98 U.S. 145, 164.

Belligerency /bəlíjərənsiy/. In international law, the status of *de facto* statehood attributed to a body of insurgents, by which their hostilities are legalized. The international status assumed by a state (*i.e.* nation) which wages war against another state. Quality of being belligerent; status of a belligerent; act or state of waging war; warfare.

Belligerent /bəlíjərənt/. In international law, as an adjective, it means engaged in lawful war. As a noun, it designates either of two nations which are actually in a state of war with each other, as well as their allies actively co-operating, as distinguished from a nation which takes no part in the war and maintains a strict indifference as between the contending parties, called a "neutral."

As a personality trait, refers to one who is overly assertive, hostile or combative.

Belligerents. A body of insurgents who by reason of their temporary organized government are regarded as conducting lawful hostilities. Also, militia, corps of volunteers, and others, who although not part of the regular army of the state, are regarded as lawful combatants provided they observe the laws of war. See also **Belligerency; Belligerent.**

Bellum /béləm/. Lat. In public law, war. An armed contest between nations; the state of those who forcibly contend with each other. *Jus belli*, the law of war.

Belong. To appertain to; to be the property of; to be a member of; to be appropriate; to own.

Belonging. That which is connected with a principal or greater thing; an appendage, an appurtenance; also, ownership. Church of the Holy Faith v. State Tax Commission, 39 N.M. 403, 48 P.2d 777, 779.

Belongings. That which belongs to one; property; possessions; a term properly used to express ownership. Ford's Adm'r v. Wade's Adm'r, 242 Ky. 18, 45 S.W.2d 818, 820. See **Personal effects.**

Below. Inferior; of inferior jurisdiction, or jurisdiction in the first instance. The court from which a cause is removed for review is called the "court *below*." Preliminary; auxiliary or instrumental.

Bail to the sheriff has been called "bail *below*," as being preliminary to and intended to secure the putting in of bail above, or special bail. See **Bail.**

Ben Avon doctrine. Due process requires opportunity for judicial determination of reasonableness of rates for public utilities set by a Public Service Commission. Ohio Valley Water Co. v. Ben Avon Borough et al., 253 U.S. 287, 40 S.Ct. 527, 64 L.Ed. 405.

Bench. A seat of judgment or tribunal for the administration of justice; the seat occupied by judges in courts; also the court itself, or the aggregate of the judges composing a court, as in the phrase "before the full bench."

The judges taken collectively, as distinguished from counsellors and advocates, who are called the bar.

The term, indicating originally the seat of the judges, came to denote the body of judges taken collectively, and also the tribunal itself, as the King's Bench.

Bench blotter. Record of arrests and other happenings kept by police.

Bench conference. A meeting at the judge's bench prior to, during or after a trial or hearing between counsel and the judge to discuss a matter pertaining to such proceeding. Commonly called to discuss questions of evidence out of hearing of jury; it may or may not be made part of the written record of the proceeding.

Benchers. In England, principal officers of each inn of court, in whom the government of such is vested.

Bench legislation. See *Judge-made law* under the title **Judge**.

Bench mark. A mark on a fixed and enduring object, indicating a particular elevation and used as a reference in topographical surveys and tidal observations. Ace Const. Co. v. U. S., 185 Ct.Cl. 487, 401 F.2d 816, 820.

Bench trial. Trial held before judge sitting without a jury; jury waived trial.

Bench warrant. Process issued by the court itself, or "from the bench," for the attachment or arrest of a person; either in case of contempt, or where an indictment has been found, or to bring in a witness who does not obey the *subpœna*.

Bene /bíyniy/. Lat. Well; in proper form; legally; sufficiently.

Benedicta est expositio quando res redimitur a destructione /bɛnədíktə èst èkspəzísh(iy)ow kwóndow ríyz rədímədər èy dəstràkshiyówniy/. Blessed is the exposition when anything is saved from destruction. It is a laudable interpretation which gives effect to the instrument, and does not allow its purpose to be frustrated.

Benefice /bénəfəs/. In ecclesiastical law, in its technical sense, this term includes ecclesiastical preferments to which rank or public office is attached, otherwise described as ecclesiastical dignities or offices, such as bishoprics, deaneries, and the like; but in popular acceptation, it is almost invariably appropriated to rectories, vicarages, perpetual curacies, district churches, and endowed chapelries. A term derived from the feudal law, in which it signified a permanent stipendiary estate, or an estate held by feudal tenure. 4 Bl.Comm. 107.

Bénéfice /bèyneyfíys/. Fr. In French law, a benefit or advantage, and particularly a privilege given by the law rather than by the agreement of the parties.

Bénéfice de discussion. Benefit of discussion. The right of a guarantor to require that the creditor should exhaust his recourse against the principal debtor before having recourse to the guarantor himself.

Bénéfice de division. Benefit of division; right of contribution as between co-sureties.

Bénéfice d'inventaire. A term which corresponds to the *beneficium inventarii* of Roman law, and substantially to the English law doctrine that the executor properly accounting is only liable to the extent of the assets received by him.

Bénéficiaire /bèyneyfiysyér/. The person in whose favor a promissory note or bill of exchange is payable; or any person in whose favor a contract of any description is executed.

Beneficial. Tending to the benefit of a person; yielding a profit, advantage, or benefit; enjoying or entitled to a benefit or profit. This term is applied both to estates (as a "beneficial interest") and to persons (as "the beneficial owner").

Beneficiary association. See **Benevolent associations**.

Beneficial enjoyment. The enjoyment which a man has of an estate in his own right and for his own benefit, and not as trustee for another.

Beneficial estate. An estate in expectancy is one where the right to the possession is postponed to a future period, and is "beneficial" where the devisee takes solely for his own use or benefit, and not as the mere holder of the title for the use of another.

Beneficial interest. Profit, benefit, or advantage resulting from a contract, or the ownership of an estate as distinct from the legal ownership or control. When considered as designation of character of an estate, is such an interest as a devisee, legatee, or donee takes solely for his own use or benefit, and not as holder of title for use and benefit of another.

Beneficial owner. Term applied most commonly to cestui que trust who enjoys ownership of the trust or estate in equity, but not legal title which remains in trustee or personal representative. Equitable as contrasted with legal owner.

One who does not have title to property but has rights in the property which are the normal incident of owning the property. The persons for whom a trustee holds title to property are the beneficial owners of the property, and the trustee has a fiduciary responsibility to them.

Beneficial power. A power which has for its object the donee of the power, and which is to be executed solely for his benefit; as distinguished from a trust power, which has for its object a person other than the donee, and is to be executed solely for the benefit of such person.

Beneficial use. The right to use and enjoy property according to one's own liking or so as to derive a profit or benefit from it, including all that makes it desirable or habitable, as light, air, and access; as distinguished from a mere right of occupancy or possession. Such right to enjoyment of property where legal title is in one person while right to such use or interest is in another. Christiansen v. Department of Social Security, 15 Wash.2d 465, 131 P.2d 189, 191.

Beneficiary /bènəfísh(iy)əry/. One who benefits from act of another. See also **Primary beneficiary; Third party beneficiary**.

Credit. A "beneficiary" of a credit is a person who is entitled under its terms to draw or demand payment. U.C.C. § 5–103(d). See also **Creditor beneficiary**.

Incidental. A person who may derive benefit from performance on contract, though he is neither the promisee nor the one to whom performance is to be rendered. Salzman v. Holiday Inns, Inc., 48 A.D.2d 258, 369 N.Y.S.2d 238, 242. See also **Incidental beneficiary**.

Insurance. The person entitled to take proceeds on death of insured.

Taxation. One who is assessed as the real owner. See also **Income beneficiary**.

Trust. As it relates to trust beneficiaries, includes a person who has any present or future interest, vested or contingent, and also includes the owner of an interest by assignment or other transfer and as it relates to a charitable trust, includes any person entitled to enforce the trust. Uniform Probate Code, § 1–201. A person named in a trust account as one for whom a party to the account is named as trustee. Uniform Probate Code, § 6–101. Person for whose benefit property is held in trust. Restatement, Second, Trusts § 3.

Beneficiary association. See **Benevolent associations**.

Beneficiary heir. In the law of Louisiana, one who has accepted the succession under the benefit of an inventory regularly made. Civ.Code La. art. 883. Also, one who may accept the succession with benefit of inventory.

Beneficio prima, or **primo [ecclesiastico habendo]** /benəfísh(iy)ow práymow (əkliyziyǽstəkow həbéndow)/. In English law, an ancient writ, which was addressed by the king to the lord chancellor, to bestow the benefice that should first fall in the royal gift, above or under a specified value, upon a person named therein.

Beneficium /benəfísh(iy)əm/. In feudal law, a benefice; a permanent stipendiary estate; the same with what was afterwards called a "fief," "feud," or "fee." It originally meant a "benefaction" from the king, usually to a noble.

In the civil law, a benefit or favor; any particular privilege. A general term applied to ecclesiastical livings. 4 Bl.Comm. 107.

Beneficium abstinendi /benəfísh(iy)əm ǽbstənénday/. In Roman law, the power of an heir to abstain from accepting the inheritance.

Beneficium cedendarum actionum /benəfísh(iy)əm sədendérəm ǽkshiyównəm/. In Roman law, the privilege by which a surety could, before paying the creditor, compel him to make over to him the actions which belonged to the stipulator, so as to avail himself of them.

Beneficium clericale /benəfísh(iy)əm klèrəkéyliy/. Benefit of clergy *(q.v.)*.

Beneficium competentiæ /benəfísh(iy)əm kòmpəténshiyiy/. In Scotch law, the privilege of competency. A privilege which the grantor of a gratuitous obligation was entitled to, by which he might retain sufficient for his subsistence, if, before fulfilling the obligation, he was reduced to indigence. In the civil law, the right which an insolvent debtor had, among the Romans, on making cession of his property for the benefit of his creditors, to retain what was required for him to live honestly according to his condition.

A defendant's privilege of being condemned only in an amount which he could pay without being reduced to a state of destitution.

Beneficium divisionis /benəfísh(iy)əm dəvíz(h)iyównəs/. In civil and Scotch law, the privilege of one of several co-sureties (cautioners) to insist upon paying only his *pro rata* share of the debt. La.Civ. Code, arts. 3045–3051.

Beneficium inventarili /bènəfísh(iy)əm ìnventériyay/. See **Benefit of inventory**.

Beneficium ordinis /benəfísh(iy)əm órdənəs/. In civil and Scotch law, the privilege of order. The privilege of a surety to require that the creditor should first proceed against the principal and exhaust his remedy against him, before resorting to the surety.

Beneficium separationis /benəfísh(iy)əm sèpərèyshiyównəs/. In the civil law, the right to have the goods of an heir separated from those of the testator in favor of creditors.

Beneficium invito non datur /benəfísh(iy)əm inváydow nòn déydər/. A privilege or benefit is not granted against one's will.

Beneficium non datum nisi propter officium /benəfísh(iy)əm nòn déydəm naysay próptər əfíshiyəm/. A remuneration [is] not given, unless on account of a duty performed.

Beneficium non datur nisi officii causa /benəfísh(iy)əm nòn déydər náysay əfíshiyay kózə/. A benefice is not granted except on account or in consideration of duty.

Beneficium principis debet esse mansurum /benəfísh(iy)əm prínsəpəs débəd ésiy mæns(y)úrəm/. The benefaction of a prince ought to be lasting.

Benefit. Advantage; profit; fruit; privilege; gain; interest. The receiving as the exchange for promise some performance or forbearance which promisor was not previously entitled to receive. Graphic Arts Finishers, Inc. v. Boston Redevelopment Authority, 357 Mass. 40, 255 N.E.2d 793, 795.

Financial assistance received in time of sickness, disability, unemployment, etc. either from insurance or public programs such as social security.

Contracts. When it is said that a valuable consideration for a promise may consist of a benefit to the promisor, "benefit" means that the promisor has, in return for his promise, acquired some legal right to which he would not otherwise have been entitled. Irving v. Irwin, 133 Cal.App. 374, 24 P.2d 215, 216; Woolum v. Sizemore, 267 Ky. 384, 102 S.W.2d 323, 324.

Eminent domain. It is a rule that, in assessing damages for private property taken or injured for public use, "special benefits" may be set off against the amount of damage found, but not "general benefits." Within the meaning of this rule, general benefits are such as accrue to the community at large, to the vicinage, or to all property similarly situated with reference to the work or improvement in question; while special benefits are such as accrue directly and solely to the owner of the land in question and not to others.

Benefit association. See **Benefit societies**.

Benefit building society. The original name for what is now more commonly called a "building society" *(q.v.)*.

Benefit certificate. A written obligation to pay the person therein named the amount specified upon the conditions therein stipulated. Also a term usually applied to policies issued by fraternal and beneficiary societies. Chandler v. New York Life Ins. Co., 194 Ark. 6, 104 S.W.2d 1060, 1061.

Benefit of bargain rule. Under such rule a defrauded purchaser may recover the difference between the real and the represented value of the property purchased. Auffenberg v. Hafley, Mo.App., 457 S.W.2d 929, 337.

In an action for fraud, plaintiff's recovery is limited to that measured by "out-of-pocket" rule, by which damages are measured by difference between purchase price of property and fair market value of same property on date of sale, unless actionable misrepresentation was warranty of value, in which case plaintiff may recover under "benefit-of-the-bargain" rule by which damages are determined by difference between actual value of property received and its value had representations as made been true. Galego v. Knudsen, 573 P.2d 313, 318, 281 Or. 43.

Benefit of cession. In the civil law, the release of a debtor from future imprisonment for his debts, which the law operates in his favor upon the surrender of his property for the benefit of his creditors.

Benefit of clergy. In its original sense, the phrase denoted the exemption which was accorded to clergymen from the jurisdiction of the secular courts, or from arrest or attachment on criminal process issuing from those courts in certain particular cases. Afterwards, it meant a privilege of exemption from the punishment of death accorded to such persons as were *clerks*, or who could read. This privilege of exemption from capital punishment was anciently allowed to clergymen only, but afterwards to all who were connected with the church, even to its most subordinate officers, and at a still later time to all persons who could read (then called "clerks"), whether ecclesiastics or laymen. It does not appear to have been extended to cases of high treason, nor did it apply to mere misdemeanors. The privilege was claimed after the person's conviction, by a species of motion in arrest of judgment, technically called "praying his clergy." As a means of testing his clerical character, he was given a psalm to read (usually, or always, the fifty-first), and, upon his reading it correctly, he was turned over to the ecclesiastical courts, to be tried by the bishop or a jury of twelve clerks. These heard him on oath, with his witnesses and compurgators, who attested their belief in his innocence. This privilege operated greatly to mitigate the extreme rigor of the criminal laws, but was found to involve such gross abuses that parliament began to enact that certain crimes should be felonies "without benefit of clergy," and finally, by the Criminal Law Act of 1827, it was altogether abolished. The act of congress of April 30, 1790, c. 9, § 31, 1 Stat. 119, provided that there should be no benefit of clergy for any capital crime against the United States, and, if this privilege formed a part of the common law of the several states before the Revolution, it no longer exists.

Sometimes used in negative sense, "without benefit of clergy", to describe status of man and woman who live together though not married to each other.

Benefit of counsel. See Counsel, right to.

Benefit of discussion. In the civil law, the right which a surety has to cause the property of the principal debtor to be applied in satisfaction of the obligation in the first instance. Civ.Code La. arts. 3045–3051.

Benefit of division. Same as *beneficium divisionis (q.v.).*

Benefit of inventory. In the civil law, the privilege which the heir obtains of being liable for the charges and debts of the succession, only to the value of the effects of the succession, by causing an inventory of these effects within the time and manner prescribed by law. Civil Code La. art. 1032.

Benefit of order. See Beneficium *(Beneficium ordinis).*

Benefit societies. Under this and several similar names, in various states, corporations which exist to receive periodical payments from members, and hold them as a fund to be loaned or given to members needing pecuniary relief.

Benerth. A feudal service rendered by the tenant to his lord with plow and cart.

Benevolence. The doing of a kind or helpful action towards another, under no obligation except an ethical one.

The love of humanity; the desire to promote its prosperity or happiness. The term includes acts of well-wishing towards others, for the promotion of general happiness, and plans actuated by love of others and a desire for their well-being. In re Peabody's Estate, 124 Misc. 338, 208 N.Y.S. 664, 671. Also beneficent; doing well.

It is a broader term than "charity" which it includes, and with which it is frequently used synonymously. "Charity" in its legal sense implies giving without consideration or expectation of return, and "benevolence" applies to any act which is prompted by or has for its object the well-being of others. State v. Texas Mut. Life Ins. Co. of Texas, Tex.Civ. App., 51 S.W.2d 405, 410.

See also **Benevolent; Charitable; Charity.**

Benevolent /bənévələnt/. Philanthropic; humane; having a desire or purpose to do good to men; intended for the conferring of benefits, rather than for gain or profit; loving others and actively desirous of their well being. In re Altman's Estate, 87 Misc. 255, 149 N.Y.S. 601, 605.

This word, as applied to objects or purposes, may refer to those which are in their nature charitable, and may also have a broader meaning and include objects and purposes not charitable in the legal sense of that word. Acts of kindness, friendship, forethought, or good-will might properly be described as benevolent. It has therefore been held that gifts to trustees to be applied for "benevolent purposes" at their discretion, or to such benevolent purposes as they could agree upon, do not create a public charity. But where the word is used in connection with other words explanatory of its meaning, and indicating the intent of the donor to limit it to purposes strictly charitable, it has been held to be synonymous with, or equivalent to, "charitable."

See also **Charitable; Charity.**

Benevolent associations. Those having a philanthropic or charitable purpose, as distinguished from such as are conducted for profit; specifically, "benefit associations" or "beneficial associations." Another name for a "benefit society," "benevolent society," and "fraternal" or "friendly society." State v. Texas Mut. Life Ins. Co. of Texas, Tex.Civ.App., 51 S.W.2d 405, 410. See also **Benevolent corporation; Charitable corporation.**

Benevolent corporation. A nonprofit corporation; created for charitable rather than for business purposes. One that ministers to all; the purpose may be anything that promotes the mental, physical, or spiritual welfare of man. The term may include a corporation to which a bequest is made to be used in the improvement of the social, physical, and economic condition of the employees of a business corporation. In re Altman's Estate, 87 Misc. 255, 149 N.Y.S. 601. See also **Charitable corporation.**

Benevolentia regis habenda /bɛnəvəlénsh(iy)ə ríyjəs həbéndə/. The form in ancient fines and submissions to purchase the king's pardon and favor in order to be restored to place, title or estate.

Benevolent society. See **Benevolent associations; Benevolent corporation.**

Benigne faciendæ sunt interpretationes chartarum, ut res magis valeat quam pereat; et quæ libet concessio fortissime contra donatorem interpretanda est /bənígniy fæshiyéndiy sənt intərprətéyshiyówniyz kartérəm, ət ríyz méyjəs væliyət kwæm péhriyət; èt kwíyləbət kənsésh(iy)ow fortísəmiy kóntrə dównətórəm intərprətǽndə èst/. Liberal interpretations are to be made of deeds, so that the purpose may rather stand than fall; and every grant is to be taken most strongly against the grantor.

Benigne faciendæ sunt interpretationes, propter simplicitatem laicorum, ut res magis valeat quam pereat; et verba intentioni, non e contra, debent inservire /bənígniy fæshiyéndiy sənt intərprətèyshiyówniyz, próptər simplìsətéydəm lèyəkórəm, ət ríyz méyjəs væliyət kwæm péhriyt; èt várbə intènshiyównay, nón èy kóntrə, débəd ìnsərváyriy/. Constructions [of written instruments] are to be made liberally, on account of the simplicity of the laity [or common people], in order that the thing [or subject-matter] may rather have effect than perish [or become void]; and words must be subject to the intention, not the intention to the words. 2 Bl.Comm. 379.

Benignior sententia in verbis generalibus seu dubiis, est præferenda /bənígn(i)yor senténsh(iy)ə in várbəs jènəréyləbəs syúw dyúwbiyəs èst prèfəréndə/. The more favorable construction is to be placed on general or doubtful expressions.

Benignius leges interpretandæ sunt quo voluntas earum conservetur /bənígn(i)yəs líyjiyz intərprətǽndiy sənt kwòw vəlántæs iyérəm kònsərvéydər/. Laws are to be more liberally interpreted, in order that their intent may be preserved.

Bequeath /bəkwíyð/. To give personal property by will to another. It therefore is distinguishable from "devise," which is properly used of realty. But if the context clearly shows the intention of the testator to use the word "bequeath" as synonymous with "devise," it may be held to pass real property. See **Bequest.**

Bequest /bəkwést/. A gift by will of personal property; a legacy. Disposition of realty in will is termed "devise." See also **Charitable bequest; Demonstrative bequest; Devise; General bequest; Legacy.**

Conditional bequest. One the taking effect or continuing of which depends upon the happening or non-occurrence of a particular event.

Executory bequest. The bequest of a future, deferred, or contingent interest in personalty.

Residuary bequest. A gift of all the remainder of the testator's personal estate, after payment of debts and legacies, etc.

Specific bequest. One whereby the testator gives to the legatee all his property of a certain class or kind; as all his pure personalty.

Berat.. Also *barat.* A warrant or patent of dignity or privilege given by an Oriental monarch.

Berbiage /bárbiyəj/. A rent paid for the pasturing of sheep.

Bernet. In Saxon law, burning; the crime of house burning, now called "arson."

Bernstein test. Form of blood test used in determining child's paternity and predicated on 4 blood types.

Berry, or **bury.** A villa or seat of habitation of a nobleman; a dwelling or mansion house; a sanctuary.

Bertillon system /bàrtiyówn sístəm/. A method of anthropometry *(q.v.),* once used for the identification of criminals and other persons, consisting of the taking and recording of a system of numerous, minute, and uniform measurements of various parts of the human body, absolutely and in relation to each other, the facial, cranial, and other angles, and of any eccentricities or abnormalities noticed in the individual.

Bes. Lat. In the Roman law, a division of the *as,* or pound, consisting of eight *unciæ,* or duodecimal parts, and amounting to two-thirds of the *as.* 2 Bl.Comm. 462 note *m.* Two-thirds of an inheritance. Eight per cent. interest.

Besaile, besayle /bèséyl/. The great-grandfather, *proavus.* 1 Bl.Comm. 186.

Besayel, besaiel, besayle /bèséyl/. In old English law, a writ which lay where a great-grandfather died seised of lands and tenements in fee-simple, and on the day of his death a stranger abated, or entered and kept out the heir. 3 Bl.Comm. 186.

Beseech. To entreat; to implore.

Besides. In addition to; moreover; also; likewise.

Besoin /bəsóyn/bəswǽn/. Fr. Need.

Besot /bəsót/. To stupefy, to make dull or senseless, to make to dote; and "to dote" is to be delirious, silly, or insane.

Best. Of the highest quality; of the greatest usefulness for the purpose intended. Most desirable, suitable, useful, or satisfactory. For example: the "best bid" of interest by a prospective depositary of school funds would not necessarily be the highest bid, but, looking to the solvency of the bidder, the bond tendered, and all the circumstances surrounding the transaction, the safety and preservation of the school fund, the "best bid" might be the lowest bid.

Best evidence. Primary evidence, as distinguished from secondary; original, as distinguished from substitutionary; the best and highest evidence of which the nature of the case is susceptible, not the highest or strongest evidence which the nature of the thing to be proved admits of. A written instrument is itself always regarded as the primary or best possible evidence of its existence and contents; a copy, or the recollection of a witness, would be secondary evidence. "Best evidence" or "primary evidence" includes the best evidence which is available to a party and procurable under the existing situation, and all evidence falling short of such standard, and which in its nature suggests there is better evidence of the same fact, is "secondary evidence." See **Best evidence rule; Original document rule; Primary evidence**.

Best evidence rule. The "best evidence rule" prohibits the introduction into evidence of secondary evidence unless it is shown that original document has been lost or destroyed or is beyond jurisdiction of court without fault of the offering party; if original document is lost, then secondary evidence is properly admissible. State v. Stephens, Mo.App., 556 S.W.2d 722, 723. Fed.R.Evid. 1002 states the basic rule as follows: "To prove the content of a writing, recording, or photograph, the original writing, recording, or photograph is required, except as otherwise provided in these rules or by Act of Congress." As to what constitutes an "original writing", see **Original**.

Bestiality. A sexual connection between a human being and an animal. State v. Poole, 59 Ariz. 44, 122 P.2d 415, 416. At common law the term "crime against nature" embraced both "sodomy" and "bestiality". See **Sodomy**.

Bestow. To give, grant, confer, or impart; not necessarily limited in meaning to "devise."

Best use. In eminent domain, the value of property considering its optimum use at a given time and hence the money which should be awarded for such governmental taking; used commonly as "highest and best use".

Bet. An agreement between two or more persons that a sum of money or other valuable thing, to which all jointly contribute, shall become the sole property of one or some of them on the happening in the future of an event at present uncertain, or according as a question disputed between them is settled in one way or the other. A contract by which two or more parties agree that a sum of money, or other thing, shall be paid or delivered to one of them on the happening or not happening of an uncertain event. See **Wager**; a term generally synonymous with bet. See also **Betting book; Betting slips**.

Betray. Act of delivering up to an enemy something of value. To divulge a matter in breach of a confidence. To deceive, seduce or lead astray. A "betrayal," as of a professional secret on the part of a physician, signifies a wrongful disclosure in violation of the trust imposed by the patient. See **Treason**.

Betrothed /bətrowðd/. One who has exchanged promises to marry. The term may be synonymous with "intended wife." See also **Engagement**.

Betrothment, bethrothal. Mutual promise of marriage; the plighting of troth; a mutual promise or contract between a man and woman competent to make it, to marry at a future time.

Better Business Bureau. Local, business-supported organizations that promote good business practices, receive complaints about specific businesses, and provide consumers with information about specific firms. The local bureaus are loosely affiliated with a national bureau.

Better equity. See **Equity**.

Betterment. An improvement put upon a property which enhances its value more than mere replacement, maintenance, or repairs. The improvement may be either temporary or permanent. Also applied to denote the additional value which a property acquires in consequence of some public improvement, as laying out or widening a street, etc. See also **Improvement**.

Betterment acts. Statutes which provide that a bona fide occupant of real estate making lasting improvements in good faith shall have a lien upon the estate recovered by the real owner to the extent that his improvements have increased the value of the land. Also called "occupying claimant acts."

Betting. Act of placing a bet or wager. See **Bet; Gambling; Pari-mutuel betting; Wager**.

Betting book. A book kept for registering bets on the result of a race as operated on race track. In a broader sense, the "betting book" is that book which enables the professional bettor to carry on his business, and to promote a race, and it includes the book, the making book and the bookmaker.

Betting slips. Part of gambling paraphernalia consisting of papers on which numbers or names of dogs or horses to be bet are written and which constitutes evidence for prosecution of illegal gaming.

Between. A space which separates. Strictly applicable only with reference to two things, but this may be understood as including cases in which a number of things are discriminated collectively as two wholes, or as taken in pairs, or where one thing is set off against a number of others. In re McShane's Will, 158 Misc. 777, 286 N.Y.S. 680, 682. Sometimes used synonymously with "among". In re Moore's Estate, 157 Pa.Super. 296, 43 A.2d 359. As a measure or indication of distance, this word has the effect of excluding the two termini. If an act is to be done "between" two certain days, it must be performed before the commencement of the latter day. In computing the time in such a case, both the days named are to be excluded.

Bewared. Eng. Expended. Before the Britons and Saxons had introduced the general use of money, they traded chiefly by exchange of wares.

Beyond a reasonable doubt. In evidence means fully satisfied, entirely convinced, satisfied to a moral certainty; and phrase is the equivalent of the words clear, precise and indubitable. In criminal case, the accused's guilt must be established "beyond a reasonable doubt," which means that facts proven must, by virtue of their probative force, establish guilt.

Beyond control. Anything or any person who, in relationship to another person is out of reach of the latter, either physically, legally or morally; for example, a child who has reached his majority is beyond the legal control of his parents. See also **Act of God**.

Beyond the seas. Beyond the limits of the United States. In England, an expression to indicate that a person was outside the United Kingdom. The Limitation Act of 1939 abolished the old procedure whereby a defendant's absence beyond the seas suspended the operation of the Statutes of Limitations.

B.F. An abbreviation for *bonum factum*, a good or proper act, deed, or decree; signifies "approved."

BIA. Bureau of Indian Affairs.

Biannually. Twice a year; semi-annually.

Bias /báyəs/. Inclination; bent; prepossession; a preconceived opinion; a predisposition to decide a cause or an issue in a certain way, which does not leave the mind perfectly open to conviction. To incline to one side. Condition of mind, which sways judgment and renders judge unable to exercise his functions impartially in particular case. As used in law regarding disqualification of judge, refers to mental attitude or disposition of the judge toward a party to the litigation, and not to any views that he may entertain regarding the subject matter involved. State ex rel. Mitchell v. Sage Stores Co., 157 Kan. 622, 143 P.2d 652, 655.

Actual bias consists in the existence of a state of mind on the part of the juror which satisfies the court, in the exercise of a sound discretion, that the juror cannot try the issues impartially and without prejudice to the substantial rights of the party challenging.

See also **Average man test; Discrimination; Prejudice**.

Bible. See **Family Bible**.

Bicameral system /bàykǽmərəl sístəm/. A term applied by Jeremy Bentham to the division of a legislative body into two chambers, as in the United States government (Senate and House).

Bid. An offer by an intending purchaser to pay a designated price for property which is about to be sold at auction. An offer to perform a contract for work and labor or supplying materials or goods at a specified price. Public contracts are frequently awarded on basis of submitted bids. See also **Invitation to bid; Let; Lowest responsible bidder; Open bid; Sealed bid**.

Term may also refer to application for another job by an employee.

Best bid. One that is not necessarily the lowest, but rather fits the best interests of the issuer of the bid; taken into consideration is the solvency of the bidder, quality of his work, reputation, etc.

Bidder. One who makes a bid. One who offers to pay a specified price for an article offered for sale at a public auction or to perform a certain contract for a specified price. As to "Responsible bidder" see that title.

Biddings. Offers of a designated price for goods or other property put up for sale at auction.

Bidding up. Raising the price for an item being sold at an auction by a series of bids, each higher than the other. If such successive bids are made collusively by persons with an interest in raising the final bid, such practice is unlawful.

Bid in. Property sold at auction is said to be "bid in" by the owner or an incumbrancer or some one else who is interested in it, when he attends the sale and makes the successful bid.

Bid off. One is said to "bid off" a thing when he bids for it at an auction sale, and it is knocked down to him in immediate succession to the bid and as a consequence of it.

By-bidding. In the law relating to sales by auction, this term is equivalent to "puffing." The practice consists in making fictitious bids for the property, under a secret arrangement with the owner or auctioneer, for the purpose of misleading and stimulating other persons who are bidding in good faith.

Competitive bidding. Bids which are submitted as the result of public notice and advertising of an intended sale or purchase.

Letting or awarding of bids. See **Let**.

Open bid. Offer to perform a contract together with the price, but with right to reduce the price to meet price quoted by others for same job.

Sealed bid. One submitted under seal, and which is not to be opened until a specified time at which all bids are to be opened and compared. Commonly required on construction contracts, to assure independence of bidding.

Upset bid. A bid made after a judicial sale, but before the successful bid at the sale has been confirmed, larger or better than such successful bid, and made for the purpose of upsetting the sale and securing to the "upset bidder" the privilege of taking the property at his bid or competing at a new sale.

Bid and asked. Price quotation for securities that are not frequently traded or are traded on the over-the-counter market. The bid quotation is the highest price a prospective buyer is willing to pay; the asked quotation is the lowest price the seller is willing to sell for.

Bid bond. Type of bond required in public construction projects which must be filed at the time of the bid and which protects the public agency in the event that the bidder refuses to enter into a contract after the award to him or withdraws his bid before the award. A type of indemnity bond.

Bid price. In market exchanges, the price a buyer is willing to pay, as contrasted with the price at which a seller is willing to sell; called the "ask price". Also, the amount specified in a bid as the amount for which the bidder will perform the work or buy the property.

Bienes /biyénes/. In Spanish law, goods; property of every description, including real as well as personal property; all things (not being persons) which may serve for the uses of man.

Bienes comunes. Common property; those things which, not being the private property of any person, are open to the use of all, such as the air, rain, water, the sea and its beaches.

Bienes gananciales. A species of community in property enjoyed by husband and wife, the property being divisible equally between them on the dissolution of the marriage; does not include what they held as their separate property at the time of contracting the marriage.

Bienes publicos. Those things which, as to property, pertain to the people or nation, and, as to their use, to the individuals of the territory or district, such as rivers, shores, ports, and public roads.

Biennial /bàyén(i)yəl/. Occurring every two years.

Biennial session. The regular session of most State legislatures, usually held in odd-numbered years; gradually being supplanted by annual sessions.

Biennium /bàyéniyəm/. A two-year period; the period for which appropriations are made in many State legislatures.

Biens /bíynz/byén(z)/. In old English law, property of every description, except estates of freehold and inheritance.

In French law, this term includes all kinds of property, real and personal. *Biens* are divided into *biens meubles*, movable property; and *biens immeubles*, immovable property. The distinction between movable and immovable property is recognized by the continental jurists, and gives rise, in the civil as well as in the common law, to many important distinctions as to rights and remedies.

Bifurcated trial /báyfərkèydəd tráy(ə)l/. Trial of issues separately, *e.g.* guilt and punishment, or guilt and sanity, in criminal trial.

The trial of the liability issue in a personal injury or wrongful death case separate from and prior to trial of the damages question. The advantage of so doing is that if the liability issue is determined in defendant's favor there is no need to try the damages question, which can be an involved one entailing expensive expert witnesses and other proof.

Bigamus /bígəməs/. In the civil law, a man who was twice married; one who at different times and successively has married two wives. One who has two wives living. One who marries a widow.

Used in ecclesiastical matters as a reason for denying benefit of the clergy.

Bigamus seu trigamus, etc., est qui diversis temporibus et successivè duas seu tres uxores habuit /bígəməs syùw trígəməs èst kwày dəvársəs tèmpórəbəs èt səksesáyviy d(y)úwəs syùw tréz əksóriyz hǽb(y)uwət/. A bigamus or trigamus, etc., is one who at different times and successively has married two or three wives.

Bigamy /bígəmiy/. The criminal offense of willfully and knowingly contracting a second marriage (or going through the form of a second marriage) while the first marriage, to the knowledge of the offender, is still subsisting and undissolved. The state of a man who has two wives, or of a woman who has two husbands, living at the same time.

A married person is guilty of bigamy, a misdemeanor, if he contracts or purports to contract another marriage, unless at the time of the subsequent marriage: (a) the actor believes that the prior spouse is dead; or (b) the actor and the prior spouse have been living apart for five consecutive years throughout which the prior spouse was not known by the actor to be alive; or (c) a Court has entered a judgment purporting to terminate or annul any prior disqualifying marriage, and the actor does not know that judgment to be invalid; or (d) the actor reasonably believes that he is legally eligible to remarry. Model Penal Code, § 230.1.

In the canon law, the term denoted the offense committed by an ecclesiastic who married two wives successively. It might be committed either by marrying a second wife after the death of a first or by marrying a widow.

See also **Pologamy.**

Big board. A popular term referring to the board showing the current prices of securities listed on the New York Stock Exchange.

Big eight. The eight largest public accounting (CPA) firms listed in alphabetical order.

Bigot. A prejudiced person; or one that is wedded to an opinion in matters of religion, race, etc.

Bilagines /bàyléyjəniyz/. By-laws of towns; municipal laws.

Bilan. A term used in Louisiana, derived from the French. A book in which bankers, merchants, and traders write a statement of all they owe and all that is due them; a balance-sheet.

Bilanciis deferendis /bəlǽnshiyəs defəréndəs/. In English law, an obsolete writ addressed to a corporation for the carrying of weights to such a haven, there to weigh the wool anciently licensed for transportation.

Bilateral contract /bàylǽdərəl kóntrækt/. A term, used originally in the civil law, but now generally adopted, denoting a contract in which both the contracting parties are bound to fulfill obligations reciprocally towards each other; as a contract of sale, where one becomes bound to deliver the thing sold, and the other to pay the price of it. A contract executory on both sides, and one which includes both rights and duties on each side. Contract formed by the exchange of promises in which the promise of one party is consideration supporting the promise of the other as contrasted with a unilateral contract which is formed by the exchange of a promise for an act. Antonucci v. Stevens Dodge, Inc., 73 Misc.2d 173, 340 N.Y.S.2d 979, 982.

Bilboes. A device used for punishment at sea, similar to the stocks (*q.v.*) on land.

Biline. A word used by Briton in the sense of "collateral." *En line biline*, in the collateral line.

Bilinguis /baylíŋgwəs/. Of a double language or tongue; that can speak two languages. A term formerly applied to a jury composed partly of Englishmen and partly of foreigners, which, by the English law, an alien party to a suit was, in certain cases, entitled to; more commonly called a "jury *de medietate linguæ.*" 3 Bl.Comm. 360.

Bill. As a legal term, this word has many meanings and applications, the most important of which are set forth below:

Bill of rights. A formal and emphatic legislative assertion and declaration of popular rights and liberties usually promulgated upon a change of government; *e.g.* the famous Bill of Rights in English history. Also the summary of the rights and liberties of the people, or of the principles of constitutional law deemed essential and fundamental, contained in many of the American state constitutions. Hamill v. Hawks, C.C.A.Okl., 58 F.2d 41, 47. That portion of Constitution guaranteeing rights and privileges to the individual; *i.e.* first ten Amendments of U.S. Constitution.

Commercial law. A written statement of the terms of a contract, or specification of the items of a transaction or of a demand. Also, a general name for any item of indebtedness, whether receivable or payable; accounts for goods sold, services rendered, or work done. As a verb, as generally and customarily used in commercial transactions, "bill" is synonymous with "charge" or "invoice." George M. Jones Co. v. Canadian Nat. R. Co., D.C.Mich., 14 F.2d 852, 855. See also *Commercial paper, infra.*

Bill-book. A book in which an account of bills of exchange and promissory notes, whether payable or receivable, is stated.

Bill-head. A printed form on which merchants and traders make out their bills and render accounts to their customers.

Bill of lading. See **Bill of lading,** *infra.*

Bill of parcels. A statement sent to the buyer of goods, along with the goods, exhibiting in detail the items composing the parcel and their several prices, to enable him to detect any mistake or omission; an invoice (*q.v.*).

Bill of sale. In contracts, a written agreement, formerly limited to one under seal, by which one person assigns or transfers his right to or interest in goods and personal chattels to another. Legal document which conveys title from seller to buyer.

Bill payable. In a merchant's accounts, all bills which he has accepted, and promissory notes which he has made, are called "bills payable," and are entered in a ledger account under that name, and recorded in a book bearing the same title. See **Account** (*Account payable*).

Bill receivable. In a merchant's accounts, all notes, drafts, checks, etc., payable to him, or of which he is to receive the proceeds at a future date, are called "bills receivable," and are entered in a ledg-

er-account under that name, and also noted in a book bearing the same title. See **Account** (*Account receivable*).

Bill rendered. A bill of items rendered by a creditor to his debtor; an "account rendered," as distinguished from "an account stated."

Grand bill of sale. In old English law, the name of an instrument used for the transfer of a ship while she is at sea. An expression which is understood to refer to the instrument whereby a ship was originally transferred from the builder to the owner, or first purchaser.

Commercial paper. A promissory obligation for the payment of money.

Bill broker. Middleman who negotiates purchase or sale of commercial paper.

Bill of credit. A bill or promissory note issued by the government, upon its faith and credit, designed to circulate in the community as money. See **Federal reserve notes; Treasury bill.**

In mercantile law, a license or authority given in writing from one person to another, very common among merchants, bankers, and those who travel, empowering a person to receive or take up money of their correspondents abroad. See also **Letter of credit.**

Bill of exchange. A three party instrument in which first party draws an order for the payment of a sum certain on a second party for payment to a third party at a definite future time. Same as "draft" under U.C.C. A check is a demand bill of exchange. See also Advance bill; Banker's acceptance; Blank bill; Clean bill; Draft; Time bill.

Foreign bill of exchange. A bill of exchange drawn in one country upon another country not governed by the same homogeneous laws, or not governed throughout by the same municipal laws. A bill of exchange drawn in one of the United States upon a person residing in another state is a foreign bill.

Common law pleading and practice.

Bill of costs. A certified, itemized statement of the amount of costs in an action or suit.

Bill of evidence. Stenographer's transcript of testimony heard at trial which may be considered on appeal as bill of exceptions. Spencer v. Commonwealth, 250 Ky. 370, 63 S.W.2d 288.

Bill of exceptions. A formal statement in writing of the objections or exceptions taken by a party during the trial of a cause to the decisions, rulings, or instructions of the trial judge, stating the objection, with the facts and circumstances on which it is founded, and, in order to attest its accuracy, signed by the judge; the object being to put the controverted rulings or decisions upon the record for the information of the appellate court. Bills of exceptions have been eliminated in civil appeals in jurisdictions which have adopted Rules of Civil Procedure tracking Fed.Rules of Civil Proc. in favor of a straight appeal with no need to claim exception after making objection at trial; *e.g.* Mass.R.Civ. Proc. 46.

Bill of particulars. A written statement or specification of the particulars of the demand for which an action at law is brought, or of a defendant's set-off against such demand (including dates, sums, and items in detail), furnished by one of the parties to the other, either voluntarily or in compliance with a judge's order for that purpose. It is designed to aid the defendant in interposing the proper answer and in preparing for trial, by giving him detailed information regarding the cause of action stated in the complaint. In jurisdictions which have adopted Rules of Civil Procedure, the bill of particulars has been replaced by various discovery devices (Fed.R. Civil P. 26 et seq.) and by motion for more definite statement (Fed.R. Civil P. 12(e)). See however *Criminal law* below with respect to bill of particulars in criminal cases.

Contracts. An obligation; a deed, whereby the obligor acknowledges himself to owe to the obligee a certain sum of money or some other thing.

Bill obligatory. A bond absolute for the payment of money. It is called also a "single bill," and differs from a promissory note only in having a seal. See *Bill penal.*

Bill of debt. An ancient term including promissory notes and bonds for the payment of money.

Bill penal. A written obligation by which a debtor acknowledges himself indebted in a certain sum, and binds himself for the payment thereof, in a larger sum, called a "penalty." Bonds with conditions have superseded such bills in modern practice. They are sometimes called bills obligatory, and are properly so called; but every bill obligatory is not a bill penal.

Bill single. A written promise to pay to a person or persons named a stated sum at a stated time, without any condition. When under seal, it is sometimes called a "bill obligatory" *(q.v.)*. It differs from a "bill penal" *(q.v.)* in that it expresses no penalty.

Criminal law.

Bill of attainder. Legislative acts, no matter what their form, that apply either to named individuals or to easily ascertainable members of a group in such a way as to inflict punishment on them without a judicial trial. United States v. Brown, 381 U.S. 437, 448–49, 85 S.Ct. 1707, 1715, 14 L.Ed. 484, 492; United States v. Lovett, 328 U.S. 303, 315, 66 S.Ct. 1073, 1079, 90 L.Ed. 1252. An act is a "bill of attainder" when the punishment is death and a "bill of pains and penalties" when the punishment is less severe; both kinds of punishment fall within the scope of the constitutional prohibition. U.S.Const. Art. I, Sec. 9, Cl. 3 (as to Congress); Art. I, Sec. 10 (as to state legislatures).

Bill of indemnity. See **Bill of indemnity**, *infra.*

Bill of indictment. A formal written document accusing a person or persons named of having committed a felony or misdemeanor, lawfully laid before a grand jury for their action upon it. See **Indictment; Presentment.**

Bill of pains and penalties. See *Bill of attainder, supra.*

Bill of particulars. Form of discovery in which the prosecution sets forth the time, place, manner and means of the commission of the crime as alleged in complaint or indictment. Fed.R.Crim.P. 7. The purpose of a "bill of particulars" is to give notice to the accused of the offenses charged in the bill of indictment so that he may prepare a defense, avoid surprise, or intelligently raise pleas of double jeopardy and the bar of the statute of limitations; it was not designed to perform the function of a discovery device. Com. v. Mervin, 230 Pa.Super. 552, 326 A.2d 602, 605.

Equity pleading and practice. The initial pleading of plaintiff or petitioner in equity action in contrast to declaration (complaint) in law actions. Under Rules of Civil Procedure, however, bill has been replaced by complaint for both equitable and legal actions because of merger of law and equity. Fed.R. Civil P. 2.

In England, in the ancient practice of the court of king's bench, the usual and orderly method of beginning an action was by a *bill*, or original bill, or plaint. This was a written statement of the plaintiff's cause of action, like a declaration or complaint, and always alleged a trespass as the ground of it, in order to give the court jurisdiction. 3 Bl.Comm. 43.

Bill for a new trial. A bill in equity in which the specific relief asked is an injunction against the execution of a judgment rendered at law, and a new trial in the action on account of some fact which would render it inequitable to enforce the judgment, but which was not available to the party on the trial at law, or which he was prevented from presenting by fraud or accident, without concurrent fraud or negligence on his own part. Superseded by motion for new trial in jurisdictions with Rules of Civil Procedure (Rule 59).

Bill for foreclosure. One which is filed by a mortgagee against the mortgagor, for the purpose of having the estate sold, thereby to obtain the sum mortgaged on the premises, with interest and costs.

Bill in aid of execution. A bill to set aside encumbrances or conveyances therein specified as fraudulent. Pape v. Pareti, 315 Ill.App. 1, 42 N.E.2d 361, 364.

Bill in nature of a bill of review. A bill in equity, to obtain a re-examination and reversal of a decree, filed by one who was not a party to the original suit, nor bound by the decree.

Bill in nature of a bill of revivor. Where, on the abatement of a suit, there is such a transmission of the interest of the incapacitated party that the title to it, as well as the person entitled, may be the subject of litigation in a court of chancery, the suit cannot be continued by a mere bill of revivor, but an original bill upon which the title may be litigated must be filed. This is called a "bill in the nature of a bill of revivor." It is founded on privity of estate or title by the act of the party. And the nature and operation of the whole act by which the privity is created is open to controversy.

Bill in nature of a supplemental bill. A bill filed when new parties, with new interests, arising from events happening since the suit was commenced, are brought before the court; such differs from a supplemental bill, which is properly applicable to those cases only where the same parties or the same interests remain before the court.

Bill in nature of interpleader. See *Bill of interpleader.*

Bill of certiorari. A bill, the object of which is to remove a suit in equity from some inferior court to the court of chancery, or some other superior court of equity, on account of some alleged incompetency of the inferior court, or some injustice in its proceedings. As an appellate vehicle, it has been replaced by appeal in jurisdictions which have adopted Rules of Appellate Procedure in civil cases. See **Certiorari.**

Bill of conformity. One filed by an executor or administrator, who finds the affairs of the deceased so much involved that he cannot safely administer the estate except under the direction of a court of chancery. This bill is filed against the creditors, generally, for the purpose of having all their claims adjusted, and procuring a final decree settling the order of payment of the assets.

Bill of discovery. A proceeding by a party against an adversary for discovery of facts within adversary's knowledge, or discovery of documents, writings, or other things within his possession or power, to be used either offensively or defensively in a pending or contemplated action. In aid of action at law is equitable remedy to enable litigant to obtain, prior to trial, such information as is in exclusive possession of adverse party and is necessary to establishment of complainant's case. Superseded by discovery rules in jurisdictions that have adopted Fed.Rules of Civil Proc. (Rules 26–37).

Bill of information. In England, where a suit is instituted on behalf of the crown or government, or of those of whom it has the custody by virtue of its prerogative, or whose rights are under its particular protection, the matter of complaint is offered to the court by way of information by the attorney or solicitor general, instead of by petition. Where a suit immediately concerns the crown or government alone, the proceeding is purely by way of information, but, where it does not do so immediately, a relator is appointed, who is answerable for costs, etc., and, if he is interested in the matter in connection with the crown or government, the proceeding is by information and bill. Informations differ from bills in little more than name and form, and the same rules are substantially applicable to both. 3 Bl.Comm. 261.

Bill of interpleader. The name of a bill in equity to obtain a settlement of a question of right to money or other property adversely claimed, in which the party filing the bill has no interest, although it may be in his hands, by compelling such adverse claimants to litigate the right or title between themselves, and relieve him from liability or litigation. Superseded by Rule 22, "Interpleader," in those jurisdictions that have adopted Rules of Civil Procedure. See **Interpleader.**

Bill of peace. One which is filed when a person has a right which may be controverted by various persons, at different times, and by different actions.

Bill of review. Proceeding in equity brought for purpose of reversing or correcting prior judgment of trial court after judgment has become final. Rogers v. Searle, Tex.Civ.App., 533 S.W.2d 433, 437. It is in the nature of a writ of error. A "bill of review," or a bill in the nature of a bill of review, are of three classes; those for error appearing on the face of the record, those for newly discovered evidence, and those for fraud impeaching the original transaction. Such bills are peculiar to courts of equity. In states where Rules of Civil Procedure are applicable, such bill is replaced by motion for relief from judgment or order (Rule 60).

Bill of revivor. One which is brought to continue a suit which has abated before its final consummation as, for example, by death, or marriage of a female plaintiff.

Bill of revivor and supplement. One which is a compound of a supplemental bill and bill of revivor, and not only continues the suit, which has abated by the death of the plaintiff, or the like, but supplies any defects in the original bill arising from subsequent events, so as to entitle the party to relief on the whole merits of his case.

Bill quia timet. A bill invoking the aid of equity "because he fears," that is, because the complainant apprehends an injury to his property rights or interests, from the fault or neglect of another. Such bills are entertained to guard against possible or prospective injuries, and to preserve the means by which existing rights may be protected from future or contingent violations; differing from injunctions, in that the latter correct past and present or imminent and certain injuries. De Carli v. O'Brien, 150 Or. 35, 41 P.2d 411, 416.

Bill to carry a decree into execution. One which is filed when, from the neglect of parties or some other cause, it may become impossible to carry a decree into execution without the further decree of the court.

Bill to perpetuate testimony. A bill in equity filed in order to procure the testimony of witnesses to be taken as to some matter not at the time before the courts, but which is likely at some future time to be in litigation. Superseded by Rule of Civil Procedure 27.

Bill to quiet possession and title. Also called a bill to remove a cloud on title (*q.v.*), and though sometimes classed with bills *quia timet* or for the cancellation of void instruments, they may be resorted to in other cases when the complainant's title is clear and there is a cloud to be removed.

Bill to suspend a decree. One brought to avoid or suspend a decree under special circumstances.

Bill to take testimony de bene esse. One which is brought to take the testimony of witnesses to a fact material to the prosecution of a suit at law which is actually commenced, where there is good cause to fear that the testimony may otherwise be lost before the time of trial. Superseded by Rule of Civil Procedure 27.

Cross-bill. One which is brought by a defendant in a suit against a plaintiff in or against other defendants in the same suit, or against both, touching the matters in question in the original bill. It is a bill brought by a defendant against a plaintiff, or other parties in a former bill depending, touching the matter in question in that bill. It is usually brought either to obtain a necessary discovery of facts in aid of the defense to the original bill, or to obtain full relief to all parties in reference to the matters of the original bill. It is to be treated as a mere auxiliary suit. A species of pleading, used for the purpose of obtaining a discovery necessary to the defense, or to obtain some relief founded on the collateral claims of the party defendant to the original suit. Such bill has been superseded by a cross-claim under Fed.R. Civil P. 13. Also, if a bill of exchange or promissory note be given in consideration of another bill or notice, it is called a "cross" or "counter" bill or note.

Supplemental bill. A bill to bring before the court matters arising after the filing of the original bill or not then known to complainant. The function of this bill has been replaced by supplemental pleadings permitted under Fed.R. Civil P. 15. See *Bill in nature of a supplemental bill.*

Legislation. The draft of a proposed law from the time of its introduction in a legislative house through all the various stages in both houses. Once introduced, a federal bill may be considered in any session of a Congress, but it dies at the end of a Congress, and it must be reintroduced as a new bill if a succeeding Congress is to consider it. The form of a proposed law before it is enacted into law by vote of the legislative body. An "Act" is the appropriate term for it after it has been acted on by, and passed by, the legislature. See also **Marking up; Omnibus bill.**

Appropriations bill. Bill covering raising and expenditure of public funds. Federal appropriations bills must originate in the House of Representatives. Art. I, Sec. 7, U.S. Const. See also **Appropriation bill.**

Authorization bill. Bill authorizing expenditure of public funds.

Clean bill. Bill coming out of committee in amended or redrafted form, making it essentially a new bill.

Engrossed bill. Bill in final form, ready to be voted on by legislature.

Enrolled bill. Bill that has been passed and forwarded to President or Governor for signature or veto.

Private bill. One dealing only with a matter of private personal or local interest. All legislative bills which have for their object some particular or private interest are so termed, as distinguished from such as are for the benefit of the whole community, which are termed "public bills."

Revenue bill. See *Appropriations bill, supra.*

Maritime law.

Bill of adventure. A written certificate by a merchant or the master or owner of a ship, to the effect that the property and risk in goods shipped on the vessel in his own name belong to another person, to whom he is accountable for the proceeds alone.

Bill of entry. Form filled out by importer for use of customs officer; describes goods, their value, etc. Permits goods to be unloaded from ship.

Bill of health. An official certificate, given by the authorities of a port from which a vessel clears, to the master of the ship, showing the state of the port, as respects the public health, at the time of sailing, and exhibited to the authorities of the port which the vessel next makes, in token that she does not bring disease. If the bill alleges that no contagious or infectious disease existed, it is called a "clean" bill; if it admits that one was suspected or anticipated, or that one actually prevailed, it is called a "touched" or a "foul" bill.

Bill of sight. When an importer of goods is ignorant of their exact quantity or quality, so that he cannot make a perfect entry of them, he may give to the customs officer a written description of them, according to the best of his information and belief. This is called a "bill of sight."

Negotiable instruments. See *Commercial paper, supra.*

Billa /bílə/. L. Lat. A bill; an original bill.

Billa cassetur, or quod billa cassetur /(kwòd) bílə kəsíydər/. (That the bill be quashed.) The form of the judgment rendered for a defendant on a plea in abatement, where the proceeding is *by bill;* that is, where the suit is commenced by *capias,* and not by original writ.

Billa excambii /bílə ekskǽmbiyay/. A bill of exchange.

Billa exonerationis /bílə egzònərèyshiyównəs/. A bill of lading.

Billa vera /bílə vírə/. (A true bill.) The indorsement anciently made on a bill of indictment by a grand jury, when they found it sufficiently sustained by evidence. See **Indictment.**

Billet. A soldier's quarters in a civilian's house; or the ticket which authorizes him to occupy them.

Billeta /bílədə/. In old English law, a bill or petition exhibited in parliament.

Billing cycle. Period of time in which creditors regularly submit bills to customers or debtors; *e.g.* 30 days.

Bill of attainder. See **Attainder; Bill** (*Criminal law*).

Bill of indemnity. A law under which a public official is protected from liability in performance of his official acts including his failure to take his official oath. An initial pleading by which the plaintiff seeks to require another (*e.g.,* insurance company) to discharge his liability to a third person.

In English law, an act of parliament, passed every session until 1869, but discontinued in and after that year, as having been rendered unnecessary by the passing of the promissory oaths act, 1868, for the relief of those who had unwittingly or unavoidably neglected to take the necessary oaths, etc., required for the purpose of qualifying them to hold their respective offices.

Bill of lading. Document evidencing receipt of goods for shipment issued by person engaged in business of transporting or forwarding goods and it includes air-bill. U.C.C. § 1–201(6). An instrument in writing, signed by a carrier or his agent, describing the freight so as to identify it, stating the name of the consignor, the terms of the contract for carriage, and agreeing or directing that the freight be delivered to the order or assigns of a specified person at a specified place. It is receipt for goods, contract for their carriage, and is documentary evidence of title to goods. Schwalb v. Erie R. Co., 161 Misc. 743, 293 N.Y.S. 842, 846.

Bills in a set. A series of bills of lading each bearing a number and providing that a certain bill is valid only if goods have not been delivered against another bill. U.C.C. § 7–304.

Clean bill. One which contains nothing in the margin qualifying the words of the bill of lading itself. Bank of America Nat. Trust & Sav. Ass'n v. Liberty Nat. Bank & Trust Co. of Oklahoma City, D.C.Okl., 116 F.Supp. 233, 238, 239.

Common law. In common law, the written evidence of a contract for the carriage and delivery of goods sent by sea for a certain freight. A written memorandum, given by the person in command of a merchant vessel, acknowledging the receipt on board the ship of certain specified goods, in good order or "apparent good order," which he undertakes, in consideration of the payment of freight, to deliver in like good order (dangers of the sea excepted) at a designated place to the consignee therein named or to his assigns.

Foul bill. Bill of lading containing notation that goods received by carrier were defective.

Negotiable bill. One which by its terms calls for goods to be delivered to bearer or to order of named persons, or where recognized in overseas trade, if it runs to named persons or assigns. U.C.C. § 7–104(1)(a)(b).

Non-negotiable bill. Document of title in which goods are consigned to named persons. U.C.C. § 7–104(2).

Ocean bill. A negotiable bill of lading used in shipment by water.

On board bill. Bill of lading which shows that loading has been completed.

Order bill. One in which it is stated that goods are consigned to order of any person named therein. See *Negotiable bill, supra;* also, **Order bill of lading.**

Overseas bill. Where the contract contemplates overseas shipment and contains a term C.I.F. or C. & F. or F.O.B. vessel, the seller unless otherwise agreed must obtain a negotiable bill of lading stating that the goods have been loaded on board or, in the case of a term C.I.F. or C. & F., received for shipment. U.C.C. § 2–323(1).

Straight bill. One in which it is stated that goods are consigned to a specified person.

Through bill. One by which a railroad contracts to transport over its own line for a certain distance carloads of merchandise or stock, there to deliver the same to its connecting lines to be transported to the place of destination at a fixed rate per carload for the whole distance. Embodies undertaking to be performed in part by persons acting as agents for issuer. U.C.C. § 7–302.

Bill of lading acts. The principal acts governing bills of lading are Article 7 of the Uniform Commercial Code, the Federal Bills of Lading Act (49 U.S.C.A. §§ 81–124), and the Carmack Amendment to the Interstate Commerce Act (49 U.S.C.A. § 20(11). See also **Harter Act.**

Bill of mortality. A written statement or account of the number of deaths which have occurred in a certain district within a given time.

Bill of pains and penalties. Statutory provision for punishment without judicial determination of guilt similar to bill of attainder except that punishment is less severe. Prohibited by U.S.Const., Art. I, § 9, cl. 3 (Congress), § 10 (States).

Bill of rights. First ten Amendments to U.S. Constitution. See also **Bill.**

Bill quia timet /bíl kwáyə tímət/. See **Quia timet.**

Bi-metallic. Pertaining to, or consisting of, two metals used as money at a fixed relative value.

Bi-metallism. The legalized use of two metals in the currency of a country at a fixed relative value *e.g.* copper and silver.

Bind. To obligate; to bring or place under definite duties or legal obligations, particularly by a bond or covenant. To affect one in a constraining or compulsory manner with a contract or a judgment. So long as a contract, an adjudication, or a legal relation remains in force and virtue, and continues to impose duties or obligations, it is said to be *"binding."* A man is *bound* by his contract or promise, by a judgment or decree against him, by his bond or covenant, by an estoppel, etc.

Binder. A written memorandum of the important terms of contract of insurance which gives temporary protection to insured pending investigation of risk by insurance company or until a formal policy is issued. Turner v. Worth Ins. Co., 106 Ariz. 132, 472 P.2d 1, 2. A receipt for earnest money or a deposit paid to secure the right to purchase a home at terms that have been agreed upon by both buyer and seller. See also **Cover note.**

Binding agreement. A contract which is enforceable such as an offer to buy or sell when person to whom it is made accepts it and communicates his acceptance. McAden v. Craig, 222 N.C. 497, 24 S.E.2d 1, 3.

Binding authority. Sources of law that must be taken into account by a judge in deciding a case; for example, statutes or decisions by a higher court of the same state on point. See **Precedent.**

Binding instruction. One in which jury is told that if they find certain conditions to be true, they should find for plaintiff or defendant, as case might be. Scott-Burr Stores Corporation v. Foster, 197 Ark. 232, 122 S.W.2d 165, 169.

Binding over. The act by which a court or magistrate requires a person to enter into a recognizance or furnish bail to appear for trial, to keep the peace, to attend as a witness, etc. Also describes act of lower court in transferring case to higher court or to grand jury after a finding of probable cause to believe that defendant committed crime.

Binding receipt or **slip.** Term refers to a limited acceptance of an application for insurance given by an authorized agent pending the ascertainment of the company's willingness to assume the burden of the proposed risk, the effect of which is to protect the applicant until the company acts upon the application, and, if it declines to accept the burden, the binding effect of the slip ceases eo instante. See **Binder.**

Bind out. To place one under a legal obligation to serve another; as to *bind out* an apprentice.

Bipartite /bàypártayt/. Consisting of, or divisible into, two parts. A term in conveyancing descriptive of an instrument in two parts, and executed by both parties.

Birretum /bərédəm/ **birretus** /bərédəs/. A cap or coif used formerly in England by judges and serjeants at law.

Birth. The act of being born or wholly brought into separate existence.

Birth certificate. A formal document which certifies as to the date and place of one's birth and a recitation of his or her parentage, as issued by an official in charge of such records. Furnishing of such is often required to prove one's age. See **Birth record.**

Birth control. Term which embraces all forms of contraception; prevention of conception.

Birth record. Official statistical data concerning dates and places of persons' birth, as well as parentage, kept by local government officials. See **Birth certificate.**

Bis /bís/. Lat. Twice.

Bisaile (also **besaile, besayel, besaiel, besayle**) /biséyl/. The father of one's grandfather or grandmother.

Bi-scot. In old English law, a fine imposed for not repairing banks, ditches, and causeways.

Bis dat qui cito dat /bís dæt kwáy sáydow dæt/. He pays twice who pays promptly.

Bishop. An ecclesiastical dignitary, being the chief of the clergy within his diocese, subject to the archbishop of the province in which his diocese is situated.

Bishopric /bíshəprìk/. In ecclesiastical law, the diocese of a bishop, or the circuit in which he has jurisdiction; the office of a bishop. 1 Bl.Comm. 377–382.

Bishop's court. In English law, an ecclesiastical court, held in the cathedral of each diocese, the judge whereof is the bishop's chancellor, who judges by the civil canon law; and, if the diocese be large, he has his commissaries in remote parts, who hold consistory courts, for matters limited to them by their commission.

Bis idem exigi bona fides non patitur; et in satisfactionibus non permittitur amplius fieri quam semel factum est /bís áydəm égzəjay bównə fáydiyz nòn páedədər; èd in sædəsfækshiyównəbəs nón pərmídədər æmpliyəs fáyəráy kwàm sémal fæktəm èst/. Good faith does not suffer the same thing to be demanded twice; and in making satisfaction [for a debt or demand] it is not allowed to be done more than once.

Bissextile /bàysékstayl/. The day which is added every fourth year (leap-year) to the month of February, in order to make the year agree with the course of the sun.

Biting rule. When first taker of conveyed property under writing submitted for construction is initially conveyed a fee title, it is then incompetent and invalid to modify, qualify, or reduce thereafter the apparent fee title of the first taker so as to reduce it to a life estate, and any gift over after death of first taker is void.

Black acre and white acre. Fictitious names used by the old writers to distinguish one parcel of land from another, to avoid ambiguity, as well as the inconvenience of a fuller description.

Black Act. The English statute 9 Geo. I, c. 22, so called because it was occasioned by the outrages committed by persons with their faces blacked or otherwise disguised, who appeared in Epping Forest, near Waltham, in Essex, and destroyed the deer there, and committed other offenses. Repealed by 7 & 8 Geo. IV, c. 27.

Black Book of the Admiralty. An English book of the highest authority in admiralty matters, generally supposed to have been compiled during the reign of Edward III. with additions of a later date. It contains the laws of Oleron, a view of crimes and offenses cognizable in the admiralty, and many other matters.

Black Book of the Exchequer. The name of an ancient book kept in the English exchequer, containing a collection of treaties, conventions, charters, etc.

Black cap. In England, the head-dress worn by the judge in pronouncing the sentence of death. It is part of the judicial full dress, and is worn by the judges on occasions of especial state.

Black code. A name given collectively to the body of laws, statutes, and rules in force in various southern states prior to 1865, which regulated the institution of slavery, and particularly those forbidding their reception at public inns and on public conveyances. Civil Rights Cases, 109 U.S. 3, 3 S.Ct. 18, 27 L.Ed. 835.

Blackjack. A short bludgeon consisting of a heavy head, as of metal, on an elastic shaft or with a flexible handle; a bludgeon-like weapon consisting of a lead slug attached to a leather thong; a small leather-covered club or billy weighted at the head and having an elastic shaft.

As a card game, another name for *vingt-et-un* (twenty-one); also, a variety of hearts in which the jack of spades counts as ten hearts.

Blackleg. A person who makes his living by frequenting race-courses and places where games of chance are played, getting the best odds, and giving the least he can, but not necessarily cheating.

Black letter law. An informal term indicating the basic principles of law generally accepted by the courts and/or embodied in the statutes of a particular jurisdiction.

Blacklist. A list of persons marked out for special avoidance, antagonism, or enmity on the part of those who prepare the list or those among whom it is intended to circulate; as where a trades-union "blacklists" workmen who refuse to conform to its rules, or where a list of insolvent or untrustworthy persons is published by a commercial agency or mercantile association.

Black Lung Benefits Act. Federal statute benefitting coal miners who are stricken with pneumoconiosis, a chronic dust disease of the lung. 30 U.S.C.A. § 902. Benefits under the Act are administered by the Department of Labor.

Blackmail. Unlawful demand of money or property under threat to do bodily harm, to injure property, to accuse of crime, or to expose disgraceful defects. This crime is commonly included under extortion statutes. See also **Extortion**; **Shakedown**.

In one of its original meanings, this term denoted a tribute paid by English dwellers along the Scottish border to influential chieftains of Scotland, as a condition of securing immunity from raids of marauders and border thieves. Also, rents payable in cattle, grain, work, and the like. Such rents were called "blackmail" *(reditus nigri),* in distinction from white rents *(blanche firmes),* which were rents paid in silver. See **Black rents**.

Black maria. A closed vehicle or van in which prisoners are carried to and from the jail, or between the court and the jail.

Black market. Illegal trading; buying and selling goods which are subject to government rationing or control, including goods which are contraband.

Black Muslim. An organization of American Negroes, founded in Detroit in 1930 by an American Negro calling himself Mohammad Elijah. To the traditional Koran the founders added the doctrine of Black Supremacy and proclaimed the desirability of maintaining (or regaining) the purity of the black race.

Black rents. In old English law, rents reserved in work, grain, provisions, or baser money than silver, in contradistinction to those which were reserved in *white* money or silver, which were termed "white rents" *(reditus albi),* or blanch farms. See **Blackmail**.

Black-Rod, Gentleman Usher of. In England, the title of a chief officer of the king, deriving his name from the *Black Rod* of office, on the top of which reposes a golden lion, which he carries. During the session of Parliament he attends on the peers, summons the Commons to the House of Lords; and to his custody all peers impeached for any crime or contempt are first committed.

Black ward. A subvassal, who held ward of the king's vassal.

Blada /bléydə/. In old English law, growing crops of grain of any kind; all manner of annual grain; harvested grain.

Bladarius /blədériyəs/. In old English law, a cornmonger; meal-man or corn-chandler; a bladier, or engrosser of corn or grain.

Blanche firme. White rent; a rent reserved, payable in silver.

Blanc seign. In Louisiana, a paper signed at the bottom by him who intends to bind himself, give acquittance, or compromise, at the discretion of the person whom he intrusts with such *blanc seign*, giving him power to fill it with what he may think proper, according to agreement.

Blank. A space left unfilled in a written document, in which one or more words or marks are to be inserted to complete the sense. Also a skeleton or printed form for any legal document, in which the necessary and invariable words are printed in their proper order, with blank spaces left for the insertion of such names, dates, figures, additional clauses, etc., as may be necessary to adapt the instrument to the particular case and to the design of the party using it.

Blank acceptance. An acceptance of a bill of exchange written on the paper before the bill is made, and delivered by the acceptor.

Blank bar. Also called the "common bar." The name of a plea in bar which in an action of trespass was put in to oblige the plaintiff to assign the certain place where the trespass was committed. It was most in practice in the common bench.

Blank bill. Bill of exchange with payee's name left blank.

Blanket bond. Generic term which may describe a bond covering a number of projects on which performance bonds are required or a bond to dissolve more than one attachment. Any bond used for multiple purposes.

Blanket insurance. See **Insurance**.

Blanket mortgage. Covers two or more assets or properties which are pledged to support the given debt.

Blanket policy. See **Insurance**.

Blanket rate. Insurance rate applied when there is more than one property or subject of insurance.

Blanket search warrant. A single warrant authorizing the search of more than one area or the seizure of everything found at a given location without specific authorization in the warrant, the latter being in violation of the requirements of the Fourth Amendment to U.S. Const. Marcus v. Search Warrants etc., 367 U.S. 717, 81 S.Ct. 1708, 6 L.Ed.2d 1127.

Blank indorsement. The indorsement of a bill of exchange or promissory note, by merely writing the name of the indorser, without mentioning any person to whom the bill or note is to be paid; called "blank," because a blank or space is left *over* it for the insertion of the name of the indorsee, or of any subsequent holder. Otherwise called an indorsement "in blank." Such indorsement causes an instrument, otherwise payable to order, to become payable to bearer and negotiable by delivery alone. U.C.C. § 3–204(2).

Blanks. A kind of white money (value 8d.), coined by Henry V in those parts of France which were then subject to England; forbidden to be current in that realm by 2 Hen. VI, c. 9.

Blank shares. "Series shares" which may vary in the relative rights and preferences as between different series but which may be fixed in articles of incorporation.

Blasphemy /blǽsfəmiy/. Any oral or written reproach maliciously cast upon God, His name, attributes, or religion. In general, blasphemy may be described as consisting in speaking evil of the Deity with an impious purpose to derogate from the divine majesty, and to alienate the minds of others from the love and reverence of God. It is purposely using words concerning God calculated and designed to impair and destroy the reverence, respect, and confidence due to Him as the intelligent creator, governor, and judge of the world. It embraces the idea of detraction, when used towards the Supreme Being, as "calumny" usually carries the same idea when applied to an individual. It is a willful and malicious attempt to lessen men's reverence of God by denying His existence, or His attributes as an intelligent creator, governor, and judge of men, and to prevent their having confidence in Him as such.

In English law, blasphemy is the offense of speaking matter relating to God, Jesus Christ, the Bible, or the Book of Common Prayer, intended to wound the feelings of mankind or to excite contempt and hatred against the church by law established, or to promote immorality.

Blended fund. In England, where a testator directs his real and personal estate to be sold, and disposes of the proceeds as forming one aggregate, this is called a "blended fund."

Blended price. As applied to milk, a price paid to producers based upon a pool average weighted by the volume of milk disposed of, according to different types of utilization. Queensboro Farm Products v. State, 175 Misc. 574, 24 N.Y.S.2d 413, 417.

Blind alley. Literally, a way from which exit is possible only by retracing the path of entry; fig., a no-win position, a dilemma.

Blind corner. Used to describe the configuration of buildings or other structures which prevent a driver approaching an intersection from being able to observe traffic coming in the direction of the intersecting way.

Blindcraft. A natural descriptive term identifying in a broad sense work of the blind, conveying the idea of the blind performing deftly at any of the various skills or trades to which their talents are applied or leaving the suggestion of dexterity and skill of the blind as well as their handiwork itself. San Francisco Ass'n for Blind v. Industrial Aid for Blind, D.C.Mo., 58 F.Supp. 995, 1001.

Blindness. Condition of one who is without sight either wholly or partially. Degrees are recognized for purpose of worker's compensation and social security benefits.

Blind selling. Selling goods without giving buyer opportunity to examine such.

Blind tiger. A place where intoxicants are sold on the sly, and contrary to the law. A "tippling-house."

Block. A square or portion of a city or town inclosed by streets, whether partially or wholly occupied by buildings or containing only vacant lots. Also used synonymous with "square." The platted portion of a city surrounded by streets. The term need not, however, be limited to blocks platted as such, but may mean an area bounded on all sides by streets or

avenues. St. Louis-San Francisco R. Co. v. City of Tulsa, Okl., C.C.A.Okl., 15 F.2d 960, 963. It must be surrounded on at least three sides by streets, which must be marked on the ground, and not simply indicated as such on a plat. See also **Lot.**

Large amount of stock or bonds sold as a unit.

Blockade. Action taken against enemy nation so as to isolate, obstruct and prevent communications, commerce, supplies, and persons from entering into or leaving such nation. Such blockades may be by sea, or land, or both.

Blockage. Recognition in the field of taxation of fact that in some instances a large block of stock cannot be marketed and turned into cash as readily as a few shares. Citizens Fidelity Bank & Trust Co. v. Reeves, Ky., 259 S.W.2d 432, 433. See **Blockage rule.**

Blockage rule. Process of determining value of large blocks of corporate stock for gift and estate tax purposes, based on the postulate that a large block of stock cannot be marketed as readily and as advantageously in price as can a few shares. Montclair Trust Co. v. Zink, Prerog., 141 N.J.Eq. 401, 57 A.2d 372, 376, 380. Application of this rule generally justifies a discount in the fair market value since the disposition of a large amount of stock at any one time may well depress the value of such shares in the market place.

Block-booking. The practice of licensing or offering for license one motion picture feature or group of features on condition that exhibitor will also license another feature or group of features released by distributor during a given period. U. S. v. Paramount Pictures, N. Y., 334 U.S. 131, 68 S.Ct. 915, 928, 92 L.Ed. 1260.

Block book system. An abstract of property assessed for taxes and also of property unrendered and of which owners were unknown, together with maps and plats. Southern Surety Co. v. Lafferty, Tex.Civ. App., 43 S.W.2d 460, 463.

Blocked account. Governmental restrictions on a bank account; usually with reference to transfers to foreign countries.

Blocked currency. Restrictions on use of currency and bank deposits (normally with respect to transfer to other countries) by the government where the currency or deposits are located.

Blocked income. Income earned by foreign taxpayer which is not subject to tax in U.S. because taxpayer is precluded in foreign country from making conversion of foreign earned income to dollars.

Block of surveys. In Pennsylvania land law, any considerable body of contiguous tracts surveyed in the name of the same warrantee, without regard to the manner in which they were originally located; a body of contiguous tracts located by exterior lines, but not separated from each other by interior lines.

Block policy. Insurance policy covering all the property of the insured against most perils.

Block to block rule. The "block to block rule" for assessing the benefits for the opening of a new street is the assessment against the lots in each block of the cost of acquiring the lands in that block. In re St. Raymona Ave. in City of New York, 175 App.Div. 518, 162 N.Y.S. 185, 188.

Blood feud. Avenging the killing of kin on the person who killed him, or on his family.

Blood grouping test. Test used in paternity and illegitimacy cases to determine whether one *could be* father of child. The test does not affirmatively establish paternity but it eliminates one who cannot be adjudicated father.

Bloodhounds. Dogs remarkable for their sense of smell and ability to follow a scent or track a human being.

Blood money. A weregild, or pecuniary mulct paid by a slayer to the relatives of his victim. Also used, in a popular sense, as descriptive of money paid by way of reward for the apprehension and conviction of a person charged with a capital crime.

Blood relations. Kindred; consanguinity; family relationship; relation by descent from a common blood ancestor. A person may be said to be "of the blood" of another who has any, however small a portion, of the blood derived from a common ancestor, thus including half blood as well as whole blood. All persons are of the blood of an ancestor who may, in the absence of other and nearer heirs, take by descent from that ancestor. See also **Relation.**

Half-blood. A term denoting the degree of relationship which exists between those who have the same father or the same mother, but not both parents in common.

Mixed blood. A person is "of mixed blood" who is descended from ancestors of different races or nationalities; but particularly, in the United States, the term denotes a person one of whose parents (or more remote ancestors) was a negro. U. S. v. First Nat. Bank of Detroit, Minn., 234 U.S. 245, 34 S.Ct. 846, 848, 58 L.Ed. 1298.

Whole blood. Kinship by descent from the same father and mother; as distinguished from *half* blood, which is the relationship of those who have one parent in common, but not both.

Blood test. See **Blood grouping test.**

Bloodwit. An amercement for bloodshed. The privilege of taking such amercements. A privilege or exemption from paying a fine or amercement assessed for bloodshed.

Bloody hand. In forest law, evidence of bloody hands or other parts of the body was one of the four kinds of circumstantial evidence of his having illegally killed deer, although he was not found in the act of chasing or hunting.

Blotter. See **Bench blotter.**

BLS. Bachelor of Library Science; Bureau of Labor Statistics.

Bludgeon. A heavy club or stick used as a weapon, commonly weighted in one end by metal. As a verb, used to inflict injury by use of it. State v. Witcher, 58 N.J.Super. 464, 156 A.2d 709, 713.

Blue chip investment. Highest quality stock or bond with minimum risk and satisfactory income or yield; commonly required by trust managers.

Blue laws. Statutes regulating entertainment activities, work, and commerce on Sundays. Such laws have their origin in colonial New England.

Blue list. Daily listing (on blue paper) of municipal bond offerings.

Blue notes. Notes accepted by a life insurance company for the amount of premiums on the policy, which provide for the continuance of the policy in force until the due date of the notes.

Blue ribbon jury. Jury consisting of highly qualified persons.

Blue sky laws. A popular name for state statutes providing for the regulation and supervision of securities offerings and sales, for the protection of citizen-investors from investing in fraudulent companies. Laws intended to stop the sale of stock in fly-by-night concerns, visionary oil wells, distant gold mines, and other like fraudulent exploitations.

A statute called a "Blue Sky Law" because it pertains to speculative schemes which have no more basis than so many feet of blue sky. State v. Cushing, 137 Me. 112, 15 A.2d 740.

Bluff. A high, steep bank, as by a river, the sea, a ravine, or a plain, or a bank or headland with a broad, steep face. To deceive by pretense or appearance of strength.

Blumba. A certifying metal tag attached to kosher meat. People on Complaint of Waller v. Jacob Branfman & Son, 147 Misc. 290, 263 N.Y.S. 629, 632.

Blunder. As applied in cases of ordinary negligence is the want of or absence of ordinary care, a failure to do what should have been done or the doing of that which should not have been done, resulting in the happening of an event or injury which could have and should have been foreseen and avoided by use of such care as a reasonably prudent person would have exercised under the same or similar circumstances. Loyd v. Pierce, Tex.Civ.App., 89 S.W.2d 1035, 1038.

Blunderbuss. A firearm intended to shoot objects at close quarters, without exact aim.

Board. An official or representative body organized to perform a trust or to execute official or representative functions or having the management of a public office or department exercising administrative or governmental functions. Commissioners of State Ins. Fund v. Dinowitz, 179 Misc. 278, 39 N.Y.S.2d 34, 38.

A committee of persons organized under authority of law in order to exercise certain authorities, have oversight or control of certain matters, or discharge certain functions of a magisterial, representative, or fiduciary character. Thus, "board of aldermen," "board of health," "board of directors," "board of works."

Group of persons with managerial, supervisory, or investigatory functions and power. See types of such boards, *infra*.

Also lodging, food, and entertainment, furnished to a guest at an inn or boarding house.

When used with reference to prisoners, as a basis for the sheriff's fee, board may be equivalent to "necessary food."

"Board," as a verb, means to receive food for a reasonable compensation, either with or without lodging. Jackson v. Engert, 453 S.W.2d 615, 618.

Boarder. One that is provided with regular meals, with or without lodging. Jackson v. Engert, 453 S.W.2d 615, 618.

Board lot. Unit of trade on a stock exchange.

Board of adjustment. Public and quasi judicial agency charged with duty to hear and determine zoning appeals. Also called "Board of Zoning Appeals" in certain cities.

Board of aldermen. The governing body of a municipal corporation. See **Aldermen**.

Board of appeals. A non-judicial, administrative tribunal which reviews the decision made by the hearing officer or by the head of the agency. See also **Board of review**.

Board of audit. A tribunal provided by statute in some states, to adjust and settle the accounts of municipal corporations.

Board of bar overseers. State board which governs licensing and discipline of attorneys.

Board of directors. The governing body of a corporation elected by the stockholders; usually made-up of officers of the corporation and outside (non-company) directors. The board is empowered to elect and appoint officers and agents to act on behalf of the corporation, declare dividends, and act on other major matters affecting the corporation. See also **Directors; Outside director**.

Board of education. A state or local agency or board organized for government and management of schools in state or municipality. The agency to which state delegates power and duty of controlling schools in school district. See also **School** *(School board or committee)*.

Board of equalization. See **Equalization**.

Board of examiners. A state agency or board appointed to examine the qualifications of applicants for license to practice a trade or profession.

Board of fire underwriters. Unincorporated voluntary associations composed exclusively of persons engaged in business of fire insurance, for consolidation and co-operation in matters affecting the business.

Board of Governors of Federal Reserve System. Seven member board, with fourteen year terms, which governs the twelve Federal Reserve Banks and branches.

The Board of Governors determines general monetary, credit, and operating policies for the System as a whole and formulates the rules and regulations necessary to carry out the purposes of the Federal Reserve Act. The Board's principal duties consist of exerting an influence over credit conditions and supervising the Federal Reserve Banks and member banks.

Board of health. A municipal or state board or commission with certain powers and duties relative to preservation and improvement of the public health.

Board of Immigration Appeals. Quasi-judicial agency within the Department of Justice which hears appeals from certain decisions of the Immigration and Naturalization Service and reviews actions of the Commissioner of Immigration and Naturalization in deporting and excluding aliens.

Board of pardons. State board, of which the governor is usually a member, authorized to review and grant pardons and clemency to convicted prisoners.

Board of Parole. See **Parole board**.

Board of Patent Appeals. Consists of Commissioner of Patents, Asst. Commissioners and examiners in chief whose responsibility is to review adverse decisions of examiners on applications for patents. 35 U.S.C.A. § 7.

Board of regents. A body of officials appointed to direct and supervise an educational institution or, in some states, the educational system of a State.

Board of registration. State boards governing licensing and discipline of professions and quasi-professions in state.

Board of review. Board authorized to review administrative agency decisions and rulings. Body authorized to review alleged improper valuation and assessment of property. In some cities, a board charged with responsibility to review alleged police brutality or excessive force. See also **Board of appeals**.

Board of supervisors. An organized committee, or body of officials, constituting part of the county government, with special charge of the county revenues.

Board of trade. An organization of merchants, manufacturers, etc., for furthering its commercial interests, advancing its prosperity, etc. Also an organization for the advancement and protection of a particular trade or line of commerce.

An exchange or association engaged in the business of buying or selling commodities; *e.g.* Chicago Board of Trade.

Boatable. A term applied in some states to minor rivers and streams capable of being navigated in small boats, skiffs, or launches, though not by steam or sailing vessels.

Boatswain /bówsən/. A seaman who superintends the work of the crew. The foreman of sailors. MaCauley v. Pacific Atlantic S. S. Co., 167 Or. 80, 115 P.2d 307, 308.

Bobbies. English name for policemen.

Bobtail driver. A person collecting and delivering laundry without being subject to complete control of employer. Ring v. City Dry Cleaners, 152 Fla. 622, 12 So.2d 593, 594.

Bobtails. Persons who conduct stores or establishments of their own where patrons may bring articles to be laundered. Schwartz v. Laundry & Linen Supply Drivers' Union, Local 187, 339 Pa. 353, 14 A.2d 438, 439.

Boc /búk/. In Saxon law, a book or writing; a deed or charter. *Boc land*, deed or charter land. *Land boc*, a writing for conveying land; a deed or charter; a land-book. The *land bocs*, or evidences of title, corresponding to modern deeds, were destroyed by William the Conqueror.

Boceras. Sax. A scribe, notary, or chancellor among the Saxons.

Boc horde /búk-hòrd/. A place where books, writings, or evidences were kept, generally in monasteries.

Boc land. In Saxon law, allodial lands held by deed or other written evidence of title.

Bodily. Pertaining to or concerning the body; of or belonging to the body or the physical constitution; not mental but corporeal. Provident Life & Accident Ins. Co. v. Campbell, 18 Tenn.App. 452, 79 S.W.2d 296.

Bodily condition. Status of human body at a given point in time as contrasted with state of mind.

Bodily exhibition. Public or semi public showing of private parts of body's anatomy; used in statutes covering obscenity and crimes against public decency; *e.g.* indecent exposure.

Bodily heirs. Heirs begotten or borne by the person referred to; lineal descendants. Progeny or issue, including children, grandchildren, and other lineal descendants. See **Heir of the body**.

Bodily infirmity. A settled disease or ailment that would probably result to some degree in general impairment of physical health and vigor. Travelers' Ins. Co. of Hartford, Conn., v. Byers, 123 Cal.App. 473, 11 P.2d 444, 446. An ailment or disorder of an established and settled character. Something that amounts to inroad on physical health or impairment of bodily or mental powers. See also **Disability.**

Bodily injury. Generally refers only to injury to the body, or to sickness or disease contracted by the injured as a result of injury. Rape of victim constitutes "bodily harm" under statute so as to make a kidnapping aggravated kidnapping. State v. Adams, 218 Kan. 495, 545 P.2d 1134, 1139. See also **Disability; Injury.**

Body. A person. Used of a natural body, or of an artificial one created by law, as a corporation. Body in the broad sense is the main central or principal part of anything as distinguished from subordinate parts. Walberg v. Probst, Cust. & Pat.App., 474 F.2d 683, 687.

The main part of the human body; the trunk. The term however has also been held to embrace all members of the person, including the head and limbs.

Also the main part of an instrument. In deeds it is spoken of as distinguished from the recitals and other introductory parts and signatures; in affidavits, from the title and jurat.

A collection of laws; that is, the embodiment of the laws in one connected statement or collection, called a "body of laws" *(q.v.)*.

See also **Corpus.**

Body corporate. A public or private corporation.

Body execution. Seizure of person by order of court to *e.g.* enforce judgment for payment of money. See **Capias ad satisfaciendum.**

Body heirs. See **Bodily** *(Bodily heirs)*; **Heir of the body.**

Body of a county. A county at large, as distinguished from any particular place within it. A county considered as a territorial whole. State v. Arthur, 39 Iowa 631; People v. Dunn, 31 App.Div. 139, 52 N.Y.S. 968.

Body of an instrument. The main and operative part; the substantive provisions, as distinguished from the recitals, title, jurat, etc.

Body of laws. An organized and systematic collection or codification of laws; *e.g.* United States Code.

Body of the offense. When applied to any particular offense, means that the particular crime charged has actually been committed by some one. Barrett v. State, 57 Okl.Cr. 259, 47 P.2d 613, 617. The corpus delicti.

Body politic or **corporate.** A social compact by which the whole people covenants with each citizen, and each citizen with the whole people, that all shall be governed by certain laws for the common good. Uricich v. Kolesar, 54 Ohio App. 309, 7 N.E.2d 413, 414. Also a term applied to a municipal corporation, school district, county or city. State or nation or public associations. Utah State Building Commission, for Use and Benefit of Mountain States Supply Co., v. Great American Indemnity Co., 105 Utah 11, 140 P.2d 763, 767.

Bogus /bówgəs/. Counterfeit; sham; imitation; as *e.g.* bogus money.

Bogus check. A check given by person upon bank in which he has no funds and which he has no reason to suppose will be honored. State v. Culver, 103 Ariz. 505, 446 P.2d 234, 236. Such act is a misdemeanor in most states.

Boilerplate. Language which is used commonly in documents having a definite meaning in the same context without variation; used to describe standard language in a legal document that is identical in instruments of a like nature. In re Pfaff's Estate, 41 Wis.2d 159, 163 N.W.2d 140. See also **Adhesion contract.**

Boiler-room transaction. High-pressure selling of stocks of doubtful value, usually over the telephone. Sometimes associated with sales of "hot-issue" securities.

Bolita tickets. Form of ticket used in game of Bolita which is a type of lottery, the winning number of which is determined by an event unconnected with the actual lottery such as a horse race. U. S. v. Robertson, C.A.Fla., 504 F.2d 289.

Bolito. A form of "lottery" which is a scheme for distribution of prizes by lot or chance. Robb v. State, Ind., 239 N.E.2d 154, 157.

Bolting. In English practice, a term formerly used in the English inns of court, but more particularly at Gray's Inn, signifying the private arguing of cases, as distinguished from *mooting*, which was a more formal and public mode of argument.

Bon. The name of a clause (*bon pour* _____, good for so much) added to a cedule or promise, where it is not in the handwriting of the signer, containing the amount of the sum which he obliges himself to pay.

Bona, *n.* /bównə/. Lat. Goods; property; possessions. In the Roman law, this term was used to designate all species of property, real, personal, and mixed, but was more strictly applied to real estate. In civil law, it includes both personal property (technically so called) and chattels real, thus corresponding to the French *biens (q.v.).* In the common law, its use was confined to the description of movable goods.

Bona confiscata /bównə kònfəskéydə/. Goods confiscated or forfeited to the imperial *fisc* or treasury. 1 Bl.Comm. 299.

Bona et catalla /bównə èt kətǽlə/. Goods and chattles; movable property. This expression includes all personal things that belong to a man.

Bona felonum /bównə fəlownəm/. In English law, goods of felons; the goods of one convicted of felony.

Bona forisfacta /bównə fòrəsfǽktə/. Goods forfeited.

Bona fugitivorum /bównə fyùwjədəvórəm/. In English law, goods of fugitives; the proper goods of him who flies for felony.

Bona immobilia /bównə ìməbíliyə/. Lands.

Bona mobilia /bównə məbíliyə/. Movables; those things which move themselves or can be transported from one place to another, and not permanently attached to a farm, heritage, or building.

Bona notabilia /bównə nòwdəbíliyə/. Notable goods; property worthy of notice, or of sufficient value to be accounted for. 2 Bl.Comm. 509.

Bona paraphernalia /bównə pæ̀rəfərnéyl(i)yə/. In the civil law, the separate property of a married woman other than that which is included in her dowry; more particularly, her clothing, jewels, and ornaments. Whiton v. Snyder, 88 N.Y. 303.

Bona peritura /bównə pèhrət(y)úrə/. Goods of a perishable nature; such goods as an executor or trustee must use diligence in disposing of and converting them into money.

Bona utlagatorum /bównə àtleygətórəm/. Goods of outlaws; goods belonging to persons outlawed.

Bona vacantia /bównə vəkǽnsh(iy)ə/. Vacant, unclaimed, or stray goods. Those things in which nobody claims a property, and which belonged, under the common law, to the finder, except in certain instances, when they were the property of the king. 1 Bl.Comm. 298.

Bona waviata /bównə wèyviyéydə/. In English law, waived goods; goods stolen and *waived*, that is, thrown away by the thief in his flight, for fear of being apprehended, or to facilitate his escape; and which go to the sovereign. 1 Bl.Comm. 296.

Bona, *adj.* /bównə/. Lat. Good. Used in numerous legal phrases of which the following are the principal:

Bona fides /bównə fáydiyz/. Good faith; integrity of dealing; honesty; sincerity; the opposite of *mala fides* and of *dolus malus.* See **Bona fide.**

Bona gestura /bównə jest(y)úrə/. Good abearance or behavior.

Bona gratia /bównə gréysh(iy)ə/. In the Roman law, by mutual consent; voluntarily. A term applied to a species of divorce where the parties separated by mutual consent; or where the parties renounced their marital engagements without assigning any cause, or upon mere pretexts.

Bona memoria /bównə məmór(i)yə/. Good memory. Generally used in the phrase *sanæ mentis et bonæ memoriæ,* of sound mind and good memory, as descriptive of the mental capacity of a testator.

Bonæ fidei /bówniy fáydiyay/. In the civil law, of good faith; in good faith.

Bonæ fidei contracts /bówniy fáydiyay kóntrækts/. In civil and Scotch law, those contracts in which equity may interpose to correct inequalities, and to adjust all matters according to the plain intention of the parties.

Bonæ fidei emptor /bówniy fáydiyay émptər/. A purchaser in good faith. One who either was ignorant that the thing he bought belonged to another or supposed that the seller had a right to sell it.

Bonæ fidei non congruit de apicibus juris disputare /bówniy fáydiyay nòn kəngrúwət dìy eypísəbəs júrəs dìspyuwtériy/. It is unbecoming to (or incompatible with good faith to) discuss (insist upon) the extreme subtleties of the law. A maxim which may be more freely rendered as meaning, "To insist on extreme subtleties of law is an encouragement to fraud."

Bonæ fidei possessor /bówniy fáydiyay pəzésər/. A possessor in good faith. One who believes that no other person has a better right to the possession than himself.

Bonæ fidei possessor in id tantum quod sese pervenerit tenetur /bówniy fáydiyay pəzésər in íd tǽntəm kwód síysìy pərvənírət tənáydər/. A possessor in good faith is liable only for that which he himself has obtained (or that which has come to him).

Bona fide /bównə fáydiy/bównə fayd/. In or with good faith; honestly, openly, and sincerely; without deceit or fraud. Merrill v. Dept. of Motor Vehicles, 71 Cal.2d 907, 80 Cal.Rptr. 89, 458 P.2d 33. Truly; actually; without simulation or pretense. Innocently; in the attitude of trust and confidence; without notice of fraud, etc. Real, actual, genuine, and not feigned. Bridgeport Mortgage & Realty Corporation v. Whitlock, 128 Conn. 57, 20 A.2d 414, 416. See also **Good faith.**

Bona fide error.　Mistake made unintentionally; inadvertently; in good faith.　Within meaning of Truth in Lending Act's exemption from liability for bona fide errors, "bona fide error" is error made in course of good-faith attempt at compliance with Act's requirements.　Mirabal v. General Motors Acceptance Corp., C.A.Ill., 537 F.2d 871, 878.

Bona fide holder for value.　An innocent or "bona fide holder for value" of negotiable paper is one who has taken it in good faith for a valuable consideration in the ordinary course of business and when it was not overdue.　One who receives negotiable paper in payment of antecedent obligations without notice of prior equities.　Under U.C.C. § 3–302, the requirements for a holder in due course are different from a mere bona fide holder for value.　See **Holder in due course**.

Bona fide judgment creditor.　One who in good faith, without fraud or collusion, recovers a judgment for money honestly due him.

Bona fide mortgage.　Essential elements of status are good faith, valuable consideration, and absence of notice.　Companaro v. Gondolfo, C.C.A.N.J., 60 F.2d 451, 452.　To constitute "bona fide mortgagee" there must be an absence of notice and payment of, or fixed liability for the consideration.　Cambridge Production Credit Ass'n v. Patrick, 140 Ohio St. 521, 45 N.E.2d 751, 755.

Bona fide operators.　Substantial, as distinguished from incidental, sporadic, or infrequent service.　Gonez v. Interstate Commerce Commission, D.C.Mass., 48 F.Supp. 286, 288.

Bona fide possessor.　One who not only supposes himself to be the true proprietor of the land, but who is ignorant that his title is contested by some other person claiming a better right to it.

Bona fide purchaser.　One who has purchased property for value without any notice of any defects in the title of the seller.　Walters v. Calderon, 25 Cal.App.3d 863, 102 Cal.Rptr. 89, 97.　One who pays valuable consideration, has no notice of outstanding rights of others, and acts in good faith.　J. C. Equipment, Inc. v. Sky Aviation, Inc., Mo.App., 498 S.W.2d 73, 75.

Bona fide purchaser for value is one who, without notice of another's claim of right to, or equity in, property prior to his acquisition of title, has paid vendor a valuable consideration.　Snuffin v. Mayo, 6 Wash.App. 525, 494 P.2d 497.

One who buys property or to whom a negotiable document of title is transferred in good faith and without notice of any defense or claim to the property or document.　U.C.C. § 7–501.　One who takes trust property for value and without notice of breach of trust and who is not knowingly part of an illegal transaction.　Restatement, Second, Trusts § 284; Uniform Probate Code § 2–202(3).

Bulk transfer.　Purchaser from transferee of bulk transfer who takes for value in good faith and without notice of any defect of non-compliance with law.　U.C.C. § 6–110.

Investment securities.　A purchaser for value in good faith and without notice of any adverse claim who takes delivery of a security in bearer form or of one in registered form issued to him or indorsed to him or in blank.　U.C.C. § 8–302.

Bona fide residence.　Residence with domiciliary intent, *i.e.*, a home in which the party actually lives.　Alburger v. Alburger, 138 Pa.Super. 339, 10 A.2d 888, 890.

Bona fide sale.　A completed transaction in which seller makes sale in good faith, for a valuable consideration without notice of any reason against the sale.

Bona fides exigit ut quod convenit fiat /bównə fáydiyz égzəjət ət kwód kənvíynət fáyət/.　Good faith demands that what is agreed upon shall be done.

Bona fides non patitur ut bis idem exigatur /bównə fáydiyz nòn péydədər ət bís áydəm ègzəgéydər/.　Good faith does not allow us to demand twice the payment of the same thing.

Bona notabilia /bównə nowdəbíliyə/.　Lat.　Notable goods.　Goods which must be accounted for in estate of decedent.　Neal v. Boykin, 132 Ga. 400, 64 S.E. 480, 482.　Includes almost every kind of property, tangible and intangible, if it has appreciable value.　In re Rowley's Estate, 178 Wash. 460, 35 P.2d 34.

Bona vacantia /bównə vəkǽnsh(iy)ə/.　Lat.　Vacant goods; unclaimed property.　Generally, personal property which escheats to state because no owner, heir or next of kin claims it.　Now includes real as well as personal property and passes to state as an incident of sovereignty.　Boswell v. Citronelle-Mobile Gathering Inc., 292 Ala. 344, 294 So.2d 428, 432.

Bond.　A certificate or evidence of a debt on which the issuing company or governmental body promises to pay the bondholders a specified amount of interest for a specified length of time, and to repay the loan on the expiration date.　In every case a bond represents debt—its holder is a creditor of the corporation and not a part owner as is the shareholder.　Commonly, bonds are secured by a mortgage.

A written obligation, made by owner of real property, to repay a loan under specific terms, usually accompanied by a mortgage placed on land as security.

A deed whereby the obligor obliges himself, his heirs, executors and administrators, to pay a certain sum of money to another at a day appointed.　Gural v. Engle, 128 N.J.L. 252, 25 A.2d 257, 260.

See also **Debenture**.

Specific types of bonds as relating to finance, surety, guaranty, appeals, performance, etc. are set forth below:

Adjustment bond.　Bonds issued upon reorganization of corporation.

Annuity bond.　See **Annuity** (Annuity bond).

Appeal bond.　Bond required to cover costs of appeal in civil cases.　See *e.g.* Fed.R.App.P. 7.

Appearance bond.　Type of bail bond required to insure presence of defendant in criminal case.　See **Bail** (Bail bond).

Arbitrage bond.　Bond posted to secure performance of arbitrage agreement; a bond which is the subject of arbitrage.　See **Arbitrage**.

Attachment bond. See that title.

Bail bond. See **Bail** *(Bail bond).*

Bearer bond. See that title.

Bid bond. See that title.

Blanket bond. See that title.

Bond and mortgage. A species of security, consisting of a bond conditioned for the repayment of a loan of money, and a mortgage of realty to secure the performance of the stipulations of the bond.

Bond coupon. Part of bond which is cut and surrendered for payment of one of successive payments of interest. See *Coupon bond.*

Bond creditor. A creditor whose debt is secured by a bond.

Bond discount. The difference between the face amount or obligation of the bond and the current market price of such bond, if selling price is lower than market price. Claussen's Inc. v. U. S., C.A.Ga., 469 F.2d 340, 345.

Bond dividend. See **Dividend.**

Bond for deed. See *Bond for title,* below.

Bond for title. An agreement to make title in the future on an executory or incomplete sale. Ingram v. Smith, 62 Ga.App. 335, 7 S.E.2d 922, 926. It is not a conveyance of legal title but only a contract to convey and may ripen into an equitable title upon payment of the consideration.

Bond issue. The totality of bonds issued at a given time. Delivery of instruments as covered by term. Vans Agnew v. Fort Myers Drainage Dist., C.C.A.Fla., 69 F.2d 244, 245.

Bond of state or local government. See *Municipal bond.*

Bond premium. The difference between the face amount or obligation of the bond and the selling price of such bond if the selling price is greater than the face amount.

Bottomry bond. Bond secured by mortgage of ships.

Callable bond. See **Callable bonds.**

Chattel mortgage bond. Bonds secured by mortgage on chattels of business.

Collateral trust bond. A bond secured by collateral deposited with a trustee. The collateral is often the stocks or bonds of companies controlled by the issuing company but may be other securities.

Completion bond. A form of surety or guaranty agreement which contains the promise of a third party, usually a bonding company, to complete or pay for the cost of completion of a construction contract if the construction contractor defaults. Bond given to insure public authority that contract once awarded will be completed as awarded within fixed period of time. Extruded Louver Corp. v. McNulty, 34 Misc.2d 566, 226 N.Y.S.2d 220, 224. See *Contract bond; Performance bond;* also, **Miller Act.**

Consolidated bond. Bond which is sufficiently large in face amount to retire two or more outstanding issues of bonds or securities.

Contract bond. A guarantee of the faithful performance of a construction contract and the payment of all material and labor costs incident thereto. A contract bond covering faithful performance is known as a "performance bond," and one covering payment of labor and materials, a "payment bond." See also *Completion bond; Performance bond.*

Convertible bond. Bond that can, at the option of the holder, be converted into stock.

Corporate bonds. See that title.

Cost bond. See *Appeal bond, supra.*

County bonds. See that title.

Coupon bond. Bond with interest coupons attached. The coupons are clipped as they come due and are presented by the holder for payment of interest.

Debenture bond. Bonds secured by general credit of government or corporation rather than by any specific property; *i.e.* bond which is not secured with collateral.

Deferred bonds. See that title.

Discount bond. See **Bond discount.**

Fidelity bond. Bond covering employer-business for loss due to embezzlement, larceny, or gross negligence by employees.

Fiduciary bond. See **Fiduciary.**

General average bond. See that title.

General mortgage bond. A bond which is secured by a blanket mortgage on the company's property, but which may be subordinate to one or more other mortgages.

General obligation bonds. Bonds backed by general tax revenues.

Gold bond. Formerly, bond containing a clause which required payment of the bonded indebtedness in gold; such clause has since been prohibited. Norman v. Baltimore & Ohio R. R. Co., 294 U.S. 240, 55 S.Ct. 407, 79 L.Ed. 885. Now bonds are dischargeable by payment in legal tender or money.

Government bond. Evidence of indebtedness issued by the government to finance its operations. Such bonds are backed solely by the credit of the government.

Guaranteed bond. A bond which has interest or principal, or both, guaranteed by a company other than the issuer.

Guaranty bond. Type of bond which combines the features of both the fidelity and surety bond and which is given to secure payment and performance.

Improvement bond. Type of bonds issued by a city, town or special authority to finance improvements within the district, with payment to be made only from the improvement fund.

Income bond. Bonds on which interest is payable only when earned and after payment of interest upon prior mortgages. In some cases unpaid interest on an income bond may accumulate as a claim against the corporation when the bond becomes due. An income bond may also be issued in lieu of preferred stock.

Indemnity bond. See that title.

Indeterminate bond. Callable bond with no set maturity date.

Industrial development bonds. Such bonds are issued by a municipality as a means of attracting private businesses. The bonds are marketed by the municipality and the proceeds used to build the private business facility. Commonly, the business leases the facility from the municipality for a total rent equal to the amount necessary to pay the interest and amortize the principal on the bonds.

Interest bond. Bond paid in lieu of interest due on other bonds.

Joint and several bond. A bond the principal and interest of which is guaranteed by two or more persons.

Joint bond. Bond executed by two or more obligors who must be joined in any action on such, as opposed to joint and several bond, on which any or all of obligors may be sued at the option of the obligee.

Judicial bonds. See that title.

Junior bond. Bonds which are subordinate in priority, in principal or interest to another issue.

Leasehold mortgage bond. A bond secured by a building constructed on leased real estate. This bond is subject to the compliance by the lessee (who issues the bond) with the terms of the lease; upon default in the terms of the lease the lessor of the leased real estate has priority over the holders of the leasehold bonds.

Liability bond. One which is intended to protect the assured from liability for damages or to protect the persons damaged by injuries occasioned by the assured as specified, when such liability should accrue, and be imposed by law, as by a court, as distinguished from an indemnity bond, whose purpose is only to indemnify the assured against actual loss by way of reimbursement for moneys paid or which must be paid.

License bond. The term "License Bond" is used interchangeably with "Permit Bond" to describe bonds required by state law, municipal ordinance, or by regulation as a condition precedent to the granting of a license to engage in a specified business or the grant of a permit to exercise a certain privilege.

Such bonds provide payment to the obligee for the loss or damage resulting from the operations permitted by law, ordinance or regulation, under which the bond is required and for violations by the licensee of the duties and obligations imposed upon him.

Mortgage bond. A bond secured by a mortgage on a property. The value of the property may or may not equal the value of the so-called mortgage bonds issued against it. See also *Leasehold mortgage bond, supra.*

Municipal bond. A bond issued by a state or a political subdivision, such as county, city, town or village. The term also designates bonds issued by state agencies and authorities. In general, interest paid on municipal bonds is exempt from federal income taxes and state and local income taxes within the state of issue. See also *Industrial development bonds, supra.*

Official bond. A bond given by a public officer, conditioned that he shall well and faithfully perform all the duties of the office. The term is sometimes made to include the bonds of executors, guardians, trustees, etc.

Passive bond. Bond which bears no interest.

Payment bond. See **Miller Act.**

Peace bond. See that title.

Penal bond. See that title.

Performance bond. Type of contract bond which protects against loss due to the inability or refusal of a contractor to perform his contract. Such are normally required on public construction projects. See *Completion bond; Contract bond, supra;* also, **Miller Act.**

Personal bond. A written document in which the obligor formally recognizes an obligation to pay money or to do a specific act; *e.g.* surrender a lost bank book when it is found.

Premium bond. See *Bond premium, supra.*

Railroad aid bonds. Bonds issued by municipal corporations to aid in the construction of railways.

Redeemable bond. See that title.

Redelivery bond. A statutory bond given by a person in whose possession attached property is found in order to regain possession of the property.

Refunding bond. See that title.

Registered bond. A bond which is registered on the books of the issuing company in the name of the owner. It can be transferred only when endorsed by the registered owner.

Removal bond. See that title.

Reorganization bond. See *Adjustment bond, supra.*

Replevin bond. **Replevin** (*Replevin bond*).

Revenue bond. Such bonds are issued by a public agency, municipal corporation, or state for purpose of raising revenue. The interest and principal on such bonds are paid from earnings; *e.g.* earnings of a municipal sports complex.

School bonds. Bonds issued by a city, town or school district for purpose of school construction.

Serial bond. Bond issue consisting of a number of bonds with different maturity dates. Bonds are issued at the same time as distinguished from series bonds which are issued at different times.

Series bonds. Groups of bonds normally issued at different times but under same indenture.

Silver bond. Bonds which require payment in silver; not used in U.S. since payment may be made in legal tender.

Simple bond. At common law, a bond without penalty; a bond for the payment of a definite sum of money to a named obligee on demand or on a day certain.

Single bond. A deed whereby the obligor obliges himself, his heirs, executors, and administrators, to pay a certain sum of money to the obligee at a day named, without terms of defeasance.

State bond. Bond issued by state, obligating state to make payment.

Straw bond. A bond upon which is used either the names of fictitious persons or those unable to pay the sum guaranteed; generally applied to insufficient bail bonds, improperly taken.

Submission bond. See that title.

Subordinated bonds or debentures. See that title.

Supersedeas bond. See that title.

Suretyship bond. Obligation of a guarantor to pay a second party upon default by a third party in the performance the third party owes to the second party.

Tax exempt bond. A bond, the receipt of income from which is not taxable, *e.g.* municipal bond *(q.v.).*

Treasury bonds. Bonds reacquired or unsold by corporation. Bonds issued by U.S. Treasury (*e.g.* U.S. Savings bonds). See also **Treasury bond.**

U.S. Savings bonds. An obligation of the United States designed to permit persons the opportunity to create savings by purchasing the bond at a reduced sum and requiring the purchaser to wait a period of time to redeem at face value.

Bondage. Slavery; involuntary personal servitude; captivity. In old English law, villenage, villein tenure. Such is prohibited by 13th Amendment to U.S. Constitution.

Bond conversion. The act of exchanging convertible bonds for preferred or common stock.

Bond discount. Sale of bonds on the market at a price less than the face amount of such. Claussen's, Inc. v. U. S., C.A.Ga., 469 F.2d 340, 345.

From the standpoint of the issuer of a bond at the issue date, the excess of the par value of a bond over its initial sales price; at later dates the excess of par over the sum of (initial) issue price plus the portion of discount already amortized. From the standpoint of a bondholder, the difference between par value and selling price when the bond sells below par.

Bonded debt. The indebtedness of a business or government which is represented by bonds payable. Indebtedness lawfully contracted for corporate purposes, payable from taxes on all property within municipality.

Bonded warehouse. See **Warehouse system.**

Bond indenture. The contract between an issuer of bonds and the bondholders.

Bond premium. The excess of the price of bonds over their face value, and generally reflects the difference between the nominal interest rate borne by such bonds and the actual or effective rate of return determined by the current market. Grace v. New York State Tax Commission, 37 N.Y.2d 193, 371 N.Y.S.2d 715, 332 N.E.2d 886.

Bond rating. System of appraising and rating the investment value of individual bond issues. Triple A (AAA) bonds have the highest rating. There are several major bond rating companies or services.

Bond redemption. Retirement of bonds upon payment. See **Redemption.**

Bondsman. A surety; one who has entered into a bond as surety; *e.g.* bail bondsman.

Bones gents /bòwn jénts/. L. Fr. In old English law, good men (of the jury).

Bonification. The remission of a tax, particularly on goods intended for export, having the same effect as a bonus or drawback. A device enabling a commodity to be exported and sold in the foreign market as if it had not been taxed. U. S. v. Passavant, 169 U.S. 16, 18 S.Ct. 219, 42 L.Ed. 644.

Boni homines /bównay hómэniyz/. In old European law, good men; a name given in early European jurisprudence to the tenants of the lord, who judged each other in the lord's courts. 3 Bl.Comm. 349.

Boni judicis est ampliare jurisdictionem /bównay júwdэsэs èst æmpliyériy jùrэsdìkshiyównэm/. It is the part of a good judge to enlarge (or use liberally) his remedial authority or jurisdiction.

Boni judicis est ampliare justitiam /bównay júwdэsэs èst æmpliyériy jэstíshiyэm/. It is the duty of a good judge to enlarge or extend justice.

Boni judicis est judicium sine dilatione mandare executioni /bównay júwdэsэs èst juwdíshiyэm sáyniy dэlèyshiyówniy mændériy ègzэkyùwshiyównay/. It is the duty of a good judge to cause judgment to be executed without delay.

Boni judicis est lites dirimere, ne lis ex lite oritur, et interest reipublicæ ut sint fines litium /bównay júwdэsэs èst láydiyz dэrímэriy, nìy láys èks láydiy órэdэr, èd íntэrэst ríyaypэ́blэsiy àt sínt fáyniyz lísh(iy)эm/. It is the duty of a good judge to prevent litigations, that suit may not grow out of suit, and it concerns the welfare of a state that an end be put to litigation.

Bonis cedere /bównэs síydэriy/. In the civil law, to make a transfer or surrender of property, as a debtor did to his creditors.

Bonis non amovendis /bównэs nòn èymэvéndэs/. A writ addressed to the sheriff, when a writ of error has been brought, commanding that the person against whom judgment has been obtained be not suffered to remove his goods till the error be tried and determined.

Bonitarian ownership /bownэtériyэn ównэrship/. In Roman law, a species of equitable title to things, as distinguished from a title acquired according to the strict forms of the municipal law; the property of a Roman citizen in a subject capable of quiritary property, acquired by a title not known to the civil law, but introduced by the prætor, and protected by his *imperium* or supreme executive power, *e.g.*, where *res mancipi* had been transferred by mere tradition.

Bono et malo /bównow èt mælow/. A special writ of jail delivery, which formerly issued of course for each particular prisoner. 4 Bl.Comm. 270.

Bonum defendentis ex integra causa; malum ex quolibet defectu /bównəm dəfendéntəs èks intégrə kózə mǽləm èks kwódləbət dəfékt(y)uw/. The success of a defendant depends on a perfect case; his loss arises from some defect.

Bonum necessarium extra terminos necessitatis non est bonum /bównəm nèsəsériyəm ékstrə tə́rmənows nəsèsətéydəs nón est bównəm/. A good thing required by necessity is not good beyond the limits of such necessity.

Bonus. A consideration or premium paid in addition to what is strictly due. A gratuity to which the recipient has no right to make a demand. Walling v. Plymouth Mfg. Corporation, C.C.A.Ind., 139 F.2d 178, 182. A premium or extra or irregular remuneration in consideration of offices performed or to encourage their performance. Willkie v. Commissioner of Internal Revenue, C.C.A.6, 127 F.2d 953, 956. A premium paid to a grantor or vendor. An advance royalty. Sneed v. Commissioner of Internal Revenue, C.C.A. Tex., 119 F.2d 767, 770. An extra consideration given for what is received, or something given in addition to what is ordinarily received by, or strictly due, the recipient. La Juett v. Coty Mach. Co., 153 Misc. 410, 275 N.Y.S. 822. An addition to salary or wages normally paid for extraordinary work. An inducement to employees to procure efficient and faithful service. Duffy Bros. v. Bing & Bing, 217 App.Div. 10, 215 N.Y.S. 755, 758. Consideration or down payment for mineral lease or transfer of oil lands. State Nat. Bank of Corpus Christi v. Morgan, Tex.Civ.App., 123 S.W.2d 1036, 1038; In re Levy, 185 Okl. 477, 94 P.2d 537, 539. Gift in recognition of officer's past successful direction of corporate affairs. Thomas v. Commissioner of Internal Revenue, C.C.A.La., 135 F.2d 378, 379. Compensation paid to professional athlete in addition to salary for signing with particular team. See also **Bonus stock; Premium.**

Bonus judex secundum æquum et bonum judicat, et æquitatem stricto juri præfert /bównəs júwdeks səkándəm íykwəm èt bównəm júwdəkət, èd èkwətéydəm stríktow júray príyfə̀rt/. A good judge decides according to what is just and good, and prefers equity to strict law.

Bonus share. See **Bonus stock,** below.

Bonus stock. Stock given as premium in connection with (to encourage) the sale of another class of securities; *e.g.* stock issued to the purchasers of bonds as an inducement to them to purchase bonds or loan money.

Shares issued for no lawful consideration. Term commonly used interchangeably with watered stock and discount stock.

Booby trap. A concealed or camouflaged device designed to be triggered by an unsuspecting victim; loosely, any device which catches a person off-guard.

Boodle. Usually applied to designate the money held to be paid or paid as a bribe for corrupt official action.

Boodling. In the slang of the day, corrupt legislative practices and corrupt influences affecting legislation.

Book. An assembly or concourse of ideas expressed in words. U. S. v. One Obscene Book Entitled "Married Love", D.C.N.Y., 48 F.2d 821, 823. A literary composition which is printed; a printed composition bound in a volume. The largest subdivisions of a treatise or other literary composition.

A bound volume consisting of sheets of paper, not printed, containing manuscript entries; such as a merchant's account-books, dockets of courts, etc.

To register or make reservation for transportation, lodging, etc. To set date and time for engagement or appointment.

Book account. A detailed statement, in the nature of debits and credits between persons; an account or record of debits and credits kept in a book. A book in which a detailed history of business transactions is entered; a record of goods sold or services rendered; a statement in detail of the transactions between parties.

Book entry. A notation, generally of figures or numbers, made in an accounting journal, consisting, in double entry bookkeeping, of debits and credits.

Bookland. In old English law, land, also called "charterland," which was held by deed under certain rents and free services, and differed in nothing from free socage land. 2 Bl.Comm. 90.

Book of original entries. A book in which a merchant enters from day to day a record of his transactions. A book kept for charging goods sold and delivered, in which the entries are made contemporaneously with the delivery of the goods. A book in which a detailed history of business transactions is entered. Nicola v. U. S., C.C.A.Pa., 72 F.2d 780, 783.

Books of account. Books in which merchants, traders, and businessmen generally keep their accounts. Entries made in the regular course of business. Nicola v. U. S., C.C.A.Pa., 72 F.2d 780, 783. Serial, continuous, and permanent memorials of business and affairs.

Book value. Accounting terminology which gives a going-concern-value for a company. It is arrived at by adding all assets and deducting all liabilities and by dividing that sum by the number of shares of common stock outstanding. The value of an outstanding share of stock of a corporation at any one time, determined by adding the par (or stated) value of the stock outstanding to the surplus applicable to that class of stock and dividing by the number of shares of that class outstanding. The valuation at which assets are carried on the books, that is, cost less reserve for depreciation.

Net tangible book value is the same as book value, except that only tangible assets are included.

Corporate books. Whatever is kept as written evidence of official doings and business transactions. First Nat. Bank of Colorado Springs v. Holt, Mo.App., 158 S.W.2d 229, 231.

Office book. See **Office.**

Booked. Engaged, destined, bound to promise or pledge oneself to make an engagement. To have travel, lodging, etc. reservations. To enter charges against accused in police register or blotter. See **Booking.**

Booking. Administrative step taken after the arrested person is brought to the police station, which involves entry of the person's name, the crime for which the arrest was made, and other relevant facts on the police "blotter," and which may also include photographing, fingerprinting, and the like.

A form of gambling commonly associated with number pools horse and dog racing when engaged in away from the track. See **Bookmaker; Bookmaking.**

Booking contract. A contract made by agents who procure contracts for appearance of acts and actors.

Bookkeeping. The art or science of recording business accounts and transactions. See also **Accounting; Book.**

Double entry bookkeeping. Accounting system which requires that in every entry there be a debit and a credit; *e.g.* on cash sale of merchandise, a debit to cash and a credit to sales.

Bookmaker. A gambler who makes book on uncertain future events. One who collects bets of others. One who establishes odds on events which are the subject of gambling.

Bookmaking. Formerly the collection of sheets of paper or other substances on which entries could be made, either written or printed. The term now commonly denotes the recording or registering of bets or wagers on any trial or contest of speed or power of endurance or selling pools. An operation which involves both the placing of bets and the paying off or collection of debts. State v. Gould, 123 N.J.Super. 444, 303 A.2d 591, 592.

Books and papers. Generic term used to describe all forms of records which are sought in a summons duces tecum, or subject to discovery under Fed.R.Civil P. 26(b)(1), 34, or Fed.R.Crim.P. 16. See also **Business records exception; Record; Shop-book rule.**

Boomage. A charge on logs for use of a boom in collecting, storing, or rafting them. A right of entry on riparian lands to fasten booms and boom sticks.

Boon days. In old English law, certain days in the year (sometimes called "due days") on which tenants in copyhold were obliged to perform corporal services for the lord.

Boosted fire. A fire wherein some inflammable substance other than that of which the building was constructed or which it contained contributed to its burning and spreading. State v. Lytle, 214 Minn. 171, 7 N.W.2d 305, 309.

Boot. Used in tax accounting to describe cash or property other than property qualifying as such for nonrecognition in an exchange of like kind of property under I.R.C. § 1031. As used in connection with reorganization, includes anything received other than stock or securities of a controlled corporation. I.R.C. §§ 355, 356(b).

Cash or property of a type not included in the definition of a nontaxable exchange. The receipt of boot will cause an otherwise taxfree transfer to become taxable to the extent of the lesser of the fair market value of such boot or the realized gain on the transfer.

Cash or other consideration used to balance an equal exchange of two properties; *e.g.* machine worth $500 plus $500 for machine worth $1000.

An old Saxon word, equivalent to "estovers".

Boothage. See **Bothagium.**

Bootlegger. One who sells, or keeps for sale, alcoholic beverages in violation of law.

Bootlegging. A popular designation for the use, possession, or transportation of liquor in violation of the law; importing the peddling and illegal sales of intoxicating liquor.

Bootstrap doctrine. The decision of a court on a special as well as a general appearance that it has jurisdiction is not subject of collateral attack but is res judicata. Peri v. Groves, 183 Misc. 579, 50 N.Y.S.2d 300, 308.

Bootstrap sale. A means by which the cash or other assets of a business are utilized by the purchaser in acquiring ownership of such business.

An arrangement resulting in tax savings by which a seller converts ordinary income from a business into capital gain from sale of corporate stock. Commissioner of Internal Revenue v. Brown, 380 U.S. 563, 85 S.Ct. 1162, 14 L.Ed.2d 75.

Booty. Property captured from the enemy in war, on land.

Bord. An old Saxon word, signifying a cottage; a house; a table.

Bordage. In old English law, a species of base tenure, by which certain "bord lands" were anciently held in England; the service was that of keeping the lord in small provisions.

Bordaria /bordériyə/. A cottage.

Bordarii /bordériyay/ or **bordimanni** /bòrdəmǽnay/. In old English law, tenants of a less servile condition than the *villani*, who had a bord or cottage, with a small parcel of land, on condition they should supply the lord with small provisions.

Bord-brigch /bórd-briych/. In Saxon law, a breach or violation of suretyship; pledge-breach, or breach of mutual fidelity.

Bordereau /bòrd(ə)rów/. In insurance, summary of transactions between agent and company.

Border search. Search conducted by immigration officials at borders of the country to prevent and to detect illegal entry. Immigration and Nationality Act, § 287(a). Almeida-Sanchez v. U. S., 413 U.S. 266, 93 S.Ct. 2535, 37 L.Ed.2d 596. Any person or thing coming into the United States is subject to search by that fact alone, whether or not there be any suspicion of illegality directed to the particular person or thing to be searched. United States v. Odland, 502 F.2d 148; Camara v. Municipal Court, 387 U.S. 523, 87 S.Ct. 1727, 18 L.Ed.2d 930.

Border warrant. Process issued for search at borders of the country for search and for arrest of illegal immigrants; no warrant necessary for preliminary stop for questioning. U. S. v. Brignoni, 422 U.S. 873, 95 S.Ct. 2574, 45 L.Ed.2d 607.

Bord-halfpenny /bòrd-héypniy/. In old English law, a customary small toll paid to the lord of a town for setting up boards, tables, booths, etc., in fairs or markets.

Bordlands. In feudal law, the demesnes which the lords kept in their hands for the maintenance of their board or table. Also lands held in bordage. Lands which the lord gave to tenants on condition of supplying him with small provisions, etc.

Bordlode /bórdlowd/. A service anciently required of tenants to carry timber out of the woods of the lord to his house; or it is said to be the quantity of food or provision which the *bordarii* or bordmen paid for their bordlands.

Bordservice. A tenure of bordlands.

Borg /bórg/. In Saxon law, a pledge, pledge giver, or surety. The name given among the Saxons to the head of each family composing a tithing or decennary, each being the pledge for the good conduct of the others. Also the contract or engagement of suretyship; and the pledge given.

Borgbriche /bórgbrìych/. A breach or violation of suretyship, or of mutual fidelity.

Borgesmon /bórgəsmən/. In Saxon law, the name given to the head of each family composing a tithing.

Born. Act of being delivered or expelled from mother's body, whether or not placenta has been separated or cord cut.

Born alive. Being the product of conception after complete expulsion or extraction from mother, irrespective of the duration of the pregnancy, which breathes or shows any other evidence of life such as beating of the heart, pulsation of the umbilical cord or definite movement of voluntary muscles, whether or not the umbilical cord has been cut or the placenta is attached. Each product of such birth is considered live born and fully recognized as a human person. Maine Rev.Stat.Ann., Tit. 22, § 1595. See also **Viable child.**

Born out of wedlock. Children whose parents are not, and have not been, married to each other regardless of marital status of either parent with respect to another. State v. Coliton, 73 N.D. 582, 17 N.W.2d 546, 549, 552. See **Illegitimate.**

Borough /bərə/bérow/. A town or township with a municipal charter. One of the five political divisions of New York City.

In old English law, a fortified town; a town of importance. In latter law, a city or town that sent members (burgesses) to Parliament. The status of many boroughs was affected by the Local Government Act of 1972.

Borough courts. In English law, private and limited tribunals, held by prescription, charter, or act of parliament, in particular districts for the convenience of the inhabitants, that they may prosecute small suits and receive justice at home. Most such courts were abolished by the Local Government Act of 1972.

Borough English. A custom prevalent in some parts of England, by which the youngest son inherits the estate in preference to his older brothers. Abolished as respects enfranchised land by the Law of Property Act (1922); and generally in regard to land by the Administration of Estates Act of 1925.

Borough fund. In English law, the revenues of a municipal borough from rents and produce of its land, houses, and stocks and supplemented where necessary by a borough rate.

Borough sessions. Courts of limited criminal jurisdiction, established in English boroughs under the municipal corporations act.

Borrasca /bəræskə/. Absence of profit, or not enough profit to pay the cost of operation, of a placer mine. Ballagh v. Williams, 50 Cal.App.2d 10, 122 P.2d 343, 344.

Borrow. To solicit and receive from another any article of property, money or thing of value with the intention and promise to repay or return it or its equivalent. If the item borrowed is money, there normally exists an agreement to pay interest for its use. In a broad sense the term means a contract for the use of money. The term may be used to express the idea of receiving something from another for one's own use. The word "loan" is the correlative of "borrow."

Borrowed capital. Term denoting various transactions between corporation and stockholders, but commonly referring to cash dividends declared by corporation and retained by it pursuant to agreement with stockholders for operating business successfully. Southport Mill v. Commissioner of Internal Revenue, C.C. A.La., 26 F.2d 17. Moneys due by corporation to another corporation used as its capital.

Borrowed employee. One who is dispatched by his employer to another becomes the other's employee for purposes of Worker's Compensation Law if the other employer exercises control over him. Otherwise, he remains employee of his first employer, and he may receive benefits under Worker's Compensation from his own employer's carrier. Avis Truck Rental v. Coggins, 129 Ga.App. 81, 198 S.E.2d 716. Before person may be considered "borrowed servant," his services must be loaned with his acquiescence or consent and he must become wholly subject to control and direction of second employer, and free during the temporary period from the control of the original employer. Foster v. Englewood Hospital Ass'n, 19 Ill.App.3d 1055, 313 N.E.2d 255, 259.

Borrowed statutes. Laws of one state or jurisdiction used by another state in deciding conflicts question involved in choice of law; *e.g.* statute of limitation of state where claim accrued as contrasted with statute of limitation of forum state. Reinhard v. Textron, Inc., Okl., 516 P.2d 1325.

Borrower. He to whom a thing or money is lent at his request. "Borrower," within automobile liability policy covering borrower of vehicle during loading and unloading, may be defined as someone who has, with permission of owner, temporary possession and use of property of another for his own purposes. Liberty Mut. Ins. Co. v. American Emp. Ins. Co., Tex., 556 S.W.2d 242, 244.

Borrowings. Generic term to describe all manners of loans from standpoint of debtor.

Borsholder /bórs-hòwldər/. In Saxon law, the borough's ealder, or headborough.

Boston interest. Interest computed by using a 30 day month rather than the exact number of days in the month.

Bote, bot /bówt/. In old English law, a recompense or compensation, or profit or advantage. Also reparation or amends for any damage done. Necessaries for the maintenance and carrying on of husbandry. An allowance; the ancient name for estovers.

House-bote. A sufficient allowance of wood from off the estate to repair or burn in the house, and sometimes termed "fire-bote;" *plow-bote* and *cart-bote* are wood to be employed in making and repairing all instruments of husbandry; and *hay-bote* or *hedge-bote* is wood for repairing of hays, hedges, or fences. The word also signifies reparation for any damage or injury done, as *man-bote*, which was a compensation or amends for a man slain, etc.

Boteless /bówtləs/. In old English law, without amends; without the privilege of making satisfaction for a crime by a pecuniary payment; without relief or remedy.

Both. The one and the other; the two without the exception of either. The term likewise has a meaning which excludes more than two mentioned subject matters. In re Turner's Estate, 171 Misc. 78, 11 N.Y.S.2d 800, 802. "Either," may mean "both." Kibler v. Parker, 191 Ark. 475, 86 S.W.2d 925, 926.

Bothagium /bowθéyjiyəm/ or **boothage** /búwθəj/. In feudal law, customary dues paid to the lord of a manor or soil, for the pitching or standing of booths in fairs or markets.

Botiler of the king. In old English law, an officer who provided the king's wines. By virtue of his office, he might choose, out of every ship laden with wines, one cask before the mast, and one behind.

Bottle club. A place where no intoxicating liquors are sold but in which a member may keep his liquor for consumption on the premises and in which mixes or so-called "set ups" are provided by the club. Mutchall v. City of Kalamazoo, 323 Mich. 215, 35 N.W.2d 245.

Bottomage. L. Fr. Bottomry.

Bottom hole contract. A form of agreement used in drilling for oil or gas and which requires a payment by owners of well to lessee of well upon the drilling to a specified depth.

Bottom land. As used in a contract to convey, means low land formed by alluvial deposits along the river, low-lying ground, a dale, valley, or intervale.

Bottomry /bódəmriy/. In maritime law, a contract by which the owner of a ship borrows for the use, equipment, or repair of the vessel, and for a definite term, and pledges the ship (or the keel or *bottom* of the ship, *pars pro toto*) as security; it being stipulated that if the ship be lost in the specified voyage, or during the limited time, by any of the perils enumerated, the lender shall lose his money.

A contract by which a ship or its freightage is hypothecated as security for a loan, which is to be repaid only in case the ship survives a particular risk, voyage, or period. The contract usually in form a bond. When the loan is not made on the ship, but on the goods on board, and which are to be sold or exchanged in the course of the voyage, the borrower's personal *responsibility* is deemed the principal security for the performance of the contract, which is therefore called *"respondentia."*

Bottomry bond. The instrument embodying the contract or agreement of bottomry. Bond with mortgage of ship as security.

Botulism /bóchəlizəm/. Food poisoning caused by a toxin which is produced by Clostridium (bacillus) botulinum.

Bouche /búwsh/búch/. Fr. The mouth. An allowance of provision. *Avoir bouche à court;* to have an allowance at court; to be in ordinary at court; to have meat and drink scotfree there.

Bouche of court, or **budge of court.** A certain allowance of provision from the king to his knights and servants, who attended him on any military expedition.

Bough of a tree. In feudal law, a symbol which gave seisin of land, to hold of the donor *in capite.*

Bought. Implies a completed transaction, a vesting of the right of title to and possession of the property sold, and also imports a valuable consideration.

Bought and sold notes. A note of the sale by a broker employed to buy and sell goods is called a "sold note," and a like note to the seller is called a "bought note."

Boulevard /búləvard/. The word originally indicated a bulwark or rampart, and afterwards applied to a public walk or road on the site of a demolished fortification. Term now generally refers to a street or highway with park-like appearance; or one specially designed for pleasure walking or driving; often landscaped. A wide street, or a street encircling a town, with sides or center for shade trees, etc. State ex rel. Copland v. City of Toledo, 75 Ohio App. 378, 62 N.E.2d 256, 258.

Boulevard rule. "Boulevard rule" commands that a driver upon approaching a "through highway" from an unfavored road must stop and yield right-of-way to all traffic already in or which may enter the intersection during the entire time the unfavored driver encroaches upon the right-of-way and that duty continues as long as he is in the intersection and until he becomes a part of the flow of favored travellers or successfully traverses the boulevard. Creaser v. Owens, 267 Md. 238, 297 A.2d 235, 236.

Boulevareism. A bargaining tactic in labor negotiations by which employer chooses a middle ground that both employer and union know will be the probable outcome before the beginning of the bargaining. N. L. R. B. v. General Elec. Co., C.A.N.Y., 418 F.2d 736, 740.

Bouncer. A term used to designate persons employed to preserve the peace in establishments such as night clubs and other places of amusement where people indulge in dancing, drinking and in gambling. Moore v. Blanchard, La.App., 35 So.2d 667, 669.

Bound. As an *adjective*, denotes the condition of being constrained by the obligations of a bond, contract, covenant, or other moral or legal obligation. See **Duty; Obligation.**

In the law of shipping, "bound to" or "bound for" denotes that the vessel spoken of is intended or designed to make a voyage to the place named.

As a *noun*, denotes a limit or boundary, or a line inclosing or marking off a tract of land. In the phrase "metes and bounds," denotes the natural or artificial marks which indicate their beginning and ending. "Bound" may signify the limit itself, and "boundary" designate a visible mark which indicates the limit. See **Boundary.**

Boundary. Every separation, natural or artificial, which marks the confines or line of division of two contiguous properties. Limits or marks of enclosures if possession be without title, or the boundaries or limits stated in title deed if possession be under a title. See also **Land boundaries; Metes and bounds; Plat map.**

Natural boundary. Any formation or product of nature which may serve to define and fix one or more of the lines inclosing an estate or piece of property.

Private boundary. An artificial boundary set up to mark the beginning or direction of a boundary line.

Public boundary. A natural boundary; a natural object or landmark used as a boundary or as a beginning point for a boundary line.

Bound bailiffs. In English law, sheriffs' officers are so called, from their being usually *bound* to the sheriff in an obligation with sureties, for the due execution of their office.

Bounded tree. A tree marking or standing at the corner of a field or estate.

Bounders. Visible marks or objects at the ends of the lines drawn in surveys of land, showing the courses and distances.

Bound over. See **Binding over.**

Bounds. The external or limiting lines, either real or imaginary, of any object or space; that which limits or circumscribes.

Bounty. A gratuity, or an unusual or additional benefit conferred upon, or compensation paid to, a class of persons. A premium given or offered to enlisted men to induce enlistment into public service. Bounty is the appropriate term where services or action of many persons are desired, and each who acts upon the offer may entitle himself to the promised gratuity (*e.g.* killing of dangerous animals). Reward is more proper in the case of a single service, which can be only once performed, and therefore will be earned only by the person or co-operative persons who succeed while others fail (*e.g.* capture of fugitive). See also **Reward.**

Bounty lands. Portions of the public domain given or donated as a bounty for services rendered, chiefly for military service.

Bourg /búrg/. In old French law, an assemblage of houses surrounded with walls; a fortified town or village. In old English law, a borough, a village.

Bourgeois /bùrzhwó/. The inhabitant of a *bourg*. A person entitled to the privileges of a municipal corporation; a burgess. A member of the middle classes.

Bourse /búrs/. Fr. An exchange; a stock exchange.

Bourse de commerce /búrs də komérs/. In the French law, an aggregation, sanctioned by government, of merchants, captains of vessels, exchange agents, and courtiers, the two latter being nominated by the government, in each city which has a *bourse*.

Bovata terræ /bowvéydə téhriy/. In old English law, as much land as one ox can cultivate. Said by some to be thirteen, by others eighteen, acres in extent. See **Carucata.**

Bow-bearer. In old English law, an under-officer of the forest, whose duty it was to oversee and true inquisition make, as well of sworn men as unsworn, in every bailiwick of the forest; and of all manner of trespasses done, either to vert or venison, and cause them to be presented, without any concealment, in the next court of attachment, etc.

Boxed weight basis. According to weight at time of packing and after wrapping. Swift & Co. v. Wallace, C.C.A.7, 105 F.2d 848, 861.

Boycott /bóykot/. Concerted refusal to do business with particular person or business in order to obtain concessions or to express displeasure with certain acts or practices of person or business. Barry v. St. Paul Fire & Marine Ins. Co., 555 F.2d 3, 7.

A conspiracy or confederation to prevent the carrying on of business, or to injure the business of any one by preventing potential customers from doing business with him or employing the representatives of said business, by threats, intimidation, coercion, etc. Such acts are prohibited by the Sherman Anti-trust Act.

Consumer boycott. Practice whereby consumers (*i.e.* customers) refrain from purchasing a particular product in protest of excessive price, offensive actions of manufacturer or producer, etc., or refrain from trading with particular business for similar reasons.

Group boycott. Concerted refusal to deal among traders with the intent or foreseeable effect of exclusion from the market of direct competitors of some of the conspirators; or, concerted refusal to deal with the intent or foreseeable effect of coercion of the trade practices of third parties. Such group boycotts are per se illegal under the Sherman Antitrust Act. Jones Knitting Corp. v. Morgan, D.C.Pa., 244 F.Supp. 235, 238.

Primary boycott. See that title.

Secondary boycott. A combination to exercise coercive pressure on customers, actual or prospective, to cause them to withhold or withdraw their patronage of a certain business or product. See also **Secondary boycott.**

Boyd rule. In a corporate reorganization, no junior security may be given participation without providing a new consideration therefor, unless all securities senior to it have received full equivalent of their rights against the estate. Phelan v. Middle States Oil Corp., D.C.N.Y., 124 F.Supp. 728, 781.

Bozero /bowsérow/. In Spanish law, an advocate; one who pleads the causes of others, or his own, before courts of justice, either as plaintiff or defendant. Called also *abogado*.

B.R. An abbreviation for *Bancus Regis* (King's Bench), or *Bancus Reginæ* (Queen's Bench). It is frequently found in the old books as a designation of that court. In more recent usage, the initial letters of the English names are ordinarily employed, *i.e.*, K.B. or Q.B.

Brabant /brəbǽnt/. A variety of the old coin known as a crocard.

Brabanter /brəbǽntər/. A mercenary soldier or bandit who figured in the Anglo-French wars of the 11th and 13th centuries, and who came from the old duchy of Brabant, now partly comprised in the provinces of Brabant in Belgium and of North Brabant in the Netherlands.

Bracery /bréysəriy/. The English statute of 32 Hen. VIII, c. 9, to prevent the buying and selling of pretended rights or titles, is commonly called "the Bill of Bracery and buying of titles."

Brachium maris /bréykiyəm mǽrəs/. An arm of the sea.

Brain death. Numerous states have enacted statutory definitions of death which include brain-related criteria. "A person shall be pronounced dead if it is determined by a physician that the person has suffered a total and irreversible cessation of brain function. There shall be independent confirmation of the death by another physician." Calif. Health & Safety Code, Section 7180 (1976).

Characteristics of brain death consist of: (1) unreceptivity and unresponsiveness to externally applied stimuli and internal needs; (2) no spontaneous movements or breathing; (3) no reflex activity; and (4) a flat electroencephalograph reading after 24 hour period of observation. Com. v. Golston, Mass., 366 N.E.2d 744. An increasing number of states have adopted this so-called "Harvard" definition of brain death, either by statute or court decision.

See also **Death** (*Natural Death Acts*).

Braking distance. Total distance required to stop a motor vehicle from time driver recognizes need to stop until vehicle is standing still. Factors which control are speed of vehicle, weather, road conditions, tires, condition of brakes, etc. Sometimes referred to as stopping distance.

Branch. An offshoot, lateral extension, or subdivision. Any member or part of a body (*e.g.* executive branch of government), or system; a department. Division, office, or other unit of business located at a different location from main office or headquarters.

A branch of a family stock is a group of persons related by descent from a common ancestor, and related to the main stock by the fact that that common ancestor descends from the original founder or progenitor.

Branch bank. Under Uniform Commercial Code, branch bank includes a separately incorporated foreign branch of bank. § 1–201. More commonly, it refers to an office of a bank physically separated from its main office, with common services and functions, and corporately part of the bank. "Branch banking" is the operation of one banking institution as the instrumentality of another, in which the relationship between them is such that they operate as a single unit. In Re Cleveland Trust Co. of Lake County, 38 Ohio St.2d 183, 311 N.E.2d 854, 859. Branch banking is not permitted in certain states.

"Branch office" of a bank or savings bank includes an office, unit, station, facility, terminal, space or receptacle at a fixed location other than a principal office, however designated, at which any business that may be conducted in a principal office of a bank or savings bank may be transacted.

Branch of the sea. This term, as used at common law, included rivers in which the tide ebbed and flowed.

Branch railroad. A lateral extension of a main line; a road connected with or issuing from a main line. Feeder lines.

Brand. A word, mark, symbol, design, term, or a combination of these, both visual and oral, used for the purpose of identification of some product or service. See also **Trade-name.**

Brandeis brief. Form of appellate brief in which economic and social surveys and studies are included along with legal principles and citations and which takes its name from Louis D. Brandeis, former Associate Justice of Supreme Court, who used such brief while practicing law.

Branding. An ancient mode of punishment by inflicting a mark on an offender with a hot iron. A recognized punishment for some military offenses. Marking of cattle for the purpose of identification.

Branks. An instrument formerly used in some parts of England for the correction of scolds; a scolding bridle.

Brassage. Government charge for coining metals; covering only the actual cost. Any profit is termed "Seignorage."

Brass knuckles or **knucks.** A weapon worn on the hand for the purposes of offense or defense, so made that in hitting with the fist considerable damage is inflicted. It is called "brass knuckles" because it was originally made of brass. The term is now used as the name of the weapon without reference to the metal of which it is made.

Brawl. A clamorous or tumultuous quarrel in a public place, to the disturbance of the public peace.

In English law, specifically, a noisy quarrel or other uproarious conduct creating a disturbance in a church or churchyard. 4 Bl.Comm. 146.

Breach. The breaking or violating of a law, right, obligation, engagement, or duty, either by commission or omission. Exists where one party to contract fails to carry out term, promise, or condition of the contract.

Breach of close. The unlawful or unwarrantable entry on another person's soil, land, or close.

Breach of contract. Failure, without legal excuse, to perform any promise which forms the whole or part of a contract. Prevention or hindrance by party to contract of any occurrence or performance requisite under the contract for the creation or continuance of a right in favor of the other party or the discharge of a duty by him. Unequivocal, distinct and absolute refusal to perform agreement.

Anticipatory breach. See **Anticipatory breach of contract.**

Constructive breach. Such breach takes place when the party bound to perform disables himself from performance by some act, or declares, before the time comes, that he will not perform. The Adamello, D.C. Va., 19 F.2d 388, 389.

Continuing breach. Such breach occurs where the state of affairs, or the specific act, constituting the breach, endures for a considerable period of time, or is repeated at short intervals.

Rights and remedies. Parts 6 and 7 of U.C.C. Article 2 cover rights and remedies of both buyer and seller on breach of contract by either. See also **Damages; Performance** (*Specific performance*).

Breach of covenant. The nonperformance of any covenant agreed to be performed, or the doing of any act covenanted not to be done.

Breach of duty. In a general sense, any violation or omission of a legal or moral duty. More particularly, the neglect or failure to fulfill in a just and proper manner the duties of an office or fiduciary employment. Every violation by a trustee of a duty which equity lays upon him, whether willful and fraudulent, or done through negligence or arising through mere oversight or forgetfulness, is a breach of duty. See **Non-support.**

Breach of pound. The breaking any pound or place where cattle or goods distrained are deposited, in order to take them back. 3 Bl.Comm. 146.

Breach of prison. Unauthorized departure of a prisoner from legal custody accomplished by the use of force. U. S. ex rel. Manzella v. Zimmerman, D.C.Pa., 71 F.Supp. 534.

Breach of privilege. An act or default in violation of the privilege of either house of parliament, of congress, or of a state legislature.

Breach of promise. Violation of a promise; chiefly used as an elliptical expression for "breach of promise of marriage."

Breach of the peace. A violation or disturbance of the public tranquillity and order. State v. Boles, 5 Conn. Cir. 22, 240 A.2d 920, 927. The offense of breaking or disturbing the public peace by any riotous, forcible, or unlawful proceeding. Breach of the peace is a generic term, and includes all violations of public peace or order and acts tending to a disturbance thereof. State v. Poinsett, 250 S.C. 293, 157 S.E.2d 570, 571, 572. One who commits a breach of the peace is guilty of disorderly conduct, but not all disorderly conduct is necessarily a "breach of the peace." City of Seattle v. Franklin, 191 Wash. 297, 70 P.2d 1049, 1051.

Term signifies disorderly, dangerous conduct disruptive of public peace. Great Atlantic & Pac. Tea Co. v. Paul, 256 Md. 643, 261 A.2d 731, 739.

See also **Peace; Peace bond.**

Breach of trust. Any act done by a trustee contrary to the terms of his trust, or in excess of his authority and to the detriment of the trust; or the wrongful omission by a trustee of any act required of him by the terms of the trust. Also the wrongful misappropriation by a trustee of any fund or property which had been lawfully committed to him in a fiduciary character. Every violation by a trustee of a duty which equity lays upon him, whether willful and fraudulent, or done through negligence, or arising through mere oversight and forgetfulness, is a "breach of trust." The term, therefore, includes every omission and commission in carrying out the trust according to its terms, of care and diligence in protecting and investing the trust property, and of using perfect good faith. A violation by the trustee of any duty which he owes to the beneficiary. Bruun v. Hanson, C.C.A.Idaho, 103 F.2d 685, 699.

Breach of trust with fraudulent intent. Larceny after trust. State v. Owings, 205 S.C. 314, 31 S.E.2d 906, 907.

Breach of warranty. In real property law and the law of insurance, the failure or falsehood of an affirmative promise or statement, or the nonperformance of an executory stipulation. As used in the law of sales, breach of warranty, unlike fraud, does not involve guilty knowledge, and rests on contract. Under Uniform Commercial Code, a violation of either an express or implied warranty for which an action in contract will lie. U.C.C. § 2–312 et seq. See **Warranty.**

Breakage. Allowance given by manufacturer to buyer for breakage damage caused while in transit or storage. Also, fractional amounts (*e.g.* pennies) due either party as for example in computing interest on loan or deposits.

Break and take. Sale of merchandise or amusement where customer pays for a chattel and a chance for another unpaid for chattel, the ticket being the opportunity for fortuitous selection of a differentiated article. Minter v. Federal Trade Commission, C.C.A.3, 102 F.2d 69, 73.

Breaking. Forcibly separating, parting, disintegrating, or piercing any solid substance. In the criminal law as to housebreaking and burglary, it means the tearing away or removal of any part of a house or of the locks, latches, or other fastenings intended to secure it, or otherwise exerting force to gain an entrance, with criminal intent; or violently or forcibly breaking out of a house, after having unlawfully entered it, in the attempt to escape. Actual "breaking" involves application of some force, though the slightest force is sufficient; *e.g.* an actual "breaking" may be made by unloosening, removing or displacing any covering or fastening of the premises, such as lifting a latch, drawing a bolt, raising an unfastened window, or pushing open a door kept closed by its own weight. Sparkman v. State, 3 Md.App. 527, 240 A.2d 328, 331. Opening of a closed and unlocked door is sufficient to constitute a "breaking" within terms of statute, so long as it is done with a burglarious intent. State v. Sanderson, Mo.App., 528 S.W.2d 527, 531. See **Burglary.**

Breaking a case. The expression by the judges of a court, to one another, of their views of a case, in order to ascertain how far they are agreed, and as preliminary to the formal delivery of their opinions. Sometimes used by crime investigators to announce the solution of a crime in the apprehension of the principal suspect.

Breaking a close. Unlawful entry upon land.

Breaking and entry. Term used to describe common law burglary which consists of breaking and entering dwelling of another in nighttime with intent to commit a felony therein. Statutory forms of burglary consist in variations of the common law crime, *e.g.* entering without breaking with intent to commit misdemeanor. See **Breaking; Burglary.**

Breaking bail. Historically, crime committed by bailee who broke open a package (bale) though no crime was committed if he converted the whole package without breaking the bulk. See **Breaking bulk.**

Breaking bulk. The offense committed by a bailee (particularly a carrier) in opening or unpacking the chest, parcel, or case containing goods intrusted to his care, and removing the goods and converting them to his own use. See also **Breaking bail.**

Breaking doors. Forcibly removing the fastenings of a house, so that a person may enter.

Breaking into. Breaking with burglarious intent. State v. Hefflin, 338 Mo. 236, 89 S.W.2d 938, 946. See **Breaking.**

Breaking jail. The act of a prisoner in effecting his escape from a place of lawful confinement. See **Breach of prison.**

Breast of the court. A metaphorical expression signifying the conscience, discretion, or recollection of the judge.

Breathalyzer test. Test to determine content of alcohol in one arrested for operating motor vehicle under influence of liquor. The results of such test, if properly administered, are admissible evidence. See **Consent** (*Implied consent*).

Breath specimen. Sample of one's breath used in testing for alcoholic content. See **Breathalyzer test.**

Bredwite /brédwət/. In Saxon and old English law, a fine, penalty, or amercement imposed for defaults in the assise of bread.

Breed. Produce (offspring) by hatching or gestation; to hatch. Miller Hatcheries v. Boyer, C.C.A.Iowa, 131 F.2d 283, 287. Number of persons of the same stock.

Brehon /bríyən/. In old Irish law, a judge. 1 Bl.Comm. 100. Brehons (*breitheamhuin*), judges.

Brehon law /bríyən ló/. The name given to the ancient system of law of Ireland as it existed at the time of its conquest by Henry II.

Brenagium /brənéyjiyəm/. A payment in bran, which tenants anciently made to feed their lords' hounds.

Brephotrophi /brèfətrówfay/. In the civil law, persons appointed to take care of houses destined to receive foundlings.

Brethren. Plural of brother; though this word, in a will, may include sisters, as well as brothers, of the person indicated; it is not necessarily limited to the masculine gender.

Brethren of Trinity House. See **Elder brethren.**

Bretts and Scotts, Laws of the. A code or system of laws in use among the Celtic tribes of Scotland down to the beginning of the fourteenth century, and then abolished by Edward I. of England.

Breve /bríyviy/. L. Lat. A writ. An original writ. A writ or precept of the king issuing out of his courts. A writ by which a person was summoned or attached to answer an action, complaint, etc., or whereby anything was commanded to be done in the courts, in order to justice, etc.

Breve de recto /bríyv(iy) dìy réktow/. A writ of right, or license for a person ejected out of an estate, to sue for the possession of it.

Breve innominatum /bríyv(iy) ənòmənéydəm/. A writ making only a general complaint, without the details or particulars of the cause of action.

Breve ita dicitur, quia rem de qua agitur, et intentionem petentis, paucis verbis breviter enarrat /bríyriy áydə dísədər kwáyə rém dìy kwéy ǽjədər, ed intènshiyównəm pətentəs, pósəs várbəs brévədər enǽrət/. A writ is so called because it briefly states, in few words, the matter in dispute, and the object of the party seeking relief.

Breve judiciale debet sequi suum originale, et accessorium suum principale /bríyviy juwdìshˈyéyliy débət sékway s(y)úwəm əhrijənéyliy, èd ǽksəsóriyəm s(y)úwəm prìn(t)səpéyliy/. A judicial writ ought to follow its original, and an accessory its principal.

Breve judiciale non cadit pro defectu formæ /bríyv(iy) jədìshiyéyliy nòn kǽdət pròw dəfékt(y)uw fórmiy/. A judicial writ fails not through defect of form.

Breve nominatum /brív(iy) no(w)mənéydəm/. A named writ. A writ stating the circumstances or details of the cause of action, with the time, place, and demand, very particularly.

Breve originale /bríyv(iy) ərijənéyliy/. An original writ; a writ which gave *origin* and commencement to a suit.

Breve perquirere /bríyv(iy) pərkwáyrəriy/. To purchase a writ or license of trial in the king's courts by the plaintiff.

Brevet /brévǝt/brǝvét/. In military law, a commission by which an officer is promoted to the next higher rank, but without conferring a right to a corresponding increase of pay.

In French law, a privilege or warrant granted by the government to a private person, authorizing him to take a special benefit or exercise an exclusive privilege. Thus a *brevet d'invention* is a patent for an invention.

Breve testatum /briyv(iy) testéydǝm/. A written memorandum introduced to perpetuate the tenor of the conveyance and investiture of lands. 2 Bl.Comm. 307.

Brevia /bríyviyǝ/. Lat. The plural of *breve*.

Brevia adversaria /bríyviyǝ ædvǝrsériyǝ/. Adversary writs; writs brought by an adversary to recover land.

Brevia amicabilia /bríyviyǝ æmǝkǝbíliyǝ/. Amicable or friendly writs; writs brought by agreement or consent of the parties.

Brevia anticipantia /bríyviyǝ æntìsǝpǽnsh(iy)ǝ/. At common law, anticipating or preventive writs. Six were included in this category, viz.: Writ of *mesne; warrantia chartœ; monstraverunt; audita querela; curia claudenda;* and *ne injuste vexes.*

Brevia de cursu /bríyviyǝ dìy kársyuw/. Writs of course. Formal writs issuing as of course.

Brevia formata /bríyviyǝ forméydǝ/. Certain writs of approved and established form which were granted of course in actions to which they were applicable, and which could not be changed but by consent of the great council of the realm.

Brevia judicialia /bríyviyǝ juwdìshiyéyliyǝ/. Judicial writs. Auxiliary writs issued from the court during the progress of an action, or in aid of the judgment.

Brevia magistralia /bríyviyǝ mæjǝstréyliyǝ/. Writs occasionally issued by the *masters* or clerks of chancery, the form of which was varied to suit the circumstances of each case.

Breviarium alaricianum /brìyviyérǝm ælǝrish(i)yéynǝm/. A compilation of Roman law made by order of Alaric II., king of the Visigoths, in Spain, and published for the use of his Roman subjects in the year 506. It is also known as *Lex Romana Visigothorum.* It became the principal, if not the only, representative of Roman law among the Franks.

Breviarium aniani /brìyviyérǝm æniyéynay/. Another name for the Brevarium Alaricianum, *(q.v.)* Anian was the referendery or chancellor of Alaric, and was commanded by the latter to authenticate, by his signature, the copies of the breviary sent to the *comites.*

Brevia selecta /bríyviyǝ sǝléktǝ/. Choice or selected writs or processes. Often abbreviated to Brev. Sel.

Brevia, tam originalia quam judicialia, patiuntur anglica nomina /bríyviyǝ tǽm ǝrijǝnéyliyǝ kwǽm juwdìshiyéyliyǝ pǽshiyántǝr ǽnglǝkǝ nó(w)mǝnǝ/. Writs, as well original as judicial, bear English names.

Breviate /bríyviyǝt/. A brief; brief statement, epitome, or abstract. A short statement of contents, accompa-

nying a bill in parliament. The name is usually applied to the famous brief of Mr. Murray (afterwards Lord Mansfield) for the complainant in the case of Penn v. Lord Baltimore, 1 Ves. 444.

Brevia testata /bríyviyǝ testéydǝ/. The name of the short memoranda early used to show grants of lands out of which the deeds now in use have grown.

Brevibus et rotulis liberandis /bríyvǝbǝs et rótyǝlǝs libǝrǽndǝs/. A writ or mandate to a sheriff to deliver to his successor, the county, and appurtenances, with the rolls, briefs, remembrance, and all other things belonging to his office.

Brewer. One who manufactures fermented liquors, for sale, from malt, wholly or in part, or from any substitute therefor.

Bribe. Any money, goods, right in action, property, thing of value, or any preferment, advantage, privilege or emolument, or any promise or undertaking to give any, asked, given, or accepted, with a corrupt intent to induce or influence action, vote, or opinion of person in any public or official capacity. A gift, not necessarily of pecuniary value, bestowed to influence the conduct of the receiver. See also **Bribery; Kickback; Solicitation of bribe.**

Bribery. The offering, giving, receiving, or soliciting of any thing of value to influence action as an official or in discharge of legal or public duty. Allen v. State, 63 Okl.Cr. 16, 72 P.2d 516, 519. The corrupt tendering or receiving of a price for official action. State v. London, 194 Wash. 458, 78 P.2d 548, 554. The receiving or offering any undue reward by or to any person concerned in the administration of public justice or a public officer to influence his behavior in office. Any gift, advantage, or emolument offered, given, or promised to, or asked or accepted by, any public officer to influence his behavior in office. Model Penal Code § 240.1. The federal statute includes "any officer or employee or person acting for or on behalf of the United States, or any department or agency or branch of government thereof," . . . in any official function". 18 U.S.C.A. § 201.

At common law, the gist of the offense was the tendency to pervert justice; the offering, giving, receiving or soliciting of anything of value to influence action as a public official; corrupt agreement induced by offer of reward. The term now, however, extends to many classes of officers and is not confined to judicial officers; it applies both to the actor and receiver, and extends to voters, legislators, sheriffs, and other classes. All persons whose official conduct is connected with the administration of the government are subjects; including persons acting under color of title to office. State v. London, 194 Wash. 458, 78 P.2d 548.

I.R.C. § 162 denies a deduction for bribes or kickbacks.

Commercial bribery. Commercial bribery, as related to unfair trade practices, is the advantage which one competitor secures over his fellow competitors by his secret and corrupt dealing with employees or agents of prospective purchasers. American Distilling Co. v. Wisconsin Liquor Co., C.C.A.Wis., 104 F.2d 582.

Bribery at elections. The offense committed by one who gives or promises or offers money or any valuable inducement to an elector, in order to corruptly induce the latter to vote in a particular way or to abstain from voting, or as a reward to the voter for having voted in a particular way or abstained from voting.

Bribour /bráybər/. One that pilfers other men's goods; a thief.

Bridewell. In England, a house of corrections.

Bridge securities. Type of security issued to finance bridges; usually secured by a lien thereon.

Brief. A written document; a letter; a writing in the form of a letter. A summary, abstract, or epitome. A condensed statement or epitome of some larger document, or of a series of papers, facts and circumstances, or propositions.

A written statement prepared by the counsel arguing a case in court. It contains a summary of the facts of the case, the pertinent laws, and an argument of how the law applies to the facts supporting counsel's position. A summary of a published opinion of a case prepared by law student. See also **Legal brief.**

Appellate brief. Written arguments by counsel required to be filed with appellate court on why the trial court acted correctly (appellee's brief) or incorrectly (appellant's brief). While the contents and form of such briefs are normally prescribed by rule of court, commonly such contain: statement of issues presented for review, statement of the case, an argument, a conclusion stating the precise relief sought. See *e.g.* Fed.Rule App.Proc. 28.

Trial brief. Document prepared for and used by attorney at trial which contains, among other things, issues to be tried, synopsis of evidence and witnesses to be presented, and case and statutory authority for the position of counsel at trial. Frequently, copies of the trial briefs are required to be furnished to the trial judge.

Brigandage /brígəndəj/. Robbery and banditry as perpetrated by a band of robbers or brigands; plundering and outlawry.

Bring. To convey to the place where the speaker is or is to be; to bear from a more distant to a nearer place; to make to come, procure, produce, draw to; to convey, carry or conduct, move. To cause to be, act, or move in a special way. The doing of something effectual. The bringing of someone to account, or the accomplishment of some definite purpose.

Bring about. To procure; implies completion. Jackson v. Thompson, Tex.Civ.App., 74 S.W.2d 1055, 1057.

Bringing money into court. The act of depositing money in the custody of a court or of its clerk or marshal, for the purpose of satisfying a debt or duty, or to await the result of an interpleader. See *e.g.* Fed.R. Civil P. 67.

Bring into. To import; to introduce.

Bring suit. To "bring" an action or suit has a settled customary meaning at law, and refers to the initiation of legal proceedings in a suit. Lake & Co. v. King

County, 4 Wash.2d 651, 104 P.2d 599, 601. A suit is "brought" at the time it is commenced. Goldenberg v. Murphy, 108 U.S. 162, 2 S.Ct. 388, 27 L.Ed. 686. "Brought" and "commenced" in statutes of limitations are commonly deemed to be synonymous. Under the Federal Rules of Civil Procedure, and also most state courts, a civil action is commenced by filing a complaint with the court. Rule 3.

Under Fed. Rules of Civil Proc., term "suit" has been replaced by "action". See Rule 2.

Bring up. Nurse, rear, and educate child until full age. In re Bamber's Estate, 147 Misc. 712, 265 N.Y.S. 798.

Bristol bargain. In English law, a contract by which A. lends B. £1,000 on good security, and it is agreed that £500, together with interest, shall be paid at a time stated; and, as to the other £500, that B., in consideration thereof, shall pay to A. £100 *per annum* for seven years.

British subject. The status conferred upon persons who are citizens of the United Kingdom and Commonwealth of Canada, Australia, New Zealand, India, etc.

British thermal unit (B.T.U.). The amount of heat required to raise a pound of water one degree Fahrenheit.

Broad interpretation. That interpretation of Constitution or statute which, brushing aside minor objections and trivial technicalities, effectuates intent of act. In re Senate Resolution No. 2 Concerning Constitutionality of House Bill No. 6, 94 Colo. 101, 31 P.2d 325, 332. A meaning given to a constitutional provision or statute which is designed to effectuate the intent of the law as contrasted with a "narrow" interpretation which may fail to do so. Giving to a law a meaning which is not necessarily included in a literal application of the words of the law.

Broadside objection. A general objection interposed without specifying grounds thereof.

Brocage /brówkəj/. The wages, commission, or pay of a broker (also called "brokerage"). Also the avocation or business of a broker.

Brocard /brówkərd/. In old English law, a legal maxim. "Brocardica Juris," the title of a small book of legal maxims, published at Paris, 1508.

Brocarius, brocator /browkériyəs/browkéydər/. In old English and Scotch law, a broker; a middleman between buyer and seller; the agent of both transacting parties.

Broken. Impoverishment. Walsh v. Kennedy, 115 Mont. 551, 147 P.2d 425, 430. See **Indigent.**

Broken lot. Odd lot; less than the usual unit of measurement or unit of sale; *e.g.* less than 100 shares of stock.

Broken stowage. In maritime law, that space in a ship which is not filled by her cargo.

Broker. An agent employed to make bargains and contracts for a compensation. A dealer in securities issued by others. White v. Financial Guarantee Corporation, 13 Cal.App.2d 93, 56 P.2d 550, 553. A middleman or negotiator between parties. A person dealing with another for sale of property. A person whose business it is to bring buyer and seller together. The term extends to almost every branch of business, to realty as well as personalty. One who is engaged for others, on a commission, to negotiate contracts relative to property. North Carolina Real Estate Licensing Board v. Aikens, 31 N.C.App. 8, 228 S.E.2d 493, 496. An agent of a buyer or a seller who buys or sells stocks, bonds, commodities, or services, usually on a commission basis.

Ordinarily, the term is applied to one acting for others but is also applicable to one in business of negotiating purchases or sales for himself.

For distinction between "commission merchant" and "broker," see **Commission merchant.** For "Factor" and "broker" as synonymous or distinguishable, see **Factor.** See also Commercial broker; Commission broker; Customs broker; Exchange broker; Pawnbroker.

Broker-agent. One licensed to act both as broker and agent.

Broker-dealer. A securities brokerage firm, usually registered with the S.E.C. and with the State in which it does business, engaging in the business of buying and selling securities to or for customers.

Insurance broker. Person who obtains insurance for individuals or companies from insurance companies or their agents. Differs from an insurance agent in that he does not represent any particular company.

Merchandise brokers. Buyers and sellers of goods and negotiators between buyer and seller, but without having the custody of the property.

Money broker. A money-changer; a scrivener or jobber; one who lends or raises money to or for others.

Note broker. Negotiators of the discount or sale of commercial paper.

Real estate broker. Persons who procure the purchase or sale of land, acting as intermediary between vendor and purchaser, and who negotiate loans on real-estate security, manage and lease estates, etc. Latta v. Kilbourn, 150 U.S. 524, 14 S.Ct. 201, 37 L.Ed. 1169. A broker employed in negotiating the sale, purchase, or exchange of lands on a commission contingent on success. A person engaged in business to such an extent that it is his vocation or partial vocation. See **Listing.**

Securities broker. Brokers employed to buy and sell for their principals stocks, bonds, government securities, etc. Any person engaged in the business of effecting transactions in securities for the account of others, but does not include a bank. Securities Exchange Act of 1934, § 3. A person engaged for all or part of his time in the business of buying and selling securities, who in the transaction concerned, acts for, or buys a security from or sells a security to a customer. U.C.C. § 8–303. See also *Broker-dealer, supra.*

Brokerage. The wages or commissions of a broker; also, his business or occupation.

Brokerage contract. A contract of agency, whereby broker is employed to make contracts of kind agreed upon in name and on behalf of his principal, and for which he is paid an agreed commission. A unilateral contract wherein the principal makes an offer which is interpreted as promise to pay broker a commission in consideration of his producing a buyer ready, able, and willing to buy the property on the principal's terms. In re Cowan's Estate, Sur., 13 N.Y.S.2d 374, 376. See also **Brokerage listing,** *infra.*

Brokerage listing. An offer of a unilateral contract, the act requested being the procuring by the broker of a purchaser ready, able and willing to buy upon the terms stated in the offer. Buckaloo v. Johnson, 14 Cal.3d 815, 122 Cal.Rptr. 745, 753, 537 P.2d 865. See also **Brokerage contract; Listing.**

Brossus /brósəs/. Bruised, or injured with blows, wounds, or other casualty.

Brothel /bróθəl/. A bawdy-house; a house of ill fame; a common habitation of prostitutes.

Brother. One person is a brother "of the whole blood" to another, the former being a male, when both are born from the same father and mother. He is a brother "of the half blood" to that other (or half-brother) when the two are born to the same father by different mothers or by the same mother to different fathers.

In the civil law, the following distinctions are observed: Two brothers who descend from the same father, but by different mothers, are called "consanguine" brothers. If they have the same mother, but are begotten by different fathers, they are called "uterine" brothers. If they have both the same father and mother, they are denominated brothers "germane."

Brother-in-law. The brother of one's spouse; the husband of one's sister; the husband of one's spouse's sister.

Brother-sister corporation. Two or more corporations owned and effectively controlled by one or more individuals, and where these corporations are involved, earnings can be transferred between them only through common shareholder or shareholders, who will be subject to progressive individual income tax. Inland Terminals, Inc. v. U. S., C.A.Md., 477 F.2d 836, 840.

Brought. Taken; carried. Past tense of "bring." See **Bring suit,** *supra.*

Brought in question upon the record. The constitutionality of an act is "brought in question upon the record" when it is clearly questioned by the allegation of any pleading, or by any other formal objection filed in the case. Brosco v. Frost, 63 R.I. 1, 6 A.2d 705, 706.

Brought to the attention of. Equivalent to the expression "made known to."

Brown decision. Supreme Court decision which declared racial segregation in public schools to be in violation of equal protection clause of Fourteenth Amendment. Brown v. Board of Education of Topeka, 347 U.S. 483, 74 S.Ct. 686, 98 L.Ed. 873. See also **Separate but equal doctrine.**

Brown decree. A decree which terminates marriage without specifying in whose favor issue as to grounds for divorce was decided. Spector v. Spector, 94 Ariz. 175, 382 P.2d 659.

Brutum fulmen /brúwdəm fálmən/. An empty noise; an empty threat. A judgment void upon its face which is in legal effect no judgment at all, and by which no rights are divested, and from which none can be obtained, and neither binds nor bars anyone. Dollert v. Pratt-Hewitt Oil Corporation, Tex.Civ.App., 179 S.W.2d 346, 348.

B.S. *Bancus Superior,* that is, upper bench. Bachelor of Science, a collegiate degree.

B.T.U. British Thermal Unit *(q.v.).*

Bubble. An extravagant or unsubstantial project for extensive operations in business or commerce, generally founded on a fictitious or exaggerated prospectus, to ensure unwary investors. Companies formed on such a basis or for such purposes are called "bubble companies". The term is chiefly used in England.

Bubble Act. English Act (1720–1825) drafted to prevent incorporation of English businesses.

Bucketing. Receipt of orders to purchase and sell stock without intention of actually executing such orders.

Bucket shop. An office or place (other than a regularly incorporated or licensed exchange) where persons engage in pretended buying and selling of securities or commodities; *e.g.* broker accepts orders to buy or sell but never actually executes such.

Budget. A balance sheet or statement of estimated receipts and expenditures. A plan for the coordination of resources and expenditures. The amount of money that is available for, required for, or assigned to a particular purpose.

A name given in England to the statement annually presented to parliament by the chancellor of the exchequer, containing the estimates of the national revenue and expenditure.

Budget system. A system by which income and expenditure for definite period are balanced.

Buffer-zone. Term used in zoning and land use law to describe area separating two different types of zones or classes of areas to make each blend more easily with each other; *e.g.* strip of land between industrial and residential areas.

Buggery. A carnal copulation against nature; a man or a woman with a brute beast, a man with a man, or man unnaturally with a woman. This term is often used interchangeably with "sodomy."

Bugging. Form of electronic surveillance by which conversations may be overheard and recorded; regulated strictly by federal and state statute for use by law enforcement officers.

Builder. One whose occupation is the building or erection of structures, the controlling and directing of construction, or the planning, constructing, remodeling and adapting to particular uses buildings and other structures. One who puts, or contracts to put, a structure into permanent form.

Building. Structure designed for habitation, shelter, storage, trade, manufacture, religion, business, education, and the like. A structure or edifice inclosing a space within its walls, and usually, but not necessarily, covered with a roof. Netter v. Scholtz, 282 Ky. 493, 138 S.W.2d 951, 953.

Building and loan association. An organization for the purpose of accumulating a fund by subscriptions and savings of its members to assist them in building or purchasing for themselves dwellings or real estate by the loan to them of the requisite money. Quasi public corporations chartered to encourage thrift and promote ownership of homes. Hopkins Federal Savings & Loan Ass'n v. Cleary, Wis., 296 U.S. 315, 56 S.Ct. 235, 237, 241, 80 L.Ed. 251. Such associations are not commercial banks, nor, in most states, are such classified as savings banks or savings institutions; though in many states such is a special type or variety of savings and loan association. See also **Savings and loan association.**

Building code. Laws, ordinances, or government regulations concerning fitness for habitation setting forth standards and requirements for the construction, maintenance, operation, occupancy, use or appearance of buildings, premises, and dwelling units. While many codes are local in nature and scope, many states have uniform codes which all local municipalities must adhere to. In addition FHA financed real estate must meet certain building code requirements.

Building is covered. Phrase in a binder or contract of temporary insurance meaning that the property shall be insured in the standard form of insurance from that instant for a reasonable time until either the policy or policies can be written out, or their issuance approved or disapproved or some other temporary impediment to the complete formal contract of insurance can be removed. Shumway v. Home Fire & Marine Ins. Co. of California, 301 Mass. 391, 17 N.E.2d 212, 214.

Building lease. A lease of land for a long term of years, at a rent called "ground rent"; the lessee covenanting to erect certain structures thereon according to specification, and to maintain the same, etc., during the term.

Building lien. The statutory lien of a materialman or contractor for the erection of a building. See **Mechanic's lien.**

Building line. A line established by municipal authority, to secure uniformity of appearance in the streets of the city, drawn at a certain uniform distance from the curb or from the edge of the sidewalk, and parallel thereto, upon which the fronts of all buildings on that street must be placed, or beyond which they are not allowed to project. Often referred to as the "set-back" requirement.

Building loan agreement. An agreement by which one undertakes to advance to another money to be used primarily in erection of buildings. Such funds are normally used by the borrower to pay the contractor, sub-contractors and materialmen; and such funds are commonly advanced in installments as the structure is completed. The lender's security is normally the structure being erected. Also called interim or construction financing.

Building permit. Authorization required by local governmental bodies for new building, or major alteration or expansion of existing structures. Building plans, estimated costs, etc., and a fee, are usually required before such is issued. Such permit is normally required to be displayed on the construction site.

Building restrictions. Regulations or restrictions (commonly in zoning ordinances) upon the type of structure that can be constructed on one's property. Such restrictions may also be created in the form of restrictive covenants in deeds.

Building society. An association in which the subscriptions of the members form a capital stock or fund out of which advances may be made to members desiring them, on mortgage security. See **Building and loan association.**

Bul. In the ancient Hebrew chronology, the eighth month of the ecclesiastical, and the second of the civil year. It has since been called *"Marshevan,"* and answers to our October.

Bulk. Unbroken packages. Merchandise which is neither counted, weighed, nor measured. The aggregate that forms a body or unit. When used in relation to sale of goods by sample, "bulk" means the whole quantity of goods sold, which is supposed to be fairly represented by the sample.

Bulk mortgage. A mortgage on property in bulk. May describe creation of security interest in several items as a whole or in bulk, or a mortgage of more than one parcel of real estate, though a bulk transfer is not a security interest subject to Art. 9 of U.C.C., § 9–111.

Bulk sale. Any transfer in bulk, and not in ordinary course of transferor's business, of a major part of the materials, supplies, merchandise or other inventory of an enterprise. U.C.C. § 6–102(1). See **Bulk Sales Acts,** *infra.*

A sale of substantially all the inventory of a trade or business to one person in one transaction. Under certain conditions, corporations making a bulk sale pursuant to a complete liquidation will recognize neither gain nor loss on such sale. I.R.C. § 337(b)(2).

Bulk Sales Acts. A class of statutes designed to prevent the defrauding of creditors by secret sale in bulk of all or substantially all of a merchant's stock of goods. Individual state bulk sales acts have been superseded by Art. 6 of U.C.C., "Bulk Transfers".

Bulk transfers. See **Bulk sale; Bulk Sales Acts,** *supra.*

Bull. In ecclesiastical law, an instrument granted by the Pope of Rome, and sealed with a seal of lead, containing some decree, commandment, or other public act, emanating from the pontiff. Bull, in this sense, corresponds with edict or letters patent from other governments.

There are three kinds of apostolical rescripts—the *brief,* the *signature,* and the *bull;* which last is most commonly used in legal matters.

Also, the term for an investor who anticipates that the stock market will rise; as contrasted with a "bear" who believes it will fall.

Bulla /búlə/. A seal used by the Roman emperors, during the lower empire; it was of four kinds,—gold, silver, wax, and lead.

Bullet. Synonymous with "shot," meaning a projectile particularly a solid ball or bullet that is not intended to fit the bore of a piece.

Bulletin. An officially published notice or announcement concerning the progress of matters of public importance and interest. A brief news item of immediate publication. The publication (organ) of an institution or association.

Bulletin des lois /bulətǽn dèy lwá/. In France, the official sheet which publishes the laws and decrees; this publication constitutes the promulgation of the law or decree.

Bull-headed. Headstrong, obstinate, unreasonably stubborn.

Bullion. Gold and silver intended to be coined.

"Bullion" encompasses, at the very least, any solid mass of uncoined gold or silver whatever its shape so long as its shape does not enhance its value. U. S. Smelting Refining & Mining Co. v. Aetna Cas. & Sur. Co., D.C.N.Y., 372 F.Supp. 489, 494.

Bullion fund. A fund of public money maintained in connection with the mints, for the purpose of purchasing precious metals for coinage, and also of enabling the mint to make returns of coins to private depositors of bullion without waiting until such bullion is actually coined.

Bull market. Securities term for a market in which prices are rising or are expected to rise.

Bull pen. A certain place of close confinement at a penitentiary.

Bum-bailiff. A person employed to dun one for a debt; a bailiff employed to arrest a debtor. Probably a vulgar corruption of "bound-bailiff" *(q.v.).*

Bumping. Displacement of a junior employee's position by a senior employee. The practice of failing to board ticketed passengers due to oversale of the scheduled flight. Mason v. Belieu, C.A.D.C., 543 F.2d 215, 219.

Bunco game /bə́ŋkow géym/. Any trick, artifice, or cunning calculated to win confidence and to deceive, whether by conversation, conduct, or suggestion. A swindling game or scheme.

Bunda /bə́ndə/. In old English law, a bound, boundary, border, or limit *(terminus, limes).*

Buoy /bóy/búwiy/. A floating object intended as a guide and warning to mariners, by marking a spot where the water is shallow, or where there is a reef or other danger to navigation, or to mark the course of a channel. Buoys are regulated by federal statutes.

Burden. Capacity for carrying cargo. Something that is carried. Something oppressive or worrisome. A burden, as on interstate commerce, means anything that imposes either a restrictive or onerous load upon such commerce.

Burden of going forward. The onus on a party to a case to refute or to explain as in the case of one who is charged with possession of stolen goods after the government has introduced evidence of the defendant's recent possession of such goods, the inference being that the defendant knew the goods to have been stolen. Barnes v. U. S., 412 U.S. 837, 846, n. 11, 93 S.Ct. 2357, 2363, 37 L.Ed.2d 380.

Burden of persuasion. The onus on the party with the burden of proof to convince the trier of fact of all elements of his case. In criminal case the burden of the government to produce evidence of all the necessary elements of the crime beyond a reasonable doubt. In re Winship, 397 U.S. 358, 364, 90 S.Ct. 1068, 1073, 25 L.Ed.2d 368.

Burden of producing evidence. The obligation of a party to introduce evidence sufficient to avoid a ruling against him on the issue. Calif.Evid.Code. Such burden is met when one with the burden of proof has introduced sufficient evidence to make out a prima facie case, though the cogency of the evidence may fall short of convincing the trier of fact to find for him. The burden of introducing some evidence on all the required elements of the crime or tort or contract to avoid the direction of a verdict against the party with the burden of proof. Stuart v. D. N. Kelley & Son, 331 Mass. 76, 117 N.E.2d 160.

Burden of proof. (Lat. *onus probandi*.) In the law of evidence, the necessity or duty of affirmatively proving a fact or facts in dispute on an issue raised between the parties in a cause. The obligation of a party to establish by evidence a requisite degree of belief concerning a fact in the mind of the trier of fact or the court.

Burden of proof is a term which describes two different concepts; first, the "burden of persuasion", which under traditional view never shifts from one party to the other at any stage of the proceeding, and second, the "burden of going forward with the evidence", which may shift back and forth between the parties as the trial progresses. Ambrose v. Wheatley, D.C.Del., 321 F.Supp. 1220, 1222.

The burden of proof may require a party to raise a reasonable doubt concerning the existence or nonexistence of a fact or that he establish the existence or nonexistence of a fact by a preponderance of the evidence, by clear and convincing proof, or by proof beyond a reasonable doubt. Except as otherwise provided by law, the burden of proof requires proof by a preponderance of the evidence. Calif.Evid.Code, § 115.

In a criminal case, all the elements of the crime must be proved by the government beyond a reasonable doubt. In re Winship, 397 U.S. 358, 90 S.Ct. 1068, 25 L.Ed.2d 368.

Term has been used to mean either the necessity of establishing a fact, that is, the burden of persuasion, or the necessity of making a prima facie showing, that is, the burden of going forward. State Farm Life Ins. Co. v. Smith, 29 Ill.App.3d 942, 331 N.E.2d 275, 278.

"Burden of establishing" a fact means the burden of persuading the triers of fact that the existence of the fact is more probable than its non-existence. U.C.C. § 1–201(8).

See also **Shifting the burden of proof.**

Bureau /byúrow/. An office for the transaction of business. A name given to the several departments of the executive or administrative branch of government, or their divisions. A specialized administrative unit. Business establishment for exchanging information, making contacts, coordinating activities, etc.

Bureaucracy /byurókrəsiy/. An organization, such as an administrative agency or the army, with the following general traits: a chain of command with fewer people at the top than at the bottom; well defined positions and responsibilities; fairly inflexible rules and procedures; "red tape"; many forms to be filled out; and delegation of authority downward from level to level.

Bureau of Customs. Federal agency charged with responsibility of collecting importing duties for the Government.

Bureau of Land Management. The Bureau of Land Management was established July 16, 1946, by the consolidation of the General Land Office (created in 1812) and the Grazing Service (formed in 1934). The Bureau manages the national resource lands (some 450 million acres) and their resources. It also administers the mineral resources connected with acquired lands and the submerged lands of the Outer Continental Shelf (OCS).

Burford doctrine. Under "Burford Doctrine" of abstention, federal courts have refrained from interfering with complex state regulatory schemes. Clutchette v. Procunier, D.C.Cal., 328 F.Supp. 767, 772.

Burgage /bárgəj/. A name anciently given to a dwelling-house in a borough town.

Burgage-tenure. In English law, one of the three species of free socage holdings; a tenure whereby houses and lands which were formerly the site of houses, in an ancient borough, are held of some lord by a certain rent. There are a great many customs affecting these tenures, the most remarkable of which is the custom of Borough English. Such tenures have been abolished.

Burgator /bərgéydər/. One who breaks into houses or inclosed places, as distinguished from one who committed robbery in the open country.

Burgbote /bárgbòwt/. In old English law, a term applied to a contribution towards the repair of castles or walls of defense, or of a borough.

Burgenses /bərjénsiyz/. In old English law, inhabitants of a *burgus* or borough; burgesses.

Burgeristh /bárgərisθ/. A word used in Domesday, signifying a breach of the peace in a town.

Burgess /bárjəs/. In English law, an inhabitant or freeman of a borough or town; a person duly and legally admitted a member of a municipal corporation. A magistrate of a borough. An elector or voter; a person legally qualified to vote at elections. The word in this sense is particularly defined by the statute 5 & 6 Wm. IV, c. 76, §§ 9, 13. A representative of a borough or town, in parliament. The term now has no local government significance.

Burgess roll. A roll, required by the St. 5 & 6 Wm. IV, c. 76, to be kept in corporate towns or boroughs, of the names of burgesses entitled to certain new rights conferred by that act.

Burgh-breche /bárg-brìych/. A fine imposed on the community of a town, for a breach of the peace, etc.

Burgh English /bárg íngləsh/. See **Borough English.**

Burgh Engloys /bárg íngloyz/. Borough English (q.v.).

Burghmote /bárgmòwt/. In Saxon law, a court of justice held semi-annually by the bishop or lord in a *burg*, which the thanes were bound to attend without summons.

Burglar. One who commits burglary.

Burglariously /bərglériyəsliy/. See **Burglariter.**

Burglariter /bərglérədər/. L. Lat. (Burglariously). In old criminal pleading, a necessary word in indictments for burglary.

Burglary. At common law, the crime of burglary consisted of a breaking and entering of a dwelling house of another in the nighttime with the intent to commit a felony therein. The modern statutory definitions of the crime are much less restrictive. For example, they commonly require no breaking and encompass entry at all times of all kinds of structures. In addition, certain state statutes classify the crime into first, second, and even third, degree burglary.

A person is guilty of burglary if he enters a building or occupied structure, or separately secured or occupied portion thereof, with purpose to commit a crime therein, unless the premises are at the time, open to the public or the actor is licensed or privileged to enter. It is an affirmative defense to prosecution for burglary that the building or structure was abandoned. Model Penal Code, § 221.1.

See also **Breaking.**

Burglary tools. Any implement which may be used to commit burglary though, of itself, it is designed for legitimate use, and possession of which is a crime if accompanied by the intent to use for such illegal purpose and the knowledge of its illegal use.

Burgomaster /bárgəmæstər/. The title given in Germany to the chief executive officer of a borough, town, or city; corresponding to our "mayor."

Burgundian law /bərgándiyən ló/. See **Lex Burgundionum.**

Burgwhar. A burgess (q.v.).

Burial. Act or process of burying a deceased person, sepulture, interment, act of depositing a dead body in the earth, in a tomb or vault, or in the water. The act of interring the human dead.

Burial insurance. A contract based on legal consideration whereby obligor undertakes to furnish obligee or one of latter's relatives at death burial reasonably worth fixed sum.

Burial place. A portion of ground set apart for or occupied by grave, or as a grave or graveyard.

Burial purposes. Continuing care, preservation, and ornamentation of the place of interment as included in term. People v. Rosehill Cemetery Co., 371 Ill. 510, 21 N.E.2d 766, 770.

Burking, burkism. Murder committed with the object of selling the cadaver for purposes of dissection, particularly and originally, by suffocating or strangling the victim.

Burning in the hand. In old English criminal law, laymen, upon being accorded the benefit of clergy, were burned with a hot iron in the brawn of the left thumb, in order that, being thus marked, they could not again claim their clergy. 4 Bl.Comm. 367. This practice was finally abolished by Stat. 19 Geo. III, c. 74; though before that time the burning was often done with a cold iron.

Bursar. A treasurer of a college.

Bursaria /bərsériyə/ or **bursary** /bársəriy/. The treasurer of collegiate or conventual bodies; or the place of receiving, paying, and accounting by the bursars. Also, monetary grant to a needy student.

Burying-ground. A place set apart for the interment of the dead; a cemetery.

Buscarl /báskàrl/. In Saxon and old English law, seamen or marines.

Bushel. A dry measure, containing four pecks, eight gallons, or thirty-two quarts. But the dimensions of a bushel, and the weight of a bushel of grain, etc., vary in the different states in consequence of statutory enactments.

Bushido /bu(w)shíydow/. *Jap.* The unwritten code of conduct of the *Samurai* demanding loyalty to superiors only, simplicity of living and military valor. Treachery and brutality against one's enemies, and self-sacrifice, blind loyalty and unquestioning obedience to one's superiors are cardinal characteristics of the code.

Business. Employment, occupation, profession, or commercial activity engaged in for gain or livelihood. Activity or enterprise for gain, benefit, advantage or livelihood. Union League Club v. Johnson, 18 Cal.2d 275, 108 P.2d 487, 490. Enterprise in which person engaged shows willingness to invest time and capital on future outcome. Doggett v. Burnet, 62 App.D.C. 103, 65 F.2d 191, 194. That which habitually busies or occupies or engages the time, attention, labor, and effort of persons as a principal serious concern or interest or for livelihood or profit.

See also Association; Company; Corporation; Doing business; Joint enterprise; Partnership; Place of business; Trade.

Business agent. Agent having some general supervision over general affairs. Person employed by union members to represent them in relations with business-employer.

Business bad debt. See **Business bad debts.**

Business corporation. A corporation organized for the purpose of carrying on a business for profit. City of St. Louis v. Smith, 325 Mo. 471, 30 S.W.2d 729, 731. See **Corporation.**

Business done in state. Business begun and completed or ended in state. Clark v. Atlantic Pipe Line Co., Tex.Civ.App., 134 S.W.2d 322, 328.

Business enterprise. Investment of capital, labor and management in an undertaking for profit; one of the recognized attributes is centralized management and control. Helvering v. Jewel Mining Co., C.C.A.8, 126 F.2d 1011, 1015.

Business expense. An item of expense incurred in carrying on a trade or business for purpose of producing income and hence deductible in computing taxable income. I.R.C. § 162(a).

Business gains. Gains from sale, exchange, or other disposition of property used in business. Fackler v. Commissioner of Internal Revenue, C.C.A.6, 133 F.2d 509, 512.

Business guest. One invited to business establishment as a guest and to whom a duty of care is owed generally greater than to a social guest, though such distinctions are becoming less acceptable in the area of torts; see *e.g.* Mounsey v. Ellard, 363 Mass. 693, 297 N.E.2d 43. See **Guest.**

Business hours. In general those hours during which persons in the community generally keep their places open for the transaction of business. Casalduc v. Diaz, C.C.A.Puerto Rico, 117 F.2d 915, 916.

Business invitee. One who is impliedly invited to premises for transacting business and to whom a duty of due care is owed. One who goes on another's premises at express or implied invitation of owner or occupant for benefit of invitor or for mutual benefit and advantage of both invitor and invitee. Campbell Sixty-Six Exp., Inc. v. Adventure Line Mfg. Co., 209 Kan. 357, 496 P.2d 1351, 1355. See **Invitee.**

Business league. An association is a business league if persons thereof have some common business interest. Underwriters' Laboratories v. Commissioner of Internal Revenue, C.C.A.7, 135 F.2d 371, 374.

Business losses. Losses from sale, exchange, or other disposition of property used in trade or business. Fackler v. Commissioner of Internal Revenue, C.C.A.6, 133 F.2d 509, 512. See also **Business bad debts.**

Business of peddling. Business of one relying on present solicitation of chance patrons for purchases of uncertain quantities and making concurring deliveries.

Business of public character. Business wherein person engaged expressly or impliedly holds himself out as engaged in business of supplying his product or service to public as a class or to limited portion of public.

Business purpose. Term used on occasion to describe the use to which property may be put or not, as in a deed's restrictive covenant. A justifiable business reason for carrying out a transaction. It has long been established that mere tax avoidance is not a business purpose. The presence of a business purpose is of crucial importance in the area of corporate readjustments.

Business records. Journals, books of account and other records which may be ordered produced as part of discovery in trial or preparation of case and generally given broad interpretation for such purposes; see *e.g.* Fed.R.Civ.Proc. Rule 26(b)(1). See also **Business entry rule; Business records exception.**

Business risk. In finance, the risk of default or variability of return arising from the type of business conducted.

Business situs. A situs acquired for tax purposes by one who has carried on a business in the state more or less permanent in its nature. A situs arising when notes, mortgages, tax sale certificates and the like are brought into the state for something more than a temporary purpose, and are devoted to some business use there and thus become incorporated with the property of the state for revenue purposes. A situs arising where possession and control of property right has been localized in some independent business or investment away from owner's domicile so that its substantial use and value primarily attach to and become an asset of the outside business. State v. Atlantic Oil Producing Co., 174 Okl. 61, 49 P.2d 534, 538.

Business trust. As distinguished from a joint-stock company, a pure "business trust" is one in which the managers are principals, and the shareholders are cestuis que trust. The essential attribute is that property is placed in the hands of trustees who manage and deal with it for use and benefit of beneficiaries. Morriss v. Finkelstein, Mo.App., 127 S.W.2d 46, 49. A "Massachusetts trust" or "common law trust." See **Massachusetts trust; Real estate investment trust.**

Business usage. See *Business purpose, supra.*

Business visitor. One who is invited or permitted to enter or remain upon the premises of another for a purpose directly or indirectly connected with the business dealings between them. Kurre v. Graham Ship by Truck Co., 136 Kan. 356, 15 P.2d 463, 465. One who comes on premises at occupant's instance for purposes connected with purpose, business, or otherwise, for which occupant uses premises. See also *Business guest; Business invitee, supra.*

Course of business. See **Course of dealing; Doing business.**

Farming business. See **Farming purposes.**

Private business. One in which capital, time, attention, labor, and intelligence have been invested for gain and profit for private benefit, purposes and use.

Public business. An element is that the business by its nature must be such that the public must use the same, or the commodities bought and sold in such manner as to affect the community at large as to supply, price, etc. See **Corporation.**

Business bad debts. A tax deduction allowed for obligations obtained in connection with a trade or business which have become either partially or completely worthless. In contrast with nonbusiness bad debts, business bad debts are deductible as business expenses. See also **Bad debt.**

Business entry rule. Exception to hearsay rule which allows introduction of entries made in usual course of business into evidence though person who made such entry is not in court. Fed.Rules Evid., Rule 803(6); 28 U.S.C.A. § 1732. See also **Business records exception.**

Business judgment rule. This rule immunizes management from liability in corporate transaction undertaken within both power of corporation and authority of management where there is reasonable basis to indicate that transaction was made in good faith. Nursing Home Bldg. Corp. v. DeHart, 13 Wash.App. 489, 535 P.2d 137, 144.

Business records exception. An exception to the "hearsay exclusion rule" that allows original, routine records (whether or not part of a "business") to be used as evidence in a trial even though they are hearsay. See also **Business entry rule.**

Busones comitatus /byuwsówniyz kò(w)mətéydəs/. In old English law, the barons of a county.

But. Except, except that, on the contrary, or, and also, yet, still.

"But for" test. Test used in determining tort liability by applying the causative criterion as to whether the plaintiff would not have suffered the wrong "but for" the action of the defendant. Today, largely discredited as a test because of the many modifications necessary in applying it.

Butler's ordinance. In English law, a law for the heir to punish waste in the life of the ancestor.

Butt. A measure of liquid capacity, equal to one hundred and eight gallons; also a measure of land.

Buttals /bádəlz/. The bounding lines of land at the end; abuttals, which see.

Butted and bounded. A phrase sometimes used in conveyancing, to introduce the boundaries of lands. See **Butts and bounds.**

Butts. In old English law, short pieces of land left unplowed at the *ends* of fields, where the plow was turned about (otherwise called "headlands") as sidelings were similarly unplowed pieces on the sides. Also a place where bowmen meet to shoot at a mark.

Butts and bounds. A phrase used in conveyancing, to describe the end lines or circumscribing lines of a certain piece of land. The phrase "metes and bounds" has the same meaning.

The angles or points where these lines change their direction. See **Abuttals.**

Buy. To acquire the ownership of property by giving an accepted price or consideration therefor; or by agreeing to do so; to acquire by the payment of a price or value; to purchase. To obtain something for a price, usually money.

Buy American acts. Federal and state statutes which require a preference for American made goods over foreign made goods in government contracts. The purpose of such acts is to protect domestic industry, goods and labor.

Buy and sell agreement. An arrangement, particularly appropriate in the case of a closely-held corporation or a partnership, whereby the surviving owners (*i.e.* shareholders or partners) or the entity (*i.e.*, corporation or partnership) agree to purchase the interest of a withdrawing or deceased owner (*i.e.*, shareholder or partner). The buy and sell agreement provides for an orderly disposition of an interest in a business and is beneficial in setting the value of such interest for inheritance and death tax purposes.

An agreement between or among part-owners of a business that under stated conditions (usually severance of employment, disability, or death), the person withdrawing or his heirs are legally obligated to sell their interest to the remaining part-owners, and the remaining part-owners are legally obligated to sell at a price fixed in the agreement either on a dollar basis or on a formula for computing the dollar value to be paid.

Entity buy and sell agreement. A buy and sell agreement whereby the entity is to purchase the withdrawing or deceased owner's interest. When the entity is a corporation, the agreement generally involves a stock redemption on the part of the withdrawing shareholder.

Buyer. One who buys; a purchaser, particularly of chattels. A person who buys or contracts to buy goods. U.C.C. § 2-103(1)(a). See also **Purchaser.**

Buyer in ordinary course of business. A person who in good faith and without knowledge that the sale to him is in violation of the ownership rights or security interest of a third party in the goods buys in ordinary course from a person in the business of selling goods of that kind but does not include a pawnbroker. "Buying" may be for cash or by exchange of other property or on secured or unsecured credit and includes receiving goods or documents of title under a pre-existing contract for sale but does not include a transfer in bulk or as security for or in total or partial satisfaction of a money debt. U.C.C. § 1-201(9).

Buyer 60 contract. A contract wherein purchaser not wishing to pay for stock purchased outright buys it at a price in excess of the market and is allowed 60 days' time to pay for stock. Herrlein v. Tocchini, 128 Cal.App. 612, 18 P.2d 73, 75.

Buyer's market. Situation where supply is greater than demand.

Buy in. See **Buying in.**

Buying dormant titles. The purchase of the rights or claims to real estate of a person who is not in possession of the land or is deceased. Such purchases were declared void by English statute (1541); and are similarly void in most states. See also **Bracery.**

Buying in. Buying of property at auction or tax or mortgage foreclosure sale by original owner or by one with interest in property.

Buying long. Purchase of stocks now with the expectation of selling them for a profit in the future.

Buying on margin. Purchase of security with payment part in cash and part by a loan. Normally, the loan is made by the broker.

By. Before a certain time; beside; close to; in close proximity; in consequence of; not later than a certain time; on or before a certain time; in conformity with; with the witness or sanction of; into the vicinity of and beyond. Through the means, act, agency or instrumentality of.

By-bidder. One employed by the seller or his agent to bid on property with no purpose to become a purchaser, so that bidding thereon may be stimulated in others who are bidding in good faith.

By-bidding. See **Bid.**

By bill, by bill without writ. In old English law, terms anciently used to designate actions commenced by original *bill*, as distinguished from those commenced by original *writ*, and applied in modern practice to suits commenced by *capias ad respondendum.* 3 Bl.Comm. 285, 286. The usual course of commencing an action in the King's Bench was by a bill of Middlesex. In an action commenced *by bill* it is not necessary to notice the form or nature of the action.

By color of office. Acts done "by color of office" are where they are of such a nature that office gives no authority to do them. State v. National Surety Co., 162 Tenn. 547, 39 S.W.2d 581, 583. See **Color of office.**

Bye-bil-wuffa. In Hindu law, a deed of mortgage or conditional sale.

By estimation. In conveyancing, a term used to indicate that the quantity of land as stated is estimated only, not exactly measured; it has the same meaning and effect as the phrase "more or less."

By God and my country. In old English criminal practice, the established formula of reply by a prisoner, when arraigned at the bar, to the question, "Culprit, how wilt thou be tried?"

By-law men. In old English law, the chief men of a town, representing the inhabitants. In an ancient deed, certain parties were described as "yeomen and *by-law men.*" They appear to have been men appointed for some purpose of limited authority by the other inhabitants, under by-laws of the corporation appointing.

By-laws. Regulations, ordinances, rules or laws adopted by an association or corporation or the like for its government. The word is also sometimes used to designate the local laws or municipal statutes of a city or town, though, more commonly the tendency is to employ the word "ordinance" exclusively for this class of enactments, reserving "by-law" for the rules adopted by corporations.

By operation of law. Effected by some positive legal rule or amendment. Terminals & Transportation Corporation v. State, 169 Misc. 703, 8 N.Y.S.2d 282, 284.

By reason of. Because of. By means, acts, or instrumentality of.

Byrnes Act. Federal law prohibiting interstate transportation of strike breakers.

Byroad. An obscure or neighborhood road, not used to any great extent by the public, yet so far a public road that the public have of right free access to it at all times. A byway.

Bystander. One who stands near; a chance looker-on; hence one who has no concern with the business being transacted. One present but not taking part, looker-on, spectator, beholder, observer.

By the by (also *Bye*). Incidentally; without new process. A term used in former English practice to denote the method of filing a declaration against a defendant who was already in the custody of the court at the suit of a different plaintiff or of the same plaintiff in another cause. It is no longer allowed.

By virtue of. By force of, by authority of, by reason of. Phillips v. Houston Nat. Bank, Houston, Tex., C.C.A. Tex., 108 F.2d 934, 936. Because of, through, or in pursuance of. For example, money received by an officer by virtue of his office is money which that officer received under the law of his office, and not in violation thereof.

C

C.—ct.—cts. These abbreviations stand for "cent" or "cents," and any one of them, placed at the top or head of a column of figures, sufficiently indicates the denomination of the figures below.

C.A.B. Civil Aeronautics Board.

Cabal /kəbǽl/. A small association for the purpose of intrigue; an intrigue. This name was given to that ministry in the reign of Charles II, formed by Clifford, Ashley, Buckingham, Arlington, and Lauderdale, who concerted a scheme for the restoration of the Pope. The initials of these five names form the word "cabal;" hence the appellation.

Cabalist /kàbalíst/. In French commercial law, a factor or broker.

Caballaria /kæ̀bəlér(i)yə/. Pertaining to a horse. It was a feudal tenure of lands, the tenant furnishing a horseman suitably equipped in time of war, or when the lord had occasion for his service.

Caballeria /kàbayeríyə/. In Spanish law, an allotment of land acquired by conquest, to a horse soldier. A quantity of land, varying in extent in different provinces. In those parts of the United States which formerly belonged to Spain, it is a lot of one hundred feet front, two hundred feet depth, and equivalent to five peonias.

Caballero /kàbayérow/kæ̀vəlyérow/. In Spanish law, a knight. So called on account of its being more honorable to go on horseback (*à caballo*) than on any other beast.

Cabana. Cabin or small house.

Cabaret /kæ̀bəréy/. A room where musical entertainment is permitted in connection with restaurant business.

Cabaret tax. Tax imposed on operation of cabaret by government authorities.

Cabinet. The advisory board or counsel of a king or other chief executive; *e.g.* President's Cabinet. The select or secret council of a prince or executive government; so called from the apartment in which it was originally held.

The President's Cabinet is a creation of custom and tradition, going back to the First President, and functions at the pleasure of the President. Its purpose is to advise the President on any matter concerning which he wishes such advice (pursuant to Article II, section 2, of the Constitution). The Cabinet is composed of the heads of the eleven executive departments—the Secretary of State, the Secretary of the Treasury, the Secretary of Defense, the Attorney General, the Secretary of the Interior, the Secretary of Agriculture, the Secretary of Commerce, the Secretary of Labor, the Secretary of Health, Education, and Welfare, the Secretary of Housing and Urban Development, and the Secretary of Transportation. Certain other officials of the executive branch have been accorded Cabinet rank. The Vice President participates in all Cabinet meetings. Others are invited from time to time for discussion of particular subjects. The Secretary to the Cabinet is designated to provide for orderly handling and followup of matters brought before the Cabinet.

Kitchen cabinet. Informal body of non-cabinet advisors which President turns to for advice.

Cabinet council. In English law, a private and confidential assembly of the most considerable ministers of state, to concert measures for the administration of public affairs; first established by Charles I.

Cabotage /kǽbədəj/. A nautical term from the Spanish, denoting strictly navigation from cape to cape along the coast without going out into the open sea. In International Law, cabotage is identified with *coasting-trade* so that it means navigating and trading along the coast between the ports thereof.

Cachepolus /kæ̀ch(iy)pólǝs/ or **cacherellas** /kæ̀chərélǝs/. An inferior bailiff, or catchpoll.

Cachet, lettres de /létrǝ də kæshéy/. Letters issued and signed by the kings of France, and countersigned by a secretary of state, authorizing the imprisonment of a person. Abolished during the revolution of 1789. See **Lettres de cachet.**

Cacicazgos /kàsiykáskows/. In Spanish-American law, property entailed on the *caciques*, or heads of Indian villages, and their descendants.

Cadastre /kədǽstər/kədástrey/. Tax inventory and assessment of real property.

Cadastu. In French law, an official statement of the quantity and value of realty made for purposes of taxation; same as *cadastre* (q.v.).

Cadaver /kədǽvər/. A dead human body; a corpse. *Cadaver nullius in bonis*, no one can have a right of property in a corpse.

Cadena /kədíynə/. In Spanish, literally, "a chain." In Spanish law, an afflictive penalty consisting of imprisonment at "hard and laborious work," originally with a chain hanging from the waist to the ankle and carrying with it the accessory penalties of civil interdiction, perpetual, absolute disqualification from office, and, in the case of "cadena temporal," surveillance by the authorities during life; sometimes described as "imprisonment in chains." The carrying of chains, however, by convicts sentenced to "cadena" has long fallen into disuse, in the Philippines, and in fact no such punishment has been inflicted since the earliest days of the military occupation of the Philippines by American troops; and so, commonly, the term has come to mean imprisonment, although it has also been contrasted with, or distinguished from, "prision," the Spanish technical name for simple imprisonment.

Cadena perpetua. Life imprisonment.

Cadena temporal. Imprisonment for a term less than life.

Cadere' /kǽdəriy/. Lat. To end; cease; fail; as in phrases such as *cadit actio* (or *breve*), the action (or writ) fails; *cadit assisa*, the assise abates; *cadit quœstio*, the discussion ends, there is no room for further argument; *cadere ab actione* (literally, to fall from an action), to fail in an action; *cadere in partem*, to become subject to a division.

To be changed; to become; to be turned into. *Cadit assisa in juratum*, the assise is changed into a jury.

Cadet /kədét/. Students in the military academy at West Point are styled "cadets;" students in the naval academy at Annapolis, "cadet midshipmen."

Younger brother or son.

In England, a younger brother; the younger son of a gentleman; particularly applied to a volunteer in the army, waiting for some post.

Cadi /kádiy/. A Turkish civil magistrate.

Cadit /kéydət/kǽdət/. Lat. It falls, abates, fails, ends, ceases. See **Cadere.**

Caduca /kəd(y)úwkə/. In the civil law, property of an inheritable quality; property such as descends to an heir. Also the lapse of a testamentary disposition or legacy. Also an escheat; escheated property.

Caducary /kəd(y)úwkəriy/. Relating to or of the nature of escheat, forfeiture, or confiscation. 2 Bl.Comm. 245.

Cæsarean operation /səzériyən/səzíriyən/. Delivery of fetus by way of abdominal incision.

Cæteris tacentibus /sédərəs təséntəbəs/. The others being silent; the other judges expressing no opinion.

Cæterorum /sèdərórəm/. When a limited administration has been granted, and all the property cannot be administered under it, administration *cæterorum* (as to the residue) may be granted.

Cafeteria plan. Type of fringe benefit plan whereby employee, in addition to receiving certain basic fringe benefits, is permitted to also select certain others up to a specified dollar amount.

Cahier /kà(hi)yéy/. In old French law, a list of grievances prepared for deputies in the states-general. A petition for the redress of grievances enumerated.

Cahoots /kəhúwts/. Partnership, teaming up, or combining efforts. City of Abilene v. Luhn, Tex.Civ.App., 65 S.W.2d 370, 371. See **Conspiracy.**

Cairns' Act. An English statute for enabling the court of chancery to award damages. Repealed as having been superseded by the Judicature Act of 1873.

Caisson disease /kéysòn dəzíyz/. A dizziness accompanied with partial paralysis of the limbs, caused by too rapid reduction of air pressure to which men have been accustomed. A condition caused by excessive air pressure wherein gas emboli or bubbles in the tissues of the body may induce severe pain and paralysis.

Calaboose /kǽləbuws/. A term used to designate a jail or prison, particularly a town or city jail or lock-up. Supposed to be a corruption of the Spanish *calabozo*, a dungeon.

Calamity. A state of extreme distress or misfortune, produced by some adverse circumstance or event. Any great misfortune or cause of loss or misery, often caused by natural forces (*e.g.* hurricane, flood, or the like). See **Act of God; Disaster.**

Calcetum, calcea /kælsíydəm/kǽlsiyə/. A causeway.

Calculated. An act intended by design to produce a certain effect or result. A thought-out, premeditated act. See **Premeditation.**

Cale. In old French law, a punishment of sailors, resembling "keelhauling."

Calefagium /kæləféyjiyəm/. In old law, a right to take fuel yearly.

Calendar. The established order of the division of time into years, months, weeks, and days; or a systematized enumeration of such arrangement; an almanac.

Calendar call. A court session given to calling the cases awaiting trial to determine the present status of each case and commonly to assign a date for trial. See also **Trial calendar.**

Calendar days. A calendar day contains 24 hours; but "calendar days" may be synonymous with "working days." Sherwood v. American Sugar Refining Co., C.C.A.N.Y., 8 F.2d 586, 588. The time from midnight to midnight. Lanni v. Grimes, 173 Misc. 614, 18 N.Y.S.2d 322, 327. So many days reckoned according to the course of the calendar.

Calendar week. A block of seven days registered on calendar beginning with Sunday and ending with Saturday. Sonoma County v. Sanborn, 1 Cal.App.2d 26, 36 P.2d 419, 422. Term may consist of any seven days of given month. Sonoma County v. Sanborn, 1 Cal.App.2d 26, 36 P.2d 419, 422.

Calendar year. The period from January 1 to December 31 inclusive. Ordinarily calendar year means 365 days except leap year, and is composed of 12 months varying in length.

Court calendar. A list of cases awaiting trial or other disposition; sometimes called "trial list" or "docket."

Special calendar. A calendar or list of causes, containing those set down specially for hearing, trial, or argument.

Calends /kǽləndz/. Among the Romans the first day of every month, being spoken of by itself, or the very day of the new moon, which usually happen together. And if *pridie*, the day before, be added to it, then it is the last day of the foregoing month, as *pridie calend. Septemb.* is the last day of August. If any number be placed with it, it signifies that day in the former month which comes so much before the month named, as the tenth calends of October is the 20th day of September; for if one reckons backwards, beginning at October, that 20th day of September makes the 10th day before October. In March, May, July, and October, the calends begin at the sixteenth day, but in other months at the fourteenth; which calends must ever bear the name of the month following, and be numbered backwards from the first day of the said following months.

Calends, Greek. A metaphorical expression for a time never likely to arrive, inasmuch as the Greeks had no calends.

Call, *n.* A request or command to come or assemble; a demand for payment of money.

Contract. As used in contract, means demand for payment of, especially by formal notice.

Conveyance. A visible natural object or landmark designated in a patent, entry, grant, or other conveyance of lands, as a limit or boundary to the land described, with which the points of surveying must correspond. Also the courses and distances designated. See also **Metes and bounds.**

Corporation law. A demand by directors upon subscribers for shares for payment of a portion or installment; in this sense, it is capable of three meanings: (1) The resolution of the directors to levy the assessment; (2) its notification to the persons liable to pay; (3) the time when it becomes payable.

Securities. An option or contract giving the holder the right to demand a stated number of shares of stock at a specified price on or before a certain fixed date. Cohn, Ivers & Co. v. Gross, 56 Misc.2d 491, 289 N.Y.S.2d 301. See also **Call option; Put.**

Call, *v.* To make a request or demand; to summon or demand by name; to demand immediate payment or at a specified time, to demand shareholders to pay additional capital; to demand the presence and participation of a number of persons by calling aloud their names, either in a pre-arranged and systematic order or in a succession determined by chance.

Callable. Option to pay before maturity on call. A bond issue, all or part of which may be redeemed by the issuing corporation under definite conditions before maturity. The term also applies to preferred shares which may be redeemed by the issuing corporation.

Callable bonds. Bonds which may be called for payment before their maturity. A bond for which the issuer reserves the right to pay a specific amount, the call price, to retire the obligation before maturity date. If the issuer agrees to pay more than the face amount of the bond when called, the excess of the payment over the face amount is the call premium.

Called upon to pay. Compelled or required to pay.

Callers. Persons employed by a motor carrier to unload truck or trailer bodies and advise checker of nature and number of items of freight unloaded. Cream v. M. Moran Transp. Lines, D.C.N.Y., 57 F.Supp. 212, 216.

Call girl. A prostitute whose bookings are normally made through the use of telephone.

Calling. One's business, occupation, profession, trade or vocation.

Calling the plaintiff. In old English law, the method of non-suiting a plaintiff who did not appear when called by the crier.

Calling to the bar. In English practice, conferring the dignity or degree of barrister at law upon a member of one of the inns of court.

Calling upon a prisoner. When a prisoner has been found guilty on an indictment, the clerk of the court addresses him and calls upon him to say why judgment should not be passed upon him.

Call loan. Loan which is callable by lender at any time; usually on 24 hours notice.

Call option. A negotiable instrument whereby writer of option, for a certain sum of money (the "premium"), grants to the buyer of option the irrevocable right to demand, within a specified time, the delivery by the writer of a specified number of shares of a stock at a fixed price (the "exercise" or "striking" price). Gordon & Co. v. Board of Governors of Federal Reserve System, D.C.Mass., 317 F.Supp. 1045, 1046. An option permitting its holder (who has paid a fee for the option) to call for a certain commodity or security at a fixed price in a stated quantity within a stated period. See **Option.**

Call patent. One whose corners are all stakes, or all but one, or whose lines were not run out and marked at time. Combs v. Combs, 238 Ky. 362, 38 S.W.2d 243, 244.

Call premium. Amount paid by issuer over par or face value upon calling a security in for payment or redemption.

Call price. Price paid corporation for redemption of securities.

Calumnia /kəlǽmniyə/. In the civil law, calumny, malice, or ill design; a false accusation; a malicious prosecution.

In the old common law, a claim, demand, challenge to jurors.

Calumniæ jusjurandum /kəlǽmniyiy jə̀sjərǽndəm/. The oath of (against) calumny. An oath imposed upon the parties to a suit that they did not sue or defend with the intention of calumniating *(calumniandi animo), i.e.,* with a malicious design, but from a firm belief that they had a good cause. The object was to prevent vexatious and unnecessary suits. It was especially used in divorce cases, though of little practical utility. A somewhat similar provision is to be bound in the requirement made in some states that the defendant shall file an affidavit of merits.

Calumniator /kəlámniyeydər/. In the civil law, one who accused another of a crime without cause; one who brought a false accusation.

Calumny /kǽləmniy/. Defamation; slander; false accusation of a crime or offense. See **Calumnia.**

Calvin's case. Calvin v. Smith, 7 Rep. 1; 2 S.T. 559, decided in 1608, in which it was held that persons born in Scotland after the accession of James I to the crown of England in 1603 were not aliens but were capable of inheriting land in England.

Calvo doctrine. The doctrine stated by the Argentine jurist, Carlos Calvo, that a government is not bound to indemnify aliens for losses or injuries sustained by them in consequence of domestic disturbances or civil war, where the state is not at fault, and that therefore foreign states are not justified in intervening, by force or otherwise, to secure the settlement of claims of their citizens on account of such losses or injuries. Such intervention, Calvo says, is not in accordance with the practice of European States towards one another, and is contrary to the principle of state sovereignty. The Calvo Doctrine is to be distinguished from the Drago Doctrine *(q.v.).*

Cambiale jus /kæmbiyéyliy jás/. The law of exchange.

Cambiator /kæmbiyéydər/. In old English law, an exchanger. *Cambiatores monetæ,* exchangers of money; money-changers.

Cambio /kámbiyow/. In Spanish law, exchange.

Cambipartia /kæmbəpársh(iy)ə/. Champerty; from *campus,* a field, and *partus,* divided.

Cambiparticeps /kæmbəpárdəsèps/. A champertor.

Cambist. In mercantile law, a person skilled in exchanges; one who trades in promissory notes or bills of exchange; a broker.

Cambium /kǽmbiyəm/. In the civil law, change or exchange. A term applied indifferently to the exchange of land, money, or debts.

    Cambium reale or *manuale* was the term generally used to denote the technical common-law exchange of lands; *cambium locale, mercantile,* or *trajectitium,* was used to designate the modern mercantile contract of exchange, whereby a man agrees, in consideration of a sum of money paid him in one place, to pay a like sum in another place.

Camera /kǽm(ə)rə/. In old English law, a chamber, room, or apartment; a judge's chamber; a treasury; a chest or coffer. Also, a stipend payable from vassal to lord; an annuity. See **In camera.**

Cameralistics /kæmərəlístəks/. The science of finance or public revenue, comprehending the means of raising and disposing of it.

Camera regis /kǽmərə riyjəs/. In old English law, a chamber of the king; a place of peculiar privileges especially in a commercial point of view. The city of London was so called.

Camerarius /kæmərériyəs/. A chamberlain; a keeper of the public money; a treasurer. Also a bailiff or receiver.

Camera scaccarii /kǽmərə skəkériyay/. The old name of the exchequer chamber.

Camera stellata /kǽmərə stəléydə/. The star chamber *(q.v.).*

Campaign /kæmpéyn/. All the things and necessary legal and factual acts done by a candidate and his adherents to obtain a majority or plurality of the votes to be cast. Running for office, or candidacy for office. Norris v. United States, C.C.A.Neb., 86 F.2d 379, 382. Any organized effort to promote a cause or to secure some definite result with any group of persons. State ex rel. Green v. City of Cleveland, Ohio App., 33 N.E.2d 35, 36.

Campartum /kæmpárdəm/. A part of a larger field or ground, which would otherwise be in gross or in common. See **Champert; Champerty.**

Campbell's (Lord) Acts. English statutes, for amending the practice in prosecutions for libel, 9 & 10 Vict., c. 93; also 6 & 7 Vict., c. 96, providing for compensation to relatives in the case of a person having been killed through negligence; also 20 & 21 Vict., c. 83, in regard to the sale of obscene books, etc.

Campers. A share; a champertor's share; a champertous division or sharing of land.

Campfight. In old English law, the fighting of two champions or combatants in the field; the judicial combat, or *duellum.*

Campum partere /kǽmpəm párdəriy/. To divide the land. See **Champerty.**

Can. As a verb, to be enabled by law, agreement, or custom; to have a right to; to have permission to. Often used interchangeably with "may."

Canal. Artificial waterway used for navigation, drainage or irrigation of land.

Cancel /kǽn(t)səl/. To obliterate; to strike or cross out. To destroy the effect of an instrument by defacing, obliterating, expunging, or erasing it. To revoke or recall; to annul or destroy, make void or invalid, or set aside. To rescind; abandon; repeal; surrender; waive; terminate. The term is sometimes equivalent to "discharge" or "pay." Debes v. Texas Nat. Bank of Beaumont, Tex.Civ.App., 92 S.W.2d 476, 479. See also Abrogation; Cancellation; Rescind; Rescission of contract; Revocation; Termination.

Cancellaria /kænsəlériyə/. Chancery; the court of chancery. *Curia cancellaria* is also used in the same sense. 4 Bl.Comm. 46.

Cancellarii angliæ dignitas est, ut secundus a rege in regno habetur /kænsəlériyay ængliyiy dígnətæs ést, ət səkándəs èy ríyjiy ìn régnow həbíydər/. The dignity of the chancellor of England is that he is deemed the second from the sovereign in the kingdom.

Cancellarius /kænsəlériyəs/. A chancellor; a scrivener, or notary. A janitor, or one who stood at the door of the court and was accustomed to carry out the commands of the judges.

In early English law, the keeper of the king's seal. In this sense only, the word chancellor seems to have been used in the English law. 3 Bl.Comm. 46.

Cancellation. To destroy the force, effectiveness, or validity of. To annul or abrogate. Defacement or mutilation of instrument. Words of revocation written across instrument.

Occurs when either party puts an end to the contract for breach by the other and its effect is the same as that of "termination" except that the cancelling party also retains any remedy for breach of the whole contract or any unperformed balance. U.C.C. § 2–106(4).

See also **Abrogation; Cancel; Revocation; Termination.**

Cancellation clause. A provision in a contract or lease which permits the parties to cancel or discharge their obligations thereunder.

Cancellatura /kænsəlóchúrə/. In old English law, a canceling.

Cancelled check. A check which bears the notation of cancellation of the drawee bank as having been paid and charged to the drawer. Used as evidence of payment of an obligation to the payee.

Cancelli /kænsélay/. The lines drawn on the face of a will or other writing, with the intention of revoking or annulling it.

Candidate. One who seeks or offers himself, or is put forward by others, for an office, privilege, or honor. State ex rel. Ranney v. Corey, Ohio App., 47 N.E.2d 799, 800. A nominee. State ex rel. Van Schoyck v. Board of Com'rs of Lincoln County, 46 N.M. 472, 131 P.2d 278, 284.

Canfara. A trial by hot iron, formerly used in England.

Cannabis /kǽnəbəs/. Commonly called marihuana; cannabis sativa L embraces all marihuana-producing cannabis. U. S. v. Honneus, C.A.Mass., 508 F.2d 566, 574. As defined in Uniform Narcotic Drug Act it embraces: (a) The dried flowering or fruiting tops of the pistillate plant Cannabis Sativa Linne from which the resin has not been extracted, (b) the resin extracted from such tops, and (c) every compound, manufacture, salt, derivative, mixture, or preparation of such resin, or of such tops from which the resin has not been extracted. See also **Marihuana.**

Cannon rule. Purchase or ownership of stock, even of a controlling interest, in a domestic corporation by a foreign corporation does not constitute doing business by the foreign parent sufficient to subject it to service of process in state of subsidiary's operation. Mid-Continent Tel. Corp. v. Home Tel. Co., D.C.Miss., 307 F.Supp. 1014, 1019.

Cannot. Denotes that one is not able (to do some act). But the term is often equivalent to "shall not."

Canon /kǽnən/. A law, rule, or ordinance in general, and of the church in particular. An ecclesiastical law or statute. A rule of doctrine or discipline. A criterion or standard of judgment. A body of principles, standards, rules, or norms.

In England, a cathedral dignitary, appointed sometimes by the Crown and sometimes by the bishop.

Canon law. A body of Roman ecclesiastical jurisprudence compiled in the twelfth, thirteenth and fourteenth centuries from the opinions of the ancient Latin fathers, the decrees of General Councils, and the decretal epistles and bulls of the Holy See. The canon law is contained in two principal parts,—the decrees or ecclesiastical constitutions made by the popes and cardinals; and the decretals or canonical epistles written by the pope, or by the pope and cardinals, at the suit of one or more persons. As the decrees set out the origin of the canon law, and the rights, dignities, and decrees of ecclesiastical persons, with their manner of election, ordination, etc., so the decretals contain the law to be used in the ecclesiastical courts. The canon law forms no part of the law of England, unless it has been brought into use and acted on there.

Canons of construction. The system of fundamental rules and maxims which are recognized as governing the construction or interpretation of written instruments.

Canons of descent. The legal rules by which inheritances are regulated, and according to which estates are transmitted by descent from the ancestor to the heir.

Canons of inheritance. The legal rules by which inheritances are regulated, and according to which estates are transmitted by descent from the ancestor to the heir. 2 Bl.Comm. 208.

Canons of judicial ethics. Standards of ethical conduct for members of the judiciary. Such were initially adopted by the American Bar Association and later by most states.

Canons of taxation. Tax criteria used in the selection of a tax base originally discussed by Adam Smith in his "Wealth of Nations." Canons of taxation include the following: equality; convenience; certainty; and economy.

Code of professional responsibility. "Canons" of the Code of Professional Responsibility are statements of axiomatic norms expressing in general terms the standards of professional conduct expected of lawyers in their relationship with the public, the legal system and with the legal profession. Such were initially adopted by the American Bar Association and later by most states.

Canonical /kənónəkəl/. Pertaining to, or in conformity to, the canons of the church.

Canonical disability. Incurable physical impotency or incapacity for copulation.

Canonical obedience. That duty which a clergyman owes to the bishop who ordained him, to the bishop in whose diocese he is beneficed, and also to the metropolitan of such bishop.

Canonicus /kənónəkəs/. In old English law, a canon.

Canonist. One versed and skilled in the canon law; a professor of ecclesiastical law.

Canonry. In English ecclesiastical law, an ecclesiastical benefice, attaching to the office of canon.

Cant. In the civil law, a method of dividing property held in common by two or more joint owners. It may be avoided by the consent of all of those who are interested, in the same manner that any other contract or agreement may be avoided.

Canterbury, Archbishop of. In English ecclesiastical law, the primate of all England; the chief ecclesiastical dignitary in the church. His customary privilege is to crown the kings and queens of England. Has also, by 25 Hen. VIII, c. 21, the power to grant dispensations.

Cantred /kǽntrəd/. In old English law, a district comprising a hundred villages; a hundred. A term used in Wales in the same sense as "hundred" is in England.

Canum /kéynəm/. In feudal law, a species of duty or tribute payable from tenant to lord, usually consisting of produce of the land.

Canvass. The act of examining and counting the returns of votes cast at a public election to determine authenticity. Personal solicitation of votes or survey to determine probable vote outcome.

Canvasser. Any of certain persons, as officers of a state, county, or district, intrusted with the duty of examining the returns of votes cast at an election. See **Canvass.**

One who, in a given town, city, or county, goes from house to house in an effort to take orders for goods; in this sense, to be distinguished from traveling salesmen.

Capable. Susceptible; competent; qualified; fitting; possessing legal power or capacity. Able, fit or adapted for. See **Capacity.**

Capacity. Legal qualification (*i.e.* legal age), competency, power or fitness. Ability to understand the nature and effects of one's acts.

The ability of a particular individual or entity to use, or to be brought into, the courts of a forum. Johnson v. Helicopter & Airplane Services Corp., D.C.Md., 404 F.Supp. 726, 729.

See also Competency; Disability; Earning capacity; Fiduciary capacity; Incapacity; Legal age; Legal capacity to sue; Mental capacity or competence; Person under disability; Standing to sue doctrine; Substantial capacity; Testamentary (*Testamentary capacity*).

Criminal capacity. Accountability for committing crime; *e.g.*, child under 7 years of age lacks criminal capacity. Application of Gault, 387 U.S. 1, 87 S.Ct. 1428, 1438, 18 L.Ed.2d 527.

Capacity defense. Generic term to describe lack of fundamental ability to be accountable for actions, as one under duress lacks the capacity to contract and hence when sued on such contract he interposes defense of lack of capacity. Similarly, a child accused of crime committed when he was under age of 7, his defense being lack of criminal capacity. As a defense, it tends to negate some essential element of the action required for responsibility. See also **Competency proceedings; Competency to stand trial; Defense; Insanity; Intoxication.**

Capax doli /kéypæks dówlay/. Lat. Capable of committing crime, or capable of criminal intent. The phrase describes the condition of one who has sufficient intelligence and comprehension to be held criminally responsible for his deeds.

Capax negotii /kéypæks nəgówshiyay/. Competent to transact affairs; having business capacity.

Cape /kéyp(iy)/. In English practice, a judicial writ, now abolished, touching a plea of lands or tenements. It was divided into *cape magnum*, or the *grand cape*, which lay before appearance to summon the tenant to answer the default, and also over to the demandant and *cape parvum*, or *petit cape*, after appearance or view granted, summoning the tenant to answer the default only. It was called a "cape," from the word with which it commenced, and a "grand cape" (or *cape magnum*) to distinguish it from the *petit cape*, which lay after appearance.

Extension of land jutting out into water as a peninsula.

Cape ad valentiam /kéypiy æd vəlénsh(iy)əm/. A species of *cape magnum.*

Capella /kəpélə/. A box, cabinet, or repository in which were preserved the relics of martyrs. A small building in which relics were preserved; an oratory or chapel.

Capers /kéypərz/. Vessels of war owned by private persons, and different from ordinary privateers only in size, being smaller.

Capias /kéypiyəs/kǽpiyəs/. Lat. "That you take." The general name for several species of writs, the common characteristic of which is that they require the officer to take the body of the defendant into custody.

In English practice, the process on an indictment when the person charged is not in custody, and in cases not otherwise provided for by statute.

See also **Cepi.**

Capias ad audiendum judicium /kéypiyəs æd odiyéndəm juwdísh(iy)əm/. A writ issued, in a case of misdemeanor, after the defendant has appeared and is found guilty, to bring him to hear judgment if he is not present when called.

Capias ad computandum /kéypiyəs æd kòmpyuwtǽndəm/. In the action of account render, after judgment of *quod computet*, if the defendant refuses to appear personally before the auditors and make his account, a writ by this name may issue to compel him. The writ is now disused.

Capias ad respondendum /kéypiyəs æd rèspondéndəm/. A judicial writ (usually simply termed a *"capias,"* and commonly appreviated to *ca. resp.*) by which actions at law were frequently commenced; and which commands the sheriff to *take* the defendant, and him safely keep, so that he may have his body before the court on a certain day, to *answer* the plaintiff in the action. It notifies defendant to defend suit and procures his arrest until security for plaintiff's claim is furnished.

Capias ad satisfaciendum /kéypiyəs æd sæedəsfèyshiyéndəm/. A writ of execution (usually termed, for brevity, a *"ca. sa."*), which commands the sheriff to *take* the party named, and keep him safely, so that he may have his body before the court on a certain day, *to satisfy* the damages or debt and damages in certain actions. It deprives the party taken of his liberty until he makes the satisfaction awarded. A body execution enabling judgment creditor in specified types of actions to cause arrest of judgment debtor and his retention in custody until he either pays judgment or secures his discharge as insolvent debtor. Perlmutter v. DeRowe, 58 N.J. 5, 274 A.2d 283, 286.

Capias extendi facias /kéypiyəs əksténday féyshiyəs/. A writ of execution issuable in England against a debtor to the crown, which commands the sheriff to "take" or arrest the body, and "cause to be extended" the lands and goods of the debtor.

Capias in withernam /kéypiyəs in wíðərnəm/. A writ, in the nature of a reprisal, which lies for one whose goods or cattle, taken under a distress, are removed from the county, so that they cannot be replevied, commanding the sheriff to seize other goods or cattle of the distrainor of equal value.

Capias pro fine /kéypiyəs pròw fáyniy/. (That you take for the fine or in mercy.) Formerly, if the verdict was for the defendant, the plaintiff was adjudged to be amerced for his false claim; but, if the verdict was for the plaintiff, then in all actions *vi et armis*, or where the defendant, in his pleading, had falsely denied his own deed, the judgment contained an award of a *capiatur pro fine;* and in all other cases the defendant was adjudged to be amerced. The insertion of the *misericordia* or of the *capiatur* in the judgment is now unnecessary. A writ in all respects an execution for collection of fine. Board of Councilmen of City of Frankfort v. Rice, 249 Ky. 771, 61 S.W.2d 614, 615.

Capias ullagatum /kéypiyəs ə̀(t)ləgéydəm/. (You take the outlaw.) In English practice, a writ which lies against a person who has been *outlawed* in an action, by which the sheriff is commanded to *take* him, and keep him in custody until the day of the return, and then present him to the court, there to be dealt with for his contempt. 3 Bl.Comm. 284.

Capiatur pro fine /kè̀ypiyéydər pròw fáyniy/. (Let him be taken for the fine.) In English practice, a clause inserted at the end of old judgment records in actions of debt, where the defendant denied his deed, and it was found against him upon his false plea, and the jury were troubled with the trial of it.

Capita /kǽpədə/. Heads, and, figuratively, entire bodies, whether of persons or animals.

Persons individually considered, without relation to others (polls); as distinguished from *stirpes* or stocks of descent. The term in this sense, making part of the common phrases, *in capita, per capita,* is derived from the civil law.

Capital. Accumulated goods, possessions, and assets, used for the production of profits and wealth. Owners' equity in a business. Often used equally correctly to mean the total assets of a business. Sometimes used to mean capital assets.

In accounting, the amount invested in a business. In economic theory there are several meanings.

"Capital" may be used to mean: capital goods, that is, the tools of production; the money available for investment, or invested; the discounted value of the future income to be received from an investment; the real or money value of total assets; money or property used for the production of wealth; sum total of corporate stock.

See also Fixed capital; Floating or circulating captial; Impaired capital; Legal capital; Stated capital.

Authorized capital. See **Stock** *(Authorized stock).*

Capital account. In accounting, the account which represents the contributions of the proprietors, partners or stockholders to which creditors may look and from which no dividends should be paid.

Capital assets. See **Assets.**

Capital case or crime. One in or for which death penalty may, but need not necessarily, be imposed.

Capital contribution. Cash, property, or services contributed by partners to partnership.

Various means by which a shareholder makes additional funds available to the corporation (*i.e.*, placed at the risk of the business) without the receipt of additional stock. Such contributions are added to the basis of the shareholder's existing stock investment and do not generate income to the corporation. I.R.C. § 118.

Capital costs. Costs for improvements to property; such are depreciable over the useful life of the improvements.

Capital expenditure. Expenditure for long term betterments or additions. Expenditure in nature of an investment for the future chargeable to capital asset account. An expenditure which should be added to the basis of the property improved. I.R.C. § 263.

Capital gains. Gain (profit) realized on sale or exchange of capital asset. I.R.C. § 1201 et seq. The excess of proceeds over cost, or other basis, from the sale of a capital asset as defined by the Internal Revenue Code.

    Long term gain. Gain (profit) realized on sale or exchange of capital asset held for more than 12 months.

    Short term gain. Gain realized on sale or exchange of capital asset which has been held for not more than 12 months.

Capital gains tax. A provision in the income tax laws that profits from the sale of capital assets are taxed at separate (lower) rates than the rate applicable to ordinary income.

Capital goods. Materials used or consumed to produce other goods.

Capital impairment. Reduction of assets of corporation below aggregate of outstanding shares of capital stock.

Capital increase. An increase not attributable to earnings.

Capital investment. Acquisition price of a "capital asset", Commissioner of Internal Revenue v. Rowan Drilling Co., C.C.A.Tex., 130 F.2d 62, 64, 65; capital stock, surplus and undivided profits, O'Connor v. Bankers Trust Co., 159 Misc. 920, 289 N.Y.S. 252,

276; money spent to increase an asset, Peerless Stages v. Commissioner of Internal Revenue, 125 F.2d 869, 871.

Capital loss. Loss on sale or exchange of capital asset.

Long term loss. Loss realized by taxpayer on sale or exchange of capital asset held for more than 12 months.

Short term loss. Loss on sale or exchange on capital asset held for not more than 12 months.

Capital market. Market for long-term investment funds.

Capital outlay. Money expended in acquiring, equipping, and promoting an enterprise.

Capital punishment. Punishment by death for capital crimes.

Capital recovery. Collection of charged-off bad debt where reserve account system is used. National Bank of Tulsa v. Oklahoma Tax Commission, 193 Okl. 529, 145 P.2d 768, 771, 772.

Capital return. In tax accounting, payments received by taxpayer which represent his cost or capital and hence not taxable as income. Commissioner v. Liftin, C.A.4th, 317 F.2d 234.

Capital stock. All shares representing ownership of a business, including preferred stock and common stock. Amount fixed by charter to be subscribed and paid in or secured to be paid in by shareholders. State ex rel. Corinne Realty Co. v. Becker, 320 Mo. 908, 8 S.W.2d 970, 971. Amount of stock that corporation may issue; amount subscribed, contributed or secured to be paid in. Haggard v. Lexington Utilities Co., 260 Ky. 261, 84 S.W.2d 84, 87. Corporate assets or property. Bates v. Daley's Inc., 5 Cal.App.2d 95, 42 P.2d 706, 709. Liability of the corporation to its shareholders, after creditors' claims have been liquidated. Valuation of the corporation as a business enterprise.

Capital stock tax. Tax on privilege of doing business. Repealed by Revenue Act of 1945, §§ 201, 202.

Capital structure. The composition of a corporation's equities; the relative proportions of short-term debt, long-term debt, and owners' equity. In finance the total of bonds (or long-term money) and ownership interests in a corporation; that is, the stock accounts and surplus. See also **Capitalization.**

Capital surplus. Property paid into corporation by shareholders in excess of capital stock liability. Surplus other than earned surplus; *i.e.* not from normal business profits.

Capital transactions. Purchases, sales and exchanges of capital assets.

Paid-in-capital. Amount paid for stock of corporation that has been sold.

Stated capital. The sum of (a) the par value of all shares with par value that have been issued, (b) the amount of the consideration received for all shares without par value that have been issued, except such part of the consideration therefor as may have been allocated to surplus in a manner permitted by law, and (c) such other amounts as have been transferred to stated capital, whether upon the distribution of shares or otherwise, minus all reductions from such sums as have been effected in a manner permitted by law and surplus. Model Bus.Corp. Act, § 2(j).

Capitale /kǽpətéyliy/. A thing which is stolen, or the value of it.

Capitalis /kǽpətéyləs/. In old English law, chief; principal; at the *head.* A term applied to persons, places, judicial proceedings, and some kinds of property.

Capitalis baro /kǽpətéyləs bǽrow/. In old English law, chief baron. *Capitalis baro scaccarii domini regis,* chief baron of the exchequer.

Capitalis custos /kǽpətéyləs kástows/. Chief warden or magistrate; mayor.

Capitalis debitor /kǽpətéyləs débədər/. The chief or principal debtor, as distinguished from a surety *(plegius).*

Capitalis dominus /kǽpətéyləs dómənəs/. Chief lord.

Capitalis justiciarius /kǽpətéyləs jəstìshiyériyəs/. The chief justiciary; the principal minister of state, and guardian of the realm in the king's absence. This office originated under William the Conqueror; but its power was greatly diminished by *Magna Charta,* and finally distributed among several courts by Edward I. 3 Bl.Comm. 38.

Capitalis justiciarius ad placita coram rege tenenda /kǽpətéyləs jəstìshiyériyəs ǽd plǽsədə kórəm ríyjiy tənéndə/. Chief justice for holding pleas before the king. The title of the chief justice of the king's bench, first assumed in the latter part of the reign of Henry III.

Capitalis justiciarius banci /kǽpətéyləs jəstìshiyériyəs bǽnsay/. Chief justice of the bench. The title of the chief justice of the (now) court of common pleas, first mentioned in the first year of Edward I.

Capitalis justiciarius totius Angliæ /kǽpətéyləs jəstìshiyériyəs towshíyəs ǽngliyiy/. Chief justice of all England. The title of the presiding justice in the court of *aula regis.* 3 Bl.Comm. 38.

Capitalis plegius /kǽpətéyləs pléjiyəs/. A chief pledge; a head borough.

Capitalis reditus /kǽpətéyləs rédədəs/. A chief rent.

Capitalist. One exclusively dependent on accumulated property, whether denoting a person of large wealth or one having an income from investments. An individual who owns all or part of an income-producing asset.

Capitalis terra /kǽpətéyləs téhrə/. A head-land. A piece of land lying at the head of other land.

Capitalization /kǽpədələzéyshən/. Capitalization represents the total amount of the various securities issued by a corporation. Capitalization may include bonds, debentures, preferred and common stock and surplus. Bonds and debentures are usually carried on the books of the issuing company in terms of their par or face value. Preferred and common shares may be carried in terms of par or stated value. Stated value may be an arbitrary figure decided upon by the directors or may represent the amount received by the company from the sale of the securities at the time of issuance.

To record an expenditure that may benefit a future period as an asset rather than to treat the expenditure as an expense of the period of its occurrence.

Capitalization method. A method of measuring values of realty for purpose of determining values of mortgages by expertly estimating the gross income which property should realize, and separately the expenses reasonably required to carry it, and thus arriving at a fair estimate of net income and using a capitalization figure or factor, expertly chosen. Depreciation must be taken into consideration in use of such method. In re New York Title & Mortgage Co. (Series B–K), 21 N.Y.S.2d 575, 594, 595.

Capitalize. To convert a periodical payment into an equivalent capital sum or sum in hand. To compute the present value of an income extended over a period of time.

Capitaneus /kæpətéyniyəs/. A tenant *in capite*. He who held his land or title directly from the king himself. A captain; a naval commander. This latter use began A.D. 1264. *Capitaneus, Admiralius.* A commander or ruler over others, either in civil, military, or ecclesiastical matters.

Capita, per /pər kǽpədə/. By heads; by the poll; as individuals. In the distribution of an intestate's personalty, the persons legally entitled to take are said to take *per capita*, that is, equal shares, when they claim, each in his own right, as in equal degree of kindred; in contradistinction to claiming by right of representation, or *per stirpes*. See **Per capita.**

Capitare /kǽpətériy/. In old law and surveys. To head, front, or abut; to touch at the head, or end.

Capitatim /kæpətéydəm/. Lat. By the head; by the poll; severally to each individual.

Capitation tax. A poll tax *(q.v.)*. A tax or imposition upon the person. It is a very ancient kind of tribute, and answers to what the Latins called *"tributum,"* by which taxes on persons are distinguished from taxes on merchandise, called *"vectigalia."*

Capite /kǽpədiy/. Lat. By the head. Tenure *in capite* was an ancient feudal tenure, whereby a man held lands of the king immediately. It was of two sorts,— the one, principal and general, or of the king as the source of all tenure; the other, special and subaltern, or of a particular subject. It is now abolished. As to distribution *per capita*, see **Capita, per.**

Capite minutus /kǽpədiy mənyúwdəs/. In the civil law, one who had suffered *capitis diminutio*, one who lost status or legal attributes.

Capitis diminutio /kǽpədəs dìmən(y)úwsh(iy)ow/. In Roman law, a diminishing or abridgment of personality; a loss or curtailment of a man's status or aggregate of legal attributes and qualifications.

Capitis diminutio maxima /kǽpədəs dìmən(y)úwsh(iy)ow mǽksəmə/. The highest or most comprehensive loss of status. This occurred when a man's condition was changed from one of freedom to one of bondage,

when he became a slave. It swept away with it all rights of citizenship and all family rights.

Capitis diminutio media /kǽpədəs dìmən(y)úwsh(iy)ow míydiyə/. A lesser or medium loss of status. This occurred where a man lost his rights of citizenship, but without losing his liberty. It carried away also the family rights.

Capitis diminutio minima /kǽpədəs dìmən(y)úwsh(iy)ow mínəmə/. The lowest or least comprehensive degree of loss of status. This occurred where a man's family relations alone were changed. It happened upon the arrogation of a person who had been his own master *(sui juris),* or upon the emancipation of one who had been under the *patria potestas*. It left the rights of liberty and citizenship unaltered.

Capititium /kæpətísh(iy)əm/. A covering for the head, mentioned in St. 1 Hen. IV, and other old statutes, which prescribe what dresses shall be worn by all degrees of persons.

Capitula /kəpíchələ/. Collections of laws and ordinances drawn up under heads of divisions. The term is used in the civil and old English law, and applies to the ecclesiastical law also, meaning chapters or assemblies of ecclesiastical persons. The *Royal and Imperial Capitula* were the edicts of the Frankish Kings and Emperors.

Capitula coronæ /kəpíchələ kərówniy/. Chapters of the crown. Chapters or heads of inquiry, resembling the *capitula itineris (infra)* but of a more minute character.

Capitula de judæis /kəpíchələ dìy juwdíyəs/. A register of mortgages made to the Jews. 2 Bl.Comm. 343.

Capitula itineris /kəpíchələ aytínərəs/. Articles of inquiry which were anciently delivered to the justices in eyre when they set out on their circuits. These schedules were designed to include all possible varieties of crime.

Capitula ruralia /kəpíchələ ruréyliyə/. Assemblies or chapters, held by rural deans and parochial clergy, within the precinct of every deanery; which at first were every three weeks, afterwards once a month, and subsequently once a quarter.

Capitulary /kəpíchələriy/. In French law, a collection and code of the laws and ordinances promulgated by the kings of the Merovingian and Carlovingian dynasties.

Any orderly and systematic collection or code of laws. See **Code.**

In ecclesiastical law, a collection of laws and ordinances orderly arranged by divisions. A book containing the beginning and end of each Gospel which is to be read every day in the ceremony of saying mass

Capitulation /kəpìchəléyshən/. The act or agreement of surrendering upon negotiated or stipulated terms.

Capituli agri /kəpíchəlay ǽgray/. Head-fields; lands lying at the head or upper end of furrows, etc.

Capitulum /kəpíchələm/. Lat. A leading division of a book or writing; a chapter; a section.

Capper /kǽpər/. A decoy or lure for purpose of swindling. Barron v. Board of Dental Examiners of California, 109 Cal.App. 382, 293 P. 144, 145.

Caprice /kəpríys/. Whim, arbitrary, seemingly unfounded motivation. Disposition to change one's mind impulsively.

Captain. A head-man; commander; commanding officer of troops, ship, etc.

Captain of the ship doctrine. This doctrine imposes liability on surgeon in charge of operation for negligence of his assistants during period when those assistants are under surgeon's control, even though assistants are also employees of hospital. This concept is an adaptation of the "borrowed servant" principle in law of agency to operating room of hospital. Thomas v. Hutchinson, 442 Pa. 118, 275 A.2d 23, 27.

Captation. In French law, the act of one who succeeds in controlling the will of another, so as to become master of it; used in an invidious sense. It was formerly applied to the first stage of the hypnotic or mesmeric trance.

Captator /kæptéydər/. A person who obtains a gift or legacy through artifice. See **Captation.**

Captio /kǽpshiyow/. In old English law and practice, a taking or seizure; arrest; receiving; holding of court.

Caption /kǽpshən/. The heading or introductory part of a pleading, motion, deposition, or other legal instrument which indicates the names of the parties, name of the court, docket or file number, title of the action, etc. Fed.R. Civil P. 10(a).

Captive. Prisoner of war.

Captive audience. Any group subject to a speaker or to a performance and which is not free to depart without adverse consequences.

Captor. In international law, one who takes or seizes property in time of war; one who takes the property of an enemy. In a stricter sense, one who takes a prize at sea. Oakes v. U. S., 174 U.S. 778, 19 S.Ct. 864, 43 L.Ed. 1169. The term also designates a belligerent who has captured the person of an enemy.

Capture. Act of catching or controlling by force, threats or strategy. In international law, the taking or wresting of property from one of two belligerents by the other. Also a taking of property by a belligerent from an offending neutral. Capture, in technical language, is a taking by military power; a *seizure* is a taking by civil authority.

Caput /kǽpət/. A head; the head of a person; the whole person; the life of a person; one's personality; status; civil condition.

At common law, a head. *Caput comitatis,* the head of the county; the sheriff; the king. A person; a life. The upper part of a town. A castle.

Capitis æstimatio /kǽpədəs èstəméysh(iy)ow/. In Saxon law, the estimation or value of the head, that is, the price or value of a man's life.

Caput anni /kǽpəd ǽnay/. The first day (or beginning) of the year.

Caput baroniæ /kǽpət bərówniyiy/. The castle or chief seat of a baron.

Caput jejunii /kǽpət jəjúwniyay/. The beginning of the Lent fast, *i.e.,* Ash Wednesday.

Caput loci /kǽpət lówsay/. The head or upper part of a place.

Caput lupinum /kǽpət lúwpənəm/. In old English law, a wolf's head. An outlawed felon was said to be *caput lupinum,* and might be knocked on the head like a wolf. 4 Bl.Comm. 284, 320.

Caput mortuum /kǽpət mórchuwəm/. A dead head; dead; obsolete.

Caput portus /kǽpət pórdəs/. In old English law, the head of a port. The town to which a port belongs, and which gives the denomination to the port, and is the head of it.

Caput, principium, et finis /kǽpət, prinsípiyəm, èt fáynəs/. The head, beginning, and end. A term applied in English law to the king, as head of parliament. 1 Bl.Comm. 188.

In civil law, it signified a person's civil condition or status, and among the Romans, consisted of three component parts or elements,—*libertas,* liberty; *civitas,* citizenship; and *familia,* family.

Caputagium /kæpətéyj(iy)əm/. In old English law, head or poll money, or the payment of it.

Caputium /kəpyúwsh(iy)əm/. In old English law, a head of land; a headland.

Carat /kǽrət/. A measure of weight for diamonds and other precious stones, equivalent to three and one-sixth grains Troy, though divided by jewelers into four parts called "diamond grains." Also a standard of fineness of gold, twenty-four carats being conventionally taken as expressing absolute purity, and the proportion of gold to alloy in a mixture being represented as so many carats.

Carcan /kárkən/. In French law, an instrument of punishment, somewhat resembling a pillory. It sometimes signifies the punishment itself.

Carcanum /karkéynəm/. A gaol; a prison.

Carcare /karkériy/. In old English law, to load; to load a vessel; to freight.

Carcatus /karkéydəs/. Loaded; freighted, as a ship.

Carcelage /kársələj/. Gaol-dues; prison-fees.

Carcer /kársər/. A prison or gaol. Strictly, a place of detention and safe-keeping, and not of punishment.

Carcer ad homines custodiendos, non ad puniendos, dari debet /kársər ǽd hóməniyz kəstòwdiyéndows, nòn ǽd pyúwniyéndows, déray débət/. A prison should be used for keeping persons, not for punishing them.

Carcer non supplicii causa sed custodiæ constitutus /kársər nòn səplísiyay kóza sèd kəstówdiyiy konstətyúwdəs/. A prison is ordained not for the sake of punishment, but of detention and guarding.

Cardholder. A member of a group such as a union wherein the card is the symbol of membership.

Care. Watchful attention; concern; custody; diligence; discretion; caution; opposite of negligence or carelessness; prudence; regard; preservation; security; support; vigilance. To be concerned with, and to attend to, the needs of oneself or another.

In the law of negligence, the amount of care demanded by the standard of reasonable conduct must be in proportion to the apparent risk. As the danger becomes greater, the actor is required to exercise caution commensurate with it. Foy v. Friedman, 280 F.2d 724.

There are three degrees of care which are frequently recognized, corresponding (inversely) to the three degrees of negligence, viz.: slight care, ordinary care, and great care. This division into three degrees of care, however, does not command universal assent.

Slight care is such as persons of ordinary prudence usually exercise about their own affairs of slight importance. Or it is that degree of care which a person exercises about his own concerns, though he may be a person of less than common prudence or of careless and inattentive disposition.

Ordinary care is that degree of care which persons of ordinary care and prudence are accustomed to use and employ, under the same or similar circumstances. Or it is that degree of care which may reasonably be expected from a person in the party's situation, that is, reasonable care. See also **Ordinary.**

Reasonable care is such a degree of care, precaution, or diligence as may fairly and properly be expected or required, having regard to the nature of the action, or of the subject-matter, and the circumstances surrounding the transaction. It is such care as an ordinarily prudent person would exercise under the conditions existing at the time he is called upon to act. Substantially synonymous with ordinary or due care.

Great care is such as persons of ordinary prudence usually exercise about affairs of their own which are of great importance; or it is that degree of care usually bestowed upon the matter in hand by the most competent, prudent, and careful persons having to do with the particular subject.

A high degree of care is not the legal equivalent of reasonable care. It is that degree of care which a very cautious, careful, and prudent person would exercise under the same or similar circumstances; a degree of care commensurate with the risk of danger.

Highest degree of care and utmost degree of care have substantially the same meaning. "Highest degree of care" only requires the care and skill exacted of persons engaged in the same or similar business. It means the highest degree required by law where human safety is at stake, and the highest degree known to the usage and practice of very careful, skillful, and diligent persons engaged in the same business by similar means or agencies.

See also **Diligence; Due care; Support.**

Careless. Absence of care; negligent; reckless.

Carena /kəríynə/. A term used in the old ecclesiastical law to denote a period of forty days.

Carence /kàróns/. In French law, lack of assets; insolvency.

Careta (spelled, also, *Carreta* and *Carecta*) /kəríydə/. A cart; a cart-load.

Caretorius /kæ̀rətóriyəs/ or **carectarius** /kæ̀rəktériyəs/. A carter.

Carga /kárgə/. In Spanish law, an incumbrance; a charge.

Cargaison /kàrgeyzó(w)n/. In French commercial law, cargo; lading.

Cargare /kargériy/. In old English law, to charge.

Cargo. The load (*i.e.* freight) of a vessel, train, truck, airplane or other carrier. See **Freight.**

Cariagium /kæ̀riyéyjiyəm/. In old English law, carriage; the carrying of goods or other things for the king.

Caristia /kərístiyə/kəríshchə/. Dearth, scarcity, dearness.

Cark. In old English law, a quantity of wool, whereof thirty made a sarplar. (The latter is equal to 2,240 pounds in weight).

Carlisle tables. Life and annuity tables, compiled at Carlisle, England, about 1780. Used by actuaries, etc.

Carload. The quantity usually contained in an ordinary freight car used for transporting the particular commodity involved. A commercial unit which by commercial usage is a single whole for purposes of sale and division. U.C.C. § 2–105(6).

Carmack Act. Amendment to Interstate Commerce Act prescribing liability of carrier for loss, damage, or injury to property carried in interstate commerce.

Carmen /kármən/. In the Roman law, literally, a verse or song. A formula or form of words used on various occasions, as of divorce.

Car mile. Movement of loaded freight car one mile.

Carnal /kárnəl/. Pertaining to the body, its passions and its appetites; animal; fleshly; sensual; impure; sexual. People v. Battilana, 52 Cal.App.2d 685, 126 P.2d 923, 928.

Carnal abuse. An act of debauchery of the female sexual organs by those of the male which does not amount to penetration; the offense commonly called statutory rape consists of carnal abuse. An injury to the genital organs in an attempt at carnal knowledge, falling short of actual penetration. Carnal knowledge of a female child of tender age includes abuse. Carnal abuse and "carnal knowledge" are synonymous in many statutes. See also **Carnal knowledge.**

Carnaliter /karnéylədər/. In old criminal law, carnally. *Carnaliter cognovit*, carnally knew. Technical words in indictments for rape; formerly held to be essential.

Carnal knowledge. Coitus; copulation; the act of a man having sexual bodily connections with a woman; sexual intercourse. Carnal knowledge of a child is unlawful sexual intercourse with a female child under the age of consent. It is a statutory crime, usually a felony. Such offense is popularly known as "statutory rape". See **Rape.**

While penetration is an essential element, there is "carnal knowledge" if there is the slightest penetration of the sexual organ of the female by the sexual organ of the male. Martinez v. People, 160 Colo. 534, 422 P.2d 44. It is not necessary that the vagina be entered or that the hymen be ruptured; the entering of the vulva or labia is sufficient. De Armond v. State, Okl.Cr., 285 P.2d 236.

Carriage. Transportation of goods, freight or passengers.

Carriage of Goods by Sea Act. Federal act governing the most important of the rights, responsibilities, liabilities and immunities arising out of the relation of issuer to holder of the ocean bill of lading, with respect to loss or damage of goods. 46 U.S.C.A. § 1300 et seq.

Carrier. Individual or organization engaged in transporting passengers or goods for hire.

"Carrier" means any person engaged in the transportation of passengers or property by land, as a common, contract, or private carrier, or freight forwarder as those terms are used in the Interstate Commerce Act, and officers, agents and employees of such carriers. 18 U.S.C.A. § 831.

See also **Certified carriers; Connecting carrier; Contract carrier.**

Common carrier. Common carriers are those that hold themselves out or undertake to carry persons or goods of all persons indifferently, or of all who choose to employ it. Merchants Parcel Delivery v. Pennsylvania Public Utility Commission, 150 Pa.Super. 120, 28 A.2d 340, 344. Those whose occupation or business is transportation of persons or things for hire or reward. Common carriers of passengers are those that undertake to carry all persons indifferently who may apply for passage, so long as there is room, and there is no legal excuse for refusal.

Private carrier. Private carriers are those who transport only in particular instances and only for those they choose to contract with.

Carrier's lien. The right to hold the consignee's cargo until payment is made for the work of transporting it.

Carroll doctrine. Rule of law to effect that existing licensee has standing to contest the grant of a competitive license because economic injury to an existing station becomes important when on the facts it spells diminution or destruction of service. Carroll Broadcasting Co. v. F. C. C., 103 U.S.App.D.C. 346, 258 F.2d 440.

Carry. To bear, bear about, sustain, transport, remove, or convey. To have or bear upon or about one's person, as a watch or weapon; locomotion not being essential. As applied to insurance, means "possess" or "hold."

Carry a member. To pay the assessments against a sick or indigent member, as of a beneficial association, the payment being made by the other members or the local lodge or camp on his behalf.

Carry an election. For a candidate to be elected, or a measure carried, at an election, he or it must receive a majority or a plurality of the legal votes cast.

Carry arms or weapons. To wear, bear, or carry them upon the person or in the clothing or in a pocket, for the purpose of use, or for the purpose of being armed and ready for offensive or defensive action in case of a conflict with another person.

Carry-back. Provision in tax law which permits taxpayer to apply net operating loss in one year to recomputation of tax of several preceding taxable years. I.R.C. § 172(b).

Carry costs. A verdict is said to carry costs when the party for whom the verdict is given becomes entitled to the payment of his costs as incident to such verdict.

Carrying away. The act of removal or asportation, by which the crime of larceny is completed, and which is essential to constitute it.

Carrying charge. Charge made by creditor, in addition to interest, for carrying installment credit. Under consumer credit protection statutes, full disclosure of all such service charges is required.

Carrying concealed weapon. Criminal offense in most all jurisdictions; though concealment is not universally an element of the crime.

Carry on trade or business. To conduct, prosecute or continue a particular avocation or business as a continuous operation or permanent occupation. The repetition of acts may be sufficient. To hold one's self out to others as engaged in the selling of goods or services. Helvering v. Highland, C.C.A.4, 124 F.2d 556, 561.

Term which has multiple meanings depending on the context, but it is commonly used in connection with the degree of activity of a foreign corporation in a given state and the consequent right of that state to regulate such enterprise and the exposure of such foreign corporation to suit within that state. In this connection, so called "long arm" statutes define what constitutes carrying on business.

Carry-over. Net operating loss for one year, which may be carried over to each of the several taxable years following the taxable year of such loss. I.R.C. § 172(b).

Carry passengers for a consideration. Transportation of persons under such conditions that operator owes them duty of carrier for hire.

Carry stock. To provide funds or credit for its payment for the period agreed upon from the date of purchase.

Carry the iron. See *Fire ordeal* under the title **Ordeal**.

Carta /kárdə/. In old English law, a charter, or deed. Any written instrument.

In Spanish law, a letter; a deed; a power of attorney.

Carta mercatoria /kárdə mərkətóriyə/. A grant (1303) to certain foreign merchants, in return for custom duties, of freedom to deal wholesale in all cities and towns of England, power to export their merchandise, and liberty to dwell where they pleased, together with other rights pertaining to speedy justice.

Cart bote /kárt bòwt/. In old English law, wood or timber which a tenant is allowed by law to take from an estate, for the purpose of repairing instruments (including necessary vehicles), of husbandry. 2 Bl. Comm. 35. See **Bote**.

Carte. In French marine law, a chart.

Carte blanche /kàrt blónsh/. A white sheet of paper; an instrument signed, but otherwise left blank. A sheet given to an agent, with the principal's signature appended, to be filled up with any contract or engagement as the agent may see fit. Term is commonly used to mean unlimited authority; full discretionary power.

Cartel /kartél/. A combination of producers of any product joined together to control its production, sale, and price, and to obtain a monopoly in any particular industry or commodity. Such exist primarily in Europe, being restricted in United States by antitrust laws. Also, an association by agreement of companies or sections of companies having common interests, designed to prevent extreme or unfair competition and allocate markets, and to promote the interchange of knowledge resulting from scientific and technical research, exchange of patent rights, and standardization of products.

An agreement between two hostile powers for the delivery of prisoners or deserters, or authorizing certain non-hostile intercourse between each other which would otherwise be prevented by the state of war; for example, agreements for intercommunication by post, telegraph, telephone, railway.

Car trust certificates, or **securities.** A class of investment securities based upon the conditional sale or hire of railroad cars or locomotives with a reservation of title or lien in the vendor or bailor until the property is paid for. See also **Equipment trust.**

Cartulary /kárchələry/. A place where papers or records are kept.

Carucage /kǽrəkəj/. In old English law, a kind of tax or tribute anciently imposed upon every plow (*carue* or plow-land) for the public service.

Carucata, carucate /kærəkéydə/kǽrəkeyt/. In old English law, a certain quantity of land used as the basis for taxation. A cartload. As much land as may be tilled by a single plow in a year and a day. A plow land of one hundred acres.

Carucatarius /kǽrəkətériyəs/. One who held lands in *carvage*, or plow-tenure.

Carue /kǽruw/. A carve of land; plow-land.

Carvage. The same as carucage (*q.v.*).

Carve. In old English law, a carucate or plow-land.

Ca. Sa. An abbreviation of *capias ad satisfaciendum*.

Casata /kəséydə/. In old English law, a house with land sufficient for the support of one family. Otherwise called *"hida,"* a hide of land, and *"familia."*

Casatus /kæzéydəs/. A vassal or feudal tenant possessing a *casata;* that is, having a house, household, and property of his own.

Case. A general term for an action, cause, suit, or controversy, at law or in equity; a question contested before a court of justice; an aggregate of facts which furnishes occasion for the exercise of the jurisdiction of a court of justice. A judicial proceeding for the determination of a controversy between parties wherein rights are enforced or protected, or wrongs are prevented or redressed; any proceeding judicial in its nature.

Criminal act requiring investigation by police. Disease or injury requiring treatment by physician.

Surveillance or inspection of residence, business, etc. by potential burglar or robber.

The word "case" may include applications for divorce, applications for the establishment of highways, applications for orders of support of relatives, and other special proceedings unknown to the common law. S. D. Warren Co. v. Fritz, 138 Me. 279, 25 A.2d 645, 648.

In ordinary usage, the word "case" means "event", "happening", "situation", "circumstances".

A statement of facts involved in a transaction or series of transactions, drawn up in writing in a technical form, for submission to a court or judge for decision or opinion. See below *Case agreed on; Case on appeal; Case reserved; Case stated.*

See also **Cause of action.**

Case agreed on. A formal written enumeration of the facts in a case, assented to by both parties as correct and complete, and submitted to the court by their agreement, in order that decision may be rendered without a trial, upon the court's conclusions of law upon the facts as stated. For agreed case, or case stated, parties must agree on all material ultimate facts on which their rights are to be determined by law.

Case made. See *Case reserved, infra.*

Case of actual controversy. The phrase in Federal Declaratory Judgment Act connotes controversy of justiciable nature, excluding advisory decree on hypothetical facts. John P. Agnew & Co., Inc. v. Hoage, 69 App.D.C. 116, 99 F.2d 349, 351. See *Cases and controversies,* below.

Case on appeal. Status of case after it leaves trial court for appellate review and is on appellate docket.

Case reserved. A statement in writing of the facts proved on the trial of a cause, drawn up and settled by the attorneys and counsel for the respective parties under the supervision of the judge, for the purpose of having certain points of law, which arose at the trial and could not then be satisfactorily decided, determined upon full argument before the court *in banc.* This is otherwise called a "special case"; and it is usual for the parties, where the law of the case is doubtful, to agree that the jury shall find a general verdict for the plaintiff, subject to the opinion of the court upon such a case to be made, instead of obtaining from the jury a special verdict.

Cases and controversies. This term, as used in the Constitution of the United States, embraces claims or contentions of litigants brought before the court for adjudication by regular proceedings established for the protection or enforcement of rights, or the prevention, redress, or punishment of wrongs; and whenever the claim or contention of a party takes such a form that the judicial power is capable of acting upon it, it has become a case or controversy. Interstate Commerce Com'n v. Brimson, 154 U.S. 447, 14 S.Ct. 1125, 38 L.Ed. 1047. The federal courts will only consider questions which arise in a "case or controversy"; i.e., only justiciable cases. Art. III, Sec. 2, U.S.Const. The case or controversy must be definite and concrete, touching the legal relations of parties having adverse interests. The questions involved must not be moot or academic, nor will the courts consider collusive actions. Aetna Life Ins. Co. v. Haworth, 300 U.S. 229, 240, 241, 57 S.Ct. 461, 464, 81 L.Ed. 617. See also **Ripeness doctrine; Standing to sue doctrine.**

Case stated. See *"Case agreed on"*, above.

Case sufficient to go to a jury. A case that has proceeded upon sufficient proof to that stage where it must be submitted to jury and not decided against the state as a matter of law. State v. McDonough, 129 Conn. 483, 29 A.2d 582, 584.

Form of action. That category into which a case falls such as contract or tort, though under Rules of Civil Procedure, all actions are "civil" actions. Fed.R. Civil P. 2.

Case in chief. That part of a trial in which the party with the initial burden of proof presents his evidence after which he rests.

Case law. The aggregate of reported cases as forming a body of jurisprudence, or the law of a particular subject as evidenced or formed by the adjudged cases, in distinction to statutes and other sources of law. See **Common law.**

Case system. A method of teaching or studying the science of the law by a study of the cases historically, or by the inductive method. It was introduced in the Law School of Harvard University in 1869–70 by Christopher C. Langdell, Dane Professor of Law.

Caseworker. Generally, a social worker whose clients are called cases and whose work is mainly in the field.

Cas fortuit /ká fortwíy/. Fr. In the law of insurance, a fortuitous event; an inevitable accident.

Cash. Money or the equivalent; usually ready money. Currency and coins, negotiable checks, and balances in bank accounts. That which circulates as money. See **Legal tender; Petty cash.**

Cash account. A record, in bookkeeping, of all cash transactions; an account of moneys received and expended.

Cash bail. Sum of money posted by a criminal defendant to insure his presence in court; used in place of surety bond and real estate. See **Bail.**

Cash basis accounting. That system of accounting which treats as income only that which is actually received and as expense only that which is actually paid out, in contrast to accrual basis which records income when due though not received and expense when incurred though not yet paid.

Cash book. In bookkeeping, an account book in which is kept a record of all cash transactions, or all cash received and expended.

Cash budget. A period-by-period statement of opening cash on hand, expected cash receipts, expected cash disbursements, and resulting expected cash balance at the end of each period.

Cash cycle. The time lapse between purchase of materials and collection of accounts receivable for finished product sold.

Cash discount. A deduction from billed price which seller allows for payment within a certain time; e.g. 10% discount for payment within 10 days.

Cash dividend. That portion of profits and surplus paid to stockholders by a corporation in form of cash. To be contrasted with "stock" dividend.

Cash equivalent doctrine. Generally, a cash basis taxpayer does not report income until cash is constructively or actually received. Under the cash equivalent doctrine, cash basis taxpayers are required to report income even though no cash is actually received in a transaction if the equivalent of cash is received e.g., property is received instead of cash in a taxable transaction.

Cash flow. The cash generated from the property. It is different than net income; cash flow looks to the amount of cash left after all payments are made, whether they are tax deductible or not. Cash receipts minus disbursements from a given asset, or group of assets, for a given period.

Cashier, *v.* To dismiss dishonorably from service.

Cashier, *n.* Executive officer of bank or trust company responsible for banking transactions. One who collects and records payments at store, restaurant, business, or the like.

Cashiered. Dismissal with ignominy or dishonor, or in disgrace.

Cashier's check. A check drawn by the bank upon itself and issued by an authorized officer of a bank, directed to another person evidencing fact that payee is authorized to demand and receive from the bank, upon presentation, the amount of money represented by the check. National Newark and Essex Bank v. Giordano, 111 N.J.Super. 347, 268 A.2d 327, 328. See also **Check.**

Cashlite. An amercement or fine; a mulct.

Cash market value. "Fair market value", "reasonable market value" or "fair cash market value" as synonymous. Housing Authority of Birmingham Dist. v. Title Guarantee Loan & Trust Co., 243 Ala. 157, 8 So.2d 835, 837. For "Fair cash market value", see that title.

Cash note. In England, a bank-note of a provincial bank or of the Bank of England.

Cash position. Degree of liquidity; amount of quick or liquid assets.

Cash price. A price payable in cash at the time of sale of property, in opposition to a barter or a sale on credit.

Cash sale. A sale for money in hand. A sale conditioned on payment concurrent with delivery. Weyerhaeuser Timber Co. v. First Nat. Bank, 150 Or. 172, 43 P.2d 1078, 1081. See **Sale; Time price differential**.

Cash surrender value. The cash surrender value of a life insurance policy is the reserve less a surrender charge. Amount which the insurer will pay upon cancellation of the policy before death. See **Cash value option**.

Cash value. The cash value of an article or piece of property is the price which it would bring at private sale (as distinguished from a forced or auction sale) the terms of sale requiring the payment of the whole price in ready money, with no deferred payments.

Actual value or market value. Fort Worth & D. N. Ry. Co. v. Sugg, Tex.Civ.App., 68 S.W.2d 570, 572. Clear market value or fair market value. Price property will bring on sale by one desiring, but not compelled, to sell to one desiring but not compelled, to purchase. Insurance Co. of North America, v. McCraw, 255 Ky. 839, 75 S.W.2d 518, 520. Saleable value. In re Lang Body Co., C.C.A.Ohio, 92 F.2d 338, 340. Value at which property would be taken in payment of just debt from solvent debtor. Bank of Fairfield v. Spokane County, 173 Wash. 145, 22 P.2d 646, 652.

See also **Actual cash value; Cash surrender value; Fair cash value; Fair market value**.

Cash value option. The right of an owner of life insurance policy to take the cash value of a policy which is a predetermined amount at a given point in time; generally limited to a specified period after default in premium payments.

Cassare. To quash; to render void; to break.

Cassation. In French law, annulling; reversal; breaking the force and validity of a judgment. A decision emanating from the sovereign authority, by which a decree or judgment in the court of last resort is broken or annulled.

Cassation, court of. (Fr. *cour de cassation*.) The highest court in France; so termed from possessing the power to quash *(casser)* the decrees of inferior courts. It is a court of appeal in criminal as well as civil cases.

Cassetur billa /kəsíydər bílə/. (Lat. That the bill be quashed.) The form of the judgment for the defendant on a plea in abatement, where the action was commenced by bill *(billa)*. 3 Bl.Comm. 303. The form of an entry made by a plaintiff on the record, after a plea in abatement, where he found that the plea could not be confessed and avoided, nor traversed nor demurred to; amounting in fact to a discontinuance of the action.

Cassetur breve /kəsíydər bríyviy/. (Lat. That the writ be quashed.) The form of the judgment for the defendant on a plea in abatement, where the action was commenced by original writ *(breve)*. 3 Bl.Comm. 303.

A judgment sometimes entered against a plaintiff at his request when, in consequence of allegations of the defendant, he can no longer prosecute his suit with effect.

Cast. To deposit formerly or officially, as to cast a ballot. The form in which a thing is constructed. To get rid of; to discard.

Cast away. Rejected; thrown away. Cast ashore or adrift, as a shipwrecked person.

Castel, or **castle.** A fortress in a town; the principal mansion of a nobleman.

Castellain /kǽstələn/. In old English law, the lord, owner, or captain of a castle; the constable of a fortified house; a person having the custody of one of the crown mansions; an officer of the forest.

Castellanus /kæstəléynəs/. A castellain; the keeper or constable of a castle.

Castellarium, castellatus /kæstəlériyəm/kæstəléydəs/. In old English law, the precinct or jurisdiction of a castle.

Castellorum operatio /kæstəlórəm opəréysh(iy)ow/. In Saxon and old English law, castle work. Service and labor done by inferior tenants for the building and upholding of castles and public places of defense. One of the three necessary charges *(trinoda necessitas)* to which all lands among the Saxons were expressly subject. Towards this some gave them personal service, and others, a contribution of money or goods. 1 Bl.Comm. 263.

Castigatory. An engine used to punish women who had been convicted of being common scolds. It was sometimes called the trebucket, tumbrel, ducking-stool, or cucking-stool.

Casting vote. Deciding vote cast by presiding officer to break tie. Act of voting by ballot or voting machine.

Castle doctrine. A man's home is his castle and, hence, he may use all manner of force including deadly force to protect it and its inhabitants from attack.

Castleguard. In feudal law, an imposition anciently laid upon such persons as lived within a certain distance of any castle, towards the maintenance of such as watched and warded the castle.

Castleguard rents. In old English law, rents paid by those that dwelt within the precincts of a castle, towards the maintenance of such as watched and warded it.

Castrensis /kæstrénsəs/. In the Roman law, relating to the camp or military service.

Castrense peculium, a portion of property which a son acquired in war, or from his connection with the camp.

Casual /kǽzh(y)uwəl/. Occurring without regularity, occasional; impermanent, as employment for irregular periods.

Happening or coming to pass without design and without being foreseen or expected; unforeseen; uncertain; unpremeditated.

Casual bettor. An occasional and irregular bettor who is not guilty of crime of engaging in betting and gambling organized and carried on as a systematic business. Bamman v. Erickson, 288 N.Y. 133, 41 N.E.2d 920, 922.

Casual deficiency of revenue. An unforeseen or unexpected deficiency, or an insufficiency of funds to meet some unforeseen and necessary expense.

Casual deficit. A deficit happening by chance or accident and without design. State Budget Commission v. Lebus, 244 Ky. 700, 51 S.W.2d 965.

Casual ejector. The nominal defendant in an action of ejectment.

Casual employment. Employment at uncertain or irregular times. Employment for short time and limited and temporary purpose. Occasional, irregular or incidental employment. Such employee does not normally receive seniority rights nor does he normally receive fringe benefits. By statute in many states, such employment may or may not be subject to worker's compensation at the election of the employer. The test is the nature of the work or the scope of the contract of employment or the continuity of employment.

Casual sale. A sale which is not made customarily or in the regular course of business; an occasional sale.

Casualty /kǽzh(y)uwəltiy/. A serious or fatal accident. A person or thing injured, lost or destroyed. A disastrous occurrence due to sudden, unexpected or unusual cause. Accident; misfortune or mishap; that which comes by chance or without design. A loss from such an event or cause; as by fire, shipwreck, lightning, etc. See also **Accident; Loss; Unavoidable casualty.**

Casualty insurance. See **Insurance**.

Casualty loss. A casualty is defined for tax purposes as "the complete or partial destruction of property resulting from an identifiable event of a sudden, unexpected or unusual nature"; *e.g.,* floods, storms, fires, auto accidents. Individuals may deduct a casualty loss only if the loss is incurred in a trade or business; in a transaction entered into for profit; or is a loss arising from fire, storm, shipwreck, or other casualty losses as itemized deductions subject to a specified nondeductible amount. Special rules are provided for the netting of casualty gains or losses.

Casu consimili /kéys(y)uw kənsíməlay/. In old English law, a writ of entry, granted where tenant by the curtesy, or tenant for life, alienated in fee, or in tail, or for another's life, which was brought by him in reversion against the party to whom such tenant so alienated to his prejudice, and in the tenant's lifetime. See **Consimili casu.**

Casu proviso /kéys(y)uw prəváyzow/. Lat. In the case provided for. A writ of entry framed under the provisions of the statute of Gloucester (6 Edw. I) c. 7, which lay for the benefit of the reversioner when a tenant in dower aliened in fee or for life.

Casus /kéysəs/. Lat. Chance; accident; an event; a case; a case contemplated.

Casus belli /kéysəs bélay/. An occurrence giving rise to or justifying war.

Casus fœderis /kéysəs fíydərəs, °fédərəs/. In international law, the case of the treaty. The particular event or situation contemplated by the treaty, or stipulated for, or which comes within its terms. In commercial law, the case or event contemplated by the parties to an individual contract or stipulated for by it, or coming within its terms.

Casus fortuitus /kéysəs forchúwədəs/. An inevitable accident, a chance occurrence, or fortuitous event. A loss happening in spite of all human effort and sagacity.

Casus fortuitus non est sperandus, et nemo tenetur devinare /kéysəs forchúwədəs nón est spərǽndəs, èt níymow təníydər dèvənériy/. A fortuitous event is not to be expected, and no one is bound to foresee it.

Casus fortuitus non est supponendus /kéysəs forchúwədəs nón est sə̀pənéndəs/. A fortuitous event is not to be presumed.

Casus major /kéysəs méyjər/. In the civil law, a casualty; an extraordinary casualty, as fire, shipwreck, etc.

Casus omissus /kéysəs əmísəs/. A case omitted; an event or contingency for which no provision is made; particularly a case not provided for by the statute on the general subject, and which is therefore left to be governed by the common law.

Casus omissus et oblivioni datus dispositioni juris communis relinquitur /kéysəs əmísəs èd əblíviyównay déydəs dìspəzishiyównay júrəs kəmyúwnəs rəlíŋkwədər/. A case omitted and given to oblivion (forgotten) is left to the disposal of the common law. A particular case, left unprovided for by statute, must be disposed of according to the law as it existed prior to such statute.

Casus omissus pro omisso habendus est /kéysəs əmísəs pròw əmísow həbéndəs ést/. A case omitted is to be held as (intentionally) omitted.

Cat. An instrument with which criminals are flogged. It consists of nine lashes of whipcord, tied to a wooden handle, and is frequently called cat-o-nine-tails. It is used where the whipping-post is retained as a mode of punishment and was formerly resorted to in the navy.

Catalepsy. Generalized condition of diminished responsiveness usually characterized by trance-like states; may occur in organic or psychological disorders or under hypnosis.

Catalla /kətǽlə/. In old English law, chattels. The word among the Normans primarily signified only beasts of husbandry, or, as they are still called, "cattle," but, in a secondary sense, the term was applied to all movables in general, and not only to these, but to whatever was not a fief or feud.

Catalla juste possessa amitti non possunt /kətǽlə jə́stiy pəzésə èymíday nòn pósənt/. Chattels justly possessed cannot be lost.

Catalla otiosa /kətǽlə òwshiyówsə/. Dead goods or chattels as distinguished from animals. Idle cattle, that is, such as were not used for working, as distinguished from beasts of the plow; called also *animalia otiosa.*

Catalla reputantur inter minima in lege /kətǽlə rep-yuwtǽntər íntər mínəmə in líyjiy/. Chattels are considered in law among the least (or minor) things.

Catallis captis nomine districtionis /kətǽləs kǽptəs nóməniy dəstrìkshiyównəs/. An obsolete writ that lay where a house was within a borough, for rent issuing out of the same, and which warranted the taking of doors, windows, etc., by way of distress.

Catallis reddendis /kætǽləs rədéndəs/. For the return of the chattels; an obsolete writ that lay where goods delivered to a man to keep till a certain day were not upon demand redelivered at the day.

Catallum /kətǽləm/. A chattel. Most frequently used in the plural form, *catalla (q.v.)*.

Catals /kǽdəlz/. Goods and chattels. See **Catalla**.

Cataneus /kətéyniyəs/. A tenant *in capite*. A tenant holding immediately of the crown.

Catascopus /kətǽskəpəs/. An old name for an archdeacon.

Catastrophe /kətǽstrəfiy/. A notable disaster; a more serious calamity than might ordinarily be understood from the term "casualty." Utter or complete failure.

Catatonic. A state found in some forms of schizophrenia, in which energy seems maintained either at a very high or very low level; changes in muscle tone allow subject to display the ability to maintain for hours either a fixed statuesque pose or a waxy flexibility of the limbs; during catatonic excitement, subject exhibits wild, blind, apparently purposeless overactivity; in catatonic stupor, subject fails to respond to, or pay attention to, external stimuli. There may be homicidal tendencies during alternating periods of excitability and stupor.

Catching bargain. See **Bargain**.

Catchings. Things caught (*e.g.* fish), and in the possession, custody, power, and dominion of the party, with a present capacity to use them for his own purposes.

Catchpoll. A name formerly given to a sheriff's deputy, or to a constable, or other officer whose duty it is to arrest persons. He was a sort of serjeant. The word is no longer in use as an official designation.

Catch time charter. One under which compensation is paid for the time the boat is actually used. Schoonmaker-Conners Co. v. New York Cent. R. Co., D.C. N.Y., 12 F.2d 314, 315.

Cater cousin. (From Fr. *Quatrecousin*.) A cousin in the fourth degree; hence any distant or remote relative.

Cathedral. In English ecclesiastical law, a tract set apart for the service of the church. The church of the bishop of the diocese, in which is his *cathedra*, or throne, and his special jurisdiction; in that respect the principal church of the diocese.

Cathedral preferments. In English ecclesiastical law, all deaneries, archdeaconries, and canonries, and generally all dignities and offices in any cathedral or collegiate church, below the rank of a bishop.

Cathedratic /kæθədrǽdək/. In English ecclesiastical law, a sum of 2*s.* paid to the bishop by the inferior clergy; but from its being usually paid at the bishop's *synod*, or visitation, it is commonly named *synodals*.

Catholic Emancipation Act. The statute of 10 Geo. IV, *c.* 7, by which Roman Catholics were restored, in general, to the full enjoyment of all civil rights, except that of holding ecclesiastical offices, and certain high appointments in the state.

Catoniana regula /kætòwniyéynə régyələ/. In Roman law, the rule which is commonly expressed in the maxim, *Quod ab initio non valet tractu temporis non convalebit*, meaning that what is at the beginning void by reason of some technical (or other) legal defect will not become valid merely by length of time. The rule applied to the institution of *hæredes*, the bequest of legacies, and such like. The rule is not without its application also in English law; *e.g.*, a married woman's will (being void when made) is not made valid merely because she lives to become a widow.

Cats and dogs. Colloquial expression for highly speculative securities.

Cattle gate. In old English law, a customary proportionate right of pasture enjoyed in common with others. A right to pasture cattle in the land of another. It was a distinct and several interest in the land, passing by lease and release.

Cattle rustling. Stealing of cattle.

CATV. Community Antenna Television Systems.

Caucasian /kokéyzhən/. Of or pertaining to the white race.

Caucus /kókəs/. A meeting of the legal voters of any political party assembled for the purpose of choosing delegates or for the nomination of candidates for office.

Cauda terræ /kódə tériy/. A land's end, or the bottom of a ridge in arable land.

Caursines /k(ə)rsənz/. Italian merchants who came into England in the reign of Henry III, where they established themselves as money lenders, but were soon expelled for their usury and extortion.

Causa /kózə/kówzə/. Lat. A cause, reason, occasion, motive, or inducement. As used with the force of a preposition, it means by virtue of, on account of, in contemplation of; *e.g. causa mortis*, in anticipation of death. A condition; a consideration; motive for performing a juristic act.

In the Civil and old English law the word signified a source, ground, or mode of acquiring property; hence a title; one's title to property. Thus, "*titulus est justa causa possidendi id quod nostrum est;*" title is the lawful ground of possessing that which is ours. Also a cause; a suit or action pending; *e.g. Causa testamentaria*, a testamentary cause. *Causa matrimonialis*, a matrimonial cause.

See also **Cause; cause of action**.

Causa causæ est causa causati /kózə kóziy èst kózə kozéyday/. The cause of a cause is the cause of the thing caused. The cause of the cause is to be considered as the cause of the effect also.

Causa causans /kózə kózænz/. The immediate cause; the last link in the chain of causation.

Causa causantis, causa est causati /kózə kozǽntəs, kózə èst kozéyday/. The cause of the thing causing is the cause of the effect.

Causa data et non secuta /kózə déydə èt nòn səkyúwdə/. In the civil law, consideration given and not followed, that is, by the event upon which it was given. The name of an action by which a thing given in the view of a certain event was reclaimed if that event did not take place.

Causa ecclesiæ publicis æquiparatur; et summa est ratio quæ pro religione facit /kózə əklíyziyiy pə́bləsəs èkwəpəréydər; èt sə́mə èst réysh(iy)ow kwìy prów rəlìjiyówniy féysət/. The cause of the church is equal to public cause; and paramount is the reason which makes for religion.

Causæ dotis, vitæ, libertatis, fisci sunt inter favorabilia in lege /kóziy dówdəs, váydiy, libərtéydəs, fískay sànt íntər féyvərəbíliyə ìn líyjiy/. Causes of dower, life, liberty, revenue, are among the things favored in law.

Causa et origo est materia negotii /kózə èd órəgow èst mətíriyə nəgówshiyay/. The cause and origin is the substance of the thing, the cause and origin of a thing are a material part of it. The law regards the original act.

Causa hospitandi /kózə hòspətǽnday/. For the purpose of being entertained as a guest.

Causa jactitationis maritagii /kózə jæktèyshiyównəs mærətéyjiyay/. A form of action which anciently lay against a party who boasted or gave out that he or she was married to the plaintiff, whereby a common reputation of their marriage might ensue. 3 Bl. Comm. 93. See **Jactitation** (*Jactitation of marriage*).

Causa list /kózə list/. See **Cause list.**

Causal relation. See **Proximate cause.**

Causa matrimonii prælocuti /kózə mætrəmówniyay prìyləkyúwday/. A writ lying where a woman has given lands to a man in fee-simple with the intention that he shall marry her, and he refuses so to do within a reasonable time, upon suitable request. Now obsolete. 3 Bl.Comm. 183.

Causam nobis significes quare /kózəm nówbəs signífəsiyz kwériy/. A writ addressed to a mayor of a town, etc., who was by the king's writ commanded to give seisin of lands to the king's grantee, on his delaying to do it, requiring him to show cause why he so delayed the performance of his duty.

Causa mortis /kózə mórdəs/. In contemplation of approaching death.

Causa mortis donatio /kózə mórdəs dənéysh(iy)ow/. See **Donatio mortis causa.**

Causa patet /kózə pǽdət/°péydət/. The reason is open, obvious, plain, clear, or manifest. A common expression in old writers.

Causa proxima /kózə próksəmə/. The immediate, nearest, or latest cause. The efficient cause; the one that necessarily sets the other causes in operation. Insurance Co. v. Boon, 95 U.S. 117, 130, 24 L.Ed. 395. See **Proximate cause.**

Causa proxima non remota spectatur /kózə próksəmə non rəmówdə spektéydər/. An efficient adequate cause being found, it must be considered the true cause unless some other independent cause is shown to have intervened between it and the result. The immediate (or direct), not the remote, cause, is looked at, or considered. For a distinction, however, between immediate and proximate cause, see **Cause; Proximate cause.**

Causare /kozériy/. In the civil and old English law, to be engaged in a suit; to litigate; to conduct a cause.

Causa rei /kózə ríyay/. In the civil law, things accessory or appurtenant. The accessions, appurtenances, or fruits of a thing; comprehending all that the claimant of a principal thing can demand from a defendant in addition thereto, and especially what he would have had, if the thing had not been withheld from him.

Causa remota /kózə rəmówdə/. A remote or mediate cause; a cause operating indirectly by the intervention of other causes.

Causa sine qua non /kózə sáyniy kwèy nón/. A necessary or inevitable cause; a cause without which the effect in question could not have happened. Hayes v. Railroad Co., 111 U.S. 228, 4 S.Ct. 369, 28 L.Ed. 410. A cause without which the thing cannot be. With reference to negligence, it is the cause without which the injury would not have occurred. See **Proximate cause.**

Causation. The fact of being the cause of something produced or of happening. The act by which an effect is produced. An important doctrine in fields of negligence and criminal law.

Causator /kozéydər/. A litigant; one who takes the part of the plaintiff or defendant in an action.

In old European law, one who manages or litigates another's cause.

Causa turpis /kózə tə́rpəs/. A base (immoral or illegal) cause or consideration.

Causa vaga et incerta non est causa rationabilis /kózə véygə èd ənsə́rdə nón est kózə ræsh(iy)ənéybələs/. A vague and uncertain cause is not a reasonable cause.

Cause, v. To be the cause or occasion of; to effect as an agent; to bring about; to bring into existence; to make to induce; to compel.

Cause, n. (Lat. *causa.*) Each separate antecedent of an event. Something that precedes and brings about an effect or a result. A reason for an action or condition. A ground of a legal action. An agent that brings something about. That which in some manner is accountable for condition that brings about an effect or that produces a cause for the resultant action or state. State v. Fabritz, 276 Md. 416, 348 A.2d 275, 280.

A suit, litigation, or action. Any question, civil or criminal, litigated or contested before a court of justice. See **Cause of action.**

See also **Causa; Causation; Concurrent causes; Contributing cause; Efficient cause; Efficient intervening cause; Good cause; Immediate cause; Intervening act; Intervening agency; Intervening cause; Legal cause; Natural and probable consequences; Negligence** *(Contributory negligence);* **Probable cause; Procuring cause; Producing cause; Proximate cause; Remote cause; Sole cause; Sufficient cause.**

Direct or immediate cause. See **Proximate cause.**

Dismissal for cause. See **For cause.**

Intervening cause. That occurrence which comes between the initial force or occurrence and the ultimate effect.

Superseding cause. That occurrence or force which not only intervenes, but which also breaks the chain of causation between the initial occurrence and the ultimate effect so as to render the initial force or occurrence causatively harmless.

See also **Concurrent causes; Efficient cause; Probable cause; Proximate cause.**

Cause in fact. That particular cause which produces an event and without which the event would not have occurred. Medallion Stores, Inc. v. Eidt, Tex.Civ. App., 405 S.W.2d 417, 422. See **Proximate cause.**

Cause list. In English practice, a printed roll of actions, to be tried in the order of their entry, with the names of the solicitors for each litigant. Similar to the calendar of causes, or docket, used in American courts.

Cause of action. The fact or facts which give a person a right to judicial relief. The legal effect of an occurrence in terms of redress to a party to the occurrence. A situation or state of facts which would entitle party to sustain action and give him right to seek a judicial remedy in his behalf. Thompson v. Zurich Ins. Co., D.C.Minn., 309 F.Supp. 1178, 1181. Fact, or a state of facts, to which law sought to be enforced against a person or thing applies. Facts which give rise to one or more relations of right-duty between two or more persons. Failure to perform legal obligation to do, or refrain from performance of, some act. Matter for which action may be maintained. Unlawful violation or invasion of right. The right which a party has to institute a judicial proceeding. See also Case; Claim; Failure to state cause of action; Justiciable controversy; Severance of actions; Splitting cause of action; Suit.

Cause of injury. That which actually produces it.

Causes célèbres /kówz səléb(rə)/. Celebrated cases. A work containing reports of the decisions of interest and importance in French courts in the seventeenth and eighteenth centuries. Secondarily, a single trial or decision is sometimes called a *"cause célèbre,"* when it is remarkable on account of the parties involved or the unusual, interesting, or sensational character of the facts.

Cause suit to be brought. Commence or begin. See Cause; Concurrent causes; Efficient cause; Probable cause; Proximate cause.

Causeway. A raised roadbed through low lands or across wet ground or water.

Causidicus /kòsídəkəs/. In the civil law, a speaker or pleader; one who argued a cause *ore tenus.* See **Advocate.**

Cautela /kódələ/. Lat. Care; caution; vigilance; prevision.

Cautio /kósh(iy)ow/. In the civil and French law, security given for the performance of any thing; bail; a bond or undertaking by way of surety. Also the person who becomes a surety.

Cautio fidejussoria /kósh(iy)ow fàydiyjəsóriyə/. Security by means of bonds or pledges entered into by third parties.

Cautio muciana /kósh(iy)ow myuwshiyéynə/. Security given by an heir or legatee, to obtain immediate possession of inheritance or legacy, for observance of a condition annexed to the bequest, where the act which is the object of the condition is one which he must avoid committing during his whole life, *e.g.,* that he will never marry, never leave the country, never engage in a particular trade, etc.

Caution. To warn, exhort, to take heed, or give notice of danger.

Cautionary instruction. That part of a judge's charge to a jury in which he instructs them to consider certain evidence only for a specific purpose, *e.g.* evidence that a criminal defendant committed crimes other than the crime for which he is on trial may be admitted to prove a scheme or to show intent as to this crime but not to prove that he committed this particular crime and such evidence requires cautionary instructions. Com. v. Campbell, Mass., 353 N.E.2d 740. Also, instruction by judge to jury to not be influenced by outside forces, or to talk about case to anyone outside of trial.

Cautione admittenda /koshiyówniy ædməténdə/. In English ecclesiastical law, a writ that lies against a bishop who holds an excommunicated person in prison for contempt, notwithstanding he offers sufficient caution or security to obey the orders and commandment of the church for the future.

Cautio pignoratitia /kósh(iy)ow pìgnərətísh(iy)ə/. Security given by pledge, or deposit, as plate, money, or other goods.

Cautio pro expensis /kósh(iy)ow pròw əkspénsəs/. Security for costs, charges, or expenses.

Cautious. Careful; prudent; circumspect; discreet in face of danger or risk.

Cautio usufructuaria /kósh(iy)ow yùwz(h)(y)uwfrəkchuwériyə/. Security, which tenants for life give, to preserve the property rented free from waste and injury.

C.A.V. An abbreviation for *curia advisari vult,* the court will be advised, will consider, will deliberate.

Caveat /kǽviyət/kéyviyət/. Lat. Let him beware. Warning to one to be careful. A formal notice or warning given by a party interested to a court, judge, or ministerial officer against the performance of certain acts within his power and jurisdiction. This process may be used in the proper courts to prevent (temporarily or provisionally) the proving of a will or the grant of administration, or to arrest the enrollment of a decree in chancery when the party intends to take an appeal, to prevent the grant of letters patent, etc.

Used in writing to warn the reader of an interpretation different from the one proposed or advanced.

Caveat actor /kǽviyəd ǽktər/. Let the doer, or actor, beware.

Caveat emptor /kǽviyəd ém(p)tər/kéyviyəd°/. Let the buyer beware. This maxim summarizes the rule that a purchaser must examine, judge, and test for himself. This maxim is more applicable to judicial sales, auctions, and the like, than to sales of consumer goods where strict liability, warranty, and other consumer protection laws protect the consumer-buyer.

Caveat emptor, qui ignorare non debuit quod jus alienum emit /kǽviyəd ém(p)tər, kwày ignərériy nòn débyuwət kwòd jás æliyíynəm émət/. Let a purchaser beware, who ought not to be ignorant that he is purchasing the rights of another. Let a buyer beware; for he ought not to be ignorant of what they are when he buys the rights of another.

Caveator /kæviyéydər/. One who files a caveat.

Caveat to will. A demand that will be produced and probated in open court. An attack on validity of alleged will.

Caveat venditor /kǽviyət véndədər/. Let the seller beware.

Caveat viator /kǽviyət viyéydər/. Let the wayfarer beware. This phrase has been used as a concise expression of the duty of a traveler on the highway to use due care to detect and avoid defects in the way.

Cavendum est a fragmentis /kævéndəm ést èy frəgméntəs/. Beware of fragments.

Cavere /kəvíriy/. Lat. In the civil and common law, to take care; to exercise caution; to take care or provide for; to provide by law; to provide against; to forbid by law; to give security; to give caution or security on arrest.

Cayagium /keyéyjiyəm/. In old English law, cayage or kayage; a toll or duty anciently paid the king for landing goods at a quay or wharf.

C.B. In English reports and legal documents, an abbreviation for common bench. Also an abbreviation for chief baron.

C.B.O.E. Chicago Board of Options Exchange.

C.C. Various terms or phrases may be denoted by this abbreviation; such as circuit court (or city or county court); criminal cases (or crown or civil or chancery cases); civil code; chief commissioner; and *cepi corpus,* I have taken his body.

C.C.; B.B. I have taken his body; bail bond entered. See **Capias** (*Capias ad respondendum).*

C.C.C. Commodity Credit Corporation.

C.C. & C. I have taken his body and he is held.

C.D. Certificate of deposit.

Ceap /chíyp/. In English law, a bargain; anything for sale; a chattel; also cattle, as being the usual medium of barter. Sometimes used instead of ceapgild *(q.v.).*

Ceapgild /chíypgìld/. Payment or forfeiture of an animal. An ancient species of forfeiture.

Cease. To stop; to become extinct; to pass away; to come to an end; to suspend or forfeit. A cessation of activity.

Cease and desist order. An order of an administrative agency or court prohibiting a person or business firm from continuing a particular course of conduct, *e.g.* Fed. Trade Commission may order a business to cease and desist from misbranding or misadvertising its products. F. T. C. v. Mandel Bros., Inc., 359 U.S. 385, 79 S.Ct. 818, 3 L.Ed.2d 893. Ruling issued in an unfair labor practice case requiring the charged party (respondent) to stop the conduct found illegal and take specified affirmative action designed to remedy the unfair labor practice.

Cede. To yield up; to assign; to grant; to surrender; to withdraw. Generally used to designate the transfer of territory from one government to another.

Cedo /síydow/. I grant. The word ordinarily used in Mexican conveyances to pass title to lands.

Cedula /O.En. sédyələ/séjələ/Sp. séyðuwla/. In old English law, a schedule. In Spanish law, an act under private signature, by which a debtor admits the amount of the debt, and binds himself to discharge the same on a specified day or on demand. Also the notice or citation affixed to the door of a fugitive criminal requiring him to appear before the court where the accusation is pending.

Cedule /sədyúwl/. In French law, the technical name of an act under private signature.

Celation /səléyshən/. Concealment of pregnancy or delivery.

Celebration of marriage /seləbréyshən əv mǽrəj/. The formal act by which a man and woman take each other for husband and wife, according to law; the solemnization of a marriage. The term is usually applied to a marriage ceremony attended with ecclesiastical functions; *i.e.* a church wedding.

Celibacy. The condition or state of life of an unmarried person, particularly of one who vows never to marry.

Celler-Kefauver Act. A federal law enacted in 1950 dealing with restrictions on mergers and expanding the Clayton Act of 1914 in this regard.

Cemetery. A graveyard; burial ground. Place or area set apart for interment of the dead. Term includes not only lots for depositing the bodies of the dead, but also avenues, walks, and grounds for shrubbery and ornamental purposes.

Cenegild /kéynəgìld/. In Saxon law, an expiatory mulct or fine paid to the relations of a murdered person by the murderer or his relations.

Cenninga. A notice given by a buyer to a seller that the things which had been sold were claimed by another, in order that he might appear and justify the sale. But the exact significance of this term is somewhat doubtful.

Censaria /sən(t)sériyə/. In old English law, a farm, or house and land let at a standing rent.

Censarii /sən(t)sériyày/. In old English law, farmers, or such persons as were liable to pay a census (tax).

Censere /sen(t)sérey/. In the Roman law, to ordain; to decree.

Censo /sén(t)sow/. In Spanish and Mexican law, an annuity, a ground rent. The right which a person acquires to receive a certain annual pension, for the delivery which he makes to another of a determined sum of money or of an immovable thing.

Censo al quitar /sén(t)sow àl kiytár/. A redeemable annuity; otherwise called "censo redimible."

Censo consignativo /sén(t)sow kənsìgnətíyvow/. A *censo (q.v.)* is called *"consignativo"* when he who receives the money assigns for the payment of the pension (annuity) the estate the fee in which he reserves.

Censo enfiteutico /sén(t)sow ènfiytéwtikow/. In Spanish and Mexican law, an emphyteutic annuity. That species of *censo* (annuity) which exists where there is a right to require of another a certain canon or pension annually, on account of having transferred to that person forever certain real estate, but reserving the fee in the land. The owner who thus transfers the land is called the *"censualisto,"* and the person who pays the annuity is called the *"censatario."*

Censor /sén(t)sər/. One who examines publications, films and the like for objectionable content. Roman officers who acted as census takers, assessors and reviewers of public morals and conduct. Officer of armed forces who reads letters and other communications of servicemen and deletes material considered to be harmful or of a danger to security. See also **Censorship; Prior restraint.**

Censo reservatio /sén(t)sow reysèrvatíyow/. In Spanish and Mexican law, the right to receive from another an annual pension by virtue of having transferred land to him by full and perfect title.

Censorship. Review of publications, movies, plays, and the like for the purpose of prohibiting the publication, distribution, or production of material deemed objectionable as obscene, indecent, or immoral. Such actions are frequently challenged as constituting a denial of freedom of press and speech. Near v. Minnesota, 283 U.S. 697, 716, 51 S.Ct. 625, 75 L.Ed. 1357; Roth v. United States, 354 U.S. 476, 77 S.Ct. 1304, 1 L.Ed.2d 1498; Miller v. California, 413 U.S. 15, 22, 93 S.Ct. 2607, 37 L.Ed.2d 419. See also **Obscenity; Prior restraint.**

Censuales /sensyuwéyliyz/. In old European law, a species of oblati or voluntary slaves of churches or monasteries; those who, to procure the protection of the church, bound themselves to pay an annual tax or quit-rent only of their estates to a church or monastery.

Censuere /sènsyuwíriy/. In Roman law, they have decreed. The term of art, or technical term for the judgment, resolution, or decree of the senate.

Censumethidus /sèn(t)səméθədəs/ or **censumorthidus** /sèn(t)səmórθədəs/. A dead rent, like that which is called "mortmain."

Censure /sénshər/. The formal resolution of a legislative, administrative, or other body reprimanding a person, normally one of its own members, for specified conduct. An official reprimand or condemnation. See also **Censor; Reprimand.**

Census /sén(t)səs/. The official counting or enumeration of people of a state, nation, district, or other political subdivision. Such contains classified information relating to social and economic conditions. City of Compton v. Adams, 33 Cal.2d 596, 203 P.2d 745, 746. The national census has been compiled decennially since 1790, and has increasingly listed a great variety of social and economic data. A primary use of such data is to apportion or reapportion legislative districts. See also **Federal census.**

In Roman law, a numbering or enrollment of the people, with a valuation of their fortunes.

In old European law, a tax, or tribute; a toll.

Census bureau. The Bureau of the Census was established as a permanent office by act of Congress on March 6, 1902 (32 Stat. 51). The major functions of the Bureau are authorized by the Constitution, which provides that a census of population shall be taken every 10 years, and by laws codified as title 13, U.S. Code. The law also provides that the information collected by the Bureau from individual persons, households, or establishments be kept strictly confidential and be used only for statistical purposes.

Census regalis /sén(t)səs rəgéyləs/. In English law, the annual revenue or income of the crown.

Cent. A coin of the United States, the least in value of those now minted. It is the hundredth part of a dollar.

Cental. A weight of 100 pounds avoirdupois, used at Liverpool for corn. Usually called *hundredweight* in the United States.

Centena /səntíynə/. A hundred. A district or division containing originally a hundred freemen, established among the Goths, Germans, Franks, and Lombards, for military and civil purposes, and answering to the Saxon "hundred." Also, in old records and pleadings, a hundred weight.

Centenarii /sèntənériyay/. Petty judges, under-sheriffs of counties, that had rule of a hundred *(centena),* and judged smaller matters among them.

Centeni /səntíynay/. The principal inhabitants of a *centena,* or district composed of different villages, originally in number a hundred, but afterwards only called by that name.

Center. This term is often used, not in its strict sense of a geographical or mathematical center, but as meaning the middle or central point or portion of anything. The center of a section of land is the intersection of a straight line from the north quarter corner to the south quarter corner with a straight line from the east quarter corner to the west quarter corner. Similarly, the center of a street intersection refers to the point where the center lines of the two streets cross. The center of the main channel of a river, is the middle of broad and distinctly defined bed of main river.

Center of gravity doctrine. Choice of law questions in conflicts of law are resolved by application of the law of the jurisdiction which has the most significant relationship to or contact with event and parties to the litigation and the issues therein. Term is used synonymously with most significant relationship theory. Mitchell v. Craft, Miss., 211 So.2d 509; Baffin Land Corp. v. Monticello Motor Inn, 70 Wash.2d 893, 425 P.2d 623, 625.

Centesima /santézama/. In Roman law, the hundredth part.

Usuriæ centesimæ. Twelve per cent. per annum; that is, a hundredth part of the principal was due each month,—the month being the unit of time from which the Romans reckoned interest. 2 Bl.Comm. 462.

Centime /sòntíym/. The name of a denomination of French money, being the one-hundredth part of a franc.

Central criminal court. Since 1834, an English court, having jurisdiction for the trial of crimes and misdemeanors committed in London and certain adjoining parts of Kent, Essex, and Sussex, and of such other criminal cases as may be sent to it out of the king's bench; superseded the "Old Bailey."

Central Intelligence Agency. An agency of the Federal government charged with responsibility of coordinating all information relating to security of the country. All such intelligence information, recommendations, etc. are reported to the National Security Council, to whom the CIA is responsible to and under the direction of.

Centralization. Concentration of power and authority in a central organization or government. For example, power and authority over national and international matters is centralized in the federal government.

Centumviri /santámvarày/. In Roman law, the name of an important court consisting of a body of one hundred and five judges. 3 Bl.Comm. 515.

Century. One hundred. A body of one hundred men. The Romans were divided into *centuries* as the English were divided into hundreds. Also a cycle of one hundred years.

Ceorl /chéyarl/. In Anglo Saxon law, a class of freemen personally free, but possessing no landed property. A tenant at will of free condition, who held land of the thane on condition of paying rent or services. A freeman of inferior rank occupied in husbandry. Under the Norman rule, this term, as did others which denoted workmen, especially those which applied to the conquered race, became a term of reproach, as is indicated by the popular signification of churl.

Cepi /síypay/. Lat. I have taken. This word was of frequent use in the returns of sheriffs when they were made in Latin, and particularly in the return to a writ of *capias*.

The full return (in Latin) to a writ of *capias* was commonly made in one of the following forms: *Cepi corpus*, I have taken the body, *i.e.*, arrested the body of the defendant; *Cepi corpus et bail*, I have taken the body and released the defendant on a bail-bond; *Cepi corpus et committitur*, I have taken the body and he has been committed (to prison); *Cepi corpus et est in custodia*, I have taken the defendant and he is in custody; *Cepi corpus et est languidus*, I have taken the defendant and he is sick, *i.e.*, so sick that he cannot safely be removed from the place where the arrest was made; *Cepi corpus et paratum habeo*, I have taken the body and have it (him) ready, *i.e.*, in custody and ready to be produced when ordered.

Cepit /síypat/. He took. This was the characteristic word employed in (Latin) writs of trespass for goods taken, and in declarations in trespass and replevin. In criminal practice, formerly a technical word necessary in an indictment for larceny.

Cepit et abduxit /síypad ad abdáksat/. He took and led away. The emphatic words in writs in trespass or indictments for larceny, where the thing taken was a living chattel, *i.e.*, an animal.

Cepit et asportavit /síypad ad æspartéyvat/. He took and carried away. Applicable in a declaration in trespass or an indictment for larceny where the defendant has carried away goods without right. 4 Bl.Comm. 231.

Cepit in alio loco /síypad an éyliyow lówkow/. In old pleading, a plea in replevin, by which the defendant alleges that he took the thing replevied in another place than that mentioned in the declaration.

Cera impressa /síra amprésa/. Lat. An impressed seal. It may include an impression made on wafers or other adhesive substances capable of receiving an impression, or even paper.

Cerebellum. Lower portion of brain below back of cerebrum concerned with muscular coordination and body equilibrium.

Cerebrum. The major frontal and upper parts of the brain which are centers of the high functions such as memory, intellect, speech, movement, sensation, etc.; consists of two hemispheres of nerve matter.

Certa debet esse intentio, et narratio, et certum fundamentum, et certa res quæ deducitur in judicium /sárda débad ésiy inténsh(iy)ow èt naréysh(iy)ow, èt sárdam fàndaméntam, èt sárda ríyz kwìy dad(y)úwsadar in juwdíshiyam/. The design and narration ought to be certain, and the foundation certain, and the matter certain, which is brought into court to be tried.

Certain. Ascertained; precise; identified; definitive; clearly known; unambiguous; or, in law, capable of being identified or made known, without liability to mistake or ambiguity, from data already given. Free from doubt.

Certain services. In feudal and old English law, such services as were stinted (limited or defined) in quantity, and could not be exceeded on any pretense; as to pay a stated annual rent, or to plow such a field for three days. 2 Bl.Comm. 61.

Certainty. Absence of doubt; accuracy; precision; definite. The quality of being specific, accurate, and distinct. See **Certain.**

Certificando de recognitione stapulæ /sərdəfəkǽndow dìy rèkəgnìshiyówniy stéypyəliy/. In English law, a writ commanding the mayor of the staple to certify to the lord chancellor a statute-staple taken before him where the party himself detains it, and refuses to bring in the same. There is a like writ to certify a statute-merchant, and in diverse other cases.

Certificate /sərtífəkət/. A written assurance, or official representation, that some act has or has not been done, or some event occurred, or some legal formality has been complied with. A written assurance made or issuing from some court, and designed as a notice of things done therein, or as a warrant or authority, to some other court, judge, or officer. A statement of some fact in a writing signed by the party certifying. A declaration in writing. A "certificate" by a public officer is a statement written and signed, but not necessarily sworn to, which is by law made evidence of the truth of the facts stated for all or for certain purposes. A document certifying that one has fulfilled the requirements of and may practice in a field. See also **Affidavit; Birth certificate; License; Permit.**

Certificate for costs. In English practice, a certificate or memorandum drawn up and signed by the judge before whom a case was tried, setting out certain facts the existence of which must be thus proved before the party is entitled, under the statutes, to recover costs.

Certificate into chancery. In English practice, a document containing the opinion of the common-law judges on a question of law submitted to them for their decision by the chancery court.

Certificate lands. In Pennsylvania, in the period succeeding the revolution, lands set apart in the western portion of the state, which might be bought with the certificates which the soldiers of that state in the revolutionary army had received in lieu of pay.

Certificate of acknowledgment. The certificate of a notary public, justice of the peace, or other authorized officer, attached to a deed, mortgage, or other instrument, setting forth that the parties thereto personally appeared before him on such a date and acknowledged the instrument to be their free and voluntary act and deed. A verification of the act of the maker of an instrument. Thane v. Dallas Joint Stock Land Bank of Dallas, Tex.Civ.App., 129 S.W.2d 795, 799.

Certificate of amendment. Document filed with state corporation authority (e.g. Secretary of State) disclosing amendment to articles of corporate organization or charter or agreement of association.

Certificate of assize. A writ granted for the re-examination or retrial of a matter passed by assize before justices. It is now entirely obsolete. 3 Bl.Comm. 389.

Certificate of authority. Document issued by state corporation authority (e.g. Secretary of State) on application of foreign corporation granting such corporation right to do business in state.

Certificate of competency. Required of business by Small Business Administration to perform a specific government procurement contract.

Certificate of convenience and necessity. Certificate of administrative agency (e.g. Public Service Commission; I.C.C.) granting operating authority for utilities and transportation companies.

Certificate of deposit. A written acknowledgment by a bank or banker of a deposit with promise to pay to depositor, to his order, or to some other person or to his order. U.C.C. § 3–104(2)(c). Document evidencing existence of a time deposit. SEC v. Fifth Ave. Coach Lines, Inc., D.C.N.Y., 289 F.Supp. 3, 31. Documents showing deposits in building and loan association in form of passbooks or any other appropriate written recital. Alter v. Security Building & Loan Co. of Defiance, 58 Ohio App. 114, 16 N.E.2d 228, 233.

Certificate of election. Issued by governor, board of elections, or other competent authority that the person or persons named have been duly elected.

Certificate of good conduct. An official written document which determines that a person is of such good conduct as to operate licensed premises, e.g. retail liquor store. City of Chattanooga v. Tenn. Alcoholic Bev. Comm., Tenn., 525 S.W.2d 470, 480.

Certificate of holder of attached property. A certificate required by statute, in some states, to be given by a third person who is found in possession of property subject to an attachment in the sheriff's hands, setting forth the amount and character of such property and the nature of the defendant's interest in it.

Certificate of incorporation. The basic instrument by which a corporation is formed (termed "articles of incorporation" in most states), under general corporation statutes, executed by several persons as incorporators and filed in some designated public office (e.g. Secretary of State) as evidence of corporate existence. Upon filing of such, corporate existence usually begins. This is properly distinguished from a "charter," which is a direct legislative grant of corporate existence and powers to named individuals. See **Articles of incorporation.**

Certificate of indebtedness. An obligation sometimes issued by corporations having practically the same force and effect as a bond, though not usually secured on any specific property. It may, however, create a lien on all the property of the corporation issuing it, superior to the rights of general creditors. Compare **Debenture.** In banking, same as a certificate of deposit; as a government security, same as a treasury certificate.

Certificate of insurance. Document evidencing fact that an insurance policy has been written and includes a statement of the coverage of the policy in general terms.

Certificate of interest. An instrument evidencing a fractional or percentage interest in oil and gas production. People v. Sidwell, 27 Cal.2d 121, 162 P.2d 913, 915.

Certificate of need. Many states have enacted certificate-of-need laws designed to combat spiraling health care costs and the unnecessary duplication and maldistribution of health care facilities and services. Under these laws, a health care provider seeking to establish or modify a health care facility or to provide new or different institutional health care services must normally apply to the appropriate state agency for a certificate of need.

Certificate of occupancy. Document certifying that premises comply with provisions of zoning and/or building ordinances. Such is often required before premises can be occupied and title transferred. Document that certifies that what has been done actually conforms substantially to approved plans and specifications. DiPasquale v. Haskins, 25 A.D.2d 490, 266 N.Y.S.2d 955, 957.

A number of cities require a "certificate of occupancy" for apartments, which aims at preventing their deterioration in the first place. After each vacancy, the apartment must be newly inspected to make sure it's up to standard.

Certificate of participation. A certificate issued instead of shares of stock to show a proportionate interest in an unincorporated business or in the ownership of debt of a corporation.

Certificate of public convenience and necessity. See **Certificate of convenience and necessity,** *supra.*

Certificate of purchase. A certificate issued by public officer to successful bidder at a judicial sale (such as a tax sale), which will entitle him to a deed upon confirmation of sale by the court, or (as the case may be) if the land is not redeemed within the time limited.

Certificate of registry. In maritime law, a certificate of the registration of a vessel according to the registry acts, for the purpose of giving her a national character.

Certificate of sale. The same as "certificate of purchase," *supra.*

Certificate of stock. A certificate of a corporation or joint-stock company that named person is owner of designated number of shares of stock. It is merely written evidence of ownership of stock, and of the rights and liabilities resulting from such ownership. It is merely a paper representation of an incorporeal right, and stands on the footing similar to that of other muniments of title.

Certificate of title. See **Insurance** (*Title insurance*).

Certificate, trial by. A mode of trial now little in use; it is resorted to in cases where the fact in issue lies out of the cognizance of the court, and the judges, in order to determine the question, are obliged to rely upon the solemn averment or information of persons in such a station as affords them the clearest and most competent knowledge of the truth.

Certification /sə̀rdəfəkéyshən/. The formal assertion in writing of some fact. The act of certifying or state of being certified. Formal designation by NLRB that a labor organization represents a majority of employees in a particular bargaining unit. See **Certificate.**

Certification mark. A mark used upon or in connection with the products or services of one or more persons other than the owner of the mark to certify regional or other origin, material, mode of manufacture, quality, accuracy or other characteristics of such goods or services or that the work or labor on the goods or services was performed by members of a union or other organization. 15 U.S.C.A. § 1127.

Certification of assize. In English practice, a writ anciently granted for the re-examining or retrial of a matter passed by assize before justices, now entirely superseded by the remedy afforded by means of a new trial. See **Certificate of assize.**

Certification of check. Certification of a check is acceptance. Where a holder procures certification the drawer and all prior indorsers are discharged. Unless otherwise agreed a bank has no obligation to certify a check. A bank may certify a check before returning it for lack of proper indorsement. If it does so the drawer is discharged. U.C.C. § 3-411. See also **Certified check.**

Certification of labor union. Declaration by labor board (*e.g.* N.L.R.B.) that a union is bargaining agent for group of employees.

Certification of questions of law. See **Certification to federal court; Certification to state court.**

Certification of record on appeal. Formal acknowledgment of questions for appellate review commonly signed by trial justice.

Certification to federal court. Method of taking case from U.S. Court of Appeals to Supreme Court in which former court may certify any question of law in any civil or criminal case as to which instructions are requested. 28 U.S.C.A. § 1254(3). Same procedure is available from Court of Claims. 28 U.S.C.A. § 1255(2).

Certification to state court. Procedure by which a Federal Court abstains from deciding a state law question until the highest court of the state has had an opportunity to rule on the question so certified by the Federal Court. Clay v. Sun Insurance Office Ltd., 363 U.S. 207, 80 S.Ct. 1222, 4 L.Ed.2d 1170. State statutes and court rules providing for such certification are generally patterned on the "Uniform Certification of Questions of Law Act."

Certificats de coutume /sèrtifiká də kuwtyúwm/. In French law, certificates given by a foreign lawyer, establishing the law of the country to which he belongs upon one or more fixed points. These certificates can be produced before the French courts, and are received as evidence in suits upon questions of foreign law.

Certified carriers. Carriers using highways of state to whom certificates of public convenience and necessity have been issued. People v. Henry, 131 Cal.App. 82, 21 P.2d 672.

Certified check. The check of a depositor drawn on a bank on the face of which the bank has written or stamped the words "accepted" or "certified" with the date and signature of a bank official. The check then becomes an obligation of the bank. The certification of a check is a statement of fact, amounting to an estoppel of the bank to deny liability; a warranty that sufficient funds are on deposit and have been set aside. It means that bank holds money to pay check and is liable to pay it to proper party. See also **Certification of check;** compare **Cashier's check.**

Certified copy. A copy of a document or record, signed and certified as a true copy by the officer to whose custody the original is intrusted.

Certified mail. Form of mail similar to registered mail by which sender may require return receipt from addressee.

Certified public accountant. See **Accountant.**

Certified question. See **Certification to federal court; Certification to state court.**

Certify. To authenticate or vouch for a thing in writing. To attest as being true or as represented. See **Certificate; Certification.**

Certiorari /sèrsh(iy)ərèray/sèrshərériy/. Lat. To be informed of. A writ of common law origin issued by a superior to an inferior court requiring the later to produce a certified record of a particular case tried therein. The writ is issued in order that the court issuing the writ may inspect the proceedings and determine whether there have been any irregularities. It is most commonly used to refer to the Supreme Court of the United States, which uses the writ of certiorari as a discretionary device to choose the cases it wishes to hear. The trend in state practice has been to abolish such writ. See also **Writ of certiorari.**

Certiorari, bill of. In English chancery practice, an original bill praying relief. It was filed for the purpose of removing a suit pending in some inferior court of equity into the court of chancery, on account of some alleged incompetency or inconvenience.

Certiorari facias /sèrsh(iy)ərèray féysh(iy)əs/. Cause to be certified. The command of a writ of certiorari.

Cert money /sárt mániy/. In old English law, head money or common fine. Money paid yearly by the residents of several manors to the lords thereof for the certain keeping of the leet (pro certo letœ); and sometimes to the hundred.

Certum est quod certum reddi potest /sárdəm èst kwòd sárdəm réday pówdəst/. That is certain which can be rendered certain.

Cesionario /sès(i)yənáriyow/. In Spanish law, an assignee.

Cess /sés/, v. In old English law, to cease, stop, determine, fail.

Cess /sés/, n. An assessment or tax. In Ireland, it was anciently applied to an exaction of victuals, at a certain rate, for soldiers in garrison.

Cessante causa, cessat effectus /səsǽntiy kózə, sésəd əféktəs/. The cause ceasing, the effect ceases.

Cessante ratione legis, cessat et ipsa lex /səsǽntiy ræshiyówniy líyjəs, sésəd əd ípsə léks/. The reason of the law ceasing, the law itself also ceases.

Cessante statu primitivo, cessat derivativus /səsǽntiy stéyt(y)uw primətáyvow sésət dərìvətáyvəs/. When the primitive or original estate determines, the derivative estate determines also.

Cessare /səsériy/. L. Lat. To cease, stop, or stay.

Cessa regnare, si non vis judicare /sésə rəgnériy sày non vís juwdəkériy/. Cease to reign, if you wish not to adjudicate.

Cessavit per biennium /səséyvət pàr bayéniyəm/. An obsolete writ, which could formerly have been sued out when the defendant had for two years ceased or neglected to perform such service or to pay such rent as he was bound to do by his tenure, and had not upon his lands sufficient goods or chattels to be distrained. It also lay where a religious house held lands on condition of performing certain spiritual services which it failed to do. 3 Bl.Comm. 232.

Cesse /sés/. An assessment or tax. A tenant of land was said to cesse when he neglected or ceased to perform the services due to the lord.

Cesser /sésər/. Neglect; a ceasing from, or omission to do, a thing. 3 Bl.Comm. 232. The determination of an estate. The determination or ending of a term, annuity, etc.

Cesser, proviso for. A provision in a settlement creating long terms that when the trusts are satisfied, the term should cease and determine. This proviso generally expresses three events: (1) The trusts never arising; (2) their becoming unnecessary or incapable of taking effect; (3) the performance of them.

Cesset executio /sésəd ègzəkyúwsh(iy)ow/. (Let execution stay.) A stay of execution; or an order for such stay; the entry of such stay on record.

Cesset processus /sésət prəsésəs/. (Let process stay.) A stay of proceedings entered on the record. Formal order for stay of process or proceedings.

Cessio /sés(h)(i)yow/. Lat. A cession; a giving up, or relinquishment; a surrender; an assignment.

Cessio bonorum /sés(h)(i)yow bənórəm/. In Roman law, cession of goods. A surrender, relinquishment, or assignment of all his property and effects made by an insolvent debtor for the benefit of his creditors. The term is commonly employed in continental jurisprudence to designate a bankrupt's assignment of property to be distributed among his creditors.

Cessio in jure /séshiyow ìn júriy/. In Roman law, a fictitious suit, in which the person who was to acquire the thing claimed (vindicabat) the thing as his own, the person who was to transfer it acknowledged the justice of the claim, and the magistrate pronounced it to be the property (addicebat) of the claimant.

Cession /séshən/. The act of ceding; a yielding or giving up; surrender; relinquishment of property or rights. The assignment, transfer, or yielding up of territory by one state or government to another. Municipality of Ponce v. Church, 210 U.S. 296, 28 S.Ct. 737, 52 L.Ed. 1068.

In ecclesiastical law, a giving up or vacating a benefice, by accepting another without a proper dispensation. 1 Bl.Comm. 392.

In the civil law, an assignment. The act by which a party transfers property to another. The surrender or assignment of property for the benefit of one's creditors. See **Cessio bonorum**.

Cessionary bankrupt. One who gives up his estate to be divided among his creditors.

Cession des biens /sèsyówn dày byén/. In French law, the voluntary or compulsory surrender which a debtor in insolvent circumstances makes of all his goods to his creditors.

Cession of goods /séshən əv gúdz/. The surrender of property; the relinquishment that a debtor makes of all his property to his creditors, when he finds himself unable to pay his debts. See **Bankruptcy proceedings.**

Cessment. An assessment, or tax.

Cessor /sésər/. One who ceases or neglects so long to perform a duty that he thereby incurs the danger of the law.

Cessure. L. Fr. A receiver; a bailiff.

C'est ascavoir /set æskəvwár/. L. Fr. That is to say, or to-wit. Generally written as one word, *cestascavoir*, *cestascavoire*.

C'est le crime qui fait la honte, et non pas l'échafaud /sèy lə kríym kiy fáy la ónt, ey nown pá leyshafó/. Fr. It is the offense which causes the shame, and not the scaffold.

Cestui, cestuy /sédiy/sè(s)twíy/. He. Used frequently in composition in law French phrases.

Cestui que trust /sédiy kə trə́st/. He who has a right to a beneficial interest in and out of an estate the legal title to which is vested in another. The person who possesses the equitable right to property and receives the rents, issues, and profits thereof; the legal estate of which is vested in a trustee. Beneficiary of trust.

Cestui que use /sédiy kə yúwz/. He for whose use and benefit lands or tenements are held by another. The *cestui que use* has the right to receive the profits and benefits of the estate, but the legal title and possession (as well as the duty of defending the same) reside in the other.

Cestui que vie /sédiy kə víy/. The person whose life measures the duration of a trust, gift, estate, or insurance contract. Person on whose life insurance is written. The person for whose life any lands, tenements, or hereditaments are held.

Cestuy que doit inheriter al père doit inheriter al fils /sè(s)twíy kə dwó ænhèriytéy owpér dwó ænhèriytéy ow fíys/. He who would have been heir to the father of the deceased shall also be heir of the son. 2 Bl.Comm. 239, 250.

Cf. An abbreviated form of the Latin word *confer*, meaning "compare." Directs the reader's attention to another part of the work, to another volume, case, etc., where contrasted, analogous, or explanatory views or statements may be found.

C. & F. or C.F. Term in sales contract means that the price so includes cost and freight to the named destination. U.C.C. § 2–320(1).

C.F. & I. or C.F.I. See **C.I.F.**

CFR. Code of Federal Regulations.

C.F.T.C. Commodity Futures Trading Commission.

Ch. This abbreviation most commonly stands for "chapter," or "chancellor," but it may also mean "chancery," or "chief."

Chacea /chéysh(iy)ə/. In old English law, a station of game, more extended than a park, and less than a forest; also the liberty of chasing or hunting within a certain district; also the way through which cattle are driven to pasture, otherwise called a "droveway."

Chacer /chèyséy/. L. Fr. To drive, compel, or oblige; also to chase or hunt.

Chafewax /chéyfwæks/. An officer in the English chancery whose duty was to prepare wax to seal the writs, commissions, and other instruments thence issuing. The office was abolished by St. 15 & 16 Vict., c. 87, § 23.

Chaffers /chæfərz/. An ancient term for goods, wares, and merchandise; hence the word *chaffering*, which is yet used for buying and selling, or beating down the price of an article.

Chaffery. Traffic; the practice of buying and selling.

Chain. As regards land measure, such equals 66 feet, 100 links, or 4 rods. See also **Land measure.**

Chain-certificate method. Method of authenticating of foreign official record. See Fed.R.Civil P. 44(a)(2).

Chain of custody. In evidence, the one who offers real evidence, such as the narcotics in a trial of drug case, must account for the custody of the evidence from the moment in which it reaches his custody until the moment in which it is offered in evidence, and such evidence goes to weight not to admissibility of evidence. Com. v. White, 353 Mass. 409, 232 N.E.2d 335.

Chain of possession. See **Chain of custody**.

Chain of title. Successive conveyances, or other forms of alienation, affecting a particular parcel of land, arranged consecutively, from the government or original source of title down to the present holder. See **Abstract of title.**

Chains and links. Used in real estate measurement; chain is 66' long or 100 links. See **Land measure**.

Chain stores. Number of stores under common name, ownership and management; normally selling same general line of merchandise or products.

Chairman. A name given to the presiding officer of an assembly, public meeting, convention, deliberative or legislative body, board of directors, committee, etc.

Chairman of committees of the whole house. In English parliamentary practice, in the commons, this officer, always a member, is elected by the house on the assembling of every new parliament. When the house is in committee on bills introduced by the government, or in committee of ways and means, or supply, or in committee to consider preliminary resolutions, it is his duty to preside.

Challenge. To object or except to; to prefer objections to a person, right, or instrument; to question formerly the legality or legal qualifications of; to invite into competition; to formally call into question the capability of a person for a particular function, or the existence of a right claimed, or the sufficiency or validity of an instrument; to call or put in question; to put into dispute; to render doubtful. For example, to challenge the personal qualification of a judge or magistrate about to preside at the trial of a cause, as on account of personal interest, his having been of counsel, bias, etc.; or to challenge a juror for cause. See **Jury challenge; Objection.**

Challenge for cause. A request from a party to a judge that a certain prospective juror not be allowed to be a member of the jury because of specified causes or reasons.

Challenge to jury array. An exception to the whole panel in which the jury are arrayed, upon account of partiality, or some default in the sheriff or other officer who arrayed the panel or made the return. A challenge to the form and manner of making up the panel. A challenge that goes to illegality of drawing, selecting, or impaneling array.

General challenge. A species of challenge for cause, being an objection to a particular juror, to the effect that the juror is disqualified from serving in any case.

Peremptory challenge. A request from a party that a judge not allow a certain prospective juror to be a member of the jury. No reason or "cause" need be stated for this type of challenge. The number of peremptory challenges afforded each party is normally set by statute or court rule; *e.g.* Fed.R.Crim.P. 24.

Challenge to fight. A summons or invitation, given by one person to another, to engage in a personal combat; a request to fight a duel.

Chamber. A room or apartment in a house. A private repository of money; a treasury. A compartment; a hollow or cavity.

Judges chambers. The private room or office of a judge; any place in which a judge hears motions, signs papers, or does other business pertaining to his office, when he is not holding a session of court. Business so transacted is said to be done "in chambers."

Legislative body. The lower chamber of a bicameral legislature is normally the larger of the two (*e.g.* House of Representatives). The upper chamber is generally the smaller (*e.g.* Senate).

Chamber business. A term applied to all such judicial business as may properly be transacted by a judge at his chambers or elsewhere, as distinguished from such as must be done by the court in session.

Chamberlain. In old English law, keeper of the chamber. Originally the chamberlain was the keeper of the treasure chamber *(camera)* of the prince or state; otherwise called "treasurer."

The name of several high officers of state in England, as the lord great chamberlain of England, lord chamberlain of the household, chamberlain of the exchequer.

The word was formerly used in some American cities as the title of an officer corresponding to "treasurer."

Chamberlaria /chèymbərlériyə/. Chamberlainship; the office of a chamberlain.

Chamber of accounts. A sovereign court, of great antiquity, in France, which took cognizance of and registered the accounts of the king's revenue; nearly the same as the English court of exchequer.

Chamber of commerce. A board or association of businessmen and merchants organized to promote the commercial interests of a locality, county, or the like, or a society of a city who meet to promote the general trade and commerce of the locality. Chambers of commerce exist in most cities, and are loosely affiliated with the national organization of the same name. Particular trades may also have their own organizations or boards to promote the interests of their own trade. Organizations with functions similar to that of chambers of commerce may be known under various other names; *e.g.* Board of Trade.

Chamber, widow's. In old English law, a portion of the effects of a deceased person, reserved for the use of his widow, and consisting of her apparel, and the furniture of her bed-chamber. This custom in London of reserving her apparel and furniture for the widow of a freeman was abolished by 19 & 20 Vict., c. 94.

Champart /shòmpár/. In French law, the grant of a piece of land by the owner to another, on condition that the latter would deliver to him a portion of the crops.

Champert /chǽmpərt/. In old English law, a share or division of land; champerty.

Champertor /chǽmpərdər/. In criminal law, one who makes or brings suits, or causes them to be moved or brought, either directly or indirectly, and maintains them at his own cost, upon condition of having a part of the gains or of the land in dispute. One guilty of champerty *(q.v.).*

Champertous /chǽmpərdəs/. Of the nature of champerty; affected with champerty.

Champerty /chǽmpərdiy/. A bargain by a stranger with a party to a suit, by which such third person undertakes to carry on the litigation at his own cost and risk, in consideration of receiving, if successful, a part of the proceeds or subject sought to be recovered. Schnabel v. Taft Broadcasting Co., Inc., Mo. App., 525 S.W.2d 819, 823. "Maintenance" consists in maintaining, supporting, or promoting the litigation of another.

Champion. A person who fights a combat in his own cause, or in place of another. At common law, the person who, in the trial by battel, fought either for the tenant or demandant. One who acts or speaks in behalf of a person, or a cause; defender; an advocate.

Champion of the king or **queen.** An ancient officer, whose duty it was at the coronation to challenge "that if any man shall deny the king's title to the crown, he is there ready to defend it in single combat".

Chance. Absence of explainable or controllable causation; accident; fortuity; hazard; result or issue of uncertain and unknown conditions or forces; risk; unexpected, unforeseen, or unintended consequence of an act. The opposite of intention, design, or contrivance. See **Act of God.**

Chance bargain. The entering into a contract for better or worse, accompanied by the taking of chances as to the true facts and situation of the thing or article bargained about. Marr v. Lawson, 290 Ky. 342, 161 S.W.2d 42, 44.

Chancellor. The name given in some states to the judge (or the presiding judge) of a court of chancery. A university president, or chief executive officer of higher education system in certain states.

Chancellor of the Exchequer. In England, an officer who formerly sat in the Court of Exchequer, but now is minister who has control over national revenues and expenditures.

Lord High Chancellor. The highest judicial functionary in England.

Chance-medley. In criminal law, a sudden affray. This word is sometimes applied to any kind of homicide by misadventure, but in strictness it is applicable to such killing only as happens in defending one's self. 4 Bl.Comm. 184.

Chancer. To adjust according to principles of equity, as would be done by a court of chancery. The practice arose in parts of New England when the courts, without equity jurisdiction, were compelled to act upon equitable principles.

Chancery. Equity; equitable jurisdiction; a court of equity; the system of jurisprudence administered in courts of equity. See **Court of Chancery; Equity.**

Chance verdict. See **Verdict.**

Chandler Act. Federal act of 1938 making major amendments to Bankruptcy Act (11 U.S.C.A.). Included in amendments was provision for a debtor to arrange payments with creditors without total liquidation of debtor's assets. See **Bankruptcy Act.**

Change, *n.* An alteration; a modification or addition; substitution of one thing for another. Exchange of money against money of a different denomination.

Change, *v.* Alter; cause to pass from one place to another; exchange; make different in some particular; put one thing in place of another; vacate.

Changed circumstances. In domestic relations law, used to show need for modification of custody or support orders. Betts v. Betts, 18 Or.App. 35, 523

P.2d 1055. Person may be estopped from exercising rights or defense if other person's circumstances have changed by reliance. Fisher v. MacDonald, 332 Mass. 727, 127 N.E.2d 484.

Change in accounting method. A change in the taxpayer's method of accounting, *e.g.,* a change from FIFO to LIFO. Such change normally requires prior approval from the Internal Revenue Service. Generally, a request to the I.R.S. must be filed within 180 days after the beginning of the taxable year of the desired change. In some instances, the permission for change will not be granted unless the taxpayer agrees to certain terms or adjustments which are prescribed by the I.R.S.

Change of beneficiary. A divesting of beneficial interest held by one person and a vesting of that interest in another.

Change of domicile. Change of abode or residence and intention to remain.

Change of grade. Usually understood as an elevation or depression of the surface of a street, or a change of the natural contour of its face so as to facilitate travel over it. It is essential that there shall have been a previously established grade and that a new grade be physically made.

Change of location. Removal from old to new location. Weber County v. Ritchie, 98 Utah 272, 96 P.2d 744. See **Change of domicile; Change of venue.**

Change of venue. The removal of a suit begun in one county or district to another county or district for trial, though the term is also sometimes applied to the removal of a suit from one court to another court of the same county or district. In criminal cases a change of venue will be permitted if for example the court feels that the defendant cannot receive a fair trial in a given venue because of prejudice. Fed.R. Crim.P. 21. In civil cases a change *may* be permitted in the interests of justice or for the convenience of the parties. 28 U.S.C.A. § 1404(a). See also **Forum non conveniens; Plea of privilege; Venue.**

Changer. In England, an officer formerly belonging to the king's mint whose business was chiefly to *exchange* coin for bullion brought in by merchants and others.

Channel. The bed in which the main stream of a river flows, rather than the deep water of the stream as followed in navigation. The deeper part of a river, harbor or strait. It may also be used as a generic term applicable to any water course, whether a river, creek, slough, or canal. The "channel" of a river is to be distinguished from a "branch".

A means of expression or communication.

Main channel. That bed of the river over which the principal volume of water flows. The main channel of a navigable stream, called for as a boundary between states, means the "thalweg", or deepest and most navigable channel as it then existed.

Natural channel. The channel of a stream as determined by the natural conformation of the country through which it flows. The floor or bed on which the water flows, and the banks on each side thereof as carved out by natural causes.

Chantry /chǽntriy/. A church or chapel endowed with lands for the maintenance of priests to say Mass daily for the souls of the donors.

Chapel. A place of worship; a lesser or inferior church, sometimes a part of or subordinate to another church.

Chapel of ease. In English ecclesiastical law, a chapel built in aid of original church for parishioners who had fixed their residence at some distance.

Private chapels. Chapels owned by private persons, and used by themselves and their families.

Proprietary chapels. In English law, those belonging to private persons who have purchased or erected them with a view to profit or otherwise.

Public chapels. In English law, chapels founded later than the church for parishioners who fixed their residence at a distance; and chapels so circumstanced were described as "chapels of ease."

Chapelry /chǽpəlriy/. The precinct and limits of a chapel. The same thing to a chapel as a parish is to a church.

Chapitre /chǽp(ə)tər/. In English law, a summary of matters to be inquired of or presented before justices in eyre, justices of assise, or of the peace, in their sessions. Also articles delivered by the justice in his charge to the inquest.

Chaplain. A clergyman officially attached to a unit of the armed services, or to some public institution, for the purpose of performing religious services.

Chapman. An itinerant vendor of small wares. A trader who trades from place to place.

Chapter. In England, a body of dignitaries called canons attached to a cathedral church and presided over by a dean. This body constitutes the council of the bishop in both spiritual and temporal affairs. Also, a local branch of a society or fraternity.

Character. The aggregate of the moral qualities which belong to and distinguish an individual person; the general result of the one's distinguishing attributes. That moral predisposition or habit, or aggregate of ethical qualities, which is believed to attach to a person, on the strength of the common opinion and report concerning him. A person's fixed disposition or tendency, as evidenced to others by his habits of life, through the manifestation of which his general reputation for the possession of a character, good or otherwise, is obtained. The estimate attached to an individual or thing in the community. The opinion generally entertained of a person derived from the common report of the people who are acquainted with him. Although "character" and "reputation" are often used synonymously, the terms are distinguishable. "Character" is what a man is, and "reputation" is what he is supposed to be in what people say he is. "Character" depends on attributes possessed, and "reputation" on attributes which others believe one to possess. The former signifies reality and the latter merely what is accepted to be reality at present. See **Bad character; Good character; Representation.**

Class or division to which claim belongs.

Character and habit. The moral traits of a person gleaned from his habitual conduct. People v. Coleman, 19 Mich.App. 250, 172 N.W.2d 512.

Character evidence. Evidence of person's moral standing in community based on reputation.

Admissability of character evidence in federal trials is governed by Fed.Evid. Rules 404 and 405, and with respect to witnesses by Rules 607–609.

Characterization. In conflicts, the classification, qualification, and interpretation of laws applicable to a case. Restatement, Second, Conflicts, § 7.

Charge, v. To impose a burden, duty, obligation, or lien; to create a claim against property; to assess; to demand; to accuse; to instruct a jury on matters of law. To impose a tax, duty, or trust. In commercial transactions, to bill or invoice; to purchase on credit. To indict or formerly accuse.

Charge, n. An incumbrance, lien, or claim; a burden or load; an obligation or duty; a liability; an accusation. A person or thing committed to the care of another. The price of, or rate for, something. See also **Charged; Charges; Floating charge; Rate; Surcharge.**

Charge to jury. The final address by judge to jury before verdict, in which he sums up the case, and instructs jury as to the rules of law which apply to its various issues, and which they must observe. The term also applies to the address of court to grand jury, in which the latter are instructed as to their duties. See also **Jury instructions.**

General charge. The charge or instruction of the court to the jury upon the case, as a whole, or upon its general features and characteristics.

Special charge. A charge or instruction given by the court to the jury, upon some particular point or question involved in the case, and usually in response to counsel's request for such instruction.

Criminal law. Accusation of a crime by a formal complaint, information or indictment.

Public charge. An indigent. A person whom it is necessary to support at public expense by reason of poverty alone or illness and poverty.

Chargeable. This word, in its ordinary acceptation, as applicable to the imposition of a duty or burden, signifies capable of being charged, subject to be charged, liable to be charged, or proper to be charged.

Charge account. System of purchasing goods and services on credit, under which customer agrees to settle or make payments on his balance within a specified time or periodically.

Revolving charge account. An arrangement between a seller and a buyer pursuant to which: (1) the seller may permit the buyer to purchase goods or services on credit either from the seller or pursuant to a seller credit card, (2) the unpaid balances of amounts financed arising from purchases and the credit service and other appropriate charges are debited to an account, (3) a credit service charge if made is not precomputed but is computed on the outstanding unpaid balances of the buyer's account from time to time, and (4) the buyer has the privilege of paying the balances in installments. Uniform Consumer Credit Code, § 2.108.

Charge and discharge. Under former equity practice, in taking an account before a master, a written statement of items for which plaintiff asked credit and a counterstatement, exhibiting claims or demands defendant held against plaintiff.

Charged. Accusation of crime by complaint, indictment, or information. With respect to "notice", a person is charged with such if he has information sufficient to apprise him of the subject, *e.g.* under land recording acts, a person is charged with notice of a lien or attachment if it is on record.

Charge des affaires, or **charge d'affaires** /shàrzhéy deyz afér(z)/ °dàfér(z)/. The title of a diplomatic representative of inferior rank. In re Baiz, 135 U.S. 403, 10 S.Ct. 854, 34 L.Ed. 222.

Charge-off. Anything manifesting intent to eliminate an item from assets. Write-off of asset or other item, *e.g.* uncollectible account receivable or debt. To treat as a loss or expense an amount originally recorded as an asset; usually the term is used when the charge is not in accord with original expectations. See **Bad debt.**

Charges. The expenses which have been incurred, or disbursements made, in connection with a contract, suit, or business transaction. See also **Charge; Costs; Fee; Fixed charges.**

Charge-sheet. A record kept at a police station to receive the names of the persons brought and given custody, the nature of the accusation, and the name of the accuser in each case.

Charging lien. A lien is a charging lien where the debt is a charge upon the specific property although it remains in the debtor's possession. See **Floor plan financing.**

Charging order. See **Order.**

Charitable. Having the character or purpose of a charity. The word "charitable", in a legal sense includes every gift for a general public use, to be applied consistent with existing laws, for benefit of an indefinite number of persons, and designed to benefit them from an educational, religious, moral, physical or social standpoint. American Soc. for Testing and Materials v. Board of Revision of Taxes, Philadelphia County, 423 Pa. 530, 225 A.2d 557. This term is synonymous with "beneficent", "benevolent", and "eleemosynary". See also **Charity; Eleemosynary.**

Charitable bequest. A bequest is charitable if its aims and accomplishments are of religious, educational, political, or general social interest to mankind and if the ultimate recipients constitute either the community as a whole or an unascertainable and indefinite portion thereof.

Charitable contributions. Contributions are deductible (subject to various restrictions and ceiling limitations) if made to qualified nonprofit charitable organizations. A cash basis taxpayer is entitled to a deduction solely in the year of payment. Accrual basis corporations may accrue contributions at year-end if payment is authorized by the Board of Directors prior to the end of the year and payment is made within time specified by I.R.C. before the end of the year. See also **Charitable organizations.**

Charitable corporation. Non-profit corporation organized for charitable purposes; *i.e.* for purpose, among other things, of promoting welfare of mankind at large, or of a community, or of some class forming part of it indefinite as to numbers and individuals and is one created for or devoted to charitable purposes. Lynch v. Spilman, 67 Cal.2d 251, 62 Cal.Rptr. 12, 18, 431 P.2d 636. Such corporations must meet certain criteria to receive tax "exempt" status. I.R.C. § 501(c)(3). See **Charitable organizations,** *infra.*

Charitable deduction. In taxes, a contribution to a qualified charity or other tax exempt institution for which taxpayer may claim a deduction on his tax return. I.R.C. § 170(c). Also applicable to trusts. I.R.C. § 512(b)(11). As regards tax exempt status of recipient organization, see **Charitable organizations.** See also **Charitable contributions.**

Charitable foundation. An organization dedicated to education, health, relief of the poor, etc.; organized for such purposes and not for profit and recognized as such for tax purposes under I.R.C. § 509(a). See also **Charitable organizations,** *infra.*

Charitable gift. See **Charitable deduction,** *supra.*

Charitable immunity. A doctrine which relieves a charity of liability in tort; long recognized, but currently most states have abrogated or restricted such immunity.

Charitable institution. One which dispenses charity to all who need and apply for it, does not provide gain or profit in private sense to any person connected with it, and does not appear to place obstacles of any character in way of those who need and would avail themselves of charitable benefits it dispenses. Distinctive features are that it has no capital stock or shareholders and earns no profits or dividends; but rather derives its funds mainly from public and private charity and holds them in trust for objects and purposes expressed in its charter. Methodist Old Peoples Home v. Korzen, 39 Ill.2d 149, 233 N.E.2d 537, 541, 542; People ex rel. Nordlund v. Association of Winnebago Home for Aged, 40 Ill.2d 91, 237 N.E.2d 533, 539.

Charitable organizations. As regards "exempt" tax status, such includes: "Corporations, and any community chest, fund, or foundation, organized and operated exclusively for religious, charitable, scientific, testing for public safety, literary, or educational purposes, or to foster national or international amateur sports competition (but only if no part of its activities involve the provision of athletic facilities or equipment), or for the prevention of cruelty to children or animals, no part of the net earnings of which inures to the benefit of any private shareholder or individual, no substantial part of the activities of which is carrying on propaganda, or otherwise attempting, to influence legislation." I.R.C. § 501(c)(3). See also Benevolent associations; Benevolent corporation; Charitable corporation; Charitable foundation; Charitable institution.

Charitable purpose. "Charitable purposes" for purpose of tax exemption has as its common element the accomplishment of objectives which are beneficial to community or area, and usually recognized charitable purposes, not otherwise limited by statute, are generally classified as: relief of poverty; advancement of education; advancement of religion; protection of health; governmental or municipal purposes; and other varied purposes the accomplishment of which is beneficial to community. Bank of Carthage v. U. S., D.C.Mo., 304 F.Supp. 77, 80.

A gift is for charitable purposes if it is for religious, scientific, charitable, literary, or educational purposes under tax law. I.R.C. § 170(c)(4). These purposes are also required for a trust to qualify as a charitable trust.

See also **Charitable deduction; Charitable use.**

Charitable remainder. A gift over after an intervening estate to a qualified charity; qualifies as a tax deduction under certain conditions.

Charitable remainder annuity trust. A trust which must pay the noncharitable income beneficiary or beneficiaries a sum certain annually, or more frequently, if desired, which is not less than 5% of the initial net fair market value of all property placed in the trust as finally determined for federal tax purposes. In re Danforth's Will, 81 Misc.2d 452, 366 N.Y.S.2d 329, 330.

Charitable trust. Fiduciary relationship with respect to property arising as a result of a manifestation of an intention to create it, and subjecting the person by whom the property is held to equitable duties to deal with the property for a charitable purpose. Restatement, Second, Trusts, § 348. See **Charitable purpose.**

Charitable use. Charitable uses are defined as those of religious, educational, political or general social interest to mankind, or as those for the relief of poverty, advancement of education or religion, or beneficial to the community generally. Thomason v. State, 245 C.A.2d 793, 54 Cal.Rptr. 229, 232. See also **Charitable purpose.**

Charity. A gift for, or institution engaged in, public benevolent purposes. A gift for benefit of indefinite number of persons under influence of religion or education, relief from disease, assisting people to establish themselves in life, or erecting or maintaining public works. Johnson v. South Blue Hill Cemetery Ass'n, Me., 221 A.2d 280, 287. A "charity", in absence of legislative definition, is attempt in good faith, spiritually, physically, intellectually, socially and economically to advance and benefit mankind in general, or those in need of advancement and benefit in particular, without regard to their ability to supply that need from other sources and without hope or expectation, if not with positive abnegation, of gain or profit by donor or by instrumentality of charity. Planned Parenthood Ass'n v. Tax Commissioner, 5 Ohio St.2d 117, 214 N.E.2d 222, 225. Se also **Benevolence; Benevolent; Charitable.**

Public charity. A charity wherein the benefit is conferred on indefinite persons composing the public or some part of the public.

Charlatan /shárlədən/. One who pretends to more knowledge or skill than he possesses; a quack; a faker.

Charre of lead. A quantity consisting of 36 pigs of lead, each pig weighing about 70 pounds.

Chart. A map used by navigators.

Charta /kárdə/. In old English law, a charter or deed; an instrument written and sealed; the formal evidence of conveyances and contracts. Also any signal or token by which an estate was held.

The term came to be applied, by way of eminence, to such documents as proceeded from the sovereign, granting liberties or privileges, and either where the recipient of the grant was the whole nation, as in the case of *Magna Charta*, or a public body, or private individual, in which case it corresponded to the modern word "charter."

In the civil law, a paper suitable for inscription of documents or books; hence, any instrument or writing.

See also **Charter.**

Charta communis /kárdə kəmyúwnəs/. In old English law, an indenture; a common or mutual charter or deed; one containing mutual covenants, or involving mutuality of obligation; one to which both parties might have occasion to refer, to establish their respective rights.

Charta cyrographata /kárdə kàyrowgræféydə/. In old English law, a chirographed charter; a charter executed in two parts, and cut through the middle *(scinditur per medium),* where the word *"cyrographum,"* or *"chirographum,"* was written in large letters. See **Chirograph.**

Charta de foresta /kárdə dìy foréstə/. A collection of the laws of the forest, made in the 9th Hen. III, and said to have been originally a part of *Magna Charta.*

The *charta de foresta* was called the Great Charter of the woodland population, nobles, barons, freemen, and slaves, loyally granted by Henry III, early in his reign (A.D. 1217). There is a difference of opinion as to the *original* charter of the forest similar to that which exists respecting the true and original Magna Carta *(q.v.),* and for the same reason, viz., that both required repeated confirmation by the kings, despite their supposed inviolability. This justifies the remark of recent historians as to the great charter that "this theoretical sanctity and this practical insecurity are shared with 'the Great Charter of Liberties' by the Charter of the Forest which was issued in 1217." It is asserted with great positiveness by Inderwick that no forest charter was ever granted by King John, but that Henry III issued the charter of 1217 (which he puts in the third year of the reign, which, however, only commenced Oct. 28, 1216), in pursuance of the promises of his father; and Lord Coke, referring to it as a charter on which the lives and liberties of the woodland population depended, says that it was confirmed at least thirty times between the death of John and that of Henry V.

Charta de una parte /kárdə dìy yúwnə párdiy/. A deed-poll; a deed of one part. Formerly used to distinguish a *deed poll*—that is, an agreement made by one party only—from a deed *inter partes.*

Charta partita /kárdə partáydə/. A charter-party.

Charta de non ente non valet /kárdə dìy non éntiy non vǽlət/. A deed of a thing not in being is not valid.

Chartæ libertatum /kárdiy libərtéydəm/chárdiy°/. The charters (grants) of liberties. These are *Magna Charta* and *Charta de Foresta*.

Charta non est nisi vestimentum donationis /kárdə non ést náysiy vèstəméntəm dənèyshiyównəs/. A deed is nothing else than the vestment of a gift.

Chartarum super fidem, mortuis testibus, ad patriam de necessitudine recurrendum est /kartérəm s(y)úwpər fáydəm, mórchuwəs téstəbəs, æd pætriyəm dìy nəsèsətyúwdəniy rèkuréndəm èst/. The witnesses being dead, the truth of charters must of necessity be referred to the country, *i.e.*, a jury.

Charte /shárt/. Fr. A chart, or plan, which mariners use at sea.

Chartel /kartél/. A variant of "cartel" (*q.v.*).

Charte-partie /shàrt-partíy/. Fr. In French marine law. A charter-party.

Charter, v. To hire, rent or lease for a temporary use; *e.g.* to hire or lease a vessel for a voyage.

Charter, n. An instrument emanating from the sovereign power, in the nature of a grant, either to the whole nation, or to a class or portion of the people, to a corporation, or to a colony or dependency, assuring to them certain rights, liberties, or powers. Such was the "Great Charter" or *"Magna Charta,"* and such also were the charters granted to certain of the English colonies in America.

A charter differs from a constitution, in that the former is granted by the sovereign, while the latter is established by the people themselves.

A city's organic law. Charter of municipal corporation consists of the creative act of incorporation, together with all those laws in force which relate to the incorporation, whether defining the powers of the corporation or regulating the mode of exercise thereof, and statute does not fail to become part of charter simply because it is not labeled as such. Opinion of the Justices, Del., 276 A.2d 736, 739.

An act of a legislature creating a corporation, or creating and defining the franchise of a corporation. Also a corporation's constitution or organic law; that is to say, the articles of incorporation taken in connection with the law under which the corporation was organized. The authority, by virtue of which an organized body acts. A contract between the state and the corporation, between the corporation and the stockholders, and between the stockholders and the state. See **Corporate charter.**

Leasing or hiring of airplane, vessel, or the like. See **Charter-party.**

In old English law, a deed or other written instrument under seal; a conveyance, covenant, or contract.

Bank charter. Document issued by governmental authority permitting a bank to operate and transact business.

Bare boat charter. Charter where ship owner only provides ship, with charterer providing personnel, insurance and other necessary materials and expenses.

Blank charter. In old English law, a document given to the agents of the crown in the reign of Richard II with power to fill up as they pleased.

Charter agreement. See **Charter party**.

Charter of affreightment. See **Affreightment**.

Gross charter. Charter where ship owner provides all personnel and equipment and incurs other expenses such as port costs.

Time charter. Charter wherein vessel is leased for specified time rather than for specified trip or voyage. See also **Time** (*Time charter*).

Chartered ship. A ship hired or freighted; a ship which is the subject-matter of a charter-party.

Charterer. One who charters (*i.e.*, hires, leases or engages) a vessel, airplane, etc. for transportation or voyage.

Charter-land. In English law, otherwise called "bookland." Property held by deed under certain rents and free services. It, in effect, differs nothing from the free socage lands, and hence have arisen most of the freehold tenants, who hold of particular manors, and owe suit and service to the same. 2 Bl.Comm. 90.

Charter-party. A contract by which a ship, or some principal part thereof, is let to a merchant for the conveyance of goods on a determined voyage to one or more places.

The term "charter party," often shortened to "charter," designates the document in which are set forth the arrangements and contractual engagements entered into when one person (the "charterer") takes over the use of the whole of a ship belonging to another (the "owner").

Chartis reddendis /kárdəs rədéndəs/. (For returning the charters.) An ancient writ which lay against one who had charters of feoffment intrusted to his keeping and refused to deliver them.

Chartophylax /kartófəlæks/. In old European law, a keeper of records or public instruments; a chartulary; a registrar.

Chase. To pursue or follow rapidly with the intention of catching or driving away. See **Fresh pursuit.**

In English law, the liberty or franchise of hunting, one's self, and keeping protected against all other persons, beasts of the chase within a specified district, without regard to the ownership of the land. The act of acquiring possession of animals *feræ naturæ* by force, cunning, or address. A privileged place for preservation of deer and beasts of the forest. It is commonly less than a forest and of larger compass than a park. Every forest is a chase, but every chase is not a forest. It differs from a park in that it is not inclosed, yet it must have certain metes and bounds. In old English law, a "common" chase was a place where all alike were entitled to hunt wild animals.

Chaste. Never voluntarily having had unlawful sexual intercourse. An unmarried woman who has had no carnal knowledge of men. New v. State, 141 Tex. Cr.R. 536, 148 S.W.2d 1099, 1101.

Chaste character. Denoting purity of mind and innocence of heart; not limited merely to unlawful sexual intercourse.

Chastity. Purity; continence. Quality or state of being chaste. It means that virtue which prevents the unlawful intercourse of the sexes; the state of purity or abstinence from unlawful sexual connection.

Chattel /chǽdəl/. An article of personal property, as opposed to real property. A thing personal and movable. It may refer to animate as well as inanimate property. See also **Goods; Property** (*Personal property*).

Personal chattel. Movable things. Personal property which has no connection with real estate.

Real chattels. Such as concern real property, such as leasehold estates; interests issuing out of, or annexed to, real estate; such chattel interests as devolve after the manner of realty. An interest in real estate less than freehold or fee. See also **Fixture.**

Chattel lien. Chattel liens exist in favor of persons expending labor, skill or materials on any chattel or furnishing storage thereof at request of owner, his agent, reputed owner, or lawful possessor. See *e.g.* **Artisan's lien.**

Chattel mortgage. A pre-Uniform Commercial Code security device whereby a security interest was taken by the mortgagee in personal property of the mortgagor. A transfer of some legal or equitable right in personal property or creation of a lien thereon as security for payment of money or performance of some other act, subject to defeasance on performance of the conditions. Such security device has generally been superseded by other types of security agreements under U.C.C. Article 9 (Secured Transactions). See **Secured transaction; Security agreement.**

Chattel paper. A writing or writings which evidence both a monetary obligation and a security interest in or a lease of specific goods. In many instances chattel paper will consist of a negotiable instrument coupled with a security agreement. When a transaction is evidenced both by such a security agreement or a lease and by an instrument or a series of instruments, the group of writings taken together constitutes chattel paper. U.C.C. § 9–105(1)(b). See **Secured transaction; Security agreement.**

Chaud-medley /shòwdmédliy/. A homicide committed in the heat of an affray and while under the influence of passion; it is thus distinguished from *chance-medley*, which is the killing of a man in a casual affray in self-defense. It has been said, however, that the distinction is of no great importance.

Chauffeur. A person employed to operate and attend motor vehicle for another.

Chauntry rents /chóntriy rénts/. In old English law, money paid to the Crown by the servants or purchasers of chauntry-lands. See **Chantry.**

Chaussée /shòwséy/. Fr. A levee of earth, made to retain the water of a river or pond; a levee made in low, wet, and swampy places to serve as a road.

Cheat, *v.* To deceive and defraud. It necessarily implies a fraudulent intent. The words "cheat and defraud" usually mean to induce a person to part with the possession of property by reason of intentionally false representations relied and acted upon by such person to his harm. They include not only the crime of false pretenses, but also all civil frauds, and include all tricks, devices, artifices, or deceptions used to deprive another of property or other right. See **Fraud.**

Cheat, *n.* Swindling; defrauding. The act of fraudulently deceiving. See **Fraud.**

Cheats, punishable at common law, were such cheats (not amounting to felony) as were effected by deceitful or illegal symbols or tokens which may affect the public at large, and against such common prudence could not have guarded.

Cheaters, or **escheators.** In old English law, officers appointed to look after the king's escheats, a duty which gave them great opportunities of fraud and oppression, and in consequence many complaints were made of their misconduct. Hence it seems that a *cheater* came to signify a fraudulent person, and thence the verb to *cheat* was derived.

Check, *v.* To control or restrain; to hold within bounds. To verify or audit, as to examine the books and records of another or a business for accuracy and proper accounting practices. Particularly used with reference to the control or supervision of one department, bureau, office, or person over another.

Check, *n.* A draft drawn upon a bank and payable on demand, signed by the maker or drawer, containing an unconditional promise to pay a sum certain in money to the order of the payee. State v. Perrigoue, 81 Wash.2d 640, 503 P.2d 1063, 1066. U.C.C. § 3–104(2)(b).

The Federal Reserve Board defines a check as "a draft or order upon a bank or banking house purporting to be drawn upon a deposit of funds for the payment at all events of a certain sum of money to a certain person therein named or to him or his order or to bearer and payable instantly on demand." It must contain the phrase "pay to the order of."

See also Bad check; Bogus check; Cancelled check; Cashier's check; Draft; Registered check; Stale check; Travelers check.

Blank check. Check which is signed by drawer but left blank as to payee and/or amount.

Cashier's check. A bank's own check drawn on itself and signed by the cashier or other authorized official. It is a direct obligation of the bank. One issued by an authorized officer of a bank directed to another person, evidencing that the payee is authorized to demand and receive upon presentation from the bank the amount of money represented by the check. A form of a check by which the bank lends its credit to the purchaser of the check, the purpose being to make it available for immediate use in banking circles. A bill of exchange drawn by a bank upon itself, and accepted by the act of issuance. In its legal effect, it is the same as a certificate of deposit, certified check or draft. An acknowledgment of a debt drawn by bank upon itself. See also **Certified check.**

Memorandum check. A check given by a borrower to a lender, for the amount of a short loan, with the understanding that it is not to be presented at the bank, but will be redeemed by the maker himself when the loan falls due. This understanding is evidenced by writing the word *"Mem."* on the check.

Personal check. An individual's own check drawn on his own account.

Post-dated check. A check which bears a date after the date of its issue. Its negotiability is not affected by being postdated and it is payable on its stated date. U.C.C. § 3–114.

Traveler's check. See **Traveler's check.**

Checkerboard system. This term, with reference to entries on lands, means one entry built on another, and a third on the second.

Check kiting. Practice of writing a check against a bank account where funds are insufficient to cover it and hoping that before it is deposited the necessary funds will have been deposited. First State Bank & Trust Co. of Edinburg v. George, Tex.Civ.App., 519 S.W.2d 198, 204. Transfer of funds between two or more banks to obtain unauthorized credit from bank during time it takes checks to clear. State v. Woodington, 31 Wis.2d 151, 142 N.W.2d 810, 820. In effect, a kite is a bad check used temporarily to obtain credit. See **Bad check.**

Check-off system. Procedure whereby employer deducts union dues directly from pay of employees and remits such sums to union.

Check register. Journal used to record checks issued.

Check-roll. In English law, a list or book, containing the names of such as are attendants on, or in the pay of, the queen or other great personages, as their household servants.

Checks and balances. Arrangement of governmental powers whereby powers of one governmental branch check or balance those of other branches. See also **Separation of powers.**

Chefe. In Anglo-Norman law, were or weregild; the price of the head or person *(capitis pretium)*.

Chemerage /shèm(ə)rázh/. In old French law, the privilege or prerogative of the eldest. A provincial term derived from *chemier.*

Chemical analysis. Any form of examination through use of chemicals as in blood tests to determine a person's sobriety, the presence of drugs, etc.

Chemier /shemyéy/. In old French law, the eldest born.

Chemin /sh(ə)mǽn/. Fr. The road wherein every man goes; the king's highway.

Cheque /chék/. A variant of check *(q.v.).*

Cherokee Nation. One of the civilized Indian tribes. See **Indian tribe.**

Chevage /chíyvəj/. In old English law, a sum of money paid by villeins to their lords in acknowledgment of their bondage. It was exacted for permission to mar-

ry, and also permission to remain without the dominion of the lord. When paid to the king, it was called subjection. *Chevage* seems also to have been used for a sum of money yearly given to a man of power for his countenance and protection as a chief or leader.

Chevantia /chəvǽnsh(iy)ə/. A loan or advance of money upon credit.

Chevisance /chévəzən(t)s/. An agreement or composition; an end or order set down between a creditor or debtor; an indirect gain in point of usury, etc.; also an unlawful bargain or contract.

Cheze. A homestead or homesfall which is accessory to a house.

Chicago Board of Trade. Exchange where futures contracts in a large number of agricultural products are transacted.

Chicane /shəkéyn/. Swindling; shrewd cunning. The use of tricks and artifice.

Chickasaw Nation. One of the civilized Indian tribes. See **Indian tribe.**

Chief. One who is put above the rest. Principal; leading; head; eminent in power or importance; the best or most important or valuable of several; paramount; of leading importance.

Declaration in chief is a declaration for the principal cause of action.

Examination in chief is the first examination of a witness by the party who produces him.

Tenant in chief. See **Chief, tenant in,** *infra.*

Chief baron. Formerly, the presiding judge of the English court of exchequer; answering to the chief justice of other courts. Superseded by Lord Chief Justice of England.

Chief clerk. The principal clerical officer of a court, bureau or department, who is generally charged, subject to the direction of his superior officer, with the superintendence of the administration of the business of the office.

Chief executive. See **Chief magistrate.**

Chief Judge. See **Chief Justice.**

Chief Justice. The presiding, most senior, or principal judge of a court.

Chief Justice of England. The formerly given to the presiding judge in the Queen's bench division of the high court of justice, and, in the absence of the lord chancellor, president of the high court, and also an *ex officio* judge of the court of appeals. Now superseded by the "Lord Chief Justice of England" who is President of the Queen's Bench Division.

Chief Justice of the Common Pleas. In England, the presiding judge in the court of common pleas, and afterwards in the common pleas division of the high court of justice, and one of the *ex officio* judges of the high court of appeal.

Chief justiciar /chíyf jəstíshiyər/. In old English law, a high judicial officer and special magistrate, who presided over the *aula regis* of the Norman kings, and who was also the principal minister of state, the second man in the kingdom, and, by virtue of his office, guardian of the realm in the king's absence. 3 Bl.Comm. 38.

Chief lord. The immediate lord of the fee, to whom the tenants were directly and personally responsible.

Chief magistrate. The head of the executive department of government of a nation, state, or municipal corporation. The President is the chief executive of the United States.

Chief office. Office of paramount importance or the leading office.

Chief pledge. In old English law, the borsholder, or chief of the borough.

Chief rents. In old English law, the annual payments of freeholders of manors; also called "quit-rents," because by paying them the tenant was freed from all other rents or services. Abolished by Law of Property Act of 1922.

Chiefrie. In feudal law, a small rent paid to the lord paramount.

Chief, tenant in. In English feudal law, all the land in the kingdom was supposed to be holden mediately or immediately of the king, who was styled the "Lord Paramount," or "Lord Above All;" and those that held immediately under him, in right of his crown and dignity, were called his tenants *"in capite"* or *"in chief,"* which was the most honorable species of tenure, but at the same time subjected the tenant to greater and more burdensome services than inferior tenures did. One who held directly of the king.

Child. Progeny; offspring of parentage. Unborn or recently born human being. Wilson v. Weaver, 358 F.Supp. 1147, 1154. At common law one who had not attained the age of fourteen years, though the meaning now varies in different statutes; *e.g.* child labor, support, criminal, etc. statutes. The term "child" or "children" may include or apply to: adopted, after-born, or illegitimate child; step-child; child by second or former marriage; issue.

See also Delinquent child; Disobedient child; Foster child; Illegitimate child; Infancy; Juvenile; Minor; Neglected child; Person; Posthumous child; Pretermitted heir; Viable child. For negligence of child, see **Parental liability.**

Childs part. A "child's part," which a widow, by statute in some states, is entitled to take in lieu of dower or the provision made for her by will, is a full share to which a child of the decedent would be entitled, subject to the debts of the estate and the cost of administration up to and including distribution.

Illegitimate child. Child born out of lawful wedlock.

Legitimate child. Child born in lawful wedlock.

Natural child. Child by natural relation or procreation. Child by birth, as distinguished from a child by adoption. Illegitimate children who have been acknowledged by the father.

Posthumous child. One born after the father's death.

Quasi-posthumous child. In the civil law, one who, born during the life of his grandfather, or other male

ascendant, was not his heir at the time he made his testament, but who by the death of his father became his heir in his life-time.

Rights of unborn child. Medical authority has recognized long since that a child is in existence (*i.e.* alive) from the moment of conception, and for many purposes its existence is recognized by the law. The criminal law regards it as a separate entity, and the law of property considers it in being for all purposes which are to its benefit, such as taking by will or descent. After its birth, it has been held that it may maintain a statutory action for the wrongful death of the parent. In addition, the child, if he is born alive, is permitted to maintain an action for the consequences of prenatal injuries, and if he dies of such injuries after birth an action will lie for his wrongful death. Many states have allowed recovery even though the injury occurred during the early weeks of pregnancy, when the child was neither viable nor quick. Sylvia v. Gobeille, 1966, 101 R.I. 76, 220 A.2d 222; Hornbuckle v. Plantation Pipe Line Co., 1956, 212 Ga. 504, 93 S.E.2d 727, conformed to 94 Ga. App.2d 328, 94 S.E.2d 523; Bennett v. Hymers, 1958, 101 N.H. 483, 147 A.2d 108; Sinkler v. Kneale, 1960, 401 Pa. 267, 164 A.2d 93; Smith v. Brennan, 1960, 31 N.J. 353, 157 A.2d 497.

Child abuse. Any form of cruelty to a child's physical, moral or mental well-being. Also used to describe form of sexual attack which may or may not amount to rape. Such acts are criminal offenses in most states. See also **Abuse** (*Female child);* **Abused and neglected children.**

Child labor laws. Network of laws on both federal and state levels prescribing working conditions for children in terms of hours and nature of work which may be performed, all designed to protect the child. See also **Fair Labor Standards Act; Working papers.**

Children's court. See **Juvenile courts.**

Child support. The legal obligation of parents to contribute to the economic maintenance, including education, of their children; enforceable in both civil and criminal contexts. In a dissolution or custody action, money paid by one parent to another toward the expenses of children of the marriage. See also **Non-support.**

Child welfare. A generic term which embraces the totality of measures necessary for a child's well being; physical, moral and mental.

Childwit. In Saxon law, the right which a lord had of taking a fine of his bondwoman gotten with child without his license.

The custom in Essex county, England, whereby every reputed father of a bastard child was obliged to pay a small fine to the lord.

Chilling a sale. The act of bidders or others who combine or conspire to suppress fair competition at a sale, for the purpose of acquiring the property at less than its fair value.

Chilling effect doctrine. In constitutional law, any law or practice which has the effect of seriously discouraging the exercise of a constitutional right, *e.g.* the right of appeal. North Carolina v. Pearce, 395 U.S. 711, 89 S.Ct. 2072, 23 L.Ed.2d 656.

Chiltern hundreds /chíltərn hə́ndrədz/. In English law, the offices of steward or bailiff of His Majesty's three Chiltern Hundreds of Stoke, Desborough, and Bonenham; or the steward of the Manor of Northsted. Chilter Hundreds is an appointment under the hand and seal of the Chancellor of the Exchequer. The stewardship of the Chiltern Hundreds is a nominal office in the gift of the crown, usually accepted by members of the house of commons desirous of vacating their seats. By law a member once duly elected to parliament is compelled to discharge the duties of the trust conferred upon him, and is not enabled at will to resign it. But by statute, if any member accepts any office of profit from the crown (except officers in the army or navy accepting a new commission), his seat is vacated. If, therefore, any member wishes to retire from the representation of the county or borough by which he was sent to parliament, he applies to the lords of the treasury for the stewardship of one of the Chiltern Hundreds, which having received, and thereby accomplished his purpose, he again resigns the office.

Chimin /chímən/. In old English law, a road, way, highway. It is either the king's highway (*chiminus regis*) or a private way. The first is that over which the subjects of the realm, and all others under the protection of the crown, have free liberty to pass, though the property in the soil itself belong to some private individual; the last is that in which one person or more have liberty to pass over the land of another, by prescription or charter. See **Chemin**.

Chiminage /chímənəj/. A toll for passing on a way through a forest; called in the civil law *"pedagium."*

Chiminus /chímənəs/. The way by which the king and all his subjects and all under his protection have a right to pass, though the property of the soil of each side where the way lieth may belong to a private man.

Chimney money, or hearth money. A tax upon chimneys or hearth; an ancient tax or duty upon houses in England, now repealed.

Chippingavel /chípəngævəl/. In old English law, a tax upon trade; a toll imposed upon traffic, or upon goods brought to a place to be sold; a toll for buying and selling.

Chirgemot, chirchgemot /chár(ch)gəmòwt/. (Also spelled Chirgemote, Chirchgemote, Circgemote, Kirkmote.) In Saxon law, an ecclesiastical assembly or court. A synod or meeting in a church or vestry.

Chirograph /káyrəgræf/. In civil and canon law, an instrument written out and subscribed by the hand of the party who made it, whether the king or a private person.

In old English law, a deed or indenture; also the last part of a fine of land, called more commonly, perhaps, the foot of the fine. An instrument of gift or conveyance attested by the subscription and crosses of the witnesses, which was in Saxon times called *"chirographum,"* and which, being somewhat changed in form and manner by the Normans, was by them styled *"charta."* Anciently when they made a chirograph or deed which required a counterpart, as we call it, they engrossed it twice upon one piece of parchment contrariwise, leaving a space between, in which they wrote in capital letters the word "chirograph," and then cut the parchment in two through the middle of the word, giving a part to each party. 2 Bl.Comm. 296.

Chirographa /kàyrógrəfə/. In Roman law, writings emanating from a single party, the debtor.

Chirographer of fines /kàyrógrəfər əv faynz/. In English law, the title of the officer of the common pleas who engrossed fines in that court so as to be acknowledged into a perpetual record.

Chirographum /kàyrógrəfəm/. In Roman law, a handwriting; that which was written with a person's own hand. An obligation which a person wrote or subscribed with his own hand; an acknowledgment of debt, as of money received, with a promise to repay. An evidence or voucher of debt; a security for debt. A right of action for debt.

Chirographum apud debitorem repertum præsumitur solutum /kàyrógrəfəm æpəd debətórəm rəpárdəm prəz(y)úwmədər səl(y)úwdəm/. An evidence of debt found in the debtor's possession is presumed to be paid.

Chirographum non extans præsumitur solutum /kàyrógrəfəm non ékstænz prəz(y)úwmədər səl(y)úwdəm/. An evidence of debt not existing is presumed to have been discharged.

Chiropody. Study and treatment of ailments of the foot.

Chiropractic, chiropractics /kàyrəpræktək(s)/. The practice of "chiropractic" is a method of detecting and correcting by manual or mechanical means structural imbalance, distortion or subluxations in the human body to remove nerve interferences where such is the result of or related to distortion, misalignment or subluxations of or in the vertebral column. Chiropractic Ass'n of New York, Inc. v. Hilleboe, 16 A.D.2d 285, 228 N.Y.S.2d 358, 360. A system of therapeutic treatment, through adjusting of articulations of human body, particularly those of the spine. Walkenhorst v. Kesler, 92 Utah 312, 67 P.2d 654, 662. The specific science that removes pressure on the nerves by the adjustment of the spinal vertebrae.

Chiropractor /káyrəpræktər/. One who practices the system of chiropractic (*q.v.*).

Chirurgeon /kàyrárjən/. The ancient denomination of a surgeon.

Chivalry. In feudal law, knight-service. Tenure in chivalry was the same as tenure by knight-service. 2 Bl.Comm. 61, 62.

Chivalry, court of. See **Court of chivalry**.

Chivalry, tenure by. Tenure by knight-service.

Choate /kówət/. That which has become perfected or ripened as *e.g.* a choate lien (*q.v.*).

Choate lien /kówət líyn/. Lien which is perfected so that nothing more need be done to make it enforcible. Identity of lienor, property subject to lien and amount of lien are all established. Walker v. Paramount

Engineering Co., C.A.Mich., 353 F.2d 445, 449; U. S. v. City of New Britain, Conn., 347 U.S. 81, 74 S.Ct. 367, 369, 98 L.Ed. 520. The lien must be definite and not merely ascertainable in the future by taking further steps. Gower v. State Tax Commission, 207 Or. 288, 295 P.2d 162.

Choice of law. In conflicts of law, the question presented in determining what law should govern. There are a number of different choice of law principles used by courts in determining the applicable law to apply; *e.g.* substantive vs. procedure distinction, center of gravity, renvoi, lex fori, grouping-of-contacts, place of most significant relationship. See also **Conflict of laws.**

Choral. In ancient times a person admitted to sit and worship in the choir; a chorister.

Chorepiscopus /kòrəpískəpəs/. In old European law, a rural bishop, or bishop's vicar.

Chose /shówz/. Fr. A thing; an article of personal property. A chose is a chattel personal, and is either in action or in possession. See **Chose in action; Chose in possession,** *infra.*

Chose local. A local thing; a thing annexed to a place, as a mill.

Chose transitory. A thing which is movable, and may be taken away or carried from place to place.

Chose in action. A thing in action and is right of bringing an action or right to recover a debt or money. Right of proceeding in a court of law to procure payment of sum of money, or right to recover a personal chattel or a sum of money by action. Gregory v. Colvin, 235 Ark. 1007, 363 S.W.2d 539, 540. A personal right not reduced into possession, but recoverable by a suit at law. A right to personal things of which the owner has not the possession, but merely a right of action for their possession. The phrase includes all personal chattels which are not in possession; and all property in action which depends entirely on contracts express or implied. A right to receive or recover a debt, demand, or damages on a cause of action *ex contractu* or for a tort or omission of a duty. Moran v. Adkerson, 168 Tenn. 372, 79 S.W.2d 44, 45. A right to recover by suit a personal chattel. Assignable rights of action ex contractu and perhaps ex delicto. Coty v. Cogswell, 100 Mont. 496, 50 P.2d 249, 250. Personalty to which the owner has a right of possession in future, or a right of immediate possession, wrongfully withheld.

Chose in possession. A personal thing of which one has possession. A thing in possession, as distinguished from a thing in action. Taxes and customs, if paid, are a chose in possession; if unpaid, a chose in action. See also **Chose in action,** *supra.*

Chosen freeholders. Name for county or township boards in certain eastern states.

Chout. In Hindu law, a fourth, a fourth part of the sum in litigation. The "Mahratta chout" is a fourth of the revenues exacted as tribute by the Mahrattas.

Chrenecruda /krìynkrúwdə/. Under the Salic law, a ceremony performed by a person who was too poor to pay his debt or fine, whereby he applied to a rich relative to pay it for him. It consisted (after certain preliminaries) in throwing green herbs upon the party, the effect of which was to bind him to pay the whole demand.

Christian. Pertaining to Jesus Christ or the religion founded by him; professing Christianity. As a noun, it signifies one who accepts and professes to live by the doctrines and principles of the Christian religion; it does not include Mohammedans, Jews, pagans, or infidels. One who believes or professes or is assumed to believe in Jesus Christ, and the truth as taught by Him.

Christianitatis curia /krìstiyǽnətéydəs kyúriyə/. The court Christian. An ecclesiastical court, as opposed to a civil or lay tribunal. See also **Court Christian.**

Christianity. The religion founded and established by Jesus Christ.

Christian name. The baptismal name as distinct from the surname. The name which is given one after his birth or at baptism, or is afterward assumed by him in addition to his family name. Such name may consist of a single letter.

Christmas Day. A festival of the Christian church, observed on the 25th of December, in memory of the birth of Jesus Christ.

Chronic /krónək/. With reference to diseases, of long duration, or characterized by slowly progressive symptoms; deepseated and obstinate, or threatening a long continuance;—distinguished from acute.

Chronic alcoholism. A medically diagnosable disease characterized by chronic, habitual or periodic consumption of alcoholic beverages resulting in the (1) substantial interference with an individual's social or economic functions in the community, or (2) the loss of powers of self-control with respect to the use of such beverages.

Church. In its most general sense, the religious society founded and established by Jesus Christ, to receive, preserve, and propagate His doctrines and ordinances. It may also mean a body of communicants gathered into church order; body or community of Christians, united under one form of government by the profession of the same faith and the observance of the same ritual and ceremonies; place where persons regularly assemble for worship; congregation; organization for religious purposes; religious society or body; the clergy or officialdom of a religious body.

Church courts. Tribunals within the structure of a church charged with adjudicating disputes of an ecclesiastical nature which may not be adjudicated in civil courts.

Church of England. The established episcopal Church of England.

Church property. Within constitutional exemption from taxation it means property used principally for religious worship and instruction. Church of the Holy Faith v. State Tax Commission, 39 N.M. 403, 48 P.2d 777, 784.

Church register. Parish record of baptisms, marriages, deaths, etc.

Church school. Church supported school providing general education in addition to religious instruction.

Churl /chárl/. In Saxon law, a freeman of inferior rank, chiefly employed in husbandry. A tenant at will of free condition, who held land from a thane, on condition of rents and services. See **Ceorl**.

Churning. Churning occurs when a broker, exercising control over the volume and frequency of trades, abuses his customer's confidence for personal gain by initiating transactions that are excessive in view of the character of account and the customer's objectives as expressed to the broker.

Ci. Fr. So; here. *Ci Dieu Vous eyde*, so help you God. *Ci devant*, heretofore. *Ci bien*, as well.

C.I.A. Central Intelligence Agency.

Cibaria /səbériyə/. Lat. In the civil law, food; victuals.

Cicatrix /səkéytrəks/síkətriks/. The mark left in the flesh or skin after the healing of a wound, and having the appearance of a seam or of a ridge of flesh.

C.I.F. This term in a sales contract means that the price includes in a lump sum the cost of the goods and the insurance and freight to the named destination.

Cigarette tax. An excise tax imposed on sale of cigarettes by both federal and state governments.

C.I.O. Congress of Industrial Organizations. Merged with AFL (American Federation of Labor) in 1955.

Cipher /sáyfər/. Ordinarily, a secret or disguised written communication, unintelligible to one without a key. As applied to telegrams, a "cipher" message is one that is unintelligible.

Cippi /sípay/. An old English law term for the stocks, an instrument in which the wrists or ankles of petty offenders were confined.

Circa /sárkə/. Lat. About; around; also, concerning; with relation to. Commonly used before a given date when the exact time is not known; as, *circa* 1800. Abbreviated *circ.* or *c.*

Circada /sərkéydə/. A tribute anciently paid to the bishop or archbishop for visiting churches.

Circar /sàrkár/. In Hindu law, head of affairs; the state or government; a grand division of a province; a headman. A name used by Europeans in Bengal to denote the Hindu writer and accountant employed by themselves, or in the public offices.

Circuit /sárkət/. Judicial divisions of the United States (*e.g.* eleven judicial circuits wherein U.S. Courts of Appeal sit) or a state, originally so called because the judges traveled from place to place within the circuit, holding court in various locations.

Circuit courts of appeals. Former name for federal intermediate appellate courts, changed in 1948 to present designation of United States Courts of Appeals. See 28 U.S.C.A. §§ 41–48.

Circuit courts. Courts whose jurisdiction extends over several counties or districts, and of which terms are held in the various counties or districts to which their jurisdiction extends.

In several of the states, the name given to a tribunal, the territorial jurisdiction of which may comprise several counties or districts, and whose sessions are held in such counties or districts alternately. These courts usually have general original jurisdiction.

Circuit paper. In English practice, a paper containing a statement of the time and place at which the several assises will be held, and other statistical information connected with the assises.

Circuitus est evitandus; et boni judicis est lites dirimere, ne lis ex lite oriatur /sərkyúwədəs èst èvətǽndəs, et bównay júwdəsəs èst láydiyz dəríməriy, nìy láys èks láydiy òriyéydər/. Circuity is to be avoided; and it is the duty of a good judge to determine litigations, lest one lawsuit arise out of another.

Circuity of action. A complex, indirect, or roundabout course of legal proceeding, making two or more actions necessary in order to effect that adjustment of rights between all the parties concerned in the transaction which, by a more direct course, might have been accomplished in a single suit. Former problems of circuity of action have been remedied by Rules of Civil Procedure.

Circular letter of credit. A letter authorizing one person to pay money or extend credit to another on the credit of the writer. Pines v. United States, C.C.A. Iowa, 123 F.2d 825, 828. See also **Letter of credit**.

Circular notes. Instruments, similar to "letters of credit," drawn by resident bankers upon their foreign correspondents, in favor of persons traveling abroad.

Circulated. A thing is "circulated" when it passes, as from one person or place to another, or spreads, as a report or tale. Willard v. State, 129 Tex.Cr.R. 384, 87 S.W.2d 269, 270.

Circulation. Transmission from person to person or place to place; *e.g.* interchange of money. Extent or degree of dissemination; *e.g.* total readers or issues sold of given publication.

Circumspecte agatis /sərkəmspéktiy əgéydəs/. The title of an English statute passed 13 Edw. I (1285) and so called from the initial words of it, the object of which was to ascertain the boundaries of ecclesiastical jurisdiction in some particulars, or, in other words, to regulate the jurisdiction of the ecclesiastical and temporal courts. See **Articles of the clergy**.

Circumstances. Attendant or accompanying facts, events or conditions. Subordinate or accessory facts; *e.g.* evidence that indicates the probability or improbability of an event.

As used in a statute for an allowance for the wife in a divorce action, having regard to the "circumstances" of the parties, it includes practically everything which has a legitimate bearing on present and prospective matters relating to the lives of both parties.

See also **Extenuating circumstances; Extraordinary cirumstances**.

Circumstantial evidence. Testimony not based on actual personal knowledge or observation of the facts in controversy, but of other facts from which deductions are drawn, showing indirectly the facts sought to be proved. People v. Yokum, 145 C.A.2d 245, 302 P.2d 406, 410. The proof of certain facts and circumstances in a given case, from which jury may infer other connected facts which usually and reasonably follow according to the common experience of mankind. Foster v. Union Starch & Refining Co., 11 Ill.App.2d 346, 137 N.E.2d 499, 502. Indirect evidence. Evidence of facts or circumstances from which the existence or nonexistence of fact in issue may be inferred. Inferences drawn from facts proved. Process of decision by which court or jury may reason from circumstances known or proved, to establish by inference the principal fact. It means that existence of principal facts is only inferred from circumstances. Twin City Fire Ins. Co. v. Lonas, 255 Ky. 717, 75 S.W.2d 348, 350.

The proof of various facts or circumstances which usually attend the main fact in dispute, and therefore tend to prove its existence, or to sustain, by their consistency, the hypothesis claimed. Or as otherwise defined, it consists in reasoning from facts which are known or proved to establish such as are conjectured to exist.

Circumstantibus, tales de. See **Tales**.

Ciric /kírək/. In Anglo-Saxon and old English law, a church.

Ciric-bryce /kírək-brìych/. Any violation of the privileges of a church.

Ciric sceat /kírək shìyt/. Church-scot, or shot; an ecclesiastical due, payable on the day of St. Martin, consisting chiefly of corn.

Cirliscus /sərlískəs/. A ceorl (q.v.).

Cista /sístə/. A box or chest for the deposit of charters, deeds, and things of value.

Citacion /siytàsyówn/. In Spanish law, citation; summons; an order of a court requiring a person against whom a suit has been brought to appear and defend within a given time. It is synonymous with the term *emplazamiento* in the old Spanish law, and the *in jus vocatio* of the Roman law.

Citatio /saytéysh(iy)ow/. Lat. A citation or summons to court.

Citatio ad reassumendam causam /saytéysh(iy)ow æd rìyəsyuwméndəm kózəm/. A summons to take up the cause. A process, in the civil law, which issued when one of the parties to a suit died before its determination for the plaintiff against the defendant's heir, or for the plaintiff's heir against the defendant, as the case might be; analogous to a bill of revivor, which is probably borrowed from this proceeding.

Citatio est de juri naturali /saytéysh(iy)ow èst dìy júriy næchəréylay/. A summons is by natural right.

Citation /saytéyshən/. A writ issued out of a court of competent jurisdiction, commanding a person therein named to appear on a day named and do something therein mentioned, or show cause why he should not.

An order, issued by the police, to appear before a magistrate or judge at a later date. Usually used for minor violations (*e.g.* traffic violations); avoids the taking of a suspect into immediate physical custody. See also **Citation of authorities.**

Citationes non concedantur priusquam exprimatur super qua re fieri debet citatio /saytèyshiyówniyz non kònsədæntər priyáskwəm èksprəméydər súwpər kwèy ríy fáyəriy débət saytéysh(iy)ow/. Citations should not be granted before it is stated about what matter the citation is to be made. (A maxim of ecclesiastical law.)

Citation of authorities. The reading, or production of, or reference to, legal authorities and precedents (such as constitutions, statutes, reported cases, and treatises), in arguments to courts, in legal text-books, law review articles, briefs, or the like to establish or fortify the propositions advanced. See also **Cite.**

Citations, law of. In Roman law, an act of Valentinian, passed A.D. 426, providing that the writings of only five jurists, viz., Papinian, Paul, Gaius, Ulpian, and Modestinus, should be quoted as authorities. The majority was binding on the judge. If they were equally divided the opinion of Papinian was to prevail; and in such a case, if Papinian was silent upon the matter, then the judge was free to follow his own view of the matter.

Citators. A set of books which provide, through letter-form abbreviations or words, the subsequent judicial history and interpretation of reported decisions, and lists of cases and legislative enactments construing, applying or affecting statutes. The most widely used set of citators is *Shepard's Citations.*

Cite. L. Fr. City; a city. *Cite de Loundr',* city of London.

Cite. To summon; to command the presence of a person; to notify a person of legal proceedings against him and require his appearance thereto. To read or refer to legal authorities, in an argument to a court or elsewhere, in support of propositions of law sought to be established. To name in citation. To mention in support, illustration, or proof of. See **Citation; Citation of authorities.**

Citizen. One who, under the Constitution and laws of the United States, or of a particular state, is a member of the political community, owing allegiance and being entitled to the enjoyment of full civil rights. All persons born or naturalized in the United States, and subject to the jurisdiction thereof, are citizens of the United States and of the state wherein they reside. U.S.Const., 14th Amend.

The term may include or apply to children of alien parents born in United States, Von Schwerdtner v. Piper, D.C.Md., 23 F.2d 862, 863; U. S. v. Minoru Yasui, D.C.Or., 48 F.Supp. 40, 54; children of American citizens born outside United States, Haaland v. Attorney General of United States, D.C.Md., 42 F.Supp. 13, 22; Indians, United States v. Hester, C.C.A.Okl., 137 F.2d 145, 147; State v. McAlhaney, 220 N.C. 387, 17 S.E.2d 352, 354; national banks, American Surety Co. v. Bank of California, C.C.A.Or., 133 F.2d 160, 162; nonresident who has qualified as administratrix of estate of deceased resident, Hunt v.

Noll, C.C.A.Tenn., 112 F.2d 288, 289. However, neither the United States nor a state is a citizen for purposes of diversity jurisdiction. Skandia American Reinsurance Corp. v. Schenck, 441 F.Supp. 715; Jizemerjian v. Dept. of Air Force, 457 F.Supp. 820. On the other hand, municipalities and other local governments are deemed to be citizens. Rieser v. District of Columbia, 563 F.2d 462. A corporation is not a citizen for purposes of privileges and immunities clause of the Fourteenth Amendment, D. D. B. Realty Corp. v. Merrill, 232 F.Supp. 629, 637.

"Citizens" are members of a political community who, in their associated capacity, have established or submitted themselves to the dominion of a government for the promotion of their general welfare and the protection of their individual as well as collective rights. Herriott v. City of Seattle, 81 Wash.2d 48, 500 P.2d 101, 109.

Citizen's arrest. A private citizen as contrasted with a police officer may, under certain circumstances, make an arrest, generally for a felony or misdemeanor amounting to a breach of the peace. A private person may arrest another: 1. For a public offense committed or attempted in his presence. 2. When the person arrested has committed a felony, although not in his presence. 3. When a felony has been in fact committed, and he has reasonable cause for believing the person arrested to have committed it. Calif.Penal Code, § 837.

Citizenship. The status of being a citizen. See **Corporate citizenship; Diversity of citizenship; Dual citizenship; Federal citizenship.**

City. A municipal corporation; in most states, of the largest and highest class. Also, the territory within the corporate limits. A political entity or subdivision for local governmental purposes; commonly headed by a mayor, and governed by a city council.

City council. The principal governmental body of a municipal corporation with power to pass ordinances, levy taxes, appropriate funds, and generally administer city government. The name of a group of municipal officers constituting primarily a legislative and administrative body, but which is often charged with judicial or quasi judicial functions, as when sitting on charges involving the removal of an officer for cause.

City courts. Court which tries persons accused of violating municipal ordinances and has jurisdiction over minor civil or criminal cases, or both.

City real estate. Property owned and used for municipal purposes. McSweeney v. Bazinet, 269 A.D. 213, 55 N.Y.S.2d 558, 561.

Civic. Pertaining to a city or citizen, or to citizenship.

Civic enterprise. A project or undertaking in which citizens of a city co-operate to promote the common good and general welfare of the people of the city.

Civil. Of or relating to the state or its citizenry. Relating to private rights and remedies sought by civil actions as contrasted with criminal proceedings.

The word is derived from the Latin civilis, a citizen. Originally, pertaining or appropriate to a member of a *civitas* or free political community; natural or proper to a *citizen*. Also, relating to the community, or to the policy and government of the citizens and subjects of a state.

As to civil Bail; Commitment; Commotion; Conspiracy; Contempt; Corporation; Death; Injury; Liberty; Obligation; Officer; Possession; Remedy; Right; and War, see those titles. See, also, the titles which follow.

Civil action. Action brought to enforce, redress, or protect private rights. In general, all types of actions other than criminal proceedings. Gilliken v. Gilliken, 248 N.C. 710, 104 S.E.2d 861, 863.

The term includes all actions, both those formerly known as equitable actions and those known as legal actions, or, in other phraseology, both suits in equity and actions at law. Thomason v. Thomason, 107 U.S.App.D.C. 27, 274 F.2d 89, 90.

In the great majority of states which have adopted rules or codes of civil procedure as patterned on the Federal Rules of Civil Procedure, there is only one form of action known as a "civil action." The former distinctions between actions at law and suits in equity, and the separate forms of those actions and suits, have been abolished. Rule of Civil Proc. 2; New York CPLR § 103(a).

See also **Penal action.**

Civil Aeronautics Board. The Civil Aeronautics Board, an independent regulatory commission, was originally established under the Civil Aeronautics Act of 1938 (52 Stat. 973) and continued by the Federal Aviation Act of 1958 (72 Stat. 731). The Board has broad authority to promote and regulate the civil air transport industry within the United States and between the United States and foreign countries in the interests of the foreign and domestic commerce of the United States, the postal service, and the national defense. Board decisions involving the domestic operations of air carriers are not subject to review or approval by the President or by any department or agency of Government, but Federal, State, or local agencies may participate in formal proceedings before the Board as parties or as intervenors. Grants of authority to operate between the United States and foreign countries require the approval of the President. Board decisions may be appealed to the United States Courts of Appeal, which have exclusive authority to affirm, modify, or set aside such orders, or to return the case to the Board for further proceedings.

Civil authority clause. Provision in fire insurance policy protecting insured from damages caused by firemen, police, and other civil authorities.

Civil bail. A bond, deposit of money or of property, to secure the release of a person who is under civil arrest for failing to pay a debt which has been reduced to court order and its effect is to insure payment of such order.

Civil Code. See **Code Civil.**

Civil commitment. A form of confinement order used in the civil context for those who are insane, alcoholic, drug addicted, etc. as contrasted with the criminal commitment of a sentence. Also applicable to confinement for failing to pay a debt which has been converted to a court order for payment; the failure to pay being contempt of court. See also **Commitment**.

Civil conspiracy. A combination of two or more persons who, by concerted action, seek to accomplish an unlawful purpose or to accomplish some purpose, not in itself unlawful, by unlawful means. Lake Mortgage Co., Inc. v. Federal Nat. Mortgage Ass'n, 159 Ind.App. 605, 308 N.E.2d 739, 744.

Civil conspiracy that gives rise to cause of action is combination of two or more persons for purpose of accomplishing by concerted action either lawful purpose by unlawful means or unlawful purpose by lawful means. Wooded Shores Property Owners Ass'n, Inc. v. Mathews, 37 Ill.App.3d 334, 345 N.E.2d 186, 192.

Civil contempt. A species of contempt of court which generally arises from a wilful failure to comply with an order of court such as an injunction as contrasted with criminal contempt which consists generally of contumelious conduct in the presence of the court. Punishment for civil contempt may be a fine or imprisonment, the object of such punishment being compliance with the order of the court. Such contempt is committed when a person violates an order of court which requires that person in specific and definite language to do or refrain from doing an act or series of acts. Lichtenstein v. Lichtenstein, C.A.Pa., 425 F.2d 1111, 1113. See also **Contempt**.

Civil Damage Acts. See **Dram Shop Acts**.

Civil death. In some states, persons convicted of serious crimes are declared to be civilly dead which means that all rights and privileges of the convicted offender including the right to contract and to sue and be sued are forfeited. See **Civil disabilities**, *infra*.

Civil disabilities. Apart from the sentence which is imposed upon a convicted offender, numerous civil disabilities are also often imposed. These disabilities, which adversely affect an offender both during his incarceration and after his release, include denial of such privileges as voting, holding public office, obtaining many jobs and occupational licenses, entering judicially-enforceable agreements, maintaining family relationships, and obtaining insurance and pension benefits. See also **Civil death**.

Civil disobedience. A form of lawbreaking employed to demonstrate the injustice or unfairness of a particular law and indulged in deliberately to focus attention on the allegedly undesirable law. See **Civil disorder**.

Civil disorder. Any public disturbance involving acts of violence by assemblages of three or more persons, which causes an immediate danger of or results in damage or injury to the property or person of any other individual. 18 U.S.C.A. § 232. See also **Riot**.

Civil fraud. In taxation, the specific intent to evade a tax which taxpayer believes to be owing is an essential element of civil fraud. May also be applied to the tort of deceit or fraud in contrast to criminal fraud.

Civilian. Private citizen, as distinguished from such as belong to the armed services, or (in England) the church. One who is skilled or versed in the civil law.

Civilis /sívələs/. Lat. Civil, as distinguished from criminal. *Civilis actio*, a civil action.

Civilista /sìvəlístə/. In old English law, a civil lawyer, or civilian.

Civiliter /səvílədər/. Civilly. In a person's civil character or position, or by civil (not criminal) process or procedure. This term is used in distinction or opposition to the word *"criminaliter,"*—criminally,—to distinguish civil actions from criminal prosecutions.

Civiliter mortuus /səvílədər mórchuwəs/. Civilly dead; dead in the view of the law. The condition of one who has lost his civil rights and capacities, and is accounted dead in law. See **Civil death**.

Civilization. A law, an act of justice, or judgment which renders a criminal process civil.

A term which covers several states of society; it is relative, and has no fixed sense, but implies an improved and progressive condition of the people, living under an organized government. It consists not merely in material achievements, in accomplishment and accumulation of wealth, or in advancement in culture, science, and knowledge, but also in doing of equal and exact justice.

Civil jury trial. Trial of civil action before a jury rather than before a judge. In suits at common law in Federal court where value in controversy exceeds $20.00, there is constitutional right to jury trial. U.S. Const., 7th Amend.; Fed.R.Civil P. 38. See also **Jury trial**.

Civil law. That body of law which every particular nation, commonwealth, or city has established peculiarly for itself; more properly called "municipal" law, to distinguish it from the "law of nature," and from international law. Laws concerned with civil or private rights and remedies, as contrasted with criminal laws.

The system of jurisprudence held and administered in the Roman empire, particularly as set forth in the compilation of Justinian and his successors,—comprising the Institutes, Code, Digest, and Novels, and collectively denominated the *"Corpus Juris Civilis,"* —as distinguished from the common law of England and the canon law. The civil law (Civil Code) is followed in Louisiana. See **Code Civil**.

Civil liability. The amenability to civil action as distinguished from amenability to criminal prosecution. A sum of money assessed either as general, special or liquidated damages; may be either single, double or treble for violation such as overcharges.

Civil liability acts. See **Dram Shop Acts**.

Civil liberties. Personal, natural rights guaranteed and protected by Constitution; *e.g.* freedom of speech, press, freedom from discrimination, etc. Body of law dealing with natural liberties, shorn of excesses which invade equal rights of others. Constitutionally, they are restraints on government. Sowers v. Ohio Civil Rights Commission, 20 Ohio Misc. 115, 252 N.E.2d 463, 476. See also **Civil Rights Acts**.

Civil nuisance. At common law, anything done to hurt or annoyance of lands, tenements, or hereditaments of another. See **Nuisance**.

Civil obligation. One which binds in law, and may be enforced in a court of justice.

Civil offense. Term used to describe violations of statutes making the act a public nuisance. Also describes an offense which is malum prohibitum and not considered reprehensible.

Civil office. A non-military public office; one which pertains to the exercise of the powers or authority of government.

Civil officer. See **Officer**.

Civil possession. See **Possession**.

Civil procedure. Body of law concerned with methods, procedures and practices in civil litigation, *e.g.* Federal Rules of Civil Procedure; Title 28 of United States Code.

Civil process. See **Process**.

Civil responsibility. The liability to be called upon to respond to an action at law for an injury caused by a delict or crime, as opposed to criminal responsibility, or liability to be proceeded against in a criminal tribunal.

Civil rights. See **Civil liberties**.

Civil Rights Acts. Federal statutes enacted after Civil War, and more recently in 1957 and 1964, intended to implement and give further force to basic personal rights guaranteed by Constitution. Such Acts prohibit discrimination based on race, color, age, or religion.

Civil rules. See **Federal Rules of Civil Procedure**.

Civil servant. See **Civil service**.

Civil service. Term generally means employment in federal, state, city and town government with such positions filled on merit as a result of competitive examinations. Such employment carries with it certain statutory rights to job security, advancement, etc. See **Civil Service Commission; Competitive civil service examination**.

Civil Service Commission. The United States Civil Service Commission (CSC) was created by act of Congress on January 16, 1883. Authority is codified under 5 U.S.C.A. § 1101.

The Civil Service Act was designed to establish a merit system under which appointments to Federal jobs are made on the basis of fitness—as determined by open and competitive examination—rather than personal preference or political considerations. Over the years, additional legislation and Executive orders have broadened the Commission's role to include such Federal personnel management activities as job classification, status and tenure, pay comparability, awards, training, labor-management relations, equal employment opportunity, health and life insurance programs, and retirement. The Commission was reorganized and restructured under the Civil Service Reform Act of 1978. Similar commissions exist in most states covering state and local public employment.

Civil side. When the same court has jurisdiction of both civil and criminal matters, proceedings of the first class are often said to be on the civil side; those of the second, on the criminal side.

Civil suits. See **Civil action**.

Civil trials. Trials of civil as distinguished from criminal cases.

Civil war. In general, any internal armed conflict between persons of same country. War Between the States in which Federal government contended against seceding Confederate states from 1861 to 1865. Also, in England, war between Parliamentarians and Royalists from 1642 to 1652.

Civil year. See **Year**.

Civis /sívəs/. Lat. In the Roman law, a citizen; as distinguished from *incola* (an inhabitant); origin or birth constituting the former, domicile the latter.

Civitas /sívətæs/. Lat. In the Roman law, any body of people living under the same laws; a state. *Jus civitatis*, the law of a state; civil law. *Civitates fœderatœ*, towns in alliance with Rome, and considered to be free. Citizenship; one of the three *status*, conditions, or qualifications of persons.

C.J. An abbreviation for chief justice; also for circuit judge.

C.J.S. Corpus Juris Secundum.

C.L. An abbreviation for civil law.

Claflin trust. A type of trust in which donor or settlor makes specific provisions for termination and the courts respect such provisions by denying the beneficiary the right to terminate. Called an indestructible trust, deriving its name from the case, Claflin v. Claflin, 149 Mass. 19, 20 N.E. 454.

Claim. To demand as one's own or as one's right; to assert; to urge; to insist. Cause of action. Means by or through which claimant obtains possession or enjoyment of privilege or thing. Demand for money or property, *e.g.* insurance claim.

Right to payment, whether or not such right is reduced to judgment, liquidated, unliquidated, fixed, contingent, matured, unmatured, disputed, undisputed, legal, equitable, secured, or unsecured; or right to an equitable remedy for breach of performance if such breach gives rise to a right to payment, whether or not such right to an equitable remedy is reduced to judgment, fixed, contingent, matured, unmatured, disputed, undisputed, secured, or unsecured. Bankruptcy Act, § 101(4).

In conflicts of law, a receiver may be appointed in any state which has jurisdiction over the defendant who owes a claim. Restatement, Second, Conflicts, § 369.

See also Antecedent claim; Cause of action; Community debt; Complaint; Counterclaim; Cross-claim; False claim; Joinder; Liability; Liquidated claim; Third party complaint. For proof of claim, see **Proof**; for joinder of claims, see **Joinder**.

Claim adjuster. Independent agent or employee of insurance company who negotiates and settles claims against the insurer. See **Adjuster; Claimant adjuster.**

Claim and delivery. Action at law for recovery of specific personal chattels wrongfully taken and detained, with damages which the taking or detention has causes. A modification of common-law action of replevin.

Claimant. One who claims or asserts a right, demand or claim. See **Claim; Plaintiff.**

Claimant adjuster. One who will obtain, secure, enforce, or establish a right, claim, or demand for an individual against an insurance company.

Claim check. Form of receipt for bailed or checked property, which normally must be surrendered when such property is recovered.

Claim in equity. In English practice, in simple cases, the summary proceeding by claim was sometimes adopted. This summary practice was created by orders 22d April, 1850. By Consolid.Ord.1860, viii, r. 4, such claims were abolished.

Claim jumping. The location on ground, knowing it to be excess ground, within the staked boundaries of another mining claim initiated prior thereto, because law governing manner of making location had not been complied with, so that location covers the workings of the prior locators. Filing of duplicate mining claims hoping that prior claim will be invalid.

Claim of cognizance or **of consuance.** An intervention by a third person, claiming jurisdiction or demanding judicature in cause, which plaintiff has commenced out of the claimant's court. Now obsolete. 2 Bl. Comm. 350, note; 3 Bl.Comm. 298.

Claim of liberty. In English practice, a suit or petition to the queen, in the former court of exchequer, to have liberties and franchises confirmed there by the attorney general.

Claim of ownership, right and title. As regards adverse possession, claim of land as one's own to hold it for oneself. Claim of right, claim of title and claim of ownership are synonymous. Claimant's intention to claim in hostility to real owner. Color of title and claim of title are synonymous. Intention of disseisor to appropriate and use land as his own, irrespective of any semblance of color, or right, or title.

Claim of right doctrine. In taxation, a payment received under a claim of right is includible in income even though there is a possibility that all or part of it may have to be returned. North American Oil Consolidated v. Burnet, 286 U.S. 417, 52 S.Ct. 613, 76 L.Ed. 1197. A judicially imposed doctrine applicable to both cash and accrual basis taxpayers which holds that an amount is includible in income upon actual or constructive receipt if the taxpayer has an unrestricted claim to such amounts.

Claim property bond. A bond filed by a defendant in cases of replevin and of execution to procure return of goods.

Claims Collection Act. Federal Act which requires that each agency of the federal government attempt to collect claims of the government (*e.g.* overpayments) arising out of the activities of the agency.

Claims court. See **Court of Claims.**

Clam /klǽm/. Lat. In the civil law, covertly; secretly.

Clam delinquentes magis puniuntur quam palam /klǽm dəliŋkwéntiyz méyjəs pyùwniyántər kwǽm pǽləm/. Those sinning secretly are punished more severely than those sinning openly.

Clamea admittenda in itinere per attornatum /kléymiyə ædməténdə in aytínəriy pàr ətòrnéydəm/. An ancient writ by which the king commanded the justices in eyre to admit the claim by attorney of a person who was in the royal service, and could not appear in person.

Clam factum id videtur esse, quod quisque, quum controversiam haberet, habiturumve se putaret, fecit /klǽm fǽktəm íd vədíydər ésiy kwòd kwískwiy, kàm kòntrəvársh(iy)əm həbírət, hǽbət(y)ərámviy síy pyətérət, fíysət/. That appears to be covertly (secretly) done, which anyone did, when he had a legal dispute, or thought he would have one.

Clamor. In old English law, a claim or complaint; an outcry; clamor.

In the civil law, a claimant; a debt; anything claimed from another; a proclamation; an accusation.

Clam, vi, aut precario /klǽm, váy, òt prəkériyow/. A technical phrase of the Roman law, meaning by force, stealth, or importunity.

Clandestine. Secret, hidden, concealed; usually for some illegal or illicit purpose. For example, a clandestine marriage is one contracted without observing the conditions precedent prescribed by law, such as publication of banns, procuring a license, or the like.

Clap. See **Gonorrhea.**

Clarendon, assize of /əsúyz əv klǽrəndən/. English statute (1166) the principal feature of which was an improvement of judicial procedure in the case of criminals. It was a part of the same scheme of reform as the Constitution of Clarendon.

Clarendon, constitutions of /kònstətyúwshənz əv klǽrəndən/. Certain statutes made in the reign of Henry II of England, at a parliament held at Clarendon (A.D. 1164), by which the king checked the power of the pope and his clergy, and greatly narrowed the exemption they claimed from secular jurisdiction. 4 Bl.Comm. 422.

Class. A group of persons, things, qualities, or activities, having common characteristics or attributes. In re Kanawha Val. Bank, 144 W.Va. 346, 109 S.E.2d 649, 670. The order or rank according to which persons or things are arranged or assorted. Also a body of persons uncertain in number.

Class action. See **Class or representative action.**

Class directors. System whereby terms of directors are staggered, thus making takeover attempt difficult.

Classes of stock. Issuance of common stock in two general classes: Class A and Class B. Normally, only one class has voting rights.

Class gift. A gift of an aggregate sum to a body of persons uncertain in number at time of gift, to be ascertained at a future time, who are all to take in equal, or other definite proportions, the share of each being dependent for its amount upon the ultimate number. In re Clarke's Estate, 460 Pa. 41, 331 A.2d 408, 410.

Classiarius /klǽsiyériyəs/. A seaman or soldier serving at sea.

Classici /klǽsəsay/. In the Roman law, persons employed in servile duties on board of vessels.

Classification. Arrangement into groups or categories on the basis of established criteria. The word may have two meanings, one primarily signifying a division required by statutes, fundamental and substantial, and the other secondary, signifying an arrangement or enumeration adopted for convenience only.

Classification of crimes. A grouping of crimes; taxonomy which may be based on the seriousness of the crime, *e.g.* felony or misdemeanor, or on the nature of the crime, *e.g.* malum prohibitum or malum in se, or on the objects of the crime, *e.g.* crimes against property or crimes against the person. Felonies and misdemeanors are also sometimes classified in state statutes as Class A, B, etc., with punishments set for each class. Crimes are also commonly classified into degrees; *e.g.*, first and second degree murder; and also as voluntary or involuntary (*e.g.* manslaughter).

Classification of risks. Term used in fire insurance to designate the nature and situation of the articles insured, and in accident insurance to the occupation of the applicant.

Classified. Grouped into classes. See **Classification**.

Classified tax. Tax system where different rates are assessed to each group of property.

Class legislation. Legislation limited in operation to certain persons or classes of persons, natural or artificial, or to certain districts of territory or state. Legislation operating upon portion of particular class of persons or things.

The term is applied to enactments which divide the people or subjects of legislation into classes, with reference either to the grant of privileges or the imposition of burdens, upon an arbitrary, unjust, or invidious principle, or which make arbitrary discriminations between those persons or things coming within the same class. Such laws commonly violate equal protection guarantees of Fourteenth Amendment.

Class or **representative action.** A class action provides a means by which, where a large group of persons are interested in a matter, one or more may sue or be sued as representatives of the class without needing to join every member of the class. This procedure is available in federal court and in most state courts under Rule of Civil Procedure 23. See also New York C.P.L.R. § 901.

There are general requirements for the maintenance of any class suit. These are that the persons constituting the class must be so numerous that it is impracticable to bring them all before the court, and the named representatives must be such as will fairly insure the adequate representation of them all. In addition, there must be an ascertainable class and there must be a well defined community of interest in the questions of law and fact involved affecting the parties to be represented. Daar v. Yellow Cab Co., 67 Cal.2d 695, 63 Cal.Rptr. 724, 731, 433 P.2d 732.

Prior to the revision of Civil Procedure Rule 23 in 1966, there were three categories of class actions, popularly known as "true", "hybrid", and "spurious." These categories no longer exist under present Rule 23.

See **Hybrid class action; Spurious class action.**

Clause /klóz/. A single paragraph or subdivision of a pleading or legal document, such as a contract, deed, will, constitution, or statute. Sometimes a sentence or part of a sentence. See **Paragraph.**

Clause potestative. In French law, the name given to the clause whereby one party to a contract reserves to himself the right to annul it.

Clause rolls. In old English law, rolls which contain all such matters of record as were committed to close writs; these rolls are preserved in the Tower.

Clausula /klóz(h)yələ/. A clause; a sentence or part of a sentence in a written instrument or law.

Clausula derogativa /klózhələ dərògətáyvə/. A clause in a will which provides that no will subsequently made is to be valid. The latter would still be valid, but there would be ground for suspecting undue influence.

Clausulæ inconsuetæ semper inducunt suspicionem /klózhəliy iŋkənswíydiy sémpər ənd(y)úwkənt səspishiyównəm/. Unusual clauses [in an instrument] always induce suspicion.

Clausula generalis de residuo non ea complectitur quæ non ejusdem sint generis cum iis quæ speciatim dicta fuerant /klózhələ jènəréyləs dìy rəzídyuwow nòn íyə kəmplékdədər kwìy nón əjásdəm sint jénərəs kàm áyəs kwìy spèshiyéydəm díktə f(y)úwərənt/. A general clause of remainder does not embrace those things which are not of the same kind with those which had been specially mentioned.

Clausula generalis non refertur ad expressa /klózhələ jènəréyləs non rəfárdər æd əksprésə/. A general clause does not refer to things expressed.

Clausula quæ abrogationem excludit ab initio non valet /klózhələ kwìy æbrəgèyshiyównəm əkskl(y)úwdət æb ənísh(iy)ow nòn vǽlət/. A clause [in a law] which precludes its abrogation is void from the beginning.

Clausula rebus sic stantibus /klózhələ ríybəs sik stǽntəbəs/. A tacit condition said to attach to all contracts meaning that they cease to be obligatory as soon as the state of facts out of which they arose has changed. This principle was used to demand payment on a contract value for value when the currency in which payment had been specified had become worthless through inflation/depreciation.

Clausula vel dispositio inutilis per præsumptionem remotam, vel causam ex post facto non fulcitur /klózhələ vèl dìspəzísh(iy)ow inyúwdələs pàr prəzàm(p)shiyównəm, rəmówdəm, vèl kózəm éks pòwst fǽktow nòn fálsədər/. A useless clause or disposition [one which expresses no more than the law by intendment would have supplied] is not supported by a remote presumption [or foreign intendment of some purpose, in regard whereof it might be material], or by a cause arising afterwards [which may induce an operation of those idle words].

Clausum /klózəm/. Lat. Close, closed up, sealed. Inclosed, as a parcel of land. A writ was either *clausum* (close) or *apertum* (open). Grants were said to be by *literæ patentæ* (open grant) or *literæ clausæ* (close grant); 2 Bl.Comm. 346. Occurring in the phrase *quare clausum fregit* it denotes in this sense only realty in which the plaintiff has some exclusive interest, whether for a limited or unlimited time or for special or for general purposes.

Clausum fregit /klózəm fríyjət/. L. Lat. (He broke the close.) In pleading and practice, technical words formerly used in certain actions of trespass, and still retained in the phrase *quare clausum fregit (q.v.)*.

Clausum paschiæ /klózəm pǽskiyiy/. In English law, the morrow of the *utas*, or eight days of Easter; the end of Easter; the Sunday after Easter-day.

Clausura /kləzhúrə/. In old English law, an inclosure. *Clausura heyœ*, the inclosure of a hedge.

Clavia /kléyviyə/. In old English law, a club or mace; tenure *per serjeantiam claviæ*, by the serjeanty of the club or mace.

Clawa. A close, or small inclosure.

Clayton Act. A Federal law enacted in 1914 as amendment to the Sherman Antitrust Act dealing with antitrust regulations and unfair trade practices. 15 U.S.C.A. §§ 12–27. The Act prohibits price discrimination, tying and exclusive dealing contracts, mergers, and interlocking directorates, where the effect may be substantially to lessen competition or tend to create a monopoly in any line of commerce.

Clean. Irreproachable; innocent of fraud or wrongdoing; free from defect in form or substance; free from exceptions or reservations. It is a very elastic adjective, however, and is particularly dependent upon context.

Clean Air Acts. Federal and state environmental statutes enacted to regulate and control air pollution.

Clean bill. Bill of exchange without documents attached.

Clean bill of health. One certifying that no contagious or infectious disease exists, or certifying as to healthy conditions generally without exception or reservation. See **Bill** *(Maritime law)*.

Clean bill of lading. One without exception or reservation as to the place or manner of stowage of the goods, and importing that the goods are to be (or

have been) safely and properly stowed under deck. One which contains nothing in the margin qualifying the words in the bill of lading itself.

Clean hands doctrine. Under "clean hands" doctrine, equity will not grant relief to a party, who, as actor, seeks to set judicial machinery in motion and obtain some remedy, if such party in his prior conduct has violated conscience or good faith or other equitable principle. Franklin v. Franklin, 365 Mo. 442, 283 S.W.2d 483, 486.

Clear. Obvious; beyond reasonable doubt; perspicuous; plain. Free from all limitation, qualification, question or shortcoming. Free from incumbrance, obstruction, burden, limitation, etc. Plain, evident, free from doubt or conjecture, unequivocal, also unincumbered. Free from deductions or drawbacks.

Clearance. In maritime law, the right of a ship to leave port. The act of clearing or leaving port. The certificate issued by the collector of a port evidencing the power of the ship to leave port. In contract for exhibition of motion pictures, the interval of time between conclusion of exhibition in one theater and commencement of exhibition at another theater. Waxmann v. Columbia Pictures Corporation, D.C.Pa., 40 F.Supp. 108, 111.

Clearance card. A letter given to an employee by his employer, at the time of his discharge or end of service, showing the cause of such discharge or voluntary quittance, the length of time of service, his capacity, and such other facts as would give to those concerned information of his former employment.

Clearance certificate. Issued to ship's captain showing that customs requirements have been made.

Clear and convincing proof. Generally, this phrase and its numerous variations mean proof beyond a reasonable, *i.e.*, a well-founded doubt. Some cases give a less rigorous, but somewhat uncertain, meaning, *viz.*, more than a preponderance but less than is required in a criminal case.

Proof which should leave no reasonable doubt in the mind of the trier of the facts concerning the truth of the matters in issue. In Interest of Jones, 34 Ill.App.3d 603, 340 N.E.2d 269, 274.

That measure or degree of proof which will produce in mind of trier of facts a firm belief or conviction as to allegations sought to be established; it is intermediate, being more than mere preponderance, but not to extent of such certainty as is required beyond reasonable doubt as in criminal cases. Fred C. Walker Agency, Inc. v. Lucas, 215 Va. 535, 211 S.E.2d 88, 92.

See also **Beyond a reasonable doubt; Burden of proof; Clear evidence or proof**.

Clear and present danger doctrine. Doctrine in constitutional law, first formulated in Schenck v. U. S., 249 U.S. 47, 39 S.Ct. 247, 63 L.Ed. 470, providing that governmental restrictions on freedoms of speech and press will be upheld if necessary to prevent grave and immediate danger to interests which government may lawfully protect.

Speech which incites to unlawful action falls outside the protection of the First Amendment where there is a direct connection between the speech and violation of the law; this is the "clear and present danger test". People v. Winston, 64 Misc.2d 150, 314 N.Y.S.2d 489, 495.

Clear annual value. The net yearly value to the possessor of the property, over and above taxes, interest on mortgages, and other charges and deductions.

Clear annuity. The devise of an annuity "clear" means an annuity free from taxes or free or clear of legacy or inheritance taxes.

Clear chance. A "clear chance" to avoid accident within meaning of last clear chance doctrine involves the element of sufficient time to appreciate peril of the party unable to extricate himself therefrom, and to take necessary steps to avoid injuring him. Klouse v. Northern Pac. Ry. Co., 50 Wash.2d 432, 312 P.2d 647, 650. See also **Last clear chance doctrine.**

Clear days. If a certain number of clear days be given for the doing of any act, the time is to be reckoned exclusively, as well of the first day as the last.

Clear evidence or proof. Evidence which is positive, precise and explicit, which tends directly to establish the point to which it is adduced and is sufficient to make out a prima facie case. It necessarily means a clear preponderance. It may mean no more than a fair preponderance of proof but may also be construed as requiring a higher degree of proof. It may convey the idea, under emphasis, of certainty, or understood as meaning beyond doubt. See also **Beyond a reasonable doubt; Clear and convincing proof.**

Clearing. The departure of a vessel from port, after complying with the customs and health laws and like local regulations. See also **Clearance; Clearance certificate.**

In banking, a method of making exchanges and settling balances, adopted among banks and bankers. See **Clearinghouse.**

Clearing account. An account containing amounts to be transferred to another account(s) before the end of the accounting period.

Clearing corporation. A corporation, all of the capital stock of which is held by or for a national securities exchange or association registered under a statute of the U.S., such as the Securities Exchange Act of 1934. U.C.C. § 8–102(3).

Clearinghouse. An association or place where banks exchange checks and drafts drawn on each other, and settle their daily balances. See U.C.C. § 4–104(d).

Clearing loan. One made to a bond dealer while an issue of bonds is being sold.

Clearings. Method of making exchanges and settling balances among banks and bankers.

Clearing title. Acts or proceedings necessary to render title marketable.

Clear legal right. A right inferable as a matter of law from uncontroverted facts.

Clearly. Visible, unmistakable, in words of no uncertain meaning. Beyond a question or beyond a reasonable doubt; honestly, straightforwardly, and frankly; plainly. Without obscurity, obstruction, entanglement, confusion, or uncertainty. Unequivocal.

Clearly erroneous. Findings when based upon substantial error in proceedings or misapplication of law, Kauk v. Anderson, C.C.A.N.D., 137 F.2d 331, 333; or when unsupported by substantial evidence, or contrary to clear weight of evidence or induced by erroneous view of the law. Gasifier Mfg. Co. v. General Motors Corporation, C.C.A.Mo., 138 F.2d 197, 199; Smith v. Porter, C.C.A.Ark., 143 F.2d 292, 294. See also **Error.**

Clearly proved. Preponderance of the evidence. Olson v. Union Oil Co. of California, 25 Cal.App.2d 627, 78 P.2d 446, 447. Proof sufficient to satisfy mind of finder of facts that its weight is such as to cause a reasonable person to accept the fact as established. In re Frihauf, 58 Wyo. 479, 135 P.2d 427, 433. See **Beyond a reasonable doubt; Clear and convincing proof,** *supra.*

Clear market price. Fair market price.

Clear market value. With regard to inheritance tax, highest price obtainable. Sum which property would bring on a fair sale by a willing seller not obliged to sell to a willing buyer not obliged to buy, or fair market value, or cash value. See **Fair market value.**

Clear reflection of income. The Internal Revenue Service has the authority to redetermine a taxpayer's income using a method which clearly reflects income if the taxpayer's method does not do so. I.R.C. § 446(b). In addition, the I.R.S. may apportion or allocate income among the various related business if income is not "clearly reflected". I.R.C. § 482.

Clear residue. Addition of income from funds, used to pay decedent's debts, administration expenses, and general legacies, to residue of estate.

Clear title. Good title; marketable title; one free from incumbrance, obstruction, burden, or limitation. Frank v. Murphy, 64 Ohio App. 501, 29 N.E.2d 41, 43. See **Marketable title.**

Clear title of record. Freedom from apparent defects, grave doubts, and litigious uncertainties. Such title as a reasonably prudent person, with full knowledge, would accept. Tull v. Milligan, 173 Okl. 131, 48 P.2d 835, 842. See **Marketable title.**

Clear view doctrine. See **Plain view doctrine.**

Clemency /klémən(t)siy/. Kindness, mercy, leniency. Used *e.g.* to describe act of governor of state when he commutes death sentence to life imprisonment, or grants pardon. See also **Amnesty; Pardon.**

Clementines /kléməntiynz/. In canon law, the collection of decretals or constitutions of Pope Clement V, made by order of John XXII, his successor, who published it in 1317.

Clement's inn. An inn of chancery. See **Inns of chancery.**

Clergy. The whole of clergymen or ministers of religion. Also an abbreviation for "benefit of clergy". See **Benefit of clergy.**

Clergyable. In old English law, allowing of, or entitled to, the benefit of clergy (*privilegium clericale*). Used of persons or crimes. 4 Bl.Comm. 371. See **Benefit of clergy**.

Clergyman. Member of the clergy. Spiritual representative of church.

Clergy privilege. Formerly, exemption given to clergy from being tried in civil courts because of availability of trial in canonical court. See **Benefit of clergy**.

Clerical. Pertaining to clergymen; or pertaining to the office or labor of a clerk. See also **Clerk; Ministerial**.

Clericale privilegium /klèhrəkéyliy prìvəlíyjiyəm/. In old English law, the clerical privilege; the privilege or benefit of clergy.

Clerical error. Generally, a mistake in writing or copying. Los Angeles Shipbuilding & Dry Dock Corporation v. Los Angeles County, 22 Cal.App.2d 418, 71 P.2d 282.

It may include error apparent on face of instrument, record, indictment or information, In re Goldberg's Estate, 10 Cal.2d 709, 76 P.2d 508, 512; error in respect of matters of record, Shotwell v. State, 135 Tex.Cr.R. 366, 120 S.W.2d 97; errors, mistakes, or omissions by clerk, writer, counsel, or judge which are not the result of exercise of judicial function, Pacific Finance Corporation of California v. La Monte, 64 Idaho 438, 133 P.2d 921, 922; Wilson v. City of Fergus Falls, 181 Minn. 329, 232 N.W. 322, 323; failure of clerk to enter order, Keller v. Cleaver, 20 Cal.App.2d 364, 67 P.2d 131, 133; omission in statutory provision, Craig v. State, 204 Ark. 798, 164 S.W.2d 1007, 1008; order fixing tax rate below statutory rate, In re Jagnow's Estate, 148 Misc. 657, 266 N.Y.S. 785, 788; placing of case on calendar without notice, New England Furniture & Carpet Co. v. Willcuts, D.C.Minn., 55 F.2d 983, 987; purported order incongruous and irrelevant to surrounding recitals, Carpenter v. Pacific Mut. Life Ins. Co. of California, 14 Cal.2d 704, 96 P.2d 796, 799; signature by judge to judgment which does not express judicial desire or intention, Bastajian v. Brown, 19 Cal.2d 209, 120 P.2d 9, 12.

As applied to judgments and decrees is a mistake or omission by a clerk, counsel, judge or printer which is not the result of exercise of judicial function. In re Humboldt River System, 77 Nev. 244, 362 P.2d 265, 267.

Clerical errors may be corrected by the court at any time of its own initiative or on the motion of any party and after such notice, if any, as the court orders. Fed.R. Civil P. 60(a).

Clerical misprision. Mistake or fraud perpetrated by clerk of court which is susceptible of demonstration by face of record, or a clerical error, which is an error by clerk in transcribing or otherwise apparent on the face of the record. Ballew v. Fowler, 285 Ky. 149, 147 S.W.2d 65, 66.

Clerical tonsure. In old English law, the having the head shaven, which was formerly peculiar to clerks, or persons in orders, and which the coifs worn by serjeants at law are supposed to have been introduced to conceal. 1 Bl.Comm. 24, note t; 4 Bl.Comm. 367.

Clerici de cancellaria; clerici de cursu /kléhrəsay dìy kænsəlériyə,°kərs(y)uw/. Clerks of the chancery. See **Cursitors**.

Clerici non ponantur in officiis /kléhrəsay nòn pənǽntər in əfís(h)iyays/. Clergymen should not be placed in offices; *i.e.*, in secular offices.

Clerici prænotarii /kléhrəsay prìynətériyay/. The six clerks in chancery.

Clerico admittendo /kléhrəkow ǽdmətÉndow/. See **Admittendo clerico**.

Clerico capto per statutum mercatorum /kléhrəkow kǽptow pər statyúwdəm mərkətórəm/. A writ for the delivery of a clerk out of prison, who was taken and incarcerated upon the breach of a statute merchant.

Clerico convicto commisso gaolæ in defectu ordinarii deliberando /kléhrəkow kənvíktow kəmísow jéyliy in dəfékt(y)uw òrdənériyay dəlibərǽndow/. An ancient writ, that lay for the delivery to his ordinary of a clerk convicted of felony, where the ordinary did not challenge him according to the privilege of clerks.

Clerico infra sacros ordines constituto, non eligendo in officium /kléhrəkow ínfrə sǽkrows órdəniyz kònstətyúwdow, nón eləjéndow, in əfís(h)iyəm/. A writ directed to those who had thrust a bailiwick or other office upon one in holy orders, charging them to release him.

Clericus /kléhrəkəs/. In old English law, a clerk or priest; a person in holy orders; a secular priest; a clerk of a court. An officer of the royal household, having charge of the receipt and payment of moneys, etc. In Roman law, a minister of religion in the Christian church; an ecclesiastic or priest. A general term, including bishops, priests, deacons, and others of inferior order. Also of the amanuenses of the judges or courts of the king.

Clericus et agricola et mercator, tempore belli, ut oret, colat, et commutet, pace fruuntur /klérəkəs èd əgríkələ èt mərkéydər, témpəriy bélay, əd órət kówləd èt kómyədəl, péysiy fruwə́ntər/. Clergymen, husbandmen, and merchants, in order that they may preach, cultivate, and trade, enjoy peace in time of war.

Clericus mercati /kléhrəkəs mərkéyday/. In old English law, clerk of the market.

Clericus non connumeretur in duabus ecclesiis /kléhrəkəs nòn kən(y)ùwməríydər in d(y)uwéybəs əklíyziyəs/. A clergyman should not be appointed to two churches.

Clericus parochialis /kléhrəkəs pəròwkiyéyləs/. In old English law, a parish clerk.

Clerigos /klériygows/. In Spanish law, clergy; men chosen for the service of God.

Clerk. Officer of court who files pleadings, motions, judgments, etc., issues process, and keeps records of court proceedings. Functions and duties of clerks of court are usually specified by statute or court rules; *e.g.* Fed.R. Civil P. 77, 79.

Person employed in public office whose duties include keeping records or accounts.

One who sells goods, waits on customers, or engages in clerical work such as bookkeeping, copying, transcribing, letter writing, tabulating, stenography, etc.

A person in holy orders; a clergyman; a cleric; an individual attached to the ecclesiastical state, and who has the clerical tonsure. See 4 Bl.Comm. 366, 367.

Clerk of arraigns. In English law, an assistant to the clerk of assise. His duties were in the crown court on circuit.

Clerk of assise. In English law, officers who officiated as associates on the circuits. They recorded all judicial proceedings done by the judges on the circuit.

Clerk of enrollments. In English law, the former chief officer of the English enrollment office (q.v.). He now forms part of the staff of the central office.

Clerk of the Crown in Chancery. See **Crown Office in Chancery**.

Clerk of the House of Commons. An officer of the English House of Commons appointed by the crown. He makes entries, remembrances, and journals of the things done and passed in the house. He signs all orders of the house, indorses the bills sent or returned to the lords, and reads whatever is required to be read in the house. He has the custody of all records and other documents.

Clerk of the market. In English law, the overseer or superintendent of a public market. In old English law, he was a *quasi* judicial officer, having power to settle controversies arising in the market between persons dealing there. Called *"clericus mercati."* 4 Bl.Comm. 275.

Clerk of the parliaments. In England, one of the chief officers of the House of Lords. He is appointed by the Crown, by letters patent. On entering office he makes a declaration to make true entries and records of the things done and passed in the parliaments, and to keep secret all such matters as shall be treated therein.

Clerk of the peace. In English law, an officer whose duties are to officiate at sessions of the peace, to prepare indictments, and to record the proceedings of the justices, and to perform a number of special duties in connection with the affairs of the county.

Clerk of the privy seal. In England, these officers attend the lord privy seal, or, in absence of the lord privy seal, the principal secretary of state. Their duty is to write and make out all things that are sent by warrant from the signet to the privy seal, and which are to be passed to the great seal; and also to make out privy seals (as they are termed) upon any special occasion of his majesty's affairs.

Clerk of the signet. An officer, in England, whose duty it is to attend on the king's principal secretary, who has the custody of the privy signet, as well for the purpose of sealing his majesty's private letters, as also grants which pass his majesty's hand by bill signed.

Clerk of the table. An official of the British House of Commons who advises the speaker on all questions of order.

Clerkship. The period which formerly must have been spent by a law-student in the office of a practicing attorney before admission to the bar. Term now generally refers to law student who clerks for an attorney, law firm, or judge, or recent law school graduate who clerks for a judge.

Clerks of indictments. Officers attached to the central criminal court in England, and to each circuit. They prepare and settle indictments against offenders, and assist the clerk of arraigns.

Clerks of records and writs. Officers formerly attached to the English court of chancery, whose duties consisted principally in sealing bills of complaint and writs of execution, filing affidavits, etc. By the judicature (officers') act, 1879, they were transferred to the central office of the supreme court, under the title of "Masters of the Supreme Court," and the office has been abolished.

Clerks of seats. In the principal registry of the probate division of the English high court, they discharge the duty of preparing and passing the grants of probate and letters of administration, take bonds from administrators, receive *caveats* against a grant being made, etc.

Cliens /klíyən(d)z/. Lat. In the Roman law, a client or dependent. One who depended upon another as his patron or protector, adviser or defender, in suits at law and other difficulties.

Client. A person who employs or retains an attorney, or counsellor, to appear for him in courts, advise, assist, and defend him in legal proceedings, and to act for him in any legal business. It should include one who disclosed confidential matters to attorney while seeking professional aid, whether attorney was employed or not.

Clientela /klàyəntíylə/. In old English law, clientship, the state of a client; and, correlatively, protection, patronage, guardianship.

Client security fund. A fund set up by many state bar associations to cover losses incurred by persons as a result of dishonest conduct of member-attorneys.

Client's privilege. Right of client to require attorney to keep secret communications made to him in the attorney-client relationship and to prevent disclosure on the witness stand. U. S. v. United Shoe Mach. Corp., D.Mass., 89 F.Supp. 357. See **Communication** *(Confidential)*.

Clifford trust. A grantor trust whereby the grantor (*i.e.*, creator) of the trust retains the right to possess again the property transferred in trust (*i.e.*, a reversionary interest is retained) upon the occurrence of an event (*e.g.*, the death of the beneficiary) or the expiration of a period of time. Unless the requirements of I.R.C. § 673 are satisfied, the income from the property placed in trust will continue to be taxed to the grantor rather than to the beneficiary. Helvering v. Clifford, 309 U.S. 331, 60 S.Ct. 554, 84 L.Ed. 788.

Clinical tests. Tests involving direct observation of the patient, including laboratory and diagnostic examinations.

Clipped sovereignty. In the relations of the several states of the United States to other nations, the states have what is termed a clipped sovereignty. Anderson v. N. V. Transandine Handelmaatschappij, Sup., 28 N.Y.S.2d 547, 552.

Clito /kláydow/. In Saxon law, the son of a king or emperor. The next heir to the throne; the Saxon adeling.

Cloere. A jail; a prison or dungeon.

Close, *v.* To finish, bring to an end, conclude, terminate, complete, wind up; as, to "close" an account, a bargain, a trial, an estate, or public books, such as tax books.

In accounting, to transfer the balance of a temporary or contra or adjunct account to the main account to which it relates.

To shut up, so as to prevent entrance or access by any person; as in statutes requiring liquor establishments to be "closed" at certain times, which further implies an entire suspension of business. To go out of business. To bar access to. To suspend or stop operations of.

Close, *n.* A portion of land, as a field, inclosed as by a hedge, fence, or other visible inclosure, or by an invisible ideal boundary founded on limit of title. The interest of a person in any particular piece of land, whether actually inclosed or not.

Close, *adj.* Closed or sealed up. Restricted to a particular class. Decided by a narrow margin.

Close copies. Copies of legal documents which might be written closely or loosely at pleasure; as distinguished from *office* copies.

Close corporation. See **Corporation**.

Closed court. A term sometimes used to designate the Common Pleas Court of England when only serjeants could argue cases, which practice persisted until 1883.

Closed-end investment trust. Trust wherein only original prescribed shares can be distributed.

Closed-end mortgage. A mortgage that does not permit additional borrowing.

Closed insurance policy. Insurance contract, the terms and rates of which cannot be changed.

Closed primary. Members of each political party participate in nominating candidates of that party, and the voters of one party are not allowed to nominate candidates for another party.

Closed season. The same as "close season" *(q.v.).*

Closed shop. Such shop exists where worker must be member of union as condition precedent to employment. Miners in General Group v. Hix, 123 W.Va. 637, 17 S.E.2d 810, 813. This practice was made unlawful by the Taft-Hartley Act. *Contrast* **Open shop.** See also **Right to work laws.**

Closed shop contract. A contract requiring employer to hire only union members and to discharge non-union members and requiring that employees, as a condition of employment, remain union members. Silva v. Mercier, Cal.App., 187 P.2d 60, 64. "Closed shop" provision in collective bargaining agreement requires membership in the contracting union before a job applicant can be employed and for the duration of his employment. Higgins v. Cardinal Mfg. Co., 188 Kan. 11, 360 P.2d 456, 461.

Closed transaction. Term used in tax law to describe a taxable event which has been consummated. For example, diminution in value of goodwill of business is not a closed transaction so as to permit deduction of the diminution of value as ordinary loss. Joffre v. U. S., D.C.Ga., 331 F.Supp. 1177.

Closed union. A labor union whose membership rolls have closed. See also **Closed shop.**

Close-hauled. In admiralty law, this nautical term means the arrangement or trim of a vessel's sails when she endeavors to make progress in the nearest direction possible towards that point of the compass from which the wind blows. But a vessel may be considered as close-hauled, although she is not quite so near to the wind as she could possibly lie.

Close jail execution. A body execution which has indorsed in or upon it the statement that the defendant ought to be confined in close jail.

Close relatives. Kinfolk who bear a close relationship to another such as mother, father, brother, sister, husband, wife and children.

Close rolls. Rolls containing the record of the close writs *(literæ clausæ)* and grants of the king, kept with the public records. 2 Bl.Comm. 346. See **Writ.**

Close season. The season of the year or period of time in which the taking of particular game or fish is prohibited, or in which all hunting or fishing is forbidden by law. See also **Fence-month.**

Close to. Near; very near; immediately adjoining.

Close writ. See **Writ.**

Closing. As regards sale of real estate, refers to the final steps of the transaction whereat the consideration is paid, mortgage is secured, deed is delivered or placed in escrow, etc. Such closings, which normally take place at a bank or savings and loan institution, are regulated by the federal Real Estate Settlement Procedures Act (RESPA). See **Closing costs; Closing statement**.

Closing argument. The final statements by the attorneys to jury or court summarizing the evidence that they think they have established and the evidence that they think the other side has failed to establish. Such is made before judge's charge to jury. Such does not constitute evidence and may be limited in time by rule of court.

In federal criminal cases, after the closing of evidence the prosecution opens the argument; the defense then replies. The prosecution is then permitted to reply in rebuttal. Fed.R.Crim.P. 29.1.

Closing costs. Expenses which must be paid in addition to the purchase price on the sale of real estate. Closing costs with respect to a debt secured by an interest in land include: (a) fees or premiums for title examination, title insurance, or similar purposes including surveys, (b) fees for preparation of a deed, settlement statement, or other documents, (c) escrows for future payments of taxes and insurance, (d) fees for notarizing deeds and other documents, (e) appraisal fees, and (f) credit reports. Uniform Consumer Credit Code, Section 1.301(5). The full disclosure of such costs is regulated by the federal Real Estate Settlement Procedures Act (RESPA).

Closing entries. In accounting, the entries that accomplish the transfer of balances in temporary accounts to the related balance sheet accounts.

Closing estates. Winding up of estates by paying legacies and inheritances, taxes, and filing necessary probate accounts.

Closing statement. Written analysis of closing of real estate transaction setting forth purchase price less deductions for such items as mortgage payoff, tax adjustments, etc. and adding credits to arrive at net amount due seller. Detailed statement is required under federal Real Estate Settlement Procedures Act (RESPA). See also **Closing argument; Closing costs.**

Cloture. Legislative rule or procedure whereby unreasonable debate (*i.e.* filibuster) is ended to permit vote to be taken.

Cloud on title. An outstanding claim or encumbrance which, if valid, would affect or impair the title of the owner of a particular estate, and on its face has that effect, but can be shown by extrinsic proof to be invalid or inapplicable to the estate in question. Best Inv. Co. v. Parkhill, Tex.Civ.App., 429 S.W.2d 531, 534. A conveyance, mortgage, judgment, tax-levy, etc., may all, in proper cases, constitute a cloud on title. Newpar Estates, Inc. v. Barilla, 161 N.Y.S.2d 950, 952. The remedy for removing a cloud on title is usually the means of an action to quiet title. See **Quiet title action.**

Clough. A valley. Also an allowance for the turn of the scale, on buying goods wholesale by weight.

C.L.P. Common law procedure, in reference to the English acts so entitled.

Club. A voluntary, incorporated or unincorporated association of persons for common purposes of a social, literary, investment, political nature, or the like. Association of persons for promotion of some common object, such as literature, science, politics, good fellowship, etc., especially one jointly supported and meeting periodically, and membership is usually conferred by ballot and carries privilege of exclusive use of club quarters, and word also applies to a building, apartment or room occupied by a club.

Club-law. Rule of violence; regulation by force; the law of arms.

Clue. Suggestion or piece of evidence which may or may not lead to solution of crime or puzzle.

Cluster zoning. Cluster zoning modifies lot size and frontage requirements on certain conditions involving setting aside of land by the developer for parks, schools, or other public needs. Steel Hill Development, Inc. v. Town of Sanbornton, C.A.N.H., 469 F.2d 956, 958. See **Planned unit development.**

Clypeus, or **clipeus** /klípiyəs/. In old English law, a shield; metaphorically one of a noble family. *Clypei prostrati,* noble families extinct.

C/o. Symbol meaning "care of".

Co. A prefix meaning with, in conjunction, joint, jointly, unitedly, and not separately, *e.g.,* cotrustees, co-executors, co-brokers. Also, an abbreviation for "county" and "company."

Co-adjutor /kòwəjúwdər/. An assistant, helper, or ally; particularly a person appointed to assist a bishop who from age or infirmity is unable to perform his duty. Also an overseer (co-adjutor of an executor), and one who disseises a person of land not to his own use, but to that of another.

Co-administrator. One who is a joint administrator with one or more others.

Coadunatio /kòwæjənéysh(iy)ow/. A uniting or combining together of persons; a conspiracy.

Co-adventurer. One who takes part with others in an adventure or in a venture or business undertaking attended with risk. Easter Oil Corporation v. Strauss, Tex.Civ.App., 52 S.W.2d 336, 344. See also **Adventure.**

Co-agent. See **Agent.**

Coal note. A species of promissory note, formerly in use in the port of London, containing the phrase "value received in coals." By the statute 3 Geo. II, c. 26, §§ 7, 8, these were to be protected and noted as inland bills of exchange. But this was repealed by the statute 47 Geo. III, sess. 2, c. 68, § 28.

Coal notice. In Pennsylvania, every deed, agreement of sale, title insurance policy and other instrument with respect to sale or conveyance of surface land, excepting mortgages or quitclaim conveyances, must include a statutory coal notice in each case involving a prior or contemporaneous severance of title to coal or right of surface support under any part of such surface land.

Co-assignee. One of two or more assignees of the same subject-matter.

Coast. The edge or margin of a country bounding on the sea. The term includes small islands and reefs naturally connected with the adjacent land, and rising above the surface of the water, but not shoals perpetually covered by water. This word is particularly appropriate to the edge of the sea, while "shore" may be used of the margins of inland waters. In precise modern usage, the term "shore" denotes line of low-water mark along mainland, while term "coast" denotes line of shore plus line where inland waters meet open sea. U. S. v. State of La., La., 363 U.S. 1, 121, 80 S.Ct. 961, 997, 4 L.Ed.2d 1025, 1096.

Coaster. A vessel plying exclusively between domestic ports, and usually engaged in domestic trade; not including pleasure yachts. Belden v. Chase, 150 U.S. 674, 14 S.Ct. 264, 37 L.Ed. 1218.

Coast Guard. The Coast Guard is responsible for enforcing Federal laws on the high seas and navigable waters of the United States and its possessions. Navigation and vessel inspection laws are specific responsibilities. Under provisions of the Federal Boating Act of 1958, Coast Guard boarding teams inspect small boats to insure compliance with required safety measures. The Coast Guard cooperates with other agencies in their law enforcement responsibilities and enforces conservation and marine environmental laws.

Coasting trade. In maritime law, commerce and navigation between different places along the coast of the United States. Commercial intercourse between different districts in different states, different districts in same state, or different places in same district, on sea-coast or on navigable river. Shannon v. Streckfus Steamers, 279 Ky. 649, 131 S.W.2d 833, 836.

Coast waters. Tide waters navigable from the ocean by sea-going craft, the term embracing all waters opening directly or indirectly into the ocean and navigable by ships coming in from the ocean of draft as great as that of the larger ships which traverse the open seas. The Britannia, 153 U.S. 130, 14 S.Ct. 795, 38 L.Ed. 660.

Coastwise. Vessels "plying coastwise" are those engaged in domestic trade, or plying between port and port in the United States.

Coat of arms. Heraldic ensigns, introduced by Richard I from the Holy Land, where they were first invented. Originally painted on shields of the Christian knights who went to the Holy Land during the crusades, to identify them. See **Insignia.**

Cocaine. A white crystaline narcotic alkaloid extracted from coca leaves. Used as a local anesthetic. A "controlled substance" as included in narcotic laws.

Cocket. In English law, a seal belonging to the customhouse, or rather a scroll of parchment, sealed and delivered by the officers of the customhouse to merchants, as a warrant that their merchandises are entered; likewise a sort of measure.

Cockpit. In England, a name which used to be given to the judicial committee of the privy council, the council-room being built on the old cockpit of Whitehall Place.

Cocksetus /kòksíydəs/. A boatman; a cockswain.

Co-conspirator. One who engages in an illegal confederacy with others. See **Conspiracy.**

Co-conspirator's rule. Under the "co-conspirator rule," all acts and declarations of members of conspiracy constitute acts and declarations of, and are therefore admissible against, each of them. Resnick v. State, Fla., 287 So.2d 24, 26. See also **Wharton Rule.**

Cocotte /kəkót/. A prostitute.

C. O. D. "Collect on delivery." These letters import the carrier's liability to the consignor to collect the cost of the goods from the consignee, and, if not collected, to return the goods to the consignor.

Code. A systematic collection, compendium or revision of laws, rules, or regulations. A private or official compilation of all permanent laws in force consolidated and classified according to subject matter. Many states have published official codes of all laws in force, including the common law and statutes as judicially interpreted, which have been compiled by code commissions and enacted by the legislatures. See also **Codification.**

Code Civil. The code which embodies the civil law of France. It was promulgated in 1804. When Napoleon became emperor, the name was changed to "Code Napoleon," by which it is still often designated though it is now officially styled by its original name of "Code Civil." A great part of the Louisiana Civil Code is derived from the Code Napoleon.

Code de commerce. A French code, enacted in 1807, as a supplement to the Code Napoleon, regulating commercial transactions, the laws of business, bankruptcies, and the jurisdiction and procedure of the courts dealing with these subjects.

Code de procedure civil. That part of the Code Napoleon which regulates the system of courts, their organization, civil procedure, special and extraordinary remedies, and the execution of judgments.

Code d'instruction criminelle. A French code, enacted in 1808, regulating criminal procedure.

Code noir. The black code. A body of laws which formerly regulated the institution of slavery in the French colonies.

Code of Justinian. The Code of Justinian (*Codex Justinianeus*) was a collection of imperial constitutions, compiled, by order of that emperor, by a commission, and promulgated A.D. 529. It comprised twelve books, and was the first of the four compilations of law which make up the *Corpus Juris Civilis.* This name is often met in a connection indicating that the entire *Corpus Juris Civilis* is intended, or, sometimes, the Digest; but its use should be confined to the *Codex.*

Code penal. The penal or criminal code of France, enacted in 1810. See also **Criminal law; Penal code.**

Co-defendant. More than one defendant being sued in the same litigation; or, more than one person charged in same complaint or indictment with same crime.

Code Napoleon. See **Code Civil.**

Code of criminal procedure. Body of federal or state law dealing with procedural aspects of trial of criminal cases; *e.g.* 18 U.S.C.A. § 3001 *et seq.* Such procedural laws are supplemented by Rules of Criminal Procedure and Rules of Evidence.

Code of Federal Regulations. The Code of Federal Regulations (CFR) is the annual cumulation of executive agency regulations published in the daily Federal Register, combined with regulations issued previously that are still in effect. Divided into 50 titles, each representing a broad subject area, individual volumes of the Code of Federal Regulations are revised at least once each calendar year and issued on a staggered quarterly basis. The CFR contains the general body of regulatory laws governing practice and procedure before federal administrative agencies.

Code of Military Justice. The Code is uniformly applicable in all its parts to the Army, the Navy, the Air Force, and the Coast Guard. It covers both the substantive and the procedural law governing military justice and its administration in all of the armed forces of the United States. The Code established a system of military courts, defines offenses, authorizes punishment, provides broad procedural guidance, and statutory safeguards which conform to the due process safeguards preserved and established by the constitution. As an additional safeguard for an accused person, the Code also provides for a system of automatic appellate review. A Court of Military Review is established within each service to review all court-martial cases where the sentence includes death, a punitive discharge, or confinement for one year or more. Appellate review in this court is automatic. No approved sentence of a courts-martial may be executed unless such findings and sentence are affirmed by a Court of Military Review. In addition, the Court of Military Appeals was established to review certain cases from all the Armed Forces. The latter Court consists of three civilian judges. Automatic review before the Court is provided for all cases in which the sentence, as affirmed by a Court of Military Review, affects a general or flag officer or extends to death. In addition, the Judge Advocate General of each service may direct that a case be reviewed by the Court. An accused may petition the Court for review. 10 U.S.C.A. § 801 et seq.

Uniform Code. Many states have adopted the Uniform Code of Military Justice, and others have adopted acts substantially following the Uniform Code.

Code of Professional Responsibility. The rules of conduct that govern the legal profession. This Code contains both general ethical guidelines and specific rules prohibiting certain actions and conduct. The Code was written by the American Bar Association and subsequently adopted by most states.

Code pleading. See **Pleadings.**

Codex. Lat. A code or collection of laws; particularly the Code of Justinian. Also a roll of volume, and a book written on paper or parchment.

Codex Gregorianus /kówdèks grəgòriyéynəs/. A collection of imperial constitutions made by Gregorius, a Roman jurist of the fifth century, about the middle of the century. It contained the constitutions from Hadrian down to Constantine.

Codex Hermogenianus /kówdèks hərməjìyniyéynəs/. A collection of imperial constitutions made by Hermogenes, a jurist of the fifth century. It was nothing more than a supplement to the Codex Gregorianus (supra), containing the constitutions of Diocletian and Maxmillian.

Codex Justinianeus /kówdèks jəstìniyéyn(iy)əs/. A collection of imperial constitutions, made by a commission of ten persons appointed by Justinian, A.D. 528.

Codex Repetitæ Prælectionis /kówdèks rèpətíshiyiy prəlèkshiyównəs/. The new code of Justinian; or the new edition of the first or old code, promulgated A.D. 534, being the one now extant.

Codex Theodosianus /kówdèks θiyədòws(h)iyéynəs/. A code compiled by the emperor Theodosius the younger, A.D. 438. 1 Bl.Comm. 81. It was a collection of all the imperial constitutions then in force. It was the only body of civil law publicly received as authentic in the western part of Europe till the twelfth century, the use and authority of the Code of Justinian being during that interval confined to the East. 1 Bl.Comm. 81.

Codex Vetus /kówdèks víydəs/. The old code. The first edition of the Code of Justinian; now lost.

Codicil. A supplement or an addition to a will; it may explain, modify, add to, subtract from, qualify, alter, restrain or revoke provisions in existing will. Such does not purport to dispose of entire estate or to contain the entire will of testator, nor does it ordinarily expressly or by necessary implication revoke in toto a prior will. In re Crooke Estate, 388 Pa. 125, 130 A.2d 185, 187.

Codicillus /kòdəsíləs/. In the Roman law, a codicil; an informal and inferior kind of will, in use among the Romans.

Codification /kòdəfəkéyshən/. The process of collecting and arranging systematically, usually by subject, the laws of a state or country, or the rules and regulations covering a particular area or subject of law or practice; *e.g.* United States Code; Code of Military Justice; Code of Federal Regulations; California Evidence Code. The end product may be called a code, revised code or revised statutes. See also **Compilation; Compiled statutes.**

Coemptio /kowém(p)shiyow/. One of the modes in which marriage was contracted among the Romans.

Co-emption. The act of purchasing the whole quantity of any commodity.

Co-equal. To be or become equal to. To have the same quantity, the same value, the same degree or rank, or the like, with. To be commensurate with. State ex rel. Com'rs of Land Office v. Board of Com'rs of Nowata County, 166 Okl. 78, 25 P.2d 1074, 1077.

Coerce /kowárs/. Compelled to compliance; constrained to obedience, or submission in a vigorous or forcible manner. See **Coercion.**

Coercion /kowárshən/. Compulsion; constraint; compelling by force or arms or threat. General Motors v. Blevins, D.C.Colo., 144 F.Supp. 381, 384. It may be actual, direct, or positive, as where physical force is used to compel act against one's will, or implied, legal or constructive, as where one party is constrained by subjugation to other to do what his free will would refuse. As used in testamentary law, any pressure by which testator's action is restrained against his free will in the execution of his testament. "Coercion" that vitiates confession can be mental as well as physical, and question is whether accused was deprived of his free choice to admit, deny, or refuse to answer. Garrity v. State of N. J., U.S.N.J., 385 U.S. 493, 87 S.Ct. 616, 618, 17 L.Ed.2d 562.

A person is guilty of criminal coercion if, with purpose to unlawfully restrict another's freedom of action to his detriment, he threatens to: (a) commit any criminal offense; or (b) accuse anyone of a criminal offense; or (c) expose any secret tending to subject any person to hatred, contempt or ridicule, or to impair his credit or business repute; or (d) take or withhold action as an official, or cause an official to take or withhold action. Model Penal Code, § 212.5.

See also **Duress; Threat.**

Co-executor. One who is a joint executor with one or more others. See also **Joint executors**.

Coffee-house. A house of entertainment where guests are supplied with coffee and other refreshments, and sometimes with lodging. Commonly serves as an informal club for its frequent guests.

Cofferer of the queen's household /kófərər əv ðə kwíynz háws-howld/. In English law, a principal officer of the royal establishment, next under the controller, who, in the countinghouse and elsewhere, had a special charge and oversight of the other officers, whose wages he paid.

Cogitationis pœnam nemo patitur /kòjətèyshiyównəs píynəm níymow pǽdədər/. No one is punished for his thoughts.

Cognac /kó(w)nyæk/. A distilled brandy, containing more than one-half of 1 per centum of alcohol. Benson v. U. S., C.C.A.Tex., 10 F.2d 309, 310.

Cognates /kógneyts/. (Lat. *cognati*.) Relations by the mother's side, or by females. A common term in Scotch law.

Cognati /kògnéyday/. Lat. In the civil law, cognates; relations by the mother's side. 2 Bl.Comm. 235. Relations in the line of the mother. Relations by or through females.

Cognatio /kògnéysh(iy)ow/. Lat. In the civil law, cognation; relationship, or kindred generally. Relationship through females, as distinguished from *agnatio*, or relationship through males. *Agnatio a patre sit, cognatio a matre.* See **Agnatio.**

In canon law, consanguinity, as distinguished from affinity. Consanguinity, as including affinity.

Cognation /kògnéyshən/. In the civil law, signifies generally the kindred which exists between two persons who are united by ties of blood or family, or both.

Civil cognation is that which proceeds alone from the ties of families, as the kindred between the adopted father and the adopted child.

Mixed cognation is that which unites at the same time the ties of blood and family, as that which exists between brothers the issue of the same lawful marriage.

Natural cognation is that which is alone formed by ties of blood; such is the kindred of those who owe their origin to an illicit connection, either in relation to their ascendants or collaterals.

Cognatus /kògnéydəs/. Lat. In the civil law, a relation by the mother's side; a cognate. A relation, or kinsman, generally.

Cognitio /kògnísh(iy)ow/. In old English law, the acknowledgment of a fine; the certificate of such acknowledgment. In the Roman law, the judicial examination or hearing of a cause.

Cognitiones /kognìshiyówniyz/. Ensigns and arms, or a military coat painted with arms.

Cognitionibus mittendis /kognìshiyównəbəs məténdəs/. In English law, a writ to a justice of the common pleas, or other, who has power to take a fine, who, having taken the fine, defers to certify it, commanding him to certify it. Now abolished.

Cognitive. The mental process of comprehension, judgment, memory and reasoning, as opposed to emotional and volitional processes.

Cognitor /kógnədər/. In the Roman law, an advocate or defender in a private cause; one who defended the cause of a person who was present.

Cognizable /kó(g)nəzəbəl/. Capable of being tried or examined before a designated tribunal; within jurisdiction of court or power given to court to adjudicate controversy. Samuel Goldwyn, Inc. v. United Artists Corporation, C.C.A.Del., 113 F.2d 703, 707.

Cognizance /kó(g)nəzən(t)s/. Jurisdiction, or the exercise of jurisdiction, or power to try and determine causes; judicial examination of a matter, or power and authority to make it. Judicial notice or knowledge; the judicial hearing of a cause; acknowledgment; confession; recognition.

Claim of cognizance or of conusance. See **Claim of cognizance or of conusance**.

Judicial cognizance. See **Judicial**.

Cognizee /kògnəzíy/. The party to whom a fine was levied. 2 Bl.Comm. 351.

Cognizor /kógnəzər/. In old conveyancing, the party levying a fine. 2 Bl.Comm. 350, 351.

Cognomen /kògnówmən/. In English law, a surname. A name added to the *nomen* proper, or name of the individual; a name descriptive of the family.

In Roman law, a man's family name.

The first name (*prænomen*) was the proper name of the individual; the second (*nomen*) indicated the *gens* or tribe to which he belonged; while the third (*cognomen*) denoted his family or house. The *agnomen* was added on account of some particular event, as a further distinction.

Cognomen majorum est ex sanguine tractum, hoc intrinsecum est; agnomen extrinsecum ab eventu /kògnówmən məjórəm èst èks sǽŋgwəniy trǽktəm, hók intrínzəkəm èst; ægnówmən ekstrínzəkəm, éks əvént(y)uw/. The cognomen is derived from the blood of ancestors, and is intrinsic; an agnomen arises from an event, and is extrinsic.

Cognovit actionem /kògnówvət ǽkshiyównəm/. (He has confessed the action). A defendant's written confession of action against him. It is usually upon condition; is supposed to be given in court; and impliedly authorizes plaintiff's attorney to sign judgment and issue execution.

Cognovit judgment /kògnówvət/. Confession of judgment by debtor. Written authority of debtor and his direction for entry of judgment against him in the event he shall default in payment. Such provision in a debt instrument or agreement permits the creditor or his attorney on default to appear in court and confers judgment against the debtor. Such agreements are prohibited, or greatly restricted, in many states; though, where permitted, the constitutionality of such has been upheld. D. H. Overmyer Co., Inc. v. Frick Co., 405 U.S. 174, 92 S.Ct. 775, 31 L.Ed.2d 124. See **Cognovit note; Judgment** (*Confession of judgment*).

Cognovit note. An extraordinary note which authorizes an attorney to confess judgment against person or persons signing it. It is written authority of a debtor and a direction by him for entry of a judgment against him if obligation set forth in note is not paid when due. Such judgment may be taken by any person holding the note, which cuts off every defense which maker of note may otherwise have and it likewise cuts off all rights of appeal from any judgment taken on it. Jones v. John Hancock Mut. Life Ins. Co., D.C.Mich., 289 F.Supp. 930, 935. See **Judgment** (*Confession of judgment*).

C.O.G.S.A. Carriage of Goods by Sea Act.

Cohabitation. To live together as husband and wife. The mutual assumption of those marital rights, duties and obligations which are usually manifested by married people, including but not necessarily dependent on sexual relations. Boyd v. Boyd, 228 Cal.App. 374, 39 Cal.Rptr. 400, 404. See also **Notorious cohabitation; Palimony.**

Cohæredes una persona censentur, propter unitatem juris quod habent /kòwhírədiyz yúwnə pərsównə sənséntər, próptər yùwnətéydəm júrəs kwòd héybənt/. Co-heirs are deemed as one person, on account of the unity of right which they possess.

Cohan Rule. Taxpayer is required to substantiate by accurate records or by sufficient evidence his claim for deduction for travel, entertainment and business gifts. I.R.C. § 274(d) (1962 Act); Cohan v. Commissioner, C.C.A.N.Y., 39 F.2d 540. Where part of expenditures by taxpayers are of deductible nature as ordinary and necessary business expense are unidentifiable, 50% of expenditures are allowed as deduction. Poletti v. C. I. R., C.A.Mo., 351 F.2d 345, 349.

Co-heir. One of several to whom an inheritance descends.

Co-heiress. A joint heiress. A woman who has an equal share of an inheritance with another woman.

Coif /kóyf/. A title given to serjeants at law, who are called "serjeants of the coif," from the coif they wear on their heads. The use of this coif at first was to cover the clerical tonsure, many of the practicing serjeants being clergymen who had abandoned their profession. It was a thin linen cover, gathered together in the form of a skull or helmet; the material being afterwards changed into white silk, and the form eventually into the black patch at the top of the forensic wig, which is now the distinguishing mark of the degree of serjeant at law.

Order of the coif. Honorary legal fraternity made up of law students with high standing in law school class.

Coin, v. To fashion pieces of metal into a prescribed shape, weight, and degree of fineness, and stamp them with prescribed devices, by authority of government, in order that they may circulate as money. Legal Tender Cases, 79 U.S. 457, 12 Wall. 457, 20 L.Ed. 287; Thayer v. Hedges, 22 Ind. 282. To invent words or phrases.

Coin, n. Pieces of gold, silver, or other metal, fashioned into a prescribed shape, weight, and degree of fineness, and stamped, by authority of government, with certain marks and devices, and put into circulation as money at a fixed value. Metal money.

Coinage. The process or the function of coining metallic money; also the great mass of metallic money in circulation.

Coinage clause. Provision in U.S. Constitution granting to Congress the power to coin money, Art. I, § 8, par. 5.

Coinsurance. A relative division of risk between the insurer and the insured, dependent upon the relative amount of the policy and the actual value of the property insured, and taking effect only when the actual loss is partial and less than the amount of the policy; the insurer being liable to the extent of the policy for a loss equal to or in excess of that amount. Insurance policies that protect against hazards such as fire or water damage often specify that the owner of the property may not collect the full amount of insurance for a loss unless the insurance policy covers at least some specified percentage, usually about 80 percent, of the replacement cost of the property. Coinsurance clauses induce the owner to carry full, or nearly-full, coverage.

Coitus. Sexual intercourse; carnal copulation; coition.

Cojudices /kòwjúwdəsiyz/. Lat. In old English law, associate judges having equality of power with others.

Coke's institutes. See **Institutes.**

Cold blood. Used in common parlance to designate a willful, deliberate, and premeditated homicide.

Cold water ordeal. The trial which was anciently used for the common sort of people, who, having a cord tied about them under their arms, were cast into a river; if they sank to the bottom until they were drawn up, which was in a very short time, then were they held guiltless; but such as did remain upon the water were held culpable, being, as they said, of the water rejected and kept up.

Colibertus /kòwləbárdəs/. In feudal law, one who, holding in free socage, was obliged to do certain services for the lord. A middle class of tenants between servile and free, who held their freedom of tenure on condition of performing certain services. Said to be the same as the *conditionales.*

Collaboration. The act of working together in a joint project; commonly used in connection with treasonably cooperative efforts with the enemy. See also **Conspiracy.**

Collapsible corporation. A corporation formed or availed of principally for the manufacture, construction, or production of property, for the purchase of property, or for the holding of stock in a corporation so formed or availed of, with a view to the sale or exchange of stock by its shareholders (whether in liquidation or otherwise), or a distribution to its shareholders, before the realization by the corporation of a substantial part of the taxable income to be derived from such property, and the realization by such shareholders of gain attributable to such property. I.R.C. §§ 337(c), 341(b)(1). These I.R.C. provisions prevent the prearranged use of a corporation to convert ordinary income into capital gain.

Collapsible partnership. A partnership formed with the intention to dissolve before any income is realized; however, the amount of money or the fair market value of any property received by a transferror partner in exchange for all or a part of his interest in the partnership attributable to unrealized receivables of the partnership, or inventory items of the partnership which have appreciated substantially in value shall be considered as an amount realized from the sale or exchange of property other than a capital asset. I.R.C. § 751(a).

Collateral, *n.* /kəlǽdərəl/. Property which is pledged as security for the satisfaction of a debt. Collateral is additional security for performance of principal obligation, or that which is by the side, and not in direct line. Shaffer v. Davidson, Wyo., 445 P.2d 13, 16. Property subject to a security interest; includes accounts, contract rights, and chattel paper which have been sold. U.C.C. § 9–105(c). See also **Collateral security.**

Collateral, *adj.* By the side; at the side; attached upon the side. Not lineal, but upon a parallel or diverging line. Additional or auxiliary; supplementary; co-operating; accompanying as a secondary fact, or acting as a secondary agent. Related to, complementary; accompanying as a co-ordinate. As to collateral Consanguinity; Descent; Estoppel; Guaranty; Issue; Limitation; Negligence; Power; Proceeding; and Warranty, see those titles. See also **Pledge; Security.**

Collateral act. Formerly, name given to any act (except the payment of money) for the performance of which a bond, recognizance, etc., was given as security.

Collateral actions. Any action which is subsidiary to another action. See **Collateral attack.**

Collateral ancestors. A phrase sometimes used to designate uncles and aunts, and other collateral ancestors, who are not strictly ancestors.

Collateral assurance. That which is made over and above the principal assurance or deed itself.

Collateral attack. With respect to a judicial proceeding, an attempt to avoid, defeat, or evade it, or deny its force and effect, in some incidental proceeding not provided by law for the express purpose of attacking it. May v. Casker, 188 Okl. 448, 110 P.2d 287, 289. An attack on a judgment in any manner other than by action or proceeding, whose very purpose is to impeach or overturn the judgment; or, stated affirmatively, a collateral attack on a judgment is an attack made by or in an action or proceeding that has an independent purpose other than impeaching or overturning the judgment. Travis v. Travis' Estate, 79 Wyo. 329, 334 P.2d 508, 510.

Collateral consanguinity. Persons are related collaterally when they have a common ancestor. See also **Collateral heir.**

Collateral contract. A contract made prior to or contemporaneous with another contract and if oral and not inconsistent with written contract is admissible within exception to parol evidence rule. High Knobb Inc. v. Allen, 205 Va. 503, 138 S.E.2d 49.

Collateral covenant. A covenant in a deed or other sealed instrument which does not pertain to the granted premises.

Collateral estoppel doctrine. Prior judgment between same parties on different cause of action is an estoppel as to those matters in issue or points controverted, on determination of which finding or verdict was rendered. E. I. duPont de Nemours & Co. v. Union Carbide Corp., D.C.Ill., 250 F.Supp. 816, 819. When an issue of ultimate fact has been determined by a valid judgment, that issue cannot be again litigated between the same parties in future litigation. City of St. Joseph v. Johnson, Mo.App., 539 S.W.2d 784, 785.

As a bar to relitigating an issue which has already been tried between the same parties or their privies, it must be pleaded affirmatively. Fed.R. Civil P. 8(c). It is applicable to criminal cases. Ashe v. Swenson, 397 U.S. 436, 443–444, 90 S.Ct. 1189, 1194, 25 L.Ed.2d 469.

See also **Issue preclusion; Res** (*Res judicata*); **Verdict, estoppel by.**

Collateral facts. Such as are outside the controversy, or are not directly connected with the principal matter or issue in dispute.

Collateral fraud. See **Fraud.**

Collateral heir. One who is not of the direct line of deceased, but comes from a collateral line, as a brother, sister, an uncle, an aunt, a nephew, a niece, or a cousin of deceased. Ferraro v. Augustine, 45 Ill. App.2d 295, 196 N.E.2d 16, 19.

Collateral impeachment. See **Collateral attack.**

Collateral inheritance tax. A tax levied upon the collateral devolution of property by will or under the intestate law.

Collateralis et socii /kəlædəréyləs èt sóws(h)iyay/. The ancient title of masters in chancery.

Collateral issues. Question or issues which are not directly involved in the matter.

Collateral kinsmen. Those who descend from one and the same common ancestor, but not from one another.

Collateral line. See **Descent.**

Collateral loan. Loan secured by pledge of specific property.

Collateral mortgage. A mortgage designed, not directly to secure an existing debt, but to secure a mortgage note pledged as collateral security for debt or succession of debts. McLendon v. Brewster, La.App., 286 So.2d 513, 516.

Collateral negligence. See **Negligence.**

Collateral note. Loan secured by pledge of specific property.

Collateral promise. A promise merely superadded to the promise of another, he remaining primarily liable.

Collateral relatives. Next of kin who are not in the direct line of inheritance, such as a cousin. See also **Collateral heir.**

Collateral security. A security given in addition to the direct security, and subordinate to it, intended to guaranty its validity or convertibility or insure its performance; so that, if the direct security fails, the creditor may fall back upon the collateral security. Concurrent security for another debt, whether antecedent or newly created and is subsidiary to the principal debt running parallel with and collateral to the debt. Shaffer v. Davidson, Wyo., 445 P.2d 13, 16.

Collateral source rule. Under this rule, if an injured person receives compensation for his injuries from a source wholly independent of the tort-feasor, the payment should not be deducted from the damages which he would otherwise collect from the tort-feasor. Kirtland & Packard v. Superior Court for County of Los Angeles, 59 Cal.App.3d 140, 131 Cal.Rptr. 418, 421. In other words, a defendant tortfeasor may not benefit from the fact that the plaintiff has received money from other sources as a result of the defendant's tort, *e.g.* sickness and health insurance.

Collateral trust bonds. Bonds of one corporation secured by its holdings of stocks, bonds, and/or notes of another corporation.

Collateral warranty. Generally applicable to real estate transactions in which a stranger warrants title and hence his warranty runs only to the covenantee, and not with the land.

Collatio bonorum /kəléysh(iy)ow bənórəm/. Lat. In the civil law, the obligation on successors to an inheritance to return to the common inheritance gifts received from the ancestor during his lifetime. A joining together or contribution of goods into a common fund. This occurs where a portion of money, advanced by the father to a son or daughter, is brought into *hotchpot*, in order to have an equal distributory share of his personal estate at his death. See **Collation.**

Collation /kəléyshən/. The comparison of a copy with its original to ascertain its correctness; or the report of the officer who made the comparison. The bringing into the estate of an intestate an estimate of the value of advancements made by the intestate to his or her children in order that the whole may be divided in accordance with the statute of descents. It is synonymous with "hotchpot."

In the civil law, the collation of goods is the supposed or real return to the mass of the succession which an heir makes of property which he received in advance of his share or otherwise, in order that such property may be divided together with the other effects of the succession. The fundamental basis of doctrine is legal presumption that ancestor intended absolute equality among his descendants in final distribution of his property, that donation by him during his lifetime to any one of them was merely advancement d'hoirie or advance on donee's hereditary share to establish him in life or for some other useful purpose, and that ancestor intended to reestablish equality among his descendants in final partition of his estate.

Collatione factâ uni post mortem alterius /kəlèyshiyówniy fǽktə yúwnay pòwst mórdəm oltíriyəs/. A writ directed to justices of the common pleas, commanding them to issue their writ to the bishop, for the admission of a clerk in the place of another presented by the crown, where there had been a demise of the crown during a suit; for judgment once passed for the king's clerk, and he dying before admittance, the king may bestow his presentation on another.

Collatione heremitagii /kəlèyshiyówniy hèrəmətéyjiyay/. In old English law, a writ whereby the king conferred the keeping of an hermitage upon a clerk.

Collation of seals. When upon the same label one seal was set on the back or reverse of the other. Comparison of seals.

Collation to a benefice /kəléyshən tùw ə bénəfəs/. In ecclesiastical law, this occurs where the bishop and patron are one and the same person, in which case the bishop cannot present the clergyman to himself, but does, by the one act of collation or conferring the benefice, the whole that is done in common cases both by presentation and institution. 2 Bl.Comm. 22.

Collatio signorum /kəléysh(iy)ow sìgnórəm/. In old English law, a comparison of marks or seals. A mode of testing the genuineness of a seal, by comparing it with another known to be genuine.

Collect. To gather together; to bring scattered things (assets, accounts, articles of property) into one mass or fund; to assemble. To receive payment.

To collect a debt or claim is to obtain payment or liquidation of it, either by personal solicitation or legal proceedings.

Collectible. Debts, obligations, demands, liabilities that one may be made to pay by means of legal process.

Collecting bank. Any bank handling the item for collection except the payor bank. U.C.C. § 4–105(d).

Collection. Indorsement "for collection." See **For collection.**

Collection of illegal fees. Collection by public official of fees in excess of those fixed by law for certain services.

Collective bargaining. As contemplated by National Labor Relations Act, is a procedure looking toward making of collective agreements between employer and accredited representative of employees concerning wages, hours, and other conditions of employment, and requires that parties deal with each other with open and fair minds and sincerely endeavor to overcome obstacles existing between them to the end that employment relations may be stabilized and obstruction to free flow of commerce prevented. National Labor Relations Act § 8(5), 29 U.S.C.A. § 158(5). Rapid Roller Co. v. National Labor Relations Board, C.C.A.7, 126 F.2d 452, 460. Negotiation between an employer and organized employees as distinguished from individuals, for the purpose of determining by joint agreement the conditions of employment. See also **Area bargaining; Labor dispute; Sixty-day notice.**

Collective bargaining agreement. Agreement between an employer and a labor union which regulates terms and conditions of employment. The joint and several contract of members of union made by officers of union as their agents. Such is enforceable by and against union in matters which affect all members alike or large classes of members, particularly those who are employees of other party to contract. Bogue Elec. Co. v. Board of Review of Division of Employment Sec. of Dept. of Labor and Industry, 21 N.J. 431, 122 A.2d 615, 618. See also **Collective labor agreement; Trade agreement.**

Collective bargaining unit. All of the employees of a single employer unless the employees of a particular department or division have voted otherwise. Re International Ass'n of Machinists, 249 Wis. 112, 23 N.W.2d 489.

Collective labor agreement. Also called "trade agreement". Bargaining agreement as to wages and conditions of work entered into by groups of employees, usually organized into a brotherhood or union on one side and groups of employers or corporations on the other side. See also **Collective bargaining agreement.**

Collective mark. A trade-mark or service mark used by the members of a cooperative, an association or other collective group or organization and includes marks used to indicate membership in a union, an association or other organization. 15 U.S.C.A. § 1127.

Collect on delivery. See **C. O. D.**

Collector. One appointed or authorized to receive taxes or other impositions, as: collector of taxes, collector of customs, etc. A person appointed by a private person to collect the debts due him.

Collector of decedent's estate. A person temporarily appointed by the probate court to collect rents, assets, interest, bills receivable, etc., of a decedent's estate, and act for the estate in all financial matters requiring immediate settlement. Such collector is usually appointed when there is protracted litigation as to the probate of the will, or as to the person to take out administration, and his duties cease as soon as an executor or administrator is qualified.

Collega /kəlíygə/. In the civil law, one invested with joint authority. A colleague; an associate.

Collegatarius /kəlègətériyəs/. Lat. In the civil law, a co-legatee.

Collegatary /kò(w)ləgéydəriy/. A co-legatee; a person who has a legacy left to him in common with other persons.

College. An organized assembly or collection of persons, established by law, and empowered to co-oper-
ate for the performance of some special function or for the promotion of some common object, which may be educational, political, ecclesiastical, or scientific in its character.

The assemblage of the cardinals at Rome is called a "college." So, in the United States, the body of presidential electors is called the "electoral college" (*q.v.*).

In the most common use of the word, it designates an institution of learning (usually incorporated) which offers instruction in the liberal arts and humanities and in scientific branches, but not in the technical arts or those studies preparatory to admission to the professions. Also applied to all kinds of institutions from universities, or departments thereof, to "business colleges," "barber colleges," etc.

In England, it is a civil corporation, company or society of men, having certain privileges, and endowed with certain revenues, founded by royal license. An assemblage of several of these colleges is called a "university."

Collegia /kəlíyjiyə/. In the civil law, the guild of a trade.

Collegialiter /kəlìyjiyéylədər/. In a corporate capacity.

Collegiate church. In English ecclesiastical law, a church built and endowed for a society or body corporate of a dean or other president, and secular priests, as canons or prebendaries in the said church; such as the churches of Westminster, Windsor, and others.

Collegium /kəlíyj(iy)əm/. Lat. In the civil law, a word having various meanings; *e.g.*, an assembly, society, or company; a body of bishops; an army; a class of men. But the principal idea of the word was that of an association of individuals of the same rank and station, or united for the pursuit of some business or enterprise. Sometimes, a corporation, as in the maxim "tres faciunt collegium" (1 Bl.Comm. 469), though the more usual and proper designation of a corporation was "universitas."

Collegium ammiralitatis /kəlíyj(iy)əm æmərælətéydəs/. The college or society of the admiralty.

Collegium est societas plurium corporum simul habitantium /kəlíyj(iy)əm èst səsáyətæs plúriyəm kórpərəm síməl hæbətænsh(iy)əm/. A college is a society of several persons dwelling together.

Collegium illicitum /kəlíyjiyəm əlísədəm/. One which abused its right, or assembled for any other purpose than that expressed in its charter.

Collegium licitum /kəlíyjiyəm lísədəm/. An assemblage or society of men united for some useful purpose or business, with power to act like a single individual.

Collide. To strike or dash against; to come into collision; to clash. Collins v. Leahy, Mo.App., 102 S.W.2d 801, 809. See **Collision.**

Colligendum bona defuncti /kòləjéndəm bównə dəfáŋktay/. See **Ad colligendum,** etc.

Collision. Striking together of two objects, one of which may be stationary. Act or instance of colliding; state of having collided. The term implies an impact or sudden contact of a moving body with an obstruction in its line of motion, whether both bodies are in motion or one stationary and the other, no matter which, in motion.

Collistrigium /kòləstríjiyəm/. The pillory.

Collocation /kòləkéyshən/. In French law, the arrangement or marshaling of the creditors of an estate in the order in which they are to be paid according to law.

Colloquium /kəlówkwiyəm/. One of the usual parts of the declaration in an action for slander. It is a general averment that the words complained of were spoken "of and concerning the plaintiff", or concerning the extrinsic matters alleged in the inducement, and its office is to connect the whole publication with the previous statement. An averment that the words in question are spoken of or concerning some usage, report, or fact which gives to words otherwise indifferent the peculiar defamatory meaning assigned to them.

Collusion /kəl(y)úwzhən/. An agreement between two or more persons to defraud a person of his rights by the forms of law, or to obtain an object forbidden by law. It implies the existence of fraud of some kind, the employment of fraudulent means, or of lawful means for the accomplishment of an unlawful purpose. Tomiyosu v. Golden, 81 Nev. 140, 400 P.2d 415, 417. A secret combination, conspiracy, or concert of action between two or more persons for fraudulent or deceitful purpose.

In divorce proceedings, collusion is an agreement between husband and wife that one of them shall commit, or appear to have committed, or be represented in court as having committed, acts constituting a cause of divorce, for the purpose of enabling the other to obtain a divorce. But it also means connivance or conspiracy in initiating or prosecuting the suit, as where there is a compact for mutual aid in carrying it through to a decree. Bizik v. Bizik, Ind. App., 111 N.E.2d 823, 828. With the enactment of "no-fault" divorce statutes by most states, agreements or acts of collusion are no longer necessary.

Collusive action. An action not founded upon an actual controversy between the parties to it, but brought for purpose of securing a determination of a point of law for the gratification of curiosity or to settle rights of third persons not parties. Such actions will not be entertained for the courts will only decide "cases or controversies". City and County of San Francisco v. Boyd, 22 Cal.2d 685, 140 P.2d 666, 669, 670. See also **Collusion.**

Collusive joinder. See **Joinder.**

Collybista /kòləbístə/. In the civil law, a money-changer; a dealer in money.

Collybum /kóləbəm/. In the civil law, exchange.

Colne. In Saxon and old English law, an account or calculation.

Colonists. Persons who have emigrated from their mother country to settle in another place but who remain loyal to mother country.

Colonus /kəlównəs/. In old European law, a husbandman; an inferior tenant employed in cultivating the lord's land. A term of Roman origin, corresponding with the Saxon ceorl.

Colony. A dependent political community, consisting of a number of citizens of the same country who have emigrated therefrom to people another, and remain subject to the mother country. Territory attached to another nation, known as the mother country, with political and economic ties; e.g. possessions or dependencies of the British Crown (e.g. thirteen original colonies of United States).

Colonial charter. A document issued by a colonial government which permits operation of a business or school or college, e.g. charters granted by England to institutions or business in this country before War of Independence.

Colonial laws. The body of law in force in the thirteen original colonies before the Declaration of Independence.

Color. An appearance, semblance, or *simulacrum*, as distinguished from that which is real. A *prima facie* or apparent right. Hence, a deceptive appearance; a plausible, assumed exterior, concealing a lack of reality; a disguise or pretext. See also **Colorable.**

In pleading, ground of action admitted to subsist in the opposite party by the pleading of one of the parties to an action, which is so set out as to be apparently valid, but which is in reality legally insufficient. A term of the ancient rhetoricians, and early adopted into the language of pleading. It was an apparent or *prima facie* right; and the meaning of the rule that pleadings in confession and avoidance should give color was that they should confess the matter adversely alleged, to such an extent, at least, as to admit some apparent right in the opposite party, which required to the encountered and avoided by the allegation of new matter. Color was either express, *i.e.* inserted in the pleading, or implied, which was naturally inherent in the structure of the pleading. Wheeler v. Nickels, 168 Or. 604, 126 P.2d 32, 36.

Colorable. That which is in appearance only, and not in reality, what it purports to be, hence counterfeit, feigned, having the appearance of truth. Windle v. Flinn, 196 Or. 654, 251 P.2d 136, 146.

Colorable alteration. One which makes no real or substantial change, but is introduced only as a subterfuge or means of evading the patent or copyright law.

Colorable cause or invocation of jurisdiction. With reference to actions for malicious prosecution, a "colorable cause or invocation of jurisdiction" means that a person, apparently qualified, has appeared before a justice and made a complaint under oath and in writing, stating some facts which in connection with other facts constitute a criminal offense or bear a similitude thereto.

Colorable claim. In bankruptcy law, a claim made by one holding the property as an agent or bailee of the bankrupt; a claim in which as a matter of law, there is no adverseness. See also **Color.**

Colorable imitation. In the law of trademarks, this phrase denotes such a close or ingenious limitation as to be calculated to deceive ordinary persons.

Colorable transaction. One presenting an appearance which does not correspond with the reality, and, ordinarily, an appearance intended to conceal or to deceive.

Colored. By common usage in America, this term, in such phrases as "colored persons," "the colored race," "colored men," and the like, is used to designate negroes or persons of the African race, including all persons of mixed blood descended from negro ancestry.

Colore officii /kəlóriy əfíshiyay/. Lat. By color of office. Officer's acts unauthorized by officer's position, though done in form that purports that acts are done by reason of official duty and by virtue of office. See also **Color of office.**

Color of authority. That semblance or presumption of authority sustaining the acts of a public officer which is derived from his apparent title to the office or from a writ or other process in his hands apparently valid and regular. See **Color of law; Color of office.**

Color of law. The appearance or semblance, without the substance, of legal right. Misuse of power, possessed by virtue of state law and made possible only because wrongdoer is clothed with authority of state, is action taken under "color of law." Atkins v. Lanning, D.C.Okl., 415 F.Supp. 186, 188.

As used in Civil Rights Act means same thing as "state action", Timson v. Weiner, D.C.Ohio, 395 F.Supp. 1344; and means pretense of law and includes actions of officers who undertake to perform their official duties, Thompson v. Baker, D.C.Ark., 133 F.Supp. 247; 42 U.S.C.A. § 1983. See **Tort** *(Constitutional tort).*

Acts "under color of any law" of a State include not only acts done by State officials within the bounds or limits of their lawful authority, but also acts done without and beyond the bounds of their lawful authority; provided that, in order for unlawful acts of an official to be done "under color of any law", the unlawful acts must be done while such official is purporting or pretending to act in the performance of his official duties; that is to say, the unlawful acts must consist in an abuse or misuse of power which is possessed by the official only because he is an official; and the unlawful acts must be of such a nature or character, and be committed under such circumstances, that they would not have occurred but for the fact that the person committing them was an official then and there exercising his official powers outside the bounds of lawful authority. 42 U.S.C.A. § 1983.

Color of office. Pretense of official right to do act made by one who has no such right. Kiker v. Pinson, 120 Ga.App. 784, 172 S.E.2d 333, 334. An act under color of office is an act of an officer who claims authority to do the act by reason of his office when the office does not confer on him any such authority. Maryland Cas. Co. v. McCormack, Ky., 488 S.W.2d 347, 352. See also **Color of law.**

Color of title. The appearance, semblance, or *simulacrum* of title. Also termed "apparent title." Any fact, extraneous to the act or mere will of the claimant, which has the appearance, on its face, of supporting his claim of a present title to land, but which, for some defect, in reality falls short of establishing it. Howth v. Farrar, C.C.A.Tex., 94 F.2d 654, 658. That which is a semblance or appearance of title, but is not title in fact or in law. McCoy v. Lowrie, 42 Wash.2d 24, 253 P.2d 415, 418. Any instrument having a grantor and grantee, and containing a description of the lands intended to be conveyed, and apt words for their conveyance, gives color of title to the lands described. Such an instrument purports to be a conveyance of the title, and because it does not, for some reason, have that effect, it passes only color or the semblance of a title.

Color of Title Act. Federal law which gives Secretary of Interior the right to issue a patent for land, exclusive of minerals, to one who has occupied it adversely and under color of right for period of time for a nominal amount of money. 43 U.S.C.A. §§ 1068–1068B.

Com. Abbreviation for "company" or "Commonwealth."

Combarones /kòmbərówniyz/. In old English law, fellow-barons; fellow-citizens; the citizens or freemen of the Cinque Ports being anciently called "barons;" the term *"combarones"* is used in this sense in a grant of Henry III, to the barons of the port of Fevresham.

Combat. A forcible encounter between two or more persons; a battle; a duel. To fight with; to struggle against.

Combaterræ /kòmbətéhrriy/. A valley or piece of low ground between two hills.

Combe. A small or narrow valley.

Combination. The union or association of two or more persons for the attainment of some common end. Albrecht v. Herald Co., C.A.Mo., 367 F.2d 517, 523. See **Joint venture.** As used in criminal context, means a conspiracy or confederation for unlawful or violent acts. See **Conspiracy.**

Combination in restraint of trade. An agreement or understanding between two or more persons, in the form of a contract, trust, pool, holding company, or other form of association, for the purpose of unduly restricting competition, monopolizing trade and commerce in a certain commodity, controlling its production, distribution, and price, or otherwise interfering with freedom of trade without statutory authority. Such combinations are prohibited by the Sherman Antitrust Act. See also **Clayton Act; Sherman Antitrust Act.**

Combination patent. Patents in which the claimed invention resides in a specific combination or arrangement of elements, rather than in the elements themselves. Kinnear-Weed Corp. v. Humble Oil & Refining Co., D.C.Tex., 150 F.Supp. 143, 162. One in which none of parts or components are new, and none are claimed as new, nor is any portion of combination less than whole claimed as new or stated to produce any given result. Borden, Inc. v. Occidental Petroleum Corp., D.C.Tex., 381 F.Supp. 1178, 1202.

Combustio /kəmbə́shch(iy)ow/. Burning. In old English law, the punishment inflicted upon apostates.

Combustio domorum /kəmbáshch(iy)ow dəmórəm/. Houseburning; arson. 4 Bl.Comm. 272.

Combustio pecuniæ /kəmbáshch(iy)ow pəkyúwniyiy/. Burning of money; the ancient method of testing mixed and corrupt money, paid into the exchequer, by melting it down.

Come. To present oneself; to appear in court.

Comes /kámz/, *v.* A word used in a pleading to indicate the defendant's presence in court.

Comes /kówmiyz/, *n.* Lat. A follower, companion, or attendant; a count or earl.

Comes and defends. This phrase, anciently used in the language of pleading, and still surviving in some jurisdictions, occurs at the commencement of a defendant's plea or demurrer; and of its two verbs the former signifies that he appears in court, the latter that he defends the action.

Comfort. Benefit, consolation, contentment, ease, enjoyment, happiness, pleasure, or satisfaction.

Comfort letter. A letter from an accounting firm stating that while certain informal procedures were followed which did not bring to light material changes in the financial statements since the date of the last audit indicated, only an audit with established auditing procedures can be relied upon to furnish such information.

Coming to rest doctrine. Under the "coming to rest doctrine" with respect to loading and unloading clauses used in automobile liability policies, coverage afforded by loading-unloading clause ceases when goods have actually come to rest and every connection of motor vehicle with process of unloading has ceased. Johnson, Drake & Piper, Inc. v. Liberty Mut. Ins. Co., D.C.Minn., 258 F.Supp. 603, 606.

Cominus /kómənəs/. Lat. Immediately; hand-to-hand; in personal contact.

Comitas /kómədəs/. Lat. Courtesy; civility; comity. An indulgence or favor granted another nation, as a mere matter of indulgence, without any claim of right made. *Comitas inter communitates;* or *comitas inter gentes;* comity between communities or nations; comity of nations.

Comitatu commisso /kòmətéyduw kəmísh(iy)ow/. In old English law, a writ or commission, whereby a sheriff was authorized to enter upon the charges of a county.

Comitatu et castro commisso /kòmətéyduw ət kǽstrow kəmísow/. A writ by which the charge of a county, together with the keeping of a castle, was committed to the sheriff.

Comitatus /kòmətéydəs/. In old English law, a county or shire; the body of a county. The territorial jurisdiction of a *comes, i.e.,* count or earl. 1 Bl.Comm. 116. An earldom. The county court, a court of great antiquity and of great dignity in early times. Also, the retinue or train of a prince or high governmental official. The retinue which accompanied a Roman proconsul to his province. The personal following of professional warriors.

Comites /kómədiyz/. Counts or earls. Attendants or followers. Persons composing the retinue of a high functionary.

Persons who are attached to the suite of a public minister.

Comites paleys /kómədiyz pæléys/. Counts or earls palatine; those who had the government of a county palatine.

Comitia /kəmísh(iy)ə/. In Roman law, an assembly, either (1) of the Roman curiæ, in which case it was called the *"comitia curiata vel calata";* or (2) of the Roman centuries, in which case it was called the *"comitia centuriata"* (called also *comitia majora*); or (3) of the Roman tribes, in which case it was called the *"comitia tributa."* Only patricians were members of the first *comitia,* and only plebians of the last; but the *comitia centuriata* comprised the entire populace, patricians and plebians both, and was the great legislative assembly passing the *leges,* properly so called, as the senate passed the *senatus consulta,* and the *comitia tributa* past the *plebiscita.* Under the *Lex Hortensia,* 287 B.C., the *plebiscitum* acquired the force of a *lex.*

Comitissa /kòmətísə/. In old English law, a countess; an earl's wife.

Comitiva /kòmətáyvə/. In old English law, the dignity and office of a *comes* (count or earl); the same with what was afterwards called *"comitatus."* Also a companion or fellow-traveler; a troop or company of robbers.

Comity /kómədiy/. Courtesy; complaisance; respect; a willingness to grant a privilege, not as a matter of right, but out of deference and good will. Recognition that one sovereignty allows within its territory to the legislative, executive, or judicial act of another sovereignty, having due regard to rights of its own citizens. Nowell v. Nowell, Tex.Civ.App., 408 S.W.2d 550, 553. In general, principle of "comity" is that courts of one state or jurisdiction will give effect to laws and judicial decisions of another state or jurisdiction, not as a matter of obligation but out of deference and mutual respect. Brown v. Babbitt Ford, Inc., 117 Ariz. 192, 571 P.2d 689, 695. See also **Full faith and credit clause.**

Comity of nations. The recognition which one nation allows within its territory to the legislative, executive, or judicial acts of another nation, having due regard both to international duty and convenience and to the rights of its own citizens or of other persons who are under the protection of its laws.

Judicial comity. The principle in accordance with which the courts of one state or jurisdiction will give effect to the laws and judicial decisions of another, not as a matter of obligation, but out of deference and respect.

Command. An order, imperative direction, or behest. To direct, with authority. Power to dominate and control.

Commandement /komònd(ə)món/. In French law, a writ served by the *huissier* pursuant to a judgment or to an executory notarial deed. Its object is to give notice to the debtor that if he does not pay the sum to which he has been condemned by the judgment, or which he engaged to pay by the notarial deed, his property will be seized and sold.

Commander in chief. One who holds supreme or highest command of armed forces. By Article II, § 2, of the Constitution it is declared that the President shall be commander in chief of the army and navy of the United States. The term implies supreme control of military operations not only with respect to strategy and tactics, but also in reference to the political and international aspects of the war.

Commandery. In old English law, a manor or chief messuage with lands and tenements thereto appertaining, which belonged to the priory of St. John of Jerusalem, in England; he who had the government of such a manor or house was styled the "commander," who could not dispose of it, but to the use of the priory, only taking thence his own sustenance, according to his degree. The manors and lands belonging to the priory of St. John of Jerusalem were given to Henry the Eighth by 32 Hen. VIII, c. 20, about the time of the dissolution of abbeys and monasteries; so that the name only of commanderies remains, the power being long since extinct.

Commanditaires /kəmǽndətérz/. Special partners; partners *en commandité*. See **Commandité.**

Commandité /komònditéy/. In French law, a partnership in which some furnish money, and others furnish their skill and labor in place of capital.

A special or limited partnership, where the contract is between one or more persons who are general partners, and jointly and severally responsible, and one or more other persons who merely furnish a particular fund or capital stock, and thence are called *"commanditaires,"* or *"commendiaires,"* or *"partners en commandité;"* the business being carried on under the social name or firm of the general partners only, composed of the names of the general or complementary partners, the partners in *commandité* being liable to losses only to the extent of the funds or capital furnished by them. The term includes a partnership containing dormant rather than special partners.

Commandment. In old English law, an authoritative order of a judge or magisterial officer. Also, the act or offense of one who commanded another to transgress the law, or do anything contrary to law, as theft, murder, or the like. Particularly applied to the act of an accessory before the fact in inciting, procuring, setting on, or stirring up another to do the fact or act. See also **Command.**

Commence. To initiate by performing the first act. To institute or start.

Civil action in most jurisdictions is commenced by filing a complaint with the court. Fed.R. Civil P. 3.

Commencement of building or improvement, within the meaning of mechanic's lien statute, is the visible commencement of actual operations on the ground for the erection of the building, which every one can readily recognize as commencement of a building, and which is done with intention to continue the work until building is completed. Diversified Mortgage Investors v. Gepada, Inc., 401 F.Supp. 682, 685.

Criminal action is commenced within statute of limitations at time preliminary complaint or information is filed with magistrate in good faith and a warrant issued thereon. Knott v. State, Okl.Cr., 387 P.2d 142, 144. A criminal prosecution is "commenced" (1) when information is laid before magistrate charging commission of crime, and a warrant of arrest is issued, or (2) when grand jury has returned an indictment. Halberstadt v. Nelson, 34 Misc.2d 472, 226 N.Y.S.2d 100, 103.

Commencement of action. See **Commence.**

Commencement of prosecution. See **Commence.**

Commenda /kəméndə/. In French law, the delivery of a benefice to one who cannot hold the legal title, to keep and manage it for a time limited and render an account of the proceeds. In commercial law, an association in which the management of the property was intrusted to individuals.

Commenda est facultas recipiendi et retinendi beneficium contra jus positivum a suprema potestate /kəméndə èst fəkáltæs rəsìpiyénday èt rèdənénday bènəfísh(iy)əm kóntrə jə́s pòzətáyvəm èy s(y)əpríymə pòwdəstéydiy/. A commendam is the power of receiving and retaining a benefice contrary to positive law, by supreme authority.

Commendam /kəméndəm/. In ecclesiastical law, the appointment of a suitable clerk to hold a void or vacant benefice or church living until a regular pastor be appointed.

In commercial law, a species of limited partnership. The limited partnership (or *société en commandité*) of the French law has been introduced into the Code of Louisiana under the title of "Partnership *in Commendam.*" Civ.Code La. art. 2810 (Civ.Code, art. 2839).

Commendatio /kòmandéysh(iy)ow/. In the civil law, commendation, praise, or recommendation, as in the maxim "simplex commendatio non obligat," meaning that mere recommendation or praise of an article by the seller of it does not amount to a warranty of its qualities.

Commendation. In feudal law, the act by which an owner of alodial land placed himself and his land under the protection of a lord, so as to constitute himself his vassal or feudal tenant.

Commendators /kómandèydərz/. Secular persons upon whom ecclesiastical benefices were bestowed; called so because the benefices were commended and intrusted to their supervision. They are merely trustees.

Commendatory. He who holds a church living or preferment *in commendam.*

Commendatory letters. In ecclesiastical law, such as are written by one bishop to another on behalf of any of the clergy, or others of his diocese traveling thither, that they may be received among the faithful, or that the clerk may be promoted, or necessaries administered to others, etc.

Commendatus /kòmandéydəs/. In feudal law, one who intrusts himself to the protection of another. A person who, by voluntary homage, put himself under the protection of a superior lord.

Comment. The expression of the judgment passed upon certain alleged facts by a person who has applied his mind to them, and who while so commenting assumes that such allegations of fact are true. The assertion of a fact is not a "comment."

Comment upon the evidence. Means that trial judge is prohibited from conveying to jury trial judge's personal opinion as to the truth or falsity of any evidence, but prohibition does not prohibit judges from giving counsel reasons for rulings on questions presented during progress of trial, or prohibit them in all cases from stating, when necessary, the facts upon which they base their conclusions. State v. Brown, 19 Wash.2d 195, 142 P.2d 257, 259, 260.

Commerce. The exchange of goods, productions, or property of any kind; the buying, selling, and exchanging of articles. Anderson v. Humble Oil and Refining Co., 226 Ga. 252, 174 S.E.2d 415, 417. The transportation of persons and property by land, water and air. Union Pacific R. Co. v. State Tax Commissioner, 19 Utah 2d 236, 429 P.2d 983, 984.

Intercourse by way of trade and traffic between different peoples or states and the citizens or inhabitants thereof, including not only the purchase, sale, and exchange of commodities, but also the instrumentalities and agencies by which it is promoted and the means and appliances by which it is carried on, and transportation of persons as well as of goods, both by land and sea. Brennan v. Titusville, 153 U.S. 289, 14 S.Ct. 829, 38 L.Ed. 719; Railroad Co. v. Fuller, 84 U.S. (17 Wall.) 568, 21 L.Ed. 710; Hoke v. United States, 227 U.S. 308, 33 S.Ct. 281, 57 L.Ed. 523. Also interchange of ideas, sentiments, etc., as between man and man.

The term "commerce" means trade, traffic, commerce, transportation, or communication among the several States, or between the District of Columbia or any Territory of the United States and any State or other Territory, or between any foreign country and any State, Territory, or the District of Columbia, or within the District of Columbia or any Territory, or between points in the same State but through any other State or any Territory or the District of Columbia or any foreign country. National Labor Relations Act, § 2.

For purposes of Fair Labor Standards Act, "commerce" means trade, commerce, transportation, transmission, or communication among several states or between any state and any place outside thereof. Wirtz v. B. B. Saxon Co., C.A.Fla., 365 F.2d 457, 460.

See also Affecting commerce; Chamber of Commerce; Interstate and foreign commerce; Interstate commerce; Interstate Commerce Act; Interstate Commerce Commission; Intrastate commerce.

Commerce among the states. Transportation from one state to another, and also all component parts of such intercourse. Dahnke-Walker Milling Co. v. Bondurant, 257 U.S. 282, 42 S.Ct. 106, 108, 66 L.Ed. 239. See **Interstate commerce.**

Commerce with foreign nations. Commerce between citizens of the United States and citizens or subject governments; commerce which, either immediately or at some stage of its progress, is extraterritorial. U. S. v. Holliday, 70 U.S. 407, 3 Wall. 407, 18 L.Ed. 182; Veazie v. Moor, 55 U.S. 568, 14 How. 568, 14 L.Ed. 545; Lord v. Steamship Co., 102 U.S. 541, 26 L.Ed. 224. The same as "foreign commerce," which see *infra.* Power of Congress to regulate "commerce with foreign nations" comprehends every species of commercial intercourse. U.S.C.A.Const. Art. I, § 8, cl. 3. Board of Trustees of University of Illinois v. U. S., Cust. & Pat.App., 289 U.S. 48, 53 S.Ct. 509, 77 L.Ed. 1025.

Commerce with Indian tribes. Commerce with individuals belonging to such tribes, in the nature of buying, selling, and exchanging commodities, without reference to the locality where carried on, though it be within the limits of a state. U. S. v. Holliday, 3 Wall. 407, 18 L.Ed. 182.

Domestic commerce. Commerce carried on wholly within the limits of the United States, as distinguished from foreign commerce. Also, commerce carried on within the limits of a single state, as distinguished from interstate commerce.

Foreign commerce. Commerce or trade between the United States and foreign countries. The term is sometimes applied to commerce between ports of two sister states not lying on the same coast, *e.g.,* New York and San Francisco.

Internal commerce. Such as is carried on between individuals within the same state, or between different parts of the same state. Now more commonly called "intrastate" commerce.

International commerce. Commerce between states or nations entirely foreign to each other.

Interstate commerce. Such as is carried on between different states of the Union or between points lying in different states. See **Interstate commerce.**

Intrastate commerce. Such as is begun, carried on, and completed wholly within the limits of a single state. Contrasted with "interstate commerce" (*q.v.*).

Commerce clause. The provision of U.S.Const. (Art. I, § 8, cl. 3) which gives Congress exclusive powers over interstate commerce. See **Commerce; Cooley Doctrine; Interstate commerce.**

Commerce court. A federal court in existence from 1910 to 1913 which had power to review and enforce determinations of the Interstate Commerce Commission.

Commerce Department. Part of executive branch of federal government headed by cabinet member (Secretary of Commerce) which is concerned with promoting domestic and international business and commerce; may also be a department of state government with similar functions.

Commercia belli /kəmárs(h)(i)yə bélay/. War contracts. Contracts between nations at war, or their subjects. Agreements entered into by belligerents, either in time of peace to take effect in the event of war, or during the war itself, by which arrangement is made for non-hostile intercourse. They may take the form of armistices, truces, capitulations, cartels, passports, safe-conducts, safeguards.

Commercial /kəmərshəl/. Relates to or is connected with trade and traffic or commerce in general; is occupied with business and commerce. Anderson v. Humble Oil & Refining Co., 226 Ga. 252, 174 S.E.2d 415, 416. Generic term for most all aspects of buying and selling.

Commercial agency. An office for the collection of debts for clients; also an agency for gathering credit information.

Commercial agent. An officer in the consular service of the United States, of rank inferior to a consul. Also used as equivalent to "commercial broker", see *infra.*

Commercial bank. An institution authorized to receive both demand and time deposits, to make loans of various types, to engage in trust services and other fiduciary funds, to issue letters of credit, to accept and pay drafts, to rent safety deposit boxes, and to engage in many similar activities, and are the only institutions authorized to receive demand deposits. U. S. v. Philadelphia Nat. Bank, D.C.Pa., 201 F.Supp. 348, 360.

Commercial bribery. A form of corrupt and unfair trade practice in which an employee accepts a gratuity to act against the best interests of his employer. People v. Davis, 33 Cr.R. 460, 160 N.Y.S. 769. May assume any form of corruption in which an employee is induced to betray his employer or to compete unfairly with a competitor. Freedman v. U. S., 437 F.Supp. 1252, 1260.

Commercial broker. One who negotiates the sale of merchandise without having the possession or control of it, being distinguished in the latter particular from a commission merchant (*q.v.*).

Commercial code. See **Uniform Commercial Code.**

Commercial corporation. One engaged in commerce in the broadest sense of that term.

Commercial court. In England, a court constituted as part of the Queen's Bench Division, to take causes and matters entered in the commercial list.

Commercial credit company. Company which extends credit and finances dealers and manufacturers.

Commercial domicile. See **Domicile.**

Commercial establishment. A place where commodities are exchanged, bought or sold. State ex rel. Kansas City Power & Light Co. v. Smith, 342 Mo. 75, 111 S.W.2d 513, 515.

Commercial frustration. Excuse of party from performance if contract depends on existence of given person or thing and such person or thing perishes, and if contract is rendered impossible by act of God, the law, or other party. Wood v. Bartolino, 48 N.M. 175, 146 P.2d 883, 885, 890. In theory it amounts to no more than a condition or term of a contract which the law implies to take the place of a covenant that it is assumed would have been inserted by the parties had the contingency which arose occurred to them at the time they made the contract. Lloyd v. Murphy, Cal. App., 142 P.2d 939, 942, 943. And doctrine is predicated upon premise of giving relief in a situation where parties could not reasonably protect themselves by terms of a contract against happening of subsequent events. Berline v. Waldschmidt, 159 Kan. 585, 156 P.2d 865, 867. Hence doctrine has no application where events were reasonably foreseeable and controllable by the parties. U.C.C. § 2–613. See **Commercial impracticability; Impossibility** (*Impossibility of performance of contract*).

Commercial impracticability. U.C.C. § 2–615 excuses either party from performing a contract where three conditions exist: (1) a contingency must occur, (2) performance must thereby be made "impracticable," and (3) the nonoccurrence of the contingency must have been a basic assumption on which the contract was made. Neal-Cooper Grain Co. v. Texas Gulf Sulphur Co., C.A.Ill., 508 F.2d 283. See also **Commercial frustration.**

Commercial insolvency. Inability of a businessman to pay his debts as they become due in the regular and ordinary course of business. See also **Bankrupt.**

Commercial instrument. See **Commercial paper.**

Commercial insurance. See **Insurance.**

Commercial law. A phrase used to designate the whole body of substantive jurisprudence (*e.g.* Uniform Commercial Code; Truth in Lending Act) applicable to the rights, intercourse, and relations of persons engaged in commerce, trade, or mercantile pursuits. See **Uniform Commercial Code.**

Commercial letter of credit. See **Letter of credit.**

Commercial motor vehicle. Those used primarily for business and industry as contrasted with pleasure vehicles, *e.g.* trucks.

Commercial name. See **Trade-name.**

Commercial paper. Bills of exchange (*i.e.* drafts), promissory notes, bank-checks, and other negotiable instruments for the payment of money, which, by their form and on their face, purport to be such instruments. U.C.C. Article 3 is the general law governing commercial paper. Term includes short-term notes issued by corporate borrowers. See also Bearer instrument; Instrument; Negotiable instruments; Note; Short term paper; Trade acceptance.

Commercial property. Income producing property (*e.g.* office buildings, apartments, etc.) as opposed to residential property.

Commercial reasonableness. May refer to goods which meet the warranty of merchantability. U.C.C. § 2–314.

Commercial set. Primary documents covering shipment of goods: invoice, bill of lading, bill of exchange, certificate of insurance.

Commercial speech doctrine. Speech that was categorized as "commercial" in nature (*i.e.* speech that advertised a product or service for profit or for business purpose) was formerly not afforded First Amendment freedom of speech protection, and as such could be freely regulated by statutes and ordinances. Valentine v. Chrestensen, 316 U.S. 52, 62 S.Ct. 920, 86 L.Ed. 1262. This doctrine, however, has been essentially abrogated. Pittsburgh Press Co. v. Pittsburgh Comm. on Human Rights, 413 U.S. 376, 93

S.Ct. 2553, 37 L.Ed.2d 669; Bigelow v. Virginia, 421 U.S. 809, 95 S.Ct. 2222, 44 L.Ed.2d 600; Virginia State Brd. of Pharmacy v. Virginia Citizen Council, 425 U.S. 748, 96 S.Ct. 1817, 48 L.Ed.2d 346.

Commercial traveler. A drummer; a traveling salesman who simply exhibits samples of goods kept for sale by his principal, and takes orders from purchasers for such goods, which goods are afterwards to be delivered by the principal to the purchasers, and payment for the goods is to be made by the purchasers to the principal on such delivery.

Commercial unit. Means such a unit of goods as by commercial usage is a single whole for purposes of sale and division of which materially impairs its character or value on the market or in use. A commercial unit may be a single article (as a machine) or a set of articles (as a suite of furniture, or an assortment of sizes) or a quantity (as a bale, gross, or carload) or any other unit treated in use or in the relevant market as a single whole. U.C.C. § 2–105(6).

Commercium /kəmə́rs(h)(i)yəm/. Lat. In the civil law, commerce; business; trade; dealings in the nature of purchase and sale; a contract.

Commercium jure gentium commune esse debet, et non in monopolium et privatum paucorum quæstum convertendum /kəmə́s(h)(i)yəm júriy jénsh(iy)əm kəmyúwniy ésiy débəd èt nón ìn mònəpów(i)yəm èt prəvéydəm pokórəm kwéstəm kònvərténdəm/. Commerce, by the law of nations, ought to be common, and not converted to monopoly and the private gain of a few.

Comminalty /kómənəltiy/. The commonalty or the people.

Comminatorium /kəmìnətóriyəm/kòmənətóriyəm/. In old practice, a clause sometimes added at the end of writs, admonishing the sheriff to be faithful in executing them.

Commingle /kəmíŋgəl/. To put together in one mass; *e.g.* to combine funds or properties into common fund or stock.

Commingling of funds. Act of fiduciary in mingling funds of his beneficiary, client, employer, or ward with his own funds. Such act is generally considered to be a breach of his fiduciary relationship. May be applied to lawyer who mixes client's funds with his own and as a result is subject to disciplinary action.

Commise /kəmíyz/. In old French law, forfeiture; the forfeiture of a fief; the penalty attached to the ingratitude of a vassal.

Commissaire /kòmisér/. In French law, a person who receives from a meeting of shareholders a special authority, viz., that of checking and examining the accounts of a manager or of valuing the *apports en nature (q.v.)*. The name is also applied to a judge who receives from a court a special mission, *e.g.*, to institute an inquiry, or to examine certain books, or to supervise the operations of a bankruptcy.

Commissaires-priseurs /kòmisér-prìyzə́r/. In French law, auctioneers, who possess the exclusive right of selling personal property at public sale in the towns

in which they are established; and they possess the same right concurrently with notaries, *greffiers,* and *huissiers,* in the rest of the arrondissement.

Commissaria lex /kòməsériyə léks/. A principle of the Roman law relative to the forfeiture of contracts.

Commissariat /kòməsériyət/. The whole body of officers who make up the commissaries' department of an army.

Commissary. One who is sent or delegated to execute some office or duty as the representative of his superior; an officer of the bishop, who exercises spiritual jurisdiction in distant parts of the diocese. A general store, especially on a military base; a lunchroom, especially at a movie or T.V. studio.

Commission. A warrant or authority or letters patent, issuing from the government, or one of its departments, or a court, empowering a person or persons named to do certain acts, or to exercise the authority of an office (as in the case of an officer in the army or navy).

The authority or instructions under which one person transacts business or negotiates for another. In a derivative sense, a body of persons to whom a commission is directed. A board or committee officially appointed and empowered to perform certain acts or exercise certain jurisdiction of a public nature or relation; as a "Public Service Commission".

An authority or writ issuing from a court, in relation to a cause before it, directing and authorizing a person or persons named to do some act or exercise some special function; usually to take the depositions of witnesses.

Civil law. A species of bailment, being an undertaking, without reward, to do something in respect to an article bailed; equivalent to "mandate".

Compensation. The recompense, compensation or reward of an agent, salesman, executor, trustee, receiver, factor, broker, or bailee, when the same is calculated as a percentage on the amount of his transactions or on the profit to the principal. Weiner v. Swales, 217 Md. 123, 141 A.2d 749, 750. Compensation to an administrator or other fiduciary for the faithful discharge of his duties.

Criminal law. Doing or perpetration of a criminal act.

Commission agent. See **Commission merchant; Factor.**

Commission broker. Member of stock or commodity exchange who executes buy and sell orders.

Commission del credere. In commercial law, exists where an agent of a seller undertakes to guaranty to his principal the payment of the debt due by the buyer. The phrase *"del credere"* is borrowed from the Italian language, in which its signification is equivalent to our word "guaranty" or "warranty."

Commissioned office. Officers in the armed forces who hold their rank by virtue of a commission from the President.

Commissioner. A person to whom a commission is directed by the government or a court. A person with a commission. An officer who is charged with the administration of the laws relating to some particular subject-matter, or the management of some bureau or agency of the government. Member of a commission or board. Specially appointed officer of court.

The administrative head of an organized professional sport.

In the commission form of municipal government, the term is applied to any of the several officers constituting the commission.

Commissioners of bail. Officers appointed to take recognizances of bail in civil cases.

Commissioners of deeds. Officers empowered by the government of one state to reside in another state, and there take acknowledgments of deeds and other papers which are to be used as evidence or put on record in the former state.

Commissioners of highways. Officers appointed in many of the states with power to take charge of the altering, opening, repair, and vacating of highways.

County commissioners. See **County.**

Court Commissioners. Term used variously to designate a lawyer appointed to hear facts and report to court. Specially appointed officer of court. A person appointed to conduct judicial sales. In admiralty, an officer appointed to hear and determine certain issues. See also **Magistrates** (*U.S. Magistrates*).

United States Commissioners. The functions of U.S. Commissioners have been taken over by U.S. Magistrates. See **Magistrates** (*U.S. Magistrates*).

Commissioner's court. In certain states, such court has jurisdiction over county affairs.

Commission government. A method of municipal government in which the legislative power is in the hands of a few persons.

Commission merchant. A term which is synonymous with "factor." It means one who receives goods, chattels, or merchandise for sale, exchange, or other disposition, and who is to receive a compensation for his services, to be paid by the owner, or derived from the sale, etc., of the goods. One whose business is to receive and sell goods for a commission, being intrusted with the possession of the goods to be sold, and usually selling in his own name. Hughes v. Young, 17 Tenn.App. 24, 65 S.W.2d 858, 864. See also **Factor.**

Broker distinguished. A "factor" or "commission merchant" is one who has the actual or technical possession of goods or wares of another for sale, while a "merchandise broker" is one who negotiates the sale of merchandise without having it in his possession or control, being simply an agent with very limited powers. Hughes v. Young, 17 Tenn.App. 24, 65 S.W.2d 858, 864.

Commission of anticipation. In English law, an authority under the great seal to collect a tax or subsidy before the day.

Commission of appraisement and sale. Where property has been arrested in an admiralty action *in rem* and ordered by the court to be sold, the order is carried out by a commission of appraisement and sale. In some cases (as where the property is to be released on bail and the value is disputed) a commission of appraisement only is required.

Commission of array. In old English law, a commission issued to send into every county officers to muster or set in military order the inhabitants. The introduction of commissions of lieutenancy, which contained, in substance, the same powers as these commissions, superseded them.

Commission of assize /kəmíshən əv əsáyz/. In English practice, a commission which formerly issued from the king, appointing certain persons as commissioners or judges of assize to hold the assizes in association with discreet knights during those years in which the justices in eyre did not come. A commission issued to judges of the high court or court of appeal, authorizing them to sit at the assizes for the trial of civil actions.

Commission of charitable uses. In old English law, this commission issued out of chancery to the bishop and others, where lands given to charitable uses were misemployed, or there was any fraud or dispute concerning them, to inquire of and redress the same, etc.

Commission of delegates. In old English law, when any sentence was given in any ecclesiastical cause by the archbishop, this commission, under the great seal, was directed to certain persons, usually lords, bishops, and judges of the law, to sit and hear an appeal of the same to the king, in the court of chancery.

Commission of partition. In the former English equity practice, this was a commission or authority issued to certain persons, to effect a division of lands held by tenants in common desiring a partition; when the commissioners reported, the parties were ordered to execute mutual conveyances to confirm the division. Commissioners appointed to make partition are in the nature of arbitrators.

Commission of rebellion. In English law, an attaching process, formerly issuable out of chancery, to enforce obedience to a process or decree; abolished in August, 1841.

Commission of review. In English ecclesiastical law, a commission formerly sometimes granted in extraordinary cases, to revise the sentence of the court of delegates. 3 Bl.Comm. 67. Now out of use, the privy council being substituted for the court of delegates, as the great court of appeal in all ecclesiastical causes.

Commission of the peace. In English law, a commission from the crown, appointing certain persons therein named, jointly and severally, to keep the *peace,* etc. Justices of the peace are appointed by special commission under the great seal; a separate commission being issued for each county and for the city of London.

Commissions. The compensation or reward paid to a factor, broker, agent, salesman, bailee, executor, trustee, receiver, etc., usually calculated as a percentage on the amount of his transactions or the amount received or expended.

Commission to examine witnesses. A commission issued out of the court in which an action is pending, to direct the taking of the depositions of witnesses who are beyond the territorial jurisdiction of the court. Fed.R. Civil P. 28.

Commit. To perpetrate, as a crime; to perform as an act; to entrust; to pledge.

To send a person to prison by virtue of a lawful authority, for any crime or contempt, or to a mental health facility, workhouse, reformatory, or the like, by authority of a court or magistrate.

To refer to a committee for action; *e.g.* a legislative bill.

Commitment. A warrant, order, or process by which court or magistrate directs ministerial officer to take person to penal institution or mental health facility. Schildhaus v. City of New York, 7 Misc.2d 859, 163 N.Y.S.2d 201, 206. Also, the act of taking or sending to the prison, mental health facility, or the like. A person is committed when he is actually sentenced to confinement by a court as contrasted with a suspended sentence or probation. See also **Mittimus.**

The proceedings directing confinement of a mentally ill or incompetent person for treatment. Commitment proceedings may be either civil or criminal; and voluntary or involuntary. Due process protections are afforded to persons involuntarily committed; *e.g.* periodic judicial review of continued confinement. Fasulo v. Arafeh, 173 Conn. 473, 378 A.2d 553. See **Civil commitment.**

Agreement or pledge to do something; *e.g.* a statement by a lender that a loan will be made under certain terms. Commitments may be of various types, that is, a conditional commitment, subject to certain items being met, or a firm commitment, which is binding on the lender without conditions.

Commitment fee. Amount paid to lender by borrower for loan commitment in addition to interest. Such are common in real estate transactions.

Committee. A person, or an assembly or board of persons, to whom the consideration, determination, or management of any matter is committed or referred, as by a court or legislature. An individual or body to whom others have delegated or committed a particular duty, or who have taken on themselves to perform it in the expectation of their act being confirmed by the body they profess to represent or act for.

In legislatures a standing committee considers all bills, resolutions, and other items of legislative business falling within the category of matters over which it has been given jurisdiction. Membership and rank on standing committees are largely determined by the seniority rule. A special (or select) committee investigates and reports on specific matters and terminates when that function has been rendered. A joint committee of a legislative body comprising two chambers is a committee consisting of representatives of each of the two houses, meeting and acting together as one committee.

Committing magistrate. An inferior judicial officer who is invested with authority to conduct the preliminary hearing of persons charged with crime, and either to discharge them for lack of sufficient prima facie evidence or to commit them to jail to await trial or (in some jurisdictions) to accept bail and release them thereon. The term is said to be synonymous with "examining court."

Committitur /kəmídədər/. An order or minute, setting forth that the person named in it *is committed* to the custody of the sheriff.

Committitur piece /kəmídədər pìys/. In old English law, an instrument in writing on paper or parchment, which charged a person, already in prison, in execution at the suit of the person who arrested him.

Commixtio /kəmíksh(iy)ow/, or **commixtion** /kəmíkshən/. In the civil law, the mixing together or confusion of things, dry or solid, belonging to different owners, as distinguished from *confusio,* which has relation to liquids.

Commodate. Exists where property is loaned gratuitously by owner for sole benefit, accommodation, and use of borrower, and specific thing loaned is to be returned. See also **Commodatum.**

Commodati actio /kòmədéyday æksh(iy)ow/. Lat. In the civil law, an action of loan; an action for a thing lent. An action given for the recovery of a thing loaned *(commodatum),* and not returned to the lender.

Commodato /kòmədátow/. In Spanish law, a contract by which one person lends gratuitously to another some object not consumable, to be restored to him in kind at a given period; the same contract as *commodatum (q.v.).*

Commodatum /kòmədéydəm/. A gratuitous loan of goods to be temporarily used by the bailee, and returned in specie. He who lends to another a thing for a definite time, to be enjoyed and used under certain conditions, without any pay or reward, is called *"commodans";* the person who receives the thing is called *"commodatarius",* and the contract is called *"commodatum".* It differs from *locatio* and *conductio,* in this: that the use of the thing is gratuitous.

Commodities /kəmódədiyz/. Those things which are useful or serviceable, particularly articles of merchandise movable in trade. Goods, wares, and merchandise of any kind; movables; articles of trade or commerce. Movable articles of value; things that are bought and sold. This word is a broader term than merchandise, and, in referring to commerce may include almost any article of movable or personal property.

Staples such as wool, cotton, etc. which are traded on a Commodity Exchange and on which there is trading in futures.

Commodities clause. A clause in the act of Congress, June 29, 1906 (49 U.S.C.A. § 1(8)), providing that it shall be unlawful for any railroad company to transport commodities (excepting timber and its manufactured products) manufactured, mined or produced by it, or under its authority, or which it may own in whole or in part, or in which it may have any interest, direct or indirect, except such articles or commodities as may be necessary and intended for its use in its business.

Commodity. See **Commodities.**

Commodity Credit Corporation. The Commodity Credit Corporation (CCC) was organized October 17, 1933, pursuant to Executive Order 6340 of October 16, 1933, under the laws of the State of Delaware, as an agency of the United States. From October 17, 1933, to July 1, 1939, the CCC was managed and operated in close affiliation with the Reconstruction Finance Corporation. On July 1, 1939, the CCC was transferred to the Department of Agriculture by the President's Reorganization Plan 1 of 1939. Approval of the Commodity Credit Corporation Charter Act on June 29, 1948 (62 Stat. 1070; 15 U.S.C.A. § 714), subsequently amended, established the CCC, effective July 1, 1948, as an agency and instrumentality of the United States under a permanent Federal charter. The purpose of CCC is to stabilize and protect farm income and prices, to assist in maintaining balanced and adequate supplies of agricultural commodities and their products, and to facilitate the orderly distribution of commodities.

Commodity future. A speculative transaction involving the sale for future delivery of a staple such as wool or cotton. See **Futures contract.**

Commodity Futures Trading Commission. The Commodity Futures Trading Commission, an independent agency of the U.S. Government, administers the Commodity Exchange Act which is designed to insure fair practices and honest dealing on the commodity futures exchanges and to provide a measure of control over speculative activity.

Commodity paper. Commercial paper representing loans secured by bills of lading or warehouse receipts covering commodities.

Commodity rate. With reference to railroads, a rate which applies to a specific commodity alone;—distinguished from a "class rate", meaning a single rate which applies to a number of articles of the same general character.

Commodum ex injuria sua nemo habere debet /kómədəm eks ənjúriyə s(y)uwə níymow həbíriy débət/. No person ought to have advantage from his own wrong.

Common, *n.* Belonging or shared equally by more than one. Of frequent occurrence. Without special or distinguishing characteristics.

An incorporeal hereditament which consists in a profit which one man has in connection with one or more others in the land of another. See **Profit** (*Profit a prende*).

Tract of land set apart by city or town for use by general public. Formerly, such land was to be used for common pasturage. Now usually called "parks."

Common appendant. In old English law, a right annexed to the possession of arable land, by which the owner is entitled to feed his beasts on the lands of another, usually of the owner of the manor of which the lands entitled to common are a part. 2 Bl.Comm. 33.

Common appurtenant. A right of feeding one's beasts on the land of another (in common with the owner or with others), which is founded on a grant, or a prescription which supposes a grant.

Common in gross, or at large. A species of common which is neither appendant nor appurtenant to *land,* but is annexed to a man's *person,* being granted to him and his heirs by deed; or it may be claimed by prescriptive right, as by a person of a church or the like corporation sole. 2 Bl.Comm. 34. It is a separate inheritance, entirely distinct from any other landed property, vested in the person to whom the common right belongs.

Common of estovers. A liberty of taking necessary wood for the use or furniture of a house or farm from off another's estate, in common with the owner or with others. 2 Bl.Comm. 35. It may be claimed, like common of pasture, either by grant or prescription.

Common of piscary. The right or liberty of fishing in another man's water, in common with the owner or with other persons. 2 Bl.Comm. 34. A liberty or right of fishing in the water covering the soil of another person, or in a river running through another's land. Hardin v. Jordan, 140 U.S. 371, 11 S.Ct. 808, 35 L.Ed. 428.

Common, tenants in. See **Tenant** (*Tenant in common*).

Common, *adj.* Usual, ordinary, accustomed; shared among several; owned by several jointly. Belonging or pertaining to many or to the majority. Generally or prevalent, of frequent or ordinary occurrence or appearance; familiar by reason of frequency. Webb v. New Mexico Pub. Co., 47 N.M. 279, 141 P.2d 333, 335. Also, usual, customary, and habitual, professed, or confessed, and used indefinitely in various terms implying illegal or criminal conduct, such as common scold, common thief, etc.

As to common Bail; Barretor; Chase; Condedit; Council; Day; Debtor; Diligence; Drunkard; Error; Fishery; Highway; Informer; Inn; Intendment of law; Intent; Jury; Labor; Nuisance; Occupant; Property; School; Scold; Seal; Sergeant; Stock; Traverse; Vouchee; Wall, see those titles.

Common ancestor. A person through whom two or more persons claim lineage.

Common appearance. The manner in which something generally appears; *e.g.* by common appearance blood is red.

Common area. In law of landlord-tenant, the portion of demised premises over which landlord retains control (*e.g.* stairs) and hence for whose condition he is liable, as contrasted with areas of which tenant has exclusive possession. Term also refers to areas in common use by residents of condominium.

Common assurances. The several modes or instruments of conveyance established or authorized by the law of England. Called "common" because thereby *every man's* estate is assured to him.

Common carrier. Any carrier required by law to convey passengers or freight without refusal if the approved fare or charge is paid in contrast to private or contract carrier. One who holds himself out to the public as engaged in business of transportation of persons or property from place to place for compensation, and who offers services to the public generally. Tilson v. Ford Motor Co., D.C.Mich., 130 F.Supp. 676, 678. Such is to be distinguished from a *contract* or *private* carrier. See **Carrier.**

Common causes or suits. A term anciently used to denote civil actions, or those depending between subject and subject, as distinguished from *pleas of the crown.*

Common condidit. See **Condedit.**

Common counts. Old forms of pleading by which pleader sets forth in account form the basis of his claim such as money had and received, goods sold and delivered, etc. Traditionally, the various forms of action of assumpsit.

Common defense. In joint trial of two or more defendants, a defense asserted by all defendants.

Common design. Community of intention between two or more persons to do an unlawful act. Generally used in criminal context to describe an action taken by two or more persons after joint planning. Actions and declarations of one participant during existence of common design are chargeable to all participants. Com. v. Dahlstrom, 345 Mass. 130, 185 N.E.2d 759. See **Combination in restraint of trade; Conspiracy.**

Common disaster. Situation in which the insured and beneficiary appear to die simultaneously with no clear indication or evidence of which died first. See **Simultaneous Death Act.**

Common disaster clause. In insurance or will, a clause that provides for an alternative beneficiary in event both the insured (testator) and beneficiary (legatee) die in a common disaster. See **Simultaneous death clause.**

Common enterprise. See **Joint enterprise.**

Common good. Generic term to describe the betterment of the general public.

Common knowledge. Information widely shared by substantial number of people. See **Judicial notice.**

Common prayer. The liturgy, or public form of prayer prescribed by the Church of England to be used in all churches and chapels, and which the clergy are enjoined to use under a certain penalty.

Common repute. The prevailing belief in a given community as to the existence of a certain fact or aggregation of facts.

Common right. A term applied to rights, privileges, and immunities appertaining to and enjoyed by all citizens equally and in common, and which have their foundation in the common law.

Common school. A public elementary school.

Common seller. A common seller of any commodity is one who sells it frequently, usually, customarily, or habitually.

Common sense. Sound practical judgment; that degree of intelligence and reason, as exercised upon the relations of persons and things and the ordinary affairs of life, which is possessed by the generality of mankind, and which would suffice to direct the conduct and actions of the individual in a manner to agree with the behavior of ordinary persons.

Common weal. The public or common good or welfare.

Commonable. Entitled to common. Commonable beasts are either beasts of the plow, as horses and oxen, or such as manure the land, as kine and sheep. Beasts not commonable are swine, goats, and the like. 2 Bl.Comm. 33.

Commonalty /kómənəltiy/. The great body of citizens; the mass of the people, excluding the nobility. The body of people composing a municipal corporation, excluding the corporate officers. The body of a society or corporation, as distinguished from the officers.

Commonance. The commoners, or tenants and inhabitants, who have the right of common or commoning in open field.

Common bar. (Otherwise called "blank bar"). A common law plea to compel the plaintiff to assign the particular place where the trespass had been committed.

Common bench. The ancient name for the English court of common pleas. Its original title appears to have been simply "The Bench", but it was designated "Common Bench" to distinguish it from the "King's Bench", and because in it were tried and determined the causes of *common* persons, *i.e.,* causes between subject and subject, in which the crown had no interest.

Common enemy doctrine. Under "common enemy doctrine" each landowner has an unqualified right, by operations on his own land, to fend off surface waters as he sees fit without being required to take into account the consequences to other landowners who also have the duty and right to protect themselves as best they can. Reutner v. Vouga, Mo.App., 367 S.W.2d 34, 41.

Commoners. In old English law, persons having a right of *common.* So called because they have a right to pasture on the waste, in common with the lord.

Common fund doctrine. This doctrine provides that private plaintiff, or his attorney, whose efforts create, discover, increase, or preserve a fund to which others also have a claim is entitled to recover from the fund the costs of his litigation, including attorneys' fees. Vincent v. Hughes Air West, Inc., C.A.Cal., 557 F.2d 759, 769.

Common humanity doctrine. Where a passenger becomes sick or is injured while en route, carrier owes duty under "common humanity doctrine" to render to passenger such reasonable care and attention as common humanity would dictate.

Common knowledge. Is what court may declare applicable to action without necessity of proof. It is knowledge that every intelligent person has. It includes matters of learning, experience, history, and facts of which judicial notice may be taken. Shelley v. Chilton's Adm'r, 236 Ky. 221, 32 S.W.2d 974, 977. See also **Judicial notice.**

Common law. As distinguished from law created by the enactment of legislatures, the common law comprises the body of those principles and rules of action, relating to the government and security of persons and property, which derive their authority solely from usages and customs of immemorial antiquity, or from the judgments and decrees of the courts recognizing, affirming, and enforcing such usages and customs; and, in this sense, particularly the ancient unwritten law of England. The "common law" is all the statutory and case law background of England and the American colonies before the American revolution. People v. Rehman, 253 C.A.2d 119, 61 Cal.Rptr. 65, 85. "Common law" consists of those principles, usage and rules of action applicable to government and security of persons and property which do not rest for their authority upon any express and positive declaration of the will of the legislature. Bishop v. U. S., D.C.Tex., 334 F.Supp. 415, 418.

As distinguished from ecclesiastical law, it is the system of jurisprudence administered by the purely secular tribunals.

Calif. Civil Code, Section 22.2, provides that the "common law of England, so far as it is not repugnant to or inconsistent with the Constitution of the United States, or the Constitution or laws of this State, is the rule of decision in all the courts of this State."

In a broad sense, "common law" may designate all that part of the positive law, juristic theory, and ancient custom of any state or nation which is of general and universal application, thus marking off special or local rules or customs.

For "Federal common law," see that title.

As a compound adjective "common-law" is understood as contrasted with or opposed to "statutory," and sometimes also to "equitable" or to "criminal." See examples below.

Common-law action. Action governed by common law, rather than statutory, equitable, or civil law.

Common-law assignments. Such forms of assignments for the benefit of creditors as were known to the common law, as distinguished from such as are of modern invention or authorized by statute.

Common-law cheat. The obtaining of money or property by means of a false token, symbol, or device; this being the definition of a cheat or "cheating" at common law.

Common-law contempt. A name sometimes applied to proceedings for contempt which are criminal in their nature, as distinguished from those which are intended as purely civil remedies ordinarily arising out of the alleged violation of some order entered in the course of a chancery proceeding.

Common-law copyright. An intangible, incorporeal right in an author of literary or artistic productions to reproduce and sell them exclusively and arises at the moment of their creation as distinguished from federal or statutory copyrights which exist for the most part only in published works. Common law copyright is perpetual while statutory copyright is for term of years. Equitable relief is available for violation of common law copyright. Edgar H. Wood Associates Inc. v. Skene, 347 Mass. 351, 197 N.E.2d 886. The distinction which formerly existed between common law copyrights and statutory copyrights was abolished by the 1976 Copyright Act revision; though § 301 of the new Act specifically preserves common law copyrights accruing prior to January 1, 1978. See also **Copyright.**

Common-law courts. In England, those administering the common law.

Common-law crime. One punishable by the force of the common law, as distinguished from crimes created by statute.

Common-law dedication. A "statutory dedication" is in nature of grant based on substantial compliance with terms of applicable statute, while "common law dedication" is generally held to rest upon doctrine of estoppel in pais. Tinaglia v. Ittzes, S.D., 257 N.W.2d 724, 729.

Common-law extortion. Corrupt collection of unlawful fee by an office under color of office.

Common-law jurisdiction. Jurisdiction of a court to try and decide such cases as were cognizable by the courts of law under the English common law. The jurisdiction of those courts which exercise their judicial powers according to the course of the common law.

Common-law larceny. See **Larceny.**

Common-law lien. One known to or granted by the common law, as distinguished from statutory, equitable, and maritime liens; also one arising by implication of law, as distinguished from one created by the agreement of the parties. It is a right extended to a person to retain that which is in his possession belonging to another, until the demand or charge of the person in possession is paid or satisfied. Whiteside v. Rocky Mountain Fuel Co., C.C.A.Colo., 101 F.2d 765, 769.

Common-law marriage. One not solemnized in the ordinary way (i.e. non-ceremonial) but created by an agreement to marry, followed by cohabitation. A consummated agreement to marry, between persons legally capable of making marriage contract, per verba de præsenti, followed by cohabitation. Such marriage requires a positive mutual agreement, permanent and exclusive of all others, to enter into a marriage relationship, cohabitation sufficient to warrant a fulfillment of necessary relationship of man and wife, and an assumption of marital duties and obligations. Marshall v. State, Okl.Cr., 537 P.2d 423, 429. Such marriages are invalid in many states; e.g. Missouri (after 1921), Indiana (after 1958), Maryland, Massachusetts, Nebraska (after 1939), Nevada, New Hampshire, New Jersey, New Mexico, New York (after 1933), North Dakota, Oregon, South Dakota (after 1959), Virginia, Washington, W. Virginia, Wisconsin, Wyoming.

Common-law trade-mark. One appropriated under common-law rules, regardless of statutes. Stratton & Terstegge Co. v. Stiglitz Furnace Co., 258 Ky. 678, 81 S.W.2d 1, 3.

Common-law trust. A business trust which has certain characteristics in common with corporations and in which trustees hold the property and manage the business and the shareholders are the trust beneficiaries or cestui que trust; sometimes known as a Massachusetts trust. See **Massachusetts trust.**

Common-law wife. A woman who was party to a common-law marriage; or one who, having lived with a man in a relation of concubinage during his life, asserts a claim, after his death, to have been his wife according to the requirements of the common law.

Common lawyer. A lawyer learned in the common law. This term is now generally obsolete.

Common market. An economic union established in 1958 which originally included Belgium, France, Italy, Luxembourg, the Netherlands and West Germany. Its official title is European Economic Community.

Common nuisance. A nuisance is a "common nuisance" or a "public nuisance", the terms being synonymous, where it affects the rights enjoyed by citizens as part of the public, that is, the rights to which every citizen is entitled. Dahlstrom v. Roosevelt Mills, Inc., 27 Conn.Sup. 355, 238 A.2d 431, 432. See also **Nuisance.**

Common pleas court. See **Court of Common Pleas.**

Common property. Property held by two or more persons in common with each other; *e.g.* as tenants in common. Portion of rented premises over which landlord retains control but which may be used by tenants such as hallways, stairways, etc. See also **Community property.**

Common recovery. In conveyancing, a species of common assurance, or mode of conveying lands by matter of record, formerly in frequent use in England. It was in the nature and form of an action at law, carried regularly through, and ending in a *recovery* of the lands against the tenant of the freehold; which recovery, being a supposed adjudication of the right, bound all persons, and vested a free and absolute fee-simple in the recoverer. 2 Bl.Comm. 357. Common recoveries were abolished by the statutes 3 & 4 Wm. IV, c. 74.

Common right. Right derivative from common law. Strother v. Lucas, 37 U.S. (12 Pet.) 410, 437, 9 L.Ed. 1137. Right peculiar to certain people is not a common right. Perdue v. Zoning Bd. of Appeals of City of Norwalk, 118 Conn. 174, 171 A. 26, 28.

Commons. The class of subjects in Great Britain exclusive of the royal family and the nobility. They are represented in parliament by the house of commons.

Part of the demesne land of a manor (or land the property of which was in the lord), which, being uncultivated, was termed the "lord's waste," and served for public roads and for common of pasture to the lord and his tenants. 2 Bl.Comm. 90.

Squares; pleasure grounds and spaces or open places for public use or public recreation owned by towns or cities—in modern usage usually called "parks."

Commons, House of. See **House** (*House of Commons*).

Common stock. Class of corporate stock which represents the ownership of the corporation. Equity stock which participates in the profits by way of dividends after preferred stockholders have been paid their dividends. Last to share in property of corporation on dissolution. Normally have voting rights. See **Stock.**

Common tenancy. Type of tenancy in which tenants hold property in common without right of survivorship. May be holding of unequal shares among tenants. Such tenancy is subject to partition. See also **Tenancy.**

Common thief. One who by practice and habit is a thief. An adjudication of a person which may be made after a person has been convicted more than once of larceny. It generally carries an additional sentence beyond that for larceny. Sometimes known as common and notorious thief.

Common trust fund. One composed of funds contributed by estates, trusts and guardianships, maintained and operated by a bank or trust company for exclusive use of its own estates, trusts and guardianships, under permission of law of state in which it is located and according to rules and regulations promulgated by Federal Reserve System. Mechanicks Nat. Bank of Concord v. D'Amours, 100 N.H. 461, 129 A.2d 859, 862. Type of trust fund in which funds of many persons are commingled for purposes of economy of administration and counselling and in which a bank or other financial institution is trustee; regulated almost entirely by statute. Several states have adopted the Uniform Common Trust Fund Act.

Commonwealth. The public or common weal or welfare. This cannot be regarded as a technical term of public law, though often used in political science. It generally designates, when so employed, a republican frame of government,—one in which the welfare and rights of the entire mass of people are the main consideration, rather than the privileges of a class or the will of a monarch; or it may designate the body of citizens living under such a government.

Sometimes it may denote the corporate entity, or the government, of a jural society (or state) possessing powers of self-government in respect of its immediate concerns, but forming an integral part of a larger government (or nation). In this latter sense, it is the official title of several of the United States (as Pennsylvania, Massachusetts, Virginia, and Kentucky), and would be appropriate to them all. In the former sense, the word was used to designate the English government during the protectorate of Cromwell.

Any of the individual States of the United States and the body of people constituting a state or politically organized community, a body politic, hence, a state, especially one constituted by a number of persons united by compact or tacit agreement under one form of government and system of laws. Detres v. Lions Bldg. Corp., C.A.Ill., 234 F.2d 596, 600.

See **Government; Nation; State.**

Commonwealth court. In Pennsylvania, the Commonwealth Court has original jurisdiction of all civil actions or proceedings against Commonwealth or its officer (except habeas corpus or postconviction relief not ancillary to its appellate jurisdiction, and eminent domain); all civil actions or proceedings by Commonwealth or any officer, except eminent domain; and under numerous specified regulatory acts. Its original jurisdiction is exclusive, except in civil actions or proceedings brought by Commonwealth or its officers, which is concurrent with common pleas.

Commorancy /kómərənsiy/. In English law, the dwelling in any place as inhabitant; which consists in usually lying there. 4 Bl.Comm. 273. In American law, it is used to denote a mere temporary residence.

Commorant /kómərənt/. Staying or abiding; dwelling temporarily in a place. One residing in a particular town, city, or district.

Commorientes /kəmòriyéntiyz/. Several persons who perish at the same time in consequence of the same calamity. See **Common** (*Common disaster*).

Commorth, or **comorth** /kómərθ/. A contribution which has gathered at marriages, and when young priests said or sung the first masses. Prohibited by 26 Hen. VIII, c. 6.

Commote /kómət/. Half a cantred or hundred in Wales, containing fifty villages. Also a great seignory or lordship, and may include one or divers manors.

Commotion /kəmówshən/. A condition of turmoil, civil unrest or insurrection. A civil commotion is an uprising among a mass of people which occasions a serious and prolonged disturbance and infraction of civil order not attaining the status of war or an armed insurrection; it is a wild and irregular action of many persons assembled together.

Commune /kəmyúwn/, *v.* To talk; to communicate.

Commune /kəmyúwniy/, *adj.* Lat. See **Communis.**

Commune /kómyuwn/, *n.* A self-governing town or village. Smallest administrative district of many European countries. The name given to the committee of the people in the French revolution of 1793; and again, in the revolutionary uprising of 1871, it signified the attempt to establish absolute self-government in Paris, or the mass of those concerned in the attempt. In old French law, it signified any municipal corporation. And in old English law, the commonalty or common people.

Small community of people, usually with common interests, who own and share property in common.

Commune concilium /kəmyúwniy kənsíl(i)yəm/. The King's Council. See **Privy council.**

Commune concilium regni /kəmyúwniy kənsíl(i)yəm régnay/. The common council of the realm. One of the names of the English parliament. See **Communitas regni angliæ.**

Commune forum /kəmyúwniy fórəm/. The common place of justice. The seat of the principal courts, especially those that are fixed.

Commune placitum /kəmyúwniy plǽsədəm/. In old English law, a common plea or civil action, such as an action of debt.

Commune vinculum /kəmyúwniy víŋkyələm/. In old English law, a common or mutual bond. Applied to the common stock of consanguinity, and to the feodal bond of fealty, as the common bond of union between lord and tenant. 2 Bl.Comm. 250; 3 Bl.Comm. 230.

Communia /kəmyúwniyə/. In old English law, common things, *res communes.* Such as running water, the air, the sea, and sea shores.

Communiæ /kəmyúwniyiy/. In feudal law on the continent of Europe, this name was given to towns enfranchised by the crown, about the twelfth century, and formed into free corporations by grants called "charters of community".

Communia placita /kəmyúwniyə plǽsədə/. In old English law, common pleas or actions; those between one subject and another, as distinguished from pleas of the crown.

Communia placita non tenenda in scaccario /kəmyúwniyə plǽsədə nòn tənéndə in skəkériyow/. An ancient writ directed to the treasurer and barons of the exchequer, forbidding them to hold pleas between common persons (*i.e.*, not debtors to the king, who alone originally sued and were sued there) in that court, where neither of the parties belonged to the same.

Communibus annis /kəmyúwnəbəs ǽnəs/. In ordinary years; on the annual average.

Communicate. To bestow, convey, make known, recount, impart; to give by way of information; to talk over; to transmit information. See also **Utter.**

Communication. Information given; the sharing of knowledge by one with another; conference; consultation or bargaining preparatory to making a contract. Intercourse; connection. Act of or system of transmitting information. A "communication" is ordinarily considered to be a deliberate interchange of thoughts or opinions between two or more persons, as distinguished from "res gestae" expressions which are spontaneously or instinctively provoked, or made while under such shock or excitement as to preclude the possibility of design. Gulf Oil Corp. v. Harris, Okl., 425 P.2d 957, 962.

Confidential communications. These are certain classes of communications, passing between persons who stand in a confidential or fiduciary relation to each other (or who, on account of their relative situation, are under a special duty of secrecy and fidelity), which the law will not permit to be divulged, or allow them to be inquired into in a court of justice, for the sake of public policy and the good order of society. Examples of such privileged relations are those of husband and wife, doctor and patient, and attorney and client. Such are privileged at the option of the spouse-witness, patient-witness, client-witness. See **Privileged communications.**

Libel or slander. As an essential element of tort liability for libel or slander, such communication (*i.e.* publication) may be either printed, written, oral, or conveyed by means of gestures, or exhibition of a picture or statue. See **Libel; Slander.**

Communi custodia /kəmyúwnay kəstówdiyə/. In English law, an obsolete writ which anciently lay for the lord, whose tenant, holding by knight's service, died, and left his eldest son under age, against a stranger that entered the land, and obtained the ward of the body.

Communi dividundo /kəmyúwnay dìvədándow/. In the civil law, an action which lies for those who have property in common, to procure a division. It lies where parties hold land in common but not in partnership.

Communio bonorum /kəmyúwn(i)yow bənorəm/. In the civil law, a community of goods.

Communis /kəmyúwnəs/, **commune** /kəmyúwniy/, *adj.* Lat. Common. See **Commune.**

Communis error facit jus /kəmyúwnəs éhrər féysət jás/. Common error, repeated many times, makes law.

Communism. A system of social organization in which goods are held in common, the opposite of the system of private property; communalism, any theory or system of social organization involving common ownership of agents of production of industry, the latter of which theories is referred to in the popular use of the word "communism" while the scientific usage sometimes conforms to the first alone and sometimes alternates between the first and second; also the principles and theories of the Communist Party. A system by which the state controls the means of production and the distribution and consumption of industrial products.

Communis opinio /kəmyúwnəs əpín(i)yow/. Common opinion; general professional opinion. According to Lord Coke (who places it on the footing of observance or usage), common opinion is good authority in law.

Communis paries /kəmyúwnəs pǽriyiyz/. In the civil law, a common or party wall.

Communis rixatrix /kəmyúwnəs ríksətrəks/. In old English law, a common scold (q.v.). 4 Bl.Comm. 168.

Communis scriptura /kəmyúwnəs skript(y)úrə/. In old English law, a common writing; a writing common to both parties; a chirograph.

Communis stipes /kəmyúwnə stáypiyz/. A common stock of descent; a common ancestor.

Communist. Member of the Communist party or movement. Adherent or advocate of Communism.

Communitas regni angliæ /kəmyúwnətǽs régnay ǽngliyiy/. The general assembly of the kingdom of England. One of the ancient names of the English parliament. 1 Bl.Comm. 148. See also **Commune concilium regni.**

Community. Neighborhood; vicinity; synonymous with locality. Conley v. Valley Motor Transit Co., C.C.A.Ohio, 139 F.2d 692, 693. People who reside in a locality in more or less proximity. A society or body of people living in the same place, under the same laws and regulations, who have common rights, privileges, or interests. Sacred Heart Academy of Galveston v. Karsch, 173 Tenn. 618, 122 S.W.2d 416, 417. It connotes a congeries of common interests arising from associations—social, business, religious, governmental, scholastic, recreational. Lukens Steel Co. v. Perkins, 70 App.D.C. 354, 107 F.2d 627, 631.

Community account. A bank account consisting of separate and community funds commingled in such manner that neither can be distinguished from the other. Smith v. Buss, 135 Tex. 566, 144 S.W.2d 529, 532.

Community antenna television (CATV). System of television reception in which signals from distant stations are picked up by large antenna and transmitted by cable to individual paying customers.

Community debt. One chargeable to the community (of husband and wife) rather than to either of the parties individually.

Community house. A house occupied by two or more persons or families. A tenement.

Community lease. Exists where a number of lessors owning interests in separate tracts execute a lease in favor of a single lessee. Howell v. Union Producing Co., C.A.Tex., 392 F.2d 95.

Community of interest. Term as applied to relation of joint adventure means interest common to both or all parties, that is, mixture or identity of interest in venture wherein each and all are reciprocally concerned and from which each and all derive material benefit and sustain a mutual responsibility. Carboneau v. Peterson, 1 Wash.2d 347, 95 P.2d 1043, 1055.

Community of profits. This term, as used in the definition of a partnership (to which a community of profits is essential), means a proprietorship in them as distinguished from a personal claim upon the other associate as much as in the other. Moore v. Williams, 26 Tex.Civ.App. 142, 62 S.W. 977.

Community property. Property owned in common by husband and wife each having an undivided one-half interest by reason of their marital status. The eight states with community property systems are: Louisiana, Texas, New Mexico, Arizona, California, Washington, Idaho, and Nevada. The rest of the states are classified as common law jurisdictions. The difference between common law and community property systems centers around the property rights possessed by married persons. In a common law system, each spouse owns whatever he or she earns. Under a community property system, one-half of the earnings of each spouse is considered by the other spouse.

Commutation /kòmyətéyshən/. Alteration; change; substitution; the act of substituting one thing for another. In criminal law, the change of a punishment to one which is less severe; as from execution to life imprisonment. In commercial law, substituting one form of payment for another.

In civil law, the conversion of the right to receive a variable or periodical payment into the right to receive a fixed or gross payment; a substitution of one sort of payment for another, or of money payment in lieu of a performance of a compulsory duty or labor. Commutation may be effected by private agreement, but it is usually done under a statute.

Commutation of taxes. Payment of a designated lump sum (permanent or annual) for the privilege of exemption from taxes, or the settlement in advance of a specific sum in lieu of an ad valorem tax.

Commutation of tithes. Signifies the conversion of tithes into a fixed payment in money.

Commutation ticket. A railroad ticket giving the holder the right to travel at a certain rate for a limited number of trips (or for an unlimited number within a certain period of time) for a less amount than would be paid in the aggregate for so many separate trips.

Commutative contract. In civil law, one in which each of the contracting parties gives and receives an equivalent; *e.g.,* the contract of sale. See **Contract.**

Commutative justice. See **Justice.**

Commuted value. The present value of a future interest in property used in taxation and in evaluating damages. Present value of future payments when discounted.

Compact, *n.* An agreement or contract between persons, nations or states. Commonly applied to working agreements between and among states concerning matters of mutual concern. A contract between parties, which creates obligations and rights capable of being enforced, and contemplated as such between the parties, in their distinct and independent characters. A mutual consent of parties concerned respecting some property or right that is the object of the stipulation, or something that is to be done or forborne. See also **Compact clause; Confederacy; Interstate compact; Treaty.**

Compact, *adj.* Closely or firmly united or packed, as the particles of solid bodies; firm; solid; dense, as a compact texture in rocks; also, lying in a narrow compass or arranged so as to economize space; having a small surface or border in proportion to contents or bulk; close, as a compact estate, or a compact order or formation of troops.

Compact clause. Art. I, Section 10, Cl. 3, of U.S. Constitution provides: "No State shall, without the consent of Congress, . . . enter into any Agreement or *Compact* with another State . . ."

Compact school district. One so closely united and so nearly adjacent to the school building that all the students residing in the district may conveniently travel from their homes to the school building and return the same day in a reasonable length of time and with a reasonable degree of comfort. People ex rel. Tudor v. Vance, 374 Ill. 415, 29 N.E.2d 673; People ex rel. Frailey v. McNeely, 376 Ill. 64, 32 N.E.2d 608, 610.

Companage. All kinds of food, except bread and drink.

Companies Clauses Consolidation Act. An English statute (8 Vict. c. 16), passed in 1845, which consolidated the clauses of previous laws still remaining in force on the subject of public companies. It is considered as incorporated into all subsequent acts authorizing the execution of undertakings of a public nature by companies, unless expressly excepted by such later acts. Its purpose is declared by the preamble to be to avoid repeating provisions as to the constitution and management of the companies, and to secure greater uniformity in such provisions.

Company. Union or association of persons for carrying on a commercial or industrial enterprise; a partnership, corporation, association, joint stock company.

Company town. A residential and commercial community opened by a company for public use and operated under color of state law. Illinois Migrant Council v. Campbell Soup Co., C.A.Ill., 519 F.2d 391. Community exists primarily because of company; with major part of housing and stores owned by company.

Company union. Union whose membership is limited to the employees of a single company. Union under company domination.

Joint stock company. An association of individuals for purposes of profit, possessing a common capital contributed by the members composing it, such capital being commonly divided into shares which each member possesses one or more, and which are transferable by the owner. One having a joint stock or capital, which is divided into numerous transferable shares, or consists of transferable stock. A partnership whereof the capital is divided, or agreed to be divided, into shares so as to be transferable without the express consent of the co-partners.

Limited company. A company in which the liability of each shareholder is limited by the number of shares he has taken, so that he cannot be called on to contribute beyond the amount of his shares. In England, the memorandum of association of such company may provide that the liability of the directors, manager, or managing director thereof shall be unlimited.

Comparable accommodation. Within the rule that it is the rent generally prevailing on the freeze date for comparable accommodations in a defense-rental area that determines rent that may be charged, two accommodations are "comparable" if they are sufficiently similar to be regarded by an expert as of substantially equal rental value or if they are sufficiently similar so that an expert taking as a standard the rent prevailing for one and making allowances for such differences as would be reflected in rental value would be able to determine the appropriate corresponding rent for the other. Sirianni v. Bowles, Em. App., 148 F.2d 343, 344.

Comparatio literarum /kòmpəréysh(iy)ow lidərérəm/. In the civil law, comparison of writings, or handwritings. A mode of proof allowed in certain cases.

Comparative. Proceeding by the method of comparison; founded on comparison; estimated by comparison.

Comparative interpretation. That method of interpretation which seeks to arrive at the meaning of a statute or other writing by comparing its several parts and also by comparing it as a whole with other like documents proceeding from the same source and referring to the same general subject.

Comparative jurisprudence. The study of the principles of legal science by the comparison of various systems of law.

Comparative negligence. Under comparative negligence statutes or doctrines, negligence is measured in terms of percentage, and any damages allowed shall be diminished in proportion to amount of negligence attributable to the person for whose injury, damage or death recovery is sought. Many states have replaced contributory negligence acts or doctrines with comparative negligence. Where negligence by both parties is concurrent and contributes to injury, recovery is not barred under such doctrine, but plaintiff's damages are diminished proportionally, provided his fault is less than defendant's, and that, by exercise of ordinary care, he could not have avoided consequences of defendant's negligence after it was or should have been apparent.

Comparative rectitude. Doctrine wherein relief by divorce is granted to the party least in fault when both have shown grounds for divorce. Weber v. Weber, 256 Ark. 549, 508 S.W.2d 725, 729.

Comparison of handwriting. A comparison by the juxtaposition of two writings, in order, by such comparison, to ascertain whether both were written by the same person.

A method of proof resorted to where the genuineness of a written document is disputed; it consists in comparing the handwriting of the disputed paper with that of another instrument which is proved or admitted to be in the writing of the party sought to be charged, in order to infer, from their identity or similarity in this respect, that they are the work of the same hand. Expert testimony with respect to such proof is permitted by Fed.Evid. Rule 702, and non-expert testimony is governed by Rule 901.

Compascuum /kəmpǽskyuwəm/. Belonging to commonage *Jus compascuum*, the right of common pasture.

Compassing. Imagining or contriving, or plotting. In English law, "compassing the king's death" is treason. 4 Bl.Comm. 76.

Compaternitas /kòmpətə́rnətæs/. In the canon law, a kind of spiritual relationship contracted by baptism.

Compaternity. Spiritual affinity, contracted by sponsorship in baptism.

Compatibility. As applied to offices, such relation and consistency between the duties of two offices that they may be held and filled by one person. Harmonious relationship as between husband and wife.

Compel. To urge forcefully; under extreme pressure. Word "compel" as used in constitutional right to be free from being compelled in a criminal case to be a witness against one's self means to be subjected to some coercion, fear, terror, inducement, trickery or threat—either physically or psychologically, blatantly or subtly; the hallmark of compulsion is the presence of some operative force producing an involuntary response. U. S. v. Escandar, C.A.Fla., 465 F.2d 438, 442.

Compellativus /kompèlətáyvəs/. An adversary or accuser.

Compelling state interest. Term used to uphold state action in the face of attack grounded on Equal Protection or First Amendment rights because of serious need for such state action. Also employed to justify state action under police power of state. Printing Industries of Gulf Coast v. Hill, 382 F.Supp. 801 (D.C.Tex.).

Compensable death. Within Worker's Compensation Acts is one which results to employee from injury by accident arising out of and in course of employment.

Compensable injury. A "compensable injury" within Worker's Compensation Act is one caused by an accident arising out of and in the course of the employment. McCauley v. Harris, 164 Neb. 216, 82 N.W.2d 30, 32; Seymour v. Journal-Star Printing Co., 174 Neb. 150, 116 N.W.2d 297, 299.

Compensacion /kòmpensas(i)yówn/. In Spanish law, compensation; set-off. The extinction of a debt by another debt of equal dignity between persons who have mutual claims on each other.

Compensating balance. The balance a borrower from a bank is required by the bank to keep on deposit.

Compensating tax. See **Use tax.**

Compensatio /kòmpənséysh(iy)ow/. Lat. In the civil law, compensation, or set-off. A proceeding resembling a set-off in the common law, being a claim on the part of the defendant to have an amount due to him from the plaintiff deducted from his demand. 3 Bl.Comm. 305.

Compensatio criminis /kòmpənséysh(iy)ow krímənəs/. (Set-off of crime or guilt). The compensation or set-off of one crime against another; the plea or defense of recrimination in a suit for a divorce; that is, that the complainant is guilty of the same kind of offense with which the respondent is charged.

Compensation. Indemnification; payment of damages; making amends; making whole; giving an equivalent or substitute of equal value. That which is necessary to restore an injured party to his former position. Remuneration for services rendered, whether in salary, fees, or commissions. Consideration or price of a privilege purchased.

Equivalent in money for a loss sustained; equivalent given for property taken or for an injury done to another; giving back an equivalent in either money which is but the measure of value, or in actual value otherwise conferred; recompense in value; recompense or reward for some loss, injury, or service, especially when it is given by statute; remuneration for the injury directly and proximately caused by a breach of contract or duty; remuneration or satisfaction for injury or damage of every description. An act which a court orders to be done, or money which a court or other tribunal orders to be paid, by a person whose acts or omissions have caused loss or injury to another, in order that thereby the person damnified may receive equal value for his loss, or be made whole in respect of his injury. Hughson Condensed Milk Co. v. State Board of Equalization, 23 Cal.App.2d 281, 73 P.2d 290, 292. See also **Damages.**

See also Commission; Daily rate of pay; Deferred compensation; Fee; Salary; Unreasonable compensation; Wages.

For "Extra compensation" and "Fair and reasonable compensation", see these titles.

Eminent domain. Payment to owners of lands taken or injured by the exercise of the power of eminent domain. See **Just compensation.**

Unemployment and worker's compensation. Payments to an unemployed or injured worker or his dependents.

Compensation period. Period fixed by unemployment or worker's compensation statutes during which unemployed or injured worker is to receive compensation.

Compensatory damages. See **Damages.**

Comperendinatio /kòmpərèndənéysh(iy)ow/. In the Roman law, the adjournment of a cause, in order to hear the parties or their advocates a second time; a second hearing of the parties to a cause.

Compertorium /kòmpərtóriyəm/. In the civil law, a judicial inquest made by delegates or commissioners to find out and relate the truth of a cause.

Comperuit ad diem /kəmpéruwət æd dáyəm/. A plea in bar of an action of a debt on a bail bond that the defendant appeared at the day required.

Compete. To contend emulously; to strive for the position, reward, profit, goal, etc., for which another is striving. To contend in rivalry. See **Competition.**

Competency. In the law of evidence, the presence of those characteristics, or the absence of those disabilities, which render a witness legally fit and qualified to give testimony in a court of justice; applied, in the same sense, to documents or other written evidence. Evidence which is admissible as being able to assist the trier of fact (*i.e.* jury) in determining questions of fact, though it may not be believed. Competency differs from credibility. The former is a question which arises before considering the evidence given by the witness; the latter concerns the degree of credit to be given to his testimony. The former denotes the personal qualification of the witness; the latter his veracity. A witness may be competent, and yet give incredible testimony; he may be incompetent, and yet his evidence, if received, be perfectly credible. Competency is for the court; credibility for the jury. Yet in some cases the term "credible" is used as an equivalent for "competent". In law of contracts, of legal age without mental disability or incapacity. See also Ability; Authority; Capacity; Competent; Competent evidence; Duly qualified; Incompetency; Power; Qualified.

Competency proceedings. Hearings conducted to determine a person's mental capacity. May be held within criminal context to determine competency to stand trial, or to be sentenced, or to determine whether at time of offense the accused was legally sane. See *e.g.* 18 U.S.C.A. §§ 4241 et seq. May be held in civil context to determine whether he or she should be committed for treatment.

Competency to stand trial. A person lacks competency to stand trial if he or she lacks capacity to understand the nature and object of the proceedings, to consult with counsel, and to assist in preparing his or her defense. Drope v. Missouri, 420 U.S. 162, 95 S.Ct. 896, 43 L.Ed.2d 103. Due process prohibits the government from prosecuting a defendant who is legally incompetent to stand trial. Drope v. Missouri, 420 U.S. 162, 95 S.Ct. 896, 43 L.Ed.2d 103; Pate v. Robinson, 383 U.S. 375, 385, 86 S.Ct. 836, 15 L.Ed.2d 815. The issue of competency is collateral to the issue of guilt and involves only the defendant's present ability to consult with his lawyer and to understand the proceedings against him. Dusky v. United States, 362 U.S. 402, 80 S.Ct. 788, 4 L.Ed.2d 824. See **Insanity.**

Competent. Duly qualified; answering all requirements; having sufficient ability or authority; possessing the requisite natural or legal qualifications; able; adequate; suitable; sufficient; capable; legally fit. A testator may be said to be "competent" if he or she understands (1) the general nature and extent of his property; (2) his relationship to the people named in the will and to any people he disinherits; (3) what a will is; and (4) the transaction of simple business affairs. See also **Capacity; Competency; Incompetency.**

Competent authority. As applied to courts and public officers, this term imports jurisdiction and due legal authority to deal with the particular matter in question.

Competent court. A court, either civil or criminal, having lawful jurisdiction.

Competent evidence. That which the very nature of the thing to be proven requires, as, the production of a writing where its contents are the subject of inquiry. Also, generally, admissible (*i.e.* relevant and material) as opposed to "incompetent" or "inadmissible" evidence. Frick v. State, Okl.Cr., 509 P.2d 135, 136. See also **Competency; Evidence; Relevant evidence.**

Competent witness. One who is legally qualified to be heard to testify in a cause. As used in statutes relating to the execution of wills, the term means a person who, at the time of making the attestation, could legally testify in court to the facts which he attests by subscribing his name to the will. See also **Competency.**

Competition. Contest between two rivals. The effort of two or more parties, acting independently, to secure the business of a third party by the offer of the most favorable terms. It is the struggle between rivals for the same trade at the same time; the act of seeking or endeavoring to gain what another is endeavoring to gain at the same time. The term implies the idea of endeavoring by two or more to obtain the same object or result. See also **Compete.**

Unfair competition in trade. See **Combination in restraint of trade; Price-fixing; Sherman Antitrust Act; Unfair competition.**

Competitive bidding. Requires that all bidders be placed on a plane of equality, and that they bid upon the same terms and conditions. State Highway Commission of Kentucky v. King, 259 Ky. 414, 82 S.W.2d 443.

Competitive civil service examination. Examination which conforms to measures or standards which are sufficiently objective to be capable of being challenged and reviewed by other examiners of equal ability and experience. Such exam may be open in which case all may take it or may be promotional in which case only those in service may compete against others in service.

Competitive traffic. Traffic which, as to any one carrier, originates at a point served also by another carrier, which other carrier handles the traffic at equal line-haul rates from origin to destination.

Competitors. Persons endeavoring to do the same thing and each offering to perform the act, furnish the merchandise, or render the service better or cheaper than his rival.

Compilation /kòmpəléyshən/. A bringing together of preexisting statutes in the form in which they appear in the books, with the removal of sections which have been repealed and the substitution of amendments in an arrangement designed to facilitate their use. A literary production composed of the works or selected extracts of others and arranged in methodical manner. *Compare* **Code; Codification.** See also **Compiled statutes; Revised statutes.**

Compile. See **Compilation.**

Compiled statutes. A collection of the statutes existing and in force in a given state; all laws and parts of laws relating to each subject-matter being brought together under one head and the whole arranged systematically, either under an alphabetical arrangement or some other plan of classification. *Compare* **Code; Codification.** See also **Revised statutes.**

Complainant. One who applies to the courts for legal redress by filing complaint (*i.e.* plaintiff). Also, one who instigates prosecution or who prefers accusation against suspected person.

Complaint. The original or initial pleading by which an action is commenced under codes or Rules of Civil Procedure. Fed.R. Civil P. 3. The pleading which sets forth a claim for relief. Such complaint (whether it be the original claim, counterclaim, cross-claim, or third-party claim) shall contain: (1) a short and plain statement of the grounds upon which the court's jurisdiction depends, unless the court already has jurisdiction and the claim needs no new grounds of jurisdiction to support it, (2) a short and plain statement of the claim showing that the pleader is entitled to relief, and (3) a demand for judgment for the relief to which he deems himself entitled. Relief in the alternative or of several different types may be demanded. Fed.R. Civil P. 8(a). The complaint, together with the summons, is required to be served on the defendant. Rule 4. See also **Counterclaim; Cross-claim; Supplemental complaint; Third party complaint.**

In criminal law, a charge, preferred before a magistrate having jurisdiction, that a person named (or an unknown person) has committed a specified offense, with an offer to prove the fact, to the end that a prosecution may be instituted. In some instances "complaint" is interchangeable with "information." The complaint is a written statement of the essential facts constituting the offense charged. It shall be made upon oath before a magistrate. Fed.R.Crim.P. 3. If it appears from the complaint that probable cause exists that the person named in the complaint committed the alleged crime, a warrant (*q.v.*) for his arrest will be issued. Fed.R.Crim.P. 4.

Complete, *v.* To finish; accomplish that which one starts out to do.

Complete, *adj.* Full; entire; including every item or element of the thing spoken of, without omissions or deficiencies; as, a "complete" copy, record, schedule, or transcript.

Perfect; consummate; not lacking in any element or particular; as in the case of a "complete legal title" to land, which includes the possession, the right of possession, and the right of property (*i.e.* fee sim-

ple title). Versailles Tp. v. Ulm, 152 Pa.Super. 384, 33 A.2d 265, 267.

Completed. Finished; nothing substantial remaining to be done; state of a thing that has been created, erected, constructed or done substantially according to contract.

Completed contract method. A method of reporting gain or loss on certain long-term contracts. Under this method of accounting, gross income and expenses are recognized in the tax year in which the contract is completed.

Complete determination of cause. Determination of every issue so as to render decree or judgment res judicata.

Complete in itself. Of a legislative act, covering entire subject; not amendatory.

Complete loss of sight. A destruction of ability to perceive, distinguish, and recognize objects to such extent that what remains will not confer any of benefits of sight or vision to practical and useful extent. Blindness.

Completeness rule. Rule of evidence which permits further use of a document to explain portion of document already in evidence. Camps v. N. Y. City Transit Authority, C.A.N.Y., 261 F.2d 320. See also **Open** (*Open the door*).

Complete operation rule. The "complete operation" doctrine holds that an unloading clause in policy covers the entire process involved in the moving of goods from the moment the goods are in the insured's possession and until they are given, at the place of destination, to the party to whom delivery is to be made. Aetna Cas. & Sur. Co. v. State Farm Mut. Auto. Ins. Co., D.C.App., 380 A.2d 1385, 1387.

Complete payment. On a contract, the final payment.

Completion. The finishing or accomplishing in full of something theretofore begun. See also **Substantial performance.**

Completion bond. See **Bond; Performance bond.**

Complex trust. A trust with elaborate provisions as distinguished from a simple trust. May refer to trust in which trustees have complete discretion as to accumulating or distributing trust income, *i.e.* trustee need not distribute income annually, or make distributions other than from income. Hay v. U. S., D.C. Tex., 263 F.Supp. 813.

Compliance. Submission; obedience; conformance.

Complicated. Consisting of many parts or particulars not easily severable in thought; hard to understand or explain; involved, intricate, confused.

Complice. One who is united with others in an ill design; an associate, confederate, accomplice, or accessory (*q.v.*). See also **Conspiracy.**

Complicity /kəmplísədiy/. A state of being an accomplice; participation in guilt. State v. Scheuering, 226 La. 660, 76 So.2d 921, 924. Involvement in crime as principal or as accessory before fact. May also refer to activities of conspirators. See **Conspiracy.**

Comply. To yield; to accommodate, or to adapt oneself to; to act in accordance with; to accept.

Composed of. Formed of; consisting of.

Composite work. Within Copyright Act means work to which a number of authors have contributed distinguishable parts.

Compositio mensurarum /kòmpəzísh(iy)ow menshərérəm/. The ordinance of measures. The title of an ancient ordinance, not printed, mentioned in the statute 23 Hen. VIII, c. 4; establishing a standard of measures. 1 Bl.Comm. 275.

Composition deed. An agreement embodying the terms of a composition between a debtor and his creditors.

Composition in bankruptcy. See **Composition with creditors.**

Composition of matter. In patent law, a substance composed of two or more different substances, without regard to form. A mixture or chemical combination of materials.

Composition of tithes, or **real composition.** This arises in English ecclesiastical law, when an agreement is made between the owner of lands and the incumbent of a benefice, with the consent of the ordinary and the patron, that the lands shall, for the future, be discharged from payment of tithes, by reason of some land or other real recompense given in lieu and satisfaction thereof. 2 Bl.Comm. 28. See **Composition with creditors.**

Composition with creditors. An agreement, made upon a sufficient consideration, between an insolvent or embarrassed debtor and his creditors, whereby the latter, for the sake of immediate or sooner payment, agree to accept a payment less than the whole amount of their claims, to be distributed *pro rata*, in discharge and satisfaction of the whole. It constitutes an agreement not only between the debtor and his creditors but also one between the creditors themselves that each shall accept the lesser sums from the assets of the embarrassed debtor. The entering into of a composition agreement is not in and of itself an act of bankruptcy. Where, however, the composition agreement expressly or secretly prefers certain creditors, the composition constitutes the second act of bankruptcy—a preferential transfer. See **Act of bankruptcy.**

Similar statutory arrangements are provided for under the Bankruptcy Act. See **Arrangement with creditors;** Assignment (*Assignment for benefit of creditors*); **Wage earner's plan.**

The difference between a common-law "composition with creditors" and a "composition in bankruptcy" is that in a composition with creditors the creditors voluntarily release the principal debtor and therefore release co-debtors, while in the case of a bankruptcy composition the discharge is by operation of law and not by act of the creditors who assent to the composition. Barker v. Ackers, 29 Cal.App.2d 162, 84 P.2d 264, 271.

"Composition" should be distinguished from "accord." The latter properly denotes an arrangement between a debtor and a single creditor for a discharge of the obligation by a part payment or on different terms. The former designates an arrangement between a debtor and the whole body of his creditors (or at least a considerable proportion of them) for the liquidation of their claims by the dividend offered.

Compositio ulnarum et perticarum /kòmpəzísh(iy)ow əlnérəm ət pə̀rdəkérəm/. The statute of ells and perches. The title of an English statute establishing a standard of measures. 1 Bl.Comm. 275.

Compos mentis /kómpəs méntəs/. Sound of mind. Having use and control of one's mental faculties.

Compos sui /kómpəs s(y)úway/. Having the use of one's limbs, or the power of bodily motion. *Si fuit ita compos sui quod itinerare potuit de loco in locum,* if he had so far the use of his limbs as to be able to travel from place to place.

Compotarius /kòmpətériyəs/. In old English law, a party accounting.

Compound, v. To compromise; to effect a composition with a creditor; to obtain discharge from a debt by the payment of a smaller sum. To put together as elements, ingredients, or parts, to form a whole; to combine, to unite. To form or make up as a composite product by combining different elements, ingredients, or parts, as to combine a medicine. See **Compounding crime.**

Compound, n. A combination of two or more elements or things by means of human agency; an artificial or synthetic product.

Compounder. In Louisiana, the maker of a composition, generally called the "amicable compounder."

Compounding a felony. See **Compounding crime.**

Compounding crime. Compounding crime consists of the receipt of some property or other consideration in return for an agreement not to prosecute or inform on one who has committed a crime. There are three elements to this offense at common law, and under the typical compounding statute: (1) the agreement not to prosecute; (2) knowledge of the actual commission of a crime; and (3) the receipt of some consideration.

The offense committed by a person who, having been directly injured by a felony, agrees with the criminal that he will not prosecute him, on condition of the latter's making reparation, or on receipt of a reward or bribe not to prosecute.

The offense of taking a reward for forbearing to prosecute a felony; as where a party robbed takes his goods again, or other amends, upon an agreement not to prosecute.

Compound interest. Interest upon interest; *i.e.,* when the interest of a sum of money is added to the principal, and then bears interest, which thus becomes a sort of secondary principal.

Compound larceny. See **Compounding crime; Larceny.**

Compra y venta /kómprə iy béntə/. In Spanish law, purchase and sale.

Comprehensive zoning plan. A general plan to control and direct the use and development of property in a municipality or in a large part thereof by dividing it into districts according to the present and potential use of the properties. Damick v. Planning and Zoning Commission of Town of Southington, 158 Conn. 78, 256 A.2d 428. See also **Planned unit development.**

Compremesso /kòmpremésow/. In Italian law, the instrument whereby parties agree to submit to arbitration a dispute between them. The equivalent of "compromissum" under the Roman Law, the principles of which have been carried into the common law and are to be found in agreements of accord and satisfaction and compromise and settlement.

Comprint. A surreptitious printing of another bookseller's copy of a work, to make gain thereby, which was contrary to common law, and is illegal. See **Infringement.**

Comprise. To comprehend; include; contain; embrace; cover.

Comprivigni /kòmprəvígnay/. In the civil law, children by a former marriage, (individually called *"privigni,"* or *"privignæ"*) considered relatively to each other. Thus, the son of a husband by a former wife, and the daughter of a wife by a former husband, are the *comprivigni* of each other.

Compromise and settlement. An arrangement arrived at, either in court or out of court, for settling a dispute upon what appears to the parties to be equitable terms, having regard to the uncertainty they are in regarding the facts, or the law and the facts together. An agreement or arrangement by which, in consideration of mutual concessions, a controversy is terminated. Putnam v. Otsego Mut. Fire Ins. Co., 41 A.D.2d 981, 343 N.Y.S.2d 736, 738.

In the civil law, an agreement whereby two or more persons mutually bind themselves to refer their legal dispute to the decision of a designated third person, who is termed "umpire" or "arbitrator."

See **Arbitration; Mediation; Settlement.**

Offer of compromise. See **Offer,** *n.*

Compromise verdict. One which is reached only by the surrender of conscientious convictions on one material issue by some jurors in return for a relinquishment of matters in their like settled opinion on another issue, and the result is one which does not hold the approval of the entire panel. See also **Allen charge; Verdict.**

Compromissarii sunt judices /kòmprəməsériyay sənt júwdəsiyz/. Arbitrators are judges.

Compromissarius /kòmprəməsériyəs/. In the civil law, an arbitrator.

Compromissum /kòmprəmísəm/. A submission to arbitration.

Compromissum ad similitudinem judiciorum redigitur /kòmprəmísəm æd sìmələtyúwdənəm jədìshiyórəm rədíjədər/. A compromise is brought into affinity with judgments.

Compte arrêté /kóm(p)t àreytéy/. Fr. An account stated in writing, and acknowledged to be correct on its face by the party against whom it is stated.

Comptroller /kóm(p)trowlər/kəntrówlər/kóntr°/. A public officer of a state or municipal corporation, or an officer of a business, charged with certain duties in relation to the fiscal affairs of the same, principally to examine and audit the accounts, to keep records, and report the financial situation from time to time. There are also officers bearing this name in the Treasury Department of the United States.

Comptroller General. Government official (head of G. A. O.) whose main function is to audit governmental agencies.

Comptroller of currency. The Office of the Comptroller of the Currency was created by act of Congress approved February 25, 1863 (12 Stat. 665), as an integral part of the national banking system. The Comptroller, as the administrator of national banks, is responsible for the execution of laws relating to national banks and promulgates rules and regulations governing the operations of national and District of Columbia banks. Approval of the Comptroller is required for the organization of new national banks, conversion of State-chartered banks into national banks, consolidations or mergers of banks where the surviving institution is a national bank, and the establishment of branches by national banks.

Compulsa /kəmpálsə/. A judicially attested copy of a testimonio.

Compulsion. Constraint; objective necessity; duress. Forcible inducement to the commission of an act. The act of compelling or the state of being compelled; the act of driving or urging by force or by physical or moral constraint; subjection to force. The compulsion which will excuse a criminal act must be present, imminent and impending and of such a nature as to induce a well-grounded apprehension of death or serious bodily harm. To constitute "compulsion" or "coercion" rendering payment involuntary, there must be some actual or threatened exercise of power possessed, or supposedly possessed, by payee over payer's person or property, from which payer has no means of immediate relief except by advancing money. See **Coercion; Duress.**

Compulsory, *n.* In ecclesiastical procedure, a compulsory is a kind of writ to compel the attendance of a witness, to undergo examination.

Compulsory, *adj.* Involuntary; forced; coerced by legal process or by force of statute.

Compulsory arbitration. That which takes place where the consent of one of the parties is enforced by statutory provisions.

Compulsory attendance. Refers to legal obligation to attend; *e.g.* school attendance is compulsory up to certain age.

Compulsory counterclaim. For claim to constitute a compulsory counterclaim, it must be logically related to original claim and arise out of same subject matter on which original claim is based; many of same factual legal issues, or offshoots of same basic controversy between parties must be involved in a compulsory counterclaim. Tasner v. Billera, D.C.Ill., 379 F.Supp. 809, 813. See Fed.R.Civil P. 13(a).

Compulsory disclosure. Term with variety of meanings; may refer to court order compelling disclosure of matters within scope of discovery rules (see Fed.R. Civil P. 26, 37, 45; Fed.R.Crim.P. 16, 17); may also refer to obligation of public officers or candidates for public office to reveal assets and income from private sources. See also **Subpoena.**

Compulsory insurance. Motor vehicle liability coverage which is required in most states as a condition to registration of such vehicle.

Compulsory nonsuit. An involuntary nonsuit. See **Nonsuit.**

Compulsory payment. One not made voluntarily, but exacted by duress, threats, the enforcement of legal process, or unconscionably taking advantage of another. May also refer to legal obligations, such as payment of taxes or support; or to creditor remedies such as garnishment or attachment.

Compulsory process. Process to compel the attendance in court of a person wanted there as a witness or otherwise; including not only the ordinary subpoena, but also a warrant of arrest or attachment if needed. See *e.g.* Fed.R. Civil P. 45. See **Bench warrant; Subpoena.**

The 6th Amend., U.S.Const., provides that the accused shall have the right to "have compulsory process for obtaining witnesses in his favor".

Compulsory sale or **purchase.** Term used to characterize the transfer of title to property under the exercise of the power of eminent domain, or by reason of judicial sale for nonpayment of taxes, or the like.

Compulsory self-incrimination. Any form of coercion, physical or psychological, which renders a confession of crime or an admission involuntary, is in violation of the 5th Amend., U.S.Const. and due process clause of 14th Amend. Such practices contravene the very basis of our criminal jurisprudence which is accusatorial not inquisitorial. Rogers v. Richmond, 365 U.S. 534, 81 S.Ct. 735, 5 L.Ed.2d 760.

Compurgator /kómpərgeydər/. One of several neighbors of a person accused of a crime, or charged as a defendant in a civil action, who appeared and swore that they believed him on his oath. 3 Bl.Comm. 341.

Computation. The act of computing, numbering, reckoning, or estimating. The account or estimation of time by rule of law, as distinguished from any arbitrary construction of the parties.

Computation of time. For purpose of calculating time under Rules of Civil Procedure, the day of the act, event or default from which the designated period of time begins to run shall not be included, though the last day of the period so computed shall be included unless it is a Saturday, Sunday or legal holiday. Fed.R. Civil P. 6(a); Fed.R.Crim.P. 45.

Computo /kəmpyúwdow/. Lat. To compute, reckon, or account. Used in the phrases *insimul computassent,* "they reckoned together," (see **Insimul**); *plene computavit,* "he has fully accounted," (see **Plene**); *quod computet,* "that he account," (see **Quod computet**).

Computus /kómpyədəs/. A writ to compel a guardian, bailiff, receiver, or accountant to yield up his accounts. It is founded on the statute Westm. 2, c. 12.

Comte /kównt/. Fr. A count or earl. In the ancient French law, the *comte* was an officer having jurisdiction over a particular district or territory, with functions partly military and partly judicial.

Con. *Adj.* A slang or cant abbreviation for confidence, as a *con* man or a *con* game.

Con. *Prep.* With.

Con-. A prefix meaning with, together.

Conatus quid sit, non definitur in jure /kənéydəs kwíd sìt nòn dèfənáydər ìn júriy/. What an attempt is, is not defined in law.

Con buena fe /kòn bwéynə féy/. In Spanish law, with (or in) good faith.

Conceal. To hide, secrete, or withhold from the knowledge of others. To withdraw from observation; to withhold from utterance or declaration; to cover or keep from sight. To hide or withdraw from observation, cover or keep from sight, or prevent discovery of. People v. Eddington, 201 Cal.App.2d 574, 20 Cal.Rptr. 122, 124.

See **Compounding crime; Harbor; Misprision of felony; Withholding of evidence.**

Accessories after the fact. A person who conceals the principal felon or the accessory before the fact is an accessory after the fact if he knows of the felony and of the identity of the felon.

Concealers /kənsíylərz/. In old English law, such as find out concealed lands; that is, lands privily kept from the king by common persons having nothing to show for them. They are called "a troublesome, disturbant sort of men; turbulent persons."

Concealment. To conceal. A withholding of something which one knows and which one, in duty, is bound to reveal. A "concealment" in law of insurance implies an intention to withhold or secrete information so that the one entitled to be informed will remain in ignorance. Indiana Ins. Co. v. Knoll, 142 Ind.App. 506, 236 N.E.2d 63, 70. See also **Conceal; Fraudulent concealment.**

Concealment may be basis of estoppel. Elements of such estoppel are concealment of material facts with knowledge thereof, ignorance thereof on part of person to whom representations are made, or from whom facts are concealed, intention that such person shall act thereon, and action induced thereby on his part. Rhoads v. Rhoads, 342 Mo. 934, 119 S.W.2d 247, 252; Rosser v. Texas Co., 173 Okl. 309, 48 P.2d 327, 330. The doctrine of "estoppel by concealment and suppression" applies only where there has been reduction to practice of invention. Bogoslowsky v. Huse, 31 C.C.P.A. (Patents) 1034, 142 F.2d 75, 76.

Conceder /kònseydéy/. Fr. In French law, to grant. See **Concession.**

Concedo /kənsíydow/. Lat. I grant. A word used in old Anglo-Saxon grants, and in statutes merchant.

Conception. The beginning of pregnancy. As to human beings, the fecundation of the female ovum by the male spermatozoon resulting in human life capable of survival and maturation under normal conditions. Also, a plan, idea, thought or design.

Conception of invention is formation in mind of inventor of definite and permanent idea of complete and operative invention as it is thereafter to be applied in practice. Radio Corp. of America v. Philco Corp., D.C.Pa., 201 F.Supp. 135, 149.

Conceptum /kənséptəm/. In the civil law, a theft *(furtum)* was called *"conceptum,"* when the thing stolen was searched for, and found upon some person in the presence of witnesses.

Concern. To pertain, relate, or belong to; be of interest or importance to; have connection with; to have reference to; to involve; to affect the interest of. People v. Photocolor Corporation, 156 Misc. 47, 281 N.Y.S. 130.

Concerning, concerned. Relating to; pertaining to; affecting; involving; being substantially engaged in or taking part in.

Concert. A person is deemed to act in concert when he acts with another to bring about some preconceived result. See **Accomplice; Conspiracy.**

Concerted action (or **plan**). Action that has been planned, arranged, adjusted, agreed on and settled between parties acting together pursuant to some design or scheme. See **Accomplice; Combination in restraint of trade; Conspiracy.**

Concert of action rule. A rule providing that an agreement by two persons to commit a particular crime cannot be prosecuted as a conspiracy when the crime is of such a nature as to necessarily require participation of two persons for its commission. Robinson v. State, 229 Md. 503, 184 A.2d 814, 820. See **Wharton Rule.**

Concessi /kənsésay/. Lat. I have granted. At common law, in a feoffment or estate of inheritance, this word does not imply a warranty; it only creates a covenant in a lease for years.

Concessimus /kənseśəməs/. Lat. We have granted. A term used in conveyances, the effect of which was to create a joint covenant on the part of the grantors.

Concessio /kənsés(h)(i)yow/. In old English law, a grant. One of the old common assurances, or forms of conveyance.

Concession. A grant, ordinarily applied to the grant of specific privileges by a government; *e.g.* French and Spanish grants in Louisiana. A voluntary grant, or a yielding to a claim or demand; rebate; abatement.

Concessio per regem fieri debet de certitudine /kənsés(h)(i)yow pàr ríyjəm fáyəray débət dìy sərdət(y)úwdəniy/. A grant by the king ought to be made from certainty.

Concessio versus concedentem latam interpretationem habere debet /kənsés(h)(i)yow vársəs kònsədéntəm léydəm intàrprətèyshiyównəm heybíriy débət/. A grant ought to have a broad interpretation (to be liberally interpreted) against the grantor.

Concessit solvere /kənsésət sólvəriy/. He granted and agreed to pay. In English law, an action of debt upon a simple contract.

Concessor /kənsésər/. In old English law, a grantor.

Concessum /kənsésəm/. Accorded; conceded. This term, frequently used in the old reports, signifies that the court admitted or assented to a point or proposition made on the argument.

Concessus /kənsésəs/. A grantee.

Conciergerie /kònsyerzhəríy/. The office or lodge of the concierge or janitor. A famous prison attached to the Palais de Justice in Paris.

Conciliation. The adjustment and settlement of a dispute in a friendly, unantagonistic manner. Used in courts before trial with a view towards avoiding trial and in labor disputes before arbitration. See **Arbitration; Court of Conciliation; Mediation; Pretrial conference; Settlement.**

Concilium /kənsíliyəm/. Lat. A council.

In Roman law, a meeting of a section of the people to consider and decide matters especially affecting itself. Also argument in a cause, or the sitting of the court to hear argument; a motion for a day for the argument of a cause; a day allowed to a defendant to present his argument; an imparlance.

Concilium ordinarium /kənsíliyəm ordənériyəm/. In Anglo-Norman times, an executive and residuary judicial committee of the *Aula Regis (q.v.).*

Concilium regis /kənsíliyəm ríyjəs/. An ancient English tribunal existing during the reigns of Edward I. and Edward II, to which were referred cases of extraordinary difficulty.

Concionator /kónshəneydər/. In old records, a common council man; a freeman called to a legislative hall or assembly.

Conclude. To finish; determine; to estop; to prevent.

Concluded. Ended; determined; estopped; prevented from.

Conclusion. The end; the termination; the act of finishing or bringing to a close. The conclusion of a declaration or complaint is all that part which follows the statement of the plaintiff's cause of action. In trial practice, it signifies making the final or concluding address to the jury or the court; *i.e.* the summation; closing argument.

Conclusion against the form of the statute. In common law pleading, the proper form for the conclusion of an indictment for an offense created by statute was the technical phrase "against the form of the statute in such case made and provided"; or, in Latin, *contra formam statuti.*

Conclusion of fact. An inference drawn from the subordinate or evidentiary facts.

Conclusion of law. Statement of court as to law applicable on basis of facts found by jury. The final judgment or decree required on basis of facts found or verdict. Peoples v. Peoples, 10 N.C.App. 402, 179 S.E.2d 138, 141. Propositions of law which judge arrives at after, and as a result of, finding certain facts in case tried without jury or an advisory jury and as to these he must state them separately in writing. Fed.R. Civil P. 52(a).

Conclusive. Shutting up a matter; shutting out all further evidence; not admitting of explanation or contradiction; putting an end to inquiry; final; irrefutable; decisive. Beyond question or beyond dispute; manifest; plain; clear; obvious; visible; apparent; indubitable; palpable.

As to conclusive proof, see **Proof.**

Conclusive evidence. That which is incontrovertible, either because the law does not permit it to be contradicted, or because it is so strong and convincing as to overbear all proof to the contrary and establish the proposition in question beyond any reasonable doubt. See **Conclusive presumption; Judicial notice; Presumption; Proof.**

Conclusive presumption. An artificially compelling force which requires trier of fact to find such fact as is conclusively presumed and which renders evidence to the contrary inadmissible. Sometimes referred to as irrebuttable presumption. See **Presumption.**

Concomitant actions. Civil actions which are brought together generally for some type of relief.

Concord. An agreement between two persons, one of whom has a right of action against the other, settling what amends shall be made for the breach or wrong. A compromise or an accord.

In the old process of levying a fine of lands, the concord was an agreement between the parties (real or feigned) in which the deforciant (or he who keeps the other out of possession) acknowledges that the lands in question are the right of complainant; and, from the acknowledgment or admission of right thus made, the party who levies the fine is called the "cognizor," and the person to whom it is levied the "cognizee." 2 Bl.Comm. 350. An agreement between two or more, upon a trespass committed, by way of amends or satisfaction for it.

Concordare leges legibus est optimus interpretandi modus /kənkərdériy líyjiyz líyjəbəs èst óptəməs əntə̀rprətǽnday mówdəs/. To make laws agree with laws is the best mode of interpreting them.

Concordat. A compact, covenant or convention between two or more independent governments.

An agreement made by a temporal sovereign with the pope, relative to ecclesiastical matters.

In French law, a compromise effected by a bankrupt with his creditors, by virtue of which he engages to pay within a certain time a certain proportion of his debts, and by which the creditors agree to discharge the whole of their claims in consideration of the same.

Concordia /kənkórdiyə/. Lat. In old English law, an agreement, or concord. The agreement or unanimity of a jury. *Compellere ad concordiam.*

Concordia discordantium canonum /kənkórdiyə dìskordǽnsh(iy)əm kǽnənəm/. The harmony of the discordant canons. A collection of ecclesiastical constitutions made by Gratian, an Italian monk, A.D.

1151; more commonly known by the name of *"Decretum Gratiani."*

Concordia parvæ res crescunt et opulentia lites /kənkórdiyə párviy ríyz kréskənt èd opyəlénsh(iy)ə láydiyz/. Small means increase by concord and litigations by opulence.

Concubinage /kənkyúwbənəj/. Living together (*i.e.* cohabitation) of persons not legally married.

Concubinatus /kənkyúwbənéydəs/. In Roman law, an informal, unsanctioned, or "natural" marriage, as contradistinguished from the *justæ nuptiæ,* or *justum matrimonium,* the civil marriage.

Concubine /kóŋkyəbàyn/. A woman who cohabits with a man to whom she is not married. A mistress. A sort of inferior wife, among the Romans, upon whom the husband did not confer his rank or quality.

Concur. To agree; accord; act together; consent. In the practice of appellate courts, a "concurring opinion" is one filed by one of the judges or justices, in which he agrees with the conclusions or the result of another opinion filed in the case (which may be either the opinion of the court or a dissenting opinion) though he states separately his views of the case or his reasons for so concurring.

In Louisiana law, to join with other claimants in presenting a demand against an insolvent estate.

Concurator /kòŋkyúrədər/. In the civil law, a joint or co-curator, or guardian.

Concurrence. A meeting or coming together; agreement or union in action; meeting of minds; union in design; consent. Babyak v. Alten, 106 Ohio App. 191, 154 N.E.2d 14, 18.

Concurrence deloyale. A term of the French law nearly equivalent to "unfair trade competition;" and used in relation to the infringement of rights secured by trade-marks, etc. It signifies a dishonest, perfidious, or treacherous rivalry in trade, or any manœuvre calculated to prejudice the good will of a business or the value of the name of a property or its credit or renown with the public, to the injury of a business competitor.

Concurrent. Running together; having the same authority; acting in conjunction; agreeing in the same act or opinion; pursuit of same course; contributing to the same event; contemporaneous. Co-operating, accompanying, conjoined, associated, concomitant, joint and equal, existing together, and operating on the same subject. United in agreement. State ex rel. School Dist. No. 8 v. Lensman, 108 Mont. 118, 88 P.2d 63, 68.

As to concurrent Covenant; Insurance; Lease; Resolution; and Writ, see those titles.

Concurrent causes. Causes acting contemporaneously and together causing injury, which would not have resulted in absence of either. Two distinct causes operating at the same time to produce a given result, which might be produced by either, are "concurrent causes"; but two distinct causes, successive and unrelated in an operation, cannot be concurring, and one will be regarded as the proximate and efficient and responsible cause, and the other will be regarded as the remote cause. See also **Cause.**

Concurrent conditions. When each party to a transaction is subject to mutual conditions precedent, these are concurrent conditions. McFadden v. Wilder, 6 Ariz.App. 60, 429 P.2d 694. See also **Conditions concurrent.**

Concurrent estates. Ownership or possession of property by two or more persons at the same time; *e.g.* joint tenancy, tenancy in common.

Concurrent interests. See **Concurrent estates.**

Concurrent jurisdiction. The jurisdiction of several different tribunals, each authorized to deal with the same subject-matter at the choice of the suitor. Authority shared by two or more legislative, judicial, or administrative officers or bodies to deal with the same subject matter. Jurisdiction exercised by different courts, at same time, over same subject matter, and within same territory, and wherein litigants may, in first instance, resort to either court indifferently. State v. Stueve, 260 Iowa 1023, 150 N.W.2d 597, 602.

Concurrent liens. Two or more liens or possessory rights in the nature of liens on the same property and possessing the same priority.

Concurrent negligence. Consists of the negligence of two or more persons concurring, not necessarily in point of time, but in point of consequence, in producing a single indivisible injury. Travelers Indemnity Co. v. Towbridge, Com.Pl., 38 Ohio Misc. 55, 311 N.E.2d 901, 905.

Concurrent power. The power of either Congress or the State legislatures, each acting independently of the other, to make laws on the same subject matter.

Concurrent sentences. Two or more terms of imprisonment, all or part of each term of which is served simultaneously and the prisoner is entitled to discharge at the expiration of the longest term specified. State ex rel. Lillemoe v. Tahash, 280 Minn. 176, 159 N.W.2d 99, 102.

Concurrent tortfeasors. Those whose independent, negligent acts combined or concurred at one point in time to injure a third party. Radford-Shelton & Associates Dental Laboratory, Inc. v. Saint Francis Hospital, Inc., Okl.App., 569 P.2d 506, 509.

Concurring opinion. A separate opinion delivered by one or more judges which agrees with the decision of the majority of the court but offering own reasons for reaching that decision. See also **Concur.**

Concurso /kənkársow/. In the law of Louisiana, the name of a suit or remedy to enable creditors to enforce their claims against an insolvent or failing debtor. Litigation or opportunity of litigation between various creditors, each claiming adversely to one another to share in a fund or an estate, object being to assemble in one accounting all claimants on the fund.

Concursus /kənkársəs/. In the civil law, a running together; a collision, as *concursus creditorum,* a conflict among creditors. A concurrence, or meeting, as *concursus actionum,* concurrence of actions. A proceeding in Louisiana similar to interpleader.

Concussio /kənkásh(iy)ow/. In the civil law, the offense of extortion by threats of violence.

Concussion. In the civil law, the unlawful forcing of another by threats of violence to give something of value. It differs from robbery, in this: That in robbery the thing is taken by force, while in concussion it is obtained by threatened violence.

Loss or alteration of consciousness from a direct, closed head injury.

Condedit /kəndíydət/. In ecclesiastical law, the name of a plea entered by a party to a libel filed in the ecclesiastical court, in which it is pleaded that the deceased made the will which is the subject of the suit, and that he was of sound mind.

Condemn. To find or adjudge guilty. To adjudge or sentence. To declare a building or ship unfit for use or occupation. To adjudge (as an admiralty court) that a vessel is a prize, or that she is unfit for service. To set apart or expropriate property for public use, in the exercise of the power of eminent domain.

Condemnation /kòndəmnéyshən/. Process of taking private property for public use through the power of eminent domain. "Just compensation" must be paid to owner for taking of such (5th Amend., U.S. Constitution). See also Constructive taking; Damages; Eminent domain; Expropriation; Just compensation; Public use; Similar sales; Take.

Admiralty law. The judgment or sentence of a court having jurisdiction and acting *in rem,* by which: (1) it is declared that a vessel which has been captured at sea as a prize was lawfully so seized and is liable to be treated as prize; or (2) that property which has been seized for an alleged violation of the revenue laws, neutrality laws, navigation laws, etc., was lawfully so seized, and is, for such cause, forfeited to the government; or (3) that the vessel which is the subject of inquiry is unfit and unsafe for navigation.

Civil law. A sentence or judgment which condemns some one to do, to give, or to pay something, or which declares that his claim or pretensions are unfounded. State v. Harr, 24 Tenn.App. 298, 143 S.W.2d 893, 895.

Excess condemnation. Taking of property not strictly needed for a public use, or taking of more property than is needed for a public use.

Inverse condemnation. Condemnation of property near a parcel so as to cause the parcel to lose much of its value. In such a case the parcel is, in effect, constructively condemned, and just compensation must be paid to the owner, even though formal eminent domain proceedings were not actually taken against that particular parcel.

Quick condemnation. Under this procedure the municipality takes immediate possession of owner's property with estimated just compensation placed in escrow until actual compensation has been ascertained.

Condemnation money. Former term for damages which the party failing in an action was adjudged or *condemned* to pay; sometimes simply called the "condemnation."

Condictio /kəndí(k)sh(iy)ow/. In Roman law, a general term for actions of a personal nature, founded upon an obligation to give or do a certain and defined thing or service. It is distinguished from *vindicatio rei,* which is an action to vindicate one's right of property in a thing by regaining (or retaining) possession of it against the adverse claim of the other party.

Condictio certi /kəndí(k)sh(iy)ow sɜ́rday/. An action which lies upon a promise to do a thing, where such promise or stipulation is certain *(si certa sit stipulatio).*

Condictio ex lege /kəndí(k)sh(iy)ow èks líyjiy/. An action arising where the law gave a remedy, but provided no appropriate form of action.

Condictio indebitati /kəndí(k)sh(iy)ow əndèbətéyday/. An action which lay to recover anything which the plaintiff had given or paid to the defendant, by mistake, and which he was not bound to give or pay, either in fact or in law.

Condictio rei furtivæ /kəndí(k)sh(iy)ow ríyay fərtáyviy/. An action which lay to recover a thing stolen, against the thief himself, or his heir.

Condictio sine causa /kəndí(k)sh(iy)ow sáyniy kózə/. An action which lay in favor of a person who had given or promised a thing without consideration *(causa).*

Conditio /kəndísh(iy)ow/. Lat. A condition.

Conditio beneficialis, quæ statum construit, benigne secundum verborum intentionem est interpretanda; odiosa autem, quæ statum destruit, stricte secundum verborum proprietatem accipienda /kəndísh(iy)ow bènəfìshiyéyləs kwìy stéydəm kónstruwət bənígniy səkə́ndəm vərbórəm intènshiyównəm èst intə̀rprətǽndə; òwdiyówsə ódəm, kwìy stéydəm déstruwət, stríktiy səkə́ndəm vərbórəm prəpràỳətéydəm əksìpiyéndə/. A beneficial condition, which creates an estate, ought to be construed favorably, according to the intention of the words; but a condition which destroys an estate is odious, and ought to be construed strictly according to the letter of the words.

Conditio dicitur, cum quid in casum incertum qui potest tendere ad esse aut non esse, confertur /kəndísh(iy)ow dísədər kə̀m kwíd ìn kéysəm insɜ́rdəm kwày pówdəst téndəriy æ̀d ésiy òt nón èsiy kənfɜ́rdər/. It is called a "condition" when something is given on an uncertain event, which may or may not come into existence.

Conditio illicita habetur pro non adjecta /kəndísh(iy)ow əlísədə həbíydər pròw non əjéktə/. An unlawful condition is deemed as not annexed.

Condition. A future and uncertain event upon the happening of which is made to depend the existence of an obligation, or that which subordinates the existence of liability under a contract to a certain future event. Provision making effect of legal instrument contingent upon an uncertain event. See also **Constructive condition; Contingency; Contingent; Proviso.**

A clause in a contract or agreement which has for its object to suspend, rescind, or modify the principal obligation, or, in case of a will, to suspend, revoke, or modify the devise or bequest. A qualification, restriction, or limitation modifying or destroying the original act with which it is connected; an event, fact, or the like that is necessary to the occurrence of some other, though not its cause; a prerequisite; a stipulation.

A qualification or restriction annexed to a conveyance of lands, whereby it is provided that in case a particular event does or does not happen, or in case the grantor or grantee does or omits to do a particular act, an estate shall commence, be enlarged, or be defeated.

An "estate on condition" arises where an estate is granted, either in fee simple or otherwise, with an express qualification annexed, whereby the estate granted shall either commence, be enlarged, or be defeated, upon performance or breach of such qualification or condition.

In insurance parlance, the printed conditions on the inside of the policy which serve generally as a limitation of risk or of liability or impose various conditions requiring compliance by the insured.

Mode or state of being; state or situation; essential quality; property; attribute; status or rank.

Civil law. Conditions in the civil law are of the following types:

The *casual* condition is that which depends on chance, and is in no way in the power either of the creditor or of the debtor. Civ.Code La. art. 2023.

A *mixed* condition is one that depends at the same time on the will of one of the parties and on the will of a third person, or on the will of one of the parties and also on a casual event. Civ.Code La. art. 2025.

The *potestative* condition is that which makes the execution of the agreement depend on an event which it is in the power of the one or the other of the contracting parties to bring about or to hinder. Civ. Code La. art. 2024.

A *resolutory* or *dissolving* condition is that which, when accomplished, operates the revocation of the obligation, placing matters in the same state as though the obligation had not existed. It does not suspend the execution of the obligation. It only obliges the creditor to restore what he has received in case the event provided for in the condition takes place. Civ.Code La. art. 2045.

A *suspensive* condition is that which depends, either on a future and uncertain event, or on an event which has actually taken place, without its being yet known to the parties. In the former case, the obligation cannot be executed till after the event; in the latter, the obligation has its effect from the day on which it was contracted, but it cannot be enforced until the event be known. Civ.Code La. art. 2043; New Orleans v. Railroad Co., 171 U.S. 312, 18 S.Ct. 875, 43 L.Ed. 178. A condition which prevents a contract from going into operation until it has been fulfilled.

Classification. Conditions are either *express* or *implied,* the former when incorporated in express terms in the deed, contract, lease, or grant; the latter, when inferred or presumed by law, from the nature of the transaction or the conduct of the parties, to have been tacitly understood between them as a part of the agreement, though not expressly mentioned.

They are *possible* or *impossible*: the former when they admit of performance in the ordinary course of events; the latter when it is contrary to the course of nature or human limitations that they should ever be performed.

They are *lawful* or *unlawful*: the former when their character is not in violation of any rule, principle, or policy of law; the latter when they are such as the law will not allow to be made.

They are *consistent* or *repugnant*: the former when they are in harmony and concord with the other parts of the transaction; the latter when they contradict, annul, or neutralize the main purpose of the "contract". Repugnant conditions are also called "insensible".

They are *affirmative* or *negative*: the former being a condition which consists in doing a thing, as provided that the lessee shall pay rent, etc.; the latter being a condition that consists in not doing a thing, as provided that the lessee shall not alien, etc.

They are *precedent* or *subsequent*. A condition precedent is one which must happen or be performed before the estate to which it is annexed can vest or be enlarged; or it is one which is to be performed before some right dependent thereon accrues, or some act dependent thereon is performed. A fact other than mere lapse of time which must exist or occur before a duty of immediate performance of a promise arises. U. S. v. Schaeffer, C.A.Wash., 319 F.2d 907, 911. A "condition precedent" is one that is to be performed before the agreement becomes effective, and which calls for the happening of some event or the performance of some act after the terms of the contract have been arrested on, before the contract shall be binding on the parties; *e.g.* under disability insurance contract, insured is required to submit proof of disability before insurer is required to pay. Sherman v. Metropolitan Life Ins. Co., 297 Mass. 330, 8 N.E.2d 892. A condition subsequent is one annexed to an estate already vested, by the performance of which such estate is kept and continued, and by the failure or non-performance of which it is defeated; or it is a condition referring to a future event, upon the happening of which the obligation becomes no longer binding upon the other party, if he chooses to avail himself of the condition. Co.Litt. 201; Carroll v. Carroll's Ex'r, 248 Ky. 386, 58 S.W.2d 670, 672. A condition subsequent is any condition which divests liability which has already attached on the failure to fulfill the condition as applied in contracts, a provision giving one party the right to divest himself of liability and obligation to perform further if the other party fails to meet condition, *e.g.*, submit dispute to arbitration. In property law, a condition which causes defeasance of estate on failure to perform, *e.g.* fee simple on condition. In lease, a provision giving lessor right to terminate for tenant's failure to perform condition.

Conditions may also be *positive* (requiring that a specified event shall happen or an act be done) and *restrictive* or *negative*, the latter being such as impose an obligation not to do a particular thing, as, that a lessee shall not alien or sub-let or commit waste, or the like.

They may be *single, copulative,* or *disjunctive.* Those of the first kind require the performance of one specified thing only; those of the second kind require the performance of divers acts or things; those of the third kind require the performance of one of several things.

Conditions may also be *independent, dependent,* or *mutual.* They belong to the first class when each of the two conditions must be performed without any reference to the other; to the second class when the performance of one condition is not obligatory until the actual performance of the other; and to the third class when neither party need perform his condition unless the other is ready and willing to perform his, or, in other words, when the mutual covenants go to the whole consideration on both sides and each is precedent to the other.

The following varieties may also be noted: A condition *collateral* is one requiring the performance of a collateral act having no necessary relation to the main subject of the agreement. A *compulsory* condition is one which expressly requires a thing to be done, as, that a lessee shall pay a specified sum of money on a certain day or his lease shall be void. *Concurrent* conditions are those which are mutually dependent and are to be performed at the same time or simultaneously. A condition *inherent* is one annexed to the rent reserved out of the land whereof the estate is made, or rather, to the estate in the land, in respect of rent.

French law. Conditions in French law are of the following types:

The following peculiar distinctions are made: (1) A condition is *casuelle* when it depends on a chance or hazard; (2) a condition is *potestative* when it depends on the accomplishment of something which is in the power of the party to accomplish; (3) a condition is *mixte* when it depends partly on the will of the party and partly on the will of others; (4) a condition is *suspensive* when it is a future and uncertain event, or present but unknown event, upon which an obligation takes or fails to take effect; (5) a condition is *resolutoire* when it is the event which undoes an obligation which has already had effect as such.

Synonymous distinguished. A "condition" is to be distinguished from a *limitation,* in that the latter may be to or for the benefit of a stranger, who may then take advantage of its determination, while only the grantor, or those who stand in his place, can take advantage of a condition. Also, a limitation ends the estate without entry or claim, which is not true of a condition. It also differs from a *conditional limitation.* In determining whether, in the case of estates greater than estates for years, the language constitutes a "condition" or a "conditional limitation," the rule applied is that, where an estate is so expressly limited by the words of its creation that it cannot endure for any longer time than until the condition happens on which the estate is to fail, this is limitation, but when the estate is expressly granted on condition in deed, the law permits it to endure beyond the time of the contingency happening, unless the grantor takes advantage of the breach of condition, by making entry. It differs also from a *covenant,* which can be made by either grantor or grantee, while only the grantor can make a condition. The chief distinction between a condition subsequent in a deed and a covenant pertains to the remedy in event of breach, which, in the former case, subjects the estate to a forfeiture, and in the latter is merely a ground for recovery of damages. A *charge* is a devise of land with a bequest out of the subject-matter, and a charge upon the devisee personally, in respect of the estate devised, gives him an estate on condition. A condition also differs from a *remainder;* for, while the former may operate to defeat the estate before its natural termination, the latter cannot take effect until the completion of the preceding estate.

Conditional. That which is dependent upon or granted subject to a condition.

As to conditional Acceptance; Appearance; Bequest; Contract; Delivery; Devise; Fee; Guaranty; Judgment; Legacy; Limitation; Obligation; Pardon and Privilege, see those titles.

Conditional assault. A threatening gesture with words accompanying it expressing a threat on condition, *e.g.* "your money or your life".

Conditional creditor. In the civil law, a creditor having a future right of action, or having a right of action in expectancy.

Conditional indorsement. See **Indorsement.**

Conditional intent. Intent to do or not to do something if some condition exists.

Conditionally privileged communication. One made in good faith on any subject matter in which the person publishing has an interest, or in reference to which he has a duty, if made to a person having a corresponding interest or duty, even though it contains matter which otherwise would be actionable. Cook v. East Shore Newspapers, 327 Ill.App. 559, 64 N.E.2d 751, 760. The essential elements of a conditionally privileged communication are good faith, an interest to be upheld, a statement limited in its scope to such purpose, a proper occasion, and publication in a proper manner to proper persons. Cook v. East Shore Newspapers, 327 Ill.App. 559, 64 N.E.2d 751.

Conditional payment. Payment of an obligation only on condition that something be done. Generally, right is reserved to demand back payment if condition fails.

Conditional promise. In law of contracts, a promise to perform based on condition; held to be valid consideration even if condition fails.

Conditional release. A discharge of obligation based on some condition, the failure of which defeats the release. Term may also be applied to a substituted form of release from custody subject to applicable statutes and rules and regulations of board of parole. Humphrey v. Wilson, D.C.Mo., 281 F.Supp. 937, 941.

Conditional right. Right to something subject to a condition, *e.g.* parent has right to chastise child on condition that the punishment is reasonable.

Conditional sale contract. Form of sales contract in which seller reserves title until buyer pays for goods, at which time, the condition having been fulfilled, title passes to buyer. Such contract under Uniform Commercial Code is a purchase money security agreement. § 9–105(h). See also **Sale.**

Conditional sentence. A sentence to confinement if defendant fails to fulfill conditions of probation.

Conditional will. A will so drawn that it takes effect only on happening of specified contingency which becomes a condition precedent to operation of will. Methodist Church of Sturgis Inc. v. Templeton, 254 Miss. 197, 181 So.2d 129.

Conditiones quælibet odiosæ; maxime autem contra matrimonium et commercium /kəndìshiyowniyz kwíyləbət òwdiyówsiy, mǽksəmiy ódəm kóntrə mǽtrəmówniyəm èt kəmársh(iy)əm/. Any conditions are odious, but especially those which are against [in restraint of] marriage and commerce.

Condition of employment. Qualification required for a particular job; circumstances under which employment may be secured. See also **Probation.**

Conditions concurrent. In contract law, conditions which must be performed by each party simultaneously; *e.g.* in a cash sale, payment for the goods and delivery are conditions concurrent. See also **Concurrent conditions.**

Conditions of sale. The terms upon which sales are made at auction; usually written or printed and exposed in the auction room at the time of sale.

Conditio præcedens adimpleri debet prius quam sequatur effectus /kəndish(iy)ow prəsíydenz ǽdimplíray debət práyəs kwǽm səkwéydər əféktəs/. A condition precedent must be fulfilled before the effect can follow.

Condominia /kòndəmíniyə/. In the civil law, co-ownerships or limited ownerships, such as *emphyteusis, superficies, pignus, hypotheca, ususfructus, usus,* and *habitatio.* These were more than mere *jura in re alienâ,* being portion of the *dominium* itself, although they are commonly distinguished from the *dominium* strictly so called.

Condominium /kòndəmíniyəm/. System of separate ownership of individual units in multiple-unit building. A single real property parcel with all the unit owners having a right in common to use the common elements with separate ownership confined to the individual units which are serially designated. Kaufman and Broad Homes of Long Island, Inc. v. Albertson, 73 Misc.2d 84, 341 N.Y.S.2d 321, 322. The condominium concept was not rooted in English common law and most condominiums in the United States are formed in accordance with specific state enabling statutes.

A condominium is an estate in real property consisting of an undivided interest in common in a portion of a parcel of real property together with a separate interest in space in a residential, industrial, or commercial building on such real property, such as an apartment, office or store. A condominium may include in addition a separate interest in other portions of such real property. Such estate may, with respect to the duration of its enjoyment, be either (1) an estate of inheritance or perpetual estate, (2) an estate for life, or (3) an estate for years, such as a leasehold or a subleasehold. Calif. Civil Code, § 783.

Condonacion /kòndownas(i)yówn/. In Spanish law, the remission of a debt, either expressly or tacitly.

Condonation /kòndənéyshən/. The conditional remission or forgiveness, by means of continuance or resumption of marital cohabitation, by one of the married parties, of a known matrimonial offense committed by the other, that would constitute a cause of divorce; the condition being that the offense shall not be repeated. Condonation to constitute valid defense in divorce action, must be free, voluntary, and not induced by duress or fraud. Condonation means pardon of offense, voluntary overlooking implied forgiveness by treating offender as if offense had not been committed. Wilson v. Wilson, 14 Ohio App.2d 148, 237 N.E.2d 421, 425. This defense has been abolished in those jurisdictions which recognize "no fault" divorce.

Condone /kəndówn/. To make condonation of.

Conduce. To contribute to as a result.

Conduct, *v.* To manage; direct; lead; have direction; carry on; regulate; do business. Scholz v. Leuer, 7 Wash.2d 76, 109 P.2d 294, 301.

Conduct, *n.* Personal behavior; deportment; mode of action; any positive or negative act.

An action or omission and its accompanying state of mind, or, where relevant, a series of acts and omissions. Model Penal Code, § 1.13.

See also **Disorderly conduct; Tortious.**

Conduct, estoppel by. See **Equitable estoppel.**

Conducti actio /kəndʌ́ktay ǽksh(iy)ow/. In the civil law, an action which the hirer (*conductor*) of a thing might have against the letter (*locator*).

Conductio /kəndʌ́ksh(iy)ow/. In the civil law, a hiring. Used generally in connection with the term *locatio,* a letting. *Locatio et conductio* (sometimes united as a compound word *"locatio-conductio"*), a letting and hiring.

Conduct money. In English practice, money paid to a witness who has been subpœnaed on a trial, sufficient to defray the reasonable expenses of going to, staying at, and returning from the place of trial.

Conductor. In the civil law, a hirer.

Conductor operarum /kəndʌ́ktər òpərérəm/. In the civil law, a person who engages to perform a piece of work for another, at a stated price.

Conductus /kəndʌ́ktəs/. A thing hired.

Conduit concept. An approach the tax law assumes in the tax treatment of certain entities and their owners. The approach permits specified tax characteristics to pass through the entity without losing their identity. Under the conduit concept, for example, long-term capital losses realized by a partnership are passed through as such to the individual partners. The same result does not materialize if the entity is a corporation. Varying forms of the conduit concept are applicable in the case of partnerships, trusts, estates, and Subchapter S corporations.

Cone. Area built up by a stream, near the mouth of a canyon of boulders, small stones, gravel, sand and other detritus.

Cone and key. In old English law, a woman at fourteen or fifteen years of age could take charge of her house and receive *cone* and *key;* that is, keep the accounts and keys. Said by Lord Coke to be *cover* and *keye,* meaning that at that age a woman knew what in her house should be kept under lock and key.

Confarreatio /kənfæriyéysh(iy)ow/. In Roman law, a sacrificial rite resorted to by marrying persons of high patrician or priestly degree, for the purpose of clothing the husband with the *manus* over his wife; the civil modes of effecting the same thing being *coemptio* (formal), and *usus mulieris* (informal).

Confectio /kənféksh(iy)ow/. The making and completion of a written instrument.

Confederacy. The association or banding together of two or more persons for the purpose of committing an act or furthering an enterprise which is forbidden by law, or which, though lawful in itself, becomes unlawful when made the object of the confederacy. More commonly called a "conspiracy."

A league or agreement between two or more independent states whereby they unite for their mutual welfare and the furtherance of their common aims. The term may apply to a union so formed for a temporary or limited purpose, as in the case of an offensive and defensive alliance; but it is more commonly used to denote that species of political connection between two or more independent states by which a central government is created, invested with certain powers of sovereignty (mostly external), and acting upon the several component states as its units, which, however, retain their sovereign powers for domestic purposes and some others. See **Compact; Confederate states; Federal government.**

Confederate states. The band of eleven states formed in 1861 which waged war against the United States in the War Between the States or Civil War.

Confederation. A league or compact for mutual support, particularly of nations, or states. Such was the colonial government during the Revolution. See **Confederacy.**

Confederation articles. See **Articles of Confederation.**

Conference. A meeting of several persons for deliberation, for the interchange of opinion, or for the removal of differences or disputes.

In the practice of legislative bodies, when the two houses cannot agree upon a pending measure, each appoints a committee of "conference," and the committees meet and consult together for the purpose of removing differences, harmonizing conflicting views, and arranging a compromise which will be accepted by both houses.

Representative assembly of a denomination; association of athletic teams.

A personal meeting between the diplomatic agents of two or more nations for the purpose of making statements and explanations that will obviate the delay and difficulty attending the more formal conduct of negotiations.

Confess. To admit as true; to assent to; to concede. To admit the truth of a charge or accusation. Usually spoken of charges of tortious or criminal conduct. See **Confession.**

Confessing error. A plea to an assignment of error, admitting the same.

Confessio /kənfés(h)(i)yow/. Lat. A confession. *Confessio in judicio,* a confession made in or before a court.

Confessio facta in judicio omni probatione major est /kənfés(h)(i)yow fǽktə in juwdísh(i)yow ómniy prəbèyshiyówniy méyjər èst/. A confession made in court is of greater effect than any proof.

Confession. A voluntary statement made by a person charged with the commission of a crime or misdemeanor, communicated to another person, wherein he acknowledges himself to be guilty of the offense charged, and discloses the circumstances of the act or the share and participation which he had in it.

A statement made by a defendant disclosing his guilt of crime with which he is charged and excluding possibility of a reasonable inference to the contrary. People v. Anderson, 236 Cal.App.2d 419, 46 Cal.Rptr. 1, 7. Voluntary statement made by one who is defendant in criminal trial at time when he is not testifying in trial and by which he acknowledges certain conduct of his own constituting crime for which he is on trial; a statement which, if true, discloses his guilt of that crime and excludes possibility of reasonable inference to contrary. People v. Beverly, 233 Cal.App.2d 702, 43 Cal.Rptr. 743, 749.

See also **Interrogation.**

Constitutional protections. See **Escobedo Rule; Mallory Rule; Miranda Rule.**

Classification of confessions. Confessions are divided into judicial and extrajudicial. The former are such as are made before a magistrate or court in the due course of legal proceedings; they include confessions made in preliminary examinations before magistrates. The latter is one made by the party out of court, or to any person, official or otherwise, when made not in the course of a judicial examination or investigation. See also **Extrajudicial.**

An *implied* confession is where the defendant does not plead guilty but indirectly admits his guilt by placing himself at the mercy of the court and asking for a light sentence. An *indirect* confession is one inferred from the conduct of the defendant. An *involuntary* confession is one induced by hope, promise, fear, violence, torture, or threat. Lyons v. State, 77 Okl.Cr. 197, 138 P.2d 142, 148; Lyons v. State, 140 P.2d 248. A *naked* confession is an admission of the guilt of the party, but which is not supported by any evidence of the commission of the crime. A *voluntary* confession is one made spontaneously by a person accused of crime, free from the influence of any extraneous disturbing cause, and in particular, not influenced, or extorted by violence, threats, or promises.

See also **Involuntary confession; Oral confession.**

Distinguished from admission. A confession is a statement admitting or acknowledging all facts necessary for conviction of the crime. An admission, on the other hand, is an acknowledgment of a fact or facts tending to prove guilt which falls short of an acknowledgment of all essential elements of the crime. Gladden v. Unsworth, 9th Cir., 396 F.2d 373, 375 n. 2; People v. Fitzgerald, 56 Cal.2d 855, 861, 17 Cal.Rptr. 129, 132, 366 P.2d 481, 484.

Confession and avoidance. A plea in confession and avoidance is one which avows and confesses the truth of the averments of fact in the complaint or declaration, either expressly or by implication, but then proceeds to allege new matter which tends to deprive the facts admitted of their ordinary legal effect, or to obviate, neutralize, or *avoid* them. Sievers v. Brown, 216 Miss. 801, 63 So.2d 217, 219.

Confession of defense. In English practice, where defendant alleges a ground of defense arising since the commencement of the action, the plaintiff may deliver confession of such defense and sign judgment for his costs up to the time of such pleading, unless it be otherwise ordered.

Confession of judgment. See **Cognovit judgment; Judgment.**

Confesso, bill taken pro. In equity practice, an order which the court of chancery makes when the defendant does not file an answer, that the plaintiff may take such a decree as the case made by his bill warrants.

Confessor. A priest who receives auricular confessions of sins from persons under his spiritual charge, and pronounces absolution upon them. The secrets of the confessional were not privileged communications at common law, but are so classified by statute or court decision in many states.

Confessoria actio /kònfesóriyə ǽksh(iy)ow/. Lat. In the civil law, an action for enforcing a servitude.

Confessus in judicio pro judicato habetur, et quodammodo sua sententia damnatur /kənfésəs in juwdísh(iy)ow pròw jùwdəkéydow həbíydər, èt kwowdǽmədow s(y)úwə senténsh(iy)ə dæmnéydər/. A person confessing his guilt when arraigned is deemed to have been found guilty, and is, as it were, condemned by his own sentence.

Confide. A synonym of the word "trust"; meaning to put into one's trust, keeping, or confidence.

Confidence. Trust; reliance; relation of trust. Reliance on discretion of another. In the construction of wills, this word is considered peculiarly appropriate to create a trust.

Confidence game. Obtaining of money or property by means of some trick, device, or swindling operation in which advantage is taken of the confidence which the victim reposes in the swindler. The elements of the crime of "confidence game" are: (1) an intentional false representation to the victim as to some present fact, (2) knowing it to be false, (3) with intent that the victim rely on the representation, (4) the representation being made to obtain the victim's confidence and thereafter his money and property, (5) which confidence is then abused by defendant. U. S. v. Brown, D.C.App., 309 A.2d 256, 257.

For distinction between false pretenses and confidence game, see **False pretenses.** See also **Flim-flam.**

Confidential. Intrusted with the confidence of another or with his secret affairs or purposes; intended to be held in confidence or kept secret; done in confidence.

Confidential communication. Privileged communications such as those between spouses, attorney-client, confessor-penitent, etc. Such are privileged at the option of the spouse-witness, client-witness and penitent-witness. Confidential communication is statement made under circumstances showing that speaker intended statement only for ears of person addressed; thus if communication is made in presence of third party whose presence is not reasonably necessary for the communication, it is not privileged. Touma v. Touma, 140 N.J.Super. 544, 357 A.2d 25, 28. See also **Communication; Privileged communications.**

Confidentiality. State or quality of being confidential; treated as private and not for publication.

Confidential relation. A fiduciary relation. It is a peculiar relation which exists between client and attorney, principal and agent, principal and surety, landlord and tenant, parent and child, guardian and ward, ancestor and heir, husband and wife, trustee and *cestui que trust*, executors or administrators and creditors, legatees, or distributees, appointor and appointee under powers, and partners and part owners. In these and like cases, the law, in order to prevent undue advantage from the unlimited confidence or sense of duty which the relation naturally creates, requires the utmost degree of good faith in all transactions between the parties. It is not confined to any specific association of parties. It appears when the circumstances make it certain that the parties do not deal on equal terms, but on the one side there is an overmastering influence, or, on the other, weakness, dependence, or trust, justifiably reposed. The mere existence of kinship does not, of itself, give rise to such relation. It covers every form of relation between parties wherein confidence is reposed by one in another, and former relies and acts upon representations of the other and is guilty of no derelictions on his own part. Peckham v. Johnson, Tex.Civ.App., 98 S.W.2d 408, 416.

Confidential relations are deemed to arise whenever two persons have come into such a relation that confidence is necessarily reposed by one and the influence which naturally grows out of the confidence is possessed by the other, and this confidence is abused or the influence is exerted to obtain an advantage at expense of confiding party. Ruebsamen v. Maddocks, Me., 340 A.2d 31, 34.

See also **Fiduciary or confidential relation.**

Confinement. State of being confined; shut in; imprisoned. Confinement may be by either a moral or a physical restraint, by threats of violence with a present force, or by physical restraint of the person.

See also **Commitment; Solitary confinement.**

Confirm. To complete or establish that which was imperfect or uncertain; to ratify what has been done without authority or insufficiently. To make firm or certain; to give new assurance of truth or certainty; to put aside past doubt; to give approval to. See also **Confirmation.**

Confirmare est id firmum facere quod prius infirmum fuit /kònfərmériy est íd fárməm féysəriy kwòd práyəs ənfárməm fyúwət/. To confirm is to make firm that which was before infirm.

Confirmare nemo potest prius quam jus ei acciderit /kònfərmériy níymow pówdəst práyəs kwæm jás íyay æksədérət/. No one can confirm before the right accrues to him.

Confirmatio /kònfərmeysh(iy)ow/. The conveyance of an estate, or the communication of a right that one hath in or unto lands or tenements, to another that hath the possession thereof, or some other estate therein, whereby a voidable estate is made sure and unavoidable, or whereby a particular estate is increased or enlarged. 2 Bl.Comm. 325.

Confirmatio chartarum /kònfərméysh(iy)ow kartárəm/. Lat. Confirmation of the charters. A statute passed in the 25 Edw. I., whereby the Great Charter is declared to be allowed as the common law; all judgments contrary to it are declared void; copies of it are ordered to be sent to all cathedral churches and read twice a year to the people; and sentence of excommunication is directed to be as constantly denounced against all those that, by word or deed or counsel, act contrary thereto or in any degree infringe it. 1 Bl.Comm. 128.

Confirmatio crescens /kònfərméysh(iy)ow krésənz/. An enlarging confirmation; one which enlarges a rightful estate.

Confirmatio diminuens /kònfərméysh(iy)ow dəmínyuwenz/. A diminishing confirmation. A confirmation which tends and serves to diminish and abridge the services whereby a tenant doth hold, operating as a release of part of the services.

Confirmatio est nulla ubi donum præcedens est invalidum /kònfərméysh(iy)ow èst nálə yúwbay dównəm prəsíyden(d)z èst invælədəm/. Confirmation is void where the preceding gift is invalid.

Confirmation. A contract, or written memorandum thereof, by which that which was infirm, difficult of proof, void, imperfect, or subject to be avoided is ratified, rendered valid and binding, made firm and unavoidable. To give formal approval. Act or process of confirming. See also **Approval; Ratification; Verification.**

A conveyance of an estate or right *in esse*, whereby a voidable estate is made sure and unavoidable, or whereby a particular estate is increased.

The ratification or approval of executive acts by a legislature or one house. In order to be valid, Presidential appointments of important officers of the United States require approval by a majority of the Senate, and treatises must be approved by two-thirds of the Senate. Art. II, § 2, U.S.Const.

A formal memorandum delivered by the customers or suppliers of a company to its independent auditor verifying the amounts shown as receivable or payable. The confirmation document is originally sent by the auditor to the customer.

Confirmation of sale. The confirmation of a judicial sale by the court which ordered it is a signification in some way (usually by the entry of an order) or the court's approval of the terms, price, and conditions of the sale.

Confirmatio omnes supplet defectus, licet id quod actum est ab initio non valuit /kònfərméysh(iy)ow ómniy sáplət dəféktəs, lísəd íd kwòd ǽktəm èst ǽb ənísh(iy)ow nòn vǽlyuwət/. Confirmation supplies all defects, though that which had been done was not valid at the beginning.

Confirmatio perficiens /kònfərméysh(iy)ow pəfíshi-yen(d)z/. A confirmation which makes valid a wrongful and defeasible title, or makes a conditional estate absolute.

Confirmat usum qui tollit abusum /kònfə́rmət yúwzəm kwày tóləd əbsárdəm/. He confirms the use [of a thing] who removes the abuse [of it].

Confirmavi /kònfərméyviy/. Lat. I have confirmed. The emphatic word in the ancient deeds of confirmation.

Confirmed credit. Means that the credit must carry the direct obligation of an agency which does business in the seller's financial market. U.C.C. § 2–325.

Confirmee /kònfərmíy/. The grantee in a deed of confirmation.

Confirming bank. A bank which engages either that it will itself honor a credit already issued by another bank or that such a credit will be honored by the issuer or a third bank. U.C.C. § 5–103.

Confirmor /kənfírmər/. The grantor in a deed of confirmation.

Confiscable /kónfiskəbəl/kənfískəbəl/. Capable of being confiscated or suitable for confiscation; liable to forfeiture.

Confiscare /kònfəskériy/. In civil and old English law, to confiscate; to claim for or bring into the fisc, or treasury.

Confiscate /kónfəskeyt/. To appropriate property to the use of the government. To adjudge property to be forfeited to the public; to seize and condemn private forfeited property to public use. To take property from enemy in time of war. See also **Confiscation; Forfeiture.**

Confiscation /kònfəskéyshən/. Act of confiscating. The seizure of private property by the government without compensation to the owner, often as a consequence of conviction for crime, or because possession or use of the property was contrary to law. The provisions of due process prohibit the confiscation of property without compensation except where the property is taken in the valid execution of the police power. See also Condemnation; Confiscate; Eminent domain; Expropriation; Forfeiture; Seizure.

Confiscation acts. Certain acts of congress enacted during the process of the civil war (1861 and 1862) in the exercise of the war powers of the government and meant to strengthen its hands and aid in suppressing the rebellion, which authorized the seizure, condemnation, and forfeiture of "property used for insurrectionary purposes".

Confiscation cases. The name given to a group of fifteen cases decided by the United States supreme court in 1868, on the validity and construction of the confiscation acts of congress. Reported in 7 Wall. 454, 19 L.Ed. 196.

Confiscatory rates. With respect to utilities, are rates which do not afford a reasonable return on value of property at time it is used in public service; rates which do not afford net return sufficient to preserve utility's property and to attract capital necessary to enable utility to discharge its public duties.

Confisk. An old form of *confiscate.*

Confitens reus /kónfəten(d)z ríyəs/. An accused person who admits his guilt.

Conflicting evidence. Evidence offered by plaintiff and defendant, or prosecutor and defendant which is inconsistent and cannot be reconciled.

Conflict of authority. A division between two or more courts (generally courts of last resort) on some legal principal or application of law. May also refer to disparity between authorities on a subject. See also **Choice of law; Conflict of laws.**

Conflict of interest. Term used in connection with public officials and fiduciaries and their relationship to matters of private interest or gain to them. Ethical problems connected therewith are covered by statutes in most jurisdictions and by federal statutes on the federal level. Generally, when used to suggest disqualification of a public official from performing his sworn duty, term "conflict of interest" refers to a clash between public interest and the private pecuniary interest of the individual concerned. Gardner v. Nashville Housing Authority of Metropolitan Government of Nashville and Davison County, Tenn., C.A. Tenn., 514 F.2d 38, 41.

Conflict of laws. Inconsistency or difference between the laws of different states or countries, arising in the case of persons who have acquired rights, incurred obligations, injuries or damages, or made contracts, within the territory of two or more jurisdictions. Hence, that branch of jurisprudence, arising from the diversity of the laws of different nations, states or jurisdictions, in their application to rights and remedies, which reconciles the inconsistency, or decides which law or system is to govern in the particular case, or settles the degree of force to be accorded to the law of another jurisdiction, (the acts or rights in question having arisen under it) either where it varies from the domestic law, or where the domestic law is silent or not exclusively applicable to the case in point. See also Center of gravity doctrine; Choice of law; Grouping of contacts; Kilberg doctrine; Lex celebrationis; Lex contractus; Lex fori; Lex loci; Lex loci celebrationis; Lex loci contractus; Lex situs; Lex solutionis; Lex validitatis; Renvoi.

Conflict of Laws is that part of the law of each state which determines what effect is given to the fact that the case may have a significant relationship to more than one state. Restatement, Second, Conflicts of Law, § 2.

Conflict of personal laws. Term used to describe conflicts within a particular state arising from application of general law to racial and religious groups which have their own laws, *e.g.* tribal laws of the Indians.

Conformed copy. An exact copy of a document on which has been written explanations of things that could not or were not copied; *e.g.* written signature might be replaced on conformed copy with notation that it was signed by the person whose signature appears on the original.

Conforming. In law of sales, goods or conduct including any part of a performance are conforming or conform to the contract when they are in accordance with the obligations under the contract. U.C.C. § 2-106(2).

Conforming use. In zoning and land use planning, a use of a structure which is in conformity with those uses permitted by the particular zoning classification of the area. Compare **Nonconforming use.**

Conformity. Correspondence in form, manner, or use; agreement; harmony; congruity.

Conformity Act, or **statute.** A term used to designate Act June 1, 1872, c. 255, § 5, 17 Stat. 197, providing that the practice, pleadings, and forms and modes of proceeding in civil causes, other than equity and admiralty causes, in the federal district courts shall conform, as near as may be, to those existing in like causes in the courts of the state within which such district courts are held. Since the adoption of the Federal Rules of Civil Procedure, 28 U.S.C.A., the Conformity Act is no longer effective. Hydraulic Press Mfg. Co. v. Williams, White & Co., C.C.A.Ill. 1947, 165 F.2d 489.

Conformity, Bill of. See **Bill** (*Equity pleading and practice*).

Conformity hearing. Hearing ordered by court to determine whether judgment or decree directed to be prepared by the prevailing party conforms with decision of court. Commonly after court makes its findings it directs prevailing party to draw judgment or decree in conformity with such findings and decision.

Confrairie /kónfrèriy/kənfrériy/. Fr. In old English law, a fraternity, brotherhood, or society.

Confreres /kónfrerz/kənfrérz/. Brethren in a religious house; fellows of one and the same society.

Confrontation. In criminal law, the act of setting a witness face to face with the prisoner, in order that the latter may make any objection he has to the witness, or that the witness may identify the accused. The constitutional right of confrontation (6th Amend.) does not mean merely that witnesses are to be made visible to the accused, but imports the constitutional privilege to cross-examine them. In fact, the essence of the right of confrontation is the right to cross examination. Davis v. Alaska, 415 U.S. 308, 94 S.Ct. 1105, 39 L.Ed.2d 347. A disruptive defendant may however lose his right to be present in the courtroom, and, as a result, lose his right to confront witnesses. Illinois v. Allen, 397 U.S. 337, 90 S.Ct. 1057, 25 L.Ed.2d 353.

Confusio /kənfyúwz(h)(i)yow/. In the civil law, the inseparable intermixture of property belonging to different owners; it is properly confined to the pouring together of fluids, but is sometimes also used of a melting together of metals or any compound formed by the irrecoverable commixture of different substances. It is distinguished from *commixtion* by the fact that in the latter case a separation may be made, while in a case of *confusio* there cannot be. 2 Bl. Comm. 405.

Confusion. This term, as used in the civil law and in compound terms derived from that source, means a blending or intermingling, and is equivalent to the term "merger" as used at common law. See also **Commingle.**

Confusion of boundaries. The title of that branch of equity jurisdiction which relates to the discovery and settlement of conflicting, disputed, or uncertain boundaries.

Confusion of debts. A mode of extinguishing a debt, by the concurrence in the same person of two qualities or adverse rights to the same thing which mutually destroy each other. This may occur in several ways, as where the creditor becomes the heir of the debtor, or the debtor the heir of the creditor, or either accedes to the title of the other by any other mode of transfer.

Confusion of goods. Results when goods belonging to two or more owners become intermixed to the point where the property of any of them no longer can be identified except as part of a mass of like goods. Johnson v. Covey, 1 Utah 2d 180, 264 P.2d 283. See also **Commingle.**

Confusion of rights. A union of the qualities of debtor and creditor in the same person. The effect of such a union is, generally, to extinguish the debt. Baylor University v. Bradshaw, Tex.Civ.App., 52 S.W.2d 1094, 1101.

Confusion of titles. A civil-law expression, synonymous with "merger," as used in the common law, applying where two titles to the same property unite in the same person.

Confute /kənfyúwt/. To prove to be false, defective, or invalid.

Con game. A swindle or any arrangement in which a person is deliberately defrauded because of his trust in the one who is swindling. See also **Confidence game; Flim-flam.**

Congé /kònjéy/kònzhéy/. Fr. In French law, permission, leave, license; a passport or clearance to a vessel; a permission to arm, equip, or navigate a vessel.

Congeable /kónjiyəbəl/. L. Fr. Lawful; permissible; allowable.

Congé d'accorder /kònzhéy dàkordéy/. Leave to accord. A permission granted by the court, in the old process of levying a fine, to the defendant to agree with the plaintiff.

Congé d'emparler /kònzhéy dòmparléy/. Leave to imparl. The privilege of an imparlance (*licentia loquendi*). 3 Bl.Comm. 299.

Congé d'eslire /kònzhéy delír/. Also spelled congé d'élire, congé délire. A permission or license from the British sovereign to a dean and chapter to elect a bishop, in time of vacation; or to an abbey or priory which is of royal foundation, to elect an abbot or prior.

Congenital. A condition present at birth.

Congildones /kòŋgildówniyz/. In Saxon law, fellow-members of a guild.

Congius /kónjiyəs/. An ancient measure containing about a gallon and a pint.

Conglomerate /kənglómərət/. A corporation that has diversified its operations usually by acquiring enterprises in widely varied industries.

Conglomerate merger. Merger among firms which operate in separate and distinct markets; *e.g.* merger of companies with different product lines. A merger in which there are no economic relationships between the acquiring and the acquired firm. Kennecott Copper Corp. v. F. T. C., C.A.10, 467 F.2d 67, 75. A merger other than a horizontal or vertical merger. U. S. v. International Tel. & Tel. Corp., D.C.Conn., 306 F.Supp. 766, 774. See also **Conglomerate; Merger.**

Congregate. To come together; to assemble; to meet.

Congregation. An assembly or gathering; specifically, an assembly or society of persons who together constitute the principal supporters of a particular parish, or habitually meet at the same church for religious exercises.

Congress /kóŋgrəs/. Formal meeting of delegates or representatives. The Congress of the United States was created by Article I, Section 1, of the Constitution, adopted by the Constitutional Convention on September 17, 1787, providing that "All legislative Powers herein granted shall be vested in a Congress of the United States, which shall consist of a Senate and House of Representatives." The first Congress under the Constitution met on March 4, 1789, in the Federal Hall in New York City. The membership then consisted of 20 Senators and 59 Representatives. See **House of Representatives; Senate.**

Congressional apportionment. See **Apportionment** (*Representatives*).

Congressional committee. A committee of the House of Representatives or of the Senate or a joint committee formed for some particular public purpose.

Congressional district. A geographical unit of a State from which one member of the House of Representatives is elected.

Congressional immunity. See **Legislative immunity.**

Congressional powers. The authority vested in the Senate and House of Representatives to enact laws, etc. as provided in U.S.Const., Art. I.

Congressional Record. Proceedings of Congress are published in the *Congressional Record*, which is issued daily when Congress is in session. Publication of the *Record* began March 4, 1873; it was the first series officially reported, printed, and published directly by the Federal Government. The Daily Digest of the *Congressional Record*, printed in the back of each issue of the *Record*, summarizes the proceedings of that day in each House, and before each of their committees and subcommittees, respectively. The Digest also presents the legislative program for each day, and at the end of the week, gives the program for the following week. Its publication was begun March 17, 1947. Members of Congress are allowed to edit their speeches before printing and may insert material never actually spoken by securing from their respective houses leave to print or to extend their remarks.

Congressman. Strictly, a member of the Congress of the United States. But the common tendency is to apply this term only to a member of the House of Representatives, as distinguished from a senator.

Congressus /kəŋgrésəs/. The extreme practical test of the truth of a charge of impotence brought against a husband by a wife. It is now disused.

Conjectio /kənjéksh(iy)ow/. In the civil law of evidence, a throwing together. Presumption; the putting of things together, with the inference drawn therefrom.

Conjectio causæ /kənjéksh(iy)ow kóziy/. In the civil law, a statement of the case. A brief synopsis of the case given by the advocate to the judge in opening the trial.

Conjectural choice, rule of /rúwl əv kənjékchərəl chóys/. Where all theories of causation rest only on conjecture, no jury question is presented.

Conjecture. A slight degree of credence, arising from evidence too weak or too remote to cause belief. Supposition or surmise. The idea of a fact, suggested by another fact; as a possible cause, concomitant, or result. An idea or notion founded on a probability without any demonstration of its truth; an idea or surmise inducing a slight degree of belief founded upon some possible, or perhaps probable fact of which there is no positive evidence. Oklahoma City v. Wilcoxson, 173 Okl. 433, 48 P.2d 1039, 1043. An explanation consistent with but not deducible as a reasonable inference from known facts or conditions. In popular use, synonymous with "guess." Also, the bringing together of the circumstances, as well as the result obtained.

Conjoint robbery. Where the act is committed by two or more persons.

Conjoints. Persons married to each other.

Conjudex /kònjúwdeks/. In old English law, an associate judge.

Conjugal /kónjəgəl/. Of or belonging to marriage or the married state; suitable or appropriate to the married state or to married persons; matrimonial; connubial.

Conjugal rights. Matrimonial rights; the right which husband and wife have to each other's society, comfort, and affection.

Conjugium /kənjúwjiyəm/. One of the names of marriage, among the Romans.

Conjuncta /kənjáŋktə/. In the civil law, things joined together or united; as distinguished from *disjuncta*, things disjoined or separated.

Conjunctim /kənjáŋktəm/. Lat. In old English law, jointly.

Conjunctim et divisim /kənjáŋktəm et dəvízəm/. L. Lat. In old English law, jointly and severally.

Conjunctio /kənjə́ŋksh(iy)ow/. In the civil law, conjunction; connection of words in a sentence.

Conjunctio mariti et feminæ est de jure naturæ /kənjə́ŋksh(iy)ow məráydy ət fémniy èst dìy júriy nəchúriy/. The union of husband and wife is of the law of nature.

Conjunctive. Connecting in a manner denoting union.

A grammatical term for particles which serve for joining or connecting together. Thus, the word "and" is called a "conjunctive," and "or" a "disjunctive," conjunction.

Conjunctive denial. Where several material facts are stated conjunctively in the complaint, an answer which undertakes to deny their averments as a whole, conjunctively stated, is called a "conjunctive denial."

Conjunctive obligation /kənjə́ŋktəv òbləgéyshən/. See **Obligation.**

Conjuratio /kònjəréysh(iy)ow/. In old English law, a swearing together; an oath administered to several together; a combination or confederacy under oath.

In old European law, a compact of the inhabitants of a commune, or municipality, confirmed by their oaths to each other and which was the basis of the commune.

Conjuration /kònjəréyshən/. In old English law, a plot or compact made by persons combining by oath to do any public harm.

The offense at common law of having conference or commerce with evil spirits, in order to discover some secret, or effect some purpose. The English Witchcraft Act of 1735, which made conjuration an offense, was repealed by the Fraudulent Mediums Act of 1951.

Conjurator /kónjərèydər/. In old English law, one who swears or is sworn with others; one bound by oath with others; a compurgator; a conspirator.

Connect. To join or fasten together as by something intervening; to associate as in occurrence or in idea; to combine; to unite or link together, as in an electrical circuit; to establish a bond or relation between; to meet or make connections for transference of passengers or change of means of communication.

Connected. Joined; united by junction, by an intervening substance or medium, by dependence or relation, or by order in a series.

Connecting carrier. One of several common carriers whose united lines or parts constitute the route over which shipment is to pass, and which participates in transportation of such shipment as a common carrier furnishing a necessary link in transportation. Herman v. Railway Exp. Agency, 17 N.J.Super. 10, 85 A.2d 284.

Connecting factors. In conflict of laws, legal categories such as the place of making a contract which serve to determine the choice of law in a particular case.

Connecting up doctrine. A thing may be put into evidence (including testimony) subject to its being connected up with later evidence that will show its relevance.

Connection. The state of being connected or joined; union by junction, by an intervening substance or medium, by dependence or relation, or by order in a series.

Connections. Relations by blood or marriage, but more commonly the relations of a person with whom one is connected by marriage. In this sense, the relations of a wife are "connections" of her husband. The term is vague and indefinite.

Connexité /konèksiytéy/. In French law, this exists when two actions are pending which, although not identical as in *lis pendens,* are so nearly similar in object that it is expedient to have them both adjudicated upon by the same judges.

Connivance /kənáyvən(t)s/. The secret or indirect consent or permission of one person to the commission of an unlawful or criminal act by another. A winking at; voluntary blindness; an intentional failure to discover or prevent the wrong; forbearance or passive consent. Pierce v. Crisp, 260 Ky. 519, 86 S.W.2d 293, 296.

As constituting defense in divorce action, is plaintiff's corrupt consent, express or implied, to offense charged against defendant. Muir v. Muir, Del.Super., 7 Terry 578, 86 A.2d 857, 858. This defense has been abolished by many states with the enactment of no-fault divorce laws.

Connive /kənáyv/. To co-operate secretly with, or to have a secret or clandestine understanding with. To take part or co-operate privily with another, to aid or abet. To look upon with secret favor; it implies both knowledge and assent, either active or passive. See **Connivance.**

Connoissement /kòneysmón/. In French law, an instrument, signed by the master of a ship or his agent, containing a description of the goods loaded on a ship, the persons who have sent them, the persons to whom they were sent, and the undertaking to transport them; similar to the English and American bill of lading.

Connubium /kən(y)úwbiyəm/. In the civil law, marriage. Among the Romans, a lawful marriage as distinguished from "concubinage" *(q.v.),* an inferior marriage.

Conociamento /konòsiyaméntow/. In Spanish law, a recognizance.

Conocimiento /konòsiym(i)yéntow/. In Spanish law, a bill of lading. In the Mediterranean ports it is called *"poliza de cargamiento."*

Conpossessio /kòmpəzésh(iy)ow/. In civil law, a joint possession.

Conquereur /kónkərər/. In Norman and old English law, the same as "conqueror" *(q.v.).*

Conqueror. In old English and Scotch law, the first purchaser of an estate; he who first brought an estate into his family, or into the family owning it. 2 Bl.Comm. 242, 243.

Conquest /kónkwest/. In feudal law, acquisition by purchase; any method of acquiring the ownership of an estate other than by descent. Also an estate acquired otherwise than by inheritance.

In international law, the acquisition of the sovereignty of a country by force of arms, exercised by an independent power which reduces the vanquished to the submission of its empire. To conquer a territory or nation by means of force.

Conquestor /kóŋkwestər/konkwéstər/. Conqueror. The title given to William of Normandy.

Conquêts /kəŋkwésts/kənkéts/. In French law, the name given to every acquisition which the husband and wife, jointly or severally, make during the conjugal community. Thus, whatever is acquired by the husband and wife, either by his or her industry or good fortune, inures to the extent of one-half for the benefit of the other. In Louisiana, these gains are called *acquêts*.

Conquisitio /kòŋkwəzísh(iy)ow/. In feudal and old English law, acquisition. 2 Bl.Comm. 242.

Conquisitor /kəŋkwəzáydər/. In feudal law, a purchaser, acquirer, or conqueror. 2 Bl.Comm. 242, 243.

Consanguineus /kònsəŋgwíniyəs/. Lat. A person related by blood; a person descended from the same common stock.

Consanguineus est quasi eodem sanguine natus /kònsəŋgwíniyəs est kwéysay iyówdəm sǽŋgwəniy néydəs/. A person related by consanguinity is, as it were, sprung from the same blood.

Consanguineus frater /kònsəŋgwíniyəs fréydər/. In civil and feudal law, a half-brother by the father's side, as distinguished from *frater uterinus,* a brother by the mother's side. 2 Bl.Comm. 231.

Consanguinity /kònsæŋgwínədiy/. Kinship; blood relationship; the connection or relation of persons descended from the same stock or common ancestor. Consanguinity is distinguished from "affinity," which is the connection existing in consequence of a marriage, between each of the married persons and the kindred of the other.

Lineal and collateral consanguinity. Lineal consanguinity is that which subsists between persons of whom one is descended in a direct line from the other, as between son, father, grandfather, greatgrandfather, and so upwards in the direct ascending line; or between son, grandson, great-grandson, and so downwards in the direct descending line. Collateral consanguinity is that which subsists between persons who have the same ancestors, but who do not descend (or ascend) one from the other. Thus, father and son are related by lineal consanguinity, uncle and nephew by collateral sanguinity.

Conscience. The moral sense; the faculty of judging the moral qualities of actions, or of discriminating between right and wrong; particularly applied to one's perception and judgment of the moral qualities of his own conduct, but in a wider sense, denoting a similar application of the standards of morality to the acts of others. The sense of right and wrong inherent in every person by virtue of his existence as a social entity; good conscience being a synonym of equity. In law, especially the moral rule which requires probity, justice, and honest dealing between man and man, as when we say that a bargain is "against conscience" or "unconscionable," or that the price paid for property at a forced sale was so inadequate as to "shock the conscience." This is also the meaning of the term as applied to the jurisdiction and principles of decision of courts of chancery, as in saying that such a court is a "court of conscience," that it proceeds "according to conscience," or that it has cognizance of "matters of conscience."

Conscience, courts of. In English law, courts, not of record, constituted by act of parliament in the city of London, and other towns, for the recovery of small debts; otherwise and more commonly called "Courts of Requests." Such courts have been superseded by county courts.

Conscience of the court. When an issue is sent out of chancery to be tried at law, to "inform the conscience of the court," the meaning is that the court is to be supplied with exact and dependable information as to the unsettled or disputed questions of fact in the case, in order that it may proceed to decide it in accordance with the principles of equity and good conscience in the light of the facts thus determined. Watt v. Starke, 101 U.S. 247, 25 L.Ed. 826.

Conscience, right of. As used in some constitutional provisions, this phrase is equivalent to religious liberty or freedom of conscience.

Conscientia dicitur a con et scio, quasi scire cum deo /kòns(h)iyénsh(iy)ə dísədər èy kón èt sáyow, kwéysay sáyriy kàm díyow/. Conscience is called from *con* and *scio*, to know, as it were, with God.

Conscientious objector. One who, by reason of religious training and belief, is conscientiously opposed to participation in war. Such person need not be a member of a religious sect whose creed forbids participation in war to be entitled to classification as a conscientious objector. U. S. v. Bowles, C.C.A.N.J., 131 F.2d 818. It is sufficient if he has a conscientious scruple against war in any form. U. S. ex rel. Phillips v. Downer, C.C.A.N.Y., 135 F.2d 521, 524, 525. Such objection must however be shown to be sincere. U. S. v. Miller, D.C.N.D., 337 F.Supp. 1402, 1403.

Conscientious scruple. A conscientious scruple against taking an oath, serving as a juror in a capital case, doing military duty, or the like, is an objection or repugnance growing out of the fact that the person believes the thing demanded of him to be morally wrong, his conscience being the sole guide to his decision; it is thus distinguished from an "objection on principle," which is dictated by the reason and judgment, rather than the moral sense, and may relate only to the propriety or expediency of the thing in question.

Conscription. Compulsory enrollment and induction into military service; drafted.

Consecrate. In ecclesiastical law, to dedicate to sacred purposes, as a bishop by imposition of hands, or a church or churchyard by prayers, etc. Consecration is performed by a bishop or archbishop.

Consecratio est periodus electionis; electio est præambula consecrationis. Consecration is the termination of election; election is the preamble of consecration.

Consecutive. Successive; succeeding one another in regular order; to follow in uninterrupted succession.

Consecutive sentences. When one sentence of confinement is to follow another in point of time, the second sentence is deemed to be consecutive. May also be applied to suspended sentences. Also called "from and after" sentences.

Consedo /konséyðow/. Sp. A term used in conveyances under Mexican law, equivalent to the English word "grant."

Conseil de famille /konséy də famíy/. In French law, a family council. Certain acts require the sanction of this body. For example, a guardian can neither accept nor reject an inheritance to which the minor has succeeded without its authority (Code Nap. 461); nor can he accept for the child a gift *inter vivos* without the like authority (Code Nap. 463).

Conseil de prudhommes /konséy də pruwdóm/. In French law, one of a species of trade tribunals, charged with settling differences between masters and workmen. They endeavor, in the first instance, to conciliate the parties. In default, they adjudicate upon the questions in dispute. Their decisions are final up to 200f. Beyond that amount, appeals lie to the tribunals of commerce.

Conseil d'état /kònséy deytá/. Council of state. One of the oldest of French institutions, its origin dating back to 1302. It decides or advises upon state questions and measures proposed for legislation, submitted to it by the President of the Republic, by the members of the Cabinet, and by Parliament.

Conseil judiciaire /kònséy zhudìs(i)yér/. In French law, when a person has been subjected to an interdiction on the ground of his insane extravagance, but the interdiction is not absolute, but limited only, the court of first instance, which grants the interdiction, appoints a council, called by this name, with whose assistance the party may bring or defend actions, or compromise the same, alienate his estate, make or incur loans, and the like.

Consensual contract /kənsénshuwəl kóntrækt/. A term derived from the civil law, denoting a contract founded upon and completed by the mere consent of the contracting parties, without any external formality or symbolic act to fix the obligation.

Consensual marriage /kənsénshuwəl mǽrəj/. Marriage resting simply on consent per verba de præsenti, between competent parties. See also **Common-law marriage.**

Consensus ad idem /kənsénsəs ǽd áydəm/. An agreement of parties to the same thing; a meeting of minds.

Consensus est voluntas plurium ad quos res pertinet, simul juncta /kənsénsəs èst vəlántæs plúriyəm ǽd kwóws ríyz párdənət, sáyməl jə́ŋktə/. Consent is the conjoint will of several persons to whom the thing belongs.

Consensus facit legem /kənsénsəs féysət líyjəm/. Consent makes the law. (A contract is law between the parties agreeing to be bound by it.)

Consensus, non concubitus, facit nuptias vel matrimonium, et consentire non possunt ante annos nubiles /kənsénsəs, nón kənkyúwbədəs, féysət népshiyəs vèl mǽtrəmówn(i)yəm, èt kònsəntáyriy nòn pósənt ǽntiy ǽnows n(y)úwbəliyz/. Consent, and not cohabitation (or coition), constitutes nuptials or marriage, and persons cannot consent before marriageable years. 1 Bl.Comm. 434.

Consensus tollit errorem /kənsénsəs tóləd ərórəm/. Consent (acquiescence) removes mistake.

Consensus voluntas multorum ad quos res pertinet, simul juncta /kənsénsəs vəlántæs məltórəm ǽd kwóws ríyz párdənət sáyməl jə́ŋktə/. Consent is the united will of several interested in one subject-matter.

Consent. A concurrence of wills. Voluntarily yielding the will to the proposition of another; acquiescence or compliance therewith. Agreement; the act or result of coming into harmony or accord. Consent is an act of reason, accompanied with deliberation, the mind weighing as in a balance the good or evil on each side. It means voluntary agreement by a person in the possession and exercise of sufficient mental capacity to make an intelligent choice to do something proposed by another. It supposes a physical power to act, a moral power of acting, and a serious, determined, and free use of these powers. Consent is implied in every agreement. It is an act unclouded by fraud, duress, or sometimes even mistake.

Willingness in fact that an act or an invasion of an interest shall take place. Restatement, Second, Torts, § 10A.

As used in the law of rape "consent" means consent of the will, and submission under the influence of fear or terror cannot amount to real consent. There must be an exercise of intelligence based on knowledge of its significance and moral quality and there must be a choice between resistance and assent. And if woman resists to the point where further resistance would be useless or until her resistance is overcome by force or violence, submission thereafter is not "consent".

See also **Acquiescence; Age of consent; Assent; Connivance; Informed consent.**

Consent decree. See **Decree.**

Consent judgment. See **Judgment.**

Express consent. That directly given, either *viva voce* or in writing. It is positive, direct, unequivocal consent, requiring no inference or implication to supply its meaning. Pacific Nat. Agricultural Credit Corporation v. Hagerman, 40 N.M. 116, 55 P.2d 667, 670.

Express or implied consent. Under motor vehicle liability insurance law providing that policy should cover any person responsible for operation of insured vehicle with insured's express or implied consent, words "express or implied consent" primarily modify not the word "operation", but the word "responsible", and imply possession of vehicle with consent of owner and responsibility to him.

Implied consent. That manifested by signs, actions, or facts, or by inaction or silence, which raise a presumption that the consent has been given. For example, when a corporation does business in a state it impliedly consents to be subject to the jurisdiction of that state's courts in the event of tortious conduct, even though it is not incorporated in that state.

Most every state has a statute implying the consent of one who drives upon its highways to submit to some type of scientific test or tests measuring the alcoholic content of the driver's blood. In addition to implying consent, these statutes usually provide that if the result of the test shows that the alcohol content exceeds a specified percentage, then a rebuttable presumption of intoxication arises.

Consentible lines /kənséntəbəl láynz/. See **Line.**

Consentientes et agentes pari pœna plectentur /kənsènshiyéntiyz èd əjéntiyz pǽriy píynə plèkténtər/. They who consent to an act, and they who do it, shall be visited with equal punishment.

Consentire matrimonio non possunt infra [ante] annos nubiles /kònsentáyriy mǽtrəmówniyow nòn pósənt ínfrə [ǽntiy] ǽnows nyúwbəliyz/. Parties cannot consent to marriage within the years of marriage [before the age of consent].

Consent judgment. See **Judgment.**

Consent jurisdiction. Parties may agree in advance to submit their controversy to a given forum, in which case the forum is the consent jurisdiction.

Consent of victim. The submission of a victim is generally no defense to a crime unless, as in the case of rape, the victim's consent negatives an element of the crime itself.

Consent rule. An entry of record by the defendant, confessing the lease, entry, and ouster by the plaintiff in an action of ejectment. A superseded instrument, in which a defendant in an action of ejectment specified for what purpose he intended to defend, and undertook to confess not only the fictitious lease, entry, and ouster, but that he was in possession.

Consent search. A search made by police after the subject of the search has consented; such consent, if freely and intelligently given, will validate a warrantless search.

Consent to be sued. Agreement in advance to be sued in a particular form. See **Cognovit judgment; Judgment** (*Confession of judgment*).

Consent to notice. In documents which treat of the requirement of notice, (*e.g.* lease) a party may consent to notice beforehand or agree that notice to some other person will satisfy the requirement of notice to him.

Consequence. The result following in natural sequence from an event which is adapted to produce, or to aid in producing, such result; the correlative of "cause". Board of Trustees of Firemen's Relief and Pension Fund for City of Tulsa v. Miller, 186 Okl. 586, 99 P.2d 146, 147. See also **Natural and probable consequences.**

Consequentæ non est consequentia /kònsəkwénshiyiy nón est kònsəkwénsh(iy)ə/. The consequence of a consequence exists not.

Consequential contempt. The ancient name for what is now known as "constructive" contempt of court. See **Contempt.**

Consequential damages. See **Damages.**

Conservator. A guardian; protector; preserver. Appointed by court to manage affairs of incompetent or to liquidate business. One who is appointed by a Court to manage the estate of a protected person. Uniform Probate Code § 1–201(6).

Conservators of the peace. Officers authorized to preserve and maintain the public peace. In England, these officers were locally elected by the people until the reign of Edward III, when their appointment was vested in the king. Their duties were to prevent and arrest for breaches of the peace, but they had no power to arraign and try the offender until about 1360, when this authority was given to them by act of parliament, and "then they acquired the more honorable appellation of justices of the peace". 1 Bl. Comm. 351.

Conserve. To save and protect from loss or damage.

Consider. To fix the mind on, with a view to careful examination; to examine; to inspect. To deliberate about and ponder over. To entertain or give heed to. See also **Considered.**

Considerable. Worthy of consideration; required to be observed. A "considerable" number, as of persons, does not necessarily mean a very great or any particular number of persons; the term "considerable" being merely relative.

Consideratio curiæ /kənsìdəréysh(iy)ow kyúriyiy/. The judgment of the court.

Consideration. The inducement to a contract. The cause, motive, price, or impelling influence which induces a contracting party to enter into a contract. The reason or material cause of a contract. Some right, interest, profit or benefit accruing to one party, or some forbearance, detriment, loss, or responsibility, given, suffered, or undertaken by the other. Richman v. Brookhaven Servicing Corp., 80 Misc.2d 563, 363 N.Y.S.2d 731, 733.

See also Adequate consideration; Failure of consideration; Fair and valuable consideration; Fair consideration; Good consideration; Inadequate consideration; Love and affection; Past consideration; Valuable consideration; Want of consideration.

Considerations are either *executed* or *executory; express* or *implied; good* or *valuable.* See definitions *infra.*

Concurrent consideration. One which arises at the same time or where the promises are simultaneous.

Continuing consideration. One consisting in acts or performances which must necessarily extend over a considerable period of time.

Equitable or moral considerations. Considerations which are devoid of efficacy in point of strict law, but are founded upon a moral duty, and may be made the basis of an express promise.

Executed or executory considerations. The former are acts done or values given before or at the time of making the contract; the latter are promises to give or do something in future.

Express or implied considerations. The former are those which are specifically stated in a deed, contract, or other instrument; the latter are those inferred or supposed by the law from the acts or situation of the parties. Express consideration is a consideration which is distinctly and specifically named in the written contract or in the oral agreement of the parties.

Good consideration. Such as is founded on natural duty and affection, or on a strong moral obligation. A consideration for love and affection entertained by and for one within degree recognized by law. Motives of natural duty, generosity, and prudence come under this class. The term is sometimes used in the sense of a consideration valid in point of law, and it then includes a valuable or sufficient as well as a meritorious consideration. Generally, however, *good* is used in antithesis to *valuable consideration (q.v.).*

Gratuitous consideration. One which is not founded upon any such loss, injury, or inconvenience to the party to whom it moves as to make it valid in law.

Illegal consideration. An act which if done, or a promise which if enforced, would be prejudicial to the public interest or contrary to law.

Implied considerations. See *Express or implied considerations, supra.*

Impossible consideration. One which cannot be performed.

Legal consideration. One recognized or permitted by the law as valid and lawful; as distinguished from such as are illegal or immoral. The term is also sometimes used as equivalent to "good" or "sufficient" consideration.

Meritorious consideration. See *Good consideration, supra.*

Moral considerations. See *Equitable or moral considerations, supra.*

Nominal consideration. One bearing no relation to the real value of the contract or article, as where a parcel of land is described in a deed as being sold for "one dollar," no actual consideration passing, or the real consideration being concealed. This term is also sometimes used as descriptive of an inflated or exaggerated value placed upon property for the purpose of an exchange.

Past consideration. An act done before the contract is made, which is ordinarily by itself no consideration for a promise. As to time, considerations may be of the past, present, or future. Those which are present or future will support a contract not void for other reasons.

Pecuniary consideration. A consideration for an act of forbearance which consists either in money presently passing or in money to be paid in the future, including a promise to pay a debt in full which otherwise would be released or diminished by bankruptcy or insolvency proceedings.

Sufficient consideration. One deemed by the law of sufficient value to support an ordinary contract between parties, or one sufficient to support the particular transaction.

Consideratum est per curiam /kənsìdəréydəm èst pər kyúriyəm/. (It is considered by the court.) The formal and ordinary commencement of a judgment.

Consideratur /kənsìdəréydər/. L. Lat. It is considered. Held to mean the same with *consideratum est.*

Considered. Deemed; determined; adjudged; reasonably regarded. For example, evidence may be said to have been "considered" when it has been reviewed by a court to determine whether any probative force should be given it.

Consign /kənsáyn/. To deliver goods to a carrier to be transmitted to a designated factor or agent. To deliver or transfer as a charge or trust. To commit, intrust, give in trust. To transfer from oneself to the care of another. To send or transmit goods to a merchant, factor, or agent for sale. To deposit with another to be sold, disposed of, or called for, whereby title does not pass until there is action of consignee indicating sale. See also **Consignment.**

Consignee /kənsàyníy/. One to whom a consignment is made. Person named in bill of lading to whom or to whose order the bill promises delivery. U.C.C. § 7–102(b).

In a commercial use, "consignee" means one to whom a consignment may be made, a person to whom goods are shipped for sale, or one to whom a carrier may lawfully make delivery in accordance with his contract of carriage, or one to whom goods are consigned, shipped, or otherwise transmitted. Power Transmission Equipment Corp. v. Beloit Corp., 55 Wis.2d 540, 201 N.W.2d 13, 15, 16.

Consignment. The act or process of consigning goods; the transportation of goods consigned; an article or collection of goods sent to a factor; goods or property sent, by the aid of a common carrier, from one person in one place to another person in another place; something consigned and shipped. Entrusting of goods to another to sell for the consignor. A bailment for sale.

The term "consignment", used in a commercial sense, ordinarily implies an agency and denotes that property is committed to the consignee for care or sale. Parks v. Atlanta News Agency, Inc., 115 Ga. App. 842, 156 S.E.2d 137, 140.

See also **Reconsignment.**

Consignment contract. Consignment of goods to another (consignee) for sale under agreement that consignee will pay consignor for any sold goods and will return any unsold goods. A bailment for sale.

Consignment sale. See **Consignment.**

Consignor /kənsáynər/. One who sends or makes a consignment; a shipper of goods. The person named in a bill of lading as the person from whom the goods have been received for shipment. U.C.C. § 7–102(c).

Consilia multorum quæruntur in magnis /kənsíliyə məltórəm kwirǽntər ìn mǽgnəs/. The counsels of many are required in great things.

Consiliarius /kənsìliyériyəs/. In the civil law, a counsellor, as distinguished from a pleader or advocate. An assistant judge. One who participates in the decisions.

Consilium /kənsíliyəm/. A day appointed to hear the counsel of both parties. A case set down for argument. It is commonly used for the day appointed for the argument of a demurrer, or errors assigned.

Consimili casu /kənsíməlay kéysyuw/. In old English law, a writ of entry, framed under the provisions of the statute Westminster 2, (13 Edw. I) c. 24, which lay for the benefit of the reversioner, where a tenant by the curtesy aliened in fee or for life. Many other new writs were framed under the provisions of this statute; but this particular writ was known emphatically by the title here defined. The writ is now practically obsolete. 3 Bl.Comm. 51.

Consist. To stand together, to be composed of or made up of. See **Consisting.**

Consistent. Having agreement with itself or something else; accordant; harmonious; congruous; compatible; compliable; not contradictory.

Consisting. Being composed or made up of. This word is not synonymous with "including", for the latter, when used in connection with a number of specified objects, always implies that there may be others which are not mentioned.

Consistor. A magistrate.

Consistorium /kònsəstóriyəm/. The state council of the Roman emperors.

Consistory. An assembly of cardinals convoked by the pope.

A tribunal (*prætorium*).

Consistory courts. In England, the courts of diocesan bishops held in their several cathedrals (before the bishop's chancellor, or commissary, who is the judge) for the trial of all ecclesiastical causes arising within their respective dioceses, and also for granting probates and administrations. From the sentence of these courts an appeal lies to the Provincial Court of the archbishop of each province respectively.

Consobrini /kònsəbráynay/. In the civil law, cousins-german, in general; brothers' and sisters' children, considered in their relation to each other.

Consociatio /kənsòws(h)iyéysh(iy)ow/. Lat. An association, fellowship, or partnership. Applied by some of the older writers to a corporation, and even to a nation considered as a body politic.

Consol. A bond that never matures but is redeemable on call.

Consolation /kònsəléyshən/. Comfort, contentment, ease, enjoyment, happiness, pleasure, satisfaction.

Consolato del mare /kònsowlátow dèl márey/. The name of a code of sea-laws, said to have been compiled by order of the kings of Arragon (or, according to other authorities, at Pisa or Barcelona) in the fourteenth century, which comprised the maritime ordinances of the Roman emperors, of France and Spain, and of the Italian commercial powers. This compilation exercised a considerable influence in the formation of European maritime law.

Consolidate. In a general sense, to unite or unify into one mass or body, as to consolidate several small school districts into a large district, or to consolidate various funds. In legislative usage, to consolidate two bills is to unite them into one. The term means something more than to rearrange or redivide.

To make solid or firm; to unite, compress, or pack together and form into a more compact mass, body, or system. To cause to become united and extinguished in a superior right or estate by both becoming vested in the same person. Swaim v. Smith, 174 Tenn. 688, 130 S.W.2d 116, 120.

See also **Commingle; Consolidation; Joinder; Merger.**

Consolidated appeal. If two or more persons are entitled to appeal from a judgment or order of a district court and their interests are such as to make joinder practicable, they may file a joint notice of appeal, or may join in appeal after filing separate timely notices of appeal, and they may thereafter proceed on appeal as a single appellant. Appeals may be consolidated by order of the court of appeals upon its own motion or upon motion of a party, or by stipulation of the parties to the several appeals. Fed.R.App.P. 3(b).

Consolidated balance sheets. See **Consolidated statements.**

Consolidated bonds. Issued to replace two or more existing issues; thus, consolidating debt into single issue.

Consolidated corporations. See **Consolidation of corporations.**

Consolidated laws. A compilation of all the laws of a State in force arranged according to subject matter. See **Code; Codification; Compilation.**

Consolidated mortgage. Unification of several outstanding mortgages.

Consolidated securities. An issue of securities sufficiently large to provide the funds to retire two or more outstanding issues of debt securities.

Consolidated statements. The financial reports for a group of affiliated corporations or enterprises, eliminating intercorporation debts and profits and showing minority stockholders' interests.

Consolidated tax returns. A procedure whereby certain affiliated corporations may file a single return, combine the tax transactions of each corporation, and arrive at a single income tax liability for the group. The election to file a consolidated return is usually binding on future years. I.R.C. §§ 1501–1505.

Consolidation. Act of consolidating, or the status of being consolidated. Unification of two or more actions. See **Consolidation of actions.**

In the *civil law*, the union of the usufruct with the estate out of which it issues, in the same person;

which happens when the usufructuary acquires the estate, or *vice versa*. In either case the usufruct is extinct.

In *ecclesiastical law,* the union of two or more benefices in one.

In *corporate law,* the combination of two or more corporations into a newly created corporation. Thus, A Corporation and B Corporation combine to form C Corporation. A consolidation may qualify as a non-taxable reorganization if certain conditions are satisfied. See also **Articles of consolidation; Consolidation of corporations; Merger.**

Consolidation of actions. The act or process of uniting several actions into one trial and judgment, by order of a court, where all the actions are between the same parties, pending in the same court, and involving substantially the same subject-matter, issues and defenses; or the court may order that one of the actions be tried, and the others decided without trial according to the judgment in the one selected.

When actions involving a common question of law or fact are pending before the court, it may order a joint hearing or trial of any or all the matters in issue in the actions; it may order all the actions consolidated; and it may make such orders concerning proceedings therein as may tend to avoid unnecessary costs or delay. Fed.R. Civil P. 42(a); New York C.P.L.R. § 602.

See also **Joinder** (*Joinder of claims*).

Consolidation of cases. See **Consolidation of actions.**

Consolidation of corporations. Occurs when two or more corporations are extinguished, and by the same process a new one is created, taking over the assets and assuming the liabilities of those passing out of existence. A unifying of two or more corporations into a single new corporation having the combined capital, franchises, and powers of all its constituents.

Merger distinguished. In a "merger", one corporation absorbs the other and remains in existence while the other is dissolved, and in a "consolidation" a new corporation is created and the consolidating corporations are extinguished. See also **Merger.**

Consonant statement. A prior declaration of a witness whose testimony has been attacked and whose credibility stands impeached, which the court will allow to be proved by the person to whom the declaration was made in order to support the credibility of the witness and which but for the existence of such impeachment would ordinarily be excluded as hearsay.

Consortio malorum me quoque malum facit /kənsórsh(iy)ow mǝlórǝm míy kwówkwiy mǽlǝm féysǝt/. The company of wicked men makes me also wicked.

Consortium /kǝnsórsh(iy)ǝm/. Conjugal fellowship of husband and wife, and the right of each to the company, society, co-operation, affection, and aid of the other in every conjugal relation. Roseberry v. Starkovich, 73 N.M. 211, 387 P.2d 321, 322; Nicholson v. Blauchette, 239 Md. 168, 210 A.2d 732, 740. Damages for loss of consortium are commonly sought in wrongful death actions, or when spouse has been seriously injured through negligence of another, or by spouse against third person alleging that he or she

has caused breaking-up of marriage. "Loss of consortium" means loss of society, affection, assistance and conjugal fellowship, and includes loss or impairment of sexual relations. Deems v. Western Maryland Ry. Co., 247 Md. 95, 231 A.2d 514, 517. Cause of action for "consortium" occasioned by injury to marriage partner, is a separate cause of action belonging to the spouse of the injured married partner and though derivative in the sense of being occasioned by injury to spouse, is a direct injury to the spouse who has lost the consortium. Peeples v. Sargent, 77 Wis.2d 612, 253 N.W.2d 459, 471. See also **Alienation of affections.**

In the civil law, a union of fortunes; a lawful Roman marriage. The joining of several persons as parties to one action.

In old English law, the term signified company or society, and in the language of pleading, as in the phrase *per quod consortium amisit,* it has substantially the same meaning, viz., the companionship or society of a wife. 3 Bl.Comm. 140.

Consortship. In maritime law, an agreement or stipulation between the owners of different vessels that they shall keep in company, mutually aid, instead of interfering with each other, in wrecking and salvage, whether earned by one vessel or both.

Conspicuous place. Within the meaning of a statute relating to the posting of notices, a "conspicuous place" means one which is reasonably calculated to impart the information in question.

Conspicuous term or **clause.** A term or clause is conspicuous when it is so written that a reasonable person against whom it is to operate ought to have noticed it. A printed heading in capitals (as: NON-NEGOTIABLE BILL OF LADING) is conspicuous. Language in the body of a form is "conspicuous" if it is in larger or other contrasting type or color. But in a telegram any stated term is "conspicuous". A term or clause is conspicuous when it is so written that a reasonable person against whom it is to operate ought to have noticed it. Whether a term or clause is "conspicuous" or not is for decision by the court. Uniform Consumer Credit Code, § 1.301(6); U.C.C. § 1–201(10).

Conspiracy /kǝnspírǝsiy/. A combination or confederacy between two or more persons formed for the purpose of committing, by their joint efforts, some unlawful or criminal act, or some act which is lawful in itself, but becomes unlawful when done by the concerted action of the conspirators, or for the purpose of using criminal or unlawful means to the commission of an act not in itself unlawful.

A person is guilty of conspiracy with another person or persons to commit a crime if with the purpose of promoting or facilitating its commission he: (a) agrees with such other person or persons that they or one or more of them will engage in conduct which constitutes such crime or an attempt or solicitation to commit such crime; or (b) agrees to aid such other person or persons in the planning or commission of such crime or of an attempt or solicitation to commit such crime. Model Penal Code, § 5.03.

Crime of conspiracy is distinct from the crime contemplated by the conspiracy (target crime), Com. v.

Dyer, 243 Mass. 472, 509, 138 N.E. 296, 314, cert. denied, 262 U.S. 751, 43 S.Ct. 700, 67 L.Ed. 1214. Some jurisdictions do not require an overt act as an element of the crime, *e.g.* Com. v. Harris, 232 Mass. 588, 122 N.E. 749.

A conspiracy may be a continuing one; actors may drop out, and others drop in; the details of operation may change from time to time; the members need not know each other or the part played by others; a member need not know all the details of the plan or the operations; he must, however, know the purpose of the conspiracy and agree to become a party to a plan to effectuate that purpose. Craig v. U. S., C.C. A.Cal., 81 F.2d 816, 822.

See also **Combination in restraint of trade; Confederacy; Wharton Rule.**

Civil conspiracy. The essence of a "civil conspiracy" is a concert or combination to defraud or cause other injury to person or property, which results in damage to the person or property of plaintiff. See also **Civil conspiracy.**

Overthrow of government. See **Sedition.**

Seditions conspiracy. See **Sedition.**

Conspiracy in restraint of trade. Term which describes all forms of illegal agreements such as boycotts, price fixing, etc., which have as their object interference with free flow of commerce and trade. See **Clayton Acts; Sherman Antitrust Act.**

Conspirators. Persons partaking in conspiracy. See **Conspiracy.**

Conspire. To engage in conspiracy. Term carries with it the idea of agreement, concurrence and combination, and hence is inapplicable to a single person or thing, and one cannot agree or conspire with another who does not agree or conspire with him. See **Conspiracy.**

Constable. An officer of a municipal corporation (usually elected) whose duties are similar to those of the sheriff, though his powers are less and his jurisdiction smaller. He is to preserve the public peace, execute the process of magistrates' courts, and of some other tribunals, serve writs, attend the sessions of the criminal courts, have the custody of juries, and discharge other functions sometimes assigned to him by the local law or by statute. Powers and duties of constables have generally been replaced by sheriffs.

In English law, public civil officer, whose proper and general duty is to keep the peace within his district, though he is frequently charged with additional duties. 1 Bl.Comm. 356. There were formerly "high," "petty," and "special" constables. In England, the functions of these special constables have been taken over by police forces.

In Medieval law, high functionary under the French and English kings, the dignity and importance of whose office was second only to that of the monarch. He was in general the leader of the royal armies, and had cognizance of all matters pertaining to war and arms, exercising both civil and military jurisdiction. He was also charged with the conservation of the peace of the nation. Thus there was a "Constable of France" and a "Lord High Constable of England." Rich v. Industrial Commission, 80 Utah 511, 15 P.2d 641, 644.

Constablewick /kánstəbəlwìk/. In English law, the territorial jurisdiction of a constable; as bailiwick is of a bailiff or sheriff.

Constabularius /kənstæbyəlériyəs/. An officer of horse; an officer having charge of foot or horse; a naval commander; an officer having charge of military affairs generally. In England his power was early diminished and restricted to those duties which related to the preservation of the king's peace. The office is now abolished except as a matter of ceremony.

Constant. Fixed or invariable; uniform. Continually recurring, regular, steady. Pfisterer v. Key, 218 Ind. 521, 33 N.E.2d 330, 335.

Constantly. In a constant manner; uniformly; continuously.

Constat /kónstət/°æt/. It is clear or evident; it appears; it is certain; there is no doubt. *Non constat,* it does not appear.

In England, a certificate which the clerk of the pipe and auditors of the exchequer made, at the request of any person who intended to plead or move in that court, for the discharge of anything. The effect of it was the certifying what appears *(constat)* upon record, touching the matter in question. An exemplification under the great seal of the enrolment of letters patent.

A certificate by an officer that certain matters therein stated appear of record.

Constat d'huissier /kònstá dwìysyéy/. In French law, an affidavit made by a *huissier,* setting forth the appearance, form, quality, color, etc., of any article upon which a suit depends.

Constate /kənstéyt/. To establish, constitute, or ordain.

"*Constating instruments*" of a corporation are its charter, organic law, or the grant of powers to it.

Constituency. The inhabitants of an electoral district.

Constituent. He who gives authority to another to act for him.

The term is used as a correlative to "attorney," to denote one who constitutes another his agent or invests the other with authority to act for him.

It is also used in the language of politics as a correlative to "representative," the constituents of a legislator being those whom he represents and whose interests he is to care for in public affairs; usually the electors of his district.

Constituent elements. The elements of a crime, tort or other type of action. Those matters which must be proved to sustain a cause of action because they constitute the action or crime.

Constituere /kònstətyúwəriy/. Lat. To appoint, constitute, establish, ordain, or undertake. Used principally in ancient powers of attorney, and now supplanted by the English word "constitute."

Constituimus /kònstətúwəməs/. A Latin term, signifying *we constitute* or *appoint.*

Constituted authorities. Officers properly appointed under the constitution for the government of the people.

Constitutio /kònstət(y)úwsh(iy)ow/. In the civil law, an imperial ordinance, decree, or constitution, distinguished from *Lex, Senatus-Consultum,* and other kinds of law and having its effect from the sole will of the emperor. An establishment or settlement. Used of controversies settled by the parties without a trial. A sum paid according to agreement.

In old English law, an ordinance or statute. A provision of a statute.

Constitutio dotis /kònstət(y)úwsh(iy)ow dówdəs/. Establishment of dower.

Constitution. The organic and fundamental law of a nation or state, which may be written or unwritten, establishing the character and conception of its government, laying the basic principles to which its internal life is to be conformed, organizing the government, and regulating, distributing, and limiting the functions of its different departments, and prescribing the extent and manner of the exercise of sovereign powers. A charter of government deriving its whole authority from the governed. The written instrument agreed upon by the people of the Union (*e.g.* United States Constitution) or of a particular state, as the absolute rule of action and decision for all departments (*i.e.* branches) and officers of the government in respect to all the points covered by it, which must control until it shall be changed by the authority which established it (*i.e.* by amendment), and in opposition to which any act or ordinance of any such department or officer is null and void. The full text of the U.S. Constitution appears at the end of this dictionary.

In a more general sense, any fundamental or important law or edict; as the Novel Constitutions of Justinian; the Constitutions of Clarendon.

Constitutional. Consistent with the constitution; authorized by the constitution; not conflicting with any provision of the constitution or fundamental law of the state. Dependent upon a constitution, or secured or regulated by a constitution; as "constitutional monarchy," "constitutional rights."

Constitutional alcalde. A person of official status under Mexican law corresponding in many respects in dignity and authority to a justice of the peace under the American system of government. Tietzel v. Southwestern Const. Co., 48 N.M. 567, 154 P.2d 238, 242.

Constitutional convention. A duly constituted assembly of delegates or representatives of the people of a state or nation for the purpose of framing, revising, or amending its constitution. Art. V of U.S. Const. provides that a Constitutional Convention may be called on application of the Legislatures of two-thirds of the states.

Constitutional court. A court named or described and expressly protected by Constitution, or recognized by name or definite description in Constitution (*e.g.* Supreme Court, as provided for in Art. III, Sec. 1 of U.S.Const.) in contrast to legislatively created courts. Commonly referred to as "Article III" courts in reference to U.S.Const.

Constitutional freedom. Generic term to describe the basic freedoms guaranteed by the Constitution such as the First Amendment freedoms of religion, speech, press and assembly together with protection under due process clause of the 14th Amendment. See also **Bill of rights, Constitutional liberty or freedom.**

Constitutional homestead. A special interest in real estate which protects it from attachment, created by constitution and available to the head of the family. Ringer v. Bryne, 183 Okl. 46, 80 P.2d 212, 214.

Constitutional law. (1) That branch of the public law of a nation or state which treats of the organization, powers and frame of government, the distribution of political and governmental authorities and functions, the fundamental principles which are to regulate the relations of government and citizen, and which prescribes generally the plan and method according to which the public affairs of the nation or state are to be administered. (2) That department of the science of law which treats of constitutions, their establishment, construction, and interpretation, and of the validity of legal enactments as tested by the criterion of conformity to the fundamental law. (3) A constitutional law is one which is consonant to, and agrees with, the constitution; one which is not in violation of any provision of the constitution of the particular state.

Constitutional liberty or freedom. Such freedom as is enjoyed by the citizens of a country or state under the protection of its constitution. The aggregate of those personal, civil, and political rights of the individual which are guaranteed by the constitution and secured against invasion by the government or any of its agencies. See also **Constitutional freedom.**

Constitutional limitations. Those provisions of a constitution which restrict the legislature in the types of laws which it may enact.

Constitutional office. A public position or office which is created by a constitution as distinguished from a statutory office which is created by an enactment of the legislature.

Constitutional officer. A governmental official whose office was created by a constitution; as contrasted with an officer whose position has been created by the legislature. One whose tenure and term of office are fixed and defined by the constitution, as distinguished from the incumbents of offices created by legislature.

Constitutional powers. See **Power.**

Constitutional protections. Those basic protections guaranteed by the Constitution such as due process, equal protection and the fundamental protections of the First Amendment, such as those touching speech, press and religion. See **Bill of rights; Constitutional freedom.**

Constitutional questions. Those legal issues which require an interpretation of the Constitution for their resolution as distinguished from those of a statutory nature.

Constitutional right. A right guaranteed to the citizens by the Constitution and so guaranteed as to prevent legislative interference therewith. See also **Constitutional freedom; Constitutional liberty or freedom; Constitutional protections.**

Constitutional tort. See **Tort.**

Constitutiones /kònstət(y)ùwshiyówniyz/. Laws promulgated, *i.e.*, enacted, by the Roman Emperor. They were of various kinds, namely, the following: (1) *Edicta;* (2) *decreta;* (3) *rescripta,* called also *"epistolæ."* Sometimes they were general, and intended to form a precedent for other like cases; at other times they were special, particular, or individual *(personales),* and not intended to form a precedent. The emperor had this power of irresponsible enactment by virtue of a certain *lex regia,* whereby he was made the fountain of justice and of mercy.

Constitutiones tempore posteriores potiores sunt his quæ ipsas præcesserunt /kònstət(y)ùwshiyówniyz témpəriy pəstìriyóriyz sánt háys kwìy ípsəs prèsəsérənt/. Later laws prevail over those which preceded them.

Constitutions of Clarendon. See **Clarendon, Constitutions of.**

Constitutions of the Forest. See **Charta** (*Charta de foresta*).

Constitutor /kónstətyùwdər/. In the civil law, one who, by a simple agreement, becomes responsible for the payment of another's debt.

Constitutum /kònstət(y)úwdəm/. In the civil law, an agreement to pay a subsisting debt which exists without any stipulation, whether of the promisor or another party. It differs from a stipulation in that it must be for an existing debt.

A day appointed for any purpose. A form of appeal.

Constitutum esse eam domum unicuique nostrum debere existimari, ubi quisque sedes et tabulas haberet, suarumque rerum constitutionem fecisset /kònst(y)úwdəm ésiy íyəm dówməm yùwnək(yuw)áykwiy nóstrəm dəbíriy əgzìstəméray, yúwbay kwískwiy síydiyz èt tǽbyələs həbírət, syùwerəmkwiy rírəm kònstət(y)ùwshiyównəm fəsísət/. It is settled that that is to be considered the home of each one of us where he may have his habitation and account-books, and where he may have made an establishment of his business.

Constraint. Act of constraining, *i.e.* state of being restrained or restricted.

Construct. To build; erect; put together; make ready for use. To adjust and join materials, or parts of, so as to form a permanent whole. To put together constituent parts of something in their proper place and order. "Construct" is distinguishable from "maintain," which means to keep up, to keep from change, to preserve. See also **Construction.**

Constructio legis non facit injuriam /kənstráksh(iy)ow líyjəs nòn féysəd ənjúriyəm/. The construction of the law (a construction made by the law) works no injury. The law will make such a construction of an instrument as not to injure a party.

Construction. The process, or the art, of determining the sense, real meaning, or proper explanation of obscure or ambiguous terms or provisions in a statute, written instrument, or oral agreement, or the application of such subject to the case in question, by reasoning in the light derived from extraneous connected circumstances or laws or writings bearing upon the same or a connected matter, or by seeking and applying the probable aim and purpose of the provision. Drawing conclusions respecting subjects that lie beyond the direct expression of the term.

The process of bringing together and correlating a number of independent entities, so as to form a definite entity.

The creation of something new, as distinguished from the repair or improvement of something already existing. The act of fitting an object for use or occupation in the usual way, and for some distinct purpose. See **Construct.**

See also Broad interpretation; Comparative interpretation; Four corners rule; Interpretation; Last antecedent rule; Literal construction; Statutory construction; Strict consideration.

Equitable construction. A construction of a law, rule, or remedy which has regard more to the equities of the particular transaction or state of affairs involved than to the strict application of the rule or remedy; that is, a liberal and extensive construction, as opposed to a literal and restrictive. See also *Liberal construction* below.

Strict and liberal construction. Strict (or literal) construction is construction of a statute or other instrument according to its letter, which recognizes nothing that is not expressed, takes the language used in its exact and technical meaning, and admits no equitable considerations or implications.

Liberal (or equitable) construction, on the other hand, expands the meaning of the statute to meet cases which are clearly within the spirit or reason of the law, or within the evil which it was designed to remedy, provided such an interpretation is not inconsistent with the language used. It resolves all reasonable doubts in favor of the applicability of the statute to the particular case. It means, not that the words should be forced out of their natural meaning, but simply that they should receive a fair and reasonable interpretation with respect to the objects and purposes of the instrument. See also *Equitable construction* above.

Construction contract. Type of contract in which plans and specifications for construction are made a part of the contract itself and commonly it is secured by performance and payment bonds to protect both subcontractors and party for whom building is being constructed.

Construction of will. Interpretation which is given to provisions of will and the law to be applied therein when there is conflict as to the meaning intended by the deceased. Such function is commonly performed by Probate court.

Constructive. That which is established by the mind of the law in its act of construing facts, conduct, circumstances, or instruments. That which has not the character assigned to it in its own essential nature, but acquires such character in consequence of the way in which it is regarded by a rule or policy of law; hence, inferred, implied, or made out by legal interpretation; the word "legal" being sometimes used here in lieu of "constructive."

As to constructive Bailment; Breaking; Contempt; Conversion; Delivery; Escape; Fraud; Larceny; Seisen; and Treason, see those titles.

Constructive adverse possession. Type of adverse possession which, under certain statutes, is characterized by payment of taxes under color of right, as distinguished from actual adverse possession in which the adverse claimant is in actual possession.

Constructive assent. An assent or consent imputed to a party from a construction or interpretation of his conduct; as distinguished from one which he actually expresses.

Constructive authority. Authority inferred or assumed to have been given because of the grant of some other antecedent authority.

Constructive breaking into a house. A breaking made out by construction of law. As where a burglar gains an entry into a house by threats, fraud, or conspiracy.

Constructive condition. Conditions in contracts which are neither expressed nor implied by the words of the contract but are imposed by law to meet the ends of justice. Restatement of Contracts, § 252. The cooperation of the parties to a contract is a constructive condition. In negotiable instruments, a promise or order otherwise unconditional is not made conditional by the fact that the instrument is subject to a constructive condition. U.C.C. § 3–105(1).

Constructive contract. A species of contracts which arise, not from the intent of the parties, but from the operation of law to avoid an injustice. These are sometimes referred to as quasi contracts or contracts implied in law as contrasted with contracts implied in fact which are real contracts expressing the intent of the parties by conduct rather than by words. Power-Matics Inc. v. Ligotti, 79 N.J.Super. 294, 191 A.2d 483, 489. An obligation created by law for reasons of justice without regard to expressions of assent by either words or acts. Power-Matics, Inc. v. Ligotti, 79 N.J.Super. 294, 191 A.2d 483, 489. See also **Contract** (*Quasi contract*).

Constructive desertion. Occurs when one spouse, through misconduct, forces the other to abandon the marital abode. Grollman v. Grollman, D.C.App., 220 A.2d 330, 332. If a spouse is forced to leave the home because of the other's conduct, the former has been constructively deserted.

Constructive dividend. If a stockholder has an unqualified right to a dividend, such a dividend is called constructive for tax purposes though he does not actually receive it because it is subject to his demand and the corporation has set it aside for this purpose. Clark v. C. I. R., C.A.9, 266 F.2d 698.

Constructive eviction. Such arises when landlord, while not actually depriving tenant of possession, has done or suffered some act by which premises are rendered untenantable. Net Realty Holding Trust v. Nelson, 33 Conn.Sup. 22, 358 A.2d 365, 367. Any disturbance of the tenant's possession by the landlord whereby the premises are rendered unfit or unsuitable for occupancy in whole or in substantial part for the purposes for which they were leased amounts to a constructive eviction, if the tenant so elects and surrenders his possession. For example, if a tenant vacates the rental property because of the absence of heat or water, he has been constructively evicted.

As the term is used with reference to breach of the covenants of warranty and of quiet enjoyment, it means the inability of the purchaser to obtain possession by reason of a paramount outstanding title.

Constructive filing. The filing of a document with a person who is the only one available to receive it, though he is not the designated person to receive it, is a constructive filing. People v. Spencer, 193 Cal. App.2d 13, 13 Cal.Rptr. 881, 883.

Constructive force. As regards robbery, a taking by force is the gist of the crime, but the force may be either actual or constructive. Constructive force is anything which produces fear sufficient to suspend the power of resistance and prevent the free exercise of the will. Actual force is applied to the body; constructive is by threatening words or gestures and operates on the mind.

Constructive fraud. Exists where conduct, though not actually fraudulent, has all actual consequences and all legal effects of actual fraud. Agair Inc. v. Shaeffer, 232 Cal.App.2d 513, 42 Cal.Rptr. 883, 886. Breach of legal or equitable duty which, irrespective of moral guilt, is declared by law to be fraudulent because of its tendency to deceive others or violate confidence. Daves v. Lawyers Sur. Corp., Tex.Civ. App., 459 S.W.2d 655, 657. See also **Fraud.**

Constructive intent. Exists where one should have reasonably expected or anticipated a particular result; *e.g.* when one does an act which is wilful and wanton resulting in injury to another, it can be said that he constructively intended the harm. Ballew v. Asheville & E. T. R. Co., 186 N.C. 704, 120 S.E. 334.

Constructive knowledge. If one by exercise of reasonable care would have known a fact, he is deemed to have had constructive knowledge of such fact; *e.g.* matters of public record. Attoe v. State Farm Mutual Auto. Ins. Co., 36 Wis.2d 539, 153 N.W.2d 575, 579. See also **Constructive notice.**

Constructive loss. One resulting from such injuries to the property, without its destruction, as render it valueless to the assured or prevent its restoration to the original condition except at a cost exceeding its value. See also **Constructive total loss.**

Constructive malice. That type of malice which the law infers from the doing of an evil act; sometimes known as implied malice.

Constructive notice. Such notice as is implied or imputed by law, as in the case of notice of documents which have been recorded in the appropriate registry of deeds or probate. Notice with which a person is charged by reason of the notorious nature of the thing to be noticed, as contrasted with actual notice of such thing.

Constructive ownership. See **Attribution.**

Constructive payment. If one charges himself with a payment and the payee has a right to demand it, it can be considered a constructive as contrasted with an actual payment; *e.g.* a check which is mailed in payment though not yet cashed is a constructive payment.

Constructive possession. A person has constructive possession of property if he has power to control and intent to control such item. Com. v. Stephens, 231 Pa.Super. 481, 331 A.2d 719, 723. Being in a position to exercise dominion or control over a thing. U. S. v. DiNovo, C.A.Ind., 523 F.2d 197, 201.

Constructive receipt of income. As applied to tax laws, is taxable income which is unqualifiedly subject to the demand of taxpayer on cash receipts and disbursements method of accounting, whether or not such income has actually been received in cash. Gounares Bros. & Co. v. U. S., D.C.Ala., 185 F.Supp. 794, 798. Under this doctrine, income which is subject to unfettered command of taxpayer and which he is free to enjoy at his option is taxed to him, despite fact that he has exercised his own choice to turn his back on that income and the doctrine is one by which form of transaction is ignored in order to get to its substance. Pittsburgh-Des Moines Steel Co. v. U. S., D.C.Pa., 360 F.Supp. 597, 599. An example would be accrued interest on a savings account. Under the constructive receipt of income concept, such interest will be taxed to a depositor in the year it is available rather than the year actually withdrawn. The fact that the depositor uses the cash basis of accounting for tax purposes makes no difference.

Constructive service of process. Form of service of process other than actual service; *e.g.* publication in newspaper is constructive service.

Constructive taking. A phrase used in the law to characterize an act not amounting to an actual appropriation of chattels, but which shows an intention to convert them to his use; as if a person intrusted with the possession of goods deals with them contrary to the orders of the owner. With respect to constructive condemnation, see **Condemnation** (*Inverse condemnation*).

Constructive total loss. In insurance, exists whenever insured item of property has lost its total usefulness and insured is deprived of its benefit totally. See also **Constructive loss.**

Constructive trust. Trust created by operation of law against one who by actual or constructive fraud, by duress or by abuse of confidence, or by commission of wrong, or by any form of unconscionable conduct, or other questionable means, has obtained or holds legal right to property which he should not, in equity and good conscience, hold and enjoy. Davis v. Howard, 19 Or.App. 310, 527 P.2d 422, 424.

A constructive trust is a relationship with respect to property subjecting the person by whom the title to the property is held to an equitable duty to convey it to another on the ground that his acquisition or retention of the property is wrongful and that he would be unjustly enriched if he were permitted to retain the property. Restatement, Second, Trusts § 1(e).

Constructive trust ex delicto. A constructive trust which is imposed on property which a fiduciary has claimed or received in violation of his duties.

Constructive willfulness. Intentional disregard of a known duty necessary to the safety of a person, and an entire absence of care for the life, the person, or the property of others, such as exhibits a conscious indifference to consequences.

Construe. To put together; to arrange or marshal the words of an instrument. To ascertain the meaning of language by a process of arrangement and inference. See **Construction.**

Constuprate /kónst(y)əpreyt/. To ravish, debauch, violate, rape.

Consuetudinarius /kònswiytyùwdənériyəs/. In ecclesiastical law, a ritual or book, containing the rites and forms of divine offices or the customs of abbeys and monasteries.

Consuetudinary law /kònswətyúwdən(ə)ry ló/. Customary law. Law derived by oral tradition from a remote antiquity.

Consuetudines /kònswətyúwdəniyz/. In old English law, customs. Thus, *consuetudines et assisa forestæ,* the customs and assise of the forest.

Consuetudines feudorum /kònswətyúwdəniyz fyuwdórəm/. (Lat. feudal customs.) A compilation of the law of feuds or fiefs in Lombardy, made A.D. 1170. It is of great authority.

Consuetudinibus et serviciis /kònswətyùwdínəbəs et sərvíshiyəs/. In old English law, a writ of right close, which lay against a tenant who deforced his lord of the rent or service due to him.

Consuetudo /kònswətyúwdow/. Lat. A custom; an established usage or practice; duties; taxes.

Consuetudo anglicana /kònswətyúwdow ængləkéynə/. The custom of England; the ancient common law, as distinguished from *lex,* the Roman or civil law.

Consuetudo contra rationem introducta potius usurpatio quam consuetudo appellari debet /kònswətyúwdow kóntrə ræshiyównəm intrədáktə pówsh(iy)əs yùwsərpéysh(iy)ow kwæm kònswətyúwdow æpəléray débət/. A custom introduced against reason ought rather to be called a "usurpation" than a "custom."

Consuetudo curiæ /kònswətyúwdow kyúriyiy/. The custom or practice of a court.

Consuetudo debet esse certa; nam incerta pro nulla habetur /kònswətyúwdow débəd ésiy sərdə, næm ìnsárdə pròw náləs heybéntər/. A custom should be certain; for an uncertain custom is considered null.

Consuetudo est altera lex /kònswətyúwdow èst æltərə léks/. Custom is another law.

Consuetudo est optimus interpres legum /kònswətyúwdow èst óptəməs intárpriyz líygəm/. Custom is the best expounder of the laws.

Consuetudo et communis assuetudo vincit legem non scriptam, si sit specialis; et interpretatur legem scriptam, si lex sit generalis /kònswətyúwdow èt kəmyúwnəs æswətyúwdow vínsət líyjəm nòn skríptəs, sày sít spèshiyéyləs; ed intàrprətéydər líyjəm skríptəm, sày sít jènəréyləs/. Custom and common usage overcomes the unwritten law, if it be special; and interprets the written law, if the law be general.

Consuetudo ex certa causa rationabili usitata privat communem legem /kònswətyúwdow èt sə́rdə kósa ræ̀shənéybəlay yúwzətéydə práyvət kəmyúwnəm líyjəm/. A custom, grounded on a certain and reasonable cause, supersedes the common law.

Consuetudo licet sit magnæ auctoritatis, nunquam tamen, præjudicat manifestæ veritati /kònswətyúwdow, líısət sìt mǽgniy oktòhrətéydəs, nə́ŋkwəm tǽmen prəjúwdəkət mæ̀nəféstiy vèhrətéyday/. A custom, though it be of great authority, should never prejudice manifest truth.

Consuetudo loci observanda est /kònswətyúwdow lówsay òbzərvǽndə ést/. The custom of a place is to be observed.

Consuetudo manerii et loci observanda est /kònswətyúwdow mənáriyay èt lówsay òbzərvǽndə èst/. A custom of a manor and place is to be observed.

Consuetudo mercatorum /kònswətyúwdow mərkətórəm/. Lat. The custom of merchants, the same with *lex mercatoria.*

Consuetudo neque injuriâ oriri neque tolli potest /kònswətyúwdow nékwiy ənjúriyə əráyray nékwiy tólay pówdəst/. Custom can neither arise from nor be taken away by injury.

Consuetudo non trahitur in consequentiam /kònswətyúwdow nòn tréy(h)ədər ən kònsəkwénsh(iy)əm/. Custom is not drawn into consequence.

Consuetudo præscripta et legitima vincit legem /kònswətyúwdow prəskríptə ət ləjídəmə vínsət líyjəm/. A prescriptive and lawful custom overcomes the law.

Consuetudo regni angliæ est lex angliæ /kònswətyúwdow régnay ǽŋgliyiy èst léks ǽŋgliyiy/. The custom of the kingdom of England is the law of England. 2 Bl.Comm. 422.

Consuetudo semel reprobata non potest amplius induci /kònswətyúwdow sémə̀l rèprowbéydə nòn pówdəst ǽmpliyəs ind(y)úwsay/. A custom once disallowed cannot be again brought forward [or relied on].

Consuetudo tollit communem legem /kònswətyúwdow tólət kəmyúwnəm líyjəm/. Custom takes away the common law.

Consuetudo vincit communem legem /kònswətyúwdow vínsət kəmyúwnəm líyjəm/. Custom overrules common law.

Consuetudo volentes ducit, lex nolentes trahit /kònswətyúwdow vəléntiyz d(y)úwsət, léks nowléntiyz tréy(h)ət/. Custom leads the willing, law compels [drags] the unwilling.

Consul /kónsəl/. An officer of a commercial character, appointed by the different nations to watch over the mercantile and tourist interests of the appointing nation and of its subjects in foreign countries. There are usually a number of consuls in every maritime country, and they are usually subject to a chief consul, who is called a "consul general." A public official residing in a foreign country responsible for developing and protecting the economic interests of his government and looking after the welfare of his government's citizens who may be traveling or residing within his jurisdiction. United States consuls form a part of the Foreign Service and are of various grades: consul general, consul, vice consul, and consular agent.

In old English law, a title of an earl.

In Roman law, during the republic, the name "consul" was given to the chief executive magistrate, two of whom were chosen annually. The office was continued under the empire, but its powers and prerogatives were greatly reduced. The name is supposed to have been derived from *consulo,* to consult, because these officers consulted with the senate on administrative measures.

Consular courts /kóns(y)ələr kórts/. Courts held by the consuls of one country, within the territory of another, under authority given by treaty, for the settlement of civil cases. In some instances they had also a criminal jurisdiction, but in this respect were subject to review by the courts of the home government. See 22 U.S.C.A. § 141. The last of the United States consular courts (Morocco) was abolished in 1956.

Consular invoice. Invoice used in foreign trade signed by consul of the country for which the shipment is destined. Such facilitates entry through destination country in that quantity, value, etc. of shipment has been pre-verified.

Consular marriage. A marriage solemnized in a foreign country by a consul or diplomatic agent of the U.S. and held to be valid in some jurisdictions.

Consulate. The residence or headquarters of a foreign consul.

Consul general. Consular officer of highest grade.

Consulta ecclesia /kənsáltə əklíyziyə/. In ecclesiastical law, a church full or provided for.

Consultary response /kənsáltəriy rəspóns/kònsəltériy°/. The opinion of a court of law on a special case.

Consultation. Act of consulting or conferring; *e.g.* patient with doctor; client with lawyer. Deliberation of persons on some subject. A conference between the counsel engaged in a case, to discuss its questions or arrange the method of conducting it.

An old writ whereby a cause which had been wrongfully removed by prohibition out of an ecclesiastical court to a temporal court was returned to the ecclesiastical court.

Consulto /kənsáltow/. Lat. In the civil law, designedly; intentionally.

Consumer /kəns(y)úwmər/. One who consumes. Individuals who purchase, use, maintain, and dispose of products and services. A member of that broad class of people who are affected by pricing policies, financing practices, quality of goods and services, credit reporting, debt collection, and other trade practices for which state and federal consumer protection laws are enacted. Consumers are to be distinguished from manufacturers (who produce goods), and wholesalers or retailers (who sell goods). See also **Purchaser.**

A buyer (other than for purposes of resale) of any consumer product, any person to whom such product is transferred during the duration of an implied or written warranty (or service contract) applicable to the product, and any other person who is entitled by the terms of such warranty (or service contract) or under applicable State law to enforce against the warrantor (or service contractor) the obligations of the warranty (or service contract). 15 U.S.C.A. § 2301.

Consumer advocate. One who is given to presenting the position of the consumer or to representing him in judicial, administrative, or legislative proceedings. See also **Omsbudsman.**

Consumer credit. Short term loans to individuals for purchase of consumer goods and services.

Consumer Credit Code. A uniform law, adopted by several states, with intent and purpose similar to that of the federal Consumer Credit Protection Act *(q.v.).*

Consumer Credit Protection Act. Federal act (commonly referred to as the Truth-in-Lending Act) enacted to safeguard the consumer in connection with the utilization of credit by requiring full disclosure of the terms and conditions of finance charges in credit transactions or in offers to extend credit, by restricting the garnishment of wages, and by regulating the use of credit cards. In addition to federal and state Truth-in-Lending Acts, several states also require by statute that consumer-loan agreements be written in plain, simplified language. See also Annual percentage rate; Equal Credit Opportunity Act; Fair Credit Billing Act; Fair Credit Reporting Acts; Truth-in-Lending Act; Uniform Consumer Credit Code.

Consumer credit sale. Any sale with respect to which consumer credit is extended or arranged by the seller. The term includes any contract in the form of a bailment or lease if the bailee or lessee contracts to pay as compensation for use a sum substantially equivalent to or in excess of the aggregate value of the property and services involved and it is agreed that the bailee or lessee will become, or for no other or for a nominal consideration has the option to become, the owner of the property upon full compliance with his obligations under the contract.

Consumer credit transaction. Credit offered or extended to a natural person, in which the money, property or service which is the subject of the transaction is primarily for personal, family, household or agricultural purposes and for which either a finance charge is or may be imposed or which, pursuant to an agreement, is or may be payable in more than four installments. "Consumer loan" is one type of "consumer credit".

Consumer debt. Debt incurred by an individual primarily for a personal, family, or household purpose. Bankruptcy Act (1978), § 101(7).

Consumer goods. Goods which are used or bought for use primarily for personal, family or household purposes. U.C.C. § 9–109(1). Such goods are not intended for resale or further use in the production of other products. Contrasted with capital goods. See also **Consumer product.**

Consumer lease. Lease of consumer goods; also may be applied to lease of dwelling as contrasted with commercial lease. Disclosure of terms in certain types of consumer leases is governed by Federal Consumer Leasing Act.

Consumer Price Index. A price index computed and issued monthly by the Bureau of Labor Statistics of the U.S. Department of Labor. The index attempts to track the price level of a group of goods and services purchased by the average consumer. Widely used to measure changes in cost of maintaining given standard of living.

Consumer product. Any tangible personal property which is distributed in commerce and which is normally used for personal, family, or household purposes (including any such property intended to be attached to or installed in any real property without regard to whether it is so attached or installed). 15 U.S.C.A. § 2301. See also **Consumer goods.**

Consumer Product Safety Commission. The Consumer Product Safety Commission is an independent federal regulatory agency established by act of October 27, 1972 (86 Stat. 1207) to administer and implement the Consumer Product Safety Act. The Commission has primary responsibility for establishing mandatory product safety standards, where appropriate, to reduce the unreasonable risk of injury to consumers from consumer products. In addition it has authority to ban hazardous consumer products. The Consumer Product Safety Act also authorizes the Commission to conduct extensive research on consumer product standards, engage in broad consumer and industry information and education programs, and establish a comprehensive Injury Information Clearinghouse.

Consumer report. Document issued by private or governmental body relative to quality of certain products, their dangers and their attributes. Document issued as to certain companies and their practices.

Consumer's cooperative. Group which purchases consumer goods for resale to its members, thus reducing costs by eliminating the middleman's profit.

Consummate /kənsámət/, *adj.* Completed; as distinguished from *initiate,* or that which is merely begun. The husband of a woman seised of an estate of inheritance becomes, by the birth of a child, tenant by the curtesy *initiate,* and may do many acts to charge the lands, but his estate is not *consummate* till the death of the wife. 2 Bl.Comm. 126, 128.

Consummate /kónsəmèyt/, *v.* To finish by completing what was intended; bring or carry to utmost point or degree; carry or bring to completion; finish; perfect; fulfill; achieve. See also **Consummation.**

Consummate lien. A term which may be used to describe the lien of a judgment when a motion for a new trial has been denied (the lien having theretofore been merely inchoate).

Consummation /kònsəméyshən/. The completion of a thing; the completion of a marriage by cohabitation (*i.e.* sexual intercourse) between spouses.

Consumption. Act or process of consuming; waste; decay; destruction. Using up of anything, as food, heat, or time.

Contagious disease. One capable of being transmitted by mediate or immediate contact.

Containerization. An efficient and economical method of handling and transporting cargo wherein a means is provided for transferring cargo from one form of transportation, such as ship, to another form of transportation, such as rail or truck without the necessity of loading and unloading the individual items each time the mode of transport changes. Sea-Land Service, Inc. v. County of Alameda, 12 Cal.3d 772, 117 Cal.Rptr. 448, 451, 528 P.2d 56.

Contamination. Condition of impurity resulting from mixture or contact with foreign substance. American Cas. Co. of Reading, Pa. v. Myrick, C.A.Tex., 304 F.2d 179, 183. See also **Adulteration.**

Contango /kòntǽŋgow/. A double bargain, consisting of a sale for cash of stock previously bought which the broker does not wish to carry, and a repurchase for the re-settlement several weeks ahead of the same stock at the same price as at the sale plus interest accrued up to the date of that settlement. The rate of interest is called a "contango" and contango days are the days during the settlement when these arrangements are in effect.

Charge by broker for carrying customer's account to next settlement day.

Contek /kəntɛ́k/. L. Fr. A contest, dispute, disturbance, opposition. *Conteckours;* brawlers; disturbers of the peace.

Contemner /kəntɛ́mnər/. One who has committed contempt of court.

Contemplate. To view or consider with continued attention; to regard thoughtfully; to have in view as contingent or probable as an end or intention. To ponder, to study, to plan, to meditate, to reflect. See **Consider.**

Contemplation. The act of the mind in considering with attention. Continued attention of the mind to a particular subject. Consideration of an act or series of acts with the intention of doing or adopting them. The consideration of an event or state of facts with the expectation that it will transpire. See **Consideration.**

Contemplation of bankruptcy. Contemplation of the breaking up of one's business or an inability to continue it. Knowledge of, and action with reference to, a condition of bankruptcy or ascertained insolvency, coupled with an intention to commit what the law declares to be an "act of bankruptcy," or to make provision against the consequences of insolvency, or to defeat the general distribution of assets which would take place under a proceeding in bankruptcy. See **Act of Bankruptcy.**

Contemplation of death. The apprehension or expectation of approaching dissolution; not that general expectation which every mortal entertains, but the apprehension which arises from some presently existing sickness or physical condition or from some impending danger. As applied to transfers of property, the phrase "in contemplation of death" means that thought of death is the impelling cause of transfer and that motive which induces transfer is of sort which leads to testamentary disposition and is practically equivalent to "causa mortis." In re Cornell's

Estate, 66 A.D. 162, 73 N.Y.S. 32; Nicholas v. Martin, 128 N.J.Eq. 344, 15 A.2d 235, 243; Pate v. C. I. R., C.C.A.8, 149 F.2d 669, 670. It has been further held however, that in determining whether transfer by decedent within three years prior to date of death was made in contemplation of death, phrase "contemplation of death" is not restricted in meaning to apprehension that death is imminent; inquiry is whether the "life" as opposed to "death" motives were the dominant controlling or impelling reasons for the transfer. Bel v. U. S., D.C.La., 310 F.Supp. 1189, 1194. For estate tax purposes, a gift by a decedent within three years ending with the date of his death is deemed made in contemplation of death. I.R.C. § 2035(b). Prior to the 1976 Tax Reform Act, such transfers were merely "presumed" to be made in contemplation of death.

Contemplation of insolvency. Knowledge of, and action with reference to, an existing or contemplated state of insolvency, with a design to make provision against its results or to defeat the operation of the insolvency laws. See **Act of bankruptcy; Contemplation of bankruptcy.**

Contemporanea expositio /kəntèmpəréyniyə èkspəzísh(iy)ow/. Lat. Contemporaneous exposition, or construction; a construction drawn from the *time* when, and the circumstances under which, the subject-matter to be construed, as a statute or custom, originated.

Contemporanea expositio est optima et fortissima in lege /kəntèmpəréyniyə èkspəzísh(iy)ow èst óptəmə èt fortísəmə in líyjiy/. Contemporaneous exposition is the best and strongest in the law. A statute is best explained by following the construction put upon it by judges who lived at the *time* it was made, or soon after.

Contempt. A willful disregard or disobedience of a public authority. See also **Civil contempt; Common-law contempt; Contempt of Congress; Contempt of court.**

Contemptibiliter /kəntèm(p)təbilədər/. Lat. Contemptuously. In old English law, contempt, contempts.

Contempt of Congress. Deliberate interference with duties and powers of Congress. Both houses of Congress may cite an individual for such contempt.

Contempt of court. Any act which is calculated to embarrass, hinder, or obstruct court in administration of justice, or which is calculated to lessen its authority or its dignity. Committed by a person who does any act in willful contravention of its authority or dignity, or tending to impede or frustrate the administration of justice, or by one who, being under the court's authority as a party to a proceeding therein, willfully disobeys its lawful orders or fails to comply with an undertaking which he has given.

Classification

Contempts are of two kinds, direct and constructive.

Direct contempts are those committed in the immediate view and presence of the court (such as insulting language or acts of violence) or so near the presence of the court as to obstruct or interrupt the due and orderly course of proceedings. These are punishable summarily. They are also called "criminal" contempts, but that term is better used in contrast with "civil" contempts. See *infra*.

Constructive (or indirect) contempts are those which arise from matters not occurring in or near the presence of the court, but which tend to obstruct or defeat the administration of justice, and the term is chiefly used with reference to the failure or refusal of a party to obey a lawful order, injunction, or decree of the court laying upon him a duty of action or forbearance. Constructive contempts were formerly called "consequential," and this term is still in occasional use.

Contempts are also classed as civil or criminal. The former are those quasi contempts which consist in the failure to do something which the party is ordered by the court to do for the benefit or advantage of another party to the proceeding before the court, while criminal contempts are acts done in disrespect of the court or its process or which obstruct the administration of justice or tend to bring the court into disrespect. A civil contempt is not an offense against the dignity of the court, but against the party in whose behalf the mandate of the court was issued, and a fine is imposed for his indemnity. But criminal contempts are offenses or injuries offered to the court, and a fine or imprisonment is imposed upon the contemnor for the purpose of punishment. Fed.R.Crim.Proc. 42.

A court of the United States has power to punish by fine or imprisonment, at its discretion, such contempt of its authority, and none other, as: (1) misbehavior of any person in its presence or so near thereto as to obstruct the administration of justice; (2) misbehavior of any of its officers in their official transactions; (3) disobedience or resistance to its lawful writ, process, order, rule, decree, or command. 18 U.S.C.A. § 401.

Contempt for failure to make discovery is governed by Fed.R. Civil P. 37(b).

Contempt power. Every court has inherent power to punish one for contempt of its judgments or decrees and for conduct within or proximate to the court which is contemptuous. See also **Contempt of Congress; Contempt of court.**

Contempt proceeding. The judicial hearing or trial conducted to determine whether one has been in contempt of court and to make an appropriate disposition. Such proceedings are sui generis and not necessarily connected to or identified with the proceeding out of which the contempt arose.

Contenementum /kəntènəméntəm/. See **Wainagium; Contentment.**

Contentious /kənténshəs/. Contested; adversary; litigated between adverse or contending parties. A judicial proceeding not merely *ex parte* in its character, but comprising attack and defense as between opposing parties, is so called. Character of being quarrelsome or belligerent.

Contentious jurisdiction. That part of jurisdiction of court that is concerned with contested matters, as opposed to voluntary, undisputed matters. In English ecclesiastical law, that branch of the jurisdiction of the ecclesiastical courts which is exercised upon adversary or *contentious* (opposed, litigated) proceedings.

Contentious possession. In stating the rule that the possession of land necessary to give rise to a title by prescription must be a "contentious" one, it is meant that it must be based on opposition to the title of the rival claimant (not in recognition thereof or subordination thereto) and that the opposition must be based on good grounds, or such as might be made the subject of litigation.

Contentment, contenement. A man's countenance or credit, which he has together with, and by reason of, his freehold; or that which is necessary for the support and maintenance of men, agreeably to their several qualities or states of life.

Comfort; consolation; ease; enjoyment; happiness; pleasure; satisfaction.

Contents and not contents. In English parliamentary law, the "contents" are those who, in the house of lords, express assent to a bill; the "not" or "non-contents" dissent.

Contents unknown. Words sometimes annexed to a bill of lading of goods in cases or other packaging. Their meaning is that the carrier only means to acknowledge that the shipment, as evidenced from the external condition of such, is in good order.

Content validation. Content validation of a test requires that an analysis of a job involved be undertaken to determine what characteristics are essential for adequate performance of that job and the job analysis is then followed by formulation of a test which accurately reflects presence or absence of these necessary qualities. Com. of Pa. v. Glickman, D.C.Pa., 370 F.Supp. 724, 737.

Conterminous /kòntə́rmənəs/. Adjacent; adjoining; having a common boundary; coterminous.

Contest, *v.* To make defense to an adverse claim in a court of law. To oppose, resist, or dispute the case made by a plaintiff or prosecutor. To strive to win or hold. To controvert, litigate, call in question, challenge. To defend, as a suit or other proceeding. See **Answer; Defense.**

Contestable clause. Provision in an insurance policy setting forth the conditions under which, or the period of time during which, the insurer may contest or void the policy.

Contestatio litis /kòntəstéysh(iy)ow láydəs/. In Roman law, contestation of suit; the framing an issue; joinder in issue. The formal act of both the parties with which the proceedings *in jure* were closed when they led to a judicial investigation, and by which the neighbors whom the parties brought with them were called to testify.

In old English law, coming to an issue; the issue so produced.

Contestatio litis eget terminos contradictarios /kòntəstéysh(iy)ow láydes íyjət tə́rmənows kòntrədiktériyows/. An issue requires terms of contradiction. To constitute an issue, there must be an affirmative on one side and a negative on the other.

Contestation of suit. In an ecclesiastical cause, that stage of the suit which is reached when the defendant has answered the libel by giving in an allegation. See also **Answer; Contest; Defense.**

Contested election. An election may be said to be contested whenever an objection is formally urged against it which, if found to be true in fact, would invalidate it. This is true both as to objections founded upon some constitutional provision and to such as are based on statutes.

Contest of will. See **Will contest.**

Context. The context of a particular sentence or clause in a statute, contract, will, etc., comprises those parts of the text which immediately precede and follow it. The context may sometimes be scrutinized, to aid in the interpretation of an obscure passage. See **Construction.**

Contiguous /kəntígyuwəs/. In close proximity; neighboring; adjoining; near in succession; in actual close contact; touching at a point or along a boundary; bounded or traversed by. The term is not synonymous with "vicinal." Ehle v. Tenney Trading Co., 56 Ariz. 241, 107 P.2d 210, 212.

Continencia /kòntinénsiyə/. In Spanish law, continency or unity of the proceedings in a cause.

Continens /kóntənənz/. In the Roman law, continuing; holding together. Adjoining buildings were said to be *continentia.*

Continental. Pertaining or relating to a continent; characteristic of a continent; as broad in scope or purpose as a continent.

Continental Congress. The first national legislative assembly in the United States, which met in 1774, in pursuance of a recommendation made by Massachusetts and adopted by the other colonies. In this Congress all the colonies were represented except Georgia. The delegates were in some cases chosen by the legislative assemblies in the states; in others by the people directly. The powers of the Congress were undefined, but it proceeded to take measures and pass resolutions which concerned the general welfare and had regard to the inauguration and prosecution of the war for independence.

Continental currency. Paper money issued under the authority of the continental congress.

Continentia /kòntənénsh(iy)ə/. In old English practice, continuance or connection. Applied to the proceedings in a cause.

Contingency /kəntínjən(t)siy/. Quality of being contingent or casual; the possibility of coming to pass; an event which may occur; a possibility; a casualty. A fortuitous event, which comes without design, foresight, or expectation. See also **Contingent.**

Contingency contract. A contract, part of performance of which at least is dependent on the happening of a contingency. Sometimes used to refer to fee arrangement with attorney who agrees to accept his fee on the contingency of a successful outcome. See **Fee.**

Contingency reserve. In accounting, a reserve set up to cover possible liability; *e.g.* possible judgment against company.

A fund created in anticipation of incidental or unforeseen expenditures.

Contingency with double aspect. A remainder is said to be "in a contingency with double aspect," when there is another remainder limited on the same estate, not in derogation of the first, but as a substitute for it in case it should fail.

Contingent /kəntínjənt/. Possible, but not assured; doubtful or uncertain; conditioned upon the occurrence of some future event which is itself uncertain, or questionable. Synonymous with provisional. This term, when applied to a use, remainder, devise, bequest, or other legal right or interest, implies that no present interest exists, and that whether such interest or right ever will exist depends upon a future uncertain event.

As to contingent Damages; Fee; Legacy; Limitation; Remainder; Trust; and Use, see those titles.

Contingent beneficiary. Person who may or will benefit if primary beneficiary dies or otherwise loses rights as beneficiary; *e.g.* person who will receive life insurance if primary beneficiary dies before insured.

Contingent claim. One which has not accrued and which is dependent on some future event that may never happen.

Contingent debt. One which is not presently fixed, but may become so in the future with the occurrence of some uncertain event. A debt in bankruptcy which may be proved and allowed and which arises out of contract. It does not encompass a tort claim on which no action or suit has been brought prior to adjudication. Resolute Ins. Co. v. Underwood, La. App., 230 So.2d 433, 435. Term may refer to debt incurred by state to which state pledges its credit and guarantees payment if revenues from funded project prove inadequate. Rochlin v. State, 112 Ariz. 171, 540 P.2d 643. See also **Contingent claim; Contingent liability.**

Contingent estate, interest or right. An estate, interest or right which depends for its effect upon an event which may or may not happen; as an estate limited to a person not *in ease,* or not yet born.

Contingent fee. See **Fee.**

Contingent fund. One set up by a municipality to pay expense items which will necessarily arise during the year but cannot appropriately be classified under any of the specific purposes for which other taxes are levied. First Nat. Bank of Norman v. City of Norman, 182 Okl. 7, 75 P.2d 1109, 1110. See also **Contingency reserve.**

Contingent interest in personal property. A future interest not transmissible to the representatives of the party entitled thereto, in case he dies before it vests in possession. Thus, if a testator leaves the income of a fund to his wife for life, and the capital of the fund to be distributed among such of his children as shall be living at her death, the interest of each child during the widow's life-time is *contingent,* and in case of his death is not transmissible to his representatives.

Contingent liability. One which is not now fixed and absolute, but which will become so in case of the occurrence of some future and uncertain event. Warren Co. v. C. I. R., C.C.A.Ga., 135 F.2d 679, 684, 685. A potential liability; *e.g.* pending lawsuit. See also **Contingent claim; Contingent debt.**

Contingent remainder. See **Remainder.**

Continual claim. In old English law, a formal claim made by a party entitled to enter upon any lands or tenements, but deterred from such entry by menaces, or bodily fear, for the purpose of preserving or keeping alive his right. It was called "continual", because it was required to be repeated once in the space of every year and day. It had to be made as near to the land as the party could approach with safety, and, when made in due form, had the same effect with, and in all respects amounted to, a legal entry. 3 Bl.Comm. 175.

Continuance. The adjournment or postponement of a session, hearing, trial, or other proceeding to a subsequent day or time. Also the entry of a continuance made upon the record of the court, for the purpose of formally evidencing the postponement, or of connecting the parts of the record so as to make one continuous whole.

Continuance nisi /kəntínyuwən(t)s náysay/. A postponement on a condition or for a specific period of time.

Continuando /kəntìnyuwǽndow/. In old pleading, a form of allegation in which the trespass, criminal offense, or other wrongful act complained of is charged to have been committed on a specified day and to have "continued" to the present time, or is averred to have been committed at divers days and times within a given period or on a specified day and on divers other days and times between that day and another. This is called "laying the time with a continuando."

Continuing. Enduring; not terminated by a single act or fact; subsisting for a definite period or intended to cover or apply to successive similar obligations or occurrences.

As to continuing Breach; Consideration; Conspiracy; Covenant; Damages; Guaranty; and Nuisance, see those titles. See also **Perpetuity.**

Continuing contract. A contract calling for periodic performances over a space of time.

Continuing jurisdiction. A doctrine invoked commonly in child custody or support cases by which a court which has once acquired jurisdiction continues to possess it for purposes of amending and modifying its orders therein. Curtis v. Gibbs, Tex., 511 S.W.2d 263.

Continuing offense. Type of crime which is committed over a span of time as, for example, a conspiracy. As to period of statute of limitation, the last act of the offense controls for commencement of the period. A "continuing offense," such that only the last act thereof within the period of the statute of limitations

need be alleged in the indictment or information, is one which may consist of separate acts or a course of conduct but which arises from that singleness of thought, purpose or action which may be deemed a single impulse. U. S. v. Benton & Co., Inc., D.C.Fla., 345 F.Supp. 1101, 1103. See also **Crime; Offense.**

Continuous. Uninterrupted; unbroken; not intermittent or occasional; so persistently repeated at short intervals as to constitute virtually an unbroken series. Connected, extended, or prolonged without cessation or interruption of sequence. Sullivan v. John Hancock Mut. Life Ins. Co. of Boston, Mo.App., 110 S.W.2d 870, 877. As to continuous "Crime" and "Easement", see those titles.

Continuous adverse use. Term is interchangeable with the term "uninterrupted adverse use".

Continuous injury. One recurring at repeated intervals, so as to be of repeated occurrence; not necessarily an injury that never ceases.

Continuously. Uninterruptedly; in unbroken sequence; without intermission or cessation; without intervening time; with continuity or continuation.

Contra. Against, confronting, opposite to; on the other hand; on the contrary.

Contra accounts. In accounting, those accounts which are related to and should be shown with their cognate accounts, *e.g.* reserve for depreciation should be shown with the asset which is being depreciated.

Contra-balance. Balance in accounts which is the opposite of the normal balance of the account; *e.g.* account receivable with credit balance.

Contraband. In general, any property which is unlawful to produce or possess. Goods exported from or imported into a country against its laws. Articles, the importation or exportation of which is prohibited by law. Smuggled goods. See also **Derivative contraband.**

Contraband of war. Certain classes of merchandise, such as arms and ammunition, which, by the rules of international law, cannot lawfully be furnished or carried by a neutral nation to either of two belligerents. If found in transit in neutral vessels, such goods may be seized and condemned for violation of neutrality.

Contra bonos mores /kóntrə bównows móriyz/. Against good morals. Contracts *contra bonos mores* are void.

Contracausator /kòntrəkozéydər/. A criminal; one prosecuted for a crime.

Contraceptive. Any device or substance which prevents fertilization of the female ovum.

Contraceptivism. The offense of distributing or prescribing contraceptives; the offense has little or no vitality today with respect to both married and unmarried persons. Baird v. Eisenstadt, 405 U.S. 438, 92 S.Ct. 1029, 31 L.Ed.2d 349.

Contract. An agreement between two or more persons which creates an obligation to do or not to do a particular thing. Its essentials are competent parties, subject matter, a legal consideration, mutuality of agreement, and mutuality of obligation. Lamoureux v. Burrillville Racing Ass'n, 91 R.I. 94, 161 A.2d 213, 215. Under U.C.C., term refers to total legal obligation which results from parties' agreement as affected by the Code. Section 1–201(11). As to sales, "contract" and "agreement" are limited to those relating to present or future sales of goods, and "contract for sale" includes both a present sale of goods and a contract to sell goods at a future time. U.C.C. § 2–106(1).

The writing which contains the agreement of parties, with the terms and conditions, and which serves as a proof of the obligation.

Contracts may be classified on several different methods, according to the element in them which is brought into prominence. The usual classifications are as follows:

Certain and hazardous. Certain contracts are those in which the thing to be done is supposed to depend on the will of the party, or when, in the usual course of events, it must happen in the manner stipulated. Hazardous contracts are those in which the performance of that which is one of its objects depends on an uncertain event.

Commutative and independent. Commutative contracts are those in which what is done, given, or promised by one party is considered as an equivalent to or in consideration of what is done, given, or promised by the other. Independent contracts are those in which the mutual acts or promises have no relation to each other, either as equivalents or as considerations.

Conditional contract. An executory contract the performance of which depends upon a condition. It is not simply an executory contract, since the latter may be an absolute agreement to do or not to do something, but it is a contract whose very existence and performance depend upon a contingency.

Consensual and real. Consensual contracts are such as are founded upon and completed by the mere agreement of the contracting parties, without any external formality or symbolic act to fix the obligation. Real contracts are those in which it is necessary that there should be something more than mere consent, such as a loan of money, deposit or pledge, which, from their nature, require a delivery of the thing *(res).* In the common law a contract respecting real property (such as a lease of land for years) is called a "real" contract.

Constructive contract. See **Constructive contract;** also *Express and implied; Quasi contract, infra.*

Cost-plus contract. See **Costs.**

Divisible and indivisible. The effect of the breach of a contract depends in a large degree upon whether it is to be regarded as indivisible or divisible; *i.e.* whether it forms a whole, the performance of every part of which is a condition precedent to bind the other party, or is composed of several independent parts, the performance of any one of which will bind

the other party *pro tanto.* The only test is whether the whole quantity of the things concerned, or the sum of the acts to be done, is of the essence of the contract. It depends, therefore, in the last resort, simply upon the intention of the parties. Integrity Flooring v. Zandon Corporation, 130 N.J.L. 244, 32 A.2d 507, 509.

When a consideration is entire and indivisible, and it is against law, the contract is void *in toto.* When the consideration is divisible, and part of it is illegal, the contract is void only *pro tanto.* Gelpcke v. Dubuque, 68 U.S. (1 Wall.) 220, 17 L.Ed. 530.

Entire and severable. An *entire* contract is one the consideration of which is entire on both sides. The entire fulfillment of the promise by either is a condition precedent to the fulfillment of any part of the promise by the other. Whenever, therefore, there is a contract to pay the gross sum for a certain and definite consideration, the contract is entire. A *severable* contract is one the consideration of which is, by its terms, susceptible of apportionment on either side, so as to correspond to the unascertained consideration on the other side, as a contract to pay a person the worth of his services so long as he will do certain work; or to give a certain price for every bushel of so much corn as corresponds to a sample.

Where a contract consists of many parts, which may be considered as parts of one whole, the contract is entire. When the parts may be considered as so many distinct contracts, entered into at one time, and expressed in the same instrument, but not thereby made one contract, the contract is a separable contract. But, if the consideration of the contract is single and entire, the contract must be held to be entire, although the subject of the contract may consist of several distinct and wholly independent items.

Entire contract clause. A provision in the insurance contract stating that the entire agreement between the insured and insurer is contained in the contract, including the application (if attached), declarations, insuring agreement, exclusions, conditions, and endorsements.

Exclusive contract. See *Requirements contract; Tying contract, infra.*

Executed and executory. Contracts are also divided into executed and executory; *executed,* where nothing remains to be done by either party, and where the transaction is completed at the moment that the arrangement is made, as where an article is sold and delivered, and payment therefor is made on the spot; *executory,* where some future act is to be done, as where an agreement is made to build a house in six months, or to do an act on or before some future day, or to lend money upon a certain interest, payable at a future time.

Express and implied. An express contract is an actual agreement of the parties, the terms of which are openly uttered or declared at the time of making it, being stated in distinct and explicit language, either orally or in writing.

An implied contract is one not created or evidenced by the explicit agreement of the parties, but inferred by the law, as a matter of reason and justice from their acts or conduct, the circumstances surrounding the transaction making it a reasonable, or even a necessary, assumption that a contract existed between them by tacit understanding.

Implied contracts are sometimes subdivided into those "implied in fact" and those "implied in law," the former being covered by the definition just given, while the latter are obligations imposed upon a person by the law, not in pursuance of his intention and agreement, either expressed or implied, but even against his will and design, because the circumstances between the parties are such as to render it just that the one should have a right, and the other a corresponding liability, similar to those which would arise from a contract between them. This kind of obligation therefore rests on the principle that whatsoever it is certain a man ought to do that the law will suppose him to have promised to do. And hence it is said that, while the liability of a party to an express contract arises directly from the contract, it is just the reverse in the case of a contract "implied in law," the contract there being implied or arising from the liability. Bliss v. Hoyt, 70 Vt. 534, 41 A. 1026; Kellum v. Browning's Adm'r, 231 Ky. 308, 21 S.W.2d 459, 465. But obligations of this kind are not properly contracts at all, and should not be so denominated. There can be no true contract without a mutual and concurrent intention of the parties. Such obligations are more properly described as "quasi contracts." See **Constructive contract;** also *Quasi contract, infra.*

Gratuitous and onerous. Gratuitous contracts are those of which the object is the benefit of the person with whom it is made, without any profit or advantage received or promised as a consideration for it. It is not, however, the less gratuitous if it proceed either from gratitude for a benefit before received or from the hope of receiving one thereafter, although such benefit be of a pecuniary nature. Onerous contracts are those in which something is given or promised as a consideration for the engagement or gift, or some service, interest, or condition is imposed on what is given or promised, although unequal to it in value. A gratuitous contract is sometimes called a contract of beneficence.

Investment contract. A contract in which one party invests money or property expecting a return on his investment. See also **Investment contract; Security.**

Joint and several. A joint contract is one made by two or more promisors, who are jointly bound to fulfill its obligations, or made to two or more promisees, who are jointly entitled to require performance of the same. A contract may be "several" as to any one of several promisors or promisees, if he has a legal right (either from the terms of the agreement or the nature of the undertaking) to enforce his individual interest separately from the other parties. Generally all contracts are joint where the interest of the parties for whose benefit they are created is joint, and separate where that interest is separate.

Mutual interest, mixed, etc. Contracts of "mutual interest" are such as are entered into for the reciprocal interest and utility of each of the parties; as sales, exchange, partnership, and the like. "Mixed" con-

tracts are those by which one of the parties confers a benefit on the other, receiving something of inferior value in return, such as a donation subject to a charge. Contracts "of beneficence" are those by which only one of the contracting parties is benefited; as loans, deposit and mandate.

Open end contract. Contract (normally sales contract) in which certain terms (*e.g.* order amount) are deliberately left open.

Output contract. A contract in which one party agrees to sell his entire output and the other agrees to buy it; it is not illusory, though it may be indefinite. See also *Requirements contract, infra.*

Parol contract. A contract not in writing, or partially in writing. At common law, a contract, though it may be in writing, not under seal. See **Parol evidence rule.**

Personal contract. A contract relating to personal property, or one which so far involves the element of personal knowledge or skill or personal confidence that it can be performed only by the person with whom made, and therefore is not binding on his executor.

Pre-contract. An obligation growing out of a contract or contractual relation, of such a nature that it debars the party from legally entering into a similar contract at a later time with any other person.

Principal and accessory. A principal contract is one entered into by both parties on their own account or in the several qualities they assume. It is one which stands by itself, justifies its own existence, and is not subordinate or auxiliary to any other. Accessory contracts are those made for assuring the performance of a prior contract, either by the same parties or by others, such as suretyship, mortgage, and pledge. Civ.Code La. art. 1771.

Quasi contract. Legal fiction invented by common law courts to permit recovery by contractual remedy in cases where, in fact, there is no contract, but where circumstances are such that justice warrants a recovery as though there had been a promise. It is not based on intention or consent of the parties, but is founded on considerations of justice and equity, and on doctrine of unjust enrichment. It is not in fact a contract, but an obligation which the law creates in absence of any agreement, when and because the acts of the parties or others have placed in the possession of one person money, or its equivalent, under such circumstances that in equity and good conscience he ought not to retain it. It is what was formerly known as the contract implied in law; it has no reference to the intentions or expressions of the parties. The obligation is imposed despite, and frequently in frustration of their intention. See also **Constructive contract.**

In the civil law, a contractual relation arising out of transactions between the parties which give them mutual rights and obligations, but do not involve a specific and express convention or agreement between them. The lawful and purely voluntary acts of a man, from which there results any obligation whatever to a third person, and sometimes a reciprocal obligation between the parties. Civ.Code La. art. 2293.

Record, specialty, simple. Contracts of record are such as are declared and adjudicated by courts of competent jurisdiction, or entered on their records, including judgments, recognizances, and statutes staple. These are not properly speaking contracts at all, though they may be enforced by action like contracts. Specialties, or special contracts, are contracts under seal, such as deeds and bonds. All others are included in the description "simple" contracts; that is, a simple contract is one that is not a contract of record and not under seal; it may be either written or oral, in either case, it is called a "parol" contract, the distinguishing feature being the lack of a seal.

Requirements contract. A contract in which one party agrees to purchase his total requirements from the other party and hence it is binding and not illusory. See also *Output contract, supra.*

Shipment contract. A contract calling for shipment of goods and in which shipment is excused if ship is lost. Texas Co. v. Hogarth Shipping Co., 256 U.S. 619, 41 S.Ct. 612, 65 L.Ed. 1123.

Special contract. A contract under seal; a specialty; as distinguished from one merely oral or in writing not sealed. But in common usage this term is often used to denote an express or explicit contract, one which clearly defines and settles the reciprocal rights and obligations of the parties, as distinguished from one which must be made out, and its terms ascertained, by the inference of the law from the nature and circumstances of the transaction. A special contract may rest in parol, and does not mean a contract by specialty; it is defined as one with peculiar provisions not found in the ordinary contracts relating to the same subject-matter.

Subcontract. A contract subordinate to another contract, made or intended to be made between the contracting parties, on one part, or some of them, and a third party (*i.e.* subcontractor). One made under a prior contract.

Where a person has contracted for the performance of certain work (*e.g.*, to build a house), and he in turn engages a third party to perform the whole or a part of that which is included in the original contract (*e.g.*, to do the carpenter work), his agreement with such third person is called a "subcontract," and such person is called a "subcontractor." The term "subcontractor" means one who has contracted with the original contractor for the performance of all or a part of the work or services which such contractor has himself contracted to perform.

Tying contract. See **Tying arrangement.**

Unconscionable contract. One which no sensible man not under delusion, duress, or in distress would make, and such as no honest and fair man would accept. Franklin Fire Ins. Co. v. Noll, 115 Ind.App. 289, 58 N.E.2d 947, 949, 950. A contract the terms of which are excessively unreasonable, overreaching and one-sided. See **Unconscionability.**

Unilateral and bilateral. A unilateral contract is one in which one party makes an express engagement or undertakes a performance, without receiving in return any express engagement or promise of performance from the other. Bilateral (or reciprocal) contracts are those by which the parties expressly enter into mutual engagements, such as sale or hire. Kling Bros. Engineering Works v. Whiting Corporation, 320 Ill.App. 630, 51 N.E.2d 1004, 1007. When the party to whom an engagement is made makes no express agreement on his part, the contract is called unilateral, even in cases where the law attaches certain obligations to his acceptance. A contract is also said to be "unilateral" when there is a promise on one side only, the consideration on the other side being executed.

Usurious contract. See **Usurious contract.**

Voidable contract. See **Voidable contract.**

Void contract. See **Void contract.**

Written contract. A "written contract" is one which in all its terms is in writing. Commonly referred to as a formal contract.

See also Adhesion contract; Agreement; Aleatory contract; Alteration of contract; Bilateral contract; Bottom hole contract; Breach of contract; Collateral contract; Compact; Constructive contract; Contingency contract; Entire output contract; Executory contract; Formal contract; Futures contract; Indemnity contract; Innominate contracts; Installment contract; Integrated contract; Investment contract; Letter contract; Letter of intent; Literal contract; Marketing contract; Novation; Oral contract; Parol evidence rule; **Privity** (*Privity of contract*); Procurement contract; Severable contract; Simulated contract; Specialty. For "liberty of contract", see **Liberty.**

Contract carrier. A carrier which furnishes transportation service to meet the special needs of shippers who cannot be adequately served by common carriers. Samardick of Grand Island-Hastings, Inc. v. B. D. C. Corp., 183 Neb. 229, 159 N.W.2d 310, 315. A transportation company that carries, for pay, the goods of certain customers only as contrasted to a common carrier that carries the goods of the public in general.

Contract clause. Provision in U.S.Const., Art. I, Sec. 10, to the effect that no state shall pass a law impairing obligation of contract. Trustees of Dartmouth College v. Woodward, 17 U.S. (4 Wheat.) 518, 4 L.Ed. 629.

Contract, estoppel by. "Estoppel by contract" is intended to embrace all cases in which there is an actual or virtual undertaking to treat a fact as settled. It means party is bound by terms of own contract until set aside or annulled for fraud, accident, or mistake. United Fidelity Life Ins. Co. v. Fowler, Tex.Civ.App., 38 S.W.2d 128, 131. There are two sorts of "estoppel by contract," estoppel to deny truth of facts agreed on and settled by force of entering into contract, and estoppel arising from acts done under or in performance of contract. Finch v. Smith, 177 Okl. 307, 58 P.2d 850, 851.

Contract for deed. An agreement by a seller to deliver the deed to the property when certain conditions have been met, such as completion of payments by purchaser. Often such contracts for deed are in turn resold.

Contract for sale of goods. Includes both a contract for present sale of goods and a contract to sell goods at a future time. U.C.C. § 2–106(1).

Contract for sale of land. A contract which calls for conveyance of interest in real estate and requires a writing signed by party sought to be charged as being within Statute of Frauds. See also **Contract for deed; Contract of sale.**

Contract implied in fact. See **Contract.**

Contract implied in law. See **Contract.**

Contraction. Abbreviation; abridgment or shortening of a word by omitting a letter or letters or a syllable, with a mark over the place where the elision occurs. This was customary in records written in the ancient "court hand," and is frequently found in the books printed in black letter.

Contract not to compete. An agreement by an employee that he will not for a stated period and within a specific geographical area compete with his employer after termination of his employment. These contracts are enforceable if the time span and area are reasonable.

Contract of affreightment. A contract for hiring a vessel. Peterson v. S. S. Wahcondah, D.C.La., 235 F.Supp. 698, 700. See also **Affreightment.**

Contract of benevolence. A contract made for the benefit of one of the contracting parties only, as a mandate or deposit.

Contract of insurance. Any contract by which one of the parties for a valuable consideration, known as a premium, assumes a risk of loss or liability that rests upon the other, pursuant to a plan for the distribution of such risk, is a contract of insurance, whatever the form it takes or the name it bears. See **Insurance; Policy of insurance.**

Contract of record. A contract of record is one which has been declared and adjudicated by a court having jurisdiction, or which is entered of record in obedience to, or in carrying out, the judgments of a court.

Contract of sale. A contract by which one of the contracting parties, called the "seller," enters into an obligation to the other to cause him to have freely, by a title of proprietor, a thing, for the price of a certain sum of money, which the other contracting party, called the "buyer," on his part obliges himself to pay. Agreement under which seller agrees to convey title to property upon payment by buyer under terms of contract. See also **Contract for deed; Contract for sale of land.**

Contractor. This term is strictly applicable to any person who enters into a contract, but is commonly reserved to designate one who, for a fixed price, undertakes to procure the performance of works or services on a large scale, or the furnishing of goods in large quantities, whether for the public or a company or individual. Such are generally classified as general contractors (responsible for entire job) and subcontractors (responsible for only portion of job; *e.g.* plumber, carpenter).

A contractor is a person who, in the pursuit of any independent business, undertakes to do a specific piece of work for other persons, using his own means and methods without submitting himself to their control in respect to all its details, and who renders service in the course of an independent occupation representing the will of his employer only as to the result of his work and not as to the means by which it is accomplished. Setzer v. Whitehurst, Ky., 339 S.W.2d 454, 456.

One who in pursuit of independent business undertakes to perform a job or piece of work, retaining in himself control of means, method and manner of accomplishing the desired result.

See also **General contractor; Independent contractor; Prime contractor.**

Contract rights. Any right to payment under a contract not yet earned by performance and not evidenced by an instrument or chattel paper. U.C.C., § 9–106.

Contract system. As applied to state prisons, this phrase signifies that the labor of the prisoners is utilized by private persons or contractors.

Contractual obligation. The obligation which arises from a contract or agreement.

Contract under seal. For centuries before the doctrine of consideration was developed, and long before informal contracts were enforced, contracts under seal were enforced. The sealed instrument required no consideration. The required formalities are: a sufficient writing, a seal, and delivery. The seal may be actual, or impressed on the paper, or merely recited by the word "seal" or "L.S."

Contractus. Lat. Contract; a contract; contracts.

Contractus bonæ fidei /kəntræktəs bówniy fáydiyày/. In Roman law, contracts of good faith. Those contracts which, when brought into litigation, were not determined by the rules of the strict law alone, but allowed the judge to examine into the *bona fides* of the transaction, and to hear equitable considerations against their enforcement. In this they were opposed to contracts *stricti juris,* against which equitable defenses could not be entertained.

Contractus civiles /kəntræktəs sívəliyz/. In Roman law, civil contracts. Those contracts which were recognized as actionable by the strict civil law of Rome, or as being founded upon a particular statute, as distinguished from those which could not be enforced in the courts except by the aid of the prætor, who, through his equitable powers, gave an action upon them. The latter were called *"contractus prœtorii."*

Contractus est quasi actus contra actum /kəntræktəs èst kwéysay æktəs kóntrə æktəm/. A contract is, as it were, act against act.

Contractus ex turpi causa, vel contra bonos mores, nullus est /kəntræktəs èks tárpay kózə, vèl kóntrə bównows móriyz, náləs est/. A contract founded on a base consideration, or against good morals, is null.

Contractus legem ex conventione accipiunt /kəntræktəs líyjəm èks kənvènshiyówniy əksípiyənt/. Contracts receive legal sanction from the agreement of the parties.

Contradict. To disprove. To prove a fact contrary to what has been asserted by a witness.

Contradiction in terms. A phrase of which the parts are expressly inconsistent, as *e.g.*, "an innocent murder"; "a fee-simple for life."

Contraescritura /kòntraèskritúrə/. In Spanish law, a counter-writing; counter-letter. A document executed at the same time with an act of sale or other instrument, and operating by way of defeasance or otherwise modifying the apparent effect and purport of the original instrument.

Contrafactio /kòntrəfǽksh(iy)ow/. Counterfeiting; as *contrafactio sigilli regis,* counterfeiting the king's seal.

Contra formam collationis /kóntrə fórməm kəlèy-shiyównəs/. In old English law, a writ that issued where lands given in perpetual alms to lay houses of religion, or to an abbot and convent, or to the warden or master of a hospital and his convent, to find certain poor men with necessaries, and do divine service, etc., were alienated, to the disherison of the house and church. By means of this writ the donor or his heirs could recover the lands.

Contra formam doni /kóntrə fórməm dównày/. Against the form of the grant. See **Formedon.**

Contra formam feoffamenti /kóntrə fórməm fíyfə-méntày/. In old English law, a writ that lay for the heir of a tenant, enfeoffed of certain lands or tenements, by charter of feoffment from a lord to make certain services and suits to his court, who was afterwards distrained for more services than were mentioned in the charter.

Contra formam statuti /kóntrə fórməm stətyúwday/. In criminal pleading. (Contrary to the form of the statute in such case made and provided.) The usual conclusion of every indictment, etc., brought for an offense created by statute.

Contrainte par corps /kòntréynt pàr kór/. In French law, the civil process of arrest of the person, which is imposed upon vendors falsely representing their property to be unincumbered, or upon persons mortgaging property which they are aware does not belong to them, and in other cases of moral heinousness.

Contra jus belli /kóntrə jás bélày/. Lat. Against the law of war.

Contra jus commune /kóntrə jás kəmyúwniy/. Against common right or law; contrary to the rule of the common law.

Contra legem facit qui id facit quod lex prohibet; in fraudem vero qui, salvis verbis legis, sententiam ejus circumvenit /kóntrə líyjəm féysət kwày íd féysət kwòd léks prəhíbət; in fródəm vírow kwày, sǽlvəs várbəs líyjəs, senténsh(iy)əm íyjəs sərkəmríynət/. He does contrary to the law who does what the law prohibits; he acts in fraud of the law who, the letter of the law being inviolate, uses the law contrary to its intention.

Contra legem terræ /kóntrə líyjəm téhriy/. Against the law of the land.

Contraligatio /kòntrəlagéysh(iy)ow/. In old English law, counter-obligation. Literally, counter-binding. *Est enim obligatio quasi contraligatio.*

Contramandatio /kòntrəmændéysh(iy)ow/. A countermanding. *Contramandatio placiti,* in old English law, was the respiting of a defendant, or giving him further time to answer, by countermanding the day fixed for him to plead, and appointing a new day; a sort of imparlance.

Contramandatum /kòntrəmændéydəm/. A lawful excuse, which a defendant in a suit by attorney alleges for himself to show that the plaintiff has no cause of complaint.

Contra negantem principia non est disputandum /kóntrə nəgǽntəm prìnsípiyə nón èst dìspyuwtǽndəm/. There is no disputing against one who denies first principles.

Contra non valentem agere nulla currit præscriptio /kóntrə nòn vəléntəm éyjəriy nə́lə kə́hrət prəskripsh(iy)ow/. No prescription runs against a person unable to bring an action.

Contra omnes gentes /kóntrə ómniyz jéntiyz/. Against all people. Formal words in old covenants of warranty.

Contra pacem /kóntrə péysəm/. Against the peace. A phrase used in the Latin forms of indictments, and also of actions for trespass, to signify that the offense alleged was committed against the public peace, *i.e.,* involved a breach of the peace. The full formula was *contra pacem domini regis,* against the peace of the lord the king. In modern pleading, in this country, the phrase "against the peace of the commonwealth" or "of the people" is used.

Contraplacitum /kòntrəplǽsədəm/. In old English law, a counter-plea.

Contrapositio /kòntrəpəzísh(iy)ow/. In old English law, a plea or answer. A counter-position.

Contra preferentem /kóntrə prèfəréntəm/. Against the party who proffers or puts forward a thing.

Contra proferentem /kóntrə pròfəréntəm/. Used in connection with the construction of written documents to the effect that an ambiguous provision is construed most strongly against the person who selected the language. U. S. v. Seckinger, 397 U.S. 203, 216, 90 S.Ct. 880, 25 L.Ed.2d 224.

Contrarients /kəntrériyənts/. This word was used in the time of Edw. II to signify those who were opposed to the government, but were neither rebels nor traitors.

Contrariorum contraria est ratio /kòntrèriyórəm kəntrériyə èst réysh(iy)ow/. The reason of contrary things is contrary.

Contrarotulator /kòntrəròwtyəléydər/kòntrərówchələeydər/. A controller. One whose business it was to observe the money which the collectors had gathered for the use of the king or the people.

Contrarotulator pipæ /kòntrəròwtyəléydər páypiy/. An officer of the exchequer that writeth out summons twice every year, to the sheriffs, to levy the rents and debts of the pipe.

Contrary. Against; opposed or in opposition to; in conflict with.

Contrary to law. Illegal; in violation of statute or legal regulations at a given time. In respect of verdict, in conflict with the law contained in court's instructions.

Contrary to the evidence. Against the evidence; against the weight of the evidence.

Contrat /kòntrá/. In French law, contracts are of the following varieties: (1) *Bilateral,* or *synallagmatique,* where each party is bound to the other to do what is just and proper; or (2) *unilateral,* where the one side only is bound; or (3) *commutatif,* where one does to the other something which is supposed to be an equivalent for what the other does to him; or (4) *aléatoire,* where the consideration for the act of the one is a mere chance; or (5) *contrat de bienfaisance,* where the one party procures to the other a purely gratuitous benefit; or (6) *contrat à titre onereux,* where each party is bound under some duty to the other.

Contra tabulas /kóntrə tǽbyələs/. In the civil law, against the will (testament).

Contratallia /kòntrətǽliyə/. In old English law, a counter-tally. A term used in the exchequer.

Contratatio rei alienæ animo furandi, est furtum /kòntrətéysh(iy)ow ríyay eyliyíyniy ǽnəmow fyərǽnday èst fárdəm/. The touching or removing of another's property, with an intention of stealing, is theft.

Contratenere /kòntrətəníriy/. To hold against; to withhold.

Contra vadium et plegium /kóntrə vǽdiyəm ət pléjiyəm/. In old English law, against gage and pledge.

Contravening equity. A right or equity, in another person, which is inconsistent with and opposed to the equity sought to be enforced or recognized.

Contravention. In French law, an act which violates the law, a treaty, or an agreement which the party has made. That infraction of the law punished by a fine which does not exceed fifteen francs and by an imprisonment not exceeding three days.

Contra veritatem lex nunquam aliquid permittit /kóntrə vərətéydəm léks nə́ŋkwəm ǽləkwəd pərmídət/. The law never suffers anything contrary to truth.

Contrectare /kòntrəktériy/. Lat. In the civil law, to handle; to take hold of; to meddle with.

In old English law, to treat. *Vel malè contrectet;* or shall ill treat.

Contrectatio /kòntrəktéysh(iy)ow/. In the civil and old English law, touching; handling; meddling. The act of removing a thing from its place in such a manner that, if the thing be not restored, it will amount to theft.

Contrectatio rei alienæ, animo furandi, est furtum /kòntrəktéysh(iy)ow ríyay èyliyíyniy, ǽnəmow fyərǽnday, èst fárdəm/. The touching or removing of another's property, with an intention of stealing, is theft.

Contrefacon /kòntrəfasón/. In French law, the offense of printing or causing to be printed a book, the copyright of which is held by another, without authority from him.

Contre-maître /kòntre-máytr(ə)/. In French marine law, the chief officer of a vessel, who, in case of the sickness or absence of the master, commanded in his place. Literally, the countermaster.

Contribute. To lend assistance or aid, or give something, to a common purpose; to have a share in any act or effect; to discharge a joint obligation. Christman v. Reichholdt, Mo.App., 150 S.W.2d 527, 532. As applied to negligence signifies causal connection between injury and negligence, which transcends and is distinguished from negligent acts or omissions which play so minor a part in producing injuries that law does not recognize them as legal causes. See **Negligence** (*Contributory negligence*).

Contributing cause. Generic term used to describe any factor which contributes to a result, though its causal nexus may not be immediate. See **Cause; Negligence** (*Contributory negligence*).

Contributing to delinquency. A criminal offense consisting of an act or omission which tends to make a child delinquent.

Contribution. Under principle of "contribution," a tortfeasor against whom a judgment is rendered is entitled to recover proportional shares of judgment from other joint tort-feasors whose negligence contributed to the injury and who were also liable to the plaintiff. Dawson v. Contractors Transport Corp., 151 U.S. App.D.C. 401, 467 F.2d 727, 729. The share of a loss payable by an insurer when contracts with two or more insurers cover the same loss. The insurer's share of a loss under a coinsurance or similar provision. The sharing of a loss or payment among several. The act of any one or several of a number of co-debtors, co-sureties, etc., in reimbursing one of their number who has paid the whole debt or suffered the whole liability, each to the extent of his proportionate share. Right of one who has discharged a common liability to recover of another also liable, the aliquot portion which he ought to pay or bear. Several states have adopted the Uniform Contribution Among Tortfeasors Act.

In the civil law, a partition by which the creditors of an insolvent debtor divide among themselves the proceeds of his property proportionably to the amount of their respective credits. Division which is made among the heirs of the succession of the debts with which the succession is charged, according to the proportion which each is bound to bear.

In maritime law, where the property of one of several parties interested in a vessel and cargo has been voluntarily sacrificed for the common safety (as by throwing goods overboard to lighten the vessel), such loss must be made good by the contribution of the others, which is termed "general average".

See also **General average contribution; Indemnity.**

Contribution clause. Insurance clause providing that where more than one policy covers loss, insurers shall share such loss proportionally in accordance with their policy limits.

Contributione facienda /kòntrəbyùwshiyówniy fæshiyǽndə/. In old English law, a writ that lay where tenants in common were bound to do some act, and one of them was put to the whole burthen, to compel the rest to make contribution.

Contribution to capital. A fund or property contributed by shareowners as financial basis for operation of corporation's business, and signifies resources whose dedication to users of the corporation is made the foundation for issuance of capital stock and which became irrevocably devoted to satisfaction of all obligations of corporation. See also **Capital.**

Contributory, *n.* A person liable to contribute to the assets of a company which is being wound up, as being a member or (in some cases) a past member thereof.

Contributory, *adj.* Joining in the promotion of a given purpose; lending assistance to the production of a given result. Said of a pension plan where employees, as well as employers, make payments to a pension fund.

As to contributory "Infringement" and "Negligence," see those titles.

Contributory cause. See **Cause; Contributing cause; Negligence** (*Contributory negligence*).

Contributory negligence. See **Negligence.**

Contrivance. Any device which has been arranged generally to deceive. An instrument or article designed to accomplish a specific objective and made by use of measure of ingenuity.

Control, *v.* To exercise restraining or directing influence over. To regulate; restrain; dominate; curb; to hold from action; overpower; counteract; govern.

Control, *n.* Power or authority to manage, direct, superintend, restrict, regulate, govern, administer, or oversee. The "control" involved in determining whether "principal and agent relationship" or "master and servant relationship" is involved must be accompanied by power or right to order or direct. Mid-Continent Petroleum Corporation v. Vicars, 221 Ind. 387, 47 N.E.2d 972.

"Control," as used in statute making it unlawful for any person to possess or control any narcotic drug, is given its ordinary meaning, namely, to exercise restraining or directing influence over, and also has been defined to relate to authority over what is not in one's physical possession. Speaks v. State, 3 Md.App. 371, 239 A.2d 600, 604.

Rule that driver must at all times have automobile under control, means having it under such control that it can be stopped before doing injury to any person in any situation that is reasonably likely to arise under the circumstances. Kindt v. Reading Co., 352 Pa. 419, 43 A.2d 145, 147.

See also **Exclusive control; Immediate control.**

Controlled company. A company, a majority of whose voting stock is held by an individual or corporation. Effective control can sometimes be exercised when less than 50 percent of the stock is owned.

Controlled substance. Any narcotic drug so designated by law; *i.e.* so designated by federal or state Controlled Substances Acts (*q.v.*).

Controlled Substance Acts. Federal and state acts (the latter modeled on the Uniform Controlled Substances Act) the purpose of which is to control the distribution, classification, sale, and use of drugs. The majority of states have such acts.

Controller. See **Comptroller.**

Controlment /kəntrólmənt/. In old English law, the controlling or checking of another officer's account; the keeping of a counter-roll.

Controver /kəntrówvər/. In old English law, an inventor or deviser of false news.

Controversy. A litigated question; adversary proceeding in a court of law; a civil action or suit, either at law or in equity; a justiciable dispute. To be a "controversy" under federal constitutional provision limiting exercise of judicial power of United States to cases and controversies there must be a concrete case admitting of an immediate and definitive determination of legal rights of parties in an adversary proceeding upon facts alleged, and claims based merely upon assumed potential invasions of rights are not enough to warrant judicial intervention. Southern Ry. Co. v. Brotherhood of Locomotive Firemen and Enginemen, D.C.Ga., 223 F.Supp. 296, 303. This term is important in that judicial power of the courts extends *only* to cases and "controversies." See **Case; Cause of action; Justiciable controversy.**

Controvert. To dispute; to deny; to oppose or contest; to take issue on.

Contubernium /kòntəbárniyəm/. In Roman law, the marriage of slaves; a permitted cohabitation.

Contumace capiendo /kòntəméysiy kæpiyéndow/. In English law, excommunication in all cases of contempt in the spiritual courts is discontinued by 53 Geo. III, c. 127, § 2, and in lieu thereof, where a lawful citation or sentence has not been obeyed, the judge shall have power, after a certain period, to pronounce such person contumacious and in contempt, and to signify the same to the court of chancery, whereupon a writ *de contumace capiendo* shall issue from that court, which shall have the same force and effect as formerly belonged, in case of contempt, to a writ *de excommunicato capiendo.* See **Excommunication.**

Contumacious conduct. Wilfully stubborn and disobedient conduct, commonly punishable as contempt of court. See **Contempt.**

Contumacy /kónt(y)əməsiy/. The refusal or intentional omission of a person who has been duly cited before a court to appear and defend the charge laid against him, or, if he is duly before the court, to obey some lawful order or direction made in the cause. In the former case it is called "presumed" contumacy; in the latter, "actual."

Contumax /kóntəmæks/. One accused of a crime who refuses to appear and answer to the charge. An outlaw.

Contumely /kóntyəməliy/. Rudeness compounded of haughtiness and contempt; scornful insolence; despiteful treatment; disdain, contemptuousness in act or speech; disgrace.

Contuse. To bruise; to injure or disorganize a part of without breaking the skin. Ansley v. Travelers Ins. Co., 27 Tenn.App. 720, 173 S.W.2d 702, 704.

Contusion. A bruise; an injury to any external part of the body by the impact of a fall or the blow of a blunt instrument, without laceration of the flesh, and either with or without a tearing of the skin, but in the former case it is more properly called a "contused wound."

Contutor /kəntyúwdər/. Lat. In the civil law, a co-tutor, or co-guardian.

Conusance /kónyəzən(t)s/. In English law, cognizance or jurisdiction. Conusance of pleas.

Conusance, claim of /kléym əv kónyəzən(t)s/. See **Cognizance.**

Conusant /kónyəzənt/. Cognizant; acquainted with; having actual knowledge; as, if a party knowing of an agreement in which he has an interest makes no objection to it, he is said to be conusant.

Conusee /kònyəzíy/. See **Cognizee.**

Conusor /kónyəzər/. See **Cognizor.**

Convalescence. Gradual recovery of health or physical strength after illness.

Convenable. In old English law, suitable; agreeable; convenient; fitting.

Convene. To call together; to cause to assemble; to convoke. In the civil law, to bring an action.

Convenience and necessity. If there is a reasonable need apparent for use of the service, and if a common carrier is not unduly interfered with, nor the public highways unduly burdened, a case of "convenience and necessity" exists with respect to an application for a license to operate as a contract motor carrier. See also **Public convenience and necessity.**

Convenient. Proper; just; suitable; fit; adapted; proper; becoming appropriate.

Convenit /kənvíynət/. Lat. In civil and old English law, it is agreed; it was agreed.

Convent. The fraternity of an abbey or priory, as *societas* is the number of fellows in a college. A religious house, now regarded as a merely voluntary association, not importing civil death.

An association or community of recluses devoted to a religious life under a superior. A body of monks, friars, or nuns, constituting one local community; now usually restricted to a convent of nuns. Sacred Heart Academy of Galveston v. Karsch, 173 Tenn. 618, 122 S.W.2d 416, 417.

Conventicle /kənvéntəkəl/. A private assembly or meeting for the exercise of religion. The word was first an appellation of reproach to the religious assemblies of Wycliffe in the reigns of Edward III, and Richard II, and was afterwards applied to a meeting of dissenters from the established church. As this word in strict propriety denotes an unlawful assembly, it cannot be justly applied to the assembling of persons in places of worship licensed according to the requisitions of law.

Conventio /kənvénsh(iy)ow/. In Canon law, the act of summoning or calling together the parties by summoning the defendant.

In Civil law, a compact, agreement, or convention. An agreement between two or more persons respecting a legal relation between them. The term is one of very wide scope, and applies to all classes of subjects in which an engagement or business relation may be founded by agreement. It is to be distinguished from the negotiations or preliminary transactions on the object of the convention and fixing its extent, which are not binding so long as the convention is not concluded.

In contracts, an agreement; a covenant.

Conventio in unum /kənvénsh(iy)ow in yúwnəm/. In the civil law, the agreement between the two parties to a contract upon the sense of the contract proposed. It is an essential part of the contract, following the pollicitation or proposal emanating from the one, and followed by the consension or agreement of the other.

Convention. An agreement or compact; *esp.* international agreement, *e.g.* Geneva Convention. An assembly or meeting of members or representatives of political, legislative, fraternal, etc. organizations.

Constitutional convention. See **Constitution.**

English law. An extraordinary assembly of the houses of lords and commons, without the assent or summons of the sovereign. It can only be justified *ex necessitate rei,* as the Parliament which restored Charles II, and that which disposed of the crown and kingdom to William and Mary. Also the name of an old writ that lay for the breach of a covenant.

Judicial convention. See **Judicial.**

Legislative and political. An assembly of delegates or representatives chosen by the people for special and extraordinary legislative purposes, such as the framing or revision of a state constitution (*i.e.* constitutional convention). Also an assembly of delegates chosen by a political party, or by the party organization in a larger or smaller territory, to nominate candidates for an approaching election.

Public and international law. A pact or agreement between states or nations in the nature of a treaty; usually applied (a) to agreements or arrangements preliminary to a formal treaty or to serve as its basis, or (b) international agreements for the regulation of matters of common interest but not coming within the sphere of politics or commercial intercourse, such as international postage or the protection of submarine cables. An agreement between states relating to trade, finance, or other matters considered less important than those usually regulated by a treaty. See **Compact; Treaty.**

Roman law. An agreement between parties; a pact. A convention was a mutual engagement between two persons, possessing all the subjective requisites of a contract, but which did not give rise to an action, nor receive the sanction of the law, as bearing an "obligation," until the objective requisite of a solemn ceremonial, (such as *stipulatio*) was supplied. In other words, convention was the informal agreement of the parties, which formed the basis of a contract, and which became a contract when the external formalities were superimposed. The division of conventions into contracts and pacts was important in the Roman law. The former were such conventions as already, by the older civil law, founded an obligation and action; all the other conventions were termed "pacts." These generally did not produce an actionable obligation. Actionability was subsequently given to several pacts, whereby they received the same power and efficacy that contracts received.

Conventional. Depending on, or arising from, the mutual agreement of parties; as distinguished from *legal,* which means created by, or arising from, the act of the law.

As to conventional Estates; Interest; Mortgage; Subrogation; and Trustees, see those titles.

Conventional lien. A lien is conventional where the lien, general or particular, is raised by the express agreement and stipulation of the parties, in circumstances where the law alone would not create a lien from the mere relation of the parties or the details of their transaction.

Conventional loan. Real estate loan not involving government participation by way of insurance (FHA) or guarantee (VA).

Conventione /kənvènshiyówniy/. The name of a writ for the breach of any covenant in writing, whether real or personal.

Conventions. This name is sometimes given to compacts or treaties with foreign countries as to the apprehension and extradition of fugitive offenders. See **Extradition.**

Conventio privatorum non potest publico juri derogare /kənvénsh(iy)ow pràyvətórəm nòn pówdəst páblǝkow júray dìyrǝgériy/. The agreement of private persons cannot derogate from public right, *i.e.,* cannot prevent the application of general rules of law, or render valid any contravention of law.

Conventio vincit legem /kənvénsh(iy)ow vínsǝt líyjǝm/. The express agreement of parties overcomes [prevails against] the law.

Conventual church. In ecclesiastical law, that which consists of regular clerks, professing some order or religion; or of dean and chapter; or other societies of spiritual men.

Conventuals /kənvénchuwǝlz/. Religious men united in a convent or religious house.

Conventus /kənvéntǝs/. Lat. A coming together; a convention or assembly. *Conventus magnatum vel procerum* (the assembly of chief men or peers) was one of the names of the English parliament. 1 Bl. Comm. 148.

In the civil law, the term meant a gathering together of people; a crowd assembled for any purpose; also a convention, pact, or bargain.

Conventus juridicus /kǝnvéntǝs jǝrídǝkǝs/. In the Roman law, a court of sessions held in the Roman provinces, by the president of the province, assisted by a certain number of counsellors and assessors, at fixed periods, to hear and determine suits, and to provide for the civil administration of the province.

Conversant. One who is in the habit of being in a particular place is said to be conversant there. Acquainted; familiar.

Conversantes /kònvǝrsǽntiyz/. In old English law, conversant or dwelling; commorant.

Conversation. Manner of living; behavior habits of life; conduct; as in the phrase "chaste life and conversation." Criminal conversation means seduction of another man's wife, considered as an actionable injury to the husband. See **Criminal** (*Criminal conversation*).

Converse. To engage in conversation; social interaction. Reversed in order or relation. The transposition of the subject and predicate in a proposition, as: "Everything is good in its place." *Converse,* "Nothing is good which is not in its place."

Conversion. An unauthorized assumption and exercise of the right of ownership over goods or personal chattels belonging to another, to the alteration of their condition or the exclusion of the owner's rights. Any unauthorized act which deprives an owner of his property permanently or for an indefinite time. Unauthorized and wrongful exercise of dominion and control over another's personal property, to exclusion of or inconsistent with rights of owner. Catania v. Garage De Le Paix, Inc., Tex.Civ.App., 542 S.W.2d 239, 241. See also **Embezzlement; Equitable conversion; Fraudulent conversion; Involuntary conversion.**

Act of exchanging a convertible security for another security. See **Convertible securities.**

Commercial instruments. An instrument is converted when: a drawee to whom it is delivered for acceptance refuses to return it on demand; or any person to whom it is delivered for payment refuses on demand either to pay or to return it; or it is paid on a forged indorsement. U.C.C. § 3–419(1).

Constructive conversion. An implied or virtual conversion, which takes place where a person does such acts in reference to the goods of another as amount in law to the appropriation of the property to himself.

Direct conversion. The act of actually appropriating the property of another to his own beneficial use and enjoyment, or to that of a third person, or destroying it, or altering its nature, or wrongfully assuming title in himself.

Equitable conversion. The exchange of property from real to personal or from personal to real, which takes place under some circumstances in the consideration of the law, such as, to give effect to directions in a will or settlement, or to stipulations in a contract, although no such change has actually taken place, and by which exchange the property so dealt with becomes invested with the properties and attributes of that into which it is supposed to have been converted. It is sometimes necessary however for certain purposes of devolution and transfer to regard the property in its changed condition as though the change has not absolutely taken place.

Conversion hysteria. A neurosis in which there is gross loss or impairment of some somatic or physical function caused by emotional conflicts, such as hysterical blindness, hysterical paralysis, hysterical tremors, hysterical limping. Used by sufferer to protect himself from anxiety.

Convertible debt. A bond or debenture or note which under certain conditions and at certain times may be converted into stock by the holder. See **Convertible securities**, *infra*.

Convertible securities. A bond, debenture or preferred share which may be exchanged by the owner for common stock or another security, usually of the same company, in accordance with the terms of the issue.

Convertible term insurance. Type of term insurance which may be changed to permanent (whole life) insurance carrying loan values, built in values, etc.

Convey. To transfer or deliver to another. To pass or transmit the title to property from one to another. To transfer property or the title to property by deed, bill of sale, or instrument under seal. Used popularly in sense of "assign", "sale", or "transfer". See **Conveyance**.

Conveyance /kənvéyən(t)s/. In its most common usage, transfer of title to land from one person, or class of persons, to another by deed. Term may also include assignment, lease, mortgage or encumbrance of land. An instrument by which some estate or interest in lands is transferred from one person to another; such as a deed, mortgage, etc. See also **Alienation; Demise; Fraudulent conveyance; Involuntary conveyance**.

Absolute or conditional conveyance. An absolute conveyance is one by which the right or property in a thing is transferred, free of any condition or qualification, by which it might be defeated or changed, as an ordinary deed of lands, in contradistinction to a mortgage, which is a conditional conveyance. Brown v. United States, C.C.A.Pa., 95 F.2d 487, 489.

Fraudulent conveyance. See **Fraudulent**.

Mesne conveyance. An intermediate conveyance; one occupying an intermediate position in a chain of title between the first grantee and the present holder.

Primary conveyances. Those by means whereof the benefit or estate is created or first arises; as distinguished from those whereby it may be enlarged, restrained, transferred, or extinguished. The term includes feoffment, gift, grant, lease, exchange, and partition, and is opposed to *derivative* conveyances, such as release, surrender, confirmation, etc. 2 Bl. Comm. 309.

Secondary conveyances. The name given to that class of conveyances which presuppose some other conveyance precedent, and only serve to enlarge, confirm, alter, restrain, restore, or transfer the interest granted by such original conveyance. 2 Bl.Comm. 324. Otherwise termed "derivative conveyances" (*q.v.*).

Voluntary conveyance. A conveyance without valuable consideration; such as a deed or settlement in favor of a wife or children.

Conveyancer. One whose business it is to prepare deeds, mortgages, examine titles to real estate, and perform other functions relating to the transfer of real property.

Conveyancing. Act of performing the various functions relating to the transfer of real property such as examination of land titles, preparation of deeds, mortgages, closing agreements, etc.

Conveyancing counsel to the court of chancery. Certain counsel, not fewer than six in number, appointed by the lord chancellor, for the purpose of assisting the court of chancery, or any judge thereof, with their opinion in matters of title and conveyancing.

Conveyor's heirs. Under common law rule, when a remainder was limited to heirs of grantor or testator, such heirs did not take a remainder; instead, the estate was considered a reversion in the grantor or testator, and hence, if heirs took at all, they would take by descent, not by purchase. This rule, known as rule of worthier title (Braswell v. Braswell, 195 Va. 971, 81 S.E.2d 560) has been abolished in many jurisdictions. See **Worthier title**.

Convicia si irascaris tua divulgas; spreta exolescunt /kənvísh(iy)ə sày àyrəskérəs tyúwə dəválgəs, spríydə èkskəléskənt/. If you be moved to anger by insults, you publish them; if despised, they are forgotten.

Convicium /kənvísh(iy)əm/. In the civil law, the name of a species of slander or injury uttered in public, and which charged some one with some act *contra bonos mores*.

Convict, v. To find a man guilty of a criminal charge, either upon a criminal trial, a plea of guilty, or a plea of nolo contendere. The word was formerly used also in the sense of finding against the defendant in a civil case.

Convict, n. One who has been adjudged guilty of a crime and is serving a sentence as a result of such conviction. A prisoner.

Convicted. See **Conviction**.

Conviction. In a general sense, the result of a criminal trial which ends in a judgment or sentence that the accused is guilty as charged.

"Conviction" and "convicted" mean the final judgment on a verdict or finding of guilty, a plea of guilty, or a plea of nolo contendere, and do not include a final judgment which has been expunged by pardon, reversed, set aside, or otherwise rendered nugatory. 18 U.S.C.A. § 4251.

The final consummation of the prosecution including the judgment or sentence, or as is frequently the case, the judgment or sentence itself. Ex parte White, 75 Okl.Cr. 204, 130 P.2d 103, 104. The stage of a criminal proceeding where the issue of guilt is determined. United States v. Locke, 409 F.Supp. 600.

A record of the summary proceedings upon any penal statute before one or more justices of the peace or other persons duly authorized, in a case where the offender has been *convicted* and sentenced.

Summary conviction. The conviction of a person (usually for a minor misdemeanor), as the result of his trial before a magistrate or court, without a jury.

Convincing proof. Such as is sufficient to establish the proposition in question, beyond hesitation, ambiguity, or reasonable doubt, in an unprejudiced mind. See **Beyond a reasonable doubt; Clear; Proof.**

Convivium /kənvíviyəm/. A tenure by which a tenant was bound to provide meat and drink for his lord at least once in the year.

Convocation. In ecclesiastical law, the general assembly of the clergy to consult upon ecclesiastical matters.

Convoy. An escort for protection, either by land or sea. A naval force for the protection of merchantships and others, during the whole voyage, or such part of it as is known to require such protection. An association for a hostile object. In undertaking it, a nation spreads over the merchant vessel an immunity from search which belongs only to a national ship. By joining a convoy every individual ship puts off her pacific character, and undertakes for the discharge of duties which belong only to the military marine, and adds to the numerical, if not to the real strength of the convoy. The Atlanta, 16 U.S. (3 Wheat.) 409, 423, 4 L.Ed. 422.

Co-obligor. A joint obligor; one bound jointly with another or others in a bond or obligation.

Cool blood. In the law of homicide, calmness or tranquility; the undisturbed possession of one's faculties and reason; the absence of violent passion, fury, or uncontrollable excitement. See also **Cooling time; Premeditation.**

Cooley doctrine. Doctrine which holds that state is deprived of all regulatory power as to subjects which "are in their nature national, or admit only of one uniform system or plan of regulation." Cooley v. Board of Wardens of Port of Philadelphia, 53 U.S. (12 How.) 299, 13 L.Ed. 996. See also **Pre-emption.**

Cooling off period. A period of time in which no action of a particular sort may be taken by either side in a dispute. For example, a period of a month after a union or a company files a grievance against the other. During this period, the union may not strike and the company may not lock-out the employees. A period of time in which a buyer may cancel a purchase; most states require a three-day cancellation period for door-to-door sales or home improvement contracts. An automatic delay in some states, in addition to ordinary court delays, between the filing of divorce papers and the divorce hearing.

Cooling time. Time to recover "cool blood" after severe excitement or provocation. Time for the mind to become so calm and sedate as that it is supposed to contemplate, comprehend, and coolly act with reference to the consequences likely to ensue.

Cooperate. To act jointly or concurrently toward a common end.

Cooperation. Action of co-operating. Association of persons for common benefit. In patent law, unity of action to a common end or a common result, not merely joint or simultaneous action.

Cooperation clause. That provision in insurance policies which requires the insured to cooperate with the insurer in defense of a claim. "Co-operation" by insured within a co-operation clause means that there shall be fair and frank disclosure of information reasonably demanded by insurer to enable it to determine whether there is genuine defense. Prudence Mut. Cas. Co. v. Dunn, 30 Ill.App.2d 469, 175 N.E.2d 286.

Cooperative /kowóp(ə)rədəv/. A corporation or association organized for purpose of rendering economic services, without gain to itself, to shareholders or members who own and control it. United Grocers, Limited v. U. S., D.C.Cal., 186 F.Supp. 724, 733. Type of business that is owned by its customers.

Cooperative generally connotes an apartment building in which owner holds title to all premises and grants rights of occupancy to particular apartments by means of proprietary leases or similar arrangements. AMR Realty Co. v. State, Bureau of Securities, 149 N.J.Super. 329, 373 A.2d 1002, 1004.

Cooperatives vary widely in character and in the manner in which they function. They have been classified along functional lines as follows: (a) consumer cooperatives (including consumer stores, housing cooperatives, utility cooperatives, and health cooperatives); (b) marketing cooperatives; (c) business purchasing cooperatives; (d) workers' productive cooperatives; (e) financial cooperatives (such as the credit union, mutual savings bank, savings and loan association, and production credit association); (f) insurance cooperatives; (g) labor unions; (h) trade associations; and (i) self-help cooperatives.

The required form for a cooperative may differ in different states; e.g. unincorporated association, cooperative association, nonprofit corporation.

See also **Consumer's cooperative; Cooperative corporation.**

Farmer's cooperative. Major function of such cooperative is to market the combined crops, produce or livestock of its farmer-owners. The cooperative attempts to sell crops and livestock at the optimum price. For example, it might store grain until the price of such rises.

Cooperative apartment. Dwelling units in a multi dwelling complex in which each owner has an interest in the entire complex and a lease of his own apartment, though he does not own his apartment as in the case of a condominium.

Cooperative association. See **Cooperative.**

Cooperative corporation. A "cooperative corporation", while having a corporate existence, is primarily an organization for purpose of providing services and profits to its members and not for corporate profit. Linnton Plywood Ass'n v. State Tax Commission, 241 Or. 1, 403 P.2d 708, 709.

Cooperative federalism. The distribution of power between national and local or state governments while each recognizes the powers of the other.

Cooperative housing. See **Cooperative apartment.**

Cooperative negligence. See **Negligence** (*Contributory negligence*).

Coopertio /kòwəpə́rsh(iy)ow/. In old English law, the head of branches of a tree cut down; though *coopertio arborum* is rather the bark of timber trees felled, and the chumps and broken wood.

Coopertus /kòwəpə́rdəs/. Covert; covered.

Co-optation /kòwoptéyshən/. A concurring choice; the election, by the members of a close corporation, of a person to fill a vacancy.

Coordinate. Equal, of the same order, rank, degree or importance; not subordinate. Empire Ins. Co. of Texas v. Cooper, Tex.Civ.App., 138 S.W.2d 159, 164. Adjusted to, in harmony with. Æolian-Skinner Organ Co. v. Shepard Broadcasting Service, C.C.A. Mass., 81 F.2d 392, 395. As to courts of "co-ordinate jurisdiction," see **Jurisdiction.**

Coordinate jurisdiction. That which is possessed by courts of equal rank, degree, or authority, equally competent to deal with the matter in question, whether belonging to the same or different systems; concurrent jurisdiction. See **Jurisdiction.**

Coordinate system. A method of land description. It uses a measurement based on an intersection of a defined north-south axis and a defined east-west axis.

Co-owner. Two or more persons who own property, real or personal. Tenants in common of property. Broad term which may describe joint tenants as well.

Coparcenary /kòwparsíynəriy/. Such estate arises where several take by descent from same ancestor as one heir, all coparceners constituting but one heir and having but one estate and being connected by unity of interest and of title. Winters Nat. Bank & Trust Co. v. Riffe, Ohio Prob., 194 N.E.2d 921, 924. A species of estate, or tenancy, which exists where lands of inheritance descend from the ancestor to two or more persons. It arose in England either by common law or particular custom. By common law, as where a person, seised in fee-simple or fee-tail, dies, and his next heirs are two or more females, his daughters, sisters, aunts, cousins, or their representatives; in this case they all inherit, and these coheirs, are then called "coparceners," or, for brevity, "parceners" only. 2 Bl.Comm. 187. By particular custom, as where lands descend, as in gavelkind, to all the males in equal degree, as sons, brothers, uncles, etc. An estate which several persons hold as one heir, whether male or female. This estate has the three unities of time, title, and possession; but the interests of the coparceners may be unequal. 2 Bl. Comm. 188.

While joint tenancies refer to persons, the idea of coparcenary refers to the estate. The title to it is always by descent. The respective shares may be unequal; as, for instance, one daughter and two granddaughters, children of a deceased daughter, may take by the same act of descent. As to strangers, the tenants' seisin is a joint one, but, as between themselves, each is seised of his or her own share, on whose death it goes to the heirs, and not by survivorship. The right of possession of coparceners is in common, and the possession of one is, in general, the possession of the others.

Coparceners /kòwparsíynərz/. Persons to whom an estate of inheritance descends jointly, and by whom it is held as an entire estate. 2 Bl.Comm. 187.

Coparticeps /kòwpárdəsèps/. In old English law, a coparcener.

Coparties. Parties having like status, such as, co-defendants. Murray v. Haverford Hospital Corp., D.C. Pa., 278 F.Supp. 5, 7.

"Co-party," within rule (F.R.C.P. 13) providing that a pleading may state as a cross-claim any claim by one party against a co-party arising out of the transaction or occurrence that is the subject matter of the original action, does not mean merely equal party, such as one of several original defendants, but applies to a third-party defendant brought into the case by an original defendant on a theory of liability over. Fogel v. United Gas Imp. Co., D.C.Pa., 32 F.R.D. 202, 204.

Copartner. One who is a partner with one or more other persons; a member of a partnership.

Copartnership. A partnership.

Copeland Act. Federal act prohibiting wage kickbacks or rebates being imposed on employees engaged in construction or repair of public buildings or works.

Copeman, or copesman. A chapman *(q.v.).*

Copesmate /kówpsmeyt/. A merchant; a partner in merchandise.

Copia /kópiyə/. Lat. In civil and old English law, opportunity or means of access.

In old English law, a copy. *Copia libelli,* the copy of a libel.

Copia libelli deliberanda /kópiyə ləbélay dəlibərǽndə/. In old English law, the name of a writ that lay where a man could not get a copy of a libel at the hands of a spiritual judge, to have the same delivered to him.

Coppa /kópə/. In English law, a crop or cock of grass, hay, or corn, divided into titheable portions, that it may be more fairly and justly tithed.

Copper and scales. See **Mancipatio.**

Coprincipal. One of two or more participants in crime who actually perpetrate crime or are present aiding and abetting person who commits crime. One of two or more persons who has appointed agents whom they have right to control.

Copula /kópyələ/. The corporal consummation of marriage. *Copula* (in logic), the link between subject and predicate contained in the verb.

Copulatio verborum indicat acceptationem in eodem sensu /kòpyələéysh(iy)ow vərbórəm índəkət ǽksəptèyshiyównəm ìn iyówdəm séns(y)uw/. Coupling of words together shows that they are to be understood in the same sense.

Copulative term. One which is placed between two or more others to join them together.

Copy. A transcript, double, imitation, or reproduction of an original writing, painting, instrument, or the like.

Under best evidence rule, a copy may not be introduced until original is accounted for. Certified copies are admissible under statutes in most jurisdictions. Similarly, photographic copies and prints from photographic films are admissible by statute.

Copies of all pleadings, motions and other papers must be served on all parties to action under Fed.R. Civil P. 5(b). Admissions concerning the genuineness of copies of documents are governed by Fed.R. Civil P. 36(a).

A duplicate is admissible in evidence to the same extent as an original unless (1) a genuine question is raised as to the authenticity of the original or (2) in the circumstances it would be unfair to admit the duplicate in lieu of the original. Fed.Evid.R. 1003.

In copyright law, "copying" of a literary work consists in exact or substantial reproduction of the original, using original as a model as distinguished from an independent production of same thing, and a "copy" is that which comes so near to original as to give every person seeing it the idea created by original and must be such that ordinary observation would cause it to be recognized as having been taken from the work of another. Turner v. Century House Pub. Co., 56 Misc.2d 1071, 290 N.Y.S.2d 637, 642.

See also **Authentication; Conformed copy; Duplicate.**

Examined copies are those which have been compared with the original or with an official record thereof.

Copyhold. In England a species of estate at will, or customary estate, the only visible title to which consisted of the copies of the court rolls, which were made out by the steward of the manor, on a tenant's being admitted to any parcel of land, or tenement belonging to the manor. It was an estate at the will of the lord, yet such a will as was agreeable to the custom of the manor, which customs were preserved and evidenced by the rolls of the several courts baron, in which they were entered. 2 Bl.Comm. 95. In a larger sense, copyhold was said to import every customary tenure (that is, every tenure pending on the particular custom of a manor), as opposed to free socage, or freehold, which later (since the abolition of knight-service) was considered as the general or common-law tenure of the country. Under the English Law of Property Act of 1922 copyholds were enfranchised and became freehold (or in certain cases leasehold).

Copyhold commissioners. Commissioners appointed to carry into effect various acts of parliament, having for their principal objects the compulsory commutation of manorial burdens and restrictions (fines, heriots, rights to timber and minerals, etc.), and the compulsory enfranchisement of copyhold lands.

Copyholder. A tenant by copyhold tenure (by copy of court-roll). 2 Bl.Comm. 95.

Privileged copyholds. Those copyhold estates which are said to be held according to the custom of the manor, and not *at the will of the lord,* as common copyholds are. They include customary freeholds and ancient demesnes.

Copyright. The right of literary property as recognized and sanctioned by positive law. An intangible, incorporeal right granted by statute to the author or originator of certain literary or artistic productions, whereby he is invested, for a limited period, with the sole and exclusive privilege of multiplying copies of the same and publishing and selling them.

Copyright protection subsists in original works of authorship fixed in any tangible medium of expression, now known or later developed, from which they can be perceived, reproduced, or otherwise communicated, either directly or with the aid of a machine or device. Works of authorship include the following categories: (1) literary works; (2) musical works, including any accompanying words; (3) dramatic works, including any accompanying music; (4) pantomimes and choreographic works; (5) pictorial, graphic, and sculptural works; (6) motion pictures and other audiovisual works; and (7) sound recordings. In no case does copyright protection for an original work of authorship extend to any idea, procedure, process, system, method of operation, concept, principle, or discovery, regardless of the form in which it is described, explained, illustrated, or embodied in such work. Copyright Act, § 102.

"Common law copyright" is that right which author has in his unpublished literary creations, a kind of property right whose extent is to give him control over first publication of his work or to prevent its publication. Hemingway's Estate v. Random House, Inc., 53 Misc.2d 462, 279 N.Y.S.2d 51, 54. See **Common-law copyright.**

See also Fair use doctrine; First sale rule; Infringement; Limited publication; Literary property; Literary work.

Copyright notice. A necessary notice in the form required by law which is placed in each published copy of the work copyrighted. Copyright Act, § 401.

Coraagium, or **coraage** /kòr(ə)éyjiyəm/. Measures of corn. An unusual and extraordinary tribute, arising only on special occasions. They are thus distinguished from services. Mentioned in connection with *hidage* and *carvage.*

Coram /kórəm/. Lat. Before; in presence of. Applied to persons only.

Coram domino rege /kórəm dómənow ríyjiy/. Before our lord the king. *Coram domino rege ubicumque tunc fuerit Angliœ,* before our lord the king wherever he shall then be in England.

Coram ipso rege /kórəm ípsow ríyjiy/. Before the king himself. The old name of the court of king's bench, which was originally held before the king in person. 3 Bl.Comm. 41.

Coram nobis /kórəm nówbəs/. In our presence; before us. The office of "writ of coram nobis" is to bring attention of court to, and obtain relief from, errors of fact, such as a valid defense existing in facts of case, but which, without negligence on defendant's part, was not made, either through duress or fraud or excusable mistake, where facts did not appear on face of record, and were such as, if known in season, would have prevented rendition of the judgment questioned. People v. Tuthill, 32 Cal.2d 819, 198 P.2d 505, 506. The essence of coram nobis is that it is addressed to the very court which renders the judgment in which injustice is alleged to have been done, in contrast to appeals or review directed to another court; the words "coram nobis", meaning "our court," as compared to the common-law writ of coram vobis," meaning "your court," clearly point this up. The writs of coram nobis and coram vobis have been abolished by Fed.R.Civil P. 60(b) and superseded by relief as provided by that rule. See also **Coram vobis; Error coram nobis; Error coram vobis; Writ of error.**

Coram non judice /kórəm nòn júwdəsiy/. In presence of a person not a judge. When a suit is brought and determined in a court which has no jurisdiction in the matter, then it is said to be *coram non judice,* and the judgment is void.

Coram paribus /kórəm pǽrəbəs/. Before the peers or freeholders. The attestation of deeds, like all other solemn transactions, was originally done only *coram paribus.* 2 Bl.Comm. 307. *Coram paribus de vicineto,* before the peers or freeholders of the neighborhood. Id. 315.

Coram sectatoribus /kórəm sèktətórəbəs/. Before the suitors.

Coram vobis /kórəm vówbəs/. Before you. A writ of error directed by a court of review to the court which tried the cause, to correct an error in fact. See **Coram nobis; Writ of error.**

Cord. A measure of wood containing 128 cubic feet, otherwise expressed as a pile of wood 8 feet long, 4 feet high, and 4 feet wide.

Co-respondent. A co-defendant. A person summoned to answer a bill, petition, or libel, together with another respondent. Used for example to designate the person charged with adultery with the respondent in a suit for divorce for that cause, and joined as a defendant with such party.

Ordinarily term "co-respondent" denotes one joined as party defendant in equity suit. Blankenship v. Blankenship, 239 Md. 498, 212 A.2d 294, 299.

Corium forisfacere /kóriyəm fòrəsféysəriy/. To forfeit one's skin, applied to a person condemned to be whipped; anciently the punishment of a servant. *Corium perdere,* the same. *Corium redimere,* to compound for a whipping.

Cornage /kórnəj/. A species of tenure in England, by which the tenant was bound to blow a horn for the sake of alarming the country on the approach of an enemy. It was a species of grand serjeanty.

Corner. A combination among the dealers in a specific commodity, or outside investors, for the purpose of buying up the greater portion of that commodity which is upon the market or may be brought to market, and holding the same back from sale, until the demand shall so far outrun the limited supply as to advance the price abnormally.

A "corner" is a condition arising when a much greater quantity of any given commodity is sold for future delivery within a given period than can be purchased in the market. The buyers, who are called in the slang of the exchanges, the "longs," then insist on delivery, and thus succeed in running up the prices

to a fictitious point, at which the deals are "rung out" between the dealers by the payment of differences, or, where the buyers insist, by actual delivery.

Lost corner. One whose location as established by the government surveyors cannot be found. The mere fact that evidence of the physical location cannot now be seen, or that no one who saw the marked corner is produced, does not necessarily make the corner a lost one.

Obliterated corner. One where no visible evidence remains of the work of the original surveyor in establishing it.

Surveying. An angle made by two boundary lines; the common end of two boundary lines, which run at an angle with each other.

Cornet. A commissioned officer of cavalry, abolished in England in 1871, and not existing in the United States army.

Corn laws. A species of protective tariff formerly in existence in England, imposing import-duties on various kinds of grain. The corn laws were abolished in 1846.

Corn Products case. Where corn products manufacturer, as an integral part of its manufacturing business and to protect itself against rises in price of raw corn, bought corn futures, accepting delivery in some cases and in other cases reselling futures upon spot purchase of corn, profits on resale of futures were taxable as ordinary income, rather than as capital gains, even though the transactions did not constitute true hedging in that there was no protection against fall in price. Corn Products Refining Co. v. Commission of Internal Revenue, 350 U.S. 46, 76 S.Ct. 20, 100 L.Ed. 29.

Corn whisky. An intoxicating whisky or liquor made from corn or containing a corn product, otherwise known as "moonshine," "white mule," "hootch," "corn liquor," "moonshine corn whisky."

Corody /kórədiy/. In old English law, a sum of money or allowance of meat, drink, and clothing due to the crown from the abbey or other religious house, whereof it was founder, towards the sustentation of such one of its servants as is thought fit to receive it. It differs from a pension, in that it was allowed towards the maintenance of any of the king's servants in an abbey; a pension being given to one of the king's chaplains, for his better maintenance, till he may be provided with a benefice. 1 Bl.Comm. 283.

Corollary. In logic, a collateral or secondary consequence, deduction, or inference.

Corona /kərównə/. The crown. *Placita coronæ;* pleas of the crown; criminal actions or proceedings, in which the crown was the prosecutor.

Corona mala /kərównə mǽlə/. In old English law, the clergy who abuse their character were so called.

Coronare /kòrənériy/. In old English law, to give the tonsure, which was done on the crown, or in the form of a crown; to make a man a priest.

Coronare filium /kòrənériy fíliyəm/. In old English law, to make one's son a priest. *Homo coronatus* was one who had received the first tonsure, as preparatory to superior orders, and the tonsure was in form of a corona, or crown of thorns.

Coronation oath. The oath administered to a sovereign at the ceremony of crowning or investing him with the insignia of royalty, in acknowledgment of his right to govern the kingdom, in which he swears to observe the laws, customs, and privileges of the kingdom, and to act and do all things conformably thereto.

Coronator /kórəneydər/. A coroner.

Coronatore eligendo /kòrənətóriy eləjéndow/. In English law, the name of a writ issued to the sheriff, commanding him to proceed to the election of a coroner.

Coronatore exonerando /kòrənətóriy egzònərǽndow/. In English law, the name of a writ for the removal of a coroner, for a cause which is to be therein assigned, as that he is engaged in other business, or incapacitated by years or sickness, or has not a sufficient estate in the county, or lives in an inconvenient part of it.

Coroner /kórənər/. Public official, of English origin, charged with duty to make inquiry into the causes and circumstances of any death which occurs through violence or suddenly and with marks of suspicion; *i.e.* unnatural death. The functions and duties of coroners have been diminished having been replaced by medical examiners. See **Coroner's inquest; Medical examiner.**

Coroner's court. In England, a tribunal of record, where a coroner holds his inquiries.

Coroner's inquest. An inquisition or examination into the causes and circumstances of any death happening by violence or under suspicious conditions, held by the coroner with the assistance of a jury. See also **Inquest.**

Corpnership. Exists when a corporation is the sole general partner in a limited partnership with numerous public investors as limited partners.

Corporale sacramentum /korpəréyliy sækrəméntəm/. In old English law, a corporal oath.

Corporal imbecility. Physical inability to perform completely the act of sexual intercourse; not necessarily congenital, and not invariably a permanent and incurable impotence.

Corporalis injuria non recipit æstimationem de futuro /korpəréyləs ənjúriyə nòn résəpət èstəmèyshiyównəm dìy fyuwchúrow/. A personal injury does not receive satisfaction from a future course of proceeding [is not left for its satisfaction to a future course of proceeding].

Corporal oath. An oath, the external solemnity of which consists in laying one's hand upon the Holy Bible while the oath is administered to him. More generally, a solemn oath.

Corporal punishment. Physical punishment as distinguished from pecuniary punishment or a fine; any kind of punishment of or inflicted on the body. The term may or may not include imprisonment, according to the context. The Supreme Court has upheld the use of reasonable corporal punishment in schools. Ingraham v. Wright, 430 U.S. 651, 97 S.Ct. 1401, 51 L.Ed.2d 711.

Corporal touch. Bodily touch; actual physical contact; manual apprehension.

Corporate. Belonging to a corporation; as a corporate name. Incorporated; as a corporate body.

Corporate agent. A natural person or a corporation who is authorized to act for a corporation as for example in the function of accepting service of process. Broadly, term includes all employees and officers of corporation who have power to bind the corporation.

Corporate alter ego, doctrine of. Means that courts ignoring forms and looking to substance will regard stockholders as owners of corporation's property, or as the real parties in interest whenever it is necessary to do so to prevent fraud which might otherwise be perpetrated, to redress a wrong which might otherwise go without redress, or to do justice which might otherwise fail. See **Piercing corporate veil.**

Corporate authorities. The title given in statutes of several states to the aggregate body of officers of a municipal corporation, or to certain of those officers (excluding the others) who are vested with authority in regard to the particular matter spoken of in the statute, as, taxation, bonded debt, regulation of the sale of liquors, etc.

Corporate body. Term is equivalent to "body corporate"; *i.e.* a corporation.

Corporate bonds. A written promise by a corporation to pay a fixed sum of money at some future time named, with stated interest payable at some fixed time or intervals, given in return for money or its equivalent received by the corporation, sometimes secured, and sometimes not.

Corporate charter. Document issued by state agency or authority (commonly Secretary of State) granting corporation legal existence and right to function (*i.e.* conduct business) as a corporation. See also **Charter; Corporate franchise.**

Corporate citizenship. Corporate status in the state of incorporation, though a foreign corporation is not a citizen for purposes of the Privileges and Immunities Clause (U.S.Const., Art. IV, § 2). Bank of Augusta v. Earle, 38 U.S. (13 Pet.) 519, 10 L.Ed. 274.

Corporate crime. Any criminal offense committed by and hence chargeable to a corporation because of activities of its officers or employees.

Corporate domicile. The domicile of a corporation is the state of its incorporation.

Corporate entity. The distinct status of a corporation which sets its existence apart from the status of its shareholders; its capacity to have a name of its own, to sue and be sued in its own name as well as the right to buy, sell, lease and mortgage its property in its own name.

Corporate excess. Term used in connection with taxation of a corporation engaged in interstate commerce by a state and meaning the proportion of fair cash value of all the shares constituting the capital stock on a given date as the value of the assets, both real and personal, employed within the state bears to the total assets of the corporation on that date. Alpha Portland Cement Co. v. Mass., 268 U.S. 203, 208, 45 S.Ct. 477, 69 L.Ed. 916.

Corporate franchise. The right to exist and do business as a corporation. The right or privilege granted by the state or government to the persons forming an aggregate corporation, and their successors, to exist and do business as a corporation and to exercise the rights and powers incidental to that form of organization or necessarily implied in the grant. See also **Corporate charter.**

Corporate liability. See **Piercing corporate veil.**

Corporate mortgage trust. Device for financing corporate activities which requires an indenture and an independent trustee for protection of holders of bonds and debentures. The trust holds security consisting of property in event of default.

Corporate name. When a corporation is formed, state statutes require that such be given a name and such name is kept on record with the proper state authority (*e.g.* Secretary of State's office). Only by and under such name may the corporation sue or be sued and do all legal acts.

Corporate officers. Those persons who fill the offices which are provided for in the charter such as president, treasurer, etc., though in a broader sense the term includes vice presidents, general manager and other officials of the corporation.

Corporate opportunity doctrine. Doctrine of "corporate opportunity" is a species of duty of fiduciary to act with undivided loyalty, and applies to acquisition of property, tangible or intangible, present or future, of person who occupies a fiduciary relationship to corporation which is in opposition to corporation. General Automotive Mfg. Co. v. Singer, 19 Wis.2d 528, 120 N.W.2d 659, 663.

Corporate purpose. In reference to municipal corporations, and especially to their powers of taxation, a "corporate purpose" is one which shall promote the general prosperity and the welfare of the municipality; or a purpose necessary or proper to carry into effect the object of the creation of the corporate body or one which is germane to the general scope of the objects for which the corporation was created or has a legitimate connection with those objects and a manifest relation thereto.

Corporate stock. Term embraces all securities issued by the corporation though it should not include bonds and debentures because these represent debt rather than stock. See **Stock.**

Corporate trustees. Those corporations which are empowered by their charter to act as trustee, such as banks and trust companies.

Corporation. An artificial person or legal entity created by or under the authority of the laws of a state or nation, composed, in some rare instances, of a single person and his successors, being the incumbents of a particular office, but ordinarily consisting of an association of numerous individuals. Such entity subsists as a body politic under a special denomination, which is regarded in law as having a personality and existence distinct from that of its several members, and which is, by the same authority, vested with the capacity of continuous succession, irrespective of changes in its membership, either in perpetuity or for a limited term of years, and of acting as a unit or single individual in matters relating to the common purpose of the association, within the scope of the powers and authorities conferred upon such bodies by law. Dartmouth College v. Woodward, 17 U.S. (4 Wheat.) 518, 636, 657, 4 L.Ed. 629; U. S. v. Trinidad Coal Co., 137 U.S. 160, 11 S.Ct. 57, 34 L.Ed. 640.

As defined in the Bankruptcy Act, "corporation" includes association having a power or privilege that a private corporation, but not an individual or a partnership, possesses; partnership association organized under a law that makes only the capital subscribed responsible for the debts of such association; joint-stock company; unincorporated company or association; or business trust; but does not include limited partnerships. Bankruptcy Act, § 101(8).

See also Affiliate company; Brother-sister corporation; Charitable corporation; Charitable organizations; Clearing corporation; Collapsible corporation; Cooperative corporation; Domestic corporation; Dormant corporation; Foreign corporation; Municipal corporation; Non-profit corporation; Non-stock corporation; Parent company; Person; Public corporations; Subchapter S corporation; Thin corporation.

Classification

According to the accepted definitions and rules, corporations are classified as follows:

Public and private. A public corporation is one created by the state for political purposes and to act as an agency in the administration of civil government, generally within a particular territory or subdivision of the state, and usually invested, for that purpose, with subordinate and local powers of legislation; such as a county, city, town, or school district. These are also sometimes called "political corporations." See **Municipal corporation.**

Private corporations are those founded by and composed of private individuals, for private purposes, as distinguished from governmental purposes, and having no political or governmental franchises or duties.

The true distinction between public and private corporations is that the former are organized for governmental purposes, the latter not. The term "public" has sometimes been applied to corporations of which the government owned the entire stock, as in the case of a state bank. But bearing in mind that "public" is here equivalent to "political," it will be apparent that this is a misnomer. Again the fact that the business or operations of a corporation may directly and very extensively affect the general public (as in the case of a railroad company or a bank or an insurance company) is no reason for calling it a public corporation. If organized by private persons for their own advantage,—or even if organized for the benefit of the public generally, as in the case of a free public hospital or other charitable institution,—it is none the less a private corporation if it does not possess governmental powers or functions. The uses may in a sense be called "public," but the corporation is "private," as much so as if the franchises were vested in a single person. Dartmouth College v. Woodward, 17 U.S. (4 Wheat.) 562, 4 L.Ed. 629. It is to be observed, however, that those corporations which serve the public or contribute to the comfort and convenience of the general public, though owned and managed by private interests, are now denominated "public-service corporations." See *infra.* Another distinction between public and private corporations is that the former are not voluntary associations (as the latter are) and that there is no contractual relation between the government and a public corporation or between the individuals who compose it.

While the above are strict distinctions between "public" and "private" corporations, in common usage the term "public" corporation is frequently used to distinquish a business corporation whose shares are traded to and among the general public as opposed to a "private" (or "close" corporation) whose shares are not so traded.

Ecclesiastical and lay. In the English law, all corporations private are divided into ecclesiastical and lay, the former being such corporations as are composed exclusively of ecclesiastics organized for spiritual purposes, or for administering property held for religious uses, such as bishops and certain other dignitaries of the church and (formerly) abbeys and monasteries. 1 Bl.Comm. 470. Lay corporations are those composed of laymen, and existing for secular or business purposes. This distinction is not recognized in American law. Corporations formed for the purpose of maintaining or propagating religion or of supporting public religious services, according to the rights of particular denominations, and incidentally owning and administering real and personal property for religious uses, are called "religious corporations," as distinguished from business corporations; but they are "lay" corporations, and not "ecclesiastical" in the sense of the English law.

Aggregate and sole. A corporation sole is one consisting of one person only, and his successors in some particular station, who are incorporated by law in order to give them some legal capacities and advantages, particularly that of perpetuity, which in their natural persons they could not have had. In this sense, the sovereign in England is a sole corporation, so is a bishop, so are some deans distinct from their several chapters, and so is every parson and vicar.

A corporation aggregate is one composed of a number of individuals vested with corporate powers; and a "corporation," as the word is used in general popular and legal speech, and as defined at the head of this title, means a "corporation aggregate."

Domestic and foreign. With reference to the laws and the courts of any given state, a "domestic" corporation is one created by, or organized under, the laws of that state; a "foreign" corporation is one created by or under the laws of another state, government, or country.

Subsidiary and parent. Subsidiary corporation is one in which another corporation (called parent corporation) owns at least a majority of the shares, and thus has control.

Other Compound and Descriptive Terms

Business corporation. One formed for the purpose of transacting business in the widest sense of that term, including not only trade and commerce, but manufacturing, mining, banking, insurance, transportation, and practically every form of commercial or industrial activity where the purpose of the organization is pecuniary profit; contrasted with religious, charitable, educational, and other like organizations, which are sometimes grouped in the statutory law of a state under the general designation of "corporations not for profit."

Brother-sister corporation. See that title.

Civil corporation. In the law of Louisiana, the term "civil" as applied to corporations, is used in a different sense, being contrasted with "religious." Civil corporations are those which relate to temporal police; such are the corporations of the cities, the companies for the advancement of commerce and agriculture, literary societies, colleges or universities founded for the instruction of youth, and the like. Religious corporations are those whose establishment relates only to religion; such are the congregations of the different religious persuasions. Civ.Code La. art. 431.

Close corporation. A corporation whose shares, or at least voting shares, are held by a single shareholder or closely-knit group of shareholders. Generally, there are no public investors and its shareholders are active in the conduct of the business. A close corporation is one which fills its own vacancies or in which power of voting is held through manipulation under fixed and virtually perpetual proxies. Brooks v. Willcuts, C.C.A.Minn., 78 F.2d 270, 273. A corporation, the stock ownership of which is not widely dispersed. Instead, a few shareholders are in control of corporate policy and are in a position to benefit personally from such policy.

Closely held corporation. See *Close corporation, supra.*

Corporation de facto. One existing under color of law and in pursuance of an effort made in good faith to organize a corporation under the statute; an association of men claiming to be a legally incorporated company, and exercising the powers and functions of a corporation, but without actual lawful authority to do so. Its elements are a law or charter authorizing such a corporation, an attempt in good faith to comply with law authorizing its incorporation, and unintentional omission of essential requirements of the law or charter, and exercise in good faith of corporate functions under the law or charter. A corporation which has been defectively formed but which is not subject to collateral attack.

Corporation de jure. That which exists by reason of full compliance by incorporators with requirements of an existing law permitting organization of such corporation.

Collapsible corporation. A corporation formed for one specific venture such as a motion picture and then collapsed, allowing tax advantages to the shareholders. I.R.C. § 341.

Corporation sole. Unusual type of corporation consisting of only one person whose successor becomes the corporation on his death or resignation; limited in the main today to bishops and heads of dioceses. See also *Aggregate and sole, supra.*

Eleemosynary corporation. Corporation with charitable functions and purposes.

Joint venture corporation. A corporation which has joined with other individuals or corporations within the corporate framework in some specific undertaking commonly found in oil, chemical, electronic and atomic fields.

Migratory corporation. A corporation, organized under laws of another state than that of incorporators' residence for purpose of doing all or greater part of their business in state of their residence or in other state than that of incorporation. Toklan Royalty Corporation v. Tiffany, 193 Okl. 120, 141 P.2d 571, 573.

Moneyed corporations are, properly speaking, those dealing in money or in the business of receiving deposits, loaning money, and exchange; but in a wider sense the term is applied to all business corporations having a money capital and employing it in the conduct of their business.

Municipal corporations. See that title.

Public-service corporations. Those whose operations serve the needs of the general public or conduce to the comfort and convenience of an entire community, such as public transportation, gas, water, and electric light companies. The business of such companies is said to be "affected with a public interest," and for that reason they are subject to legislative regulation and control to a greater extent than corporations not of this character. See also *Quasi public corporation, infra.*

Non-stock corporation. Type of corporation where ownership is not recognized by stock; *e.g.* municipal corporation.

Not-for-profit corporation. A corporation formed for some charitable or benevolent purpose and not for profit making and generally organized under special statutes for this purpose.

Professional corporation. In most states such may be organized by those rendering personal services to public of a type which requires a license or other legal authorization and which prior to such statutory authorization could not be performed by a corporation. Includes, but is not limited to, public accountants, certified public accountants, chiropractors, osteopaths, physicians, surgeons, dentists, podiatrists, chiropodists, architects, veterinarians, optometrists, and attorneys at law. Tax benefits are one of several reasons for professional incorporation. Incorporation does not alter professional responsibility or privilege nor does it insulate principal from malpractice liability.

Quasi corporation. A term applied to those bodies, or municipal societies, which, though not vested with the general powers of corporations, are yet recognized, by statutes or immemorial usage, as persons, or aggregate corporations, with precise duties, which may be enforced, and privileges, which may be maintained, by suits at law. "Quasi corporation" is a phrase used to designate bodies which possess a limited number of corporate powers, and which are low down in the scale or grade of corporate existence, and is generally applied to a body which exercises certain functions of a corporate character, but which has not been created a corporation by any statute, general or special. There is a well-defined and marked distinction between municipal corporations proper and political or quasi corporations. Cities, towns, and villages are municipal corporations proper, while counties, townships, school districts, road districts, and the like are quasi corporations. See *Quasi public corporation,* below.

Quasi public corporation. This term is sometimes applied to corporations which are not strictly public, in the sense of being organized for governmental purposes, but whose operations contribute to the comfort, convenience, or welfare of the general public, such as telegraph and telephone companies, gas, water, and electric light companies, and irrigation companies. More commonly and more correctly styled "public-service corporations."

There is a large class of private corporations which on account of special franchises conferred on them owe a duty to the public which they may be compelled to perform. This class of corporations is known as public service corporations, and in legal phraseology as "quasi public corporations," or corporations affected with a public interest. A "quasi public corporation" may be said to be a private corporation which has given to it certain powers of a public nature, such, for instance, as the power of eminent domain, in order to enable it to discharge its duties for the public benefit, in which respect it differs from an ordinary private corporation, the powers of which are given and exercised for the exclusive advantage of its stockholders.

The term is also applied to corporations of that class sometimes called "quasi municipal corporations," such as school districts, irrigation districts, township, etc.

Subchapter S corporation. A small business corporation which, under certain conditions, may elect to have its undistributed taxable income taxed to its shareholders. I.R.C. § 1371 *et seq.* If major significance is the fact that Subchapter S status usually avoids the corporate income tax, and corporate losses can be claimed by the shareholders.

Spiritual corporations. Corporations, the members of which are entirely spiritual persons, and incorporated as such, for the furtherance of religion and perpetuating the rights of the church.

Trading corporations. A commercial corporation engaged in buying and selling. The word "trading," is much narrower in scope than "business," as applied to corporations, and though a trading corporation is a business corporation, there are many business corporations which are not trading companies. Dartmouth College v. Woodward, 17 U.S. (4 Wheat.) 669, 4 L.Ed. 629.

Tramp corporations. Companies chartered in one state without any intention of doing business therein, but which carry on their business and operations wholly in other states.

Corporation Act. In English law, the statute 13 Car. II, St. 2, c. 1; by which it was provided that no person should thereafter be elected to office in any corporate town that should not, within one year previously, have taken the sacrament of the Lord's Supper, according to the rites of the Church of England; and every person so elected was also required to take the oaths of allegiance and supremacy. 4 Bl.Comm. 58. This statute is now repealed.

Corporation courts. Formerly, certain courts in Virginia described as follows: "For each city of the state, there shall be a court called a 'corporation court,' to be held by a judge, with like qualifications and elected in the same manner as judges of the county court."

Corporator. A member of a corporation aggregate. Seaborn v. Wingfield, 56 Nev. 260, 48 P.2d 881, 883. See **Incorporator.**

Corporeal /kərpóriyəl/. A term descriptive of such things as have an objective, material existence; perceptible by the senses of sight and touch; possessing a real body. Opposed to incorporeal and spiritual. There is a distinction between "corporeal" and "corporal." The former term means "possessing a body," that is, tangible, physical, material; the latter means "relating to or affecting a body," that is, bodily, external. Corporeal denotes the nature or physical existence of a body; corporal denotes its exterior or the co-ordination of it with some other body. Hence we speak of "corporeal hereditaments," but of "corporal punishment," "corporal touch," "corporal oath," etc.

Corporeal hereditaments /kərpóriyəl hərédədəmənts/. See **Hereditaments.**

Corporeal property. Such as affects the senses, and may be seen and handled, as opposed to incorporeal property, which cannot be seen or handled, and exists only in contemplation. Thus a house is corporeal, but the annual rent payable for its occupation is incorporeal. Corporeal property is, if movable, capable of manual transfer: if immovable, possession of it may be delivered up. But incorporeal property cannot be so transferred, but some other means must be adopted for its transfer, of which the most usual is an instrument in writing.

In Roman law, the distinction between things corporeal and incorporeal rested on the sense of touch; tangible objects only were considered corporeal. In modern law, all things which may be perceived by any of the bodily senses are termed corporeal, although a common definition of the word includes merely that which can be touched and seen.

Corpore et animo /kórpəriy əd ǽnəmow/. Lat. By the body and by the mind; by the physical act and by the mental intent.

Corps diplomatique /kór dìpləmatíyk/. In international law, ambassadors and diplomatic persons at any court or capital.

Corpse /kórps/. The dead body of a human being.

Corpus /kórpəs/. Lat. Body; an aggregate or mass (of men, laws, or articles); physical substance, as distinguished from intellectual conception; the principal sum or capital, as distinguished from interest or income. The main body or principal of a trust.

A substantial or positive fact, as distinguished from what is equivocal and ambiguous. The *corpus delicti* (body of an offense) is the fact of its having been actually committed.

A corporeal act of any kind (as distinguished from *animus* or mere intention), on the part of him who wishes to acquire a thing, whereby he obtains the physical ability to exercise his power over it whenever he pleases. The word occurs frequently in this sense in the civil law.

As proof, it consists of showing that there exists the object of the crime (dead body in homicide case), and that such resulted from criminal act of some person. In some jurisdictions, it cannot be proved by confession of defendant in the first instance but only after extrinsic evidence (of the elements) has been offered. Downey v. People, 121 Colo. 307, 215 P.2d 892. In other states, confessional evidence is admissible in the first instance. See *Corpus delicti,* below.

Corpus comitatus /kórpəs kòmətéydəs/. The body of a county. The whole county, as distinguished from a part of it, or any particular place in it.

Corpus corporatum /kórpəs kòrpəréydəm/. A corporation; a corporate body, other than municipal.

Corpus cum causa /kórpəs kəm kózə/. (The body with the cause.) An English writ which issued out of chancery, to remove both the *body* and the record, touching the *cause* of any man lying in execution upon a judgment for debt, into the king's bench, there to remain until he satisfied the judgment.

Corpus delicti /kórpəs dəlíktay/. The body of a crime. The body (material substance) upon which a crime has been committed, *e.g.,* the corpse of a murdered man, the charred remains of a house burned down. In a derivative sense, the substance or foundation of a crime; the substantial fact that a crime has been committed. The "corpus delicti" of a crime is the body or substance of the crime, which ordinarily includes two elements: the act and the criminal agency of the act. State v. Edwards, 49 Ohio St.2d 31, 358 N.E.2d 1051, 1055.

Corpus pro corpore /kórpəs pròw kórpəriy/. In old records, body for body. A phrase expressing the liability of manucaptors.

Corpus humanum non recipit æstimationem /kórpəs hyəméynəm nòn résəpəd èstəmèyshiyównəm/. The human body does not admit of valuation.

Corpus juris /kórpəs júrəs/. A body of law. A term used to signify a book comprehending several collections of law. There are two principal collections to which this name is given; the *Corpus Juris Civilis,* and the *Corpus Juris Canonici.* Also name of an encyclopædic statement of the principles of American law; *e.g. Corpus Juris Secundum.*

Corpus juris canonici /kórpəs júrəs kənónəsay/. The body of the canon law. A compilation of the canon law, comprising the decrees and canons of the Roman Church, constituting the body of ecclesiastical law of that church.

Corpus juris civilis /kórpəs júrəs sívələs/. The body of the civil law. The system of Roman jurisprudence compiled and codified under the direction of the emperor Justinian, in A.D. 528–534. This collection comprises the Institutes, Digest (or Pandects), Code, and Novels. The name is said to have been first applied to this collection early in the seventeenth century.

Correct attest. These words, used before the signatures of bank directors to reports made to the commissioner of banking, mean not alone to bear witness, but to affirm to be true or genuine, and such words are appropriately used for the affirmation of persons in their official capacity to attest the truth of a writing.

Corrected policy. Policy issued after investigation of risk to correct misstatements in policy first issued.

Correction. Discipline, treatment and rehabilitation of offenders through confinement, parole, probation, counseling, etc. See also **Correctional system.**

Correctional institutions. A generic term describing prisons, jails, reformatories and other places of correction and detention.

Correctional system. Network of governmental agencies concerned with prisons, jails, houses of correction and reformatories; may also refer to pardon and parole systems.

Correction, house of. A prison for the reformation of petty or juvenile offenders.

Corrector of the staple. In old English law, a clerk belonging to the staple, to write and record the bargains of merchants there made.

Corregidor /koréyhidòr/kərégədòr/. In Spanish law, a magistrate who took cognizance of various misdemeanors, and of civil matters.

Correi /kòwríyay/. Lat. In the civil law, co-stipulators; joint stipulators.

Correi credendi /kòwríyay krədénday/. In the civil and Scotch law, joint creditors; creditors *in solido.*

Correlative /kərélədiv/. Having a mutual or reciprocal relation, in such sense that the existence of one necessarily implies the existence of the other. *Father* and *son* are correlative terms, as are *claim* and *duty.*

Correlative rights. Refers to doctrine which is applied to owners of land and their rights to use of their land with respect to rights of adjoining or lower riparian landowners in water or oil. Alameda County Water District v. Niles Sand & Gravel Co. Inc., 37 Cal. App.3d 924, 112 Cal.Rptr. 846.

Correspondence. Interchange of written communications. The letters written by a person and the answers written by the one to whom they are addressed. The agreement of things with one another.

Correspondence audit. An audit conducted by the Internal Revenue Service through the use of the mail.

Typically, the I.R.S. writes to the taxpayer requesting the verification of a particular deduction or exemption. The completion of a special form or the remittance of copies of records or other support is all that is requested of the taxpayer.

Correspondent. A securities firm, bank or other financial organization which regularly performs services for another in a place or market to which the other does not have direct access. Securities firms may have correspondents in foreign countries or on exchanges of which they are not members. Bank which serves as agent for another bank; carries deposit balance for bank in another city.

Correspondent bank. See **Correspondent.**

Corroborate /kəróbəreyt/. To strengthen; to add weight or credibility to a thing by additional and confirming facts or evidence. The testimony of a witness is said to be corroborated when it is shown to correspond with the representation of some other witnesses, or to comport with some facts otherwise known or established. See **Corroborating evidence.**

Corroborating evidence /kəróbəreydiŋ évədəns/. Evidence supplementary to that already given and tending to strengthen or confirm it. Additional evidence of a different character to the same point. Edwards v. Edwards, Tenn.App., 501 S.W.2d 283, 289. In some jurisdictions, corroborating evidence of an accomplice to the crime is given much weight. People v. Baker, 16 Ill.2d 364, 158 N.E.2d 1.

Corrupt. Spoiled; tainted; vitiated; depraved; debased; morally degenerate. As used as a verb, to change ones morals and principles from good to bad.

Corruption. An act done with an intent to give some advantage inconsistent with official duty and the rights of others. The act of an official or fiduciary person who unlawfully and wrongfully uses his station or character to procure some benefit for himself or for another person, contrary to duty and the rights of others. See **Bribe; Extortion.**

Corruption of blood. In English law, the consequence of *attainder,* being that the attainted person could neither inherit lands or other hereditaments from his ancestor, nor retain those he already had, nor transmit them by descent to any heir, because his blood was considered in law to be corrupted. Avery v. Everett, 110 N.Y. 317, 18 N.E. 148. This was abolished by St. 3 & 4, Wm. IV, c. 106, and 33 & 34 Vict., c. 23, and is unknown in America. Const.U.S., Art. III, § 3.

Corruptly. When used in a statute, this term, generally imports a wrongful design to acquire some pecuniary or other advantage.

Corrupt motive doctrine. Doctrine invoked in assessing crimes like bribery to determine motive of gift or payment.

Corrupt practices acts. Federal and state statutes regulating campaign contributions and expenditures.

Corselet /kórslət/. Ancient armor which covered the body.

Corse-present /kórs prèzənt/. In old English law, a mortuary, thus termed because, when a mortuary became due on the death of a man, the best or second-best beast was, according to custom, offered or presented to the priest, and carried with the corpse. In Wales a corse-present was due upon the death of a clergyman to the bishop of the diocese, till abolished by 12 Anne St. 2, c. 6. 2 Bl.Comm. 426.

Corsned /kórsnèd/. In Saxon law, the morsel of exe cration. A species of ordeal in use among the Saxons, performed by eating a piece of bread over which the priest had pronounced a certain imprecation. If the accused ate it freely, he was pronounced innocent; but, if it stuck in his throat, it was considered as a proof of his guilt. 4 Bl.Comm. 345.

Cortes /kórtes/kortéz/. The name of the legislative assemblies, the parliament or congress, of Spain and Portugal.

Cortis /kórdəs/. A court or yard before a house.

Cortularium /kòrchəlériyəm/, or **cortarium** /kortériyəm/. In old records, a yard adjoining a country farm.

Corvée /korvéy/. In French law, gratuitous labor exacted from the villages or communities, especially for repairing roads, constructing bridges.

Corvée seigneuriale /korvéy seynyə̀riyál/. Services due the lord of the manor.

Cosa juzgada /kówsa huwsgáða/. In Spanish law, a cause or matter adjudged (*res judicata*).

Cosas comunes /kówsas komúwne(y)s/. In Spanish law, a term corresponding to the *res communes* of the Roman law, and descriptive of such things as are open to the equal and common enjoyment of all persons and not to be reduced to private ownership, such as the air, the sea, and the water of running streams.

Cosbering /kózbəriŋ/. See **Coshering**.

Cosduna /kózduwnə/. In feudal law, a custom or tribute.

Cosen, cozen /kázən/. In old English law, to cheat.

Cosenage /káz(ə)naj/. (Also spelled "Cosinage," "Cousinage.") In old English law, a writ that lay for the heir where the *tresail*, *i.e.*, the father of the *besail*, or great-grandfather, was seised of lands in fee at his death, and a stranger entered upon the land and abated. 3 Bl.Comm. 186. Kindred; cousinship; relationship; affinity. 3 Bl.Comm. 186.

Cosening /káz(ə)niŋ/. In old English law, an offense, mentioned in the old books, where anything was done deceitfully, whether belonging to contracts or not, which could not be properly termed by any special name. The same as the *stellionatus* of the civil law. 4 Bl.Comm. 158.

Coshering /kóshəriŋ/. In old English law, a feudal prerogative or custom for lords to lie and feast themselves at their tenants' houses.

Cosmopathic /kòzməpǽθək/. Open to the access of supernormal knowledge or emotion supposedly from a preternatural world; applied to methods of healing.

Cost. Expense; price. The sum or equivalent expended, paid or charged for something. Expenses awarded by court to prevailing party. See *e.g.* Fed.R.Civil P. 54(d). See also **Actual cost; Costs; Net cost; Rate.**

Cost accounting. That branch of accounting which deals with methods and systems of compiling and analyzing costs in selling and manufacturing. Classifying, summarizing, recording, reporting, and allocating current or predicted costs.

Cost basis. In accounting, the value placed on an asset in a financial statement in terms of its cost; used in determining capital gains or losses.

Cost bond. See **Costs**, *infra.*

Cost contract. See *Cost-plus contract*, *infra.*

Cost depletion. In accounting and taxation, depletion computed in oil production without reference to discovery or percentage depletion. Magale v. U. S., 118 Ct.Cl. 183, 93 F.Supp. 1004.

Cost-plus contract. One which fixes the amount to be paid the contractor on a basis, generally, of the cost of the material and labor, plus an agreed percentage thereof as profits. Such contracts are used when costs of production or construction are unknown or difficult to ascertain in advance.

Costs of collection. Strictly, expenses involved in endeavoring to make collection, as of a promissory note; but as used in or with reference to such notes, the phrase is synonymous with attorney's fees. There is commonly a provision to this effect in such notes. It does not refer to costs of suit, which are recoverable by law.

Imputed cost. A value expressing cost which is derived from or based on factors other than actual cost records; estimated costs.

Cost and freight (C.A.F.). Quoted sales price includes cost of goods and freight but not insurance or other special charges.

Co-stipulator. A joint promisor.

Cost of living clause. A provision, commonly in labor agreements, and also in certain pension or retirement programs, giving an automatic wage or benefit increase tied in some way to cost-of-living rises in the economy. Cost of living is usually measured by the Consumer Price Index (CPI) (*q.v.*).

Costs. A pecuniary allowance, made to the successful party (and recoverable from the losing party), for his expenses in prosecuting or defending an action or a distinct proceeding within an action. Fed.R.Civil P. 54(d); Fed.R.App.P. 39. Generally, "costs" do not include attorney fees unless such fees are by a statute denominated costs or are by statute allowed to be recovered as costs in the case. Fees and charges required by law to be paid to the courts or some of their officers, the amount of which is fixed by statute or court rule; *e.g.* filing and service fees. See also **Closing costs; Fee; Security for costs; Service charge.**

Bill of costs. A certified, itemized statement of the amount of costs in an action or suit.

Cost bond, or bond for costs. A bond given by a party to an action to secure the eventual payment of such costs as may be awarded against him. A bond which may be required of an appealing party in a civil case; *e.g.* Fed.R.App.P. 7. Purpose of bond is to cover appellee's costs in event of affirmance of judgment.

Costs de incremento. Increased costs, costs of increase. Costs adjudged by the court in addition to those assessed by the jury.

Costs of the day. Costs which are incurred in preparing for the trial of a cause on a specified *day*, consisting of witnesses' fees, and other fees of attendance.

Costs to abide event. When an order is made by an appellate court reversing a judgment, with "costs to abide the event," the costs intended by the order include those of the appeal, so that, if the appellee is finally successful, he is entitled to tax the costs of the appeal.

Final costs. Such costs as are to be paid at the end of the suit. Costs, the liability for which depends upon the final result of the litigation.

Interlocutory costs. Costs accruing upon proceedings in the intermediate stages of a cause, as distinguished from final costs; such as the costs of motions.

Security for costs. A security which a defendant in an action may require of a plaintiff who does not reside within the jurisdiction of the court, for the payment of such costs as may be awarded to the defendant. See also *Cost bond, supra.*

Statutory costs. Amounts awarded for various phases of litigation that are fixed by statute. Word "costs" generally refers to statutory fees to which officers, witnesses, jurors and others are entitled for their services in an action and which statutes authorize to be taxed and included in the judgment. Terry v. Burger, 6 Ohio App.2d 53, 216 N.E.2d 383.

Costs, insurance and freight (C.I.F.). Quoted sales price which includes cost of goods, freight and insurance.

Costumbre /kostúmbre(y)/. In Spanish law, custom; an unwritten law established by usage, during a long space of time.

Co-sureties /kòwshúrədiyz/. Joint sureties; two or more sureties to the same obligation.

Cotenancy. A tenancy by several distinct titles but by unity of possession, or any joint ownership or common interest with its grantor. The term is broad enough to comprise both tenancy in common and joint tenancy.

Coterelli /kòdərélay/. Anciently, a kind of peasantry who were outlaws; robbers.

Coterellus /kòdəréləs/. In feudal law, a cottager; a servile tenant, who held in mere villenage; his person, issue, and goods were disposable at the lord's pleasure. A coterellus, therefore, occupied a less favorable position than a cotarius (*q.v.*), for the latter held by socage tenure.

Coterie /kòwdəríy/. A fashionable association, or a knot of persons forming a particular circle. The origin of the term was purely commercial, signifying an association, in which each member furnished his part, and bore his share in the profit and loss.

Cotland. In old English law, land held by a cottager, whether in socage or villenage.

Cotsethla /kòtséθlə/kòtsétlə/. In old English law, the little seat or mansion belonging to a small farm.

Cotsethland /kòtséθlænd/. The seat of a cottage with the land belonging to it.

Cotsetus /kòtsíydəs/. A cottager or cottage-holder who held by servile tenure and was bound to do the work of the lord.

Cottage. Dwelling of farm laborer or small farmer. Small vacation house. In English law, a small dwellinghouse that has no land belonging to it.

Cottier tenancy /kódiyər ténənsiy/. A species of tenancy in Ireland, constituted by an agreement in writing, and subject to the following terms: That the tenement consists of a dwelling-house with not more than half an acre of land; at a rental not exceeding a specified sum a year; the tenancy to be for not more than a month at a time; the landlord to keep the house in good repair.

Cotton notes. Receipts given for each bale of cotton received on storage by a public warehouse.

Cotuchans. A term used in Domesday for peasants, boors, husbandmen.

Couchant /káwchənt/. Lying down; squatting. *Couchant and levant* (lying down and rising up) is a term applied to animals trespassing on the land of one other than their owner, for one night or longer. 3 Bl.Comm. 9.

Coucher, or **courcher** /káwchər/. A factor who continues abroad for traffic; also the general book wherein any corporation, etc., register their acts.

Coulisse /kùlíys/. The stockbrokers' curb market in Paris.

Council. An assembly of persons for the purpose of concerting measures of state or municipal policy. The legislative body in the government of cities or boroughs. An advisory body selected to aid the executive; *i.e.* a body appointed to advise and assist the governor in his executive or judicial capacities or both. See also **City council; Legislative council; Metropolitan council.**

Common Council. In American law, the lower or more numerous branch of the legislative assembly of a city. In English law, the councillors of the city of London. The parliament, also, was anciently called the "common council of the realm."

Privy Council. See that title.

Select Council. The name given, in some states, to the upper house or branch of the council of a city.

Council of conciliation. In England, by the Acts 30 & 31 Vict., c. 105, power was given for the crown to grant licenses for the formation of councils of conciliation and arbitration, consisting of a certain number of masters and workmen in any trade or employment, having power to hear and determine all questions between masters and workmen which may be submitted to them by both parties, arising out of or with respect to the particular trade or manufacture, and incapable of being otherwise settled. They have power to apply to a justice to enforce the performance of their award. The members are elected by persons engaged in the trade.

Council of the bar. A body composed of members of the English bar which governs the bar. It hears complaints against barristers and reports its findings with recommendations to the benchers of the Inn of Court of which the barrister is a member, who alone can act.

Council of the north. In England, a court instituted by Henry VIII, in 1537, to administer justice in Yorkshire and the four other northern counties. Under the presidency of Stratford, the court showed great rigor, bordering, it is alleged, on harshness. It was abolished by 16 Car. I, the same act which abolished the Star Chamber.

Counsel /káwn(t)səl/. Attorney or counsellor (q.v.).

Advice and assistance given by one person to another in regard to a legal matter, proposed line of conduct, claim, or contention.

The words "counsel" and "advise" may be, and frequently are, used in criminal law to describe the offense of a person who, not actually doing the felonious act, by his will contributed to it or procured it to be done. See **Aid and abet.**

See also **Legislative counsel; Of counsel.**

Junior counsel. The younger of the counsel employed on the same side of a case, or the one lower in standing or rank, or who is intrusted with the less important parts of the preparation or trial of the cause.

Counsellor. An attorney; lawyer. Member of the legal profession who gives legal advice and handles the legal affairs of client, including, if necessary, appearing on his or her behalf in civil, criminal, or administrative actions and proceedings.

Counsel of record. Attorney whose appearance has been filed with court papers.

Counsel, right to. Constitutional right of criminal defendant to court appointed attorney if he is financially unable to retain private counsel; guaranteed by Sixth and Fourteenth Amendments to U.S. Constitution, and as well by court rule (Fed.R.Crim.P. 44), and statute (18 U.S.C.A. § 3006A). Such right to counsel exists with respect to felonies (Gideon v. Wainright, 372 U.S. 335, 83 S.Ct. 792); misdemeanors when the sentence is to a jail term (Argersinger v. Hemlin, 407 U.S. 25, 92 S.Ct. 2006), and to juvenile delinquency proceedings (In re Gault, 387 U.S. 1, 87 S.Ct. 1428). The extent of this right extends from the time that judicial proceedings have been initiated against the accused, whether by way of formal charge, preliminary hearing, indictment, information, or arraignment (Brewer v. Williams, 430 U.S. 387, 97 S.Ct. 1232), through to sentencing (Mempa v. Rhay, 389 U.S. 128, 88 S.Ct. 254) and appeal (Douglas v. California, 372

U.S. 353, 83 S.Ct. 814). "Counsel" however within Sixth Amendment does not include a lay person but refers only to person authorized to practice law. U. S. v. Grismore, C.A.Colo., 546 F.2d 844, 847. See also critical stage; Effective assistance of counsel; Escobedo Rule; Miranda Rule; Public defender.

Count, v. In pleading, to declare; to recite; to state a case; to narrate the facts constituting a plaintiff's cause of action. To plead orally; to plead or argue a case in court; to recite or read in court; to recite a count in court.

Count, n. In pleading, the plaintiff's statement of his cause of action. The different parts of a declaration, each of which, if it stood alone, would constitute a ground for action. This term is no longer used in pleading under Rules of Civil Procedure. Used also to signify the several parts of an indictment, each charging a distinct offense. Fed.R.Crim.P. 7.

"Count" and "charge" when used relative to allegations in an indictment or information are synonymous. State v. Puckett, 39 N.M. 511, 50 P.2d 964, 965.

A separate and independent claim. A civil petition or a criminal indictment may contain several counts.

An earl.

Common counts. Certain general counts or forms inserted in a declaration in an action to recover a money debt, not founded on the circumstances of the individual case, but intended to guard against a possible variance, and to enable the plaintiff to take advantage of any ground of liability which the proof may disclose, within the general scope of the action.

The various forms of an action of assumpsit. In the action of *assumpsit*, these counts are as follows: For goods sold and delivered, or bargained and sold; for work done; for money lent; for money paid; for money received to the use of the plaintiff; for interest; or for money due on an account stated.

General count. One stating in a general way the plaintiff's claim.

Money counts. A species of common counts, so called from the subject-matter of them; embracing the *indebitatus assumpsit* count for money lent and advanced, for money paid and expended, and for money had and received, together with the *insimul computassent* count, or count for money due on an account stated.

Omnibus count. A count which combines in one all the money counts with one for goods sold and delivered, work and labor, and an account stated.

Several counts. Where a plaintiff has several distinct causes of action, he is allowed to pursue them cumulatively in the same action, subject to certain rules which the law prescribes. See *e.g.* Fed.R. Civil P. 8(e).

Special count. As opposed to the common counts, in pleading, a special count is a statement of the actual facts of the particular case, or a count in which the plaintiff's claim is set forth with all needed particularity.

Countee. In old English law, the most eminent dignity of a subject before the Conquest. He was *præfectus* or *præpositus comitatus*, and had the charge and custody of the county; but this authority is now vested in the sheriff.

Countenance. In old English law, credit; estimation. Also, encouragement; aiding and abetting.

Counter, *adj.* Adverse; antagonistic; opposing or contradicting; contrary.

Counter-affidavit. An affidavit made and presented in contradiction or opposition to an affidavit which is made the basis or support of a motion or application.

Counter-bond. Bond which indemnifies a surety. See *Counter-security.*

Counterclaim. See that title.

Counter-deed. A secret writing, either before a notary or under a private seal, which destroys, invalidates, or alters a public one.

Counter-letter. A species of instrument of defeasance common in the civil law. It is executed by a party who has taken a deed of property, absolute on its face, but intended as security for a loan of money, and by it he agrees to reconvey the property on payment of a specified sum. The two instruments, taken together, constitute what is known in Louisiana as an "*antichresis*" *(q.v.).*

Counter-mark. A sign put upon goods already marked; also the several marks put upon goods belonging to several persons, to show that they must not be opened, but in the presence of all the owners or their agents.

Counter-plea. See **Plea.**

Counter-security. A security given to one who has entered into a bond or become surety for another; a countervailing bond of indemnity.

Counterclaim. A claim presented by a defendant in opposition to or deduction from the claim of the plaintiff. Fed.R. Civil P. 13. If established, such will defeat or diminish the plaintiff's claim. Under federal rule practice, and also in most states, counterclaims are either compulsory (required to be made) or permissive (made at option of defendant).

A counterclaim may be any cause of action in favor of one or more defendants or a person whom a defendant represents against one or more plaintiffs, a person whom a plaintiff represents or a plaintiff and other persons alleged to be liable. New York C.P. L.R. § 39019(a).

For requisite content of counterclaim under Federal Rules of Civil Procedure, see **Complaint.** *Compare* **Cross-claim.** See also **Offset; Recoupment; Set-off; Transaction or occurrence test.**

Compulsory counterclaim. A pleading shall state as a counterclaim any claim which at the time of serving the pleading the pleader has against any opposing party, if it arises out of the transaction or occurrence that is the subject matter of the opposing party's claim and does not require for its adjudication the presence of third parties of whom the court cannot acquire jurisdiction. But the pleader need not state the claim if (1) at the time the action was commenced the claim was the subject of another pending action, or (2) the opposing party brought suit upon his claim by attachment or other process by which the court did not acquire jurisdiction to render a personal judgment on that claim. Fed.R. Civil P. 13(a).

Permissive Counterclaim. A pleading may state as a counterclaim any claim against an opposing party not arising out of the transaction or occurrence that is the subject matter of the opposing party's claim. Fed.R. Civil P. 13(b).

Counterfeit /káwntərfit/. To forge; to copy or imitate, without authority or right, and with a view to deceive or defraud, by passing the copy or thing forged for that which is original or genuine. Most commonly applied to the fraudulent and criminal imitation of money or securities. 18 U.S.C.A. § 471 et seq. Counterfeit in common parlance signifies fabrication of false image or representation; counterfeiting an instrument means falsely making it; and in its broadest sense means making of copy without authority or right and with view to deceive or defraud by passing copy as original or genuine. Smith v. State, 7 Md.App. 457, 256 A.2d 357, 360, 361. See also **False making; Falsify; Forgery; Imitation.**

Counterfeit coin. Coin not genuine, but resembling or apparently intended to resemble or pass for genuine coin, including genuine coin prepared or altered so as to resemble or pass for coin of a higher denomination.

Counterfeiter. One who unlawfully makes base coin in imitation of the true metal, or forges false currency, or any instrument of writing, bearing a likeness and similitude to that which is lawful and genuine, with an intention of deceiving and imposing upon another.

Counter-fesance. The act of forging.

Counter letter. An agreement to reconvey where property has been passed by absolute deed with the intention that it shall serve as security only.

Countermand. A change or revocation of orders, authority, or instructions previously issued. It may be either express or implied; the former where the order or instruction already given is explicitly annulled or recalled; the latter where the party's conduct is incompatible with the further continuance of the order or instruction, as where a new order is given inconsistent with the former order.

Counter offer. A statement by the offeree which has the legal effect of rejecting the offer and of proposing a new offer to the offeror. Restatement of Contracts, § 60. However, the provisions of U.C.C. § 2–207(1)(2) modifies this principle of contract law as regards sales of goods by providing that the "additional terms are to be construed as proposals for addition to the contract."

Counterpart. In conveyancing, the corresponding part of an instrument; a duplicate or copy. Where an instrument of conveyance, as a lease, is executed in parts, that is, by having several copies or duplicates made and interchangeably executed, that which is executed by the grantor is usually called the "original," and the rest are "counterparts"; although, where all the parties execute every part, this renders them all originals. See **Duplicate.**

Counterpart writ. A copy of the original writ, authorized to be issued to another county when the court has jurisdiction of the cause by reason of the fact that some of the defendants are residents of the county or found therein.

Counter-rolls. In English law, the rolls which sheriffs have with the coroners, containing particulars of their proceedings, as well of appeals as of inquests, etc.

Countersign. As a noun, the signature of a secretary or other subordinate officer to any writing signed by the principal or superior to vouch for the authenticity of it.

As a verb, to sign in addition to the signature of another in order to attest the authenticity.

Counter-signature. See **Countersign**.

Countervail. To counterbalance; to avail against with equal force or virtue; to compensate for, or serve as an equivalent of or substitute for.

Countervailing equity. See **Equity**.

Countervail livery. At common law, a release was a form of transfer of real estate where some right to it existed in one person but the actual possession was in another; and the possession in such case was said to "countervail livery," that is, it supplied the place of and rendered unnecessary the open and notorious delivery of possession required in other cases.

Counteur /kàwntyúr/. In the time of Edward I, a pleader; also called a *Nurrator*, and *Serjeant-Counteur*. See **Countors**.

Countez /káwntìyz/. L. Fr. Count, or reckon. In old practice, a direction formerly given by the clerk of a court to the crier, after a jury was sworn, to *number* them; and which Blackstone says was given in his time, in good English, "count these." 4 Bl.Comm. 340, note (*u*).

Countors /káwntərz/. Advocates, or serjeants at law, whom a man retains to defend his cause and speak for him in court, for their fees.

Country. The territory occupied by an independent nation or people, or the inhabitants of such territory. In the primary meaning "country" denotes the population, the nation, the state, or the government, having possession and dominion over a territory.

Rural, as distinguished from urban areas.

Country whence he came. Within statute providing for deportation of aliens means country of alien's nativity, where domicile has not been acquired elsewhere. Immigration Act 1924, § 13, 8 U.S.C.A. § 213; Schenck ex rel. Capodilupo v. Ward, C.C.A.Mass., 80 F.2d 422, 426. But deportation to "country whence alien came" would be complied with if the alien was returned to political dominion in exile and control of country from whence he came. Delany v. Moraitis, C.C.A.Md., 136 F.2d 129–133.

County. The largest territorial division for local government in state. Its powers and importance vary from state to state. In certain New England states, it exists mainly for judicial administration. In Louisiana, the equivalent unit is called a parish. Counties are held in some jurisdictions to be municipal corporations, and are sometimes said to be involuntary municipal corporations. Other cases, seeking to distinguish between the two, hold that counties are agencies or political subdivisions of the state for governmental purposes, and not, like municipal corporations, incorporations of the inhabitants of specified regions for purposes of local government. Counties are also said to be merely quasi corporations. Jefferson County ex rel. Grauman v. Jefferson County Fiscal Court, 274 Ky. 91, 118 S.W.2d 181, 184.

Body of the county. The county at large, as distinguished from any particular place within it. A county considered as a territorial whole.

County affairs. Those relating to the county in its organic and corporate capacity and included within its governmental or corporate powers.

County attorney. Attorney employed by county to represent it in civil matters; also, the prosecuting attorney in many counties.

County auditor. County official whose responsibility is examination of accounts and financial records of the county.

County board. The administrative body which governs a county.

County board of equalization. A body created for the purpose of equalizing values of property subject to taxation.

County board of supervisors. A body of town and city officers acting for and on behalf of county in such matters as have been turned over to them by law.

County bonds. Broadly, any bonds issued by county officials to be paid for by a levy on a special taxing district, whether or not coextensive with the county.

County business. All business pertaining to the county as a corporate entity. All business of the county, and any other business of such county connected with or interrelated with the business of any other county properly within the jurisdiction of the county commissioners' court.

County commissioners. Officers of a county, charged with a variety of administrative and executive duties, but principally with the management of the financial affairs of the county, its police regulations, and its corporate business. Sometimes the local laws give them limited judicial powers. In some states they are called "supervisors".

County courts. The powers and jurisdiction of such courts are governed by state constitutions or statutes; some with strictly administrative, or strictly judicial functions, or a combination of both; some with only criminal jurisdiction, or only civil, or both; some have exclusive jurisdictions, others concurrent jurisdiction; such jurisdictional powers may, in addition, be either general or specific.

County officers. Those whose general authority and jurisdiction are confined within the limits of the county in which they are appointed, who are appointed in and for a particular county, and whose duties apply only to that county, and through whom the county performs its usual political functions. Public officers who fill a position usually provided for in the organization of counties and county governments, and are selected by the county to represent it continuously and as part of the regular and permanent administration of public power in carrying out certain acts with the performance of which it is charged in behalf of the public.

County palatine. A term bestowed upon certain counties in England, the lords of which in former times enjoyed especial privileges. They might pardon treasons, murders, and felonies. All writs and indictments ran in their names, as in other counties in the king's; and all offenses were said to be done against their peace, and not, as in other places, *contra pacem domini regis.* But these privileges have in modern times nearly disappeared.

County powers. Such only as are expressly provided by law or which are necessarily implied from those expressed.

County property. That which a county is authorized to acquire, hold, and sell.

County purposes. Those exercised by the county acting as a municipal corporation. As regards the rate of taxation, all purposes for which county taxation may be levied. Test whether a tax is levied for county purposes is whether it is for strictly county uses, for which county or its inhabitants alone would benefit, or is it for a purpose in which entire state is concerned and will profit.

County road. One which lies wholly within one county, and which is thereby distinguished from a state road, which is a road lying in two or more counties.

County-seat. A county-seat or county-town is the chief town of a county, where the county buildings and courts are located and the county business transacted.

County supervisors. See *County commissioners, supra.*

County tax. Tax exclusively for county purposes, in which state has no sovereign interest or responsibility, and which has no connection with duties of county in its relation to state.

County-town. The county-seat; the town in which the seat of government of the county is located.

County warrant. An order or warrant drawn by some duly authorized officer of the county, directed to the county treasurer and directing him to pay out of the funds of the county a designated sum of money to a named individual, or to his order or to bearer.

Foreign county. Any county having a judicial and municipal organization separate from that of the county where matters arising in the former county are called in question, though both may lie within the same state or country.

Coup d'etat /kùwdeytá/. Political move to overthrow existing government by force.

Coupled with an interest. This phrase, in the law of agency, has reference to a writing creating, conveying to, or vesting in the agent an interest in the estate or property which is the subject of the agency, as distin-

guished from the proceeds or profits resulting from the exercise of the agency.

Coupons. Interest and dividend certificates; also those parts of a commercial instrument which are to be cut, and which are evidence of something connected with the contract mentioned in the instrument. They are generally attached to certificates of loan, where the interest is payable at particular periods, and, when the interest is paid, they are cut off and delivered to the payor. That portion of a bond redeemable at a specified date for interest payment.

Coupons are written contracts for the payment of a definite sum of money on a given day, and being drawn and executed in a form and mode for the purpose, that they may be separated from the bonds and other instruments to which they are usually attached, it is held that they are negotiable and that a suit may be maintained on them without the necessity of producing the bonds. Each matured coupon upon a negotiable bond is a separable promise, distinct from the promises to pay the bonds or the other coupons, and gives rise to a separate cause of action. Thompson v. Perrine, 106 U.S. 589, 1 S.Ct. 564, 27 L.Ed. 298.

Coupon bonds. Bonds to which are attached coupons for the several successive installments of interest to maturity.

Coupon notes. Promissory notes with coupons attached, the coupons being notes for interest written at the bottom of the principal note, and designed to be cut off severally and presented for payment as they mature.

Coupon securities. Usually provides for the payment of principal to the bearer thereof, and for payment of an installment of interest to the bearer of the respective interest coupons upon presentation thereof upon their respective due dates. Coupon securities are usually in the denomination of $1,000. Ownership of the security and/or coupons is transferred by delivery thereof. Such a security is negotiable under the Uniform Commercial Code. U.C.C. §§ 8–105, 8–302.

Cour de cassation /kúr də kasasyówn/. The supreme judicial tribunal of France, having appellate jurisdiction only.

Course. In surveying, the direction of a line with reference to a meridian.

Course of business. What is usually and normally done in the management of trade or business. See also **Course of dealing; Regular course of business.**

In Worker's Compensation Acts, the usual course of business of the employer covers the normal operations which form part of the ordinary business carried on, and not including incidental and occasional operations having for their purpose the preservation of the premises or the appliances used in the business.

Commercial paper is said to be transferred, or sales alleged to have been fraudulent may be shown to have been made, "in the course of business," or "in the usual and ordinary course of business," when the circumstances of the transaction are such as usually and ordinarily attend dealings of the same kind and do not exhibit any signs of haste, secrecy, or fraudulent intention.

Course of dealing. A sequence of previous acts and conduct between the parties to a particular transaction which is fairly to be regarded as establishing a common basis of understanding for interpreting their expressions and other conduct. U.C.C. § 1–205(1). See also **Usage** (*Usage of trade*).

Course of employment. Those words as applied to compensation for injuries within the purview of Worker's Compensation Acts, refer to the time, place, and circumstances under which the accident takes place. A worker is in course of employment when, within time covered by employment, he is doing something which he might reasonably do while so employed at proper place. Generally, in order that an injury may arise out of and in the course of employment, it must be received while the worker is doing the duty he is employed to perform and also as a natural incident of the work flowing therefrom as a natural consequence and directly connected therewith.

The expression "in the course of his employment", in the rule that an employer is liable for the torts of his employee done in the course of his employment, means while engaged in the service of the employer while engaged generally in the employer's work, as distinguished from acts done when the employee steps outside of his employment to do an act for himself, not connected with his employer's business.

State statutes and decisions differ as to the types and scope of activities which fall within "course of employment".

See also **Deviation; Scope of employment.**

Course of river. The course of a river is a line parallel with its banks. The term is not synonymous with the "current" of the river.

Course of the voyage. By this term is understood the regular and customary track, if such there be, which a ship takes in going from one port to another, and the shortest way.

Course of trade. What is customarily or ordinarily done in the management of trade or business. See also **Course of business.**

Course of vein. In mining, the "course of the vein" appearing on the surface is the course of its apex, which is generally inclined and undulated and departs more or less materially from the strike.

Course of vessel. In navigation, the "course" of a vessel is her apparent course, and not her heading at any given moment. It is her actual course.

Courses and distances. A method or form for describing real estate in deeds and mortgages by setting forth the distances in one direction as a boundary, followed by other distances and the direction thereof until the entire parcel has been described. See also **Metes and bounds.**

Court. A space which is uncovered, but which may be partly or wholly inclosed by buildings or walls. When used in connection with a street, indicates a short street, blind alley, or open space like a short street inclosed by dwellings or other buildings facing thereon.

A legislative assembly. Parliament is called in the old books a court of the king, nobility, and commons assembled. This meaning of the word has also been retained in the titles of some deliberative bodies, such as the "General Court" of Massachusetts, *i.e.,* the legislature.

The person and suit of the sovereign; the place where the sovereign sojourns with his regal retinue, wherever that may be. The English government is spoken of in diplomacy as the court of St. James, because the palace of St. James is the official palace.

An organ of the government, belonging to the judicial department, whose function is the application of the laws to controversies brought before it and the public administration of justice. The presence of a sufficient number of the members of such a body regularly convened in an authorized place at an appointed time, engaged in the full and regular performance of its functions. A body in the government to which the administration of justice is delegated. A body organized to administer justice, and including both judge and jury. An incorporeal, political being, composed of one or more judges, who sit at fixed times and places, attended by proper officers, pursuant to lawful authority, for the administration of justice. An organized body with defined powers, meeting at certain times and places for the hearing and decision of causes and other matters brought before it, and aided in this, its proper business, by its proper officers, viz., attorneys and counsel to present and manage the business, clerks to record and attest its acts and decisions, and ministerial officers to execute its commands, and secure due order in its proceedings.

The words "court" and "judge," or "judges," are frequently used in statutes as synonymous. When used with reference to orders made by the court or judges, they are to be so understood.

General Classification

Courts may be classified and divided according to several methods, the following being the more usual:

Appellate courts. Such courts review decisions of inferior courts, and may be either intermediate appellate courts (court of appeals) or supreme courts. See **Court of Appeals; Supreme Court.**

Article III courts. See **Constitutional court.**

Civil and criminal courts. The former being such as are established for the adjudication of controversies between individual parties, or the ascertainment, enforcement, and redress of private rights; the latter, such as are charged with the administration of the criminal laws, and the punishment of wrongs to the public. While in some states there are both civil and criminal courts, in most states the trial court is a *court of general jurisdiction (q.v.).*

Court above, court below. In appellate practice, the "court above" is the one to which a cause is removed for review, whether by appeal, writ of error, or certiorari; while the "court below" is the one from which the case is removed (normally the trial court).

Court in bank (en banc). A meeting of all the judges of a court, usually for the purposes of hearing arguments on demurrers, motions for new trial, etc., as distinguished from sessions of the same court presided over by a single judge or panel of judges. See *Full court, infra.*

Court of competent jurisdiction. One having power and authority of law at the time of acting to do the particular act. One having jurisdiction under the Constitution and/or laws to determine the question in controversy.

Court of general jurisdiction. A court having unlimited trial jurisdiction, both civil and criminal, though its judgments and decrees are subject to appellate review. A superior court; a court having full jurisdiction within its own jurisdictional area.

Court of limited jurisdiction. Court with jurisdiction over only certain types of matters; *e.g.* probate or juvenile court. When a court of general jurisdiction proceeds under a special statute, it is a "court of limited jurisdiction" for the purpose of that proceeding, and its jurisdiction must affirmatively appear.

Court of original jurisdiction. Courts where actions are initiated and heard in first instance.

Court of record. A court that is required to keep a record of its proceedings, and that may fine or imprison. Such record imports verity and cannot be collaterally impeached.

De facto court. One established, organized, and exercising its judicial functions under authority of a statute apparently valid, though such statute may be in fact unconstitutional and may be afterwards so adjudged; or a court established and acting under the authority of a *de facto* government.

Equity courts and law courts. The former being such as possess the jurisdiction of a chancellor, apply the rules and principles of chancery (*i.e.* equity) law, and follow the procedure in equity; the latter, such as have no equitable powers, but administer justice according to the rules and practice of the common law. Under Rules of Civil Procedure, however, equity and law have been merged at the procedural level, and as such this distinction no longer exists in the federal courts nor in most state courts, though equity substantive jurisprudence remains viable. Fed.R.Civil P. 2. See **Court of Chancery; Court of Equity.**

Full court. A session of a court, which is attended by all the judges or justices composing it. See *Court in bank, infra.*

Spiritual courts. In English law, the ecclesiastical courts, or courts Christian. 3 Bl.Comm. 61. See **Ecclesiastical courts.**

Superior and inferior courts. The former being courts of general original jurisdiction in the first instance, and which exercise a control or supervision over a system of lower courts, either by appeal, error, or *certiorari;* the latter being courts of small or restricted jurisdiction, and subject to the review or correction of higher courts. Sometimes the former term is used to denote a particular group or system of courts of high powers, and all others are called "inferior courts".

Trial courts. Generic term for courts where civil actions or criminal proceedings are first commenced at the state level such are variously called municipal, circuit, superior, district, or county courts. At the federal level, the U.S. district courts are the trial courts.

As to the division of courts according to their *jurisdiction,* see **Jurisdiction.**

As to several names or kinds of courts not specifically described in the titles immediately following, see **Admiralty court, Arches Court, Appellate court, Bankruptcy proceedings** (*Bankruptcy court*), **Circuit courts, City courts, Commonwealth court, Consistory courts, Constitutional court, Consular courts, County** (*County court*), **Court-baron, Court of High Commission, Customs Court, District** (*District courts*), **Ecclesiastical courts, Family court, Federal courts, Forest courts, Instance court, Insular courts, International Court of Justice, Justice's court, Kangaroo court, Land court, Legislative courts, Maritime court, Mayor's court, Military courts, Moot court, Municipal courts, Orphans' court, Police court, Prerogative court, Prize court, Probate court, Superior** (*Superior courts*), **Supreme court, Surrogate court, Tax court, United States courts.**

Court administrator. Generally, a non-judicial officer whose responsibility is the administration of the courts as to budgets, calendars and non-judicial personnel.

Court-baron. In English law, a court which, although not one of record, was incident to every manor, and could not be severed therefrom. It was ordained for the maintenance of the services and duties stipulated for by lords of manors, and for the purpose of determining actions of a personal nature, where the debt or damage was under forty shillings. *Customary court-baron* was one appertaining entirely to copyholders. 3 Bl.Comm. 33. *Freeholders' court-baron* was one held before the freeholders who owed suit and service to the manor. It was the court-baron proper.

Court calendar. A list of cases for trial or appellate argument prepared for a given period of time as a week, month or even a term of the sitting of the court. Such may include scheduling of motions and other pretrial matters. See also **Docket.**

Court Christian. The ecclesiastical courts in England often so called, as distinguished from the civil courts. 1 Bl.Comm. 83; 3 Bl.Comm. 64.

Court commissioner. A person appointed by a judge to take testimony and find facts or to carry out some specific function connected with a case, such as selling property which is the subject of a petition to partition. See also **Commissioner; Court administrator; Master; Referee.**

Court en banc /kùrt om bóŋk/. See **Court** (*Court in bank*).

Courtesy. See **Curtesy.**

Court for Consideration of Crown Cases Reserved. In England, a court established by St. 11 & 12, Vict., c. 78, composed of such of the judges of the superior courts of Westminister as were able to attend, for the consideration of questions of law reserved by any judge in a court of oyer and terminer, gaol delivery, or quarter sessions, before which a prisoner had been found guilty by verdict. Such question is stated in the form of a special case. 4 Steph. The trial judge was empowered to "state a case" for the opinion of that court. He could not be compelled to do so, and only a question of law could be raised. If the court considered that the point had been wrongly decided at the trial, the conviction would be quashed. By Act of 1907, the Court of Criminal Appeal was created and the Court for Crown Cases Reserved was abolished.

Court for Divorce and Matrimonial Causes. This court was established by St. 20 & 21, Vict., c. 85, which transferred to it all jurisdiction then exercisable by any ecclesiastical court in England, in matters matrimonial, and also gave it new powers. The court consisted of the lord chancellor, the three chiefs, and three senior puisne judges of the common-law courts, and the judge ordinary, who together constituted, and still constitute, the "full court." The judge ordinary heard almost all matters in the first instance. By the judicature act, 1873, § 3, the jurisdiction of the court was transferred to the supreme court of judicature.

Court for the Correction of Errors. The name of a court having jurisdiction for review, by appeal or writ of error. The name was formerly used in New York and South Carolina.

Court for the Relief of Insolvent Debtors. In English law, a local court which had its sittings in London only, which received the petitions of insolvent debtors, and decided upon the question of granting a discharge. Abolished by the Bankruptcy Act of 1861.

Court for the Trial of Impeachments. A tribunal empowered to try any officer of government or other person brought to its bar by the process of impeachment. In England, the house of lords constitutes such a court; in the United States, the senate; and in the several states, usually the upper house of the legislative assembly. See also **Impeachment.**

Court-hand. In old English practice, the peculiar hand in which the records of courts were written from the earliest period down to the reign of George II. Its characteristics were great strength, compactness, and undeviating uniformity; and its use undoubtedly gave to the ancient record its acknowledged superiority over the modern, in the important quality of durability.

The writing of this hand, with its peculiar abbreviations and contractions, constituted, while it was in use, an art of no little importance, being an indispensable part of the profession of "clerkship," as it was called. Two sizes of it were employed, a large and a small hand; the former, called "great court-hand," being used for initial words or clauses, the *placita* of records, etc.

Court-house. The building occupied for the public sessions of a court, with its various offices. The building occupied and appropriated according to law for the holding of courts.

Court, Hundred. See **Hundred Court.**

Court-Lands. Domains or lands kept in the lord's hands to serve his family.

Court-Leet. The name of an English court of record held once in the year, and not oftener, within a particular hundred, lordship, or manor, before the steward of the leet; being the king's court granted by charter to the lords of those hundreds or manors. Its office was to view the frankpledges, that is, the freemen within the liberty; to present by jury crimes happening within the jurisdiction; and to punish trivial misdemeanors.

Court-Martial. A military court, convened under authority of government and the Uniform Code of Military Justice, 10 U.S.C.A. § 801 et seq., for trying and punishing offenses committed by members of the armed forces. Courts-martial are courts of law and courts of justice although they are not part of the Federal Judiciary established under Article III of the Constitution. They are legislative criminal courts established in the Armed Forces under the Constitutional Power of Congress to regulate the Armed Forces. Their jurisdiction is entirely penal and disciplinary. They may be convened by the President, Secretaries of Military Departments and by senior commanders specifically empowered by law. The type (*e.g.* summary, special, or general) and composition of courts-martial varies according to the gravity of offenses. Courts-martial are ad hoc bodies empowered to try only persons who are made constitutionally amenable to such trial by Act of Congress for offenses punishable under the Uniform Code of Military Justice. Generally they are designed to deal with the internal affairs of the military when summary command discipline is inadequate to achieve corrective results, but they have concurrent jurisdiction with civil courts over a wide range of civil offenses. Appeals are to the Court of Military Appeals.

Court of Admiralty. A court having jurisdiction of admiralty and maritime matters; such jurisdiction being possessed by federal district courts. See **Admiralty Court.**

High Court of Admiralty. In English law, this was a court which exercised jurisdiction in prize cases, and had general jurisdiction in maritime causes, on the instance side. Its proceedings were usually *in rem,* and its practice and principles derived in large measure from the civil law. The judicature acts of 1873 transferred all the powers and jurisdiction of this tribunal to the probate, divorce, and admiralty division of the high court of justice. The Justice Act of 1970 established a new Admiralty Court as part of the Queens Bench Division of the High Court.

Court of Ancient Demesne. In English law, a court of peculiar constitution, held by a bailiff appointed by the king, in which alone the tenants of the king's demesne could be impleaded.

Court of Appeal, His Majesty's. Formerly, the chief appellate tribunal of England. It was established by the judicature acts of 1873 and 1875, and invested with the jurisdiction formerly exercised by the court of appeal in chancery, the exchequer chamber, the judicial committee of the privy council in admiralty and lunacy appeals, and with general appellate jurisdiction from the high court of justice.

Court of Appeals. In those states with courts of appeals, such courts are usually intermediate appellate courts. In New York, Maryland, and the District of Columbia, however, such are the highest appellate courts. In West Virginia the Supreme Court of Appeals is the court of last resort. Alabama, Oklahoma, Tennessee, and Texas have Courts of Criminal Appeals, with those in Oklahoma and Texas being the highest appellate courts for criminal matters. Alabama, Oklahoma, and Texas have Courts of Civil Appeals, which are intermediate appellate courts. See also **Supreme Court.**

The United States is divided into eleven federal judicial circuits in each of which there is established a court of appeals known as the United States Court of Appeals for the circuit. 28 U.S.C.A. §§ 41, 43. See **Courts of Appeals, U.S.**

Court of Appeals in Cases of Capture. A court erected by act of congress under the articles of confederation which preceded the adoption of the Constitution. It had appellate jurisdiction in prize causes.

Court of Archdeacon. The most inferior of the English ecclesiastical courts, from which an appeal generally lies to that of the bishop (*i.e.*, to the Consistory Court). Such court is now virtually obsolete.

Court of Assistants. Formerly a court in Massachusetts organized in 1630, consisting of the governor, deputy governor and assistants. It exercised the whole power both legislative and judicial of the colony and an extensive chancery jurisdiction as well.

Court of Attachments. In old English law, the lowest of the three courts held in the forests. It has fallen into total disuse. It was held before the verderers of the forest once in every forty days, to view the attachments by the foresters for offences against the vert and the venison. It had cognizance only of small trespasses. Larger ones were enrolled and heard by the Justices in Eyre.

Court of Audience. An ecclesiastical court, in which the primates once exercised in person a considerable part of their jurisdiction. Such courts, which existed in England for both the Archbishop of Canterbury and York, have long since been disused.

Court of Augmentation. An English court created in the time of Henry VIII (27 Hen. VIII, c. 27), with jurisdiction over the property and revenue of certain religious foundations, which had been made over to the king by act of parliament, and over suits relating to the same. It was called "The Court of the Augmentations of the Revenues of the King's Crown" (from the *augmentation* of the revenues of the crown derived from the suppression of the monasteries), and was dissolved in the reign of Queen Mary, but the Office of Augmentation remained long after; the records of the court are now at the Public Record Office.

Court of Bankruptcy. Federal court established in each judicial district, as an adjunct to the U.S. district court for such district, with general jurisdiction over bankruptcy matters. 28 U.S.C.A. §§ 151, 1471.

Court of Brotherhood. In old English law, an assembly of the mayors or other chief officers of the principal towns of the Cinque Ports in England, originally administering the chief powers of those ports, now almost extinct.

Court of Chancery. A court administering equity and proceeding according to the forms and principles of equity. In England, prior to the judicature acts, the style of the court possessing the largest equitable powers and jurisdiction was the "high court of chancery." In some of the United States, the title "court of chancery" is applied to a court possessing general equity powers, distinct from the courts of law. Courts of chancery (equity courts) have been abolished by all states that have adopted Rules of Civil Procedure. See also **Court of Equity.**

Court of Chivalry. In English law, the name of a court anciently held as a court of honor merely, before the earl-marshal, and as a criminal court before the lord high constable, jointly with the earl-marshal. But it is also said that this court was held by the constable, and after that office reverted to the crown in the time of Henry VIII, by the earl-marshal. It had jurisdiction as to contracts and other matters touching deeds of arms or war, as well as pleas of life or member. It also corrected encroachments in matters of coat-armor, precedency, and other distinctions of families. It is now grown entirely out of use (except for one case in 1955, after a lapse of 200 years) on account of the feebleness of its jurisdiction and want of power to enforce its judgments, as it could neither fine nor imprison, not being a court of record.

Court of Civil Appeals. Such exist as intermediate appellate courts in Alabama, Oklahoma, and Texas. The Texas Court of Civil Appeals has appellate jurisdiction of cases decided in district and county courts.

Court of Claims. This federal court was established on February 25, 1855 (10 Stat. 612; 28 U.S.C.A. § 171); its jurisdiction is set forth in 28 U.S.C.A. §§ 1491–1506. The court has original jurisdiction to render judgment upon any claim against the United States founded upon the Constitution, upon any act of Congress, upon any regulation of an executive department, upon any expressed or implied contracts with the United States, and for liquidated or unliquidated damages in cases not sounding in tort. A growing number of states also have courts of claims (*e.g.* Illinois, Michigan, New York, Ohio).

Court of Common Pleas. In English law, one of the four superior courts at Westminster, which existed up to the passing of the judicature acts. It was also styled the "Common Bench". It was one of the courts derived from the breaking up of the *aula regis*, and had exclusive jurisdiction of all real actions and of *communia placita*, or common pleas, *i.e.*, between subject and subject. It was presided over by a chief justice with four puisne judges (later five, by virtue of 31 & 32, Vict., c. 125, § 11, subsec. 8). Appeals lay anciently to the king's bench, but afterwards to the exchequer chamber. See 3 Bl.Comm. 37, *et seq.* Its jurisdiction was altogether confined to civil matters, having no cognizance in criminal cases, and was concurrent with that of the queen's bench and exchequer in personal actions and ejectment. In the United States, such courts exist in Pennsylvania wherein all civil and criminal actions are begun (except such as are brought before courts of inferior jurisdiction). Most such courts have been abolished, however, their jurisdiction being transferred to district, circuit, or superior courts.

Court of Conciliation. A court which proposes terms of adjustment, so as to avoid litigation; *e.g.* conciliation between debtor and creditor over disputed debt. May also function to aid in resolving marital disputes. See also **Small Claims Court.**

Court of Conscience. The same as courts of request *(q.v.).* This name was also frequently applied to the courts of equity or of chancery, not as name but as a description. See also **Conscience.**

Court of Convocation. In English ecclesiastical law, a court, or assembly, comprising all the high officials of each province and representatives of the minor clergy. It was in the nature of an ecclesiastical parliament; and, so far as its judicial functions extend, it had jurisdiction of cases of heresy, schism, and other purely ecclesiastical matters. An appeal was to the king in council.

Court of County Commissioners. In some states, a court of record in each county.

Court of Criminal Appeals. See **Court of Appeals.**

Court of Customs and Patent Appeals. See **Customs and Patent Appeals Court.**

Court of Delegates. An English tribunal composed of delegates appointed by royal commission, and formerly the great court of appeal in all ecclesiastical causes. The powers of the court were, by 2 & 3 Wm. IV, c. 92, transferred to the privy council. 3 Bl. Comm. 66. A commission of review was formerly granted, in extraordinary cases, to revise a sentence of the court of delegates, when that court had apparently been led into material error.

Court of Equity. A court which has jurisdiction in equity, which administers justice and decides controversies in accordance with the rules, principles, and precedents of equity, and which follows the forms and procedure of chancery; as distinguished from a court having the jurisdiction, rules, principles, and practice of the common law. Equity courts have been abolished in all states which have adopted Rules of Civil Procedure; law and equity actions having been merged procedurally into a single form of "civil action". Fed.R. Civil P. 2. See also **Court of Chancery.**

Court of Error. An expression formerly applied especially in England to the court of exchequer chamber and the house of lords, as taking cognizance of *error* brought. It was formerly applied in some of the United States (*e.g.* Connecticut) to the court of last resort in the state; and in its most general sense denotes any court having power to review the decisions of lower courts on appeal, error, *certiorari,* or other process. See **Court of Appeals.**

Court of Errors and Appeals. Formerly, the court of last resort in the states of New Jersey and New York.

Court of Exchequer /kòrd əv èkschékər/. In English law, a very ancient court of record, set up by William the Conqueror as a part of the *aula regis,* and afterwards one of the four superior courts at Westminster. It was, however, inferior in rank to both the king's bench and the common pleas. It was presided over by a chief baron and four puisne barons. It was originally the king's treasury, and was charged with keeping the king's accounts and collecting the royal revenues. But pleas between subject and subject were anciently heard there, until this was forbidden by the *Articula super Chartas* (1290), after which its jurisdiction as a court only extended to revenue cases arising out of the non-payment or withholding of debts to the crown. But the privilege of suing and being sued in this court was extended to the king's accountants, and later, by the use of a convenient fiction to the effect that the plaintiff was the king's debtor or accountant, the court was thrown open to all suitors in personal actions. The exchequer had formerly both an equity side and a common-law side, but its equity jurisdiction was taken away by the statute 5, Vict., c. 5 (1842), and transferred to the court of chancery. The judicature act (1873) transferred the business and jurisdiction of this court to the "Exchequer Division" of the "High Court of Justice" and by Orders in Council under Sec. 32 of that Act the Exchequer Division was in turn merged in the Queen's Bench Division.

Court of Exchequer Chamber /kòrd əv èkschékər chéymbər/. The name of a former English court of appeal, intermediate between the superior courts of common law and the house of lords. When sitting as a court of appeal from any one of the three superior courts of common law, it was composed of judges of the other two courts. 3 Bl.Comm. 56, 57. By the judicature act (1873) the jurisdiction of this court was transferred to the court of appeal.

Court of Faculties /kòrd əv fǽkəltiyz/. A tribunal of the archbishop in England. It does not hold pleas in any suits, but grants special dispensations, and creates rights to pews, monuments, and other mortuary matters. It has also various other powers as given by the Ecclesiastical Licenses Act of 1533.

Court of First Instance. A court of original or primary jurisdiction, *e.g.* trial court. Courts of this title may be found in the jurisprudence of the Philippine Islands.

Court of General Quarter Sessions of the Peace. Formerly, a court of criminal jurisdiction in New Jersey.

In English law, a court of criminal jurisdiction held in each county once in every quarter of a year, but in the county of Middlesex twice a month. When held at other times than quarterly, the sessions were called "general sessions of the peace." Quarter sessions were abolished by the Courts Act of 1971, with most jurisdiction transferred to the Crown Court *(q.v.).*

Court of General Sessions. The name given in some states to a court of general original jurisdiction in criminal cases.

Court of Great Sessions in Wales. A court formerly held in Wales; abolished by 11 Geo. IV, and 1 Wm. IV, c. 70 (1830) and the Welsh judicature incorporated with that of England.

Court of Guestling. In old English law, an assembly of the members of the Court of Brotherhood *(supra)* together with other representatives of the corporate members of the Cinque Ports, invited to sit with the mayors of the seven principal towns.

Court of High Commission. In English law, an ecclesiastical court of formidable jurisdiction, for the vindication of the peace and dignity of the church, by reforming, ordering, and correcting the ecclesiastical state and persons, and all manner of errors, heresies, schisms, abuses, offenses, contempts, and enormities. 3 Bl.Comm. 67. It was erected by St. 1 Eliz., c. 1 (1588), and abolished by 16 Car. I, c. 11 (1688).

Court of Honor. In old English law, a court having jurisdiction to hear and redress injuries or affronts to a man's honor or personal dignity, of a nature not cognizable by the ordinary courts of law, or encroachments upon his rights in respect to heraldry, coat-armor, right of precedence, and the like. It was one of the functions of the Court of Chivalry *(q.v.)* in England to sit and act as a court of honor. 3 Bl. Comm. 104.

The name is also given in some European countries to a tribunal of army officers (more or less distinctly recognized by law as a "court") convened for the purpose of inquiring into complaints affecting the honor of brother officers and punishing derelictions from the code of honor and deciding on the causes and occasions for fighting duels, in which officers are concerned, and the manner of conducting them.

Court of Hustings. In English law, the county court of London, held before the mayor, recorder, and sheriff, but of which the recorder, is, in effect, the sole judge. No actions can be brought in this court that are merely personal. Since the abolition of all real and mixed actions except ejectment, the jurisdiction of this court has fallen into comparative desuetude.

Formerly, a local court in some parts of Virginia.

Court of Inquiry. In English law, a court sometimes appointed by the crown to ascertain whether it be proper to resort to extreme measures against a person charged before a court-martial. Also a court for hearing the complaints of private soldiers.

In American law, formerly, a court constituted by authority of the articles of war, invested with the power to examine into the nature of any transaction of, or accusation or imputation against, any officer or soldier, when demanded by him. Rev.St. § 1342, arts. 115, 116. Repealed by Act June 4, 1920, c. 227, § 4, 41 Stat. 812. They were not strictly courts, having no power to try and determine guilt or innocence. They were rather agencies created by statute to investigate facts and report thereon. They could not compel the attendance of witnesses nor require them to testify.

In Texas when a judge of any county or district court of this state, acting in his capacity as magistrate, has good cause to believe that an offense has been committed against the laws of this state, he may summon and examine any witness in relation thereto in accordance with the rules hereinafter provided, which procedure is defined as a "Court of Inquiry".

Court of Justice Seat. In English law, the principal of the forest courts. Called also Court of the Chief Justice in Eyre *(q.v.)*.

Court of King's (or Queen's) Bench. In English law, the supreme court of common law in the kingdom; merged in the high court of justice under the judicature act of 1873, § 16. It was one of the successors of the *curia regis* and received its name, it is said,

because the king formerly sat in it in person. During the reign of a queen it was called the Queen's Bench, and during Cromwell's Protectorate it was called the Upper Bench.

Court of law. In a wide sense, any duly constituted tribunal administering the laws of the state or nation; in a narrower sense, a court proceeding according to the course of the common law and governed by its rules and principles, as contrasted with a "court of equity *(q.v.)*."

Court of Magistrates and Freeholders. The name of a court formerly established in South Carolina for the trial of slaves and free persons of color for criminal offenses.

Court of Marshalsea /kòrd əv márshəlsìy/. In English law, the court or seat of the marshal. A court originally held before the steward and marshal of the king's house, instituted to administer justice between the king's domestic servants. It had jurisdiction of all trespasses committed within the verge of the king's court, where one of the parties was of the royal household; and of all debts and contracts, when both parties were of that establishment. It was abolished by 12 & 13, Vict., c. 101, § 13 (1849).

Court of Military Appeals. This court was established pursuant to the act approved May 5, 1950, as amended (64 Stat. 129, 82 Stat. 178, 1342; 10 U.S.C.A. § 867), as the final appellate tribunal to review court-martial convictions of all the services. It is exclusively an appellate criminal court. The Court, consisting of three civilian judges appointed by the President, is called upon to exercise jurisdiction as to questions of law in all cases affecting a general or flag officer, or extending to death; questions certified to the Court by the Judge Advocates General of the armed services, and by the General Counsel of the Department of Transportation, acting for the Coast Guard; petitions by accused who have received a sentence of a year or more confinement, and/or a punitive discharge.

Court of Nisi Prius /kòrd əv náysay práyəs/. Though this term is frequently used as a general designation of any court exercising general, original jurisdiction in civil cases (being used interchangeably with "trial-court"), it belonged as a legal title only to a court which formerly existed in the city and county of Philadelphia, and which was presided over by one of the judges of the supreme court of Pennsylvania. This court was abolished by the constitution of 1874. See **Assize; Courts of Assize and Nisi Prius; Nisi prius.**

Court of Ordinary. In Georgia such courts formerly had exclusive and general jurisdiction over probate of wills; granting letters testamentary, or of administration, and revocation of same; management, disposition and distribution of estate of decedents, idiots, lunatics and insane persons and of all such other matters and things as appertain or relate to same; appointment and removal of guardians of minors and persons of unsound mind and all controversies as to right of guardianship; receiving and hearing applications for homestead and exemption and granting same; and concurrently with judge of the county court, jurisdiction in binding out of orphans and apprentices, and all controversies between master and apprentice. The Probate Court now has jurisdiction over such matter.

Court of Orphans /kòrd əv órfənz/. In Maryland and Pennsylvania, a court, elsewhere known as a "Probate" or "Surrogates" court, with general jurisdiction over matters of probate and administration of estates, orphans, wards, and guardians.

Court of Oyer and Terminer /kòrd əv óyər ənd tármənər/. In England, formerly, a court for the trial of cases of treason and felony. The commissioners of assise and *nisi prius* were judges selected by the king and appointed and authorized under the great seal, including usually two of the judges at Westminster, and sent out twice a year into most of the counties of England, for the trial (with a jury of the county) of causes then depending at Westminster, both civil and criminal. They sat by virtue of several commissions, each of which, in reality, constituted them a separate and distinct court. The commission of *oyer and terminer* gave them authority for the trial of treasons and felonies; that of *general gaol delivery* empowers them to try every prisoner then in gaol for whatever offense, so that, altogether, they possessed full criminal jurisdiction. The assize courts have since been abolished and replaced by the Crown Court.

In American law, this name was generally used (sometimes, with additions) as the title, or part of the title, of a state court of criminal jurisdiction, or of the criminal branch of a court of general jurisdiction, being commonly applied to such courts as may try *felonies,* or the higher grades of crime. Such courts existed in Delaware and Pennsylvania. They were abolished in New York and New Jersey in 1895.

Court of Oyer and Terminer and General Gaol (or Jail) Delivery /kòrd əv óyər ənd tármənər ænd jénərəl jéyl dəlívəriy/. In American law, formerly, a court of criminal jurisdiction in the state of Pennsylvania. It was held at the same time with the court of quarter sessions, as a general rule, and by the same judges. Pa.Const. art. 5, § 1.

In English law, formerly a tribunal for the examination and trial of criminals. Such jurisdiction is now in the Crown Court.

Court of Palace at Westminster. In England, this court had jurisdiction of personal actions arising within twelve miles of the palace at Whitehall. Abolished by 12 & 13, Vict., c. 101. See **Court of the Steward and Marshal.**

Court of Passage. In England, an inferior court, possessing a very ancient jurisdiction over causes of action arising within the borough of Liverpool. It appears to have been also called the "Borough Court of Liverpool." It had the same jurisdiction in admiralty matters as the Lancashire county court. Such court was abolished by the Courts Act of 1971.

Court of Peculiars /kòrd əv pəkyúwlyərz/. A spiritual court in England, being a branch of, and annexed to, the Court of Arches. It has a jurisdiction over all those parishes dispersed through the province of Canterbury, in the midst of other dioceses, which are exempt from the ordinary's jurisdiction, and subject to the metropolitan only. All ecclesiastical causes

arising within these *peculiar* or exempt jurisdictions are originally cognizable by this court, from which an appeal lies to the Court of Arches. Most of such courts have been abolished by legislation. See also **Arches Court.**

Court of Piepoudre /kòrd əv pàypówdər/. (Also spelled Pipowder, Pie Powder, Py-Powder, Piedpoudre, etc.) The lowest (and most expeditious) of the courts of justice known to the older law of England. It is supposed to have been so called from the dusty feet of the suitors. It was a court of record incident to every fair and market, was held by the steward, and had jurisdiction to administer justice for all commercial injuries and minor offenses done in that same fair or market (not a preceding one). An appeal lay to the courts at Westminster. This court long ago fell into disuse. 3 Bl.Comm. 32.

Court of Pleas. In England, a court of the county palatine of Durham, having a local common-law jurisdiction. It was abolished by the judicature act, which transferred its jurisdiction to the high court. 3 Bl. Comm. 79.

Court of Policies of Assurance. In England, a court established by statute 43 Eliz., c. 12 (1601), to determine in a summary way all causes between merchants, concerning policies of insurance. The court was formally abolished by Stat. 26 & 27, Vict., c. 125 (1863). 3 Bl.Comm. 74.

Court of Private Land Claims. A federal court created by act of Congress in 1891 (26 Stat. 854), to hear and determine claims by private parties to lands within the public domain, where such claims originated under Spanish or Mexican grants, and had not already been confirmed by Congress or otherwise adjudicated. The existence and authority of this court were to cease and determine at the end of the year 1895.

Court of Probate. In England, the name of a court established in 1857, under the probate act of that year (20 & 21 Vict., c. 77), to be held in London, to which court was transferred the testamentary jurisdiction of the ecclesiastical courts. The probate court was merged in the Supreme Court of Judicature in 1873, and its jurisdiction is now split between the Chancery and Family divisions.

In American law, a court existing in many states having jurisdiction over the probate of wills, the grant of administration, and the supervision of the management and settlement of the estates of decedents, including the collection of assets, the allowance of claims, and the distribution of the estate. In some states the probate courts also have jurisdiction of the estates of minors, including the appointment of guardians and the settlement of their accounts, and of the estates of lunatics, habitual drunkards, and spendthrifts. And in some states these courts possess a limited jurisdiction in civil and criminal cases. They are also called in some jurisdictions "Orphans' courts" (*e.g.* Maryland, Pennsylvania) and "Surrogate's courts" (*e.g.* N.Y.).

Court of Pypowder, Py-Powder, or **Py-Powders** /kòrd əv pàypáwdər(z)/. See **Court of Piepoudre.**

Court of Quarter Sessions of the Peace. Formerly, a court of criminal jurisdiction in the state of Pennsylvania, having power to try misdemeanors, and exercising certain functions of an administrative nature.

Court of Queen's Bench. See **Court of King's Bench.**

Court of Record. See **Court,** *supra.*

Court of Regard. One of the forest courts, in England, held every third year, for the lawing or expedition of dogs, to prevent them from running after deer. It has long since been obsolete. 3 Bl.Comm. 71, 72.

Court of Sessions. Courts of criminal jurisdiction existing in only a few states.

Court of Shepway. A court held before the lord warden of the Cinque Ports. A writ of error lay from the mayor and jurats of each port to the lord warden in this court, and thence to the queen's bench. The civil jurisdiction of the Cinque Ports was abolished by 18 & 19 Vict., c. 48.

Court of Special Sessions. A generic term, applicable to those courts which have no stated terms and are not continuous, but which are organized only for the trial of each particular case and become *functus officio* when judgment is rendered therein.

Court of Stannaries /kòrd əv stǽnəriyz/. In English law, a court established in Devonshire and Cornwall, for the administration of justice among the miners and tinners, that they might not be drawn away from their business to attend suits in distant courts. The stannary court was a court of record, with a special jurisdiction. By the Stannaries Court (Abolition) Act of 1896 their jurisdiction was transferred to country courts.

Court of Star Chamber. This was an English court of very ancient origin, but new-modeled by St. 3 Hen. VII, c. 1, and 21 Hen. VIII, c. 20, consisting of divers lords, spiritual and temporal, being privy councillors, together with two judges of the courts of common law, without the intervention of any jury. The jurisdiction extended legally over riots, perjury, misbehavior of sheriffs, and other misdemeanors contrary to the laws of the land; yet it was afterwards stretched to the asserting of all proclamations and orders of state, to the vindicating of illegal commissions and grants of monopolies; holding for honorable that which it pleased, and for just that which it profited, and becoming both a court of law to determine civil rights and a court of revenue to enrich the treasury. It was finally abolished by Car. I, c. 10, to the general satisfaction of the Habeas Corpus Act of 1640.

Court of Survey. A court for the hearing of appeals by owners or masters of ships, from orders for the detention of unsafe ships, made by the English board of trade, under the Merchant Shipping Act, 1876, § 6.

Court of Sweinmote /kòrd əv swéynmowt/. (Spelled, also, *Swainmote, Swain-gemote.*) Saxon, *swang,* an attendant, a freeholder, and *mote* or *gemote,* a meeting. In England, one of the old forest courts, held before the verderers, as judges, by the steward, thrice in every year, the sweins or freeholders within the forest composing the jury. This court had jurisdiction to inquire into grievances and oppressions committed by the officers of the forest, and also to receive and try presentments certified from the court of attachments, certifying the cause, in turn, under the seals of the jury, in case of conviction, to the court of justice seat for the rendition of judgment.

Court of the Chief Justice in Eyre. In England, the highest of the courts of the forest, held every three years, by the chief justice, to inquire of purprestures or encroachments, assarts, or cultivation of forest land, claims to franchises, parks, warrens, and vineyards in the forest, as well as claims of the hundred, claims to the goods of felons found in the forest, and any other civil questions that might arise within the forest limits. But it had no criminal jurisdiction, except of offenses against the forest laws. It was called also the court of justice seat. After the Restoration, the forest laws fell into disuse. The office was abolished in 1817.

Court of the Clerk of the Market. An English court of inferior jurisdiction formerly held in every fair or market for the punishment of misdemeanors committed therein. The jurisdiction over weights and measures formerly exercised was taken away by Stat. 526 Will. IV, c. 63.

Court of the Coroner. In England, formerly a court of record to inquire, when any one died in prison, or came to a violent or sudden death, by what manner he came to his end. 4 Bl.Comm. 274. Such functions are now performed by the coroner or by a coroner's inquest. See **Coroner.**

Court of the Counties Palatine. In English law, a species of private court which formerly appertained to the counties palatine of Lancaster and Durham.

Court of the Duchy of Lancaster. In England, a court of special jurisdiction, held before the chancellor of the duchy or his deputy, concerning all matters of equity relating to lands holden of the king in right of the duchy of Lancaster. 3 Bl.Comm. 78. Though not formerly abolished, such court has not sat since 1835.

Court of the Earl Marshal. In the reign of William the Conqueror the marshal was next in rank to the constable, in command of the army. When the constable's office ceased, his duties devolved upon the earl marshal. The military Court of the Constable came to be known as the Marshal's Court, or, in its modern form, Court-Martial. Aside from its criminal jurisdiction, it had much to do with questions relating to fiefs and military tenures, though not to property rights involved therein. See **Constable Court of Chivalry; Court-Martial.**

Court of the Lord High Admiral. In the earlier part of the 14th century, the Admiral possessed a disciplinary jurisdiction over his fleet. After 1340 it is reasonable to suppose that the Admiral could hold an independent court and administer justice in piracy and other maritime cases. There were at first several admirals and several courts. From the early 15th century there was one Lord High Admiral and one Court of Admiralty.

Court of the Lord High Steward. In English law, a court formerly instituted for the trial, during the recess of parliament, of peers indicted for treason or felony, or for misprision of either. This court was not a permanent body, but was created when occasion required and for the time being, only; and the lord high steward, so constituted, with such of the temporal lords as may take the proper oath, and act, constituted the court. Privilege of peerage was abolished by Sec. 30 of the Criminal Justice Act of 1948.

Court of the Lord High Steward of the Universities. In English law, a court constituted for the trial of scholars or privileged persons connected with the university at Oxford or Cambridge who were indicted for treason, felony, or mayhem. 3 Bl.Comm. 83.

Court of the Official Principal. This court, the Court of the "Official Principal" of the Archbishop of Canterbury, is more commonly called the Arches Court, or Court of the Arches. See **Arches Court.**

Court of the Steward and Marshal. A high court, formerly held in England by the steward and marshal of the king's household, having jurisdiction of all actions against the king's peace within the bounds of the household for twelve miles, which circuit was called the "verge." It had also jurisdiction of actions of debt and covenant, where both the parties were of the household. This court was created by Charles I, and abolished in 1849. It was held in the borough of Southwark, and was called also the "palace court," having jurisdiction of all personal actions arising within twelve miles of the royal palace of Whitehall, exclusive of London.

Court of the Steward of the King's Household. In English law, a court which had jurisdiction of all cases of treason, misprision of treason, murder, manslaughter, bloodshed, and other malicious strikings whereby blood is shed, occurring in or within the limits of any of the palaces or houses of the king, or any other house where the royal person is abiding. It was created by statute 33 Hen. VIII, c. 12, but long ago fell into disuse. 4 Bl.Comm. 276, 277.

Court of Wards and Liveries. A court of record, established in England in the reign of Henry VIII. For the survey and management of the valuable fruits of tenure, a court of record was created by St. 32 Hen. VIII, c. 46, called the "Court of the King's Wards." To this was annexed, by St. 33 Hen. VIII, c. 22, the "Court of Liveries;" so that it then became the "Court of Wards and Liveries." This court was not only for the management of "wards," properly so called, but also of idiots and natural fools in the king's custody, and for licenses to be granted to the king's widows to marry, and fines to be made for marrying without his license. It was abolished by St. 12 Car. II, c. 24.

Court packing plan. An attempt by President F. D. Roosevelt in 1937 to replace those justices of the U.S. Supreme Court who did not subscribe to his social philosophy with men whose views were consonant with his.

Court reporter. A person who transcribes by shorthand or stenographically takes down testimony during court proceedings, or at trial related proceedings such as depositions. If an appeal is to be taken wherein an official record is required, the reporter prepares an official transcript from his or her record. A reporter may also constitute the person responsible for publication of the opinions of the court; sometimes called "Reporter of Decisions".

Court rolls. In England, the rolls of a manor, containing all acts relating thereto. While belonging to the lord of the manor, they are not in the nature of public books for the benefit of the tenant. Under the law of Property Act of 1922 copyholds became freeholds and manorial rights were extinguished subject to the provisions therein contained.

Court room. That portion of a courthouse in which the actual proceedings (*i.e.* trial, motions, etc.) take place. Compare **Chamber.**

Court rule. Regulations with the force of law governing practice and procedure in the various courts. They may cover all procedures in a trial court system (*e.g.* Federal Rules of Civil and Criminal Procedure), or govern only procedures before a specific court (*e.g.* U.S. Supreme Court Rules), or only certain aspects of procedure (*e.g.* Federal Rules of Evidence), or they may be so called housekeeping rules which govern internal court practices and procedures. Most states have adopted in whole, or substantially, the Federal Rules of Civil Procedure to govern their trial courts. Also, a growing number of states have adopted Rules of Criminal Procedure and Rules of Appellate Procedure modeled after the Federal Rules of Criminal and Appellate Procedure. In addition, a number of states have adopted Rules of Evidence patterned on the Federal Rules of Evidence.

Courts martial. See **Court-martial.**

Courts of Appeals, U. S. Intermediate appellate courts created by Congress in 1891 and known until 1948 as United States Circuit Courts of Appeals, sitting in ten numbered circuits and the District of Columbia. Normally cases are heard by divisions of three judges sitting together, but on certain matters all the judges of a circuit may hear a case. Courts of Appeals have appellate jurisdiction over most cases decided by United States District Courts and review and enforce orders of many federal administrative bodies. The decisions of the courts of appeals are final except as they are subject to discretionary review on appeal by the Supreme Court. 28 U.S.C.A. § 1291. See also **Temporary Emergency Court of Appeals.**

Courts of Assize and Nisi Prius /kòrts əv əsáyz ænd náysay práyəs/. Courts in England composed of two or more commissioners, called "judges of assize" (or of "assize and *nisi prius*"), who were twice in every year sent by the king's special commission, on circuits all round the kingdom, to try, by a jury of the respective counties, the truth of such matters of fact as were there under dispute in the courts of Westminster Hall. With the establishment of the Crown Court (1971), these courts were abolished.

Courts of Record. Those courts whose proceedings are permanently recorded, and which have the power to fine or imprison for contempt.

Courts of Request. Inferior courts, in England, having local jurisdiction in claims for small debts, established in various parts of the kingdom by special acts of parliament. They were superseded in 1846 by the county courts.

Courts of the Forest. Courts held for the enforcement of the forest laws. See **Forest Courts.**

Courts of the Franchises. Jurisdictions in the early Norman period which rested upon royal grants—often assumed. Edward I, in 1274, sent out commissioners to enquire by what warrant different landowners were exercising their *jura regalia.* There were many varieties of lesser franchises. Some of these franchises were recognized as existing by the County Courts Acts, 1846–1888.

Courts of the United States. "Court of the United States" means any of the following courts: the Supreme Court of the United States, a United States court of appeals, a United States district court, the District of Columbia Court of Appeals, the Superior Court of the District of Columbia, the District Court of Guam, the District Court of the Virgin Islands, the United States Court of Claims, the United States Court of Customs and Patent Appeals, the Tax Court of the United States, the Customs Court, bankruptcy courts, and the Court of Military Appeals. 28 U.S. C.A. § 451. Also, the senate sitting as a court of impeachment.

Courts of Westminster Hall. The superior courts, both of law and equity, were for centuries fixed at Westminster, an ancient palace of the monarchs of England. Formerly, all the superior courts were held before the king's capital justiciary of England, in the *aula regis,* or such of his palaces wherein his royal person resided, and removed with his household from one end of the kingdom to another. This was found to occasion great inconvenience to the suitors to remedy which it was made an article of the great charter of liberties, both of King John and King Henry III, that "common pleas should no longer follow the king's court, but be held in some certain place," in consequence of which they have ever since been held (a few necessary removals in times of the plague excepted) in the palace of Westminster only.

Court system. The network of courts in a particular jurisdiction; *e.g.* trial, appellate, juvenile, land, etc., courts.

Courtyard. A corrupted form of "curtilage", signifying a space of land about a dwelling house, which not only might be inclosed, but within which appurtenant buildings and structures might be erected.

Cousin /kázən/. Kindred in the fourth degree, being the issue (male or female) of the brother or sister of one's father or mother.

Those who descend from the brother or sister of the father of the person spoken of are called "paternal cousins", "maternal cousins" are those who are descended from the brothers or sisters of the mother. Cousins-german are first cousins.

First cousins. Cousins-german; the children of one's uncle or aunt.

Quarter cousin. Properly, a cousin in the fourth degree, but the term has come to express any remote degree of relationship, and even to bear an ironical signification in which it denotes a very trifling degree of intimacy and regard. Often corrupted into "cater" cousin.

Second cousins. Persons who are related to each other by descending from the same great-grandfather or great-grandmother. The children of one's first cousins are his second cousins. These are sometimes called "first cousins once removed."

Cousinage. See **Cosenage.**

Coustom. (Fr. Coutum.) Custom; duty; toll; tribute. See **Custom and usage.**

Coustoumier /kùwt(y)um(i)yéy/. (Otherwise spelled *"Coustumier"* or *"Coutumier."*) In old French law, a collection of customs, unwritten laws, and forms of procedure. Two such volumes are of especial importance in juridical history, viz., the *Grand Coustumier de Normandie,* and the *Coutumier de France* or *Grand Coutumier.*

Couthutlaugh /kúwθətlò/. A person who willingly and knowingly received an outlaw, and cherished or concealed him; for which offense he underwent the same punishment as the outlaw himself.

Couverture /kùwvertyúr/. In French law, the deposit ("margin") made by the client in the hands of the broker, either of a sum of money or of securities, in order to guaranty the broker for the payment of the securities which he purchases for the client.

Covenable /kávənəbəl/kónəbəl/. A French word signifying convenient or suitable; as convenably endowed. Anciently written "convenable."

Covenant /kávənənt/. An agreement, convention, or promise of two or more parties, by deed in writing, signed, and delivered, by which either of the parties pledges himself to the other that something is either done, or shall be done, or shall not be done, or stipulates for the truth of certain facts. At common law, such agreements were required to be under seal. The term is currently used primarily with respect to promises in conveyances or other instruments relating to real estate.

In its broadest usage, means any contract.

The name of a common-law form of action *ex contractu,* which lies for the recovery of damages for breach of a covenant, or contract under seal.

General Classification

Covenants may be classified according to several distinct principles of division:

Absolute or conditional. An absolute covenant is one which is not qualified or limited by any condition.

Affirmative or negative. The former being those in which the party binds himself to the existence of a present state of facts as represented or to the future performance of some act; while the latter are those in which the covenantor obliges himself *not* to do or perform some act.

Declaratory or obligatory. The former being those which serve to limit or direct uses; while the latter are those which are binding on the party himself.

Dependent, concurrent, and independent. Covenants are either dependent, concurrent, or mutual and independent. The first depends on the prior performance of some act or condition, and, until the condition is performed, the other party is not liable to an action on his covenant. In the second, mutual acts are to be performed at the same time; and if one party is ready, and offers to perform his part, and the other neglects or refuses to perform his, he who is ready and offers has fulfilled his engagement, and may maintain an action for the default of the other, though it is not certain that either is obliged to do the first act. The third sort is where either party may recover damages from the other for the injuries he may have received by a breach of the covenants in his favor; and it is no excuse for the defendant to allege a breach of the covenants on the part of the plaintiff. Mutual and independent covenants are such as do not go to the whole consideration on both sides, but only to a part, and where separate actions lie for breaches on either side to recover damages for the injury sustained by breach.

Covenants are dependent where performance by one party is conditioned on and subject to performance by the other, and in such case the party who seeks performance must show performance or a tender or readiness to perform on his part; but covenants are independent when actual performance of one is not dependent on another, and where, in consequence, the remedy of both sides is by action.

Disjunctive covenants. Those which are for the performance of one or more of several things at the election of the covenantor or covenantee, as the case may be.

Executed or executory. The former being such as relate to an act already performed; while the latter are those whose performance is to be future.

Express or implied. The former being those which are created by the express words of the parties to the deed declaratory of their intention, while implied covenants are those which are inferred by the law from certain words in a deed which imply (though they do not express) them. An implied covenant is one which may reasonably be inferred from whole agreement and circumstances attending its execution. Anderson v. Britt, Ky., 375 S.W.2d 258, 260. Express covenants are also called covenants "in deed," as distinguished from covenants "in law."

General or specific. The former relate to land generally and place the covenantee in the position of a specialty creditor only; the latter relate to particular lands and give the covenantee a lien thereon.

Inherent and collateral. The former being such as immediately affect the particular property, while the latter affect some property collateral thereto or some matter collateral to the grant or lease. A covenant inherent is one which is conversant about the land, and knit to the estate in the land; as, that the thing demised shall be quietly enjoyed, shall be kept in repair, or shall not be aliened. A covenant collateral is one which is conversant about some collateral thing that doth nothing at all, or not so immediately, concern the thing granted; as to pay a sum of money in gross, etc.

Joint or several. The former bind both or all the covenantors together; the latter bind each of them separately. A covenant may be both joint and several at the same time, as regards the covenantors; but, as regards the covenantees, they cannot be joint and several for one and the same cause, but must be either joint or several only. Covenants are usually joint or several according as the interests of the covenantees are such; but the words of the covenant, where they are unambiguous, will decide, although, where they are ambiguous the nature of the interests as being joint or several is left to decide.

Principal and auxiliary. The former being those which relate directly to the principal matter of the contract entered into between the parties; while auxiliary covenants are those which do not relate directly to the principal matter of contract between the parties, but to something connected with it.

Real and personal. A real covenant is one which binds the heirs of the covenantor and passes to assignees or purchasers; a covenant the obligation of which is so connected with the realty that he who has the latter is either entitled to the benefit of it or is liable to perform it; a covenant which has for its object something annexed to, or inherent in, or connected with, land or other real property, and runs with the land, so that the grantee of the land is invested with it and may sue upon it for a breach happening in his time.

Transitive or intransitive. The former being those personal covenants the duty of performing which passes over to the representatives of the covenantor; while the latter are those the duty of performing which is limited to the covenantee himself, and does not pass over to his representative.

Other Compound and Descriptive Terms

Continuing covenant. One which indicates or necessarily implies the doing of stipulated acts successively or as often as the occasion may require; as, a covenant to pay rent by installments, to keep the premises in repair or insured, to cultivate land, etc.

Full covenants. As this term is commonly used, it includes: covenants for seisin, for right to convey, against incumbrances, for quiet enjoyment, sometimes for further assurance, and almost always of warranty, this last often taking the place of the covenant for quiet enjoyment, and indeed in many states being the only covenant in practical use.

Restrictive covenants. See that title.

Separate covenant. A several covenant; one which binds the several covenantors each for himself, but not jointly.

Usual covenants. An agreement on the part of a seller of real property to give the usual covenants binds him to insert in the grant covenants of "seisin," "quiet enjoyment," "further assurance," "general warranty," "right to convey," and "against incumbrances." Collectively they are called covenants for title to distinguish them from restrictive covenants. See *Covenants for title,* below.

Specific Covenants

Covenants against incumbrances. A covenant that there are no incumbrances on the land conveyed. A stipulation against all rights to or interests in the land which may subsist in third persons to the diminution of the value of the estate granted.

Covenant appurtenant. A covenant which is connected with land of the grantor, and not in gross. A covenant running with the land and binding heirs, executors and assigns of the immediate parties.

Covenant for further assurance. An undertaking, in the form of a covenant, on the part of the vendor of real estate to do such further acts for the purpose of perfecting the purchaser's title as the latter may reasonably require. This covenant is deemed of great importance, since it relates both to the vendor's title of and to the instrument of conveyance to the vendee, and operates as well to secure the performance of all acts necessary for supplying any defect in the former as to remove all objections to the sufficiency and security of the latter.

Covenant for possession. A covenant by which the grantee or lessee is granted possession.

Covenant for quiet enjoyment. An assurance against the consequences of a defective title, and of any disturbances thereupon. A covenant that the tenant or grantee of an estate shall enjoy the possession of the premises in peace and without disturbance by hostile claimants.

Covenants for title. Covenants usually inserted in a conveyance of land, on the part of the grantor, and binding him for the completeness, security, and continuance of the title transferred to the grantee. They comprise covenants for seisin, for right to convey, against incumbrances, or quiet enjoyment, sometimes for further assurance, and almost always of warranty.

Covenant in gross. Such as do not run with the land.

Covenant not to compete. An agreement, generally part of a contract of employment or a contract to sell a business, in which the covenantor agrees for a specific period of time and within a particular area to refrain from competition with the covenantee.

Covenant not to sue. A covenant by one who had a right of action at the time of making it against another person, by which he agrees not to sue to enforce such right of action.

Covenant of non-claim. A covenant formerly sometimes employed, particularly in the New England states, and in deeds of extinguishment of ground rents in Pennsylvania, that neither the vendor, nor his heirs, nor any other person, etc., shall claim any title in the premises conveyed.

Covenant of right to convey. An assurance by the covenantor that the grantor has sufficient capacity and title to convey the *estate* which he by his deed undertakes to convey.

Covenant of seisin. An assurance to the purchaser that the grantor has the very estate in quantity and quality which he purports to convey.

Covenant of warranty. An assurance by the grantor of an estate that the grantee shall enjoy the same without interruption by virtue of paramount title.

Covenant running with land. A covenant which goes with the land, as being annexed to the estate, and which cannot be separated from the land, and transferred without it. A covenant is said to run with the land, when not only the original parties or their representatives, but each successive owner of the land, will be entitled to its benefit, or be liable (as the case may be) to its obligation. Or, in other words, it is so called when either the liability to perform it or the right to take advantage of it passes to the assignee of the land. One which touches and concerns the land itself, so that its benefit or obligation passes with the ownership. Local Federal Savings & Loan Ass'n of Oklahoma City v. Eckroat, 186 Okl. 660, 100 P.2d 261, 262. Essentials of a "covenant running with the land" are that the grantor and grantee must have intended that the covenant run with the land, the covenant must affect or concern the land with which it runs, and there must be privity of estate between party claiming the benefit and the party who rests under the burden. Greenspan v. Rehberg, 56 Mich. App. 310, 224 N.W.2d 67, 73.

Covenant running with title. A covenant which goes with the title. Stipulation in a lease granting to lessee the option of renewing it for another specified period was such a covenant. See also *Covenants for title, supra.*

Covenant to convey. A covenant by which the covenantor agrees to convey to the covenantee a certain estate, under certain circumstances.

Covenant to renew. An executory contract, giving lessee the right to renew on compliance with the terms specified in the renewal clause, if any, or, if none, on giving notice, prior to termination of the lease, of his desire to renew, whereupon the contract becomes executed as to him.

Covenant to stand seised. A conveyance adapted to the case where a person seised of land in possession, reversion, or vested remainder, proposes to convey it to his wife, child, or kinsman. In its terms it consists of a covenant by him, in consideration of his natural love and affection, to stand seised of the land to the use of the intended transferee. Before the statute of uses this would merely have raised a use in favor of the covenantee; but by that act this use is converted into the legal estate, and the covenant therefore operates as a conveyance of the land to the covenantee. It is now almost obsolete.

Covenantee /kàvənəntíy/. The party to whom a covenant is made.

Covenantor /kávənəntər/. The party who makes a covenant.

Covenants performed. In Pennsylvania practice, this was the name of a plea to the action of covenant whereby the defendant, upon informal notice to the plaintiff, was allowed to give anything in evidence which he might have pleaded. With the addition of the words "absque hoc" it amounted to a denial of the allegations of the declaration; and the further addition of "with leave," etc., imported an equitable defense, arising out of special circumstances, which the defendant meant to offer in evidence. This plea was abolished in 1887.

Covent. A contraction, in the old books, of the word "convent."

Coventry Act. The name given to the statute 22 & 23 Car. II, c. 1, which provided for the punishment of assaults with intent to maim or disfigure a person. It was so named from its being occasioned by an assault on Sir John Coventry in the street as was supposed, for some obnoxious words uttered by him in parliament. 4 Bl.Comm. 207.

Cover. To protect by means of insurance; sometimes orally pending issuance of policy. See also **Binder; Cover note.**

The right of a buyer, after breach by a seller, to purchase goods in substitution for those due from the seller if such purchase is made in good faith and without unreasonable delay. The buyer may then recover as damages the difference between the cost of cover and the contract price plus any incidental and consequential damages but less expenses saved in consequence of the seller's breach. U.C.C. § 2–712(1), (2).

Coverage. In insurance, amount and extent of risk covered by insurer.

Cover-all clause. A provision in a document which purportedly embraces all eventualities of which the parties are aware as possibilities.

Cover into. The phrase "covered into the treasury," as used in acts of Congress and the practice of the United States Treasury Department, means that money has actually been paid into the treasury in the regular manner, as distinguished from merely depositing it with the treasurer. U. S. v. Johnston, 124 U.S. 236, 8 S.Ct. 446, 31 L.Ed. 389.

Cover note. Written statement by insurance agent that coverage is in effect. Distinguished from binder which is prepared by company.

Covert /kávərt/. Covered, protected, sheltered. A covert act is a concealed, not apparent act.

Covert baron, or **covert de baron** /kávərt (də) bǽrən/. Under the protection of a husband; married. *La feme que est covert de baron,* the woman which is covert of a husband.

Coverture /kávərchər/. The condition or state of a married woman. Sometimes used elliptically to describe the legal disability which formerly existed from a state of coverture.

Cover-up. To conceal. As a crime, the act of concealing or hiding something wrong or criminal. See also **Harbor; Misprision of felony.**

Covin /kávən/. A secret conspiracy or agreement between two or more persons to injure or defraud another.

Covinous /kávənəs/. Deceitful; fraudulent; having the nature of, or tainted by covin.

Cowardice. Pusillanimity; fear; misbehavior through fear in relation to some duty to be performed.

C.P. An abbreviation for common pleas.

C.P.A. Certified Public Accountant.

C.R. An abbreviation for *curia regis;* also for chancery reports.

Craft. Generally, any boat, ship or vessel.

A trade or occupation of the sort requiring skill and training, particularly manual skill combined with a knowledge of the principles of the art. Also the body of persons pursuing such a calling; a guild.

Guile, artful cunning, trickiness. Not a legal term in this sense, though often used in connection with such terms as "fraud" and "artifice."

Craft union. A labor union all of whose members do the same kind of work (*i.e.* trade) such as plumbing or carpentry for different employers and industries.

Cranage. A liberty to use a crane for drawing up goods and wares of burden from ships and vessels, at any creek of the sea, or wharf, unto the land, and to make a profit of doing so. It also signifies the money paid and taken for the service.

Crank. A term vulgarly applied to a person of eccentric, ill-regulated, and unpractical mental habits; an ill-tempered person.

Crassus /krǽsəs/. Large; gross; excessive; extreme. *Crassa ignorantia* /krǽsə ignərǽnsh(iy)ə/ gross ignorance.

Crassa negligentia /krǽsə nègləjénsh(iy)ə/. Gross neglect; absence of ordinary care and diligence.

Crastino /krǽstənow/. Lat. On the morrow, the day after. In old English law, the return-day of writs; because the first day of the term was always some saint's day, and writs were returnable on the day after.

Crave. To ask or demand; as to crave oyer. See **Oyer.**

Craven /kréyvən/. In old English law, a word of disgrace and obloquy, pronounced on either champion, in the ancient trial by battle, proving recreant, *i.e.,* yielding.

Crazy. Non-medical, lay expression or description for a broken, shattered, or deranged condition of the mind; insane.

Creamer. A foreign merchant, but generally taken for one who has a stall in a fair or market.

Creamus /kriyéyməs/. Lat. We create. One of the words by which a corporation in England was formerly created by the king. 1 Bl.Comm. 473.

Creance /kreyón(t)s/. In French law, a claim; a debt; also belief, credit, faith.

Creancer /kríyənsər/. One who trusts or gives credit; a creditor.

Creansor /kríyənsər/. A creditor.

Create. To bring into being; to cause to exist; to produce; as, to create a trust, to create a corporation.

Credentials /krədénshəlz/. Documentary evidence of a person's authority; commonly in the form of letters, licenses or certificates which on their face indicate the authority and capacity of the bearer.

Credibility. Worthiness of belief; that quality in a witness which renders his evidence worthy of belief. After the competence of a witness is allowed, the consideration of his *credibility* arises, and not before. As to the distinction between *competency* and *credibility,* see **Competency.** See also **Character; Reputation.**

Credible. Worthy of belief; entitled to credit. See **Competency; Character; Reputation.**

Credible person. One who is trustworthy and entitled to be believed. In law and legal proceedings, one who is entitled to have his oath or affidavit accepted as reliable, not only on account of his good reputation for veracity, but also on account of his intelligence, knowledge of the circumstances, and disinterested relation to the matter in question. Also one who is competent to testify. Burleson v. State, 131 Tex. Cr.R. 576, 100 S.W.2d 1019, 1020.

Credible witness. One who is competent to give evidence; also one who is worthy of belief. Burleson v. State, 131 Tex.Cr.R. 576, 100 S.W.2d 1019, 1020. See **Credibility,** *supra.*

Credibly informed. The statement in a pleading or affidavit, that one is "credibly informed and verily believes" such and such facts, means that, having no direct personal knowledge of the matter in question, he has derived his information in regard to it from authentic sources or from the statements of persons who are not only "credible," in the sense of being trustworthy, but also informed as to the particular matter or conversant with it.

Credit. The ability of a business or person to borrow money, or obtain goods on time, in consequence of the favorable opinion held by the particular lender as to solvency and reliability. In re Ford, D.C.Wash., 14 F.2d 848, 849. Time allowed to the buyer of goods by the seller, in which to make payment for them. The correlative of a *debt;* that is, a debt considered from the creditor's standpoint, or that which is incoming or due *to* one. That which is due to a person, as distinguished from debit, that which is due by him. Claim or cause of action for specific sum of money.

"Credit" means the right granted by a creditor to a debtor to defer payment of debt or to incur debt and defer its payment. Uniform Consumer Credit Code, Section 1.301(7).

In accounting, as a noun, an entry on the right-hand side of an account. As a verb, to make an entry on the right-hand side of an account. Records increases in liabilities, owners' equity, and revenues; and decreases in assets and expenses.

In taxation, an amount which may be subtracted from the computed tax itself in contrast to a deduction which is generally subtracted from gross income to arrive at adjusted gross income or taxable income.

See also Confirmed credit; Credit line; Fair Credit Reporting Act; Installment credit; Investment tax credit; Letter of credit; Notation credit; Open credit; Open-end credit; Revocable credit; Revolving credit; Tax credit.

Bank credit. Money bank owes or will lend individual or person.

Bill of credit. See **Bill.**

Consumer credit. See Consumer credit; Consumer Credit Code; Consumer Credit Protection Act; Consumer credit sale; Consumer credit transaction; Credit card; Fair Credit Reporting Acts; Fair Credit Billing Act; Equal Credit Opportunity Act; Truth-in-lending Act.

Credit insurance. See **Insurance.**

Extortionate credit. See **Extortion; Loanshark.**

Line of credit. See **Line.**

Open credit. See **Open credit; Open-end credit.**

Credit advertising. An advertisement which aids, promotes or assists directly or indirectly the extension of credit. Federal and state statutes regulate such advertising.

Credit bureau. Establishments which make a business of collecting information relating to the credit, character, responsibility and reputation of individuals and businesses, for the purpose of furnishing the information (*i.e.* credit reports) to subscribers (*i.e.* merchants, banks, suppliers, etc.). Practices of credit bureaus are regulated by federal (*e.g.* Fair Credit Reporting Act) and often state statutes. See also **Credit rating; Credit report.**

Credit card. Any card, plate, or other like credit device existing for the purpose of obtaining money, property, labor or services on credit. The term does not include a note, check, draft, money order or other like negotiable instrument. Federal (*e.g.* Consumer Credit Protection Act) and often state statutes regulate the issuance and use of credit cards.

Credit card crime. A person commits an offense if he uses a credit card for the purpose of obtaining property or services with knowledge that: (1) the card is stolen or forged; or (2) the card has been revoked or cancelled; or (3) for any other reason his use of the card is unauthorized. Model Penal Code, § 224.6.

Credit disclosure. See **Annual percentage rate; Consumer Credit Protection Act; Truth-in-Lending Act.**

Credited. The alternative to paid. Lynchburg Trust & Savings Bank v. Commissioner of Internal Revenue, C.C.A.4, 68 F.2d 356, 358.

Credit foncier /krèydíy fònsyéy/. A company or corporation formed for the purpose of carrying out improvements, by means of loans and advances on real estate security.

Credit insurance. A contract whereby the insurer promises, in consideration of a premium paid, and subject to specified conditions as to the persons to whom credit is to be extended, to indemnify the insured, wholly or in part, against loss that may result from the death, disability, or insolvency of persons to whom he may extend credit within the term of the insurance. The requirement of such, as well as the full disclosure of the terms and cost of such, is regulated by federal and often state statutes.

Credit life, accident, and health insurance. Term insurance on lives of debtors, with the creditors of the insured debtor as beneficiary. The amount payable on death of insured debtor is an amount at least sufficient to discharge debtor's indebtedness; and in event of total permanent disability an amount is payable which is at least sufficient to meet installment payments on debtor's indebtedness as they mature during the period of disability. Superior Life Ins. Co. v. U. S., D.C.S.C., 322 F.Supp. 921, 924.

Credit line. In banking and commerce, that amount of money or merchandise which a banker or supplier agrees to supply to a person on credit and generally agreed to in advance. The limit of money which may be borrowed or merchandise purchased on credit.

In motion pictures, the preliminary statement which gives the names of the players, producer, director, etc. May also refer to similar acknowledgments of contributors or assistants in authorship of books, production of plays, or the like.

Credit memorandum. A document used by a seller to inform a buyer that the buyer's account receivable is being credited (reduced) because of errors, returns, or allowances.

Credit mobilier /krèydíy mòwbìylyéy/. A company or association formed for carrying on a banking business or for the construction of public works, building or railroads, operation of mines, or other such enterprises, by means of loans or advances on the security of personal property.

Creditor. A person to whom a debt is owing by another person who is the "debtor." Rooney v. Inheritance Tax Commission of Kansas, 143 Kan. 143, 53 P.2d 500, 501. One who has a right to require the fulfillment of an obligation or contract. Murphy v. Jos. Hollander, Inc., 131 N.J.L. 165, 34 A.2d 780, 783. One to whom money is due, and, in ordinary acceptation, has reference to financial or business transactions. The antonym of "debtor." Erickson v. Grande Ronde Lumber Co., 162 Or. 556, 92 P.2d 170, 177.

The word is susceptible of latitudinous construction. In its broad sense the word means one who has any legal liability upon a contract, express or implied, or in tort; in its narrow sense, the term is limited to one who holds a demand which is certain and liquidated. In statutes the term has various special meanings, dependent upon context, purpose of statute, etc.

The term "creditor," within the common-law and statutes that conveyances with intent to defraud creditors shall be void, includes every one having right to require the performance of any legal obligation, contract, or guaranty, or a legal right to damages growing out of contract or tort, and includes not merely the holder of a fixed and certain present debt, but every one having a right to require the performance of any legal obligation, contract, or guaranty, or a legal right to damages growing out of contract or tort, and includes one entitled to damages for breach of contract to convey real estate, notwithstanding the abandonment of his action for specific performance.

Under U.C.C., term includes a general creditor, a secured creditor, a lien creditor and any representative of creditors, including an assignee for the benefit of creditors, a trustee in bankruptcy, a receiver in equity and an executor or administrator of an insolvent debtor's or assignor's estate. U.C.C. § 1–201(12).

Under Bankruptcy Act, term includes entity that has a claim against the debtor that arose at the time of or before the order for relief concerning the debtor. Bankruptcy Act, § 101(9).

Classification

A creditor may be called a "simple contract creditor," a "specialty creditor," a "bond creditor," or otherwise, according to the nature of the obligation giving rise to the debt.

Attaching creditor. One who has caused an attachment to be issued and levied on property of his debtor.

Certificate creditor. A creditor of a municipal corporation who receives a certificate of indebtedness for the amount of his claim, there being no funds on hand to pay him.

Confidential creditor. A term sometimes applied to creditors of a failing debtor who furnished him with the means of obtaining credit to which his real circumstances did not entitle him, thus involving loss to other creditors not in his confidence.

Creditor at large. One who has not established his debt by the recovery of a judgment or has not otherwise secured a lien on any of the debtor's property.

Domestic creditor. One who resides in the same state or country in which the debtor has his domicile or his property.

Double creditor. See that title.

Execution creditor. One who, having recovered a judgment against the debtor for his debt or claim, has also caused an execution to be issued thereon.

Foreign creditor. One who resides in a state or country foreign to that where the debtor has his domicile or his property.

General creditor. A creditor at large *(supra)*, or one who has no lien or security for the payment of his debt or claim.

Joint creditors. Persons jointly entitled to require satisfaction of the same debt or demand.

Judgment creditor. See that title.

Junior creditor. One whose claim or demand accrued at a date later than that of a claim or demand held by another creditor, who is called correlatively the "senior" creditor. Creditor whose claim ranks below other creditors in rights to the debtor's property. For example, a creditor with an unperfected security interest in a property is a junior creditor to one holding a perfected security interest.

Lien creditor. A creditor who has acquired a lien on the property involved by attachment, levy or the like and includes an assignee for benefit of creditors from the time of assignment, and a trustee in bankruptcy from the date of the filing of the petition or a receiver in equity from the time of appointment. U.C.C. § 9–301. See also **Lien creditor.**

Preferred creditor. See that title.

Principal creditor. One whose claim or demand very greatly exceeds the claims of all other creditors in amount is sometimes so called.

Secondary creditors. One whose claim is secondary to preferred creditor(s).

Secured creditor. See **Secured creditor;** also, *Lien creditor, supra.*

Single creditor. See that title.

Subsequent creditor. One whose claim or demand accrued or came into existence after a given fact or transaction, such as the recording of a deed or mortgage or the execution of a voluntary conveyance. See also *Junior creditor, supra.*

Warrant creditor. A creditor of a municipal corporation to whom is given a municipal warrant for the amount of his claim, because there are no funds in hand to pay it.

Creditor beneficiary. A third person to whom performance of promise comes in satisfaction of legal duty. Where performance of a promise in a contract will benefit a person other than the promisee, that person is a creditor beneficiary if no purpose to make a gift appears from the terms of the promise in view of the accompanying circumstances and performance of the promise will satisfy an actual or supposed or asserted duty of the promisee to the beneficiary, or a right of the beneficiary against the promisee which has been barred by the Statute of Limitations or by a discharge in bankruptcy, or which is unenforceable because of the Statute of Frauds. Restatement of Contracts, § 133(1)(b).

Creditor's bill or **suit.** Equitable proceeding brought to enforce payment of debt out of property or other interest of debtor which cannot be reached by ordinary legal process. Sackin v. Kersting, 105 Ariz. 464, 466 P.2d 758. By use of the creditor's bill, a judgment creditor can reach any nonexempt property interest of the debtor that is alienable or assignable under state law. A suit by judgment creditor in equity for purpose of reaching property which cannot be reached by execution at law. A proceeding to enforce the security of a judgment creditor against the property or interests of his debtor. This action proceeds upon the theory that the judgment is in the nature of a lien, such as may be enforced in equity. Under rules of civil procedure, such action is simply a civil action in which demand is made for this type of equitable relief because of the merger of law and equity. Fed.R. Civil P. 2.

Creditor's claim. Generic term to describe any right which a creditor has against his debtor. For recovery in bankruptcy, they must be provable. See also **Claim.**

Creditors' meeting. In bankruptcy, first meeting of creditors and equity security holders. Bankruptcy Act, § 341. See also **Meeting of creditors.**

Creditorum appellatione non hi tantum accipiuntur qui pecuniam crediderunt, sed omnes quibus ex qualibet causa debetur /krèdətórəm æpəlèyshiyówniy nòn háy tǽntəm əksìpiyántər kwày pəkyúwniyəm krèdədírənt, sèd ómniyz kwíbəs èks kwéyləbət kózə dəbíydər/. Under the head of "creditors" are included, not alone those who have lent money, but all to whom from any cause a debt is owing.

Credit rating. The evaluation of a person's or business' ability and past performance in paying debts. Generally established by a credit bureau and used by merchants, suppliers and bankers to determine whether a loan should be granted or a line of credit given. Reports of credit ratings are regulated by the federal Fair Credit Reporting Act.

Credit report. A document from a credit bureau setting forth a credit rating and pertinent financial data concerning a person or a company and used by banks, merchants, suppliers and the like in evaluating a credit risk. Credit reports are regulated by the federal Fair Credit Reporting Act.

Creditrix /krédətrìks/. A female creditor.

Credits. A term of universal application to obligations due and to become due. Colbert v. Superior Confection Co., 154 Okl. 28, 6 P.2d 791, 793. See also **Credit; Tax credit.**

Credit sale. A sale in which the buyer is permitted to pay for the goods at a later time, as contrasted with a cash sale. Any sale with respect to which consumer credit is extended or arranged by the seller. The term includes any contract in the form of a bailment or lease if the bailee or lessee contracts to pay as compensation for use a sum substantially equivalent to or in excess of the aggregate value of the property and services involved and it is agreed that the bailee or lessee will become, or for no other or for a nominal consideration has the option to become, the owner of the property upon full compliance with his obligations under the contract. See also **Installment sale.**

Credit slip. A document generally given by stores and suppliers when a person returns merchandise and which permits the customer to purchase another item, or receive the equivalent in cash or open credit for future purchases, in return for the credit extended by the slip.

Credit union. Cooperative association that uses money deposited by a closed group of persons (*e.g.* fellow employees) and lends it out again to persons in the same group at favorable interest notes. Credit unions are commonly regulated by state banking boards or commissions.

Creed. The word "creed" has been defined as "confession or articles of faith," "formal declaration of religious belief," "any formula or confession of religious faith," and "a system of religious belief." Cummings v. Weinfeld, 177 Misc. 129, 30 N.Y.S.2d 36, 38.

Creek. A small stream less than a river. The term imports a recess, cove, bay, or inlet in the shore of a river, and not a separate or independent stream; though it is sometimes used in the latter meaning.

Cremation. The act or practice of reducing a corpse to ashes by means of extreme heat or fire. See also **Dead body.**

Crementum comitatus /krəméntəm komətéydəs/. The increase of a county. The sheriffs of counties anciently answered in their accounts for the improvement of the king's rents, above the *viscontiel* rents, under this title.

Crepare oculum /krəpériy ókyələm/. In Saxon law, to put out an eye; which had a pecuniary punishment of fifty shillings annexed to it.

Crepusculum /krəpáskyələm/. Twilight. In the common law of burglary, this term means the presence of sufficient light to discern the face of a man; such light as exists immediately before the rising of the sun or directly after its setting.

Crescente malitia crescere debet et pœna /krəséntiy məlísh(iy)ə krésəriy débəd èt píynə/. Vice increasing, punishment ought also to increase.

Crest. A term used in heraldry; it signifies the devices set over a coat of arms. High point of an action or process. Highest or upper edge, prominence, level, or limit.

Cretio /kríysh(iy)ow/. Lat. In the civil law, a certain number of days allowed an heir to deliberate whether he would take the inheritance or not.

Crew. Usually referred to and is primarily thought of as those who are on board and aiding in the navigation; *e.g.* flight crew, ship's crew. The aggregate of seamen who man a ship or vessel, including the master and officers; or it may mean the ship's company, exclusive of the master, or exclusive of the master and all other officers.

Crew does not have an absolutely unvarying legal significance or any well-defined factual significance. Schantz v. American Dredging Co., C.C.A.Pa., 138 F.2d 534, 537.

Crew list. A list of the crew of a vessel or aircraft; one of a ship's or aircraft's papers. This instrument is required by statute and sometimes by treaties. 46 U.S.C.A. §§ 322, 323.

Crier /kráyər/. An officer of a court, who makes proclamations. His principal duties are to announce the opening of the court and its adjournment and the fact that certain special matters are about to be transacted, to announce the admission of persons to the bar, to call the names of jurors, witnesses, and parties, to announce that a witness has been sworn, to proclaim silence when so directed, and generally to make such proclamations of a public nature as the judges order. An auctioneer (cryer). See also **Bailiff.**

Criez la peez /kráyiyz lə píys/. Rehearse the concord, or peace. A phrase used in the ancient proceedings for levying fines. It was the form of words by which the justice before whom the parties appeared directed the serjeant or countor in attendance to recite or *read aloud* the *concord* or agreement between the parties, as to the lands intended to be conveyed.

Crim. Con. An abbreviation for "criminal conversation," denoting adultery.

Crime. A positive or negative act in violation of penal law; an offense against the State or United States.

"Crime" and "misdemeanor", properly speaking, are synonymous terms; though in common usage "crime" is made to denote such offenses as are of a more serious nature.

A crime may be defined to be any act done in violation of those duties which an individual owes to the community, and for the breach of which the law has provided that the offender shall make satisfaction to the public. A crime or public offense is an act committed or omitted in violation of a law forbidding or commanding it, and to which is annexed, upon conviction, either, or a combination of the following punishments: (1) death; (2) imprisonment; (3) fine; (4) removal from office; or (5) disqualification to hold and enjoy any office of honor, trust, or profit. While many crimes have their origin at common law, most have been created by statute; and, in many states, such have been codified. In addition, there are both state and federal crimes (as to the latter, see Title 18, U.S.C.A.).

See also Classification of crimes; Compounding crime; Continuing offense; Criminal; Degrees of crime; Federal crimes; Felony; Inchoate crimes; Instantaneous crime; Lesser included offense; Misdemeanor; Offense; Petty offense; Political crime; Serious crime.

General Classification

Crimes are classified for various purposes, the principal classification being that which divides crimes into felonies and misdemeanors. Other classifications are: (a) crimes which are *mala in se* versus crimes *mala prohibita;* (b) infamous crimes versus crimes which are not infamous; (c) crimes involving moral turpitude versus those which do not involve moral turpitude; (d) major crimes versus petty crimes; and (e) common law crimes versus statutory crimes.

Capital crime. See **Capital** *(adj.).*

Common law crimes. Such crimes as are punishable by the force of the common law, as distinguished from crimes created by statute.

Continuous crime. One consisting of a continuous series of acts, which endures after the period of consummation, as, the offense of carrying concealed weapons. In the case of instantaneous crimes, the statute of limitations begins to run with the consummation, while in the case of continuous crimes it only begins with the cessation of the criminal conduct or act.

Crime against law of nations. Term which is understood to include crimes which all nations agree to punish such as murder and rape.

Crime against nature. Deviate sexual intercourse per os or per anum between human beings who are not husband and wife and any form of sexual intercourse with an animal. Model Penal Code, § 213.0. Crime of buggery or sodomy.

Crime against property. Term used to describe a crime, the object of which is property as contrasted with person; *e.g.* larceny.

Crime insurance. See **Insurance.**

Crime of omission. Any offense, the gravamen of which is the failure to act when there is an obligation to act. May amount to manslaughter if the failure is wilful, wanton and reckless.

Crime of violence. Crimes of violence include voluntary manslaughter, murder, rape, mayhem, kidnaping, robbery, burglary or housebreaking in the nighttime, extortion accompanied by threats of violence, assault with a dangerous weapon or assault with intent to commit any offense punishable by imprisonment for more than one year, arson punishable as a felony, or an attempt or conspiracy to commit any of the foregoing offenses. 18 U.S.C.A. § 4251.

Crimes mala in se. Crimes mala in se embrace acts immoral or wrong in themselves, such as burglary, larceny, arson, rape, murder, and breaches of peace.

Crimes mala prohibita. Crimes mala prohibita embrace things prohibited by statute as infringing on others' rights, though no moral turpitude may attach, and constituting crimes only because they are so prohibited.

Felony. See **Felony.**

Infamous crime. A crime which entails infamy upon one who has committed it. The term "infamous"— *i.e.,* without fame or good report—was applied at common law to certain crimes, upon the conviction of which a person became incompetent to testify as a witness, upon the theory that a person would not commit so heinous a crime unless he was so depraved as to be unworthy of credit. These crimes are treason, felony, and the *crimen falsi.* A crime punishable by imprisonment in the state prison or penitentiary, with or without hard labor, is an infamous crime, within the provision of the fifth amendment of the constitution that "no person shall be held to answer for a capital or otherwise infamous crime unless on a presentment or indictment of a grand jury." Mackin v. U. S., 117 U.S. 348, 6 S.Ct. 777, 29 L.Ed. 909; Brede v. Powers, 263 U.S. 4, 44 S.Ct. 8, 68 L.Ed. 132. It is not the character of the crime but the nature of the punishment which renders the crime "infamous." Whether an offense is infamous depends on the punishment which may be imposed therefor, not on the punishment which was imposed. United States v. Moreland, 258 U.S. 433, 42 S.Ct. 368, 370, 66 L.Ed. 700.

Misdemeanor. See **Misdemeanor.**

Organized crime. Term used to describe that form of crime which is the product of groups and organizations as contrasted with the crime planned and committed by individuals without organizational backing; gambling and narcotics are common subjects of organized crime.

Quasi crimes. This term embraces all offenses not crimes or misdemeanors, but that are in the nature of crimes. A class of offenses against the public which have not been declared crimes, but wrongs against the general or local public which it is proper should be repressed or punished by forfeitures and penalties. This would embrace all *qui tam* actions and forfeitures imposed for the neglect or violation of a public duty. A *quasi* crime would not embrace an indictable offense, whatever might be its grade, but simply forfeitures for a wrong done to the public, whether voluntary or involuntary, where a penalty is given, whether recoverable by criminal or civil process. Also, offenses for which some person other than the actual perpetrator is responsible, the perpetrator being presumed to act by command of the responsible party. Sometimes, injuries which have been unintentionally caused. D.W.I. (driving while intoxicated) offenses are sometimes classified as *quasi* crimes.

Statutory crimes. Those created by statutes, as distinguished from such as are known to, or cognizable by, the common law.

Crime Control Act. Shortened name for Omnibus Crime Control and Safe Streets Act of 1968 (18 U.S. C.A.); a multifaceted federal law designed to curb crime.

Crime statistic. Those figures compiled by federal and state agencies showing the incidence of various types of crime on a geographical basis.

Crimen /kráymən/. Lat. Crime. Also an accusation or charge of crime.

Crimen furti /kráymən fə́rday/. The crime or offense of theft.

Crimen incendii /kráymən ənséndiyay/. The crime of burning, which included not only the modern crime of arson, but also the burning of a man, a beast, or other chattel.

Crimen innominatum /kráymən ənòmənéydəm/. The nameless crime; the crime against nature; sodomy or buggery.

Crimen raptus /kráymən rǽptəs/. The crime of rape.

Crimen roberiæ /kráymən rəbáriyiy/. The offense of robbery.

Flagrans crimen; Locus criminis; Particeps criminis. See those titles.

Crimen falsi /kráymən fól(t)say/. Term generally refers to crimes in the nature of perjury or subornation of perjury, false statement, criminal fraud, embezzlement, false pretense, or any other offense which involves some element of deceitfulness, untruthfulness, or falsification bearing on witness' propensity to testify truthfully. Government of Virgin Islands v. Toto, C.A.Virgin Islands, 529 F.2d 278, 282.

At *common law,* any crime which rendered the perpetrator incompetent to be a witness, such as forgery, perjury, subornation of perjury and other crimes affecting the administration of justice.

In the *civil law,* the crime of falsifying; which might be committed either by writing, as by the forgery of a will or other instrument; by words, as by bearing false witness, or perjury; and by acts, as by counterfeiting or adulterating the public money, dealing with false weights and measures, counterfeiting seals, and other fraudulent and deceitful practices.

Crimen falsi dicitur, cum quis illicitus, cui non fuerit ad hæc data auctoritas, de sigillo regis, rapto vel invento, brevia, cartasve consignaverit /kráymən fóltsay dísədər, kæ̀m kwís əlísədəs, k(yúw)ay nòn fyúwərəd ǽd híyk déydə októhrətæs, diy səjílow ríyjəs, rǽptow vèl invéntow, bríyviyə kartǽsviy kònsignéyvərət/. The crime of forgery is when any one illicitly, to whom power has not been given for such purposes, has signed writs or charters with the king's seal, either stolen or found.

Crimen læsæ majestatis /kráymən líyziy mæ̀jəsətéydəs/. The crime of *lese-majesty,* or injuring majesty or royalty; high treason. The term was used by the older English law writers to denote any crime affecting the king's person or dignity.

It is borrowed from the civil law, in which it signified the undertaking of any enterprise against the emperor or the republic.

Crimen læsæ majestatis omnia alia crimina excedit quoad pœnam /kráymən líyziy mæ̀jəstéydəs ómniyə éyliyə krímənə əksíydət kwówæd píynəm/. The crime of treason exceeds all other crimes in its punishment.

Crimen omnia ex se nata vitiat /kráymən ómniyə èks síy néydə víshiyət/. Crime vitiates everything which springs from it.

Crimen trahit personam /kráymən tréy(h)ət pərsównəm/. The crime carries the person (*i.e.*, the commission of a crime gives the courts of the place where it is committed jurisdiction over the person of the offender).

Criminal, *n.* One who has committed a criminal offense; one who has been legally convicted of a crime; one adjudged guilty of crime. See also **Dangerous criminal; Habitual criminal.**

Criminal, *adj.* That which pertains to or is connected with the law of crimes, or the administration of penal justice, or which relates to or has the character of crime. Of the nature of or involving a crime.

Criminal abortion. See **Abortion.**

Criminal act. Commission of a crime.

Criminal action. Proceeding by which person charged with a crime is brought to trial and either found not guilty or guilty and sentenced. An action, suit, or cause instituted to punish an infraction of the criminal laws. See also **Penal action.**

Criminal anarchy. The doctrine that organized government should be overthrown by force and violence or other unlawful means. The advocacy of such doctrine has been made a felony. Whitney v. California, 274 U.S. 357, 47 S.Ct. 641, 71 L.Ed. 1095; 18 U.S.C.A. § 2384.

Criminal Appeals Act. Federal Act which allows the United States to appeal to a court of appeals from certain judgments, orders, or rulings of district courts. 18 U.S.C.A. § 3731.

Criminal attempt. Crime of a criminal attempt consists of an attempt to commit the crime and some step or overt act towards commission of the crime. State v. Harvill, 106 Ariz. 386, 476 P.2d 841. A substantial step towards a criminal offense with specific intent to commit that particular crime. A criminal attempt is defined as an overt act done in pursuance of intent to do a specific thing, tending to the end but falling short of complete accomplishment of it; such overt act must be sufficiently proximate to intended crime to form one of natural series of acts which intent requires for its full execution. Com. v. McCloskey, 234 Pa.Super. 577, 341 A.2d 500, 503. See also **Attempt.**

Criminal behavior. Conduct which causes any social harm which is defined and made punishable by law.

Criminal capacity. Legal qualifications necessary to commit a crime such as voluntariness of the act, age and mental condition. See also **Capacity; Insanity.**

Criminal charge. An accusation of crime, formulated in a written complaint, information, or indictment, and taking shape in a prosecution.

Criminal conspiracy. An agreement or confederacy of two or more persons to do a criminal or unlawful act or to do a lawful act in an unlawful or criminal manner. In many jurisdictions, an overt act in furtherance of the confederacy is required. See also **Conspiracy.**

Criminal contempt. A crime which consists in the obstruction of judicial duty generally resulting in an act done in the presence of the court; *e.g.* contumelious conduct directed to the judge or a refusal to answer questions after immunity has been granted. Conduct directed against the majesty of the law or the dignity and authority of the court or judge acting judiciously, whereas a "civil contempt" ordinarily consists in failing to do something ordered to be done by a court in a civil action for the benefit of an imposing party therein. Sullivan v. Sullivan, 16 Ill. App.3d 549, 306 N.E.2d 604, 605. See also **Contempt.**

Criminal conversation. Defilement of the marriage bed, sexual intercourse of an outsider with husband or wife, or a breaking down of the covenant of fidelity. Tort action based on adultery, considered in its aspect of a civil injury to the husband or wife entitling him or her to damages; the tort of debauching or seducing of a wife or husband. Often abbreviated to *crim. con.* Statutes in several states prohibit actions for criminal conversation. See **Alienation of affections; Heart-balm statutes.**

Criminal forfeiture. The taking by the government of property because of its involvement in a crime; *e.g.* an automobile used to smuggle narcotics; gun used in hunting without license or out of season. See also, **Confiscate; Forfeiture; Seizure.**

Criminal fraud. In taxation, the attempt to evade the payment of lawfully due taxes by willfully filing a false or fraudulent tax return. I.R.S. §§ 7201, 7207. In other contexts, the crime of larceny by false pretenses or larceny by trick.

Criminal gross negligence. Gross negligence is culpable or criminal when accompanied by acts of commission or omission of a wanton or willful nature, showing a reckless or indifferent disregard of the rights of others, under circumstances reasonably calculated to produce injury, or which make it not improbable that injury will be occasioned, and the offender knows or is charged with knowledge of the probable result of his acts; "culpable" meaning deserving of blame or censure. See also *Criminal negligence, infra.*

Criminal insanity. See **Insanity.**

Criminal instrumentality rule. Where the wrong is accomplished by a crime, the crime and not the negligent act of the party which made it possible is the "proximate cause". Foutch v. Alexandria Bank & Trust Co., 177 Tenn. 348, 149 S.W.2d 76, 85.

Criminal intent. The intent to commit a crime; malice, as evidenced by a criminal act; an intent to deprive or defraud the true owner of his property. Includes those consequences which represent the very purpose for which an act is done, regardless of the likelihood of occurrence, or are known to be substantially certain to result, regardless of desire. May be general or specific intent; mens rea. See also **Mens rea; Specific intent.**

Criminal jurisdiction. Power of tribunal to hear and dispose of criminal cases.

Criminal laws. See **Penal code; Penal laws.**

Criminal libel. Criminal libel is the malicious publication of durable defamation. The malicious defamation of a person made public by any printing or writing tending to provoke him to wrath and to deprive him of the benefits of public confidence and social intercourse. It is a misdemeanor at common law and also under modern statutes unless it has been made a felony which is not common. Four elements are included: (1) defamation, (2) durable, (3) publication and (4) malice. It should be noted however that criminal sanctions for defamation of public officials is subject to same constitutional limitations as for civil actions. Garrison v. State of Louisiana, 379 U.S. 64, 85 S.Ct. 209, 13 L.Ed.2d 125. See also **Libel.**

Criminal malversion. A broad category of corrupt official practices. Jimenez v. Aristeguieta, C.A.Fla., 311 F.2d 547, 562.

Criminal mischief. A species of wilful and malicious injury to property made punishable by statutes in most jurisdictions.

Criminal motive. Something in the mind or that condition of the mind which incites to action or induces action, or gives birth to a purpose. Distinguishable from intent which represents the immediate object in view while motive is the ulterior intent.

Criminal negligence. That failure to use the degree of care required to avoid criminal consequences. Sometimes equated erroneously with wanton and reckless conduct. See *Criminal gross negligence, supra;* also, **Negligence.**

Criminal non-support. The wilful and unreasonable failure to support one whom the law requires a person to support (*i.e.* spouse and children). See **Nonsupport; Support.**

Criminal proceeding. One instituted and conducted for the purpose either of preventing the commission of crime, or for fixing the guilt of a crime already committed and punishing the offender; as distinguished from a "civil" proceeding, which is for the redress of a private injury. Strictly, a "criminal proceeding" means some step taken before a court against some person or persons charged with some violation of the criminal law. See also **Criminal procedure.**

Criminal process. Process which issues to compel a person to answer for a crime or misdemeanor; *e.g.* arrest warrant. See also **Indictment; Information; Process; Warrant.**

Criminal prosecution. An action or proceeding instituted in a proper court on behalf of the public, for the purpose of securing the conviction and punishment of one accused of crime.

Criminal syndicalism. Any doctrine or precept advocating, teaching or aiding and abetting the commission of crime of sabotage or unlawful acts of force and violence or unlawful methods of terrorism as a means of accomplishing a change in industrial ownership or control or affecting any political change. Gitlow v. New York, 268 U.S. 652, 45 S.Ct. 625, 69 L.Ed. 1138. The advocacy of sabotage, violence, terrorism, or other unlawful methods for revolutionary purposes. See also **Syndicalism.**

Criminal trespass. The offense committed by one who, without license or privilege to do so, enters or surreptitiously remains in any building or occupied structure. Model Penal Code, § 221.2. Offense is committed when a person without effective consent enters or remains on property or in building of another knowingly or intentionally or recklessly when he had notice that entry was forbidden or received notice to depart but failed to do so. Day v. State, Tex.Cr.App., 532 S.W.2d 302, 306.

Criminalist. One versed in criminal law, one addicted to criminality, and, also, a psychiatrist dealing with criminality. People v. Taylor, 152 Cal.App.2d 29, 312 P.2d 731, 734; Douglas v. State, 42 Ala.App. 314, 163 So.2d 477, 486.

Criminalistics. The science of crime detection, based upon the application of chemistry, physics, physiology, psychology, and other sciences. See also **Criminology.**

Criminaliter /krìmənéylədər/. Lat. Criminally. This term is used, in distinction or opposition to the word *"civiliter,"* civilly, to distinguish a criminal liability or prosecution from a civil one.

Criminalization. The rendering of an act criminal and hence punishable by the government in a proceeding in its name.

Criminal justice system. The network of courts and tribunals which deal with criminal law and its enforcement.

Criminal law. The substantive criminal law is that law which for the purpose of preventing harm to society, (a) declares what conduct is criminal, and (b) prescribes the punishment to be imposed for such conduct. It includes the definition of specific offenses and general principles of liability. Substantative criminal laws are commonly codified into criminal or penal codes; *e.g.* U.S.C.A. Title 18, California Penal Code, Model Penal Code. *Compare* **Criminal procedure.**

Criminal procedure. Criminal procedure is concerned with the *procedural* steps through which a criminal case passes, commencing with the initial investigation of a crime and concluding with the unconditional release of the offender. Generic term to describe the network of laws and rules which govern the procedural administration of criminal justice; *e.g.* laws and court rules (*e.g.* Rules of Criminal Procedure) governing arrest, search and seizure, bail, etc. Compare **Criminal law.** See also **Code of criminal procedure.**

Criminal protector. An accessory after the fact to a felony. Skelly v. U. S., 10th Cir., 76 F.2d 483. One who aids or harbors a felon after the commission of a crime.

Criminal registration. Statutes in certain jurisdictions require that persons who are convicted felons register with the police so that their presence in the community will be known at all times. Lambert v. California, 355 U.S. 225, 78 S.Ct. 240, 2 L.Ed.2d 228.

Criminal sanctions. Punishments attached to conviction of crimes such as fines, probation and sentences. See also **Civil death.**

Criminal statutes or codes. Federal and state laws enacted by legislative bodies which define, classify, and set forth punishments for specific crimes; *e.g.* Title 18 of United States Code; Model Penal Code.

Crimina morte extinguuntur /krímənə mórdiy èks-tiŋgwántər/. Crimes are extinguished by death.

Criminate. To charge one with crime; to furnish ground for a criminal prosecution; to implicate, accuse, or expose a person to a criminal charge. A witness cannot be compelled to answer any question which has a tendency to *criminate* him. See **Self-incrimination.**

Criminology. The science which treats of crimes and their prevention and punishment.

Crimp. One who decoys and plunders sailors under cover of harboring them.

Crippling. The word "crippling" is equivalent of words "physical disability" and is defined as to deprive of use of limbs, particularly of leg or foot, to deprive of strength, activity or capability for service or use and to disable.

Crisis. A crucial point or situation in the course of things; a turning point; a very tense moment; an unstable or crucial time.

Critical stage. Critical stage in a criminal proceeding at which accused is entitled to counsel is one in which a defendant's rights may be lost, defenses waived, privileges claimed or waived, or in which the outcome of the case is otherwise substantially affected. See Mempa v. Rhay, 389 U.S. 128, 88 S.Ct. 254. Test of "critical stage" of criminal proceeding as it relates to right to counsel is whether proceeding either requires or offers opportunity to take procedural step which will have prejudicial effects in later proceedings, or whether events transpire that are likely to prejudice ensuing trial. Miller v. State of S. C., D.C.S.C., 309 F.Supp. 1287, 1290. See also **Counsel, right to; Custodial interrogation.**

Crocia /króws(h)iyə/. The *crosier*, or pastoral staff.

Crociarius /kròwsiyériyəs/. A cross-bearer, who went before the prelate.

Croft. A little close adjoining a dwelling-house, and inclosed for pasture and tillage or any particular use. A small place fenced off in which to keep farm-cattle. The word is now entirely obsolete.

Croises /króyzəz/króyziyz/. Pilgrims; so called as wearing the sign of the *cross* on their upper garments. The knights of the order of St. John of Jerusalem, created for the defense of the pilgrims.

Croiteir. A crofter; one holding a croft.

Crook. A person given to crooked or fraudulent practices; a swindler, sharper, thief, forger, or the like. Term "crook" has been defined as a professional rogue; a criminal; or one consorting with criminals; a person recognized by the authorities as belonging to the criminal class.

Crooked. Deviating from rectitude or uprightness; not straightforward; dishonest; wrong; perverse. A "crook" is a dishonest person; one who is crooked in conduct; a tricky or underhand schemer; a thief or swindler.

Crop. Products of the soil, as are annually grown, raised, and harvested. Growing crops are considered "goods" under U.C.C. § 2–105(1). Term includes fruit grown on trees, and grass used for pasturage. See also **Growing crop.**

Crop insurance. See **Insurance.**

Cropper. See **Sharecropper.**

Cross. A mark made by persons who are unable to write, to stand instead of a signature. A mark usually in the form of an X, by which voters are commonly required to express their selection. There are four principal forms of the cross: The St. Andrew's cross, which is made in the form of an X; the Latin cross, †, as used in the crucifixion; St. Anthony's cross, which is made in the form of a T; and the Greek cross, +, which is made by the intersection at right angles of lines at their center point.

As an adjective, the word is applied to various demands and proceedings which are connected in subject-matter, but opposite or contradictory in purpose or object.

As a verb it means to pass or extend from one side to the other, as to cross a stream. People v. Hawkins, 51 Cal.App.2d Supp. 781, 124 P.2d 691, 692.

Cross-action. An action brought by one who is defendant in a suit against the party who is plaintiff in such suit, or against a co-defendant, upon a cause of action growing out of the same transaction which is there in controversy, whether it be a contract or tort. An independent suit brought by defendant against plaintiff or co-defendant. See also **Counterclaim; Cross-claim; Cross-complaint.**

Cross appeal. An appeal by the appellee. In the federal courts a cross appeal is argued with the initial appeal of the appellant. Fed.R.App.P. 34(d). See also **Appeal.**

Cross-claim. Cross-claims against co-parties are governed in the federal district courts and in most state trial courts by Rule of Civil Procedure 13(g): "A pleading may state as a cross-claim any claim by one party against a co-party arising out of the transaction or occurrence that is the subject matter either of the original action or of a counterclaim therein or relating to any property that is the subject matter of the original action. Such cross-claim may include a claim that the party against whom it is asserted is or may be liable to the cross-claimant for all or part of a claim asserted in the action against the cross-claimant." See also New York C.P.L.R. § 3019(b).

For requisite content of cross-claim under Rules of Civil Procedure, see **Complaint.** See also **Cross-complaint; Transaction or occurrence test.**

Counterclaim distinguished. "Cross-claims" are litigated by parties on the same side of the main litigation, while "counterclaims" are litigated between opposing parties to the principal action. Resource Engineering, Inc. v. Siler, 94 Idaho 935, 500 P.2d 836, 840.

Cross collateral. Security given by both parties to a contract or undertaking for performance or payment.

Cross-complaint. A defendant or cross-defendant may file a cross-complaint setting forth either or both of the following: (a) Any cause of action he has against any of the parties who filed the complaint against him. (b) Any cause of action he has against a person alleged to be liable thereon, whether or not such person is already a party to the action, if the cause of action asserted in his cross-complaint, (1) arises out of the same transaction, occurrence, or series of transactions or occurrences as the cause brought against him or (2) asserts a claim, right, or interest in the property or controversy which is the subject of the cause brought against him. Calif. Code of Civil Proc. § 428.10. See also **Cross-claim.**

Cross-demand. Where a person against whom a demand is made by another, in his turn makes a demand against that other, these mutual demands are called "cross-demands." A *set-off* is a familiar example. See also **Counterclaim.**

Crossed check. See **Check.**

Cross-errors. Errors being assigned by the respondent in a writ of error; the errors assigned on both sides are called "cross-errors."

Cross-examination. The examination of a witness upon a trial or hearing, or upon taking a deposition, by the party opposed to the one who produced him, upon his evidence given in chief, to test its truth, to further develop it, or for other purposes. The examination of a witness by a party other than the direct examiner upon a matter that is within the scope of the direct examination of the witness. Generally the scope of examination is limited to matters covered on direct examination. Fed.R. Civil P. 43(b).

Crossing. A portion of a street over which pedestrians may lawfully cross from one side to the other. With reference to railroads, that portion of the right of way covered by intersection with a street or highway. In a broader sense, the term includes embankments constructed as necessary approaches to a railroad track, and approaches or embankments reasonably necessary to enable crossings or bridges to be used. For **"Farm Crossing"**, see that title.

Cross interrogatory. A party to an action who has been interrogated may serve cross questions on all other parties. Fed.R. Civil P. 31(a).

Cross-licensing. Permission or right to use a thing or property given in exchange between two or more parties. Exchange of licenses by two or more patent holders in order that each may use or benefit from the patents of the other.

Cross remainder. Cross remainders are remainders which are so limited after particular estates to two or more persons in several parcels of land, or in several undivided shares in the same parcel of land, that, on the determination of the particular estates in any of the several parcels of undivided shares, they remain over to the other grantees, and the reversioner or ulterior remainderman is not let in until the determination of all of the particular estates. Hartford Nat. Bank & Trust Co. v. Harvey, 143 Conn. 233, 121 A.2d 276.

Crown. The sovereign power and position of a monarch. An ornamental badge of regal power worn on the head by sovereign princes. The word is frequently used when speaking of the sovereign himself, or the rights, duties, and prerogatives belonging to him. Also a silver coin of the value of five shillings.

Crown cases. In English law, criminal prosecutions on behalf of the crown, as representing the public; causes in the criminal courts.

Crown cases reserved. In English law, questions of law arising in criminal trials at the assizes (otherwise than by way of demurrer), and not decided there, but reserved for the consideration of the court of criminal appeal. Superseded by criminal division of Court of Appeal.

Crown court. In England, such court was established by Courts Act of 1971, superseding the former assize courts and courts of quarter sessions. It is part of the Supreme Court with jurisdiction throughout England and Wales, and is a superior court of record.

Crown debts. In England, debts due the crown, which are put, by various statutes, upon a different footing from those due to a subject. Bankruptcy does not discharge such debts unless Commissioners of the Treasury certify in writing their consent to discharge.

Crown lands. The demesne lands of the crown. In England and Canada, lands belonging to the sovereign personally or to the government or nation, as distinguished from such as have passed into private ownership.

Crown law. Criminal law in England is sometimes so termed, the crown being always the prosecutor in criminal proceedings.

Crown office. In England, the criminal side of the former court of king's bench. The king's attorney in this court was called "master of the crown office". Now the Crown Office and Associates' Department of the Central Office of the Supreme Court.

Crown office in chancery. Formerly one of the offices of the English high court of chancery; later transferred to the high court of justice. The principal official, the clerk of the crown, was an officer of parliament, and of the lord chancellor, in his nonjudicial capacity, rather than an officer of the courts of law.

Crown paper. A paper containing the list of criminal cases, which await the hearing or decision on the Crown side of the Queen's Bench Division.

Crown side. That jurisdiction of Queen's Bench Division by which it takes jurisdiction of criminal cases.

Crown solicitor. In England, the solicitor to the treasury acts, in state prosecutions, as solicitor for the crown in preparing the prosecution. Public prosecutions are now handled either by the Director of Public Prosecutions or by police or some other public authority.

Cruce signati /krúwsiy sàynéydiy/. In old English law, signed or marked with a cross. Pilgrims to the holy land, or crusaders; so called because they wore the sign of the cross upon their garments.

Crude. A flexible term depending largely on context. In natural state; raw; unrefined; not artificially altered; unfinished. Vulgar.

Cruel and inhuman treatment. As ground for divorce, consists of unwarranted and unjustifiable conduct on part of defendant causing other spouse to endure suffering and distress, thereby destroying peace of mind and making living with such spouse unbearable, completely destroying real purpose and object of matrimony. Welling v. Welling, 144 Ind.App. 182, 245 N.E.2d 173, 176.

Cruel and unusual punishment. See **Corporal punishment; Punishment.**

Cruelty. The intentional and malicious infliction of physical or mental suffering upon living creatures, particularly human beings; or, as applied to the latter, the wanton, malicious, and unnecessary infliction of pain upon the body, or the feelings and emotions; abusive treatment; inhumanity; outrage.

Chiefly used in the law of divorce, in such phrases as "cruel and abusive treatment," "cruel and barbarous treatment," or "cruel and inhuman treatment" *(q.v.).* In domestic relations, term includes mental injury as well as physical. Williams v. Williams, 351 Mich. 210, 213, 88 N.W.2d 483, 484. Generally, single act of cruelty is not sufficient for divorce—there must be course of cruel conduct over period of time, Richardson v. Richardson, 258 S.C. 135, 187 S.E.2d 528. This ground for divorce is of limited importance with the enactment by most states of no-fault divorce laws.

See also **Legal cruelty; Mental anguish; Mental cruelty.**

Cruelty to animals. The infliction of physical pain, suffering, or death upon an animal, when not necessary for purposes of training or discipline or (in the case of death) to procure food or to release the animal from incurable suffering, but done wantonly, for mere sport, for the indulgence of a cruel and vindictive temper, or with reckless indifference to its pain.

A person commits a misdemeanor if he purposely or recklessly: (1) subjects any animal to cruel mistreatment; or (2) subjects any animal in his custody to cruel neglect; or (3) kills or injures any animal belonging to another without legal privilege or consent of the owner. Model Penal Code, § 250.11.

Cruelty to children. Most jurisdictions have "battered child" statutes in which both emotional and physical injuries are embraced in the term "cruelty." See also **Child abuse.**

Legal cruelty. See **Legal cruelty.**

Crush. To break by means of pressure; to compress or bruise between two hard bodies; to squeeze or force by pressure so as to destroy the natural condition, shape, or integrity of the parts, or to force together into a mass. To defeat.

Cry. To call out aloud; to proclaim; to publish; to sell at auction. A clamor raised in the pursuit of an escaping felon. See **Hue and cry.**

Cry de pais, or **cri de pais** /kráy də péyz/. The hue and cry raised by the people in ancient times, where a felony had been committed and the constable was absent.

Cryer /kráyər/. An auctioneer. One who calls out aloud; one who publishes or proclaims. See **Crier.**

Crypta /kríptə/. A chapel or oratory underground, or under a church or cathedral.

C.S.C. Civil Service Commission.

C.T.A. An abbreviation for *cum testamento annexo,* in describing a species of administration.

Cucking-stool. An engine of correction for common scolds, which in the Saxon language is said to signify the scolding-stool, though now it is frequently corrupted into *ducking-stool,* because the judgment was that, when the woman was placed therein, she should be plunged in the water for her punishment. It was also variously called a "trebucket," "tumbrel," or "castigatory." 4 Bl.Comm. 169.

Cuckold. A man whose wife is unfaithful; the husband of an adulteress. It is explained that the word alludes to the habit of the female cuckold, which lays her eggs in the nests of other birds to be hatched by them. To make a cuckold of a man is to seduce his wife.

Cueillette. A term of French maritime law. See **A cueillette.**

Cui ante divortium /kyúway æntiy dəvórsh(iy)əm /k(w)áy°/. (L. Lat. The full phrase was, *Cui ipsa ante divortium contradicere non potuit,* whom she before the divorce could not gainsay). A writ which anciently lay in favor of a woman who had been divorced from her husband, to recover lands and tenements which she had in fee-simple, fee-tail, or for life, from him to whom her husband had aliened them during marriage, when she could not gainsay it. 3 Bl.Comm. 183. Abolished in 1833.

Cui bono /kyúway bównow/k(w)áy°/k(w)áy°/. For whose good; for whose use or benefit. "*Cui bono* is ever of great weight in all agreements." Sometimes translated, for what good, for what useful purpose.

Cuicunque aliquis quid concedit concedere videtur et id, sine quo res ipsa esse non potuit /k(w)ùw)aykáŋkwiy ǽləkwəs kwíd kənsíydət kənsíydəriy vədíydər èt íd sáyniy kwòw ríyz ípsə ésiy nòn póduwət/. Whoever grants anything to another is supposed to grant that also without which the thing itself would be of no effect.

Cui in vita /kyúway ən váydə/. (L. Lat. The full phrase was, *Cui in vita sua ipsa contradicere non potuit,* whom in his lifetime she could not gainsay). A writ of entry which lay for a widow against a person to whom her husband had in his lifetime aliened her lands. It was a method of establishing the fact of death, being a trial with witnesses, but without a jury. The object of the writ was to avoid a judgment obtained against the husband by confession or default. It was rendered obsolete in England by force of 32 Hen. VIII, c. 28, § 6.

Cui jurisdictio data est, ea quoque concessa esse videntur, sine quibus jurisdictio explicari non potest /k(y úw)ay jùrəsdíksh(iy)ow déydə èst, íyə kwówkwiy kənsésə ésiy vədéntər, sáyniy kwíbəs jùrəsdíksh(iy)ow èkspləkéray nòn pówdəst/. To whomsoever a jurisdiction is given, those things also are supposed to be granted, without which the jurisdiction cannot be exercised. The grant of jurisdiction implies the grant of all powers necessary to its exercise.

Cui jus est donandi, eidem et vendendi et concedendi jus est /kyúway jás èst dənǽnday iyáydəm èt vəndénday èt kònsədénday jás èst/. He who has the right of giving has also the right of selling and granting.

Cuilibet in arte sua perito est credendum /kyuwáylibəd in árdiy syúwə pəráydow èst krədéndəm/. Any person skilled in his peculiar art or profession is to be believed [i.e., when he speaks of matters connected with such art]. Credence should be given to one skilled in his peculiar profession.

Cuilibet licet juri pro se introducto renunciare /kyuwáyləbət láysət júriy pròw síy intrədáktow rənànsiyériy/. Any one may waive or renounce the benefit of a principle or rule of law that exists only for his protection.

Cui licet quod majus, non debet quod minus est non licere /kyúway láysət kwòd méyjəs, nòn débət kwòd máynəs èst nòn ləsíriy/. He who is allowed to do the greater ought not to be prohibited from doing the less. He who has authority to do the more important act ought not to be debarred from doing what is of less importance.

Cui pater est populus non habet ille patrem /kyúway péydər əst pópyələs nòn héybəd íliy pǽtrəm/. He to whom the people is father has not a father.

Cuique in sua arte credendum est /kyuwáykwiy ìn s(y)úwə árdiy krədéndəm èst/. Everyone is to be believed in his own art.

Cujus est commodum ejus debet esse incommodum /kyúwjəs èst kóm-əwdəm íyjəs débəd ésiy ìnkóməwdəm/. Whose is the advantage, his also should be the disadvantage.

Cujus est dare, ejus est disponere /kyúwjəs èst dériy, íyjəs èst dəspównəriy/. Whose it is to give, his it is to dispose; or, "the bestower of a gift has a right to regulate its disposal."

Cujus est divisio, alterius est electio /kyúwjəs èst dəvízh(iy)ow oltíriyəs èst əléksh(iy)ow/. Whichever [of two parties] has the division [of an estate], the choice [of the shares] is the other's. In partition between coparceners, where the division is made by the eldest, the rule in English law is that she shall choose her share last. 2 Bl.Comm. 189.

Cujus est dominium ejus est periculum /kyúwjəs èst dəmíniyəm íyjəs èst pəríkyələm/. The risk lies upon the owner of the subject.

Cujus est instituere, ejus est abrogare /kyúwjəs èst ìnstətyúwəriy íyjəs èst ǽbrəgériy/. Whose right it is to institute, his right it is to abrogate.

Cujus est solum, ejus est usque ad cœlum /kyúwjəs èst sówləm, íyjəs èst áskwiy ǽd síyləm/. Whose is the soil, his it is up to the sky. He who owns the soil, or surface of the ground, owns, or has an exclusive right to, everything which is upon or above it to an indefinite height. 2 Bl.Comm. 18; 3 Bl.Comm. 217.

Cujus est solum, ejus est usque ad cœlum et ad inferos /kyúwjəs èst sówləm, íyjəs èst áskwiy ǽd síyləm əd ǽd ínfərows/. To whomsoever the soil belongs, he owns also to the sky and to the depths. The owner of a piece of land owns everything above and below it to an indefinite extent.

Cujus juris (i.e., jurisdictionis) est principale, ejusdem juris erit accessorium /kyúwjəs júrəs est prinsəpéyliy, iyjásdəm júrəs éhrət ǽksəsóriyəm/. An accessory matter is subject to the same jurisdiction as its principal.

Cujus per errorem dati repetitio est, ejus consulto dati donatio est /kyúwjəs pər ərórəm déyday rèpətísh(iy)ow èst, íyjəs kənsáltow déyday dənéysh(iy)ow èst/. He who gives a thing by mistake has a right to recover it back; but, if he gives designedly, it is a gift.

Cujusque rei potissima pars est principium /kyuwjáskwiy ríyay pətísəmə párz èst prìnsípiyəm/. The chiefest part of everything is the beginning.

Culagium /kəléyjiyəm/. In old records, the laying up a ship in a dock, in order to be repaired.

Cul de sac /kál də sǽk/. (Fr. the bottom of a sack.) A blind alley; a street which is open at one end only. A street closed at one end. Beckham v. State, 64 Cal. App.2d 487, 149 P.2d 296, 300.

Culpa /kálpə/. Lat. A term of the civil law, meaning fault, neglect, or negligence. There are three degrees of culpa, lata culpa, gross fault or neglect; levis culpa, ordinary fault or neglect; levissima culpa, slight fault or neglect, and the definitions of these degrees are precisely the same as those in our law. This term is to be distinguished from dolus, which means fraud, guile, or deceit.

Culpabilis /kəlpéybələs/. Lat. In old English law, guilty. Culpabilis de intrusione, guilty of intrusion. Non culpabilis (abbreviated to non cul.), the plea of "not guilty." See **Culprit.**

Culpability /kàlpəbílədiy/. Blameworthiness. Except in cases of absolute liability, a person's criminal culpability requires a showing that he acted purposely, knowingly, recklessly or negligently, as the law may require, with respect to each material element of the offense. Model Penal Code, § 2.02(1).

Culpable /kálpəbəl/. Blamable; censurable; criminal; involving the breach of a legal duty or the commission of a fault. That which is deserving of moral blame.

As to culpable Homicide; Ignorance; Neglect; Negligence; and Wantonness, see those titles.

Culpa caret qui scit sed prohibere non potest /kálpə kǽrət kwày sít sèd pròwhəbíriy nòn pówdəst/. He is clear of blame who knows, but cannot prevent.

Culpa est immiscere se rel ad se non pertinenti /kálpə èst əmísəriy siy ríyay ǽd síy nòn pàrdənéntay/. It is a fault for any one to meddle in a matter not pertaining to him.

Culpa in contrahendo /kálpə in kòntrəhéndow/. Term used to describe the liability which attaches to breach of contract, especially a breach by the offeror after the offeree has begun performance in a unilateral contract and is stopped by the offeror before completion of the performance which is also the acceptance of the offer in a unilateral contract.

Culpa lata dolo æquiparatur /kálpə léydə dówlow èkwəpəréydər/. Gross negligence is held equivalent to intentional wrong.

Culpa tenet [teneat] suos auctores /kálpə ténət s(y)úwows òktóriyz/°téniyət°/. Misconduct binds [should bind] its own authors. It is a never-failing axiom that every one is accountable only for his own delicts.

Culprit. One accused or charged with commission of crime. Also, commonly used to mean one guilty of a crime or fault.

Blackstone believes this term to be an abbreviation of the old forms of arraignment, whereby, on the prisoner's pleading not guilty, the clerk would respond, *"culpabilis, prit"*, *i.e.*, he is guilty and the crown is ready. It was (he says) the *viva voce* replication by the clerk, on behalf of the crown, to the prisoner's plea of *non culpabilis; prit* being a technical word, anciently in use in the formula of joining issue. 4 Bl.Comm. 339. The ordinary derivation is from *culpa*.

Cultivator. A cropper. See **Sharecropper.**

Cultura /kəltyúrə/. A parcel of arable land.

Culvertage /kálvərdəj/. In old English law, a base kind of slavery. The confiscation or forfeiture which takes place when a lord seizes his tenant's estate.

Cum actio fuerit mere criminalis, institui poterit ab initio criminaliter vel civiliter /kàm ǽksh(iy)ow fyúwərət míriy krìmənéyləs, instìtyuway pódərəd æb ənísh(iy)ow krìmənéylədər vèl səvúlədər/. When an action is merely criminal, it can be instituted from the beginning either criminally or civilly.

Cum adsunt testimonia rerum, quid opus est verbis? /kàm ǽdsənt tèstəmówniyə rírəm, kwìd ówpəs èst várbəs/. When the proofs of facts are present, what need is there of words?

Cum aliquis renunciaverit societati, solvitur societas /kàm ǽləkwis rənànsiyéyvərət səsìyətéyday, sólvədər səsáyətæ̀s/. When any partner renounces the partnership, the partnership is dissolved.

Cum confitente sponte mitius est agendum /kàm kònfəténtiy spóntiy mísh(iy)əs èst əjéndəm/. One confessing willingly should be dealt with more leniently.

Cum copula /kàm kópyələ/. Lat. With copulation, *i.e.*, sexual intercourse. Used in speaking of the validity of a marriage contracted "per verba de futuro cum copula," that is, with words referring to the future (a future intention to have the marriage solemnized) and consummated by sexual connection.

Cum de lucro duorum quæritur, melior est causa possidentis /kàm dìy l(y)úwkrow dyuwórəm kwírədər, míyliyər èst kózə pəsìdiyéntəs/. When the question is as to the gain of two persons, the cause of him who is in possession is the better.

Cum dividend /kyúwm dívədènd/. Means that when a share of stock is sold after a dividend is declared, the buyer has the right to the dividend; *lit.*, with dividend. See also **Dividend** (*Cumulative dividend*).

Cum duo inter se pugnantia reperiuntur in testamento, ultimum ratum est /kàm d(y)úwow íntər sìy pəgnǽnsh(iy)ə rəpàriyántər ìn testəméntow, áltəməm réydəm èst/. Where two things repugnant to each other are found in a will, the last shall stand.

Cum duo jura concurrunt in una persona æquum est ac si essent in duobus /kám d(y)úwow júrə kənkárənt ìn yúwnə pərsównə íykwəm èst æ̀k sày ésənt ìn d(y)uwówbəs/. When two rights meet in one person, it is the same as if they were in two persons.

Cum grano salis /kàm gréynow séyləs/kúm grǽnow sǽləs/. (With a grain of salt.) With allowance for exaggeration.

Cum in corpore dissentitur, apparet nullam esse acceptionem /kàm in kórpəriy dəséntədər, əpǽrət náləm ésiy əksèpshiyównəm/. When there is a disagreement in the substance, it appears that there is no acceptance.

Cum in testamento ambigue aut etiam perperam scriptum est benigne interpretari et secundum id quod credibile est cogitatum credendum est /kàm in tèstəméntow æmbígyuwiy òt ésh(iy)əm párpərəm skríptəm èst bənígniy intàrprətéray èt səkándəm íd kwòd krədíbəliy èst kòjətéydəm krədéndəm èst/. Where an ambiguous, or even an erroneous, expression occurs in a will, it should be construed liberally, and in accordance with the testator's probable meaning.

Cum legitimæ nuptiæ factæ sunt, patrem liberi sequuntur /kàm ləjídəmiy nápshiyiy fǽktiy sànt, pǽtrəm líbəray səkwántər/. Children born under a legitimate marriage follow the condition of the father.

Cum onere /kàm ównəriy/. With the burden; subject to an incumbrance or charge. What is taken *cum onere* is taken subject to an existing burden or charge.

Cum par delictum est duorum, semper oneratur petitor et melior habetur possessoris causa /kàm pár dəlíktəm èst d(y)uwórəm, sémpər ownəréydər pédədər èt míyl(i)yər həbíydər pòwzesórəs kózə/. When both parties are in fault the plaintiff must always fail, and the cause of the person in possession be preferred.

Cum pertinentiis /kàm pərdənénshiyəs/. With the appurtenances.

Cum quod ago non valet ut ago, valeat quantum valere potest /kám kwòd éygow nòn vǽləd àd éygow, vǽliyət kwóntəm vəlíriy pówdəst/. When that which I do is of no effect as I do it, it shall have as much effect as it can; *i.e.*, in some other way.

Cum rights. *Lit.* with rights; a share of stock sold under conditions which permit the buyer to buy new stock of the issuer in a stated amount.

Cum testamento annexo /kàm testəméntow ənéksow/. L. Lat. With the will annexed. A term applied to administration granted where a testator makes an incomplete will, without naming any executors, or where he names incapable persons, or where the executors named refuse to act. If the executor has died, an administrator *de bonis non cum testamento annexo* (of the goods not [already] administered upon with the will annexed) is appointed. Often abbreviated d. b. n. c. t. a.

Cumulative /kyúmyələdəv/. Additional; heaping up; increasing; forming an aggregate. The word signifies that two things are to be added together, instead of one being a repetition or in substitution of the other.

As to cumulative Dividend, and Punishment, see those titles.

Cumulative evidence. Additional or corroborative evidence to the same point. That which goes to prove what has already been established by other evidence. See also **Corroborating evidence.**

Cumulative legacies. Legacies given in addition to a prior legacy, as when one legacy is given in a will and another legacy is given to the same person in a codicil. See also **Legacy.**

Cumulative offense. One which can be committed only by a repetition of acts of the same kind but committed on different days or times.

Cumulative preferred dividend. Dividend on preferred stock which, if declared at the end of a particular year, must be paid before any common stock dividend is paid. See also **Dividend.**

Cumulative remedy. A remedy created by statute in addition to one which still remains in force. Wulff-Hansen & Co. v. Silvers, Cal.App., 120 P.2d 677, 680.

Cumulative sentence. Any sentence which is to take effect after the expiration of a prior sentence; also known as "from and after" sentence. See also **Sentence.**

Cumulative voting. Type of voting in which a stockholder may cast as many votes for directors as he has shares of stock multiplied by the number of directors to be elected. The stockholder may cast all his votes for one or more but fewer than all the directors on the slate, and hence, minority representation is promoted. Cumulative voting is *required* under the corporate laws of some states, and is *permitted* in most states.

A system of minority representation which is used for the election of members of the lower house of the Illinois legislature. Each voter has three votes which he may lump together on one candidate or distribute among two or three candidates as he chooses.

Cunades /kuwnáðes/. In Spanish law, affinity; alliance; relation by marriage.

Cuneator /kyúwniyeydər/. *Lat.* /kyùwniyéydər/. A coiner. *Cuneare* /kyùwniyériy/, to coin. *Cuneus* /kyúwniyəs/, the die with which to coin. *Cuneata* /kyùwniyéydə/, coined.

Cunnilingus /kànəlíŋgəs/. An act of sex committed with the mouth and the female sexual organ.

Cur. A common abbreviation of *curia.*

Cura /kyúrə/. Lat. Care; charge; oversight; guardianship. In the civil law a species of guardianship which commenced at the age of puberty (when the guardianship called "tutela" expired), and continued to the completion of the twenty-fifth year.

Curagulos /kyuréygyələs/. One who takes care of a thing.

Curate /kyúrət/. In ecclesiastical law, an incumbent who has the *cure* of souls, but now generally restricted to signify the spiritual assistant of a rector or vicar in his *cure.* An officiating temporary minister in the English church, who represents the proper incumbent; being regularly employed either to serve in his absence or as his assistant, as the case may be. He may be temporary or stipendiary or perpetual.

Curateur /kyùratyúr/. In French law, a person charged with supervising the administration of the affairs of an emancipated minor, giving him advice, and assisting him in the important acts of such administration.

Curatio /kyəréyshow/. In the civil law, the power or duty of managing the property of him who, either on account of infancy or some defect of mind or body, cannot manage his own affairs. The duty of a curator or guardian.

Curative /kyúrədəv/. Intended to cure (that is, to obviate the ordinary legal effects or consequences of) defects, errors, omissions or irregularities. The word is defined as relating to, or employed in, the cure of diseases; tending to cure; a remedy.

Curative admissibility of evidence. As applied to evidence, curative admissibility is the doctrine that an opponent may reply with similar evidence whenever it is needed for removing an unfair prejudice which might otherwise have ensued. Biener v. St. Louis Public Service Co., Mo.App., 160 S.W.2d 780, 786. In some jurisdictions, an opponent may counter or answer evidence which has been admitted without objection though otherwise inadmissible to cure the effect of such evidence. This rule is not of universal application or acceptance.

Curative statute. A law, retrospective in effect, which is designed to remedy some legal defect in previous transactions. A form of retrospective legislation which reaches back into the past to operate upon past events, acts or transactions in order to correct errors and irregularities and to render valid and effective many attempted acts which would otherwise be ineffective for the purpose intended. As applied to conveyances they supply one or more ingredients of a legal act which the parties intended to perform but which they failed to accomplish completely or which they executed only imperfectly.

Curator /kyárədər/kyəréydər/. A temporary guardian or conservator appointed by the court to care for the property or person or both of an incompetent, spendthrift, or a minor. One in charge of museum, art gallery, or the like.

In Louisiana, a person appointed to take care of the estate of an absentee.

Curator ad hoc /kyəréydər æd hók/. A guardian or other person appointed to take charge or care of a single matter or transaction; a special guardian.

Curator ad litem /kyəréydər əd láydəm/. Guardian for the suit or action.

Curator bonis /kyəréydər bównəs/. In the civil law, a guardian or trustee appointed to take care of *property* in certain cases; as for the benefit of creditors.

Curatorship. The office of a curator or guardian. *Compare* **Tutorship.**

Curatrix /kyəréytrəks/. A woman who has been appointed to the office of curator; a female guardian.

Curatus non habet titulum /kyəréydəs nòn héybət tityələm/. A curate has no title [to tithes].

Cure. The act of healing; restoration to health from disease, or to soundness after injury.

Under rule that a vessel and her owner must provide maintenance, and "cure" for seaman injured or falling ill while in service, "cure" is care, including nursing and medical attention during such period as the duty continues. Calmar S. S. Corporation v. Taylor, 303 U.S. 525, 58 S.Ct. 651, 653, 82 L.Ed. 993. See also **Maintenance and cure.**

The right of a seller under U.C.C. to correct a non-conforming delivery of goods to buyer within the contract period. § 2–508.

Cure by verdict. In common law pleading, the rectification or rendering nugatory of a defect in the pleadings by the rendition of a verdict; the court presuming after a verdict, that the particular thing omitted or defectively stated in the pleadings was duly proved at the trial. This function is served by Rule of Civil Procedure 15 which permits amendment of pleadings to conform to the evidence.

Cure of souls. In ecclesiastical law, the ecclesiastical or spiritual charge of a parish, including the usual and regular duties of a minister in charge.

Curfew. A law (commonly an ordinance) which imposes on people (particularly children) the obligation to remove themselves from the streets on or before a certain time of night.

An institution supposed to have been introduced into England by order of William the Conqueror, which consisted in the ringing of a bell or bells at eight o'clock at night, at which signal the people were required to extinguish all lights in their dwellings, and to put out or rake up their fires, and retire to rest, and all companies to disperse. The word is probably derived from the French *couvre feu,* to cover the fire. The curfew is spoken of in 1 Social England 373, as having been ordained by William I, in order to prevent nightly gatherings of the people of England. But the custom is evidently older than the Norman; for we find an order of King Alfred that the inhabitants of Oxford should at the ringing of that bell cover up their fires and go to bed. And there is evidence that the same practice prevailed at this period in France, Normandy, Spain, and probably in most of the other countries of Europe. It was doubtless intended as a precaution against fires, which were very frequent and destructive when most houses were built of wood. It appears to have met with so much opposition that in 1103 we find Henry I, repealing the enactment of his father on the subject; and Blackstone says that, though it is mentioned a century afterwards, it is rather spoken of as a time of night then as a still subsisting custom. Shakespeare frequently refers to it in the same sense.

Curia /kyúriyə/. In old European law, a court. The palace, household, or retinue of a sovereign. A judicial tribunal or court held in the sovereign's palace. A court of justice. The civil power, as distinguished from the ecclesiastical. A manor; a nobleman's house; the hall of a manor. A piece of ground attached to a house; a yard or courtyard. A lord's court held in his manor. The tenants who did suit and service at the lord's court. A manse.

In Roman law, a division of the Roman people, said to have been made by Romulus. They were divided into three tribes, and each tribe into ten *curiæ,* making thirty *curiæ* in all. The place or building in which each *curia* assembled to offer sacred rites. The place of meeting of the Roman senate; the senate house. The senate house of a province; the place where the *decuriones* assembled. See **Decurio.**

Curia admiralitatis /kyúriyə ædmərælətéydəs/. The court of admiralty.

Curia advisari vult /kyúriyə ædvəséray vólt/. L. Lat. The court will advise; the court will consider. A phrase frequently found in the reports, signifying the resolution of the court to suspend judgment in a cause, after the argument, until they have deliberated upon the question, as where there is a new or difficult point involved. It is commonly abbreviated to *cur. adv. vult,* or *c. a. v.*

Curia baronis, or **baronum** /kyúriyə bərównəs/°bərównəm/. In old English law, a court-baron.

Curia cancellariæ officina justitiæ /kyúriyə kænsəlériyiy ofəsáynə jəstíshiyiy/. The court of chancery is the workshop of justice.

Curia christianitatis /kyúriyə krìstiyænətéydəs/. The ecclesiastical court.

Curia claudenda /kyúriyə klodéndə/. The name of a writ to compel another to make a fence or wall, which he was bound to make, between his land and the plaintiff's. Now obsolete.

Curia comitatus /kyúriyə kòmətéydəs/. The county court *(q.v.).*

Curia domini /kyúriyə dómənay/. In old English law, the lord's court, house, or hall, where all the tenants met at the time of keeping court.

Curia magna /kyúriyə mǽgnə/. In old English law, the great court; one of the ancient names of parliament.

Curia majoris /kyúriyə məjórəs/. In old English law, the mayor's court.

Curia militum /kyúriyə mílədəm/. A court so called, anciently held at Carisbrook Castle, in the Isle of Wight.

Curia palatii /kyúriyə pəléyshiyay/. In old English law, the palace court. It was abolished by 12 & 13 Vict., c. 101.

Curia parliamenti suis propriis legibus subsistit /kyúriyə pàrl(y)əméntay syúwəs prówpriyəs líyjəbəs səbsístət/. The court of parliament is governed by its own laws.

Curia pedis pulverizati /kyúriyə píydəs pòlvərəzéyday/. In old English law, the court of *piedpoudre* or *piepouders.* See **Court of Piepoudre.**

Curia personæ /kyúriyə pərsówniy/. In old records, a parsonage-house, or manse.

Curia regis /kyúriyə ríyjəs/. The king's court. A term applied to the *aula regis,* the *bancus,* or *communis bancus,* and the *iter* or *eyre,* as being courts of the king, but especially to the *aula regis* (which title see).

Curing title. Removal of defects from land title which render such unmarketable. "Clearing", "curing", "straightening out", or "removing cloud from" title denotes acts or proceedings necessary to render title marketable. See **Action to quiet title.**

Curiosa et captiosa interpretatio in lege reprobatur /kyúriyówsə èt kæpshiyówsə intɜ̀rprətéysh(iy)ow ìn líyjiy rèprəbéydər/. A curious [overnice or subtle] and captious interpretation is reprobated in law.

Curnock /kɜ́rnək/. In old English law, a measure containing four bushels or half a quarter of corn.

Currency. Coined money and such banknotes or other paper money as are authorized by law and do in fact circulate from hand to hand as the medium of exchange. See also **Blocked currency; Comptroller of Currency; Current money; Legal tender.**

Current. Running; now in transit; present existence; now in progress; whatever is at present in course of passage, as "the current month." American Fruit Growers v. United States, C.C.A.Cal., 105 F.2d 722, 726. Most recent; up-to-date.

A continuous movement in the same direction, as a fluid stream. Buckeye Incubator Co. v. Blum, D.C. Ohio, 17 F.2d 456, 458.

Passing in time or belonging to the time actually passing. Now passing or present in its course, as the current month, and as applied to current obligations it denotes the obligations then passing or present in its progress, the service rendered and the compensation therefor measured by the time of the occurrence of the event.

The word "current", when used as an adjective, has many meanings, and definition depends largely on word which it modifies, or subject-matter with which it is associated. Commissioner of Internal Revenue v. Keller, C.C.A., 59 F.2d 499, 501.

Current account. An open, running, or unsettled account between two parties.

Current assets. Any property that will be converted into cash in the normal operation of business at an early date, usually within one year. Short-term assets.

Current expenses. Ordinary, regular, recurring, and continuing expenditures for the maintenance of property, the carrying on of a business, an office, municipal government, etc.

Current funds. Cash and other assets readily convertible into cash. Money which circulates as legal tender. Formerly, this phrase meant gold or silver, or something equivalent thereto, and convertible at pleasure into coin money. Bull v. First National Bank, 123 U.S. 105, 8 S.Ct. 62, 31 L.Ed. 97. See **Current money.**

Current income. Income which is due within the present accounting period.

Current liabilities. A liability that will be paid in the normal operation of a business at an early date, usually within one year, normally by expending current assets. The phrase "current liability" carries with it the idea of a liability that is presently enforceable. Warren Co. v. Commissioner of Internal Revenue, C.C.A.Ga., 135 F.2d 679, 684, 685.

Current maintenance. The expense occasioned in keeping the physical property in the condition required for continued use during its service life. Lindheimer v. Illinois Bell Telephone Co., 292 U.S. 151, 54 S.Ct. 658, 78 L.Ed. 1182.

Current market value. The value of an asset which may be realized by liquidation within the present accounting period. Present value which may be realized in an arms length transaction between a willing buyer and a willing seller. See also **Fair market value.**

Current money. The currency of the country; whatever is intended to and does actually circulate as currency; every species of coin or currency. In this phrase the adjective "current" is not synonymous with "convertible". It is employed to describe money which passes from hand to hand, from person to person, and circulates through the community, and is generally received. Money is current which is received as money in the common business transactions, and is the common medium in barter and trade. See also **Currency; Legal tender.**

Current obligations. The word "current" means passing in time or belonging to the time actually passing, now passing, present in its course, as the current month, and as applied to current obligations it denotes the obligations then passing or present in its progress, the service rendered and the compensation therefor measured by the time of the occurrence of the event. Pecos Mercantile Co. v. Texlite, Inc., Tex. Civ.App., 65 S.W.2d 811, 812. One presently enforceable and not past due. Naylor v. Gutteridge, Tex.Civ. App., 430 S.W.2d 726, 733.

Current price. This term means the same as "market value", "market price", "going price", the price that runs or flows with the market. See also **Current market value; Fair market value.**

Current revenues. See **Current income.**

Current value. See **Current market value; Fair market value.**

Current wages. Such as are paid periodically, or from time to time as the services are rendered or the work is performed; more particularly, wages for the current period, hence not including such as are past-due or deferred. See also **Minimum wage.**

Current year. The year now running. Ordinarily, a calendar year in which the event under discussion took place; though the current fiscal year of a business may run from July 1st to June 30th, or some other twelve month period.

Curriculum. The set of studies or courses for a particular period, designated by a school or branch of a school.

Currit quatuor pedibus /kə́hrət kwóduwər pédəbəs/. L. Lat. It runs upon four feet; or, as sometimes expressed, it runs upon all fours. A phrase used in arguments to signify the entire and exact application of a case quoted. "It does not follow that they run *quatuor pedibus.*"

Currit tempus contra desides et sui juris contemptores /kə́rət témpəs kóntrə díysədiyz èt syúway júrəs kòntem(p)tóriyz/. Time runs against the slothful and those who neglect their rights.

Cursing. Malediction; imprecation; execration; profane words intended to convey hate and to invoke harm; swearing.

Cursitor baron /kə́rsədər bǽrən/. In old English law, an officer of the court of exchequer, who is appointed by patent under the great seal to be one of the barons of the exchequer. The office was abolished by St. 19 & 20 Vict., c. 86.

Cursitors /kə́rsədərz/. In old English law, clerks in the chancery office, whose duties consisted in drawing up those writs which were of course, *de cursu,* whence their name. They were abolished by St. 5 & 6 Wm. IV, c. 82.

Cursor /kə́rsər/. An inferior officer of the papal court.

Cursory examination /kə́rs(ə)riy əgzǽmənéyshən/. An inspection for defects visible or ascertainable by ordinary examination; contrasted from a thorough examination.

Cursus curiæ est lex curiæ /kə́rsəs kyúriyiy èst léks kyúriyiy/. The practice of the court is the law of the court.

Curtail. To cut off the end or any part of; hence to shorten, abridge, diminish, lessen, or reduce; and term has no such meaning as abolish. State v. Edwards, 207 La. 506, 21 So.2d 624, 625.

Curtesy /kə́rdəsiy/. The estate to which by common law a man is entitled, on the death of his wife, in the lands or tenements of which she was seised in possession in fee-simple or in tail during her coverture, provided they have had lawful issue born alive which might have been capable of inheriting the estate. It is a freehold estate for the term of his natural life.

In some jurisdictions, there is no requirement that issue be born of the union. The estate has gradually lost much of its former value and now in some jurisdictions it attaches only to the real estate which the wife owns at death, rather than to the real estate owned by the wife during the marriage, while in others it has been abolished or otherwise materially altered.

Initiate and consummate. Curtesy initiate is the interest which a husband has in his wife's estate after the birth of issue capable of inheriting, and before the death of the wife; after her death, it becomes an estate "by the curtesy consummate." Hopper v. Gurtman, 126 N.J. 263, 18 A.2d 245, 246, 250.

Curtilage /kə́rdələj/. The inclosed space of ground and buildings immediately surrounding a dwellinghouse. United States v. Vlahos, D.C.Or., 19 F.Supp. 166, 169; State v. Aragon, 89 N.M. 91, 547 P.2d 574, 579.

A piece of ground commonly used with the dwelling house. A small piece of land, not necessarily inclosed, around the dwelling house, and generally includes the buildings used for domestic purposes in the conduct of family affairs. A courtyard or the space of ground adjoining the dwelling house necessary and convenient and habitually used for family purposes and the carrying on of domestic employments. A piece of ground within the common inclosure belonging to a dwelling house, and enjoyed with it, for its more convenient occupation.

For search and seizure purposes includes those outbuildings which are directly and intimately connected with the habitation and in proximity thereto and the land or grounds surrounding the dwelling which are necessary and convenient and habitually used for family purposes and carrying on domestic employment. State v. Hanson, 113 N.H. 689, 313 A.2d 730, 732.

Curtiles terræ /kərtáyliyz téhriy/. In old English law, court lands. See **Court lands.**

Curtillium /kərtíl(i)yəm/. A curtilage *(q.v.);* the area or space within the inclosure of a dwellinghouse.

Curtis /kə́rdəs/. A garden; a space about a house; a house, or manor; a court, or palace; a court of justice; a nobleman's residence.

Custa /kə́stə/, **custagium** /kèstéyj(iy)əm/, **custantia** /kəstǽnsh(iy)ə/. Costs.

Custode admittendo, custode amovendo /kə́stədiy ǽdməténdow, kə́stədiy èymərvéndow/. Writs for the admitting and removing of guardians.

Custodes /kəstówdiyz/. In Roman law, guardians; observers; inspectors. Persons who acted as inspectors of elections, and who counted the votes given.

In old English law, keepers; guardians; conservators.

Custodes libertatis angliæ auctoritate parliamenti /kəstówdiyz libərtéydəs ǽngliyiy oktòrətéydiy pàrl(y)əméntay/. The style in which writs and all judicial processes were made out during the great revolution, from the execution of King Charles I, till Oliver Cromwell was declared protector.

Custodes pacis /kəstówdiyz péysəs/. Guardians of the peace. 1 Bl.Comm. 349.

Custodial arrest. Confinement or detention by police or government authorities during which a person is entitled to certain warnings as to his rights when questioned. Miranda v. Arizona, 384 U.S. 436, 86 S.Ct. 1602, 16 L.Ed.2d 694. See **Custodial interrogation.**

Custodia legis /kəstówdiyə líyjəs/. In the custody of the law. Doctrine of "custodia legis" provides that when personal property is repossessed under writ of replevin, property is considered to be in custody of the court, though actual possession may be in either of the parties to the replevin action, and that property remains in custody of court until judgment in replevin action finally determines whether replevining party or prior holder is entitled to possession. Brunswick Corp. v. J & P, Inc., C.A.Okl., 424 F.2d 100, 102.

Custodial interrogation. Custodial interrogation, requiring that defendant be advised of his constitutional rights, means questioning initiated by law enforcement officers after person has been taken into custody or otherwise deprived of his freedom in any significant way; custody can occur without formality of arrest and in areas other than in police station. Miranda v. Arizona, 384 U.S. 436, 86 S.Ct. 1602, 16 L.Ed.2d 694; Brewer v. Williams, 430 U.S. 387, 97 S.Ct. 1232. See **Miranda Rule.**

Custodiam lease /kəstówdiyəm líys/. In old English law, a grant from the crown under the exchequer seal, by which the custody of lands, etc., seised in the king's hands, was demised or committed to some person as custodee or lessee thereof.

Custodian. General term to describe anyone who has charge or custody of property, papers, etc.

Custody. The care and control of a thing or person. The keeping, guarding, care, watch, inspection, preservation or security of a thing, carrying with it the idea of the thing being within the immediate personal care and control of the person to whose custody it is subjected. Immediate charge and control, and not the final, absolute control of ownership, implying responsibility for the protection and preservation of the thing in custody. Also the detainer of a man's person by virtue of lawful process or authority.

The term is very elastic and may mean actual imprisonment or physical detention or mere power, legal or physical, of imprisoning or of taking manual possession. Term "custody" within statute requiring that petitioner be "in custody" to be entitled to federal habeas corpus relief does not necessarily mean actual physical detention in jail or prison but rather is synonymous with restraint of liberty. U. S. ex rel. Wirtz v. Sheehan, D.C.Wis., 319 F.Supp. 146, 147. Accordingly, persons on probation or released on own recognizance have been held to be "in custody" for purposes of habeas corpus proceedings.

See **Chain of custody; Custodial interrogation; Protective custody.**

Custody account. A type of agency account in which the custodian has the obligation to preserve and safekeep the property entrusted to him for his principal.

Custody of children. The care, control and maintenance of a child which may be awarded by a court to one of the parents as in a divorce or separation proceeding. A number of states have adopted the Uniform Child Custody Jurisdiction Act. See also **Guardianship.**

Custody of the law. Property is in the custody of the law when it has been lawfully taken by authority of legal process, and remains in the possession of a public officer (as a sheriff) or an officer of a court (as a receiver) empowered by law to hold it. See **Forfeiture; Seizure.**

Custom and usage. A usage or practice of the people, which, by common adoption and acquiescence, and by long and unvarying habit, has become compulsory, and has acquired the force of a law with respect to the place or subject-matter to which it relates. It results from a long series of actions, constantly repeated, which have, by such repetition and by unin-

terrupted acquiescence, acquired the force of a tacit and common consent. Louisville & N. R. Co. v. Reverman, 243 Ky. 702, 49 S.W.2d 558, 560. An habitual or customary practice, more or less widespread, which prevails within a geographical or sociological area; usage is a course of conduct based on a series of actual occurrences. Corbin-Dykes Elec. Co. v. Burr, 18 Ariz.App. 101, 500 P.2d 632, 634.

Parol evidence rule does not bar evidence of custom or usage to explain or supplement a contract or memorandum of the parties. U.C.C. § 2–203.

Classification. Customs are general, local or particular. *General* customs are such as prevail throughout a country and become the law of that country, and their existence is to be determined by the court. Or as applied to usages of trade and business, a general custom is one that is followed in all cases by all persons in the same business in the same territory, and which has been so long established that persons sought to be charged thereby, and all others living in the vicinity, may be presumed to have known of it and to have acted upon it as they had occasion. *Local* customs are such as prevail only in some particular district or locality, or in some city, county, or town. *Particular* customs are nearly the same, being such as affect only the inhabitants of some particular district.

Usage distinguished. "Usage" is a repetition of acts, and differs from "custom" in that the latter is the law or general rule which arises from such repetition; while there may be usage without custom, there cannot be a custom without a usage accompanying or preceding it. U. S. for Use of E & R Const. Co., Inc. v. Guy H. James Const. Co., D.C.Tenn., 390 F.Supp. 1193, 1209. See also **Usage.**

Customarily. Means usually, habitually, according to the customs; general practice or usual order of things; regularly. Fuller Brush Co. v. Industrial Commission of Utah, 99 Utah 97, 104 P.2d 201, 203.

Customary. According to custom or usage; founded on, or growing out of, or dependent on, a custom (*q.v.*); ordinary; usual; common.

Customary court-baron. See **Court-baron.**

Customary dispatch. Due diligence according to lawful, reasonable and well-known custom of port or ports involved. Context and conditions existing or contemplated will, of course, affect the meaning of the phrase. Taisho Kaiun Kabushiki Kaisha v. Gano Moore Co., D.C.Del., 14 F.2d 985, 986.

Customary estates. Estates which owe their origin and existence to the custom of the manor in which they are held. 2 Bl.Comm. 149.

Customary freehold. In old English law, a variety of copyhold estate, the evidences of the title to which are to be found upon the court rolls; the entries declaring the holding to be according to the custom of the manor, but it is not said to be at the will of the lord. The incidents are similar to those of common or pure copyhold.

Customary interpretation. See **Interpretation.**

Customary services. Such as are due by ancient custom or prescription only.

Customary tenants. Tenants holding by custom of the manor.

Custom duties. Taxes on the importation and exportation of commodities. The tariff or tax assessed upon merchandise, imported from, or exported to a foreign country.

Tax levied by federal government on goods shipped into U.S., though in other countries it may include export taxes as well. See also **Customs.**

Customer. One who regularly or repeatedly makes purchases of, or has business dealings with, a tradesman or business. Aiken Mills v. United States, D.C. S.C., 53 F.Supp. 524, 526; Arkwright Corporation v. United States, D.C.Mass., 53 F.Supp. 359, 361. Ordinarily, one who has had repeated business dealings with another. A buyer, purchaser, consumer or patron.

In banking, any person having an account with a bank or for whom a bank has agreed to collect items and includes a bank carrying an account with another bank. U.C.C. § 4–104(e). As to letters of credit, a buyer or other person who causes an issuer to issue credit or a bank which procures issuance or confirmation on behalf of that bank's customer. U.C.C. § 5–103(g).

Customers' goods. The words "customers' goods," as used in statement of claim on fire policy referring to merchandise destroyed as "customers' goods," in their ordinary sense, mean goods belonging to insured's customers in his custody as a bailee for the purpose of his trade.

Customers' man. One who has duty to greet customers of broker, when they appear in office on business, to assist them in placing their orders, and generally to see that their wants are taken care of. Fenner & Beane v. Lincoln, Tex.Civ.App., 101 S.W.2d 305, 308. An employee of a brokerage house who solicits or processes orders from the investing public for the purchase and sale of commodities and securities to be executed upon various commodities and securities exchanges. Such persons also give investment advice to customers about the purchase and sale of securities. Clothier v. Beane, 187 Okl. 693, 105 P.2d 752, 756.

Custome serra prise stricte /kástə séhrə práyz(iy) stríkt(iy)/. Custom shall be taken [is to be construed] strictly.

Custom-house. The house or office where commodities are entered for importation or exportation; where the duties, bounties, or drawbacks payable or receivable upon such importation or exportation are paid or received; and where ships are cleared out, etc. A public establishment for the inspection and assessment of duties on imported goods. See also **Bureau of Customs; Customs broker; Customs Service.**

Custom-house broker. One whose occupation it is, as an agent, to arrange entries and other custom-house papers, or transact business, at any port of entry, relating to the importation or exportation of goods, wares, or merchandise. A person authorized by the commissioners of customs to act for parties, at their option, in the entry or clearance of ships and the transaction of general business.

Customs. This term is usually applied to those taxes which are payable upon goods and merchandise imported or exported. Pollock v. Trust Co., 158 U.S. 601, 15 S.Ct. 912, 39 L.Ed. 1108. The duties, toll, tribute, or tariff payable upon merchandise exported or imported. See also **Custom duties; Custom-house; Customs Service.**

Customs and Patent Appeals Court. This court was established in 1929 under Article III of the Constitution of the United States as successor to the United States Court of Customs Appeals (28 U.S.C.A. § 211). The jurisdiction of the court is nationwide and includes (1) appeals from the United States Customs Court (28 U.S.C.A. § 1541), (2) appeals from the United States Patent and Trademark Office (28 U.S. C.A. § 1542), (3) appeals from the United States International Trade Commission (28 U.S.C.A. § 1543), (4) appeals from the Secretary of Commerce under the Educational, Scientific, and Cultural Materials Importation Act (28 U.S.C.A. § 1544), (5) appeals from the Secretary of Agriculture under the Plant Variety Protection Act (28 U.S.C.A. § 1545), and (6) petitions for extraordinary writs under the All Writs Act (28 U.S.C.A. § 1651(a)). Judgments of the court are final and conclusive unless reviewed by the Supreme Court on writ of certiorari. See also **Customs Court.**

Customs broker. Licensed agent or broker whose function is to handle the process of clearing goods through customs.

Customs Court. A court created in 1890 as the Board of United States General Appraisers and given its present name in 1926. The court has exclusive jurisdiction of civil actions arising under the tariff laws including those involving the appraised value of imported merchandise; classification and rate and amount of duties chargeable; exclusion of merchandise from entry of delivery under any provisions of customs laws; liquidation or reliquidation of an entry, or a modification thereof; refusal to pay a claim for drawback. 28 U.S.C.A. § 1582.

Customs duty. See **Custom duties.**

Customs House. See **Custom-house; Customs Service.**

Customs Service. The United States Customs Service collects the revenue from imports and enforces customs and related laws and also administers the Tariff Act of 1930, as amended, and other customs laws. Some of the responsibilities which the Customs Service is specifically charged with are as follows: properly assessing and collecting customs duties, excise taxes, fees, and penalties due on imported merchandise; interdicting and seizing contraband, including narcotics and illegal drugs; processing persons, carriers, cargo, and mail into and out of the United States; administering certain navigation laws; detecting and apprehending persons engaged in fraudulent practices designed to circumvent customs and related laws; protecting American business and labor by enforcing statutes and regulations such as the Antidumping Act; countervailing duty; copyright, patent, and trademark provisions; quotas; and marking requirements for imported merchandise. See also **Bureau of Customs; Custom-house.**

Custos /kástəs/. Lat. A custodian, guard, keeper, or warden; a magistrate.

Custos brevium /kástəs bríyviyəm/. In England, the keeper of the writs. A principal clerk belonging to the courts of queen's bench and common pleas, whose office it was to keep the writs returnable into those courts. The office was abolished by 1 Wm. IV, c. 5.

Custos ferarum /kástəs fərérəm/. A gamekeeper.

Custos horrei regii /kástəs hóhriyay ríyjiyay/. In old English law, protector of the royal granary. 2 Bl. Comm. 394.

Custos maris /kástəs mǽrəs/. In old English law, warden of the sea. The title of a high naval officer among the Saxons and after the Conquest, corresponding with *admiral*.

Custos morum /kástəs mórəm/. The guardian of morals. The court of queen's bench has been so styled.

Custos placitorum coronæ /kástəs plǽsətórəm kərówniy/. In old English law, keeper of the pleas of the crown. Cowell supposes this office to have been the same with the *custos rotulorum*. But it seems rather to have been another name for "coroner."

Custos rotulorum /kástəs ròchəlórəm/. Keeper of the rolls. An officer in England who had the custody of the rolls or records of the sessions of the peace, and also of the commission of the peace itself. He was always a justice of the quorum in the county where appointed and was the principal civil officer in the county. 1 Bl.Comm. 349; 4 Bl.Comm. 272.

Custos spiritualium /kástəs spìrəchuwéyliyəm/. In English ecclesiastical law, keeper of the spiritualities. He who exercised the spiritual jurisdiction of a diocese during the vacancy of the see.

Custos statum hæredis in custodia existentis meliorem, non deteriorem, facere potest /kástəs stéydəm həríydəs ìn kəstówdiyə ègzəsténtəs mìyliyórəm, nòn dətìriyórəm, féysəriy pówdəst/. A guardian can make the estate of an existing heir under his guardianship better, not worse.

Custos temporalium /kástəs tèmpəréyliyəm/. In English ecclesiastical law, the person to whom a vacant see or abbey was given by the king, as supreme lord. His office was, as steward of the goods and profits, to give an account to the escheator, who did the like to the exchequer.

Custos terræ /kástəs téhriy/. In old English law, guardian, warden, or keeper of the land.

Custuma antiqua sive magna /kástʃəmə æntáykwə sáyviy mǽgnə/. (Lat. Ancient or great duties.) In old English law, the duties on wool, sheepskin, or woolpelts and leather exported were so called, and were payable by every merchant, stranger as well as native, with the exception that merchant strangers paid one-half as much again as natives. 1 Bl.Comm. 314.

Custuma parva et nova /kástʃəmə párvə èt nówvə/. (Small and new customs.) Imposts of 3d. in the pound, due formerly in England from merchant strangers only, for all commodities, as well imported as exported. This was usually called the "aliens duty," and was first granted in 31 Edw. I. 1 Bl.Comm. 314.

Cut. To penetrate, separate or lacerate as with a sharp instrument. To shorten or reduce in content, time or amount. To divide into parts or segments. One's share of something.

Cuth, couth /kúwθ/. Sax. Known, knowing. *Uncuth,* unknown. See **Couthutlaugh; Uncuth.**

Cuthred /káθrəd/. A knowing or skillful counsellor.

Cut-over land. Land which has been logged; from which desired timber has been removed.

Cutpurse /kátpàrs/. One who steals by the method of cutting purses; a common practice in old England when men wore their purses at their girdles, as was once the custom.

Cutter of the tallies /kádər əv ðə tǽliyz/. In old English law, an officer in the exchequer, to whom it belonged to provide wood for the tallies, and to cut the sum paid upon them, etc.

CWAS. Contractor Weighted Average Share In Cost Risk.

Cwt. A hundred-weight.

Cy /síy/. In law French, here. (*Cy-apres* /síyəpréy/, hereafter; *cy-devant* /síy dəvón/, heretofore.) Also as, so.

Cycle. A measure of time; a space in which the same revolutions begin again; a periodical space of time.

Cyne-bot /kínəbowt/, or **cyne-gild** /kínəgild/. In feudal law, the portion belonging to the nation of the mulct for slaying the king, the other portion or *were* being due to his family.

Cynebote /kínəbòwt/. A mulct anciently paid by one who killed another, to the kindred of the deceased.

Cyphonism /sáyfənizəm/. That kind of punishment used by the ancients, and later by the Chinese, called by Staunton the "wooden collar," by which the neck of the malefactor is bent or weighed down.

Cy-pres /sìypréy/. As near as (possible). The rule of *cy-pres* is a rule for the construction of instruments in equity, by which the intention of the party is carried out *as near as may be,* when it would be impossible or illegal to give it literal effect. Thus, where a testator attempts to create a perpetuity, the court will endeavor, instead of making the devise entirely void, to explain the will in such a way as to carry out the testator's general intention as far as the rule against perpetuities will allow. So in the case of bequests to charitable uses; and particularly where the language used is so vague or uncertain that the testator's design must be sought by construction.

Equitable power which makes it possible for court to carry out testamentary trust established for particular charitable purpose if testator has expressed general charitable intent, and for some reason his purpose cannot be accomplished in manner specified in the will. In re Gatlin's Estate, 16 C.A.3d 644, 94 Cal.Rptr. 295, 296.

Cyricbryce /chár(ə)chbrìych/. A breaking into a church.

Cyricsceat /chár(ə)chshìyt/. (From *cyric,* church, and *sceat,* a tribute). In Saxon law, a tribute or payment due to the church.

Cyrographarius /sàyrəgrəfériyəs/. In old English law, a cyrographer; an officer of the *bancus,* or court of common bench.

Cyrographum /sayrógrəfəm/. A chirograph.

Czar /zár/(t)sár/. (Also written *zar, tsar, tzar,* etc.) The title of the former emperors of Russia, derived from the old Slavonic *cesar,* king or emperor, which, although long held to be derived from the Roman title *Caesar,* is almost certainly of Tartar origin. The Slavonic word ultimately represents the Latin *Caesar,* but came through the medium of a Germanic language in which the word had the general sense "emperor."

In the beginning of the 10th century the Bulgarian prince Symeon assumed this title, which remained attached to the Bulgarian crown. In 1346 it was adopted by Stephen Duschan, king of Serbia. Among the Russians the Byzantine emperors were so called, as were also the khans of the Mongols that ruled in Russia. Ivan III, grand prince of Moscow, held the title, and Ivan IV, the Terrible, in 1547, caused himself to be crowned as czar. In 1721 the Senate and clergy conferred on Peter I, in the name of the nation, the title Emperor of Russia, for which in Russia the Latin word *imperator* is used. Peter the Great introduced the title *imperator,* "emperor," and the official style then became "Emperor of all the Russias, Tsar of Poland, and Grand Duke of Finland"; but the Russian popular appellation continued to be *tsar* (the preferable modern spelling). The last tsar was Nicholas II, who abdicated on March 15, 1917, and was later executed.

D

The letter "D" is used as an abbreviation for a number of words, the more important and usual of which are as follows:

1. *Digestum*, or *Digesta*, that is, the Digest or Pandects in the Justinian collections of the civil law. Citations to this work are sometimes indicated by this abbreviation, but more commonly by "Dig."

2. *Dictum*. A remark or observation, as in the phrase *"obiter dictum" (q.v.)*.

3. *Demissione*. "On the demise." An action of ejectment is entitled "Doe *d.* Stiles v. Roe;" that is, "Doe, on the demise of Stiles, against Roe."

4. *"Doctor."* As in the abbreviated forms of certain academical degrees. "M.D.," "doctor of medicine;" "LL.D.," "doctor of laws;" "D.C.L.," "doctor of civil law"; "J.D.," "juris doctor."

5. *"District."* Thus, "U. S. Dist. Ct. W. D. Pa." stands for United States District Court for the Western *District* of Pennsylvania.

In the Roman system of notation, this letter stands for five hundred; and, when a horizontal dash or stroke is placed above it, it denotes five thousand.

Dabis? dabo /déybəs? déybow/. Lat. (Will you give? I will give.) In the Roman law, one of the forms of making a verbal stipulation.

Dacion /dasyówn/. In Spanish law, the real and effective delivery of an object in the execution of a contract.

Dactylography /dæktəlógrəfiy/. Dactylography is the scientific study of finger prints as a means of identification.

Daily. Every day; every day in the week; every day in the week except one. A newspaper which is published six days in each week has been held to be a "daily" newspaper.

Daily balances; average daily balance. The various balances for the different days in the period for which interest is to be paid, and the "average daily balance" for the interest period means the sum of these daily balances divided by the number of days in the interest period.

Daily occupation. The same as "usual occupation". International Brotherhood of Boiler Makers, Iron Shipbuilders & Helpers of America v. Huval, 133 Tex. 136, 126 S.W.2d 476, 478.

Daily rate of pay. Obtained by multiplying hourly rate by number of hours in normal working day, though actual number of hours worked may be fewer.

Dale and sale. Fictitious names of places, used in the English books, as examples "The manor of *Dale* and the manner of *Sale,* lying both in Vale."

Dalus, dailus, dailia /déyləs, déyliyə(s)/. A certain measure of land; such narrow slips of pasture as are left between the plowed furrows in arable land.

Damage. Loss, injury, or deterioration, caused by the negligence, design, or accident of one person to another, in respect of the latter's person or property. The word is to be distinguished from its plural, "damages", which means a compensation in money for a loss or damage. An injury produces a right in them who have suffered any damage by it to demand reparation of such damage from the authors of the injury. By damage we understand every loss or diminution of what is a man's own, occasioned by the fault of another. The harm, detriment, or loss sustained by reason of an injury. See also **Damages; Injury; Loss**.

Damage-cleer. In old English law, a fee assessed of the tenth part in the common pleas, and the twentieth part in the queen's bench and exchequer, out of all damages exceeding five marks recovered in those courts, in actions upon the case, covenant, trespass, etc., wherein the damages were uncertain; which the plaintiff was obliged to pay to the prothonotary or the officer of the court wherein he recovered, before he could have execution for the damages. This was originally a gratuity given to the prothonotaries and their clerks for drawing special writs and pleadings; but it was taken away by statute, since which, if any officer in these courts took any money in the name of damage-cleer, or anything in lieu thereof, he forfeited treble the value.

Damage feasant or **faisant** /dǽmaj fíyzənt/. Doing damage. A term formerly applied to a person's cattle or beasts found upon another's land, doing damage by treading down the grass, grain, etc. 3 Bl.Comm. 7, 211. This phrase seems to have been introduced in the reign of Edward III, in place of the older expression *"en son damage"* (in damno suo).

Damages. A pecuniary compensation or indemnity, which may be recovered in the courts by any person who has suffered loss, detriment, or injury, whether to his person, property, or rights, through the unlawful act or omission or negligence of another. A sum of money awarded to a person injured by the tort of another. Restatement, Second, Torts, § 12A.

Damages may be compensatory or punitive according to whether they are awarded as the measure of actual loss suffered or as punishment for outrageous conduct and to deter future transgressions. Nominal damages are awarded for the vindication of a right where no real loss or injury can be proved. Generally, punitive or exemplary damages are awarded only if compensatory or actual damages have been sustained.

Compensatory or actual damages consist of both general and special damages. General damages are the natural, necessary, and usual result of the wrongful act or occurrence in question. Special damages are those "which are the natural, but not the necessary and inevitable result of the wrongful act."

See also **Injury; Just compensation; Loss; Pain and suffering.**

Actual damages. Real, substantial and just damages, or the amount awarded to a complainant in compensation for his actual and real loss or injury, as opposed on the one hand to "nominal" damages, and on the other to "exemplary" or "punitive" damages. Synonymous with "compensatory damages" and with "general damages."

Civil Damage Acts. See **Dram Shop Acts.**

Compensatory damages. Compensatory damages are such as will compensate the injured party for the injury sustained, and nothing more; such as will simply make good or replace the loss caused by the wrong or injury. Damages awarded to a person as compensation, indemnity, or restitution for harm sustained by him. Northwestern Nat. Cas. Co. v. McNulty, C.A.Fla., 307 F.2d 432, 434.

Consequential damages. Such damage, loss or injury as does not flow directly and immediately from the act of the party, but only from some of the consequences or results of such act. Richmond Redevelopment and Housing Authority v. Laburnum Const. Corp., 195 Va. 827, 80 S.E.2d 574, 580. Damages which arise from intervention of special circumstances not ordinarily predictable. Roanoke Hospital Ass'n v. Doyle & Russell, Inc., 215 Va. 796, 214 S.E.2d 155, 160. Those losses or injuries which are a result of an act but are not direct and immediate. Consequential damages resulting from a seller's breach of contract include any loss resulting from general or particular requirements and needs of which the seller at the time of contracting had reason to know and which could not reasonably be prevented by cover or otherwise, and injury to person or property proximately resulting from any breach of warranty. U.C.C. § 2–715(2).

Continuing damages. Such as accrue from the same injury, or from the repetition of similar acts, between two specified periods of time.

Criminal damage. Criminal damage to property is by means other than by fire or explosive: (a) Willfully injuring, damaging, mutilating, defacing, destroying, or substantially impairing the use of any property in which another has an interest without the consent of such other person; or (b) Injuring, damaging, mutilat-

ing, defacing, destroying, or substantially impairing the use of any property with intent to injure or defraud an insurer or lienholder. See **Arson.**

Damages ultra. Additional damages claimed by a plaintiff not satisfied with those paid into court by the defendant.

Direct damages. Direct damages are such as follow immediately upon the act done. Damages which arise naturally or ordinarily from breach of contract; they are damages which, in ordinary course of human experience, can be expected to result from breach. Roanoke Hospital Ass'n v. Doyle & Russell, Inc., 215 Va. 796, 214 S.E.2d 155, 160.

Excessive damages. Damages awarded by a jury which are grossly in excess of the amount warranted by law on the facts and circumstances of the case; unreasonable or outrageous damages. See **Remittitur.**

Excess liability damages. A cause of action in tort by an insured against his liability carrier for the negligent handling of settlement negotiations which result in a judgment against the insured in excess of his policy limits. G. A. Stowers Furniture Co. v. American Indemnity Co., Tex.Com.App., 15 S.W.2d 544.

Exemplary or punitive damages. Exemplary damages are damages on an increased scale, awarded to the plaintiff over and above what will barely compensate him for his property loss, where the wrong done to him was aggravated by circumstances of violence, oppression, malice, fraud, or wanton and wicked conduct on the part of the defendant, and are intended to solace the plaintiff for mental anguish, laceration of his feelings, shame, degradation, or other aggravations of the original wrong, or else to punish the defendant for his evil behavior or to make an example of him, for which reason they are also called "punitive" or "punitory" damages or "vindictive" damages. Unlike compensatory or actual damages, punitive or exemplary damages are based upon an entirely different public policy consideration—that of punishing the defendant or of setting an example for similar wrongdoers, as above noted. In cases in which it is proved that a defendant has acted willfully, maliciously, or fraudulently, a plaintiff may be awarded exemplary damages in addition to compensatory or actual damages. Damages other than compensatory damages which may be awarded against person to punish him for outrageous conduct. Wetherbee v. United Ins. Co. of America, 18 C.A.3d 266, 95 Cal.Rptr. 678, 680.

Expectancy damages. As awarded in actions for nonperformance of contract, such damages are calculable by subtracting the injured party's actual dollar position as a result of the breach from that party's projected dollar position had performance occurred. The goal is to ascertain the dollar amount necessary to ensure that the aggrieved party's position after the award will be the same—to the extent money can achieve the identity—as if the other party had performed. Alover Distrib., Inc. v. Kroger Co., C.A.Ill., 513 F.2d 1137, 1140; Pletz v. Christian Herald Ass'n, C.A.Tex., 486 F.2d 94, 97.

Fee damages. Damages sustained by and awarded to an abutting owner of real property occasioned by the construction and operation of an elevated railroad in a city street, are so called, because compensation is made to the owner for the injury to, or deprivation of, his easements of light, air, and access, and these are parts of the fee.

Future damages. See **Future damages**.

General damages. Such as the law itself implies or presumes to have accrued from the wrong complained of, for the reason that they are its immediate, direct, and proximate result, or such as necessarily result from the injury, or such as did in fact result from the wrong, directly and proximately, and without reference to the special character, condition, or circumstances of the plaintiff. Myers v. Stephens, 43 Cal.Rptr. 420, 433, 233 C.A.2d 104.

Inadequate damages. Damages are called "inadequate," within the rule that an injunction will not be granted where adequate damages at law could be recovered for the injury sought to be prevented, when such a recovery at law would not compensate the parties and place them in the position in which they formerly stood.

Incidental damages. Under U.C.C. § 2–710, such damages include any commercially reasonable charges, expenses or commissions incurred in stopping delivery, in the transportation, care and custody of goods after the buyer's breach, in connection with the return or resale of the goods or otherwise resulting from the breach. Also, such damages, resulting from a seller's breach of contract, include expenses reasonably incurred in inspection, receipt, transportation and care and custody of goods rightfully rejected, any commercially reasonable charges, expenses or commissions in connection with effecting cover and any other reasonable expense incident to the delay or other breach. U.C.C. § 2–715(1).

Irreparable damages. In the law pertaining to injunctions, damages for which no certain pecuniary standard exists for measurement. Damages not easily ascertainable at law. With reference to public nuisances which a private party may enjoin, the term includes wrongs of a repeated and continuing character, or which occasion damages estimable only by conjecture, and not by any accurate standard.

Land damages. A term sometimes applied to the amount of compensation to be paid for land taken under the power of eminent domain or for injury to, or depreciation of, land adjoining that taken. See **Just compensation**; also, *Severance damages, infra,* this topic.

Limitation of damages. Provision in contract or agreement by which parties agree in advance as to the amount or limit of damages for breach. U.C.C. § 2–718. See also *Liquidated damages and penalties,* below.

Liquidated damages and penalties. The term is applicable when the amount of the damages has been ascertained by the judgment in the action, or when a specific sum of money has been expressly stipulated by the parties to a bond or other contract as the amount of damages to be recovered by either party for a breach of the agreement by the other. Stein v. Bruce, 366 S.W.2d 732, 735. The purpose of a penalty is to secure performance, while the purpose of stipulating damages is to fix the amount to be paid in lieu of performance. The essence of a penalty is a stipulation as in terrorem while the essence of liquidated damages is a genuine covenanted preestimate of such damages.

Liquidated damages is the sum which party to contract agrees to pay if he breaks some promise and, which having been arrived at by good faith effort to estimate actual damage that will probably ensue from breach, is recoverable as agreed damages if breach occurs. In re Plywood Co. of Pa., C.A.Pa., 425 F.2d 151, 154.

Damages for breach by either party may be liquidated in the agreement but only at an amount which is reasonable in the light of the anticipated or actual harm caused by the breach, the difficulties of proof of loss, and the inconvenience or nonfeasibility of otherwise obtaining an adequate remedy. A term fixing unreasonably large liquidated damages is void as a penalty. U.C.C. § 2–718(1).

Mitigation of damages. Although the law of damages contemplates full and just compensation for negligently inflicted injuries, the law likewise prescribes, as a reciprocal principle, that a tortfeasor should not sustain liability for those damages not attributable to the injury producing event. Consequently, a plaintiff may not recover damages for the effects of an injury which reasonably could have been avoided or substantially ameliorated. This limitation on recovery is generally denominated as "mitigation of damages" or "avoidance of consequences." Mitigation of damages or avoidance of consequences arises only after the injury producing event has occurred.

Necessary damages. A term said to be of much wider scope in the law of damages than "pecuniary." It embraces all those consequences of an injury usually denominated "general" damages, as distinguished from special damages; whereas the phrase "pecuniary damages" covers a smaller class of damages within the larger class of "general" damages.

Nominal damages. Nominal damages are a trifling sum awarded to a plaintiff in an action, where there is no substantial loss or injury to be compensated, but still the law recognizes a technical invasion of his rights or a breach of the defendant's duty, or in cases where, although there has been a real injury, the plaintiff's evidence entirely fails to show its amount.

Pecuniary damages. Such as can be estimated in and compensated by money; not merely the loss of money or salable property or rights, but all such loss, deprivation, or injury as can be made the subject of calculation and of recompense in money. See also **Pecuniary loss.**

Presumptive damages. A term occasionally used as the equivalent of "exemplary" or "punitive" damages.

Prospective damages. Damages which are expected to follow from the act or state of facts made the basis of a plaintiff's suit; damages which have not yet accrued, at the time of the trial, but which, in the nature of things, must necessarily, or most probably, result from the acts or facts complained of.

Proximate damages. Proximate damages are the immediate and direct damages and natural results of the act complained of, and such as are usual and might have been expected. Remote damages are those attributable immediately to an intervening cause, though it forms a link in an unbroken chain of causation, so that the remote damage would not have occurred if its elements had not been set in motion by the original act or event.

Punitive damages. See *Exemplary or punitive damages, supra.*

Remote damages. The unusual and unexpected result, not reasonably to be anticipated from an accidental or unusual combination of circumstances—a result beyond which the negligent party has no control.

Severance damages. In condemnation, where the property condemned constitutes only a part of an owner's interest, the owner is entitled to just compensation, not only for the fair market value of the interest actually taken, but also such additional amount as will be equivalent to the diminution or lowering, if any, of the fair market value of the owner's interest in the land which was not taken, due to the severance therefrom of the interest which was taken.

Special damages. Those which are the actual, but not the necessary, result of the injury complained of, and which in fact follow it as a natural and proximate consequence in the particular case, that is, by reason of special circumstances or conditions. Twin Coach Co. v. Chance Vought Aircraft Inc., 2 Storey 588, 163 A.2d 278, 286. Special damages must be specially pleaded and proved. Fed.R. Civil P. 9(g).

Speculative damages. Prospective or anticipated damages from the same acts or facts constituting the present cause of action, but which depend upon future developments which are contingent, conjectural, or improbable.

Statutory damages. Damages resulting from statutorily created causes of actions, as opposed to actions at common law; *e.g.* wrongful death and survival actions; actions under tort claims acts; under § 504 of the federal Copyright Act, a copyright owner has the right to collect statutory damages in lieu of actual damages for copyright infringement.

Substantial damages. A sum, assessed by way of damages, which is worth having; opposed to nominal damages, which are assessed to satisfy a bare legal right. Considerable in amount and intended as a real compensation for a real injury.

Temporary damages. Damages allowed for intermittent and occasional wrongs, such as injuries to real estate, where cause thereof is removable or abatable.

Treble damages. See **Treble damages.**

Unliquidated damages. Such as are not yet reduced to a certainty in respect of amount, nothing more being established than the plaintiff's right to recover; or such as cannot be fixed by a mere mathematical calculation from ascertained data in the case.

Damage to person. The measure of injury, physical, mental and emotional, as a result of another's action or omission, whether such action or omission be intentional or negligent. "Damage" and "injury" are commonly used interchangeably, but they are different to extent that injury is what is actually suffered

while damage is the measure of compensation for such suffering. See **Damage; Injury; Loss.**

Damage to property. Injury to property and generally does not include conversion of such property or taking of such property by public authority. Wandermere Corp. v. State, 79 Wash.2d 688, 488 P.2d 1088. See also **Damage.**

Damaiouse /dǽmiyəs/. In old English law, causing damage or loss, as distinguished from *torcenouse,* wrongful.

Dame. In English law, the legal designation of the wife of a knight or baronet.

Damn, *v.* /dǽm/. To invoke condemnation, curse, swear, condemn to eternal punishment, or consign to perdition.

Damna /dǽmnə/. Damages, both inclusive and exclusive of costs.

Damnatus /dæmnéydəs/. In old English law, condemned; prohibited by law; unlawful. *Damnatus coitus,* an unlawful sexual connection.

Damnification /dæmnəfəkéyshən/. That which causes damage or loss.

Damnify /dǽmnəfay/. To cause damage or injurious loss to a person or put him in a position where he must sustain it. A surety is "damnified" when a judgment has been obtained against him.

Damni injuriæ actio /dǽmnay injúriyiy ǽksh(iy)ow/. An action given by the civil law for the damage done by one who intentionally injured the slave or beast of another.

Damnosa hæreditas /dæmnówsə həríydətæs/. In the civil law, a losing inheritance; an inheritance that was a charge, instead of a benefit.

The term has also been metaphorically applied to that species of property of a bankrupt which, so far from being valuable, would be a charge to the creditors; for example, a term of years where the rent would exceed the revenue.

Damnum /dǽmnəm/. Lat. Damage; the loss or diminution of what is a man's own, either by fraud, carelessness, or accident.

Damnum absque injuria /dǽmnəm ǽbskwiy injúriyə/. Loss, hurt, or harm without injury in the legal sense; that is, without such breach of duty as is redressible by an action. A loss which does not give rise to an action for damages against the person causing it.

Damnum emergens /dǽmnəm əmárjen(d)z/. *Lit.,* damage arising. Actual damage or loss as contrasted with future loss or expectancy.

Damnum fatale /dǽmnəm fətéyliy/. Fatal damage; damage from fate; loss happening from a cause beyond human control *(quod ex fato contingit),* or an act of God, for which bailees are not liable; such as shipwreck, lightning, and the like. The civilians included in the phrase "*damnum fatale*" all those accidents which are summed up in the common-law expression, "Act of God or public enemies;" though, perhaps, it embraced some which would not now be admitted as occurring from an irresistible force. See **Act of God.**

Damnum infectum /dǽmnəm inféktəm/. In Roman law, damage not yet committed, but threatened or impending. A preventive interdict might be obtained to prevent such damage from happening; and it was treated as a *quasi-delict,* because of the imminence of the danger.

Damnum rei amissae /dǽmnəm ríyay əmísiy/. In the civil law, a loss arising from a payment made by a party in consequence of an error of law.

Damnum sine injuriâ esse potest /dǽmnəm sáyniy injúriyə ésiy pówdəst/. There may be damage or injury inflicted without any act of injustice.

Dan. Anciently the better sort of men in England had this title; so the Spanish *Don.* The old term of honor for men, as we now say Master or Mister.

Danegelt, danegeld /déyngèld/. A tribute originally of 1s. and afterwards of 2s., which came to be imposed upon every hide of land through the realm, levied by the Anglo-Saxons, for maintaining (it is supposed) such a number of forces as were thought sufficient to clear the British seas of Danish pirates, who greatly annoyed their coasts, or to buy off the ravages of Danish invaders. It continued a tax until the time of Stephen, and was one of the rights of the crown. The Danegeld was levied as a land tax by the Norman kings; it disappears under that name after 1163, but in fact continued under the name of *tallage.*

Danelage /déynlèy, déynlò/. A system of laws, introduced by the Danes on their invasion and conquest of England, which was principally maintained in some of the midland counties, and also on the eastern coast. 1 Bl.Comm. 65; 4 Bl.Comm. 411.

Danger. Jeopardy; exposure to loss or injury; peril. State v. Londe, 345 Mo. 185, 132 S.W.2d 501, 506. See also **Apparent danger; Dangerous; Hazard; Hazardous risk; Imminent danger; Peril; Risk; Unavoidable dangers.**

Dangeria /dænjíriyə/. In old English law, a money payment made by forest-tenants, that they might have liberty to plow and sow in time of pannage, or mast feeding.

Danger invites rescue. Term used in law of torts and, in limited manner, in law of crimes to describe where liability is borne by one who creates dangerous condition for one person when another person comes to his rescue and is injured. The liability to the second person is founded on this maxim. Krauth v. Geller, 54 N.J.Super. 442, 149 A.2d 271.

Dangerous. Attended with risk; perilous; hazardous; unsafe. See also **Danger.**

Dangerous criminal. One convicted of a particularly heinous crime or one who has escaped or tried to escape from penal confinement by use of force of an aggravated character. Such criminals may be segregated within prison.

Dangerous instrumentality. Anything which has the inherent capacity to place people in peril, either in itself (*e.g.* dynamite), or by a careless use of it (*e.g.*

boat). Green v. Ross, D.C.Fla., 338 F.Supp. 365, 367. Due care must be exercised in using to avoid injury to those reasonably expected to be in proximity. Pendleton Woolen Mills v. Vending Associates, 195 Neb. 46, 237 N.W.2d 99. In certain cases, absolute liability may be imposed. See also **Dangerous weapon; Deadly weapon; Strict liability.**

Dangerous machine. A machine is "dangerous" in such sense that the employer is required to guard it, if, in the ordinary course of human affairs, danger may be reasonably anticipated from the use of it without protection.

Dangerous occupation. Term used to describe hazardous work for purposes of worker's compensation laws, and in wage and hour and child labor laws.

Dangerous per se. A thing that may inflict injury without the immediate application of human aid or instrumentality.

Dangerous place. One where there is considerable risk, or danger, or peril; one where accidents or injuries are very apt to occur. Henri v. Rocky Mountain Packing Corp., 113 Utah 415, 196 P.2d 487, 489.

Dangerous-tendency test. Propensity of person or animal to inflict injury; used in dog bite cases to describe viscious habits of dog. Frazier v. Stone, 515 S.W.2d 766 (Mo.App.).

Dangerous weapon. One dangerous to life; one by the use of which a fatal wound may probably or possibly be given. As the manner of use enters into the consideration as well as other circumstances, the question is often one of fact for the jury, but not infrequently one of law for the court. See also **Assault with dangerous or deadly weapon; Dangerous instrumentality; Deadly weapon.**

Dangers of navigation. See **Dangers of the river; Dangers of the sea,** *infra.*

Dangers of the river. This phrase, as used in bills of lading, means only the natural accidents incident to river navigation, and does not embrace such as may be avoided by the exercise of that skill, judgment, or foresight which are demanded from persons in a particular occupation. It includes dangers arising from unknown reefs which have suddenly formed in the channel, and are not discoverable by care and skill.

Dangers of the sea. The expression "dangers of the sea" means those accidents peculiar to navigation that are of an extraordinary nature, or arise from irresistible force or overwhelming power, which cannot be guarded against by the ordinary exertions of human skill and prudence. Hibernia Ins. Co. v. Transp. Co., 120 U.S. 166, 7 S.Ct. 550, 30 L.Ed. 621.

Danism /dǽnizəm/. The act of lending money or usury.

Dans et retinens, nihil dat /dǽnz ət rédənènz náyəl dǽt/. One who gives and yet retains does not give effectually. Or, one who gives, yet retains [possession], gives nothing.

Dare /dériy/. Lat. In the civil law, to transfer property. When this transfer is made in order to discharge a debt, it is *datio solvendi animo*; when in order to receive an equivalent, to create an obligation, it is *datio contrahendi animo*; lastly, when made *donandi animo*, from mere liberality, it is a gift, *dono datio*.

Dare ad remanentiam /dériy æd rèmənénsh(iy)əm/. To give away in fee, or forever.

Darraign /dəréyn/. To clear a legal account; to answer an accusation; to settle a controversy.

Darrein /dəréyn/. L. Fr. Last.

Darrein continuance /dəréyn kəntínyuwən(t)s/. The last continuance.

Darrein presentment /dəréyn prəséntmənt/. In old English law, the last presentment. See Assise of darrein presentment.

Darrein seisin /dəréyn síyzən/. Last seisin. A plea at common law which in some cases lay for the tenant in a writ of right.

Dartmouth College Case. Dartmouth College v. Woodward, 17 U.S. 518, 4 Wheat. 518, 4 L.Ed. 629, held that a college charter was a contract within the constitutional provision against state legislatures' prohibiting impairment of the obligation of contract. Art. I, Sec. 10, U.S.Const. Although *Dartmouth College* involved a charitable and educational institution, the Supreme Court readily expanded the principles announced in the opinion to corporate charters issued for business purposes. Consequently, the decision protected industrial and financial corporations from much government regulation.

Dash. The em dash (—) or the en dash (–) is often used to indicate the omission of the intermediate terms of a series which are to be supplied in reading, being thus often equivalent to * * * inclusive; thus Mark iv, 3–20 (that is, verses 3 to 20, inclusive); the years 1880–1888 (that is, 1880 to 1888).

Data. Organized information generally used as the basis for an adjudication or decision. Commonly, organized information, collected for specific purpose.

In old practice and conveyancing, the date of a deed; the time when it was *given*; that is, executed. Grounds whereon to proceed; facts from which to draw a conclusion.

Date. The specification or mention, in a written instrument, of the time (day, month and year) when it was made (executed). Also the time so specified.

The word is derived from the Latin word "datum" meaning given and is defined as the time given or specified—in some way ascertained and fixed. The time when an instrument was made, acknowledged, delivered or recorded; the clause or memorandum which specifies that fact; and the time from which its operation is to be reckoned.

That part of a deed or writing which expresses the day of the month and year in which it was made or given.

The primary signification of *date* is not time in the abstract, nor time taken absolutely, but time given or specified; time in some way ascertained and fixed. When we speak of the date of a deed, date of issue of a bond or date of a policy, we do not mean the time

when it was actually executed, but the time of its execution as given or stated in the deed itself. The date of an item, or of a charge in a book-account, is not necessarily the time when the article charged was, in fact, furnished, but rather the time given or set down in the account, in connection with such charge. And so the expression "the date of the last work done, or materials furnished," in a mechanic's lien law, may be taken, in the absence of anything in the act indicating a different intention, to mean the time when such work was done or materials furnished, as specified in the plaintiff's written claim.

The precise meaning of date, however, depends upon context, since there are numerous instances when it means actual as distinguished from conventional time.

See also **Antedate; Backdating; Post-date.**

Date certaine /dát sèrtéyn/. In Franch law, a deed is said to be a *date certaine* (fixed date) when it has been subjected to the formality of registration. After this formality has been complied with, the parties to the deed cannot by mutual consent change the date thereof.

Date of bankruptcy. Under Bankruptcy law, time at which court declares a person a bankrupt. Usually coincides with date of filing in case of voluntary petition. See also **Date of cleavage.**

Date of cleavage. The date of filing voluntary petition of bankruptcy and hence the cut-off date as to dischargeability of debts in bankruptcy. Only those debts, with some exceptions, which exist at this time are dischargeable in bankruptcy.

Date of injury. Means inception date of the injury and is regarded as coincident with date of occurrence or happening of accident which caused such injury. Indemnity Ins. Co. of North America v. Williams, 129 Tex. 51, 99 S.W.2d 905, 907.

Date of issue. When applied to notes, bonds, etc., of series, usually means an arbitrary date fixed as beginning of term for which they run, without reference to precise time when convenience or state of market may permit their sale or delivery; date which bonds and stocks bear, and not date when they were actually issued in sense of being signed and delivered and put into circulation. Whetstone v. City of Stuttgart, 193 Ark. 88, 97 S.W.2d 641, 643.

The words in life insurance policy have been held not to mean the date of actual execution or the delivery date, but the date set forth in the policy itself. Potts v. Metropolitan Life Ins. Co., 133 Pa.Super. 397, 2 A.2d 870, 872.

Date of maturity. Day on which a debt falls due as in the case of a promissory note, bond or other evidence of indebtedness.

Datio /déysh(iy)ow/. In the civil law, a giving, or act of giving. *Datio in solutum*; a giving in payment; a species of accord and satisfaction. Called, in modern law, "dation."

Dation /déyshən/. In the civil law, a gift; a giving of something. It is not exactly synonymous with "donation," for the latter implies generosity or liberality in making a gift, while dation may mean the giving of something to which the recipient is already entitled.

Dation en paiement /déyshən ən péymənt/dasyówn òn pèymón/. In French law, a giving by the debtor and receipt by the creditor of something in payment of a debt, instead of a sum of money. It is somewhat like the accord and satisfaction of the common law.

Dative /déydəv/. A word derived from the Roman law, signifying "appointed by public authority." Thus, in Scotland, an executor-dative is an executor appointed by a court; corresponding or equivalent to an English *administrator* or "administrator with the will annexed". In old English law, in one's gift; that may be given and disposed of at will and pleasure.

Da tua dum tua sunt, post mortem tunc tua non sunt /déy t(y)úwə dəm t(y)úwə sənt, pòwst mórdəm tənk t(y)úwə nón sənt/. Give the things which are yours whilst they are yours; after death they are not yours.

Datum /déydəm/. A first principle; a thing given; a date.

Datur digniori /déydər dìgniyóray/. It is given to the more worthy.

Daughter. Female offspring.

Daughter-in-law. Wife of one's son.

Davis-Bacon Act. Federal law which deals with rate of pay for laborers and mechanics on public buildings and public works. 40 U.S.C.A. § 276a.

Day. 1. A period of time consisting of twenty-four hours and including the solar day and the night.

2. The period of time during which the earth makes one revolution on its axis. Long v. City of Wichita Falls, 142 Tex. 202, 176 S.W.2d 936, 938, 939.

3. The space of time which elapses between two successive midnights. Long v. City of Wichita Falls, 142 Tex. 202, 176 S.W.2d 936, 938, 939.

4. The whole or any part of period of 24 hours from midnight to midnight. Talbott v. Caudill, 248 Ky. 146, 58 S.W.2d 385.

5. That portion of time during which the sun is above the horizon, and, in addition, that part of the morning and evening during which there is sufficient light for the features of a man to be reasonably discerned. U. S. v. Martin, D.C.Mass., 33 F.2d 639, 640. Compare **Nighttime.**

6. An artificial period of time, computed from one fixed point to another twenty-four hours later, without any reference to the prevalence of light or darkness.

7. The period of time, within the limits of a natural day, set apart either by law or by common usage for the transaction of particular business or the performance of labor; as in banking, in laws regulating the hours of labor, in contracts for so many "days work," and the like, the word "day" may signify six, eight, ten, or any number of hours.

8. In practice and pleading, a particular time assigned or given for the appearance in court, the return of process, etc.

Artificial day. The time between the rising and setting of the sun; that is, day or daytime as distinguished from night.

Astronomical day. The period of twenty-four hours beginning and ending at noon.

Banking day. See **Banking day.**

Calendar days. See **Calendar.**

Civil day. The solar day, measured by the diurnal revolution of the earth, and denoting the interval of time which elapses between the successive transits of the sun over the same hour circle, so that the "civil day" commences and ends at midnight.

Clear days. See **Clear.**

Common days. In old English practice, an ordinary day in court.

Daytime. See **Daytime.**

Judicial day. A day proper for the transaction of business in court. One on which the court may lawfully sit, excluding Sundays, holidays, and other days specifically excluded by statute or court rule. Fed.R.Civil P. 77.

Law day. Currently, May 1st of each year is designated "Law Day" and is observed in schools, public assemblies, and courts, in honor and respect of our legal system.

The day prescribed in a bond, mortgage, or defeasible deed for payment of the debt secured thereby; maturity date.

Natural day. Properly the period of twenty-four hours from midnight to midnight. Though sometimes taken to mean the daytime or time between sunrise and sunset.

Solar day. A term sometimes used as meaning that portion of the day when the sun is above the horizon, but properly it is the time between two complete (apparent) revolutions of the sun, or between two consecutive positions of the sun over any given terrestrial meridian, and hence, according to the usual method of reckoning, from noon to noon at any given place.

Day-book. A tradesman's account book; a book in which all the occurrences of the day are set down. It is usually a book of original entries.

Day certain. A fixed or appointed day; a specified particular day; a day in term.

Day in court. The right and opportunity afforded a person to litigate his claims, seek relief, or defend his rights in a competent judicial tribunal.

The time appointed for one whose rights are called judicially in question, or liable to be affected by judicial action, to appear in court and be heard in his own behalf. This phrase, as generally used, means not so much the time appointed for a hearing as the opportunity to present one's claims or rights in a proper forensic hearing before a competent tribunal.

A litigant has his "day in court" when he has been duly cited to appear and has been afforded an opportunity to appear and to be heard. Cohen v. City of Houston, Tex.Civ.App., 185 S.W.2d 450, 452; In re Hampton's Estate, 55 Cal.App.2d 543, 131 P.2d 565, 573.

Daylight. See **Daytime.**

Daylight saving time. Time each year from Spring through Fall when clocks are set ahead one hour to give people more daylight at end of working day. Daylight saving time is one hour later than Standard Time for the locality.

Day of atonement. See **Yom Kippur.**

Day order. An order to buy or sell a security or commodity on a particular day and if such sale does not take place, the order expires.

Day-rule, or **day-writ.** In English law, a permission granted to a prisoner to go out of prison, for the purpose of transacting his business, as to hear a case in which he was concerned at the assizes, etc. Abolished by 5 & 6 Vict., c. 22, § 12 (1842).

Days in bank. (L. Lat. *dies in banco.*) In old English law, certain stated days in term appointed for the appearance of parties, the return of process, etc., originally peculiar to the court of common pleas, or bench (bank), as it was anciently called. 3 Bl.Comm. 277.

By the common law, the defendant was allowed three full days in which to make his appearance in court, exclusive of the day of appearance or return-day named in the writ; 3 Bl.Comm. 278. Upon his appearance, time was usually granted him for pleading; and this was called giving him day, or, as it was more familiarly expressed, a continuance. 3 Bl. Comm. 316. When the suit was ended by discontinuance or by judgment for the defendant, he was discharged from further attendance, and was said to go thereof *sine die*, without day. See **Continuance.**

Daysman. An arbitrator, umpire, or elected judge.

Days of grace. A number of days allowed, as a matter of favor or grace, to a person who has to perform some act, or make some payment, after the time originally limited for the purpose has elapsed.

In old practice, three days allowed to persons summoned in the English courts, beyond the day named in the writ, to make their appearance; the last day being called the *"quarto die post".* 3 Bl.Comm. 278.

In mercantile law, a certain number of days (generally three) allowed to the maker or acceptor of a bill, draft, or note, in which to make payment, after the expiration of the time expressed in the paper itself. Originally these days were granted only as a matter of *grace* or favor, but the allowance of them became an established custom of merchants, and was sanctioned by the courts (and in some cases prescribed by statute), so that they are now demandable as of right. Bell v. Bank, 115 U.S. 373, 6 S.Ct. 105, 29 L.Ed. 409; Renner v. Bank, 9 Wheat. 581, 6 L.Ed. 166.

See also **Grace period.**

Daytime. The time during which there is the light of day, as distinguished from night or nighttime. That portion of the full twenty-four day in which a man's countenance is visible by natural light and, hence, that portion of the day which is distinguished from nighttime in crime of burglary; nighttime being the period between one hour after sunset and one hour before sunrise. Model Penal Code, § 221.0(2). Word "daytime" as used in statutory crime of breaking and entering a dwelling in the daytime means that time of day when there is sufficient daylight so as to be able to discern the features of another by natural sunlight. State v. Briggs, 161 Conn. 283, 287 A.2d 369, 373.

Under Fed.R.Crim.Proc. 41(h), relating to search and seizure, "daytime" means the hours from 6:00 a. m. to 10:00 p. m.

See also **Nighttime.**

Daywere. In old English law, a term applied to land, and signifying as much arable ground as could be plowed up in one day's work.

D.B. Abbreviation for Doomsday Book.

D.B.A. Abbreviation for "doing business as."

D.B.E. An abbreviation for *de bene esse* (q.v.).

D.B.N. An abbreviation for *de bonis non*; descriptive of a species of administration.

D.C. An abbreviation standing either for "District Court," or "District of Columbia."

DDB. Double-declining-balance depreciation. See **Depreciation.**

De /díy/. A Latin preposition, signifying of; by; from; out of; affecting; concerning; respecting.

Deacon /díykən/. In ecclesiastical law, a minister or servant in the church, whose office is to assist the priest in divine service and the distribution of the sacrament. It is the lowest degree of holy orders in the Church of England.

De acquirendo rerum dominio /díy ækwəréndow rírəm dəmín(i)yow/. Of (about) acquiring the ownership of things.

Dead asset. Worthless asset which has no realizable value; *e.g.* uncollectable account receivable.

Dead beat. Slang term for one who fails to pay his debts.

Dead body. A corpse. The body of a human being, deprived of life.

Dead-born. A dead-born child is to be considered as if it had never been conceived or born; in other words, it is presumed it never had life, it being a maxim of the common law that *mortuus exitus non est exitus* (a dead birth is no birth). This is also the doctrine of the civil law.

Dead freight. The amount paid by a charterer for that part of the vessel's capacity which he does not occupy although he has contracted for it.

Deadhead. A term formerly applied to persons other than the officers, agents, or employees of a railroad company who were permitted by the company to travel on the road without paying any fare therefor.

Dead letter. A term sometimes applied to a law that has become obsolete by long disuse, and also to a letter that is undeliverable by the postal service because of insufficient address or postage and absence of return address.

Deadlocked jury. See **Dynamite instruction.**

Deadly force. Force likely or intended to cause death or great bodily harm; may be reasonable or unreasonable, depending on the circumstances.

Deadly weapon. Any firearm, or other weapon, device, instrument, material or substance, whether animate or inanimate, which in the manner it is used or is intended to be used is known to be capable of producing death or serious bodily injury. Model Penal Code, § 210.0.

Such weapons or instruments as are made and designed for offensive or defensive purposes, or for the destruction of life or the infliction of injury. One which, from the manner used, is calculated or likely to produce death or serious bodily injury. Austin v. State, Fla.App., 336 So.2d 480, 481.

See also **Dangerous weapon; Malicious assault with deadly weapon.**

Deadly weapon per se. A weapon which of itself is deadly or one which would ordinarily result in death by its use; *e.g.* gun. Baylor v. State, 151 Tex.Cr.R. 365, 208 S.W.2d 558, 561.

Dead man's part. In English law, that portion of the effects of a deceased person which, by the custom of London and York, is allowed to the administrator; being, where the deceased leaves a widow and children, one-third; where he leaves only a widow or only children, one-half; and, where he leaves neither, the whole. This portion the administrator was wont to apply to his own use, till the statute 1 Jac. II, c. 17, declared that the same should be subject to the statute of distributions. 2 Bl.Comm. 518.

Dead man's statute. An evidential disqualification which renders inadmissible oral promises or declarations of a dead person when offered in support of their claims by those who bring claims against the estate of the dead person. The last vestige of the disqualification of witnesses by reason of interest as this existed at common law, though many states admit such testimony under certain statutory conditions. The standard type of state dead man statute would be applicable under Fed.R.Evid. 601 only if testimony of the witness concerned claims or defenses, or elements thereof, which were governed by state law.

De admensuratione /dìy ædmènshərèyshiyówniy/. Of admeasurement. Thus, *de admensuratione dotis* was a writ for the admeasurement of dower, and *de admensuratione pasturæ* was a writ for the admeasurement of pasture.

Dead-pledge. A mortgage, *mortuum vadium.*

Dead rent. In English law, a rent payable on a mining lease in addition to a royalty, so called because it is payable although the mine may not be worked.

Dead stock. Goods in inventory for which there is no market.

Dead storage. The storage, especially of automobiles in public garages, where automobiles not in use are to remain uninterruptedly for a time, sometimes for the season.

Dead time. Time which does not count for any purpose, *e.g.* time for which a person is not paid wages, or time when employee is not working due to no fault of his own (*e.g.* because of machinery breakdown), or time for which a prisoner does not get credit in serving his sentence.

Dead use. A future use.

De advisamento consilii nostri /dìy ædvàyzəméntow kənsíliyay nóstray/. L. Lat. With or by the advice of our council. A phrase used in the old writs of summons to parliament.

De æquitate /dìy èkwətéydiy/. In equity, *de jure stricto, nihil possum vendicare, de æquitate tamen, nullo modo hoc obtinet;* in strict law. I can claim nothing, but in equity this by no means obtains.

De æstimato /dìy èstəméydow/. In Roman law, one of the innominate contracts, and, in effect, a sale of land or goods at a price fixed (*æstimato*), and guarantied by some third party, who undertook to find a purchaser.

De ætate probanda /dìy iytéydiy prowbǽndə/. For proving age. A writ which formerly lay to summon a jury in order to determine the age of the heir of a tenant *in capite* who claimed his estate as being of full age.

Deafforest /dìyəfóhrəst/. See **Disafforest.**

Deaf person. Any person whose hearing is so seriously impaired as to prohibit the person from understanding oral communications when spoken in a normal conversational tone. See Ga. Code Ann. § 99–4001.

Deal, *n.* An arrangement to attain a desired result by a combination of interested parties; the prime object being usually the purchase, sale, or exchange of property for a profit. Also, an act of buying and selling; a bargain to purchase at a favorable price. See **Bargain.**

Deal, *v.* To traffic; to transact business; to bargain or trade. Also, to act between two persons, to intervene, or to have to do with.

As to dealing in futures, see **Futures contract.**

Dealer. In the popular sense, one who buys to sell; not one who buys to keep, or makes to sell. One who purchases goods for resale to final customers.

The term "dealer" means any person engaged in the business of buying and selling securities for his own account, through a broker or otherwise, but does not include a bank, or any person insofar as he buys or sells securities for his own account, either individually or in some fiduciary capacity, but not as a part of a regular business. Securities Exchange Act of 1934, § 3.

Dealer's talk. The puffing of goods to induce the sale thereof; not regarded in law as fraudulent unless accompanied by some artifice to deceive the purchaser and throw him off his guard or some concealment of intrinsic defects not easily discoverable. See **Puffing.**

Dealings. Transactions in the course of trade or business.

De allocatione facienda /dìy æləkèyshiyówniy fèys(h)iyéndə/. *Breve.* Writ for making an allowance. An old writ directed to the lord treasurer and barons of the exchequer, for allowing certain officers (as collectors of customs) in their accounts certain payments made by them.

De alto et basso /dìy æltow èt bæsow/. Of high and low. A phrase anciently used to denote the absolute submission of all differences to arbitration.

De ambitu /dìy æmbətyuw/. Lat. Concerning bribery. A phrase descriptive of the subject-matter of several of the Roman laws; as the *Lex Aufidia*, the *Lex Pompeia*, the *Lex Tullia*, and others. See **Ambitus**.

De ampliori gratia /dìy æmpliyóray gréysh(iy)ə/. Of more abundant or especial grace.

Dean. Administrative or academic head of school, college or university. There may be several kinds of deans in larger schools (*e.g.* dean of student affairs, academic dean) and also deans of specific schools within university. Administrator in charge of counseling and disciplining students in college or secondary school.

In England, an ecclesiastical dignitary who presides over the chapter of a cathedral, and is next in rank to the bishop. So called from having been originally appointed to superintend *ten* canons or prebendaries. 1 Bl.Comm. 382.

De anno bissextili /dìy ænow bàysekstáylay/. Of the bissextile or leap year. The title of a statute passed in the twenty-first year of Henry III, which in fact, however, is nothing more than a sort of writ or direction to the justices of the bench, instructing them how the extraordinary day in the leap year was to be reckoned in cases where persons had a day to appear at the distance of a year, as on the essoin *de malo lecti*, and the like. It was thereby directed that the additional day should, together with that which went before, be reckoned only as one, and so, of course, within the preceding year.

De annua pensione /dìy ænyuwə pènshiyówniy/. *Breve.* Writ of annual pension. An ancient writ by which the king, having a yearly pension due him out of an abbey or priory for any of his chaplains, demanded the same of the abbot or prior, for the person named in the writ.

De annuo reditu /dìy ænyuwow rédətyuw/. For a yearly rent. A writ to recover an annuity, no matter how payable, in goods or money.

Dean of the Arches. In England, the presiding judge of the Court of Arches.

De apostata capiendo /dìy æpostéydə kæpiyéndow/. *Breve.* Writ for taking an apostate. A writ which anciently lay against one who, having entered and professed some order of religion, left it and wandered up and down the country, contrary to the rules of his order, commanding the sheriff to apprehend him and deliver him again to his abbot or prior.

De arbitratione facta /dìy àrbətrèyshiyówniy fæktə/. (Lat. Of arbitration had.) A writ formerly used when an action was brought for a cause which had been settled by arbitration.

De arrestandis bonis ne dissipentur /dìy ærəstændəs bównəs níy dəsəpéntər/. An old writ which lay to seize goods in the hands of a party during the pendency of a suit, to prevent their being made away with.

De arrestando ipsum qui pecuniam recepit /dìy ærəstændow ípsəm kwày pəkyúwniyəm rəsíypət/. A writ which lay for the arrest of one who had taken the king's money to serve in the war, and hid himself to escape going.

De asportatis religiosorum /dìy æspartéydəs rəlìjiyowsórəm/. Concerning the property of religious persons carried away. The title of the statute 35 Edward I, passed to check the abuses of clerical possessions, one of which was the waste they suffered by being drained into foreign countries.

De assisa proroganda /dìy əsáyzə pròwrəgændə/. (Lat. For proroguing assise.) A writ to put off an assise, issuing to the justices, where one of the parties is engaged in the service of the king.

Death. The cessation of life; permanent cessations of all vital functions and signs. Numerous states have enacted statutory definitions of death which include brain-related criteria.

See also **Contemplation of death; Presumption of death; Simultaneous Death Act; Wrongful death action.**

Brain death. See **Brain death**; also *Natural Death Acts,* below.

Civil death. See **Civil death**.

Death benefits. Amount paid under insurance policy on death of insured. A payment made by an employer to the beneficiary or beneficiaries of a deceased employee on account of the death of the employee.

Death by wrongful act. Statutory action arising from act to which law attaches absolute liability as in the case of serving unwholesome food that results in death, the action for which may be brought by personal representative of deceased. See also **Wrongful death statutes**.

Death certificate. Official document issued by Register of Deaths or some other public official which certifies that a person has died. Generally such certificate specifies the cause of death, and is commonly required to be signed by the attending or an examining physician. Fed.Evid.R. 803(9) provides a hearsay exception for admissibility of death certificates.

Death duty. See *Death taxes, infra.*

Death penalty. Supreme penalty exacted as punishment for murder and other capital crimes; held not to be, under all circumstances, cruel and unusual punishment within prohibitions of 8th and 14th Amends., U.S.Const. Gregg v. Georgia, 428 U.S. 153, 96 S.Ct. 2909, 49 L.Ed.2d 859.

Death records. Official records of deaths kept by town or city Register of Deaths or by some other public official with like functions. See *Death certificate, supra.*

Death sentence. See *Death penalty, supra.*

Death taxes. Generic term to describe all taxes imposed on property or on transfer of property at death of owner. Includes estate and inheritance taxes. See **Estate tax; Inheritance tax.**

Death warrant. A warrant from the proper executive authority appointing the time and place for the execution of the sentence of death upon a convict judicially condemned to suffer that penalty.

Fetal death. See **Fetal death.**

Instantaneous death. Term to describe death following accident within a very short time such as 15–20 minutes; such concept is important in death actions in which a claim is made for pain and suffering.

Natural death. A death which occurs by the unassisted operation of natural causes, as distinguished not only from "civil death", but also from "unnatural" (*e.g.* violent) death.

Natural Death Acts. Such statutes (*e.g.* Cal. Health & Safety Code § 7185 *et seq.*) authorize an adult to make a written directive instructing his physician to withhold life-sustaining procedures in the event of a terminal condition. In the directive, which is to be executed in a prescribed manner and made a part of the patient's medical records, the declarant directs that if he has been certified by two physicians as being afflicted with a terminal condition, he is to be permitted to die naturally. The Act removes all civil or criminal liability from physicians who act in accordance with its provisions. See also **Brain death.**

Presumptive death. That which is presumed from proof of a long continued absence unheard from and unexplained. The general rule, as provided by state statutes, is that the presumption of the duration of life ceases at the expiration of seven years from the time when the person was last known to be living; and after the lapse of that period there is a presumption of death.

Violent death. One caused or accelerated by the interference of human agency; distinguished from "natural death."

Death on High Seas Act. Federal Act which provides for a pecuniary recovery for death "caused by wrongful act, neglect or default occurring on the high seas beyond a marine league from the shore of any state [territory or dependency]." 41 U.S.C.A. § 761 *et seq.* Mobil Oil Corp. v. Higginbotham, 98 S.Ct. 2010, 56 L.Ed.2d 581.

Deathsman. The executioner; hangman; person that executes capital punishment.

Death's part. See **Dead man's part.**

Death trap. A structure or situation involving imminent risk of death or a place apparently safe but actually very dangerous to life. Benson v. Missouri, K. & T. R. Co., Tex.Civ.App., 200 S.W.2d 233, 240.

De attornato recipiendo /dìy ætərnéydow rəsìpiyén-dow/. A writ which lay to the judges of a court, requiring them to receive and admit an attorney for a party.

De audiendo et terminando /dìy òdiyéndow èt tèrmənǽndow/. For hearing and determining; to hear and determine. The name of a writ, or rather commission granted to certain justices to hear and determine cases of heinous misdemeanor, trespass,

riotous breach of the peace, etc. See **Oyer and Terminer.**

De averiis captis in withernamium /dìy əvǽriyəs kǽptəs ən wìðərnéymiyəm/. Writ for taking cattle in withernam. A writ which lay where the sheriff returned to a *pluries* writ of replevin that the cattle or goods, etc., were eloined, etc.; by which he was commanded to take the cattle of the defendant in withernam (or reprisal), and detain them until he could replevy the other cattle. See **Withernam.**

De averiis replegiandis /dìy əvǽriyəs rəplìyjiyǽndəs/. A writ to replevy beasts. 3 Bl.Comm. 149.

De banco /dìy bǽŋkow/. Of the bench. A term formerly applied in England to the justices of the court of common pleas, or "bench," as it was originally styled.

Debarment. To bar, exclude or preclude from having or doing something. Exclusion from government contracting and subcontracting. See also **Disbarment.**

Debasement. Reducing the weight of gold and silver in coins of standard value or of increasing the amount of alloy in such coins. Such has the effect of reducing the intrinsic value.

Debauch /dəbóch/. To corrupt one's manners; to make lewd; to mar or spoil; to entice; and, when used of a woman, to seduce, or corrupt with lewdness. Originally, the term had a limited signification, meaning to entice or draw one away from his work, employment, or duty; and from this sense its application has enlarged to include the corruption of manners and violation of the person. In its modern legal sense, the word carries with it the idea of "carnal knowledge," aggravated by assault, violent seduction, ravishment. See also **Debauchery.**

Debauchery /dəbóchəriy/. In general, excessive indulgence in sensual pleasures; in a narrower sense, sexual immorality or excesses, or the unlawful indulgence of lust.

De bene esse /dìy bíyniy ésiy/də bíyniy°/. Conditionally; provisionally; in anticipation of future need. A phrase applied to proceedings which are taken *ex parte* or provisionally, and are allowed to stand as *well done* for the present, but which may be subject to future exception or challenge, and must then stand or fall according to their intrinsic merit and regularity.

Examination de bene esse. A provisional examination of a witness; an examination of a witness whose testimony is important and might otherwise be lost, held out of court and before the trial, with the proviso that the deposition so taken may be used on the trial in case the witness is unable to attend in person at that time or cannot be produced. See *e.g.* Fed.R.Civil P. 26, 27.

Debenture /dəbénchər/. A promissory note or bond backed by the general credit of a corporation and usually not secured by a mortgage or lien on any specific property.

Certificate issued by customs to an importer for the deduction or refund of duties on merchandise imported and then exported by such importer.

Convertible debenture. Debenture which may be changed or converted into some other security (*e.g.* stock) usually at the option of the holder.

Convertible subordinated debenture. Debenture which is subject or subordinate to prior payment of other indebtedness but which may be converted into another form of security.

Sinking fund debenture. Debenture which is secured by periodic payments into sinking fund, commonly managed by trustee for purpose of retiring such debt.

Subordinate debenture. Debenture which is subject to or subordinate to prior payment of other indebtedness.

Debenture bond. Bonds not secured by any specific property but issued against the general credit of a corporation of government.

Debenture indenture. An indenture containing obligations not secured by a mortgage or other collateral; a key instrument in the process of long term debt financing for general business corporations. Its effect is to put the debenture-holder in substantially the same practical position as a bondholder secured by a first mortgage.

Debenture stock. In England, a stock or fund representing money borrowed by a company or public body and charged on the whole or part of its property. An issue of stock usually irredeemable and transferable in any amount, not including a fraction of a pound. The terminability and fixity in amount of debentures being inconvenient to lenders led to their being in many cases superseded by debenture stock.

Debet esse finis litium /débəd ésiy fáynəs lísh(iy)əm/. There ought to be an end of suits; there should be some period put to litigation.

Debet et detinet /débəd èt dédənət/. (Lat. He owes and detains.) Words anciently used in the original writ (and now, in English, in the plaintiff's declaration), in an action of debt, where it was brought by one of the original contracting parties who personally gave the credit, against the other who personally incurred the debt, or against his heirs, if they were bound to the payment; as by the obligee against the obligor, by the landlord against the tenant, etc. The declaration, in such cases, states that the defendant *"owes* to," as well as *"detains* from," the plaintiff the debt or thing in question; and hence the action is said to be "in the *debet et detinet*". Where the declaration merely states that the defendant *detains* the debt (as in actions by and against an executor for a debt due to or from the testator), the action is said to be "in the *detinet*" alone. 3 Bl.Comm. 155.

Debet quis juri subjacere ubi delinquit /débət kwìs júray səbjǽsəriy yúwbay dəlíŋkwət/. One [every one] ought to be subject to the law [of the place] where he offends.

Debet sine breve /débət sáyniy bríyviy/. (Lat. He owes without declaration filed.) Used in relation to a confession of judgment.

Debet sua cuique domus esse perfugium tutissimum /débət syúwə kyuwáykwiy dówməs ésiy pərfyúwjiyəm tyùwtísəməm/. Every man's house should be a perfectly safe refuge.

De bien et de mal /də byén ey də mǽl/. L. Fr. For good and evil. A phrase by which a party accused of a crime anciently put himself upon a jury, indicating his entire submission to their verdict; also the name of the special writ of jail delivery formerly in use in England, which issued for each particular prisoner, of course. It was superseded by the general commission of jail delivery.

De biens le mort /də bíynz lə mór(t)/. L. Fr. Of the goods of the deceased.

De bigamis /dìy bígəməs/. Concerning men twice married. The title of the English statute 4 Edw. I, St. 3; so called from the initial words of the fifth chapter.

Debile fundamentum fallit opus /débəliy fàndəméntəm fǽləd ówpəs/. A weak foundation frustrates [or renders vain] the work [built upon it]. When the foundation fails, all goes to the ground; as, where the cause of action fails, the action itself must of necessity fail.

Debit /débət/. A sum charged as due or owing. An entry made on the asset side of a ledger or account. The term is used in book-keeping to denote the left side of the ledger, or the charging of a person or an account with all that is supplied to or paid out for him or for the subject of the account. Also, the balance of an account where it is shown that something remains due to the party keeping the account.

As a noun, an entry on the left-hand side of an account. As a verb, to make an entry on the left-hand side of an account. Records increases in assets and expenses, and decreases in liabilities, owners' equity, and revenues.

Debita laicorum /débədə lèyəkórəm/. L. Lat. In old English law, debts of the laity, or of lay persons. Debts recoverable in the civil courts.

Debita sequuntur personam debitoris /débədə səkwántər pərsównəm dèbətórəs/. Debts follow the person of the debtor; that is, they have no locality, and may be collected wherever the debtor can be found.

Debit balance. Accounting condition where there is an excess of debit over credit entries.

Debitor /débədər/. In the civil and old English law, a debtor.

Debitor non præsumitur donare /débədər nòn prəzyúwmədər dənériy/. A debtor is not presumed to make a gift. Whatever disposition he makes of his property is supposed to be in satisfaction of his debts. Where a debtor gives money or goods, or grants land to his creditor, the natural presumption is that he means to get free from his obligation, and not to make a present, unless donation be expressed.

Debitorum pactionibus creditorum petitio nec tolli nec minui potest /dèbətórəm pǽksh(iy)ównəbəs kredətórəm pətísh(iy)ow nèk tólay nèk míyuway pówdəst/. The rights of creditors can neither be taken away nor diminished by agreements among (or of) the debtors.

Debitrix /débətrəks/. A female debtor.

Debitum /débədəm/. Something due, or owing, a debt.

Debitum et contractus sunt nullius loci /débədəm èt kəntrǽktə sànt nəláyəs lówsay/. Debt and contract are of [belong to] no place; have no particular locality. The obligation in these cases is purely personal, and actions to enforce it may be brought anywhere.

Debitum in præsenti solvendum in futuro /débədəm in prəzéntay sòlvéndəm in fyəchúrow/. A debt or obligation complete when contracted, but of which the performance cannot be required till some future period.

Debitum sine brevi /débədəm sáyniy bríyvay/. L. Lat. Debt without writ; debt without a declaration. In old practice, this term denoted an action begun by original bill, instead of by writ. In modern usage, it is sometimes applied to a debt evidenced by confession of judgment without suit. The equivalent Norman-French phrase was "*debit sans breve.*" Both are abbreviated to *d.s.b.*

De bone memorie /dìy bówniy mém:əriy/. L. Fr. Of good memory; of sound mind.

De bonis asportatis /dìy bównəs æspərtéydəs/. For goods taken away; for taking away goods. The action of trespass for taking personal property is technically called "trespass *de bonis asportatis.*"

De bonis non /dìy bównəs nón/. An abbreviation of *De bonis non administratis (q.v.).*

De bonis non administratis /dìy bównəs nòn əd-mìnəstréydəs/. Of the goods not administered. When an administrator is appointed to succeed another, who has left the estate partially unsettled, he is said to be granted "administration *de bonis non;*" that is, of the goods not already administered.

De bonis non amovendis /dìy bównəs nòn èym-avéndəs/. Writ for not removing goods. A writ anciently directed to the sheriffs of London, commanding them, in cases where a writ of error was brought by a defendant against whom a judgment was recovered, to see that his *goods* and chattels were safely kept *without being removed*, while the error remained undetermined, so that execution might be had of them, etc.

De bonis propriis /dìy bównəs prówpriyəs/. Of his own goods. The technical name of a judgment against an administrator or executor to be satisfied from his own property, and not from the estate of the deceased, as in cases where he has been guilty of a *devastavit* or of a false plea of *plene administravit.*

De bonis testatoris, or **intestati** /dìy bównəs tès-tətórəs/°ìntestéyday/. Of the goods of the testator, or intestate. A term applied to a judgment awarding execution against the property of a testator or intestate, as distinguished from the individual property of his executor or administrator.

De bonis testatoris ac si /dìy bównəs tèstətórəs æk sáy/. (Lat. From the goods of the testator, *if he has any,* and, if *not, from those of the executor.*) A judgment rendered where an executor falsely pleads any matter as a release, or, generally, in any case where he is to be charged in case his testator's estate is insufficient.

De bono et malo /dìy bównow et mǽlow/. See **De Bien et De Mal.**

De bono gestu /dìy bównow jéschuw/. For good behavior; for good abearance.

Debt. A sum of money due by certain and express agreement. A specified sum of money owing to one person from another, including not only obligation of debtor to pay but right of creditor to receive and enforce payment. State v. Ducey, 25 Ohio App.2d 50, 266 N.E.2d 233, 235. Liability on a claim. Bankruptcy Act, § 101(11).

A fixed and certain obligation to pay money or some other valuable thing or things, either in the present or in the future. In a still more general sense, that which is due from one person to another, whether money, goods, or services. In a broad sense, any duty to respond to another in money, labor, or service; it may even mean a moral or honorary obligation, unenforceable by legal action. Also, sometimes an aggregate of separate debts, or the total sum of the existing claims against a person or company. Thus we speak of the "national debt", the "bonded debt" of a corporation, etc.

Active debt. One due to a person. Used in the civil law.

Ancestral debt. One of an ancestor which the law compels the heir to pay.

Antecedent debt. See that title.

Bad debt. Uncollectible account receivable. Under National Bank Act, an unsecured debt on which interest or payment is past due for at least six months. See also **Bad debt; Bad debt reserve.**

Bonded debt. Debt represented by bonds. See **Bonded debt.**

Common-law action. The name of a common-law action which lies to recover a certain specific sum of money, or a sum that can readily be reduced to a certainty. It is thus distinguished from *assumpsit,* which lies as well where the sum due is uncertain as where it is certain, and from *covenant,* which lies only upon contracts evidenced in a certain manner.

It is said to lie in the *debet* and *detinet* (when it is stated that the defendant owes and detains), or in the *detinet* (when it is stated merely that he detains). Debt in the *detinet* for goods differs from detinue, because it is not essential in this action, as in detinue, that the specific property in the goods should have been vested in the plaintiff at the time the action is brought.

Consumer debt. See **Consumer debt.**

Contingent debt. See **Contingent debt.**

Convertible debt. Debt which may be changed or converted by creditor into another form of security, *e.g.* shares of stock. See **Debenture** (*Convertible debenture*).

Debt by simple contract. A debt or demand founded upon a verbal or implied contract, or upon any written agreement that is not under seal.

Debt by specialty or special contract. A debt due, or acknowledged to be due, by some deed or instrument under seal; as a deed of covenant or sale, a lease reserving rent, or a bond or obligation. 2 Bl.Comm. 465.

Debt of record. A debt which appears to be due by the evidence of a court of record, as by a judgment or recognizance. 2 Bl.Comm. 465.

Existing debt. See **Existing debt.**

Floating debt. Short-term or current debt, not represented by securities.

Fraudulent debt. A debt created by fraud. Such a debt implies confidence and deception. It implies that it arose out of a contract, express or implied, and that fraudulent practices were employed by the debtor, by which the creditor was defrauded.

Funded debt. Debt represented by bonds or other securities.

General debt. See that title.

Hypothecary debt. One which is a lien upon an estate.

Installment debt. Debt which is to be repaid in installments; *e.g.* retail installment contract.

Judgment debt. See **Judgment debt.**

Legal debts. Those that are recoverable in a court of law, as debt on a bill of exchange, a bond, or a simple contract.

Liquid debt. One which is immediately and unconditionally due. See also **Liquidated debt.**

Mutual debts. Money due on both sides between two persons. Such debts must be due to and from same persons in same capacity. Cross debts in the same capacity and right, and of the same kind and quality.

Passive debt. A debt upon which, by agreement between the debtor and creditor, no interest is payable, as distinguished from *active* debt; *i.e.,* a debt upon which interest is payable. As used in another sense, a debt is "active" or "passive" according as the person of the creditor or debtor is regarded; a passive debt being that which a man owes; an active debt that which is owing to him. In this meaning every debt is both active and passive; active as regards the creditor, passive as regards the debtor.

Preferential debts. See that title.

Privileged debt. One which is to be paid before others in case a debtor is insolvent; *e.g.* secured debt.

Proof of debt. See **Proof.**

Public debt. That which is due or owing by the government of a state or nation.

Secured debt. Debt secured by collateral; *e.g.* by mortgage, securities, deed, etc. See **Secured transaction.**

Simple contract debt. At common law, one where the contract upon which the obligation arises is neither ascertained by matter of record nor yet by deed or special instrument, but by mere oral evidence the most simple of any, or by notes unsealed, which are capable of a more easy proof, and therefore only better than a verbal promise. 2 Bl.Comm. 466.

Specialty debt. See *Debt by specialty or special contract, supra.*

Debt adjusting. Debt adjusting is engaging in the business of making contracts, express or implied, with a debtor whereby the debtor agrees to pay a certain amount of money periodically to the person engaging in the debt adjusting business who shall for a consideration distribute the same among certain specified creditors. See also **Debt pooling; Wage earner's plan.**

Debt adjustment. Settlement of dispute regarding debt obligation by compromise and adjustment. Term also refers to adjustment of debts of an individual with regular income as provided for under Chapter 13 of the Bankruptcy Act. See also **Compromise and settlement; Debt pooling; Wage earner's plan.**

Debt cancellation. Under federal tax law, discharge or cancellation of indebtedness ordinarily results in income to debtor when he settles debt for less than amount which he owes. I.R.C. § 61(a)(12). See **Bankruptcy.**

Debt consolidation. See **Debt pooling**.

Debtee. A person to whom a debt is due; a creditor.

Debt-equity ratio. Total liabilities divided by total equities.

Debt financing. Raising funds by issuing bonds or notes. Contrasted with equity financing which is raising funds by issuing and selling stocks. Corporate borrowing of money, generally on a long term basis for acquiring working capital or for retiring current indebtedness.

Debt limitations. Ceiling placed on amount of borrowings by individuals, corporations or governments. Certain state constitutions prohibit deficit spending by government.

Debtor. One who owes a debt; he who may be compelled to pay a claim or demand; anyone liable on a claim, whether due or to become due. First Nat. Bank & Trust Co. in Macon v. Kunes, 128 Ga.App. 565, 197 S.E.2d 446, 449.

"Debtor" means "the person who owes payment or other performance of the obligation secured, whether or not he owns or has rights in the collateral, and includes the seller of accounts or chattel paper. Where the debtor and the owner of the collateral are not the same person, the term 'debtor' means the owner of the collateral in any provision of the Article dealing with the collateral, the obligor in any provision dealing with the obligation, and may include both where the context so requires." U.C.C. § 9–105(1)(d).

Person or municipality concerning which a bankruptcy case has been commenced. Bankruptcy Act, § 101(12).

See also **Absconding debtor; Joint debtors.**

Judgment debtor. One who owes money as a result of a judgment in favor of a creditor.

Debtor's Act of 1869. The English statute 32 & 33 Vict. c. 62, abolishing imprisonment for debt in England, and for the punishment of fraudulent debtors. Not to be confounded with the Bankruptcy Act of 1869.

Debt pooling. Arrangement by which debtor adjusts many debts by distributing his assets among several creditors, who may or may not agree to take less than is owed; or, an arrangement by which debtor agrees to pay in regular installments a sum of money to one creditor who agrees to discharge all his debts. Such activities may constitute unauthorized practice of law (as in *e.g.* Mass.), and may, as well, be an act of bankruptcy. See **Act of bankruptcy; Arrangement with creditors; Assignment** (*Assignment for benefit of creditors*); **Wage earner's plan.**

Debt security. Any form of corporate security reflected as debt on the books of the corporation in contrast to equity securities such as stock; *e.g.* bonds, notes and debentures are debt securities.

Debt service. The interest and charges currently payable on a debt, including principal payments.

De cætero /dìy síydərow/. Henceforth.

De calceto reparando /dìy kǽlsədow rèpərǽndow/. Writ for repairing a causeway. An old English writ by which the sheriff was commanded to distrain the inhabitants of a place to repair and maintain a causeway, etc.

Decalogue /dékəlòg/. The ten commandments which, according to Exodus XX, 1–18, were given by God to Moses. The Jews called them the "Ten Words," hence the name.

Decanatus /dèkənéydəs/. A deanery. A company of ten persons. Also (and in this sense sometimes spelled Decania, or Decana), a town or tithing, consisting originally of ten families of freeholders. Ten tithings compose a hundred. 1 Bl.Comm. 114.

Decania /dəkéyniyə/. The office, jurisdiction, territory, or command of a *decanus*, or dean.

Decanus /dəkéynəs/. In ecclesiastical and old European law, an officer having supervision over *ten;* a dean. A term applied not only to ecclesiastical, but to civil and military, officers. *Decanus monasticus;* a monastic dean, or dean of a monastery; an officer over ten monks. *Decanus in majori ecclesiæ;* dean of a cathedral church, presiding over ten prebendaries. *Decanus episcopi;* a bishop's or rural dean, presiding over ten clerks or parishes. *Decanus friborgi;* dean of a friborg. An officer among the Saxons who presided over a friborg, tithing, decennary, or association of ten inhabitants; otherwise called a "tithing man," or "borsholder," his duties being those of an inferior judicial officer. *Decanus militaris;* a military officer having command of ten soldiers.

In Roman law, an officer having the command of a company or "mess" of ten soldiers. Also an officer at Constantinople having charge of the burial of the dead.

De capitalibus dominis feodi /dìy kæpətéyləbəs dómənay fíy(ə)day/. Of the chief lords of the fee.

Decapitation. The act of beheading. A mode of capital punishment by cutting off the head.

De capite minutis /dìy kǽpədiy mənyúwdəs/. Of those who have lost their *status*, or civil condition. The name of a title in the Pandects. See **Capitis deminutio.**

De cartis reddendis /dìy kárdəs rədéndəs/. For restoring charters. A writ to secure the delivery of charters or deeds; a writ of detinue.

De catallis reddendis /dìy kətǽləs rədéndəs/. For restoring chattels. A writ to secure the return specifically of chattels detained from the owner.

De cautione admittenda /dìy kòshiyowniy ædməténdə/. Writ to take caution or security. A writ which anciently lay against a bishop who held an excommunicated person in prison for his contempt, notwithstanding he had offered sufficient security (*idoneam cautionem*) to obey the commands of the church; commanding him to take such security and release the prisoner.

Decease, n. Death; not including civil death. See **Death.**

Decease, v. To die; to depart life, or from life.

Deceased. A dead person.

Decedent. A deceased person, especially one who has lately died. Etymologically the word denotes a person who is *dying,* but it has come to be used in law as signifying any deceased person, testate or intestate.

Decedent's estate. Property, both real and personal, which person possesses at the time of his death, and title to it descends immediately to his heirs upon his death subject to the control of the probate court for the purposes of paying debts and claims and after distribution the estate ceases to exist. Mathey v. Mathey, 109 Mont. 467, 98 P.2d 373, 375.

Deceit. A fraudulent and deceptive misrepresentation, artifice, or device, used by one or more persons to deceive and trick another, who is ignorant of the true facts, to the prejudice and damage of the party imposed upon. To constitute "deceit," the statement must be untrue, made with knowledge of its falsity or with reckless and conscious ignorance thereof, especially if parties are not on equal terms, made with intent that plaintiff act thereon or in a manner apparently fitted to induce him to act thereon, and plaintiff must act in reliance on the statement in the manner contemplated, or manifestly probable, to his injury. See also **Fraud; Misrepresentation; Reliance.** For larceny by deceit, see **Larceny.**

In old English law, the name of an original writ, and the action founded on it, which lay to recover damages for any injury committed *deceitfully,* either in the name of another (as by bringing an action in another's name, and then suffering a nonsuit, whereby the plaintiff became liable to costs), or by a fraudulent warranty of goods, or other personal injury committed contrary to good faith and honesty. Also the name of a judicial writ which formerly lay to recover lands which had been lost by default by the tenant in a real action, in consequence of his not having been summoned by the sheriff, or by the collusion of his attorney.

Decem tales /désəm téyliyz/. Ten such; or ten tales, jurors. In practice, the name of a writ which issued in England, where, on a trial at bar, *ten* jurors were necessary to make up a full panel, commanding the sheriff to summon the requisite number. 3 Bl.Comm. 364.

Decemviri litibus judicandis /dəsémvəray láydəbəs jùwdəkǽndəs/. Lat. In the Roman law, ten persons (five senators and five *equites*) who acted as the council or assistants of the prætor, when he decided on matters of law.

Decency. Propriety of action, speech, dress, etc.

Decenna /dəsénə/. In old English law, a tithing or decennary; the precinct of a frank-pledge; consisting of ten freeholders with their families.

Decennarius /dèsənériyəs/. Lat. One who held one-half a virgate of land. One of the ten freeholders in a *decennary*. *Decennier*. One of the *decennarii*, or ten freeholders making up a tithing. 1 Bl.Comm. 114.

Decennary /dəsénəriy/. At common law a tithing, composed of ten neighboring families. 1 Bl.Comm. 114.

Deception. The act of deceiving; intentional misleading by falsehood spoken or acted. Synonymous with fraud. Jackman v. Mau, 78 C.A. 234, 177 P.2d 599, 605. Knowingly and willfully making a false statement or representation, express or implied, pertaining to a present or past existing fact. See also **Bait and switch; Deceit; Fraud; Misrepresentation.**

Deceptione /dəsèpshiyówny/. An old writ which lay properly against one that deceitfully did anything in the name of another, for one that was damaged thereby. It was either original or judicial.

Deceptis non decipientibus, jura subveniunt /dəséptəs nón dəsìpiyéntəbəs, júrə sàbvíyniyənt/. The laws help persons who are deceived, not those deceiving.

Deceptive sales practices. As term is used in consumer protection statutes, may import less than common law fraud in sale of goods or services though there must be some measure of deceit. Slaney v. Westwood Auto Inc., 366 Mass. 688, 322 N.E.2d 768, 779. See *e.g.* **Bait and switch.**

De certificando /dìy sàrdəfəkǽndow/. A writ requiring a thing to be certified. A kind of *certiorari*.

De certiorando /dìy sàrsh(iy)ərǽndow/. A writ for certifying. A writ directed to the sheriff, requiring him to certify to a particular fact.

Decessus /dəsésəs/. In the civil and old English law, death; departure.

Decet tamen principem servare leges quibus ipse servatus est /díysət tǽmən prín(t)səpəm sərvériy líyjiyz kwíbəs ípsiy sərvéydəs èst/. It behooves, indeed, the prince to keep the laws by which he himself is preserved.

De champertia /dìy kæmpársh(iy)ə/. Writ of champerty. A writ directed to the justices of the bench, commanding the enforcement of the statute of *champertors*.

De char et de sank /də chár èy dəsǽŋ(k)/. L. Fr. Of flesh and blood. *Affaire rechat de char et de sank.* Words used in claiming a person to be a villein, in the time of Edward II.

De chimino /dìy kímənow/. A writ for the enforcement of a right of way.

De cibariis utendis /dìy səbériyəs yuwténdəs/. Of victuals to be used. The title of a sumptuary statute passed 10 Edw. III, St. 3, to restrain the expense of entertainments.

Decide. To arrive at a determination. To "decide" includes the power and right to deliberate, to weigh the reasons for and against, to see which preponderate, and to be governed by that preponderance. See **Decision.**

Decies tantum /déshiyiyz tǽntəm/. Ten times as much. The name of an ancient writ that was used against a juror who had taken a bribe in money for his verdict. The injured party could thus recover ten times the amount of the bribe.

Decimæ /désəmiy/. In ecclesiastical law, tenths, or tithes. The tenth part of the annual profit of each living, payable formerly to the pope. There were several valuations made of these livings at different times. The *decimæ* (tenths) were appropriated to the crown, and a new valuation established, by 26 Hen. VIII, c. 3. 1 Bl.Comm. 284. See **Tithes.**

Decimæ debentur parocho /désəmiy dəbéntər pərówkow/. Tithes are due to the parish priest.

Decimæ de decimatis solvi non debent /désəmiy dìy dèsəméydəs sólvay nón débənt/. Tithes are not to be paid from that which is given for tithes.

Decimæ de jure divino et canonica institutione pertinent ad personam /désəmiy dìy júriy dəváynow èt kənónəkə ìnstətyùwshiyówniy párdənət ǽd pərsównəm/. Tithes belong to the parson by divine right and canonical institution.

Decimæ non debent solvi, ubi non est annua renovatio; et ex annuatis renovantibus simui semei /désəmiy nòn débənt sólvay, yúwbay nón èst ǽnyuwə rènəvéysh(iy)ow; éd èks ǽnyuwéydəs rènəvǽntəbəs sáyməl séməl/. Tithes ought not to be paid where there is not an annual renovation, and from annual renovations once only.

Decimation. The punishing of every tenth soldier by lot, for mutiny or other failure of duty. This was termed *"decimatio legionis"* by the Romans. Sometimes only the twentieth man was punished (*vicesimatio*), or the hundredth (*centesimatio*).

Decipi quam fallere est tutius /désəpay kwǽm fǽləriy èst tyúwsh(iy)əs/. It is safer to be deceived than to deceive.

Decision. A determination arrived at after consideration of facts, and, in legal context, law. A popular rather than technical or legal word; a comprehensive term having no fixed, legal meaning. It may be employed as referring to ministerial acts as well as to those that are judicial or of a judicial character.

A determination of a judicial or quasi judicial nature. A judgment or decree pronounced by a court in settlement of a controversy submitted to it and by way of authoritative answer to the questions raised before it. The term is broad enough to cover both final judgments and interlocutory orders. And though sometimes limited to the sense of judgment, the term is at other times understood as meaning simply the first step leading to a judgment; or as an order for judgment. The word may also include various rulings, as well as orders. U. S. v. Thompson, 251 U.S. 407, 40 S.Ct. 289, 291, 64 L.Ed. 333.

The findings of fact and conclusions of law which must be in writing and filed with the clerk. Wilcox v. Sway, 69 Cal.App.2d 560, 160 P.2d 154, 156.

"Decision" is not necessarily synonymous with "opinion." A decision of the court is its judgment; the opinion is the reasons given for that judgment, or the expression of the views of the judge. But the two words are sometimes used interchangeably.

See also Decree; Final decision; Finding; Judgment; Opinion; Order; Verdict.

Decision on merits. A decision determining the validity of a written instrument or passing on a controversy with respect to the interpretation thereof which bars subsequent suit on same cause of action. Eulenberg v. Torley's Inc., 56 Cal.App.2d 653, 133 P.2d 15, 17.

Decisive, or decisory, oath. See **Oath.**

De clamea admittenda in itinere per attornatum /dìy kléymiyə ǽdmətèndə in aytínəriy pər ǽtərnéydəm/. See **Clamea admittenda,** etc.

Declarant. A person who makes a declaration.

Declaration. In common-law pleading, the first of the pleadings on the part of the plaintiff in an action at law, being a formal and methodical specification of the facts and circumstances constituting his cause or action. It commonly comprises several sections or divisions, called "counts", and its formal parts follow each other in this general order: Title, venue, commencement, cause of action, counts, conclusion. The declaration, at common law, answers to the "libel" in ecclesiastical and admiralty law, the "bill" in equity, the "petition" in civil law, the "complaint" in code and rule pleading, and the "count" in real actions. The term "complaint" is used in the federal courts and in all states that have adopted Rules of Civil Procedure.

In law of evidence, an unsworn statement or narration of facts made by party to the transaction, or by one who has an interest in the existence of the facts recounted. Also, similar statements made by a person since deceased, which are admissible in evidence in some cases, contrary to the general rule, e.g., "dying declarations" (q.v.). See also Declaration against interest, infra.

Listing by person entering United States of merchandise or other goods brought into country by him.

A document by the owner of property which is recorded in order to establish a legal order upon the property, such as a condominium (by a declaration of condominium or master deed), a system of cross-easements (by a declaration of easements) or a homeowners association (by declaration of covenants, restrictions and easements).

Declaration against interest. Such declarations are evidence of the fact declared, and are therefore distinct from admissions, which amount to a waiver of proof. They are statements which, when made, conflict with the pecuniary or proprietary interest of the person making them, or so far tend to subject him to civil or criminal liability, or to render invalid a claim by him against another, that a reasonable man in his position would not have made the statement unless he believed it to be true. Fed.Evid.R. 804(b)(3) excepts such statements from the hearsay rule.

Declaration in chief. A declaration for the principal cause of action.

Declaration of dividend. The act of a corporation in setting aside a portion of its net or surplus income for distribution among the stockholders according to their respective interests. First Nat. Bank & Trust Co. v. Glenn, D.C.Ky., 36 F.Supp. 552, 554. See also **Dividend.**

Declaration of homestead. Statement filed with proper state or local official or agency showing property ownership for purposes of securing homestead exemption rights. It is merely an act of the owner whereby he avails himself of, and secures, a right or privilege given him by statute; it is neither a conveyance nor a contract, and there is no transfer of, or change in, title, nor any agreement of transfer or change. U. S. Fidelity & Guaranty Co. v. Alloway, 173 Wash. 404, 23 P.2d 408. See also **Homestead.**

Declaration of Independence. A formal declaration or announcement, promulgated July 4, 1776, by the Congress of the United States of America, in the name and behalf of the people of the colonies, asserting and proclaiming their independence of the British crown, vindicating their pretensions to political autonomy, and announcing themselves to the world as a free and independent nation.

Declaration of intention. A declaration made by an alien, as a preliminary to naturalization, before a court of record, to the effect that it is his intention in good faith to become a citizen of the United States, and to renounce forever all allegiance and fidelity to any foreign prince, potentate, state, or sovereignty whereof at the time he may be a citizen or subject. 8 U.S.C.A. § 731.

Declaration of legitimacy. Formal pronouncement that a person is a legitimate child.

Declaration of pain. Exception to hearsay rule which permits testimony of out of court statement consisting of declarant's exclamation of present pain. Fed. Evid.R. 803(3).

Declaration of right. See **Bill of Rights.**

Declaration of state of mind. Exception to hearsay rule which permits testimony of out of court statement concerning person's state of mind, e.g. "I am sad". Fed.Evid.R. 803(3).

Declaration of trust. The act by which the person who holds the legal title to property or an estate acknowledges and declares that he holds the same in trust to the use of another person or for certain specified purposes. The name is also used to designate the deed or other writing embodying such a declaration.

Declaration of war. A public and formal proclamation by a nation, through its executive or legislative department, that a state of war exists between itself and another nation, and forbidding all persons to aid or assist the enemy.

An act of Congress is necessary to the commencement of a foreign war and is in itself a "declaration" and fixes the date of the war. Rosenau v. Idaho Mut. Ben. Ass'n, 65 Idaho 408, 145 P.2d 227, 230. See Art. I, Sec. 8, cl. 11, U.S. Const.

Dying declarations. Statements made by a person who is lying at the point of death, and is conscious of his approaching death, in reference to the manner in which he received the injuries of which he is dying, or other immediate cause of his death, and in reference to the person who inflicted such injuries or the connection with such injuries of a person who is charged or suspected of having committed them; which statements are admissible in evidence in a trial for homicide (and occasionally, at least in some jurisdictions, in other cases) where the killing of the declarant is the crime charged to the defendant. Shepard v. U. S., Kan., 290 U.S. 96, 54 S.Ct. 22, 78 L.Ed. 196.

Generally, the admissibility of such declarations is limited to use in prosecutions for homicide; but is admissible on behalf of accused as well as for prosecution.

In a prosecution for homicide or in a civil action or proceeding, a statement made by a declarant while believing that his death was imminent, concerning the cause or circumstances of what he believed to be his impending death is not excluded by the hearsay rule. Fed.Evid.R. 804(b)(2).

Self-serving declaration. One made by a party in his own interest at some time and place out of court; not including testimony which he gives as witness at the trial.

Declaration date. The day on which directors of a corporation declare a dividend as contrasted with date on which the dividend is actually paid.

Declaration of estimated tax. A procedure whereby non-wage earner individuals and corporations are required to file declarations of estimated tax and make periodic installment payments of such. Such requirements assure current collection of taxes from taxpayers whose incomes are not taxed by means of payroll withholdings. I.R.C. §§ 6015, 6154.

Declaration of Paris. The name given to an agreement announcing four important rules of international law effected between the principal European powers at the Congress of Paris in 1856. These rules are: (1) Privateering is and remains abolished; (2) the neutral flag covers enemy's goods, except contraband of war; (3) neutral goods, except contraband of war, are not liable to confiscation under a hostile flag; (4) blockades, to be binding, must be effective.

Declaration of Taking Act. Federal law governing taking of private property for public use under eminent domain. 40 U.S.C.A. §§ 58a–258e; U. S. v. Miller, 317 U.S. 369, 63 S.Ct. 276, 87 L.Ed. 336.

Declarator of trust. A common law action resorted to against a trustee who holds property upon titles *ex facie* for his own benefit.

Declaratory. Explanatory; designed to fix or elucidate what before was uncertain or doubtful.

Declaratory action. See **Declaratory judgment**.

Declaratory judgment. Statutory (see **Declaratory Judgment Act**) remedy for the determination of a justiciable controversy where the plaintiff is in doubt as to his legal rights. A binding adjudication of the rights and status of litigants even though no consequential relief is awarded. Brimmer v. Thomson,

Wyo., 521 P.2d 574, 579. Such judgment is conclusive in a subsequent action between the parties as to the matters declared and, in accordance with the usual rules of issue preclusion, as to any issues actually litigated and determined. Seaboard Coast Line R. Co. v. Gulf Oil Corp., C.A.Fla., 409 F.2d 879.

Declaratory Judgment Act. Federal statute enacted in 1934, 28 U.S.C.A. § 2201, which permits bringing of complaint for a declaration of rights if there is an actual controversy between the parties. The judgment is binding as to present and future rights of the parties to the action. See Fed.R.Civil P. 57. Most states have statutes of a like or similar nature; many of which are patterned on The Uniform Declaratory Judgments Act. See also **Declaratory judgment.**

Declaratory part of a law. That which clearly defines rights to be observed and wrongs to be eschewed.

Declaratory statute. One enacted for the purpose of removing doubts or putting an end to conflicting decisions in regard to what the law is in relation to a particular matter. It may either be expressive of the common law, 1 Bl.Comm. 86; In re Ungaro's Will, 88 N.J.Eq. 25, 102 A. 244, 246, or may declare what shall be taken to be the true meaning and intention of a previous statute, though in the latter case such enactments are more commonly called "expository statutes." McMahon v. Maddox, Tex.Civ.App., 297 S.W. 310, 312. A statute enacted to put an end to a doubt as to what is the common law, or the meaning of another statute, and which declares what it is and ever has been. Nelson v. Sandkamp, 227 Minn. 177, 34 N.W.2d 640, 642.

Declare. To make known, manifest, or clear. To signify, to show in any manner either by words or acts. To publish; to utter; to announce clearly some opinion or resolution. To solemnly assert a fact before witnesses, *e.g.*, where a testator *declares* a paper signed by him to be his last will and testament. See **Declaration.**

De claro die /dìy klérow dáy(iy)/. By daylight.

De clauso fracto /dìy klózow frǽktow/. Of close broken; of breach of close. See **Clausum fregit.**

De clerico admittendo /dìy kléhrəkow ǽdməténdow/. See **Admittendo clerico.**

De clerico capto per statutum mercatorium deliberando /dìy kléhrəkow kǽptow pàr stəchúwdəm màrkətóriyəm dəlìbərǽndow/. Writ for delivering a clerk arrested on a statute merchant. A writ for the delivery of a clerk out of prison, who had been taken and imprisoned upon the breach of a statute merchant.

De clerico convicto deliberando /dìy kléhrəkow kənvíktow dəlìbərǽndow/. See **Clerico convicto,** etc.

De clerico infra sacros ordines constituto non eligendo in officium /dìy kléhrəkow ínfrə sǽkrows órdəniyz kònstətyúwdow nòn èləjéndow ìn əfís(h)iyəm/. See **Clerico infra sacros,** etc.

De clero /dìy klírow/. Concerning the clergy. The title of the statute 25 Edw. III, St. 3; containing a variety of provisions on the subject of presentations, indictments of spiritual persons, and the like.

Declination. Document filed in court by a fiduciary who chooses not to serve in his named capacity. At common law, a plea to the courts' jurisdiction on the ground that the judge is personally interested in the suit.

Declinatoires /deyklìynatwárz/. In French law, pleas to the jurisdiction of the court; also of *lis pendens,* and of *connexité (q.v.).*

Declinatory exceptions /dəkláynətòriy əksépshəns/. Such dilatory exceptions as merely decline the jurisdiction of the judge before whom the action is brought. A plea to the jurisdiction *rationæ personæ.*

Declinatory plea /dəkláynətòriy plíy/. In English practice, the plea of sanctuary, or of benefit of clergy, before trial or conviction. 4 Bl.Comm. 333. Now abolished.

Decline. A failing process, a tendency to a worse state; to become gradually impaired; a falling off or downward tendency. Also, to refuse or reject.

Decoctor /dəkóktər/. In the Roman law, a bankrupt; a spendthrift; a squanderer of public funds.

Decollatio /dìykoléysh(iy)ow/. In old English and Scotch law, decollation; the punishment of beheading.

De combustione domorum /dìy kəmbàshchiyówniy dəmórəm/. Of house burning. One of the kinds of appeal formerly in use in England.

De communi dividundo /dìy kəmyúwnay dìvədándow/. For dividing a thing held in common. The name of an action given by the civil law.

De comon droit /də kómən dróyt/. L. Fr. Of common right; that is, by the common law.

Decomposed. A state of decomposition. A separation into components; specifically, decay or dissolution. In re Vetter, Cust. & Pat.App., 96 F.2d 999, 1000.

De computo /dìy kómpyədow/. Writ of account. A writ commanding a defendant to render a reasonable account to the plaintiff, or show cause to the contrary. The foundation of the modern action of account.

De concilio curiæ /dìy kənsíliyow kyúriyiy/. By the advice (or direction) of the court.

Deconfes. In French law, a name formerly given to those persons who died without confession, whether they refused to confess or whether they were criminals to whom the sacrament was refused.

De conflictu legum /dìy kənflíktow líygəm/. Concerning the conflict of laws. The title of several works written on that subject.

De conjunctim feoffatis /dìy kənjáŋktəm fìyféydəs/. Concerning persons jointly enfeoffed, or seised. The title of the statute 34 Edw. I, which was passed to prevent the delay occasioned by tenants in novel disseisin, and other writs, pleading that some one else was seised jointly with them.

De consanguineo, and **de consanguinitate** /dìy kònsæŋgwíniyow/dìy kònsæŋgwìnətéydiy/. Writs of cosinage (q.v.).

De consilio /dìy kənsíliyow/. In old criminal law, of counsel; concerning counsel or advice to commit a crime.

De consilio curiæ /dìy kənsiliyow kyúriyiy/. By the advice or direction of the court.

De continuando assisam /dìy kəntìnyuwǽndow əsáyzəm/. Writ to continue an assise.

De contumace capiendo /dìy kòntyəméysiy kæpiyéndow/. Writ for taking a contumacious person. A writ which issues out of the English court of chancery, in cases where a person has been pronounced by an ecclesiastical court to be contumacious, and in contempt. It is a commitment for contempt.

De copia libelli deliberanda /dìy kówpiyə ləbélay dəlìbərǽndə/. Writ for delivering the copy of a libel. An ancient writ directed to the judge of a spiritual court, commanding him to *deliver* to a defendant a *copy* of the libel filed against him in such court. The writ in the register was directed to the Dean of the Arches, and his commissary.

De coronatore eligendo /dìy kòrənatóriy èləjéndow/. Writ for electing a coroner. A writ issued to the sheriff in England, commanding him to proceed to the election of a coroner, which is done in full county court, the freeholders being the electors.

De coronatore exonerando /dìy kòrənatóriy əgzònərǽndow/. Writ for discharging or removing a coroner. A writ by which a coroner in England may be removed from office for some cause therein assigned. 1 Bl.Comm. 348.

De corpore comitatus /dìy kórpəriy kòmətéydəs/. From the body of the county at large, as distinguished from a particular neighborhood *(de vicineto).* 3 Bl.Comm. 360. Used with reference to the composition of a jury.

De corrodio habendo /dìy kərówdiyow həbéndow/. Writ for having a corody. A writ to exact a corody from a religious house. See **Corody.**

Decoy. To inveigle, entice, tempt, or lure; as, to decoy a person within the jurisdiction of a court so that he may be served with process, or to decoy a fugitive criminal to a place where he may be arrested without extradition papers, or to decoy one away from his place of residence for the purpose of kidnapping him and as a part of that act. In all these uses the word implies enticement or luring by means of some fraud, trick, or temptation, but excludes the idea of force.

Decoy letter. A letter prepared and mailed for the purpose of detecting a criminal, particularly one who is perpetrating frauds upon the postal or revenue laws.

Decree. The judgment of a court of equity or chancery, answering for most purposes to the judgment of a court of law. A decree in equity is a sentence or order of the court, pronounced on hearing and understanding all the points in issue, and determining the rights of all the parties to the suit, according to equity and good conscience. It is a declaration of the court announcing the legal consequences of the facts found. With the procedural merger of law and equity in the federal and most state courts under the Rules of Civil Procedure, the term "judgment" has generally replaced "decree". See Fed.R. Civil P. 54(a). See also **Decision; Judgment; Order.**

General Classification

Decrees in equity are either *final* or *interlocutory*. A final decree is one which fully and finally disposes of the whole litigation, determining all questions raised by the case, and leaving nothing that requires further judicial action. An interlocutory decree is a provisional or preliminary decree, which is not final and does not determine the suit, but directs some further proceedings preparatory to the final decree. It is a decree pronounced for the purpose of ascertaining matter of law or fact preparatory to a final decree. Where something more than the ministerial execution of the decree as rendered is left to be done, the decree is interlocutory, and not final, even though it settles the equities of the bill. Lodge v. Twell, 135 U.S. 232, 10 S.Ct. 745, 34 L.Ed. 153. The difficulty of exact definition is mentioned in McGourkey v. Ry. Co., 146 U.S. 536, 13 S.Ct. 170, 36 L.Ed. 1079.

Consent decree. Agreement by defendant to cease activities asserted as illegal by government (*e.g.* deceptive advertising practices as alleged by F.T.C.). Upon approval of such agreement by the court the government's action against the defendant is dropped. Also, a decree entered in an equity suit on consent of both parties; it is not properly a judicial sentence, but is in the nature of a solemn contract or agreement of the parties, made under the sanction of the court, and in effect an admission by them that the decree is a just determination of their rights upon the real facts of the case, if such facts had been proved. It binds only the consenting parties; and is not binding upon the court.

Decree nisi /dəkríy náysay/. A provisional decree, which will be made absolute on motion unless cause be shown against it. Interlocutory judgment or decree in divorce action. In English practice, it is the order made by the court for divorce, on satisfactory proof being given in support of a petition for dissolution of marriage; it remains imperfect for a certain period (which period may be shortened by the court), and then, unless sufficient cause be shown, it is made absolute on motion, and the dissolution takes effect, subject to appeal. It effects a conditional divorce, becoming absolute only upon the happening of a prescribed contingency.

Decree of distribution. An instrument by which heirs receive property of a deceased; it is a final determination of the parties to a proceeding.

Decree of insolvency. One entered in a probate court, declaring the estate in question to be insolvent, that is, that the assets are not sufficient to pay the debts in full.

Decree of nullity. One entered in a suit for the annulment of a marriage, and adjudging the marriage to have been null and void *ab initio.* See **Nullity.**

Decree pro confesso. One entered in a court of equity in favor of the complainant where the defend-

ant has made no answer to the bill and its allegations are consequently taken "as confessed." It is merely an admission of the allegations of the bill well pleaded.

Deficiency decree. In a mortgage foreclosure suit, a decree for the balance of the indebtedness after applying the proceeds of a sale of the mortgaged property to such indebtedness.

For "Execution of decree," see **Execution.**

Decreet absolvitor /dəkríyd əbzólvədər/. A decree dismissing a claim, or acquitting a defendant.

Decreet arbitral /dəkríyd árbətrəl/. An award of arbitrators.

Decreet cognitionis causâ /dəkríyt kognìshiyównəs kózə/. When a creditor brings his action against the heir of his debtor in order to constitute the debt against him and attach the lands, and the heir appears and renounces the succession, the court then pronounces a decree *cognitionis causâ.*

Decreet condemnator /dəkríyt kòndəmnéydər/. One where the decision is in favor of the plaintiff.

Decreet of valuation of teinds /dəkríyd əv vǽl-yuwéyshən əv tíyndz/. A sentence of the court of sessions (who are now in the place of the commissioners for the valuation of teinds), determining the extent and value of teinds.

Decrementum maris /dèkrəméntəm mǽrəs/. Lat. In old English law, decrease of the sea; the receding of the sea from the land. See **Reliction.**

Decrepit /dəkrépət/. This term designates a person who is disabled, incapable, or incompetent, either from physical or mental weakness or defects, whether produced by age or other causes, to such an extent as to render the individual comparatively helpless in a personal conflict with one possessed of ordinary health and strength. Lutz v. State, 147 Tex.Cr.R. 236, 179 S.W.2d 979, 980. The term includes a blind man. Lewing v. State, 135 Tex.Cr.R. 485, 121 S.W.2d 599, 600.

Decreta /dəkríydə/. In the Roman law, judicial sentences given by the emperor as supreme judge.

Decreta conciliorum non ligant reges nostros /dəkríydə kənsìliyórəm nòn lígənt ríyjiyz nóstrows/. The decrees of councils bind not our kings.

Decretal /dəkríydəl/. The granting or denying of remedy sought. State v. Reagan County Purchasing Co., Tex.Civ.App., 186 S.W.2d 128, 134.

Decretal order /dəkríydəl órdər/. A preliminary order that determines no question upon the merits and establishes no right.

Decretals /dəkríydəlz/. In ecclesiastical law, letters of the pope, written at the suit or instance of one or more persons, determining some point or question in ecclesiastical law, and possessing the force of law, within the Roman Catholic Church. The decretals form the second part of the body of canon law.

This is also the title of the second of the two great divisions of the canon law, the first being called the "Decree" (decretum).

Decreto /deykréytow/. In Spanish colonial law, an order emanating from some superior tribunal, promulgated in the name and by the authority of the sovereign, in relation to ecclesiastical matters.

Decretum /dəkríydəm/. In the civil law, a species of imperial constitution, being a judgment or sentence given by the emperor upon hearing of a cause *(quod imperator cognoscens decrevit)*.

In canon law, an ecclesiastical law, in contradistinction to a secular law *(lex)*.

Decretum gratiani /dəkríydəm grèyshiyéynay/. Gratian's decree, or *decretum*. A collection of ecclesiastical law in three books or parts, made in the year 1151, by Gratian, a Benedictine monk of Bologna, being the oldest as well as the first in order of the collections which together form the body of the Roman canon law. 1 Bl.Comm. 82.

Decriminalization. An official act generally accomplished by legislation, in which an act or omission, formerly criminal, is made non-criminal and without punitive sanctions.

Decrowning. The act of depriving of a crown.

Decry. To cry down; to deprive of credit; to deprecate, disparage or belittle. "The king may at any time *decry* or cry down any coin of the kingdom, and make it no longer current." 1 Bl.Comm. 278.

De cujus /dìy kyúwjəs/. Lat. From whom. A term used to designate the person by, through, from, or under whom another claims.

De curia claudenda /dìy kyúriyə klodéndə/. An obsolete writ, to require a defendant to fence in his court or land about his house, where it was left open to the injury of his neighbor's freehold.

Decurio /dəkyúriyow/. Lat. A decurion. In the provincial administration of the Roman empire, the decurions were the chief men or official personages of the large towns. Taken as a body, the decurions of a city were charged with the entire control and administration of its internal affairs; having powers both magisterial and legislative.

De cursu /dìy kə́rsyuw/. Of course. The usual, necessary, and formal proceedings in an action are said to be *de cursu;* as distinguished from *summary* proceedings, or such as are incidental and may be taken on summons or motion. Writs *de cursu* are such as are issued of course, as distinguished from prerogative writs.

De custode admittendo /dìy kəstówdiy æ̀dməténdow/. Writ for admitting a guardian.

De custode amovendo /dìy kəstówdiy èyməvéndow/. Writ for removing a guardian.

De custodia terræ et hæredis /dìy kəstówdiyə téhriy èt həríydəs/. Writ of ward, or writ of right of ward. A writ which lay for a guardian in knight's service or in socage, to recover the possession and custody of the infant, or the *wardship of the land and heir.* 3 Bl. Comm. 141.

Dedbana /dédbeynə/. In Saxon law, an actual homicide or manslaughter.

De debito /dìy débədow/. A writ of debt.

De debitore in partes secando /dìy debətóriy ìn pártiyz səkǽndow/. In Roman law; "Of cutting a debtor in pieces." This was the name of a law contained in the Twelve Tables, the meaning of which has occasioned much controversy. Some commentators have concluded that it was literally the privilege of the creditors of an insolvent debtor (all other means failing) to cut his body into pieces and distribute it among them. Others contend that the language of this law must be taken figuratively, denoting a cutting up and apportionment of the debtor's *estate*.

De deceptione /dìy dəsèpshiyówniy/. A writ of deceit which lay against one who acted in the name of another whereby the latter was damnified and deceived.

De deoneranda pro rata portionis /dìy diyòwnərǽndə pròw réydə pòrshiyównəs/. Writ that lay where one was distrained for rent that ought to be paid by others proportionably with him.

Dedi /díyday/. (Lat. I have given.) A word used in deeds and other instruments of conveyance when such instruments were made in Latin, and anciently held to imply a warranty of title.

Dedicate. To appropriate and set apart one's private property to some public use; as to make a private way public by acts evincing an intention to do so.

Dedication. The appropriation of land, or an easement therein, by the owner, for the use of the public, and accepted for such use by or on behalf of the public. Such dedication may be express where the appropriation is formally declared, or by implication arising by operation of law from the owner's conduct and the facts and circumstances of the case. Varallo v. Metropolitan Government of Nashville and Davidson County, Tenn.App., 508 S.W.2d 342, 346. A deliberate appropriation of land by its owner for any general and public uses, reserving to himself no other rights than such as are compatible with the full exercise and enjoyment of the public uses to which the property has been devoted. Longley v. City of Worcester, 304 Mass. 580, 24 N.E.2d 533, 537; Consolidated Realty Co. v. Richmond Hotel & Building Co., 253 Ky. 463, 69 S.W.2d 985.

See also **Dedication and reservation,** below.

By adverse user. A dedication may arise from an adverse exclusive use by the public under a claim of right with the knowledge, actual or imputed, and acquiescence of the owner.

Common-law or statutory. A common-law dedication is one made as above described, and may be either express or implied. A statutory dedication is one made under and in conformity with the provisions of a statute regulating the subject, and is of course necessarily express. An "express common-law dedication" is one where the intent is expressly manifested, such as by ordinary deeds, recorded plats not executed pursuant to statute or defectively certified so as not to constitute a statutory dedication. Board of Com'rs of Garfield County v. Anderson, 167 Okl. 253, 29 P.2d 75, 78.

Copyright law. The first publication of a work, without having secured a copyright, is a dedication of it to the public; that having been done, any one may republish it. Deward & Rich v. Bristol Savings & Loan Corporation, C.C.A.Va., 120 F.2d 537, 540 (partial publication).

Express or implied. A dedication may be express, as where the intention to dedicate is expressly manifested by a deed or an explicit oral or written declaration of the owner, or some other explicit manifestation of his purpose to devote the land to the public use. An implied dedication may be shown by some act or course of conduct on the part of the owner from which a reasonable inference of intent may be drawn, or which is inconsistent with any other theory than that he intended a dedication.

Dedication and reservation. The dedicator may impose reasonable conditions, restrictions and limitations, and compliance therewith is essential unless waived. Dedicator may reserve a new right in himself by way of implied grant and may include rights personal or rights appurtenant to the land. At common law, a reservation in a dedication is not perpetual.

Dedication-day. The feast of dedication of churches, or rather the feast day of the saint and patron of a church, which was celebrated not only by the inhabitants of the place, but by those of all the neighboring villages, who usually came there; and such assemblies were allowed as lawful. It was usual for the people to feast and to drink on those days.

De die in diem /dìy dáyiy in dáyəm/. From day to day.

Dedi et concessi /díyday èt kənsésay/. I have given and granted. The operative words of conveyance in ancient charters of feoffment, and deeds of gift and grant; the English *"given and granted"* being still the most proper, though not the essential, words by which such conveyances are made. 2 Bl.Comm. 53, 316, 317.

Dedimus et concessimus /dédəməs èt kənsésəməs/. (Lat. We have given and granted.) Words used by the king, or where there were more grantors than one, instead of *dedi et concessi.*

Dedimus potestatem /dédəməs pòwdəstéydəm/. (We have given power.) In old English practice, a writ or commission issuing out of chancery, empowering the persons named therein to perform certain acts, as to administer oaths to defendants in chancery and take their answers, to administer oaths of office to justices of the peace, etc. 3 Bl.Comm. 447. It was anciently allowed for many purposes not now in use, as to make an attorney, to take the acknowledgment of a fine, etc.

In the United States, a commission to take testimony was sometimes termed a *"dedimus potestatem."*

Dedimus potestatem de attorno faciendo /dédəməs pòwdəstéydəm dìy ətárnow fèys(h)iyéndow/. In old English practice, a writ, issued by royal authority, empowering an attorney to appear for a defendant. Prior to the statute of Westminster 2, a party could not appear in court by attorney without this writ.

Dedition /dədíshən/. The act of yielding up anything; surrender.

Dedititii /dìydəshíshiyay/. In Roman law, criminals who had been marked in the face or on the body with fire or an iron, so that the mark could not be erased, and subsequently manumitted.

De diversis regulis juris antiqui /dìy dəvársəs régyələs júrəs æntáykway/. Of divers rules of the ancient law. A celebrated title of the Digests, and the last in that collection. It consists of two hundred and eleven rules or maxims.

De dolo malo /dìy dówlo mǽlow/. Of or founded upon fraud. See **Actio de dolo malo.**

De domo reparanda /dìy dówmow rèpərǽndə/. A writ which lay for one tenant in common to compel his cotenant to contribute towards the repair of the common property.

De donis /dìy dównəs/. Concerning gifts (or more fully, *de donis conditionalibus,* concerning conditional gifts). The name of a celebrated English statute, passed in the thirteenth year of Edw. I, and constituting the first chapter of the statute of Westm. 2, by virtue of which estates in fee-simple conditional (formerly known as *"dona conditionalia"*) were converted into estates in fee-tail and rendered inalienable, thereby strengthening the power of the nobles. 2 Bl.Comm. 112.

De dote assignanda /dìy dówdiy æsəgnǽndə/. Writ for assigning dower. A writ which lay for the widow of a tenant *in capite,* commanding the king's escheater to cause her dower to be assigned to her.

De dote unde nihil habet /dìy dówdiy ándiy náyəl héybət/. A writ of dower which lay for a widow where no part of her dower had been assigned to her. It is not much used; but a form closely resembling it was sometimes used in the United States.

Deductible. That which may be taken away or subtracted. An item which may be subtracted from income for tax purposes, such as a deductible debt, In re Hermann's Estate, 349 Pa. 230, 36 A.2d 804, 806; a deductible expense, Pacific Southwest Realty Co. v. McColgan, 53 Cal.App.2d 549, 128 P.2d 86, 87; or, a deductible loss, Helvering v. Gordon, C.C.A.4, 134 F.2d 685, 689; Bickerstaff v. Commissioner of Internal Revenue, C.C.A.Ga., 128 F.2d 366, 367. See also **Deduction.**

The portion of an insured loss to be borne by the insured before he is entitled to recovery from the insurer. See **Deductible clause.**

Deductible clause. Clause in insurance policy providing that insured will absorb first part of loss (*e.g.* first $100) with insurer paying the excess.

Deduction. That which is deducted; the part taken away; abatement; as deductions from gross income in arriving at net income for tax purposes.

In the civil law, a portion or thing which an heir has a right to take from the mass of the succession before any partition takes place. Civil Code La. art. 1358.

See also **Charitable deduction; Orphan's deduction.**

Itemized deductions. Those expenses which are allowed as deductions from adjusted gross income, itemized in detail under their appropriate captions, and subtracted to arrive at income subject to tax. I.R.C. §§ 161–188.

Standard deduction. An option allowed taxpayers by which they can deduct a certain percentage from adjusted gross income instead of itemizing their expenses (deductions). I.R.C. § 144(a).

Deduction for new. In marine insurance, an allowance or drawback credited to the insurers on the cost of repairing a vessel for damage arising from the perils of the sea insured against. This allowance is usually one-third, and is made on the theory that the parts restored with new materials are better in that proportion than they were before the damage.

Deductions in respect of a decedent. Deductions accrued to the point of death but not recognizable on the final income tax return of a decedent because of the method of accounting used. Such items are allowed as deductions on the death tax return and on the income tax return of the estate or the heir. An example of a deduction in respect of a decedent would be interest expense accrued up to the date of death by a cash basis debtor.

Deed. A conveyance of realty; a writing signed by grantor, whereby title to realty is transferred from one to another. National Fire Ins. Co. v. Patterson, 170 Okl. 593, 41 P.2d 645, 647. A written instrument, signed, and delivered, by which one person conveys land, tenements, or hereditaments to another.

At common law, a *sealed* instrument, containing a contract or covenant, delivered by the party to be bound thereby, and accepted by the party to whom the contract or covenant runs. 2 Bl.Comm. 295. A writing under seal by which lands, tenements, or hereditaments are conveyed for an estate not less than freehold. 2 Bl.Comm. 294. It is no longer necessary that the instrument be sealed.

See also Ancient deed; Bargain and sale deed; Contract for deed; Quitclaim deed; Sheriff's deed; Special warranty deed; Tax deed; Trust (*Trust deed*); Warranty deed.

Deed absolute. Deed which conveys absolute title as contrasted with mortgage deed which is defeasible on fulfillment of mortgage conditions.

Deed for a nominal sum. In effect the same as a deed of gift. Bertelsen v. Bertelson, 49 Cal.App.2d 479, 122 P.2d 130, 133.

Deed indented, or indenture. In common-law conveyancing, a deed executed or purporting to be executed in parts, between two or more parties, and distinguished by having the edge of the paper or parchment on which it is written indented or cut at the top in a particular manner. This was formerly done at the top or side, in a line resembling the teeth of a saw; a formality derived from the ancient practice of dividing chirographs; but the cutting is now made either in a waving line, or more commonly by notching or nicking the paper at the edge. 2 Bl. Comm. 295, 296.

Deed in fee. A deed conveying the title to land in fee simple with the usual covenants.

Deed of covenant. Covenants are sometimes entered into by a separate deed, for title, or for the indemnity of a purchaser or mortgagee, or for the production of title-deeds. A covenant with a penalty is sometimes taken for the payment of a debt, instead of a bond with a condition, but the legal remedy is the same in either case.

Deed of distribution. Deed of fiduciary by which real estate of decedent is conveyed.

Deed of gift. A deed executed and delivered without consideration.

Thus a conveyance to church mission board for which board agreed to educate a relative of grantors for the ministry should grantors die before his education was completed, was not a strict "deed of gift". Forbes v. Board of Missions of M. E. Church, South, 17 Cal.2d 332, 110 P.2d 3, 7.

Deed of release. One releasing property from the incumbrance of a mortgage or similar pledge upon payment or performance of the conditions. More specifically, where a deed of trust to one or more trustees has been executed, pledging real property for the payment of a debt or the performance of other conditions, substantially as in the case of a mortgage, a deed of release is the conveyance executed by the trustees, after payment or performance, for the purpose of divesting themselves of the legal title and revesting it in the original owner.

Deed of separation. An instrument by which, through the medium of some third person acting as trustee, provision is made by a husband for separation from his wife and for her separate maintenance.

Deed of settlement. A deed formerly used in England for the formation of joint stock companies constituting certain persons trustees of the partnership property and containing regulations for the management of its private affairs. They are now regulated by articles of association.

Deed of trust. An instrument in use in some states, taking the place and serving the uses of a mortgage, by which the legal title to real property is placed in one or more trustees, to secure the repayment of a sum of money or the performance of other conditions. Though differing in form from mortgage, it is essentially a security. In re Title Guaranty Trust Co., Mo.App., 113 S.W.2d 1053, 1057. See also **Mortgage; Potomac mortgages; Trust** (*Trust deed*).

Deed poll. A deed which is made by one party only. A deed in which only the party making it executes it or binds himself by it as a deed. It was originally so called because the edge of the paper or parchment was *polled* or cut in a straight line, wherein it was distinguished from a deed indented or indenture. As to a special use of this term in Pennsylvania in colonial times, see Herron v. Dater, 120 U.S. 464, 7 S.Ct. 620, 624, 30 L.Ed. 748 (citing Evans v. Patterson, 71 U.S. 224, 4 Wall. 224, 18 L.Ed. 393).

Deed to lead uses. A common law deed made before a fine or common recovery, to show the object thereof.

Defeasible deed. A deed containing a condition subsequent the happening of which will cause title to the property to revert to the grantor or to go to some third party.

Gratuitous deed. One made without consideration. See *Deed of gift.*

Deed, estoppel by. "Estoppel by deed" is a bar which precludes one party to a deed and his privies from asserting as against the other party and his privies any right or title in derogation of the deed or from denying the truth of any material facts asserted in it. Denny v. Wilson County, 198 Tenn. 677, 281 S.W.2d 671, 675. Such estoppel precludes a party from denying a certain fact recited in deed executed or accepted by him in an action brought on the deed by party who would be detrimentally affected by such denial. Cleveland Boat Service v. City of Cleveland, 102 Ohio App. 255, 130 N.E.2d 421, 425.

De ejectione custodiæ /dìy əjèkshiyówniy kəstówdiyiy/. A writ which lay for a guardian who had been forcibly ejected from his wardship.

De ejectione firmæ /dìy əjèkshiyówniy fármiy/. A writ which lay at the suit of the tenant for years against the lessor, reversioner, remainderman, or stranger who had himself deprived the tenant of the occupation of the land during his term. 3 Bl.Comm. 199. By a gradual extension of the scope of this form of action its object was made to include not only damages for the unlawful detainer, but also the possession for the remainder of the term, and eventually the possession of land generally. And, as it turned on the right of possession, this involved a determination of the right of property, or the title, and thus arose the modern action of ejectment.

Deem. To hold; consider; adjudge; believe; condemn; determine; treat as if; construe.

Deemed transferor. The person holding an interest in a trust the expiration of which will lead to the imposition of a generation-skipping tax. Assume, for example, GF creates a trust, income payable to S (GF's son) for life and, upon S's death, remainder to GS (GF's grandson). Upon S's death, he will be the "deemed transferor" and the trust will be included in his gross estate for purposes of determining the generation-skipping transfer tax. I.R.S. § 2612. See **Generation-skipping trust.**

Deep Rock doctrine. Insider claims to corporate assets are sometimes subordinated to other obligations during reorganization or liquidation as a matter of equity. S.E.C. v. S & P Nat. Corp., 360 F.2d 741.

De escæta /dìy əschíydə/. Writ of escheat. A writ which a lord had, where his tenant died without heir, to recover the land.

De escambio monetæ /dìy əskæmbiyow məníydiy/. A writ of exchange of money. An ancient writ to authorize a merchant to make a bill of exchange (*literas cambitorias facere*).

De essendo quietum de tolonio /dìy əséndow kwayíydəm dìy təlówniyow/. A writ which lay for those who were by privilege free from the payment of toll, on their being molested therein.

De essonio de malo lecti /dìy əsówniyow dìy mǽlow léktay/. A writ which issued upon an essoin of *malum lecti* being cast, to examine whether the party was in fact sick or not.

De estoveriis habendis /dìy èstəvíriyəs həbéndəs/. Writ for having estovers. A writ which lay for a wife divorced *a mensa et thoro*, to recover her alimony or estovers. 1 Bl.Comm. 441.

De estrepamento /dìy əstrèpəméntow/. A writ which lay to prevent or stay waste by a tenant, during the pendency of a suit against him to recover the lands.

De eu et trene /də yúw èy tréyn/. L. Fr. Of water and whip of three cords. A term applied to a neife, that is, a bond woman or female villein, as employed in servile work, and subject to corporal punishment.

De eve et de treve /də év èy də trév/. A law French phrase, equivalent to the Latin *de avo et de tritavo*, descriptive of the ancestral rights of lords in their villeins. Literally, "from grandfather and from great-grandfather's great-grandfather." It occurs in the Year Books.

De excommunicato capiendo /dìy èkskəmyùwnəkéydow kæpiyéndow/. A writ commanding the sheriff to arrest one who was excommunicated, and imprison him till he should become reconciled to the church. 3 Bl.Comm. 102.

De excommunicato deliberando /dìy èkskəmyùwnəkéydow dəlìbərǽndow/. A writ to deliver an excommunicated person, who had made satisfaction to the church, from prison. 3 Bl.Comm. 102.

De excommunicato recapiendo /dìy èkskəmyùwnəkéydow rəkæpiyéndow/. Writ for retaking an excommunicated person, where he had been liberated from prison without making satisfaction to the church, or giving security for that purpose.

De excusationibus /dìy əkskyùwzèyshiyównəbəs/. "Concerning excuses." This is the title of book 27 of the Pandects (in the *Corpus Juris Civilis*). It treats of the circumstances which excuse one from filling the office of tutor or curator. The bulk of the extracts are from Modestinus.

De executione facienda in withernamium /dìy èksəkyùwshiyówiy fæs(h)iyéndə ìn wìðərnéymiyəm/. Writ for making execution in withernam. A species of *capias in withernam*.

De executione judicii /dìy eksəkyùwshiyówniy juwdíshiyay/. A writ directed to a sheriff or bailiff, commanding him to do execution upon a judgment.

De exemplificatione /dìy əgzèmpləfəkèyshiyówniy/. Writ of exemplification. A writ granted for the exemplification of an original.

De exoneratione sectæ /dìy əgzònərèyshiyówniy séktiy/. Writ for exoneration of suit. A writ that lay for the king's ward to be discharged of all suit to the county court, hundred, leet, or court-baron, during the time of his wardship.

De expensis civium et burgensium /dìy əkspénsəs síviyəm ət bərjénsiyəm/. An obsolete writ addressed to the sheriff to levy the expenses of every citizen and burgess of parliament.

De expensis militum levandis /dìy əkspénsəs mílədəm ləvǽndəs/. Writ for levying the expenses of knights. A writ directed to the sheriff for levying the allowance for knights of the shire in parliament.

Deface. To mar or destroy the face (that is, the physical appearance of written or inscribed characters as expressive of a definite meaning) of a written instrument, signature, inscription, etc., by obliteration, erasure, cancellation, or superinscription, so as to render it illegible or unrecognizable. To mar, injure or spoil. State v. Kasnett, 30 Ohio App.2d 77, 283 N.E.2d 636, 638. See **Cancel; Mar; Mutilation; Obliteration.**

Also used in respect of injury to monument, buildings and other structures. So, to deface the flag carries the meaning of dishonor, which imputes a lively sense of shaming or an equivalent acquiescent callousness. State v. Schlueter, 127 N.J.L. 496, 23 A.2d 249, 251. See also **Defile; Desecrate.**

De facto /diy fǽktow/. In fact, in deed, actually. This phrase is used to characterize an officer, a government, a past action, or a state of affairs which must be accepted for all practical purposes, but is illegal or illegitimate. Thus, an office, position or status existing under a claim or color of right such as a de facto corporation. In this sense it is the contrary of *de jure,* which means rightful, legitimate, just, or constitutional. Thus, an officer, king, or government *de facto* is one who is in actual possession of the office or supreme power, but by usurpation, or without lawful title; while an officer, king, or governor *de jure* is one who has just claim and rightful title to the office or power, but has never had plenary possession of it, or is not in actual possession. MacLeod v. United States, 229 U.S. 416, 33 S.Ct. 955, 57 L.Ed. 1260. A wife *de facto* is one whose marriage is voidable by decree, as distinguished from a wife *de jure,* or lawful wife. But the term is also frequently used independently of any distinction from *de jure;* thus a blockade *de facto* is a blockade which is actually maintained, as distinguished from a mere paper blockade. *Compare* **De jure.**

As to *de facto* Corporation; Court; Domicile; Government, and Officer, see those titles.

In old English law it means respecting or concerning the principal act of a murder, which was technically denominated *factum.*

De facto adoption. An agreement to adopt according to statutory procedures in a given state which will ripen into de jure adoption when the petition is properly presented. In The Matter of The Estate of Schultz, 220 Or. 350, 348 P.2d 22. An equitable adoption *(q.v.).*

De facto contract /diy fǽktow kóntrækt/. One which has purported to pass the property from the owner to another but is defective in some element.

De facto court. See **Court.**

De facto government. One that maintains itself by a display of force against the will of the rightful legal government and is successful, at least temporarily, in overturning the institutions of the rightful legal government by setting up its own in lieu thereof. Wortham v. Walker, 133 Tex. 255, 128 S.W.2d 1138, 1145.

De facto judge. A judge who functions under color of authority but whose authority is defective in some procedural form. Riley v. Bradley, 252 Ala. 282, 41 So.2d 641.

De facto marriage. A marriage in which the parties live together as husband and wife under color of validity but which is defective for reasons of form, etc.

De facto officer. One who, while in actual possession of the office, is not holding such in a manner prescribed by law. Trost v. Tynatishon, 12 Ill.App.3d 406, 299 N.E.2d 14.

De facto segregation. Segregation which is inadvertent and without assistance of school authorities and not caused by any state action but rather by social, economic and other determinates. DeFunis v. Odegaard, 82 Wash.2d 11, 507 P.2d 1169.

De faire échelle /də fér eyshél/. In French law, a clause commonly inserted in policies of marine insurance, equivalent to a license to touch and trade at intermediate ports.

Defalcation /diyfolkéyshən/. The act of a defaulter; act of embezzling; failure to meet an obligation; misappropriation of trust funds or money held in any fiduciary capacity; failure to properly account for such funds. Commonly spoken of officers of corporations or public officials.

Also set-off, recoupment or counterclaim. The diminution of a debt or claim by deducting from it a smaller claim held by the debtor or payor. See **Defalk.**

Defalk. To set off one claim against another; to deduct a debt due to one from a debt which one owes. This verb corresponds only to the second meaning of "defalcation" as given above; *i.e.* a public officer or trustee who misappropriates or embezzles funds in his hands is *not* said to "defalk."

De falso judicio /diy fólsow juwdíshiyow/. Writ of false judgment.

De falso moneta /diy fólsow məníydə/. Of false money. The title of the English statute 27 Edw. I, ordaining that persons importing certain coins, called "pollards," and "crokards," should forfeit their lives and goods, and everything they could forfeit.

Defamacast /dəféyməkæst/. Defamation by broadcast. American Broadcasting-Paramount Theatres, Inc. v. Simpson, 106 Ga.App. 230, 126 S.E.2d 873, 879.

Defamation. Holding up of a person to ridicule, scorn or contempt in a respectable and considerable part of the community; may be criminal as well as civil. Includes both libel and slander.

Defamation is that which tends to injure reputation; to diminish the esteem, respect, goodwill or confidence in which the plaintiff is held, or to excite adverse, derogatory or unpleasant feelings or opinions against him. Statement which exposes person to contempt, hatred, ridicule or obloquy. McGowen v. Prentice, La.App., 341 So.2d 55, 57. The unprivileged publication of false statements which naturally and proximately result in injury to another. Wolfson v. Kirk, Fla.App., 273 So.2d 774, 776.

A communication is defamatory if it tends so to harm the reputation of another as to lower him in the estimation of the community or to deter third persons from associating or dealing with him. The meaning of a communication is that which the recipient correctly, or mistakenly but reasonably, understands that it was intended to express. Restatement, Second, Torts §§ 559, 563.

See also **Actionable per quod; Actionable per se; Journalist's privilege; Libel; Slander**.

Defamatory. Calumnious; containing defamation; injurious to reputation; libelous; slanderous. See **Defamation**.

Defamatory libel. Written, permanent form of defamation as contrasted with slander which is oral defamation. See **Libel**.

Defamatory per quod /dəfǽmətòriy pàr kwód/. In respect of words, those which require an allegation of facts, aside from the words contained in the publication, by way of innuendo, to show wherein the words used libel the plaintiff. See **Actionable per quod**.

Defamatory per se /dəfǽmətòriy pàr síy/. In respect of words, those which by themselves, and as such, without reference to extrinsic proof, injure the reputation of the person to whom they are applied. Conrad v. Allis-Chalmers Mfg. Co., 228 Mo.App. 817, 73 S.W.2d 438, 446. See **Actionable per se**.

Defames /dəféymiyz/. L. Fr. Infamous.

Default. By its derivation, a failure. Meadows v. Continental Assur. Co., C.C.A.Tex., 89 F.2d 256. An omission of that which ought to be done. Town of Milton v. Bruso, 111 Vt. 82, 10 A.2d 203, 205. Specifically, the omission or failure to perform a legal or contractual duty, Easterwood v. Willingham, Tex.Civ. App., 47 S.W.2d 393, 395; to observe a promise or discharge an obligation (*e.g.* to pay interest or principal on a debt when due), Bradbury v. Thomas, 135 Cal.App. 435, 27 P.2d 402; or to perform an agreement, Eastman v. Morgan, D.C.N.Y., 43 F.Supp. 637, 641. The term also embraces the idea of dishonesty, and of wrongful act, Greco v. S. S. Kresge Co., 277 N.Y. 26, 12 N.E.2d 557, 562; or an act of omission discreditable to one's profession, Hilkert v. Canning, 58 Ariz. 290, 119 P.2d 233, 236.

Under the U.C.C. "default" is left undefined, §§ 9–501–507, though it is precisely what the parties agree that it is. Borochoff Properties, Inc. v. Howard Lumber Co., 115 Ga.App. 691, 155 S.E.2d 651.

Default-judgment. Under Rules of Civil Procedure, when a party against whom a judgment for affirmative relief is sought has failed to plead (*i.e.* answer) or otherwise defend, he is in default and a judgment by default may be entered either by the clerk or the court. Rule 55. See also **Judgment**.

Defaulter. One who is in default. One who misappropriates money held by him in an official or fiduciary character, or fails to account for such money.

Defeasance /dəfíyzən(t)s/. An instrument which defeats the force or operation of some other deed or estate. A collateral deed made at the same time with a feoffment or other conveyance, containing certain conditions, upon the performance of which the estate then created may be *defeated* or totally undone. 2 Bl.Comm. 327.

An instrument accompanying a bond, recognizance, or judgment, containing a condition which, when per-

formed, defeats it. See also **Defeasance clause; Defeasible**.

Defeasance clause. That provision in a mortgage which assures the revesting of title in the mortgagor when all the terms and conditions of the mortgage have been met. A clause which permits the mortgagor-borrower to defeat the temporary and conditional conveyance by discharging the debt and thus causing a release of any interests in the real estate.

Defeasible. Subject to be defeated, annulled, revoked, or undone upon the happening of a future event or the performance of a condition subsequent, or by a conditional limitation. Usually spoken of estates and interests in land. For instance, a mortgagee's estate is defeasible (liable to be defeated) by the mortgagor's equity of redemption.

Defeasible fee. An estate in fee that is liable to be defeated by some future contingency; *e.g.,* a vested remainder which might be defeated by the death of the remainderman before the time fixed for the taking effect of the devise. Giltner's Trustee v. Talbott, 253 Ky. 474, 69 S.W.2d 981.

Defeasible title. One that is liable to be annulled or made void, but not one that is already void or an absolute nullity.

Defeasibly vested remainder. Gift over to remainderman which, though not subject to condition precedent as in the case of a contingent remainder, is subject to divestment on the happening of a condition subsequent.

Defeasive. Describes counterclaim which, if it prevails, will defeat right of plaintiffs to recover. Hayden v. Collins, 90 Utah 238, 63 P.2d 223, 225.

Defeat. To prevent, frustrate, or circumvent; as in the phrase "hinder, delay, or defeat creditors." To overcome or prevail against in any contest; as in speaking of the "defeated party" in an action at law, or "defeated candidate" in an election. Norcop v. Jordan, 216 Cal. 764, 17 P.2d 123, 124.

To annul, undo, or terminate; as, a title or estate. See **Defeasible**.

Defect. The want or absence of some legal requisite; deficiency; imperfection; insufficiency. Galloway v. City of Winchester, 299 Ky. 87, 184 S.W.2d 890, 892, 893. The want or absence of something necessary for completeness or perfection; a lack or absence of something essential to completeness; a deficiency in something essential to the proper use for the purpose for which a thing is to be used. See also **Apparent defects; Defective; Hidden defect; Latent defect**.

Fatal defect. Of such serious nature as to nullify contract.

Latent defect. One which is not apparent to buyer by reasonable observation.

Patent defect. One which is apparent to buyer on normal observation.

Defect in highway or **street.** Ordinarily anything in the condition of state of highway or street that renders it unreasonably safe for travel. Payne v. State Highway Commission, 136 Kan. 561, 16 P.2d 509, 511.

Defective. Lacking in some particular which is essential to the completeness, legal sufficiency, or security of the object spoken of; as a "defective" service of process or return of service. A product is "defective" if it is not fit for the ordinary purposes for which such articles are sold and used. Manieri v. Volkswagenwerk, A.G., 151 N.J.Super. 422, 376 A.2d 1317, 1322. See also **Defect; Warranty.**

Defective condition. A product is in a defective condition unreasonably dangerous to the user when it has a propensity for causing physical harm beyond that which would be contemplated by the ordinary user or consumer who purchases it, with the ordinary knowledge common to the foreseeable class of users as to its characteristics. A product is not defective or unreasonably dangerous merely because it is possible to be injured while using it. Moomey v. Massey-Ferguson, Inc., C.A.N.M., 429 F.2d 1184. See **Strict liability.**

Defective execution. Failure to comply with requirements in executing document with the result that document is legally inadequate or defective.

Defective pleadings. Complaint, answer, cross-claim, counterclaim, etc. which fail to meet minimum standards of sufficiency or accuracy in form or substance. Such defects may usually be cured by amendment. Fed.R.Civil P. 15.

Defective record. May refer to record on appeal which does not conform to requisites of appellate rules. May also refer to state of title to real estate based on defects on the record in registry of deeds.

Defective title. With respect to negotiable paper within U.C.C. Article 3 (§ 3–201) the title of a person who obtains instrument or any signature thereto by fraud, duress, or force and fear, or other unlawful means, or for an illegal consideration, or when he negotiates it in breach of faith or under such circumstances as amount to fraud.

Defective verdict. Verdict lacking legitimacy because of some irregularity or inadequacy and hence one on which a judgment may not be based.

Defect of form. An imperfection in the style, manner, arrangement, or non-essential parts of a legal instrument, plea, indictment, etc., as distinguished from a "defect of substance" *(q.v.)*.

Defect of parties. Insufficiency of the parties before a court in any given proceeding to give it jurisdiction and authority to decide the controversy, arising from the omission or failure to join plaintiffs or defendants who should have been brought in. Rules of Civil Procedure have relaxed some of the former rigidity in requirements of joinder, but not all. Fed.R.Civ.P., Rules 19, 20. See **Joinder.**

Defect of substance. An imperfection in the body or substantive part of a legal instrument, plea, indictment, etc., consisting in the omission of something which is essential to be set forth. Sweeney v. Greenwood Index-Journal Co., D.C.S.C., 37 F.Supp. 484, 487.

Defectus /dəféktəs/. Lat. Defect; default; want; imperfection; disqualification.

Challenge propter defectum. A challenge to a juror on account of some legal disqualification, such as infancy, etc. See **Challenge.**

Defectus sanguinis. Failure of the blood, *i.e.,* failure or want of issue.

Defend. To prohibit or forbid. To deny. To contest and endeavor to defeat a claim or demand made against one in a court of justice. To oppose, repel, or resist. To protect, to shield, to make a stand for, or uphold by force or argument. To vindicate, to maintain or keep secure, to guaranty, to agree to indemnify. To represent defendant in administrative, civil or criminal proceeding. See also **Defense.**

Defendant. The person defending or denying; the party against whom relief or recovery is sought in an action or suit or the accused in a criminal case. See also **Joint defendants; Nominal defendant.**

Defendare /dèfəndériy/. To answer for; to be responsible for.

Defendemus /dèfədíyməs/. Lat. A word used in grants and donations, which binds the donor and his heirs to defend the donee, if any one go about to lay any incumbrance on the thing given other than what is contained in the deed of donation.

Defender. (Fr.) To deny; to defend; to conduct a suit for a defendant; to forbid; to prevent; to protect. See **Public defender.**

In Scotch and canon law, a defendant.

Defendere se per corpus suum /dəféndəriy síy pər kórpəs s(y)úwəm/. To offer duel or combat as a legal trial and appeal. Abolished by 59 Geo. III, § 46. See **Battel.**

Defendere unica manu /dəféndəriy (sìy) yúwnəkə mǽn(y)uw/. To wage law; a denial of an accusation upon oath. See **Wager of law.**

Defender of the faith. A peculiar title belonging to the sovereign of England, as that of "Catholic" to the king of Spain, and that of "Most Christian" to the king of France. These titles were originally given by the popes of Rome; and that of *Defensor Fidei* was first conferred by Pope Leo X on King Henry VIII, as a reward for writing against Martin Luther; and the bull for it bears date *quinto Idus Octob.,* 1521.

Defendit vim et injuriam /dəféndət vím èd injúriyəm/. He defends the force and injury.

Defendour /dèyfondúr/. L. Fr. A defender or defendant; the party accused in an appeal.

Defeneration /dəfènəréyshən/. The act of lending money on usury.

Defenestration /dìyfenəstréyshən/. Act of throwing something or somebody out of a window.

Defense. That which is offered and alleged by the party proceeded against in an action or suit, as a reason in law or fact why the plaintiff should not recover or establish what he seeks. That which is put forward to diminish plaintiff's cause of action or defeat recovery. Evidence offered by accused to defeat criminal charge.

A response to the claims of the other party, setting forth reasons why the claims should not be granted. The defense may be as simple as a flat denial of the other party's factual allegations or may involve entirely new factual allegations. In the latter situation, the defense is an affirmative defense. Under Rules of Civil Procedure, many defenses may be raised by motion as well as by answer (Rule 12(b)), while others must be pleaded affirmatively (Rules 8(c), (9). See **Affirmative defense; Answer; Equitable defense; Justification.**

As regards defense to criminal charge, such defenses include alibi, consent, "corporate" liability defenses, de minimis infraction, duress, entrapment, ignorance or mistake, infancy, insanity, intoxication, law enforcement authority, necessity, protection of property, public duty, legal impossibility, self defense and protection of others.

Defense also means the forcible repelling of an attack made unlawfully with force and violence, such as the defense of one's person or property or nation in time of war. See **Self-defense.**

Affidavit of defense. See **Affidavit.**

Frivolous defense. One which at first glance can be seen to be merely pretensive, setting up some ground which cannot be sustained by argument. On motion, such defense may be ordered stricken from the pleadings. Fed.R.Civil P. 12(f).

Legal defense. A defense which is complete and adequate in point of law. A defense which may be set up in court of law, as distinguished from an "equitable defense", which is cognizable only in a court of equity or court possessing equitable powers. This later distinction is no longer applicable with the procedural merger of law and equity under Rules of Civil Procedure.

Meritorious defense. One going to the merits, substance, or essentials of the case, as distinguished from dilatory or technical objections.

Partial defense. One which goes only to a part of the cause of action, or which only tends to mitigate the damages to be awarded.

Peremptory defense. A defense which insists that the plaintiff never had the right to institute the suit, or that, if he had, the original right is extinguished or determined.

Personal defense. In negotiable instruments law, a defense which, though not good as against a holder in due course, is good against certain parties, because of their participation in or knowledge of certain transactions or facts from which such defense arises. Such defenses include all defenses that are not real or absolute defenses. U.C.C. § 3–305.

Pretermitted defense. One which was available to a party and of which he might have had the benefit if he had pleaded it in due season, but which cannot afterwards be heard as a basis for affirmative relief.

Real defense. In negotiable instruments law, a defense inherent in the res and therefore good against anyone seeking to enforce the instrument, even a holder in due course. Real defenses include infancy, and such other incapacity, or duress, or illegality of the transaction, as renders the obligation of the party

a nullity, and fraud in the factum. These defenses are good even against a holder in due course because, where they exist, no contract was formed. U.C.C. § 3–305(2).

Self defense. See **Self-defense.**

Sham defense. A false or fictitious defense, interposed in bad faith, and manifestly untrue, insufficient, or irrelevant on its face.

Defense attorney. Lawyer who files appearance in behalf of defendant and represents such in civil or criminal case. See **Public defender.**

Defense au fond en droit /deyfóns ow fónd òn dr(w)ó/. (Called, also, *defense en droit*). A demurrer.

Defense au fond en fait /deyfóns ow fónd òn féy/. The general issue.

Defense bonds. United States Savings Bonds.

Defense of habitation. In criminal law, right to use force to defend one's home; interposed in criminal case in defense of crime. See **Defense of property.**

Defense of insanity. In criminal cases, an affirmative defense interposed to prove that defendant lacked essential mental capacity which is required for criminal responsibility. Model Penal Code, § 4.01. Fed.R. Crim.P. 12.2 requires the defendant to notify the prosecutor prior to trial of intention to assert such defense. See **Insanity.**

Defense of property. Affirmative defense in criminal case consisting of justified force in protecting one's property though such force must be reasonable under all circumstances.

Defensiva /dèfənsáyvə/. In old English law, a lord or earl of the marches, who was the warden and defender of his country.

Defensive allegation. In English ecclesiastical law, a species of pleading, where the defendant, instead of denying the plaintiff's charge upon oath, has any circumstances to offer in his defense. This entitles him, in his turn to the plaintiff's answer upon oath, upon which he may proceed to proofs as well as his antagonist. 3 Bl.Comm. 100.

Defenso /dəfén(t)sow/. In old England, that part of any open field or place that was allotted for corn or hay, and upon which there was no common or feeding, was anciently said to be *in defenso;* so of any meadow ground that was laid in for hay only. The same term was applied to a wood where part was inclosed or fenced, to secure the growth of the underwood from the injury of cattle.

Canon law. The advocate or patron of a church. An officer who had charge of the temporalities of the church.

Civil law. A defender; one who assumed the defense of another's case in court. Also an advocate. A tutor or curator.

Old English law. A guardian, defender, or protector. The defendant in an action. A person vouched in to warranty.

Defensor civitatis /dəfén(t)sər sìvətéydəs/. Defender or protector of a city or municipality. An officer under the Roman empire, whose duty it was to protect the people against the injustice of the magistrates, the insolence of the subaltern officers, and the rapacity of the money-lenders. He had the powers of a judge, with jurisdiction of pecuniary causes to a limited amount, and the lighter species of offenses. He had also the care of the public records, and powers similar to those of a notary in regard to the execution of wills and conveyances.

Defensor fidei /dəfén(t)sər fáydiyày/. Defender of the faith. See **Defender**.

Defensum /dəfén(t)səm/. A prohibition. An inclosure of land; any fenced ground. See **Defenso**.

Defer. Delay; put off; remand; postpone to a future time. The term does not have, however, the meaning of abolish, Moore v. Sampson County, 220 N.C. 232, 17 S.E.2d 22, 23, or omit, United States v. Murine Co., C.C.A.Ill., 90 F.2d 549, 551.

Deferral. Act of delaying, postponing or putting off.

Deferral period. Time span within which payment of expense, premium, interest, or the like, is delayed or in which income is postponed. See also **Grace period.**

Deferred annuity. An annuity in which the terms require payment to the annuitant at a time after the purchase date, as for example when the annuitant reaches a certain age or after the expiration of a stated term. See **Annuity**.

Deferred bonds. Bonds which carry a provision that interest payments are postponed for a certain period of time.

Deferred charge. Expense not chargeable currently on the profit and loss statement and which is carried on the balance sheet, as for example discount on bonds. Expenditure not recognized as an expense of the period when made but carried forward as an asset to be written off in future periods, such as for advance rent payments or insurance premiums.

Deferred claims. Claims which are postponed to a future date or to a subsequent accounting period.

Deferred compensation. Compensation which will be taxed when received or upon the removal of certain restrictions upon receipt and not when earned. An example would be contributions by an employer to a qualified pension or profit-sharing plan on behalf of an employee. Such contributions will not be taxed to the employee until the funds are made available or distributed to the employee (*e.g.*, upon retirement), at which time the recipient will likely be in a lower tax bracket.

Nonqualified deferred compensation plans. Compensation arrangements which are frequently offered to executives. Such plans may include stock options, restricted stock, etc. Generally, an executive may defer the recognition of taxable income to future periods and the employer does not receive a tax deduction until the employee is required to include the compensation in income.

Deferred credits. Credit items which are required to be spread over subsequent accounting period such as premium on bonds issued.

Deferred income. Income received in advance but not yet earned, such as prepaid rent or insurance. Income taken on the books but not credited until a later accounting period.

Deferred lien. Lien postponed or delayed in its effect until a future time as contrasted with a present lien; usually possessory in nature.

Deferred payments. Payments of principal or interest postponed to a future time; installment payments. See also **Deferred income**.

Deferred sentence. A sentence, the pronouncement of which has been postponed. It does not operate as a suspension of sentence. See **Probation.**

Deferred stock. See **Stock**.

Defiance /dəfáyən(t)s/. A contemptuous opposition or disregard openly expressed in words or action. State v. Mohar, 169 Wash. 368, 13 P.2d 454, 455. A provoking to combat, a challenge, a declaration of hostilities. Anderson-Berney Bldg. Co. v. Lowry, Tex.Civ. App., 143 S.W.2d 401, 403. Defiant challenge or opposition to authority.

Deficiency. A lack, shortage or insufficiency. The amount by which the income tax imposed exceeds the amount shown as the tax by the taxpayer upon his return, or otherwise owed by the taxpayer. As defined in the Internal Revenue Code is the amount of tax imposed less any amount that may have been reported by the taxpayer on his returns; where there has been no return filed, the deficiency is the amount of tax due. Laing v. U. S., Ky. & Vt., 423 U.S. 161, 96 S.Ct. 473, 480, 46 L.Ed.2d 416. See also **Deficiency assessment; Deficiency notice**.

That part of a debt secured by mortgage not realized from sale of mortgaged property. A judgment or decree for the amount of such deficiency is called a "deficiency judgment" or "decree." See **Deficiency judgment**.

Deficiency assessment. In taxation, difference between tax as computed by taxpayer and tax due as computed and assessed by taxing authorities. See also **Deficiency.**

Deficiency bill. In parliamentary practice, an appropriation bill covering items of expense omitted from the general appropriation bill or bills, or for which insufficient appropriations were made. If intended to cover a variety of such items, it is commonly called a "general deficiency bill"; if intended to make provision for expenses which must be met immediately, or which cannot wait the ordinary course of the general appropriation bills, it is called an "urgent deficiency bill."

Deficiency judgment. In mortgage law, imposition of personal liability on mortgagor for unpaid balance of mortgage debt after foreclosure has failed to yield full amount of due debt. In re Pittsburgh-Duquesne Development Co., C.A.Pa., 482 F.2d 243, 246. May also apply to debt due after repossession of personal property subject to security interest. See also **Judgment**.

Deficiency notice. Notice of tax deficiency (90 day letter) which is mailed to taxpayer and which is prerequisite to jurisdiction of Tax Court. I.R.C. § 6212. See also **Ninety day letter.**

Deficiency suits. In mortgage law, action to recover difference between debt and amount realized on foreclosure. See also **Deficiency judgment**.

May also apply to petition in Tax Court following receipt of deficiency notice (90 day letter). I.R.C. § 6212.

Deficit. An excess of expenditures over revenues. Loss in operation of business. Something wanting, generally in the accounts of one intrusted with money, or in the money received by him. The term is broad enough to cover defalcation, misappropriation, shrinkage, or costs, and, in its popular meaning, signifies deficiency from any cause.

In accounting, opposite of surplus on balance sheet. May represent accumulated losses.

Deficit spending. Expenditures in excess of income; usually from borrowed funds rather than from actual revenues or surplus.

De fide et officio judicis non recipitur quæstio, sed de scientia, sive sit error juris, sive facti /dìy fáydiy èd əfíshiyow júwdəsəs nòn rəsípədər kwés(h)ch(iy)ow, sèd dìy sayénsh(iy)ə, sáyviy sìd éhrər júrəs sáyviy fæktay/. Concerning the fidelity and official conduct of a judge, no question is [will be] entertained; but [only] concerning his knowledge, whether the error [committed] be of law or of fact. The *bona fides* and honesty of purpose of a judge cannot be questioned, but his decision may be impugned for error either of law or fact. The law doth so much respect the certainty of judgments, and the credit and authority of judges, that it will not permit any error to be assigned which impeacheth them in their *trust* and *office,* and in willful abuse of the same; but only in ignorance and mistaking either of the law, or of the case and matter of fact. Thus, it cannot be assigned for error that a judge did that which he ought not to do; as that he entered a verdict for the plaintiff, where the jury gave it for the defendant.

De fidei læsione /dìy fáydiyay lìyz(h)iyówniy/. Of breach of faith or fidelity.

Defile. To corrupt purity or perfection of; to debase; to make ceremonially unclean; to pollute; to sully; to dishonor. State v. Kasnett, 30 Ohio App.2d 77, 283 N.E.2d 636, 638. To debauch, deflower, or corrupt the chastity of a woman. The term does not necessarily imply force or ravishment, nor does it connote previous immaculateness. The term, when used in a statute penalizing any person who shall publicly defile any flag of the United States, has the meaning of dishonor, State v. Schlueter, 127 N.J.L. 496, 23 A.2d 249, 251; and means to make filthy or to make ceremonially unclean and refers to physical defilement, State v. Hodsdon, Del.Super., 289 A.2d 635, 638. See also **Desecrate.**

Defilement /dəfáylmənt/. Uncleanness; impurity; corruption of morals or conduct.

Define. To explain or state the exact meaning of words and phrases; to state explicitly; to limit; to deter-

mine essential qualities of; to determine the precise signification of; to settle; to establish or prescribe authoritatively; to make clear. Walling v. Yeakley, C.C.A.Colo., 140 F.2d 830, 832. To declare that a certain act shall constitute an offense is defining that offense. U. S. v. Arjona, 120 U.S. 479, 7 S.Ct. 628, 30 L.Ed. 728. See also **Definition.**

To "define" with respect to space, means to set or establish its boundaries authoritatively; to mark the limits of; to determine with precision or to exhibit clearly the boundaries of; to determine the end or limit; to fix or establish the limits. It is the equivalent to declare, fix or establish. Seeking out what exists already is not "defining." Redlands Foothill Groves v. Jacobs, D.C.Cal., 30 F.Supp. 995, 1004.

De fine force /dìy fáyniy fórs/. L. Fr. Of necessity; of pure necessity. See **Fine force.**

De fine non capiendo pro pulchre placitando /dìy fáyniy nòn kæpiyéndow pròw pólkriy plæsətændow/. A writ prohibiting the taking of fines for beau pleader.

De fine pro redisseisina capiendo /dìy fáyniy pròw rìydəsíysənə kæpiyéndow/. A writ which lay for the release of one imprisoned for a re-disseisin, on payment of a reasonable fine.

De finibus levatis /dìy fáynəbəs ləvéydəs/. Concerning fines levied. The title of the English statute 27 Edw. I, requiring fines thereafter to be levied, to be read openly and solemnly in court.

Definite. Fixed, determined, defined, bounded.

Definite sentence. Sentence calling for imprisonment for specified number of years as contrasted with indeterminate sentence which leaves duration to prison authorities (*e.g.* parole boards) and good behavior of prisoner. Also called "determinate sentence".

Definitio /dèfənísh(iy)ow/. Lat. Definition, or more strictly, limiting or bounding; as in the maxim of the civil law: *Omnis definitio periculosa est, parum est enim ut non subverti possit, i.e.,* the attempt to bring the law within the boundaries of precise definitions is hazardous, as there are but few cases in which such a limitation cannot be subverted.

Definition. A description of a thing by its properties; an explanation of the meaning of a word or term. The process of stating the exact meaning of a word by means of other words. Such a description of the thing defined, including all essential elements and excluding all nonessential, as to distinguish it from all other things and classes. See also **Define.**

Definitive. That which finally and completely ends and settles a controversy. For example, a definitive sentence or judgment as opposed to an interlocutory judgment.

Definitive sentence. See **Definite sentence**.

Deflect. To turn aside, to deviate from a straight or horizontal line or from a proper position, to swerve.

Defloration /dìyfləréyshən/. Seduction or debauching. The act by which a woman is deprived of her virginity.

Deforce. In old English law, to withhold wrongfully; to withhold the possession of lands from one who is lawfully entitled to them. 3 Bl.Comm. 172.

Deforcement. Deforcement is where a man wrongfully holds lands to which another person is entitled. It therefore includes disseisin, abatement, discontinuance, and intrusion. But it is applied especially to cases, not falling under those heads, where the person entitled to the freehold has never had possession. 3 Bl.Comm. 172. Also, to detain dower from widow.

Deforciant /diyfórshənt/. One who wrongfully keeps the owner of lands and tenements out of the possession of them. 2 Bl.Comm. 350.

Deforciare /dəfòrs(h)iyériy/. L. Lat. To withhold lands or tenements from the rightful owner. This is a word of art which cannot be supplied by any other word.

Deforciatio /dəfòrs(h)iyéysh(iy)ow/. L. Lat. In old English law, a distress, distraint, or seizure of goods for satisfaction of a lawful debt.

De forisfactura maritagii /dìy fòrəsfækchúrə mærətéyjiyay/. Writ of forfeiture of marriage.

Deformity. A deformed or misshapen condition; an unnatural growth, or a distorted or misshapen part or member; disfigurement, as a bodily deformity.

Defossion /dəfóshən/. The punishment of being buried alive.

De frangentibus prisonam /dìy frænjéntəbəs prízənəm/. Concerning those that break prison. The title of the English statute 1 Edw. II, ordaining that none from thenceforth who broke prison should have judgment of life or limb for breaking prison only, unless the cause for which he was taken and imprisoned required such a judgment if he was lawfully convicted thereof.

Defraud. To make a misrepresentation of an existing material fact, knowing it to be false or making it recklessly without regard to whether it is true or false, intending one to rely and under circumstances in which such person does rely to his damage. To practice fraud; to cheat or trick. To deprive a person of property or any interest, estate, or right by fraud, deceit, or artifice. See also **Collusion; Deceit; Fraud; Material fact; Misrepresentation.**

Intent to defraud means an intention to deceive another person, and to induce such other person, in reliance upon such deception, to assume, create, transfer, alter or terminate a right, obligation or power with reference to property.

Defraudation. Privation by fraud.

Defunct. Having ceased to exist; no longer operative. Deceased; a deceased person. A business which has ceased to function.

Defunctus /dəfə́ŋ(k)təs/. Lat. Dead. "Defunctus sine prole," dead without (leaving) issue.

De furto /dìy fárdow/. Of theft. One of the kinds of criminal appeal formerly in use in England.

Degaster /dèygæstéy/. L. Fr. To waste.

De gestu et fama /dìy jéschuw ət féymə/. Of behavior and reputation. An old writ which lay in cases where a person's conduct and reputation were impeached.

Degradation. A deprivation of dignity; dismissal from rank or office; act or process of degrading. Moral or intellectual decadence; degeneration; deterioration.

An ecclesiastical censure, whereby a clergyman is divested of his holy orders. There are two sorts by the canon law,—one *summary,* by word only; the other *solemn,* by stripping the party degraded of those ornaments and rights which are the ensigns of his degree. Degradation is otherwise called "deposition," but the canonists have distinguished between these two terms, deeming the former as the greater punishment of the two. There was likewise a degradation of a lord or knight at common law, and also by act of parliament.

Degradations /dègrədéyshənz/. A term for waste in the French law.

Degrade. See **Degradation.**

Degrading. Reviling; holding one up to public obloquy; lowering a person in the estimation of the public; exposing to disgrace, dishonor, or contempt.

De gratia /dìy gréysh(iy)ə/. Of grace or favor, by favor. *De speciali gratia,* of special grace or favor.

Degree. Extent, measure or scope of an action, condition or relation. Legal extent of guilt or negligence. Title conferred on graduates of school, college, or university. The state or civil condition of a person.

The grade or distance one thing may be removed from another; *i.e.,* the distance, or number of removes, which separates two persons who are related by consanguinity. Thus we speak of a brother as being in the second degree of kindred.

Degree of proof. That measure of cogency required to prove a case depending upon the nature of the case. In a criminal case such proof must be beyond a reasonable doubt, whereas in most civil cases such proof is by a fair preponderance of the evidence. See also **Burden of proof; Proof** (*Proof beyond a reasonable doubt*).

Degrees of crime. A division or classification of one specific crime into several grades or *stadia* of guilt, according to the circumstances attending its commission. For example, in most states there are degrees of murder as "first" and "second" degree murder. Also, a division of crimes generally. Thus, a *felony* is punishable by imprisonment in state prison whereas a *misdemeanor* carries a maximum punishment of a short term sentence to a jail or house of correction and/or a fine. In some jurisdictions there are also petty misdemeanors. In addition, criminal codes in certain states classify felonies and misdemeanors into classes (*e.g.* class A, B, etc.) with corresponding punishment or sentencing categories. See also **Crime.**

Degrees of kin. The relationship between a deceased and the survivors which govern descent and distribution. See also **Descent.**

Degrees of negligence. The different grades of negligence which govern the liability of persons; *e.g.* ordinary negligence as contrasted with gross negligence. See **Negligence.**

De hærede deliberando illi qui habet custodiam terræ /dìy həríydiy dəlìbərǽndow ílay kwày héybət kəstówdiyəm téhriy/. Writ for delivering an heir to him who has wardship of the land. A writ directed to the sheriff, to require one that had the body of him that was ward to another to deliver him to the person whose ward he was by reason of his land.

De hærede rapto et abducto /dìy həríydiy rǽptow əd əbdǽktow/. Writ concerning an heir ravished and carried away. A writ which anciently lay for a lord who, having by right the wardship of his tenant under age could not obtain his body, the same being carried away by another person.

De hæretico comburendo /dìy hərédəkow kòmb(y)əréndow/. (Lat. For burning a heretic.) An ancient writ which formerly issued from the secular courts for the execution, by burning, of a heretic, who had been convicted in the ecclesiastical courts of heresy, had abjured, and had relapsed into heresy. 4 Bl.Comm. 46. See **Hæretico comburendo.**

De homagio respectuando /dìy həméyjiyow rəspèkchuwǽndow/. A writ for respiting or postponing homage.

De homine capto in withernam /dìy hóm’əniy kǽptow ən wíðərnəm/. (Lat. For taking a man in withernam.) A writ to take a man who had carried away a bondman or bondwoman into another country beyond the reach of a writ of replevin.

De homine replegiando /dìy hóm’əniy rəplìyjiyiyǽndow/. (Lat. For replevying a man.) A writ which lies to replevy a man out of prison, or out of the custody of a private person, upon giving security to the sheriff that the man shall be forthcoming to answer any charge against him. 3 Bl.Comm. 129. This writ has been superseded almost wholly, in modern practice, by that of *habeas corpus*; but it is still used, in some of the states, in an amended and altered form.

Dehors /dəhór/dìyhórz/. L. Fr. Out of; without; beyond; foreign to; unconnected with. Blackford v. Anderson, 226 Iowa 1138, 286 N.W. 735, 746. *Dehors* the record; foreign to the record. 3 Bl.Comm. 387.

De identitate nominis /dìy ədèntətéydiy nómənəs/. A writ which lay for one arrested in a personal action and committed to prison under a mistake as to his identity, the proper defendant bearing the same name.

Dei gratia /díyay gréysh(iy)ə/. Lat. By the grace of God. A phrase used in the formal title of a king or queen, importing a claim of sovereignty by the favor or commission of God. In ancient times it was incorporated in the titles of inferior officers (especially ecclesiastical), but in later use was reserved as an assertion of "the divine right of kings."

De iis qui ponendi sunt in assisis /dìy áyəs kwày pənénday sènt ən əsáyzəs/. Of those who are to be put on assises. The title of a statute passed 21 Edw. I, defining the qualifications of jurors.

Dei judicium /díyay juwdísh(iy)əm/. The judgment of God. The old Saxon trial by ordeal, so called because it was thought to be an appeal to God for the justice of a cause, and it was believed that the decision was

according to the will and pleasure of Divine Providence.

De incremento /dìy iŋkrəméntow/. Of increase; in addition. Costs *de incremento,* or costs of increase, are the costs adjudged by the court in civil actions, *in addition* to the damages and nominal costs found by the jury.

De ingressu /dìy əŋgrés(h)uw/. A writ of entry.

De injuria /dìy injúriyə/. Of [his own] wrong. In the technical language of common law pleading, a replication *de injuria* is one that may be made in an action of tort where the defendant has admitted the acts complained of, but alleges, in his plea, certain new matter by way of justification or excuse. By this replication the plaintiff avers that the defendant committed the grievances in question "of his own wrong, and without any such cause," or motive or excuse, as that alleged in the plea *(de injuria sua propria absque tali causa);* or, admitting part of the matter pleaded, "without the rest of the cause" alleged *(absque residuo causœ).* In form it is a species of traverse, and it is frequently used when the pleading of the defendant, in answer to which it is directed, consists merely of matter of excuse of the alleged trespass, grievance, breach of contract, or other cause of action. Its comprehensive character in putting in issue all the material facts of the defendant's plea has also obtained for it the title of the general replication. Such technical pleading no longer exists under current rules practice.

De inofficioso testamento /dìy ìnəfis(h)iyówsow tèstəméntow/. Concerning an inofficious or undutiful will. A title of the civil law.

De integro /dìy íntəgrow/. Anew; a second time. As it was before.

De intrusione /dìy əntrùwzhiyówniy/. A writ of intrusion; where a stranger entered after the death of the tenant, to the injury of the reversioner.

Dejacion /dèyhasyówn/. In Spanish law, surrender; release; abandonment; *e.g.,* the act of an insolvent in surrendering his property for the benefit of his creditors, of an heir in renouncing the succession, the abandonment of insured property to the underwriters.

De jactura evitanda /dìy jæktyúrə èvətǽndə/. For avoiding a loss. A phrase applied to a defendant, as *de lucro captando* is to a plaintiff.

Dejeration /dìyjəréyshən/. A taking of a solemn oath.

De jure /dìy júriy/. Descriptive of a condition in which there has been total compliance with all requirements of law. Of right; legitimate; lawful; by right and just title. In this sense it is the contrary of *de facto* (q.v.). It may also be contrasted with *de gratia,* in which case it means "as a matter of right," as *de gratia* means "by grace or favor." Again it may be contrasted with *de æquitate;* here meaning "by law," as the latter means "by equity."

De jure corporation. Corporation which has been created as result of compliance with all of the constitutional or statutory requirements of state of incorporation. Harris v. Stephens Wholesome Bldg. Supply Co. Inc., 54 Ala.App. 405, 309 So.2d 115.

De jure decimarum, originem ducens de jure patronatus, tunc cognitio spectat at legem civilem, i.e., communem. With regard to the right of tithes deducing its origin from the right of the patron, then the cognizance of them belongs to the civil law; that is, the common law.

De jure government. See **Government.**

De jure judices, de facto juratores respondent /dìy júriy júwdəsiyz, dìy fǽktow jùrətóriyz rəspóndənt/. The judges find the law, the jury the facts.

De jure segregation. Generally refers to segregation directly intended or mandated by law or otherwise issuing from an official racial classification or in other words to segregation which has or had the sanction of law.

Term comprehends any situation in which the activities of school authorities have had a racially discriminatory impact contributing to the establishment or continuation of a dual system of schools, while "de facto segregation" is limited to that which is inadvertent and without the assistance or collusion of school authorities. State ex rel. Citizens Against Mandatory Bussing v. Brooks, 80 Wash.2d 121, 492 P.2d 536, 542.

De la pluis beale, or **belle** /də la pl(y)úw bél/. L. Fr. Of the most fair. A term applied to a species of dower, which was assigned out of the fairest of the husband's tenements.

De latere /dìy lǽdəriy/. From the side; on the side; collaterally; of collaterals.

Delatio /dəléysh(iy)ow/. In the civil law, an accusation or information.

Delator /dəléydər/. An accuser; an informer; a sycophant.

Delatura /dələchúrə/. In old English law, the reward of an informer.

Delay. To retard; obstruct; put off; postpone; defer; procrastinate; prolong the time of or before; hinder; interpose obstacles; as, when it is said that a conveyance was made to "hinder and delay creditors." The term does not necessarily, though it may, imply dishonesty or involve moral wrong.

Delay rental. Rent, usually on oil and gas leases, paid for additional time in which to utilize land. It does not depend on oil or gas produced, does not exhaust substance of land, and resembles a bonus payment, which is an advance royalty. Commissioner of Internal Revenue v. Wilson, C.C.A.Tex., 76 F.2d 766, 769; State v. Magnolia Petroleum Co., Tex.Civ.App., 173 S.W.2d 186, 190.

Del bien estre /dèl bíyn é(s)trə/. L. Fr. In old English practice, of well being; of form. The same as *de bene esse.*

Del credere /dèl kréydərey/. An agreement by which a factor, when he sells goods on credit, for an additional commission (called a "*del credere* commission"), guaranties the solvency of the purchaser and his

performance of the contract. Such a factor is called a "*del credere* agent." He is a mere surety, liable to his principal only in case the purchaser makes default. Agent who is obligated to indemnify his principal in event of loss to principal as result of credit extended by agent to third party.

Delectus personæ /dəléktəs pərsówniy/. Lat. Choice of the person. Johnston v. Winn, Tex.Civ.App., 105 S.W.2d 398, 400. By this term is understood the right of a partner to exercise his choice and preference as to the admission of any new members to the firm, and as to the persons to be so admitted, if any. The doctrine is equally applicable to close and family corporations and is exemplified in the use of restrictions for the transfer of shares of stock.

Delegata potestas non potest delegari /dèləgéydə pətéstæs nòn pówdəst dèləgéray/. A delegated power cannot be delegated.

Delegate. A person who is delegated or commissioned to act in the stead of another. Landro v. Pacific Atlantic S. S. Co., D.C.Wash., 30 F.Supp. 538, 539. A person to whom affairs are committed by another; an attorney.

A person elected or appointed to be a member of a representative assembly. Usually spoken of one sent to a special or occasional assembly or convention. Person selected by a constituency and authorized to act for it at a party or State convention. See also **Delegation.**

Delegates, the high court of. In English law, formerly the court of appeal from the ecclesiastical and admiralty courts. Abolished upon the judicial committee of the privy council being constituted the court of appeal in such cases.

Delegation. A sending away; a putting into commission; the assignment of a debt to another; the intrusting another with a general power to act for the good of those who depute him; a body of delegates. The transfer of authority by one person to another. The act of making or commissioning a delegate.

The body of delegates from a State to a national nominating convention or from a county to a State or other party convention. The whole body of delegates or representatives sent to a convention or assembly from one district, place, or political unit are collectively spoken of as a "delegation."

In civil law, a species of novation which consists in the change of one debtor for another, when he who is indebted substitutes a third person who obligates himself in his stead to the creditor, or to the person appointed by him so that the first debtor is acquitted and his obligation extinguished, and the creditor contents himself with the obligation of the second debtor. Delegation is essentially distinguished from any other species of novation, in this: that the former demands the consent of all three parties, but the latter that only of the two parties to the new debt. Delegation is novation effected by the intervention of another person whom the debtor, in order to be liberated from his creditor, gives to such creditor, or to him whom the creditor appoints; and such person so given becomes obliged to the creditor in the place of the original debtor. *Perfect delegation* exists when the debtor who makes the obligation is discharged by the creditor. *Imperfect delegation* exists when the creditor retains his rights against the original debtor.

Delegation of powers. Transfer of authority by one branch of government in which such authority is vested to some other branch or administrative agency.

U.S. Constitution delegates different powers to the executive, legislative and judicial branches of government. Exercise by the executive branch of the powers delegated to the legislative branch offends this separation and delegation of powers and hence is unconstitutional. Schechter Poultry Corp. v. U. S., 295 U.S. 495, 55 S.Ct. 837, 79 L.Ed. 1570. Certain powers may not be delegated from one branch of government to another such as the judicial powers or such congressional powers as power to declare war, impeach, or admit new states.

For distinction between delegated powers and various other types of constitutional powers, see **Power** *(Constitutional powers).*

De legatis et fidei commissis /dìy ləgéydəs èt fáydiyay kəmísəs/. Of legacies and trusts. The name of a title of the Pandects.

Delegatus non potest delegare /dèləgéydəs nòn pówdəst dèləgériy/. A delegate cannot delegate; an agent cannot delegate his functions to a subagent without the knowledge or consent of the principal; the person to whom an office or duty is delegated cannot lawfully devolve the duty on another, unless he be expressly authorized so to do.

Delete /dəlíyt/. To erase; to remove; to strike out.

Deleterious /dèlətíriyəs/. Hurtful, morally or physically; injurious, as influence; poisonous; unwholesome.

De libera falda /dìy líbərə fóldə/. Writ of free fold. A species of *quod permittat.*

De libera piscaria /dìy líbərə pəskériyə/. Writ of free fishery. A species of *quod permittat.*

Deliberate, v. To weigh, ponder, discuss, regard upon, consider. To examine and consult in order to form an opinion. To weigh in the mind; to consider the reasons for and against; to consider maturely; reflect upon, as to deliberate a question; to weigh the arguments for and against a proposed course of action. People v. Thomas, 25 Cal.2d 880, 156 P.2d 7, 17, 18. See also **Deliberation.**

Deliberate, *adj.* Well advised; carefully considered; not sudden or rash; circumspect; slow in determining. Willful rather than merely intentional. Formed, arrived at, or determined upon as a result of careful thought and weighing of considerations, as a deliberate judgment or plan. Carried on coolly and steadily, especially according to a preconceived design; given to weighing facts and arguments with a view to a choice or decision; careful in considering the consequences of a step; slow in action; unhurried; characterized by reflection; dispassionate; not rash. People v. Thomas, 25 Cal.2d 880, 156 P.2d 7, 17, 18.

By the use of this word, in describing a crime, the idea is conveyed that the perpetrator weighs the motives for the act and its consequences, the nature of the crime, or other things connected with his intentions, with a view to a decision thereon; that he carefully considers all these, and that the act is not suddenly committed. It implies that the perpetrator must be capable of the exercise of such mental powers as are called into use by deliberation and the consideration and weighing of motives and consequences. See also **Deliberation; Premeditation.**

Deliberately. Willfully; with premeditation; intentionally; purposely; in cold blood. Averheart v. State, 158 Ark. 639, 238 S.W. 620, 621.

Deliberate speed. Phrase used in mandate to desegregate public schools and means such speed as is consistent with the welfare of all people of the state, with the maintenance of law and order and with the preservation, if possible, of the common school system. Calhoun v. Members of Bd. of Ed., City of Atlanta, D.C.Ga., 188 F.Supp. 401, 404; Brown v. Board of Education, 347 U.S. 483, 74 S.Ct. 686, 98 L.Ed. 873.

Deliberation. The act or process of deliberating. The act of weighing and examining the reasons for and against a contemplated act or course of conduct or a choice of acts or means. As used in context of an essential element of first-degree murder, is a weighing in the mind of consequences of course of conduct, as distinguished from acting upon a sudden impulse without exercise of reasoning powers. Davis v. State, 251 Ark. 771, 475 S.W.2d 155, 156. See also **Deliberate; Premeditation.**

De libero passagio /dìy líbərow pəséyjiow/. Writ of free passage. A species of *quod permittat.*

De libertate probanda /dìy lìbərtéydiy prəbǽndə/. Writ for proving liberty. A writ which lay for such as, being demanded for villeins or niefs, offered to prove themselves free.

De libertatibus allocandis /dìy lìbərtéydəbəs ǽləkǽndəs/. A writ of various forms, to enable a citizen to recover the liberties to which he was entitled.

De licentia transfretandi /dìy ləsénsh(iy)ə trǽnsfrətǽnday/. Writ of permission to cross the sea. An old writ directed to the wardens of the port of Dover, or other seaport in England, commanding them to permit the persons named in the writ to cross the sea from such port, on certain conditions.

Delict. Criminal offense; tort; a wrong.

In Roman law this word, taken in its most general sense, is wider in both directions than our English term "tort." On the one hand, it includes those wrongful acts which, while directly affecting some individual or his property, yet extend in their injurious consequences to the peace or security of the community at large, and hence rise to the grade of crimes or misdemeanors. These acts were termed in the Roman law "public delicts;" while those for which the only penalty exacted was compensation to the person primarily injured were denominated "private delicts." On the other hand, the term appears to have included injurious actions which transpired without any malicious intention on the part of the doer. A quasi delict in Roman law was an act whereby a person, without malice, but by fault, negligence, or imprudence not legally excusable, caused injury to another. They were four in number, viz.: (1) *Qui judex litem suam fecit,* being the offense of partiality or excess in the *judex* (juryman). (2) *Dejectum effusumve aliquid,* being the tort committed by one's servant in emptying or throwing something out of an attic or upper story upon a person passing beneath. (3) *Damnum infectum,* being the offense of hanging dangerous articles over the heads of persons passing along the king's highway. (4) Torts committed by one's agents in the course of their employment.

Delictual fault /dəlíkchuwəl fólt/. An act, productive of obligations, which takes place between persons juridically strangers to each other; it supposes the absence of obligation and its result is the creation of one. Reserve Ins. Co. v. Fabre, 243 La. 982, 149 So.2d 413, 416.

Delictum /dəlíktəm/. Lat. A delict, tort, wrong, injury, or offense. Actions *ex delicto* are such as are founded on a tort, as distinguished from actions on contract.

Culpability, blameworthiness, or legal delinquency. The word occurs in this sense in the maxim, "*In pari delicto melior est condito defendentis*".

A challenge of a juror *propter delictum* is for some crime or misdemeanor that affects his credit and renders him infamous. 3 Bl.Comm. 363.

Delimit. To mark or lay out the limits or boundary line of a territory or country; to fix or to mark the limits of; to demarcate; to limit; bound. Walling v. Yeakley, C.C.A.Colo., 140 F.2d 830, 832.

Delimitation. The act of fixing, marking off, or describing the limits or boundary line of a territory, country, authority, right, statutory exception or the like. See **Delimit**.

Delinquency. Failure, omission, violation of law or duty. State or condition of one who has failed to perform his duty or obligation.

Delinquency charges. As used in the commercial credit field, generally refer to specific pecuniary sums that are assessed against the borrower solely because of his failure to make his payment in timely manner. Johnson v. McCrackin-Sturman Ford, Inc., C.A.Pa., 527 F.2d 257, 265.

Delinquent, *n.* He who has been guilty of some crime, offense, or failure of duty or obligation.

Delinquent, *adj.* As applied to a debt or claim, it means simply due and unpaid at the time appointed by law or fixed by contract; as, a delinquent tax.

Delinquent child. An infant of not more than specified age who has violated criminal laws or engages in disobedient, indecent or immoral conduct, and is in need of treatment, rehabilitation, or supervision. In re Garner, 230 Pa.Super. 426, 326 A.2d 581, 584. Defined by a state statute as: A child who (A) violates any federal or state law, or municipal or local ordinance; or (B) without just cause runs away from his parental home or other properly authorized and lawful place of abode; or (C) is beyond the control of his parents, parent, guardian or other custodian; or (D) has engaged in indecent or immoral conduct; or (E) has been habitually truant or, while in school, has been continuously and overtly defiant of school rules

and regulations; or (F) has violated any lawful order of court. See 18 U.S.C.A. § 5001 et seq. See also **Disobedient child.**

With respect to parental liability for acts of delinquent child, see **Parental liability.**

Delinquent taxes. Past due and unpaid taxes.

Delirium /dəlíriyəm/. Disturbed mental state characterized by a combination of motor restlessness displaying excitement, confusion, incoherence, perplexity, and disorientation, in combination with a dream-like state and some sensory disturbance, such as hallucinations and delusions. Sometimes caused by an infection or a toxic chemical substance.

Delirium febrile /dəlíriyəm fébrəliy/. A form of mental aberration incident to fevers, and sometimes to the last stages of chronic diseases.

Delirium tremens /dəlíriyəm tríymən(d)z/. A delirium due to alcohol (Korsakow's Syndrome) or other drug poisoning or withdrawal, or to dietary metabolic deprivation resulting from sudden abstinence from alcohol.

Delist. The process by which the privileges of a security listed on an exchange are suspended for failure to meet the requirements of listing. Such delisting may be permanent or temporary.

Deliverance. The verdict rendered by a jury.

At common law, a writ allowed a plaintiff in replevin, where the defendant has obtained judgment for return of the goods, by default or nonsuit, in order to have the same distress again delivered to him, on giving the same security as before. 3 Bl.Comm. 150.

Delivery. The act by which the res or substance thereof is placed within the actual or constructive possession or control of another. Poor v. American Locomotive Co., C.C.A.Ill., 67 F.2d 626, 630. What constitutes delivery depends largely on the intent of the parties. It is not necessary that delivery should be by manual transfer. Jones v. Young, Tex.Civ.App., 539 S.W.2d 901, 904. See also **Drop shipment delivery; Misdelivery.**

Absolute and conditional. An absolute delivery, as distinguished from conditional delivery or delivery in escrow, is one which is complete upon the actual transfer of the instrument from the possession of the grantor. A conditional delivery is one which passes the thing subject to delivery from the possession of the grantor, but is not to be completed by possession of the grantee, or a third person as his agent, until the happening of a specified event. One of the exceptions to parol evidence rule which permits introduction of evidence to the effect that document was delivered on condition that something be done and it is understood that document does not become operative until such action be taken.

Actual and constructive. Actual delivery consists in the giving real possession to the vendee or his servants or special agents who are identified with him in law and represent him. It is a formal immediate transfer of the property to the vendee.

Constructive delivery is a general term, comprehending all those acts which, although not truly conferring a real possession of the thing sold on the vendee, have been held, by construction of law, equivalent to acts of real delivery. A constructive delivery of personalty takes place when the goods are set apart and notice given to the person to whom they are to be delivered, or when, without actual transfer of the goods or their symbol, the conduct of the parties is such as to be inconsistent with any other supposition than that there has been a change in the nature of the holding. "Constructive delivery" is a term comprehending all those acts which, although not truly conferring a real possession of the vendee, have been held by construction of law equivalent to acts of real delivery. Lakeview Gardens, Inc. v. State ex rel. Schneider, Kan., 557 P.2d 1286, 1290. See also *Symbolical delivery, infra.*

Commercial law. Delivery with respect to instruments, documents of title, chattel paper or securities means voluntary transfer of possession. U.C.C. § 1–201(14).

Deed. The final and absolute transfer of a deed, properly executed, to the grantee, or to some person for his use, in such manner that it cannot be recalled by the grantor. Controlling factor in determining if there has been delivery of a deed is the intention of the grantor; to constitute "delivery" the deed must be placed in the hands of the grantee or within his control, with the intention that it is to become presently operative as a conveyance. Jones v. Young, 539 S.W.2d 901, 904.

Delivery bond. A bond given upon the seizure of goods (as under the revenue laws) conditioned for their restoration to the defendant, or the payment of their value, if so adjudged.

Delivery in escrow. Transfer physically of something such as a deed to escrow agent to be held on some condition which is not inconsistent with the primary transaction and which is to be released on the occurrence of some specific event or happening. See **Escrow.**

Delivery order. A written order to deliver goods directed to a warehouseman, carrier or other person who in the ordinary course of business issues warehouse receipts or bills of lading. U.C.C. § 7–102(1)(d). The primary function of the delivery order is to aid in the breaking down into smaller lots of one large lot of goods (whether fungible or otherwise) which is represented by one bill of lading.

Drugs. In the context of illegal transfer of drugs, "deliver" means the actual, constructive, or attempted transfer from one person to another of a controlled substance. State v. Medina, 87 N.M. 394, 534 P.2d 486, 489.

Gift. "Delivery" for purposes of creating a gift consists of irrevocable surrender of dominion and control over the subject matter of the gift. Bray v. Illinois Nat. Bank of Springfield, 37 Ill.App.3d 286, 345 N.E.2d 503, 505.

Second delivery. The legal delivery by the depositary of a deed placed in escrow.

Symbolical delivery. The constructive delivery of the subject-matter of a sale, where it is cumbersome or inaccessible, by the actual delivery of some article which is conventionally accepted as the symbol or representative of it, or which renders access to it possible, or which is the evidence of the purchaser's title to it; as the key of a warehouse, or a bill of lading of goods on shipboard.

De lunatico inquirendo /dìy l(y)uwnǽdəkow ìŋkwərén-dow/. The name of a writ directed to the sheriff, directing him to inquire by good and lawful men whether the party charged is a lunatic or not.

Delusion. False, unshakeable belief which is (a) contrary to fact, (b) inappropriate to the person's education, intelligence or culture, and (c) adhered to in spite of tangible evidence that it is false. A reality judgment which cannot be accepted by people of the same class, education, race and period of life as the person who expresses it and which cannot be changed by logical argument or evidence against it. Three common delusions are: (1) delusions of persecution; (2) delusions of grandeur; and (3) delusions of personal unworthiness. The first two are common to schizophrenia. Delusion appears to spring from a distorted world view created by the subject in order to satisfy his inner needs or to reconcile conflicting elements of his personality. See **Insane delusion.**

Dem. An abbreviation for "demise"; *e.g., Doe dem. Smith,* Doe, on the demise of Smith.

De magna assisa eligenda /dìy mǽgnə əsáyzə èləjéndə/. A writ by which the grand assise was chosen and summoned.

Demain. See **Demesne.**

De majori et minori non variant jura /dìy məjóray èt mənóray nòn vǽriyənt júrə/. Concerning greater and less laws do not vary.

De malo /dìy mǽlow/. Of illness. This phrase was frequently used to designate several species of essoin (*q.v.*), such as *de malo lecti,* of illness in bed; *de malo veniendi,* of illness (or misfortune) in coming to the place where the court sat; *de malo villœ,* of illness in the town where the court sat.

Demand, *v.* To claim as one's due; to require; to ask relief. To summon; to call in court.

Demand, *n.* The assertion of a legal right; a legal obligation asserted in the courts. An imperative request preferred by one person to another, under a claim of right, requiring the latter to do or yield something or to abstain from some act. A debt or amount due. An asking with authority, claiming or challenging as due. Smith v. Municipal Court of Glendale Judicial Dist., Los Angeles County, 167 Cal. App.2d 534, 334 P.2d 931.

The seeking after a commodity or service. It is not something static, but necessarily contains the idea of "competition" and a realization that markets are as much limited by sales efforts as by capacity to produce. Mendota Coal & Coke Co. v. Eastern Ry. & Lumber Co., C.C.A.Wash., 53 F.2d 77, 82.

See also **Call; Liquidated demand; On demand; Payable on demand.**

Cross-demand. A demand that is preferred by one party to an action in opposition to a demand already preferred against him by his adversary. See **Counterclaim; Cross-claim.**

Demand clause. Provision in note which allows holder to compel full payment if maker fails to meet any installment. See *Demand note.*

Demand deposits. Any bank deposit which the depositor may demand (withdraw) at any time in contrast to time deposit which requires depositor to wait the specified time before withdrawing or pay a penalty for early withdrawal. Funds accepted by bank subject to immediate withdrawal; such represent largest element in money supply of the United States. U. S. v. Philadelphia Nat. Bank, D.C.Pa., 201 F.Supp. 348, 360.

Demand draft. Sight draft; draft payable on demand.

Demand loan. Loan which may be called by lender at any time because there is no fixed maturity date. See *Demand note.*

Demand note. A note which expressly states that it is payable on demand, on presentation or at sight; a note in which no time for payment is expressed. Cassity v. Cassity, 147 Kan. 411, 76 P.2d 862, 866; Kent v. Lampman, 59 Cal.App.2d 407, 139 P.2d 57, 59; Tarlton v. Johnson, Mo.App., 138 S.W.2d 49, 52. A note issued, accepted or indorsed when overdue, as regards person so issuing, accepting or indorsing it. Nees v. Hagan, 22 Tenn.App. 78, 118 S.W.2d 566, 568.

Legal demand. A demand properly made, as to form, time, and place, by a person lawfully authorized.

Personal demand. A demand for payment of a bill or note, made upon the drawer, acceptor or maker, in person.

Demandant /dəmǽndənt/. The plaintiff or party suing in a real action.

Demandress /dəmǽndrəs/. A female demandant.

De manucaptione /dìy mæ̀nəkæ̀pshiyówniy/. Writ of manucaption, or mainprise. A writ which lay for one who, being taken and imprisoned on a charge of felony, had offered bail, which had been refused; requiring the sheriff to discharge him on his finding sufficient mainpernors or bail.

De manutenendo /dìy mæ̀nətənéndow/. Writ of maintenance. A writ which lay against a person for the offense of maintenance.

Demarcation. The marking of a boundary line on the ground by physical means or a cartographic representation. State ex rel. Buckson v. Pennsylvania R. Co., Del., 267 A.2d 455, 459.

Demeanor /dəmíynər/. As respects a witness or other person, relates to physical appearance; outward bearing or behavior. Faircloth v. State, 44 Ala.App. 295, 208 So.2d 66, 70. It embraces such facts as the tone of voice in which a witness' statement is made, the hesitation or readiness with which his answers are given, the look of the witness, his carriage, his evidences of surprise, his gestures, his zeal, his bearing, his expression, his yawns, the use of his eyes, his furtive or meaning glances, or his shrugs, the pitch of his voice, his self-possession or embarrassment, his air of candor or seeming levity. Rains v. Rains, 17 N.J.Misc. 310, 8 A.2d 715, 717.

Demeanor evidence. Species of real evidence consisting of behavior of witness on the witness stand and which may be considered by trier of fact on issue of credibility.

Demease /dəmíyz/. In old English law, death.

De medietate linguæ /dìy mìydiyətéydiy líŋgwiy/. Of the half tongue; half of one tongue and half of another. This phrase describes that species of jury which, at common law, was allowed in both civil and criminal cases where one of the parties was an alien, not speaking or understanding English. It was composed of six English denizens or natives and six of the alien's own countrymen.

De medio /dìy míydiyow/. A writ in the nature of a writ of right, which lay where upon a subinfeudation the *mesne* (or middle) lord suffered his under-tenant or tenant *paravail* to be distrained upon by the lord paramount for the rent due him from the *mesne* lord.

De melioribus damnis /dìy miyliyórəbəs dǽmnəs/. Of or for the better damages. A term used in practice to denote the election by a plaintiff against which of several defendants (where the damages have been assessed separately) he will take judgment.

Judgment *de melioribus damnis* (of, or for, the better damages). Where, in an action against several persons for a joint tort, the jury by mistake sever the damages by giving heavier damages against one defendant than against the others the plaintiff may cure the defect by taking judgment for the greater damages (*de melioribus damnis*) against that defendant, and entering a *nolle prosequi* (*q.v.*) against the others.

Demens /díymen(d)z/. One whose mental faculties are enfeebled; one who has lost his mind; distinguished from *amens,* one totally insane.

Demented /dəméntəd/. Of unsound mind.

Dementenant en avant /də mè(y)ntənónt òn əvón(t)/. L. Fr. From this time forward.

Dementia /dəménsh(iy)ə/. Form of mental disorder in which cognitive and intellectual functions of the mind are prominently affected; impairment of memory is early sign; total recovery not possible since organic cerebral disease is involved. See also **Insanity.**

Dementia praecox /dəménsh(iy)ə príykòks/. A term used to include a wide range of mental disorders which occur in early life. It is also called adolescent insanity and schizophrenia. Dementia praecox includes three types, namely, primary dementia, catatonia, and hebephrenia. See also **Insanity.**

De mercatoribus /dìy mərkətórəbəs/. "Concerning merchants." The name of an English statute passed in the eleventh year of Edw. I (1233), more commonly called the "Statute of Acton Burnel," authorizing the recognizance by statute merchant. 2 Bl.Comm. 161.

Demesne /dəmíyn/dəméyn/. Domain; dominical; held in one's own right, and not of a superior; not allotted to tenants.

In the language of pleading, own; proper; original. Thus, *son assault demesne,* his own assault, his assault originally or in the first place.

Ancient demesne. See **Ancient.**

Demesne as of fee. A man is said to be seised *in his demesne as of fee* of a corporeal inheritance, because he has a property, *dominicum* or *demesne,* in the *thing* itself. But when he has no dominion in the thing itself, as in the case of an incorporeal hereditament, he is said to be *seised* as of fee, and not in his *demesne* as of fee. 2 Bl.Comm. 106.

Demesne lands. In old English law, those lands of a manor not granted out in tenancy, but reserved by the lord for his own use and occupation. Lands set apart and appropriated by the lord for his own private use, as for the supply of his table, and the maintenance of his family; the opposite of *tenemental* lands. Tenancy and demesne, however, were not in every sense the opposites of each other; lands held for years or at will being included among demesne lands, as well as those in the lord's actual possession. 2 Bl.Comm. 90.

Demesne lands of the crown. That share of lands reserved to the crown at the original distribution of landed property, or which came to it afterwards by forfeiture or otherwise. 1 Bl.Comm. 286.

Demesnial. Pertaining to a *demesne.*

De minimis non curat lex. The law cares not for small things.

Demi /démiy-/. Fr. Half; the half. Used chiefly in composition.

As to demi Mark; Official; Vill, see those titles.

Demidietas /dèmiydáyətæs/. In old records, a half or moiety.

De minimis doctrine. See **De minimis non curat lex.**

De minimis non curat lex /díy mínəməs nòn kyúrət léks/. The law does not care for, or take notice of, very small or trifling matters. The law does not concern itself about trifles.

De minis /díy mínəs/. Writ of threats. A writ which lay where a person was threatened with personal violence, or the destruction of his property, to compel the offender to keep the peace.

Deminutio /dìymən(y)úwsh(iy)ow/. In the civil law, a taking away; loss or deprivation. See **Capitis diminutio.**

Demi-sangue, or **demy-sangue** /démiysæŋ(k)/. Half-blood.

Demise, *v.* To convey or create an estate for years or life. To lease; to bequeath or transmit by succession or inheritance.

Demise, *n.* A conveyance of an estate to another for life, for years, or at will (most commonly for years); a lease. Originally a posthumous grant. Commonly a lease or conveyance for a term of years; sometimes applied to any conveyance in fee, for life, or for years. "Demise" is synonymous with "lease" or "let". The use of the term in a lease imports a convenant for quiet enjoyment, Evans v. Williams, 291 Ky. 484, 165 S.W.2d 52, 55; Sixty-Third & Halsted Realty Co. v. Chicago City Bank & Trust Co., 299 Ill.App. 297, 20 N.E.2d 162, 167; and implies a covenant by lessor of good right and title to make the lease, Evans v. Williams, 291 Ky. 484, 165 S.W.2d 52, 55.

The word is also used as a synonym for "decease" or "death". In England it is especially employed to denote the death of the sovereign.

Demise and redemise. In conveyancing, mutual leases made from one party to another on each side, of the same land, or something out of it; as when A. grants a lease to B. at a nominal rent (as of a pepper corn), and B. redemises the same property to A. for a shorter time at a real, substantial rent.

Demise charter. Under a demise charter, there is but a hiring of the vessel, under which no title passes to the charterer but merely the right to possess and control it for a limited period. McGahern v. Koppers Coal Co., C.C.A.Pa., 108 F.2d 652, 653. One under which control of vessel is taken from owner and vested in the charterer. F. Jacobus Transp. Co. v. Gallagher Bros. Sand & Gravel Corp., D.C.N.Y., 161 F.Supp. 507, 511. There must be relinquishment of all control over ship, barge or scow. B. W. King, Inc. v. Consolidated Iron & Metal Co., D.C.N.Y., 310 F.Supp. 471, 474.

Demise of the crown. The natural dissolution of the king is generally so called; an expression which signifies merely a transfer of property. By demise of the crown we mean only that, in consequence of the disunion of the king's natural body from his body politic, the kingdom is transferred or demised to his successor, and so the royal dignity remains perpetual. 1 Bl.Comm. 249.

Several demises. In English practice, in the action of ejectment, it was formerly customary, in case there were any doubt as to the legal estate being in the plaintiff, to insert in the declaration several demises from as many different persons; but this was rendered unnecessary by the provisions of the common-law procedure acts.

Single demise. A declaration in ejectment might contain either one demise or several. When it contained only one, it was called a "declaration with a single demise."

Demised premises. That property, or portion of a property which is leased to a tenant.

Demisi /dəmáyzay/. Lat. I have demised or leased. *Demisi, concessi, et ad firmam tradidi;* have demised, granted, and to farm let. The usual operative words in ancient leases, as the corresponding English words are in the modern forms. 2 Bl.Comm. 317, 318.

Demissio /dəmísh(iy)ow/. L. Lat. A demise or letting. Chiefly used in the phrase *ex demissione* (on the demise), which formed part of the title of the cause in the old actions of ejectment, where it signified that the nominal plaintiff (a fictitious person) held the estate "on the demise" of, that is, by a lease from, the real plaintiff.

De mittendo tenorem recordi /díy məténdow tənórəm rəkórday/. A writ to send the tenor of a record, or to exemplify it under the great seal.

Demobilization. The dismissal of an army or body of troops from active service.

Democracy. That form of government in which the sovereign power resides in and is exercised by the whole body of free citizens directly or indirectly through a system of representation, as distinguished from a monarchy, aristocracy, or oligarchy.

De moderata misericordia capienda /dìy modəréydə mìzərəkórdiyə kæpiyéndə/. Writ for taking a moderate amercement. A writ, founded on *Magna Charta* (c. 14), which lay for one who was excessively amerced in a court not of record, directed to the lord of the court, or his bailiff, commanding him *to take a moderate amercement* of the party.

De modo decimandi /dìy mówdow dèsəmǽnday/. Of a *modus* of tithing. A term applied in English ecclesiastical law to a prescription to have a special manner of tithing. 2 Bl.Comm. 29.

De molendino de novo erecto non jacet prohibitio /dìy məléndənow dìy nówvow əréktow nòn jéysət pròw-(h)əbísh(iy)ow/. A prohibition lies not against a newly-erected mill.

Demolish. To throw or pull down; to raze; to destroy the fabrication of; to pull to pieces; hence to ruin or destroy. Star Mfg. Co. v. Quarries, 172 Okl. 550, 46 P.2d 497, 498. To destroy totally or to commence the work of total destruction with the purpose of completing the same.

Demonetization /dìymonədəzéyshən/. The disuse of a particular metal for purposes of coinage. The withdrawal of the value of a metal as money. For example, in the United States gold has been demonetized.

Demonstrate. To teach by exhibition of samples; to derive from admitted premises by steps of reasoning which admit of no doubt; to prove indubitably. To show or prove value or merits by operation, reasoning, or evidence.

Demonstratio /dèmənstréysh(iy)ow/. Lat. Description; addition; denomination. Occurring often in the phrase, *"Falsa demonstratio non nocet"* (a false description does not harm). 2 Bl.Comm. 382.

Demonstration. Description; pointing out. That which is said or written to designate a thing or person. Show or display of attitudes toward a person, cause, or issue. See also **False demonstration.**

Demonstrative bequest. A testamentary gift which, by its terms, must be paid from a specific fund; *e.g.* bequest of one thousand dollars to be paid from testator's shares of stock in X Corporation. Hence, it is partly a general bequest and partly a specific bequest. See also **Legacy.**

Demonstrative evidence. That evidence addressed directly to the senses without intervention of testimony. Real ("thing") evidence such as the gun in a trial of homicide or the contract itself in the trial of a contract case. Evidence apart from the testimony of witnesses concerning the thing. Such evidence may include maps, diagrams, photographs, models, charts, medical illustrations, X-rays.

Demonstrative legacy. See **Legacy.**

Demonstrator. One who stands, walks or parades in public in support of a cause to inform the public of the legitimacy of the cause and to enlist support for such cause.

De morte hominis nulla est cunctatio longa /dìy mórdiy hómənəs nàlə èst kənktéysh(iy)ow lóŋgə/. Where the death of a human being is concerned [in a matter of life and death], no delay is [considered] long.

Demotion. A reduction to lower rank or grade, or to lower type of position. See also **Degradation.**

Demur /dəmár/. To present a demurrer; to take an exception to the sufficiency in point of law of a pleading or state of facts alleged. See **Demurrer.**

Demurrable /dəmárəbəl/. Subject to a demurrer. A pleading, petition, or the like, is said to be demurrable when it does not state such facts as support the claim, prayer, or defense put forward.

Demurrage /dəmárəj/. In maritime law, the sum which is fixed by the contract of carriage, or which is allowed, as remuneration to the owner of a ship for the detention of his vessel beyond the number of days allowed by the charter-party for loading and unloading or for sailing. Also the detention of the vessel by the freighter beyond such time. With respect to railroads a charge exacted by a carrier from a shipper or consignee on account of a failure on the latter's part to load or unload cars within the free time prescribed by the applicable tariffs; the purpose of the charge is to expedite the loading and unloading of cars, thus facilitating the flow of commerce, which is in the public interest. St. Louis, Southwestern Ry. Co. v. Mays, D.C.Ark., 177 F.Supp. 182, 183. Demurrage is extended freight and is the amount payable for delays by receiver in loading or unloading cargo; it is stipulated damages for detention. Hellenic Lines, Limited v. Director General of India Supply Mission for and on Behalf of Union of India, D.C. N.Y., 319 F.Supp. 821, 831.

Demurrage lien. Carrier's right to possession of goods for unpaid demurrage charges.

Demurrant /dəmárənt/. One who demurs; the party who, in pleading, interposes a demurrer.

Demurrer. An allegation of a defendant, which, admitting the matters of fact alleged by complaint or bill (equity action) to be true, shows that as they are therein set forth they are insufficient for the plaintiff to proceed upon or to oblige the defendant to answer; or that, for some reason apparent on the face of the complaint or bill, or on account of the omission of some matter which ought to be contained therein, or for want of some circumstances which ought to be attendant thereon, the defendant ought not to be compelled to answer. The formal mode of disputing the sufficiency in law of the pleading of the other side. In effect it is an allegation that, even if the facts as stated in the pleading to which objection is taken be true, yet their legal consequences are not such as to put the demurring party to the necessity of answering them or proceeding further with the cause. An assertion that complaint does not set forth a cause of action upon which relief can be granted, and it admits, for purpose of testing sufficiency of complaint, all properly pleaded facts, but not conclusions of law. Balsbaugh v. Rowland, 447 Pa. 423, 290 A.2d 85, 87. A legal objection to the sufficiency of a pleading, attacking what appears on the face of the document. People v. Hale, 232 Cal.App.2d 112, 42

Cal.Rptr. 533, 538. See Calif. Code of Civil Proc. § 430.10. See also **Demurrer to evidence.**

By Federal Rules of Civil Procedure (adopted in whole or part in most states) demurrers, pleas and exceptions for insufficiency of a pleading are abolished. Rule 7(c). Every defense in law shall be made by motion or by answer; motions going to jurisdiction, venue, process, or failure to state a claim are to be disposed of before trial, unless the court orders otherwise. Objections to the pleadings by means of demurrer still exists however in certain states; see *e.g.* Calif. Code of Civil Proc. § 430.10 et seq.

Classification of Demurrers

General demurrer. A *general* demurrer is a demurrer framed in general terms, without showing specifically the nature of the objection, and which is usually resorted to where the objection is to matter of substance. Thus, a demurrer on the ground that the complaint sets forth no cause of action is a general demurrer (see *e.g.* Calif. Code of Civil Proc. § 430.-10(e)), and a motion to dismiss a bill on ground that there is no equity apparent on the face thereof or that court has no jurisdiction is treated as a general demurrer.

A general demurrer to an indictment challenges only matters of form and substance appearing on its face. It is one which raises an objection that averments are insufficient in law to support the action or defense without specifying any particular cause or defect, and is sufficient only to reach matters of substance.

The Federal Rules equivalent to a general demurrer is a motion to dismiss for failure to state a claim on which relief may be granted. Fed.R. Civil P. 12(b).

Special demurrer. A *special* demurrer goes merely to structure or form of pleading which it attacks, and usually only to some portion thereof, and must distinctly specify wherein defect lies. Cameron v. Evans Securities Corp., 119 Cal.App. 164, 6 P.2d 272, 274. It is one which excepts to the sufficiency of the pleadings on the opposite side, and shows specifically the nature of the objection, and the particular ground of the exception. Johanson v. Cudahy Packing Co., 107 Utah 114, 152 P.2d 98, 105. See *e.g.* Calif. Code of Civil Proc. §§ 430.50, 430.60. The Federal Rules analogue of the special demurrer is the motion to make more definite and certain. Fed.R. Civil P. 12(e).

Speaking demurrer. A *speaking* demurrer is one which, in order to sustain itself, requires the aid of a fact not appearing on the face of the pleading objected to, or, in other words, which alleges or assumes the existence of a fact not already pleaded, and which constitutes the ground of objection and is condemned both by the common law and the code system of pleading. Preston A. Blair Co. v. Rose, 56 Idaho 114, 51 P.2d 209, 212. A speaking demurrer is one which alleges some new matter, not disclosed by the pleading against which the demurrer is aimed and not judicially known or legally presumed to be true.

Parol demurrer. A *parol* demurrer (not properly a demurrer at all) was a staying of the pleadings; a suspension of the proceedings in an action during the nonage of an infant, especially in a real action. Now abolished. 3 Bl.Comm. 300.

Demurrer book. A record of the issue on a demurrer at law, containing a transcript of the pleadings, with proper entries; and intended for the use of the court and counsel on the argument.

Demurrer ore tenus. An objection to the introduction of any evidence on the ground that the complaint or petition fails to state a cause of action. Peerless Fixture Co. v. Frick, Mo.App., 133 S.W.2d 1089, 1090. This name is sometimes given to a ruling on an objection to evidence, but is not properly a demurrer at all. It should be considered as a general demurrer only.

Demurrer to evidence. This proceeding is analogous to a demurrer to a pleading. It is an objection or exception by one of the parties in an action at law, to the effect that the evidence which his adversary produced is insufficient in point of law (whether true or not) to make out his case or sustain the issue. The practice has been largely superseded by motions for nonsuit and directed verdict. Thus, a motion to nonsuit, a motion to dismiss at close of plaintiff's evidence for failure to prove essential facts, and a defendant's motion for a directed verdict, made at close of the evidence, have been held to be equivalent to a "demurrer to the evidence" for insufficiency to sustain a verdict for plaintiff. A motion to exclude evidence has the effect of a demurrer to the evidence, the chief points of difference being the stage of the proceeding at which each is available and the consequences resulting from deferring the motion to exclude. Thornhill v. Thornhill, 172 Va. 553, 2 S.E.2d 318, 319.

Demurrer to interrogatories. Where a witness objects to a question propounded (particularly on the taking of a deposition) and states his reason for objecting or refusing to answer, it is called a "demurrer to the interrogatory," though the term cannot here be understood as used in its technical sense.

Demy sanke, or **demy sangue** /démiy sǽŋ(k)/. Half-blood. A corruption of *demi-sang.*

Den and strond /dén ən(d) strónd/. In old English law, liberty for ships or vessels to run aground, or come ashore (strand themselves).

Denariate /dənériyət/. In old English law, as much land as is worth one penny *per annum.*

Denarii /dənériyay/. An ancient general term for any sort of *pecunia numerata,* or ready money. The French use the word *"denier"* in the same sense,— *payer de ses propres deniers.*

Denarius Dei /dənériyəs díyay/. (Lat. "God's penny.") Earnest money; money given as a token of the completion of a bargain. It differs from *arrhœ* in this: that *arrhœ* is a part of the consideration, while the *denarius Dei* is no part of it. The latter was given away in charity; whence the name.

Denationalization. As applied to a person, the act of depriving him of national rights or status. As applied to an industry or function, the act of returning it to private ownership and control after a period of national or sovereign ownership and control.

De nativo habendo /diy néydəvow həbéndow/. A writ which lay for a lord directed to the sheriff, commanding him to apprehend a fugitive villein, and restore him, with all his chattels, to the lord.

De natura brevium /dìy nəchúrə bríyviyəm/. (Lat.) Concerning the nature of writs. The title of more than one textbook of English Mediæval law. See **Register of writs.**

Denial. A traverse in the pleading of one party of an allegation of fact set up by the other; a defense. Under Rules of Civil Procedure, denials must be specific and directed at the particular allegations controverted. Denials may be made in part or in whole, but, in the main should be specific and "fairly meet the substance of the averments denied." Fed.R. Civil P. 8(b).

General and specific. In code pleading, a general denial is one which puts in issue all the material averments of the complaint or petition, and permits the defendant to prove any and all facts tending to negative those averments or any of them. A specific denial is a separate denial applicable to one particular allegation of the complaint. An answer by way of a general denial is the equivalent of, and substitute for, the general issue under the common-law system of pleading. It gives to the defendant the same right to require the plaintiff to establish by proof all the material facts necessary to show his right to a recovery as was given by that plea.

Denier /dənáyər/. L. Fr. In old English law, denial; refusal. *Denier* is when the rent (being demanded upon the land) is not paid.

Denier a dieu /dənyéy a dyúw/. In French law, earnest money; a sum of money given in token of the completion of a bargain. The phrase is a translation of the Latin *denarius Dei (q.v.).*

Denization /dènəzéyshən/. The act of making one a denizen; the conferring of the privileges of citizenship upon an alien born. See **Denizen.**

Denize /dənáyz/. To make a man a denizen or citizen.

Denizen /dénəzən/. In English law, a person who, being an alien born, has obtained, *ex donatione regis,* letters patent to make him an English subject,—a high and incommunicable branch of the royal prerogative. A denizen is in a kind of middle state between an alien and a natural-born subject, and partakes of the *status* of both of these. The term is used to signify a person who, being an alien by birth, has obtained letters patent making him an English subject. The king may denize, but not naturalize, a man; the latter requiring the consent of parliament, as under the naturalization act, 1870, 33 & 34 Vict., c. 14. A denizen holds a position midway between an alien and a natural-born or naturalized subject, being able to take lands by purchase or devise (which an alien could not until 1870 do), but not able to take lands by descent (which a natural-born or naturalized subject may do). The denizen becomes a British subject from the date of the letters while a naturalized person is placed in a position equivalent to that of a natural-born subject. Naturalization of aliens is now governed by British Nationality Act.

In American law, a dweller; a stranger admitted to certain rights in a foreign country or as one who lives

habitually in a country but is not a native born citizen; one holding a middle state between an alien and a natural born subject. One who has some relation to the enemy nation which is not lost by the alien's presence within the United States. United States ex rel. Zdunic v. Uhl, C.C.A.N.Y., 137 F.2d 858, 861; United States ex rel. D'Esquiva v. Uhl, C.C.A. N.Y., 137 F.2d 903, 905. Thus, one who lived and worked in Austria in 1938 at time Germany obtained control of Austrian government, and continued to live there until leaving for the United States in 1939, at which time he was issued a German passport, was a "denizen" of Germany, within Enemy Alien Act. United States ex rel. Zdunic v. Uhl, D.C.N.Y., 47 F.Supp. 520.

A denizen, in the primary, but obsolete, sense of the word, is a natural-born subject of a country.

Denman's (Lord) Act /(lòrd) dénmənz ǽkt/. An English statute, for the amendment of the law of evidence (6 & 7 Vict., c. 85), which provides that no person offered as a witness shall thereafter be excluded by reason of incapacity, from crime or interest, from giving evidence.

Denman's (Mr.) Act /(místər) dénmənz ǽkt/. An English statute, for the amendment of procedure in criminal trials (28 & 29 Vict., c. 18), allowing counsel to sum up the evidence in criminal as in civil trials, provided the prisoner be defended by counsel.

Denombrement /dənòbrəmón/. In French feudal law, a minute or act drawn up, on the creation of a fief, containing a description of the fief, and all the rights and incidents belonging to it.

Denominatio fieri debet a dignioribus /dənòmənéysh(iy)ow fáyəray débəd èy dìgniyórəbəs/. Denomination should be made from the more worthy.

Denomination. The act of naming. A society of individuals known by the same name, usually a religious society.

Denominational, *adj.* /dənòmənéyshənəl/. Of, or pertaining to, a denomination; sectarian.

Denominational institution. Institution controlled or operated by a religious sect or organization and hence forbidden to receive governmental aid because of constitutional separation of church and state.

De nomine proprio non est curandum cum in substantia non erretur; quia nomina mutabilia sunt, res autem immobiles /dìy nómaniy prówpriyow nón èst kyərǽndəm kàm in səbstǽnsh(iy)ə nòn əríydər, kwáyə nómənə myùwdəbĺiyə sànt, ríyz ódəm imówbəliyz/. As to the proper name, it is not to be regarded where it errs not in substance, because names are changeable, but things immutable.

De non apparentibus, et non existentibus, eadem est ratio /dìy nòn æpəréntəbəs et nòn ègzəsténtəbəs iyéydəm èst réysh(iy)ow/. As to things not apparent, and those not existing, the rule is the same.

De non decimando /dìy nòn desəmǽndow/. Of not paying tithes. A term applied in English ecclesiastical law to a prescription or claim to be entirely discharged of tithes, and to pay no compensation in lieu of them. 2 Bl.Comm. 31.

De non procedendo ad assisam /dìy nòn pròwsədéndow æd əsáyzəm/. A writ forbidding the justices from holding an assise in a particular case.

De non residentia clerici regis /dìy nòn rezədénsh(iy)ə klérəsay ríyjəs/. An ancient writ where a parson was employed in the royal service, etc., to excuse and discharge him of non-residence.

De non sane memorie /dìy nòn séyniy məmóriyiy/°sǽniy méməriy/. L. Fr. Of unsound memory or mind; a phrase synonymous with *non compos mentis*.

Denounce. To declare (an act or thing) to be a crime and prescribe a punishment for it. To pronounce or condemn something as being evil or morally wrong. The word is also used (not technically but popularly) as the equivalent of "accuse" or "inform against."

The term is frequently used in regard to treaties, indicating the act of one nation in giving notice to another nation of its intention to terminate an existing treaty between the two nations. The French *dénoncer* means to declare, to lodge an information against.

Denouncement. An application to the authorities for a grant of the right to work a mine, either on the ground of new discovery, or on the ground of forfeiture of the rights of a former owner, through abandonment or contravention of the mining law. Castillero v. U. S., 67 U.S. 17, 2 Black 17, 17 L.Ed. 360; Stewart v. King, 85 Or. 14, 166 P. 55, 56. An application for the acquisition of land for mining purposes, under certain rules prescribed by Mexican laws. The application is called the "denouncement," and, when approved by the Mexican government, is called "concession" or "title," sometimes "patent." It is then a grant given by the government to use the land applied for, for the purpose of mining, and is called the "title." Winningham v. Dyo, Tex.Com.App., 48 S.W.2d 600, 603.

In Spanish and Mexican law, a judicial proceeding for the forfeiture of land held by an alien.

De novi operis nunciatione /dìy nówvay ówpərəs nànsiyèyshiyówniy/. In the civil law, a form of interdict or injunction which lies in some cases where the defendant is about to erect a "new work" *(q.v.)* in derogation or injury of the plaintiff's rights.

De novo /dìy nówvow/. Anew; afresh; a second time. A *venire de novo* is a writ for summoning a jury for the second trial of a case which has been sent back from above for a new trial.

De novo hearing. See **Hearing de novo.**

De novo trial. Trying a matter anew; the same as if it had not been heard before and as if no decision had been previously rendered. Farmingdale Supermarket, Inc. v. U. S., D.C.N.J., 336 F.Supp. 534, 536.

De nullo, quod est sua natura indivisibile, et divisionem non patitur, nullam partem habebit vidua, sed satisfaciat ei ad valentiam /dìy nálow, kwód èst s(y)úwə nət(y)úrə indivəzíbəliy èt dəvìz(h)iyównəm nòn pǽdədər, náləm párdəm həbíybət víd(y)uwə, sèd sǽdəsféyshiyət íyay æd vəlénshiyəm/. A widow shall have no part of that which in its own nature is indivisible, and is not susceptible of division, but let the heir satisfy her with an equivalent.

De nullo tenemento, quod tenetur ad terminum, fit homagii, fit tamen inde fidelitatis sacramentum /dìy nálow tènəméntow, kwòd təníydər æd tə́rmənəm, fít həméyjiyay, fít tǽmən índiy fədìylətéydəs sǽkrəméntəm/. In no tenement which is held for a term of years is there an avail of homage; but there is the oath of fealty.

Denumeration. The act of present payment.

Denunciation. Act of denouncing.

In the civil law, the act by which an individual informs a public officer, whose duty it is to prosecute offenders, that a crime has been committed.

The giving of an information in the ecclesiastical courts by one who was not the accuser.

Denuntiatio /dənə̀nsiyéysh(iy)ow/. In old English law, a public notice or summons.

Deny. To traverse. To give negative answer or reply to. To refuse to grant or accept. To refuse to grant a petition or protest. Safeway Stores v. Brown, Em. App., 138 F.2d 278, 280. See **Denial.**

Deodand /díyədæ̀nd/. (L. Lat. *Deo dandum,* a thing to be given to God.) In English law, any personal chattel which was the immediate occasion of the death of any reasonable creature, and which was forfeited to the crown to be applied to *pious* uses, and distributed in alms by the high almoner.

De odio et atia /dìy ówdiyow ed éysh(iy)ə/. A writ anciently called *"breve de bono et malo,"* addressed to the sheriff to inquire whether a man committed to prison upon suspicion of murder were committed on just cause of suspicion, or only upon malice and ill will *(propter odium et atiam);* and, if upon the inquisition, due cause of suspicion did not appear, then there issued another writ for the sheriff to admit him to bail. 3 Bl.Comm. 128.

De office /d(ə) owfíys/. L. Fr. Of office; in virtue of office; officially; in the discharge of ordinary duty.

De onerando pro rata portione /dìy ò̀wnərǽndow pròw réydə pòrshiyówniy/. Writ for charging according to a rateable proportion. A writ which lay for a joint tenant, or tenant in common, who was distrained for more rent than his proportion of the land came to.

De pace et legalitate tenenda /dìy péysiy èt ləgæ̀lətéydiy tənéndə/. For keeping the peace, and for good behavior.

De pace et plagis /dìy péysiy èt pléyjəs/. Of peace (breach of peace), and wounds. One of the kinds of criminal appeal formerly in use in England, and which lay in cases of assault, wounding, and breach of the peace.

De pace et roberia /dìy péysiy èt ròbáriyə/. Of peace [breach of peace] and robbery. One of the kinds of criminal appeal formerly in use in England, and which lay in cases of robbery and breach of the peace.

De parco fracto /dìy párkow frǽktow/. A writ or action for damages caused by a pound-breach *(q.v.)*. It has long been obsolete. 3 Bl.Comm. 146.

Depart. To go away from; leave; die.

De partitione facienda /dìy partìshiyówniy fèys(h)iyéndə/. A writ which lay to make partition of lands or tenements held by several as coparceners, tenants in common, etc.

Department. One of the territorial divisions of a country. The term is chiefly used in this sense in France, where the division of the country into departments is somewhat analogous, both territorially and for governmental purposes, to the division of an American state into counties.

One of the major administrative divisions of the executive branch of the government usually headed by an officer of cabinet rank; *e.g.* Department of State. Generally, a branch or division of governmental administration. Also, a division of a business, or of something comparable thereto. U. S. v. Elgin, J. & E. Ry. Co., Ill., 298 U.S. 492, 56 S.Ct. 841, 80 L.Ed. 1300.

Department of State. See **State Department.**

Departure. A deviation or divergence, from a standard rule, measurement or course of conduct.

A variance between pleading and proof. Kintner v. U. S., C.C.A.Colo., 71 F.2d 961, 962. In common law pleading, the statement of matter in a replication, rejoinder, or subsequent pleading, as a cause of action or defense, which is not pursuant to the previous pleading of the same party, and which does not support and fortify it. Under Rules of Civil Procedure, no provision is made for "departure" but there are liberal amendment provisions. Fed.R. Civil P. 15.

See also **Variance.**

Departure in despite of court. In old English practice, the tenant in a real action, having once appeared, was considered as constructively present in court until again called upon. Hence if, upon being demanded, he failed to appear, he was said to have "departed in despite [*i.e.*, contempt] of the court."

Depeculation. In English law, a robbing of the prince or commonwealth; an embezzling of the public treasure.

Dependable, *adj.* Trustworthy or reliable, Anderson v. Wyoming Development Co., 60 Wyo. 417, 154 P.2d 318, 340; evidence, Taylor v. Latimer, D.C.Mo., 47 F.Supp. 236, 238.

Dependence. A state of looking to another for support, maintenance, food, clothing, comfort and protection of a home and care. Soderstrom v. Missouri Pac. R. Co., Mo.App., 141 S.W.2d 73, 79. See **Dependent.**

Dependency. A territory distinct from the country in which the supreme sovereign power resides, but belonging rightfully to it, and subject to the laws and regulations which the sovereign may think proper to prescribe. Posadas v. National City Bank of N. Y., Phil. Islands, 296 U.S. 497, 56 S.Ct. 349, 350, 80 L.Ed. 351. It differs from a *colony,* because it is not settled by the citizens of the sovereign or mother state; and from *possession,* because it is held by other title than that of mere conquest.

A relation between two persons, where one is sustained by another or looks to or relies on aid of another for support or for reasonable necessaries consistent with dependent's position in life. See **Dependent.**

Dependent, *n.* One who derives his or her main support from another. Means relying on, or subject to, someone else for support; not able to exist or sustain oneself, or to perform anything without the will, power, or aid of someone else. Fox-Vliet Wholesale Drug Co. v. Chase, Okl., 288 P.2d 391, 393. Generally, for worker's compensation purposes, "dependent" is one who relies on another for support or favor and one who is sustained by another. Industrial Indem. Co. v. Industrial Acc. Commission, 243 Cal.App.2d 700, 52 Cal.Rptr. 647, 651, 653. One who has relied upon decedent for support and who has reasonable expectation that such support will continue. Wheat v. Red Star Exp. Lines, 156 Conn. 245, 240 A.2d 859, 862, 863. See also **Lawful dependents.**

Dependent, *adj.* Deriving existence, support, or direction from another; conditioned, in respect to force or obligation, upon an extraneous act or fact.

Dependent conditions. Mutual covenants which go to the whole consideration on both sides.

Dependent contract. One which depends or is conditional upon another. One which it is not the duty of the contractor to perform until some obligation contained in the same agreement has been performed by the other party.

Dependent covenant. See **Covenant.**

Dependent promise. One which it is not the duty of the promisor to perform until some obligation contained in the same agreement has been performed by the other party.

Dependent relative revocation. The doctrine which regards as mutually dependent the acts of one destroying a will and thereupon substituting another instrument for distribution of estate, when both acts are result of one plan, so that, if second act, through incompleteness or other defect, fails to accomplish its intended purpose, and it thereby becomes evident that testator was misled when he destroyed his will, act of destruction is regarded as bereft of intent of revocation and way for probate of destroyed will is opened. In re Cuneo's Estate, 60 Cal.2d 196, 32 Cal.Rptr. 409, 412, 384 P.2d 1.

Depending. Pending or undetermined; in progress.

In patent law, a convenient means of saying that the parts of a device were so attached as to have a right-angle relationship to each other, not a gravitational hanging of one part upon another. Alemite Mfg. Corporation v. Rogers Products Co., C.C.A.N.J., 42 F.2d 648, 651.

De perambulatione facienda /dìy pəræmbyəlèyshiyówniy fæs(h)iyéndə/. A writ which lay where there was a dispute as to the boundaries of two adjacent lordships or towns, directed to the sheriff, commanding him to take with him twelve discreet and lawful knights of his county and make the perambulation and set the bounds and limits in certainty.

Depesas /dəpéysəs/°-z/. In Spanish-American law, spaces of ground in towns reserved for commons or public pasturage.

De pignore surrepto furti, actio /ǽksh(iy)ow dìy pignóriy səréptow fárday/. In the civil law, an action to recover a pledge stolen.

De placito /dìy plǽsədow/. Of a plea; of or in an action. Formal words used in declarations and other proceedings, as descriptive of the particular action brought.

De plagis et mahemio /dìy pléyjəs èt məhíymiyow/. Of wounds and mayhem. The name of a criminal appeal formerly in use in England, in cases of wounding and maiming. See **Appeal**.

De plano /dìy pléynow/. Lat. On the ground; on a level. A term of the Roman law descriptive of the method of hearing causes, when the prætor stood on the ground with the suitors, instead of the more formal method when he occupied a bench or tribunal; hence informal, or summary.

De plegiis acquietandis /dìy pliyjiyəs əkwàyətǽndəs/. Writ for acquitting or releasing pledges. A writ that lay for a surety, against him for whom he had become surety for the payment of a certain sum of money at a certain day, where the latter had not paid the money at the appointed day, and the surety was compelled to pay it.

Depletable economic interest. The interest in mineral land which is subject to depletion by the removal of the minerals by operation of an oil well, mine, or the like. Spalding v. U. S., C.C.A.Cal., 97 F.2d 697, 700; U. S. v. Spalding, C.C.A.Cal., 97 F.2d 701, 704. See **Depletion**.

Deplete. To reduce or lessen, as by use, exhaustion, or waste. McKnight v. U. S., C.C.A.Cal., 78 F.2d 931, 933.

Depletion. An emptying, exhausting or wasting of assets. A reduction during taxable year of oil, gas or other mineral deposits or reserves (i.e. wasting assets) as result of production. The process by which the cost or other basis of a natural resource (e.g., an oil and gas interest) is recovered upon extraction and sale of the resource. The two ways to determine the depletion allowance are the cost and percentage (or statutory) methods. Under the cost method, each unit of production sold is assigned a portion of the cost or other basis of the interest. This is determined by dividing the cost or other basis by the total units expected to be recovered. Under the percentage (or statutory) method the tax law provides a special percentage factor for different types of minerals and other natural resources. This percentage is multiplied by the gross income from the interest to arrive at the depletion allowance. I.R.S. §§ 613 and 613A.

Depletion allowance. See **Depletion**.

Depletion deduction. See **Depletion**.

Depletion reserve. In accounting, a charge to income to reflect the decrease in value of a wasting asset such as an oil well.

De ponendo sigillum ad exceptionem /dìy pənéndow səjíləm æd əksèpshiyównəm/. Writ for putting a seal to an exception. A writ by which justices were formerly commanded to put their seals to exceptions taken by a party in a suit.

Deponent /dəpównənt/. One who deposes (that is, testifies) to the truth of certain facts; one who gives under oath testimony which is reduced to writing; one who makes oath to a written statement. One whose deposition is given. A witness; an affiant. See **Depose; Deposition**.

Depopulatio agrorum /dìypopyəléysh(iy)ow əgrórəm/. In old English law, the crime of destroying, ravaging, or laying waste a country. 4 Bl.Comm. 373.

Depopulation. In old English law, a species of waste by which the population of the kingdom was diminished. Depopulation of houses was a public offense.

Deportatio /dìyportéysh(iy)ow/. Lat. In the civil law, a kind of banishment, where a condemned person was sent or carried away to some foreign country, usually to an island (in insulam deportatur), and thus taken out of the number of Roman citizens.

Deportation. Banishment to a foreign country, attended with confiscation of property and deprivation of civil rights. A punishment derived from the deportatio (q.v.) of the Roman law.

The transfer of an alien, excluded or expelled, from the United States to a foreign country. Petition for Milanovic, D.C.N.Y., 162 F.Supp. 890, 892. The removal or sending back of an alien to the country from which he came because his presence is deemed inconsistent with the public welfare, and without any punishment being imposed or contemplated. The list of grounds for deportation are set forth at 8 U.S.C.A. § 1251, and the procedures are provided for in §§ 1252–1254. See also **Banishment**.

Depose. To make a deposition; to give evidence in the shape of a deposition; to make statements which are written down and sworn to; to give testimony which is reduced to writing by a duly-qualified officer and sworn to by the deponent. See **Deponent; Deposition**.

To deprive an individual of a public employment or office against his will. The term is usually applied to the deprivation of all authority of a sovereign.

In ancient usage, to testify as a witness; to give evidence under oath.

Deposit, v. To commit to custody, or to lay down; to place; to put; to let fall (as sediment). Jefferson County ex rel. Grauman v. Jefferson County Fiscal Court, 273 Ky. 674, 117 S.W.2d 918, 924. To lodge for safe-keeping or as a pledge to intrust to the care of another. White v. Greenlee, 330 Mo. 135, 49 S.W.2d 132, 134.

Deposit, n. A bailment of goods to be kept by the bailee without reward, and delivered according to the object or purpose of the original trust. In general, an act by which a person receives the property of another, binding himself to preserve it and return it in kind. The delivery of chattels by one person to another to keep for the use of the bailor. The giving of the possession of personal property by one person to another, with his consent, to keep for the use and benefit of the first or of a third person. Something intrusted to the care of another, either for a permanent or a temporary disposition.

Money lodged with a person as an earnest or security for the performance of some contract, to be forfeited if the depositor fails in his undertaking. It may be deemed to be part payment, and to that extent may constitute the purchaser the actual owner of the estate.

The act of placing money in the custody of a bank or banker, for safety or convenience, to be withdrawn at the will of the depositor or under rules and regulations agreed on. Also, the money so deposited, or the credit which the depositor receives for it. Deposit, according to its commonly accepted and generally understood meaning among bankers and by the public, includes not only deposits payable on demand and subject to check, but deposits not subject to check, for which certificates, whether interest-bearing or not, may be issued, payable on demand, or on certain notice, or at a fixed future time.

A quantity of ore or other mineral substances occurring naturally in the earth; as, a deposit of gold, oil, etc.

See **Bailment; Escrow.**

General Classification

According to the classification of the civil law, deposits are of the following several sorts: (1) *Necessary,* made upon some sudden emergency, and from some pressing necessity; as, for instance, in case of a fire, a shipwreck, or other overwhelming calamity, when property is confided to any person whom the depositor may meet without proper opportunity for reflection or choice, and thence it is called *"miserabile depositum."* (2) *Voluntary,* which arises from the mere consent and agreement of the parties. The common law has made no such division. The civilians again divide deposits into "simple deposits," made by one or more persons having a common interest, and "sequestrations," made by one or more persons, each of whom has a different and adverse interest in controversy touching it; and these last are of two sorts,—"conventional," or such as are made by the mere agreement of the parties without any judicial act; and "judicial," or such as are made by order of a court in the course of some proceeding. Thus, under Louisiana statutes, it is said that the difference between "sequestration" and "deposit" is that the former may have for its object both movable and immovable property, while the latter is confined to movables.

There is another class of deposits called "involuntary," which may be without the assent or even knowledge of the depositor; as lumber, etc., left upon another's land by the subsidence of a flood. An "involuntary" deposit is one made by the accidental leaving or placing of personal property in the possession of any person without negligence on the part of the owner. Another class of deposits is called "irregular," as when a person, having a sum of money which he does not think safe in his own hands, confides it to another, who is to return to him, not the same money, but a like sum when he shall demand it. A *regular* deposit is a strict or special deposit; a deposit which must be returned *in specie; i.e.,* the thing deposited must be returned. A *quasi* deposit is a kind of implied or involuntary deposit, which takes place where a party comes lawfully to the possession of another person's property, by finding it. Particularly with reference to money, deposits are also classed as *general* or *special.* A general deposit is where the money deposited is not itself to be returned, but an equivalent in money (that is, a like sum) is to be returned. It is equivalent to a loan, and the money deposited becomes the property of the depositary. A special deposit is a deposit in which the identical thing deposited is to be returned to the depositor. The particular object of this kind of deposit is safekeeping. In banking law, this kind of deposit is contrasted with a "general" deposit, as above; but in the civil law it is the antithesis of an "irregular" deposit. A *gratuitous* or *naked* deposit is a bailment of goods to be kept for the depositor without hire or reward on either side, or one for which the depositary receives no consideration beyond the mere possession of the thing deposited. Properly and originally, all deposits are of this description; for according to the Roman law, a bailment of goods for which hire or a price is to be paid, is not called "depositum" but "locatio." If the owner of the property pays for its custody or care, it is a "locatio custodiæ;" if, on the other hand, the bailee pays for the use of it, it is "locatio rei." (See **Locatio.**) But in the modern law, a gratuitous or naked deposit is distinguished from a "deposit for hire," in which the bailee is to be paid for his services in keeping the article. There is also a *specific* deposit, which exists where money or property is given to a bank for some specific and particular purpose, as a note for collection, money to pay a particular note, or property for some other specific purpose.

See also **Certificate of deposit; Involuntary deposit.** For bank deposit, see **Bank.**

Demand deposit. Bank deposit which may be withdrawn at any time by the depositor, without prior notice to bank. Compare *"Time deposit", infra.*

Deposit box. Commonly referred to as safe deposit box in which a person may keep valuables. See **Safe deposit box.**

Deposit company. A company whose business is the safe-keeping of securities or other valuables deposited in boxes or safes in its building which are leased to the depositors. See **Depositary; Depository.**

Deposit in court. Person who acknowledges liability but is in doubt as to whom the liability runs may pay into court the sum of money representing his liability and be bound by the court's determination of who is entitled to it. See *e.g.* Fed.R. Civil P. 67. May also embrace payment into court pursuant to court order as in the case of rent pending outcome of eviction case.

Deposit insurance. Insurance coverage (*e.g.* Federal Deposit Insurance Corporation) for bank depositors protecting them from loss resulting from bank failure. See **Deposit Insurance Corporation.**

Deposit of title-deeds. A method of pledging real property as security for a loan, by placing the title-deeds of the land in the keeping of the lender as pledgee.

Deposit premium. The initial premium paid by the insured on a provisional basis pending a premium adjustment in the case of policies subject to adjustment.

Deposit ratio. Ratio of total deposits to total capital.

Deposit slip. An acknowledgment that the amount named therein has been received by the bank. It is a receipt intended to furnish evidence as between the depositor and depositary that on a given date there was deposited the sum named therein, the time of deposit, and amount deposited, being also shown.

Time deposit. Bank deposit which is to remain for specified period of time, or on which notice must be given to bank before withdrawal.

Depositary. The party or institution (*e.g.* bank or trust company) receiving a deposit. One with whom anything is lodged in trust, as "depository" is the place where it is put. A trustee; fiduciary; one to whom goods are bailed to be held without recompense. The obligation on the part of the depositary is that he keep the thing with reasonable care, and, upon request, restore it to the depositor, or otherwise deliver it, according to the original trust. This term should not be confused with "depository" which is the physical place of deposit.

Deposit Insurance Act. Federal act creating Federal Deposit Insurance Corporation (F.D.I.C.) to insure deposits of qualifying banks. 12 U.S.C.A. § 1811 et seq. See **Deposit Insurance Corporation.**

Deposit Insurance Corporation. Independent federal agency (Federal Deposit Insurance Corporation) created to insure bank deposits up to a specified amount in national and most state banks, including commercial and mutual savings banks, and to protect depositors from hazards of bank closings.

Deposition. The testimony of a witness taken upon interrogatories, not in open court, but in pursuance of a commission to take testimony issued by a court, or under a general law or court rule on the subject, and reduced to writing and duly authenticated, and intended to be used upon the trial of a civil action or criminal prosecution. A discovery device by which one party asks oral questions of the other party or of a witness for the other party. The person who is deposed is called the deponent. The deposition is conducted under oath outside of the courtroom, usually in one of the lawyer's offices. A transcript— word for word account—is made of the deposition. Testimony of witness, taken in writing, under oath or affirmation, before some judicial officer in answer to questions or interrogatories. Fed.R. Civil P. 26 et seq.; Fed.R.Crim.P. 15. See also **Discovery; Interrogatories.**

In ecclesiastical law, the act of depriving a clergyman, by a competent tribunal, of his clerical orders, to punish him for some offense and to prevent his acting in future in his clerical character.

Oral deposition. Form of discovery by addressing questions orally to person interrogated. Fed.R. Civil Proc. 30.

Written questions. Form of discovery in which written questions are addressed to person interrogated. Fed.R. Civil Proc. 31.

Deposition de bene esse /dèpəzíshən dìy bíyniy ésiy/. Testimony to be read at the trial, so far as relevant and competent, as though the witness were present in court. Milprint, Inc. v. Macleod Laboratories, 127 N.J.L. 333, 22 A.2d 566, 567.

Deposito /deypósiytow/. In Spanish law, deposit; the species of bailment so called.

A real contract by which one person confides to the custody of another an object on the condition that it shall be returned to him whenever he shall require it.

Depositor. One who makes a deposit. One who delivers and leaves money with a bank on his order or subject to check.

Depository. The place where a deposit (*q.v.*) is placed and kept; *e.g.* bank, trust company. Place where something is deposited or stored as for safekeeping or convenience. Perkins v. State, 61 Wis.2d 341, 212 N.W.2d 141, 146.

This term should not be confused with "depositary" which is the person or institution taking responsibility for the deposit, rather than the place itself.

United States depositories are banks selected and designated to receive deposits of the public funds (*e.g.* taxes) of the United States.

Depositum /dəpózədəm/. Lat. In the civil law, one of the forms of the contract of bailment, being a naked bailment of goods to be kept for the use of the bailor without reward. See **Deposit.**

One of the four real contracts specified by Justinian, and having the following characteristics: (1) The depositary or depositee is not liable for negligence, however extreme, but only for fraud, *dolus;* (2) the property remains in the depositor, the depositary having only the possession. *Precarium* and *sequestre* were two varieties of the *depositum.*

De post disseisina /dìy pówst dəsíyzənə/. Writ of post disseisin. A writ which lay for him who, having recovered lands or tenements by *præcipe quod reddat,* on default, or reddition, was again disseised by the former disseisor.

Dépôt /dèypów/. In French law, the *depositum* of the Roman and the deposit of the English law. It is of two kinds, being either (1) *dépôt* simply so called, and which may be either voluntary or necessary, and (2) *séquestre,* which is a deposit made either under an agreement of the parties, and to abide the event of pending litigation regarding it, or by virtue of the direction of the court or a judge, pending litigation regarding it.

De prærogativa regis /dìy prərogətáyva ríyjəs/. The English statute 17 Edw. I, St. 1, c. 9, defining the prerogatives of the crown on certain subjects, but especially directing that the king shall have ward of the lands of idiots, taking the profits without waste, and finding them necessaries.

De præsenti /dìy prəzéntay/. Of the present; in the present tense. See **Per verba de præsenti.**

Deprave. To defame; to corrupt morally; vilify; exhibit contempt for. In England it was a criminal offense to "deprave" the Lord's Supper or the Book of Common Prayer.

Depraved mind. An inherent deficiency of moral sense and rectitude, equivalent to statutory phrase "depravity of heart" defined as highest grade of malice. A corrupt or perverted mind. As required for conviction of second-degree murder, is one which is indifferent to the life of others. Jones v. State, 70 Wis.2d 41, 233 N.W.2d 430, 435. Such state of mind is equatable with malice in commonly understood sense of ill will, hatred, spite or evil intent. Weaver v. State, Fla.App., 220 So.2d 53, 60.

Depreciable life. For an asset, the time period over which depreciable cost is to be allocated. For tax returns, depreciable life may be shorter than estimated service life.

Depreciation /dəprìyshiyéyshən/. A fall in value; reduction of worth. The deterioration, or the loss or lessening in value, arising from age, use, and improvements, due to better methods. A decline in value of property caused by wear or obsolescence and is usually measured by a set formula which reflects these elements over a given period of useful life of property. State Highway Commission v. Tubbs, 147 Mont. 296, 411 P.2d 739, 744. Consistent, gradual process of estimating and allocating cost of capital investments over estimated useful life of asset in order to match cost against earnings. Coca-Cola Bottling Co. of Baltimore v. U. S., 203 Ct.Cl. 18, 487 F.2d 528, 534. The write-off for tax purposes of the cost or other basis of a tangible asset over its estimated useful life. As to intangible assets, see **Amortization.** As to natural resources, see **Depletion.** See also **Annual depreciation; Asset Depreciation Range; Recapture of depreciation; Useful life.**

Depreciation Methods

Accelerated depreciation. Various methods of depreciation that yield larger deductions in the earlier years of the life of an asset than the straight-line method. Examples include the double declining-balance and the sum of the years' digits methods of depreciation.

Accrued depreciation. See **Accrued depreciation.**

Declining balance method. Under the declining balance method, the annual depreciation allowance is computed by multiplying the undepreciated cost of the asset each year by a uniform rate up to double the straight-line rate or 150 percent, as the case may be.

Double declining method. Spreading the initial cost of a capital asset over time by deducting in each period double the percentage recognized by the straight-line method and applying that double percentage to the undepreciated balance existing at the start of each period. No salvage value is used in the calculation.

Original cost method. Amortization of asset based on its cost, less salvage value.

Replacement cost method. Amortization of asset in which value is fixed in terms of replacement cost.

Sinking fund method. A process of recovering the value of an asset by setting up a sinking fund.

Straight-line method. Under the straight-line method of depreciation, the cost or other basis (*e.g.,* fair market value in the case of donated assets) of the asset, less its estimated salvage value, if any, is determined first; then this amount is distributed in equal amounts over the period of the estimated useful life of the asset. Taking the initial cost of a capital asset, deducting the expected salvage value at the time it is expected to be discarded, and spreading the difference in equal installments per unit of time over an estimated life of the asset.

Sum-of-the-year's digits method. Under this method, the annual depreciation allowance is computed by multiplying the depreciable cost basis (cost less salvage value) by a constantly decreasing fraction. The numerator of the fraction is represented by the remaining years of useful life of the asset at the beginning of each year, and the denominator is always represented by the sum of the years' digits of useful life at the time of acquisition.

Unit method. Amortization method in which the amount of the investment is divided by the estimated total number of revocable units and this results in the unit cost which is multiplied by the number of units sold during the year and the final figure is the dollar amount of the amortization or depreciation.

Depreciation reserve. An account kept on the books, as of a public utility, to offset the depreciation of the property due to time and use. It does not represent the actual depreciation of its properties which is to be deducted from the reproduction cost new to ascertain the present value for rate purposes; but only what observation and experience suggest as likely to happen, with a margin over. In taxation, when gain is realized on disposition of depreciable property the gain must be reported as ordinary income, not capital gain, to the extent of depreciation previously taken as a deduction. I.R.C. §§ 1245, 1250.

Depredation /dèprədéyshən/. The act of plundering, robbing, or pillaging. Deal v. U. S., 274 U.S. 277, 47 S.Ct. 613, 615, 71 L.Ed. 1045.

In French law, pillage, waste, or spoliation of goods, particularly of the estate of a decedent.

Depression. A period of economic stress; usually accompanied by poor business conditions and high unemployment. McCuiston v. Haggard, 21 Tenn.App. 277, 109 S.W.2d 413. In economic parlance, a "depression" is more severe than a "recession".

A hole or hollow. Rice v. Kansas City, Mo.App., 16 S.W.2d 659, 661.

Mental syndrome manifested by sense of inadequacy, self-depreciation, melancholy, and guilt feelings.

Depressive reaction. Mental or emotional condition, precipitated by some external factor and manifested by guilt, self-depreciation, psychomotor retardation, defection and/or sense of inadequacy; generally considered to be a neurosis.

Deprivation /dèprəvéyshən/. A taking away or confiscation; as the deprivation of a constitutional right or the taking of property under eminent domain without due process of law (*i.e.* without just compensation). See also **Deprivation of property.**

Deprivation of property. Due process guaranty which is abridged when government takes private property without just compensation except under extraordinary circumstances of the police power, though for deprivation of property there is not required an actual, physical taking for private or public use. See **Condemnation; Eminent domain; Expropriation; Just compensation; Taking.**

Deprive permanently. To "deprive permanently" means to: (a) Take from the owner the possession, use or benefit of his property, without an intent to restore the same; or (b) Retain property without intent to restore the same or with intent to restore it to the owner only if the owner purchases or leases it back, or pays a reward or other compensation for its return; or (c) Sell, give, pledge or otherwise dispose of any interest in property or subject it to the claim of a person other than the owner.

De procedendo ad judicium /dìy prò(w)səséndow æd juwdísh(iy)əm/. An old English writ proceeding out of chancery and ordering the judges of any court to proceed to judgment. 3 Bl.Comm. 109.

De proprietate probanda /dìy prəprày ətéydiy prəbǽndə/. Writ for proving property. An old English writ directed to the sheriff, to inquire of the property or goods distrained, where the defendant in an action of replevin claims the property. 3 Bl.Comm. 148.

Deputize. To appoint a deputy; to appoint or commission one to act as deputy to an officer. In a general sense, the term is descriptive of empowering one person to act for another in any capacity or relation, but in law it is almost always restricted to the substitution of a person appointed to act for an officer of the law.

Deputy. A substitute; a person duly authorized by an officer to exercise some or all of the functions pertaining to the office, in the place and stead of the latter. One appointed to substitute for another with power to act for him in his name or behalf. A substitute for another and is empowered to act for him in his name and behalf in all matters in which principal may act. Williams v. Ferrentino, Fla.App., 199 So.2d 504, 511.

Deputy consul. See **Consul.**

Deputy sheriff. One appointed to act in the place and stead of the sheriff in the official business of the latter's office. A *general* deputy (sometimes called "undersheriff") is one who, by virtue of his appointment, has authority to execute all the ordinary duties of the office of sheriff, and who executes process without any special authority from his principal. A *special* deputy, who is an officer *pro hac vice,* is one appointed for a special occasion or a special service, as, to serve a particular writ or to assist in keeping the peace when a riot or tumult is expected or in progress. He acts under a specific and not a general appointment and authority.

Deputy steward. In English law steward of a manor could depute or authorize another to hold a court; and the acts done in a court so holden were as legal as if the court had been holden by the chief steward in person. So an under steward or deputy could authorize another as subdeputy, *pro hac vice,* to hold a court for him; such limited authority not being inconsistent with the rule *delegatus non potest delegare.*

Special deputy. One appointed to exercise some special function or power of the official or person for whom he is appointed. See also *Deputy sheriff, above.*

De quarantina habenda /dìy kwòrəntáynə həbéndə/. At common law, a writ which a widow entitled to quarantine might sue out in case the heir or other persons ejected her. It seems to have been a summary process, and required the sheriff, if no just cause were shown against it, speedily to put her into possession.

De quibus sur disseisin /dìy kwíbəs sèr dəsíyzən/. An ancient writ of entry.

De quo /dìy kwów/ and **de quibus** /dìy kwíbəs/. Of which. Formal words in the simple writ of entry, from which it was called a writ of entry "in the *quo,*" or "in the *quibus.*"

De quota litis /dìy kwówdə láydəs/. In the civil law, a contract by which one who has a claim difficult to recover agrees with another to give a part, for the purpose of obtaining his services to recover the rest.

Deraign /dəréyn/. To prove; to vindicate; to disprove allegations.

Derangement. See **Insanity.**

De raptu virginum /dìy rǽpt(y)uw várjənəm/. Of the ravishment of maids. The name of an appeal formerly in use in England in cases of rape.

De rationabilibus divisis /dìy ræshənəbíləbəs dəváyzəs/. Writ for fixing reasonable boundaries. A writ which lay to settle the boundaries between the lands of persons in different towns, where one complained of encroachment.

De rationabili parte bonorum /dìy ræsh(iy)ənéybəlay párdiy bənórəm/. A writ which lay for the widow (and children) of a deceased person against his executors, to recover a third part of the deceased's personalty, after payment of his debts, or to recover their reasonable part or share of his goods. 2 Bl.Comm. 492.

Derecho /deréychow/. In Spanish law, law or right. *Derecho comun,* common law. The civil law is so called. A right. *Derechos,* rights. Also, specifically, an impost laid upon goods or provisions, or upon persons or lands, by way of tax or contribution.

De recordo et processu mittendis /dìy rəkórdow èt prəsésyuw məténdəs/. Writ to send the record and process of a cause to a superior court; a species of writ of error.

De recto /dìy réktow/. Writ of right. See **Writ of right.**

De recto de advocatione /dìy réktow dìy ædvəkèy-shiyówniy/. Writ of right of advowson. An old English writ which lay for one who had an estate in an advowson to him and his heirs in fee-simple, if he were disturbed to present. Abolished by St. 3 & 4 Wm. IV, c. 27.

De recto de rationabili parte /dìy réktow dìy ræshənéybəlay párdiy/. Writ of right, of reasonable part. An old English writ which lay between privies in blood, as between brothers in gavelkind, or between sisters or other coparceners for lands in fee-simple, where one was deprived of his or her share by another. Abolished by St. 3 & 4 Wm. IV, c. 27.

De recto patens /diy réktow péytèn(d)z/. Writ of right patent.

De redisseisina /diy rìydəsíyzənə/. Writ of redisseisin. A writ which lay where a man recovered by assise of novel disseisin land, rent, or common, and the like, and was put in possession thereof by verdict, and afterward was disseised of the same land, rent, or common, by him by whom he was disseised before.

Derelict /dérəlikt/. Forsaken; abandoned; deserted; cast away. Personal property abandoned or thrown away by the owner in such manner as to indicate that he intends to make no further claim thereto. "Dereliction" or "renunciation" of property at sea as well as on land requires both the intention to abandon and external action. The No. 105, C.C.A.Fla., 97 F.2d 425, 426.

Land left uncovered by the receding of water from its former bed. See **Dereliction.**

A boat or vessel found entirely deserted or abandoned on the sea without hope or intention of recovery or return by the master or crew, whether resulting from wreck, accident, necessity, or voluntary abandonment. When a vessel, without being abandoned, is no longer under the control or direction of those on board (as where part of the crew are dead, and the remainder are physically and mentally incapable of providing for their own safety), she is said to be *quasi derelict.* When the crew have left their vessel temporarily, with the intention of returning to resume possession, she is not technically a derelict, but is what may be termed a "quasi derelict."

Dereliction /dèrəlíkshən/. The gaining of land from the water, in consequence of the sea shrinking back below the usual water mark; the opposite of *alluvion (q.v.).* Mexico Beach Corp. v. St. Joe Paper Co., 97 So.2d 708, 710. Also, land left dry by running water retiring imperceptibly from one of its shores and encroaching on the other. See **Accretion; Reliction.**

In the civil law, the voluntary abandonment of goods by the owner, without the hope or the purpose of returning to the possession.

De reparatione facienda /diy rèpərèyshiyówniy fæs(h)iyéndə/. A writ by which one tenant in common sought to compel another to aid in repairing the property held in common.

De rescussu /diy rəskásyuw/. Writ of rescue or rescous. A writ which lay where cattle distrained, or persons arrested, were rescued from those taking them.

De retorno habendo /diy rətórnow həbéndow/. For having a return; to have a return. A term applied to the judgment for the defendant in an action of replevin, awarding him a return of the goods replevied; and to the writ or execution issued thereon. 3 Bl.Comm. 149. Applied also to the sureties given by the plaintiff on commencing the action.

D.E.R.I.C. An abbreviation used for *De ea re ita censuere* (concerning that matter have so decreed), in recording the decrees of the Roman senate.

De rien culpable /də ríyn kálpəbəl/. L. Fr. Guilty of nothing; not guilty.

Derivative. Coming from another; taken from something preceding; secondary. That which has not its origin in itself, but owes its existence to something foregoing. Anything obtained or deduced from another.

Derivative action. A suit by a shareholder to enforce a corporate cause of action. The corporation is a necessary party, and the relief which is granted is a judgment against a third person in favor of the corporation. Price v. Gurney, Ohio, 324 U.S. 100, 65 S.Ct. 513, 516, 89 L.Ed. 776. An action is a derivative action when the action is based upon a primary right of the corporation, but is asserted on its behalf by the stockholder because of the corporation's failure, deliberate or otherwise, to act upon the primary right. Lehrman v. Godebaux Sugars, 207 Misc. 314, 138 N.Y.S.2d 163, 168. Procedure in such actions in federal courts is governed by Fed.R. Civil P. 23.1.

Derivative contraband. Items of property not otherwise illegal but subject to forfeiture according to use to which they are put. Kane v. McDaniel, D.C.Ky., 407 F.Supp. 1239, 1242.

Derivative conveyances. Conveyances which presuppose some other conveyance precedent, and only serve to enlarge, confirm, alter, restrain, restore, or transfer the interest granted by such original conveyance. They are releases, confirmations, surrenders, assignments, and defeasances. 2 Bl.Comm. 324.

Derivative evidence. Evidence which is derived or spawned from other illegally obtained evidence is inadmissible because of the primary taint. See **Fruit of poisonous tree doctrine.**

Derivative suit. See **Derivative action.**

Derivative tort. Tort liability may be imposed on a principal for wrong committed by agent and to this extent the principal's liability is derivative.

Derive. To receive from a specified source or origin. Crews v. Commissioner of Internal Revenue, C.C. A.10, 89 F.2d 412, 416. To proceed from property, sever from capital, however invested or employed, and to come in, receive or draw by taxpayer for his separate use, benefit, and disposal. Staples v. United States, D.C.Pa., 21 F.Supp. 737, 739.

Derived. Received from specified source.

Derogation /dèrəgéyshən/. The partial repeal or abolishing of a law, as by a subsequent act which limits its scope or impairs its utility and force. Distinguished from *abrogation,* which means the entire repeal and annulment of a law.

Derogation from grant. Provision in an instrument of transfer such as a deed which diminishes or militates against the grant itself.

Derogatory clause. In a will, this is a sentence or secret character, inserted by the testator, of which he reserves the knowledge to himself, with a condition that no will he may make thereafter should be valid, unless this clause be inserted word for word. This is done as a precaution to guard against later wills being extorted by violence, or otherwise improperly obtained. Such a provision is anomalous.

Derogatur legi, cum pars detrahitur; abrogatur legi, cum prorsus tollitur /dèrəgéydər líyjay, kəm párz dətréy(h)ədər; æbrəgéydər líyjay, kəm prórsəs tólədər/. To derogate from a law is to take away part of it; to abrogate a law is to abolish it entirely.

Desafuero /dèysaf(u)wérow/. In Spanish law, an irregular action committed with violence against law, custom, or reason.

De salva gardia /dìy sǽlvə gárdiyə/. A writ of safeguard allowed to strangers seeking their rights in English courts, and apprehending violence or injury to their persons or property.

De salvo conductu /dìy sǽlvow kəndə́kt(y)uw/. A writ of safe conduct.

Desamortizacion /dèysamòrtiysasyówn/. In Mexican law, the *desamortizacion* of property is to take it out of mortmain (dead hands); that is, to unloose it from the grasp, as it were, of ecclesiastical or civil corporations. The term has no equivalent in English.

De sa vie /də sà víy/. L. Fr. Of his or her life; of his own life; as distinguished from *pur autre vie,* for another's life.

De scaccario /dìy skəkériyow/. Of or concerning the exchequer. The title of a statute passed in the fifty-first year of Henry III.

Descend. To pass by succession; as when the estate vests by operation of law in the heirs immediately upon the death of the ancestor. The term, as used in some statutes, includes an acquisition by devise. Cordon v. Gregg, 164 Or. 306, 101 P.2d 414, 415. To pass down from generation to generation. To go or pass to; often used as a word of transfer. As used in wills, the word is often regarded as a general expression equivalent to the words "go to" or "belong to," and as indicating a passing of title by the force of the will rather than of the statute. See **Descent.**

Descendent. Those persons who are in the blood stream of the ancestor. Term means those descended from another, persons who proceed from a body of another such as a child or grandchild, to the remotest degree; it is the opposite of "ascendants". Bassett v. Merlin, Inc., Fla.App., 304 So.2d 543, 544. In the plural, the term means issue, offspring or posterity in general. Also, all those to whom an estate descends, whether it be in a direct or collateral line from the intestate. See **Descent.**

Lineal descendent. One who is in the line of descent from the ancestor. The term may include an adopted child.

Descender. Descent; in the descent. See **Formedon.**

Descendibility of future interests. Legal suitability of a future interest such as a remainder or executory interest to pass by inheritance on death of the holder.

Descendible. Capable of passing by descent, or of being inherited or transmitted by devise (spoken of estates, titles, offices, and other property).

Descent. Hereditary succession. Succession to the ownership of an estate by inheritance, or by any act of law, as distinguished from "purchase." Title by descent is the title by which one person, upon the death of another, acquires the real estate of the latter as his heir at law. 2 Bl.Comm. 201. The title by inheritance is in all cases called descent, although by statute law the title is sometimes made to ascend.

The division among those legally entitled thereto of the real property of intestates.

See also **Per capita; Per stirpes.**

Classification

Descents are of two sorts, *lineal* and *collateral.* Lineal descent is descent in a direct or right line, as from father or grandfather to son or grandson. Collateral descent is descent in a collateral or oblique line, that is, up to the common ancestor and then down from him, as from brother to brother, or between cousins. They are also distinguished into *mediate* and *immediate* descends. But these terms are used in different senses. A descent may be said to be a mediate or immediate descent of the estate or right; or it may be said to be mediate or immediate, in regard to the mediateness or immediateness of the pedigree or consanguinity. Thus, a descent from the grandfather, who dies in possession, to the grandchild, the father being then dead, or from the uncle to the nephew, the brother being dead, is, in the former sense, in law, immediate descent, although the one is collateral and the other lineal; for the heir is in the *per,* and not in the *per* and *cui.* On the other hand, with reference to the line of pedigree or consanguinity, a descent is often said to be immediate, when the ancestor from whom the party derives his blood is immediate, and without any intervening link or degrees; and mediate, when the kindred is derived from him *mediante altero,* another ancestor intervening between them. Thus a descent in lineals from father to son is in this sense immediate; but a descent from grandfather to grandson, the father being dead, or from uncle to nephew, the brother being dead, is deemed mediate; the father and the brother being, in these latter cases, the *medium deferens,* as it is called, of the descent or consanguinity.

Descent was denoted, in the Roman law, by the term *"successio,"* which is also used by Bracton, from which has been derived the *succession* of the Scotch and French jurisprudence.

Line of Descent

The order or series of persons who have descended one from the other or all from a common ancestor, considered as placed in a line of succession in the order of their birth, the line showing the connection of all the blood-relatives.

Collateral line. A line of descent connecting persons who are not directly related to each other as ascendants or descendants, but whose relationship consists in common descent from the same ancestor.

Direct line. A line of descent traced through those persons only who are related to each other directly as ascendants or descendants.

Maternal line. A line of descent or relationship between two persons which is traced through the mother of the younger.

Paternal line. A similar line of descent traced through the father.

Descent cast. The devolving of realty upon the heir on the death of his ancestor intestate.

Another name for what was formerly called a "descent which tolls entry." When a person had acquired land by disseisin, abatement, or intrusion, and died seised of the land, the descent of it to his heir took away or tolled the real owner's right of entry, so that he could only recover the land by an action.

Describe. To narrate, express, explain, set forth, relate, recount, narrate, depict, delineate, portray. Of land, to give the metes and bounds.

Description. A delineation or account of a particular subject by the recital of its characteristic accidents and qualities.

A written enumeration of items composing an estate, or of its condition, or of titles or documents; like an inventory, but with more particularity, and without involving the idea of an appraisement.

An exact written account of an article, mechanical device, or process which is the subject of an application for a patent.

A method of pointing out a particular person by referring to his relationship to some other person or his character as an officer, trustee, executor, etc.

That part of a conveyance, advertisement of sale, etc., which identifies the land or premises intended to be affected.

A fair portrayal of the chief features of the proposed law in words of plain meaning, so that it can be understood by the persons entitled to vote. Sawyer Stores v. Mitchell, 103 Mont. 148, 62 P.2d 342, 348.

That part of affidavit for search warrant describing the place to be searched.

For description of criminal suspect, see **Lineup.**

See also **Identification.**

Descriptio personæ /dəskrípsh(iy)ow pərsówniy/. Lat. Description of the person. By this is meant a word or phrase used merely for the purpose of identifying or pointing out the person intended, and not as an intimation that the language in connection with which it occurs is to apply to him only in the official or technical character which might appear to be indicated by the word. Forrester v. Cantley, 227 Mo. App. 325, 51 S.W.2d 550, 551.

In wills, it sometimes happens that the word heir is used as a *descriptio personæ.* A legacy "to the eldest son" of A would be a designation of the person.

Descriptive. Containing a description; serving or aiming to describe; having the quality of representing. Sawyer Stores v. Mitchell, 103 Mont. 148, 62 P.2d 342, 348. See also **Identification.**

If trademark imparts information directly, it is "descriptive"; if it stands for an idea which requires some operation of the imagination connected with the goods, it is "suggestive"; the information imparted may concern a characteristic, quality or ingredient of the product. Union Carbide Corp. v. Ever-Ready, Inc., C.A.Ill., 531 F.2d 366, 378.

De scutagio habendo /dìy skyuwtéyjiyow həbéndow/. Writ for having (or to have) escuage or scutage. A writ which anciently lay against tenants by knight-service, to compel them to serve in the king's wars or send substitutes or to pay escuage; that is a sum of money. The same writ lay for one who had already served in the king's army, or paid a fine instead, against those who held of him by knight-service, to recover his escuage or scutage.

De se bene gerendo /dìy sìy bíyniy jəréndow/. For behaving himself well; for his good behavior.

Desecrate. To violate sanctity of, to profane, or to put to unworthy use. A person commits a misdemeanor if he purposely desecrates any public monument or structure, or place of worship or burial, or if he purposely desecrates the national flag or any other object of veneration by the public or a substantial segment thereof in any public place. Offense consists of defacing, damaging, polluting or otherwise physically mistreating in a way that the actor knows will outrage the sensibilities of persons likely to observe or discover his action. Model Penal Code, § 250.9. See also **Deface; Defile.**

De secta ad molendinum /dìy séktə æd məléndənəm/. Of suit to a mill. An old English writ which lay to compel one to continue his custom (of grinding) at a mill. 3 Bl.Comm. 235.

Desegregation. The judicial mandate eliminating color of a person as a basis for disqualification to attend the school of his or her choice or to work at place of employment of his or her choice. See **Brown decision; Discrimination.**

Desert. To leave or quit with an intention to cause a permanent separation; to forsake utterly; to abandon. It is essentially willful in nature.

Desertion. The act by which a person abandons and forsakes, without justification, or unauthorized, a station or condition of public, social, or family life, renouncing its responsibilities and evading its duties. A willful abandonment of an employment or duty in violation of a legal or moral obligation.

Criminal desertion is a husband's or wife's abandonment or willful failure without just cause to provide for the care, protection or support of a spouse who is in ill health or necessitous circumstances.

See also **Abandonment; Desertion and nonsupport; Non-support.**

Adoption. As used in statute providing that parental consent to adoption is not required when parent has wilfully deserted child evinces settled purpose to forego, abandon, or desert all parental duties and parental rights in child. Moody v. Voorhies, 257 Or. 105, 475 P.2d 579, 581.

Constructive desertion. That arising where an existing cohabitation is put an end to by misconduct of one of the parties, provided such misconduct is itself a ground for divorce. For example, where one spouse, by his or her words, conduct, demeanor, and attitude produces an intolerable condition which forces the other spouse to withdraw from the joint habitation to a more peaceful one. West v. West, 264 Ky. 826, 95 S.W.2d 789, 790.

Divorce law. As a ground for divorce, an actual abandonment or breaking off of matrimonial cohabitation, by either of the parties, and a renouncing or refusal of the duties and obligations of the relation, with an intent to abandon or forsake entirely and not to return to or resume marital relations, occurring without legal justification either in the consent or the wrongful conduct of the other party. The elements of offense of "desertion" as ground for divorce are a voluntary intentional abandonment of one party by the other, without cause or justification and without consent of party abandoned. See also *Constructive desertion, supra;* **Desertion and nonsupport,** *infra.*

Maritime law. The act by which a seaman deserts and abandons a ship or vessel, in which he had engaged to perform a voyage, before the expiration of his time, and without leave. By desertion, in the maritime law, is meant, not a mere unauthorized absence from the ship without leave, but an unauthorized absence from the ship, with an intention not to return to her service, or, as it is often expressed, *animo non revertendi;* that is, with an intention to desert. The Cripple Creek, D.C.Pa., 52 F.Supp. 710, 712 (strike); The Youngstown, C.C.A.La., 110 F.2d 968, 970. Desertion, within statute providing for forfeiture of wages of deserting seaman, consists of seaman's unconsented abandonment of duty by quitting ship before termination of engagement specified in articles he signed, without justification and with intention of not returning. Petition of Russo, D.C. Cal., 232 F.Supp. 650, 651.

Military law. Any member of the armed forces who —(1) without authority goes or remains absent from his unit, organization, or place of duty with intent to remain away therefrom permanently; (2) quits his unit, organization, or place of duty with intent to avoid hazardous duty or to shirk important service; or (3) without being regularly separated from one of the armed forces enlists or accepts an appointment in the same or another one of the armed forces without fully disclosing the fact that he has not been regularly separated, or enters any foreign armed service except when authorized by the United States; is guilty of desertion. Code of Military Justice, 10 U.S.C.A. § 885.

Non-support. Desertion is frequently accompanied by non-support, which may be a crime. See also **Desertion and non-support; Non-support.**

Obstinate desertion. See **Obstinate desertion.**

Desertion and non-support. While both desertion and non-support go hand in hand in many cases, they are distinguishable because a man may be guilty of desertion and not guilty of non-support. The converse is also true because a man may be guilty of wilfully failing to support though he remains in the marital home. See also **Desertion; Non-support.**

Deserving. Worthy or meritorious, without regard to condition or circumstances. In no sense of the word is it limited to persons in need of assistance, or objects which come within the class of charitable uses.

Deshonora /dèysonóra/. In Spanish law, dishonor; injury; slander.

Design. To form plan or scheme of, conceive and arrange in mind, originate mentally, plan out, contrive. Also, the plan or scheme conceived in mind and intended for subsequent execution; preliminary conception of idea to be carried into effect by action; contrivance in accordance with preconceived plan. A project, an idea. As a term of art, the giving of a visible form to the conceptions of the mind, or invention.

In evidence, purpose or intention, combined with plan, or implying a plan in the mind.

In patent law, the drawing or depiction of an original plan or conception for a novel pattern, model, shape, or configuration, to be used in the manufacturing or textile arts or the fine arts, and chiefly of a decorative or ornamental character. "Design patents" are contrasted with "utility patents," but equally involve the exercise of the inventive or originative faculty. Design, in the view of the patent law, is that characteristic of a physical substance which, by means of lines, images, configuration, and the like, taken as a whole, makes an impression, through the eye, upon the mind of the observer. The essence of a design resides not in the elements individually, nor in their method of arrangement, but in the total ensemble—in that indefinable whole that awakens some sensation in the observer's mind. Impressions thus imparted may be complex or simple. But whatever the impression, there is attached in the mind of the observer, to the object observed, a sense of uniqueness and character.

Designate. To indicate, select, appoint, nominate, or set apart for a purpose or duty, as to designate an officer for a command. To mark out and make known; to point out; to name; indicate. New Haven Federation of Teachers v. New Haven Bd. of Ed., 27 Conn.Sup. 298, 237 A.2d 373, 380. See also **Identification.**

Designating petition. Means used to designate a candidate for a party nomination at a primary election or for election to party position.

Designatio justiciariorum est a rege; jurisdictio vero ordinaria a lege. The appointment of justices is by the king, but their ordinary jurisdiction by the law.

Designation. An addition to a name, as of title, profession, trade, or occupation, to distinguish the person from others. A description or descriptive expression by which a person or thing is denoted in a will without using the name. Also, an appointment or assignment, as to a particular office. The act of pointing out, distinguishing by marks of description, or calling by a distinctive title. See also **Identification.**

Designatio personæ /dèzəgnéysh(iy)ow pərsówniy/. The description of a person or a party to a deed or contract. See also **Descriptio personæ.**

Designatio unius est exclusio alterius, et expressum facit cessare tacitum /dèzəgnéysh(iy)ow yuwnáyəs èst əksklúwzh(iy)ow oltíriyəs, èd əksprésəm féysət səsériy tǽsədəm/. The specifying of one is the exclusion of another, and that which is expressed makes that which is understood to cease. (The appointment or designation of one is the exclusion of the other; and that which is expressed prevails over that which is implied.)

Designed. Contrived or taken to be employed for a particular purpose. Fit, adapted, prepared, suitable, appropriate. Intended, adapted, or designated. The term may be employed as indicating a bad purpose with evil intent.

Designedly. Sometimes equivalent to the words "wilfully," "knowingly," "unlawfully," and "feloniously."

De similibus ad similia eadem ratione procedendum est /dìy səmíləbəs ǽd səmíliyə iyéydəm rèyshiyówniy pròwsədéndəm ést/. From like things to like things we are to proceed by the same rule or reason [*i.e.*, we are allowed to argue from the analogy of cases].

De similibus idem est judicandum /dìy səmíləbəs áydəm èst juwdəkǽndəm/. Of [respecting] like things [in like cases], the judgment is to be the same.

Desire. To ask, to request. Ordinarily, to wish for more or less earnestly. Sometimes, to empower or authorize. According to context or circumstances, the word may import a request or even a demand.

This term, used in a will in relation to the management and distribution of property, has been interpreted by the courts with different shades of meaning, varying from the mere expression of a preference to a positive command. The word "desire" may be as effective as if the word "devise" or "bequeath" had been used. Drinkard v. Hughes, Tex.Civ.App., 32 S.W.2d 935, 936.

Desistement /dəsístmənt/. The name of a doctrine under which the court, in construing a foreign will, applies the law of the forum on the theory that there is a hiatus.

Deslinde /dèyslíyndey/. A term used in the Spanish law, denoting the act by which the boundaries of an estate or portion of a country are determined.

Desmemoriados /dèysmemòriyáðows/. In Spanish law, persons deprived of memory.

De son tort /də sówn tór(t)/. L. Fr. Of his own wrong. An *executor de son tort* is an executor of his own wrong. A person who assumes to act as executor of an estate without any lawful warrant or authority, but who, by his intermeddling, makes himself liable as an executor to a certain extent. If a stranger takes upon him to act as executor without any just authority, he is called in law an "executor of his own wrong," *de son tort.* 2 Bl.Comm. 507.

De son tort demesne /də sówn tór(t) dəmíyn/. Of his own wrong. The law French equivalent of the Latin phrase *de injuria (q.v.).*

Despitus /déspədəs/. Contempt. A contemptible person.

Despoil /dəspóyl/. This word involves, in its signification, violence or clandestine means by which one is deprived of that which he possesses.

Despojar /dèyspowhár/. A possessory action of the Mexican law. It is brought to recover possession of immovable property, of which one has been despoiled *(despojado)* by another. See also **Despoil.**

Desponsation /dəspònséyshən/. The act of betrothing persons to each other.

Desposorio /dèspowsóriyow/. In Spanish law, espousals; mutual promises of future marriage.

Despot. This word, in its original and most simple acceptation, signifies *master and supreme lord;* it is synonymous with monarch. A ruler with absolute power and authority, but taken in bad sense, as it is usually employed, it signifies a tyrant. In some nations, despot is the title given to the sovereign, as king is given in others.

Despotism /déspədizəm/. That abuse of government where the sovereign power is not divided, but united and unlimited in the hands of a single man, whatever may be his official title. It is not, properly, a form of government.

"Despotism" is not exactly synonymous with "autocracy," for the former involves the idea of tyranny or abuse of power, which is not necessarily implied by the latter. Every despotism is autocratic; but an autocracy is not necessarily despotic.

Dessaisissement /dèseysìysmón/. In French law, when a person is declared bankrupt, he is immediately deprived of the enjoyment and administration of all his property; this deprivation, which extends to all his rights, is called "dessaisissement."

De statuto mercatorio /dìy stətyúwdow màrkətériyow/. The writ of statute merchant.

De statuto stapulæ /dìy stətyúwdow stéypəliy/. The writ of statute staple.

Destination. The purpose to which it is intended an article or a fund shall be applied. Act of appointing or setting aside for a purpose. A testator gives a destination to a legacy when he prescribes the specific use to which it shall be put. Place to which something is sent; place set for end of journey; terminal point to which one directs his course.

Destination bill. Instead of issuing a bill of lading to the consignor at the place of shipment a carrier may at the request of the consignor procure the bill to be issued at destination or at any other place designated in the request. Upon request of anyone entitled as against the carrier to control the goods while in transit and on surrender of any outstanding bill of lading or other receipt covering such goods, the issuer may procure a substitute bill to be issued at any place designated in the request. U.C.C. § 7–305.

Destination contract. Contract between seller and buyer by which risk of loss passes to buyer upon seller's tender of goods at destination. U.C.C. § 2–509(1)(b).

Destination du père de famille /dèstənasyówn dyùw pér də fəmíy/. A use which owner has intentionally established on one part of his property in favor of another part, and which is equal to a title with respect to perpetual and apparent servitudes thereon.

Destitute. Not possessing necessaries of life; in condition of extreme want; bereft; lacking possessions and resources. Destitute of Bennington County by Van Santvoord v. Henry W. Putnam Memorial Hospital, 125 Vt. 289, 215 A.2d 134, 138. See also **Indigent.**

Destitute or necessitous circumstances. Circumstances in which one needs the necessaries of life, which cover not only primitive physical needs, things absolutely indispensable to human existence and decency, but those things, also, which are in fact necessary to the particular person left without support.

Destroy. Term is susceptible of applications in a variety of contexts, but in general, it means to ruin completely and may include a taking. State v. Robinson, 266 Minn. 166, 123 N.W.2d 812. To ruin the structure, organic existence or condition of a thing; to demolish; to injure or mutilate beyond possibility of use; to nullify. State by Clark v. Wolkoff, 250 Minn. 504, 85 N.W.2d 401, 410.

As used in policies of insurance, leases, and in maritime law, and under various statutes, this term is often applied to an act which renders the subject useless for its intended purpose, though it does not literally demolish or annihilate it.

In relation to wills, contracts, and other documents, the term "destroy" does not import the annihilation of the instrument or its resolution into other forms of matter, but a destruction of its legal efficacy, which may be by cancellation, obliterating, tearing into fragments, etc.

Destructibility. Capability of being destroyed by some action or turn of events or by operation of law.

Destructibility of contingent remainders. Doctrine dealing with future interest which may be destroyed by failure of condition. Such destructible future interest as a contingent remainder is subject to Rule Against Perpetuities unlike future interest which is destructible by act of the grantor or owner of present estate.

Destructible trust. Trust susceptible of being terminated or destroyed by happening of certain events or by operation of law.

Desuetude /dèswət(y)úwd/. Disuse; cessation or discontinuance of use, especially in the phrase, "to fall into desuetude." Applied to obsolete statutes.

De superoneratione pasturæ /dìy sùwpərownərèy-shiyówniy pæschúriy/. Old English writ of surcharge of pasture. A judicial writ which lay for him who was impleaded in the county court, for surcharging a common with his cattle, in a case where he was formerly impleaded for it in the same court, and the cause was removed into one of the courts at Westminster.

De tabulis exhibendis /dìy tǽbyələs ègzəbéndəs/. Of showing the tablets of a will.

Detachiare /dətǽshyériy/. To seize or take into custody another's goods or person by writ of attachment or course of law.

Detail, *v.* To enumerate minutely, specify, particularize.

Detail, *n.* An individual part, an item, a particular.

One who belongs to the army, but is only detached, or set apart, for the time to some particular duty or service, and who is liable at any time to be recalled to his place in the ranks.

Detain. To retain as the possession of personalty. To arrest, to check, to delay, to hinder, to hold, or keep in custody, to retard, to restrain from proceeding, to stay, to stop. People v. Smith, 17 Cal.App.2d 468, 62 P.2d 436, 438; State v. King, 303 S.W.2d 930, 934. See **Confinement; Custody.**

Detainer. The act (or the juridical fact) of withholding from a person lawfully entitled the possession of land or goods, or the restraint of a man's personal liberty against his will; detention. The wrongful keeping of a person's goods is called an "unlawful detainer" although the original taking may have been lawful. See also **Forcible detainer; Unlawful detainer.**

Detainment. Act of detaining. This term is used in policies of marine insurance, in the clause relating to "arrests, restraints, and detainments." The last two words are construed as equivalents, each meaning the effect of superior force operating directly on the vessel.

De tallagio non concedendo /dìy təléyjiyow nòn kònsədéndow/. Of not allowing talliage. The name given to the English statutes 25 and 34 Edw. I, restricting the power of the king to grant talliage.

Detection. A discovery or laying open of that which was hidden; investigation.

Detective. One whose business it is to detect criminals or discover matters of secret and pernicious import for the protection of the public. Such may be either a private detective engaged by an individual, or a member of a police force.

Detector. Device which reveals the presence of electric waves or radioactivity or the presence of metal or indicates the presence of eavesdropping equipment ("bug"). See also **Lie detector; Wiretapping.**

De tempore cujus contrarium memoria hominum non existit /dìy témpəriy kyúwjəs kəntrériyəm məmóriyə hómənəm nòn əgzístət/. From time whereof the memory of man does not exist to the contrary.

De tempore in tempus et ad omnia tempora /dìy témpəriy in témpəs èd æd ómniyə témpərə/. From time to time, and at all times.

De temps dont memorie ne court /də tón dòwn méməriy nə kúr/. L. Fr. From time whereof memory runneth not; time out of memory of man.

Detentio /dəténshow/. In the civil law, that condition of fact under which one can exercise his power over a corporeal thing at his pleasure, to the exclusion of all others. It forms the substance of possession in all its varieties.

Detention. The act of keeping back or withholding, either accidentally or by design, a person or thing. See **Confinement; Detain; Detainer; Preventive detention.**

Detention hearing. Judicial or quasi judicial proceeding used to determine the propriety of detaining a person on bail or a juvenile in a shelter facility. P. F. M. v. District Court In and For County of Adams, 184 Colo. 393, 520 P.2d 742.

Detention in a reformatory. A punishment or measure of prevention where a juvenile offender is sentenced to be sent to a reformatory school, to be there detained for a certain period of time.

Deter. To discourage or stop by fear. To stop or prevent from acting or proceeding by danger, difficulty, or other consideration which disheartens or countervails the motive for the act.

Deterioration. With respect to a commodity, consists of a constitutional hurt or impairment, involving some degeneration in the substance of the thing, such as that arising from decay, corrosion, or disintegration. With respect to values or prices, a decline.

Determinable. Liable to come to an end upon the happening of a certain contingency. Susceptible of being determined, found out, definitely decided upon, or settled.

As to determinable **Fee** and **Freehold,** see those titles.

Determinate. That which is ascertained; what is particularly designated.

Determinate hospitalization. Fixed period of hospitalization pursuant to civil commitment.

Determinate obligation. See **Obligation.**

Determinate sentence. Sentence to confinement for a fixed period as specified by statute as contrasted with an indeterminate sentence, the duration of which is only partly governed by statute; the duration of the latter, in the main, being governed by behavior of prisoner.

Determination. The decision of a court or administrative agency. It implies an ending or finality of a controversy or suit. Piccone v. U. S., 186 Ct.Cl. 752, 407 F.2d 866, 873. The ending or expiration of an estate or interest in property, or of a right, power, or authority. The coming to an end in any way whatever.

Also, an estimate. As respects an assessment, the term implies judgment and decision after weighing the facts.

See also **Decision; Decree; Finding; Judgment; Opinion.**

Determination letter. Document issued by a District Director of Internal Revenue Service which consists of an opinion as to the tax significance of a past or prospective transaction. Determination letters are most frequently used to clarify employee status, to determine whether a retirement or profit-sharing plan "qualifies" under the Internal Revenue Code, and to determine the tax exempt status of certain non-profit organizations.

Determinism. A philosophy which teaches that human behavior is governed, in the main, by pre-existing conditions such as environment and family patterns and leaves no room for freedom of the will.

Deterrent. Anything which impedes or has a tendency to prevent; *e.g.* punishment is a "deterrent" to crime.

De theolonio /dìy θiyəlówniyow/. A writ which lay for a person who was prevented from taking toll.

Detinet /dédənət/. Lat. He detains. In old English law, a species of action of debt, which lay for the specific recovery of goods, under a contract to deliver them.

An action of *debt* is said to be in the *detinet* when it is alleged merely that the defendant withholds or unjustly detains from the plaintiff the thing or amount demanded.

An action of *replevin* is said to be in the *detinet* when the defendant retains possession of the property until after judgment in the action.

Detinue /dédən(y)uw/. A form of action which lies for the recovery, *in specie,* of personal chattels from one who acquired possession of them lawfully, but retains it without right, together with damages for the detention. Possessory action for recovery of personal chattels unjustly detained. Durst v. Durst, 232 Md. 311, 193 A.2d 26.

The action of *detinue* is defined in the old books as a remedy founded upon the delivery of goods by the owner to another to keep, who afterwards refuses to redeliver them to the bailor; and it is said that, to authorize the maintenance of the action, it is necessary that the defendant should have come lawfully into the possession of the chattel, either by delivery to him or by finding it. In fact, it was once understood to be the law that *detinue* does not lie where the property had been tortiously taken. But it is, upon principle, very unimportant in what manner the defendant's possession commenced, since the gist of the action is the wrongful detainer, and not the original taking.

It is only incumbent upon the plaintiff to prove property in himself, and possession in the defendant. The action of *detinue* is proper in every case where the owner prefers recovering the specific property to damages for its conversion, and no regard is had to the manner in which the defendant acquired the possession.

Detinue of goods in frank marriage /dédən(y)uw əv gúdz in fræŋk mǽrəj/. A writ formerly available to a wife after a divorce, for the recovery of the goods given with her in marriage.

Detinuit /dətínyuwət/. An action of replevin is said to be in the *detinuit* when the plaintiff acquires possession of the property claimed by means of the writ. The right to retain is, of course, subject in such case to the judgment of the court upon his title to the property claimed.

Detour. A temporary turning aside from usual or regular route, course or procedure or from a task or employment. See also **Deviation.**

A temporary road or a longer road in temporary use because of an obstruction or state of disrepair on regularly used road.

Detournement. The misappropriation by a servant of funds the property of his master; fraudulent abstraction of documents; or "abus de confiance" which is fraudulently misusing or spending to anybody's prejudice goods, cash, bills, documents, or contracts handed over for a special object. See also **Embezzlement.**

Detraction. The removal of property from one state to another upon a transfer of the title to it by will or inheritance.

De transgressione /dìy trænzgreshiyówniy/. A writ of trespass.

De transgressione, ad audiendum et terminandum /dìy trænzgreshiyówniy, æd òdiyendəm èt tàrmənǽndəm/. A writ or commission for the hearing and determining any outrage or misdemeanor.

Detriment. Any loss or harm suffered in person or property; *e.g.*, the consideration for a contract may consist not only in a payment or other thing of value given, but also in loss or "detriment" suffered by the promisee. In that connection, "detriment" means that the promisee has, in return for the promise, forborne some legal right which he otherwise would have been entitled to exercise, or that he has given up something which he had a right to keep, or done something which he had a right not to do. Irving v. Irwin, 133 Cal.App. 374, 24 P.2d 215. See **Consideration; Legal detriment.**

Detrimental reliance. Response by promisee by way of act to offer of promisor in a unilateral contract. See also **Promissory estoppel.**

Detriment to promisee. In contracts, consideration offered by promisee to promisor, especially in a unilateral contract which calls for an act from the promisee though the promisor may revoke his offer before the completion of the act. See also **Consideration; Culpa in contrahendo.**

Detunicari /dətyùwnəkéray/. To discover or lay open to the world.

De una parte /dìy yúwnə párdiy/. A deed *de una parte* is one where only one party grants, gives, or binds himself to do a thing to another. It differs from deed *inter partes (q.v.).*

Deuterogamy /d(y)ùwdərógəmiy/. The act, or condition, of one who marries after the death of a former wife or husband.

De uxore rapta et abducta /dìy əksóriy rǽptə ed əbdǽktə/. Old English writ which lay where a man's wife had been ravished and carried away. A species of writ of trespass. 3 Bl.Comm. 139.

Devadiatus, or **divadiatus** /dəvædiyéydəs/. In old English law, an offender without sureties or pledges.

Devaluation. Reduction in value of a currency or of a standard monetary unit.

Devastation. Wasteful use of the property of a deceased person, as for extravagant funeral or other unnecessary expenses. 2 Bl.Comm. 508.

Devastaverunt /dəvæstəvírənt/. They have wasted. A term applied in old English law to waste by executors and administrators, and to the process issued against them therefor. See **Devastavit.**

Devastavit /dèvəstéyvət/. Lat. He has wasted. The act of an executor or administrator in wasting the goods of the deceased; mismanagement of the estate by which a loss occurs. A breach of trust or misap-

propriation of assets held in a fiduciary character; any violation or neglect of duty by an executor or administrator, involving loss to the decedent's estate, which makes him personally responsible to heirs, creditors, or legatees.

De vasto /dìy vǽstow/. Writ of waste. Old English writ which might be brought by him who had the immediate estate of inheritance in reversion or remainder, against the tenant for life, in dower, by curtesy, or for years, where the latter had committed *waste* in lands; calling upon the tenant to appear and show cause why he committed waste and destruction in the place named, to the disinherison *(ad exhœredationem)* of the plaintiff. 3 Bl.Comm. 227, 228. Abolished by St. 3 & 4 Wm. IV, c. 27.

De ventre inspiciendo /dìy véntriy ənspìs(h)iyéndow/. A common law writ to inspect the body, where a woman feigned to be pregnant, to see whether she was with child. It lay for the heir presumptive to examine a widow suspected to be feigning pregnancy in order to enable a supposititious heir to obtain the estate. 1 Bl.Comm. 456. It lay also where a woman sentenced to death pleaded pregnancy. 4 Bl.Comm. 395. This writ was also formerly recognized in America. See **Matrons, jury of.**

De verbo in verbum /dìy várbow ən várbəm/. Word for word. Literally, from word to word.

Deviation. Departure from established or usual conduct or ideology. A change made in the progress of a work from the original terms or design or method agreed upon. Ward v. City of Monrovia, 16 Cal.2d 815, 108 P.2d 425, 429. A voluntary departure by railroad carrier, without necessity or reasonable cause, from the regular or usual route or from a stipulated or customary mode of carriage. Ward v. Gulf, M. & N. R. Co., 23 Tenn.App. 533, 134 S.W.2d 917, 924. A wandering from the way, variation from the common way, from an established rule, standard, or position. S. J. Groves & Sons Co. v. West Virginia Turnpike Commission, D.C.W.Va., 164 F.Supp. 816, 821.

In employment, departure of employee from his course of employment and duties to employer for purposes entirely personal. Such term comes into use and is applied in workers' compensation cases and in actions against employer by third persons for injuries caused by employee. See also **Scope of employment.**

In insurance, term refers to variance from the risks insured against, as described in the policy, without necessity or just cause, after the risk has begun. Such deviation may void the liability or responsibility of the insurer.

A voluntary, unnecessary or unexcused departure without reasonable cause from the course of the voyage insured, or an unreasonable delay in pursuing the voyage, or the commencement of an entirely different voyage. The Chester Valley, C.C.A.La., 110 F.2d 592, 594; The Willdomino v. Citro Chemical Co. of America, 272 U.S. 718, 47 S.Ct. 261, 262, 71 L.Ed. 491.

Deviation doctrine. In wills and trusts, principle which permits variation from terms of trust where circumstances are such that purposes of trust would otherwise be defeated. Connecticut Bank & Trust Co. v. Johnson Memorial Hospital, 30 Conn.Sup. 1, 294 A.2d 586, 591. In agency, principle which permits agent to vary activity slightly from scope of master's permission. Johnson v. Maryland Casualty Co., C.C.A.Wis., 125 F.2d 337.

Deviation well survey. Examination permitted under Fed.Rules Civ.Proc., Rule 34 to determine whether a well is bottomed under another person's land. Williams v. Continental Oil Co., C.A.Okl., 215 F.2d 4.

Device. An invention or contrivance; any result of design; as in the phrase "gambling device," which means a machine or contrivance of any kind for the playing of an unlawful game of chance or hazard. A plan or project; a scheme to trick or deceive; a stratagem or artifice, as in the laws relating to fraud and cheating. Also, an emblem, pictorial representation, or distinguishing mark or sign of any kind; as in the laws prohibiting the marking of ballots used in public elections with "any device."

In patent law, a plan or contrivance, or an application, adjustment, shaping, or combination of materials or members, for the purpose of accomplishing a particular result or serving a particular use, chiefly by mechanical means and usually simple in character or not highly complex, but involving the exercise of the inventive faculty.

De vicineto /díy vəsínədow/. From the neighborhood, or vicinage. 3 Bl.Comm. 360. A term applied to a jury.

De vi laica amovenda /díy váy léyəkə èyməvéndə/. Writ of (or for) removing lay force. A writ which lay where two parsons contended for a church, and one of them entered into it with a great number of *laymen*, and held out the other *vi et armis;* then he that was holden out had this writ directed to the sheriff, that he remove the force.

Devilling /dévəliŋ/. A term used in London of a barrister recently admitted to the bar, who assists a junior barrister in his professional work, without compensation and without appearing in any way in the matter.

Devil on the neck. An instrument of torture, formerly used to extort confessions, etc. It was made of several irons, which were fastened to the neck and legs, and wrenched together so as to break the back.

Devisable. Capable of being devised.

Devisavit vel non /dèvəzéyvət vèl nón/. The name of an issue sent out of a court of chancery, or one which exercises chancery jurisdiction, to a court of law, to try the validity of a paper asserted and denied to be a will, to ascertain whether or not the testator did devise, or whether or not that paper was his will.

Devise /dəváyz/. A testamentary disposition of land or realty, a gift of real property by the last will and testament of the donor. When used as a noun, means a testamentary disposition of real or personal property and when used as a verb, means to dispose of real or personal property by will. Uniform Probate Code, § 1–201(7). See also **Bequest; Executory devise; Legacy.**

To contrive; plan; scheme; invent; prepare.

Classification

Devises are *contingent* or *vested;* that is, after the death of the testator. Contingent, when the vesting of any estate in the devisee is made to depend upon some future event, in which case, if the event never occur, or until it does occur, no estate vests under the devise. But, when the future event is referred to merely to determine the time at which the devisee shall come into the use of the estate, this does not hinder the vesting of the estate at the death of the testator. Devises are also classed as *general* or *specific.* A general devise is one which passes lands of the testator without a particular enumeration or description of them; as, a devise of "all my lands" or "all my other lands." In a more restricted sense, a general devise is one which grants a parcel of land without the addition of any words to show how great an estate is meant to be given, or without words indicating either a grant in perpetuity or a grant for a limited term; in this case it is construed as granting a life estate. Specific devises are devises of lands particularly specified in the terms of the devise, as opposed to general and residuary devises of land, in which the local or other particular descriptions are not expressed. For example, "I devise my Hendon Hall estate" is a specific devise; but "I devise all my lands," or, "all my other lands," is a *general* devise or a *residuary* devise. But all devises are (in effect) specific, even residuary devises being so. At common law, all devises of land were deemed to be "specific" whether the land was identified in the devise or passed under the residuary clause. A *conditional* devise is one which depends upon the occurrence of some uncertain event, by which it is either to take effect or be defeated. An *executory* devise of lands is such a disposition of them by will that thereby no estate vests at the death of the devisor, but only on some future contingency. It differs from a remainder in three very material points: (1) That it needs not any particular estate to support it; (2) that by it a fee-simple or other less estate may be limited after a fee-simple; (3) that by this means a remainder may be limited of a chattel interest, after a particular estate for life created in the same. 2 Bl.Comm. 172. In a stricter sense, a limitation by will of a future contingent interest in lands, contrary to the rules of the common law. A limitation by will of a future estate or interest in land, which cannot, consistently with the rules of law, take effect as a remainder. A future interest taking effect as a fee in derogation of a defeasible fee devised or conveyed to the first taker, when created by will, is an "executory devise," and, when created by deed, is a "conditional limitation," and in either event is given effect as a shifting or springing use.

The estates known as a contingent remainder and an "executory devise" are both interests or estates in land to take effect in the future and depend upon a future contingency; an "executory devise" being an interest which the rules of law do not permit to be created in conveyances, but allow in case of wills. It follows a fee estate created by a will. A contingent remainder may be created by will or other conveyance and must follow a particular or temporary estate created by the same instrument of conveyance.

Lapsed devise. A devise which fails, or takes no effect, in consequence of the death of the devisee before the testator; the subject-matter of it being considered as not disposed of by the will.

Residuary devise. A devise of all the residue of the testator's real property, that is, all that remains over and above the other devises. See also general definition above.

Devisee /dəvàyzíy/. The person to whom lands or other real property are devised or given by will. In the case of a devise to an existing trust or trustee, or to a trustee on trust described by will, the trust or trustee is the devisee and the beneficiaries are not devisees. Uniform Probate Code, § 1–201(8).

Residuary devisee. The person named in a will, who is to take all the real property remaining over and above the other devises.

Devisor /dəváyzər/. A giver of lands or real estate by will; the maker of a will of lands; a testator.

Devoir /dəvóy(ə)r/dəvwár/. Fr. Duty. It is used in the statute of 2 Rich. II, c. 3, in the sense of duties or customs.

Devolution. The transfer or transition from one person to another of a right, liability, title, estate, or office. Transference of property from one person to another. Hermann v. Crossen, Ohio App., 160 N.E.2d 404, 408. See also **Descent.**

In ecclesiastical law, the forfeiture of a right or power (as the right of presentation to a living) in consequence of its non-user by the person holding it, or of some other act or omission on his part, and its resulting transfer to the person next entitled.

Devolve /dəvólv/. To pass or be transferred from one person to another; to fall on, or accrue to, one person as the successor of another; as a title, right, office, liability. The term is said to be peculiarly appropriate to the passing of an estate from a person dying to a person living. See **Descent; Devolution.**

Devy /dəváy/. L. Fr. Dies; deceases.

De warrantia chartæ /dìy wohrǽnsh(iy)ə kárdiy/. Writ of warranty of charter. A writ which lay for him who was enfeoffed, with clause of warranty [in the charter of feoffment], and was afterwards impleaded in an assise or other action, in which he could not *vouch* or call to warranty; in which case he might have this writ against the feoffor, or his heir, to compel him to warrant the land unto him. Abolished by St. 3 & 4 Wm. IV, c. 27.

De warrantia diei /dìy worǽnsh(iy)ə dàyíyay/. A writ that lay where a man had a day in any action to appear in proper person, and the king at that day, or before, employed him in some service, so that he could not appear at the day in court. It was directed to the justices, that they should not record him to be in default for his not appearing.

Dextrarius /dèkstrériyəs/. One at the right hand of another.

Dextras dare /dékstrəs dériy/. To shake hands in token of friendship; or to give up oneself to the power of another person.

Diaconate /diyǽkənət/day°/. The office of a deacon.

Diaconus /diyǽkənəs/. A deacon.

Diagnosis /dàyəgnówsəs/. A medical term, meaning the discovery of the source of a patient's illness or the determination of the nature of his disease from a study of its symptoms. The art or act of recognizing the presence of disease from its symptoms, and deciding as to its character, also the decision reached, for determination of type or condition through case or specimen study or conclusion arrived at through critical perception or scrutiny. A "clinical diagnosis" is one made from a study of the symptoms only, and a "physical diagnosis" is one made by means of physical measure, such as palpation and inspection.

Diagnostic tests. Tests to determine and identify the nature of a disease; including laboratory and exploratory tests.

Dialectics /dàyəléktəks/. That branch of logic which teaches the rules and modes of reasoning.

Diallage /dayǽləjiy/. A rhetorical figure in which arguments are placed in various points of view, and then turned to one point.

Dialogus de scaccario /dayǽləgəs dìy skəkériyow/. In old English law, dialogue of or about the exchequer. An ancient treatise on the court of exchequer, attributed by some to Gervase of Tilbury, by others to Richard Fitz Nigel, bishop of London in the reign of Richard I. It is quoted by Lord Coke under the name of Ockham.

Dianatic /dàyənǽdək/. A logical reasoning in a progressive manner, proceeding from one subject to another.

Diarium /dayériyəm/. Daily food, or as much as will suffice for the day.

Diatim /dayéydəm/. In old records, daily; every day; from day to day.

Dica /dáykə/. In old English law, a tally for accounts, by number of cuts (*taillees*), marks, or notches. See **Tallia; Tally.**

Dicast /dáykæst/. An officer in ancient Greece answering in some respects to our juryman, but combining, on trials had before them, the functions of both judge and jury. The dicasts sat together in numbers varying, according to the importance of the case, from one to five hundred.

Di colonna /dìy kolónə/. In maritime law, the contract which takes place between the owner of a ship, the captain, and the mariners, who agree that the voyage shall be for the benefit of all. The term is used in the Italian law.

Dicta /díktə/. Opinions of a judge which do not embody the resolution or determination of the court. Expressions in court's opinion which go beyond the facts before court and therefore are individual views of author of opinion and not binding in subsequent cases. State ex rel. Foster v. Naftalin, 246 Minn. 181, 74 N.W.2d 249. See also **Dictum.**

Dictate. To order or instruct what is to be said or written. To pronounce, word by word, what is meant to be written by another. See **Dictation.**

Dictation. In Louisiana, this term is used in a technical sense, and means to pronounce orally what is destined to be written at the same time by another. It is used in reference to nuncupative wills. The dictation of a will refers to the substance, and not the style, and it is sufficient if the will, as written, conveys the identity of thought expressed by the testator, though not the identity of words used by him.

Dictator. One in whom supreme authority in any line is invested, one who rules autocratically, and one who prescribes for others authoritatively, and offer oppressively. Houston Printing Co. v. Hunter, Tex. Civ.App., 105 S.W.2d 312, 317.

In Roman law, a magistrate invested with unlimited power, and created in times of national distress and peril. Among the Romans, he continued in office for six months only, and had unlimited power and authority over both the property and lives of the citizens.

Dictores. Arbitrators.

Dictum /díktəm/. A statement, remark, or observation. *Gratis dictum;* a gratuitous or voluntary representation; one which a party is not bound to make. *Simplex dictum;* a mere assertion; an assertion without proof.

The word is generally used as an abbreviated form of *obiter dictum,* "a remark by the way;" that is, an observation or remark made by a judge in pronouncing an opinion upon a cause, concerning some rule, principle, or application of law, or the solution of a question suggested by the case at bar, but not necessarily involved in the case or essential to its determination; any statement of the law enunciated by the court merely by way of illustration, argument, analogy, or suggestion. Statements and comments in an opinion concerning some rule of law or legal proposition not necessarily involved nor essential to determination of the case in hand are obiter dicta, and lack the force of an adjudication. Wheeler v. Wilkin, 98 Colo. 568, 58 P.2d 1223, 1226. *Dicta* are opinions of a judge which do not embody the resolution or determination of the court, and made without argument, or full consideration of the point, are not the professed deliberate determinations of the judge himself.

In old English law, *dictum* meant an arbitrament, or the award of arbitrators.

In French law, the report of a judgment made by one of the judges who has given it.

Dictum de Kenilworth. The edict or declaration of Kenilworth. An edict or award between King Henry III, and all the barons and others who had been in arms against him; and so called because it was made at Kenilworth Castle in Warwickshire, in the fifty-first year of his reign, containing a composition of five years' rent for the lands and estates of those who had forfeited them in that rebellion.

Die, *v.* To expire; cease to live; the equivalent to the phrase "lose his life." See also **Death.**

Diei dictio /dayíyay díksh(iy)ow/. Lat. In Roman law, this name was given to a notice promulgated by a magistrate of his intention to present an impeachment against a citizen before the people, specifying the day appointed, the name of the accused, and the crime charged.

Diem clausit extremum /dáyəm klózəd əkstríyməm/. (Lat. He has closed his last day, *i.e.* died.) A writ which formerly lay on the death of a tenant *in capite,* to ascertain the lands of which he died seised, and reclaim them into the king's hands. It was directed to the king's escheators.

A writ awarded out of the exchequer after the death of a crown debtor, the sheriff being commanded by it to inquire by a jury when and where the crown debtor died, and what chattels, debts, and lands he had at the time of his decease, and to take and seize them into the crown's hands.

Dies /dáyiyz/. Lat. A day; days. Days for appearance in court. Provisions or maintenance for a day. The king's rents were anciently reserved by so many days' provisions.

Dies amoris /dáyiz əmórəs/. A day of favor. The name given to the appearance day of the term on the fourth day, or *quarto die post.* It was the day given by the favor and indulgence of the court to the defendant for his appearance, when all parties appeared in court, and had their appearance recorded by the proper officer.

Dies a quo /dáyiz èy kwów/. (The day from which.) In the civil law. The day from which a transaction begins; the commencement of it; the conclusion being the *dies ad quem.*

Dies cedit /dáyiz síydət/. The day begins; *dies venit,* the day has come. Two expressions in Roman law which signify the vesting or fixing of an interest, and the interest becoming a present one.

Dies communes in banco /dáyiz kəmyúwniyz ìn bæŋkow/. Regular days for appearance in court; called, also "common return-days."

Dies datus /dáyiz déydəs/. A day given or allowed (to a defendant in an action); amounting to a continuance. But the name was appropriate only to a continuance before a declaration filed; if afterwards allowed, it was called an "imparlance."

Dies datus in banco /dáyiz déydəs ìn bæŋkow/. A day given in the *bench* (or court of common pleas). A day given in bank, as distinguished from a day at *nisi prius.*

Dies datus partibus /dáyiz déydəs párdəbəs/. A day given to the parties to an action; an adjournment or continuance.

Dies datus prece partium /dáyiz déydəs príysiy párshəm/. A day given on the prayer of the parties.

Dies dominicus /dáyiz dəmínəkəs/. The Lord's day; Sunday.

Dies dominicus non est juridicus /dáyiz dəmínəkəs nón èst jərídəkəs/. Sunday is not a court day, or day for judicial proceedings, or legal purposes.

Dies excrescens /dáyiz əkskríysən(d)z/. In old English law, the added or increasing day in leap year.

Dies fasti /dáyiz fæstay/. In Roman law, days on which the courts were open, and justice could be legally administered; days on which it was lawful for the prætor to pronounce *(fari)* the *three* words "*do*", *"dico", "addico".* Hence called *"triverbial* days," answering to the *dies juridici* of the English law.

Dies feriati /dáyiyz fəriyéyday/. In the civil law, holidays.

Dies gratiæ /dáyiyz gréyshiyiy/. In old English practice, a day of grace, courtesy, or favor. The *quarto die post* was sometimes so called.

Dies inceptus pro completo habetur /dáyiyz ənséptəs pròw kəmplíydow həbíydər/. A day begun is held as complete.

Dies incertus pro conditione habetur /dáyiyz ənsárdəs pròw kəndìshiyówniy həbíydər/. An uncertain day is held as a condition.

Dies intercisi /dáyiyz ìntərsáyzay/. In Roman law, divided days; days on which the courts were open for a part of the day.

Dies juridicus /dáyiyz jərídəkəs/. A lawful day for the transaction of judicial or court business; a day on which the courts are or may be open for the transaction of business.

Dies legitimus /dáyiyz ləjídəməs/. In the civil and old English law, a lawful or law day; a term day; a day of appearance.

Dies marchiæ /dáyiyz márkiyiy/. In old English law, the day of meeting of English and Scotch, which was annually held on the marches or borders to adjust their differences and preserve peace.

Dies nefasti /dáyiyz nìyfǽstay/. In Roman law, days on which the courts were closed, and it was unlawful to administer justice; answering to the *dies non juridici* of the English law.

Dies non /dáyiyz nón/. An abbreviation of *Dies non juridicus (q.v.).*

Dies non juridicus /dáyiyz nòn jərídəkəs/. A day not juridical; not a court day. A day on which courts are not open for business, such as Sundays and some holidays.

Dies pacis /dáyiyz péysəs/. (Days of peace.) The year was formerly divided into the days of the peace of the church and the days of the peace of the king, including in the two divisions all the days of the year.

Dies solaris /dáyiyz səlérəs/. In old English law, a solar day, as distinguished from what was called *"dies lunaris"* (a lunar day); both composing an artificial day. See **Day.**

Dies solis /dáyiyz sówləs/. In the civil and old English law, Sunday (literally, the day of the sun).

Dies utiles /dáyiyz yúwdəliyz/. Juridical days; useful or available days. A term of the Roman law, used to designate those especial days occurring within the limits of a prescribed period of time upon which it was lawful, or possible, to do a specific act.

Diet. A general legislative assembly is sometimes so called on the continent of Europe.

Dieta /dayíydə/. A day's journey; a day's work; a day's expenses.

Di. et fi. /dáy ət fáy/(dəléktow èt fədíylay)/. L. Lat. In old writs, an abbreviation of *dilecto et fideli* (to his beloved and faithful).

Dieu et mon droit /dyúw ey mòn dr(w)ó/. Fr. God and my right. The motto of the royal arms of England, first assumed by Richard I.

Dieu son acte /dyúw sòn ákt/. L. Fr. In old law, God his act; God's act. An event beyond human foresight or control. See **Act of God.**

Die without issue. See **Dying without issue.**

Diffacere /dəféysəriy/. To destroy; to disfigure or deface.

Difference. In an agreement for submission to arbitration, a disagreement or dispute. As respects contract specifications or material described therein, a state of being unlike. Disagreement in opinion, interpretation or conclusion. Instance or cause of disagreement. See also **Disagreement.**

Difforciare /dəfòrs(h)(i)yériy/. In old English law, to deny, or keep from one. *Difforciare rectum,* to deny justice to any one, after having been required to do it.

Diffuse. To spread widely; scatter; disperse.

Digama, or **digamy** /dígəmiy/. Second marriage; marriage to a second wife after the death of the first, as "bigamy," in law, is having two wives at once. Originally, a man who married a widow, or married again after the death of his wife, was said to be guilty of bigamy.

Digest. A collection or compilation, embodying the chief matter of numerous books, articles, court decisions, etc. in one, disposed under proper heads or titles, and usually by an alphabetical arrangement, for facility in reference.

An index to reported cases, providing brief statements of court holdings or facts of cases, which is arranged by subject and subdivided by jurisdiction and courts. See *American Digest System; Special digests,* below.

As a legal term, "digest" is to be distinguished from "abridgment." The latter is a summary or epitome of the contents of a single work, in which, as a rule, the original order or sequence of parts is preserved, and in which the principal labor of the compiler is in the matter of consolidation. A digest is wider in its scope; is made up of quotations or paraphrased passages, and has its own system of classification and arrangement. An "index" merely points out the places where particular matters may be found, without purporting to give such matters *in extenso.* A "treatise" or "commentary" is not a compilation, but an original composition, though it may include quotations and excerpts.

A reference to the "Digest," or "Dig.," is often understood to designate the Digest (or Pandects) of the Justinian collection; that being the digest *par eminence,* and the authoritative compilation of the Roman law.

American Digest System. The American Digest System is a subject classification scheme whereby decisions that were reported chronologically in the various units of the National Reporter System are rearranged by subject, bringing together all cases on a similar point of law. The system divides the subject of law into seven main classes. Each class is then divided into sub-classes and then each sub-class into topics. There are over 400 topics, each of which corresponds to a legal concept. The system consists of a Century Digest (1658–1896), eight Decennial Digests (1897–1905, 1906–1915, 1916–1925, 1926–1935, 1936–1945, 1946–1955, 1956–1966, and 1966–1976), and the General Digest, 5th Series (1976 to date). The American Digest System is the master index to all reported case law. See also *Special digests, infra.*

Special digests. Decisions included in the American Digest System are as well included in special digests covering the federal courts and also in regional and state digests. The "U.S. Supreme Court Digest" covers decisions from the U.S. Supreme Court. The Federal Digest (cases decided prior to 1939), Modern Federal Practice Digest (1939–1961), and West's Federal Practice Digest (1961 to date) cover federal court cases. State court decisions from geographical areas are also published in "Regional Digests" (Atlantic, North Western, Pacific, South Eastern, Southern Digests). Also, individual "State Digests" are published for most all states.

Digesta /dəjéstə/. Digests. One of the titles of the Pandects of Justinian.

Digests. The ordinary name of the Pandects of Justinian, which are now usually cited by the abbreviation "Dig." instead of "Ff.," as formerly. Sometimes called "Digest," in the singular. See also **Digest.**

Dignitary. In canon law, a person holding an ecclesiastical benefice or dignity, which gave him some preeminence above mere priests and canons. To this class exclusively belonged all bishops, deans, archdeacons, etc.; but it now includes all the prebendaries and canons of the church.

Dignity. In English law, an honor; a title, station, or distinction of honor. Dignities are a species of incorporeal hereditaments, in which a person may have a property or estate. 2 Bl.Comm. 37; 1 Bl.Comm. 396.

Dijudication /dàyjuwdəkéyshən/. Judicial decision or determination.

Dilacion /dìylasyówn/. In Spanish law, a space of time granted to a party to a suit in which to answer a demand or produce evidence of a disputed fact.

Dilapidation. A species of ecclesiastical waste which occurs whenever the incumbent suffers any edifices of his ecclesiastical living to go to ruin or decay. It is either voluntary, by pulling down, or permissive, by suffering the church, parsonage-houses, and other buildings thereunto belonging, to decay. And the remedy for either lies either in the spiritual court, where the canon law prevails, or in the courts of common law. It is also held to be good cause of deprivation if the bishop, parson, or other ecclesiastical person dilapidates buildings or cuts down timber growing on the patrimony of the church, unless for necessary repairs; and that a writ of prohibition will also lie against him in the common-law courts. 3 Bl.Comm. 91.

The term is also used, in the law of landlord and tenant, to signify the neglect of necessary repairs to a building, or suffering it to fall into a state of decay, or the pulling down of the building or any part of it.

Dilationes in lege sunt odiosæ /dəlèyshiyówniyz ìn líyjiy sànt owdiyówsiy/. Delays in law are odious.

Dilatory /dílət(ò)riy/. Tending or intended to cause delay or to gain time or to put off a decision.

Dilatory defense. In chancery practice, one the object of which is to dismiss, suspend, or obstruct the suit, without touching the merits, until the impediment or obstacle insisted on shall be removed. 3 Bl.Comm. 301, 302. See also **Dilatory pleas.**

Dilatory exceptions. Such as do not tend to defeat the action, but only to retard its progress.

Dilatory pleas. A class of defenses at common law, founded on some matter of fact not connected with the merits of the case, but such as might exist without impeaching the right of action itself. They were either pleas to the *jurisdiction,* showing that, by reason of some matter therein stated, the case was not within the jurisdiction of the court; or pleas in *suspension,* showing some matter of temporary incapacity to proceed with the suit; or pleas in *abatement,* showing some matter for abatement or quashing the declaration. Davis v. Thiede, 138 Ind.App. 537, 203 N.E.2d 835.

Diligence. Vigilant activity; attentiveness; or care, of which there are infinite shades, from the slightest momentary thought to the most vigilant anxiety. Attentive and persistent in doing a thing; steadily applied; active; sedulous; laborious; unremitting; untiring. National Steel & Shipbuilding Co. v. U. S., 190 Ct.Cl. 247, 419 F.2d 863, 875.

The civil law is in perfect conformity with the common law. It lays down three degrees of diligence,—ordinary (*diligentia*); extraordinary (*exactissima diligentia*); slight (*levissima diligentia*).

There may be a high degree of diligence, a common degree of diligence, and a slight degree of diligence, with their corresponding degrees of negligence. Common or ordinary diligence is that degree of diligence which men in general exercise in respect to their own concerns; high or great diligence is of course extraordinary diligence, or that which very prudent persons take of their own concerns; and low or slight diligence is that which persons of less than common prudence, or indeed of any prudence at all, take of their own concerns.

See also **Care.**

Due diligence. Such a measure of prudence, activity, or assiduity, as is properly to be expected from, and ordinarily exercised by, a reasonable and prudent man under the particular circumstances; not measured by any absolute standard, but depending on the relative facts of the special case.

Extraordinary diligence. That extreme measure of care and caution which persons of unusual prudence and circumspection use for securing and preserving their own property or rights.

Great diligence. Such a measure of care, prudence, and assiduity as persons of unusual prudence and discretion exercise in regard to any and all of their own affairs, or such as persons of ordinary prudence exercise in regard to very important affairs of their own.

High diligence. The same as great diligence.

Low diligence. The same as slight diligence.

Necessary diligence. That degree of diligence which a person placed in a particular situation must exercise in order to entitle him to the protection of the law in respect to rights or claims growing out of that situation, or to avoid being left without redress on account of his own culpable carelessness or negligence.

Ordinary diligence is that degree of care which men of common prudence generally exercise in their affairs, in the country and the age in which they live.

Reasonable diligence. A fair, proper and due degree of care and activity, measured with reference to the particular circumstances; such diligence, care, or attention as might be expected from a man of ordinary prudence and activity.

Special diligence. The measure of diligence and skill exercised by a good business man in his particular specialty, which must be commensurate with the duty to be performed and the individual circumstances of the case; not merely the diligence of an ordinary person or non-specialist.

Diligent. Attentive and persistent in doing a thing; steadily applied; active; sedulous; laborious; unremitting; untiring.

Diligent inquiry. Such inquiry as a diligent man, intent upon ascertaining a fact, would ordinarily make, and it is inquiry made with diligence and good faith to ascertain the truth, and must be an inquiry as full as the circumstances of the situation will permit. Liepelt v. Baird, 17 Ill.2d 428, 161 N.E.2d 854, 857.

Diligiatus /dəlìjiyéydəs/. (Fr. *De lege ejectus*, Lat.) Outlawed.

Dillon's Rule. Rule used in construction of statutes delegating authority to local government: " . . . [A] municipal corporation possesses and can exercise the following powers and no others: First, those granted in express words; second, those necessarily implied or necessarily incident to the powers expressly granted; third, those absolutely essential to the declared objects and purposes of the corporation— not simply convenient, but indispensable . . . " Merriam v. Moody's Executors, 25 Iowa 163, 170 (1868).

Dilution doctrine. Concept most applicable where subsequent user used the trademark of prior user for a product so dissimilar from the product of the prior user and there is no likelihood of confusion of the products or sources but where the use of the trademark by the subsequent user will lessen uniqueness of the prior user's mark with the possible future result that a strong mark may become a weak mark. Holiday Inns, Inc. v. Holiday Out in America, C.A. Fla., 481 F.2d 445, 450.

Dimidia, dimidium, dimidius /dəmídiyə(m)/dəmíydiyə(s)/. Half; a half; the half.

Dimidietas /dìmədáyətæs/. The moiety or half of a thing.

Diminished capacity. See **Diminished responsibility doctrine.**

Diminished responsibility doctrine /dəmínəsht rəspòn-səbílədiy dóktrən/. Term used to refer to lack of capacity to achieve state of mind requisite for commission of crime. McGuire v. Superior Court for Los Angeles County, 274 Cal.App. 583, 79 Cal.Rptr. 155, 161. The concept of diminished responsibility, also known as partial insanity, permits the trier of fact to regard the impaired mental state of the defendant in mitigation of the punishment or degree of the offense even though the impairment does not qualify as insanity under the prevailing test. A number of courts have adopted the concept. In some jurisdictions, mental retardation and extremely low intelligence will, if proved, serve to reduce first degree murder to manslaughter. See also **Insanity.**

Diminutio /dìmən(y)úwsh(iy)ow/. In the civil law, diminution; a taking away; loss or deprivation. *Diminutio capitis*, loss of *status* or condition. See **Capitis diminutio.**

Diminution /dìmən(y)úwshən/. Incompleteness. Act or process of diminishing, taking away, or lessening. A word signifying that the record sent up from an inferior to a superior court for review is incomplete, or not fully certified.

Diminution in value. Rule of damages which provides for difference between "before" and "after" value of property which has been damaged or taken. Big Rock Mountain Corp. v. Stearns-Roger Corp., C.A. S.D., 388 F.2d 165, 168.

Diminution of damages. See **Mitigation of damages.**

Dimisi /dəmáysay/. In old conveyancing, I have demised. *Dimisi, concessi, et ad firmam tradidi*, have demised, granted, and to farm let. The usual words of operation in a lease. 2 Bl.Comm. 317, 318.

Dimisit /dəmáysət/. In old conveyancing, [he] has demised. See **Dimisi.**

Dimissoriæ litteræ /dìməsóriyiy lídəriy/. In the civil law, letters dimissory or dismissory, commonly called "apostles" (*quæ vulgo apostoli dicuntur*). See **Apostoli, Apostles.**

Dimissory letters /dím. əsòriy lédərz/. Where a candidate for holy orders has a title of ordination in one diocese in England, and is to be ordained in another, the bishop of the former diocese gives letters dimissory to the bishop of the latter to enable him to ordain the candidate.

Dinarchy /dáynarkiy/. A government of two persons.

Diocesan /dayósəsən/. Belonging to a diocese; a bishop, as he stands related to his own diocese.

Diocesan courts. In English law, the consistorial courts of each diocese, exercising general jurisdiction of all matters arising locally within their respective limits, with the exception of places subject to *peculiar* jurisdiction, and administering the other branches of the ecclesiastical law.

Diocesan mission. A mission which does missionary work in single diocese.

Diocese /dáyəsəs/. The territorial extent of a bishop's jurisdiction. The circuit of every bishop's jurisdiction.

Dioichia /dayíykiyə/. The district over which a bishop exercised his spiritual functions.

Diploma. In the civil law, a royal charter; letters patent granted by a prince or sovereign. Instrument conferring some honor, privilege, or authority. Commonly used to denote document given by educational institution on graduation and awarding of degree.

Diplomacy. The art and practice of conducting negotiations between foreign governments for the attainment of mutually satisfactory political relations. Negotiation or intercourse between nations through their representatives. The rules, customs, and privileges of representatives at foreign courts.

Diplomatic agent. In international law, a general name for all classes of persons charged with the negotiation, transaction, or superintendence of the diplomatic business of one nation with that of another. See also **Ambassador.**

Diplomatic relations. Established and formal communications and acknowledgment between one country and another in which diplomatic agents are exchanged.

Diplomatics. The science of diplomas, or of ancient writings and documents. The art of judging of ancient charters, public documents, diplomas, etc., and discriminating the true from the false.

Dipsomania /dìpsəméyn(i)yə/. A mental disease characterized by an uncontrollable desire for intoxicating drinks. An irresistible impulse to indulge in intoxication, either by alcohol or other drugs.

Dipsomaniac /dìpsəméyniyæk/. A person subject to dipsomania. One who has an irresistible desire for alcoholic liquors. See **Insanity.**

Diptycha /díptikə/. Diptychs; tablets of wood, metal, or other substance, used among the Romans for the purpose of writing, and folded like a book of two leaves. The diptychs of antiquity were especially employed for public registers. They were used in the Greek, and afterwards in the Roman, church, as registers of the names of those for whom supplication was to be made, and are ranked among the earliest monastic records.

Direct, *v.* To point to; guide; order; command; instruct. To advise; suggest; request.

Direct, *adj.* Immediate; proximate; by the shortest course; without circuity; operating by an immediate connection or relation, instead of operating through a medium; the opposite of *indirect.* Carter v. Carter Coal Co., App.D.C., 298 U.S. 238, 56 S.Ct. 855, 80 L.Ed. 1160.

In the usual or natural course or line; immediately upwards or downwards; as distinguished from that which is out of the line, or on the side of it. In the usual or regular course or order, as distinguished from that which diverts, interrupts, or opposes. The opposite of cross, contrary, collateral or remote.

Without any intervening medium, agency or influence; unconditional.

Direct action. An action by insured directly against insurer rather than against tortfeasor's indemnity policy. Hand v. Northwestern Nat. Ins. Co., 255 Ark. 802, 502 S.W.2d 474. Action by a stockholder to enforce right of action existing in him as contrasted with a derivative suit in behalf of corporation. Citizens Nat'l Bank of St. Petersburg v. Peters, Fla.App., 175 So.2d 54, 56.

Direct and proximate cause. See **Direct cause.**

Direct attack. A direct attack on a judgment or decree is an attempt, for sufficient cause, to have it annulled, reversed, vacated, corrected, declared void, or enjoined, in a proceeding instituted for that specific purpose, such as an appeal, writ of error, bill of review, or injunction to restrain its execution; distinguished from a collateral attack, which is an attempt to impeach the validity or binding force of the judgment or decree as a side issue or in a proceeding instituted for some other purpose. Ernell v. O'Fiel, Tex.Civ.App., 441 S.W.2d 653, 655. A direct attack on a judicial proceeding is an attempt to void or correct it in some manner provided by law.

Direct cause. That which sets in motion train of events which brings about result without intervention of any force operating or working actively from new and independent source; or, as one without which the injury would not have happened. Norbeck v. Mutual of Omaha Ins. Co., 3 Wash.App. 582, 476 P.2d 546, 547. See **Cause; Proximate cause.**

Direct charge-off method. A method of accounting for bad debts whereby a deduction is permitted only when an account becomes partially or completely worthless.

Direct contempt. Those contempts committed within the presence of the court, or so near the court as to interrupt its proceedings. Ex parte Tarpley, 293 Ala. 137, 300 So.2d 409, 413. See **Contempt.**

Direct costs. Cost of direct material and labor, and variable overhead incurred in producing a product.

Directed verdict. In a case in which the party with the burden of proof has failed to present a prima facie case for jury consideration, the trial judge may order the entry of a verdict without allowing the jury to consider it, because, as a matter of law, there can be only one such verdict. Fed.R. Civil P. 50(a). In a criminal case, the judge may render a judgment of acquittal in favor of defendant. Fed.R. Crim.P. 29. See also **Verdict.**

Direct estoppel. Form of estoppel by judgment where issue has been actually litigated and determined in action between same parties based upon same cause of action. Napper v. Anderson et al., C.A.Tex., 500 F.2d 634, 636.

Direct evidence. Evidence in form of testimony from a witness who actually saw, heard or touched the subject of interrogation. State v. Baker, 249 Or. 549, 438 P.2d 978, 980. Evidence, which if believed, proves existence of fact in issue without inference or presumption. State v. McClure, Mo.App., 504 S.W.2d

664, 668. That means of proof which tends to show the existence of a fact in question, without the intervention of the proof of any other fact, and is distinguished from circumstantial evidence, which is often called "indirect." Direct evidence means evidence which in the first instance applies directly to the factum probandum, or which immediately points to a question at issue, or is evidence of the precise fact in issue and on trial by witnesses who can testify that they saw the acts done or heard the words spoken which constituted the precise fact to be proved.

Evidence that directly proves a fact, without an inference or presumption, and which in itself, if true, conclusively establishes that fact. Calif.Evid.Code.

Direct examination. The first interrogation or examination of a witness, on the merits, by the party on whose behalf he is called. The first examination of a witness upon a matter that is not within the scope of a previous examination of the witness. Calif.Evid. Code.

This is to be distinguished from an examination *in pais,* or on the *voir dire,* which is merely preliminary, and is had when the competency of the witness is challenged; from the cross-examination, which is conducted by the adverse party; and from the redirect examination which follows the cross-examination, and is had by the party who first examined the witness.

Direct injury. A wrong which directly results in the violation of a legal right and which must exist to permit a court to determine the constitutionality of an act of Congress.

Direct interest. A direct interest, such as would render the interested party incompetent to testify in regard to the matter, is an interest which is certain, and not contingent or doubtful. A matter which is dependent alone on the successful prosecution of an execution cannot be considered as uncertain, or otherwise than direct, in this sense.

Direction. The act of governing; management; superintendence. Denton v. Yazoo & M. V. R. Co., Miss., 284 U.S. 305, 52 S.Ct. 141, 142, 76 L.Ed. 310. Also the body of persons (called "directors") who are charged with the management and administration of a corporation or institution.

The charge or instruction given by the court to a jury upon a point of law arising or involved in the case, to be by them applied to the facts in evidence. See **Jury instructions.**

The clause of a bill in equity containing the address of the bill to the court.

That which is imposed by directing; a guiding or authoritative instruction; order; command. Hughes v. Van Bruggen, 44 N.M. 534, 105 P.2d 494, 496.

The line or course upon which anything is moving or aimed to move.

Direct line. See **Descent.**

Direct loss. One resulting immediately and proximately from the occurrence and not remotely from some of the consequences or effects thereof. See **Loss.**

Directly. In a direct way without anything intervening; not by secondary, but by direct, means.

Director. One who, or that which directs; as one who directs or regulates, guides or orders; a manager or superintendent, or a chief administrative official. State ex inf. McKittrick v. Bode, 342 Mo. 162, 113 S.W.2d 805, 808. See **Directors.**

Director of the Mint. An officer having the control, management, and superintendence of the United States Mint and its branches. He is appointed by the President, by and with the advice and consent of the senate.

Directors. Persons appointed or elected according to law, authorized to manage and direct the affairs of a corporation or company. The whole of the directors collectively form the board of directors.

Board of directors. See **Board of directors.**

Inside director. Director who is an employee, officer or major stockholder of corporation.

Interlocking director. Person who is a director of more than one corporation having allied interests. See **Interlocking directorate.**

Outside director. Non-employee director with no, or only mimimal, direct interest in corporation.

Directory, *adj.* A provision in a statute, rule of procedure, or the like, which is a mere direction or instruction of no obligatory force, and involving no invalidating consequence for its disregard, as opposed to an imperative or mandatory provision, which must be followed. The general rule is that the prescriptions of a statute relating to the performance of a public duty are so far directory that, though neglect of them may be punishable, yet it does not affect the validity of the acts done under them, as in the case of a statute requiring an officer to prepare and deliver a document to another officer on or before a certain day.

A "directory" provision in a statute is one, the observance of which is not necessary to the validity of the proceeding to which it relates; one which leaves it optional with the department or officer to which it is addressed to obey or not as he may see fit. Generally, statutory provisions which do not relate to essence of thing to be done, and as to which compliance is matter of convenience rather than substance are "directory," while provisions which relate to essence of thing to be done, that is, matters of substance, are "mandatory." Rodgers v. Meredith, 274 Ala. 179, 146 So.2d 308, 310.

Under a general classification, statutes are either "mandatory" or "directory," and, if mandatory, they prescribe, in addition to requiring the doing of the things specified, the result that will follow if they are not done, whereas, if directory, their terms are limited to what is required to be done. A statute is mandatory when the provision of the statute is the essence of the thing required to be done; otherwise, when it relates to form and manner, and where an act is incident, or after jurisdiction acquired, it is directory merely.

Directory trust. Where, by the terms of a trust, the fund is directed to be vested in a particular manner till the period arrives at which it is to be appropriated, this is called a "directory trust." It is distinguished from a discretionary trust, in which the trustee has a discretion as to the management of the fund.

Directory, *n.* Book containing names, addresses, and occupations of inhabitants of city. Also any list or compilation, usually in book or pamphlet form, of persons, professional organizations, firms or corporations forming some class separate and distinct from others, *e.g.* telephone directory, lawyer's directory, hotel directory, etc.

Direct payment. One which is absolute and unconditional as to the time, amount, and the persons by whom and to whom it is to be made.

Direct placement. With respect to securities offerings, the negotiation by a borrower, such as an industrial or utility company, directly with the lender, such as a life insurance company or group of companies, for an entire issue of securities. No underwriter is involved and the transaction is exempt from SEC filing.

Direct selling. Selling directly to customer rather than to distributor or dealer; or to retailer rather than to wholesaler.

Direct tax. One that is imposed directly upon property, according to its value. It is generally spoken of as a property tax or an ad valorem tax. Distinguishable from an indirect tax which is levied upon some right or privilege.

Diribitores /dìrəbətóriyz/. In Roman law, officers who distributed ballots to the people, to be used in voting.

Diriment impediments /dírəmənt əmpédəmənts/. In canon law, absolute bars to marriage, which would make it null *ab initio*.

Disability. The want of legal capability to perform an act. Term is generally used to indicate an incapacity for the full enjoyment of ordinary legal rights; thus, persons under age, insane persons, and convicts are said to be under disability. Sometimes the term is used in a more limited sense, as when it signifies an impediment to marriage, or the restraints placed upon clergymen by reason of their spiritual avocations, or lack of legal qualifications to hold office.

As used in connection with Workers' Compensation Acts, disability is a composite of (1) actual incapacity to perform the tasks usually encountered in one's employment and the wage loss resulting therefrom, and (2) physical impairment of the body that may or may not be incapacitating. Russell v. Bankers Life Co., 46 Cal.App.3d 405, 120 Cal.Rptr. 627, 633.

Statutory definition of a "disability," for social security benefits purposes, imposes three requirements: (1) that there be a medically determinable physical or mental impairment which can be expected to result in death or meets the duration aspect set forth; (2) that there be an inability to engage in any substantial gainful activity; and (3) that the inability be by reason of the impairment. Pierce v. Gardner, C.A.Ill., 388 F.2d 846, 847. Inability to work without some pain or discomfort does not necessarily satisfy test of disability. DeFontes v. Celebrezze, 226 F.Supp. 327, 330 (D.C.R.I.).

Absence of competent physical, intellectual, or moral powers; impairment of earning capacity; loss of physical function that reduces efficiency; inability to work. Rorabaugh v. Great Eastern Casualty Co., 117 Wash. 7, 200 P.2d 587, 590.

Under Uniform Probate Code, an incapacitated person is one who is impaired by reason of physical disability.

See also Capacity; Civil disabilities; Incapacity; Incompetency; Loss of earning capacity; Person under disability; Temporary disability.

General Classification

Disability may be either *general* or *special;* the former when it incapacitates the person for the performance of all legal acts of a general class, or giving to them their ordinary legal effect; the latter when it debars him from one specific act. Disability may also be either *personal* or *absolute;* the former where it attaches to the particular person, and arises out of his *status,* his previous act, or his natural or juridical incapacity; the latter where it originates with a particular person, but extends also to his descendants or successors. The term *civil* disability is used as equivalent to *legal* disability, both these expressions meaning disabilities or disqualifications created by positive law, as distinguished from *physical* disabilities. A *physical* disability is a disability or incapacity caused by physical defect or infirmity, or bodily imperfection, or mental weakness or alienation; as distinguished from *civil* disability, which relates to the civil *status* or condition of the person, and is imposed by the law.

Partial disability. Under workers' compensation law, incapacity in part from returning to work performed before accident.

Permanent disability. Incapacity forever from returning to work formerly performed before accident, though this incapacity may be either total or partial. See also **Permanent disability.**

Temporary disability. Temporary, as distinguished from permanent, disability is a condition that exists until the injured employee is as far restored as the permanent character of the injuries will permit.

Total disability. Total disability to follow insured's usual occupation arises where he is incapacitated from performing any substantial part of his ordinary duties, though still able to perform a few minor duties and be present at his place of business. "Total disability" within an accident policy does not mean absolute physical disability to transact any business pertaining to insured's occupation, but disability from performing substantial and material duties connected with it. The term may also apply to any impairment of mind or body rendering it impossible for insured to follow continuously a substantially gainful occupation without seriously impairing his health, the disability being permanent when of such nature as to render it reasonably certain to continue throughout the lifetime of insured. See also **Permanent disability; Wholly disabled.**

Disability clause. Provision in insurance policy calling for waiver of premiums during period of disability.

Disability compensation. Payments from public or private funds to one during period of disability and incapacity from work; *e.g.* social security or workers' compensation disability benefits.

Disability insurance. Insurance coverage purchased to protect insured during periods of incapacity from working. Often purchased by professionals.

Disability retirement. Plan of retirement which is invoked when person covered is disabled from working to normal retirement age or increased benefits when person retires because of disability.

Disable. Ordinarily, to take away the ability of, to render incapable of proper and effective action. Federal Union Life Ins. Co. of Cincinnati, Ohio v. Richey's Adm'x, 256 Ky. 262, 75 S.W.2d 767, 768. See **Civil death; Disability.**

In the old language of pleading, to disable is to take advantage of one's own or another's disability. Thus, it was an express maxim of the common law that the party shall "not disable himself"; but "this disability to disable himself * * * is personal."

Disabled person. Person who lacks legal capacity to act *sui juris* or one who is physically or mentally disabled from acting in his own behalf or from pursuing his normal occupation. See **Civil death; Disability.**

Disabling restraints. Restraints on alienation of property which are normally void as against public policy. Lohmann v. Adams, Okl., 540 P.2d 552, 556.

Disabling statutes. English acts of parliament, restraining and regulating the exercise of a right or the power of alienation; the term is specially applied to 1 Eliz., c. 19, and similar acts restraining the power of ecclesiastical corporations to make leases.

Disadvocare. To deny a thing.

Disaffirm. To repudiate; to revoke a consent once given; to recall an affirmance. To refuse one's subsequent sanction to a former act; to disclaim the intention of being bound by an antecedent transaction.

Disaffirmance. The repudiation of a former transaction. The refusal by one who has the legal power to refuse (as in the case of a voidable contract), to abide by his former acts, or accept the legal consequences of them. It may either be "express" (in words) or "implied" from acts inconsistent with a recognition of validity of former transaction.

Disafforest /dìsəfóhrəst/. To restore to their former condition lands which have been turned into forests. To remove from the operation of the forest laws. 2 Bl.Comm. 416.

Disagreement. Difference of opinion or want of uniformity or concurrence of views; as, a disagreement among the members of a jury, among the judges of a court, or between arbitrators.

The refusal by a grantee, lessee, etc., to accept an estate, lease, etc., made to him. The annulling of a thing that had essence before. No estate can be vested in a person against his will. Consequently, no one can become a grantee, etc., without his *agreement.* The law implies such an agreement until the contrary is shown, but his disagreement renders the grant, etc., inoperative.

Disallow. To refuse to allow, to deny the need or validity of, to disown or reject.

Disalt /dəsólt/. To disable a person.

Disappropriation. In ecclesiastical law, this is where the appropriation of a benefice is severed, either by the patron presenting a clerk or by the corporation which has the appropriation being dissolved. 1 Bl. Comm. 385.

Disapprove. To pass unfavorable judgment upon; to refuse official approbation to; to disallow; to decline to sanction; to refuse to confirm, ratify or consent to.

Disaster. For common disaster, see **Common.**

Disaster loss. If a casualty is sustained in an area designated as a disaster area by the President of the U.S., the casualty is designated a disaster loss. In such an event, the disaster loss may be treated as having occurred in the taxable year immediately preceding the taxable year in which the disaster actually occurred. Thus, immediate tax benefits are provided to victims of a disaster. See **Casualty loss.**

Disavow /dìsəváw/. To repudiate the unauthorized acts of an agent; to deny the authority by which he assumed to act.

Disbarment. Act of court in suspending attorney's license to practice law. See also **Debarment.**

Disbocatio /dìsbəkéysh(iy)ow/. In old English law, a conversion of wood grounds into arable or pasture; an assarting. See **Assart.**

Disbursement /dìsbə́rsmənt/. To pay out, commonly from a fund. To make payment in settlement of a debt or account payable.

D.I.S.C. Domestic International Sales Corporation.

Discarcare /dìskarkériy/. In old English law, to discharge, to unload; as a vessel. *Carcare et discarcare;* to charge and discharge; to load and unload.

Discargare /dìskargériy/. In old European law, to discharge or unload, as a wagon.

Disceptio causæ /dəsépsh(iy)ow kóziy/. In Roman law, the argument of a cause by the counsel on both sides.

Discharge. To release; liberate; annul; unburden; disincumber; dismiss. To extinguish an obligation; terminate employment of person; release, as from prison, confinement or military service.

Discharge is a generic term; its principal species are rescission, release, accord and satisfaction, performance, judgment, composition, bankruptcy, merger.

As applied to demands, claims, rights of action, incumbrances, etc., to discharge the debt or claim is to extinguish it, to annul its obligatory force, to satisfy it. And here also the term is generic; thus a debt, a mortgage, a legacy, may be discharged by payment or performance, or by any act short of that, lawful in itself, which the creditor accepts as sufficient. U.C.C. § 3–601 et seq. governs discharge of commercial instruments. To discharge a person is to liberate him from the binding force of an obligation, debt, or claim.

See also **Release.**

Bankruptcy. The release of a bankrupt from all of his debts which are provable in bankruptcy, except such as are excepted by the Bankruptcy Act. The discharge of the bankrupt is the step which regularly follows the adjudication of bankruptcy and the administration of his estate. By it the debtor is released from the obligation of all his debts which were or might be proved in the proceedings, so that they are no longer a charge upon him, and so that he may thereafter engage in business and acquire property without its being liable for the satisfaction of such former debts.

Contract. To cancel the obligation of a contract; to make an agreement or contract null and inoperative. As a noun, the word means the act or instrument by which the binding force of a contract is terminated, irrespective of whether the contract is carried out to the full extent contemplated (in which case the discharge is the result of *performance*) or is broken off before complete execution.

Criminal law. The act by which a person in confinement, held on an accusation of some crime or misdemeanor, is set at liberty.

Equity practice. In the process of accounting before a master in chancery, the *discharge* is a statement of expenses and counter-claims brought in and filed, by way of set-off, by the accounting defendant; which follows the *charge* in order.

Jury. To discharge a jury is to relieve them from any further consideration of a cause. This is done when the continuance of the trial is, by any cause, rendered impossible; also when the jury, after deliberation, has rendered a verdict or cannot agree on a verdict.

Military discharge. The release or dismissal of a soldier, sailor, or marine, from further military service, either at the expiration of his term of enlistment, or previous thereto on special application therefor, or as a punishment. An "honorable" discharge is one granted at the end of an enlistment and accompanied by an official certificate of good conduct during the service. A "dishonorable" discharge is a dismissal from the service for bad conduct or as a punishment imposed by sentence of a court-martial for offenses against the military law. There is also in occasional use a form of "discharge without honor," which implies censure, but is not in itself a punishment.

Mortgage. Formal document which recites that a mortgage debt has been satisfied and which is generally recorded in Registry of Deeds or in other appropriate place for recording deeds to real estate.

Dischargeable claim. In bankruptcy, a claim which is barred by bankrupt's discharge if properly scheduled.

Disciplinary proceedings. Proceedings which are brought against attorney to secure his censure, suspension or disbarment.

Discipline. Instruction, comprehending the communication of knowledge and training to observe and act in accordance with rules and orders.

Correction, chastisement, punishment, penalty. Rules and regulations.

Disclaimer. The repudiation or renunciation of a claim or power vested in a person or which he had formerly alleged to be his. The refusal, or rejection of an estate or right offered to a person. The disavowal, denial, or renunciation of an interest, right, or property imputed to a person or alleged to be his. Also the declaration, or the instrument, by which such disclaimer is published.

The rejection, refusal, or renunciation of a claim, power, or property. I.R.C. § 2518 sets forth the conditions required to avoid gift tax consequences as the result of a disclaimer.

See also **Refusal; Renunciation; Repudiation.**

Estates. The act by which a party refuses to accept an estate which has been conveyed to him.

Patents. When the title and specifications of a patent do not agree, or when part of that which it covers is not strictly patentable, because neither new nor useful, the patentee is empowered, with leave of the court, to enter a disclaimer of any part of either the title or the specification, and the disclaimer is then deemed to be part of the letters patent or specification, so as to render them valid for the future.

Pleading. In common law pleading, a renunciation by the defendant of all claim to the subject of the demand made by the plaintiff's bill.

Warranty. Words or conduct which tend to negate or limit warranty in sale of goods and which in certain instances must be conspicuous and refer to specific warranty to be excluded. U.C.C. § 2–316.

Disclose. To bring into view by uncovering; to expose; to make known; to lay bare; to reveal to knowledge; to free from secrecy or ignorance, or make known. See **Discovery.**

Disclosure. Act of disclosing. Revelation; the impartation of that which is secret or not fully understood.

In patent law, the specification; the statement of the subject-matter of the invention, or the manner in which it operates.

Under Truth in Lending Act is a term of art which refers to the manner in which certain information (*e.g. total* cost of loan), deemed basic to an intelligent assessment of a credit transaction, shall be conveyed to the consumer. Doggett v. Ritter Finance Co. of Louisa, D.C.Va., 384 F.Supp. 150, 153.

See **Compulsory disclosure; Discovery; Freedom of Information Act; Full disclosure; Subpoena.**

Disclosure by parties. Term sometimes used in law of deceit or fraud as to the obligation of parties to reveal fact which is material if its revelation is necessary because of the position of the parties to each other. See also **Material fact.**

Discommon /dìskómən/. To deprive commonable lands of their commonable quality, by inclosing and appropriating or improving them.

Discontinuance /dìskəntínyuwən(t)s/. Ending, causing to cease, ceasing to use, giving up, leaving off. Refers to the termination or abandonment of a project, structure, highway, or the like.

The cessation of the proceedings in an action where the plaintiff voluntarily puts an end to it, either by giving notice in writing to the defendant before any step has been taken in the action subsequent to the answer, or at any other time by order of the court of a judge. A non-suit; dismissal. Under Rules practice, "dismissal" is appropriate term for discontinuance; may be voluntary or involuntary and may effect counterclaim, cross claim or third party claim. Costs may be assessed. Fed.R. Civil P. 41.

In common law pleading, that technical interruption of the proceedings in an action which follows where a defendant does not answer the whole of the plaintiff's declaration, and the plaintiff omits to take judgment for the part unanswered.

Discontinuance of an estate. The termination or suspension of an estate-tail, in consequence of the act of the tenant in tail, in conveying a larger estate in the land than he was by law entitled to do. 2 Bl.Comm. 275; 3 Bl.Comm. 171. An alienation made or suffered by tenant in tail, or by any that, is seised in *autre droit,* whereby the issue in tail, or the heir or successor, or those in reversion or remainder, are driven to their action, and cannot enter. The cesser of a seisin under an estate, and the acquisition of a seisin under a new and necessarily a wrongful title.

Disconvenable /dìskənvíynəbəl/. L. Fr. Improper; unfit.

Discount. In a general sense, an allowance or deduction made from a gross sum on any account whatever. In a more limited and technical sense, the taking of interest in advance.

Discount means a deduction from an original price or debt, allowed for paying promptly or in cash. Benner Tea Co. v. Iowa State Tax Commission, 252 Iowa 843, 109 N.W.2d 39, 40.

A discount by a bank means a drawback or deduction made upon its advances or loans of money, upon negotiable paper or other evidences of debt payable at a future day, which are transferred to the bank. Although the discounting of notes or bills, in its most comprehensive sense, may mean lending money and taking notes in payment, yet, in its more ordinary sense, the discounting of such means advancing a consideration for a bill or note, deducting or discounting the interest which will accrue for the time the note has to run. Discounting by a bank means lending money upon a note, and deducting the interest or premium in advance. That step in lending transaction where interest on loan is taken in advance by deducting amount therefor for term of loan, giving borrower face value of obligation less interest. Russell v. Lumbermen's Mortg. Co., Com.Pl., 27 Ohio Misc. 171, 273 N.E.2d 803, 804.

See also **Rebate; Rediscount; Rediscount rate.**

Quantity discount. Allowed manufacturers or wholesalers for purchases in large amounts. Robinson Patman Act requires that such be justified by savings of seller.

Trade discount. Price reduction to different classes of customers; *e.g.* discount given by lumber dealers to builders and contractors.

Discount bond. A bond sold for less than face or maturity value. No interest is paid annually, but all interest accrues to the maturity date when it is paid.

Discount broker. A bill broker; one who discounts bills of exchange and promissory notes, and advances money on securities.

Discount market. Segment of the money market in which banks and other financial institutions trade commercial paper.

Discount rate. Percentage of the face amount of commercial paper which a holder pays when he transfers such paper to a financial institution for cash or credit. Rate charged for discounting loan. See **Discount; Rediscount rate.**

The discount rate is the rate charged Federal Reserve System member banks for borrowing from the country's district Federal Reserve banks. The rate, which is set by the Federal Reserve Board, controls the supply of money available to banks for lending.

Discount shares. Shares of stock issued as fully paid and nonassessable for less than the full lawful consideration. Such shares might be treated as void, voidable, assessable or subject to creditor claims.

Discount stock. See **Discount shares.**

Discover. To uncover that which was hidden, concealed, or unknown from every one. To get first sight or knowledge of; to get knowledge of what has existed but has not theretofore been known to the discoverer. Shellmar Products Co. v. Allen-Qualley Co., C.C.A.Ill., 87 F.2d 104, 108. Under U.C.C., refers to knowledge rather than reason to know. U.C.C. § 1–201(25). See also **Discovery; Notice.**

Discovered peril doctrine. The doctrine of discovered peril is regarded as a limitation of, or an exception to, the general rule of contributory negligence precluding a plaintiff's recovery. It is founded on considerations of public policy, deduced from humanitarian principles, which impose a moral duty upon everyone to avoid injuring another unnecessarily. The three essential elements which comprise the doctrine of discovered peril are: (1) the exposed condition brought about by the negligence of the plaintiff, (2) the actual discovery by defendant or his agents of plaintiff's perilous situation in time to have averted the injury by use of all means at their command commensurate with their own safety, and (3) failure thereafter to use such means. The party raising the issue of discovered peril must also prove that the opposing party's negligent conduct was a proximate cause of the injuries he sustained. Welch v. Ada Oil Co., Tex.Civ. App., 302 S.W.2d 175, 179.

Discovert /dìskávərt/. Not married; not subject to the disabilities of a coverture. It applies equally to a maid and a widow.

Discovery. In a general sense, the ascertainment of that which was previously unknown; the disclosure or coming to light of what was previously hidden; the acquisition of notice or knowledge of given acts or facts; as, in regard to the "discovery" of fraud affecting the running of the statute of limitations, or the granting of a new trial for newly "discovered" evidence.

International law. As the foundation for a claim of national ownership or sovereignty, discovery is the finding of a country, continent, or island previously unknown, or previously known only to its uncivilized inhabitants.

Mining claim. See **Mining location.**

Patent law. The finding out some substance, mechanical device, improvement, or application, not previously known. It is something less than invention, and may be the result of industry, application, or be perhaps merely fortuitous. A. O. Smith Corporation v. Petroleum Iron Works Co. of Ohio, C.C.A.Ohio, 73 F.2d 531, 538.

Trial practice. The pre-trial devices that can be used by one party to obtain facts and information about the case from the other party in order to assist the party's preparation for trial. Under Federal Rules of Civil Procedure (and in states which have adopted rules patterned on such), tools of discovery include: depositions upon oral and written questions, written interrogatories, production of documents or things, permission to enter upon land or other property, physical and mental examinations and requests for admission. Rules 26–37. Term generally refers to disclosure by defendant of facts, deeds, documents or other things which are in his exclusive knowledge or possession and which are necessary to party seeking discovery as a part of a cause of action pending, or to be brought in another court, or as evidence of his rights or title in such proceeding. Hardenbergh v. Both, 247 Iowa 153, 73 N.W.2d 103, 106.

Discovery and inspection in federal *criminal* cases is governed by Fed.R.Crim.P. 16.

See also Deposition; Fishing trip or expedition; Good cause; Inspection; Interrogatories; Jencks Act or Rule; Perpetuating testimony; Work product rule.

Discovery, bill of. In equity pleading, a bill for the discovery of facts resting in the knowledge of the defendant, or of deeds or writings, or other things in his custody or power; but seeking no relief in consequence of the discovery, though it may pray for a stay of proceedings at law until the discovery is made.

Discovery rule. The "discovery rule" is, generally, that cause of action for medical malpractice will not be held to accrue until patient knows, or, in exercise of reasonable diligence, should have known of the alleged malpractice. Owens v. White, C.A.Idaho, 380 F.2d 310, 313.

Discovery vein. See **Vein.**

Discredit. To destroy or impair the credibility of a person; to impeach; to lessen the degree of credit to be accorded to a witness or document, as by impugning the veracity of the one or the genuineness of the other; to disparage or weaken the reliance upon the testimony of a witness, or upon documentary evidence, by any means whatever. See **Impeachment.**

Discreetly. Prudently; judiciously; with discernment.

Discrepancy. A difference between two things which ought to be identical, as between one writing and another; a variance *(q.v.).* Also discord, discordance, dissonance, dissidence, unconformity, disagreement, difference.

Discretely. Separately; disjunctively.

Discretio est discernere per legem quid sit justum /diskrésh(iy)ow èst dəsárnəriy pàr líyjəm kwíd sit jástəm/. Discretion is to know through law what is just.

Discretio est scire per legem quid sit justum /diskrésh(iy)ow èst sáyriy pàr líyjəm kwíd sit jástəm/. Discretion consists in knowing what is just in law.

Discretion. When applied to public functionaries, discretion means a power or right conferred upon them by law of acting officially in certain circumstances, according to the dictates of their own judgment and conscience, uncontrolled by the judgment or conscience of others. As applied to public officers means power to act in an official capacity in a manner which appears to be just and proper under the circumstances. Application of Blackburn, 206 Misc. 393, 134 N.Y.S.2d 138, 142, 144.

In criminal law and the law of torts, it means the capacity to distinguish between what is right and wrong, lawful or unlawful, wise or foolish, sufficiently to render one amenable and responsible for his acts.

Wise conduct and management; cautious discernment, especially as to matters of propriety and self-control; prudence; circumspection; wariness.

See **Discretionary acts.**

Judicial and legal discretion. These terms are applied to the discretionary action of a judge or court, and mean discretion bounded by the rules and principles of law, and not arbitrary, capricious, or unrestrained. It is not the indulgence of a judicial whim, but the exercise of judicial judgment, based on facts and guided by law, or the equitable decision of what is just and proper under the circumstances. It is a legal discretion to be exercised in discerning the course prescribed by law and is not to give effect to the will of the judge, but to that of the law. The exercise of discretion where there are two alternative provisions of law applicable, under either of which court could proceed. A liberty or privilege to decide and act in accordance with what is fair and equitable under the peculiar circumstances of the particular case, guided by the spirit and principles of the law. Manekas v. Allied Discount Co., 6 Misc.2d 1079, 166 N.Y.S.2d 366, 369.

Discretionary account. An account in which customer gives broker discretion, as to purchase and sales of securities or commodities, including selection, timing, and price to be paid or received. Stevens v. Abbott, Proctor and Paine, D.C.Va., 288 F.Supp. 836, 839.

Discretionary acts. Those acts wherein there is no hard and fast rule as to course of conduct that one must or must not take and, if there is clearly defined rule, such would eliminate discretion. Elder v. Anderson, 205 Cal.App.2d 326, 23 Cal.Rptr. 48, 51. Option open to judges and administrators to act or not as they deem proper or necessary and such acts or refusal to act may not be overturned without a showing of abuse of discretion, which means an act or failure to act that no conscientious person acting reasonably could perform or refuse to perform. One which requires exercise in judgment and choice and involves what is just and proper under the circumstances. Burgdorf v. Funder, 246 Cal.App.2d 443, 54 Cal.Rptr. 805.

Discretionary damages. Those which are measureable by enlightened conscience of impartial jurors.

Discretionary power. One which is not imperative or, if imperative, the time, manner, or extent of execution of which is left to donee's discretion. The power to do or to refrain from doing a certain thing. City of San Antonio v. Zogheib, Tex.Civ.App., 70 S.W.2d 333, 334.

Discretionary review. Form of appellate review which is not a matter of right but rather of discretion; *e.g.* appeal to U.S. Supreme Court. See **Certiorari.**

Discretionary trusts. Such as are not marked out on fixed lines, but allow a certain amount of discretion in their exercise. Those which cannot be duly administered without the application of a certain degree of prudence and judgment. Trusts where the trustee or another party has the right to accumulate (rather than pay out) the income for each year. Depending on the terms of the trust instrument, such income may be accumulated for future distributions to the income beneficiaries or added to corpus for the benefit of the remainderman.

Discrimination. In constitutional law, the effect of a statute or established practice which confers particular privileges on a class arbitrarily selected from a large number of persons, all of whom stand in the same relation to the privileges granted and between whom and those not favored no reasonable distinction can be found. Unfair treatment or denial of normal privileges to persons because of their race, age, nationality or religion. A failure to treat all persons equally where no reasonable distinction can be found between those favored and those not favored. Baker v. California Land Title Co., D.C.Cal., 349 F.Supp. 235, 238, 239.

Federal statutes prohibit discrimination in employment on basis of sex, age, race, nationality or religion; *e.g.* Title VII of 1964 Civil Rights Act, Age Discrimination in Employment Act, Equal Pay Act, Sex Discrimination in Employment Based on Pregnancy Act. Other federal acts, as supplemented by court decisions, prohibit discrimination in voting rights, housing, extension of credit, public education, and access to public facilities.

With reference to common carriers, a breach of the carrier's duty to treat all shippers alike, and afford them equal opportunities to market their product. A carrier's failure to treat all alike under substantially similar conditions.

See also Bias; Equal protection clause; Equal protection of the law; Price discrimination; Redlining; Reverse discrimination.

Discussion. In the civil law, a proceeding, at the instance of a surety, by which the creditor is obliged to exhaust the property of the principal debtor, towards the satisfaction of the debt, before having recourse to the surety; and this right of the surety is termed the "benefit of discussion."

Disease. Deviation from the healthy or normal condition of any of the functions or tissues of the body. An alteration in the state of the body or of some of its organs, interrupting or disturbing the performance of the vital functions, and causing or threatening pain and weakness. Illness; sickness; disorder; malady; bodily infirmity. An illness or an abnormal state having a definite pattern of symptoms. See also **Industrial disease; Occupational disease.**

Disentailing deed /dìsəntéyliŋ díyd/. In English law, an enrolled assurance barring an entail, pursuant to 3 & 4 Wm. IV, c. 74.

Disentailing statutes. Statutes dealing with or prohibiting the barring of the entail in a fee tail conveyance.

Disentailment. Act of barring the entail created by fee tail conveyance and consisting of a deed absolute in fee simple by the tenant in tail. In this case the grantee took the fee simple and the entail or right of the first born of the tenant in tail took nothing on the death of the tenant in tail.

Disfigurement. That which impairs or injures the beauty, symmetry, or appearance of a person or thing; that which renders unsightly, misshapen, or imperfect, or deforms in some manner. See **Maim.**

Disfranchise. To deprive of the rights and privileges of a free citizen; to deprive of chartered rights and immunities; to deprive of any franchise, as of the right of voting in elections, etc. In any election where the party system furnishes the means by which the citizen's right of suffrage is made effective, denial of his party's right to participate in the election accomplishes the "disfranchisement of voters" or compels them, if they vote, to vote for representatives of political parties other than that to which they belong, and the deprivation of the right of selection is a deprivation of the right of franchise. Communist Party of United States of America v. Peek, 20 Cal.2d 536, 127 P.2d 889, 894.

Disfranchisement. The act of disfranchising. The act of depriving a member of a corporation of his right as such, by expulsion. It differs from amotion *(q.v.)* which is applicable to the removal of an officer from office, leaving him his rights as a member.

In a more popular sense, the taking away of the elective franchise (that is, the right of voting in public elections) from any citizen or class of citizens.

Disgavel /dìsgǽvəl/. In English law, to deprive lands of that principal quality of gavelkind tenure by which they descend equally among all the sons of the tenant.

Disgrace. Ignominy; shame; dishonor.

Disgrading. In old English law, the depriving of an order or dignity.

Disguise, *v.* /dəskáyz/. To change the guise or appearance of, especially to conceal by unusual dress; to hide by a counterfeit appearance. To obscure the existence or true state or character of a person or thing.

Disguise, *n.* A counterfeit habit; a dress intended to conceal the person who wears it. Anything worn upon the person with the intention of so altering the wearer's appearance that he shall not be recognized by those familiar with him, or that he shall be taken for another person.

Disherison /dìshé(h)razən/. Disinheritance; depriving one of an inheritance. Obsolete term.

Disheritor /dìshéhrədər/. One who disinherits, or puts another out of his freehold. Obsolete term.

Dishonesty. Disposition to lie, cheat or defraud; untrustworthiness; lack of integrity.

Dishonor. To refuse to accept or pay a draft or to pay a promissory note when duly presented. An instrument is dishonored when a necessary or optional presentment is duly made and due acceptance or payment is refused, or cannot be obtained within the prescribed time, or in case of bank collections, the instrument is seasonably returned by the midnight deadline; or presentment is excused and the instrument is not duly accepted or paid. U.C.C. § 3–507(1); § 4–210. See also **Notice of dishonor; Protest.**

As respects the flag, to deface or defile, imputing a lively sense of shaming or an equivalent acquiescent callousness. State v. Schlueter, 127 N.J.L. 496, 23 A.2d 249, 251. See **Deface; Defile.**

Disincarcerate /dìsiŋkársərèyt/. To set at liberty, to free from prison.

Disinfected. Made free from injurious or contagious diseases. Immunization.

Disinherison /dìsinhé(h)rəzən/. In the civil law, the act of depriving a forced heir of the inheritance which the law gives him. Disinherison is a testamentary disposition and not a mere penalty for lack of filial respect, but such a testamentary disposition is not self-operative and something more than its mere appearance in a will is required to give it effect.

Disinheritance /dìsinhéhrədən(t)s/. The act by which the owner of an estate deprives a person, who would otherwise be his heir, of the right to inherit it.

Disinter /dìsintár/. To exhume, unbury, take out of the grave.

Disinterested. Not concerned, in respect to possible gain or loss, in the result of the pending proceedings or transactions; impartial, not biased or prejudiced.

Disinterested witness. One who has no interest in the cause or matter in issue, and who is lawfully competent to testify.

Disintermediation. When free market interest rates exceed the regulated interest ceiling for time deposits, some depositors withdraw their funds and invest them elsewhere at a higher interest rate. This process is known as "disintermediation."

Disjunctim /dəsjáŋktəm/. Lat. In the civil law, separately; severally. The opposite of *conjunctim (q.v.).*

Disjunctive allegation. A statement in a pleading or indictment which expresses or charges a thing alternatively, with the conjunction "or"; for instance, an averment that defendant "murdered or caused to be murdered", etc., would be of this character.

Disjunctive term. One which is placed between two contraries, by the affirming of one of which the other is taken away; it is usually expressed by the word "or".

Dislocation. To put out of proper place.

Disloyal. Not true to; unfaithful.

Dismes /dáymz/. Tenths; tithes *(q.v.).* The original form of "dime," the name of the American coin.

Dismiss. To send away; to discharge; to discontinue; to dispose of; to cause to be removed temporarily or permanently; to relieve from duty. To dismiss an action or suit without any further consideration or hearing.

Dismissal. An order or judgment finally disposing of an action, suit, motion, etc., without trial of the issues involved. Such may be either voluntary or involuntary. Fed.R. Civil P. 41.

A release or discharge from employment.

Involuntary dismissal. Under rules practice, may be accomplished on court's own motion for lack of prosecution or on motion of defendant for lack of prosecution or failure to introduce evidence of facts on which relief may be granted. Fed.R. Civil P. 41(b).

Voluntary dismissal. Under rules practice, may be accomplished by plaintiff without leave of court if filed before answer or by stipulation signed by all parties after answer is filed. Fed.R. Civil P. 41(a).

Dismissal and nonsuit. Termination of case because of plaintiff's failure to prosecute or plaintiff's desire to discontinue.

Dismissal compensation. The payment of a specific sum, made by employer to employee for permanently terminating employment. Also called severance or separation pay.

Dismissal for cause. See **For cause.**

Dismissal without prejudice. Dismissal without prejudice to the right of the complainant to sue again on the same cause of action. The effect of the words "without prejudice" is to prevent the decree of dismissal from operating as a bar to a subsequent suit.

Dismissal with prejudice. An adjudication on the merits, and final disposition, barring the right to bring or maintain an action on the same claim or cause. It is res judicata as to every matter litigated.

Dismissed for want of equity. A phrase used to indicate a decision on the merits, as distinguished from one based upon some formal defect. The dismissal may be because the averments of complainant's bill have been found untrue in fact, or because they are insufficient to entitle complainant to the relief sought. Reinman v. Little Rock, 237 U.S. 171, 35 S.Ct. 511, 513, 59 L.Ed. 900.

Dismortgage /dìsmórgəj/. To redeem from mortgage. See **Redemption.**

Disobedience. See **Civil disobedience; Civil disorder.**

Disobedient child. Child who may be adjudicated delinquent in some jurisdictions under law governing stubborn children. May be subject of petition as child in need of social services. Child who wilfully refuses to honor requests of parents or legal guardian or other person in whose custody he is. See also **Delinquent child.**

Disorder. Turbulent or riotous behavior; immoral or indecent conduct. The breach of the public decorum and morality. See also Breach of the peace; Civil disobedience; Civil disorder; Riot; Unlawful assembly.

A slight, partial, and temporary physical ailment. Pacific Mut. Life Ins. Co. v. McCombs, 188 Ark. 52, 64 S.W.2d 333.

Disorderly. Contrary to the rules of good order and behavior; violative of the public peace or good order; turbulent, riotous, or indecent.

Disorderly conduct. A term of loose and indefinite meaning (except when defined by statutes), but signifying generally any behavior that is contrary to law, and more particularly such as tends to disturb the public peace or decorum, scandalize the community, or shock the public sense of morality. An offense against public morals, peace or safety. State v. Cherry, 185 Neb. 103, 173 N.W.2d 887, 888.

A person is guilty of disorderly conduct if, with purpose to cause public inconvenience, annoyance or alarm, or recklessly creating a risk thereof, he: (a) engages in fighting or threatening, or in violent or tumultuous behavior; or (b) makes unreasonable noise or offensively coarse utterance, gesture or display, or addresses abusive language to any person present; or (c) creates a hazardous or physically offensive condition by any act which serves no legitimate purpose of the actor. Model Penal Code, § 250.2.

See also **Breach of the peace.**

Disorderly house. House or place where residents or inhabitants behave in such a manner as to become a nuisance to the neighborhood. One where acts are performed which tend to corrupt morals of community or promote breaches of peace. Payne v. U. S., D.C.Mun.App., 171 A.2d 509, 511. It has a wide meaning, and includes bawdy houses, gambling houses, houses of prostitution and places of a like character. At common law, it was misdemeanor to keep such house. Burgess v. Johnson, 223 Ga. 427, 156 S.E.2d 78. Under current laws, such activity, generally, would constitute a breach of the peace or disorderly conduct. The *specific* acts (*e.g.* prostitution) might also be crimes.

Disorderly persons. Such as are dangerous or hurtful to the public peace and welfare by reason of their misconduct or vicious habits, and are therefore amenable to police regulation. The phrase is chiefly used in statutes, and the scope of the term depends on local regulations. One who violates peace and good order of society.

Disorderly picketing. See **Unlawful picketing.**

Disorientation. Inability to identify time, place or surroundings.

Disparagare /dìspæragériy/. In old English law, to bring together those that are unequal (*dispares conferre*); to connect in an indecorous and unworthy manner; to connect in marriage those that are unequal in blood and parentage.

Disparagatio /dìspæragéysh(iy)ow/. In old English law, disparagement. *Hæredes maritentur absque disparagatione,* heirs shall be married without disparagement.

Disparagation /dìspæragéyshan/. L. Fr. Disparagement; the matching an heir, etc., in marriage, under

his or her degree or condition, or against the rules of decency.

Disparage /dəspǽrəj/. To connect unequally; to match unsuitably. To discredit one's person or property.

Disparagement /dəspǽrəjmənt/. In old English law, an injury by union or comparison with some person or thing of inferior rank or excellence. To discredit by marriage below one's class. Marriage without *disparagement* was marriage to one of suitable rank and character.

Matter which is intended by its publisher to be understood or which is reasonably understood to cast doubt upon the existence or extent of another's property in land, chattels or intangible things, or upon their quality.

Disparagement of goods. A statement about a competitor's goods which is untrue or misleading and is made to influence or tends to influence the public not to buy. Aerosonic Corp. v. Trodyne Corp., 402 F.2d 223, 231.

Disparagement of title. Actionably tortious detraction from title for which person may be required to respond in damages. Injurious falsehood in which aspersion is cast on person's title to property. Publication made without privilege or justification of matter that is untrue and disparaging to another's property in land, chattels or intangible things under such circumstances as would lead reasonable man to foresee that conduct of third person as purchaser or lessee thereof might be determined thereby and results in pecuniary loss from impairment of vendability thus caused. Hill v. Allan, 259 Cal.App.2d 470, 66 Cal. Rptr. 676, 689.

Disparaging instructions. Jury charge which tends to detract or defame person or party to litigation.

Disparity. Marked difference in quantity or quality between two things or among many things.

Dispatch. A sending off, completion or settlement with speed.

In maritime law, diligence, due activity, or proper speed in the discharge of a cargo; the opposite of delay. *Customary dispatch* is such as accords with the rules, customs, and usages of the port where the discharge is made. *Dispatch money* is in the nature of a reward to charterer of ship for loading or unloading in shorter time than provided for or than stipulated as "lay days", The West Nosska, D.C.N.Y., 2 F.Supp. 547. *Quick dispatch* is speedy discharge of cargo without allowance for the customs or rules of the port or for delay from the crowded state of the harbor or wharf.

Dispauper /dìspópər/. When a person, by reason of his poverty, is admitted to sue *in formâ pauperis,* and afterwards, before the suit be ended, acquires any lands, or personal estate, or is guilty of anything whereby he is liable to have this privilege taken from him, then he loses the right to sue *in formâ pauperis,* and is said to be dispaupered.

Dispel. To drive away by scattering, to clear away, to banish, to dissipate.

Dispensary. Place where a drug is prepared or distributed.

Dispensatio est mali prohibiti provida relaxatio, utilitate seu necessitate pensata; et est de jure domino regi concessa, propter impossibilitatem prævidendi de omnibus particularibus /dìspenséysh(iy)ow èst mǽlay prəhíbəday prəváydə rèlækséysh(iy)ow, yuwtìlətéydiy s(y)ùw nəsèsətéydiy pen(t)séydə, èd ést dìy júriy dómənow ríyjay kən(t)sésəs, próptər impòsəbìlətéydəm prìyvədénday dìy ómnəbəs partìkyəlérəbəs/. A dispensation is the provident relaxation of a *malum prohibitum* weighed from utility or necessity; and it is conceded by law to the king on account of the impossibility of foreknowledge concerning all particulars.

Dispensatio est vulnus, quod vulnerat jus commune /dìspenséysh(iy)ow èst válnəs kwòd válnəræt jás kəmyúwniy/. A dispensation is a wound, which wounds common law.

Dispensation. An exemption from some laws; a permission to do something forbidden; an allowance to omit something commanded; the canonistic name for a license. A relaxation of law for the benefit or advantage of an individual. In the United States, no power exists, except in the legislature, to dispense with law; and then it is not so much a dispensation as a change of the law. See also **Exemption.**

Dispense. Etymologically, "dispense" means to weigh out, pay out, distribute, regulate, manage, control, etc., but when used with "with," it has, among other meanings, that of "doing without," and "doing away with," being synonymous with "abolish."

Dispersonare /dispèrsənériy/. To scandalize or disparage.

Displace. To crowd out; to take the place of. Ford v. Department of Water and Power of City of Los Angeles, 4 Cal.App.2d 526, 41 P.2d 188, 189.

Displaced person. Person left homeless in his own country because of war.

Displacement. Shifting of emotional emphasis from one object to another as a means of disguising or avoiding unacceptable ideas or tendencies.

Display. An opening or unfolding, exhibition, manifestation, ostentatious show, exhibition for effect, parade. 20th Century Lites v. Goodman, 64 Cal.App.2d Supp. 938, 149 P.2d 88, 91.

As applied to printing, means a varying arrangement of lines, as by the use of unequal lengths or different styles or sizes of type faces; also matter thus printed. Display advertising means advertising not under specific headings in newspapers, magazines and trade papers. Rust v. Missouri Dental Board, 348 Mo. 616, 155 S.W.2d 80, 85.

Dispono /dìspównow/. Lat. To dispose of, grant, or convey. *Disponet,* he grants or alienates. *Jus disponendi,* the right of disposition, *i.e.,* of transferring the title to property.

Disposable earnings. That portion of person's income which he is free to spend or invest as he sees fit after payment of taxes and other obligations.

Disposable portion. That portion of a man's property which he is free to dispose of by will to beneficiaries other than his wife and children. By the ancient common law, this amounted to one-third of his estate if he was survived by both wife and children. 2 Bl.Comm. 492. In the civil law (by the *Lex Falcidia*) it amounted to three-fourths.

Disposal. Sale, pledge, giving away, use, consumption or any other disposition of a thing. To exercise control over; to direct or assign for a use; to pass over into the control of someone else; to alienate, bestow, or part with.

Dispose of. To alienate or direct the ownership of property, as disposition by will. Used also of the determination of suits. To exercise finally, in any manner, one's power of control over; to pass into the control of someone else; to alienate, relinquish, part with, or get rid of; to put out of the way; to finish with; to bargain away. Often used in restricted sense of "sale" only, or so restricted by context.

Disposing capacity or **mind.** These are alternative or synonymous phrases in the law of wills for "sound mind," and "testamentary capacity" (*q.v.*).

Disposition. Act of disposing; transferring to the care or possession of another. The parting with, alienation of, or giving up property.

In criminal procedure, the sentencing or other final settlement of a criminal case.

With respect to a mental state, means an attitude, prevailing tendency, or inclination.

Disposition hearing. Judicial proceeding in which a criminal defendant is sentenced or otherwise disposed of.

Disposition without trial. The sentencing or other treatment of a criminal defendant who has pleaded guilty or admitted to sufficient facts for finding of guilty without a trial on the merits.

Dispositive facts. Jural facts, or those acts or events that create, modify or extinguish jural relations.

Dispossess. To oust from land by legal process; to eject, to exclude from realty.

Dispossession. Ouster; a wrong that carries with it the amotion of possession. An act whereby the wrongdoer gets the actual occupation of the land or hereditament. It includes abatement, intrusion, disseisin, discontinuance, deforcement.

Dispossess proceedings. Summary process by a landlord to oust the tenant and regain possession of the premises for nonpayment of rent or other breach of the conditions of the lease. See also **Ejectment; Eviction; Forcible entry and detainer; Process** (*Summary process*).

Disprove. To refute; to prove to be false or erroneous; not necessarily by mere denial, but by affirmative evidence to the contrary.

Dispunishable. In old English law, not answerable. Not punishable; *e.g.* "This murder is dispunishable."

Disputable presumption. A species of evidence that may be accepted and acted upon when there is no other evidence to uphold contention for which it stands; and when evidence is introduced supporting such contention, evidence takes place of presumption, and there is no necessity for indulging in any presumption. A rule of law to be laid down by the court, which shifts to the party against whom it operates the burden of evidence merely. City of Montpelier v. Town of Calais, 114 Vt. 5, 39 A.2d 350, 356. See **Presumption.**

Disputatio fori /dìspyuwtéysh(iy)ow fóray/. In the civil law, discussion or argument before a court.

Dispute. A conflict or controversy; a conflict of claims or rights; an assertion of a right, claim, or demand on one side, met by contrary claims or allegations on the other. The subject of litigation; the matter for which a suit is brought and upon which issue is joined, and in relation to which jurors are called and witnesses examined. See **Cause of action; Claim; Controversy; Justiciable controversey; Labor dispute.**

Disqualify. To divest or deprive of qualifications; to incapacitate; to render ineligible or unfit, as, in speaking of the "disqualification" of a judge by reason of his interest in the case, of a juror by reason of his holding a fixed preconceived opinion, or of a candidate for public office by reason of non-residence, lack of statutory age, previous commission of crime, etc.

Disrate /dìsréyt/. In maritime law, to deprive a seaman or petty officer of his "rating" or rank; to reduce to a lower rate or rank.

Disrationare, or **dirationare** /dì(s)rèyshənériy/. To justify; to clear one's self of a fault; to traverse an indictment; to disprove.

Disregard. To treat as unworthy of regard or notice; to take no notice of; to leave out of consideration; to ignore; to overlook; to fail to observe.

Disrepair. The state of being in need of repair or restoration after decay or injury.

Disrepute. Loss or want of reputation; ill character; disesteem; discredit.

Disruptive conduct. Disorderly or contemptuous conduct generally within the framework of a judicial or quasi judicial proceeding. See **Contempt.**

Dissection /dəsékshən/. The act of cutting into pieces an animal or vegetable for the purpose of ascertaining the structure and use of its parts. The anatomical examination of a dead body by cutting into pieces or exscinding one or more parts or organs. The process of separating tissues along their natural lines of separation from each other; the act of separating into constituent parts for the purpose of critical examination.

Disseise /dəsíyz/. To dispossess; to deprive.

Disseisee /dəsìyzíy/. One who is wrongfully put out of possession of his lands; one who is disseised.

Disseisin /dəsíyzən/. Dispossession; a deprivation of possession; a privation of seisin; a usurpation of the right of seisin and possession, and an exercise of such powers and privileges of ownership as to keep out or displace him to whom these rightfully belong. It is a wrongful putting out of him that is seised of the freehold, not, as in *abatement* or *intrusion,* a wrong-

ful entry, where the possession was vacant, but an attack upon him who is in actual possession, and turning him out. It is an ouster from a freehold in deed, as abatement and intrusion are ousters in law.

When one man invades the possession of another, and by force or surprise turns him out of the occupation of his lands, this is termed a "disseisin," being a deprivation of that actual seisin or corporal possession of the freehold which the tenant before enjoyed. In other words, a disseisin is said to be when one enters intending to usurp the possession, and to oust another from the freehold. To constitute an entry a disseisin, there must be an ouster of the freehold, either by taking the profits or by claiming the inheritance.

Equitable disseisin is where a person is wrongfully deprived of the equitable seisin of land, *e.g.,* of the rents and profits.

Disseisin by election is where a person alleges or admits himself to be disseised when he has not really been so.

Disseisinam satis facit, qui uti non permittit possessorem, vel minus commode, licet omnino non expellat /dəsíyzənəm sǽdəs féysət kwày yúwday nòn pərmídət pòwzesórəm, vèl máynəs kómədiy, láysəd omnáynow nòn əkspélət/. He makes disseisin enough who does not permit the possessor to enjoy, or makes his enjoyment less beneficial, although he does not expel him altogether.

Disseisitrix /dəsíyzətrəks/. A female disseisor; a disseisoress.

Disseisitus /dəsíyzədəs/. One who has been disseised.

Disseisor /dəsíyzər/. One who puts another out of the possession of his lands wrongfully. A settled trespasser on the land of another. Flinn v. Blakeman, 254 Ky. 416, 71 S.W.2d 961, 968.

Disseisoress /dəsíyzərəs/. A woman who unlawfully puts another out of his land.

Dissemble /dəsémbəl/. To conceal by assuming some false appearance.

Dissensus /dəsén(t)səs/. Lat. In the civil law, the mutual agreement of the parties to a simple contract obligation that it shall be dissolved or annulled; technically, an undoing of the *consensus* which created the obligation.

Dissent /dəsént/. Contrariety of opinion; refusal to agree with something already stated or adjudged or to an act previously performed.

The term is most commonly used to denote the explicit disagreement of one or more judges of a court with the decision passed by the majority upon a case before them. In such event, the non-concurring judge is reported as "dissenting." A dissent may or may not be accompanied by an opinion.

Ecclesiastical law. A refusal to conform to the rites and ceremonies of the established church.

Dissenter. One who dissents.

Dissentiente /dəsènshiyéntiy/dəsèntiyéntiy/. (Lat. dissenting.) Used with the name or names of one or more judges, it indicates a dissenting opinion in a case. *Nemine dissentiente* /némənay/. No one dissenting; unanimous.

Dissignare /dìsəgnériy/. In old law, to break open a seal.

Dissimulatione tollitur injuria. /dəsìmyəlèyshiyówniy tólədə injúriyə/. An injury is extinguished by the forgiveness or reconcilement of the party injured.

Dissipate. To destroy or waste, as to expend funds foolishly. Also, to break up a crowd. See also **Drain.**

Dissolute. Loosed from restraint, unashamed, lawless, loose in morals and conduct, recklessly abandoned to sensual pleasures, profligate, wanton, lewd, debauched.

Dissolution. Act or process of dissolving; termination; winding up.

Contracts. The dissolution of a contract is the cancellation or abrogation of it by the parties themselves, with the effect of annulling the binding force of the agreement, and restoring each party to his original rights. In this sense it is frequently used in the phrase "dissolution of a partnership." See *Partnership, infra,* this topic.

Corporation. The dissolution of a corporation is the termination of its existence as a body politic. This may take place in several ways; as by act of the legislature, where that is constitutional; by surrender or forfeiture of its charter; by expiration of its charter by lapse of time; by proceedings for winding it up under the law; by loss of all its members or the reduction below the statutory limit; by bankruptcy. Bruun v. Katz Drug Co., 351 Mo. 731, 173 S.W.2d 906, 909. See also **Articles of dissolution; Liquidation.**

Marriage. The act of terminating a marriage; divorce; but the term does not include annulment. Deihl v. Jones, 170 Tenn. 217, 94 S.W.2d 47, 48. See **Divorce.**

Partnership. The dissolution of a partnership is the relation of the partners caused by any partner ceasing to be associated in the carrying on as distinguished from the winding up of the business. Uniform Partnership Act, § 29.

Dissolution of parliament. The crown may dissolve parliament either in person or by proclamation; the dissolution is usually by proclamation, after a prorogation.

Dissolve. To terminate; abrogate; cancel; annul; disintegrate. To release or unloose the binding force of anything. As to "dissolve a corporation," see **Dissolution.**

Dissolving bond. A bond given to obtain the dissolution of a legal writ or process, particularly an attachment or an injunction, and conditioned to indemnify the opposite party or to abide the judgment to be given.

Dissuade. In criminal law, to advise and procure a person not to do an act.

To dissuade a witness from giving evidence against a person indicted is an indictable offense at common law.

Distance. A straight line along a horizontal plane from point to point and is measured from the nearest point of one place to the nearest point of another.

Distill. To subject to a process of distillation, *i.e.,* vaporizing the more volatile parts of a substance and then condensing the vapor so formed. In law, the term is chiefly used in connection with the manufacture of intoxicating liquors.

Distilled liquor or **distilled spirits.** A term which includes all potable alcoholic liquors obtained by the process of distillation (such as whisky, brandy, rum, and gin).

Distiller. One who produces distilled spirits (*i.e.* alcoholic liquors) or who brews or makes mash, wort, or wash, fit for distillation or for the production of spirits, or who, by any process of evaporization, separates alcoholic spirit from any fermented substance.

Distillery. A place or building where alcoholic liquors are distilled or manufactured.

Distinct. Clear to the senses or mind; easily perceived or understood; plain; unmistakable. Evidently not identical; observably or decidedly different.

Distinguished by nature or station; not the same; different in the place or the like; separate; individual; that which is capable of being distinguished; actually divided or apart from other things. Gavin v. Webb, Tex.Civ.App., 99 S.W.2d 372, 379.

Distincte et aperte /dəstíŋktiy èd əpárdiy/. In old English practice, distinctly and openly. Formal words in writs of error, referring to the return required to be made to them.

Distinctively. Characteristically, or peculiarly, but not necessarily exclusively.

Distinguish. To point out an essential difference; to prove a case cited as applicable, inapplicable.

Distinguishing mark. A birth mark, scar, or other like feature which distinguishes a person. A mark on a ballot which takes away its secrecy. Any deliberate marking of ballot by voter that is not made in attempt to indicate his choice of candidates and which is also effective as mark by which his ballot may be distinguished.

Distort. To twist out of natural or regular shape; to twist aside physically; to force or put out of true posture; to wrest, or deform.

Distracted person. A term used in the statutes of certain states to express a state of insanity.

Distractio /dəstrǽksh(iy)ow/. Lat. In the civil law, a separation or division into parts; also an alienation or sale. Sometimes applied to the act of a guardian in appropriating the property of his ward.

Distractio bonorum /dəstrǽksh(iy)ow bənórəm/. The sale at retail of the property of an insolvent estate, under the management of a curator appointed in the interest of the creditors, and for the purpose of realizing as much as possible for the satisfaction of their claim.

Distraction rule. If plaintiff's attention is diverted from known danger by a sufficient cause, under this rule the question of contributory negligence is for jury.

Distractio pignoris /dəstrǽksh(iy)ow pəgnórəs/. The sale of a thing pledged or hypothecated, by the creditor or pledgee, to obtain satisfaction of his claim on the debtor's failure to pay or redeem.

Distrahere /dəstréy(h)əriy/. To sell; to draw apart; to dissolve a contract; to divorce.

Distrain. To take as a pledge property of another, and keep it until he performs his obligation or until the property is replevied by the sheriff. Remedy used to secure an appearance in court, payment of rent, performance of services, etc. Also, any detention of personal property, whether lawful or unlawful, for any purpose. See **Distraint; Distress.**

Distrainer or **distrainor.** He who seizes property under a distress.

Distraint. Seizure; the act of distraining or making a distress. The inchoate right and interest which a landlord has in the property of a tenant located on the demised premises. Upon a tenant's default, a landlord may in some jurisdictions distrain upon the tenant's property, generally by changing the locks and giving notice, and the landlord will then have a lien upon the goods. The priority of the lien will depend on local law. See **Distress.**

Distress. A common-law right of landlord, now regulated by statute, to seize a tenant's goods and chattels in a nonjudicial proceeding to satisfy an arrears of rent. Van Ness Industries, Inc. v. Claremont Painting & Decorating Co., 129 N.J.Super. 507, 324 A.2d 102, 104.

The taking of goods and chattels out of the possession of a wrong-doer into the custody of the party injured to procure a satisfaction for a wrong committed; as for non-payment of rent. The taking of personal property by way of pledge, to enforce the performance of something due from the party distrained upon. Hall v. Marshall, 145 Or. 221, 27 P.2d 193. The taking of a defendant's goods, in order to compel an appearance in court.

Certain state statutes, insofar as they authorize distress for rents by landlords, have been held to be unconstitutional. See *e.g.* Van Ness Industries v. Claremont Painting, 129 N.J.Super. 507, 324 A.2d 102.

The seizure of personal property to enforce payment of taxes, to be followed by its public sale if the taxes are not voluntarily paid; also the thing taken by distraining, *i.e.* that which is seized to procure satisfaction.

See **Landlord's warrant.**

Distress infinite. At common law, one that had no bounds with regard to its quantity, and could be repeated from time to time, until the stubbornness of the party was conquered. Such were distresses for realty or suit of court, and for compelling jurors to attend. 3 Bl.Comm. 231.

Distress warrant. A writ authorizing an officer to make a distraint; particularly, a writ authorizing the levy of a distress on the chattels of a tenant for non-payment of rent.

A power of attorney by which landlord delegates exercise of his right to his duly authorized agent. In re Koizim, D.C.N.J., 52 F.Supp. 357, 358.

Grand distress, writ of. A writ formerly issued in England in the real action of *quare impedit,* when no appearance had been entered after the attachment; it commanded the sheriff to distrain the defendant's lands and chattels in order to compel appearance. It is no longer used, 23 & 24 Vict., c. 126, § 26, having abolished the action of *quare impedit,* and substituted for it the procedure in an ordinary action.

Second distress. A supplementary distress for rent in arrear, allowed by law in some cases, where the goods seized under the first distress are not of sufficient value to satisfy the claim.

Distress and danger. The "distress" and "danger" to which a ship needs to be exposed to entitle its rescuer to salvage need not be actual or immediate, or the danger imminent and absolute. It is sufficient if at the time the assistance is rendered, the ship has encountered any damage or misfortune which might possibly expose her to destruction if the services were not rendered, or if a vessel is in a situation of actual apprehension though not of actual danger.

Distressed goods. Goods sold at a distressed sale.

Distressed property. Property that must be sold because of mortgage foreclosure or on probate of insolvent estate.

Distressed sale. Form of liquidation sale (*e.g.* "going out of business" sale) in which the seller receives less for his goods than he would under normal selling conditions.

Distributable net income (DNI). The measure that limits the amount of the distributions from estates and trusts that the beneficiaries thereof will have to include in income. Also, DNI limits the amount that estates and trusts can claim as a deduction for such distributions. I.R.C. § 643(a).

Distribute. To deal or divide out in proportion or in shares. See **Distribution.**

Distributee /dəstrìbyuwtíy/. An heir; a person entitled to share in the distribution of an estate. This term is used to denote one of the persons who is entitled, under the statute of distributions, to the personal estate of one who is dead intestate. See also **Beneficiary.**

Distribution. The giving out or division among a number, sharing or parceling out, allotting, dispensing, apportioning.

Probate. The apportionment and division, under authority of a court, of the remainder of the estate of an intestate, after payment of the debts and charges, among those who are legally entitled to share in the same. See **Distributive share.**

Securities offering. A public offering of securities of an issuer, whether by an underwriter, statutory underwriter or by the issuer itself. Such offering may be *controlled, i.e.* an offering to the public of securities by selling stockholders or an issuer through a broker-dealer acting as an underwriter for such persons pursuant to a formal underwriting arrangement;

or *uncontrolled, i.e.* an offering to the public of securities by selling stockholders on a random basis through any number of brokers who are willing to assist such persons; or an offering to the public by such persons without the use of a broker.

Statutes of distribution. State laws prescribing the manner of the distribution of the estate of an intestate among his heirs or relatives.

Distribution in kind. A transfer of property "as is." If, for example, a corporation distributes land to its shareholders, a distribution in kind has taken place. A sale of land followed by a distribution of the cash proceeds would not be a distribution in kind of the land. See also **Like-kind exchange.**

Distribution in liquidation. Distribution of assets upon dissolution of corporation. Liquidating dividend is amount distributed in complete or partial liquidation of corporation and such amount is treated as in full payment for the stock of the corporation. I.R.C. § 331(a).

Distributive. That which exercises or accomplishes distribution; that which apportions, divides, and assigns in separate items or shares.

Distributive clause. That provision in trust which governs distribution of income and ultimate distributions or gifts over.

Distributive deviation. Distribution of principal to income beneficiaries for whom income is inadequate, without the consent of the remaindermen who are entitled to receive the entire principal at a later time under the terms of the trust.

Distributive finding of the issue. The jury are bound to give their verdict for that party who, upon the evidence, appears to them to have succeeded in establishing his side of the issue. But there are cases in which an issue may be found distributively, *i.e.*, in part for plaintiff, and in part for defendant. Thus, in an action for goods sold and work done, if the defendant pleaded that he never was indebted, on which issue was joined, a verdict might be found for the plaintiff as to the goods, and for the defendant as to the work. See also **Comparative negligence.**

Distributive justice. See **Justice.**

Distributive share. The share or portion which a given heir receives on the legal distribution of an intestate estate; or from a dissolved partnership. Helvering v. Enright's Estate, 312 U.S. 636, 61 S.Ct. 777, 781, 85 L.Ed. 1093. Sometimes, by an extension of meaning, the share or portion assigned to a given person on the distribution of any estate or fund, as, under an assignment for creditors or under insolvency proceedings.

Distributor. Any individual, partnership, corporation, association, or other legal relationship which stands between the manufacturer and the retail seller in purchases, consignments, or contracts for sale of consumer goods. A wholesaler.

District. One of the territorial areas into which an entire state or country, county, municipality or other political subdivision is divided, for judicial, political, electoral, or administrative purposes. State ex rel. Schur v. Payne, 57 Nev. 286, 63 P.2d 921, 925.

The circuit or territory within which a person may be compelled to appear. Circuit of authority; province.

As to Fire; Judicial; Land; Levee; Metropolitan; Mineral; Mining; Road; School; and Tax (*Taxing district*), districts, see those titles.

Congressional district. Geographical district of state which may send (vote) a representative to U.S. Congress.

District attorney. The prosecuting officer of the United States government in each of the federal judicial districts. Also, under the state governments, the prosecuting officer who represents the state in each of its judicial districts. In some states, where the territory is divided, for judicial purposes, into sections called by some other name than "districts," the same officer is denominated "prosecuting attorney", "county attorney" or "state's attorney." See also **United States Attorney.**

District clerk. The clerk of a district court of either a state or the United States.

District courts. Each state is comprised of one or more federal judicial districts, and in each district there is a district court. 28 U.S.C.A. § 81 *et seq.* The United States district courts are the trial courts with general Federal jurisdiction. Each State has at least one district court, though many have several judicial districts (*e.g.* northern, southern, middle districts) or divisions. There is also a United States district court in the District of Columbia. In addition, the Commonwealth of Puerto Rico has a United States district court with jurisdiction corresponding to that of district courts in the various States. Only one judge is usually required to hear and decide a case in a district court, but in some kinds of cases it is required that three judges be called together to comprise the court (28 U.S.C.A. §§ 2281, 2284). In districts with more than one judge, the judge senior in commission who has not reached his seventieth birthday acts as the chief judge.

Also, name for inferior state courts of record having general jurisdiction.

District judge. The judge of a United States district court; also, in some states, the judge of a district court of the state.

District parishes. Ecclesiastical divisions of parishes in England, for all purposes of worship, and for the celebration of marriages, christenings, churchings, and burials, formed at the instance of the queen's commissioners for building new churches.

Legislative district. Geographical district which may send (vote) a representative to the state legislature.

Districting. Term refers to defining lines of electoral districts. Moolenaar v. Todman, D.C.Virgin Islands, 317 F.Supp. 226, 231. See **Reapportionment.**

Districtio /distríksh(iy)ow/. Lat. A distress; a distraint.

District of Columbia. A territory situated on the Potomac river, and being the seat of government of the United States. It was originally ten miles square, and was composed of portions of Maryland and Virginia ceded by those states to the United States; but in

1846 the tract coming from Virginia was retroceded. Legally it is neither a state nor a territory, but is made subject, by the Constitution, to the exclusive jurisdiction of Congress.

Distringas /dəstríŋgəs/. In English practice, a writ formerly directed to the sheriff of the county in which a defendant resided or had any goods or chattels, commanding him to *distrain* upon the goods and chattels of the defendant for forty shillings, in order to compel his appearance. This writ issued in cases where it was found impracticable to get at the defendant personally, so as to serve a summons upon him.

A *distringas* was also used in equity, as the first process to compel the appearance of a corporation aggregate.

A form of execution in the actions of detinue and assise of nuisance.

Distringas juratores /dəstríŋgəs jùrətóriyz/. In old English law, a writ commanding the sheriff to have the bodies of the jurors, or to *distrain* them by their lands and goods, that they may appear upon the day appointed. It issued at the same time with the *venire,* though in theory afterwards, founded on the supposed neglect of the juror to attend.

Distringas nuper vice comitem /dəstríŋgəs n(y)úwpər váysiy kómədəm/. In old English law, a writ to distrain the goods of one who lately filled the office of sheriff, to compel him to do some act which he ought to have done before leaving the office; as to bring in the body of a defendant, or to sell goods attached under a fi. fa.

Distringas vice comitem /dəstríŋgəs váysiy kómədəm/. In old English law, a writ of *distringas,* directed to the coroner, issued against a sheriff if he neglected to execute a writ of *venditioni exponas.*

Distringere /dìstrínjəriy/. In feudal and old English law, to distrain; to coerce or compel.

Disturb. To throw into disorder; to move from a state of rest or regular order; to interrupt a settled state of; to throw out of course or order.

Disturbance. Any act causing annoyance, disquiet, agitation, or derangement to another, or interrupting his peace, or interfering with him in the pursuit of a lawful and appropriate occupation or contrary to the usages of a sort of meeting and class of persons assembled that interferes with its due progress or irritates the assembly in whole or in part. See **Disturbance of peace; Riot.**

At common law, a wrong done to an incorporeal hereditament by hindering or disquieting the owner in the enjoyment of it. Blackstone enumerated five types of such disturbances: Disturbances of franchises, common, tenure, ways, and patronage. 3 Bl. Comm. 235.

Disturbance of common. At common law, the doing any act by which the right of another to his common is incommoded or diminished; as where one who has no right of common puts his cattle into the land, or where one who has a right of common puts in cattle which are not commonable, or surcharges the common; or where the owner of the land, or other person, incloses or otherwise obstructs it.

Disturbance of franchise. The disturbing or incommoding a man in the lawful exercise of his franchise, whereby the profits arising from it are diminished. 3 Bl.Comm. 236.

Disturbance of patronage. The hindrance or obstruction of a patron from presenting his clerk to a benefice. 3 Bl.Comm. 242.

Disturbance of peace. Interruption of the peace, quiet, and good order of a neighborhood or community, particularly by unnecessary and distracting noises. Conduct which tends to annoy all good citizens and which does in fact annoy anyone present not favoring it. Com. v. Orlando, Mass., 359 N.E.2d 810. In some jurisdictions (*e.g.* Calif.) term includes an affray. See also **Breach of the peace; Disorderly conduct; Riot.**

Disturbance of public meetings. It was a misdemeanor at common law to be guilty of conduct which tended to disturb a public assembly, though the prosecution, in most instances, was required to prove that the disturbance was caused wantonly or wilfully. In most jurisdictions there is statutory crime for such conduct and the disturbance need not be so turbulent as to constitute a riot.

Disturbance of public or **religious worship.** Any acts or conduct which interfere with the peace and good order of an assembly of persons lawfully met together for religious exercises.

Disturbance of tenure. In the law of tenure, disturbance was where a stranger, by menaces, force, persuasion, or otherwise, caused a tenant to leave his tenancy; or this disturbance of tenure was an injury to the lord for which an action could lie.

Disturbance of ways. This happened where a person who had a right of way over another's ground by grant or prescription was obstructed by inclosures or other obstacles, or by plowing across it by which means he could not enjoy his right of way, or at least in so commodious a manner as he might have done. 3 Bl.Comm. 241.

Ditching, diking, or **tiling.** Every kind of work necessary to convert parts of arid lands, particularly sagebrush lands, into farms and orchards,—the word "diking" as applied to arid regions implying a leveling of the land, and the term "clearing land" as applied to arid regions covered with sagebrush meaning not only the removal or the destruction of the brush but the plowing or breaking up of the roots as well.

Divers /dáyvərs/. Various, several, sundry; a collective term grouping a number of unspecified persons, objects, or acts.

Diversion. A turning aside or altering the natural course or route of a thing. The term is chiefly applied to the unauthorized change or alteration of a water course to the prejudice of a lower riparian, or to the unauthorized use of funds.

Diversion program. A disposition of a criminal defendant either before or after adjudication of guilt in which the court directs the defendant to participate in a work or educational program as part of a probation.

Diversité des courts /divèrsətéy dèy kúr(t)s/. A treatise on courts and their jurisdiction, written in French in the reign of Edward III as is supposed, and by some attributed to Fitzherbert. It was first printed in 1525, and again in 1534.

Diversity /dəvársədiy/. In criminal pleading at common law, a plea by the prisoner in bar of execution, alleging that he was not the same who was attainted, upon which a jury was immediately impaneled to try the collateral issue thus raised, viz., the identity of the person, and not whether he was guilty or innocent, for that had been already decided. 4 Bl.Comm. 396.

Diversity jurisdiction. See **Diversity of citizenship.**

Diversity of citizenship. A phrase used with reference to the jurisdiction of the federal courts, which, under U.S.Const. Art. III, § 2, extends to cases between citizens of different states, designating the condition existing when the party on one side of a lawsuit is a citizen of one state, and the party on the other side is a citizen of another state, or between a citizen of a state and an alien. The requisite jurisdictional amount must, in addition, be met. 28 U.S.C.A. § 1332. See **Outcome test.**

Divert /dəvárt/. To turn aside; to turn out of the way; to alter the course of things. Usually applied to water-courses or to the unauthorized use of funds. See **Diversion.**

Dives /dáyviyz/. In the practice of the English chancery division, "dives costs" are costs on the ordinary scale, as opposed to the costs formerly allowed to a successful pauper suing or defending *in formâ pauperis,* which consisted only of his costs out of pocket.

Divest. Equivalent to devest *(q.v.).*

Divestitive fact /dəvéstədəv fǽkt/. Any act or event that extinguishes or modifies a jural relation.

Divestiture /dəvéstəchər/. In anti-trust law, the order of court to a defendant *(e.g.* corporation) to divest itself of property, securities or other assets. U. S. v. E. I. duPont de Nemours and Co., 366 U.S. 316, 81 S.Ct. 1243, 6 L.Ed.2d 318.

Divestment. In property law, the cutting short of an interest prior to its normal termination. Restatement of Property, § 16(b).

Divide. To cut into parts, disunite, separate, keep apart. The term is synonymous with distribute.

Divide and pay over rule. Substance of such rule is that when the only words of gift are found in direction to divide or pay at a future time, use of such words imports a condition of survival, but if postponement of payment is for purpose of letting in an intermediate estate, then interest shall be deemed vested at death of testator and class of legatee is to be determined as of that date for futurity is not annexed to substance of the gift. In re Bogart's Will, 62 Misc.2d 114, 308 N.Y.S.2d 594, 602.

Divided court. Appellate court whose opinion or decision is not unanimous in a particular case. See also **Division of opinion.**

Dividend. The payment designated by the board of directors of a corporation to be distributed pro rata among the shares outstanding. On preferred shares, it is generally a fixed amount. On common shares, the dividend varies with the fortunes of the company and the amount of cash on hand, and may be omitted if business is poor or the directors determine to withhold earnings to invest in plant and equipment. Sometimes a company will pay a dividend out of past earnings even if it is not currently operating at a profit. See also **Allocation of dividends.**

Accumulated dividend. A cumulative dividend which has not been paid when due.

Asset dividend. Dividend paid in the form of an asset of the company; normally a product. See *Property dividend, infra.*

Bond dividend. Type of dividend distribution which is rare but one in which the shareholder receives bonds instead of scrip, property or money.

Cash dividend. See that title.

Consent dividend. For purposes of avoiding or reducing the penalty tax on the unreasonable accumulation of earnings or the personal holding company tax, a corporation may declare a consent dividend. In a consent dividend no cash or property is distributed to the shareholders although the corporation obtains a dividends paid deduction. The consent dividend is taxed to the shareholders and increases the basis in their stock investment.

Constructive dividend. A taxable benefit derived by a shareholder from his or her corporation although such benefit was not designated as a dividend. Examples include unreasonable compensation, excessive rent payments, bargain purchases of corporate property, and shareholder use of corporate property. The pass-through of undistributed taxable income (*i.e.,* UTI) to the shareholders of a Subchapter S corporation sometimes is referred to as a constructive dividend. Constructive dividends generally are a problem limited to closely-held corporations.

Cumulative dividend. A dividend that if not paid annually (or periodically as provided in the stock certificate) will ultimately have to be paid before any common stock dividend can be paid. The arrearage is said to accumulate.

Deferred dividend. One declared, but due to be paid at some future date.

Deficiency dividend. Once the IRS has established a corporation's liability for the personal holding company tax in a prior year, the tax may be reduced or avoided by the issuance of a deficiency dividend under I.R.C. § 547. The deficiency dividend procedure is not available in cases where the deficiency was due to fraud with intent to evade tax or to a willful failure to file the appropriate tax return [§ 547(g)]. Nor does the deficiency dividend procedure avoid the usual penalties and interest applicable for failure to file a return or pay a tax.

Dividend addition. Something added to the policy in the form of paid-up insurance, and does not mean unapportioned assets or surplus. The term does not refer to dividends added directly to the loan value. Anderson v. Liberty Life Ins. Co. of Topeka, 149 Kan. 447, 87 P.2d 499, 502.

Ex-dividend. Term used by stock brokers, meaning that a sale of corporate stock does not carry with it the seller's right to receive his proportionate share of a dividend already declared and shortly payable. See **Ex-dividend.**

Extra dividend. One paid in addition to regular dividends; normally because of exceptional profits of corporation during dividend period.

Extraordinary dividend. See that title.

Liquidation dividend. See that title.

Nimble dividend. Dividend paid out of net profits when the corporate capital is impaired. Model Bus. Corp.Act, § 40(a).

Noncumulative dividends. See that title.

Passed dividend. Dividend not paid when due by company which has history of paying regular dividends.

Preferred dividend. One paid on the preferred stock of a corporation. A dividend paid to one class of shareholders in priority to that paid to another.

Property dividend. Consists of a portion of corporate property paid to shareholders instead of cash or corporate stock. See *Asset dividend, supra.*

Scrip dividend. One paid in scrip, or in certificates of the ownership of a corresponding amount of capital stock of the company thereafter to be issued. Dividend paid in a short term promissory note which, in effect, divides profits but enables the corporation to postpone actual distribution of cash. Billingham v. E. P. Gleason Mfg. Co., 101 A.D. 476, 91 N.Y.S. 1046.

Stock dividend. One paid in stock, that is, not in money, but in a proportional number of shares of the capital stock of the company, which is ordinarily increased for this purpose to a corresponding extent. A stock dividend is not in the ordinary sense a dividend, which is a cash distribution to stockholders of profits on their investments, but rather it is an increase in the number of shares declared out of profits, the increased number representing exactly the same property as was represented by the smaller number of shares.

Year-end dividend. Type of extra dividend paid at end of fiscal year with amount dependent on profits. See also *Extra dividend, supra.*

Dividenda /dìvədéndə/. An indenture; one counterpart of an indenture.

Dividend income. Species of gross income derived from dividend distribution and subject to tax. I.R.C. §§ 61(a)(7), 301(c).

Dividends received deduction. A deduction allowed a corporate shareholder for dividends received from a domestic corporation. The deduction usually is 85 percent of the dividends received but could be 100 percent if an affiliated group is involved. I.R.C. §§ 243–246.

Dividend yield. The current annual dividend divided by the market price per share.

Divinare /dìvənériy/. Lat. To divine; to conjecture or guess; to foretell. *Divinatio,* a conjecturing or guessing.

Divine laws. Those ascribed to God. See **Natural law.**

Divine right of kings. The right of a king to rule as posited by the patriarchal theory of government, especially under the doctrine that no misconduct and no dispossession can forfeit the right of a monarch or his heirs to the throne, and to the obedience of the people. This theory was in its origin directed, not against popular liberty, but against papal and ecclesiastical claims to supremacy in temporal as well as spiritual affairs.

Divine service. Divine service was the name of a feudal tenure, by which the tenants were obliged to do some special divine services in certain; as to sing so many masses, to distribute such a sum in alms, and the like. It differed from tenure in *frankalmoign,* in this: that, in case of the tenure by divine service, the lord of whom the lands were holden might distrain for its nonperformance, whereas, in case of *frankal moign,* the lord has no remedy by distraint for neglect of the service, but merely a right of complaint to the visitor to correct it.

Divisa /dəváyzə/. In old English law, a device, award, or decree; also a devise; also bounds or limits of division of a parish or farm, etc. Also a court held on the boundary, in order to settle disputes of the tenants.

Divisible. That which is susceptible of being divided.

Divisible contract. One which is in its nature and purposes susceptible of division and apportionment, having two or more parts in respect to matters and things contemplated and embraced by it, not necessarily dependent on each other nor intended by the parties so to be.

Divisible divorce. Decree of divorce may be divided as between provisions for support and alimony and provisions dissolving the marriage. Doctrine applied in cases under full faith and credit clause in connection with effect of foreign divorce on support provisions. Rymanowski v. Rymanowski, 105 R.I. 89, 249 A.2d 407.

Divisible obligation. See **Obligation.**

Divisible offense. One that includes one or more offenses of lower grade, *e.g.,* murder includes assault, battery, assault with intent to kill, and other offenses.

Divisim /dəváyzəm/. In old English law, severally; separately.

Division. Act of distributing among a number. Portion of territorial area marked off for a particular purpose. Operating or administrative unit of government, court, business, or school system. Condition of being divided in opinion. Major military unit. Separation of members of a legislative body to take a vote. See also **Range.**

Division, action for. Action to compel obligee to divide his claim against debtors and collect as if each debtor were liable only for his portion. Central Bank v. Winn Farmers Co-op., La.App., 299 So.2d 442, 445.

Divisional courts. Courts in England, consisting of two or (in special cases) more judges sitting to transact certain kinds of business which cannot be disposed of by one judge. There exist divisional courts of the Queen's Bench Division, Chancery Division, and Family Division.

Divisional securities. Special type of securities issued to finance particular projects.

Division of opinion. In the practice of appellate courts, this term denotes such a disagreement among the judges that there is not a majority in favor of any one view, and hence no decision can be rendered on the case. But it also commonly denotes a division into two classes, one of which may comprise a majority of the judges; as when we speak of a decision having proceeded from a "divided court." See also **Divided court.**

Division of powers. See **Separation of powers.**

Divisum imperium /dəváyzəm ìmpíriyəm/. Lat. A divided jurisdiction. Applied, *e.g.*, to the jurisdiction of courts of common law and equity over the same subject.

Divorce. The legal separation of man and wife, effected by the judgment or decree of a court, and either totally dissolving the marriage relation, or suspending its effects so far as concerns the cohabitation of the parties.

See also Alimony; Equitable distribution; Ex parte divorce; Legislative divorce; Living separate and apart; Mail order divorce; Mexican divorce; Migratory divorce; Rabbinical divorce.

Divorce a mensa et thoro /dəvórs èy ménsə èt θórow/. A divorce from table and bed, or from bed and board. A partial or qualified divorce, by which the parties are separated and forbidden to live or cohabit together, without affecting the marriage itself.

Divorce a vinculo matrimonii /dəvórs èy víŋkyəlow mætrəmówniyay/. A divorce from the bond of marriage. A total divorce of husband and wife, dissolving the marriage tie, and releasing the parties wholly from their matrimonial obligations.

Divorce by consent. Type of no-fault divorce in which parties are not required to prove fault or grounds for divorce beyond a showing of irretrievable breakdown of marriage or irreconcilable differences. The majority of states have no-fault divorce in one form or another.

Divorce from bed and board. See *Divorce a mensa et thoro, supra.*

Foreign divorce. A divorce obtained out of the state or country where the marriage was solemnized.

Limited divorce. A divorce from bed and board; or a judicial separation of husband and wife not dissolving the marriage tie. See also **Separation of spouses.**

No-fault divorce. See *Divorce by consent, supra.*

Parliamentary divorce. A divorce decreed by the British Parliament or by a legislative act in contrast to a divorce granted by a court. See **Lady's friend.**

Divorce proctors. Person, generally an attorney, appointed to protect children or the interests of the state in a divorce action. Uniform Marriage and Divorce Act, § 310.

Divortium dicitur a divertendo, quia vir divertitur ab uxore /dəvórsh(iy)əm dísədər èy dàyvərténdow, kwáyə vár dəvárdədər æb əksóriy/. Divorce is called from *divertendo,* because a man is diverted from his wife.

Divulge /dəvəlj/. To disclose or make known, as to divulge secret or classified information.

Dixième /dìyz(i)yém/. Fr. Tenth; the tenth part. An income tax payable to the crown.

D. J. An abbreviation for "District Judge."

Do /dów/. Lat. I give. The ancient and aptest word of feoffment and of gift.

Dock, v. To curtail or diminish, as to dock a person's wages for, *e.g.* lateness or poor work.

Dock, n. The cage or inclosed space in a criminal court where prisoners stand when brought in for trial.

Dockage. A charge against vessels for the privilege of mooring to the wharves or in the slips. A pecuniary compensation for the use of a dock while a vessel is undergoing repairs. See also **Demurrage; Moorage.**

Docket, v. To abstract and enter in a book. To make a brief entry of any proceeding in a court of justice in the docket.

Docket, n. A minute, abstract, or brief entry; or the book containing such entries. A formal record, entered in brief, of the proceedings in a court of justice. A book containing an entry in brief of all the important acts done in court in the conduct of each case, from its inception to its conclusion. The name of "docket" or "trial docket" is sometimes given to the list or calendar of causes set to be tried at a specified term, prepared by the clerks for the use of the court and bar.

General Classification

An *appearance* docket is one in which the appearances in actions are entered, containing also a brief abstract of the successive steps in each action. A *bar* docket is an unofficial paper consisting of a transcript of the docket for a term of court, printed for distribution to members of the bar. An *execution* docket is a list of the executions sued out or pending in the sheriff's office. A *judgment* docket is a list or docket of the judgments entered in a given court, methodically kept by the clerk or other proper officer, open to public inspection, and intended to afford official notice to interested parties of the existence or lien of judgments. See also **Judgment docket; Preferred dockets.**

Civil docket. Fed.R. Civil P. 79(a), and analogous state rules, requires that the clerk keep a "civil docket" of all actions pending before the court. Actions shall be assigned consecutive file numbers. The file number of each action shall be noted on the folio of the docket whereon the first entry of the actions is made. All papers filed with the clerk, all process issued and returns made thereon, all appearances, orders, verdicts, and judgments shall be entered chronologically in the civil docket on the folio assigned to the action and shall be marked with its file number. The entry of an order or judgment shall show the date the entry is made. When in an action trial by jury has been properly demanded or ordered the clerk shall enter the word "jury" on the folio assigned to that action.

Docket fee. An attorney's fee, of a fixed sum, chargeable with or as a part of the costs of the action, for the attorney of the successful party; so called because chargeable on the docket, not as a fee for making docket entries.

Dock-master. In England, an officer invested with powers within the docks, and a certain distance therefrom, to direct the mooring and removing of ships, so as to prevent obstruction to the dock entrances.

Dock warrant. In English law, a warrant given by dock-owners to the owner of merchandise imported and warehoused on the dock, upon the faith of the bills of lading, as a recognition of his title to the goods. It is a negotiable instrument, and, like a bill of lading, it passes by indorsement and delivery, and transfers the absolute right to the goods described in it. See also **Document** (*Document of title*); **Warehouse receipt.**

Doctor, *v.* To prescribe or treat medically or to treat as a doctor or physician.

Doctor, *n.* A learned man; one qualified to give instruction of the higher order in a science or art, particularly, one who has received the highest academical degree in his art or faculty, as, a doctor of laws, medicine, or theology. In colloquial language, however, the term is practically restricted to practitioners of medicine; *i.e.* physicians, surgeons.

Doctor-patient privilege. In law of evidence, right of patient to exclude from evidence communications made by him to his physician; not recognized in all jurisdictions and limited in others; *e.g.* to communications to psychotherapist.

Doctrinal interpretation. See **Interpretation.**

Doctrine. A rule, principle, theory, or tenet of the law; as, the doctrine of merger, the doctrine of relation, etc.

Document. An instrument on which is recorded, by means of letters, figures, or marks, the original, official, or legal form of something, which may be evidentially used. In this sense the term "document" applies to writings; to words printed, lithographed, or photographed; to maps or plans; to seals, plates, or even stones on which inscriptions are cut or engraved. In the plural, the deeds, agreements, title-papers, letters, receipts, and other written instruments used to prove a fact. As used as a verb, to support with documentary evidence or authorities.

Within meaning of the best evidence rule, document is any physical embodiment of information or ideas; *e.g.* a letter, a contract, a receipt, a book of account, a blueprint, or an X-ray plate. Strico v. Cotto, 67 Misc.2d 636, 324 N.Y.S.2d 483, 486.

See also **Instrument.**

Ancient documents. Deeds, wills, and other writings more than thirty years (twenty years under Fed. Evid.R. 803(16)) old are so called; they are presumed to be genuine without express proof, when coming from the proper custody.

Commercial law. Under U.C.C., any paper including document of title, security, invoice, certificate, notice of default and the like. U.C.C. § 5–103.

Conflicts of law. (1) Whether a right is embodied in a document is determined by the law which governs the right. (2) As between persons who are not both parties to the conveyance, (a) the effect of a conveyance of a right embodied in a document depends upon the effect of the conveyance of the document; and (b) the effect of a conveyance of an interest in a document in which a right is embodied is determined by the law that would be applied by the courts of the state where the document was at the time of the conveyance. These courts would usually apply their own local law in determining such questions. Restatement, Second, Conflicts, § 249.

Document of title. Includes bill of lading, dock warrant, dock receipt, warehouse receipt or order for the delivery of goods, and also any other document which in the regular course of business or financing is treated as adequately evidencing that the person in possession of it is entitled to receive, hold and dispose of the document and the goods it covers. To be a document of title a document must purport to be issued by or addressed to a bailee and purport to cover goods in the bailee's possesion which are either identified or are fungible portions of an identified mass. U.C.C. § 1–201(15). See also **Negotiable document of title.**

Foreign document. One which was prepared or executed in, or which comes from, a foreign state or country.

Judicial documents. Proceedings relating to litigation. They are divided into (1) judgments, decrees, and verdicts; (2) depositions, examinations, and inquisitions taken in the course of a legal process; (3) writs, warrants, pleadings, etc., which are incident to any judicial proceedings.

Public document. A state paper, or other instrument of public importance or interest, issued or published by authority of congress or a state legislature. Also any document or record, evidencing or connected with the public business or the administration of public affairs, preserved in or issued by any department of the government. One of the publications printed by order of congress or either house thereof. Broadly any document open to public inspection.

Documentary credit. Credit which is extended on documents of title or other legal documents.

Documentary draft. A "documentary draft" or a "documentary demand for payment" is one the honor of which is conditioned upon the presentation of a document or documents. "Document" means any paper including document of title, security, invoice, certificate, notice of default and the like. U.C.C. § 5–103(b).

Documentary draft means any negotiable or non-negotiable draft with accompanying documents, securities or other papers to be delivered against honor of the draft. U.C.C. § 4–104(f).

Check with accompanying documents which are to be delivered when payment is made is "documentary draft." Wiley v. Peoples Bank & Trust Co., C.A. Miss., 438 F.2d 513, 516.

Documentary evidence. Evidence derived from conventional symbols (such as letters) by which ideas are represented on material substances. Such evidence as is furnished by written instruments, inscriptions, documents of all kinds, and also any inanimate objects admissible for the purpose, as distinguished from "oral" evidence, or that delivered by human beings viva voce. People v. Purcell, 22 Cal.App.2d 126, 70 P.2d 706, 709.

Documentary instructions. Term for written agreement between importer and exporter covering disposition of the various documents relating to the shipment, and disposition of the goods.

Documentary originals rule. See **Best evidence.**

Documentary stamp. Stamp required by federal (prior to 1968) and state law to be affixed to deeds and other documents of transfer before they may be recorded, the cost of which is generally governed by the consideration recited in the document. Federal Revenue Stamps were abolished in 1968.

Documentation. See **Authorities.**

DOD. Department of Defense.

Do, dico, addico /dów, díkow, ədíkow/. Lat. I give, I say, I adjudge. Three words used in the Roman law, to express the extent of the civil jurisdiction of the prætor. *Do* denoted that he *gave* or granted actions, exceptions, and judices; *dico,* that he pronounced judgment; *addico,* that he adjudged the controverted property, or the goods of the debtor, etc., to the plaintiff.

DOE. Department of Energy.

Doed-bana /dédbèynə/. In Saxon law, the actual perpetrator of a homicide.

Doe, John. The name of the fictitious plaintiff in certain types of actions; *e.g.* ejectment action. See also **John Doe.**

Dog-draw. In old English forest law, the manifest deprehension of an offender against venison in a forest, when he was found drawing after a deer by the scent of a hound led in his hand; or where a person had wounded a deer or wild beast, by shooting at him, or otherwise, and was caught with a dog drawing after him to receive the same.

Dog-Latin. The Latin of illiterate persons. Latin words put together on the English grammatical system.

Dogma. Definite authoritative opinions or tenets. Formally stated and proclaimed doctrines on faith or morals. In the civil law, a word occasionally used as descriptive of an ordinance of the senate.

DOHSA. Death on High Seas Act.

Doing. The formal word by which *services* were reserved and expressed in old conveyances; as "rendering" (reddendo) was *expressive* of *rent.*

Doing business. Within statutes on service of process on foreign corporations, means equivalent to carrying on, conducting or managing business. A foreign corporation is "doing business", making it amenable to process within state, if it does business therein in such a manner as to warrant the inference that it is present there. Or that it has subjected itself to the jurisdiction and laws in which the service is made. The doing of business is the exercise in the state of some of the ordinary functions for which the corporation was organized. What constitutes "doing business" depends on the facts in each particular case. The general rule is that the business need only have certain "minimum contacts" with the state to make it amenable to process in that state. International Shoe Co. v. State of Washington, 326 U.S. 310, 66 S.Ct. 154, 90 L.Ed. 95. And, such contacts may be as minimal as selling a single insurance contract. McGee v. International Life Insurance Co., 355 U.S. 220, 78 S.Ct. 199, 2 L.Ed.2d 223; Hanson v. Denckla, 357 U.S. 235, 78 S.Ct. 1228, 2 L.Ed.2d 1283. See also **Minimal contacts.**

The determination as to what constitutes "doing business" may differ as to whether the term is being used with reference to amenability to service of process or to taxation, and also may vary in definition from state to state.

Doitkin, or **doit** /dóyt(kən)/. A base coin of small value prohibited by Henry the Fifth. We still retain the phrase, in the common saying, when we would undervalue a man, that he is not worth a doit.

Do, lego. Lat. I give, I bequeath; or I give and bequeath. The formal words of making a bequest or legacy, in the Roman law. The expression is literally retained in modern wills.

Dolg /dólg/. Sax. A wound.

Dolg-bote /dólgbòwt/. A recompense for a scar or wound.

Doli. Lat. See **Dolus.**

Doli capax /dówlay kéypæks/. Capable of malice or criminal intention; having sufficient discretion and intelligence to distinguish between right and wrong, and so to become amenable to the criminal laws.

Doli incapax /dówlay ìnkéypæks/. Incapable of criminal intention or malice; not of the age of discretion; not possessed of sufficient discretion and intelligence to distinguish between right and wrong to the extent of being criminally responsible for his actions.

Dollar. The money unit employed in the United States of the value of one hundred cents, or of any combination of coins totalling 100 cents.

Dollar averaging. Investment term for practice of purchasing a fixed dollar amount of a given security at regular intervals.

Dolo /dówlow/. In Spanish law, bad or mischievous design.

Dolo facit qui petit quod redditurus est /dówlow féysət kwáy pédət kwòd rèdətúrəs èst/. He acts with guile who demands that which he will have to return.

Dolo malo pactumse non servaturum /dówlow mǽlow pæktámsiy nòn sərvət(y)úrəm/. An agreement induced by fraud cannot stand.

Dolosus versatur in generalibus /dəlówsəs vərséydər ìn jènəréyləbəs/. A person intending to deceive deals in general terms.

Dolum ex indiciis perspicuis probari convenit /dówləm èks ìndíshiyəs pərspíkyuwəs prowbéray kənvíynət/. Fraud should be proved by clear tokens.

Dolus /dówləs/. In the civil law, guile; deceitfulness; malicious fraud. A fraudulent address or trick used to deceive some one; a fraud. Any subtle contrivance by words or acts with a design to circumvent.

Such acts or omissions as operate as a deception upon the other party, or violate the just confidence reposed by him, whether there be a deceitful intent *(malus animus)* or not.

Fraud, willfulness, or intentionality. In that use it is opposed to *culpa,* which is negligence merely, in greater or less degree. The policy of the law may sometimes treat extreme *culpa* as if it were *dolus,* upon the maxim *culpa dolo comparatur.* A person is always liable for *dolus* producing damage, but not always for *culpa* producing damage, even though extreme.

Dolus auctoris non nocet successori /dówləs òktórəs nòn nósət səksəsóray/. The fraud of a predecessor prejudices not his successor.

Dolus bonus, dolus malus /dówləs bownəs/dówləs mǽləs/. In a wide sense, the Roman law distinguishes between "good," or rather "permissible" *dolus* and "bad" or fraudulent *dolus.* The former is justifiable or allowable deceit; it is that which a man may employ in self-defense against an unlawful attack, or for another permissible purpose, as when one dissembles the truth to prevent a lunatic from injuring himself or others. The latter exists where one intentionally misleads another or takes advantage of another's error wrongfully, by any form of deception, fraud, or cheating.

Dolus circuitu non purgatur /dówləs sərkyúwəduw nòn pərgéydər/. Fraud is not purged by circuity.

Dolus dans locum contractui /dówləs dǽn(d)z lówkəm kəntrǽkchuwày/. Fraud (or deceit) giving rise to the contract; that is, a fraudulent misrepresentation made by one of the parties to the contract, and relied upon by the other, and which was actually instrumental in inducing the latter to enter into the contract.

Dolus est machinatio, cum aliud dissimulat aliud agit /dówləs èst mǽkənéysh(iy)ow kàm ǽliyəd dəsímyələt ǽliyəd éyjət/. Deceit is an artifice, since it pretends one thing and does another.

Dolus et fraus nemini patrocinentur, (patrocinari derent) /dówləs èt frós némənay pǽtrowsənéntər (°pǽtrowsənéray débənt)/. Deceit and fraud shall excuse or benefit no man.

Dolus latet in generalibus /dówləs léydət in jènəréyləbəs/. Fraud lurks in generalities.

Dolus versatur in generalibus /dówləs vərséydər in jènəréyləbəs/. Fraud deals in generalities.

Domain. The complete and absolute ownership of land; a paramount and individual right of property in land. Also the real estate so owned. The inherent sovereign power claimed by the legislature of a state, of controlling private property for public uses, is termed the "right of eminent domain." See **Condemnation; Eminent domain.**

National domain is sometimes applied to the aggregate of the property owned directly by a nation. Public domain embraces all lands, the title to which is in the United States, including as well land occupied for the purposes of federal buildings, arsenals, dockyards, etc., as land of an agricultural or mineral character not yet granted to private owners.

Sphere of influence. Range of control or rule; realm.

Dombec, domboc /dówmbùk/. (Sax. From *dom,* judgment, and *bec, boc,* a book.) Dome-book or doombook. A name given among the Saxons to a code of laws. Several of the Saxon kings published *dombocs,* but the most important one was that attributed to Alfred. This is sometimes confounded with the celebrated *Domesday-Book.* See **Dome-book; Domesday.**

Dombrowski doctrine. Rule enunciated in Dombrowski v. Pfister, 380 U.S. 479, 85 S.Ct. 1116, 14 L.Ed.2d 22, to the effect that a person is entitled to an injunction in a federal court to prevent state officers from prosecuting or threatening to prosecute him under a state statute which is so broad and vague that it interferes with rights guaranteed by the First Amendment, U.S. Constitution.

Dome. (Sax.) Doom; sentence; judgment. An oath. The homager's oath in the black book of Hereford.

Dome-book. A book or code said to have been compiled under the direction of Alfred, for the general use of the whole kingdom of England; containing, as is supposed, the principal maxims of the common law, the penalties for misdemeanors, and the forms of judicial proceedings. It is said to have been extant so late as the reign of Edward IV, but is now lost. 1 Bl.Comm. 64, 65.

Domesday, domesday-book. (Sax.) An ancient record made in the time of William the Conqueror, and later remaining in the English exchequer, consisting of two volumes of unequal size, containing minute and accurate surveys of the lands in England. 2 Bl.Comm. 49, 50. The work was begun by five justices in each county in 1081, and finished in 1086.

Domesmen /dówmzmən/. (Sax.) In old English law, an inferior kind of judge. Men appointed to doom (judge) in matters in controversy. Suitors in a court of a manor in ancient demesne, who were judges there.

Domestic, *n.* A household servant.

Domestic, *adj.* Pertaining, belonging, or relating to a home, a domicile, or to the place of birth, origin, creation, or transaction.

As to domestic Administrators; Attachment; Commerce; Corporation; Creditor; Factor; Fixture; Judgment; and Manufacture, see those titles.

Domestic animals. Such as are habituated to live in or about the habitations of men, or such as contribute to the support of a family. Tamed animals; *e.g.* horses, sheep, dogs.

Domesticated. Made domestic or converted to domestic use; *e.g.* taming of wild horse.

Domestic authority. The right of parents and, by extension, the right of teachers, to discipline and compel obedience to their lawful commands from their children; formerly extended to authority of husbands over their wives.

Domestic bill. Draft which is payable in the state in which it is drawn, as contrasted with a foreign bill which is payable in another state.

Domestic corporation. When a corporation is organized and chartered in a particular state, it is considered a domestic corporation of that state. Term is used in contrast to foreign corporation which has been incorporated in another state, territory or country. For tax purposes, a corporation created or organized in the U.S. or under the law of the U.S. or any state or territory. I.R.C. §§ 4920(a)(5), 7701(a)(4).

Domestic courts. Those existing and having jurisdiction at the place of the party's residence or domicile.

Domestic exports. Goods originally grown, produced, or manufactured in the United States, in contrast to goods originally imported and then re-exported.

Domestic International Sales Corporation (DISC). A U.S. corporation, usually a subsidiary, whose income is primarily attributable to exports. Income tax on 50 percent of a DISC's income is usually deferred for a long period. Generally, this results in a lower overall corporate tax for the parent than would otherwise be incurred.

Domestic jurisdiction. Power of court over a person or action within its district or state.

Domestic relations. That branch or discipline of the law which deals with matters of the household or family, including divorce, separation, custody, support and adoption.

Domestic servant. A person hired or employed primarily for the performance of household duties and chores, the maintenance of the home, and the care, comfort and convenience of members of the household. Hardware Dealers Mut. Fire Ins. Co. v. King, Tex.Civ.App., 408 S.W.2d 790, 791. See also **Domestic.**

Domesticus /dǝméstǝkǝs/. In old European law, a *seneschal,* steward, or *major domo;* a judge's assistant; an assessor *(q.v.).*

Domicellus /dòmǝsélǝs/. In old English law, a better sort of servant in monasteries; also an appellation of a king's bastard.

Domicile. That place where a man has his true, fixed, and permanent home and principal establishment, and to which whenever he is absent he has the intention of returning. Smith v. Smith, 206 Pa.Super. 310, 213 A.2d 94. The permanent residence of a person or the place to which he intends to return even though he may actually reside elsewhere. A person may have more than one residence but only one domicile. The legal domicile of a person is important since it, rather than the actual residence, often controls the jurisdiction of the taxing authorities and determines where a person may exercise the privilege of voting and other legal rights and privileges. The established, fixed, permanent, or ordinary dwellingplace or place of residence of a person, as distinguished from his temporary and transient, though actual, place of residence. It is his legal residence, as distinguished from his temporary place of abode; or his home, as distinguished from a place to which business or pleasure may temporarily call him. See also **Residence.**

"Citizenship," "habitancy," and "residence" are severally words which in particular cases may mean precisely the same as "domicile," while in other uses may have different meanings.

"Residence" signifies living in particular locality while "domicile" means living in that locality with intent to make it a fixed and permanent home. Schreiner v. Schreiner, Tex.Civ.App., 502 S.W.2d 840, 843.

For purpose of federal diversity jurisdiction, "citizenship" and "domicile" are synonymous. Hendry v. Masonite Corp., C.A.Miss., 455 F.2d 955.

See also **Abode.**

Commercial domicile. A domicile acquired by the maintenance of a commercial establishment.

Corporate domicile. Place considered by law as center of corporate affairs and place where its functions are discharged.

Domicile of choice. The essentials of "domicile" of choice are the fact of physical presence at a dwelling place and the intention to make that place home. New York Trust Co. v. Riley, 24 Del.Ch. 354, 16 A.2d 772, 776, 783, 785.

Domicile of origin. The home of the parents. That which arises from a man's birth and connections. The domicile of the parents at the time of birth, or what is termed the "domicile of origin," constitutes the domicile of an infant, and continues until abandoned, or until the acquisition of a new domicile in a different place. Struble v. Struble, Tex.Civ.App., 177 S.W.2d 279, 283.

Domicile of succession. As distinguished from a commercial, political, or forensic domicile, the actual residence of a person within some jurisdiction, of such a character as shall, according to the well-established principles of public law, give direction to the succession of his personal estate.

Domicile of trustee. Jurisdiction which appoints trustee is domicile of trustee.

Elected domicile. The domicile of parties fixed in a contract between them for the purposes of such contract.

Foreign domicile. A domicile established by a citizen or subject of one sovereignty within the territory of another.

Matrimonial domicile. The place where a husband and wife have established a home, in which they reside in the relation of husband and wife, and where the matrimonial contract is being performed.

Municipal domicile. One which as distinguished from "national domicile" and "quasi national domicile" (see those titles, *infra*), has reference to residence in a county, township, or municipality.

National domicile. The domicile of a person, considered as being within the territory of a particular nation, and not with reference to a particular locality or subdivision of a nation.

Natural domicile. The same as domicile of origin or domicile by birth.

Necessary domicile. That kind of domicile which exists by operation of law, as distinguished from voluntary domicile or domicile of choice.

Quasi national domicile. One involving residence in a state. See also *National domicile, supra.*

Domiciled /dómǝsǝld/dómǝsàyld/. Established in a given domicile; belonging to a given state or jurisdiction by right of domicile.

Domiciliary /dòmǝsîl(i)yǝriy/. Pertaining to domicile; relating to one's domicile. Existing or created at, or connected with, the domicile of a suitor or of a decedent.

Domiciliary administration. Administration in state where person was domiciled at time of death is deemed principal or primary administration and is ordinarily termed "domiciliary administration." First Nat. Bank v. Blessing, 231 Mo.App. 288, 98 S.W.2d 149, 151.

Domiciliate /dòmǝsîliyeyt/. To establish one's domicile; to take up one's fixed residence in a given place. To establish the domicile of another person whose legal residence follows one's own.

Domiciliation /dòmǝsìliyéyshǝn/. In Spanish law, the acquisition of domiciliary rights and status, nearly equivalent to naturalization, which may be accomplished by being born in the kingdom, by conversion to the Catholic faith there, by taking up a permanent residence in some settlement and marrying a native woman, and by attaching oneself to the soil, purchasing or acquiring real property and possessions.

Domicilium /dòmǝsîl(i)yǝm/. Lat. Domicile (q.v.).

Domigerium /dòmǝjériyǝm/. In old English law, power over another; also danger.

Domina (dame) /dómǝnǝ/. A title given to honorable women, who anciently, in their own right of inheritance, held a barony.

Dominant estate or tenement /dómǝnǝnt ǝstéyt/. That to which a servitude or easement is due, or for the benefit of which it exists. A term used in the civil and Scotch law, and later in ours, relating to servitudes, meaning the tenement or subject in favor of which the service is constituted; as the tenement over which the servitude extends is called the "servient tenement." That particular parcel of land that is benefited as a result of an easement on a servient estate.

Dominant theme. Within meaning of requirement that before any material can be found to be obscene the dominant theme of material taken as a whole must appeal to prurient interest in sex means prevailing, governing, influencing or controlling idea. State ex rel. Dowd v. "Pay the Baby Sitter", Com.Pl., 31 Ohio Misc. 208, 287 N.E.2d 650, 654.

Dominate /dómǝnèyt/. To master, to rule, or to control. Humble Oil & Refining Co. v. National Labor Relations Board, C.C.A.5, 113 F.2d 85, 88, 90.

Dominatio /dòmǝnéysh(iy)ow/. In old English law, lordship.

Dominical. That which denotes the Lord's day, or Sunday.

Dominicide /dǝmínǝsàyd/. The act of killing one's lord or master.

Dominicum /dǝmínǝkǝm/. Lat. Domain; demain; demesne. A lordship. That of which one has the lordship or ownership. That which remains under the lord's immediate charge and control. In Domesday Book it meant the home farm as distinguished from the holdings of the tenants.

Property; domain; anything pertaining to a lord. In ecclesiastical law, a church, or any other building consecrated to God.

Dominicum antiquum /dǝmínǝkǝm æntáykwǝm/. In old English law, ancient demesne.

Dominio /domíyniyow/. Sp. In Spanish law, a term corresponding to and derived from the Latin *dominium (q.v.)*. *Dominio alto,* eminent domain; *dominio directo,* immediate ownership; *dominio utile,* beneficial ownership.

Dominion. Generally accepted definition of "dominion" is perfect control in right of ownership. The word implies both title and possession and appears to require a complete retention of control over disposition. Eastex Aviation, Inc. v. Sperry & Hutchinson Co., C.A.Tex., 522 F.2d 1299, 1307. Title to an article of property which arises from the power of disposition and the right of claiming it.

Sovereignty; as the dominion of the seas or over a territory.

In the civil law, with reference to the title to property which is transferred by a sale of it, dominion is said to be either "proximate" or "remote," the former being the kind of title vesting in the purchaser when he has acquired both the ownership and the possession of the article, the latter describing the nature of his title when he has legitimately acquired the ownership of the property but there has been no delivery.

See also **Ownership; Title.**

Dominium /dǝmíniyǝm/. In the civil and old English law, ownership; property in the largest sense, including both the right of property and the right of possession or use.

The mere right of property, as distinguished from the possession or usufruct. The right which a lord had in the fee of his tenant.

Sovereignty or dominion. *Dominium maris,* the sovereignty of the sea.

Dominium directum /dǝmíniyǝm dǝréktǝm/. In the civil law, strict ownership; that which was founded on strict law, as distinguished from equity. In later law, property without use; the right of a landlord. In feudal law, right or proper ownership; the right of a superior or lord, as distinguished from that of his vassal or tenant. The title or property which the sovereign in England is considered as possessing in all the lands of the kingdom, they being holden either immediately or mediately of him as lord paramount.

Dominium directum et utile /dǝmíniyǝm dǝréktǝm èt yúwdǝliy/. The complete and absolute dominion in property; the union of the title and the exclusive use.

Dominium eminens /dəmíniyəm émənèn(d)z/. Eminent domain.

Dominium non potest esse in pendenti /dəmíniyəm nòn pówdest ésiy in pèndéntay/. Lordship cannot be in suspense, *i.e.*, property cannot remain in abeyance.

Dominium plenum /dəmíniyəm plíynəm/. Full ownership; the union of the *dominium directum* with the *dominium utile.*

Dominium utile /dəmíniyəm yúwdəliy/. In the civil law, equitable or prætorian ownership; that which was founded on equity. In later law, use without property; the right of a tenant. In feudal law, useful or beneficial ownership; the usufruct, or right to the use and profits of the soil, as distinguished from the *dominium directum (q.v.)* or ownership of the soil itself; the right of a vassal or tenant.

Domino volente /dómənow vəléntiy/. Lat. The owner being willing; with the consent of the owner.

Dominus /dómənəs/. In feudal and ecclesiastical law, a lord, or feudal superior. *Dominus rex,* the lord the king; the king's title as lord paramount. *Dominus capitalis,* a chief lord. *Dominus medius,* a mesne or intermediate lord. *Dominus ligius,* liege lord or sovereign.

Lord or sir; a title of distinction. It usually denoted a knight or clergyman; and was sometimes given to a gentleman of quality, though not a knight, especially if he were lord of a manor.

The owner or proprietor of a thing, as distinguished from him who uses it merely. A master or principal, as distinguished from an agent or attorney.

In the civil law, a husband; a family.

Dominus capitalis loco hæredis habetur, quoties per defectum vel delictum extinguitur sanguis sui tenentis /dómənəs kæpətéyləs lówkow həríydəs həbíydər, kwówshiyiyz pər dəféktəm vèl dəlíktəm ekstíŋgwədər sǽŋgwəs s(y)úway tənéntəs/. The supreme lord takes the place of the heir, as often as the blood of the tenant is extinct through deficiency or crime.

Dominus litis /dómənəs láydəs/. Lat. The master of the suit; *i.e.*, the person who was really and directly interested in the suit as a party, as distinguished from his attorney or advocate. But the term is also applied to one who, though not originally a party, has made himself such, by intervention or otherwise, and has assumed entire control and responsibility for one side, and is treated by the court as liable for costs. Virginia Electric & Power Co. v. Bowers, 181 Va. 542, 25 S.E.2d 361, 363.

Dominus navis /dómənəs néyvəs/. In the civil law, the owner of a vessel.

Dominus non maritabit pupillum nisi semel /dómənəs nòn mærətéybət pyuwpíləm náysay séməl/. A lord cannot give a ward in marriage but once.

Dominus rex nullum habere potest parem, multo minus superiorem /dómənəs réks nʌ́ləm həbíriy pówdəst pǽrəm, mʌ́ltow máynəs səpìriyórəm/. The king cannot have an equal, much less a superior.

Domitæ /dómədiy/. Lat. Tame; domesticated; not wild. Applied to domestic animals, in which a man may have an absolute property. 2 Bl.Comm. 391.

Dommages intérêts. In French law, damages.

Domo reparanda /dówmow rèpərǽndə/. A writ that lay for one against his neighbor, by the anticipated fall of whose house he feared a damage and injury to his own.

Dom. Proc. An abbreviation of *Domus Procerum* or *Domo Procerum;* the house of lords in England. Sometimes expressed by the letters D. P.

Domus /dówməs/. Lat. In the civil and old English law, a house or dwelling; a habitation. Shreveport Long Leaf Lumber Co. v. Wilson, D.C.La., 38 F.Supp. 629, 631. See **Domicile.**

Domus conversorum /dówməs kònvərsórəm/. An ancient house built or appointed by King Henry III for such Jews as were converted to the Christian faith; but King Edward III, who expelled the Jews from the kingdom, deputed the place for the custody of the rolls and records of the chancery.

Domus dei /dówməs díyay/. The house of God; a name applied to many hospitals and religious houses.

Domus procerum /dó(w)məs pró(w)sərəm/. The house of lords, abbreviated into *Dom. Proc.,* or *D. P.*

Domus sua cuique est tutissimum refugium /dówməs s(y)úwə k(yu)wáykwiy èst tyuwtísəməm rəfyúwjiyəm/. To every man his own house is his safest refuge. The house of every one is to him as his castle and fortress, as well for his defense against injury and violence as for his repose. A man's dwellinghouse is his castle, not for his own personal protection merely, but also for the protection of his family and his property therein.

Domus tutissimum cuique refugium atque receptaculum sit /dówməs tyuwtísəməm k(yu)wáykwiy rəfyúwjiyəm ǽtkwiy rəsèptǽkyələm sít/. A man's house should be his safest refuge and shelter. The habitation of each one is an inviolable asylum for him. A maxim of the Roman law.

Dona clandestina sunt semper suspiciosa /dównə klǽndəstáynə sənt sémpər səspìshiyówsə/. Clandestine gifts are always suspicious.

Donari videtur, quod nullo jure cogente conceditur /dòwnéray vədíydər kwòd nálow júriy kəjéntiy kənsíydədər/. A thing is said to be given when it is yielded otherwise than by virtue of right (that is considered to be given which is granted when no law compels).

Donatarius /dòwnətériyəs/. A donee; one to whom something is given. See **Donee.**

Donated stock. Securities given to a corporation by its own stockholders commonly for resale.

Donated surplus. Contribution of assets to a corporation generally in the form of stock from its stockholders.

Donatio /dòwnéysh(iy)ow/. Lat. A gift. A transfer of the title to property to one who receives it without paying for it. The act by which the owner of a thing voluntarily transfers the title and possession of the same from himself to another person, without any consideration.

By the civil law (adopted into the English and American law) donations are either *inter vivos* (between living persons) or *mortis causa* (in anticipation of death). As to these forms, see *infra*. A *donatio* or gift as between living persons is called *donatio mera* or *pura* when it is a simple gift without compulsion or consideration, that is, resting solely on the generosity of the donor, as in the case of most charitable gifts. It is called *donatio remuneratoria* when given as a reward for past services, but still not under any legal compulsion, as in the case of pensions and land-grants. It is called *donatio sub modo* (or *modalis*) when given for the attainment of some special object or on condition that the donee shall do something not specially for the benefit of the donor, as in the case of the endowment of hospitals, colleges, etc., coupled with the condition that they shall be established and maintained. The following terms are also used: *Donatio conditionalis,* a conditional gift; *donatio relata,* a gift made with reference to some service already done, *donatio stricta et coarctura,* a restricted gift, as an estate tail.

Donatio inofficiosa /dòwnéysh(iy)ow ìnəfis(h)iyówsə/. An inofficious (undutiful) gift; a gift of so great a part of the donor's property that the birthright portion of his heirs is diminished.

Donatio inter vivos /dòwnéysh(iy)ow íntər váyvows/. A gift between the living. The ordinary kind of gift by one person to another. A term derived from the civil law. A donation *inter vivos* (between living persons) is an act by which the donor divests himself at present and irrevocably of the thing given in favor of the donee who accepts it.

There are three kinds of "donations inter vivos", namely, "gratuitous donations", "onerous donations", and "remunerative donations", the first being based on mere liberality, the second being burdened with charges imposed by the donee, and the third being recompense for services rendered. White v. White, La.App., 7 So.2d 255, 257.

Donatio mortis causa /dòwnéysh(iy)ow mórdəs kózə/. A gift made by a person in sickness, who, apprehending his death, delivers, or causes to be delivered, to another the possession of any personal goods, to keep as his own in case of the donor's decease. The civil law defines it to be a gift under apprehension of death; as when anything is given upon condition that, if the donor dies, the donee shall possess it absolutely, or return it if the donor should survive or should repent of having made the gift, or if the donee should die before the donor. A gift in view of death is one which is made in contemplation, fear, or peril of death, and with intent that it shall take effect only in case of the death of the giver. A donation *mortis causa* (in prospect of death) is an act to take effect when the donor shall no longer exist, by which he disposes of the whole or a part of his property, and which is revocable. See **Contemplation of death.**

Donation. A gift (*q.v.*). See **Donatio.**

In ecclesiastical law, a mode of acquiring a benefice by deed of gift alone, without presentation, institution, or induction.

Donation lands. Lands granted from the public domain to an individual as a bounty, gift, or donation; partic-ularly, in early Pennsylvania history, lands thus granted to soldiers of the revolutionary war.

Donatio non præsumitur /downéysh(iy)ow nòn prəz-(y)úwmədər/. A gift is not presumed.

Donationum alia perfecta, alia incepta et non perfecta, ut si donatio lecta fuit et concessa, ac traditio nondum fuerit subsecuta /dənèyshiyównəm éyl(i)yə pərfékta, éyl(i)yə inéptə èt nón pərféktə, àt sày downéysh(iy)ow léktə fyúwəd èt kən(t)sésə, æk trədísh(iy)ow nóndəm fyúwərət sòbsəkyúwdə/. Some gifts are perfect, others incipient and not perfect as if a gift were read and agreed to, but delivery had not then followed.

Donatio perficitur possessione accipientis /downéysh(iy)ow pərfísədər pəzèshiyówniy əksìpiyéntəs/. A gift is perfected [made complete] by the possession of the receiver. A gift is incomplete until possession is delivered.

Donatio principis intelligitur sine præjudicio tertii /downéysh(iy)ow prínsəpəs ìntəléjədər sáyniy prìyjuwdísh(iy)ow társhiyày/. A gift of the prince is understood without prejudice to a third party.

Donatio propter nuptias /downéysh(iy)ow próptər nápshiyəs/. A gift on account of marriage. In Roman law, the bridegroom's gift to the bride in anticipation of marriage and to secure her *dos* was called *"donatio ante nuptias";* but by an ordinance of Justinian such gift might be made after as well as before marriage, and in that case it was called *"donatio propter nuptias."*

Donative advowson /dównədəv ədváwzən/. In ecclesiastical law, a species of advowson, where the benefice is conferred on the clerk by the patron's deed of donation, without presentation, institution, or induction. 2 Bl.Comm. 23.

Donative trust. May be created by transfer of property in trust as gift for benefit of another person or by proper declaration of legal owner of property that he will hold it in trust for another's benefit and does not require payment of any consideration by the beneficiary. Elbert v. Waples-Platter Co., Tex.Civ.App., 156 S.W.2d 146, 150, 151.

Donator /dòwnéydər/. A donor; one who makes a gift (*donatio*).

Donatorius /dòwnətóriyəs/. A donee; a person to whom a gift is made; a purchaser.

Donator nunquam desinit possidere, antequam donatorius incipiat possidere /downéydow nánkwəm désənət pòsədíriy æntəkwəm dòwnətóriyəs in(t)sípiyət pòsədíriy/. The donor never ceases to possess, until the donee begins to possess.

Donatory /dównət(ò)riy/. The person on whom the king bestows his right to any forfeiture that has fallen to the crown.

Done. Completed; brought to an end; over.

Donec /dównek/. Lat. As long as; while; until; within a certain time.

Donec probetur in contrarium /dównek prowbíydər ìn kəntrériyəm/. [Given] until proof to the contrary.

Donee. One to whom a gift is made or a bequest given. One who is invested with a power of appointment; the party executing a power, otherwise called the "appointer." He to whom lands or tenements are given in tail. In old English law, he to whom lands were given; the party to whom a *donatio* was made.

Donee beneficiary. In a third party contract, the person who takes the benefit of the contract though there is no privity between him and the contracting parties.

Donee of power. The person to whom the settlor or donor of a power of appointment gives such power to be exercised. In the case of a special power, in favor of a limited class such as members of a family, or, in the case of a general power, in favor of any one including the donee himself.

Donis, Statute de /stǽchuwt dìy dównǝs/. See **De Donis.**

Donneur d'aval /dònǝ́r davál/. In French law, guarantor of negotiable paper other than by indorsement.

Donor. The party conferring a power. One who makes a gift. One who creates a trust. He who gives lands or tenements to another in tail. In old English law, he by whom lands were given to another; the party making a *donatio*.

Donum /dównǝm/. Lat. In the civil law, a gift; a free gift. The difference between *donum* and *munus* is said to be that *donum* is more general, while *munus* is specific.

Doomsday-book. See **Domesday-book.**

Door closing doctrine. The principle invoked when a loop-hole in a law is closed by a statute or decision.

Dope. Any thick liquid or pasty preparation, as of opium for medicinal purposes, of grease for a lubricant, etc., and in popular meaning signifies opium derivative, ranging from harmless concoction to most powerful narcotics containing heroin or opium as ingredient.

Dormant. Literally, sleeping; hence, inactive; in abeyance; unknown; concealed; silent.

Dormant claim. One which is in abeyance.

Dormant corporation. An inactive but legal corporation which is capable of being activated, but is presently not operating.

Dormant execution. One which a creditor delivers to the sheriff with directions to levy only, and not to sell, until further orders, or until a junior execution is received.

Dormant judgment. One which has not been satisfied, nor extinguished by lapse of time, but which has remained so long unexecuted that execution cannot now be issued upon it without first reviving the judgment, or one which has lost its lien on land from the failure to issue execution on it or take other steps to enforce it within the time limited by statute. See **Judgment; Revival.**

Dormant partner. See **Partner.**

Dormiunt aliquando leges, nunquam moriuntur /dórmiyǝnt ǽlǝkwóndow líyjiyz, nǽŋkwǝm mòriyántǝr/. The laws sometimes sleep, never die.

Dorsum /dórsǝm/. Lat. The back. *In dorso recordi,* on the back of the record.

Dos /dóws/. In Roman law, dowry; a wife's marriage portion; all that property which on marriage is transferred by the wife herself or by another to the husband with a view of diminishing the burden which the marriage will entail upon him. It is of three kinds. *Profectitia dos* is that which is derived from the property of the wife's father or paternal grandfather. That *dos* is termed *adventitia* which is not *profectitia* in respect to its source, whether it is given by the wife from her own estate or by the wife's mother or a third person. It is termed *receptitia dos* when accompanied by a stipulation for its reclamation by the constitutor on the termination of the marriage.

In old English law, the portion given to the wife by the husband at the church door, in consideration of the marriage; dower; the wife's portion out of her deceased husband's estate in case he had not endowed her.

Dos de dote peti non debet /dóws dìy dówdiy péday nòn débǝt/. Dower ought not to be demanded of dower. A widow is not dowable of lands assigned to another woman in dower.

Dos rationabilis /dóws ræshǝnéybǝlǝs/. A reasonable marriage portion. A reasonable part of her husband's estate, to which every widow is entitled, of lands of which her husband may have endowed her on the day of marriage. Dower, at common law. 2 Bl.Comm. 134.

Dos rationabilis vel legitima est cujuslibet mulieris de quocunque tenemento tertia pars omnium terrarum et tenementorum, quæ vir suus tenuit in dominio suo ut de feodo, etc. /dóws ræshǝnéybǝlǝs vèl lǝjídǝmǝ èst kyuwjáslǝbǝt myùwliyírǝs dìy kwowkáŋkwiy tènǝméntow társhiyǝ párz ómniyǝm tehrérǝm èt tènǝmentórǝm, kwìy vár s(y)úwǝs tényuwǝd in dǝmín(i)yow s(y)úwow ǝ̀t dìy fyúwdow/. Reasonable or legitimate dower belongs to every woman of a third part of all the lands and tenements of which her husband was seised in his demesne, as of fee, etc.

Dossier /dòs(i)yéy/dós(i)yèy/. Fr. A brief; a bundle of papers.

Dot. (A French word, adopted in Louisiana.) The fortune, portion, or dowry which a woman brings to her husband by the marriage.

DOT. Department of Transportation.

Dotage /dówdǝj/. Senility. That feebleness of the mental faculties which proceeds from old age. It is a diminution or decay of that intellectual power which was once possessed. Also called "second childhood." Relating to woman's marriage dowry.

Dotal /dówdǝl/. Relating to the *dos* or portion of a woman; constituting her portion; comprised in her portion.

Dotalitium /dòwtǝlíshiyǝm/. In canon and feudal law, dower.

Dotal property /dówdəl própərdiy/. In the civil law, in Louisiana, property which the wife brings to the husband to assist him in bearing the expenses of the marriage establishment. Extradotal property, otherwise called "paraphernal property," is that which forms no part of the dowry. Fleitas v. Richardson, 147 U.S. 550, 13 S.Ct. 495, 37 L.Ed. 276. See also **Community.**

Dotation /dòwtéyshən/. The act of giving a dowry or portion; endowment in general, including the endowment of a hospital or other charitable institution.

Dote /dówtey/, *n.* In Spanish law, the marriage portion of a wife. The property which the wife gives to the husband on account of marriage, or for the purpose of supporting the matrimonial expenses.

Dote, *v.* To be besotted, delirious, silly, or insane.

Dote assignanda /dówdiy æsəgnǽndə/. A writ which lay for a widow, when it was judicially ascertained that a tenant to the king was seised of tenements in fee or fee-tail at the day of his death, and that he held of the king in chief. In such case the widow might come into chancery, and then make oath that she would not marry without the king's leave, and then she might have this writ. These widows were called the "king's widows."

Dote unde nihil habet /dówdiy ə́ndiy náy(h)əl héybət/. "Dower from whence she has nothing." An English writ which lay for a widow to whom no dower had been assigned.

Doti lex favet; præmium pudoris est; ideo parcatur /dówday léks féyvət, príymiyəm pədórəs èst, ídiyow parkéydər/. The law favors dower; it is the reward of chastity; therefore let it be preserved.

Dotis administratio /dówdəs ədmìnəstréysh(iy)ow/. Admeasurement of dower, where the widow holds more than her share, etc.

Dotissa /dowtísə/. A dowager.

Double. Twofold; acting in two capacities or having two aspects; multiplied by two. This term has ordinarily the same meaning in law as in popular speech. The principal compound terms into which it enters are noted below.

Double adultery. Adultery committed by two persons each of whom is married to another as distinguished from "single" adultery, where one of the participants is unmarried.

Double assessment. The imposition of same tax, by same taxing power, upon same subject matter. Aragon v. Empire Gold Mining & Milling Co., 47 N.M. 299, 142 P.2d 539, 541.

Double commissions. Commissions or fees paid by both seller and buyer or paid to the same person in different capacities, such as executor and trustee.

Double complaint /dábəl kəmpléynt/, **double quarrel** /°kwóhrəl/ or **duplex querela** /d(y)úwpleks kwəríylə/. A grievance made known by a clerk or other person, to the archbishop of the province, against the ordinary, for delaying or refusing to do justice in some cause ecclesiastical, as to give sentence, institute a clerk, etc. It is termed a "double complaint," because it is most commonly made against both the judge and him at whose suit justice is denied or delayed; the effect whereof is that the archbishop, taking notice of the delay, directs his letters, under his authentical seal, to all clerks of his province, commanding them to admonish the ordinary, within a certain number of days, to do the justice required, or otherwise to appear before him or his official, and there allege the cause of his delay; and to signify to the ordinary that if he neither perform the thing enjoined, nor appear nor show cause against it, he himself, in his court of audience, will forthwith proceed to do the justice that is due. In current usage, a complaint in the nature of an appeal from the ordinary to his next immediate superior, as from a bishop to an archbishop. This complaint is available to a clergyman who, having been presented to a living, is refused institution by the ordinary. See **Duplicity.**

Double costs. See **Costs.**

Double creditor. One who has a lien on two funds.

Double damages. See **Damages.**

Double eagle. A gold coin of the United States of the value of twenty dollars.

Double entry. A system of bookkeeping, in which the entries are posted twice into the ledger, once as a credit and once as a debit.

Double hearsay. A statement made outside of court is hearsay when introduced in court to prove the truth of the statement. However, certain exceptions permit the introduction of hearsay if the out-of-court statement was made on the personal knowledge of the declarant as in the case of a declaration of a deceased person. If such statement of the deceased person was not made on his personal knowledge, the hearsay would be double or totem pole hearsay.

Double house. A building having accommodations for two families, divided vertically instead of horizontally. Also called "duplex".

Double indemnity. Payment of twice the basic benefit in event of loss resulting from specified causes or under specified circumstances. Provision in life insurance contract requiring payment of twice the face amount of the policy by the insurer in the event of death by accidental means.

Double insurance. Exists where the same person is insured by several insurers separately in respect to the same subject and interest.

Double jeopardy. Common-law and constitutional (Fifth Amendment) prohibition against a second prosecution after a first trial for the same offense. People v. Wheeler, 271 Cal.App. 205, 79 Cal.Rptr. 842, 845, 271 C.A.2d 205. The evil sought to be avoided is double trial and double conviction, not necessarily double punishment. Breed et al. v. Jones, 421 U.S. 519, 95 S.Ct. 1779, 44 L.Ed.2d 346. See also **Jeopardy; Same evidence test.**

Double patenting. The test respecting "double patenting" is whether the claims of both patents, when properly construed in the light of the descriptions given, define essentially the same things. Occurs only when claims of two patents issued to one applicant are the same.

Double plea, double pleading. See **Duplicity; Plea; Pleadings.**

Double proof. Species of evidence required for conviction of certain crimes in which the government must offer corroboration.

Double recovery. Recovery which represents more than the total maximum loss which all parties have sustained.

Double rent. In English law, rent payable by a tenant who continues in possession after the time for which he has given notice to quit, until the time of his quitting possession.

Doubles. Letters-patent.

Double standard. Set of principles which permit greater opportunity for one class of people than another and commonly based on differences such as sex, race or color and hence invidious standards which may offend equal protection of law to the discriminated minority. See **Discrimination.**

Double taxation. The taxing of the same item or piece of property twice to the same person, or taxing it as the property of one person and again as the property of another, but this does not include the imposition of different taxes concurrently on the same property or income (e.g. federal and state income taxes), nor the taxation of the same piece of property to different persons when they hold different interests in it or when it represents different values in their hands, as when both the mortgagor and mortgagee of property are taxed in respect to their interests in it, or when a tax is laid upon the profits of a corporation and also upon the dividends paid to its shareholders. "Double taxation" means taxing twice for the same purpose in the same year some of the property in the territory in which the tax is laid without taxing all of it. Diefendorf v. Gallet, 51 Idaho 619, 10 P.2d 307, 315; Amarillo-Pecos Valley Truck Lines v. Gallegos, 44 N.M. 120, 99 P.2d 447, 451. To constitute "double taxation," two taxes must be imposed on same property by same governing body during same taxing period and for same taxing purpose. Second St. Properties, Inc. v. Fiscal Court of Jefferson County, Ky., 445 S.W.2d 709, 715.

Double tax rule. Collections made in taxable year on sales made in prior years, and which had already been taxed in prior years. Hoover-Bond Co. v. Denman, C.C.A.Ohio, 59 F.2d 909, 910.

Double use. In patent law, an application of a principle or process, previously known and applied, to some new use, but which does not lead to a new result or the production of a new article.

Double value. In old English law, a penalty on a tenant holding over after his landlord's notice to quit. By 4 Geo. II, c. 28, § 1, it is enacted that if any tenant for life or years hold over any lands, etc., after the determination of his estate, after demand made, and notice in writing given, for delivering the possession thereof, by the landlord, or the person having the

reversion or remainder therein, or his agent thereunto lawfully authorized, such tenant so holding over shall pay to the person so kept out of possession at the rate of *double* the yearly value of the lands, etc., so detained, for so long a time as the same are detained.

Double voucher. In old English law, this was when a common recovery was had, and an estate of freehold was first conveyed to any indifferent person against whom the *proecipe* was brought, and then he vouched the tenant in tail, who vouched over the common vouchee. For, if a recovery were had immediately against a tenant in tail, it barred only the estate in the premises of which he was then actually seised, whereas, if the recovery were had against another person, and the tenant in tail were vouchee, it barred every latent right and interest which he might have in the lands recovered. 2 Bl.Comm. 359.

Double waste. When a tenant bound to repair suffers a house to be wasted, and then unlawfully fells timber to repair it, he is said to commit double waste.

Double will. A will in which two persons join, each leaving his property and estate to the other, so that the survivor takes the whole. See **Reciprocal wills.**

Doubt, *v.* To question or hold questionable.

Doubt, *n.* Uncertainty of mind; the absence of a settled opinion or conviction; the attitude of mind towards the acceptance of or belief in a proposition, theory, or statement, in which the judgment is not at rest but inclines alternately to either side.

Reasonable doubt. This is a term often used, probably pretty well understood, but not easily defined. It does not mean a mere possible doubt, because everything relating to human affairs, and depending on moral evidence, is open to some possible or imaginary doubt. It is that state of the case which, after the entire comparison and consideration of all the evidence, leaves the minds of jurors in that condition that they cannot say they feel an abiding conviction to a moral certainty of the truth of the charge. If upon proof there is reasonable doubt remaining, the accused is entitled to the benefit of it by an acquittal; for it is not sufficient to establish a probability, though a strong one, arising from the doctrine of chances, that the fact charged is more likely to be true than the contrary, but the evidence must establish the truth of the fact to a reasonable and moral certainty, *i.e.* a certainty that convinces and directs the understanding and satisfies the reason and judgment of those who are bound to act conscientiously upon it. This is proof beyond reasonable doubt; because if the law, which mostly depends upon considerations of a moral nature, should go further than this, and require absolute certainty, it would exclude circumstantial evidence altogether.

Proof "beyond a reasonable doubt" is not beyond all possible or imaginary doubt, but such proof as precludes every reasonable hypothesis except that which it tends to support. It is proof "to a moral certainty"; such proof as satisfies the judgment and consciences of the jury, as reasonable men, and applying their reason to the evidence before them, that the crime charged has been committed by the defendant, and so satisfies them as to leave no other reasonable conclusion possible.

A "reasonable doubt" is such a doubt as would cause a reasonable and prudent man in the graver and more important affairs of life to pause and hesitate to act upon the truth of the matter charged. But a reasonable doubt is not a mere possibility of innocence, nor a caprice, shadow, or speculation as to innocence not arising out of the evidence or the want of it.

Doubtful title. One as to the validity of which there exists some doubt, either as to matter of fact or of law; one which invites or exposes the party holding it to litigation. Barrett v. McMannis, 153 Kan. 420, 110 P.2d 774, 778. Distinguished from a "marketable" title, which is of such a character that the courts will compel its acceptance by a purchaser who has agreed to buy the property or has bid it in at public sale. See **Marketable title.**

Doun /dówn/. L. Fr. A gift. Otherwise written *"don"* and *"done."* The thirty-fourth chapter of Britton is entitled *"De Douns."*

Do ut des /dów àt díyz/. Lat. I give that you may give; I give [you] that you may give [me]. A formula in the civil law, constituting a general division under which those contracts (termed "innominate") were classed in which something was *given* by one party as a consideration for something *given* by the other.

Do ut facias /dów àt féys(h)(i)yəs/. Lat. I give that you may do; I give [you] that you may do or make [for me]. A formula in the civil law, under which those contracts were classed in which one party *gave* or agreed to give money, in consideration the other party *did* or performed certain work. In this and the foregoing phrase, the conjunction *"ut"* is not to be taken as the technical means of expressing a consideration. In the Roman usage, this word imported a *modus,* that is, a qualification; while a consideration *(causa)* was more aptly expressed by the word *"quia."*

Dovetail seniority. Combining two or more seniority lists (usually of different companies being merged) into a master seniority list, with each employee keeping the seniority he had previously acquired even though he may thereafter be employed by a new employer.

Dowable /dáwəbəl/. Subject to be charged with dower; as dowable lands. Entitled or entitling to dower. Thus, a dowable interest in lands is such as entitles the owner to have such lands charged with dower.

Dowager /dáwəjər/. A widow who is endowed, or who has a jointure in lieu of dower. Widow holding property or a title received from her deceased husband. In England, this is a title or addition given to the widows of princes, dukes, earls, and other noblemen, to distinguish them from the wives of the heirs, who have right to bear the title. 1 Bl.Comm. 224.

Dowager-queen /dáwəjər kwíyn/. The widow of the king. As such she enjoys most of the privileges belonging to her as queen consort. It is not treason to conspire her death or violate her chastity, because the succession to the crown is not thereby endangered. No man, however, can marry her without a special license from the sovereign, on pain of forfeiting his lands or goods. 1 Bl.Comm. 233.

Dower. The provision which the law makes for a widow out of the lands or tenements of her husband, for her support and the nurture of her children. 2 Bl.Comm. 130; In re Miller's Estate, 44 N.M. 214, 100 P.2d 908, 911. A species of life-estate which a woman is, by law, entitled to claim on the death of her husband, in the lands and tenements of which he was seised in fee during the marriage, and which her issue, if any, might by possibility have inherited. The life estate to which every married woman is entitled on death of her husband, intestate, or, in case she dissents from his will, one-third in value of all lands of which husband was beneficially seized in law or in fact, at any time during coverture.

Dower has been abolished in the majority of the states and materially altered in most of the others.

See also **Inchoate dower.**

Dower ad ostium ecclesiæ /dáwər æd óstiyəm əklíyzi-yiy/. Dower at the church door or porch. An ancient kind of dower in England, where a man (being tenant in fee-simple, of full age), openly *at the church door,* where all marriages were formerly celebrated, after affiance made and troth plighted between them, *endowed* his wife with the whole of his lands, or such quantity as he pleased, at the same time specifying and ascertaining the same. 2 Bl.Comm. 133.

Dower by common law. The ordinary kind of dower in English and American law, consisting of a life interest in one-third of the lands of which the husband was seised in fee at any time during the coverture. 2 Bl.Comm. 132.

Dower by custom. A kind of dower in England, regulated by custom, where the quantity allowed the wife different from the proportion of the common law; as that the wife should have half the husband's lands; or, in some places, the whole; and, in some, only a quarter. 2 Bl.Comm. 132.

Dower de la plus belle (de la pluis beale) /dáwər də la plyùw bél/. L. Fr. Dower of the fairest [part]. A species of ancient English dower, incident to the old tenures, where there was a guardian in chivalry, and the wife occupied lands of the heir as guardian in socage. If the wife brought a writ of dower against such guardian in chivalry, he might show this matter, and pray that the wife might be endowed *de la plus belle* of the tenement in socage. This kind of dower was abolished with the military tenures. 2 Bl.Comm. 132.

Dower ex assensu patris /dáwər èks əséns(h)(y)uw pǽtrəs/. Dower by the father's assent. A species of dower *ad ostium ecclesiæ,* made when the husband's father was alive, and the son, by his consent expressly given, endowed his wife with parcel of his father's lands. 2 Bl.Comm. 133.

Dower unde nihil habet /dáwər əndiy náy(h)əl héybət/. A writ of right which lay for a widow to whom no dower had been assigned.

Dow Jones Average. A stock market performance indicator that consists of the price movements in the top 30 industrial companies in the United States.

Dowle stones. Stones dividing lands, etc.

Dowment. In old English law, endowment; dower.

Down payment. The portion of purchase price which is generally required to be paid at time purchase and sale agreement is signed and is generally paid in cash or its equivalent. An amount of money paid to the seller at the time of sale, which represents only a part of the total cost. See also **Earnest money.**

Dowress /dáw(ə)rəs/. A woman entitled to dower; a tenant in dower.

Dowry. The property which a woman brings to her husband in marriage; also sometimes called a "portion." See **Dos.**

Dozen peers /dázən pírz/. Twelve peers assembled at the instance of the barons, in the reign of Henry III, to be privy counselors, or rather conservators of the kingdom.

D. P. An abbreviation for *Domus Procerum,* the house of lords.

Dr. An abbreviation for "doctor". Also, in commercial usage, for "debtor," indicating the items or particulars in a bill or in an account-book chargeable against the person to whom the bill is rendered or in whose name the account stands, as opposed to "Cr." ("Credit" or "creditor"), which indicates the items for which he is given credit.

Drachma /drǽkmə/. A term employed in old pleadings and records, to denote a groat.

An Athenian silver coin, of the value of about fifteen cents.

Draconian laws /drəkówniyən lóz/. A code of laws prepared by Draco, the celebrated lawgiver of Athens. These laws were exceedingly severe, and the term is now sometimes applied to any laws of unusual harshness.

Draff. Waste matter, sweepings, refuse, lees, or dregs. In weighing commodities the term signifies dust and dirt, and not what is generally meant by "draught" or "draft" *(q.v.).*

Draft. A written order by the first party, called the drawer, instructing a second party, called the drawee (such as a bank), to pay a third party, called the payee. An order to pay a sum certain in money, signed by a drawer, payable on demand or at a definite time, and to order or bearer. People v. Norwood, 26 Cal.App.3d 148, 103 Cal.Rptr. 7, 11. An unconditional order drawn by drawer on drawee to the order of the payee; same as a bill of exchange. U.C.C. § 3–104. See also Check; Documentary draft; Redraft; Sight draft; Trade acceptance.

A tentative, provisional, or preparatory writing out of any document (as a will, contract, lease, etc.) for purposes of discussion and correction, which is afterwards to be copied out in its final shape.

Also, a small arbitrary deduction or allowance made to a merchant or importer, in the case of goods sold by wright or taxable by weight, to cover possible loss of weight in handling or from differences in scales.

Bank draft. One drawn by one bank on another.

Clean draft. One which has no shipping documents attached.

Documentary draft. One to which various shipping documents are attached.

Overdraft. Writing a check for more money than is in account.

Sight draft. One which is payable on presentation or demand.

Time draft. One payable a certain number of days after sight or after presentation for acceptance. The number of days must be specified.

Draft board. Federal agency that registers, classifies and selects men for compulsory military service.

Draftsman. Any one who draws or frames a legal document, *e.g.,* a will, conveyance, pleading, etc. One who draws plans and specifications for machinery, structures, etc.

Dragnet clause. Provision in a mortgage in which mortgagor gives security for past and future advances as well as present indebtedness.

Drago doctrine. The principle asserted by Luis Drago, Minister of Foreign Affairs of the Argentine Republic, in a letter to the Argentine Minister at Washington, December 29, 1902, that the forcible intervention of states to secure the payment of public debts due to their citizens from foreign states is unjustifiable and dangerous to the security and peace of the nations of South America. The subject was brought before the Conference by the United States and a Convention was adopted in which the contracting powers agreed, with some restrictive conditions, not to have recourse to armed force for the recovery of contract debts claimed by their nationals against a foreign state. See **Calvo doctrine.**

Drain, *v.* To conduct water from one place to another, for the purpose of drying the former. To make dry; to draw off water; to rid land of its superfluous moisture by adapting or improving natural water courses and supplementing them, when necessary, by artificial ditches. To "drain," in its larger sense, includes not only the supplying of outlets and channels to relieve the land from water, but also the provision of ditches, drains, and embankments to prevent water from accumulating.

To totally consume or exhaust.

Drain, *n.* A trench or ditch to convey water from wet land; a channel through which water may flow off. The word has no technical legal meaning. Any hollow space in the ground, natural or artificial, where water is collected and passes off, is a ditch or drain.

Also, sometimes, the easement or servitude (acquired by grant or prescription) which consists in the right to drain water through another's land. See **Drainage rights.**

Public drainage way. The land reserved or dedicated for the installation of storm water sewers or drainage ditches, or required along a natural stream or watercourse for preserving the channel and providing for the flow of water to safeguard the public against flood damage, sedimentation, and erosion.

Drainage district. A political subdivision of the state, created for the purpose of draining and reclaiming wet and overflowed land, as well as to preserve the public health and convenience.

Drainage rights. A landowner may not obstruct or divert the natural flow of a watercourse or natural drainage course to the injury of another. In urban areas, "natural drainage course" is narrowly interpreted to include only streams with well-defined channels and banks. In rural areas, the term is more broadly construed, apparently including the flow and direction of diffused surface waters. Chamberlin v. Ciaffoni, 373 Pa. 430, 436, 437, 96 A.2d 140, 143. See also **Water** (*Water rights*).

Dram. A drink of some substance containing alcohol; something which can produce intoxication. An apothecary system measurement of fluid, roughly equivalent to 4 or 5 cc, or one teaspoonful.

Drama. A term descriptive of any representation in which a story is told, a moral conveyed, or the passions portrayed, whether by words and actions combined, or by mere actions alone.

Dramatic composition. In copyright law, a literary work setting forth a story, incident, or scene from life, in which, however, the narrative is not related, but is represented by a dialogue and action; may include a descriptive poem set to music, or a pantomime.

Dram-shop. A drinking establishment where liquors are sold to be drunk on the premises; a bar or saloon.

Dram Shop Acts. Many states have Dram Shop or Civil Liability Acts which impose liability on the seller of intoxicating liquors (which may or may not include beer), when a third party is injured as a result of the intoxication of the buyer where the sale has caused or contributed to such intoxication. Some acts apply to gifts as well as sales. Such acts protect the third party not only against injuries resulting directly from affirmative acts of the intoxicated man, such as resulting from negligent operation of vehicle or assault and battery, but also against the loss of family support due to injuries to the man himself.

Draw, *v.* To draw a firearm or deadly weapon is to point it intentionally. To draw a bead on; to bring into line with the bead or fore sight of a rifle and the hind sight; to aim at.

To draw a bill of exchange, check, or draft, is to write (or cause it to be written) and sign it; to make, as a note.

To compose and write out in due form, as, a deed, complaint, petition, memorial, etc.

To draw a jury is to select the persons who are to compose it, either by taking their names successively, but at hazard, from the jury box, or by summoning them individually to attend the court.

In old criminal practice, to drag (on a hurdle) to the place of execution. Anciently no hurdle was allowed, but the criminal was actually dragged along the road to the place of execution. A part of the ancient punishment of traitors was to be thus drawn. 4 Bl.Comm. 92, 377.

To withdraw money; *i.e.,* to take out money from a bank, treasury, or other depository in the exercise of a lawful right and in a lawful manner. To periodically advance money on a construction loan agreement. See also **Drawing account.**

Drawback. In the customs laws, an allowance made by the government upon the duties due on imported merchandise when the importer, instead of selling it here, re-exports it; or the refunding of such duties if already paid. This allowance amounts, in some cases, to the whole of the original duties; in others, to a part only. See 19 U.S.C.A. § 1313.

Drawee. The person on whom a bill or draft is drawn. A person to whom a bill of exchange or draft is directed, and who is requested to pay the amount of money therein mentioned. The drawee of a check is the bank on which it is drawn.

When drawee accepts, he engages that he will pay the instrument according to its tenor at the time of his engagement or as completed. U.C.C. § 3–413(1).

Drawer. The person who draws a bill or draft. The drawer of a check is the person who signs it.

The drawer engages that upon dishonor of the draft and any necessary notice of dishonor or protest, he will pay the amount of the draft to the holder or to any indorser who takes it up. The drawer may disclaim this liability by drawing without recourse, U.C.C. § 3–413(2).

Drawing account. Fund of money from which salesmen or other employees may draw in anticipation of earnings or commissions; may be used to pay current expenses.

Drawing lots. An act in which selection is based on pure chance and in which the result depends upon the particular lot which is drawn. See also **Lottery**

Drawlatches /drólǽchəz/. Thieves; robbers.

Drayage. A charge for the local transportation of property. Similar to cartage.

Dred Scott Case. The case in which the United States Supreme Court held that descendants of Africans who were imported into this country, and sold as slaves, were not included nor intended to be included under the word "Citizens" in the Constitution, whether emancipated or not, and remained without rights or privileges except such as those which the government might grant them. Dred Scott v. Sandford, 60 U.S. (19 How.) 393, 15 L.Ed. 691.

Dreit-dreit /dríyt-dríyt/. Droit-droit. (Also written without the hyphen.) Double right. A union of the right of possession and the right of property. 2 Bl.Comm. 199.

Drenches, or **drenges.** In Saxon law, tenants *in capite.* They are said to be such as, at the coming of William the Conqueror, being put out of their estates, where afterwards restored to them, on their making it appear that they were the true owners thereof, and neither *in auxilio* or *consilio* against him.

Drengage /dréŋ(g)əj/. The tenure by which the drenches, or drenges, held their lands. A variety of feudal tenure by *serjeanty (q.v.),* often occurring in the northern counties of England, involving a kind of general service.

Driftland, drofland, or **dryfland.** A Saxon word, signifying a tribute or yearly payment made by some tenants to the king, or their landlords, for driving their cattle through a manor to fairs or markets.

Drifts of the forest. In old English law, a view or examination of what cattle were in a forest, chase, etc., that it could be known whether such be surcharged or not; and whose the beasts were, and whether they were commonable. These drifts were made at certain times in the year by the officers of the forest, when all cattle were driven into some pound or place inclosed, for the before mentioned purposes, and also to discover whether any cattle of strangers be there, which ought not to common.

Drift-stuff. This term signifies, not goods which are the subject of salvage, but matters floating at random, without any known or discoverable ownership, which, if cast ashore, will probably never be reclaimed, but will, as a matter of course, accrue to the riparian proprietor.

Drinking-shop. A place where intoxicating liquors are sold to be drunk on the premises; a bar or saloon.

Drip. A species of easement or servitude obligating one man to permit the water falling from another man's house to fall upon his own land.

Drive-it-yourself cars. A term used to describe automobiles which their owners, as a regular business, rent out for hire without furnishing drivers. More commonly termed "rental" or "leased" cars.

Driver. A person actually doing driving, whether employed by owner to drive or driving his own vehicle.

Driver's license. The certificate or license issued by a state which authorizes a person to operate a motor vehicle. Generally, a written and driving examination is required for obtaining such.

Driving. To urge forward under guidance, compel to go in a particular direction, urge onward, and direct the course of.

Driving while intoxicated (DWI). An offense committed by one who operates a motor vehicle while under the influence of intoxicating liquor or drugs. A showing of complete intoxication is not required. State statutes specify levels of blood alcohol content at which a person is presumed to be under the influence of intoxicating liquor. See **Consent** (*Implied consent*); **Drunk-o-meter.**

Drofland /drówflənd/. In old English law, a quit rent, or yearly payment, formerly made by some tenants to the king, or their landlords, for *driving* their cattle through a manor to fairs or markets.

Droit Fr. /dr(w)ó, Engl. /dróyt/. In French law, right, justice, equity, law, the whole body of law; also a right.

This term exhibits the same ambiguity which is discoverable in the German equivalent, *"recht"* and the English word *"right."* On the one hand, these terms answer to the Roman *"jus,"* and thus indicate law in the abstract, considered as the foundation of all rights, or the complex of underlying moral principles which impart the character of justice to all positive law, or give it an ethical content. Taken in this abstract sense, the terms may be adjectives, in which case they are equivalent to "just," or nouns, in which case they may be paraphrased by the expressions "justice," "morality," or "equity." On the other hand, they serve to point out *a* right; that is, a power, privilege, faculty, or demand, inherent in one person, and incident upon another. In the latter signification, *droit* (or *recht* or *right*) is the correlative of "duty" or "obligation." In the former sense, it may be considered as opposed to wrong, injustice, or the absence of law. *Droit* has the further ambiguity that it is sometimes used to denote the existing body of law considered as one whole, or the sum total of a number of individual laws taken together. See **Jus; Recht; Right.**

A person was said to have *droit droit, plurimum juris,* and *plurimum possessionis,* when he had the freehold, the fee, and the property in him.

In old English law, law; right; a writ of right.

Autre droit. The right of another.

Droit-close /dròyt klóws/. An ancient writ, directed to the lord of ancient demesne on behalf of those of his tenants who held their lands and tenements by charter in fee-simple, in fee-tail, for life, or in dower.

Droit common /dròyt kómən/. The common law.

Droit coutumier /drwó kùwtyuwmyéy/. Common law.

Droit d'accession /drwó daksèsyówn/. That property which is acquired by making a new species out of the material of another. It is equivalent to the Roman *"specificatio."*

Droit d'accroissement /drwó dakr(o)wàsmón/. The right which an heir or legatee has of combining with his own interest in a succession the interest of a coheir or colegatee who either refuses to or cannot accept his interest.

Droit d'aubaine /drwó dowbé(y)n/. A rule by which all the property of a deceased foreigner, whether movable or immovable, was confiscated to the use of the state, to the exclusion of his heirs, whether claiming *ab intestato* or under a will of the deceased. Finally abolished in 1819.

Droit de bris /drwó dəbríy/. A right formerly claimed by the lords of the coasts of certain parts of France, to shipwrecks, by which not only the property, but the persons of those who were cast away, were confiscated for the prince who was lord of the coast. Otherwise called *"droit de bris sur le naufrage."* This right prevailed chiefly in Bretagne, and was solemnly abrogated by Henry III as duke of Normandy, Aquitaine, and Guienne, in a charter granted A.D. 1226, preserved among the rolls at Bordeaux.

Droit de détraction /drwó də dèytraksyówn/. A tax upon the removal from one state or country to another of property acquired by succession or testamentary disposition; it does not cover a tax upon the succession to or transfer of property. *Cf.* Duties of detraction.

Droit de garde /drwó də gárd/. In French feudal law, right of ward. The guardianship of the estate and person of a noble vassal, to which the king, during his minority, was entitled.

Droit de gîte /drwó də zhíyt/. In French feudal law, the duty incumbent on a *roturier,* holding lands within the royal domain, of supplying board and lodging to the king and to his suite while on a royal progress.

Droit de greffe /drwó də gréf/. In old French law, the right of selling various offices connected with the custody of judicial records or notarial acts. A privilege of the French kings.

Droit de maîtrise drwó d(ə) meytríyz/. In old French law, a charge payable to the crown by any one who, after having served his apprenticeship in any commercial guild or brotherhood, sought to become a master workman in it on his own account.

Droit de naufrage /drwó d(ə) nowfrázh/. The right of a seigneur, who owns the seashore, or the king, when a vessel is wrecked, to take possession of the wreckage and to kill the crew or sell them as slaves.

Droit de prise /drwó d(ə) príyz/. In French feudal law, the duty (incumbent on a *roturier*) of supplying to the king on credit, during a certain period, such articles of domestic consumption as might be required for the royal household.

Droit de quint /drwó də kǽn(t)/. In French feudal law, a relief payable by a noble vassal to the king as his *seigneur*, on every change in the ownership of his fief.

Droit de suite /drwó də swíyt/. The right of a creditor to pursue the debtor's property into the hands of third persons for the enforcement of his claim.

Droit d'exécution /drwó dèkseykyùwsyówn/. The right of a stockbroker to sell the securities bought by him for account of a client, if the latter does not accept delivery thereof. The same expression is also applied to the sale by a stockbroker of securities deposited with him by his client, in order to guaranty the payment of operations for which the latter has given instructions.

Droit-droit. A double right; that is, the right of possession and the right of property. These two rights were, by the theory of our ancient law, distinct; and the above phrase was used to indicate the concurrence of both in one person, which concurrence was necessary to constitute a complete title to land.

Droit écrit /drwót eykríy/. In French law, the written law. The Roman civil law, or *Corpus Juris Civilis.*

Droit international /drwót ænternàsyownál/. International law.

Droit maritime /drwó màriytíym/. Maritime law.

Droit naturel /drwó natyurél/. The law of nature.

Droit ne done pluis que soit demaunde /drwó nə dón pwíy kə swó dèymondéy/. The law gives not more than is demanded.

Droit ne poet pas morier /drwó nə pyúw pà mouríy/. Right cannot die.

Droits civils /drwó sivíl/. This phrase in French law denotes private rights, the exercise of which is independent of the *status (qualité)* of citizen. Foreigners enjoy them; and the extent of that enjoyment is determined by the principle of reciprocity. Conversely, foreigners may be sued on contracts made by them in France.

Droits of admiralty /dróyts əv ǽdmərəltiy/. Rights or perquisites of the admiralty. A term applied to goods found derelict at sea. Applied also to property captured in time of war by non-commissioned vessels of a belligerent nation. In England, it has been usual in maritime wars for the government to seize and condemn, as droits of admiralty, the property of an enemy found in her ports at the breaking out of hostilities. The power to exercise such a right has not been delegated to, nor has it ever been claimed by, the United States government.

Droitural /dróychərəl/. What belongs of right; relating to right; as real actions are either droitural or possessory,—*droitural* when the plaintiff seeks to recover the property.

Dromones, dromos, dromunda /drəmówniyz, drówmowz, drəmándə/. These were at first high ships of great burden, but afterwards those which we now call "men-of-war."

Drop. In English practice, when the members of a court are equally divided on the argument showing cause against a rule *nisi*, no order is made, *i.e.,* the rule is neither discharged nor made absolute, and the rule is said to *drop.* In practice, there being a right to appeal, it has been usual to make an order in one way, the junior judge withdrawing his judgment.

Drop-letter. A letter addressed for delivery in the same city or district in which it is posted.

Drop shipment delivery. Shipment of goods directly from manufacturer to dealer or consumer rather than first to wholesaler, though wholesaler still earns profit because he took order for such.

Drop shipper. Type of wholesaler described above.

Drove. A number of animals collected and driven together in a body; a flock or herd of cattle in process of being driven, indefinite as to number, but including at least several.

Drover's pass. A free pass given by a railroad company, accepting a drove of cattle for transportation, to the drover who accompanies and cares for the cattle on the train.

Drug. An article intended for use in the diagnosis, cure, mitigation, treatment, or prevention of disease in man or other animals and any article other than food intended to affect the structure or any function of the body of man or other animals. 21 U.S.C.A. § 321(g)(1). The general name of substances used in medicine; any substance, vegetable, animal, or mineral, used in the composition or preparation of medicines; any substance used as a medicine. See **Controlled Substance Acts.**

Drug abuse. State of chronic or periodic intoxication detrimental to the individual and to society, produced by the repeated consumption of a drug, natural or synthetic. See also **Drug dependence.**

The voluntary, habitual, and excessive use of drugs is a ground for divorce in many states.

Drug addict. A person subject to drug abuse. See **Drug abuse; Drug dependence.**

Drug dependence. Habituation to, abuse of, and/or addiction to a chemical substance.

Druggist. A dealer in drugs; one whose business is to mix, compound, dispense, and sell drugs.

Drugless healer. Any person who practises or holds himself out in any way as practising the treatment of any ailment, disease, defect, or disability of the human body by manipulation, adjustment, manual or electrotherapy, or by any similar method. State v. Houck, 32 Wash.2d 681, 203 P.2d 693, 699. See **Chiropractor.**

Drummer. A term applied to commercial agents who travel for wholesale merchants and supply the retail trade with goods or take orders for goods to be shipped to the retail dealer. Term most commonly refers to traveling salesmen. See also **Commercial traveler.**

Drungarius /dràŋgériyəs/. In old European law, the commander of a *drungus*, or band of soldiers. Applied also to a naval commander.

Drungus /dráŋgəs/. In old European law, a band of soldiers (*globus militum*).

Drunk. Intoxicated. A person is "drunk" when he is so far under the influence of liquor that his passions are visibly excited or his judgment impaired, or when his brain is so far affected by liquor that his intelligence, sense-perceptions, judgment, continuity of thought or of ideas, speech, and coordination of volition with muscular action (or some of these faculties or processes) are impaired or not under normal control.

Drunkard. One who is habitually intoxicated. A "common" drunkard is defined by statute in some states as a person who has been convicted of drunkenness (or proved to have been drunk) a certain number of times within a limited period. Elsewhere the word "common" in this connection is understood as being equivalent to "habitual."

Drunkenness. State of intoxication. The condition of a person whose mind is affected by the consumption of intoxicating drinks; the state of one who is "drunk." The effect produced upon the mind or body by drinking intoxicating liquors to such an extent that the normal condition of the subject is changed and his capacity for rational action and conduct is substantially lessened. See also **Driving while intoxicated; Intoxication.**

While some states have decriminalized public drunkenness (*e.g.* Mass.), there is no constitutional infirmity in a criminal statute which penalizes being drunk in public. Powell v. Texas, 392 U.S. 514, 88 S.Ct. 2145, 20 L.Ed.2d 1254.

Drunk-o-meter. Device used for measuring blood alcohol content by chemical analysis of the breath. The results of such tests are generally used in prosecutions for drunk driving or operating a vehicle under the influence of liquor. See **Consent** (*Implied consent*); **Driving while intoxicated.**

Dry, *adj.* In the vernacular, this term means desiccated or free from moisture; but, in legal use, it signifies formal or nominal, without imposing any duty or responsibility, or unfruitful, without bringing any profit or advantage; *e.g.* dry trust.

Dry, *n.* Term used to designate a person who is opposed to allowing the sale of intoxicating liquors; a prohibitionist, in contradistinction to a "wet," or anti-prohibitionist.

Dry check. Synonymous with "cold check", and "hot check". Elder v. Evatt, Tex.Civ.App., 154 S.W.2d 684, 685.

Dry-cræft. Witchcraft; magic.

Dry exchange. In English law, a term formerly in use, said to have been invented for the purpose of disguising and covering usury; something being pretended to pass on both sides, whereas, in truth, nothing passed but on one side, in which respect it was called "dry."

Dry hole clause. Provision in gas or oil well lease dealing with payment of rent in event of drilling a dry hole. Sunac Petroleum Corp. v. Parkes, Tex., 416 S.W.2d 798.

Dry mortgage. One which creates a lien on land for the payment of money, but does not impose any personal liability upon the mortgagor, collateral to or over and above the value of the premises.

Dry receivership. Receivership wherein there is no equity to be administered for general creditors, even if action is in statutory form.

Dry rent. Rent seck; a rent reserved without a clause of distress.

Dry state. State wherein sale of intoxicating liquors is prohibited.

Dry trust. A passive trust; one which requires no action on the part of the trustee beyond turning over money or property to the *cestui que trust.*

Dual business. Such business must show units of substantial separateness and completeness, such as might be maintained as an independent business and capable of producing profit in and of themselves.

Dual citizenship. Status of citizens of United States who reside within a state; *i.e.*, persons who are born or naturalized in the U.S. are citizens of the U.S. and the state wherein they reside.

Dual court system. Term descriptive of Federal and State court systems of United States.

Dual purpose doctrine. The dual purpose doctrine is that if the work of an employee creates a necessity for travel, he is in the course of his employment while doing that work even though at the same time he is serving some purpose of his own. Snowden v. Orscheln Bros. Truck Lines, Inc., Mo.App., 446 S.W.2d 494, 496. Doctrine is that injury during trip which serves both business and personal purpose is within course of employment if trip involves performance of service for employer which would have caused trip to be taken by someone even if it had not coincided with personal journey. Stoskin v. Board of Ed. of Montgomery County, 11 Md.App. 355, 274 A.2d 397, 400.

Duarchy /d(y)úwàrkiy/. A form of government where two reign jointly.

Duas uxores eodem tempore habere non licet /d(y)úwəs əksóriyz iyówdəm témpəriy həbíriy nòn láysət/. It is not lawful to have two wives at the same time. 1 Bl.Comm. 436.

Dubitante /d(y)ùwbətǽntiy/. Doubting. Term is affixed to the name of a judge, in the reports, to signify that he doubted the decision rendered.

Dubitatur /d(y)ùwbətéydər/. It is doubted. A word frequently used in the reports to indicate that a point is considered doubtful.

Dubitavit /d(y)ùwbətéyvət/. Doubted.

Ducat /də́kət/. A foreign coin, varying in value in different countries.

Ducatus /dəkéydəs/. In feudal and old English law, a duchy, the dignity or territory of a duke.

Duces tecum /d(y)úwsiyz tíykəm/. (Lat. Bring with you.) The name of certain species of writs, of which the *subpoena duces tecum* is the most usual, requiring a party who is summoned to appear in court to bring with him some document, piece of evidence, or other thing to be used or inspected by the court. See **Subpoena**.

Duces tecum licet languidus /d(y)úwsiyz tíykəm láysət lǽngwədəs/. (Bring with you, although sick.) In practice, an ancient writ, now obsolete, directed to the sheriff, upon a return that he could not bring his prisoner without danger of death, he being *adeo languidus* (so sick); whereupon the court granted a *habeas corpus* in the nature of a *duces tecum licet languidus*.

Duchy Court of Lancaster. A tribunal of special jurisdiction, held before the chancellor of the duchy, or his deputy, concerning all matters of equity relating to lands holden of the crown in right of the duchy of Lancaster; which is a thing very distinct from the county palatine (which has also its separate chancery, for sealing of writs, and the like), and comprises much territory which lies at a vast distance from it; as particularly a very large district surrounded by the city of Westminster. The proceedings in this court are the same as were those on the equity side of the court of chancery, so that it seems not to be a court of record; and, indeed, it has been holden that the court of chancery has a concurrent jurisdiction with the duchy court, and may take cognizance of the same causes. Although not formerly abolished, this court has not sat since 1835.

Duchy of Lancaster /də́chiy əv lǽŋkəstər/. Those lands which formerly belonged to the dukes of Lancaster, and now belong to the crown in right of the duchy. The duchy is distinct from the county palatine of Lancaster, and includes not only the county, but also much territory at a distance from it, especially the Savoy in London and some land near Westminster. 3 Bl.Comm. 78.

Ducking-stool. See **Castigatory**.

Ducroire /dyuwkrwóhr/. In French law, guaranty; equivalent to *del credere* (which see).

Due. Just; proper; regular; lawful; sufficient; reasonable, as in the phrases "due care," "due process of law," "due notice."

Owing; payable; justly owed. That which one contracts to pay or perform to another; that which law or justice requires to be paid or done.

Owed, or owing, as distinguished from payable. A debt is often said to be *due* from a person where he is the party owing it, or primarily bound to pay, whether the time for payment has or has not arrived. The same thing is true of the phrase "due and owing."

Payable. A bill or note is commonly said to be *due* when the time for payment of it has arrived.

The word "due" always imports a fixed and settled obligation or liability, but with reference to the time for its payment there is considerable ambiguity in the use of the term, the precise signification being determined in each case from the context. It may mean that the debt or claim in question is now (presently or immediately) matured and enforceable, or that it matured at some time in the past and yet remains unsatisfied, or that it is fixed and certain but the day appointed for its payment has not yet arrived. But commonly, and in the absence of any qualifying expressions, the word "due" is restricted to the first of these meanings, the second being expressed by the term "overdue," and the third by the word "payable."

Due and proper care. That degree of care which is required of one for prevention of the accident. See **Due care**.

Due and reasonable care. Care which reasonably prudent man would exercise under same or similar circumstances. See **Due care**.

Due bill. Written acknowledgment of a debt, or promise to pay. See **I.O.U.**

Due care. Just, proper, and sufficient care, so far as the circumstances demand it; the absence of negligence. That care which an ordinarily prudent person would have exercised under the same or similar circumstances. Strickland v. Hughes, 2 N.C.App. 395, 163 S.E.2d 24, 26. "Due care" is care proportioned to any given situation, its surroundings, peculiarities, and hazards. It may and often does require extraordinary care. "Due care," "reasonable care," and "ordinary care" are often used as convertible terms.

This term, as usually understood in cases where the gist of the action is the defendant's negligence, implies not only that a party has not been negligent or careless, but that he has been guilty of no violation of law in relation to the subject-matter or transaction which constitutes the cause of action.

Due compensation. For condemned land is the value of land taken and the damages, if any, which result to him as a consequence of the taking without considering either general benefits or injuries. See **Just compensation**.

Due consideration. To give such weight or significance to a particular factor as under the circumstances it seems to merit, and this involves discretion. United States ex rel. Maine Potato Growers & Shippers Ass'n v. Interstate Commerce Commission, 66 App. D.C. 398, 88 F.2d 780, 783. As regards sufficient consideration in contract law, see **Consideration**.

Due course holder. See **Holder in due course**.

Due course of law. This phrase is synonymous with "due process of law," or "the law of the land," and the general definition thereof is "law in its regular course of administration through courts of justice". See **Due process of law.**

Due date. In general, the particular day on or before which something must be done to comply with law or contractual obligation.

Due diligence. See **Diligence.**

Due influence. Influence obtained by persuasion and argument or by appeals to the affections. In re Chamberlain's Estate, Cal.App., 109 P.2d 449, 452. See also **Coercion; Duress.**

Duel. A duel is any combat with deadly weapons fought between two or more persons, by previous agreement or upon a previous quarrel.

Dueling. The fighting of two persons, one against the other, at an appointed time and place, upon a precedent quarrel. If death results, the crime is murder. It differs from an affray in this, that the latter occurs on a sudden quarrel, while the former is always the result of design.

Duellum /d(y)uwéləm/. The trial by battel or judicial combat. See **Battel.**

Due notice. Sufficient, legally prescribed notice. Notice reasonably intended, and with the likelihood of, reaching the particular person or public. No fixed rule can be established as to what shall constitute "due notice." "Due" is a relative term, and must be applied to each case in the exercise of the discretion of the court in view of the particular circumstances. See **Notice.**

Due posting. Stamping and placing letter in United States mail.

Due process clause. Two such clauses are found in the U.S. Constitution, one in the 5th Amendment pertaining to the federal government, the other in the 14th Amendment which protects persons from state actions. There are two aspects: procedural, in which a person is guaranteed fair procedures and substantive which protects a person's property from unfair governmental interference or taking. Similar clauses are in most state constitutions. See **Due process of law.**

Due process of law. Law in its regular course of administration through courts of justice. Due process of law in each particular case means such an exercise of the powers of the government as the settled maxims of law permit and sanction, and under such safeguards for the protection of individual rights as those maxims prescribe for the class of cases to which the one in question belongs. A course of legal proceedings according to those rules and principles which have been established in our systems of jurisprudence for the enforcement and protection of private rights. To give such proceedings any validity, there must be a tribunal competent by its constitution—that is, by the law of its creation—to pass upon the subject-matter of the suit; and, if that involves merely a determination of the personal liability of the defendant, he must be brought within its jurisdiction by service of process within the state, or his volun-

tary appearance. Pennoyer v. Neff, 95 U.S. 733, 24 L.Ed. 565. Due process of law implies the right of the person affected thereby to be present before the tribunal which pronounces judgment upon the question of life, liberty, or property, in its most comprehensive sense; to be heard, by testimony or otherwise, and to have the right of controverting, by proof, every material fact which bears on the question of right in the matter involved. If any question of fact or liability be conclusively presumed against him, this is not due process of law.

An orderly proceeding wherein a person is served with notice, actual or constructive, and has an opportunity to be heard and to enforce and protect his rights before a court having power to hear and determine the case. Kazubowski v. Kazubowski, 45 Ill.2d 405, 259 N.E.2d 282, 290. Phrase means that no person shall be deprived of life, liberty, property or of any right granted him by statute, unless matter involved first shall have been adjudicated against him upon trial conducted according to established rules regulating judicial proceedings, and it forbids condemnation without a hearing. Pettit v. Penn, La. App., 180 So.2d 66, 69. The concept of "due process of law" as it is embodied in Fifth Amendment demands that a law shall not be unreasonable, arbitrary, or capricious and that the means selected shall have a reasonable and substantial relation to the object being sought. U. S. v. Smith, D.C.Iowa, 249 F.Supp. 515, 516. Fundamental requisite of "due process" is the opportunity to be heard, to be aware that a matter is pending, to make an informed choice whether to acquiesce or contest, and to assert before the appropriate decision-making body the reasons for such choice. Trinity Episcopal Corp. v. Romney, D.C.N.Y., 387 F.Supp. 1044, 1084. Aside from all else, "due process" means fundamental fairness. Pinkerton v. Farr, W.Va., 220 S.E.2d 682, 687.

The essential elements of due process of law are notice and opportunity to be heard and to defend in orderly proceeding adapted to nature of case, and the guarantee of due process requires that every man have protection of day in court and benefit of general law. Di Maio v. Reid, 132 N.J.L. 17, 37 A.2d 829, 830. Daniel Webster defined this phrase to mean a law which hears before it condemns, which proceeds on inquiry and renders judgment only after trial. Wichita Council No. 120 of Security Ben. Ass'n v. Security Ben. Assn., 138 Kan. 841, 28 P.2d 976, 980; J. B. Barnes Drilling Co. v. Phillips, 166 Okl. 154, 26 P.2d 766. This constitutional guaranty demands only that law shall not be unreasonable, arbitrary, or capricious, and that means selected shall have real and substantial relation to object. Nebbia v. People of State of New York, N. Y., 291 U.S. 502, 54 S.Ct. 505, 78 L.Ed. 940; North American Co. v. Securities & Exchange Commission, C.C.A.2, 133 F.2d 148, 154.

See also **Procedural due process; Substantive due process.**

Due process rights. All rights which are of such fundamental importance as to require compliance with due process standards of fairness and justice.

Due proof. Within insurance policy requirements, term means such a statement of facts, reasonably verified, as, if established in court, would prima facie require payment of the claim, and does not mean some particular form of proof which the insurer arbitrarily demands. National Life Ins. Co. v. White, D.C.Mun. App., 38 A.2d 663, 666. Sufficient evidence to support or produce a conclusion; adequate evidence. See **Burden of proof; Proof.**

Due regard. Consideration in a degree appropriate to demands of the particular case. Willis v. Jonson, 279 Ky. 416, 130 S.W.2d 828, 832.

Dues. Certain payments; rates or taxes. As applied to clubs and other membership organizations, refers to sums paid toward support and maintenance of same and as a requisite to retain membership.

Due to. Expressions "sustained by," "caused by," "due to," "resulting from," "sustained by means of," "sustained in consequence of," and "sustained through" have been held to be synonymous. Federal Life Ins. Co. v. White, Tex., 23 S.W.2d 832, 834.

Duke. In English law, is a title of nobility, ranking immediately next to the Prince of Wales. It is only a title of dignity. Conferring it does not give any domain, territory, or jurisdiction over the place whence the title is taken. *Duchess,* the consort of a duke.

Duke of Exeter's Daughter. The name of a rack in the Tower, so called after a minister of Henry VI, who sought to introduce it into England.

Duke of York's Laws. A body of laws compiled in 1665 for the government of the colony of New York.

Dulocracy /d(y)ùwlókrəsiy/. A government where servants and slaves have so much license and privilege that they domineer.

Duly. In due or proper form or manner; according to legal requirements. Regularly; properly; suitable; upon a proper foundation, as distinguished from mere form; according to law in both form and substance. Welborn v. Whitney, 190 Okl. 630, 126 P.2d 263, 266; Cromwell v. Slaney, C.C.A.Mass., 65 F.2d 940, 941; Zechiel v. Firemen's Fund Ins. Co., C.C.A.Ind., 61 F.2d 27, 28. See **Due process of law.**

Duly ordained minister of religion. Person who has been ordained in accordance with the ceremonial, ritual, or discipline of a recognized church, religious sect, or religious organization, to teach and preach its doctrines and to administer its rites and ceremonies and public worship, and who customarily performs those duties. In re Rogers, D.C.Tex., 47 F.Supp. 265, 266.

Duly qualified. Being "duly qualified" to fill an office, in the constitutional sense and in the ordinary acceptation of the words, means that the officer shall possess every qualification; that he shall in all respects comply with every requisite before entering on duties of the office; and that he shall be bound by oath or affirmation to support the Constitution, and to perform the duties of the office with fidelity.

Dum /dám/. Lat. While; as long as; until; upon condition that; provided that.

Dumb-bidding. In sales at auction, when the minimum amount which the owner will take for the article is written on a piece of paper, and placed by the owner under an object, and it is agreed that no bidding shall

avail unless equal to that, this is called "dumb-bidding."

Dum bene se gesserit /dəm bíyniy sìy jésərət/. While he shall conduct himself well; during good behavior. Expressive of a tenure of office not dependent upon the pleasure of the appointing power, nor for a limited period, but terminable only upon the death or misconduct of the incumbent.

Dum fervet opus /dəm fə́rvəd ówpəs/. While the work glows; in the heat of action.

Dum fuit infra ætatem /dəm fyúwəd ínfrə ìytéydəm/. (While he was within age.) In old English practice, a writ of entry which formerly lay for an infant after he had attained his full age, to recover lands which he had aliened in fee, in tail, or for life, during his infancy; and, after his death, his heir had the same remedy.

Dum fuit in prisona /dəm fyúwəd in prízənə/. In old English law, a writ which lay for a man who had aliened lands under duress by imprisonment, to restore to him his proper estates. Abolished by St. 3 & 4 Wm. IV, c. 27.

Dummodo /dəmówdow/. Provided; provided that. A word of limitation in the Latin forms of conveyances, of frequent use in introducing a reservation; as in reserving a rent.

Dummy, n. One who purchases property and holds legal title for another, usually to conceal the identity of the true owner; a straw man. Space 6⅓ feet in width between street railroad tracks.

Dummy, adj. Sham; make-believe; pretended; imitation. Person who serves in place of another, or who serves until the proper person is named or available to take his place (*e.g.* dummy corporate directors; dummy owners of real estate).

Dummy corporation. Corporation formed for sham purposes and not for conduct of legitimate business; *e.g.* formed for sole reason of avoiding personal liability.

Dummy director. One to whom (usually) a single share of stock in a corporation is transferred for the purpose of qualifying him as a director of the corporation, in which he has no real or active interest. One who is a mere figurehead and in effect discharges no duties.

Dummy stockholder. One who holds shares of stock in his name for the benefit of the true owner whose name is generally concealed. See also **Streetname.**

Dum non fuit compos mentis /də́m nòn fyúwət kómpəs méntəs/. In old English law, the name of a writ which the heirs of a person who was *non compos mentis,* and who aliened his lands, might have sued out to restore him to his rights. Abolished by 3 & 4 Wm. IV, c. 27.

Dump. To put or throw down with more or less of violence; to unload. To drop down; to deposit something in a heap or unshaped mass. To sell abroad at less than price sold at home. See **Dumping Act.**

Dumping. The act of selling in quantity at a very low price or practically regardless of the price; also, selling goods abroad at less than the market price at home. See **Dumping Act.**

The act of forcing a product such as cotton on the market during the short gathering season.

Dumping Act. Federal law which provides that the Secretary of Treasury is required to notify U.S. Tariff Commission whenever he determines that foreign merchandise is being or is likely to be sold in U.S. or elsewhere at less than its fair value and Tariff Commission shall determine the injury to U.S. industry. If such imports are determined to be injurious to domestic sales of like products, such imports may be ordered stopped. 19 U.S.C.A. § 160.

Dum recens fuit maleficium /də̀m ríysèn(d)z fyúwət mǽləfísh(iy)əm/. While the offense was fresh. A term employed in the old law of appeal of rape.

Dum sola /də̀m sówlə/. While sole, or single. *Dum sola fuerit,* while she shall remain sole. *Dum sola et casta vixerit,* while she lives single and chaste. Words of limitation in old conveyances. Also applied generally to an unmarried woman in connection with something that was or might be done during that condition.

Dun. A demand for payment (*e.g.* dun letter) to a delinquent debtor.

Dungeon. Such an underground prison or cell as was formerly placed in the strongest part of a fortress. A dark or subterraneous prison.

Dunio. A double; a kind of base coin less than a farthing.

Dunnage. Pieces of wood placed against the sides and bottom of the hold of a vessel, to preserve the cargo from the effect of leakage, according to its nature and quality. There is considerable resemblance between dunnage and ballast. The latter is used for trimming the ship, and bringing it down to a draft of water proper and safe for sailing. Dunnage is placed under the cargo to keep it from being wetted by water getting into the hold, or between the different parcels to keep them from bruising and injuring each other. Padding in shipping container to prevent breakage.

Duodecemvirale judicium /d(y)ùwowdèsəmvəréyliy juwdísh(iy)əm/. The trial by twelve men, or by jury. Applied to juries *de medietate linguæ.*

Duodecima manus /d(y)ùwowdésəmə mǽnəs/. Twelve hands. The oaths of twelve men, including himself, by whom the defendant was allowed to make his law. 3 Bl.Comm. 343.

Duodena /d(y)uwədíynə/. In old records, a jury of twelve men.

Duodena manu /d(y)uwədíynə mǽn(y)uw/. A dozen hands, *i.e.,* twelve witnesses to purge a criminal of an offense.

Duo non possunt in solido unam rem possidere /d(y)úwow nòn pósənt in sólədow yúwnəm rém pòsədíriy/. Two cannot possess one thing in entirety.

Duopoly /d(y)uwópəliy/. A condition in the market in which there are only two producers or sellers of a given product.

Duorum in solidum dominium vel possessio esse non potest /d(y)uwórəm in sólədəm dəmíniyəm vèl pəzésh(iy)ow ésiy nòn pówdəst/. Ownership or possession in entirety cannot be in two persons of the same thing.

Duosony /d(y)uwósəniy/. A condition of the market in which there are only two buyers of a given product.

Duo sunt instrumenta ad omnes res aut confirmandas aut impugnandas, ratio et authoritas /dyúwow sə̀nt instrəméntə ǽd ómniyz ríyz òt kònfərmǽndəs òt impəgnǽndəs, réysh(iy)ow èt oθóhrətǽs/. There are two instruments for confirming or impugning all things,—reason and authority.

Dupla /d(y)úwplə/. In the civil law, double the price of a thing.

Duplex house. A dwelling which has accommodations for two families, without regard to whether such accommodations are identical or not. The units may be either adjacent to each other or on separate floors.

Duplex querela /d(y)úwplèks kwəríylə/. A double complaint. An ecclesiastical proceeding, which is in the nature of an appeal. See **Double complaint.**

Duplex valor maritagii /d(y)úwplèks vǽlər mǽrətéyjiyay/. In old English law, double the value of the marriage. While an infant was in ward, the guardian had the power of tendering him or her a suitable match, without disparagement, which if the infants refused, they forfeited the value of the marriage to their guardian, that is, so much as a jury would assess or any one would give to the guardian for such an alliance; and, if the infants married themselves without the guardian's consent, they forfeited double the value of the marriage. 2 Bl.Comm. 70.

Duplicate, *v.* To douple, repeat, copy, make, or add a thing exactly like a preceding one; reproduce exactly.

Duplicate, *n.* A "duplicate" is a counterpart produced by the same impression as the original, or from the same matrix, or by means of photography, including enlargements and miniatures, or by mechanical or electronic re-recording, or by chemical reproduction, or by other equivalent techniques which accurately reproduces the original. Fed.R.Evid. 1001.

That which exactly resembles or corresponds to something else; another, correspondent to the first; hence, a copy; transcript; counterpart; an original instrument repeated; a document the same as another in essential particulars. The term is also frequently used to signify a new original, made to take the place of an instrument that has been lost or destroyed, and to have the same force and effect. See also **Copy.**

In England, the ticket given by a pawnbroker to the pawner of a chattel.

Duplicate taxation. See **Double taxation.**

Duplicate will. A term used where a testator executes two copies of his will, one to keep himself, and the other to be deposited with another person. Upon application for probate of a duplicate will, both copies must be deposited in the registry of the court of probate. The execution of duplicate wills is undesirable because if the testator desires to revoke his will, he must be careful to comply with the laws of revocation as to both wills. See also **Reciprocal wills.**

Duplicatio /d(y)ùwpləkéysh(iy)ow/. In the civil law, the defendant's answer to the plaintiff's replication; corresponding to the rejoinder of the common law.

Duplicationem possibilitatis lex non patitur /d(y)ùwpləkèyshiyównəm pòsəbìlətéydəs léks nòn tólədər/. The law does not allow the doubling of a possibility.

Duplicatum jus /d(y)ùwpləkéydəm jás/. Double right.

Duplicitous /d(y)ùwplísədəs/. A pleading which joins in one and the same count different grounds of action of different nature, or of the same nature, to enforce a single right to recovery, or which is based on different theories of the defendant's liability. Such duplicity was not permitted in common law pleading, but is allowed under Rule of Civil Procedure 8(e). In an information, the joinder of separate and distinct offenses in one and the same count. State v. Seward, 163 Kan. 136, 181 P.2d 478, 480. See **Duplicity.**

Duplicitous appeal. Appeal from two separate judgments or from judgment and order or from two independent orders, both of which are appealable. City of Duncan v. Abrams, 171 Okl. 619, 43 P.2d 720, 723.

Duplicity. The technical fault in common law pleading of uniting two or more causes of action in one count in a writ, or two or more grounds of defense in one plea, or two or more breaches in a replication, or two or more offenses in the same count of an indictment, or two or more incongruous subjects in one legislative act, or two or more controverted ultimate issues submitted in a single special issue. Such duplicity of pleading in civil actions is permitted under Rule of Civil Procedure 8(e).

Rule of "duplicity" prohibits the simultaneous charging of several distinct, unrelated crimes in one indictment. Mechling v. Stayton, D.C.Va., 361 F.Supp. 770, 772.

Deliberate deception or double dealing.

Dupuytren's contraction. A pathological condition involving the palmar fascia of the hands.

Durable leases. Leases reserving a rent payable annually, with right of re-entry for nonpayment of the same, and for the term "as long as grass grows or water runs," or equivalent terms.

Dura mater /d(y)úrə méydər/. The tough, membranous, outer covering of the brain and spinal cord.

Durante /d(y)ərǽntiy/. Lat. During. A word of limitation in old conveyances.

Durante absentia /d(y)ərǽntiy əbsénsh(iy)ə/. During absence. In some jurisdictions, administration of a decedent's estate is said to be granted *durante absentia* in cases where the absence of the proper proponents of the will, or of an executor, delays or imperils the settlement of the estate.

Durante bene placito /d(y)ərǽntiy bíyniy plǽsədow/. During good pleasure. The ancient tenure of English judges was *durante bene placito.* 1 Bl.Comm. 267, 342.

Durante minore ætate /d(y)ərǽntiy mənóriy iytéydiy/. During minority. 2 Bl.Comm. 503. Words taken from the old form of letters of administration.

Durante viduitate /d(y)ərǽntiy vəjùwətéydiy/. During widowhood. 2 Bl.Comm. 124. *Durante casta viduitate,* during chaste widowhood.

Durante virginitate /d(y)ərǽntiy vərjìnətéydiy/. During virginity (so long as she remains unmarried).

Durante vita /d(y)ərǽntiy váydə/. During life.

Duration. Extent, limit or time. The portion of time during which anything exists.

Interest. The period of time during which an interest in property lasts.

Trust. The period of time during which a trust exists before its termination.

Duress. Duress consists in any illegal imprisonment, or legal imprisonment used for an illegal purpose, or threats of bodily or other harm, or other means amounting to or tending to coerce the will of another, and actually inducing him to do an act contrary to his free will. Heider v. Unicume, 142 Or. 410, 20 P.2d 384, 385. Duress may also include the same injuries, threats, or restraint exercised upon the man's wife, child, or parent. Distinguishable from undue influence because in the latter, the wrongdoer is generally in a fiduciary capacity or in a position of trust and confidence with respect to the victim of the undue influence.

A condition where one is induced by wrongful act or threat of another to make contract under circumstances which deprive him of exercise of his free will. Hyde v. Lewis, 25 Ill.App.3d 495, 323 N.E.2d 533, 537. Includes any conduct which overpowers will and coerces or constrains performance of an act which otherwise would not have been performed. Williams v. Rentz Banking Co., 112 Ga.App. 384, 145 S.E.2d 256, 258.

As a defense to a civil action, it must be pleaded affirmatively. Fed.R.Civil P. 8(c).

One who, under the pressure of an unlawful threat from another human being to harm him (or to harm a third person), commits what would otherwise be a crime may, under some circumstances, be justified in doing what he did and thus not be guilty of the crime in question.

See also **Coercion; Extortion; Undue influence.**

Duress of goods. Where the act consists of a tortious seizure or detention of property from the person entitled to it, and requires some act as a condition for its surrender, the act is "duress of goods". Sistrom v. Anderson, 51 Cal.App.2d 213, 124 P.2d 372, 376.

Duress of imprisonment. The wrongful imprisonment of a person, or the illegal restraint of his liberty, in order to compel him to do some act. 1 Bl.Comm. 130, 131, 136, 137.

Duressor /d(y)ərésər/. One who subjects another to duress; one who compels another to do a thing, as by menace.

Duress per minas /d(y)ərés pàr máynəs/. Duress by threats. The use of threats and menaces to compel a person, by the fear of death, or grievous bodily harm, as mayhem or loss of limb, to do some lawful act, or to commit a misdemeanor. 1 Bl.Comm. 130; 4 Bl. Comm. 30. See **Metus.**

Durham /də́hrəm/. A county palatine in England, the jurisdiction of which was vested in the Bishop of Durham until the statute 6 & 7 Wm. IV, c. 19 vested it as a separate franchise and royalty in the crown. The jurisdiction of the Durham Court of Pleas was transferred to the Supreme Court of Judicature by the Judicature Act of 1873.

Durham rule. The irresistible impulse test of criminal responsibility. The rule states that when there is some evidence that the accused suffered from a diseased or defective mental condition at the time the unlawful act was committed the accused is not criminally responsible if it is found beyond a reasonable doubt that the act was the product of such mental abnormality. Durham v. United States, C.A.D.C., 214 F.2d 862, 875.

Under the Durham Rule, to find a defendant not guilty by reason of insanity or mental irresponsibility, the jury must find (1) that he was suffering from a diseased (or defective) mental condition at the time of the commission of the act charged and (2) that there was a causal relation between such disease or defective condition and the act. State v. Jones, 84 Wash.2d 823, 529 P.2d 1040, 1044.

See also **Insanity.**

During. Throughout the course of; throughout the continuance of; in the time of; after the commencement and before the expiration of. Continental Bank & Trust Co. of N. Y. v. Chemical Bank & Trust Co., 51 N.Y.S.2d 903, 909.

During good behavior. While defendant, whose sentence had been suspended, was obedient to the state law.

During the hours of service. Working-hours plus reasonable periods for ingress and egress. See also **Course of employment.**

During the trial. Period beginning with swearing of jury and ending with rendition of verdict. Period commencing with presentation of indictment by grand jury to court and terminating with final judgment.

Dustuck /dʌ́stək/. A term used in Hindostan for a passport, permit, or order from the English East Indian Company. It generally meant a permit under their seal exempting goods from the payment of duties.

Dutch auction. See **Auction.**

Dutch lottery. Also known as the "class lottery." As distinguished from the "Genoese lottery" (q.v.), it is a scheme in which the number and value of the prizes are regularly estimated, all the ticket holders are interested at once in the play, and chance determines whether a prize or a blank falls to a given number.

Duties. In its most usual signification this word is the synonym of imposts or customs; i.e. tax on imports; but it is sometimes used in a broader sense, as including all manner of taxes, charges, or governmental impositions. See also **Customs; Most favored nation clause; Tariff; Toll; Tonnage duty.**

Duties of detraction. Taxes levied upon the removal from one state to another of property acquired by succession or testamentary disposition. Fredrickson v. Louisiana, 23 How. 445, 16 L.Ed. 577; In re Strobel's Estate, 5 App.Div. 621, 39 N.Y.S. 169. Cf. **Droit de détraction.**

Duties on imports /d(y)úwdiyz òn ímpòrts/. This term signifies not merely a duty on the act of importation, but a duty on the thing imported. It is not confined to a duty levied while the article is entering the country, but extends to a duty levied after it has entered the country.

Duty. A human action which is exactly conformable to the laws which require us to obey them. Legal or moral obligation. Obligatory conduct or service. Mandatory obligation to perform. Huey v. King, 220 Tenn. 189, 415 S.W.2d 136. See also **Obligation.**

A thing due; that which is due from a person; that which a person owes to another. An obligation to do a thing. A word of more extensive signification than "debt," although both are expressed by the same Latin word "debitum." Sometimes, however, the term is used synonymously with debt.

Those obligations of performance, care, or observance which rest upon a person in an official or fiduciary capacity; as the duty of an executor, trustee, manager, etc.

In negligence cases term may be defined as obligation, to which law will give recognition and effect, to conform to particular standard of conduct toward another. Rasmussen v. Prudential Ins. Co., 277 Minn. 266, 152 N.W.2d 359, 362. The word "duty" is used throughout the Restatement of Torts to denote the fact that the actor is required to conduct himself in a particular manner at the risk that if he does not do so he becomes subject to liability to another to whom the duty is owed for any injury sustained by such other, of which that actor's conduct is a legal cause. Restatement, Second, Torts § 4. See **Care;**

Due care.

In its use in jurisprudence, this word is the correlative of right. Thus, wherever there exists a right in any person, there also rests a corresponding duty upon some other person or upon all persons generally.

It also denotes a tax or impost due to the government upon the importation or exportation of goods. See also **Customs; Tariff; Toll; Tonnage duty.**

See also **Legal duty; Obligation.**

Judicial duty. See **Judicial.**

Duty of tonnage. A charge upon a vessel as an instrument of commerce for entering, lying in or leaving a port, and includes all taxes and duties, regardless of name or form. Marine Lighterage Corporation v. Luckenbach S. S. Co., 139 Misc. 612, 248 N.Y.S. 71, 72.

Duty of water. Such a quantity of water necessary when economically conducted and applied to land without unnecessary loss as will result in the successful growing of crops.

Duty to act. Obligation to take some action to prevent harm to another and for failure of which there may or may not be liability in tort depending upon the circumstances and the relationship of the parties to each other. See **Emergency doctrine; Humanitarian doctrine.**

Duumviri /d(y)uwə́mvərày/. (From *duo,* two, and *viri,* men.) A general appellation among the ancient Romans, given to any magistrates elected in pairs to fill any office, or perform any function.

Duumviri municipales were two annual magistrates in the towns and colonies, having judicial powers.

Duumviri navales were officers appointed to man, equip, and refit the navy.

Dux /də́ks/. A military governor of a province. A military officer having charge of the borders or frontiers of the empire, called *"dux limitis."* At this period, the word began to be used as a title of honor or dignity.

In Roman law, a leader or military commander. The commander of an army.

In feudal and old European law, duke; a title of honor, or order of nobility. 1 Bl.Comm. 397.

Dwell. To have an abode; to reside; to inhabit; to live in a place. More than mere physical presence is sometimes required. It must be in conformity with law. Kaplan v. Tod, 267 U.S. 228, 45 S.Ct. 257, 69 L.Ed. 585. To delay, to pause or linger. To abide as a permanent residence or for a time. Term is synonymous with inhabit, live, sojourn, reside, stay, rest. See also **Domicile; Residence.**

Dwelling. The house or other structure in which a person or persons live; a residence; abode; habitation; the apartment or building, or group of buildings, occupied by a family as a place of residence. Structure used as place of habitation.

In conveyancing, includes all buildings attached to or connected with the house. In criminal law (*e.g.* burglary), means a building or portion thereof, a tent, a vehicle or other enclosed space which is used or intended for use as a human habitation, home or residence.

Dwelling defense. In most jurisdictions, a person in his dwelling is permitted to use even deadly force to protect himself, his household and the house itself from attack on the principle that a person's house is his castle. State v. Couch, 52 N.M. 127, 193 P.2d 405.

D.W.I. In genealogical tables, a common abbreviation for "died without issue." Also, abbreviation for offense of "driving while intoxicated *(q.v.)*."

Dyer Act. National Motor Vehicle Theft Act (1919) which makes it a criminal offense to transport a stolen motor vehicle in interstate or foreign commerce knowing it to be stolen or to receive or conceal such a motor vehicle in interstate or foreign commerce knowing it to be stolen, though knowledge of its interstate transportation is not essential to guilt. Odom v. U. S., C.A.Fla., 377 F.2d 853. 18 U.S.C.A. § 2312.

Dying declaration. See **Declaration.**

Dying without issue. Dying without a child either before or after the decedent's death. At common law this phrase imports an indefinite failure of issue, and not a dying without issue surviving at the time of the death of the first taker. But this rule has been changed in many decisions, with many states having held that the expression "dying without issue," and like expressions, have reference to the time of the death of the party, and not to an indefinite failure of issue. See also **Failure of issue.**

Dying without children imports not a failure of issue at any indefinite future period, but a leaving no children at the death of the legatee. The law favors vesting of estates, and limitation such as "dying without issue," refers to a definite period, fixed in will, rather than to an indefinite failure of issue. Where context is such as to show clearly that testator intended the phrase "die without issue" to mean that, if first taker die without issue during life of testator, the second taker shall stand in his place and prevent a lapse, the words "die without issue" are taken to mean death during life of testator. Martin v. Raff, 114 Ind.App. 507, 52 N.E.2d 839, 845.

Dynamite instruction. Further instruction given by the trial judge to jury when the jury have reported an inability to agree on a verdict in a criminal case. In the further instructions, the judge advises them of their obligation to consider the opinions of their fellow jurors and to yield their own views where possible. Allen v. United States, 164 U.S. 492, 17 S.Ct. 154, 41 L.Ed. 528. This type of jury instruction (also called "Allen charge") is prohibited in certain states; *e.g.* California, People v. Gainer, 19 Cal.3d 835, 566 P.2d 997, 139 Cal.Rptr. 861. See also **Allen charge.**

Dynasty /dáynəstiy/dínəstiy/. A succession of rules in the same line or family. Powerful and influential group or family which continues in existence for a considerable time.

Dysnomy /dísnəmy/. Bad legislation; the enactment of bad laws.

Dyspareunia /dìspərúwniyə/. Incapacity of a woman to sustain the act of sexual intercourse except with great difficulty and pain; anaphrodisia.

E

E. As an abbreviation, this letter may stand for "Exchequer," "English," "Edward," "Equity," "East," "Eastern," "Easter," or "Ecclesiastical." A Latin preposition, meaning from, out of, after, or according. It occurs in many Latin phrases; but (in this form) only before a consonant.

Ea. Sax. The water or river; also the mouth of a river on the shore between high and low water-mark.

Each. A distributive adjective pronoun, which denotes or refers to every one of the persons or things mentioned; every one of two or more persons or things, composing the whole, separately considered. The effect of this word, used in the covenants of a bond, is to create a several obligation. The word "any" is equivalent to "each." Conerty v. Richtsteig, 308 Ill. App. 321, 31 N.E.2d 351.

Eadem causa diversis rationibus coram judicibus ecclesiasticis et secularibus ventilatur /iyéydəm kózə dəvársəs ræshiyównəbəs kórəm juwdísəbəs əklìyziyǽstəsəs èt sèkyəlérəbəs vèntəléydər/. The same cause is argued upon different principles before ecclesiastical and secular judges.

Eadem est ratio, eadem est lex /iyéydəm èst réysh(iy)ow, iyéydəm èst léks/. The same reason, the same law.

Eadem mens præsumitur regis quæ est juris et quæ esse debet, præsertim in dubiis /iyéydəm mén(d)z prəz(y)úwmədər ríyjəs kwíy èst júrəs èt kwíy ésiy débət, prəzárdəm ìn d(y)úwbiyəs/. The mind of the sovereign is presumed to be coincident with that of the law, and with that which it ought to be, especially in ambiguous matters.

Ea est accipienda interpretatio, quæ vitio caret /íyə èst əksìpiyéndə intàrprətéysh(iy)ow kwìy vísh(iy)ow kǽrət/. That interpretation is to be received [or adopted] which is free from fault [or wrong]. The law will not intend a wrong.

Eagle. A gold coin of the United States of the value of ten dollars.

Ea intentione /íyə intènshiyówniy/. With that intent. Held not to make a condition, but a confidence and trust.

Ealder /éldər/, or **ealding** /éldiŋ/. In old Saxon law, an elder or chief.

Ealderman /éldərmən/, or **ealdorman** /óldərmən/. The name of a Saxon magistrate; alderman; analogous to *earl* among the Danes, and *senator* among the Romans. See **Alderman.**

Ealdor-biscop /éldərbìshəp/. An archbishop.

Ealdorburg /éldərbàrg/. Sax. The metropolis; the chief city. Obsolete.

Ealhorda /éylhòrdə/. Sax. The privilege of assising and selling beer. Obsolete.

Ea quæ, commendandi causa, in venditionibus dicuntur, si palam appareant, venditorem non obligant /íyə kwìy, kòməndǽnday kózə, ìn vendìshiyównəbəs dəkántər, sày pǽləm əpǽriyənt, vèndətórəm nòn óbləgənt/. Those things which are said on sales, in the way of commendation, if [the qualities of the thing sold] appear openly, do not bind the seller.

Ea quæ dari impossibilia sunt, vel quæ in rerum natura non sunt, pro non adjectis habentur /íyə kwìy déray impòsəbíliyə sònt, vèl kwìy in rírəm nətyúrə nòn sánt pròw nón əjéktəs həbéntər/. Those things which are impossible to be given, or which are not in the nature of things, are regarded as not added [as no part of an agreement].

Ea quæ in curia nostra rite acta sunt debitæ executioni demandari debent /íyə kwìy ìn kyúriyə nóstrə ráydiy ǽktə sònt débədiy èksəkyùwshiyównay dəmǽndéray débənt/. Those things which are properly transacted in our court ought to be committed to a due execution.

Ea quæ raro accidunt non temere in agendis negotiis computantur /íyə kwìy rérow ǽksədənt nòn təmíriy ìn əjéndəs nəgówshiyəs kòmpyətǽntər/. Those things which rarely happen are not to be taken into account in the transaction of business without sufficient reason.

Earl. A title of nobility, formerly the highest in England, now the third, ranking between a marquis and a viscount, and corresponding with the French *"comte"* and the German *"Graf."* The title originated with the Saxons, and is the most ancient of the English peerage. William the Conqueror first made this title hereditary, giving it in fee to his nobles; and allotting them for the support of their state the third penny out of the sheriff's court, issuing out of all pleas of the shire, whence they had their ancient title "shiremen." At present the title is accompanied by no territory, private or judicial rights, but merely confers nobility and an hereditary seat in the house of lords.

Earldom. The dignity or jurisdiction of an earl. The dignity only remains now, as the jurisdiction has been given over to the sheriff. 1 Bl.Comm. 339.

Earles-penny, or **earl's penny.** Money given in part payment. See **Earnest.**

Earlier maturity rule. The rule under which bonds first maturing are entitled to priority when sale of security is not sufficient to satisfy all obligations. Scherk v. Newton, C.C.A.Colo., 152 F.2d 747, 749.

Earl Marshal of England. A great officer of state who had anciently several courts under his jurisdiction, as the court of chivalry and the court of honor. Under him is the herald's office, or college of arms. He was also a judge of the Marshalsea court, now abolished. This office is of great antiquity, and has been for several ages hereditary in the family of the Howards. 3 Bl.Comm. 68, 103.

Ear-mark. A mark put upon a thing to distinguish it from another. Originally and literally, a mark upon the ear; a mode of marking sheep and other animals.

Property is said to be *ear-marked* when it can be identified or distinguished from other property of the same nature.

To set apart from others.

Money has no ear-mark, but it is an ordinary term for a privy mark made by any one on a coin.

Ear-mark rule. Rule that through the process of commingling money or deposit with the funds of a bank it loses its identity, with the resultant effect of defeating the right of preference over general creditors.

Earn. To acquire by labor, service or performance. Hartford Electric Light Co. v. McLaughlin, 131 Conn. 1, 37 A.2d 361, 363. To merit or deserve.

Earned income. Income (*e.g.* wages, salaries, or fees) derived from labor, professional service, or entrepreneurship as opposed to income derived from invested capital (*e.g.* rents, dividends, interest). The distinction, however, for tax purposes has lost much of its original importance. See also **Earnings; Income.**

Earned income credit. A refundable tax credit on earned income up to a certain amount for low income workers who maintain a household for dependent children. The amount of credit is reduced on a dollar for dollar basis if earned income (or adjusted gross income) is greater than such amount.

Earned premium. In insurance, that portion of the premium properly allocable to policy period which has expired. An "earned premium" is difference between premium paid by insured and portion returnable to him by insurance company on cancellation of policy during its term. Price v. Guaranty Nat. Ins. Co., Okl., 456 P.2d 108, 111.

Earned surplus. That species of surplus which has been generated from profits as contrasted with paid-in surplus. Term relates to net accumulation of profits; it is a part of surplus that represents net earnings, gains or profits, after deduction of all losses, but has not been distributed as dividends, or transferred to stated capital or capital surplus, or applied to other purposes permitted by law. Conine v. Leikam, Okl., 570 P.2d 1156, 1160.

Earner. One whose personal efforts produce income (*e.g.* wage earner) or who owns property which produces it, or combination of both. Wells v. Commissioner of Internal Revenue, C.C.A.Minn., 63 F.2d 425, 430.

Earnest. The payment of a part of the price of goods sold, or the delivery of part of such goods, for the purpose of binding the contract. A token or pledge passing between the parties, by way of evidence, or ratification of the sale. See **Earnest money.**

Earnest money. A sum of money paid by a buyer at the time of entering a contract to indicate the intention and ability of the buyer to carry out the contract. Normally such earnest money is applied against the purchase price. Often the contract provides for forfeiture of this sum if the buyer defaults. A deposit of part payment of purchase price on sale to be consummated in future. McGuire v. Andre, 259 Ala. 109, 65 So.2d 185, 190. Import of term "earnest money" in real estate contract is that when comparatively small sum is paid down, it is an assurance that party is in earnest and good faith and that if his being in earnest and good faith fails, it will be forfeited. Mortenson v. Financial Growth, Inc., 23 Utah 2d 54, 456 P.2d 181, 184.

Earning capacity. Term refers to capability of worker to sell his labor or services in any market reasonably accessible to him, taking into consideration his general physical functional impairment resulting from his accident, any previous disability, his occupation, age at time of injury, nature of injury and his wages prior to and after the injury. Sims v. Industrial Commission, 10 Ariz.App. 574, 460 P.2d 1003, 1006. Term does not necessarily mean the actual earnings that one who suffers an injury was making at the time the injuries were sustained, but refers to that which, by virtue of the training, the experience, and the business acumen possessed, an individual is capable of earning.

Fitness, readiness and willingness to work, considered in connection with opportunity to work.

Earning power. See **Earning capacity.**

Earnings. Income. That which is earned; *i.e.* money earned from performance of labor, services, sale of goods, etc. The price of services performed; the reward from labor or the price received for personal services, whether in money or chattels. The fruit or reward of labor; the fruits of the proper skill, experience, and industry; the gains of a person derived from his services or labor without the aid of capital; money or property gained or merited by labor, service, or the performance of something. Term is broader in meaning than "wages." See also Commissions; Compensation; Dividend; Gross earnings; Income; Premium; Retained earnings; Salary; Wages.

Gross earnings. Total income before deducting expenditures. Receipts from employment of capital, without deduction for expenses incurred. See also **Income.**

Net earnings. Net earnings (income) are the excess of the gross earnings over the expenditures incurred in producing them. Such may be determined before or after deduction of income taxes. See also **Income.**

Surplus earnings. See **Surplus.**

Earnings and profits. A tax concept peculiar to corporate taxpayers which measures economic capacity to make a distribution to shareholders that is not a return of capital. Such a distribution will result in dividend income to the shareholders to the extent of the corporation's current and accumulated earnings and profits.

Earnings per share. One common measure of the value of common stock. The figure is computed by dividing the net earnings (after interest and prior dividends) by the number of shares of common stock.

Earnings report. Businesses' statement of profit and loss.

Earth. Soil of all kinds, including gravel, clay, loam, and the like, in distinction from the firm rock.

Ear-witness. In the law of evidence, one who attests or can attest anything as heard by himself. See also **Voiceprint.**

Ease. Comfort, consolation, contentment, enjoyment, happiness, pleasure, satisfaction.

Easement. A right of use over the property of another. Traditionally the permitted kinds of uses were limited, the most important being rights of way and rights concerning flowing waters. The easement was normally for the benefit of adjoining lands, no matter who the owner was (an easement appurtenant), rather than for the benefit of a specific individual (easement in gross). The land having the right of use as an appurtenance is known as the dominant tenement and the land which is subject to the easement is known as the servient tenement.

A right in the owner of one parcel of land, by reason of such ownership, to use the land of another for a special purpose not inconsistent with a general property in the owner.

An interest which one person has in the land of another. A primary characteristic of an easement is that its burden falls upon the possessor of the land from which it issued and that characteristic is expressed in the statement that the land constitutes a servient tenement and the easement a dominant tenement. Potter v. Northern Natural Gas Co., 201 Kan. 528, 441 P.2d 802, 805. An interest in land in and over which it is to be enjoyed, and is distinguishable from a "license" which merely confers personal privilege to do some act on the land. Logan v. McGee, Miss., 320 So.2d 792, 793.

See also **Affirmative easement; Non-continuous easement; Prescriptive easement.**

Access easement. See **Access.**

Affirmative easement. One where the servient estate must permit something to be done thereon, as to pass over it, or to discharge water on it.

Apparent easement. One the existence of which appears from the construction or condition of one of the tenements, so as to be capable of being seen or known on inspection.

Appendent easement. See *Appurtenant easement,* infra.

Appurtenant easement. An incorporeal right which is attached to a superior right and inheres in land to which it is attached and is in the nature of a covenant running with the land. Fort Dodge, D. M. & S. Ry. v. American Community Stores Corp., 256 Iowa 1344, 131 N.W.2d 515, 521. There must be a dominant estate and servient estate. An easement interest which attaches to the land and passes with it. First Nat. Bank of Amarillo v. Amarillo Nat. Bank, Tex.Civ. App., 531 S.W.2d 905, 907. An "incorporeal right" which is attached to and belongs with some greater and superior right or something annexed to another thing more worthy and which passes as incident to it and is incapable of existence separate and apart from the particular land to which it is annexed.

Discontinuing easement. Discontinuous, non-continuous, or non-apparent easements are those the enjoyment of which can be had only by the interference of man, as, a right of way or a right to draw water.

Easement by estoppel. Easement which is created when landlord voluntarily imposes apparent servitude on his property and another person, acting reasonably, believes that servitude is permanent and in reliance upon that belief does something that he would not have done otherwise or refrains from doing something that he would have done otherwise. U. S. v. Thompson, D.C.Ark., 272 F.Supp. 774, 784.

Easement by necessity. Such arises by operation of law when land conveyed is completely shut off from access to any road by land retained by grantor or by land of grantor and that of a stranger. Tarr v. Watkins, 180 Cal.App. 362, 4 Cal.Rptr. 293, 296.

Easement by prescription. A mode of acquiring title to property by immemorial or long-continued enjoyment, and refers to personal usage restricted to claimant and his ancestors or grantors.

Easement in gross. An easement in gross is not appurtenant to any estate in land or does not belong to any person by virtue of ownership of estate in other land but is mere personal interest in or right to use land of another; it is purely personal and usually ends with death of grantee. Shingleton v. State, 260 N.C. 451, 133 S.E.2d 183, 185.

Easement of access. Right of ingress and egress to and from the premises of a lot owner to a street appurtenant to the land of the lot owner.

Easement of convenience. One which increases the facility, comfort, or convenience of the enjoyment of the dominant estate, or of some right connected with it.

Easement of natural support. Easement which creates right of lateral support to land in its natural condition entitling the holder thereof to have his land held in place from the sides by neighboring land.

Easement of necessity. One in which the easement is indispensable to the enjoyment of the dominant estate.

Equitable easements. The special easements created by derivation of ownership of adjacent proprietors from a common source, with specific intentions as to buildings for certain purposes, or with implied privileges in regard to certain uses, are sometimes so called. A name frequently applied to building restrictions in a deed.

Implied easement. One which the law imposes by inferring the parties to a transaction intended that result, although they did not express it. Schwob v. Green, Iowa, 215 N.W.2d 240, 242. An easement resting upon the principle that, where the owner of two or more adjacent lots, sells a part thereof, he grants by implication to the grantee all those apparent and visible easements which are necessary for the reasonable use of the property granted, which at the time of the grant are used by the owner of the entirety for the benefit of the part granted. One not expressed by parties in writing but arises out of existence of certain facts implied from the transaction. Wagner v. Fairlamb, 151 Colo. 481, 379 P.2d 165, 167.

Intermittent easement. One which is usable or used only at times, and not continuously.

Negative easement. Those where the owner of the servient estate is prohibited from doing something otherwise lawful upon his estate, because it will affect the dominant estate (as interrupting the light and air from the latter by building on the former). As to *"Reciprocal negative easement,"* see that title, *infra.*

Private or public easements. A private easement is one in which the enjoyment is restricted to one or a few individuals, while a public easement is one the right to the enjoyment of which is vested in the public generally or in an entire community; such as an easement of passage on the public streets and highways or of navigation on a stream.

Quasi easement. An "easement," in the proper sense of the word, can only exist in respect of two adjoining pieces of land occupied by different persons, and can only impose a negative duty on the owner of the servient tenement. Hence an obligation on the owner of land to repair the fence between his and his neighbor's land is not a true easement, but is sometimes called a *"quasi* easement."

Reciprocal negative easement. If the owner of two or more lots, so situated as to bear the relation, sells one with restrictions of benefit to the land retained, the servitude becomes mutual, and, during the period of restraint, the owner of the lot or lots retained can do nothing forbidden to the owner of the lot sold; this being known as the doctrine of "reciprocal negative easement."

Secondary easement. One which is appurtenant to the primary or actual easement. Every easement includes such "secondary easements," that is, the right to do such things as are necessary for the full enjoyment of the easement itself.

East. In the absence of other words qualifying its meaning, the word "east" describing boundaries means due east. Livingston Oil & Gas Co. v. Shasta Oil Co., Tex.Civ.App., 114 S.W.2d 378, 381. The general direction of sunrise. Point directly opposite to west. See also **Easterly.**

Easter. A feast of the Christian church held in memory of the Saviour's resurrection. The Greeks and Latins call it "pascha" (passover), to which Jewish feast our Easter answers. This feast has been annually celebrated since the time of the apostles, and is one of the most important festivals in the Christian calendar, being that which regulates and determines the times of all the other movable feasts.

Easterling. A coin struck by Richard II which is supposed by some to have given rise to the name of "sterling," as applied to English money.

Easterly. This word, when used alone, will be construed to mean "due east." But that is a rule of necessity growing out of the indefiniteness of the term, and has no application where other words are used for the purpose of qualifying its meaning. Where such is the case, it means precisely what the qualifying word makes it mean. See also **East.**

Easter-offerings, or **Easter-dues.** In English law, small sums of money paid to the parochial clergy by the parishioners at Easter as a compensation for personal tithes, or the tithe for personal labor; recoverable under 7 & 8 Wm. III, c. 6, before justices of the peace.

Easter term. In English law, formerly one of the four movable terms of the courts, but afterwards a fixed term, beginning on the 15th of April and ending on the 8th of May in every year, though sometimes prolonged so late as the 13th of May, under St. 11 Geo. IV, and 1 Wm. IV, c. 70. From November 2, 1875, the division of the legal year into terms was abolished so far as concerns the administration of justice.

East Greenwich. The name of a royal manor in the county of Kent, England; mentioned in royal grants or patents, as descriptive of the tenure of free socage.

East India Company. Originally established for prosecuting the trade between England and India, which they acquired a right to carry on exclusively. The company's political affairs became of more importance than their commerce. In 1858, by 21 & 22 Vict., c. 106, the government of the territories of the company was transferred to the crown. The company was finally dissolved in 1874.

Eastinus. An easterly coast or country.

Eastman formula. In determining fixed charges under railroad reorganization plan, the "Eastman Formula" is that such charges should not exceed 80 per cent. of the net available for interest in the three worst years of the last ten. In re Denver & R. G. W. R. Co., D.C.Colo., 38 F.Supp. 106, 110.

Eat inde sine die /íyəd índiy sáyniy dáy(iy)/. Words used on the acquittal of a defendant, or when a prisoner is to be discharged, *that he may go thence without a day, i.e.,* be dismissed without any further continuance or adjournment.

Eaves-drip. The drip or dropping of water from the eaves of a house on the land of an adjacent owner; the easement of having the water so drip, or the servitude of submitting to such drip; the same as the *stillicidium* of the Roman law. See **Stillicidium.**

Eavesdropping. Eavesdropping is knowingly and without lawful authority: (a) Entering into a private place with intent to listen surreptitiously to private conversations or to observe the personal conduct of any other person or persons therein; or (b) Installing or using outside a private place any device for hearing, recording, amplifying, or broadcasting sounds originating in such place, which sounds would not ordinarily be audible or comprehensible outside, without the consent of the person or persons entitled to privacy therein; or (c) Installing or using any device or equipment for the interception of any telephone, telegraph or other wire communication without the consent of the person in possession or control of the facilities for such wire communication. Such activities are regulated by state and federal statutes, and commonly require a court order.

At common law, the offense of listening under walls or windows, or the *eaves* of a house, and thereupon to frame slanderous and mischievous tales. 4 Bl.Comm. 168. It was a misdemeanor at common law.

See also **Pen register; Wiretapping.**

Ebba. In old English law, ebb. *Ebba et fluctus;* ebb and flow of tide; ebb and flood. The time occupied by one ebb and flood was anciently granted to persons essoined as being beyond sea, in addition to the period of forty days.

Ebb and flow. The coming in and going out of tide. An expression used formerly to denote the limits of admiralty jurisdiction.

Ebdomadarius /(h)èbdomədériyəs/. In ecclesiastical law, an officer in cathedral churches who supervised the regular performance of divine service, and prescribed the particular duties of each person in the choir.

Eberemorth, eberemors, eberemurder. See **Aberemurder.**

Ebriety /əbráyədiy/. Drunkenness; alcoholic intoxication.

Ecce modo mirum, quod femina fert breve regis, non nominando virum, conjunctum robore legis /éksiy mówdow máyrəm, kwòd fémənə fə́rt bríyviy ríyjəs, nón nòmənǽndow vérəm, kənjə́ŋktəm rówbəriy líyjəs/. Behold, indeed, a wonder! that a woman has the king's writ without naming her husband, who by law is united to her.

Eccentricity. Personal or individual peculiarities of mind and disposition which markedly distinguish the subject from the ordinary, normal, or average types of men, but do not amount to mental unsoundness or insanity.

Ecclesia /əklíyz(i)yə/. Lat. An assembly. A Christian assembly; a church. A place of religious worship. In the law, generally, the word is used to denote a place of religious worship, and sometimes a parsonage.

Ecclesia ecclesiæ decimas solvere non debet /əklíyz(i)yə əklíyz(h)(i)yiy désəməs sólvəriy nòn débət/. A church ought not to pay tithes to a church.

Ecclesiæ magis favendum est quam personæ /əklíyz(i)yə méyjəs fəvéndəm èst kwǽm pərsówniy/. The church is to be more favored than the parson (or an individual).

Ecclesiæ sculptura /əklíyz(i)yiy skə̀lpchúrə/. The image or sculpture of a church in ancient times was often cut out or cast in plate or other metal, and preserved as a religious treasure or relic, and to perpetuate the memory of some famous churches.

Ecclesia est domus mansionalis omnipotentis dei /əklíyz(i)yə èst dówməs mænshənéyləs òmnəpówténtəs díyay/. The church is the mansionhouse of the Omnipotent God.

Ecclesia est infra ætatem et in custodia domini regis, qui tenetur jura et hæreditates ejusdem manu tenere et defendere /əklíyz(i)yə èst ínfrə ətéydəm èd ín kəstówdiyə dómənay ríyjəs kwày təníydər júrə èt hərèdətéydiyz iyjə́sdəm mæn(y)uw təníriy èt dəféndəriy/. The church is under age, and in the custody of the king, who is bound to uphold and defend its rights and inheritances.

Ecclesia fungitur vice minoris; meliorem conditionem suam facere potest, deteriorem nequaquam /əklíyz(i)yə fə́njədər váysiy mənórəs; mìyliyórəm kəndìshiyównəm s(y)úwəm fǽsəriy pówdəst, dətìriyórəm nəkwéykwəm/. The church enjoys the privilege of a minor; it can make its own condition better, but not worse.

Ecclesia non moritur /əklíyz(i)yə nòn mórədər/. The church does not die.

Ecclesiarch /əklíyziyark/. The ruler of a church.

Ecclesiastic /əklìyziyǽstək/. A clergyman; a priest; a man consecrated to the service of the church; as, a bishop, a priest, a deacon.

Ecclesiastical /əklìyziyǽstəkəl/. Pertaining to anything belonging to or set apart for the church, as distinguished from "civil" or "secular," with regard to the world.

Ecclesiastical authorities. In England, the clergy, under the sovereign, as temporal head of the church, set apart from the rest of the people or laity, in order to superintend the public worship of God and the other ceremonies of religion, and to administer spiritual counsel and instruction. The several orders of the clergy are: (1) Archbishops and bishops; (2) deans and chapters; (3) archdeacons; (4) rural deans; (5) parsons (under whom are included appropriators) and vicars; (6) curates. Church-wardens or sidesmen, and parish clerks and sextons, inasmuch as their duties are connected with the church, may be considered to be a species of ecclesiastical authorities. See **Ecclesiastical courts.**

Ecclesiastical commissioners. In England, a body corporate, erected by St. 6 & 7 Wm. IV, c. 77, empowered to suggest measures conducive to the efficiency of the established church, to be ratified by orders in council. As a body, Ecclesiastical Commissioners have been dissolved and their functions, rights, property, etc. vested in Church Commissioners.

Ecclesiastical corporation. See **Corporation.**

Ecclesiastical council. In New England, formerly a church court or tribunal, having functions partly judicial and partly advisory, appointed to determine questions relating to church discipline, orthodoxy, standing of ministers, controversies between ministers and their churches, differences and divisions in churches, and the like.

Ecclesiastical courts (called, also, "Courts Christian"). A generic name for certain courts having cognizance mainly of spiritual matters. A system of courts in England, held by authority of the sovereign, and having jurisdiction over matters pertaining to the religion and ritual of the established church, and the rights, duties, and discipline of ecclesiastical persons as such. They are as follows: The Archdeacon's Court (now practically obsolete), Consistory Court, Provincial Courts (*i.e.* Court of Arches of Canterbury and Chancery Court of York), Court of Faculties, and Court of Final Appeal (Judicial Committee of the Privy Council).

Ecclesiastical division of England. This is a division into provinces, dioceses, archdeaconries, rural deaneries, and parishes.

Ecclesiastical jurisdiction. Jurisdiction over ecclesiastical cases and controversies; such as appertains to the ecclesiastical courts.

Ecclesiastical law. The body of jurisprudence administered by the ecclesiastical courts of England; derived, in large measure, from the canon and civil law. As now restricted, it applies mainly to the affairs, and the doctrine, discipline, and worship, of the established church.

Ecclesiastical matter. One that concerns doctrine, creed, or form of worship of the church, or the adoption and enforcement within a religious association of needful laws and regulations for the government of the membership, and the power of excluding from such associations those deemed unworthy of membership. Olear v. Haniak, 235 Mo.App. 249, 131 S.W.2d 375, 380.

Ecclesiastical things. This term, as used in the canon law, includes church buildings, church property, cemeteries, and property given to the church for the support of the poor or for any other pious use.

Ecdicus /éktəkəs/. The attorney, proctor, or advocate of a corporation.

Échantillon /èyshontiyówn/. In French law, one of the two parts or pieces of a wooden tally. That in possession of the debtor is properly called the "tally," the other *"échantillon."*

Echevin. In French law, a municipal officer corresponding with alderman or burgess, and having in some instances a civil jurisdiction in certain causes of trifling importance.

Echolalia /èkowléyliyə/°læliyə/. The constant and senseless repetition of particular words or phrases, recognized as a sign or symptom of insanity or of aphasia.

Echouement /èyshuwmón/. In French marine law, stranding.

Ecology. In general, the study or science of the relationships between organisms and their environments; study of the environment. See **Ecosystems.**

Economic discrimination. Any form of discrimination within the field of commerce such as a boycott of a particular product or price fixing. See **Boycott; Price discrimination; Price-fixing.**

Economic obsolescence. Loss of desirability and useful life of property due to economic developments (*e.g.* deterioration of neighborhood or zoning change) rather than deterioration (functional obsolescence). Term as used with respect to valuation of property for taxation is a loss of value brought about by conditions that environ a structure such as a declining location or down-grading of a neighborhood resulting in reduced business volume. Piazza v. Town Assessor of Town of Porter, 16 A.D.2d 863, 228 N.Y.S.2d 397, 398. See also **Obsolescence.**

Economic strike. Refusal to work because of dispute over wages, hours or working conditions or other conditions of employment. N. L. R. B. v. Transport Co. of Tex., C.A.Tex., 438 F.2d 258. An economic strike is one neither prohibited by law nor by collective bargaining agreement nor caused by employer unfair labor practices, but is typically for purpose of enforcing employer compliance with union collective bargaining demands, and economic strikers possess more limited reinstatement rights than unfair labor practice strikers. N. L. R. B. v. Transport Co. of Tex., C.A.Tex., 438 F.2d 258, 262.

Economic waste. An overproduction or excessive drilling of oil or gas.

Economy. Frugality; prudent expenditure of money or use of resources. Not synonymous with "parsimony." Includes that which pertains to the satisfaction of man's needs. D'Arcy v. Snell, 162 Or. 351, 91 P.2d 537, 540. Economic structure of country.

E contra /ìy kóntrə/. From the opposite; on the contrary.

E converso /ìy kənvə́rsow/. Conversely. On the other hand; on the contrary. Equivalent to *e contra.*

Ecosystems. The totality of cycles and processes which constitute the ecology system.

Ecumenical /ékyəménəkəl/ìykyəménəkəl/. General; universal; as an ecumenical council.

Edderbreche /édərbrìych/. In Saxon law, the offense (now obsolete) of hedge-breaking.

Edge lease. One located on the edge of an oil bearing structure. Carter Oil Co. v. Mitchell, C.C.A.Okl., 100 F.2d 945, 947.

Edict. A formal decree, command, or proclamation. A positive law promulgated by the sovereign of a country, and having reference either to the whole land or some of its divisions, but usually relating to affairs of state. It differs from a "public proclamation," in that it enacts a new statute, and carries with it the authority of law, whereas the latter is, at most, a declaration of a law before enacted. In Roman law, sometimes, a citation to appear before a judge. A "special edict" was a judgment in a case; a "general edict" was in effect a statute. See **Decree; Edictum; Mandate.**

Edicts of Justinian /íydìkts əv jəstín(i)yən/. Thirteen constitutions or laws of this prince, found in most editions of the *Corpus Juris Civilis,* after the Novels. Being confined to matters of police in the provinces of the empire, they have long since been of little use.

Edictum /ədíktəm/. In the Roman law, an edict; a mandate, or ordinance. An ordinance, or law, enacted by the emperor without the senate; belonging to the class of *constitutiones principis.* An edict was a mere voluntary constitution of the emperor; differing from a rescript, in not being returned in the way of answer; and from a decree, in not being given in judgment; and from both, in not being founded upon solicitation.

A general order published by the prætor, on entering upon his office, containing the system of rules by which he would administer justice during the year of his office.

Edictum annuum /ədíktəm ǽnyuwəm/. The annual edict or system of rules promulgated by a Roman prætor immediately upon assuming his office, setting forth the principles by which he would be guided in determining causes during his term of office.

Edictum perpetuum /ədíktəm pərpéchuwəm/. The perpetual edict. A compilation or system of law in fifty books, digested by Julian, from the prætor's edicts and other parts of the *Jus Honorarium.* All the remains of it which have come down to us are the extracts of it in the Digests.

Edictum provinciale /ədíktəm prəvìnshiyéyliy/. An edict or system of rules for the administration of justice, similar to the edict of the prætor, put forth by the proconsuls and proprætors in the provinces of the Roman Empire.

Edictum Theodorici /ədíktəm θìyədəráysay/. This is the first collection of law that was made after the downfall of the Roman power in Italy. It was promulgated by Theodoric, king of the Ostrogoths, at Rome in A.D. 500. It consists of 154 chapters, in which we recognize parts taken from the Code and Novellæ of Theodosius, from the Codices Gregorianus and Hermogenianus, and the Sententiæ of Paulus. The edict was doubtless drawn up by Roman writers, but the original sources are more disfigured and altered than in any other compilation. This collection of law was intended to apply both to the Goths and the Romans, so far as its provisions went; but, when it made no alteration in the Gothic law, that law was still to be in force.

Edictum tralatitium /ədíktəm trælətísh(iy)əm/. Where a Roman prætor, upon assuming office, did not publish a wholly new edict, but retained the whole or a principal part of the edict of his predecessor (as was usually the case) only adding to it such rules as appeared to be necessary to adapt it to changing social conditions or juristic ideas, it was called "edictum tralatitium."

Edition. The total number of copies of a publication printed from a single typesetting or at one specified time. May also refer to the form which a publication takes such as a hardbound or paperback edition. Also, the means of identifying the various versions of a given publication; *e.g.* first, second, etc. edition. One of the several issues of a newspaper for a single day.

Editor. One who directs or supervises the policies, content and contributions of a newspaper, magazine, book, work of reference, or the like. The term is held to include not only the person who writes, edits or selects the articles for publication, but he who publishes a paper and puts it in circulation. Pennoyer v. Neff, 95 U.S. 721, 24 L.Ed. 565.

Editus /édədəs/. In old English law, put forth or promulgated, when speaking of the passage of a statute; and brought forth, or born, when speaking of the birth of a child.

Edmunds Act. An act of Congress of March 22, 1882, punishing polygamy.

Educate. To give proper moral, as well as intellectual and physical, instruction. To prepare and fit oneself for any calling or business, or for activity and usefulness in life.

Education. Comprehends not merely the instruction received at school or college, but the whole course of training; moral, religious, vocational, intellectual, and physical. Education may be particularly directed to either the mental, moral, or physical powers and faculties, but in its broadest and best sense it relates to them all. Acquisition of all knowledge tending to train and develop the individual. See also **Board of education.**

Educational expenses. Employees may deduct education expenses if such items are incurred either (1) to maintain or improve existing job related skills or (2) to meet the express requirements of the employer or the requirements imposed by law to retain employment status. Such expenses are not deductible if the education is (1) required to meet the minimum educational requirements for the taxpayer's job or (2) the education qualifies the individual for a new trade or business. Ronald F. Weiszmann v. Commissioner of Internal Revenue, 443 F.2d 29.

Educational institution. A school, seminary, college, university, or other educational establishment, not necessarily a chartered institution. As used in a zoning ordinance, the term may include not only buildings, but also all grounds necessary for the accomplishment of the full scope of educational instruction, including those things essential to mental, moral, and physical development. Commissioners of District of Columbia v. Shannon & Luchs Const. Co., 57 App.D.C. 67, 17 F.2d 219, 220.

Educational purposes. Term as used in constitutional and statutory provisions exempting property so used from taxation, includes systematic instruction in any and all branches of learning from which a substantial public benefit is derived, and is not limited to such school properties as would relieve some substantial educational burden from the state. McKee v. Evans, Alaska, 490 P.2d 1226, 1230.

E.E.O.C. Equal Employment Opportunity Commission.

Effect, *v.* To do; to produce; to make; to bring to pass; to execute; enforce; accomplish.

Effect, *n.* That which is produced by an agent or cause; result; outcome; consequence. State by Clark v. Wolkoff, 250 Minn. 504, 85 N.W.2d 401, 410. The result which an instrument between parties will produce in their relative rights, or which a statute will produce upon the existing law, as discovered from the language used, the forms employed, or other materials for construing it. The operation of a law, of an agreement, or an act. The phrases "take effect," "be in force," "go into operation," etc., are used interchangeably.

With effect. With success; as, to prosecute an action with effect.

Effecting loan. To bring about a loan. To accomplish, fulfill, produce or make a loan. It means the result or consequence of bringing into operation a loan; while "renewal" is not a loan, but an extension of the time of payment.

Effective assistance of counsel. Conscientious, meaningful representation wherein accused is advised of his rights and honest, learned and able counsel is given a reasonable opportunity to perform task assigned to him. State v. Williams, Iowa, 207 N.W.2d 98, 104. See **Counsel, right to.**

Effective possession. See **Constructive possession.**

Effective procuring cause. The "effective procuring cause" of sale of realty is ordinarily the broker who first secures the serious attention of the customer and is instrumental in bringing the parties together. See **Cause; Efficient cause; Proximate cause.**

Effects. Personal estate or property; though the term may include both real and personal property. See **Personal effects.**

Effectus sequitur causam /əféktəs síykwədər kózəm/. The effect follows the cause.

Effet. In France an "effet" is a bill of exchange; "effets" means goods, movables, chattels. In re Steimes' Estate, 150 Misc. 279, 270 N.Y.S. 339.

Effets mobiliers /əféts mòwbəlírz/. Funds or stocks. In re Steimes' Estate, 150 Misc. 279, 270 N.Y.S. 339.

Efficient. Causing an effect; particularly the result or results contemplated. Adequate in performance or producing properly a desired effect. Spotts v. Baltimore & O. R. Co., C.C.A.Ind., 102 F.2d 160, 162.

Efficient cause. The working cause; that cause which produces effects or results. An intervening cause, which produces results which would not have come to pass except for its interposition, and for which, therefore, the person who set in motion the original chain of causes is not responsible. Southland-Greyhound Lines v. Cotten, Tex.Civ.App., 55 S.W.2d 1066, 1069. The cause which originates and sets in motion the dominating agency that necessarily proceeds through other causes as mere instruments or vehicles in a natural line of causation to the result. That cause of an injury to which legal liability attaches. The "proximate cause." Hillis v. Home Owners' Loan Corporation, 348 Mo. 601, 154 S.W.2d 761, 764. The phrase is practically synonymous with "procuring cause." Buhrmester v. Independent Plumbing & Heating Supply Co., Mo.App., 151 S.W.2d 509, 513. The immediate agent in the production of an effect. Armijo v. World Ins. Co., 78 N.M. 204, 429 P.2d 904, 906.

The proximate cause of an injury is the efficient cause, the one that necessarily sets the other causes in operation, and, where a wrongful act puts other forces in operation which are natural and which the act would reasonably and probably put in action, the party who puts in force the first efficient cause will be responsible in damages for the injury proved, although immediately resulting from the other force so put in motion.

See also **Proximate cause.**

Efficient intervening cause. An intervening efficient cause is a new and independent force, which breaks the causal connection between the original wrong and the injury, and is the proximate cause of the injury. Thus, the original negligent actor is not liable for an injury that could not have been foreseen or reasonably anticipated as the probable consequence of his negligent act, and would not have resulted from it had not the intervening efficient cause interrupted the natural sequence of events, turned aside their course, and produced the injury. Coyle v. Stopak, 165 Neb. 594, 86 N.W.2d 758, 768; Knuth v. Singer, 174 Neb. 182, 116 N.W.2d 291, 295. See also **Proximate cause.**

Effigy /éfəjiy/. The figure or corporeal representation of a person.

Efflux /éfləks/. The running, as of a prescribed period of time to its end; expiration by lapse of time. Particularly applied to the termination of a lease by the expiration of the term for which it was made.

Effluxion of time /əflə́kshən əv táym/. When this phrase is used in leases, conveyances, and other like deeds, or in agreements expressed in simple writing, it indicates the conclusion or expiration of an agreed term of years specified in the deed or writing, such conclusion or expiration arising in the natural course of events, in contradistinction to the determination of the term by the acts of the parties or by some unexpected or unusual incident or other sudden event.

Efforcialiter /əfòrs(h)iyéylədər/. Forcibly; applied to military force.

Effort. An attempt; an endeavor; a struggle directed to the accomplishment of an object.

Effraction /əfrǽkshən/. A breach made by the use of force.

Effractor /əfrǽktər/. One who breaks through; one who commits a burglary.

Effusio sanguinis /əfyúwz(h)(i)yow sǽngwənəs/. In old English law, the shedding of blood; the mulct, fine, wite, or penalty imposed for the shedding of blood, which the king granted to many lords of manors. See **Bloodwit.**

E.g. An abbreviation of *exempli gratia.* For the sake of an example.

Ego /íygow/. I; myself. This term is used in forming genealogical tables, to represent the person who is the object of inquiry.

The part of the conscious personality which has the task of balancing the demands of the real world and maintaining harmony between the *id* (instinctual drives) and the *superego* (morality of the conscience);

that portion of the total personality noticeable to others which maintains contact with the environment of the outer world.

See also **Alter ego.**

Ego, talis /íygow, téyləs/. I, such a one. Words used in describing the forms of old deeds.

Egrediens et exeuns /əgríydiyèn(d)z èd éksiyàn(d)z/. In old pleading, going forth and issuing out of (land).

Egress /íygrès/. The path by which a person goes out; exit. The means or act of going out. Often used interchangeably with the word "access." C. Hacker Co. v. City of Joliet, 196 Ill.App. 415, 423.

Egyptians. Derivative name in old England for "gypsies"; a wandering, nomadic people without permanent abode, living in tents or other shelters, pretending to tell fortunes of others.

Eia, or Ey. An island.

Eighteenth Amendment. The amendment to the U.S. Constitution added in 1919 which prohibited the manufacture, sale, transportation and exportation of intoxicating liquors in all the States and Territories of the United States and which was repealed in 1933 by the Twenty-first Amendment.

Eighth Amendment. The amendment to the U.S. Constitution added in 1791 which prohibits excessive bail, excessive fines and cruel and unusual punishment.

Eight hour laws. Statutes (*e.g.* Adamson Act; Fair Labor Standards Act) which established eight hours as the length of a day's work, prohibited work beyond this period, and required payment of overtime for work in excess of this period. See **Wage and Hour Laws.**

Eigne /éyn/. L. Fr. Eldest; eldest-born. The term is of common occurrence in the old books. Thus, *bastard eigne* means an illegitimate son whose parents afterwards marry and have a second son for lawful issue, the latter being called *mulier puisne* (afterborn). *Eigne* is probably a corrupt form of the French *"aîné."* 2 Bl.Comm. 248.

Eignesse /èynés/. See **Esnecy.**

Ei incumbit probatio, qui dicit, non qui negat; cum per rerum naturam factum negantis probatio nulla sit /íyay inkámbət prəbéysh(iy)ow kwày dísət, nón kwày négət; kám pàr rírəm nət(y)úrəm fæktəm nəgæntəs prəbéysh(iy)ow nálə sìt/. The proof lies upon him who affirms, not upon him who denies; since, by the nature of things, he who denies a fact cannot produce any proof.

Einecia /əníysiyə/. Eldership. See **Esnecy.**

Einetius /əníysh(iy)əs/. In English law, the oldest; the first-born.

Ei nihil turpe, cui nihil satis /íyay náy(h)əl tárpiy, k(yúw)ay náy(h)əl sædəs/. To him to whom nothing is enough, nothing is base.

Eire, or eyre /ér/. In old English law, a journey, route, or circuit. Justices *in eire* were judges who were sent by commission, every seven years, into various counties to hold the assizes and hear pleas of the crown. 3 Bl.Comm. 58.

Eirenarcha /àyrənárkə/. A name formerly given to a justice of the peace. In the Digests, the word is written *"irenarcha."*

Eisdem modis dissolvitur obligatio quæ nascitur ex contractu, vel quasi, quibus contrahitur /iyáysdəm mówdəs dəzólvədər òbləgéysh(iy)ow kwìy næsədər èks kəntrækt(y)uw, vèl kwéysay, kwíbəs kəntréy(h)ədər/. An obligation which arises from contract, or *quasi* contract, is dissolved in the same ways in which it is contracted.

Eisne /éyn/. The senior; the oldest son. Spelled also, *"eigne," "einsne," "aisne," "eign."*

Eisnetia, einetia /ə(z)níysh(iy)ə/. The share of the oldest son. The portion acquired by primogeniture.

Either. Each of two; the one and the other; one or the other of two alternatives; one of two. Often used, however, with reference to more than two, in which case it may mean "each" or "any."

Eject. To cast, or throw out; to oust, or dispossess; to put or turn out of possession. To expel or thrust forcibly, as disorderly patrons.

Ejecta /əjéktə/. In old English law, a woman ravished or deflowered, or cast forth from the virtuous.

Ejection. A turning out of possession.

Ejectione custodiæ /əjèkshiyówniy kəstówdiyiy/. In old English law, ejectment of ward. This phrase, which is the Latin equivalent for the French *"ejectment de garde,"* was the title of a writ which lay for a guardian when turned out of any land of his ward during the minority of the latter. It lay to recover the land or person of his ward, or both.

Ejectione firmæ /əjèkshiyówniy fármiy/. Ejection, or ejectment of farm. The name of a writ or action of trespass, which lay at common law where lands or tenements were let for a term of years, and afterwards the lessor, reversioner, remainder-man, or any stranger *ejected* or ousted the lessee of his term, *ferme*, or *farm* (*ipsum a firma ejecit*). In this case the latter might have his writ of *ejection*, by which he recovered at first damages for the trespass only, but it was afterwards made a remedy to recover back the term itself, or the remainder of it, with damages. 3 Bl.Comm. 199. It is the foundation of the modern action of ejectment.

Ejectment. At common law, this was the name of a mixed action (springing from the earlier personal action of *ejectione firmæ*) which lay for the recovery of the possession of land, and for damages for the unlawful detention of its possession. The action was highly fictitious, being in theory only for the recovery of a term for years, and brought by a purely fictitious person, as lessee in a supposed lease from the real party in interest. The latter's title, however, had to be established in order to warrant a recovery, and the establishment of such title, though nominally a mere incident, was in reality the object of the action. Hence this convenient form of suit came to be adopted as the usual method of trying titles to land. 3 Bl.Comm. 199; French v. Robb, 67 N.J.Law 260, 51 A. 509. In England, since the Judicature Act of 1852, ejectment has given place to a new action for the recovery of land.

The common law action for ejectment has been materially modified by statute in most states and may come under the title of action to recover possession of land, action for summary process, action for eviction, or forcible entry and detainer action.

Ejectment is an action to restore possession of property to the person entitled to it. Not only must the plaintiff establish a right to possession in himself, but he must also show that the defendant is in wrongful possession. If the defendant has only trespassed on the land, the action is for trespass (*i.e.* damages).

See also **Eviction; Forcible entry and detainer; Process** (*Summary process*).

Ejectment bill. A bill in equity brought merely for the recovery of real property, together with an account of the rents and profits, without setting out any distinct ground of equity jurisdiction; hence demurrable.

Equitable ejectment. A proceeding brought to enforce specific performance of a contract for the sale of land, and for some other purposes, which is in form an action of ejectment, but is in reality a substitute for a bill in equity.

Justice ejectment. A statutory proceeding for the eviction of a tenant holding over after termination of the lease or breach of its conditions.

Ejector. One who ejects, puts out, or dispossesses another.

Casual ejector. The nominal defendant in an action of ejectment; so called because, by a fiction of law peculiar to that action, he is supposed to come casually or by accident upon the premises and to eject the lawful possessor. 3 Bl.Comm. 203.

Ejectum /əjéktəm/. That which is thrown up by the sea. Also jetsam, wreck, etc.

Ejectus /əjéktəs/. In old English law, a whore-monger.

Ejercitoria /eyhèrsiytóriyə/. In Spanish law, the name of an action lying against a ship's owner, upon the contracts or obligations made by the master for repairs or supplies. It corresponds to the *actio exercitoria* of the Roman law.

Ejidos /eyhíyðows/. In Spanish law, commons; lands used in common by the inhabitants of a city, pueblo, or town, for pasture, wood, threshing-ground, etc.

Ejuration /ìyjəréyshən/. Renouncing or resigning one's place.

Ejusdem generis /iyjásdəm jénərəs/. Of the same kind, class, or nature. In the construction of laws, wills, and other instruments, the "ejusdem generis rule" is, that where general words follow an enumeration of persons or things, by words of a particular and specific meaning, such general words are not to be construed in their widest extent, but are to be held as applying only to persons or things of the same general kind or class as those specifically mentioned. U. S. v. LaBrecque, D.C.N.J., 419 F.Supp. 430, 432; Aleksich v. Industrial Accident Fund, 116 Mont. 127, 151 P.2d 1016, 1021. The rule, however, does not necessarily require that the general provision be limited in its scope to the identical things specifically named. Nor does it apply when the context manifests a contrary intention.

Under "ejusdem generis" canon of statutory construction, where general words follow the enumeration of particular classes of things, the general words will be construed as applying only to things of the same general class as those enumerated. Campbell v. Board of Dental Examiners, 53 Cal.App.3d 283, 125 Cal.Rptr. 694, 696.

Ejus est interpretari cujus est condere /íyjəs èst intərprətéray kyúwjəs èst kóndəriy/. It is his to interpret whose it is to enact.

Ejus est nolle, qui potest velle /íyjəs èst nóliy, kwày pówdəst véliy/. He who can will [exercise volition], has a right to refuse to will [to withhold consent]. This maxim is sometimes written, *Ejus est non nolle qui potest velle,* and is translated, "He may consent tacitly who may consent expressly."

Ejus est periculum cujus est dominium aut commodum /íyjəs èst pəríkyələm kyúwjəs èst dəmíniyəm òt kóməwdəm/. He who has the dominion or advantage has the risk.

Ejus nulla culpa est, cui parere necesse sit /íyjəs nálə kálpə èst, k(yúw)ay pərériy nəsésiy sít/. No guilt attaches to him who is compelled to obey. Obedience to existing laws is a sufficient extenuation of guilt before a civil tribunal.

Elaborare /əlǽbərériy/. In old European law, to gain, acquire, or purchase, as by labor and industry.

Elaboratus /əlǽbəréydəs/. Property which is the acquisition of labor.

Elder brethren. A distinguished body of men, elected as masters of Trinity House, an institution incorporated in the reign of Henry VIII, charged with numerous important duties relating to the marine, such as the superintendence of light-houses. The full title of the corporation is Elder Brethren of the Holy and Undivided Trinity.

Elder title. A title of earlier date, but coming simultaneously into operation with a title of younger origin, is called the "elder title," and prevails.

Eldest. Oldest; first born; one with greatest seniority.

Electa una via, non datur recursus ad alteram /əléktə yuwnə váyə, nòn déydər rəkársəs æd óltərəm/. He who has chosen one way cannot have recourse to another.

Elected. The word "elected," in its ordinary signification, carries with it the idea of a vote, generally popular, sometimes more restricted, and cannot be held the synonym of any other mode of filling a position.

Electio est interna libera et spontanea separatio unius rei ab alia, sine compulsione, consistens in animo et voluntate /əléksh(iy)ow èst intárnə líbərə èt spòntəníyə sèpəréysh(iy)ow yənáyəs ríyay æb éyliyə, sáyniy kəmpàlsiyówniy, kənsísten(d)z ìn ǽnəmow èt vòləntéydiy/. Election is an internal, free, and spontaneous separation of one thing from another, without compulsion, consisting in intention and will.

Election. The act of choosing or selecting one or more from a greater number of persons, things, courses, or rights. The choice of an alternative. The internal, free, and spontaneous separation of one thing from another, without compulsion, consisting in intention and will. The selection of one person from a specified class to discharge certain duties in a state, corporation, or society. With respect to the choice of persons to fill public office or the decision of a particular public question or public policy the term means in ordinary usage the expression by vote of the will of the people or of a somewhat numerous body of electors. "Election" ordinarily has reference to a choice or selection by electors, while "appointment" refers to a choice or selection by an individual.

The choice which is open to a debtor who is bound in an alternative obligation to select either one of the alternatives.

The choice, by the prosecution, upon which of several counts in an indictment (charging distinct offenses of the same degree, but not parts of a continuous series of acts) it will proceed.

See also **Certificate of election; Equitable election; Free and clear.**

Election at large. Election in which a public official is selected from a major election district rather than a minor subdivision within the larger unit.

Election of defenses. The selection of a particular defense on which to rest in contesting a claim or in defending a criminal charge.

Election of remedies. The liberty of choosing (or the act of choosing) one out of several means afforded by law for the redress of an injury, or one out of several available forms of action. An "election of remedies" arises when one having two coexistent but inconsistent remedies chooses to exercise one, in which event he loses the right to thereafter exercise the other. Doctrine provides that if two or more remedies exist which are repugnant and inconsistent with one another, a party will be bound if he has chosen one of them. Melby v. Hawkins Pontiac, Inc., 13 Wash.App. 745, 537 P.2d 807, 810. See also **Equitable election.**

General election. One for a definite purpose, regularly reoccurring at fixed intervals without any requirements other than the lapse of time. Bolin v. Superior Court In and For Maricopa County, 85 Ariz. 131, 333 P.2d 295, 298. One at which the officers to be elected are such as belong to the general government; that is, the general and central political organization of the whole state, as distinguished from an election of officers for a particular locality only. Also, one held for the selection of an officer after the expiration of the full term of the former officer; thus distinguished from a *special* election, which is one held to supply a vacancy in office occurring before the expiration of the full term for which the incumbent was elected.

One that regularly recurs in each election precinct of the state on a day designated by law for the selection of officers, or is held in such entire territory pursuant to an enactment specifying a single day for the ratification or rejection of one or more measures submitted to the people by the Legislature, and not for the election of any officer. One that is held throughout the entire state or territory. An election for the choice of a national, state, judicial, district, municipal, county or township official, required by law to be held regularly at a designated time, to fill a new office or a vacancy in an office at the expiration of the full term thereof.

In statutes, the term may include a primary election.

See also *Regular election, infra.*

Law of wills. A widow's election is her choice of whether she will take under the will or under the statute; that is, whether she will accept the provision made for her in the will, and acquiesce in her husband's disposition of his property, or disregard it and claim what the law allows her. Logan v. Logan, Tex.Civ.App., 112 S.W.2d 515, 518. An "election under the will" means that a legatee or devisee under a will is put to the choice of accepting the beneficial interest offered by the donor in lieu of some estate which he is entitled to, but which is taken from him by the terms of the will. See also **Election by spouse; Equitable election.**

Off-year election. Election conducted at a time other than the presidential election year.

Presidential election. See U.S.Const. Amends. XII, XX, XXII–XXVI.

Primary election. An election by the voters of a ward, precinct, or other small district, belonging to a particular party, of representatives or delegates to a convention which is to meet and nominate the candidates of their party to stand at an approaching municipal or general election. Also, an election to select candidates for office by a political organization, the voters being restricted to the members or supporters of such organization. An election, preliminary in nature, the purpose being to narrow in number the candidates that will appear on the final, official ballot.

Recall election. Election where voters have opportunity to remove public official from elected office.

Regular election. One recurring at stated times fixed by law. A general, usual, or stated election. When applied to elections, the terms "regular" and "general" are used interchangeably and synonymously. The word "regular" is used in reference to a general election occurring throughout the state. See also *General election, supra.*

Special election. An election for a particular emergency or need, conducted in the interval between regularly scheduled elections in order to fill a vacancy arising by death of the incumbent of the office, decide a question submitted on an initiative referendum, or recall petition, etc. In determining whether an election is special or general, regard must be had to the subject-matter as well as date of the election, and, if an election occurs throughout state uniformly by direct operation of law, it is a "general election," but, if it depends on employment of special preliminary proceeding peculiar to process which may or may not occur, and the election is applicable only to a restricted area less than whole state, it is a "special election."

Election board. A board of inspectors or commissioners appointed in each election precinct by government (*e.g.* county or city) authorities responsible for determining whether individual voters are qualified, supervising the polling, and often ascertaining and reporting the results. Local, city or town agency which is charged with the conduct of elections.

Election by spouse. Statutory provision that a surviving spouse may choose as between taking that which is provided for her in her husband's will, claiming dower or taking her statutorily prescribed share. Such election may be presented if the will leaves the spouse less than she would otherwise receive by statute. This election may also be taken if the spouse seeks to set aside a will which contains a provision to the effect that an attempt to contest the will defeats the rights of one to take under the will. See also **Election** (*Law of wills*); **Equitable election.**

Election contest. A contest in behalf of one who has failed of success in election against right of one who has been declared or determined by proper authority to have been successful. Election contest involves matter of going behind election returns and inquiring into qualifications of electors, counting of ballots, and other matters affecting validity of ballots. Vance v. Johnson, 238 Ark. 1009, 386 S.W.2d 240, 242.

Election district. A subdivision of territory, whether of state, county, or city, the boundaries of which are fixed by law, for convenience in local or general elections.

Election, doctrine of. When a third person has contracted with an agent without knowing of the agency, and thereafter the third person discovers the agency and the identity of the principal, the third person may enforce the contract against the agent or against the principal at his election, but not against both. This is known as the doctrine of election.

Election dower. A name sometimes given to the provision which a law or statute makes for a widow in case she "elects" to reject the provision made for her in the will and take what the statute accords. Stanton v. Leonard, 344 Mo. 998, 130 S.W.2d 487, 489. See **Election** (*Law of wills*); **Election by spouse.**

Electiones fiant rite et libere sine interruptione aliqua /ələ̀kshiyówniyz fáyənt ráydiy èt líbəriy sáyniy ìntərə̀pshiyówniy ǽləkwə/. Elections should be made in due form, and freely, without any interruption.

Election, estoppel by. An estoppel which arises by a choice between inconsistent remedies. See **Election** (*Election of remedies*).

An estoppel predicated on a voluntary and intelligent action or choice of one of several things which is inconsistent with another, the effect of the estoppel being to prevent the party so choosing from afterwards reversing his election or disputing the state of affairs or rights of others resulting from his original choice.

The doctrine of "estoppel by election" against beneficiary who has elected to take favorable provisions of will from objecting to other provisions of will applies only where will undertakes to bestow a gift and also deprive donee of a prior existing right, thus confronting devisee with alternative of accepting devise and renouncing prior right or of retaining latter and renouncing devise. Mason & Mason v. Brown, Tex.Civ.App., 182 S.W.2d 729, 733.

Election judges. In English law, judges of the high court selected in pursuance of Parliamentary Elections Act of 1868, and Judicature Act of 1925, for the trial of election petitions. See **Election board.**

Election of remedies. See **Election.**

Election petitions. In England, petitions for inquiry into the validity of elections of members of parliament when it is alleged that the return of a member is invalid for bribery or any other reason.

Election returns. The report made to the board of canvassers or election board of the number of votes cast for each candidate or proposition voted upon by those charged by law with the duty of counting or tallying the votes for or against the respective candidates or propositions.

Electio semel facta, et placitum testatum non patitur regressum /əléksh(iy)ow séməl fǽktə èt plǽsədəm testéydəm nòn pǽdədər rəgrésəm/. Election once made, and plea witnessed (or intent shown), suffers not a recall.

Elective. Dependent upon choice; bestowed or passing by election. Also pertaining or relating to elections; conferring the right or power to vote at elections.

Elective franchise. The right of voting at public elections. The privilege of qualified voters to cast their ballots for the candidates they favor at elections authorized by law as guaranteed by Fifteenth and Nineteenth Amendments to Constitution, and by federal voting rights acts.

Elective office. One which is to be filled by popular election. One filled by the direct exercise of the voters' franchise in contrast to an appointive office.

Elective share. See **Election** (*Law of wills*); **Election by spouse.**

Elector. A duly qualified voter; one who has a vote in the choice of any officer; a constituent. One who elects or has the right of choice, or who has the right to vote for any functionary, or for the adoption of any measure. In a narrower sense, one who has the general right to vote, and the right to vote for public officers. One authorized to exercise the elective franchise.

One of the persons chosen to comprise the "electoral college" (*q.v.*).

Also, the title of certain German princes who had a voice in the election of the Holy Roman Emperors. The office of elector in some instances became hereditary and was connected with territorial possessions.

Sometimes, one who exercises the right of election in equity.

Registered qualified elector. One possessing the constitutional qualifications, and registered under the registration statute.

Electoral. Pertaining to electors or elections; composed or consisting of electors. See **Electoral college.**

Electoral college. The college or body of electors of a state chosen to elect the president and vice-president; also, the whole body of such electors, composed of the electoral colleges of the several states. See U.S. Const. Amend. XII.

Electoral process. Generic term for methods by which persons are elected to public office; voting.

Electronic surveillance. See **Eavesdropping; Wiretapping.**

Eleemosynæ /èləmósəniy/. Possessions belonging to the church.

Eleemosyna regis, and **eleemosyna aratri,** or **carucarum** /èləmósənə ríyjəs/°əréytray/°kǽrəkérəm/. A penny which King Ethelred ordered to be paid for every plow in England towards the support of the poor.

Eleemosynaria /èləmòsənériyə/. The place in a religious house where the common alms were deposited, and thence by the almoner distributed to the poor. In old English law, the *aumerie, aumbry,* or *ambry;* words still used in common speech in the north of England, to denote a pantry or cupboard. The office of almoner.

Eleemosynarius /èləmòsənériyəs/. In old English law, an almoner, or chief officer, who received the eleemosynary rents and gifts, and in due method distributed them to pious and charitable uses.

The name of an officer (lord almoner) of the English kings, in former times, who distributed the royal alms or bounty.

Eleemosynary /èləmósənè(h)riy/èliyəmózənè(h)riy/. Relating or devoted to charity; given in charity; having the nature of alms. United Community Services v. Omaha Nat. Bank, 162 Nev. 786, 77 N.W.2d 576, 582. See **Charity; Charitable.**

Eleemosynary corporation. A private corporation created for charitable and benevolent purposes. Charitable corporation. See also **Charitable organizations.**

Eleemosynary defense. Term used to describe defense available in some jurisdictions for charitable corporations and institutions when they are sued in tort; though such tort immunity has been abrogated or greatly restricted in many states.

Eleganter /èləgǽntər/. In the civil law, accurately; with discrimination.

Elegit /əlíyjət/. (Lat. He has chosen.) This was the name, in English practice, of a writ of execution first given by the statute of Westm. 2 (13 Edw. I, c. 18) either upon a judgment for a debt or damages or upon the forfeiture of a recognizance taken in the king's court. It was so called because it was in the choice or election of the plaintiff whether he would sue out this writ or a fi. fa. By it the defendant's goods and chattels were appraised and all of them (except oxen and beasts of the plow) were delivered to the plaintiff, at such reasonable appraisement and price, in part satisfaction of his debt. If the goods were not sufficient, then the moiety of his freehold lands, which he had at the time of the judgment given, were also to be delivered to the plaintiff, to hold till out of the rents and profits thereof the debt be levied, or till the defendant's interest be expired. During this period the plaintiff was called "tenant by *elegit,*" and his estate, an "estate by *elegit.*" Such writ was abolished by Administration of Justice Act of 1956.

Element. Material; substance; ingredient; factor.

Also, one of the simple substances or principles of which, according to early natural philosophers, the physical universe is composed, the four elements pointed out by Empedocles being fire, air, water, earth. See **Elements.**

Elements. The forces of nature. Violent or severe weather. The ultimate undecomposable parts which unite to form anything. Popularly, fire, air, earth, and water, anciently supposed to be the four simple bodies of which the world was composed. Often applied in a particular sense to wind and water, as "the fury of the elements." Fire and water as elements included in the expression "damages by the elements" means the same thing as "damages by the act of God."

Elements of crime. Those constituent parts of a crime which must be proved by the prosecution to sustain a conviction.

Eleventh Amendment. The Amendment to the U.S. Constitution, added in 1798, which provides that the judicial power of the U.S. shall not extend to any suit in law or equity, commenced or prosecuted against one of the United States by citizens of another state, or by citizens or subjects of any foreign state.

Eligible. Fit and proper to be chosen; qualified to be elected. Capable of serving, legally qualified to serve. Capable of being chosen, as a candidate for office. Also, qualified and capable of holding office. See also **Capacity.**

Elimination. In old English law, the act of banishing or turning out of doors; rejection.

Elinguation /iylìngwéyshən/. The punishment of cutting out the tongue.

Elisors /əláyzərz/. Electors or choosers. Persons appointed by the court to execute writs of *venire,* in cases where both the sheriff and coroner are disqualified from acting, and whose duty is to *choose*—that is, name and return—the jury. 3 Bl.Comm. 355.

Persons appointed to execute *any* writ, in default of the sheriff and coroner, are also called "elisors." An elisor may be appointed to take charge of a jury retiring to deliberate upon a verdict, when both sheriff and coroner are disqualified or unable to act.

Elkins Act. Federal Act (1903) which strengthened the Interstate Commerce Act by prohibiting rebates and other forms of preferential treatment to large shippers.

Ell. A measure of length answering to the modern yard. 1 Bl.Comm. 275. See also **Meter.**

Ellenborough's Act /élənbrəz ǽkt/. An English statute (43 Geo. III, c. 58) punishing offenses against the person.

Ellipsis /əlípsəs/. Omission of words or clauses necessary to complete the construction, but not necessary to convey the meaning.

Elogium /əlówjiyəm/. In the civil law, a will or testament.

Eloigne /əlóyn/. (Fr. *éloigner,* to remove to a distance; to remove afar off.) A return to a writ of replevin, when the chattels have been removed out of the way of the sheriff.

Eloignment /əlóynmənt/. The getting a thing or person out of the way; or removing it to a distance, so as to be out of reach.

Elongata /ǝlòŋgéydǝ/ìyloŋgéydǝ/. Eloigned; carried away to a distance. The old form of the return made by a sheriff to a writ of replevin, stating that the goods or beasts had been *eloigned;* that is, carried to a distance, to places to him unknown. 3 Bl.Comm. 148. The word *eloigne* is sometimes used as synonymous with *elongata.*

Elongatus /ìyloŋgéydǝs/. Eloigned. A return made by a sheriff to a writ *de homine replegiando,* stating that the party to be replevied has been eloigned, or conveyed out of his jurisdiction. 3 Bl.Comm. 129.

Elongavit /ìyloŋgéyvǝt/. In England, where in a proceeding by foreign attachment the plaintiff has obtained judgment of appraisement, but by reason of some act of the garnishee the goods cannot be appraised (as where he has removed them from the city, or has sold them, etc.), the serjeant-at-mace returns that the garnishee has eloigned them, *i.e.,* removed them out of the jurisdiction, and on this return (called an "elongavit") judgment is given for the plaintiff that an inquiry be made of the goods eloigned. This inquiry is set down for trial, and the assessment is made by a jury after the manner of ordinary issues.

Elopement. The act of a wife who voluntarily deserts her husband to go away with and cohabit with another man. The departure of a married woman from her husband and dwelling with an adulterer. Also, the act of a man in going away with a woman who has voluntarily left her husband, to indulge in sexual intercourse with her.

In a more popular sense, the act of an unmarried woman in secretly leaving her home with a man, especially with a view to marriage without her parents' consent.

Elsewhere. In another place; in any other place. The term does not always mean literally any other place whatever, but may be more or less limited by the context.

In shipping articles, this term, following the designation of the port of destination, must be construed either as void for uncertainty or as subordinate to the principal voyage stated in the preceding words.

Eluviation /ǝl(y)ùwviyéyshǝn/. Movement of soil caused by excessive water in soil.

Emanations. The act of coming or flowing forth from something. That which flows or comes forth from something. An effluence.

Emancipated minor. A person under 18 years of age who is totally self-supporting.

Emancipation. The act by which one who was unfree, or under the power and control of another, is rendered free, or set at liberty and made his own master.

The term is principally used with reference to the emancipation of a minor child by its parents, which involves an entire surrender of the right to the care, custody, and earnings of such child as well as a renunciation of parental duties. Glover v. Glover, 44 Tenn.App. 712, 319 S.W.2d 238, 241. The emancipation may be express, as by voluntary agreement of parent and child, or implied from such acts and conduct as import consent, and it may be conditional or absolute, complete or partial. Complete emancipa-

tion is entire surrender of care, custody, and earnings of child, as well as renunciation of parental duties. And a "partial emancipation" frees a child for only a part of the period of minority, or from only a part of the parent's rights, or for some purposes, and not for others.

There is no fixed age when a child becomes emancipated (though it is usually upon reaching majority); it does not automatically occur on reaching majority. Turner v. McCune, Mass.App., 357 N.E.2d 942.

In Roman law, the enfranchisement of a son by his father, which was anciently done by the formality of an imaginary sale. This was abolished by Justinian, who substituted the simpler proceeding of a manumission before a magistrate.

Emancipation proclamation. An executive proclamation, issued January 1, 1863, by Abraham Lincoln, declaring that all persons held in slavery in certain designated states and districts were and should remain free.

Embargo /ǝmbárgow/. A proclamation or order of government, usually issued in time of war or threatened hostilities, prohibiting the departure of ships or goods from some or all ports until further order. Government order prohibiting commercial trade with individuals or businesses of other nations. Legal prohibition on commerce.

The temporary or permanent sequestration of the property of individuals for the purposes of a government, *e.g.,* to obtain vessels for the transport of troops, the owners being reimbursed for this forced service.

Embassador. See **Ambassador.**

Embassy /émbǝsiy/ or **Embassage** /émbǝsǝj/. Mission, function, business, or official residence of an ambassador. Body of diplomatic representatives headed by ambassador. See **Ambassador.**

Ember Days. In ecclesiastical law, those days which the ancient fathers called *"quatuor tempora jejunii"* are of great antiquity in the church. They are observed on Wednesday, Friday, and Saturday next after Quadragesima Sunday, or the first Sunday in Lent, after Whitsuntide, Holyrood Day, in September, and St. Lucy's Day, about the middle of December. Our almanacs call the weeks in which they fall the "Ember Weeks," and they are now chiefly noticed on account of the ordination of priests and deacons; because the canon appoints the Sundays next after the Ember weeks for the solemn times of ordination, though the bishops, if they please, may ordain on any Sunday or holiday.

Embezzlement. To "embezzle" means willfully to take, or convert to one's own use, another's money or property, of which the wrongdoer acquired possession lawfully, by reason of some office or employment or position of trust. The elements of "embezzlement" are that there must be relationship such as that of employment or agency between the owner of the money and the defendant, the money alleged to have been embezzled must have come into the possession of defendant by virtue of that relationship and there must be an intentional and fraudulent appropriation or conversion of the money. State v.

Thyfault, 121 N.J.Super. 487, 297 A.2d 873, 879. The fraudulent conversion of the property of another by one who has lawful possession of the property and whose fraudulent conversion has been made punishable by statute. See also **Conversion.**

Emblemata triboniani /emblémədə trəbòwniyéynay/. In the Roman law, alterations, modifications, and additions to the writings of the older jurists, selected to make up the body of the Pandects, introduced by Tribonian and his associates who constituted the commission appointed for that purpose, with a view to harmonize contradictions, exscind obsolete matter, and make the whole conform to the law as understood in Justinian's time, were called by this name.

Emblements /émbləmənts/. Crops annually produced by labor of tenant. Corn, wheat, rye, potatoes, garden vegetables, and other crops which are produced annually, not spontaneously, but by labor and industry. Finley v. McClure, 222 Kan. 637, 567 P.2d 851, 853. The doctrine of emblements denotes the right of a tenant to take and carry away, after his tenancy has ended, such annual products of the land as have resulted from his own care and labor. See **Fructus industriales.**

Emblers de gentz /émblərz də jénts/. L. Fr. A stealing from the people. The phrase occurs in the old English rolls of parliament: "Whereas divers murders, *emblers de gentz,* and robberies are committed," etc.

Embolism /émbəlizəm/. The mechanical obstruction of an artery or capillary by some body traveling in the blood current, as, a blood-clot (embolus), a globule of fat or an air bubble.

Embolus /émbələs/. In case of wounds is a product of coagulation of the blood or blood clot. A plug which floats along until it becomes lodged so as to obstruct the passage of the blood. It consists usually of a clot or fibrin, a shred from a morbid growth, a globule of fat, air bubbles, or a microorganism. An embolus or floating particle by attaching itself or becoming wedged may form a thrombosis or occlusion.

Embraceor /əmbréysər/. A person guilty of the offense of embracery *(q.v.).*

Embracery /əmbréysəriy/. The crime of attempting to influence a jury corruptly to one side or the other, by promises, persuasions, entreaties, entertainments, *douceurs,* and the like. The person guilty of it is called an "embraceor." This is both a state and federal (18 U.S.C.A. §§ 1503, 1504) crime.

Emenda /əméndə/. Amends; something given in reparation for a trespass; or, in old Saxon times, in compensation for an injury or crime.

Emendare /ìyməndériy/. In Saxon law, to make amends or satisfaction for any crime or trespass committed; to pay a fine; to be fined. *Emendare se,* to redeem, or ransom one's life, by payment of a weregild.

Emendatio /èməndéysh(iy)ow/. In old English law, amendment, or correction. The power of amending and correcting abuses, according to certain rules and measures.

In Saxon law, a pecuniary satisfaction for an injury; the same as *emenda (q.v.).*

Emendatio panis et cerevisiæ /èməndéysh(iy)ow pǽnəs èt sərəvíz(h)iyiy/. In old English law, the power of supervising and correcting the weights and measures of bread and ale (assising bread and beer).

E mera gratia /iy mírə gréysh(iy)ə/. Out of mere grace or favor.

Emerge /əmə́rj/. To arise; to come to light.

Emergency. A sudden unexpected happening; an unforeseen occurrence or condition; perplexing contingency or complication of circumstances; a sudden or unexpected occasion for action; exigency; pressing necessity. Emergency is an unforeseen combination of circumstances that calls for immediate action. State v. Perry, 29 Ohio App.2d 33, 278 N.E.2d 50, 53. See also **Emergency doctrine; Sudden emergency doctrine.**

Emergency Court of Appeals. Court created during World War II to review orders of the Price Control Administrator. It was abolished in 1953. This court was established again in 1970 under Section 211 of the Economic Stabilization Act to handle primarily wage and price control matters.

Emergency doctrine. Under the doctrine variously referred to as the "emergency," "imminent peril," or "sudden peril" doctrine, when one is confronted with a sudden peril requiring instinctive action, he is not, in determining his course of action, held to the exercise of the same degree of care as when he has time for reflection, and in the event that a driver of a motor vehicle suddenly meets with an emergency which naturally would overpower the judgment of a reasonably prudent and careful driver, so that momentarily he is thereby rendered incapable of deliberate and intelligent action, and as a result injures a third person, he is not negligent, provided he has used due care to avoid meeting such an emergency and, after it arises, he exercises such care as a reasonably prudent and capable driver would use under the unusual circumstances. Sandberg v. Spoelstra, 46 Wash.2d 776, 285 P.2d 564, 568.

In an emergency situation when medical service is required for an adult who by virtue of his physical condition is incapable of giving consent, or with respect to a child, whose parent or other guardian is absent, and thus incapable of giving consent, the law implies the consent required to administer emergency medical services. This is a good defense to an action of tort for an alleged battery.

Emergency employment doctrine. A regularly employed servant possesses implied authority to engage an assistant to aid in performing a task, within scope of servant's duties in case of emergency rendering it absolutely necessary to obtain such assistance, and without which emergency conditions could not be overcome by servant or any of his coemployees in regular service of their common master. Hall v. O. C. Whitaker Co., 143 Tex. 397, 185 S.W.2d 720, 722, 723.

Emergent year. The epoch or date whence any people begin to compute their time.

Emigrant /émagrant/. One who leaves his country for any reason, with intention to not return, with design to reside elsewhere. See also **Immigrant.**

Emigrant agent. One engaged in the business of hiring laborers for work outside the country or state.

Emigration. The act of removing from one country to another, with intention to not return. It is to be distinguished from "expatriation" which means the abandonment of one's country and renunciation of one's citizenship in it, while emigration denotes merely the removal of person and property to another country. The former is usually the consequence of the latter. Emigration is also sometimes used in reference to the removal from one section to another of the same country. See also **Deportation; Immigration.**

Emigré. Person forced to emigrate for political reasons. See also **Deportation.**

Eminence /émənən(t)s/. An honorary title given to cardinals. They were called *"illustrissimi"* and *"reverendissimi"* until the pontificate of Urban VIII.

Eminent domain /émənənt dəméyn/. The power to take private property for public use by the state, municipalities, and private persons or corporations authorized to exercise functions of public character. Housing Authority of Cherokee National of Oklahoma v. Langley, Okl., 555 P.2d 1025, 1028. Fifth Amendment, U.S. Constitution.

In the United States, the power of eminent domain is founded in both the federal (Fifth Amend.) and state constitutions. However, the Constitution limits the power to taking for a public purpose and prohibits the exercise of the power of eminent domain without just compensation to the owners of the property which is taken. The process of exercising the power of eminent domain is commonly referred to as "condemnation", or, "expropriation".

The right of eminent domain is the right of the state, through its regular organization, to reassert, either temporarily or permanently, its dominion over any portion of the soil of the state on account of public exigency and for the public good. Thus, in time of war or insurrection, the proper authorities may possess and hold any part of the territory of the state for the common safety; and in time of peace the legislature may authorize the appropriation of the same to public purposes, such as the opening of roads, construction of defenses, or providing channels for trade or travel. Eminent domain is the highest and most exact idea of property remaining in the government, or in the aggregate body of the people in their sovereign capacity. It gives a right to resume the possession of the property in the manner directed by the constitution and the laws of the state, whenever the public interest requires it.

See also Adequate compensation; Condemnation; Constructive taking; Damages; Expropriation; Fair market value; Just compensation; Larger parcel; Public use; Take.

Expropriation. The term "expropriation" (used *e.g.* in Louisiana) is practically synonymous with the term "eminent domain". Tennessee Gas Transmission Co. v. Violet Trapping Co., La.App., 200 So.2d 428, 433.

Partial taking. The taking of part of an owner's property under the laws of eminent domain. Compensation must be based on damages or benefits to the remaining property, as well as the part taken. See **Condemnation.**

Emissary /émǝsèriy/. A person sent upon a mission as the agent of another; also a secret agent sent to ascertain the sentiments and designs of others, and to propagate opinions favorable to his employer. See **Ambassador; Diplomat.**

Emission. The discharge, ejection or throwing out of; *e.g.* a pollutant from a factory or any secretion or other matter from the body.

Emit. To put forth or send out; to issue. "No state shall *emit* bills of credit." Art. 1, § 10, U.S. Const.

To give forth with authority; to give out or discharge; to put into circulation. See **Bill** (*Bill of credit*).

Emolument /əmólyəmənt/. The profit arising from office or employment; that which is received as a compensation for services, or which is annexed to the possession of office as salary, fees, and perquisites. Any perquisite, advantage, profit, or gain arising from the possession of an office. McLean v. United States, 226 U.S. 374, 38 S.Ct. 122, 124, 57 L.Ed. 260; State ex rel. Todd v. Reeves, 196 Wash. 145, 82 P.2d 173, 175.

Emotion. A strong feeling of hate, love, sorrow and the like arising within a person and not as a result, necessarily, of conscious activity of the mind.

Emotional insanity. The species of mental aberration produced by a violent excitement of the emotions or passions, though the reasoning faculties may remain unimpaired. A passion, effecting for a space of time complete derangement of accused's intellect, or an impulse, which his mind is not able to resist, to do the act. Fannon v. Commonwealth, 295 Ky. 817, 175 S.W.2d 531, 533. See **Insanity.**

Empalement /əmpéylmənt/. In ancient law, a mode of inflicting punishment, by thrusting a sharp pole up the fundament.

Empannel. See **Impanel.**

Emparlance. See **Imparlance.**

Emparnours /əmpárnərz/. L. Fr. Undertakers of suits.

Emperor. The title of the sovereign ruler of an empire. This designation was adopted by the rulers of the Roman world after the decay of the republic, and was assumed by those who claimed to be their successors in the "Holy Roman Empire," as also by Napoleon. The sovereigns of Japan and Morocco are often, though with little propriety, called emperors. In western speech the former sovereigns of Turkey and China were called emperors.

The title "emperor" seems to denote a power and dignity superior to that of a "king." It appears to be the appropriate style of the executive head of a federal government, constructed on the monarchial principle, and comprising in its organization several distinct kingdoms or other *quasi* sovereign states; as was the case with the German empire from 1871 to 1918. The proper meaning of *emperor* is the chief of a confederation of states of which kings are members. In general, an *emperor* is the holder of a sovereignty extending over conquered or confederated peoples, a *king* is ruler of a single people.

Emphasizing facts. A jury instruction is said to emphasize facts which may contain sufficient facts to authorize a verdict, but nevertheless some fact or facts are selected from the evidence and mentioned in such a way as to indicate to the jury that they have especial importance when that is not justified. Robinson v. Ross, Mo., 47 S.W.2d 122, 125.

Emphyteusis /èmfətyúwsəs/. In the Roman and civil law, a contract by which a landed estate was leased to a tenant, either in perpetuity or for a long term of years, upon the reservation of an annual rent or *canon,* and upon the condition that the lessee should improve the property, by building, cultivating, or otherwise, and with a right in the lessee to alien the estate at pleasure or pass it to his heirs by descent, and free from any revocation, re-entry, or claim of forfeiture on the part of the grantor, except for nonpayment of the rent. 3 Bl.Comm. 232.

The right granted by such a contract (*jus emphyteuticum,* or *emphyteuticarium*). The real right by which a person is entitled to enjoy another's estate as if it were his own, and to dispose of its substance, as far as can be done without deteriorating it.

Emphyteuta /èmfətyúwdə/. In the civil law, the person to whom an *emphyteusis* is granted; the lessee or tenant under a contract of *emphyteusis.*

Emphyteuticus /èmfətyúwdəkəs/. In the civil law, founded on, growing out of, or having the character of, an *emphyteusis;* held under an *emphyteusis.* 3 Bl.Comm. 232.

Empire. The dominion or jurisdiction of an emperor; the region over which the dominion of an emperor extends; imperial power; supreme dominion; sovereign command.

Empiric /əmpírək/. A practitioner in medicine or surgery, who proceeds on experience only, without science or legal qualification; a quack.

Empirical. That which is based on experience, experiment, or observation.

Emplazamiento /emplàsimyéntow/. In Spanish law, a summons or citation, issued by authority of a judge, requiring the person to whom it is addressed to appear before the tribunal at a designated day and hour.

Emplead. To indict; to prefer a charge against; to accuse.

Emploi /òmplwá/. In French law, equitable conversion. When property covered by the *régime dotal* is sold, the proceeds of the sale must be reinvested for the benefit of the wife. It is the duty of the purchaser to see that the price is so reinvested.

Employ. To engage in one's service; to hire; to use as an agent or substitute in transacting business; to commission and intrust with the performance of certain acts or functions or with the management of one's affairs; and, when used in respect to a servant or hired laborer, the term is equivalent to hiring, which implies a request and a contract for a compensation. Tennessee Coal Iron & R. Co. v. Muscoda Local No. 123, Ala., 321 U.S. 590, 64 S.Ct. 698, 703, 705, 88 L.Ed. 949. To make use of, to keep at work, to entrust with some duty. See also **Employment.**

Employed. Term signifies both the act of doing a thing and the being under contract or orders to do it. To give employment to; to have employment.

Employee. A person in the service of another under any contract of hire, express or implied, oral or written, where the employer has the power or right to control and direct the employee in the material details of how the work is to be performed. Riverbend Country Club v. Patterson, Tex.Civ.App., 399 S.W.2d 382, 383. One who works for an employer; a person working for salary or wages.

Generally, when person for whom services are performed has right to control and direct individual who performs services not only as to result to be accomplished by work but also as to details and means by which result is accomplished, individual subject to direction is an "employee".

"Servant" is synonymous with "employee". Gibson v. Gillette Motor Transport, Tex.Civ.App., 138 S.W.2d 293, 294; Tennessee Valley Appliances v. Rowden, 24 Tenn.App. 487, 146 S.W.2d 845, 848. However, "employee" must be distinguished from "independent contractor," "officer," "vice-principal," "agent," etc.

The term is often specially defined by statutes (*e.g.* workers' compensation acts; Fair Labor Standards Act), and whether one is an employee or not within a particular statute will depend upon facts and circumstances.

For **"Executive employees"**, see that title. See also **Borrowed employee; Servant.**

Employer. One who employs the services of others; one for whom employees work and who pays their wages or salaries. The correlative of "employee."

Employers' liability acts. Statutes (*e.g.* Federal Employers' Liability Act; Workers' Compensation Acts) defining or limiting the occasions and the extent to which employers shall be liable in damages for injuries to their employees occurring in the course of the employment, and particularly abolishing the common-law rule that the employer is not liable if the injury is caused by the fault or negligence of a fellow servant.

Employment. Act of employing or state of being employed; that which engages or occupies; that which consumes time or attention; also an occupation, profession, trade, post or business. Hinton v. Columbia River Packers' Ass'n, C.C.A.Or., 117 F.2d 310. Includes the doing of the work and a reasonable margin of time and space required in passing to and from the place where the work is to be done. California Casualty Indemnity Exchange v. Industrial Accident Commission, 21 Cal.2d 751, 135 P.2d 158, 161; Park Utah Consol. Mines Co. v. Industrial Commission, 103 Utah 64, 133 P.2d 314, 317. Activity in which person engages or is employed; normally, on a day-to-day basis. See also **Casual employment; Course of employment; Seasonable employment.**

Employment agency. Business operated by a person, firm or corporation engaged in procuring, for a fee, employment for others and employees for employers. The fee may be paid by either the employer or the employee, depending upon the terms of the agreement. See also **Finder.**

Employment contract. An agreement or contract between employer and employee in which the terms and conditions of one's employment are provided.

Emporium /əmpóriyəm/. A place for wholesale trade in commodities carried by sea. The name is sometimes applied to a seaport town, but it properly signifies only a particular place in such a town.

Empower. A grant of authority rather than a command of its exercise. In re Whiteman's Will, 268 App.Div. 591, 52 N.Y.S.2d 723, 725. See **Power.**

Empresarios /èmpreysáriyows/. In Mexican law, undertakers or promoters of extensive enterprises, aided by concessions or monopolistic grants from government; particularly, persons receiving extensive land grants in consideration of their bringing emigrants into the country and settling them on the lands, with a view of increasing the population and developing the resources of the country. U. S. v. Maxwell Land-Grant Co., 121 U.S. 325, 7 S.Ct. 1015, 30 L.Ed. 949.

Emprestido /èmpreystíyðow/. In Spanish law, a loan. Something lent to the borrower at his request.

Emptio /ém(p)sh(iy)ow/. In the Roman and civil law, the act of buying; a purchase.

Emptio bonorum /ém(p)sh(iy)ow bənórəm/. A species of forced assignment for the benefit of creditors; being a public sale of an insolvent debtor's estate whereby the purchaser succeeded to all his property, rights, and claims, and became responsible for his debts and liabilities to the extent of a quota fixed before the transfer.

Emptio et venditio /ém(p)sh(iy)ow èt vəndísh(iy)ow/. Purchase and sale; sometimes translated "emption and vendition." The name of the contract of sale in the Roman law. Sometimes made a compound word, *emptio-venditio.*

Emptio rei speratæ /ém(p)sh(iy)ow ríyay spəréydiy/. A purchase in the hope of an uncertain future profit; the purchase of a thing not yet in existence or not yet in the possession of the seller, as, the cast of a net or a crop to be grown, and the price of which is to depend on the actual gain. On the other hand, if the price is fixed and not subject to fluctuation, but is to be paid whether the gain be greater or less, it is called *emptio spei.*

Emptor /ém(p)tər/. Lat. A buyer or purchaser. Used in the maxim *"caveat emptor,"* let the buyer beware; *i.e.,* the buyer of an article must be on his guard and take the risks of his purchase. See **Caveat emptor.**

Emptor emit quam minimo potest, venditor vendit quam maximo potest /ém(p)tər émət kwæm mínəmow pówdəst, véndədər véndət kwæm mæksəmow pówdəst/. The buyer purchases for the lowest price he can; the seller sells for the highest price he can.

Emtio /ém(p)sh(iy)ow/. In the civil law, purchase. This form of the word is used in the Digests and Code. See **Emptio.**

Emtor /ém(p)tər/. In the civil law, a buyer or purchaser; the buyer.

Emtrix /ém(p)trəks/. In the civil law, a female purchaser; the purchaser.

Enable. To give power to do something; to make able. In the case of a person under disability as to dealing with another, "enable" has the primary meaning of removing that disability; not of conferring a compulsory power as against that other.

Enabling Act. See **Enabling statute.**

Enabling clause. That portion of a statute or constitution which gives to governmental officials the right to put it into effect and to enforce such. See **Enforcement powers.**

Enabling power. When the donor of a power, who is the owner of the estate, confers upon persons not seised of the fee the right of creating interests to take effect out of it, which could not be done by the donee of the power unless by such authority, this is called an "enabling power." See also **Power of appointment.**

Enabling statute. Term applied to any statute enabling persons or corporations to do what before they could not. It is applied to statutes which confer new powers. See also **Enabling clause.**

The English Act of 32 Henry VIII, c. 28, by which tenants in tail, husbands seised in right of their wives, and others were empowered to make leases for their lives or for twenty-one years, which they could not do before. 2 Bl.Comm. 319.

Enach. In Saxon law, the satisfaction for a crime; the recompense for a fault.

Enact. To establish by law; to perform or effect; to decree. The common introductory formula in making statutory laws is, *"Be it enacted."* See **Enacting clause.**

Enacting clause. A clause at the beginning of a statute which states the authority by which it is made. That part of a statute which declares its enactment and serves to identify it as an act of legislation proceeding from the proper legislative authority. Various formulas are used for this clause, such as "Be it enacted by the people of the state of Illinois represented in general assembly," "Be it enacted by the senate and house of representatives of the United States of America in congress assembled," "The general assembly do enact," etc.

Enactment. The method or process by which a bill in the Legislature becomes a law.

Enajenacion /eynàheynasyówn/. In Spanish and Mexican law, alienation; transfer of property. The act by which the property in a thing, by lucrative title, is transferred, as a donation; or by onerous title, as by sale or barter. In a more extended sense, the term comprises also the contracts of emphyteusis, pledge, and mortgage, and even the creation of a servitude upon an estate.

En arere /èn ərír/. L. Fr. In time past.

En autre droit /ən ówtrə dróyt/òn ówtrə dr(w)ó/. In the right of another. See **Autre droit.**

En banc /ən bæŋk/òn bóŋk/. L. Fr. In the bench. Full bench. Refers to a session where the entire membership of the court will participate in the decision rather than the regular quorum. In other countries, it is common for a court to have more members than are usually necessary to hear an appeal. In the United States, the Circuit Courts of Appeal usually sit in panels of judges but for important cases may expand the bench to a larger number, when they are said to be sitting *en banc.* See Fed.R.App.P. 35. An appellate court in which all the judges who are necessary for a quorum are sitting as contrasted with a session of such court presided over by a single justice or panel of justices.

En bloc /òn blók/. As a unit; as a whole.

Enbrever /ənbríyvər/. L. Fr. To write down in short; to abbreviate, or, in old language, *imbreviate;* to put into a schedule.

En brevet /òn brəvéy/. In French law, an *acte* is said to be *en brevet* when a copy of it has not been recorded by the notary who drew it.

Enceinte /ònsǽnt/. Pregnant. See **Pregnancy.**

Encheson /ənchíyzən/. The occasion, cause, or reason for which anything is done.

Enclose. See **Inclose.**

Enclosure /ənklówzhər/. See **Inclosure.**

Encomienda /enkòwmiyéndə/. In Spanish law, a grant from the crown to a private person of a certain portion of territory in the Spanish colonies, together with the concession of a certain number of the native inhabitants, on the feudal principle of commendation. Also a royal grant of privileges to the military orders of Spain.

Encourage. In criminal law, to instigate; to incite to action; to give courage to; to inspirit; to embolden; to raise confidence; to make confident; to help; to forward; to advise. See **Aid and abet.**

Encroach. To enter by gradual steps or stealth into the possessions or rights of another; to trespass or intrude. To gain or intrude unlawfully upon the lands, property, or authority of another.

Encroachment. An illegal intrusion in a highway or navigable river, with or without obstruction. Hartford Elec. Light Co. v. Water Resources Commission, 162 Conn. 89, 291 A.2d 721, 730. An encroachment upon a street or highway is a fixture, such as a wall or fence, which illegally intrudes into or invades the highway or incloses a portion of it, diminishing its width or area, but without closing it to public travel.

In the law of easements, where the owner of an easement alters the dominant tenement, so as to impose an additional restriction or burden on the servient tenement, he is said to commit an encroachment.

Encumbrance. Any right to, or interest in, land which may subsist in another to diminution of its value, but consistent with the passing of the fee. Knudson v. Weeks, D.C.Okl., 394 F.Supp. 963, 976. A claim, lien, charge, or liability attached to and binding real property; *e.g.* a mortgage; judgment lien; mechanics' lien; lease; security interest; easement or right of way; accrued and unpaid taxes.

End. Object; intent; result; goal; termination point. Things are construed according to the end.

Endeavor. To exert physical and intellectual strength toward the attainment of an object. A systematic or continuous effort. Thompson v. Corbin, Tex.Civ. App., 137 S.W.2d 157, 159.

En déclaration de simulation /òn dèklarasyówn də sìm(y)əlasyówn/. A form of action used in Louisiana. Its object is to have a contract declared judicially a simulation and a nullity, to remove a cloud from the title, and to bring back, for any legal purpose, the thing sold to the estate of the true owner.

En demeure /òn dəmyúr/. In default. Used in Louisiana of a debtor who fails to pay on demand according to the terms of his obligation.

Endenzie, or **endenizen** /əndénəzən/. To make free; to enfranchise.

End lines. In mining law, the end lines of a claim, as platted or laid down on the ground, are those which mark its boundaries on the shorter dimension, where it crosses the vein, while the "side lines" are those which mark its longer dimension, where it follows the course of the vein. But with reference to extra-lateral rights, if the claim as a whole crosses the vein, instead of following its course, the end lines will become side lines and vice versa.

Endocarditis /èndowkardáydəs/. An inflammation of the living membrane of the heart.

End of will. Point in will at which dispositive provisions terminate. In re Coyne's Estate, 349 Pa. 331, 37 A.2d 509, 510. Such is normally followed by attestation clauses.

Endorsement. See **Indorsement.**

Endorsee. See **Indorsee.**

Endorser. See **Indorser.**

Endow. To give a dower; to bestow upon; to make pecuniary provision for.

Endowment. Transfer, generally as a gift, of money or property to an institution for a particular purpose such as a gift to a hospital for medical research. The act of settling a fund, or permanent pecuniary provision, for the maintenance of a public institution, charity, college, etc.

The assignment of dower; the setting off a woman's dower. 2 Bl.Comm. 135.

Endowment insurance. See **Insurance.**

Endowment policy. Insurance policy under which insurer agrees to pay insured a stated sum at end of definite period, or, if insured dies before end of such period, to pay amount to person designated as beneficiary. Spellacy v. American Life Ins. Ass'n, 144 Conn. 346, 131 A.2d 834, 838.

Endurance. State or capability of lasting; continuance; or act or instance of bearing or suffering. A continuing or the power of continuing under pain, hardship, or distress without being overcome. Sufferance; as beyond endurance. State ex rel. Adams v. Crowder, 46 N.M. 20, 120 P.2d 428, 431.

Enemy. Adversary; *e.g.* military adversary.

Enemy alien. An alien residing or traveling in a country which is at war with the country of which he is a national. Enemy aliens may be interned or restricted.

Enemy belligerent. Citizens who associate themselves with the military arm of an enemy government and enter the United States bent on hostile acts. Ex parte Quirin, App.D.C., 317 U.S. 1, 63 S.Ct. 2, 15, 87 L.Ed. 3.

Enemy's property. In international law, and particularly in the usage of prize courts, this term designates any property which is engaged or used in illegal intercourse with the public enemy, whether belonging to an ally or a citizen, as the illegal traffic stamps it with the hostile character and attaches to it all the penal consequences.

Public enemy. A nation at war with the United States; also every citizen or subject of such nation. Term however does not generally include robbers, thieves, private depredators, or riotous mobs. The term has acquired, in the vocabulary of journalism and civic indignation, a more extended meaning, denoting a particularly notorious offender against the criminal laws, especially one who seems more or less immune from successful prosecution, or a social, health or economic condition or problem affecting the public at large, which is difficult to abate or control.

Energy, Department of. The Department of Energy (DOE) provides the framework for a comprehensive and balanced national energy plan through the coordination and administration of the energy functions of the Federal Government. The Department is responsible for the research, development, and demonstration of energy technology; the marketing of Federal power; energy conservation; the nuclear weapons program; regulation of energy production and use; pricing and allocation; and a central energy data collection and analysis program.

En eschange il covient que les estates soient egales. In an exchange it is desirable that the estates be equal.

En fait /òn féy/. Fr. In fact; in deed; actually.

Enfeoff /ènfíyf/ənféf/. To invest with an estate by feoffment. To make a gift of any corporeal hereditaments to another. See **Feoffment.**

Enfeoffment /ənfíyfmənt/. The act of investing with any dignity or possession; also the instrument or deed by which a person is invested with possessions.

Enforce. To put into execution; to cause to take effect; to make effective; as, to enforce a particular law, a writ, a judgment, or the collection of a debt or fine; to compel obedience to. See *e.g.* **Attachment; Execution; Garnishment.**

Enforcement. The act of putting something such as a law into effect; the execution of a law; the carrying out of a mandate or command. See also **Enforcement powers.**

Enforcement of Foreign Judgments Act. One of the uniform laws adopted by several states which gives the holder of a foreign judgment essentially the same rights to levy and execution on his judgment as the holder of a domestic judgment. The Act defines a "foreign judgment" as any judgment, decree, or order of a court of the United States or of any other court which is entitled to full faith and credit in the state. See also **Full faith and credit clause.**

Enforcement powers. The 13th, 14th, 15th, 19th, 23rd, 24th, and 26th Amendments to U.S.Const. each contain clauses granting to Congress the power to enforce by appropriate legislation the provisions of such Amendments.

Enfranchisement. The act of making free (as from slavery); giving a franchise or freedom to; investiture with privileges or capacities of freedom, or municipal or political liberty. Conferring the privilege of voting upon classes of persons who have not previously possessed such. See also **Franchise.**

Enfranchisement of copyholds. In English law, the conversion of copyhold into freehold tenure, by a conveyance of the fee-simple of the property from the lord of the manor to the copyholder, or by a release from the lord of all seigniorial rights, etc., which destroys the customary descent, and also all rights and privileges annexed to the copyholder's estate.

Engage. To employ or involve one's self; to take part in; to embark on.

Engaged in commerce. To be "engaged in commerce" for purposes of Fair Labor Standards Act and Federal Employers' Liability Act, an employee must be actually engaged in the movement of commerce or the services he performs must be so closely related thereto as to be for all practical purposes an essential part thereof, rather than an isolated local activity. McLeod v. Threlkeld, Tex., 319 U.S. 491, 63 S.Ct. 1248, 1251, 1252, 87 L.Ed. 1538; Boutell v. Walling, C.C.A.Mich., 148 F.2d 329, 331. See also **Commerce.**

Engaged in employment. To be rendering service for employer under terms of employment, and is more than being merely hired to commence work. Walling v. Consumers Co., C.C.A.Ill., 149 F.2d 626, 629.

Engagement. A contract or agreement characterized by exchange of mutual promises; *e.g.* engagement to marry.

Engagement to marry. A promise or undertaking by a man to marry a woman, for breach of which, formerly, there was a cause of action in many jurisdictions. These actions today have lost favor and are not available in most states. Such actions were called heart balm suits. See **Heart balm statutes.**

Engender. To cause, to bring about, to excite, to occasion, to call forth.

Engineering. The art and science by which mechanical properties of matter are made useful to man in structures and machines. Employers' Liability Assur. Corporation v. Accident & Casualty Ins. Co. of Winterthur, Switzerland, C.C.A.Ohio, 134 F.2d 566, 569.

Engleshire /ínglǝshriy/. A law was made by Canute, for the preservation of his Danes, that, when a man was killed, the hundred or town should be liable to be amerced, unless it could be proved that the person killed was an Englishman. This proof was called "Engleshire."

En gros /òn grów/òŋ°/. Fr. In gross; total; by wholesale.

Engrossment. To copy in final draft. Drafting of resolution or bill just prior to final vote upon same in legislature. Buying up or securing enough of a commodity to obtain a monopoly, so as to resell at higher price; *i.e.* to corner market in such commodity. Preparing deed for execution.

Enhanced. Made greater; *e.g.* in value or attractiveness. This word, taken in an unqualified sense, is synonymous with "increased," and comprehends any increase of value, however caused or arising.

Enheritance. L. Fr. Inheritance.

Enitia pars /ənísh(iy)ə párz/. The share of the eldest. A term of the English law descriptive of the lot or share chosen by the eldest of coparceners when they make a voluntary partition. The first choice (*primer election*) belongs to the eldest.

Enitia pars semper præferenda est propter privilegium ætatis /ənísh(iy)ə párz sémpər prèfəréndə ést próptər prìvəlíyjiyəm ətéydəs/. The part of the elder sister is always to be preferred on account of the privilege of age.

Enjoin. To require; command; positively direct. To require a person, by writ of injunction, to perform, or to abstain or desist from, some act. See **Injunction; Restraining order.**

Enjoy. To have, possess, and use with satisfaction; to occupy or have benefit of.

Enjoyment. The exercise of a right; the possession and fruition of a right, privilege or incorporeal hereditament. Comfort, consolation, contentment, ease, happiness, pleasure and satisfaction.

Adverse enjoyment. The possession or exercise of an easement under a claim of right against the owner of the land out of which such easement is derived.

Quiet enjoyment. Covenant for. See **Covenant.**

En juicio /èn huwíys(i)yow/. Span. Judicially; in a court of law; in a suit at law.

Enlarge. To make larger; to increase; to extend a time limit; to grant further time. Also to set at liberty one who has been imprisoned or in custody.

Enlarger l'estate /ənlár jər ləstéyt/. A species of release which inures by way of enlarging an estate, and consists of a conveyance of the ulterior interest to the particular tenant; as if there be tenant for life or years, remainder to another in fee, and he in remainder releases all his right to the particular tenant and his heirs, this gives him the estate in fee.

Enlarging. Extending, expanding, or making more comprehensive.

Enlistment. Voluntary entry into one of the armed services other than as a commissioned officer.

En masse /òn mǽs/°más/. Fr. In a mass; in a lump; in bulk; at wholesale.

En mort mayne /ən mórt méyn/. L. Fr. In a dead hand; in mortmain.

Enoc Arden doctrine. The legal principles involved when a person leaves his spouse under such circumstances and for such a period of time as to make the other spouse believe that he is dead with the result that the remaining spouse marries another only to discover later the return of her first husband. Generally, in most states, it is safer for the remaining spouse to secure a divorce before marrying again.

Enormia /ənórmiyə/. In old practice and pleading, unlawful or wrongful acts; wrongs. *Et alia enormia,* and other wrongs. This phrase constantly occurs in the old writs and declarations of trespass.

Enormous. Aggravated; excessively large. Written "enormious," in some of the old books. *Enormious* is where a thing is made without a rule or against law.

En owel main /ən áwəl méyn/. L. Fr. In equal hand. The word *"owel"* occurs also in the phrase *"owelty* of partition."

Enpleet /ənplíyt/. Ancient for implead.

Enquête, or **enquest** /òŋkét/əŋkwést/. In canon law, an examination of witnesses, taken down in writing, by or before an authorized judge, for the purpose of gathering testimony to be used on a trial.

En recouvrement /òn reykùwvrəmón/. Fr. In French law, an expression employed to denote that an indorsement made in favor of a person does not transfer to him the property in the bill of exchange, but merely constitutes an authority to such person to recover the amount of the bill.

Enrégistrement /onrèyzhistrəmón/. In French law, registration. A formality which consists in inscribing on a register, specially kept for the purpose by the government, a summary analysis of certain deeds and documents. At the same time that such analysis is inscribed upon the register, the clerk places upon the deed a memorandum indicating the date upon which it was registered, and at the side of such memorandum an impression is made with a stamp.

Enroll. To register; to record; to enter on the rolls of a court; to transcribe.

Enrolled. Registered; recorded. Generally speaking, terms "registered" and "enrolled" are used to distinguish certificates granted to two classes of vessels; registry is for purpose of declaring nationality of vessel engaged in foreign trade, and enrollment evidences national character of a vessel engaged in coasting trade or home traffic. R. C. Craig Ltd. v. Ships of the Sea Inc., D.C.Ga., 401 F.Supp. 1051, 1056.

Enrolled bill. The final copy of a bill or joint resolution which has passed both houses of a legislature and is ready for signature. In legislative practice, a bill which has been duly introduced, finally passed by both houses, signed by the proper officers of each, approved by the governor (or President) and filed by the secretary of state.

Enrolled bill rule. Under "enrolled bill rule" it is conclusively presumed that statute, as authenticated and deposited in Secretary of State's office, is precisely same as enacted by Legislature and courts will not go behind enrolled bill. Nueces County v. King, Tex.Civ.App., 350 S.W.2d 385, 387. Under this rule, once an election which is had on question of adoption of statute is sanctioned by law and is held, it is then too late to question the steps or legal procedure by which the measure got on the ballot.

Enrollment. Act of recording, enrolling, or registering.

Enrollment of vessels. The recording and certification of vessels employed in coastwise or inland navigation; as distinguished from the "registration" of vessels employed in foreign commerce.

En route /òn rúwt/. Fr. On the way; in the course of a voyage or journey; in course of transportation.

Enschedule /ənskéjəl/. To insert in a list, account, or writing.

Enseal /ənsíyl/. To seal. *Ensealing* is still used as a formal word in conveyancing.

Enserver /ènsárvər/. L. Fr. To make subject to a service or servitude.

Ens legis /én(d)z líyjəs/. L. Lat. A creature of the law; an artificial being, as contrasted with a natural person. Applied to corporations, considered as deriving their existence entirely from the law.

Ensue /əns(y)úw/. To follow after; to follow in order or train of events.

Entail, *v.* To settle or limit the succession to real property; to create an estate tail.

Entail, *n.* A fee abridged or limited to the issue, or certain classes of issue, instead of descending to all the heirs.

Break or bar an entail. To free an estate from the limitations imposed by an entail and permit its free disposition, anciently by means of a fine or common recovery, but later by deed in which the tenant and next heir join.

Quasi entail. An estate *pur autre vie* may be granted, not only to a man and his heirs, but to a man and the heirs of his body, which is termed a *"quasi* entail;" the interest so granted not being properly an estate-tail (for the statute *De Donis* applies only where the subject of the entail is an estate of inheritance), but yet so far in the nature of an estate-tail that it will go to the heir of the body as special occupant during the life of the *cestui que vie*, in the same manner as an estate of inheritance would descend, if limited to the grantee and the heirs of his body.

Entailed. Settled or limited to specified heirs, or in tail.

Entailed money. Money directed to be invested in realty to be entailed.

Entailment. An interference with and curtailment of the ordinary rules pertaining to devolution by inheritance; a limitation and direction by which property is to descend different from the course which it would take if the creator of the entailment, grantor or testator, had been content that the estate should devolve in regular and general succession to heirs at law in the statutory order of precedence and sequence.

Entencion /ənténshən/. In old English law, the plaintiff's count or declaration.

Entendment. The old form of *intendment (q.v.)* derived directly from the French, and used to denote the true meaning or signification of a word or sentence; that is, the understanding or construction of law.

Enter. To form a constituent part; to become a part or partaker; to impenetrate; share or mix with, as, tin "enters" into the composition of pewter. Bedford v. Colorado Fuel & Iron Corporation, 102 Colo. 538, 81 P.2d 752, 755. To go or come into a place or condition; to make or effect an entrance; to cause to go into or be received into. Hancock v. State, Tex.Cr. App., 363 S.W.2d 273, 275.

In the law of real property, to go upon land for the purpose of taking possession of it. In strict usage, the entering is preliminary to the taking possession but in common parlance the entry is now merged in the taking possession. See **Entry.**

To place anything before a court, or upon or among the records, in a formal and regular manner, and usually in writing; as to "enter an appearance," to "enter a judgment." In this sense the word is nearly equivalent to setting down formally in writing, in either a full or abridged form. See **Appearance; Docket; Entering judgments; Entry.**

Enterceur /èntərsyú(wə)r/. L. Fr. A party challenging (claiming) goods; he who has placed them in the hands of a third person.

Entering. Generally synonymous with "recording". In re Labb, D.C.N.Y., 42 F.Supp. 542, 544.

Entering judgments. The formal entry of the judgment on the rolls or records (*e.g.* civil docket) of the court, which is necessary before bringing an appeal or an action on the judgment. The entering of judgment is a ministerial act performed by the clerk of court by means of which permanent evidence of judicial act in rendering judgment is made a record of the court. Knox v. Long, 152 Tex. 291, 257 S.W.2d 289, 291. Under some statutes or court rules, the entering consists merely in the filing of a judgment with the clerk, while under others the entry of a judgment consists in the recording of it in the judgment book or civil docket. Fed.R.Civil P. 55, 58, 79.

The "entry" of a judgment consists in recording of it in the judgment book, and there can be no record of a judgment until so entered. Wilson v. Los Angeles County Emp. Ass'n, 127 Cal.App.2d 285, 273 P.2d 824, 828.

Entry of judgment differs from rendition of judgment. "Rendition" of a judgment is the judicial act of the court in pronouncing the sentence of the law upon the facts in controversy. The "entry" is a ministerial act, which consists in entering upon the record a statement of the final conclusion reached by the court in the matter, thus furnishing external and incontestable evidence of the sentence given, and designed to stand as a perpetual memorial of its action.

Enterprise. A venture or undertaking especially one involving financial commitment. Sizemore v. Hall, 148 Kan. 233, 80 P.2d 1092, 1095. To find existence of "enterprise" within Fair Labor Standards Act, there must be related activities, unified operation or common control, and common business purpose. Brennan v. Arnheim & Neely, Inc., U.S.Pa., 410 U.S. 512, 93 S.Ct. 1138, 1142, 35 L.Ed.2d 463. See also **Joint enterprise.**

Entertainment expenses. Such expenses are deductible only if they are directly related or associated with business. Various restrictions and documentation requirements have been imposed by the Internal Revenue Code and Regulations upon the deductibility of entertainment expenses to prevent abuses.

Entice. To wrongfully solicit, persuade, procure, allure, attract, draw by blandishment, coax or seduce. To lure, induce, tempt, incite, or persuade a person to do a thing. Berger v. Levy, 5 Cal.App.2d 544, 43 P.2d 610, 611. Enticement of a child is inviting, persuading or attempting to persuade a child to enter any vehicle, building, room or secluded place with intent to commit an unlawful sexual act upon or with the person of said child.

Entire. Whole; without division, separation, or diminution; unmingled; complete in all its parts; not participated in by others.

Entire act. The words "entire act" as used in the rule of statutory construction that it is the duty of the court to examine the entire act means the caption, the body of the act, and the emergency clause. Anderson v. Penix, 138 Tex. 596, 161 S.W.2d 455, 459.

Entire balance of my estate. The residue.

Entire blood. Relations of the "entire blood" are those derived not only from the same ancestor, but from the same couple of ancestors. In re Skidmore's Estate, 148 Misc. 569, 266 N.Y.S. 312.

Entire contract. See **Contract.**

Entire day. This phrase signifies an undivided day, not parts of two days. An entire day must have a legal, fixed, precise time to begin, and a fixed, precise time to end. A day, in contemplation of law, comprises all the twenty-four hours, beginning and ending at twelve o'clock at night; *e.g.,* in a statute requiring the closing of all liquor establishments during "the entire day of any election," etc., this phrase means the natural day of twenty-four hours, commencing and terminating at midnight. See also **Day.**

Entire interest. The whole interest or right, without diminution. See **Fee simple.**

Entire loss of sight. In respect of one eye, or both, means substantial blindness, not necessarily absolute. See **Blindness.**

Entirely without understanding. Inability to comprehend nature and effect of transaction involved, not necessarily absolute imbecility, idiocy or mental incapacity.

Entire output contract. Promise to deliver one's entire output (*i.e.* production) to the other. If no other detriment can be located, it will be found in the promisor's having surrendered his privilege of selling elsewhere. Such agreements are governed by U.C.C. § 2–306.

Entire tenancy. A sole possession by one person, called "severalty," which is contrary to several tenancy, where a joint or common possession is in one or more.

Entirety. The whole, in contradistinction to a moiety or part only. When land is conveyed to husband and wife, they do not take by moieties, but both are seised of the *entirety*. Parceners, on the other hand, have not an *entirety* of interest, but each is properly entitled to the whole of a distinct moiety. 2 Bl.Comm. 188. See **Estate by the entirety.**

The word is also used to designate that which the law considers as one whole, and not capable of being divided into parts. Thus, a judgment, it is held, is an *entirety,* and, if void as to one of the two defendants, cannot be valid as to the other. Also, if a contract is an *entirety,* no part of the consideration is due until the whole has been performed.

Entire use, benefit, etc. These words in the *habendum* of a trust-deed for the benefit of a married woman are equivalent to the words "sole use," or "sole and separate use," and consequently her husband takes nothing under such deed.

Entitle. In its usual sense, to entitle is to give a right or legal title to. Schmidt v. Gibbons, 101 Ariz. 222, 418 P.2d 378, 380. To qualify for; to furnish with proper grounds for seeking or claiming. In ecclesiastical law, to entitle is to give a title or ordination as a minister.

Entitlement. Right to benefits, income or property which may not be abridged without due process.

Entity. A real being; existence. An organization or being that possesses separate existence for tax purposes. Examples would be corporations, partnerships, estates and trusts. The accounting entity for which accounting statements are prepared may not be the same as the entity defined by law.

An existence apart, such as a corporation in relation to its stockholders.

Entity includes person, estate, trust, governmental unit. Bankruptcy Act, § 101(14).

See also **Legal entity.**

Entrance. Door, opening or passage for entering.

Entrap. To catch, to entrap, to ensnare; hence, to catch by artifice. To involve in difficulties or distresses; to catch or involve in contradictions.

Entrapment. The act of officers or agents of the government in inducing a person to commit a crime not contemplated by him, for the purpose of instituting a criminal prosecution against him. According to the generally accepted view, a law enforcement official, or an undercover agent acting in cooperation with such an official, perpetrates an entrapment when, for the purpose of obtaining evidence of a crime, he originates the idea of the crime and then induces another person to engage in conduct constituting such a crime when the other person is not otherwise disposed to do so. Sorrells v. U. S., 287 U.S. 435, 53 S.Ct. 210, 77 L.Ed. 413; Sherman v. U. S., 356 U.S. 369, 78 S.Ct. 819, 2 L.Ed.2d 848.

A public law enforcement official or a person acting in cooperation with such an official perpetrates an entrapment if for the purpose of obtaining evidence of the commission of an offense, he induces or encourages another person to engage in conduct constituting such offense by either: (a) making knowingly false representations designed to induce the belief that such conduct is not prohibited; or (b) employing methods of persuasion or inducement which create a substantial risk that such an offense will be committed by persons other than those who are ready to commit it. Model Penal Code, § 2.13.

Entreaty. Beseeching, or suppliant, or prayerful in nature. In re Sloan's Estate, 7 Cal.App.2d 319, 46 P.2d 1007, 1018.

Entrebat. L. Fr. An intruder or interloper.

Entrega /entréyga/. Span. Delivery.

Entrepôt /òntərpów/òntrəpów/. A warehouse or magazine for the deposit of goods. In France, a building or place where goods from abroad may be deposited, and from whence they may be withdrawn for exportation to another country, without paying a duty.

Entrepreneur /òntərprənə́r/°n(y)u(wə)r/òntrə°/. One who, on his own, initiates and assumes the financial risks of a new enterprise and who undertakes its management.

Entrust. To give over to another something after a relation of confidence has been established. To deliver to another something in trust or to commit something to another with a certain confidence regarding his care, use or disposal of it. Humphries v. Going, D.C.N.C., 59 F.R.D. 583, 587.

Entrusting. The transfer of possession of goods to a merchant who deals in goods of that type and who may in turn transfer such goods and all rights therein to a purchaser in the ordinary course of business. U.C.C. § 2–403(2)(3).

Entry. The act of making or entering a record; a setting down in writing of particulars; or that which is entered; an item. Generally synonymous with "recording." In re Labb, D.C.N.Y., 42 F.Supp. 542, 544. See also **Enroll.**

Enter, in practice, means to place anything before court, or upon or among records, and is nearly equivalent to setting down formally in writing, either in full or abridged form but it may be used as meaning simply to file or duly deposit. Neiman v. City of Chicago, 37 Ill.App.2d 309, 185 N.E.2d 358, 365.

Passage leading into a house or other building or to a room; a vestibule.

The act of a merchant, trader, or other businessman in recording in his account-books the facts and circumstances of a sale, loan, or other transaction. The books in which such memoranda are first (or originally) inscribed are called "books of original entry," and are *prima facie* evidence for certain purposes.

In copyright law, depositing with the register of copyrights the printed title of a book, pamphlet, etc., for the purpose of securing copyright on the same. Copyright Act, § 408.

In criminal law, entry is the unlawful making one's way into a dwelling or other house, for the purpose of committing a crime therein. In cases of burglary, the least entry with the whole or any part of the body, hand, or foot, or with any instrument or weapon, introduced for the purpose of committing a felony, is sufficient to complete the offense. See also **Breaking.**

In customs law, the entry of imported goods at the custom house consists in submitting them to the inspection of the revenue officers, together with a statement or description of such goods, and the original invoices of the same, for the purpose of estimating the duties to be paid thereon.

See also **False entry; Forcible entry; Illegal entry; Journal entry.**

Entry of judgment. See **Entering judgments.**

Open entry. An entry upon real estate, for the purpose of taking possession, which is not clandestine nor effected by secret artifice or stratagem, and (in some states by statute) one which is accomplished in the presence of two witnesses.

Re-entry. The resumption of the possession of leased premises by the landlord on the tenant's failure to pay the stipulated rent or otherwise to keep the conditions of the lease. See **Ejectment.**

Right of entry. See **Right of entry.**

Entry ad communem legem /éntriy æd kəmyúwnəm líyjəm/. Entry at common law. The name of a writ of entry which lay for a reversioner after the alienation and death of the particular tenant for life, against him who was in possession of the land.

Entry ad terminum qui præteriit /éntriy æd tə́rmənəm kwày prətéhriyət/. The writ of entry *ad terminum qui præteriit* lies where a man leases land to another for a term of years, and the tenant holds over his term. And if lands be leased to a man for the term of another's life, and he for whose life the lands are leased dies, and the lessee holds over, then the lessor shall have this writ.

Entry for marriage in speech. A writ of entry *causa matrimonii præloquuti* existed in old English law where lands or tenements were given to a man upon condition that he would take the donor to be his wife within a certain time, and he did not espouse her within the said term, or espoused another woman, or made himself priest.

Entry in casu consimili /éntriy in kéyz(y)uw kənsíməlay/. In old English law, a writ of entry *in casu consimili* existed where a tenant for life or by the curtesy alienated in fee.

Entry in regular course of business. A record setting forth a fact or transaction made by one in the ordinary and usual course of one's business, employment, office or profession, which it was the duty of the enterer in such manner to make, or which was commonly and regularly made, or which it was convenient to make, in the conduct of the business to which such entry pertains.

Entry of cause for trial. In old English practice, the proceeding by a plaintiff in an action who had given notice of trial, depositing with the proper officer of the court the *nisi prius* record, with the panel of jurors annexed, and thus bringing the issue before the court for trial.

Entry of judgment. See **Entering judgments.**

Entry on the roll. In old English practice, the parties to an action, personally or by their counsel, used to appear in open court and make their mutual statements *vivâ voce,* instead of as at the present day delivering their mutual pleadings, until they arrived at the issue or precise point in dispute between them. During the progress of this oral statement, a minute of the various proceedings was made on parchment by an officer of the court appointed for that purpose. The parchment then became the record; in other words, the official history of the suit. Long after the practice of oral pleading had fallen into disuse, it continued necessary to enter the proceedings in like manner upon the parchment roll, and this was called "entry on the roll," or making up the "issue roll." But by a rule of H.T. 4 Wm. IV, the practice of making up the issue roll was abolished; and it was only necessary to make up the issue in the form prescribed for the purpose by a rule of H.T. 1853, and to deliver the same to the court and to the opposite party. The issue which was delivered to the court was called the *"nisi prius record;"* and that was regarded as the official history of the suit, in like manner as the issue roll formerly was. Under later practice, the issue roll or *nisi prius record* consisted of the papers delivered to the court, to facilitate the trial of the action, these papers consisting of the pleadings simply, with the notice of trial.

A future interest created in a transferor who conveys an estate on condition subsequent.

Entry, right of. See **Right of entry.**

Entry, writ of. In old English practice, this was a writ made use of in a form of real action brought to recover the possession of lands from one who wrongfully withheld the same from the demandant. Its object was to regain the *possession* of lands of which the demandant, or his ancestors, had been unjustly deprived by the tenant of the freehold, or those under whom he claimed, and hence it belonged to the *possessory* division of real actions. It decided nothing with respect to the *right of property,* but only restored the demandant to that situation in which he was (or by law ought to have been) before the dispossession committed. 3 Bl.Comm. 180. It was usual to specify in such writs the degree or degrees within which the writ was brought, and it was said to be "in the *per* " or "in the *per and cui*," according as there had been one or two descents or alienations from the original wrongdoer. If more than two such transfers had intervened, the writ was said to be "in the *post.*" 3 Bl.Comm. 181. See **Writ of entry.**

Enumerated. This term is often used in law as equivalent to "mentioned specifically," "designated," or "expressly named or granted"; as in speaking of "enumerated" governmental powers, items of property, or articles in a tariff schedule.

Enumerated powers. The powers specifically delegated by the Constitution to some branch or authority of the national government, and which are not denied to that government or reserved to the States or to the people. The powers specifically given to Congress are enumerated in Article I of U.S. Constitution. See also **Powers** (*Constitutional powers*).

Enumeratio infirmat regulam in casibus non enumeratis /ən(y)ùwməréysh(iy)ow ənfə́rmət régyələm ən kéyzəbəs nòn ən(y)ùwməréydəs/. Enumeration disaffirms the rule in cases not enumerated.

Enumeratio unius est exclusio alterius /ən(y)ùwməréysh(iy)ow yənáyəs èst əksklúwzh(iy)ow òltíriyəs/. The specification of one thing is the exclusion of a different thing. A maxim more generally expressed in the form *"expressio unius est exclusio alterius" (q.v.).*

Enumerators /ən(y)úmərèydərz/. Persons appointed to collect census papers or schedules.

Enure. To operate or take effect. To serve to the use, benefit, or advantage of a person. A release to the tenant for life *enures* to him in reversion; that is, it has the same effect for him as for the tenant for life. Often written "inure."

En ventre sa mere /òn vóntrə sà mér/. L. Fr. In its mother's womb. A term descriptive of an unborn child. For some purposes the law regards an infant *en ventre* as in being. It may take a legacy; have a guardian; an estate may be limited to its use, etc. 1 Bl.Comm. 130. LaBlue v. Specker, 358 Mich. 558, 100 N.W.2d 445, 447.

En vie /òn víy/. L. Fr. In life; alive.

Environment. The totality of physical, economic, cultural, aesthetic, and social circumstances and factors which surround and affect the desirability and value of property and which also affect the quality of peoples' lives. The surrounding conditions, influences or forces which influence or modify. U. S. v. Amadio, C.A.Ind., 215 F.2d 605, 611.

Environmental impact statements. Documents which are required by federal and state laws to accompany proposals for major projects and programs that will likely have an impact on the surrounding environment. See 42 U.S.C.A. § 4332.

Environmental Protection Agency. The federal Environmental Protection Agency was created in 1970 to permit coordinated and effective governmental action on behalf of the environment. EPA endeavors to abate and control pollution systematically, by proper integration of a variety of research, monitoring, standard setting, and enforcement activities. As a complement to its other activities, EPA coordinates and supports research and antipollution activities by State and local governments, private and public groups, individuals, and educational institutions. EPA also reinforces efforts among other Federal agencies with respect to the impact of their operations on the environment, and it is specifically charged with making public its written comments on environmental impact statements and with publishing its determinations when those hold that a proposal is unsatisfactory from the standpoint of public health or welfare or environmental quality. See also **National Environmental Policy Act.**

Envoy. A diplomat of the rank of minister or ambassador sent by a country to the government of a foreign country to execute a special mission or to serve as a permanent diplomatic representative.

Eodem ligamine quo ligatum est dissolvitur /iyówdəm ləgéyməniy kwòw ləgéydəm èst dəzólvədər/. A bond is released by the same formalities with which it is contracted.

Eodem modo quo quid constituitur, dissolvitur /iyówdəm mówdow kwòw kwíd kònstətyúwədər, dəzólvədər/. In the manner in which [by the same means by which] a thing is constituted, is it dissolved.

Eo die /íyow dáy(iy)/. Lat. On that day; on the same day.

E.O.E. Errors and omissions excepted. Vernon Metal & Produce Co. v. Joseph Joseph & Bros. Co., 212 App.Div. 358, 209 N.Y.S. 6, 11.

Eo instanti /íyow ənstǽntay/. Lat. At that instant; at the very or same instant; immediately. 1 Bl.Comm. 196, 249; 2 Bl.Comm. 168. Also written *eo instante*.

Eo intuitu /íyow ənt(y)úwəduw/. Lat. With or in that view; with that intent or object.

Eo loci /íyow lówsay/. Lat. In the civil law, in that state or condition; in that place *(eo loco)*.

E.O.M. *Abbr.* End of month. Payment terms in sale contract.

Eo nomine /íyow nómən iy/. Lat. Under that name; by that appellation. *Perinde ac si eo nomine tibi tradita fuisset,* just as if it had been delivered to you by that name.

Eoth. In Saxon law, an oath.

EPA. Environmental Protection Agency.

Epidemic. This term, in its ordinary and popular meaning, applies to any disease which is widely spread or generally prevailing at a given place and time. Bethlehem Steel Co. v. Industrial Accident Commission, 21 Cal.2d 742, 135 P.2d 153, 157; Martin v. Springfield City Water Co., Mo.App., 128 S.W.2d 674, 679.

Epilepsy /épəlèpsiy/. Epilepsy, a disruption of the normal rhythm of the brain, is an occasional, periodic, excessive and disorderly discharge of nerve cells in the brain. The discharge is chemical-electrical in nature. While the discharge itself is hidden, it manifests itself in various forms of visible activity, called seizures. The type of seizures will vary according to the location of the discharge in the brain, and the spread of the charge from cell to cell. In many cases, seizures are so mild (a brief twitch, a momentary attention loss) that they are not recognized. Even when they are, they have a minimal effect. A major convulsion which the public tends immediately to associate with epilepsy is only one of a number of seizure types.

E pili ana /éy pìyliy ána/. Hawaiian. Adjoining.

Epimenia /èpəmíyniyə/. Expenses or gifts.

Epiphany /əpífəniy/. A Christian festival, otherwise called the "Manifestation of Christ to the Gentiles," observed on the 6th of January, in honor of the appearance of the star to the three *magi,* or wise men, who came to adore the Messiah, and bring him presents. It is commonly called "Twelfth Day."

Epiphyseal separation /èpəfəsíyəl separéyshən/. Not a bone fracture in true sense, but a separation of the fibers and cartilaginous tissues which attach the epiphysis to the femur.

Epiphyseitis /èpəfiziyáydəs/. Inflammation of an epiphysis—a process of bone attached for a time to another bone by cartilage.

Epiphysis /əpífəsəs/. Part or process of a bone which ossifies separately and subsequently becomes ankylosed (to grow together into one) into the main part of the bone.

Epiqueya /èpiykéyə/. In Spanish law, a term synonymous with "equity" in one of its senses, and defined as "the benignant and prudent interpretation of the law according to the circumstances of the time, place, and person."

Episcopacy /əpískəpəsiy/. The office of overlooking or overseeing; the office of a bishop, who is to overlook and oversee the concerns of the church. A form of church government by diocesan bishops.

Episcopalia /əpìskəpéyl(i)yə/. In ecclesiastical law, synodals, pentecostals, and other customary payments from the clergy to their diocesan bishop, formerly collected by the rural deans.

Episcopalian /əpìskəpéylyən/. Of or pertaining to episcopacy, or to the Episcopal Church.

Episcopate /əpískəpət/. A bishopric. The dignity or office of a bishop.

Episcoporum ecdicus /əpìskəpórəm ékdəkəs/. Bishop's proctors; church lawyers.

Episcopus /əpískəpəs/. In the civil law, an overseer; an inspector. A municipal officer who had the charge and oversight of the bread and other provisions which served the citizens for their daily food. Vicat. In medieval history, a bishop; a bishop of the Christian church.

Episcopus alterius mandato quam regis non tenetur obtemperare /əpískəpəs oltíriyəs mændéydow kwæm ríyjəs nòn təníydər obtèmpərériy/. A bishop needs not obey any mandate save the king's.

Episcopus puerorum /əpískəpəs pyùwərórəm/. It was an old custom that upon certain feasts some lay person should plait his hair, and put on the garments of a bishop, and in them pretend to exercise episcopal jurisdiction, and do several ludicrous actions, for which reason he was called "bishop of the boys;" and this custom obtained in England long after several constitutions were made to abolish it.

Episcopus teneat placitum, in curia christianitatis, de iis quæ mere sunt spiritualia /əpískəpəs téniyət plǽsədəm in kyúriyə krìstiyǽnətéydəs, dìy iyəs kwìy míriy sɔ̀nt spìrəchuwéyl(i)yə/. A bishop may hold plea in a Court Christian of things merely spiritual.

Epistola /əpístələ/. A letter; a charter; an instrument in writing for conveyance of lands or assurance of contracts.

Epistolæ /əpístəliy/. In the civil law, rescripts; opinions given by the emperors in cases submitted to them for decision. Answers of the emperors to petitions. The answers of counsellors *(juris-consulti)*, as Ulpian and others, to questions of law proposed to them, were also called *"epistolæ."*

Opinions written out. The term originally signified the same as *literæ.*

E pluribus unum /ìy pl(y)úrəbəs yúwnəm/. One out of many. The motto of the United States of America.

Epoch /épək/íypòk/. The time at which a new computation is begun; the time whence dates are numbered.

E.P.S. Earnings per share.

Equal. Alike; uniform; on the same plane or level with respect to efficiency, worth, value, amount, or rights. Word "equal" as used in law implies not identity but duality and the use of one thing as the measure of another. Poindexter v. Willis, 23 Ohio Misc. 199, 256 N.E.2d 254, 260.

Equal and uniform taxation. Taxes are said to be "equal and uniform" when no person or class of persons in the taxing district, whether it be a state, county, or city, is taxed at a different rate than are other persons in the same district upon the same value or the same thing, and where the objects of taxation are the same, by whomsoever owned or whatsoever they may be. Weatherly Independent School Dist. v. Hughes, Tex.Civ.App., 41 S.W.2d 445, 447.

Equal Credit Opportunity Act. Federal Act prohibiting a creditor from discriminating against any applicant on the basis of race, color, religion, national origin, age, sex or marital status with respect to any aspect of a credit transaction. 15 U.S.C.A. § 1691 et seq.

Equal degree. Persons are said to be related to a decedent "in equal degree" when they are all removed by an equal number of steps or degrees from the common ancestor.

Equal Employment Opportunity Commission. The Equal Employment Opportunity Commission (EEOC) was created by Title VII of the Civil Rights Act of 1964 (78 Stat. 241; 42 U.S.C.A. § 2000a), and became operational July 2, 1965. The purposes of the Commission are to end discrimination based on race, color, religion, age, sex, or national origin in hiring, promotion, firing, wages, testing, training, apprenticeship, and all other conditions of employment; and to promote voluntary action programs by employers, unions, and community organizations to put equal employment opportunity into actual operation.

Equality. The condition of possessing substantially the same rights, privileges, and immunities, and being liable to substantially the same duties. "Equality" guaranteed under equal protection clause is equality under the same conditions and among persons similarly situated; classifications must not be arbitrary and must be based upon some difference in classes having substantial relation to legitimate objects to be accomplished. Boyne v. State ex rel. Dickerson, 80 Nev. 160, 390 P.2d 225, 227. See **Equal protection clause; Equal protection of the law.**

Equalization. The act or process of making equal or bringing about conformity to a common standard.

The process of equalizing assessments or taxes, as performed by "boards of equalization" in various states, consists in comparing the assessments made by the local officers of the various counties or other taxing districts within the jurisdiction of the board and reducing them to a common and uniform basis, increasing or diminishing by such percentage as may be necessary, so as to bring about, within the entire territory affected, a uniform and equal ratio between the assessed value and the actual cash value of property. The term is also applied to a similar process of leveling or adjusting the assessments of individual taxpayers, so that the property of one shall not be assessed at a higher (or lower) percentage of its market value than the property of another. Adjusting the value of property assessed to conform to its real value. County of Sacramento v. Assessment Appeals Board Number 2 of Sacramento County, 32 Cal.App.3d 654, 108 Cal.Rptr. 434, 441. See also **Equal protection of the law.**

Equalization board. Local governmental agency whose function is to supervise the equalization of taxes as among various properties and as among various districts to bring about an equitable distribution of tax burdens.

Equalization of taxes. See **Equalization.**

Equalize. To make equal, to cause to correspond, or be like in amount or degree, as compared with something. Los Angeles County v. Ransohoff, 24 Cal. App.2d 238, 74 P.2d 828, 830; De Mille v. Los Angeles County, 25 Cal.App. 506, 77 P.2d 905, 906.

Equally divided. Provision in will that property shall be "equally divided," or divided "share and share alike" means that the property shall be divided per capita and not per stirpes. However, these phrases may be so modified by other parts of the will as to require distribution per stirpes.

Equal Pay Act. Federal law which mandates same pay for all persons who do same work without regard to sex, age, etc.

Equal protection clause. That provision in 14th Amendment to U.S. Constitution which prohibits a State from denying to any person within its jurisdiction the equal protection of the laws. "Equal protection" clause of Federal Constitution requires that persons under like circumstances be given equal protection in the enjoyment of personal rights and the prevention and redress of wrongs. In re Adoption of Richardson, 251 C.A.2d 222, 59 Cal.Rptr. 323, 334. See also **Equal protection of the law.**

Equal protection of the law. The constitutional guarantee of "equal protection of the laws" means that no person or class of persons shall be denied the same protection of the laws which is enjoyed by other persons or other classes in like circumstances in their lives, liberty, property, and in their pursuit of happiness. People v. Jacobs, 27 Cal.App.3d 246, 103 Cal. Rptr. 536, 543; 14th Amend., U.S. Const.

The equal protection of the laws of a state is extended to persons within its jurisdiction, within the meaning of the constitutional requirement, when its courts are open to them on the same conditions as to others, with like rules of evidence and modes of procedure, for the security of their persons and property, the prevention and redress of wrongs, and the enforcement of contracts; when they are subjected to no restrictions in the acquisition of property, the enjoyment of personal liberty, and the pursuit of happiness, which do not generally affect others; when they are liable to no other or greater burdens and charges than such as are laid upon others; and when no different or greater punishment is enforced against them for a violation of the laws.

"Equal protection," with respect to classification for taxation purposes, does not require identity of treatment, but only (1) that classification rests on real and not feigned differences, (2) that the distinction have some relevance to purpose for which classification is made, and (3) that the different treatments be not so disparate, relative to difference in classification, as to be wholly arbitrary. Walters v. City of St. Louis, Mo., 347 U.S. 231, 74 S.Ct. 505, 509, 98 L.Ed. 660.

Equal Rights Amendment. Proposed amendment to U.S. Constitution which provides that: "Equality of rights under the law shall not be denied or abridged by the United States or by any State on account of sex."

Equal Time Act. If licensee of broadcasting facility permits a legally qualified candidate for public office to use facility for broadcasting, he shall afford equal opportunities to all other such candidates for that office. 47 U.S.C.A. § 315.

Eques /íykwìyz/. Lat. In Roman and old English law, a knight.

Equilocus /èkwəlówkəs/. An equal.

Equinoxes /íykwənòksəz/ékw°/. The two periods of the year (vernal equinox about March 21st, and autumnal equinox about September 22d) when the time from the rising of the sun to its setting is equal to the time from its setting to its rising.

Equip. To furnish for service or against a need or exigency; to fit out; to supply with whatever is necessary to efficient action in any way. Synonymous with furnish.

Equipment. Furnishings, or outfit for the required purposes. Whatever is needed in equipping; the articles comprised in an outfit; equippage. Department of Treasury, Gross Income Tax Division v. Ranger-Cook, Inc., 114 Ind.App. 107, 49 N.E.2d 548, 550; Farm & Home Saving & Loan Ass'n of Missouri v. Empire Furniture Co., Tex.Civ.App., 87 S.W.2d 1111, 1112.

Under U.C.C., goods include "equipment" if they are used or bought for use primarily in business (including farming or a profession) or by a debtor who is a non-profit organization or a governmental subdivision or agency or if the goods are not included in the definitions of inventory, farm products or consumer goods. U.C.C. § 9–109(2).

Equipment trust. Financing device commonly used by railroads by which equipment is purchased from the manufacturer by a trustee who provides a substantial portion of the purchase price, the railroad providing the balance. The trustee then leases the equipment to the railroad which pays a rental fee consisting of interest, amortization for serial retirement and trustee's fee.

Equipment trust certificate. A type of security, generally issued by a railroad, to pay for new equipment. Title to the equipment, such as a locomotive, is held by a trustee until the notes are paid off. An equipment trust certificate is usually secured by a first claim on the equipment.

Equitable. Just; conformable to the principles of justice and right. Existing in equity; available or sustainable in equity, or upon the rules and principles of equity.

As to equitable Assets; Construction; Conversion; Easement; Ejectment; Estate; Garnishment; Levy; Mortgage; Title, and Waste, see those titles.

Equitable abstention doctrine. A court may refrain from exercising jurisdiction which it possesses in the interest of comity between courts and between states as in the case of actions involving the affairs of a foreign corporation or foreign land. Doctrine also applies to case of Federal court's refraining from interfering with decision of state administrative agency's decision on a local matter. Allegheny Airlines, Inc. v. Penn. Public Utility Comm., D.C.Pa., 319 F.Supp. 407.

Equitable action. One seeking an equitable remedy or relief; though in the federal and most state courts, with the procedural merger of law and equity, there is now *procedurally* only one type of action—a "civil action." Fed.R. Civil P. 2.

Equitable adjustment theory. In settlement of federal contract disputes, contracting officer should make fair adjustment within a reasonable time before contractor is required to settle with his subcontractors, suppliers and other creditors. Roberts v. U. S., 174 Ct.Cl. 940, 357 F.2d 938.

Equitable adoption. "Equitable adoption" refers to situation involving oral contract to adopt child, fully performed except that there was no statutory adoption, and in which rule is applied for benefit of child in determination of heirship upon death of person contracting to adopt. Barlow v. Barlow, 170 Colo. 465, 463 P.2d 305, 308. In certain jurisdictions, a child has rights of inheritance from person who has contracted to adopt him but has not done so. Dunn v. Richardson, D.C.Ark., 336 F.Supp. 649, 654.

Equitable assignment. An assignment which, though invalid at law, will be recognized and enforced in equity; *e.g.,* an assignment of a chose in action, or of future acquisitions of the assignor. Stewart v. Kane, Mo.App., 111 S.W.2d 971, 974. In order to work an "equitable assignment", there must be an absolute appropriation by the assignor of the debt or fund sought to be assigned. Sneesby v. Livington, 182 Wash. 229, 46 P.2d 733, 735.

Equitable conversion. A doctrine commonly applied when death intervenes between the signing of an agreement to sell real estate and the date of transfer of title resulting in treating land as personalty and personalty as land under certain circumstances. It takes place when a contract for sale of realty becomes binding on parties. Lampman v. Sledge, Tex. Civ.App., 502 S.W.2d 957, 959. See also **Conversion.**

Equitable defense. Formerly, a defense which was only available in a court of equity. With the procedural merger of law and equity however, equitable defenses can be raised along with legal defenses in same action. Fed.R. Civil P. 8.

Equitable distribution. No-fault divorce statutes in certain states (*e.g.* New Jersey) grant courts the power to distribute equitably upon divorce all property legally and beneficially acquired during marriage by husband and wife, or either of them, whether legal title lies in their joint or individual names.

Equitable doctrine of approximation. This doctrine differs from "Cy pres doctrine" in purpose and application. The last mentioned doctrine applies where an apparent charitable intention has failed, whether by an incomplete disposition at the outset or by subsequent inadequacy of the original object, and its purpose is to give a cy pres or proximate application to testator's intention, whereas the "equitable doctrine of approximation" merely authorizes a court to vary the details of administration, in order to preserve the trust, and carry out the general purpose of the donor.

Equitable election. Under this doctrine, a person cannot accept benefits accruing to him by a will and at the same time refuse to recognize validity of will in other respects, but doctrine may not be applied to prejudice of third parties. Luttrell v. Luttrell, 4 Ohio App.2d 305, 212 N.E.2d 641, 642. The choice to be made by a person who may, under a will or other instrument, have either one of two alternative rights or benefits, but not both. Peters v. Bain, 133 U.S. 670, 10 S.Ct. 354, 33 L.Ed. 696. The obligation imposed upon a party to choose between two inconsistent or alternative rights or claims, in cases where there is clear intention of the person from whom he derives one that he should not enjoy both. Dakan v. Dakan, 125 Tex. 305, 83 S.W.2d 620, 624. A choice shown by an overt act between two inconsistent rights, either of which may be asserted at the will of the chooser alone. Bierce v. Hutchins, 205 U.S. 346, 27 S.Ct. 524, 51 L.Ed. 828. See also **Election** (*Law of wills*).

Equitable estoppel. The doctrine by which a person may be precluded by his act or conduct, or silence when it is his duty to speak, from asserting a right which he otherwise would have had. Mitchell v. McIntee, 15 Or.App. 85, 514 P.2d 1357, 1359. The effect of voluntary conduct of a party whereby he is precluded from asserting rights against another who has justifiably relied upon such conduct and changed his position so that he will suffer injury if the former is allowed to repudiate the conduct. American Bank & Trust Co. v. Trinity Universal Ins. Co., 251 La. 445, 205 So.2d 35, 40.

Elements or essentials of such estoppel include change of position for the worse by party asserting estoppel, Malone v. Republic Nat. Bank & Trust Co., Tex.Civ.App., 70 S.W.2d 809, 812; conduct by party estopped such that it would be contrary to equity and good conscience for him to allege and prove the truth, Rody v. Doyle, 181 Md. 195, 29 A.2d 290, 293; false representation or concealment of facts, Clark v. Na-

tional Aid Life Ass'n, 177 Okl. 137, 57 P.2d 832, 833; Antrim Lumber Co. v. Wagner, 175 Okl. 564, 54 P.2d 173, 176; ignorance of party asserting estoppel of facts and absence of opportunity to ascertain them, Fipps v. Stidham, 174 Okl. 473, 50 P.2d 680, 684; injury from declarations, acts, or omissions of party were he permitted to gainsay their truth, Fleishbein v. Western Auto Supply Agency, 19 Cal.App.2d 424, 65 P.2d 928; Roberts v. Friedell, 218 Minn. 88, 15 N.W.2d 496, 500; intention that representation should be acted on, Consolidated Cut Stone Co. v. Seidenbach, 181 Okl. 578, 75 P.2d 442, 452; knowledge, actual or constructive, of facts by party estopped, Antrim Lumber Co. v. Wagner, 175 Okl. 564, 54 P.2d 173, 176; Lillywhite v. Coleman, 46 Ariz. 523, 52 P.2d 1157, 1160; misleading person to his prejudice. United States, for Use and Benefit of Noland Co., v. Wood, C.C.A.Va., 99 F.2d 80, 82; omission, misconduct or misrepresentation misleading another; reliance upon representation or conduct of person sought to be estopped, Wilkinson v. Lieberman, 327 Mo. 420, 37 S.W.2d 533, 536; George W. Armbruster, Jr., Inc. v. City of Wildwood, D.C.N.J., 41 F.2d 823, 829.

Estoppel in pais and equitable estoppel are convertible terms, Brown v. Corn Exchange Nat. Bank & Trust Co., 136 N.J.Eq. 430, 42 A.2d 474, 480.

Equitable interest. The interest of a beneficiary under a trust is considered equitable as contrasted with the interest of the trustee which is a legal interest because the trustee has legal as contrasted with equitable title. Restatement, Second, Trusts, § 2f. See also **Equitable ownership.**

Equitable lien. A right, not existing at law, to have specific property applied in whole or in part to payment of a particular debt or class of debts. Morrison Flying Service v. Deming Nat. Bank, C.A.N.M., 404 F.2d 856, 861. An equitable lien arises either from a written contract which shows an intention to charge some particular property with a debt or obligation or is implied and declared by a court of equity out of general considerations of right and justice as applied to relations of the parties and circumstances of their dealings. Owensboro Banking Co. v. Lewis, 269 Ky. 277, 106 S.W.2d 1000, 1004; Clark v. Armstrong & Murphy, 180 Okl. 514, 72 P.2d 362, 365, 366.

Equitable life estate. An interest in real or personal property which lasts for the life of the holder of the estate and which is equitable as contrasted with legal in its creation as in the case of a beneficiary of a trust who has a life estate under the trust.

Equitable mortgage. Any agreement to post certain property as security before the security agreement is formalized. If a person transfers property by deed absolute to his creditor as security for a debt with the mutual understanding that such property will be reconveyed by the creditor on the repayment of the debt, a court of equity will consider such a deed a mortgage, though an innocent purchaser for value from the creditor can cut off the equitable rights of the debtor. See also **Mortgage.**

Equitable ownership. The ownership interest of one who has equitable as contrasted with legal ownership of property as in the case of a trust beneficiary.

Ownership rights which are protected in equity. See also **Equitable interest.**

Equitable recoupment. Rule of the law which diminishes the right of a party invoking legal process to recover a debt, to the extent that he holds money or property of his debtor, to which he has no moral right, and it is ordinarily a defensive remedy going only to mitigation of damages. Doctrine of "equitable recoupment" provides that, at least in some cases, a claim for a refund of taxes barred by a statute of limitations may nevertheless be recouped against a tax claim of the government. May Dept. Stores Co. v. City of Pittsburgh, Pa.Cmwlth., 376 A.2d 309, 313.

Equitable redemption. The act or process by which a mortgagor redeems his property after payment of the mortgage debt. The purchase of the equity of redemption after foreclosure has commenced. See **Equity of redemption.**

Equitable relief. That species of relief sought in a court with equity powers as, for example, in the case of one seeking an injunction or specific performance instead of money damages.

Equitable rescission. Rescission decreed by court of equity, as distinguished from "legal rescission" which is effected by restoration or offer to restore.

Equitable restraint doctrine. Under this doctrine, federal courts will not intervene to enjoin a pending state criminal prosecution absent a strong showing of bad faith and irreparable injury. Samuels v. Mackell, 401 U.S. 66, 91 S.Ct. 764, 27 L.Ed.2d 688; Boyle v. Landry, 401 U.S. 77, 91 S.Ct. 758, 27 L.Ed.2d 696; Perez v. Ledesma, 401 U.S. 82, 91 S.Ct. 674, 27 L.Ed.2d 701; Dyson v. Stein, 401 U.S. 200, 91 S.Ct. 769, 27 L.Ed.2d 78; Byrne v. Karalexis, 401 U.S. 216, 91 S.Ct. 777, 27 L.Ed.2d 792.

Equitable right. Right cognizable within court of equity as contrasted with legal right enforced in court of law; though under rules practice in most states and in the federal courts there has been a merger procedurally between actions at law and equity. Fed.R. Civil P. 2.

Equitable servitudes. A restriction on the use of land enforceable in court of equity. It is broader than a covenant running with the land because it is an interest in land.

Equitable title. See **Equitable ownership.**

Equitable waste. Injury to the corpus of property inconsistent with good management or husbandry and recognized by a court of equity but not by a court of law.

Equitas sequitur legem /íykwətæs sékwədər líyjəm/. Equity follows the law.

Equity. Justice administered according to fairness as contrasted with the strictly formulated rules of common law. It is based on a system of rules and principles which originated in England as an alternative to the harsh rules of common law and which were based on what was fair in a particular situation. One sought relief under this system in courts of equity rather than in courts of law. The term "equi-ty" denotes the spirit and habit of fairness, justness, and right dealing which would regulate the intercourse of men with men. Gilles v. Department of Human Resources Development, 11 Cal.3d 313, 113 Cal.Rptr. 374, 380, 521 P.2d 110. Equity is a body of jurisprudence, or field of jurisdiction, differing in its origin, theory, and methods from the common law; though procedurally, in the federal courts and most state courts, equitable and legal rights and remedies are administered in the same court.

A system of jurisprudence collateral to, and in some respects independent of, "law"; the object of which is to render the administration of justice more complete, by affording relief where the courts of law are incompetent to give it, or to give it with effect, or by exercising certain branches of jurisdiction independently of them.

See **Equity, courts of.**

Countervailing equity. A contrary and balancing equity; an equity or right opposed to that which is sought to be enforced or recognized, and which ought not to be sacrificed or subordinated to the latter, because it is of equal strength and justice, and equally deserving of consideration.

Latent or secret equity. An equitable claim or right, the knowledge of which has been confined to the parties for and against whom it exists, or which has been concealed from one or several persons interested in the subject-matter.

Natural equity. A term sometimes employed in works on jurisprudence, possessing no very precise meaning, but used as equivalent to justice, honesty, or morality in business relations, or man's innate sense of right dealing and fair play. Inasmuch as equity, as now administered, is a complex system of rules, doctrines, and precedents, and possesses, within the range of its own fixed principles, but little more elasticity than the law, the term "natural equity" may be understood to denote, in a general way, that which strikes the ordinary conscience and sense of justice as being fair, right, and equitable, in advance of the question whether the technical jurisprudence of the chancery courts would so regard it.

Perfect equity. An equitable title or right which lacks nothing to its completeness as a legal title or right except the formal conveyance or other investiture which would make it cognizable at law; particularly, the equity or interest of a purchaser of real estate who has paid the purchase price in full and fulfilled all conditions resting on him, but has not yet received a deed or patent.

Real estate. The remaining interest belonging to one who has pledged or mortgaged his property, or the surplus of value which may remain after the property has been disposed of for the satisfaction of liens. The amount or value of a property above the total liens or charges. The difference of the fair market value and debt in property; thus, an equity of $5,000 may come about by having fair market value property of $20,-000 with debt of $15,000. The term came from the development in English courts of equity of the right of an owner of property to redeem his property even after a foreclosure, which right came to be known as the equity of redemption. The existence of the right was predicated on the property being of far greater value than the debt owed to the party that foreclosed.

Equity acts in personam. A basic principle of law of equity to the effect that equity grants relief in the form of personal decrees as contrasted with law which awards money damages. A necessary corollary of this principle is that equity requires personal jurisdiction to grant its relief.

Equity, bill in. The name given to the original pleading in an equity case. However, under current rules practice in most states, the "bill" has been replaced by a complaint with the procedural merger of law and equity. Fed.R. Civil P. 2.

Equity, courts of. Courts which administer justice according to the system of equity, and according to a peculiar course of procedure or practice. Frequently termed "courts of chancery." With the procedural merger of law and equity in the federal and most state courts, equity courts have been abolished.

Equity financing. Raising of capital by corporation by issuing (selling) stock. This is contrasted with "debt financing" which is the raising of capital by issuing bonds or borrowing money.

Equity follows the law. Equity adopts and follows the rules of law in all cases to which those rules may, in terms, be applicable. Equity, in dealing with cases of an equitable nature, adopts and follows the analogies furnished by the rules of law. A leading maxim of equity jurisprudence, which, however, is not of universal application, but liable to many exceptions.

Equity jurisdiction. In a general sense, the jurisdiction belonging to a court of equity, but more particularly the aggregate of those cases, controversies, and occasions which form proper subjects for the exercise of the powers of a chancery court.

In the federal and most state courts there has been a merger procedurally between law and equity actions (*i.e.*, the same court has jurisdiction over *both* legal and equitable matters) and, hence, a person seeking equitable relief brings the same complaint as in a law action and simply demands equitable relief instead of (or in addition to) money damages. Fed.R. Civil P. 2.

"Equity jurisdiction," in its ordinary acceptation, as distinguished on the one side from the general power to decide matters at all, and on the other from the jurisdiction "at law" or "common-law jurisdiction," is the power to hear certain kinds and classes of civil causes according to the principles of the method and procedure adopted by the court of chancery, and to decide them in accordance with the doctrines and rules of equity jurisprudence, which decision may involve either the determination of the equitable rights, estates, and interests of the parties to such causes, or the granting of equitable remedies. In order that a cause may come within the scope of the equity jurisdiction, one of two alternatives is essential; either the primary right, estate, or interest to be maintained, or the violation of which furnishes the cause of action, must be equitable rather than legal; or the remedy granted must be in its nature purely equitable, or if it be a remedy which may also be given by a court of law, it must be one which, under the facts and circumstances of the case, can only be made complete and adequate through the equitable modes of procedure. Norback v. Board of Directors of Church Extension Soc., 84 Utah 506, 37 P.2d 339.

Equity jurisprudence. That portion of remedial justice which is exclusively administered by courts of equity as distinguished from courts of common law. More generally speaking, the science which treats of the rules, principles, and maxims which govern the decisions of a court of equity, the cases and controversies which are considered proper subjects for its cognizance, and the nature and form of the remedies which it grants.

Equity looks upon that as done which ought to have been done. Equity will treat the subject-matter, as to collateral consequences and incidents, in the same manner as if the final acts contemplated by the parties had been executed exactly as they ought to have been; not as the parties might have executed them.

Equity of a statute. By this phrase is intended the rule of statutory construction which admits within the operation of a statute a class of cases which are neither expressly named nor excluded, but which, from their analogy to the cases that are named, are clearly and justly within the spirit and general meaning of the law; such cases are said to be "within the equity of the statute."

Equity of partners. A term used to designate the right of each of them to have the firm's property applied to the payment of the firm's debts.

Equity of redemption. The right of the mortgagor of an estate to redeem the same after it has been forfeited, at law, by a breach of the condition of the mortgage, upon paying the amount of debt, interest and costs. Brown v. United States, C.C.A.Pa., 95 F.2d 487, 489. A right a mortgagor is given to redeem his property from default; period from the time of default until foreclosure proceedings are begun.

Equity ratio. Stockholders' equity divided by total assets.

Equity security. As defined in Bankruptcy Act, § 101(15), term includes: (A) share in a corporation, whether or not transferable or denominated "stock", or similiar security; (B) interest of a limited partner in a limited partnership; or (C) warrant or right, other than a right to convert, to purchase, sell, or subscribe to a share, security, or interest of a kind specified in subparagraph (A) or (B).

Equity shares. Shares of any class of stock, whether or not preferred as to dividends or assets, having unlimited dividend rights.

Equity suffers not a right without a remedy. Graselli Chemical Company v. Ætna Explosives Co., 164 C.C.A. 380, 252 F. 456.

Equity term. An equity term of court is one devoted exclusively to equity business, that is, in which no criminal cases are tried nor any cases requiring the impaneling of a jury. See **Equity, courts of.**

Equity to a settlement. The equitable right of a wife, when her husband sues in equity for the reduction of her equitable estate to his own possession, to have the whole or a portion of such estate settled upon herself and her children. Also a similar right recognized by the equity courts as directly to be asserted against the husband. Also sometimes called the "wife's equity."

Equivalent, *adj.* Equal in value, force, measure, volume, power, and effect or having equal or corresponding import, meaning or significance; alike, identical. Salt Lake County v. Utah Copper Co., C.C.A.Utah, 93 F.2d 127, 132; Nahas v. Nahas, 59 Nev. 220, 90 P.2d 223, 224.

Equivalents doctrine. In patent law, doctrine of "equivalents" means that if two devices do the same work in substantially the same way and accomplish substantially the same result, they are the same, even though they differ in name, form or shape. Fife Mfg. Co. v. Stanford Engineering Co., D.C.Ill., 193 F.Supp. 226, 232. Principle of law evolved to protect patentee from devices which differ merely in name, form or shape and thereby to prevent an unauthorized person from reaping benefits of another's inventive genius. Fraser v. Continental Realty Corp., D.C.W. Va., 356 F.Supp. 704, 705. Patentee may invoke doctrine of "equivalency" to proceed against producer of device, if it performs substantially same function in substantially the same way to obtain the same result. Ceramic Tilers Supply, Inc. v. Tile Council of America, Inc., C.A.Cal., 378 F.2d 283, 286.

Equivocal. Having a double or several meanings or senses. Synonymous with "ambiguous". See **Ambiguity.**

Equuleus /əkwúwliyəs/. A kind of rack for extorting confessions.

Erastians /ərǽstiyən(d)z/. The followers of Erastus. The sect obtained much influence in England, particularly among common lawyers in the time of Selden. They held that offenses against religion and morality should be punished by the civil power, and not by the censures of the church or by excommunication.

Erasure. The obliteration of words or marks from a written instrument by rubbing, scraping, or scratching them out. Also the place in a document where a word or words have been so removed. The term is sometimes used for the removal of parts of a writing by any means whatever, as by cancellation; but this is not an accurate use.

Erasure of record. Procedure by which a person's criminal record may be sealed or destroyed if certain conditions are met. This is commonly provided for by statute for juvenile records.

Within statute providing that all police and court records shall be erased upon acquittal of the accused, word "erased" means at the very least nondisclosure. Lechner v. Holmberg, 165 Conn. 152, 328 A.2d 701, 707. See also **Expungement of record.**

Erciscundus /ərsəskǽndəs/. In the civil law, to be divided. *Judicium familiæ erciscundæ,* a suit for the partition of an inheritance. An ancient phrase derived from the Twelve Tables.

Erect. In England, one of the formal words of incorporation in royal charters. "We do, incorporate, *erect,*

ordain, name, constitute, and establish." "Construct" is synonymous with "erect".

Erection. Raising up; building; a completed building; to build; construct; set up. There is a distinction between "erection" and maintenance. Turturro v. Calder, 307 Mass. 159, 29 N.E.2d 744, 746.

Ergo /ə́rgow/. Lat. Therefore; hence; because.

Ergolabi /ərgowléybay/. In the civil law, undertakers of work; contractors.

Erie v. Tompkins. The landmark case holding that in an action in the Federal court, except as to matters governed by the U.S. Constitution and Acts of Congress, the law to be applied in any case is the law of the State in which the Federal Court is situated. 304 U.S. 64, 58 S.Ct. 817, 82 L.Ed. 1188. This case overruled Swift v. Tyson, 41 U.S. 1, 16 Pet. 1, 10 L.Ed. 865, which held that there was a body of federal general common law to be applied in such cases.

Erigimus /əríjəməs/. We erect. One of the words by which a corporation may be created in England by the king's charter. 1 Bl.Comm. 473.

E.R.I.S.A. Employment Retirement Income Security Act. Federal Act governing the funding, vesting and administration of pension plans.

Ermine /ə́rmən/. By metonymy, this term is used to describe the office or functions of a judge, whose state robe, lined with ermine, is emblematical of purity and honor without stain.

Erosion. To wear away by the action of water, wind, or other elements. The gradual eating away of the soil by the operation of currents or tides. Distinguished from *submergence,* which is the disappearance of the soil under the water and the formation of a navigable body over it.

Erotomania /əròdəméyn(i)yə/. See **Insanity.**

Errant. Wandering; itinerant; applied to justices on circuit, and bailiffs at large, etc.

Erratum /ərǽdəm/əréydəm/. Lat. Error. Used in the Latin formula for assigning errors, and in the reply thereto, "in nullo est erratum," *i.e.,* there was no error, no error was committed.

Erroneous. Involving error; deviating from the law. This term is not generally used as designating a corrupt or evil act. See **Error.**

Erroneous assessment. Refers to an assessment that deviates from the law and is therefore invalid, and is a defect that is jurisdictional in its nature, and does not refer to the judgment of the assessing officer in fixing the amount of valuation of the property. In re Blatt, 41 N.M. 269, 67 P.2d 293, 301.

Erroneous judgment. One rendered according to course and practice of court, but contrary to law, upon mistaken view of law, or upon erroneous application of legal principles.

Erroneous or illegal tax. One levied without statutory authority, or upon property not subject to taxation, or by some officer having no authority to levy the tax, or one which in some other similar respect is illegal.

Erronice /ərównəsiy/. Lat. Erroneously; through error or mistake.

Error. A mistaken judgment or incorrect belief as to the existence or effect of matters of fact, or a false or mistaken conception or application of the law. Such a mistaken or false conception or application of the law to the facts of a cause as will furnish ground for a review of the proceedings upon a writ of error. A mistake of law, or false or irregular application of it, such as vitiates the proceedings and warrants the reversal of the judgment.

Error is also used as an elliptical expression for "writ of error"; as in saying that *error* lies; that a judgment may be reversed *on error*. See **Writ of error**.

See also **Ignorance; Mistake; Plain error rule**.

Assignment of errors. A specification of the errors upon which the appellant will rely in seeking to have the judgment of the lower court reversed, vacated, modified, or a new trial ordered. See *e.g.* Fed.R.App. P. 28.

Clerical error. See **Clerical error**.

Error apparent of record. Plain, fundamental error that goes to the foundation of the action irrespective of the evidence; an obvious misapprehension of the applicable law. Parks v. Parks, 68 App.D.C. 363, 98 F.2d 235, 236.

Fundamental error. In appellate practice, error which goes to the merits of the plaintiff's cause of action, and which will be considered on review, whether assigned as error or not, where the justice of the case seems to require it. Error of such character as to render judgment void. Error in law apparent on the face of the record; *e.g.* court lacked jurisdiction. See *Reversible error*, infra. See also **Plain error rule**.

Harmful error. Error which more probably than improbably affected the verdict or judgment prejudicially to the party complaining. See *Fundamental error; Reversible error*, this topic. See also **Plain error rule**.

Harmless error. In appellate practice, an error committed in the progress of the trial below, but which was not prejudicial to the rights of the party assigning it, and for which, therefore, the court will not reverse the judgment, as, where the error was neutralized or corrected by subsequent proceedings in the case, or where, notwithstanding the error, the particular issue was found in that party's favor, or where, even if the error had not been committed, he could not have been legally entitled to prevail. Error which is not sufficient in nature or effect to warrant reversal, modification, or retrial. Fed.R.Crim.P. 52 provides: "Any error, defect, irregularity or variance which does not affect substantial rights shall be disregarded."

Invited error. In appellate practice, the principle of "invited error" is that if, during the progress of a cause, a party requests or moves the court to make a ruling which is actually erroneous, and the court does so, that party cannot take advantage of the error on appeal or review.

Reversible error. In appellate practice, such an error as warrants the appellate court in reversing the judgment before it; substantial error, that which reason-ably might have prejudiced the party complaining. See *Fundamental error*, supra. See also **Plain error rule**.

Error coram nobis /éhrər kórəm nówbəs/. Error committed in the proceedings "before us"; *i.e.*, error assigned as a ground for reviewing, modifying, or vacating a judgment in the same court in which it was rendered. A writ to bring before the court that pronounced judgment errors in matters of fact which had not been put in issue or passed on and were material to validity and regularity of legal proceeding itself. Hiawassee Lumber Co. v. United States, C.C. A.N.C., 64 F.2d 417, 418. See **Coram nobis**.

Error coram vobis /éhrər kórəm vówbəs/. Error in the proceedings "before you"; words used in a writ of error directed by an appellate court to the court which tried the cause. See **Coram vobis**.

Errores ad sua principia referre, est refellere /əróriyz æd s(y)úwə prənsíp(i)yə rəfəriy, èst rəféləriy/. To refer errors to their sources is to refute them. To bring errors to their beginning is to see their last.

Errores scribentis nocere non debent /əróriyz skrəbéntəs nósəriy nòn débənt/. The mistakes of the writer ought not to harm.

Error fucatus nuda veritate in multis, est probabilior; et sæpenumero rationibus vincit veritatem error /éhrər fyəkéydəs nyúwdə vèhrətéydiy ìn máltəs èst pròbəbíliyər; èt síypiyn(y)úwmərow ræshiyównəbəs vínsət vèhrətéydəm éhrər/. Error artfully disguised [or colored] is, in many instances, more probable than naked truth; and frequently error overwhelms truth by [its show of] reasons.

Error in exercise of jurisdiction. Error in determination of questions of law or fact on which the court's jurisdiction in particular case depends. Burgess v. Nail, C.C.A.Okl., 103 F.2d 37, 43.

Error in fact. Error in fact occurs when, by reason of some fact which is unknown to the court and not apparent on the record (*e.g.*, infancy, or death of one of the parties), it renders a judgment void or voidable. Such occurs when some fact which really exists is unknown, or some fact is supposed to exist which really does not. Schwartz v. Kominski, 25 Ill.App.3d 789, 324 N.E.2d 91, 93.

Error in law. An error of the court in applying the law to the case on trial, *e.g.*, in ruling on the admission of evidence, or in charging the jury. See also **Error**.

Error in vacuo /éhrər ìn vǽkyuwow/. Error in adverse ruling without adverse effect is "error in vacuo" which may subject the erring judge to criticism but not the case to re-trial. See **Error** (*Harmless error*).

Error juris nocet /éhrər júrəs nósət/. Error of law injures. A mistake of the law has an injurious effect; that is, the party committing it must suffer the consequences.

Error nominis /éhrər nómənəs/. Error of name. A mistake of detail in the name of a person; used in contradistinction to error *de personâ*, a mistake as to identity.

Error nominis nunquam nocet, si de identitate rei constat /éhrər nómənəs nǽŋkwəm nósət, sáy dìy ədèntətéydiy ríyay kónstət/. A mistake in the name of a thing is never prejudicial, if it be clear as to the identity of the thing itself [where the thing intended is certainly known]. This maxim is applicable only where the means of correcting the mistake are apparent on the face of the instrument to be construed.

Error of fact. See Error in fact.

Error of law. See Error in law.

Error qui non resistitur approbatur /éhrər kwày nón rəzístədər ǽprowbéydər/. An error which is not resisted or opposed is approved.

Errors excepted /éhrərz əkséptəd/. A phrase appended to an account stated, in order to excuse slight mistakes or oversights.

Error, writ of. See Writ of error.

Erthmiotum. In old English law, a meeting of the neighborhood to compromise differences among themselves; a court held on the boundary of two lands.

Erubescit lex filios castigare parentes /ərəbésət léks fíliyows kǽstəgériy pəréntiyz/. The law blushes when children correct their parents.

Escalator clause. In union contract, a provision that wages will rise or fall depending on some standard like the cost of living index. In lease, provision that rent may be increased to reflect increase in real estate taxes, operating costs, and even increases in Consumer Price Index. In construction contract, clause authorizing contractor to increase contract price should costs of labor or materials increase.

Clause in leases or contracts executed subject to price control regulations. Under this clause, in the case of a lease, the landlord is authorized to collect the maximum rent permissible under rent regulations in force at time of execution of the lease. The escalator part of the clause of the lease consists in the provision that in the event that the rent regulations are modified during the term of the lease, the tenant will pay the increased rental following the allowance thereof. See also Cost-of-living clause.

Escambio /əskǽmbiyow/. In old English law, a writ of exchange. A license in the shape of a writ, formerly granted to an English merchant to draw a bill of exchange on another in foreign parts.

Escambium /əskǽmbiyəm/. An old English law term, signifying exchange.

Escape. The departure or deliverance out of custody of a person who was lawfully imprisoned before he is entitled to his liberty by the process of law. The voluntarily or negligently allowing any person lawfully in confinement to leave. To flee from; to avoid; to get away, as to flee to avoid arrest. The voluntary departure from lawful custody by a prisoner with the intent to evade the due course of justice. People v. Rivera, Colo.App., 542 P.2d 90, 92. See 18 U.S.C.A. § 751 et seq.

Escape clause. Provision in a contract or other document permitting party or parties to avoid liability or performance under certain conditions. For example, international tariff containing clause that tariff will be changed if imports covered by such cause harm to domestic industries producing like goods. An "escape clause" is one that provides for avoidance of liability when there is other valid insurance. Chamberlin v. Smith, 72 C.A.3d 835, 140 Cal.Rptr. 493, 500.

Escape period. Term generally applied to provision in union contracts in connection with maintenance of membership clauses permitting workers to withdraw from the union during a certain period near the end of the contract period and before the start of the next contract period.

Escape warrant. In English practice, this was a warrant granted to retake a prisoner committed to the custody of the king's prison who had escaped therefrom. It was obtained on affidavit from the judge of the court in which the action had been brought, and was directed to all the sheriffs throughout England, commanding them to retake the prisoner and commit him to gaol when and where taken, there to remain until the debt was satisfied.

Escapio quietus /əskéypiyow kwiyíydəs/. In old English law, delivered from that punishment which by the laws of the forest lay upon those whose beasts were found upon forbidden land.

Escapium /əskéypiyəm/. That which comes by chance or accident.

Eschæta derivatur a verbo gallico eschoir, quod est accidere, quia accidit domino ex eventu et ex insperato /əschíydə dèhrəvéydər èy várbow gǽləkow əs(h)wár, kwód èst æksídəriy kwáyə ǽksədət dómənow èks əvént(y)uw èd éks insèpəréydow/. Escheat is derived from the French word *"eschoir,"* which signifies to happen, because it falls to the lord from an event and from an unforeseen circumstance.

Eschætæ vulgo dicuntur quæ decidentibus iis quæ de rege tenent, cum non existit ratione sanguinis hæres, ad fiscum relabuntur /əschíydiy vólgow dəkántər kwìy dèsədéntəbəs áyəs kwìy dìy ríyjiy ténənt kám nón əgzístət rǽshiyówniy sǽŋgwənəs híriyz æd fískəm rèləbántər/. Those things are commonly called "escheats" which revert to the exchequer from a failure of issue in those who hold of the king, when there does not exist any heir by consanguinity.

Escheat /əs(h)chíyt/. A reversion of property to the state in consequence of a want of any individual competent to inherit.

Escheat at feudal law was the right of the lord of a fee to re-enter upon the same when it became vacant by the extinction of the blood of the tenant. This extinction might either be *per defectum sanguinis* or else *per delictum tenentis,* where the course of descent was broken by the corruption of the blood of the tenant. As a fee might be holden either of the crown or from some inferior lord, the escheat was not always to the crown. The word "escheat", in this country, merely indicates the preferable right of the state to an estate left vacant, and without there being any one in existence able to make claim thereto.

Escheator /əs(h)chíydər/. In English law, the name of an officer who was appointed in every county to look after the escheats which fell due to the king in that particular county, and to certify the same into the exchequer. An escheator could continue in office for one year only, and was not re-eligible until three years. There does not appear to exist any such officer at the present day.

Escheat, writ of. A writ which anciently lay for a lord, to recover possession of lands that had escheated to him.

Escheccum /əs(h)chékəm/. In old English law, a jury or inquisition.

Escobedo Rule /èskəbíydow ruwl/. Where police investigation begins to focus on a particular suspect, the suspect is in custody, the suspect requests and is denied counsel, and the police have not warned him of his right to remain silent, the accused has been denied assistance of counsel and no statement elicited during such interrogation may be used in a criminal trial. Escobedo v. State of Illinois, 378 U.S. 478, 490, 491, 84 S.Ct. 1758, 12 L.Ed.2d 977. See also **Miranda Rule.**

Escot /əskót/. In England, a tax formerly paid in boroughs and corporations towards the support of the community, which is called "scot and lot."

Escribano /èyskriybánow/. In Spanish law, an officer, resembling a notary in French law, who has authority to set down in writing, and verify by his attestation, transactions and contracts between private persons, and also judicial acts and proceedings.

Escritura /èyskriytúra/. In Spanish law, a written instrument. Every deed that is made by the hand of a public *escribano,* or notary of a corporation or council *(concejo),* or sealed with the seal of the king or other authorized persons.

Escroquerie /e(s)kròwkeríy/. Fr. Fraud, swindling, cheating.

Escrow. A writing, deed, money, stock, or other property delivered by the grantor, promisor or obligor into the hands of a third person, to be held by the latter until the happening of a contingency or performance of a condition, and then by him delivered to the grantee, promisee or obligee. A system of document transfer in which a deed, bond, or funds is delivered to a third person to hold until all conditions in a contract are fulfilled; *e.g.* delivery of deed to escrow agent under installment land sale contract until full payment for land is made.

Escrow account. A bank account generally held in the name of the depositor and an escrow agent which is returnable to depositor or paid to third person on the fulfillment of escrow condition; *e.g.* funds for payment of real estate taxes are commonly paid into escrow account of bank-mortgagor by mortgagee.

Escrow deposit. See **Escrow account.**

Escrowl /eskrówl/. In old English law, an escrow; a scroll. "And deliver the deed to a stranger, as an escrowl."

Escuage /éskyuwəj/. In feudal law, service of the shield. One of the varieties of tenure in knight's service, the duty imposed being that of accompanying

the king to the wars for forty days, at the tenant's own charge, or sending a substitute. In later times, this service was commuted for a certain payment in money, which was then called "escuage certain." 2 Bl.Comm. 74, 75.

Esketores /èskətóriyz/. Robbers, or destroyers of other men's lands and fortunes.

Eskipper, eskippare /èskəpér(iy)/. To ship.

Eskippeson /(ə)skíp(ə)sən/. Shippage, or passage by sea. Spelled, also, *"skippeson."*

Eslisors /əláyzərz/. See **Elisors.**

Esne /ézniy/. In old English law, a hireling of servile condition.

Esnecy /é(s)nəsiy/. Seniority; the condition or right of the eldest; the privilege of the eldest-born. Particularly used of the privilege of the eldest among coparceners to make a first choice of purparts upon a voluntary partition.

E.S.O.P. Employee Stock Ownership Plan.

Espedient /espèyðiyént/. In Spanish law, a junction of all the separate papers made in the course of any one proceeding and which remains in the office at the close of it.

Espera /éspərə/. A period of time fixed by law or by a court within which certain acts are to be performed, *e.g.,* the production of papers, payment of debts, etc.

Espionage. Espionage, or spying, has reference to the crime of "gathering, transmitting or losing" information respecting the national defense with intent or reason to believe that the information is to be used to the injury of the United States, or to the advantage of any foreign nation. 18 U.S.C.A. § 793; Rosenberg v. United States, 346 U.S. 273, 73 S.Ct. 1152, 97 L.Ed. 1609. See **Internal security acts.**

Espionage Act. Federal law which punishes espionage, spying, and related crimes. 18 U.S.C.A. § 793 *et seq.*

Esplees /əsplíyz/. An old term for the products which the ground or land yields; as the hay of the meadows, the herbage of the pasture, corn of arable fields, rent and services, etc. The word has been anciently applied to the land itself.

Espousals /əspáwzəlz/. A mutual promise between a man and a woman to marry each other at some other time. It differs from a marriage, because then the contract is completed.

Espurio /espúriyow/. In Spanish law, a spurious child; one begotten on a woman who has promiscuous intercourse with many men.

Esq. Abbreviation for Esquire.

Esquire /éskway(ə)r/əskwáy(ə)r/. In English law, a title of dignity next above gentleman, and below knight. Also a title of office given to sheriffs, serjeants, and barristers at law, justices of the peace, and others.

In United States, title commonly appended after name of attorney; *e.g.* John J. Jones, Esquire.

Essence. That which is indispensable. The gist or substance of any act; the vital constituent of a thing; that without which a thing cannot be itself. Norman v. Department of Labor and Industries, 10 Wash.2d 180, 116 P.2d 360, 362.

Essence of the contract. Any condition or stipulation in a contract which is mutually understood and agreed by the parties to be of such vital importance that a sufficient performance of the contract cannot be had without exact compliance with it is said to be "of the essence of the contract." See also **Basis of bargain.**

Essendi quietum de tolonio /əsénday kwiyíydəm dìy təlówniyow/. A writ to be quit of toll; it lies for citizens and burgesses of any city or town who, by charter or prescription, ought to be exempted from toll, where the same is exacted of them.

Essential. Indispensably necessary; important in the highest degree; requisite. That which is required for the continued existence of a thing.

Essential governmental duties. Those duties which framers of Constitution intended each member of union would assume in functioning under form of government guaranteed by Constitution. Commissioner of Internal Revenue v. Stilwell, C.C.A.7, 101 F.2d 588, 591.

Essoin, *v.* /əsóyn/. In old English practice, to present or offer an excuse for not appearing in court on an appointed day in obedience to a summons; to cast an essoin. This was anciently done by a person whom the party sent for that purpose, called an "essoiner."

Essoin, *n.* /əsóyn/. In old English law, an excuse for not appearing in court at the return of the process. Presentation of such excuse. Essoin was not now allowed at all in personal actions. 3 Bl.Comm. 278, note.

Essoin day /əsóyn dèy/. In England, formerly the first general return-day of the term, on which the courts sat to receive essoins, *i.e.*, excuses for parties who did not appear in court, according to the summons of writs. 3 Bl.Comm. 278. By St. 11 Geo. IV, and 1 Wm. IV, c. 70, § 6, these days were done away with, as a part of the term.

Essoin de malo villæ /əsóyn dìy mǽlow víliy/. When the defendant is in court the first day; but gone without pleading, and being afterwards surprised by sickness, etc., cannot attend, but sends two essoiners, who openly protest in court that he is detained by sickness in such a village, that he cannot come *pro lucrari* and *pro perdere;* and this will be admitted, for it falls on the plaintiff to prove whether the essoin is true or not.

Essoiniator /əsóyniyèydər/. A person who made an essoin.

Essoin roll /əsóyn ròwl/. In England, a roll upon which essoins were formerly entered, together with the day to which they were adjourned.

Establish. This word occurs frequently in the Constitution of the United States, and it is there used in different meanings: (1) To settle firmly, to fix unalterably; as to establish justice, which is the avowed object of the Constitution. (2) To make or form; as to establish uniform laws governing naturalization or bankruptcy. (3) To found, to create, to regulate; as: "Congress shall have power to establish post-offices." (4) To found, recognize, confirm, or admit; as: "Congress shall make no law respecting an establishment of religion." See **Establishment clause.** (5) To create, to ratify, or confirm, as: "We, the people . . . do ordain and establish this Constitution." Ware v. U. S., 71 U.S. (4 Wall.) 617, 18 L.Ed. 389.

To settle, make or fix firmly; place on a permanent footing; found; create; put beyond doubt or dispute; prove; convince. Wells Lamont Corp. v. Bowles, Em.App., 149 F.2d 364, 366. To enact permanently. To bring about or into existence.

Establishment. Place of business. Public or private institution. State of being established.

Establishment clause. That provision of the First Amendment to U.S. Constitution which provides that "Congress shall make no law respecting an establishment of religion, or prohibiting the free exercise thereof . . . ". Such language prohibits a state or the federal government from setting up a church, or passing laws which aid one, or all, religions, or giving preference to one religion, or forcing belief or disbelief in any religion. Everson v. Board of Education, 330 U.S. 1, 67 S.Ct. 504, 91 L.Ed. 711; McCollum v. Brd. of Education, 333 U.S. 203, 68 S.Ct. 461, 92 L.Ed. 649.

Estadal /èstədál/. In Spanish America, a measure of land of sixteen square varas, or yards.

Estadia (or Sobrestadia) /èstaðíya (sòwbreystaðíya)/. In Spanish law, delay in a voyage, or in the delivery of cargo, caused by the charterer or consignee, for which demurrage is payable. The time for which the party who has chartered a vessel, or is bound to receive the cargo, has to pay demurrage on account of his delay in the execution of the contract.

Est aliquid quod non oportet etiam si licet; quicquid vero non licet certe non oportet /èst ǽləkwid kwòd nón əpórdət éshiyəm sày lísət; kwíkwid vírow nòn lísət sərdiy nòn əpórdət/. There is that which is not proper, even though permitted; but whatever is not permitted is certainly not proper.

Estandard /əstǽndərd/. L. Fr. A standard (of weights and measures). So called because it stands constant and immovable, and hath all other measures coming towards it for their conformity.

Est ascavoir /éy asavwóhr/. It is to be understood or known; "it is to-wit."

Estate. The degree, quantity, nature, and extent of interest which a person has in real and personal property. An estate in lands, tenements, and hereditaments signifies such interest as the tenant has therein. 2 Bl.Comm. 103. The condition or circumstance in which the owner *stands* with regard to his property. Boyd v. Sibold, 7 Wash.2d 279, 109 P.2d 535, 539. In this sense, "estate" is commonly used in conveyances in connection with the words "right," "title," and "interest," and is, in a great degree, synonymous with all of them.

The total property of whatever kind that is owned by a decedent prior to the distribution of that property in accordance with the terms of a will, or, when there is no will, by the laws of inheritance in the state of domicile of the decedent. It means, ordinarily, the whole of the property owned by anyone, the realty as well as the personalty. As used in connection with the administration of decedents' estates, term includes property of a decedent, trust or other person as such property exists from time to time during the administration, and hence may include probate assets as well as property passing by intestacy. Uniform Probate Code, § 1–201(11).

In its broadest sense, the social, civic, or political condition or standing of a person; or a class of persons considered as grouped for social, civic, or political purposes.

Common Law Classifications

Estates may be either *absolute* or *conditional.* An absolute estate is a full and complete estate, or an estate in lands not subject to be defeated upon any condition. In this phrase the word "absolute" is not used legally to distinguish a fee from a life-estate, but a qualified or conditional fee from a fee simple. A conditional estate is one, the existence of which depends upon the happening or not happening of some uncertain event, whereby the estate may be either originally created, or enlarged, or finally defeated. Estates are also classed as *executed* or *executory.* The former is an estate whereby a present interest passes to and resides in the tenant, not dependent upon any subsequent circumstance or contingency. They are more commonly called "estates in possession." 2 Bl.Comm. 162. An estate where there is vested in the grantee a present and immediate right of present or future enjoyment. An executory estate is an estate or interest in lands, the vesting or enjoyment of which depends upon some future contingency. Such estate may be an *executory devise,* or an *executory remainder,* which is the same as a contingent remainder, because no present interest passes. A *contingent* estate is one which depends for its effect upon an event which may or may not happen, as, where an estate is limited to a person not yet born. *Conventional* estates are those freeholds not of inheritance or estates for life, which are created by the express acts of the parties, in contradistinction to those which are legal and arise from the operation of law. A *dominant* estate, in the law of easements, is the estate for the benefit of which the easement exists, or the tenement whose owner, as such, enjoys an easement over an adjoining estate. An *expectant* estate is one which is not yet in possession, but the enjoyment of which is to begin at a future time; a present or vested contingent right of future enjoyment. Examples are remainders and reversions. A *future* estate is an estate which is not now vested in the grantee, but is to commence in possession at some future time. It includes remainders, reversions, and estates limited to commence *in futuro* without a particular estate to support them, which last are not good at common law, except in the case of chattel interests. 2 Bl.Comm. 165. An estate limited to commence in possession at a future day, either without the intervention of a precedent estate, or on the determination by lapse of time, or otherwise, of a precedent estate created at the same time. A *particular* estate is a limited estate which is taken out of the fee, and which precedes a remainder; as an estate for years to A., remainder to B. for life; or an estate for life to A., remainder to B. in tail. This precedent estate is called the "particular estate," and the tenant of such estate is called the "particular tenant." 2 Bl.Comm. 165. A *servient* estate, in the law of easements, is the estate upon which the easement is imposed or against which it is enjoyed; an estate subjected to a burden or servitude for the benefit of another estate. A *settled* estate, in English law, is one created or limited under a settlement; that is, one in which the powers of alienation, devising, and transmission according to the ordinary rules of descent are restrained by the limitations of the settlement. A *vested* estate is one in which there is an immediate right of present enjoyment or a present fixed right of future enjoyment; an estate as to which there is a person in being who would have an immediate right to the possession upon the ceasing of some intermediate or precedent estate. An *original* estate is the first of several estates, bearing to each other the relation of a particular estate and a reversion. An original estate is contrasted with a *derivative* estate; and a derivative estate is a particular interest carved out of another estate of larger extent.

"Estate" and "heirs" are not equivalent terms, Martin v. Hale, 167 Tenn. 438, 71 S.W.2d 211, 214; Abraham v. Abraham, 245 App.Div. 302, 280 N.Y.S. 825.

As to Homestead; Movable; Real; Residuary; Separate, and Trust (*Trust estate*), see those titles. See also Augmented estate; Beneficial estate; Gross estate; Joint estate; Life estate; Net estate; Residuary estate; Vested estate.

For the names and definitions of the various kinds of estates in land, see the different titles below.

Landed estate or property. See **Landed estate or property.**

Qualified estate. Interests in real property which are not absolute and unconditional including fee tail, estates on condition, estates on limitation, and estates on conditional limitation. Carpender v. City of New Brunswick, 135 N.J.Eq. 397, 39 A.2d 40, 43.

Small estate. In some jurisdictions, there is an informal procedure for administration of small estates of decedents less structured than ordinary probate and administration. Normally, the services of an attorney are not required. Uniform Probate Code, § 3–1201 *et seq.*

Estate ad remanentiam /əstéyd ǽd rèmənénsh(iy)əm/. An estate in fee-simple.

Estate at sufferance. The interest of a tenant who has come rightfully into possession of lands by permission of the owner, and continues to occupy the same after the period for which he is entitled to hold by such permission. 2 Bl.Comm. 150. The estate arises where one comes into possession of land by lawful title, but keeps it afterwards without any title at all, and the original entry need not have been under lease or as a tenant of the dispossessing landlord.

Estate at will. A species of estate less than freehold, where lands and tenements are let by one man to another, to have and to hold at the will of the lessor;

and the tenant by force of this lease obtains possession. 2 Bl.Comm. 145. Or it is where lands are let without limiting any certain and determinate estate. The estate arises where lands or tenements are expressly demised by one person to another to be held during the joint wills of both parties, or it may arise by implication of law wherever one person is put in possession of another's land with the owner's consent, but under an agreement which does not suffice to create in the tenant an estate of freehold or for years.

Estate by elegit. See **Elegit.**

Estate by entirety. See **Estate by the entirety.**

Estate by purchase. One acquired in any other method than descent. See also **Purchase.**

Estate by statute merchant. In England, an estate whereby the creditor, under the custom of London, retained the possession of all his debtor's lands until his debts were paid. See **Statute** (*Statute merchant*).

Estate by statute staple. See **Staple** (*Statute staple*).

Estate by the curtesy. See **Curtesy.**

Estate by the entirety. Called also estate in entirety, or estate by the entireties. An estate in joint tenancy, plus the unity of the marital relation. A form of co-ownership of realty or personalty held by husband and wife in which there is unity of estate, unity of possession and unity of control of entire property, and on death of one, survivor takes estate under original conveyance. In re Gallagher's Estate, 352 Pa. 476, 43 A.2d 132, 133. A common-law estate, based on the doctrine that husband and wife are one, and that a conveyance of real property to husband and wife creates but one estate. An estate held by husband and wife together so long as both live, and, after the death of either, by the survivor. It is an estate held by husband and wife by virtue of a title acquired by them jointly after marriage. A creature of the common law created by legal fiction based wholly on the common-law doctrine that husband and wife are one, and hence a conveyance to husband and wife created only one estate, and each was owner of the whole estate, and neither could dispose of it without the consent of the other, and on the death of one survivor was the owner in fee simple. Alexander v. Alexander, 154 Or. 317, 58 P.2d 1265, 1270, 1271.

Type of joint estate which may be held only by two persons who are married to each other at the time that the estate is created and which does not admit of partition, though, on divorce, it automatically becomes an estate in common unless the parties provide otherwise.

An "estate by entireties" resembles a "joint tenancy" in that there is a right of survivorship in both, but such an estate is distinguishable from a joint tenancy in that the latter may be invested in any number of natural persons each of whom is seized of an undivided moiety of the whole, whereas a "tenancy by entirety" is vested in two persons only, who in law are regarded as only one, and each of whom becomes seized of the estate as a whole. Heffner v. White, 113 Ind.App. 296, 45 N.E.2d 342, 346.

See also **Community property; Entirety; Tenancy** (*Joint tenancy*).

Estate duty. A duty formerly imposed in England (act of 1894) upon the principal value of all property which passed on death. Such duty was replaced in 1975 by a capital transfer tax.

Estate for life. See **Life estate.**

Estate for years. A species of estate less than freehold, where a man has an interest in lands and tenements, and a possession thereof, by virtue of such interest, for some fixed and determinate period of time; as in the case where lands are leased for the term of a certain number of years, agreed upon between the lessor and the lessee. Blackstone calls this estate a "contract" for the possession of lands or tenements for some determinate period. 2 Bl.Comm. 140. Estates for years embrace all terms limited to endure for a definite and ascertained period, however short or long the period may be; they embrace terms for a fixed number of weeks or months or for a single year, as well as for any definite number of years, however great. Also called "tenancy for a term".

Estate from period to period. An estate continuing for successive periods of a year, or successive periods of a fraction of a year, unless it is terminated. Pitney-Bowes Postage Meter Co. v. United States, D.C. Conn., 57 F.Supp. 365, 366. Also called "tenancy from period to period"; or "periodic estate".

Estate from year to year. An example of an "estate for years" (*q.v.*). It exists in cases where the parties stipulate for it, and also where the parties by their conduct have placed themselves in the relation of landlord and tenant without adopting any other term. If a tenant has been allowed to hold over after the expiration of his term in such a way as to preclude the possibility of his becoming a tenant on sufferance, it is a tenancy from year to year. It was originally a development of a tenancy at will, by which the tenancy was terminable only at the time of the year at which it began, and on notice.

Estate in common. An estate in lands held by two or more persons, with interests accruing under different titles; or accruing under the same title, but at different periods; or conferred by words of limitation importing that the grantees are to take in distinct shares. See also **Tenancy** (*Tenancy in common*).

Estate in coparcenary /əstéyd ən kowpárs(ə)nəriy/. See **Coparcenary.**

Estate in dower. See **Dower.**

Estate in expectancy. One which is not yet in possession, but the enjoyment of which is to begin at a future time. An estate giving a present or vested contingent right of future enjoyment. One in which the right to pernancy of the profits is postponed to some future period. Such are estates in remainder and reversion.

Estate in fee simple. See **Fee simple.**

Estate in fee-tail. See **Tail, estate in.**

Estate in joint tenancy. See **Tenancy.**

Estate in lands. Property one has in lands, tenements or hereditaments, or conditions or circumstances in which tenant stands as to his property. Tallman v.

Eastern Illinois & Peoria R. Co., 379 Ill. 441, 41 N.E.2d 537, 540. See **Estate.**

Estate in remainder. See **Remainder.**

Estate in reversion. See **Reversion.**

Estate in severalty /əstéyd ən sévrəltiy/. An estate held by a person in his own right only, without any other person being joined or connected with him in point of interest, during his estate. This is the most common and usual way of holding an estate. 2 Bl.Comm. 179.

Estate in vadio /əstéyd ən vǽdiyow/. An estate in gage or pledge. 2 Bl.Comm. 157. See **Mortgage.**

Estate less than freehold. An estate for years, estate at will, or estate at sufferance.

Estate of freehold. See **Freehold.**

Estate of inheritance. An estate which may descend to heirs. Administration & Trust Co. v. Catron, 171 Tenn. 268, 102 S.W.2d 59, 60. A species of freehold estate in lands, otherwise called a "fee," where the tenant is not only entitled to enjoy the land for his own life, but where, after his death, it is passed by the law upon the persons who successively represent him *in perpetuum,* according to a certain established order of descent.

Estate on condition. See **Estate upon condition.**

Estate on conditional limitation. An estate conveyed to one person so that, upon occurrence or failure of occurrence of some contingent event, whether conditional or limitative, the estate shall depart from original grantee and pass to another. Carpender v. City of New Brunswick, 135 N.J.Eq. 397, 39 A.2d 40, 43.

Estate on limitation /əstéyd òn lìmətéyshən/. An estate originated by the use of words denoting duration of time, such as while, during, so long as, and the like and when designated limitative event happens, such estate ends naturally without any re-entry and property reverts to grantor. Carpender v. City of New Brunswick, 135 N.J.Eq. 397, 39 A.2d 40, 43. Sometimes referred to as "base fee", "qualified fee", "determinable fee", or "fee simple defeasible". Lehigh Valley R. Co. v. Chapman, 35 N.J. 177, 171 A.2d 653, 657.

Estate planning. That branch of the law which, in arranging a person's property and estate, takes into account the laws of wills, taxes, insurance, property, and trusts so as to gain maximum benefit of all laws while carrying out the person's own wishes for the disposition of his property upon his death.

Éstate pur autre vie /əstéyt pər ówtrə váy/. See **Pur autre vie.**

Estates of the realm. The lords spiritual, the lords temporal, and the commons of Great Britain. 1 Bl. Comm. 153. Sometimes called the "three estates." Inasmuch as the lords spiritual had no separate assembly or negative in their political capacity, some authorities reduce the estates in Great Britain to two, the lords and commons. Generally in feudal Europe there were three estates: the clergy, nobles, and commons. In England (until about the 14th century) the three estates of the realm were the clergy, barons, and knights. In legal practice the lords spiritual and lords temporal are usually collectively designated under the one name *lords.*

Estate subject to a conditional limitation. The distinction between an estate upon condition subsequent and an "estate subject to a conditional limitation" is that in former words creating condition do not originally limit term, but merely permit its termination upon happening of contingency, while in latter words creating it limit continuation of estate to time preceding happening of contingency. Johnson v. Lane, 199 Ark. 740, 135 S.W.2d 853, 866.

Estate tail. See **Tail, estate in.**

Estate tail, quasi. When a tenant for life grants his estate to a man and his heirs, as these words, though apt and proper to create an estate tail, cannot do so, because the grantor, being only tenant for life, cannot grant *in perpetuum,* therefore they are said to create an estate tail *quasi,* or improper.

Estate tax. A tax imposed on the right to transfer property by death. Thus, an estate tax is levied on the decedent's estate and not on the heir receiving the property. A tax levied on right to transmit property, while "inheritance tax" is levied on right to receive property. Allen v. Flournoy, 26 Cal.App.3d 774, 103 Cal.Rptr. 275, 277. The tax is based on value of the whole estate less certain deductions. I.R.C. § 2001 *et seq.* See also **Inheritance tax; Unified transfer tax.**

Many states have adopted the "Uniform Interstate Compromise of Death Taxes Act" or the "Uniform Interstate Arbitration of Death Taxes Act."

Estate upon condition. An estate in lands, the existence of which depends upon the happening or not happening of some uncertain event, whereby the estate may be either originally created, or enlarged, or finally defeated. 2 Bl.Comm. 151. An estate having a qualification annexed to it, by which it may, upon the happening of a particular event, be created, or enlarged, or destroyed. United States v. 1,010.8 Acres, More or Less, Situate in Sussex County, Del., D.C.Del., 56 F.Supp. 120, 127.

Estate upon condition expressed. An estate granted, either in fee-simple or otherwise, with an express qualification annexed, whereby the estate granted shall either commence, be enlarged, or be defeated upon performance or breach of such qualification or condition. 2 Bl.Comm. 154. An estate which is so expressly defined and limited by the words of its creation that it cannot endure for any longer time than till the contingency happens upon which the estate is to fail.

Estate upon condition implied. An estate having a condition annexed to it inseparably from its essence and constitution, although no condition be expressed in words. 2 Bl.Comm. 152.

Est autem jus publicum et privatum, quod ex naturalibus præceptis aut gentium, aut civilibus est collectum; et quod in jure scripto jus appellatur, id in lege angliæ rectum esse dicitur /ést òdəm jás pə́bləkəm èt prəvéydəm, kwòd èks næ̀tyəréyləbəs prəséptəs òt jénsh(iy)əm òt səvíləbəs èst kəléktəm; èt kwód ìn júriy skríptow jás ǽpəléydər, íd in líyjiy ǽngliyiy réktəm èst dísədər/. Public and private law is that which is collected from natural precepts, on the one hand of nations, on the other of citizens; and that which in the civil law is called *"jus,"* that, in the law of England, is said to be right.

Est autem vis legem simulans /ést òdəm vís líyjəm símyəlæn(d)z/. Violence may also put on the mask of law.

Estendard, estendart, or standard /(ə)stǽndərd/. An ensign for horsemen in war.

Ester in judgment. L. Fr. To appear before a tribunal either as plaintiff or defendant.

Estimate. A valuing or rating by the mind, without actually measuring, weighing, or the like. A rough or approximate calculation only. United States v. Foster, C.C.A.Iowa, 131 F.2d 3, 7. Act of appraising or valuing. Determination of approximate cost or return.

This word is used to express the mind or judgment of the speaker or writer on the particular subject under consideration. It implies a calculation or computation, as to *estimate* the gain or loss of an enterprise.

Estimated tax. Tax computed in the first instance without fully accurate and complete information but which is filed only as a preliminary matter to be followed by a final tax return. Tax payments are made in instalments based on the estimate and then credited to taxpayer when he files his final return. Federal law dictates when declarations of estimated tax must be filed (*e.g.* quarterly). I.R.C. § 6015(a). Declarations and payment of estimated taxes are normally made by non-wage earners since, unlike wage earners, their taxes are not withheld from each paycheck by the employer. See also **Declaration of estimated tax.**

Estimated useful life. The period over which an asset will be used by a particular taxpayer. Although such period cannot be longer than the estimated physical life of an asset, it could be shorter if the taxpayer does not intend to keep the asset until it wears out. Assets such as goodwill do not have an estimated useful life. The estimated useful life of an asset is essential to measuring the annual tax deduction for depreciation and amortization and in determining the amount of any investment tax credit allowable.

Estin doctrine. The principle of law enunciated in Estin v. Estin, 334 U.S. 541, 68 S.Ct. 1213, 92 L.Ed. 1561 to the effect that a divorce decree is divisible and, while full faith and credit must be given to a decree as to the termination of the marriage, no full faith and credit is required as to that portion of the decree ordering support for the wife unless the court entering the order had personal jurisdiction of the husband.

Est ipsorum legislatorum tanquam viva vox /ést ipsórəm lèjəslətórəm tǽŋkwəm váyvə vóks/. The voice of the legislators themselves is like the living voice; that is, the language of a statute is to be understood and interpreted like ordinary spoken language.

Estop. To stop, bar, or impede; to prevent; to preclude. See **Embargo; Estoppel; Injunction.**

Estoppel /əstópəl/. "Estoppel" means that party is prevented by his own acts from claiming a right to detriment of other party who was entitled to rely on such conduct and has acted accordingly. Graham v. Asbury, 112 Ariz. 184, 540 P.2d 656, 658. An estoppel arises when one is concluded and forbidden by law to speak against his own act or deed. Gural v. Engle, 128 N.J.L. 252, 25 A.2d 257, 261. An inconsistent position, attitude or course of conduct may not be adopted to loss or injury of another. Brand v. Farmers Mut. Protective Ass'n of Texas, Tex.Civ. App., 95 S.W.2d 994, 997. See Restatement, Agency, Second § 8B.

Estoppel is a bar or impediment which precludes allegation or denial of a certain fact or state of facts, in consequence of previous allegation or denial or conduct or admission, or in consequence of a final adjudication of the matter in a court of law. It operates to put party entitled to its benefits in same position as if thing represented were true. May v. City of Kearney, 145 Neb. 475, 17 N.W.2d 448, 458. Under law of "estoppel" where one of two innocent persons must suffer, he whose act occasioned loss must bear it. Buxbaum v. Assicurazioni Generali, 175 Misc. 785, 25 N.Y.S.2d 357, 360; Sackenreuther v. Winston, Tex.Civ.App., 137 S.W.2d 93, 96. Elements or essentials of estoppel include change of position of parties so that party against whom estoppel is invoked has received a profit or benefit or party invoking estoppel has changed his position to his detriment.

Estoppel is or may be based on acceptance of benefits, Rhodus v. Geatley, 347 Mo. 397, 147 S.W.2d 631, 637, 638, 639; Harjo v. Johnston, 187 Okl. 561, 104 P.2d 985, 992, 998; actual or constructive fraudulent conduct, Peterson v. Hudson Ins. Co., 41 Ariz. 31, 15 P.2d 249, 252; admissions or denials by which another is induced to act to his injury, Wabash Drilling Co. v. Ellis, 230 Ky. 769, 20 S.W.2d 1002, 1004; agreement on and settlement of facts by force of entering into contract, Masterson v. Bouldin, Tex.Civ. App., 151 S.W.2d 301, 307; In re Schofield's Estate, 101 Colo. 443, 73 P.2d 1381; assertion of facts on which another relies; assumption of position which, if not maintained, would result in injustice to another; concealment of facts, Greer v. Franklin Life Ins. Co., Tex.Civ.App., 109 S.W.2d 305, 315; Rosser v. Texas Co., 173 Okl. 309, 48 P.2d 327, 330; conduct or acts amounting to a representation or a concealment; consent to copyright infringement, whether express or implied from long acquiescence with knowledge of the infringement, Edwin L. Wiegand Co. v. Harold E. Trent Co., C.C.A.Pa., 122 F.2d 920, 925; election between rights or remedies, Mason & Mason v. Brown, Tex.Civ.App., 182 S.W.2d 729, 733; inaction, Utah State Building Commission, for Use and Benefit of Mountain States Supply Co. v. Great American Indemnity Co., 105 Utah 11, 140 P.2d 763, 771, 772; Hankins v. Waddell, 26 Tenn.App. 71, 167 S.W.2d 694, 696; laches; language or conduct which has induced another to act, Brown v. Federal Land Bank of Houston, Tex.Civ.App., 180 S.W.2d 647, 652.

Estoppels at common law are sometimes said to be of three kinds: (1) by deed; (2) by matter of record; (3) by matter *in pais.* The first two are also called legal estoppels, as distinguished from the last kind, known as equitable estoppels.

For Acquiescence, estoppel by; Collateral attack; Contract, estoppel by; Deed, estoppel by; Election, estoppel by; Equitable estoppel; In pais, estoppel; Judgment, estoppel by; Judicial estoppel; Laches, estoppel by; Legal estoppel; Negligence, estoppel by; Promissory estoppel; Quasi estoppel; Record, estoppel by; Representation, estoppel by; Silence, estoppel by; and Verdict, estoppel by, see those titles.

Acts and declarations. An "estoppel by acts and declarations" is such as arises from the acts and declarations of a person by which he designedly induces another to alter his position injuriously to himself.

Estoppel by deed. A grantor in a warranty deed who does not have title at the time of the conveyance but who subsequently acquires title is estopped from denying that he had title at the time of the transfer and such after-acquired title inures to the benefit of the grantee or his successors. See also **Deed, estoppel by.**

Estoppel by judgment. Term means that when a fact has been agreed on, or decided in a court of record, neither of the parties shall be allowed to call it in question, and have it tried over again at any time thereafter, so long as judgment or decree stands unreversed. Humphrey v. Faison, 247 N.C. 127, 100 S.E.2d 524, 529. Final adjudication of material issue by a court of competent jurisdiction binds parties in any subsequent proceeding between or among them, irrespective of difference in forms or causes of action. Mansker v. Dealers Transport Co., 160 Ohio St. 255, 116 N.E.2d 3, 6. See also **Judgment, estoppel by.**

Estoppel certificate. A signed statement by a party, such as a tenant or a mortgagee, certifying for the benefit of another party that a certain statement of facts is correct as of the date of the statement, such as that a lease exists, that there are no defaults and that rent is paid to a certain date. Delivery of the statement by the tenant prevents (estops) the tenant from later claiming a different state of facts.

Estoppel in pais. The doctrine by which a person may be precluded by his act or conduct, or silence when it is his duty to speak, from asserting a right which he otherwise would have had. Mitchell v. McIntee, 15 Or.App. 85, 514 P.2d 1357, 1359. See also **Equitable estoppel.**

Misrepresentation. See **Representation, estoppel by.**

Pleading. Pleader must allege and prove not only that person sought to be estopped made misleading statements and representations but that pleader actually believed and relied on them and was misled to his injury thereby. Stanolind Oil & Gas Co. v. Midas Oil Co., Tex.Civ.App., 173 S.W.2d 342, 345.

Under rules practice in most states, and in the federal courts, estoppel is an affirmative defense which must be pleaded. Fed.R. Civil P. 8(c).

Ratification distinguished. The substance of "estoppel" is the inducement of another to act to his prejudice. The substance of "ratification" is confirmation after conduct.

By ratification party is bound because he intended to be, while under "estoppel" he is bound because other party will be prejudiced unless the law treats him as legally bound. Carlile v. Harris, Tex.Civ.App., 38 S.W.2d 622. See **Ratification.**

Res judicata distinguished. A prior judgment between same parties, which is not strictly res judicata because based upon different cause of action, operates as an "estoppel" only as to matters actually in issue or points controverted. Ætna Life Ins. Co. of Hartford, Conn. v. Martin, C.C.A.Ark., 108 F.2d 824, 827; Cunningham v. Oklahoma City, 188 Okl. 466, 110 P.2d 1102, 1104. In a later action upon a different cause of action a judgment operates as an "estoppel" only as to such issues in second action as were actually determined in the first action. Lorber v. Vista Irr. Dist., C.C.A.Cal., 127 F.2d 628, 634. The doctrine of "res judicata" is a branch of law of "estoppel". Krisher v. McAllister, 71 Ohio App. 58, 47 N.E.2d 817, 819. The plea of "res judicata" is in its nature an "estoppel" against the losing party from again litigating matters involved in previous action, but the plea does not have that effect as to matters transpiring subsequently. Fort Worth Stockyards Co. v. Brown, Tex.Civ.App., 161 S.W.2d 549, 555. See **Res** (*Res judicata*).

Waiver distinguished. Waiver is voluntary surrender or relinquishment of some known right, benefit or advantage; estoppel is the inhibition to assert it. In insurance law, however, the two terms are commonly used interchangeably. See **Waiver.**

Estover /əstówvər/. The right or privilege which a tenant has to furnish himself with so much wood from the demised premises as may be sufficient or necessary for his fuel, fences, and other agricultural operations. 2 Bl.Comm. 35.

An allowance made to a person out of an estate or other thing for his or her support, as for food and raiment.

An allowance (more commonly called "alimony") granted to a woman divorced *a mensa et thoro,* for her support out of her husband's estate. 1 Bl.Comm. 441.

Estoveria sunt ardendi, arandi, construendi et claudendi /èstəvíriyə sànt ardénday, ərǽnday, kònstruwénday èt klòdénday/. Estovers are of fire-bote, plow-bote, house-bote, and hedge-bote.

Estoveriis habendis /èstəvíriyəs həbéndəs/. A writ (now obsolete) for a wife judicially separated to recover her alimony or estovers.

Est quiddam perfectius in rebus licitis /ést kwídəm pərféksh(iy)əs ìn ríybəs lísədəs/. There is something more perfect in things allowed.

Estray /əstréy/. An estray is an animal that has escaped from its owner, and wanders or strays about; usually defined, at common law, as a wandering animal whose owner is unknown. An animal cannot be an estray when on the range where it was raised, and permitted by its owner to run, and especially when the owner is known to the party who takes it up.

The term is also used of flotsam at sea.

Estreat, *v.* /əstríyt/. To take out a forfeited recognizance from the recordings of a court, and return it to the court to be prosecuted. See **Estreat,** *n.*

Estreat, *n.* (From Lat. *extractum.*) In English law, a copy or extract from the book of estreats, that is, the rolls of any court, in which the amercements or fines, recognizances, etc., imposed or taken by that court upon or from the accused, are set down, and which are to be levied by the bailiff or other officer of the court. A true copy or duplicate of some original writing or record, and especially of fines and amercements imposed by a court, *extracted* from the record, and certified to a proper officer or officers authorized and required to collect them.

Estreciatus /əstrìys(h)iyéydəs/. Straightened, as applied to roads.

Estrepe /əstríyp/. To strip; to despoil; to lay waste; to commit waste upon an estate, as by cutting down trees, removing buildings, etc. To injure the value of a reversionary interest by stripping or spoiling the estate.

Estrepement /əstríypmənt/. A species of aggravated waste, by stripping or devastating the land, to the injury of the reversioner, and especially pending a suit for possession.

Estrepement, writ of. A common-law writ of waste, which lay in particular for the reversioner against the tenant for life, in respect of damage or injury to the land committed by the latter. As it was only auxiliary to a real action for recovery of the land, and as equity afforded the same relief by injunction, the writ fell into disuse in England, and was abolished by 3 & 4 Wm. IV, c. 27.

Estuary /és(h)chəwèhriy/. That part of the mouth or lower course of a river flowing into the sea which is subject to tide; especially, an enlargement of a river channel toward its mouth in which the movement of the tide is very prominent.

Et. And. The introductory word of several Latin and law French phrases formerly in common use.

Et adjournatur /éd ædjərnéydər/. And it is adjourned. A phrase used in the old reports, where the argument of a cause was adjourned to another day, or where a second argument was had.

Et al. /èd ǽl/. An abbreviation for *et alii,* "and others." The singular is "et alius" (*q.v.*). It may also mean "and another" in the singular.

The abbreviation et al. (sometimes in the plural written *et als.*) is often affixed to the name of the person first mentioned, where there are several plaintiffs, grantors, persons addressed, etc.

Where the words "et al." are used in a judgment against defendants, the quoted words include all defendants. Williams v. Williams, 25 Tenn.App. 290, 156 S.W.2d 363, 369.

Et alii è contra /èd éyliyay ìy kóntrə/. And others on the other side. A phrase constantly used in the Year Books, in describing a joinder in issue.

Et alius /èd éyliyəs/. And another.

Et allocatur /èd ǽləkéydər/. And it is allowed.

Et cetera (or etc.) /et sédərə/. And others; and other things; and others of like character; and others of the like kind; and the rest; and so on; and so forth. In its abbreviated form *(etc.)* this phrase is frequently affixed to one of a series of articles or names to show that others are intended to follow or understood to be included. So, after reciting the initiatory words of a set formula, or a clause already given in full, *etc.* is added, as an abbreviation, for the sake of convenience. And other things of like kind or purpose as compared with those immediately theretofore mentioned.

Et de ceo se mettent en le pays. L. Fr. And of this they put themselves upon the country.

Et de hoc ponit se super patriam /èt dìy hók pównət síy s(y)úwpər pǽtriyəm/. And of this he puts himself upon the country. The formal conclusion of a common-law plea in bar by way of traverse. 3 Bl.Comm. 313. The literal translation is retained in the modern form.

Et ei legitur in hæc verba /èd íyay líyjədər ən híyk várbə/. L. Lat. And it is read to him in these words. Words formerly used in entering the prayer of oyer on record.

Eternal security. The doctrine of "eternal security" means that once one becomes a Christian or has been "regenerated" his future conduct, no matter what it may be, will not jeopardize his salvation. Ashman v. Studebaker, 115 Ind.App. 73, 56 N.E.2d 674, 678.

Et habeas ibi tunc hoc breve /èt héybiyəs íbay tə̀nk hók bríyviy/. And have you then there this writ. The formal words directing the return of a writ. The literal translation was retained in the later form of a considerable number of writs.

Et habuit /èt hǽbyuwət/. And he had it, a common phrase in the Year Books, expressive of the allowance of an application or demand by a party.

Ethics. Of or relating to moral action, conduct, motive or character; as, ethical emotion; also, treating of moral feelings, duties or conduct; containing precepts of morality; moral. Professionally right or befitting; conforming to professional standards of conduct. Kraushaar v. La Vin, 181 Misc. 508, 42 N.Y.S.2d 857, 859.

Legal ethics. See **Canon** (*Canons of judicial ethics*); **Code of Professional Responsibility; Legal ethics.**

Et hoc paratus est verificare /et hók pəréydəs èst vèhrəfəkériy/. And this he is prepared to verify. The Latin form of concluding a plea in confession and avoidance; that is, where the defendant has confessed all that the plaintiff has set forth, and has pleaded new matter in avoidance. These words were used, when the pleadings were in Latin, at the conclusion of any pleading which contained new affirmative matter. They expressed the willingness or readiness of the party so pleading to establish by proof the matter alleged in his pleading. A pleading which concluded in that manner was technically said to "conclude with a verification," in contradistinction to a pleading which simply denied matter alleged by the opposite party, and which for that reason was said to "conclude to the country," because the party merely put himself upon the country, or left the matter to the jury.

Et hoc petit quod inquiratur per patriam /et hók pédət kwòd iŋkwəréydər pàr pǽtriyəm/. And this he prays may be inquired of by the country. The conclusion of a plaintiff's pleading, tendering an issue to the country. Literally translated in the modern forms.

Et inde petit judicium /ed índiy pédət juwdísh(iy)əm/. And thereupon [or thereof] he prays judgment. A clause at the end of pleadings, praying the judgment of the court in favor of the party pleading. It occurs as early as the time of Bracton, and is literally translated in the modern forms.

Et inde producit sectam /ed índiy prəd(y)úwsət séktəm/. And thereupon he brings suit. The Latin conclusion of a declaration, except against attorneys and other officers of the court. 3 Bl.Comm. 295.

Etiquette of the profession /édəkət əv ðə prəféshən/. The code of honor agreed on by mutual understanding and tacitly accepted by members of the legal profession, especially by the bar. See **Code of Professional Responsibility; Legal ethics.**

Et modo ad hunc diem /et mówdow ǽd háŋk dáyəm/. Lat. And now at this day. This phrase was the formal beginning of an entry of appearance or of a continuance. The equivalent English words are still used in this connection.

Et non /èt nón/. Lat. And not. A technical phrase in pleading, which introduces the negative averments of a special traverse. It has the same force and effect as the words *absque hoc*, "without this," and is occasionally used instead of the latter.

Et seq. /èt səkwéntiyz/et səkwénsh(iy)ə/. An abbreviation for *et sequentes* (masculine and feminine plural) or *et sequentia* (neuter), "and the following." Thus a reference to "p. 1, *et seq.*" means "page first and the following pages." Also abbreviated "et sqq.," which is preferred by some authorities for a reference to more than one following page.

Et sic /èt sík/. And so. In the Latin forms of pleading these were the introductory words of a special conclusion to a plea in bar, the object being to render it positive and not argumentative; as *et sic nil debet*.

Et sic ad judicium /èt sík ǽd juwdíshiyəm/. And so to judgment.

Et sic ad patriam /èt sík ǽd pǽtriyəm/. And so to the country. A phrase used in the Year Books, to record an issue to the country.

Et sic fecit /èt sík féysət/. And he did so.

Et sic pendet /èt sík péndət/. And so it hangs. A term used in the old reports to signify that a point was left undetermined.

Et sic ulterius /èt sík àltíriyəs/. And so on; and so further; and so forth.

Et ux /èd ə́ks(ər)/. An abbreviation for *et uxor,*—"and wife." Where a grantor's wife joins him in the conveyance, it is sometimes expressed (in abstracts, etc.) to be by "A. B. *et ux.*"

Euclidian. Type of general zoning ordinance which excludes apartment houses, businesses, retail shops and the like from a residential zone; name is derived from case of Village of Euclid, Ohio et al. v. Ambler Realty Co., 272 U.S. 365, 47 S.Ct. 114, 71 L.Ed. 303.

Eum qui nocentem infamat, non est æquum et bonum ob eam rem condemnari; delicta enim nocentium nota esse oportet et expedit /íyəm kwày nəséntəm inféymət nón èst íykwəm èt bównəm òb íyəm rém kòndemnéray; dəlíkta íynəm nəsénsh(iy)əm nówdə ésiy əpórdət èd ékspədət/. It is not just and proper that he who speaks ill of a bad man should be condemned on that account; for it is fitting and expedient that the crimes of bad men should be known. 1 Bl.Comm. 125.

Eundo et redeundo /iyə́ndow èt rèdiyə́ndow/. Lat. In going and returning. Applied to vessels.

Eundo, morando, et redeundo /iyə́ndow, mərǽndow, èt rèdiyə́ndow/. Lat. Going, remaining, and returning. A person who is privileged from arrest (as a witness, legislator, etc.) is generally so privileged *eundo, morando, et redeundo;* that is, on his way to the place where his duties are to be performed, while he remains there, and on his return journey.

Eunomy /yúwnəmiy/. Equal laws and a well-adjusted constitution of government.

Eunuch /yúwnək/. A male of the human species who has been castrated.

Euphoria /yuwfóriyə/. Exaggerated feeling of physical and emotional well-being not consonant with apparent stimuli or events; usually of psychologic origin, but also seen in organic brain diseases, or toxic and drug induced states.

Eurodollar /yúrowdòlər/. A dollar in U.S. currency on deposit in a bank abroad, especially in a bank in Europe.

Euthanasia /yùwθənéyzhə/. The act or practice of painlessly putting to death persons suffering from incurable and distressing disease as an act of mercy.

Evarts Act. See **Judiciary acts.**

Evasion. An act of eluding, dodging, or avoiding, or avoidance by artifice. City of Wink v. Griffith Amusement Co., 129 Tex. 40, 100 S.W.2d 695, 701. A subtle endeavoring to set aside truth or to escape the punishment of the law. Tax "evasion" is to be distinguished from tax "avoidance," the former meaning the illegal nonpayment of taxes due, the latter referring to the legal reduction or nonpayment of taxes through allowable deductions, exemptions, etc.

Evasive. Tending or seeking to evade; elusive; shifting; as an *evasive* argument or plea. If a pleading to which a responsive pleading is required is evasive, a party may make motion for a more definite statement. Fed.R.Civil P. 12(e).

Evasive answer. One which consists in refusing either to admit or to deny a matter in a direct, straight-forward manner as to which the person is necessarily presumed to have knowledge. Under Fed.R.Civil P. 37, an evasive answer is considered and treated as a failure to answer, for which a party may on motion seek a court order compelling answers to discovery questions.

Eve. Evening. The period immediately preceding an important event.

Even. Nothing due or owing on either side; neither a profit nor loss; *i.e.* breaking even.

Evening. The closing part of the day and beginning of the night; in a strict sense, from sunset till dark. In common speech, the latter part of the day and the earlier part of the night, until bedtime. The period between sunset or the evening meal and ordinary bedtime. See also **Nighttime.**

Evenings. In old English law, the delivery at evening or night of a certain portion of grass, or corn, etc., to a customary tenant, who performs the service of cutting, mowing, or reaping for his lord, given him as a gratuity or encouragement.

Event. The consequence of anything; the issue or outcome of an action as finally determined; that in which an action, operation, or series of operations, terminates. Noteworthy happening or occurrence. Something that happens.

Distinguished from an act in that an act is the product of the will whereas an event is an occurrence which takes place independent of the will such as an earthquake or flood.

See also **Fortuitous event.**

Eventus est qui ex causa sequitur; et dicitur eventus quia ex causis evenit /əvéntəs èst kwáy èks kózə sékwədər, èt dísədər əvéntəs kwáyə èks kózəs évənət/. An event is that which follows from the cause, and is called an "event" because it eventuates from causes.

Eventus varios res nova semper habet /əvéntəs vériyows ríyz nówvə sémpər héybət/. A new matter always produces various events.

Evergreen contract. A contract which renews itself from year to year in lieu of notice by one of the parties to the contrary. Chemplex Co. v. Tauber Oil Co., D.C.Iowa, 309 F.Supp. 904, 908.

Every. Each one of all; all the separate individuals who constitute the whole, regarded one by one. The term is sometimes equivalent to "all"; and sometimes to "each".

Every other thing. This phrase, as used in requiring employer to furnish safe place of employment and to do "every other thing" reasonably necessary to protect employees, relates to things of same kind that employer must necessarily do in making place safe.

Evesdroppers. See **Eavesdropping.**

Evict. In civil law, to recover anything from a person by virtue of the judgment of a court or judicial sentence. See **Eviction.**

Eviction. Dispossession by process of law; the act of depriving a person of the possession of land or rental property which he has held or leased. Act of turning a tenant out of possession, either by re-entry or legal proceedings, such as an action of ejectment. Deprivation of lessee of possession of premises or disturbance of lessee in beneficial enjoyment so as to cause

tenant to abandon the premises (the latter being constructive conviction). Estes v. Gatliff, 291 Ky. 93, 163 S.W.2d 273, 276.

See also Actual eviction; Constructive eviction; Ejectment; Forcible entry and detainer; Notice to quit; Partial eviction; Retaliatory eviction; Total eviction.

Evidence. Any species of proof, or probative matter, legally presented at the trial of an issue, by the act of the parties and through the medium of witnesses, records, documents, exhibits, concrete objects, etc., for the purpose of inducing belief in the minds of the court or jury as to their contention. Taylor v. Howard, 111 R.I. 527, 304 A.2d 891, 893.

Testimony, writings, material objects, or other things presented to the senses that are offered to prove the existence or nonexistence of a fact. Calif. Evid.Code.

All the means by which any alleged matter of fact, the truth of which is submitted to investigation, is established or disproved. Any matter of fact, the effect, tendency, or design of which is to produce in the mind a persuasion of the existence or nonexistence of some matter of fact. That which demonstrates, makes clear, or ascertains the truth of the very fact or point in issue, either on the one side or on the other. That which tends to produce conviction in the mind as to existence of a fact. The means sanctioned by law of ascertaining in a judicial proceeding the truth respecting a question of fact.

As a part of procedure "evidence" signifies those rules of law whereby it is determined what testimony should be admitted and what should be rejected in each case, and what is the weight to be given to the testimony admitted. See **Evidence rules.**

For Presumption as evidence, see **Presumption;** Proof and evidence distinguished, see **Proof;** Testimony as synonymous or distinguishable, see **Testimony;** View as evidence, see **View.**

See also Adminicular evidence; Aliunde; Autoptic evidence; Best evidence; Beyond a reasonable doubt; Circumstantial evidence; Competent evidence; Conclusive evidence; Conflicting evidence; Corroborating evidence; Cumulative evidence; Demeanor evidence; Demonstrative evidence; Derivative evidence; Direct evidence; Documentary evidence; Extrajudicial evidence; Extraneous evidence; Extrinsic evidence; Fabricated evidence; Fact; Fair preponderance of evidence; Hearsay; Illegally obtained evidence; Immaterial evidence; Incompetent evidence; Incriminating evidence; Inculpatory; Independent source rule; Indirect evidence; Indispensable evidence; Inference; Laying foundation; Legal evidence; Legally sufficient evidence; Limited admissibility; Material evidence; Mathematical evidence; Moral evidence; Narrative evidence; Newly-discovered evidence; Offer of proof; Opinion evidence; Oral evidence; Original document rule; Parol evidence rule; Partial evidence; Past recollection recorded; Perpetuating testimony; Physical fact rule; Positive evidence; Preliminary evidence; Preponderance; Presumption; Presumptive evidence; Prima facie evidence; Primary evidence; Prior inconsistent statements; Privileged evidence; Probable evidence; Probative evidence; Probative facts; Proof; Proper evidence; Real evidence; Reasonable inference rule; Rebuttal evidence; Relevant evidence; Satisfactory evidence; Scintilla of evidence; Secondary evidence; Second-hand evidence; State's evidence; Substantial evidence; Substantive evidence; Substitutionary evidence; Sufficiency of evidence; Traditionary evidence; View; Weight of evidence; Withholding of evidence.

There are, generally speaking, two types of evidence from which a jury may properly find the truth as to the facts of a case. One is direct evidence— such as the testimony of an eyewitness. The other is indirect or circumstantial evidence—the proof of a chain of circumstances pointing to the existence or non-existence of certain facts. As a general rule, the law makes no distinction between direct and circumstantial evidence, but simply requires that the jury find the facts in accordance with the preponderance of all the evidence in the case, both direct and circumstantial.

Autoptic evidence. Type of evidence presented in court which consists of the thing itself and not the testimony accompanying its presentation. Articles offered in evidence which the judge or jury can see and inspect. Real evidence as contrasted with testimonial evidence; *e.g.* in contract action, the document purporting to be the contract itself, or the gun in a murder trial.

Character evidence. Evidence of a person's character or traits is admissible under certain conditions in a trial, though, as a general rule, evidence of character traits are not competent to prove that a person acted in conformity therewith on a particular occasion. Fed.Evid.R. 404.

Curative admissibility. See **Curative.**

Exculpatory evidence. A defendant in a criminal case is entitled to evidence in possession or control of the government if such evidence tends to indicate his innocence or tends to mitigate his criminality if he demands it and if the failure to disclose it results in a denial of a fair trial. U. S. v. Agurs, 427 U.S. 97, 96 S.Ct. 2392, 49 L.Ed.2d 342. Disclosure of evidence by the government is governed by Fed.R.Crim.P. 16.

Expert evidence. Testimony given in relation to some scientific, technical, or professional matter by experts, *i.e.*, persons qualified to speak authoritatively by reason of their special training, skill, or familiarity with the subject. See also **Expert witness.**

Identification evidence. See **Exemplars.**

Illegally obtained evidence. See Exclusionary rule; Miranda Rule; Mapp v. Ohio; McNabb-Mallory Rule; Motion to suppress; Poisonous tree doctrine.

Inculpatory evidence. Evidence tending to show a person's involvement in a crime; incriminating evidence.

Irrelevant evidence. Evidence is irrelevant if it is not so related to the issues to be tried and if it has no logical tendency to prove the issues. See also *Relevant evidence, infra.*

Material evidence. See *Relevant evidence, infra.*

Oral evidence. See **Testimony.**

Original evidence. See **Original; Original document rule.**

Preponderance of the evidence. A standard of proof (used in many civil suits) which is met when a party's evidence on a fact indicates that it is "more likely than not" that the fact is as the party alleges it to be. See **Fair preponderance of evidence.**

Proffered evidence. Evidence, the admissibility or inadmissibility of which is dependent upon the existence or nonexistence of a preliminary fact. Calif. Evid.Code.

Relevant evidence. Evidence having any tendency to make the existence of any fact that is of consequence to the determination of the action more probable or less probable than it would be without the evidence. Fed.Evid.R. 401. Evidence, including evidence relevant to the credibility of a witness or hearsay declarant, having any tendency in reason to prove or disprove any disputed fact that is of consequence to the determination of the action. Calif.Evid.Code. Evidence which bears a logical relationship to the issues in a trial or case.

Tangible evidence. Physical evidence; evidence that can be seen or touched, *e.g.*, documents, weapons. Testimonial evidence is evidence which can be heard, *e.g.*, the statements made by anyone sitting in the witness box. See **Demonstrative evidence.**

Evidence by inspection. Such evidence as is addressed directly to the senses without intervention of testimony. Tangible; physical evidence. See **Demonstrative evidence.**

Evidence codes. Statutory provisions governing admissibility of evidence and burden of proof at hearings and trials. See also **Evidence rules**, *infra.*

Evidence completed. Exists where both sides have offered testimony and rested, or where plaintiff has rested and defendant has made motion for finding on plaintiff's case and stands on motion and declines to offer evidence. Merriam v. Sugrue, D.C.Mun.App., 41 A.2d 166, 167.

Evidence, law of. The aggregate of rules and principles regulating the burden of proof, admissibility, relevancy, and weight and sufficiency of evidence in legal proceedings. See **Evidence codes; Evidence rules.**

Evidence of debt. A term applied to written instruments or securities for the payment of money, importing on their face the existence of a debt. See **Bonds.**

Evidence of insurability satisfactory to company. Evidence which would satisfy a reasonable person experienced in the life insurance business that insured was in an insurable condition. Bowie v. Bankers Life Co., C.C.A.Colo., 105 F.2d 806, 808.

Evidence of title. A deed or other document establishing the title to property, especially real estate.

Evidence reasonably tending to support verdict. Means evidence that is competent, relevant, and material, and which to rational and impartial mind naturally leads, or involuntarily tends to lead, to conclusion for which there is valid, just, and substantial reason. Kelly v. Oliver Farm Equipment Sales Co., 169 Okl. 269, 36 P.2d 888, 891.

Means some legal evidence tending to prove every material fact in issue as to which the party in whose favor the verdict was rendered had the burden of proof. Nicolai-Neppach Co. v. Smith, 154 Or. 450, 58 P.2d 1016, 1024.

Evidence rules. Rules which govern the admissibility of evidence at hearings and trials, *e.g.* Federal Rules of Evidence; Uniform Rules of Evidence; Maine Rules of Evidence. In certain states evidence rules are codified (*e.g.* California Evidence Code) or otherwise set forth in statutes (*e.g.* state statutes commonly govern admissibility of confidential communications).

Evidence to support findings. Substantial evidence or such relevant evidence as a reasonable mind might accept as adequate to support a conclusion and enough to justify, if the trial were to a jury, a refusal to direct a verdict when the conclusion sought to be drawn from it is one of fact for jury. Jordan v. Craighead, 114 Mont. 337, 136 P.2d 526, 528.

Evident. Clear to the understanding and satisfactory to the judgment; manifest; plain; obvious; conclusive. Noticeable; apparent to observation.

Proof evident. See **Proof.**

Evidentia /èvədénsh(iy)ə/. L. Evidence.

Evidentiary /èvədénsh(ə)riy/°chəriy/°iyèriy/. Having the quality of evidence; constituting evidence; evidencing. A term introduced by Bentham, and, from its convenience, adopted by other writers.

Evidentiary fact. Those facts which are necessary for determination of the ultimate facts; they are the premises upon which conclusions of ultimate facts are based. Womack v. Industrial Comm., 168 Colo. 364, 451 P.2d 761, 764. Facts which furnish evidence of existence of some other fact.

Evidentiary harpoon. Exists where prosecution through its witnesses successfully places before jury improper evidence, such as previous arrests and convictions of defendant, in situations where such evidence would not be admissible. Kramer v. State, 258 Ind. 257, 317 N.E.2d 203, 207.

Evidently. Means in an evident manner; perceptibly, clearly, obviously, plainly. It is employed to express the idea of full-proof conviction. Tennes v. Tennes, 320 Ill.App. 19, 50 N.E.2d 132, 139.

Evocation. In French law, the withdrawal of a cause from the cognizance of an inferior court, and bringing it before another court or judge. In some respects this process resembles the proceedings upon *certiorari.*

Evolution statute. Legislative enactment which forbids teaching of evolution in schools and which has been held unconstitutional as violative of the Establishment Clause of First Amend., U.S.Const. Epperson v. Arkansas, 393 U.S. 97, 89 S.Ct. 266, 21 L.Ed.2d 228.

Ewage /yúwəj/. (L. Fr. *Ewe,* water.) In old English law, toll paid for water passage. The same as *aquage* or *aquagium.*

Ewbrice /yúwbrìych/. Adultery; spouse-breach; marriage-breach.

Ewry /yúw(ə)riy/. An office in the royal household where the table linen, etc., is taken care of.

Ex /éks/. A latin preposition meaning from, out of, by, on, on account of, or according to.

A prefix, denoting removal, cessation or former. Prefixed to the name of an office, relation, *status,* etc., it denotes that the person spoken of once occupied that office or relation, but does so no longer, or that he is now *out* of it. Thus, *ex*-mayor, *ex*-partner, *ex*-judge.

A prefix which is equivalent to "without," "reserving," or "excepting." In this use, probably an abbreviation of "except." Thus, *ex*-interest, *ex*-coupons, *ex*-dividend.

Also used as an abbreviation for "exhibit."

Ex abundanti /èks əbэ̀ndǽntay/. Out of abundance; abundantly; superfluously; more than sufficient.

Ex abundanti cautela /èks əbэ̀ndǽntay kotíylə/. Lat. Out of abundant caution.

Exaction. The wrongful act of an officer or other person in compelling payment of a fee or reward for his services, under color of his official authority, where no payment is due. See also **Extortion.**

Exactor. In the civil law, a gatherer or receiver of money; a collector of taxes. In old English law, a collector of the public moneys; a tax gatherer. Thus, *exactor regis* was the name of the king's tax collector, who took up the taxes and other debts due the treasury.

Ex adverso /èks ədvэ́rsow/. On the other side. Applied to opposing counsel.

Ex æquitate /èks iykwэtéydiy/. According to equity; in equity.

Ex æquo et bono /èks íykwow èt bównow/. A phrase derived from the civil law, meaning, in justice and fairness; according to what is just and good; according to equity and conscience. 3 Bl.Comm. 163.

Ex altera parte /èks óltərə párdiy/. Of the other part.

Examen /əgzéymən/. L. Lat. A trial. *Examen computi,* the balance of an account.

Examination. An investigation; search; inspection; interrogation.

Abstract of title. An investigation of the abstract of title made by or for a person who intends to purchase real estate, to ascertain the history and present condition of the title to such land, and its status with reference to liens, incumbrances, clouds, etc. to determine if marketable title exists.

Bankruptcy. Questioning of bankrupt during course of bankruptcy proceedings (first meeting of creditors) concerning extent of his debts and assets, conduct of his business, the cause of his bankruptcy, his dealings with his creditors and other persons, the amount, kind, and whereabouts of his property, and all matters which may affect the administration and settlement of his estate. Bankruptcy Act, § 343.

Criminal procedure. An investigation by a magistrate of a person who has been charged with crime and arrested, or of the facts and circumstances which are alleged to have attended the crime, in order to ascertain whether there is sufficient ground to hold him to bail for his trial by the proper court. The preliminary hearing to determine whether person charged with having committed a crime should be held for trial. See **Court of Inquiry; Examining court; Examining trial; Preliminary hearing.**

Discovery. See **Deposition; Discovery; Interrogatories.**

Invention. An inquiry made at the patent-office, upon application for a patent, into the novelty and utility of the alleged invention, and as to its interfering with any other patented invention. 35 U.S.C.A. § 36.

Witnesses. The examination of a witness consists of the series of questions put to him by a party to the action, or his counsel, for the purpose of bringing before the court and jury in legal form the knowledge which the witness has of the facts and matters in dispute, or of probing and sifting his evidence previously given.

See also Cross-examination; Direct examination; Leading question; Preliminary hearing; Re-cross examination; Redirect examination; Reexamination; Separate examination. As regards examination of witnesses prior to trial, see **Deposition; Interrogatories.** As regards compulsory examination, see **Subpoena.**

Examined copy. A copy of a record, public book, or register, and which has been compared with the original.

Examiner. Officer or other person authorized to conduct an examination (*e.g.* bank examiner) or appointed by court to take testimony of witnesses.

An officer appointed by the court to take testimony in causes pending in that court; *e.g.* a master, auditor, referee.

An officer in the patent-office charged with the duty of examining the patentability of inventions for which patents are asked.

For "Special examiner," see that title. See also **Auditor; Inspector; Master; Referee.**

Examiners, bar. Persons appointed to test law graduates to ascertain their qualifications to practice law. Such test is called "bar examination."

Examining board. Generally, a board composed of public or quasi public officials who are responsible for conducting tests and examinations for those applying for licenses.

Examining court. A lower court which conducts preliminary examinations to determine probable cause and set bail before a criminal defendant is bound over to the grand jury. See **Court of inquiry; Preliminary hearing.**

Examining trial. A preliminary hearing to determine whether there exists probable cause for binding one over to the grand jury. See also **Preliminary hearing.**

Exannual roll /èksǽnyuwəl rówl/. In old English practice, a roll into which (in the old way of exhibiting sheriffs' accounts) the illeviable fines and desperate debts were transcribed, and which was *annually* read to the sheriff upon his accounting, to see what might be gotten.

Ex antecedentibus et consequentibus fit optima interpretatio /èks æntəsədéntəbəs èt kònsəkwéntəbəs fit óptəmə əntàrprətéysh(iy)ow/. A passage in a statute is best interpreted by reference to what precedes and what follows it. The best interpretation [of a part of an instrument] is made from the antecedents and the consequents [from the preceding and following parts]. The law will judge of a deed or other instrument, consisting of divers parts or clauses, by looking at the whole; and will give to each part its proper office, so as to ascertain and carry out the intention of the parties. The whole instrument is to be viewed and compared in all its parts, so that every part of it may be made consistent and effectual.

Ex arbitrio judicis /èks arbítriyow júwdəsəs/. At, in, or upon the discretion of the judge. 4 Bl.Comm. 394. A term of the civil law.

Ex assensu curiæ /èks əséns(y)uw kyúriyiy/. By or with the consent of the court.

Ex assensu patris /èks əséns(y)uw pǽtrəs/. By or with the consent of the father. A species of dower *ad ostium ecclesiæ*, during the life of the father of the husband; the son, by the father's consent expressly given, endowing his wife with parcel of his father's lands. Abolished in England by 3 & 4 Wm. IV, c. 105, § 13.

Ex assensu suo /èks əséns(y)uw s(y)úwow/. With his assent. Formal words in judgments for damages by default.

Ex bonis /èks bównəs/. Of the goods or property. A term of the civil law, distinguished from *in bonis*, as being descriptive of or applicable to property not in actual possession.

Excambiator /əkskǽmbiyèydər/. An exchanger of lands; a broker. Obsolete.

Excambium /əkskǽmbiyəm/. An exchange; a place where merchants meet to transact their business; also an equivalent in recompense; a recompense in lieu of dower *ad ostium ecclesiæ*.

Ex cathedra /èks kǽθədrə/°kəθíydrə/. From the chair. Originally applied to the decisions of the popes from their *cathedra*, or chair. Hence, authoritative; having the weight of authority.

Ex causa /èks kózə/. L. Lat. By title.

Excellency. Title sometimes given to the chief executive of a state or of the nation; also to members of hierarchy of church.

Except. But for; only for; not including; other than; otherwise than; to leave out of account or consideration. See **Exception.**

Excepting. As used in a deed, the terms "reserving" and "excepting" are used interchangeably, and their technical meaning will give way to the manifest intent. Porter v. Warner-Caldwell Oil Co., 183 Okl. 1, 80 P.2d 252, 253. The words "reserving" and "excepting," although strictly distinguishable, may be used interchangeably or indiscriminately. Stephens v. Kentucky Valley Distilling Co., 275 Ky. 705, 122 S.W.2d 493, 496.

Exceptio /əksépsh(iy)ow/. An exception, plea, or objection. In civil law, a plea by which the defendant admits the cause of action, but alleges new facts which, provided they be true, totally or partially answer the allegations put forward on the other side; thus distinguished from a mere traverse of the plaintiff's averments. In this use, the term corresponds to the common-law plea in confession and avoidance. Such answers to the "defense" or "plea" of the common law. An allegation and defense of a defendant by which the plaintiff's claim or complaint is defeated, either according to strict law or upon grounds of equity. In a stricter sense, the exclusion of an action that lay in strict law, on grounds of equity *(actionis jure stricto competentis ob æquitatem exclusio)*. A kind of limitation of an action, by which it was shown that the action, though otherwise just, did not lie in the particular case. A species of defense allowed in cases where, though the action as brought by the plaintiff was in itself just, yet it was unjust as against the particular party sued.

Exceptio dilatoria /əksépsh(iy)ow dìlətóriyə/. A dilatory exception; called also *"temporalis"* (temporary); one which defeated the action for a time *(quæ ad tempus nocet)*, and created delay *(et temporis dilationem tribuit)*; such as an agreement not to sue within a certain time, as five years.

Exceptio doli mali /əksépsh(iy)ow dówlay mǽlay/. An exception or plea of fraud.

Exceptio domminii /əksépsh(iy)ow dəmíniyay/. A claim of ownership set up in an action for the recovery of property not in the possession of the plaintiff.

Exceptio dotis cautæ non numeratæ /əksépsh(iy)ow dówdəs kódiy nòn n(y)ùwməréydiy/. A defense to an action for the restitution of a dowry that it was never paid, though promised, available upon the dissolution of the marriage within a limited time.

Exceptio ejus rei cujus petitur dissolutio nulla est /əksépsh(iy)ow íyjəs ríyay kyúwjəs pédədər dìsəl(y)úwsh(iy)ow nálə èst/. A plea of that matter the dissolution of which is sought [by the action] is null [or of no effect].

Exceptio falsi omnium ultima /əksépsh(iy)ow fólsay ómniyəm áltəmə/. A plea denying a fact is the last of all.

Exceptio firmat regulam in casibus non exceptis /əksépsh(iy)ow fə́rmət régyələm ən kéysəbəs nòn əkséptəs/. An exception affirms the rule in cases not excepted.

Exceptio firmat regulam in contrarium /əksépsh(iy)ow fə́rmət régyələm ìn kəntrériyəm/. An exception proves an opposite rule. See **Exceptio probat regulam.**

Exceptio in factum /əksépsh(iy)ow ìn fǽktəm/. An exception on the fact. An exception or plea founded on the peculiar circumstances of the case.

Exceptio in personam /əksépsh(iy)ow ìn pərsównəm/. A plea or defense of a personal nature, which may be alleged only by the person himself to whom it is granted by the law.

Exceptio in rem /əksépsh(iy)ow ìn rém/. A plea or defense not of a personal nature, but connected with the legal circumstances on which the suit is founded, and which may therefore be alleged by any party in interest, including the heirs and sureties of the proper or original debtor.

Exceptio jurisjurandi /əksépsh(iy)ow jùrəsjərǽnday/. An exception of oath; an exception or plea that the matter had been sworn to. This kind of exception was allowed where a debtor, at the instance of his creditor *(creditore deferente)*, had sworn that nothing was due the latter, and had notwithstanding been sued by him.

Exceptio metus /əksépsh(iy)ow médəs/. An exception or plea of fear or compulsion. Answering to the modern plea of duress.

Exception. Act of excepting or excluding from a number designated or from a description; that which is excepted or separated from others in a general rule or description; a person, thing, or case specified as distinct or not included; an act of excepting, omitting from mention or leaving out of consideration. Express exclusion of something from operation of contract or deed. An "exception" operates to take something out of thing granted which would otherwise pass or be included. Christman v. Emineth, N.D., 212 N.W.2d 543, 552.

Objection to order or ruling of trial court. A formal objection to the action of the court, during the trial of a cause, in refusing a request or overruling an objection; implying that the party excepting does not acquiesce in the decision of the court, but will seek to procure its reversal, and that he means to save the benefit of his request or objection in some future proceeding. Under rules practice in the federal and most state courts, the need for claiming an exception to evidence or to a ruling to preserve appellate rights has been eliminated in favor of an objection. Fed.R. Civil P. 46.

See also Challenge; Dilatory exceptions; General exception; Objection; Peremptory exceptions; Special exception.

Bill of exceptions. See **Bill.**

Deed. An exception withdraws from operation of deed part of thing granted which would otherwise pass to grantee.

Insurance policy. An exclusion of one or more risks. Kirkby v. Federal Life Ins. Co., C.C.A.Mich., 35 F.2d 126, 128. The object of an exception is to exclude that which otherwise would be included, to take special cases out of a general class, or to guard against misinterpretation.

"Reservation" and "proviso" compared. A "reservation" creates some new right in grantor while an "exception" withholds from grant title to some part of property which would otherwise pass. Clark v. Pauley, 291 Ky. 637, 165 S.W.2d 161, 162. A reservation does not affect the description of the property conveyed, but retains to the grantor some right upon

the property, as an easement, whereas an exception operates upon the description and withdraws from the description the excepted property. Moore v. Davis, 273 Ky. 838, 117 S.W.2d 1033, 1035. A "reservation" is always of something taken back out of that which is clearly granted, while an "exception" is of some part of the estate not granted at all. Lewis v. Standard Oil Co. of California, C.C.A.Cal., 88 F.2d 512, 514. An exception *exempts,* absolutely, from the operation of an engagement or an enactment; a proviso, properly speaking, defeats their operation, *conditionally.* An exception takes out of an engagement or enactment something which would otherwise be part of the subject-matter of it; a proviso avoids them by way of defeasance or excuse. Reservation reserves to grantor some new interest out of thing granted, while exception excludes from operation of grant some existing part of estate. Petty v. Griffith, Mo., 165 S.W.2d 412, 414; U. S. v. 1,010.8 Acres, More or Less, Situate in Sussex County, Del., D.C. Del., 56 F.Supp. 120, 128.

It has also been held however that a "proviso" and an "exception" are substantially the same thing, and that the terms are frequently used interchangeably for synonymous terms. Victory Oil Co. v. Hancock Oil Co., 270 P.2d 604, 611.

Compare also **Variance.**

Statutory laws. An exception in a statute is a clause designed to reserve or exempt some individuals from the general class of persons or things to which the language of the act in general attaches. The office of an "exception" in a statute is to except something from the operative effect of a statute or to qualify or restrain the generality of the substantive enactment to which it is attached, and it is not necessarily limited to the section of the statute immediately following or preceding. Gatliff Coal Co. v. Cox, C.C.A. Ky., 142 F.2d 876, 882. Two statutes relating to same subject must be read together, and provisions of one having special application to particular subject will be deemed an "exception" to other statute general in its terms. Eagleton v. Murphy, 348 Mo. 949, 156 S.W.2d 683, 685. See **Grandfather clause.**

Exceptional circumstances. Conditions which are out of the ordinary course of events; unusual or extraordinary circumstances. Lack of original jurisdiction to hear and determine a case constitutes "exceptional circumstance" as basis for raising question for the first time on habeas corpus. Wesley v. Schneckloth, 55 Wash.2d 90, 346 P.2d 658, 660.

Exceptio non adimpleti contractus /əksépsh(iy)ow nòn ædəmplíyday kəntrǽktəs/. An exception in an action founded on a contract involving mutual duties or obligations, to the effect that the plaintiff is not entitled to sue because he has not performed his own part of the agreement.

Exceptio non solutæ pecuniæ /əksépsh(iy)ow nòn səl(y)úwdiy pəkyúwniyiy/. A plea that the debt in suit was not discharged by payment (as alleged by the adverse party) notwithstanding an acquittance or receipt given by the person to whom the payment is stated to have been made.

Exceptio nulla est versus actionem quæ exceptionem perimit /əksépsh(iy)ow nálə èst vérsəs ǽkshiyównəm

kwìy əksèpshiyówniy pérəmət/. There is [can be] no plea against an action which destroys [the matter of] the plea.

Exceptio pacti conventi /əksépsh(iy)ow pǽktay kənvéntay/. An exception of compact; an exception or plea that the plaintiff had agreed not to sue.

Exceptio pecuniæ non numeratæ /əksépsh(iy)ow pəkyúwniyiy nòn n(y)ùwməréydiy/. An exception or plea of money not paid; a defense which might be set up by a party who was sued on a promise to repay money which he had never received.

Exceptio peremptoria /əksépsh(iy)ow pərèmtóriyə/. A peremptory exception; called also *"perpetua,"* (perpetual); one which forever destroyed the subject-matter or ground of the action *(quæ semper rem de qua agitur perimit);* such as the *exceptio doli mali,* the *exceptio metus,* etc.

Exceptio plurium concubentium /əksépsh(iy)ow pl(y)úriyəm kònkyuwbénsh(iy)əm/. The plea or defense of several lovers (*i.e.* multiple access) in paternity actions. Yarmark v. Strickland, Fla.App., 193 So.2d 212.

Exceptio probat regulam /əksépsh(iy)ow prówbət régyələm/. The exception proves the rule. Sometimes quoted with the addition *"de rebus non exceptis"* ("so far as concerns the matters not excepted").

Exceptio quæ firmat legem, exponit legem /əksépsh(iy)ow kwìy fármət líyjəm, əkspównət líyjəm/. An exception which confirms the law explains the law.

Exceptio quoque regulam declarat /əksépsh(iy)ow kwówkwiy régyələm dəklérət/. The exception also declares the rule.

Exceptio rei judicatæ /əksépsh(iy)ow ríyay jùwdəkéydiy/. An exception or plea of matter adjudged; a plea that the subject-matter of the action had been determined in a previous action.

Exceptio rei venditæ et traditæ /əksépsh(iy)ow ríyay véndədiy èt trǽdədiy/. An exception or plea of the sale and delivery of the thing. This exception presumes that there was a valid sale and a proper tradition; but though, in consequence of the rule that no one can transfer to another a greater right than he himself has, no property was transferred, yet because of some particular circumstance the real owner is estopped from contesting it.

Exceptio semper ultimo ponenda est /əksépsh(iy)ow sémpər ə́ltəmow pənéndə èst/. An exception should always be put last.

Exceptio senatusconsulti macedoniani /əksépsh(iy)ow sənèydəskənsə́ltay mæsədòwniyéynay/. A defense to an action for the recovery of money loaned, on the ground that the loan was made to a minor or person under the paternal power of another; so named from the decree of the senate which forbade the recovery of such loans.

Exceptio senatusconsulti velleiani /əksépsh(iy)ow sənèydəskənsə́ltay vèliyéynay/. A defense to an action on a contract of suretyship, on the ground that the surety was a woman and therefore incapable of becoming bound for another; so named from the decree of the senate forbidding it.

Exceptio temporis /əksépsh(iy)ow témpərəs/. An exception or plea analogous to that of the statute of limitations in our law; viz., that the time prescribed by law for bringing such actions has expired.

Exceptis excipiendis /əkséptəs əksìpiyéndəs/. Lat. With all necessary exceptions.

Exceptor. In old English law, a party who entered an exception or plea.

Except right of way. Recitals "less the right of way" and "except right of way" in granting clause of deed have well-defined accepted certain and unambiguous meaning by which grantor conveys entire interest in servient estate and at same time expressly recognizes and acknowledges dominant estate. Jennings v. Amerada Petroleum Corporation, 179 Okl. 561, 66 P.2d 1069, 1071.

Excerpta /əksárptə/ or **excerpts** /éksərpts/. Extracts.

Ex certa scientia /èks sárdə sayénsh(iy)ə/. Of certain or sure knowledge. These words were anciently used in patents, and imported full knowledge of the subject-matter on the part of the king.

Excess. Act or amount which goes beyond that which is usual, proper, or necessary. Degree or amount by which one thing or number exceeds another. See also **Excessive.**

Excess clause. In insurance policy, such clause provides for insurer's liability up to limits of policy covering excess loss only after exhaustion of other valid insurance. Underground Const. Co., Inc. v. Pacific Indem. Co., 49 Cal.App.3d 62, 122 Cal.Rptr. 330, 333.

Excess condemnation. Taking more property under condemnation than is actually needed. See **Condemnation.**

Excess insurance. That amount of insurance coverage which is beyond the dollar amount of coverage of one carrier but which is required to pay a particular loss as distinguished from "other insurance" which may be used to pay or contribute to the loss. See also **Excess policy.**

Excess jurisdiction. Such exists where a court, having jurisdiction of persons and subject matter of the case before it, exceeds its power in trial of such case by dealing with matters about which it is without power or authority to act; and error in court's ruling is not synonymous with ruling in excess of jurisdiction. Robrock v. Robrock, 105 Ohio App. 25, 151 N.E.2d 234, 239.

Excessive. Greater than what is usual or proper. A general term for what goes beyond just measure or amount. Austin St. Ry. Co. v. Oldham, Tex.Civ.App., 109 S.W.2d 235, 237. Tending to or marked by excess, which is the quality or state of exceeding the proper or reasonable limit or measure.

Excessive assessment. A tax assessment grossly disproportionate as compared with other assessments. Southern California Telephone Co. v. Los Angeles County, 45 Cal.App.2d 111, 113 P.2d 773, 776.

Excessive bail. The 8th Amendment to the U.S. Constitution prohibits excessive bail. Bail in a sum more than will be reasonably sufficient to prevent evasion of the law by flight or concealment; bail which is per se unreasonably great and clearly disproportionate to the offense involved, or shown to be so by the special circumstances of the particular case. Blunt v. U. S., 322 A.2d 579. See also Bail Reform Act, 18 U.S.C.A. § 3146.

Excessive damages. See **Damages.**

Excessive drunkenness. Drunkenness is excessive where a party is so far deprived of his reason and understanding as to render him incapable of understanding character and consequences of his act. See **Driving while intoxicated.**

Excessive fine or **penalty.** The 8th Amendment to the U.S. Constitution prohibits excessive fines. A state may not constitutionally imprison a person for inability to pay a fine if he would not have been imprisoned on a showing of ability to pay the fine and on payment of the fine. Tate v. Short, 401 U.S. 395, 91 S.Ct. 668, 28 L.Ed.2d 130. Any fine or penalty which seriously impairs the capacity of gaining a business livelihood. See **Corporal punishment; Excessive punishment; Punishment.**

Excessive force. That amount of force which is beyond the need and circumstances of the particular event or which is not justified in the light of all the circumstances as in the case of deadly force to protect property as contrasted with protecting life. See **Self defense.**

Excessively. To excess.

Excessively intoxicated. Exists where one is so intoxicated as to be so far deprived of his reason and understanding as to render him incapable of knowing the character and consequences of his act. See **Driving while intoxicated.**

Excessive punishment. Any sentence or fine which does not commensurate with the gravity of the offense or the criminal record of the defendant. Excessive length of a sentence may be cruel and unusual punishment within the meaning of the prohibition in the 8th Amendment, U.S. Constitution. Weems v. U. S., 217 U.S. 349, 30 S.Ct. 544, 54 L.Ed. 793. See **Corporal punishment; Excessive fine or penalty; Punishment.**

Excessive speed. Automobile's speed is "excessive" whenever it places car beyond driver's control.

Excessive verdict. A verdict which is result of passion or prejudice. Babb v. Murray, 26 Cal.App.2d 153, 79 P.2d 159, 160. The test of whether a verdict is "excessive" is whether the amount thereof is such as to shock the conscience of the court. Scheidegger v. Thompson, Mo.App., 174 S.W.2d 216, 222. See **Remittitur.**

Excessivum in jure reprobatur. Excessus in re qualibet jure reprobatur communi /èksesáyvəm ìn júriy rèprəbéydər. eksésəs ìn ríy kwéyləbət júriy rèprəbéydər kəmyúwhay/. Excess in law is reprehended. Excess in anything is reprehended at common law.

Excess of jurisdiction. A case in which court has initially proceeded properly within its jurisdiction but steps out of jurisdiction in making of some order or in the doing of some judicial act. Olson v. District Court of Salt Lake County, 93 Utah 145, 71 P.2d 529, 534. Acts which exceed defined power of court in any instance. Abelleira v. District Court of Appeal, Third Dist., 17 Cal.2d 280, 109 P.2d 942, 948. A departure by a court from those recognized and established requirements of law, however close apparent adherence to mere form in method of procedure, which has the effect of depriving one of a constitutional right, is an "excess of jurisdiction." Wuest v. Wuest, 53 Cal.App.2d 339, 127 P.2d 934, 937.

Excess or surplus water. Water which is flowing in stream in addition to what may be termed adjudicated waters. Any water not needed for reasonable beneficial uses of those having prior rights is "excess or surplus water". City of Pasadena v. City of Alhambra, 33 Cal.2d 908, 207 P.2d 17, 28.

Excess policy. One that provides that the insurer is liable only for the excess above and beyond that which may be collected on other insurance. Brownsville Fabrics, Inc. v. Gulf Ins. Co., Tex.Civ.App., 550 S.W.2d 332, 337.

Excess profits tax. Tax levied on profits which are beyond the normal profits of a business and generally imposed in times of national emergency such as war to discourage profiteering. The Internal Revenue Code also imposes a tax on corporations who accumulate an unreasonable surplus of profits rather than paying such out as dividends. I.R.C. § 531 et seq. See **Accumulated earnings tax.**

Exchange. To barter; to swap. To part with, give or transfer for an equivalent. Kessler v. United States, C.C.A.Pa., 124 F.2d 152, 154. Act of giving or taking one thing for another. United States v. Paine, D.C. Mass., 31 F.Supp. 898, 900; Kessler v. United States, C.C.A.Pa., 124 F.2d 152, 154. Contract by terms of which specific property is given in consideration of the receipt of property other than money. Capps v. Mines Service, 175 Or. 248, 152 P.2d 414, 416. Mutual grant of equal interests, the one in consideration of the other. Hale v. Helvering, 66 App.D.C. 242, 85 F.2d 819, 821, 822. Mutual transfer of property other than for money although one of parties may pay a sum of money in addition to property. Transaction in which one piece of property, usually something other than money or its equivalent, is given in return for another piece of property. Hadley Falls Trust Co. v. United States, C.C.A.Mass., 110 F.2d 887, 891. Transfer of property for other property. Helvering v. Nebraska Bridge Supply & Lumber Co., C.C.A.Ark., 115 F.2d 288, 290. Transfer of property for property or some value other than money. Burger-Phillips Co. v. Commissioner of Internal Revenue, C.C.A.Ala., 126 F.2d 934, 936. Transfers of enduring interests and not such as must immediately be reconveyed in fulfillment of preconceived plan. Morgan v. Helvering, C.C.A.N.Y., 117 F.2d 334, 336. The criterion in determining whether a transaction is a sale or an exchange is whether there is a determination of value of things exchanged, and if no price is set for either property it is an "exchange". Gruver v. Commissioner of Internal Revenue, C.C.A.D.C., 142 F.2d 363, 366. The

mutual transfers must be in kind, and any transaction into which money enters, either as the consideration or as a basis of measure is excluded. Hoovel v. State, 125 Tex.Cr.R. 545, 69 S.W.2d 104, 108; Trenton Cotton Oil Co. v. C. I. R., C.C.A.Tenn., 147 F.2d 33, 36. Reciprocal transfers. Helvering v. William Flaccus Oak Leather Co., 313 U.S. 247, 61 S.Ct. 878, 880, 85 L.Ed. 1310; Harwick v. Commissioner of Internal Revenue, C.C.A.Minn., 133 F.2d 732, 737.

Commerce or trade in goods, currency, or commercial paper.

Any organization, association, or group of persons, incorporated or not, which constitutes, maintains, or provides a market place or facilities for bringing together purchasers and sellers of securities, and includes the market place and facilities maintained by such an exchange. A major stock and bond exchange is the New York Stock Exchange. Similar exchanges exist for the trading of commodities; *e.g.* New York Commodities Exchange; Minneapolis Grain Exchange; Chicago Board of Trade. Trading in securities is controlled by the Securities and Exchange Commission; trading in commodities by the Commodity Futures Trading Commission.

For Arbitration of exchange; Dry exchange; First of exchange, and Owelty of exchange, see those titles. For "Bill of exchange," see **Bill.** See also **Barter.**

Commercial law. A negotiation by which one person transfers to another funds which he has in a certain place, either at a price agreed upon or which is fixed by commercial usage. The process of settling accounts or debts between parties residing at a distance from each other, without the intervention of money, by exchanging orders or drafts, called bills of exchange. The payment of debts in different places by an exchange or transfer of credits. The profit which arises from a maritime loan, when such profit is a percentage on the money lent, considering it in the light of money lent in one place to be returned in another, with a difference in amount in the sum borrowed and that paid, arising from the difference of time and place.

Conveyancing. A mutual grant of equal interests (in lands or tenements), the one in consideration of the other.

Like kind exchange. See **Like-kind exchange.**

Nontaxable exchange. Exists where property is transferred to a corporation in exchange for stock or securities in corporation and where transferors immediately after exchange are in control of corporation through ownership of 80 per cent of all other classes of stock of corporation. Commissioner of Internal Revenue v. Cement Investors, C.C.A.Colo., 122 F.2d 380, 383.

Exchange broker. One who negotiates bills of exchange drawn on foreign countries or on other places in the same country. One who makes and concludes bargains for others in matters of money or merchandise.

Exchange offer. In a bilateral contract, such constitutes part of the consideration for the ultimate contract when such offer is accepted.

Exchange rate. The value of one country's money in terms of the value of another country's currency (*e.g.* dollar vs. pound). See also **Foreign exchange rate; Rate** (*Rate of exchange*).

Exchequer /èkschékər/. That department of the English government which has charge of the collection of the national revenue; the treasury department.

It is said to have been so named from the chequered cloth, resembling a chess-board, which anciently covered the table there, and on which, when certain of the king's accounts were made up, the sums were marked and scored with counters. 3 Bl. Comm. 44.

For "Court of Exchequer" and "Court of Exchequer Chamber," see those titles.

Exchequer bills. Bills of credit issued in England by authority of parliament.

Instruments issued at the exchequer, under the authority, for the most part, of acts of parliament passed for the purpose, and containing an engagement on the part of the government for repayment of the principal sums advanced with interest.

Exchequer division. A division of the English high court of justice, to which the special business of the court of exchequer was specially assigned by section 34 of the judicature act of 1873. Merged in the queen's bench division from and after 1881, by order in council under section 31 of that act.

Excise. A tax imposed on the performance of an act, the engaging in an occupation, or the enjoyment of a privilege. Rapa v. Haines, Ohio Com.Pl., 101 N.E.2d 733, 735. Tax laid on manufacture, sale, or consumption of commodities or upon licenses to pursue certain occupations or upon corporate privileges. In current usage the term has been extended to include various license fees and practically every internal revenue tax except the income tax.

Excise lieu property tax. Tax on gross premiums received and collected by designated classes of insurance companies. United Pacific Ins. Co. v. Bakes, 57 Idaho 537, 67 P.2d 1024, 1029.

Excise tax. See Excise.

Excited utterance. In evidence, a statement relating to a startling event or condition made while the declarant was under the stress of excitement caused by the event or condition. It is an exception to the hearsay rule. Fed.Evid. Rule 803(2); State v. Emery, 4 Or. App. 527, 480 P.2d 445, 447. See also **Fresh complaint rule; Spontaneous declarations.**

Exclusa /əksklúwzə/. In old English law, a sluice to carry off water; the payment to the ford for the benefit of such a sluice.

Exclusion. Denial of entry or admittance.

Evidence. The action by the trial judge in which he excludes from consideration by the trier of fact whatever he rules is not admissible as evidence. See also **Exclusionary Rule.**

Gift tax. The amount which a donor may transfer by gift each year without tax consequences. I.R.C. § 2503(b).

Insurance. In insurance policy, "exclusion" is provision which eliminates coverage where were it not for exclusion, coverage would have existed. Kansas-Nebraska Natural Gas Co., Inc. v. Hawkeye-Security Ins. Co., 195 Neb. 658, 240 N.W.2d 28, 31. Provision in policy specifying the situations, occurrences or persons not covered by the policy.

Witness. A trial judge may, under certain circumstances, sequester witnesses and require that they be kept apart from other witnesses until they are called to testify.

Exclusionary Rule. This rule commands that where evidence has been obtained in violation of the privileges guaranteed by the U.S. Constitution, the evidence must be excluded at the trial. Evidence which is obtained by an unreasonable search and seizure is excluded from evidence under the Fourth Amendment, U.S. Constitution and this rule is applicable to the States. Mapp v. Ohio, 367 U.S. 643, 81 S.Ct. 1684, 6 L.Ed.2d 1081. See also Counsel, right to; Illegally obtained evidence; Independent source rule. **Miranda Rule; Motion to suppress; Suppression of evidence; Suppression hearing.**

Exclusionary zoning. Any form of zoning ordinance which tends to exclude specific classes of persons or businesses from a particular district or area.

Exclusive. Appertaining to the subject alone, not including, admitting, or pertaining to any others. Sole. Shutting out; debarring from interference or participation; vested in one person alone.

Exclusive agency. Grant to agent of exclusive right to sell within a particular market or area. A contract to give an "exclusive agency" to deal with property is ordinarily interpreted as not precluding competition by the principal generally, but only as precluding him from appointing another agent to accomplish the result. Navy Gas & Supply Co. v. Schoech, 105 Colo. 374, 98 P.2d 860, 861, 863. The grant of an "exclusive agency to sell," that is, the exclusive right to sell the products of a wholesaler in a specified territory, ordinarily is interpreted as precluding competition in any form within designated area. Navy Gas & Supply Co. v. Schoech, 105 Colo. 374, 98 P.2d 860, 861.

Exclusive agency listing. Agreement between a property owner and a real estate broker whereby the owner promises to pay a fee or commission to broker if his real property is sold during the listing period, regardless of whether the broker is responsible for the sale. Carlson v. Zane, 261 Cal.App.2d 399, 67 Cal.Rptr. 747, 749. See also **Exclusive right** (*Exclusive right to sell*); **Listing.**

Exclusive agent. An agent who has exclusive right to sell within a particular market or area. See also **Exclusive agency.**

Exclusive contract. A contract by which one binds himself to sell to or buy from only one person for his total requirements. See **Entire output contract; Exclusive dealing arrangements.**

Exclusive control. The "exclusive control" of thing causing accident, applies to right of control of instrumentality causing injury. Gerhart v. Southern California Gas Co., 56 Cal.App.2d 425, 132 P.2d 874, 877. Under the rule "of exclusive control", where a thing is shown to be under management of defendant or his servants, and accident is such as in ordinary course does not happen if those having management use proper care, it affords reasonable evidence in absence of explanation that the accident arose from want of care. Mack v. Reading Co., 377 Pa. 135, 103 A.2d 749, 751.

Exclusive dealing arrangements. At common law, generally, agreements to deal exclusively with one seller or buyer were upheld, but under the Sherman Act as well as the Clayton and Federal Trade Commission Acts, such agreements are usually illegal.

Exclusive franchise. See **Exclusive agency.**

Exclusive jurisdiction. That power which a court or other tribunal exercises over an action or over a person to the exclusion of all other courts. That forum in which an action must be commenced because no other forum has the jurisdiction to hear and determine the action. For example, by statute, actions brought under the Securities Exchange Act *must* be brought in federal district court.

Exclusive and concurrent jurisdiction. The federal courts have original and exclusive jurisdiction over certain actions (*e.g.* controversies between two or more states) and concurrent jurisdiction with that of state courts in others (*e.g.* actions between citizens of different states).

Exclusive license. Exclusive right granted by patent holder to licensee to use, manufacture, and sell patented article. Permission to do thing and contract not to give leave to any one else to do same thing. Overman Cushion Tire Co. v. Goodyear Tire & Rubber Co., C.C.A.N.Y., 59 F.2d 998, 999. A license which binds licensor not to enlarge thereafter the scope of other licenses already granted, or increase the number of licenses, is an "exclusive license". Mechanical Ice Tray Corporation v. General Motors Corporation, C.C.A.N.Y., 144 F.2d 720, 725. See also **Exclusive agency; License.**

Exclusive licensee. One granted exclusive right and license to use, manufacture, and sell patented article. Deitel v. Chisholm, C.C.A.N.Y., 42 F.2d 172, 173. One having exclusive right to use patented method and apparatus in designated territory. Paul E. Hawkinson Co. v. Carnell, C.C.A.Pa., 112 F.2d 396, 398.

Exclusive listing. See **Exclusive agency listing.**

Exclusively. Apart from all others; only; solely; substantially all or for the greater part. To the exclusion of all others; without admission of others to participation; in a manner to exclude. Standard Oil Co. of Texas v. State, Tex.Civ.App., 142 S.W.2d 519, 521, 522, 523.

Exclusively used. The phrase in provision exempting from taxation properties exclusively used for religious worship, for schools or for purposes purely charitable, has reference to primary and inherent as over against a mere secondary and incidental use. Salvation Army v. Hoehn, Mo., 354 Mo. 107, 188 S.W.2d 826, 830.

Exclusive ownership. Ownership free from any kind of legal or equitable interest in any one else. See **Fee simple.**

Exclusive possession. Exclusive possession by adverse possessor means that adverse possessor must show an exclusive dominion over the land and an appropriation of it to his own use and benefit. Vernon's Ann.Civ.St. art. 5510. W. T. Carter & Bro. v. Holmes, 131 Tex. 365, 113 S.W.2d 1225, 1226. Possession may be "exclusive" so as to entitle possessor to title by adverse possession, notwithstanding that the land is subject to exercise of easement by private party. Young v. City of Lubbock, Tex.Civ.App., 130 S.W.2d 418, 420.

Exclusive right. An exclusive right is one which only the grantee thereof can exercise, and from which all others are prohibited or shut out.

Exclusive right to sell. An "exclusive right to sell" agreement listing real property for sale prohibits the owner from selling his property either by himself or through another broker without liability while the property is listed with the original broker. Foltz v. Begnoche, 222 Kan. 383, 565 P.2d 592, 595. See **Exclusive agency listing.**

Exclusive use. As used in law authorizing registration of trade-marks, means exclusive use not only of specific mark but also any other confusingly similar mark or term. McKesson & Robbins v. Charles H. Phillips Chemical Co., C.C.A.Conn., 53 F.2d 1011.

Exclusive use, as essential element of acquisition of easement by prescription, means that exercise of right shall not be dependent upon similar right in others, but use may be shared with owner of servient estate. White v. Wheatland Irr. Dist., Wyo., 413 P.2d 252, 260. Exclusive use, for purpose of establishing a right in easement by adverse user, does not mean use to exclusion of use by all others, but exclusive use under claim of right requires only that right claimed by adverse user be not dependent on right of any one else to use way and may be established by common user thereof with owner of servient land and without any subjective claim of right. Feldman v. Knapp, 196 Or. 453, 250 P.2d 92, 102.

Ex colore /éks kəlóriy/. By color; under color of; under pretense, show, or protection of. Thus, *ex colore officii,* under color of office.

Ex comitate /éks komətéydiy/. Out of comity or courtesy.

Excommengement /èkskəménjmənt/. Excommunication *(q.v.).*

Ex commodato /éks komədéydow/. From or out of loan. A term applied in the old law of England to a right of action arising out of a loan *(commodatum).*

Excommunication. In old English law, a sentence of censure pronounced by one of the spiritual courts for offenses falling under ecclesiastical cognizance. It is described as two-fold: (1) The lesser excommunication, which is an ecclesiastical censure, excluding the party from the sacraments; (2) the greater, which excludes him from the company of all Christians. Formerly, too, an excommunicated man was under various civil disabilities. He could not serve upon juries, or be a witness in any court; neither could he bring an action to recover lands or money due to him. These penalties were abolished in England by St. 53 Geo. III, c. 127.

Excommunicato capiendo /èkskəmyùwnəkéydow kæ̀piyéndow/. In ecclesiastical law, a writ issuing out of chancery, founded on a bishop's certificate that the defendant had been excommunicated, and requiring the sheriff to arrest and imprison him, returnable to the king's bench.

Excommunicato deliberando /èkskəmyùwnəkéydow dəlìbərǽndow/. In old English law, a writ to the sheriff for delivery of an excommunicated person out of prison, upon certificate from the ordinary of his conformity to the ecclesiastical jurisdiction.

Excommunicato interdicitur omnis actus legitimus, ita quod agere non potest, nec aliquem convenire, licet ipse ab aliis possit conveniri /èkskəmyùwnəkéydow ìntərdísədər ómnəs ǽktəs ləjídəməs, áydə kwòd ǽjəriy nòn pówdəst, nèk ǽləkwem kònvənáyriy, lísəd ípsiy æ̀b éyliyəs pósət kònvənáyray/. Every legal act is forbidden an excommunicated person, so that he cannot act, nor sue any person, but he may be sued by others.

Excommunicato recapiendo /èkskəmyùwnəkéydow rəkæ̀piyéndow/. A writ commanding that persons excommunicated, who for their obstinacy had been committed to prison, but were unlawfully set free before they had given caution to obey the authority of the church, should be sought after, retaken, and imprisoned again.

Ex comparatione scriptorum /èks kòmpərèyshiyówniy skriptórəm/. By a comparison of writings or handwritings. A term in the law of evidence.

Ex concessis /èks kənsésəs/. From the premises granted. According to what has been already allowed.

Ex consulto /èks kənsóltow/. With consultation or deliberation.

Ex continenti /éks kòntiniyéntay/. Immediately; without any interval or delay; incontinently. A term of the civil law.

Ex contractu /éks kəntrǽkt(y)uw/. From or out of a contract. In both the civil and the common law, rights and causes of action are divided into two classes,—those arising *ex contractu* (from a contract), and those arising *ex delicto* (from a delict or tort). 3 Bl.Comm. 117. Where cause of action arises from breach of a promise set forth in contract, the action is *"ex contractu"*, but where it arises from a breach of duty growing out of contract, it is *"ex delicto"*. Eads v. Marks, 39 C.2d 807, 249 P.2d 257, 260. See also **Ex delicto.**

Exculpate /ékskəlpeyt/əkskə́lpeyt/. Term is employed in sense of excuse of justification. State v. Langdon, 46 N.M. 277, 127 P.2d 875, 876.

Exculpatory /ekskə́lpət(o)riy/. Clearing or tending to clear from alleged fault or guilt; excusing. Baird v. State, 246 S.W.2d 192, 195.

Exculpatory clause. Such clause in favor of a trustee in will implies that trustee has power which he purports to execute, and it exculpates him where this power is exercised in good faith. In re Wacht's Estate, Sur., 32 N.Y.S.2d 871, 897.

Exculpatory statement. A statement which tends to justify, excuse or clear the defendant from alleged fault or guilt. State v. Cobb, 2 Ariz.App. 71, 406 P.2d 421, 423.

Ex curia /èks kyúriyə/. Out of court; away from the court.

Excusable. Admitting of excuse or palliation. As used in the law, this word implies that the act or omission spoken of is on its face unlawful, wrong, or liable to entail loss or disadvantage on the person chargeable, but that the circumstances attending it were such as to constitute a legal "excuse" for it, that is, a legal reason for withholding or foregoing the punishment, liability, or disadvantage which otherwise would follow. See **Justification; Legal excuse.**

Excusable assault. One committed by accident or misfortune in doing any lawful act by lawful means, with ordinary caution and without any unlawful intent. People v. O'Connor, 82 App.Div. 55, 81 N.Y.S. 555. See *e.g.* **Self defense.**

Excusable homicide. See **Homicide.**

Excusable neglect. In practice, and particularly with reference to the setting aside of a judgment taken against a party through his "excusable neglect," this means a failure to take the proper steps at the proper time, not in consequence of the party's own carelessness, inattention, or willful disregard of the process of the court, but in consequence of some unexpected or unavoidable hindrance or accident, or reliance on the care and vigilance of his counsel or on promises made by the adverse party. As used in rule (*e.g.* Fed.R.Civil P. 6(b)) authorizing court to permit an act to be done after expiration of the time within which under the rules such act was required to be done, where failure to act was the result of "excusable neglect", quoted phrase is ordinarily understood to be the act of a reasonably prudent person under the same circumstances. Conlan v. Conlan, Ky., 293 S.W.2d 710, 712.

Excusat aut extenuat delictum in capitalibus quod non operatur idem in civilibus /əkskyúwzəd òt əkstényuwət dəlíktəm in kæ̀pətéyləbəs kwòd nón opəréydər áydəm in səvíləbəs/. That may excuse or palliate a wrongful act in capital cases which would not have the same effect in civil injuries.

Excusatio /èkskyəzéysh(iy)ow/. In the civil law, an excuse or reason which exempts from some duty or obligation.

Excusator /èkskyuwzéydər/. In English law, an excuser. In old German law, a defendant; he who utterly denies the plaintiff's claim.

Excusatur quis quod clameum non opposuerit, ut si toto tempore litigii fuit ultra mare quacunque occasione /èkskyuwzéydər kwís kwòd kléymiyəm nòn əpòz(y)uwérət, ət sày tówdow témpəriy lətíjiyay fyúwəd últrə mǽriy kweykáŋkwiy əkèyzhiyówniy/. He is excused who does not bring his claim, if, during the whole period in which it ought to have been brought, he has been beyond sea for any reason.

Excuse. A reason alleged for doing or not doing a thing. A matter alleged as a reason for relief or exemption from some duty or obligation. That which is offered as a reason for being excused, or a plea offered in extenuation of a fault or irregular deportment. It is that plea or statement made by the accused which arises out of the state of facts constituting and relied on as the cause. See also **Defense.**

Excuss. To seize and detain by law.

Excussio /əkskə́s(h)(i)yow/. In civil law, a diligent prosecution of a remedy against a debtor. The exhausting of a remedy against a principal debtor before resorting to his sureties. Translated "discussion" *(q.v.).*

Ex debito justitiae /èks débədow jəstíshiyiy/. From or as a debt of justice; in accordance with the requirement of justice; of right; as a matter of right. The opposite of *ex gratia (q.v.).* 3 Bl.Comm. 48, 67.

Ex defectu sanguinis /èks dəfékt(y)uw sǽŋgwənəs/. From failure of blood; for want of issue.

Ex delicto /èks dəlíktow/. From a delict, tort, fault, crime, or malfeasance. In both the civil and the common law, obligations and causes of action are divided into two classes—those arising *ex contractu* (out of a contract), and those *ex delicto.* The latter are such as grow out of or are founded upon a wrong or tort, e.g., trespass, trover, replevin. See also **Ex contractu.**

Where cause of action arises from breach of a promise set forth in contract, the action is "ex contractu", but where it arises from a breach of duty growing out of contract, it is "ex delicto". Eads v. Marks, 39 Cal.2d 807, 249 P.2d 257, 260.

Ex delicto non ex supplicio emergit infamia /èks dəlíktow nón èks səplísh(iy)ow əmárjəd ənféymiyə/. Infamy arises from the crime, not from the punishment.

Ex delicto trusts. Trusts which are created for illegal purposes, the most common of which are trusts created to prevent creditors of the settlor from collecting their claims out of the property.

Ex demissione /éks dəmìs(h)iyówniy/. (Commonly abbreviated *ex dem.*) Upon the demise. A phrase forming part of the title of the old action of ejectment.

Ex directo /èks dəréktow/. Directly; immediately.

Ex diuturnitate temporis, omnia praesumuntur solemniter esse acta /èks dàyətə̀rnətéydiy témpərəs, ómniyə prìyzyəmántər səlémnədər ésiy ǽktə/. From length of time [after lapse of time] all things are presumed to have been done in due form.

Ex dividend. A synonym for "without dividend." The buyer of a stock selling ex-dividend does not receive the recently declared dividend. Said of a stock at the time when the declared dividend becomes the property of the person who owned the stock on the record date. The payment date follows the ex-dividend date. When stock is sold ex dividend, the seller, not the buyer, has the right to the next dividend which has been declared but not paid.

Ex dolo malo /èks dówlo mǽlow/. Out of fraud; out of deceitful or tortious conduct. A phrase applied to obligations and causes of action vitiated by fraud or deceit.

Ex dolo malo non oritur actio /èks dówlow mǽlow nòn órədər ǽksh(iy)ow/. Out of fraud no action arises; fraud never gives a right of action. No court will lend its aid to a man who founds his cause of action upon an immoral or illegal act.

Ex donationibus autem feoda militaria vel magnum serjeantium non continentibus oritur nobis quoddam nomen generale, quod est socagium /èks dənèy-shiyównəbəs ódəm fyúwdə mìlətériyə vèl mǽgnəm sàrjiyǽnsh(iy)əm nón kòntənéntəbəs órədər nówbəs kwódəm nówmən jènəréyliy, kwód èst səkéyj(iy)-əm/. From grants not containing military fees or grand serjeanty, a kind of general name is used by us, which is "socage."

Exeat /éksiyət/. A permission which a bishop grants to a priest to go out of his diocese; also leave to go out generally. For **Ne Exeat,** see that title.

Execute. To complete; to make; to sign; to perform; to do; to follow out; to carry out according to its terms; to fulfill the command or purpose of. To perform all necessary formalities, as to make and sign a contract, or sign and deliver a note. See also **Execution.**

Executed. Completed; carried into full effect; already done or performed; signed; taking effect immediately; now in existence or in possession; conveying an immediate right or possession. Act or course of conduct carried to completion. Term imports idea that nothing remains to be done. The opposite of *executory.* See also **Execution.**

Executed consideration. A consideration which is wholly performed. An act done or value given before the making of the agreement.

Executed contract. Contract which has been performed. If performed in part, it is partially executed (executory); if entirely performed, it is fully or wholly executed. See also **Contract; Executed oral agreement; Executory contract.**

Executed estate. Estate in property which is vested. See **Estate.**

Executed fine. The fine *sur cognizance de droit, come ceo que il ad de son done;* or a fine upon acknowledgment of the right of the cognizee, as that which he has of the gift of the cognizor. Abolished in England by 3 & 4 Wm. IV, c. 74.

Executed gift. See **Gift.**

Executed note. Promissory note which has been signed and delivered.

Executed oral agreement. An oral agreement is not "executed" unless it has been fully performed by both parties. Walther v. Occidental Life Ins. Co., 40 Cal. App.2d 160, 104 P.2d 551, 554.

Executed remainder. See **Remainder.**

Executed sale. See **Sale.**

Executed trust. See **Trust.**

Executed use. See **Use.**

Executio /èksəkyúwsh(iy)ow/. Lat. The doing or following up of a thing; the doing a thing completely or thoroughly; management or administration.

In old practice, execution; the final process in an action.

Executio bonorum /èksəkyúwsh(iy)ow bənórəm/. In old English law, management or administration of goods. *Ad ecclesiam et ad amicos pertinebit executio bonorum*, the execution of the goods shall belong to the church and to the friends of the deceased.

Executio est executio juris secundum judicium /èksəkyúwsh(iy)ow èst èksəkyúwsh(iy)ow júrəs səkándəm juwdísh(iy)əm/. Execution is the execution of the law according to the judgment.

Executio est finis et fructus legis /èksəkyúwsh(iy)ow èst fáynəs èt fráktəs líyjəs/. Execution is the end and fruit of the law.

Executio juris non habet injuriam /èksəkyúwsh(iy)ow júrəs nòn héybəd ənjúriyəm/. The execution of law does no injury.

Execution. Carrying out some act or course of conduct to its completion. Northwest Steel Rolling Mills v. Commissioner of Internal Revenue, C.C.A.Wash., 110 F.2d 286, 290. Completion of an act. Putting into force. The completion, fulfillment, or perfecting of anything, or carrying it into operation and effect.

Execution of contract includes performance of all acts necessary to render it complete as an instrument and imports idea that nothing remains to be done to make complete and effective contract. Travelers Ins. Co. v. Chicago Bridge & Iron Co., Tex.Civ.App., 442 S.W.2d 888, 895.

Execution upon a money judgment is the legal process of enforcing the judgment, usually by seizing and selling property of the debtor. See *Writ of execution,* infra.

Execution is a process in action to carry into effect the directions in a decree or judgment. Foust v. Foust, 47 Cal.2d 121, 302 P.2d 11, 13.

Body execution. An order of court which commands the officer to take the body of the defendant or debtor; generally to bring him before court to pay debt. A capias.

Writ of execution. Formal process issued by court generally evidencing the debt of the defendant to the plaintiff and commanding the officer to take the property of the defendant in satisfaction of the debt. Unless the court directs otherwise, the process to enforce a money judgment shall be a writ of execution. Fed.R. Civil P. 69. A writ of execution is a written demand to bailiff, directing him to execute the judgment of the court. Miami Motor Sales v. Singleton, Ohio Mun., 94 N.E.2d 819, 822. Process issuing from a court in a civil action authorizing the sheriff or other competent officer to carry out the court's decision in favor of the prevailing party.

For "Attachment execution," see **Attachment.** For "Testatum execution", see **Testatum.** See also Alias execution; Dormant execution; General execution; Judgment execution; Junior execution; Special execution.

Execution creditor. See **Creditor.**

Executione faciendâ in withernamium /èksəkyùwshiyówniy fǽshiyéndə in wìðərnéymiyəm/. A writ that lay for taking cattle of one who has conveyed the cattle of another out of the county, so that the sheriff cannot replevy them.

Executione judicii /èksəkyùwshiyówniy juwdíshiyay/. A writ directed to the judge of an inferior court to do execution upon a judgment therein, or to return some reasonable cause wherefore he delays the execution.

Executioner. Person who executes (*i.e.* carries out) capital punishment.

Execution lien. An execution lien may be created by service of execution, levy upon real estate, and filing of a certificate of levy in the proper office of county in which real estate is located. Reconstruction Finance Corporation v. Maley, C.C.A.Ill., 125 F.2d 131, 135.

Execution of instrument. Completion of instrument, including signing and delivery. Execution includes performance of all acts necessary to render instrument complete and of every act required to give instrument validity or to carry it into effect. Northwest Steel Rolling Mills v. Commissioner of Internal Revenue, C.C.A.Wash., 110 F.2d 286, 290. "Execution" of written contract includes signing, unconditional delivery by promisor, and acceptance by promisee. Coen v. American Surety Co. of New York, C.C.A.Mo., 120 F.2d 393, 397.

Execution of judgment or **decree.** See **Execution.**

Execution parée /èkseykyuwsyówn pàréy/. In French law, a right founded on an act passed before a notary, by which the creditor may immediately, without citation or summons, seize and cause to be sold the property of his debtor, out of the proceeds of which to receive his payment. It imports a confession of judgment, and is not unlike a warrant of attorney.

Execution sale. A sale by a sheriff or other ministerial officer under the authority of a writ of execution which he has levied on property of the debtor. See also **Judicial sale.**

Executive. As distinguished from the legislative and judicial departments (*i.e.* branches) of government, the executive dpeartment is that which is charged with the detail of carrying the laws into effect and securing their due observance. See also **Executive department; Executive powers.**

The word "executive" is also used as an impersonal designation of the chief executive officer of a state or nation. Term also refers to upper level management of business. See also **Executive employees.**

Executive administration, or **ministry.** A political term in England, applicable to the higher and responsible class of public officials by whom the chief departments of the government of, the kingdom are administered.

Executive agency. A department of the executive branch of government such as the Army and Air Force Exchange Service whose activities are subject to statutes and whose contracts are subject to judicial review. W. B. Fishburn Cleaners Inc. v. Army &

Air Force Exchange Service, D.C.Tex., 374 F.Supp. 162, 165.

Executive agreement. A treaty-like agreement with another country in which the President may bind the country without submission to the Senate (as in the case of a treaty). State of Russia v. National City Bank of N. Y., C.C.A.N.Y., 69 F.2d 44, 48; United States v. Belmont, 301 U.S. 324, 57 S.Ct. 758, 81 L.Ed. 1134.

Executive capacity. Duties in such capacity relate to active participation in control, supervision, and management of business. Arkansas Amusement Corporation v. Kempner, C.C.A.Ark., 57 F.2d 466, 473; Wilkinson v. Noland Co., D.C.Va., 40 F.Supp. 1009, 1012.

Executive clemency. The power of the chief executive (*i.e.* President or a governor) to pardon or commute a criminal sentence as, for example, the power to reduce the death penalty to life imprisonment. Art. II, § 2, U.S.Const. See also **Clemency.**

Executive committee. In business, the body which directly manages the operations between meetings of the board of directors; commonly consisting of the principal officers and directors.

Executive department. That branch of government charged with carrying out the laws enacted by the legislature. The President is the chief executive officer of the country and the governor is chief executive officer of a state. Used to describe that branch of the government in contrast to the other two branches; *i.e.* legislative and judicial. See Art. II, U.S.Const.

Executive employees. Persons whose duties include some form of managerial authority, actually directing the work of other persons. Persons whose duties relate to active participation in control, supervision and management of business, or who administer affairs, or who direct, manage, execute or dispense. Steiner v. Pleasantville Constructors, 181 Misc. 798, 46 N.Y.S.2d 120, 123. The term executive employee carries the idea of supervision of or control over ordinary employees. Ralph Knight, Inc. v. Mantel, C.C.A.Mo., 135 F.2d 514, 517.

Executive officer. An officer of the executive department of government; one in whom resides the power to execute the laws; one whose duties are to cause the laws to be executed and obeyed. Petzak v. Graves, 33 Wis.2d 175, 147 N.W.2d 294, 297. Officers who are neither judicial nor legislative are executive officers. Spivey v. State, 69 Okl.Cr. 397, 104 P.2d 263, 277. One who assumes command or control and directs course of business, or some part thereof, and who outlines duties and directs work of subordinate employees. President and vice president of corporation are executive officers. Emmerglick v. Philip Wolf, Inc., C.C.A.N.Y., 138 F.2d 661, 662.

Executive order. An order or regulation issued by the President or some administrative authority under his direction for the purpose of interpreting, implementing, or giving administrative effect to a provision of the Constitution or of some law or treaty. To have the effect of law, such orders must be published in the Federal Register.

Executive order Indian reservation. Reservation created by order of President withdrawing land within its boundaries from settlement or making other disposition of it under public land laws of United States. Santa Rita Oil & Gas Co. v. Board of Equalization, 101 Mont. 268, 54 P.2d 117, 122.

Executive pardon. An executive act of grace exempting an individual from punishment for a crime he has committed. Such presidential power is authorized by Art. II, § 2, U.S.Const. Similar powers are afforded to governors by state constitutions. See also **Executive clemency; Pardon.**

Executive powers. Power to execute laws. The enumerated powers of the President are provided for in Article II of the U.S.Const. Executive powers of governors are provided for in state constitutions. The executive powers vested in governors by state constitutions include the power to execute the laws, that is, to carry them into effect, as distinguished from the power to make the laws and the power to judge them. Tucker v. State, 218 Ind. 614, 35 N.E.2d 270, 291. See also **Executive order.**

Executive privilege. Executive privilege, based on constitutional doctrine of separation of powers, exempts the executive from disclosure requirements applicable to the ordinary citizen or organization where such exemption is necessary to the discharge of highly important executive responsibilities involved in maintaining governmental operations, and extends not only to military and diplomatic secrets but also to documents integral to an appropriate exercise of the executive's domestic decisional and policy making functions, that is, those documents reflecting the frank expression necessary in intra-governmental advisory and deliberative communications. Black v. Sheraton Corp. of America, D.C.D.C., 371 F.Supp. 97, 100. However, need for confidentiality of high level communications cannot, without more, sustain an absolute unqualified presidential privilege of immunity from judicial process under all circumstances. U. S. v. Nixon, 418 U.S. 683, 94 S.Ct. 3090, 3106, 3107, 41 L.Ed.2d 1039. See also **Privilege.**

Executive session. Executive session of a board or governmental body is a session closed to the public.

Executor /əgzékədər/. A person appointed by a testator to carry out the directions and requests in his will, and to dispose of the property according to his testamentary provisions after his decease. A person who either expressly or by implication is appointed by a testator to carry out testator's directions concerning the dispositions he makes under his will. In re Silverman's Estate, 6 Ill.App.3d 225, 285 N.E.2d 548, 550.

"Personal representative" includes "executor." Uniform Probate Code, § 1–201. Compare **Administrator.**

For Co-executor; General executor; Instituted executor; Joint executors; Limited executor; Special executor and Substituted executor, see those titles.

Civil Law

A ministerial officer who executed or carried into effect the judgment or sentence in a cause.

Ecclesiastical Law

Executor à lege constitutus. An executor appointed by law; the ordinary of the diocese.

Executor ab episcopo constitutus, or *executor dativus.* An executor appointed by the bishop; an administrator to an intestate.

Executor à testatore constitutus. An executor appointed by a testator. Otherwise termed *"executor testamentarius;"* a testamentary executor.

An *executor to the tenor.* One who, though not directly constituted executor by the will, is therein charged with duties in relation to the estate which can only be performed by the executor.

Executor by substitution. A successor executor appointed by testator entitled to succeed to administration of estate following resignation of first executor who had partially administered upon such estate. In re Stahl's Estate, 113 Ind.App. 29, 44 N.E.2d 529, 532.

Executor creditor. See **Creditor**.

Executor dative. See **Dative**.

Executor de son tort. See **De son tort**.

Executor lucratus /èksəkyúwdər l(y)uwkréydəs/. An executor who has assets of his testator who in his life-time made himself liable by a wrongful interference with the property of another.

Executorship. Office held by an executor.

Executory /əgzékyətòriy/. That which is yet to be executed or performed; that which remains to be carried into operation or effect; incomplete; depending upon a future performance or event. The opposite of *executed*.

As to executory Bequests; Contracts; Devise; Estates; Remainder; Trust, and Use, see those titles.

Executory accord. An agreement for the future discharge of an existing claim by a substituted performance; it is the promised performance that is to discharge the existing claim, not the promise to render performance. Elliot v. Whitney, 215 Kan. 256, 524 P.2d 699, 703. Two principal categories of compromise agreements are "executory accord", providing for acceptance in future of stated performance in satisfaction of claim, and "substituted contract" which itself is accepted as substitution for and extinguishment of existing claim. Johnson v. Utile, 86 Nev. 593, 472 P.2d 335, 337.

Executory consideration. A consideration which is to be performed after the contract for which it is a consideration is made.

Executory contract. A contract that has not as yet been fully completed or performed. A contract the obligation (performance) of which relates to the future. Wagstaff v. Peters, 203 Kan. 108, 453 P.2d 120, 124. *Compare* **Executed contract**.

Executory contract to sell. Contract under which something remains to be done by either party before delivery and passing of title. Martin v. John Clay & Co., Mo.App., 167 S.W.2d 407, 411.

Executory devise. Devise of a future estate, and, if the executory devisee dies before the event happens, the estate goes to the heir at the time of the event, and not to the heir at the time of the death of the devisee. The happening of the contingency determines who is to take the estate, and until that time no one has an interest to transmit. By the earlier common law it was an established rule that a devise of lands, without words of limitation, conferred upon the devisee an estate for life only. An exception was soon recognized in the case of a will, so that an estate in fee could be given without the use of the technical words required in a conveyance or deed. The gift in such case was known as an "executory devise."

Executory interests. A general term, comprising all future estates and interests in land or personalty, other than reversions and remainders.

A contingent future interest which: (a) cannot qualify as a remainder; (b) is always in favor of a conveyee, and; (c) takes effect when the contingency happens as a springing use or shifting use under the Statute of Uses (1535), or Statute of Wills (1540).

Executory limitation. A limitation of a future interest by deed or will; if by will, it is also called an "executory devise."

Executory process. A civil law process which can be resorted to in the following cases, namely: (1) When the right of the creditor arises from an act importing confession of judgment, and which contains a privilege or mortgage in his favor; (2) when the creditor demands the execution of a judgment which has been rendered by a tribunal different from that within whose jurisdiction the execution is sought. An accelerated procedure, summary in nature, by which holder of a mortgage or privilege evidenced by an authentic act importing a confession of judgment seeks to effect an ex parte seizure and sale of the subject property, without previous citation, contradictory hearing or judgment. Cameron Brown South, Inc. v. East Glen Oaks, Inc., La.App., 341 So.2d 450, 457.

Executory sale. See **Sale**.

Executory trust. Under this type of trust a further conveyance or settlement is to be made by the trustee. The test as to whether a trust is an "executory trust" is to determine whether settlor has acted as his own conveyancer and defines precisely the settlement to be made, and, if he has, the word "heirs" is one of limitation, and if he has not, the trust is executory, and the word "heirs" is a word of purchase, and the persons coming within such definition have an interest in the property. Sutliff v. Aydelott, 373 Ill. 633, 27 N.E.2d 529, 532.

Executory unilateral accord. An offer to enter a contract.

Executory warranties. Such arise where insured undertakes to perform some executory stipulation, as that certain acts will be done, or that certain facts will continue to exist.

Executress /əgzékyətrəs/. A female executor.

Executrix /əgzékyətriks/. Female executor. A woman who has been appointed by will to execute such will or testament.

Exedos /èyhéyðows/. See **Ejidos.**

Exempla illustrant non restringunt legem /egzémplə iləstrənt nòn rəstríŋgənt líyjəm/. Examples illustrate, but do not restrain, the law.

Exemplars /əgzémplərz/. Nontestimonial identification evidence taken from defendant; *e.g.* fingerprints, blood samples, voiceprints, lineup identification, handwriting samples.

Exemplary damages /əgzémpləriy dǽməjəz/. Damages on an increased scale, awarded to plaintiff over and above what will barely compensate him for his property loss, where wrong done to him was aggravated by circumstances of violence, oppression, malice, fraud, or wanton and wicked conduct on part of defendant. Goines v. Pennsylvania R. R., 208 Misc. 103, 143 N.Y.S.2d 576, 583. See also **Damages** *(Exemplary or punitive damages).*

Exemplification. An official transcript of a document from public records, made in form to be used as evidence, and authenticated or certified as a true copy. See **Certified copy.**

Exemplificatione /əgzèmpləfəkèyshiyówniy/. A writ granted for the exemplification or transcript of an original record.

Exemplified copy. Copy of document which has been authenticated. See **Certified copy.**

Exempli gratia /əgzémplay gréysh(iy)ə/. For the purpose of example, or for instance. Often abbreviated "ex. gr." or "*e.g.*"

Exemplum /əgzémpləm/. In the civil law, copy; a written authorized copy. This word is also used in the modern sense of example—*ad exemplum constituti singulares non trahi,* exceptional things must not be taken for examples.

Exempt. To release, discharge, waive, relieve from liability. To relieve, excuse, or set free from a duty or service imposed upon the general class to which the individual exempted belongs; as to exempt from military service.

To relieve certain classes of property from liability to sale on execution, or from taxation, or from bankruptcy or attachment.

See also **Exemption; Exemption laws.**

Exemption. Freedom from a general duty or service; immunity from a general burden, tax, or charge. Immunity from certain legal obligations, as jury duty, military service, or the payment of taxes.

A privilege allowed by law to a judgment debtor, by which he may hold property to a certain amount or certain classes of property, free from all liability to levy and sale on execution or attachment.

Property exempt in bankruptcy proceedings is provided for under Bankruptcy Act § 522.

Term used for various amounts subtracted from gross income to determine taxable income; *e.g.* personal tax exemptions for self and dependents. I.R.C. § 151 *et seq.*

See also **Immunity.**

Exemption laws. Laws which provide that a certain amount or proportion of a debtor's property shall be exempt from execution and bankruptcy. Bankruptcy Act, § 522.

Exemption, words of. It is a maxim of law that words of exemption are not to be construed to import any liability; the maxim *expressio unius exclusio alterius,* or its converse, *exclusio unius inclusio alterius,* not applying to such a case.

Ex empto /èks ém(p)tow/. Out of purchase; founded on purchase. A term of the civil law, adopted by Bracton.

Exempts. Persons who are not bound by law, but excused from the performance of duties imposed upon others.

Exempt transactions. Those dealings in securities which fall outside the scope of Securities Act of 1933 and Securities Exchange Act.

Exennium /əkséniyəm/. In old English law, a gift; a new year's gift.

Exequatur /èksəkwéydər/. Lat. Let it be executed.

An "exequatur" is a written official recognition and authorization of consular officer, issued by government to which he is accredited. Doyle v. Fleming, D.C.Canal Zone, 219 F.Supp. 277, 283.

In French practice, this term is subscribed by judicial authority upon a transcript of a judgment from a foreign country, or from another part of France, and authorizes the execution of the judgment within the jurisdiction where it is so indorsed.

Exercise. To make use of. Thus, to exercise a right or power is to do something which it enables the holder to do; *e.g.* exercising option to purchase stock.

To put in action or practice, to carry on something, to transact. See **Performance.**

Exercised dominion. Open acts and conduct relative to land as evidence claim of the right of absolute possession, use, and ownership. Whelan v. Henderson, Tex.Civ.App., 137 S.W.2d 150, 153.

Exercise of judgment. Exercise of sound discretion, that is, discretion exercised, not arbitrarily or willfully, but with regard to what is right and equitable. United States v. Beckman, C.C.A.Pa., 104 F.2d 260, 262.

Exercitalis /əgzàrsətéyləs/. A soldier; a vassal.

Exercitoria actio /əgzàrsətóriyə ǽksh(iy)ow/. In the civil law, an action which lay against the employer of a vessel *(exercitor navis)* for the contracts made by the master.

Exercitorial power /əgzàrsətóriyəl páwər/. The trust given to a ship-master.

Exercitor navis /əgzàrsədər néyvəs/. Lat. The temporary owner or charterer of a ship.

Exercitual /ègzərsíchuwəl/. In old English law, a heriot paid only in arms, horses, or military accouterments.

Exercitus /əgzársədəs/. In old European law, an army; an armed force. The term was absolutely indefinite as to number. It was applied, on various occasions, to a gathering of forty-two armed men, of thirty-five, or even of four.

Ex facie /èks féys(h)iyiy/. From the face; apparently; evidently. A term applied to what appears on the face of a writing.

Ex facto /èks fæktow/. From or in consequence of a fact or action; actually. Usually applied to an unlawful or tortious act as the foundation of a title, etc. Sometimes used as equivalent to *"de facto."*

Ex facto jus oritur /èks fæktow jás óradar/. The law arises out of the fact. A rule of law continues in abstraction and theory, until an act is done on which it can attach and assume as it were a body and shape.

Exfestucare /eksfèstakériy/. In old English law, to abdicate or resign; to resign or surrender an estate, office, or dignity, by the symbolical delivery of a staff or rod to the alienee.

Ex fictione juris /èks fikshiyówniy júras/. By a fiction of law.

Exfrediare /èksfriydiyériy/. To break the peace; to commit open violence.

Ex frequenti delicto augetur pœna /èks frakwéntay dalíktow ojíydar píyna/. Punishment increases with increasing crime.

Ex gratia /èks gréysh(iy)a/. Out of grace; as a matter of grace, favor, or indulgence; gratuitous. A term applied to anything accorded as a favor; as distinguished from that which may be demanded *ex debito*, as a matter of right.

Ex gratia payment. Payment made by one who recognizes no legal obligation to pay but who makes payment to avoid greater expense as in the case of a settlement by an insurance company to avoid costs of suit. A payment without legal consideration.

Ex gravi querela /èks gréyvay kwaríyla/. (From or on the grievous complaint.) In old English practice, the name of a writ (so called from its initial words) which lay for a person to whom any lands or tenements in fee were devised by will (within any city, town, or borough wherein lands were devisable by custom), and the heir of the devisor entered and detained them from him. Abolished by St. 3 & 4 Wm. IV, c. 27, § 36.

Exhaustion of administrative remedies /agzós(h)chan av admínastradav rémadiyz/. This doctrine requires that where an administrative remedy is provided by statute, relief must first be sought by exhausting such remedies before the courts will act. McKart v. U. S., 395 U.S. 185, 89 S.Ct. 1657, 23 L.Ed.2d 194.

Exhaustion of state remedies. Under the "exhaustion of state remedies" doctrine, a petition for habeas corpus by a state prisoner will be entertained by a federal court only after all state remedies have been exhausted. U. S. ex rel. Pennise v. Fay, 210 F.Supp. 275.

Exhibere /ègzabíriy/. To present a thing corporeally, so that it may be handled. To appear personally to conduct the defense of an action at law.

Exhibit, *v.* To show or display; to offer or present for inspection. To produce anything in public, so that it may be taken into possession. To present; to offer publicly or officially; to file of record. To administer; to cause to be taken, as medicines. To submit to a court or officer in course of proceedings.

Exhibit, *n.* A paper or document produced and exhibited to a court during a trial or hearing, or to a commissioner taking depositions, or to auditors, arbitrators, etc., as a voucher, or in proof of facts, or as otherwise connected with the subject-matter, and which, on being accepted, is marked for identification and annexed to the deposition, report, or other principal document, or filed of record, or otherwise made a part of the case.

Paper, document, chart, map, or the like, referred to and made a part of an affidavit, pleading or brief.

An item of physical/tangible evidence which is to be or has been offered to the court for inspection.

Exhibits may be included as a part of the appendix to appellate briefs. See Fed.R.App.P. 30(e).

Exhibitio billæ /ègzabísh(iy)ow bíliy/. Lat. Exhibition of a bill. In old English practice, actions were instituted by presenting or exhibiting a bill to the court, in cases where the proceedings were by bill; hence this phrase is equivalent to "commencement of the suit."

Exhibition. See **Exhibit.**

Exhibitionism. Indecent exposure of sexual organs. See **Indecent.**

Exhibition value. "Minimum sale" or "exhibition value" is interchangeably used with term "price expectancy" in moving picture industry, denoting minimum receipts which distributors expect to realize from exhibition of pictures. Export & Import Film Co. v. B. P. Schulberg Productions, 125 Misc. 756, 211 N.Y.S. 838, 839.

Exhumation /èks(h)yuwméyshan/ègz(y)uw°/. Disinterment; the removal from the earth of anything previously buried therein, particularly a human corpse.

Ex hypothesi /èks hàypóθasay/. By the hypothesis; upon the supposition; upon the theory or facts assumed.

Exidos /èyhíyðows/. See **Ejidos.**

Exigence /égzajan(t)s/ or **exigency** /égzajansiy/agzí°/. Demand, want, need, imperativeness. Something arising suddenly out of the current of events; any event or occasional combination of circumstances, calling for immediate action or remedy; a pressing necessity; a sudden and unexpected happening or an unforeseen occurrence or condition. Los Angeles County v. Payne, 8 Cal.2d 563, 66 P.2d 658, 663. State of being urgent or exigent; pressing need or demand; also, case requiring immediate attention, assistance, or remedy; critical period or condition, pressing necessity. State v. Rubion, Tex.Civ.App., 292 S.W.2d 650, 657. See **Exigent circumstances,** *infra.*

Exigency of a bond. That which the bond demands or exacts, *i.e.,* the act, performance, or event upon which it is conditioned.

Exigency of a writ. The command or imperativeness of a writ; the directing part of a writ; the act or performance which it commands.

Exigendary /èksəjéndəriy/. In English law, an officer who makes out exigents. See **Exigenter.**

Exigent, /éksəjənt/ **exigi facias** /éksəjay féys(h)iyəs/. L. Lat. In English practice, a judicial writ made use of in the process of outlawry, commanding the sheriff to *demand* the defendant (or *cause him to be demanded, exigi faciat*), from county court to county court, until he be outlawed; or, if he appear, then to take and have him before the court on a day certain in term, to answer to the plaintiff's action. 3 Bl.Comm. 283, 284. Outlawry has long been obsolete. See **Allocatur exigent.**

Exigent circumstances. The "exigent circumstances" test permits police to make warrantless entry to effect an arrest when exigencies of situation make that course imperative. Vance v. State of N. C., C.A.N.C., 432 F.2d 984, 990. Exception to rule requiring search warrant is presence of exigent or emergency-like circumstances as for example presence of weapons in a motor vehicle stopped on highway and such exigent circumstances permit warrantless search and seizure. Chambers v. Maroney, 399 U.S. 42, 90 S.Ct. 1975, 26 L.Ed.2d 419.

Exigenter /éksəjentər/. An officer of the English court of common pleas, whose duty it was to make out the *exigents* and proclamations in the process of outlawry. Abolished by St. 7 Wm. IV, and 1 Vict., c. 30.

Exigent list. A phrase used to indicate a list of cases set down for hearing upon various incidental and ancillary motions and rules.

Exigent search. See **Exigent circumstances.**

Exigible /éksəjəbəl/. Demandable; requirable.

Exigible debt /éksəjəbəl dét/. A liquidated and demandable or matured claim.

Exigi facias /éksəjay féyshiyəs/. That you cause to be demanded. The emphatic words of the Latin form of the writ of *exigent.* They are sometimes used as the name of that writ.

Exile /égzayl/éksayl/. Banishment; the person banished.

Exilium /əgzíliyəm/. Lat. In old English law: (1) Exile; banishment from one's country. (2) Driving away; despoiling. The name of a species of waste, which consisted in driving away tenants or vassals from the estate; as by demolishing buildings, and so compelling the tenants to leave, or by enfranchising the bond servants, and unlawfully turning them out of their tenements.

Exilium est patriæ privatio, natalis soli mutatio, legum nativarum amissio /əgzíliyəm èst pǽtriyiy prəvéysh(iy)ow, nətéyləs sówlay myuwtéysh(iy)ow, líygəm nèydəvérəm əmísh(iy)ow/. Exile is a privation of country, a change of natal soil, a loss of native laws.

Ex industria /èks indʌ́striyə/. With contrivance or deliberation; designedly; on purpose.

Ex integro /èks íntəgrow/. Anew; afresh.

Exist. To live; to have life or animation; to be in present force, activity, or effect at a given time, as in speaking of "existing" contracts, creditors, debts, laws, rights, or liens. To be or continue to be. State v. Sawtooth Men's Club, 59 Idaho 616, 85 P.2d 695, 698.

Existimatio /əgzìstəméysh(iy)ow/. In the civil law, the civil reputation which belonged to the Roman citizen, as such. Called a state or condition of unimpeached dignity or character *(dignitatis inlæsæ status);* the highest standing of a Roman citizen. Also the decision or award of an arbiter.

Existing claim. Claim which has arisen and is pending.

Existing debt. To have an "existing debt" it is sufficient if there is an absolute debt owing though the period for its payment may not yet have arrived. A tax may be a "debt" within meaning of agreement to assume "existing debts". Shepard v. Commissioner of Internal Revenue, C.C.A.Ill., 101 F.2d 595, 598. Within provision of Uniform Fraudulent Conveyance Act which defines "insolvency", an "existing debt" is an existing legal liability, whether matured or unmatured, liquidated or unliquidated, absolute, fixed or contingent. Baker v. Geist, 457 Pa. 73, 321 A.2d 634, 636.

Existing disease. A chronic or definite affliction such as would be embraced in the common understanding and meaning of the term "diseased" or "sick." Browning v. Equitable Life Assur. Soc. of United States, 94 Utah 532, 72 P.2d 1060, 1074.

Existing person. A child conceived, but not born, is to be deemed an "existing person" so far as may be necessary for its interests in the event of its subsequent birth.

Exit /égzət/. Lat. It goes forth. This word is used in docket entries as a brief mention of the issue of process. Thus, *"exit fi. fa."* denotes that a writ of *fieri facias* has been issued in the particular case. The *"exit of a writ"* is the fact of its issuance.

Way out; opposite of entrance. See **Egress.**

Exitus /éksədəs/. Children; offspring. The rents, issues, and profits of lands and tenements. An export duty. The conclusion of the pleadings.

Exit wound. A term used in medical jurisprudence to denote the wound made by a weapon on the side where it emerges, after it has passed completely through the body, or through any part of it.

Ex justa causa /èks jʌ́stə kózə/. From a just or lawful cause; by a just or legal title.

Exlegalitas /èksləgéylətæs/. In old English law, outlawry.

Exlegalitus /èksləgéylədəs/. He who is prosecuted as an outlaw.

Exlegare /èksləgériy/. In old English law, to outlaw; to deprive one of the benefit and protection of the law *(exuere aliquem beneficio legis).*

Ex lege /èks líyjiy/. By the law; by force of law; as a matter of law.

Ex legibus /èks líyjəbəs/. According to the laws. A phrase of the civil law, which means according to the intent or spirit of the law, as well as according to the words or letter.

Exlex /ékslèx/. In old English law, an outlaw; *qui est extra legem*, one who is *out* of the *law's* protection.

To relieve from responsibility, duty, or obligation. To clear from guilt; *i.e.* dropping criminal charges against accused.

Ex licentia regis /èks ləsénsh(iy)ə ríyjəs/. By the king's license. 1 Bl.Comm. 168, note.

Ex locato /èks ləkéydow/. From or out of lease or letting. A term of the civil law, applied to actions or rights of action arising out of the contract of *locatum*. Adopted at an early period in the law of England.

Ex maleficio /èks mælfísh(i)yow/. Defined variously as from or growing out of wrongdoing; tortious; tortiously; growing out of, or founded on, misdoing or tort; on account of misconduct; by virtue of or out of an illegal act. Synonymous with "malfeasance". Lucas v. Central Missouri Trust Co., 350 Mo. 593, 166 S.W.2d 1053, 1056. This term is frequently used in the civil law as the synonym of *"ex delicto" (q.v.),* and is thus contrasted with *"ex contractu".* In this sense it is of more rare occurrence in the common law.

Ex maleficio non oritur contractus /èks mæləfísh(i)yow nòn órədər kəntræktəs/. A contract cannot arise out of an act radically vicious and illegal.

Ex malis moribus bonæ leges natæ sunt /èks mæləs mórəbəs bówniy líyjiyz néydiy sónt/. Good laws arise from evil morals, *i.e.,* are necessitated by the evil behavior of men.

Ex malitia /èks məlísh(iy)ə/. From malice; maliciously. In the law of libel and slander, this term imports a publication that is false and without legal excuse.

Ex mero motu /èks mírow mówduw/. Of his own mere motion; of his own accord; voluntarily and without prompting or request. In England, royal letters patent which are granted at the crown's own instance, and without request made, are said to be granted *ex mero motu.* When a court interferes, of its own motion, to object to an irregularity, or to do something which the parties are not strictly entitled to, but which will prevent injustice, it is said to act *ex mero motu,* or *ex proprio motu,* or *sua sponte,* all these terms being here equivalent.

Ex mora /èks mórə/. A term of the civil law, meaning from or in consequence of delay. Interest is allowed *ex mora;* that is, where there has been delay in repaying a sum borrowed.

Ex more /èks móriy/. According to custom.

Ex multitudine signorum, colligitur identitas vera /èks mòltət(y)úwdəniy signórəm, kəlíjədər ədéntətæs vírə/. From a great number of signs or marks, true identity is gathered or made up. A thing described by a great number of marks is easily identified, though, as to some, the description may not be strictly correct.

Ex mutuo /èks myúwchuwow/. From or out of loan. In the old law of England, a debt was said to arise *ex*

mutuo when one lent another anything which consisted in number, weight, or measure.

Ex necessitate /èks nəsèsətéydiy/. Of necessity.

Ex necessitate legis /èks nəsèsətéydiy líyjəs/. From or by necessity of law. 4 Bl.Comm. 394.

Ex necessitate rei /èks nəsèsətéydiy ríyay/. From the necessity or urgency of the thing or case.

Ex nihilo nihil fit /èks náy(h)əlow náy(h)əl fít/. From nothing nothing comes.

Ex nudo pacto non oritur [nascitur] actio /èks n(y)úwdow pæktow nòn órədər ækshiyow/ °næs(h)ədər/. Out of a nude or naked pact [that is, a bare parol agreement without consideration] no action arises. Out of a promise neither attended with particular solemnity (such as belongs to a specialty) nor with any consideration no legal liability can arise. A parol agreement, without a valid consideration, cannot be made the foundation of an action. A leading maxim both of the civil and common law.

Ex officio /èks əfísh(iy)ow/. From office; by virtue of the office; without any other warrant or appointment than that resulting from the holding of a particular office. Powers may be exercised by an officer which are not specifically conferred upon him, but are necessarily implied in his office; these are *ex officio.* Thus, a judge has *ex officio* the powers of a conservator of the peace.

Ex officio information /èks əfísh(iy)ow ìnfərméyshən/. In English law, a criminal information filed by the attorney general *ex officio* on behalf of the crown, in the court of king's bench, for offenses more immediately affecting the government, and to be distinguished from informations in which the crown is the nominal prosecutor.

Ex officio justices. Judges who serve in a particular capacity by reason of their office as a judge who serves on a commission or board because the law requires a particular judge to serve thereon and not because he is selected for such post. May also refer to one who exercises judicial functions by reason of his office.

Ex officio services /èks əfísh(iy)ow sárvəsəs/. Services which the law annexes to a particular office and requires the incumbent to perform.

Exoine. In French law, an act or instrument in writing which contains the reasons why a party in a civil suit, or a person accused, who has been summoned, agreeably to the requisitions of a decree, does not appear. The same as "Essoin" *(q.v.).*

Exonerate /əgzónəreyt/. To exculpate.

Exoneration /əgzònəréyshən/. The removal of a burden, charge, responsibility, or duty. Right to be reimbursed by reason of having paid that which another should be compelled to pay while "indemnity" generally is based upon contract, express or implied, and means compensation for loss already sustained. Uptagrafft v. U. S., C.A.Va., 315 F.2d 200, 203.

Exoneratione sectæ /əgzònərèyshiyówniy séktiy/. A writ that formerly lay for the crown's ward, to be free from all suit to the county court, hundred court, leet, etc., during wardship.

Exoneratione sectæ ad curiam baron /əgzònərèy-shiyówniy séktiy æd kyúriyəm bǽrən/. A writ of the same nature as that last above described, issued by the guardian of the crown's ward, and addressed to the sheriffs or stewards of the court, forbidding them to distrain him, etc., for not doing suit of court, etc.

Exoneretur /əgzònəríydər/. Lat. Let him be relieved or discharged. An entry made on a bailpiece, whereby the surety is relieved or discharged from further obligation, when the condition is fulfilled by the surrender of the principal or otherwise.

Exorbitant /əgzórbədənt/. Deviating from the normal or customary course, or going beyond the rule of established limits of right or propriety.

Exordium /əgzórdiyəm/. The beginning or introductory part of a speech or document.

Ex pacto illicito non oritur actio /èks pǽktow əlísədow nòn órədər ǽksh(iy)ow/. From an illegal contract an action does not arise.

Ex parte /èks párdiy/. On one side only; by or for one party; done for, in behalf of, or on the application of, one party only.

A judicial proceeding, order, injunction, etc., is said to be *ex parte* when it is taken or granted at the instance and for the benefit of one party only, and without notice to, or contestation by, any person adversely interested.

"*Ex parte*," in the heading of a reported case, signifies that the name following is that of the party upon whose application the case is heard.

Ex parte divorce. Divorce proceeding in which only one spouse participates or one in which the other spouse does not appear. The validity of such divorce depends upon the nature of the notice given to the absent spouse.

Ex parte hearing. Hearings in which the court or tribunal hears only one side of the controversy.

Ex parte injunction. An injunction which issues from a court which has heard only one side, the moving side, of the controversy.

Ex parte investigation. An investigation conducted about a person who is not personally contacted or questioned.

Ex parte materna /èks párdiy mətárnə/. On the mother's side; of the maternal line.

Ex parte paterna /èks párdiy pətárnə/. On the father's side; of the paternal line.

Ex parte proceeding. Any judicial or quasi judicial hearing in which only one party is heard as in the case of a temporary restraining order.

Ex parte revocation. The withdrawal or revocation of a license or other authority from a person without that person's participation or without notice and opportunity to be heard and defend.

Expatriation /ekspèytriyéyshən/. The voluntary act of abandoning one's country, and becoming the citizen or subject of another.

Ex paucis dictis intendere plurima possis /èks pósəs díktəs ənténdəriy pl(y)úrəmə pósəs/. You can imply many things from few expressions.

Ex paucis plurima concipit ingenium /èks pósəs pl(y)úrəmə kənsípəd ənjíyn(i)yəm/. From a few words or hints the understanding conceives many things.

Expect. To await; to look forward to something intended, promised, or likely to happen.

Expectancy. That which is expected or hoped for. The condition of being deferred to a future time, or of dependence upon an expected event. Contingency as to possession or enjoyment. With respect to the time of their enjoyment, estates may either be in possession or in expectancy; and of expectancies there are two sorts,—one created by the act of the parties, called a "remainder;" the other by act of law, called a "reversion." Expectancy as applied to property, is contingency as to possession, that which is expected or hoped for. At most it is a mere hope or expectation, contingent upon the will and pleasure of the landowner, and hardly reaches the height of a property right, much less a vested right, because where there is no obligation, there is no right. It is a possibility for which a party may under certain circumstances properly hope for or expect.

Expectancy of life. With respect to life annuities, the share or number of years of life which a person of a given age may, upon an equality of chance, expect to enjoy. See **Actuarial table; Mortality tables.**

Expectancy tables. See **Actuarial table; Mortality tables.**

Expectant. Contingent as to enjoyment. Having relation to, or dependent upon, a contingency. See **Contingent.**

Expectant estates. See **Estate in expectancy.**

Expectant heir /əkspéktənt ér/. A person who has the expectation of inheriting property or an estate, but small present means.

Expectant right. A contingent right, not vested; one which depends on the continued existence of the present condition of things until the happening of some future event. Pearsall v. Great Northern R. Co., 161 U.S. 646, 16 S.Ct. 705, 40 L.Ed. 838. A right is contingent, not vested, when it comes into existence only on an event or condition which may not happen.

Expectation of life. See **Actuarial table; Expectancy of life; Mortality tables.**

Expedient. Apt and suitable to end in view. Werner v. Biederman, 64 Ohio App. 423, 28 N.E.2d 957, 959. Whatever is suitable and appropriate in reason for the accomplishment of a specified object.

Expediente /ekspèyðiyéntey/. An historical record of proceedings in connection with grant of land by the sovereign. State v. Balli, Tex.Civ.App., 173 S.W.2d 522, 526. In Mexican law, a term including all the papers or documents constituting a grant or title to land from government.

Expediment /əkspédəmənt/. The whole of a person's goods and chattels, bag and baggage.

Expedite. To hasten; to make haste; to speed.

Expediter /ékspədàydər/. An employee whose duty is to see that shortage in material at one point in a plant is remedied by delivery of the needed material from another part of the plant where it is stacked or stored.

Expeditio /èkspədísh(iy)ow/. An expedition; an irregular kind of army.

Expeditio brevis /èkspədísh(iy)ow bríyvəs/. In old practice, the service of a writ.

Expedition. A sending forth or setting forth for the execution of some object of consequence. Speed or promptness in performance. An important journey or excursion for a specific purpose; as, a military or exploring expedition; also, the body of persons making such an excursion. Equitable Life Assur. Soc. of United States v. Dyess, 194 Ark. 1023, 109 S.W.2d 1263, 1265. A journey, march, or voyage generally of several or many persons for definite purpose, such as a military or exploring expedition or a trading expedition to the African coast. The word carries an implication of a military exploit or of an exploration into remote regions or over new routes. Day v. Equitable Life Assur. Soc. of U. S., C.C.A.Colo., 83 F.2d 147, 149.

Expeditious /èkspədíshəs/. Possessed of, or characterized by, expedition or efficiency and rapidity in action; performed with, or acting with, expedition; quick; speedy.

Expedit reipublicæ ne sua re quis male utatur /ékspədət rìyaypábləsiy níy s(y)úwə ríy kwìs mǽliy yúwdədər/. It is for the interest of the state that a man should not enjoy his own property improperly (to the injury of others).

Expedit reipublicæ ut sit finis litium /ékspədət rìyaypábləsiy ət sít fáynəs lísh(iy)əm/. It is for the advantage of the state that there be an end of suits; it is for the public good that actions be brought to a close. This maxim belongs to the law of all countries.

Expel. In regard to trespass and other torts, this term means to eject, to put out, to drive out, and generally with an implication of the use of force. See also **Ejectment; Eviction.**

Expend. To pay out, lay out, consume, use up; normally implying receiving something in return.

Expendable. That which is consumed in its use over a short period of time such as expenses for day to day operations which are charged as expenses to current income as contrasted with payments for long term or capital improvements. Not essential or critical to preserve.

Expendere /əkspéndəriy/. The word "expense" had its origin in the Latin word "expendere"; "ex" meaning "out," and "pendere" meaning "to weigh."

Expenditors /əkspéndədərz/. Paymasters. Those who expend or disburse certain taxes.

Expenditure. Spending or payment of money; the act of expending, disbursing, or laying out of money; payment. *Compare* **Appropriation.** See also **Expense.** As regards "Capital expenditure" see **Capital.**

Expensæ litis /əkspénsiy láydəs/. Costs or expenses of the suit, which are generally allowed to the successful party.

Expense. That which is expended, laid out or consumed. An outlay; charge; cost; price. The expenditure of money, time, labor, resources, and thought. See also **Costs; Fee.**

Accrued expense. One which has been incurred in a given period but not yet paid.

Business expense. One which is directly related to one's business as contrasted with personal expenses incurred for personal and family reasons. See *Tax deduction, infra.*

Current expense. Normal expense incurred, for example, in daily operations of a business. See *Operating expenses, infra.*

Operating expenses. The cost of operating an income producing property, such as rent, wages, utilities, and similar day to day expenses, as well as taxes, insurance, and a reserve for depreciation.

Ordinary expense. See **Ordinary.**

Out of pocket expenses. A direct expense which requires the immediate outlay of cash in contrast to an accrued expense.

Prepaid expense. Payment of rent, interest, insurance, or like expenses, prior to actual due date. Cash basis as well as accrual basis taxpayers are generally required to capitalize prepayments for rent, insurance, etc. that cover more than one year. Deductions are taken during the period the benefits are received.

Tax deduction. Certain expenses such as those directly related to production of income are deductions from gross income for tax purposes.

Expense in carrying on business. Usual or customary expenditure in course of conducting business during the year. Whitney v. Commissioner of Internal Revenue, C.C.A.N.Y., 73 F.2d 589, 591.

Expense ratio. Proportion or ratio of expenses to income.

Expenses of administration. As used in Internal Revenue Code, means obligations incurred after decedent's death by his representatives in administering his estate. Mayer v. Reinecke, D.C.Ill., 28 F.Supp. 334, 339. See **Administration expense.**

Expenses of family. Medical and funeral expenses are "expenses of the family" within meaning of statute making expenses of family chargeable upon property of both husband and wife. Hansen v. Hayes, 175 Or. 358, 154 P.2d 202, 205. Under such a statute the term includes not only merchandise used by family as a whole, but also expenses, such as medical aid, hospital services and burial attendance, incurred or supplied for one of the spouses. In re De Nisson's Guardianship, 197 Wash. 265, 84 P.2d 1024, 1026.

Expenses of receivership. Includes allowances to receivers' counsel, master's fees, appraisers' fees, auditors' fees, and rent and other expenses incurred by receivers in conducting business.

Expenses of the state. Within constitutional provision for raising revenue has reference to general operating expenses of state government for fiscal year.

Expensis militum non levandis /əkspénsəs məlísh(iy)əm nòn ləvǽndəs/. An ancient writ to prohibit the sheriff from levying any allowance for knights of the shire upon those who held lands in ancient demesne.

Experience. A state, extent, or duration of being engaged in a particular study or work; the real life as contrasted with the ideal or imaginary. A word implying skill, facility, or practical wisdom gained by personal knowledge, feeling, and action, and also the course or process by which one attains knowledge or wisdom.

Experience rating. In insurance, a method of determining rates by using the loss experience of the insured over a period of time.

Experientia per varios actus legem facit. Magistra rerum experientia /əkspìriyénsh(iy)ə pàr vériyows ǽctəs líyjəm fíysət. məjístrə rírəm əkspiydiyénsh(iy)ə/. Experience by various acts makes law. Experience is the mistress of things.

Experiment. A trial or special test or observation made to confirm or disprove something doubtful. The process of testing.

Expert. One who is knowledgeable in specialized field, that knowledge being obtained from either education or personal experience. Midtown Properties, Inc. v. George F. Richardson, Inc., 139 Ga.App. 182, 228 S.E.2d 303, 307. One who by habits of life and business has peculiar skill in forming opinion on subject in dispute. Brown v. State, 140 Ga.App. 160, 230 S.E.2d 128, 131. See **Expert testimony; Expert witness.**

Expert testimony. Opinion evidence of some person who possesses special skill or knowledge in some science, profession or business which is not common to the average man and which is possessed by the expert by reason of his special study or experience. Board of Ed. of Claymont Special School Dist. v. 13 Acres of Land in Brandywine Hundred, Del.Super., 11 Terry 387, 131 A.2d 180, 184. Testimony given in relation to some scientific, technical, or professional matter by experts, i.e., persons qualified to speak authoritatively by reason of their special training, skill, or familiarity with the subject. Evidence of persons who are skilled in some art, science, profession, or business, which skill or knowledge is not common to their fellow men, and which has come to such experts by reason of special study and experience in such art, science, profession, or business.

If scientific, technology, or other specialized knowledge will assist the trier of fact to understand the evidence or to determine a fact in issue, a witness qualified as an expert by knowledge, skill, experience, training, or education, may testify thereto in the form of an opinion or otherwise. Fed.Evid.R. 702, 703. See also **Expert witness.**

Expert witness. One who by reason of education or specialized experience possesses superior knowledge respecting a subject about which persons having no particular training are incapable of forming an accurate opinion or deducing correct conclusions. Kim Mfg., Inc. v. Superior Metal Treating, Inc., Mo.App., 537 S.W.2d 424, 428. A witness who has been qualified as an expert and who thereby will be allowed (through his/her answers to questions posted) to assist the jury in understanding complicated and technical subjects not within the understanding of the average lay person. One possessing, with reference to particular subject, knowledge not acquired by ordinary persons. One skilled in any particular art, trade, or profession, being possessed of peculiar knowledge concerning the same, and one who has given subject in question particular study, practice, or observation. One who by habits of life and business has peculiar skill in forming opinion on subject in dispute. See also **Expert testimony; Hypothetical question.**

Expilare /èkspəlériy/. In the civil law, to spoil; to rob or plunder. Applied to inheritances.

Expilatio /èkspəléysh(iy)ow/. In the civil law, the offense of unlawfully appropriating goods belonging to a succession. It is not technically theft *(furtum)* because such property no longer belongs to the decedent, nor to the heir, since the latter has not yet taken possession. In the common law, the grant of letters testamentary, or letters of administration, relates back to the time of the death of the testator or intestate; so that the property of the estate is vested in the executor or administrator from that period.

Expilator /ékspəlèydər/. In the civil law, a robber; a spoiler or plunderer.

Expiration. Cessation; termination from mere lapse of time, as the expiration of a lease, insurance policy, statute, and the like. Coming to close; termination or end.

The term "expiration," as in an insurance policy, refers to termination of the policy by lapse of time covering the policy period, while "cancellation" refers to termination of the policy by act of either or both parties prior to ending of the policy period.

Expire. See **Expiration.**

Explees /ə(k)splíyz/. See **Esplees.**

Expleta /əksplíydə/, **expletia** /əksplíysh(iy)ə/, or **explecia** /əksplíys(h)(i)yə/. The rents and profits of an estate.

Explicatio /èkspləkéysh(iy)ow/. In the civil law, the fourth pleading; equivalent to the surrejoinder of the common law.

Explicit. Not obscure or ambiguous, having no disguised meaning or reservation. Clear in understanding.

Exploitation /èksploytéyshən/. Act or process of exploiting, making use of, or working up. Utilization by application of industry, argument, or other means of turning to account, as the exploitation of a mine or a forest. State Finance Co. v. Hamacher, 171 Wash. 15, 17 P.2d 610, 613. Taking unjust advantage of another for one's own advantage or benefit.

Exploration. The examination and investigation of land supposed to contain valuable minerals, by drilling, boring, sinking shafts, driving tunnels, and other means, for the purpose of discovering the presence of ore and its extent.

Explorator /éksplərèydər/. A scout, huntsman, or chaser.

Export, v. To carry or to send abroad. Canton R. Co. v. Rogan, 340 U.S. 511, 71 S.Ct. 447, 449, 95 L.Ed. 488. To send, take, or carry an article of trade or commerce out of the country. To transport merchandise from one country to another in the course of trade. To carry out or convey goods by sea. Transportation of goods from United States to foreign country. West India Oil Co. v. Sancho, C.C.A.Puerto Rico, 108 F.2d 144, 147. See also **Re-export.**

Export, n. A thing or commodity exported. More commonly used in the plural.

Exportation. The act of sending or carrying goods and merchandise from one country to another. A severance of goods from mass of things belonging to United States with intention of uniting them to mass of things belonging to some foreign country. Matson Nav. Co. v. State Bd. of Equalization, 136 Cal.2d 577, 289 P.2d 73, 77.

Export declaration. Document which contains details of export shipment and required by federal law.

Export-Import Bank. Independent agency of federal government whose function is to aid in financing exports and imports.

Export quotas. Amounts of specific goods which may be exported. Such quotas are set by the federal government for purposes of national defense, economic stability, price support, etc.

Exports clause. Provision in U.S.Const., Art. I, Sec. 10, Cl. 2, limiting power of states to impose duties or imposts on imports or exports.

Export tax. Tax levied upon merchandise and goods shipped out of a country. Tax levied upon right to export or upon goods because of fact that they are being exported or intended to be exported. Virgo Corp. v. Paiewonsky, D.C.Virgin Islands, 251 F.Supp. 279, 283.

Expose, v. To show publicly; to display; to offer to the public view, as, to "expose" goods to sale, to "expose" a tariff or schedule of rates, to "expose" misconduct of public or quasi-public figures.

To place in a position where the object spoken of is open to danger, or where it is near or accessible to anything which may affect it detrimentally; as, to "expose" a child, or to expose oneself or another to a contagious disease or to danger or hazard of any kind.

For indecent exposure, see **Indecent.**

Exposé /əkspówz/èkspowzéy/. Fr. A statement; account; recital; explanation. The term is used in diplomatic language as descriptive of a written explanation of the reasons for a certain act or course of conduct. Exposure of discreditable matter concerning a person, government, etc.

Expositio /èkspəzísh(iy)ow/. Lat. Explanation; exposition; interpretation.

Exposition. Explanation; interpretation.

Exposition de part. In French law, the abandonment of a child, unable to take care of itself, either in a public or private place.

Expositio quæ ex visceribus causæ nascitur, est aptissima et fortissima in lege /èkspəzísh(iy)ow kwìy èks vəséhrəbəs kóziy nǽsədər èst æptísəmə èt fortísəmə ìn líyjiy/. That kind of interpretation which is born [or drawn] from the bowels [or vitals] of a cause is the aptest and most forcible in the law.

Expository statute. A law that is enacted to explain the meaning of a previously enacted law. Such statutes are often expressed thus: "The true intent and meaning of an act passed * * * be and is hereby declared to be"; "the provisions of the act shall not hereafter extend"; or "are hereby declared and enacted not to apply", and the like. This is a common mode of legislation.

Ex post facto /éks pòwst fǽktow/. After the fact; by an act or fact occurring after some previous act or fact, and relating thereto; by subsequent matter; the opposite of *ab initio.* Thus, a deed may be good *ab initio,* or, if invalid at its inception, may be confirmed by matter *ex post facto.*

Ex post facto law /éks pòwst fǽktow ló/. A law passed after the occurrence of a fact or commission of an act, which retrospectively changes the legal consequences or relations of such fact or deed. By Art. I, § 10 of U.S.Const., the states are forbidden to pass "any ex post facto law." Most all state constitutions contain similar prohibitions against ex post facto laws.

An "ex post facto law" is defined as a law which provides for the infliction of punishment upon a person for an act done which, when it was committed, was innocent; a law which aggravates a crime or makes it greater than when it was committed; a law that changes the punishment or inflicts a greater punishment than the law annexed to the crime when it was committed; a law that changes the rules of evidence and receives less or different testimony than was required at the time of the commission of the offense in order to convict the offender; a law which, assuming to regulate civil rights and remedies only, in effect imposes a penalty or the deprivation of a right which, when done, was lawful; a law which deprives persons accused of crime of some lawful protection to which they have become entitled, such as the protection of a former conviction or acquittal, or of the proclamation of amnesty; every law which, in relation to the offense or its consequences, alters the situation of a person to his disadvantage. Wilensky v. Fields, Fla., 267 So.2d 1, 5.

Exposure. The act or state of exposing or being exposed. See **Exposé.**

For "Indecent exposure," see **Indecent.**

Exposure of child. Placing child in such a place or position as to leave it unprotected against danger to its health or life or subject it to the peril of severe suffering or serious bodily harm.

Exposure of person. In criminal law, such an intentional exposure, in a public place, of the naked body or the private parts as is calculated to shock the feelings of chastity or to corrupt the morals of the community. See also **Indecent** (*Indecent exposure*).

Ex præcedentibus et consequentibus optima fit interpretatio /èks prèsədéntəbəs èt kònsəkwéntəbəs óptəmə fid əntàrprətéysh(iy)ow/. The best interpretation is made from the context.

Express. Clear; definite; explicit; plain; direct; unmistakable; not dubious or ambiguous. Declared in terms; set forth in words. Directly and distinctly stated. Made known distinctly and explicitly, and not left to inference. Minneapolis Steel & Machinery Co. v. Federal Surety Co., C.C.A.Minn., 34 F.2d 270, 274. Manifested by direct and appropriate language, as distinguished from that which is inferred from conduct. The word is usually contrasted with "implied."

As to express Condition; Consent; Consideration; Contracts; Covenants; Dedication; Emancipation; Invitation; Malice; Notice; Obligation; Trust; Waiver; and Warranty, see those titles.

Express abrogation. Abrogation by express provision or enactment; the repeal of a law or provision by a subsequent one, referring directly to it. Express abrogation is that literally pronounced by the law either in general terms, as when a final clause abrogates or repeals all laws contrary to the provisions of the new one, or in particular terms, as when it abrogates certain preceding laws which are named.

Express active trust. See **Trust.**

Expressa nocent, non expressa non nocent /əksprésə nósənt, nón əksprèsə nón nòsənt/. Things expressed are [may be] prejudicial; things not expressed are not. Express words are sometimes prejudicial, which, if omitted, had done no harm.

Expressa non prosunt quæ non expressa proderunt /əksprésə nòn prówsənt kwiy nón əksprèsə prədírənt/. The expression of things of which, if unexpressed, one would have the benefit, is useless. Things expressed may be prejudicial which when not expressed will profit.

Express assumpsit /əksprés əsám(p)sət/. An undertaking to do some act, or to pay a sum of money to another, manifested by express terms. An undertaking made orally, by writing not under seal, or by matter of record, to perform act or to pay sum of money to another. Holcomb v. Kentucky Union Co., 262 Ky. 192, 90 S.W.2d 25, 27; Anderson v. Biesman & Carrick Co., 287 Ill.App. 507, 4 N.E.2d 639, 640, 641.

Express authority. Authority delegated to agent by words which expressly authorize him to do a delegable act. Authority distinctly, plainly expressed, orally or in writing. Ulen v. Knecttle, 50 Wyo. 94, 58 P.2d 446, 449. Authority which is directly granted to or conferred upon agent in express terms. That authority which principal intentionally confers upon his agent by manifestations to him. Epstein v. Corporacion Peruana de Vapores, D.C.N.Y., 325 F.Supp. 535, 537.

That which confers power to do a particular identical thing set forth and declared exactly, plainly, and directly with well-defined limits. An authority given in direct terms, definitely and explicitly, and not left to inference or implication, as distinguished from authority which is general, implied, or not directly stated or given.

Express color. In old English law, an evasive form of special pleading in a case where the defendant ought to plead the general issue. Abolished by the common-law procedure act, 1852, 15 & 16 Vict., c. 76, § 64.

Express common-law dedication. See **Dedication.**

Express company. A firm or corporation engaged in the business of transporting parcels or other movable property, in the capacity of common carriers, and especially undertaking the safe carriage and speedy delivery of small but valuable packages of goods and money.

Express conditions. See **Condition.**

Express contract. See **Contract.**

Express dissatisfaction. Where will declares that any one expressing dissatisfaction with its provisions should forfeit his interest, "dissatisfaction" is legally "expressed" when beneficiary contests or objects in legal proceeding to enforcement of any provision of will.

Expressed. Means stated or declared in direct terms; set forth in words; not left to inference or implication. Anderson v. Board of Ed. of School Dist. No. 91, 390 Ill. 412, 61 N.E.2d 562, 567. See **Express.**

Expressio eorum quæ tacite insunt nihil operatur /əksprésh(iy)ow iyórəm kwiy tǽsədiy ínsənt náy(h)əl òpəréydər/. The expression or express mention of those things which are tacitly implied avails nothing. A man's own words are void, when the law speaks as much. Words used to express what the law will imply without them are mere words of abundance.

Expression, freedom of. One of the basic freedoms guaranteed by the First Amendment of U.S.Const. and by most state constitutions. Such is equivalent to freedom of speech, press, or assembly.

Expressio unius est exclusio alterius /əksprésh(iy)ow yənáyəs èst əksklúwz(h)(i)yow oltíriyəs/. A maxim of statutory interpretation meaning that the expression of one thing is the exclusion of another. Burgin v. Forbes, 293 Ky. 456, 169 S.W.2d 321, 325; Newblock v. Bowles, 170 Okl. 487, 40 P.2d 1097, 1100. Mention of one thing implies exclusion of another. When certain persons or things are specified in a law, contract, or will, an intention to exclude all others from its operation may be inferred. Under this maxim, if statute specifies one exception to a general rule or assumes to specify the effects of a certain provision, other exceptions or effects are excluded.

Expressio unius personæ est exclusio alterius /əksprésh(iy)ow yənáyəs pərsówniy èst əksklúwz(h)(i)yow oltíriyəs/. The mention of one person is the exclusion of another.

Expressly. In an express manner; in direct or unmistakable terms; explicitly; definitely; directly. Le Ballister v. Redwood Theatres, 1 Cal.App.2d 447, 36 P.2d 827; St. Louis Union Trust Co. v. Hill, 336 Mo. 17, 76 S.W.2d 685, 689. The opposite of impliedly. Bolles v. Toledo Trust Co., 144 Ohio St. 195, 58 N.E.2d 381, 396.

Express malice. Express malice for purposes of first degree murder includes malice, formed design or intention to kill or to do great bodily harm, and sedate and deliberate mind of which that intention is the product. State v. Gardner, 7 Storey 588, 203 A.2d 77, 80. As used with respect to libel, means publication of defamatory material in bad faith, without belief in the truth of the matter published, or with reckless disregard of the truth or falsity of the matter. Barlow v. International Harvester Co., 95 Idaho 881, 522 P.2d 1102, 1113. See also **Malice.**

Express permission. Within statute respecting automobile owner's liability, includes prior knowledge of intended use and affirmative and active consent thereto.

Express private trust. See **Trust.**

Express repeal. Abrogation or annulment of previously existing law by enactment of subsequent statute declaring that former law shall be revoked or abrogated.

Express republication. Occurs with respect to will when testator repeats ceremonies essential to valid execution, with avowed intention of republishing will.

Express request. That which occurs when one person commands or asks another to do or give something, or answers affirmatively when asked whether another shall do a certain thing.

Express terms. Within provision that qualified acceptance, in "express terms," varies effect of draft, "express terms" means clear, unambiguous, definite, certain, and unequivocal terms.

Express trust. See **Trust.**

Expressum facit cessare tacitum /əksprésəm féysət səsériy tǽsədəm/. That which is expressed makes that which is implied to cease [that is, supersedes it, or controls its effect]. Thus, an implied covenant in a deed is in all cases controlled by an express covenant. Where a law sets down plainly its whole meaning the court is prevented from making it mean what the court pleases. Munro v. City of Albuquerque, 48 N.M. 306, 150 P.2d 733, 743.

Expressum servitium regat vel declaret tacitum /əksprésəm sərvísh(iy)əm ríygət vèl dèklərérət tǽsədəm/. Let service expressed rule or declare what is silent.

Express warranty. See **Warranty.**

Expromissio /èksprəmís(h)(i)yow/. In the civil law, the species of novation by which a creditor accepts a new debtor, who becomes bound instead of the old, the latter being released.

Expromissor /èksprəmísər/. In the civil law, a person who assumes the debt of another, and becomes solely liable for it, by a stipulation with the creditor. He differs from a surety, inasmuch as this contract is one of novation, while a surety is jointly liable with his principal.

Expromittere /èksprəmídəriy/. In the civil law, to undertake for another with the view of becoming liable in his place.

Expropriation. A taking, as under eminent domain. This term is also used in the context of a foreign government taking an American industry located in the foreign country. In Louisiana, the word has the same general meaning as eminent domain.

A voluntary surrender of rights or claims; the act of divesting oneself of that which was previously claimed as one's own, or renouncing it. In this sense it is the opposite of "appropriation."

See also **Condemnation; Eminent domain.**

Ex proprio motu /èks prówpriyow mówduw/. Of his own accord. See **Ex mero motu.**

Ex proprio vigore /èks prówpriyow vəgóriy/. By their or its own force.

Ex provisione hominis /èks prəvìz(h)iyówniy hómənəs/. By the provision of man. By the limitation of the party, as distinguished from the disposition of the law.

Ex provisione mariti /èks prəvìz(h)iyówniy mǽrəday/. From the provision of the husband.

Expulsion. A putting or driving out. Ejectment; banishment; a cutting off from the privileges of an institution or society permanently. The act of depriving a member of a corporation, legislative body, assembly, society, commercial organization, etc., of his membership in the same, by a legal vote of the body itself, for breach of duty, improper conduct, or other sufficient cause. Also, in the law of torts and of landlord and tenant, an eviction or forcible putting out. See Deportation; Ejectment; Eviction; Expel; Forcible entry and detainer; **Summary** (*Summary process*).

Expunge /əkspʌ́nj/. To destroy; blot out; obliterate; erase; efface designedly; strike out wholly. The act of physically destroying information—including criminal records—in files, computers, or other depositories.

Expungement of record. Process by which record of criminal conviction is destroyed or sealed after expiration of time. See also **Erasure** (*Erasure of record*).

Expurgation /èkspərgéyshən/. The act of purging or cleansing, as where a book is published without its obscene passages.

Expurgator /ékspərgèydər/. One who corrects by expurging.

Ex quasi contractu /èks kwéysày kəntrǽkchuw/. From *quasi* contract.

Ex rel. See **Ex relatione.**

Ex relatione /èks rəlèyshiyówniy/. Upon relation or information.

Legal proceedings which are instituted by the attorney general (or other proper person) in the name and behalf of the state, but on the information and at the instigation of an individual who has a private interest in the matter, are said to be taken "on the relation" *(ex relatione)* of such person, who is called the "relator." Such a cause is usually entitled thus: "State *ex rel.* Doe *v.* Roe."

In the books of reports, when a case is said to be reported *ex relatione,* it is meant that the reporter derives his account of it, not from personal knowledge, but from the relation or narrative of some person who was present at the argument.

Ex rights. Literally, without rights. Stock sold ex rights is sold without privileged subscription rights to a current new issue by a corporation.

Ex rigore juris /èks rəgóriy júrəs/. According to the rigor or strictness of law; in strictness of law.

Exrogare /èksrəgériy/. (From *ex,* from, and *rogare,* to pass a law.) In Roman law, to take something from an old law by a new law.

Ex scriptis olim visis /èks skríptəs ówləm váyzəs/. From writings formerly seen. A term used as descriptive of that kind of proof of handwriting where the knowledge has been acquired by the witness having seen letters or other documents professing to be the handwriting of the party, and having afterwards communicated personally with the party upon the contents of those letters or documents, or having otherwise acted upon them by written answers, producing further correspondence or acquiescence by the party in some matter to which they relate, or by the witness transacting with the party some business to which they relate, or by any other mode of communication between the party and the witness which, in the ordinary course of the transactions of life, induces a reasonable presumption that the letters or documents were the handwriting of the party.

Ex ship. See **Ship.**

Ex statuto /èks stəchúwdow/. According to the statute.

Ex stipulatu actio /èks stipyəléyduw ǽksh(iy)ow/. In the civil law, an action of stipulation. An action given to recover marriage portions.

Ex tempore /èks témpəriy/. From or in consequence of time; by lapse of time. *Ex diuturno tempore,* from length of time. Without preparation or premeditation.

Extend. Term lends itself to great variety of meanings, which must in each case be gathered from context. It may mean to expand, enlarge, prolong, lengthen, widen, carry or draw out further than the original limit; *e.g.,* to extend the time for filing an answer, to extend a lease, term of office, charter, railroad track, etc. Keetch v. Cordner, 90 Utah 423, 62 P.2d 273, 277. To stretch out or to draw out Crane Enamelware Co. v. Smith, 168 Tenn. 203, 76 S.W.2d 644; Loeffler v. Federal Supply Co., 187 Okl. 373, 102 P.2d 862, 864. See also **Extension; Renewal.**

Extended. A lengthening out of time previously fixed and not the arbitrary setting of a new date. Stretched, spread, or drawn out.

Extended coverage clause. Provision in insurance policy which carries protection for hazards beyond those covered in the basic policy. See also **Omnibus clause.**

Extended insurance. An option to use dividend to procure extended insurance is one to procure extension of term of insurance from date to which premiums have been paid, without further payment. Williams v. Union Central Life Ins. Co., Tex., 291 U.S. 170, 54 S.Ct. 348, 78 L.Ed. 711.

Extendi facias /əksténday féys(h)(i)yəs/. Lat. You cause to be extended. In English practice, the name of a writ of execution (derived from its two emphatic words); more commonly called an "extent."

Extension. An increase in length of time (*e.g.* of expiration date of lease, or due date of note).

The word "extension" ordinarily implies the existence of something to be extended. State v. Graves, 352 Mo. 1102, 182 S.W.2d 46, 51.

A part constituting an addition or enlargement, as an annex to a building or an extension to a house. Addition of existing facilities. Enlargement of main body; addition of something smaller than that to which it is attached; to cause to reach or continue as from point to point; to lengthen or prolong. That property of a body by which it occupies a portion of space. Newark Stove Co. v. Gray & Dudley Co., D.C.Tenn., 39 F.Supp. 992, 993.

Bankruptcy. An extension proposal is an agreement on part of creditors that they will extend time within which their claims are probably to be paid, in full as to secured creditors, on terms proposed by debtor and approved by court. Heldstab v. Equitable Life Assur. Soc. of United States, C.C.A.Kan., 91 F.2d 655, 658.

Commercial law. An allowance of additional time for the payment of debts. An agreement between a debtor and his creditors, by which they allow him further time for the payment of his liabilities. A creditor's indulgence by giving a debtor further time to pay an existing debt.

Lease. The word "extension," when used in its proper and usual sense in connection with a lease, means a prolongation of the previous leasehold estate. The distinction between "extension" and "renewal" of lease is chiefly that, in the case of renewal, a new lease is requisite, while, in the case of extension, the same lease continues in force during additional period upon performance of stipulated act. An option for renewal implies giving of new lease on same terms as old lease, while an option for extension contemplates a continuance of old lease for a further period.

Patents. Extension of life of patent for an additional statutorily allowed period.

Time. Extensions of time in civil actions are governed by Fed.R. Civil P. 6, in criminal actions by Fed.R.Crim.P. 45, and in appeals by Fed.R.App.P. 26.

Extension agreements. Those agreements which provide for further time in which performance of the basic agreement may be performed.

Extension or renewal of note. Takes place when parties agree upon valuable consideration for maturity of debt on day subsequent to that provided in original contract. Elk Horn Bank & Trust Co. v. Spraggins, 182 Ark. 27, 30 S.W.2d 858, 859.

Extensive. Widely extended in space, time, or scope; great or wide or capable of being extended.

Extensores /èkstənsóriyz/. In old English law, extenders or appraisers. The name of certain officers appointed to appraise and divide or apportion lands. It was their duty to make a survey, schedule, or inventory of the lands, to lay them out under certain heads, and then to ascertain the value of each, as preparatory to the division or partition.

Extent. Amount; scope; range; magnitude.

In old English law, a writ of execution issuing from the exchequer upon a debt due the crown, or upon a debt due a private person, if upon recognizance or statute merchant or staple, by which the sheriff was directed to appraise the debtor's lands, and, instead of selling them, to set them off to the creditor for a term during which the rental will satisfy the judgment. It was so called because the sheriff was to cause the lands to be appraised at their full extended value before he delivers them to the plaintiff. The term was at one time used in the various states of the United States to denote writs which give the creditor possession of the debtor's lands for a limited time till the debt be paid.

Extenta manerii /əksténtə məníriyày/. (The extent or survey of a manor.) The title of English statute passed 4 Edw. I, St. 1; being a sort of direction for making a *survey* or terrier of a manor, and all its appendages.

Extent in aid. In old English law, that kind of extent which issued at the instance and for the benefit of a debtor to the crown for the recovery of a debt due to himself. This writ was much abused, owing to some peculiar privileges possessed by crown-debtors, and its use was regulated by Stat. 57 Geo. III, c. 117. 3 Bl.Comm. 419. Abolished by Crown Proceedings Act (1947). The writ formerly used by a debtor of the king against his debtor to enforce the right of preference given to him because of his indebtedness to the king. United States Fidelity & Guaranty Co. v. Carter, 161 Va. 381, 170 S.E. 764, 768.

Extent in chief. In old English law, a summary process by which the king's action was commenced against his debtor and his body, personal property (tangible and intangible), and lands at once seized for the satisfaction of the king's debt. The principal kind of extent, issuing at the suit of the crown, for the recovery of the crown's debt. Abolished by Crown Proceedings Act (1947). An adverse proceeding by the king, for the recovery of his own debt.

Extent of such payment. Under statute extending right of subrogation to Federal Deposit Insurance Corporation, phrase "to the extent of such payment" is equivalent to term "pro tanto" or words "as to the portion of the deposit paid". Federal Deposit Ins. Corporation v. Citizens State Bank of Niangua, C.C.A.Mo., 130 F.2d 102, 103.

Extenuate /əkstényuweyt/. To lessen; to palliate; to mitigate.

Extenuating circumstances. Such as render a delict or crime less aggravated, heinous, or reprehensible than it would otherwise be, or tend to palliate or lessen its guilt. Such circumstances may ordinarily be shown in order to reduce the punishment or damages. See also **Extraordinary circumstances.**

Extenuation. That which renders a crime or tort less heinous than it would be without it. It is opposed to aggravation. See **Extenuating circumstances.**

Exterior. On the outside, external, pertaining to the outside part. Northwestern Casualty & Surety Co. v. Barzune, Tex.Civ.App., 42 S.W.2d 100, 103. The surface outside.

External. Apparent, outward, visible from the outside, patent, exterior, capable of being perceived. Acting from without, as the external surface of a body; physical or corporeal, as distinguished from mental or moral. Provident Life & Accident Ins. Co. v. Campbell, 18 Tenn.App. 452, 79 S.W.2d 292, 296. In double indemnity clause of life policy, the term "external" applies to the force or means and not to the injury. Hanna v. Rio Grande Nat. Life Ins. Co., Tex.Civ.App., 181 S.W.2d 908, 911.

External, violent and accidental means. Death through "external, violent and accidental means" necessarily implies that death did not result indirectly from disease or bodily infirmity. Mutual Life Ins. Co. of New York v. Hassing, C.C.A.10, 134 F.2d 714, 716.

Exterritoriality. The privilege of those persons (such as foreign ministers) who, though temporarily resident within a country, are not subject to the operation of its laws. The exemption from the operation of the ordinary laws of the country accorded to foreign monarchs temporarily within the country and their retinue, to diplomatic agents and the members of their household, and to others of similar position and rank. See **Capitulation; Extraterritoriality.**

Exterus /ékstərəs/. Lat. A foreigner or alien; one born abroad. The opposite of *civis.*

Exterus non habet terras /ékstərəs nòn héybət téhrəs/. An alien holds no lands.

Ex testamento /èks tèstəméntow/. From, by, or under a will. The opposite of *ab intestato (q.v.).*

Extinct. Extinguished. No longer in existence or use. Lacking a claimant. A rent is said to be extinguished when it is destroyed and put out. See **Extinguishment.**

Extincto subjecto, tollitur adjunctum /əkstíŋktow səbjéktow tólədər əjáŋktəm/. When the subject [or substance] is extinguished, the incident [or adjunct] ceases. Thus, when the business for which a partnership has been formed is completed, or brought to an end, the partnership itself ceases.

Extinguish. To bring or put an end to. Onondaga Water Service Corporation v. Crown Mills, Inc., 132 Misc. 848, 230 N.Y.S. 691, 698. To terminate or cancel. To put out, quench, stifle, as to extinguish a fire or flame. See also **Cancellation; Termination.**

Extinguishment. The destruction or cancellation of a right, power, contract, or estate. The annihilation of a collateral thing or subject in the subject itself out of which it is derived. See **Cancellation.**

"Extinguishment" is sometimes confounded with "merger," though there is a clear distinction between them. "Merger" is only a mode of extinguishment, and applies to estates only under particular circumstances; but "extinguishment" is a term of general application to rights, as well as estates. "Extinguishment" connotes the end of a thing, precluding the existence of future life therein; in "mergers" there is a carrying on of the substance of the thing, except that it is merged into and becomes a part of a separate thing with a new identity. McRoberts v. McRoberts, 177 Okl. 156, 57 P.2d 1175, 1177.

Extinguishment of common. In English law, loss of the right to have common, which could happen from various causes.

Extinguishment of copyhold. In English law, a copyhold is said to be extinguished when the freehold and copyhold interests unite in the same person and in the same right, which may be either by the copyhold interest coming to the freehold or by the freehold interest coming to the copyhold.

Extinguishment of debts. This takes place by payment; by accord and satisfaction; by novation, or the substitution of a new debtor; by merger, when the creditor recovers a judgment or accepts a security of a higher nature than the original obligation; by a release; and where one of the parties, debtor or creditor, makes the other his executor. See also **Bankruptcy.**

Extinguishment of legacy. This occurs in case the identical thing bequeathed is not in existence, or has been disposed of so that it does not form part of the testator's estate, at the time of his death. See **Ademption.**

Extinguishment of lien. Discharge by operation of law.

Extinguishment of rent. If a person have a yearly rent of lands, and afterwards purchase those lands, so that he has as good an estate in the land as in the rent, the rent is extinguished. Rent may also be extinguished by conjunction of estates, by confirmation, by grant, by release, and by surrender.

Extinguishment of ways. This is usually effected by unity of possession, as if a man had a way over the close of another, and he purchased that close, the way is extinguished.

Extirpation /èkstərpéyshən/. In English law, a species of destruction or waste, analogous to estrepement. See **Estrepement.**

Extirpatione /èkstərpèyshiyówniy/. A judicial writ, either before or after judgment, that lay against a person who, when a verdict was found against him for land, etc., maliciously overthrew any house or extirpated any trees upon it.

Extorsively /əkstórsəvliy/. A technical word used in indictments for extortion.

Extort. To compel or coerce, as a confession or information by any means serving to overcome one's power of resistance, thus making the confession or admis-sion involuntary. To gain by wrongful methods; to obtain in an unlawful manner, as to compel payments by means of threats of injury to person, property, or reputation. To exact something wrongfully by threats or putting in fear. The natural meaning of the word "extort" is to obtain money or other valuable thing either by compulsion, by actual force, or by the force of motives applied to the will, and often more overpowering and irresistible than physical force. See also **Extortion,** *infra.*

Extortio est crimen quando quis colore officii extorquet quod non est debitum, vel supra debitum, vel ante tempus quod est debitum /ekstórsh(iy)ow èst kráymən kwóndow kwis kəlóriy əfíshiyay əkstórkwət kwòd nón èst débədəm, vèl s(y)úwprə débədəm, vèl æntiy témpəs kwód èst débədəm/. Extortion is a crime when, by color of office, any person extorts that which is not due, or more than is due, or before the time when it is due.

Extortion. The obtaining of property from another induced by wrongful use of actual or threatened force, violence, or fear, or under color of official right. 18 U.S.C.A. § 871 et seq.; § 1951.

A person is guilty of theft by extortion if he purposely obtains property of another by threatening to: (1) inflict bodily injury on anyone or commit any other criminal offense; or (2) accuse anyone of a criminal offense; or (3) expose any secret tending to subject any person to hatred, contempt or ridicule, or to impair his credit or business repute; or (4) take or withhold action as an official, or cause an official to take or withhold action; or (5) bring about or continue a strike, boycott or other collective unofficial action, if the property is not demanded or received for the benefit of the group in whose interest the actor purports to act; or (6) testify or provide information or withhold testimony or information with respect to another's legal claim or defense; or (7) inflict any other harm which would not benefit the actor. Model Penal Code, § 223.4.

See also **Blackmail; Hobbs Act; Loan sharking; Shakedown.** With respect to "Larceny by extortion", see **Larceny.**

Extortionate credit. See **Loanshark.**

Ex tota materia emergat resolutio /èks tówdə mətíriyə əmárgət rèzəl(y)úwsh(iy)ow/. The explanation should arise out of the whole subject-matter; the exposition of a statute should be made from all its parts together.

It has also been defined as corrupt demanding or receiving by a person in office of a fee for services which should be performed gratuitously; or, where compensation is permissible, of a larger fee than the law justifies, or a fee not due.

Term applies to persons who exact money either for the performance of a duty, the prevention of injury, or the exercise of influence, and covers the obtaining of money or other property by operating on fear or credulity, or by promise to conceal the crimes of others. Term in comprehensive or general sense signifies any oppression under color of right, and in strict or technical sense signifies unlawful taking by any officer, under color of office, of any money or thing of value not due him, more than is due, or before it is due.

See also **Blackmail; Hobbs Act; Loanshark; Shakedown.**

For the distinction between "extortion" and "exaction," see **Exaction.**

Extra /ékstrə/. A Latin preposition, occurring in many legal phrases, and meaning beyond, except, without, out of, outside. Additional.

Extra allowance. In New York practice, a sum in addition to costs, which may, in the discretion of the court, be allowed to the successful party in cases of unusual difficulty. Hascall v. King, 54 App.Div. 441, 66 N.Y.S. 1112.

Extra commercia /ékstrə kəmársh(i)(i)yə/. Property once dedicated to public use is "extra commercia".

Extract, *v.* To draw out or forth; to pull out from a fixed position.

Extract, *n.* A portion or segment of a writing.

Extracta curiæ /əkstrǽktə kyúriyiy/. In old English law, the issues or profits of holding a court, arising from the customary fees, etc.

Extradition. The surrender by one state or country to another of an individual accused or convicted of an offense outside its own territory and within the territorial jurisdiction of the other, which, being competent to try and punish him, demands the surrender. U.S.Const., Art. IV, § 2; 18 U.S.C.A. § 3181 *et seq.* Most states have adopted the Uniform Criminal Extradition Act. See also **Interstate rendition; Rendition.**

Extra dividend. Dividend paid by corporation in cash or stock beyond that which is regularly paid. See also **Ex dividend; Extraordinary dividend.**

Extra-dotal property. In Louisiana this term is used to designate that property which forms no part of the dowry of a woman, and which is also called "paraphernal property." Fleitas v. Richardson, 147 U.S. 550, 13 S.Ct. 495, 37 L.Ed. 276.

Extra feodum /ékstrə fíy(ə)dəm/. Out of his fee; out of the seigniory, or not holden of him that claims it.

Extrahazardous. In the law of insurance, means conditions of special and unusual danger.

Extrahura /èkstrəhyúrə/. In old English law, an animal wandering or straying about, with an owner; an estray.

Extrajudicial /èkstrəjuwdíshəl/. That which is done, given, or effected outside the course of regular judicial proceedings. Not founded upon, or unconnected with, the action of a court of law, as *e.g.* extrajudicial evidence, or an extrajudicial oath.

That which, though done in the course of regular judicial proceedings, is unnecessary to such proceedings, or interpolated, or beyond their scope; as an extrajudicial opinion *(dictum).*

That which does not belong to the judge or his jurisdiction, notwithstanding fact that he takes cognizance of it.

Extrajudicial confession /èkstrəjuwdíshəl kənféshən/. See **Confession.**

Extrajudicial evidence. That which is used to satisfy private persons as to facts requiring proof.

Extrajudicial oath. One taken not in the course of judicial proceedings, or taken without any authority of law, though taken formally before a proper person.

Extrajudicial statement. Any utterance, written or oral, made outside of court. It is governed by the hearsay rule and its exceptions when offered in court as evidence.

Extra judicium /ékstrə jədísh(iy)əm/. Extrajudicial; out of the proper cause; out of court; beyond the jurisdiction. See **Extrajudicial.**

Extra jus /ékstrə jəs/. Beyond the law; more than the law requires.

Extralateral right. In mining law, the right of the owner of a mining claim duly located on the public domain to follow, and mine, any vein or lode the apex of which lies within the boundaries of his location on the surface, notwithstanding the course of the vein on its dip or downward direction may so far depart from the perpendicular as to extend beyond the planes which would be formed by the vertical extension downwards of the side lines of his location.

Extra legem /ékstrə líyjəm/. Out of the law; out of the protection of the law.

Extra legem positus est civiliter mortuus /ékstrə líyjəm pózədəs èst səvílədər mórchuwəs/. He who is placed out of the law is civilly dead. International Bank v. Sherman, 101 U.S. 403, 25 L.Ed. 866.

Extramural /èkstrəmyúrəl/. As applied to the powers of a municipal corporation, its "extramural" powers are those exercised outside the corporate limits, as distinguished from "intramural".

Extranational. Beyond the territorial and governing limits of a country. See also **Extraterritorial.**

Extraneous evidence. With reference to a contract, deed, will, or any writing, extraneous evidence is such as is not furnished by the document itself, but is derived from outside sources; the same as evidence *aliunde.* See also **Aliunde; Parol evidence rule.**

Extraneous offense. One that is extra, beyond, or foreign to the offense for which the party is on trial. Ridinger v. State, 146 Tex.Cr.R. 286, 174 S.W.2d 319, 320.

Extraneous questions. Issues which are beyond or beside the point to be decided.

Extraneus /əkstréyniyəs/. In old English law, one foreign born; a foreigner.

In Roman law, an heir not born in the family of the testator. Those of a foreign state. The same as *alienus.*

Extraneus est subditus qui extra terram, *i.e.*, potestatem regis natus est /əkstréyniyəs èst səbdədəs kwày ékstrə téhrəm, íd èst, pòwdəstéydəm ríyjəs néydəs èst/. A foreigner is a subject who is born out of the territory, *i.e.*, government of the king.

Extraordinary. Out of the ordinary; exceeding the usual, average, or normal measure or degree; beyond or out of the common order or rule; not usual, regular, or of a customary kind; remarkable; uncommon; rare. Courtney v. Ocean Accident & Guaranty Corporation, 346 Mo. 703, 142 S.W.2d 858, 861. The word is both comprehensive and flexible in meaning. Beyond or out of the common order or method; exceeding the ordinary degree; not ordinary; unusual; employed for an exceptional purpose or on a special occasion. As a noun it is defined as something extraordinary, especially, an extraordinary expense or allowance. State v. Rogers, 142 Kan. 841, 52 P.2d 1185, 1195.

Extraordinary designates an accident, casualty, occurrence or risk of a class or kind other than those which ordinary experience or prudence would foresee, anticipate or provide for. Western & Atlantic Ry. Co. v. Hassler, 92 Ga.App. 278, 88 S.E.2d 559, 562.

Extraordinary average. A contribution by all the parties concerned in a commercial voyage, either as to the vessel or cargo, toward a loss sustained by some of the parties in interest for the benefit of all.

Extraordinary care. Synonymous with greatest care, utmost care, highest degree of care. See **Care; Diligence; Negligence.**

Extraordinary circumstances. Factors of time, place, etc., which are not usually associated with a particular thing or event; out of the ordinary factors. See also **Extenuating circumstances.**

Extraordinary danger. Danger or risk of employment, not ordinarily incident to the service. The "extraordinary circumstances" justifying federal equitable intervention in pending state criminal prosecution must be extraordinary in the sense of creating an extraordinary pressing need for immediate federal equitable relief, not merely in the sense of presenting a highly unusual factual situation. Kugler v. Helfant, N.J., 421 U.S. 117, 95 S.Ct. 1524, 1531, 44 L.Ed.2d 15. See also **Extraordinary hazard.**

Extraordinary dividend. Dividend of corporation which is nonrepetitive and generally paid at irregular time because of some unusual corporate event (*e.g.* unusually high profits). An "extraordinary dividend" is distinguished from an "ordinary dividend" or "regular dividend" in that it is not declared from ordinary profits arising out of regular course of business of corporation and is generally declared by reasons of unusually large income or unexpected increment in capital assets due to fortuitous conditions or circumstances occurring outside of activities and control of corporation but advantageous to corporation either in stepping up its product and sales or in giving added value to its property. In re Bank of N. Y. & Fifth Ave. Bank, 105 N.Y.S.2d 211, 217, 222. See also **Extra dividend.**

Cash disbursements by "wasting asset" companies are apportioned as "extraordinary dividends" where they represent, in part at least, distribution of proceeds of capital assets.

Extraordinary expenses. This term in a constitutional provision that the state may incur indebtedness for extraordinary expenses, means other than ordinary expenses and such as are incurred by the state for the promotion of the general welfare, compelled by some unforeseen condition which is not regularly provided for by law, such as flood, famine, fire, earthquake, pestilence, war, or any other condition that will compel the state to put forward its highest endeavors to protect the people, their property, liberty, or lives.

Extraordinary flood. One of those unexplained occurrences whose coming is not foreshadowed by the usual course of nature, and whose magnitude and destructiveness could not have been anticipated or provided against by the exercise of ordinary foresight. Jensen v. Buffalo Drainage Dist. of Cloud County, 148 Kan. 712, 84 P.2d 961, 965. One of such unusual occurrence that it could not have been foreseen by men of ordinary experience and prudence.

Extraordinary grand jury. Such jury is limited in scope of its investigation which may not go beyond terms of executive proclamation, and examination of witness must be confined within those terms, and must not be used as a means of disclosing or intermeddling with extraneous matters.

Extraordinary hazard. One not commonly associated with a job or undertaking. If hazards are increased by what other employees do, and injured employee has no part in increasing them, they are "extraordinary". Stone v. Howe, 92 N.H. 425, 32 A.2d 484, 487. See also **Extraordinary risk.**

Extraordinary remedies. The writs of *mandamus, quo warranto, habeas corpus,* and some others are often classified or termed "extraordinary remedies," in contradistinction to the ordinary remedy by action.

Under Rules practice in most states, most extraordinary "writs" have been abolished. In any action seeking relief formerly obtainable under any such writ, the procedure shall follow that of a regular action.

Extraordinary repairs. Within the meaning of a lease, such as are made necessary by some unusual or unforeseen occurrence which does not destroy the building but merely renders it less suited to the use for which it was intended. Courtney v. Ocean Accident & Guaranty Corporation, 346 Mo. 703, 142 S.W.2d 858, 861. In lease provisions for "extraordinary" repairs, word "extraordinary" means beyond or out of common order of rule, not the usual, customary or regular kind, not ordinary. Atlanta & St. A. B. Ry. Co. v. Chilean Nitrate Sales Corp., D.C.Fla., 277 F.Supp. 242, 246.

Extraordinary risk. An "extraordinary risk" is one lying outside of the sphere of the normal, arising out of conditions not usual in the business. It is one which is not normally and necessarily incident to the employment. It is one which may be obviated by the exercise of reasonable care by the employer. See also **Extraordinary hazard.**

Extraordinary session. A legislative session, called usually by the governor, which meets in the interval between regular sessions. In most States such sessions are limited to the consideration of matters specified in the governor's call. See also **Extra session,** *supra.*

Extraordinary storm. One which is not necessarily an unprecedented one, but one that happens so rarely that it is unusual and not ordinarily to be expected. Oklahoma City v. Evans, 173 Okl. 586, 50 P.2d 234, 238. See also **Extraordinary flood.**

Extraordinary writs. See **Extraordinary remedies.**

Extraparochial /èkstrəpərówkiyəl/. In English law, out of a parish; not within the bounds or limits of any parish.

Extrapolation. The process of estimating an unknown number outside the range of known numbers. Term sometimes used in cases when a court deduces a principle of law from another case.

Extra præsentiam mariti /ékstrə prəzénsh(iy)əm mǽrəday/. Out of her husband's presence.

Extra quatuor maria /ékstrə kwóduwər mǽriyə/. Beyond the four seas; out of the kingdom of England.

Extra regnum /ékstrə régnəm/. Out of the realm.

Extra session. After a Legislature has adjourned or prorogued, it may be recalled for an additional session by the Governor to deal with matters which could not be considered during the regular term. Also, a court may provide additional court sessions to eliminate or reduce a case backlog. See also **Extraordinary session.**

Extraterritorial. Beyond the physical and juridical boundaries of a particular state or country. See **Extraterritoriality.**

Extraterritoriality. The extraterritorial operation of laws; that is, their operation upon persons, rights, or jural relations, existing beyond the limits of the enacting state or nation, but still amenable to its laws. A term used, especially formerly, to express, in lieu of the word exterritoriality the exemption from the obligation of the laws of a state granted to foreign diplomatic agents, warships, etc. The term is used to indicate jurisdiction exercised by a nation in other countries by treaty, or by its own ministers or consuls in foreign lands. Crime is said to be extraterritorial when committed in a state or country other than that of the forum in which the party is tried.

Extraterritorial jurisdiction. Juridical power which extends beyond the physical limits of a particular state or country. See **Long-arm statutes.**

Extra territorium /ékstrə tèhrətóriyəm/. Beyond or without the territory.

Extra territorium jus dicenti impune non paretur /ékstrə tèhrətóriyəm jə́s dəséntay ìmpyúwniy nòn pəríydər/. One who exercises jurisdiction out of his territory is not obeyed with impunity. He who exercises judicial authority beyond his proper limits cannot be obeyed with safety.

Extravagantes /èkstrəvəgǽntiyz/. In canon law, those decretal epistles which were published after the Clementines. They were so called because at first they were not digested or arranged with the other papal constitutions, but seemed to be, as it were, detached from the canon law. They continued to be called by the same name when they were afterwards inserted in the body of the canon law. The first extravagantes are those of Pope John XXII, successor of Clement V. The last collection was brought down to the year 1483, and was called the "Common Extravagantes," notwithstanding that they were likewise incorporated with the rest of the canon law.

Extra viam /ékstrə váyəm/. Outside the way. In common law pleading, where the defendant in trespass pleaded a right of way in justification, and the replication alleged that the trespass was committed outside the limits of the way claimed, these were the technical words to be used.

Extra vires /ékstrə váyriyz/. Beyond powers. See **Ultra** (Ultra vires).

Extra work. As used in connection with construction contract, means work done not required in performance of the contract, i.e. something done or furnished in addition to or in excess of the requirement of the contract. Work entirely outside and independent of contract—something not required or contemplated in its performance.

Extra work, for which a contractor is entitled to charge additional compensation, depends on construction of the original contract, and generally means only labor and materials not contemplated by or embraced in terms of the original contract. Trinity Builders, Inc. v. Schaff, N.D., 199 N.W.2d 914, 918. Such work is usually defined as being work not foreseen at time of entrance into contract. W. R. Ferguson, Inc. v. William A. Berbusse, Jr., Inc., Del.Super., 216 A.2d 876, 879. Materials and labor not contemplated by the contract, but which are required by changes in the plans and specifications made after the contract had been entered into, are "extra work". Collins v. Hall, Tex.Civ.App., 161 S.W.2d 311, 314.

Extreme. At the utmost point, edge, or border; most remote. Last; conclusive. Greatest, highest, strongest, or the like. Immoderate; violent.

Extreme case. One in which the facts or the law or both reach the outer limits of probability; desperate.

Extreme cruelty. Extreme cruelty authorizing divorce may consist of personal injury or physical violence or it may be acts or omissions of such character as to destroy peace of mind or impair bodily or mental health of person upon whom inflicted or be such as to destroy the objects of matrimony. Schlueter v. Schlueter, 158 Neb. 233, 62 N.W.2d 871, 876.

Extreme low tide. Tides which are lower than lower low. State v. Edwards, 188 Wash. 467, 62 P.2d 1094, 1095.

Extremis /(ìn) əkstríyməs/. When a person is sick, beyond the hope of recovery, and near death, he is said to be in *extremis.*

Extremis probatis, præsumuntur media /əkstríyməs prəbéydəs, prìyzyəmántər míydiyə/. Extremes being proved, intermediate things are presumed.

Extremity. The furthest point, section, or part. Limb of the body (hand or foot). Extreme danger or need. Desperate act or measure.

Extrinsic. Foreign; from outside sources; *dehors.* As to "Extrinsic fraud", see **Fraud.**

Grounds for quashing of indictment may be matters "intrinsic" to the pleading, as defects apparent upon its face. United States v. Frankfeld, D.C.D.C., 38 F.Supp. 1018, 1019.

Extrinsic ambiguity. In a written contract, such is an uncertainty which does not arise by the terms of the instrument itself, but is created by some collateral matter not appearing in the instrument. Pacific Indemnity Co. v. California Electric Works, 29 Cal. App.2d 260, 84 P.2d 313, 320.

Extrinsic evidence. External evidence, or that which is not contained in the body of an agreement, contract, and the like. Extrinsic evidence is also said to be evidence not legitimately before the tribunal in which the determination is made. See **Parol evidence rule.**

Ex turpi causa non oritur actio /èks tárpay kózə nòn órədər ǽksh(iy)ow/. Out of a base [illegal, or immoral] consideration, an action does [can] not arise.

Ex turpi contractu actio non oritur /èks tárpay kəntrǽkchuw ǽksh(iy)ow nòn órədər/. From an immoral or iniquitous contract an action does not arise. A contract founded upon an illegal or immoral consideration cannot be enforced by action.

Exuere patriam /əgz(y)úwəriy pǽtriyəm/. To throw off or renounce one's country or native allegiance; to expatriate one's self.

Exulare /ègzəlériy/. In old English law, to exile or banish. *Nullus liber homo, exuletur, nisi,* etc., no freeman shall be exiled, unless, etc.

Ex una parte /èks yúwnə párdiy/. Of one part or side; on one side.

Ex uno disces omnes /èks yúwnow dísiyz ómniyz/. From one thing you can discern all.

Exuperare /egz(y)ùwpərériy/. To overcome; to apprehend or take.

Ex utraque parte /èks yuwtréykwiy párdiy/. On both sides.

Ex utrisque parentibus conjuncti /èks yuwtrískwiy pəréntəbəs kənjə́ŋktay/. Related on the side of both parents; of the whole blood.

Ex visceribus /èks vəséhrəbəs/. From the bowels. From the vital part, the very essence of the thing. *Ex visceribus verborum,* from the mere words and nothing else.

Ex visitatione Dei /èks vìzəteyshiyówniy díyay/. By the dispensation of God; by reason of physical incapacity. Anciently, when a prisoner, being arraigned, stood silent instead of pleading, a jury was impaneled to inquire whether he obstinately stood mute or was dumb *ex visitatione Dei.*

Also by natural, as distinguished from violent, causes. When a coroner's inquest finds that the death was due to disease or other natural cause, it is frequently phrased *"ex visitatione Dei."*

Ex visu scriptionis /èks váysyuw skrìpshiyównəs/. From sight of the writing; from having seen a person write. A term employed to describe one of the modes of proof of handwriting.

Ex vi termini /èks váy tə́rmənay/. From or by the force of the term. From the very meaning of the expression used. 2 Bl.Comm. 109, 115.

Ex voluntate /èks vòləntéydiy/. Voluntarily; from free will or choice.

Ex warrants. A security is traded ex warrants when sold without warrants which have been retained by seller.

Eyde /éyd/. Aid; assistance; relief. A subsidy.

Eyewitness. A person who could testify as to what he had seen. Wigginton v. Order of United Commercial Travelers of America, C.C.A.Ind., 126 F.2d 659, 662, 665, 666, 667. One who saw the act, fact, or transaction to which he testifies. Distinguished from an ear-witness *(auritus).* Pannell v. Sovereign Camp, W. O. W., 171 Tenn. 245, 102 S.W.2d 50, 52. Persons able to testify from their observation. Hayes v. Stunkard, 233 Iowa 582, 10 N.W.2d 19.

Eyewitness identification. Type of evidence by which one who has seen the event testifies as to the person or persons involved from his own memory of the event. See also **Lineup.**

Eygne /éyn/. The same as "eigne" *(q.v.).*

Eyre /ér/. A journey; a court of itinerant justices.

Justices in eyre were judges commissioned in Anglo-Norman times in England to travel systematically through the kingdom, once in seven years, holding courts in specified places for the trial of certain descriptions of causes.

Eyrer /érər/. L. Fr. To travel or journey; to go about or itinerate.

F

F. Under the old English criminal law, this letter was branded upon felons upon their being admitted to clergy; as also upon those convicted of fights or frays, or falsity. Federal Reporter, First Series.

F.2d. Federal Reporter, Second Series.

F.A.A. Federal Aviation Administration. In maritime insurance means: "Free of all average", denoting that the insurance is against total loss only.

Fabrica /fǽbrəkə/. In old English law, the making or coining of money.

Fabricare /fæbrəkériy/. Lat. To make. Used in old English law of a lawful coining, and also of an unlawful making or counterfeiting of coin. Used in an indictment for forging a bill of lading.

Fabricate. To invent; to devise falsely.

Fabricated evidence. Evidence manufactured or arranged after the fact, and either wholly false or else warped and discolored by artifice and contrivance with a deceitful intent. To fabricate evidence is to arrange or manufacture circumstances or *indicia,* after the fact committed, with the purpose of using them as evidence, and of deceitfully making them appear as if accidental or undesigned. To devise falsely or contrive by artifice with the intention to deceive. Such evidence may be wholly forged and artificial, or it may consist in so warping and distorting real facts as to create an erroneous impression in the minds of those who observe them and then presenting such impression as true and genuine. See also **Fabricated fact.**

Fabricated fact. In the law of evidence, a fact existing only in statement, without any foundation in truth. An actual or genuine fact to which a false appearance has been designedly given; a physical object placed in a false connection with another, or with a person on whom it is designed to cast suspicion. See also **Deceit; Fraud.**

Fabric lands. In old English law, lands given towards the maintenance, rebuilding, or repairing of cathedral and other churches.

Fabula /fǽbyələ/. In old European law, a contract or formal agreement; particularly used in the Lombardic and Visigothic laws to denote a marriage contract or a will.

Face. The surface of anything, especially the front, upper, or outer part or surface. That which particularly offers itself to the view of a spectator. The words of a written paper in their apparent or obvious meaning, as, the face of a note, bill, bond, check, draft, judgment record, or contract. The face of a judgment for which it was rendered exclusive of interest. Cunningham v. Great Southern Life Ins. Co., Tex.Civ.App., 66 S.W.2d 765, 773.

Face amount. The face amount of an instrument is that shown by the mere language employed, and excludes any accrued interest. See **Face of instrument; Face value.**

Face amount insured by the policy. Within statute relating to extended life insurance, means the amount which is, in all events, payable under the policy as straight life insurance without regard to additional features such as accident or disability insurance. Wilkins v. Metropolitan Life Ins. Co., 350 Mo. 185, 165 S.W.2d 858, 861, 862; Wilkins v. Metropolitan Life Ins. Co., 236 Mo.App. 586, 159 S.W.2d 354, 356. See also **Face of policy; Face value.**

Face of instrument. That which is shown by the language employed, without any explanation, modification, or addition from extrinsic facts or evidence. Investors' Syndicate v. Willcuts, D.C.Minn., 45 F.2d 900, 902. Thus, if the express terms of the paper disclose a fatal legal defect, it is said to be "void on its face." Regarded as an evidence of debt, the face of an instrument is the principal sum which it expresses to be due or payable, without any additions in the way of interest or costs.

Face of judgment. The sum for which it was rendered, exclusive of interest.

Face of policy. A phrase which, as used in a statute forbidding life insurance policies to contain provision for any mode of settlement at maturity of less value than the amount insured on the "face of the policy," does not mean merely the first page, but denotes the entire insurance contract contained in the policy, including a rider attached and referred to on the first page. See also **Face value.**

Face of record. The entire record in a case, not merely what the judgment recites. Every part of trial proceedings reserved in courts of record under direction of court for purpose of its records. Permian Oil Co. v. Smith, 129 Tex. 413, 107 S.W.2d 564, 566. The "face of the record" means, in a criminal case, the indictment and the verdict. See also **Record.**

Facere /féysəriy/. Lat. To do; to make. Thus, *facere defaltam,* to make default; *facere duellum,* to make the duel, or make or do battle; *facere finem,* to make or pay a fine; *facere legem,* to make one's law; *facere sacramentum,* to make oath.

Face value. The value stated on the face of a security or insurance policy. This is the value at maturity or death. The value upon which interest is computed. The value which can be ascertained from the language of the instrument without aid from extrinsic facts or evidence. Investors' Syndicate v. Willcuts, D.C.Minn., 45 F.2d 900, 902. See also **Face amount.**

Facial disfigurement. That which impairs or injures the beauty, symmetry, or appearance of a person. That which renders unsightly, misshapen or imperfect or deforms in some manner. Ferguson v. State Highway Department, 197 S.C. 520, 15 S.E.2d 775, 778.

Facias /féys(h)(i)yəs/. That you cause.

Occurring in the phrases *"scire facias"* (that you cause to know), *"fieri facias"* (that you cause to be made), etc. Used also in the phrases *Do ut facias* (I give that you may do), *Facio ut facias* (I do that you may do), two of the four divisions of considerations made by Blackstone, 2 Comm. 444. See **Facio ut des; Facio ut facias.**

Facie. See **Facies.**

Faciendo /fèys(h)iyéndow/. In doing or paying; in some activity.

Facies /féys(h)iy(iy)z/. Lat. The face or countenance; the exterior appearance or view; hence, contemplation or study of a thing on its external or apparent side. Thus, *prima facie* means at the first inspection, on a preliminary or exterior scrutiny. When we speak of a *"prima facie* case," we mean one which, on its own showing, on a first examination, or without investigating any alleged defenses, is apparently good and maintainable.

Facilitate. To free from difficulty or impediment. Pon Wing Quong v. United States, C.C.A.Cal., 111 F.2d 751, 756. To make easier or less difficult; free more or less completely from obstruction or hindrance; lessen the labor of. United States v. One Dodge Coupe, Motor No. D14–105424, Serial No. 30284066, D.C.N.Y., 43 F.Supp. 60, 61. See also **Facilitation; Facilities.**

Facilitation. In criminal law, the act of making it easier for another to commit crime; *e.g.* changing of cars to evade police officer who has suspect under surveillance and thus to enable a clandestine transfer of contraband to take place would constitute "facilitation" within forfeiture statute. U. S. v. One (1) Chevrolet Corvette Auto. Serial No. 194371S121113, C.A. Fla., 496 F.2d 210, 212.

Facilities. That which promotes the ease of any action, operation, transaction, or course of conduct. The term normally denotes inanimate means rather than human agencies, though it may also include animate beings such as persons, people and groups thereof. Cheney v. Tolliver, 234 Ark. 973, 356 S.W.2d 636, 638.

The word "facilities" embraces anything which aids or makes easier the performance of the activities involved in the business of a person or corporation. Hartford Electric Light Co. v. Federal Power Commission, C.C.A.2, 131 F.2d 953, 960, 961, 962.

A name formerly given to certain notes of some of the banks in the state of Connecticut, which were made payable in two years after the close of the war of 1812. Springfield Bank v. Merrick, 14 Mass. 322.

Facility. Something that is built or installed to perform some particular function, but it also means something that promotes the ease of any action or course of conduct. Raynor v. American Heritage Life Ins. Co., 123 Ga.App. 247, 180 S.E.2d 248, 250. See also **Facilities.**

Facility of payment clause. Appointment by insured and beneficiary of persons authorized to receive payment. French v. Lanham, 61 App.D.C. 56, 57 F.2d 422. It confers on insurer an option as to whom it will make payment, Metropolitan Life Ins. Co. v. Brown for Use and Benefit of Fleming, 25 Tenn.App. 514, 160 S.W.2d 434, 438; Rohde v. Metropolitan Life Ins. Co., 233 Mo.App. 865, 111 S.W.2d 1006. Such clause in group policy giving employer under certain contingencies power to designate beneficiary controls only where no other beneficiary is named. Potter v. Young, 193 Ark. 957, 104 S.W.2d 802, 804.

Facinus quos inquinat æquat /fǽsənəs kwòws íŋkwənəd íykwət/. Guilt makes equal those whom it stains.

Facio ut des /féys(h)(i)yow ət díyz/. Lat. I do that you may give. A species of contract in the civil law (being one of the *innominate* contracts) which occurs when a man agrees to perform anything for a price either specifically mentioned or left to the determination of the law to set a value on it; as when a servant hires himself to his master for certain wages or an agreed sum of money. 2 Bl.Comm. 445. Also, the consideration of that species of contract.

Facio ut facias /féys(h)(i)yow ət féys(h)(i)yəs/. Lat. I do that you may do. The consideration of that species of contract in the civil law, or the contract itself (being one of the *innominate* contracts), which occurs when I agree with a man to do his work for him if he will do mine for me; or if two persons agree to marry together, or to do any other positive acts on both sides; or it may be to forbear on one side in consideration of something done on the other. 2 Bl.Comm. 444.

Facsimile /fæksíməliy/. An exact copy, preserving all the marks of the original.

Facsimile probate. In England, where the construction of a will may be affected by the appearance of the original paper, the court will order the probate to pass in *facsimile,* as it may possibly help to show the meaning of the testator.

Facsimile signature. One which has been prepared and reproduced by some mechanical or photographic process. Many states have adopted the Uniform Facsimile Signatures of Public Officials Act.

Fact. A thing done; an action performed or an incident transpiring; an event or circumstance; an actual occurrence; an actual happening in time space or an event mental or physical; that which has taken place. City of South Euclid v. Clapacs, 6 Ohio Misc. 101, 213 N.E.2d 828, 832. A fact is either a state of things, that is, an existence, or a motion, that is, an event. The quality of being actual; actual existence or occurrence.

Evidence. A circumstance, event or occurrence as it actually takes or took place; a physical object or appearance, as it usually exists or existed. An actual and absolute reality, as distinguished from mere supposition or opinion. A truth, as distinguished from fiction or error. "Fact" means reality of events or things the actual occurrence or existence of which is to be determined by evidence. Peoples v. Peoples, 10 N.C.App. 402, 179 S.E.2d 138, 141. Under Rule of Civil Procedure 41(b), providing for motion for dismissal at close of plaintiff's evidence in nonjury case on ground that upon the facts and the law plaintiff has shown no right to relief, the "facts" referred to are the prima facie facts shown by plaintiff's evidence viewed in light most favorable to him. Schad v. Twentieth Century-Fox Film Corporation, C.C.A. Pa., 136 F.2d 991, 993.

Fact and law distinguished. "Fact" is very frequently used in opposition or contrast to "law". Thus, questions of *fact* are for the jury; questions of *law* for the court. Fraud *in fact* consists in an actual intention to defraud, carried into effect; while fraud imputed by *law* arises from the man's conduct in its necessary relations and consequences. A "fact", as distinguished from the "law", may be taken as that out of which the point of law arises, that which is asserted to be or not to be, and is to be presumed or proved to be or not to be for the purpose of applying or refusing to apply a rule of law. Hinckley v. Town of Barnstable, 311 Mass. 600, 42 N.E.2d 581, 584. Law is a principle; fact is an event. Law is conceived; fact is actual. Law is a rule of duty; fact is that which has been according to or in contravention of the rule. See **Fact question.**

See also Collateral facts; Dispositive facts; Evidentiary fact; Fabricated fact; Fact question; **Finding** *(Finding of fact)*; Material fact; **Principal** *(Principal fact)*; Ultimate facts.

Facta /fǽktə/. In old English law, deeds. *Facta armorum,* deeds or feats of arms; that is, jousts or tournaments.

Facta sunt potentiora verbis /fǽktə sənt pətènshiyórə várbəs/. Deeds [or facts] are more powerful than words.

Facta tenent multa quæ fieri prohibentur /fǽktə ténənt máltə kwìy fáyərày pròwhəbéntər/. Deeds contain many things which are prohibited to be done.

Fact finding board. A group or committee appointed by business or government to investigate and report facts concerning some event or situation.

Factio testamenti /fǽksh(iy)ow tèstəméntay/. In the civil law, the right, power, or capacity of making a will; called *"factio activa."*

The right or capacity of taking by will; called *"factio passiva."*

Fact material to risk. See **Material fact.**

Facto /fǽktow/. In fact; by an act; by the act or fact. *Ipso facto,* by the act itself; by the mere effect of a fact, without anything superadded, or any proceeding upon it to give it effect.

Facto et animo /fǽktow èd ǽnəmow/. In fact and intent.

Factor. A commercial agent, employed by a principal to sell merchandise consigned to him for that purpose, for and in behalf of the principal, but usually in his own name, being entrusted with the possession and control of the goods, and being remunerated by a commission, commonly called "factorage." A commercial agent to whom the possession of personalty is entrusted by or for the owner, to be sold, for a compensation, in pursuance of the agent's usual trade or business, with title to goods remaining in principal and the "factor" being merely a bailee for the purposes of the agency. Neild v. District of Columbia, 71 App.D.C. 306, 110 F.2d 246, 259. See also **Commission merchant.**

Any circumstance or influence which brings about or contributes to a result such as a factor of production.

Broker and factor distinguished. A factor differs from a "broker" in that he is entrusted with the possession, management, and control of the goods (which gives him a special property in them); while a broker acts as a mere intermediary without control or possession of the property. A factor may buy and sell in his own name, as well as in that of the principal, while a broker, as such, cannot ordinarily buy or sell in his own name.

Factorage /fǽkt(ə)rəj/. The wages, allowance, or commission paid to a factor for his services. The business of a factor.

Factoring. Sale of accounts receivable of a firm to a factor at a discounted price. The purchase of accounts receivable from a business by a factor who thereby assumes the risk of loss in return for some agreed discount. Manhattan Factoring Corp. v. Orsburn, 238 Ark. 947, 385 S.W.2d 785, 790.

A system involving notice to the trade debtors, confined principally to the textile industry. Corn Exchange Nat. Bank & Trust Co., Philadelphia v. Klauder, 318 U.S. 434, 63 S.Ct. 679, 682, 87 L.Ed. 884.

Factorizing process. A process by which the effects of a debtor are attached in the hands of a third person. More commonly termed "trustee process", "garnishment", and process by "foreign attachment".

Factors' acts. The name given to several English statutes (6 Geo. IV, c. 94; 5 & 6 Vict., c. 39; 40 & 41 Vict., c. 39) by which a factor was enabled to make a valid pledge of the goods, or of any part thereof, to one who believed him to be the *bona fide* owner of the goods. Similar legislation is not uncommon in the United States.

Factor's lien. The right (usually provided by statute) of a factor to keep possession of his principal's merchandise until the latter has settled his account with him.

Factory acts. Laws enacted for the purpose of regulating the hours of work, and the health and safety conditions. See *e.g.* **Fair Labor Standards Act; Occupational Safety and Health Act; Wage and Hour Laws.**

Factory prices. The prices at which goods may be bought at the factories, as distinguished from the prices of goods bought in the market after they have passed into the hands of wholesalers or retailers.

Fact question. Those issues in a trial or hearing which concern facts or events and whether such occurred and how they occurred as contrasted with issues and questions of law. Fact questions are for the jury, unless the issues are presented at a bench trial, while law questions are decided by the judge. Fact questions and their findings are generally not appealable though rulings of law are subject to appeal.

Facts. See **Fact.**

Facts incomplete. A certificate of trial judge to bill of exceptions not certifying to correctness of any recital therein and only certifying that the bill is "facts incomplete", that is, not finished, not perfect, defective, verifies nothing and brings nothing before the Court of Appeals for review. Loving v. Kamm, Ohio App., 34 N.E.2d 591.

Facts in issue. Those matters of fact on which the plaintiff proceeds by his action, and which the defendant controverts in his defense. Under civil rule practice in the federal courts, and in most state courts, the facts alleged in the initial complaint are usually quite brief, with the development of additional facts being left to discovery and pretrial conference.

Facts well pleaded. Those of a substantive nature necessary to the framing of the issue submitted. Bushman v. Barlow, 321 Mo. 1052, 15 S.W.2d 329, 331.

Factum /fǽktəm/. A fact, event, doing. A statement of facts.

Civil law. Fact; a fact; a matter of fact, as distinguished from a matter of law.

French law. A memoir which contains concisely set down the fact on which a contest has happened, the means on which a party founds his pretensions, with the refutation of the means of the adverse party.

Old English law. A deed; a person's act and deed. A culpable or criminal act; an act not founded in law. Anything stated or made certain; a deed of conveyance; a written instrument under seal: called, also, *charta.* 2 Bl.Comm. 295. A fact; a circumstance; particularly a fact in evidence. *Factum probandum* (the fact to be proved).

Old European law. A portion or allotment of land; otherwise called a hide, *bovata,* etc.

Testamentary law. The execution or due execution of a will. The *factum* of an instrument means not merely the signing of it, and the formal publication or delivery, but proof that the party well knew and understood the contents thereof, and did give, will, dispose, and do, in all things, as in the said will is contained. Weatherhead's Lessee v. Baskerville, 52 U.S. (11 How.) 329, 13 L.Ed. 717.

Factum a judice quod ad ejus officium non spectat non ratum est /fǽktəm èy júwdəsiy, kwòd ǽd íyjəs əfísh(iy)əm nòn spéktət, nòn réydəm èst/. An action of a judge which relates not to his office is of no force.

Factum cuique suum non adversario, nocere debet /fǽktəm k(yuw)áykwiy s(y)úwəm nòn ædvərsériyow, nósəriy débət/. A party's own act should prejudice himself, not his adversary.

Factum infectum fieri nequit /fǽktəm ənféktəm fáyəráy nékwət/. A thing done cannot be undone.

Factum juridicum /fǽktəm jərídəkəm/. A juridical fact. Denotes one of the factors or elements constituting an obligation.

Factum negantis nulla probatio sit /fǽktəm nəgǽntəs nálə prəbéysh(iy)ow sít/. There is no proof incumbent upon him who denies a fact.

"Factum" non dicitur quod non perseverat /fǽktəm nòn dísədər kwòd nòn pərsəvírət/. That is not called a "deed" which does not continue operative. That is not said to be done which does not last.

Factum probandum /fǽktəm prəbǽndəm/. Lat. In the law of evidence, the fact to be proved; a fact which is in issue, and to which evidence is to be directed.

Factum probans /fǽktəm prówbæn(d)z/. A probative or evidentiary fact; a subsidiary or connected fact tending to prove the principal fact in issue; a piece of circumstantial evidence.

Factum unius alteri noceri non debet /fǽktəm yənáyəs óltəray nəsíriy nòn débət/. The deed of one should not hurt another.

Facultas probationum non est angustanda /fəkáltæs prəbèyshiyównəm nòn est ǽngəstǽndə/. The power of proofs [right of offering or giving testimony] is not to be narrowed.

Facultative compensation /fǽkəltèydəv kòmpənséyshən/. That which operates by the will of the parties, when one of them removes an obstacle preventing compensation, resulting from the dispositions of the law.

Facultative reinsurance /fǽkəltèydəv rìyənshúrən(t)s/. Under type designated "facultative", the reinsurer has the option of accepting the tendered part of the original insurer's risk. Lincoln Nat. Life Ins. Co. v. State Tax Commission, 196 Miss. 82, 16 So.2d 369.

Faculties /fǽkəltiyz/. Abilities; powers; capabilities. In the law of divorce, the capability of the husband to render a support to the wife in the form of alimony, whether temporary or permanent, including not only his tangible property, but also his income and his ability to earn money. See **Allegation of faculties.**

Faculties, Court of. In English ecclesiastical law, a jurisdiction or tribunal belonging to the archbishop. It does not hold pleas in any suits, but creates rights to pews, monuments, and particular places, and modes of burial. It has also various powers under 25 Hen. VIII, c. 21, in granting licenses of different descriptions, as a license to marry, a faculty to erect an organ in a parish church, to level a church-yard, to remove bodies previously buried. Faculties are also granted by Consistory Courts.

Faculties, Master of the. An official in the archdiocese of Canterbury who is head of the Court of Faculties. See **Arches Court.**

Faculty. Ability; power; capability. Teaching staff of school. See also **Faculties.**

Faderfium /fáðərfiyəm/. In old English law, a marriage gift coming from the father or brother of the bride.

Fade the game. Means that spectators of a game of "craps" bet on the success of actual participants. Sullivan v. State, 146 Tex.Cr.R. 79, 171 S.W.2d 353.

Fæder-feoh /fáðərfiy/. In old English law, the portion brought by a wife to her husband, and which reverted to a widow, in case the heir of her deceased husband refused his consent to her second marriage; *i.e.*, it reverted to her family in case she returned to them.

Fæsting-men /fǽstiŋmèn/. Approved men who were strong-armed; *habentes homines* or rich men, men of substance; pledges or bondsmen, who, by Saxon custom, were bound to answer for each other's good behavior.

Faggot. A badge worn in early times by persons who had recanted and abjured what was then adjudged to be heresy, as an emblem of what they had merited.

Faggot vote. A term applied in England to votes manufactured by nominally transferring land to persons otherwise disqualified from voting for members of parliament. A faggot vote occurred where a man was formally possessed of a right to vote for members of parliament, without possessing the substance which the vote should represent; as if he was enabled to buy a property, and at the same moment mortgage it to its full value, for the mere sake of the vote.

Faida /fáyðə/. In Saxon law, malice; open and deadly hostility; deadly feud. The word designated the enmity between the family of a murdered man and that of his murderer, which was recognized, among the Teutonic peoples, as justification for vengeance taken by any one of the former upon any one of the latter.

Fail. Fault, negligence, or refusal. Fall short; be unsuccessful or deficient. Fading health. See **Extremis.**

Fail also means: involuntarily to fall short of success or the attainment of one's purpose; to become insolvent and unable to meet one's obligations as they mature; to become or be found deficient or wanting; to keep or cease from an appointed, proper, expected, or required action, Romero v. Department of Public Works, 17 Cal.2d 189, 109 P.2d 662, 665; to lapse, as a legacy which has never vested or taken effect; to leave unperformed; to omit; to neglect; to be wanting in action. See also **Failure; Lapse.**

Failing circumstances. Insolvency, that is, the lack of sufficient assets to pay one's debts. A person (or a corporation or institution) is said to be in failing circumstances when he is about to fail, that is, when he is actually insolvent and is acting in contemplation of giving up his business because he is unable to carry it on.

A bank is in "failing circumstances" when, from any cause, it is unable to pay its debts in the ordinary or usual course of business, Sanders v. Owens, Mo. App., 47 S.W.2d 132, 134; when in state of uncertainty as to whether it will be able to sustain itself, depending on favorable or unfavorable contingencies, over which its officers have no control. Graf v. Allen, 230 Mo.App. 721, 74 S.W.2d 61, 66. See also **Failure to meet obligations.**

Faillite /fayíyt/. In French law, bankruptcy; failure; the situation of a debtor who finds himself unable to fulfill his engagements.

Failure. Abandonment or defeat. Failure of duty or obligation. Lapse. Deficiency, want, or lack; ineffectualness; inefficiency as measured by some legal standard; an unsuccessful attempt. See also **Fail; Lapse.**

Failure of consideration. As applied to notes, contracts, conveyances, etc., this term does not necessarily mean a want of consideration, but implies that a consideration, originally existing and good, has since become worthless or has ceased to exist or been extinguished, partially or entirely. It means that sufficient consideration was contemplated by the parties at time contract was entered into, but either on account of some innate defect in the thing to be given or nonperformance in whole or in part of that which the promisee agreed to do or forbear nothing of value can be or is received by the promisee. Holcomb v. Long Beach Inv. Co., 129 Cal.App. 285, 19 P.2d 31, 36. It occurs where the thing expected to be received by one party and given by the other party cannot be or has not been given without fault of the party contracting to give it.

Failure to execute a promise the performance of which has been exchanged for performance by other party. Taliaferro v. Davis, 216 Cal.App.2d 398, 31 Cal.Rptr. 164, 172.

Failure of evidence. See **Failure of proof.**

Failure of good behavior. As enumerated in statute as ground for removal of a civil service employee, means behavior contrary to recognized standards of propriety and morality, misconduct or wrong conduct. State ex rel. Ashbaugh v. Bahr, 68 Ohio App. 308, 40 N.E.2d 677, 680, 682.

Failure of issue. Dying without children. The failure at a fixed time, or the total extinction, of issue to take an estate limited over by an executory devise. A definite failure of issue is when a precise time is fixed by the will for the failure of issue, as in the case where there is a devise to one, but if he dies without issue or lawful issue living at the time of his death, etc. An indefinite failure of issue is the period when the issue or descendants of the first taker shall become extinct, and when there is no longer any issue of the issue of the grantee, without reference to any particular time or any particular event. See also **Dying without issue.**

Failure of justice. The defeat of a particular right, or the failure of reparation for a particular wrong, from the lack or inadequacy of a legal remedy for the enforcement of the one or the redress of the other. The term is also colloquially applied to the miscarriage of justice which occurs when the result of a trial is so palpably wrong as to shock the moral sense. See also **Miscarriage of justice.**

Failure of proof. A "failure of proof" consists in failure to prove the cause of action or defense in its entire scope and meaning. Breslin-Griffitt Carpet Co. v. Asadorian, Mo.App., 145 S.W.2d 494, 496.

Where evidence is such as would support either of two contradictory inferences, or presumptions, respecting the ultimate facts, there is a "failure of proof". Muesenfechter v. St. Louis Car Co., Mo. App., 139 S.W.2d 1102, 1106.

See **Directed verdict; Failure to state cause of action; Non obstante verdicto; Summary judgment.**

Failure of record. Failure of the defendant to produce a record which he has alleged and relied on in his plea.

Failure of title. The inability or failure of a vendor to make good title to the whole or a part of the property which he has contracted to sell. See also **Cloud on title; Curing title; Marketable title.**

Failure of trust. The lapsing or nonefficiency of a proposed trust, by reason of the defect or insufficiency of the deed or instrument creating it, or on account of illegality, indefiniteness, or other legal impediment.

Failure otherwise than upon merits. Phrase imports some action by court by which plaintiff is defeated without a trial upon the merits; *e.g.* judgment on pleadings, summary judgment.

Failures in revenue. Terms "casual deficits" and "failures in revenue," within provision authorizing legislature to contract debt to meet such deficits, are synonymous. State Budget Commission v. Lebus, 244 Ky. 700, 51 S.W.2d 965.

Failure to bargain collectively. An employer's refusal to discuss with union, as employees' bargaining agency, questions involving conditions of employment and interpretation of contract constitutes a "failure to bargain collectively" with union. Rapid Roller Co. v. National Labor Relations Board, C.C.A.7, 126 F.2d 452, 459.

Failure to make delivery. Misdelivery or nondelivery. This phrase is fully adequate to cover all cases where delivery has not been made as required. Georgia, F. & A. Ry. Co. v. Blish Milling Co., 241 U.S. 190, 36 S.Ct. 541, 543, 60 L.Ed. 948.

Failure to meet obligations. Bank's failure to pay depositors on demand constitutes "failure to meet obligations" in most cases. Where bank closed its doors and ceased to transact business or make transfers of capital stock, and thereafter ordinary deposits could not be drawn out and checks in process of collection were dishonored, returned unpaid, was "failure to meet obligations". State of Ohio ex rel. Squire v. Union Trust Co. of Pittsburgh, 137 Pa.Super. 75, 8 A.2d 476, 480. See also **Failing circumstances; Insolvency.**

Failure to perform. As regards reciprocal promises, allegation of defendant's "failure to perform" when demanded is equivalent to allegation of "refusal to perform," unless performance by plaintiff is condition precedent to cause of action. Brooks v. Scoville, 81 Utah 163, 17 P.2d 218, 220.

Failure to state cause of action. Failure of the plaintiff to allege enough facts in the complaint. Even if the plaintiff proved all the facts alleged in the complaint, the facts would not establish a cause of action entitling the plaintiff to recover against the defendant. The motion to dismiss for failure to state a cause of action is sometimes referred to as (a) a demurrer (*e.g.* California) or (b) a failure to state a claim upon which relief can be granted. Fed.R.Civ.P. 12(b). See also **Directed verdict; Summary judgment.**

Failure to testify. In criminal trial, defendant is not required to testify and such failure may not be commented on by judge or prosecution because of protection of Fifth Amendment, U.S.Const. Griffin v. California, 380 U.S. 609, 85 S.Ct. 1229, 14 L.Ed.2d 106. See also **Self incrimination.**

Faint (or feigned) action. In old English practice, an action was so called where the party bringing it had no title to recover, although the words of the writ were true. See also **Feigned action.**

Faint pleader. A fraudulent, false, or collusive manner of pleading to the deception of a third person.

Fair. Having the qualities of impartiality and honesty; free from prejudice, favoritism, and self-interest. Just; equitable; even-handed; equal, as between conflicting interests. See also **Equitable; Reasonable.**

A gathering of buyers and sellers for purposes of exhibiting and sale of goods; usually accompanied by amusements, contests, entertainment, and the like.

In England, a greater species of market; a privileged market. It is an incorporeal hereditament, granted by royal patent, or established by prescription presupposing a grant from the crown. A public mart or place of buying or selling. 1 Bl.Comm. 274. In the earlier English law, the franchise to hold a fair conferred certain important privileges; and fairs, as legally recognized institutions, possessed distinctive legal characteristics. Most of these privileges and characteristics, however, are now obsolete. In America, fairs, in the ancient technical sense, are unknown, and, in the modern and popular sense, they are entirely voluntary and nonlegal, and transactions arising in or in connection with them are subject to the ordinary rules governing sales, etc.

Fair and impartial jury. Means that every member of the jury must be a fair and impartial juror. City of San Antonio v. McKenzie Const. Co., 136 Tex. 315, 150 S.W.2d 989, 993. See **Fair and impartial trial.**

Fair and impartial trial. One where accused's legal rights are safeguarded and respected. Raney v. Commonwealth, 287 Ky. 492, 153 S.W.2d 935, 937, 938. A fair and impartial trial by a jury of one's peers contemplates counsel to look after one's defense, compulsory attendance of witnesses, if need be, and a reasonable time in the light of all prevailing circumstances to investigate, properly prepare, and present the defense. One wherein defendant is permitted to be represented by counsel and neither witnesses nor counsel are intimidated. One wherein no undue advantage is taken by the district attorney or any one else. People v. Nationwide News Service, 172 Misc. 752, 16 N.Y.S.2d 277, 279. One wherein witnesses of litigants are permitted to testify under rules of court within proper bounds of judicial discretion, and under law governing testimony of witnesses with right in parties to testify, if qualified, and of counsel to be heard. It requires that the jury chosen to sit in judgment shall have no fixed opinion concerning the guilt or innocence of one on trial. Baker v. Hudspeth, C.C.A.Kan., 129 F.2d 779, 782, 783. There must not only be fair and impartial jury, and learned and upright judge, but there should be atmosphere of calm in which witnesses can deliver their testimony without fear and intimidation, in which attorneys can assert accused's rights freely and fully, and in which the truth may be received and given credence without fear of violence. Raney v. Commonwealth, 287 Ky. 492, 153 S.W.2d 935, 937, 938. See also **Fair trial; Impartial jury.**

Fair and proper legal assessment. Such as places the value of property on a fair, equal, and uniform basis with other property of like character and value throughout the county and state.

Fair and reasonable value. See **Fair market value; Fair value; Just compensation.**

Fair and valuable consideration. One which is a substantial compensation for the property conveyed, or which is reasonable, in view of the surrounding circumstances and conditions, in contradistinction to an inadequate consideration. Lucas v. Coker, 189 Okl. 95, 113 P.2d 589, 590. See also **Fair market value; Fair value; Just compensation.**

Fair averaging. In tax assessment, means average, typical of amount and price of goods acquired over twelve month period. Sears Roebuck & Co. v. State Tax Commission, 214 Md. 550, 136 A.2d 567.

Fair cash market value. Terms "cash market value", "fair market value", "reasonable market value" or "fair cash market value" are substantially synonymous. Fort Worth & D. N. Ry. Co. v. Sugg, Tex.Civ. App., 68 S.W.2d 570, 572.

Fair cash value. The phrase is practically synonymous with "reasonable value," "fair market value," and "actual cash value," meaning the fair or reasonable cash price for which the property can be sold on the market. Fair cash value for property tax purposes is interpreted as meaning "fair market value" or price that property would bring at a sale where both parties are willing, ready and able to do business and under no duress to do so. Consolidation Coal Co. v. Property Tax Appeal Bd. of Dept. of Local Government Affairs, 29 Ill.App.3d 465, 331 N.E.2d 122, 126.

For tax purposes "fair cash value", means the highest price the property would bring free of incumbrances, at a fair and voluntary private sale for cash. Commonwealth v. Sutcliffe, 287 Ky. 809, 155 S.W.2d 243, 245. The price that an owner willing but not compelled to sell ought to receive from one willing but not compelled to buy. Assessors of Quincy v. Boston Consolidated Gas Co., 309 Mass. 60, 34 N.E.2d 623, 626. The price that the property would bring at a voluntary sale where the owner is ready, willing and able to sell but not compelled to do so. In re 168 Adams Bldg. Corporation, C.C.A.Ill., 105 F.2d 704, 708. The price which someone will pay for it in open market.

See also **Fair market value; Fair value; Just compensation.**

Fair comment. A term used in the law of libel, applying to statements made by a writer in an honest belief of their truth, relating to official acts, even though the statements are not true in fact. Defense of "fair comment" is not destroyed by circumstance that jury may believe that the comment is logically unsound, but it suffices that a reasonable man may honestly entertain such opinion, on facts found. Cohalan v. New York Tribune, 172 Misc. 20, 15 N.Y.S.2d 58, 60, 61. Fair comment must be based on facts truly stated, must not contain imputations of corrupt or dishonorable motives except as warranted by the facts, and must be honest expression of writer's real opinion. Cohalan v. New York World-Telegram Corporation, 172 Misc. 1061, 16 N.Y.S.2d 706, 712; Hall v. Binghamton Press Co., 263 A.D. 403, 33 N.Y.S.2d 840, 848. Imputation to official of corrupt or dishonorable motives is justified as "fair comment" if it is inference which fair-minded man might reasonably draw from facts. Tanzer v. Crowley Pub. Corporation, 240 App.Div. 203, 268 N.Y.S. 620.

See also **Fairness or equal time doctrine.**

Fair competition. Open, equitable, just competition, which is fair as between competitors and as between any of them and his customers. See **Clayton Act; Sherman Antitrust Act.**

Fair consideration. A fair equivalent. One which, under all the circumstances, is honest, reasonable, and free from suspicion. Full and adequate consideration. Good-faith satisfaction of an antecedent debt. One which fairly represents the value of the property transferred. One which is not disproportionate to the value of the property conveyed. See also **Adequate consideration; Fair cash value; Fair market value; Fair value; Just compensation.**

Fair Credit Billing Act. Federal Act designed to facilitate settlement of billing error disputes and to make credit card companies more responsible for the quality of merchandise purchased by cardholders. 15 U.S. C.A. § 1666 et seq.

Fair Credit Reporting Acts. *Federal Act.* This law represents the first Federal regulation of the vast consumer reporting industry, covering all credit bureaus, investigative reporting companies, detective and collection agencies, lenders' exchanges, and computerized information reporting companies. The purpose of this Act is to insure that consumer reporting activities are conducted in a manner that is fair and equitable to the affected consumer, upholding his right to privacy as against the informational demands of others. The consumer is given several important new rights, including the right to notice of reporting activities, the right to access to information contained in consumer reports, and the right to correction of erroneous information that may have been the basis for a denial of credit, insurance, or employment. 15 U.S.C.A. § 1681 et seq.

State Acts. Typical state acts cover consumer's rights against credit investigatory agencies; prohibit reporting of obsolete information; require that person giving credit disclose to consumer that report is being obtained, and require reporting agency to make copy available to consumer.

Fair equivalent. As used in statute providing that fair consideration is given for property exchanged at fair equivalent means value at time of conveyance. "Equivalent" means equal in worth or value; "fair" means equitable as a basis for exchange; reasonable; a fair value.

Fair hearing. One in which authority is fairly exercised; that is, consistently with the fundamental principles of justice embraced within the conception of due process of law. Contemplated in a fair hearing is the right to present evidence, to cross examine, and to have findings supported by evidence.

Fair hearing of an alien's right to enter the United States means a hearing before the immigration officers in accordance with the fundamental principles that inhere in due process of law, and implies that alien shall not only have a fair opportunity to present evidence in his favor, but shall be apprised of the evidence against him, so that at the conclusion of the hearing he may be in a position to know all of the evidence on which the matter is to be decided; it being not enough that the immigration officials meant to be fair.

The test of a "fair hearing" before the National Labor Relations Board is whether the issues were clearly defined, so that the employer could address itself to the charges made against it. National Labor Relations Board v. Air Associates, C.C.A.N.Y., 121 F.2d 586, 591.

See also **Fair trial.**

Fair knowledge or skill. A reasonable degree of knowledge or measure of skill.

Fair Labor Standards Act. Federal Act (1938) which set a minimum standard wage (periodically increased by later statutes) and a maximum work week of 40 hours in industries engaged in interstate commerce. Such Act also prohibited the labor of children under 16 in most employments, and under 18 in dangerous occupations. The Act created the Wage and Hour Division in the Department of Labor.

Fairly. Equitably, honestly, impartially, reasonably. Looney v. Elliott, Tex.Civ.App., 52 S.W.2d 949, 952. Justly; rightly. With substantial correctness. "Fairly merchantable" conveys the idea of mediocrity in quality, or something just above it. See also **Equitable; Fair.**

Fair market price. See **Fair market value.**

Fair market value. The amount at which property would change hands between a willing buyer and a willing seller, neither being under any compulsion to buy or sell and both having reasonable knowledge of the relevant facts. By fair market value is meant the price in cash, or its equivalent, that the property would have brought at the time of taking, considering its highest and most profitable use, if then offered for sale in the open market, in competition with other similar properties at or near the location of the property taken, with a reasonable time allowed to find a purchaser. State, by Commissioner of Transp. v. Cooper Alloy Corp., 136 N.J.Super. 560, 347 A.2d 365, 368. Fair market value is the price that the asset would bring by bona fide bargaining between well-informed buyers and sellers at the date of acquisition.

Usually the fair market price will be the price at which bona fide sales have been consummated for assets of like type, quality, and quantity in a particular market at the time of acquisition. The amount of money which purchaser who is willing but not obligated to buy would pay owner who is willing but not obligated to sell, taking into consideration all uses to which the land is adapted and might in reason be applied. Arkansas State Highway Commission v. DeLaughter, 250 Ark. 990, 468 S.W.2d 242, 247.

Synonymous or identical terms are: Actual cash value, Stiles v. Commissioner of Internal Revenue, C.C.A.Fla., 69 F.2d 951, 952; actual value, Appeals of Matson, 152 Pa.Super. 424, 33 A.2d 464, 465; cash market value, West Texas Hotel Co. v. City of El Paso, Tex.Civ.App., 83 S.W.2d 772, 775; fair cash market value, Housing Authority of Birmingham Dist. v. Title Guarantee Loan & Trust Co., 243 Ala. 157, 8 So.2d 835, 837; fair cash value, Commissioner of Corporations and Taxation v. Boston Edison Co., 310 Mass. 674, 39 N.E.2d 584, 593; market value, Fort Worth & D. N. Ry. Co. v. Sugg, Tex.Civ.App., 68 S.W.2d 570, 572; United States v. 3969.59 Acres of Land, D.C.Idaho, 56 F.Supp. 831, 837; reasonable market value, Housing Authority of Birmingham Dist. v. Title Guarantee Loan & Trust Co., 243 Ala. 157, 8 So.2d 835, 837; true cash value, Appeals of Matson, 152 Pa.Super. 424, 33 A.2d 464, 465; value, United States v. 3969.59 Acres of Land, D.C.Idaho, 56 F.Supp. 831, 837.

See also **Fair value.**

Fairness or **equal time doctrine.** This doctrine imposes affirmative responsibilities on the broadcaster to provide coverage of issues of public importance which is adequate and which fairly reflects differing viewpoints. Columbia Broadcasting System, Inc. v. Democratic National Committee, Dist.Col., 412 U.S. 94, 93 S.Ct. 2080, 2089, 36 L.Ed.2d 772. Section of Federal Communications Act which provides that major advocates of both sides of political and public issues should be given fair or equal opportunity to broadcast their viewpoints. 47 U.S.C.A. § 315. See also **Equal Time Act.**

Fair on its face. A tax deed "fair on its face," is one which cannot be shown to be illegal without extraneous evidence. Denny v. Stevens, 52 Wyo. 253, 73 P.2d 308, 310. A process fair on its face does not mean that it must appear to be perfectly regular or in all respects in accord with proper practice and after the most approved form, but that it shall apparently be process lawfully issued and such as the officer may lawfully serve, and a process is fair on its face which proceeds from a court, magistrate, or body having authority of law to issue process of that nature and which is legal in form and on its face contains nothing to notify or fairly apprise the officer that it is issued without authority.

Fair persuasion. Argument, exhortation, or entreaty addressed to a person without threat of physical harm or economic loss, or persistent molestation or harassment or material and fraudulent misrepresentations. City of Reno v. Second Judicial District Court in and for Washoe County, 59 Nev. 416, 95 P.2d 994, 998.

Fair play. Equity, justice and decency in dealings with another. See **Equity.**

Fair pleader. See **Beau pleader.**

Fair preponderance of evidence. Evidence sufficient to create in the minds of the triers of fact the conviction that the party upon whom is the burden has established its case. The greater and weightier evidence; the more convincing evidence. Belmont Hotel v. New Jersey Title Guaranty & Trust Co., 22 N.J.Misc. 261, 37 A.2d 681, 682. Such a superiority of evidence on one side that the fact of its outweighing the evidence on the other side can be perceived if the whole evidence is fairly considered. Such evidence as when weighed with that which is offered to oppose it, has more convincing power in the minds of the jury. The term conveys the idea of something more than a preponderance. The term is not a technical term, but simply means that evidence which outweighs that which is offered to oppose it, and does not necessarily mean the greater number of witnesses.

Fair rent. A reasonable rent. Shapiro v. Goldstein, 113 Misc. 258, 185 N.Y.S. 234.

Fair return on investment. A net return upon fair value of property. State ex rel. City of St. Louis v. Public Service Commission, 341 Mo. 920, 110 S.W.2d 749, 778. A "fair return" is to be largely measured by usual returns in like investments in the same vicinity over the same period of time. Natural Gas Pipeline Co. of America v. Federal Power Commission, C.C.A. Ill., 120 F.2d 625, 633, 634. Reasonable profit on sale or holding of investment assets. A fair return on value of property used and useful in carrying on the enterprise, performing the service or supplying the thing for which the rates are paid. Lubin v. Finkelstein, 82 N.Y.S.2d 329, 335. Term is generally used in reference to setting of rates for public utilities.

Fair sale. In foreclosure and other judicial proceedings, this means a sale conducted with fairness and impartiality as respects the rights and interests of the parties affected. A sale at a price sufficient to warrant confirmation or approval when it is required.

Fair trade laws. State statutes which permit manufacturers or distributors of namebrand goods to fix minimum retail prices. Following a series of court decisions striking down such statutes, Congress in 1976 repealed such statutes.

Fair trial. A hearing by an impartial and disinterested tribunal; a proceeding which hears before it condemns, which proceeds upon inquiry, and renders judgment only after trial consideration of evidence and facts as a whole. A basic constitutional guarantee contained implicitly in the Due Process Clause of Fourteenth Amendment, U.S. Constitution.

A legal trial or one conducted in all material things in substantial conformity to law. Stacey v. State, 79 Okl.Cr. 417, 155 P.2d 736, 739. A trial which insures substantial justice. A trial without prejudice to the accused. An orderly trial before an impartial jury and judge whose neutrality is indifferent to every factor in trial but that of administering justice. One conducted according to due course of law. A trial before an impartial judge, an impartial jury, and in an atmosphere of judicial calm. In such trial the judge may and should direct and control the proceedings, and may exercise his right to comment on the evidence, yet he may not extend his activities so far as to become in effect either an assisting prosecutor or a thirteenth juror. Goldstein v. U. S., C.C.A.Mo., 63

F.2d 609, 613. An adequate hearing and an impartial tribunal, free from any interest, bias, or prejudice. The Reno, C.C.A.N.Y., 61 F.2d 966, 968. See also **Fair and impartial trial.**

Fair use doctrine. "Fair use" is privilege in other than owner of copyright to use copyrighted material in reasonable manner without consent, notwithstanding monopoly granted to the owner. Meeropol v. Nizer, D.C.N.Y., 361 F.Supp. 1063, 1067. Section 107 of the Copyright Act sets forth factors to be considered in determining whether the use made in any particular case is "fair use."

Fair value. Present market value; such sum as the property will sell for to a purchaser desiring to buy, the owner wishing to sell; such a price as a capable and diligent business man could presently obtain from the property after conferring with those accustomed to buy such property; the amount the property would bring at a sale on execution shown to have been in all respects fair and reasonable; the fair market value of the property as between one who wants to purchase and one who wants to sell the property. Where no definite market value can be established and expert testimony must be relied on, fair valuation is the amount which the property ought to give to a going concern as a fair return, if sold to some one who is willing to purchase under ordinary selling conditions. In determining "fair valuation" of property, court should consider all elements entering into the intrinsic value, as well as the selling value, and also the earning power of the property. In re Gibson Hotels, D.C.W.Va., 24 F.Supp. 859, 863. In determining depreciation, "fair value" implies consideration of all factors material in negotiating sale and purchase of property, such as wear, decay, deterioration, obsolescence, inadequacy, and redundancy. Idaho Power Co. v. Thompson, D.C.Idaho, 19 F.2d 547, 566. Price which a seller, willing but not compelled to sell, would take, and a purchaser, willing but not compelled to buy, would pay. Price which buyers of the class which would be interested in buying property would be justified in paying for it. In re Crane's Estate, 344 Pa. 141, 23 A.2d 851, 855.

Within provision of business corporation act for determination of fair value of dissenting stockholder's shares, "fair value" means intrinsic value. Santee Oil Co., Inc. v. Cox, 265 S.C. 270, 217 S.E.2d 789, 793. Among elements to be considered in arriving at "fair value" or "fair cash value" of stock of a stockholder who dissents from a sale of corporate assets are its market value, net asset value, investment value, and earning capacity. Lucas v. Pembroke Water Co., 205 Va. 84, 135 S.E.2d 147, 150.

"Actual value," "market value," "fair value," and the like, are commonly used as convertible terms. See also **Fair market value.**

Fait /féyt/. L. Fr. Anything done. A deed; act; fact. A deed lawfully executed.

Fait accompli. Factor deed accomplished, presumably irreversible.

Fait enrolle /féyt ònrówl/. A deed enrolled, as a bargain and sale of freeholds.

Faith. Confidence; credit; reliance. Thus, an act may be said to be done "on the faith" of certain representations.

Belief; credence; trust. Thus, the Constitution provides that "full faith and credit" shall be given to the judgments of each state in the courts of the others.

Purpose; intent; sincerity; state of knowledge or design. This is the meaning of the word in the phrases "good faith" and "bad faith." See **Good faith.**

Faithful. Honest; loyal; trustworthy; reliable; allegiant; conscientious. Wright v. Fidelity & Deposit Co. of Maryland, 176 Okl. 274, 54 P.2d 1084, 1087.

As used in the rule that executors must be "faithful," means that they must act in good faith. In re McCafferty's Will, 147 Misc. 179, 264 N.Y.S. 38. Where a public officer gives a bond for the "faithful" discharge of his duties, "faithful" implies that he has assumed that measure of responsibility laid on him by law had no bond been given. London & Lancashire Indemnity Co. of America v. Community Savings & Loan Ass'n, 102 Ind.App. 665, 4 N.E.2d 688, 693.

Faithfully. Conscientious diligence or faithfulness in meeting obligations, or just regard of adherence to duty, or due observance of undertaking of contract. Commonwealth v. Polk, 256 Ky. 100, 75 S.W.2d 761, 765. Diligently, and without unnecessary delay. Truthfully, sincerely, accurately.

As used in bonds of public and private officers, this term imports not only honesty, but also a punctilious discharge of all the duties of the office, requiring competence, diligence, and attention, without any malfeasance or nonfeasance, aside from mere mistakes.

Fait juridique /féy zhyùridíyk/. In French law, a juridical fact. One of the factors or elements constitutive of an obligation.

Faitours /féytərz/. Idle persons; idle livers; vagabonds.

Fake. To make or construct falsely. A "faked alibi" is a made, manufactured, or false alibi. Something that is not what it purports to be; counterfeit. An imposter. See **Counterfeit; Forgery.**

Faker. A petty swindler.

Fakir /fèykír/féykər/. A term applied among the Mohammedans to a kind of religious ascetic or beggar, whose claim is that he "is in need of mercy, and poor in the sight of God, rather than in need of worldly assistance."

Sometimes spelled *faqueer* or *fakeer*. It is commonly used to designate a person engaged in some useless or dishonest business. Fake is also so used and also to designate the quality of such business. A street peddler who disposes of worthless wares, or of any goods above their value, by means of any false representation, trick, device, lottery, or game of chance.

Falcarious. See **Falsarius.**

Falcidia /fòlsídiyə/fǽl°/. In Spanish law, the Falcidian portion; the portion of an inheritance which could not be legally bequeathed away from the heir, viz., one-fourth.

Falcidian law /fòlsídiyən ló/fǽl°/. In Roman law, a law on the subject of testamentary disposition. It was enacted by the people during the reign of Augustus, in the year of Rome 714, on the proposition of the tribune Falcidius. By this law, the testator's right to burden his estate with legacies was subjected to an important restriction. It prescribed that no one could bequeath more than three-fourths of his property in legacies, and that the heir should have at least one-fourth of the estate, and that, should the testator violate this prescript, the heir may have the right to make a proportional deduction from each legatee, so far as necessary.

A similar principle exists in Louisiana. See **Legitime.** In some of the states the statutes authorizing bequests and devises to charitable corporations limit the amount which a testator may give, to a certain fraction of his estate.

Falcidian portion /fòlsídiyən pórshən/fǽl°/. That portion of a testator's estate which, by the Falcidian law, was required to be left to the heir, amounting to at least one-fourth. See also **Legitime.**

Faldworth. In Saxon law, a person reckoned old enough to become a member of the decennary, and so subject to the law of frank-pledge.

Falk-land. See **Folc-land.**

Fall. One of the four seasons of the year, embracing, in the Northern Hemisphere, the three months commencing with the 1st of September and terminating with the last day of November. Autumn.

To come within limits, scope, or jurisdiction of something. To decrease in value. To recede, as a depression or recession in the economy.

Fallo /fá(l)yow/. In Spanish law, the final decree or judgment given in a controversy at law.

Fallopian tube. An essential part of the female reproductive system, consisting of a narrow conduit, some four inches in length, that extends on each side of a woman's body from the base of the womb to the ovary upon that side.

Fallow /fǽlow/. Barren or unproductive. May v. American Trust Co., 135 Cal.App. 385, 27 P.2d 101. Not pregnant.

Fallow-land. Land plowed, but not sown, and left uncultivated for a time after successive crops. Land tilled, but left unseeded during the growing season.

Fallum. In old English law, an unexplained term for some particular kind of land.

Falsa demonstratio /fólsə dèmənstréysh(iy)ow/. In the civil law, false designation; erroneous description of a person or thing in a written instrument.

Falsa demonstratione legatum non perimi /fólsə dèmənstrèyshiyówniy ləgéydəm nòn péhrəmay/. A bequest is not rendered void by an erroneous description.

Falsa demonstratio non nocet, cum de corpore (persona) constat /fólsə dèmənstréysh(iy)ow nòn nósət, kàm dìy kórpəriy (pərsównə) kónstət/. False description does not injure or vitiate, provided the thing or person intended has once been sufficiently described. Mere false description does not make an instrument inoperative.

Falsa grammatica non vitiat concessionem /fólsə grəmǽdəkə nòn víshiyət kənsès(h)iyównəm/. False or bad grammar does not vitiate a grant. Neither false Latin nor false English will make a deed void when the intent of the parties doth plainly appear.

Falsa moneta /fólsə məníydə/. In the civil law, false or counterfeit money.

Falsa orthographia non vitiat chartam, concessionem /fólsə òrθəgrǽfiyə nòn víshiyət kárdəm, °kənsès(h)iyównəm/. False spelling does not vitiate a deed.

Falsare /fòlsériy/. In old English law, to counterfeit. *Quia falsavit sigillum,* because he counterfeited the seal.

Falsarius (or falcarious) /fòlsériyəs/. A counterfeiter.

False. Not true. State v. Arnett, 338 Mo. 907, 92 S.W.2d 897, 900; Sentinel Life Ins. Co. v. Blackmer, C.C.A.Colo., 77 F.2d 347, 352. Term also means: artificial, Sentinel Life Ins. Co. v. Blackmer, C.C.A. Colo., 77 F.2d 347, 352; assumed or designed to deceive, Sentinel Life Ins. Co. v. Blackmer, C.C.A. Colo., 77 F.2d 347, 352; North American Accident Ins. Co. v. Tebbs, C.C.A.Utah, 107 F.2d 853, 855; contrary to fact, In re Davis, 349 Pa. 651, 37 A.2d 498, 499; counterfeit, Sentinel Life Ins. Co. v. Blackmer, C.C.A.Colo., 77 F.2d 347, 352; North American Accident Ins. Co. v. Tebbs, C.C.A.Utah, 107 F.2d 853, 855; deceitful; deliberately and knowingly false, People v. Mangan, 140 Misc. 783, 252 N.Y.S. 44, 52; designedly untrue, W. T. Rawleigh Co. v. Brantley, 97 Miss. 244, 19 So.2d 808, 811; erroneous, Gilbert v. Inter-Ocean Casualty Co. of Cincinnati, Ohio, 41 N.M. 463, 71 P.2d 56, 59; hypocritical; sham; feigned, Sentinel Life Ins. Co. v. Blackmer, C.C.A.Colo., 77 F.2d 347, 352; North American Accident Ins. Co. v. Tebbs, C.C.A.Utah, 107 F.2d 853, 855; incorrect, State v. Arnett, 338 Mo. 907, 92 S.W.2d 897, 900; intentionally untrue, In re Venturella, D.C.Conn., 25 F.Supp. 332, 333; In re Cleveland, D.C.Mich., 40 F.Supp. 343; not according to truth or reality, State v. Arnett, 338 Mo. 907, 92 S.W.2d 897, 900; North American Accident Ins. Co. v. Tebbs, C.C.A.Utah, 107 F.2d 853, 855; not genuine or real, North American Accident Ins. Co. v. Tebbs, C.C.A.Utah, 107 F.2d 853, 855; uttering falsehood; unveracious; given to deceit; dishonest, Wilensky v. Goodyear Tire & Rubber Co., C.C.A.Mass., 67 F.2d 389, 390; wilfully and intentionally untrue, In re Brown, D.C.N.Y., 37 F.Supp. 526, 527; North American Accident Ins. Co. v. Tebbs, C.C.A.Utah, 107 F.2d 853, 855.

The word "false" has two distinct and well-recognized meanings: (1) intentionally or knowingly or negligently untrue; (2) untrue by mistake or accident, or honestly after the exercise of reasonable care. Metropolitan Life Ins. Co. v. Adams, D.C.Mun.App., 37 A.2d 345, 350. A thing is called "false" when it is done, or made, with knowledge, actual or constructive, that it is untrue or illegal, or is said to be done falsely when the meaning is that the party is in fault for its error. A statement (including a statement in a claim or document), is "false" if it was untrue by the person making it, or causing it to be made.

See also Alteration; Bogus; Counterfeit; Falsely; False representation; Falsify; Forgery; Fraud; Perjury.

False action. See **Feigned action.**

False and fraudulent. To amount to actionable "false and fraudulent representations", they must have been as to existing fact or known by one making them, from his superior knowledge, to have been untrue when made. Burlison v. Weis, Mo.App., 152 S.W.2d 201, 203. See **False representation; Fraud.**

False answer. In pleading, a sham answer; one which is false in the sense of being a mere pretense set up in bad faith and without color of fact. Such answer may be ordered stricken on motion. Fed.R. Civil P. 12(f).

False arrest. Such arrest consists in unlawful restraint of an individual's personal liberty or freedom of locomotion. Johnson v. Jackson, 43 Ill.App.2d 251, 193 N.E.2d 485, 489. An arrest without proper legal authority is a false arrest and because an arrest restrains the liberty of a person it is also false imprisonment. The gist of the tort is protection of the personal interest in freedom from restraint of movement. Neither ill will nor malice are elements of the tort, but if these elements are shown, punitive damages may be awarded in addition to compensatory or nominal damages.

False character. In England, the offense of personating the master or mistress of a servant, or any representative of such master or mistress, and giving a false character to the servant.

False checks. Offense of obtaining money by means and use of a check upon a bank, in which the drawer at the time had no funds or credit with which to meet the same, and which he had no reason to believe would honor such check upon presentation at said bank for payment. See also **Kiting.**

False claim. A statement or a claim which is not true.

It is a criminal offense to make or present a false, fictitious or fraudulent claim against the federal government. 18 U.S.C.A. § 287; 31 U.S.C.A. § 231 et seq.

Falsedad /fàlsəyðád/. In Spanish law, falsity; an alteration of the truth; deception; fraud.

False decretals. A collection of canon law, dated about the middle of the 9th century, probably by a Frankish ecclesiastic who called himself Isadon. It continued to be the chief repertory of the canon law till the 15th century when its untrustworthy nature was demonstrated.

False demonstration. An erroneous description of a person or thing in a written instrument. Where description of person or thing in will is partly true and partly false, if part which is true describes subject or object of gift with sufficient certainty, untrue part may be rejected and gift sustained, under doctrine of "false demonstration." In re Heins' Estate, 132 Cal. App. 131, 22 P.2d 549.

False entry. An untrue statement of items of account by written words, figures, or marks. One making an original false entry makes a false entry in every book which is made up in regular course from the entry or entries from the original book of entry.

An entry in books of a bank or trust company which is intentionally made to represent what is not true or does not exist, with intent either to deceive its officers or a bank examiner or to defraud the bank or trust company. Agnew v. U. S., 165 U.S. 36, 17 S.Ct. 235, 41 L.Ed. 624.

False fact. In the law of evidence, a feigned, simulated, or fabricated fact; a fact not founded in truth, but existing only in assertion; the deceitful semblance of a fact. See **Perjury.**

Falsehood. A statement or assertion known to be untrue, and intended to deceive. A willful act or declaration contrary to the truth. It is committed either by the wilful act of the party, or by dissimulation, or by words. A fabrication. Werner v. Southern Cal. Associated Newspapers, Cal.App., 206 P.2d 952, 961. See **Perjury.**

False impersonation. To impersonate another falsely, and in such assumed character to do any act whereby any benefit might accrue to the offender or to another person. People v. Horkans, 109 Colo. 177, 123 P.2d 824. See also **False personation.**

False imprisonment. See **False arrest; Imprisonment; Probable cause.**

False instrument. A counterfeit; one made in the similitude of a genuine instrument and purporting on its face to be such. See also **Counterfeit; False making; Forgery.**

False judgment. In old English law, a writ which lay when a false judgment had been pronounced in a court not of record, as a county court, court baron, etc.

In old French law, the defeated party in a suit had the privilege of accusing the judges of pronouncing a false or corrupt judgment, whereupon the issue was determined by his challenging them to the combat or *duellum.* This was called the "appeal of false judgment."

False Latin. When law proceedings were written in Latin, if a word were significant though not good Latin, then an indictment, declaration, or fine should not be made void by it; but if the word were not Latin, nor allowed by the law, and it were in a material point, it made the whole void.

False lights and signals. Lights and signals falsely and maliciously displayed for the purpose of bringing a vessel into danger.

Falsely. In a false manner, erroneously, not truly, perfidiously or treacherously. Dombroski v. Metropolitan Life Ins. Co., 126 N.J.L. 545, 19 A.2d 678, 680. Knowingly affirming without probable cause.

The word "falsely", particularly in a criminal statute, suggests something more than a mere untruth and includes perfidiously or treacherously or with intent to defraud. United States v. Achtner, C.C.A. N.Y., 144 F.2d 49, 52. Commonly used in the sense of designedly untrue and deceitful, and as implying an intention to perpetrate some treachery or fraud. As applied to making or altering a writing in order to make it forgery, implies that the paper or writing is not genuine; that in itself it is false or counterfeit. See also **False.**

Falsely impersonate. To falsely impersonate may mean to pretend to be a particular person without lawful authority. People v. Horkans, 109 Colo. 177, 123 P.2d 824, 826. See also **False personation; Personate.**

Falsely make. To make an instrument which has no original as such and no genuine maker whose work is copied, although in form it may resemble a type of recognized security. Pines v. United States, C.C.A. Iowa, 123 F.2d 825, 828. See **Counterfeit; Forgery.**

False making. An essential element of forgery, where material alteration is not involved. Term has reference to manner in which writing is made or executed rather than to its substance or effect. A falsely made instrument is one that is fictitious, not genuine, or in some material particular something other than it purports to be and without regard to truth or falsity of facts stated therein. Wright v. U. S., C.A.Ariz., 172 F.2d 310, 311. See also **Counterfeit; Forgery.**

False news. Spreading false news, whereby discord may grow between the queen of England and her people, or the great men of the realm, or which may produce other mischiefs, seems to have been a misdemeanor, under St. 3 Edw. I, c. 34.

False oath. To defeat discharge in bankruptcy "false oath" must contain all the elements involved in "perjury" at common law, namely, an intentional untruth in matter material to a material issue. It must have been knowingly and fraudulently made. In re Stone, D.C.N.H., 52 F.2d 639, 641. See also **Perjury.**

False personation. The criminal offense of falsely representing some other person and acting in the character thus unlawfully assumed, in order to deceive others, and thereby gain some profit or advantage, or enjoy some right or privilege belonging to the one so personated, or subject him to some expense, charge, or liability. See also **False impersonation; Personate.**

False plea. See **Sham** *(Sham pleading).*

False pretenses. False pretenses, a statutory crime, although defined in slightly different ways in the various jurisdictions, consists in most jurisdictions of these elements: a false representation of a material present or past fact which causes the victim to pass title to his property to the wrongdoer, who (a) knows his representation to be false and (b) intends thereby to defraud the victim.

Essential elements of offense of "false pretenses", as defined by statute, are design, false pretense, intent to defraud, obtaining of signature, and character of instrument signed as one the false making of which would be punishable as forgery. State v. Pullen, 252 Iowa 1324, 110 N.W.2d 328, 331. False pretense is representation of some fact or circumstance which is not true and is calculated to mislead; representation may be implied from conduct or may consist of concealment or nondisclosure where there is duty to speak, and may consist of any acts, work, symbol or token calculated and intended to deceive. Bright v. Sheriff, Washoe County, 90 Nev. 168, 521 P.2d 371, 373.

Other definitions of "false pretenses" include: false representation of existing fact or condition by which a party obtains property of another; false representation of existing fact, whether by oral or written words or conduct, calculated to deceive, intended to deceive, and does in fact deceive, whereby one person obtains value from another without compensation; false representation of existing or past fact calculated to induce confidence on part of one to whom representation is made, and accompanied by or blended with a promise to do something in future, State v. Parkinson, 181 Wash. 69, 41 P.2d 1095, 1097; false representation of existing fact, made with knowledge of falsity, with intent that party to whom it is made should act upon it, and acted upon by such party to his detriment; false representation of past or existing fact, made with knowledge of falsity, with intent to deceive and defraud, and which is adapted to deceive person to whom made.

Larceny distinguished. In larceny owner has no intention to part with his property, although he may intend to part with possession, while in false pretenses the owner does intend to part with the property but it is obtained from him by fraud. The intention of owner of property not to part with title when relinquishing possession of property is vital point to be determined in distinguishing between "larceny by fraud" and obtaining property by "false pretenses". Dobson v. State, 74 Okl.Cr. 341, 126 P.2d 95, 101.

False representation. A "false representation" in order to be actionable must consist of a statement of fact which is untrue, such statement must have been made with intent to defraud and for the purpose of inducing another to act upon it, and he must have in fact relied on such statement and must have been induced thereby to act to his injury or damage. Household Finance Corp. v. Christian, 8 Wis.2d 53, 98 N.W.2d 390, 392. To maintain an action for damages for "false representation," the plaintiff, in substance, must allege and must prove by a preponderance of the evidence the following elements: (1) What representation was made; (2) that it was false; (3) that the defendant knew it was false, or else made it without knowledge as a positive statement of known fact; (4) that the plaintiff believed the representation to be true; (5) that the plaintiff relied on and acted upon the representation; (6) that the plaintiff was thereby injured; and (7) the amount of the damages.

See also **Deceit; Fraud; Material fact; Reliance.**

False return. See **Return.**

False statement. As used in bankruptcy statute provision concerning discharge, these words denote or connote guilty scienter on part of bankrupt. In re Krulewitch, D.C.N.J., 60 F.2d 1039, 1041; Wilensky v. Goodyear Tire & Rubber Co., C.C.A.Mass., 67 F.2d 389, 390. They mean an incorrect statement made or acquiesced in with knowledge of incorrectness or with reckless indifference to actual facts and with no reasonable ground to believe it correct. International Shoe Co. v. Lewine, C.C.A.Miss., 68 F.2d 517, 518. Statement knowingly false, or made recklessly without honest belief in its truth, and with purpose to mislead or deceive. Third Nat. Bank v. Schatten, C.C.A.Tenn., 81 F.2d 538, 540; In re Venturella, D.C. Conn., 25 F.Supp. 332. They mean more than errone-

ous or untrue and import intention to deceive. Schapiro v. Tweede Footwear Corporation, C.C.A.Pa., 131 F.2d 876, 878.

Under statutory provision making it unlawful for officer or director of corporation to make any false statement in regard to corporation's financial condition, the phrase means something more than merely untrue or erroneous, but implies that statement is designedly untrue and deceitful, and made with intention to deceive person to whom false statement is made or exhibited.

See also **Deceit; Fraud; Material fact; Perjury; Reliance.**

False swearing. A person who makes a false statement under oath or equivalent affirmation, or swears or affirms the truth of such a statement previously made, when he does not believe the statement to be true, is guilty of a misdemeanor if: (a) the falsification occurs in an official proceeding; or (b) the falsification is intended to mislead a public servant in performing his official function. Model Penal Code, § 241.2.

The essential elements of "false swearing" consist in willfully, knowingly, absolutely and falsely swearing under oath or affirmation on a matter concerning which a party could legally be sworn and on oath administered by one legally authorized to administer it. Smith v. State, 66 Ga.App. 669, 19 S.E.2d 168, 169. It must appear that matter sworn to was judicially pending or was being investigated by grand jury, or was a subject on which accused could legally have been sworn, or on which he was required to be sworn. Capps v. Commonwealth, 294 Ky. 743, 172 S.W.2d 610, 611. See also **Perjury.**

False token. In criminal law, a false document or sign of the existence of a fact, in general, used for the purpose of fraud. Device used to obtain money by false pretenses. See **Counterfeit; False weights.**

False verdict. See **Verdict.**

False weights. False weights and measures are such as do not comply with the standard prescribed by the state or government, or with the custom prevailing in the place and business in which they are used.

Falsi crimen /fólsay kráymən/. Fraudulent subornation or concealment, with design to darken or hide the truth, and make things appear otherwise than they are. It is committed (1) by words, as when a witness swears falsely; (2) by writing, as when a person antedates a contract; (3) by deed, as selling by false weights and measures. See **Crimen falsi.**

Falsification. See **Falsify.**

Falsify. To counterfeit or forge; to make something false; to give a false appearance to anything. To make false by mutilation, alteration, or addition; to tamper with, as to falsify a record or document. The word "falsify" may be used to convey two distinct meanings—either that of being intentionally or knowingly untrue, made with intent to defraud, or mistakenly and accidentally untrue. Washer v. Bank of America Nat. Trust & Savings Ass'n, 21 Cal.2d 822, 136 P.2d 297, 301. See also **Alteration; Counterfeit; False; Forgery.**

To disprove; to prove to be false or erroneous; to avoid or defeat. Spoken of verdicts, appeals, etc.

Falsifying a record. A high offense against public justice, punishable in England by 24 & 25 Vict. c. 98, §§ 27, 28, and in the United States, generally, by statute.

Falsity. Term implies more than erroneous or untrue; it indicates knowledge of untruth.

Falsonarius /fòlsənériyəs/. A forger; a counterfeiter.

Falso retorno brevium /fólsow rətórnow bríyviyəm/. In old English law, a writ which formerly lay against the sheriff who had execution of process for false returning of writs.

Falsum /fólsəm/. Lat. In the civil law, a false or forged thing; a fraudulent simulation; a fraudulent counterfeit or imitation, such as a forged signature or instrument. Also falsification, which may be either by falsehood, concealment of the truth, or fraudulent alteration, as by cutting out or erasing part of a writing.

Falsus /fólsəs/. Lat. False; fraudulent; erroneous; deceitful; mistaken. In the sense of "deceiving" or "fraudulent," it is applied to persons in respect to their acts and conduct, as well as to things; and in the sense of "erroneous," it is applied to persons on the question of personal identity.

Falsus in uno, falsus in omnibus /fólsəs ìn yúwnow, fólsəs ìn ómnəbəs/. False in one thing, false in everything. Dawson v. Bertolini, 70 R.I. 325, 38 A.2d 765, 768.

The doctrine means that if testimony of a witness on a material issue is willfully false and given with an intention to deceive, jury may disregard all the witness' testimony. Hargrave v. Stockloss, 127 N.J.L. 262, 21 A.2d 820, 823. The maxim deals only with weight of evidence. It does not relieve jury from passing on credibility of the whole testimony of a false swearing witness or excuse jury from weighing the whole testimony. State v. Willard, 346 Mo. 773, 142 S.W.2d 1046, 1052. It is a mere rule of evidence affirming a rebuttable presumption of fact, under which the jury must consider all the evidence of the witness, other than that which is found to be false, and it is their duty to give effect to so much of it, if any, as is relieved from the presumption against it and found to be true. It is not a rule of the law of evidence, but is merely an aid in weighing and sifting of evidence. Dawson v. Bertolini, 70 R.I. 325, 38 A.2d 765, 768. It is particularly applied to the testimony of a witness who, if he is shown to have sworn falsely in one detail, may be considered unworthy of belief as to all the rest of his evidence.

Fama /féymə/. Lat. Fame; character, reputation; report of common opinion.

Famacide /féyməsàyd/. A killer of reputation; a slanderer.

Fama, fides et oculus non patiuntur ludum /féymə, fáydiyz èd ókyələs nòn pædiyántər l(y)úwdəm/. Fame, faith, and eyesight do not suffer a cheat.

Fama quæ suspicionem inducit, oriri debet apud bonos et graves, non quidem malevolos et maledicos, sed providas et fide dignas personas, non semel sed sæpius, quia clamor minuit et defamatio manifestat /féymə kwìy səspìshiyównəm ind(y)úwsət, əráyray débəd ǽpəd bównows èt gréyviyz, nòn kwídəm məlévəlows èt məlédəkows, sèd prəváydəs èt fáydiy dígnəs pərsównəs, nòn séməl sed síypiyəs, kwáyə klǽmər mínyuwət èt dèfəméysh(iy)ow mǽnəféstət/. Report, which induces suspicion, ought to arise from good and grave men; not, indeed, from malevolent and malicious men, but from cautious and credible persons; not only once, but frequently, for clamor diminishes, and defamation manifests.

Familia /fəmíl(i)yə/. *Old English law.* A household; the body of household servants; a quantity of land, otherwise called *"mansa,"* sufficient to maintain one family.

Roman law. A household; a family. Family right; the right or status of being the head of a family, or of exercising the *patria potestas* over others. This could belong only to a Roman citizen who was a "man in his own right."

Spanish law. A family, which might consist of domestics or servants.

Familiæ emptor /fəmíliyiy ém(p)tər/. In Roman law, an intermediate person who purchased the aggregate inheritance when sold *per æs et libram,* in the process of making a will under the Twelve Tables. This purchaser was merely a man of straw, transmitting the inheritance to the *hœres* proper.

Familiæ erciscundæ /fəmíliyiy àrsəskándiy/. In Roman law, an action for the partition of the aggregate succession of a *familia,* where that devolved upon *cohœredes.* It was also applicable to enforce a contribution towards the necessary expenses incurred on the *familia.*

Familiar. Fair or reasonable knowledge of, or acquaintance with. Closeness; intimacy.

Familiares regis /fəmìliyériyz ríyjəs/. Persons of the king's household. The ancient title of the "six clerks" of chancery in England.

Familiarity. Close or reasonable acquaintance with or knowledge of.

Family. The meaning of word "family" necessarily depends on field of law in which word is used, purpose intended to be accomplished by its use, and facts and circumstances of each case. LeRoux v. Edmundson, 276 Minn. 120, 148 N.W.2d 812, 814. Most commonly refers to group of persons consisting of parents and children; father, mother and their children; immediate kindred, constituting fundamental social unit in civilized society. People v. Hasse, 57 Misc.2d 59, 291 N.Y.S.2d 53, 55. A collective body of persons who live in one house and under one head or management. A group of blood-relatives; all the relations who descend from a common ancestor, or who spring from a common root. A group of kindred persons. Hartley v. Bohrer, 52 Idaho 72, 11 P.2d 616, 618. Husband and wife and their children, wherever they may reside, and whether they dwell together or not. Franklin Fire Ins. Co. v. Shadid, Tex.Com.App., 68 S.W.2d 1030, 1032.

The word conveys the notion of some relationship, blood or otherwise. Collins v. Northwest Casualty Co., 180 Wash. 347, 39 P.2d 986, 989. In restricted sense, the word "family" may be used interchangeably with household. Collins v. Northwest Casualty Co., 180 Wash. 347, 39 P.2d 986, 989.

When used in constitution of benefit society, declaring its purpose among others as that of aiding the families of members, the word means such persons as habitually reside under one roof and form one domestic circle, or such persons as are dependent on each other for support or among whom there is legal or equitable obligation to furnish support and in its widest scope it would include all descendants of a common progenitor. Logan v. St. Louis Police Relief Ass'n, Mo.App., 133 S.W.2d 1048, 1049, 1050.

As used in context of uninsured motorist insurance coverage, "family" is not confined to those who stand in a legal or blood relationship, but rather should include those who live within the domestic circle of, and are economically dependent on, the named insured (e.g. foster child or ward). Brokenbaugh v. N. J. Manufacturers Ins. Co. et al., 158 N.J.Super. 424, 386 A.2d 433.

Descent and descendants. The word "family" may mean all descendants of a common progenitor, Logan v. St. Louis Police Relief Ass'n, Mo.App., 133 S.W.2d 1048, 1049, 1050; In re Lund's Estate, 26 Cal.2d 472, 159 P.2d 643, 645; or, those who are of the same lineage, or descend from one common progenitor.

Homestead and exemption laws. To constitute family there must be one whom law designates or recognizes as head of family who by natural ties or by legal or moral obligation is under duty to support others of the household. Owens v. Altsheller & Co., 263 Ky. 727, 93 S.W.2d 844, 846. To constitute persons living with another in same house a "family", it must appear that they are being supported by that other in whole or in part, and are dependent on him therefor, and that he is under a natural or moral obligation to render such support.

Household. Those who live in same household subject to general management and control of the head thereof. Family and household are substantially synonymous terms for certain purposes.

Support. A "family" is a collection of persons living together under one head, under such circumstances or conditions that the head is under a legal or moral obligation to support the other members, and the other members are dependent upon him or her for support. Hurt v. Perryman, 173 Tenn. 646, 122 S.W.2d 426, 427. Those entitled by law to look to person for support and protection, In re Fulton's Estate, 15 Cal.App.2d 202, 59 P.2d 508, 510. See also **Dependent.**

Wills. As respects construction of will, the word "family" denotes a group of persons related to each other by marriage or blood living together under a single roof and comprising a household whose head is usually the father or husband, but the word is not one of inflexible meaning and its significance to a large extent depends upon the context and the purpose for which it is employed. For example, the word "family" has been held to include those who have left father's home and have married and established their own homes when context and purpose indicate such significance should be attributed to the word. Magill v. Magill, 317 Mass. 89, 56 N.E.2d 892, 894, 896.

When the word "family" is used to designate those entitled to receive a legacy, the intended meaning of the word depends upon the context of the will and upon a showing as to whom were the objects of the testator's bounty by reason of kinship or friendship.

Family allowance. Consists of certain amount of decedent's property allocated for the support of the widow and children during the period of estate administration.

Family arrangement. A term denoting an agreement between a father and his children, or between the heirs of a deceased father, to dispose of property, or to partition it in a different manner than that which would result if the law alone directed it, or to divide up property without administration. In these cases, frequently, the mere relation of the parties will give effect to bargains otherwise without adequate consideration. See also **Family settlement.**

Family automobile doctrine. In a number of jurisdictions, when an automobile is maintained by the owner thereof for the general use and convenience of his or her family, such owner is liable for the negligence of a member of the family, having general authority to drive the car, while it is being used as such family car; that is, for the pleasure or convenience of the family or a member of it. This doctrine has been rejected, superseded, or limited in its application, in most states.

The doctrine rests upon the basis that the automobile is furnished by the husband in his individual capacity and as common-law head of the family for the use of the family, and not as the agent of the community. Under the doctrine, a father furnishing automobile for pleasure and convenience of family makes the use of automobile by family his business and any member of family driving automobile with father's express or implied consent is the father's agent and the father is liable for the member's negligence. Donn v. Kunz, 52 Ariz. 219, 79 P.2d 965, 966, 967.

See also **Family group; Family purpose doctrine,** which are synonymous terms.

Family Bible. A Bible containing a record of the births, marriages, and deaths of the members of a family.

Family car doctrine. See **Family automobile doctrine.**

Family council. See **Family arrangement; Family meeting; Conseil de famille.**

Family court. Such courts exist in several states. While the jurisdiction of such courts will differ somewhat from state to state, typically this court will have jurisdiction over: (1) child abuse and neglect proceedings, (2) support proceedings, (3) proceedings to determine paternity and for support of children born out of wedlock, (4) proceedings permanently to terminate custody by reason of permanent neglect, (5) proceedings concerning juvenile delinquency and whether a person is in need of supervision, and (6) family offenses proceedings. The family court may be a division or department of a court of general jurisdiction.

Family disturbance. Generic term used to describe any crime, tort or disorder within or touching the family.

Family expense statutes. State statutes which permit charge against property of husband or wife for debts connected with family such as rent, groceries, clothing, and tuition.

As used in tax law, expenses incurred for personal, living or family purposes for which no deduction may be claimed. I.R.C. § 262.

Family group. Within purview of the family automobile doctrine, is not confined to persons related to the owner, but includes members of the collective body of persons living in his household for whose convenience the car is maintained and who have authority to use it. See also **Family automobile doctrine; Family purpose doctrine,** which are synonymous terms.

Family law. Branch or specialty of law, also denominated "domestic relations" law, concerned with such subjects as divorce, separation, paternity, custody, support and child care. See also **Family court.**

Family meeting. In Louisiana, an advisory jury called to aid court in determining matters or affairs in which members of family are concerned. An institution of the laws of Louisiana, being a council of the relatives (or, if there are no relatives, of the friends) of a minor, for the purpose of advising as to his affairs and the administration of his property. It corresponds to the "conseil de famille" of French law.

Family partnership. In tax law, partnership consisting of members of family and such members shall include only a spouse, ancestors and lineal descendants. I.R.C. § 704(e).

Family physician. A physician who regularly attends and is consulted by the members of the family as their medical adviser; but he need not attend in all cases or be consulted by all the members of the family.

Family purpose doctrine. A doctrine that the owner of a car, who gives it over to the use of his family and permits it to be operated by the members thereof, is liable for the injuries inflicted while being operated by a member of the family. Turoff v. Burch, 60 App.D.C. 221, 50 F.2d 986, 987. Under "family purpose" doctrine where one purchases and maintains automobile for comfort, convenience, pleasure, entertainment and recreation of his family, any member thereof operating automobile will be regarded as agent or servant of the owner and owner will be held liable for injuries sustained by third person by reason of negligent operation of vehicle by member of family. Freeland v. Freeland, 152 W.Va. 332, 162 S.E.2d 922, 925. This doctrine has been rejected, or limited in its application, in many states. See also **Family automobile doctrine** and **Family group,** which are synonymous terms.

Family service rule. See **Family automobile doctrine.**

Family settlement. An agreement between members of a family settling the distribution of family property among them. Fitzgerald v. Nelson, 159 Or. 264, 79 P.2d 254, 255. An arrangement or an agreement, between heirs of a deceased person, by which they agree on distribution or management of estate without administration by court having jurisdiction of such administration proceedings. Wright v. Salt-

marsh, 174 Okl. 226, 50 P.2d 694, 703. An agreement made between a father and his son or children or between brothers to dispose of property in a different manner from that which would otherwise take place. Peterson v. Hegna, 158 Minn. 289, 197 N.W. 484, 487. A term of practically the same signification as "family arrangement" *(q.v.).*

Famosus /fəmówsəs/. In the civil and old English law, relating to or affecting injuriously the character or reputation; defamatory; slanderous; scandalous.

Famosus libellus /fəmówsəs ləbéləs/. A libelous writing. A term of the civil law denoting that species of *injuria* which corresponds nearly to libel or slander.

Fanatic. A religious or political enthusiast; a person entertaining extravagant notions, or affected by excessive zeal or enthusiasm, especially upon religious or political subjects.

Fanciful trade-name. Trade-names are "fanciful" when they do not, by their usual and ordinary meaning, denote or describe products to which they are applied, but indicate their purpose by application and association. Skinner Mfg. Co. v. General Foods Sales Co., D.C.Neb., 52 F.Supp. 432, 445.

Fanega /fanéygə/. In Spanish law, a measure of land varying in different provinces, but in the Spanish settlements in America consisting of 6,400 square varas or yards.

Fannie Mae. See **Federal National Mortgage Association.**

Faqueer /fəkír/. See **Fakir.**

Fardel of land /fárdəl əv lænd/. In old English law, the fourth part of a yard-land.

Farding-deal. The fourth part of an acre of land.

Fare. A voyage, journey, or passage. The transportation charge paid by passenger. A paying passenger.

As used in connection with interstate transportation means a rate of charge for the carriage of passengers, as approved by the proper governmental agency. Krause v. Pacific Mut. Life Ins. Co. of California, 141 Neb. 844, 5 N.W.2d 229, 232.

Farleu (or Farley) /fàrlyúw/fárliy/. Money paid by tenants in lieu of a heriot. It was often applied to the best chattel, as distinguished from *heriot,* the best beast.

Farlingarii /fàrləngériyay/. Whoremongers; adulterers.

Farm, *n.* A tract of land devoted to agriculture, pasturage, stock raising, or some allied industry. Includes dairy, stock, and poultry farms.

The original meaning of the word was rent; a term; a lease of lands; a leasehold interest, and by a natural transition it came to mean the land out of which the rent or lease issued.

A letting out of the collection of taxes and revenues for a fixed sum.

See also **Farmer.**

Farm, *v.* To lease or let; to demise or grant for a limited term and at a stated rental. To carry on business or occupation of farming.

Farm Credit Administration. The Farm Credit Administration, an independent agency, supervises and co-ordinates activities of the cooperative Farm Credit System. The System is comprised of Federal land banks and Federal land bank associations, Federal intermediate credit banks and production credit associations, and banks for cooperatives. Initially capitalized by the United States, the entire System is now owned by its users.

Farm crossing. A roadway over or under a railroad track for the purpose of reaching land cut off by the track.

Farmer. A cultivator; a husbandman; an agriculturist, Kaslovitz v. Reid, C.C.A.Utah, 128 F.2d 1017, 1018; one engaged in agricultural pursuits as a livelihood or business. Skinner v. Dingwell, C.C.A.Iowa, 134 F.2d 391, 393; one engaged in dairy farming and in production of poultry or livestock, Leonard v. Bennett, C.C.A.Or., 116 F.2d 128, 131, 132, 134; one engaged in the business of cultivating land or employing it for the purpose of husbandry, Kaslovitz v. Reid, C.C.A. Utah, 128 F.2d 1017, 1018; one living on his farm from revenue thereof and personally operating it on large scale as his primary activity, In re Lindsay, D.C.Tex., 41 F.Supp. 948, 950, 951; one personally engaged in farming, Shyvers v. Security-First Nat. Bank of Los Angeles, C.C.A.Cal., 108 F.2d 611, 612, 613; In re Davis, D.C.Iowa, 22 F.Supp. 12, 13; one primarily engaged in agricultural pursuits, Leonard v. Bennett, C.C.A.Or., 116 F.2d 128, 131, 132, 134; one who cultivates a considerable tract of land in some one of the usual recognized ways of farming, Kaslovitz v. Reid, C.C.A.Utah, 128 F.2d 1017, 1018; Mattison v. Dunlap, 191 Okl. 168, 127 P.2d 140, 141; one who cultivates a farm either as owner or lessee, Kaslovitz v. Reid, C.C.A.Utah, 128 F.2d 1017, 1018; one who cultivates a farm, whether the land be his own or another's; one who directs the business of a farm and works at farm labor, Kaslovitz v. Reid, C.C.A.Utah, 128 F.2d 1017, 1018; Stoner v. New York Life Ins. Co., Mo.App., 90 S.W.2d 784, 795; one who expends his energies and production efforts in tilling the soil, raising crops and marketing them, thereby promoting his financial interest and advancement, Kaslovitz v. Reid, C.C.A.Utah, 128 F.2d 1017, 1018; one who is devoted to the tillage of the soil, Kaslovitz v. Reid, C.C.A.Utah, 128 F.2d 1017, 1018; one who is primarily, personally, and bona fide engaged in farming although he does not spend all of his time therein, work farm without assistance, or refrain from engaging in secondary activities, In re Lindsay, D.C.Tex., 41 F.Supp. 948, 950, 951.

Person that received more than 80 percent of his gross income during the taxable year immediately preceding commencement of bankruptcy proceeding from a farming operation owned or operated by such person. Bankruptcy Act, § 101(17).

See also **Husbandman.**

One who assumes the collection of the public revenues, taxes, excise, etc., for a certain commission or percentage; as a *farmer* of the revenues.

Farming operation. Term includes farming, tillage of the soil, dairy farming, ranching, production or raising of crops, poultry, or livestock, and production of poultry or livestock products in an unmanufactured state. Bankruptcy Act, § 101(18).

Farming products. All things are considered as "farming products" or "agricultural products" which have a situs of their production upon the farm and which are brought into condition for uses of society by labor of those engaged in agricultural pursuits as contradistinguished from manufacturing or other industrial pursuits.

Crops or livestock or supplies used or produced in farming operations or products of crops or livestock in their unmanufactured states, if they are in the possession of a debtor engaged in farming operations. U.C.C. § 9–109(3).

Farming purposes. These words are not limited in meaning to mere cultivation of soil and maintenance of improvements thereon for such purposes, but include raising of livestock, as well as production of farm crops directly from soil. State v. Superior Court for Walla Walla County, 168 Wash. 142, 10 P.2d 986, 987. See **Farming operation.**

Farm labor or **laborer.** Agricultural employment and farm labor are used as practically synonymous and include all farm work and work incidental thereto. Smythe v. Phoenix, 63 Idaho 585, 123 P.2d 1010, 1012.

One employed as a laborer on a farm, especially one who does all kinds of farm work; one employed in or about business of farming. One employed on a farm in customary types of farm work or employed and paid directly by a farmer in transporting his raw produce. Cedarburg Fox Farms v. Industrial Commission, 241 Wis. 604, 6 N.W.2d 687, 689, 690. One who devotes his time to ordinary farm labor as gainful occupation with some reasonable degree of regularity and continuity. One who labors on a farm in raising crops or livestock, or in doing general farm work.

See also **Agricultural labor; Farmer.**

Farm let. Technical words in a lease creating a term for years. Operative words in a lease, which strictly mean to let upon payment of a certain rent in farm; *i.e.,* in agricultural produce. See also **Fee-farm; Fee-farm rent.**

Farm out. To let for a term at a stated rental. To turn over for performance or care. To exhaust farm land by continuous raising of single crop.

Among the Romans the collection of revenue was farmed out, and the same system existed in France before the revolution of 1789; in England the excise taxes were farmed out, and thereby their evils were greatly aggravated. The farming of the excise was abolished in Scotland by the union, having been before that time abandoned in England. In all these cases the custom gave rise to great abuse and oppression of the people, and in France most of the farmers-general, as they were called, perished on the scaffold.

Farmout agreement. Under standard "farmout agreement" whereby natural gas producer-lessee agrees to assign leases, farmout operator drills at his own expense and upon completion of commercial well becomes owner of working interest and usually operates well or arranges for its operation, the assignor retaining a royalty. Northern Natural Gas Co. v. Grounds, D.C.Kan., 292 F.Supp. 619, 628.

Farm products. See **Farming products.**

Farm-to-market roads. Within act designating purposes for which road funds were allotted to counties, held to mean county public highways leading directly to, or intersecting, state highways leading to markets. Hastings v. Pfeiffer, 184 Ark. 952, 43 S.W.2d 1073, 1074.

Faro /férow/fǽrow/. A game of cards in which all the other players play against the banker or dealer, staking their money upon the order in which the cards will lie and be dealt from the pack.

Farrier /fǽriyər/. Occupation of shoeing horses.

Farthing /fárðiŋ/. The fourth part of an English penny.

Farthing of gold. An ancient English coin, containing in value the fourth part of a noble.

Farthing of land. A great quantity of land, differing much from farding-deal *(q.v.)*.

Farvand. Standing by itself, this word signifies "passage by sea or water". In charter-parties, it means voyage or passage by water.

Fas /fǽs/. Lat. Right; justice; the divine law. In primitive times it was the will of the gods, embodied in rules regulating not only ceremonials but the conduct of all men.

F.A.S. Free alongside. Term used in sales price quotations, indicating that the price includes all costs of transportation and delivery of the goods alongside the ship. See U.C.C. § 2–319(2).

Fast bill of exceptions. A former practice in Georgia in injunction suits and similar cases, meaning to bring the case up for review with great expedition.

Fast-day. A day of fasting and penitence, or of mortification by religious abstinence.

Fastermans, fastermannes, or **fastingmen** /fǽstərmənz/ fǽstiŋmèn/. Men in repute and substance; pledges, sureties, or bondsmen, who, according to the Saxon polity, were *fast* bound to answer for each other's peaceable behavior.

Fast estate. See **Estate.**

Fasti /fǽstay/. In Roman law, lawful. *Dies fasti,* lawful days; days on which justice could lawfully be administered by the prætor.

Fatal errors. Harmful errors; reversible errors. Such only as may reasonably be held to have worked substantial injury or prejudice to complaining party. Such errors generally afford party right to new trial, as contrasted with "harmless" errors which do not. See **Error.**

Fatal injury. A term embracing injuries resulting in death, which, as used in accident and disability insurance policies is distinguished from "disability," which embraces injuries preventing the insured from performing the work in which he is usually employed, but not resulting in death.

Fatal variance. A variance tending to mislead defendant in making defense or one preventing plea of former jeopardy. Burke v. U. S., C.C.A.Cal., 58 F.2d 739, 741. A variance in order to be "fatal" must be substantial and material. Whittier v. Leifert, 72 N.D. 528, 9 N.W.2d 402, 405; Miller v. Arliskas, 324 Ill. App. 588, 58 N.E.2d 743. It must be misleading or serve so as to substantially and materially mislead the adverse party. Lorenz v. Santa Monica City High School Dist., 51 Cal.App.2d 393, 124 P.2d 846, 851.

A fatal variance is a failure to prove material allegations contained in information; it is a failure of proof. Davis v. State, 241 Ark. 646, 242 Ark. 43, 411 S.W.2d 531, 534.

The general rule with respect to proof of time when an offense is committed is that there is no "fatal variance" from the allegation that it was committed on a particular date, to show that it was actually committed on or about or near that date unless the variance results in misleading defendant so as to prevent him from making his defense to the charge or to deprive him of the benefit of a plea of former jeopardy in event of another trial for the same offense. People v. Tracy, 50 Cal.App.2d 460, 123 P.2d 138, 140, 141.

See also **Variance.**

Fatetur facinus qui judicium fugit /fətíydər fǽsənəs kwày jədísh(iy)əm fyúwjət/. He who flees judgment confesses his guilt.

Father. A male parent. He by whom a child is begotten. Natural father; procreator of a child. For "Putative father," see that title.

As used in law, this term may (according to the context and the nature of the instrument) include a putative as well as a legal father, also a stepfather, an adoptive father, or a grandfather, but is not as wide as the word "parent," and cannot be so construed as to include a female.

As used in statute providing that father may inherit from his illegitimate children, includes heirs of the father. State v. Chavez, 42 N.M. 569, 82 P.2d 900, 906.

A priest of the clergy.

Father-in-law. The father of one's wife or husband.

Fathom. A nautical measure of six feet in length. Occasionally used as a superficial measure of land and in mining, and in that case it means a square fathom or thirty-six square feet.

Fatua mulier /fǽchuwə myúwl(i)yər/. A whore; prostitute.

Fatuitas /fəchúwətæs/. In old English law, fatuity; idiocy.

Fatum /féydəm/. Lat. Fate; a superhuman power; an event or cause of loss, beyond human foresight or means of prevention.

Fatuum judicium /fǽchuwəm jədísh(iy)əm/. A foolish judgment or verdict. As applied to the latter it is one rather false by reason of folly than criminally so, or as amounting to perjury.

Fatuus /fǽchuwəs/. An idiot or fool. Foolish; silly; absurd; indiscreet; or ill considered. See **Fatuum judicium.**

Fatuus, apud jurisconsultos nostros, accipitur pro non compos mentis; et fatuus dicitur, qui omnino desipit /fǽtyuwəs, ǽpəd jùrəskənsáltows nóstrows, æksípədər pròw nón kómpəs méntəs; et fǽtyuwəs dísədər kwày omnáynow désəpət/. Fatuous, among our jurisconsults, is understood for a man not of right mind; and he is called *"fatuus"* who is altogether foolish.

Fatuus præsumitur qui in proprio nomine errat /fǽchuwəs prəz(y)úwmədər kwày in prówpriyow nóməniy éhrət/. A man is presumed to be simple who makes a mistake in his own name.

Faubourg /fówbùrg/fowbúr/. In French law, and in Louisiana, a district or part of a town adjoining the principal city; a suburb.

Fauces terræ /fósiyz téhriy/. (Jaws of the land.) Narrow headlands and promontories, inclosing a portion or arm of the sea within them.

Fault. Negligence; an error or defect of judgment or of conduct; any deviation from prudence, duty, or rectitude; any shortcoming, or neglect of care or performance resulting from inattention, incapacity, or perversity; a wrong tendency, course, or act; bad faith or mismanagement; neglect of duty. Continental Ins. Co. v. Sabine Towing Co., C.C.A.Tex., 117 F.2d 694, 697.

The word "fault" connotes an act to which blame, censure, impropriety, shortcoming or culpability attaches. Kersey Mfg. Co. v. Rozic, 207 Pa.Super. 182, 215 A.2d 323, 325.

Wrongful act, omission or breach. U.C.C. § 1-201(16).

See also **Negligence; No fault; Pari delicto; Tort.**

Fauntleroy doctrine. In Fauntleroy v. Lum, 210 U.S. 230, 28 S.Ct. 641, 52 L.Ed. 1039, the U.S. Supreme Court held that a state must give full faith and credit to a judgment of a sister state if such state had jurisdiction to render it even though the judgment is based on an original cause of action which is illegal in the state in which enforcement is sought.

Fautor /fódər/. *Old English law.* A favorer or supporter of others; an abettor. A partisan. One who encouraged resistance to the execution of process.

Spanish law. Accomplice; the person who aids or assists another in the commission of a crime.

Faux /fów/. *Civil law.* The fraudulent alteration of the truth. The same with the Latin *falsum* or *crimen falsi.*

French law. A falsification or fraudulent alteration or suppression of a thing by words, by writings, or by acts without either. *Faux* may be understood in three ways. In its most extended sense it is the alteration of truth, with or without intention; it is nearly synonymous with "lying." In a less extended sense, it is the alteration of truth, accompanied with fraud, *mutatio veritatis cum dolo facta.* And lastly, in a narrow, or rather the legal, sense of the word, when it is a question to know if the *faux* be a crime, it is the fraudulent alteration of the truth in those cases ascertained and punished by the law.

Old English law. False; counterfeit. *Faux action,* a false action. *Faux money,* counterfeit money. *Faux peys,* false weights. *Faux serement,* a false oath.

Favor, *n.* An act of kindness or generosity, as distinguished from one that is inspired by regard for justice, duty, or right. Friendly regard shown towards another. Bias; partiality; lenity; prejudice. See **Challenge.**

Favor, *v.* To regard with favor; to aid or to have the disposition to aid; to show partiality or unfair bias towards; practically synonymous with "support."

Favorabilia in lege sunt fiscus, dos, vita, libertas /fèyvərəbíl(i)yə in líyjiy sənt fískəs, dóws, váydə, líbərtæs/. Things favorably considered in law are the treasury, dower, life, liberty.

Favorabiliores rei, potius quam actores, habentur /fèyvərəbìliyóriyz ríyay, pówsh(iy)əs kwæm októriyz, həbéntər/. The condition of the defendant must be favored, rather than that of the plaintiff.

Favorabiliores sunt executiones aliis processibus quibuscunque /fèyvərəbìliyóriyz sənt èksəkyùwshiyówniyz ǽliyəs prəsésəbəs kwibəskə́ŋkwiy/. Executions are preferred to all other processes whatever.

Favored beneficiary. Within rule that confidential relations and activity by favored beneficiary in the execution of the will raises a prima facie presumption of undue influence, is one who in the circumstances has been favored over others having equal claims to testator's bounty. Mindler v. Crocker, 245 Ala. 578, 18 So.2d 278, 281.

Favored nation. See **Most favored nation clause.**

Favores ampliandi sunt; odia restringenda /fəvóriyz æmpliyǽnday sənt; ówdiyə rìystrinjéndə/. Favors are to be enlarged; things hateful restrained.

Favoritism. Invidious preference and selection based on friendship and factors other than merit. See **Nepotism; Patronage.**

Favor legitimationis /féyvər ləjìdəmèyshiyownəs/. Favor of legitimacy; in conflicts of law, principle which is invoked in cases of children's status of legitimacy.

Favor matrimonii /féyvər mætrəmówniyay/. Favor of marriage. In conflicts of law, principle invoked to uphold a marriage.

Favor negotii /féyvər nəgówshiyay/. In conflicts of laws, legal principle which favors agreement of the parties against a construction which would render an agreement illegal or unenforceable.

Favor paternitatis /féyvər pətə̀rnətéydəs/. Favor of paternity. Legal principle which is invoked to uphold paternity of child.

Favor solutionis /féyvər səl(y)uwshiyównəs/. In conflicts, a rule of interpretation of a contract in terms of the applicable law governing performance.

Favor testamenti /féyvər tèstəméntay/. In conflicts, general rule favoring the validity of a will.

F.B.I. Federal Bureau of Investigation.

F.C.A. Federal Credit Administration.

F.C.C. Federal Communications Commission.

F.C.I.C. Federal Crop Insurance Corporation. See **Insurance.**

F.D.A. Federal Drug Administration.

F.D.I.C. Federal Deposit Insurance Corporation.

Feal /fíy(ə)l/. Faithful; truthful; true. Tenants by knight service swore to their lords to be *feal* and *leal*; *i.e.*, faithful and loyal. *Feal homager,* faithful subject.

Fealty /fíy(ə)ltiy/. In feudal law, fidelity; allegiance to the feudal lord of the manor; the feudal obligation resting upon the tenant or vassal by which he was bound to be faithful and true to his lord, and render him obedience and service. This fealty was of two sorts: that which is general, and is due from every subject to his prince; the other special, and required of such only as in respect of their fee are tied by this oath to their landlords.

Fealty signifies fidelity, the phrase "feal and leal" meaning simply "faithful and loyal." Tenants by knights' service and also tenants in socage were required to take an oath of fealty to the king or others, their immediate lords; and fealty was one of the conditions of their tenure, the breach of which operated a forfeiture of their estates.

Although foreign jurists considered fealty and homage as convertible terms, because in some continental countries they were blended so as to form one engagement, yet they were not to be confounded in our country, for they did not imply the same thing, *homage* being the acknowledgment of tenure, and *fealty,* the vassal oath of fidelity, being the essential feudal bond, and the animating principle of a feud, without which it could not subsist.

Fear. Apprehension of harm; dread; consciousness of approaching danger. Mental response to threat. Profound reverence and awe.

Feasance /fíyzən(t)s/. A doing; the doing of an act; a performing or performance. See **Malfeasance; Misfeasance; Nonfeasance.**

Feasant /fíyzənt/. Doing, or making, as, in the term "damage feasant" (doing damage or injury), spoken of cattle straying upon another's land.

Feasible. Capable of being done, executed, affected or accomplished. Reasonable assurance of success. See **Possible.**

Feasor /fíyzər/. Doer; maker. *Feasors del estatute,* makers of the statute. Also used in the compound term, "tort-feasor," one who commits or is guilty of a tort.

Feasts. Certain established festivals or holidays in the ecclesiastical calendar. These days were anciently used as the dates of legal instruments, and in England the quarter-days, for paying rent, are four feast-days. The terms of the courts, in England, before 1875, were fixed to begin on certain days determined with reference to the occurrence of four of the chief feasts.

Featherbedding. The name given to employee practices which create or spread employment by unnecessarily maintaining or increasing the number of employees used, or the amount of time consumed, to work on a particular job. It may take the form of minimum-crew regulations on the railroad, make-work rules such as the setting and prompt destruction of unneeded "bogus" type in the newspaper industry, stand-by pay for musicians when a radio station broadcasts music from phonograph records, or production ceilings for work on the assembly line or at the construction site. Most of these practices stem from a desire on the part of employees for job security in the face of technological improvements. In addition to job security, employees often justify such practices as required by minimum standards of health and safety (*e.g.,* minimum-crew and production-ceiling limitations).

F.E.C.A. Federal Employees' Compensation Act.

Feciales /fiyshiyéyliyz/. Among the ancient Romans, that order of priests who discharged the duties of ambassadors. Subsequently their duties appear to have related more particularly to the declaring of war and peace.

Fecial law /fíyshəl ló/. The nearest approach to a system of international law known to the ancient world. It was a branch of Roman jurisprudence, concerned with embassies, declarations of war, and treaties of peace. It received this name from the *feciales (q.v.),* who were charged with its administration.

Federal. Belonging to the general government or union of the states. Founded on or organized under the Constitution of the United States. Pertaining to the national government of the United States. Of or constituting a government in which power is distributed between a central authority (*i.e.* federal government) and a number of constituent territorial units (*i.e.* states). See also **Federal government.**

A league or compact between two or more states, to become united under one central government. See **Federation.**

Federal Acts. Statutes enacted by Congress, relating to matters within authority delegated to federal government by U.S. Constitution.

Federal Aviation Administration. The Federal Aviation Administration (FAA), formerly the Federal Aviation Agency, became a part of the Department of Transportation in 1967 as a result of the Department of Transportation Act (80 Stat. 932). The Federal Aviation Administration is charged with regulating air commerce to foster aviation safety; promoting civil aviation and a national system of airports; achieving efficient use of navigable airspace; and developing and operating a common system of air traffic control and air navigation for both civilian and military aircraft.

Federal Bureau of Investigation. The FBI (established in 1908) is charged with investigating all violations of Federal laws with the exception of those which have been assigned by legislative enactment or otherwise to some other Federal agency. The FBI's jurisdiction includes a wide range of responsibilities in the criminal, civil, and security fields. Among these are espionage, sabotage, and other subversive activities; kidnaping; extortion; bank robbery; interstate transportation of stolen property; civil rights matters; interstate gambling violations; fraud against the Government; and assault or killing the President or a Federal officer. Cooperative services of the FBI for other duly authorized law enforcement agencies include fingerprint identification, laboratory services, police training, and the National Crime Information Center.

Federal census. A census of each state or territory or of a certain state or of any subdivision or portion of any state, provided it is taken by and under the direction and supervision of the Census Bureau of the United States, and approved and certified by it as the census of that state or subdivision. See **Census.**

Federal citizenship. Rights and obligations accruing by reason of being a citizen of the United States. State or status of being a citizen of the United States.

A person born or naturalized in the United States and subject to the jurisdiction thereof is a citizen of the United States and of the State wherein he resides. Fourteenth Amend., U.S. Const.

See also **Citizenship; Naturalization.**

Federal common law. A body of a decisional law developed by the federal courts untrammeled by state court decisions. O'Brien v. Western Union Telegraph Co., C.C.A.Mass., 113 F.2d 539, 541. The application of federal common law was restricted by Erie R. Co. v. Tompkins, 304 U.S. 64, 58 S.Ct. 817, 82 L.Ed. 1188, which held that the federal courts are required to apply state law except as to cases governed by the U.S. Constitution and Acts of Congress, thereby overruling Swift v. Tyson, 41 U.S. (16 Pet.) 1, 10 L.Ed. 865. See **Swift v. Tyson case.**

Federal Communications Commission. The Federal Communications Commission was created by the Communications Act of 1934 to regulate interstate and foreign communications by wire and radio in the public interest. It was assigned additional regulatory jurisdiction under the provisions of the Communications Satellite Act of 1962. The scope of its regulatory powers includes radio and television broadcasting) telephone, telegraph, and cable television operation; two-way radio and radio operators; and satellite communication.

Federal courts. The courts of the United States as created either by Art. III of U.S. Const., or by Congress. See specific courts; *e.g.* **Court of Appeals; Court of Claims; District** *(District courts);* **Supreme Court; Three-judge courts.**

Federal crimes. Those acts which have been made criminal by federal law. There are no federal common law crimes though many federal statutes have incorporated the elements of common law crimes. Most federal crimes are codified in Title 18 of the United States Code; though other Code Titles also include specific crimes.

Federal Deposit Insurance Corporation. The F.D.I.C. is an independent agency within the executive branch of the Government. The management of the Corporation is vested in a Board of Directors consisting of three members, one of whom is the Comptroller of the Currency, and two of whom are appointed by the President, with the advice and consent of the Senate. Appointive members serve 6-year terms, and one serves as Chairman of the Board of Directors. The Corporation insures, up to the statutory limitation, the deposits in national banks, in State banks which are members of the Federal Reserve System, and in State banks which apply for Federal Deposit Insurance and meet certain prescribed qualifications.

Federal Employees' Compensation Act. Type of workers' compensation plan for federal employees by which payments are made for death or disability sustained in performance of duties of employment. 5 U.S.C.A. § 8101 *et seq.*

Federal Employer's Liability Act. Federal workers' compensation law which protects employees of railroads engaged in interstate and foreign commerce. 45 U.S.C.A. § 51 *et seq.* Payments are made for death or disability sustained in performance of duties of employment.

Federal government. The system of government administered in a nation formed by the union or confederation of several independent states.

In strict usage, there is a distinction between a *confederation* and a *federal government.* The former term denotes a league or permanent alliance between several states, each of which is fully sovereign and independent, and each of which retains its full dignity, organization, and sovereignty, though yielding to the central authority a controlling power for a few limited purposes, such as external and diplomatic relations. In this case, the component states are the units, with respect to the confederation, and the central government acts upon them, not upon the individual citizens. In a *federal government,* on the other hand, the allied states form a union,—not, indeed, to such an extent as to destroy their separate organization or deprive them of *quasi* sovereignty with respect to the administration of their purely local concerns, but so that the central power is erected into a true national government, possessing sovereignty both external and internal,—while the administration of national affairs is directed, and its effects felt, not by the separate states deliberating as units, but by the people of all, in their collective capacity, as citizens of the nation. The distinction is expressed, by the German writers, by the use of the two words *"Staatenbund"* and *"Bundesstaat;"* the former denoting a league or confederation of states, and the latter a federal government, or state formed by means of a league or confederation.

See also **Federal.**

Federal Home Loan Bank Board. The board which charters and regulates federal savings and loan associations, and controls the system of Federal Home Loan Banks.

Federal Home Loan Banks. Banks created under the Federal Home Loan Bank Act of 1932, for the purpose of keeping a permanent supply of money available for home financing. The banks are controlled by the Federal Home Loan Bank Board. Savings and loans, insurance companies, and other similar companies making long term mortgage loans may become members of the Federal Home Loan Bank System, and thus may borrow from one of twelve regional banks throughout the country.

Federal Home Loan Mortgage Corporation. A federal agency which purchases first mortgages (both conventional and federally insured) from members of the Federal Reserve System, and the Federal Home Loan Bank System. Commonly called "Freddie Mac."

Federal Housing Administration. This federal agency, established by Congress in 1934, insures mortgage loans made by FHA-approved lenders on homes that meet FHA standards in order to make mortgages more desirable investments for lenders.

Federal instrumentality. A means or agency used by the federal government. Capitol Building & Loan Ass'n v. Kansas Commission of Labor and Industry, 148 Kan. 446, 83 P.2d 106, 107. A government agency immune from state control. Waterbury Sav. Bank v. Danaher, 128 Conn. 78, 20 A.2d 455, 458. See **Administrative agency.**

Federal Insurance Contributions Act. Federal Act imposing social security tax on employees, self employed, and employers. Under the F.I.C.A. the employer matches the tax paid by the employee. These taxes fund the social security and medicare programs.

Federalism. Term which includes interrelationships among the states and relationship between the states and the federal government.

Federalist Papers. A series of 85 essays by Alexander Hamilton, James Madison and John Jay, expounding and advocating the adoption of the Constitution of the United States. All but six of the essays were first published in the "Independent Journal" of New York City from October, 1787, to April, 1788.

Federal Judicial Code. This Code, comprising Title 28 of the United States Code, is concerned with the organization, jurisdiction, venue, and procedures of the federal court system. Also covered by this Code is the Department of Justice as well as court officers and personnel.

Federal jurisdiction. Powers of federal courts founded on U.S. Constitution (Article III) and Acts of Congress (e.g. Title 28 of United States Code). See **Diversity of citizenship; Federal question; Jurisdiction.**

Federal Land Banks. Regional banks established by Congress to provide mortgage loans to farmers. See **Federal Home Loan Banks.**

Federal laws. See **Federal acts.**

Federal Maritime Commission. The Federal Maritime Commission regulates the waterborne foreign and domestic offshore commerce of the United States, assures that United States international trade is open to all nations on fair and equitable terms, and guards against unauthorized monopoly in the waterborne commerce of the United States. This is accomplished through maintaining surveillance over steamship conferences and common carriers by water; assuring that only the rates on file with the Commission are charged; approving agreements between persons subject to the Shipping Act; guaranteeing equal treatment to shippers and carriers by terminal operators, freight forwarders, and other persons subject to the shipping statutes; and ensuring that adequate levels of financial responibility are maintained for indemnification of passengers or oil spill cleanup.

Federal Mediation and Conciliation Service. The Federal Mediation and Conciliation Service helps prevent disruptions in the flow of interstate commerce caused by labor-management disputes by providing media-

tors to assist disputing parties in the resolution of their differences. The Service can intervene on its own motion or by invitation of either side in a dispute. Mediators have no law enforcement authority and rely wholly on persuasive techniques. The Service also helps provide qualified third party neutrals as factfinders or arbitrators.

Federal National Mortgage Association. Organized in 1938 to provide a secondary mortgage market for purchase and sale of mortgages guaranteed by Veterans Administration and those insured under Federal Housing Administration. The short name for this association is "Fannie Mae".

Federal Power Commission. The Federal Power Commission issues permits and licenses for non-Federal hydroelectric power projects; regulates the rates and other aspects of interstate wholesale transactions in electric power and natural gas; issues certificates for interstate gas sales and construction and operation of interstate pipeline facilities; conducts continuing investigations of the electric power and natural gas pipeline industries and their relationships to national programs and objectives, including conservation and efficient utilization of resources; requires maximum protection of our environment in the construction of new hydroelectric projects and natural gas transmission lines consistent with the Nation's needs for adequate and reliable electric power and natural gas services; and allocates resources consistent with the public interest under the Federal Power Act and the Natural Gas Act. The Federal Power Commission was terminated in 1977, with its functions taken over by the Department of Energy, and, within the DOE, by the Federal Energy Regulatory Commission.

Federal pre-emption. The U.S. Constitution and acts of Congress have given to the federal government exclusive power over certain matters such as interstate commerce and sedition to the exclusion of state jurisdiction. Occurs where federal law so occupies the field that state courts are prevented from asserting jurisdiction. State v. McHorse, 85 N.M. 753, 517 P.2d 75, 79. See also **Pre-emption.**

Federal question. Cases arising under Constitution of United States, Acts of Congress, or treaties, and involving their interpretation and application, and of which jurisdiction is given to federal courts, are commonly described as involving a "federal question." See 28 U.S.C.A. § 1331 with respect to "federal question" jurisdiction of federal courts.

Federal Register. The Federal Register, published daily, is the medium for making available to the public Federal agency regulations and other legal documents of the executive branch. These documents cover a wide range of Government activities. An important function of the Federal Register is that it includes proposed changes (rules, regulations, standards, etc.) of governmental agencies. Each proposed change published carries an invitation for any citizen or group to participate in the consideration of the proposed regulation through the submission of written data, views, or arguments, and sometimes by oral presentations. Such regulations and rules as finally approved appear thereafter in the Code of Federal Regulations.

Federal regulations. See **Code of Federal Regulations; Federal Register.**

Federal Reporter. The Federal Reporter (consisting of a First and Second series) publishes opinions of the below listed federal courts:

1880–1932

    Circuit Court of Appeals

    District Courts

    U.S. Court of Customs and Patent Appeals

    Court of Claims of the U.S.

    Court of Appeals of the District of Columbia

1932–present

    U.S. Courts of Appeals

    U.S. Court of Customs and Patent Appeals

1942–61, 1972–present

    U.S. Emergency Court of Appeals

1960–present

    U.S. Court of Claims

    See also **Federal Supplement.**

Federal Reserve Act. Law which created Federal Reserve banks which act as agents in maintaining money reserves, issuing money in the form of bank notes, lending money to banks, and supervising banks. Administered by Federal Reserve Board *(q.v.).*

Federal Reserve Banks. See **Federal Reserve Act; Federal Reserve Board of Governors; Federal Reserve System.**

Federal Reserve Board of Governors. The seven-member Board of Governors, appointed by the President and confirmed by the Congress, sets reserve requirements for member banks, reviews and approves the discount-rate actions of regional Federal Reserve Banks, sets ceilings on the rates of interest that banks can pay on time and savings deposits, and issues regulations. Members also sit on the Federal Open Market Committee—the principal instrument for implementing the Board's national monetary policy.

Federal reserve notes. Form of currency issued by Federal Reserve Banks in the likeness of noninterest bearing promissory note payable to bearer on demand. The federal reserve note (*e.g.* one, five, ten, etc. dollar bill) is the most widely used paper currency. Such have replaced silver and gold certificates which were backed by silver and gold. Such reserve notes are direct obligations of the United States.

Federal Reserve System. Network of twelve central banks to which most national banks belong and to which state chartered banks may belong. Membership rules require investment of stock and minimum reserves. The Federal Reserve System was established in 1913 to give the country an elastic currency, provide facilities for discounting commercial paper and to improve the supervision of banking.

    The System consists of five parts: the Board of Governors in Washington; the 12 Federal Reserve Banks, their branches and other facilities situated throughout the country; the Federal Open Market Committee; the Federal Advisory Council; and the member commercial banks, which include all national banks and State-chartered banks that have voluntarily joined the System.

Federal Rules Act. Act of 1934 granting U.S. Supreme Court power to adopt Federal Rules of Civil Procedure. See 28 U.S.C.A. §§ 2071, 2072. Additional power to prescribe rules is provided for by 28 U.S. C.A. § 2075 (Bankruptcy Rules), § 2076 (Evidence Rules) and 18 U.S.C.A. § 3771 (Criminal Rules).

Federal Rules Decisions. Reporter which publishes federal court decisions which construe or apply the Federal Rules of Civil, Criminal and Appellate Procedure, as well as Federal Rules of Evidence.

Federal Rules of Appellate Procedure. These rules govern procedure in appeals to United States courts of appeals from the United States district courts and the Tax Court of the United States; in proceedings in the courts of appeals for review or enforcement of orders of administrative agencies, boards, commissions and officers of the United States; and in applications for writs or other relief which a court of appeals or a judge thereof is competent to give. Certain states have adopted appellate rules patterned on such federal rules.

Federal Rules of Civil Procedure. Body of procedural rules which govern all civil actions in U.S. District Courts and after which most of the states have modeled their own rules of procedure. These rules were promulgated by the U.S. Supreme Court in 1938 under power granted by Congress, and have since been frequently amended. Such rules also govern bankruptcy proceedings in the bankruptcy courts; and, Supplemental Rules, in addition to main body of rules, govern admiralty and maritime actions.

Federal Rules of Criminal Procedure. Procedural rules which govern all criminal proceedings in the U.S. District Courts, and, where specified, before U.S. Magistrates. Such rules were promulgated by the U.S. Supreme Court in 1945 under power granted by Congress, and have since been frequently amended. Several states have adopted criminal rules patterned on the federal criminal rules.

Federal Rules of Evidence. Rules which govern the admissability of evidence at trials in the Federal Courts and before U.S. Magistrates. Several states have adopted Evidence Rules patterned on these federal rules.

Federal statutes. See **Federal Acts.**

Federal Supplement. The Federal Supplement publishes opinions of the below listed federal courts:

1932–present

    U.S. District Courts

1932–1960

    U.S. Court of Claims

1949–present

    U.S. Customs Court (vol. 135).

    See also **Federal Reporter.**

Federal Tort Claims Act. The government of the United States may not be sued in tort without its consent. That consent was given in the Federal Tort Claims Act (1946), which largely abrogated the federal government's immunity from tort liability and established the conditions for suits and claims against the federal government. The Act preserves governmental immunity with respect to the traditional categories of intentional torts, and with respect to acts or omissions which fall within the "discretionary function or duty" of any federal agency or employee. See also **Governmental immunity; Sovereign immunity.**

Federal Trade Commission. Agency of the federal government created in 1914. The Commission's principal functions are to promote free and fair competition in interstate commerce through prevention of general trade restraints such as price-fixing agreements, false advertising, boycotts, illegal combinations of competitors and other unfair methods of competition. See also **Clayton Act; Robinson-Patman Act; Sherman Antitrust Act.**

Federation. A joining together of states or nations in a league or association; the league itself. See also **Compact; Federal; Federal government.**

An unincorporated association of persons for a common purpose.

Fee. A charge fixed by law for services of public officers or for use of a privilege under control of government. Fort Smith Gas Co. v. Wiseman, 189 Ark. 675, 74 S.W.2d 789, 790. A recompense for an official or professional service or a charge or emolument or compensation for a particular act or service. A fixed charge or perquisite charged as recompense for labor; reward, compensation, or wage given to a person for performance of services or something done or to be done.

See also **Base** *(Base fee)*; **Commitment** *(Commitment fee)*; **License fee; Poundage fees; Retainer.**

Attorney fees. Numerous federal statutes provide for the award of attorney fees to the prevailing party; *e.g.* 25% of award in social security disability claim actions. See *Contingent fees, infra;* also, **American Rule; Minimum fee schedules; Suit** *(Suit money).*

Contingent fees. Arrangement between attorney and client whereby attorney agrees to represent client with compensation to be a percentage of the amount recovered; *e.g.* 25% if case is settled, 30% if case goes to trial. Frequently used in personal injury actions. Such fees are often regulated by court rule or statute depending on the type of action and amount of recovery.

Docket fees. See **Docket.**

Estates

An estate of inheritance without condition, belonging to the owner, and alienable by him or transmissible to his heirs absolutely and simply, and is an absolute estate in perpetuity and the largest possible estate a man can have, being, in fact, allodial in its nature. Stanton v. Sullivan, 63 R.I. 216, 7 A.2d 696, 698, 699. See also **Fee simple.**

Ordinarily, word "fee" or "fee simple" is applied to an estate in land, but term is applicable to any kind of hereditament, corporeal or incorporeal, and is all the property in thing referred to or largest estate therein which person may have. In re Forsstrom, 44 Ariz. 472, 38 P.2d 878, 888.

A freehold estate in lands, held of a superior lord, as a reward for services, and on condition of rendering some service in return for it. The true meaning of the word "fee" is the same as that of "feud" or "fief," and in its original sense it is taken in contradistinc-

tion to "allodium," which latter is defined as a man's own land, which he possesses merely in his own right, without owing any rent or service to any superior. 2 Bl.Comm. 105.

In modern English tenures, "fee" signifies an estate of inheritance, being the highest and most extensive interest which a man can have in a feud; and when the term is used simply, without any adjunct, or in the form "fee-simple," it imports an absolute inheritance clear of any condition, limitation, or restriction to particular heirs, but descendible to the heirs general, male or female, lineal or collateral. 2 Bl.Comm. 106.

Base fee. A determinable or qualified fee; an estate having the nature of a fee, but not a fee simple absolute.

Conditional fee. An estate restrained to some particular heirs, exclusive of others, Blume v. Pearcy, 204 S.C. 409, 29 S.E.2d 673, 674, as to the heirs of a man's body, by which only his lineal descendants were admitted, in exclusion of collateral; or to the heirs male of his body, in exclusion of heirs female, whether lineal or collateral. It was called a "conditional fee," by reason of the condition expressed or implied in the donation of it that, if the donee died without such particular heirs, the land should revert to the donor. The term includes a fee that is either to commence or determine on some condition; and is sometimes used interchangeably with "base fee," that is, one to determine or be defeated on the happening of some contingent event or act.

Determinable fee. Also called a "base" or "qualified" fee. One which has a qualification subjoined to it, and which must be determined whenever the qualification annexed to it is at an end. An estate in fee which is liable to be determined by some act or event expressed on its limitation to circumscribe its continuance, or inferred by law as bounding its extent. An estate which may last forever is a "fee," but if it may end on the happening of a merely possible event, it is a "determinable," or "qualified fee."

Determinable fee or fee simple. Estate created with special limitation which delimits duration of estate in land.

Fee damages. See **Damages.**

Fee expectant. A name sometimes applied to an estate created where lands are given to a man and his wife and the heirs of their bodies. See also Frank-Marriage.

Fee simple. See **Fee simple.**

Fee simple defeasible. Title created in trustees where legal title in fee simple to active trust estate is by will placed in trustees who are required to distribute property in fee simple upon happening of event. Also called a "determinable fee", "base fee", or "qualified fee". Kanawha Val. Bank v. Hornbeck, 151 W.Va. 308, 151 S.E.2d 694, 700.

Great fee. In feudal law, the designation of a fee held directly from the crown.

Knight's fee. See **Knight's fee.**

Limited fee. An estate of inheritance in lands, which is clogged or confined with some sort of condition or qualification. Such estates are based on qualified fees, conditional fees, and fees-tail. The term is opposed to "fee-simple."

Plowman's fee. In old English law, was a species of tenure peculiar to peasants or small farmers, somewhat like gavelkind, by which the lands descended in equal shares to all the sons of the tenant.

Qualified fee. In English law, a fee having a qualification subjoined thereto, and which must be determined whenever the qualification annexed to it is at an end; otherwise termed a "base fee." An interest which may continue forever, but is liable to be determined, without the aid of a conveyance, by some act or event, circumscribing its continuance or extent. An interest given to a man *and certain of his heirs* at the time of its limitation.

Quasi fee. An estate gained by wrong.

Feed. To lend additional support; to strengthen *ex post facto.* Similarly, a subsequent title acquired by the mortgagor is said "to feed the mortgage."

Fee-farm. A species of tenure, where land is held of another in perpetuity at a yearly rent, without fealty, homage, or other services than such as are specially comprised in the feoffment. It corresponds very nearly to the *"emphyteusis"* of the Roman law. Fealty, however, was incident to a holding in fee-farm, according to some authors.

Fee-farm is where an estate in fee is granted subject to a rent in fee of at least one-fourth of the value of the lands at the time of its reservation. Such rent appears to be called "fee-farm" because a grant of lands reserving so considerable a rent is indeed only letting lands to farm in fee-simple, instead of the usual method of life or years. Fee-farms are lands held in fee to render for them annually the true value, or more or less; so called because a farm rent is reserved upon a grant in fee. Such estates are estates of inheritance. They are classed among estates in fee-simple. No reversionary interest remains in the lessor, and they are therefore subject to the operation of the legal principles which forbid restraints upon alienation in all cases where no feudal relation exists between grantor and grantee.

Fee-farm rent. The rent reserved on granting a fee-farm. It might be one-fourth or one-third the value of the land. Fee-farm rent is a rent-charge issuing out of an estate in fee; a perpetual rent reserved on a conveyance in fee-simple.

Fee simple.

Absolute. A fee simple absolute is an estate limited absolutely to a man and his heirs and assigns forever without limitation or condition. An absolute or fee-simple estate is one in which the owner is entitled to the entire property, with unconditional power of disposition during his life, and descending to his heirs and legal representatives upon his death intestate. Such estate is unlimited as to duration, disposition, and descendibility. Slayden v. Hardin, 257 Ky. 685, 79 S.W.2d 11, 12.

The estate which a man has where lands are given to him and to his heirs absolutely without any end or limit put to his estate. 2 Bl.Comm. 106. The word "fee," used alone, is a sufficient designation of this species of estate, and hence "simple" is not a necessary part of the title, but it is added as a means of clearly distinguishing this estate from a fee-tail or from any variety of conditional estates. Fee-simple signifies a pure fee; an absolute estate of inheritance clear of any condition or restriction to particular heirs, being descendible to the heirs general, whether male or female, lineal or collateral. It is the largest estate and most extensive interest that can be enjoyed in land.

Conditional. Type of transfer in which grantor conveys fee simply on condition that something be done or not done. A defeasible fee which leaves grantor with right of entry for condition broken, which right may be exercised by some action on part of grantor when condition is breached.

At common law an estate in fee simple conditional was a fee limited or restrained to some particular heirs, exclusive of others. But the statute "De donis" converted all such estates into estates tail. 2 Bl. Comm. 110.

Defeasible. Type of fee grant which may be defeated on the happening of an event. An estate which may last forever, but which may end upon the happening of a specified event, is a "fee simple defeasible". Newbern v. Barnes, 3 N.C.App. 521, 165 S.E.2d 526, 530.

Determinable. A "fee simple determinable" is created by conveyance which contains words effective to create a fee simple and, in addition, a provision for automatic expiration of estate on occurrence of stated event. Selectmen of Town of Nahant v. U. S., D.C.Mass., 293 F.Supp. 1076, 1978.

Fee simple title. See **Fee simple.**

Fee tail. A freehold estate in which there is a fixed line of inheritable succession limited to the issue of the body of the grantee or devisee, and in which the regular and general succession of heirs at law is cut off. Coleman v. Shoemaker, 147 Kan. 689, 78 P.2d 905, 907.

An estate tail; an estate of inheritance given to a man and the heirs of his body, or limited to certain classes of particular heirs. It corresponds to the *feudum talliatum* of the feudal law, and the idea is believed to have been borrowed from the Roman law, where, by way of *fidei commissa,* lands might be entailed upon children and freedmen and their descendants, with restrictions as to alienation. For the varieties and special characteristics of this kind of estate, see **Tail, Estate in.**

Fegangi /fəgǽnjay/. In old English law, a thief caught while escaping with the stolen goods in his possession.

Fehmgerichte /féymgərìktə/. The name given to certain secret tribunals which flourished in Germany from the end of the twelfth century to the middle of the sixteenth, usurping many of the functions of the governments which were too weak to maintain law and order, and inspiring dread in all who came within their jurisdiction. Such a court existed in Westphalia (though with greatly diminished powers) until finally suppressed by Jerome Bonaparte in 1811.

Feigned /féynd/. Fictitious; pretended; supposititious; simulated.

Feigned accomplice. One who pretends to consult and act with others in the planning or commission of a crime, but only for the purpose of discovering their plans and confederates and securing evidence against them.

Feigned action. An action, now obsolete, brought on a pretended right, when the plaintiff has no true cause of action, for some illegal purpose. In a feigned action the words of the writ are true. It differs from *false action,* in which case the words of the writ are false. See also **Feigned issue.**

Feigned diseases. Simulated or pretended illness. Diseases are generally feigned from one of three causes, —fear, shame, or the hope of gain.

Feigned issue. A proceeding, now obsolete, whereby parties, by consent, could have matter determined by jury without actually bringing action. See also **Feigned action.**

FELA. Federal Employers' Liability Act.

Felagus /fəléygəs/. In Saxon law, one bound for another by oath; a sworn brother. A friend bound in the decennary for the good behavior of another. One who took the place of the deceased. Thus, if a person was murdered, the recompense due from the murderer went to the *felagus* of the slain, in default of parents or lord.

Feld. A field; in composition, wild.

Fele, feal. L. Fr. Faithful. See **Feal.**

Fellow. A co-worker; a partaker or sharer of; a companion; one with whom we consort; one joined with another in some legal *status* or relation; a member of a college or corporate body.

Fellow-heir. A co-heir; partner of the same inheritance.

Fellow servant. One who serves and is controlled by the same master. Walsh v. Eubanks, 183 Ark. 34, 34 S.W.2d 762, 764. Those engaged in the same common pursuit, under the same general control. Those who derive authority and compensation from the same common source, and are engaged in the same general business, though it may be in different grades or departments of it. Southern Ry. Co. v. Taylor, 57 App.D.C. 21, 16 F.2d 517, 519. When servants are employed and paid by the same master, and their duties are such as to bring them into such relation that negligence of one in doing his work may injure other in performance of his, then they are engaged in the same common business, and are "fellow servants." See also **Employee.**

Fellow servant rule. A common law doctrine, now generally abrogated by workers' compensation acts and Federal Employers' Liability Act, that in an action for damages brought against an employer by an injured employee the employer may allege that the negligence of another employee was partly or wholly responsible for the accident resulting in the injury and, thus reducing or extinguishing his own liability.

Felo de se /félow dìy síy/. Killing of self; suicide.

Felon /félən/. Person who commits or has committed a felony *(q.v.).*

Felonia /fəlówniyə/. Felony. The act or offense by which a vassal forfeited his fee. *Per feloniam,* with a criminal intention.

Felonia, ex vi termini significat quodlibet capitale crimen felleo animo perpetratum /fəlówniyə, èks váy tármənay, səgnífəkæt kwódləbət kǽpətéyliy kráymən félliyow ǽnəmow pərpətréydəm/. Felony, by force of the term, signifies any capital crime perpetrated with a malignant mind.

Felonia implicatur in qualibet proditione /fəlówniyə ìmpləkéydər in kwéyləbət prədìshiyówniy/. Felony is implied in every treason.

Felonice /fəlównəsiy/. Feloniously.

Felonious /fəlówn(i)yəs/. A technical word of law which means done with intent to commit crime, *i.e.* criminal intent. Of the grade or quality of a felony, as, for example, a felonious assault *(q.v.).* Malicious; villainous; traitorous; malignant. Proceeding from an evil heart or purpose. Wickedly and against the admonition of the law; unlawfully. See also **Felony; Feloniously.**

Felonious assault. Such an assault upon the person as, if consummated, would subject the party making it, upon conviction, to the punishment of a felony, that is, to imprisonment. Aggravated assault as contrasted with simple assault.

Felonious entry. Type of statutory burglary. See **Burglary.**

Felonious homicide. Killing of human being without justification or excuse. See **Homicide; Manslaughter; Murder; Premeditation.**

Felonious intent. An act of the will in which one forms his desire to commit a felony.

Feloniously. Of, pertaining to, or having, the quality of felony. Proceeding from an evil heart or purpose; done with a deliberate intention of committing a crime. Golden v. Commonwealth, 245 Ky. 19, 53 S.W.2d 185, 186. Without color of right or excuse. Malignantly; maliciously. Acting with a felonious intent; *i.e.* acting with intent to commit a felony. See also **Felonious.**

Felonious taking. As used in the crimes of larceny and robbery, it is the taking with intent to steal.

Felony. A crime of a graver or more serious nature than those designated as misdemeanors; *e.g.* aggravated assault (felony) as contrasted with simple assault (misdemeanor). Under federal law, and many state statutes, any offense punishable by death or imprisonment for a term exceeding one year. 18 U.S.C.A. § 1. Many state penal or criminal codes define felony status crimes, and certain states in turn also have various classes of felonies (*e.g.* Class A, B, C, etc.) with varying sentences for each class.

At common law, an offense occasioning total forfeiture of either land or goods to which capital or other punishment might be superadded according to degree of guilt. At early common law the term was applied to describe the more serious offenses cognizable in the royal courts, conviction for which entailed forfeiture of life, limb and chattels and escheat of lands to the felon's lord after a year and a day in the king's hands. Subsequently, however, the classification was so greatly enlarged that many offenses not involving moral turpitude were included therein. In re Donegan, 282 N.Y. 285, 26 N.E. 260, 261. This term meant originally the state of having forfeited lands and goods to the crown upon conviction for certain offenses, and then, by transition, any offense upon conviction for which such forfeiture followed, in addition to capital or any other punishment prescribed by law; as distinguished from a "misdemeanor," upon conviction for which no forfeiture followed. In feudal law, the term meant an act or offense on the part of the vassal, which cost him his fee, or in consequence of which his fee fell into the hands of his lord; that is, became forfeited. (See **Felonia.**) Perfidy, ingratitude, or disloyalty to a lord.

Felony, compounding of. See **Compounding crime.**

Forcible felony. Forcible felony includes any treason, murder, voluntary manslaughter, rape, robbery, burglary, arson, kidnapping, aggravated battery, aggravated sodomy and any other felony which involves the use or threat of physical force or violence against any person.

Misprision of felony. See **Misprision.**

Reducible felony. A felony upon conviction of which the offender may be punished as for a misdemeanor, upon recommendation of the jury.

Felony murder doctrine. At common law, one whose conduct brought about an unintended death in the commission or attempted commission of a felony was guilty of murder. While some states still follow the common law rule, today the law of felony murder varies substantially throughout the country, largely as a result of efforts to limit the scope of the rule. Jurisdictions have limited the rule in one or more of the following ways: (1) by permitting its use only as to certain types of felonies; (2) by more strict interpretation of the requirement of proximate or legal cause; (3) by a narrower construction of the time period during which the felony is in the process of commission; (4) by requiring that the underlying felony be independent of the homicide.

Female. The sex which conceives and gives birth to young. Also a member of such sex. The term is generic, but may have the specific meaning of "woman," if so indicated by the context.

Feme, femme /fém/. L. Fr. A woman. Also, a wife, as in the phrase *"baron et feme".*

Feme covert /fém kávərt/. A married woman. Generally used in reference to the former legal disabilities of a married woman, as compared with the condition of a *feme sole.*

Feme sole /fém sówl/. A single woman, including those who have been married, but whose marriage has been dissolved by death or divorce, and, for most purposes, those women who are judicially separated from their husbands.

Feme sole trader /fém sówl tréydər/. In old English law, a married woman, who, by the custom of London, trades on her own account, independently of her husband; so called because, with respect to her trad-

ing, she is the same as a *feme sole.* The term is applied also to women deserted by their husbands, who do business as *femes sole.*

Femicide /fémasàyd/. The killing of a woman. One who kills a woman.

Feminine /fémanən/. Of or belonging to females.

Femme couleur libre /fám kùwlár líybrə/. Up to the time of Civil War, term applied to all persons not of the white race, including Indians.

Fence, n. A hedge, structure, or partition, erected for the purpose of inclosing a piece of land, or to divide a piece of land into distinct portions, or to separate two contiguous estates. An enclosure about a field or other space, or about any object; especially an enclosing structure of wood, iron or other materials, intended to prevent intrusion from without or straying from within.

A colloquial characterization of a receiver of stolen property.

Fence county. A county where the stock law has not been adopted. McKenzie v. Powell, 68 Ga.App. 285, 22 S.E.2d 735, 736.

Fence-month, or **defense-month.** In old English law, a period of time, occurring in the middle of summer, during which it was unlawful to hunt deer in the forest, that being their fawning season. Probably so called because the deer were then *defended* from pursuit or hunting.

Fencing patents. Patents procured in an effort to broaden the scope of the invention beyond the article or process which is actually intended to be manufactured or licensed. Special Equipment Co. v. Coe, 79 U.S.App.D.C. 133, 144 F.2d 497, 499.

Feneration /fènəréyshən/. Usury; the gain of interest; the practice of increasing money by lending. Sometimes applied to interest on money lent.

Fengeld /féngèld/. In Saxon law, a tax or imposition, exacted for the repelling of enemies.

Fenian /fíyniyən/. A champion, hero, giant. This word, in the plural, is generally used to signify invaders or foreign spoilers. A member of an organization of persons of Irish birth, resident in the United States, Canada, and elsewhere, having for its aim the overthrow of English rule in Ireland.

Feod /fyúwd/. The same as *feud* or *fief.* 2 Bl.Comm. 45.

Feodal /fyúwdəl/. Belonging to a fee or feud; feudal. More commonly used by the old writers than *feudal.*

Feodal actions /fyúwdəl ǽkshənz/. Real actions. 3 Bl.Comm. 117.

Feodality /fyuwdǽlədiy/. Fidelity or fealty. See **Fealty.**

Feodal system /fyúwdəl sìstəm/. See **Feudal system.**

Feodarum (or feudaram) consuetudines /fyùwdérəm kònswət(y)úwdəniyz/. The customs of feuds. The name of a compilation of feudal laws and customs made at Milan in the twelfth century. It is the most ancient work on the subject, and was always regarded, on the continent of Europe, as possessing the highest authority.

Feodary /fyúwdəriy/. In England, an officer of the court of wards, appointed by the master of that court, under 32 Hen. VIII, c. 26, whose business it was to be present with the escheator in every county at the finding of offices of lands, and to give evidence for the king, as well concerning the value as the tenure; and his office was also to survey the land of the ward, after the office found, and to rate it. He also assigned the king's widows their dower; and received all the rents, etc.

Feodatory, or **feudatory** /fyúwdət(ə)riy/. In feudal law, the grantee of a *feod, feud,* or fee; the vassal or tenant who held his estate by feudal service. Blackstone uses *"feudatory."* 2 Bl.Comm. 46.

Feodi firma /fyúwday fármə/. In old English law, fee-farm *(q.v.).*

Feodi firmarius /fyúwday fərmériyəs/. The lessee of a fee-farm.

Feodum /fyúwdəm/. This word (meaning a feud or fee) is the one most commonly used by the older English law-writers, though its equivalent, *"feudum" (q.v.),* is used generally by the more modern writers and by the *feudal* law-writers. There were various classes of *feoda,* among which may be enumerated the following: *Feodum laicum,* a lay fee. *Feodum militare,* a knight's fee. *Feodum improprium,* an improper or derivative fee. *Feodum proprium,* a proper and original fee, regulated by the strict rules of feudal succession and tenure. *Feodum simplex,* a simple or pure fee; fee-simple. *Feodum talliatum,* a fee-tail.

In old English law, a seigniory or jurisdiction. A fee, a perquisite or compensation for a service.

Feodum antiquum /fyúwdəm æntáykwəm/. A feud which devolved upon a vassal from his intestate ancestor.

Feodum est quod quis tenet ex quacunque causa sive sit tenementum sive redditus /fyúwdəm èst kwòd kwís ténəd èks kweykə́ŋkwiy kózə sáyviy sìt tenəméntəm sáyviy rédədəs/. A fee is that which any one holds from whatever cause, whether tenement or rent.

Feodum nobile /fyúwdəm nówbəliy/. A fief for which the tenant did guard and owed homage.

Feodum novum /fyúwdəm nówvəm/. A feud acquired by a vassal himself.

Feodum simplex quia feodum idem est quod hæreditas, et simplex idem est quod legitimum vel purum; et sic feodum simplex idem est quod hæreditas legitima vel hæreditas pura /fyúwdəm símpleks kwàyə fyúwdəm áydəm èst kwòd hərédətæs, et símpleks áydəm èst kwòd ləjidəməm vèl pyúrəm; et sik fyúwdəm simpleks áydəm èst kwòd hərédətæs ləjídəmə vèl hərédətæs pyúrə/. A fee-simple, so called because fee is the same as inheritance, and simple is the same as lawful or pure; and thus fee-simple is the same as a lawful inheritance, or pure inheritance.

Feodum talliatum, *i.e.,* **hæreditas in quandam certitudinem limitata** /fyúwdəm tæliyéydəm, ìd ést, həríydətæs

in kwóndəm sàrtət(y)úwdənəm lìmətéydə/. Fee-tail, *i.e.,* an inheritance limited in a definite descent.

Feoffamentum /fiy(ə)fəméntəm/. A feoffment.

Feoffare /fiy(ə)fériy/. To enfeoff; to bestow a fee. The bestower was called *"feoffator,"* and the grantee or feoffee, *"feoffatus."*

Feoffator /fiy(ə)féydər/. In old English law, a feoffer or feoffor; one who gives or bestows a fee; one who makes a feoffment.

Feoffatus /fiy(ə)féydəs/. In old English law, a feoffee; one to whom a fee is given, or a feoffment made.

Feoffee /fəfíy/fiyfíy/. He to whom a fee is conveyed.

Feoffee to uses /fəfíy tə yúwsəz/fiyfíy°/. A person to whom land was conveyed for the use of a third party. (The latter was called *"cestui que use."*) One holding the same position with reference to a use that a trustee does to a trust. He answers to the *hæres fiduciarius* of the Roman law.

Feoffment /féfmənt/fíyf°/. The gift of any corporeal hereditament to another, operating by transmutation of possession, and requiring, as essential to its completion, that the seisin be passed, which might be accomplished either by investiture or by livery of seisin. A gift of a freehold interest in land accompanied by livery of seisin. The essential part is the livery of seisin. Also the deed or conveyance by which such corporeal hereditament is passed.

A feoffment originally meant the grant of a *feud* or *fee;* that is, a barony or knight's fee, for which certain services were due from the feoffee to the feoffor. By custom it came afterwards to signify also a grant (with livery of seisin) of a free inheritance to a man and his heirs, referring rather to the perpetuity of the estate than to the feudal tenure. It was for ages the only method (in ordinary use) for conveying the freehold of land in possession, but has now fallen in great measure into disuse, even in England, having been almost entirely supplanted by some of that class of conveyances founded on the statute law of the realm.

Feoffment to uses /féfmənt tə yúwsəz/fíyf°/. A feoffment of lands to one person to the use of another. In such case the feoffee was bound in conscience to hold the lands according to the use, and could himself derive no benefit. Sometimes such feoffments were made to the use of the feoffer. The effect of such conveyance was entirely changed by the statute of uses.

Feoffor /féfər/fíyfər/. The person making a feoffment, or enfeoffing another in fee.

Feoh /fíy/. This Saxon word meant originally cattle, and thence property or money, and, by a second transition, wages, reward, or fee. It was probably the original form from which the words "feod," "feudum," "fief," "feu," and "fee" (all meaning a feudal grant of land) have been derived.

Feorme /fárm/. A certain portion of the produce of the land due by the grantee to the lord according to the terms of the charter.

Feræ bestiæ /fíriy bés(h)chiyiy/. Wild beasts.

Feræ naturæ /fíriy nəchúriy/. Lat. Of a wild nature or disposition. Animals which are by nature wild are so designated, by way of distinction from such as are naturally tame, the latter being called *"domitæ naturæ."*

Ferdella terræ /fərdélə téhriy/. A fardel-land; ten acres; or perhaps a yard-land.

Ferdfare. Sax. A summons to serve in the army. An acquittance from going into the army.

Ferdingus. A term denoting, apparently, a freeman of the lowest class, being named after the *cotseti.*

Ferdwite. In Saxon law, an acquittance of manslaughter committed in the army; also a fine imposed on persons for not going forth on a military expedition.

Feria /fíriyə/. In old English law, a weekday; a holiday; a day on which process could not be served; a fair; a ferry.

Feriæ /fíriyiy/. In Roman law, holidays; generally speaking, days or seasons during which free-born Romans suspended their political transactions and their lawsuits, and during which slaves enjoyed a cessation from labor.

All *feriæ* were thus *dies nefasti.* All *feriæ* were divided into two classes,—*"feriæ publicæ"* and *"feriæ privatæ."* The latter were only observed by single families or individuals, in commemoration of some particular event which had been of importance to them or their ancestors.

Numerous festivals were called by this name in the early Roman empire. In the later Roman empire the single days occurring at intervals of a week apart, commencing with the seventh day of the ecclesiastical year, were so called.

Ferial days /fíriəl déyz/. Originally and properly, days free from labor and pleading; holidays.

Ferita /féhrədə/. In old European law, a wound; a stroke.

Ferling /fárliŋ/. In old records, the fourth part of a penny; also the quarter of a ward in a borough.

Ferlingata /fərliŋgéydə/. A fourth part of a yard-land.

Ferlingus, or **ferlingum** /fərliŋgəs, fárliŋgəm/. A furlong.

Ferm, or **fearm** /fárm, fárm/. A house or land, or both, let by lease.

Ferme /fárm, fárm/. A farm; a rent; a lease; a house or land, or both, taken by indenture or lease.

Fermentation. A decomposition produced in an organic substance by the physiological action of a living organism, or by certain unorganized agents.

Fermented liquors. Beverages produced by, or which have undergone, a process of alcoholic fermentation, to which they owe their intoxicating properties, including beer, wine, hard cider, and the like, but not spirituous or distilled liquors.

Fermer, fermor /fármər, fármər/. A lessee; a farmer. One who holds a term, whether of lands or an incorporeal right, such as customs or revenue.

Fermier /fèrmyéy/. In French law, one who farms any public revenue.

Fermisona. In old English law, the winter season for killing deer.

Fermory /fármriy, fármɔriy/. In old records, a place in monasteries, where they received the poor *(hospicio excipiebant),* and gave them provisions *(ferm, firma).* Hence the modern *infirmary,* used in the sense of a hospital.

Fernigo. In old English law, a waste ground, or place where fern grows.

Ferrator. A farrier *(q.v.).*

Ferri /féhray/. In the civil law, to be borne; that is on or about the person. This was distinguished from *portari* (to be carried), which signified to be carried on an animal.

Ferriage /féhriyəj/. The toll or fare paid for the transportation of persons and property across a ferry. Literally speaking, it is the price or fare fixed by law for the transportation of the traveling public, with such goods and chattels as they may have with them, across a river, bay, or lake.

Ferry. Commercial transportation of people, vehicles, goods, etc. across body of water. Also, boat or vessel used in such transportation. In law it is treated as a franchise, and defined as the exclusive right to carry passengers and freight across a river, lake or arm of the sea, or to connect a continuous line of road leading from one side of the water to the other. Canadian Pac. Ry. Co. v. U. S., C.C.A.Wash., 73 F.2d 831, 832.

A continuation of the highway from one side of the water over which it passes to the other, for transportation of passengers or of travelers with their vehicles and such other property as they may carry or have with them. U. S. v. Puget Sound Nav. Co., D.C. Wash., 24 F.Supp. 431, 432.

A liberty to have a boat on a stream, river, arm of the sea, lake, or other body of water for the transportation of passengers and vehicles with their contents, for a reasonable toll. Sometimes limited to the landing place. State Highway Commission v. Smith, 250 Ky. 269, 62 S.W.2d 1044.

Whether a boat is a "ferry" and comprises a continuous part of the road or highway depends on length of run, type of ship, whether it was operated under state franchise or federal certificate of convenience, whether it was equipped to carry cargo, extent to which service to passengers is emphasized and extent to which its use is necessitated by lack of land transportation. Alaska S. S. Co. v. Federal Maritime Commission, C.A.Wash., 399 F.2d 623, 628.

A *public* ferry is one to which all the public have the right to resort, for which a regular fare is established, and the ferryman is a common carrier, bound to take over all who apply, and bound to keep his ferry in operation and good repair.

A *private* ferry is one mainly for the use of the owner, and though he may take pay for ferriage, he does not follow it as a business. His ferry is not open to the public at its demand, and he may or may not keep it in operation.

Ferry franchise. The public grant of a right to maintain a ferry at a particular place; a right conferred to land at a particular point and secure toll for the transportation of persons and property from that point across the stream. A grant to a named person empowering him to continue an interrupted land highway over the interrupting waters. U. S. v. Puget Sound Nav. Co., D.C.Wash., 24 F.Supp. 431, 432.

Ferryman. One employed in taking persons across a lake, river or stream, in boats or other vessels, at a ferry.

Festa in cappis /féstə in kǽpəs/. In old English law, grand holidays, on which choirs wore caps.

Festinatio justitiæ est noverca infortunii /fèstənéysh(iy)ow jəstíshiyiy èst nəvérkə inforchúwniyay/. Hasty justice is the stepmother of misfortune.

Festing-man. In old English law, a bondsman; a surety; a frank-pledge, or one who was surety for the good behavior of another. Monasteries enjoyed the privilege of being "free from festing-men," which means that they were "not bound for any man's forthcoming who should transgress the law." See **Frank-pledge.**

Festing-penny. Earnest given to servants when hired or retained.

Festinum remedium /féstənəm rəmíydiyəm/. Lat. A speedy remedy. A term applied to those cases where the remedy for the redress of an injury is given without any unnecessary delay. The action of dower is *festinum remedium.* The writ of assise was also thus characterized (in comparison with the less expeditious remedies previously available) by the statute of Westminster 2 (13 Edw. I, c. 24.)

Festuca /fèstyúwkə/. In Frankish law, a rod or staff or (as described by other writers) a stick, on which imprecatory runs were cut, which was used as a gage or pledge of good faith by a party to a contract, or for symbolic delivery in the conveyance or quit-claim of land, before a court of law, anterior to the introduction of written documents by the Romans.

Festum /féstəm/. A feast, holiday, or festival. *Festum stultorum* /féstəm stəltórəm/, the feast of fools.

Fetal death. The death of a child not yet born. Death in utero of a fetus weighing 500 grams or more. This weight corresponds roughly to a fetus of twenty weeks or more (gestational age), *i.e.* a viable fetus.

Death is defined in the following context: after expulsion, the fetus does not breathe or show any other evidence of life, such as the beating of the heart, pulsation of the umbilical cord, or definite movement of voluntary muscles.

Feticide /fíydəsàyd/. Destruction of the fetus; the act by which criminal abortion is produced. See also **Abortion; Prolicide.**

Fettering. The act of shackling or placing manacles on another.

Fetters /fédərz/. Chains or shackles for the feet; irons used to secure the legs of convicts, unruly prisoners, etc. Similar chains securing the wrists are called "handcuffs".

Fetus /fíydəs/. An unborn child. The unborn offspring of any viviparous animal; specifically the unborn offspring in the post embryonic period after major structures have been outlined (in man from seven or eight weeks after fertilization until birth).

Feud. *Feudal law.* An estate in land held of a superior on condition of rendering him services. 2 Bl.Comm. 105. An inheritable right to the use and occupation of lands, held on condition of rendering services to the lord or proprietor, who himself retains the property in the lands.

In this sense the word is the same as "feod", "feodum", "feudum", "fief", or "fee".

Saxon and old German law. An enmity, or species of private war, existing between the family of his slayer. In Scotland and the north of England, a combination of all the kin to revenge the death of any of the blood upon the slayer and all his race. See **Faida.**

Feuda /fyúwdə/. Feuds or fees.

Feudal /fyúwdəl/. Pertaining to feuds or fees; relating to or growing out of the feudal system or feudal law; having the quality of a feud, as distinguished from "allodial."

Feudal actions. An ancient name for real actions, or such as concern real property only. 3 Bl.Comm. 117.

Feudal courts. In the 12th century a lord *qua* lord had the right to hold a court for his tenants. In the 13th century, they became of less importance for three reasons: The feudal principle would have led to a series of courts one above the other, and the dominions of the large landowners were usually scattered, so that great feudal courts became impossible. The growth of the jurisdiction of the king's court removed the necessity for feudal courts. All the incidents of the feudal system came to be regarded in a commercial spirit—as property. Its jurisdiction became merely appendant to landowning.

Feudalism. The feudal system; the aggregate of feudal principles and usages. The social, political, and economic system that dominated the major European nations between the ninth and fifteenth centuries. The system was based upon a servile relationship between a "vassal" and a "lord." The vassal paid homage and service to the lord and the lord provided land and protection to the vassal. See also **Feudal system.**

Feudalize /fyúwdəlàyz/. To reduce to a feudal tenure; to conform to feudalism.

Feudal law. The body of jurisprudence relating to feuds; the real-property law of the feudal system; the law anciently regulating the property relations of lord and vassal, and the creation, incidents, and transmission of feudal estates.

The body of laws and usages constituting the "feudal law" was originally customary and unwritten, but a compilation was made in the twelfth century, called "Feodarum Consuetudines," which has formed the basis of later digests. The feudal law prevailed over Europe from the twelfth to the fourteenth century, and was introduced into England at the Norman Conquest, where it formed the entire basis of the law of real property until comparatively modern times. Survivals of the feudal law, to the present day, so affect and color that branch of jurisprudence as to require a certain knowledge of the feudal law in order to better comprehend modern tenures and rules of real-property law.

See also **Feudal system.**

Feudal possession. The equivalent of "seisin" under the feudal system.

Feudal system. The system of feuds. A political and social system which prevailed throughout Europe during the eleventh, twelfth, and thirteenth centuries, and is supposed to have grown out of the peculiar usages and policy of the Teutonic nations who overran the continent after the fall of the Western Roman Empire, as developed by the exigencies of their military domination, and possibly furthered by notions taken from the Roman jurisprudence.

It was introduced into England, in its completeness, by William I, A.D. 1085, though it may have existed in a rudimentary form among the Saxons before the Conquest. It formed the entire basis of the real-property law of England in medieval times; and survivals of the system, in modern days, so modify and color that branch of jurisprudence, both in England and America, that many of its principles require for their complete understanding a knowledge of the feudal system. The feudal system originated in the relations of a military chieftain and his followers, or king and nobles, or lord and vassals, and especially their relations as determined by the bond established by a grant of *land* from the former to the latter. From this it grew into a complete and intricate complex of rules for the tenure and transmission of real estate, and of correlated duties and services; while, by tying men to the land and to those holding above and below them, it created a close-knit hierarchy of persons, and developed an aggregate of social and political institutions.

Feudal tenures. The tenures of real estate under the feudal system, such as knight-service, socage, villenage, etc.

Feudary /fyúwdəriy/. A tenant who holds by feudal tenure (also spelled "feodatory" and "feudatory"). Held by feudal service. Relating to feuds or feudal tenures.

Feudbote /fyúwdbòwt/. A recompense for engaging in a feud, and the damages consequent, it having been the custom in ancient times for all the kindred to engage in their kinsman's quarrel.

Feude /fyúwd/. An occasional early form of "feud" in the sense of private war or vengeance. See **Feud.**

Feudist /fyúwdəst/. A writer on feuds, as Cujacius.

Feudo /feyúwðow/. In Spanish law, feud or fee.

Feudorum liber /fyùwdórəm láybər/. The Books of Feuds. A compilation of feudal law, prepared by order of the emperor Frederick I, and published at Milan in 1170. It comprised five books, of which only the first two are now extant with fragmentary portions of the others, printed at the end of modern editions of the Corpus Juris Civilis.

Feudorum libri /fyùwdórəm láybray/. The Books of Feuds published during the reign of Henry III, about the year 1152. The particular customs of Lombardy as to feuds began about the year 1152 to be the standard of authority to other nations by reason of the greater refinement with which that branch of learning had been there cultivated. This compilation was probably known in England, but does not appear to have had any other effect than to influence English lawyers to the more critical study of their own tenures, and to induce them to extend the learning of real property so as to embrace more curious matter of similar kind.

Feudum /fyúwdəm/. L. Lat. A feud, fief, or fee. A right of using and enjoying forever the lands of another, which the lord grants on condition that the tenant shall render fealty, military duty, and other services. It is not properly the land, but a right in the land.

This form of the word is used by the feudal writers. The earlier English writers generally prefer the form *feodum.* There was an older word *feum.* Its use by the Normans is exceedingly obscure. "Feudal" was not in their vocabulary. Usually it denoted a stretch of land, rarely a tenure or mass of rights. It came to be applied to every person who had heritable rights in land.

Feudum antiquum /fyúwdəm æntáykwəm/. An ancient feud or fief; a fief descended to the vassal from his ancestors. 2 Bl.Comm. 212, 221. A fief which ancestors had possessed for more than four generations.

Feudum apertum /fyúwdəm əpárdəm/. An open feud or fief; a fief resulting back to the lord, where the blood of the person last seised was utterly extinct and gone or where the tenant committed a crime, or gave other legal cause.

Feudum francum /fyúwdəm frǽŋkəm/. A free feud. One which was noble and free from talliage and other subsidies to which the *plebeia feuda* (vulgar feuds) were subject.

Feudum hauberticum /fyúwdəm hobárdəkəm/. A fee held on the military service of appearing fully armed at the *ban* and *arriere ban.*

Feudum improprium /fyúwdəm imprówpriyəm/. An improper or derivative feud or fief.

Feudum individuum /fyúwdəm ìndəvíjuwəm/. An indivisible or impartible feud or fief; descendible to the eldest son alone.

Feudum laicum /fyúwdəm léyəkəm/. A lay fee.

Feudum ligium /fyúwdəm líjiyəm/. A liege feud or fief; a fief held immediately of the sovereign; one for which the vassal owed fealty to his lord against all persons. 1 Bl.Comm. 367.

Feudum maternum /fyúwdəm mətárnəm/. A maternal fief; a fief descended to the feudatory from his mother. 2 Bl.Comm. 212.

Feudum militare /fyúwdəm mìlətériy/. A knight's fee, held by knight service and esteemed the most honorable species of tenure. 2 Bl.Comm. 62.

Feudum nobile /fyúwdəm nówbəliy/. A fee for which the tenant did guard and owed fealty and homage.

Feudum novum /fyúwdəm nówvəm/. A new feud or fief; a fief which began in the person of the feudatory, and did not come to him by succession. 2 Bl. Comm. 212.

Feudum novum ut antiquum /fyúwdəm nówvəm əd æntáykwəm/. A new fee held with the qualities and incidents of an ancient one. 2 Bl.Comm. 212.

Feudum paternum /fyúwdəm pətárnəm/. A fee which the paternal ancestors had held for four generations. One descendible to heirs on the paternal side only. 2 Bl.Comm. 223. One which might be held by males only.

Feudum proprium /fyúwdəm prówpriyəm/. A proper, genuine, and original feud or fief; being of a purely military character, and held by military service. 2 Bl.Comm. 57, 58.

Feudum talliatum /fyúwdəm tæliyéydəm/. A restricted fee. One limited to descend to certain classes of heirs. 2 Bl.Comm. 112, note.

Feu et lieu /fyúw èy lyúw/. Fr. In old French and Canadian law, hearth and home. A term importing actual settlement upon land by a tenant.

Feu holding /fyúw hówldiŋ/. A holding by tenure of rendering grain or money in place of military service.

Feum /fíyəm/. An older form of *feudum*.

Few. Not many; of small number. U. S. v. Margolis, C.C.A.N.J., 138 F.2d 1002, 1003. An indefinite expression for a small or limited number. Indicating a small number of units or individuals which constitute a whole. A relative term of great elasticity of meaning.

Ff. A Latin abbreviation for "Fragmenta," designating the Digest or Pandects in the *Corpus Juris Civilis* of Justinian; so called because that work is made up of fragments or extracts from the writings of numerous jurists.

F.G.A. In marine insurance means: "Free from general average"; also, sometimes, "foreign general average." The precise meaning of this abbreviation must be gathered from the context. See **Average; General average contribution.**

FHA. Federal Housing Administration.

FHLB. Federal Home Loan Bank. A Federal System which loans money to members of savings and loan associations. See **Federal Home Loan Banks.**

FHLBB. Federal Home Loan Bank Board.

FHLMC. Federal Home Loan Mortgage Corporation.

Fiancer. L. Fr. To pledge one's faith.

Fianza /fiyánsə/. Sp. In Spanish law, trust, confidence, and correlatively a legal duty or obligation arising therefrom. The term is sufficiently broad in meaning to include both a general obligation and a restricted liability under a single instrument. But in a special sense, it designates a surety or guarantor, or the contract or engagement of suretyship; the contract by which one person engages to pay the debt of another if the latter should fail to do so.

Fiat /fáyæt, fáyət/. (Lat. "Let it be done.") In old English practice, a short order or warrant of a judge or magistrate directing some act to be done; an authority issuing from some competent source for the doing of some legal act.

One of the proceedings in the English bankruptcy practice, being a power, signed by the lord chancellor, addressed to the court of bankruptcy, authorizing the petitioning creditor to prosecute his complaint before it. By the statute 12 & 13 Vict., c. 116, fiats were abolished.

Arbitrary or authoritative order or decision.

Joint fiat. In old English law, a fiat in bankruptcy, issued against two or more trading partners.

Fiat justitia /fáyət jəstísh(iy)ə/. Let justice be done. On a petition to the king for his warrant to bring a writ of error in parliament, he writes on the top of the petition, *"Fiat justitia,"* and then the writ of error is made out, etc.

Fiat justitia, ruat cœlum /fáyət jəstísh(iy)ə, rúwət síyləm/. Let right be done, though the heavens should fall.

Fiat money. Paper currency not backed by gold or silver.

Fiat prout fieri consuevit (nil temere novandum) /fáyət prówət fáyəray kənswíyvət, níl téməriy nəvændəm/. Let it be done as it hath used to be done (nothing must be rashly innovated).

Fiat ut petitur /fáyəd ət pédədər/. Let it be done as it is asked. A form of granting a petition.

Fiaunt /fáyònt/. An order; command. See **Fiat.**

FICA. Federal Insurance Contributions Act. The law that sets "Social Security" taxes and benefits.

Fictio /fíksh(iy)ow/. In Roman law, a fiction; an assumption or supposition of the law. Such was properly a term of pleading, and signified a false averment on the part of the plaintiff which the defendant was not allowed to traverse; as that the plaintiff was a Roman citizen, when in truth he was a foreigner. The object of the fiction was to give the court jurisdiction.

Fictio cedit veritati. Fictio juris non est ubi veritas /fíksh(iy)ow siydət vèhrətéyday. fíksh(iy)ow júrəs nón èst yúwbay véhrətæs/. Fiction yields to truth. Where there is truth, fiction of law exists not.

Fictio est contra veritatem, sed pro veritate habetur /fíksh(iy)ow èst kóntrə vèhrətéydəm, séd pròw vèhrətéydiy həbíydər/. Fiction is against the truth, but it is to be esteemed truth.

Fictio juris non est ubi veritas /fíksh(iy)ow júrəs nón èst yúwbay véhrətæs/. Where truth is, fiction of law does not exist.

Fictio legis inique operatur alicui damnum vel injuriam /fíksh(iy)ow líyjəs ínəkwiy òpəréydər ælək(yúw)ay dæmnəm vèl injúriyəm/. A legal fiction does not properly work loss or injury. Fiction of law is wrongful if it works loss or injury to anyone.

Fictio legis neminem lædit /fíksh(iy)ow líyjəs némənəm líydət/. A fiction of law injures no one. 3 Bl.Comm. 43.

Fiction of law. An assumption or supposition of law that something which is or may be false is true, or that a state of facts exists which has never really taken place. An assumption, for purposes of justice, of a fact that does not or may not exist. A rule of law which assumes as true, and will not allow to be disproved, something which is false, but not impossible. Ryan v. Motor Credit Co., 30 N.J.Eq. 531, 23 A.2d 607, 621.

These assumptions are of an innocent or even beneficial character, and are made for the advancement of the ends of justice. They secure this end chiefly by the extension of procedure from cases to which it is applicable to other cases to which it is not strictly applicable, the ground of inapplicability being some difference of an immaterial character.

See also **Legal fiction**.

Estoppels distinguished. Fictions are to be distinguished from estoppels; an estoppel being the rule by which a person is precluded from asserting a fact by previous conduct inconsistent therewith on his own part or the part of those under whom he claims, or by an adjudication upon his rights which he cannot be allowed to question.

Presumptions distinguished. Fictions are to be distinguished from presumptions of law. By the former, something known to be false or unreal is assumed as true; by the latter, an inference is set up, which may be and probably is true, but which, at any rate, the law will not permit to be controverted. It may also be said that a presumption is a rule of law prescribed for the purpose of getting at a certain conclusion, though arbitrary, where the subject is intrinsically liable to doubt from the remoteness, discrepancy, or actual defect of proofs.

Fictitious. Founded on a fiction; having the character of a fiction; pretended; counterfeit. Feigned, imaginary, not real, false, not genuine, nonexistent. Arbitrarily invented and set up, to accomplish an ulterior object.

Fictitious action. An action brought for the sole purpose of obtaining the opinion of the court on a point of law, not for the settlement of any actual controversy between the parties. See **Declaratory judgment; Feigned action; Feigned issue**.

Fictitious name. A counterfeit, alias, feigned, or pretended name taken by a person, differing in some essential particular from his true name (consisting of Christian name and patronymic), with the implication that it is meant to deceive or mislead. See also **Alias**.

Fictitious payee. Negotiable instrument is drawn to fictitious payee whenever payee named in it has no right to it, and its maker does not intend that such payee shall take anything by it; whether name of payee used by maker is that of person living or dead or one who never existed is immaterial. Goodyear Tire & Rubber Co. of California v. Wells Fargo Bank & Union Trust Co., 1 Cal.App.2d 694, 37 P.2d 483. The test is not whether the named payee is "fictitious" but whether the signer intends that he shall have no interest in the instrument. U.C.C. § 3–405.

Fictitious person. A person, who, though named as payee in a check has no right to it or its proceeds because the drawer of it so intended. Johnston v. Exchange Nat. Bank of Tampa, 152 Fla. 228, 9 So.2d 810, 811, 812. See **Fictitious payee**.

Fictitious plaintiff. A person appearing in the writ, complaint, or record as the plaintiff in a suit, but who in reality does not exist, or who is ignorant of the suit and of the use of his name in it. It is a contempt of court to sue in the name of a fictitious party.

Fictitious promise. See **Promise**.

Fide-commissary /fáydiy kóm0əsèhriy/. A term derived from the Latin *"fidei-commissarius,"* and occasionally used by writers on equity jurisprudence as a substitute for the law French term *"cestui que trust,"* as being more elegant and euphonious. See Brown v. Brown, 83 Hun. 160, 31 N.Y.S. 650.

Fidei-commissarius /fáydiyay kòməsériyəs/. In the civil law, this term corresponds nearly to our *"cestui que trust."* It designates a person who has the real or beneficial interest in an estate or fund, the title or administration of which is temporarily confided to another.

Fidei-commissum /fáydiyay kəmísəm/. In the civil law, a species of trust; being a gift of property (usually by will) to a person, accompanied by a request or direction of the donor that the recipient will transfer the property to another, the latter being a person not capable of taking directly under the will or gift. Elements of "fidei commissum" are that donee or legatee is invested with title and charged or directed to convey it to another or to make particular disposition of it. Succession of Abraham, La.App., 136 So.2d 471, 478.

Fide-jubere /fáydiy jəbíriy/ fáydiy júwbiyz? fáydiy júwbiyow/. In the civil law, to order a thing upon one's faith; to pledge one's self; to become surety for another. *Fide-jubes? Fide-jubeo:* Do you pledge yourself? I do pledge myself. One of the forms of stipulation.

Fide-jussio /fáydiy jásh(iy)ow/. An act by which any one binds himself as an additional security for another. This giving security does not destroy the liability of the principal, but adds to the security of the surety.

Fide-jussor /fáydiy jásər/. In Roman law, a guarantor; one who becomes responsible for the payment of another's debt, by a stipulation which binds him to discharge it if the principal debtor fails to do so. 3 Bl.Comm. 108. He differs from a co-obligor in this, that the latter is equally bound to a debtor, with his principal, while the former is not liable till the principal has failed to fulfil his engagement. The obligation of the fide-jussor was an accessory contract; for, if the principal obligation was not previously contracted, his engagement then took the name of mandate. The sureties taken on the arrest of a defendant, in the court of admiralty, were formerly denominated *"fide jussors."* 3 Bl.Comm. 108.

Fidelitas /fədíylətæs/. Fealty; fidelity. See **Fealty**.

Fidelitas. De nullo tenemento, quod tenetur ad terminum, fit homagii; fit tamen inde fidelitatis sacramen-

tum /fədélətæs. Dìy nálow tènəméntow, kwòd təníydər æd tármənəm, fit həméyjiyay; fít tǽmən fədèlətéydəs sǽkrəméntəm/. Fealty. For no tenement which is held for a term is there the oath of homage, but there is the oath of fealty.

Fidelity and guaranty insurance. A contract of fidelity or guaranty insurance is one whereby the insurer, for a valuable consideration, agrees, subject to certain conditions, to indemnify the insured against loss consequent upon the dishonesty or default of a designated person. Guaranty insurance, used in its broad sense, also includes credit insurance, and title insurance, as well as the numerous forms of surety bonds.

The contract partakes of the nature both of insurance and of suretyship. Hence, even in the absence of terms so providing, the contract is avoided by the failure of the insured to disclose to the insurer, at the time of making the contract, any known previous acts of dishonesty on the part of the employee, or any dishonest practices that may occur during the currency of the policy. But the insured is not required to give notice of mere irregularities not involving moral turpitude; nor, in the absence of agreement to that effect, does the insured owe to the insurer any duty of watching the conduct and accounts of the employee concerned.

Fidelity bond. Contract of fidelity insurance. Runcie v. Corn Exchange Bank Trust Co., Sup., 6 N.Y.S.2d 616, 620. A guaranty of personal honesty of officer furnishing indemnity against his defalcation or negligence. Phillips v. Board of Education of Pineville, 283 Ky. 173, 140 S.W.2d 819, 822. A contract whereby, for a consideration, one agrees to indemnify another against loss arising from the want of honesty, integrity, or fidelity of an employee or other person holding a position of trust. Liberty Mut. Ins. Co. v. Thunderbird Bank, 25 Ariz.App. 201, 542 P.2d 39, 41. See also **Bond; Fidelity and guaranty insurance; Insurance.**

Fidelity insurance. See **Fidelity and guaranty insurance; Insurance.**

Fidem mentiri /fáydəm mèntáyray/. Lat. To betray faith or fealty. A term used in feudal and old English law of a feudatory or feudal tenant who does not keep that fealty which he has sworn to the lord.

Fide-promissor /fàydiy prəmísər/. See **Fide-jussor.**

Fides /fáydiyz/. Lat. Faith; honesty; confidence; trust; veracity; honor. Occurring in the phrases *"bona fides"* (good faith), *"mala fides"* (bad faith), and *"uberrima fides"* (the utmost or most abundant good faith).

Fides est obligatio conscientiæ alicujus ad intentionem alterius /fáydiyz èst òbləgéysh(iy)ow kònshiyénshiyiy ǽləkyúwjəs æd intènshiyównəm oltíriyəs/. A trust is an obligation of conscience of one to the will of another.

Fides facta /fáydiyz fǽktə/. Among the Franks and Lombards undertakings were guaranteed by "making one's faith"—*fides facta*. This was symbolized by such formal acts as the giving of a rod; in suretyship giving the "festuca" or "vadium."

Fides servanda est /fáydiyz sərvǽndə èst/. Faith must be observed. An agent must not violate the confidence reposed in him.

Fides servanda est; simplicitas juris gentium prævaleat /fáydiyz sərvǽndə èst, sìmplísətǽs júrəs jénsh(iy)əm prəvǽliyət/. Faith must be kept; the simplicity of the law of nations must prevail. A rule applied to bills of exchange as a sort of sacred instruments.

Fiducia /fəd(y)úwsh(iy)ə/. In Roman law, an early form of mortgage or pledge, in which both the title and possession of the property were passed to the creditor by a formal act of sale (properly with the solemnities of the transaction known as *mancipatio*), there being at the same time an express or implied agreement on the part of the creditor to reconvey the property by a similar act of sale provided the debt was duly paid; but on default of payment, the property became absolutely vested in the creditor without foreclosure and without any right of redemption.

Fiducial. An adjective having the same meaning as "fiduciary;" as, in the phrase "public or fiducial office."

Fiduciarius hæres /fəd(y)ùwshiyériyəs híriyz/. See **Fiduciary heir.**

Fiduciarius tutor /fəd(y)ùwshiyériyəs t(y)úwdər/. In Roman law, the elder brother of an emancipated *pupillus*, whose father had died leaving him still under fourteen years of age.

Fiduciary /fəd(y)úwsh(iy)əry/. The term is derived from the Roman law, and means (as a noun) a person holding the character of a trustee, or a character analogous to that of a trustee, in respect to the trust and confidence involved in it and the scrupulous good faith and candor which it requires. A person having duty, created by his undertaking, to act primarily for another's benefit in matters connected with such undertaking. As an adjective it means of the nature of a trust; having the characteristics of a trust; analogous to a trust; relating to or founded upon a trust or confidence.

A person or institution who manages money or property for another and who must exercise a standard of care in such management activity imposed by law or contract; *e.g.* executor of estate; receiver in bankruptcy; trustee. A trustee, for example, possesses a fiduciary responsibility to the beneficiaries of the trust to follow the terms of the trust and the requirements of applicable state law. A breach of fiduciary responsibility would make the trustee liable to the beneficiaries for any damage caused by such breach.

The status of being a fiduciary gives rise to certain legal incidents and obligations, including the prohibition against investing the money or property in investments which are speculative or otherwise imprudent.

Many states have adopted the Uniform Fiduciaries Act; Uniform Management of Institutional Funds Act; and the Uniform Simplification of Fiduciary Security Transfers Act.

See also **Fiduciary capacity; Fiduciary or confidential relation.**

Foreign fiduciary. A trustee, executor, administrator, guardian or conservator appointed by a jurisdiction other than the one in which he is acting.

Fiduciary bond. Type of surety bond required by court to be filed by trustees, administrators, executors, guardians, and conservators to insure proper performance of their duties.

Fiduciary capacity. One is said to act in a "fiduciary capacity" or to receive money or contract a debt in a "fiduciary capacity," when the business which he transacts, or the money or property which he handles, is not his own or for his own benefit, but for the benefit of another person, as to whom he stands in a relation implying and necessitating great confidence and trust on the one part and a high degree of good faith on the other part. The term is not restricted to technical or express trusts, but includes also such offices or relations as those of an attorney at law, a guardian, executor, or broker, a director of a corporation, and a public officer.

Fiduciary contract. An agreement by which a person delivers a thing to another on the condition that he will restore it to him.

Fiduciary debt. A debt founded on or arising from some confidence or trust as distinguished from a "debt" founded simply on contract. Montgomery v. Phillips Petroleum Co., Tex.Civ.App., 49 S.W.2d 967, 973.

Fiduciary heir. The Roman laws called a fiduciary heir the person who was instituted heir, and who was charged to deliver the succession to a person designated by the testament.

Fiduciary or **confidential relation.** A very broad term embracing both technical fiduciary relations and those informal relations which exist wherever one man trusts in or relies upon another. One founded on trust or confidence reposed by one person in the integrity and fidelity of another. A "fiduciary relation" arises whenever confidence is reposed on one side, and domination and influence result on the other; the relation can be legal, social, domestic, or merely personal. Heilman's Estate, Matter of, 37 Ill.App.3d 390, 345 N.E.2d 536, 540. Such relationship exists when there is a reposing of faith, confidence and trust, and the placing of reliance by one upon the judgment and advice of the other. Williams v. Griffin, 35 Mich.App. 179, 192 N.W.2d 283, 285.

An expression including both technical fiduciary relations and those informal relations which exist whenever one man trusts and relies upon another. It exists where there is special confidence reposed in one who in equity and good conscience is bound to act in good faith and with due regard to interests of one reposing the confidence. A relation subsisting between two persons in regard to a business, contract, or piece of property, or in regard to the general business or estate of one of them, of such a character that each must repose trust and confidence in the other and must exercise a corresponding degree of fairness and good faith. Out of such a relation, the law raises the rule that neither party may exert influence or pressure upon the other, take selfish advantage of his trust, or deal with the subject-matter of the trust in such a way as to benefit himself or prejudice the other except in the exercise of the utmost good faith and with the full knowledge and consent of that other, business shrewdness, hard bargaining, and astuteness to take advantage of the forgetfulness or negligence of another being totally prohibited as between persons standing in such a relation to each other. Examples of fiduciary relations are those existing between attorney and client, guardian and ward, principal and agent, executor and heir, trustee and *cestui que trust,* landlord and tenant, etc.

Fief /fíyf/. A fee, feod, or feud.

Fief d'haubert (or d'hauberk) /fíyf dòwbér(k)/. Fr. In Norman feudal law, a fief or fee held by the tenure of knight-service; a knight's fee. 2 Bl.Comm. 62. A fee held on the military tenure of appearing fully armed on the *ban* and *arrière-ban.*

Fief-tenant /fíyf ténənt/. In old English law, the holder of a fief or fee; a feeholder or freeholder.

Fiel /fiyéyl/. In Spanish law, a sequestrator; a person in whose hands a thing in dispute is judicially deposited; a receiver.

Field. Open area of land; commonly used for cultivation or pasturage.

Fieldad /fiyeyldád/. In Spanish law, sequestration. This is allowed in six cases by the Spanish law where the title to property is in dispute.

Field-ale, or **filkdale** /fíyldeyl/. An ancient custom in England, by which officers of the forest and bailiffs of hundreds had the right to compel the hundred to furnish them with ale.

Field audit. See **Audit.**

Field book. A description of the courses and distances of the lines, and of the corners of the lots of the town as they were surveyed, and as they appear by number and division on the town plan.

Field Code. The original New York Code brought into being by David Dudley Field in 1848 calling for simplification of civil procedure. This Code served as the model for future state civil procedure codes and rules.

Field notes. A description of a survey.

Field office. A branch or subsidiary office of a government agency apart from the central office. See also **Branch office.**

Field reeve. In old English law, an officer elected by the owners of a regulated pasture to keep in order the fences, ditches, etc., on the land, to regulate the times during which animals are to be admitted to the pasture, and generally to maintain and manage the pasture subject to the instructions of the owners.

Field vision. The general vision used in catching in sight, following and locating objects;—distinguished from "binocular vision" *(q.v.).*

Field warehouse receipt. Document issued by warehouseman evidencing receipt of goods which have been stored. Such may be used as collateral for loans. See also **Field warehousing; Warehouse receipt.**

Field warehousing. Arrangement whereby wholesaler, manufacturer, or merchant finances his business through pledge of goods remaining on his premises and it is limited type of warehousing as distinguished from public warehouse. Lawrence Warehouse Co. v. McKee, C.A.Fla., 301 F.2d 4, 6. An arrangement whereby a pledgor may have necessary access to the pledged goods, while the goods are actually in the custody and control of a third person, acting as a warehouseman on the pledgor's premises. Field warehousing is often employed as a security device in inventory financing where the financer or secured party desires to maintain close control over the borrower's inventory and have the advantages of being a pledgee of the property. The device is employed in financing manufacturers or wholesalers in seasonal industries and is also useful where the manufactured products must be aged or cured or where they are accumulated over a period of time and then disposed of all at once.

Field work. Work in the field, specifically the task of gathering data from the field. Includes the sphere of practical operation, as of an organization or enterprise; also, the place or territory where direct contacts as with a clientele may be made, or whereby practical, first-hand knowledge may be gained. Sphere of action or place of contest, either literally or figuratively; hence, any scene of operations or opportunity for activity. State ex rel. McPherson v. Snell, 168 Or. 153, 121 P.2d 930, 937.

Fierding courts /fírdiŋ kórts/. Ancient Gothic courts of an inferior jurisdiction, so called because *four* were instituted within every inferior district or hundred. 3 Bl.Comm. 34.

Fieri /fáyəray/. Lat. To be made; to be done. See **In fieri.**

Fieri facias /fáyəray féys(h)(i)yəs/. Lat. Means that you "cause (it) to be done." A writ of execution commanding the sheriff to levy and make the amount of a judgment from the goods and chattels of the judgment debtor.

Fieri facias de bonis ecclesiasticis /fáyəray féys(h)(i)yəs dìy bównəs əklìyziyǽstəsəs/. When a sheriff to a common *fi. fa.* returns *nulla bona,* and that the defendant is a beneficed clerk, not having any lay fee, a plaintiff may issue a *fi. fa. de bonis ecclesiasticis,* addressed to the bishop of the diocese or to the archbishop (during the vacancy of the bishop's see), commanding him to make of the ecclesiastical goods and chattels belonging to the defendant within his diocese the sum therein mentioned.

Fieri facias de bonis testatoris /fáyəray féys(h)(i)yəs dìy bównəs tèstətórəs/. The writ issued on an ordinary judgment against an executor when sued for a debt due by his testator. If the sheriff returns to this writ *nulla bona,* and a *devastavit (q.v.),* the plaintiff may sue out a *fieri facias de bonis propriis,* under which the goods of the executor himself are seized.

Fieri feci /fáyəray fíysay/. Means I have caused to be made. The return made by a sheriff or other officer to a writ of *fieri facias,* where he has collected the whole, or a part, of the sum directed to be levied. The return, as actually made, is expressed by the word "Satisfied" indorsed on the writ.

Fieri non debet (debuit), sed factum valet /fáyəray nòn débət, sèd fǽktəm vǽlət/°débyuwət°/. It ought not to be done, but [if] done, it is valid.

Fi. Fa. /fáy féy/. An abbreviation for *fieri facias (q.v.).*

FIFO. First-in, first-out; an inventory flow assumption by which ending inventory cost is determined from most recent purchases and cost of goods sold is determined from oldest purchases including beginning inventory. *Contrast* with **Last-in, first-out (LIFO).**

Fifteenth Amendment. Amendment to U.S. Constitution, ratified by the States in 1870, guaranteeing all citizens the right to vote regardless of race, color, or previous condition of servitude. Congress was given the power to enforce such rights by appropriate legislation.

Fifteenths /fiftíynθs/. In old English law, this was originally a tax or tribute, levied at intervals by act of parliament, consisting of one-fifteenth of all the movable property of the subject or personalty in every city, township, and borough. Under Edward III, the taxable property was assessed, and the value of its fifteenth part (then about £29,000) was recorded in the exchequer, whence the tax, levied on that valuation, continued to be called a "fifteenth," although as the wealth of the kingdom increased, the name ceased to be an accurate designation of the proportion of the tax to the value taxed. 1 Bl.Comm. 309.

Fifth Amendment. Amendment to U.S. Constitution providing that no person shall be required to answer for a capital or otherwise infamous offense unless on indictment or presentment of a grand jury except in military cases; that no person will suffer double jeopardy; that no person will be compelled to be a witness against himself; that no person shall be deprived of life, liberty or property without due process of law and that private property will not be taken for public use without just compensation.

Fifth degree of kinship. The degree of kinship between a deceased intestate and the children of decedent's first cousin, sometimes designated as "first cousins once removed", is in the "fifth degree". Simonton v. Edmunds, 202 S.C. 397, 25 S.E.2d 284, 285.

Fifty decisions. Ordinances of Justinian (529–532) upon the authority of which all moot points were settled in the preparation of the second edition of the Code.

Fight. Hostile encounter; either physical or verbal in nature. To oppose or attempt to prevent combat or battle, as hostile encounter or engagement between opposing forces, suggesting primarily the notion of a brawl or unpremeditated encounter, or that of a pugilistic combat. Gitlow v. Kiely, D.C.N.Y., 44 F.2d 227, 232. See also **Affray.**

Fighting words. Fighting words, which may constitutionally be prohibited, are words directed to the person of the hearer which would have a tendency to cause acts of violence by the person to whom, individually, the remark is addressed. Conchito v. City of Tulsa, Okl.Cr., 521 P.2d 1384, 1388.

The "freedom of speech" protected by the Constitution is not absolute at all times and under all circumstances and there are well-defined and narrowly limited classes of speech, the prevention and punishment of which does not raise any constitutional problem, including the lewd and obscene, the profane, the libelous, and the insulting or "fighting words" which by their very utterance inflict injury or tend to incite an immediate breach of the peace. Chaplinsky v. New Hampshire, 315 U.S. 568, 62 S.Ct. 766, 86 L.Ed. 1031.

Fightwite. Sax. A mulct or fine for making a quarrel to the disturbance of the peace. A payment to a lord possessing soc over a place where a wrong was done.

Figures. Artificial representations of a form, as in sculpture, drawing, or painting, especially the human body represented by art of any king. People v. Eastman, 89 Misc. 596, 152 N.Y.S. 314, 317.

Numerals; number symbols. They are either Roman, made with letters of the alphabet: *e.g.* "MDCCLXXVI"; or they are Arabic: *e.g.* "1776".

Filacer /fíləsər/fíləzər/. In England an officer of the superior courts at Westminster, whose duty it was to file the writs on which he made process. There were fourteen filacers, and it was their duty to make out all original process. The office was abolished in 1837.

Filare /fəlériy/. In old English practice, to file.

Filching /fílchiŋ/fílshiŋ/. To steal money, commonly of little value, secretly or underhandedly. Peck v. Bez, W.Va., 40 S.E.2d 1, 10.

File, *n.* A record of the court. Milton v. United States, C.C.A.La., 105 F.2d 253, 255. A paper is said to be filed when it is delivered to the proper officer, and by him received to be kept on file as a matter of record and reference. But, in general, "file," or "the files," is used loosely to denote the official custody of the court or the place in the offices of a court where the records and papers are kept. The "file" in a cause includes the original complaint and all pleadings and papers belonging thereto. See also **Docket; Record.**

File, *v.* To lay away and arrange in order, pleadings, motions, instruments, and other papers for preservation and reference. To deposit in the custody or among the records of a court. To deliver an instrument or other paper to the proper officer or official for the purpose of being kept on file by him as a matter of record and reference in the proper place. It carries the idea of permanent preservation as a public record. In re Gubelman, C.C.A.N.Y., 10 F.2d 926, 929; City of Overland Park v. Nikias, 209 Kan. 643, 498 P.2d 56, 59. See also **Record.**

Constructive filing. See that title.

Filing officer. The person in charge of the office (*e.g.* office or department of Secretary of State) in which a financing statement must be filed to perfect a security interest under the Uniform Commercial Code. U.C.C. § 9–401.

Filing with court. Fed.R.Civil P. 5 requires that all papers after the complaint required to be served upon a party shall be filed with the court (*i.e.* clerk or judge) either before service or within a reasonable time thereafter.

Filed. See **File.**

File wrapper estoppel. Under doctrine of "file wrapper estoppel," if, in order to obtain patent, inventor restricts what he has claimed, he is thereafter bound by that surrender which may be readily ascertained by an examination of the file wrapper. Fraser v. Continental Realty Corp., D.C.W.Va., 356 F.Supp. 704, 706. Means that the inventor had earlier given up certain claims with respect to his patent that he is now attempting to assert through the doctrine of equivalents in order to establish a basis for his charge that the patent has been infringed. Systematic Tool & Machine Co. v. Oalter Kidde & Co., Inc., D.C.Pa., 390 F.Supp. 178, 200.

Filiation /filiyéyshən/. Judicial determination of paternity. The relation of child to father.

In the civil law, the descent of son or daughter, with regard to his or her father, mother, and their ancestors.

Filiation proceeding. A special statutory proceeding, criminal in form, but in the nature of a civil action to enforce a civil obligation or duty specifically for the purpose of establishing parentage and the putative father's duty to support his illegitimate child. State v. Morrow, 158 Or. 412, 75 P.2d 737, 738, 739, 744.

Filibuster. Tactics designed to obstruct and delay legislative action by prolonged and often irrelevant speeches on the floor of the House or Senate. See also **Cloture;** a means of cutting off filibustering.

Filing. See **Constructive filing; File.**

Filiolus (or filious) /filiyówləs/. In old records, a godson.

Filius /fíliyəs/. Lat. A son; a child. As distinguished from heir, *filius* is a term of nature, *hæres* a term of law. In the civil law the term was used to denote a child generally. A distinction was sometimes made, in the civil law, between *"filii"* and *"liberi";* the latter word including grandchildren (*nepotes*), the former not.

Filius est nomen naturæ, sed hæres nomen juris /fíliyəs èst nówmən nəchúriy sèd híriyz nówmən júrəs/. Son is a name of nature, but heir is a name of law.

Filius familias /fíliyəs fəmíliyəs/. In the civil law, the son of a family; an unemancipated son.

Filius in utero matris est pars viscerum matris /fíliyəs in yúwdərow méytrəs èst párz vísərəm méytrəs/. A son in the mother's womb is part of the mother's vitals.

Filius mulieratus /fíliyəs myùwl(i)yəréydəs/. In old English law, the eldest legitimate son of a woman, who previously had an illegitimate son by his father. Otherwise called *"mulier."* 2 Bl.Comm. 248.

Filius nullius /fíliyəs nəláyəs/°náliyəs/. An illegitimate child; son of nobody.

Filius populi /fíliyəs pópyələy/. A son of the people. Natural child.

Fill. To make full; to complete; to satisfy or fulfill; to possess and perform the duties of; to occupy the whole capacity or extent of, so as to leave no space vacant.

Filthy. Dirty, vulgar, indecent, obscene, lewd, offensive to the moral sense, morally depraving, debasing. Containing or covered with filth. See **Obscene.**

Filum /fáyləm/. Lat. In old practice, a file, *i.e.,* a thread or wire on which papers were strung, that being the ancient method of filing. An imaginary thread or line passing through the middle of a stream or road, as in the titles following.

Filum aquæ /fáyləm ǽkwiy/. A thread of water; a line of water; the middle line of a stream of water, supposed to divide it into two equal parts, and constituting in many cases the boundary between the riparian proprietors on each side. *Medium filum* is sometimes used with no additional meaning. Cf. **Thalweg.**

Filum forestæ /fáyləm fəréstiy/. The border of the forest. 2 Bl.Comm. 419. Manw. *Purlieu.*

Filum viæ /fáyləm váyiy/. The thread or middle line of a road. The boundary between the owners of the land on each side of a road.

Fin /fǽn/. Fr. An end, or limit; a limitation, or period of limitation.

Final. Last; conclusive; decisive; definitive; terminated; completed. In its use in reference to legal actions, this word is generally contrasted with "interlocutory." See also **Final decision; Final judgment.**

As to final Costs; Decree; Injunction; Judgment; Order; Process; Recovery; Sentence, and Settlement, see those titles.

Final appealable order. To constitute a "final, appealable order" the order must terminate the litigation and finally determine, fix and dispose of the parties' rights as to the issues in the suit. Myers v. Myers, 9 Ill.Dec. 603, 51 Ill.App.3d 830, 366 N.E.2d 1114, 1121.

Final architect's certificate. One which is issued after a job is done and which finally determines the rights of the parties as to money and disputes.

Final award. One which conclusively determines the matter submitted and leaves nothing to be done except to execute and carry out terms of award. Trollope v. Jeffries, 55 Cal.App.3d 816, 128 Cal.Rptr. 115, 120.

Final decision. One which leaves nothing open to further dispute and which sets at rest cause of action between parties. Judgment or decree which terminates action in court which renders it. One which settles rights of parties respecting the subject-matter of the suit and which concludes them until it is reversed or set aside. The filing of signed findings and conclusions and order for judgment. Synonymous with final judgment or decree. In re Tiffany, 252 U.S. 32, 40 S.Ct. 239, 240, 64 L.Ed. 443. Also, a decision from which no appeal or writ of error can be taken. U. S. v. Tod, C.C.A.N.Y., 1 F.2d 246, 251. "Final decision" which may be appealed is one that ends litigation on merits and leaves nothing for courts to do but execute judgment. Kappelmann v. Delta Air Lines, Inc., 176 U.S.App.D.C. 163, 539 F.2d 165, 168. See also Final decision rule; Final disposition; Final judgment; Interlocutory Appeals Act; Judgment *(Final judgment)*; Res *(Res judicata).*

Final decision rule. Appeals to federal courts of appeals from U.S. district courts must be from "final decisions" of district courts. 28 U.S.C.A. § 1291. In other words, the courts of appeals lack jurisdiction over nonfinal judgments. The object of this restriction is to prevent piecemeal litigation which would otherwise result from the use of interlocutory appeals. See, however, **Interlocutory Appeals Act.**

Final decree. See **Final decision; Final judgment.**

Final determination. See **Final decision.**

Final disposition. Such a conclusive determination of the subject-matter that after the award, judgment, or decision is made nothing further remains to fix the rights and obligations of the parties, and no further controversy or litigation can arise thereon. Quarture v. Allegheny County, 141 Pa.Super. 356, 14 A.2d 575, 578. It is such an award that the party against whom it is made can perform or pay it without any further ascertainment of rights or duties. See **Final decision.**

Final hearing. Describes that stage of proceedings relating to the determination of a subject matter upon its merits as distinguished from those of preliminary or interlocutory nature.

Finalis concordia /fənéyləs kəŋkórd(i)yə/. A final or conclusive agreement.

Finality rule. See **Final decision rule.**

Final judgment. One which finally disposes of rights of parties, either upon entire controversy or upon some definite and separate branch thereof. Casati v. Aero Marine Management Co., Inc., 43 Ill.App.3d 1, 1 Ill. Dec. 544, 356 N.E.2d 826, 833. Judgment is considered "final" only if it determines the rights of the parties and disposes of all of the issues involved so that no future action by the court will be necessary in order to settle and determine the entire controversy. Howard Gault & Son, Inc., v. First Nat. Bank of Hereford, Tex.Civ.App., 523 S.W.2d 496, 498. See also **Final decision; Judgment.**

Final judgment rule. See **Final decision rule.**

Final order. One which terminates the litigation between the parties and the merits of the case and leaves nothing to be done but to enforce by execution what has been determined. Richerson v. Jones, C.A. Pa., 551 F.2d 918, 921. See also **Final decision.**

Final passage. The vote on a passage of a bill or resolution in either house of the legislature after it has received the prescribed number of readings and has been subjected to such action as is required by the fundamental law governing the body or its own rule.

Final receiver's receipt. An acknowledgment by the government that it has received full payment for public land, that it holds the legal title in trust for the entryman, and will in due course issue to him a patent.

Final settlement. In probate proceeding, a direct adjudication that the estate is fully administered; that the administrator has completely executed his trust and has accounted for all moneys received as the law requires. In re Braun's Estate, 140 Kan. 188, 34 P.2d 94, 95.

The final determination of amount due contractor by proper governmental authority. Consolidated Indemnity & Insurance Co. v. W. A. Smoot & Co., C.C.A.Va., 57 F.2d 995, 996.

With respect to final settlement in a real estate transaction, see **Closing.**

Final submission. Exists when nothing remains to be done to render submission complete. Where the whole case, both requested instructions and evidence, is submitted to the court for its ruling and the court takes the case under advisement, there is a "final submission" of the entire case. Piatt v. Helm & Overly Realty Co., 342 Mo. 772, 117 S.W.2d 327, 329.

Finance. As a verb, to supply with funds through the issuance of stocks, bonds, notes, or mortgages; to provide with capital or loan money as needed to carry on business.

Finance is concerned with the value of the assets of the business system and the acquisition and allocation of the financial resources of the system.

Finance charge. The consideration for privilege of deferring payment of purchase price. The amount however denominated or expressed which the retail buyer contracts to pay or pays for the privilege of purchasing goods or services to be paid for by the buyer in installments; it does not include the amounts, if any, charged for insurance premiums, delinquency charges, attorney's fees, court costs, collection expenses or official fees. The cost of credit which is regulated in most jurisdictions by statute; *e.g.* federal and state "truth-in-lending" statutes require full disclosure of finance charges on credit agreements, billing statements, and the like.

Finance committee. A committee of the U.S. Senate with functions and powers similar to that of the Ways and Means Committee of the House. In business, an executive level committee, commonly made up of members of board of directors, responsible for major financial decisions of business.

Financial. Fiscal. Relating to finances.

Financial institutions. Means any organization authorized to do business under state or federal laws relating to financial institutions, including, without limitation, banks and trust companies, savings banks, building and loan associations, savings and loan companies or associations, and credit unions. Uniform Probate Code, § 6–101(3).

Financial interest. An interest equated with money or its equivalent.

Financially able. Solvent; able to pay debts and expenses as due. Means purchaser must be able to command the necessary funds to close the deal within the required time. Hersh v. Garau, 218 Cal. 460, 23 P.2d 1022. Credit worthy. See also **Financial responsibility acts; Solvency.**

Financial reports. See **Annual report; Financial statement; Profit and loss statement.**

Financial responsibility. Term commonly used in connection with motor vehicle insurance equivalents. See also **Financial responsibility acts.**

Financial responsibility acts. State statutes which require owners of motor vehicles to produce proof of financial accountability as a condition to acquiring a license and registration so that judgments rendered against them arising out of the operation of the vehicles may be satisfied.

Financial statement. Any report summarizing the financial condition or financial results of an organization on any date or for any period. The two principal types of financial statements are the balance sheet and the profit and loss statement. See also **Annual report.**

Financial worth. The value of one's property less what he owes, or the value of his resources less his liabilities.

Financier. A person or financial institution employed in the economical management and application of money. One skilled in matters appertaining to the judicious investment, loaning, and management of money affairs. Person or institution that financially backs business ventures.

Financing agency. A bank, finance company or other person who in the ordinary course of business makes advances against goods or documents of title or who by arrangement with either the seller or the buyer intervenes in ordinary course to make or collect payment due or claimed under the contract for sale, as by purchasing or paying the seller's draft or making advances against it or by merely taking it for collection whether or not documents of title accompany the draft. "Financing agency" includes also a bank or other person who similarly intervenes between persons who are in the position of seller and buyer in respect to the goods. U.C.C. § 2–104.

Financing statement. Under the Uniform Commercial Code, a financing statement is used under Article 9 to reflect a public record that there is a security interest or claim to the goods in question to secure a debt. The financing statement is filed by the security holder with the Secretary of State, or similar public body, and as such becomes public record. See also **Secured transaction; Security interest.**

Find. To come upon by seeking or by effort. Shields v. Shields, 115 Mont. 146, 139 P.2d 528, 530. To discover; to determine; to locate; to ascertain and declare.

To announce a conclusion upon a disputed fact or state of facts; as a jury is said to "find a will." To determine a controversy in favor of one of the parties; as a jury "finds for the plaintiff." See also **Finding.**

Fin de non recevoir /fǽn də nòn rəsèyvwár/. In French law, an exception or plea founded on law, which, without entering into the merits of the action, shows that the plaintiff has no right to bring it, either because the time during which it ought to have been brought has elapsed, which is called "prescription," or that there has been a compromise, accord and satisfaction, or any other cause which has destroyed the right of action which once subsisted.

Finder. With respect to a securities issue, refers to one who brings together an issuer and an underwriter; in connection with mergers, refers to one who brings two companies together. May also refer to one who secures mortgage financing for borrower; or one who locates a particular type of executive or professional for a corporation; or one who locates a particular type of business acquisition for a corporation.

Finder's fee. Amount charged for bringing lender and borrower or issuer and underwriter together, or for performing other types of services described under "Finder" supra. A finder's fee for a securities issue may be stock or a combination of cash and stock.

Finding. The result of the deliberations of a jury or a court. A decision upon a question of fact reached as the result of a judicial examination or investigation by a court, jury, referee, coroner, etc. A recital of the facts as found. The word commonly applies to the result reached by a judge or jury. See also **Decision; Judgment; Verdict.**

Finding of fact. Determinations from the evidence of a case, either by court or an administrative agency, concerning facts averred by one party and denied by another. Kozsdiy v. O'Falton Bd. of Fire and Police Com'rs, 31 Ill.App.3d 173, 334 N.E.2d 325, 329. A determination of a fact by the court, averred by one party and denied by the other, and founded on evidence in case. C.I.T. Corp. v. Elliott, 66 Idaho 384, 159 P.2d 891, 897. A conclusion by way of reasonable inference from the evidence. Barker v. Narragansett Racing Ass'n, 65 R.I. 489, 16 A.2d 495, 497. Also the answer of the jury to a specific interrogatory propounded to them as to the existence or non-existence of a fact in issue. Conclusion drawn by trial court from facts without exercise of legal judgment.

Findings of fact shall not be set aside unless clearly erroneous. Fed.R. Civil P. 52(a). The court may amend, or make additional findings, on motion of a party. Fed.R. Civil P. 52(b).

A *general* finding by a court is a general statement that the facts are in favor of a party or entitle him to judgment. It is a complete determination of all matters, and is a finding of every special thing necessary to be found to sustain the general finding.

A *special* finding is a specific setting forth of the ultimate facts established by the evidence and which are determinative of the judgment which must be given. It is only a determination of the ultimate facts on which the law must be determined. A special finding may also be said to be one limited to the fact issue submitted.

Finding of law. Term applies to rulings of law made by court in connection with findings of fact; such findings or rulings of law are subject to appellate review.

Fine, *v.* To impose a pecuniary punishment or mulct. To sentence a person convicted of an offense to pay a penalty in money.

Fine, *n.* A pecuniary punishment imposed by lawful tribunal upon person convicted of crime or misdemeanor. A pecuniary penalty. It may include a forfeiture or penalty recoverable in a civil action, and, in criminal convictions, may be in addition to imprisonment. See also **Penalty.**

Conveyancing. An amicable composition or agreement of a suit, either actual or fictitious, by leave of the court, by which the lands in question become, or are acknowledged to be, the right of one of the parties. Hitz v. Jenks, 123 U.S. 297, 8 S.Ct. 143, 31 L.Ed. 156. Fines were abolished in England by St. 3 & 4 Wm. IV, c. 74, substituting a disentailing deed. A fine is so called because it puts an *end* not only to the suit thus commenced, but also to all other suits and controversies concerning the same matter. The party who parted with the land, by acknowledging the right of the other, was said to *levy* the fine, and was called the "cognizor" or "conusor," while the party who recovered or received the estate was termed the "cognizee" or "conusee," and the fine was said to be levied to him.

Executed fine. See **Executed.**

Tenure law. A money payment made by a feudal tenant to his lord. The most usual fine was that payable on the admittance of a new tenant, but there was also due in some manors fines upon alienation, on a license to demise the lands, or on the death of the lord, or other events.

Fine and recovery act. The English statutes 3 & 4 Wm. IV, c. 74, abolishing fines and recoveries.

Fine anullando levato de tenemento quod fuit de antiquo dominico /fáyniy ænəlǽndow ləvéydow dìy tènəméntow kwòd fyúwət dìy æntáykwow dəmínəkow/. An abolished writ for disannulling a fine levied of lands in ancient demesne to the prejudice of the lord.

Fine capiendo pro terris /fáyniy kæpiyéndow pròw téhrəs/. An obsolete writ which lay for a person who, upon conviction by jury, had his lands and goods taken, and his body imprisoned, to be remitted his imprisonment, and have his lands and goods redelivered to him, on obtaining favor of a sum of money, etc.

Fine for alienation. A fine anciently payable upon the alienation of a feudal estate and substitution of a new tenant. It was payable to the lord by all tenants holding by knight's service or tenants *in capite* by socage tenure. Abolished in England by 12 Car. II, c. 24. 2 Bl.Comm. 71, 89.

Fine-force. An absolute necessity or inevitable constraint.

Fine for endowment. A fine anciently payable to the lord by the widow of a tenant, without which she could not be endowed of her husband's lands. Abolished in England under Henry I, and by *Magna Charta.* 2 Bl.Comm. 135.

Finem facere /fáynəm fǽsəriy/. To make or pay a fine.

Fine non capiendo pro pulchre placitando /fáyniy nòn kæpiyéndow pròw pɔ́lkriy plǽsətǽndow/. An obsolete writ to inhibit officers of courts to take fines for fair pleading.

Fine pro redisseisinâ capiendo /fáyniy pròw rèdəsíyzənə kæpiyéndow/. An old writ that lay for the release of one imprisoned for a redisseisin, on payment of a reasonable fine.

Fine rolls. See **Oblate Rolls.**

Fines le roy /fáynz lə róy/. In old English law, the king's fines. Fines formerly payable to the king for any contempt or offense, as where one committed any trespass, or falsely denied his own deed, or did anything in contempt of law.

Fine sur cognizance de droit, cum ceo que il ad de son done /fáyn sòr kəgnáyzən(t)s də dróyt, kòm síyow kwìy il æd də sòn dówn/. A fine upon acknowledgment of the right of the cognizeè as that which he hath of the gift of the cognizor. By this the deforciant acknowledged in court a former feoffment or gift in possession to have been made by him to the plaintiff. 2 Bl.Comm. 352.

Fine sur cognizance de droit tantum /fáyn sòr kəgnáyzən(t)s də dróyt tǽntəm/. A fine upon acknowledgment of the right merely, and not with the circumstance of a *preceding gift* from the cognizor. This was commonly used to pass a *reversionary* interest which was in the cognizor, of which there could be no feoffment supposed. 2 Bl.Comm. 353.

Fine sur concessit /fáyn sòr kənsésət/. A fine upon *concessit* (he hath granted). A species of fine, where the cognizor, in order to make an end of disputes, though he acknowledged no precedent right, yet *granted* to the cognizee an estate *de novo,* usually for life or years, by way of supposed composition. 2 Bl.Comm. 353.

Fine sur done grant et render /fáyn sòr dówn grǽnt èy réndər/. A double fine, comprehending the fine *sur cognizance de droit come ceo* and the fine *sur concessit.* It might be used to convey particular limitations of estates, whereas the fine *sur cognizance de droit come ceo,* etc., conveyed nothing but an absolute estate, either of inheritance, or at least freehold. In this last species of fines, the cognizee, after the right was acknowledged to be in him, granted back again or rendered to the cognizor, or perhaps to a stranger, some other estate in the premises. 2 Bl.Comm. 353.

Fingerprints. See **Anthropometry.**

Finire /fənáyriy/. In old English law, to fine, or pay a fine. To end or finish a matter.

Finis /fáynəs/. Lat. An end; a fine; a boundary or terminus; a limit. Also in L. Lat., a fine *(q.v.).*

Finis est amicabilis compositio et finalis concordia ex concensu et concordia domini regis vel justiciarum /fáynəs èst æməkéybələs kòmpəzísh(iy)ow èt fənéyləs kənkórdiyə èks kən(t)sén(t)syuw èt kənkórdiyə dómənay ríyjəs vèl jəstìshiyérəm/. A fine is an amicable settlement and decisive agreement by consent and agreement of our lord, the king, or his justices.

Finis finem litibus imponit /fáynəs fáynəm lídəbəs impównət/. A fine puts an end to litigation.

Finis rei attendendus est /fáynəs ríyay ætəndéndəs èst/. The end of a thing is to be attended to.

Finis unius diei est principium alterius /fáynəs yənáyəs dayíyay èst prinsípiyəm oltíriyəs/. The end of one day is the beginning of another.

Finitio /fənísh(iy)ow/. An ending; death, as the end of life.

Finium regundorum actio /fáyniyəm rəgòndórəm ǽksh(iy)ow/. In the civil law, action for regulating boundaries. The name of an action which lay between those who had lands bordering on each other, to settle disputed boundaries.

Finors /fáynərz/. Those that purify gold and silver, and part them by fire and water from coarser metals. In the English statute of 4 Hen. VII, c. 2, they are also called "parters."

Firdfare. Sax. In old English law, a summoning forth to a military expedition *(indictio ad profectionem militarem).*

Firdiringa. Sax. A preparation to go into the army.

Firdsocne. Sax. In old English law, exemption from military service.

Firdwite. In old English law, a fine for refusing military service *(mulcta detrectantis militiam).* A mulct or penalty imposed on military tenants for their default in not appearing in arms or coming to an expedition.

A fine imposed for murder committed in the army; an acquittance of such fine.

Fire. The effect of combustion. The juridical meaning of the word does not differ from the vernacular. The word "fire," as used in insurance policies, does not have the technical meaning developed from analysis of its nature, but more nearly the popular meaning, being an effect rather than an elementary principle, and is the effect of combustion, being equivalent to ignition or burning. A destructive burning.

To dismiss or discharge from a position or employment.

Firearm. An instrument used in the propulsion of shot, shell, or bullets by the action of gunpowder exploded within it. A weapon which acts by force of gunpowder. This word comprises all sorts of guns, fowling-pieces, blunderbusses, pistols, etc. In addition, grenade shells, fuses, and powder may be considered "firearm" even though disassembled. U. S. v. Shafer, C.A.Ill., 445 F.2d 579, 583.

The term "firearm" means any weapon which is designed to or may readily be converted to expel any projectile by the action of an explosive; or the frame or receiver of any such weapon. 18 U.S.C.A. § 232.

Firearms Acts. Statutes (federal and state) imposing criminal penalties for illegal possession, sale and use of firearms; *e.g.* possession without license; carrying concealed weapon.

Firebare /fáy(ə)rbèr/. A beacon or high tower by the seaside, wherein are continual lights, either to direct vessels in the night, or to give warning of the approach of an enemy.

Firebote /fáy(ə)rbòwt/. Allowance of wood or *estovers* to maintain competent firing for the tenant. A sufficient allowance of wood to burn in a house.

Firebug. A popular phrase referring to persons guilty of the crime of arson; commonly understood to mean an incendiary, pyromaniac, or arsonist.

Fire district. One of the districts into which a city may be divided for the purpose of more efficient service by the fire department in the extinction of fires.

Fire insurance. See **Insurance.**

Fire marshal or **warden.** Official whose duties include supervision of firefighting and fire prevention for a state, county, city or town.

Fire ordeal. See **Ordeal.**

Fire sale. Sale of merchandise at reduced prices because of damage by fire or water; commonly, any sale at reduced prices, especially one brought about by an emergency. Fire sales are often regulated by statute or ordinance to protect the public-buyer from deceptive sales practices.

Firm. Business entity or enterprise. Unincorporated business. Partnership of two or more persons. See also **Firm name.**

Binding; fixed; final; definite.

Firma /fárma/. In old English law, the contract of lease or letting; also the rent (or farm) reserved upon a lease of lands, which was frequently payable in provisions, but sometimes in money, in which latter case it was called *"alba firma,"* white rent.

A tribute or custom paid towards entertaining the king for one night.

Firma burgi /fárma bárjay/. The right, in medieval days, to take the profits of a borough, paying for them a fixed sum to the crown or other lord of the borough.

Firma feodi /fárma fyúwday/ °fíy(a)day/. In old English law, a farm or lease of a fee; a fee-farm.

Firman /fármæn/. A Turkish word denoting a decree or grant of privileges, or passport to a traveler. A passport granted by the Great Mogul to captains of foreign vessels to trade within the territories over which he has jurisdiction; a permit.

Firmaratio /fármaréysh(iy)ow/. The right of a tenant to his lands and tenements.

Firmarium /fármériyam/. In old records, a place in monasteries, and elsewhere, where the poor were received and supplied with food. Hence the word "infirmary."

Firmarius /fármériyas/. L. Lat. A fermor. A lessee of a term. *Firmarii* comprehend all such as hold by lease for life or lives or for year, by deed or without deed.

Firm bid. Offer which contains no conditions which may defeat acceptance and which by its terms remains open and binding until accepted or rejected.

Firme /fárm/. In old records, a farm.

Firmior et potentior est operatio legis quam dispositio hominis /fármiyar èt paténshiyar èst aparéysh(iy)ow líyjas kwæm dìspazísh(iy)ow hómanas/. The operation of the law is firmer and more powerful [or efficacious] than the disposition [or will] of man.

Firmitas /fármatæs/. In old English law, an assurance of some privilege, by deed or charter.

Firmly. A statement that an affiant "firmly believes" the contents of the affidavit imports a strong or high degree of belief, and is equivalent to saying that he "verily" believes it. The operative words in a bond or recognizance, that the obligor is held and "firmly bound," are equivalent to an acknowledgment of indebtedness and promise to pay.

Firm name. The name or title under which company transacts its business.

Firm offer. An offer by a merchant to buy or sell goods in a signed writing which by its terms give assurance that it will be held open is not revocable, for lack of consideration, during the time stated or if no time is stated for a reasonable time, but in no event may such period of irrevocability exceed three months; but any such term of assurance on a form supplied by the offeree must be separately signed by the offeror. U.C.C. § 2–205. A binding; definite offer.

Firmura /fármyara/. In old English law, liberty to scour and repair a mill-dam, and carry away the soil, etc.

First. Preceding all others; foremost; used as an ordinal of one, as earliest in time or succession or foremost in position; in front of or in advance of all others. Colgate-Palmolive-Peet Co. v. U. S., C.C.A. Del., 130 F.2d 913, 915. Initial; senior; leading; chief; entitled to priority or preference above others.

As to first Cousin; Distress, and Mortgage, see those titles.

First Amendment. Amendment to U.S. Constitution guaranteeing basic freedoms of speech, religion, press, and assembly and the right to petition the government for redress of grievances.

First blush. By the phrase "first blush," within the rule that damages, to justify reversal, must be so great as to strike the mind at first blush as having been superinduced by passion or prejudice on the part of the jury, is meant that immediately the judicial mind is shocked and surprised at the great disproportion of the size of the verdict to what the facts of the case would authorize. Cole & Crane v. May, 185 Ky. 135, 214 S.W. 885, 887.

First-class. Of the most superior or excellent grade or kind; belonging to the head or chief or numerically precedent of several classes into which the general subject is divided; *e.g.* first class mail.

First-class misdemeanant. Under the English prisons act (28 & 29 Vict., c. 126, § 67) prisoners in the county, city, and borough prisons convicted of misdemeanors, and not sentenced to hard labor, were divided into two classes, one of which was called the "first division;" and it was in the discretion of the court to order that such a prisoner be treated as a misdemeanant of the first division, usually called "first-class misdemeanant," and as such not to be deemed a criminal prisoner, *i.e.,* a prisoner convicted of a crime.

First-class title. A marketable title, shown by a clean record, or at least not depending on presumptions that must be overcome or facts that are uncertain. See also **Marketable title.**

First degree murder. Murder committed with deliberately premeditated malice aforethought, or with extreme atrocity or cruelty, or in the commission or attempted commission of a crime punishable with death or imprisonment for life, is murder in the first degree. State v. McLaughlin, 286 N.C. 597, 213 S.E.2d 238, 244. See also **Murder; Premeditation.**

First devisee /fə́rst dəvàyzíy/°dèvəzíy/. The person to whom the estate is first given by the will; term "next devisee" referring to the person to whom the remainder is given.

First fruits. In English ecclesiastical law, the first year's whole profits of every benefice or spiritual living, anciently paid by the incumbent to the pope, but afterwards transferred to the fund called "Queen Anne's Bounty," for increasing the revenue from poor livings.

In feudal law, one year's profits of land which belonged to the king on the death of a tenant *in capite;* otherwise called *"primer seisin."* One of the incidents to the old feudal tenures. 2 Bl.Comm. 66, 67.

Firsthand knowledge. Information or knowledge gleaned directly from its source; *e.g.* eyewitness to a homicide.

First heir. The person who will be first entitled to succeed to the title to an estate after the termination of a life estate or estate for years.

First impression case. First examination. First presentation to a court for examination or decision. A case is said to be "of the first impression" when it presents an entirely novel question of law for the decision of the court, and cannot be governed by any existing precedent.

First in, first out. See **FIFO.**

First lien. One which takes priority or precedence over all other charges or encumbrances upon the same piece of property, and which must be satisfied before such other charges are entitled to participate in the proceeds of its sale. See also **First mortgage.**

First meeting. As used in a statute providing that, for insulting words or conduct to reduce homicide to manslaughter, killing must occur immediately or at "first meeting" after slayer is informed thereof, quoted words mean first time parties are in proximity under such circumstances as would enable slayer to act in the premises.

First meeting of creditors. In bankruptcy, the initial meeting called by the court for the examination of the bankrupt (*i.e.* debtor). Bankruptcy Act, § 341.

First mortgage. The senior mortgage which, by reason of its position, has priority over all junior encumbrances. The holder of the first or senior mortgage has priority right to payment on default. See also **Mortgage.**

First of exchange. Where a set of bills of exchange is drawn in duplicate or triplicate, for greater safety in their transmission, all being of the same tenor, and the intention being that the exceptance and payment of any one of them (the first to arrive safely) shall cancel the others of the set, they are called individually the "first of exchange," "second of exchange," etc.

First offender. One who has never before been convicted of a crime and, hence, one generally given special consideration in the disposition of his case. For example, first offenders of less serious crimes often receive suspended sentences or are placed on probation.

First policy year. In insurance, the year beginning with the first issuance of the insurance policy. This phrase in a statute eliminating suicide of insured after such year as defense, means year for which policy, annually renewed, was first issued.

First purchaser. In the law of descent, this term signifies the ancestor who first acquired (in any other manner than by inheritance) the estate which still remains in his family or descendants.

First return. The "first return", within statute as to depletion deduction is a first return listing items of gross income and deductions arising out of the property. Commissioner of Internal Revenue v. Alta Mines, C.C.A.Colo., 139 F.2d 580, 582.

First sale rule. Under the "first sale" doctrine where a copyright owner parts with title to a particular copy of his copyrighted work, he divests himself of his exclusive right to vend that particular copy, and vendee is not restricted by statute from further transfers of that copy. U. S. v. Drebin, C.A.Cal., 557 F.2d 1316, 1326.

First vested estate. Refers to first estate to vest in heirs after death of ancestor.

Fisc /físk/. A treasury of a kingdom, nation, state, or other governmental body. An Anglicized form of the Latin *"fiscus"* (which see).

Fiscal. In general, having to do with financial matters; *i.e.* money, taxes, public or private revenues, etc. Belonging to the fisc, or public treasury. Relating to accounts or the management of revenue. Of or pertaining to the public finances of a government or private finances of business.

Fiscal agent. Generally, a bank which collects and disburses money and serves as a depository of private and public funds in behalf of another.

Fiscal court. Formerly, a ministerial and executive body in some states.

Fiscal judge. A public officer named in the laws of the Ripuarians and some other Germanic peoples, apparently the same as the *"Graf", "reeve", "comes",* or *"count",* and so called because charged with the collection of public revenues, either directly or by the imposition of fines.

Fiscal officers. Those charged with the collection and distribution of public money, as, the revenues of a state (State Treasurer), county, or municipal corporation. In private corporation, officers directly charged with duty to oversee financial transactions such as treasurer and comptroller.

Fiscal period. In accounting, that space of time for which financial statements are prepared such as a year, a month or a quarter. See also **Accounting period; Fiscal year.**

Fiscal year. A period of twelve consecutive months chosen by a business as the accounting period for annual reports. A corporation's accounting year. Due to the nature of their particular business, some companies do not use the calendar year for their bookkeeping. A typical example is the department store which finds December 31 too early a date to close its books after Christmas sales. For that reason many stores close their accounting year January 31. Their fiscal year, therefore, runs from February 1 of one year through January 31 of the next. The fiscal year of other companies may run from July 1 through the following June 30. Most companies, though, operate on a calendar year basis. See also **Accounting period.**

Fiscus /fískəs/. *Roman law.* The treasury of the prince or emperor, as distinguished from *"ærarium,"* which was the treasury of the state. This distinction was not observed in France. In course of time the *fiscus* absorbed the ærarium and became the treasury of the state. The treasury or property of the state, as distinguished from the private property of the sovereign.

English law. The king's treasury, as the repository of forfeited property. The treasury of a noble, or of any private person.

Fish Commissioner. A public officer of the United States, created by act of congress of February 9, 1871, R.S. § 4395, whose duties principally concerned the preservation and increase throughout the country of fish suitable for food. Office of Commissioner of Fisheries was abolished and functions were transferred to the U.S. Fish and Wildlife Service.

Fishery. Business or process of catching, processing, or selling fish. A hatchery or place for catching fish.

A right or liberty of taking fish at a particular place or waters. A species of incorporeal hereditament, anciently termed "piscary," of which there are several kinds:

Common fishery. A fishing ground where all persons have a right to take fish. Not to be confounded with "common of fishery," as to which see **Common, n.**

Free fishery. A franchise in the hands of a subject, existing by grant or prescription, distinct from an ownership in the soil. It is an exclusive right, and applies to a public navigable river, without any right in the soil.

Right of fishery. The general and common right of the citizens to take fish from public waters, such as the sea, great lakes, etc. Shively v. Bowlby, 152 U.S. 1, 14 S.Ct. 548, 38 L.Ed. 331. Such rights are restricted however by federal and state laws that establish fishing seasons, licensing requirements, etc.

Several fishery. A fishery of which the owner is also the owner of the soil, or derives his right from the owner of the soil. 2 Bl.Comm. 39, 40. One by which the party claiming it has the right of fishing, independently of all other, so that no person can have a coextensive right with him in the object claimed; but

a partial and independent right in another, or a limited liberty, does not derogate from the right of the owner.

Fishgarth. A dam or weir in a river for taking fish.

Fishing trip or expedition. Using the courts to find out information beyond the fair scope of the lawsuit. The loose, vague, unfocused questioning of a witness or the overly broad use of the discovery process. Discovery sought on general, loose, and vague allegations, or on suspicion, surmise, or vague guesses. The scope of discovery may be restricted by protective orders as provided for by Fed.Rule Civil P. 26(c).

Fish royal. These were the whale and the sturgeon, which, when thrown ashore or caught near the coast of England, became the property of the king by virtue of his prerogative and in recompense for his protecting the shore from pirates and robbers. Some authorities include the porpoise.

Fistuca, or **festuca** /fəstyúwkə/. In old English law, the rod or wand, by the delivery of which the property in land was formerly transferred in making a feoffment. Called, also, *"baculum," "virga,"* and *"fustis."* See **Festuca.**

Fit. Suitable or appropriate. Conformable to a duty. Adapted to, designed, prepared.

Fitness for particular purpose. Where the seller at the time of contracting has reason to know any particular purpose for which the goods are required and that the buyer is relying on the seller's skill or judgment to select or furnish suitable goods, there is, unless excluded or modified, an implied warranty that the goods shall be fit for such purpose. U.C.C. § 2–315. See also **Warranty.**

Fitz. A Norman word, meaning "son." It is used in law and genealogy; as *Fitzherbert,* the son of Herbert; *Fitzjames,* the son of James; *Fitzroy,* the son of the king. It was originally applied to illegitimate children.

Five-Mile Act. An English act of parliament, passed in 1665, against non-conformists, whereby ministers of that body who refused to take the oath of non-resistance were prohibited from coming within five miles of any corporate town, or place where they had preached or lectured since the passing of the act of oblivion in 1660, nullified by act of 1689.

Fix. Adjust or regulate; determine; settle; make permanent. Term imports finality; stability; certainty; definiteness. See also **Firm.**

To liquidate or render certain. To fasten a liability upon one. To transform a possible or contingent liability into a present and definite liability.

Fixed. Prices are "fixed" when they are mutually agreed upon. United States v. Masonite Corporation, 316 U.S. 265, 62 S.Ct. 1070, 1076, 86 L.Ed. 1461. See **Fixed prices; Price-fixing.**

Fixed assets. Plant assets. Property used in operating a business which will not be consumed or converted into cash or its equivalent during the current accounting period; *e.g.* machinery, land, buildings. Contrasted with liquid assets; *e.g.* cash, securities.

Fixed bail. Setting the amount and terms of bail.

Fixed capital. The amount of money which is permanently invested in the business. May also refer to capital invested in fixed assets (land, buildings, machinery, etc.). Cost of total plant and general equipment. Lindheimer v. Illinois Bell Telephone Co., Ill., 292 U.S. 151, 54 S.Ct. 658, 78 L.Ed. 1182.

Fixed charges. The expenses that have to be borne whether any business is done or not. The chief items are the company's interest on bonds, certain taxes levied by the government, insurance payments, and depreciation due to obsolescence.

Fixed costs. See **Fixed charges.**

Fixed debt. A more or less permanent form of debt commonly evidenced by bonds or debenture. See also **Fixed indebtedness; Fixed liabilities.**

Fixed expenses. See **Fixed charges.**

Fixed fee. Term commonly used in construction contracts which provide for payment of costs plus a predetermined amount as a fee.

Fixed income. That species of income which does not fluctuate over a period of time such as interest on bonds and debentures or dividends from preferred stock as contrasted with dividend income from common stock. May also refer to income received by retiree from pension, annuity, or other form of fixed retirement benefit or income.

Fixed indebtedness. An established or settled indebtedness; not contingent. State ex rel. Hawkins v. State Board of Examiners, 97 Mont. 441, 35 P.2d 116, 120. See **Fixed debt; Fixed liabilities.**

Fixed liabilities. Those certain and definite as to both obligation and amount; e.g. interest on bonds or mortgage. Long term liabilities. See also **Fixed debt.**

Fixed opinion. A conviction, bias, or prejudgment as to guilt or liability disqualifying juror to impartially consider whole evidence and apply free from bias law as given in charge by court.

Fixed price contract. Type of contract in which buyer agrees to pay seller a definite, predetermined price.

Fixed prices. Prices established (i.e. mutually agreed upon) between wholesalers or retailers for sale or resale of materials, goods, or products. Agreements to fix prices are generally prohibited by state and federal statutes. See **Price-fixing.**

Fixed salary. One which is definitely ascertained and prescribed as to amount and time of payment, and does not depend upon the receipt of fees or other contingent emoluments; though not necessarily a salary which cannot be changed by competent authority. Established or settled, to remain for a time.

Fixture. An article in the nature of personal property which has been so annexed to the realty that it is regarded as a part of the land. Leawood Nat. Bank of Kansas City v. City Nat. Bank & Trust Co. of Kansas City, Mo.App., 474 S.W.2d 641, 644. That which is fixed or attached to something permanently as an appendage, and not removable.

A thing is deemed to be affixed to land when it is attached to it by roots, imbedded in it, permanently resting upon it, or permanently attached to what is thus permanent, as by means of cement, plaster, nails, bolts, or screws. Ordinarily, requisites are actual annexation to realty, or something appurtenant thereto, appropriation to use or purpose of realty, and intention to make article permanent accession to property as gathered from nature of articles affixed, relation and situation of person making annexation, structure and mode of annexation, and purpose or use for which it has been made.

Goods are fixtures when they become so related to particular real estate that an interest in them arises under real estate law; e.g., a furnace affixed to a house or other building; counters permanently affixed to the floor of a store; a sprinkler system installed in a building. U.C.C. § 9–313(1)(a).

Agricultural fixtures. Those annexed for the purpose of farming. In re Shelar, D.C.Pa., 21 F.2d 136, 138.

Trade fixtures. Articles placed in or attached to rented buildings by the tenant, to prosecute the trade or business for which he occupies the premises, or to be used in connection with such business, or promote convenience and efficiency in conducting it. Such chattels as merchants usually possess and annex to the premises occupied by them to enable them to store, handle, and display their goods, which are generally removable without material injury to the premises.

Flaco. A place covered with standing water.

Flag. A national standard on which are certain emblems; an ensign; a banner. It is carried by soldiers, ships, etc., and commonly displayed at forts, businesses and many other suitable places.

In common parlance, the word "flag," when used as denoting a signal, does not necessarily mean the actual use of a flag, but by figure of speech the word is used in the secondary sense and signifies a signal given as with a flag, that is to say, as by a waving of the hand for the purpose of communicating information.

Flag desecration. Flagrant misuse of flag punishable by statutes in most jurisdictions; though such statutes must meet constitutional tests in balancing state's interest in protecting the flag from disgrace and the individual's right to freedom of speech (symbolic). Spence v. State of Washington, 418 U.S. 405, 94 S.Ct. 2727, 41 L.Ed.2d 842. See also **Defile.**

Flag, duty of the. This was an ancient ceremony in acknowledgment of British sovereignty over the British seas, by which a foreign vessel struck her flag and lowered her top-sail on meeting the British flag.

Flag, law of. In maritime law, the law of that nation or country whose flag is flown by a particular vessel. A shipowner who sends his vessel into a foreign port gives notice by his flag to all who enter into contracts with the master that he intends the law of that flag to regulate such contracts, and that they must either submit to its operation or not contract with him.

Flag of convenience. Practice of registering a merchant vessel with a country that has favorable (i.e. less restrictive) safety requirements, registration fees, etc.

Flag of the United States. By the act entitled "An act to establish the flag of the United States," (Rev.St. §§ 1791, 1792), it was provided that, "from and after the fourth day of July next, the flag of the United States be thirteen horizontal stripes, alternate red and white; that the union be twenty stars, white in a blue field; that, on the admission of every new state into the Union, one star be added to the union of the flag; and that such addition shall take effect on the fourth day of July then next succeeding such admission." See 4 U.S.C.A. §§ 1, 2.

Flag of truce. A white flag displayed by one of two belligerent parties to notify the other party that communication and a cessation of hostilities are desired.

Flagrans /fléygræ̀n(d)z/. Lat. Burning; raging; in actual perpetration.

Flagrans bellum /fléygræ̀n(d)z béləm/. A war actually going on.

Flagrans crimen /fléygræ̀n(d)z kráymən/. In Roman law, a fresh or recent crime. This term designated a crime in the very act of its commission, or while it was of recent occurrence.

Flagrant delit /flagrón deylíy/. In French law, a crime which is in actual process of perpetration or which has just been committed.

Flagrante bello /fləgræntiy bélow/. During an actual state of war.

Flagrante delicto /fləgræntiy dəlíktow/. In the very act of committing the crime. 4 Bl.Comm. 307.

Flagrantly against evidence /fléygrəntliy əgénst évədən(t)s/. Without any substantial support in evidence. Williams v. Commonwealth, 276 Ky. 754, 125 S.W.2d 221, 223. So much against weight of evidence as to shock conscience and clearly indicate passion and prejudice of jury.

Flagrant necessity /fléygrənt nəsésədiy/. A case of urgency rendering lawful an otherwise illegal act, as an assault to remove a man from impending danger.

Flash check. A check drawn upon a banker by a person who has no funds at the banker's and knows that such is the case. Such act is a crime. Also called check kiting.

Flat. A place covered with water too shallow for navigation with vessels ordinarily used for commercial purposes. The space between high and low water mark along the edge of an arm of the sea, bay, tidal river, etc.

A floor or separate division of a floor, fitted for housekeeping and designed to be occupied by a single family. An apartment on one floor. A floor or story in a building. A building, the various floors of which are fitted up as flats, either residential or business.

In insurance, a policy without coinsurance provision; a provision for termination of renewal policy within short period after anniversary date without charge to insured.

In finance, stock is sold flat when no provision is made for adjusting accrued dividends.

Flat bond. Bond which includes accrued interest in the price.

Flat money. Paper money which is not backed by gold or silver but issued by order of the government. Also called "fiat" money. See **Federal reserve notes.**

Flat rate. Fixed amount paid each period without regard to actual amount of electricity, gas, etc. used in that particular period.

Flattery. False or excessive praise; insincere complimentary language or conduct.

Fledwite /flédwət/. In old English law, a discharge or freedom from amercements where one, having been an outlawed fugitive, came to the place of our lord of his own accord.

The liberty to hold court and take up the amercements for beating and striking.

The fine set on a fugitive as the price of obtaining the king's freedom.

Flee from justice. Removing one's self from or secreting one's self within jurisdiction wherein offense was committed; or leaving one's home, residence, or known place of abode, or concealing one's self therein, with intent, in either case, to avoid detection or punishment for some public offense. Streep v. U. S., 160 U.S. 128, 16 S.Ct. 244, 40 L.Ed. 365. See also **Extradition; Flight from justice; Fugitive.**

Fleet. A place where the tide flows; a creek, or inlet of water. A company of ships or navy. A prison in London (so called from a river or ditch formerly in its vicinity), abolished by 5 & 6 Vict., c. 22. See **Fleta.**

Flee to the wall. A metaphorical expression, used in connection with homicide done in self-defense, signifying the exhaustion of every possible means of escape, or of averting the assault, before killing the assailant.

Fleet policy. In insurance, a blanket policy which covers a number of vehicles owned by the same insured.

Flem. In Saxon and old English law, a fugitive bondman or villein.

The privilege of having the goods and fines of fugitives.

Flemene frit, flemenes frinthe, or **flymena frynthe** /flíymən frít, flíymənz frínθ, fláymənə frínθ/. A corrupt pseudo-archaic form is *flemens-firth,* representing the old law Latin form, *flemenaferth,* of the Anglo-Saxon *flyman fyrmth* or *flymena fyrmth.* The reception or relief of a fugitive or outlaw.

Flemeswite /flíymzwət/. The possession of the goods of fugitives.

Flet. In Saxon law, land; a house; home.

Fleta /flíydə/. The name given to an ancient treatise on the laws of England, founded mainly upon the writings of Bracton and Glanville, and supposed to have been written in the time of Edw. I. The author is unknown, but it is surmised that he was a judge or learned lawyer who was at that time confined in the Fleet prison, whence the name of the book.

Flexible participation bank night. A scheme whereby some method is employed by means of which some persons obtain chances to win without purchasing theater tickets. Commonwealth v. Lund, 142 Pa.Super. 208, 15 A.2d 839, 842.

Flexible participation scheme. A scheme whereby sum of money is given to member of audience holding registered number drawn from a hopper at theater. The scheme is one form of a lottery. Commonwealth v. Lund, 142 Pa.Super. 208, 15 A.2d 839, 846.

Flichwite /flíchwət/. In Saxon law, a fine on account of brawls and quarrels.

Flight from justice. The evading of the course of justice by voluntarily withdrawing one's self in order to avoid arrest or detention, or the institution or continuance of criminal proceedings, regardless of whether one leaves jurisdiction. Also comprehends continued concealment. See also **Flee from justice; Fugitive.**

Flim-flam. A form of bunco or confidence game. Commonwealth v. Townsend, 149 Pa.Super. 337, 27 A.2d 462, 463. Procedure variously known as "flim-flam", "faith and trust" or "confidence game" essentially is performed by two operators, ostensibly strangers to each other, by persuading victim to turn over to one of operators a sum of money to demonstrate his trustworthiness as prerequisite to obtaining some easy money and, after victim has turned over his money, operators disappear and victim receives nothing. Few v. U. S., D.C.App., 248 A.2d 125.

Flipping. Colloquial term for refinancing of consumer loans.

Float. Checks that have been credited to the depositor's bank account, but not yet debited to the drawer's bank account. The time between when a check is written and when such check is actually deducted from bank account. In banking practice, checks and other items in the process of collection. In manufacturing, the amount of goods in the process of production, usually measured in terms of the number of units in process divided by the number of finished units produced per average day and expressed as, for example, "six days float." In finance, the unsold part of a security issue or the number of shares actively traded. See also **Kiting.**

To let a given currency "float" is to allow it to freely establish its own value as against other currencies (*i.e.* exchange rate) by the law of supply and demand.

In land law, especially in the western states, a certificate authorizing the entry, by the holder, of a certain quantity of land not yet specifically selected or located. Wisconsin Cent. R. Co. v. Price County, 133 U.S. 496, 10 S.Ct. 341, 33 L.Ed. 687.

Floatage. See **Flotsam.**

Floater policy. In insurance, policy which is issued to cover items which have no fixed location such as jewelry or other items of personal property worn or carried about by the insured. See also **Floating policy.**

Floating charge. A continuing charge on the assets of the company creating it, but permitting the company to deal freely with the property in the usual course of business until the security holder shall intervene to enforce his claim. Pennsylvania Co. for Insurance on

Lives and Granting Annuities v. United Railways of Havana & Regla Warehouses, D.C.Me., 26 F.Supp. 379, 387, 388. See also **Floating lien.**

Floating debt. Liabilities (exclusive of bonds) payable on demand or at an early date; *e.g.* accounts payable; bank loans.

Floating easement. Easement for right-of-way which, when created, is not limited to any specific area on servient tenement. City of Los Angeles v. Howard, 53 Cal.Rptr. 274, 276, 244 C.A.2d 538.

Floating interest rate. Rate of interest that is not fixed but which varies depending upon the existing rate in the money market.

Floating lien. Security interest under which borrower pledges security for present and future advances. John Miller Supply, Inc. v. Western State Bank, 55 Wis.2d 385, 199 N.W.2d 161, 163. Such security is not only in inventory or accounts of the debtor in existence at the time of the original loan, but also in his after-acquired inventory or accounts. U.C.C. § 9–204(4).

Floating or **circulating capital**. Capital retained for the purpose of meeting current expenditures. The capital which is consumed at each operation of production and reappears transformed into new products. Capital in the form of current, as opposed to fixed, assets.

Floating policy. Insurance policy intended to supplement specific insurance on property and attaches only when the latter ceases to cover the risk, and the purpose of such policy is to provide indemnity for property which cannot, because of its frequent change in location and quantity, be covered by specific insurance. Davis Yarn Co. v. Brooklyn Yarn Dye Co., 293 N.Y. 236, 56 N.E.2d 564, 570. See also **Floater policy.**

Floating stock. The act or process by which stock is issued and sold. See also **Issue.**

Floating zone. A floating zone is a special detailed use district of undetermined location in which the proposed kind, size and form of structures must be preapproved. It is legislatively predeemed compatible with area in which it eventually locates if specified standards are met and the particular application is not unreasonable. Sheridan v. Planning Bd. of City of Stamford, 159 Conn. 1, 266 A.2d 396, 404.

Flode-mark. Flood-mark, high-water mark. The mark which the sea, at flowing water and highest tide, makes on the shore.

Flogging. Thrashing or beating with a whip or lash.

Flood. An inundation of water over land not usually covered by it. Water which inundates area of surface of earth where it ordinarily would not be expected to be. Stover v. U. S., D.C.Cal., 204 F.Supp. 477, 485. See also **Act of God; Flood water.**

Ordinary and extraordinary floods. Extraordinary or unprecedented floods are floods which are of such unusual occurrence that they could not have been foreseen by men of ordinary experience and prudence. Ordinary floods are those, the occurrence of which may be reasonably anticipated from the general experience of men residing in the region where such floods happen.

Flood water. Waters which escape from stream or other body of water and overflow adjacent territory, under conditions which do not usually occur. Everett v. Davis, 18 Cal.2d 289, 115 P.2d 821, 823, 824. Flood water is the extraordinary overflow of rivers and streams. Keys v. Romley, 64 Cal.2d 396, 50 Cal.Rptr. 273, 275, 412 P.2d 529. Waters which escape from a watercourse in great volume and flow over adjoining lands in no regular channel. Kennecott Copper Corp. v. McDowell, 100 Ariz. 276, 413 P.2d 749, 752.

Floor. A term used metaphorically, in parliamentary practice, to denote the exclusive right to address the body in session. A member who has been recognized by the chairman, and who is in order, is said to "have the floor", until his remarks are concluded. Similarly, the "floor of the house" means the main part of the hall where the members sit, as distinguished from the galleries, or from the corridors or lobbies.

Trading area where stocks and commodities are bought and sold on exchanges.

The lower limit; *e.g.* minimum wages; lowest price stock will be permitted to fall before selling.

In England, the floor of a court is that part between the judge's bench, and the front row of counsel. Litigants appearing in person, in the high court or court of appeal, are supposed to address the court from the floor.

Floored. An automobile is "floored" when it is financed under a trust receipt, floor plan financing agreement, or similar title retention document, whereby retail dealer obtains possession of automobile from distributor for exhibition and sale through payment to distributor by finance company. Commercial Credit Co. v. Barney Motor Co., 10 Cal.2d 718, 76 P.2d 1181, 1183. See **Floor plan financing.**

Floor plan financing. Arrangement for the lending of money to an automobile dealer, or other supplier of goods, so that he may purchase cars, or other articles, to include in his inventory; the loan being secured by the automobile or other goods while in the dealer's possession, and is gradually reduced as the cars or other merchandise are sold. Harlan v. U. S., 160 Ct.Cl. 209, 312 F.2d 402, 406.

Floor plan rule. Rule by which an owner who has placed an automobile on the floor of a retail dealer's showroom for sale is estopped to deny the title of an innocent purchaser from such dealer in the ordinary retail dealing, without knowledge of any conflicting claim. Mutual Finance Co. v. Municipal Emp. Union Local No. 1099, 110 Ohio App. 341, 165 N.E.2d 435.

Floor trader. Member of stock or commodity exchange who trades on floor for his own account.

Florin /flóhrən/. A coin originally made at Florence with the value of about two English shillings.

Flotage /flówdəjəz/. See **Flotsam.**

Floterial district /flòwtíriyəl dístrəkt/. One formed by combining two or more legislative districts, each of

which elects its own representatives, into larger district for the election at large of one additional representative. In re Apportionment Law Senate Joint Resolution No. 1305, 1972 Regular Session, Fla., 263 So.2d 797, 804.

Flotsam, flotsan /flótsəm/. A name for the goods which float upon the sea when cast overboard for the safety of the ship, or when a ship is sunk. Distinguished from "jetsam" (goods deliberately thrown over to lighten ship) and "ligan".

Floud-marke. In old English law, high-water mark; flood-mark.

Flowage. The natural flow or movement of water from an upper estate to a lower one is a servitude which the owner of the latter must bear, though the flowage be not in a natural water course with well defined banks.

Flower bond. Type of U.S. Savings Bond which may be cashed in at par to pay Federal estate taxes.

Flowing lands. Imports raising and setting back water on another's land, by a dam placed across a stream or water course which is the natural drain and outlet for surplus water on such land.

FLSA. Fair Labor Standards Act.

Fluctuating clause. Type of escalator provision which is inserted in some long term contracts to allow for increase in costs during the contract period. See also **Escalator clause.**

Fluctus /flə́ktəs/. Flood; flood-tide.

Flume. Primarily a stream or river, but usually used to designate an artificial channel applied to some definite use, and may mean either an open or a covered aqueduct.

Flumen /fl(y)úwmən/. In Roman law, a servitude which consists in the right to conduct the rain-water, collected from the roof and carried off by the gutters, onto the house or ground of one's neighbor. Also a river or stream. In old English law, flood; flood-tide.

Flumina et portus publica sunt, ideoque jus piscandi omnibus commune est /fl(y)úwmənə èt pórdəs pə́bləkə sə̀nt, ìdiyówkwiy jə́s piskǽnday ómnəbəs kəmyúwniy èst/. Rivers and ports are public; therefore the right of fishing there is common to all.

Fluminæ volucres /fl(y)úwməniy vəl(y)úwkriyz/. Wild fowl; waterfowl.

Fluvius /fl(y)úwviyəs/. Lat. A river; a public river; flood; flood-tide.

Fluxus /flə́ksəs/. In old English law, flow. *Per fluxum et refluxum maris*, by the flow and reflow of the sea.

Fly for it. Anciently, it was the custom in a criminal trial to inquire after a verdict, "Did he fly for it?" After the verdict, even if not guilty, forfeiture of goods followed conviction upon such inquiry. Abolished by 7 & 8 Geo. IV, c. 28.

Flyma /fláymə(n)/. In old English law, a runaway; fugitive; one escaped from justice, or who has no "hlaford."

Flyman-frymth /fláymǝn frímθ/. See **Flemene frit.**

Fly-power. A written assignment in blank, whereby, on being attached to a stock certificate, the stock may be transferred.

FMC. Federal Maritime Commission.

FMCS. Federal Mediation and Conciliation Service.

FMW. Fair market value.

FNMA. Federal National Mortgage Association.

FOB. Free on board some location (for example, FOB shipping point; FOB destination); the invoice price includes delivery at seller's expense to that location. Title to goods usually passes from seller to buyer at the FOB location. U.C.C. § 2–319(1).

Focage /fówkǝj/. House-bote; fire-bote.

Focale /fówkǝl/. In old English law, firewood. The right of taking wood for the fire. Fire-bote.

Fodder /fódǝr/. Food for horses or cattle. In feudal law, the term also denoted a prerogative of the prince to be provided with corn, etc., for his horses by his subjects in his wars.

Fodertorium /fòdǝrtóriyǝm/. Provisions to be paid by custom to the royal purveyors.

Foderum /fódǝrǝm/. See **Fodder.**

Fodina. A mine.

Fœdus /fíydǝs/. In international law, a treaty; a league; a compact.

Fœminæ ab omnibus officiis civilibus vel publicis remotæ sunt /fémǝniy æb ómnǝbǝs ǝfís(h)iyǝs sǝvílǝbǝs vèl páblǝsǝs rǝmówdiy sǝnt/. Women are excluded from all civil and public charges or offices.

Fœminæ non sunt capaces de publicis officiis /fémǝniy nón sǝnt kǝpéysiyz diy páblǝsǝs ǝfís(h)iyǝs/. Women are not admissible to public offices.

Fœmina viro co-operta /fémǝnǝ váyro kòw(ow)párdǝ/. A married woman; a *feme covert.*

Fœneration /fiynǝréyshǝn/. Lending money at interest; the act of putting out money to usury.

Fœnus /fíynǝs/. Lat. In the civil law, interest on money; the lending of money on interest.

Fœnus nauticum /fíynǝs nódǝkǝm/. Nautical or maritime interest.

Fœnus unciarium /fíynǝs àn(t)siyériyǝm/. Interest of one-twelfth, that is, interest amounting annually to one-twelfth of the principal, hence at the rate of eight and one-third per cent. per annum. This was the highest legal rate of interest in the early times of the Roman republic. An extraordinary rate of interest agreed to be paid for the loan of money on the hazard of a voyage; sometimes called *"usura maritima."* 2 Bl.Comm. 458. The extraordinary rate of interest, proportioned to the risk, demanded by a person, lending money on a ship, or on "bottomry," as it is termed. The agreement for such a rate of interest is also called *"fœnus nauticum."*

Fœticide /fíydǝsàyd/. See **Feticide.**

Fœtura /fǝchúrǝ/. In the civil law, the produce of animals, and the fruit of other property, which are acquired to the owner of such animals and property by virtue of his right.

Fœtus /fíydǝs/. An unborn child. An infant *in ventre sa mère.*

Fog. In maritime law, any atmospheric condition (including not only fog properly so called, but also mist or falling snow) which thickens the air, obstructs the view, and so increases the perils of navigation.

Fogagium /fǝgéyjiyǝm/. In old English law, foggage or fog; a kind of rank grass of late growth, and not eaten in summer.

Foi /fóy/f(w)éy/fwá/. In French feudal law, faith; fealty.

FOIA. Freedom of Information Act.

Foiterers /fóydǝrǝrz/féy°/. Vagabonds.

Folc-gemote /fówkgǝmòwt/. (Spelled, also, *folkmote, folcmote, folkgemote;* from *folc,* people, and *gemote,* an assembly.) In Saxon law, a general assembly of the people in a town or shire. It appears to have had judicial functions of a limited nature, and also to have discharged political offices, such as deliberating upon the affairs of the commonwealth or complaining of misgovernment, and probably possessed considerable powers of local self-government. The name was also given to any sort of a popular assembly.

Folc-land /fówklænd/. In Saxon law, land of the folk or people. Land belonging to the people or the public. Folc-land was the property of the community. In might be occupied in common, or possessed in severalty; and, in the latter case, it was probably parceled out to individuals in the folc-gemote or court of the district, and the grant sanctioned by the freemen who were there present. But, while it continued to be folc-land, it could not be alienated in perpetuity; and therefore, on the expiration of the term for which it had been granted, it reverted to the community, and was again distributed by the same authority. It was subject to many burdens and exactions from which boc-land was exempt.

Folc-mote /fówkmòwt/. A general assembly of the people, under the Saxons. See **Folc-gemote.**

Folc-right /fówkràyt/. The common right of all the people. 1 Bl.Comm. 65, 67.

The *jus commune,* or common law, mentioned in the laws of King Edward the Elder, declaring the same equal right, law, or justice to be due to persons of all degrees.

Foldage. A privilege possessed in some places by the lord of a manor, which consisted in the right of having his tenant's sheep to feed on his fields, so as to manure the land. The name of foldage is also given in parts of Norfolk to the customary fee paid to the lord for exemption at certain times from this duty.

Fold-course. In English law, land to which the sole right of folding the cattle of others is appurtenant.

Sometimes it means merely such right of folding. The right of folding on another's land, which is called "common foldage."

Fold-soke. A feudal service which consisted in the obligation of the tenant not to have a fold of his own but to have his sheep lie in the lord's fold.

Folgarii /fəlgériyay/. Menial servants; followers.

Folgere /fówljər/. In old English law, a freeman, who had no house or dwelling of his own, but was the follower or retainer of another *(heorthfœst),* for whom he performed certain predial services.

Folgers /fówljərz/. Menial servants or followers.

Folgoth. Official dignity.

Folie brightique /folíy bràytíyk/. See **Insanity.**

Folie circulaire /folíy sìrkyuwlér/. See **Insanity.**

Folio. A leaf of a book or manuscript. A page number. In the ancient lawbooks it was the custom to number the leaves, instead of the pages; hence a folio would include both sides of the leaf, or two pages. The references to these books are made by the number of the folio, the letters *"a"* and *"b"* being added to show which of the two pages is intended.

A large size of book, the page being obtained by folding the sheet of paper once only in the binding. Many of the ancient lawbooks are folios.

When used in connection with legal documents, it formerly meant a certain number of words varying from 72 to 100, but generally in the United States it consisted of 100. Such was used as a unit for measuring the text length of the legal instrument.

Placing a serial number on each leaf or page of printed matter.

Folk-land; folk-mote /fówklænd/fówkmòwt/. See **Folc-land; Folc-gemote.**

Follow. To conform to, comply with, or be fixed or determined by; as in the expressions "costs follow the event of the suit," "the *situs* of personal property follows that of the owner," "the offspring follows the mother" *(partus sequitur ventrem).* To go, proceed, or come after. To seek to obtain; to accept as authority.

Fonds de commerce. Fr. Goods of commerce, and trade.

Fonds et biens. Fr. In French law, goods and effects; including realty.

Fonds perdus. In French law, a capital is said to be invested *à fonds perdus* when it is stipulated that in consideration of the payment of an amount as interest, higher than the normal rate, the lender shall be repaid his capital in this manner. The borrower, after paying the interest during the period determined, is free as regards the capital itself.

Fonsadera /fònsaðérə/. In Spanish law, any tribute or loan granted to the king for the purpose of enabling him to defray the expenses of a war.

Fontana /fontǽnə/. A fountain or spring.

Food and Drug Administration. An agency within the Department of Health, Education, and Welfare established to set safety and quality standards for foods, drugs, cosmetics, and other household substances sold as consumer products. Among the basic tasks of the FDA are research, inspection and licensing of drugs for manufacturing and distribution. This agency is in charge of administering Food, Drug and Cosmetic Act *(q.v.).*

Food, Drug and Cosmetic Act. Federal Act of 1938 prohibiting the transportation in interstate commerce of adulterated or misbranded food, drugs and cosmetics. Act is administered by Food and Drug Administration.

Foot. A measure of length containing twelve inches or one-third of a yard. The base, bottom, or foundation of anything; and, by metonomy, the end or termination; as the foot of a fine. The terminal part of the leg. That part of leg at or below ankle joint; including the arch. Trustees for Arch Preserver Shoe Patents v. James McCreery & Co., Cust. & Pat.App., 49 F.2d 1068, 1071. See also **Foundation.**

Foot acre. One acre of coal one foot thick.

Foot-frontage rule. Under rule, assessment is confined to actual frontage on line of improvement, and depth of lot, number or character of improvements, or value thereof, is immaterial.

Footgeld /fútgèld/. In the forest law, an amercement for not cutting out the ball or cutting off the claws of a dog's feet (expeditating, him). To be quit of *footgeld* is to have the privilege of keeping dogs in the forest *unlawed* without punishment or control.

Foot of the fine. At common law, the fifth part of the conclusion of a fine. It includes the whole matter, reciting the names of the parties, day, year, and place, and before whom it was acknowledged or levied. 2 Bl.Comm. 351.

Foot pound. A unit of energy, or work, equal to work done in raising one pound avoirdupois against the force of gravity to the height of one foot.

Footprints. In the law of evidence, impressions made upon earth, snow, or other surface by the feet of persons, or by the shoes, boots, or other covering of the feet.

For. Fr. In French law, a tribunal. *Le for interieur,* the interior forum; the tribunal of conscience.

In behalf of, in place of, in lieu of, instead of, representing, as being which, or equivalent to which, and sometimes imports agency. Medler v. Henry, 44 N.M. 63, 97 P.2d 661, 662. During; throughout; for the period of, as, where a notice is required to be published "for" a certain number of weeks or months. Duration, when put in connection with time. Progressive Building & Loan Ass'n v. McIntyre, 169 Tenn. 491, 89 S.W.2d 336, 337.

In consideration for; as an equivalent for; in exchange for; in place of; as where property is agreed to be given "for" other property or "for" services.

Belonging to, exercising authority or functions within, as where one describes himself as "a notary public in and for the said county."

By reason of; with respect to; for benefit of; for use of; in consideration of. The cause, motive or occasion of an act, state or condition. American Ins. Co. v. Naylor, 103 Colo. 461, 87 P.2d 260, 265. Used in sense of "because of," "on account of," or "in consequence of." Kelly v. State Personnel Board of California, 31 Cal.App.2d 443, 88 P.2d 264, 266. By means of, or growing out of.

It connotes the end with reference to which anything is, acts, serves, or is done. In consideration of which, in view of which, or with reference to which, anything is done or takes place. In direction of; with view of reaching; with reference to needs, purposes or uses of; appropriate or adapted to; suitable to purpose, requirement, character or state of.

For account of. Language introducing name of person entitled to receive proceeds of indorsed note or draft. Equitable Trust Co. of New York v. Rochling, 275 U.S. 248, 48 S.Ct. 58, 59, 72 L.Ed. 264.

Foraker Act /fórəkər ǽkt/. A name usually given to the act of congress of April 12, 1900, 31 Stat.L. 77, c. 191 (48 U.S.C.A. § 731 et seq.), which provided civil government for Puerto Rico. See Downes v. Bidwell, 182 U.S. 244, 390, 21 S.Ct. 770, 45 L.Ed. 1088.

Foraneus /fəréyniyəs/. One from without; a foreigner; a stranger.

Forathe. In forest law, one who could make oath, *i.e.*, bear witness for another.

Forbalca /fórbò(l)kə/. In old records, a forebalk; a balk (that is, an unplowed piece of land) lying forward or next the highway.

Forbannitus /fòrbǽnədəs/. A pirate; an outlaw; one banished.

Forbarrer. L. Fr. To bar out; to preclude; hence, to estop.

Forbatudus. In old English law, the aggressor slain in combat.

Forbearance. Act by which creditor waits for payment of debt due him by debtor after it becomes due. Upton v. Gould, 64 Cal.App.2d 814, 149 P.2d 731, 733. A delay in enforcing rights. Indulgence granted to a debtor.

Refraining from action. The term is used in this sense in general jurisprudence, in contradistinction to "act."

Within usury law, term signifies contractual obligation of lender or creditor to refrain, during given period of time, from requiring borrower or debtor to repay loan or debt then due and payable. Hafer v. Spaeth, 22 Wash.2d 378, 156 P.2d 408, 411.

As regards forbearance as a form of consideration, see **Consideration.**

For cause. With respect to removal from office "for cause", means for reasons which law and public policy recognize as sufficient warrant for removal and such cause is "legal cause" and not merely a cause which the appointing power in the exercise of discretion may deem sufficient. State ex rel. Nagle v. Sullivan, 98 Mont. 425, 40 P.2d 995, 998. They do not mean removal by arbitrary or capricious action but

there must be some cause affecting and concerning ability and fitness of official to perform duty imposed on him. The cause must be one in which the law and sound public policy will recognize as a cause for official no longer occupying his office. Napolitano v. Ward, D.C.Ill., 317 F.Supp. 79, 81.

Force. Power dynamically considered, that is, in motion or in action; constraining power, compulsion; strength directed to an end. Commonly the word occurs in such connections as to show that unlawful or wrongful action is meant; *e.g.* forcible entry.

Power statically considered; that is at rest, or latent, but capable of being called into activity upon occasion for its exercise. Efficacy; legal validity. This is the meaning when we say that a statute or a contract is "in force."

In old English law, a technical term applied to a species of accessary before the fact.

See also **Constructive force; Excessive force; Intervening force; Reasonable force.**

Deadly force. Force which the actor uses with the purpose of causing or which he knows to create a substantial risk of causing death or serious bodily harm. Purposely firing a firearm in the direction of another person or at a vehicle in which another person is believed to be constitutes deadly force. A threat to cause death or serious bodily harm, by the production of a weapon or otherwise, so long as the actor's purpose is limited to creating an apprehension that he will use deadly force if necessary, does not constitute deadly force. Model Penal Code, § 3.11.

Unlawful force. Force, including confinement, which is employed without the consent of the person against whom it is directed and the employment of which constitutes an offense or actionable tort or would constitute such offense or tort except for a defense (such as the absence of intent, negligence, or mental capacity; duress; youth; or diplomatic status) not amounting to a privilege to use the force. Assent constitutes consent, within the meaning of this Section, whether or not it otherwise is legally effective, except assent to the infliction of death or serious bodily harm. Model Penal Code, § 3.11.

Force and arms. A phrase used in common law pleading in declarations of trespass and in indictments, but now unnecessary, to denote that the act complained of was done with violence.

Force and fear. Called also *"vi metuque"* means that any contract or act extorted under the pressure of force *(vis)* or under the influence of fear *(metus)* is voidable on that ground, provided, of course, that the force or the fear was such as influenced the party.

Forced heirs. Those persons whom the testator or donor cannot deprive of the portion of his estate reserved for them by law, except in cases where he has a just cause to disinherit them.

Forced sale. A sale made at the time and in the manner prescribed by law, in virtue of execution issued on a judgment already rendered by a court of competent jurisdiction; a sale made under the process of the court, and in the mode prescribed by law. A sale which is not the voluntary act of the owner, such as to satisfy a debt, whether of a mortgage, judgment, tax lien, etc. Sale brought about in shorter time than normally required because of creditor's action. See also **Fire sale; Foreclosure; Judicial sale; Sheriff's sale.**

Force majesture /fórs màzhəstyúr/. Includes lightnings, earthquakes, storms, flood, sunstrokes, freezing, etc., wherein latter two can be considered hazards in contemplation of employer within compensation acts. See also **Act of God; Vis major.**

Force majeure /fórs màzhúr/°məzhár/. Fr. In the law of insurance, superior or irresistible force. Such clause is common in construction contracts to protect the parties in the event that a part of the contract cannot be performed due to causes which are outside the control of the parties and could not be avoided by exercise of due care. See also **Act of God; Vis major.**

Forces /fórsəz/. The military and naval power of the country.

Forcheapum /fòrchíypəm/. Pre-emption; forestalling the market.

Forcible. Effected by force used against opposition or resistance; obtained by compulsion or violence. Offutt v. Liberty Mut. Ins. Co., 251 Md. 262, 247 A.2d 272, 276.

Forcible detainer. A summary, speedy and adequate statutory remedy for obtaining possession of premises by one entitled to actual possession. Casa Grande Trust Co. v. Superior Court In and For Pinal County, 8 Ariz.App. 163, 444 P.2d 521, 523. Exists where one originally in rightful possession of realty refuses to surrender it at termination of his possessory right. Sayers & Muir Service Station v. Indian Refining Co., 266 Ky. 779, 100 S.W.2d 687, 689. Forcible detainer may ensue upon a peaceable entry, as well as upon a forcible entry; but it is most commonly spoken of in the phrase "forcible entry and detainer." See also **Ejectment; Eviction; Forcible entry and detainer; Process** (*Summary process*).

Forcible entry. At common law, violently taking possession of lands and tenements with menaces, force, and arms, against the will of those entitled to the possession, and without the authority of law. 4 Bl. Comm. 148. Entry accompanied with circumstances tending to excite terror in the occupant, and to prevent him from maintaining his rights. Barbee v. Winnsboro Granite Corporation, 190 S.C. 245, 2 S.E.2d 737, 739. Angry words and threats of force may be sufficient. Calidino Hotel Co. of San Bernardino v. Bank of America Nat. Trust & Savings Ass'n, 31 Cal.App.2d 295, 87 P.2d 923, 931.

Every person is guilty of forcible entry who either (1) by breaking open doors, windows, or other parts of a house, or by any kind of violence or circumstance of terror, enters upon or into any real property; or (2) who, after entering peaceably upon real property, turns out by force, threats, or menacing conduct the party in possession. Code Civil Proc.Cal. § 1159.

In many states, an entry effected without consent of rightful owner, or against his remonstrance, or under circumstances which amount to no more than a mere trespass, is now technically considered "forcible," while a detainer of the property consisting merely in the refusal to surrender possession after a lawful demand, is treated as a "forcible" detainer, the "force" required at common law being now supplied by a mere fiction.

See **Ejectment; Eviction; Forcible detainer; Forcible entry and detainer; Process** (*Summary process*).

Forcible entry and detainer. A summary proceeding for restoring to possession of land one who is wrongfully kept out or has been wrongfully deprived of the possession. Wein v. Albany Park Motor Sales Co., 312 Ill.App. 357, 38 N.E.2d 556, 559. See also **Ejectment; Eviction; Forcible detainer; Process** (*Summary process*).

Forcible rape. Aggravated form of statutory rape made punishable by statute. See also **Rape.**

Forcible trespass. An invasion of the rights of another with respect to his personal property, of the same character, or under the same circumstances, which would constitute a "forcible entry and detainer" of real property at common law. It consists in taking or seizing the personal property of another by force, violence, or intimidation or in forcibly injuring it. There must be actual violence used, or such demonstration of force as is calculated to intimidate or tend to a breach of the peace. It is not necessary that the person be actually put in fear.

For collection. A form of indorsement on a note or check where it is not intended to transfer title to it or to give it credit or currency, but merely to authorize the transferee to collect the amount of it. Such an indorsement is restrictive. U.C.C. § 3–205(c).

Forda /fórdə/. In old records, a ford or shallow, made by damming or penning up the water.

Fordal /fórdəl/. A butt or headland, jutting out upon other land.

Fordanno /fòrdǽnow/. In old European law, he who first assaulted another.

Fore /fór/. Sax. Before. Fr. Out.

Foreclose /fòrklówz/. To shut out; to bar; to terminate. Method of terminating mortgagor's right of redemption. Hibernia Savings & Loan Soc. v. Lauffer, 41 Cal.App.2d 725, 107 P.2d 494, 497. See also **Foreclosure.**

Foreclosure /fòrklówzhər/. To shut out, to bar, to destroy an equity of redemption. Anderson v. Barr, 178 Okl. 508, 62 P.2d 1242, 1246. A termination of all rights of the mortgagor or his grantee in the property covered by the mortgage. The process by which a mortgagor of real or personal property, or other owner of property subject to a lien, is deprived of his interest therein. Procedure by which mortgaged property is sold on default of mortgagor in satisfaction of mortgage debt.

In common usage, refers to enforcement of lien, trust deed, or mortgage in any method provided by law.

Statutory foreclosure. The term is sometimes applied to foreclosure by execution of a power of sale contained in the mortgage, without recourse to the courts, as it must conform to the provisions of the statute regulating such sales.

Strict foreclosure. A decree of strict foreclosure of a mortgage finds the amount due under the mortgage, orders its payment within a certain limited time, and provides that, in default of such payment, the debtor's right and equity of redemption shall be forever barred and foreclosed; its effect is to vest the title of the property absolutely in the mortgagee, on default in payment, without any sale of the property.

Foreclosure decree. Properly speaking, a decree ordering the strict foreclosure of a mortgage; but the term is also loosely and conventionally applied to a decree ordering the sale of the mortgaged premises and the satisfaction of the mortgage out of the proceeds.

Foreclosure sale. A sale of mortgaged property to obtain satisfaction of the mortgage out of the proceeds, whether authorized by a decree of the court or by a power of sale contained in the mortgage. See also **Forced sale.**

Foregift /fórgìft/. A premium for a lease.

Foregoers /fòrgówərz/. Royal purveyors.

Forehand rent. In English law, rent payable in advance; or, more properly, a species of premium or bonus paid by the tenant on the making of the lease, and particularly on the renewal of leases by ecclesiastical corporations.

Foreign. Belonging to another nation or country; belonging or attached to another jurisdiction; made, done, or rendered in another state or jurisdiction; subject to another jurisdiction; operating or solvable in another territory; extrinsic; outside; extraordinary. Nonresident person, corporation, executor, etc.

As to foreign Administrator; Assignment; Attachment; Bill *(Bill of exchange)*; Charity; Commerce; Corporation; County; Creditor; Divorce; Document; Domicile; Factor; Judgment; Jury; Minister; Plea; Port; State; Vessel, and Voyage, see those titles.

Foreign agent. Person who registers with the federal government as a lobbyist representing the interests (*e.g.* import quotas, tourism, foreign aid) of a foreign nation or corporation.

Foreign answer. In old English practice, an answer which was not triable in the county where it was made.

Foreign apposer /fóhrən əpówzər/. In England, an officer in the exchequer who examines the sheriff's *estreats*, comparing them with the records, and apposes (interrogates) the sheriff as to each particular sum therein.

Foreign bill of exchange. Bill of exchange which is drawn in one state and payable in another state or country. See also **Bill** *(Bill of exchange).*

Foreign coins. Coins issued as money under the authority of a foreign government. As to their valuation in the United States, see 31 U.S.C.A. § 372.

Foreign commerce. Trade between persons in the United States and those in a foreign country. See also **Commerce; Foreign trade.**

Foreign consulate. The office or headquarters of a consul who represents a foreign country in the United States.

Foreign corporation. A corporation doing business in one state though chartered or incorporated in another state is a foreign corporation as to the first state, and, as such, is required to consent to certain conditions and restrictions in order to do business in such first state. Under federal tax laws, a foreign corporation is one which is not organized under the laws of one of the states or territories of the United States. I.R.C. § 7701(a)(5). Service of process on foreign corporations is governed by Fed.R.Civil P. 4. See also **Corporation.**

Foreign courts. The courts of a foreign state or nation. In the United States, this term is frequently applied to the courts of one of the states when their judgments or records are introduced in the courts of another.

Foreign diplomatic or **consular offices.** Officials appointed by a foreign government to protect the interest of its nationals in the United States. See also **Foreign agent.**

Foreign dominion. In English law, this means a country which at one time formed part of the dominions of a foreign state or potentate, but which by conquest or cession has become a part of the dominions of the British crown.

Foreigner. In old English law, this term, when used with reference to a particular city, designated any person who was not an inhabitant of that city. According to later usage, it denotes a person who is not a citizen or subject of the state or country of which mention is made, or any one owing allegience to a foreign state or sovereign.

Person belonging to or under citizenship of another country.

Foreign exchange. Conversion of the money of one country into its equal of another country. Process by which money of one country is used to pay balances due in another country.

Foreign exchange rate. The rate or price for which the currency of one country may be exchanged for the money of another country. See also **Float.**

Foreign immunity. With respect to jurisdictional immunity of foreign nations, see 28 U.S.C.A. § 1602 et seq.

Foreign judgment. See **Judgment.**

Foreign jurisdiction. Any jurisdiction foreign to that of the forum; *e.g.* of a sister state or another country. Also the exercise by a state or nation of jurisdiction beyond its own territory. Long-arm service of process is a form of such foreign or extraterritorial jurisdiction. See also 28 U.S.C.A. § 1330.

Foreign laws. The laws of a foreign country, or of a sister state. In conflicts of law, the legal principles of jurisprudence which are part of the law of a sister state or nation. Foreign laws are additions to our own laws, and in that respect are called *"jus receptum".*

Foreign money. The currency or medium of exchange of a foreign country. See also **Foreign exchange.**

Foreign personal representative. A personal representative of another jurisdiction. Uniform Probate Code, § 1–201(14).

Foreign proceeding. Proceeding, whether judicial or administrative and whether or not under bankruptcy law, in a foreign country in which the debtor's domicile, residence, principal place of business, or principal assets were located at the commencement of such proceeding, for the purpose of liquidating an estate, adjusting debts by composition, extension, or discharge, or effecting a reorganization. Bankruptcy Act § 101(19).

Foreign receiver. An official receiver appointed by a court of another state or nation.

Foreign representative. Duly selected trustee, administrator, or other representative of an estate in a foreign proceeding. Bankruptcy Act § 101(20).

Foreign service. The United States Foreign Service conducts relations with foreign countries through its representatives at embassies, missions, consulates general, consulates, and consular agencies throughout the world. These representatives and agencies report to the State Department.

Feudal law. In feudal law, was that whereby a mesne lord held of another, without the compass of his own fee, or that which the tenant performed either to his own lord or to the lord paramount out of the fee. Foreign service seems also to have been used for knight's service, or escuage uncertain.

Foreign service of process. Service of process for the acquisition of jurisdiction by a court in the United States upon a person in a foreign country is prescribed by Fed.R.Civil P. 4(i) and 28 U.S.C.A. § 1608. Service of process on foreign corporations is governed by Fed.R.Civil P. 4(d)(3).

Foreign states. Nations which are outside the United States. Term may also refer to another state; *i.e.* a sister state.

The term "foreign nations," as used in a statement of the rule that the laws of foreign nations should be proved in a certain manner, should be construed to mean all nations and states other than that in which the action is brought; and hence one state of the Union is foreign to another, in the sense of that rule.

A "foreign state" within statute providing for expatriation of American citizen who is naturalized under laws of foreign state is a country which is not the United States, or its possession or colony, an alien country, other than our own. Kletter v. Dulles, D.C. D.C., 111 F.Supp. 593, 598.

Foreign substance. Substance occurring in any part of the body or organism where it is not normally found, usually introduced from without. Adams v. Great Atlantic & Pacific Tea Co., 251 N.C. 565, 112 S.E.2d 92, 94. A "foreign substance" within rule that a cause of action against physician who leaves a foreign substance in body does not begin until patient discovers or should have discovered the presence of such substance includes drugs and medicine which are introduced into the body and which are not organically connected or naturally related. Rothman v. Silber, 83 N.J.Super. 192, 199 A.2d 86, 89, 92.

Foreign tax credit or **deduction.** Both individual taxpayers and corporations may claim a foreign tax credit on income earned and subject to tax in a foreign country or U.S. possession. As an alternative to the credit, a deduction may be taken for the foreign taxes paid.

Foreign trade. Commercial interchange of commodities between different countries; export and import trade. Standard Oil Co. of New Jersey v. United States, 29 Cust. & Pat.App. 82, 120 F.2d 340, 342. See also **Foreign commerce.**

Foreign trade zone. Zones or areas established in states wherein component parts for electric products, watches, automobiles, etc. may be imported initially duty free; such duty being postponed until the finished product enters the larger American market.

Foreign will. Will of person not domiciled within state at time of death. De Tray v. Hardgrove, Tex.Com. App., 52 S.W.2d 239, 240.

Forejudge. In old English law and practice, to expel from court for some offense or misconduct. When an officer or attorney of a court was expelled for any offense, or for not appearing to an action by bill filed against him, he was said to be *forejudged the court.*

To deprive or put out of a thing by the judgment of a court. To condemn to lose a thing.

To expel or banish.

Forejudger. In English practice, a judgment by which a man is deprived or *put out* of a thing; a judgment of expulsion or banishment.

Foreman or **foreperson.** The presiding member of a grand or petit jury, who speaks or answers for the jury.

Person designated by employer-management to direct work of employees; superintendent, overseer.

Fore-matron /fórmèytrən/. In a jury of women this word corresponds to the foreman of a jury.

Forensic. Belonging to courts of justice.

Forensic medicine. That science which teaches the application of every branch of medical knowledge to the purposes of the law; hence its limits are, on the one hand, the requirements of the law, and, on the other, the whole range of medicine. Anatomy, physiology, medicine, surgery, chemistry, physics, and botany lend their aid as necessity arises; and in some cases all these branches of science are required to enable a court of law to arrive at a proper conclusion on a contested question affecting life or property.

Forensic pathology. That branch of medicine dealing with diseases and disorders of the body in relation to legal principles and cases.

Forensic psychiatry. That branch of medicine dealing with disorders of the mind in relation to legal principles and cases.

Forensis /farén(t)səs/. In Civil law, belonging to or connected with a court; forensic. *Forensis homo,* an advocate; a pleader of causes; one who practices in court.

Fore-oath /fóròwθ/. Before the Norman Conquest, an oath required of the complainant in the first instance (in the absence of manifest facts) as a security against frivolous suits.

Foreschoke. Foresaken; disavowed.

Foreseeability. The ability to see or know in advance; hence, the reasonable anticipation that harm or injury is a likely result of acts or omissions. Emery v. Thompson, 347 Mo. 494, 148 S.W.2d 479, 480. "Foreseeability" element of proximate cause is established by proof that actor, as person of ordinary intelligence and prudence, should reasonably have anticipated danger to others created by his negligent act, whether by event which occurred or some similar event, without regard to what actor believed would occur or anticipation as to just how injuries would grow out of dangerous situation created by him. Clark v. Waggoner, Tex., 452 S.W.2d 437, 439. As necessary element of proximate cause means that wrongdoer is not responsible for consequence which is merely possible, but is responsible only for consequence which is probable according to ordinary and usual experience. Wyatt v. Motsenbocker, Tex.Civ.App., 360 S.W.2d 543, 546.

Foreshore. The strip of land that lies between the high and low water marks and that is alternately wet and dry according to the flow of the tide. According to the medium line between the greatest and least range of tide (spring tides and neap tides). See also **Shore.**

Foresight. Heedful thought for the future; reasonable anticipation of result of certain acts or omissions. Emery v. Thompson, 347 Mo. 494, 148 S.W.2d 479.

Forest. A tract of land covered with trees and one usually of considerable extent.

In old English law, a certain territory of wooded ground and fruitful pastures, privileged for wild beasts and fowls of forest, chase, and warren, to rest and abide in the safe protection of the prince for his princely delight and pleasure, having a peculiar court and officers. A royal hunting-ground which lost its peculiar character with the extinction of its courts, or when the franchise passed into the hands of a subject. The word is also used to signify a franchise or right, being the right of keeping, for the purpose of hunting, the wild beasts and fowls of forest, chase, park, and warren, in a territory or precinct of woody ground or pasture set apart for the purpose.

Forestage /fóhrəstəj/. In old English law, a duty or tribute payable to the king's foresters.

Forestagium /fòhrəstéyjiyəm/. In old English law, a duty or tribute payable to the king's foresters.

Forestall. In old English law, to intercept or obstruct a passenger on the king's highway. To beset the way of a tenant so as to prevent his coming on the premises. 3 Bl.Comm. 170. To intercept a deer on his way to the forest before he can regain it.

Forestaller. In old English law, obstruction; hindrance; the offense of stopping the highway; the hindering a tenant from coming to his land; intercepting a deer before it can regain the forest. Also one who forestalls; one who commits the offense of forestalling. 3 Bl.Comm. 170.

Forestalling. Obstructing the highway. Intercepting a person on the highway.

Forestalling the market. Securing control of commodities on way to market.

The act of the buying or contracting for any merchandise or provision on its way to the market, with the intention of selling it again at a higher price; or dissuading of persons from bringing their goods or provisions there; or persuading them to enhance the price when there. This was formerly an indictable offense in England, but is now abolished by St. 7 & 8 Vict., c. 24.

Forestarius /fòhrəstériyəs/. In English law, a forester. An officer who takes care of the woods and forests. *De forestario apponendo,* a writ which lay to appoint a forester to prevent further commission of waste when a tenant in dower had committed waste.

Forest courts. In English law, courts instituted for the government of the king's forest in different parts of the kingdom, and for the punishment of all injuries done to the king's deer or *venison,* to the *vert* or greensward, and to the *covert* in which such deer were lodged. They consisted of the courts of attachments, of regard, of sweinmote, and of justice-seat. Such courts are now obsolete. 3 Bl.Comm. 71.

Forester. In old English law, a sworn officer of the *forest,* appointed by the king's letters patent to walk the forest, watching both the vert and the venison, attaching and presenting all trespassers against them within their own bailiwick or walk. These letters patent were generally granted during good behavior; but sometimes they held the office in fee.

Person trained in forestry; employee of U.S. Forest Service.

Forest law. The system or body of old law relating to the royal forests. The last of the forest laws were repealed by the Wild Creatures and Forest Laws Act of 1971.

Forfang /fórfæŋ/. In old English law, the taking of provisions from any person in fairs or markets before the royal purveyors were served with necessaries for the sovereign. Also the seizing and rescuing of stolen or strayed cattle from the hands of a thief, or of those having illegal possession of them; also the reward fixed for such rescue.

Forfeit /fórfət/. To lose, or lose the right to, by some error, fault, offense, or crime; or to subject, as property, to forfeiture or confiscation. To lose, in consequence of breach of contract, neglect of duty, or offense, some right, privilege, or property to another or to the State. United States v. Chavez, C.C.A.N.M., 87 F.2d 16, 19. To incur a penalty; to become liable to the payment of a sum of money, as the consequence of a certain act.

To lose an estate, a franchise, or other property belonging to one, by the act of the law, and as a consequence of some misfeasance, negligence, or omission. It is a deprivation (that is, against the will of the losing party), with the property either transferred to another or resumed by the original grantor.

See also **Forfeiture; Seizure.**

Forfeitable. Liable to be forfeited; subject to forfeiture for non-user, neglect, crime, etc.

Forfeiture /fórfəchər/. Something to which the right is lost by the commission of a crime or fault or the losing of something by way of penalty. Ridgeway v. City of Akron, Ohio App., 42 N.E.2d 724, 726. A deprivation or destruction of a right in consequence of the nonperformance of some obligation or condition. Loss of some right or property as a penalty for some illegal act. Loss of property or money because of breach of a legal obligation.

A punishment annexed by law to some illegal act or negligence in the owner of land, tenements, or hereditaments whereby he loses all interest therein. Hammond v. Johnson, 94 Utah 20, 66 P.2d 894, 900.

The loss of a corporate franchise or charter in consequence of some illegal act, or of malfeasance or nonfeasance.

In old English law, the loss of land by a tenant to his lord, as the consequence of some breach of fidelity. The loss of goods or chattels, as a punishment for some crime or misdemeanor in the party forfeiting, and as a compensation for the offense and injury committed against him to whom they are forfeited.

See also **Default; Foreclosure; Forfeit; Seizure.** For Criminal forfeiture, see **Criminal.**

Forfeiture of bond. A failure to perform the condition upon which obligor was to be excused from the penalty in the bond. Hall v. Browning, 71 Ga.App. 835, 32 S.E.2d 424, 427. With respect to a bail bond, occurs when the accused fails to appear for trial.

Forfeiture of marriage. A penalty incurred by a ward in chivalry who married without the consent or against the will of the guardian.

Forfeitures Abolition Act. Another name for the felony act of 1870, abolishing forfeitures for felony in England.

Forgabulum, or **forgavel** /fòrgǽbyələm/. A quit-rent; a small reserved rent in money.

Forge. To fabricate by false imitation. Carter v. State, 135 Tex.Cr.R. 457, 116 S.W.2d 371, 377. To fabricate, construct, or prepare one thing in imitation of another thing, with the intention of substituting the false for the genuine, or otherwise deceiving and defrauding by the use of the spurious article. To counterfeit or make falsely. Especially, to make a spurious written instrument with the intention of fraudulently substituting it for another, or of passing it off as genuine; or to fraudulently alter a genuine instrument to another's prejudice; or to sign another person's name to a document, with a deceitful and fraudulent intent. See **Counterfeiting; Forgery; Fraud.**

Forgery. A person is guilty of forgery if, with purpose to defraud or injure anyone, or with knowledge that he is facilitating a fraud or injury to be perpetrated by anyone, the actor: (a) alters any writing of another without his authority; or (b) makes, completes, executes, authenticates, issues or transfers any writing so that it purports to be the act of another who did not authorize that act, or to have been executed at a time or place or in a numbered sequence other than was in fact the case, or to be a copy of an original when no such original existed; or (c) utters any writing which he knows to be forged in a manner specified in paragraph (a) or (b). Model Penal Code, § 224.1.

Crime includes both act of forging handwriting of another and act of uttering as true and genuine any forged writing knowing same to be forged with intent to prejudice, damage or defraud any person. State v. May, 93 Idaho 343, 461 P.2d 126, 129. Crime is committed when one makes or passes a false instrument with intent to defraud, and the element of loss or detriment is immaterial. People v. McAffery, 182 Cal.App.2d 486, 6 Cal.Rptr. 333, 337. The false making of an instrument, which purports on face of it to be good and valid for purposes for which it was created, with a design to defraud any person or persons. State v. Goranson, 67 Wash.2d 456, 408 P.2d 7, 9. The fraudulent making of a false writing having apparent legal significance. Nelson v. State, 224 Md. 374, 167 A.2d 871, 873.

See also Alteration; Counterfeit; False making; Falsify; Fraud; Imitation; Raised check.

Evidence. The fabrication or counterfeiting of evidence. The artful and fraudulent manipulation of physical objects, or the deceitful arrangement of genuine facts or things, in such a manner as to create an erroneous impression or a false inference in the minds of those who may observe them.

Forherda /fórhə̀rdə/. In old English records, a herdland, headland, or foreland.

For hire or **reward.** To transport passengers or property for a fare, charge, or rate to be paid by such passengers, or persons for whom such property is transported, to owner or operator. Michigan Consol. Gas Co. v. Sohio Petroleum Co., 321 Mich. 102, 32 N.W.2d 353, 356. See also **Carrier.**

Fori disputationes /fóray dìspyətèyshiyówniyz/. In the civil law, discussions or arguments before a court.

Forinsecus /fərínsəkəs/. Lat. Foreign; exterior; outside; extraordinary.

Servitium forinsecum, the payment of aid, scutage, and other extraordinary military services. *Forinsecum manerium,* the manor, or that part of it which lies outside the bars or town, and is not included within the liberties of it.

Forinsic /fərínsək/. In old English law, exterior; foreign; extraordinary. In feudal law, the term "forinsic services" comprehended the payment of extraordinary aids or the rendition of extraordinary military services, and in this sense was opposed to "intrinsic services."

Foris /fórəs/. Lat. Abroad; out of doors; on the outside of a place; without; extrinsic.

Forisbanitus /fórəsbǽnədəs/. In old English law, banished.

Forisfacere /fòrəsféysəriy/. Lat. To forfeit; to lose an estate or other property on account of some criminal or illegal act. To confiscate.

To act beyond the law, *i.e.,* to transgress or infringe the law; to commit an offense or wrong; to do any act against or beyond the law.

Forisfacere, *i.e.,* extra legem seu consuetudinem facere /fòrəsféysəriy, íd èst, ékstrə líyjəm syùw kònswətyúwdənəm féysəriy/. *Forisfacere, i.e.,* to do something beyond law or custom.

Forisfactum /fòrəsfǽktəm/. Forfeited. *Bona forisfacta,* forfeited goods. A crime.

Forisfactura /fòrəsfǽkchúrə/. A crime or offense through which property is forfeited. A fine or punishment in money.

Forfeiture; the loss of property or life in consequence of crime.

Forisfactura plena /fòrəsfǽkchúrə plíynə/. A forfeiture of all a man's property. Things which were forfeited.

Forisfactus /fòrəsfǽktəs/. A criminal. One who has forfeited his life by commission of a capital offense.

Forisfactus servus /fòrəsfǽktəs sárvəs/. A slave who has been a free man, but has forfeited his freedom by crime.

Forisfamiliare /fòrəsfəmìliyériy/. In old English and Scotch law, literally, to put out of a family *(foris familiam ponere)*. To portion off a son, so that he could have no further claim upon his father. To emancipate, or free from paternal authority.

Forisfamiliated /fòrəsfəmíliyeydəd/. In old English law, portioned off. A son was said to be forisfamiliated *(forisfamiliari)* if his father assigned him part of his land, and gave him seisin thereof, and did this at the request or with the free consent of the son himself, who expressed himself satisfied with such portion.

Forisfamiliatus /fòrəsfəmìliyéydəs/. In old English law, put out of a family; portioned off; emancipated; forisfamiliated.

Forisjudicatio /fòrəsjùwdəkéysh(iy)ow/. In old English law, forejudger. A forejudgment. A judgment of court whereby a man is put out of possession of a thing.

Forisjudicatus /fòrəsjùwdəkéydəs/. Forejudged; sent from court; banished. Deprived of a thing by judgment of court.

Forisjurare /fòrəsjərériy/. To forswear; to abjure; to abandon.

Provinciam forisjurare /prəvínsh(iy)əm fòrəsjərériy/. To forswear the country.

Forisjurare parentilam /fòrəsjərériy pəréntələm/. To remove oneself from parental authority. The person who did this lost his rights as heir.

Forjudge /fòrjáj/. See **Forejudge.**

Forjurer. L. Fr. In old English law, to forswear; to abjure.

Forjurer royalme. To abjure the realm.

Form. A model or skeleton of an instrument to be used in a judicial proceeding or legal transaction, containing the principal necessary matters, the proper technical terms or phrases and whatever else is necessary to make it formally correct, arranged in proper and methodical order, and capable of being adapted to the circumstances of the specific case.

In contradistinction to "substance," "form" means the legal or technical manner or order to be observed in legal instruments or juridical proceedings, or in the construction of legal documents or processes. Antithesis of "substance."

Common form, solemn form. See **Probate.**

Form of the statute. This expression means the words, language, or frame of a statute, and hence the inhibition or command which it may contain; used in the phrase (in criminal pleading) "against the form of the statute in that case made and provided."

Forms of action. This term is the general designation of the various species or kinds of personal actions known to the common law, such as trover, trespass, debt, *assumpsit*, etc., and also to the general classification of actions as those in "equity" or "law". These differ in their pleadings and evidence, as well as in the circumstances to which they are respectively applicable. Under Rules of Civil Procedure (applicable in federal and most state courts) there is now only one form of action known as a "civil action," Fed.R.Civ.Proc., Rule 2. See also **Forms of action.**

Matter of form. In pleadings, indictments, affidavits, conveyances, etc., matter of form (as distinguished from matter of substance) is all that relates to the mode, form, or style of expressing the facts involved, the choice or arrangement of words, and other such particulars, without affecting the substantial validity or sufficiency of the instrument, or without going to the merits.

Forma. Lat. Form; the prescribed form of judicial proceedings.

Forma dat esse /fórmə dǽt ésiy/. Form gives being. Called "the old physical maxim."

Forma et figura judicii /fórmə èt figyúrə juwdíshiyay/. The form and shape of judgment or judicial action. 3 Bl.Comm. 271.

Formal. Relating to matters of form; as, "formal defects"; inserted, added, or joined *pro forma.* See **Form; Parties.**

Formal contract. A *written* contract or agreement as contrasted with an *oral* or informal contract or agreement. Historically, a formal contract was under seal; though this is generally no longer required. See also **Contract.**

Forma legalis forma essentialis /fórmə ləgéyləs fórmə əsènshiyéyləs/. Legal form is essential form.

Formalities. In England, robes worn by the magistrates of a city or corporation, etc., on solemn occasions.

Formality. The conditions, in regard to method, order, arrangement, use of technical expressions, performance of specific acts, etc., which are required by the law in the making of contracts or conveyances, or in the taking of legal proceedings, to insure their validity and regularity. Term generally refers to "procedure" in contrast to "substance".

Formal parties. See **Parties.**

Forma non observata, infertur adnullatio actus /fórmə nòn òbzərvéydə, infárdər ǽdnəléysh(iy)ow ǽktəs/. Where form is not observed, a nullity of the act is inferred. Where the law prescribes a form, the nonobservance of it is fatal to the proceeding, and the whole becomes a nullity.

Forma pauperis /fórmə pópərəs/. See **Appeal in forma pauperis; In forma pauperis.**

Formata /forméydə/. In canon law, canonical letters.

Formata brevia /forméydə bríyviyə/. Formed writs; writs of form. See **Brevia formata.**

Formed action. An action for which a set form of words is prescribed, which must be strictly adhered to. Such are now generally obsolete.

Formed design. In criminal law, and particularly with reference to homicide, this term means a deliberate and fixed intention to kill, whether directed against a particular person or not. See also **Premeditation.**

Formedon /fórmədòn/. An ancient writ in English law which was available for one who had a right to lands or tenements by virtue of a gift in tail. It was in the nature of a writ of right, and was the highest action that a tenant in tail could have; for he could not have an absolute writ of right, that being confined to such as claimed in fee-simple, and for that reason this writ of formedon was granted to him by statute and was emphatically called "his" writ of right. The writ was distinguished into three species, viz.: Formedon in the descender, in the remainder, and in the reverter. It was abolished in England by St. 3 & 4 Wm. IV, c. 27. 3 Bl.Comm. 191.

Formedon in the descender /fórmədòn in ðə dəséndər/. A writ of formedon which lay where a gift was made in tail, and the tenant in tail aliened the lands or was disseised of them and died, for the heir in tail to recover them, against the actual tenant of the freehold. 3 Bl.Comm. 192.

Formedon in the remainder /fórmədòn in ðə rəméyndər/. A writ of formedon which lay where a man gave lands to another for life or in tail, with remainder to a third person in tail or in fee, and he who had the particular estate died without issue inheritable, and a stranger intruded upon him in remainder, and kept him out of possession. In this case he in *remainder,* or his heir, was entitled to this writ. 3 Bl.Comm. 192.

Formedon in the reverter /fórmədòn in ðə rəvárdər/. A writ of formedon which lay where there was a gift in tail, and afterwards, by the death of the donee or his heirs without issue of his body, the reversion fell in upon the donor, his heirs or assigns. In such case, the *reversioner* had this writ to recover the lands. 3 Bl.Comm. 192.

Former acquittal /fórmər əkwiydəl/. See **Autrefois.**

Former adjudication. An adjudication in a former action. Either a final determination of the rights of the parties or an adjudication of certain questions of fact. Johnson v. Fontana County Fire Protection Dist., 15 Cal.2d 380, 101 P.2d 1092, 1097; Johnson v. Fontana County Fire Protection Dist., Cal.App., 87 P.2d 426, 430. See **Res** *(Res judicata).*

Former jeopardy. Also called "double jeopardy." Plea of "former jeopardy," that a man cannot be tried for the offense more than once, is fundamental common law and constitutional right of defendant, affording protection against his being again tried for the same offense, and not against the peril of second punishment. Fifth Amendment of U.S.Const. However, prosecution by both the state and federal govern-ments is not barred by the constitutional protection against double jeopardy. Bartkus v. Illinois, 359 U.S. 121, 79 S.Ct. 676, 3 L.Ed.2d 684.

Former proceedings. Term used in reference to action taken earlier and its result in determining whether present proceeding is barred by res judicata.

Former recovery. Recovery in a former action. See **Res** *(Res judicata).*

Former statements. As used in evidence, declarations made by a party or witness at an earlier time. Fed. Evid.R. 613.

Former testimony. In evidence, testimony given by party or witness at an earlier trial or hearing and which, under certain conditions, may be used in present proceeding. Fed.Evid.R. 613.

Forms of action. Forms of action governed common law pleading and were the procedural devices used to give expression to the theories of liability recognized by the common law. Failure to analyze the cause of action properly, to select the proper theory of liability and to choose the appropriate procedural mechanism or forms of action could easily result in being thrown out of court. A plaintiff had to elect his remedy in advance and could not subsequently amend his pleadings to conform to his proof or to the court's choice of another theory of liability. According to the relief sought, actions have been divided into three categories: real actions were brought for the recovery of real property; mixed actions were brought to recover real property and damages for injury to it; personal actions were brought to recover debts or personal property, or for injuries to personal, property, or contractual rights. The common law actions are usually considered to be eleven in number: trespass, trespass on the case, trover, ejectment, detinue, replevin, debt, covenant, account, special assumpsit, and general assumpsit.

Under the Rules of Civil Procedure (applicable in the federal and most state courts) there is now only one form of action known as a "civil action". Fed.R. Civil P., Rule 2.

Formula. In common-law practice, a set form of words used in judicial proceedings. In the civil law, an action.

Formula deal. An agreement between motion picture distributors and independent or affiliated circuits to exhibit a feature in all theatres at specified percentage of national gross receipts realized from such feature by all theatres in the United States. U. S. v. Paramount Pictures, D.C.N.Y., 66 F.Supp. 323, 333, 347.

Formulæ /fórmyəliy/. In Roman law, when the *legis actiones* were proved to be inconvenient, a mode of procedure called *"per formulas"* (i.e., by means of *formulæ),* was gradually introduced, and eventually the *legis actiones* were abolished by the Lex Æbutia, B.C. 164, excepting in a very few exceptional matters. The *formulæ* were four in number, namely: (1) The *Demonstratio,* wherein the plaintiff stated, *i.e.,* showed, the facts out of which his claim arose; (2) the *Intentio,* where he made his claim against the defendant; (3) the *Adjudicatio,* wherein the judex was directed to assign or adjudicate the property or any portion or portions thereof according to the rights of the parties; and (4) the *Condemnatio*, in which the judex was authorized and directed to condemn or to acquit according as the facts were or were not proved. These *formulæ* were obtained from the magistrate *(in jure)*, and were thereafter proceeded with before the judex *(in judicio)*.

Formula instruction. A jury instruction intended to be complete statement of law upon which jury may base verdict. Harvey v. Aceves, 115 Cal.App. 333, 1 P.2d 1043, 1045. An instruction which advises the jury that under certain facts therein hypothesized their verdict should be for one of the parties. McFatridge v. Harlem Globe Trotters, 69 N.M. 271, 365 P.2d 918, 922. See **Jury instructions.**

Formularies /fórmyələ̀riyz/. Collections of *formulæ*, or forms of forensic proceedings and instruments used among the Franks, and other early continental nations of Europe.

Fornagium /fòrnéyjiyəm/. The fee taken by a lord of his tenant, who was bound to bake in the lord's common oven *(in furno domini)*, or for a commission to use his own.

Fornication. Unlawful sexual intercourse between two unmarried persons. Further, if one of the persons be married and the other not, it is fornication on the part of the latter, though adultery for the former. In some jurisdictions, however, by statute, it is adultery on the part of both persons if the woman is married, whether the man is married or not. This offense is very seldom enforced. See also **Illicit cohabitation.**

Fornix /fórnəks/. Lat. A brothel; fornication.

Foro /fórow/. In Spanish law, the place where tribunals hear and determine causes,—*exercendarum litium locus.*

Foros /fórows/. In Spanish law, emphyteutic rents.

Forprise /fórpràyz/. An exception; reservation; excepted; reserved. Anciently, a term of frequent use in leases and conveyances. In another sense, the word is taken for any exaction.

For purpose of. With the intention of.

Forschel. A strip of land lying next to the highway.

Forspeaker /fòrspíykər/. An attorney or advocate in a cause.

Forspeca /fòrspíykə/. In old English law, prolocutor; paranymphus.

Forstal /fòrstól/. See **Forestall.**

Forstellarius est pauperum depressor et totius communitatis et patriæ publicus inimicus /forstəlériyəs èst pópərəm dəprésər èt tòwsh(íy)əs kəmyùwnətéydəs èt pǽtriyiy pə́bləkəs ìnəmáykəs/. A forestaller is an oppressor of the poor, and a public enemy of the whole community and country.

Forswear /fòrswér/. In criminal law, to make oath to that which the deponent knows to be untrue. This term is wider in its scope than "perjury," for the latter, as a technical term, includes the idea of the oath being taken before a competent court or officer, and relating to a material issue, which is not implied by the word "forswear."

Fort. This term means something more than a mere military camp, post, or station. The term implies a fortification, or a place protected from attack by some such means as a moat, wall, or parapet.

Fortalice, or **fortelace** /fórdələs/. A fortress or place of strength, which anciently did not pass without a special grant.

Fortaxed /fòrtǽkst/. Wrongly or extortionately taxed.

For that. In pleading, words used to introduce the allegations of a declaration. "For that" is a positive allegation; "For that whereas" is a recital. Such words are not required in federal court pleadings nor in the majority of states that have adopted Rules of Civil Procedure.

For that whereas. In pleading, formal words introducing the statement of the plaintiff's case, by way of recital, in his declaration, in all actions except trespass. In trespass, where there was no recital, the expression used was, "For that." Such words are not required in federal court pleadings nor in the majority of states that have adopted Rules of Civil Procedure.

Forthcoming bond. A bond conditioned on the forthcoming of property to answer such judgment as may be entered. If the property be forthcoming, no liability ensues. U. S. Fidelity & Guaranty Co. v. Sabath, 286 Ill.App. 320, 3 N.E.2d 330, 335. A bond given to a sheriff who has levied on property, conditioned that the property shall be forthcoming, *i.e.,* produced, when required. On the giving of such bond, the goods are allowed to remain in the possession of the debtor.

Forthwith. Immediately; without delay; directly; within a reasonable time under the circumstances of the case; promptly and with reasonable dispatch. U. S. ex rel. Carter v. Jennings, D.C.Pa., 333 F.Supp. 1392, 1397. Within such time as to permit that which is to be done, to be done lawfully and according to the practical and ordinary course of things to be performed or accomplished. The first opportunity offered.

Fortia /fórsh(iy)ə/. Force. In old English law, force used by an accessory, to enable the principal to commit a crime, as by binding or holding a person while another killed him, or by aiding or counseling in any way, or commanding the act to be done.

Fortia frisca /fórsh(iy)ə f006rískə/. Fresh force *(q.v.).*

Fortility /fòrtílədiy/. In old English law, a fortified place; a castle; a bulwark.

Fortior /fórshiyər/. Lat. Stronger. A term applied, in the law of evidence, to that species of presumption, arising from facts shown in evidence, which is strong enough to shift the burden of proof to the opposite party.

Fortior est custodia legis quam hominis /fórshiyər èst kəstówdiyə líyjəs kwæm hómənəs/. The custody of the law is stronger than that of man.

Fortior et potentior est dispositio legis quam hominis /fórshiyər èt pəténshiyər èst dìspəzísh(iy)ow líyjəs kwæm hómənəs/. The disposition of the law is of greater force and effect than that of man. The law in some cases overrides the will of the individual, and renders ineffective or futile his expressed intention or contract.

Fortiori /fòrshiyóray/. See **A fortiori.**

Fortis /fórdəs/. Lat. Strong. *Fortis et sana,* strong and sound; staunch and strong; as a vessel.

Fortlett /fórtlət/. A place or port of some strength; a little fort.

Fortuit /fòrtwíy/. In French law, accidental; fortuitous. *Cas fortuit,* a fortuitous event. *Fortuitement,* accidentally; by chance; casually.

Fortuitous /forchúwədəs/. Happening by chance or accident. Occurring unexpectedly, or without known cause. Accidental; undesigned; adventitious. Resulting from unavoidable physical causes.

Fortuitous collision /forchúwədəs kəlízhən/. In maritime law, the accidental running foul of vessels.

Fortuitous event /forchúwədəs əvént/. An event happening by chance or accident. That which happens by a cause which cannot be resisted. An unforeseen occurrence, not caused by either of the parties, nor such as they could prevent.

Fortuna /fòrchúwnə/. Lat. Fortune; also treasure-trove.

Fortunam faciunt judicem /fòrchúwnəm féys(h)iyənt júwdəsəm/. They make fortune the judge. Spoken of the process of making partition among co-parceners by drawing lots for the several purparts.

Fortune teller. One who professes to tell future events in the life of another.

In English law, persons pretending or professing to tell fortunes, and punishable as rogues and vagabonds or disorderly persons. 4 Bl.Comm. 62.

Fortunium /fòrchúwniyəm/. In old English law, a tournament or fighting with spears, and an appeal to fortune therein.

Forty. In land laws and conveyancing, in those regions where grants, transfers, and deeds are made with reference to the subdivisions of the government survey, this term means forty acres of land in the form of a square, being the tract obtained by quartering a section of land (640 acres) and again quartering one of the quarters.

Forty-days court. In old English forest law, the court of attachment in forests, or woodmote court.

Forum /fórəm/. Lat. A court of justice, or judicial tribunal; a place of jurisdiction; a place of litigation. Place where remedy is pursued. See also **Venue.**

In Roman law, the market place, or public paved court, in the city of Rome, where such public business was transacted as the assemblies of the people and the judicial trial of causes and where also elections, markets, and the public exchange were held.

Forum actus /fórəm æktəs/. The forum of the act. The forum of the place where the act was done which is now called in question.

Forum conscientiæ /fórəm kòns(h)iyénshiyiy/. The forum or tribunal of conscience.

Forum contentiosum /fórəm kəntènshiyówzəm/. A contentious forum or court; a place of litigation; the ordinary court of justice, as distinguished from the tribunal of conscience. 3 Bl.Comm. 211.

Forum contractus /fórəm kəntræktəs/. The forum of the contract; the court of the place where a contract is made; the place where a contract is made, considered as a place of jurisdiction.

Forum conveniens /fórəm kənvíyn(i)yèn(d)z/. The state or judicial district in which an action may be most appropriately brought, considering the best interest of the parties and the public. See, in contradistinction, **Forum non conveniens.**

Forum domesticum /fórəm dəméstəkəm/. A domestic forum or tribunal. The visitatorial power is called a *"forum domesticum,"* calculated to determine, *sine strepitu,* all disputes that arise within themselves.

Forum domicilii /fórəm dò(w)məsíliyay/. The forum or court of the domicile; the domicile of a defendant, considered as a place of jurisdiction.

Forum ecclesiasticum /fórəm əklìyziyæstəkəm/. An ecclesiastical court. The spiritual jurisdiction, as distinguished from the secular.

Forum ligeantiæ rei /fórəm lìjiyænshiyiy ríyay/. The forum of defendant's allegiance. The court or jurisdiction of the country to which he owes allegiance.

Forum non conveniens /fórəm nòn kənvíyn(i)yèn(d)z/. Term refers to discretionary power of court to decline jurisdiction when convenience of parties and ends of justice would be better served if action were brought and tried in another forum. Johnson v. Spider Staging Corp., 87 Wash.2d 577, 555 P.2d 997, 999, 1000. See 28 U.S.C.A. § 1404.

The doctrine is patterned upon the right of the court in the exercise of its powers to refuse the imposition upon its jurisdiction of the trial of cases even though the venue is properly laid if it appears that for the convenience of litigants and witnesses and in the interest of justice the action should be instituted in another forum where the action might have been brought. Hayes v. Chicago, R. I. & P. R. Co., D.C.Minn., 79 F.Supp. 821, 824. The doctrine presupposes at least two forums in which the defendant is amenable to process and furnishes criteria for choice between such forums. Wilson v. Seas Shipping Co., D.C.Pa., 78 F.Supp. 464, 465; Neal v. Pennsylvania R. Co., D.C.N.Y., 77 F.Supp. 423, 424. The application of the doctrine rests in the sound discretion of the court and the factors to be considered in the doctrine are the private interests of the litigant and the interest of the public. Cullinan v. New York Cent. R. Co., D.C.N.Y., 83 F.Supp. 870, 871. And a court, either state or federal, will generally decline to interfere with or control by injunction or otherwise the management of internal affairs of a corporation organized under the laws of another state, leaving controversies as to such matters to courts of state of domicile. Garrett v. Phillips Petroleum Co., Tex.Civ. App., 218 S.W.2d 238, 240; Murray v. Union Pac. R. Co., D.C.Ill., 77 F.Supp. 219; Kelley v. American Sugar Refining Co., C.C.A.Mass., 139 F.2d 76; Tiuoli Realty v. Interstate Circuit, C.C.A.Tex., 167 F.2d 155; Rogers v. Guaranty Trust Co., 288 U.S. 123, 53 S.Ct. 295, 77 L.Ed. 652.

The rule is an equitable one embracing the discretionary power of a court to decline to exercise jurisdiction which it has over a transitory cause of action when it believes that the action may be more appropriately and justly tried elsewhere. Leet v. Union Pac. R. Co., 25 Cal.2d 605, 155 P.2d 42, 44. In determining whether doctrine should be applied, court should consider relative ease of access to sources of proof, availability of compulsory process for attendance of unwilling witnesses, cost of obtaining attendance of willing witnesses, possibility of view of premises, and all other practical problems that make trial easy, expeditious and inexpensive. Di Lella v. Lehigh Val. R. Co., D.C.N.Y., 7 F.R.D. 192, 193.

Forum originis /fórəm əríjənəs/. The court of one's nativity. The place of a person's birth, considered as a place of jurisdiction.

Forum regium /fórəm ríyj(iy)əm/. The king's court.

Forum rei /fórəm ríyay/. This term may mean either (1) the forum of the defendant, that is, of his residence or domicile; or (2) the forum of the *res* or thing in controversy, that is, of the place where the property is situated. The ambiguity springs from the fact that *rei* may be the genitive of either *reus* or *res*.

Forum rei gestæ /fórəm ríyay jéstiy/. The forum or court of a *res gesta* (thing done); the place where an act is done, considered as a place of jurisdiction and remedy.

Forum rei sitæ /fórəm ríyay sáydiy/. The court where the thing in controversy is situated. The place where the subject-matter in controversy is situated, considered as a place of jurisdiction.

Forum seculare /fórəm sèkyəlériy/. A secular, as distinguished from an ecclesiastical or spiritual, court.

Forum shopping. Such occurs when a party attempts to have his action tried in a particular court or jurisdiction where he feels he will receive the most favorable judgment or verdict.

For use. For the benefit or advantage of another. Thus, where an assignee is obliged to sue in the name of his assignor, the suit is entitled "A. *for use* of B. v. C." For enjoyment or employment without destruction. A loan "for use" is one in which the bailee has the right to use and enjoy the article, but without consuming or destroying it, in which respect it differs from a loan "for consumption."

For value. See **Holder.**

For value received. See **Value** (*Value received*).

Forward. To send forward; to send toward the place of destination; to transmit. To ship goods by common carrier. See **Forwarder.**

Forwarder. Person or business whose business it is to receive goods for further handling by way of warehousing, packing, carload shipping, delivery, etc. See **Forwarding agent; Freight forwarder.**

Forwarding agent. Freight forwarder who assembles less than carload shipments (small shipments) into carload shipments, thus taking advantage of lower freight rates. Company or individual whose business it is to receive and ship merchandise for others. See **Forwarder.**

For whom it may concern. Phrase creates presumption of intention on part of named insured to cover any persons who may have an insurable interest in the property.

Fossa /fósə/. In the civil law, a ditch; a receptacle of water, made by hand.

In old English law, a ditch. A pit full of water, in which women committing felony were drowned. A grave or sepulcher.

Fossagium /fòséyj(iy)əm/. In old English law, the duty levied on the inhabitants for repairing the moat or ditch round a fortified town.

Fossatorum operatio /fòsətórəm òpəréysh(iy)ow/. In old English law, fosse-work; or the service of laboring, done by inhabitants and adjoining tenants, for the repair and maintenance of the ditches round a city or town, for which some paid a contribution, called *"fossagium."*

Fossatum /fəséydəm/. A dyke, ditch, or trench; a place inclosed by a ditch; a moat; a canal.

Fosterage /fóstəraj/. Care of a foster child, brother, sister, parent, etc.—one considered as holding the relationship indicated in consequence of nursing and rearing, though not related by blood. In re Norman's Estate, 209 Minn. 19, 295 N.W. 63, 66.

Foster child. Child whose care, comfort, education and upbringing has been left to persons other than his natural parents. See **Foster parent.**

Foster home. A home for children without parents or who have been taken from their parents.

Fostering. An ancient custom in Ireland, in which persons put away their children to fosterers. Fostering was held to be a stronger alliance than blood, and the foster children participated in the fortunes of their foster fathers.

Fosterland. Land given, assigned, or allotted to the finding of food or victuals for any person or persons; as in monasteries for the monks, etc.

Fosterlean /fóstərliyn/. The remuneration fixed for the rearing of a foster child; also the jointure of a wife.

Foster parent. One who has performed the duties of a parent to the child of another by rearing the child as his own child. See **Foster child.**

Foul bill of lading. Type of bill of lading which shows on its face that the goods were damaged or that there was a shortage at the time of shipment.

Found. A person is said to be "found" within a state for purposes of service of process when actually present therein. But only if a person is in a place voluntarily and not by reason of plaintiff's fraud, artifice, or trick for purpose of obtaining service. Shields v. Shields, 115 Mont. 146, 139 P.2d 528, 530, 531. It does not necessarily mean physical presence; *e.g.* defendant who, after removal of action for breach of contract to federal court, entered general appearance, defended on the merits, and filed counterclaim, was "found" in the district. Freeman v. Bee Mach. Co., Mass., 319 U.S. 448, 63 S.Ct. 1146, 1149, 87 L.Ed. 1509. As applied to a corporation it is necessary that it be doing business in such state through an officer or agent or by statutory authority in such manner as to render it liable then to suit and to constructive or substituted service of process. A corporation is "found" in a district for venue purposes if it is subject to personal jurisdiction in that district. Stith v. Manor Baking Co., D.C.Mo., 418 F.Supp. 150, 155.

Foundation. Permanent fund established and maintained by contributions for charitable, educated, religious or other benevolent purpose. An institution or association given to rendering financial aid to colleges, schools and charities and generally supported by gifts for such purposes.

The founding or building of a college or hospital. The incorporation or endowment of a college or hospital is the foundation; and he who endows it with land or other property is the founder. Dartmouth College v. Woodward, 17 U.S. (4 Wheat.) 518, 4 L.Ed. 629; Seagrave's Appeal, 125 Pa. 362, 17 A. 412; Union Baptist Ass'n v. Huhn, 7 Tex.Civ.App. 249, 26 S.W. 755.

Preliminary questions to witness to establish admissibility of evidence, *i.e.* "laying foundation" for admissibility. Fed.Evid.R. 104.

See also **Charitable foundation; Endowment.**

Founded. Based upon; arising from, growing out of, or resting upon; as in the expressions "founded in fraud," "founded on a consideration," "founded on contract," and the like.

Founded on. To serve as a base or basis for.

Founder. The person who endows an eleemosynary corporation or institution, or supplies the funds for its establishment. See **Foundation.**

Founders' shares. In English Company Law, shares issued to the founders of (or vendors to) a public company as a part of the consideration for the business, or concession, etc., taken over, and not forming a part of, the ordinary capital. As a rule, such shares only participate in profits after the payment of a fixed minimum dividend on paid-up capital.

Foundling. A deserted or abandoned infant; a child found without a parent or guardian, its relatives being unknown.

Foundling hospitals. Charitable institutions which exist in many European countries for taking care of infants forsaken by their parents, such being generally the offspring of illegal connections.

Four /fúr/. Fr. In old French law, an oven or bakehouse. *Four banal,* an oven, owned by the seignior of the estate, to which the tenants were obliged to bring their bread for baking. Also the proprietary right to maintain such an oven.

Fourcher /fùrshéy/. Fr. To fork. This was a method of delaying an action anciently resorted to by defendants when two of them were joined in the suit. Instead of appearing together, each would appear in turn and cast an essoin for the other, thus postponing the trial.

Four corners. The face of a written instrument.

Four corners rule. Under "four corners rule", intention of parties, especially that of grantor, is to be gathered from instrument as a whole and not from isolated parts thereof. Davis v. Andrews, Tex.Civ.App., 361 S.W.2d 419, 423.

Fourierism /fúriyərizəm/fór°/. A form of socialism.

Four seas. The seas surrounding England. These were divided into the Western, including the Scotch and Irish; the Northern, or North sea; the Eastern, being the German ocean; the Southern, being the British channel.

Fourteenth Amendment. The Fourteenth Amendment of the Constitution of the United States, ratified in 1868, creates or at least recognizes for the first time a citizenship of the United States, as distinct from that of the states; forbids the making or enforcement by any state of any law abridging the privileges and immunities of citizens of the United States; and secures all "persons" against any state action which results in either deprivation of life, liberty, or property without due process of law, or, in denial of the equal protection of the laws. This Amendment also contains provisions concerning the apportionment of representatives in Congress.

Fourth Amendment. Amendment of the U.S. Constitution guaranteeing people the right to be secure in their homes and property against unreasonable searches and seizures and providing that no warrants shall issue except upon probable cause and then only as to specific places to be searched and persons and things to be seized. See **Probable cause; Search.**

Fourth estate. The journalistic profession (*i.e.* the press). Term has its source from a reference to the reporters' gallery of the British Parliament whose influence on public policy was said to equal that of Parliament's three traditional estates, the clergy, nobility, and commons.

Fox's Libel Act. In English law, this was the statute 52 Geo. III, c. 60, which secured to juries, upon the trial of indictments for libel, the right of pronouncing a general verdict of guilty or not guilty upon the whole matter in issue, and no longer bound them to find a verdict of guilty on proof of the publication of the paper charged to be a libel, and of the sense ascribed to it in the indictment.

Foy /fóy/f(w)éy/fwá/. L. Fr. Faith; allegiance; fidelity.

F.P.A. In maritime insurance: "Free from particular average". See **Average.**

F.P.C. Federal Power Commission.

F.P.R. Federal Procurement Regulations.

Fr. A Latin abbreviation for "fragmentum," a fragment, used in citations to the Digest or Pandects in the *Corpus Juris Civilis* of Justinian, the several extracts from juristic writings of which it is composed being so called.

Fractio /fræksh(iy)ow/. Lat. A breaking; division; fraction; a portion of a thing less than the whole.

Fraction. A breaking, or breaking up; a fragment or broken part; a portion of a thing, less than the whole.

Fractional. As applied to tracts of land, particularly townships, sections, quarter sections, and other divisions according to the government survey, and also mining claims, this term means that the exterior boundary lines are laid down to include the whole of such a division or such a claim, but that the tract in question does not measure up to the full extent or include the whole acreage, because a portion of it is cut off by an overlapping survey, a river or lake, or some other external interference. Any irregular division whether containing more or less than conventional amount of acreage.

Fractional share. That part or portion of a share of stock indicated on a right or warrant as subject to purchase by the exercise of such right.

Fractional share formula. See **Marital deduction.**

Fractionem diei non recipit lex /frækshiyównəm dayíyay nòn résəpət léks/. The law does not take notice of a portion of a day.

Fraction of a day. A portion of a day. The dividing a day. Generally, the law does not allow the fraction of a day.

Fractitium /fræktísh(iy)əm/. Arable land. Mon. Angl.

Fractura navium /frækchúrə néyv(i)yəm/. Lat. The breaking or wreck of ships; the same as *naufragium* (*q.v.*).

Fragmenta /frægméntə/. Lat. Fragments. A name sometimes applied (especially in citations) to the Digest or Pandects in the *Corpus Juris Civilis* of Justinian, as being made up of numerous extracts or "fragments" from the writings of various jurists.

Frais /fréy/. Fr. Expense; charges; costs. *Frais d'un procès,* costs of a suit.

Frais de justice /fréy də zhustíys/. In French and Canadian law, costs incurred incidentally to the action.

Frais jusqu'à bord /fréy jəskà bór(d)/. Fr. In French commercial law, expenses to the board; expenses incurred on a shipment of goods, in packing, cartage, commissions, etc., up to the point where they are actually put on board the vessel.

Framed. When used to describe evidence, word is generally accepted as implying that willful perjurers, suborned by and conspiring with parties in interest to litigation, are swearing or have sworn to matters without any basis in fact. Tri-State Transit Co. of Louisiana v. Westbrook, 207 Ark. 270, 180 S.W.2d 121, 125. Incrimination of person on false evidence. See also **Entrapment.**

Frame-up. Conspiracy or plot, especially for evil purpose, as to incriminate person on false evidence. See **Entrapment.**

Franc aleu /frónk alyúw/. In French feudal law, an allod; a free inheritance; or an estate held free of any services except such as were due to the sovereign.

Franchilanus /frænkəléynəs/. A freeman. A free tenant.

Franchise. A special privilege conferred by government on individual or corporation, and which does not belong to citizens of country generally of common right. Artesian Water Co. v. State Dept. of Highways and Transp., Del.Super., 330 A.2d 432, 439. In England it is defined to be a royal privilege in the hands of a subject.

A privilege granted or sold, such as to use a name or to sell products or services. The right given by a manufacturer or supplier to a retailer to use his products and name on terms and conditions mutually agreed upon.

In its simplest terms, a franchise is a license from owner of a trademark or trade name permitting another to sell a product or service under that name or mark. More broadly stated, a "franchise" has evolved into an elaborate agreement under which the franchisee undertakes to conduct a business or sell a product or service in accordance with methods and procedures prescribed by the franchisor, and the franchisor undertakes to assist the franchisee through advertising, promotion and other advisory services. H & R Block, Inc. v. Lovelace, 208 Kan. 538, 493 P.2d 205, 211.

Corporate franchise. See that title. See also **Charter.**

Elective franchise. The right of suffrage; the right or privilege of voting in public elections. Such right is guaranteed by Fifteenth, Nineteenth, and Twenty-fourth Amendments to U.S. Constitution.

Exclusive franchise. See **Exclusive agency.**

General and special. The charter of a corporation is its "general" franchise, while a "special" franchise consists in any rights granted by the public to use property for a public use but with private profit.

Sports franchise. As granted by a professional sports association, it is a privilege to field a team in a given geographic area under the auspices of the league that issues it. It is merely an incorporeal right.

Tax treatment. A franchise is an agreement which gives the transferee the right to distribute, sell, or provide goods, services, or facilities, within a specified area. The cost of obtaining a franchise may be amortized over the life of the agreement. In general, a franchise is a capital asset and results in capital gain or loss if all significant powers, rights or continuing interests are transferred pursuant to the sale of a franchise.

Franchise appurtenant to land. Usually a franchise is not regarded as real property or land and is not included in the term "tenement;" but it is sometimes characterized or classified as real property or as property of the nature of real property when exercised in connection with real property, and is, in terms, classified as real property, real estate, or land by some statutes.

Franchise clause. Provision in casualty insurance policy to the effect that the insurer will pay those claims only over a stated amount and that the insured is responsible for all damage under the agreed amount. This clause differs from a deductible provision in that the insured bears the loss in every claim up to the deductible amount whereas, under the franchise clause, once the claim exceeds the agreed amount, the insurer pays the entire claim.

Franchised dealer. A retailer who sells the product of a manufacturer or supplier under an agreement or franchise which generally protects the territory for the retailer and provides advertising and promotion support to him.

Franchise tax. A tax on the franchise of a corporation, that is, on the right and privilege of carrying on business in the character of a corporation, for the purposes for which it was created, and in the conditions which surround it. City of Poplar Bluff v. Poplar Bluff Loan and Bldg. Ass'n, Mo.App., 369 S.W.2d 764, 766.

Though the value of the franchise, for purposes of taxation, may be measured by the amount of business done, or the amount of earnings or dividends, or by the total value of the capital or stock of the corporation in excess of its tangible assets, a franchise tax is not a tax on either property, capital, stock, earnings, or dividends. Home Ins. Co. v. New York, 134 U.S. 594, 10 S.Ct. 593, 33 L.Ed. 1025; Greene v. Louisville & I. R. Co., 244 U.S. 499, 37 S.Ct. 673, 678, 61 L.Ed. 1280.

Francia /fræns(h)(i)yə/. France.

Francigena /frænsəjíynə/. A man born in France. A designation formerly given to aliens in England. See **Frenchman.**

Franc tenancier /fróŋk tenònsyéy/. In French law, a freeholder.

Francus /fræŋkəs/. L. Lat. Free; a freeman; a Frank.

Francus bancus /fræŋkəs bǽŋkəs/. Free-bench (q.v.).

Francus homo /fræŋkəs hówmow/. In old European law, a free man.

Francus plegius /fræŋkəs pléjiyəs/. In old English law, a frank pledge, or free pledge. See **Frank-pledge.**

Francus tenens /fræŋkəs ténən(d)z/. A freeholder. See **Frank-tenement.**

Frank, v. To send matter through the public mails free of postage, by a personal or official privilege. See **Franking privilege.**

Frank, adj. In old English law, free. Occurring in several compounds.

Frankalmoign /fræŋkælmóyn/. In English law, free alms. A spiritual tenure whereby religious corporations, aggregate or sole, held lands of the donor to them and their successors forever. They were discharged of all other except religious services, and the

trinoda necessitas. It differs from tenure by divine service, in that the latter required the performance of certain divine services, whereas the former, as its name imports, is free. Such type tenures were abolished by the Administration of Estates Act of 1925.

Frank bank. In old English law, free bench. See **Free-bench.**

Frank-chase. A liberty of free chase enjoyed by any one, whereby all other persons having ground within that compass are forbidden to cut down wood, etc., even in their own demesnes, to the prejudice of the owner of the liberty. See **Chase.**

Frank-fee. Freehold lands exempted from all services, but not from homage; lands held otherwise than in ancient demesne. That which a man holds to himself and his heirs, and not by such service as is required in ancient demesne, according to the custom of the manor.

Frank ferm. In English law, a species of estate held in socage, said by Britton to be "lands and tenements whereof the nature of the fee is changed by feoffment out of chivalry for certain yearly services, and in respect whereof neither homage, ward, marriage, nor relief can be demanded." 2 Bl.Comm. 80.

Frank-fold. In old English law, free-fold; a privilege for the lord to have all the sheep of his tenants and the inhabitants within his seigniory, in his fold, in his demesnes, to manure his land.

Franking privilege. The privilege of sending certain matter through the public mails without payment of postage, in pursuance of a personal or official privilege. The privilege granted to members of Congress to send out a certain amount of mail under signature without charge. See 39 U.S.C.A. § 321 et seq.

Frank-law. An obsolete expression signifying the rights and privileges of a citizen, or the liberties and civic rights of a freeman.

Frankleyn /fræŋklən/. (Spelled, also, "Francling" and "Franklin".) A freeman; a freeholder; a gentleman.

Frank-marriage. In old English law, a species of entailed estates. When tenements are given by one to another, together with a wife, who is a daughter or cousin of the donor, to hold in frank-marriage, the donees shall have the tenements to them and the heirs of their two bodies begotten, *i.e.*, in special tail. The word "frank-marriage," *ex vi termini*, both creates and limits an inheritance, not only supplying words of descent, but also terms of procreation. The donees are liable to no service except fealty, and a reserved rent would be void, until the fourth degree of consanguinity be passed between the issues of the donor and donee, when they were capable by the law of the church of intermarrying. 2 Bl.Comm. 115.

Frank-pledge. In old English law, a pledge or surety for freemen; that is, the pledge, or corporate responsibility, of all the inhabitants of a tithing for the general good behavior of each free-born citizen above the age of fourteen, and for his being forthcoming to answer any infraction of the law. A pledge of surety to the sovereign for the collective good conduct of a group.

Frank-tenant. A freeholder.

Frank-tenement. In English law, a free tenement, freeholding, or freehold. 2 Bl.Comm. 61, 62, 104. Used to denote both the tenure and the estate.

F.R.A.P. Federal Rules of Appellate Procedure.

Frater /fréydər/. In the civil law, a brother. *Frater consanguineus,* a brother having the same father, but born of a different mother. *Frater uterinus,* a brother born of the same mother, but by a different father. *Frater nutricius,* a bastard brother.

Frater fratri uterino non succedet in hæreditate paterna /fréydər frǽtray yùwdəráynow nòn səksíydət in hərìydətéydiy pətárnə/. A brother shall not succeed a uterine brother in the paternal inheritance. 2 Bl. Comm. 223. A maxim of the common law of England, now superseded.

Frateria /frətír(i)yə/. In old records, a fraternity, brotherhood, or society of religious persons, who were mutually bound to pray for the good health and life, etc., of their living brethren, and the souls of those that were dead.

Fraternal. Brotherly; relating or belonging to a fraternity or an association of persons formed for mutual aid and benefit, but not for profit. In re Mason Tire & Rubber Co., 56 App.D.C. 170, 11 F.2d 556, 557.

Fraternal benefit association or **society.** One whose members have adopted the same, or a very similar, calling, avocation, or profession, or who are working in unison to accomplish some worthy object, and who for that reason have banded themselves together as an association or society to aid and assist one another, and to promote the common cause. Alpha Rho Alumni Ass'n v. City of New Brunswick, 126 N.J.L. 233, 18 A.2d 68, 70. An association having a representative form of government and a lodge system with a ritualistic form of work for the meeting of its chapters, or other subordinate bodies. Fain v. Feldman, 191 Ga. 519, 13 S.E.2d 179, 181. A society or voluntary association organized and carried on for the mutual aid and benefit of its members, not for profit; which ordinarily has a lodge system, a ritualistic form of work, and a representative government, makes provision for the payment of death benefits, and (sometimes) for benefits in case of accident, sickness, or old age, the funds therefor being derived from dues paid or assessments levied on the members.

Fraternal insurance. The form of life (or accident) insurance furnished by a fraternal beneficial association, consisting in the payment to a member, or his heirs in case of death, of a stipulated sum of money, out of funds raised for that purpose by the payment of dues or assessments by all the members of the association.

Fraternal lodge. See **Fraternal benefit association or society.**

Fraternia /frətárn(i)yə/. A fraternity or brotherhood.

Fraternity. A body of men associated for their common interest, business or pleasure. Woman's Club of Little Falls v. Township of Little Falls, 20 N.J.Misc.

278, 26 A.2d 739, 741; Alpha Rho Alumni Ass'n v. City of New Brunswick, 126 N.J.L. 233, 18 A.2d 68, 71.

In American colleges, a student organization, either a nationally chartered society comprising many affiliated chapters or a single chapter in one institution, formed chiefly to promote friendship and welfare among the members, and usually having secret rites and a name consisting of Greek letters. Woman's Club of Little Falls v. Township of Little Falls, 20 N.J.Misc. 278, 26 A.2d 739, 741; Alpha Rho Alumni Ass'n v. City of New Brunswick, 126 N.J.L. 233, 18 A.2d 68, 71.

Fratres conjurati /frǽtriyz kònjəréyday/. Sworn brothers or companions for the defense of their sovereign, or for other purposes.

Fratres pyes /frǽtriyz páyz/. In old English law, certain friars who wore white and black garments.

Fratriage /frǽtriyəj/. A younger brother's inheritance.

Fratricide /frǽtrəsáyd/. One who has killed a brother or sister; also the killing of a brother or sister.

Fraud. An intentional perversion of truth for the purpose of inducing another in reliance upon it to part with some valuable thing belonging to him or to surrender a legal right. A false representation of a matter of fact, whether by words or by conduct, by false or misleading allegations, or by concealment of that which should have been disclosed, which deceives and is intended to deceive another so that he shall act upon it to his legal injury. Any kind of artifice employed by one person to deceive another. Goldstein v. Equitable Life Assur. Soc. of U. S., 160 Misc. 364, 289 N.Y.S. 1064, 1067. A generic term, embracing all multifarious means which human ingenuity can devise, and which are resorted to by one individual to get advantage over another by false suggestions or by suppression of truth, and includes all surprise, trick, cunning, dissembling, and any unfair way by which another is cheated. Johnson v. McDonald, 170 Okl. 117, 39 P.2d 150. "Bad faith" and "fraud" are synonymous, and also synonyms of dishonesty, infidelity, faithlessness, perfidy, unfairness, etc.

Elements of a cause of action for "fraud" include false representation of a present or past fact made by defendant, action in reliance thereupon by plaintiff, and damage resulting to plaintiff from such misrepresentation. Citizens Standard Life Ins. Co. v. Gilley, Tex.Civ.App., 521 S.W.2d 354, 356.

It consists of some deceitful practice or willful device, resorted to with intent to deprive another of his right, or in some manner to do him an injury. As distinguished from negligence, it is always positive, intentional. It comprises all acts, omissions, and concealments involving a breach of a legal or equitable duty and resulting in damage to another. And includes anything calculated to deceive, whether it be a single act or combination of circumstances, whether the suppression of truth or the suggestion of what is false, whether it be by direct falsehood or by innuendo, by speech or by silence, by word of mouth, or by look or gesture. Fraud, as applied to contracts, is the cause of an error bearing on a material part of the contract, created or continued by artifice, with design to obtain some unjust advantage to the one party, or to cause an inconvenience or loss to the other.

See also Actionable fraud; Badges of fraud; Cheat; Civil fraud; Collusion; Constructive fraud; Deceit; False pretenses; False representation; Intrinsic fraud; Mail fraud; Material fact; Misrepresentation; Promissory fraud; Reliance.

Actionable fraud. See **Actionable.**

Actual or constructive fraud. Fraud is either *actual* or *constructive.* Actual fraud consists in deceit, artifice, trick, design, some direct and active operation of the mind; it includes cases of the intentional and successful employment of any cunning, deception, or artifice used to circumvent or cheat another. It is something said, done, or omitted by a person with the design of perpetrating what he knows to be a cheat or deception. Constructive fraud consists in any act of commission or omission contrary to legal or equitable duty, trust, or confidence justly reposed, which is contrary to good conscience and operates to the injury of another. Or, as otherwise defined, it is an act, statement or omission which operates as a virtual fraud on an individual, or which, if generally permitted, would be prejudicial to the public welfare, and yet may have been unconnected with any selfish or evil design. Or, constructive frauds are such acts or contracts as, though not originating in any actual evil design or contrivance to perpetrate a positive fraud or injury upon other persons, are yet, by their tendency to deceive or mislead other persons, or to violate private or public confidence, or to impair or injure the public interests, deemed equally reprehensible with actual fraud. Constructive fraud consists in any breach of duty which, without an actually fraudulent intent, gains an advantage to the person in fault, or any one claiming under him, by misleading another to his prejudice, or to the prejudice of any one claiming under him; or, in any such act or omission as the law specially declares to be fraudulent, without respect to actual fraud.

Extrinsic fraud. Fraud which is collateral to the issues tried in the case where the judgment is rendered. Type of deceit which may form basis for setting aside a judgment as for example a divorce granted ex parte because the plaintiff-spouse falsely tells the court he or she is ignorant of the whereabouts of the defendant-spouse. Patrick v. Patrick, 245 N.C. 195, 95 S.E.2d 585.

Fraud in fact or in law. Fraud is also classified as *fraud in fact* and *fraud in law.* The former is actual, positive, intentional fraud. Fraud disclosed by matters of fact, as distinguished from constructive fraud or fraud in law. Fraud in law is fraud in contemplation of law; fraud implied or inferred by law; fraud made out by construction of law, as distinguished from fraud found by a jury from matter of fact; constructive fraud *(q.v.).*

Fraud in the inducement. Fraud connected with underlying transaction and not with the nature of the contract or document signed.

Intrinsic fraud. That which pertains to issue involved in original action or where acts constituting fraud were, or could have been, litigated therein. Fahrenbruch v. People ex rel. Taber, 169 Colo. 70, 453 P.2d 601. Perjury is an example of intrinsic fraud.

Larceny. See **Larceny** *(Larceny by fraud or deception).*

Legal or positive fraud. Fraud is also said to be *legal* or *positive.* The former is fraud made out by legal construction or inference, or the same thing as constructive fraud. Positive fraud is the same thing as actual fraud. Nocatee Fruit Co. v. Fosgate, C.C.A. Fla., 12 F.2d 250, 252. See also **Legal fraud.**

Statute of frauds. See **Frauds, Statute of.**

Tax fraud. Tax fraud falls into two categories: civil and criminal. Under civil fraud, the IRS may impose as a penalty an amount equal to 50% of the underpayment. Fines and/or imprisonment are prescribed for conviction of various types of criminal tax fraud. Both civil and criminal fraud require a specific intent on the part of the taxpayer to evade the tax; mere negligence will not be enough. Criminal fraud requires the additional element of wilfulness (*i.e.,* done deliberately and with evil purpose). In actual practice, it becomes difficult to distinguish between the degree of intent necessary to support criminal, as opposed to civil, fraud. In both situations, however, the IRS has the burden of proving fraud.

Fraudare /frŏdériy/. Lat. In the civil law, to deceive, cheat, or impose upon; to defraud.

Fraud order. A name given to orders issued by the postmaster general, for preventing the use of the mails as an agency for conducting schemes for obtaining money or property by means of false or fraudulent pretenses, etc. The fraud order is issued to the postmaster of the office through which the person affected by it receives his mail. It forbids the postmaster to pay any postal money order to the specified person, and instructs the postmaster to return all letters to the senders if practicable, or if not, to the dead letter office, stamped in either case with the word "fraudulent." The method of testing the validity of the fraud order is to apply to the federal court for an injunction to restrain the postmaster from executing it. The decision of the postmaster-general is not the exercise of a judicial function; if he exceeds his jurisdiction, the party injured may have relief in equity. Degge v. Hitchcock, 229 U.S. 162, 33 S.Ct. 639, 57 L.Ed. 1135.

Frauds, Statute of. This is the common designation of a very celebrated English statute (29 Car. II, c. 3), passed in 1677, which has been adopted, in a more or less modified form, in nearly all of the United States. Its chief characteristic is the provision that no suit or action shall be maintained on certain classes of contracts or engagements unless there shall be a note or memorandum thereof in writing signed by the party to be charged or by his authorized agent. Its object was to close the door to the numerous frauds and perjuries. It is more fully named as the "statute of frauds and perjuries."

Uniform Commercial Code. U.C.C. § 2–201 provides that a contract for the sale of goods for the price of $500 or more is not enforceable by way of action or defense unless there is some writing sufficient to indicate that a contract for sale has been made between the parties and signed by the party against whom enforcement is sought or by his authorized agent or broker.

Fraudulent. Based on fraud; proceeding from or characterized by fraud; tainted by fraud; done, made, or effected with a purpose or design to carry out a fraud. See also **False and fraudulent.**

A statement, or claim, or document, is "fraudulent" if it was falsely made, or caused to be made, with the intent to deceive.

To act with "intent to defraud" means to act willfully, and with the specific intent to deceive or cheat; ordinarily for the purpose of either causing some financial loss to another, or bringing about some financial gain to oneself.

Fraudulent alienation. In a general sense, the transfer of property with an intent to defraud creditors, lienors, or others. In a particular sense, the act of an administrator who wastes the assets of the estate by giving them away or selling at a gross undervalue.

Fraudulent alienee /frójələnt èyl(i)yəníy/. One who knowingly receives from an administrator assets of the estate under circumstances which make it a fraudulent alienation on the part of the administrator.

Fraudulent banking. Receipt of deposit by banker who knows that bank is insolvent at the time.

Fraudulent claims. See **False claim.**

Fraudulent concealment. The hiding or suppression of a material fact or circumstance which the party is legally or morally bound to disclose. The employment of artifice planned to prevent inquiry or escape investigation and to mislead or hinder the acquisition of information disclosing a right of action; acts relied on must be of an affirmative character and fraudulent. Fundunburks v. Michigan Mut. Liability Co., 63 Mich.App. 405, 234 N.W.2d 545, 547. The test of whether failure to disclose material facts constitutes fraud is the existence of a duty, legal or equitable, arising from the relation of the parties; failure to disclose a material fact with intent to mislead or defraud under such circumstances being equivalent to an actual "fraudulent concealment." Fraudulent concealment justifying a rescission of a contract is the intentional concealment of some fact known to the party charged, which is material for the party injured to know to prevent being defrauded; the concealment of a fact which one is bound to disclose being the equivalent of an indirect representation that such fact does not exist. See **Material fact.**

Fraudulent conversion. Receiving into possession money or property of another and fraudulently withholding, converting, or applying the same to or for one's own use and benefit, or to use and benefit of any person other than the one to whom the money or property belongs. See **Conversion.**

Fraudulent conveyance. A conveyance or transfer of property, the object of which is to defraud a creditor, or hinder or delay him, or to put such property beyond his reach. Dean v. Davis, 242 U.S. 438, 37 S.Ct. 130, 61 L.Ed. 419. Conveyance made with intent to avoid some duty or debt due by or incumbent on person making transfer. As constituting an act of bankruptcy, a gift or transfer of the bankrupt's property for little or no consideration at a time when the bankrupt is insolvent, or one which renders bankrupt's capital unreasonably small, or one made by bankrupt who believes that he will not be able to meet maturing obligations, or one made with actual intent to hinder and delay his creditors. Many states have adopted the Uniform Fraudulent Conveyances Act.

Fraudulent intent. Such intent exists where one, either with a view of benefitting himself or misleading another into a course of action, makes a representation which he knows to be false or which he does not believe to be true. In re Orenduff, D.C.Okl., 226 F.Supp. 312, 314.

Fraudulent or **dishonest act.** One which involves bad faith, a breach of honesty, a want of integrity, or moral turpitude. Hartford Acc. & Indem. Co. v. Singer, 185 Va. 620, 39 S.E.2d 505, 507, 508.

Fraudulent preferences. See **Preference.**

Fraudulent representation. A false statement as to material fact, made with intent that another rely thereon, which is believed by other party and on which he relies and by which he is induced to act and does act to his injury, and statement is fraudulent if speaker knows statement to be false or if it is made with utter disregard of its truth or falsity. Osborne v. Simmons, Mo.App., 23 S.W.2d 1102, 1104. As basis for civil action, establishment of representation, falsity, scienter, deception, and injury, are generally required. See also **Deceit; Fraud; Material fact; Misrepresentation.**

Fraudulent sale. See **Sale.**

Fraudulent transfers. See **Fraudulent conveyance.**

Fraunc, fraunche, fraunke /fróŋk/. See **Frank.**

Fraunchise /frónchəz/frǽnchàyz/. L. Fr. A franchise.

Fraus /frós/. Lat. Fraud. More commonly called, in the civil law, *"dolus,"* and *"dolus malus"* (q.v.). A distinction, however, was sometimes made between *"fraus"* and *"dolus"*; the former being held to be of the most extensive import.

Fraus dans locum contractui /frós dǽn(d)z lówkəm kəntrǽkchuway/. A misrepresentation or concealment of some fact that is material to the contract, and had the truth regarding which been known the contract would not have been made as made, is called a "fraud *dans locum contractui"*; i.e., a fraud occasioning the contract, or giving place or occasion for the contract.

Fraus est celare fraudem /frós èst səlériy fródəm/. It is a fraud to conceal a fraud.

Fraus est odiosa et non præsumenda /frós èst òwdiyówsə èt nón prìyz(y)əméndə/. Fraud is odious, and not to be presumed.

Fraus et dolus nemini patrocinari debent /frós èt dówləs némənay pǽtrəsənériy débənt/. Fraud and deceit should defend or excuse no man.

Fraus et jus nunquam cohabitant /frós èt jás náŋkwəm kòwhǽbədənt/. Fraud and justice never dwell together.

Fraus latet in generalibus /frós lǽdət ìn jènəréyləbəs/. Fraud lies hid in general expressions.

Fraus legis /frós líyjəs/. Lat. In the civil law, fraud of law; fraud upon law. See **In fraudem legis.**

Fraus meretur fraudem /frós məríydər fródəm/. Fraud merits fraud.

Fray /fréy/. See **Affray.**

F.R.B. Federal Reserve Board.

F.R.C.P. Federal Rules of Civil Procedure.

F.R.D. Federal Rules Decisions.

Frectum /fréktəm/. In old English law, freight. *Quoad frectum navium suarum,* as to the freight of his vessels.

Freddie Mac. See **Federal Home Loan Mortgage Corporation.**

Frednite. In old English law, a liberty to hold courts and take up the fines for beating and wounding. To be free from fines.

Fredstole /fríθstùwl/. Sanctuaries; seats of peace.

Fredum /fríydəm/. A fine paid for obtaining pardon when the peace had been broken. A sum paid the magistrate for protection against the right of revenge.

Fredwit, or **fredwite** /fríθwət/. A liberty to hold courts and take up the fines for beating and wounding.

Free. Not subject to legal constraint of another.

Unconstrained; having power to follow the dictates of his own will. Not subject to the dominion of another. Not compelled to involuntary servitude. Used in this sense as opposed to "slave."

Not bound to service for a fixed term of years; in distinction to being bound as an apprentice. Enjoying full civic rights. Available to all citizens alike without charge; as a free school.

Not despotic; assuring liberty; defending individual rights against encroachment by any person or class; instituted by a free people; said of governments, institutions, etc.

Certain, and also consistent with an honorable degree in life; as free services, in the feudal law.

Confined to the person possessing, instead of being shared with others; as a free fishery.

Not engaged in a war as belligerent or ally; neutral, as in the maxim: "Free ships make free goods."

See also **Freedom.**

Free alms. The name of a species of tenure. See **Frank almoigne.**

Free alongside (FAS). In price quotations, means that the price includes all costs of transportation and delivery of the goods alongside of the ship. See U.C.C. § 2–319(2–4).

Free and clear. The title to property is said to be "free and clear" when it is not incumbered by any liens; but it is said that an agreement to convey land "free and clear" is satisfied by a conveyance passing a good (*i.e.* marketable) title.

Free and equal. As used in a constitutional provision that election shall be free and equal, the word "free" means that every one entitled to vote should have a reasonable opportunity to do so, a reasonable manner of doing so, etc., and the word "equal" means that every vote cast should have its decisive effect in the selection or choice to be made at the election. The term means that the voter shall not be physically restrained in the exercise of his right of franchise, by either civil or military authority, and that every voter shall have the same right as every other voter. Asher v. Arnett, 280 Ky. 347, 132 S.W.2d 772, 775. It is the essence of free elections that the right of suffrage be untrammeled and unfettered, and that the ballot represent and express the electors' own intelligent judgment and conscience, and there can be no "free election" unless there is freedom of opinion. An election to be free must be without coercion of any description or any deterrent from the elector's exercise of his free will by means of any intimidation or influence whatever, although there is no violence or physical coercion.

Free-bench. In old English law, a widow's dower out of copyholds to which she was entitled by the custom of some manors. It was regarded as an excrescence growing out of the husband's interest, and was a continuance of his estate.

Free-bord. In old records, an allowance of land over and above a certain limit or boundary, as so much beyond or without a fence. The right of claiming that quantity.

Free chapel. In English ecclesiastical law, a place of worship, so called because not liable to the visitation of the ordinary. It is always of royal foundation, or founded at least by private persons to whom the crown has granted the privilege.

Free course. In admiralty law, a vessel having the wind from a favorable quarter is said to sail on a "free course," or said to be "going free" when she has a fair (following) wind and her yards braced in.

Freedman. In Roman law, one who was set free from a state of bondage; an emancipated slave. The word was used in the same sense in the United States, respecting negroes who were formerly slaves.

Freedom. The state of being free; liberty; self-determination; absence of restraint; the opposite of slavery.

The power of acting, in the character of a moral personality, according to the dictates of the will, without other check, hindrance, or prohibition than such as may be imposed by just and necessary laws and the duties of social life. See **Liberty.**

The prevalence, in the government and constitution of a country, of such a system of laws and institutions as secure civil liberty to the individual citizen.

Freedom of association. Right guaranteed by First Amendment of U.S. Constitution. See **Association.**

Freedom of choice. Freedom of choice to attend school of choice in unitary, integrated school system, devoid of any de jure segregation means the maximum amount of freedom and clearly understood choice in bona fide unitary system where schools are not white schools or Negro schools, but just schools. Hall v. St. Helena Parish School Bd., D.C.La., 268 F.Supp. 923, 926.

Freedom of expression. Right guaranteed by First Amendment of U.S. Constitution; includes freedom of religion, speech, and press. See also **Liberty**.

Freedom of Information Act. The Freedom of Information Act (5 U.S.C.A. § 552) provides for making information held by Federal agencies available to the public unless it comes within one of the specific categories of matters exempt from public disclosure. Virtually all agencies of the executive branch of the Federal Government have issued regulations to implement the Freedom of Information Act. These regulations inform the public where certain types of information may be readily obtained, how other information may be obtained on request, and what internal agency appeals are available if a member of the public is refused requested information. This Act is designed to prevent abuse of discretionary power of federal agencies by requiring them to make public certain information about their workings and work product.

Freedom of press. Right guaranteed by First Amendment of U.S. Constitution. Such right includes freedom from prior restraint of publication. See **Censor; Censorship; Gag order; Liberty; Prior restraint**.

Freedom of religion. Freedom to individually believe and to practice or exercise one's belief. In re Elwell, 55 Misc.2d 252, 284 N.Y.S.2d 924, 930. This First Amendment protection embraces the concept of freedom to believe and freedom to act, the first of which is absolute, but the second of which remains subject to regulation for protection of society. Oney v. Oklahoma City, C.C.A.Okl., 120 F.2d 861, 865. Such freedom means not only that civil authorities may not intervene in affairs of church; it also prevents church from exercising its authority through state. Eastern Conference of Original Free Will Baptists of N. C. v. Piner, 267 N.C. 74, 147 S.E.2d 581, 583. See also **Establishment clause; Free exercise clause**.

Freedom of speech. Right guaranteed by First Amendment of U.S. Constitution. See also **Fighting words; Liberty; Speech or debate clause**.

Freedom of the city. In English law, this phrase signifies immunity from county jurisdiction, and the privilege of corporate taxation and self-government held under a charter from the crown. This freedom is enjoyed of right, subject to the provision of the charter, and is often conferred as an honor on princes and other distinguished individuals. The freedom of a city carries the parliamentary franchise. The rights and privileges possessed by the burgesses or freemen of a municipal corporation under the old English law; now of little importance, and conferred chiefly as a mark of honor.

The phrase has no place in American law, and as frequently used in addresses of welcome made to organizations visiting an American city, particularly by mayors, has no meaning whatever except as an expression of good will.

Free election. Exists where each voter is allowed to cast his ballot as his own conscience dictates. See **Free and equal**, *supra*.

Free enterprise. The right to conduct a legitimate business for profit. Lafayette Dramatic Productions v. Ferentz, 305 Mich. 193, 9 N.W.2d 57, 62.

Free entry, egress, and regress. An expression used to denote that a person has the right to go on land again and again as often as may be reasonably necessary. Thus, in the case of a tenant entitled to emblements.

Free exercise clause. First Amendment to U.S. Constitution provides that "Congress shall make no law respecting an establishment of religion, or prohibiting the free exercise thereof." See also **Establishment clause; Freedom of religion; Liberty**.

Free fishery. See **Fishery**.

Freehold. An estate for life or in fee. Intermountain Realty Co. v. Allen, 60 Idaho 228, 90 P.2d 704, 706. A "freehold estate" is a right of title to land. Cohn v. Litwin, 311 Ill.App. 55, 35 N.E.2d 410, 413. An estate in land or other real property, of uncertain duration; that is, either of inheritance or which may possibly last for the life of the tenant at the least (as distinguished from a leasehold); and held by a free tenure (as distinguished from copyhold or villeinage).

An estate to be a freehold must possess these two qualities: (1) Immobility, that is, the property must be either land or some interest issuing out of or annexed to land; and (2) indeterminate duration, for, if the utmost period of time to which an estate can endure be fixed and determined, it cannot be a freehold.

Freehold *in deed* is the real possession of land or tenements in fee, fee-tail, or for life. Freehold *in law* is the right to such tenements before entry. The term has also been applied to those offices which a man holds in fee or for life.

Determinable freeholds are estates for life, which may determine upon future contingencies before the life for which they are created expires, as if an estate be granted to a woman during her widowhood, or to a man until he be promoted to a benefice. In these and similar cases, whenever the contingency happens,—when the widow marries, or when the grantee obtains the benefice,—the respective estates are absolutely determined and gone. Yet, while they subsist, they are reckoned estates for life; because they may by possibility last for life, if the contingencies upon which they are to determine do not sooner happen. 2 Bl.Comm. 121.

Freehold in law is a freehold which has descended to a man, upon which he may enter at pleasure, but which he has not entered on.

Freeholder. One having title to realty; either of inheritance or for life; either legal or equitable title. A person who possesses a freeholder estate; *i.e.* the owner of a freehold.

Freehold land societies. Societies in England designed for the purpose of enabling mechanics, artisans, and other workingmen to purchase at the least possible price a piece of freehold land of a sufficient yearly value to entitle the owner to the elective franchise for the county in which the land is situated.

Free ice. All ice in navigable streams not included within that authorized to be appropriated is sometimes called "free" ice, and does not belong to the adjacent riparian owners, but to the person who first appropriates it. Hudson River Ice Co. v. Brady, 158 App.Div. 142, 142 N.Y.S. 819, 821.

Free law. A term formerly used in England to designate the freedom of civil rights enjoyed by freemen. It was liable to forfeiture on conviction of treason or an infamous crime.

Freeman. A person in the possession and enjoyment of all the civil and political rights accorded to the people under a free government.

In the Roman law, it denoted one who was either born free or emancipated, and was the opposite of "slave." In feudal law, it designated an allodial proprietor, as distinguished from a vassal or feudal tenant. (And so in Pennsylvania colonial law.) In old English law, the word described a freeholder or tenant by free services; one who was not a villein. The term later referred to a member of a city or borough having the right of suffrage, or a member of any municipal corporation invested with full civic rights.

Freeman's roll. A list of persons admitted as burgesses or freemen for the purposes of the rights reserved by the municipal corporation act. Distinguished from the Burgess Roll. The term was used, in early colonial history, in some of the American colonies.

Free men. Before the Norman Conquest, a free man might be a man of small estate dependent on a lord. Every man, not himself a lord, was bound to have a lord or be treated as unworthy of a free man's right. Among free men there was a difference in their estimation for *Wergild.* See **Homo liber.**

Free on board (FOB). In sales price quotation, means generally that the seller assumes all responsibilities and costs up to the point of delivery, including insurance, transportation, etc. See U.C.C. § 2–319.

The term "F.O.B." is an abbreviation for "free on board" and means that seller will deliver subject matter contracted for, on certain conveyance, without expense to buyer. Tyson v. Seaport Grain, Inc., Tex. Civ.App., 388 S.W.2d 731, 735.

Free port. An area or section of a port set aside for handling of foreign goods without entering customs.

Free press. See **Freedom of press.**

Free services. In feudal and old English law, such feudal services as were not unbecoming the character of a soldier or a freeman to perform; as to serve under his lord in the wars, to pay a sum of money, and the like.

Free shareholders. The free shareholders of a building and loan association are subscribers to its capital stock who are not borrowers from the association.

Free ships. In international law, ships of a neutral nation. The phrase "free ships shall make free goods" is often inserted in treaties, meaning that goods, even though belonging to an enemy, shall not be seized or confiscated, if found in neutral ships.

Free socage. See **Socage.**

Free tenure. Tenure by free services; freehold tenure.

Free time. Period that railroad car or vessel may remain unloaded before demurrage charges begin.

Free trade zone. See **Foreign trade zone.**

Free warren. See **Warren.**

Freeze-out. Action taken by persons in control of corporation resulting in termination of a shareholder's interest, and term implies a purpose to enforce a liquidation or sale of other stockholder's shares, not incident to some other wholesome business goal. Miller v. Steinbach, D.C.N.Y., 268 F.Supp. 255, 270. The use of corporate control vested in the statutory majority of shareholders or the board of directors to eliminate minority shareholders from the enterprise or to reduce to relevant insignificance their voting power or claims on corporate assets. It implies a purpose to force upon the minority shareholder a change which is not incident to any other business goal of the corporation. Gabhart v. Gabhart, Ind., 370 N.E.2d 345, 353. See also **Squeeze-out.**

Freight. The price or compensation paid for the transportation of goods by a carrier. Name also applied to goods transported by such carriers. See also **Freight rate.**

Dead freight. Money payable by a person who has chartered a ship and only partly loaded her, in respect of the loss of freight caused to the ship-owner by the deficiency of cargo.

Freight booking. Making of specific arrangements for the transportation of goods in advance. See **Forwarding agent; Freight forwarder.**

Freighter. One who charters a ship to transport cargo; also, the vessel so chartered. The party by whom a vessel is engaged or chartered; otherwise called the "charterer." In French law, the owner of a vessel is called the "freighter" *(fréteur);* the merchant who hires it is called the "affreighter" *(affréteur).*

Freight forwarder. One who in the ordinary course of business assembles and consolidates small shipments into a single lot and assumes responsibility for transportation of such property from point of receipt to point of destination. Mercury Motor Express, Inc. v. Brinke, C.A.Fla., 475 F.2d 1086, 1090. Freight forwarders collect and consolidate less than carload or less than truckload shipments and secure common carrier transportation for the long haul movement of property owned by individual shippers by carload or truckload. National Motor Freight Traffic Ass'n v. U. S., D.C.D.C., 253 F.Supp. 661, 663.

Freight mile. The equivalent of one ton of goods *(i.e.* freight) carried one mile.

Freight rate. The transportation charge for goods carried based on number of pieces carried, or the weight, or the mileage, or the value of the goods, or a combination thereof.

Freight then pending. Earnings of the voyage. The C. F. Coughlin, D.C.N.Y., 25 F.Supp. 649, 650.

Frenchman. In early times, in English law, this term was applied to every stranger or "outlandish" man.

French pool. A system of gambling, especially on horse races, now generally known as "pari mutuel" *(q.v.).*

Frendlesman /fréndləsmən/. Sax. An outlaw. So called because of his outlawry he was denied all help of friends after certain days.

Frendwite /fréndwàyt/. In old English law, a mulct or fine exacted from him who harbored an outlawed friend.

Freneticus /frənédəkəs/. In old English law, a madman, or person in a frenzy.

Freoborgh /fríybòrg/. A free-surety, or free-pledge. See **Frank-pledge.**

Freoling /fríyliŋ/. (Sax. *freoh,* free, plus *ling,* progeny.) A freeman born. See **Frilingi.**

Frequent /frəkwént/, *v.* To visit often; to resort to often or habitually.

Frequenter /frəkwéntər/. Any person not an employee who may go in or be in place of employment or public building under circumstances which render him other than trespasser.

Frequentia actus multum operatur /frəkwénsh(iy)ə æktəs məltəm òpəréydər/. The frequency of an act effects much. A continual usage is of great effect to establish a right.

Frère /frér/. Fr. A brother. *Frère eyne,* elder brother. *Frère puisne,* younger brother.

Fresca /fréskə/. In old records, fresh water, or rain and land flood.

Fresh. Immediate; recent; following without any material interval.

Fresh complaint rule. The fresh complaint rule provides that in certain sexual assault cases proof that the alleged victim complained of the criminal act within a reasonable time after it occurred to a person she would ordinarily turn to for help or advice is admissible to bolster the credibility of the victim. State v. Tirone, 64 N.J. 222, 314 A.2d 601.

Fresh disseisin /frésh dəsíyzən/. By the ancient common law, where a man had been disseised, he was allowed to right himself by force, by ejecting the disseisor from the premises, without resort to law, provided this was done forthwith, while the disseisin was *fresh (flagrante disseisina).*

Freshet /fréshət/. A flood, or overflowing of a river, by means of rains or melted snow; an inundation.

Fresh fine. In old English law, a fine that had been levied within a year past.

Fresh pursuit. Refers to common-law right of police officer to cross jurisdictional lines in order to arrest a felon. Carson v. Pape, 15 Wis.2d 300, 112 N.W.2d 693, 697. Several states have adopted the Uniform Extra-Territorial Arrest on Fresh Pursuit Act. Basically, the law permits a police officer, of a State which has enacted the Act, to enter a State, which has enacted a similar Act, if he is in fresh pursuit and he can continue in fresh pursuit, of a person in order to arrest him on the ground that he had committed a felony in the State of the pursuing officer. The officer has the same powers of arrest and to hold in custody as the law enforcement officials of the State that he has entered.

One from whom property has been taken may use reasonable force to retake it if such force is used immediately after the taking. Sometimes referred to as hot pursuit.

Fresh start adjustment. For persons dying after 1976, normally the decedent's income tax basis in property will carry over to the estate of heirs. The "fresh start" adjustment, however, permits an addition to basis for the appreciation attributable to the period from the date the property was acquired by the decedent to December 31, 1976. The "fresh start" adjustment is only allowed for purposes of determining income tax gain on the later disposition of the property by the estate or heirs. I.R.S. § 1023.

Fresh suit. In old English law, immediate and unremitting pursuit of an escaping thief. "Such a present and earnest following of a robber as never ceases from the time of the robbery until apprehension."

Fret. Fr. In French marine law, freight.

Fréter /freytéy/. Fr. In French marine law, to freight a ship; to let it.

Fréteur /freytyúr/. Fr. In French marine law, freighter. The owner of a ship, who lets it to the merchant.

Frettum, frectum /fré(k)təm/. In old English law, the freight of a ship; freight money.

Fretum /fríydəm/. Lat. A strait.

Friars /fráyərz/. An order of religious persons, of whom there were four principal branches, viz.: (1) Minors, Grey Friars, or Franciscans; (2) Augustines; (3) Dominicans, or Black Friars; (4) White Friars, or Carmelites, from whom the rest descend.

Friburgh /fríybərg/. (Also, Frithborg, Frithborgh, Friborg, Froborg, and Freoburgh.) (Sax.) A kind of frank-pledge whereby the principal men were bound for themselves and servants.

Fribusculum /frəbáskyələm/. In the civil law, a temporary separation between husband and wife, caused by a quarrel or estrangement, but not amounting to a divorce, because not accompanied with an intention to dissolve the marriage.

Fridborg, frithborg /fríðbòrg/. Frank-pledge. Security for the peace.

Fridhburgus /friðbárgəs/. In old English law, a kind of frank-pledge, by which the lords or principal men were made responsible for their dependents or servants.

Friend. One favorably disposed. Ned v. Robinson, 181 Okl. 507, 74 P.2d 1156. Varying in degree from greatest intimacy to acquaintance more or less casual. United States Trust Co. of Newark v. Montclair Trust Co., 133 N.J.Eq. 579, 33 A.2d 901, 903. See also **Next friend.**

Friendless man. In old English law, an outlaw; so called because he was denied all help of friends.

Friendly fire. Fire burning in place where it was intended to burn, although damages may result. Progress Laundry & Cleaning Co. v. Reciprocal Exchange, Tex.Civ.App., 109 S.W.2d 226, 227.

Friendly societies. In English law, associations supported by subscription, for the relief and maintenance of the members, or their wives, children, relatives, and nominees, in sickness, infancy, advanced age, widowhood, etc. The statutes regulating these societies were consolidated and amended by St. 38 & 39 Vict., c. 60.

Friendly suit. A suit brought by a creditor against an executor or administrator, being really a suit by the executor or administrator, in the name of a creditor, against himself, in order to compel the creditors to take an equal distribution of the assets. Also any suit instituted by agreement between the parties to obtain the opinion of the court upon some doubtful question in which they are interested. See also **Amicable action.**

Friend of the court. See **Amicus curiæ.**

Frilingi /frəlínjay/. Persons of free descent, or freemen born; the middle class of persons among the Saxons. See **Freoling.**

Fringe benefits. Side benefits which accompany or are in addition to a person's employment such as paid insurance, recreational facilities, profit-sharing plans, paid holidays and vacations, etc. Such benefits are in addition to regular salary or wages and are a matter of bargaining in union contracts. See also **Cafeteria plan; Perquisites.**

Frisk. A pat-down search of a suspect by police, designed to discover weapons, not to recover contraband. The scope of a frisk has been limited by the courts to be less than a full-scale search. In determining whether a police officer had a basis for initiating a frisk, there are two matters to be considered. One concerns whether the officer had a sufficient degree of suspicion that the party frisked was armed and dangerous, and the other whether the officer was rightfully in the presence of the party frisked so as to be endangered if that person was armed. Terry v. Ohio, 392 U.S. 1, 88 S.Ct. 1868, 20 L.Ed.2d 889. The running of hands rapidly over another's person, as distinguished from "search," which is to strip and examine contents more particularly. Kalwin Business Men's Ass'n v. McLaughlin, 126 Misc. 698, 214 N.Y.S. 99, 102. See also **Stop.**

Frith. Sax. Peace, security, or protection. This word occurs in many compound terms used in Anglo-Saxon law.

Frithborg /fríθbòrg/. Frank-pledge.

Frithbote /fríθbòwt/. A satisfaction or fine, for a breach of the peace.

Frithbreach /fríθbrìych/. The breaking of the peace.

Frithgar /fríθvàr/. The year of jubilee, or of meeting for peace and friendship.

Frithgilda /fríθgìldə/. Guildhall; a company or fraternity for the maintenance of peace and security; also a fine for breach of the peace.

Frithman /fríθmæ̀n/. A member of a company or fraternity.

Frithsocne /fríθsòwkən/. Surety of defense. Jurisdiction of the peace. The franchise of preserving the peace. Also spelled *"frithsoken."*

Frithsplot /fríθsplòt/. A spot or plot of land, encircling some stone, tree, or well, considered sacred, and therefore affording sanctuary to criminals.

Frithstool /fríθstùwl/. The stool of peace. A stool or chair placed in a church or cathedral, and which was the symbol and place of sanctuary to those who fled to it and reached it.

Frivolous. Of little weight or importance. A pleading is "frivolous" when it is clearly insufficient on its face, and does not controvert the material points of the opposite pleading, and is presumably interposed for mere purposes of delay or to embarrass the opponent. Frivolous pleadings may be amended to proper form, or ordered stricken, under federal and state Rules of Civil Procedure.

Frivolous appeal. One in which no justiciable question has been presented and appeal is readily recognizable as devoid of merit in that there is little prospect that it can ever succeed. Brooks v. General Motors Assembly Division, Mo.App., 527 S.W.2d 50, 53.

From. As used as a function word, implies a starting point, whether it be of time, place, or condition; and meaning having a starting point of motion, noting the point of departure, origin, withdrawal, etc., as he traveled "from" New York to Chicago. Silva v. MacAuley, 135 Cal.App. 249, 26 P.2d 887. One meaning of "from" is "out of". Word "from" or "after" an event or day does not have an absolute and invariable meaning, but each should receive an inclusion or exclusion construction according to intention with which such word is used. Acme Life Ins. Co. v. White, Tex.Civ.App., 99 S.W.2d 1059, 1060. Words "from" and "to," used in contract, may be given meaning to which reason and sense entitles them, under circumstances of case. Woodruff v. Adams, 134 Cal.App. 490, 25 P.2d 529.

From one place to another. From premises owned by one person to premises owned by another person in some legal subdivision or from one legal subdivision to another.

From person. Includes taking from presence of person assaulted as well as taking of property in actual contact with person of one robbed.

From, through, or **under.** The term refers to origin or devolution of property, and unless some title to or interest therein has been derived by assignment or otherwise from party adverse to decedent's estate, statute barring testimony is inapplicable.

From time to time. Occasionally, at intervals, now and then. See **From.**

Front. Forepart, as opposed to the back or rear. Any side or face of a building is a front, although the word is more commonly used to denote the entrance side. In re McInerney, 47 Wyo. 258, 34 P.2d 35, 43. As applied to a bare lot, it is that side of lot towards which, in ordinary circumstances, house, when built, will most likely face, and very general usage of building houses with their main entrance toward shorter street line results in common understanding that this is side intended when front of lot is referred to.

Frontage. Frontage denotes line of property on street. Jagendorf v. City of Memphis, Tenn., 520 S.W.2d 333, 335. Extent of front along road or street. Tzeses v. Barbahenn, 125 N.J.L. 643, 17 A.2d 539, 540. Space available for erection of buildings, and does not include cross streets or space occupied by sidewalk or any ornamental spaces in plat between sidewalks and curb. The expense of local improvements made by municipal corporations (such as paving, curbing, and sewering) is generally assessed on abutting property owners in proportion to the "frontage" of their lots on the street or highway, and an assessment so levied being called a "frontage assessment."

Front foot. Measurement used in assessing and apportioning cost of public improvements; *e.g.* curbs, sewers, sidewalks, streets. As respects assessment, synonymous with "abutting foot." See also **Frontage.** *Front-foot rule.* One by which cost of improvement is to be apportioned among several properties in proportion to their frontage on improvement and without regard to benefits conferred.

Frontier. In international law, that portion of the territory of any country which lies close along the border line of another country, and so "fronts" or faces it. Border between two countries. The term means something more than the boundary line itself, and includes a tract or strip of country, of indefinite extent, contiguous to the line.

Fronting and abutting. Very often, "fronting" signifies abutting, adjoining, or bordering on, depending largely on the context. Rombauer v. Compton Heights Christian Church, 328 Mo. 1, 40 S.W.2d 545, 551. As used in statutes relating to assessment for improvements, property between which and the improvement there is no intervening land.

Front wages. Type of prospective compensation paid to a victim of job discrimination without harm to incumbent employees until the victim achieves the position that he would have attained but for the illegal and discriminatory act. See also **Back pay award.**

Frozen account. An account in which no activity is permitted until a court order is lifted.

Frozen assets. Those assets of a business which cannot be readily sold without injuring the capital structure of the business in contrast to liquid assets which are readily convertible into cash.

Frozen snake. A term used to impute ingratitude and held libelous, the court taking judicial notice of its meaning without an innuendo.

Fructuarius /frə̀kchuwériyəs/. Lat. In the civil law, one who had the usufruct of a thing; *i.e.,* the use of the fruits, profits, or increase, as of land or animals. Bracton applies it to a lessee, fermor, or farmer of land, or one who held lands *ad firmam,* for a farm or term.

Fructus /frə́ktəs/. Lat. In the civil law, fruit, fruits; produce; profit or increase; the organic productions of a thing. The right to the fruits of a thing belonging to another. The compensation which a man receives from another for the use or enjoyment of a thing, such as interest or rent.

Fructus augent hæreditatem /frə́ktəs ógənt hərèdətéydəm/. The yearly increase goes to enhance the inheritance.

Fructus civiles /frə́ktəs sívəliyz/. All revenues and recompenses which, though not *fruits,* properly speaking, are recognized as such by the law. The term includes such things as the rents and income of real property, interest on money loaned, and annuities.

Fructus fundi /frə́ktəs fə́nday/. The fruits (produce or yield) of land.

Fructus industriales /frə́ktəs əndə̀striyéyliyz/. Industrial fruits, or fruits of industry. Those fruits of a thing, as of land, which are produced by the labor and industry of the occupant, as crops of grain; as distinguished from such as are produced solely by the powers of nature. Emblements are so called in the common law. Annual crops obtained by yearly labor and cultivation. Term includes those plants which are sown annually and grown primarily by manual labor such as wheat, corn and vegetables. Key v. Loder, D.C.Mun.App., 182 A.2d 60, 61.

Fructus legis /frə́ktəs líyjəs/. The fruit of the law, *i.e.* execution.

Fructus naturales /frə́ktəs næ̀chəréyliyz/. Those products which are produced by the powers of nature alone; as wool, metals, milk, the young of animals. Term includes any plant which has perennial roots, such as trees, shrubs and grasses. Key v. Loder, D.C.Mun.App., 182 A.2d 60, 61.

Fructus pecudum /frə́ktəs pékyədəm/. The produce or increase of flocks or herds.

Fructus pendentes /frə́ktəs pendéntiyz/. Hanging fruits; those not severed. The fruits united with the thing which produces them. These form a part of the principal thing.

Fructus pendentes pars fundi videntur /frə́ktəs pendéntiyz párz fə́nday vədéntər/. Hanging fruits make part of the land.

Fructus perceptos villæ non esse constat /frə́ktəs pərséptows víliy nòn ésiy kónstət/. Gathered fruits do not make a part of the farm.

Fructus rei alienæ /frə́ktəs ríyay æ̀liyíyniy/. The fruits of another's property; fruits taken from another's estate.

Fructus separati /frə́ktəs sèpəréyday/. Separate fruits; the fruits of a thing when they are separated from it.

Fructus stantes /frə́ktəs stǽntiyz/. Standing fruits; those not yet severed from the stalk or stem.

Fruges /frújiyz/. In the civil law, anything produced from vines, underwood, chalk-pits, stone-quarries.

Grains and leguminous vegetables. In a more restricted sense, any esculent growing in pods.

Fruit. The produce of a tree or plant which contains the seed or is used for food. The edible reproductive body of a seed plant. The effect or consequence of an act or operation.

Civil fruits. In the civil law *(fructus civiles)* are such things as the rents and income of real property, the interest on money loaned, and annuities. Rents and revenues of an immovable.

Fruit fallen. In old English law, the produce of any possession detached therefrom, and capable of being enjoyed by itself. Thus, a next presentation, when a vacancy has occurred, is a fruit fallen from the advowson.

Natural fruits. In the civil law, the produce of the soil, or of fruit-trees, bushes, vines, etc., which are edible or otherwise useful or serve for the reproduction of their species. The term is used in contradistinction to "artificial fruits," *i.e.,* such as by metaphor or analogy are likened to the fruits of the earth. Of the latter, interest on money is an example.

Fruit and the tree doctrine. The courts have held that an individual who earns income from his property or services cannot assign that income to another. For example, a father cannot assign his earnings from commissions to his son and escape income tax on such amount.

Fruit of poisonous tree doctrine. Evidence which is spawned by or directly derived from an illegal search or illegal interrogation is generally inadmissible against the defendant because of its original taint, though knowledge of facts gained independently of the original and tainted search is admissible. Wong Sun v. U. S., 371 U.S. 471, 83 S.Ct. 407, 9 L.Ed.2d 441. This doctrine is to the effect that an unlawful search taints not only evidence obtained at the search, but facts discovered by process initiated by the unlawful search. This doctrine is generally applied to cases involving searches in violation of the Fourth Amendment to the Constitution right against unlawful searches and seizures, but it can be applied to searches in violation of a statutory right. Duncan v. State, 278 Ala. 145, 176 So.2d 840, 865.

Fruits of crime. In the law of evidence, material objects acquired by means and in consequence of the commission of crime, and sometimes constituting the subject-matter of the crime. See also **Fruit of poisonous tree doctrine.**

Frumenta quæ sata sunt solo cedere intelliguntur /frəméntə kwíy séydə sənt sówlow síydəriy intèləgántər/. Grain which is sown is understood to form a part of the soil.

Frumentum /frəméntəm/. In the civil law, grain. That which grows in an ear.

Frumgyld /frámgild/. Sax. The first payment made to the kindred of a slain person in recompense for his murder.

Frumstoll /frámstòl/. Sax. In Saxon law, a chief seat, or mansion house.

Frusca terra /fráskə téhrə/. In old records, uncultivated and desert ground.

Frussura /frəshúrə/. A breaking; plowing.

Frustra /frástrə/. Lat. Without effect, in vain, to no purpose, uselessly; without reason or cause, groundlessly; in error.

Frustra agit qui judicium prosequi nequit cum effectu /frástə éyjət kwày jədísh(iy)əm prósəkway nékwət kəm əfékchuw/. He sues to no purpose who cannot prosecute his judgment with effect [who cannot have the fruits of his judgment].

Frustra [vana] est potentia quæ nunquam venit in actum /frástrə èst pəténshiyə kwiy nə́ŋkwəm víynəd in ǽktəm/véynə°/. That power is to no purpose which never comes into act, or which is never exercised.

Frustra expectatur eventus cujus effectus nullus sequitur /frástrə èkspektéydər əvéntəs kyúwjəs əféktəs nə́ləs sékwədər/. An event is vainly expected from which no effect follows.

Frustra feruntur leges nisi subditis et obedientibus /frástrə fərántər líyjiyz náysay sə́bdədəs èd əbìydiyéntəbəs/. Laws are made to no purpose, except for those that are subject and obedient.

Frustra fit per plura, quod fieri potest per pauciora /frástrə fít pər pl(y)úrə, kwòd fáyəray pówdəst pər pòsiyórə/. That is done to no purpose by many things which can be done by fewer. The employment of more means or instruments for effecting a thing than are necessary is to no purpose.

Frustra legis auxilium invocat [quærit] qui in legem committit /frástrə líyjəs ogzíl(i)yəm invówkət kwày ən líyjəm kəmídət/°kwírət°/. He vainly invokes the aid of the law who transgresses the law.

Frustra petis quod mox es restiturus /frástrə pédəs kwòd móks ès rèstət(y)úrəs/. In vain you ask that which you will have immediately to restore.

Frustra petis quod statim alteri reddere cogeris /frástrə pédəs kwòd stǽdəm óltəray rédəriy kójərəs/. You ask in vain that which you might immediately be compelled to restore to another.

Frustra probatur quod probatum non relevat /frástrə prəbéydər kwòd prəbéydəm nòn réləvət/. That is proved to no purpose which, when proved, does not help.

Frustration of contract. Where, from nature of contract and surrounding circumstances, parties from beginning must have known it could not be fulfilled unless, when time thereof arrived, some particular condition continued to exist, under doctrine of "frustration", in absence of warranty that such condition of things shall exist, contract is to be construed as subject to implied condition that parties shall be excused in case, before breach, performance becomes impossible or purpose frustrated from such condition ceasing to exist without default of either. Johnson v. Atkins, 53 Cal.App.2d 430, 127 P.2d 1027, 1028, 1029, 1030. This doctrine provides, generally, that where existence of a specific thing is, either by terms of contract or in contemplation of parties, necessary for performance of a promise in the contract, duty to perform promise is discharged if thing is no longer in existence at time for performance. Glidden Co. v. Hellenic Lines, Limited, C.A.N.Y., 275 F.2d 253, 255. See U.C.C. § 2–615; see also **Commercial impracticability.**

Frustration of purpose doctrine. This doctrine excuses a promisor in certain situations when the objectives of contract have been utterly defeated by circumstances arising after formation of agreement, and performance is excused under this rule even though there is no impediment to actual performance. Hess v. Dumouchel Paper Co., 154 Conn. 343, 225 A.2d 797, 801.

Frustrum terræ /frə́strəm téhriy/. A piece or parcel of land lying by itself.

Frymith /fráymiθ/. In old English law, the affording harbor and entertainment to any one.

Frythe. Sax. In old English law, a plain between woods. An arm of the sea, or a strait between two lands.

F.Supp. Federal Supplement.

F.T.C. Federal Trade Commission.

Fuage, fouage, or **feuage** /fyúwəj/. Hearth money. A tax laid upon each fireplace or hearth. An imposition of a shilling for every hearth, levied by Edward III in the dukedom of Aquitaine. 1 Bl.Comm. 324.

Fuer /fyúwər/. In old English law, flight. It was of two kinds: (1) *Fuer in fait,* or *in facto,* where a person did apparently and corporally flee; (2) *fuer in ley,* or *in lege,* when, being called in the county court, he did not appear, which legal interpretation makes flight.

Fuero /fwérow/. In Spanish law, a law; a code.

A general usage or custom of a province, having the force of law. *Ir contra fuero,* to violate a received custom.

A grant of privileges and immunities. *Conceder fueros,* to grant exemptions.

A charter granted to a city or town. Also designated as *"cartas pueblas."*

An act of donation made to an individual, a church, or convent, on certain conditions.

A declaration of a magistrate, in relation to taxation, fines, etc.

A charter granted by the sovereign, or those having authority from him, establishing the franchises of towns, cities, etc.

A place where justice is administered. A peculiar *forum,* before which a party is amenable.

The jurisdiction of a tribunal, which is entitled to take cognizance of a cause; as *fuero ecclesiastico, fuero militar.*

Fuero de castilla /fwérow ðè kastíy(ly)a/. The body of laws and customs which formerly governed the Castilians.

Fuero de correos y caminos /fwérow ðè koréyows ìy kamíynows/. A special tribunal taking cognizance of all matters relating to the post office and roads.

Fuero de guerra /fwérow ðè géra/. A special tribunal taking cognizance of all matters in relation to persons serving in the army.

Fuero de marina /fwérow ðè maríyna/. A special tribunal taking cognizance of all matters relating to the navy and to the persons employed therein.

Fuero municipal /fwérow muwnìysiypál/. The body of laws granted to a city or town for its government and the administration of justice.

Fuero viejo /fwérow v(i)yéyhow/. The title of a compilation of Spanish law, published about A.D. 992.

Fugacia /fyəgéysh(iy)ə/. A chase.

Fugam fecit /fyúwgəm fíysət/. Lat. He has made flight; he fled. A clause inserted in an inquisition, in old English law, meaning that a person indicted for treason or felony had fled. The effect of this was to make the party forfeit his goods absolutely, and the profits of his lands until he had been pardoned or acquitted.

Fugator /fyəgéydər/. In old English law, a privilege to hunt.

A driver. *Fugatores carrucarum,* drivers of wagons.

Fugitation /fyùwjətéyshən/. When a criminal does not obey the citation to answer, the court pronounces sentence of fugitation against him, which induces a forfeiture of goods and chattels to the crown.

Fugitive. One who flees; used in criminal law with the implication of a flight, evasion, or escape from arrest, prosecution, or imprisonment. See **Extradition; Fugitive from justice; Rendition.**

Fugitive Felon Act. A federal statute which makes it a felony to flee across the state line for the purpose of avoiding prosecution or confinement for a state felony or attempted felony, or to avoid giving testimony in a state felony case. 18 U.S.C.A. § 1073. See **Extradition.**

Fugitive from justice. A person who, having committed a crime, flees from jurisdiction of court where crime was committed or departs from his usual place of abode and conceals himself within the district. A person who, having committed or been charged with crime in one state, has left its jurisdiction and is found within territory of another state when it is sought to subject him to criminal process of former state. King v. Noe, 244 S.C. 344, 137 S.E.2d 102, 103. See also **Extradition; Rendition.**

Fugitive's goods. Under the old English law, where a man fled for felony, and escaped, his own goods were not forfeited as *bona fugitivorum* until it was found by proceedings of record (*e.g.* before the coroner in the case of death) that he fled for the felony.

Fugitive slave law. Acts of Congress passed in 1793 and 1850 (prior to abolition of slavery) providing for the surrender and deportation of slaves who escaped from their masters and fled into the territory of another state, generally a "free" state.

Fugitivus /fyùwjətáyvəs/. In the civil law, a fugitive; a runaway slave.

Fugue /fyúwg/. Period of memory loss during which subject functions almost as if normal, but concerning which he has no subsequent recollection. See **Automatism.**

Full. Abundantly provided, sufficient in quantity or degree, complete, entire, and detailed. Having no open space. Ample, perfect, mature, not wanting in any essential quality.

Full age. The age of legal majority; legal age.

Full answer. In pleading, a complete and meritorious answer, not wanting in any essential requisite. Frizell v. Northern Trust Co. of Chicago, Ill., 144 Kan. 481, 61 P.2d 1344, 1345, 1346.

Full blood. Relations of the "full blood," "whole blood," or "entire blood" are those derived not only from the same ancestor, but from the same couple of ancestors.

Full cash value. See **Fair market value.**

Full copy. In equity practice, a complete and unabbreviated transcript of a bill or other pleading, with all indorsements, and including a copy of all exhibits.

Full court. In practice, a court *en banc.* A court duly organized with all the judges present. Court containing permissible complement of judges, as distinguished from a quorum of two. Textile Mills Securities Corporation v. Commissioner of Internal Revenue, 314 U.S. 326, 62 S.Ct. 272, 277, 86 L.Ed. 249. See **En banc.**

Full cousin. Son or daughter of one's uncle or aunt.

Full covenants. See **Covenant.**

Full coverage. Type of insurance protection which covers all losses with no deductible amount and which covers to the full amount.

Full crew laws. Laws which regulate the number of railroad employees who are required to man trains.

Full defense. In common law pleading, the formula of defense in a plea, stated at length and without abbreviation, thus: "And the said C.D., by E.F., his attorney, comes and defends the force (or wrong) and injury when and where it shall behoove him, and the damages, and whatsoever else he ought to defend, and says," etc. Such technical pleading is no longer required under federal or state Rules of Civil Procedure.

Full disclosure. Term used in variety of legal contexts, *e.g.* a fiduciary who participates in a transaction for his own benefit is required to fully reveal the details of such. In consumer law, the obligation to reveal all details of a transaction to the consumer; *e.g.* federal and state Truth-in-Lending Acts. Also, federal election laws require candidates to make full disclosure of the extent and source of their campaign contributions. See also **Compulsory disclosure.**

Full faith and credit clause. The clause of the U.S. Constitution (Art. IV, Sec. 1) which provides that the various states must recognize legislative acts, public records, and judicial decisions of the other states within the United States. There are exceptions to this, a major one being that a state need not recognize a divorce decree of a state where neither spouse was a legal resident. Doctrine means that a state must accord the judgment of a court of another state the same credit that it is entitled to in the courts of that state. Morphet v. Morphet, 263 Or. 311, 502 P.2d 255, 260. A judgment or record shall have the

same faith, credit, conclusive effect, and obligatory force in other states as it has by law or usage in the state from whence taken. Christmas v. Russell, 72 U.S. (5 Wall.) 290, 18 L.Ed. 475; McElmoyle v. Cohen, 38 U.S. (13 Pet.) 312, 10 L.Ed. 177; Pennsylvania Fire Ins. Co. of Philadelphia v. Gold Issue Min. & Mill. Co., 243 U.S. 93, 37 S.Ct. 344, 61 L.Ed. 610. See also **Comity; Fauntleroy doctrine.**

Full hearing. Embraces not only the right to present evidence, but also a reasonable opportunity to know the claims of the opposing party, and to meet them. Morgan v. U. S., 304 U.S. 1, 58 S.Ct. 773, 776, 777, 82 L.Ed. 1129. One in which ample opportunity is afforded to all parties to make, by evidence and argument, a showing fairly adequate to establish the propriety or impropriety from the standpoint of justice and law of the step asked to be taken. Akron, C. & Y. Ry. Co. v. U. S., 261 U.S. 184, 43 S.Ct. 270, 67 L.Ed. 605; Boston & M. R. R. v. U. S., D.C.Mass., 208 F.Supp. 661, 669.

Full indorsement. See **Indorsement.**

Full jurisdiction. Complete jurisdiction over a given subject-matter or class of actions without any exceptions or reservations. See **Jurisdiction.**

Full life. Life in fact and in law. See **In full life.**

Full name. The first, middle and surname of a person, or the first name, middle initial and surname. May also refer to name under which a person is known in the community.

Full-paid stock. Stock on which no further payments can be demanded by the issuing company.

Full powers. A document issued by the government of a nation empowering its diplomatic agent to conduct special business with a foreign government.

Full proof. In the civil law, proof by two witnesses, or a public instrument. Evidence which satisfies the minds of the jury of the truth of the fact in dispute, to the entire exclusion of every reasonable doubt. See **Prima facie; Proof.**

Full right. The union of a good title with actual possession.

Full settlement. Implies an adjustment of all pending matters, the mutual release of all prior obligations existing between the parties. Hickox v. Hickox, Tex. Civ.App., 151 S.W.2d 913, 918.

Full value. See **Fair market value.**

Fully administered. The English equivalent of the Latin phrase *"plene administravit";* being a plea by an executor or administrator that he has completely and legally disposed of all the assets of the estate, and has nothing left out of which a new claim could be satisfied.

Fumage /fyúməj/. In old English law, the same as *fuage,* or smoke farthings. 1 Bl.Comm. 324. See **Fuage.**

Function. Derived from Latin "functus," the past participle of the verb "fungor" which means to perform, execute, administer. The nature and proper action of anything; activity appropriate to any business or profession. Rosenblum v. Anglim, D.C.Cal., 43 F.Supp. 889, 892. Office; duty; fulfillment of a definite end or set of ends by the correct adjustment of means. The occupation of an office. By the performance of its duties, the officer is said to fill his function. The proper activities or duties of municipality. Bean v. City of Knoxville, 180 Tenn. 448, 175 S.W.2d 954, 955.

Functional claim. One which claims function. In re Tucker, Cust. & Pat.App., 46 F.2d 214, 216. See **Claim.**

Functional depreciation. Such results from necessary replacement of equipment before it is worn out, by reason of invention and improved machinery, equipment, etc. which render more efficient and satisfactory service. See **Functional obsolescence.**

Functional disease. One which prevents, obstructs, or interferes with the due performance of its special functions by any organ of the body, without anatomical defect or abnormality in the organ itself. Distinguished from "organic" disease, which is due to some injury to, or lesion or malformation in, the organ in question.

Functional obsolescence. The need for replacement because a structure or equipment has become inefficient or out-moded because of improvements developed since its original construction or production. The loss of value due to inherent deficiencies within the property. Fisher-New Center Co. v. Michigan State Tax Commission, 380 Mich. 340, 157 N.W.2d 271, 279.

Functionary. A public officer or employee. An officer of a private corporation is also sometimes so called.

Functus officio /fǝ́ŋktǝs ǝfish(iy)ow/. Lat. A task performed. Board of School Trustees of Washington City Administrative Unit v. Benner, 222 N.C. 566, 24 S.E.2d 259, 263. Having fulfilled the function, discharged the office, or accomplished the purpose, and therefore of no further force or authority. Applied to an officer whose term has expired and who has consequently no further official authority; and also to an instrument, power, agency, etc., which has fulfilled the purpose of its creation, and is therefore of no further virtue or effect. Holmes v. Birmingham Transit Co., 270 Ala. 215, 116 So.2d 912, 919.

Fund. To capitalize with a view to the production of interest. Also, to put into the form of bonds, stocks, or other securities, bearing regular interest, and to provide or appropriate a fund or permanent revenue for the payment thereof. An asset or group of assets set aside for a specific purpose. To fund a debt is to pledge a specific fund to keep down the interest and reduce the principal.

A generic term and all-embracing as compared with term "money," etc., which is specific. A sum of money or other liquid assets set apart for a specific purpose, or available for the payment of debts or claims.

In the plural, this word has a variety of slightly different meanings, as follows: moneys and much more, such as notes, bills, checks, drafts, stocks and bonds, and in broader meaning may include property

of every kind. State v. Finney, 141 Kan. 12, 40 P.2d 411, 421. Money in hand, assets, cash, money available for the payment of a debt, legacy, etc. Corporate stocks or government securities; in this sense usually spoken of as the "funds." Assets, securities, bonds, or revenue of a state or government appropriated for the discharge of its debts. Generally, working capital; sometimes used to refer to cash or to cash and marketable securities.

See also Contingent fund; Current funds; Funded; Funding; General fund; Mutual fund; Revolving fund.

Funded debt. As applied to states or municipal corporations, a funded debt is one for the payment of which (interest and principal) some fund is appropriated, either specifically, or by provision made for future taxation and the *quasi* pledging in advance of the public revenue. As applied to the financial management of corporations (and sometimes of estates in course of administration or properties under receivership) funding means the borrowing of a sufficient sum of money to discharge a variety of floating or unsecured debts, or debts evidenced by notes or secured by bonds but maturing within a short time, and creating a new debt in lieu thereof, secured by a general mortgage, a series of bonds, or an issue of stock, generally maturing at a more remote period, and often at a lower rate of interest. The new debt thus substituted for the pre-existing debts is called the "funded debt." This term is very seldom applied to the debts of a private individual; but when so used it must be understood as referring to a debt embodied in securities of a permanent character and to the payment of which certain property has been applied or pledged. See also **Funded.**

Funding system. The practice of borrowing money to defray the expenses of government, and creating a "sinking fund," designed to keep down interest, and to effect the gradual reduction of the principal debt. See *Sinking fund,* infra.

General fund. This phrase, in many states, is a collective designation of all the assets of the state which furnish the means for the support of government and for defraying the discretionary appropriations of the legislature. Such are distinguished from assets of a special character, such as the school fund. See also **General fund.**

General revenue fund. As used in connection with municipal finances, term refers to the fund out of which the usual, ordinary, running, and incidental expenses of a municipality are paid.

No funds. This term denotes a lack of assets or money for a specific use. It is the return made by a bank to a check drawn upon it by a person who has no deposit to his credit there; also by an executor, trustee, etc., who has no assets for the specific purpose.

Public funds. An untechnical name for (1) the revenue or money of a government, state, or municipal corporation; (2) the bonds, stocks, or other securities of a national or state government. Money, warrants, or bonds, or other paper having a money value, and belonging to the state, or to any county, city, incorporated town or school district. The term applies to funds of every political subdivision of state wherein taxes are levied for public purposes. Ætna Casualty & Surety Co. v. Bramwell, D.C.Or., 12 F.2d 307, 309.

Revolving fund. Usually, a renewable credit over a defined period. In simple parlance it relates usually to a situation where a banker or merchant extends credit for a certain amount which can be paid off from time to time and then credit is again given not to exceed the same amount. It may also mean a fund, which, when reduced, is replenished by new funds from specified sources. Term may refer to a revolving charge account.

Sinking fund. The aggregate of sums of money (as those arising from particular taxes or sources of revenue) set apart and invested, usually at fixed intervals, for the extinguishment of the debt of a government or corporation, by the accumulation of interest. A fund arising from particular taxes, imposts, or duties, which is appropriated towards the payment of the interest due on a public loan and for the gradual payment of the principal. A fund created for extinguishing or paying a funded debt.

Sinking fund tax. A tax raised to be applied to the payment of interest on, and principal of public loan.

Fundamental error. See **Error; Plain error rule.**

Fundamental fairness doctrine. Due process of law as applied to judicial procedure. See **Due process of law.**

Fundamental law. The law which determines the constitution of government in a nation or state, and prescribes and regulates the manner of its exercise. The organic law of a nation or state; its constitution.

Fundamental rights. Those which have their origin in the express terms of the Constitution or which are necessarily to be implied from those terms. Sidle v. Majors, 264 Ind. 206, 341 N.E.2d 763, 769. See *e.g.* **Bill of rights.**

Fundamus /fəndéyməs/. We found. One of the words by which a corporation may be created in England. 1 Bl.Comm. 473.

Fundatio /fəndéysh(iy)ow/. Lat. A founding or foundation. Particularly applied to the creation and endowment of corporations. As applied to eleemosynary corporations such as colleges and hospitals, it is said that *"fundatio incipiens"* is the incorporation or grant of corporate powers, while *"fundatio perficiens"* is the endowment or grant or gift of funds or revenues. Dartmouth College v. Woodward, 17 U.S. (4 Wheat.) 518, 4 L.Ed. 629.

Fundator /fəndéydər/. A founder (*q.v.*).

Funded. Said of a pension plan or other obligation when funds have been set aside for meeting the obligation when it becomes due. See also **Fund** (*Funded debt*).

Funded pension plan. One containing sufficient funds as contributed by corporation to meet current and future retirement benefit obligations. The Employee Retirement Income Security Act (ERISA) regulates funding of pension plans.

Funding. Process of financing capital expenditures by issuing long term debt obligations or by converting short term obligations into long term obligations to finance current expenses. See also **Fund.**

Fundi patrimoniales /fənday pætrəməniyéyliyz/. Lands of inheritance.

Fundi publici /fənday páblǝsay/. Public lands.

Fundus /fəndəs/. In the civil and old English law, land; land or ground generally; land, without considering its specific use; land, including buildings generally; a farm.

Funeral expenses. Money expended in procuring the interment, cremation, or other disposition of a corpse, including suitable monument, perpetual care of burial lot and entertainment of those participating in wake.

Fungibiles res /fənjíbəliyz ríyz/. Lat. In the civil law, fungibile things. See that title.

Fungibles. Goods of which each particle is identical with every other particle, such as grain and oil. Mississippi State Tax Commission v. Columbia Gulf Transmission Co., 249 Miss. 88, 161 So.2d 173, 178. With respect to goods or securities, those of which any unit is, by nature or usage of trade, the equivalent of any other like unit. U.C.C. § 1–201(17); *e.g.,* a bushel of wheat or other grain.

Movable goods which may be estimated and replaced according to weight, measure, and number. Things belonging to a class, which do not have to be dealt with *in specie.*

Where a thing which is the subject of an obligation (which one man is bound to deliver to another) must be delivered *in specie,* the thing is not fungible; that very individual thing, and not another thing of the same or another class, in lieu of it, must be delivered. Where the subject of the obligation is a thing of a given class, the thing is said to be fungible; *i.e.,* the delivery of any object which answers to the generic description will satisfy the terms of the obligation.

Fur /fər/. Lat. A thief. One who stole secretly or without force or weapons, as opposed to robber.

Furandi animus /fyərǽnday ǽnəməs/. Lat. An intention of stealing.

Furca /fərkə/. In old English law, a fork. A gallows or gibbet.

Furca et flagellum /fərkə èt fləjéləm/. Gallows and whip. *Tenure ad furcam et flagellum,* tenure by gallows and whip. The meanest of servile tenures, where the bondman was at the disposal of his lord for life and limb.

Furca et fossa /fərkə èt fósə/. Gallows and pit, or pit and gallows. A term used in ancient charters to signify a jurisdiction of punishing thieves, viz., men by hanging, women by drowning.

Furian law /fyúriyən ló/. See **Lex Furia Caninia.**

Furigeldum /fyùrəjéldəm/. A fine or mulct paid for theft.

Furiosi nulla voluntas est /fyəriyówsay nálə vəlántæs ést/. A madman has no will.

Furlingus /fərlíŋgəs/. A furlong, or a furrow one-eighth part of a mile long.

Furlong. A measure of length, being forty poles, or one-eighth of a mile.

Furlough /fə́rlow/. A leave of absence. Smith v. Sovereign Camp, W. O. W., 204 S.C. 193, 28 S.E.2d 808, 811. A temporary leave of absence to one in the armed service of the country, or to a government official or an employee, indicating some voluntary act on part of employee as contrasted with the phrase "lay-off" which contemplates action by employer. Jones v. Metropolitan Life Ins. Co., 156 Pa.Super. 156, 39 A.2d 721, 725. Also the document granting leave of absence.

Fur manifestus /fə́r mænəféstəs/. In the civil law, a manifest thief. A thief who is taken in the very act of stealing.

Furnage. See **Fornagium; Four.**

Furnish. To supply, provide, or equip, for accomplishment of a particular purpose. As used in the liquor laws, "furnish" means to provide in any way, and includes giving as well as selling.

Furniture. This term includes that which furnishes, or with which anything is furnished or supplied; whatever must be supplied to a house, a room, place of business, or public building or the like, to make it habitable, convenient, or agreeable; goods, vessels, utensils, and other appendages necessary or convenient for housekeeping; whatever is added to the interior of a house or apartment, for use or convenience.

Furor brevis /fyúrər bríyvəs/. A sudden transport of passion.

Furor contrahi matrimonium non sinit, quia consensu opus est /fyúrər kəntréyhay mætrəmówn(i)yəm nòn sínət, kwáyə kənsénshuw ówpəs èst/. Insanity prevents marriage from being contracted, because consent is needed. 1 Bl.Comm. 439.

Furst and fondung. In old English law, time to advise or take counsel.

Furta /fə́rdə/. A right derived from the king as supreme lord of a state to try, condemn, and execute *thieves* and felons within certain bounds or districts of an honour, manor, etc.

Further. Not a word of strict legal or technical import, and may be used to introduce negation or qualification of some precedent matter, but generally when used as an adverb it is word of comparison, and means "additional," and is equivalent to "moreover, or furthermore, something beyond what has been said or likewise, or also." Wider, or fuller, or something new. Occasionally it may mean any, future, or other.

Further advance. A second or subsequent loan of money to a mortgagor by a mortgagee, either upon the same security as the original loan was advanced upon, or an additional security. Equity considers the arrears of interest on a mortgage security converted into principal, by agreement between the parties, as a further advance. See also **Future advance clause; Future advances.**

Furtherance. Act of furthering, helping forward, promotion, advancement, or progress. Maryland Casualty Co. v. Smith, Tex.Civ.App., 40 S.W.2d 913, 914.

Further assurance, covenant for. See **Covenant.**

Further hearing, or **further proceedings.** Hearing at another time; additional hearing; new trial; or other proceedings directed by appellate court. Not a new proceeding but rather a continuation of an existing proceeding.

Further instructions. Additional instructions given to jury after they have once been instructed and have retired. Such may be requested by jury during course of deliberations when, for example, the jury is uncertain as to the applicable law.

Further maintenance of action, plea to. A plea grounded upon some fact or facts which have arisen since the commencement of the suit, and which the defendant puts forward for the purpose of showing that the plaintiff should not further maintain his action. Such plea is obsolete under federal and state Rules of Civil Procedure.

Furtive /fə́rdəv/. Stealthily; by secret or stealth.

Furtum /fə́rdəm/. Lat. Theft. The fraudulent appropriation to one's self of the property of another, with an intention to commit theft without the consent of the owner. The thing which has been stolen.

Furtum conceptum /fə́rdəm kənséptəm/. In Roman law, the theft which was disclosed where, upon searching any one in the presence of witnesses in due form, the thing stolen was discovered in his possession.

Furtum est contrectatio rei alienæ fraudulenta, cum animo furandi, invito illo domino cujus res illa fuerat /fə́rdəm èst kòntrektéysh(iy)ow ríyay æliyíyniy fròdyuwléntə, kàm ǽnəmow f(y)ərǽnday, ənváydow ílow dómənow kyúwjəs ríyz ílə fyúwərət/. Theft is the fraudulent handling of another's property, with an intention of stealing, against the will of the proprietor, whose property it was.

Furtum manifestum /fə́rdəm mænəféstəm/. Open theft. Theft where a thief is caught with the property in his possession.

Furtum non est ubi initium habet detentionis per dominium rei /fə́rdəm nón èst yúwbay ənísh(iy)əm héybət dətènshiyównəs pàr dəmín(i)yəm ríyay/. There is no theft where the foundation of the detention is based upon ownership of the thing.

Furtum oblatum /fə́rdəm əbléydəm/. In the civil law, offered theft. *Oblatum furtum dicitur cum res furtiva ab aliquo tibi oblata sit, eaque apud te concepta sit.* Theft is called *"oblatum"* when a thing stolen is offered to you by any one, and found upon you.

Fuse plug levees. Under Mississippi Flood Control Act lower points for possible flood spillways were designated "fuse plug levees." U. S. v. Sponenbarger, Ark., 308 U.S. 256, 60 S.Ct. 225, 227, 84 L.Ed. 230.

Fust. See **Fuz.**

Fustigatio /fə̀stəgéysh(iy)ow/. In old English law, a beating with stick or clubs; one of the ancient kinds of punishment of malefactors.

Fustis /fə́stəs/. In old English law, a staff, used in making livery of seisin.

   A baton, club, or cudgel.

Futhwite, or **fithwite.** A fine for fighting or breaking the peace.

Future acquired property. See **After acquired property.**

Future advance clause. A clause in an open-end mortgage or deed of trust which allows the borrower to borrow additional sums at a future time, secured under the same instrument and by the same real property security.

Future advances. Money lent after a security interest has attached and secured by the original security agreement. U.C.C. § 9–204(5). See also **Further advance.**

Future damages. Those sums awarded to an injured party for, among other things, residuals or future effects of an injury which have reduced the capability of an individual to function as a whole man, future pain and suffering, loss or impairment of earning capacity, and future medical expenses. Jordan v. Bero, W.Va., 210 S.E.2d 618, 631.

Future earnings. Earnings which, if it had not been for injury, could have been made in future, but which were lost as result of injury. Nowlin v. Kansas City Public Service Co., Mo.App., 58 S.W.2d 324.

Future estate. See **Estate.**

Future goods. Goods which are not both existing and identified. A purported present sale of such goods operates as a contract to sell. U.C.C. § 2–105(2).

Future interests. Interests in land or other things in which the privilege of possession or of enjoyment is future and not present. Commissioner of Internal Revenue v. Wells, C.C.A.6, 132 F.2d 405, 407. An interest that will come into being at some future point in time. It is distinguished from a present interest which is already in existence. Assume, for example, that D transfers securities to a newly created trust. Under the terms of the trust instrument, income from the securities is to be paid each year to W for her life, with the securities passing to S upon her death. W has a present interest in the trust since she is currently entitled to receive the income from the securities. S has a future interest since he must wait for W's death to benefit from the trust.

Future performance. In contracts, execution which is due in the future; deferred performance.

Futures contract. A present right to receive at future date a specific quantity of given commodity for fixed price. Clayton Brokerage Co. of St. Louis, Inc. v. Mouer, Tex.Civ.App., 520 S.W.2d 802, 804. Commodity futures contracts are commitments to buy or sell commodities at a specified time and place in the future. The price is established when the contract is made in open auction on a futures exchange. Only a small percentage of futures trading actually leads to delivery of a commodity, for a contract may change hands or be liquidated before the delivery date. Participants fall into two categories: commercial hedgers who use futures to minimize price risks inherent in their marketing operations and speculators who, employing venture capital, seek profits through price changes. Both purchase contracts with only a small margin payment. Futures prices are an indication of the direction of prices based on current market conditions. Such exchanges and transactions are regulated by the federal Commodity Futures Trading Commission. See also **Option.**

Futures trading. The buying and selling of futures contracts, commonly in commodities. See **Futures contract.**

Futuri /f(y)əchúray/. Lat. Those who are to be. Part of the commencement of old deeds. *"Sciant præsentes et futuri, quod ego talis, dedi et concessi,"* etc. (Let all men now living and to come know that I, A. B., have, etc.).

Fuz, or **fust** /fə́st/. A Celtic word, meaning a wood or forest.

F.W.C. Free Woman of Color. Up to the time of Civil War, term applied to all persons not of the white race, including Indians.

Fyhtwite /fáytwət/. One of the fines incurred for homicide.

Fynderinga. (Sax.) An offense or trespass for which the fine or compensation was reserved to the king's pleasure. Its nature is not known.

Fyrd /fə́rd/. Sax. In Anglo-Saxon law, the military array or land force of the whole country. Contribution to the fyrd was one of the imposts forming the *trinoda necessitas.* (Also spelled "ferd" and "fird.")

Fyrdfare /fə́rdfèr/. A summoning forth to join a military expedition; a summons to join the *fyrd* or army.

Fyrdsocne or **fyrdsoken** /fə́rdsòwkən/. Exemption from military duty; exemption from service in the *fyrd.*

Fyrdwite /fə́rdwət/. A fine imposed for neglecting to join the *fyrd* when summoned. Also a fine imposed for murder committed in the army; also an acquittance of such fine.

G

GAAP. Generally accepted accounting principles.

GAAS. Generally accepted auditing standards.

Gabel /gəbél/. An excise; a tax on movables; a rent, custom, or service. A tax, impost, or excise duty, especially in continental Europe. Formerly, in France, such term referred specifically to the tax on salt, but also applied to taxes on other industrial products.

Land gabel. See **Land gabel.**

Gabella /gəbélə/. The Law Latin form of *"gabel,"* *(q.v.).* Also, in Teutonic and early English history, the peasantry constituting a village or hamlet; the holdings of such a group of freemen and serfs, or of either. The original significance of the word seems to be in its indication of a small rent-paying community, the rents being rendered in kind or in labor.

Gablatores /gæblətóriyz/. Persons who paid *gabel,* rent, or tribute.

Gablum /gǽbləm/. A rent; a tax.

Gabulus denariorum /gǽbyələs dənèriyórəm/. Rent paid in money.

Gadsden Purchase. A term commonly applied to the territory acquired by the United States from Mexico by treaty of December 30, 1853, known as the Gadsden Treaty.

Gafol /gǽvəl/. The same word as "gabel" or "gavel." Rent; tax; interest of money.

Gage, v. In old English law, to pawn or pledge; to give as security for a payment or performance; to wage or wager.

Gage, n. In old English law, a pawn or pledge; something deposited as security for the performance of some act or the payment of money, and to be forfeited on failure or non-performance.

A mortgage is a *dead-gage* or pledge; for, whatsoever profit it yields, it redeems not itself, unless the whole amount secured is paid at the appointed time.

In French law, the contract of pledge or pawn; also the article pawned.

Gager de deliverance /géyjər də dəlívərən(t)s/. In old English law, when he who has distrained, being sued, has not delivered the cattle distrained, then he shall not only avow the distress, but *gager deliverance, i.e.,* put in surety or pledge that he will deliver them.

Gager del ley /géyjər dèl léy/. Wager of law *(q.v.).*

Gag order. An unruly defendant at trial may constitutionally be bound and gagged to prevent further interruptions in the trial. Illinois v. Allen, 397 U.S. 337, 90 S.Ct. 1057, 25 L.Ed.2d 353. Term may also refer to an order by the court, in a trial with a great deal of notoriety, directed to attorneys and witnesses, to not discuss the case with reporters—such order being felt necessary to assure the defendant of a fair trial. Term may also refer to orders of the court directed to reporters to not report court proceedings, or certain aspects thereof. Such latter type orders have been struck down by the Supreme Court as being an unconstitutional obstruction of freedom of the press. See Nebraska Press Ass'n. v. Stuart, 427 U.S. 539, 96 S.Ct. 2791.

Gain. Profits; winnings; increment of value. Difference between receipts and expenditures; pecuniary gain. Difference between cost and sale price. Appreciation in value or worth of securities or property.

Excess of revenues over expenses from a specific transaction. Frequently used in the context of describing a transaction not part of a firm's typical, day-to-day operations.

"Gain derived from capital" is a gain, profit, or something of exchangeable value proceeding from the property, severed from the capital however invested, and received or drawn by claimant for his separate use, benefit, and disposal. Commissioner of Internal Revenue v. Simmons Gin Co., C.C.A.10, 43 F.2d 327, 328.

See also Acquire; Acquisition; Capital *(Capital gains);* Income; Profit; Return.

Gainage. At common law, the gain or profit of tilled or planted land, raised by cultivating it; and the draught, plow, and furniture for carrying on the work of tillage by the baser kind of *sokemen* or *villeins.*

Gainery. At common law, tillage, or the profit arising from it, or from the beasts employed therein.

Gainful. Profitable, advantageous, or lucrative.

Gainful employment or **occupation.** In general, any calling, occupation, profession or work which one may profitably pursue. Within disability clause of policy, term means ordinary employment of particular insured, or such other employment, if any, as insured may fairly be expected to follow. Mutual Life Ins. Co. of New York v. Barron, 198 Ga. 1, 30 S.E.2d 879, 882.

Gainor. In old English law, a sokeman; one who occupied or cultivated arable land.

Gaius, institutes of /ínstətyùwts əv géyəs/. See **Institutes.**

Gale. In English law, the payment of rent, tax, duty, or annuity. The right is a license or interest in the nature of real estate, conditional on the due payment of rent and observance of the obligations imposed on the galee. It follows the ordinary rules as to the devolution and conveyance of real estate. The galee pays the crown a rent known as a "galeage rent," "royalty," or some similar name, proportionate to the quantity of minerals taken from the mine or quarry.

Galea /gǽliyə/. In old records, a piratical vessel; a galley.

Gallon. A liquid measure containing 231 cubic inches, or four quarts; the standard gallon of the United States. The imperial gallon contains about 277, and the ale gallon 282, cubic inches. The metric equivalent is 3.785 liters.

Gallows. A scaffold; a beam laid over either one or two posts, from which persons sentenced to capital punishment are hanged.

Gamalis /gəméyləs/. A child born in lawful wedlock; also one born to betrothed but unmarried parents.

Gambler. One who follows or practices games of chance or skill, with the expectation and purpose of thereby winning money or other property. See **Gambling.**

Gambling. The dealing, operating, carrying on, conducting, maintaining or exposing for pay of any game. Making a bet. To plan, or game, for money or other stake; hence to stake money or other thing of value on an uncertain event. It involves, not only chance, but a hope of gaining something beyond the amount played. Gambling consists of a consideration, an element of chance, and a reward. In re Gaming Devices Seized at American Legion Post No. 109, 197 Pa.Super. 10, 176 A.2d 115, 122. The elements of gambling are payment of a price for a chance to win a prize. Boies v. Bartell, 82 Ariz. 217, 310 P.2d 834, 837. Gambling is regulated by state and federal statutes. See e.g. 18 U.S.C.A. §§ 1081 et seq., 1955. See also Bet; Bookmaking; Game of chance; Gaming; Lottery; Wager.

Gambling device. Such device, apparatus, and the like, as is used and employed for gambling, in the sense that in using it, money or the like is staked, wagered, won, or lost as a direct result of its employment or operation. A machine, implement, or contrivance of any kind for the playing of an unlawful game of chance or hazard. See **Slot machine.**

Gambling place. Any place, room, building, vehicle, tent or location which is used for any of the following: Making and settling bets; receiving, holding, recording or forwarding bets or offers to bet; conducting lotteries; or playing gambling devices.

Gambling policy. In life insurance, one issued to a person, as beneficiary, who has no pecuniary interest in the life insured. Otherwise called a "wager policy." Such policies are generally illegal or not otherwise written by insurance companies because of the absence of an insurable interest.

Game. Wild birds and beasts. The word includes all game birds, game fowl, and game animals. State ex rel. Sofeico v. Hefferman, 41 N.M. 219, 67 P.2d 240, 246. A sport, pastime or contest. A contrivance which has for its object to furnish sport, recreation, or amusement. Ex parte Williams, 127 Cal.App. 424, 16 P.2d 172, 173. See **Gaming.**

Game-keeper. One who has the care of keeping and preserving the game in a reserve, forest, or the like.

Game laws. Federal and state laws passed for the preservation of game, usually forbidding the killing and capturing of specified game during certain seasons, or by certain described means, or by restricting the number and type of game that may be killed or trapped in season. See 16 U.S.C.A. § 661 et seq., 18 U.S.C.A. § 41 et seq. See also **Lacey Act; Open season.**

Game of chance. One in which result as to success or failure depends less on skill and experience of player than on purely fortuitous or accidental circumstances incidental to game or manner of playing it or device or apparatus with which it is played, but not under control of player. Kansas City v. Caresio, Mo., 447 S.W.2d 535, 537. See also **Lottery.**

Gaming. The practice or act of gambling. An agreement between two or more persons to play together at a game of chance for a stake or wager which is to become the property of the winner, and to which all contribute. See **Gambling.**

Gaming contracts. See **Wager.**

Gaming device. See **Gambling device.**

Gaming house. See **Gambling place.**

Gananciales /gənànsiyáleys/. A Spanish term, used as either a noun or adjective, and applied to property acquired during marriage. Discussed in Sanchez v. Bowers, C.C.A.N.Y., 70 F.2d 715, 716. See **Ganancial property,** supra.

Ganancial property /gənǽnshəl própərdiy/. In Spanish law, a species of community in property enjoyed by husband and wife, the property being divisible between them equally on a dissolution of the marriage. See **Community property.**

Ganancias /gənansíyəs/. In Spanish law, gains or profits.

Gang. Any company of persons who go about together or act in concert; in modern use, mainly for criminal purposes.

Gangiatori /gǽnj(iy)ətóray/. Officers in ancient times whose business it was to examine weights and measures.

Gangster. A member of a gang of criminals, thieves, or the like.

Ganser syndrome /gánzər síndròwm/gǽn(t)sər°/. A setting in which questions are given nonsensical answers from which a hidden relevancy may be inferred. This is observed in prisoners who wish to gain leniency by simulating mental clouding.

Gantelope /gǽntlowp/góntlət/. (Pronounced "gaunt-lett".) A military punishment, in which the criminal running between the ranks receives a lash from each man. This was called "running the gauntlett."

GAO. General Accounting Office.

Gaol /jéy(ə)l/. A now obsolete term (of English origin) for a prison for temporary confinement; a jail; a place for the confinement of offenders against the law. As distinguished from "prison," it is said to be a place for temporary or provisional confinement, or for the punishment of the lighter offenses and misdemeanors. See also **Jail.**

Gaol delivery. In old criminal law, the delivery or clearing of a gaol of the prisoners confined therein, by trying them. Also, the clearing of a gaol by the escape of the prisoners. Such term is of English origin.

Gaoler /jéylər/. A variant of "jailer" (q.v.).

Gaol liberties, gaol limits /jéy(ə)l líbərdiyz/°límǝts/. A district around a gaol, defined by limits, within which prisoners are allowed to go at large on giving security to return. It is considered a part of the gaol.

Garandia, or **garantia** /gərǽndiyə/gərǽnsh(iy)ə/. A warranty.

Garantie /gárontíy/. In French law, this word corresponds to warranty or covenants for title in English law. In the case of a sale this *garantie* extends to two things: (1) Peaceful possession of the thing sold; and (2) absence of undisclosed defects (*défauts cachés*).

Garathinx /gǽrəθiŋks/. In old Lombardic law, a gift; a free or absolute gift; a gift of the whole of a thing.

Garauntor /gǽrəntər/. L. Fr. In old English law, a warrantor of land; a vouchee; one bound by a warranty to defend the title and seisin of his alienee, or, on default thereof, and on eviction of the tenant, to give him other lands of equal value.

Garba /gárbə/. In old English law, a bundle or sheaf. *Blada in garbis,* corn or grain in sheaves.

Garba sagittarum /gárbə sæjətérəm/. A sheaf of arrows, containing twenty-four. Otherwise called *"schaffa sagittarum."*

Garble. In English statutes, to sort or cull out the good from the bad in spices, drugs, etc.

Garbler of spices. An ancient officer in the city of London, who might enter into any shop, warehouse, etc., to view and search drugs and spices, and garble and make clean the same, or see that it be done.

Gard, or **garde.** L. Fr. Wardship; care; custody; also the ward of a city.

Gardein /gárdən/. A keeper; a guardian.

Garden. A small piece of land, appropriated to the cultivation of herbs, fruits, flowers, or vegetables.

Gardia /gárd(i)yə/. L. Fr. Custody; wardship.

Gardianus /gàrdiyéynəs/. In old English law, a guardian, defender, or protector. In feudal law, *gardio.* A warden. *Gardianus ecclesiæ,* a churchwarden.

Garene /gəríyn/. L. Fr. A warren; a privileged place for keeping animals.

Garnestura /gàrnəst(y)úrə/. In old English law, victuals, arms, and other implements of war, necessary for the defense of a town or castle.

Garnish, *n.* In English law, money paid by a prisoner to his fellow-prisoners on his entrance into prison.

Garnish, *v.* To warn or summon. To issue process of garnishment against a person.

Garnishee. One garnished; a person against whom process of garnishment is issued; one who has money or property in his possession belonging to a defendant, or who owes the defendant a debt, which money, property, or debt is attached. A person who owes a debt to a judgment debtor, or a person other than the judgment debtor who has property in his possession or custody in which a judgment debtor has an interest.

Garnishment. A statutory proceeding whereby person's property, money, or credits in possession or under control of, or owing by, another are applied to payment of former's debt to third person by proper statutory process against debtor and garnishee. Beggs v. Fite, 130 Tex. 46, 106 S.W.2d 1039, 1042. Satisfaction of an indebtedness out of property or credits of debtor in possession of, or owing by, a third person. Frank F. Fasi Supply Co. v. Wigwam Inv. Co., D.C.Hawaii, 308 F.Supp. 59, 61. An ancillary remedy in aid of execution to obtain payment of a judgment. First Nat. Bank in Chester v. Conner, Mo.App., 485 S.W.2d 667, 671. It is an incident to or an auxiliary of judgment rendered in principal action, and is resorted to as a means of obtaining satisfaction of judgment by reaching credits or property of judgment debtor.

Due process requirements of Fourteenth Amendment, U.S.Const., requires notice and an opportunity to be heard before pre-judgment garnishment of wages. Sniadach v. Family Finance Corp. of Bay View et al., 395 U.S. 337, 89 S.Ct. 1820, 23 L.Ed.2d 349. Garnishment is regulated by both state and federal (*e.g.* Consumer Credit Protection Act) statutes.

See also **Attachment execution.**

Garnistura /gàrnəst(y)úrə/. In old English law, garniture; whatever is necessary for the fortification of a city or camp, or for the ornament of a thing.

Garroting. A method of inflicting the death penalty on convicted criminals practiced in Spain, Portugal, and some Spanish-American countries, consisting in strangulation by means of an iron collar which is mechanically tightened about the neck of the sufferer, sometimes with the variation that a sharpened screw is made to advance from the back of the apparatus and pierce the base of the brain. Also, any form of strangling resorted to to overcome resistance or induce unconsciousness.

Garsumme /gársəm/. In old English law, an amerciament or fine.

Garter. The mark of the highest order of English knighthood, ranking next after the nobility. This military order of knighthood is said to have been first instituted by Richard I, at the siege of Acre, where he caused twenty-six knights who firmly stood by him to wear thongs of blue leather about their legs.

Garth. In English law, a yard; a little close or homestead in the north of England. A dam or wear in a river, for the catching of fish.

Gasoline tax. Excise imposed on sale of gasoline by both Federal and state governments.

Gas sold. Term used in leases of natural gas wells to describe gas which is actually sold to others and it does not necessarily include all gas used in production. Southland Royalty Co. v. Pan American Petro Corp., Tex., 378 S.W.2d 50.

Gastaldus /gəstǽldəs/. A temporary governor of the country. A bailiff or steward.

Gastine /gətíyn/. L. Fr. Waste or uncultivated ground.

Gas used. Term used in leases for natural gas to describe quantity of gas employed or consumed though not necessarily sold while operating a well. Southland Royalty Co. v. Pan American Petro Corp., Tex., 378 S.W.2d 50.

GATT. General Agreement on Tariffs and Trade. A multi-lateral international agreement that requires foreign products to be accorded no less favorable treatment under the laws than that accorded domestic products.

Gaudies /gódiyz/. A term used in the English universities to denote double commons.

Gaugeator /gəjiyéydər/. A gauger.

Gauger. In England, a surveying officer under the customs, excise, and internal revenue laws, appointed to examine all tuns, pipes, hogsheads, barrels and tierces of wine, oil, and other liquids, and to give them a mark of allowance, as containing lawful measure. There are also private gaugers in large seaport towns, who are licensed by government to perform the same duties.

Gaugetum /gəjíydəm/. A gauge or gauging; a measure of the contents of any vessel.

Gault, Application of. Landmark Supreme Court case guaranteeing to a defendant in a juvenile proceeding the right of confrontation, the privilege against self incrimination, prior notice of the complaint, and the right to counsel. Application of Gault, 387 U.S. 1, 87 S.Ct. 1428, 18 L.Ed.2d 527.

Gavel. In English law, custom; tribute; toll; yearly rent; payment of revenue; of which there were anciently several sorts; as *gavel-corn, gavel-malt, oat-gavel, gavel fodder*, etc.

Gavelbred. Rent reserved in bread, corn, or provision; rent payable in kind.

Gavelcester. A certain measure of rent-ale.

Gavelet /gǽvələt/. An obsolete English writ. An ancient and special kind of *cessavit*, used in Kent and London for the recovery of rent.

Gavelgeld /gǽvəlgèld/. That which yields annual profit or toll. The tribute or toll itself.

Gavelherte. A service of plowing performed by a customary tenant.

Gaveling men. Tenants who paid a reserved rent, besides some customary duties to be done by them.

Gavelkind. A species of socage tenure common in Kent, in England, where the lands descend to all the sons, or heirs of the nearest degree, together; may be disposed of by will; do not escheat for felony; may be aliened by the heir at the age of fifteen; and dower and curtesy is given of half the land.

Gavella /gəvélə/. See **Gabella**.

Gavel-man. A tenant liable to the payment of gavel or tribute.

Gavelmed /gǽvəlmìyd/. A customary service of mowing meadow-land or cutting grass (*consuetudo falcandi*).

Gavelrep /gǽvəlrìyp/. Bedreap or bidreap; the duty of reaping at the bid or command of the lord.

Gavelwerk /gǽvəlwèrk/. A customary service, either *manuopera*, by the person of the tenant, or *carropera*, by his carts or carriages.

Gazette /gəzét/. The official publication of the English government, also called the "London Gazette." It is evidence of acts of state, and of everything done by the Queen in her political capacity. Orders of adjudication in bankruptcy are required to be published therein; and the production of a copy of the "Gazette," containing a copy of the order of adjudication, is evidence of the fact, and of the date thereof.

See also **Official Gazette** (*Patent Office*).

Gdn. Equivalent to guardian.

Gebocced. An Anglo-Saxon term, meaning "conveyed."

Gebocian. In Saxon law, to convey; to transfer *boc* land (book-land or land held by charter). The grantor was said to *gebocian* the alienee.

Gebrauchsmuster /gəbráwksmùstər/. A patent, issued in accordance with law of Germany. Permutit Co. v. Graver Corporation, D.C.Ill., 37 F.2d 385, 390.

Gebur /gəbúr/. (Sax.) A boor. His services varied in different places—to work for his lord two or more days a week; to pay gafols in money, barley, etc.; to pay hearth money, etc. He was a tenant with a house and a yard land or virgate or two oxen.

Geburscript /gəbúrskrìpt/. In old English law, neighborhood or adjoining district.

Geburus /gəbúrəs/. In old English law, a country neighbor; an inhabitant of the same *geburscript*, or village.

Geld. In Saxon law, money or tribute. A mulct, compensation, value, price. *Angeld* was the single value of a thing; *twigeld*, double value, etc. So, *weregeld* was the value of a man slain; *orfgeld*, that of a beast. A land tax of so much per hide or carucate. The compensation for a crime.

Geldabilis /geldéybələs/. In old English law, taxable; geldable.

Geldable /géldəbəl/. Liable to pay geld; liable to be taxed.

Gelding. A horse that has been castrated, and which is thus distinguished from the horse in his natural and unaltered condition. A "ridgling" (a half-castrated horse) is not a gelding, but a horse, within the denomination of animals in the statutes.

Gelt. As a verb, an alternative form of the past tense of "geld," commonly "gelded." See **Gelding.** As a noun, used incorrectly for *geld (q.v.).*

Gemma /jémə/. Lat. In the civil law, a gem; a precious stone. Gems were distinguished by their transparency; such as emeralds, chrysolites, amethysts.

Gemot /gəmówt/. In Saxon law, a meeting or moot; a convention; a public assemblage. These were of several sorts, such as the *witena-gemot,* or meeting of the wise men; the *folc-gemot,* or general assembly of the people; the *shire-gemot,* or county court; the *burg-gemot,* or borough court; the *hundred-gemot,* or hundred court; the *hali-gemot,* or court-baron; the *hal-mote,* a convention of citizens in their public hall; the *holy-mote,* or holy court; the *swein-gemote,* or forest court; the *ward-mote,* or ward court.

Genealogy /jìyniyólǝjiy/. The summary history or table of a family, showing how the persons there named are connected together.

Genearch /jéniyàrk/. The head of a family.

Geneath /gǝníyθ/. In Saxon law, a villein, or agricultural tenant *(villanus villicus);* a hind or farmer *(firmarius rusticus).*

Gener /jénǝr/. Lat. In the civil law, a son-in-law; a daughter's husband.

General. From Latin word genus. It relates to the whole kind, class, or order. Leuthold v. Brandjord, 100 Mont. 96, 47 P.2d 41, 45. Pertaining to or designating the genus or class, as distinguished from that which characterizes the species or individual; universal, not particularized, as opposed to special; principal or central, as opposed to local; open or available to all, as opposed to select; obtaining commonly, or recognized universally, as opposed to particular; universal or unbounded, as opposed to limited; comprehending the whole or directed to the whole, as distinguished from anything applying to or designed for a portion only. Extensive or common to many.

As a noun, the word is the title of a principal officer in the army, usually one who commands a whole army, division, corps, or brigade. In the United States army, the rank of "general" is one of the highest, next to the commander in chief (*i.e.* President), and is only occasionally created. The officers next in rank are lieutenant general, major general, and brigadier general.

As to general Acceptance; Administration of estates; Agent; Appearance; Assignment; Average; Benefit; Challenge; Character; Charge; Covenant; Creditor; Customs; Damages; Demurrer; Denial; Deposit; Devise; Election; Finding; Franchise; Fund; Gaol delivery; Guaranty; Guardian; Imparlance; Insurance; Intent; Issue; Legacy; Letter of credit; Malice; Meeting; Monition; Mortgage; Occupant; Orders; Owner; Partnership; Power; Property; Replication; Restraint of trade; Retainer; Return day; Rule; Session; Ship; Statute; Tail; Tenancy; Term; Traverse; Usage; Verdict; Warrant; and Warranty, see those titles.

General Accounting Office. The General Accounting Office of the federal government has the following basic purposes: assist the Congress, its committees, and its members to carry out their legislative and oversight responsibilities, consistent with its role as an independent nonpolitical agency in the legislative branch; carry out legal, accounting, auditing, and claims settlement functions with respect to Federal Government programs and operations as assigned by the Congress; and make recommendations designed to make Government operations more efficient and effective. The GAO is under the control and direction of the Comptroller General of the United States and the Deputy Comptroller General of the United States, appointed by the President with the advice and consent of the Senate for a term of 15 years.

General agency business. One engaged in such general agency business is one not engaged as agent for single firm or person, but holding himself out to public as being engaged in business of being agent. Comer v. State Tax Commission of New Mexico, 41 N.M. 403, 69 P.2d 936, 939.

General appearance. Consent to the jurisdiction of the court and a waiver of all jurisdictional defects except the competency of the court. Johnson v. Zoning Bd. of Appeals of Town of Branford, 166 Conn. 102, 347 A.2d 53, 56. In a general appearance defendant submits his person to jurisdiction of court by appearing himself or by duly authorized representative. Buehne v. Buehne, 190 Kan. 666, 378 P.2d 159, 164. See also **Appearance.**

General assembly. Title of legislative body in many states. See also **Legislature.**

The policy making body of the United Nations. It is composed of from one to five delegates from each member nation, although each member nation has but one vote.

The highest "judicatory" of the Presbyterian church, representing in one body all of the particular churches of the denomination. Trustees of Pencader Presbyterian Church in Pencader Hundred v. Gibson, 26 Del.Ch. 375, 22 A.2d 782, 788.

General assignment for benefit of creditors. A transfer of legal and equitable title to all debtor's property to trustee, with authority to liquidate debtor's affairs and distribute proceeds equitably to creditors. Central Fibre Products Co. v. Hardin, C.C.A.Tex., 82 F.2d 692, 694. See also **Assignment** (*Assignment for benefit of creditors*).

General assumpsit /jén(ǝ)rǝl ǝsǝ́m(p)sǝt/. An action of assumpsit brought upon the promise or contract implied by law in certain cases. Holcomb v. Kentucky Union Co., 262 Ky. 192, 90 S.W.2d 25, 28.

General average. See **Average; General average contribution.**

General average bond. Type of bond required by master of ship as security for general average contribution before master delivers the cargo.

General average contribution. Contribution by all parties in sea adventure to make good loss sustained by one of their number on account of sacrifices voluntarily made of part of ship or cargo to save residue, or for extraordinary expenses necessarily incurred by one or more of parties for general benefit of all interests embarked in general enterprise. S. C. Loveland Co. v. U. S., D.C.Pa., 207 F.Supp. 450, 451.

General average loss. Loss at sea commonly sustained when cargo is thrown overboard to save ship. Such loss is generally shared by shipowner and owners of cargo. See **General average contribution; Jettison.**

General average statement. Statement of account and admission on shipowner's part as to amount due cargo owner.

General benefits. Such benefits in a condemnation case are those produced by the improvement which a property owner may enjoy in the future in common with all other property owners in the area, which benefits may not be considered to reduce the compensation due. State, by Com'r of Transp. v. Interpace Corp., 130 N.J.Super. 322, 327 A.2d 225, 229.

General bequest. One not segregated or withdrawn from estate under terms of will but to be paid in money or property as latter directs. Gift payable out of general assets of estate, not amounting to a bequest of particular thing or money. Feder v. Weissman, 81 Nev. 668, 409 P.2d 251, 252.

General building scheme. One under which owner of large tract of land divides it into building lots, to be sold to different persons for separate occupancy by deeds which contain uniform covenants restricting the use which the several grantees may make of their premises. Besch v. Hyman, 221 App.Div. 455, 223 N.Y.S. 231, 233.

General circulation. That of a general newspaper only, as distinguished from one of a special or limited character. It is not determined by number of subscribers but by the diversity of subscribers and general nature of subject matter.

General contractor. One who contracts for the construction of an entire building or project, rather than for a portion of the work. The general contractor hires subcontractors (*e.g.* plumbing, electrical, etc.), coordinates all work, and is responsible for payment to subcontractors. Also called "prime" contractor.

General Court. The name given to the legislature of Massachusetts and of New Hampshire, in colonial times, and subsequently by their constitutions; so called because the colonial legislature of Massachusetts grew out of the general court or meeting of the Massachusetts Company.

General court martial. See **Court-Martial.**

General credit. The character of a witness as one generally worthy of credit. A distinction is sometimes made between this and "particular credit," which may be affected by proof of particular facts relating to the particular action. See also **General reputation.**

General debt. Debt of a governmental unit legally payable from general revenues and backed by the full faith and credit of the governmental unit.

General denial. See **General plea.**

Generale /jènəréyliy/. The usual commons in a religious house, distinguished from *pietantiœ*, which on extraordinary occasions were allowed beyond the commons.

Generale dictum generaliter est interpretandum /jènəréyliy díktəm jènəréylədər èst intàrprətǽndəm/. A general expression is to be interpreted generally.

General election. An election held in the state at large. A regularly recurring election to select officers to serve after the expiration of the full terms of their predecessors. See also **Election.**

Generale nihil certum implicat /jènəréyliy náy(h)əl sárdəm ímpləkət/. A general expression implies nothing certain. A general recital in a deed has not the effect of an estoppel.

General estate. Customarily, the entire estate held by a person in his individual capacity.

Generale tantum valet in generalibus, quantum singulare in singulis /jènəréyliy tǽntəm véyləd in jènəréyləbəs, kwóntəm sìngyəlériy in síngyələs/. What is general is of as much force among general things as what is particular is among things particular.

General exception. General exception is an objection to a pleading, or any part thereof, for want of substance, while a special exception is an objection to the form in which a cause of action is stated. Exception taken at trial of case in which the exceptor does not specify the grounds or limitations of his objection. See also **Demurrer.**

General execution. A writ commanding an officer to satisfy a judgment out of any personal property of the defendant. If authorizing him to levy only on certain specified property, the writ is sometimes called a "special" execution.

General executor. One whose power is not limited either territorially or as to the duration or subject of his trust. One who is to have charge of the whole estate, wherever found, and administer it to a final settlement.

General fee conditional. A grant to a person and heirs of his body. Blume v. Pearcy, 204 S.C. 409, 29 S.E.2d 673, 674.

General field. Several distinct lots or pieces of land inclosed and fenced in as one common field.

General fund. Assets and liabilities of a nonprofit entity not specifically earmarked for other purposes. The primary operating fund of a governmental unit. See also **Fund.**

Generalia præcedunt, specialia sequuntur /jènəréyliyə prìysíydənt spèshiyéyliyə səkwántər/. Things general precede, things special follow.

Generalia specialibus non derogant /jènəréyliyə spèshiyéyləbəs nòn dérəgənt/. General words do not derogate from special.

Generalia sunt præponenda singularibus /jènəréyliyə sànt prìpənéndə singyəlérəbəs/. General things are to precede particular things.

Generalia verba sunt generaliter intelligenda /jènəréyliyə várbə sànt jènəréylədər intèləjéndə/. General words are to be understood generally, or in a general sense.

Generalibus specialia derogant /jènəréyləbəs spes(h)iyéyl(i)yə dérəgənt/. Special things take from generals.

General improvement. Exists where primary purpose and effect of improvement is to benefit public generally, though it may incidentally benefit property owners in particular locality.

General Inclosure Act. The English statute, 41 Geo. III, c. 109, which consolidated a number of regulations as to the inclosure of common fields and waste lands.

General indorsement. See **Indorsement.**

General intangibles. Any personal property (including things in action) other than goods, accounts, contract rights, chattel paper, documents and instruments. U.C.C. § 9–106.

General interest. In regard to admissibility of hearsay evidence, a distinction is sometimes made between "public" and "general" interest, the term "public" being strictly applied to that which concerns every member of the state, and the term "general" being confined to a lesser, though still a considerable, portion of the community.

Generalis clausula non porrigitur ad ea quæ antea specialiter sunt comprehensa /jènəréyləs klózyələ nòn pəríjədər æd íyə kwìy æntiyə spèshiyéylədər sànt kòmprəhén(t)sə/. A general clause does not extend to those things which are previously provided for specially. Therefore, where a deed at the first contains special words, and afterwards concludes in general words, both words, as well general as special, shall stand.

Generalis regula generaliter est intelligenda /jènəréyləs régyələ jènəréylədər èst intèləjéndə/. A general rule is to be understood generally.

General jurisdiction. Such as extends to all controversies that may be brought before a court within the legal bounds of rights and remedies; as opposed to *special* or *limited* jurisdiction, which covers only a particular class of cases, or cases where the amount in controversy is below a prescribed sum, or which is subject to specific exceptions. The terms "general" and "special," applied to jurisdiction, indicate the difference between a legal authority extending to the whole of a particular subject and one limited to a part; and, when applied to the terms of court, the occasion upon which these powers can be respectively exercised. See also **Jurisdiction.**

General Land Office. Formerly an office of the United States government, being a division of the Department of the Interior, having charge of all executive action relating to the public lands, including their survey, sale or other disposition, and patenting; originally constituted by Act of Congress in 1812. The General Land Office and the U.S. Grazing Service were consolidated into the Bureau of Land Management under the Department of the Interior by 1946 Reorganization Plan No. 3, § 403. See **Bureau of Land Management.**

General law. A law that affects the community at large. A general law as contradistinguished from one that is special or local, is a law that embraces a class of subjects or places, and does not omit any subject or place naturally belonging to such class. A law, framed in general terms, restricted to no locality, and operating equally upon all of a group of objects, which, having regard to the purposes of the legislation, are distinguished by characteristics sufficiently marked and important to make them a class by themselves, is not a special or local law, but a general law. A law that relates to a subject of a general nature, or that affects all people of state, or all of a particular class, while one relating to particular persons or things of a class is a "special law". Albuquerque Metropolitan Arroyo Flood Control Authority v. Swinburne, 74 N.M. 487, 394 P.2d 998, 1000.

General lien. A general lien is a right to detain a chattel, etc., until payment be made, not only of any debt due in respect of the particular chattel, but of any balance that may be due on general account in the same line of business.

Generally Accepted Accounting Principles (GAAP). The conventions, rules and procedures necessary to define accepted accounting practices at a particular time; includes both broad and specific guidelines. The source of such principles is the Financial Accounting Standards Board.

Generally Accepted Auditing Standards. The standards, as opposed to particular procedures, promulgated by the AICPA which concern the auditor's professional qualities and the judgment exercised by him in the performance of his examination and in his report.

General manager. One having general direction and control of corporation's affairs, and who may do everything which corporation could do in transaction of its business. Continental Supply Co. v. Forrest E. Gilmore Co. of Texas, Tex.Civ.App., 55 S.W.2d 622. A manager for all general purposes of the corporation.

General partner. One of two or more persons who associate to carry on business as co-owners for profit and who are personally liable for all debts of the partnership. Uniform Partnership Act, § 6(1), (15). To be contrasted with "limited" partner. See **Partner.**

General plea. Type of pleading such as a general denial which controverts *all* of the averments of the preceding pleading (*e.g.* of the complaint). See Fed.R. Civil P. 8(b).

General power of appointment. One exercisable in favor of any person the donee may select. Johnstone v. Commissioner of Internal Revenue, C.C.A.9, 76 F.2d 55, 57.

General reputation. In evidence, testimony concerning the repute in which a person is held in the community; *e.g.* peaceable, law abiding citizen.

Criminal defendant may show his good character by proof of his "real character", that is, those peculiar qualities which individual is supposed to possess and which distinguish him from others and denote what a man really is, not what he is reputed to be, or by proof of his "general reputation" which is based on speech of his associates and is sum of opinions generally entertained concerning what is reputed or understood to be the estimate of person's character in community in which he moves or resides. State v. Hobbs, Iowa, 172 N.W.2d 268, 271.

See **Character; Reputation.**

General Services Administration. Federal agency created to manage government property and records. The GSA supervises construction and operation of buildings, procurement and distribution of supplies, disposal of surplus property, traffic and communications facilities, stockpiling of strategic and critical materials, and management of automatic data processing resources program.

General taxes. Those imposed by and paid to state which return taxpayer no special benefit other than the protection afforded him and his property by government, and promotion of programs which have for their benefit the welfare of all. A tax, imposed solely or primarily for purpose of raising revenue and merely granting person taxed right to conduct business or profession.

General welfare. General term used to describe the government's concern for the health, peace, morals, and safety of its citizens.

General welfare clause. The provision of the U.S. Constitution (Art. I, Sec. 8, Cl. 1) which declares that Congress may tax and pay debts in order to provide for the "general welfare of the United States."

General words. Such words of a descriptive character as are used in conveyances in order to convey, not only the specific property described but also all kinds of easements, privileges, and appurtenances which may possibly belong to the property conveyed. Such words are in general unnecessary; but are properly used when there are any easements or privileges reputed to belong to the property not legally appurtenant to it.

Generatio /jènəréysh(iy)ow/. The issue or offspring of a mother-monastery.

Generation. May mean either a degree of removal in computing descents, or a single succession of living beings in natural descent. Average span of time between birth of parents and that of their offspring. Group of people born and living contemporaneously.

Generation-skipping tax. The transfer tax imposed upon a generation-skipping trust. A transfer which bypasses a generation younger than the transferor and, therefore, avoids the imposition of one transfer tax. For example, a grandmother gives property to her grandchildren. By by-passing the children, a transfer tax is avoided. If the property had been given to the children and they later pass it (by gift or death) to the grandchildren, no generation skipping takes place. A generation-skipping tax may be imposed if the generation-skipping approach utilizes the trust device. See **Generation-skipping trust.**

Generation-skipping trust. A trust which skips a transfer tax on a generation of beneficiaries younger than the grantor of the trust. In the classic situation, D creates a trust with income payable to his children for life and remainder to the grandchildren upon the death of the children. Until the Tax Reform Act of 1976 enacted new Code §§ 2601–2603 and 2611–2614, there was no transfer tax imposed upon the death of D's children. Thus, one generation (*i.e.*, D's children) was able to avoid both the gift and death tax when the trust property passed to the grandchildren. Under the new law, barring certain exceptions, the trust must pay a transfer tax on the death of the children as if the trust corpus had been included in their gross estates. See **Deemed transferor.**

Generic. Relating to or characteristic of a whole group or class; general, as opposed to specific or special.

Generic name. The "established name" of a drug; its chemical name, a common name, or an official name used in an official compendium. Abbott Laboratories v. Celebrezze, C.A.Del., 352 F.2d 286, 287. See also **Name.**

Generosa /jènərówsə/. Gentlewoman.

Generosi filius /jènərówsay fíliyəs/. The son of a gentleman. Generally abbreviated *"gen. fil."*

Generosus /jènərówsəs/. Lat. Gentleman; a gentleman.

Geneva Convention. An international agreement for the conduct of nations at war drafted in 1864 and ratified by nearly every country. It provides, among other things, that a belligerent shall give proper care to enemy sick or wounded, that the Red Cross shall be the emblem of the sanitary service; and that hospitals and ambulances with their personnel shall be respected and protected. Revisions have brought the convention into accord with newer scientific discoveries and methods of warfare.

Geniculum /jəníkyələm/. A degree of consanguinity.

Genoese lottery /jènowíyz lódəriy/. Also known as the "numerical" lottery. As distinguished from the "class" lottery (see the title **Dutch lottery**), it is a scheme by which, out of 90 consecutive numbers, five are to be selected or drawn by lot. The players have fixed on certain numbers, wagering that one, two, or more of them will be drawn among the five, or that they will appear in a certain order.

Gens /jén(d)z/. Lat. In Roman law, a tribe or clan; a group of families, connected by common descent and bearing the same name, being all free-born and of free ancestors, and in possession of full civic rights.

Gens de justice /zhón(d)z də justíys/. In French law, officers of a court.

Gentes /jéntiyz/. Lat. People. *Contra omnes gentes,* against all people. Words used in the clause of warranty in old deed.

Gentiles /jèntáyliyz/. In Roman law, the members of a *gens* or common tribe.

Gentleman. In its English origin, this term formerly referred to a man of noble or gentle birth; one belonging to the landed gentry; a man of independent means; all above the rank of Yeomen.

Gentlemen's agreement. Generally an unsigned and unenforceable agreement made between parties who expect its performance because of good faith.

Genuine. As applied to notes, bonds, and other written instruments, this term means that they are truly what they purport to be, and that they are not false, forged, fictitious, simulated, spurious, or counterfeit. U.C.C. § 1–201(18).

Genuine issue. Genuine issues which will preclude entry of summary judgment are issues which can be sustained by substantial evidence. Riss & Co. v. Association of Am. Railroads, D.C.D.C., 190 F.Supp. 10, 17. As used in rule that burden of proving absence of material fact so that no "genuine issue" is left for jury determination is on movant for summary judgment, means a real as opposed to a false or colorable issue. Byrd v. Leach, Fla.App., 226 So.2d 866, 868. A "genuine issue of fact" precluding summary judgment exists whenever there is slightest doubt as to facts. Seliga Shoe Stores, Inc. v. City of Maplewood, Mo.App., 558 S.W.2d 328, 331. See Fed. R.Civil P. 56(c).

Genus /jíynəs/. In the civil law, a general class or division, comprising several species. *In toto jure generi per speciem derogatur, et illud potissimum habetur quod ad speciem directum est,* throughout the law, the species takes from the genus, and that is most particularly regarded which refers to the species.

A man's lineage, or direct descendants.

In logic, it is the first of the universal ideas, and is when the idea is so common that it extends to other ideas which are also universal; *e.g.,* incorporeal hereditament is *genus* with respect to a *rent,* which is *species.*

George-noble. An English gold coin, value 6s. 8d.

Gerechtsbode /gərék(t)sbòwd(ə)/. In old New York law, a court messenger or constable.

Gerefa /gəríyfə/. In Saxon law, greve, reve, or reeve; a ministerial officer of high antiquity in England; answering to the *grave* or *graf (grafio)* of the early continental nations. The term was applied to various grades of officers, from the *scyre-gerefa, shire-grefe,* or *shire-reve,* who had charge of the county (and, whose title and office have been perpetuated in the modern "sheriff"), down to the *tungerefa,* or town-reve, and lower.

Gerens /jéhrən(d)z/. Bearing. *Gerens datum,* bearing date.

German. Whole, full, or own, in respect to relationship or descent. Brothers-german, as opposed to half-brothers, are those who have both the same father and mother. Cousins-german are "first" cousins; that is, children of brothers or sisters.

Germane /jərméyn/. In close relationship, appropriate, relative, pertinent. State ex rel. Riley v. District Court of Second Judicial Dist. in and for Silver Bow County, 103 Mont. 576, 64 P.2d 115, 119.

Germanus /jərméynəs/. Lat. Descended of the same stock, or from the same couple of ancestors; of the whole or full blood.

Gerontocomi /jèhrəntəkówmay/. In the civil law, officers appointed to manage hospitals for the aged poor.

Gerontocomium /jèhrəntəkówmiyəm/. In the civil law, an institution or hospital for taking care of the old.

Gerrymander /jéhriymændər/géhr°/. A name given to the process of dividing a state or other territory into the authorized civil or political divisions, but with such a geographical arrangement as to accomplish an ulterior or unlawful purpose, as, for instance, to secure a majority for a given political party in districts where the result would be otherwise if they were divided according to obvious natural lines.

Gersumarius /jərsəmériyəs/. In old English law, finable; liable to be amerced at the discretion of the lord of a manor.

Gersume /gérsəm/. In old English law, expense; reward; compensation; wealth. It is also used for a fine or compensation for an offense.

Gest. In Saxon law, a guest. A name given to a stranger on the *second night* of his entertainment in another's house. *Twanight gest.*

Gestation. The time during which a woman carries a fetus in her womb, from conception to birth. But, as used in medical authorities, this phrase does not mean the actual number of days from conception to birth. Dazey v. Dazey, 50 Cal.App.2d 15, 122 P.2d 308, 309.

Gestio /jés(h)ch(iy)ow/. In the civil law, behavior or conduct. Management or transaction. *Negotiorum gestio,* the doing of another's business; an interference in the affairs of another in his absence, from benevolence or friendship, and without authority.

Gestio pro hærede /jés(h)ch(iy)ow pròw həríydiy/. Behavior as heir. This expression was used in the Roman law, and adopted in the civil law and Scotch law, to denote conduct on the part of a person appointed heir to a deceased person, or otherwise entitled to succeed as heir, which indicates an intention to enter upon the inheritance, and to hold himself out as heir to creditors of the deceased; as by receiving the rents due to the deceased, or by taking possession of his title-deeds, etc. Such acts will render the heir liable to the debts of his ancestor.

Gestor /jéstòr/. In the civil law, one who acts for another, or transacts another's business.

Gestu et fama /jést(y)uw èt féymə/. An ancient and obsolete writ resorted to when a person's good behavior was impeached.

Gestum /jéstəm/. Lat. In Roman law, a deed or act; a thing done. Some writers affected to make a distinction between *"gestum"* and *"factum."* But the best authorities pronounced this subtile and indefensible.

Gesture. Motion of the body calculated to express a thought or used for emphasis. An act used as a sign of feeling, such as a gesture of friendship.

Get. To receive; gain possession of; obtain; to prevail or have influence on.

Under Hebraic law, evidence of the granting of a divorce. A bill of divorce among the Jews which is drawn in the Aramaic language, uniformly worded and carefully written by a proper scribe, and after proper ceremonies and questionings by the rabbi, especially as to whether both parties agree to the divorce, the husband hands to the wife in the presence of ten witnesses.

Gewineda /gəwínədə/. In Saxon law, the ancient convention of the people to decide a cause.

Gewitnessa /gəwítnəsə/. In Saxon and old English law, the giving of evidence.

Gewrite /gəráydiy/. In Saxon law, deeds or charters; writings.

Gibbet. A gallows; the post on which malefactors are hanged, or on which their bodies are exposed. It differs from a common gallows, in that it consists of one perpendicular post, from the top of which proceeds one arm, except it be a double gibbet, which is formed in the shape of the Roman capital T.

Gibbet law. Lynch law; in particular a custom anciently prevailing in the parish of Halifax, England, by which the free burghers held a summary trial of any one accused of petit larceny, and, if they found him guilty, ordered him to be decapitated.

Gideon v. Wainwright. Landmark Supreme Court decision which held that provision guaranteeing a criminal defendant the assistance of counsel under the Sixth Amendment, U.S.Const., is binding on the states in state proceedings through the due process provision of the Fourteenth Amendment. 372 U.S. 335, 83 S.Ct. 792, 9 L.Ed.2d 799. See also **Counsel, right to.**

Gift. A voluntary transfer of property to another made gratuitously and without consideration. Bradley v. Bradley, Tex.Civ.App., 540 S.W.2d 504, 511. Essential requisites of "gift" are capacity of donor, intention of donor to make gift, completed delivery to or for donee, and acceptance of gift by donee.

In tax law, a payment is a gift if it is made without conditions, from detached and disinterested generosity, out of affection, respect, charity or like impulses, and not from the constraining force of any moral or legal duty or from the incentive of anticipated benefits of an economic nature.

An *absolute gift,* or gift inter vivos, as distinguished from a testamentary gift, or one made in contemplation of death, is one by which the donee becomes in the lifetime of the donor the absolute owner of the thing given, whereas a *donatio mortis causa* leaves the whole title in the donor, unless the event occurs (the death of the donor) which is to divest him.

The only important difference between a "gift" and a "voluntary trust" is that in the case of a gift the thing itself passes to the donee, while in the case of a trust the actual, beneficial, or equitable title passes to the cestui que trust, while the legal title is transferred

to a third person, or retained by the person creating it. In re Alberts' Estate, 38 Cal.App.2d 42, 100 P.2d 538, 540.

In old English law, a conveyance of lands in tail; a conveyance of an estate tail in which the operative words are "I give," or "I have given." 2 Bl.Comm. 316.

See also Anatomical gift; Annual exclusion; Endowment; Symbolic delivery; Taxable gift; Vested gift.

Antenuptial gift. Voluntary transfer of property before a marriage from one spouse to another, commonly made in exchange for a waiver of rights to property after the marriage.

Class gift. See **Gift to a class.**

Gift in contemplation of death. In taxation, a gift made by donor within three years of his death is considered part of his gross estate for estate tax purposes. I.R.C. § 2035(b).

More broadly, a gift by a donor immediately before his death while he has knowledge of his impending death. See also **Gift causa mortis.**

Testamentary gift. Voluntary transfer of property to take effect upon the death of the donor.

Gift causa mortis /gíft kózə mórdəs/. A gift of personal property made in expectation of donor's death and on condition that donor die as anticipated. Antos v. Bocek, 9 Ariz.App. 368, 452 P.2d 533, 534. A "gift causa mortis" is effected only if the following conditions are met: the donor must be stricken with some disorder which makes death imminent, death of donor must ensue as a result of the disorder existing at time the gift was made without any intervening perfect recovery, gift must have been made to take effect only in event of donor's death by his existing disorder, and there must have been an actual delivery of the subject of the donation to the donee. In re Vardalos' Estate, 24 Ill.App.3d 520, 320 N.E.2d 568, 571. See also **Gift** *(Gift in contemplation of death), supra.*

Gift deed. A deed for a nominal sum or for love and affection. Bertelsen v. Bertelson, 49 Cal.App.2d 479, 122 P.2d 130, 133.

Gift enterprise. A scheme for the division or distribution of articles to be determined by chance amongst those who have taken shares in the scheme. A sporting artifice by which, for example, a merchant or tradesman sells his wares for their market value, but, by way of inducement, gives to such purchaser a ticket which entitles him to a chance to win certain prizes to be determined after the manner of a lottery.

Gift inter vivos /gíft íntər váyvows/. Gifts between the living, which are perfected and become absolute during lifetime of donor and donee. Neal v. Neal, 194 Ark. 226, 106 S.W.2d 595, 600. An immediate, voluntary, and gratuitous transfer of personalty by one to another. Tilton v. Mullen, 101 Ohio App. 129, 137 N.E.2d 125, 128, 130. The essentials of an inter vivos gift are; (1) donative intention; (2) delivery to donee; in the case of a chose in action not capable of delivery, the donor must during his lifetime strip himself of all dominion over the thing taken; (3) acceptance by donee. In re Posey's Estate, 89 N.J. Super. 293, 214 A.2d 713, 719.

Gift in trust. Gift made in such manner that the donee acquires legal title for the beneficial enjoyment of the cestui que trust.

Gift over. A gift to one for life, and from and after his death to another. Broadly, any transfer of property to take effect after the termination of an intermediate estate or estates such as a life estate, *e.g.* to A for life, remainder to B.

Gift splitting. Under this tax provision when a married man gives away his property, he may, if his spouse consents, treat the gift as though he had given away half of the property and his spouse had given away the other half. The net effect of the privilege of splitting gifts, which is optional and not mandatory, is to double the gift tax exclusions and exemptions, and by treating the gift as a gift by each spouse of half of the amount actually given away to cause the gift to be taxed in a lower bracket. I.R.C. § 2513.

Gifts to Minors Act. A Uniform Act adopted by most states providing for a means of transferring property (usually stocks and bonds) to a minor. The designated custodian of the property has the legal right to act on behalf of the minor without the necessity of a guardianship. Generally, the custodian possesses the right to change investments (*e.g.,* sell one type of stock and buy another), apply the income from the custodial property to the minor's support, and even terminate the custodianship. In this regard, however, the custodian is acting in a fiduciary capacity on behalf of the minor. The custodian could not, for example, appropriate the property for his or her own use because it belongs to the minor. During the period of the custodianship, the income from the property is taxed to the minor. The custodianship terminates when the minor reaches legal age. One of the primary reasons for making gifts to minors pursuant to the requirements of the Uniform Act is to receive favorable tax treatment.

Gift tax. A tax imposed on the transfer of property by gift. Such tax is imposed upon the donor of a gift and is based on the fair market value of the property on the date of the gift. See also **Tax.**

Gift to a class. A gift of aggregate sum to body of persons uncertain in number at time of gift, to be ascertained at future time, who are all to take in equal shares, or some other definite proportion; share of each being dependent for its amount upon ultimate number taking. See also **Class gift.**

Gild. In Saxon law, a tax or tribute.

A fine, mulct, or amerciament; a satisfaction or compensation for an injury.

In old English law, a fraternity, society, or company of persons combined together, under certain regulations, and with the king's license, and so called because its expenses were defrayed by the *contributions* (*geld, gild*) of its members. In other words, a corporation; called, in Latin, "*societas,*" "*collegium,*" "*fratria,*" "*fraternitas,*" "*sodalitium,*" "*adunatio;*" and, in foreign law, "*gildonia.*" There were various kinds of these gilds, as merchant or commercial gilds, religious gilds, and others. See **Gilda mercatoria; Guild.**

A friborg, or decennary; called, by the Saxons, "*gyldscipes,*" and its members, "*gildones*" and "*congildones.*"

Gildable /gíldəbəl/. In old English law, taxable, tributary, or contributory; liable to pay tax or tribute.

Gilda mercatoria /gíldə mə̀rkətóriyə/. In old English law, a gild merchant, or merchant gild; a gild, corporation, or company of merchants.

Gild-hall. See **Guildhall.**

Gildo /gíldow/. In Saxon law, members of a *gild* or decennary. Oftener spelled "congildo."

Gild-rent. In old English law, certain payments made to the crown from any gild or fraternity.

Gill. A measure of capacity, equal to one-fourth of a pint.

Gilour /gáylər/. L. Fr. A cheat or deceiver. Applied in Britton to those who sold false or spurious things for good, as pewter for silver or laten for gold.

Gilt edge. As applied to commercial paper, a colloquialism, meaning of the best quality or highest price, first class; but not implying that a note which is not gilt edge is not collectible, or that the maker is irresponsible. Also, a bond or other security issue with the highest rating (*i.e.* highest investment quality).

Ginnie Mae. Government National Mortgage Association.

Girante /jirántey/. An Italian word, which signifies the drawer of a bill. It is derived from "*girare,*" to draw.

Girth. In Saxon and old English law, a measure of length, equal to one yard, derived from the girth or circumference of a man's body.

Gisement /jáyzmənt/. L. Fr. Agistment; cattle taken in to graze at a certain price; also the money received for grazing cattle.

Giser /jáyzər/. L. Fr. To lie. *Gist en le bouche,* it lies in the mouth. *Le action bien gist,* the action well lies. *Gisant,* lying.

Gisetaker /jáyztèykər/. An agister; a person who takes cattle to graze.

Gisle /gáyzəl/. In Saxon law, a pledge. *Fredgisle,* a pledge of peace. *Gislebert,* an illustrious pledge.

Gist /jíst/. In common law pleading, the essential ground or object of the action in point of law, without which there would be no cause of action. The cause for which an action will lie or the ground or foundation of a suit without which it would not be maintainable; the essential ground or object of the suit without which there is no cause of action. This term is no longer used in those states that have adopted Rules of Civil Procedure, nor in the federal courts.

Give. To transfer ownership or possession without compensation. To bestow upon another gratuitously or without consideration. See also **Gift.**

Give and bequeath. These words, in a will, import a benefit in point of right, to take effect upon the decease of the testator and proof of the will, unless it is made in terms to depend upon some contingency or condition precedent.

Give bail. To furnish or post bail or security for one's appearance. See **Bail.**

Give color. To admit an apparent or colorable right in the opposite party. In common law pleading, a plea of confession and avoidance had to give color to the affirmative averments of the complaint, or it would be fatally defective. The "giving color" was simply the absence of any denials, and the express or silent admission that the declaration, as far as it went, told the truth. See **Color.**

Give judgment. To render, pronounce, or declare the judgment of the court in an action at law; not spoken of a judgment obtained by confession.

Give notice. To communicate to another, in any proper or permissible legal manner, information or warning of an existing fact or state of facts or (more usually) of some intended future action; *e.g.* tenant giving landlord thirty day notice of termination of tenancy; employee giving employer two weeks notice of intention to quit; to give notice of appeal to appellee. See also **Notice.**

Giver. A donor; he who makes a gift.

Give time. Extending the period at which, by the contract between them, the principal debtor was originally liable to pay the creditor. Buffalo Forge Co. v. Fidelity & Casualty Co. of New York, 142 Misc. 647, 256 N.Y.S. 329, 334.

Give way. In the rules of navigation, one vessel is said to "give way" to another when she deviates from her course in such a manner and to such an extent as to allow the other to pass without altering her course.

Giving in payment. In Louisiana law, a phrase (translating the Fr. "*dation en paiement*") which signifies the delivery and acceptance of real or personal property in satisfaction of a debt, instead of a payment in money. Civil Code La. art. 265.

Gladius /glǽdiyəs/. Lat. A sword. An ancient emblem of defense. Hence the ancient earls or *comites* (the king's attendants, advisers, and associates in his government) were made by being girt with swords (*gladio succincti*).

The emblem of the executory power of the law in punishing crimes. 4 Bl.Comm. 177.

In old Latin authors, and in the Norman laws, this word was used to signify supreme jurisdiction (*jus gladii*).

Glaive /gléyv/. A sword, lance, or horseman's staff. One of the weapons allowed in a trial by combat.

Gleaning. The gathering of grain after reapers, or of grain left ungathered by reapers. Held not to be a right at common law.

Glebæ ascriptitii /glíybiy æskriptíshiyay/. In old English law, villein-socmen, who could not be removed from the land while they did the service due.

Glebe /glíyb/. In Ecclesiastical law, the land possessed as part of the endowment or revenue of a church or ecclesiastical benefice.

In Roman law, a clod; turf; soil. Hence, the soil of an inheritance; an agrarian estate. *Servi addicti glebæ* were serfs attached to and passing with the estate.

Gliscywa. In Saxon law, a fraternity.

Glos /glós/. Lat. In the civil law, a husband's sister.

Gloss. An interpretation, consisting of one or more words, interlinear or marginal; an annotation, explanation, or comment on any passage in the text of a work, for purposes of elucidation or amplification.

Glossa /glósə/. Lat. A gloss, explanation, or interpretation.

The *glossæ* of the Roman law are brief illustrative comments or annotations on the text of Justinian's collections, made by the professors who taught or lectured on them about the twelfth century (especially at the law school of Bologna), and were hence called "*glossators.*" These glosses were at first inserted in the text with the words to which they referred, and were called "*glossæ interlineares;*" but afterwards they were placed in the margin, partly at the side, and partly under the text, and called "*glossæ marginales.*" A selection of them was made by Accursius, between A.D. 1220 and 1260, under the title of "*glossa Ordinaria,*" which is of the greatest authority.

Glossator /gloséydər/. In the civil law, a commentator or annotator. A term applied to the professors and teachers of the Roman law in the twelfth century, at the head of whom was Irnerius.

Glossa viperina est quæ corrodit viscera textus /glósə vàypəráynə èst kwíy kərówdət vísərə tékstəs/. It is a poisonous gloss which corrupts the essence of the text.

Gloucester, Statute of /stǽchuwd əv glóstər/. The English statute of 6 Edw. I, c. 1, A.D. 1278. It takes its name from the place of its enactment, and was the first statute giving costs in actions.

Gloves /glávz/. In England, it was an ancient custom on a maiden assize, when there was no offender to be tried, for the sheriff to present the judge with a pair of white gloves. It was an immemorial custom to remove the glove from the right hand on taking oath.

Glove silver. In old English law, extraordinary rewards formerly given to officers of courts, etc.; money formerly given by the sheriff of a county in which no offenders are left for execution to the clerk of assize and judges' officers.

G.N.M.A. Government National Mortgage Association (Ginnie Mae).

GNP. Gross National Product.

Go. To be dismissed from a court. To issue from a court. "The court said a *mandamus* must *go.*"

Go bail. To assume the responsibility of a surety on a bail-bond.

God and my country. The answer formerly made by a prisoner, when arraigned, in answer to the question, "How will you be tried?" In the ancient practice he had the choice (as appears by the question) whether to submit to the trial by ordeal (by God) or to be tried by a jury (by the country); and it is probable that the original form of the answer was, "By God *or* my country," whereby the prisoner averred his innocence by declining neither of the modes of trial.

God-bote. An ecclesiastical or church fine paid for crimes and offenses committed against God.

God-gild. That which is offered to God or his service.

God's penny. In old English law, earnest-money; money given as evidence of the completion of a bargain. This name is probably derived from the fact that such money was given to the church or distributed in alms.

Go fifty-fifty. Division into halves of something under discussion by the parties at the time. Boyer v. Bowles, 310 Mass. 134, 37 N.E.2d 489, 493.

Go hence. To depart from the court; with the further implication that a suitor who is directed to "go hence" is dismissed from further attendance upon the court in respect to the suit or proceeding which brought him there, and that he is finally denied the relief which he sought, or, as the case may be, absolved from the liability sought to be imposed upon him.

Going. In various compound phrases (as those which follow) this term implies either motion, progress, active operation, or present and continuous validity and efficacy.

Going and coming rule. Under this rule, employees who suffer injuries while going to and returning from work are generally excluded from the benefits of the Worker's Compensation Act. Wiley Mfg. Co. v. Wilson, 30 Md.App. 87, 351 A.2d 487, 490. Under the "going and coming" rule, an employee who is going to or coming from work is generally not, during such times, considered to be acting in the course or scope of his employment for purpose of applying the doctrine of respondeat superior. Sherar v. B and E Convalescent Center, 49 C.A.3d 227, 122 Cal.Rptr. 505, 506.

Going before the wind. In the language of mariners and in the rules of navigation, a vessel is said to be going "before the wind" when the wind is free as respects her course, that is, comes from behind the vessel or over the stern, so that her yards may be braced square across. She is said to be "going off large" when she has the wind free on either tack, that is, when it blows from some point abaft the beam or from the quarter.

Going concern. An enterprise which is being carried on as a whole, and with some particular object in view. The term refers to an existing solvent business, which is being conducted in the usual and ordinary way for which it was organized. When applied to a corporation, it means that it continues to transact its ordinary business. A firm or corporation which, though financially embarrassed, continues to transact its ordinary business. City and County of Denver v. Denver Union Water Co., 246 U.S. 178, 38 S.Ct. 278, 62 L.Ed. 649.

Going concern value. The value which inheres in a plant where its business is established, as distinguished from one which has yet to establish its business. East Bay Water Co. v. McLaughlin, D.C.Cal., 24 F.Supp. 222, 226. The value of the assets of a business as a going, active concern, rather than merely as items of property which would be the case in a liquidation sale. Such value includes goodwill.

Going into effect of act. Becoming operative as a law. State ex rel. Bishop v. Board of Education of Mt. Orab Village School Dist., Brown County, 139 Ohio St. 427, 40 N.E.2d 913, 919.

Going off large. See **Going before the wind.**

Going price. The prevalent market price; the current market value of the article in question at the time and place of sale. See **Fair market value.**

Going private. Causing of a class of equity securities to be delisted from a national securities exchange or the causing of a class of equity securities which is authorized to be quoted in an inter-dealer quotation system of a registered national securities exchange to cease to be so authorized. Nearly all attempts to go private utilize variations of one or more of a limited number of basic techniques. These include (in probable order of frequency): (1) A cash tender offer by the issuer, its management or an affiliated entity; (2) a merger or consolidation of the issuer with, or the sale of its assets to, another corporation controlled by management of the issuer; (3) an exchange offer (almost always involving a debt security) by the issuer, its management or an affiliated entity; and (4) a reverse stock split.

Going public. Term used to describe the process by which a corporation issues its first stock for public purchase. Also, when a private corporation becomes a public corporation. Said of a business when its shares become traded to the general public, rather than being closely held by relatively few stockholders.

Going through the bar. The act of the chief of an English common-law court in demanding of every member of the bar, in order of seniority, if he has anything to move. This was done at the sitting of the court each day in term, except special paper days, crown paper days in the queen's bench, and revenue paper days in the exchequer. On the last day of term this order is reversed, the first and second time round. In the exchequer the postman and tubman are first called on.

Going to the country. When a party, under the common-law system of pleading, finished his pleading by the words "and of this he puts himself upon the country," this was called "going to the country." It was the essential termination of a pleading which took issue upon a material fact in the preceding pleading.

Going value. See **Going concern value.**

Going witness. One who is about to take his departure from the jurisdiction of the court, although only into a state or country under the general sovereignty; as from one to another of the United States.

Gold bond. One payable in gold coin or its equivalent, which means any money acceptable to United States government in payment of debts due it.

Gold clause. Provision formerly found in contracts, bonds and mortgages calling for payment in gold, though such clause is void today. Norman v. Baltimore & Ohio R. Co., 294 U.S. 240, 55 S.Ct. 407, 79 L.Ed. 885.

Golden Rule argument. "Golden Rule" type of argument, by which jurors are urged to place themselves or members of their families or friends in place of person who has been offended and to render verdict as if they or either of them or member of their families or friends was similarly situated, is improper in both civil and criminal cases. Lycans v. Com., Ky., 562 S.W.2d 303.

Goldsmiths' notes. Bankers' cash notes (*i.e.*, promissory notes given by a banker to his customers as acknowledgments of the receipt of money) were originally called in London "goldsmiths' notes," from the circumstance that all the banking business in England was originally transacted by goldsmiths.

Gold standard. A monetary system in which every form of currency is convertible on demand into its legal equivalent in gold or gold coin. The United States adopted the gold standard in 1900 and terminated it in 1934.

Goldwit. A mulct or fine in gold.

Gomashtah /gəmáshtə/. In Hindu law, an agent; a steward; a confidential factor; a representative.

Good. Valid; sufficient in law; effectual; unobjectionable; sound; responsible; solvent; able to pay an amount specified.

Of a value corresponding with its terms; collectible. A note is said to be "good" when the payment of it at maturity may be relied on.

Good abearing. See **Abearance.**

Good and clear record title, free from all incumbrances. A title which on the record itself can be again sold as free from obvious defects and substantial doubts, and differs from a "good, marketable title," which is an actual title, but which may be established by evidence independently of the record.

Good and valid. Reliable, sufficient, and unimpeachable in law; adequate; responsible.

Good and workmanlike manner. In a manner generally considered skillful by those capable of judging such work in the community of the performance.

Good behavior. Orderly and lawful conduct; behavior such as is proper for a peaceable and law-abiding citizen. "Good behavior," as used in an order suspending sentence upon a defendant during good behavior, means merely conduct conformable to law, or to the particular law theretofore breached.

Under some state penal systems, each day of "good behavior" by a prisoner reduces his or her sentence by one day. See also **Goodtime allowance.**

Good cause. Substantial reason, one that affords a legal excuse. Legally sufficient ground or reason. Phrase "good cause" depends upon circumstances of individual case, and finding of its existence lies largely in discretion of officer or court to which decision is committed. Wilson v. Morris, Mo., 369 S.W.2d 402, 407. "Good cause" is a relative and highly abstract term, and its meaning must be determined not only by verbal context of statute in which term is employed but also by context of action and procedures involved in type of case presented. Wray v. Folsom,

D.C.Ark., 166 F.Supp. 390, 394, 395. See also **Probable cause.**

Discovery. "Good cause" for discovery is present if information sought is material to moving party's trial preparation. Daniels v. Allen Industries, Inc., 391 Mich. 398, 216 N.W.2d 762, 766. "Good cause" requirement for discovery and production of documents is ordinarily satisfied by a factual allegation showing that requested documents are necessary to establishment of the movant's claim or that denial of production would cause moving party hardship or injustice. Black v. Sheraton Corp. of America, D.C.D.C., 47 F.R.D. 263, 273. Under a 1970 amendment to Fed.R. Civil P. 34, however, "good cause" is no longer required to be shown for production of documents and things. Federal Rule 35(a) does, however, require that "good cause" be shown for order requiring physical or mental examination, as does Rule 26(c) for protective orders to restrict scope of discovery.

Quitting employment. "Good cause" for leaving one's employment is such good cause as would compel a reasonably prudent person to quit under similar circumstances. Chamblee v. Employment Division, Or.App., 541 P.2d 165, 167.

Unemployment compensation. "Good cause" within statute denying unemployment compensation benefits if claimant has refused without good cause to accept an offer of suitable work is that cause that to an ordinary intelligent man is a justifiable reason for doing or not doing a certain particular thing. Wallace v. Bureau of Unemployment Compensation, Ohio Com.Pl., 160 N.E.2d 580, 582.

Good character. Sum or totality of virtues of a person which generally forms the basis for one's reputation in the community, though his reputation is distinct from his character. See **Character; Reputation.**

Good conduct. See **Certificate of good conduct.**

Good consideration. Any benefit conferred, or agreed to be conferred, upon the promisor, by any other person, to which the promisor is not lawfully entitled, or any prejudice suffered, or agreed to be suffered, by such person, other than such as he is at the time of consent lawfully bound to suffer, as an inducement to the promisor, is a good consideration for a promise. That consideration or detriment which the law considers valid and to this extent "good" does not refer to moral goodness. See **Consideration.**

Good faith. Good faith is an intangible and abstract quality with no technical meaning or statutory definition, and it encompasses, among other things, an honest belief, the absence of malice and the absence of design to defraud or to seek an unconscionable advantage, and an individual's personal good faith is concept of his own mind and inner spirit and, therefore, may not conclusively be determined by his protestations alone. Doyle v. Gordon, 158 N.Y.S.2d 248, 259, 260. Honesty of intention, and freedom from knowledge of circumstances which ought to put the holder upon inquiry. An honest intention to abstain from taking any unconscientious advantage of another, even through technicalities of law, together with absence of all information, notice, or benefit or belief of facts which render transaction unconscientious. In common usage this term is ordinarily used to describe that state of mind denoting honesty of purpose, freedom from intention to defraud, and, generally speaking, means being faithful to one's duty or obligation. Efron v. Kalmanovitz, 249 Cal.App. 187, 57 Cal.Rptr. 248, 251. See **Bona fide.**

Commercial law. Honesty in fact in the conduct or transaction concerned. U.C.C. § 1–201(19). In the case of a merchant, honesty in fact and the observance of reasonable commercial standards of fair dealing in the trade. U.C.C. § 2–103(1)(b).

Good faith purchaser. Those who buy without notice of circumstances which would put a person of ordinary prudence on inquiry as to the title of seller.

Good health. Good health, as employed in insurance contract, ordinarily means a reasonably good state of health. It means that the applicant has no grave, important, or serious disease, and is free from any ailment that seriously affects the general soundness and healthfulness of the system. A mere temporary indisposition not tending to weaken or undermine constitution does not render a person in "bad health". It does not mean a condition of perfect health.

Good jury. A jury of which the members are selected from the list of special jurors.

Good, merchantable abstract of title. An abstract showing a good title, clear from incumbrances, and not merely an abstract of matters of record affecting the title, made by one engaged in the business of making abstracts in such form as is customary, as passing current among persons buying and selling real estate and examining titles. See also **Marketable title.**

Good order. Goods or property are in "good order" when they are in acceptable condition under all the circumstances. See **Merchantability.**

Good record title. A "good record title," without words of limitation, means that the proper records shall show an unincumbered, fee-simple title, the legal estate in fee, free and clear of all valid claims, liens, and incumbrances. See also **Marketable title.**

Good repute. An expression, synonymous with and meaning only "of good reputation." See **Reputation.**

Goodright, goodtitle. The fictitious plaintiff in the old action of ejectment, most frequently called "John Doe," was sometimes called "Goodright" or "Goodtitle."

Goods. A term of variable content and meaning. It may include every species of personal property or it may be given a very restricted meaning.

Items of merchandise, supplies, raw materials, or finished goods. Sometimes the meaning of "goods" is extended to include all tangible items, as in the phrase "goods and services."

All things (including specially manufactured goods) which are movable at the time of identification to the contract for sale other than the money in which the price is to be paid, investment securities and things in action. Also includes the unborn of animals and growing crops and other identified things attached to realty as fixtures. U.C.C. § 2–105(1). All things treated as movable for the purposes of a contract of storage or transportation. U.C.C. § 7–102(1)(f).

As used with reference to collateral for security interest, goods include all things which are movable at the time the security interest attaches or which are fixtures. Section 9–105(1)(h) of the 1972 U.C.C.; § 9–105(1)(f) of the 1962 U.C.C.

See also **Confusion of goods; Future goods; Identification of goods.**

Capital goods. The equipment and machinery used in production of other goods or services.

Consumer goods. Goods which are used or bought for use primarily for personal, family or household purposes. U.C.C. § 9–109(1). See also **Consumer goods.**

Durable goods. Goods which have a reasonably long life and which are not generally consumed in use; *e.g.* refrigerator.

Fungible goods. Goods, every unit of which is similar to every other unit in the mass; *e.g.* uniform goods such as coffee, grain, etc. U.C.C. § 1–201.

Hard goods. Consumer durable goods. See *Durable goods, supra.*

Soft goods. Generally consumer goods such as wearing apparel, curtains, etc., in contrast to hard goods.

Good Samaritan doctrine. One who sees a person in imminent and serious peril through negligence of another cannot be charged with contributory negligence, as a matter of law, in risking his own life or serious injury in attempting to effect a rescue, provided the attempt is not recklessly or rashly made. Jobst v. Butler Well Servicing, Inc., 190 Kan. 86, 372 P.2d 55, 59. Under doctrine, negligence of a volunteer rescuer must worsen position of person in distress before liability will be imposed. U. S. v. DeVane, C.A.Fla., 306 F.2d 182, 186. This protection from liability is provided by statute in most states.

Goods and chattels. This phrase is a general denomination of personal property, as distinguished from real property. In the law of wills, the term "goods and chattels" will, unless restrained by the context, pass all the personal estate.

Goods sold and delivered. A phrase frequently used in the action of *assumpsit,* when the sale and delivery of goods furnish the cause.

Goods, wares, and merchandise. A general and comprehensive designation of such chattels and goods as are ordinarily the subject of traffic and sale. The phrase is used in the statute of frauds, and is sometimes found in pleadings and other instruments.

Goodtime allowance. "Good time" is awarded for good conduct and reduces period of sentence which prisoner must spend in prison although it does not reduce the period of the sentence itself. Carothers v. Follette, D.C.N.Y., 314 F.Supp. 1014, 1026, 1027. Credit allowed on the sentence which is given for satisfactory conduct in prison. Introduced as an incentive for inmates, it has become practically automatically awarded. It may reduce the minimum or maximum sentence or both. See also **Good behavior.**

Good title. One free from reasonable doubt, that is, not only a valid title in fact, but one that can again be sold to a reasonable purchaser or mortgaged to a person of reasonable prudence. MacGowan v. Gaines, 127 Vt. 477, 253 A.2d 121, 123. A title free from litigation, palpable defects and grave doubts. See also **Marketable title.**

Good will. The favor which the management of a business wins from the public. Seneca Hotel Co. v. U. S., Ct.Cl., 42 F.2d 343, 344. The fixed and favorable consideration of customers arising from established and well-conducted business. Colton v. Duvall, 254 Mich. 346, 237 N.W. 48, 49. The favorable consideration shown by the purchasing public to goods known to emanate from a particular source. White Tower System v. White Castle System of Eating Houses Corporation, C.C.A.Mich., 90 F.2d 67, 69. Good will is an intangible asset. Something in business which gives reasonable expectancy of preference in race of competition. In re Witkind's Estate, 167 Misc. 885, 4 N.Y.S.2d 933, 947. The custom or patronage of any established trade or business; the benefit or advantage of having established a business and secured its patronage by the public. The advantage or benefit which is acquired by an establishment, beyond the mere value of the capital, stocks, funds, or property employed therein, in consequence of the general public patronage and encouragement which it receives from constant or habitual customers, on account of its local position, or common celebrity, or reputation for skill or affluence or punctuality, or from other accidental circumstances or necessities, or even from ancient partialities or prejudices. And as property incident to business sold, favor vendor has won from public, and probability that all customers will continue their patronage. It means every advantage, every positive advantage, that has been acquired by a proprietor in carrying on his business, whether connected with the premises in which the business is conducted, or with the name under which it is managed, or with any other matter carrying with it the benefit of the business.

The excess of cost of an acquired firm or operating unit over the current or fair market value of net assets of the acquired unit. Informally used to indicate the value of good customer relations, high employee morale, a well-respected business name, etc. which are expected to result in greater than normal earning power.

The ability of a business to generate income in excess of a normal rate on assets due to superior managerial skills, market position, new product technology, etc. In the purchase of a business, good will represents the difference between the purchase price and the value of the net assets. Good will is an intangible asset which possesses an indefinite life and cannot, therefore, be amortized for Federal income tax purposes.

Gore. In old English law, a small, narrow slip of ground. In modern land law, a small triangular piece of land, such as may be left between surveys which do not close. In some of the New England states (as Maine and Vermont) the term is applied to a subdivision of a county, having a scanty population and for that reason not organized as a town.

Gossipred /gósəprèd/. In canon law, compaternity; spiritual affinity.

Go to. In a statute, will, or other instrument, a direction that property shall "go to" a designated person means that it shall pass or proceed to such person, vest in and belong to him.

Go to protest. Commercial paper is said to "go to protest" when it is dishonored by non-payment or non-acceptance. See also **Protest.**

Govern. To direct and control the actions or conduct of, either by established laws or by arbitrary will; to direct and control, rule, or regulate, by authority. To be a rule, precedent, law or deciding principle for.

Governing body. Governing body of institution, organization or territory means that body which has ultimate power to determine its policies and control its activities. Student Bar Ass'n Bd. of Governors of School of Law, University of North Carolina at Chapel Hill v. Byrd, N.C., 239 S.E.2d 415, 421.

Government. From the Latin *gubernaculum.* Signifies the instrument, the helm, whereby the ship to which the state was compared, was guided on its course by the "gubernator" or helmsman, and in that view, the government is but an agency of the state, distinguished as it must be in accurate thought from its scheme and machinery of government.

In the United States, government consists of the executive, legislative, and judicial branches in addition to administrative agencies. In a broader sense, includes the federal government and all its agencies and bureaus, state and county governments, and city and township governments.

The system of polity in a state; that form of fundamental rules and principles by which a nation or state is governed, or by which individual members of a body politic are to regulate their social actions. A constitution, either written or unwritten, by which the rights and duties of citizens and public officers are prescribed and defined, as a monarchical government, a republican government, etc. The sovereign or supreme power in a state or nation. The machinery by which the sovereign power in a state expresses its will and exercises its functions; or the framework of political institutions, departments, and offices, by means of which the executive, judicial, legislative, and administrative business of the state is carried on.

The whole class or body of officeholders or functionaries considered in the aggregate, upon whom devolves the executive, judicial, legislative, and administrative business of the state.

In a colloquial sense, the United States or its representatives, considered as the prosecutor in a criminal action; as in the phrase, "the government objects to the witness."

The regulation, restraint, supervision, or control which is exercised upon the individual members of an organized jural society by those invested with authority; or the *act* of exercising supreme political power or control.

See also **De facto government; Federal government; Judiciary; Legislature; Seat of government.**

Federal government. The government of the United States of America, as distinguished from the governments of the several states.

Local government. The government or administration of a particular locality; especially, the governmental authority of a municipal corporation, as a city or county, over its local and individual affairs, exercised in virtue of power delegated to it for that purpose by the general government of the state or nation.

Mixed government. A form of government combining some of the features of two or all of the three primary forms, viz., monarchy, aristocracy, and democracy.

Republican government. One in which the powers of sovereignty are vested in the people and are exercised by the people, either directly, or through representatives chosen by the people, to whom those powers are specially delegated. In re Duncan, 139 U.S. 449, 11 S.Ct. 573, 35 L.Ed. 219; Minor v. Happersett, 88 U.S. (21 Wall.) 162, 22 L.Ed. 627.

Governmental. Of, pertaining to, or proceeding from government.

Governmental act. An act in exercise of police power or in exercise of constitutional, legislative, administrative, or judicial powers conferred on federal, state or local government for benefit of public. A step physically taken by persons capable of exercising the sovereign authority of the foreign nation. Banco de Espana v. Federal Reserve Bank of New York, C.C.A. N.Y., 114 F.2d 438, 444. Any action of the federal government, or of a state, within its constitutional power. Graves v. People of State of New York ex rel. O'Keefe, N.Y., 306 U.S. 466, 59 S.Ct. 595, 596, 83 L.Ed. 927. See also **Governmental activity; Governmental functions.**

Governmental activity. A function of government in providing for its own support or in providing services to the public; *e.g.* taxation and the collection of taxes. Goble v. Zolot, 144 Neb. 70, 12 N.W.2d 311, 312. Generally, when a municipality's activity is for advantage of state as a whole, or is in performance of a duty imposed by sovereign power, activity is "public" and "governmental." Department of Treasury v. City of Evansville, Ind., 223 Ind. 435, 60 N.E.2d 952, 955. See **Governmental act; Governmental functions.**

Governmental agency. A subordinate creature of federal, state or local government created to carry out a governmental function or to implement a statute or statutes. For example, the Federal Trade Commission was created and functions to implement and enforce the Federal Trade Commission Act and various other federal antitrust and consumer protection laws. See also **Administrative agency; Governmental subdivision.**

Governmental agents. Those performing services and duties of a public character for benefit of all citizens of community. The term includes firemen and policemen. Miller v. City of Albany, 158 Misc. 720, 287 N.Y.S. 889, 891.

Governmental body. See **Administrative agency; Governmental agency; Governmental subdivision.**

Governmental duties. Those duties of a municipality that have reference to some part or element of the state's sovereignty granted it to be exercised for the benefit of the public, and all other duties are "proprietary". Those duties that the framers of the Constitution intended each member of the union of states would assume in order adequately to function under the form of government guaranteed by the Constitution. First State Bank of Gainesville v. Thomas, D.C.Tex., 38 F.Supp. 849, 851. See also **Governmental functions.**

Governmental enterprise. A project or undertaking by the government of a more or less permanent nature, such as a drainage district. Rorick v. United States Sugar Corporation, C.C.A.Fla., 120 F.2d 418, 421.

Governmental facility. A building or institution provided by the government to care for a specified need, such as a courthouse or county jail. Haney v. Town of Rainelle, 125 W.Va. 397, 25 S.E.2d 207, 211.

Governmental functions. The functions of a municipality which are essential to its existence, in sense of serving public at large, and are to be distinguished from those which are private, which are not necessary to its existence, and which enure to advantage of its inhabitants. City of New Rochelle v. State, 34 Misc.2d 454, 228 N.Y.S.2d 279, 282. Activities which are carried on by city, pursuant to state requirement, in discharge of state's obligation for health, safety or general welfare of public generally, or which are voluntarily assumed by city for benefit of public generally rather than for its own citizens, are performed in governmental capacity and as "governmental function". Sarmiento v. City of Corpus Christi, Tex.Civ. App., 465 S.W.2d 813, 816, 818.

Where duty involves general public benefit not in nature of corporate or business undertaking for corporate benefit and interest of municipality, function is "governmental," whether duty be directly imposed or voluntarily assumed. Those conferred upon municipality as local agency of prescribed and limited jurisdiction to be employed in administering the affairs of the state and promoting the public welfare generally. State ex rel. Gebhardt v. City Council of Helena, 102 Mont. 27, 55 P.2d 671, 673, 675.

Governmental immunity. The federal, state and local governments are not amenable to actions in tort except in cases in which they have consented to be sued. The federal government under the Federal Tort Claims Act has waived its immunity in certain cases "in the same manner and to the same extent as a private individual under like circumstances." 28 U.S. C.A. §§ 1346(b), 2674. Most states have also waived governmental immunity to various degrees at both the state and municipal government levels. See **Federal Tort Claims Act.**

Governmental instrumentality. Any agency constitutionally or legislatively created. See **Administrative agency; Governmental agency; Governmental subdivision.**

Governmental interests. In conflicts of law, term used to describe the particular governmental policies of a jurisdiction in terms of whether its law or another law should be applied in a choice of law issue.

Governmental powers. The totality of power which reposes in a government enabling it to carry out its proper functions as a sovereign. General powers of federal government are enumerated in U.S. Constitution; powers of state governments in state constitutions; municipal governments in charters.

Governmental privileges. See **Governmental secrets.**

Governmental purpose. One which has for its objective the promotion of the public health, safety, morals, general welfare, security, prosperity and contentment of the inhabitants of a given political division. See also **Governmental functions.**

Governmental secrets. In evidence, a privilege exists which protects the government from revealing military or diplomatic secrets or other information the disclosure of which would be contrary to the public interest. U. S. v. Reynolds, 345 U.S. 1, 73 S.Ct. 528, 97 L.Ed. 727. See also **Executive privilege.**

Governmental subdivision. An agency created to carry out a governmental purpose or function. See **Administrative agency; Governmental agency.**

Governmental survey. General mapping out by government of towns, sections, quarter sections, etc.; sometimes known as congressional survey. See also **Government survey system.**

Governmental trusts. Type of charitable trust used for erection and maintenance of public buildings and for the promotion of purposes which are of a character sufficiently beneficial to the community to justify permitting property to be devoted forever to their accomplishment. Restatement, Second, Trusts, §§ 373, 374.

Government annuities societies. Societies formed in England under 3 & 4 Wm. IV, c. 14, 7 & 8 Vict., c. 83, 16 & 17 Vict., c. 45, and 27 & 28 Vict., c. 43, to enable the industrious classes to make provisions for themselves by purchasing, on advantageous terms, a government annuity for life or term of years.

Government bonds. See **Bond.**

Government contract. See **Procurement contract.**

Government de facto. A government of fact. A government actually exercising power and control, as opposed to the true and lawful government; a government not established according to the constitution of the nation, or not lawfully entitled to recognition or supremacy, but which has nevertheless supplanted or displaced the government *de jure.* A government deemed unlawful, or deemed wrongful or unjust, which, nevertheless, receives presently habitual obedience from the bulk of the community.

There are several degrees of what is called *"de facto* government." Such a government, in its highest degree, assumes a character very closely resembling that of a lawful government. This is when the usurping government expels the regular authorities from their customary seats and functions, and establishes itself in their place, and so becomes the actual government of a country. The distinguishing characteristic of such a government is that adherents to it in war against the government *de jure* do not incur the penalties of treason; and, under certain limitations, obligations assumed by it in behalf of the country or otherwise will, in general, be respected by the government *de jure* when restored. Such a government

might be more aptly denominated a "government of paramount force," being maintained by active military power against the rightful authority of an established and lawful government; and obeyed in civil matters by private citizens. They are usually administered directly by military authority, but they may be administered, also, by civil authority, supported more or less by military force. Thorington v. Smith, 75 U.S. (8 Wall.) 1, 19 L.Ed. 361.

Government de jure /gávərnmənt diy júriy/. A government of right; the true and lawful government; a government established according to the constitution of the nation, and lawfully entitled to recognition and supremacy and the administration of the nation, but which is actually cut off from power or control. A government deemed lawful, or deemed rightful or just, which, nevertheless, has been supplanted or displaced; that is to say, which receives not presently (although it received formerly) habitual obedience from the bulk of the community.

Government immunity. See **Governmental immunity.**

Government instrumentality doctrine. The doctrine that government instrumentalities are tax exempt.

Government National Mortgage Association. Agency of Federal government (division of HUD) which, among its other functions, makes a market for higher risk loans by acquiring such from lenders who would otherwise not make such mortgage loans. Referred to as "Ginnie Mae."

Government of laws. Fundamental principle of American jurisprudence which requires decisions of courts to be based on laws, statutory and common law, irrespective of the character of the litigants and the personal predelictions of the judges.

Government survey system. A type of legal description whereby the United States is generally divided into checks or tracts of ground. These are further broken down by smaller descriptions, such as metes and bounds. See also **Governmental survey; Metes and bounds.**

Government tort. A wrong perpetrated by the government through an employee or agent or instrumentality under its control which may or may not be actionable depending upon whether there is governmental tort immunity. Tort actions against the federal government are governed by the Federal Tort Claims Act; many states also have Tort Claims Acts. See **Governmental immunity.**

Governor. The chief executive official of a state in the United States, and territories of the United States; and also of the chief magistrate of some colonies, provinces, and dependencies of other nations. Governors serve terms ranging from two to four years; are usually restricted to two terms in office; possess veto powers, powers to call special sessions of legislature, powers to pardon and reprieve, and many other appointive, administrative, and financial powers. See also **Lieutenant governor.**

Go without day. Words used to denote that a party is dismissed by the court. He is said to go without day, because there is no day appointed for him to appear again.

GPO. Government Printing Office. Such office prints and publishes laws, regulations, forms, etc. of federal government.

Grace. A favor or indulgence as distinguished from a right. See also **Days of grace; Grace, days of; Grace period; Of grace.**

Grace, days of. Time of indulgence granted to an acceptor or maker for the payment of his bill of exchange or note. It was originally a gratuitous favor (hence the name), but custom has rendered it a legal right. See also **Days of grace; Grace period.**

Grace period. In insurance law, a period beyond the due date of premium (usually 30 or 31 days) during which insurance is continued in force and during which payment may be made to keep policy in good standing. The grace period for payment of premium does not contemplate free insurance or operate to continue the policy in force after it expires by agreement of the parties. Miller v. Travelers Ins. Co., 143 Pa.Super. 270, 17 A.2d 907, 909.

Gradatim /grədéydəm/. In old English law, by degrees or steps; step by step; from one degree to another.

Grade, v. To establish a level by mathematical points and lines, and then to bring the surface of the street or highway to the level by the elevation or depression of the natural surface to the line fixed. To bring property to the level of an abutting highway. Nassau County v. O'Connell, Sup., 37 N.Y.S.2d 1009, 1012.

Grade, n. Used in reference to streets: (1) The line of the street's inclination from the horizontal; (2) a part of a street inclined from the horizontal. The hypothetical line to which the work is to be constructed. Musto-Keenan Co. v. City of Los Angeles, 139 Cal. App. 506, 34 P.2d 506, 509. The street wrought to the line.

"Grades of crime" in legal parlance are understood as higher or lower in grade or degree, according to the measure of punishment attached and meted out on conviction and the consequences resulting to the party convicted; e.g. first, second or, third degree murder.

Quality, value, relative position, rank, status, or standing. Mossman v. Chicago & Southern Air Lines, 236 Mo.App. 282, 153 S.W.2d 799, 801, 802.

Grade crossing. A place where a railroad is crossed at grade by a public or private road, or by another railroad, or where one highway crosses another.

Graded offense. One for which offender is subject to a more severe penalty for a higher grade than for a lower grade of offense according to terms of statute; e.g. first degree murder, as opposed to second or third degree; aggravated as opposed to simple assault.

Graduate. One who has received a degree, or other evidence of completion, from a grade school, high school, trade or vocational school, college, university, graduate or professional school, or the like.

Graduated lease. A type of lease arrangement which provides that rent will vary depending upon future contingencies, such as the amount of traffic or gross income produced.

Graduated tax. Tax structured so that the rate increases as the amount of income of taxpayer increases. For example, the federal income tax is a graduated tax.

Gradus /gréydəs/. In the civil and old English law, a measure of space. A degree of relationship.

A step or degree generally; e.g., gradus honorum, degrees of honor. A pulpit; a year; a generation.

A port; any place where a vessel can be brought to land.

Gradus parentelæ /gréydəs pərəntíyliy/. A pedigree; a table of relationship.

Graffarius /grəfériyəs/. In old English law, a graffer, notary, or scrivener.

Graffer /grǽfər/. A notary or scrivener. The word is a corruption of the French "greffier" (q.v.).

Graffium /grǽfiyəm/. A writing-book, register, or cartulary of deeds and evidences.

Grafio /gréyf(i)yow/. A baron, inferior to a count. A fiscal judge. An advocate.

Graft. The popular meaning is the fraudulent obtaining of public money unlawfully by the corruption of public officers. Smith v. Pure Oil Co., 278 Ky. 430, 128 S.W.2d 931, 933. Advantage or personal gain received because of peculiar position or superior influence of one holding position of trust and confidence without rendering compensatory services, or dishonest transaction in relation to public or official acts, and sometimes implies theft, corruption, dishonesty, fraud, or swindle, and always want of integrity. See also **Bribery.**

A term used in equity to denote the confirmation, by relation back, of the right of a mortgagee in premises to which, at the making of the mortgage, the mortgagor had only an imperfect title, but to which the latter has since acquired a good title.

Grain. In Troy weight, the twenty-fourth part of a pennyweight. Any kind of corn sown in the ground.

Grainage. An ancient duty in London under which the twentieth part of salt imported by aliens was taken.

Grain rent. A payment for the use of land in grain or other crops; the return to the landlord paid by sharecroppers or persons working the land on shares.

Grammar school. In England, this term designates a school in which such instruction is given as will prepare the student to enter a college or university, and in this sense the phrase was used in the Massachusetts Colonial Act of 1647, requiring every town containing a hundred householders to set up a "grammar school." But in American usage the term usually denotes a school, intermediate between the primary school and the high school.

Grammatica falsa non vitiat chartam /grəmǽdəkə fólsə nòn víshiyət kárdəm/. False grammar does not vitiate a deed.

Grammatophylacium /grǽmədəfəléysh(iy)əm/. (Græco-Lat.) In the civil law, a place for keeping writings or records.

Gramme /grǽm/. The unit of weight in the metric system. The gramme is the weight of a cubic centimeter of distilled water at the temperature of 4° C. It is equal to 15.4341 grains troy, or 5.6481 drachms avoirdupois.

Granatarius /grǽnətér(i)yəs/. In old English law, an officer having charge of a granary.

Grand, n. Jargon term for one thousand dollars.

As to grand Assize; Bill of sale; Cape; Distress; Jury; Larceny; Serjeanty, see those titles.

Grandchild. Generally, child of one's child. Descendant of second degree.

Grand coutumier /gròn kuwtyuwmyéy/. A collection of customs, laws, and forms of procedure in use in early times in France. See **Coustoumier.**

Grand days. In English practice, certain days in the terms, which are solemnly kept in the inns of court and chancery, viz., Candlemas day in Hilary term, Ascension day in Easter, St. John the Baptist day in Trinity, and All Saints in Michaelmas; which are *dies non juridici.* They are days set apart for peculiar festivity; the members of the respective inns being on such occasions regaled at their dinner in the hall, with more than usual sumptuousness.

Grandfather. The father of either of one's parents.

Grandfather clause. Provision in a new law or regulation exempting those already in or a part of the existing system which is being regulated. An exception to a restriction that allows all those already doing something to continue doing it even if they would be stopped by the new restriction. A clause introduced into several of the constitutions of the southern states, limiting the right to vote to those who can read and write any article of the constitution of the United States, and have worked or been regularly employed in some lawful employment for the greater part of the year next preceding the time they offer to register unless prevented from labor or ability to read or write by physical disability, or who own property assessed at three hundred dollars upon which the taxes have been paid; but excepting those who have served in the army or navy of the United States or in the Confederate States in time of war, their lawful descendants in every degree, and persons of good character who understand the duties and obligations of citizenship under a republican form of government.

One of the original purposes of the "grandfather" clause of the Motor Carrier Act was to permit the continued operation of carrier businesses already established prior to passage of the Act. Transamerican Freight Lines v. United States, D.C.Del., 51 F.Supp. 405, 409.

Grand jury. See **Jury.**

Grand jury investigation. Investigations conducted by a grand jury into possible wrongdoing. Generally, such are conducted under the aegis of the prosecuting official and they may or may not result in indictments. See **Jury** *(Grand jury).*

Grandmother. The mother of either of one's parents.

Grand remonstrance. A constitutional document passed by the British House of Commons in November, 1641. It was in the nature of an appeal to the country, setting forth political grievances. It consisted of a preamble of 20 clauses and the body of the remonstrance with 206 clauses, each of which was voted separately. Its first remedial measure was against papists; its second demanded that all illegal grievances and exactions should be presented and punished at the sessions and assizes and that judges and justices should be sworn to the due execution of the Petition of Rights and other laws. The third was a series of precautions to prevent the employment of evil councillors.

Grange. A farm furnished with barns, granaries, stables, and all conveniences for husbandry.

Grangearius /grèynj(iy)ériyəs/. A keeper of a grange or farm.

Granger Cases. A name applied to six cases decided by the supreme court of the United States in 1876, which are reported in Munn v. Illinois, 94 U.S. 113, 24 L.Ed. 77; Chicago, B. & Q. R. Co. v. Iowa, 94 U.S. 155, 24 L.Ed. 94; Peik v. Ry. Co., 94 U.S. 164, 24 L.Ed. 97; Chicago, M. & St. P. R. Co. v. Ackley, 94 U.S. 179, 24 L.Ed. 99; Winona & St. Peter R. Co. v. Blake, 94 U.S. 180, 24 L.Ed. 99; those most frequently cited being Munn v. Illinois, and C., B. & Q. R. Co. v. Iowa. They are so called because they arose out of an agitation commenced by the grangers which resulted in the enactment of statutes for the regulation of the tolls and charges of common carriers, warehousemen, and the proprietors of elevators. The enforcement of these acts was resisted and their constitutionality questioned. The supreme court affirmed the common-law doctrine that private property appropriated by the owner to a public use is thereby subjected to public regulation. They also held that the right of regulation was not restrained by the prohibition of the fourteenth amendment of the federal constitution against the taking by the states of private property without due process of law.

Grangia /gréynj(iy)ə/. A grange.

Grant. To bestow; to confer upon some one other than the person or entity which makes the grant. Porto Rico Ry., Light & Power Co. v. Colom, C.C.A.Puerto Rico, 106 F.2d 345, 354. To bestow or confer, with or without compensation, a gift or bestowal by one having control or authority over it, as of land or money. Palmer v. U. S. Civil Service Commission, D.C.Ill., 191 F.Supp. 495, 537.

A conveyance; *i.e.* transfer of title by deed or other instrument. Dearing v. Brush Creek Coal Co., 182 Tenn. 302, 186 S.W.2d 329, 331. Transfer of property real or personal by deed or writing. Commissioner of Internal Revenue v. Plestcheeff, C.C.A.9, 100 F.2d 62, 64, 65. A generic term applicable to all transfers of real property, including transfers by operation of law as well as voluntary transfers. White v. Rosenthal, 140 Cal.App. 184, 35 P.2d 154, 155. A technical term made use of in deeds of conveyance of lands to import a transfer. A deed for an incorporeal interest such as a reversion.

As distinguished from a mere license, a grant passes some estate or interest, corporeal or incorporeal, in the lands which it embraces.

To give or permit as a right or privilege; *e.g.* grant of route authority to a public carrier.

By the word "grant," in a treaty, is meant not only a formal grant, but any concession, warrant, order, or permission to survey, possess, or settle, whether written or parol, express, or presumed from possession. Such a grant may be made by law, as well as by a patent pursuant to a law. Bryan v. Kennett, 113 U.S. 179, 5 S.Ct. 407, 28 L.Ed. 908.

In England, an act evidenced by letters patent under the great seal, granting something from the king to a subject.

Land grant. See **Land grant.**

Office grant. See **Office.**

Private land grant. A grant by a public authority vesting title to public land in a private (natural) person.

Public grant. A grant from the public; a grant of a power, license, privilege, or property, from the state or government to one or more individuals, contained in or shown by a record, conveyance, patent, charter, etc.

Grant and to freight let. Operative words in a charter party, implying the placing of the vessel at the disposition of the charterer for the purposes of the intended voyage, and generally, transferring the possession.

Grant, bargain, and sell. Operative words in conveyances of real estate.

Grantee. One to whom a grant is made.

Grant-in-aid. Sum of money given by a governmental agency to a person or institution for a specific purpose such as education or research.

Granting clause. That portion of a deed or instrument of conveyance which contains the words of transfer of a present interest. New Home Building Supply Co. v. Nations, 259 N.C. 681, 131 S.E.2d 425.

Grant of patent. Written transfer of rights to an invention or of a right to use or sell the thing patented. See also **License; Patent.**

Grant of personal property. A method of transferring personal property, distinguished from a gift by being always founded on some consideration or equivalent. Its proper legal designation is an "assignment," or "bargain and sale."

Grantor. The person by whom a grant is made. A transferor of property. The creator of a trust is usually designated as the grantor of the trust.

Grantor-grantee index. Master index, as kept in county recorder's office, to all recorded instruments. Such index contains the volume and page number where the specific instrument can be located in the record books.

Grantor's lien. Lien which exists for payment of purchase money when title is transferred. Kosters v. Hoover, 69 App.D.C. 66, 98 F.2d 595, 596. Such lien arises when vendor has conveyed title to vendee without receiving full consideration. Birnbaum v. Rollerama, Inc., 232 N.Y.S.2d 188, 191.

Grantor trusts. Trusts whereby the grantor retains control over the income or corpus, or both, to such an extent that such grantor will be treated as the owner of the property and its income for income tax purposes. The result is to make the income from a grantor trust taxable to the grantor and not to the beneficiary who receives it. I.R.C. §§ 671–677.

Grant to uses. The common grant with uses superadded, which became the favorite mode of transferring realty in England.

Grantz /grónts/grǽndz/. In old English law, noblemen or grandees.

Grass. Jargon name for marihuana.

Grass hearth /grǽs hàrθ/. In old English records, the grazing or turning up the earth with a plow. The name of a customary service for inferior tenants to bring their plows, and do one day's work for their lords.

Grasson, or **grassum** /grǽsəm/. A fine paid upon the transfer of a copyhold estate. See **Gressume.**

Grass week. In old England, rogation week, so called anciently in the inns of court and chancery.

Grass widow. A slang term for a woman separated from her husband by abandonment or prolonged absence; a woman living apart from her husband. A divorcee.

Gratian. Italian monk, circa 1151, who made a compilation of canon law.

Gratification. A gratuity; a recompense or reward for services or benefits, given voluntarily, without solicitation or promise.

Gratis /gréydəs/grǽdəs/. Without reward or consideration. Done or received freely or gratuitously.

Gratis dictum /gréydəs díktəm/. A voluntary assertion; a statement which a party is not legally bound to make, or in which he is not held to precise accuracy.

Gratuitous. Given or granted without valuable or legal consideration. A term applied to deeds of conveyance and to bailments and other contracts.

In old English law, voluntary; without force, fear, or favor.

As to gratuitous Bailment; Contract; Deposit, see those titles. See also **Gratis.**

Gratuitous allowance. A pension. Moran v. Firemen's and Policemen's Pension Fund Commission of Jersey City, 20 N.J.Misc. 479, 28 A.2d 885, 887; State ex rel. Parker v. Board of Education of City of Topeka, 155 Kan. 754, 129 P.2d 265, 267.

Gratuitous bailee. Person to whom possession of personal property is transferred and who furnishes no consideration for such transfer and hence is required to use great care to avoid liability for negligence. One responsible for goods entrusted to him when goods are damaged or lost through his gross negligence. Christensen v. Dady, 238 Ark. 577, 383 S.W.2d 283, 285.

Gratuitous guest. In automobile law, a person riding at invitation of owner or authorized agent without payment of a consideration or fare. Hart v. Hogan, 173 Wash. 598, 24 P.2d 99. See **Guest.**

Gratuitous licensee. Person who has permission though not an invitation to come on to the property of another and who has furnished no consideration for such permission. He is not an invitee, though, because of the permission, he is not a trespasser.

Gratuitous passenger. See **Gratuitous guest; Guest.**

Gratuitous promise. Promise made by one who has not received consideration for it.

Gratuity. Something acquired without bargain or inducement. State ex rel. Stafford v. Fox-Great Falls Theatre Corporation, 114 Mont. 52, 132 P.2d 689, 697. Something given freely or without recompense; a gift. Something voluntarily given in return for a favor or especially a service, hence, a bounty; a tip; a bribe. McCook v. Long, 193 Ga. 299, 18 S.E.2d 488, 490.

Gravamen /grəvéymən/. The material part of a grievance, indictment, charge, etc. Williamson v. Pacific Greyhound Lines, 67 Cal.App.2d 250, 153 P.2d 990, 991. The burden or gist of a charge; the grievance or injury specially complained of.

In English Ecclesiastical law, a grievance complained of by the clergy before the bishops in convocation.

Gravatio /grəvéysh(iy)ow/. In old English law, an accusation or impeachment.

Grave. An excavation in earth in which a dead body is or is to be buried, or place for interment of a corpse, such as a tomb, or a sepulcher.

Graven dock. A "graven dock" is distinguished from a "floating dock," in that it is permanently attached to, and in that manner is, a part of land. Manufacturers' Liability Ins. Co. v. Hamilton, 129 Misc. 665, 222 N.Y.S. 394.

Graveyard. A cemetery; a place for the interment of dead bodies; sometimes defined in statutes as a place where a minimum number of persons (as "six or more") are buried.

Graveyard insurance. A term applied to insurances fraudulently obtained (as, by false personation or other means) on the lives of infants, very aged persons, or those in the last stages of disease. Also occasionally applied to an insurance company which writes wager policies, takes extra-hazardous risks, or otherwise exceeds the limits of prudent and legitimate business.

Gravis /gréyvəs/grǽvəs/. Grievous; great. *Ad grave damnum,* to the grievous damage.

Gravius /gréyviyəs/. A graf; a chief magistrate or officer. A term derived from the more ancient "*grafio,*" and used in combination with various other words, as an official title in Germany; as *Margravius, Rheingravius, Landgravius,* etc.

Gravius est divinam quam temporalem lædere majestatem /gréyviyəs èst dəváynəm kwǽm tèmpəréyləm líydəriy mæjəstéydəm/. It is more serious to hurt divine than temporal majesty.

Gray's inn. An inn of court. See **Inns of court.**

Great. Considerable in magnitude, power, importance, intensity or degree. Thompson v. Anderson, 107 Utah 331, 153 P.2d 665, 666. As used in various compound legal terms, this word generally means extraordinary, that is, exceeding the common or ordinary measure or standard, in respect to physical size, or importance, dignity, etc.

For *presumption great,* see **Proof.** As to great Care; Pond; Seal; Tithes; see those titles.

Great bodily injury. The term "great bodily injury" as used in statute stating when an assault and battery becomes aggravated, is not susceptible of precise definition, but implies an injury of a graver and more serious character than ordinary battery. Herrington v. State, Okl.Cr., 352 P.2d 931, 933.

Great charter. *Magna Charta (q.v.).*

Great-grandchildren. Children of one's grandchildren.

Great Law, The. "The Body of Laws of the Province of Pennsylvania and Territories thereunto belonging, Past at an Assembly held at Chester *alias* Upland, the 7th day of the tenth month, called 'December,' 1682." This was the first code of laws established in Pennsylvania, and is justly celebrated for the provision in its first chapter for liberty of conscience.

Great tithes. In ecclesiastical law, the more valuable tithes: as, corn, hay, and wood. See **Tithes.**

Great writ of liberty. The writ of "habeas corpus and subjiciendum", issuing at common law out of courts of Chancery, King's Bench, Common Pleas, and Exchequer. See **Habeas corpus.**

Gree. Satisfaction for an offense committed or injury done.

Greek cross. See **Cross.**

Greek kalends. A colloquial expression to signify a time indefinitely remote, there being no such division of time known to the Greeks.

Greenback. The popular name applied to United States treasury issues.

Green cloth. In old English law, a board or court of justice held in the countinghouse of the king's (or queen's) household, and composed of the lord steward and inferior officers. It takes its name from the green cloth spread over the board at which it is held.

Green River ordinance. Type of local licensing law which protects persons from unwanted peddlers and salespersons who call on homes and business establishments. Green River v. Bunger, 50 Wyo. 52, 70, 58 P.2d 456, 462.

Green wax. In English law, the name of the estreats in the exchequer, delivered to the sheriff under the seal of that court which was impressed upon green wax.

Greffiers /gréf(i)yərz/grèfyéy/. In French law, registrars, or clerks of the courts. They are officials attached to the courts to assist the judges in their duties. They keep the minutes, write out the judgments, orders, and other decisions given by the tribunals, and deliver copies thereof to applicants.

Gregorian code. The code or collection of constitutions made by the Roman jurist Gregorius. See **Codex Gregorianus.**

Gregorian epoch. The time from which the Gregorian calendar or computation dates; *i.e.,* from the year 1582.

Gremio /greymíyow/. In Spanish law, a guild; an association of workmen, artificers, or merchants following the same trade or business; designed to protect and further the interests of their craft.

Gremium /gríym(i)yəm/. Lat. The bosom or breast; hence, derivatively, safeguard or protection. In English law, an estate which is in abeyance is said to be *in gremio legis* /ìn gríym(i)yow líyjəs/; that is, in the protection or keeping of the law.

Grenville Act. The statute 10 Geo. III, c. 16, by which the jurisdiction over parliamentary election petitions was transferred from the whole house of commons to select committees.

Gressume /grés(y)əm/. In English law, a customary fine due from a copyhold tenant on the death of the lord. Spelled also *"grassum," "grossome,"* and *"gressame."*

Greva /gríyvə/. In old records, the seashore, sand, or beach.

Greve /gríyv/. A word of power or authority.

Grievance. In labor law, a complaint filed by an employee regarding working conditions and for resolution of which there is procedural machinery provided in the union contract. An injury, injustice or wrong which gives ground for complaint because it is unjust, discriminatory, and oppressive. See **Complaint.**

Grieved. Aggrieved.

Grievous. Causing grief or sorrow, painful, afflictive, hard to bear, offensive, harmful.

Grith. In Saxon law, peace; protection.

Grithbrech, or **grithbreche** /gríθbrìych/. Breach of the peace.

Grithstole /gríθstùwl/. A place of sanctuary.

Groat /grówt/. An English silver coin (value four pence) issued from the fourteenth to the seventeenth century.

Grocer /grówsər/. In old English law, a merchant or trader who *engrossed* all vendible merchandise; an engrosser.

Grog-shop. A liquor saloon, bar, liquor store, or dramshop; a place where intoxicating liquor is sold.

Gross. Great; culpable; general; absolute. A thing *in gross* exists in its own right, and not as an appendage to another thing. Before or without diminution or deduction. Whole; entire; total; as the gross sum, amount, weight—opposed to net. State v. Hallenberg-Wagner Motor Co., 341 Mo. 771, 108 S.W.2d

398, 401. Not adjusted or reduced by deductions or subtractions. Contrast with **Net.**

Out of all measure; beyond allowance; flagrant; shameful; as a gross dereliction of duty, a gross injustice, gross carelessness or negligence. State Board of Dental Examiners v. Savelle, 90 Colo. 177, 8 P.2d 693, 697. Such conduct as is not to be excused.

As to gross Adventure; Average; Fault; Weight, see those titles.

Gross alimony. The terms "alimony in gross" and "gross alimony" are applied to an amount agreed upon or determined in full or in lieu of all alimony, and such amount is frequently payable in installments. Whitney v. Whitney, 15 Ill.App.2d 425, 146 N.E.2d 800, 804. See also **Alimony.**

Gross earnings. Total receipts of a person or business before deductions and expenses. Rambin v. Continental Ins. Co., La.App., 186 So.2d 861. See also **Gross income.**

Grosse aventure /gròws avontyúr/. Fr. In French marine law, the contract of bottomry.

Gross estate. The property owned or previously transferred by a decedent that will be subject to the Federal death tax. It can be distinguished from the probate estate which is property actually subject to administration by the administrator or executor of an estate. I.R.C. §§ 2031–2044. See also **Adjusted gross estate.**

Gross income. Under I.R.C. Section 61(a) gross income means all income from whatever source derived, including (but not limited to) the following items: (1) Compensation for services, including fees, commissions, and similar items; (2) Gross income derived from business; (3) Gains derived from dealings in property; (4) Interest; (5) Rents; (6) Royalties; (7) Dividends; (8) Alimony and separate maintenance payments; (9) Annuities; (10) Income from life insurance and endowment contracts; (11) Pensions; (12) Income from discharge of indebtedness; (13) Distributive share of partnership gross income; (14) Income in respect of a decedent; and (15) Income from an interest in an estate or trust. See Heard v. C. I. R., C.A.Mo., 326 F.2d 962, 966.

In the case of a manufacturing or merchandising business, gross income means gross profit (*i.e.,* gross sales or gross receipts less cost of goods sold).

Adjusted gross income. A determination peculiar to individual taxpayers. Generally, it represents gross income less business expenses, expenses attributable to the production of rent or royalty income and the long-term capital gain deduction.

Gross income multiplier. Valuation technique used to estimate the valuation of real property. For example, the gross income times a given gross income multiplier to produce the estimated value.

Gross income tax. Levy on total receipts of business without allowance for expenses and deductions.

Any tax imposed on gross receipts; may include retail sales tax and general sales tax.

Gross interest. Total interest payment by borrower including administrative, service, and insurance charges.

Gross lease. See **Lease.**

Gross margin. The difference between the amount of sales after returns and allowances and the cost of goods sold.

Gross misdemeanor. Classification of a type of crime which, while not a felony, is ranked as a serious misdemeanor.

Gross National Product (GNP). The market value within a nation for a year of all goods and services produced as measured by final sales of goods and services to individuals, corporations, and governments plus the excess of exports over imports. The total market value of the output of all goods and services of a country without doublecounting, divided into four main categories: consumption, gross private domestic investment, government purchases of goods and services, and net exports (exports minus imports).

Gross neglect of duty. Type of serious nonfeasance or failure to attend to one's duties, either public or private. See **Desertion; Non-support.**

Gross negligence. See **Negligence.**

Grossome /grówsəm/. In old English law, a fine, or sum of money paid for a lease. Supposed to be a corruption of *gersuma (q.v.)*. See **Gressume.**

Gross premium. Net premium plus loading for expenses and contingencies; *i.e.,* the net premium represents the cost of insurance. Fox v. Mutual Ben. Life Ins. Co., C.C.A.Mo., 107 F.2d 715, 719.

Gross profit. The difference between sales and the cost of goods sold before allowance for operating expenses and income taxes. See also **Gross income.**

Gross receipts. Term refers to the total amount of money or the value of other considerations received from selling property or from performing services. New Mexico Enterprises, Inc. v. Bureau of Revenue, App., 86 N.M. 799, 528 P.2d 212, 213. See also **Gross income.**

Gross receipts tax. See **Gross income tax.**

Gross revenue. Receipts of a business before deductions for any purpose except those items specifically exempted. Public Service Co. v. City and County of Denver, 153 Colo. 396, 387 P.2d 33, 36.

Gross sales. Total of all sales at invoice prices, not reduced by discounts, allowances, returns, or other adjustments.

Gross spread. In finance the difference between the price paid by an investment banker for an issue and the price paid by the buying public.

Gross stress reaction. A term employed for an acute emotional reaction incident to severe environmental stress.

Gross up. To add back to the value of the property or income received the amount of the tax that has been deducted. In the case of gifts made after 1976 and included in the gross estate when the donor dies within three years of the gift, any gift tax paid on the transfer is added to the fair market value of the property on the appropriate death tax valuation date. Thus, the gift property is "grossed-up" for any such gift tax. I.R.C. § 2035. Process by which U.S. corporations add pre-foreign tax income in federal income tax returns in order to acquire credit against federal taxes for foreign income taxes paid.

Ground. Soil; earth; the earth's surface appropriated to private use and under cultivation or susceptible of cultivation.

A foundation or basis; points relied on; *e.g.* "ground" for bringing civil action, or charging criminal defendant, or foundation for admissibility of evidence. See also **Ground of action.**

Groundage. Old custom or tribute paid for the standing of shipping in port. See also **Demurrage.**

Ground landlord. The grantor of an estate on which a ground-rent is reserved.

Ground lease. A lease of vacant land, or land exclusive of any buildings on it, or unimproved real property. Usually a net lease. See also **Ground rent; Lease.**

Ground of action. The basis of a suit; the foundation or fundamental state of facts on which an action rests (*e.g.* negligence; breach of contract); the real object of the plaintiff in bringing his suit. See also **Cause of action.**

Ground rent. Rent paid to owner of land for use of property; normally to construct building on such. Generally, rent is paid for a long-term lease (*e.g.* 99 year lease) with lessor retaining title to land. Such long-term lease is commonly renewable. Office buildings, hotels, and similar large structures in cities are commonly built on land under such types of ground leases.

A perpetual rent reserved to himself and his heirs, by the grantor of land in fee-simple, out of the land conveyed. It is in the nature of an emphyteutic rent. Also, in English law, rent paid on a building lease.

Ground water. Water in the subsoil or of a spring or shallow well.

Ground writ. Prior to the English common-law procedure act, 1852, c. 121 a *ca. sa.* or *fi. fa.* could not be issued into a county different from that in which the venue in the action was laid, without first issuing a writ, called a "ground writ," into the latter county, and then another writ, which was called a "*testatum* writ," into the former.

Group annuity. Type of pension plan for employees under a master plan or contract in which employer each year buys a deferred annuity for each qualified employee.

Group boycott. A concerted refusal by traders to deal with other traders. Such is unlawful per se because it restrains freedom of parties to the boycott independently to decide whether to deal with boycotted party. A single trader's refusal to deal with another does not constitute a group boycott. Arzee Supply Corp. of Conn., v. Ruberoid Co., D.C.Conn., 222 F.Supp. 237, 242.

A group action to coerce third parties to conform to pattern of conduct desired by group or to secure third parties' removal from competition. Jones Knitting Corp. v. Morgan, D.C.Pa., 244 F.Supp. 235, 238.

Grouping of contacts. In conflict of laws, when choice-of-law issue arises, court will apply the law of the jurisdiction most intimately concerned with the outcome of the litigation; also known as "center of gravity" approach or doctrine. Industrial Credit Co. v. J. A. D. Const. Co., 29 A.D.2d 952, 289 N.Y.S.2d 243.

Group insurance. A contract of group insurance is one between insurer and employer for benefit of employees. Crawford v. Metropolitan Life Ins. Co., Mo. App., 167 S.W.2d 915, 924. In its nature, group insurance is similar, if not identical, with that form of insurance known as "term" insurance. See **Insurance.**

Group libel. See **Libel.**

Growing crop. Lit. A crop in the process of growth; though decisions differ as to whether such must be above the surface of the soil, and as to whether matured crops are "growing" crops. The cases as well differ as to whether pasturage grass is a growing crop. Growing crops are personal property. Estate of Ruwe v. Ruwe, 190 Neb. 663, 211 N.W.2d 610, 613.

Growth half-penny. In old English law, a rate paid in some places for the tithe of every fat beast, ox, or other unfruitful cattle.

Growth stock. Type of security characterized by the prospect of increase in market value, but not necessarily with a good dividend return.

Gruarii /gruwériyay/. The principal officers of a forest.

Grub stake. In mining law, a contract between two parties by which one undertakes to furnish the necessary provisions, tools, and other supplies, and the other to prospect for and locate mineral lands and stake out mining claims thereon, the interest in the property thus acquired inuring to the benefit of both parties, either equally or in such proportion as their agreement may fix.

G.S.A. General Services Administration.

Guadalupe Hidalgo, Treaty of /tríydiy əv gwàdəlúwpey hi(y)dálgow/. A treaty between the United States and Mexico, terminating the Mexican War, dated February 2, 1848. See **Gadsden Purchase.**

Guadia /(g)wéydiyə/. In old European law, a pledge. A custom. Spelled also "wadia."

Guarantee. One to whom a guaranty is made. This word is also used, as a noun, to denote the contract of guaranty or the obligation of a guarantor, and, as a verb, to denote the action of assuming the responsibilities of a guarantor.

Guarantee clause. That provision in a contract, deed, mortgage, etc. by which one person promises to pay the obligation of another. Also, the provision in Art. IV, § 4, U.S.Const., in which the federal government guarantees to every state a republican form of government and the protection of the federal government in the event of domestic violence.

Guaranteed payment. See **Payment guaranteed.**

Guaranteed stock. See **Stock.**

Guarantee stock. Guarantee stock of a building and loan association is a fixed non-withdrawal investment which guarantees to all other investors in the association a fixed rate of dividend or interest. Stumph v. Wheat Belt Building & Loan Ass'n of Pratt, 148 Kan. 25, 79 P.2d 896, 899.

Guarantor. He who makes a guaranty. One who becomes secondarily liable for another's debt or performance in contrast to a strict surety who is primarily liable with the principal debtor. See also **Surety.**

Guaranty, v. To undertake collaterally to answer for the payment of another's debt or the performance of another's duty, liability, or obligation; to assume the responsibility of a guarantor; to warrant. See **Guaranty, n.**

Guaranty, n. A collateral agreement for performance of another's undertaking. An undertaking or promise that is collateral to primary or principal obligation and that binds guarantor to performance in event of nonperformance by the principal obligor. Commercial Credit Corp. v. Chisholm Bros. Farm Equipment Co., 96 Idaho 194, 525 P.2d 976, 978.

A promise to answer for payment of debt or performance of obligation if person liable in first instance fails to make payment or perform obligation. An undertaking by one person to be answerable for the payment of some debt, or the due performance of some contract or duty, by another person, who himself remains liable to pay or perform the same. A promise to answer for the debt, default, or miscarriage of another person.

A guaranty is a contract that some particular thing shall be done exactly as it is agreed to be done, whether it is to be done by one person or another, and whether there be a prior or principal contractor or not. An undertaking by one person that another shall perform his contract or fulfill his obligation, or that, if he does not, the guarantor will do it for him. A guarantor of a bill or note is said to be one who engages that the note shall be paid, but is not an indorser or surety.

The contract of a guarantor is his own separate contract. It is in the nature of a warranty by him that the thing guarantied to be done by the principal shall be done, not merely an engagement jointly with the principal to do the thing. The original contract of the principal is not his contract, and he is not bound to take notice of its non-performance. See **Suretyship** (contract of); also Collateral guaranty, below.

Synonyms

The terms guaranty and suretyship are sometimes used interchangeably; but they should not be confounded. The distinction between contract of suretyship and contract of guaranty is whether or not the undertaking is a joint undertaking with the principal or a separate and distinct contract; if it is the former it is one of "suretyship", and if the latter, it is one of "guaranty". General Finance Corp. of Atlanta, Northeast v. Welborn, 98 Ga.App. 280, 105 S.E.2d 386, 389.

Guaranty and *warranty* are derived from the same root, and are in fact etymologically the same word, the "g" of the Norman French being interchangeable with the English "w." They are often used colloquially and in commercial transactions as having the same signification, as where a piece of machinery or the produce of an estate is "guarantied" for a term of years, "warranted" being the more appropriate term in such a case. A distinction is also sometimes made in commercial usage, by which the term "guaranty" is understood as a collateral warranty (often a conditional one) against some default or event in the future, while the term "warranty" is taken as meaning an absolute undertaking *in præsenti,* against the defect, or for the quantity or quality contemplated by the parties in the subject-matter of the contract. But in strict legal usage the two terms are widely distinguished in this, that a warranty is an absolute undertaking or liability on the part of the warrantor, and the contract is void unless it is strictly and literally performed, while a guaranty is a promise, entirely collateral to the original contract, and not imposing any primary liability on the guarantor, but binding him to be answerable for the failure or default of another. See **Warranty.**

Absolute guaranty. An unconditional undertaking by a guarantor that debtor will pay debt or perform the obligation. An unconditional promise of payment or performance of principal contract on default of principal debtor or obligor. Robey v. Walton Lumber Co., 17 Wash.2d 242, 135 P.2d 95, 102.

Collateral guaranty. A contract by which the guarantor undertakes, in case the principal fails to do what he has promised or undertaken to do, to pay damages for such failure; distinguished from an engagement of suretyship in this respect, that a surety undertakes to do the very thing which the principal has promised to do, in case the latter defaults.

Conditional guaranty. One which depends upon some extraneous event, beyond the mere default of the principal, and generally upon notice of the guaranty, notice of the principal's default, and reasonable diligence in exhausting proper remedies against the principal.

Continuing guaranty. One relating to a future liability of the principal, under successive transactions, which either continue his liability or from time to time renew it after it has been satisfied.

Special guaranty. A guaranty which is available only to the particular person to whom it is offered or addressed; as distinguished from a *general* guaranty, which will operate in favor of any person who may accept it.

Guaranty company. A corporation authorized to transact the business of entering into contracts of guaranty and suretyship; as one which, for fixed premiums, becomes surety on judicial bonds, fidelity bonds, and the like.

Guaranty bond. See **Bond.**

Guaranty clause. See **Guarantee clause.**

Guaranty fund. Statutes have made provision for depositors' guaranty funds to be raised, in whole or in part, by assessments on banks and to be used to pay the depositors of an insolvent bank. Noble State Bank v. Haskell, 219 U.S. 104, 31 S.Ct. 186, 55 L.Ed. 112; Shallenberger v. Bank, 219 U.S. 114, 31 S.Ct. 189, 55 L.Ed. 117; Assaria State Bank v. Dolley, 219 U.S. 121, 31 S.Ct. 189, 55 L.Ed. 123; Abilene Nat. Bank v. Dolley, 228 U.S. 1, 33 S.Ct. 409, 57 L.Ed. 707. Most bank deposits are insured to a specified limit by the Federal Deposit Insurance Corporation *(q.v.).*

Guaranty insurance. See **Insurance.**

Guardage. A state of wardship.

Guardian. A person lawfully invested with the power, and charged with the duty, of taking care of the person and managing the property and rights of another person, who, for defect of age, understanding, or self-control, is considered incapable of administering his own affairs. One who legally has the care and management of the person, or the estate, or both, of a child during its minority.

Classification

A *testamentary* guardian is one appointed by the deed or last will of the child's father or mother; while a guardian *by election* is one chosen by the infant himself in a case where he would otherwise be without one.

A *general* guardian is one who has the general care and control of the person and estate of his ward; while a *special* guardian is one who has special or limited powers and duties with respect to his ward, *e.g.,* a guardian who has the custody of the estate but not of the person, or vice versa, or a guardian *ad litem.*

A *domestic* guardian is one appointed at the place where the ward is legally domiciled; while a *foreign* guardian derives his authority from appointment by the courts of another state, and generally has charge only of such property as may be located within the jurisdiction of the power appointing him.

A *guardian ad litem* is a special guardian appointed by the court to prosecute or defend, in behalf of an infant or incompetent, a suit to which he is a party, and such guardian is considered an officer of the court to represent the interests of the infant or incompetent in the litigation. Kossar v. State, 13 Misc.2d 941, 179 N.Y.S.2d 71, 73, 76, 79.

A *guardian by estoppel* is one who assumes to act as guardian without legal authority; similar to a guardian de son tort.

A *guardian by nature* is the father, and, on his death, the mother, of a child. Daniels v. Metropolitan Life Ins. Co., 135 Pa.Super. 450, 5 A.2d 608, 611. This guardianship extends only to the custody of the person of the child to the age of majority. Sometimes called "natural guardian".

A *guardian by statute or testamentary guardian* is a guardian appointed for a child by the deed or last will of the father, and who has the custody both of his person and estate until the attainment of full age. This kind of guardianship is founded on the statute of 12 Car. II, c. 24, and has been extensively adopted in this country. 1 Bl.Comm. 462.

A *guardian for nurture* is the father, or, at his decease, the mother, of a child. This kind of guardianship at common law extended only to the person, and determined when the infant arrived at the age of fourteen. 1 Bl.Comm. 461.

Guardian in chivalry. In the tenure by knight's service, in the feudal law, if the heir of the feud was under the age of twenty-one, being a male, or fourteen, being a female, the lord was entitled to the wardship (and marriage) of the heir, and was called the "guardian in chivalry." This wardship consisted in having the custody of the body and lands of such heir, without any account of the profits. 2 Bl.Comm. 67.

Guardian in socage. At the common law, this was a species of guardian who had the custody of lands coming to the infant by descent, as also of the infant's person, until the latter reached the age of fourteen. Such guardian was always "the next of kin to whom the inheritance cannot possibly descend." 1 Bl.Comm. 461.

Natural guardian. The father of a child, or the mother if the father be dead.

Guardian de son tort, sometimes described as "quasi guardian" or "guardian by estoppel," is one who assumes to act as guardian without valid authority. Similar to *guardian by estoppel.*

Guardian of the peace /gárd(i)yən əv ðə píys/. A warden or conservator of the peace.

Guardian of the poor. In English law, a person elected by the ratepayers of a parish to have the charge and management of the parish work-house or union.

Guardian of the spiritualities /gárd(i)yən əv ðə spìri-chuwǽlədiyz/. In England, the person to whom the spiritual jurisdiction of any diocese is committed during the vacancy of the see.

Guardian of the temporalities /gárd(i)yən əv ðə tèmpərǽlədiyz/. The person to whose custody a vacant see or abbey was committed by the crown.

Guardian or warden of the cinque ports /gárd(i)yən əv ðə sìŋk pórts/wórdən°/. A magistrate who has the jurisdiction of the ports or havens which are called the "Cinque Ports" (*q.v.*). This office was first created in England, in imitation of the Roman policy, to strengthen the sea-coasts against enemies, etc.

Guardianship. The office, duty, or authority of a guardian. Also the relation subsisting between guardian and ward. See **Guardian; Ward.**

Guardianus /gàrdiyéynəs/. A guardian, warden, or keeper.

Guarentigio /gàrentíyhiyow/. In Spanish law, a written authorization to a court to enforce the performance of an agreement in the same manner as if it had been decreed upon regular legal proceedings.

Guarnimentum /gàrnəméntəm/. In old European law, a provision of necessary things. A furnishing or garnishment.

Guastald. In old English law, one who had the custody of the royal mansions.

Gubernator /gyùwbərnéydər/. Lat. In Roman law, the pilot or steersman of a ship.

Guerpi, Guerpy. L. Fr. Abandoned; left; deserted.

Guerra, guerre /gér(ə)/. War.

Guest. A person receiving lodging for pay at inn, motel, or hotel on general undertaking of keeper thereof. A traveler who lodges with the consent of the keeper or owner.

Guest is a person who is received and entertained at one's home, club, etc., and who is not a regular member. Stadelmann v. Glen Falls Ins. Co. of Glen Falls, 5 Mich.App. 536, 147 N.W.2d 460, 463.

A "guest" in an automobile is one who takes ride in automobile driven by another person, merely for his own pleasure or on his own business, and without making any return or conferring any benefit on automobile driver. Guest is used to denote one whom owner or possessor of vehicle invites or permits to ride with him as gratuity, without any financial return except such slight benefits as are customarily extended as part of ordinary courtesies of road. Rothwell v. Transmeier, 206 Kan. 199, 477 P.2d 960, 963, 966. See **Guest statute.**

Business guest. See **Business.**

Guest statute. A "guest," under provisions of guest statute, is a recipient of the voluntary hospitality of the driver or owner, that is, one who is invited or permitted by owner or possessor of automobile to ride with owner-possessor as a gratuity. Walker v. Bounds, Tex.Civ.App., 510 S.W.2d 392, 394.

Many states have statutes referred to as "automobile guest statutes," which provide that operators of automobiles shall only be liable for injuries to guests carried gratuitously for gross or willful negligence, willful or wanton misconduct, or the like, with a further provision in some statutes continuing liability for want of ordinary care in case of hosts operating automobiles while intoxicated. In recent years however there has been a trend towards repealing or delimiting such statutes.

While a typical guest statute excludes all non-paying guests from suing the host-driver or owner for damages arising out of the host-driver's ordinary negligence, certain statutes are more narrow in their scope; *e.g.* precluding only those guests without payment who are related within the second degree of consanguinity or affinity to the owner or operator from suing.

Guidage /gáydəj/. In old English law, that which was given for safe conduct through a strange territory, or another's territory. The office of guiding of travelers through dangerous and unknown ways.

Guidon de la mer /gìydówn də là mér/. The name of a treatise on maritime law, by an unknown author, supposed to have been written about 1671 at Rouen, and considered, in continental Europe, as a work of high authority.

Guild. A voluntary association of persons, pursuing the same trade, art, profession or business, such as printers, goldsmiths, artists, wool merchants, etc., united under a distinct organization of their own, analogous to that of a corporation, regulating the affairs of their trade or business by their own laws and rules, and aiming, by cooperation and organization, to protect and promote the interests of their common vocation. Goodman v. Federal Trade Commission, C.A.9, 244 F.2d 584, 594.

In medieval history these fraternities or guilds played an important part in the government of some states; as at Florence, in the thirteenth and following centuries, where they chose the council of government of the city. The word is said to be derived from the Anglo-Saxon *"gild"* or *"geld,"* a tax or tribute, because each member of the society was required to pay a tax towards its support.

Guildhall. The hall or place of meeting of a guild, or gild.

The place of meeting of a municipal corporation. The mercantile or commercial gilds of the Saxons are supposed to have given rise to the present municipal corporations of England, whose place of meeting is still called the "Guildhall."

Guildhall sittings. The sittings held in the Guildhall of the city of London for city of London causes.

Guild rents. In England, rents payable to the crown by any guild, or such as formerly belonged to religious guilds, and came to the crown at the general dissolution of the monasteries.

Guillotine /gílətiyn/gìyətíyn/. An instrument for decapitation, used in France for the infliction of the death penalty on convicted criminals, consisting, essentially, of a heavy and weighted knife-blade moving perpendicularly between grooved posts, which is made to fall from a considerable height upon the neck of the sufferer, immovably fixed in position to receive the impact.

Guilt. In criminal law, that quality which imparts criminality to a motive or act, and renders the person amenable to punishment by the law. Responsibility for offense. That disposition to violate the law which has manifested itself by some act already done. The opposite of innocence.

Guilty. Having committed a crime or tort; the word used by an accused in pleading to an indictment when he confesses the crime of which he is charged, and by the jury in convicting. Responsible for a delinquency, crime, or other offense, and the connotation of such word is "evil", "wrongdoing", or "culpability". Hilkert v. Canning, 58 Ariz. 290, 119 P.2d 233, 236.

Guilty plea. Formal admission in court as to guilt which a defendant may make if he or she does so intelligently and voluntarily; *i.e.* accused can only make such plea after he or she has been fully advised of rights and court has determined that accused understands such rights and is making plea voluntarily. Boykin v. Alabama, 395 U.S. 238, 89 S.Ct. 1709, 23 L.Ed.2d 274. See also **Plea bargaining.**

Guilty verdict. Formal pronouncement by jury that they adjudge the defendant guilty of the offense charged.

Guinea /gíniy/. A coin formerly issued by the English mint, but all these coins were called in the time of Wm. IV. The word now means only the sum of £1 1 *s.,* in which denomination the fees of counsel are always given.

Gun. Portable firearm such as a rifle, pistol, revolver, shotgun, carbine, etc.

Gwalstow. A place of execution.

Gwayf /gwéyf/. In old English law, waif, or waived; that which has been stolen and afterwards dropped in the highway for fear of a discovery.

Gyltwite, or **guiltwit** /gíltwət/. Sax. Compensation for fraud or trespass.

Gynecocracy. Government by a woman; a state in which women are legally capable of the supreme command; *e.g.* in Great Britain (Queen).

Gyves /jáyvs/. Fetters or shackles for the legs.

H

H. This letter, as an abbreviation, stands for Henry (a king of that name) in the citation of English statutes. In the Year Books, it is used as an abbreviation for Hilary term. In tax assessments and other such official records, "h" may be used as an abbreviation for "house".

H.A. An abbreviation for *hoc anno*, this year, in this year.

Habe, or **have.** Lat. A form of the salutatory expression *"Ave"* (hail) in the titles of the constitutions of the Theodosian and Justinian Codes.

Habeas corpora juratorum /héybiyəs kórpərə jùrətórəm/. In old English law, a writ commanding the sheriff to bring up the persons of jurors, and, if need were, to distrain them of their lands and goods, in order to insure or compel their attendance in court on the day of trial of a cause. It issued from the Common Pleas, and served the same purpose as a *distringas juratores* in the King's Bench. Such writ was abolished by the C.L.P. Act, 1852, § 104.

Habeas corpus /héybiyəs kórpəs/héybiyz°/. Lat. (You have the body.) The name given to a variety of writs (of which these were anciently the emphatic words), having for their object to bring a party before a court or judge. In common usage, and whenever these words are used alone, they are usually understood to mean the *habeas corpus ad subjiciendum* (see *infra*). U. S. v. Tod, 263 U.S. 149, 44 S.Ct. 54, 57, 68 L.Ed. 221. The primary function of the writ is to release from unlawful imprisonment. People ex rel. Luciano v. Murphy, 160 Misc. 573, 290 N.Y.S. 1011. The office of the writ is not to determine prisoner's guilt or innocence, and only issue which it presents is whether prisoner is restrained of his liberty by due process. Ex parte Presnell, 58 Okl.Cr. 50, 49 P.2d 232.

Initially, the writ only permitted a prisoner to challenge a state conviction on constitutional grounds that related to the jurisdiction of the state court. But the scope of the inquiry was gradually expanded, and Fay v. Noia, 372 U.S. 391, 83 S.Ct. 822, 9 L.Ed.2d 837, concluded that the writ now extends to all constitutional challenges.

See also **Post-conviction remedies** with respect to review of sentence of federal prisoner.

Habeas corpus acts. The English statute of 31 Car. II, c. 2, is the original and prominent *habeas corpus* act. It was amended and supplemented by St. 56 Geo. III,

c. 100. Similar statutes have been enacted in all the United States. This act is regarded as the great constitutional guaranty of personal liberty. See Art. I, § 9, U.S.Const.; 28 U.S.C.A. § 2241 et seq.

Habeas corpus ad deliberandum et recipiendum /héybiyəs kórpəs æd dəlìbərǽndəm èt rəsìpiyéndəm/. A writ which is issued to remove, for trial, a person confined in one county to the county or place where the offense of which he is accused was committed. Thus, it has been granted to remove a person in custody for contempt to take his trial for perjury in another county.

Habeas corpus ad faciendum et recipiendum /héybiyəs kórpəs æd fæs(h)iyéndəm èt rəsìpiyéndəm/. A writ issuing in civil cases to remove the cause, as also the body of the defendant, from an inferior court to a superior court having jurisdiction, there to be disposed of. It is also called *"habeas corpus cum causa."*

Habeas corpus ad prosequendum /héybiyəs kórpəs æd pròsəkwéndəm/. A writ which issues when it is necessary to remove a prisoner in order to *prosecute* in the proper jurisdiction wherein the fact was committed. State ex rel. Deeb v. Fabisinski, 111 Fla. 454, 152 So. 207, 210.

Habeas corpus ad respondendum /héybiyəs kórpəs æd rèspondéndəm/. A writ which is usually employed in civil cases to remove a person out of the custody of one court into that of another, in order that he may be sued and answer the action in the latter.

Habeas corpus ad satisfaciendum /héybiyəs kórpəs æd sædəsfæs(h)iyéndəm/. In English practice, a writ which issues when a prisoner has had judgment against him in an action, and the plaintiff is desirous to bring him up to some superior court, to charge him with process of execution.

Habeas corpus ad subjiciendum /héybiyəs kórpəs æd səbjìs(h)iyéndəm/. A writ directed to the person detaining another, and commanding him to produce the body of the prisoner, or person detained. This is the most common form of habeas corpus writ, the purpose of which is to test the legality of the detention or imprisonment; not whether he is guilty or innocent. This writ is guaranteed by U.S.Const. Art. I, § 9, and by state constitutions. See also 28 U.S.C.A. § 2241 et seq.

This is the well-known remedy in England and the United States for deliverance from illegal confinement, called by Sir William Blackstone the most celebrated writ in the English law, and the great and efficacious writ in all manner of illegal confinement. 3 Bl.Comm. 129. The "great writ of liberty," issuing at common law out of courts of Chancery, King's Bench, Common Pleas, and Exchequer.

Habeas corpus ad testificandum /héybiyəs kórpəs æd tèstəfəkǽndəm/. The writ, meaning "you have the body to testify", used to bring up a prisoner detained in a jail or prison to give evidence before the court. Hottle v. District Court in and for Clinton County, 233 Iowa 904, 11 N.W.2d 30, 34; 3 Bl.Comm. 130.

Habeas corpus cum causa /héybiyəs kórpəs kəm kózə/. (You have the body, with the cause.) Another name for the writ of *habeas corpus ad faciendum et recipiendum (q.v.).*

Habemus optimum testem, confitentem reum /həbíyməs óptəməm téstəm, kənfədéntəm ríyəm/. We have the best witness,—a confessing defendant.

Habendum clause /həbéndəm klòz/. Portion of deed beginning with the words "To have and to hold". Bannin v. Peck, 266 App.Div. 209, 41 N.Y.S.2d 668, 670. The clause usually following the granting part of the premises of a deed, which defines the extent of the ownership in the thing granted to be held and enjoyed by the grantee. New York Indians v. U. S., 170 U.S. 1, 18 S.Ct. 531, 42 L.Ed. 927. The office of the "habendum" is properly to determine what estate or interest is granted by the deed, though office may be performed by the premises, in which case the habendum may lessen, enlarge, explain, or qualify, but not totally contradict or be repugnant to, estate granted in the premises. Claridge v. Phelps, 105 Ind.App. 344, 11 N.E.2d 503, 504.

Habendum et tenendum /həbéndəm èt tənéndəm/. In old conveyancing "to have and to hold". Formal words in deeds of land from a very early period.

Habentes homines /həbéntiyz hóməniyz/. In old English law, rich men; literally, having men. The same with *fœsting-men (q.v.).*

Habere /həbíriy/. Lat. In the civil law, to have. Sometimes distinguished from *tenere* (to hold), and *possidere* (to possess); *habere* referring to the right, *tenere* to the fact, and *possidere* to both.

Habere facias possessionem /həbíriy féys(h)iyəs pəzès(h)iyównəm/. Lat. That you cause to have possession. The name of the process commonly resorted to by the successful party in an action of ejectment, for the purpose of being placed by the sheriff in the actual possession of the land recovered. It is commonly termed simply *"habere facias,"* or *"hab. fa."*

Habere facias seisinam /həbíriy féys(h)iyəs síyzənəm/. L. Lat. That you cause to have seisin. The writ of execution in real actions, directing the sheriff to cause the demandant to have seisin of the lands recovered. It was the proper process for giving seisin of a freehold, as distinguished from a chattel interest in lands.

Habere facias visum /həbíriy féys(h)iyəs váyzəm/. Lat. That you cause to have a view. A writ to cause the sheriff to take a view of lands or tenements.

Habere licere /həbíriy ləsíriy/. Lat. In Roman law, to allow [one] to have [possession]. This phrase denoted the duty of the seller of property to allow the purchaser to have the possession and enjoyment. For a breach of this duty, an *actio ex empto* might be maintained.

Habeto tibi res tuas /həbíydow tíbay ríyz tyúwəs/. Lat. Have or take your effects to yourself. One of the old Roman forms of divorcing a wife.

Habilis /hǽbələs/. Lat. Fit; suitable; active; useful (of a servant). Proved; authentic (of Book of Saints). Fixed; stable (of authority of the king).

Habit. A disposition or condition of the body or mind acquired by custom or a usual repetition of the same act or function. The customary conduct, to pursue which one has acquired a tendency, from frequent repetition of the same acts. Knickerbocker Life Ins. Co. v. Foley, 105 U.S. 350, 26 L.Ed. 1055. Course of behavior of a person regularly repeated in like circumstances. Evidence of a specific habit may be admissible to show specific conduct or acts within the sphere of the developed habit. Fed.Evid. R. 406. See also **Custom and usage; Habitual.**

Habitability. Condition of premises which permits inhabitant to live free of serious defects to health and safety.

Warranty of habitability. In most states, either by statute or case law, every landlord is held to impliedly warrant that the residential premises rented are fit for human habitation (*i.e.* free of violations of building and sanitary codes) at the time of the inception of the tenancy, and will continue as such during the term. Boston Housing Authority v. Hemingway et al., 363 Mass. 184, 293 N.E.2d 831; Hinson v. Delis, 26 Cal.App.3d 62, 102 Cal.Rptr. 661; Uniform Residential Landlord and Tenant Law, § 2.104. See also **Home Owners Warranty.**

Habitable repair. A covenant by a lessee to "put the premises into habitable repair" binds him to put them into such a state that they may be occupied, not only with safety, but with reasonable comfort, for the purposes for which they are taken. See **Habitability.**

Habitancy. That fixed place of abode to which a person intends to return habitually when absent. Owens v. Huntling, C.C.A.Or., 115 F.2d 160, 162. Settled dwelling in a given place; fixed and permanent residence there. Place of abode, settled dwelling; residence; house. Moore v. Tiller, Ky., 409 S.W.2d 813, 815.

It is difficult to give an exact definition of "habitancy." In general terms, one may be designated as an "inhabitant" of that place which constitutes the principal seat of his residence, of his business, pursuits, connections, attachments, and of his political and municipal relations. The term, therefore, embraces the fact of residence at a place, together with the intent to regard it and make it a home. The act and intent must concur.

See also **Domicile; Residence.**

Habitant. Fr. In French and Canadian law, a resident tenant; a settler; a tenant who kept hearth and home on the seigniory. A native of Canada of French descent, particularly of the peasant or farming class.

Habitatio /hæbətéysh(iy)ow/. Lat. In the civil law, the right of dwelling; the right of free residence in another's house.

Habitation. Place of abode; dwelling place; residence.

In the civil law, the right of a person to live in the house of another without prejudice to the property. It differed from a usufruct, in this: that the usufructuary might apply the house to any purpose, as of a store or manufactory; whereas the party having the right of habitation could only use it for the residence of himself and family.

See **Domicile; Habitancy; Residence.**

Habitual. Customary, usual, of the nature of a habit. Synonyms are customary, common, regular; while its antonyms are unusual, unwonted, extraordinary, rare. Illinois Bankers Life Ass'n v. Theodore, 47 Ariz. 314, 55 P.2d 806, 811. Formed or acquired by or resulting from habit; frequent use or custom. See also **Habit.**

Habitual criminal. A recidivist (q.v.). A legal category created by statute in many states by which severe penalties ranging up to life imprisonment can be imposed on criminals convicted of any crime the third or fourth time. In general, habitual offender statutes impose greater sentences on offender for repeated crimes, with life imprisonment being imposed upon commission of several felonies.

Habitual drunkenness or **intoxication.** One who frequently and repeatedly becomes intoxicated by excessive indulgence in intoxicating liquor so as to acquire a fixed habit and an involuntary tendency to become intoxicated as often as the temptation is presented, even though he remains sober for days or even weeks at a time. A person given to inebriety or the excessive use of intoxicating drink, who has lost the power or the will, by frequent indulgence, to control his appetite for it. The custom or habit of getting drunk; the constant indulgence in stimulants, whereby intoxication is produced; not the ordinary use, but the habitual use of them; the habit should be actual and confirmed, but need not be continuous, or even of daily occurrence. That degree of intemperance from the use of intoxicating drinks which disqualifies the person a great portion of the time from properly attending to business, or which would reasonably inflict a course of great mental anguish upon the innocent party.

Habitually. Customarily; by frequent practice or use. It does not mean entirely or exclusively.

Hable. L. Fr. In old English law, a port or harbor; a station for ships.

Hacienda /(h)às(i)yénda/hòsiyéndə/. In Spanish law, the public domain; the royal estate; the aggregate wealth of the state. The science of administering the national wealth; public economy.

Also an estate or farm belonging to a private person. A royal estate.

Had. As used in a statute providing that no suit, action or proceeding to foreclose a mortgage or trust deed shall be had or maintained, "had" means commenced or begun.

Hadbote /hǽdbowt/. In Saxon law, a recompense or satisfaction for the violation of holy orders, or violence offered to persons in holy orders.

Hadd. In Hindu law, a boundary or limit. A statutory punishment defined by law, and not arbitrary.

Haderunga /hǽdərə́ŋgə/. In old English law, hatred; ill will; prejudice, or partiality.

Respect or distinction of persons.

Hadgonel. In old English law, a tax or mulct.

Hæc est conventio /híyk èst kənvénsh(iy)ow/. Lat. This is an agreement. Words with which agreements anciently commenced.

Hæc est finalis concordia /híyk èst fənéyləs kənkórd(i)yə/. L. Lat. This is the final agreement. The words with which the foot of a fine commenced.

Hæreda /hər_iydə/. In Gothic law, a tribunal answering to the English court-leet or hundred court.

Hærede abducto /həríydiy əbdáktow/. An ancient writ that lay for the lord, who, having by right the wardship of his tenant under age, could not obtain his person, the same being carried away by another person.

Hærede deliberando alteri qui habet custodium terræ /həríydiy dəlìbərǽndow óltəray kwày héybət kəstówdiyəm téhriy/. An ancient writ, directed to the sheriff, to require one that had the body of an heir, being in ward, to deliver him to the person whose ward he was by reason of his land.

Hæredem deus facit, non homo /həríydəm díyəs fèysət, nòn hówmow/. God makes the heir, not man.

Hærede rapto /həríydiy rǽptow/. An ancient writ that lay for the ravishment of the lord's ward.

Hæredes /həríydiyz/. Lat. In the civil law, heirs. The plural of hæres (q.v.).

Hæredes proximi /həríydiyz próksəmay/. Nearest or next heirs. The children or descendants of the deceased.

Hæredes remotiores /həríydiyz rəmòwshiyóriyz/. More remote heirs. The kinsmen other than children or descendants.

Hæredes sui et necessarii /həríydiyz syúway èt nèsəsériyay/. In Roman law, own and necessary heirs; i.e., the lineal descendants of the estate-leaver. They were called "necessary" heirs, because it was the law that made them heirs, and not the choice of either the decedent or themselves. But since this was also true of slaves (when named "heirs" in the will) the former class was designated "sui et necessarii," by way of distinction, the word "sui" denoting that the necessity arose from their relationship to the decedent.

Hæredipeta /hìrədípədə/. Lat. In old English law, a seeker of an inheritance; hence, the next heir to lands.

Hæredipetæ suo propinquo vel extraneo periculoso sane custodi nullus committatur /hìrədípədə s(y)úwow prəpíŋkwow vèl ekstréyniyow pərikyəlówsow séyniy kəstówday nə́ləs kòmətéydər/. To the next heir, whether a relation or a stranger certainly a dangerous guardian, let no one be committed.

Hæreditas /hərédətæs/. In *Roman law,* the *hæreditas* was a universal succession by law to any deceased person, whether such person had died testate or intestate, and whether in trust *(ex fideicommisso)* for another or not. The like succession according to Prætorian law was *bonorum possessio.*

In *old English law,* an estate transmissible by descent; an inheritance.

Hæreditas, alia corporalis, alia incorporalis; corporalis est, quæ tangi potest et videri; incorporalis quæ tangi non potest nec videri /hərédətæs éyl(i)yə kòrpəréyləs éyl(i)yə ínkorpəréyləs; kòrpəréyləs èst, kwìy tǽnjay pówdəst èt vədíray; ínkorpəréyləs kwìy tǽnjay nón pówdəst nèk vədíray/. An inheritance is either corporeal or incorporeal. Corporeal is that which can be touched and seen; incorporeal, that which can neither be touched nor seen.

Hæreditas damnosa /hərédətæs dæmnówsə/. A burdensome inheritance; one which would be a burden instead of a benefit, that is, the debts to be paid by the heir would exceed the assets.

Hæreditas est successio in universum jus quod defunctus habuerit /hərédətæs èst səksés(h)(i)yow ìn yùwnəvársəm jás kwòd dəfántəs həbyúwərət/. Inheritance is the succession to every right which the deceased had.

Hæreditas jacens /hərédətæs jéysən(d)z/. In civil law, a prostrate or vacant inheritance. The inheritance left to a voluntary heir was so called so long as he had not manifested, either expressly or by silence, his acceptance or refusal of the inheritance. So long as no one had acquired the inheritance, it was termed *"hæreditas jacens";* and this, by a legal fiction, represented the person of the decedent. The estate of a person deceased, where the owner left no heirs or legatee to take it, called also *"caduca";* an escheated estate. The term has also been used in English law to signify an estate in abeyance; that is, after the ancestor's death, and before assumption of heir. An inheritance without legal owner, and therefore open to the first occupant.

Hæreditas legitima /hərédətæs ləjídəmə/. A succession or inheritance devolving by operation of law (intestate succession) rather than by the will of the decedent.

Hæreditas luctuosa /hərédətæs làkchuwówsə/. A sad or mournful inheritance or succession; as that of a parent to the estate of a child, which was regarded as disturbing the natural order of mortality *(turbato ordine mortalitatis).* It was sometimes termed *tristis successio.*

Hæreditas nihil aliud est, quam successio in universum jus, quod defunctus habuerit /hərédətæs náy(h)əl ǽliyəd èst, kwæm səksésh(iy)ow ìn yùwnəvársəm jás, kwòd dəfáŋktəs həbyúwərət/. The right of inheritance is nothing else than the faculty of succeeding to all the rights of the deceased.

Hæreditas nunquam ascendit /hərédətæs náŋkwəm əséndət/. An inheritance never ascends. 2 Bl.Comm. 211. A maxim of feudal origin, and which invariably prevailed in the law of England down to the passage of the statute 3 & 4 Wm. IV, c. 106, § 6, by which it was abrogated.

Hæreditas testamentaria /hərédətæs tèstəmentériyə/. Testamentary inheritance, that is, succession to an estate under and according to the last will and testament of the decedent.

Hæredum appellatione veniunt hæredes hæredum in infinitum /həríydəm ǽpəlèyshiyówniy véniyənt həríydiyz həríydəm ìn ìnfənáydəm/. By the title of heirs, come the heirs of heirs to infinity.

Hæres /híriyz/. In *Roman law,* the heir, or universal successor in the event of death. The heir is he who actively or passively succeeds to the entire property of the estate-leaver. He is not only the successor to the rights and claims, but also to the estate-leaver's debts, and in relation to his estate is to be regarded as the identical person of the estate-leaver, inasmuch as he represents him in all his active and passive relations to his estate.

The institution of the *hæres* was the essential characteristic of a *testament:* if this was not done, the instrument was called a *codicillus.* The office, powers, and duties of the *hæres,* in Roman law, were much more closely assimilated to those of a modern *executor* than to those of an heir at law. Hence "heir" is not at all an accurate translation of *"hæres,"* unless it be understood in a special technical sense.

In *Common law,* an heir; he to whom lands, tenements, or hereditaments by the act of God and right of blood to descend, of some estate of inheritance.

Hæres astrarius /híriyz əstrériyəs/. In old English law, an heir in actual possession of the house of his ancestor.

Hæres de facto /híriyz dìy fæktow/. In old English law, heir from fact; that is, from the disseisin or other act of his ancestor, without or against right. An heir in fact, as distinguished from an heir *de jure,* or by law.

Hæres est alter ipse, et filius est pars patris /híriyz èst óltər ípsiy èt fíliyəs, èst párz pǽtrəs/. An heir is another self, and a son is part of the father.

Hæres est aut jure proprietatis aut jure representationis /híriyz èst òt júriy prəpràyətéydəs òt júriy rèprəzəntèyshiyównəs/. An heir is either by right of property, or right of representation.

Hæres est eadem persona cum antecessore /híriyz èst iyéydəm pərsównə kəm æntəsəsóriy/. An heir is the same person with his ancestor.

Hæres est nomen collectivum /híriyz èst nówmən kòləktáyvəm/. "Heir" is a collective name or noun.

Hæres est nomen juris; filius est nomen naturæ /híriyz èst nówmən jurəs, fíliyəs èst nówmən nəchúriy/. "Heir" is a name or term of law; "son" is a name of nature.

Hæres est pars antecessoris /híriyz èst párz æntəsəsórəs/. An heir is a part of the ancestor. So said because the ancestor, during his life, bears in his body (in judgment of law) all his heirs.

Hæres ex asse /híriyz èks ǽsiy/. In the civil law, an heir to the whole estate; a sole heir.

Hæres extraneus /híriyz əkstréyniyəs/. In the civil law, a strange or foreign heir; one who was not subject to the power of the testator, or person who made him heir. *Qui testatoris juri subjecti non sunt, extranei hœredes appellantur.*

Hæres factus /híriyz fǽktəs/. In the civil law, an heir made by will; a testamentary heir; the person created universal successor by will. Otherwise called *"hæres ex testamento,"* and *"hæres institutus."*

Hæres fideicommissarius /híriyz fídiyaykòməsériyəs/. In the civil law, the person for whose benefit an estate was given to another (termed *"hœres fiduciarius,"* q.v.) by will. Answering nearly to the *cestui que trust* of the English law.

Hæres fiduciarius /híriyz fədùws(h)iyériyəs/. A fiduciary heir, or heir in trust; a person constituted heir by will, in trust for the benefit of another, called the *"fideicommissarius."*

Hæres hæredis mei est meus hæres /híriyz həríydəs míyay èst. míyəs híriyz/. The heir of my heir is my heir.

Hæres institutus /híriyz ìnstətyúwdəs/. A testamentary heir; one appointed by the will of the decedent.

Hæres legitimus /híriyz ləjídəməs/. A lawful heir; one pointed out as such by the marriage of his parents.

Hæres legitimus est quem nuptiæ demonstrant /híriyz ləjídəməs èst kwèm nápshiyiy dəmónstrənt/. He is a lawful heir whom marriage points out as such; who is born in wedlock.

Hæres minor uno et viginti annis non respondebit, nisi in casu dotis /híriyz máynər yúwnow èt vəjíntay ǽnəs nòn rèspondíybət náysay ìn kéysyuw dówdəs/. An heir under twenty-one years of age is not answerable, except in the matter of dower.

Hæres natus /híriyz néydəs/. In the civil law, an heir born; one born heir, as distinguished from one made heir *(hæres factus, q.v.);* an heir at law, or by intestacy *(ab intestato);* the next of kin by blood, in cases of intestacy.

Hæres necessarius /híriyz nèsəsériyəs/. In the civil law, a necessary or compulsory heir. This name was given to the heir when, being a slave, he was named "heir" in the testament, because on the death of the testator, whether he would or not, he at once became free, and was compelled to assume the heirship.

Hæres non tenetur in Anglia ad debita antecessoris reddenda, nisi per antecessorem ad hoc fuerit obligatus, præterquam debita regis tantum /híriyz nòn təníydər ìn ǽngliyə ǽd débədə ǽntəsəsórəs rədéndə, náysay pər ǽntəsəsórəm ǽd hók fyúwərəd òbləgéydəs prətárkwəm débədə ríjəs tǽntəm/. In England, the heir is not bound to pay his ancestor's debts, unless he be bound to it by the ancestor, except debts due to the king. However, by 3 & 4 Wm. IV, c. 104, he is now liable.

Hæres rectus /híriyz réktəs/. In old English law, a right heir.

Hæres suus /híriyz s(y)úwəs/. In the civil law, a man's *own* heir; a decedent's proper or natural heir. This name was given to the lineal descendants of the deceased. Persons who were in the power of the testator but became *sui juris* at his death. Those descendants who were under the power of the deceased at the time of his death, and who are most nearly related to him.

Hæretare /hèhrətériy/. In old English law, to give a right of inheritance, or make the donation hereditary to the grantee and his heirs.

Hæretico comburendo /hərédəkow kòmbyəréndow/. The English statute 2 Hen. IV, c. 15, *de hæretico comburendo,* was the first penal law enacted against heresy, and imposed the penalty of death by burning against all heretics who relapsed or who refused to abjure their opinions. This statute was repealed by the statute 29 Car. II, c. 9. This was also the name of a writ for the purpose indicated.

Hafne /héyvən/. A haven or port.

Hafne courts /héyvən kórts/. Haven courts; courts anciently held in certain ports in England.

Hagne /héyk/hǽg/. A little handgun. A misspelling of *hague.*

Hagnebut /hǽkbət/hǽg°/. A handgun of a larger description than the hagne.

Hague Tribunal /héyg trəbyúwnəl/. The Court of Arbitration established by the Hague Peace Conference of 1899. The object of the establishment was to facilitate the immediate recourse to arbitration for the settlement of international differences by providing a permanent court, "accessible at all times, and acting, in default of agreement to the contrary between the parties, in accordance with the rules of procedure inserted in the present convention." The court was given jurisdiction over all arbitration cases, provided the parties did not agree to institute a special tribunal. An international Bureau was likewise established to serve as a registry for the court and to be the channel of communications relative to the meetings of the court. The court, although called "permanent," is really so only in the fact that there is a permanent list of members from among whom the arbitrators in a given case are selected. At the Second Hague Conference of 1907, apart from minor changes made in the court, it was provided that, of the two arbitrators appointed by each of the parties, only one should be a national of the appointing state.

Haia /héyə/. In old English law, a park inclosed. A hedge.

Hakh /hák/. Truth; the true God; a just or legal prescriptive right or claim; a perquisite claimable under established usage by village officers.

Hakhdar /hákdàr/. The holder of a right.

Halakar /hálakàr/. The realization of the revenue.

Half. One of two equal parts into which anything may be divided. Hoyne v. Schneider, 138 Kan. 545, 27 P.2d 558. A moiety.

Half blood. See **Blood relations.**

Half brother, half sister. Persons who have the same father, but different mothers; or the same mother, but different fathers.

Half cent. A copper coin of the United States, of the value of five mills, and of the weight of ninety-four grains. The coinage of these was discontinued in 1857.

Half defense. See **Defense**.

Half dime. A silver (now nickel) coin of the United States, of the value of five cents.

Half dollar. A silver (now only partially silver) coin of the United States, of the value of fifty cents, or one-half the value of a dollar.

Half eagle. A gold coin of the United States, of the value of five dollars. No longer in general circulation.

Half endeal or **halfen-deal** /hàf°/hòfəndýl/. A moiety or half of a thing.

Half-kineg /hàfkínəg/. In Saxon law, half-king (*semirex*). A title given to the aldermen of all England.

Half-mark. A noble, or six shillings and eight pence in English money.

Half nephew or **half niece.** Son or daughter of a half brother or half sister.

Half pilotage. Compensation for services which a pilot has put himself in readiness to perform, by labor, risk, and cost, and has offered to perform, at half the rate he would have received if the services had actually been performed. Gloucester Ferry Co. v. Pennsylvania, 114 U.S. 196, 5 S.Ct. 826, 29 L.Ed. 158.

Half-proof. In the civil law, proof by one witness, or a private instrument. Or *prima facie* proof, which yet was not sufficient to found a sentence or decree.

Half-seal. That which was formerly used in the English chancery for sealing of commissions to delegates, upon any appeal to the court of delegates, either in ecclesiastical or marine causes.

Half section. The half of a section of land according to the divisions of the government survey, laid off either by a north-and-south or by an east-and-west line, and containing 320 acres.

Half-timer. A child who, by the operation of the English factory and education acts, was employed for less than the full time in a factory or workshop, in order that he might attend some "recognized efficient school."

Half-tongue. A jury half of one *tongue* or nationality and half of another.

Halfway house. Loosely structured institution designed to rehabilitate persons who have left a hospital or prison or who, for personal reasons, need help in readjusting. Such houses, for example, assist a recently discharged prisoner in making the often difficult transition from prison to civilian life.

Half year. In legal computation, the period of one hundred and eighty-two days; the odd hours being rejected.

Halifax law /hæləfæks ló/. A synonym for lynch law, or the summary (and unauthorized) trial of a person accused of crime and the infliction of death upon him; from the name of the parish of Halifax, in England, where anciently this form of private justice was practised by the free burghers in the case of persons accused of stealing; also called "gibbet law."

Haligemot, or **halimote** /hælə(gə)mòwt/. In Saxon law, the meeting of a hall (*conventus aulæ*), that is, a lord's court; a court of a manor, or court-baron. So called from the *hall*, where the tenants or freemen met, and justice was administered. It was sometimes used to designate a convention of citizens in their public hall and was also called folkmote and hallmote. The word *halimote* rather signifies the lord's court or a court baron held in a manor in which the differences between the tenants were determined. Furthermore, it seems to have been a common practice for a wealthy abbey to keep a court, known as a *halimote*, on each of its manors, while in addition to these manorial courts it kept a central court, a *libera curia* for all its greater freehold tenants.

Halimas /hæləməs/. In English law, the feast of All Saints, on the 1st of November; one of the cross-quarters of the year, was computed from Halimas to Candlemas.

Hall. A building or room of considerable size, used as a place for the meeting of public assemblies, conventions, courts, etc.; as, the city hall, the town hall.

In old English law, a name given to many manor-houses because the magistrate's court was held in the hall of his mansion; a chief mansion-house.

Hence, *hall day*, a court day.

Hallage /hóləj/. In old English law, a fee or toll due for goods or merchandise vended in a hall. A toll due to the lord of a fair or market, for such commodities as were vended in the common hall of the place.

Hallazco /(h)a(l)yáskow/. In Spanish law, the finding and taking possession of something which previously had no owner, and which thus becomes the property of the first occupant.

Halle-gemote /hólgəmòwt/. In Saxon law, haligemot (*q.v.*).

Hallmark. An official stamp affixed by the goldsmiths upon articles made of gold or silver as an evidence of genuineness, and hence used to signify any mark of genuineness.

Hallmoot /hólmòwt/. See **Haligemot**.

Hallucination /həl(y)ùwsənéyshən/. An apparently real sensory perception (auditory or visual) without any real external stimuli to cause it; commonly experienced by psychotics. It may occur with relation to any of the special senses, *e.g.* hearing sounds or seeing things that do not exist. The perception by any of the senses of an object which has no existence. The conscious recognition of a sensation of sight, hearing, feeling, taste, or smell which is not due to any impulse received by the perceptive apparatus from without, but arises within the perceptive apparatus itself.

Hallucinogenic drug. Drugs that induce hallucinations, such as mescaline, LSD, and the like.

Halmote /hólmòwt/. See **Haligemot.**

Halved notes. Payment notes which are torn in half, one half of each note being given to seller when order is placed, the other half, when the goods are delivered.

Halymote /hǽləmòwt/. A holy or ecclesiastical court. It was anciently held on Sunday next before St. Thomas' day, and therefore called the *"holymote"*, or holy court.

Halywercfolk /hǽləwàrkfówk/. Sax. In old English law, tenants who held land by the service of repairing or defending a church or monument, whereby they were exempt from feudal and military services. Especially in the county of Durham, those who held by service of defending the corpse of St. Cuthbert.

Ham. In England, a place of dwelling; a homeclose; a little narrow meadow. A house or little village.

Hama /héymə/. In English law, a piece of land.

Hamel, hameleta, or **hamleta** /hǽməl/hǽmlədə/. A hamlet.

Hamesecken /héymsèkən/. In old English law, the crime of housebreaking or burglary. See also **Hamsocne.**

Hamfare /hǽmfèr/. (Sax. From *ham,* a house.) In Saxon law, an assault made in a house; a breach of the peace in a private house. This word by some is said to signify the freedom of a man's house. See also **Hamsocne.**

Hamlet. A small village; a part or member of a vill. It is the diminutive of *"ham",* a village. A "village" or "hamlet" in a rural community may be no more than a store, a school, a church, and a few residences.

Hammer. Metaphorically, a forced sale or sale at public auction. "To bring to the hammer", *i.e.* to put up for sale at auction. "Sold under the hammer", *i.e.* sold by an officer of the law or by an auctioneer. See also **Forced sale.**

Hammurabi, Code of. Set of laws once considered the oldest promulgation of laws in human history prepared by Babylonian king, 1792–1750 B.C. (circa).

Hamsocne /hǽmsòwkən/. In Saxon law, the word is variously spelled *hamsoca, hamsocna, haimsuken, hamesaken, hamsocn.* The right of security and privacy in a man's house. The breach of this privilege by a forcible entry of a house is breach of the peace.

Among the Anglo-Saxons it was breaking into a house; perhaps the time of the day was not an element. See also **Hamesecken.**

Hanaper /hǽnəpər/. In old English law, a hamper or basket in which were kept the writs of the court of chancery relating to the business of a subject, and their returns; equivalent to the Roman *fiscus.* The fees accruing on writs, etc., were there kept.

Hanaper-office /hǽnəpər ófəs/. An office formerly belonging to the common-law jurisdiction of the court of chancery, so called because all writs relating to the business of a subject, and their returns, were formerly kept in a hamper, *in hanaperio.*

Hand. A measure of length equal to four inches, used in measuring the height of horses.

A person's signature.

In anatomical usage the hand, or manus, includes the phalanges, or fingers and thumb; the metacarpus, or hand proper; and the carpus, or wrist; but in popular usage the wrist is often excluded.

An instrumental part; *e.g.* "he had a hand in the crime". One who performs some work or labor; *e.g.* a "hired hand". To give assistance; *e.g.* to lend a "hand".

In the plural, the term may be synonymous with "possession"; as, the "hands" of an executor, garnishee, etc.

In old English law, an oath. For the meaning of the terms "strong hand" and "clean hands," see those titles.

Handbill. A written or printed notice displayed, handed out, or posted, to inform those concerned of something to be done or some event. Posting and distribution of handbills is regulated by ordinance or statute in most localities.

Handborow. In Saxon law, a hand pledge; a name given to the nine pledges in a decennary or friborg; the tenth or chief, being called *"headborow" (q.v.).* So called as being an inferior pledge to the chief.

Handcuffs. See **Fetters.**

Hand down. To announce or file an opinion in a cause. Used originally and properly of the opinions of appellate courts transmitted to the court below; but in later usage the term is employed more generally with reference to any decision by a court upon a case or point reserved for consideration.

Hand-fasting. In old English law, betrothment.

Hand-grith. Peace or protection given by the king with his own hand; used in the laws of Henry I.

Handhabend, or **hand-habende** /hǽndhǽbənd/. In Saxon law, one having a thing in his hand, that is, a thief found having the stolen goods in his possession. Jurisdiction to try such thief.

Handle. To control, direct, to deal with, to act upon, to perform some function with regard to or to have passed through one's hands, to buy and sell, or to deal or trade in. State ex rel. Bell v. Phillips Petroleum Co., 349 Mo. 360, 160 S.W.2d 764, 769. To manage or operate.

Hand money. Money paid in hand to bind a bargain; earnest money, when it is in cash.

Handsale. Anciently, among the northern European nations, shaking of hands was held necessary to bind a bargain,—a custom still retained in verbal contracts. A sale thus made was called "handsale" *(venditio per mutuam manum complexionem).* In process of time the same word was used to signify the price or earnest money which was given immediately after the shaking of hands, or instead thereof. 2 Bl.Comm. 448.

Handsel. Handsale, or earnest money.

Handwriting. The chirography of a person; the cast or form of writing peculiar to a person, including the size, shape, and style of letters, tricks of penmanship, and whatever gives individuality to his writing, distinguishing it from that of other persons. Anything written by hand; an instrument written by the hand of a person, or a specimen of his writing.

Handwriting, considered under the law of evidence, includes not only the ordinary writing of one able to write, but also writing done in a disguised hand, or in cipher, and a mark made by one able or unable to write. For nonexpert opinion as to genuineness of handwriting, as based on familiarity not required for purposes of litigation, see Fed.Evid. R. 901(b)(2).

Handwriting exemplars. Samples of one's handwriting required in criminal cases involving forgery, kidnapping, etc., for comparison purposes.

Compelling grand jury witness to produce handwriting and printing exemplars, to be used solely as standard of comparison in order to determine whether witness was author of certain writings, does not violate Fifth Amendment privilege although privilege might be asserted if government should seek more than physical characteristics of handwriting as by seeking to obtain written answers to incriminating questions or a signature on incriminating statement. U.S.C.A.Const. Amend. 5. U. S. v. Mara, 410 U.S. 19, 93 S.Ct. 774, 35 L.Ed.2d 99.

Hang. In old practice, to remain undetermined. Thus, the present participle means pending; during the pendency. Remaining undetermined.

Hanged, drawn and quartered. A method of executing traitors in England, said to have been introduced in 1241. The traitor was carried on a sled, or hurdle to the gallows (formerly dragged there tied to the tail of a horse); hanged till half dead and then cut down; his entrails cut out and burnt; his head cut off and his body to be divided into quarters, which, with his head, were hung in some public place. In practice the executioner usually cut out the heart and held it up to view.

Hanging. As a form of capital punishment, means suspension by neck until dead. Such means of capital punishment is seldom used in United States.

Hanging in chains. In atrocious cases it was at one time usual, in England, for the court to direct a murderer, after execution, to be hanged upon a gibbet in chains near the place where the murder was committed. Its legality was declared by acts in 1751 and 1828, and abolished by 4 & 5 Wm. IV, c. 26.

Hangman. An executioner. One who executes condemned criminals by hanging.

Hangwite /hǽŋwət/. In Saxon law, a fine for illegal hanging of a thief, or for allowing him to escape. Immunity from such fine.

Hanse /hǽn(t)s/hánzə/. In Germany, formerly an alliance or confederation among merchants or cities, for the good ordering and protection of the commerce of its members. An imposition upon merchandise.

Hanseatic /hǽnsiyǽdək/. Pertaining to a hance or commercial alliance; but, generally, the union of the Hanse Towns is the one referred to, as in the expression the "Hanseatic League."

Hanse Towns /hǽn(t)s táwnz/. The collective name of certain German cities, including Lübeck, Hamburg, and Bremen, which formed an alliance for the mutual protection and furtherance of their commercial interests, in the twelfth century. The powerful confederacy thus formed was called the "Hanseatic League." The league framed and promulgated a code of maritime law, which was known as the "Laws of the Hanse Towns," or *Jus Hanseaticum Maritimum.*

The years 1356 to 1377 marked the zenith of the league's power. The league gradually declined till, in 1669, the last general assembly was held and Lübeck, Hamburg and Bremen were left alone to preserve the name and small inheritance of the "Hansa."

Hanse Towns, laws of the /lóz əv ðə hǽn(t)s táwnz/. The maritime ordinances of the Hanseatic towns, first published in German at Lübeck, in 1597, and in May, 1614, revised and enlarged.

Hantelod, or **hantelode** /hǽntəlòwd/. In old European law, an arrest, or attachment.

Haole /háwliy/. White foreign. Refers to rank rather than to race. International Longshoremen's & Warehousemen's Union v. Ackerman, D.C.Hawaii, 82 F.Supp. 65, 76.

Hap. To catch. Thus, "hap the rent," "hap the deed-poll," were formerly used.

Happiness. Comfort, consolation, contentment, ease, enjoyment, pleasure, satisfaction. The constitutional right of men to pursue their "happiness" means the right to pursue any lawful business or vocation, in any manner not inconsistent with the equal rights of others, which may increase their prosperity, or develop their faculties, so as to give to them their highest enjoyment. Butchers' Union Co. v. Crescent City Co., 111 U.S. 746, 4 S.Ct. 652, 28 L.Ed. 585.

Harassment. Used in variety of legal contexts to describe words, gestures and actions which tend to annoy, alarm and abuse (verbally) another person. A person commits a petty misdemeanor if, with purpose to harass another, he: (1) makes a telephone call without purpose of legitimate communication; or (2) insults, taunts or challenges another in a manner likely to provoke violent or disorderly response; or (3) makes repeated communications anonymously or at extremely inconvenient hours, or in offensively coarse language; or (4) subjects another to an offensive touching; or (5) engages in any other course of alarming conduct serving no legitimate purpose of the actor. Model Penal Code, § 250.4.

The federal Fair Debt Collection Practices Act prohibits harassment by debt collectors. 15 U.S.C.A. § 1692c et seq.

Harbinger /hárbənjər/. In England, an officer of the royal household.

Harbor, *n.* A haven, or a space of deep water so sheltered by the adjacent land as to afford a safe anchorage for ships. A port or haven for ships; a sheltered place, natural or artificial, on the coast of a sea, lake, or other body of water. A place of security and comfort; a refuge. See also **Haven.**

Harbor, *v.* To afford lodging to, to shelter, or to give a refuge to. To clandestinely shelter, succor, and protect improperly admitted aliens. Susnjar v. U. S., C.C.A.Ohio, 27 F.2d 223, 224. To receive clandestinely and without lawful authority a person for the purpose of so concealing him that another having a right to the lawful custody of such person shall be deprived of the same. Or, in a less technical sense, it is the reception of persons improperly. It may be aptly used to describe the furnishing of shelter, lodging, or food clandestinely or with concealment, and under certain circumstances, may be equally applicable to those acts divested of any accompanying secrecy. Harboring a criminal is a crime under both federal and state statutes.

Harbor line. A line marking the boundary of a certain part of a public water which is reserved for a harbor. The line beyond which wharves and other structures cannot be extended.

Hard cases. A phrase used to indicate judicial decisions which, to meet a case of hardship to a party, are not entirely consonant with the true principle of the law. It is said of such: "Hard cases make bad law."

Hard labor. A punishment, additional to mere imprisonment, sometimes imposed upon convicts sentenced to a penitentiary for serious crimes, or for misconduct while in prison.

Hard money. Lawful coined money.

Hardship. In general, privation, suffering, adversity. As used in zoning statutes as grounds for variance, it refers to fact that zoning ordinance or restriction as applied to a particular property is unduly oppressive, arbitrary or confiscatory. St. Onge v. City of Concord, 95 N.H. 306, 63 A.2d 221.

The severity with which a proposed construction of the law would bear upon a particular case, founding, sometimes, an argument against such construction, which is otherwise termed the "argument *ab inconvenienti.*" See **Hard cases.**

Harm. The existence of loss or detriment in fact of any kind to a person resulting from any cause. See also **Damages; Injury; Physical injury.**

Harmful. As used in connection with foods, means noxious, hurtful, pernicious, likely to cause illness or damage. See also **Adulteration.**

As used in connection with errors committed at trial, it means that rights were seriously affected; an appellate court will consider harmful error but not harmless error. See also **Error; Harmless error; Plain error rule.**

Harmless error. An error which is trivial or formal or merely academic and was not prejudicial to the substantial rights of the party assigning it, and in no way affected the final outcome of the case. State v. Johnson, 1 Wash.App. 553, 463 P.2d 205, 206. Doctrine which permits an appellate court to affirm a conviction in spite of error appearing in record. State v. Michelli, La., 301 So.2d 577, 579.

Harmless error is not a ground for granting a new trial or for setting aside a verdict or for vacating, modifying or otherwise disturbing a judgment or order, unless such refusal appears to the court inconsistent with substantial justice. Fed.R.Civil P. 61. Any error, defect, irregularity or variance which does not affect substantial rights will be disregarded by court. Fed.R.Crim.P. 52.

See also **Error.**

Harmonic plane. The zero adopted by the United States Coast and Geodetic Survey of the Department of Commerce upon which its tidal tables, charts, and maps are based. It is an arbitrary plane, and, in Puget Sound, is the lowest plane of the tide recognized by that department.

Harmonize. See **Harmony.**

Harmony. The phrase "in harmony with" is synonymous with "in agreement, conformity, or accordance with."

Haro, harron /hǽrow/. Fr. In Norman and early English law, an outcry, or hue and cry after felons and malefactors.

Harter Act. A name commonly applied to the act of Congress of February 13, 1893, c. 105, providing: (§ 1) that agreements in a bill of lading relieving the owner, etc., of a vessel sailing between the United States and foreign ports, from liability for negligence or fault in proper loading, storage, custody, care, or delivery of merchandise, are void (46 U.S.C.A. § 190); (§ 2) that no bill of lading shall contain any agreement whereby the obligations of the owner to exercise due diligence, properly equip, man, provision and outfit a vessel and make it seaworthy, and whereby the obligations of the master, etc., carefully to handle, store, care for and deliver the cargo, are in any way lessened, weakened or avoided (46 U.S.C.A. § 191); (§ 3) that if the owner shall exercise due diligence to make such vessel in all respects seaworthy and properly manned, equipped and supplied, neither the vessel nor her owners, etc., shall be liable for loss resulting from faults or errors in navigation or management, nor for losses arising from dangers of the sea, acts of God, or public enemies, or the inherent defect of the thing carried, or insufficiency of package, or seizure under legal process, or any act or omission of the shipper of the goods, or from saving or attempting to save life at sea, or deviation in rendering such service (46 U.S.C.A. § 192).

Harvesting. The act or process of gathering of crops of any kind. Also the quantity or yield of a crop.

Hashish. Drug which is formed of resin scraped from the flowering top of the cannabis plant, as distinguished from marijuana which consists of the chopped leaves and stems of the cannabis plant.

Haspa /hǽspə/. In old English law, the hasp of a door; by which livery of seisin might anciently be made, where there was a house on the premises.

Hasta /hǽstə/. Lat. A spear. In the Roman law, a spear was the sign of a public sale of goods or sale by auction. Hence the phrase *"hastæ subjicere"* (to put under the spear) meant to put up at auction.

In feudal law, a spear, the symbol used in making investiture of a fief.

Hatch Act. Federal statute which prohibits federal, state, and local employees from partaking in certain types of political activities.

Hat money. In maritime law, primage; a small duty paid to the captain and mariners of a ship.

Hauber /ówbər/. O. Fr. A high lord; a great baron.

Haul. To pull or draw with force; to drag; to transport by hauling.

Haula. See **Aula.**

Haulage royalty /hólaj róyəltiy/. Damages at a certain amount per ton for coal from adjacent lands hauled through subterranean passageways of lessor's land. Quality Excelsior Coal Co. v. Reeves, 206 Ark. 713, 177 S.W.2d 728, 732.

Haustus /hóstəs/. Lat. In the civil law, a species of servitude, consisting in the right to draw water from another's well or spring, in which the *iter* (right of way to the well or spring), so far as it is necessary, is tacitly included.

Have. Lat. A form of the salutatory expression *"Ave,"* used in the titles of some of the constitutions of the Theodosian and Justinian Codes.

Have. Imports ownership, and has been defined to mean "to keep," "to hold in possession," "to own." To bear (children).

Have and hold. A common phrase in conveyancing, derived from the *habendum et tenendum* of the old common law. See **Habendum et tenendum.**

Haven. A place of a large receipt and safe riding of ships, so situate and secured by the land circumjacent that the vessels thereby ride and anchor safely, and are protected by the adjacent land from dangerous or violent winds; as Milford Haven, Plymouth Haven, and the like. Lowndes v. Board of Trustees, 153 U.S. 1, 14 S.Ct. 758, 38 L.Ed. 615. A place of refuge. See also **Harbor.**

Hawker. An itinerant or traveling salesman who carries goods about in order to sell them, and who actually sells them to purchasers, in contradistinction to a trader who has goods for sale and sells them in a fixed place of business. A hawker or peddler usually sells his goods in the public streets, or from door-to-door, and commonly is required to have a license.

Formerly, a peddler who used beast of burden to carry wares and who cried out merits of wares in street. City of Washington v. Reed, 229 Mo.App. 1195, 70 S.W.2d 121, 122. See **Hawking; Peddler.**

Hawking. The act of offering goods for sale from door-to-door, or on the streets by outcry or by attracting the attention of persons by exposing goods in a public place, or by placards, labels, or signals. The business of peddling or hawking is distinct from that of a manufacturer selling his own products, and those who raise or produce what they sell, such as farmers and butchers, are not peddlers or hawkers.

Hay-bote /héybòwt/. In old English law, another name for "hedge-bote," being one of the estovers allowed to a tenant for life or years, namely, material for repairing the necessary hedges or fences of his grounds, or for making necessary farming utensils. 2 Bl.Comm. 35.

Hayward. In old English law, an officer appointed in the lord's court to keep a common herd of cattle of a town; so called because he was to see that they did not break or injure the hedges of inclosed grounds. His duty was also to impound trespassing cattle, and to guard against poundbreaches.

Hazard. A risk or peril, assumed or involved, whether in connection with contract relation, employment, personal relation, sport or gambling. A danger or risk lurking in a situation which by change or fortuity develops into an active agency of harm. Hough v. Contributory Retirement Appeal Board, 309 Mass. 534, 36 N.E.2d 415, 417, 418. Exposure to the chance of loss or injury. Caminetti v. Guaranty Union Life Ins. Co., 52 Cal.App.2d 330, 126 P.2d 159, 163. A game of chance or wagering.

In insurance law, the risk, danger, or probability that the event insured against may happen, varying with the circumstances of the particular case.

In old English law, an unlawful game at dice, those who play at it being called "hazardors."

See also **Dangerous; Extraordinary hazard; Risk.**

Moral hazard. In fire insurance, the risk or danger of the destruction of the insured property by fire, as measured by the character and interest of the insured owner, his habits as a prudent and careful man or the reverse, his known integrity or his bad reputation, and the amount of loss he would suffer by the destruction of the property or the gain he would make by suffering it to burn and collecting the insurance.

Hazardor /hǽzərdər/. In old English law, one who played at a hazard, *i.e.,* an unlawful game of dice.

Hazardous. Exposed to or involving danger; perilous; risky; involving risk of loss. Caminetti v. Guaranty Union Life Ins. Co., 52 Cal.App.2d 330, 126 P.2d 159, 162, 163.

The terms "hazardous", "extra-hazardous", "specially hazardous", and "not hazardous" are well-understood technical terms in the business of insurance, having distinct and separate meanings. See **Extraordinary hazard.**

Hazardous contract. See **Contract.**

Hazardous employment. High risk and extra perilous work. When used in context of worker's compensation, it refers to employment which requires employer to carry worker's compensation coverage or its equivalent regardless of the number of employees.

Hazardous insurance. Insurance effected on property which is in unusual or peculiar danger of destruction by fire, or on the life of a man whose occupation exposes him to special or unusual perils.

Hazardous negligence. See **Negligence.**

Hazar-zamin. A bail or surety for the personal attendance of another.

H.B. House Bill; a bill in the process of going through the House of Representatives on its way to becoming a law.

H.B.M. An abbreviation for His (or Her) Britannic Majesty.

H.C. An abbreviation for house of commons, or for *habeas corpus.*

He. Properly a pronoun of the masculine gender, but usually used and construed in status to include both sexes as well as corporations. May be read "they". Buono v. Yankee Maid Dress Corporation, C.C.A. N.Y., 77 F.2d 274, 278.

Head. Chief; leading; principal; the upper part or principal source of a stream.

The principal person or chief of any agency, bureau, organization, corporation, or firm.

Headborough. In Saxon law, the head or chief officer of a borough; chief of the frank-pledge tithing or decennary. This office was afterwards, when the petty constableship was created, united with that office.

Head money. A sum of money reckoned at a fixed amount for each head (person) in a designated class. Particularly (1) a capitation or poll tax. (2) A bounty offered by the laws of the United States for each person on board an enemy's ship or vessel, at the commencement of a naval engagement, which shall be sunk or destroyed by a ship or vessel of the United States of equal or inferior force, the same to be divided among the officers and crew in the same manner as prize money. A similar reward is offered by the British statutes. (3) The tax or duty imposed by act of congress of Aug. 3, 1882, on owners of steamships and sailing vessels for every immigrant brought into the United States. Head Money Cases, 112 U.S. 580, 5 S.Ct. 247, 28 L.Ed. 798. (4) A bounty or reward formerly paid to one who pursued and killed a bandit or outlaw and produced his head as evidence; the offer of such a reward being popularly called "putting a price on his head". See **Bounty; Reward.**

Headnote. A brief summary of a legal rule or significant facts in a case, which, among other headnotes applicable to the case, precedes the printed opinion in reports. A syllabus to a reported case; a summary of the points decided in the case, which is placed at the head or beginning of the opinion. See also **Syllabus.**

Head of family or **household.** An individual who actually supports and maintains in one household one or more individuals who are closely connected with him by blood relationship, relationship by marriage, or by adoption, and whose right to exercise family control and provide for the dependent individuals is based upon some moral or legal obligation. Miller v. Glenn, D.C.Ky., 47 F.Supp. 794, 796, 797.

The Internal Revenue Code gives preferential tax rates to heads of family or household if they meet the criteria of the statute (*e.g.* if he or she contributed over half the cost of maintaining the household during the taxable year). An unmarried individual who maintains a household for another and satisfies certain conditions set forth in I.R.C. § 2(b). Such status enables the taxpayer to use a set of income tax rates that are lower than those applicable to other unmarried individuals but higher than those applicable to surviving spouses and married persons filing a joint return.

A term used in homestead and exemption laws to designate a person who maintains a family; a householder. Not necessarily a husband or father, but any person who has charge of, supervises, supports, maintains, and manages the affairs of the household or the collective body of persons residing together and constituting the family. The term may thus include an abandoned wife maintaining minor children or a bachelor supporting his parents.

Head of stream. The highest point on the stream which furnishes a continuous stream of water, not necessarily the longest fork or prong. The source of a stream. See also **Headstream.**

Headright. Under the Allotment Act (Act Cong. June 28, 1906 [34 Stat. 539]), creating a trust fund from all tribal funds which included funds from sale of tribal lands, funds allowed on claims against the United States and received from tribal oil, gas, and mineral rights, each allottee owned his pro rata share of the trust fund, and this pro rata beneficial interest is commonly called a "headright."

Headright certificate. In the laws of the republic of Texas, a certificate issued under authority of an act of 1839, which provided that every person immigrating to the republic between October 1, 1837, and January 1, 1840, who was the head of a family and actually resided within the government with his or her family should be entitled to a grant of 640 acres of land, to be held under such a certificate for three years, and then conveyed by absolute deed to the settler, if in the meantime he had resided permanently within the republic and performed all the duties required of citizens.

Head-silver. In old English law, a name sometimes given to a Common Fine (*q.v.*). By a payment of a certain sum of money to the lord, litigants might try their suits nearer home.

Headstream. Stream that is the source of a river. See also **Head of stream.**

Head tax. Tax of flat amount per person.

Heafodweard. In old English law, one of the services to be rendered by a thane, or a geneath or villein, the precise nature of which is unknown.

Healer. One who heals or cures; specifically, one who professes to cure bodily diseases without medicine or any material means, according to the tenets and practices of so-called "Christian Science," whose beliefs and practices are founded on their religious convictions.

Healgemote /héylgəmòwt/. In Saxon law, a court-baron; an ecclesiastical court; Haligemot (*q.v.*).

Healing act. Another name for a curative act or statute.

Healsfang /héylsfàŋ/. In Saxon law, a sort of pillory, by which the head of the culprit was caught between two boards, as feet are caught in a pair of stocks. It was very early disused, no mention of it occurring in the laws of the Saxon Kings.

Health. State of being hale, sound, or whole in body, mind or soul, well being. Freedom from pain or sickness. See **Healthy.**

Bill of health. See **Bill.**

Board of health. See **Board.**

Health laws. Laws, ordinances, or codes prescribing sanitary standards and regulations, designed to promote and preserve the health of the community.

Health officer. The officer charged with the execution and enforcement of health laws, *e.g.* Surgeon General. The powers and duties of health officers are regulated by federal, state and local laws.

Public health. As one of the objects of the police power of the state, the "public health" means the prevailingly healthful or sanitary condition of the general body of people or the community in mass, and the absence of any general or widespread disease or cause of mortality. The wholesome sanitary condition of the community at large. Many cities have "Public Health Departments" or agencies of similar function and status. Federal laws dealing with health are administered by the Department of Health, Education and Welfare.

Sound health. See **Sound.**

Healthy. Free from disease, injury, or bodily ailment, or any state of the system peculiarly susceptible or liable to disease or bodily ailment.

Hearing. Proceeding of relative formality (though generally less formal than a trial), generally public, with definite issues of fact or of law to be tried, in which witnesses are heard and parties proceeded against have right to be heard, and is much the same as a trial and may terminate in final order. It is frequently used in a broader and more popular significance to describe whatever takes place before magistrates clothed with judicial functions and sitting without jury at any stage of the proceedings subsequent to its inception, and to hearings before administrative agencies as conducted by a hearing examiner or Administrative Law Judge.

The introduction and admissibility of evidence is usually more lax in a hearing than in a civil or criminal trial.

An *adversary* hearing exists when both parties are present at the hearing arguing their respective positions. An *ex parte* hearing exists when only one party is present at the hearing.

Hearings are extensively employed by both legislative and administrative agencies and can be adjudicative or merely investigatory. Adjudicative hearings can be appealed in a court of law. Congressional committees often hold hearings prior to enactment of legislation; these hearings are then important sources of legislative history.

See also **Detention hearing; Fair hearing; Full hearing; Omnibus hearing.**

Ex parte hearing. See **Ex parte.**

Final hearing. See **Final.**

In criminal law. The examination of a prisoner charged with a crime or misdemeanor, and of the witnesses for the accused. See *Preliminary hearing, infra.*

Preliminary examination. The examination of a person charged with crime, before a magistrate or judge. See *Preliminary hearing, infra.*

Preliminary hearing. In criminal law, synonymous with "preliminary examination". The hearing given to a person accused of crime, by a magistrate or judge, exercising the functions of a committing magistrate, to ascertain whether there is evidence to warrant and require the commitment and holding to bail of the persons accused. It is in no sense a trial for the determination of accused's guilt or innocence, but simply a course of procedure whereby a possible abuse of power may be prevented, and accused discharged or held to answer, as the facts warrant. See Fed.R.Crim.P. 5.1.

Unfair hearing. See that title.

Hearing de novo /híriŋ dìy nówvow/. Generally, a new hearing or a hearing for the second time, contemplating an entire trial in same manner in which matter was originally heard and a review of previous hearing. On hearing "de novo" court hears matter as court of original and not appellate jurisdiction. Collier & Wallis v. Astor, 9 Cal.2d 202, 70 P.2d 171, 173.

Hearing examiner. Generally, a civil service employee of an administrative agency whose responsibility is to conduct hearings on matters within the agency's jurisdiction. Now called "Administrative Law Judge" (*q.v.*) in the federal government.

Hearing officer. See **Administrative law judge.**

Hearsay. A statement, other than one made by the declarant while testifying at the trial or hearing offered in evidence to prove the truth of the matter asserted. Fed.R.Evid. 801(c). "Hearsay evidence" is evidence of a statement that was made other than by a witness while testifying at the hearing and that is offered to prove the truth of the matter stated. Calif. Evid.Code.

Hearsay evidence is testimony in court of a statement made out of the court, the statement being offered as an assertion to show the truth of matters asserted therein, and thus resting for its value upon the credibility of the out-of-court asserter. Mutyambizi v. State, 33 Md.App. 55, 363 A.2d 511, 518. Evidence not proceeding from the personal knowledge of the witness, but from the mere repetition of what he has heard others say. That which does not derive its value solely from the credit of the witness, but rests mainly on the veracity and competency of other persons. The very nature of the evidence shows its weakness, and it is admitted only in specified cases from necessity.

There are numerous exceptions to the hearsay exclusion; see *e.g.* Fed.R.Evid. 803, 804.

See also **Double hearsay.**

Heart balm statutes. State statutes abolishing right of action for alienation of affections, breach of promise to marry, criminal conversation, and seduction of person over legal age of consent.

Hearth money. A tax levied in England by St. 14 Car. II, c. 10, consisting of two shillings on every hearth or stove in the kingdom. It was extremely unpopular, and was abolished by 1 W. & M., St. 1, c. 10. This tax was otherwise called "chimney money."

Hearth silver. In old English law, a species of *modus* or composition for tithes; viz.: a prescription for cutting down and using for fuel the tithe of wood.

Heat of passion. In criminal law, a state of violent and uncontrollable rage engendered by a blow or certain other provocation given, which will reduce a homicide from the grade of murder to that of manslaughter. Passion or anger suddenly aroused at the time by some immediate and reasonable provocation, by words or acts of one at the time. The term includes an emotional state of mind characterized by anger, rage, hatred, furious resentment or terror. State v. Lott, 207 Kan. 602, 485 P.2d 1314, 1317.

Heave to. In maritime parlance and admiralty law, to stop a sailing vessel's headway by bringing her head "into the wind," that is, in the direction from which the wind blows. A steamer is said to be "hove to" when held in such a position that she takes the heaviest seas upon her quarter.

Hebberthef /hébərθèyf/. In Saxon law, the privilege of having the goods of a thief, and the trial of him, within a certain liberty.

Hebdomad /hébdəmæd/. A week; a space of seven days.

Hebephrenia /hìybəfríyn(i)yə/. Psychotic form of schizophrenia featuring regression into silly, deteriorated, or infantile behavior and mannerisms.

Hebote. The king's edict commanding his subjects into the field.

Heda. A small haven, wharf, or landing place. See **Harbor; Haven.**

Hedagium /hədéyjiyəm/. In old English law, a toll or customary dues at the hithe or wharf, for landing goods, etc., from which exemption was granted by the crown to some particular persons and societies.

Hedging. A means by which traders and exporters of grain or other products, and manufacturers who make contracts in advance for the sale of their goods, secure themselves against the fluctuations of the market by counter-contracts for the purchase or sale of an equal quantity of the product or of the material of manufacture. Whorley v. Patton-Kjose Co., 90 Mont. 461, 5 P.2d 210, 214. A means by which a party who deals in the purchase of commodities in large quantities for actual delivery at some future time insures itself against unfavorable changes in the price of such commodities by entering into compensatory arrangements or counterbalancing transactions on the other side. Ralston Purina Co. v. McFarland, C.A.N.C., 550 F.2d 967, 970.

Safeguarding one's self from loss on a bet or speculation by making compensatory arrangements on the other side. Whorley v. Patton-Kjose Co., 90 Mont. 461, 5 P.2d 210, 214.

Heedless. Term is almost as strong as word "reckless" and includes the element of disregard of the rights or safety of others. Thoughtless; inconsiderate.

Hegemony /həjémɔniy/héjəmòwniy/həgéʸ/. The leadership of one among several independent confederate states.

Heir /ér/. See **Heirs.**

Heir apparent. An heir whose right of inheritance is indefeasible, provided he outlive the ancestor; as in England the eldest son, or his issue, who must, by the course of the common law, be heir to the father whenever he happens to die. One who, before the death of the ancestor, is next in the line of succession, provided he be heir to the ancestor whenever he happens to die. See also **Apparent heir.**

Heir at law. At common law, he who, after his ancestor dies intestate, has a right to all lands, tenements, and hereditaments which belonged to him or of which he was seised. The same as "heir general."

"Heirs at law," as the term is used in wrongful death statute, means lineal descendants. Howlett v. Greenberg, 34 Colo.App. 356, 530 P.2d 1285, 1287.

A deceased person's "heirs at law" are those who succeed to his estate of inheritance under statutes of descent and distribution, in absence of testamentary disposition, and not necessarily his heirs at common law, who are persons succeeding to deceased's realty in case of his intestacy. In re Towndrow's Will, 47 N.M. 173, 138 P.2d 1001, 1003.

See also **Heir, legal.**

Heir beneficiary. In the civil law, one who has accepted the succession under the benefit of an inventory regularly made.

Heirs are divided into two classes, according to the manner in which they accept the successions left to them, to-wit, unconditional and beneficiary heirs. Unconditional heirs are those who inherit without any reservation, or without making an inventory, whether their acceptance be express or tacit. Beneficiary heirs are those who have accepted the succession under the benefit of an inventory regularly made. Civ.Code La. art. 883. If the heir apprehend that the succession will be burdened with debts beyond its value, he accepts with benefit of inventory, and in that case he is responsible only for the value of the succession. See **Beneficiary.**

Heir by adoption. By statute in most all jurisdictions, an adopted child takes all the rights of succession to intestate property as those of a natural born child unless a contrary intention is clearly expressed. Statutes differ however as to whether such adopted child may in addition inherit from its natural parents or family.

Heir by custom. In old English law, one whose right of inheritance depends upon a particular and local custom, such as gavelkind, or borough English.

Heir by devise. One to whom lands are devised by will; a devisee of lands. Answering to the *hæres factus* (*q.v.*) of the civil law.

Heir collateral. One who is not lineally related to the decedent, but is of collateral kin; *e.g.*, his uncle, cousin, brother, nephew.

Heir conventional. In the civil law, one who takes a succession by virtue of a contract or settlement entitling him thereto.

Heirdom /érdəm/. Succession by inheritance.

Heiress /érəs/. A female heir to a person having an estate of inheritance. When there are more than one, they are called "co-heiresses," or "co-heirs."

Heir expectant. See **Heir apparent.**

Heir, forced. One who cannot be disinherited. See **Forced heirs.**

Heir general. An heir at law. The ordinary heir by blood, succeeding to all the lands.

Heir hunter. Those whose business or occupation consists in tracking down missing heirs.

Heir, irregular. In Louisiana, irregular heirs are those who are neither testamentary nor legal, and who have been established by law to take the succession. See Civ.Code La. art. 878. When there are no direct or collateral relatives surviving the decedent, and the succession consequently devolves upon the surviving husband or wife, or illegitimate children, or the state, it is called an "irregular succession."

Heir, legal. In the civil law, a legal heir is one who takes the succession by relationship to the decedent and by force of law. This is different from a testamentary or conventional heir, who takes the succession in virtue of the disposition of man. See Civ. Code La. arts. 877, 879. The term is also used in American law in substantially the same sense, that is, the person to whom the law would give the decedent's property, real and personal, if he should die intestate. In legal strictness, the term signifies one who would inherit real estate, but it is also used to indicate one who would take under the statute of distribution. See also **Heir at law.**

Heirless estate. The property of one who dies intestate leaving no heirs in which case there generally is escheat (q.v.).

Heirlooms /érlùwmz/. In general, valued possessions of great sentimental value passed down through generations within a family.

In old English law, such goods and chattels as, contrary to the nature of chattels, shall go by special custom to the heir along with the inheritance, and not to the executor. The termination "loom" (Sax.) signifies a limb or member; so that an heirloom is nothing else but a limb or member of the inheritance. They are generally such things as cannot be taken away without damaging or dismembering the freehold; such as deer in a park, doves in a cote, deeds and charters, etc.

Heir, male. In English law, the nearest male blood-relation of the decedent, unless further limited by the words "of his body," which restrict the inheritance to sons, grandsons, and other male descendants in the right line.

Heir of the blood. An inheritor who succeeds to the estate by virtue of consanguinity with the decedent, either in the ascending or descending line, including illegitimate children, but excluding husbands, wives, and adopted children.

Heir of the body. An heir begotten or borne by the person referred to, or a child of such heir; any lineal descendant of the decedent, excluding a surviving husband or wife, adopted children, and collateral relations; bodily heir. May be used in either of two senses: In their unrestricted sense, as meaning the persons who from generation to generation become entitled by descent under the entail; and in the sense of heirs at law, or those persons who are descendants of him whom the statute of descent appoints to take intestate estate.

Heir presumptive. The person who, if the ancestor should die immediately, would, in the present circumstances of things, be his heir, but whose right of inheritance may be defeated by the contingency of some nearer heir being born; as a brother or nephew, whose presumptive succession may be destroyed by the birth of a child.

In Louisiana, the presumptive heir is he who is the nearest relation of the deceased capable of inheriting. This quality is given to him before the decease of the person from whom he is to inherit, as well as after the opening of the succession, until he has accepted or renounced it. La.Civ.Code, art. 880.

Heir, pretermitted. One who, except for an unambiguous act of the ancestor, would take his property on his death. See also **Pretermitted heir.**

Heirs /érz/. At common law, the person appointed by law to succeed to the estate in case of intestacy. One who inherits property, whether real or personal. A person who succeeds, by the rules of law, to an estate in lands, tenements, or hereditaments, upon the death of his ancestor, by descent and right of relationship. One who would receive his estate under statute of descent and distribution. Faulkner's Guardian v. Faulkner, 237 Ky. 147, 35 S.W.2d 6, 7. Moreover, the term is frequently used in a popular sense to designate a successor to property either by will or by law. Word "heirs" is no longer limited to designated character of estate as at common law. Jay v. Dollarhide, 3 Cal.App.3d 1001, 84 Cal.Rptr. 538, 547.

Word "heirs" is a technical term and is used to designate persons who would, by statute, succeed to an estate in case of intestacy. Wells Fargo Bank v. Title Ins. & Trust Co., 22 Cal.App.3d 295, 99 Cal.Rptr. 464, 466.

Bodily laws. See **Heir of the body.**

Civil law. A universal successor in the event of death. He who actively or passively succeeds to the entire property or estate, rights and obligations, of a decedent, and occupies his place.

The term is indiscriminately applied to all persons who are called to the succession, whether by the act of the party or by operation of law. The person who is created universal successor by a will is called the "testamentary heir;" and the next of kin by blood is, in cases of intestacy, called the "heir at law," or "heir by intestacy." The executor of the common law in many respects corresponds to the testamentary heir of the civil law. Again, the administrator in many respects corresponds with the heir by intestacy. By the common law, executors and administrators have no right except to the personal estate of the deceased; whereas the heir by the civil law is authorized to administer both the personal and real estate. The term "heir" has several significations. Sometimes it refers to one who has formally accepted a succession and taken possession thereof; sometimes to one who is called to succeed, but still retains the faculty of accepting or renouncing, and it is frequently used as applied to one who has formally renounced.

Collateral heir. See that title.

Joint heirs. Co-heirs. The term is also applied to those who are or will be heirs to both of two designated persons at the death of the survivor of them, the word "joint" being here applied to the ancestors rather than the heirs.

Known heirs. See that title.

Lawful heirs. See **Heir at law; Heir, legal.**

Legitimate heirs. Children born in lawful wedlock and their descendants, not including collateral heirs or issue in indefinite succession.

Lineal heir. See **Lineal heir.**

Natural heirs. Heirs by consanguinity as distingushed from heirs by adoption, and also as distinguished from collateral heirs.

Right heir. This term was formerly used, in the case of estates tail, to distinguish the preferred heir, to whom the estate was limited, from the heirs in general, to whom, on the failure of the preferred heir and his line, the remainder over was usually finally limited. With the abolition of estates tail, the term has fallen into disuse, but when still used, in modern law, it has no other meaning than "heir at law."

Heirs and assigns. Ordinarily words of limitation and not of purchase. At common law, the words were essential to conveyance granting title in fee simple, and though they are unnecessary for that or any purpose under statute when used in wills or deeds, words still have that meaning.

Heirs at law shall not be disinherited by conjecture, but only by express words or necessary implication. Maxim which means that ancestor must clearly cut off heir and that such disinheritance is not lightly inferred.

Heirship /érshəp/. The quality or condition of being heir, or the relation between the heir and his ancestor. It is a legal right, regulated by law, to be enjoyed subject to the provisions of the statute.

Heir special. In English law, the issue in tail, who claims *per formam doni;* by the form of the gift.

Heirs per stirpes. See **Per stirpes.**

Heir testamentary. In the civil law, one who is named and appointed heir in the testament of the decedent. This name distinguishes him from a *legal* heir (one upon whom the law casts the succession), and from a *conventional* heir (one who takes it by virtue of a previous contract or settlement).

Heir unconditional. In the civil law and in Louisiana, one who inherits without any reservation, or without making an inventory, whether his acceptance be express or tacit. Distinguished from *heir beneficiary.* La.Civ.Code, art. 882.

Held. In reference to the decision of a court, decided. See also **Hold.**

Hell. The name formerly given in England to a place under the exchequer chamber, where the king's debtors were confined.

Helsing. A Saxon brass coin, of the value of a half-penny.

Hemiplegia /hèməplíyjiyə/. Unilateral paralysis; paralysis of one side of the body, commonly due to a lesion in the brain, but sometimes originating from the spinal cord, as in "Brown-Sequard's paralysis," unilateral paralysis with crossed *anœsthesia.* In the cerebral form, the *hemiplegia* is sometimes "alternate" or crossed, that is, occurring on the opposite side of the body from the initial lesion. Paralysis of half of the body, as of both legs or of both arms, or an arm and leg. Gray v. United States, C.C.A.Ark., 109 F.2d 728, 729.

Henceforth /hén(t)sfòrθ/. A word of futurity, which, as employed in legal documents, statutes, and the like, always imports a continuity of action or condition from the present time forward, but excludes all the past.

Henchman. A page; an attendant; servant; a herald. A loyal and trusted follower. A footman; one who holds himself at the bidding of another. It has come to mean here a political follower; used in a rather bad sense. Gates v. State, 140 Tex.Cr.R. 228, 143 S.W.2d 780, 783, 784. Member of criminal gang.

Henfare. In old English law, a fine for flight on account of murder.

Henghen /héŋən/. In Saxon law, a prison, a gaol, or house of correction.

Hengwyte /héŋwət/. Sax. In old English law, an acquittance from a fine for hanging a thief.

Henricus Vetus /henráykəs víydəs/. Henry the Old, or Elder. King Henry I is so called in ancient English chronicles and charters, to distinguish him from the subsequent kings of that name.

Heordfæte, or **Hedefæst.** In Saxon law, a master of a family, keeping house, distinguished from a lower class of freemen, viz., *folgeras (folgarii),* who had no habitations of their own, but were house-retainers of their lords.

Heordpenny /hárdpèniy/. Peter-pence *(q.v.).*

Heordwerch /hárdwòrk/. In Saxon law, the service of herdsman, done at the will of their lord.

Hepburn Act. The name commonly given to an act of Congress (1906), amending §§ 1, 6, 14, 15, 16 and 20 of the Interstate Commerce Act. Such Act increased the jurisdiction of the I.C.C. to include pipelines; prohibited free passes except to employees; prohibited common carriers from transporting any products, except timber, in which they had an interest; required joint tariffs and uniform system of accounts.

Heptarchy /héptàrkiy/. A government exercised by seven persons, or a nation divided into seven governments. In the year 560, seven different monarchies had been formed in England by the German tribes, namely, that of Kent by the Jutes; those of Sussex, Wessex, and Essex by the Saxons; and those of East

Anglia, Bernicia, and Deira by the Angles. To these were added, about the year 586, an eighth, called the "Kingdom of Mercia," also founded by the Angles, and comprehending nearly the whole of the heart of the kingdom. These states formed what has been designated the "Anglo-Saxon Octarchy," or more commonly, though not so correctly, the "Anglo-Saxon Heptarchy," from the custom of speaking of Deira and Bernicia under the single appellation of the "Kingdom of Northumberland."

Herald. In ancient law, a herald was a diplomatic messenger who carried messages between kings or states, and especially proclamations of war, peace, or truce. In English law, a herald is an officer whose duty is to keep genealogical lists and tables, adjust armorial bearings, and regulate the ceremonies at royal coronations and funerals.

Heraldry /héhrəldriy/. The art, office, or science of heralds. Also an old and obsolete abuse of buying and selling precedence in the paper of causes for hearing.

Heralds' College. In England, an ancient royal corporation, first instituted by Richard III, in 1483. It comprised three kings of arms, six heralds, and four marshals or pursuivants of arms, together with the earl marshal and a secretary. The heralds' books, compiled when progresses were solemnly and regularly made into every part of the kingdom, to inquire into the state of families, and to register such marriages and descents as were verified to them upon oath, are allowed to be good evidence of pedigrees. The heralds' office is still allowed to make grants of arms and to permit change of names.

Herbage /(h)árbəj/. In English law, an easement or liberty, which consists in the right to pasture cattle on another's ground.

Herciscunda /(h)ərsəskándə/. In the civil law, to be divided. *Familia herciscunda,* an inheritance to be divided. *Actio familiæ herciscundæ,* an action for dividing an inheritance. *Erciscunda* is more commonly used in the civil law.

Herd, *n.* An indefinite number, more than a few, of cattle, sheep, horses, or other animals of the larger sorts, assembled and kept together as one drove and under one care and management. Boland v. Cecil, 65 Cal.App.2d Supp. 832, 150 P.2d 819, 822.

Herd, *v.* To tend, take care of, manage, and control a herd of cattle or other animals, implying something more than merely driving them from place to place.

Herder. One who herds or has charge of a herd of cattle, in the senses above defined.

Herdwerch, heordwerch /hárdwərk/. In old English law, herdsmen's work, or customary labor, done by shepherds and inferior tenants, at the will of the lord.

Hereafter. A word of futurity, always used in statutes and legal documents as indicative of future time, excluding both the present and the past.

Herebannum /hèrəbǽnəm/. In old English law, a proclamation summoning the army into the field. A mulct or fine for not joining the army when summoned. A tax or tribute for the support of the army.

Herebote /hérbòwt/. In old English law, the royal edict summoning the people to the field.

Heredad /(h)èreyðád/. In Spanish law, a piece of land under cultivation; a cultivated farm, real estate; an inheritance or heirship.

Heredad yacente /(h)èreyðád yaséntey/. From Lat. "*Hæreditas jacens*" (q.v.). In Spanish law, an inheritance not yet entered upon or appropriated.

Heredero /(h)èreyðérow/. In Spanish law, heir; he who, by legal or testamentary disposition, succeeds to the property of a deceased person. "*Hæres censeatur cum defuncto una eademque persona.*"

Hereditagium /hərèdətéyj(iy)əm/. In Sicilian and Neapolitan law, that which is held by hereditary right; the same with *hereditamentum (hereditament)* in English law.

Hereditaments /hərédədəmənts/hèhrədídəmənts/. Things capable of being inherited, be it corporeal or incorporeal, real, personal, or mixed, and including not only lands and everything thereon but also heirlooms, and certain furniture which, by custom, may descend to the heir together with the land. Things which may be directly inherited, as contrasted with things which go to the personal representative of a deceased. Denver Joint Stock Land Bank of Denver v. Dixon, 57 Wyo. 523, 122 P.2d 842, 846.

At common law corporeal hereditaments were physical objects, comprehended under the term land, and were said to lie in livery, while incorporeal hereditaments existed only in contemplation of law, were said to lie in grant and were affiliated with chattel interests.

Corporeal hereditaments. Substantial permanent objects which may be inherited. The term "land" will include all such.

Incorporeal hereditaments. Anything, the subject of property, which is inheritable and not tangible or visible. A right issuing out of a thing corporate (whether real or personal) or concerning or annexed to or exercisable within the same. A right growing out of, or concerning, or annexed to, a corporeal thing, but not the substance of the thing itself.

Hereditary /hərédət(èh)riy/. That which is the subject of inheritance. Genetically transmitted or transmittable from parent to offspring.

Hereditary right to the crown. The crown of England, by the positive constitution of the kingdom, has ever been descendible, and so continues, in a course peculiar to itself, yet subject to limitation by parliament; but, notwithstanding such limitation, the crown retains its descendible quality, and becomes hereditary in the prince to whom it is limited. 1 Bl.Comm. 191.

Hereditary succession. Inheritance by law, title by descent; the title whereby a person, on the death of his ancestor, acquires his estate by right of representation as his heir at law.

Heredity /hərédədiy/. Inheritance. That biological law by which all living beings tend to repeat themselves in their descendants. The transmission through genes of characteristics from parents to children.

Herefare /hérəfèr/. Sax. A going into or with an army; a going out to war *(profectio militaris);* an expedition.

Heregeat /hériyət/. A heriot *(q.v.).*

Heregeld /hérəgèld/. Sax. In old English law, a tribute or tax levied for the maintenance of an army.

Heremones /hèrəmówniyz/. Followers of an army.

Herenach /hérənæk/. An archdeacon.

Heres /híriyz/. Heir; an heir. A form of *hæres,* very common in the civil law. See **Hæres.**

Hereslita, heressa, heressiz. A hired soldier who departs without license.

Heresy /héhrəsiy/. In English law, an offense against religion, consisting not in a total denial of Christianity, but of some of its essential doctrines, publicly and obstinately avowed. Opinion or doctrine contrary to church dogma. An opinion on divine subjects devised by human reason, openly taught, and obstinately maintained. This offense is now subject only to ecclesiastical correction, and is no longer punishable by the secular law.

Heretoch /hértòk/. A general, leader, or commander; also a baron of the realm.

Heretofore. This word simply denotes time past, in distinction from time present or time future, and has no definite and precise signification beyond this.

Hereunder. A word of reference in a document or law, directing attention to matter therein which follows in such document or is contained therein.

Herge. In Saxon law, offenders who joined in a body of more than thirty-five to commit depredations.

Heriot /hériyət/. In English law, a customary tribute of goods and chattels, payable to the lord of the fee on the decease of the owner of the land. Heriots are divided into heriot *service* and heriot *custom.* The former expression denotes such as are due upon a special reservation in a grant or lease of lands, and therefore amount to little more than a mere rent; the latter arise upon no special reservation whatever, but depend solely upon immemorial usage and custom.

Herischild /hérəshìld/. In old English law, a species of military service, or knight's fee.

Heriscindium /hèrəsíndiyəm/. A division of household goods.

Herislit /hérəslìyt/. Laying down of arms. Desertion from the army.

Heristal /hérəstòl/. The station of an army; the place where a camp is pitched.

Heritable bond /héhrədəbəl bónd/. A bond for a sum of money to which is added, for further security of the creditor, a conveyance of land or heritage to be held by the creditor as pledge.

Heritable obligation /héhrədəbəl òbləgéyshən/. In Louisiana, an obligation is heritable when the heirs and assigns of one party may enforce the performance against the heirs of the other. Civ.Code La. art. 1997.

Heritable security /héhrədəbəl səkyúrədiy/. Security constituted by heritable property.

Heritage /héhrədəj/. In the civil law, every species of immovable which can be the subject of property; such as lands, houses, orchards, woods, marshes, ponds, etc., in whatever mode they may have been acquired, either by descent or purchase.

Hermandad /èrmandád/. In Spanish law, a fraternity formed among different towns and villages to prevent the commission of crimes, and to prevent the abuses and vexations to which they were subjected by men in power.

Hermaphroditus tam masculo quam feminæ comparatur, secundum prævalentiam sexus incalescentis /hərmǽfrədáydəs tæm mǽskyəlow kwǽm fémʒniy kòmpəréydər, səkándəm prèvəlénsh(iy)əm séksəs ìnkæləséntəs/. An hermaphrodite is to be considered male or female according to the predominance of the exciting sex.

Hermeneutics /hàrmən(y)úwdəks/. The science or art of construction and interpretation. By the phrase "legal hermeneutics" is understood the systematic body of rules which are recognized as applicable to the construction and interpretation of legal writings.

Hermer /hármər/. A great lord.

Hermogenian Code /hərməjíyniyən kówd/. See **Codex Hermogenianus.**

Hernescus /hərnéskəs/. A heron.

Heroin. Narcotic drug which is a derivative of opium and whose technical name is diacetyl-morphine. It is classified as a Class A substance for criminal purposes and the penalty for its possession is severe.

Heroud, heraud /hérə(l)d/. L. Fr. A herald.

Herus /(h)írəs/. Lat. A master. *Servus facit ut herus det,* the servant does [the work] in order that the master may give [him the wages agreed on]. *Herus dat ut servus facit,* the master gives [or agrees to give, the wages], in consideration of, or with a view to, the servant's doing [the work]. 2 Bl.Comm. 445.

Hesia /híyz(h)(i)yə/. An easement.

Hetærarcha /hèdərárkə/. The head of a religious house; the head of a college; the warden of a corporation.

Hetæria /hətíriyə/. In Roman law, a company, society, or college.

Heuvelborh /hyúwvəlbor(k)/. Sax. In old English law, a surety *(warrantus).*

HEW. Department of Health, Education and Welfare.

He who comes into a court of equity must come with clean hands. See **Clean hands doctrine.**

He who has committed iniquity shall not have equity. See **Clean hands doctrine.**

He who is silent when conscience requires him to speak shall be debarred from speaking when conscience requires him to be silent. A maxim of equity invoked when a person who has a duty to speak and to disclose a matter is silent so as to conceal that which should be revealed but who seeks equitable relief against him to whom it should have been disclosed.

He who seeks equity must do equity. This expression means that the party asking the aid of a court for equitable relief must stand in a conscientious relation toward his adversary and the transaction from which his claim arises must be fair and just and the relief must not be harsh and oppressive upon defendant. Jacklich v. Baer, 57 Cal.App.2d 684, 135 P.2d 179, 184. This maxim provides that court will not confer equitable relief on party seeking its aid, unless he has acknowledged and conceded or will admit and provide for all equitable rights, claims, and demands justly belonging to adverse party and growing out of or necessarily involved in subject matter of controversy. Bates v. Dana, 345 Mo. 311, 133 S.W.2d 326, 329. It is in pursuance of this maxim that equity enforces the right of the wife's equity to a settlement.

He who will have equity done to him must do equity to the same person. This maxim of equity provides that conduct which, by itself, is not illegal or even morally reprehensible but which is contrary to principles of equity will bar one who seeks equitable relief from one against whom such conduct is directed.

Hidage /háydəj/. In old English law, an extraordinary tax formerly payable to the crown for every hide of land. This taxation was levied, not in money, but provision of armor, etc.

Hidalgo /(h)iyðálgow/. In Spanish law, a noble; a person entitled to the rights of nobility. By *hidalgos* are understood men chosen from good situations in life *(de buenos lugures)*, and possessed of property *(algo)*.

Hidalguia /(h)iyðàlgíyə/. In Spanish law, nobility by descent or lineage.

Hidden asset. Asset carried on books at a substantially reduced value; its market value being greater than its book value.

Hidden defect. Type of deficiency in property which is not discoverable by reasonable inspection and for which a lessor or seller is generally liable if such defect causes harm to a user. See also **Defect; Latent defect.**

Hide. In old English law, a measure of land, being as much as could be worked with one plow. It is variously estimated at from 60 to 100 acres, but was probably determined by local usage. Another meaning was as much land as would support one family or the dwellers in a mansion-house. Also a house; a dwelling-house. A hide was anciently employed as a unit of taxation.

Hidel /háydəl/. In old English law, a place of protection; a sanctuary.

Hidgild /háydgìld/. A sum of money paid by a villein or servant to save himself from a whipping.

Hierarchy /háy(ə)ràrkiy/. Originally, government by a body of priests. Now, the body of officers in any church or ecclesiastical institution, considered as forming an ascending series of ranks or degrees of power and authority, with the correlative subjection, each to the one next above. Derivatively, any body of persons organized or classified according to authority, position, rank, or capacity.

High. This term, as used in various compound legal phrases, is sometimes merely an addition of dignity, not importing a comparison; but more generally it means exalted, either in rank or location, or occupying a position of superiority, and in a few instances it implies superiority in respect to importance, size, or frequency or publicity of use, *e.g.,* "high seas," "highway."

As to high Bailiff; Constable; Crime; Justice; Justiciar; License; Prerogative writs; Probability (*High probability rule*); School; Sea; Sheriff; Tide; Treason; Water-mark, see those titles.

High Commission Court. See **Court of High Commission.**

High Court of Admiralty. See **Court of Admiralty.**

High Court of Delegates. See **Court of Delegates.**

High Court of Errors and Appeals. See **Court of Errors and Appeals.**

High Court of Parliament. See **Parliament.**

High degree of care and diligence. See **Care.**

High degree of negligence. See **Negligence** (*Gross*).

Higher and lower scale. In the practice of the English supreme court of judicature there were two scales regulating the fees of the court and the fees which solicitors were entitled to charge. The lower scale applied (unless the court otherwise ordered) to the following cases: All causes and matters assigned by the judicature acts to the king's bench, or the probate, divorce, and admiralty divisions; all actions of debt, contract, or tort; and in almost all causes and matters assigned by the acts to the chancery division in which the amount in litigation was under £1,000. The higher scale applied in all other causes and matters, and also in actions falling under one of the above classes, but in which the principal relief sought to be obtained was an injunction.

Highest and best use. In real estate valuation (*e.g.* in condemnation proceedings) the use of land which will bring the greatest economic return over a given time.

Highest degree of care. A standard of care exacted in some jurisdictions of common carriers of passengers. The standard is relative, not absolute, and is sometimes regarded as no more than reasonable care measured by the circumstances.

Highest proved value. In an action of trover the amount which the jury from a consideration of all the evidence, may find to be the highest value of the property during the period between the conversion and the trial.

Highgrading. The practice, in mining vernacular, of stealing ore. People v. Siderius, 29 Cal.App.2d 361, 84 P.2d 545, 547.

Highness. A title of honor given to princes. The kings of England, before the time of James I were not usually saluted with the title of "Majesty", but with that of "Highness". The children of crowned heads generally receive the title of "Highness".

High seas. That portion of ocean which is beyond the territorial jurisdiction of any country. See also **Sea.**

High water line or **mark.** The line on the shore to which high tide rises under normal weather conditions. High-water mark is generally computed as a mean or average high tide and not as extreme height of water. Carolina Beach Fishing Pier, Inc. v. Town of Carolina Beach, 277 N.C. 297, 177 S.E.2d 513, 516. High water mark of navigable river is line to which high water ordinarily reaches and is not line reached by water in unusual floods; it is that line below which soil is unfit for vegetation or agricultural purposes. State v. Bonelli Cattle Co., 108 Ariz. 258, 495 P.2d 1312, 1314.

Highway. A free and public roadway, or street; one which every person has the right to use. In popular usage, refers to main public road connecting towns or cities. In broader sense, refers to any main route on land, water, or in the air. Its prime essentials are the right of common enjoyment on the one hand and the duty of public maintenance on the other. Robinson v. Faulkner, 163 Conn. 365, 306 A.2d 857, 861.

The term "highway," as generally understood, does not have a restrictive or a static meaning, but it denotes ways laid out or constructed to accommodate modes of travel and other related purposes that change as customs change and as technology develops, and the term "highway," as it is generally understood, includes areas other than and beyond the boundaries of the paved surface of a roadway. Opinion of the Justices to the Senate, Mass., 352 N.E.2d 197, 201.

Commissioners of Highways. Public officers appointed in states, counties and municipalities to take charge of constructing, altering, repairing and vacating of highways within their respective jurisdictions.

Common highway. A road to be used by the community at large for any purpose of transit or traffic.

Highway acts, or laws. The body or system of laws governing the laying out, construction, repair, and use of highways.

Highway crossing. A place where the track of a railroad crosses the line of a highway.

Highwayman. A bandit; one who robs travelers upon the highway. Anderson v. Hartford Accident & Indemnity Co., 77 Cal.App. 641, 247 P. 507, 510. See also **Hijacking.**

Highway-rate. In English law, a tax for the maintenance and repair of highways, chargeable upon the same property that is liable to the poorrate.

Highway robbery. See **Hijacking; Robbery.**

Highway tax. A tax for and applicable to the making and repair of highways.

Highway toll. See **Toll.**

Public highway. One under the control of and maintained by public authorities for use of the general public.

Higler /híglər/. In English law, a hawker or peddler. A person who carries from door to door, and sells by retail, small articles of provisions, and the like.

Higuela /(h)iygéylə/. In Spanish law, a receipt given by an heir of a decedent, setting forth what property he has received from the estate.

H.I.H. His (or her) Imperial Highness.

Hiis testibus /háys téstəbəs/. Words formerly used in deeds, signifying *these being witness.* They have been disused since Henry VIII.

Hijacking. Robbery of goods while in transit, commonly from trucks. May involve robbery of only goods, or of both vehicle and goods.

Hilary Rules /híləriy rúwlz/. A collection of orders and forms extensively modifying the pleading and practice in the English superior courts of common law, established in Hilary term, 1834.

Hilary term. In English law, a term of court, beginning on the 11th and ending on the 31st of January in each year. Superseded (1875) by Hilary sittings, which begin January 11th, and end on the Wednesday before Easter.

Hilton doctrine. In civil procedure, rule that in a dispute between parties to an oil and gas lease, royalty holders who would lose their rights if the lease to the defendant was terminated are regarded as indispensable parties to the proceeding challenging the lease. Hilton v. Atlantic Refining Co., C.A.Tex., 327 F.2d 217.

Hindeni homines /hìndíynay hóməniyz/. A society of men. The Saxons ranked men into three classes, and valued them, as to satisfaction for injuries, etc., according to their class. The highest class were valued at 1,200s., and were called *"twelf hindmen"*; the middle class at 600s., and called *"sexhindmen"*; the lowest at 200s., called *"twyhindmen".* Their wives were termed "hindas."

Hinder. Obstruct or impede.

Hine, or **hind.** In old English law, a husbandry servant.

Hinefare /háyn(d)fèr/. In old English law, the loss or departure of a servant from his master.

Hinegeld /háyn(d)gèld/. A ransom for an offense committed by a servant.

Hipoteca /(h)ìypowtéyka/. In Spanish law, a mortgage of real property.

Hirciscunda /(h)ə̀rsəskə́ndə/. See **Herciscunda.**

Hire, *v.* To purchase the temporary use of a thing, or to arrange for the labor or services of another for a stipulated compensation. See also **Employ; Rent.** Compare **Lease.**

Hire, *n.* Compensation for the use of a thing, or for labor or services. State v. Kenyon, Inc., Tex.Civ. App., 153 S.W.2d 195, 197. Act of hiring. A bailment in which compensation is to be given for the use of a thing, or for labor and services about it.

Hirer. One who hires a thing, or the labor or services of another person. See also **Employer.**

Hiring. See **Hire.**

Hiring at will. A general or indefinite hiring. Long v. Forbes, 58 Wyo. 533, 136 P.2d 242, 246.

Hiring hall. Agency or office operated by union, or by employer and union, to provide and place employees for specific jobs.

His. This pronoun, generically used, may refer to a person of either sex. Its use in a written instrument, in referring to a person whose Christian name is designated therein by a mere initial, is not conclusive that the person referred to is a male; it may be shown by parol that the person intended is a female.

His Excellency. In English law, the title of a viceroy, governor general, ambassador, or commander in chief.

In American law, this title is given to the governor of Massachusetts by the constitution of that state; and it is commonly given, as a title of honor and courtesy, to the governors of the other states and to the president of the United States and also to certain members of the clergy. It is also customarily used by foreign ministers in addressing the secretary of state in written communications.

His Honor. A title given by the Constitution of Massachusetts to the lieutenant governor of that commonwealth. Mass.Const. part 2, c. 2, § 2, art. 1. It is also customarily given to some inferior magistrates, as the mayor of a city.

Hissa /hísə/. A lot or portion; a share of revenue or rent.

His testibus /háys téstəbəs/. Lat. These being witnesses. The attestation clause in old deeds and charters. See **Hiis testibus.**

Historical cost. Acquisition or original cost.

Historic bay. "Historic bays" are those over which a coastal nation has traditionally asserted and maintained dominion with the acquiescence of foreign nations. Warner v. Dunlap, C.A.R.I., 532 F.2d 767, 770.

Historic site. Any building, structure, area or property that is significant in the history, architecture, archeology or culture of a State, its communities or the Nation and has been so designated pursuant to statute. Such structures cannot be altered without permission of the appropriate authorities.

Hit and run accident. Collision generally between motor vehicle and pedestrian or with another vehicle in which the operator of vehicle leaves scene without identifying himself. Such an act is a crime.

Hitherto. In legal use, this term always restricts the matter in connection with which it is employed to a period of time already passed.

H.L. House of Lords.

Hlafæta /(h)láfiytə/. Sax. A servant fed at his master's cost.

Hlaford /(h)lǽvərd/. Sax. A lord.

Hlafordsocna /(h)lǽvərdsòwknə/. Sax. A lord's protection.

Hlafordswice /(h)lǽvərdzwàys/. Sax. In Saxon law, the crime of betraying one's lord (proditio domini); treason.

Hlasocna /(h)lǽsòwknə/. Sax. The benefit of the law.

Hlothbote /(h)lóθbòwt/. In Saxon law, a fine for being present at an unlawful assembly.

Hlothe /(h)lówθ/. In Saxon law, an unlawful assembly from eight to thirty-five, inclusive.

Hoarding. Act of holding and acquiring goods in short supply beyond the reasonable needs of the person so holding. See also **Profiteering.**

Fence enclosing house and materials while builders are at work.

Hobblers /hóblərz/. In old English law, light horsemen or bowmen; also certain tenants, bound by their tenure to maintain a little light horse for giving notice of any invasion, or such like peril, towards the seaside.

Hobbs Act. Federal anti-racketeering act making it a crime to interfere with interstate commerce by extortion, robbery, or physical violence. 18 U.S.C.A. § 1951. Racketeering offenses are defined in 18 U.S.C.A. § 1961. See **Racketeering.**

Hobby. An activity not engaged in for profit. I.R.C. § 183. See **Hobby loss.**

Hobby loss. A nondeductible loss arising from a personal hobby as contrasted with an activity engaged in for profit. Generally, the law provides a presumption that an activity is engaged in for profit if gross profits are earned during any 2 or more years during a 5 year period. I.R.S. § 183.

Hoc /hók/. Lat. This. Hoc intuitu, with this expectation. Hoc loco, in this place. Hoc nomine, in this name. Hoc titulo, under this title. Hoc voce, under this word.

Hoc paratus est verificare /hók pəréydəs èst verəfəkériy/. Lat. This he is ready to verify.

Hoc quidem perquam durum est, sed ita lex scripta est /hók kwáydəm pərkwəm dyúrəm èst, sèd áydə léks skríptə èst/. Lat. This indeed is exceedingly hard, but so the law is written; such is the written or positive law. An observation quoted by Blackstone as used by Ulpian in the civil law; and applied to cases where courts of equity have no power to abate the rigor of the law.

Hoc servabitur quod initio convenit /hók sərvéybədər kwòd ənísh(iy)ow kənvíynət/. This shall be preserved which is useful in the beginning.

Hodge-Podge Act. A name applied to a statute which comprises a medley of incongruous subjects.

Hoghenhyne /hówənhàyn(d)/. In Saxon law, a houseservant. Any stranger who lodged three nights or more at a man's house in a decennary was called "hoghenhyne," and his host became responsible for his acts as for those of his servant.

Hold, v. 1. To possess in virtue of a lawful title; as in the expression, common in grants, "to have and to hold," or in that applied to notes, "the owner and holder."

2. To be the grantee or tenant of another; to take or have an estate from another. Properly, to have an estate on condition of paying rent, or performing service.

3. To adjudge or decide, spoken of a court, particularly to declare the conclusion of law reached by the court as to the legal effect of the facts disclosed.

4. To maintain or sustain; to be under the necessity or duty of sustaining or proving; as when it is said that a party "holds the affirmative" or negative of an issue in a cause.

5. To bind or obligate; to restrain or constrain; to keep in custody or under an obligation; as in the phrases "hold to bail," "hold for court," "held and firmly bound," etc.

6. To administer; to conduct or preside at; to convoke, open, and direct the operations of; as to hold a court, hold pleas, etc.

7. To prosecute; to direct and bring about officially; to conduct according to law; as to hold an election.

8. To possess; to occupy; to be in possession and administration of; as to hold office.

9. To keep; to retain; to maintain possession of or authority over.

See also **Ownership; Possession.**

Hold over. To retain possession as tenant of property leased, after the end of the term. To continue in possession of an office and continue to exercise its functions, after the end of the officer's lawful term.

Hold pleas. To hear or try causes. 3 Bl.Comm. 35, 298.

Hold, n. In old English law, tenure. A word constantly occurring in conjunction with others, as *freehold, leasehold, copyhold,* etc., but rarely met with in the separate form.

Holder. The holder of a bill of exchange, promissory note, check, or other commercial paper, is the person who has legally acquired possession of the same, by indorsement or delivery, and who is entitled to receive payment of the instrument. Person who is in possession of a document of title or an instrument or an investment security drawn, issued or endorsed to him or to his order, or to bearer or in blank. U.C.C. § 1–201(20).

Holder for value. A holder who has given a valuable consideration for the document of title, instrument or investment security which he has in his possession. A holder takes an instrument for value: (a) to the extent that the agreed consideration has been performed or that he acquires a security interest in, or a lien on, the instrument otherwise than by legal process; or (b) when he takes the instrument in payment of, or as security for, an antecedent claim against any person whether or not the claim is due; or (c) when he gives a negotiable instrument for it or makes an irrevocable commitment to a third person. U.C.C. § 3–303.

Holder in due course. A holder who takes an instrument for value, in good faith, and without notice that it is overdue or has been dishonored or of any defense against or claim to it on the part of any person. A payee may be a holder in due course. A holder does not become a holder in due course of an instrument by purchase of it at a judicial sale or by taking it under legal process, or by acquiring it in taking over an estate, or by purchasing it as part of a bulk transaction not in regular course of business of the transferor. A purchaser of a limited interest can be a holder in due course only to the extent of the interest purchased. U.C.C. § 3–302. Kaw Valley State Bank & Trust Co. v. Riddle, 219 Kan. 550, 549 P.2d 927, 933.

A holder in due course of a consumer credit contract (*i.e.* consumer paper) is subject to all claims and defenses which the debtor (buyer) could assert against the seller of the goods or services obtained pursuant to the credit contract or with the proceeds thereof. 16 CFR § 433.1 et seq.

Holder in good faith. One who takes property or an instrument without knowledge of any defect in its title.

Hold harmless agreement. A contractual arrangement whereby one party assumes the liability inherent in a situation, thereby relieving the other party of responsibility. Such agreements are typically found in leases, and easements. Agreement or contract in which one party agrees to hold the other without responsibility for damage or other liability arising out of the transaction involved. See also **Guaranty; Indemnity; Surety.**

Holding. The legal principle to be drawn from the opinion (decision) of the court. Opposite of dictum (*q.v.*). Also, general term for property, securities, etc. owned by person or corporation. See also **Dicta.**

In English law, a piece of land held under a lease or similar tenancy for agricultural, pastoral, or similar purposes.

Holding company. A company that confines its activities to owning stock in, and supervising management of, other companies. A holding company usually owns a controlling interest in (more than 50 percent of the voting stock) the companies whose stock it holds. A corporation that controls the voting power of other individual corporations for the purpose of united action.

Personal holding company. One formed (usually for tax reasons) by an individual or small group of individuals for the purpose of holding investments and receiving the income therefrom. See also **Holding company tax; Personal holding company.**

Holding company tax. Tax on undistributed personal holding company income after allowable deductions for dividends paid, etc. I.R.C. § 545.

Holding period. In taxation, that period of time in which a capital asset must be held to determine whether gain or loss from its sale or exchange is long term or short term. I.R.C. §§ 1222–1223.

Holdings. Extent of ownership of investments (real estate, securities, etc.).

Holdover tenant. A tenant who retains possession after the expiration of a lease, or after a tenancy at will has been terminated.

Holiday. A religious festival; a day set apart for commemorating some important event in history; a day of exemption from labor. A day upon which the usual operations of business are suspended and the courts closed, and, generally, no legal process is served. In addition to national holidays (*e.g.* Fourth of July), there are also state holidays (*e.g.* "Bunker Hill" holiday in Massachusetts).

Legal holiday. See **Legal holiday.**

Public holiday. A legal holiday (*q.v.*).

Statutory holidays. Most states observe the same holidays as those observed by the federal government (see 5 U.S.C.A. § 6103). There are variations however, *e.g.*, several states do not celebrate Columbus Day, several states do not observe the National Memorial Day, while many other states have special holidays commemorating historical events, the birthdays of state or regional heros, religious festival days, or other occasions deemed worthy of celebration. See also **Legal holiday.**

Holografo /(h)òwlógrafow/. In Spanish law, a holograph. An instrument (particularly a will) wholly in the handwriting of the person executing it; or which, to be valid, must be so written by his own hand.

Holograph /hó(w)ləgræf/. A will or deed written entirely by the testator or grantor with his own hand and not witnessed (attested). State laws vary widely with respect to the status of self-written "holographic" wills. Some states categorically refuse to recognize any will not meeting the formal statutory requirements relating to attestation clause, witnesses, etc. Others will recognize a holographic will if all or certain portions are in the handwriting of the testator. And many states that do not recognize holographic wills executed by their own citizens within their borders will nevertheless recognize such wills if valid under other jurisdictions. Under the Uniform Probate Code (as adopted by several states), such will is valid, whether or not witnessed, if the signature and the material provisions are in the handwriting of the testator. § 2–503.

Holy Orders. In ecclesiastical law, the orders of bishops (including archbishops), priests, and deacons in the Church of England. The Roman canonists had the orders of bishop (in which the pope and archbishops were included), priest, deacon, subdeacon, psalmist, acolyte, exorcist, reader, ostiarius. One of the seven sacraments of the Roman Catholic Church.

Homage /(h)óməj/. In feudal law, a service (or the ceremony of rendering it) which a tenant was bound to perform to his lord on receiving investiture of a fee, or succeeding to it as heir, in acknowledgment of the tenure. It is described as the most honorable service of reverence that a free tenant might do to his lord. The ceremony was as follows: The tenant, being ungirt and with bare head, knelt before the lord, the latter sitting, and held his hands extended and joined between the hands of the lord, and said: "I become your man [*homo*] from this day forward, of life and limb and earthly honor, and to you will be faithful and loyal, and bear you faith, for the tenements that I claim to hold of you, saving the faith that I owe unto our sovereign lord the king, so help me God." The tenant then received a kiss from the lord. Homage could be done only to the lord himself. "Homage" is to be distinguished from "fealty," another incident of feudalism, and which consisted in the solemn oath of fidelity made by the vassal to the lord, whereas homage was merely an acknowledgment of tenure. If the homage was intended to include fealty, it was called "liege homage;" but otherwise it was called "simple homage."

Homage ancestral. In feudal law, homage was called by this name where a man and his ancestors had immemorially held of another and his ancestors by the service of homage, which bound the lord to warrant the title, and also to hold the tenant clear of all services to superior lords. If the tenant aliened in fee, his alienee was a tenant by homage, but not by homage ancestral. 2 Bl.Comm. 300.

Homage jury. In feudal law, a jury in a court-baron, consisting of tenants that do homage, who are to inquire and make presentments of the death of tenants, surrenders, admittances, and the like.

Homage liege /(h)óməj líyj/. In feudal law, that kind of homage which was due to the sovereign alone as supreme lord, and which was done without any saving or exception of the rights of other lords.

Homager /(h)óməjər/. In feudal law, one who does or is bound to do homage.

Homagio respectuando /həméyj(iy)ow rəspèkchuwǽndow/. A writ to the escheator commanding him to deliver seisin of lands to the heir of the king's tenant, notwithstanding his homage not done.

Homagium /həméyj(iy)əm/. L. Lat. Homage (*q.v.*).

Homagium ligium /həméyj(iy)əm láyj(iy)əm/. In feudal law, liege homage; that kind of homage which was due to the sovereign alone as supreme lord, and which was done without any saving or exception of the rights of other lords. So called from *ligando* (binding), because it could not be renounced like other kinds of homage.

Homagium, non per procuratores nec per literas fieri potuit, sed in propria persona tam domini quam tenentis capi debet et fieri /həméyj(iy)əm, nón pər pròkyurətóriyz nék pər lídərəs fáyəray póduwət, sèd in prówpriyə pərsównə tæm dómənay kwæm tənéntəs kǽpay débəd èt fáyəray/. Homage cannot be done by proxy, nor by letters, but must be paid and received in the proper person, as well of the lord as the tenant.

Homagium planum /həméyj(iy)əm pléynəm/. In feudal law, plain homage; a species of homage which bound him who did it to nothing more than fidelity, without any obligation either of military service or attendance in the courts of his superior.

Homagium reddere /həméyj(iy)əm rédəriy/. In feudal law, to renounce homage. This was when a vassal made a solemn declaration of disowning and defying his lord; for which there was a set form and method prescribed by the feudal laws.

Homagium simplex /həméyj(iy)əm símpləks/. In feudal law, simple homage; that kind of homage which was merely an acknowledgment of tenure, with a saving of the rights of other lords.

Hombre bueno /(h)ómbrey bwéynow/. In Spanish law, the judge of a district. Also an arbitrator chosen by the parties to a suit. Also a man in good standing; one who is competent to testify in a suit.

Home. One's own dwelling place; the house in which one lives; especially the house in which one lives with his family; the habitual abode of one's family; a dwelling house. Mann v. Haines, 146 Kan. 988, 73 P.2d 1066, 1072. That place in which one in fact resides with the intention of residence, or in which he has so resided, and with regard to which he retains residence or to which he intends to return. Place where a person dwells and which is the center of his domestic, social and civil life. Restatement of Conflicts, Second, § 12. "Home", within statute permitting deduction for income tax purposes of amounts expended for meals and lodging while away from home, means "tax home", which is person's principal place of business or employment. Egan v. U. S., D.C.Del., 325 F.Supp. 1227, 1230. See also **Domicile; Residence; Tax home.**

Home brew. An intoxicating beverage made at home or on general premises. Moonshine.

Home loan bank. See **Federal Home Loan Banks.**

Home Loan Bank Board. See **Federal Home Loan Bank Board.**

Home ne sera puny pur suer des briefes en court le roy, soit il a droit ou a tort. A man shall not be punished for suing out writs in the king's court, whether he be right or wrong.

Home office. The department of state through which the English sovereign administers most of the internal affairs of the kingdom, especially the police, and communicates with the judicial functionaries. As applied to a corporation, its principal office or corporate headquarters.

Homeowner's association. An association of people who own homes in a given area, formed for the purpose of improving or maintaining the quality of the area.

An association formed by a land developer or the builder of condominiums or planned unit developments. The builder's participation as well as the duties of the association are controlled by statute in certain states. Such non-profit associations are commonly formed pursuant to a restrictive covenant or a declaration of restrictions.

Homeowners policy. In insurance, multi-peril type policy available to homeowners, combining coverage for fire, water, burglary, liability, etc.

Home Owners Warranty (HOW). A warranty and insurance protection program offered by many home builders in the United States. The program was developed by the Home Owners Warranty Corporation, a subsidiary of the National Association of Home Builders. The major provisions of the program are that a new home is protected for ten years against major structural defects. Similar warranty protection is provided by statute in many states.

Home port. In maritime law, the home port of a vessel is either the port where she is registered or enrolled, or the port at or nearest to which her owner usually resides, or, if there be more than one owner, the port at or nearest to which the husband, or acting and managing owner resides. But for some purposes any port where the owner happens at the time to be with his vessel is its home port.

Under the shipping laws, every vessel has what is called her "home port," to which she belongs, and which constitutes her legal abiding place or residence, regardless of her actual absence therefrom. 46 U.S.C.A. § 17, provides that "every vessel, except as hereinafter provided, shall be registered by the collector of the collection district which includes the port to which such vessel shall belong at the time of her registry, which port shall be deemed to be that at or nearest to which the owner if there be but one or, if more than one, the husband or acting and managing owner of such vessel usually resides."

See also **Port.**

Home port doctrine. Under "home-port" doctrine vessels engaged in interstate and foreign commerce are taxable at their home port only. Scandinavian Airlines System, Inc. v. Los Angeles County, 56 Cal.2d 11, 14 Cal.Rptr. 25, 29, 363 P.2d 25. Under "home port doctrine" a vessel plying the high seas may be taxed at its full value in its home port or in true domicile of its owner, and no other jurisdiction, including those ports visited by the vessel during its voyages, has power to tax it. Star-Kist Foods, Inc. v. Byram, 241 C.A.2d 313, 50 Cal.Rptr. 381, 382, 385.

Where repairs have been made, or necessaries furnished to a foreign ship, or to a ship in a port of the State to which she does not belong, the general maritime law, following the civil law, gives the party a lien on the ship itself for his security; and he may well maintain a suit in rem in the Admiralty to enforce his right. But in respect to repairs and necessaries in the port or State to which the ship belongs, the case is governed altogether by the municipal law of that State; and no lien is implied, unless it is recognized by that law. The General Smith, 17 U.S. (4 Wheat.) 438, 442, 4 L.Ed. 609.

Home rule. Constitutional provision or type of legislative action which results in providing local cities and towns with a measure of self government if such local government accepts terms of the state legislation. See also **Local option.**

Home rule charter. The organizational plan or framework of a municipal corporation, analogous to a constitution of a state or nation, drawn by the municipality itself and adopted by popular vote of its people.

Homestead. The dwelling house and the adjoining land where the head of the family dwells; the home farm. The fixed residence of the head of a family, with the land and buildings surrounding the main house.

Technically, and under the modern homestead laws, an artificial estate in land, devised to protect the possession and enjoyment of the owner against the claims of his creditors, by withdrawing the property from execution and forced sale, so long as the land is occupied as a home. See *Homestead exemption laws, infra.*

Homestead corporations. Corporations organized for the purpose of acquiring lands in large tracts, paying off incumbrances thereon, improving and subdividing them into homestead lots or parcels, and distributing them among the shareholders, and for the accumulation of a fund for such purposes.

Homestead entry. See **Entry.**

Homestead exemption laws. Laws passed in most of the states allowing a householder or head of a family to designate a house and land as his homestead, and exempting the same homestead from execution for his general debts. Property tax exemptions (for all or part of the tax) are also available in some states for homesteaded property. Statutory requirements to establish a homestead may include a formal declaration to be recorded.

Homestead right. The personal right to the beneficial, peaceful and uninterrupted use of the home property free from claims of creditors.

Probate homestead. A homestead set apart by the court for the use of a surviving husband or wife and the minor children out of the common property, or out of the real estate belonging to the deceased.

Homicidal. Pertaining, relating, or impelling to homicide, as a homicidal mania.

Homicide. The killing of one human being by the act, procurement, or omission of another. The act of a human being in taking away the life of another human being. A person is guilty of criminal homicide if he purposely, knowingly, recklessly or negligently causes the death of another human being. Criminal homicide is murder, manslaughter or negligent homicide. Model Penal Code, § 210.1. See **Manslaughter; Murder.**

Homicide is not necessarily a crime. It is a necessary ingredient of the crimes of murder and manslaughter, but there are other cases in which homicide may be committed without criminal intent and without criminal consequences, as, where it is done in the lawful execution of a judicial sentence, in self-defense, or as the only possible means of arresting an escaping felon. The term "homicide" is neutral; while it describes the act, it pronounces no judgment on its moral or legal quality. People v. Connors, 13 Misc. 582, 35 N.Y.S. 472. See *Excusable homicide; Justifiable homicide, infra.*

Classification

Homicide is ordinarily classified as "justifiable," "excusable," and "felonious." For the definitions of these terms, and of some other compound terms, see *infra.*

Culpable homicide. Described as a crime varying from the very lowest culpability, up to the very verge of murder.

Excusable homicide. The killing of a human being, either by misadventure or in self-defense. "Excusable homicide" consists of a perpetrator's acting in a manner which the law does not prohibit, such as self-defense or accidental homicide. Law v. State, 21 Md.App. 13, 318 A.2d 859, 869. The name itself imports some fault, error, or omission, so trivial, however, that the law excuses it from guilt of felony, though in strictness it judges it deserving of some little degree of punishment. It is of two sorts,—either *per infortunium,* by misadventure, or *se defen-*

dendo, upon a sudden affray. Homicide *per infortunium* is where a man, doing a lawful act, without any intention of hurt, unfortunately kills another; but, if death ensue from any unlawful act, the offense is manslaughter, and not misadventure. Homicide *se defendendo* is where a man kills another upon a sudden affray, merely in his own defense, or in defense of his wife, child, parent, or servant, and not from any vindictive feeling. See **Self-defense.**

Felonious homicide. The wrongful killing of a human being, of any age or either sex, without justification or excuse in law; of which offense there are two degrees, manslaughter and murder.

Homicide by misadventure. The accidental killing of another, where the slayer is doing a lawful act, unaccompanied by any criminally careless or reckless conduct. The same as "homicide *per infortunium.*"

Homicide by necessity. A species of justifiable homicide, because it arises from some unavoidable necessity, without any will, intention, or desire, and without any inadvertence or negligence in the party killing, and therefore without any shadow of blame. See **Self-defense.**

Homicide per infortunium. Homicide by misfortune, or accidental homicide; as where a man doing a lawful act without any intention of hurt, accidentally kills another; a species of excusable homicide.

Homicide se defendendo. Homicide in self-defense; the killing of a person in self-defense upon a sudden affray, where the slayer had no other possible (or, at least, probable) means of escaping from his assailant. A species of excusable homicide.

Justifiable homicide. Such as is committed intentionally, but without any evil design, and under such circumstances of necessity or duty as render the act proper, and relieve the party from any shadow of blame; as where a sheriff lawfully executes a sentence of death upon a malefactor, or where the killing takes place in the endeavor to prevent the commission of felony which could not be otherwise avoided, or, as a matter of right, such as self-defense or other causes provided for by statute. See **Self-defense.**

Negligent homicide. Criminal homicide constitutes negligent homicide when it is committed negligently. Model Penal Code, § 210.4. See **Self-defense.**

Reckless homicide. See that title.

Vehicular homicide. Vehicular homicide is the killing of a human being by the operation of an automobile, airplane, motorboat or other motor vehicle in a manner which creates an unreasonable risk of injury to the person or property of another and which constitutes a material deviation from the standard of care which a reasonable person would observe under the same circumstances.

Homicidium /hòməsáydiyəm/. Lat. Homicide *(q.v.).*

Homicidium ex casu, homicide by accident.

Homicidium ex justitia, homicide in the administration of justice, or in the execution of the sentence of the law.

Homicidium ex necessitate, homicide from inevitable necessity, as for the protection of one's person or property.

Homicidium ex voluntate, voluntary or willful homicide.

Hominatio /hòmənéysh(iy)ow/. The mustering of men; the doing of homage.

Homine capto in withernamium /hómǝniy kǽptow ìn wìðǝrnéymiyǝm/. A writ to take him that had taken any bond man or woman, and led him or her out of the country, so that he or she could not be replevied according to law.

Homine eligendo /hómǝniy èlǝjéndow/. In old English law, a writ directed to a corporation, requiring the members to make choice of a man to keep one part of the seal appointed for statutes merchant, when a former is dead, according to the statute of Acton Burnell.

Homine replegiando /hómǝniy rǝplìyjiyǽndow/. In old English law, a writ which lay to replevy a man out of prison, or out of the custody of any private person, in the same manner that chattels taken in distress may be replevied.

Homines /hómǝniyz/. Lat. In feudal law, men; feudatory tenants who claimed a privilege of having their causes, etc., tried only in their lord's court.

Homines ligii /hómǝniyz láyjiyay/. Liege men; feudal tenants or vassals, especially those who held immediately of the sovereign. 1 Bl.Comm. 367.

Hominum causa jus constitutum est /hómǝnǝm kózǝ jás kònstǝtúwdǝm èst/. Law is established for the benefit of man.

Homiplagium /hòmǝpléyjiyǝm/. In old English law, the maiming of a man.

Homme /óm/. Fr. Man; a man. The term "man" as sometimes used may include a woman or women.

Hommes de fief. Fr. In feudal law, men of the fief; feudal tenants; the peers in the lords' courts.

Hommes feodaux. Fr. Feudal tenants; the same with *hommes de fief (q.v.).*

Homo /hówmow/. Lat. A man; a human being, male or female; a vassal, or feudal tenant; a retainer, dependent, or servant.

Homo chartularius /hówmow kàrchǝlériyǝs/. A slave manumitted by charter.

Homo commendatus /hówmow kòmǝndéydǝs/. In feudal law, one who surrendered himself into the power of another for the sake of protection or support. See **Commendation.**

Homo ecclesiasticus /hówmow ǝklìyziyǽstǝkǝs/. A church vassal; one who was bound to serve a church, especially to do service of an agricultural character.

Homo exercitalis /hówmow ǝgzàrs(h)ǝtéylǝs/. A man of the army *(exercitus);* a soldier.

Homo feodalis /hówmow fyuwdéylǝs/. A vassal or tenant; one who held a fee *(feodum),* or part of a fee.

Homo fiscalis, or **fiscalinus** /hówmow fǝskéylǝs/°fìskǝláynǝs/. A servant or vassal belonging to the treasury or *fiscus.*

Homo francus /hówmow frǽŋkǝs/. In old English law, a freeman. A Frenchman.

Homo ingenuus /hówmow injényuwǝs/. A freeman. A free and lawful man. A yeoman.

Homo liber /hówmow láybǝr/. A free man; a freeman lawfully competent to act as juror. An allodial proprietor, as distinguished from a vassal or feudatory. This was the sense of the term in the laws of the barbarous nations of Europe.

Homo ligius /hówmow láyj(iy)ǝs/. A liege man; a subject; a king's vassal. The vassal of a subject.

Homologacion /(h)òwmowlowgàs(i)yówn/. In Spanish law, the tacit consent and approval inferred by law from the omission of the parties, for the space of ten days, to complain of the sentences of arbitrators, appointment of syndics, or assignees of insolvents, settlements of successions, etc. Also the approval given by the judge of certain acts and agreements for the purpose of rendering them more binding and executory.

Homologare /hòmǝlǝgériy/. In the civil law, to confirm or approve; to consent or assent; to confess.

Homologate /hǝmólǝgeyt/. In civil law, to approve; to confirm; as a court *homologates* a proceeding. See **Homologation.** Literally, to use the *same words* with another; to say the like. To assent to what another says or writes.

Homologation /hǝmòlǝgéyshǝn/. In the civil law, approbation; confirmation by a court of justice; a judgment which orders the execution of some act.

In English law, an estoppel *in pais.*

Homo novus /hówmow nówvǝs/. In feudal law, a new tenant or vassal; one who was invested with a new fee. Also one who, after conviction of a crime, had been pardoned, thus "making a new man of him."

Homonymiæ /hòmǝnímiyiy/. A term applied in the civil law to cases where a law was repeated, or laid down in the same terms or to the same effect, more than once. Cases of iteration and repetition.

Homo pertinens /hówmow pǝrdǝnǝn(d)z/. In feudal law, a feudal bondman or vassal; one who *belonged* to the soil *(qui glebœ adscribitur).*

Homo potest esse habilis et inhabilis diversis temporibus /hówmow pówdǝst ésiy hǽbǝlǝs èd ínhæbǝlǝs dǝvárs ǝs tempórǝbǝs/. A man may be capable and incapable at different times.

Homo regius /hówmow ríyj(iy)ǝs/. A king's vassal.

Homo romanus /hówmow rǝméynǝs/. A Roman. An appellation given to the old inhabitants of Gaul and other Roman provinces, and retained in the laws of the barbarous nations.

Homo trium litterarum /hówmow tráyǝm lìdǝrérǝm/. A man of the three letters; that is, the three letters, "f," "u," "r;" the Latin word *fur* meaning "thief."

Homo vocabulum est naturæ; persona juris civilis /hówmow vǝkǽbyǝlǝm èst nǝchúriy, pǝrsównǝ júrǝs sívǝlǝs, °sǝváylǝs/. Man *(homo)* is a term of nature; person *(persona)* of civil law.

Hondhabend /hóndhæbənd/. Sax. Having in hand. See **Handhabend.**

Honeste vivere /(h)ənéstiy vívəriy/. Lat. To live honorably, creditably, or virtuously. One of the three general precepts to which Justinian reduced the whole doctrine of the law, the others being *alterum non lœdere* (not to injure others), and *suum cuique tribuere* (to render to every man his due).

Honestus /(h)ənéstəs/. Lat. Of good character or standing. *Coram duobus vel pluribus viris legalibus et honestis,* before two or more lawful and good men.

Honi /(h)ówniy/. See **Hony.**

Honor, *v.* To accept a bill of exchange, or to pay a note, check, or accepted bill, at maturity and according to its tenor. To pay or to accept and pay, or where a credit so engages to purchase or discount a draft complying with the terms of the draft. U.C.C. § 1–201(21). See also **Dishonor.**

Honor, *n.* In old English law, a seigniory of several manors held under one baron or lord paramount. Also those dignities or privileges, degrees of nobility, knighthood, and other titles, which flow from the crown as the fountain of honor.

In America, the customary title of courtesy given to judges, and occasionally to some other officers; as, "his honor," "your honor," "honorable".

Act of honor. When a bill has been protested, and a third person wishes to take it up, or accept it, for the "honor" (credit) of one or more of the parties, the notary draws up an instrument, evidencing the transaction, which is called by this name. Such acts of honor have been eliminated by the U.C.C.

Honor courts. In old English law, tribunals held within honors or seigniories.

Office of honor. As used in constitutional and statutory provisions, this term denotes a public office of considerable dignity and importance, to which important public trusts or interests are confided, but which is not compensated by any salary or fees, being thus contrasted with an "office of profit."

Honorable. A title of courtesy given in England to the younger children of earls, and the children of viscounts and barons; and, collectively, to the house of commons. In America, the word is used as a title of courtesy for various classes of officials and judges, but without any clear lines of distinction.

Honorable discharge. A formal final judgment passed by the government upon the entire military record of a soldier, and an authoritative declaration by the government that he has left the service in a status of honor. Zearing v. Johnson, 10 Cal.App.2d 654, 52 P.2d 1019, 1020. Full veterans benefits are only given to those with an "honorable discharge" status.

Honorarium /ònərériyəm/. In the civil law, an honorary or free gift; a gratuitous payment, as distinguished from hire or compensation for service; a lawyer's or counsellor's fee.

A voluntary reward for that for which no remuneration could be collected by law. Cunningham v. Commissioner of Internal Revenue, C.C.A., 67 F.2d 205. A voluntary donation, in consideration of services which admit of no compensation in money.

Honorarium jus /ònərériyəm jás/. Lat. In Roman law, the law of the prætors and the edicts of the ædiles.

Honorary. As applied to public offices and other positions of responsibility or trust, this term means either that the office or title is bestowed upon the incumbent as a mark of honor or compliment, without intending to charge him with the active discharge of the duties of the place, or else that he is to receive no salary or other compensation in money, the honor conferred by the incumbency of the office being his only reward. In other contents or usages, it means attached to or growing out of some honor or dignity or honorable office, or else it imports an obligation or duty growing out of honor or trust only, as distinguished from legal accountability.

Honorary canons. Those without emolument.

Honorary feuds. In old English law, titles of nobility, descendible to the eldest son, in exclusion of all the rest. 2 Bl.Comm. 56.

Honorary services. In feudal law, special services to be rendered to the king in person, characteristic of the tenure by grand serjeanty; such as to carry his banner, his sword, or the like or to be his butler, champion, or other officer, at his coronation.

Honorary trust. See **Trust.**

Honorary trustees. Trustees to preserve contingent remainders, so called because they are bound, in honor only, to decide on the most proper and prudential course.

Honoris respectum /(h)ənórəs rəspéktəm/. By reason of honor or privilege. See **Challenge.**

Hontfongenethef /hòntfóŋənθéyf/. In Saxon law, a thief taken with *hondhabend; i.e.,* having the thing stolen in his hand.

Hony /(h)ówniy/. L. Fr. Shame; evil; disgrace. *Hony soit qui mal y pense,* evil be to him who evil thinks. Preferably written *honi.* See **Garter.**

Hootch. Slang for intoxicating liquor illicitly distilled for beverage purposes. State v. Cook, 318 Mo. 1233, 3 S.W.2d 365, 369. Also called "moonshine."

Hope, *v.* A desire or expectation. As used in a will, this term is a precatory word, rather than mandatory or dispositive, but it is sufficient, in proper cases, to create a trust in or in respect to the property spoken of.

Hoppo. A Chinese term for a collector; an overseer of commerce.

Horæ juridicæ or **judiciæ** /hóriy jərídəsiy/°juwdíshiyiy/. Hours during which the judges sat in court to attend to judicial business.

Hora non est multum de substantia negotii, licet in appello de ea aliquando fiat mentio /hórə nón èst máltəm dìy səbstǽnshiyə nəgówshiyay, láysəd ìn əpélow dìy íyə ǽləkwóndow fáyət ménsh(iy)ow/. The hour is not of much consequence as to the substance of business, although in appeal it is sometimes mentioned.

Horca /(h)órka/. In Spanish law, a gallows; the punishment of hanging.

Hordera /hórdərə/. In old English law, a treasurer.

Horderium /hordíriyəm/. In old English law, a hoard; a treasurer, repository.

Horizontal merger. Acquisition of one company by another company producing same product or similar product and selling it in same geographic market. U. S. v. International Tel. & Tel. Corp., D.C.Conn., 306 F.Supp. 766, 774. See **Merger.**

Horizontal price-fixing contracts. Agreements between producers, wholesalers, or retailers as to sale or resale prices. Such agreements are prohibited by federal and state antitrust laws. See also **Price-fixing.**

Horizontal property acts. Statutes dealing with cooperatives and condominiums.

Hornbook. A primer; a book explaining the basics, fundamentals or rudiments of any science or branch of knowledge. The phrase "horn-book law" is a colloquial designation of the rudiments or general principles of law.

Popular reference to a series of textbooks which review various fields of law in summary, narrative form, as opposed to casebooks which are designed as primary teaching tools and include many reprints of court opinions.

Horner. A narcotic addict who inhales or snuffs heroin rather than one who takes it by injection. People v. Carner, 117 Cal.App.2d 362, 255 P.2d 835, 836.

Horngled. Sax. In old English law, a tax within a forest, paid for horned beasts.

Hornswoggle. To triumph over; overcome; beat; bedevil.

Horn tenure. In old English law, tenure by cornage; that is, by the service of winding a horn when the Scots or other enemies entered the land, in order to warn the king's subjects. This was a species of grand serjeanty. 2 Bl.Comm. 74.

Hors de son fee. Out of his fee. In old common law pleading, this was the name of a plea in an action for rent or services, by which the defendant alleged that the land in question was out of the compass of the plaintiff's fee.

Horse power. A unit of power capable of lifting 33,000 pounds a foot a minute.

Hospes /hóspiyz/. Lat. A guest.

Hospes generalis /hóspiyz jènəréyləs/. A great chamberlain.

Hospital. An institution for the treatment and care of sick, wounded, infirm, or aged persons; generally incorporated, and then of the class of corporations called "eleemosynary" or "charitable." Also the building used for such purpose. Hospitals may be either public or private, and may be limited in their functions or services; e.g. children's hospital.

Base hospital. One established at a definite military or naval base of operations.

Field hospital. One set up near the field of operations. It is generally equipped to care for emergency cases and can be moved readily.

Hospitallers. The knights of a religious order, so called because they built a hospital at Jerusalem, wherein pilgrims were received. All their lands and goods in England were given to the sovereign by 32 Hen. VIII, c. 24.

Hospitator. A host or entertainer. *Hospitator communis.* An innkeeper. *Hospitator magnus.* The marshal of a camp.

Hospitia /hòspísh(iy)ə/. Inns. *Hospitia communia,* common inns. *Hospitia curiœ,* inns of court. *Hospitia cancellariœ,* inns of chancery.

Hospiticide /həspídəsàyd/. One that kills his guest or host.

Hospitium /hòspísh(iy)əm/. An inn; a household.

Host. L. Fr. An army. A military expedition; war.

Hostage. An innocent person held captive by one who threatens to kill or harm him if his demands are not met. A person who is given into the possession of the enemy, in time of war, his freedom (or life) to stand as security for the performance of some contract or promise made by the belligerent power giving the hostage with the other.

Hostelagium /hòstəléyj(iy)əm/. A right to receive lodging and entertainment, anciently reserved by lords in the houses of their tenants.

Hosteler. An innkeeper. See also **Hostler.**

Hostes /hóstiyz/. Lat. Enemies. *Hostes humani generis,* enemies of the human race; *i.e.,* pirates.

Hostes sunt qui nobis vel quibus nos bellum decernimus; cæteri proditores vel prædones sunt /hóstiyz sənt kwày nówbəs vèl kwíbəs nòws béləm dəsárnəməs; sédəray pròwdətóriyz vèl prədówniyz sənt/. Enemies are those with whom we declare war, or who declare it against us; all others are traitors or pirates.

Hosticide /hóstəsàyd/. One who kills an enemy.

Hostilaria, hospitalaria /hòs(pə)təláriyə/. A place or room in religious houses used for the reception of guests and strangers.

Hostile. Having the character of an enemy; standing in the relation of an enemy. Feeling or displaying enmity or antagonism such as a hostile witness. See **Hostile or adverse witness.**

Within requirement for adverse possession that possession be asserted in hostile manner, "hostile" means that it is asserted against claim of ownership of all others, including record owner, but does not mean that adverse possessor display a subjective evil intent or emotion against title owner. Steller v. David, Del.Super., 257 A.2d 391, 395.

Hostile embargo. One laid upon the vessels of an actual or prospective enemy.

Hostile fire. In fire insurance law, a fire which breaks out in place not anticipated; fire which escapes into area not expected. One which becomes uncontrollable or breaks out from where it was intended to be and becomes hostile element. Reliance Ins. Co. v. Naman, 118 Tex. 21, 6 S.W.2d 743, 744.

Hostile or **adverse witness.** A witness who manifests so much hostility or prejudice under examination in chief that the party who has called him, or his representative, is allowed to cross-examine him, *i.e.,* to treat him as though he had been called by the opposite party. When a party calls a hostile witness, an adverse party, or a witness identified with an adverse party, interrogation may be by leading questions. Fed.Evid. R. 611.

Hostile possession. See **Possession.**

Hostility. State of enmity between individuals or nations. An act or series of acts displaying antagonism. Hostile act or state. Acts of war.

Hostler /hóstlər/. In Norman and old English law, this was the title of the officer in a monastery charged with the entertainment of guests. It was also applied (until about the time of Queen Elizabeth) to an innkeeper, and afterwards, when the keeping of horses at livery became a distinct occupation, to the keeper of a livery stable, and then (under the modern form "ostler") to the groom in charge of the stables of an inn.

Hot blood. In criminal law, condition of one whose passions have been aroused to an uncontrollable degree and whose homicide may be reduced, therefore, from murder to manslaughter. See also **Heat of passion.**

Hot cargo. In labor law, goods produced or handled by employer with whom union has dispute.

Hot cargo agreement. Voluntary agreement between union and neutral employer by which latter agrees to exert pressure on another employer with whom union has a dispute. N. L. R. B. v. Amalgamated Lithographers of America, C.C.A.Ind., 309 F.2d 31. See **Landrum-Griffin Act.**

Hotchpot. The blending and mixing property belonging to different persons, in order to divide it equally. Anciently applied to the mixing and blending of lands given to one daughter in frank marriage, with those descending to her and her sisters in fee-simple, for the purpose of dividing the whole equally among them; without which the daughter who held in frank marriage could have no share in the lands in fee-simple. 2 Bl.Comm. 190.

    Hotchpot, or the *putting in hotchpot,* is applied in modern law to the throwing the amount of an advancement made to a particular child, in real or personal estate, into the common stock, for the purpose of a more equal division, or of equalizing the shares of all the children. This answers to or resembles the *collatio bonorum,* or *collation* of the civil law.

Hotel. A "hotel" is a building held out to the public as a place where all transient persons who come will be received and entertained as guests for compensation and it opens its facilities to the public as a whole rather than limited accessibility to a well-defined private group. Ambassador Athletic Club v. Utah State Tax Commission, 27 Utah 2d 377, 496 P.2d 883.

Hotel divorce. Form of collusive divorce in which by agreement of both spouses, one spouse stages a fake adultery scene.

Hot issue. See **Issue** *(Securities).*

Hot pursuit. See **Fresh pursuit.**

Hot-water ordeal. In old English law, this was a test, in cases of accusation, by hot water; the party accused and suspected being appointed by the judge to put his arms up to the elbows in seething hot water, which, after sundry prayers and invocations, he did, and was, by the effect which followed, judged guilty or innocent.

Hour. The twenty-fourth part of a natural day; sixty minutes of time.

    Office hours. See **Office.**

Hours of labor. Time period in which employees work and which is governed in part by state and federal (*e.g.* Adamson Act; Fair Labor Standards Act) laws enacted under police power insofar as such legislation deals with the safety and welfare of laborers and the public.

House. Structure that serves as living quarters for one or more persons or families. See also **Curtilage; Domicile; Home; Residence.**

    A legislative assembly, or (where the bicameral system obtains) one of the two branches of the legislature; as the "house of lords" or "house of representatives". Also a quorum of a legislative body.

    The name "house" is also given to some collections of men other than legislative bodies, to some public institutions, and (colloquially) to mercantile firms or joint-stock companies.

    Ancient house. In old English law, one which has stood long enough to acquire an easement of support against the adjoining land or building.

    Bawdy house. A brothel; a house maintained for purposes of prostitution.

    Disorderly house. See that title.

    Duplex house. A double house.

    Dwelling house. See **Dwelling.**

    House-bote. In old English law, a species of estovers, belonging to a tenant for life or years, consisting in the right to take from the woods of the lessor or owner such timber as may be necessary for making repairs upon the house.

    House-burning. See **Arson.**

    House-duty. In England, a tax on inhabited houses imposed by 14 & 15 Vict., c. 36, in lieu of window-duty, which was abolished.

    House of Commons. One of the constituent houses of the British parliament, composed of representatives of the counties, cities, and boroughs. The lower house, so called because the commons of the realm, that is, the knights, citizens, and burgesses returned to parliament, representing the whole body of the commons, sit there. See also *House of Lords, infra.*

    House of correction. A reformatory. A place for the confinement of juvenile offenders, or those who have committed crimes of lesser magnitude.

House of Delegates. The official title of the lower branch of the legislative assembly of several of the states, *e.g.,* Maryland and Virginia.

House of ill fame. A bawdy house; house of prostitution; a brothel; a dwelling allowed by its chief occupant to be used as a resort of persons desiring unlawful sexual intercourse. People v. Lee, 307 Mich. 743, 12 N.W.2d 418, 421. See **Bawdy-house.**

House of Lords. The upper chamber of the British parliament. It comprises the lords spiritual and the lords temporal, and a certain number of Scotch peers. The House of Lords is also the court of final appeal in most civil cases and has jurisdiction over impeachment. See also *House of Commons, supra.*

House of refuge. A prison for juvenile delinquents. A house of correction or reformatory.

House of Representatives. See **House of Representatives.**

House of worship. A building or place set apart for and devoted to the holding of religious services or exercises or public worship; a church or chapel or place similarly used.

Mansion house. See **Mansion-house.**

Public house. An inn or tavern; a house for the entertainment of the public, or for the entertainment of all who come lawfully and pay regularly. A place of public resort, particularly for purposes of drinking or gaming. In a more general sense, any house made public by the occupation carried on in it and the implied invitation to the public to enter, such as inns, taverns, drinking saloons, gambling houses, and perhaps also shops and stores. This term is now generally obsolete.

Search and seizure. "Houses," within purview of Fourth Amendment, includes curtilage. Everhart v. State, 274 Md. 459, 337 A.2d 100, 111.

Tippling house. A place where intoxicating liquors are sold to be drunk on the premises.

Houseage. A fee paid for housing goods by a carrier, or at a wharf, etc.

Housebreaking. Burglary. Breaking and entering a dwelling-house with intent to commit any felony therein. See **Burglary.**

Under some statutes housebreaking may consist in "breaking out" of a house after access had been gained without breaking.

House counsel. Lawyer who acts as attorney for business though carried as an employee of that business and not as an independent lawyer. Generally, such lawyer advises business on day to day matters. Larger businesses have legal departments with attorneys assigned to specialized areas of law affecting their particular business; *e.g.* labor law, taxes, personal injury litigation, corporate law, etc.

Household, *adj.* Belonging to the house and family; domestic.

Household, *n.* A family living together. Schurler v. Industrial Commission, 86 Utah 284, 43 P.2d 696, 699. Those who dwell under the same roof and compose a family. A man's family living together constitutes his household, though he may have gone to another state.

Term "household" is generally synonymous with "family" for insurance purposes, and includes those who dwell together as a family under the same roof. Van Overbeke v. State Farm Mut. Auto. Ins. Co., 303 Minn. 387, 227 N.W.2d 807, 810. Generally, the term "household" as used in automobile policies is synonymous with "home" and "family." Bartholet v. Berkness, 291 Minn. 123, 189 N.W.2d 410, 412.

For **"Family,"** see that title.

Householder. The occupier of a house. More correctly, one who keeps house with his or her family; the head or master of a family. Berghean v. Berghean, 113 Ind.App. 412, 48 N.E.2d 1001, 1003. One who has a household; the head of a household. See also **Head of family or household.**

House law. A peculiar type of regulatory code, now largely obsolete, promulgated by the head of a royal or noble family, or of a prominent private family, governing intra-family relationships and acts with respect to policies of marriage, disposition of property, inheritance and the like. Usually these codes had no legal authority but were enforced within the family by sufficient personal and economic sanctions.

House of prostitution. See **Bawdy house.**

House of Representatives. The House of Representatives of Congress comprises 435 representatives. The number representing each State is determined by population but every State is entitled to at least one representative. Members are elected by the people by district for 2-year terms, all terms running for the same period. Representatives must be at least 25 years of age, citizens of United States for at least seven years, and live in the state they represent. Art. I, § 2 of U.S.Const.

Housing code. See **Building code.**

Housing courts. Such courts exist in several cities in Massachusetts. These courts deal primarily with disputes concerning rental housing and hear actions relating to enforcement of, or disputes concerning sanitary, building and fire codes.

HOW. See **Home Owners Warranty.**

H.R. House of Representatives.

H.R. 10 Plans. See **Keogh Plan.**

H.T. An abbreviation for *hoc titulo,* this title, or under this title; used in references to books.

Huckster /hákstər/. A petty hawker or peddler.

Hucusque /həkə́skwiy/. In old pleading, hitherto.

HUD. Department of Housing and Urban Development.

Hude-geld /háy(n)dgèld/. In old English law, an acquittance for an assault upon a trespassing servant. Also, the price on one's skin, or the money paid by a servant to save himself from a whipping.

Hue and cry. In old English law, a loud outcry with which felons (such as robbers, burglars, and murderers) were anciently pursued, and which all who heard it were bound to take up, and join in the pursuit, until the malefactor was taken. 4 Bl.Comm. 293. A written proclamation issued on the escape of a felon from prison, requiring all officers and police to assist in retaking him.

Hughes doctrine. Name is derived from case of Trans World Airlines, Inc. v. Hughes, C.A.N.Y., 449 F.2d 51, reversed on other grounds, 409 U.S. 363, 93 S.Ct. 647, 34 L.Ed.2d 577, in which court held that defendant's default had the effect of admitting that the conduct described in complaint violated antitrust laws and caused damage, though not necessarily in the amount alleged.

Hui /húwiy/. Under the law of Hawaii, an association of persons in the ownership of land, members of which ordinarily hold the property as tenants in common. De Fries v. Scott, C.C.A.Hawaii, 268 F.2d 952.

Huissiers /wìsyéy/. In French law, marshals; ushers; process-servers; sheriff's officers. Ministerial officers attached to the courts, to effect legal service of process required by law in actions, to issue executions, etc., and to maintain order during the sitting of the courts.

Hulks. A place of punishment for convicts in England, abandoned with the reform in the punishment of convicts which began in England about 1840.

Humanitarian doctrine. Doctrine evolved from Missouri (Wonnack v. Missouri Pacific R. Co., 337 Mo. 1160, 88 S.W.2d 368) in which a plaintiff is relieved of responsibility for his negligence if he can show that the defendant (generally one operating a train or motor vehicle while plaintiff is pedestrian) had last opportunity to avoid the accident. It is only when plaintiff comes into a position of imminent, impending and immediate danger in which injury to plaintiff is reasonably certain if the existing circumstances remain unchanged that the "humanitarian doctrine" seizes upon the situation and imposes upon defendant a duty to thereafter exercise proper care to avoid the threatened injury. Finch v. Kegevic, Mo.App., 486 S.W.2d 515, 518, 519, 521. Only a very few states follow this doctrine.

See also **Imminent peril; Last clear chance doctrine.**

Hundred. Under the Saxon organization of England, each county or shire comprised of an indefinite number of *hundreds,* and each hundred containing ten *tithings,* or groups of ten families of freeholders or frankpledges. The hundred was governed by a high constable, and had its own court; but its most remarkable feature was the corporate responsibility of the whole for the crimes or defaults of the individual members. The introduction of this plan of organization into England is commonly ascribed to Alfred, but the idea, as well of the collective liability as of the division, was probably known to the ancient German peoples, as we find the same thing established in the Frankish kingdom under Clothaire, and in Denmark. 1 Bl.Comm. 115; 4 Bl.Comm. 411.

Hundredarius /hàndrədériyəs/. In old English law, a hundredary or hundredor. A name given to the chief officer of a hundred, as well as to the freeholders who composed it.

Hundredary /hàndrədèriy/. The chief or presiding officer of a hundred.

Hundred Court. In English law, a larger court-baron, being held for all the inhabitants of a particular *hundred,* instead of a manor. The free suitors were the judges, and the steward the registrar, as in the case of a court-baron. It was not a court of record, and resembled a court-baron in all respects except that in point of territory it was of greater jurisdiction. These courts no longer exist. 3 Bl.Comm. 34, 35.

Hundredes earldor, or **hundredes man** /hàndrədz órldər/ hàndrədzmən/. The presiding officer in the hundred court.

Hundred-fecta /hàndrəd fèktə/. The performance of suit and service at the hundred court.

Hundred gemote /hàndrəd gəmòwt/. Among the Saxons, a meeting or court of the freeholders of a hundred, which assembled, originally, twelve times a year, and possessed civil and criminal jurisdiction and ecclesiastical powers.

Hundred lagh /hàndrəd lò/. The law of the hundred, or hundred court; liability to attend the hundred court.

Hundredors /hàndrədərz/. In English law, the inhabitants or freeholders of a hundred, anciently the suitors or judges of the hundred court. Persons impaneled or fit to be impaneled upon juries, dwelling within the hundred where the cause of action arose. It was formerly necessary to have some of these upon every panel of jurors. 3 Bl.Comm. 359, 360. The term "hundredor" was also used to signify the officer who had the jurisdiction of a hundred, and held the hundred court, and sometimes the bailiff of a hundred.

Hundred penny. In old English law, a tax collected from the hundred, by the sheriff or lord of the hundred.

Hundred rolls. In England, rolls embodying the result of investigations made by the commissioners in 1274 as to usurpations of the royal rights.

Hundred secta /hàndrəd sèktə/. The performance of suit and service at the hundred court.

Hundred setena /hàndrəd sətìynə/. In Saxon law, the dwellers or inhabitants of a hundred.

Hundredweight. A denomination of weight containing, according to the English system, 112 pounds; but in this country, generally, it consists of 100 pounds avoirdupois.

Hung jury. A jury so irreconcilably divided in opinion that they cannot agree upon any verdict. See **Dynamite instruction.**

Huntley hearing. In New York, a separate proceeding in a criminal case wherein the admissibility of an accused's extrajudicial statements is determined. People v. Huntley, 15 N.Y.2d 72, 255 N.Y.S.2d 838, 204 N.E.2d 179.

Hurdereferst /hárdərfərst/. A domestic; one of a family.

Hurt. In such phrases as "to the hurt or annoyance of another," or "hurt, molested, or restrained in his person or estate," this word is not restricted to physical injuries, but includes also mental pain, as well as discomfort or annoyance. See also **Damage; Injury.**

Hurto /(h)úrtow/. In Spanish law, theft.

Husband. A married man; one who has a lawful wife living. The correlative of "wife."

Etymologically, the word signified the "house bond;" the man who, according to Saxon ideas and institutions, held around him the family, for whom he was in law responsible.

Husbandman. A farmer, a cultivator or tiller of the ground. The word "farmer" is colloquially used as synonymous with "husbandman", but originally meant a tenant who cultivates *leased* ground.

Husband of a ship. See **Ship** (*Ship's husband*).

Husbandria /hàzbəndríyə/. In old English law, husbandry.

Husbandry. Agriculture; farming; cultivation of the soil for food. Farming, in the sense of operating land to raise crops and livestock. State ex rel. Boynton v. Wheat Farming Co., 137 Kan. 697, 22 P.2d 1093. Care of household. Careful management of resources.

Husband-wife privilege. Term refers to privilege extended to confidential marital communications. While state statutes vary, in general such provide that a spouse has a privilege to refuse to disclose, and to prevent the other from disclosing, a confidential communication made while spouses were married. There are certain exceptions to this privilege, the major one being where one spouse is the victim of a crime by the other.

Husband-wife tort actions. The common law rule, carried forward by statute in many states, prohibits tort actions between spouses. The current trend however is to abolish this interspousal immunity doctrine, thus permitting such suits between spouses. Some states have abolished the doctrine only insofar as automobile tort actions.

Husbrec /húwsbrèyk/. In Saxon law, the crime of housebreaking or burglary.

Huscarle /húwskàrl/. In old English law, a house servant or domestic; a man of the household. A king's vassal, thane, or baron; an earl's man or vassal.

Husfastne /húwsfæ̀s(t)ən/. He who holds house and land.

Husgablum /húwsgæ̀bləm/. In old English law, house rent; or a tax or tribute laid upon a house.

Hush-money. A colloquial expression to designate a bribe to hinder information; pay to secure silence.

Hustings. Council; court; tribunal. Apparently so called from being held within a building, at a time when other courts were held in the open air. It was a local court. The county court in the city of London bore this name. There were hustings at York, Winchester, Lincoln, and in other places similar to the London hustings. Also the raised place from which candidates for seats in parliament address the constituency, on the occasion of their nomination. Courts of Husting in England no longer exist.

Hutesium et clamor /hyətíyz(h)(i)yəm èt klǽmər/. Hue and cry.

H.V. An abbreviation for *hoc verbo* or *hac voce*, this word, under this word; used references to dictionaries and other works alphabetically arranged.

Hybrid class action. Term refers to type of actions where the right to be enforced is several but the object of the action is the adjudication of claims which do or may affect specific property in the action. Eastham v. Public Emp. Retirement Ass'n Bd., 89 N.M. 399, 553 P.2d 679, 682.

Hybrid security. Type of security which, in the form of a debenture, contains elements of indebtedness and elements of equity stock. J. S. Biritz Const. Co. v. C. I. R., C.A.Mo., 387 F.2d 451, 455.

Hypnotism. The act of inducing artificially a state of sleep or trance in a subject by means of verbal suggestion by the hypnotist or by the subject's concentration upon some object. It is generally characterized by extreme responsiveness to suggestions from the hypnotist.

Hypobolum /həpóbələm/. In the civil law, the name of the bequest or legacy given by the husband to his wife, at his death, above her dowry.

Hypochondria; hypomania /hàypəkóndriyə, hìpə°/hàypəméyn(i)yə, hìpə°/. See **Insanity.**

Hypotheca /hàypəθíykə, hìpə°/. "Hypotheca" was a term of the Roman law, and denoted a pledge or mortgage. As distinguished from the term *"pignus,"* in the same law, it denoted a mortgage, whether of lands or of goods, in which the subject in pledge remained in the possession of the mortgagor or debtor; whereas in the *pignus* the mortgagee or creditor was in the possession. Such an hypotheca might be either express or implied; express, where the parties upon the occasion of a loan entered into express agreement to that effect; or implied, as, *e.g.*, in the case of the stock and utensils of a farmer, which were subject to the landlord's right as a creditor for rent; whence the Scotch law of hypothec.

The word has suggested the term "hypothecate," as used in the mercantile and maritime law of England. Thus, under the factor's act, goods are frequently said to be "hypothecated;" and a captain is said to have a right to hypothecate his vessel for necessary repairs.

Hypothecaria actio /həpòθəkériyə ǽksh(iy)ow/. Lat. In the civil law, an hypothecary action; an action for the enforcement of an *hypotheca*, or right of mortgage; or to obtain the surrender of the thing mortgaged.

Hypothecarii creditores /həpòθəkériyay krèdətóriyz/. Lat. In the civil law, hypothecary creditors; those who loaned money on the security of an *hypotheca* (*q.v.*).

Hypothecary action /həpóθəkèhriy ǽkshən/. The name of an action allowed under the civil law for the enforcement of the claims of a creditor by the contract of hypotheca. Lovell v. Cragin, 136 U.S. 130, 10 S.Ct. 1024, 34 L.Ed. 372.

An hypothecary action is a real action, which the creditor brings against the property which has been hypothecated to him by his debtor, in order to have it seized and sold for the payment of his debt. La. Code of Civil Procedure, Arts. 2378, 3721 et seq. In the hypothecary action proper, there is no pursuit of the person; the thing mortgaged is the debtor, and the action is directed against it. In this sense, the action is real.

Hypothecate /həpóθəkèyt/. To pledge property as security or collateral for a debt. Generally, there is no physical transfer of the pledged property to the lender; nor is the lender given title to the property; though he has the right to sell the pledged property upon default. Moore v. Wardlaw, C.C.A.Tex., 522 S.W.2d 552, 554. See also **Pledge; Rehypothecation.**

Hypothecation bond /həpòθəkéyshən bònd/. A bond given in the contract of bottomry or *respondentia*.

Hypothèque /ìypowték/. In French law, hypothecation; a mortgage on real property; the right vested in a creditor by the assignment to him of real estate as security for the payment of his debt, whether or not it be accompanied by possession.

It corresponds to the mortgage of real property in English law, and is a real charge, following the property into whosesoever hands it comes. It may be *légale*, as in the case of the charge which the state has over the lands of its accountants, or which a married woman has over those of her husband; *judiciaire*, when it is the result of a judgment of a court of justice; and *conventionelle*, when it is the result of an agreement of the parties.

Hypothesis /həpóθəsəs/. A supposition, assumption, or theory; a theory set up by the prosecution, on a criminal trial, or by the defense, as an explanation of the facts in evidence, and a ground for inferring guilt or innocence, as the case may be, or as indicating a probable or possible motive for the crime.

Hypothetical question. A combination of assumed or proved facts and circumstances, stated in such form as to constitute a coherent and specific situation or state of facts, upon which the opinion of an expert is asked, by way of evidence on a trial. A hypothetical question is a form of question framed in such a manner as to call for an opinion from an expert based on a series of assumptions claimed to have been established as fact by the evidence in a case. It should be so framed as to recite all the facts in evidence which are relevant to the formation of an opinion and then, assuming the facts recited to be true, the witness should be asked whether he is able to form an opinion therefrom and if so to state his opinion. McMurrey v. State, 145 Tex.Cr.R. 439, 168 S.W.2d 858, 860; Fed.Evid. R. 703, 705.

Hypothetical yearly tenancy. The basis, in England, of rating lands and hereditaments to the poor-rate, and to other rates and taxes that are expressed to be leviable or assessable in like manner as the poor-rate.

Hysteria. Disorder of the psychoneurotic system characterized by disturbances of the psychic, sensory, motor, and visceral functions. Extreme emotionalism, commonly characterized by attention-seeking, impulsive demonstrations.

Hysteropotmoi. Those who, having been thought dead, had, after a long absence in foreign countries, returned safely home; or those who, having been thought dead in battle, had afterwards unexpectedly escaped from their enemies and returned home. These, among the Romans, were not permitted to enter their own houses at the door, but were received at a passage opened in the roof.

Hysterotomy /hìstəródəmiy/. The Cæsarean operation. See **Cæsarean operation.**

I

Ib. See **Ibidem**.

Ibidem /íbədəm/əbáydəm/. Lat. In the same place; in the same book; on the same page, etc. Abbreviated to *"ibid."* or *"ib."*

Ibi semper debet fieri triatio ubi juratores meliorem possunt habere notitiam /íbay sémpər débət fáyəray triyéysh(iy)ow yúwbay jùrətóriyz pósənt həbíriy nətísh(iy)əm/. A trial should always be had where the jurors can be the best informed.

I.C.C. Interstate Commerce Commission.

I—ctus. An abbreviation for *"jurisconsultus,"* one learned in the law; a jurisconsult. See **Jurisconsultus**.

Ictus orbis /íktəs órbəs/. A maim, a bruise, or swelling; any hurt without cutting the skin. When the skin is cut, the injury is called a "wound."

Id. See **Idem**.

I.D. Identification.

Id certum est quod certum reddi potest /ìd sárdəm èst kwòd sárdəm réday pówdəst/. That is certain which can be made certain. 2 Bl.Comm. 143; 1 Bl.Comm. 78.

Id certum est quod certum reddi potest, sed id magis certum est quod de semetipso est certum /ìd sárdəm èst kwòd sárdəm réday pówdəst, sèd íd méyjəs sárdəm èst kwòd dìy sìymədípsow èst sárdəm/. That is certain which can be made certain, but that is more certain which is certain of itself.

Idem /áydəm/. Lat. The same; used to indicate a reference previously made. According to Lord Coke, *"idem"* has two significations, *sc., idem syllabis seu verbis* (the same in syllabus or words), and *idem re et sensu* (the same in substance and in sense).

Idem agens et patiens esse non potest /áydəm éyjən(d)z èt péysh(iy)ən(d)z ésiy nòn pówdəst/. The same person cannot be both agent and patient; *i.e.,* the doer and person to whom the thing is done.

Idem est facere, et non prohibere cum possis; et qui non prohibit, cum prohibere possit, in culpa est (aut jubet) /áydəm èst féysəriy èt nón pròwhəbíriy, kàm pósəs, èt kwáy nòn prów(h)əbət kàm pròwhəbíriy pósət ìn kálpə èst/. To commit, and not to prohibit when in your power, is the same thing; and he who does not prohibit when he can prohibit is in fault, or does the same as ordering it to be done.

Idem est nihil dicere, et insufficienter dicere /áydəm èst náy(h)əl dísəriy èt ìnsəfis(h)iyéntər dísəriy/. It is the same thing to say nothing, and to say a thing insufficiently. To say a thing in an insufficient manner is the same as not to say it at all. Applied to the plea of a prisoner.

Idem est non esse, et non apparere /áydəm èst nòn ésiy èt nòn æpəríriy/. It is the same thing not to be as not to appear. Not to appear is the same thing as not to be.

Idem est non probari et non esse; non deficit jus, sed probatio /áydəm èst nòn prəbéray èt nòn ésiy, nòn défəsət jás sèd prəbéysh(iy)ow/. What is not proved and what does not exist are the same; it is not a defect of the law, but of proof.

Idem est scire aut scire debere aut potuisse /áydəm èst sáyriy òt sáyriy dəbíriy òt pòduwísiy/. To be bound to know or to be able to know is the same as to know.

Idem per idem /áydəm pər áydəm/. The same for the same. An illustration of a kind that really adds no additional element to the consideration of the question.

Idem semper antecedenti proximo refertur /áydəm sémpər æntəsədéntay próksəmow rəfárdər/. "The same" is always referred to its next antecedent.

Idem sonans /áydəm sównæn(d)z/. Sounding the same or alike; having the same sound. A term applied to names which are substantially the same, though slightly varied in the spelling, as "Lawrence" and "Lawrance," and the like. State v. Culbertson, 6 N.C.App. 327, 170 S.E.2d 125, 127. Under the rule of "idem sonans," variance between allegation and proof of a given name is not material if the names sound the same or the attentive ear finds difficulty in distinguishing them when pronounced. Martin v. State, Tex.Cr.App., 541 S.W.2d 605, 606.

Two names are said to be *"idem sonantes"* if the attentive ear finds difficulty in distinguishing them when pronounced, or if common and long-continued usage has by corruption or abbreviation made them identical in pronunciation. The rule of *"idem sonans"* is that absolute accuracy in spelling names is not required in a legal document or proceedings either civil or criminal; that if the name, as spelled in the document, though different from the correct spelling thereof, conveys to the ear, when pronounced according to the commonly accepted methods, a sound practically identical with the correct name as commonly pronounced, the name thus given is a sufficient identification of the individual referred to, and no advantage can be taken of the clerical error. The doctrine of *"idem sonans"* has been much enlarged by decisions, to conform to the growing rule that a variance, to be material, must be such as has misled the opposite party to his prejudice.

Identical. Exactly the same for all practical purposes.

Identification. Proof of identity. The proving that a person, subject, or article before the court is the very same that he or it is alleged, charged, or reputed to be; as where a witness recognizes the prisoner as the same person whom he saw committing the crime; or where handwriting, stolen goods, counterfeit coin, etc., are recognized as the same which once passed under the observation of the person identifying them. See also **Authentication; Line-up; Mug book.**

The requirement of identification as a condition precedent to admissability is satisfied by evidence sufficient to support a finding that the matter in question is what its proponent claims. Fed.Evid.R. 901.

See also **Authentication; Eyewitness identification; Label; Lineup; Voiceprint.**

Identification of goods. The buyer obtains a special property and an insurable interest in goods by identification of existing goods as goods to which the contract refers even though the goods so identified are non-conforming and he has an option to return or reject them. Such identification can be made at any time and in any manner explicitly agreed to by the parties. U.C.C. § 2–501.

Identitas vera colligitur ex multitudine signorum /ədéntətæs víra kəlíjədər èks màltətyúwdəniy səgnórəm/. True identity is collected from a multitude of signs.

Identitate nominis /ədèntətéydiy nómənəs/. In English law, an ancient writ (now obsolete) which lay for one taken and arrested in any personal action, and committed to prison, by mistake for another man of the same name.

Identity. *Evidence.* Sameness; the fact that a subject, person, or thing before a court is *the same* as it is represented, claimed, or charged to be. See **Authentication; Identification.**

Patent Law. Such sameness between two designs, inventions, combinations, etc., as will constitute the one an infringement of the patent granted for the other. To constitute "identity of invention," and therefore infringement, not only must the result obtained be the same, but, in case the means used for its attainment is a combination of known elements, the elements combined in both cases must be the same, and combined in the same way, so that each element shall perform the same function; provided that the differences alleged are not merely colorable according to the rule forbidding the use of known equivalents. Electric Railroad Signal Co. v. Hall Railroad Signal Co., 114 U.S. 87, 5 S.Ct. 1069, 29 L.Ed. 96. "Identity of design" means sameness of appearance, or, in other words, sameness of effect upon the eye,— not the eye of an expert, but of an ordinary intelligent observer. Smith v. Whitman Saddle Co., 148 U.S. 674, 13 S.Ct. 768, 37 L.Ed. 606.

Identity of interests. In civil procedure, an amendment (addition) of a party will be allowed if the party sought to be joined is so closely related in business operations or other activities that the institution of an action against one serves as notice of litigation to the other, and hence the amendment will relate back. Grooms v. Greyhound Corp., C.A.Ohio, 287 F.2d 95; Fed.R.Civil P. 15(c). See also **Identity of parties; Privity.**

Identity of parties. Refers to condition of persons in relation to each other so that a former judgment against one bars action against others because of res adjudicata; hence, same parties and those in privity are so barred. See **Res** (*Res judicata*).

Ideo /áydiyow/. Lat. Therefore.

Ideo consideratum est /áydiyow kənsìdəréydəm èst/. Lat. Therefore it is considered. These were the words used at the beginning of the entry of judgment in an action, when the forms were in Latin. They are also used as a name for that portion of the record.

Ides /áydz/. A division of time among the Romans. In March, May, July, and October, the Ides were on the 15th of the month; in the remaining months, on the 13th. This method of reckoning is still retained in the chancery of Rome, and in the calendar of the breviary.

Id est /íd èst/. Lat. That is. Commonly abbreviated *"i.e."*

Idiochira /ìdiyowkáyrə/. Græco-Lat. In the civil law, an instrument privately executed, as distinguished from such as were executed before a public officer.

Idiocy, idiopathic insanity /íd(i)yəsiy, ìdiyowpǽθək ìnsǽnədiy/. See **Insanity.**

Idiota /idiyówdə/. In the civil law, an unlearned, illiterate, or simple person. A private man; one not in office.

Idiota inquirendo, writ de /rít dìy ìdiyówdə iŋkwəréndow/. This is the name of an old writ which directs the sheriff to inquire whether a man be an idiot or not. The inquisition is to be made by a jury of twelve men. And, if the man were found an idiot, the profits of his lands and the custody of his person might be granted by the king to any subject who had interest enough to obtain them. 1 Bl.Comm. 303.

Idoneitas /ìdəníyətæs/. In old English law, ability or fitness (of a person).

Idoneum se facere; idoneare se /idówniyəm sìy féysəriy/idənériy sìy/. To purge one's self by oath of a crime of which one is accused.

Idoneus /idówniyəs/. Lat. In the civil and common law, sufficient; competent; fit or proper; responsible; unimpeachable. *Idoneus homo,* a responsible or solvent person; a good and lawful man. Sufficient; adequate; Satisfactory. *Idonea cautio,* sufficient security.

Id perfectum est quod ex omnibus suis partibus constat /íd pərféktəm èst kwód èks ómnəbəs s(y)úwəs párdəbəs kónstət/. That is perfect which consists of all its parts.

Id possumus quod de jure possumus /íd pósəməs kwòd dìy júriy pósəməs/. We may do only that which by law we are allowed to do.

Id quod est magis remotum, non trahit ad se quod est magis junctum, sed e contrario in omni casu /íd kwòd èst méyjəs rəmówdəm, nòn tréy(h)əd æd síy kwód èst méyjəs jə́ŋktəm, sèd íy kəntrériyow ìn ómnay kéys(y)uw/. That which is more remote does not draw to itself that which is nearer, but the contrary in every case.

Id quod nostrum est sine facto nostro ad alium transferri non potest /íd kwòd nóstrəm èst sáyniy fǽktow nóstrow æd éyl(i)yəm trǽnsfəray nòn pówdəst/. That which is ours cannot be transferred to another without our act.

Id solum nostrum quod debitis deductis nostrum est /íd sówləm nóstrəm kwòd débədəs dədáktəs nóstrəm èst/. That only is ours which remains to us after deduction of debts.

I.e. An abbreviation for *"id est,"* that is; that is to say.

If. In deeds and wills, this word, as a rule, implies a condition precedent, unless it is controlled by other words. Hughes v. John Hancock Mut. Life Ins. Co., 163 Misc. 31, 297 N.Y.S. 116, 122.

I.F.B. Invitation for Bids.

Ignis judicium /ígnəs jədísh(iy)əm/. Lat. The old judicial trial by fire.

Ignitegium /ìgnətíyj(iy)əm/. In old English law, the curfew, or evening bell. See **Curfew.**

Ignominy /ígnəmìniy/. Public disgrace; infamy; reproach; dishonor. Ignominy is the opposite of esteem.

Ignoramus /ìgnəréyməs/. Lat. "We are ignorant;" "We ignore it." Formerly the grand jury wrote this word on bills of indictment when, after having heard the evidence, they thought the accusation against the prisoner was groundless, intimating that, though the facts might possibly be true, the truth did not appear to them; but now they usually write in English the words "No bill", "Not a true bill," or "Not found," if that is their verdict. But they are still said to *ignore* the bill.

Ignorance. The want or absence of knowledge, unaware or uninformed.

Ignorance *of law* is want of knowledge or acquaintance with the laws of the land in so far as they apply to the act, relation, duty, or matter under consideration. Ignorance *of fact* is want of knowledge of some fact or facts constituting or relating to the subject-matter in hand.

Ignorance is not a state of the mind in the sense in which sanity and insanity are. When the mind is ignorant of a fact, its condition still remains sound; the power of thinking, of judging, of willing, is just as complete before communication of the fact as after.

The essence or texture, so to speak, of the mind, is not, as in the case of insanity, affected or impaired. Ignorance of a particular fact consists in this: that the mind, although sound and capable of healthy action, has never acted upon the fact in question, because the subject has never been brought to the notice of the perceptive faculties.

Synonyms

"Ignorance" and "error" or "mistake" are not convertible terms. The former is a lack of information or absence of knowledge; the latter, a misapprehension or confusion of information, or a mistaken supposition of the possession of knowledge. Error as to a fact may imply ignorance of the truth; but ignorance does not necessarily imply error.

General Types

Culpable ignorance is that which results from a failure to exercise ordinary care to acquire knowledge, and knowledge which could be acquired by the exercise of ordinary care is by law imputed to the person and he is held to have constructive knowledge. Luck v. Buffalo Lakes, Tex.Civ.App., 144 S.W.2d 672, 676.

Essential ignorance is ignorance in relation to some essential circumstance so intimately connected with the matter in question, and which so influences the parties, that it induces them to act in the business.

Involuntary ignorance is that which does not proceed from choice, and which cannot be overcome by the use of any means of knowledge known to a person and within his power; as the ignorance of a law which has not yet been promulgated.

Nonessential or accidental ignorance is that which has not of itself any necessary connection with the business in question, and which is not the true consideration for entering into the contract.

Voluntary ignorance exists when a party might, by taking reasonable efforts, have acquired the necessary knowledge. For example, every man might acquire a knowledge of the laws which have been promulgated.

Ignorantia /ìgnərǽnsh(iy)ə/. Lat. Ignorance; want of knowledge. Distinguished from mistake (error), or wrong conception. Divided by Lord Coke into *ignorantia facti* (ignorance of fact) and *ignorantia juris* (ignorance of law). And the former, he adds, is twofold—*lectionis et linguæ* (ignorance of reading and ignorance of language).

Ignorantia eorum quæ quis scire tenetur non excusat /ìgnərǽnsh(iy)ə iyórəm kwiy kwís sáyriy təníydər nòn əksk(y)úwzət/. Ignorance of those things which one is bound to know excuses not.

Ignorantia facti excusat /ìgnərǽnsh(iy)ə fǽktay əkskyúwzət/. Ignorance of fact excuses or is a ground of relief. Acts done and contracts made under mistake or ignorance of a material fact are voidable and relievable in law and equity.

Ignorantia facti excusat, ignorantia juris non excusat /ìgnərǽnsh(iy)ə fǽktay əkskyúwzət, ìgnərǽnsh(iy)ə júrəs nòn əkskyúwzət/. Ignorance of the fact excuses; ignorance of the law excuses not. Every man must be taken to be cognizant of the law; otherwise there is no saying to what extent the excuse of ignorance may not be carried.

Ignorantia juris quod quisque tenetur scire, neminem excusat /ìgnərǽnsh(iy)ə júrəs kwòd kwískwiy təníydər sáyriy, némənəm əkskyúwzət/. Ignorance of the [or a] law, which every one is bound to know, excuses no man. A mistake in point of law is, in criminal cases, no sort of defense. And, in civil cases, ignorance of the law, with a full knowledge of the facts, furnishes no ground, either in law or equity, to rescind agreements, or reclaim money paid, or set aside solemn acts of the parties.

Ignorantia juris sui non præjudicat juri /ìgnərǽnsh(iy)ə júris s(y)úway nòn prəjúwdəkət júray/. Ignorance of one's right does not prejudice the right.

Ignorantia legis neminem excusat /ìgnərǽnsh(iy)ə líyjəs némənəm əkskyúwzət/. Ignorance of law excuses no one.

Ignorantia præsumitur ubi scientia non probatur /ìgnərǽnsh(iy)ə prəz(y)úwmədər yúwbay sayénsh-(iy)ə nòn prəbéydər/. Ignorance is presumed where knowledge is not proved.

Ignorare legis est lata culpa /ìgnərériy líyjəs èst léydə kə́lpə/. To be ignorant of the law is gross neglect.

Ignoratio elenchi /ìgnəréysh(iy)ow əléŋkay/. Lat. A term of logic, sometimes applied to pleadings and to arguments on appeal, which signifies a mistake of the question, that is, the mistake of one who, failing to discern the real question which he is to meet and answer, addresses his allegations or arguments to a collateral matter or something beside the point.

Ignoratis terminis artis, ignoratur et ars /ìgnəréydəs tə́rmənəs árdəs, ígnəréydər èd árz/. Where the terms of an art are unknown, the art itself is unknown also.

Ignore. To be ignorant of, or unacquainted with. To disregard willfully; to refuse to recognize; to decline to take notice of.

To reject as groundless, false or unsupported by evidence; as when a grand jury *ignores* a bill of indictment.

Ignoscitur ei qui sanguinem suum qualiter redemptum voluit /ìgnósədər íyay kwày sǽŋgwənəm s(y)úwəm kwóladər rədém(p)təm vól(y)uwət/. The law holds him excused from obligation who chose to redeem his blood (or life) upon any terms. Whatever a man may do under the fear of losing his life or limbs will not be held binding upon him in law. 1 Bl.Comm. 131.

Ikbal. Acceptance (of a bond, etc.).

Ikbal dawa. Confession of judgment.

Ikrah. Compulsion; especially constraint exercised by one person over another to do an illegal act, or to act contrary to his inclination.

Ikrar. Agreement, assent, or ratification.

Ikrar nama. A deed of assent and acknowledgment.

Ill. In old pleading, bad; defective in law; null; naught; the opposite of good or valid.

Illegal. Against or not authorized by law.

Illegal entry. An alien is guilty of illegal entry if: (1) he enters at the wrong time or place in the country, or (2) eludes an examination by immigration officers, or (3) obtains entry by fraud. 8 U.S.C.A. § 1325.

Illegal interest. Usury; interest at a higher rate than the law allows.

Illegality /ìləgǽlədiy/. That which is contrary to the principles of law, as contradistinguished from mere rules of procedure.

Illegally obtained evidence. Evidence which is obtained in violation of defendant's rights because officers had no warrant and no probable cause to arrest or because the warrant was defective and no valid grounds existed for seizure without a warrant. Evidence secured in violation of statutes or constitutional guarantee against unreasonable searches, U.S. Constitution, 4th Amendment. Such evidence is inadmissible in criminal trial of victim of such search. Mapp v. Ohio, 367 U.S. 643, 81 S.Ct. 1684, 6 L.Ed.2d 1081. See **Exclusionary Rule; Fruit of poisonous tree.**

Illegal per se. Unlawful in and of itself and not because of some extraneous circumstance, *e.g.* a contract to assassinate a public official.

Illegal trade. Such traffic or commerce as carried on itn violation of federal, state, or local laws; *e.g.* trade in violation of antitrust laws; trade in stolen goods.

Illegitimacy /ìləjídəməsiy/. The condition before the law, or the social status, of an illegimate child; condition of one whose parents were not intermarried at the time of his or her birth.

Illegitimate /ìləjídəmət/. That which is contrary to law; term is usually applied to children born out of lawful wedlock. See **Illegitimate child.**

Illegitimate child. Child who is born at a time when his parents, though alive, are not married to each other. Such child however is legitimate if they were married after his conception and before his birth. Home of Holy Infancy v. Kaska, Tex., 397 S.W.2d 208. While the laws with respect to inheritance are changing, the majority of states still provide that while the illegitimate child has a right to inherit from its mother, such illegitimate child does not have a similar right to inherit from its natural father. Trimble v. Gordon, 430 U.S. 762, 97 S.Ct. 1459, 52 L.Ed.2d 31. See also **Person.**

Ill fame. Evil repute; notorious bad character. Houses of prostitution, gaming houses, and other such disorderly places are called "houses of ill fame," and a person who frequents them is a person of ill fame.

Illicenciatus /ìləsènsiyéydəs/. In old English law, without license.

Illicit /əlísət/. Not permitted or allowed; prohibited; unlawful; as an illicit trade; illicit intercourse.

Illicit cohabitation. The living together as man and wife of two persons who are not lawfully married, with the implication that they habitually practice fornication. Thomas v. United States, D.C.Mass., 14 F.2d 228, 229. At common law and by statutes in many states, living together either in adultery or fornication is a crime, though at common law such cohabitation had to be open and notorious so as to cause a public scandal. Such statutes are seldom enforced.

Illicit connection. Unlawful sexual intercourse. See **Illicit relations.**

Illicit distillery. One carried on without a compliance with the provisions of the laws of the United States relating to the distribution and taxation of spirituous liquor.

Illicit relations. Any form of unlawful sexual intercourse such as fornication or adultery. See **Illicit cohabitation.**

Illicit trade. Policies of marine insurance usually contain a covenant of warranty against "illicit trade", meaning thereby trade which is forbidden, or declared unlawful, by the laws of the country where the cargo is to be delivered.

Illicitum collegium /əlísədəm kəlíyj(i)yəm/. Lat. An illegal corporation.

Illinois land trust. See **Land trust.**

Illiteracy. The condition of one who cannot read or write and, in general, of one who is unlettered or unlearned.

Illness. Sickness, disease or disorder of body or mind. In insurance law, a disease or ailment of such a character as to affect the general soundness and healthfulness of the system seriously, and not a mere temporary indisposition which does not tend to undermine or weaken the constitution of the insured. Zogg v. Bankers' Life Co. of Des Moines, Iowa, C.C. A.W.Va., 62 F.2d 575, 578. For mental illness, see **Insanity.** See also **Serious illness.**

Illocable /ìló(w)kəbəl/. Incapable of being placed out or hired.

Illud /íləd/. Lat. That.

Illud, quod alias licitum non est, necessitas facit licitum; et necessitas inducit privilegium quoad jura privata /íləd kwòd éyliyəs lísədəm nòn èst nəsésətæs féysət lísədəm; èt nəsésətæs ənd(y)úwsət prìvəlíyj(iy)əm kwówæd júrə prəvéydə/. That which is otherwise not permitted, necessity permits; and necessity makes a privilege as to private rights.

Illud, quod alteri unitur, extinguitur, neque amplius per se vacare licet /íləd, kwòd óltəray yúwnədər, əkstíŋgwədər, nékwiy æmpliyəs pər síy vəkériy láysət/. That which is united to another is extinguished, nor can it be any more independent.

Illusion /əl(y)uwzhən/. Distorted or misinterpreted sensory impression which, in contrast to hallucinations, arises from an actual stimulus, i.e., shadow is taken to be a man, specks on window are seen as a swarm of mosquitos. Prevalent in delirious states. The misinterpretation of a real, external sensory experience.

An image or impression in the mind, excited by some external object addressing itself to one or more of the senses, but which, instead of corresponding with the reality, is perverted, distorted, or wholly mistaken, the error being attributable to the imagination of the observer, not to any defect in the organs of sense. See **Hallucination.**

Illusory /əl(y)úwsəriy/°uwz°/. Deceiving by false appearances; nominal, as distinguished from substantial; fallacious; illusive. Bolles v. Toledo Trust Co., 144 Ohio St. 195, 58 N.E.2d 381, 390.

Illusory appointment. Nominal, overly restrictive or conditional transfer of property under power of appointment; lacking in substantial existence.

Formerly the appointment of a merely nominal share of the property to one of the objects of a power, in order to escape the rule that an exclusive appointment could not be made unless it was authorized by the instrument creating the power, was considered illusory and void in equity. This rule has been abolished in England. Brown v. Fidelity Union Trust Co., 126 N.J.Eq. 406, 9 A.2d 311. See **Illusory Appointment Act.**

Illusory Appointment Act. This English statute provided that no appointment made after its passing (July 16, 1830), in exercise of a power to appoint property, real or personal, among several objects, shall be invalid, or impeached in equity, on the ground that an unsubstantial, illusory, or nominal share only was thereby appointed, or left unappointed, to devolve upon any one or more of the objects of such power; but that the appointment shall be valid in equity, as at law. See now Law of Property Act (1925), § 158.

Illusory promise. A purported promise that actually promises nothing because it leaves to speaker the choice of performance or nonperformance. When promise is illusory, there is no actual requirement upon promisor that anything be done because promisor has an alternative which, if taken, will render promisee nothing. When provisions of supposed promise leave promisor's performance optional or entirely within discretion, pleasure and control of promisor, the promise is illusory. Interchange Associates v. Interchange Inc., 16 Wash.App. 359, 557 P.2d 357, 358.

An illusory promise is an expression cloaked in promissory terms, but which, upon closer examination, reveals that the promisor has really not committed himself to anything. If performance of an apparent promise is entirely optional with the provisor, the promise is illusory.

Illusory trust. Where a settlor in form either declares himself trustee of, or transfers to a third party, property in trust, but by the terms of the trust, or by his dealings with the trust property, in substance exercises so much control over the trust property that it is clear that he did not intend to relinquish any of his rights in the trust property, the trust is invalid as illusory. An "illusory trust" is a trust arrangement which takes the form of a trust, but because of powers retained in the settlor has no real substance and in reality is not a completed trust. In re Herron's Estate, Fla.App., 237 So.2d 563, 566.

Illustrious /əlástriyəs/. The prefix to the title of a prince of the blood in England.

Imagine. In old English law, in cases of treason the law made it a crime to imagine the death of the king. But, in order to complete the crime, this act of the mind must have been demonstrated by some overt act. The terms "imagining" and "compassing" are in this connection synonymous. 4 Bl.Comm. 78.

Imbargo. An old form of "embargo" *(q.v.)*.

Imbecility. See **Insanity**.

Imbezzle. An occasional or obsolete form of "embezzle" *(q.v.)*.

Imbracery. See **Embracery**.

Imitation. The making of one thing in the similitude or likeness of another; as, counterfeit coin is said to be made "in imitation" of the genuine.

An imitation of a trademark is that which so far resembles the genuine trademark as to be likely to induce the belief that it is genuine, whether by the use of words or letters similar in appearance or in sound, or by any sign, device, or other means.

The test of "colorable imitation" is, not whether a difference may be recognized between the names of two competing articles when placed side by side, but whether the difference will be recognized by the purchaser with no opportunity for comparison. The Best Foods v. Hemphill Packing Co., D.C.Del., 5 F.2d 355, 357.

See **Counterfeit; Forgery**.

Immaterial. Not material, essential, or necessary; not important or pertinent; not decisive; of no substantial consequence; without weight; of no material significance. See also **Impertinence; Irrelevancy: Irrelevant allegation**. *Compare* **Material; Material fact; Relevant**.

Immaterial averment. In pleading, an averment alleging with needless particularity or unnecessary circumstances what is material and necessary, and which might properly have been stated more generally, and without such circumstances and particulars; or, in other words, a statement of unnecessary particulars in connection with and as descriptive of what is material. Such immaterial matter may be ordered stricken from the pleading. Fed.R.Civil P. 12(f). See also **Irrelevant allegation**.

Immaterial evidence. Evidence which lacks probative weight and is unlikely to influence the tribunal in resolving the issue before it. Such evidence is commonly objected to by opposing counsel, and disallowed by the court. See also **Irrelevancy; Irrelevant**. *Compare* **Relevant evidence**.

Immaterial facts. Those which are not essential to the right of action or defense. See **Immaterial averment**. *Compare* **Material fact**.

Immaterial issue. In pleading, an issue taken on an immaterial point; that is, a point not proper to decide the action.

Immaterial variance. Discrepancy between the pleading and proof of a character so slight that the adverse party cannot say that he was misled thereby. See also **Variance**.

Immediacy. The state or quality of being immediately and directly perceived; urgency; occurring without delay.

Immediate. Present; at once; without delay; not deferred by any interval of time. In this sense, the word, without any very precise signification, denotes that action is or must be taken either instantly or without any considerable loss of time. A reasonable time in view of particular facts and circumstances of case under consideration. Next in line or relation; directly connected; not secondary or remote. Not separated in respect to place; not separated by the intervention of any intermediate object, cause, relation, or right. Thus we speak of an action as prosecuted for the "immediate benefit" of A., of a devise as made to the "immediate issue" of B., etc.

Immediate cause. The last of a series or chain of causes tending to a given result, and which, of itself, and without the intervention of any further cause, directly produces the result or event. A cause may be immediate in this sense, and yet not "proximate;" and conversely, the proximate cause (that which directly and efficiently brings about the result) may not be immediate. The familiar illustration is that of a drunken man falling into the water and drowning. His intoxication is the proximate cause of his death, if it can be said that he would not have fallen into the water when sober; but the immediate cause of death is suffocation by drowning. See also **Proximate cause**.

Immediate control. Such constant control as would enable driver to instantly govern vehicle's movements, including the power to stop within a distance in which such a vehicle, in good mechanical condition, driven by a reasonably skillful driver, and traveling at a lawful rate of speed, could be stopped.

Immediate danger. Definition of "immediate danger" as part of humanitarian doctrine contemplates that there be some inexorable circumstance, situation or agency bearing down on plaintiff with reasonable probability of danger prior to negligent act of defendant. Curran v. Bi-State Development Agency, Mo. App., 522 S.W.2d 98, 100. See also **Imminent danger; Imminent peril**.

Immediate descent. See **Descent**.

Immediately. Without interval of time, without delay, straightway, or without any delay or lapse of time. Drumbar v. Jeddo-Highland Coal Co., 155 Pa.Super. 57, 37 A.2d 25, 27. The words "immediately" and "forthwith" have generally the same meaning. They are stronger than the expression "within a reasonable time" and imply prompt, vigorous action without any delay. Alsam Holding Co. v. Consolidated Taxpayers' Mut. Ins. Co., 4 N.Y.S.2d 498, 505, 167 Misc. 732.

Immediate notice. As required by policy as for proof of loss means within a reasonable time. Lydon v. New York Life Ins. Co., C.C.A.Mo., 89 F.2d 78, 82.

Immemorial. Beyond human memory; time out of mind.

Immemorial possession. In Louisiana, possession of which no man living has seen the beginning, and the existence of which he has learned from his elders. Civ.Code La. art. 766.

Immemorial usage. A practice which has existed time out of mind; custom; prescription.

Immeubles /imyúwblə/. Fr. These are, in French law, the immovables of English law. Things are *immeubles* from any one of three causes: (1) From their own nature, *e.g.,* lands and houses; (2) from their destination, *e.g.,* animals and instruments of agriculture when supplied by the landlord; or (3) by the object to which they are annexed, *e.g.,* easements.

Immigrant. An alien in a country except, in United States, one within a specified class within the Immigration and Nationality Act. 8 U.S.C.A. § 1101(a)(15). One who leaves a country to permanently settle in another.

Immigration. The coming into a country of foreigners for purposes of permanent residence. The correlative term "emigration" denotes the act of such persons in leaving their former country.

Immigration and Nationality Act. A comprehensive federal law which deals with immigration, naturalization and exclusion of aliens. 8 U.S.C.A. § 1101 *et seq.*

Immigration and Naturalization Service. Such Service is responsible for administering the immigration and naturalization laws relating to the admission, exclusion, deportation, and naturalization of aliens. Specifically, the Service inspects aliens to determine their admissibility into the United States; adjudicates requests of aliens for benefits under the law; guards against illegal entry into the United States; investigates, apprehends, and removes aliens in this country in violation of the law; and examines alien applicants wishing to become citizens.

Immigration Appeals Board. The Board of Immigration Appeals, the highest administrative tribunal in the immigration field, is charged with the interpretation and administration of the immigration laws. The Board has jurisdiction, defined by regulation, to hear appeals from certain decisions of the Immigration and Naturalization Service. Most of the cases reaching the Board consist of appeals from formal orders of the Service's Immigration Judges entered in due process deportation hearings against aliens. These usually also involve applications by aliens for discretionary relief from deportation.

Imminent. Near at hand; mediate rather than immediate; close rather than touching; impending; on the point of happening; threatening; menacing; perilous.

Imminent danger. In relation to homicide in self-defense, this term means immediate danger, such as must be instantly met, such as cannot be guarded against by calling for the assistance of others or the protection of the law. Or, as otherwise defined, such an appearance of threatened and impending injury as would put a reasonable and prudent man to his instant defense. See **Self-defense.**

Imminently dangerous article. One that is reasonably certain to place life or limb in peril. Employers' Liability Assur. Corporation v. Columbus McKinnon Chain Co., D.C.N.Y., 13 F.2d 128.

Imminent peril. Such peril under humanitarian doctrine means certain, immediate, and impending, and not remote, uncertain, or contingent; and likelihood or bare possibility of injury is not sufficient to create "imminent peril." Hastings v. Coppage, Mo., 411 S.W.2d 232, 236. That position of danger to the plaintiff in which—if the existing circumstances remain unchanged—injury to him is reasonably certain. Elam v. Allbee, Mo.App., 432 S.W.2d 379, 381. See also **Emergency doctrine; Humanitarian doctrine.**

Immiscere /imísəriy/. Lat. In the civil law, to mix or mingle with; to meddle with; to join with.

Immobilia situm sequuntur /iməbíl(i)yə sáydəm səkwántər/. Immovable things follow their site or position; are governed by the law of the place where they are fixed. Cf. Mobilia Sequuntur Personam.

Immobilis /imówbələs/. Lat. Immovable. *Immobilia* or *res immobiles,* immovable things, such as lands and buildings.

Immoderate /imódərət/. Exceeding just, usual, or suitable bounds; not within reasonable limits.

Immoral. Contrary to good morals; inconsistent with the rules and principles of morality; inimical to public welfare according to the standards of a given community, as expressed in law or otherwise. Morally evil; impure; obscene; unprincipled; vicious; or dissolute. U. S. v. One Book, Entitled "Contraception," by Marie C. Stopes, D.C.N.Y., 51 F.2d 525, 527.

Immoral act or **conduct.** Within rules authorizing disbarment of attorney is that conduct which is willful, flagrant, or shameless, and which shows a moral indifference to the opinions of the good and respectable members of the community. Warkentin v. Kleinwachter, 166 Okl. 218, 27 P.2d 160.

Immoral consideration. One contrary to good morals, and therefore invalid. Contracts based upon an immoral consideration are generally void.

Immoral contracts. Contracts founded upon considerations *contra bonos mores* are void.

Immorality. That which is *contra bonos mores.* See **Immoral.**

Immovables. In the civil law, property which, from its nature, destination, or the object to which it is applied, cannot move itself, or be removed.

In conflicts of law, refers to land and those things so firmly attached thereto that they may be regarded as part of it and the law of the situs governs in choice of law. Restatement, Second, Conflict of Laws, § 223.

Immunity. Exemption, as from serving in an office, or performing duties which the law generally requires other citizens to perform; *e.g.* exemption from paying taxes. Freedom from duty or penalty. Special privilege. See also Exemption; Judicial immunity; Legislative immunity; Parent-child immunity; Privilege; Sovereign immunity.

Governmental tort immunity. The federal, and derivatively, the state and local governments are free from liability for torts committed except in cases in which they have consented by statute to be sued; *e.g.* Federal Tort Claims Act; state tort claims acts. Most states, either by statute or court decision, have abolished or greatly restricted the doctrine of sovereign immunity at both the state and local levels.

The Supreme Court has held that local governments can be sued directly under 42 U.S.C.A. § 1983 for monetary, declaratory, or injunctive relief where "the action that is alleged to be unconstitutional implements or executes a policy statement, ordinance, regulation, or decision officially adopted and promulgated by that body's officers." Monell v. Department of Social Services of N. Y., 429 U.S. 1071, 97 S.Ct. 807, 50 L.Ed.2d 789.

See also **Governmental immunity; Sovereign immunity.**

Immunity from prosecution. By state and federal statutes, a witness may be granted immunity from prosecution for his or her testimony (*e.g.* before grand jury). States either adopt the "use" or the "transactional" immunity approach. The federal government replaced the later with the former approach in 1970. The distinction between the two is as follows: "Use immunity" prohibits witness' compelled testimony and its fruits from being used in any manner in connection with criminal prosecution of the witness; on the other hand, "transactional immunity" affords immunity to the witness from prosecution for offense to which his compelled testimony relates.

Protection from prosecution must be commensurate with privilege against self incrimination, but it need not be any greater and hence a person is entitled only to protection from prosecution based on the use and derivative use of his testimony; he is not constitutionally entitled to protection from prosecution for everything arising from the illegal transaction which his testimony concerns (transactional immunity). Kastigar v. U. S., 406 U.S. 441, 92 S.Ct. 1653, 32 L.Ed.2d 212.

Interspousal immunity. See **Husband-wife tort actions.**

Property law. A freedom on the part of one person against having a given legal relation altered by a given act or omission to act on the part of another person. Restatement of Property, § 4.

Immunization. The condition of being, or the act rendering one, immunized or protected, especially from communicable diseases.

Impacted area. An "impacted area" is an area whose school population has been burdened because of attendance by a large number of federal employees' children and which may at the same time be losing school tax revenue because of the United States Government's immunity from land taxes. Douglas Independent School Dist. v. Jorgenson, D.C.S.D., 293 F.Supp. 849, 850.

Impact rule. Rule formerly prevailing in many jurisdictions which required a blow or impact from without as a condition for recovering damages in negligence for emotional distress. Such rule has been abandoned in most jurisdictions today.

Impair. To weaken, to make worse, to lessen in power, diminish, or relax, or otherwise affect in an injurious manner.

Impaired capital. Condition of a business when the surplus account shows a negative balance and hence the capital is reduced below its value from when the stock was issued.

Impairing the obligation of contracts. A law which impairs the obligation of a contract is one which renders the contract in itself less valuable or less enforceable, whether by changing its terms and stipulations, its legal qualities and conditions, or by regulating the remedy for its enforcement.

To "impair the obligation of a contract", within prohibition of Art. I, § 10, U.S.Const., is to weaken it, lessen its value, or make it worse in any respect or in any degree, and any law which changes the intention and legal effect of the parties, giving to one a greater and to the other a less interest or benefit, or which imposes conditions not included in the contract or dispenses with the performance of those included, impairs the obligation of the contract.

A statute "impairs the obligation of a contract" when by its terms it nullifies or materially changes existing contract obligations.

Impanel. The act of the clerk of the court in making up a list of the jurors who have been selected for the trial of a particular cause. All the steps of ascertaining who shall be the proper jurors to sit in the trial of a particular case up to the final formation.

Imparcare /ìmparkériy/. In old English law, to impound. To shut up, or confine in prison. *Inducti sunt in carcerem et imparcati,* they were carried to prison and shut up.

Imparl /əmpárl/. To have license to settle a litigation amicably; to obtain delay for adjustment.

Imparlance /əmpárlən(t)s/. In early practice, imparlance meant time given to either of the parties to an action to answer the pleading of the other. It thus amounted to a continuance of the action to a further day. Literally the term signified leave given to the parties to *talk together; i.e.,* with a view to settling their differences amicably. But in modern practice it denotes a time given to the defendant to plead.

A *general imparlance* is the entry of a general prayer and allowance of time to plead till the next term, without reserving to the defendant the benefit of any exception; so that after such an imparlance the defendant cannot object to the jurisdiction of the court, or plead any matter in abatement. This kind of imparlance is always from one term to another.

A *general special imparlance* contains a saving of all exceptions whatsoever, so that the defendant after this may plead not only in abatement, but he may also plead a plea which affects the jurisdiction of the court, as privilege. He cannot, however, plead a tender, and that he was always ready to pay, because by craving time, he admits that he is not ready, and so falsifies his plea.

A *special imparlance* reserves to the defendant all exceptions to the writ, bill, or count; and therefore after it the defendant may plead in abatement, though not to the jurisdiction of the court.

Impartial. Favoring neither; disinterested; treating all alike; unbiased; equitable, fair, and just.

Impartial expert. Witness appointed by tribunal for unbiased opinion on matter addressed to the court. Commonly, Worker's Compensation Board will appoint an impartial physician to examine and report his findings to Board. Similar usage of experts is made in social security disability hearings.

Impartial jury. The provision of the Bill of Rights (Sixth Amendment to Const. of U.S.) requiring that the accused shall have a fair trial by an impartial jury, means that the jury must be not partial, not favoring one party more than another, unprejudiced, disinterested, equitable, and just, and that the merits of the case shall not be prejudged. Term refers to a jury which is of impartial frame of mind at beginning of trial, is influenced only by legal and competent evidence produced during trial, and bases its verdict upon evidence connecting defendant with the commission of the crime charged. Durham v. State, 182 Tenn. 577, 188 S.W.2d 555, 558.

For "Fair and impartial jury", and "Fair and impartial trial", see those titles.

Impartible feud /ìmpárdəbəl fyúwd/. See **Feudum individuum.**

Impeach. To accuse; to charge a liability upon; to sue. To dispute, disparage, deny, or contradict; as, to impeach a judgment or decree, or impeach a witness; or as used in the rule that a jury cannot "impeach their verdict". To proceed against a public officer for crime or misfeasance, before a proper court, by the presentation of a written accusation called "articles of impeachment". See **Impeachment.**

Impeachment. A criminal proceeding against a public officer, before a *quasi* political court, instituted by a written accusation called "articles of impeachment"; for example, a written accusation by the House of Representatives of the United States to the Senate of the United States against the President, Vice President, or an officer of the United States. Such federal power of impeachment is provided for in Art. II, § 4 of the Constitution. Under Art. I, § 2, cl. 5, the House of Representatives "shall have the sole Power of Impeachment", and under § 3, cl. 6, "The Senate shall have the sole Power to try all Impeachments".

Articles of impeachment. The formal written allegation of the causes for an impeachment, answering the same purpose as an indictment in an ordinary criminal proceeding.

Collateral impeachment. See **Collateral attack.**

Impeachment of verdict. Attack on verdict because of alleged improprieties in the jury's deliberations or conduct.

Impeachment of witness. To call in question the veracity of a witness, by means of evidence adduced for such purpose, or the adducing of proof that a witness is unworthy of belief. McWethy v. Lee, 1 Ill.App.3d 80, 272 N.E.2d 663, 666. In general, though there are variations from state to state, a witness may be impeached with respect to prior inconsistent statements, contradiction of facts, bias, or character. A witness, once impeached, may be rehabilitated with evidence supporting credibility. State v. Peterson, Iowa, 219 N.W.2d 665, 671.

Fed.R.Civil P. 32(a)(1) permits the use at trial of a witness's prior deposition to discredit or impeach testimony of the deponent as a witness.

Fed.Evid.R. 607 provides that the "credibility of a witness may be attached by any party, including the party calling him." Rule 608 governs impeachment by evidence of character and conduct of witness, and Rule 609 impeachment by evidence of conviction of crime.

See also **Jenks Act** or **Rule; Prior inconsistent statements.**

Impechiare /əmpìychiyə́riy/. To impeach, to accuse, or prosecute for felony or treason.

Impede. To obstruct; hinder; check; delay.

Impediens /ìmpíydiyèn(d)z/. In old English practice, one who hinders; an impedient. The defendant or deforciant in a fine was sometimes so called.

Impedimento /impèyðiméntow/. In Spanish law, a prohibition to contract marriage, established by law between certain persons.

Impediments /impédəmənts/. Disabilities, or hindrances to the making of contracts, such as infancy, want of reason, etc.

Civil law. Absolute impediments are those which prevent the person subject to them from marrying at all, without either the nullity of marriage or its being punishable. *Dirimant impediments* are those which render a marriage void; as where one of the contracting parties is unable to marry by reason of a prior undissolved marriage. *Prohibitive impediments* are those which do not render the marriage null, but subject the parties to a punishment. *Relative impediments* are those which regard only certain persons with respect to each other; as between two particular persons who are related within the prohibited degrees.

Impediment to marriage. Legal obstacle to contracting a valid marriage such as relationship of blood within prohibited degree of consanguinity between parties. See also **Impediments.**

Impeditor /impédədər/. In old English law, a disturber in the action of *quare impedit.*

Impensæ /ìmpénsiy/. Lat. In the civil law, expenses; outlays. Divided into necessary (*necessariæ*), useful (*utiles*), and tasteful or ornamental (*voluptuariæ*).

Imperative. Mandatory. See **Directory.**

Imperator /impəréydər/. Emperor. The title of the Roman emperors, and also of the Kings of England before the Norman conquest. 1 Bl.Comm. 242. See **Emperor.**

Imperfect. As used in various legal compound terms, this word means defective or incomplete; wanting in some legal or formal requisite; wanting in legal sanction or effectiveness; as in speaking of imperfect "obligations," "ownership," "rights," "title," "usufruct," or "war." See those nouns.

Imperii majestas est tutelæ salus /impíriyay məjéstæs èst t(y)uwtíyliy sǽləs/. The majesty of the empire is the safety of its protection.

Imperitia /ìmpərísh(iy)ə/. Lat. Unskillfulness; want of skill.

Imperitia culpæ adnumeratur /ìmpərísh(iy)ə kálpiy ədn(y)ùwməréydər/. Want of skill is reckoned as *culpa*; that is, as blamable conduct or neglect.

Imperitia est maxima mechanicorum pœna /ìmpərísh(iy)ə ést mǽksəmə məkǽnəkórəm píynə/. Unskillfulness is the greatest punishment of mechanics [that is, from its effect in making them liable to those by whom they are employed]. The word *"pœna"* in some translations is erroneously rendered "fault."

Imperium /ìmpíriyəm/. The right to command, which includes the right to employ the force of the state to enforce the laws. This is one of the principal attributes of the power of the executive.

Impersonalitas /ìmpərsənéylətæs/. Lat. Impersonality. A mode of expression where no reference is made to any person, such as the expression *"ut dicitur"* (as is said).

Impersonalitas non concludit nec ligat /ìmpərsənéylətæs nòn kənkl(y)úwdət nèk lígət/. Impersonality neither concludes nor binds.

Impersonation. False impersonation is representing oneself to be a public officer or employee or a person licensed to practice or engage in any profession or vocation for which a license is required by state law with knowledge that such representation is false. The act of pretending or representing oneself to be another, commonly a crime if the other is a public official or police officer. People v. Vaughn, 196 Cal. App.2d 622, 16 Cal.Rptr. 711. See also **Personate.**

Impertinence. Irrelevancy; the fault of not properly pertaining to the issue or proceeding. The introduction of any matters into a bill, complaint, answer, or other pleading or proceeding in a suit, which are not properly before the court for decision, at any particular stage of the suit. Harrison v. Perea, 168 U.S. 311, 18 S.Ct. 129, 42 L.Ed. 478. See **Impertinent.**

A question propounded to a witness, or evidence offered or sought to be elicited, is called "impertinent" when it has no logical bearing upon the issue, is not necessarily connected with it, or does not belong to the matter in hand. See also **Immaterial evidence; Irrelevant.**

Impertinent. That which does not belong to a pleading, interrogatory, or other proceeding; out of place; superfluous; irrelevant. A term applied to matter not necessary to constitute the cause of action or ground of defense. Such matter may be ordered stricken from the pleading. Fed.R.Civil P. 12(f). See also **Immaterial averment; Surplusage.**

Impescare /ìmpəskériy/. In old records, to impeach or accuse. *Impescatus*, impeached.

Impetitio vasti /ìmpətísh(iy)ow vǽstay/. Impeachment of waste (*q.v.*).

Impetrare /ìmpətrériy/. In old English practice, to obtain by request, as a writ or privilege. This application of the word seems to be derived from the civil law.

Impetration /ìmpətréyshən/. In old English law, the obtaining anything by petition or entreaty. Particularly, the obtaining of a benefice from Rome by solicitation, which benefice belonged to the disposal of the king or other lay patron.

Impier /ímpay(ə)r/. Umpire (*q.v.*).

Impierment /impérmənt/. Impairing or prejudicing.

Impignorata /əmpìgnəréydə/. Pledged; given in pledge (*pignori data);* mortgaged.

Impignoration /əmpìgnəréyshən/. The act of pawning or putting to pledge.

Impius et crudelis judicandus est qui libertati non favet /ímpiyəs èt krədíyləs jùwdəkǽndəs èst kwày lìbərtéyday nòn féyvət/. He is to be judged impious and cruel who does not favor liberty.

Implacitare /implæsətériy/. Lat. To implead; to sue.

Implead. To sue; to prosecute. To bring new party into action on ground that new party is, or may be, liable to party who brings him in, for all or party of the subject matter claim. Fed.R.Civil P. 14. See **Third-party practice.**

Impleader. Procedure by which party is impleaded. See **Implead; Third-party practice; Vouching-in.**

Implements /ímpləmənts/. Such things as are used or employed for a trade, or furniture of a house. Particularly applied to tools, utensils, instruments of labor; as the implements of trade or of farming.

Implication. Intendment or inference, as distinguished from the actual expression of a thing in words. In a will, an estate may pass by mere *implication,* without any express words to direct its course.

An inference of something not directly declared, but arising from what is admitted or expressed. Act of implying or condition of being implied.

"Implication" is also used in the sense of "inference"; *i.e.,* where the existence of an intention is inferred from acts not done for the sole purpose of communicating it, but for some other purpose.

See also **Inference.**

Implied. This word is used in law in contrast to "express"; *i.e.,* where the intention in regard to the subject-matter is not manifested by explicit and direct words, but is gathered by implication or necessary deduction from the circumstances, the general language, or the conduct of the parties. Term differs from "inferred" to the extent that the hearer or reader "infers" while the writer or speaker "implies".

As to implied Abrogation; Agreement; Assumpsit; Condition; Confession; Consent; Consideration; Contract; Covenant; Dedication; Easement; Invitation; Malice; Notice; Obligation; Power; Trust; Use; Waiver; and Warranty, see those titles.

Implied assertions. Statements which, while not expressed, may be deduced from what is written or spoken.

Implied authority. In law of agency, power given by principal to agent which necessarily follows from the express authority given though such power is not expressly asserted. Actual authority may be either express or implied, "implied authority" being that which is necessary, usual and proper to accomplish or perform the main authority expressly delegated to an agent. Clark v. Gneiting, 95 Idaho 10, 501 P.2d 278, 280.

Implied consent. See **Consent.**

Implied intent. Intent which necessarily arises from language used in an instrument or from conduct of parties.

Implied promise. Fiction which the law creates to render one liable on contract theory so as to avoid fraud or unjust enrichment. See also **Equitable estoppel.**

Implied reservation. Type of easement created by grantor for benefit of land retained by him and not included in conveyance. Wolek v. Di Feo, 60 N.J.Super. 324, 159 A.2d 127.

Implied reservation of water doctrine. When Federal Government withdraws its land from public domain and reserves it for a federal purpose, the government, by implication, reserves appurtenant water then unappropriated to the extent needed to accomplish the purpose of the reservation. However, it reserves only that amount of water necessary to fulfill the purpose of the reservation, and no more. Cappaert v. U. S., 426 U.S. 128, 96 S.Ct. 2062, 2071, 48 L.Ed.2d 523.

Implied warranty. See **Warranty.**

Import. See **Importation.**

Importation. The act of bringing goods and merchandise into a country from a foreign country. Cunard Steamship Co. v. Mellon, 262 U.S. 100, 43 S.Ct. 504, 67 L.Ed. 894.

Import-export clause. Provision in U.S. Constitution, Art. 1, § 10, cl. 2, to the effect that no state shall, without the consent of Congress, lay imposts or duties on imports or exports, except what may be absolutely necessary for executing its inspection laws.

Import quota. The precise quantity of specific goods which a country will permit to be imported at a given time. Such quotas are set by the government to protect domestic businesses from excessive importation of competitive goods. See also **Most favored nation clause.**

Imports clause. See **Import-export clause.**

Importunity. Pressing solicitation; urgent request; application for a claim or favor which is urged with troublesome frequency or pertinacity.

Impose. To levy or exact as by authority; to lay as a burden, tax, duty or charge.

Imposition. An impost; tax; contribution. Unreasonable request or burden. Act of imposing.

Impossibility. That which, in the constitution and course of nature or the law, no man can do or perform.

Impossibility is of the following several sorts:

An act is *physically* impossible when it is contrary to the course of nature. Such an impossibility may be either *absolute, i.e.,* impossible in any case, (*e.g.,* to stop earth rotation) or *relative* (sometimes called "impossibility in fact"), *i.e.,* arising from the circumstances of the case (*e.g.,* for A. to make a payment to B., he being a deceased person). To the latter class belongs what is sometimes called "*practical* impossibility,*" which exists when the act *can* be done, but only at an excessive or unreasonable cost. An act is *legally* or juridically impossible when a rule of law makes it impossible to do it; *e.g.,* for A. to make a valid will before his majority. This class of acts must not be confounded with those which are possible, although forbidden by law, as to commit a theft. An act is *logically* impossible when it is contrary to the nature of the transaction, as where A. gives property to B. expressly for his own benefit, on condition that he transfers it to C. See also **Legal impossibility.**

Impossibility of performance of contract. As absolving party from liability for nonperformance, means not only strict impossibility, but impracticability because of extreme and unreasonable difficulty, expense, injury or loss involved. Total inability of party to perform for either subjective or objective reasons and under certain circumstances, though not all, such impossibility may be a defense. Jones v. Servel, Inc., 135 Ind.App. 171, 186 N.E.2d 689.

It is now recognized that a thing is impossible in legal contemplation when it is not practicable; and a thing is impracticable when it can only be done at an excessive and unreasonable cost. Transatlantic Fin. Corp. v. United States, 363 F.2d 312, 315. When the issue is raised, the court is asked to construct a condition of performance based on changed circumstances, a process which involves at least three reasonably definable steps. First, a contingency—something unexpected—must have occurred. Second, the risk of the unexpected occurrence must not have been allocated either by agreement or by custom. Finally, occurrence of the contingency must have rendered performance commercially impracticable. Although impossibility or impracticability of performance may arise in many different ways, the tendency has been to classify the cases into several categories. These are: 1) Destruction, deterioration or unavailability of the subject matter or the tangible means of performance; 2) Failure of the contemplated mode of delivery or payment; 3) Supervening prohibition or prevention by law; 4) Failure of the intangible means of performance and 5) Death or illness. The basic U.C.C. sections dealing with impossibility of performance are §§ 613, 615. See in this regard, **Commercial frustration; Commercial impracticability.**

Impossible contract. One which the law will not hold binding upon the parties, because of the natural or legal impossibility of the performance by one party of that which is the consideration for the promise of the other.

Impossibilium nulla obligatio est /əmpòsəbíl(i)yəm nə́lə òbləgéysh(iy)ow èst/. There is no obligation to do impossible things.

Imposter. One who pretends to be somebody other than who he is, with intent to deceive; a faker, charlatan; mountebank. See also **Impersonation; Personate.**

Imposts. Taxes, duties, or impositions levied for divers reasons. Crew Levick Co. v. Commonwealth of Pennsylvania, 245 U.S. 292, 38 S.Ct. 126, 62 L.Ed. 295. Generic term for taxes. See **Duty.**

Impotence. Inability to copulate. Properly used of the male; but it has also been used synonymously with "sterility." Impotency as a ground for divorce means want of *potentia copulandi* or incapacity to consummate the marriage, and not merely incapacity for procreation. Reed v. Reed, 26 Tenn.App. 690, 177 S.W.2d 26, 27.

Impotentia excusat legem /ìmpəténsh(iy)ə əkskyúwzət líyjəm/. The impossibility of doing what is required by the law excuses from the performance.

Impotentiam, property propter /própərdiy próptər ìmpəténsh(iy)əm/. A qualified property, which may subsist in animals *feræ naturæ* on account of their inability, as where hawks, herons, or other birds build in a person's trees, or conies, etc., make their nests or burrows in a person's land, and have young there, such person has a qualified property in them till they can fly or run away, and then such property expires.

Impound. To shut up stray animals or distrained goods in a pound. To seize and take into the custody of the law or of a court. Thus, a court will sometimes *impound* a suspicious document produced at a trial or a vehicle or other item used in commission of a crime. See also **Confiscate; Seizure.**

Impound account. Accumulated funds (normally collected monthly from mortgagor or trustor) held by a lender for payment of taxes, insurance, or other periodic debts against real property. The lender pays the tax bill, premium, etc. from the accumulated funds when due. See also **Escrow.**

Impracticability. The term "impracticability" in federal rule providing for class action if class is so numerous that joinder of all members is impracticable does not mean "impossibility" but only the difficulty of inconvenience of joining all members of the class. Union Pac. R. Co. v. Woodahl, D.C.Mont., 308 F.Supp. 1002, 1008. See also **Commercial frustration; Commercial impracticability; Impossibility.**

Imprescriptibility. The state or quality of being incapable of prescription; not of such a character that a right to it can be gained by prescription.

Imprescriptible rights. Such rights as a person may use or not, at pleasure, since they cannot be lost to him by the claims of another founded on prescription.

Impression, case of first. One without a precedent; one presenting a wholly new state of facts; one involving a question never before determined.

Impressment. A power possessed by the English crown of taking persons or property to aid in the defense of the country, with or without the consent of the persons concerned. It is usually exercised to obtain hands for the royal ships in time of war, by taking seamen engaged in merchant vessels, but in former times impressment of merchant ships was also practiced. The admiralty issues protections against impressment in certain cases, either under statutes passed in favor of certain callings or voluntarily.

Imprest fund. Petty cash fund used by business for small, routine expenses.

Imprest money. Money paid on enlisting or impressing soldiers or sailors.

Impretiabilis /əmprèshiyéybələs/. Lat. Beyond price; invaluable.

Imprimatur /ìmprəméydər/. Lat. Let it be printed. A license or allowance, granted by the constituted authorities, giving permission to print and publish a book. This allowance was formerly necessary, in England, before any book could lawfully be printed, and in some other countries is still required.

Imprimere /impríməriy/. To press upon; to impress or press; to imprint or print.

Imprimery /impríməriy/. In some of the ancient English statutes this word is used to signify a printing-office, the art of printing, a print or impression.

Imprimis /impráyməs/. Lat. In the first place; first of all.

Imprison. To put in a prison; to put in a place of confinement. To confine a person, or restrain his liberty, in any way.

Imprisonment. The act of putting or confining a man in prison. The restraint of a man's personal liberty; coercion exercised upon a person to prevent the free exercise of his powers of locomotion. It is not a necessary part of the definition that the confinement should be in a place usually appropriated to that purpose; it may be in a locality used only for the specific occasion; or it may take place without the actual application of any physical agencies of restraint (such as locks or bars), as by verbal compulsion and the display of available force. Every confinement of the person is an "imprisonment," whether it be in a prison, or in a private house, or even by forcibly detaining one in the public streets. Any unlawful exercise or show of force by which person is compelled to remain where he does not wish to be. McKendree v. Christy, 29 Ill.App.2d 866, 172 N.E.2d 380, 381. See also **Solitary confinement.**

False imprisonment. The unlawful arrest or detention of a person without warrant, or by an illegal warrant, or a warrant illegally executed, and either in a prison or a place used temporarily for that purpose, or by force and constraint without confinement. False imprisonment consists in the unlawful detention of the person of another, for any length of time, whereby he is deprived of his personal liberty. Dupler v. Seubert, 69 Wis.2d 626, 230 N.W.2d 626, 631. The unlawful detention of the occupant of an automobile may be accomplished by driving so rapidly that he cannot alight.

A person commits a misdemeanor if he knowingly restrains another unlawfully so as to interfere substantially with his liberty. Model Penal Code, § 212.-3.

The tort of "false imprisonment" is the nonconsensual, intentional confinement of a person, without lawful privilege, for an appreciable length of time, however short. City of Newport Beach v. Sasse, 9 Cal.App.3d 803, 88 Cal.Rptr. 476, 480.

Impristi /ìmprístay/. Adherents; followers. Those who side with or take the part of another, either in his defense or otherwise.

Improbable. Unlikely to be true, or to occur, not to be readily believed. Johnson v. Tregle, La.App., 8 So.2d 755, 758.

Improper. Not suitable; unfit; not suited to the character, time, and place. Godbey v. Godbey, 70 Ohio App. 455, 44 N.E.2d 810, 813. Not in accordance with fact, truth, or right procedure and not in accord with propriety, modesty, good taste, or good manners. Landry v. Daley, D.C.Ill., 280 F.Supp. 968, 970.

Improper cumulation of actions. In common law pleading, an attempt to join in one proceeding inconsistent causes of action. Toms v. Nugent, La.App., 12 So.2d 713, 715. This is permitted under Rule of Civil Procedure 8(e)(2).

Improper feuds. In old English law, these were derivative feuds; as, for instance, those that were originally bartered and sold to the feudatory for a price, or were held upon base or less honorable services, or upon a rent in lieu of military service, or were themselves alienable, without mutual license, or descended indifferently to males or females.

Improper influence. Undue influence *(q.v.)*.

Improperly obtained evidence. See **Illegally obtained evidence.**

Impropriate rector. In ecclesiastical law, commonly signifies a lay rector as opposed to a spiritual rector; just as impropriate tithes are tithes in the hands of a lay owner, as opposed to appropriate tithes, which are tithes in the hands of a spiritual owner.

Impropriation. In ecclesiastical law, the annexing an ecclesiastical benefice to the use of a lay person, whether individual or corporate, in the same way as *appropriation* is the annexing of any such benefice to the proper and perpetual use of some spiritual corporation, whether sole or aggregate, to enjoy forever.

Improve. To meliorate, make better, to increase the value or good qualities of, mend, repair, as to "improve" a street by grading, parking, curbing, paving, etc.

Improved land. Real estate whose value has been increased by addition of sewers, roads, utilities, and the like.

Improved value. Appraisal term encompassing the total value of land and improvements rather than the separate values of each.

Improvement. A valuable addition made to property (usually real estate) or an an,elioration in its condition, amounting to more than mere repairs or replacement, costing labor or capital, and intended to enhance its value, beauty or utility or to adapt it for new or further purposes. Generally, buildings, but may also include any permanent structure or other development, such as a street, sidewalks, sewers, utilities, etc. An expenditure to extend the useful life of an asset or to improve its performance over that of the original asset. Such expenditures are capitalized as part of the asset's cost. Contrast with **Mainte-**

nance and **Repair.** See also **Betterment; Internal improvements; Leasehold improvements.**

In the law of patents, an addition to, or modification of, a previous invention or discovery, intended or claimed to increase its utility or value. Steiner Sales Co. v. Schwartz Sales Co., C.C.A.Utah, 98 F.2d 999, 1010. It includes two necessary ideas: the idea of a complete and practical operative art or instrument and the idea of some change in such art or instrument not affecting its essential character but enabling it to produce its appropriate results in a more perfect or economical manner.

Improvement bonds. See **Bond.**

Improvidence. As used in a statute excluding one found incompetent to execute the duties of an administrator by reason of improvidence, means that want of care and foresight in the management of property which would be likely to render the estate and effects of the intestate unsafe, and liable to be lost or diminished in value, in case the administration should be committed to the improvident person.

Improvidently. A judgment, decree, rule, injunction, etc., when given or rendered without adequate consideration by the court, or without proper information as to all the circumstances affecting it, or based upon a mistaken assumption or misleading information or advice, is sometimes said to have been "improvidently" given or issued.

Impruiare /imprùwiyériy/. In old English law, to improve land. *Impruiamentum,* the improvement so made of it.

Impubes /ìmpyúwbiyz/. Lat. In the civil law, a minor under the age of puberty; a male under fourteen years of age; a female under twelve.

Impulse. Sudden urge or inclination; thrusting or impelling force within a person. See also **Insanity; Irresistible impulse.**

Impunitas continuum affectum tribuit delinquendi /ìmpyúwnətæs kəntínyuwəm əféktəm tríbyuwət dèləŋkwénday/. Impunity confirms the disposition to commit crime.

Impunitas semper ad deteriora invitat /ìmpyúwnətæs sémpər æd dətìriyórə ənváydət/. Impunity always invites to greater crimes.

Impunity. Exemption or protection from penalty or punishment. See also **Immunity.**

Imputability. The state or condition rendering one chargeable for an act. Liability or responsibility for conduct or omission. See **Liability.**

Imputatio /ìmpyətéysh(iy)ow/. Lat. In the civil law, legal liability.

Imputation of payment. In the civil law, the application of a payment made by a debtor to his creditor.

Imputed. As used in legal phrases, this word means attributed vicariously; that is, an act, fact, or quality is said to be "imputed" to a person when it is ascribed or charged to him, not because he is personally cognizant of it or responsible for it, but because another person is, over whom he has control or for whose acts or knowledge he is responsible. See also **Estoppel.**

Imputed cost. See **Cost.**

Imputed income. See **Income.**

Imputed interest. See **Interest.**

Imputed knowledge. This phrase is sometimes used as equivalent to "implied notice," *i.e.*, knowledge attributed or charged to a person because the facts in question were open to his discovery and it was his duty to inform himself as to them. In law of agency, notice of facts brought to the attention of an agent within the scope of his authority or employment is chargeable to his principal in most cases. See **Imputed notice.**

Imputed negligence. The negligence of one person may be chargeable to another depending upon the relationship of the parties, as for example, the negligence of an agent acting within the scope of his employment is chargeable to the principal. Negligence which is not directly attributable to the person himself, but which is the negligence of a person who is in privity with him, and with whose fault he is chargeable. See also **Negligence.**

Imputed notice. Information as to a given fact or circumstance charged or attributed to a person, and affecting his rights or conduct on the ground that actual notice was given to some person whose duty was to report it to the person to be affected, as, his agent or his attorney of record. See also **Notice.**

In. In the law of real estate, this preposition is used to denote the fact of seisin, title, or possession, and serves as an elliptical expression for some such phrase as "in possession," or as an abbreviation for "*in*titled" or "*in*vested with title."

An elastic preposition in other cases, expressing relation of presence, existence, situation, inclusion, action, etc.; inclosed or surrounded by limits, as in a room; also meaning for, in and about, on, within etc.; and is synonymous with expressions "in regard to", "respecting", "with respect to", and "as is".

In action. Attainable or recoverable by action; not in possession. A term applied to property of which a party has not the possession, but only a right to recover it by action. Things in action are rights of personal things, which nevertheless are not in possession. See **Chose in action.**

Inadequate. Insufficient; disproportionate; lacking in effectiveness or in conformity to a prescribed standard or measure.

Inadequate consideration. One not adequate or equal in value to the thing conveyed. Farrell v. Third Nat. Bank, 20 Tenn.App. 540, 101 S.W.2d 158, 163.

Inadequate damages. See **Damages.**

Inadequate price. A term applied to indicate the want of a sufficient consideration for a thing sold, or such a price as would ordinarily be entirely incommensurate with its intrinsic value.

Inadequate remedy at law. Within the meaning of the rule that equity will not entertain a suit if there is an adequate remedy at law, this does not mean that there must be a failure to collect money or damages at law, but the remedy is considered inadequate if it is, in its nature and character, unfitted or not adapted to the end in view, as, for instance, when the relief sought is preventive (*e.g.* injunction) rather than compensatory. Cruickshank v. Bidwell, 176 U.S. 73, 20 S.Ct. 280, 44 L.Ed. 377.

Inadmissible. That which, under the established rules of law, cannot be admitted or received; *e.g.*, parol evidence to contradict a written contract; evidence obtained from illegal search and seizure; certain types of hearsay evidence.

In adversum /in ædvársəm/. Against an adverse, unwilling, or resisting party. "A decree not by consent, but *in adversum.*"

Inadvertence. Heedlessness; lack of attention; want of care; carelessness; failure of a person to pay careful and prudent attention to the progress of a negotiation or a proceeding in court by which his rights may be affected. Used chiefly in statutory and rule enumerations of the grounds on which a judgment or decree may be vacated or set aside; as, "mistake, inadvertence, surprise, or excusable neglect." Fed.R. Civil P. 60(b). State ex rel. Regis v. District Court of Second Judicial Dist. in and for Silver Bow County, 102 Mont. 74, 55 P.2d 1295, 1298.

In ædificatio /in iydəfəkéysh(iy)ow/. Lat. In the civil law, building on another's land with one's own materials, or on one's own land with another's materials.

In æquali jure /in əkwéylay júriy/. In equal right; on an equality in point of right.

In æquali jure melior est conditio possidentis /in əkwéylay júriy míyliyər èst kəndísh(iy)ow pəsìdiyéntəs/. In [a case of] equal right the condition of the party in possession is the better.

In æquali manu /in əkwéylay mǽnyuw/. In equal hand; held equally or indifferently between two parties. Where an instrument was deposited by the parties to it in the hands of a third person, to keep on certain conditions, it was said to be held *in æquali manu.*

In æqua manu /in íykwə mǽnyuw/. In equal hand.

Inalienable /inéyl(i)yənəbəl/. Not subject to alienation; the characteristic of those things which cannot be bought or sold or transferred from one person to another, such as rivers and public highways, and certain personal rights; *e.g.*, liberty.

Inalienable interests. Type of interest in property which cannot be sold or traded.

Inalienable rights. Rights which are not capable of being surrendered or transferred without the consent of the one possessing such rights. Morrison v. State, Mo.App., 252 S.W.2d 97, 101.

In alieno solo /in æliyíynow sówlow/. In another's land.

In alio loco /in éyl(i)yow lówkow/. In another place.

In alta proditione nullus potest esse accessorius sed principalis solummodo /ìn ǽltə prədìshiyówniy náləs pówdəst ésiy æksəsóriyəs sèd prìnsəpéyləs sòwləmówdow/. In high treason no one can be an accessory but only principal.

In alternativis electio est debitoris /ìn oltàrnətáyvəs əléksh(iy)ow èst dèbətórəs/. In alternatives the debtor has the election.

In ambigua voce legis ea potius accipienda est significatio quæ vitio caret, præsertim cum etiam voluntas legis ex hoc colligi possit /ìn æmbígyuwə vówsiy líyjəs íyə pówsh(iy)əs əksìpiyéndə èst sìgnəfəkéysh(iy)ow kwiy vísh(iy)ow kérət, prəsárdəm kæm ésh(iy)əm vəlántæs líyjəs èks hók kóləjày pósət/. In an ambiguous expression of law, that signification is to be preferred which is consonant with equity, especially when the spirit of the law can be collected from that.

In ambiguis casibus semper præsumitur pro rege /ìn æmbígyuwəs kéysəbəs sémpər prəz(y)úwmədər pròw ríyjiy/. In doubtful cases the presumption is always in favor of the king.

In ambiguis orationibus maxime sententia spectanda est ejus qui eas protulisset /ìn æmbígyuwəs əreyshiyównəbəs mǽksəmiy sènténsh(iy)ə spèktǽndə èst íyjəs kwày íyəs pròwdəlísət/. In ambiguous expressions, the intention of the person using them is chiefly to be regarded.

In ambiguo /ìn æmbígyuwow/. In doubt.

In ambiguo sermone non utrumque dicimus sed id duntaxat quod volumus /ìn æmbígyuwow sərmówniy nòn yuwtrǽmkwiy dísəməs sèd id dàntǽksət kwòd vól(y)əməs/. When the language we use is ambiguous, we do not use it in a double sense, but in the sense in which we mean it.

In anglia non est interregnum /ìn ǽngliyə nón est ìntərégnəm/. In England there is no interregnum.

In aperta luce /ìn əpárdə l(y)úwsiy/. In open daylight; in the day-time.

In apicibus juris /ìn əpísəbəs júrəs/. Among the subtleties or extreme doctrines of the law.

In arbitrium judicis /ìn arbítriyəm júwdəsəs/. At the pleasure of the judge.

In arcta et salva custodia /ìn árktə èt sǽlvə kəstówd(i)yə/. In close and safe custody.

In articulo /ìn artíkyəlow/. In a moment; immediately.

In articulo mortis /ìn artíkyəlow mórdəs/. In the article of death; at the point of death.

In atrocioribus delictis punitur affectus licet non sequatur effectus /ìn ətròws(h)iyórəbəs dəlíktəs pyúwnədər əféktəs láysət nòn səkwéydər əféktəs/. In more atrocious crimes the intent is punished, though an effect does not follow.

Inauguration. The act of installing or inducting into office with formal ceremonies, as the coronation of a sovereign, the inauguration of a president or governor, or the consecration of a prelate. A word applied by the Romans to the ceremony of dedicating a temple, or raising a man to the priesthood, after the *augurs* had been consulted.

In autre droit /ìn ówtrə dróyt/. L. Fr. In another's right. As representing another. An executor, administrator, or trustee sues *in autre droit*.

In banc. See **En banc.**

In banco /ìn bǽnkow/. In bank; in the bench. A term applied to proceedings in the court in bank, as distinguished from the proceedings at *nisi prius*. Also, in the English court of common bench. See **Banc; En banc.**

In being. In existence or life at a given moment of time, as, in the phrase "life or lives in being" in the rule against perpetuities. An unborn child may, in some circumstances be considered as "in being."

In blank. A term applied to the indorsement of a bill or note where it consists merely of the indorser's name, without restriction to any particular indorsee. U.C.C. § 3–204(2).

Inblaura /ìnblóhrə/. In old records, profit or product of ground.

Inboard. In maritime law, and particularly with reference to the stowage of cargo, this term is contrasted with "outboard." It does not necessarily mean under deck, but is applied to a cargo so piled or stowed that it does not project over the "board" (side or rail) of the vessel.

In bonis /ìn bównəs/. Among the goods or property; in actual possession. *In bonis defuncti*, among the goods of the deceased.

Inborh /ínbòrg/. In Saxon law, a security, pledge, or *hypotheca*, consisting of the chattels of a person unable to obtain a personal "borg," or surety.

Inbound common. An uninclosed common, marked out, however, by boundaries.

In bulk. As a whole; as an entirety, without division into items or physical separation in packages or parcels. See also **Bulk.**

Inc. Incorporated.

In cahoots /ìn kəhúwts/. Jointly interested in property; or, common participants in enterprise or illegal act.

In camera /ìn kǽm(ə)rə/. In chambers; in private. A cause is said to be heard *in camera* either when the hearing is had before the judge in his private chambers or when all spectators are excluded from the courtroom.

In camera inspection. Under certain circumstances, a trial judge may inspect a document which counsel wishes to use at trial in his chambers before ruling on its admissibility or its use; *e.g.* grand jury testimony.

In camera proceedings. Trial or hearing held in a place not open to the public such as the judge's lobby or chambers.

Incapacitated person. Any person who is impaired by reason of mental illness, mental deficiency, physical illness or disability, advanced age, chronic use of drugs, chronic intoxication, or other cause (except minority) to the extent that he lacks sufficient understanding or capacity to make or communicate responsible decisions concerning his person. Uniform Probate Code, § 5–101. See also **Incapacity.**

Incapacity. Want of capacity; want of power or ability to take or dispose; want of legal ability to act. Inefficiency; incompetency; lack of adequate power. The quality or state of being incapable, want of capacity, lack of physical or intellectual power, or of natural or legal qualification; inability, incapability, disability, incompetence. Bole v. Civil City of Ligonier, 130 Ind.App. 362, 161 N.E.2d 189, 194.

Legal incapacity. This expression implies that the person in view has the right vested in him, but is prevented by some impediment from exercising it; as in the case of minors, committed persons, prisoners, etc. See **Civil death; Minority.**

Total incapacity. In Workers' Compensation Acts, such disqualification from performing the usual tasks of a worker that he or she cannot procure and retain employment. Incapacity for work is total not only so long as the injured employee is unable to do any work of any character, but also while he remains unable, as a result of his injury, either to resume his former occupation or to procure remunerative employment at a different occupation suitable to his impaired capacity. Such period of total incapacity may be followed by a period of partial incapacity, during which the injured employee is able both to procure and to perform work at some occupation suitable to his then-existing capacity, but less remunerative than the work in which he was engaged at the time of his injury. That situation constitutes "partial incapacity." Synonymous with "total disability."

In capita /in kǽpədə/. To the heads; by heads or polls. Persons succeed to an inheritance *in capita* when they individually take equal shares. So challenges to individual jurors are challenges *in capita,* as distinguished from challenges to the array. See also **Challenge; Per capita.**

In capite /in kǽpədiy/. In chief. Tenure *in capite* was a holding directly from the king.

Incarceration /inkàrsəréyshən/. Imprisonment; confinement in a jail or penitentiary. See **Imprisonment.**

In case. If; in the event.

In casu extremæ necessitatis omnia sunt communia /in kéys(y)uw əkstríymiy nəsèsətéydəs ómniyə sént kəmyúwn(i)yə/. In cases of extreme necessity, everything is in common.

In casu proviso /in kéys(y)uw prəváyzow/. In a (or the) case provided. *In tali casu editum et provisum,* in such case made and provided.

Incaute factum pro non facto habetur /ìnkódiy fǽktəm pròw nón fǽktow həbíydər/. A thing done unwarily (or unadvisedly) will be taken as not done.

Incendiary /insénd(i)yəriy/. A house-burner; one guilty of arson; one who maliciously and willfully sets another person's building on fire.

Incendium ære alieno non exuit debitorem /insénd(i)yəm íriy æliyiýnow nòn égzyuwət dèbətórəm/. A fire does not release a debtor from his debt.

Inception. Commencement; opening; initiation. The beginning of the operation of a contract or will, or of a note, mortgage, lien, etc.; the beginning of a cause or suit in court. Oriental Hotel Co. v. Griffiths, 88 Tex. 574, 33 S.W. 652.

Incertæ personæ /insárdiy pərsówniy/. Uncertain persons, as posthumous heirs, a corporation, the poor, a juristic person, or persons who cannot be ascertained until after the execution of a will.

Incerta pro nullis habentur /insárdə pròw nə́ləs həbéntər/. Uncertain things are held for nothing.

Incerta quantitas vitiat actum /insárdə kwóntətæs víshiyəd ǽktəm/. An uncertain quantity vitiates the act.

Incest. The crime of sexual intercourse or cohabitation between a man and woman who are related to each other within the degrees wherein marriage is prohibited by law.

A person is guilty of incest, a felony of the third degree, if he knowingly marries or cohabits or has sexual intercourse with an ancestor or descendant, a brother or sister of the whole or half blood [or an uncle, aunt, nephew or niece of the whole blood]. "Cohabit" means to live together under the representation or appearance of being married. The relationships referred to herein includes blood relationships without regard to legitimacy, and relationship of parent and child by adoption. Model Penal Code, § 230.2.

Incestuosi /insèschuwówsay/. Those offspring incestuously begotten.

Incestuous adultery. The elements of this offense are that defendant, being married to one person, has had sexual intercourse with another related to the defendant within the prohibited degrees.

Incestuous bastards. Incestuous bastards are those who are produced by the illegal connection of two persons who are relations within the degrees prohibited by law.

Inch. A measure of length, containing one-twelfth part of a foot; originally supposed equal to three barleycorns. Its metric equivalent is 2.540 centimeters.

Inch of candle. A mode of sale at one time in use among merchants. A notice was first given upon the exchange, or other public place, as to the time of sale. The goods to be sold were divided into lots, printed papers of which, and the conditions of sale, were then published. When the sale took place, a small piece of candle, about an inch long was kept burning, and the last bidder, when the candle went out, was entitled to the lot or parcel for which he bid.

In charge of. Means in the care or custody of, or intrusted to the management or direction of. See **Guardian; Ward.**

Inchartare /ìnkartériy/. To give, or grant, and assure anything by a written instrument.

In chief. Principal; primary; directly obtained. A term applied to the evidence obtained from a witness upon his examination in court by the party producing him; *i.e.* direct examination of witness.

Tenure in chief, or *in capite,* is a holding directly of the king or chief lord.

Inchmaree clause. In marine insurance, provision in policy protecting one from perils resulting from negligence of master, or from any latent defect in machinery or hull, charterer, mariners, engineers and pilots.

Inchoate /inkówǝt/. Imperfect; partial; unfinished; begun, but not completed; as a contract not executed by all the parties. State ex rel. McCubbin v. McMillian, Mo.App., 349 S.W.2d 453, 462.

Inchoate crimes. An incipient crime which generally leads to another crime. An assault has been referred to as an inchoate battery, though the assault is a crime in and of itself. The Model Penal Code classifies attempts, solicitation and conspiracy as such. §§ 5.01–5.03.

Inchoate dower. A wife's interest in the lands of her husband during his life, which may become a right of dower upon his death. A contingent claim or possibility of acquiring dower by outliving husband and arises, not out of contract, but as an institution of law constituting a mere chose in action incapable of transfer by separate grant but susceptible of extinguishment, which is effected by wife joining with husband in deed, which operates as release or satisfaction of interest and not as conveyance.

Inchoate instrument. Instruments which the law requires to be registered or recorded are said to be "inchoate" prior to registration, in that they are then good only between the parties and privies and as to persons having notice.

Inchoate interest. An interest in real estate which is not a present interest, but which may ripen into a vested estate, if not barred, extinguished, or divested.

Inchoate lien. The lien of a judgment, from the day of its entry, subject to be defeated by its vacation, becoming a consummate lien if the motion for a new trial is thereafter overruled; such lien then relating back to the original entry of the judgment.

Inchoate right. In patent law, the right of an inventor to his invention while his application is pending which matures as "property" when the patent issues. Mullins Mfg. Co. v. Booth, C.C.A.Mich., 125 F.2d 660, 664.

Incident. Used both substantively and adjectively of a thing which, either usually or naturally and inseparably, depends upon, appertains to, or follows another that is more worthy. Used as a noun, it denotes anything which inseparably belongs to, or is connected with, or inherent in, another thing, called the "principal". Also, less strictly, it denotes anything which is usually connected with another, or connected for some purposes, though not inseparably. Thus, the right of alienation is incident to an estate in fee-simple, though separable in equity.

Incidental. Depending upon or appertaining to something else as primary; something necessary, appertaining to, or depending upon another which is termed the principal; something incidental to the main purpose. The Robin Goodfellow, D.C.Wash., 20 F.2d 924, 925.

Incidental beneficiary. A person is not a beneficiary of a trust if the settlor does not manifest an intention to give him a beneficial interest, although he may incidentally benefit from the performance of the trust. Restatement, Second, Trusts, § 126.

Incidental damages. See **Damages.**

Incidental powers. The term "incidental powers," within the rule that a corporation possesses only those powers which its charter confers upon it, either expressly or as incidental to its existence, means such powers as are directly and immediately appropriate to the execution of the powers expressly granted and exist only to enable the corporation to carry out the purpose of its creation.

Incidental to arrest. To be "incidental to an arrest" search must be limited to premises where arrest is made, be contemporaneous with arrest, have definite object, and be reasonable in scope. People v. Davis, 231 C.A.2d 180, 41 Cal.Rptr. 617, 619, 620.

Incidental to employment. A risk is "incidental to employment" within Worker's Compensation Act, when it belongs to or is connected with what a worker has to do in fulfilling the duties of his or her employment.

Incidental use. In zoning, use of premises which is dependent on or affiliated with the principal use of such premises. Needham v. Winslow Nurseries, Inc., 330 Mass. 95, 111 N.E.2d 453.

Incident of ownership. An element of ownership or degree of control over a life insurance policy. The retention by an insured of an incident of ownership in a life insurance policy will cause the policy proceeds to be included in his or her gross estate upon death. I.R.C. § 2042(2).

In estate taxation, if decedent retains control or right in property, as for example the right to change beneficiary of insurance policy, the property falls into his gross estate for estate tax purposes. In re Lumpkin's Estate, C.A.Tex., 474 F.2d 1092.

Incidere /insídəriy/. Lat. In the civil and old English law, to fall into; to fall out; to happen; to come to pass. To fall upon or under; to become subject or liable to. *Incidere in legem,* to incur the penalty of a law.

Incipitur /insípədər/. Lat. It is begun; it begins. In old practice, when the pleadings in an action at law, instead of being recited at large on the issue-roll, were set out merely by their commencements, this was described as entering the *incipitur; i.e.,* the beginning.

Incite /insáyt/. To arouse; urge; provoke; encourage; spur on; goad; stir up; instigate; set in motion; as, to "incite" a riot. Also, generally, in criminal law to instigate, persuade, or move another to commit a crime; in this sense nearly synonymous with "abet".

Inciter. In criminal law, an aider or abettor; an accessory.

Incivile /insívəliy/. Lat. Irregular; improper; out of the due course of law.

Incivile est, nisi tota lege perspecta, una aliqua particula ejus proposita, judicare, vel respondere /insívəliy èst, náysay tówdə líyjiy pərspéktə, yúwnə ǽləkwə partíkyələ íyjəs prəpózədə, jùwdəkériy, vèl rəspòndíriy/. It is improper, without looking at the whole of a law, to give judgment or advice, upon a view of any one clause of it.

Incivile est, nisi tota sententia inspecta, de aliqua parte judicare /insívəliy èst, náysay tówdə sənténsh(iy)ə inspéktə, dìy ǽləkwə párdiy jùwdəkériy/. It is irregular, or legally improper, to pass an opinion upon any part of a sentence, without examining the whole.

In civilibus ministerium excusat, in criminalibus non item /in səvíləbəs mìnəstíriyəm əkskyúwzət, ìn krìmənéyləbəs nòn áydəm/. In civil matters agency (or service) excuses, but not so in criminal matters.

Incivism /ínsəvìzəm/. Unfriendliness to the state or government of which one is a citizen.

In claris non est locus conjecturis /in klérəs nón èst lówkəs kònjəkt(y)úrəs/. In things obvious there is no room for conjecture.

Inclausa /inklózə/. In old records, a home close or inclosure near the house.

Inclose. To surround; to encompass; to bound; fence, or hem in, on all sides. To shut up.

Inclosed lands. Lands which are actually inclosed and surrounded with fences.

Inclosure. In old English law, act of freeing land from rights of common, commonable rights, and generally all rights which obstruct cultivation and the productive employment of labor on the soil.

Land surrounded by some visible obstruction. An artificial fence around one's estate. See **Close.**

Include. (Lat. *Inclaudere,* to shut in, keep within.) To confine within, hold as in an inclosure, take in, attain, shut up, contain, inclose, comprise, comprehend, embrace, involve. Term may, according to context, express an enlargement and have the meaning of *and* or *in addition to,* or merely specify a particular thing already included within general words theretofore used. "Including" within statute is interpreted as a word of enlargement or of illustrative application as well as a word of limitation. Premier Products Co. v. Cameron, 240 Or. 123, 400 P.2d 227, 228.

Included offense. In criminal law, a crime which is part of another crime; *e.g.* included in every murder is assault and battery. One which is established by proof of the same or less than all of the facts, or a less culpable mental state, or both, than that which is required to establish commission of offense charged. People v. Lyons, 26 Ill.App.3d 193, 324 N.E.2d 677, 680. To be an "included offense", all elements of the lesser offense must be contained in the greater offense, the greater containing certain elements not contained in the lesser. Gaskin v. State, 244 Ark. 541, 426 S.W.2d 407, 409.

Inclusio unius est exclusio alterius /inklúwzh(iy)ow yənáyəs èst əksklúwzh(iy)ow oltíriyəs/. The inclusion of one is the exclusion of another. The certain designation of one person is an absolute exclusion of all others. Burgin v. Forbes, 293 Ky. 456, 169 S.W.2d 321, 325.

Inclusive. Embraced; comprehended; comprehending the stated limits or extremes. Opposed to "exclusive."

Inclusive survey. In land law, one which includes within its boundaries prior claims excepted from the computation of the area within such boundaries and excepted in the grant.

Incola. Lat. In the civil law, an inhabitant; a dweller or resident. Properly, one who has transferred his domicile to any country.

Incolas domicilium facit /ínkələs dòməsíl(i)yəm féysət/. Residence creates domicile.

Income. The return in money from one's business, labor, or capital invested; gains; profits, salary, wages, etc.

The gain derived from capital, from labor or effort, or both combined, including profit or gain through sale or conversion of capital. Income is not a gain accruing to capital or a growth in the value of the investment, but is a gain, a profit, something of exchangeable value, proceeding from the property, severed from the capital, however invested or employed, and coming in, being derived, that is, received or drawn by the recipient for his separate use, benefit, and disposal. Goodrich v. Edwards, 255 U.S. 527, 41 S.Ct. 390, 65 L.Ed. 758. The true increase in amount of wealth which comes to a person during a stated period of time.

See also Allocation of income; Blocked income; Clear reflection of income; Constructive receipt of income; Deferred income; Earned income; Earnings; Fixed income; Gross income; Net income; Net operating income; Personal income; Profit; Split income; Taxable income; Unearned income.

Accrued income. Income earned during a certain accounting period but not paid or received.

Deferred income. Income received before it is earned, such as rents received in one accounting period for use of the premises in the following period.

Earned income. Income derived from one's own labor or through active participation in a business as distinguished from income from, for example, dividends or investments. See also **Earnings.**

Fixed income. That type of income which is stable over a considerable period of time such as a pension or annuity.

Gross income. The total income of a business or individual before deductions; including salary, commissions, royalties, gains from dealings in property, interest, dividends, etc. I.R.C. § 61.

Imputed income. Value assigned to property or income, sometimes artificially for tax purposes, as in the case of a non-interest bearing or low interest bearing loan between persons or organizations related to each other. I.R.C. § 483. The value of property enjoyed by the taxpayer as part of his salary; *e.g.* use of home provided by employer to employee.

Net (business) income. Net profit of business arrived at by deducting operating expenses and taxes from gross profit.

Nonoperating income. Income of a business from investments and not from operations.

Operating income. Income derived from operations of business in contrast to income from investments.

Ordinary income. See **Ordinary.**

Personal income. In taxation, the total of income received by individuals from all sources.

Unearned income. Income derived from investments, rental property, etc., as distinguished from income derived from personal labor.

Income averaging. Method of computing income tax by an individual who has unusually large income in the current taxable year as compared with the four prior years, whereby the taxpayer may elect to have the excess taxed as if it had been received ratably over a five year period. This tax provision (I.R.C. § 1301 et seq.) benefits such taxpayers as athletes and actors whose incomes might be very high in a given year in contrast to prior years.

Income basis. Method of computing the rate of return on a security based on the dividend or interest and on the price paid rather than on its face or par value.

Income beneficiary. The party entitled to income from property. A typical example would be a trust where A is to receive the income for life with corpus or principal passing to B upon A's death. In this case, A would be the income beneficiary of the trust.

Income in respect of decedent. Income earned by a decedent at the time of death but not reportable on the final income tax return because of the method of accounting utilized. Typically it includes any accrued income to date of death for cash basis decedent/taxpayer. Estate of Rose, 465 Pa. 53, 348 A.2d 113, 116. Such income is included in the gross estate and will be taxed to the eventual recipient (*i.e.,* either the estate or heirs). The recipient will, however, be allowed an income tax deduction for the death tax attributable to the income. I.R.C. § 691.

In estate taxation, term refers to inclusion of certain income in estate as if it had been collected by decedent in his or her lifetime, Grill v. U. S., 157 Ct.Cl. 804, 303 F.2d 922, 927 *e.g.* payments received toward satisfaction of a right or expectancy created almost entirely through the efforts or status of the decedent and which, except for his death and without further action on his part, the decedent would have realized as gross income.

Income property. Property which produces income; *e.g.* rental property. Such property can be either residential, commercial, or industrial.

Income statement. The statement of revenues, expenses, gains, and losses for the period ending with net income (or loss) for the period.

Income tax. A tax on the yearly profits arising from property, business pursuits, professions, trades, or offices. A tax on a person's income, wages, salary, commissions, emoluments, profits, and the like, or the excess thereof over a certain amount. Tax levied by the U.S. Government, and by some state governments, on taxpayer's income. Such may be either a corporate or individual income tax. See also **Tax.**

Income tax deficiency. Exists whenever taxpayer has failed to pay sufficient taxes on income, notwithstanding lack of determination by commissioner or his agents. Moore v. Cleveland Ry. Co., C.C.A.Ohio, 108 F.2d 656, 659. See **Deficiency notice; Ninety day letter.**

Income tax return. Forms required by taxing authority to be completed by taxpayer, disclosing all items necessary for computation of tax and the computation itself. See also **Return.**

In commendam /in kəméndəm/. In commendation; as a commended living. See **Commenda.**

A term applied in Louisiana to a limited partnership, answering to the French *"en commandite".*

In commodato hæc pactio, ne dolus præstetur, rata non est /in kòmədéydow híyk pǽksh(iy)ow, niy dówləs prəstíydər, réydə nòn ést/. In the contract of loan, a stipulation not to be liable for fraud is not valid.

Incommodum non solvit argumentum /inkómədəm nòn sólvəd àrgyəméntəm/. An inconvenience does not destroy an argument.

In common. Shared in respect to title, use, or enjoyment; without apportionment or division into individual parts. Held by several for the equal advantage, use, or enjoyment of all. See **Condominium.**

In communi /in kəmyúwnay/. In common.

Incommunicado. Status of person who appears or travels without disclosing his true identity.

Incommunication. In Spanish law, the condition of a prisoner who is not permitted to see or to speak with any person visiting him during his confinement. A person accused cannot be subjected to this treatment unless it be expressly ordered by the judge, for some grave offense, and it cannot be continued for a longer period than is absolutely necessary. This precaution is resorted to for the purpose of preventing the accused from knowing beforehand the testimony of the witnesses, or from attempting to corrupt them and concert such measures as will efface the traces of his guilt. As soon, therefore, as the danger of his doing so has ceased, the interdiction ceases likewise.

Incommutable. Not capable of or entitled to be commuted. See **Commutation.**

Incompatibility. Incapability of existing or being exercised together. As ground for divorce, refers to such deep and irreconcilable conflict in personalities or temperments of parties as makes it impossible for them to continue normal marital relationship. Such conflict of personalities and dispositions must be so deep as to be irreconcilable and irremediable. Berry v. Berry, 215 Kan. 47, 523 P.2d 342, 345; Burch v. Burch, C.A.Virgin Islands, 195 F.2d 799, 806, 807. Such condition is a ground for divorce in states with no-fault divorce statutes.

Incompetency. Lack of ability, legal qualification, or fitness to discharge the required duty. A relative term which may be employed as meaning disqualification, inability or incapacity and it can refer to lack of legal qualifications or fitness to discharge the required duty and to show want of physical or intellectual or moral fitness. County Bd. of Ed. of Clarke County v. Oliver, 270 Ala. 107, 116 So.2d 566, 567. See also **Incapacity; Insanity.**

Incompetent evidence. Evidence which is not admissible under the established rules of evidence; *e.g.* Fed. Rules of Evidence. Evidence which the law does not permit to be presented at all, or in relation to the particular matter, on account of lack of originality or of some defect in the witness, the document, or the nature of the evidence itself.

Incomplete transfer. A transfer made by a decedent during lifetime which, because of certain control or enjoyment retained by the transferor, will not be considered complete for Federal death tax purposes. Thus, some or all of the fair market value of the property transferred will be included in the transferor's gross estate. I.R.C. §§ 2036–2038.

Inconclusive. That which may be disproved or rebutted; not shutting out further proof or consideration. Applied to evidence and presumptions. See **Presumption.**

In conjunction with /ìn kənjə́ŋkshən wíθ/. In association with.

In conjunctivis, oportet utramque partem essə veram /ìn kònjəŋktáyvəs, əpórdət yuwtrǽmkwiy párdəm ésiy vírəm/. In conjunctives it is necessary that each part be true. In a condition consisting of divers parts in the copulative, both parts must be performed.

In consideratione inde /ìn kənsìdərèyshiyówniy índiy/. In consideration thereof.

In consideratione legis /ìn kənsìdərèyshiyówniy líyjəs/. In consideration or contemplation of law; in abeyance.

In consideratione præmissorum /ìn kənsìdərèyshiyówniy prèməsórəm/. In consideration of the premises.

In consimili casu /ìn kənsíməlay kéys(y)uw/. See **Consimili casu.**

In consimili casu, consimile debet esse remedium /ìn kənsíməlay kéys(y)uw, kənsíməliy débəd ésiy rəmíyd(i)yəm/. In a similar case the remedy should be similar.

Inconsistent. Mutually repugnant or contradictory; contrary, the one to the other, so that both cannot stand, but the acceptance or establishment of the one implies the abrogation or abandonment of the other; as, in speaking of "inconsistent defenses," or the repeal by a statute of "all laws inconsistent herewith." Berry v. City of Fort Worth, Tex.Civ.App., 110 S.W.2d 95, 103.

In conspectu ejus /ìn kənspékt(y)uw íyjəs/. In his sight or view.

In consuetudinibus, non diuturnitas temporis sed soliditas rationis est consideranda /ìn kònswət(y)uwdínəbəs, nòn dàyətárnətæs témpərəs sèd səlídətæs rèyshiyównəs èst kənsìdərǽndə/. In customs, not length of time, but solidity of reason, is to be considered. The antiquity of a custom is to be less regarded than its reasonableness.

In contemplation of death. In taxation and property law, a transaction, commonly a transfer or gift of property, made by the donor with a view towards his death. For federal estate tax purposes, a transfer made within three years of the decedent's death is deemed to be made in contemplation of death and the value of the property is included in his or her estate for such tax purposes. I.R.C. § 2035(b).

Incontestability clause. A clause in a life or health insurance policy providing that after the policy has been in force for a given length of time (*e.g.* two or three years) the insurer shall not be able to contest it as to statements contained in the application; and, in the case of health insurance, the provision also states that no claim shall be denied or reduced on the grounds that a condition not excluded by name at the time of issue existed prior to the effective date.

Incontinence /inkóntənən(t)s/. Want of chastity; indulgence in unlawful carnal connection.

In continenti /ìn kòntənéntay/. Immediately; without any interval or intermission. Sometimes written as one word *"incontinenti."*

In contractibus, benigna; in testamentis, benignior; in restitutionibus, benignissima interpretatio facienda est /ìn kəntrǽktəbəs, bənígnə, ìn tèstəméntəs, bənígniyər, in rèstət(y)ùwshiyównəbəs, bənìgnísəmə intərprətéysh(iy)ow fæs(h)iyéndə èst/. In contracts, the interpretation is to be liberal; in wills, more liberal; in restitutions, most liberal.

In contractibus, rei veritas potius quam scriptura perspici debet /ìn kəntrǽktəbəs, ríyay véhrətæs pówsh(iy)əs kwæm skriptyúrə pə́rspəsay débət/. In contracts, the truth of the matter ought to be regarded rather than the writing.

In contractibus, tacite insunt [veniunt] quæ sunt moris et consuetudinis /ìn kəntrǽktəbəs, tǽsədiy ínsənt kwìy sə̀nt mórəs èt kònswət(y)úwdənəs/°víyn(i)yənt°/. In contracts, matters of custom and usage are tacitly implied. A contract is understood to contain the customary clauses, although they are not expressed.

In contrahenda venditione, ambiguum pactum contra venditorem interpretandum est /ìn kòntrəhéndə vəndìshiyówniy æmbígyuwəm pǽktəm kóntrə vèndətórəm intə̀rprətǽndəm èst/. In the contract of sale, an ambiguous agreement is to be interpreted against the seller.

Inconvenience. In the rule that statutes should be so construed as to avoid "inconvenience," this means, as applied to the public, the sacrifice or jeopardizing of important public interests or hampering the legitimate activities of government or the transaction of public business, and, as applied to individuals, serious hardship or injustice.

In conventionibus, contrahentium voluntas potius quam verba spectari placuit /ìn kənvènshiyównəbəs, kòntrəhénsh(iy)əm vəlántæs pówsh(iy)əs kwǽm və́rbə spektéray plǽk(y)uwət/. In agreements, the intention of the contracting parties, rather than the words used, should be regarded.

Incopolitus /ìnkəpólədəs/. A proctor or vicar.

Incorporalia bello non adquiruntur /ìnkorpəréyl(i)yə bélow nòn ædkwəréntər/. Incorporeal things are not acquired by war.

Incorporamus /inkòrpəréyməs/. We incorporate. One of the words by which a corporation may be created in England. 1 Bl.Comm. 473.

Incorporate. To create a corporation; to confer a corporate franchise upon determinate persons. See **Incorporation.**

To declare that another document shall be taken as part of the document in which the declaration is made as much as if it were set out at length therein. See **Incorporation by reference.**

Incorporated law society. In England, a society of attorneys and solicitors whose function it is to carry out the acts of parliament and orders of court with reference to articled clerks; to keep an alphabetical roll of solicitors; to issue certificates to persons duly admitted and enrolled, and to exercise a general control over the conduct of solicitors in practice, and to bring cases of misconduct before the judges.

Incorporation. The act or process of forming or creating a corporation. The formation of a legal or political body, with the quality of perpetual existence and succession, unless limited by the act of incorporation. Abbott v. Limited Mut. Compensation Ins. Co., 30 Cal.App.2d 157, 85 P.2d 961, 964. Incorporation procedure and requisites are governed by state statutes; many of which are patterned on the Model Business Corporation Act.

In the civil law, the union of one domain to another.

See also **Articles of incorporation; Certificate of incorporation.**

Incorporation by reference. The method of making one document of any kind become a part of another separate document by referring to the former in the latter, and declaring that the former shall be taken and considered as a part of the latter the same as if it were fully set out therein. If the one document is copied at length in the other, it is called "actual incorporation."

Incorporator. Person who joins with others to form a corporation and the successors of those who actually sign the papers of incorporation.

In corpore /ìn kórpəriy/. In body or substance; in a material thing or object.

Incorporeal /ìnkərpóriyəl/. Without body; not of material nature; the opposite of "corporeal" *(q.v.).*

Incorporeal chattels. A class of incorporeal rights growing out of or incident to things *personal;* such as patent-rights and copyrights.

Incorporeal hereditaments. See **Hereditaments.**

Incorporeal property. In the civil law, that which consists in legal right merely. The same as choses in action at common law.

Incorporeal rights. Rights to intangibles, such as legal actions, rather than rights to property (rights to possession or use of land).

Incorporeal things. In the civil law, things which can neither be seen nor touched, such as consist in rights only, such as the mind alone can perceive.

Incorrigible /inkórəjəbəl/. Incapable of being corrected, reformed, amended, or improved. With respect to juvenile offenders, unmanageable by parents or guardians. Shinn v. Barrow, Tex.Civ.App., 121 S.W.2d 450, 451. See **Delinquent child; Disobedient child.**

Incorruptible /ìnkərÁptəbəl/. That which cannot be affected by immoral or debasing influences, such as bribery or the hope of gain or advancement.

Increase. Enlargement, growth, development, increment, addition, accession, extension, production, profit, interest, issue. The produce of land; the offspring of animals.

Increase, affidavit of. Affidavit of payment of increased costs, produced on taxation.

Increase, costs of. In old English law, it was formerly a practice with the jury to award to the successful party in an action the nominal sum of 40s. only for his costs; and the court assessed by their own officer the actual amount of the successful party's costs; and the amount so assessed, over and above the nominal sum awarded by the jury, was thence called "costs of increase." The practice has now wholly ceased.

Increment /íŋkrəmənt/. An increasing in quantity, number, value, etc. That which is gained or added; the act or process of increasing, augmenting, or growing; enlargement, that which is added; increase; opposed to decrement. In re Corning's Will, 160 Misc. 434, 289 N.Y.S. 1101, 1103.

Incremental cost. Additional or increased costs. As applied to cost of gas, includes cost of gas to distributors plus transportation costs and taxes. Fuels Research Council Inc. v. Federal Power Commission, C.A.Ill., 374 F.2d 842.

Incrementum /ìŋkrəméntəm/. Lat. Increase or improvement, opposed to *decrementum* or abatement.

In criminalibus, probationes debent esse luce clariores /in krìmənéyləbəs, prəlèyshiyowniyz débənt ésiy l(y)úwsiy klæriyóriyz/. In criminal cases, the proofs ought to be clearer than light.

In criminalibus, sufficit generalis malitia intentionis, cum facto paris gradus /in krìmənéyləbəs, sÁfəsət jènəréyləs məlísh(iy)ə intènshiyównəs kəm fæktow pærəs gréydəs/. In criminal matters or cases, a general malice of intention is sufficient [if united], with an act of equal or corresponding degree.

In criminalibus, voluntas reputabitur pro facto /in krìmənéyləbəs vəlántæs rèpyətéybədər pròw fæktow/. In criminal acts, the will will be taken for the deed.

Incriminate /inkríməneyt/. To charge with crime; to expose to an accusation or charge of crime; to involve oneself or another in a criminal prosecution or the danger thereof; as, in the rule that a witness is not bound to give testimony which would tend to incriminate him. In re Dendy, Tex.Civ.App., 175 S.W.2d 297, 302. See **Self-incrimination.**

Incriminating admission. An acknowledgment of facts tending to establish guilt.

Incriminating circumstance. A fact or circumstance, collateral to the fact of the commission of a crime, which tends to show either that such a crime has been committed or that some particular person committed it.

Incriminating evidence. Evidence which tends to establish guilt of the accused or from which, with other evidence, his or her guilt may be inferred.

Incrimination. See **Incriminate; Self-incrimination.**

Incriminatory statement. A statement which tends to establish guilt of the accused or from which, with other facts, his guilt may be inferred, or which tends to disprove some defense.

Incroachment /inkrówchmənt/. An unlawful gaining upon the right or possession of another. See **Encroachment; Trespass.**

In cujus rei testimonium /ìn kyúwjəs ríyay tèstəmówn(i)yəm/. In testimony whereof. The initial words of the concluding clause of ancient deeds in Latin, literally translated in the English forms.

Inculpate /inkálpeyt/íŋkəlpeyt/. To impute blame or guilt; to accuse; to involve in guilt or crime. See **Incriminate.**

Inculpatory /inkálpət(ò)riy/. In the law of evidence, going or tending to establish guilt; intended to establish guilt; criminative. People v. White, 35 Cal. App.2d 61, 94 P.2d 617, 621. See also **Incriminate.**

Incumbent /inkámbənt/. A person who is in present possession of an office; one who is legally authorized to discharge the duties of an office. Hilliard v. Park, 212 Tenn. 588, 370 S.W.2d 829, 839.

In ecclesiastical law, the term signifies a clergyman who is in possession of a benefice.

Incumber. See **Encumbrance.**

Incumbrance. See **Encumbrance.**

Incumbrances, covenant against. See **Covenant.**

Incur. To have liabilities cast upon one by act or operation of law, as distinguished from contract, where the party acts affirmatively. To become liable or subject to.

Incurable disease. Any disease which has reached an incurable stage in the patient afflicted therewith, according to general state of knowledge of the medical profession. Disease for which there is no known cure.

Incurramentum /inkàrəméntəm/. L. Lat. The liability to a fine, penalty, or amercement.

In custodia legis /ìn kəstówd(i)yə líyjəs/. In the custody or keeping of the law.

Inde /índiy/. Lat. Thence; thenceforth; thereof; thereupon; for that cause.

Indebitatus /indèbətéydəs/. Lat. Indebted. *Nunquam indebitatus,* never indebted. The title of the plea substituted in England for *nil debet.*

Indebitatus assumpsit /indèbətéydəs əsám(p)sət/. Lat. Being indebted, he promised or undertook. That form of the action of *assumpsit* in which the declaration alleges a debt or obligation to be due from the defendant, and then avers that, in consideration thereof, he promised to pay or discharge the same.

Indebiti solutio /indébəday səl(y)úwsh(iy)ow/. Lat. In the civil and Scotch law, a payment of what is not due. When made through ignorance or by mistake, the amount paid might be recovered back by an action termed *"conditio indebiti."*

Indebitum /indébədəm/. In the civil law, not due or owing.

Indebtedness. The state of being in debt, without regard to the ability or inability of the party to pay the same. The owing of a sum of money upon a certain and express agreement. Obligations yet to become due constitute indebtedness, as well as those already due. And in a broad sense and in common understanding the word may mean anything that is due and owing.

Indecent. Offensive to common propriety; offending against modesty or delicacy; grossly vulgar; obscene; lewd; unseemly; unbecoming; indecorous; unfit to be seen or heard. See **Obscene.**

Indecent assault. The act of a male person taking indecent liberties with the person of a female, without her consent and against her will, but with no intent to commit the crime of rape.

Indecent exhibition. Any exhibition *contra bonos mores,* as the taking a dead body for the purpose of dissection or public exhibition.

Indecent exposure. Exposure to sight of the private parts of the body in a lewd or indecent manner in a public place. It is an indictable offense at common law, and by statute in states. Term refers to exhibition of those private parts which instinctive modesty, human decency or self-respect require shall be kept covered in presence of others; exposure of person becomes indecent when it occurs at such time and place where reasonable man knows or should know his act will be open to observation of others. State v. Borchard, 24 Ohio App.2d 95, 264 N.E.2d 646, 650.

A person commits a misdemeanor if, for the purpose of arousing or gratifying sexual desire of himself or of any person other than his spouse, he exposes his genitals under circumstances in which he knows his conduct is likely to cause affront or alarm. Model Penal Code, § 213.5.

Indecent liberties. In the statutory offense of "taking indecent liberties with the person of a female child," this phrase means such liberties as the common sense of society would regard as indecent and improper. According to some authorities, it involves an assault or attempt at sexual intercourse, but according to others, it is not necessary that the liberties or familiarities should have related to the private parts of the child. See **Obscene.**

Indecent publications. Such as are offensive to modesty and delicacy; obscene; lewd; tending to the corruption of morals. Dunlop v. U. S., 165 U.S. 486, 17 S.Ct. 375, 41 L.Ed. 799. See **Obscene.**

Public indecency. This phrase has no fixed legal meaning, is vague and indefinite, and cannot, in itself, imply a definite offense. The courts, by a kind of judicial legislation, in England and the United States, have usually limited the operation of the term to public displays of the naked person, the publication, sale, or exhibition of obscene books and prints, or the exhibition of a monster,—acts which have a direct bearing on public morals, and affect the body of society. Irven v. State, 138 Tex.Cr.R. 368, 136 S.W.2d 608, 609. See **Obscene;** also, *Indecent exposure, supra.*

Indecimable /ìndés(ə)məbəl/. In old English law, that which is not titheable, or liable to pay tithe.

Inde datæ leges ne fortior omnia posset /índiy déydiy líyjiyz nìy fórsh(iy)ər ómn(i)yə pósət/. Laws are made to prevent the stronger from having the power to do everything.

Indefeasible /ìndəfíyzəbəl/. That which cannot be defeated, revoked, or made void. This term is usually applied to an estate or right which cannot be defeated.

Indefensus /ìndəfén(t)səs/. Lat. In old English practice, undefended; undenied by pleading. A defendant who makes no defense or plea.

Indefinite. Without fixed boundaries or distinguishing characteristics; not definite, determinate, or precise.

Indefinite failure of issue. A failure of issue not merely at the death of the party whose issue are referred to, but at any subsequent period, however remote. A failure of issue whenever it shall happen, sooner or later, without any fixed, certain, or definite period within which it must happen.

Indefinite legacy. See **Legacy.**

Indefinite number. A number which may be increased or diminished at pleasure.

Indefinitum æquipollet universali /ìndéfənáydəm èkwəpólət yùwnəvərséylay/. The undefined is equivalent to the whole.

Indefinitum supplet locum universalis /ìndèfənáydəm sáplət lówkəm yùwnəvərséyləs/. The undefined or general supplies the place of the whole.

In delicto /ìn dəlíktow/. In fault. See **In pari delicto.**

Indemnification. See **Indemnify; Indemnity.**

Indemnify /indémnəfày/. To restore the victim of a loss, in whole or in part, by payment, repair, or replacement. To save harmless; to secure against loss or damage; to give security for the reimbursement of a person in case of an anticipated loss falling upon him. To make good; to compensate; to make reimbursement to one of a loss already incurred by him. Several states by statute have provided special funds for compensating crime victims. See also **Hold harmless agreement; Indemnity; Reparation; Restitution; Subrogation.**

Indemnis /indémnəs/. Lat. Without hurt, harm, or damage; harmless.

Indemnitee /indèmnətíy/. The person who, in a contract of indemnity, is to be indemnified or protected by the other.

Indemnitor /indémnədər/. The person who is bound, by an indemnity contract, to indemnify or protect the other.

Indemnity /indémnədiy/. A collateral contract or assurance, by which one person engages to secure another against an anticipated loss or to prevent him from being damnified by the legal consequences of an act or forbearance on the part of one of the parties or of some third person. Term pertains to liability for loss shifted from one person held legally responsible to another person. Boyle v. Burt, Iowa, 179 N.W.2d 513, 515.

The term is also used to denote a compensation given to make the person whole from a loss already sustained; as where the government gives indemnity for private property taken by it for public use. It means, also, restitution or reimbursement. See **Condemnation; Eminent domain; Expropriation; Just compensation.**

A legislative act, assuring a general dispensation from punishment or exemption from prosecution to persons involved in offenses, omissions of official duty, or acts in excess of authority, is called an indemnity; strictly it is an act of indemnity.

See also **Contribution; Double indemnity; Indemnify; Subrogation.**

Indemnity against liability. A contract to indemnify when liability of person indemnified arises, irrespective of whether person indemnified has suffered actual loss. Indemnity against loss, on the other hand, does not render indemnitor liable until person indemnified makes payment or sustains loss. See also **Subrogation.**

Indemnity bond. A bond for the payment of a penal sum conditioned to be void if the obligor shall indemnify and save harmless the obligee against some anticipated loss. It is generally given to provide reimbursement for loss resulting from breach of trust or failure of employee or agents to perform duties.

Indemnity contract. A contract between two parties whereby the one undertakes and agrees to indemnify the other against loss or damage arising from some contemplated act on the part of the indemnitor, or from some responsibility assumed by the indemnitee, or from the claim or demand of a third person, that is, to make good to him such pecuniary damage as he may suffer.

Indemnity insurance. See **Insurance.**

Indemnity lands. Lands granted to railroads, in aid of their construction, being portions of the public domain, to be selected in lieu of other parcels embraced within the original grant, but which were lost to the railroad by previous disposition or by reservation for other purposes.

Indemnity policy. As distinguished from general liability policy, a policy on which no action can be maintained except to indemnify for money actually paid. See *Indemnity insurance* and *Liability insurance* under **Insurance.**

Indenization /indènəzéyshən/. The act of making a denizen, or of naturalizing.

Indent, n. A certificate or indented certificate issued by the government of the United States at the close of the Revolution for the principal or interest of the public debt.

Indent, v. To cut in a serrated or wavy line. In old conveyancing, if a deed was made by more parties than one, it was usual to make as many copies of it as there were parties, and each was cut or indented (either in acute angles, like the teeth of a saw, or in a wavy line) at the top or side, to tally or correspond with the others, and the deed so made was called an "indenture". Anciently, both parts were written on the same piece of parchment, with some word or letters written between them through which the parchment was cut, but afterwards, the word or letters being omitted, indenting came into use, the idea of which was that the genuineness of each part might be proved by its fitting into the angles cut in the other. But at length even this was discontinued, and eventually the term served only to give name to the species of deed executed by two or more parties, as opposed to a deed-poll *(q.v.)*. 2 Bl.Comm. 295.

Indenture /indénchər/. A written agreement under which bonds and debentures are issued, setting forth maturity date, interest rate, and other terms. A deed to which two or more persons are parties, and in which these enter into reciprocal and corresponding grants or obligations towards each other; whereas a deed-poll is properly one in which only the party making it executes it, or binds himself by it as a deed, though the grantors or grantees therein may be several in number. See **Indent, v.**

Indenture means mortgage, deed of trust, or indenture, under which there is outstanding a security, other than a voting-trust certificate, constituting a claim against the debtor, a claim secured by a lien on any of the debtor's property, or an equity security of the debtor. Bankruptcy Act, § 101(22).

Indenture of a fine. In old English law, indentures made and engrossed at the chirographer's office and delivered to the cognizor and the cognizee, usually beginning with the words: *"Hæc est finalis concordia."* And then reciting the whole proceedings at length. 2 Bl.Comm. 351.

Indenture of trust. See **Trust indenture.**

Indenture trustee. Person or institution named in a trust indenture and charged with holding legal title to the trust property and with carrying out the terms of the indenture. Trustee under an indenture. Bankruptcy Act, § 101(23).

Independence. The state or condition of being free from dependence, subjection, or control. Political independence is the attribute of a nation or state which is entirely autonomous, and not subject to the government, control, or dictation of any exterior power.

Independent. Not dependent; not subject to control, restriction, modification, or limitation from a given outside source.

Independent adjuster. A person, firm or corporation who holds himself or itself out for employment to more than one insurance company, is not a regular employee of the company, does not work exclusively for one company and is paid in each case assigned for time consumed and expenses incurred.

Independent advice. Concerning a trust deed or will which must be shown where a fiduciary relationship exists, means that the donor had the preliminary benefit of conferring fully and privately upon the subject of his intended gift with a person who was not only competent to inform him correctly as to its legal effect, but who was, furthermore, so disassociated from the interests of the donee as to be in a position to advise with the donor impartially and confidentially as to the consequences to himself of his proposed benefaction.

Independent contract. See **Contract.**

Independent contractor. Generally, one who, in exercise of an independent employment, contracts to do a piece of work according to his own methods and is subject to his employer's control only as to end product or final result of his work. Hammes v. Suk, 291 Minn. 233, 190 N.W.2d 478, 480, 481. One who renders service in course of independent employment or occupation, and who follows employer's desires only as to results of work, and not as to means whereby it is to be accomplished. Sparks v. L. D. Folsom Co., 217 Cal.App.2d 279, 31 Cal.Rptr. 640, 643; Housewright v. Pacific Far East Line Inc., 229 Cal.App.2d 259, 40 Cal.Rptr. 208, 212; Dowling v. Mutual Life Ins. Co. of New York, La.App., 168 So.2d 107, 112.

An independent contractor is a person who contracts with another to do something for him but who is not controlled by the other nor subject to the other's right to control with respect to his physical conduct in the performance of the undertaking. He may or may not be an agent. Restatement, Second, Agency, § 2.

Independent covenant. See **Covenant.**

Independenter se habet assecuratio a viaggio navis /indəpèndéntər sìy héybət əsèkyəréysh(iy)ow èy viyéyj(iy)ow néyvəs/. The voyage insured is an independent or distinct thing from the voyage of the ship.

Independent significance. An act or document is said to have independent legal significance so as to carry out the wishes of the testator or decedent if it is not executed solely to avoid the requirements of a will; and, hence, what may appear to be a testamentary disposition without observing the requirements of the statutes on wills will be given effect.

Independent source rule. In connection with evidence, if the evidence to be introduced can be traced to a source independent of the originally illegally obtained fruits of interrogation or arrest, it is admissible. Wong Sun v. U. S., 371 U.S. 471, 83 S.Ct. 407, 9 L.Ed.2d 441.

Indestructible trust. A trust which, inter alia, does not permit the invasion of principal by the trustees but which provides for income to A for life, with remainder to A's son's issue and for failure to A's daughter or issue. Application of Renn, 177 Misc. 95, 29 N.Y. S.2d 410, 412.

Indeterminate. That which is uncertain, or not particularly designated.

Indeterminate conditional release. Type of release from penal confinement after fulfillment of conditions but subject to revocation for breach of conditions of release. See also **Parole.**

Indeterminate obligation. See **Obligation.**

Indeterminate sentence. A sentence to imprisonment for the maximum period defined by law, subject to termination by the parole board or other agency at any time after service of the minimum period. Such a sentence is invalid unless specifically authorized by statute.

A sentence of imprisonment the duration of which is not fixed by the court but is left to the determination of penal authorities within minimum and maximum time limits fixed by the court of law. See also **Sentence.**

Index. A book containing references, alphabetically arranged, to the contents of a series or collection of volumes; or an addition to a single volume or set of volumes containing such references to its contents.

Index animi sermo /índəks ǽnəmay sə́rmow/. Language is the exponent of the intention. The language of a statute or instrument is the best guide to the intention.

Index offenses. The term designating the seven classes of offenses reported annually by the FBI in its Uniform Crime Reports. They include: willful homicide, forcible rape, robbery, burglary, aggravated assault, larceny over a specified amount, and motor vehicle theft.

Indian Claims Commission. The Indian Claims Commission hears and determines claims against the United States on behalf of any Indian tribe, band, or other identifiable group of American Indians residing within the United States.

Indian country. Part of public domain set apart for use, occupancy and protection of Indian peoples. Youngbear v. Brewer, 415 F.Supp. 807, 809. See **Indian land; Indian reservation; Indian tribal property.**

Indian lands. Real property ceded to the U.S. by Indians, commonly to be held in trust for Indians. See **Indian country; Indian reservation; Indian tribal property; Indian tribe.**

Indian reservation. A part of public domain set aside by proper authority for use and occupation of tribe or tribes of Indians. United States v. Parton, D.C.N.C., 46 F.Supp. 843, 844. An Indian reservation consists of lands validly set apart for use of Indians, under superintendence of the government which retains title to the land. Healing v. Jones, D.C.Ariz., 210 F.Supp. 125, 180. See also **Executive order Indian reservation.**

Indian title. Claim of Indian tribes of right, because of immemorial occupancy, to occupy certain territory to exclusion of any other Indians. Northwestern Bands of Shoshone Indians v. U. S., Ct.Cl., 324 U.S. 335, 65 S.Ct. 690, 692, 89 L.Ed. 985. Permissive right of occupancy granted by federal government to aboriginal possessors of the land; it is mere possession not specifically recognized as ownership and may be extinguished by federal government at any time. U. S. v. Gemmill, C.A.Cal., 535 F.2d 1145, 1147.

Indian tribal property. Property in which an Indian tribe has a legally enforceable interest. Such term refers to real property, the title to which is vested in United States but held in trust for the Indian tribe. Such property, depending on context in which the term is used, may or may not be "public property" of the United States. Chief Seattle Properties, Inc. v. Kitsap County, 86 Wash.2d 7, 541 P.2d 699, 704.

Indian tribe. A separate and distinct community or body of the aboriginal Indian race of men found in the United States. Montoya v. U. S., 180 U.S. 261, 21 S.Ct. 358, 45 L.Ed. 521. An "Indian tribe" within meaning of Indian Nonintercourse Act is a body of Indians of the same or similar race, united in a community under one leadership or government, and inhabiting a particular, though sometimes ill-defined, territory. Mashpee Tribe v. New Seabury Corp., D.C. Mass., 427 F.Supp. 899, 902.

Indicare /ìndəkériy/. Lat. In the civil law, to show or discover. To fix or tell the price of a thing. To inform against; to accuse.

Indicatif. An abolished English writ by which a prosecution was in some cases removed from a court-christian to the queen's bench.

Indication. In the law of evidence, a sign or token; a fact pointing to some inference or conclusion. See **Inference.**

Indicative evidence. This is not evidence properly so called, but the mere suggestion of evidence proper, which may possibly be procured if the suggestion is followed up. See **Inference.**

Indicavit /ìndəkéyvət/. In old English practice, a writ of prohibition that lies for a patron of a church, whose clerk is sued in the spiritual court by the clerk of another patron, for tithes amounting to a fourth part of the value of the living. 3 Bl.Comm. 91. So termed from the emphatic word of the Latin form.

Indicia /indís(h)(i)yə/. Signs; indications. Circumstances which point to the existence of a given fact as probable, but not certain. For example, "*indicia* of partnership" are any circumstances which would induce the belief that a given person was in reality, though not ostensibly, a member of a given firm.

The term is much used in the civil law in a sense nearly or entirely synonymous with circumstantial evidence. It denotes facts which give rise to inferences, rather than the inferences themselves.

Indicia of title. Generally, a document evidencing title to property, real or personal; *e.g.* carbon copy of bill of sale to automobile. Edwards v. Central Motor Co., 38 Tenn.App. 577, 277 S.W.2d 413, 416.

Indicium /indís(h)(i)yəm/. In the civil law, a sign or mark. A species of proof, answering very nearly to the circumstantial evidence of the common law.

Indict /indáyt/. See **Indictment**.

Indictable /indáydəbəl/. Subject to being indicted. An offense, the nature of which is proper or necessary to be prosecuted by process of indictment. Indictable offenses embrace common-law offenses or statutory offenses the punishments for which are infamous.

Indictable offense. Any criminal offense for which a person may properly be indicted or complained of.

Indicted /indáydəd/. Charged in an indictment with a criminal offense. See **Jury; Indictment.**

Indictee /ìndaytíy/. A person indicted.

Indictio /indíksh(iy)ow/. In old public law, a declaration; a proclamation. *Indictio belli*, a declaration or indiction of war. An indictment.

Indictment /indáytmənt/. An accusation in writing found and presented by a grand jury, legally convoked and sworn, to the court in which it is impaneled, charging that a person therein named has done some act, or been guilty of some omission, which by law is a public offense, punishable on indictment. A formal written accusation originating with a prosecutor and issued by a grand jury against a party charged with a crime. An indictment is referred to as a "true bill", whereas failure to indict is called a "no bill".

An indictment is merely a charge which must be proved at trial beyond a reasonable doubt before defendant may be convicted. U. S. v. Zovluck, D.C. N.Y., 274 F.Supp. 385, 390. An indictment is only an accusation, it is the physical means by which a defendant is brought to trial, its sole purpose is to identify defendant's alleged offense, and it is not evidence that offense charged was committed and may not be considered as evidence by jury during its deliberations. U. S. v. Glaziou, C.A.N.Y., 402 F.2d 8, 15.

An offense which may be punished by death shall be prosecuted by indictment. An offense which may be punished by imprisonment for a term exceeding one year or at hard labor shall be prosecuted by indictment or, if indictment is waived, it may be prosecuted by information. Any other offense may be prosecuted by indictment or by information. Fed. R.Crim.P. 7.

See also **Information; Presentment.**

Joinder of indictments. See **Joinder.**

Joint indictment. When several offenders are joined in the same indictment, as when principals in the first and second degree, and accessories before and after the fact, are all joined in the same indictment.

Indictment de felony est contra pacem domini regis, coronam et dignitatem suam, in genere et non in individuo; quia in Anglia non est interregnum /indáytmənt dìy félǝniy èst kóntrǝ péysǝm dómǝnǝy ríyjǝs, kǝrównǝm èt dìgnǝtéydǝm s(y)úwǝm, ìn jéneriy èt nón in ìndǝvídyuwow, kwáyǝ ìn ǽngliyǝ nón èst intǝrégnǝm/. Indictment for felony is against the peace of our lord the king, his crown and dignity in general, and not against his individual person; because in England there is no interregnum.

Indictor /indáydǝr/. He who causes another to be indicted. The latter is sometimes called the "indictee."

In diem /in dáyǝm/. For a day; for the space of a day. See also **Per diem.**

Indifferent. Impartial; unbiased; disinterested.

Indigena /indíjǝnǝ/. In old English law, a subject born; one born within the realm, or naturalized by act of parliament. The opposite of *"alienigena" (q.v.).*

Indigent /índǝjǝnt/. In a general sense, one who is needy and poor, or one who has not sufficient property to furnish him a living nor anyone able to support him to whom he is entitled to look for support. Term commonly used to refer to one's financial ability, and ordinarily indicates one who is destitute of means of comfortable subsistence so as to be in want. Powers v. State, 194 Kan. 820, 402 P.2d 328, 332.

Indigent defendant. A person indicted or complained of who is without funds or ability to hire a lawyer to defend him and who, in most instances, is entitled to appointed counsel, consistent with the protection of the Sixth and Fourteenth Amendments to U.S.Const. Gideon v. Wainwright, 372 U.S. 335, 83 S.Ct. 792, 9 L.Ed.2d 799; Fed.R.Crim.P. 44. See also **Counsel, right to; Pauper's oath.**

Indignity /indígnǝdiy/. In the law of divorce, a species of cruelty addressed to the mind, sensibilities, self-respect, or personal honor of the subject, rather than to the body. "Indignities" justifying grant of divorce may consist of vulgarity unmerited reproach, habitual contumely, studied neglect, intentional incivility, manifest disdain, abusive language, or malignant ridicule. Hargrove v. Hargrove, Pa.Super., 381 A.2d 143, 148. See **Mental cruelty.**

Indirect. Not direct in relation or connection; not having an immediate bearing or application; not related in the natural way. Almost always used in law in opposition to "direct," though not the only antithesis of the latter word, as the terms "collateral" and "cross" are sometimes used in contrast with "direct."

As to indirect Confession; Contempt, and Tax, see those titles.

Indirect evidence. Such evidence which only tends to establish the issue by proof of various facts sustaining by their consistency the hypothesis claimed. It consists of both inferences and presumptions. Proof of collateral circumstances, from which a fact in controversy, not directly attested to by direct evidence (witnesses or documents), may be inferred. Proof of some other fact or facts from which, taken either singly or collectively, existence of particular fact in question may be inferred as necessary or probable consequence. United Textile Workers of America, AFL–CIO, Local Union No. 120 v. Newberry Mills, Inc., D.C.S.C., 238 F.Supp. 366, 372. See also **Circumstantial evidence; Inference; Presumption.**

Indirect tax. A tax upon some right or privilege or corporate franchise; *e.g.* privilege tax; franchise tax. Madison Suburban Utility Dist. of Davidson County

v. Carson, 191 Tenn. 300, 232 S.W.2d 277, 280. A tax laid upon the happening of an event as distinguished from its tangible fruits. Chickering v. Commissioner of Internal Revenue, C.C.A.Mass., 118 F.2d 254, 258.

In disjunctivis sufficit alteram partem esse veram /ín dìsjəŋ(k)táyvəs səfəsət óltərəm párdəm ésiy víram/. In disjunctives it is sufficient that either part be true. Where a condition is in the disjunctive, it is sufficient if either part be performed.

Indispensable. That which cannot be spared, omitted, or dispensed with.

Indispensable evidence. That without which a particular fact cannot be proved.

Indispensable parties. One without whose presence no adequate judgment can be entered determining rights of parties before a court. Insurance Co. of North America v. Allied Crude Vegetable Oil Refining Corp., 89 N.J.Super. 518, 215 A.2d 579, 588. Those who have such an interest in the controversy that the court cannot render a final decree without affecting their interests. Ohmart v. Dennis, 188 Neb. 260, 196 N.W.2d 181, 184. Those without whom the action cannot proceed, and must be joined even if by such joinder the court loses jurisdiction over the controversy. Milligan v. Anderson, C.A.Okl., 522 F.2d 1202, 1205. Fed.R.Civil P. 19. See **Joinder** (*Joinder of parties*); **Parties.**

Indistanter /ìndəstǽntər/. Forthwith; without delay.

Inditee /ìndaytíy/. L. Fr. In old English law, a person indicted.

Individual. As a noun, this term denotes a single person as distinguished from a group or class, and also, very commonly, a private or natural person as distinguished from a partnership, corporation, or association; but it is said that this restrictive signification is not necessarily inherent in the word, and that it may, in proper cases, include artificial persons. See also **Person.**

As an adjective, "individual" means pertaining or belonging to, or characteristic of, one single person, either in opposition to a firm, association, or corporation, or considered in his relation thereto.

Individual assets. In the law of partnership, property belonging to a member of a partnership as his separate and private property, apart from the assets or property belonging to the firm as such or the partner's interest therein.

Individual debts. Such as are due from a member of a partnership in his private or personal capacity, as distinguished from those due from the firm or partnership.

Individually. Separately and personally, as distinguished from jointly or officially, and as opposed to collective or associate action or common interest.

Individual proprietorship. See **Sole proprietorship.**

Individual retirement account (I.R.A.). Employees not covered by qualified pension or profit-sharing plans are permitted to set aside a certain percent of their income per year (not to exceed a statutorily set amount) in an individual retirement trust account.

The amount set aside can be deducted by the employee and will be subject to income tax only upon withdrawal. Specific statutory requirements are established for the establishment of the trust, contributions, and withdrawal of such amounts with penalties provided for failure to comply. I.R.C. § 408(a). See also **Keogh Plan.**

Individual system of location. A term formerly used in some states to designate the location of public lands by surveys, in which the land called for by each warrant was separately surveyed.

Indivisible. Not susceptible of division or apportionment; inseparable; entire. Thus, a contract, covenant, consideration, etc., may be divisible or indivisible; *i.e.,* separable or entire. See also **Contract.**

Indivisum /ìndəváyzəm/. Lat. That which two or more persons hold in common without partition; undivided.

Indorsee /əndòrsíy/ìndorsíy/. The person to whom a negotiable instrument, promissory note, bill of lading, etc., is assigned by indorsement.

Indorsee in due course. An indorsee in due course is one who, in good faith, in the ordinary course of business, and for value, before its apparent maturity or presumptive dishonor, and without knowledge of its actual dishonor, acquires a negotiable instrument duly indorsed to him, or indorsed generally, or payable to the bearer.

Indorsement /əndórsmənt/. The act of a payee, drawee, accommodation indorser, or holder of a bill, note, check, or other negotiable instrument, in writing his name upon the back of the same, with or without further or qualifying words, whereby the property in the same is assigned and transferred to another. U.C.C. § 3–202 *et seq.*

An indorsement must be written by or on behalf of the holder and on the instrument or on a paper so firmly affixed thereto as to become a part thereof. An indorsement is effective for negotiation only when it conveys the entire instrument or any unpaid residue. If it purports to be of less it operates only as a partial assignment. U.C.C. § 3–202.

Accommodation indorsement. In the law of negotiable instruments, one made by a third person without any consideration, but merely for the benefit of the holder of the instrument, or to enable the maker to obtain money or credit on it. Unless otherwise explained, it is understood to be a loan of the indorser's credit without restriction. Accommodation indorser is not liable to party accommodated. U.C.C. § 3–415.

Blank indorsement. One made by the mere writing of the indorser's name on the back of the note or bill, without mention of the name of any person in whose favor the indorsement is made, but with the implied understanding that any lawful holder may fill in his own name above the indorsement if he so chooses. An indorsement in blank specifies no particular indorsee and may consist of a mere signature. An instrument payable to order and indorsed in blank becomes payable to bearer and may be negotiated by delivery alone until specially indorsed. The holder may convert a blank indorsement into a special indorsement by writing over the signature of the indorser in blank any contract consistent with the character of the indorsement. U.C.C. § 3–204(2), (3).

Conditional indorsement. One by which the indorser annexes some condition (other than the failure of prior parties to pay) to his liability. The condition may be either present or subsequent. Special indorsement with additional words of condition. U.C.C. § 3–205(a).

Full indorsement. One by which the indorser orders the money to be paid to some particular person by name; it differs from a blank indorsement, which consists merely in the name of the indorser written on the back of the instrument.

General indorsement. See *Blank indorsement, supra.*

Qualified indorsement. One which restrains or limits, or qualifies or enlarges, the liability of the indorser, in any manner different from what the law generally imports as his true liability, deducible from the nature of the instrument. Stover Bank v. Welpman, Mo. App., 284 S.W. 177, 180. A transfer of a bill or promissory note to an indorsee, without any liability to the indorser. Accomplished by adding after signature words such as "without recourse" or the like. U.C.C. § 3–414(1).

Restrictive indorsement. One which stops the negotiability of the instrument, or which contains such a definite direction as to the payment as to preclude the indorsee from making any further transfer of the instrument. An indorsement is restrictive which either: (a) is conditional; or (b) purports to prohibit further transfer of the instrument; or (c) includes the words "for collection", "for deposit", "pay any bank", or like terms signifying a purpose of deposit or collection; or (d) otherwise states that it is for the benefit or use of the indorser or of another person. U.C.C. § 3–205.

Special indorsement. A special indorsement specifies the person to whom or to whose order it makes the instrument payable. Any instrument specially indorsed becomes payable to the order of the special indorsee and may be further negotiated only by his indorsement. U.C.C. § 3–204(1).

Unauthorized indorsement. One made without actual, implied or apparent authority and includes a forgery. U.C.C. §§ 1–201, 3–404.

Without recourse. See *Qualified indorsement, supra.*

Indorser /əndórsər/. He who indorses; *i.e.*, being the payee or holder, writes his name on the back of a negotiable instrument. One who signs his name as payee on the back of a check to obtain the cash or credit represented on its face.

In dorso /in dórsow/. On the back. 2 Bl.Comm. 468. *In dorso recordi*, on the back of the record. Hence the English *indorse, indorsement,* etc.

In dubiis, benigniora præferenda sunt /in d(y)úwbiyəs, bənìgniyórə prèfəréndə sənt/. In doubtful cases, the more favorable views are to be preferred; the more liberal interpretation is to be followed.

In dubiis, magis dignum est accipiendum /in d(y)úwbiyəs, méyjəs dígnəm èst əksìpiyéndəm/. In doubtful cases, the more worthy is to be accepted.

In dubiis, non præsumitur pro testamento /in d(y)úwbiyəs, nòn prəz(y)úwmədər pròw tèstəméntow/. In cases of doubt, the presumption is not in favor of a will.

In dubio /in d(y)úwbiyow/. In doubt; in a state of uncertainty, or in a doubtful case.

In dubio, hæc legis constructio quam verba ostendunt /in d(y)úwbiyow, hìyk líyjəs kənstráksh(iy)ow kwæm vә́rbə əsténdənt/. In a case of doubt, that is the construction of the law which the words indicate.

In dubio, pars mitior est sequenda /in d(y)úwbiyow, párz máysh(iy)ər èst səkwéndə/. In doubt, the milder course is to be followed.

In dubio, pro lege fori /in d(y)úwbiyow, pròw líyjiy fóray/. In a doubtful case, the law of the forum is to be preferred. "A false maxim."

In dubio, sequendum quod tutius est /in d(y)úwbiyow, səkwéndəm kwòd t(y)úwsh(iy)əs èst/. In doubt, the safer course is to be adopted.

Indubitable proof /ind(y)úwbədəbəl prúwf/. Evidence which is not only found credible, but is of such weight and directness as to make out the facts alleged beyond a doubt. See **Prima facie.**

Induce. To bring on or about, to affect, cause, to influence to an act or course of conduct, lead by persuasion or reasoning, incite by motives, prevail on. See also **Seduce.**

Inducement. In contracts, the benefit or advantage which the promisor is to receive from a contract is the inducement for making it. In criminal evidence, motive; that which leads or tempts to the commission of crime.

Induciæ /ind(y)úws(h)iyiy/. In international law, a truce; a suspension of hostilities; an agreement during war to abstain for a time from warlike acts.

Induct. To put in enjoyment or possession, especially to introduce into possession of an office or benefice, with customary ceremonies. To bring in, initiate; to put formally in possession; to enter formerly into military service; to inaugurate or install. See **Induction.**

Inductio /ində́ksh(iy)ow/. Lat. In the civil law, obliteration, by drawing the pen over the writing.

Induction. Act or process of inducting; *e.g.* process of inducting civilian into military service.

Inducti sunt in carcerem et imparcati /ində́ktay sə́nt in kársərəm èd ìmparkéyday/. See **Imparcare.**

Indulto /indáltow/. In Ecclesiastical law, a dispensation granted by the pope to do or obtain something contrary to the common law.

In old Spanish law, the condonation or remission of the punishment imposed on a criminal for his offense. This power was exclusively vested in the king.

Indument /indyúwmənt/. Endowment (*q.v.*).

In duplo /in d(y)úwplow/. In double. *Damna in duplo*, double damages.

Industrial disease. In law of worker's compensation, physical disorder which is caused by or is incident to particular occupation. Lumbermen's Mut. Cas. Co. v. Rozan, 92 N.H. 328, 30 A.2d 474, 475. See also **Occupational disease.**

Industrial goods. Goods which are destined and designed to produce other goods as contrasted with consumer goods.

Industrial relations. Term includes all phases of relations between employer and employee, including collective bargaining, safety, employee benefits, etc.

Industriam, per /pər ində́striyəm/. Lat. A qualified property in animals *feræ naturæ* may be acquired *per industriam, i.e.,* by a man's reclaiming and making them tame by art, industry, and education; or by so confining them within his own immediate power that they cannot escape and use their natural liberty.

Industry. Any department or branch of art, occupation, or business conducted as a means of livelihood or for profit; especially, one which employs much labor and capital and is a distinct branch of trade. Dessen v. Department of Labor and Industries of Washington, 190 Wash. 69, 66 P.2d 867, 869.

In eadem causa /ìn iyéydəm kózə/. In the same state or condition.

Inebriate /əníybriyət/. A person under the influence of or addicted to the use of intoxicating liquors.

Ineligibility. Disqualification or legal incapacity to be elected to an office or appointed to a particular position. Thus, an alien or naturalized citizen is ineligible to be elected president of the United States. This incapacity arises from various causes, and a person may be incapable of being elected to one office who may be elected to another; the incapacity may also be perpetual or temporary. See also **Incapacity.**

In emulationem vicini /ìn èm(y)əlèyshiyównəm vəsáynay/. In envy or hatred of a neighbor. Where an act is done, or action brought, solely to hurt or distress another, it is said to be *in emulationem vicini.*

In eo quod plus sit, semper inest et minus /ìn íyow kwòd plə́s sít, sémpər ínèst èt máynəs/. In the greater is always included the less also.

In equity. In a court of equity, as distinguished from a court of law; in the purview, consideration, or contemplation of equity; according to the doctrines of equity. See **Equitable; Equity.**

Inescapable peril. Within last clear chance doctrine, means peril which the plaintiff is helpless to avoid by his own efforts, but which requires action on part of defendant to avert it. Melenson v. Howell, 344 Mo. 1137, 130 S.W.2d 555, 560.

In esse /ìn ésiy/. In being. Actually existing. Distinguished from *in posse,* which means "that which is not, but may be." A child before birth is *in posse;* after birth, *in esse.*

Inesse potest donationi, modus, conditio sive causa; ut modus est; si conditio; quia causa /inésiy pówdəst dənèyshiyównay, mówdəs, kəndísh(iy)ow sáyviy kózə; ə́t mówdəs èst; sáy kəndísh(iy)ow; kwáyə kózə/. In a

gift there may be manner, condition, and cause; as *[ut]* introduces a manner; if *[si]*, a condition; because *[quia]*, a cause.

In est de jure /ìnèst dìy júriy/. (Lat.) It is implied of right or by law.

In evidence. Included in the evidence already adduced. The "facts in evidence" are such as have already been proved in the cause.

Inevitable. Incapable of being avoided; fortuitous; transcending the power of human care, foresight, or exertion to avoid or prevent, and therefore suspending legal relations so far as to excuse from the performance of contract obligations, or from liability for consequent loss.

Inevitable accident. An unavoidable accident; one produced by an irresistible physical cause; an accident which cannot be prevented by human skill or foresight, but results from natural causes, such as lightning or storms, perils of the sea, inundations or earthquakes, or sudden death or illness. By irresistible force is meant an interposition of human agency, from its nature and power absolutely uncontrollable.

An accident is "inevitable", so as to preclude recovery on ground of negligence, if person by whom it occurs neither has nor is legally bound to have sufficient power to avoid it or prevent its injuring another. Stephens v. Virginia Elec. & Power Co., 184 Va. 94, 34 S.E.2d 374, 377.

The highest degree of caution that can be used is not required. It is enough that it is reasonable under the circumstances; such as is usual in similar cases, and has been found by long experience to be sufficient to answer the end in view,—the safety of life and property. Inevitable accident is only when the disaster happens from natural causes, without negligence or fault on either side, and when both parties have endeavored, by every means in their power, with due care and caution, and with a proper display of nautical skill, to prevent the occurrence of the accident. The Philip J. Kenny, C.C.A.N.J., 60 F.2d 457, 458.

See also **Act of God.**

In excambio /ìn əkskǽmb(i)yow/. In exchange. Formal words in old deeds of exchange.

Inexcusable neglect. Such neglect which will preclude setting aside of default judgment, implies something more than the unintentional inadvertence or neglect common to all who share the ordinary frailties of mankind. Montez v. Tonkawa Village Apartments, 215 Kan. 59, 523 P.2d 351, 356.

In execution and pursuance of /ìn èksəkyúwshən ǽnd pərs(y)úwəns òv/. Words used to express the fact that the instrument is intended to carry into effect some other instrument, as in case of a deed in execution of a power.

In exitu /ìn égzət(y)uw/. In issue. *De materia in exitu,* of the matter in issue.

In expositione instrumentorum, mala grammatica, quod fieri potest, vitanda est /ìn èkspəzìshiyówniy ìnstrəməntórəm, mǽlə grəmǽdəkə, kwòd fáyəray pówdəst, vətǽndə èst/. In the construction of instruments, bad grammar is to be avoided as much as possible.

In extenso /ìn əksténsow/. In extension; at full length; from beginning to end, leaving out nothing.

In extremis /ìn əkstríyməs/. In extremity; in the last extremity; in the last illness. *Agens in extremis*, being in extremity. Declarations *in extremis*, dying declarations. In extremis does not always mean in articulo mortis. In re Mallery's Will, 127 Misc. 784, 217 N.Y.S. 489, 492.

In facie curiæ /ìn féys(h)iy(iy) kyúriy(iy)/. In the face of the court.

In facie ecclesiæ /ìn féys(h)iy(iy) əklíyziy(iy)/. In the face of the church. A term applied in the law of England to marriages, which are required to be solemnized in a parish church or public chapel, unless by dispensation or license.

In faciendo /ìn fèys(h)iyéndow/. In doing; in feasance; in the performance of an act.

In fact. Actual, real; as distinguished from implied or inferred. Resulting from the acts of parties, instead of from the act or intendment of law.

In facto /ìn fǽktow/. In fact; in deed. *In facto dicit*, in fact says.

In facto quod se habet ad bonum et malum, magis de bono quam de malo lex intendit /ìn fǽktow kwòd sìy héybəd ǽd bównəm èt mǽləm, méyjəs dìy bównow kwǽm dìy mǽlow léks ənténdət/. In an act or deed which admits of being considered as both good and bad, the law intends more from the good than from the bad; the law makes the more favorable construction.

Infamia /inféym(i)yə/. Lat. Infamy; ignominy or disgrace.

By *infamia juris* is meant infamy established by law as the consequence of crime; *infamia facti* is where the party is supposed to be guilty of such crime, but it has not been judicially proved.

Infamis /inféyməs/. Lat. In Roman law, a person whose right of reputation was diminished (involving the loss of some of the rights of citizenship) either on account of his infamous avocation or because of conviction for crime.

Infamous /ínfəməs/. Shameful or disgraceful. Possessing notorious reputation. Famous or well known in a derogatory sense.

Infamous crime. See **Crime.**

Infamous punishment. See **Punishment.**

Infamy /ínfəmiy/. Condition of being infamous. A qualification of a man's legal status produced by his conviction of an infamous crime and the consequent loss of honor and credit, which, at common law, rendered him incompetent as a witness, and by statute in some jurisdictions entails other disabilities. See **Civil death.**

Infancy. Minority; the state of a person who is under the age of legal majority,—at common law, twenty-one years; now, generally 18 years. According to the sense in which this term is used, it may denote the condition of the person merely with reference to his years, or the contractual disabilities which non-age entails, or his status with regard to other powers or relations.

At common law, children under the age of seven are conclusively presumed to be without criminal capacity, those who have reached the age of fourteen are treated as fully responsible, while as to those between the ages of seven and fourteen there is a rebuttable presumption of criminal incapacity. Many states have made some change by statute in the age of criminal responsibility for minors. In addition, all jurisdictions have adopted juvenile court legislation providing that some or all criminal conduct by those persons under a certain age (usually eighteen) must or may be adjudicated in the juvenile court rather than in a criminal prosecution.

See also **Child; Minor.**

Infangenthef /infǽŋənθìyf/. In old English law, a privilege of lords of certain manors to judge any thief taken within their fee. See **Outfangthef.**

Infans /ínfǽn(d)z/. Lat. In the civil law, a child under the age of seven years; so called *"quasi impos fandi"* (as not having the faculty of speech).

Infant. See **Child; Infancy; Minor.**

Infantia /infǽnsh(iy)ə/. Lat. In the civil law, the period of infancy between birth and the age of seven years.

Infanticide /infǽntəsàyd/. The murder or killing of an infant soon after its birth. The fact of the birth distinguishes this act from "feticide" or "procuring abortion," which terms denote the destruction of the *fetus* in the womb. See also **Prolicide.**

Infanzon /ìnfansówn/. In Spanish law, a person of noble birth, who exercises within his domains and inheritance no other rights and privileges than those conceded to him.

In favorabilibus magis attenditur quod prodest quam quod nocet /ìn fèyvərəbíləbəs méyjəs əténdədər kwòd prówdèst kwæm kwòd nósət/. In things favored, what profits is more regarded than what prejudices.

In favorem libertatis /ìn fəvórəm lìbərtéydəs/. In favor of liberty.

In favorem vitæ /ìn fəvórəm váydiy/. In favor of life.

In favorem vitæ, libertatis, et innocentiæ, omnia præsumuntur /ìn fəvórəm váydiy, lìbərtéydəs, èd inəsénshiyiy, ómniyə prìyzyəmántər/. In favor of life, liberty, and innocence, every presumption is made.

Infensare curiam /ìnfənsériy kyúriyəm/. Lat. An expression applied to a court when it suggested to an advocate something which he had omitted through mistake or ignorance.

In feodo /ìn fyúwdow/. In fee. *Seisitus in feodo*, seised in fee.

Infeoffment /ìnfíyfmənt/°féf°/. The act or instrument of feoffment.

Inference. In the law of evidence, a truth or proposition drawn from another which is supposed or admitted to be true. A process of reasoning by which a fact or proposition sought to be established is deduced as a logical consequence from other facts, or a state of facts, already proved or admitted. Com. v. Whitman, 199 Pa.Super. 631, 186 A.2d 632, 633. Inferences are deductions or conclusions which with reason and common sense lead the jury to draw from facts which have been established by the evidence in the case.

An inference is a deduction of fact that may logically and reasonably be drawn from another fact or group of facts found or otherwise established in the action. Calif.Evid.Code.

See also **Reasonable inference rule.** *Compare* **Presumption.**

Inference on inference, rule of. Means that one presumption or inference may not be based upon another. McManimen v. Public Service Co. of Northern Illinois, 317 Ill.App. 649, 47 N.E.2d 385.

Inferential. In the law of evidence, operating in the way of inference; argumentative. Presumptive evidence is sometimes termed "inferential".

Inferential facts. Such as are established not directly by testimony or other evidence, but by inferences or conclusions drawn from the evidence.

Inferior. One who, in relation to another, has less power and is below him; one who is bound to obey another. He who makes the law is the superior; he who is bound to obey it, the inferior.

Inferior court. This term may denote any court subordinate to the chief appellate tribunal in the particular judicial system (*e.g.* trial court); but it is also commonly used as the designation of a court of special, limited, or statutory jurisdiction, whose record must show the existence and attaching of jurisdiction in any given case, in order to give presumptive validity to its judgment.

Infeudation /ìnfyuwdéyshən/. The placing in possession of a freehold estate; also the granting of tithes to laymen.

Inficiari /infis(h)iyéray/. Lat. In the civil law, to deny; to deny one's liability; to refuse to pay a debt or restore a pledge; to deny the allegation of a plaintiff; to deny the charge of an accuser.

Inficiatio /infis(h)iyéysh(iy)ow/. Lat. In the civil law, denial; the denial of a debt or liability; the denial of the claim or allegation of a party plaintiff.

In fictione juris semper æquitas existit /ìn fìkshiyówniy júrəs sémpər íykwətæs əgzístət/. In the fiction of law there is always equity; a legal fiction is always consistent with equity.

Infidel. One who does not believe in the existence of a God who will reward or punish in this world or in that which is to come. One who professes no religion that can bind his conscience to speak the truth. One who does not recognize the inspiration or obligation of the Holy Scriptures, or generally recognized features of the Christian religion.

Infidelis /ìnfədíyləs/°dél°/. In old English law, an infidel or heathen.

In feudal law, one who violated fealty.

Infidelitas /ìnfədélətæs/. In feudal law, infidelity; faithlessness to one's feudal oath.

Infidelity. Unfaithfulness in marriage; usually referring to commission of adultery by one spouse.

Infiduciare /ìnfəd(y)ùws(h)iyériy/. In old European law, to pledge property.

In fieri /ìn fáyəray/. In being made; in process of formation or development; hence, incomplete or inchoate. Legal proceedings are described as *in fieri* until judgment is entered.

Infiht /ínfayt/. Sax. An assault made on a person inhabiting the same dwelling.

In fine /ìn fáyn(iy)/. Lat. At the end. Used, in references, to indicate that the passage cited is at the *end* of a book, chapter, section, etc.

Infinitum in jure reprobatur /ìnfənáydəm ìn júriy rèprəbéydər/. As applied to litigation, that which is endless is reprobated in law.

Infirm. Weak, feeble. Lacking moral character or weak of health. The testimony of an "infirm" witness may be taken *de bene esse* in some circumstances. See also **Incapacity.**

Infirmative. In the law of evidence, having the quality of diminishing force; having a tendency to weaken or render infirm. Exculpatory is used by some authors as synonymous.

Infirmative consideration. In the law of evidence, a consideration, supposition, or hypothesis of which the criminative facts of a case admit, and which tends to weaken the inference or presumption of guilt deducible from them.

Infirmative fact. In the law of evidence, a fact set up, proved, or even supposed, in opposition to the criminative facts of a case, the tendency of which is to weaken the force of the inference of guilt deducible from them.

Infirmative hypothesis. A term sometimes used in criminal evidence to denote an hypothesis or theory of the case which assumes the defendant's innocence, and explains the criminative evidence in a manner consistent with that assumption.

Infirmity. Disability; feebleness. In an application for insurance an ailment or disease of a substantial character, which apparently in some material degree impairs the physical condition and health of the applicant and increases the chance of his death or sickness and which if known, would have been likely to deter the insurance company from issuing the policy. See also **Incapacity.**

Influence. Power exerted over others. To affect, modify or act upon by physical, mental or moral power, especially in some gentle, subtle, and gradual way. State v. Robertson, 241 La. 249, 128 So.2d 646, 648. See also **Undue influence.**

Informal. Deficient in legal form; inartificially drawn up.

Informal contract. Generally refers to an oral contract as contrasted with a written contract or specialty instrument.

Informality. Want of legal form.

Informal proceedings. Proceedings less formal than a normal trial; *e.g.* small claims or conciliation court, hearings, etc. Those conducted without prior notice to interested persons by an officer of the Court acting as registrar for probate of a will or appointment of a personal representative. Uniform Probate Code, § 1–201(19).

Informant. See **Informer.**

In forma pauperis /ìn fórmə pópərəs/. In the character or manner of a pauper. Describes permission given to a poor person (*i.e.* indigent) to proceed without liability for court fees or costs. An indigent will not be deprived of his rights to litigate and appeal; if the court is satisfied as to his indigence he may proceed without incurring costs or fees of court. Fed.R. Crim.P. 44. See also **Indigent defendant.**

Information. An accusation exhibited against a person for some criminal offense, without an indictment. An accusation in the nature of an indictment, from which it differs only in being presented by a competent public officer on his oath of office, instead of a grand jury on their oath. A written accusation made by a public prosecutor, without the intervention of a grand jury. Salvail v. Sharkey, 108 R.I. 63, 271 A.2d 814, 817. In most states the information may be used in place of a grand jury indictment to bring a person to trial. As regards federal crimes, see Fed.R.Crim.P. 7. See also **Arraignment; Indictment.** As to joinder of informations, see **Joinder.**

Information and belief. A standard legal term which is used to indicate that the allegation is not based on the firsthand knowledge of the person making the allegation, but that person nevertheless, in good faith, believes the allegation to be true. See **Probable cause.**

Informed consent. A person's agreement to allow something to happen (such as surgery) that is based on a full disclosure of facts needed to make the decision intelligently; *i.e.,* knowledge of risks involved, alternatives, etc. Informed consent is the name for a general principle of law that a physician has a duty to disclose what a reasonably prudent physician in the medical community in the exercise of reasonable care would disclose to his patient as to whatever grave risks of injury might be incurred from a proposed course of treatment, so that a patient, exercising ordinary care for his own welfare, and faced with a choice of undergoing the proposed treatment, or alternative treatment, or none at all, may intelligently exercise his judgment by reasonably balancing the probable risks against the probable benefits. Ze Barth v. Swedish Hospital Medical Center, 81 Wash.2d 12, 499 P.2d 1, 8.

Informer. A person who informs or prefers an accusation against another, whom he suspects of the violation of some penal statute. An undisclosed person who confidentially volunteers material information of law violations to officers and does not include persons who supply information only after being interviewed by police officers, or who give information as witnesses during course of investigation. Gordon v. U. S., C.A.Fla., 438 F.2d 858, 874. Rewards for information obtained from informers is provided for by 18 U.S.C.A. § 3059.

Informer's privilege. Government's privilege to withhold from disclosure identity of persons who furnish government with information as to violations of law. City of Burlington, Vt. v. Westinghouse Elec. Corp., D.C.D.C., 246 F.Supp. 839, 843.

In foro /ìn fórow/. In a (or the) forum, court, or tribunal.

In foro conscientiæ /ìn fórow kòns(h)iyénshiy(iy)/. In the tribunal of conscience; conscientiously, considered from a moral, rather than a legal, point of view.

In foro contentioso /ìn fórow kəntènshiyówsow/. In the forum of contention or litigation.

In foro ecclesiastico /ìn fórow əklìyziyǽstəkow/. In an ecclesiastical forum; in the ecclesiastical court.

In foro sæculari /ìn fórow sèkyəléray/. In a secular forum or court.

Infortunium, homicide per /hómǝsayd pɔ̀r ìnfɔrtyúwn-(i)yəm/. Where a man doing a lawful act, without intention of hurt, unfortunately kills another.

Infra /ínfrə/. (Lat.) Below, under, beneath, underneath. The opposite of *supra,* above. Thus, we say, *primo gradu est*—supra, *pater, mater,* infra, *filius, filia:* in the first degree of kindred in the ascending line, above is the father and the mother, below, in the descending line, son and daughter.

In another sense, this word signifies *within;* as, *infra corpus civitatis,* within the body of the country; *infra præsidia,* within the guards. So of time, *during: infra furorem,* during the madness. This use is not classical. The use of *infra* for *intra* seems to have sprung up among the barbarians after the fall of the Roman empire.

Infra ætatem /ínfrə ǝtéydǝm/. Under age; not of age. Applied to minors.

Infra annos nubiles /ínfrə ǽnows n(y)úwbǝliyz/. Under marriageable years; not yet of marriageable age.

Infra annum /ínfrə ǽnǝm/. Under or within a year.

Infra annum luctus /ínfrə ǽnǝm lə́ktəs/. (Within the year of mourning.) The phrase is used in reference to the marriage of a widow within a year after her husband's death, which was prohibited by the civil law.

Infra brachia /ínfrə bréyk(i)yə/. Within her arms. Used of a husband *de jure,* as well as *de facto.* Also *inter brachia.* It was in this sense that a woman could only have an appeal for murder of her husband *inter brachia sua.*

Infra civitatem /ínfrə sìvǝtéydǝm/. Within the state.

Infra corpus comitatus /ínfrə kórpǝs kòmǝtéydǝs/. Within the body (territorial limits) of a county. In English law, waters which are *infra corpus comitatus* are exempt from the jurisdiction of the admiralty.

Infraction. A breach, violation, or infringement; as of a law, a contract, a right or duty. A violation of a statute for which the only sentence authorized is a fine and which violation is expressly designated as an infraction.

Infra dignitatem curiæ /ínfrə dìgnətéydəm kyúriy(iy)/. Beneath the dignity of the court; unworthy of the consideration of the court. Where a bill in equity is brought upon a matter too trifling to deserve the attention of the court, it is demurrable, as being *infra dignitatem curiæ.*

Infra furorem /ínfrə fyərórəm/. During madness; while in a state of insanity.

Infra hospitium /ínfrə hospísh(iy)əm/. Within the inn. When a traveler's baggage comes *infra hospitium, i.e.,* in the care and under the custody of the innkeeper, the latter's liability attaches. Davidson v. Madison Corporation, 231 App.Div. 421, 247 N.Y.S. 789, 795.

Infra jurisdictionem /ínfrə jùrəsdìkshiyównəm/. Within the jurisdiction.

Infra præsidia /ínfrə prəsíd(i)yə/. Within the protection; within the defenses. In international law, when a prize, or other captured property, is brought into a port of the captors, or within their lines, or otherwise under their complete custody, so that the chance of rescue is lost, it is said to be *infra præsidia.*

In fraudem creditorum /in fródəm krèdətórəm/. In fraud of creditors; with intent to defraud creditors.

In fraudem legis /in fródəm líyjəs/. In fraud of the law. With the intent or view of evading the law.

Infringement /infrínjmənt/. A breaking into; a trespass or encroachment upon; a violation of a law, regulation, contract, or right. Used especially of invasions of the rights secured by patents, copyrights, and trademarks. See also **Encroachment; Trespass.**

Contributory infringement. The intentional aiding of one person by another in the unlawful making or selling of a patented invention; usually done by making or selling one part of the patented invention, or one element of the combination, with the intent and purpose of so aiding.

Criminal infringement. Any person who infringes a copyright willfully and for purposes of commercial advantage or private financial gain is subject to a fine and/or imprisonment. Copyright Act, § 506.

Infringement of copyright. Unauthorized use of copyrighted material; *i.e.* use without permission of copyright holder. In determining whether there is a copyright infringement, and not a "fair use" exemption, the factors to be considered include: (1) the purpose and character of the use, including whether such use is of a commercial nature or is for nonprofit educational purposes; (2) the nature of the copyrighted work; (3) the amount and substantiality of the portion used in relation to the copyrighted work as a whole; and (4) the effect of the use upon the potential market for or value of the copyrighted work. Copyright Act, § 107.

Remedies for copyright infringement include injunctive relief, impounding and disposition of infringing articles, and recovery of actual damages and profits. In lieu of actual damages, the federal Copyright Act provides for statutory damages which will vary as to whether the infringement was willful or unintentional. Copyright Act, § 504.

See also **Fair use doctrine.**

Infringement of patent. The unauthorized making, using, or selling for practical use, or for profit, of an invention covered by a valid claim of a patent during the life of the patent. It may involve any one or all of the acts of making, using, and selling. Phillips Electronic & Pharmaceutical Industries Corp. v. Thermal & Electronics Industries, Inc., D.C.N.J., 311 F.Supp. 17, 39. To constitute infringement of a patent claim there must be present in the infringing device or combination every element of such claim or its equivalent, so combined as to produce substantially the same result operating in substantially the same way. Montgomery Ward and Co. v. Clair, C.C.A.Mo., 123 F.2d 878, 881.

Infringement of trademark. The unauthorized use or colorable imitation of the mark already appropriated by another, on goods of a similar class. Northam Warren Corporation v. Universal Cosmetic Co., C.C. A.Ill., 18 F.2d 774, 775. It exists if words or designs used by defendant are identical with or so similar to plaintiff's that they are likely to cause confusion, or deceive or mislead others. McGraw-Hill Pub. Co. v. American Aviation Associates, 73 App.D.C. 131, 117 F.2d 293, 294; Seattle Street Railway & Municipal Employees Relief Ass'n v. Amalgamated Ass'n of Street, Electric Railway & Motor Coach Employees of America, 3 Wash.2d 520, 101 P.2d 338, 344; California Fruit Growers Exchange v. Windsor Beverages, C.C.A.Ill., 118 F.2d 149, 152.

Infringer. One who infringes the rights secured by copyright, patent or trademark holders. One who affixes the trademark of another to similar articles in such way that his use of it is liable to cause confusion in the trade, or is calculated to mislead purchasers and induce them to buy infringer's articles as goods of the other thus depriving the latter of the full benefit of his property. James Heddon's Sons v. Millsite Steel & Wire Works, C.C.A.Mich., 128 F.2d 6, 8.

In full. Relating to the whole or *full* amount; as a receipt in full. Complete; giving all details.

In full life. Continuing in both physical and civil existence; that is, neither actually dead nor *civiliter mortuus.*

In futuro /in f(y)əchúrow/. In future; at a future time; the opposite of *in præsenti.*

In generalibus versatur error /in jènəréyləbəs vərséydər éhrər/. Error dwells in general expressions.

In generali passagio /in jènəréylay pəséyj(iy)ow/. In the general passage; that is, on the journey to Palestine with the general company or body of Crusaders. This term was of frequent occurrence in the old law of essoins, as a means of accounting for the absence of the party, and was distinguished from *simplex passagium,* which meant that he was performing a pilgrimage to the Holy Land alone.

In genere /ìn jénəriy/. In kind; in the same *genus* or class; the same in quantity and quality, but not individually the same. In the Roman law, things which may be given or restored *in genere* are distinguished from such as must be given or restored *in specie;* that is, identically.

Ingenuitas /ìnjən(y)úwətæs/. Lat. Freedom; liberty; the state or condition of one who is free. Also liberty given to a servant by manumission.

Ingenuitas regni /ìnjən(y)úwətæs régnay/. In old English law, the freemen, yeomanry, or commonalty of the kingdom. Applied sometimes also to the barons.

Ingenuus /injényuwəs/. In Roman law, a person who, immediately that he was born, was a free person. He was opposed to *libertinus*, or *libertus*, who, having been born a slave, was afterwards manumitted or made free. It is not the same as the English law term *"generosus"*, which denoted a person not merely free, but of good family. There were no distinctions among *ingenui;* but among *libertini* there were (prior to Justinian's abolition of the distinctions) three varieties, namely: Those of the highest rank, called *"Cives Romani";* those of the second rank, called *"Latini Juniani";* and those of the lowest rank, called *"Dediticii"*.

Ingratitude. In Roman law, ingratitude was accounted a sufficient cause for revoking a gift or recalling the liberty of a freedman. Such is also the law of France with respect to the first case. But the English and American law has left the matter entirely to the moral sense. Ungrateful.

In gremio legis /ìn gríym(i)yow líyjəs/. In the bosom of the law; in the protection of the law; in abeyance.

Ingress. The act, or right of, entering. Access; entrance.

Ingress, egress, and regress. These words express the right (*e.g.* of a lessee) to enter, go upon, and return from the lands in question.

Ingressu /ingrés(y)uw/. In English law, an ancient writ of entry, by which the plaintiff or complainant sought an entry into his lands. Abolished in 1833.

Ingressus /ingrésəs/. In old English law, ingress; entry. The relief paid by an heir to the lord was sometimes so called.

In gross. In a large quantity or sum; without deduction, division, or particulars; by wholesale. At large, in one sum; not annexed to or dependent upon another thing. Common in gross is such as is neither appendant nor appurtenant to land, but is annexed to a man's person. See also **In bulk.**

Ingrossator /ingrəséydər/. In old English law, an engrosser. *Ingrossator magni rotuli* /ingrəséydər mǽgnay róchələy/, engrosser of the great roll; called "clerk of the pipe".

Ingrossing. The act of making a fair and perfect copy of any document from a rough draft of it, in order that it may be executed or put to its final purpose. See **Engross.**

Inhabit. Synonymous with dwell, live, reside, sojourn, stay, rest. See also **Domicile; Residence.**

Inhabitant. One who resides actually and permanently in a given place, and has his domicile there. Ex parte Shaw, 145 U.S. 444, 12 S.Ct. 935, 36 L.Ed. 768.

The words "inhabitant," "citizen," and "resident," as employed in different constitutions to define the qualifications of electors, means substantially the same thing; and, in general, one is an inhabitant, resident, or citizen at the place where he has his domicile or home. But the terms "resident" and "inhabitant" have also been held not synonymous, the latter implying a more fixed and permanent abode than the former, and importing privileges and duties to which a mere resident would not be subject. A corporation can be an inhabitant only in the state of its incorporation. Sperry Products v. Association of American Railroads, C.C.A.N.Y., 132 F.2d 408, 411. See also **Domicile, Residence.**

In hac parte /ìn hǽc párdiy/. In this behalf; on this side.

In hæc verba /ìn híyk várbə/. In these words; in the same words.

In hæredes non solent transire actiones quæ pœnales ex maleficio sunt /ìn həríydiyz nòn sówlənt trænzáyriy ǽkshiyówniyz kwìy pənéyliyz èks əfísh(iy)ow sànt/. Penal actions arising from anything of a criminal nature do not pass to heirs.

Inhere /inhír/. To exist in and inseparable from something else; to stick fast. To be inherent.

Inherently dangerous. Danger inhering in instrumentality or condition itself at all times, so as to require special precautions to prevent injury; not danger arising from mere casual or collateral negligence of others with respect thereto under particular circumstances. Brown v. City of Craig, 350 Mo. 836, 168 S.W.2d 1080, 1082. An object which has in itself the potential for causing harm or destruction, against which precautions must be taken. Dangerous per se, without requiring human intervention to produce harmful effects; *e.g.*, explosives.

Product is "inherently dangerous" where danger of an injury arises from product itself, and not from defect in product. General Bronze Corp. v. Kostopulos, 203 Va. 66, 122 S.E.2d 548, 551. An activity is "inherently dangerous" when it is probable or likely that injurious consequences will attend doing of work. Reeves v. John A. Cooper Co., D.C.Ark., 304 F.Supp. 828, 832.

See also **Strict liability.**

Inherent or latent defect. Fault or deficiency in a thing which is not easily discoverable and which is fixed in the object itself and not from without. See **Latent defect.**

Inherent powers /inhírənt páwərz/. An authority possessed without its being derived from another. A right, ability, or faculty of doing a thing, without receiving that right, ability, or faculty from another. Powers originating from the nature of government or sovereignty, *i.e.*, powers over and beyond those explicitly granted in the Constitution or reasonably to be implied from express grants. See also **Power.**

Inherent powers of a court. Those reasonably necessary for administration of justice. State ex rel. Gentry v. Becker, 351 Mo. 769, 174 S.W.2d 181, 183; Ex parte Wetzel, 243 Ala. 130, 8 So.2d 824, 825.

Inherent right. One which abides in a person and is not given from something or someone outside itself. A right which a person has because he is a person.

Inheretrix /inhéhrətriks/. The old term for "heiress".

Inherit /inhéhrət/. To take by inheritance; to take as heir on death of ancestor; to take by descent from ancestor; to take or receive, as right or title, by law from ancestor at his decease. In re Buell's Estate, 167 Or. 295, 117 P.2d 832, 836. Acquisition of property by descent and distribution. The word is also used in its popular sense, as the equivalent of to take or receive. See also **Inheritance.**

Inheritable blood. Blood which has the purity (freedom from attainder) and legitimacy necessary to give its possessor the character of a lawful heir. That which is capable of being the medium for the transmission of an inheritance.

Inheritance /inhéhrədən(t)s/. That which is inherited or to be inherited. Property which descends to heir on the intestate death of another. An estate or property which a man has by descent, as heir to another, or which he may transmit to another, as his heir. See **Bequest; Descent; Heirs; Legacy.**

Civil law. The succession of the heir to all the rights and property of the estate-leaver. It is either testamentary, where the heir is created by will, or *ab intestato,* where it arises merely by operation of law.

Inheritance tax. Tax imposed upon the privilege of receiving property from a decedent at death as contrasted with an estate tax which is imposed on the privilege of transmitting property at death. A tax on the transfer or passing of estates or property by legacy, devise, or intestate succession; not a tax on the property itself, but on the right to acquire it by descent or testamentary gift. *Compare* **Estate tax.**

Inhibition /in(h)əbíshən/. Restraining or holding back.

In Ecclesiastical law, a writ issuing from a superior ecclesiastical court, forbidding an inferior judge to proceed further in a cause pending before him. In this sense it is closely analogous to the writ of *prohibition* at common law. Also the writ of a bishop or ecclesiastical judge that a clergyman shall cease from taking any duty.

In old English law, the name of a writ which forbids a judge from further proceeding in a cause pending before him; it was in the nature of a prohibition.

In the civil law, a prohibition which the law makes or a judge ordains to an individual. See **Immigration.**

In his enim quæ sunt favorabilia animæ, quamvis sunt damnosa rebus, fiat aliquando extentio statuti /ìn hís énəm kwìy sànt fèyvərəbíl(i)yə ǽnəmiy, kwǽmvəs sànt dæmnówsə ríybəs, fáyəd ǽləkwǽndow əksténsh(iy)ow stəchúwday/. In things that are favorable to the spirit, though injurious to property, an extension of the statute should sometimes be made.

In his quæ de jure communi omnibus conceduntur, consuetudo alicujus patriæ vel loci non est allegenda /ìn hís kwíy dìy júriy kəmyúwnay ómnəbəs kònsədántər, kònswət(y)úwdow ǽləkyúwjəs pǽtriyiy vèl lówsay

nón èst ǽləjéndə/. In those things which by common right are conceded to all, the custom of a particular district or place is not to be alleged.

In hoc /ìn hók/. In this; in respect to this.

Inhonestus /ìnhənéstəs/. In old English law, unseemly; not in due order.

Inhuman treatment. In the law of divorce, such mental or physical cruelty or severity as endangers the life or health of the party to whom it is addressed, or creates a well-founded apprehension of such danger. The phrase commonly employed in statutes is "cruel and inhuman treatment," from which it may be inferred that "inhumanity" is an extreme or aggravated "cruelty." Such treatment commonly constitutes a ground for divorce. See also **Cruelty; Mental cruelty.**

In iisdem terminis /ìn iyáysdəm tármənəs/. In the same terms.

In iis quæ sunt meræ facultatis nunquam præscribitur /ìn áyəs kwìy sànt míriy fǽkəltéydəs nə́ŋkwəm prəskríbədər/. Prescription does not run against a mere power or faculty to act.

In individuo /ìn indəvíd(y)uwow/. In the distinct, identical, or individual form; *in specie.*

In infinitum /ìn infənáydəm/. Infinitely; indefinitely. Imports indefinite succession or continuance.

In initio /ìn əním(iy)ow/. In or at the beginning. *In initio litis,* at the beginning, or in the first stage of the suit.

In integrum /ìn əntégrəm/. To the original or former state.

In invidiam /ìn ənvíd(i)yəm/. To excite a prejudice.

In invitum /ìn ənváydəm/. Against an unwilling party; against one not assenting. A term applied to proceedings against an adverse party, to which he does not consent.

In ipsis faucibus /ìn ípsəs fósəbəs/. In the very throat or entrance. *In ipsis faucibus* of a port, actually entering a port.

Iniquissima pax est anteponenda justissimo bello /ìnikwísəmə pǽks èst ǽntəpənéndə jə̀stísəmow bélow/. The most unjust peace is to be preferred to the justest war.

Iniquum est alios permittere, alios inhibere mercaturam /ináykwəm èst éyl(i)yows pərmídəriy, éyl(i)yows ìn(h)əbíriy màrkəchúrəm/. It is inequitable to permit some to trade and to prohibit others.

Iniquum est aliquem rei sui esse judicem /ənáykwəm èst ǽləkwəm ríyay s(y)úway ésiy júwdəsəm/. It is wrong for a man to be a judge in his own cause.

Iniquum est ingenuis hominibus non esse liberam rerum suarum alienationem /ənáykwəm èst injényuwəs həmínəbəs nòn ésiy líbərəm rírəm s(y)uwérəm èyliyèyshiyównəm/. It is unjust that freemen should not have the free disposal of their own property.

Initial. That which begins or stands at the beginning. The first letter of a man's name.

Initial carrier. In the law of bailments, the carrier who first receives the goods and begins the process of their transportation, afterwards delivering them to another carrier for the further prosecution or completion of their journey. But it has also been defined as the one contracting with the shipper, and not necessarily the one whose line constitutes the first link in transportation.

Initiate. Commence; start; originate; introduce; inchoate. *Curtesy initiate* is the interest which a husband has in the wife's lands after a child is born who may inherit, but before the wife dies. To propose for approval—as schedule of rates. Idaho Power Co. v. Thompson, D.C.Idaho, 19 F.2d 547, 579.

Initiation fee. The sum paid on joining an organization or club for privileges of membership. Derby v. U. S., D.C.Mass., 17 F.2d 119, 120.

Initiative. An electoral process whereby designated percentages of the electorate may initiate legislative or constitutional changes through the filing of formal petitions to be acted on by the legislature or the total electorate. The power of the people to propose bills and laws, and to enact or reject them at the polls, independent of legislative assembly. Hughes v. Bryan, Okl., 425 P.2d 952, 954. Not all state constitutions provide for initiative. See also **Referendum.**

In itinere /in aytínəriy/. In eyre; on a journey or circuit. In old English law, the justices *in itinere* (or in eyre) were those who made a circuit through the kingdom once in seven years for the purposes of trying causes. In course of transportation; on the way; not delivered to the vendee. In this sense the phrase is equivalent to *"in transitu."*

Iniurcolleguia /ìynyùrkalyéygiyə/. A body of Soviet lawyers in Moscow organized and constituted pursuant to statute under jurisdiction and control of the U.S.S.R. Ministry of Justice for the purpose of exclusive representation of Soviet nationals in foreign legal matters. In re Mitzkel's Estate, 36 Misc.2d 671, 233 N.Y.S.2d 519, 524; In re Kapocius' Estate, 36 Misc.2d 1087, 234 N.Y.S.2d 346, 348.

In judgment. In a court of justice; in a seat of judgment.

In judiciis, minori ætati succurritur /in jədís(h)iyəs, mənóray ətéyday səkə́rədər/. In courts or judicial proceedings, infancy is aided or favored.

In judicio /in jədís(h)(i)yow/. In Roman law, in the course of an actual trial; before a judge *(judex).* A cause, during its preparatory stages, conducted before the prætor, was said to be *in jure;* in its second stage, after it had been sent to a *judex* for trial, it was said to be *in judicio.*

In judicio non creditur nisi juratis /in jədís(h)(i)yow nòn krédədər náysay jəréydəs/. In a trial, credence is given only to those who are sworn.

Injunction. A prohibitive, equitable remedy issued or granted by a court at the suit of a party complainant, directed to a party defendant in the action, or to a party made a defendant for that purpose, forbidding the latter to do some act, or to permit his servants or agents to do some act, which he is threatening or attempting to commit, or restraining him in the continuance thereof, such act being unjust and inequitable, injurious to the plaintiff, and not such as can be adequately redressed by an action at law. A judicial process operating in personam, and requiring person to whom it is directed to do or refrain from doing a particular thing. Gainsburg v. Dodge, 193 Ark. 473, 101 S.W.2d 178, 180. Fed.R.Civil P. 65. See also **Temporary restraining order.**

Interlocutory injunction. Interlocutory injunctions are those issued at any time during the pendency of the litigation for the short-term purpose of preventing irreparable injury to the petitioner prior to the time that the court will be in a position to either grant or deny permanent relief on the merits. In accordance with their purpose, interlocutory injunctions are limited in duration to some specified length of time, or at the very outside, to the time of conclusion of the case on the merits. Within the category of interlocutory injunctions there are two distinct types which must be considered individually. The first is generally referred to as a preliminary injunction, and includes any interlocutory injunction granted after the respondent has been given notice and the opportunity to participate in a hearing on whether or not that injunction should issue. The second is generally referred to as a temporary restraining order, and differs from a preliminary injunction primarily in that it is issued ex parte, with no notice or opportunity to be heard granted to the respondent. Temporary restraining orders supply the need for relief in those situations in which the petitioner will suffer irreparable injury if relief is not granted immediately, and time simply does not permit either the delivery of notice or the holding of a hearing. Fed.R.Civil P. 65.

Mandatory injunction. One which (1) commands the defendant to do some positive act or particular thing; (2) prohibits him from refusing (or persisting in a refusal) to do or permit some act to which the plaintiff has a legal right; or (3) restrains the defendant from permitting his previous wrongful act to continue operative, thus virtually compelling him to undo it.

Permanent injunction. One intended to remain in force until the final termination of the particular suit.

Perpetual injunction. An injunction which finally disposes of the suit, and is indefinite in point of time.

Preliminary injunction. An injunction granted at the institution of a suit, to restrain the defendant from doing or continuing some act, the right to which is in dispute, and which may either be discharged or made perpetual, according to the result of the controversy, as soon as the rights of the parties are determined. Fed.R.Civil P. 65.

Preventive injunction. One which prohibits the defendant from doing a particular act or commands him to refrain from it.

Prohibitory injunction. An order of a court in the form of a judgment which directs one not to do a certain thing; sometimes called a restraining order.

Provisional injunction. Another name for a preliminary or temporary injunction or an injunction pendente lite.

Restraining order. See **Order; Restraining order; Temporary restraining order.**

Temporary injunction. A preliminary or provisional injunction, or one granted pendente lite; as opposed to a final or perpetual injunction. See also **Temporary restraining order.**

In jure /ìn júriy/. In law; according to law.

In the Roman practice, the procedure in an action was divided into two stages. The first was said to be *in jure;* it took place before the prætor, and included the formal and introductory part and the settlement of questions of law. The second stage was committed to the *judex,* and comprised the investigation and trial of the facts; this was said to be *in judicio.*

Injure. To violate the legal right of another or inflict an actionable wrong. To do harm to, damage, or impair. To hurt or wound, as the person; to impair the soundness of, as health. Ziolkowski v. Continental Casualty Co., 284 Ill.App. 505, 1 N.E.2d 410, 412. As applied to a building, "injure" means to materially impair or destroy any part of the existing structure. See **Injury.**

In jure alterius /ìn júriy oltíriyəs/. In another's right.

In jure, non remota causa sed proxima spectatur /ìn júriy, nòn rəmówdə kózə sèd próksəmə spèktéydər/. In law, the proximate, and not the remote, cause is regarded.

In jure proprio /ìn júriy prówpriyow/. In one's own right.

Injures graves /ínjəriyz gréyvz/ænzhyúr gráv/. Fr. In French law, grievous insults or injuries, including personal insults and reproachful language, constituting a just cause of divorce.

Injuria /ənjúr(i)yə/. Lat. Injury; wrong; the privation or violation of right.

Injuria absque damno /ənjúr(i)yə æbskwiy dǽmnow/. Injury or wrong without damage. A wrong done, but from which no loss or damage results, and which, therefore, will not sustain an action.

Injuria fit ei cui convicium dictum est, vel de eo factum carmen famosum /ənjúr(i)yə fit íyay k(yúw)ay kənvís(h)(i)yəm díktəm èst, vèl dìy íyow fǽktəm kármən fəmówsəm/. An injury is done to him of whom a reproachful thing is said, or concerning whom an infamous song is made.

Injuria illata judici, seu locum tenenti regis, videtur ipsi regi illata maxime si fiat in exercentem officium /ənjúr(i)yə əléydə júwdəsay, s(y)ùw lówkəm tənéntay ríyjəs, vədíydər ípsay ríyjay əléydə mǽksəmiy sày fáyət ìn ègzərséntəm əfísh(iy)əm/. An injury offered to a judge, or person representing the king, is considered as offered to the king himself, especially if it be done in the exercise of his office.

Injuria non excusat injuriam /ənjúr(i)yə nòn əkskyúwzəd ənjúr(i)yəm/. One wrong does not justify another.

Injuria non præsumitur /ənjúr(i)yə nòn prəz(y)úwmədər/. Injury is not presumed. Cruel, oppressive, or tortious conduct will not be presumed.

Injuria propria non cadet in beneficium facientis /ənjúr(i)yə prówpriyə nòn kéydəd ən bènəfísh(iy)əm fǽs(h)(i)yéntəs/. One's own wrong shall not fall to the advantage of him that does it. A man will not be allowed to derive benefit from his own wrongful act.

Injuria servi dominum pertingit /ənjúr(i)yə sə́rvay dómənəm pərtínjət/. The master is liable for injury done by his servant.

Injurious falsehood. In law of slander and libel, a defamation which does actual damage. See **Libel; Slander.**

Injurious words /ənjúriyəs wə́rdz/. Slander, or libelous words. See **Libel; Slander.**

Injury. Any wrong or damage done to another, either in his person, rights, reputation, or property. The invasion of any legally protected interest of another. Restatement, Second, Torts, § 7.

Absolute injuries. Injuries to those rights which a person possesses as being a member of society.

Accidental injury. A bodily injury by accident.

Within worker's compensation acts, one which occurs in the course of the employment, unexpectedly, and without the affirmative act or design of the employee; it being something which is unforeseen and not expected by the person to whom it happens. Any injury to an employee in the course of his employment due to any occurrence referable to a definite time, and of the happening of which he can give notice to his employer, regardless of whether the injury is a visible hurt from external force, or disease or infection induced by sudden and castastrophic exposure. Lerner v. Rump Bros., 212 App.Div. 747, 209 N.Y.S. 698, 701. The term is to receive a broad and liberal construction with a view to compensating injured employés where injury resulted through some accidental means, was unexpected and undesigned and may be the result of mere mischance or miscalculation as to effect of voluntary action. It includes an accident causing injury to the physical structure of the body, notwithstanding a natural weakness predisposing to injury. The words indicate, not so much the existence of an accident, but rather the idea that the injury was unexpected or unintended.

See also Accident; Compensable injury; Continuous injury; Damages; Disability; Great bodily injury; Harm; Loss; Malicious injury; Pain and suffering; Pecuniary injury.

Bodily injury. Physical pain, illness or any impairment of physical condition. "Serious bodily injury" means bodily injury which creates a substantial risk of death or which causes serious, permanent disfigurement, or protracted loss or impairment of the function of any bodily member or organ. Model Penal Code, § 210.0.

Civil injury. Injuries to person or property, resulting from a breach of contract, delict, or criminal offense, which may be redressed by means of a civil action. An infringement or privation of the civil rights which belong to individuals considered as individuals.

Irreparable injury. This phrase does not mean such an injury as is beyond the possibility of repair, or beyond possible compensation in damages, or necessarily great damage, but includes an injury, whether great or small, which ought not to be submitted to, on the one hand, or inflicted, on the other; and which, because it is so large or so small, or is of such constant and frequent occurrence, or because no certain pecuniary standard exists for the measurement of damages, cannot receive reasonable redress in a court of law. Wrongs of a repeated and continuing character, or which occasion damages that are estimated only by conjecture, and not by any accurate standard, are included. The remedy for such is commonly in the nature of injunctive relief. "Irreparable injury" justifying an injunction is that which cannot be adequately compensated in damages or for which damages cannot be compensable in money. Caffery v. Powell, La.App., 320 So.2d 223, 226. Contrast *Reparable injury,* infra.

Permanent injury. An injury that, according to every reasonable probability, will continue throughout the remainder of one's life.

Personal injury. In a narrow sense, a hurt or damage done to a man's *person,* such as a cut or bruise, a broken limb, or the like, as distinguished from an injury to his property or his reputation. The phrase is chiefly used in this connection with actions of tort for negligence and under worker's compensation statutes. But the term is also used (chiefly in statutes) in a much wider sense, and as including any injury which is an invasion of personal rights, and in this signification it may include such injuries to the person as libel or slander, criminal conversation, malicious prosecution, false imprisonment, and mental suffering. Gray v. Wallace, 319 S.W.2d 582.

In worker's compensation acts, "personal injury" means any harm or damage to the health of an employee, however caused, whether by accident, disease, or otherwise, which arises in the course of and out of his employment, and incapacitates him in whole or in part. The occurrence of disability or impairment. Such includes the aggravation of a preexisting injury.

Private injuries. Infringements of the private or civil rights belonging to individuals considered as individuals.

Public injuries. Breaches and violations of rights and duties which affect the whole community as a community.

Real injury. A *real injury* is inflicted by any act by which a person's honor or dignity is affected.

Relative injuries. Injuries to those rights which a person possesses in relation to the person who is immediately affected by the wrongful act done.

Reparable injury. The general principle is that an injury, the damage from which is merely in the nature of pecuniary loss, and can be exactly and fully repaired by compensation in money, is a "reparable injury". Contrast *Irreparable injury, supra.*

Verbal injury. See **Libel; Slander.**

Injustice. The withholding or denial of justice. In law, almost invariably applied to the act, fault, or omission of a court, as distinguished from that of an individual. "Fraud" is deception practiced by the party; "injustice" is the fault or error of the court. They are not equivalent words in substance, or in a statute authorizing a new trial on a showing of fraud or injustice. Fraud is always the result of contrivance and deception; injustice may be done by the negligence, mistake, or omission of the court itself. Silvey v. U. S., 7 Ct.Cl. 305, 324.

Injustum est, nisi tota lege inspecta, de una aliqua ejus particula proposita judicare vel respondere /injə́stəm èst, náysay tówdə líyjíy ənspéktə, diy yúwnə ǽləkwə íyjəs partík(y)ələ prəpózədə jùwdəkériy vél rèspondíriy/. It is unjust to decide or respond as to any particular part of a law without examining the whole of the law.

In jus vocare /ìn jə́s vòwkériy/. To call, cite, or summon to court. *In jus vocando,* summoning to court.

In kind. Of the same species or category. In the same kind, class, or genus. A loan is returned "in kind" when not the identical article, but one corresponding and equivalent to it, is given to the lender. See **Distribution in kind; In genere; Like-kind exchange.**

Inlagare /ìnləgériy/. In old English law, to restore to protection of law. To restore a man from the condition of outlawry. Opposed to *utlagare.*

Inlagation /ìnləgéyshən/. Restoration to the protection of law. Restoration from a condition of outlawry.

Inlagh /ínlò/. A person within the law's protection; contrary to *utlagh,* an outlaw.

Inland. Within a country, state or territory; within the interior part of a land mass.

In old English law, inland was used for the demesne *(q.v.)* of a manor; that part which lay next or most convenient for the lord's mansion-house, as within the view thereof, and which, therefore, he kept in his own hands for support of his family and for hospitality; in distinction from outland or utland, which was the portion let out to tenants.

Inland bill of exchange. A bill of which both the drawer and drawee reside within the same state or country. Otherwise called a "domestic bill," and distinguished from a "foreign bill." See **Bill.**

Inland navigation. Within the meaning of the legislation of congress upon the subject, this phrase means navigation upon inland waters *(q.v.).*

Inland trade. Trade wholly carried on at home; as distinguished from foreign commerce. See **Commerce.**

Inland waters. Such waters as canals, lakes, rivers, watercourses, inlets and bays, within, or partly within, the United States, exclusive of the open sea, though the water in question may open or empty into the ocean. United States v. Steam Vessels of War, 106 U.S. 607, 1 S.Ct. 539, 27 L.Ed. 286.

Inlantal, inlantale /ínlæntəl, ìnlæntéyliy/. Demesne or inland, opposed to *delantal,* or land tenanted.

Inlaughe /ínlò/. Sax. In old English law, under the law *(sub lege),* in a frank-pledge, or decennary.

Inlaw. To place under the protection of the law.

In law. In the intendment, contemplation, or inference of the law; implied or inferred by law; existing in law or by force of law. See **In fact.**

In laws. Persons related by marriage rather than blood; *e.g.* relationship of parents of wife to husband.

In lecto mortali /ìn léktow mòrtéylay/. On the deathbed.

In liberam elemosinam /ìn líbərəm ìyləmósənəm/. In free alms. Land given for a charitable motive was said to be so given. See **Frankalmoign.**

In lieu of /ìn lyúw əv/. Instead of; in place of; in substitution of.

In limine /ìn líməniy/. On or at the threshold; at the very beginning; preliminarily. See **Motion in limine.**

In litem /ìn láydəm/. For a suit; to the suit.

In loco /ìn lówkow/. In place; in lieu; instead; in the place or stead.

In loco parentis /ìn lówkow pəréntəs/. In the place of a parent; instead of a parent; charged, factitiously, with a parent's rights, duties, and responsibilities.

In majorem cautelam /ìn məjórəm kòtíyləm/. For greater security.

In majore summa continetur minor /ìn məjóriy sə́mə kòntəníydər máynər/. In the greater sum is contained the less.

In malam partem /ìn mǽləm párdəm/. In a bad sense, so as to wear an evil appearance.

In maleficiis voluntas spectatur, non exitus /ìn mǽləfís(h)iyəs vəlántǽs spèktéydər, nòn égzədəs/. In evil deeds regard must be had to the intention, and not to the result.

In maleficio, ratihabitio mandato comparatur /ìn mǽləfís(h)(i)ỳow, rèydayhəbísh(iy)ow mǽndéydow kòmpəréydər/. In a case of malfeasance, ratification is equivalent to command.

Inmate. A person confined to a prison, penitentiary, or the like. A person who lodges or dwells in the same house with another, occupying different rooms, but using the same door for passing in and out of the house.

In maxima potentia minima licentia /ìn mǽksəmə pəténsh(iy)ə mínəmə ləsénsh(iy)ə/. In the greatest power there is the least freedom.

In medias res /ìn míydiyəs ríyz/. Into the heart of the subject, without preface or introduction.

In mercibus illicitis non sit commercium /ìn mə́rsəbəs əlísədəs nón sìt kəmárs(h)(i)yəm/. There should be no commerce in illicit or prohibited goods.

In mercy. To be in mercy is to be at the discretion of the king, lord, or judge in respect to the imposition of a fine or other punishment.

In misericordia /ìn mìzərəkórd(i)yə/. The entry on the record where a party was in mercy was, *"Ideo in misericordia,"* etc. Sometimes *"misericordia"* means the being quit of all amercements.

In mitiori sensu /ìn mìshiyóray séns(y)uw/. In the milder sense; in the less aggravated acceptation.

In actions of slander, it was formerly the rule that, if the words alleged would admit of two constructions, they should be taken in the less injurious and defamatory sense, or *in mitiori sensu.*

In modum assisæ /ìn mówdəm əsáyziy/. In the manner or form of an assize. *In modum juratæ,* in manner of a jury.

In mora /ìn mórə/. In default; literally, in delay. In the civil law, a borrower who omits or refuses to return the thing loaned at the proper time is said to be *in mora.*

In mortua manu /ìn mórchuwə mǽnyuw/. Property owned by religious societies was said to be held *in mortua manu,* or in mortmain, since religious men were *civiliter mortui.*

Inn. A public lodging establishment. A lodging house where all who conduct themselves properly, and who are able and ready to pay for their entertainment, are received, if there is accommodation for them, and who, while there, are supplied at a reasonable charge with their meals, their lodging, and such services and attention as are necessarily incident to the use of the house as a temporary home. A place where the public will be received and accommodations provided to guests for compensation. Edwards v. City of Los Angeles, 48 Cal.App.2d 62, 119 P.2d 370, 373, 374. A hotel, tavern, motel, or hostel.

Innamium /ìnéymiyəm/. In old English law, a pledge.

Innavigability. In insurance law, the condition of being *innavigable (q.v.).* The term is also applied to the condition of streams which are not large enough or deep enough, or are otherwise unsuited, for navigation.

Innavigable. As applied to streams, not capable of or suitable for navigation; impassable by ships or vessels. As applied to vessels in the law of marine insurance, it means unfit for navigation; so damaged by misadventures at sea as to be no longer capable of making a voyage.

Inner barrister. A serjeant or king's counsel, in England, who is admitted to plead within the bar.

Innings. In old records, lands recovered from the sea by draining and banking.

Innkeeper. One who keeps an inn, hotel, motel or house for the lodging and entertainment of travelers.

Innocence. The absence of guilt. See also **Presumption of innocence.**

Innocent. Free from guilt; acting in good faith and without knowledge of incriminatory circumstances, or of defects or objections.

Innocent agent. In criminal law, one who, being ignorant of any unlawful intent on the part of his principal, is merely the instrument of the guilty party in committing an offense; one who does an unlawful act at the solicitation or request of another, but who, from defect of understanding or ignorance of the inculpatory facts, incurs no legal guilt.

Innocent conveyances. A technical term of the old English law of conveyancing, used to designate such conveyances as may be made by a leasehold tenant without working a forfeiture. These are said to be lease and re-lease, bargain and sale, and, in case of a life-tenant, a covenant to stand seised.

Innocent purchaser. One who, by an honest contract or agreement, purchases property or acquires an interest therein, without knowledge, or means of knowledge sufficient to charge him in law with knowledge, of any infirmity in the title of the seller. Treit v. Oregon Auto. Ins. Co., 262 Or. 549, 499 P.2d 335, 336. Person is "innocent purchaser" when he purchases without notice, actual or constructive, of any infirmity and pays valuable consideration and acts in good faith. Morehead v. Harris, 262 N.C. 330, 137 S.E.2d 174, 182, 185. See also **Good faith purchaser.**

Innocent trespass. A trespass to land, committed, not recklessly, but through inadvertence or mistake, or in good faith, under an honest belief that the trespasser was acting within his legal rights.

Innocent trespasser. One who enters another's land unlawfully, but inadvertently or unintentionally, or in the honest, reasonable belief of his own right so to do, and removes sand or other material therefrom, is an "innocent trespasser." Restatement, Second, Torts, § 164.

Innominate /inóməneyt/. In the civil law, not named or classed; belonging to no specific class; ranking under a general head. A term applied to those contracts for which no certain or precise remedy was appointed, but a general action on the case only.

Innominate contracts. Literally, are the "unclassified" contracts of Roman law. They are contracts which are neither *re, verbis, literis,* nor *consensu* simply, but some mixture of or variation upon two or more of such contracts. They are principally the contracts of *permutatio, de æstimato, precarium,* and *transactio.*

In nomine Dei, Amen /in nóməniy díyay, èymén/. In the name of God, Amen. A solemn introduction, anciently used in wills and many other instruments. The translation is often used in wills at the present day.

Innotescimus /inətésəməs/. Lat. We make known. A term formerly applied to letters patent, derived from the emphatic word at the conclusion of the Latin forms. It was a species of exemplification of charters of feoffment or other instruments not of record.

In novo casu, novum remedium apponendum est /in nówvow kéys(y)uw, nówvəm rəmíyd(i)yəm æpənéndəm èst/. A new remedy is to be applied to a new case.

Innoxiare /ənòks(h)iyériy/. In old English law, to purge one of a fault and make him innocent.

Inns of Chancery. So called because anciently inhabited by such clerks as chiefly studied the framing of writs, which regularly belonged to the cursitors, who were officers of the Court of Chancery. There were nine of them,—Clement's, Clifford's, and Lyon's Inn; Furnival's, Thavies', and Symond's Inn; New Inn; and Barnard's and Staples' Inn. These were formerly preparatory colleges for students, and many entered them before they were admitted into the inns of court. They consist chiefly of solicitors, and possess corporate property, hall, chambers, etc., but perform no public functions like the inns of court.

Inns of Court. These are certain private unincorporated associations, in the nature of collegiate houses, located in London, and invested with the exclusive privilege of calling men to the bar; that is, conferring the rank or degree of a barrister. They were founded probably about the beginning of the fourteenth century. The principal inns of court are the Inner Temple, Middle Temple, Lincoln's Inn, and Gray's Inn. (The two former originally belonged to the Knights Templar; the two latter to the earls of Lincoln and Gray respectively.) These bodies now have a "common council of legal education," for giving lectures and holding examinations. The inns of chancery, distinguishable from the foregoing, but generally classed with them under the general name, are the buildings known as "Clifford's Inn," "Clement's Inn," "New Inn," "Staples' Inn," and "Barnard's Inn." They were formerly a sort of collegiate houses in which law students learned the elements of law before being admitted into the inns of court, but they have long ceased to occupy that position. The Inns of Court (governed by officers called "benches") hold the exclusive privilege of conferring the degree of barrister-at-law which is required to practice as an advocate or counsel in the superior courts.

In nubibus /in n(y)úwbəbəs/. In the clouds; in abeyance; in custody of law. *In nubibus, in mare, in terrâ, vel in custodiâ legis,* in the air, sea, or earth, or in the custody of the law. In case of abeyance, the inheritance is figuratively said to rest *in nubibus,* or *in gremio legis.*

Innuendo /inyuwéndow/. This Latin word (commonly translated "meaning") was the technical beginning of that clause in a declaration or indictment for slander or libel in which the meaning of the alleged libelous words was explained, or the application of the language charged to the plaintiff was pointed out; hence it gave its name to the whole clause. Indirect or subtle implication in words or expression, usually derogatory.

An "innuendo" in pleading in libel action is a statement by plaintiff of construction which he puts upon words which are alleged to be libelous and which meaning he will induce jury to adopt at trial. Its function is to set a meaning upon words or language of doubtful or ambiguous import which alone would not be actionable.

The word is also used (though more rarely) in other species of pleadings, to introduce an explanation of a preceding word, charge, or averment. Guide Pub. Co. v. Futrell, 175 Va. 77, 7 S.E.2d 133, 138.

In nullius bonis /in nəláyəs bównəs/. Among the goods or property of no person; belonging to no person, as treasure-trove and wreck were anciently considered.

In nullo est erratum /in nálow èst əréydəm/. In nothing is there error. The name of the common plea or joinder in error, denying the existence of error in the record or proceedings; which is in the nature of a demurrer, and at once refers the matter of law arising thereon to the judgment of the court.

**In obscura voluntate manumittentis, favendum est liber-
tati** /ìn əbskyúrə vòləntéydiy mæn(y)əməténdəs,
fəvéndəm èst lìbərtéyday/. Where the expression of
the will of one who seeks to manumit a slave is
ambiguous, liberty is to be favored.

**In obscuris, inspici solere quod verisimilius est, aut quod
plerumque fieri solet** /ìn əbskyúrəs, ínspəsay səlíriy
kwòd vèhrəsəmíliyəs èst, òt kwód plərámkwiy fáyəray
sówlət/. In obscure cases, we usually look at what is
most probable, or what most commonly happens.

In obscuris, quod minimum est sequimur /ìn əbskyúrəs,
kwód mínəmən èst sékwəmər/. In obscure or doubtful cases, we follow that which is the least.

In odium spoliatoris /ìn ówd(i)yəm spòwl(i)yətórəs/. In
hatred of a despoiler, robber, or wrongdoer.

In odium spoliatoris omnia præsumuntur /ìn ówd(i)yəm
spòwl(i)yətórəs ómniyə prìyz(y)əmántər/. To the prejudice (in condemnation) of a despoiler all things are
presumed; every presumption is made against a
wrongdoer.

Inofficiosum /ìnəfis(h)iyówsəm/. In the civil law, inofficious; contrary to natural duty or affection. Used
of a will of a parent which disinherited a child without just cause, or that of a child which disinherited a
parent, and which could be contested by *querela
inofficiosi testamenti.*

Inofficious testament /ìnəfíshəs téstəmənt/. A will not
in accordance with the testator's natural affection
and moral duties. But particularly, in the civil law, a
will which deprives the heirs of that portion of the
estate to which they law entitles them, and of which
they cannot legally be disinherited. A testament contrary to the natural duty of the parent, because it
totally disinherited the child, without expressly giving
the reason therefor.

Inofficiocidad /ìnowfiysiyòwsiyòðád/. In Spanish law,
everything done contrary to a duty or obligation assumed, as well as in opposition to the piety and
affection dictated by nature: *inofficiosum dicitur id
omne quod contra pietatis officium factum est.* The
term applies especially to testaments, donations,
dower, etc., which may be either revoked or reduced
when they affect injuriously the rights of creditors or
heirs.

**In omni actione ubi duæ concurrunt districtiones, vide-
licet, in rem et in personam, illa districtio tenenda est
quæ magis timetur et magis ligat** /ìn ómnay
æ̀kshiyówniy yúwbay d(y)úwiy kənkáhrənt
distrìkshiyówniyz, vàydiylísəd in rém èt in
pərsównəm, ílə distríksh(iy)ow tənéndə èst kwìy
méyjəs təmíydər èt méyjəs lígət/. In every action
where two distresses concur, that is, *in rem* and *in
personam,* that is to be chosen which is most dread-
ed, and which binds most firmly.

In omnibus /ìn ómnəbəs/. In all things; on all points.
"A case parallel *in omnibus.*"

**In omnibus contractibus, sive nominatis sive innomina-
tis, permutatio continetur** /ìn ómnəbəs kəntrǽtəbəs,
sáyviy nòmənéydəs sáyviy ínomənéydəs, pə̀rmyuw-
téysh(iy)ow kòntəníydər/. In all contracts, whether
nominate or innominate, an exchange [of value, *i.e.*, a
consideration] is implied.

**In omnibus obligationibus in quibus dies non ponitur,
præsenti die debetur** /ìn ómnəbəs òbləgèyshiyównəbəs
ìn kwíbəs dáyiz nòn pównədər, prəzéntay dáyiy
dəbíydər/. In all obligations in which a date is not
put, the debt is due on the present day; the liability
accrues immediately.

**In omnibus [fere] pœnalibus judiciis, et ætati et impru-
dentiæ succurritur** /ìn ómnəbəs (fíriy) pənéyləbəs
jədíshiyəs, èd ətéyday èd impruwdénshiy(iy)
səkáhrədər/. In nearly all penal judgments, immaturi-
ty of age and imbecility of mind are favored.

**In omnibus quidem, maxime tamen in jure, æquitas
spectanda sit** /ìn ómnəbəs kwáydəm mǽksəmiy
téymən ìn júriy, íykwətæs spèktǽndə sìt/. In all
things, but especially in law, equity is to be regarded.

In omni re nascitur res quæ ipsam rem exterminat /ìn
ómnay ríy nǽsədər ríyz kwìy ípsəm rém əkstár-
mənət/. In everything there arises a thing which
destroys the thing itself. Everything contains the
element of its own destruction.

Inops consilii /ínops kən(t)síliyay/. Lat. Destitute of
counsel; without legal counsel. A term applied to
the acts or condition of one acting without legal
advice, as a testator drafting his own will.

Inordinatus /inòrdənéydəs/. An intestate.

In pacato solo /ìn pəkéydow sówlow/. In a country
which is at peace.

In pace Dei et regis /ìn péysiy díyay èt ríyjəs/. In the
peace of God and the king. Formal words in old
appeals of murder.

In pais /ìn péy(s)/. This phrase, as applied to a legal
transaction, primarily means that it has taken place
without legal proceedings. Thus a widow was said to
make a request *in pais* for her dower when she
simply applied to the heir without issuing a writ. So
conveyances are divided into those by matter of record and those by matter *in pais.* In some cases,
however, "matters *in pais*" are opposed not only to
"matters of record," but also to "matters in writing,"
i.e., deeds, as where estoppel by deed is distinguished
from estoppel by matter *in pais.* See also **Pais.**

In pais, estoppel /əstópəl ìn péy(s)/. An estoppel not
arising from deed or record or written contract. The
doctrine is that a person may be precluded by his act
or conduct or silence, when it is his duty to speak,
from asserting a right which he otherwise would have
had. Marshall v. Wilson, 175 Or. 506, 154 P.2d 547,
551. The effect of a party's voluntary conduct
whereby ‚he is precluded from asserting rights as
against another person who has in good faith relied
upon such conduct and has been led thereby to
change his condition for the worse and who acquires
some corresponding right of property or contract.
Oswego Falls Corporation v. City of Fulton, 148 Misc.
170, 265 N.Y.S. 436.

Elements or fundamentals of "estoppel in pais"
include admission, statement, or act inconsistent with
claim afterwards asserted, National Match Co. v. Empire Storage & Ice Co., 227 Mo.App. 1115, 58 S.W.2d
797; change of position to loss or injury of party
claiming estoppel, Malloy v. City of Chicago, 369 Ill.
97, 15 N.E.2d 861, 865; circumstances such that par-

ty estopped knew or should have known facts to be otherwise or pretended to know facts which he did not know; false representation or concealment of material facts, Pickens v. Maryland Casualty Co., 141 Neb. 105, 2 N.W.2d 593, 596; inducement to alter position; intention that false representation or concealment be acted on, Malloy v. City of Chicago, 369 Ill. 97, 15 N.E.2d 861, 865; Peterson v. City of Parsons, 139 Kan. 701, 33 P.2d 715, 720; knowledge of facts, by party to be estopped, Darling Stores v. Fidelity-Bankers Trust Co., 178 Tenn. 165, 156 S.W.2d 419, 424; Peterson v. City of Parsons, 139 Kan. 701, 33 P.2d 715, 720; lack of knowledge or means of knowledge of party claiming estoppel, Sinclair Refining Co. v. Jenkins Petroleum Process Co., C.C.A.Me., 99 F.2d 9, 13, 14; misleading of one person by another person to his prejudice or injury, Garmon v. Davis, 63 Ga.App. 815, 12 S.E.2d 209, 211; Current News Features v. Pulitzer Pub. Co., C.C.A. Mo., 81 F.2d 288, 292; prejudice or loss or injury to party claiming estoppel, City of St. Louis v. Mississippi River Fuel Corporation, D.C.Mo., 57 F.Supp. 549, 554; In re Bremer's Estate, 141 Neb. 251, 3 N.W.2d 411, 413, 414; reliance by one party on belief induced by other party, Strand v. State, 16 Wash.2d 107, 132 P.2d 1011, 1016.

See also **Equitable estoppel.**

In paper. In old English law, a term formerly applied to the proceedings in a cause before the record was made up. Probably from the circumstance of the record being always on parchment. The opposite of "on record."

In pari causa /ìn pǽray kózə/°péray°/. In an equal cause. In a cause where the parties on each side have equal rights.

In pari causa possessor potior haberi debet /ìn pǽray kózə pəzésər pówsh(iy)ər həbíray débət/. In an equal cause he who has the possession should be preferred.

In pari delicto /ìn pǽray dəlíktow/°péray°/. In equal fault; equally culpable or criminal; in a case of equal fault or guilt. A person who is *in pari delicto* with another differs from a *particeps criminis* in this, that the former term always includes the latter, but the latter does not always include the former.

In pari delicto potior est conditio possidentis [defendentis] /ìn pǽray dəlíktow pówsh(iy)ər èst kəndísh(iy)ow pòsədéntəs/°dəfèndéntəs/. In a case of equal or mutual fault [between two parties] the condition of the party in possession [or defending] is the better one. Where each party is equally in fault, the law favors him who is actually in possession. Where the fault is mutual, the law will leave the case as it finds it.

In pari materia /ìn pǽray mətír(i)yə/. Upon the same matter or subject. Statutes *in pari materia* are to be construed together. "Statutes in pari materia" are those relating to the same person or thing or having a common purpose. Undercofler v. L. C. Robinson & Sons, Inc., 111 Ga.App. 411, 141 S.E.2d 847, 849.

In patiendo /ìn pæshiyéndow/. In suffering, permitting, or allowing.

In pectore judicis /ìn péktəriy júwdəsəs/. In the breast of the judge. A phrase applied to a judgment.

In pejorem partem /ìn pəjórəm párdəm/. In the worst part; on the worst side.

Inpeny and outpeny /ínpeniy ǽnd áwtpeniy/. In old English law, a customary payment of a penny on entering into and going out of a tenancy (*pro exitu de tenura, et pro ingressu*).

In perpetuam rei memoriam /ìn pərpéchuwəm ríyay məmóriyəm/. In perpetual memory of a matter; for preserving a record of a matter. Applied to depositions taken in order to preserve the testimony of the deponent.

In perpetuity /ìn pərpəchúwədiy/. Endless duration; forever.

In perpetuum rei testimonium /ìn pərpéchuwəm ríyay tèstəmówn(i)yəm/. In perpetual testimony of a matter; for the purpose of declaring and settling a thing forever.

In person. A party, plaintiff or defendant, who sues out a complaint, writ or other process, or appears to conduct his case in court himself, instead of through a solicitor or counsel, is said to act and appear *in person*. See Pro se.

In personam /ìn pərsównəm/. Against the person. Action seeking judgment against a person involving his personal rights and based on jurisdiction of his person, as distinguished from a judgment against property (*i.e.* in rem). Type of jurisdiction or power which a court may acquire over the defendant himself in contrast to jurisdiction over his property. See also **In personam jurisdiction; In rem; Jurisdiction in personam.**

In personam actio est, qua cum eo agimus qui obligatus est nobis ad faciendum aliquid vel dandum /ìn pərsównəm ǽksh(iy)ow èst, kwéy kèm íyow ǽjəməs kwày òbləgéydəs èst nówbəs æd fèys(h)iyéndəm ǽləkwìd vèl dǽndəm/. The action *in personam* is that by which we sue him who is under obligation to us to do something or give something.

In personam jurisdiction. Power which a court has over the defendant himself in contrast to the court's power over the defendant's interest in property (quasi in rem) or power over the property itself (in rem). A court which lacks personal jurisdiction is without power to issue an in personam judgment. Pennoyer v. Neff, 95 U.S. 714, 24 L.Ed. 565. See also **In rem; Jurisdiction in personam.**

In pios usus /ìn páyəs yúwzəs/. For pious uses; for religious purposes. 2 Bl.Comm. 505.

In plena vita /ìn plíynə váydə/. In full life.

In pleno comitatu /ìn plíynow kòmətéyd(y)uw/. In full county court. 3 Bl.Comm. 36.

In pleno lumine /ìn plíynow l(y)úwməniy/. In public; in common knowledge; in the light of day.

In pœnalibus causis benignius interpretandum est /ìn pənéyləbəs kózəs bənígn(i)yəs intòrprətǽndəm èst/. In penal causes or cases, the more favorable interpretation should be adopted.

In posse /ìn pósiy/. In possibility; not in actual existence. See **In esse.**

In potestate parentis /ìn pòwdəstéydiy pəréntəs/. In the power of a parent. 2 Bl.Comm. 498.

In præmissorum fidem /ìn prèməsórəm fáydəm/. In confirmation or attestation of the premises. A notarial phrase.

In præparatoriis ad judicium favetur actori /ìn prèpərətóriyəs æd juwdísh(iy)əm fəvíydər æktóray/. In things preceding judgment the plaintiff is favored.

In præsenti /ìn prəzéntay/. At the present time. 2 Bl.Comm. 166. Used in opposition to *in futuro.* Van Wyck v. Knevals, 106 U.S. 360, 1 S.Ct. 336, 27 L.Ed. 201.

In præsentia majoris potestatis, minor potestas cessat /ìn prəzénsh(iy)ə məjórəs pòwdəstéydəs, máynər pətéstæs sésət/. In the presence of the superior power, the inferior power ceases. The less authority is merged in the greater.

In prender /ìn préndər/. L. Fr. In taking. A term applied to such incorporeal hereditaments as a party entitled to them was to *take* for himself; such as common. 3 Bl.Comm. 15. See **In render.**

In pretio emptionis et venditionis, naturaliter licet contrahentibus se circumvenire /ìn présh(iy)ow ém(p)sh(iy)ównəs èt vəndishiyównəs, næchəréylədər láysət kòntrəhéntəbəs síy sàrkəmvənáyriy/. In the price of buying and selling, it is naturally allowed to the contracting parties to overreach each other.

In primis /ìn práyməs/ìmpr°/. In the first place. A phrase used in argument.

In principio /ìn prənsíp(i)yow/. At the beginning.

In promptu /ìn próm(p)t(y)uw/ìmpr°/. In readiness; at hand. Usually written impromptu.

In propria causa nemo judex /ìn prówpriyə kózə níymow júwdəks/. No one can be judge in his own cause.

In propria persona /ìn prówpriyə pərsównə/. In one's own proper person. It was formerly a rule in pleading that pleas to the jurisdiction of the court must be plead *in propria persona,* because if pleaded by attorney they admit the jurisdiction, as an attorney is an officer of the court, and he is presumed to plead after having obtained leave, which admits the jurisdiction. See **Pro se.**

Inquest. The inquiry by a coroner or medical examiner, sometimes with the aid of a jury, into the manner of the death of any one who has been slain, or has died suddenly or by violence or in prison.

A body of men appointed by law to inquire into certain matters. The grand jury is sometimes called the "grand inquest." The judicial inquiry made by a jury summoned for the purpose is called an "inquest." The finding of such men, upon an investigation, is also called an "inquest."

See also **Inquisition.**

Coroner's inquest. See **Coroner.**

Inquest, arrest of. See **Arrest.**

Inquest jury. See **Jury.**

Inquest of office. In old English practice, an inquiry made by the king's (or the queen's) officer, his sheriff, coroner, or escheator, *virtute officii,* or by writ sent to them for that purpose, or by commissioners specially appointed, concerning any matter that entitles the king to the possession of lands or tenements, goods or chattels; as to inquire whether the king's tenant for life died seised, whereby the reversion accrues to the king; whether A., who held immediately of the crown, died without heir, in which case the lands belong to the king by escheat; whether B. be attainted of treason, whereby his estate is forfeited to the crown; whether C., who has purchased land, be an alien, which is another cause of forfeiture, etc. 3 Bl.Comm. 258. These *inquests of office* were most frequent in practice during the continuance of the military tenures; and were devised by law as an authentic means to give the king his right by solemn matter of record. Id. 258, 259. Sometimes simply termed *"office,"* as in the phrase "office found" *(q.v.).* Atlantic & P. R. Co. v. Mingus, 165 U.S. 413, 17 S.Ct. 348, 41 L.Ed. 770.

Inquilinus /ìnkwəláynəs/. In Roman law, a tenant; one who hires and occupies another's house; but particularly, a tenant of a hired house in a city, as distinguished from *colonus,* the hirer of a house or estate in the country.

Inquirendo /ìŋkwəréndow/. An authority given to some official person to institute an inquiry concerning the crown's interests.

Inquiry court. See **Court of inquiry; Inquest.**

Inquiry, writ of. A common law writ (now obsolete), sued out by a plaintiff in a case where the defendant had let the proceedings go by default, and an interlocutory judgment had been given for damages generally, where the damages did not admit of calculation. It issued to the sheriff of the county in which the *venue* was laid, and commanded him to inquire, by a jury of twelve men, concerning the amount of damages. The sheriff thereupon tried the cause in his sheriff's court, and some amount was always returned to the court. But the return of the inquest merely informed the court, which could, if it chose, in all cases assess damages and thereupon give final judgment.

Inquisitio /ìŋkwəzísh(iy)ow/. In old English law, an inquisition or inquest. *Inquisitio post mortem,* an inquisition after death. An inquest of office held, during the continuance of the military tenures, upon the death of every one of the king's tenants, to inquire of what lands he died seised, who was his heir, and of what age, in order to entitle the king to his marriage, wardship, relief, primer seisin, or other advantages, as the circumstances of the case might turn out. 3 Bl.Comm. 258. *Inquisitio patriæ,* the inquisition of the country; the ordinary jury, as distinguished from the grand assise.

Inquisition /ìnkwəzíshən/. An inquiry or inquest; particularly, an investigation of certain facts made by a sheriff, together with a jury impaneled by him for the purpose. The instrument of writing on which their decision is made is also called an inquisition. In its broadest sense, "inquisition," includes any judicial inquiry. See **Inquest.**

Inquisition after death. See **Inquest; Inquisitio.**

Inquisitor /ənkwízədər/. A designation of sheriffs, coroners *super visum corporis,* and the like, who have power to inquire into certain matters.

In Ecclesiastical law, the name of an officer who is authorized to inquire into heresies, and the like, and to punish them. A judge.

In quo quis delinquit, in eo de jure est puniendus /ìn kwów kwís dəlíŋkwət, ìn íyow dìy júriy èst pyùwniyéndəs/. In whatever thing one offends, in that is he rightfully to be punished. The punishment shall have relation to the nature of the offense.

In re /ìn ríy/. In the affair; in the matter of; concerning; regarding. This is the usual method of entitling a judicial proceeding in which there are not adversary parties, but merely some *res* concerning which judicial action is to be taken, such as a bankrupt's estate, an estate in the probate court, a proposed public highway, etc. It is also sometimes used as a designation of a proceeding where one party makes an application on his own behalf, but such proceedings are more usually entitled *"Ex parte ____."*

In rebus /ìn ríybəs/. (Lat.) In things, cases, or matters.

In rebus manifestis, errat qui auctoritates legum allegat; quia perspicua vera non sunt probanda /ìn ríybəs mænəféstəs, éhrət kwày octòrətéydiyz líygəm ǽləgət; kwáyə pərspíkyuwə vírə nón sònt prəbǽndə/. In clear cases, he mistakes who cites legal authorities; for obvious truths are not to be proved. Applied to cases too plain to require the support of authority; "because," says the report, "he who endeavors to prove them obscures them."

In rebus quæ sunt favorabilia animæ, quamvis sunt damnosa rebus, fiat aliquando extensio statuti /ìn ríybəs kwìy sònt fèyvərəbíl(iy)ə ǽnəmiy, kwǽmvəs sònt dæmnówsə ríybəs, fáyəd ǽləkwǽndow əksténsh(iy)ow stətyúwday/. In things that are favorable to the spirit, though injurious to things, an extension of a statute should sometimes be made.

In re communi melior est conditio prohibentis /ìn ríy kəmyúwnay míyl(i)yər èst kəndísh(iy)ow pròwhəbéntəs/. In common property the condition of the one prohibiting is the better. In other words, either co-owner has a right of veto against the acts of the other. Gulf Refining Co. of Louisiana v. Carroll, 145 La. 299, 82 So. 277, 279.

In re communi neminem dominorum jure facere quicquam, invito altero, posse /ìn ríy kəmyúwnay némənəm dòmənórəm júriy féysəriy kwáykwəm, ənváydow óltərow, pósiy/. One co-proprietor can exercise no authority over the common property against the will of the other. In other words, either co-owner has a right of veto against the acts of the other.

In re communi potior est conditio prohibentis /ìn ríy kəmyúwnay pówsh(iy)ər èst kəndísh(iy)ow pròwhəbéntəs/. In a partnership the condition of one who forbids is the more favorable.

In re dubia, benigniorem interpretationem sequi, non minus justius est quam tutius /ìn ríy d(y)úwbiyə, bənìgniyórəm əntèrprətèyshiyównəm sékway, nòn máynəs jǽst(i)yəs èst kwǽm tyúwsh(iy)əs/. In a doubtful matter, to follow the more liberal interpretation is not less the juster than the safer course.

In re dubia, magis inficiatio quam affirmatio intelligenda /ìn ríy d(y)úwbiyə, méyjəs ənfis(h)iyéysh(iy)ow kwǽm ǽfərméysh(iy)ow əntèləjéndə/. In a doubtful matter, the denial or negative is to be understood [or regarded], rather than the affirmative.

In regard to /ìn rəgárd tùw/. Concerning; relating to; in respect of; with respect to; about. Hart v. Hart, 181 Iowa 527, 164 N.W. 849, 850.

In re lupanari, testes lupanares admittentur /ìn ríy l(y)ùwpənéray, téstiyz l(y)ùwpənériyz ǽdməténtər/. In a matter concerning a brothel, prostitutes are admitted as witnesses.

In rem /ìn rém/. A technical term used to designate proceedings or actions instituted *against the thing,* in contradistinction to personal actions, which are said to be *in personam.*

An "action in rem" is a proceeding that takes no cognizance of owner but determines right in specific property against all of the world, equally binding on everyone. Flesch v. Circle City Excavating & Rental Corp., 137 Ind.App. 695, 210 N.E.2d 865, 868. It is true that, in a strict sense, a proceeding *in rem* is one taken directly against property, and has for its object the disposition of property, without reference to the title of individual claimants; but, in a larger and more general sense, the terms are applied to actions between parties, where the direct object is to reach and dispose of property owned by them, or of some interest therein. Such are cases commenced by attachment against the property of debtors, or instituted to partition real estate, foreclose a mortgage, or enforce a lien. Pennoyer v. Neff, 95 U.S. 714, 24 L.Ed. 565. In the strict sense of the term, a proceeding "in rem" is one which is taken directly against property or one which is brought to enforce a right in the thing itself.

Actions in which the court is required to have control of the thing or object and in which an adjudication is made as to the object which binds the whole world and not simply the interests of the parties to the proceeding. Flesch v. Circle City Excavating & Rental Corp., 137 Ind.App. 695, 210 N.E.2d 865.

See also **In personam; In rem jurisdiction; Quasi in rem.**

Judgment in rem. See that title.

Quasi in rem. A term applied to proceedings which are not strictly and purely *in rem,* but are brought against the defendant personally, though the real object is to deal with particular property or subject property to the discharge of claims asserted; for example, foreign attachment, or proceedings to foreclose a mortgage, remove a cloud from title, or effect a partition. Freeman v. Alderson, 119 U.S. 185, 7 S.Ct. 165, 30 L.Ed. 372. An action in which the basis of jurisdiction is the defendant's interest in property, real or personal, which is within the court's power, as distinguished from in rem jurisdiction in which the court exercises power over the property itself, not simply the defendant's interest therein.

In rem actio est per quam rem nostram quæ ab alio possidetur petimus, et semper adversus eum est qui

rem possidet. The action *in rem* is that by which we seek our property which is possessed by another, and is always against him who possesses the property.

In rem jurisdiction. Power over a thing possessed by a court which allows it to seize and hold the object for some legal purpose; *e.g.* boat on which narcotics are found. Calero Toledo v. Pearson Yacht Leasing Co., 416 U.S. 663, 94 S.Ct. 2080, 40 L.Ed.2d 452. See also **Jurisdiction in rem; Jurisdiction quasi in rem.**

In rem mortgage. Foreclosure of mortgage is in the nature of an in rem proceeding but it approximates more closely a quasi in rem action because it is directed to the extinguishment of the rights of mortgagor as well as all others.

In render. A thing is said to lie *in render* when it must be rendered or given by the tenant; as rent. It is said to lie *in prender* when it consists in the right in the lord or other person to *take* something. See **In prender.**

In re pari potiorem causam esse prohibentis constat /ìn ríy péray pòwshiyórəm kózəm ésiy pròwhəbéntəs kónstət/. In a thing equally shared [by several] it is clear that the party refusing [to permit the use of it] has the better cause. A maxim applied to partnerships, where one partner has a right to withhold his assent to the acts of his copartner.

In re propria iniquum admodum est alicui licentiam tribuere sententiæ /ìn ríy prówpriyə ənáykwəm ǽdmədəm èst ǽlək(yuw)ay ləsénsh(iy)əm trəbyúwəriy senténshiy(iy)/. It is extremely unjust that any one should be judge in his own cause.

In republica maxime conservanda sunt jura belli /ìn rəpábləkə mǽksəmiy kònsərvǽndə sànt júrə bélay/. In a state the laws of war are to be especially upheld.

In rerum natura /ìn rírəm nəchúrə/. In the nature of things; in the realm of actuality; in existence. In a dilatory plea, an allegation that the plaintiff is not *in rerum natura* is equivalent to averring that the person named is fictitious. 3 Bl.Comm. 301.

In respect of decedent. See **Income in respect of decedent.**

In restitutionem, non in pœnam hæres succedit /ìn rèstət(y)ùwshiyównəm, nón ìn píynəm híriyz səksíydət/. The heir succeeds to the restitution, not to the penalty. An heir may be compelled to make restitution of a sum unlawfully appropriated by the ancestor, but is not answerable criminally, as for a penalty.

In restitutionibus benignissima interpretatio facienda est /ìn rèstət(y)ùwshiyównəbəs bènəgnísəmə intàrprətéysh(iy)ow fèys(h)iyéndə èst/. The most benignant interpretation is to be made in restitutions.

Inroll. A form of "enroll," used in the old books. See **Enroll.**

Inrollment. See **Enrollment.**

I.N.S. Immigration and Naturalization Service.

Insane delusion. An "insane delusion" is a conception of a disordered mind which imagines facts to exist of which there is no evidence and belief in which is adhered to against all evidence and argument to contrary, and which cannot be accounted for on any reasonable hypothesis. In re Nigro's Estate, 243 Cal. App.2d 152, 52 Cal.Rptr. 128, 133.

Insanity. The term is a social and legal term rather than a medical one, and indicates a condition which renders the affected person unfit to enjoy liberty of action because of the unreliability of his behavior with concomitant danger to himself and others. The term is more or less synonymous with mental illness or psychosis. In law, the term is used to denote that degree of mental illness which negates the individual's legal responsibility or capacity.

Insanity as Defense to Crime

There are various tests used by the courts to determine criminal responsibility, or lack thereof, of a defendant who asserts the defense that he or she was insane at the time of the crime. The test as provided in Section 4.01 of the Model Penal Code is as follows: "A person is not responsible for criminal conduct if at the time of such conduct as a result of mental disease or defect he lacks substantial capacity either to appreciate the criminality (wrongfulness) of his conduct or to conform his conduct to the requirements of law." This test, as defined by the American Law Institute, has been adopted (sometimes with slight modifications) by a number of states and also in the various Federal Courts of Appeal.

If a defendant intends to rely upon the defense of insanity at the time of the alleged crime, he is required to notify the attorney for the government of such intention. Fed.R.Crim.P. 12.2.

See also Automatism; Diminished responsibility doctrine; Durham rule; Irresistible impulse; M'Naghten Rule; and Right and wrong test, for various other tests used by courts to determine criminal responsibility of defendant who asserts insanity defense. See also Competency; Incompetency; Insane delusion; Lucid interval; Lunacy; Melancholia; Sanity hearing; Substantial capacity; Uncontrollable impulse.

Insanity as Affecting Capacity

Capacity to make a will includes an intelligent understanding of the testator's property, its extent and items, and of the nature of the act he is about to perform, together with a clear understanding and purpose as to the manner of its distribution and the persons who are to receive it. Lacking these, the testator is not mentally competent. The presence of insane delusions is not inconsistent with testamentary capacity, if they are of such a nature that they cannot reasonably be supposed to have affected the dispositions made by the will; and the same is true of the various forms of monomania and of all kinds of eccentricity and personal idiosyncrasy. But imbecility, senile dementia, and all forms of systematized mania which affect the understanding and judgment generally disable the person from making a valid will. To constitute "senile dementia," incapacitating one to make a will, there must be such a failure of the mind as to deprive the testator of intelligent action. See also **Capacity.**

As a ground for voiding or annulling a contract or conveyance, insanity does not mean a total deprivation of reason, but an inability, from defect of perception, memory, and judgment, to do the act in question or to understand its nature and consequences. The insanity must have entered into and induced the particular contract or conveyance; it must appear that it was not the act of the free and untrammeled mind, and that on account of the diseased condition of the mind the person entered into a contract or made a conveyance which he would not have made if he had been in the possession of his reason.

Most state statutes provide for annulment of a marriage because of insanity. Insanity sufficient to justify the annulment of a marriage means such a want of understanding at the time of the marriage as to render the party incapable of assenting to the contract of marriage. Also, under most state statutes, insanity, if sufficient in degree and/or duration, constitutes a ground for divorce. In general, the same degree of mental capacity which enables a person to make a valid deed or will is sufficient to enable him to marry.

As a ground for restraining the personal liberty of the person (i.e. commitment), it may be said in general that the form of insanity from which he suffers should be such as to make his going at large a source of danger to himself or to others, though this matter is largely regulated by statute, and in many places the law permits the commitment of persons whose insanity does not manifest itself in homicidal or other destructive forms of mania, but who are incapable of caring for themselves and their property or who are simply fit subjects for treatment in hospitals and other institutions specially designed for the care of such patients. See **Commitment.**

To constitute insanity such as will authorize the appointment of a guardian or conservator, there must be such a deprivation of reason and judgment as to render him incapable of understanding and acting with discretion in the ordinary affairs of life; a want of sufficient mental capacity to transact ordinary business and to take care of and manage his property and affairs.

Insanity as a plea or proceeding to avoid the effect of the statute of limitations means practically the same thing as in relation to the appointment of a guardian. On the one hand, it does not require a total deprivation of reason or absence of understanding. On the other hand, it does not include mere weakness of mind short of imbecility. It means such a degree of derangement as renders the subject incapable of understanding the nature of the particular affair and his rights and remedies in regard to it and incapable of taking discreet and intelligent action. The time of sanity required in order to allow the statute to begin to run is such as will enable the party to examine his affairs and institute an action, and is for the jury.

There are a few other legal rights or relations into which the question of insanity enters, such as the capacity of a witness or of a voter; but they are governed by the same general principles. The test is capacity to understand and appreciate the nature of the particular act and to exercise intelligence in its performance. A witness must understand the nature and purpose of an oath and have enough intelligence and memory to relate correctly the facts within his knowledge. So a voter must understand the nature of the act to be performed and be able to make an intelligent choice of candidates. In either case, eccentricity, feeble-mindedness not amounting to imbecility, or insane delusions which do not affect the matter in hand, do not disqualify. District of Columbia v. Armes, 107 U.S. 519, 2 S.Ct. 840, 27 L.Ed. 618.

Insanus est qui, abjecta ratione, omnia cum impetu et furore facit /inséynəs èst kwáy əbjéktə rèyshiyówniy ómniyə kàm ímpəduw èt fyəróriy féysət/. He is insane who, reason being thrown away, does everything with violence and rage.

In satisfactionibus non permittitur amplius fieri quam semel factum est /ìn sædəsfækshiyównəbəs nòn pərmídədər æmpliyəs fáyəray kwæm séməl fæktəm èst/. In payments, more must not be received than has been received once for all.

Inscribed. Entered (e.g. a name) on a list or in a register. Type of government bonds, such as Series E, whose records are kept by the Federal Reserve Bank rather than by the Treasury Dept.

Inscribere /inskríbəriy/. Lat. In the civil law, to subscribe an accusation. To bind one's self, in case of failure to prove an accusation, to suffer the same punishment which the accused would have suffered had he been proved guilty.

Inscriptio /inskrípsh(iy)ow/. Lat. In the civil law, a written accusation in which the accuser undertakes to suffer the punishment appropriate to the offense charged, if the accused is able to clear himself of the accusation.

Inscription. In evidence, anything written or engraved upon a metallic or other solid substance, intended for great durability; as upon a tombstone, pillar, tablet, medal, ring, etc.

The entry of a mortgage, lien, or other document at large in a book of public records; corresponding to "recording" or "registration."

In civil law, an engagement which a person who makes a solemn accusation of a crime against another enters into that he will suffer the same punishment, if he has accused the other falsely, which would have been inflicted upon him had he been guilty.

Inscriptiones /inskrìpshiyówniyz/. The name given by the old English law to any written instrument by which anything was granted.

Insecure. Unsafe and dangerous. Not secure or safe; not certain. Impairment or loss of security. See **Acceleration clause; Insecurity clause.**

Insecurity clause. Provision in contract that allows a creditor to make an entire debt come due if there is good reason to believe that the debtor cannot or will not pay. See also **Acceleration clause.**

In separali /ìn sèpəréylay/. In several; in severalty.

Insider. With respect to federal regulation of purchase and sale of securities, refers to anyone who has knowledge of facts not available to the general public. 15 U.S.C.A. § 78p(a). See also Insider information; Insider reports; Insider trading; Rule 10b–5; Short swing profits; Tippees.

Insider as contemplated in bankruptcy proceedings is defined in Bankruptcy Act, § 101(25).

Insider information. Information about a company's financial situation that is obtained before the public obtains it. True inside information is usually only known by corporate officials or other "insiders." See also **Insider.**

Insider reports. Monthly reports required by Securities and Exchange Commission from directors, officers and stockholders of their transactions in stock of which they own more than 10% of such shares.

Insider trading. Buying and selling of corporate shares by officers, directors and stockholders who own more than 10% of the stock of a corporation listed on a national exchange. Such transactions must be reported monthly to Securities and Exchange Commission. See also **Insider reports.**

Insidiatores viarum /insìdiyətóriyz vayérəm/. Lat. Highwaymen; persons who lie in wait in order to commit some felony or other misdemeanor.

Insignia /insígn(i)yə/. Ensigns or arms; distinctive marks; badges; *indicia;* characteristics.

Insiliarius /insìliyériyəs/. An evil counsellor.

Insilium /insíl(i)yəm/. Evil advice or counsel.

In simili materia /in símələy mətír(i)yə/. Dealing with the same or a kindred subject-matter.

Insimul /ínsəməl/. Lat. Together; jointly.

Insimul computassent /ínsəməl kòmpyətǽsənt/. They accounted together. In common law pleading, the name of the count in *assumpsit* upon an account stated; it being averred that the parties had settled their accounts together, and defendant engaged to pay plaintiff the balance.

Insimul tenuit /ínsəməl tényuwət/. One species of the writ of *formedon* brought against a stranger by a coparcener on the possession of the ancestor, etc.

Insinuacion /iynsìynuwasyówn/. In Spanish law, the presentation of a public document to a competent judge, in order to obtain his approbation and sanction of the same, and thereby give it judicial authenticity. Escriche.

Insinuare /insìnyuwériy/. Lat. In the civil law, to put into; to deposit a writing in court, answering nearly to the modern expression "to file." *Si non mandatum actis insinuatum est,* if the power or authority be not deposited among the records of the court. To declare or acknowledge before a judicial officer; to give an act an official form.

Insinuatio /insìnyuwéysh(iy)ow/. Lat. In old English law, information or suggestion. *Ex insinuatione,* on the information.

Insinuation. To hint or suggest doubt or suspicion.

In the civil law, the transcription of an act on the public registers like our recording of deeds. It was not necessary in any other alienation but that appropriated to the purpose of donation.

Insinuation of a will. In the civil law, the first production of a will, or the leaving it with the registrar, in order to its probate.

In solido /ìn sólədow/. In the civil law, for the whole; as a whole. An obligation *in solido* is one where each of the several obligors is liable for the whole; that is, it is joint and several. Henderson v. Wadsworth, 115 U.S. 264, 6 S.Ct. 40, 29 L.Ed. 377. Possession *in solidum* is exclusive possession. When several persons obligate themselves to the obligee by the terms *"in solido,"* or use any other expressions which clearly show that they intend that each one shall be separately bound to perform the whole of the obligation, it is called an "obligation *in solido"* on the part of the obligors.

In solidum /ìn sólədəm/. For the whole. *Si plures sint fidejussores, quotquot erunt numero, singuli in solidum tenentur,* if there be several sureties, however numerous they may be, they are individually bound for the whole debt. *In parte sive in solidum,* for a part or for the whole.

In solo /ìn sówlow/. In the soil or ground. *In solo alieno,* in another's ground. *In solo proprio,* in one's own ground.

Insolvency. The condition of a person who is insolvent; inability to pay one's debts; lack of means to pay one's debts. Such a relative condition of a man's assets and liabilities that the former, if all made immediately available, would not be sufficient to discharge the latter. Or the condition of a person who is unable to pay his debts as they fall due, or in the usual course of trade and business. Adams v. Richardson, Mo., 337 S.W.2d 911, 916. In general, state insolvency laws have been superseded by the Federal Bankruptcy Act. See **Bankruptcy.**

"Insolvency" under the Bankruptcy Act is defined in § 101(26).

Under U.C.C., a person is insolvent who either has ceased to pay his debts in the ordinary course of business or cannot pay his debts as they fall due or is insolvent within the meaning of the Federal Bankruptcy Law. U.C.C. § 1–201(23).

In specie /ìn spíys(h)iy(iy)/. Specific; specifically. Thus, to decree performance *in specie* is to decree specific performance. In kind; in the same or like form. A thing is said to exist *in specie* when it retains its existence as a distinct individual of a particular class.

Inspectator. A prosecutor or adversary.

Inspection. To examine; scrutinize; investigate; look into; check over; or view for the purpose of ascertaining the quality, authenticity or conditions of an item, product, document, residence, business, etc. See also **Freedom of Information Act; In camera inspection; Privacy Acts.**

Discovery practice. Rights of parties in civil actions to inspect papers, documents, land, etc. of opposing party are governed by Fed.R. Civil P. 26 and 34. Similar rights of prosecutor and defendant in criminal cases are governed by Fed.R.Crim.P. 16. See also **Inspection of documents; Jencks Act.**

Reasonable inspection. As relates to duty of employer to provide employee with proper instrumentalities with which to work, does not mean such an inspection as would necessarily or infallibly disclose a defect if one existed, but only such inspection as reasonably prudent man, in the exercise of ordinary care, would make.

Inspection laws. Laws authorizing and directing the inspection and examination of various kinds of merchandise intended for sale, especially food, with a view to ascertaining its fitness for use, and excluding unwholesome or unmarketable goods from sale, and directing the appointment of official inspectors for that purpose; *e.g.* grain or meat inspection laws. Patapsco Guano Co. v. Board of Agriculture, 171 U.S. 345, 18 S.Ct. 862, 43 L.Ed. 191. State and federal inspection laws may also be concerned with employment safety conditions (*e.g.* Occupational Safety and Health Act (OSHA)); building construction safety (*e.g.* building ordinances); health conditions of restaurants or food processors; and safety conditions of motor vehicles.

If a resident refuses permission to a fire, health, building, etc. inspector to inspect the premises, a search warrant will be required. Camara v. Municipal Court of etc. San Francisco, 387 U.S. 523, 87 S.Ct. 1727, 18 L.Ed.2d 930. A warrant is likewise required for inspection of business premises by OSHA inspectors. Marshall v. Barlow's, Inc., 436 U.S. 307, 98 S.Ct. 1816, 56 L.Ed.2d 305.

See also **Freedom of Information Act; Privacy Act.**

Inspection of documents. This phrase refers to the right of a party, in a civil action, to inspect and make copies of documents which are essential or material to the maintenance of his cause, and which are either in the custody of an officer of the law or in the possession of the adverse party. Fed.R. Civil P. 26 and 34. Such opportunity for inspection in criminal cases is afforded both the prosecutor and defendant under Fed.R.Crim.P. 16.

Inspection rights. Buyer of goods has right to inspect them before payment or acceptance at any reasonable place and time and in any reasonable manner. U.C.C. § 2–513(1). See also **Inspection.**

With respect to discovery in civil actions, Fed.R. Civil P. 26 and 34 affords a party the right to inspect documents, records, land, etc. of the other party. Similar rights are afforded the prosecutor and defendant under Fed.R.Crim.P. 16.

Inspection searches. Administrative searches conducted by local or state authorities for health or building law enforcement must be based on a warrant issued on probable cause. Camara v. Municipal Court of etc. San Francisco, 387 U.S. 523, 87 S.Ct. 1727, 18 L.Ed.2d 930. A warrant is likewise required for inspection of business premises by OSHA inspectors. Marshall v. Barlow's, Inc., 436 U.S. 307, 98 S.Ct. 1816, 56 L.Ed.2d 305.

Inspection, trial by. A mode of trial formerly in use in England, by which the judges of a court decided a point in dispute, upon the testimony of their own senses, without the intervention of a jury. This took place in cases where the fact upon which issue was taken must, from its nature, be evident to the court from ocular demonstration, or other irrefragable proof; and was adopted for the greater expedition of a cause.

Inspector. The name given to certain officers whose duties are to examine and inspect things over which they have jurisdiction. Officers whose duty it is to examine the quality of certain articles of merchandise, food, weights and measures, working conditions of business, structural soundness of building, etc.; *e.g.* federal grain or meat inspectors; OSHA inspectors; building inspectors; health inspectors. See also **Inspection laws.**

Inspectorship, deed of. In old English law, an instrument entered into between an insolvent debtor and his creditors, appointing one or more persons to inspect and oversee the winding up of such insolvent's affairs on behalf of the creditors.

Inspeximus /inspéksəməs/. (Lat.) We have seen. A word sometimes used in letters patent, reciting a grant, *inspeximus* such former grant, and so reciting it verbatim; it then grants such further privileges as are thought convenient.

Install. To place in a seat, give a place to; to set, place, or instate in an office, rank, or order, etc. To set up or fix in position for use or service.

Installation. The ceremony of inducting or investing with any charge, office, or rank, as the placing a bishop into his see, a dean or prebendary into his stall or seat, or a knight into his order. The act by which an officer is put in public possession of the place he is to fill. The President of the United States, or a governor, is installed into office, by being sworn agreeably to the constitution and laws.

Installment. Partial payment of a debt or collection of a receivable. Different portions of the same debt payable at different successive periods as agreed. Partial payments on account of a debt due. Kenney v. Los Feliz Inv. Co., 121 Cal.App. 378, 9 P.2d 225, 228.

Installment contract. Type of agreement calling for periodic performances and payments.

An "installment contract" is one which requires or authorizes the delivery of goods in separate lots to be separately accepted, even though the contract contains a clause "each delivery is a separate contract" or its equivalent. U.C.C. § 2–612.

See **Installment land contract; Installment sale; Retail installment contract.**

Installment credit. Commercial arrangement in which buyer undertakes to pay in more than one payment and seller agrees to sell on such basis and in which a finance charge may be exacted. Such agreements are commonly subject to statutory disclosure regulation; *e.g.* Truth-in-Lending laws. See also **Annual percentage rate.**

Installment land contract. Type of contract by which buyer is required to make periodic payments towards purchase price of land and only on the last payment is the seller required to deliver a deed. Also called a "contract for deed" or "long-term land contract." See also **Land contract.**

Installment loan. A loan made to be repaid in specified, usually equal, amounts over a certain number of months. The contract specifies the amount and method of payment. Consumer installment loan contracts are subject to disclosure requirements of Truth-in-Lending Act *(q.v.)*. See also **Annual percentage rate; Balloon payment; Installment credit; Installment sale.**

Installment method. A method of accounting enabling a taxpayer to spread the recognition of gain on the sale of property over the payout period. Under this elective procedure, the seller computes the gross profit percentage from the sale (*i.e.,* the gain divided by the selling price) and applies it to each payment received to arrive at the gain to be recognized. I.R.C. § 453.

Installment plan. Commercial sales arrangement by which goods are sold and buyer pays for them in periodic payments. See also **Installment contract; Installment credit; Installment loan; Installment sale.**

Installment sale. Commercial arrangement by which buyer makes initial down payment and signs a contract for payment of the balance in installments over a period of time. In accounting for such sales, the seller may either account for the profits on basis of each installment payment received or the entire amount in the period of the sale; in latter case, reserves are established for bad debts, collection expenses and costs of reconditioning returned merchandise. See also **Installment contract; Installment credit; Installment loan; Installment method.**

Retail installment sale. The sale of goods or the furnishing of services by a retail seller to a retail buyer for a deferred payment price payable in installments. Retail installment sales contracts are governed with respect to disclosure of terms and finance charges by Truth-in-Lending Act *(q.v.)*. See also **Annual percentage rate.**

Instance court. In English law, that division or department of the court of admiralty which exercised all the ordinary admiralty jurisdiction, with the single exception of prize cases, the latter belonging to the branch called the "Prize Court." Now part of High Court.

Instancia /iynstánsiya/. In Spanish law, the institution and prosecution of a suit from its commencement until definitive judgment. The first instance, *"primera instancia,"* is the prosecution of the suit before the judge competent to take cognizance of it at its inception; the second instance, *"secunda instancia,"* is the exercise of the same action before the court of appellate jurisdiction; and the third instance, *"tercera instancia,"* is the prosecution of the same suit, either by an application of revision before the appellate tribunal that has already decided the cause, or before some higher tribunal, having jurisdiction of the same.

Instans est finis unius temporis et principium alterius /ínstæn(d)z èst fáynəs yənáyəs témpərəs èt prin(t)síp(i)yəm oltíriyəs/. An instant is the end of one time and the beginning of another.

Instant. Present, current, as instant case.

Instantaneous crime. An "instantaneous" crime is one which is fully consummated or completed in and by a single act (such as arson or murder) as distinguished from one which involves a series or repetition of acts.

Instantaneous death. See **Death.**

Instanter /instǽntər/. Immediately; instantly; forthwith; without delay. Trial *instanter* was had where a prisoner between attainder and execution pleaded that he was not the same who was attainted. When a party was ordered to plead *instanter,* he was required to plead the same day. The term was usually understood to mean within twenty-four hours.

Instantly. Immediately; directly; without delay; at once.

Instar /ínstàr/. Lat. Likeness; the likeness, size, or equivalent of a thing. *Instar dentium,* like teeth. *Instar omnium,* equivalent or tantamount to all.

In statu quo /in stéyt(y)uw kwów/°stæt(y)°/. In the condition in which it was. Status quo.

Instigate /ínstəgeyt/. To stimulate or goad to an action, especially a bad action; one of its synonyms is "abet". Hughes v. Van Bruggen, 44 N.M. 534, 105 P.2d 494, 499. See **Aid and abet; Entrapment.**

Instigation /ìnstəgéyshən/. Incitation; urging; solicitation. The act by which one incites another to do something, as to commit some crime or to commence a suit. See **Aid and abet; Entrapment.**

In stipulationibus cum quæritur quid actum sit verba contra stipulatorem interpretanda sunt /in stìpyəlèyshiyównəbəs kàm kwírədər kwíd ǽktəm sít vǿrbə kóntrə stìpyələtórəm intàrprətǽndə sànt/. In the construction of agreements words are interpreted against the person using them. Thus, the construction of the *stipulatio* is against the stipulator, and the construction of the *promissio* against the promissor.

In stipulationibus, id tempus spectatur quo contrahimus /in stìpyəlèyshiyównəbəs íd témpəs spèktéydər kwów kəntrǽhəməs/. In stipulations, the time when we contract is regarded.

Instirpare /ìnstərpériy/. To plant or establish.

In stirpes /in stǿrpiyz/. In the law of intestate succession, according to the roots or stocks; by representation; as distinguished from succession *per capita.* See **Per stirpes; Per capita.**

Institor /ínstədər/. Lat. In the civil law, a clerk in a store; an agent.

Institoria actio /ìnstətór(i)yə ǽksh(iy)ow/. Lat. In the civil law, the name of an action given to those who had contracted with an institor *(q.v.)* to compel the principal to performance.

Institorial power /ìnstətór(i)yəl páwər/. In the civil law, the charge given to a clerk to manage a shop or store.

Institute, *v.* To inaugurate or commence, as to institute an action. Post v. U. S., 161 U.S. 583, 16 S.Ct. 611, 40 L.Ed. 816. To set up; to originate; to start; to introduce. To nominate, constitute, or appoint, as to institute an heir by testament. See **Institution.**

Institute, *n.* Act of instituting; something that is instituted. A principle recognized as authoritative; also the organization which drafts and authors such authoritative principles; *e.g.* American Law Institute. See also **Institution.**

In the civil law, a person named in the will as heir, but with a direction that he shall pass over the estate to another designated person, called the "substitute."

Instituted executor. An instituted executor is one who is appointed by the testator without any condition.

Institutes. A name sometimes given to textbooks containing the elementary principles of jurisprudence, arranged in an orderly and systematic manner. For example, the Institutes of Justinian, of Gaius, of Lord Coke.

Institutes of Gaius. An elementary work of the Roman jurist Gaius; important as having formed the foundation of the Institutes of Justinian *(q.v.).* These Institutes were discovered by Niebuhr in 1816, in a *codex rescriptus* of the library of the cathedral chapter at Verona, and were first published at Berlin in 1820.

Institutes of Justinian. One of the four component parts or principal divisions of the *Corpus Juris Civilis,* being an elementary treatise on the Roman law, in four books. This work was compiled from earlier sources (resting principally on the Institutes of Gaius), by a commission composed of Tribonian and two others, by command and under direction of the emperor Justinian, and was first published November 21, A.D. 533.

Institutes of Lord Coke. The name of four volumes by Lord Coke, published A.D. 1628. The first is an extensive comment upon a treatise on tenures, compiled by Littleton, a judge of the common pleas, *temp.* Edward IV. This comment is a rich mine of valuable common-law learning, collected and heaped together from the ancient reports and Year Books, but greatly defective in method. It is usually cited by the name of "Co. Litt.," or as "1 Inst." The second volume is a comment upon old acts of parliament, without systematic order; the third a more methodical treatise on the pleas of the crown; and the fourth an account of the several species of courts. These are cited as 2, 3, or 4 "Inst.," without any author's name.

Theophilus' Institutes. A paraphrase of Justinian, made, it is believed, soon after A.D. 533. This paraphrase maintained itself as a manual of law until the eighth or tenth century. This text was used in the time of Hexabiblos of Harmenipulus, the last of the Greek jurists. It is also conjectured that Theophilus was not the editor of his own paraphrase, but that it was drawn up by some of his pupils after his explanations and lectures, inasmuch as it contains certain barbarous phrases, and the texts of the manuscripts vary greatly from each other.

Institutio hæredis /ìnstət(y)úwsh(iy)ow həríydəs/. Lat. In Roman law, the appointment of the *hæres* in the will. It corresponds very nearly to the nomination of an executor in English law. Without such an appointment the will was void at law, but the *prætor* (*i.e.,* equity) would, under certain circumstances, carry out the intentions of the testator.

Institution. The commencement or inauguration of anything, as the commencement of an action. The first establishment of a law, rule, rite, etc. Any custom, system, organization, etc., firmly established. An elementary rule or principle. See also **Institute.**

An establishment, especially one of eleemosynary or public character or one affecting a community. An established or organized society or corporation. It may be private in its character, designed for profit to those composing the organization, or public and charitable in its purposes, or educational (*e.g.* college or university). In re Peabody's Estate, 21 Cal.App.2d 690, 70 P.2d 249, 250. A foundation, as a literary or charitable institution. Prescott Courier v. Board of Sup'rs of Yavapai County, 49 Ariz. 423, 67 P.2d 483, 486.

Civil law. The appointment of an heir; the act by which a testator nominates one or more persons to succeed him in all his rights active and passive.

Political law. A law, rite, or ceremony enjoined by authority as a permanent rule of conduct or of government. An organized society, established either by law or the authority of individuals, for promoting any object, public or social.

A system or body of usages, laws, or regulations, of extensive and recurring operation, containing within itself an organism by which it effects its own independent action, continuance, and generally its own further development. Its object is to generate, effect, regulate, or sanction a succession of acts, transactions, or productions of a peculiar kind or class. We are likewise in the habit of calling single laws or usages "institutions," if their operation is of vital importance and vast scope, and if their continuance is in a high degree independent of any interfering power.

Practice. Commencement of civil action or criminal prosecution. See **Commence.**

Public institution. One which is created and exists by law or public authority, for benefit of public in general; *e.g.,* a public hospital, charity, college, university, etc.

Institutiones /ìnstət(y)ùwshiyówniyz/. Lat. Works containing the elements of any science; institutions or institutes. One of Justinian's principal law collections, and a similar work of the Roman jurist Gaius, are so entitled. See **Institutes.**

Instruct. To convey information as a client to an attorney, or as an attorney to a counsel, or as a judge to a jury. To authorize one to appear as advocate; to give a case in charge to the jury.

Instructions to jury. See **Jury instructions.**

Instrument. A written document; a formal or legal document in writing, such as a contract, deed, will, bond, or lease. A negotiable instrument (defined in U.C.C. § 3–104), or a security (defined in U.C.C. § 8–102) or any other writing which evidences a right to the payment of money and is not itself a security agreement or lease and is of a type which is in ordinary course of business transferred by delivery with any necessary indorsement or assignment. U.C.C. § 9–105(1).

Anything reduced to writing, a document of a formal or solemn character, a writing given as a means of affording evidence. A document or writing which gives formal expression to a legal act or agreement, for the purpose of creating, securing, modifying, or terminating a right. A writing executed and delivered as the evidence of an act or agreement. Moore v. Diamond Dry Goods Co., 47 Ariz. 128, 54 P.2d 553, 554. Anything which may be presented as evidence to the senses of the adjudicating tribunal.

See also **Bearer instrument; Bill; Commercial paper; Negotiable instruments; Note.**

Instrumenta /ìnstrəméntə/. Lat. That kind of evidence which consists of writings not under seal; as court-rolls, accounts, and the like.

Instrumental. Serviceable, helpful; serving as a means or agent; something by which an end is achieved.

Instrumentality rule. Under this rule, corporate existence will be disregarded where a corporation (subsidiary) is so organized and controlled and its affairs so conducted as to make it only an adjunct and instrumentality of another corporation (parent corporation), and parent corporation will be responsible for the obligations of its subsidiary. Taylor v. Standard Gas & Electric Co., C.C.A.Okl., 96 F.2d 693, 704.

The so-called "instrumentality" or "alter ego" rule states that when a corporation is so dominated by another corporation that the subservient corporation becomes a mere instrument and is really indistinct from controlling corporation, then the corporate veil of dominated corporation will be disregarded, if to retain it results in injustice. National Bond Finance Co. v. General Motors Corp., D.C.Mo., 238 F.Supp. 248, 255.

Instrument of appeal. The document by which an appeal is brought in an English matrimonial cause from the president of the probate, divorce, and admiralty division to the full court. It is analogous to a petition.

Instrument of evidence. Instruments of evidence are the *media* through which the evidence of facts, either disputed or required to be proved, is conveyed to the mind of a judicial tribunal; and they comprise persons and living things as well as writings. Demonstrative evidence.

Insubordination. State of being insubordinate; disobedience to constituted authority. Refusal to obey some order which a superior officer is entitled to give and have obeyed. Term imports a wilful or intentional disregard of the lawful and reasonable instructions of the employer. Porter v. Pepsi-Cola Bottling Co. of Columbia, 247 S.C. 370, 147 S.E.2d 620, 622.

Insufficiency of evidence to support verdict. This phrase in a motion for new trial, or for judgment notwithstanding the verdict, means that there is some evidence, but not enough in light of the evidence to the contrary to support a verdict. Arnold v. Haskins, 347 Mo. 320, 147 S.W.2d 469, 472. It means that there is no evidence which ought reasonably to satisfy jury that fact to be proved is established. Shtevelan v. Metropolitan Life Ins. Co., 162 Misc. 835, 295 N.Y.S. 735, 736.

Insufficient. Not sufficient; inadequate to some need, purpose, or use; wanting in needful value, ability, or fitness; incompetent; unfit, as insufficient food; insufficient means. It is the antonym of "sufficient." Nissen v. Miller, 44 N.M. 487, 105 P.2d 324, 325.

Insula /íns(y)ələ/. Lat. An island; a house not connected with other houses, but separated by a surrounding space of ground.

Insular courts. Federal courts established by Congress with jurisdiction over insular possessions of the United States.

Insular possessions. Island territories of the U.S., *e.g.* Puerto Rico.

Insulation period. The sixty days immediately preceding the expiration of a collective bargaining agreement when no representation petition may be filed. This is to permit the employer and incumbent union the opportunity to negotiate a new contract without rival claims for recognition.

Insuper /íns(y)úwpər/. Lat. Moreover; over and above.

An old English exchequer term, applied to a charge made *upon* a person in his account.

Insurable. Capable of being insured against loss, damage, death, etc.; proper to be insured; affording a sufficient ground for insurance. Greenberg v. Continental Casualty Co., 24 Cal.App.2d 506, 75 P.2d 644, 649.

Insurable interest. Such a real and substantial interest in specific property as will prevent a contract to indemnify the person interested against its loss from being a mere wager policy. Such an interest as will make the loss of the property of pecuniary damage to the insured. A right, benefit, or advantage arising out of the property or dependent thereon, or any liability in respect thereof, or any relation thereto or concern therein, of such a nature that it might be so affected by the contemplated peril as to directly damnify the insured. Generally, an "insurable interest" exists where insured derives pecuniary benefit or advantage by preservation and continued existence of property or would sustain pecuniary loss from its destruction. Hinojosa v. Allstate Ins. Co., Tex.Civ. App., 520 S.W.2d 936, 938.

In the case of life insurance, a reasonable expectation of pecuniary benefit from the continued life of another; also, a reasonable ground, founded upon the relation of the parties to each other, either pecuniary or of blood or affinity, to expect some benefit or advantage from the continuance of the life of the assured. Connecticut Mut. Life Insurance Co. v. Schaefer, 94 U.S. 457, 460, 24 L.Ed. 251. Essential thing being that policy be obtained in good faith, not for purpose of speculating on hazard of life in which insured has no interest. Alexander v. Griffith Brokerage Co., 228 Mo.App. 773, 73 S.W.2d 418, 423.

Insurable value. Value of property for insurance purposes. Based on the value of the property, less indestructible parts (land) for fire insurance. For title insurance purposes, the sales price (market value) is used.

Insurance. A contract whereby, for a stipulated consideration, one party undertakes to compensate the other for loss on a specified subject by specified perils. The party agreeing to make the compensation is usually called the "insurer" or "underwriter;" the other, the "insured" or "assured;" the agreed consideration, the "premium;" the written contract, a "policy;" the events insured against, "risks" or "perils;" and the subject, right, or interest to be protected, the "insurable interest." A contract whereby one undertakes to indemnify another against loss, damage, or liability arising from an unknown or contingent event and is applicable only to some contingency or act to occur in future. An agreement by which one party for a consideration promises to pay money or its equivalent or to do an act valuable to other party upon destruction, loss, or injury of something in which other party has an interest.

See also Insurable interest; Lloyd's insurance; Lloyd's of London; Loss; Named insured; Partial limitation; Participation; Policy of insurance; Premium; Pro rata clause; Reinsurance; Replacement insurance; **Self-insurance.**

Classification

Accident insurance. Form of insurance which undertakes to indemnify the assured against expense, loss of time, and suffering resulting from accidents causing him physical injury, usually by payment at a fixed rate per month while the consequent disability lasts, and sometimes including the payment of a fixed sum to his heirs in case of his death by accident within the term of the policy. See also *Casualty insurance.*

Accounts receivable insurance. Insurance coverage designed to protect against inability to collect because of damage to records which support the accounts.

Additional insured. A person other than the named insured, such as the insured's spouse, who is protected under the terms of the contract.

Air travel insurance. Form of life insurance which may be purchased by air travelers according to the terms of which the face value of the policy is paid to the named beneficiary in the event of death resulting from a particular flight.

All-risk insurance. Type of insurance policy which ordinarily covers every loss that may happen, except by fraudulent acts of the insured. Miller v. Boston Ins. Co., 218 A.2d 275, 278, 420 Pa. 566. Type of policy which protects against all risks and perils except those specifically enumerated.

Annuity insurance. An insurance contract calling for periodic payments to the insured or annuitant for a stated period or for life.

Assessment insurance. A species of mutual insurance in which the policyholders are assessed as losses are incurred. A contract by which payments to insured are not unalterably fixed, but dependent on collection of assessments necessary to pay amounts insured, while an "old-line policy" unalterably fixes premiums and definitely and unchangeably fixes insurer's liability.

Automobile insurance may embrace insurance against loss of or damage to a motor vehicle caused by fire, windstorm, theft, collision, or other insurable hazards, and also against legal liability for personal injuries or damage to property resulting from operation of the vehicle. Policy of indemnity to protect the operator and owner from liability to third persons as a result of the operation of the automobile. See also *Collision insurance;* and *No-fault auto insurance, infra,* this topic.

Business insurance. Type of insurance which protects a business on the disability or death of a key employee. See also *Key man life insurance, infra.*

Business interruption insurance. Type of insurance which protects a business from losses due to inability to operate because of fire or other hazards.

Casualty insurance. That type of insurance that is primarily concerned with losses caused by injuries to persons and legal liability imposed upon the insured for such injury or for damage to the property of others.

Coinsurance. Provision in a policy that the liability of the insurer is limited to that proportion of the loss which the amount of insurance bears to a particular percentage of the value of property at the time of the loss. See also **Coinsurance.**

Collision insurance. A form of automobile insurance that covers loss to the insured vehicle from its collision with another vehicle or object, but not covering bodily injury or liability also arising out of the collision. Type of coverage which protects insured for damage to his own property in an accident as contrasted with liability insurance which protects him in an action or claim for loss to another's property.

See also *Convertible collision insurance, infra.*

Commercial insurance. Indemnity agreements, in the form of insurance bonds or policies, whereby parties to commercial contracts are to a designated extent guaranteed against loss by reason of a breach of contractual obligations on the part of the other contracting party. To this class belong policies of contract credit and title insurance.

Comprehensive insurance. See *All risk insurance, supra.*

Concurrent insurance. Insurance coverage under two or more similar policies of varying dates and amounts.

Convertible collision insurance. Type of collision coverage generally carrying lower premium but requiring higher premium after first loss or claim; an alternative form of deductible collision coverage.

Convertible insurance. A policy that may be changed to another form by contractual provision and without evidence of insurability. Usually used to refer to term life insurance convertible to permanent insurance.

Convertible life insurance. Generally a form of term life insurance which gives the insured the right to change policy to permanent life insurance without medical examination.

Cooperative insurance. Type of non-stock mutual insurance in which the policyholders are the owners; may be assessable or nonassessable.

Credit insurance. Type of insurance protection against losses due to death, disability, insolvency or bankruptcy of debtor. Policy covers balance of debt due, with proceeds payable to creditor. Commonly offered by banks and other lenders. Terms and conditions of such are regulated by federal and state statutes; *e.g.* Truth-in-Lending laws.

Crime insurance. Type of insurance which protects insured from losses due to criminal acts against insured such as burglary, etc. Such insurance is sponsored by federal government for residents of certain high-crime localities.

Crop insurance. Insurance coverage against financial loss due to destruction of agricultural products resulting from rain, hail, and other elements of nature. Such insurance is sponsored by Federal Crop Insurance Corporation.

Decreasing term insurance. A term insurance policy where the premiums are uniform throughout its life, but the face value of the policy declines. Sometimes called a home protection plan because the face value declines much in the same way a mortgage due on a house declines. A form of life insurance that provides a death benefit of amount declining throughout the term of the contract to zero at the end of the term.

Deposit insurance. Federally sponsored (Federal Deposit Insurance Corp.) insurance coverage against loss of deposits due to bank closings.

Employer's liability insurance. In this form of insurance the risk insured against is the liability of the assured to make compensation or pay damages for an accident, injury, or death occurring to a servant or other employee in the course of his employment, either at common law or under statutes imposing such liability on employers. Coverage which protects employer as to claims not covered under worker's compensation insurance.

Endowment insurance. Type of protection which combines life insurance and investment so that if the insured outlives the policy the face value is paid to him. If he does not outlive it, the face value is paid to his beneficiary.

Errors and omissions insurance. Insurance that indemnifies the insured for any loss sustained because of an error or oversight on his part.

Excess insurance. Coverage against loss in excess of a stated amount or in excess of coverage provided under another insurance contract.

Extended term insurance. A non-forfeiture provision in most policies which continues the existing amount of life insurance for as long a period of time as the contract's cash value will purchase term coverage.

Family income insurance. Type of term insurance designed to give maximum coverage during the period of maximum family dependency.

Fidelity insurance. Form of insurance in which the insurer undertakes to guaranty the fidelity of an officer, agent, or employee of the assured, or rather to indemnify the latter for losses caused by dishonesty or a want of fidelity on the part of such a person. See also **Fidelity and guaranty insurance.**

Fire insurance. A contract of insurance by which the underwriter, in consideration of the premium, undertakes to indemnify the insured against all losses in his houses, buildings, furniture, ships in port, or merchandise, by means of accidental fire happening within a prescribed period. See also **Loss payable clause; Pro rata distribution clause.**

First party insurance. Insurance which applies to the insured's own property or person.

Fleet policy insurance. Type of blanket policy covering a number of vehicles of the same insured; *e.g.* covers pool or fleet of vehicles owned by business.

Floater insurance. A form of insurance that applies to moveable property whatever its location, if within the territorial limits imposed by the contract.

Fraternal insurance. The form of life or accident insurance furnished by a fraternal beneficial association, consisting in the undertaking to pay to a member, or his heirs in case of death, a stipulated sum of money, out of funds raised for that purpose by the payment of dues or assessments by all the members of the association.

Government insurance. Life insurance underwritten and offered by Federal government to war veterans. See also *National service life insurance; War risk insurance, infra.*

Group insurance. A form of insurance whereby individual lives of a group of persons, usually employees, are in consideration of a flat periodical premium based on average age and paid either by employer in whole or partially by both employer and employee, insured each in a definite sum so long as insured remains in such employment and the premiums are paid. Holland v. Lincoln Nat. Life Ins. Co., 45 N.J.Super. 66, 131 A.2d 428, 429. Coverage of number of individuals by means of single or blanket policy. McFarland v. Business Men's Assur. Co. of America, 105 Ga.App. 209, 124 S.E.2d 432, 433. Type of insurance (life, medical, dental, automobile, legal) offered to employees or other homogeneous group under a single master policy. Generally, each employee receives a certificate of participation instead of a policy.

Group-term life insurance. Life insurance coverage permitted by an employer for a group of employees. Such insurance is renewable on a year-to-year basis and does not accumulate in value (*i.e.,* no cash surrender value is built up). The premiums paid by the employer on such insurance are not taxed to an employee on coverage of up to a specified amount per year.

Guaranty or fidelity insurance. A contract whereby one, for a consideration, agrees to indemnify another against loss arising from the want of integrity or fidelity of employees and persons holding positions of trust, or embezzlements by them, or against the insolvency of debtors, losses in trade, loss by non-payment of notes, or against breaches of contract.

Hail insurance. Type of insurance which provides protection against loss of crops, grain, etc. because of hail storms. See also *Crop insurance, supra.*

Health insurance. A contract or agreement whereby an insurer is obligated to pay or allow a benefit of pecuniary value with respect to the bodily injury, disablement, sickness, death by accident or accidental means of a human being, or because of any expense relating thereto, or because of any expense incurred in prevention of sickness, and includes every risk pertaining to any of the enumerated risks.

Homeowners insurance. Policy insuring individuals against any, some, or all of the risks of loss to personal dwellings or the contents thereof or the personal liability pertaining thereto.

Indemnity insurance. Insurance which provides indemnity against loss, in contrast to contracts which provide for indemnity against liability. The latter are known as liability contracts or policies, and the former as indemnity contracts or policies.

Inland marine insurance. Originally, a form of insurance protection for goods transported other than on the ocean. Now, term applies to a variety of coverages on floating personal property and to general liability as a bailee.

Joint life insurance. Form of life insurance on two or more persons and payable on the death of the first to die.

Key man life insurance. Type of life insurance written on the life of an important or key officer or employee in a business organization. The business is the beneficiary and is entitled to the proceeds on his death. See also **Key man insurance**.

Level premium insurance. Type of insurance in which the cost is spread evenly over the premium paying period.

Liability insurance. Insurance that covers suits against the insured for such damages as injury or death to other drivers or passengers, property damage, and the like. It is insurance for those damages for which the driver can be held liable.

Liability insurance is that form of insurance which indemnifies against liability on account of injuries to the person or property of another. It is distinguished from "indemnity insurance" (see that title, *supra*), and may be issued to cover the liability of, for example, carriers, contractors, employers, landlords, manufacturers, drivers.

Life insurance. A contract between the holder of a policy and an insurance company (*i.e.,* the carrier) whereby the company agrees, in return for premium payments, to pay a specified sum (*i.e.,* the face value or maturity value of the policy) to the designated beneficiary upon the death of the insured.

That kind of insurance in which the risk contemplated is the death of a particular person; upon which event (if it occurs within a prescribed term, or, according to the contract, whenever it occurs) the insurer engages to pay a stipulated sum to the legal representatives of such person, or to a third person having an insurable interest in the life of such person.

See also **Life insurance proceeds; Life insurance trust;** *Term insurance* (this topic).

Group life insurance. Type of life insurance commonly offered by companies to their employees in which there is a master insurance contract providing life insurance benefits to each covered employee who holds a certificate indicating his participation.

Limited payment life insurance. Type of life insurance for which premiums are payable for a definite period after which the policy is fully paid.

Straight life insurance or whole life insurance is insurance for which premiums are collected so long as the insured may live, whereas, term insurance is insurance which promises payment only within a stipulated term covered by the policy; though such term policies are commonly renewed each term. The premium for whole life insurance remains the same whereas the premium for term insurance increases with the age of the insured, *i.e.* as the risk increases. Also, whole life policies build up cash reserves, whereas term policies do not. See also *Term insurance.*

Limited policy insurance. Type of coverage which offers protection against specific perils or accidents and against no others.

Major medical insurance. Insurance protection against large medical, surgical and hospital expenses of the insured.

Malpractice insurance. Type of liability insurance which protects professional people (*e.g.* doctors, lawyers, accountants) against claims of negligence brought against them.

Manual rating insurance. Type of insurance in which the premium is set from a manual classifying types of risk on a general basis such as a particular industry without reference to the individual case.

Marine insurance. A contract whereby one party, for a stipulated premium, undertakes to indemnify the other against certain perils or sea-risks to which his ship, freight, and cargo, or some of them, may be exposed during a certain voyage, or a fixed period of time. An insurance against risks connected with navigation, to which a ship, cargo, freightage, profits, or other insurable interest in movable property may be exposed during a certain voyage or a fixed period of time. See also *Inland marine insurance, supra.*

Mortgage insurance. Insurance from which the benefits are intended by the policyowner to pay off the balance due on a mortgage upon the death of the insured or to meet the payments on a mortgage as they fall due in case of the death or disability of the insured. Insurance against loss to the mortgagees in the event of default and a failure of the mortgaged property to satisfy the balance owing plus costs of foreclosure.

National service life insurance. Life insurance on servicemen. The contract is between the U.S. Government and private insurers for benefit of servicemen.

No-fault auto insurance. Type of automobile insurance in which claims for personal injury (and sometimes property damage) are made against the claimant's own insurance company (no matter who was at fault) rather than against the insurer of the party at fault. Under such state "no-fault" statutes only in cases of serious personal injuries and high medical costs may the injured bring an action against the other party or his insurer. No-fault statutes vary from state to state in terms of scope of coverage, threshold amounts, etc.

Nonassessable insurance. Type of insurance in which the rate of premium is guaranteed and no additional assessments may be made against the policyholder.

Old line life insurance. Insurance on a level or flat rate plan where, for a fixed premium payable without condition at stated intervals, a certain sum is to be paid upon death without condition.

Ordinary life insurance. Whole life and permanent insurance as distinguished from term, group and industrial insurance.

Paid-up insurance. Insurance policy on which all premiums have been paid and on which no further premiums are due and for which benefits company is liable.

Participating insurance. Type of insurance issued by a mutual company on which policyholder may participate in dividend distributions.

Partnership insurance. Life insurance on lives of partners designed to enable surviving partners to buy out deceased partner's estate. Life or health insurance sold to a partnership, usually for guaranteeing business continuity in case of disability or death of a partner.

Product liability insurance. Type of liability coverage which protects manufacturers and suppliers from claims for accidents arising out of the use of their products.

Public liability insurance. Insurance liability protection against claims arising out of the insured's property, conduct or the conduct of his agent.

Reciprocal insurance. Type of insurance plan administered by an exchange rather than an insurance company and in which each insured is the insurer of the other members of the plan.

Renewable term insurance. Type of term insurance in which the premiums are level during each term, but increases at each *new* term with the age of the insured. The insured generally has the right to renew for additional terms without a medical examination.

Retirement income insurance. Type of insurance in which the insurer guarantees payment of the policy if the insured dies before a certain age and an annuity if the insured survives beyond the specified period.

Self insurance. Plan in which the insured (*e.g.* business) places aside in a fund sufficient sums to cover liability losses that may be sustained. Commonly, under such plan the business will self-insure itself up to a certain amount and then carry regular liability insurance to cover any excesses.

Single premium insurance. Type of policy on which the insured makes but one premium payment.

Social insurance. A comprehensive welfare plan established by law, generally compulsory in nature, and based on a program which spreads the cost of benefits among the entire population rather than on individual recipients. The federal government began to use social insurance programs in 1935 with the passage of the Social Security Act. The basic federal and state approaches to social insurance presently in use are: Old Age, Survivors, and Disability Insurance (*i.e.* social security); Medicare and Medicaid; unemployment insurance; and worker's compensation.

Split dollar insurance. Type of insurance in which the insurer divides the premium dollar between life insurance protection and investment for the benefit of the insured.

Step-rate premium insurance. Type of insurance in which the premium may vary from time to time at the option of the insurer.

Surety and fidelity insurance. Form of insurance which more approximates a bond which protects the insured against dishonesty of employees, agents and the public.

Term insurance. Form of pure life insurance having no cash surrender value and generally furnishing insurance protection for only a specified or limited period of time; though such policy is usually renewable from term to term. See also *Convertible life; Decreasing term; Extended term; Family income; Group term; Renewable term insurance, supra.*

Title insurance. Insurance against loss or damage resulting from defects or failure of title to a particular parcel of realty, or from the enforcement of liens existing against it at the time of the insurance. This form of insurance is taken out by a purchaser of the property or one loaning money on mortgage, and is furnished by companies specially organized for the purpose, and which keep complete sets of abstracts or duplicates of the records, employ expert title-examiners, and prepare conveyances and transfers of all sorts. A "certificate of title" furnished by such a company is merely the formally expressed professional opinion of the company's examiner that the title is complete and perfect (or otherwise, as stated), and the company is liable only for a want of care, skill, or diligence on the part of its examiner; whereas an "insurance of title" warrants the validity of the title in any and all events. It is not always easy to distinguish between such insurance and a "guaranty of title" given by such a company, except that in the former case the maximum limit of liability is fixed by the policy, while in the latter case the undertaking is to make good any and all loss resulting from defect or failure of the title.

Trust insurance. A trust, the res of which consists in whole or in part of insurance policies.

Unemployment insurance. Form of taxation collected from business to fund unemployment payments and benefits.

War risk insurance. Insurance offered by the federal government to protect persons against wartime loss of vessels and property on the high seas, and death or injury while in the armed forces. Insurance covering damage caused by acts of war. War risk insurance refers to those contracts which were brought into being by the United States government during the first World War to replace ordinary life and accident insurance which was no longer available to those in the hazardous occupation of military service. See also *National service life insurance, supra.*

Worker's compensation insurance. Type of protection purchased by employers to cover payments to employees who are injured in accidents arising out of and in the course of their employment; governed by statutes in all jurisdictions. See also *Employer's liability insurance, supra.*

Other Insurance Terms

Blanket policy. Policy covering more than one type of property in one location, or one or more types of property at more than one location.

Comprehensive coverage. A simple and convenient form of indemnity now commonly available in contracts of automobile insurance. It includes not only the conventional coverages against loss caused by fire, theft, wind, water, or malicious mischief, but is generally designed to protect against all damage to the insured vehicle except collision or upset.

Concurrent insurance. That which to any extent insures the same interest against the same casualty, at the same time, as the primary insurance, on such terms that the insurers would bear proportionately the loss happening within the provisions of both policies.

Contract of insurance. See **Contract of insurance.**

Double insurance. See **Double.**

Excess insurance. See *Excess insurance, supra.*

General and special insurance. In marine insurance, a general insurance is effected when the perils insured against are such as the law would imply from the nature of the contract considered in itself and supposing none to be specified in the policy. In the case of special insurance, further perils (in addition to implied perils) are expressed in the policy.

Insurance adjuster. One undertaking to ascertain and report the actual loss to the subject-matter of insurance due to the peril insured against. The adjuster also settles claims against the insurer. Such adjuster may be employed either by the insurer or the insured. See **Adjuster.**

Insurance agent. Person authorized to represent insurer in dealing with third parties in matters relating to insurance. American Casualty Co. of Reading, Pa. v. Ricas, 179 Md. 627, 22 A.2d 484, 487. An agent employed by an insurance company to solicit insurance business. Agents of insurance companies are called "general agents" when clothed with the general oversight of the companies' business in a state or large section of country, and "local agents" when their functions are limited and confined to some particular locality. See also *Insurance broker, infra.*

Insurance broker. One who acts as middleman between insured and company, and who solicits insurance from public under no employment from any special company and places order of insurance with company selected by insurer or, in absence of any selection, with company selected by such broker. Broker is agent for insured though at same time for some purposes he may be agent for insurer, and his acts and representations within scope of his authority as such agent are binding on insured. An "insurance agent" is tied to his company, whereas an "insurance broker" is an independent middleman not tied to a particular company. Osborn v. Ozlin, Va., 310 U.S. 53, 60 S.Ct. 758, 761, 84 L.Ed. 1074.

Insurance commissioner. A public officer in most states, whose duty is to supervise the business of insurance as conducted in the state by foreign and domestic companies, for the protection and benefit of policy-holders, and especially to issue licenses, approve rates, make periodical examinations into the condition of such companies, and receive, file, and publish periodical statements of their business as furnished by them.

Insurance company. A corporation or association whose business is to make contracts of insurance. They are generally either mutual companies or stock companies. A "mutual" insurance company is one whose fund for the payment of losses consists not of capital subscribed or furnished by outside parties, but of premiums mutually contributed by the parties insured, or in other words, one in which all persons insured become members of the association and contribute either cash or assessable premium notes, or both, to a common fund, out of which each is entitled to indemnity in case of loss. A "stock" company is one organized according to the usual form of business corporations, having a capital stock divided into shares, which, with current income and accumulated surplus, constitutes the fund for the payment of losses, policy-holders paying fixed premiums and not being members of the association unless they also happen to be stockholders. See also **Joint stock insurance company.**

Insurance policy. See **Policy of insurance.**

Insurance premium. The consideration paid by insured to insurer for insurance protection. Alyea-Nichols Co. v. U. S., D.C.Ill., 12 F.2d 998, 1005. See **Premium.**

Insurance rating. Process by which the premium for a policy is set after considering the risks involved.

Insurance trust. An agreement between insured and trustee, whereby proceeds of policy are paid directly to trustee for investment and distribution to designated beneficiaries in manner and at such time as insured has directed in trust agreement. See also **Trust.**

Interinsurance. Insurance system whereby several individuals, partnerships, or corporations, through common attorney in fact, underwrite one another's risks against loss under agreement that underwriters act separately and severally. Hoopeston Canning Co. v. Cullen, 318 U.S. 313, 63 S.Ct. 602, 604, 87 L.Ed. 777. It is distinguishable from all other forms of insurance, in that every insured is interinsurer, and every insurer is insured.

Loss. See **Loss.**

Mutual insurance. That form of insurance provided by mutual companies. An essential characteristic of a mutual insurance company is collective and entire ownership and control by its members, all of whom must be policyholders. A mutual company may collect cash premiums from members in advance or it may assess members to pay losses and overhead. An insurance company can be mutual even though policyholders are not subject to assessment. To be a mutual insurance company, it is also essential that the company provide insurance to its members substantially at cost. Ohio Farmers Indemnity Co. v. Commissioner of Internal Revenue, C.C.A.Ohio, 108 F.2d 665; Union Ins. Co. v. Hoge, 62 U.S. (21 How.) 35, 16 L.Ed. 61; Mutual Fire Ins. Co. of Germantown v. United States, 142 F.2d 344.

Over-insurance. Insurance effected upon property, either in one or several companies, to an amount which, separately or in the aggregate, exceeds the actual value of the property. See *Excess insurance.*

Reinsurance. Insurance of an insurer; a contract by which an insurer procures a third person (usually another insurance company) to insure it against loss or liability, or a portion of such, by reason of the original insurance.

Umbrella policy. A type of supplemental insurance policy that extends normal automobile liability limits to *e.g.* $1 million or more for a relatively small additional premium.

Under-insurance. Insurance coverage for less than the value of the property. Under such policy, coverage for loss or damage to property will be reduced by percentage of underinsurance.

Insure. To make sure or secure, to guarantee, as, to insure safety to any one. To engage to indemnify a person against pecuniary loss from specified perils or possible liability. To provide insurance. See also **Underwrite.**

Insured. The person who obtains or is otherwise covered by insurance on his health, life, or property. The "insured" in a policy is not limited to the insured named in the policy, but applies to anyone who is insured under the policy. Midwest Contractors Equipment Co. v. Bituminous Cas. Corp., 112 Ill. App.2d 134, 251 N.E.2d 349, 352. The owner of a policy of insurance. Detrick v. Aetna Cas. & Sur. Co., Iowa, 158 N.W.2d 99, 104.

Insurer. The underwriter or insurance company with whom a contract of insurance is made. The one who assumes risk or underwrites a policy, or the underwriter or company with whom contract of insurance is made. National Securities, Inc. v. Johnson, 14 Ariz.App. 31, 480 P.2d 368, 370.

Insurgent. One who participates in an insurrection; one who opposes the execution of law by force of arms, or who rises in revolt against the constituted authorities. An enemy.

Insurrection. A rebellion, or rising of citizens or subjects in resistance to their government. Insurrection consists in any combined resistance to the lawful authority of the state, with intent to cause the denial thereof, when the same is manifested, or intended to be manifested, by acts of violence. It is a federal crime to incite, assist, or engage in a rebellion or insurrection against the United States. 18 U.S.C.A. § 2383. See also **Internal security acts.**

Intakes. In old English law, temporary inclosures made by customary tenants of a manor under a special custom authorizing them to inclose part of the waste until one or more crops have been raised on it.

In tali casu editum et provisum /ìn téylay kéys(y)uw édədəm èt prəváyzəm/. See **In casu proviso.**

Intangible asset. Such values as accrue to a going business as goodwill, trademarks, copyrights, franchises, or the like. A nonphysical, noncurrent asset which exists only in connection with something else, as the goodwill of a business.

Intangible property. As used chiefly in the law of taxation, this term means such property as has no intrinsic and marketable value, but is merely the representative or evidence of value, such as certificates of stock, bonds, promissory notes, and franchises. See **Intangible asset.**

Intangibles. Property that is a "right" rather than a physical object. Examples would be patents, stocks, bonds, goodwill, trademarks, franchises, and copyrights. See **Amortization; General intangibles; Intangible asset.**

Intangibles tax. In certain states such tax is imposed on every resident for right to exercise following privileges: (a) Signing, executing and issuing intangibles; (b) selling, assigning, transferring, renewing, removing, consigning, mailing, shipping, trading in and enforcing intangibles; (c) receiving income, increase, issues and profits of intangibles; (d) transmitting intangibles by will or gift or under state laws of descent; (e) having intangibles separately classified for taxes.

Integer /íntəjər/. Lat. Whole; untouched. *Res integra* /ríyz íntəgrə/ means a question which is new and undecided.

Integrated bar. The act of organizing the bar of a state into an association, membership in which is a condition precedent to the right to practice law. Integration is generally accomplished by enactment of a statute conferring authority upon the highest court of the state to integrate the bar, or by rule of court in the exercise of its inherent power.

Integrated contract. Contract which contains within its four corners the entire agreement of the parties and parol evidence tending to contradict, amend, etc., is inadmissible; the parties having made the contract the final expression of their agreement.

An agreement is integrated where the parties thereto adopt the writing or writings as the final and complete expression of the agreement and an "integration" is the writing or writings so adopted. Wilson v. Viking Corporation, 134 Pa.Super. 153, 3 A.2d 180, 183.

Integrated property settlements. Contract commonly made on separation or divorce of spouses wherein the parties intend that the contract become part of the court order, decree or judgment.

Integrated writing. The writing or writings adopted by the parties to an agreement as the final and complete expression of the agreement. Restatement, Contracts, § 228; Pettett v. Cooper, 62 Ohio App. 377, 24 N.E.2d 299, 302. See also **Integrated contract.**

Integration. The act or process of making whole or entire. Bringing together different groups (as races) as equals.

Horizontal integration. Combination of two or more businesses of the same type such as manufacturers of the same type of products. Such combinations may violate antitrust laws under certain conditions. See also **Merger.**

Vertical integration. Combination of two or more businesses on different levels of operation such as manufacturing, wholesaling and retailing the same product. See also **Merger.**

Integrity. As used in statutes prescribing the qualifications of public officers, trustees, etc., this term means soundness or moral principle and character, as shown by one person dealing with others in the making and performance of contracts, and fidelity and honesty in the discharge of trusts; it is synonymous with "probity," "honesty," and "uprightness."

Intelligibility. In pleading, the statement of matters of fact directly (excluding the necessity of inference or argument to arrive at the meaning) and in such appropriate terms, so arranged, as to be comprehensible by a person of common or ordinary understanding. "Each averment of a pleading shall be simple, concise, and direct." Fed.R. Civil P. 8(e).

Intemperance. Habitual intemperance is that degree of intemperance from the use of intoxicating liquor which disqualifies the person a great portion of the time from properly attending to business, or which would reasonably inflict a course of great mental anguish upon an innocent party. Habitual or excessive use of liquor. See **Intoxication.**

Intend. To design, resolve, propose. To plan for and expect a certain result. To apply a rule of law in the nature of presumption; to discern and follow the probabilities of like cases. See also **Intent.**

Intendant. One who has the charge, management, or direction of some office, department, or public business.

Used in the constitutional and statutory law of some European governments to designate a principal officer of state corresponding to the cabinet or secretaries of the various departments of the United States government, as, "intendant of marine," "intendant of finance."

Intended to be recorded. Phrase used in conveyances, when reciting some other conveyance which has not yet been recorded, but which forms a link in the chain of title.

Intended use doctrine. In product liability cases, two factors are considered: the marketing scheme of the maker, and the foreseeability of the risks which are inherent in the product when used for the purposes intended. Helene Curtis Industries, Inc. v. Pruitt, C.A.Tex., 385 F.2d 841.

Intendente /ìntendéntey/. In Spanish law, the immediate agent of the minister of finance, or the chief and principal director of the different branches of the revenue, appointed in the various departments in each of the provinces into which the Spanish monarchy is divided.

Intendment of law. The true meaning, the correct understanding or intention of the law. A presumption or inference made by the courts.

Common intendment. The natural and usual sense; the common meaning or understanding; the plain meaning of any writing as apparent on its face without straining or distorting the construction.

Intent. Design, resolve, or determination with which person acts. Witters v. United States, 70 U.S.App. D.C. 316, 106 F.2d 837, 840. Being a state of mind, is rarely susceptible of direct proof, but must ordinarily be inferred from the facts. It presupposes knowledge. Reinhard v. Lawrence Warehouse Co., 41 Cal. App.2d 741, 107 P.2d 501, 504. A mental attitude which can seldom be proved by direct evidence, but must ordinarily be proved by circumstances from which it may be inferred. State v. Gantt, 26 N.C. App. 554, 217 S.E.2d 3, 5. A state of mind existing at the time a person commits an offense and may be shown by act, circumstances and inferences deducible therefrom. State v. Evans, 219 Kan. 515, 548 P.2d 772, 777.

The word "intent" is used throughout the Restatement of Torts, 2nd, to denote that the actor desires to cause consequences of his act, or that he believes that the consequences are substantially certain to result from it. Sec. 8A.

Intent and motive should not be confused. Motive is what prompts a person to act, or fail to act. Intent refers only to the state of mind with which the act is done or omitted.

See also Aforethought; Constructive intent; Intention; Larcenous intent; Legislative intent; Malice aforethought; Manifestation of intention; Premeditation; Predatory intent; Presumed intent; Specific intent; Wilful.

Common intent. The natural sense given to words.

Criminal intent. See **Criminal.**

General intent. In criminal law, the intent to do that which the law prohibits. It is not necessary for the prosecution to prove that the defendant intended the precise harm or the precise result which eventuated.

Specific intent. In criminal law, the intent to accomplish the precise act which the law prohibits; *e.g.* assault with intent to rape.

Transferred intent. In tort law, if A, intending to strike B, misses B and hits C instead, the intent to strike B is transferred and supplies the necessary intent for the tort against C. See also **Transferred intent, doctrine of.**

Intentio /inténsh(iy)ow/. Lat. In the civil law, the formal complaint or claim of a plaintiff before the prætor.

In old English law, a count or declaration in a real action *(narratio).*

Intentio cæca mala /inténsh(iy)ow síyka mǽla/. A blind or obscure meaning is bad or ineffectual. Said of a testator's intention.

Intentio inservire debet legibus, non leges intentioni /inténsh(iy)ow insarváyriy débat líyjabas, nòn líyjiyz intènshiyównay/. The intention [of a party] ought to be subservient to [or in accordance with] the laws, not the laws to the intention.

Intentio mea imponit nomen operi meo /inténsh(iy)ow míya impównat nówman óparay míyow/. My intent gives a name to my act.

Intention. Determination to act in a certain way or to do a certain thing. Meaning; will; purpose; design.

"Intention," when used with reference to the construction of wills and other documents, means the sense and meaning of it, as gathered from the words used therein. When used with reference to civil and criminal responsibility, a person who contemplates any result, as not unlikely to follow from a deliberate act of his own, may be said to intend that result, whether he desires it or not. See also **Four corners rule; Intent.**

Intentione /intènshiyówniy/. In old English law, a writ that lay against him who entered into lands after the death of a tenant in dower, or for life, etc., and held out to him in reversion or remainder.

Intent to kill. An element in certain aggravated assaults and batteries which requires the prosecution to prove the intent to kill in addition to the other elements of the assault and battery. See **Aggravated assault; Malice aforethought; Premeditation.**

Inter /íntər. Lat. Among; between.

Inter alia /íntər éyl(i)yə/°æliyə/. Among other things. A term anciently used in pleading, especially in reciting statutes, where the whole statute was not set forth at length. *Inter alia enactatum fuit,* among other things it was enacted.

Inter alias causas acquisitionis, magna, celebris, et famosa est causa donationis /íntər éyl(i)yəs kózəs ækwəzìshiyównəs, mǽgnə, séləbrəs, èt fəmówsə èst kózə dənèyshiyównəs/. Among other methods of acquiring property, a great, much-used, and celebrated method is that of gift.

Inter alios /íntər éyliyəs/. Between other persons; between those who are strangers to a matter in question.

Inter alios res gestas aliis non posse præjudicium facere sæpe constitutum est /íntər éyliyəs ríyz jéstəs ǽliyəs nòn pósiy prəjùwdəkǽndəm fǽsəriy síypiy kònstətyúwdəm èst/. It has been often settled that things which took place between other parties cannot prejudice.

Inter apices juris /íntər éypəsiyz júrəs/. Among the subtleties of the law. See **Apex juris.**

Inter arma silent leges /íntər ármə sáylənt líyjiyz/. In time of war the laws are silent. It applies as between the state and its external enemies; and also in cases of civil disturbance where extrajudicial force may supersede the ordinary process of law.

Inter brachia /íntər bréykiyə/. Between her arms.

Inter cæteros /íntər sédərows/. Among others; in a general clause; not by name *(nominatim).* A term applied in the civil law to clauses of disinheritance in a will.

Intercalare /intərkəlériy/. Lat. In the civil law, to introduce or insert among or between others; to introduce a day or month into the calendar; to intercalate.

Intercedere /intərsíydəriy/. Lat. In the civil law, to become bound for another's debt.

Intercept. "Intercept" means the aural acquisition of the contents of any wire or oral communication through the use of any electronic, mechanical, or other device. 18 U.S.C.A. § 2510. See **Eavesdropping; Wiretapping.**

Interception. Within Federal Communications Act, prohibiting interception of communication by wire or radio, indicates taking or seizure by the way or before arrival at destined place, and does not ordinarily connote obtaining of what is to be sent before, or at the moment, it leaves the possession of the proposed sender, or after, or at the moment, it comes into possession of intended receiver. Communications Act of 1934, § 605, 47 U.S.C.A. § 605; Goldman v. United States, N.Y., 316 U.S. 129, 62 S.Ct. 993, 995, 86 L.Ed. 1322. See **Eavesdropping; Wiretapping.**

Interchangeably. By way of exchange or interchange. This term properly denotes the method of signing deeds, leases, contracts, etc., executed in duplicate, where each party signs the copy which he delivers to the other.

Inter conjuges /íntər kónjəgiyz/. Between husband and wife.

Intercourse. Communication; literally, a *running* or passing *between* persons or places; commerce; sexual relations.

Interdict /íntərdìkt/. A prohibitory decree.

Ecclesiastical law. An ecclesiastical censure, by which divine services (*i.e.* sacraments) are prohibited to be administered either to particular persons or in particular places.

Roman and civil law. A decree of the prætor by means of which, in certain cases determined by the edict, he himself directly commanded what should be done or omitted, particularly in causes involving the right of possession or a *quasi* possession. In the modern civil law, interdicts are regarded precisely the same as actions, though they give rise to a summary proceeding.

Interdicts are either prohibitory, restorative, or exhibitory; the first being a prohibition, the second a decree for restoring possession lost by force, the third a decree for the exhibiting of accounts, etc.

An interdict was distinguished from an "action" (*actio*), properly so called, by the circumstance that the prætor himself decided in the first instance (*principaliter*), on the application of the plaintiff, without previously appointing a *judex*, by issuing a decree commanding what should be done, or left undone. It might be adopted as a remedy in various cases where a regular action could not be maintained, and hence interdicts were at one time more extensively used than were the *actiones* themselves. Afterwards, however, they fell into disuse, and in the time of Justinian were generally dispensed with.

Interdiction /intərdíkshən/. *French law.* Every person who, on account of insanity, has become incapable of controlling his own interests, can be put under the control of a guardian, who shall administer his affairs with the same effect as he might himself. Such a person is said to be *"interdit,"* and his *status* is described as "interdiction."

Civil law. A judicial decree, by which a person is deprived of the *exercise* of his civil rights.

French-Canadian law. A proceeding instituted for the purpose of obtaining a curator of the person and property, and includes the calling of a family council and a petition to the court or its prothonotary, followed by a hearing.

International law. An "interdiction of commercial intercourse" between two countries is a governmental prohibition of commercial intercourse, intended to bring about an entire cessation for the time being of all trade whatever. The Edward, 1 Wheat. 272, 4 L.Ed. 86.

Interdiction of fire and water. Banishment by an order that no man should supply the person banished with fire or water, the two necessaries of life.

Interdum evenit ut exceptio quæ prima facie justa videtur, tamen inique noceat /intárdəm əvíynət əd əksépsh(iy)ow kwiy práymə féyshiy(iy) jə́stə vədíydər, tǽmən ənáykwiy nósiyət/. It sometimes happens that a plea which seems *prima facie* just, nevertheless is injurious and unequal.

Interesse /ìntərésiy/. Lat. Interest. The interest of money; also an interest in lands.

Interesse termini. An interest in a term. That species of interest or property which a lessee for years acquires in the lands demised to him, before he has actually become possessed of those lands; as distinguished from that property or interest vested in him by the demise, and also reduced into possession by an actual entry upon the lands and the assumption of ownership therein, and which is then termed an "estate for years."

Pro interesse suo. For his own interest; according to, or to the extent of, his individual interest. Used (in practice) to describe the intervention of a party who comes into a suit for the purpose of protecting interests of his own which may be involved in the dispute between the principal parties or which may be affected by the settlement of their contention.

Interest. The most general term that can be employed to denote a right, claim, title, or legal share in something. In its application to lands or things real, it is frequently used in connection with the terms "estate," "right," and "title." More particularly it means a right to have the advantage accruing from anything; any right in the nature of property, but less than title.

The word "interest" is used throughout the Restatement of Torts, 2d, to denote the object of any human desire. Sec. 1.

The word "interest" is used in the Restatement of Property both generically to include varying aggregates of rights, privileges, powers and immunities and distributively to mean any one of them. Sec. 5.

See also Adverse interest; Against interest; Beneficial interest; Contingent interest in personal property; Community of interest; Compelling state interest; Compound interest; Conflict of interest; Coupons; Equitable interest; Executory interests; Future interests; Identity of interests; Insurable interest; Leasehold interest; Legal interest; Lessee's interest; Lessor's interest; New York interest; Ownership; Pecuniary interest; Possessory interest; Public interest; Security interest; Senior interest; Terminable interest; Usury; Vested interest.

Absolute interest. Person has absolute interest in property when such is so completely vested in individual that no contingency can deprive him of it without his consent. So, too, he is the owner of such absolute interest who must necessarily sustain the loss if the property is destroyed. See also **Fee simple; Title.**

Easement. An easement is an "interest" in land and involves the title. Allen v. Smith, Mo.App., 375 S.W.2d 874, 878.

For use of money. Interest is the compensation allowed by law or fixed by the parties for the use or forbearance or detention of money. Rosen v. U. S., C.A.Pa., 288 F.2d 658, 660. Basic cost of borrowing money or buying on installment contract. Payments a borrower pays a lender for the use of the money. A corporation pays interest on its bonds to the bondholders.

Accrued interest. Interest earned but not yet paid. See also **Accruing interest.**

Accumulated interest. Interest on bonds and other debts which is due or overdue but not yet paid.

Boston interest. See **Boston interest.**

Compound interest. Interest upon interest; *i.e.* interest paid on principal plus accrued interest. Exists where accrued interest is added to the principal sum, and the whole treated as a new principal for the calculation of the interest for the next period. Interest added to principal as interest becomes due and thereafter made to bear interest. Wieland v. Loon, 79 S.D. 608, 116 N.W.2d 391, 393.

Conventional interest. Interest at the rate agreed upon and fixed by the parties themselves, as distinguished from that which the law would prescribe in the absence of an explicit agreement.

Excessive interest. See **Usury.**

Ex-interest. In the language of stock exchanges, a bond or other interest-bearing security is said to be sold "ex-interest" when the seller reserves to himself the interest already accrued and payable (if any) or the interest accruing up to the next interest day.

Gross interest. The total interest paid by the borrower which includes administrative costs and expenses to lender.

Interest rate. See **Interest rate.**

Interest upon interest. See *Compound interest, infra.*

Legal interest. See **Legal interest.**

New York interest. Computation of interest on the exact number of days in a month and not on a thirty day month. See also **Boston interest.**

Nominal interest. The interest stated on the security and not the rate based on the price of the security.

Ordinary interest. Interest computed entirely on the principal with no interest computed on the interest past due.

Simple interest. That which is paid for the principal or sum lent, at a certain rate or allowance, made by law or agreement of parties. Interest calculated on principal where interest earned during periods before maturity of the loan is neither added to the principal nor paid to the lender. That paid on the principal lent as distinguished for compound interest which is interest paid on unpaid interest. B. F. Saul Co. v. West End Park North, Inc., 250 Md. 707, 246 A.2d 591, 598.

Imputed interest. In taxation, taxable income resulting from purchase at a bargain of assets for less than their fair value; such occurs when one is so placed as to take advantage of an opportunity not available to others. An estimated charge for interest for use of capital though no cash payment is provided. See also **Cost** *(Imputed cost).*

In the case of certain long-term sales of property, the Internal Revenue Service has the authority to convert some of the gain from the sale into interest income if the contract does not provide for a minimum rate of interest to be paid by the purchaser. The application of this procedure has the effect of forcing the seller to recognize less long-term capital gain and more ordinary income (*i.e.,* interest income).

Insurance. See **Insurable interest.**

Intervention. Word "interest" as used in provision of Federal Rule of Civil Procedure that on timely application anyone shall be permitted to intervene in an action when representation of his "interest" by existing parties is or may be inadequate and he is or may be bound by judgment in action means specific legal or equitable interest in chose. Toles v. U. S., C.A. N.M., 371 F.2d 784, 785, 786. See Fed.R.Civil P. 24.

Interest sufficient to support intervention as of right must be significant, must be direct rather than contingent, and must be based on a right which belongs to the proposed intervenor rather than to an existing party to the suit. Vazman, S. A. v. Fidelity Intern. Bank., D.C.N.Y., 418 F.Supp. 1084, 1085. An "interest" in the subject of an action so as to render the holder thereof a necessary party or a proper intervenor does not include a mere, consequential, remote or conjectural possibility of being in some manner affected by the result of the action but must be such a direct claim upon the subject matter of the action that the holder will either gain or lose by direct operation of the judgment to be rendered. Bunting v. McDonnell Aircraft Corp., Mo., 522 S.W.2d 161, 169.

Penalty. Interest is exaction for past-due obligations and in essence is in the nature of a penalty; it is compensation for delay in payment. Wayne Tp. in Passaic County v. Ricmin, Inc., 124 N.J.Super. 509, 308 A.2d 27, 30. See also **Penalty.**

Interest equalization tax. Tax imposed on each acquisition by a U.S. person of stock of a foreign issuer, or of a debt obligation of a foreign obligor if such obligation has a period remaining to maturity of a year or more. I.R.C. § 4911(a).

Interest rate. The percentage of an amount of money which is paid for its use for a specified time. Commonly expressed as an annual percentage rate (APR). See **Annual percentage rate; Truth-in-Lending Act; Usury.**

Prime rate. The most favorable interest rates charged by a commercial bank on short-term loans to its best (*i.e.* most credit worthy) customers.

Interest reipublicæ ne maleficia remaneant impunita /íntərèst rìyaypábləsiy níy mǽləfís(h)(i)yə rəmǽniyənt ìmpyənáydə/. It concerns the state that crimes remain not unpunished.

Interest reipublicæ ne sua quis male utatur /íntərèst rìyaypábləsiy níy s(y)úwə kwìs mǽliy yətéydər/. It concerns the state that persons do not misuse their property.

Interest reipublicæ quod homines conserventur /íntərèst rìyaypábləsiy kwód hóməniyz kònsərvéntər/. It concerns the state that [the lives of] men be preserved.

Interest reipublicæ res judicatas non rescindi /íntərèst rìyaypábləsiy ríyz juwdəkéydəs nòn rəsínday/. It concerns the state that things adjudicated be not rescinded. It is matter of public concern that solemn adjudications of the courts should not be disturbed.

Interest reipublicæ suprema hominum testamenta rata haberi /íntərèst rìyaypábləsiy s(y)əpríymə hómənəm tèstəméntə réydə həbíray/. It concerns the state that men's last wills be held valid (or allowed to stand).

Interest reipublicæ ut carceres sint in tuto /íntərèst rìyaypábləsiy ət kársəriyz sìnt in t(y)úwdow/. It concerns the state that prisons be safe places of confinement.

Interest (imprimis) reipublicæ ut pax in regno conservetur, et quæcunque paci adversentur provide declinentur /íntərèst əmpráyməs rìyaypábləsiy ət pǽks in régnow kònsərvéydər èt kwiykə́ŋkwiy péysay ǽdvərséntər prəváydiy dèklənéntər/. It especially concerns the state that peace be preserved in the kingdom, and that whatever things are against peace be prudently avoided.

Interest reipublicæ ut quilibet re sua bene utatur /íntərèst rìyaypábləsiy ət kwáyləbət ríy s(y)úwə bíyniy yətéydər/. It is the concern of the state that every one uses his property properly.

Interest reipublicæ ut sit finis litium /íntərèst rìyaypábləsiy ət sít fáynəs láysh(iy)əm/. It concerns the state that there be an end of lawsuits. It is for the general welfare that a period be put to litigation.

Interfere. To check; hamper; hinder; infringe; encroach; trespass; disturb; intervene; intermeddle; interpose. To enter into, or to take part in, the concerns of others. People ex rel. Benefit Ass'n of Railway Employees v. Miner, 387 Ill. 393, 56 N.E.2d 353, 356.

Interference. In patent law, this term designates a collision between rights claimed or granted; that is, where a person claims a patent for the whole or any integral part of the ground already covered by an existing patent or by a pending application. Term refers to Patent Office proceeding designed to determine priority of invention between two or more parties claiming same subject matter. Philco Corp. v. Radio Corp. of America, D.C.Del., 276 F.Supp. 24, 26. See **Infringement.**

Interim /íntərəm/. Lat. In the meantime; meanwhile; temporary; between. An assignee *ad interim* is one appointed between the time of bankruptcy and appointment of the regular assignee. See also **Interlocutory.**

Interim committitur /íntərəm kəmídədər/. "In the meantime, let him be committed." An order of court (or the docket-entry noting it) by which a prisoner is committed to prison and directed to be kept there until some further action can be taken, or until the time arrives for the execution of his sentence.

Interim curator /íntərəm kyəréydər/°kyùrədər/. In old English law, a person appointed by justices of the peace to take care of the property of a felon convict, until the appointment by the crown of an administrator or administrators for the same purpose.

Interim financing. A short-term loan usually obtained to pay for construction costs of building or house, with final financing to be covered by mortgage.

Interim officer. One appointed to fill the office during a temporary vacancy, or during an interval caused by the absence or incapacity of the regular incumbent.

Interim order. One made in the meantime, and until something is done.

Interim receipt. A receipt for money paid by way of premium for a contract of insurance for which application is made. If the risk is rejected, the money is refunded, less the *pro rata* premium.

Interim statements. In accounting, statements issued for periods less than the regular, annual accounting period. Most corporations are required to issue interim statements on a quarterly basis.

Interinsurance exchange /ìntərinshúrən(t)s əkschéynj/. Reciprocal exchange (*q.v.*).

Interior Department. Executive level department of federal government overseeing agencies concerned with Indian affairs, mining, fish and wildlife, geologic research, land management, national parks and monuments, territories, flood control, conservation, public works, and related areas. See also **Bureau of Land Management.**

Interlaqueare /ìntərlækwiyériy/. In old English practice, to link together, or interchangeably. Writs were called "interlaqueata" where several were issued against several parties residing in different counties, each party being summoned by a separate writ to warrant the tenant, together with the other warrantors.

Interlineation. The act of writing between the lines of an instrument; also what is written between lines. See also **Interpolate.**

Interlining. The practice whereby a carrier, whose certificated routes do not reach the shipment destination, transfers the shipment to another carrier for delivery. Gilbertville Trucking Co. v. U. S., Mass., 371 U.S. 115, 83 S.Ct. 217, 221, 9 L.Ed.2d 177. See also **Joint through rate.**

Interlocking directorate. A board of directors linked with that of another corporation by interlocking directors so that the businesses managed by them are to some degree under one control. Jack Tar of Ark., Inc. v. National Wells Television, Inc., 234 Ark. 306, 351 S.W.2d 848, 850.

Situation where places or seats on boards of directors of several different corporations or banks are filled by the same persons. This situation has the potential for antitrust violations (where *e.g.* the corporations or banks are competitors) and as such is controlled by Clayton Act (Sec. 8), 15 U.S.C.A. § 19.

Interlocutory /ìntərlók(y)ədəriy/. Provisional; interim; temporary; not final. Something intervening between the commencement and the end of a suit which decides some point or matter, but is not a final decision of the whole controversy.

As to interlocutory Costs; Decree; Injunction; Judgment; Order; and Sentence, see those titles. See also **Intermediate order.**

Interlocutory appeal. An appeal of a matter which is not determinable of the controversy, but which is necessary for a suitable adjudication of the merits. See also **Final decision rule.**

Interlocutory Appeals Act. Federal Act which grants discretion to the courts of appeals to review any interlocutory order whatever in a civil case if the trial (*i.e.* federal district court) judge, in making the order, has stated in writing that the order involves a controlling question of law as to which there is substantial ground for difference of opinion and that an immediate appeal from the order may materially advance the ultimate termination of litigation. 28 U.S.C.A. § 1292(b).

Interloper. Persons who interfere or intermeddle into business to which they have no right. Persons who enter a country or place to trade without license. One who meddles in affairs which are none of his business and for which he has no responsibility; an intruder; an intermeddler. Encroachment on rights of others.

Intermarriage. See **Miscegenation.**

Intermeddle. To interfere wrongly with property or the conduct of business affairs officiously or without right or title. See also **Interfere; Interloper.**

Not a technical legal term, but sometimes used with reference to the acts of an executor *de son tort* or a *negotiorum gestor* in the civil law.

Intermediary. An arbitrator or mediator. A broker; one who is employed to negotiate a matter between two parties, and who for that purpose may be agent of both; *e.g.* insurance broker. See also **Finder.**

Intermediary bank. Any bank to which an item is transferred in the course of collection except the depositary or payor bank. U.C.C. § 4–105(c).

Intermediate. Intervening; interposed during the progress of a suit, proceeding, business, etc., or between its beginning and end. See **Interlocutory; Intervention.**

Intermediate account. In probate law, an account of an executor, administrator, or guardian filed subsequent to his first or initial account and before his final account. An account filed with the court for the purpose of disclosing the acts of the person accounting and the state or condition of the fund in his hands, and not made the subject of a final judicial settlement.

Intermediate courts. Those courts which have general jurisdiction, either trial or appellate or both, but which are below the court of last resort in the jurisdiction.

Intermediate order. An order made between the commencement of the action and its final determination, incident to and during its progress, which does not determine the cause but only some intervening matter relating thereto; one that is not directly appealable. See **Interlocutory.**

In terminis terminantibus /in tə́rmənəs tə̀rmənǽntəbəs/. In terms of determination; exactly in point. In express or determinate terms.

Intermittent easement. See **Easement.**

Intermittent stream. A stream, the flow of which in the state of nature is interrupted either from time to time during the year or at various places along its course, or both. U. S. v. Fallbrook Public Utility Dist., D.C. Cal., 109 F.Supp. 28, 78.

Intermixture of goods. Confusion of goods; the confusing or commingling together of goods belonging to different owners in such a way that the property of no particular owner can be separately identified or extracted from the mass. See also **Confusion of goods.**

Intern. To restrict or confine a person or group of persons, particularly in time of war (*e.g.* enemy aliens). An advanced student or recent graduate in a professional field; one trained in a profession allied to medicine who undergoes a period of practical clinical experience prior to practicing his profession. Regents of University of Mich. v. Michigan Employment Relations Commission, 38 Mich.App. 55, 195 N.W.2d 875, 878. See also **Internment.**

Internal. Relating to the interior; comprised within boundary lines; of interior concern or interest; domestic, as opposed to foreign.

Internal act. That which transpires within a person or organization or government as contrasted with a happening outside such.

Internal affairs doctrine. In context of labor and international law, matters dealing with crew of foreign ships and employer. Windward Shipping (London) Limited v. American Radio Ass'n, AFL–CIO, Tex.Civ. App., 482 S.W.2d 675, 681.

Internal affairs of corporation. In conflicts, the rights and liabilities of a corporation are determined by the local law of the state which has the most significant relationship to the occurrence and the parties. Restatement, Second, Conflicts, § 302(1). Such affairs are generally left to courts of the state of incorporation.

Internal commerce. See **Commerce.**

Internal improvements. With reference to governmental policy and constitutional provisions restricting taxation or the contracting of public debts, this term means works of general public utility or advantage, designed to promote facility of intercommunication, trade, and commerce, the transportation of persons and property, or the development of the natural re-sources of the state, such as railroads, public highways, turnpikes, and canals, bridges, the improvement of rivers and harbors, systems of artificial irrigation, and the improvement of water powers; but it does not include the building and maintenance of state institutions.

Internal police. A term sometimes applied to the police power, or power to enact laws in the interest of the public safety, health, and morality, which is inherent in the legislative authority of each state, is to be exercised with reference only to its domestic affairs and its own citizens, and is not surrendered to the federal government. See also **Police power.**

Internal revenue. Governmental revenues from internal sources by way of taxes as contrasted with revenues from customs and foreign sources.

Internal Revenue Code (I.R.C.). That body of law which codifies all federal tax laws including income, estate, stamp, gift, excise, etc. taxes. Such laws comprise Title 26 of U.S. Code, and are implemented by Treasury Regulations and Revenue Rulings.

Internal Revenue Service. The Internal Revenue Service (I.R.S.) is responsible for administering and enforcing the internal revenue laws, except those relating to alcohol, tobacco, firearms, explosives, and wagering. Basic I.R.S. activities include providing taxpayer service and education; determination, assessment, and collection of internal revenue taxes; determination of pension plan qualification and exempt organization status; and preparation and issuance of rulings and regulations to interpret the provisions of the Internal Revenue Code.

Internal security. That branch of law and government (*e.g.* CIA, FBI) dealing with measures to protect the country from subversive activities.

Internal security acts. Federal Acts (Smith Act, 18 U.S.C.A. §§ 2385, 2386; McCarran Act, 50 U.S.C.A. § 781 et seq.) controlling and making illegal subversive activities of communist organizations and other groups whose purpose is to overthrow or disrupt the government.

Internal waters. Such as lie wholly within the body of the particular state or country. See also **Inland waters.**

International agreements. Treaties and other agreements of a contractual character between different countries or organizations of states (foreign) creating legal rights and obligations between the parties.

International commerce. See **Commerce.**

International Court of Justice. Judicial arm of the United Nations. It has jurisdiction to give advisory opinions on matters of law and treaty construction when requested by the General Assembly, Security Council or any other international agency authorized by the General Assembly to petition for such opinion. It has jurisdiction, also, to settle legal disputes between nations when voluntarily submitted to it. Its judgments may be enforced by the Security Council. Its jurisdiction and powers are defined by statute, to which all member states of the U.N. are parties. Judges of such court are elected by the General Assembly and Security Council of U.N.

International jurisdiction. Power of a court or other organization to hear and determine matters between different countries or persons of different countries or foreign states. See **International Court of Justice.**

International law. The law which regulates the intercourse of nations; the law of nations. The customary law which determines the rights and regulates the intercourse of independent nations in peace and war.

International Monetary Fund. Agency of United Nations established to stabilize international exchange and promote balanced international trade.

International Shoe Case. Due process requires that a foreign corporation be "present" within a state by a measure of minimal activity within the state for suits to be maintained against it in the state. International Shoe Co. v. State of Washington, etc., 326 U.S. 310, 66 S.Ct. 154, 90 L.Ed. 95. See also McGee v. International Life Ins. Co., 355 U.S. 220, 78 S.Ct. 199, 2 L.Ed.2d 223; Hanson v. Denckla, 357 U.S. 235, 78 S.Ct. 1228, 2 L.Ed.2d 1283. See **Minimal contacts.**

Internment. The detainment or confinement of enemy aliens or persons suspected of disloyalty in specially designated areas; *e.g.* Japanese during World War II. Johnson v. Eisentrager, 339 U.S. 763, 70 S.Ct. 936, 94 L.Ed. 1255.

Internuncio /ìntərnə́ns(h)(i)yow/. A minister of a second order, charged with the affairs of the papal court in countries where that court has no nuncio.

Internuncius /ìntərnə́ns(h)(i)yəs/. A messenger between two parties; a go-between. Applied to a broker, as the agent of both parties.

Inter pares /íntər périyz/. Between peers; between those who stand on a level or equality, as respects diligence, opportunity, responsibility, etc.

Inter partes /íntər párdiyz/. Between parties. Instruments in which two persons unite, each making conveyance to, or engagement with, the other, are called "papers *inter partes.*"

Judgment inter partes. See **Judgment in personam.**

Interpellate /ìntərpéleyt/°pəléyt/. To address with a question, especially when formal and public; originally used with respect to proceedings in the French legislature. Used in reference to questions by the court to counsel during an argument.

Interpellation /ìntərpəléyshən/. In the civil law, the act by which, in consequence of an agreement, the party bound declares that he will not be bound beyond a certain time.

Interplea /íntərplìy/. A plea by which a person sued in respect to property disclaims any interest in it and demands that rival claimants shall litigate their titles between themselves and relieve him from responsibility. See **Interpleader.**

A statutory proceeding, serving as a substitute for the action of replevin, by which a third person intervenes in an action of attachment, sets up his own title to the specific property attached, and seeks to recover the possession of it.

Interpleader. When two or more persons claim the same thing (or fund) of a third, and he, laying no claim to it himself, is ignorant which of them has a right to it, and fears he may be prejudiced by their proceeding against him to recover it, he may join such claimants as defendants and require them to interplead their claims so that he may not be exposed to double or multiple liability. A defendant exposed to similar liability may obtain such interpleader by way of cross-claim or counterclaim. Interpleader in federal court is governed by the federal Interpleader Act, 28 U.S.C.A. § 1335, and Fed.R. Civil P. 22. Similar statutes and court rules govern interpleader in state courts.

Statutory interpleader. A federal statutory right (28 U.S.C.A. § 1335) whereby disinterested stakeholder from whom several people claim same proceeds may require claimants to litigate matter among themselves without embroiling stakeholder. Glens Falls Ins. Co. v. Strom, D.C.Cal., 198 F.Supp. 450, 455.

Interpol. International Criminal Police Organization; a coordinating group for international law enforcement.

Interpolate /intárpəleyt/. To insert (additional or false) words in a complete instrument or document, thus altering meaning of such. See also **Interlineation.**

Interpolated terminal reserve. The method used in valuing insurance policies for gift and death tax purposes when the policies are not paid-up at the time of their transfer.

Interpolation /intàrpəléyshən/. The act of interpolating; the words interpolated. See also **Interlineation; Interpretation.**

Interposition /intàrpəzíshən/. The doctrine that a state, in the exercise of its sovereignty, may reject a mandate of the federal government deemed to be unconstitutional or to exceed the powers delegated to the federal government. The doctrine denies constitutional obligation of states to respect Supreme Court decisions with which they do not agree. Bush v. Orleans Parish School Bd., D.C.La., 188 F.Supp. 916. The concept is based on the 10th Amendment of the Constitution of the United States reserving to the states powers not delegated to the United States. Historically, the doctrine emanated from Chisholm v. Georgia, 2 U.S. (Dall.) 419, wherein the state of Georgia, when sued in the Supreme Court by a private citizen of another state, entered a remonstrance and declined to recognize the court's jurisdiction. The U.S. Supreme Court rejected this doctrine of interposition in Cooper v. Aaron, 358 U.S. 1, 78 S.Ct. 1401, 3 L.Ed.2d 5.

Interpret. To construe; to seek out the meaning of language; to translate orally from one tongue to another.

Interpretare et concordare leges legibus, est optimus interpretandi modus /intàrprətériy èt kòŋkərdériy líyjiyz líyjəbəs, èst óptəməs intàrprətǽnday mówdəs/. To interpret, and [in such a way as] to harmonize laws with laws, is the best mode of interpretation.

Interpretatio chartarum benigne facienda est, ut res magis valeat quam pereat /intàrprətéysh(iy)ow kartérəm bənígniy fèys(h)iyéndə èst át ríyz méyjəs vǽliyət kwǽm péhriyət/. The interpretation of deeds is to be liberal, that the thing may rather have effect than fail.

Interpretatio fienda est ut res magis valeat quam pereat /intə̀rprətéysh(iy)ow fayéndə èst ə́t ríyz méyjəs vǽliyət kwǽm péhriyət/. Such an interpretation is to be adopted that the thing may rather stand than fall.

Interpretation. The art or process of discovering and ascertaining the meaning of a statute, will, contract, or other written document. The discovery and representation of the true meaning of any signs used to convey ideas.

It is said to be either "legal," which rests on the same authority as the law itself, or "doctrinal," which rests upon its intrinsic reasonableness. Legal interpretation may be either "authentic," when it is expressly provided by the legislator, or "usual," when it is derived from unwritten practice. Doctrinal interpretation may turn on the meaning of words and sentences, when it is called "grammatical," or on the intention of the legislator, when it is described as "logical." When logical interpretation stretches the words of a statute to cover its obvious meaning, it is called "extensive;" when, on the other hand, it avoids giving full meaning to the words, in order not to go beyond the intention of the legislator, it is called "restrictive."

As to *strict* and *liberal* interpretation, see **Construction.** See also **Broad interpretation; Last antecedent rule.**

Construction distinguished. In the strict usage of this term, "construction" is a term of wider scope than "interpretation;" for, while the latter is concerned only with ascertaining the sense and meaning of the subject-matter, the former may also be directed to explaining the legal effects and consequences of the instrument in question. Hence interpretation precedes construction, but stops at the written text. Interpretation and construction of written instruments are not the same. A rule of construction is one which either governs the effect of an ascertained intention, or points out what the court should do in the absence of express or implied intention, while a rule of interpretation is one which governs the ascertainment of the meaning of the maker of the instrument. In re Union Trust Co., 89 Misc. 69, 151 N.Y.S. 246, 249.

These two terms are however, commonly used interchangeably.

Close or strict interpretation (interpretatio restricta) is adopted if just reasons, connected with the formation and character of the text, induce us to take the words in their narrowest meaning. This species of interpretation has generally been called "literal."

Extensive interpretation (interpretatio extensiva, called, also, "liberal interpretation") adopts a more comprehensive signification of the word.

Extravagant interpretation (interpretatio excedens) is that which substitutes a meaning evidently beyond the true one. It is therefore not genuine interpretation.

Free or unrestricted interpretation (interpretatio soluta) proceeds simply on the general principles of interpretation in good faith, not bound by any specific or superior principle.

Limited or restricted interpretation (interpretatio limitata) is when we are influenced by other principles than the strictly hermeneutic ones.

Predestined interpretation (interpretatio predestinata) takes place if the interpreter, laboring under a strong bias of mind, makes the text subservient to his preconceived views or desires. This includes artful interpretation *(interpretatio vafer),* by which the interpreter seeks to give a meaning to the text other than the one he knows to have been intended.

In the civil law, *authentic* interpretation of laws is that given by the legislator himself, which is obligatory on the courts. *Customary* interpretation (also called "usual") is that which arises from successive or concurrent decisions of the court on the same subject-matter, having regard to the spirit of the law, jurisprudence, usages, and equity; as distinguished from "authentic" interpretation, which is that given by the legislator himself.

Interpretation clause. A section of a statute which defines the meaning of certain words occurring frequently in the other sections.

Interpretatio talis in ambiguis semper fienda est ut evitetur inconveniens et absurdum /intə̀rprətéysh(iy)ow tǽləs in æmbígyuwəs sémpər fayéndə èst ət èvətíydər inkənvíyn(i)yen(d)z èd əbsə́rdəm/. In cases of ambiguity, such an interpretation should always be made that what is inconvenient and absurd may be avoided.

Interpreter. A person sworn at a trial to interpret the evidence of a foreigner or a deaf and dumb person to the court.

Inter quatuor parietes /íntər kwóduwər pəráyədiyz/. Between four walls.

Inter regalia /íntər rəgéyl(i)yə/. In English law, among the things belonging to the sovereign. Among these are rights of salmon fishing, mines of gold and silver, forests, forfeitures, casualties of superiority, etc., which are called *"regalia minora,"* and may be conveyed to a subject. The *regalia majora* include the several branches of the royal prerogative, which are inseparable from the person of the sovereign.

Interregnum /intərégnəm/. An interval between reigns. The period which elapses between the death of a sovereign and the election of another. The vacancy which occurs when there is no government.

Interrogation. In criminal law, process of questions propounded by police to person arrested or suspected to seek solution of crime. Such person is entitled to be informed of his rights, including right to have counsel present, and the consequences of his answers. If the police fail or neglect to give these warnings, the questions and answers are not admissible in evidence at the trial or hearing of the arrested person. Miranda v. State of Arizona, 384 U.S. 436, 86 S.Ct. 1602, 16 L.Ed.2d 694. See also **Confession; Custodial interrogation; Miranda Rule.**

Custodial interrogation. Questioning initiated by law enforcement officers after a person has been taken into custody or otherwise deprived of his freedom of action in any significant way. See also **Miranda Rule.**

Interrogatoire /ìnterogatwár/. In French law, an act which contains the interrogatories made by the judge to the person accused, on the facts which are the object of the accusation, and the answers of the accused.

Interrogatories /ìntərógət(ò)riyz/. A set or series of written questions drawn up for the purpose of being propounded to a party, witness, or other person having information of interest in the case.

A discovery device consisting of written questions about the case submitted by one party to the other party or witness. The answers to the interrogatories are usually given under oath, *i.e.*, the person answering the questions signs a sworn statement that the answers are true. Fed.R. Civil P. 33.

The court may submit to the jury, together with appropriate forms for a general verdict, written interrogatories upon one or more issues of fact the decision of which is necessary to a verdict. See Fed.R. Civil P. 49.

See also **Discovery; Special interrogatories.**

In terrorem /in tèhrórəm/. Lit. In fright or alarm or terror. In terror or warning; by way of threat. Applied to legacies given upon condition that the recipient shall not dispute the validity or the dispositions of the will; such a condition being usually regarded as a mere threat. See **In terrorem clause.**

In terrorem clause. A provision in a document such as a lease or will designed to frighten a beneficiary or lessee into doing or not doing something; *e.g.* clause in a will providing for revocation of a bequest or devise if the legatee or devisee contests the will. A condition "in terrorem" is a provision in a will which threatens beneficiaries with forfeiture of their legacies and bequests should they contest validity or dispositions of will. Taylor v. Rapp, 217 Ga. 654, 124 S.E.2d 271, 272.

In terrorem populi /in tèhrórəm pópyəlay/. Lat. To the terror of the people. A technical phrase formerly necessary in indictments for riots.

Interruptio /ìntərə́psh(iy)ow/. Lat. Interruption. A term used both in the civil and common law of prescription.

Interruptio multiplex non tollit præscriptionem semel obtentam /ìntərə́psh(iy)ow mə́ltəplèks nòn tólət prəskrípshiyównəm sémal əbténtəm/. Frequent interruption does not take away a prescription once secured.

Interruption. A break in continuity or uniformity. The occurrence of some act or fact, during the period of prescription, which is sufficient to arrest the running of the statute of limitations. It is said to be either "natural" or "civil," the former being caused by the act of the party; the latter by the legal effect or operation of some fact or circumstance. Interruption of the possession is where the right is not enjoyed or exercised continuously; interruption of the right is where the person having or claiming the right ceases the exercise of it in such a manner as to show that he does not claim to be entitled to exercise it.

Inter rusticos /íntər rə́stəkows/. Among the illiterate or unlearned.

Intersection. As applied to a street or highway means the space occupied by two streets at the point where they cross each other. Space common to both streets or highways, formed by continuing the curb lines. Western Union Tel. Co. v. Dickson, 27 Tenn.App. 752, 173 S.W.2d 714, 718.

Point of intersection of two roads is the point where their middle lines intersect. But the term may also mean the point which each of two approaching vehicles will reach at the same moment. "Intersection" may also apply where street or highway runs into but without crossing another; *e.g.* a "T" intersection.

Inter se or **inter sese** /íntər síy(siy)/. Lat. Among or between themselves; used to distinguish rights or duties between two or more parties from their rights or duties to others.

Interspousal. Between husband and wife.

Interspousal immunity. See **Husband-wife tort actions.**

Interstate. Between two or more states; between places or persons in different states; concerning or affecting two or more states politically or territorially. See also **Intrastate commerce.**

Interstate agreements. See **Interstate compact.**

Interstate and foreign commerce. Commerce between a point in one State and a point in another State, between points in the same State through another State or through a foreign country, between points in a foreign country or countries through the United States, and commerce between a point in the United States and a point in a foreign country or in a Territory or possession of the United States, but only insofar as such commerce takes place in the United States. The term "United States" means all the States and the District of Columbia. 18 U.S.C.A. § 831.

Interstate commerce. Traffic, intercourse, commercial trading, or the transportation of persons or property between or among the several states of the Union, or from or between points in one state and points in another state; commerce between two states, or between places lying in different states. Gibbons v. Ogden, 22 U.S. (9 Wheat.) 1, 6 L.Ed. 23; Wabash, etc. R. Co. v. Illinois, 118 U.S. 557, 7 S.Ct. 4, 30 L.Ed. 244. It comprehends all the component parts of commercial intercourse between different states. Furst v. Brewster, 282 U.S. 493, 51 S.Ct. 295, 296, 75 L.Ed. 478. See **Balancing of interests.**

Interstate Commerce Act. The act of congress of February 4, 1887 (49 U.S.C.A. § 1 *et seq.*), designed to regulate commerce between the states, and particularly the transportation of persons and property, by carriers, between interstate points, prescribing that charges for such transportation shall be reasonable and just, prohibiting unjust discrimination, rebates, draw-backs, preferences, pooling of freights, etc., requiring schedules of rates to be published, establishing a commission to carry out the measures enacted, and prescribing the powers and duties of such commission and the procedure before it.

Interstate Commerce Commission. The I.C.C. was created by Congress to regulate, in the public interest, carriers subject to the Interstate Commerce Act which are engaged in transportation in interstate commerce and in foreign commerce to the extent that it takes place within the United States. Surface transportation under the Commission's jurisdiction includes railroads, trucking companies, bus lines, freight forwarders, water carriers, oil pipelines, transportation brokers, and express agencies. The regulatory laws vary with the type of transportation; however, they generally involve certification of carriers seeking to provide transportation for the public, rates, adequacy of service, purchases, and mergers. The I.C.C. assures that the carriers it regulates will provide the public with rates and services that are fair and reasonable.

Interstate compact. A voluntary agreement between two or more states which is designed to meet common problems of the parties concerned. Compacts on major matters must receive the consent of the U.S. Congress as specified in Article I, Section 10 of the Constitution. They usually relate to such things as conservation, boundary problems, education, port control, flood control, and penal matters.

Interstate extradition. The reclamation and surrender, according to due legal proceedings, of a person who, having committed a crime in one of the states of the Union, has fled into another state to evade justice or escape prosecution. Art. IV, § 2, U.S.Const. See **Extradition; Interstate rendition.**

Interstate Land Sales Full Disclosure Act. Federal Act (15 U.S.C.A. § 1701 et seq.), the purpose of which is to provide purchasers and lessees of undeveloped land with the information they need in order to make an informed decision with regard to the land being sold or leased. As indicated by its title, this is a "disclosure" act.

Interstate law. That branch of law which affords rules and principles for the determination of controversies between citizens of different states in respect to mutual rights or obligations, in so far as the same are affected by the diversity of their citizenship or by diversity in the laws or institutions of the several states.

Interstate rendition. Right of one state to demand from asylum state surrender of a fugitive from justice from the demanding state when the fugitive is found in the asylum state. Art. IV, § 2, U.S.Const. Application of Dugger, 17 Ariz.App. 297, 497 P.2d 413. Nearly all states have adopted the Uniform Criminal Extradition Act. See **Extradition.**

Interval ownership. Type of ownership of second (*i.e.* vacation) home whereby the property is owned for only an interval (*e.g.* two weeks or a month) of the year. Each owner receives a deed covering his interval period.

Intervening act. Such act of third person in order to break chain of causation and obviate liability for original breach of duty must be a superseding cause and one which original wrongdoer was not bound to anticipate as the natural or ordinary result of his acts. Littell v. Argus Production Co., C.C.A.Kan., 78 F.2d 955, 957. See also **Intervening cause.**

Intervening agency. To render an original wrong a remote cause, an "intervening agency" must be independent of such wrong, adequate to produce the injury, so interrupting the natural sequence of events as to produce a result different from what would have been produced, and one that could not have been reasonably expected from the original wrong. An independent "intervening agency" which will protect the original wrongdoer must be the efficient cause of the injury of which complaint is made, and not a negligent act or omission of such agency concurring with or succeeding the original negligence permitted by the original wrongdoer to continue and which in the natural course of events results in such injury. In short, the result prevented by the intervening agency must be the injury complained of, and not the requital for that injury. Swanson v. Slagal, 212 Ind. 394, 8 N.E.2d 993, 1000. See also **Intervening cause.**

Intervening cause. The "intervening cause," which will relieve of liability for an injury, is an independent cause which intervenes between the original wrongful act or omission and the injury, turns aside the natural sequence of events, and produces a result which would not otherwise have followed and which could not have been reasonably anticipated. An act of an independent agency which destroys the causal connection between the negligent act of the defendant and the wrongful injury; the independent act being the immediate cause, in which case damages are not recoverable because the original wrongful act is not the proximate cause. An "intervening efficient cause" is a new and independent force which breaks the causal connection between the original wrong and injury, and itself becomes direct and immediate cause of injury. Phillabaum v. Lake Erie & W. R. Co., 315 Ill. 131, 145 N.E. 806, 808.

In criminal law, a cause which comes between an antecedent and a consequence; it may be either independent or dependent, but in either case it is sufficient to negate criminal responsibility.

See also **Intervening act; Intervening agency.**

Intervening damages. See **Damages.**

Intervening force. One which actively operates in producing harm to another after the actor's negligent act or omission has been committed. Walborn v. Epley, 148 Pa.Super. 417, 24 A.2d 668, 671; American Mut. Liability Ins. Co. v. Buckley & Co., C.C.A.Pa., 117 F.2d 845, 847.

Intervenor. An intervenor is a person who voluntarily interposes in an action or other proceeding with the leave of the court. See **Intervention.**

Intervention. The procedure by which a third person, not originally a party to the suit, but claiming an interest in the subject matter, comes into the case, in order to protect his right or interpose his claim. The grounds and procedure are usually defined by various state statutes or Rules of Civil Procedure; *e.g.*, Fed.R. Civil P. 24. Intervention may exist either as a matter of right (Rule 24(a)) or at the discretion of the court (Rule 24(b)).

In English ecclesiastical law, the proceeding of a third person, who, not being originally a party to the suit or proceeding, but claiming an interest in the subject-matter in dispute, in order the better to protect such interest, interposes his claim. Stillwell Hotel Co. v. Anderson, 16 Cal.App.2d 636, 61 P.2d 71, 72.

Inter virum et uxorem /íntər váyrəm èd əksórəm/. Between husband and wife.

Inter vivos /íntər váyvows/. Between the living; from one living person to another. Where property passes by conveyance, the transaction is said to be *inter vivos,* to distinguish it from a case of succession or devise. So an ordinary gift from one person to another is called a "gift *inter vivos,*" to distinguish it from a gift made in contemplation of death *(mortis causa)* or a testamentary gift.

Inter vivos gift. Gift made when donor is living and provides that gift take effect while donor is living as contrasted with testamentary gift which is to take effect on death of donor (testator).

Inter vivos transfer. A transfer of property during the life of the owner. To be distinguished from testamentary transfers where the property passes at death.

Inter vivos trust. Trust created during lifetime of settlor and to become effective in his lifetime as contrasted with a testamentary trust which takes effect at death of settlor or testator. See also **Trust.**

Intestabilis /ìntestéybələs/. Lat. A witness incompetent to testify.

Intestable. One who has not testamentary capacity; *e.g.,* an infant, lunatic, or person civilly dead.

Intestacy /intéstəsiy/. The state or condition of dying without having made a valid will, or without having disposed by will of a part of his property.

In testamentis plenius testatoris intentionem scrutamur /in tèstəméntəs plíyniyəs tèstətórəs intènshiyównəm skrùwtéymər/. In wills we more especially seek out the intention of the testator.

In testamentis plenius voluntates testantium interpretantur /in tèstəméntəs plíyniyəs vòləntéydiyz tèstǽnsh(iy)əm intàrprətǽntər/. In wills the intention of testators is more especially regarded.

In testamentis ratio tacita non debet considerari, sed verba solum spectari debent; adeo per divinationem mentis a verbis recedere durum est /in tèstəméntəs réysh(iy)ow tǽsədə nòn débət kənsidəréray, sèd vərbə sówləm spèktéray débənt, ǽdiyow pàr dìvənèyshiyównəm méntəs èy várbəs rəsíydəriy d(y)úrəm èst/. In wills an unexpressed meaning ought not to be considered, but the words alone ought to be looked to; so hard is it to recede from the words by guessing at the intention.

Intestate. Without making a will. A person is said to die intestate when he dies without making a will, or dies without leaving anything to testify what his wishes were with respect to the disposal of his property after his death. The word is also often used to signify the person himself. Thus, in speaking of the property of a person who died intestate, it is common to say "the intestate's property;" *i.e.,* the property of the person dying in an intestate condition. *Compare* **Testate.**

Intestate laws. State statutes which provide and prescribe the devolution of estates of persons who die without disposing of their estates by will.

Intestate succession. A succession is called "intestate" when the deceased has left no will, or when his will has been revoked or annulled as irregular.

Intestato /ìntestéydow/. Lat. In the civil law, intestate; without a will.

Intestatus /ìntestéydəs/. Lat. In the civil and old English law, an intestate; one who dies without a will.

Intestatus decedit, qui aut omnino testamentum non fecit; aut non jure fecit; aut id quod fecerat ruptum irritumve factum est; aut nemo ex eo hæres exstitit. A person dies intestate who either has made no testament at all or has made one not legally valid; or if the testament he has made be revoked, or made useless; or if no heir has come forward.

In testimonium /in tèstəmówn(i)yəm/. Lat. In witness; in evidence whereof.

In the course of employment. The phrase "in the course of" employment, as used in workers' compensation acts, relates to time, place and circumstances under which accident occurred, and means injury happened while worker was at work in his or her employer's service. Peter Kiewitt Sons' Co. v. Industrial Commission, 88 Ariz. 164, 354 P.2d 28, 30.

Intimacy /íntəməsiy/. As generally applied to persons, it is understood to mean a proper, friendly relation of the parties, but it is frequently used to convey the idea of an improper relation.

Intimate. Close in friendship or acquaintance, familiar, near, confidential. Atkins Corporation v. Tourny, 6 Cal.2d 206, 57 P.2d 480, 484. To communicate indirectly; to hint or suggest.

Intimation. In the civil law, a notification to a party that some step in a legal proceeding is asked or will be taken. Particularly, a notice given by the party taking an appeal, to the other party, that the court above will hear the appeal.

Intimidation. Unlawful coercion; extortion; duress; putting in fear.

To take, or attempt to take, "by intimidation" means willfully to take, or attempt to take, by putting in fear of bodily harm. Such fear must arise from the willful conduct of the accused, rather than from some mere temperamental timidity of the victim; however, the fear of the victim need not be so great as to result in terror, panic, or hysteria.

Intitle. An old form of *"entitle."*

Into. A preposition signifying to the inside of; within It expresses entrance, or a passage from the outside of a thing to its interior, and follows verbs expressing motion. It has been held equivalent to, or synonymous with, "at," "inside of," and "to," and has been distinguished from the words "from" and "through."

Intol and uttol. Toll or custom paid for things imported and exported, or bought in and sold out.

In totidem verbis /in tòwdáydəm várbəs/. In so many words; in precisely the same words; word for word.

In toto /in tówdow/. In the whole; wholly; completely; as the award is void *in toto*.

In toto et pars continetur /ìn tówdow èt párz kòntəníydər/. In the whole the part also is contained.

Intoxicated. Affected by an intoxicant, under the influence of an intoxicating liquor. Taylor v. Joyce, 4 Cal.App.2d 612, 41 P.2d 967, 968. See **Intoxication.**

Intoxicating liquor. Any liquor used as a beverage, and which, when so used in sufficient quantities, ordinarily or commonly produces entire or partial intoxication. Any liquor intended for use as a beverage or capable of being so used, which contains alcohol, either obtained by fermentation or by the additional process of distillation, in such proportion that it will produce intoxication when imbibed in such quantities as may practically be drunk. Frisvold v. Leahy, 15 Cal.App.2d 752, 60 P.2d 151, 153. See also **Alcoholic liquors.**

Intoxication. Term comprehends situation where, by reason of drinking intoxicants, an individual does not have the normal use of his physical or mental faculties, thus rendering him incapable of acting in the manner in which an ordinarily prudent and cautious man, in full possession of his faculties, using reasonable care, would act under like conditions. Hendy v. Geary, 105 R.I. 419, 252 A.2d 435, 441.

A disturbance of mental or physical capacities resulting from the introduction of substances into the body. Model Penal Code, § 2.08.

The fact that a person charged with a crime was in an intoxicated condition at the time the alleged crime was committed is a defense only if such condition was involuntarily produced and rendered such person substantially incapable of knowing or understanding the wrongfulness of his conduct and of conforming his conduct to the requirements of law. An act committed while in a state of voluntary intoxication is not less criminal by reason thereof, but when a particular intent or other state of mind is a necessary element to constitute a particular crime, the fact of intoxication may be taken into consideration in determining such intent or state of mind.

Under most state statutes dealing with driving while intoxicated, "intoxication" includes such by alcohol or by drug or by both.

Confirmed habits of intoxication caused by voluntary and excessive use of liquor is a ground for divorce under many state divorce statutes.

See also **Habitual drunkenness; Intemperance.**

Public intoxication. Public intoxication is being on a highway or street or in a public place or public building while under the influence of intoxicating liquor, narcotics or other drug to the degree that one may endanger himself or other persons or property, or annoy persons in his vicinity.

Intoximeter. A trade name for scientific breath testing device that operates on assumption that concentration of blood alcohol bears fixed relation to concentration of alcohol in the deep lung, or alveolar air. Also commonly called breathalyzer test.

Intra /íntrə/. Lat. In; near; within. *"Infra"* or *"inter"* has taken the place of *"intra"* in many of the more modern Latin phrases.

Intra anni spatium /íntrə ǽnay spéysh(iy)əm/. Within the space of a year.

In traditionibus scriptorum, non quod dictum est, sed quod gestum est, inspicitur /in trədishiyownəbəs skriptórəm, nón kwòd díktəm èst, sèd kwòd jéstəm èst, ənspísədər/. In the delivery of writings, not what is said, but what is done, is looked to.

Intra fidem /íntrə fáydəm/. Within belief; credible.

In trajectu /in trəjékt(y)uw/. In the passage over; on the voyage over.

Intraliminal /intrəlímənəl/. In mining law, the term "intraliminal rights" denotes the right to mine, take, and possess all such bodies or deposits of ore as lie within the four planes formed by the vertical extension downward of the boundary lines of the claim; as distinguished from "extraliminal," or more commonly "extralateral," rights.

Intra luctus tempus /íntrə lə́ktəs témpəs/. Within the time of mourning.

Intra moenia /íntrə míyn(i)yə/. Within the walls (of a house). A term applied to domestic or *menial* servants.

Intramural. Within the walls. Existing within. The confines of an institution or governmental body. The powers of a municipal corporation are "intramural" and "extramural"; the one being the powers exercised within the corporate limits, and the other being those exercised without.

In transitu /in trǽnzət(y)uw/. In transit; on the way or passage; while passing from one person or place to another. In the course of transportation.

Intra parietes /íntrə pəráyədiyz/. Between walls; among friends; out of court; without litigation.

Intra præsidia /íntrə prəsíd(i)yə/. Within the defenses. See **Infra præsidia.**

Intra quatuor maria /íntrə kwóduwər mǽriyə/. Within the four seas.

Intrastate commerce. Commerce within a state, as opposed to commerce between states (*i.e.* interstate). See also **Balancing of interests; Commerce;** *compare* **Interstate commerce.**

Intra vires /íntrə váyriyz/. An act is said to be *intra vires* ("within the power") of a person or corporation when it is within the scope of his or its powers or authority. It is the opposite of *ultra vires (q.v.).*

Intrinsecum servitium /əntrínzəkəm sərvísh(iy)əm/. Lat. In old English law, common and ordinary duties with the lord's court.

Intrinsic. Internal; inherent. Pertaining to the essential nature of a thing.

Intrinsic fraud. That fraud which occurs within framework of actual conduct of trial and pertains to and affects determination of issues presented therein, and it may be accomplished by perjury, or by use of false or forged instruments, or by concealment or misrepresentation of evidence. Auerbach v. Samuels, 10 Utah 2d 152, 349 P.2d 1112, 1114. Fraud is "intrinsic fraud" where judgment is founded on fraudulent instruments or perjured evidence or the fraudulent actions pertain to an issue involved in original action and litigated therein. Alleghany Corp. v. Kirby, D.C. N.Y., 218 F.Supp. 164, 183.

Species of fraud which renders the document void as, for example, an instrument signed by one who had neither knowledge nor reasonable opportunity to obtain knowledge of its character or its essential terms, is not enforceable even by a holder in due course because such fraud is intrinsic. U.C.C. § 3-305(2)(c).

Intrinsic value. The true, inherent and essential value of thing, not depending upon accident, place or person but same everywhere and to everyone. King v. U. S., D.C.Colo., 292 F.Supp. 767, 776. The value of the thing itself, rather than any special features which make its market value different.

Introduction. The part of a writing which sets forth preliminary matter, or facts tending to explain the subject.

Intromission. Introduction; admission.

In English law, term means dealings in stock, goods, or cash of a principal coming into the hands of his agent, to be accounted for by the agent to his principal.

Intruder. One who enters upon land without either right of possession or color of title. In a more restricted sense, a stranger who, on the death of the ancestor, enters on the land, unlawfully, before the heir can enter. Williams v. Alt, 226 N.Y. 283, 123 N.E. 499, 500. Also one who intrudes on office and assumes to exercise its functions without legal title or color of right thereto. State ex rel. City of Republic v. Smith, 345 Mo. 1158, 139 S.W.2d 929, 933; Alleger v. School Dist. No. 16, Newton County, Mo.App., 142 S.W.2d 660, 663. See **Encroachment; Intrusion; Trespass.**

Intrusion. Act of wrongfully entering upon or taking possession of property of another. See also **Encroachment; Trespass.**

At common law, a species of injury by ouster or amotion of possession from the freehold, being an entry of a stranger, after a particular estate of freehold is determined, before him in remainder or reversion. Boylan v. Deinzer, 45 N.J.Eq. 485, 18 A. 119, 121.

Intrust. To confer a trust upon; to deliver to another something in trust or to commit something to another with a certain confidence regarding his care, use or disposal of it. See also **Bailment; Fiduciary; Trust.**

Intuitus /ǝntyúwǝdǝs/. Lat. A view; regard; contemplation. *Diverso intuitu (q.v.),* with a different view.

Inundation. To flood or swamp. The overflow of waters by coming out of their natural bed or confines. See also Backwater; Flood; Water; Water course.

Inure /inyúr/. To take effect; to result. In property law, to come to the benefit of a person or to fix his interest therein.

Inurement /inyúrmǝnt/. Useful, beneficial; serving to the use or benefit of a person or thing. Dickerson v. Colgrove, 100 U.S. 578, 25 L.Ed. 618.

Inutilis labor et sine fructu non est effectus legis /inyúwdǝlǝs léybǝr èt sáyniy frǝ́kt(y)uw nón èst ǝféktǝs líyjǝs/. Useless and fruitless labor is not the effect of law. The law forbids such recoveries whose ends are vain, chargeable, and unprofitable.

In utroque jure /in yǝtrówkwiy júriy/. In both laws; *i.e.,* the civil and canon law.

Invadiare /invèydiyériy/. To pledge or mortgage lands.

Invadiatio /invèydiyéysh(iy)ow/. A pledge or mortgage.

Invadiatus /invèydiyéydǝs/. One who is under pledge; one who has had sureties or pledges given for him.

Invalid. Vain; inadequate to its purpose; not of binding force or legal efficacy; lacking in authority or obligation. See also **Illegal; Void; Voidable.**

Invasion. An encroachment upon the rights of another. The incursion of an army for conquest or plunder. Act of invading; intrusion; encroachment.

Invasiones /invèyz(h)iyówniyz/. The inquisition of serjeanties and knights' fees.

Invasion of corpus principal. Payments made from the sum created to generate income (*e.g.* trust res) and not from the income so generated.

Invasion of privacy. The unwarranted appropriation or exploitation of one's personality, publicizing one's private affairs with which public has no legitimate concern, or wrongful intrusion into one's private activities, in such a manner as to cause mental suffering, shame or humiliation to person of ordinary sensibilities. Shorter v. Retail Credit Co., D.C.S.C., 251 F.Supp. 329, 330. Violation of right which one has to be left alone and unnoticed if he so chooses. Such invasion may constitute an actionable tort. See **Eavesdropping; Privacy Acts.**

Invecta et illata /invéktǝ èd ǝléydǝ/. Lat. In the civil law, things carried in and brought in. Articles brought into a hired tenement by the hirer or tenant, and which became or were pledged to the lessor as security for the rent.

Inveigle. To "inveigle" means to lure or entice or lead astray, by false representations or promises, or other deceitful means.

Inveniens libellum famosum et non corrumpens punitur /invíyn(i)yèn(d)z lǝbélǝm fǝmówsǝm èt nón kǝrǝ́mpǝn(d)z pyúwnǝdǝr/. He who finds a libel and does not destroy it is punished.

Invent. To find out something new; to devise, contrive, and produce something not previously known or existing, by the exercise of independent investigation and experiment; particularly applied to machines, mechanical appliances, compositions, and patentable inventions of every sort. To create. E. W. Bliss Co.

v. United States, 248 U.S. 37, 39 S.Ct. 42, 43, 63 L.Ed. 112. See also **Invention; Patent.**

Inventio /invénsh(iy)ow/. In the civil law, finding; one of the modes of acquiring title to property by occupancy.

In old English law, a thing found; as goods or treasure-trove. The plural, *"inventiones,"* is also used.

Invention. In patent law, the act or operation of finding out something new; the process of contriving and producing something not previously known or existing, by the exercise of independent investigation and experiment. Also the article or contrivance or composition so invented. Smith v. Nichols, 88 U.S. (21 Wall.) 112, 22 L.Ed. 566; Hollister v. Mfg. Co., 113 U.S. 59, 5 S.Ct. 717, 28 L.Ed. 901.

Invention is a concept; a thing involved in the mind; it is not a revelation of something which exists and was unknown, but is creation of something which did not exist before, possessing elements of novelty and utility in kind and measure different from and greater than what the art might expect from skilled workers. Pursche v. Atlas Scraper & Engineering Co., C.A.Cal., 300 F.2d 467, 472. The finding out—the contriving, the creating of something which did not exist, and was not known before, and which can be made useful and advantageous in the pursuits of life, or which can add to the enjoyment of mankind. Not every improvement is invention; but to entitle a thing to protection it must be the product of some exercise of the inventive faculties and it must involve something more than what is obvious to persons skilled in the art to which it relates. Mere adaptation of known process to clearly analogous use is not invention. Firestone Tire and Rubber Co. v. U. S. Rubber Co., C.C.A.Ohio, 79 F.2d 948, 952, 953.

Inventive skill has been defined as that intuitive faculty of the mind put forth in the search for new results, or new methods, creating what had not before existed, or bringing to light what lay hidden from vision; it differs from a suggestion of that common experience which arose spontaneously and by a necessity of human reasoning in the minds of those who had become acquainted with the circumstances with which they had to deal. Hollister v. Mfg. Co., 113 U.S. 59, 5 S.Ct. 717, 28 L.Ed. 901. Invention, in the nature of improvements, is the double mental act of discerning, in existing machines, processes or articles, some deficiency, and pointing out the means of overcoming it.

For "Examination of invention", see **Examination.** See also **Patent.**

Inventiones /invènshiyówniyz/. See **Inventio.**

Inventor. One who invents or has invented. One who finds out or contrives some new thing; one who devises some new art, manufacture, mechanical appliance, or process; one who invents a patentable contrivance. See **Invention.**

Inventory. A detailed list of articles of property; a list or schedule of property, containing a designation or description of each specific article; quantity of goods or materials on hand or in stock; an itemized list of the various articles constituting a collection, estate, stock in trade, etc., with their estimated or actual

values. In law, the term is often applied to such a list made by an executor, administrator, or assignee in bankruptcy.

Goods held for sale or lease or furnished under contracts of service; also, raw materials, work in process or materials used or consumed in a business. U.C.C. § 9–109(4). Also, written schedule of such goods.

In ventre sa mere /ìn véntriy sà mér/. L. Fr. In his mother's womb; spoken of an unborn child.

Inventus /invéntəs/. Lat. Found. *Thesaurus inventus*, treasure-trove. *Non est inventus*, [he] is not found.

In veram quantitatem fidejussor teneatur, nisi pro certa quantitate accessit /ìn vírəm kwòntətéydəm fàydiyjə́sər tèniyéydər, náysay pròw sə́rdə kwòntətéydiy əksésət/. Let the surety be holden for the true quantity, unless he agree for a certain quantity.

In verbis, non verba, sed res et ratio, quærenda est /ìn várbəs nòn várbə, sèd ríyz èt réysh(iy)ow, kwəréndə èst/. In the construction of words, not the mere words, but the thing and the meaning, are to be inquired after.

Inveritare /invèhrətériy/. To make proof of a thing.

Inverse condemnation. A cause of action against a government agency to recover the value of property taken by the agency, though no formal exercise of the power of eminent domain has been completed. Lincoln Loan Co. v. State, By and Through State Highway Commission, Or.App., 536 P.2d 450, 451.

Inverse order of alienation doctrine. Under this doctrine, mortgage or other lienor, where land subject to lien has been aliened in separate parcels successively, shall satisfy his lien out of land remaining in grantor or original owner if possible, and, if that be insufficient, he shall resort to parcels aliened in inverse order of their alienation. Fidelity & Casualty Co. of New York v. Massachusetts Mut. Life Ins. Co., C.C.A. N.C., 74 F.2d 881, 884.

Invest. See **Investment.**

Investigate. To follow up step by step by patient inquiry or observation. To trace or track; to search into; to examine and inquire into with care and accuracy; to find out by careful inquisition; examination; the taking of evidence; a legal inquiry. See also **Discovery; Inspection.**

Investigatory powers. Authority conferred on governmental agencies to inspect and compel disclosure of facts germane to the investigation. See also **Inquest; Inspection laws; Search-warrant; Subpoena.**

Investitive fact /invésdədəv fǽkt/. The fact by means of which a right comes into existence; *e.g.*, a grant of a monopoly; the death of one's ancestor.

Investiture /invéstəchər/. A ceremony which accompanied the grant of lands in the feudal ages, and consisted in the open and notorious delivery of possession in the presence of the other vassals, which perpetuated among them the *æra* of their new acquisition at the time when the art of writing was very little known; and thus the evidence of the property was reposed in the memory of the neighborhood, who, in case of disputed title, were afterwards called upon to decide upon it.

In Ecclesiastical law, investiture is one of the formalities by which the election of a bishop is confirmed by the archbishop.

Investment. An expenditure to acquire property or other assets in order to produce revenue; the asset so acquired. The placing of capital or laying out of money in a way intended to secure income or profit from its employment. Securities & Exchange Commission v. Wickham, D.C.Minn., 12 F.Supp. 245, 247. To purchase securities of a more or less permanent nature, or to place money or property in business ventures or real estate, or otherwise lay it out, so that it may produce a revenue or income. See also **Investment contract.**

To clothe one with the possession of a fief or benefice. See **Investiture.**

For "Capital investment", see **Capital.** See also **Legal investments; Legal list; Prudent Man Rule.**

Investment advisor. Any person who, for compensation, engages in the business of advising others, either directly or through publications or writings, as to the value of securities or as to the advisability of investing in, purchasing, or selling securities, or who, for compensation and as a part of a regular business, issues or promulgates analyses or reports concerning securities. Uniform Securities Act, § 401(f).

Investment Advisors Act. Federal statute which regulates activities of those who furnish investment advice and counselling. 15 U.S.C.A. § 80b. The Act is administered by the Securities and Exchange Commission.

Investment banker. An underwriter, the middleman between the corporation issuing new securities and the public. The usual practice is for one or more investment bankers to buy outright from a corporation a new issue of stocks or bonds. The group forms a syndicate to sell the securities to individuals and institutions. Investment bankers also distribute very large blocks of stocks or bonds—perhaps held by an estate. Thereafter the market in the security may be over-the-counter or on a stock exchange.

Investment banking. Underwriting and selling primarily new issues of stocks and bonds to investors. See **Investment banker.**

Investment bill. Type of bill of exchange purchased at a discount and intended to be held to maturity in the form of an investment.

Investment company. Any issuer which: (1) is or holds itself out as being engaged primarily, or proposes to engage primarily, in the business of investing, reinvesting, or trading in securities; (2) is engaged or proposes to engage in the business of issuing face-amount certificates of the installment type, or has been engaged in such business and has any such certificates outstanding; or (3) is engaged or proposes to engage in the business of investing, reinvesting, owning, holding, or trading in securities, and owns or proposes to acquire investment securities having a value exceeding 40 percentum of the value of such issuer's total assets (exclusive of Government securities and cash items) on an unconsolidated basis. Investment Company Act, § 3.

A company or trust which uses its capital to invest in other companies. There are two principal types: the closed-end and the open-end, or mutual fund. Shares in closed-end investment companies are readily transferable in the open market and are bought and sold like other shares. Capitalization of these companies remains the same unless action is taken to change. Open-end funds sell their own new shares to investors, stand ready to buy back their old shares, and are not listed. Open-end funds are so called because their capitalization is not fixed; they issue more shares as demanded. See also **Mutual fund.**

Investment Company Act. Federal statute passed in 1940 which regulates investment companies. 15 U.S. C.A. § 80a–1 et seq. See **Investment company.**

Investment contract. A contract, transaction or scheme whereby a person invests his money in a common enterprise and is led to expect profits solely from the efforts of the promoter or a third party. S. E. C. v. W. J. Howey Co., 328 U.S. 293, 298, 66 S.Ct. 1100, 1103, 90 L.Ed. 1244, 1249. The placing of capital or laying out of money in a way intended to secure income or profit from its employment. State by Spannaus v. Coin Wholesalers, Inc., Minn., 250 N.W.2d 583.

To fall within scope of the federal securities acts an "investment contract" must involve three elements: (1) an investment of money, (2) in a common enterprise, and (3) an expectation of profits solely from the efforts of others. Hector v. Wiens, C.A.Mont., 533 F.2d 429, 432.

Investment credit. See **Investment tax credit.**

Investment property. Generally, any property purchased for the primary purpose of profit. The profit may be from income or from resale.

Investment security. Under U.C.C., an instrument issued in bearer or registered form as a type commonly recognized as a medium for investment and evidencing a share or other interest in the property or enterprise of the issuer. § 8–102(1)(a). See also **Investment contract; Security.**

Investment tax credit. Federal legislation designed to stimulate investment by business in capital goods and equipment by allowing a percentage of the purchase price as a credit against corporate taxes due and not merely as a deduction from taxable income. See also **Recapture of investment tax credit.**

Investment trust. A company which sells its own stock and invests the money in stocks, real estate, and other investments. See also **Mutual fund; Real estate investment trust.**

In vinculis /ìn víŋk(y)ələs/. In chains; in actual custody. Applied also, figuratively, to the condition of a person who is compelled to submit to terms which oppression and his necessities impose on him.

Inviolability /ìnvàyələbílədiy/. The attribute of being secured against violation. Safe from trespass or assault.

Inviolate. Intact; not violated; free from substantial impairment. Com. v. Almeida, 362 Pa. 596, 68 A.2d 595.

In viridi observania /ìn vírəday òbzərvǽnsh(iy)ə/. Present to the minds of men, and in full force and operation.

Invitation. In the law of negligence, and with reference to trespasses on realty, invitation is the act of one who solicits or incites others to enter upon, remain in, or make use of, his property or structures thereon, or who so arranges the property or the means of access to it or of transit over it as to induce the reasonable belief that he expects and intends that others shall come upon it or pass over it. Thus the proprietor of a store, theatre or amusement park "invites" the public to come upon his premises for such purposes as are connected with its intended use.

The differences in duties of care owed as between and among licensees, business guests and social guests have been eliminated in many jurisdictions so that today reasonable care is owed to all lawful visitors and this phrase includes all but trespassers. Mounsey v. Ellard, 363 Mass. 693, 297 N.E.2d 43.

An invitation may be *express*, when the owner or occupier of the land by words invites another to come upon it or make use of it or of something thereon; or it may be *implied* when such owner or occupier by acts or conduct leads another to believe that the land or something thereon was intended to be used as he uses them, and that such use is not only acquiesced in by the owner or occupier, but is in accordance with the intention or design for which the way or place or thing was adapted and prepared and allowed to be used.

See also **Attractive nuisance doctrine; Invitee.**

Invitation to bid. Type of advertisement used by one who desires bids to be submitted for a particular job; it usually contains sufficient specifications to permit an intelligent bid.

Invited error. Underlying basis for rule of "invited error" is that where one party offers inadmissible evidence, which is received, opponent may then offer similar facts whose only claim to admission is that they negative or explain or counterbalance prior inadmissible evidence, presumably upon the same fact, subject or issue. Wynn v. Sundquist, 259 Or. 125, 485 P.2d 1085, 1090. See also **Error.**

Invitee. A person is an "invitee" on land of another if (1) he enters by invitation, express or implied, (2) his entry is connected with the owner's business or with an activity the owner conducts or permits to be conducted on his land and (3) there is mutuality of benefit or benefit to the owner. Madrazo v. Michaels, 1 Ill.App.2d 583, 274 N.E.2d 635, 638.

The leading English case of Indermaur v. Dames laid down the rule that as to those who enter premises upon business which concerns the occupier, and upon his invitation express or implied, the latter is under an affirmative duty to protect them, not only against dangers of which he knows, but also against those which with reasonable care he might discover. The case has been accepted in all common law jurisdictions, and the invitee, or as he is sometimes called the business visitor, is placed upon a higher footing than a licensee. The typical example, of course, is the customer in a store. There is however a conflict of decisions as to whether certain visitors are to be included in the definition of invitee. The minority view is that there must be some economic benefit to the occupier before his duty to the visitor attaches. The majority view holds however that the basis of liability is not any economic benefit to the occupier, but a representation to be implied when he encourages others to enter to further a purpose of his own, that reasonable care has been exercised to make the place safe for those who come for that purpose; *e.g.* persons attending free public lectures, persons using municipal parks, playgrounds, libraries and the like. The element of "invitation" however must exist.

See also **Licensee; Public invitee.**

Invito /inváydow/. Lat. Being unwilling. Against or without the assent or consent.

Invito beneficium non datur /inváydow bènəfísh(i)yəm nòn déydər/. A benefit is not conferred on one who is unwilling to receive it; that is to say, no one can be compelled to accept a benefit.

In vocibus videndum non a quo sed ad quid sumatur /in vówsəbəs vədéndəm nòn éy kwów sèd ǽd kwíd səméytər/. In discourses, it is to be considered not from what, but to what, it is advanced.

Invoice. A written account, or itemized statement of merchandise shipped or sent to a purchaser, consignee, factor, etc., with the quantity, value or prices and charges annexed, and may be as appropriate to a consignment or a memorandum shipment as it is to a sale. Joseph B. Cooper & Son, Inc. v. Finlay Depts., Inc., 11 Misc.2d 382, 174 N.Y.S.2d 265, 269. Document showing details of a sale or purchase transaction. A list sent to a purchaser, factor, consignee, etc., containing the items, together with the prices and charges of merchandise sent or to be sent to him. A writing made on behalf of an importer, specifying the merchandise imported, and its true cost or value. See also **Consular invoice.**

Invoice book. A book in which invoices are copied.

Involuntary. Without will or power of choice; opposed to volition or desire. An involuntary act is that which is performed with constraint *(q.v.)* or with repugnance, or without the will to do it. An action is involuntary, then, which is performed under duress, force, or coercion.

As to involuntary Bankruptcy; Indebtedness; Nonsuit; and Trust, see those titles.

Involuntary alienation. A loss of or parting with property by attachment, levy, sale for taxes or other debts. See also **Involuntary conveyance.**

Involuntary confession. Confession is "involuntary" if it is not the product of an essentially free and unrestrained choice of its maker or where maker's will is overborne at the time of the confession. People v. Pickerel, 32 Ill.App.3d 822, 336 N.E.2d 778, 780. Term refers to confessions that are extracted by any threats of violence, or obtained by direct or implied promises, or by exertion of improper influence. Phillips v. State, Okl.Cr., 330 P.2d 209, 214. See also **Interrogation.**

Involuntary conversion. The loss or destruction of property through theft, casualty, or condemnation. Any gain realized on an involuntary conversion can, at the taxpayer's election, be considered nonrecognizable for Federal income tax purposes if the owner reinvests the proceeds within a prescribed period of time in property that is similar or related in service or use. I.R.C. § 1033.

Involuntary conversion for federal income tax purposes must result from (1) destruction of property in whole or in part; or (2) theft; or (3) actual seizure; or (4) requisition or condemnation or threat or imminence of requisition or condemnation. Hitke v. C. I. R., C.A.Ill., 296 F.2d 639, 643, 644.

Involuntary conveyance. A transfer of real property without the consent of the owner, such as in a divorce, in condemnation, etc. See also **Involuntary alienation; Sheriff's sale.**

Involuntary deposit. In the law of bailments, one made by the accidental leaving or placing of personal property in the possession of another, without negligence on the part of the owner, or, in cases of fire, shipwreck, inundation, riot, insurrection, or the like extraordinary emergencies, by the owner of personal property committing it out of necessity to the care of any person.

Involuntary discontinuance. A discontinuance is involuntary where, in consequence of technical omission, mispleading, or the like, the suit is regarded as out of court, as where the parties undertake to refer a suit that is not referable, or omit to enter proper continuances.

Involuntary lien. A lien, such as a tax lien, judgment lien, etc., which attaches to property without the consent of the owner, rather than a mortgage lien, to which the owner agrees.

Involuntary manslaughter. The unlawful killing of a human being in the commission of an unlawful act not amounting to felony, or in the commission of a lawful act which might produce death in an unlawful manner, or without due caution and circumspection. An unlawful homicide, unintentionally caused by an act which constitutes such disregard of probable harmful consequences to another as to constitute wanton or reckless conduct. Com. v. McCauley, 355 Mass. 554, 246 N.E.2d 425, 428. See also **Manslaughter.**

Involuntary payment. One obtained by fraud, oppression, or extortion, or to avoid the use of force to coerce it, or to obtain the release of the person or property from detention.

Involuntary servitude. The condition of one who is compelled by force, coercion, or imprisonment, and against his will, to labor for another, whether he is paid or not. Ex parte Wilson, 114 U.S. 417, 5 S.Ct. 935, 29 L.Ed. 89; In re Slaughterhouse Cases, 83 U.S. (16 Wall.) 69, 21 L.Ed. 394; Robertson v. Baldwin, 165 U.S. 275, 17 S.Ct. 326, 41 L.Ed. 715. Slavery, peonage, or compulsory labor for debts; all of which are prohibited by the 13th Amendment, U.S.Const.

Involuntary transfer. See **Involuntary conveyance.**

Involuntary trust. An implied trust which arises because the law imposes trust-like consequences on certain transactions where, for example, an agent breaches his fiduciary duty and buys property in his own name which rightfully should have been purchased for the benefit of his principal (constructive trust) or A supplies the funds for purchase of property by B with the understanding that A will own it but title will be taken in the name of B (resulting trust).

In witness whereof /ìn wítnəs (h)wèróv/. The initial words of the concluding clause in deeds: "In witness whereof the said parties have hereunto set their hands", etc. A translation of the Latin phrase *"in cujus rei testimonium"*.

Iota. The minutest quantity possible. Iota is the smallest Greek letter. The word "jot" is derived therefrom.

IOU. A memorandum of debt, consisting of these letters ("I owe you"), a sum of money and the debtor's signature, is termed an "IOU".

Ipsæ leges cupiunt ut jure regantur /ípsiy líyjiyz kyúwpiyənt ət júriy rəgǽntər/. The laws themselves require that they should be governed by right.

Ipse /ípsiy/. Lat. He himself; the same; the very person.

Ipse dixit /ípsiy díksət/. He himself said it; a bare assertion resting on the authority of an individual.

Ipsissimis verbis /ìpsísəməs várbəs/. In the identical words; opposed to "substantially".

Ipso facto /ípsow fǽktow/. By the fact itself; by the mere fact. By the mere effect of an act or a fact.

Ipso jure /ípsow júriy/. By the law itself; by the mere operation of law.

IRA. Individual Retirement Account.

Ira furor brevis est /áyrə fyúrər bríyvəs èst/. Anger is a short insanity.

Ira motus /áyrə mówdəs/. Lat. Moved or excited by anger or passion. A term sometimes formerly used in the plea of *son assault demesne*.

IRAN. Individual Retirement Annuity.

IRB. Individual Retirement Bond.

I.R.C. Internal Revenue Code.

I.R.D. Income in respect of decedent.

Ire ad largum /áyriy æ̀d lárgəm/. Lat. To go at large; to escape; to be set at liberty.

Iron-safe clause. A clause in policies of fire insurance, requiring the insured to preserve his books and inventory in an iron or fireproof safe, or in some secure place not exposed to a fire which would destroy the building. This provision casts on the insured the responsibility for the loss of books and records if due to the wrongful act or negligence of himself or his employees in failing to comply with the requirement.

Irrational. Unreasonable, foolish, illogical, absurd; a person may be irrational in such sense, and still not be insane in the legal sense.

Irreconcilable differences. No-fault ground for dissolution of marriage under many state divorce statutes. See also **Irretrievable breakdown of marriage.**

Irrecusable /ìrəkyúwzəbəl/. A term used to indicate a certain class of contractual obligations recognized by the law which are imposed upon a person without his consent and without regard to any act of his own. They are distinguished from recusable obligations which are the result of a voluntary act on the part of a person on whom they are imposed by law. A clear example of an irrecusable obligation is the obligation imposed on every man not to strike another without some lawful excuse. A recusable obligation is based upon some act of a person bound, which is a condition precedent to the genesis of the obligation. These terms were first suggested by Prof. Wigmore in 8 Harv.Law Rev. 200.

Irregular. Not according to rule; improper or insufficient, by reason of departure from the prescribed course.

As to irregular Deposit; Indorsement; Process; and Succession, see those titles.

Irregularity. The doing or not doing that, in the conduct of a suit at law, which, conformably with the practice of the court, ought or ought not to be done. Violation or nonobservance of established rules and practices. The want of adherence to some prescribed rule or mode of proceeding; consisting either in omitting to do something that is necessary for the due and orderly conducting of a suit, or doing it in an unseasonable time or improper manner. The technical term for every defect in mechanics of proceedings, or the mode of conducting an action or defense, as distinguishable from defects in pleadings. Term is not synonymous with "illegality."

In Canon law, any impediment which prevents a man from taking holy orders.

Irregular judgment. One rendered contrary to the course and practice of the court. Duplin County v. Ezzell, 223 N.C. 531, 27 S.E.2d 448, 450.

Irrelevancy. The absence of the quality of relevancy, as in evidence or pleadings. The quality or state of being inapplicable or impertinent to a fact or argument. Irrelevancy, in an answer, consists in statements which are not material to the decision of the case; such as do not form or tender any material issue. Such irrelevancy in pleadings may be stricken on motion of party. Fed.R.Civil P. 12(f). See also **Immaterial; Irrelevant; Irrelevant allegation.**

Irrelevant. Not relevant; immaterial; not relating or applicable to the matter in issue; not supporting the issue or fact to be proved. Evidence is irrelevant where it has no tendency to prove or disprove any issue of fact involved. Irrelevant evidence is commonly objected to and disallowed at trial. Fed. Evid.R. 402. See also **Immaterial; Impertinence; Irrelevancy.**

Irrelevant allegation. One which has no substantial relation to the controversy between the parties to the suit, and which cannot affect the decision of the court. Wayte v. Bowker Chemical Co., 196 App.Div. 665, 187 N.Y.S. 276, 277; Commander Milling Co. v. Westinghouse Electric and Mfg. Co., C.C.A.Minn., 70

F.2d 469, 472. The test of any allegation being whether it tends to constitute a cause of action or a defense. Isaacs v. Salomon, 159 App.Div. 675, 144 N.Y.S. 876, 877. See also **Immaterial argument.**

An allegation is irrelevant, where the issue made by its denial has no effect upon the cause of action or no connection with the allegation. In this connection, "redundant" is almost a synonym for "irrelevant". Irrelevant matters may be stricken from pleadings on motion of party. Fed.R.Civil P. 12(f).

Irrelevant answer. See **Answer.**

Irreparable damages. See **Damages.**

Irreparable harm. See **Injury** *(Irreparable injury).*

Irreparable injury. See **Injury.**

Irrepleviable /ìrəpléviyəbəl/. That cannot be replevied or delivered on sureties. Spelled, also, "irreplevisable" /ìrəplévəzəbəl/.

Irresistible force. A term applied to such an interposition of human agency as is, from its nature and power, absolutely uncontrollable; as the inroads of a hostile army.

Irresistible impulse. As used as insanity defense, an "irresistible impulse" means an impulse to commit an unlawful or criminal act which cannot be resisted or overcome because mental disease has destroyed the freedom of will, the power of self-control, and the choice of actions. Snider v. Smyth, D.C.Va., 187 F.Supp. 299, 302. The "irresistible impulse" test for insanity is a test which is broader than the M'Naghten test. Under the "irresistible impulse" test a person may avoid criminal responsibility even though he is capable of distinguishing between right and wrong, and is fully aware of the nature and quality of his acts, provided that he establishes that he was unable to refrain from acting. Com. v. Walzack, 468 Pa. 210, 360 A.2d 914, 919. See also **Insanity; M'Naghten Rule.**

Irretrievable breakdown of marriage. As a no-fault ground for divorce means one in which either or both spouses are unable or unwilling to cohabit and for which there are no prospects for reconciliation. Harwell v. Harwell, 233 Ga. 89, 209 S.E.2d 625. In some jurisdictions, the sole ground for so-called no-fault divorce. See also **Irreconcilable differences.**

Irrevocable. That which cannot be revoked or recalled. Commissioner of Internal Revenue v. Strong Mfg. Co., C.C.A.Ohio, 124 F.2d 360, 363.

Irrevocable letter of credit. A confirmed irrevocable letter of credit, irrevocable letter, or a confirmed credit is a contract to pay on compliance with its terms, and needs no formal acknowledgment or acceptance other than is therein stated. See also **Letter of credit.**

Irrigation company. A private corporation, authorized and regulated by statute in several states, having for its object to acquire exclusive rights to the water of certain streams or other sources of supply, and to convey it by means of ditches or canals through a region where it can be beneficially used for agricultural purposes, and either dividing the water among stockholders, or making contracts with consumers, or furnishing a supply to all who apply at fixed rates.

Irrigation district. A public and quasi-municipal corporation authorized by law in several states, comprising a defined region or area of land which is susceptible of one mode of irrigation from a common source and by the same system of works. These districts are created by proceedings in the nature of an election under the supervision of a court, and are authorized to purchase or condemn the lands and waters necessary for the system of irrigation proposed and to construct necessary canals and other works, and the water is apportioned ratably among the landowners of the district.

Irrogare /ìrəgériy/. Lat. In the civil law, to impose or set upon, as a fine. To inflict, as a punishment. To make or ordain, as a law.

Irrotulatio /əròchəléysh(iy)ow/. L. Lat. An enrolling; a record.

I.R.S. Internal Revenue Service.

Is. This word, although normally referring to the present; often has a future meaning, but is not synonymous with "shall have been." It may have, however, a past signification, as in the sense of "has been."

Island. A piece of land surrounded by water. Land in a navigable stream which is surrounded by water only in times of high water is not an island within the rule that the state takes title to newly formed islands in navigable streams.

Isolated sale. Isolated sale which does not entail implied warranty of merchantability is one which occurs only once or at least very infrequently within ordinary course of business. McHugh v. Carlton, D.C.S.C., 369 F.Supp. 1271, 1277.

Is qui cognoscit /ís kwày kəgnó(w)sət/. Lat. The cognizor in a fine. *Is cui cognoscitur* /ís k(yúw)ay kəgnósədər/, the cognizee.

Issei /íysèy/. Jap. A term used to describe alien Japanese residing in the United States.

Issuable. Leading or tending to, or producing, an issue; relating to an issue or issues.

Issuable defense. In common law pleading, a technical expression meaning a plea to the merits, properly setting forth a legal defense, as distinguished from a plea in abatement, or any plea going only to delay the case.

Issuable plea. In common law pleading, a plea to the merits; a traversable plea. A plea such that the adverse party can join issue upon it and go to trial. It is true a plea in abatement is a plea, and if it be properly pleaded, issues may be found on it. In the ordinary meaning of the word "plea", and of the word "issuable," such pleas may be called "issuable pleas," but, when these two words are used together, "issuable plea," or "issuable defense," they have a technical meaning, to-wit, pleas to the merits.

Issuable terms. In the former practice of the English courts, Hilary term and Trinity term were called "issuable terms," because the issues to be tried at the assizes were made up at those terms. But the distinction was superseded by the provisions of the judicature acts of 1873 and 1875.

Issue, v. To send forth; to emit; to promulgate; as, an officer issues orders, process issues from a court. To put into circulation; as, the treasury issues notes. To send out, to send out officially; to deliver, for use, or authoritatively; to go forth as authoritative or binding. When used with reference to writs, process, and the like the term is ordinarily construed as importing delivery to the proper person, or to the proper officer for service, etc. With respect to securities, refers to act or process of offering stocks or bonds for sale to public or institutional investors.

In financial parlance the term "issue" seems to have two phases of meaning. "Date of issue" when applied to notes, bonds, etc., of a series, usually means the arbitrary date fixed as the beginning of the term for which they run, without reference to the precise time when convenience or the state of the market may permit of their sale or delivery. When the securities are delivered to the purchaser, they will be "issued" to him, which is the other meaning of the term.

In commercial law, means the first delivery of an instrument to a holder or a remitter. U.C.C. § 1–102(1)(a).

Issue, n. The act of issuing, sending forth, emitting or promulgating; the giving a thing its first inception; as the issue of an order or a writ.

See also **Date of issue**.

Pleading and Practice

A single, certain, and material point, deduced by the allegations and pleadings of the parties, which is affirmed on the one side and denied on the other. A fact put in controversy by the pleadings; such may either be issues of law or fact. An "issue" is a disputed point or question to which parties to action have narrowed their several allegations and upon which they are desirous of obtaining either decision of court on question of law or of court or jury on question of fact. Muller v. Muller, 235 Cal.App.2d 341, 45 Cal.Rptr. 182, 184.

Real or *feigned.* A real or actual issue is one formed in a regular manner in a regular suit for the purpose of determining an actual controversy. A feigned issue is one made up by direction of the court, upon a supposed case, for the purpose of obtaining the verdict of a jury upon some question of fact collaterally involved in the cause. Such issues are generally ordered by a court of equity, to ascertain the truth of a disputed fact. They are also used in courts of law, by the consent of the parties, to determine some disputed rights without the formality of pleading; and by this practice much time and expense are saved in the decision of a cause. The name is a misnomer, inasmuch as the *issue* itself is upon a real, material point in question between the parties, and the circumstances only are fictitious.

Ultimate issue. Signifies either such an issue as within itself is sufficient and final for the disposition of the entire case or one which in connection with other issues will serve such end. First State Bank of Seminole v. Dillard, Tex.Civ.App., 71 S.W.2d 407, 410.

See also Failure of issue; Feigned issue; Genuine issue; Issue of fact; Issue of law; Issue preclusion; Lawful issue; Legal issue; Ultimate issue.

Descendant's Estates

All persons who have descended from a common ancestor. Offspring; progeny; descent; lineage; lineal descendants. In this sense, the word includes not only a child or children, but all other descendants in whatever degree, and it is so construed generally in deeds. But, when used in wills, it is, of course, subject to the rule of construction that the intention of the testator, as ascertained from the language used by him; and hence issue may, in such a connection, be restricted to children, or to descendants living at the death of the testator, where such an intention clearly appears.

The term "issue" and "descendants" have been held to be co-extensive and interchangeable. In re Radt's Will, 6 Misc.2d 716, 167 N.Y.S.2d 817, 818.

The word "issue" in a will is generally a word of limitation, and when so used, is sometimes said to be equivalent to "heirs of the body". But it has been pointed out in other cases that this word is not as strong a word of limitation as the words "heirs of the body", and yields readily to a context indicating its use as a work of purchase.

The term is commonly held to include only legitimate issue. Large v. National City Bank of Cleveland, Ohio Prob., 170 N.E.2d 309, 312; *contra* Will of Hoffman, 53 A.D.2d 55, 385 N.Y.S.2d 49. The general rule in most states is that the illegitimate child may inherit from his mother but not from his father, but may inherit from both if legitimated.

Many state intestacy statutes provide that an adopted child is "issue" of his or her adopted parents.

Securities

Any of a corporation's securities offered for sale at a certain time, or the act or process of distributing (*i.e.* offering) such for sale. A class or series of bonds, debentures, etc., comprising all that are emitted at one and the same time. See also Distribution; Issuer; Offering; Prospectus; Underwriter; When issued.

Hot issue. A public offering where securities, after their initial sale to the public, are resold in the open market at prices substantially higher than the original public offering price.

New issue. A stock or bond sold by a corporation for the first time. Proceeds may be used to retire outstanding securities of the company, for new plant or equipment, or for additional working capital.

Issue of fact. An issue of fact arises when a fact is maintained by one party and is controverted by the other in the pleadings. General Elec. Co. v. Employment Relations Bd., 3 Wis.2d 227, 88 N.W.2d 691, 701. An issue which arises upon a denial in the answer of a material allegation of the complaint or in the reply of a material allegation in the answer.

Issue of law. An issue of law arises where evidence is undisputed and only one conclusion can be drawn therefrom. Chaison v. Stark, Tex.Civ.App., 29 S.W.2d 500, 503. An issue of law arises upon a demurrer to the complaint or answer, or to some part thereof. Calif.C.C.P. § 589.

In making motion for summary judgment, party must show that only issues of law exist for court to consider; *i.e.* must show that there is no genuine issue of material facts. Fed.R.Civil P. 56.

In pleading, an issue upon matter of law, or consisting of matter of law, being produced by a demurrer on the one side, and a joinder in demurrer on the other. The term "issue" may be so used as to include one of law raised by demurrer to the complaint, as well as one raised by answer.

Issue preclusion. Term means that when a particular issue has already been litigated, further litigation of same issue is barred. Hawkeye Sec. Ins. Co. v. Ford Motor Co., Iowa, 199 N.W.2d 373, 379. As it relates to civil actions, concept of "issue preclusion" is in substance that any fact, question or matter in issue and directly adjudicated or necessarily involved in determination of action before court of competent jurisdiction in which judgment or decree is rendered on merits, is conclusively settled by judgment therein and cannot be relitigated in any future action between parties or privies, either in same court or court of concurrent jurisdiction, while judgment remains unreversed or unvacated by proper authority, regardless of whether claim or cause of action, purpose or subject matter of two suits is same. Palma v. Powers, D.C.Ill., 295 F.Supp. 924, 933. See also **Collateral estoppel doctrine; Res** (*Res judicata*).

Issuer. With respect to obligations on or defenses to a security, "issuer" includes a person who: (a) places or authorizes the placing of his name on a security (otherwise than as authenticating trustee, registrar, transfer agent or the like) to evidence that it represents a share, participation or other interest in his property or in an enterprise or to evidence his duty to perform an obligation evidenced by the security; or (b) directly or indirectly creates fractional interests in his rights or property which fractional interests are evidenced by securities; or (c) becomes responsible for or in place of any other person described as an issuer in this section. U.C.C. § 8–201(1). Every person who issues or proposes to issue any securities; generally the legal entity owning the securities and which has the responsibility for causing the same to be offered publicly or privately.

Bank or other person issuing a credit. U.C.C. § 5–103(1)(c).

A bailee who issues a document except that in relation to an unaccepted delivery order it means the person who orders the possessor of goods to deliver. Issuer includes any person for whom an agent or employee purports to act in issuing a document if the agent or employee has real or apparent authority to issue documents, notwithstanding that the issuer received no goods or that the goods were misdescribed or that in any other respect the agent or employee violated his instructions. U.C.C. § 7–102(g).

Issue roll. In English practice, a roll upon which the issue in actions at law was formerly required to be entered, the roll being entitled of the term in which the issue was joined. It was not, however, the practice to enter the issue at full length, if triable by the country, until after the trial, but only to make an *incipitur* on the roll. It was abolished by the rules of Hilary Term, 1834.

Issues and profits. As applied to real estate, comprehend every available return therefrom, whether it arise above or below the surface. "Issues" are goods and profits of the land. Costanzo v. Harris, 71 Wash.2d 254, 427 P.2d 963, 965.

Ita est /áydə èst/. Lat. So it is; so it stands. In modern civil law, this phrase is a form of attestation added to exemplifications from a notary's register when the same are made by the successor in office of the notary who made the original entries.

Ita lex scripta est /áydə léks skríptəm èst/. Lat. So the law is written. The law must be obeyed notwithstanding the apparent rigor of its application. 3 Bl. Comm. 430. We must be content with the law as it stands, without inquiring into its reasons. 1 Bl. Comm. 32.

Ita semper fiat relatio ut valeat dispositio /áydə sémpər fáyət rəléysh(iy)ow ət vǽliyət dispəzísh(iy)ow/. Let the interpretation be always such that the disposition may prevail.

Ita te Deus adjuvet /áydə tíy díyəs ǽjəvət/. Lat. So help you God. The old form of administering an oath in England, generally in connection with other words, thus: *Ita te Deus adjuvet, et sacrosancta Dei Evangelia*, So help you God, and God's holy Evangelists. *Ita te Deus adjuvet et omnes sancti*, So help you God and all the saints.

Ita utere tuo ut alienum non lædas /áydə yúwdəriy t(y)úwow əd ǽliyíynəm nòn líydəs/. Use your own property and your own rights in such a way that you will not hurt your neighbor, or prevent him from enjoying his. Frequently written *"Sic utere tuo"*, etc. (*q.v.*).

Item /áydəm/. Also; likewise; in like manner; again; a second time. This word was formerly used to mark the beginning of a new paragraph or division after the first, whence is derived the common application of it to denote a separate or distinct particular of an account or bill. One of the portions, equal or unequal, into which anything is divided, or regarded as divided; something less than a whole; a number, quantity, mass, or the like, regarded as going to make up, with others or another, a larger number, quantity, mass, etc., whether actually separate or not; a piece, fragment, fraction, member or constituent. A separate entry in an account or a schedule, or a separate particular in an enumeration of a total. An "item" in an appropriation is an indivisible sum of money dedicated to a stated purpose. Commonwealth v. Dodson, 176 Va. 281, 11 S.E.2d 120, 124, 127, 130, 131.

Any instrument for the payment of money, though not negotiable; but not money. U.C.C. § 4–104(1)(g).

Itemize. To set down by items. To state each item or article separately. Used commonly with reference to tax accounting.

Itemized deductions. Certain personal expenditures allowed by the Internal Revenue Code as deductions *from* adjusted gross income if an individual taxpayer chooses not to use the standard deduction and total itemized deductions exceed the standard deduction (zero bracket amount). Examples include certain medical expenses, interest on home mortgages, state sales taxes, and charitable contributions.

Iter /áydər/. Lat. In the civil law, a way; a right of way belonging as a servitude to an estate in the country (*prædium rusticum*). The right of way was of three kinds: (1) *iter*, a right to walk, or ride on horseback, or in a litter; (2) *actus*, a right to drive a beast or vehicle; (3) *via*, a full right of way, comprising right to walk or ride, or drive beast or carriage. Or, as some think, they were distinguished by the width of the objects which could be rightfully carried over the way; *e.g.*, *via*, 8 feet; *actus*, 4 feet, etc.

In old English law, a journey, especially a circuit made by a justice in eyre, or itinerant justice, to try causes according to his own mission.

In maritime law, a way or route. The route or direction of a voyage; the route or way that is taken to make the voyage assured. Distinguished from the voyage itself.

Iteratio /ìdəréysh(iy)ow/. Lat. Repetition. In the Roman law, a bonitary owner might liberate a slave, and the quiritary owner's repetition (*iteratio*) of the process effected a complete manumission.

Iter est jus eundi, ambulandi hominis; non etiam jumentum agendi vel vehiculum /áydər èst jás iyánday, ǽmbyəlǽnday hómənəs, nòn íysh(iy)əm jəméntəm əjénday vèl vəhík(y)ələm/. A way is the right of going or walking, and does not include the right of driving a beast of burden or a carriage.

Itinera /aytínərə/. Eyres, or circuits.

Itinerant. Wandering or traveling from place to place; formerly applied to justices who made circuits. Also applied in various statutory and municipal laws (in the sense of traveling from place to place) to certain classes of merchants, traders, and salesmen.

Itinerant peddling. The going about of a merchant from place to place, meeting and dealing with his customers where he finds them. Good Humor Corporation v. City of New York, 264 App.Div. 620, 36 N.Y.S.2d 85, 91.

Itinerant vendor. This term is variously defined in statutes; *e.g.*, a person engaged in transient business either in one locality or in traveling from place to place selling goods. See also **Hawker; Peddler.**

J

J. The initial letter of the words "judge" and "justice," for which it frequently stands as an abbreviation. Thus, "J.A.," judge advocate; "J.J.," junior judge; "L.J.," law judge; "A.L.J.," administrative law judge; "P.J.," president judge; "F.J.," first judge; "A.J.," associate judge; "C.J.," chief justice or judge; "J.P.," justice of the peace; "JJ.," judges or justices; "J.C.P.," justice of the common pleas; "J. K.B.," justice of the king's bench; "J.Q.B.," justice of the queen's bench; "J.U.B.," justice of the upper bench.

Jac. An abbreviation for *"Jacobus"*, the Latin form of the name James; used principally in citing statutes enacted in the reigns of the English kings of that name; *e.g.*, "St. 1, Jac. II."

Jacens /jéysən(d)z/. Lat. Lying in abeyance, as in the phrase *"hæreditas jacens"*, which is an inheritance or estate lying vacant or in abeyance prior to the ascertainment of the heir or his assumption of the succession.

Jacens hæreditas /jéysən(d)z həríydətæs/. See **Hæreditas jacens.**

Jack. A kind of defensive coat-armor worn by horsemen in war; not made of solid iron, but of many plates fastened together. Some tenants were bound by their tenure to find it upon invasion.

Jacobus /jəkówbəs/. A gold coin an inch and three-eighths in diameter, in value about twenty-five shillings, so called from James I., in whose reign it was first coined. It was also called *broad, laurel*, and *broad-piece*. Its value is sometimes put at twenty-four shillings, but Macaulay speaks of a salary of eight thousand Jacobuses as equivalent to ten thousand pounds sterling.

Jactitation /jæktətéyshən/. Boasting of something which is challenged by another. A false boasting; a false claim; assertions repeated to the prejudice of another's right.

The species of defamation or disparagement of another's title to real estate known at common law as "slander of title" comes under the head of jactitation, and in some jurisdictions (as in Louisiana) a remedy for this injury is provided under the name of an "action of jactitation."

Jactitation of marriage. In English ecclesiastical law, the boasting or giving out by a party that he or she is married to some other, whereby a common reputa-

tion of their matrimony may ensue. To defeat that result, the person may be put to a proof of the actual marriage, failing which proof, he or she is put to silence about it. 3 Bl.Comm. 93. The High Court has jurisdiction over such actions.

Jactitation of tithes. In English ecclesiastical law, the boasting by a man that he is entitled to certain tithes, to which he has legally no title.

Jactivus /jæktáyvəs/. Lost by default; tossed away.

Jactura /jækt(y)úrə/. In the civil law, a throwing of goods overboard in a storm; jettison. Loss from such a cause.

Jactus /jæktəs/. A throwing of goods overboard to lighten or save the vessel, in which case the goods so sacrificed are a proper subject for general average. See **Jettison.**

Jactus lapilli /jæktəs ləpílay/. The throwing down of a stone. One of the modes, under the civil law, of interrupting prescription. Where one person was building on another's ground, and in this way acquiring a right by *usucapio*, the true owner challenged the intrusion and interrupted the prescriptive right by throwing down one of the stones of the building before witnesses called for the purpose.

Jail. A gaol; a prison; a building designated by law, or regularly used, for the confinement of persons held in lawful custody. A place of confinement that is more than a police station lockup and less than a prison. It is usually used to hold persons either convicted of misdemeanors (minor crimes) or persons awaiting trial. See also **Gaol.**

Jail delivery. See **Gaol.**

Jailer. A keeper or warden of a prison or jail.

Jailhouse lawyer. Inmate of a penal institution who spends his time reading the law and giving legal assistance and advice to inmates.

Jail liberties. See **Gaol.**

Jamunlingi, jamundilingi. Freemen who delivered themselves and property to the protection of a more powerful person, in order to avoid military service and other burdens. Also a species of serfs among the Germans. The same as *commendati*.

Janus-faced. An argument looking in both directions at the same time, *e.g.*, urging jurors not to be swayed by

748

sympathy, but adding that any sympathy should be in favor of the arguing counsel's client. Davis v. Franson, 141 Cal.App.2d 263, 296 P.2d 600, 606.

Jaques. In old English law, small money.

Jason clause. Clause in bills of lading which obligates cargo owners to contribute in general average in cases of danger, damage, or disaster resulting from faults or errors in navigation or in management of vessel, her machinery or appurtenances, provided that shipowner shall have exercised due diligence to make vessel in all respects seaworthy, and to have her properly manned, equipped, and supplied. Merklen v. Johnson & Higgins, D.C.N.Y., 3 F.Supp. 897, 898.

Javelin-men /jǽv(ə)lənmèn/. In old English law, yeomen retained by the sheriff to escort the judge of assize.

Jay walking. Proceeding diagonally across a street intersection. Also, crossing a street between intersections, or at a place other than a crosswalk.

J.D. Short for "Juris Doctor" or "Doctor of Jurisprudence." This is now the basic law degree, replacing the "LL.B." in the late 1960's.

Jedburgh justice /jédbərə jə́stəs/. Summary justice inflicted upon a marauder or felon without a regular trial, equivalent to "lynch law." So called from a Scotch town, near the English border, where raiders and cattle lifters were often summarily hung. Also written "Jeddart" /jédərt/ or "Jedwood" /jédwəd/ justice.

Jencks Act or Rule. A criminal defendant in the Federal Court is entitled to access to government documents for assistance in cross-examination of witnesses in order to impeach for prior inconsistent statements. Jencks v. U. S., 353 U.S. 657, 77 S.Ct. 1007, 1 L.Ed.2d 1103. Following this case, a federal statute was enacted to the same effect; 18 U.S.C.A. § 3500.

Jeofaile /jéfèyl/. L. Fr. I have failed; I am in error. An error or oversight in pleading.

Jeopardy. Danger; hazard; peril.

The danger of conviction and punishment which the defendant in a criminal action incurs when a valid indictment has been found, and a petit jury has been impaneled and sworn to try the case and give a verdict in a court of competent jurisdiction. Hanley v. State, 83 Nev. 461, 434 P.2d 440, 442. The condition of a person when he is put upon trial, before a court of competent jurisdiction, upon an indictment or information which is sufficient in form and substance to sustain a conviction, and a jury has been charged with his deliverance. For purpose of prohibition against double jeopardy, a court proceeding which may result in incarceration places a person, adult or juvenile, in "jeopardy." Fain v. Duff, C.A. Fla., 488 F.2d 218, 225.

The terms "jeopardy of life and liberty for the same offense," "jeopardy of life or limb," "jeopardy for the same offense," "in jeopardy of punishment," and other similar provisions used in the various constitutions, are to be construed as meaning substantially the same thing.

See also **Double jeopardy; Former jeopardy; Legal jeopardy.**

Jeopardy assessment. If the collection of a tax appears in question, the IRS may assess and collect the tax immediately without the usual formalities. Also, the IRS has the power to terminate a taxpayer's taxable year before the usual date if it feels that the collection of the tax may be in peril because the taxpayer plans to leave the country.

Jetsam /jétsəm/. Goods which, by the act of the owner, have been voluntarily cast overboard from a vessel, in a storm or other emergency, to lighten the ship. See also **Jactus; Jettison.**

Jettison /jédəsən/. The act of throwing overboard from a vessel part of the cargo, in case of extreme danger, to lighten the ship. The thing or things so cast out; jetsam. A carrier by water may, when in case of extreme peril it is necessary for the safety of the ship or cargo, throw overboard, or otherwise sacrifice, any or all of the cargo or appurtenances of the ship. Throwing property overboard for such purpose is called "jettison," and the loss incurred thereby is called a "general average loss." See also **Jactus; Jetsam.**

Jetty. A projection of stone or other material serving as a protection against the waves.

Jeux de bourse /zhúw də búrs/. Fr. In French law, speculation in the public funds or in stocks; gambling speculations on the stock exchange; dealings in "options" and "futures."

A kind of gambling or speculation, which consists of sales and purchases which bind neither of the parties to deliver the things which are the object of the sale, and which are settled by paying the difference in the value of the things sold between the day of the sale and that appointed for delivery of such things.

J.N.O.V., Abr. Judgment non obstante veredicto; judgment notwithstanding verdict. See **Non obstante veredicto.**

Job. The whole of a thing which is to be done. A specific task or piece of work to be done for a set fee or compensation. Employment position. Criminal act (*e.g.* robbery).

Jobber. One who buys and sells goods for others. One who buys or sells on the stock exchange; a dealer in stocks, shares, or securities. One who buys and sells articles in bulk and resells them to dealers. A merchant buying and selling in job lots. In general, a wholesaler; one who buys and sells small lots; a middleman. Person who does piecework. See also **Middleman.**

Jocelet /jós(ə)lət/. A little manor or farm.

Jocus /jówkəs/. In old English law, a game of hazard.

Jocus partitus /jówkəs párdədəs/. In old English practice, a divided game, risk, or hazard. An arrangement which the parties to a suit were anciently sometimes allowed to make by mutual agreement upon a certain hazard, as that one should lose if the case turned out in a certain way, and, if it did not, that the other should gain.

John Doe. A fictitious name frequently used to indicate a person for the purpose of argument or illustration, or in the course of enforcing a fiction in the law. The name which was usually given to the fictitious lessee of the plaintiff in the mixed action of ejectment. He was sometimes called "Goodtitle." So the Romans had their fictitious personages in law proceedings, as *Titius, Seius.*

The name "John Doe" is, and for some centuries has been, used in legal proceedings as a fictitious name to designate a party until his real name can be ascertained. State v. Rossignol, 22 Wash.2d 19, 153 P.2d 882, 885.

Join. To unite; to come together; to combine or unite in time, effort, action; to enter into an alliance.

Joinder. Joining or coupling together; uniting two or more constituents or elements in one; uniting with another person in some legal step or proceeding; union; concurrence.

The consent to an agreement or document by a party who has an interest in the subject matter of the agreement or document, but who is not himself an active party to the agreement or document.

Collusive joinder. The joinder of a defendant, commonly a nonresident, for purpose of removal to or conferring jurisdiction on a Federal Court. Bentley v. Halliburton Oil Well Cementing Co., D.C.Tex., 174 F.2d 788, 791.

Compulsory joinder. A person must be joined in an action if complete relief cannot be afforded the parties without his joinder or if his interest is such that grave injustice will be done without him. Fed.R. Civ.P. 19(a). See *Joinder of parties, below.*

Joinder in demurrer. In common law pleading, when a defendant in an action tenders an issue of law (called a "demurrer"), the plaintiff, if he means to maintain his action, must accept it, and this acceptance of the defendant's tender, signified by the plaintiff in a set form of words, is called a "joinder in demurrer."

Joinder in issue. In common law pleading, a formula by which one of the parties to a suit joins in or accepts an issue in fact tendered by the opposite party. Also called *"similiter".*

Joinder in pleading. In common law pleading, accepting the issue, and mode of trial tendered, either by demurrer, error, or issue, in fact, by the opposite party.

Joinder of claims. Under rules practice, a party asserting a claim to relief as an original claim, counterclaim, cross claim or third party claim may join as many claims as he has against an opposing party whether they are legal or equitable. Fed.R.Civ.P. 18(a); New York C.P.L.R. § 601.

Joinder of defendants. Two or more defendants may be charged in the same indictment or information if they are alleged to have participated in the same act or transaction or in the same series of acts or transactions constituting an offense or offenses. Such defendants may be charged in one or more counts together or separately and all of the defendants need not be charged in each count. Fed.R.Crim.Proc. 8(b).

Joinder of error. In proceedings on a writ of error in criminal cases, the joinder of error is a written denial of the errors alleged in the assignment of errors. It answers to a joinder of issue in an action.

Joinder of indictments or informations. The court may order two or more indictments or informations or both to be tried together if the offenses, and the defendants if there is more than one, could have been joined in a single indictment or information. The procedure shall be the same as if the prosecution were such single indictment or information. Fed.R. Crim.P. 13.

Joinder of issue. The act by which the parties to a cause arrive at that stage of it in their pleadings, that one asserts a fact to be so, and the other denies it.

Joinder of offenses. Two or more offenses may be charged in the same indictment or information in a separate count for each offense if the offenses charged, whether felonies or misdemeanors or both, are of the same or similar character or are based on the same act or transaction or on two or more acts or transactions connected together or constituting parts of a common scheme or plan. Fed.R.Crim.Proc. 8(a).

Joinder of parties. The act of uniting as parties to an action all persons who have the same rights or against whom rights are claimed, as either co-plaintiffs or co-defendants. Fed.R.Civil P. 19 and 20.

Necessary and indispensible parties. Prior to 1966 the federal, and most state, courts used classifications to determine if a person should or must be joined in an action. The label "indispensible" was used if the connection to the action of the absentee party was so close that the action should be dismissed unless the party was joined. The label "necessary" was used if the party was one who ought to be joined if this was possible. These classifications proved unsatisfactory and in 1966 Fed.Rule of Civil Proc. 19 was replaced with a new Rule 19, "Joinder of Persons needed for Just Adjudication." Rule 19(a) defines the class of persons who are needed for just adjudication. If an absentee meets this test, and is subject to process, the court must require that he be joined. If the absentee is needed for just adjudication and is not subject to process, Rule 19(b) states the factors to be considered in deciding whether to proceed in his absence or to dismiss the action.

Proper parties. If a party has some relation to the action, but it is not so close as to make him a person needed for just adjudication within Rule of Civil Proc. 19(a), he is a "proper" party, and the plaintiff has an option whether to join him if the tests of Rule 20 are met.

Joinder of remedies. Whenever a claim is one theretofore cognizable only after another claim has been prosecuted to a conclusion, the two claims may be joined in a single action; but the court will grant relief in that action only in accordance with the relative substantive rights of the parties. In particular, a plaintiff may state a claim for money and a claim to have set aside a conveyance fraudulent as to him, without first having obtained a judgment establishing the claim for money. Fed.R.Civ.P. 18(b).

Misjoinder. The improper joining together of parties to a suit, as plaintiffs or defendants, or of different causes of action. Misjoinder, however, is not a ground for dismissal. The improper party is merely dropped on motion of any party or on courts own motion. Fed.R.Civil P. 21. Relief from prejudicial joinder of offenses or defendants in an indictment or information is permitted under Fed.R.Crim.P. 14.

Misjoinder in a criminal prosecution is the charging in separate counts of separate and distinct offenses arising out of wholly different transactions having no connection or relation with each other. Optner v. U. S., C.C.A.Mich., 13 F.2d 11, 13.

Nonjoinder. The omission to join some person as party to a suit, whether as plaintiff or defendant, who ought to have been so joined. An omitted party may be added on motion of any party or on courts own motion. Fed.R.Civil P. 21.

Permissive joinder. All persons may join in one action as plaintiffs if they assert any right to relief jointly, severally, or in the alternative in respect of or arising out of the same transaction, occurrence, or series of transactions or occurrences and if any question of law or fact common to all these persons will arise in the action. All persons (and any vessel, cargo or other property subject to admiralty process in rem) may be joined in one action as defendants if there is asserted against them jointly, severally, or in the alternative, any right to relief in respect of or arising out of the same transaction, occurrence, or series of transactions or occurrences and if any questions of law or fact common to all defendants will arise in the action. A plaintiff or defendant need not be interested in obtaining or defending against all the relief demanded. Judgment may be given for one or more of the plaintiffs according to their respective rights to relief, and against one or more defendants according to their respective liabilities. Fed.R.Civ.P. 20(a).

Joint. United; combined; undivided; done by or against two or more unitedly; shared by or between two or more; coupled together in interest or liability.

The term is used to express a common property interest enjoyed or a common liability incurred by two or more persons. Thus, it is one in which the obligors (being two or more in number) bind themselves jointly but not severally, and which must therefore be prosecuted in a joint action against them all; distinguished from "joint and several" obligation.

As to joint Ballot; Committee; Contract; Covenant; Creditor; Fiat; Fine; Indictment; Obligation; Obligee; Obligor; Owner; Rate; Resolution; Session; Tenancy; Tenant; Trespass; Trespasser; Trustee; Will, see those titles. As to joint-stock banks, see **Bank**; joint-stock company, see **Company**; joint-stock corporation, see **Corporation**.

Joint account. An account in two or more names. Harbour v. Harbour, 207 Ark. 551, 181 S.W.2d 805, 807.

Joint action. An action brought by two or more as plaintiffs or against two or more as defendants. See **Joinder**.

Joint adventure. Any association of persons to carry out a single business enterprise for profit, for which purpose they combine their property, money, effects, skill, and knowledge. A "joint adventure" exists where there is a special combination of two or more persons jointly seeking to profit in some specific venture without actual partnership or corporate designation; it is an association of persons to carry out a single business enterprise for profit, for which purpose they combine their property, money, effects, skill, and knowledge. Fulton v. Fulton, Mo.App., 528 S.W.2d 146, 155. See also **Community of interest; Joint enterprises; Joint venture.**

Joint and several contracts. Contracts in which the parties bind themselves both individually and as a unit (jointly).

Joint and several liability. A liability is said to be joint and several when the creditor may sue one or more of the parties to such liability separately, or all of them together at his option. A joint and several bond or note is one in which the obligors or makers bind themselves both jointly and individually to the obligee or payee, so that all may be sued together for its enforcement, or the creditor may select one or more as the object of his suit. Term also refers to the liability of joint tortfeasors. See **Contribution; Joint tort-feasors.**

Such liability permits the Internal Revenue Service to collect a tax from one or all of several taxpayers. A husband and wife that file a joint income tax return usually are collectively or individually liable for the full amount of the tax liability.

Joint authorship. As to literary property, such exists where there is a common design to the execution of which several persons contribute. Mere alterations, additions or improvements, whether with or without the sanction of the author, will not entitle the person making them to claim to be a joint author of the work. Joint labor in furtherance of a common design. Edward B. Marks Music Corporation v. Jerry Vogel Music Co., D.C.N.Y., 140 F.2d 266, 267.

Joint bank account. An account in the names of two or more persons who have equal right to it, generally with the right of survivorship.

Joint cause of action. See **Joinder**.

Joint debtors. Persons united in a joint liability or indebtedness. Two or more persons jointly liable for the same debt.

Joint debtors' acts. Statutes enacted in many of the states, which provide that judgment may be given for or against one or more of several defendants, and that, "in an action against several defendants, the court may, in its discretion, render judgment against one or more of them, leaving the action to proceed against the others, whenever a several judgment is proper". The name is also given to statutes providing that where an action is instituted against two or more defendants upon an alleged joint liability, and some of them are served with process, but jurisdiction is not obtained over the others, the plaintiff may still proceed to trial against those who are before the court, and, if he recovers, may have judgment against all of the defendants whom he shows to be jointly liable. Hall v. Lanning, 91 U.S. 160, 168, 23 L.Ed. 271.

Joint defendants. Persons who are sued and tried together. In criminal law, persons who are indicted for the same crime and tried together. See **Joinder; Trial.**

Joint enterprise. Also called "common enterprise". The joint prosecution of common purpose under such circumstances that each has authority express or implied to act for all in respect to the control, means or agencies employed to execute such common purpose. Elements necessary to constitute a "joint enterprise" are: (1) an agreement among the group's members, either express or implied; (2) a common purpose that the group intends to carry out; (3) community of pecuniary interest among members of the group in that purpose; and (4) an equal right to a voice in control and direction of the enterprise which gives an equal right of control. Fredrickson v. Kluever, 82 S.D. 579, 152 N.W.2d 346, 348. See also **Joint adventure; Joint venture.**

Joint estate. Joint estate involves unity of interest, unity of title, unity of time, and unity of possession, and joint tenants must have the same interest accruing under the same conveyance, commencing at the same time, and held under the same undivided possession. Mosser v. Dolsay, 132 N.J.Eq. 121, 27 A.2d 155. See also **Joint tenancy.**

Joint executors. Co-executors; two or more who are joined in the execution of a will. See also **Coexecutor.**

Joint feasors in pari delicto /jóynt fíyzərz in péray dəlíktow/. Phrase means as between persons who by concert of action intentionally commit the wrong complained of; there is no right of contribution. Commercial Cas. Ins. Co. v. Leonard, 210 Ark. 575, 196 S.W.2d 919, 920.

Joint indictment. See **Indictment.**

Joint inventions. These are made when two or more persons jointly work or collaborate in devising and putting into practical form the subject-matter of patent. Altoona Publix Theatres v. American Tri-Ergon Corporation, C.C.A.Pa., 72 F.2d 53, 56.

Jointist. A person established in a definite place of business, for the purpose of illegally selling intoxicants. One who opens up, conducts, or maintains any place for the unlawful sale of intoxicating liquors.

Joint liability. One wherein joint obligor has right to insist that co-obligor be joined as a codefendant with him, that is, that they be sued jointly. Schram v. Perkins, D.C.Mich., 38 F.Supp. 404, 407. See **Contribution; Joinder.**

Joint lives. This expression is used to designate the duration of an estate or right which is granted to two or more persons to be enjoyed so long as they both (or all) shall live. As soon as one dies, the interest determines.

Jointly. Unitedly, combined or joined together in unity of interest or liability. Soderberg v. Atlantic Lighterage Corporation, D.C.N.Y., 15 F.2d 209. In a joint manner; in concert; not separately; in conjunction. To be or become liable to a joint obligation. Kaspar American State Bank v. Oul Homestead Ass'n, 301 Ill.App. 326, 22 N.E.2d 785, 786; Creighton v. Continental Roll & Steel Foundry Co., 155 Pa.Super. 165,

38 A.2d 337, 342. Participated in or used by two or more, held or shared in common.

Jointly acquired property. Property accumulated by joint industry of husband and wife during marriage. See also **Community property.**

Jointly and severally. See **Joint and several contracts; Joint and several liability.**

Jointly owned property. See **Community property; Joint bank account; Joint tenancy.**

Joint negligence. In case of "joint negligence" of several people, proximately causing accident, they act together in concert and either do something together which they should not do or fail to do something which they are together obligated to do under circumstances. Russo v. Aucoin, La.App., 7 So.2d 744, 747. See also **Contribution; Joint tort-feasors.**

Joint offense. One offense committed by two or more persons jointly. Crime committed by the participation of two or more persons. See **Conspiracy.**

Joint policy. Insurance on lives of spouses, for benefit of survivor. O'Boyle v. Home Life Ins. Co. of America, D.C.Pa., 20 F.Supp. 33, 36.

Joint rate. See **Joint through rate; Rate.**

Jointress, jointuress. A woman who has an estate settled on her by her husband, to hold during her life, if she survives him.

Joint return. See **Joint tax return.**

Joint-stock association. An unincorporated business enterprise with ownership interests represented by shares of stock. It was recognized at common law and by statute is generally treated as an entity for certain purposes.

Joint-stock company. See **Joint-stock association.**

Joint stock insurance company. An insurance company having a subscribed capital and policyholders having nothing to do with management. Ohio Farmers Indemnity Co. v. Commissioner of Internal Revenue, C.C.A.Ohio, 108 F.2d 665, 667.

Joint tax return. Tax return filed for federal or state taxes by a husband and wife together and each is individually liable. Such return includes the income of both spouses, though one spouse need not have any income. It is normally more beneficial from a tax standpoint for spouses to file a joint return than separate returns.

Joint tenancy. See **Tenancy.**

Joint through rate. Transportation charge applicable from a point on one transportation line to a point on another transportation line. Occurs when freight is to be shipped to its destination by more than one carrier.

Joint tort. Where two or more persons owe to another the same duty and by their common neglect such other is injured, the tort is "joint." See **Joint negligence; Joint tort-feasors.**

Joint tort-feasors. Term refers to two or more persons jointly or severally liable in tort for the same injury to person or property. American Tobacco Co. v. Transport Corp., D.C.Va., 277 F.Supp. 457, 461. Those persons who have acted in concert in their tortious conduct and are, accordingly, jointly and severally liable. Those who act together in committing wrong, or whose acts if independent of each other, unite in causing single injury. Bowen v. Iowa Nat. Mut. Ins. Co., 270 N.C. 486, 155 S.E.2d 238, 242. Several states have adopted the Uniform Contribution Among Tortfeasors Act. See also **Contribution.**

Joint trial. The trial of two or more persons for the same or similar offenses conducted within the framework of one trial. See also **Joinder; Trial.**

Jointure. A freehold estate in lands or tenements secured to the wife, and to take effect on the decease of the husband, and to continue during her life at the least, unless she be herself the cause of its determination. Property provision for wife, made prior to marriage, in lieu of dower.

Joint venture. A legal entity in the nature of a partnership engaged in the joint prosecution of a particular transaction for mutual profit. Tex-Co Grain Co. v. Happy Wheat Growers, Inc., Tex.Civ.App., 542 S.W.2d 934, 936. An association of persons jointly undertaking some commercial enterprise. It requires a community of interest in the performance of the subject matter, a right to direct and govern the policy in connection therewith, and duty, which may be altered by agreement, to share both in profit and losses. Russell v. Klein, 33 Ill.App.3d 1005, 339 N.E.2d 510, 512.

A one-time grouping of two or more persons in a business undertaking. Unlike a partnership, a joint venture does not entail a continuing relationship among the parties. A joint venture is treated like a partnership for Federal income tax purposes.

See also **Community of interest; Joint adventure; Joint enterprise.**

Joint venture corporation. See **Corporation.**

Joint verdict. Jury verdict covering more than one party to the action and combining two or more verdicts in one. See also **Verdict.**

Joint will. See **Will.**

Joker. In political usage, a clause in legislation that is ambiguous or apparently immaterial, inserted to render it inoperative or uncertain without arousing opposition at the time of passage.

Jones Act. Federal statute passed in 1920 which provides that a seaman injured in the course of his employment by the negligence of the owner, master or fellow crew members can recover damages for his injuries. 46 U.S.C.A. § 688. Similar remedies are available under the Act to the personal representative of a seaman killed in the course of his employment. See also **Longshoremen's and Harbor Workers' Compensation Act.**

Jornale /jornéyliy/jur°/. In old English law, as much land as could be plowed in one day.

Josh. To ridicule or tease, or make fun of in a joke, to lure or tease by misrepresenting the facts.

Jouir /zhùwír/. A French word, meaning to enjoy; to have enjoyment of; or to possess.

Jour /zhúr/júr/. A French word, signifying "day."

Jour en banc /júr ən bǽŋk/. A day *in banc.* Distinguished from *"jour en pays"* (a day in the country), otherwise called *"jour en nisi prius."*

Jour in court /júr ən kórt/. In old practice, day in court; day to appear in court; appearance day. "Every process gives the defendant a day in court."

Journal. A daily book; a book in which entries are made or events recorded from day to day. The place where transactions are recorded as they occur. The book of original entry.

In maritime law, the journal (otherwise called "log" or "log-book") is a book kept on every vessel, which contains a brief record of the events and occurrences of each day of a voyage, with the nautical observations, course of the ship, account of the weather, etc. In the system of double-entry bookkeeping, the journal is an account-book into which are transcribed, daily or at other intervals, the items entered upon the day-book, for more convenient posting into the ledger. In the usage of legislative bodies, the journal is a daily record of the proceedings of either house. It is kept by the clerk, and in it are entered the appointments and actions of committees, introduction of bills, motions, votes, resolutions, etc., in the order of their occurrence.

Journal entry. A recording in a journal of equal debits and credits, with, when necessary, an explanation of the transaction.

Journal entry rule. Regularity of enactment of statute may be inquired into by examining legislative journals.

Journalists' privilege. In the law of defamation, a publisher is protected in actions of defamation if the publication constitutes fair comment on the subject of public officers and employees in matters of public concern. Such privilege is qualified and hence is lost on proof of malice which, in this context, consists in publishing material either knowing it to be false or heedless in the reckless disregard of whether it is true or false when, in fact, it is false. New York Times Co. v. Sullivan, 376 U.S. 254, 84 S.Ct. 710, 11 L.Ed.2d 686. See also **Shield laws.**

Journeyman. A craftsman who has progressed through an apprenticeship and is qualified in his trade.

Journeys account. In English practice, a new writ which the plaintiff was permitted to sue out within a reasonable time after the abatement, without his fault, of the first writ. This time was computed with reference to the number of days which the plaintiff must spend in *journeying* to reach the court; hence the name of *journeys account,* that is, journeys *accomptes* or *counted.*

Joyriding. The temporary taking of an automobile without intent to deprive owner permanently of the vehicle. People v. Rivera, 185 Colo. 337, 524 P.2d 1082, 1083.

Jubere /jəbíriy/. Lat. In the civil law, to order, direct, or command. The word *jubeo* (I order), in a will, was called a "word of direction," as distinguished from "precatory words." To assure or promise. To decree or pass a law.

Judex /júwdèks/. Lat. In Roman law, a private person appointed by the prætor, with the consent of the parties, to try and decide a cause of action commenced before him. He received from the prætor a written formula instructing him as to the legal principles according to which the action was to be judged. Hence the proceedings before him were said to be *in judicio,* as those before the prætor were said to be *in jure.* A judge who conducted the trial from beginning to end; *magistratus.*

The practice of calling in *judices* was disused before Justinian's time: therefore, in the Code, Institutes, and Novels, *judex* means judge in its modern sense. The term *judex* is used with very different significations at different periods of Roman law.

In later and modern civil law, a judge.

In old English law, a juror. A judge, in modern sense, especially—as opposed to *justiciarius, i.e.,* a common-law judge—to denote an ecclesiastical judge.

Judex ad quem /júwdèks æd kwém/. A judge to whom an appeal is taken.

Judex æquitatem semper spectare debet /júwdèks ìykwətéydəm sémpər spektériy débət/. A judge ought always to regard equity.

Judex ante oculos æquitatem semper habere debet /júwdèks æntiy ókyəlows ìykwətéydəm sémpər həbíriy débət/. A judge ought always to have equity before his eyes.

Judex a quo /júwdèks èy kwów/. In civil law, the judge *from* whom, as *judex ad quem* is the judge *to* whom, an appeal is made or taken.

Judex bonus nihil ex arbitrio suo faciat, nec proposito domesticæ voluntatis, sed juxta leges et jura pronunciet /júwdèks bównəs náy(h)əl èks arbítriyow s(y)úwow féysh(iy)ət, nek prəpózədow dəméstəsiy vòləntéydəs, sèd júkstə líyjiyz èt júrə prənánshiyət/. A good judge should do nothing of his own arbitrary will, nor on the dictate of his personal inclination, but should decide according to law and justice.

Judex damnatur cum nocens absolvitur /júwdèks dæmnéydər kàm nósən(d)z əbzólvədər/. The judge is condemned when a guilty person escapes punishment.

Judex datus /júwdèks déydəs/. In Roman law, a judge given, that is, assigned or appointed, by the prætor to try a cause.

Judex debet judicare secundum allegata et probata /júwdèks débət jùwdəkériy səkándəm æləgéydə èt prəbéydə/. The judge ought to decide according to the allegations and the proofs.

Judex delegatus /júwdèks dèləgéydəs/. A delegated judge; a special judge.

Judex est lex loquens /júwdèks èst léks lówkwèn(d)z/. A judge is the law speaking [the mouth of the law].

Judex fiscalis /júwdèks fəskéyləs/. A fiscal judge; one having cognizance of matters relating to the *fiscus (q.v.).*

Judex habere debet duos sales,—salem sapientiæ, ne sit insipidus; et salem conscientiæ, ne sit diabolus /júdèks həbíriy débət d(y)úwows séyliyz: séyləm sæpiyénshiyiy nìy síd ənsípədəs èt séyləm kòns(h)iyenshiyiy, nìy sít diyǽbələs/. A judge should have two salts,—the salt of wisdom, lest he be insipid [or foolish]; and the salt of conscience, lest he be devilish.

Judex non potest esse testis in propria causa /júwdèks nòn pówdəst ésiy téstəs ìn prówpriyə kózə/. A judge cannot be a witness in his own cause.

Judex non potest injuriam sibi datam punire /júwdèks nòn pówdəst ənjúriyəm síbay déydəm pyənáyriy/. A judge cannot punish a wrong done to himself.

Judex non reddit plus quam quod petens ipse requirit /júwdèks nòn rédət plás kwæm kwód pédən(d)z ípsiy rəkwáyrət/. A judge does not give more than what the complaining party himself demands.

Judex ordinarius /júwdèks òrdənér(i)yəs/. In the civil law, an ordinary judge; one who had the right of hearing and determining causes as a matter of his own proper jurisdiction (*ex propria jurisdictione*), and not by virtue of a delegated authority. According to Blackstone judices ordinarii determined only questions of fact. 3 Bl.Comm. 315.

Judex pedaneus /júwdèks pədéyniyəs/. In Roman law, inferior judge; deputy judge. The judge who was commissioned by the prætor to hear a cause was so-called, from the low seat which he anciently occupied at the foot of the prætor's tribunal.

Judex quæstionis /júwdèks kwès(h)chiyównəs/. A magistrate who decided the law of a criminal case, when the prætor himself did not sit as a magistrate. The director of the criminal court under the presidency of the prætor.

Judex selectus /júwdèks səléktəs/. A select or selected *judex* or judge. The judges in criminal suits selected by the prætor. These *judices selecti* were used in criminal causes, and between them and modern *jurors* many points of resemblance have been noticed; 3 Bl.Comm. 366.

Judge. An officer so named in his commission, who presides in some court; a public officer, appointed to preside and to administer the law in a court of justice; the chief member of a court, and charged with the control of proceedings and the decision of questions of law or discretion. Todd v. U. S., 158 U.S. 278, 15 S.Ct. 889, 39 L.Ed. 982. A public officer who, by virtue of his office, is clothed with judicial authority. State ex rel. Mayer v. City of Cincinnati, 60 Ohio App. 119, 19 N.E.2d 902. Presiding officer of court. State v. Horn, 336 Mo. 524, 79 S.W.2d 1044, 1045. Any officer authorized to function as or for judge in doing specified acts. In re Roberts' Estate, 49 Cal. App.2d 71, 120 P.2d 933, 937.

"Judge", "justice", and "court" are often used synonymously or interchangeably.

See also **Magistrate.**

Judge advocate. An officer of the Judge Advocate General's Corps of the Army or the Navy or an officer of the Air Force or the Marine Corps who is designated as a judge advocate. 10 U.S.C.A. § 801.

In American usage, the term "judge advocate" no longer refers to any of the parties involved in a court-martial. Instead, it refers to the principal legal adviser on the staff of a military commander (usually with a more definitive title, such as Staff Judge Advocate, Post Judge Advocate, or Command Judge Advocate) or, more broadly, to any officer in the Judge Advocate General's Corps or Department (*i.e.*, branch) of one of the U.S. armed forces. British usage is different.

Judge advocate corps. Staff of Judge Advocate General.

Judge Advocate General. Senior legal officer and chief legal advisor of the Army, Navy, and Air Force and, except when the Coast Guard is operating as a service in the Navy, the General Counsel of the Department of Transportation. 10 U.S.C.A. § 801.

Judge de facto. One who holds and exercises the office of a judge under color of lawful authority and by a title valid on its face, though he has not full right to the office, as where he was appointed under an unconstitutional statute, or by an usurper of the appointing power, or has not taken the oath of office.

Judge-made law. A phrase used to indicate judicial decisions which construe away the meaning of statutes, or find meanings in them the legislature never intended. It is perhaps more commonly used as meaning, simply, the law established by judicial precedent and decisions. Laws having their source in judicial decisions as opposed to laws having their source in statutes or administrative regulations.

Judge pro tempore /jəj pròw témpəriy/. One appointed for the term or some part thereof, during which time he exercises all the functions of the regular judge. State ex rel. Hodshire v. Bingham, 218 Ind. 490, 33 N.E.2d 771.

Judge's minutes, or notes. Memoranda usually taken by a judge, while a trial is proceeding, of the testimony of witnesses, or documents offered or admitted in evidence, of offers of evidence, and whether it has been received or rejected, and the like matters.

Judge trial. Trial conducted before a judge without a jury. Jury waived trial; bench trial; non-jury trial.

Judgment. A sense of knowledge sufficient to comprehend nature of transaction. Thomas v. Young, 57 App.D.C. 282, 22 F.2d 588, 590. An opinion or estimate. McClung Const. Co. v. Muncy, Tex.Civ.App., 65 S.W.2d 786, 790. The formation of an opinion or notion concerning some thing by exercising the mind upon it. Cleveland Clinic Foundation v. Humphrys, C.C.A.Ohio, 97 F.2d 849, 857.

The official and authentic decision of a court of justice upon the respective rights and claims of the parties to an action or suit therein litigated and submitted to its determination. The final decision of the court resolving the dispute and determining the rights and obligations of the parties. The law's last word in a judicial controversy, it being the final determination by a court of the rights of the parties upon matters submitted to it in an action or proceeding. Towley v. King Arthur Rings, Inc., 40 N.Y.2d 129, 386 N.Y.S.2d 80, 351 N.E.2d 728, 730. Conclusion of law upon facts found or admitted by the parties or upon their default in the course of the suit. Decision or sentence of the law, given by a court of justice or other competent tribunal, as the result of proceedings instituted therein, Allegheny County v. Maryland Casualty Co., C.C.A.Pa., 132 F.2d 894, 897; State v. Siglea, 196 Wash. 283, 82 P.2d 583, 584. Decision or sentence of the law pronounced by the court and entered upon its docket, minutes or record. Determination of a court of competent jurisdiction upon matters submitted to it. State ex rel. Curran v. Brookes, 142 Ohio St. 107, 50 N.E.2d 995, 998. Determination or sentence of the law, pronounced by a competent judge or court, as the result of an action or proceeding instituted in such court, affirming that, upon the matters submitted for its decision, a legal duty or liability does or does not exist.

Term "judgment" under rules practice includes "decree". Fed.R.Civ.P. 54(a). Terms "decision" and "judgment" are commonly used interchangeably.

The term "judgment" is also used to denote the reason which the court gives for its decision; but this is more properly denominated an "opinion."

An award may be in the nature of, or equivalent of, a judgment. Traders & General Ins. Co. v. Baker, Tex.Civ.App., 111 S.W.2d 837, 839, 840; Holliday v. Salling, 54 Ariz. 496, 97 P.2d 221, 223. Also, an order may be a judgment. Traders & General Ins. Co. v. Baker, Tex.Civ.App., 111 S.W.2d 837, 839, 840; State v. Thierfelder, 114 Mont. 104, 132 P.2d 1035, 1037; State v. McNichols, 62 Idaho 616, 115 P.2d 104, 107; Baumgartner v. United States, C.C.A.Mo., 138 F.2d 29, 33.

See also Amendment of judgment; Decree; Entering judgments; Judgment in rem; Judgment quasi in rem; Rendition of judgment; Simulated judgment; Vacation of judgment; Void judgment.

Specific Types of Judgments

Agreed judgment. A judgment entered on agreement of the parties, which receives the sanction of the court, and it constitutes a contract between the parties to the agreement, operates as an adjudication between them and when court gives the agreement its sanction, becomes a judgment of the court. Traveler's Ins. Co. v. U. S., D.C.Tex., 283 F.Supp. 14, 28.

Alternative judgment. One that by its terms might be satisfied by doing either of several acts at the election of the party or parties against whom the judgment is rendered and from whom performance is by the judgment required. A judgment for one thing or another which does not specifically and in a definite manner determine the rights of the parties.

Appealable judgment. One which disposes of all parties and issues in case. Chuning v. Calvert, Mo.App., 452 S.W.2d 580, 582. See also *Final judgment, infra.*

Arrest of judgment. See **Arrest of judgment.**

Assets in futuro, judgment of. One against an executor or heir, who holds at the time no property on which it can operate.

Cognovit actionem. See **Cognovit actionem.**

Cognovit judgment. See **Cognovit judgment;** also, *Confession of judgment,* below.

Conditional judgment. One whose force depends upon the performance of certain acts to be done in the future by one of the parties; as, one which may become of no effect if the defendant appears and pleads according to its terms, or one which orders the sale of mortgaged property in a foreclosure proceeding unless the mortgagor shall pay the amount decreed within the time limited.

Confession of judgment. At common law, judgment entered where defendant, instead of entering plea, confessed action, or withdrew plea and confessed action. Judgment where a defendant gives the plaintiff a cognovit or written confession of the action by virtue of which the plaintiff enters judgment. The act of a debtor in permitting judgment to be entered against him by his creditor, for a stipulated sum, by a written statement to that effect or by warrant of attorney, without the institution of legal proceedings of any kind; voluntary submission to court's jurisdiction. O'Hara v. Manley, 140 Pa.Super. 39, 12 A.2d 820, 822. Such agreements for confession of judgment are void in many states; *e.g.* Mass.G.L. c. 231, § 13A.

The negotiability of an instrument is not affected by a term authorizing a confession of judgment if the instrument is not paid when due. U.C.C. § 3–112.

See also **Cognovit judgment.**

Consent judgment. A judgment, the provisions and terms of which are settled and agreed to by the parties to the action. Hargis v. Hargis, 252 Ky. 198, 66 S.W.2d 59; Matthews v. Looney, 132 Tex. 313, 123 S.W.2d 871, 872. See also **Consent** *(Consent decree);* and *Agreed judgment, supra.*

Contradictory judgment. A judgment which has been given after the parties have been heard, either in support of their claims or in defense. Used in Louisiana to distinguish such judgments from those rendered by default.

Declaratory judgment. See **Declaratory judgment.**

Default and inquiry, judgment by. It establishes right of action of kind properly pleaded in complaint, determines right of plaintiff to recover at least nominal damages and costs, and precludes defendant from offering any evidence on execution of inquiry to show that plaintiff has no right of action. Such type judgment is obsolete.

Default judgment. A judgment rendered in consequence of the non-appearance of the defendant. Fed. R.Civil P. 55(a). One entered upon the failure of a party to appear or plead at the appointed time. The term is also applied to judgments entered under statutes or rules of court, for want of affidavit of defense, plea, answer, and the like, or for failure to take some required step in the cause.

Judgments rendered on defendant's default are: Judgment *by default;* Judgment by *non sum informatus;* judgment *nil dicit.* Judgments rendered on plaintiff's default are: Judgment of *non pros.* (from *non prosequitur)* and judgment of *nonsuit* (from *non sequitur,* or *ne suit pas).*

Deficiency judgment. A judgment in favor of a creditor for the difference between the amount of the indebtedness and the amount derived from the judicial sale held in order to satisfy the indebtedness. Cameron Brown South, Inc. v. East Glen Oaks, Inc., La.App., 341 So.2d 450, 456. See also **Deficiency judgment.**

De melioribus damnis. See **De melioribus damnis.**

Demurrer, judgment on. Such concludes party demurring, because by demurring, a party admits the facts alleged in the pleadings of his adversary and relies on their insufficiency in law. See **Demurrer.**

Dismissal, judgment of. See **Dismissal.**

Domestic judgment. A judgment is *domestic* in the courts of the same state or country where it was originally rendered; in other states or countries it is called *foreign.* See *Foreign judgment, infra.*

Dormant judgment. One which has not been satisfied or extinguished by lapse of time, but which has remained so long unexecuted that execution cannot now be issued upon it without first reviving the judgment. Or one which has lost its lien on land from the failure to issue execution on it or take other steps to enforce it within the time limited by statute.

Execution of judgment. See **Execution of judgment or decree.**

Face of judgment. See **Face of judgment.**

Final judgment. One which puts an *end* to an action at law by declaring that the plaintiff either has or has not entitled himself to recover the remedy he sues for. So distinguished from *interlocutory* judgments. A judgment which disposes of the subject-matter of the controversy or determines the litigation as to all parties on its merits. A judgment which terminates all litigation on the same right. Appeals in federal courts will only lie from "final" judgments. 28 U.S. C.A. § 1291. **See Final decision; Final decision rule.**

Foreign judgment. One rendered by the courts of a state or country politically and judicially distinct from that where the judgment or its effect is brought in question. One pronounced by a tribunal of a foreign country, or of a sister state. Grover & B. Sewing Mach. Co. v. Radcliffe, 137 U.S. 287, 11 S.Ct. 92, 34 L.Ed. 670. Several states have adopted the Uniform Foreign Money Judgments Recognition Act, and also the Uniform Enforcement of Foreign Judgments Act.

General verdict subject to a special case, judgment on. Where at the trial the parties agree on the facts and the only question is one of law and a verdict pro forma is taken and the jury find for the plaintiff generally but subject to the opinion of the court on a special case.

In personam or inter partes. See **Judgment in personam or inter partes.**

In rem. See **Judgment in rem.**

Interlocutory judgment. One given in the progress of a cause upon some plea, proceeding, or default which is only intermediate and does not finally determine or complete the suit. One which determines some preliminary or subordinate point or plea, or settles some step, question, or default arising in the progress of the cause, but does not adjudicate the ultimate rights of the parties, or finally put the case out of court. Thus, a judgment or order passed upon any provisional or accessory claim or contention is, in general, merely interlocutory, although it may finally dispose of that particular matter. An "interlocutory judgment" is one which reserves or leaves some further question or direction for future determination. State ex rel. Great Am. Ins. Co. v. Jones, Mo., 396 S.W.2d 601, 603. See **Interlocutory appeal.**

Judgment notwithstanding verdict. See **Non obstante veredicto.**

Judgment of conviction. A judgment of conviction shall set forth the plea, the verdict or findings, and the adjudication and sentence. If the defendant is found not guilty or for any other reason is entitled to be discharged, judgment shall be entered accordingly. The judgment shall be signed by the judge and entered by the clerk. Fed.R.Crim.P. 32(b).

Judgment on pleadings. After the pleadings are closed but within such time as not to delay the trial, any party may move for judgment on the pleadings. If, on a motion for judgment on the pleadings, matters outside the pleadings are presented to and not excluded by the court, the motion shall be treated as one for summary judgment and disposed of as provided in Rule 56, and all parties shall be given reasonable opportunity to present all material made pertinent to such a motion by Rule 56. Fed.R.Civ.P. 12(c). This device resembles closely a demurrer to the extent that it attacks the pleadings on the same basis as a demurrer.

Junior judgment. One which was rendered or entered after the rendition or entry of another judgment, on a different claim, against the same defendant.

Merits, judgment on. One rendered after argument and investigation, and when it is determined which party is in the right, as distinguished from a judgment rendered upon some preliminary or formal or merely technical point, or by default and without trial. A decision that was rendered on the basis of the evidence introduced. Normally, a judgment based solely on some procedural error is not a judgment on the merits. The latter kind of judgment is often referred to as a "dismissal without prejudice." A party who has received a judgment on the merits cannot bring the same suit again. A party whose case has been dismissed without prejudice can bring the same suit again so long as the procedural errors are corrected (*i.e.*, cured) in the later action.

Money judgment. One which adjudges the payment of a sum of money, as distinguished from one directing an act to be done or property to be restored or transferred. A judgment, or any part thereof, for a sum of money or directing the payment of a sum of money. For enforcement or satisfaction of money judgment, see **Execution.** Several states have adopted the Uniform Foreign Money Judgments Recognition Act.

Nihil dicit. See **Nihil dicit.**

Nil capiat per breve or per billa (that he take nothing by his writ, or by his bill). A judgment in favor of the defendant upon an issue raised upon a declaration or peremptory plea.

Nil dicit, judgment by. Judgment for plaintiff rendered when defendant has appeared but has failed to answer or when answer has been withdrawn or abandoned and no further defense is made. Bredeson v. Merrill Lynch, Pierce, Fenner & Smith, Inc., Tex.Civ. App., 513 S.W.2d 110, 112. At common law, it may be taken against defendant who omits to plead or answer whole or any separable substantial portion of declaration. It amounts to judgment by confession with reference to cause of action states. Grand Lodge Brotherhood of Railroad Trainmen v. Ware, Tex.Civ.App., 73 S.W.2d 1076, 1077. Under current rules practice, such judgment is substantially identical with default judgment. See also **Nihil dicit.**

Nisi. At common law, judgment nisi was a judgment entered on the return of the nisi prius record, which, according to the terms of the postea indorsed thereon was to become absolute unless otherwise ordered by the court within the first four days of the next succeeding term. See also **Nisi; Show cause order.**

Nolle prosequi, judgment of. One entered against plaintiff when, after appearance and before judgment, he declares that he will not further prosecute his suit. Merchants Mut. Casualty Co. v. Kiley, 92 N.H. 323, 30 A.2d 681, 683. See also **Nolle prosequi.**

Non obstante veredicto. See **Non obstante veredicto.**

Non pros. (Non prosequitur [he does not follow up, or pursue]). See **Non prosequitur.**

Nonsuit. See **Nonsuit.**

Non sum informatus. See **Non sum informatus.**

Notwithstanding verdict. See **Non obstante verdicto.**

Nul tiel record. See **Nul tiel record.**

Nunc pro tunc. One entered on a day subsequent to the time at which it should have been entered, as of the latter date. See **Nunc pro tunc.**

Offer of judgment. Before trial, a party defending against a claim may serve upon the adverse party an offer to allow judgment to be taken against him for the money or property or to the effect specified in his offer, with costs then accrued. If after service of the offer the adverse party serves written notice that the offer is accepted, either party may then file the offer and notice of acceptance together with proof of service thereof and thereupon the clerk shall enter judgment. Fed.R.Civil P. 68.

Personal judgment. One imposing on the defendant a personal liability to pay it, and which may therefore be satisfied out of any of his property which is within the reach of process, as distinguished from one which may be satisfied only out of a particular fund or the proceeds of particular property. Judgments in which court has personal jurisdiction over parties. State v. Dreyer, 188 Kan. 270, 362 P.2d 55, 57.

Pro retorno habendo. A judgment that the party have a return of the goods.

Quod computet. See **Quod computet.**

Quod partes replacitent. See **Quod partes replacitent.**

Quod partitio fiat. Interlocutory judgment in a writ of partition, that partition be made.

Quod recuperet. See **Quod recuperet.**

Relicta verificatione. See **Relicta verificatione.**

Repleader, judgment of. See **Repleader.**

Respondeat ouster. When the issue in law arises on a dilatory plea, and is determined for the plaintiff, the judgment is only that the defendant "do answer over," called a judgment of *respondeat ouster;* it is interlocutory only.

Retraxit. See **Retraxit.**

Revival of judgment. See **Revival.**

Stet processus. See **Stet processus.**

Summary judgment. See **Summary judgment.**

Verdict, judgment on. The most usual of the judgments upon facts found, and is for the party obtaining the verdict. See also **Verdict.**

Warrant of attorney. See **Warrant.**

Judgment book. A book required to be kept by the clerk, among the records of the court, for the entry of judgments. Such is called a "civil docket" or "criminal docket" in the federal and many state courts. Fed.R.Civil P. 79; Fed.R.Crim.P. 55. See also **Judgment docket.**

Judgment creditor. One who has obtained a judgment against his debtor, under which he can enforce execution. A person in whose favor a money judgment is entered or a person who becomes entitled to enforce it. Owner of an unsatisfied judgment.

Judgment debt. One which is evidenced by matter of record. A debt, whether on simple contract or by specialty, for the recovery of which judgment has been entered up, either upon a *cognovit* or upon a warrant of attorney or as the result of a successful action.

Judgment debtor. A person against whom judgment has been recovered, and which remains unsatisfied. The term has been construed to include a judgment debtor's successors in interest.

Judgment docket. A list or docket of the judgments entered in a given court, methodically kept by the clerk or other proper officer, open to public inspection, and intended to afford official notice to interested parties of the existence or lien of judgments. See Fed.R.Civ.P. 79; Fed.R.Crim.P. 55. See also **Docket; Judgment book.**

Judgment, estoppel by. The estoppel raised by the rendition of a valid judgment by a court having jurisdiction. The essence of estoppel by judgment is that there has been a judicial determination of a fact. Price v. Clement, 187 Okl. 304, 102 P.2d 595, 597. It rests upon principles forbidding one to relitigate matter in dispute between parties which has been determined by competent court, on ground that record of judgment imports absolute verity. Where subsequent proceeding is on same cause of action between same parties a former adjudication is conclusive. Kimpton v. Spellman, 351 Mo. 674, 173 S.W.2d 886. Ordinarily, "estoppel" of judgment does not extend to matters not expressly adjudicated. Sonken-Galamba Corporation v. Atchison, T. & S. F. Ry. Co., C.C.A. Mo., 124 F.2d 952, 956; and a judgment or decree

without prejudice does not work an "estoppel". In re McDermott, C.C.A.Ill., 115 F.2d 582, 584. See also **Collateral estoppel doctrine; Issue preclusion; Judicial estoppel; Res** (*Res judicata*).

Judgment execution. The formal or written evidence of the judgment which commands the officer to seize the goods and property of the judgment debtor to satisfy the judgment. Procedure on execution is governed by Fed.R.Civil P. 69. See **Execution.**

Judgment file. The docket in which the entry of a judgment is recorded and preserved as a permanent court record. Fed.R.Civ.P. 79; Fed.R.Crim.P. 55. See also **Docket; Judgment docket.**

Judgment in personam or **inter partes** /jǝ́jmǝnt in pǝrsównǝm/ °íntǝr párdiyz/. A judgment against a particular person, as distinguished from a judgment against a thing or a right or *status.*

Judgment in rem. An adjudication pronounced upon the status of some particular thing or subject matter, by a tribunal having competent authority. Booth v. Copley, 283 Ky. 23, 140 S.W.2d 662, 666. It is founded on proceeding instituted against or on some thing or subject matter whose status or condition is to be determined, Eureka Building & Loan Ass'n v. Shultz, 139 Kan. 435, 32 P.2d 477, 480; or one brought to enforce a right in the thing itself, Federal Land Bank of Omaha v. Jefferson, 229 Iowa 1054, 295 N.W. 855, 857; Hobbs v. Lenon, 191 Ark. 509, 87 S.W.2d 6, 11. It operates directly upon the property. Hobbs v. Lenon, 191 Ark. 509, 87 S.W.2d 6, 11; Guild v. Wallis, 150 Or. 69, 40 P.2d 737, 742. It is a solemn declaration of the status of some person or thing. Jones v. Teat, Tex.Civ.App., 57 S.W.2d 617, 620. It is binding upon all persons in so far as their interests in the property are concerned. Booth v. Copley, 283 Ky. 23, 140 S.W.2d 662, 666; Hobbs v. Lenon, 191 Ark. 509, 87 S.W.2d 6, 11. See also **Judgment quasi in rem.**

Judgment in retraxit /jǝ́jmǝnt in rǝtrǽksǝt/. A judgment which is usually based upon and follows a settlement out of court, and like a judgment on the merits is a bar and estops plaintiff from again proceeding in another suit on same cause of action. Steele v. Beaty, 215 N.C. 680, 2 S.E.2d 854, 856, 857. See **Retraxit.**

Judgment lien. A lien binding the real estate of a judgment debtor, in favor of the holder of the judgment, and giving the latter a right to levy on the land for the satisfaction of his judgment to the exclusion of other adverse interests subsequent to the judgment. Right to subject land of judgment debtor to satisfaction of judgment. A charge on or attachment of property of one who owes a debt and is subject to a judgment thereon. See also **Execution.**

Judgment note. A promissory note (also called cognovit note) embodying an authorization to an attorney, or to a designated attorney, or to the holder, or the clerk of the court, to enter an appearance for the maker and confess a judgment against him for a sum therein named, upon default of payment of the note. Such are invalid in many states. See **Judgment** (*Confession of judgment*).

Judgment of his peers. A term of expression borrowed from Magna Charta and means trial by jury. Ex parte Wagner, 58 Okl.Cr. 161, 50 P.2d 1135, 1139.

Judgment paper. In English practice, a sheet of paper containing an *incipitur* of the pleadings in an action at law, upon which final judgment is signed by the master.

Judgment proof. Descriptive of all persons against whom judgments for money recoveries are of no effect; *e.g.*, persons who are insolvent, who do not have sufficient property within the jurisdiction of the court to satisfy the judgment, or who are protected by statutes which exempt wages and property from execution.

Judgment quasi in rem. A judgment based on the court's jurisdiction over the defendant's interest in property within the jurisdiction of the court and not on the court's jurisdiction over the person of the defendant (in personam) or over the thing itself (in rem).

Judgment record. In English practice, a parchment roll, on which are transcribed the whole proceedings in the cause, deposited and filed of record in the treasury of the court, after signing of judgment. In American practice, the record is signed, filed, and docketed by the clerk. See Fed.R.Civil P. 79. See also **Docket; Judgment docket.**

Judgment recovered. A plea by a defendant that the plaintiff has already recovered that which he seeks to obtain by his action. This was formerly a species of sham plea, often put in for the purpose of delaying a plaintiff's action. Under current rules practice, the defense of prior judgment would be raised as an affirmative defense. Fed.R.Civ.P. 8(c).

Judgment roll. See **Roll.**

Judgment void on its face. A judgment or order is "void on its face" when its invalidity is apparent upon inspection of judgment roll. Application of Behymer, 130 Cal.App. 200, 19 P.2d 829, 830.

Judicandum est legibus, non exemplis /jùwdəkǽndəm èst líyjəbəs nòn əgzémpləs/. Judgment is to be given according to the laws, not according to examples or precedents.

Judicare /jùwdəkériy/. Lat. In the civil and old English law, to judge; to decide or determine judicially; to give judgment or sentence.

Judicatio /jùwdəkéysh(iy)ow/. Lat. In the civil law, judging; the pronouncing of sentence after hearing a cause.

Judicatories /júwdəkətòriyz/juwdíkət(o)riyz/. The term as used designates that department of government which it was intended should interpret and administer the laws.

Judicature. The state or profession of those officers who are employed in administering justice; the judiciary. A judicatory, tribunal, or court of justice. Jurisdiction; the right of judicial action; the scope or extent of jurisdiction.

Judicature acts (England). The acts under which the present system of courts in England was organized and is continued.

The statutes of 36 & 37 Vict., c. 66, and 38 & 39 Vict., c. 77, which went into force November 1, 1875, with amendments in 1877, 40 & 41 Vict., c. 9; 1879, 42 & 43 Vict., c. 78; and 1881, 44 & 45 Vict., c. 68, made very important changes in the organization of, and methods of procedure in, the superior courts of England, consolidating them together so as to constitute one supreme court of judicature, consisting of two divisions,—her majesty's high court of justice, having chiefly original jurisdiction; and her majesty's court of appeal, whose jurisdiction is chiefly appellate.

See also **Judiciary Acts.**

Judices /júwdəsiyz/. Lat. Judges. See **Judex.**

Judices non tenentur exprimere causam sententiæ suæ /júwdəsiyz nòn tənéntər əkspráyməriy kózəm senténshiy(iy) s(y)úwiy/. Judges are not bound to explain the reason of their sentence.

Judices ordinarii /júwdəsiyz òrdənériyay/. Lat. Plural of *judex ordinarius (q.v.).*

Judices pedanei /júwdəsiyz pədéyniyay/. Lat. Plural of *judex pedaneus (q.v.).*

Judices selecti /júwdəsiyz səléktay/. Lat. Plural of *judex selectus (q.v.).*

Judicia; judicia publica /jədís(h)(i)yə/°pábləkə/. Lat. In Roman law. Judicial proceedings; trials. *Judicia publica,* criminal trials. See also **Judicium.**

Judicia in curia regis non adnihilentur, sed stent in robore suo quousque per errorem aut attinctum adnullentur /jədís(h)(i)yə in kyúriyə ríyjəs nòn ədnày(y)əléntər, sèd stént ìn rəbóriy s(y)úwow kwowǽskwiy pàr ərórəm òd ətíŋ(k)təm ǽdnəléntər/. Judgments in the king's court are not to be annihilated, but to remain in force until annulled by error or attaint.

Judicia in deliberationibus crebro maturescunt, in accelerato processu nunquam /jədís(h)(i)yə in dəlíbərèyshiyównəbəs kríybrow mæchəréskənt, ìn əksèləréydow prəsés(h)uw nə́ŋkwəm/. Judgments frequently become matured by deliberations, never by hurried process or precipitation.

Judicial. Belonging to the office of a judge; as judicial authority. Relating to or connected with the administration of justice; as a judicial officer. Having the character of judgment or formal legal procedure; as a judicial act. Proceeding from a court of justice; as a judicial writ, a judicial determination. Involving the exercise of judgment or discretion; as distinguished from *ministerial.*

Of or pertaining or appropriate to the administration of justice, or courts of justice, or a judge thereof, or the proceedings therein; as, judicial power, judicial proceedings. State v. Freitag, 53 Idaho 726, 27 P.2d 68.

As to judicial Action; Confession; Day; Discretion; Document; Estoppel; Evidence; Factor; Mortgage; Notice; Process; Record; Sale; Sequestration; Writ, see those titles. As to quasi judicial, see that title.

Judicial act. An act which involves exercise of discretion or judgment. It is also defined as an act by court or magistrate touching rights of parties or property brought before it or him by voluntary appearance, or by prior action of ministerial officers. An act by member of judicial department in construing law or applying it to a particular state of facts. State ex rel. Tharel v. Board of Com'rs of Creek County, 188 Okl. 184, 107 P.2d 542, 549. An act of administrative board if it goes to determination of some right, protection of which is peculiar office of courts. Belk's Dept. Store v. Guilford County, 222 N.C. 441, 23 S.E.2d 897, 902. An act which imposes burdens or confers privileges according to finding of some person or body whether a general rule is applicable or according to discretionary judgment as to propriety. An act which undertakes to determine a question of right or obligation or of property as foundation on which it proceeds. The action of judge in trying a cause and rendering a decision. Application of Gleit, 178 Misc. 198, 33 N.Y.S.2d 629, 630, 631.

Rendition or pronouncement of a judgment is a judicial act and entry thereof a ministerial act. Peoples Electric Co-op. v. Broughton, 191 Okl. 229, 127 P.2d 850, 853; O'Brien v. New York Edison Co., D.C.N.Y., 26 F.Supp. 290, 291; Bailer v. Dowd, 219 Ind. 624, 40 N.E.2d 325, 327. But if there are matters requiring exercise of court's discretion, entry of decree is judicial act. Stewart v. Superior Court in and for Los Angeles County, 3 Cal.App.2d 702, 40 P.2d 529.

See also **Decision; Decree; Judgment; Order.**

Judicial action. An adjudication upon rights of parties who in general appear or are brought before tribunal by notice or process, and upon whose claims some decision or judgment is rendered. Action of a court upon a cause, by hearing it, and determining what shall be adjudged or decreed between the parties, and with which is the right of the case.

Judicial activism. Judicial philosophy which motivates judges to depart from strict adherence to judicial precedent in favor or progressive and new social policies which are not always consistent with the restraint expected of appellate judges. It is commonly marked by decisions calling for social engineering and occasionally these decisions represent intrusions into legislative and executive matters.

Judicial acts. See **Judiciary Acts.**

Judicial admission. See **Admission.**

Judicial Article. Article III of the U.S.Const. which creates the U.S. Supreme Court; vests in Congress the right to create inferior courts; provides for life tenure for Federal Court judges; and specifies the powers and jurisdiction of the Federal Courts. See **Judicial branch; Judicial power; Judicial system; Judiciary Acts.**

Judicial authority. The power and authority appertaining to the office of a judge. Jurisdiction; the official right to hear and determine questions in controversy.

Judicial bonds. Generic term for bonds required by court for appeals, costs, attachment, injunction, etc.

Judicial branch. Branch of state and federal government whose function it is to interpret, construe, apply, and generally administer and enforce the laws. This branch, together with the executive and legislative branches forms our tripartite form of federal and state government. See **Judicial Article; Judicial power; Judicial system; Judiciary Acts.**

Judicial business. Such as involves the exercise of judicial power, or the application of the mind and authority of a court to some contested matter, or the conduct of judicial proceedings, as distinguished from such ministerial and other acts, incident to the progress of a cause, as may be performed by the parties, counsel, or officers of the court without application to the court or judge. See **Judicial act; Judicial action.**

Judicial Code. See **Federal Judicial Code.**

Judicial cognizance. Judicial notice, or knowledge upon which a judge is bound to act without having it proved in evidence. See **Judicial notice.**

Judicial comity. Principle in accordance with which courts of one state or jurisdiction give effect to laws and judicial decisions of another state out of deference and respect, not obligation. See also **Full faith and credit clause.**

Judicial council. Provision is made in 28 U.S.C.A. § 332 for the Chief Judge of each Circuit Court of Appeal to call a council of all the judges of the circuit twice each year. The primary function of the councils is to assure expeditious and effective administration of the business of the courts.

Judicial cy pres /jədíshəl sìy préy/. Doctrine of "judicial cy pres" is a principle of construction based on a judicial finding of donor's intention as applied to new conditions. Rohlff v. German Old People's Home, 143 Neb. 636, 10 N.W.2d 686, 691. When only minor features of a trust for charity become impossible or impracticable of performance and it cannot properly be said that general scheme of testator has failed, doctrine of "judicial cy pres" operates to avoid failure of charity. Noel v. Olds, 78 U.S.App.D.C. 155, 138 F.2d 581, 586, 587. See also **Cy-pres.**

Judicial decision. Application by a court or tribunal exercising judicial authority of competent jurisdiction of the law to a state of facts proved, or admitted to be true, and a declaration of the consequences which follow. In re Knofler's Estate, 73 Ohio App. 383, 52 N.E.2d 667, 668. See also **Decision; Decree; Judgment; Opinion; Order.**

Judicial declaration of law. A rule adopted as the basis of decision of issues involved. Trustees of Phillips Exeter Academy v. Exeter, 90 N.H. 472, 27 A.2d 569, 577.

Judicial department. See also **Judicial branch.**

Judicial dictum /juwdíshəl díktəm/. A dictum made by a court or judge in the course of a judicial decision or opinion. Com. v. Paine, 207 Pa. 45, 56 A. 317. See **Dictum.**

Judicial discretion. Term is a broad and elastic one which is equated with sound judgment of court to be exercised according to rules of law. People v. Russel, 70 Cal.Rptr. 210, 215, 448 P.2d 794. The option the trial judge has in doing or not doing a thing that cannot be demanded by a litigant as an absolute right. Kasper v. Helfrich, Mo.App., 421 S.W.2d 66, 69. See also **Judicial duty.**

Judicial district. One of the circuits or precincts into which a state is commonly divided for judicial purposes; a court of general original jurisdiction being usually provided in each of such districts, and the boundaries of the district marking the territorial limits of its authority; or the district may include two or more counties, having separate and independent county courts, but in that case they are presided over by the same judge.

Judicial duty. One that requires exercise of judgment or choice of alternatives in its performance. One that requires exercise of judgment or decision of a question of fact. State ex rel. Coast Holding Co. v. Ekwall, 144 Or. 672, 26 P.2d 52. One that requires use of discretion or examination of evidence and decision of questions of law and fact. One that legitimately pertains to an officer in judicial department. Harding v. McCullough, 236 Iowa 556, 19 N.W.2d 613, 617; Ex parte Lewis, 328 Mo. 843, 42 S.W.2d 21, 22. See also **Judicial act; Judicial action; Judicial discretion.**

Judicial errors. Errors into which the court itself falls are "judicial errors." An error of this character occurs when the judgment rendered is erroneous in some particular, requiring it to be changed. See **Error.**

Judicial estoppel. Under doctrine of "judicial estoppel," a party is bound by his judicial declarations and may not contradict them in a subsequent proceeding involving same issues and parties. Sailes v. Jones, 17 Ariz.App. 593, 499 P.2d 721, 726. Under this doctrine, a party who by his pleadings, statements or contentions, under oath, has assumed a particular position in a judicial proceeding is estopped to assume an inconsistent position in a subsequent action. Yarber v. Pennell, Tex.Civ.App., 443 S.W.2d 382, 384. The doctrine of "judicial estoppel" is the doctrine of the conclusiveness of the judgments. State v. Ohio Oil Co., Tex.Civ.App., 173 S.W.2d 470, 478, 479. See also **Judgment, estoppel by; Res** (Res judicata).

Judicial evidence. The means, sanctioned by law, of ascertaining in a judicial proceeding the truth respecting a question. See **Evidence.**

Judicial function. The exercise of the judicial faculty or office. The capacity to act in the specific way which appertains to the judicial power, as one of the powers of government. The term is used to describe generally those modes of action which appertain to the judiciary as a department of organized government, and through and by means of which it accomplishes its purposes and exercises its peculiar powers. See also **Judicial act; Judicial action; Judicial business.**

Judicial immunity. The absolute protection from civil liability arising out of the discharge of judicial functions which every judge enjoys. C. M. Clark Ins. Agency, Inc. v. Reed, D.C.Tex., 390 F.Supp. 1056. Under doctrine of "judicial immunity," a judge is not subject to liability for any act committed within the exercise of his judicial function; the immunity is absolute in that it is applicable even if the actions of the judicial official are taken in bad faith. C. M. Clark Ins. Agency, Inc. v. Reed, D.C.Tex., 390 F.Supp. 1056, 1060.

Judicial inquiry. Such inquiry investigates, declares, and enforces liabilities as they stand on present or past facts and under laws supposed already to exist. Oklahoma Gas & Electric Co. v. Wilson & Co. of Oklahoma, C.C.A.Okl., 54 F.2d 596, 598.

Judicial knowledge. Knowledge of that which is so notorious that everybody, including judges, knows it, and hence need not be proved. Ex parte Ferguson, 112 Tex.Cr.R. 152, 15 S.W.2d 650, 652. See **Judicial notice.**

Judicial legislation. See **Judge-made law.**

Judicial lien. One obtained by judgment, levy, sequestration, or other legal or equitable process or proceeding. Bankruptcy Act, § 101(27).

Judicial notice. The act by which a court, in conducting a trial, or framing its decision, will, of its own motion, and without the production of evidence, recognize the existence and truth of certain facts, having a bearing on the controversy at bar, which, from their nature, are not properly the subject of testimony, or which are universally regarded as established by common notoriety, e.g., the laws of the state, international law, historical events, the constitution and course of nature, main geographical features, etc. The cognizance of certain facts which judges and jurors may properly take and act upon without proof, because they already know them. Fed.Evid.Rule 201.

Judicial oath. See **Oath.**

Judicial office. Offices which relate to the administration of justice; and which should be exercised by persons of sufficient skill and experience in the duties which appertain to them. A general term including courts of record and courts not of record.

Judicial officer. A judge or magistrate. The term, in the popular sense, applies generally to any officer of a court, but in the strictly legal sense applies only to an officer who determines causes between parties or renders decision in a judicial capacity. One who exercises judicial function. Adams v. State, 214 Ind. 603, 17 N.E.2d 84. A person in whom is vested authority to decide causes or exercise powers appropriate to a court.

Judicial opinion. A term synonymous with what has been adjudged or decreed and final in its character. See **Decision; Decree; Judgment; Opinion; Order.**

Judicial order. One which involves exercise of judicial discretion and affects final result of litigation. Happy Coal Co. v. Brashear, 263 Ky. 257, 92 S.W.2d 23, 27. See also **Decision; Decree; Judgment; Order.**

Judicial power. The authority exercised by that department of government which is charged with declaration of what law is and its construction. The authority vested in courts and judges, as distinguished from the executive and legislative power. Courts have general powers to decide and pronounce a judgment and carry it into effect between two persons and parties who bring a case before it for decision; and also such specific powers as contempt powers, power to control admission and disbarment of attorneys, power to adopt rules of court, etc.

A power involving exercise of judgment and discretion in determination of questions of right in specific cases affecting interests of person or property, as distinguished from ministerial power involving no discretion. Inherent authority not only to decide, but to make binding orders or judgments. Fewel v. Fewel, 23 Cal.2d 431, 144 P.2d 592, 594. Power to decide and pronounce a judgment and carry it into effect between persons and parties who bring a case before court for decision. Power that adjudicates upon and protects the rights and interests of persons or property, and to that end declares, construes and applies the law.

The primary source of powers of federal courts is provided in Art. III of U.S.Const., and Judiciary Act of 1789 (Title 28 of U.S.Code). See **Judiciary Acts.**

Judicial proceeding. Any proceeding wherein judicial action is invoked and taken. Mannix v. Portland Telegram, 144 Or. 172, 23 P.2d 138. Any proceeding to obtain such remedy as the law allows. Any step taken in a court of justice in the prosecution or defense of an action. A general term for proceedings relating to, practiced in, or proceeding from, a court of justice; or the course prescribed to be taken in various cases for the determination of a controversy or for legal redress or relief. A proceeding in a legally constituted court. A proceeding wherein there are parties, who have opportunity to be heard, and wherein the tribunal proceeds either to a determination of facts upon evidence or of law upon proved or conceded facts. See also **Trial.**

Judicial question. One proper for the determination of a court of justice, as distinguished from moot questions or from such questions as belong to the decision of the legislative or executive departments of government and with which the courts will not interfere, called "political" or "legislative" questions.

Judicial records. Dockets or records of judicial proceedings; a judgment is a judicial record. Little v. Stevens, 23 Cal.App.3d 112, 99 Cal.Rptr. 885, 886; Fed.R.Civil P. 79. See **Docket; Judgment docket; Judgment record.**

Judicial remedy. Such as is administered by the courts of justice, or by judicial officers empowered for that purpose by the constitution and laws of the state or nation. See also **Remedy.**

Judicial reprieve. See **Reprieve.**

Judicial review. Form of appeal from an administrative body to the courts for review of either the findings of fact, or of law, or of both. See also **Appeal.**

Judicial Review Act. Federal statute which sets forth scope of review of decisions of federal administrative agencies. 28 U.S.C.A. §§ 2341–2351.

Judicial sale. Sale conducted under a judgment, order, or supervision of a court as in a sale under a petition for partition of real estate or an execution. A "judicial sale" is one which must be based upon an order

or a decree of a court directing the sale. Petition of Acchione, 425 Pa. 23, 227 A.2d 816, 821, 823. A sale in a bankruptcy proceeding is a "judicial sale". In re Dennis Mitchell Industries, Inc., D.C.Pa., 280 F.Supp. 433, 436. See also **Execution sale; Sale; Sheriffs' sale; Tax sale.**

Judicial self-restraint. Self-imposed discipline by judges in deciding cases without permitting themselves to indulge their own personal views or ideas which may be inconsistent with existing decisional or statutory law.

Judicial separation. A separation of man and wife by decree of court, less complete than an absolute divorce. A "limited divorce" or a "divorce a mensa et thoro."

Judicial system. Entire network of courts in a particular jurisdiction. The federal judicial system consists of the Supreme Court, Courts of Appeals, District Courts, and specialized courts such as the Court of Claims, Court of Customs and Patent Appeals, etc. See also **Judiciary** (n).

Judicia posteriora sunt in lege fortiora /jədís(h)(i)yə pəstìriyórə sənt in líyjiy fòrsh(iy)órə/. The later decisions are the stronger in law.

Judiciary, *adj.* /jədísh(iy)əriy/. Pertaining or relating to the courts of justice, to the judicial department of government, or to the administration of justice.

Judiciary, *n.* That branch of government invested with the judicial power; the system of courts in a country; the body of judges; the bench. That branch of government which is intended to interpret, construe and apply the law. Board of Com'rs of Wyandotte County v. General Securities Corporation, 157 Kan. 64, 138 P.2d 479, 487. See also **Judicial system.**

Judiciary Acts. The Judiciary Article (Art. III) of the U.S. Constitution created a Supreme Court and "such inferior courts as the Congress may from time to time ordain or establish". The First Congress established such inferior federal courts under the Judiciary Act of 1789. Subsequent major judiciary acts include the following: Act of 1875 granting federal question jurisdiction; Act of 1891 (Evarts Act) establishing circuit courts of appeals and fixing the outline of the contemporary scheme of federal appellate review; Act of 1911 enacting the Federal Judicial Code (which was recodified in 1948 and 1958); Act of 1925 (Judges' Bill) further narrowing the scope of discretionary review by certiorari of the Supreme Court.

Judicia sunt tanquam juris dicta, et pro veritate accipiuntur /jədís(h)(i)yə sənt tǽŋkwəm júrəs díktə, èt pròw vèhrətéydiy əksìpiyántər/. Judgments are, as it were, the sayings of the law, and are received as truth.

Judiciis posterioribus fides est adhibenda /jədís(h)iyəs pəstìriyórəbəs fáydiyz èst ǽdhəbéndə/. Faith or credit is to be given to the later judgments.

Judici officium suum excedenti non paretur /júwdəsay əfísh(iy)əm s(y)úwəm èksədéntay nòn pəríydər/. A judge exceeding his office (or jurisdiction) is not to be obeyed. Said of void judgments.

Judiciously. Directed by sound judgment. Shivers v. Stovall, Tex.Civ.App., 75 S.W.2d 276, 279.

Judici satis pœna est, quod Deum habet ultorem /júwdəsay séydəs píynə èst kwòd díyəm héybəd əltórəm/. It is punishment enough for a judge that he has God as his avenger.

Judicis est in pronuntiando sequi regulam, exceptione non probata /júwdəsəs èst in prənəns(h)iyǽndow sékway régyələm, əksèpshiyówniy nòn prəbéydə/. The judge in his decision ought to follow the rule, when the exception is not proved.

Judicis est judicare secundum allegata et probata /júwdəsəs èst jùwdəkériy səkándəm ǽləgéydə èt prəbéydə/. It is the duty of a judge to decide according to facts alleged and proved.

Judicis est jus dicere, non dare /júwdəsəs èst jás dísəriy, non dériy/°dáysəriy°/. It is the province of a judge to declare the law, not to give it.

Judicis officium est opus diei in die suo perficere /júwdəsəs əfísh(iy)əm èst ówpəs dàyíyay in dáyiy s(y)úwow pərfísəriy/. It is the duty of a judge to finish the work of each day within that day.

Judicis officium est ut res, ita tempora rerum, quærere /júwdəsəs əfísh(iy)əm èst ət ríyz, áydə témpərə rírəm, kwírəriy/. It is the duty of a judge to inquire into the times of things, as well as into things themselves.

Judicium /jədís(h)(i)yəm/. Lat. Judicial authority or jurisdiction; a court or tribunal; a judicial hearing or other proceeding; a verdict or judgment; a proceeding before a judex or judge.

Judicium a non suo judice datum nullius est momenti /jədís(h)(i)yəm èy nón s(y)úwow júwdəsiy déydəm nəláyəs èst məméntay/. A judgment given by one who is not the proper judge is of no force.

Judicium capitale /jədís(h)(i)yəm kǽpətéylíy/. In old English law, judgment of death; capital judgment. Called, also, "*judicium vitæ amissionis*," judgment of loss of life.

Judicium Dei /jədís(h)(i)yəm díyay/. In old English and European law, the judgment of God; otherwise called "*divinum judicium,*" the "divine judgment." A term particularly applied to the ordeals by fire or hot iron and water, and also to the trials by the cross, the Eucharist, and the corsned, and the *duellum* or trial by battle *(q.v.)*, it being supposed that the interposition of Heaven was directly manifest, in these cases, in behalf of the innocent.

Judicium est quasi juris dictum /jədís(h)(i)yəm èst kwéysay júrəs díktəm/. Judgment is, as it were, a declaration of law.

Judicium non debet esse illusorium; suum effectum habere debet /jədís(h)(i)yəm nòn débəd ésiy ìl(y)uwzóriyəm; s(y)úwəm əféktəm həbíriy débət/. A judgment ought not to be illusory; it ought to have its proper effect.

Judicium parium /jədís(h)(i)yəm pǽriyəm/. In old English law, judgment of the peers; judgment of one's peers: trial by jury.

Judicium (semper) pro veritate accipitur /jədís(h)(i)yəm (sémpər) pròw vèhrətéydiy əksípidər/. A judgment is always taken for truth [that is, as long as it stands in force it cannot be contradicted].

Judicium redditur in invitum /jədís(h)(i)yəm rédədər in ənváydəm/. Judgment is given against one, whether he will or not.

Juge. In French law, a judge.

Juge de paix /zhyúwz də péy/. An inferior judicial functionary, appointed to decide summarily controversies of minor importance, especially such as turn mainly on questions of fact. He has also the functions of a police magistrate.

Juge d'instruction. See **Instruction.**

Jugerum /jəgírəm/. An acre. As much as a yoke (jugum) of oxen could plow in one day.

Jugulator /jágyəlèydər/. In old records, a cutthroat or murderer.

Jugum /júwgəm/. Lat. In the civil law, a yoke; a measure of land; as much land as a yoke of oxen could plow in a day.

Jugum terræ /júwgəm téhriy/. In old English law, a yoke of land; half a plow-land.

Juicio /huwíysiyow/. In Spanish law, a trial or suit.

Juicio de apeo /huwíysiyow dèy apéyow/. The decree of a competent tribunal directing the determining and marking the boundaries of lands or estates.

Juicio de concurso de acreedores /huwíysiyow dey konkúrsow dey akrèyeyðóreys/. The judgment granted for a debtor who has various creditors, or for such creditors, to the effect that their claims be satisfied according to their respective form and rank, when the debtor's estate is not sufficient to discharge them all in full.

Julian law /júwl(i)yən ló/. See **Lex Julia.**

Jump bail. To abscond, withdraw, or secrete one's self, in violation of the obligation of a bail bond.

Junior. Younger. Lower in rank, tenure, preference, or position.

This has been held to be no part of a man's name, but an addition by use, and a convenient distinction between a father and son of the same name.

As to junior Barrister; Counsel; Creditor; Judgment; Writ, see those titles.

Junior execution. One which was issued after the issuance of another execution, on a different judgment, against the same defendant.

Junior interest. A legal right which is subordinate to another's right as applied to property; *e.g.* a second mortgage is subordinate to a first mortgage. See also **Creditor** (*Junior creditor*).

Junior lien. Lien which is subordinate to prior lien. See **Lien.**

Junior mortgage. A mortgage which is subordinate to another mortgage, called the priority or prior mortgage. See **Mortgage.**

Junk. Worn out and discarded material in general that may be turned to some use. City of Chicago v.

Iroquois Steel & Iron Co., 284 Ill.App. 561, 1 N.E.2d 241, 243; Ex parte Scott, 130 Tex.Cr.R. 29, 91 S.W.2d 748, 749. Articles that have outlived their usefulness in their original form, and are commonly gathered up and sold to be converted into another product, either of the same or of a different kind; *e.g.* old iron, or other base metals, old rope, rags, waste paper, etc., and empty bottles, and all articles discarded or no longer used as a manufactured article composed of any one or more of the materials mentioned.

Junket. An arrangement or arrangements the primary purpose of which is to induce any person to gamble at a licensed casino hotel and pursuant to which, and as consideration for which, a certain portion of the cost of transportation, food, lodging, and entertainment for said person is directly or indirectly paid by a casino licensee or employee or agent thereof.

Jura /júrə/. Lat. Plural of "jus." Rights; laws.

Jura ecclesiastica limitata sunt infra limites separatos /júrə əklìyziyǽstəkə lìmətéydə sènt ínfrə límədiyz sepəréydows/. Ecclesiastical laws are limited within separate bounds.

Jura eodem modo destituuntur quo constituuntur /júrə iyówdəm mówdow dəstìchuwǽntər kwòw kənstìchuwǽntər/. Laws are abrogated by the same means [authority] by which they are made.

Jura fiscalia /júrə fəskéyl(i)yə/. In English law, fiscal rights; rights of the exchequer.

Jura in re /júrə ìn ríy/. In the civil law, rights in a thing; rights which, being separated from the *dominium*, or right of property, exist independently of it, and are enjoyed by some other person than him who has the *dominium*.

Jural /júrəl/. Pertaining to natural or positive right, or to the doctrines of rights and obligations; as "jural relations." Of or pertaining to jurisprudence; juristic; juridical.

Recognized or sanctioned by positive law; embraced within, or covered by, the rules and enactments of positive law. Founded in law; organized upon the basis of a fundamental law, and existing for the recognition and protection of rights.

The "jural sphere" is to be distinguished from the "moral sphere;" the latter denoting the whole scope or range of ethics or the science of conduct, the former embracing only such portions of the same as have been made the subject of legal sanction or recognition.

The term "jural society" is used as the synonym of "state" or "organized political community."

Jural cause. A matter or item involving law as contrasted with social obligations or ethics. A judicial matter.

Jura majestatis /júrə mǽjəstéydəs/. Rights of sovereignty or majesty; a term used in the civil law to designate certain rights which belong to each and every sovereignty and which are deemed essential to its existence.

Juramentæ corporales /jurəméntiy kòrpəréyliyz/. Lat. Corporal oaths, *q.v.*

Juramentum /jurəméntəm/. Lat. In the civil law, an oath.

Juramentum calumniæ /jurəméntəm kəlámniyiy/. In the civil and canon law, the oath of calumny. An oath imposed upon both parties to a suit, as a preliminary to its trial, to the effect that they are not influenced by malice or any sinister motives in prosecuting or defending the same, but by a belief in the justice of their cause. It was also required of the attorneys and proctors.

Juramentum corporalis /jurəméntəm kòrpəréyləs/. A corporal oath. See **Corporal oath.**

Juramentum est indivisibile; et non est admittendum in parte verum et in parte falsum /jurəméntəm èst ìndivəzíbəliy èt nón èst ǽdməténdəm ìn párdiy víram èd ìn párdiy fólsəm/. An oath is indivisible; it is not to be held partly true and partly false.

Juramentum in litem /jurəméntəm ìn láydəm/. In the civil law, an assessment oath; an oath, taken by the plaintiff in an action, that the extent of the damages he has suffered, estimated in money, amounts to a certain sum, which oath, in certain cases, is accepted in lieu of other proof.

Juramentum judiciale /jurəméntəm juwdìshiyéyliy/. In the civil law, an oath which the judge, of his own accord, defers to either of the parties. It is of two kinds: *First,* that which the judge defers for the decision of the cause, and which is understood by the general name *"juramentum judiciale,"* and is sometimes called "suppletory oath," *juramentum suppletorium; second,* that which the judge defers in order to fix and determine the amount of the condemnation which he ought to pronounce, and which is called *"juramentum in litem."*

Juramentum necessarium /jurəméntəm nèsəsériyəm/. In Roman law, a compulsory oath. A disclosure under oath, which the prætor compelled one of the parties to a suit to make, when the other, applying for such an appeal, agreed to abide by what his adversary should swear.

Juramentum voluntarium /jurəméntəm vòləntériyəm/. In Roman law, a voluntary oath. A species of appeal to conscience, by which one of the parties to a suit, instead of proving his case, offered to abide by what his adversary should answer under oath.

Jura mixti dominii /júrə míkstay dəmíniyay/. In old English law, rights of mixed dominion. The king's right or power of jurisdiction was so termed.

Jura naturæ sunt immutabilia /júrə nət(y)úriy sènt imyùwdəbíl(i)yə/. The laws of nature are unchangeable.

Jura novit curia /júrə nówvət kyúriyə/. The court knows the laws; the court recognizes rights.

Jura personarum /júrə pèrsənérəm/. Rights of persons; the rights of persons. Rights which concern and are annexed to the persons of men.

Jura prædiorum /júrə prìydiyórəm/. In the civil law, the rights of estates.

Jura publica anteferenda privatis /júrə pə́bləkə æ̀ntəfəréndə prəvéydəs/. Public rights are to be preferred to private.

Jura publica ex privato [privatis] promiscue decidi non debent /júrə pə́bləkə èks prəvéydow prəmískyuwiy dəsáyday nòn débənt/°èks prəvéydəs°/. Public rights ought not to be decided promiscuously with private.

Jurare /jərériy/. Lat. To swear; to take an oath.

Jurare est Deum in testem vocare, et est actus divini cultus /jərériy èst díyəm in téstəm vəkériy èd èst ǽktəs dəváynay kə́ltəs/. To swear is to call God to witness, and is an act of religion.

Jura regalia /júrə rəgéyl(i)yə/. In English law, royal rights or privileges.

Jura regia /júrə ríyj(iy)ə/. In English law, royal rights; the prerogatives of the crown.

Jura regis specialia non conceduntur per generalia verba /júrə ríyjəs speshiyéyl(i)yə nòn kònsədə́ntər pə̀r jènəréyl(i)yə və́rbə/. The special rights of the king are not granted by general words.

Jura rerum /júrə rírəm/. Rights of things; the rights of things; rights which a man may acquire over external objects or things, unconnected with his person.

Jura sanguinis nullo jure civili dirimi possunt /júrə sǽŋgwənəs nə́low júriy sívəlay dírəmay pósənt/. The right of blood and kindred cannot be destroyed by any civil law.

Jura summi imperii /júrə sə́may əmpíriyay/. Rights of supreme dominion; rights of sovereignty.

Jurat /júrət/. Certificate of officer or person before whom writing was sworn to. In common use term is employed to designate certificate of competent administering officer that writing was sworn to by person who signed it. Stearn v. Board of Elections of Cuyahoga County, 14 Ohio St.2d 175, 237 N.E.2d 313, 317. The clause written at the foot of an affidavit, stating when, where, and before whom such affidavit was sworn. U. S. v. McDermott, 140 U.S. 151, 11 S.Ct. 746, 35 L.Ed. 391; U. S. v. Julian, 162 U.S. 324, 16 S.Ct. 801, 40 L.Ed. 984. See also **Affidavit; Verification.**

Jurata /jəréydə/. In old English law, a jury of twelve men sworn. Especially, a jury of the common law, as distinguished from the *assisa.*

The jury clause in a *nisi prius* record, so called from the emphatic words of the old forms: *"Jurata ponitur in respectum,"* the jury is put in respite.

See also **Jurat.**

Juration /jəréyshən/. The act of swearing; the administration of an oath.

Jurato creditur in judicio /jəréydow krédədər in jədísh(iy)ow/. He who makes oath is to be believed in judgment.

Jurator /jəréydər/. A juror; a compurgator *(q.v.).*

Juratores debent esse vicini, sufficientes, et minus suspecti /jùrətóriyz débənt ésiy vəsáynay, səfis(h)iyéntiyz, èt máynəs səspéktay/. Jurors ought to be neighbors of sufficient estate, and free from suspicion.

Juratores sunt judices facti /jùrətóriyz sə́nt júwdəsiyz fǽktay/. Juries are the judges of fact.

Jurats /júræts/. In English law, officers in the nature of aldermen, sworn for the government of many corporations.

Jure /júriy/. Lat. By right; in right; by the law.

Jure belli /júriy bélay/. By the right or law of war.

Jure civili /júriy sívəlay/. By the civil law.

Jure coronæ /júriy kərówniy/. In right of the crown.

Jure divino /júriy dəváynow/. By divine right.

Jure ecclesiæ /júriy əklíyziy(iy)/. In right of the church.

Jure emphyteutico /júriy èmfətyúwdəkow/. By the right or law of *emphyteusis.* See **Emphyteusis.**

Jure gentium /júriy jénsh(iy)əm/. By the law of nations.

Jure naturæ æquum est neminem cum alterius detrimento et injuria fieri locupletiorem /júriy nəchúriy íykwəm èst némənəm kə̀m oltíriyəs dètrəméntow èd ənjúriyə fáyəray lòwkəplìyshiyórəm/. By the law of nature it is not just that any one should be enriched by the detriment or injury of another.

Jure representationis /júriy rèprəzentèyshiyównəs/. By right of representation; in the right of another person.

Jure uxoris /júriy əksórəs/. In right of a wife.

Juridical /jərídəkəl/. Relating to administration of justice, or office of a judge.

Regular; done in conformity to the laws of the country and the practice which is there observed.

Juridical day. Day on which court is in session. Black v. National Bank of Kentucky, 226 Ky. 152, 10 S.W.2d 629, 630.

Juridicus /jərídəkəs/. Lat. Relating to the courts or to the administration of justice; juridical; lawful.

Juri non est consonum quod aliquis accessorius in curia regis convincatur antequam aliquis de facto fuerit attinctus /júray nón èst kónsənəm kwòd ǽləkwəs æ̀ksəsóriyəs in kyúriyə ríyjəs kònviŋkéydər ǽntiykwəm ǽləkwəs dìy fǽktow fyúwərəd ətíŋktəs/. It is not consonant to justice that any accessory should be convicted in the king's court before any one has been attainted of the fact.

Juris /júrəs/. Lat. Of right; of law.

Juris affectus in executione consistit /júrəs əféktəs in èksəkyùwshiyówniy kənsístət/. The effect of the law consists in the execution.

Jurisconsult /jùrəskónsəlt/°kənsə́lt/. A jurist; a person skilled in the science of law, particularly of international or public law.

Jurisconsultus /jùrəskənsáltəs/. Lat. In Roman law, an expert in juridical science; a person thoroughly versed in the laws, who was habitually resorted to, for information and advice, both by private persons as his clients, and also by the magistrates, advocates, and others employed in administering justice. Abbreviated *i–ctus.*

Jurisdictio est potestas de publico introducta, cum necessitate juris dicendi /jùrəsdíksh(iy)ow èst pətéstæs dìy páblǝkow ìntrədə́ktə, kə̀m nəsèsǝtéydiy júrǝs dǝsénday/. Jurisdiction is a power introduced for the public good, on account of the necessity of dispensing justice.

Jurisdiction. The word is a term of large and comprehensive import, and embraces every kind of judicial action. Federal Land Bank of Louisville, Ky., v. Crombie, 258 Ky. 383, 80 S.W.2d 39, 40. It is the authority by which courts and judicial officers take cognizance of and decide cases. Board of Trustees of Firemen's Relief and Pension Fund of City of Marietta v. Brooks, 179 Okl. 600, 67 P.2d 4, 6; State v. True, Me., 330 A.2d 787. The legal right by which judges exercise their authority. Max Ams, Inc. v. Barker, 293 Ky. 698, 170 S.W.2d 45, 48. It exists when court has cognizance of class of cases involved, proper parties are present, and point to be decided is within powers of court. United Cemeteries Co. v. Strother, 342 Mo. 1155, 119 S.W.2d 762, 765; Harder v. Johnson, 147 Kan. 440, 76 P.2d 763, 764. Power and authority of a court to hear and determine a judicial proceeding. In re De Camillis' Estate, 66 Misc.2d 882, 322 N.Y.S.2d 551, 556. The right and power of a court to adjudicate concerning the subject matter in a given case. Biddinger v. Fletcher, 224 Ga. 501, 162 S.E.2d 414, 416.

Areas of authority; the geographic area in which a court has power or types of cases it has power to hear.

Scope and extent of jurisdiction of federal courts is governed by 28 U.S.C.A. § 1251 et seq.

For Ancillary; Appellate; Concurrent; Contentious; Continuing; Coordinate; Criminal; Equity; Exclusive; Foreign; General; International; Legislative; Limited; Military; Pendent; Plenary; Primary; Probate; Special; Subject-matter; Summary; Territorial; and Voluntary jurisdiction, see those titles. See also Excess of jurisdiction; Jurisdiction in personam; Jurisdiction in rem; Jurisdiction of the subject matter; Jurisdiction quasi in rem; Lack of jurisdiction. For original jurisdiction, see **Original.** For diversity jurisdiction, see **Diversity of citizenship.** For federal question jurisdiction, see **Federal question.** For jurisdiction over nonresidents or foreign corporations, see **Long arm statutes; Minimal contacts.**

Jurisdictional. Pertaining or relating to jurisdiction; conferring jurisdiction; showing or disclosing jurisdiction; defining or limiting jurisdiction; essential to jurisdiction.

Jurisdictional amount. Amount involved in the particular case, Shabotzky v. Massachusetts Mut. Life Ins. Co., D.C.N.Y., 21 F.Supp. 166, 167; sum of all claims that are properly joined, Gray v. Blight, C.C.A.Colo., 112 F.2d 696, 700; value of the object sought to be attained in the litigation, Mountain States Power Co. v. City of Forsyth, D.C.Mont., 41 F.Supp. 389, 390; Ronzio v. Denver & R. G. W. R. Co., C.C.A.Utah, 116 F.2d 604, 606. The jurisdiction of the trial court is commonly limited by the amount in controversy in the particular action; *e.g.* the requisite jurisdictional amounts for federal question and diversity of citizenship jurisdiction in the federal district courts are set forth in 28 U.S.C.A. §§ 1331, 1332.

Jurisdictional dispute. The competing claims made to an employer by different unions that each of their members are entitled to perform certain specific work. There must be evidence of a threat of coercive action for the N.L.R.B. to conduct a hearing and make an assignment of the work.

Jurisdictional facts. Those matters of fact which must exist before the court can properly take jurisdiction of the particular case, as, that the defendant has been properly served with process, that the amount in controversy exceeds a certain sum, that the parties are citizens of different states, etc. Noble v. Union River Logging Railroad Co., 147 U.S. 165, 13 S.Ct. 271, 37 L.Ed. 123. See **Jurisdictional statement; Jurisdiction clause.**

Jurisdictional limits. The constitutional or statutory parameters within which judicial power may be exercised such as limits based on the monetary value of the action. See **Jurisdictional amount.**

Jurisdictional plea. Form of answer addressed to the issue of whether the court has the power over the defendant or over the subject matter of the litigation; *e.g.* Fed.R.Civ.P. 12(b)(1), (2).

Jurisdictional statement. In some states, a statement required to set forth the amount claimed to be in controversy so as to permit a court of general jurisdiction to hear the case without remanding it to an inferior court. See also **Jurisdiction clause.**

Jurisdiction clause. A pleading which sets forth a claim for relief, whether an original claim, counterclaim, crossclaim, or third party claim, shall contain "a short and plain statement of the grounds upon which the court's jurisdiction depends, unless the court already has jurisdiction and the claim needs no new grounds to support it." Fed.R.Civ.P. 8(a).

In equity practice, that part of a bill which is intended to give jurisdiction of the suit to the court, by a general averment that the acts complained of are contrary to equity, and tend to the injury of the complainant, and that he has no remedy, or not a complete remedy, without the assistance of a court of equity, is called the "jurisdiction clause."

See also **Jurisdictional statement.**

Jurisdiction in personam. Power which a court has over the defendant's person and which is required before a court can enter a personal or in personam judgment. Pennoyer v. Neff, 95 U.S. 714, 24 L.Ed. 565. It may be acquired by an act of the defendant within a jurisdiction under a law by which the defendant impliedly consents to the personal jurisdiction of the court, *e.g.* operation of a motor vehicle on the highways of state confers jurisdiction of operator and owner on courts of state. Hess v. Pawloski, 274 U.S. 352, 47 S.Ct. 632, 71 L.Ed. 1091. A judgment in personam brings about a merger of the original cause of action into the judgment and thereafter the action is upon the judgment and not on the original cause of action. See also **In personam.**

Jurisdiction in rem. Power of a court over a thing so that its judgment is valid as against the rights of every person in the thing, *e.g.* a judgment or decree of registration of title to land. See also **In rem; Jurisdiction quasi in rem.**

Jurisdiction of the subject matter. Power of a particular court to hear the type of case that is then before it. Davis v. Davis, 9 Ill.App.3d 922, 293 N.E.2d 399, 405; People ex rel. Scott v. Janson, 10 Ill.App.3d 787, 295 N.E.2d 140, 144; Alfaro v. Meagher, 27 Ill.App.3d 292, 326 N.E.2d 545, 548. Term refers to jurisdiction of court over class of cases to which particular case belongs, Honea v. Graham, Tex.Civ.App., 66 S.W.2d 802, 804; McFarlin v. McFarlin, 384 Ill. 428, 51 N.E.2d 520, 521; Ferree v. Ferree, 285 Ky. 825, 149 S.W.2d 719, 721; jurisdiction over the nature of the cause of action and relief sought, Mid-City Bank & Trust Co. v. Myers, 343 Pa. 465, 23 A.2d 420, 423; or the amount for which a court of limited jurisdiction is authorized to enter judgment.

A court is without authority to adjudicate a matter over which it has no jurisdiction even though the court possesses jurisdiction over the parties to the litigation; *e.g.* a court of limited criminal jurisdiction has no power to try a murder indictment and its judgment therein would be void and of no effect because it lacks subject matter jurisdiction.

Jurisdiction over person. The legal power of the court to render a personal judgment against a party to an action or a proceeding. Imperial v. Hardy, La., 302 So.2d 5, 7. See **Jurisdiction in personam.**

Jurisdiction quasi in rem. The power of a court over the defendant's interest in property, real or personal, within the geographical limits of the court. The court's judgment or decree binds only the defendant's interest and not the whole world as in the case of jurisdiction in rem. The original cause of action is not merged in the judgment as in the case of a judgment predicated on personal jurisdiction.

Juris et de jure /júrəs èt dìy júriy/. Of law and of right.

A presumption *juris et de jure*, or an irrebuttable presumption, is one which the law will not suffer to be rebutted by any counter-evidence, but establishes as conclusive; while a presumption *juris tantum* is one which holds good in the absence of evidence to the contrary, but may be rebutted.

Juris et seisinæ conjunctio /júrəs èt síyzəniy kənjáŋ(k)sh(iy)ow/. The union of seisin or possession and the right of possession, forming a complete title. 2 Bl. Comm. 199, 311.

Juris ignorantia est cum jus nostrum ignoramus /júrəs ìgnəráensh(iy)ə èst kàm jás nóstrəm ìgnəréyməs/. It is ignorance of the law when we do not know our own rights.

Jurisinceptor /jùrəsənséptər/. Lat. A student of the civil law.

Jurisperitus /jùrəspəráydəs/. Lat. Skilled or learned in the law.

Juris positivi /júrəs pòzətáyvay/. Of positive law; a regulation or requirement of positive law, as distinguished from natural or divine law.

Juris præcepta sunt hæc: honeste vivere; alterum non lædere; suum cuique tribuere /júrəs prəséptə sànt híyk: (h)onéstiy vívəriy; óltərəm nòn líydəriy; s(y)úwəm k(yuw)áykwiy trəbyúwəriy/. These are the precepts of the law: To live honorably; to hurt nobody; to render to every one his due.

Juris privati /júrəs prəvéyday/. Of private right; subjects of private property.

Jurisprudence. The philosophy of law, or the science which treats of the principles of positive law and legal relations.

In the proper sense of the word, "jurisprudence" is the science of law, namely, that science which has for its function to ascertain the principles on which legal rules are based, so as not only to classify those rules in their proper order, and show the relation in which they stand to one another, but also to settle the manner in which new or doubtful cases should be brought under the appropriate rules. Jurisprudence is more a formal than a material science. It has no direct concern with questions of moral or political policy, for they fall under the province of ethics and legislation; but, when a new or doubtful case arises to which two different rules seem, when taken literally, to be equally applicable, it may be, and often is, the function of jurisprudence to consider the ultimate effect which would be produced if each rule were applied to an indefinite number of similar cases, and to choose that rule which, when so applied, will produce the greatest advantage to the community.

For **Comparative jurisprudence** and **Medical jurisprudence**, see those titles. For equity jurisprudence, see **Equity.**

Jurisprudentia /jùrəspruwdénsh(iy)ə/. Lat. In the civil and common law, jurisprudence, or legal science.

Jurisprudentia est divinarum atque humanarum rerum notitia, justi atque injusti scientia /jùrəspruwdénsh(iy)ə èst dìvənérəm ǽtkwiy hyùwmənérəm rírəm nowtísh(iy)ə, jə́stay ǽtkwiy injə́stay sayénsh(iy)ə/. Jurisprudence is the knowledge of things divine and human, the science of what is right and what is wrong.

Jurisprudentia legis communis angliæ est scientia socialis et copiosa /jùrəspruwdénsh(iy)ə líyjəs kəmyúwnəs ǽngliyiy èst sayénsh(iy)ə sòws(h)iyéyləs èt kòwpiyówsə/. The jurisprudence of the common law of England is a science social and comprehensive.

Juris publici /júrəs pə́bləsay/. Of common right; of common or public use; such things as, at least in their own use, are common to all the king's subjects; as common highways, common bridges, common rivers, and common ports.

Jurist. One who is versed or skilled in law; answering to the Latin *"jurisperitus" (q.v.).* A legal scholar.

The term is commonly applied to those who have distinguished themselves by their writings on legal subjects or to judges.

Juristic /jərístək/. Pertaining or belonging to, or characteristic of, jurisprudence, or a jurist, or the legal profession.

Juristic act. One designed to have a legal effect, and capable thereof. An act of a private individual directed to the origin, termination, or alteration of a right.

Juris utrum /júrəs yúwtrəm/. In English law, an abolished writ which lay for the parson of a church whose predecessor had alienated the lands and tenements thereof.

Juror. Member of jury. In addition to regular jurors, term includes special and alternate jurors.

Alternate juror. Additional juror impanelled in case of sickness or disability of another juror; generally in trials of expectedly long duration. Fed.R.Civil P. 47(b).

Juror designate. A juror who has been drawn as a juror. Summers v. State ex rel. Boykin, 66 Ga.App. 648, 19 S.E.2d 28, 31.

Juror's book. A list of persons qualified to serve on juries. See also **Jury-list.**

Jury. A certain number of men and women selected according to law, and *sworn (jurati)* to inquire of certain matters of fact, and declare the truth upon evidence to be laid before them. This definition embraces the various subdivisions of juries; as *grand jury, petit jury, common jury, special jury, coroner's jury, sheriff's jury (q.v.).*

A jury is a body of persons temporarily selected from the citizens of a particular district, and invested with power to present or indict a person for a public offense, or to try a question of fact. See also **Trier of fact.**

Advisory jury. A body of jurors impanelled to hear a case in which the parties have no right to a jury trial. The judge remains solely responsible for the findings and he may accept or reject the jury's verdict. Fed. R.Civil P. 39(c). See also **Advisory jury.**

Challenge to jury. See **Jury challenge.**

Common jury. The ordinary kind of jury (*i.e.* petit jury) by which issues of fact are generally tried, as distinguished from a *special jury (q.v.).*

Deadlocked jury. See *Hung jury, infra.*

Fair and impartial jury. See **Fair and impartial jury.**

Foreign jury. A jury obtained from a county or jurisdiction other than that in which issue was joined.

Grand jury. A jury of inquiry who are summoned and returned by the sheriff to each session of the criminal courts, and whose duty is to receive complaints and accusations in criminal cases, hear the evidence adduced on the part of the state, and find bills of indictment in cases where they are satisfied a trial ought to be had. They are first sworn, and instructed by the court. This is called a "grand jury" because it comprises a greater number of jurors than the ordinary trial jury or "petit jury." At common law, a grand jury consisted of not less than twelve nor more than twenty-three men.

Body of citizens, the number of whom varies from state to state, whose duties consist in determining whether probable cause exists that a crime has been committed and whether an indictment (true bill)

should be returned against one for such a crime. If the grand jury determines that probable cause does not exist, it returns a "no bill." It is an accusatory body and its function does not include a determination of guilt.

Federal Grand Jury. Every grand jury impaneled before any district court shall consist of not less than sixteen nor more than twenty-three persons. If less than sixteen of the persons summoned attend, they shall be placed on the grand jury, and the court shall order the marshal to summon, either immediately or for a day fixed, from the body of the district, and not from the bystanders, a sufficient number of persons to complete the grand jury. 18 U.S.C.A. § 3321; Fed.R.Crim.P. 6.

See also **Inquest; Special grand jury.**

Hung jury. A jury which is unable to agree on a verdict after a suitable period of deliberation; a deadlocked jury. The result is a mistrial of the case.

Impanelling of jury. See **Impanel.**

Impartial jury. See **Impartial jury.**

Inquest jury. A jury of inquest is a body of persons summoned from the citizens of a particular district before the sheriff, coroner, or other ministerial officers, to inquire of particular facts. See **Inquest.**

Jury instructions. See **Jury instructions.**

Jury size. While at common law, and traditionally, a jury consisted of 12 members, there is no constitutional infirmity or deficiency in a jury of less than twelve; and it is not uncommon for state and Federal district court juries to consist of six persons, instead of twelve (*e.g.* Dist. of Mass.). Colgrove v. Battin, 413 U.S. 149, 93 S.Ct. 2448, 37 L.Ed.2d 522. Also, in federal district courts, and many state courts, the parties may stipulate that the jury shall consist of any number less than twelve. Fed.R.Civil P. 48; Fed. R.Crim.P. 23.

Petit jury. The ordinary jury for the trial of a civil or criminal action; so called to distinguish it from the grand jury.

Polling of jury. See **Polling the jury.**

Sequestration of jury. In some cases of great notoriety, the trial judge will order the jury to be isolated from the public (*e.g.* confined to area of hotel while trial not in session) for the duration of the trial to prevent tampering and exposure to trial publicity. In these cases the jurors are always in the custody of the court.

Special jury. A jury ordered by the court, on the motion of either party, in cases of unusual importance or intricacy. Called, from the manner in which it is constituted, a "struck jury." See **Striking a jury.**

At common law, a jury composed of persons above the rank of ordinary freeholders; usually summoned to try questions of greater importance than those usually submitted to common juries.

Traverse jury. See **Traverse.**

Trial jury. The jury participating in the trial of a given case; or a jury summoned and impaneled for the trial of a case, and in this sense a petit jury as distinguished from a grand jury. A body of persons returned from the citizens of a particular district before a court or officer of competent jurisdiction, and sworn to try and determine, by verdict, a question of fact.

Jury-box. The place in court (strictly an inclosed place) where the jury sits during the trial of a cause.

Jury challenge. *Challenge for cause.* In most jurisdictions, each party to the litigation has right to a certain number of peremptory challenges to jurors at the time of impanelling. In addition, a party has the right to challenge a juror by furnishing a satisfactory reason why such juror should not be seated such as bias or knowledge of the case. Unlike the peremptory challenge for which no reason need be given, the party challenging a juror for cause must satisfy the trial judge that his reasons are compelling. See *e.g.* Fed.R.Crim.P. 24. See also **Challenge.**

Challenge to array. A challenge to the entire jury venire based on such grounds as systematic exclusion of women, blacks, young persons, etc. in the selection process.

Peremptory challenge. A challenge to a juror at the time of impanelling for which no reason need be advanced; in most jurisdictions each party is entitled to a certain number of such challenges in addition to challenges for cause. See *e.g.* Fed.R.Crim.P. 24.

Jury commissioner. An officer charged with the duty of selecting the names to be put into the jury wheel, or of drawing the panel of jurors for a particular term of court. Local official responsible for collecting lists of qualified prospective jurors for submission to court.

Jury instructions. A direction given by the judge to the jury concerning the law of the case; a statement made by the judge to the jury informing them of the law applicable to the case in general or some aspect of it; an exposition or the rules or principles of law applicable to the case or some branch or phase of it, which the jury are bound to accept and apply. Attorneys for both sides normally furnish judge with suggested instructions. Fed.R.Civil P. 51; Fed.R.Crim.P. 30. Many states have model or pattern jury instructions which are required to be used, or substantially followed, by the trial judge.

See also Allen charge; Argumentative instruction; Cautionary instruction; Charge (Charge to jury); Dynamite instruction; Golden Rule argument. For request for instructions, see **Request.**

Additional instructions. If during the course of deliberations the jury is unclear about a particular point of law or aspect of the evidence it may request the court for additional or supplementary instructions.

Mandatory instruction. A mandatory instruction unequivocally charges the jury that if jurors find from preponderance of evidence that certain set of facts exists, jurors must find for one party and against the other. City of Evansville v. Rinehart, 142 Ind.App. 164, 233 N.E.2d 495, 499; Vance v. Wells, 129 Ind. App. 659, 159 N.E.2d 586, 590. Mandatory instructions are those which attempt to set up a factual situation and direct jury to a certain result and they are to be distinguished from instructions which mere-

ly state propositions of law without incorporating a factual situation. LaNoux v. Hagar, Ind.App., 308 N.E.2d 873, 878.

Peremptory instruction. An instruction given by a court to a jury which the latter must obey implicitly; as an instruction to return a verdict for the defendant, or for the plaintiff, as the case may be. See also *Mandatory instruction,* above.

Jury-list. A paper containing the names of jurors impaneled to try a cause, or the names of all the jurors summoned to attend court.

Jury of matrons. See **Matrons, jury of.**

Jury panel. The group of prospective jurors who are summoned to appear on a stated day and from which a grand jury or petit jury is chosen. See **Jury; Jury-list.**

Jury polling. See **Polling the jury.**

Jury process. The process by which a jury is summoned in a cause, and by which their attendance is enforced. See also **Impanel.**

Jury questions. In general, term refers to questions of fact which are peculiarly within the province of the jury as contrasted with questions of law which must be decided by the judge. Term may also refer to special questions or interrogatories which the court may direct to the jury for a special verdict. Fed.R. Civil P. 49. See also **Voir dire.**

Jury Selection and Service Act. Federal Act (1968) to insure non-discrimination in federal jury selection and service. 28 U.S.C.A. § 1861.

Jury summation. See **Closing argument.**

Jury trial. Trial of matter or cause before jury as opposed to trial before judge. Such right is guaranteed with respect to criminal cases by Art. III, Sec. 2, cl. 3 of U.S.Const., and with respect to "suits at common law, where the value in controversy shall exceed twenty dollars" by the Seventh Amendment. Such right is also preserved by rule of court (*e.g.* Fed.R.Civil P. 38) and by the Fifth Amendment which provides *inter alia* for indictment by grand jury, and the Sixth Amendment which contains further specifications respecting jury trial in criminal cases. In addition, state constitutions provide for right to jury trial and the Supreme Court has held that the Fourteenth Amendment guarantees a right of jury trial in all state criminal cases which—were they to be tried in federal court—would come within the Sixth Amendment's guarantee. Duncan v. Louisiana, 391 U.S. 145, 88 S.Ct. 1444, 20 L.Ed.2d 491.

The right to "jury trial" of controverted issues implies a trial by an impartial and qualified jury. Alexander v. R. D. Crier & Sons Co., 181 Md. 415, 30 A.2d 757, 759.

See also **Trial.**

Jury wheel. Physical device or electronic system for the storage and random selection of the names or identifying numbers of prospective jurors. A machine containing the names of persons qualified to serve as grand and petit jurors, from which, in an order determined by the hazard of its revolutions, are drawn a sufficient number of such names to make up the panels for a given term of court.

Jurywoman. Member of a jury of matrons.

Jus /jə́s/. Lat. In Roman law, right; justice; law; the whole body of law; also a right. The term is used in two meanings:

1. *"Jus"* means "law," considered in the abstract; that is, as distinguished from any specific enactment, the science or department of learning, or *quasi* personified factor in human history or conduct or social development, which we call, in a general sense, "the law." Or it means the law taken as a system, an aggregate, a whole; "the sum total of a number of individual laws taken together." Or it may designate some one particular system or body of particular laws; as in the phrases *"jus civile," "jus gentium," "jus prœtorium."*

2. In a second sense, *"jus"* signifies "a right;" that is, a power, privilege, faculty, or demand inherent in one person and incident upon another; or a capacity residing in one person of controlling, with the assent and assistance of the state, the actions of another. This is its meaning in the expressions *"jus in rem," "jus accrescendi," "jus possessionis."*

It is thus seen to possess the same ambiguity as the words *"droit," "recht,"* and "right" *(q.v.).*

Within the meaning of the maxim that *"ignorantia juris non excusat"* (ignorance of the law is no excuse), the word *"jus"* is used to denote the general law or ordinary law of the land, and not a private right.

Some further meanings of the word are:

An action, or, rather, those proceedings in the Roman action which were conducted before the prætor.

Power or authority. *Sui juris,* in one's own power; independent. *Alieni juris,* under another's power.

The profession *(ars)* or practice of the law. *Jus ponitur pro ipsa arte.*

A court or judicial tribunal *(locus in quo redditur jus).*

Jus abstinendi /jə́s æ̀bstənénday/. The right of renunciation; the right of an heir, under the Roman law, to renounce or decline the inheritance, as, for example, where his acceptance, in consequence of the necessity of paying the debts, would make it a burden to him.

Jus abutendi /jə́s æbyəténday/. The right to abuse. By this phrase is understood the right to do exactly as one likes with property, or having full dominion over property.

Jus accrescendi /jə́s æ̀krəsénday/. The right of survivorship. In re Brogan's Estate, 165 Misc. 111, 300 N.Y.S. 447, 455. The right of the survivor or survivors of two or more joint tenants to the tenancy or estate, upon the death of one or more of the joint tenants. In re Capria's Estate, 89 Misc. 101, 151 N.Y.S. 385, 386.

Jus accrescendi inter mercatores, pro beneficio commercii, locum non habet /jə́s æ̀krəsénday íntər màrkətóriyz, pròw benəfís(h)(i)yow kəmársiyay, lówkəm nòn héybət/. The right of survivorship has no place between merchants, for the benefit of commerce.

There is no survivorship in cases of partnership, as there is in joint-tenancy.

Jus accrescendi præfertur oneribus /jə́s æ̀krəsénday prəfárdər ónérəbəs/. The right of survivorship is preferred to incumbrances. Hence no dower or curtesy can be claimed out of a joint estate.

Jus accrescendi præfertur ultimæ voluntati /jə́s æ̀krəsénday prəfárdər áltəmiy voləntéyday/. The right of survivorship is preferred to the last will. A devise of one's share of a joint estate, by will, is no severance of the jointure; for no testament takes effect till after the death of the testator, and by such death the right of the survivor (which accrued at the original creation of the estate, and has therefore a priority to the other) is already vested. 2 Bl.Comm. 186.

Jus actus /jə́s ǽktəs/. In Roman law, a rural servitude giving to a person a passage for carriages, or for cattle.

Jus ad rem /jə́s æd rém/. A term of the civil law, meaning "a right to a thing;" that is, a right exercisable by one person over a particular article of property in virtue of a contract or obligation incurred by another person in respect to it, and which is enforceable only against or through such other person. It is thus distinguished from *jus in re,* which is a complete and absolute dominion over a thing available against all persons. Mire v. Sunray DX Oil Co., D.C.La., 285 F.Supp. 885, 889.

The disposition of writers is to use the term *"jus ad rem"* as descriptive of a right without possession, and *"jus in re"* as descriptive of a right accompanied by possession. Or, in a somewhat wider sense, the former denotes an inchoate or incomplete right to a thing; the latter, a complete and perfect right to a thing. The Carlos F. Roses, 177 U.S. 655, 20 S.Ct. 803, 44 L.Ed. 929.

In canon law, a right to a thing. An inchoate and imperfect right, such as is gained by nomination and institution; as distinguished from *jus in re* or complete and full right, such as is acquired by corporal possession. 2 Bl.Comm. 312.

Jus Ælianum /jə́s iyliyéynəm/. A body of laws drawn up by Sextus Ælius, and consisting of three parts, wherein were explained, respectively: (1) The laws of the Twelve Tables; (2) the interpretation of and decisions upon such laws; and (3) the forms of procedure. In date, it was subsequent to the *jus Flavianum (q.v.).*

Jus æquum /jə́s íykwəm/. A term used by the Romans to express the adaptation of the law to the circumstances of the individual case as opposed to *jus strictum (q.v.).*

Jus æsneciæ /jə́s əsníys(h)iyiy/. The right of primogeniture *(q.v.).*

Jus albinatus /jə́s ælbənéydəs/. The *droit d'aubaine (q.v.).* See **Albinatus jus.**

Jus angariæ /jə́s æŋgériyiy/. See **Angaria; Angary, right of.**

Jus aquæductus /jə́s æ̀kwədáktəs/. In the civil law, the name of a servitude which gives to the owner of land the right to bring down water through or from the land of another.

Jus aquæ haustus /jós ǽkwiy hóstəs/. In Roman law, a rural servitude giving to a person a right of watering cattle on another's field, or of drawing water from another's well.

Jus banci /jós bǽnsay/. In old English law, the right of bench. The right or privilege of having an elevated and separate *seat of judgment,* anciently allowed only to the king's judges, who hence were said to administer *high* justice *(summam administrant justitiam).*

Jus belli /jós bélay/. The law of war. The law of nations as applied to a state of war, defining in particular the rights and duties of the belligerent powers themselves, and of neutral nations. That which may be done without injustice with regard to an enemy.

Jus bellum dicendi /jós béləm dəsénday/. The right of proclaiming war.

Jus canonicum /jós kənónəkəm/. The canon law.

Jus civile /jós sívəliy/. Civil law. The system of law peculiar to one state or people. Particularly, in Roman law, the civil law of the Roman people, as distinguished from the *jus gentium.* The term is also applied to the body of law called, emphatically, the "civil law." See also **Civil law.**

The *jus civile* and the *jus gentium* are distinguished in this way. All people ruled by statutes and customs use a law partly peculiar to themselves, partly common to all men. The law each people has settled for itself is peculiar to the state itself, and is called *"jus civile,"* as being peculiar to that very state. The law, again, that natural reason has settled among all men, —the law that is guarded among all peoples quite alike,—is called the *"jus gentium,"* and all nations use it as if law. The Roman people, therefore, use a law that is partly peculiar to itself, partly common to all men.

But this is not the only, or even the general, use of the words. What the Roman jurists had chiefly in view, when they spoke of *"jus civile,"* was not local as opposed to cosmopolitan law, but the old law of the city as contrasted with the newer law introduced by the prætor *(jus prætorium, jus honorarium).* Largely, no doubt, the *jus gentium* corresponds with the *jus prætorium;* but the correspondence is not perfect.

Jus civile est quod sibi populus constituit /jós sívəliy èst kwód síbay pópyələs kənstít(y)uwət/. The civil law is what a people establishes for itself.

Jus civitatus /jós sivətéydəs/. The right of citizenship; the freedom of the city of Rome. It differs from *jus quiritium,* which comprehended all the privileges of a free native of Rome. The difference is much the same as between "denization" and "naturalization".

Jus cloacæ /jós klowéysiy/°klówəsiy/. In the civil law, the right of sewerage or drainage. An easement consisting in the right of having a sewer, or of conducting surface water, through the house or over the ground of one's neighbor.

Jus commune /jós kəmyúwniy/. In the Civil law, common right; the common and natural rule of right, as opposed to *jus singulare (q.v.).*

In English law, the common law, answering to the Saxon *"folcright."*

Jus constitui oportet in his quæ ut plurimum accidunt non quæ ex inopinato /jós kənstíchuway əpórdət ìn hís kwìy ət plúrəməm ǽksədənt nón kwìy èks inòpənéydow/. Laws ought to be made with a view to those cases which happen most frequently, and not to those which are of rare or accidental occurrence.

Jus coronæ /jós kərówniy/. In English law, the right of the crown, or to the crown; the right of succession to the throne.

Jus cudendæ monetæ /jós kədéndiy məníydiy/. In old English law, the right of coining money.

Jus curialitatis /jós kyùriyælətéydəs/. In English law, the right of curtesy.

Jus dare /jós dériy/. To give or to make the law; the function and prerogative of the legislative department.

Jus deliberandi /jós dəlìbərǽnday/. In the civil law the right of deliberating. A term granted by the proper officer at the request of him who is called to the inheritance (the heir), within which he has the right to investigate its condition and to consider whether he will accept or reject it.

Jus descendit, et non terra /jós dəséndəd, èt nón téhrə/. A right descends, not the land.

Jus devolutum /jós dəvəl(y)úwdəm/. The right of the church of presenting a minister to a vacant parish, in case the patron shall neglect to exercise his right within the time limited by law.

Jus dicere /jós dáysəriy/. To declare the law; to say what the law is. The province of a court or judge.

Jus dicere, et non jus dare /jós dáysəriy, èt nòn jós dériy/. To declare the law, not to make it.

Jus disponendi /jós dìspənénday/. The right of disposing. An expression used either generally to signify the right of alienation, as when we speak of depriving a married woman of the *jus disponendi* over her separate estate, or specially in the law relating to sales of goods, where it is often a question whether the vendor of goods has the intention of reserving to himself the *jus disponendi; i.e.,* of preventing the ownership from passing to the purchaser, notwithstanding that he (the vendor) has parted with the possession of the goods.

Jus distrahendi /jós dìstrəhénday/. The right of sale of goods pledged in case of non-payment. See **Distress; Pledge.**

Jus dividendi /jós dìvədénday/. The right of disposing of realty by will.

Jus duplicatum /jós d(y)ùwpləkéydəm/. A double right; the right of possession united with the right of property; otherwise called *"droit-droit."* 2 Bl.Comm. 199.

Jus edicere or **jus edicendi** /jós ədáysəriy/jós ìydəsénday/. The right to issue edicts. It belonged to all the higher magistrates, but special interest is attached to the prætorian edicts in connection with the history of Roman law.

Jus est ars boni et æqui /jás èst árz bównay èd íykway/. Law is the science of what is good and just.

Jus est norma recti; et quicquid est contra normam recti est injuria /jás èst nórmə réktay, èt kwí(d)kwid èst kóntrə nórməm réktay èst ənjúr(i)yə/. Law is a rule of right; and whatever is contrary to the rule of right is an injury.

Jus et fraus nunquam cohabitant /jás èt frós nánˌkwəm kowhǽbədənt/. Right and fraud never dwell together.

Jus ex injuria non oritur /jás èks ənjúr(i)yə nòn órədər/. A right does (or can) not rise out of a wrong.

Jus ex non scripto /jás èks nón skríptow/. Law constituted by custom or such usage as indicates the tacit consent of the community.

Jus falcandi /jás fòlkǽnday/. The right of mowing or cutting. The right of cutting wood.

Jus feciale /jás fes(h)iyéyliy/. In Roman law, the law of arms, or of heralds. A rudimentary species of international law founded on the rites and religious ceremonies of the different peoples.

Jus fiduciarium /jás fəd(y)uws(h)iyérəm/. In the civil law, a right in trust; as distinguished from *jus legitimum,* a legal right. 2 Bl.Comm. 328.

Jus fluminum /jás fl(y)úwmənəm/. In the civil law, the right to the use of rivers.

Jus fodiendi /jás fò(w)diyénday/. In the civil and old English law, a right of digging on another's land.

Jus futurum /jás fyəchúrəm/. In the civil law, a future right; an inchoate, incipient, or expectant right, not yet fully vested. It may be either *"jus delatum,"* when the subsequent acquisition or vesting of it depends merely on the will of the person in whom it is to vest, or *"jus nondum delatum,"* when it depends on the future occurrence of other circumstances or conditions.

Jus gentium /jás jénsh(iy)əm/. The law of nations. That law which natural reason has established among all men is equally observed among all nations, and is called the "law of nations," as being the law which all nations use. Although this phrase had a meaning in the Roman law which may be rendered by our expression "law of nations," it must not be understood as equivalent to what we now call "international law," its scope being much wider. It was originally a system of law, or more properly equity, gathered by the early Roman lawyers and magistrates from the common ingredients in the customs of the old Italian tribes,—those being the nations, *gentes,* whom they had opportunities of observing,—to be used in cases where the *jus civile* did not apply; that is, in cases between foreigners or between a Roman citizen and a foreigner. The principle upon which they proceeded was that any rule of law which was common to all the nations they knew of must be intrinsically consonant to right reason, and therefore fundamentally valid and just. From this it was an easy transition to the converse principle, viz., that any rule which instinctively commended itself to their sense of justice and reason must be a part of the *jus gentium.* And

so the latter term came eventually to be about synonymous with "equity" (as the Romans understood it), or the system of prætorian law.

Jurists frequently employed the term *"jus gentium privatum"* to denote private international law, or that subject which is otherwise styled the "conflict of laws"; and *"jus gentium publicum"* for public international law, or the system of rules governing the intercourse of nations with each other as persons.

Jus gladii /jás glǽdiyay/. The right of the sword; the executory power of the law; the right, power, or prerogative of punishing for crime. 4 Bl.Comm. 177.

Jus habendi /jás həbénday/. The right to have a thing. The right to be put in actual possession of property.

Jus habendi et retinendi /jás həbénday èt rèdənénday/. A right to have and to retain the profits, tithes, and offerings, etc., of a rectory or parsonage.

Jus hæreditatis /jás hərèdətéydəs/. The right of inheritance.

Jus hauriendi /jás hohriyénday/. In the civil and old English law, the right of drawing water.

Jus honorarium /jás (h)ònərériyəm/. The body of Roman law, which was made up of edicts of the supreme magistrates, particularly the prætors.

Jus honorum /jás (h)ənórəm/. In Roman law, the right of holding offices. See **Jus suffragii.**

Jus imaginis /jás əmǽjənəs/. In Roman law, the right to use or display pictures or statues of ancestors; somewhat analogous to the right, in English law, to bear a coat of arms.

Jus immunitatis /jás əmyùwnətéydəs/. In the civil law, the law of immunity or exemption from the burden of public office.

Jus incognitum /jás inkógnədəm/. An unknown law. This term is applied by the civilians to obsolete laws.

Jus individuum /jás indəvídyuwəm/. An individual or indivisible right; a right incapable of division.

Jus in personam /jás in pərsównəm/. A right against a person; a right which gives its possessor a power to oblige another person to give or procure, to do or not to do, something.

Jus in re /jás in ríy/. A right in a thing. Denver Joint Stock Land Bank of Denver v. Dixon, 57 Wyo. 523, 122 P.2d 842, 847. A right existing in a person with respect to an article or subject of property, inherent in his relation to it, implying complete ownership with possession, and available against all the world.

See **Jus ad rem.**

Jus in re aliena /jás in ríy èyliyíynə/. An easement on servitude, or right in, or arising out of, the property of another.

Jus in re inhæret ossibus usufructuarii /jás in ríy inhírət ósəbəs yùwz(h)uwfrəktériyay/. A right in the thing cleaves to the person of the usufructuary.

Jus in re propria /jás in ríy prówpriyə/. The right of enjoyment which is incident to full ownership or property, and is often used to denote the full ownership or property itself. It is distinguished from *jus in re alienâ,* which is a mere easement or right in or over the property of another.

Jus italicum /jós ətǽləkəm/. A term of the Roman law descriptive of the aggregate of rights, privileges, and franchises possessed by the cities and inhabitants of Italy, outside of the city of Rome, and afterwards extended to some of the colonies and provinces of the empire, consisting principally in the right to have a free constitution, to be exempt from the land tax, and to have the title to the land regarded as Quiritarian property.

Jus itineris /jós aytínərəs/. In Roman law, a rural servitude giving to a person the right to pass over an adjoining field, on foot or horseback.

Jus jurandi forma verbis differt, re convenit; hunc enim sensum habere debet: ut deus invocetur /jós jərǽnday fórmə vərbəs dífərt, ríy kənvíynət; həŋk íyəm sénsəm həbíriy débəd: ət díyəs invəsíydər/. The form of taking an oath differs in language, agrees in meaning; for it ought to have this sense; that the deity is invoked.

Jus jurandum /jós jərǽndəm/. Lat. An oath.

Jus jurandum inter alios factum nec nocere neo prodesse debet /jós jərǽndəm íntər ǽliyows fǽktəm nèk nəsíriy nèk prədésiy débət/. An oath made between others ought neither to hurt nor profit.

Jus Latii /jós léyshiyay/. In Roman law, the right of Latium or of the Latins.

The principal privilege of the Latins seems to have been the use of their own laws, and their not being subject to the edicts of the prætor, and that they had occasional access to the freedom of Rome, and a participation in her sacred rites.

Jus Latium /jós léysh(iy)əm/. In Roman law, a rule of law applicable to magistrates in Latium. It was either *majus Latium* or *minus Latium,*—the *majus Latium* raising to the dignity of Roman citizen not only the magistrate himself, but also his wife and children; the *minus Latium* raising to that dignity only the magistrate himself.

Jus legitimum /jós ləjídəməm/. A legal right. In the civil law, a right which was enforceable in the ordinary course of law.

Jus liberorum /jós lìbərórəm/. In Roman law, the privilege conferred upon a woman who had three or four children.

Jus mariti /jós mǽrəday/. The right of a husband; especially the right which a husband acquires to his wife's movable estate by virtue of the marriage.

Jus merum /jós mírəm/. In old English law, mere or bare right; the mere right of property in lands, without either possession or even the right of possession.

Jus moribus constitutum /jós mórəbəs kònstətyúwdəm/. See **Jus ex non scripto.**

Jus naturæ /jós nəchúriy/. The law of nature. See **Jus naturale.**

Jus naturale /jós nǽchəréyliy/. The natural law, or law of nature; law, or legal principles, supposed to be discoverable by the light of nature or abstract reasoning, or to be taught by nature to all nations and men alike; or law supposed to govern men and peoples in a state of nature, *i.e.,* in advance of organized governments or enacted laws. See **Natural law.**

This concept originated with the philosophical jurists of Rome, and was gradually extended until the phrase came to denote a supposed basis or substratum common to all systems of positive law, and hence to be found, in greater or less purity, in the laws of all nations. And, conversely, they held that if any rule or principle of law was observed in common by all peoples with whose systems they were acquainted, it must be a part of the *jus naturale,* or derived from it. Thus the phrases *"jus naturale"* and *"jus gentium"* came to be used interchangeably.

Jus naturale est quod apud homines eandem habet potentiam /jós nǽchəréyliy èst kwód ǽpəd hóməniyz iyǽndəm héybət pəténsh(iy)əm/. Natural right is that which has the same force among all mankind.

Jus navigandi /jós nǽvəgǽnday/. The right of navigating or navigation; the right of commerce by ships or by sea.

Jus necis /jós níysəs/. In Roman law, the right of death, or of putting to death. A right which a father anciently had over his children. See **Jus vitæ necisque.**

Jus non habenti tute non paretur /jós nòn həbéntay t(y)úwdiy nòn pəríydər/. One who has no right cannot be safely obeyed.

Jus non patitur ut idem bis solvatur /jós nòn pǽdədər əd áydəm bís sòlvéydər/. Law does not suffer that the same thing be twice paid.

Jus non sacrum /jós nòn sǽkrəm/. In Roman law, that portion of the *jus publicum* which regulated the duties of magistrates.

Non-sacred law; that which dealt with the duties of civil magistrates, the preservation of public order, and the rights and duties of persons in their relation to the state. It was analogous to that which would now be called the police power.

Jus non scriptum /jós nòn skríptəm/. The unwritten law.

Jus offerendi /jós òfərénday/. In Roman law, the right of subrogation, that is, the right of succeeding to the lien and priority of an elder creditor on tendering or paying into court the amount due to him.

Jus oneris ferendi /jós ównərəs fərénday/. An urban servitude in the Roman law, the owner of which had the right of supporting and building upon the house wall of another.

Jus pascendi /jós pæsénday/. In the civil and old English law, the right of pasturing cattle.

Jus patronatus /jós pǽtrənéydəs/. In English ecclesiastical law, the right of patronage; the right of presenting a clerk to a benefice.

A commission from the bishop, where two presentations are offered upon the same avoidance, directed usually to his chancellor and others of competent learning, who are to summon a jury of six clergymen and six laymen to inquire into and examine who is the rightful patron. 3 Bl.Comm. 246.

Jus personarum /jás pàrsənérəm/. Rights of persons. Those rights which, in the civil law, belong to persons as such, or in their different characters and relations; as parents and children, masters and servants, etc.

Jus pœnitendi /jás pènəténday/. In Roman law, the right of rescission or revocation of an executory contract on failure of the other party to fulfill his part of the agreement.

Jus portus /jás pórdəs/. In maritime law, the right of port or harbor.

Jus possessionis /jás pəzèshiyównəs/. The right of possession.

Jus possidendi /jás pòsədénday/. The right of possessing, which is the legal consequence of ownership. It is to be distinguished from the *jus possessionis (q.v.),* which is a right to possess which may exist without ownership.

Jus postliminii /jás pòwstləmíniyay/. In the civil law, the right of postliminy; the right or claim of a person who had been restored to the possession of a thing, or to a former condition, to be considered as though he had never been deprived of it.

In International law, the right by which property taken by an enemy, and recaptured or rescued from him by the fellow-subjects or allies of the original owner, is restored to the latter upon certain terms.

Jus præsens /jás príyzèn(d)z/. In the civil law, a present or vested right; a right already completely acquired.

Jus prætorium /jás prətóriyəm/. In the civil law, the discretion of the prætor, as distinct from the *leges*, or standing laws. 3 Bl.Comm. 49. That kind of law which the prætors introduced for the purpose of aiding, supplying, or correcting the civil law, for the public benefit. Called, also *"jus honorarium" (q.v.).*

Jus precarium /jás prəkériyəm/. In the civil law, a right to a thing held for another, for which there was no remedy by legal action, but only by entreaty or request. 2 Bl.Comm. 328.

Jus presentationis /jás prèzəntèyshiyównəs/. The right of presentation.

Jus privatum /jás prəvéydəm/. Private law; the law regulating the rights, conduct, and affairs of individuals, as distinguished from "public" law, which relates to the constitution and functions of government and the administration of criminal justice. The right of a person acquiring title to lands under navigable waters to fill in such lands, making upland out of foreshore, and thus extinguishing *jus publicum,* subject to right of sovereign to make public improvements on tide water for benefit of commerce. Arnold's Inn, Inc. v. Morgan, 63 Misc.2d 279, 310 N.Y.S.2d 541, 547.

Also private ownership, or the right, title, or dominion of a private owner, as distinguished from *"jus publicum,"* which denotes public ownership, or the ownership of property by the government, either as a matter of territorial sovereignty or in trust for the benefit and advantage of the general public. In this sense, a state may have a double right in given property, *e.g.,* lands covered by navigable waters within its boundaries, including both *"jus publicum,"* a sovereign or political title, and *"jus privatum,"* a proprietary ownership.

Jus projiciendi /jás prəjìs(h)iyénday/. In the civil law, the name of a servitude which consists in the right to build a projection, such as a balcony or gallery, from one's house in the open space belonging to one's neighbor, but without resting on his house.

Jus proprietatis /jás prəpràyətéydəs/. The right of property, as distinguished from the *jus possessionis* or right of possession.

Jus protegendi /jás pròwdəjénday/. In the civil law, the name of a servitude. It is a right by which a part of the roof or tiling of one house is made to extend over the adjoining house.

Jus protimeseos /jás pròwtəmíysiyòs/. The right of pre-emption of a landlord in case the tenant wishes to dispose of his rights as a perpetual lessee. *Pactum protimeseos* was the right of pre-emption to the seller; *i.e.* in case the buyer should sell, he must sell to the former seller.

Jus publicum /jás pábləkəm/. Public law, or the law relating to the constitution and functions of government and its officers and the administration of criminal justice. Also public ownership, or the paramount or sovereign territorial right or title of the state or government. The right shared by all to navigate on waters covering foreshore at high tide and, at low tide, to have access across foreshore to waters for fishing, bathing or any other lawful purpose. Arnold's Inn, Inc. v. Morgan, 63 Misc.2d 279, 310 N.Y. S.2d 541. See **Jus privatum.**

It implies a right in a sovereign or public capacity to be exercised for the interest or benefit of the state or the public, as distinguished from the exercise in a proprietary capacity of a right of the sovereign or a right possessed by an individual in common with the public.

Sovereign's right of jurisdiction and dominion for governmental purposes over all lands and waters within its territorial limits, including tidal waters and their bottoms, is sometimes termed *"jus publicum."*

Jus publicum et privatum quod ex naturalibus præceptis aut gentium aut civilibus est collectum; et quod in jure scripto jus appellatur, id in lege Angliæ rectum esse dicitur /jás pábləkəm èt prəvéydəm kwòd èks nætyəréyləbəs prəséptəs òt jénsh(iy)əm òt səvíləbəs èst kəléktəm, èt kwód ìn júriy skríptow jás æpəléydər, ìd ìn líyjiy ængliyiy réktəm ésiy dísədər/. Public and private law is that which is collected from natural principles, either of nations or in states; and that which in the civil law is called *"jus,"* in the law of England is said to be "right."

Jus publicum privatorum pactis mutari non potest /jás pábləkəm pràyvətórəm pæktəs myuwtéray nòn pówdəst/. A public law or right cannot be altered by the agreements of private persons.

Jus quæsitum /jós kwəzáydəm/. A right to ask or recover; for example, in an obligation there is a binding of the obligor, and a *jus quæsitum* in the obligee.

Jus quiritium /jós kwəráysh(iy)əm/. The old law of Rome, that was applicable originally to patricians only, and, under the Twelve Tables, to the entire Roman people, was so called, in contradistinction to the *jus prætorium (q.v.)*, or equity.

Jus recuperandi /jós rək(y)ùwpərǽnday/. The right of recovering [lands].

Jus representationis /jós rèprəzentèyshiyównəs/. The right of representing or standing in the place of another, or of being represented by another.

Jus rerum /jós rírəm/. The law of things. The law regulating the rights and powers of persons over things; how property is acquired, enjoyed, and transferred.

Jus respicit æquitatem /jós réspəsət èkwətéydəm/. Law regards equity.

Jus sacrum /jós sǽkrəm/. In Roman law, that portion of the public law which was concerned with matters relating to public worship and including the regulation of sacrifices and the appointment of priests. There was a general division of the *jus publicum* into *jus sacrum* and *jus non sacrum (q.v.)*.

Jus sanguinis /jós sǽŋgwənəs/. The right of blood. The principle that a person's citizenship is determined by the citizenship of the parents. See **Jus soli.**

Jus scriptum /jós skríptəm/. In English law, written law, or statute law, otherwise called *"lex scripta,"* as distinguished from the common law, *"lex non scripta."* 1 Bl.Comm. 62.

In Roman law, all law that was actually committed to writing, whether it had originated by enactment or by custom, in contradistinction to such parts of the law of custom as were not committed to writing.

Jus singulare /jós sìŋgyəlériy/. In the civil law, a peculiar or individual rule, differing from the *jus commune,* or common rule of right, and established for some special reason.

Jus soli /jós sówlay/. The law of the place of one's birth as contrasted with *jus sanguinis,* the law of the place of one's descent or parentage. The principle that a person's citizenship is determined by place of birth rather than by the citizenship of one's parents. It is of feudal origin.

Jus spatiandi /jós spèyshiyǽnday/. A right of way over land by the public by uses merely for the purposes of recreation and instruction.

Jus stapulæ /jós stéypyəliy/. In old European law, the law of staple; the right of staple. A right or privilege of certain towns of stopping imported merchandise, and compelling it to be offered for sale in their own markets.

Jus stillicidii vel fluminis recipiendi /jós stìləsídiay vèl fl(y)úwmənəs rəsìpiyénday/. In Roman law, an urban servitude giving the owner a right to project his roof over the land of another or to open a house drain upon it.

Jus strictum /jós stríktəm/. Strict law; law interpreted without any modification, and in its utmost rigor.

Jus suffragii /jós səfréyjiyay/. In Roman law, the right of voting. This and the *jus honorum (q.v.)* were the public rights of the Roman citizen.

Jus superveniens auctori accrescit successori /jós s(y)uwpərvíyn(i)yèn(d)z októray əkrésət səksesóray/. A right growing to a possessor accrues to the successor.

Just. Conforming to or consonant with what is legal or lawful; legally right; lawful. National Surety Corporation v. Mullins, 262 Ky. 465, 90 S.W.2d 707, 708. Correct, true, due. Wisdom v. Board of Sup'rs of Polk County, 236 Iowa 669, 19 N.W.2d 602, 606. Equitable. Carter v. Carter, 181 Okl. 204, 73 P.2d 404, 405. Reasonable. National Surety Corporation v. Mullins, 262 Ky. 465, 90 S.W.2d 707, 708; Wisdom v. Board of Sup'rs of Polk County, 236 Iowa 669, 19 N.W.2d 602, 606. Right; in accordance with law and justice. See also **Equitable.**

Justa causa /jóstə kózə/. In the civil law, a just cause; a lawful ground; a legal transaction of some kind.

Just cause. A cause outside legal cause, which must be based on reasonable grounds, and there must be a fair and honest cause or reason, regulated by good faith. Dubois v. Gentry, 182 Tenn. 103, 184 S.W.2d 369, 371. Fair, adequate, reasonable cause. In re Municipal Garage in and for City of Utica, 141 Misc. 15, 252 N.Y.S. 18, 32. Legitimate cause; legal or lawful ground for action; such reasons as will suffice in law to justify the action taken. Boston Elevated Ry. Co. v. Commonwealth, 310 Mass. 528, 39 N.E.2d 87, 112, 124. See **Cause of action.**

Under provision that no license shall be revoked without "just cause," the words imply that charges should be made and notice of hearing given and an opportunity to be heard afforded. Carroll v. California Horse Racing Board, 16 Cal.2d 164, 105 P.2d 110, 111.

Just cause of provocation. That which will constitute the homicide murder in the second degree, as distinguished from a lawful provocation, which will reduce it to manslaughter. State v. McCracken, 341 Mo. 697, 108 S.W.2d 372, 376.

Just compensation. Compensation which is fair to both the owner and the public when property is taken for public use through condemnation (eminent domain). Consideration is taken of such criteria as the cost of reproducing the property, its market value, and the resulting damage to the remaining property of the owner. The Fifth Amendment to the U.S. Constitution provides that no private property shall be taken for public use, without "just compensation." Within Fifth Amendment provision that private property shall not be taken for public use without just compensation, "just compensation" means the full monetary equivalent of the property taken. U. S. v. Reynolds, Ky., 397 U.S. 14, 90 S.Ct. 803, 805, 25 L.Ed.2d 12.

As regards property taken for public use, the term is comprehensive and includes all elements, Jacobs v. U. S., Ala., 290 U.S. 13, 54 S.Ct. 26, 78 L.Ed. 142;

Metropolitan Water Dist. of Southern California v. Adams, 16 Cal.2d 676, 107 P.2d 618, 621, but does not exceed market value. Sigurd City v. State, 105 Utah 278, 142 P.2d 154, 158; U. S. v. Waterhouse, C.C.A. Hawaii, 132 F.2d 699, 703. It means a settlement which leaves one no poorer or richer than he was before the property was taken. U. S. ex rel. Tennessee Valley Authority v. Indian Creek Marble Co., D.C.Tenn., 40 F.Supp. 811, 818, 819. Adequate compensation. State v. Hale, Tex.Civ.App., 96 S.W.2d 135, 141; In re Board of Sup'rs of Chenango County, Co.Ct., 6 N.Y.S.2d 732, 739. Fair market value. Cameron Development Co. v. United States, C.C.A. Fla., 145 F.2d 209, 210; U. S. ex rel. and for Use of Tennessee Valley Authority v. Davis, D.C.Tenn., 41 F.Supp. 595, 597, 598; United States v. Certain Parcels of Land in City of Baltimore, Parcel No. 12, D.C.Md., 43 F.Supp. 687, 689. Full and perfect equivalent of the property taken. Housing Authority of Shreveport v. Green, 200 La. 463, 8 So.2d 295, 298; U. S. v. 2.4 Acres of Land, More or Less, in Lake County, Ill., C.C.A.Ill., 138 F.2d 295, 297. It is the value of property taken at time of taking, United States v. 813.96 Acres of Land in Ouachita County, Ark., D.C.Ark., 45 F.Supp. 535, 538; Danforth v. U. S., Mo., 308 U.S. 271, 60 S.Ct. 231, 236, 84 L.Ed. 240; plus compensation for delay in payment, Kieselbach v. Commissioner of Internal Revenue, 317 U.S. 399, 63 S.Ct. 303, 305, 87 L.Ed. 358; or consequential damages to the owner, In re Board of Water Supply of City of New York, 277 N.Y. 452, 14 N.E.2d 789; or value of use of property from date of taking possession to date of judgment if possession is taken by condemnor prior to judgment. Los Angeles County Flood Control Dist. v. Hansen, 48 Cal.App.2d 314, 119 P.2d 734, 735. It requires that the owner be put in as good position pecuniarily as he would otherwise have been. Kansas City Southern Ry. Co. v. Commissioner of Internal Revenue, C.C.A.Ark., 52 F.2d 372, 379; In re Gratiot Ave., City of Detroit, 294 Mich. 569, 293 N.W. 755, 757; U. S. ex rel. and for Use of Tennessee Valley Authority v. Powelson, C.C.A.N.C., 118 F.2d 79, 87. Interest is recoverable in eminent domain proceedings as part of "just compensation" when payment is not contemporaneous with the taking. New Hampshire Water Resources Bd. v. Pera, 108 N.H. 18, 226 A.2d 774, 775, 776. Michigan Consol. Gas Co. v. Muzeck, 8 Mich.App. 329, 154 N.W.2d 667, 671. Market value at time of taking; *i.e.* highest price for which property considered at its best and most profitable use can be sold in open market by willing seller to willing buyer, neither acting under compulsion and both exercising reasonable judgment. State Highway Commission v. American Memorial Parks, Inc., 82 S.D. 231, 144 N.W.2d 25, 27. See also **Similar sales.**

On government's cancellation of contract, "just compensation" recoverable consists of such sum as in court's judgment will fairly compensate contractor. Enright v. U. S., 73 Ct.Cl. 416, 54 F.2d 182, 190. It is the value of contract at time of cancellation, not profits which it would have produced. De Laval Steam Turbine Co. v. U. S., 284 U.S. 61, 52 S.Ct. 78, 79, 76 L.Ed. 168.

Just debts. As used in a will or a statute, this term means legal, valid, and incontestable obligations, not including such as are barred by the statute of limita-

tions or voidable at the election of the party. Jones' Ex'r v. Jones, 275 Ky. 753, 122 S.W.2d 779, 780.

Jus tertii /jós társhiyay/. The right of a third party.

A tenant, bailee, etc., who pleads that the title is in some person other than his landlord, bailor, etc., is said to set up a *jus tertii.* Dempsey Oil & Gas Co. v. Citizens' Nat. Bank, 110 Okl. 39, 235 P. 1104, 1107.

Jus testamentorum pertinet ordinario /jós tèstəmentórəm pərdənəd òrdənériyow/. The right of testaments belongs to the ordinary.

Justice, v. To do justice, to see justice done; to summon one to do justice.

Justice, n. Title given to judges, particularly to judges of U.S. and state supreme courts, and as well to judges of appellate courts. The U.S. Supreme Court, and most state supreme courts are composed of a chief justice and several associate justices.

Proper administration of laws. In Jurisprudence, the constant and perpetual disposition of legal matters or disputes to render every man his due.

In Feudal law, jurisdiction; judicial cognizance of causes or offenses. *High* justice was the jurisdiction or right of trying crimes of every kind, even the highest. This was a privilege claimed and exercised by the great lords or barons of the middle ages. *Low* justice was jurisdiction of petty offenses.

See also **Miscarriage of justice; Obstructing justice.**

Justice Department. One of the executive departments of the federal government, headed by the Attorney General. The chief purposes of the Department of Justice are to enforce the federal laws, to furnish legal counsel in federal cases, and to construe the laws under which other departments act. It conducts all suits in the Supreme Court in which the United States is concerned, supervises the federal penal institutions, and investigates and detects violations against federal laws. It represents the government in legal matters generally, rendering legal advice and opinions, upon request, to the President and to the heads of the executive departments. The Attorney General supervises and directs the activities of the U.S. attorneys and marshals in the various judicial districts. See **Attorney General.**

Justice in eyre /jástəs ìn ér/. From the old French word *"eire,"* i.e., a journey. Those justices who in ancient times were sent by commission into various counties, to hear more especially such causes as were termed "pleas of the crown," were called "justices in eyre." They differed from justices in oyer and terminer, inasmuch as the latter were sent to one place, and for the purpose of trying only a limited number of special causes; whereas the justices in eyre were sent through the various counties, with a more indefinite and general commission. In some respects they resembled our present justices of assize, although their authority and manner of proceeding differed much from them. In England, such justices made a circuit every seven years throughout the Kingdom to try causes.

Justicements /jástəsmənts/. An old general term for all things appertaining to justice.

Justice of the peace. A judicial magistrate (of English origin) of inferior rank having (usually) jurisdiction limited to that prescribed by statute in civil matters (*e.g.* performance of marriages) and jurisdiction over minor criminal offenses, committing more serious crimes to higher courts. Trend in most states has been to abolish office and courts of justice of the peace, transferring their powers and functions to other courts; *e.g.* municipal or district courts. See **Justice's courts.**

Justicer /jástəsər/. The old form of *justice.*

Justice's clerk. An amanuensis of the justice. A justice of the peace is regarded as his own clerk, and, in making entries on his docket, he acts in a ministerial capacity. State ex rel. Morris Bldg. & Inv. Co. v. Brown, 228 Mo.App. 760, 72 S.W.2d 859, 862.

Justice's courts. Inferior tribunals, not of record, with limited jurisdiction, both civil and criminal, held by justices of the peace. The trend has been to abolish such courts, transferring their powers and functions to other courts; *e.g.* municipal or district courts.

Justice seat. In old English law, the principal court of the forest, held before the chief justice in eyre, or chief itinerant judge or his deputy; to hear and determine all trespasses within the forest, and all claims of franchises, liberties, and privileges, and all pleas and causes whatsoever therein arising. 3 Bl.Comm. 72.

Justiceship. Rank or office of a justice.

Justices of assize /jástəsəz əv əsáyz/. These justices, or, as they were sometimes called, "justices of *nisi prius,*" were judges of the superior English courts, who went on circuit into the various counties of England and Wales for the purpose of disposing of such causes as were ready for trial at the assizes. See **Assise.**

Justices of gaol delivery. In old English law, those justices who were sent with a commission to hear and determine all causes appertaining to persons, who, for any offense, had been cast into gaol. Part of their authority was to punish those who let to mainprise those prisoners who were not bailable by law, and they seem formerly to have been sent into the country upon this exclusive occasion, but afterwards had the same authority given them as the justices of assize.

Justices of laborers. In old English law, justices appointed to redress the frowardness of laboring men, who would either be idle or have unreasonable wages.

Justices of nisi prius /jástəsəz əv náysay práyəs/. In old English law, this title was usually coupled with that of *justices of assize;* the judges of the superior courts acting on their circuits in both these capacities. See **Assise.**

Justices of oyer and terminer /jástəsəz əv óyər ænd tə́rmənər/. In England, certain persons appointed by the king's commission, among whom were usually two judges of the courts at Westminster, and who went twice in every year to every county of the kingdom (except London and Middlesex), and, at what was usually called the "assizes," heard and determined all treasons, felonies, and misdemeanors. See **Oyer and terminer.**

Justices of the bench. In England, the justices of the court of common bench or common pleas.

Justices of the forest. In old English law, officers who had jurisdiction over all offenses committed within the forest against vert or venison. The court wherein these justices sat and determined such causes was called the "justice seat of the forest." They were also sometimes called the "justices in eyre of the forest." See **Forest courts.**

Justices of the hundred. Hundredors; lords of the hundreds. In old English law, they who had the jurisdiction of hundreds and held the hundred courts. See **Hundred Court.**

Justices of the quorum. See **Quorum.**

Justices of trail-baston. See **Trail-baston.**

Justiciable /jəstísh(iy)əbəl/. Matter appropriate for court review. See **Justiciable controversy.**

Justiciable controversy. A controversy in which a claim of right is asserted against one who has an interest in contesting it. A question as may properly come before a tribunal for decision. Duart Mfg. Co. v. Philad Co., D.C.Del., 30 F.Supp. 777, 779, 780. Courts will only consider a "justiciable" controversy, as distinguished from a hypothetical difference or dispute or one that is academic or moot. Aetna Life Ins. Co. v. Haworth, 300 U.S. 227, 239, 57 S.Ct. 461, 463, 81 L.Ed. 617. Term refers to real and substantial controversy which is appropriate for judicial determination, as distinguished from dispute or difference of contingent, hypothetical or abstract character. Guimarin & Doan, Inc. v. Georgetown Textile & Mfg. Co., 249 S.C. 561, 155 S.E.2d 618, 621. See **Case.**

Justiciar /jəstísh(iy)ər/. In old English law, a judge or justice. One of several persons learned in the law, who sat in the *aula regis,* and formed a kind of court of appeal in cases of difficulty. Also spelled *justicier.*

Justiciarii itinerantes /jəstìs(h)iyériyay aytìnərǽntiyz/. In old English law, justices in eyre, who formerly went from county to county to administer justice. They were so called to distinguish them from justices residing at Westminster, who were called *"justicii residentes".*

Justiciarii residentes /jəstìs(h)iyériyay rèzədéntiyz/. In old English law, justices or judges who usually resided in Westminster. They were so called to distinguish them from justices in eyre.

Justiciary /jəstísh(iy)əry/. An old name for a judge or justice. The word is formed on the analogy of the Latin *"juriciarius"* and French *"justicier",* and is a variant of *justiciar (q.v.).*

Justiciatus /jəstìshiyéydəs/. Judicature; prerogative.

The proceeding by which bail establishes the ability to perform the undertaking of the bond or recognizance.

Justicier. Fr. See **Justiciar.**

Justicies /jəstís(h)iy(iy)z/. In old English law, a writ directed to the sheriff, empowering him, for the sake of dispatch, to try an action in his county court for a larger amount than he has the ordinary power to do.

It is so called because it is a commission to the sheriff to do the party justice, the word itself meaning, "You may do justice to ___". 3 Bl.Comm. 36.

Justifiable. Rightful; defensible; warranted or sanctioned by law; that which can be shown to be sustained by law, as justifiable homicide. See **Homicide; Justifiable homicide.**

Justifiable cause. Justifiable cause for prosecution is well-founded belief of person of ordinary caution, prudence, and judgment in existence of facts essential to prosecution. See also **Probable cause.**

Justifiable homicide. Killing of another in self-defense when danger of death or serious bodily injury exists. An act which the law positively enjoins upon the perpetrator or positively permits him to perform, such as a capital crime execution or the prevention of a crime or escape by a proper officer. Law v. State, 21 Md.App. 13, 318 A.2d 859, 869. See **Self defense.**

Justification. Just, lawful excuse or reason for act or failing to act. A maintaining or showing a sufficient reason in court why the defendant did what he is called upon to answer, particularly in an action of libel and as a defense to criminal charges of assault or homicide (*e.g.* self defense).

Justification is a procedure with common-law origins by which a surety must demonstrate to the satisfaction of the court that it has sufficient ability to perform its obligations. Matthews v. IMC Mint Corp., C.A.Utah, 542 F.2d 544, 546.

Justification means explanation with supporting data. American Export-Isbrandtsen Lines, Inc. v. Federal Maritime Commission, 135 U.S.App.D.C. 181, 417 F.2d 749, 752. Term means maintaining or showing a sufficient reason in court why the defendant did what he is called upon to answer or, just cause or excuse, just, lawful excuse for act, reasonable excuse. Young Women's Christian Ass'n of Princeton, N. J. v. Kugler, D.C.N.J., 342 F.Supp. 1048, 1062.

See also **Legal excuse.**

Justificators /jástəfəkèydər/. A kind of compurgators (*q.v.*), or those who by oath justified the innocence or oaths of others; as in the case of wager or law.

Justifying bail. Consists in the requirement of proving the sufficiency of bail or sureties in point of property, etc. See **Bail** (*Bail point scale*).

Jus tigni immittendi /jás tígnay iməténday/. In Roman law, an urban servitude which gave the right of inserting a beam into the wall of another.

Justinianist /jəstín(i)yənəst/. A civilian; one who studies the civil law.

Justinian's institutes /jəstín(i)yən(d)z ínstət(y)ùwts/. See **Institutes.**

Justitia /jəstísh(iy)ə/. Lat. Justice. A jurisdiction, or the office of a judge.

Justitia debet esse libera, quia nihil iniquis venali justitia; plena, quia justitia non debet claudicare; et celeris, quia dilatio est quædam negatio /jəstísh(iy)ə débəd ésiy líbərə, kwáyə náy(h)əl əníkwiyəs vənéylay jəstísh(iy)ə; plíynə, kwíyə jəstísh(iy)ə nòn débət klòdəkériy, èt sélərəs, kwáyə dəléysh(iy)ow èst kwíydəm nəgéysh(iy)ow/. Justice ought to be free, because nothing is more iniquitous than venal justice; full, because justice ought not to halt; and speedy, because delay is a kind of denial.

Justitia est constans et perpetua voluntas jus suum cuique tribuendi /jəstísh(iy)ə èst kónstæn(d)z èt pərpéchuwə vəlántæs jás s(y)úwəm k(yuw)áykwiy trìb(y)uwénday/. Justice is a steady and unceasing disposition to render to every man his due.

Justitia est duplex, viz., severe puniens et vere præveniens /jəstísh(iy)ə èst d(y)úwpleks viz: səvíriy pyúwn(i)yèn(d)z èt víriy prəvíyn(i)yèn(d)z/. Justice is double; punishing severely, and truly preventing.

Justitia est virtus excellens et altissimo complacens /jəstísh(iy)ə èst vártəs éksələn(d)z èd æltísəmow kəmpléysən(d)z/. Justice is excellent virtue and pleasing to the most high.

Justitia firmatur solium /jəstísh(iy)ə fərméydər sówliyəm/. By justice the throne is established.

Justitia nemini neganda est /jəstísh(iy)ə némənay nəgǽndə èst/. Justice is to be denied to none.

Justitia non est neganda non differenda /jəstísh(iy)ə nón èst nəgǽndə, nón dífəréndə/. Justice is neither to be denied nor delayed.

Justitia non novit patrem nec matrem; solam veritatem spectat justitia /jəstísh(iy)ə nòn nówvət pǽtrəm nèk méytram; sówləm vèhrətéydəm spéktət jəstísh(iy)ə/. Justice knows not father nor mother; justice looks at truth alone.

Justitia piepoudrous. Speedy justice.

Justitium /jəstísh(iy)əm/. Lat. In the civil law, a suspension or intermission of the administration of justice in courts; vacation time.

Justness. Conformity to truth, propriety, accuracy, or the like. John W. Masury & Son v. Bisbee Lumber Co., 49 Ariz. 443, 68 P.2d 679, 693.

As used in statute providing for acknowledgment of "justness" of claim to remove bar of limitations, refers to moral obligation. John W. Masury & Son v. Bisbee Lumber Co., 49 Ariz. 443, 68 P.2d 679, 693.

Just prior. Immediately preceding; just before; without appreciable lapse of time before. Jackson v. McCrary, Tex.Civ.App., 148 S.W.2d 942, 944. It means before the time and connotes nearness in point of time. Salmons v. Dun & Bradstreet, Mo.App., 153 S.W.2d 556, 562, modified on other grounds 349 Mo. 498, 162 S.W.2d 245. It means some period of time before. Hoelzel v. Chicago, R. I. & P. Ry. Co., 337 Mo. 61, 85 S.W.2d 126, 129.

Jus tripertitum /jás tràypərtáydəm/. In Roman law, a name applied to the Roman law of wills, in the time of Justinian, on account of its three-fold derivation, viz., from the prætorian edict, from the civil law, and from the imperial constitutions.

Jus triplex est,—propietatis, possessionis, et possibilitatis /jás trípleks èst: prəprày
ətéydəs pəzèshiyównəs èt pòsəbilətéydəs/. Right is three-fold,—of property, of possession, and of possibility.

Jus trium liberorum /jə́s tráyəm làybərórəm/. In Roman law, a right or privilege allowed to the parent of three or more children. These privileges were an exemption from the trouble of guardianship, priority in bearing offices, and a treble proportion of corn.

Just title. By the term "just title," in cases of prescription, is meant a title which the possessor may have received from any person whom he honestly believed to be the real owner, provided the title were such as to transfer the ownership of the property. Davis v. Gaines, 104 U.S. 386, 400, 26 L.Ed. 757; B. Fernandez & Bros. v. Ayllon, 266 U.S. 144, 45 S.Ct. 52, 69 L.Ed. 209. One good against all the world. See **Marketable title.**

Justum non est aliquem antenatum mortuum facere bastardum, qui pro tota vita sua pro legitimo habetur /jə́stəm nón èst ǽləkwəm æntənéydəm mórchuwəm féysəriy bæstárdəm, kwáy pròw tówdə váydə s(y)úwə pròw ləjídəmow həbíydər/. It is not just to make a bastard after his death one elder born who all his life has been accounted legitimate.

Just value. In taxation, the fair, honest, and reasonable value of property, without exaggeration or depreciation; its actual market value. See also **Fair market value.**

Jus utendi /jə́s yuwténday/. The right to use property without destroying its substance. It is employed in contradistinction to the *jus abutendi.*

Jus venandi et piscandi /jə́s vənǽnday èt piskǽnday/. The right of hunting and fishing.

Jus vendit quod usus approbavit /jə́s véndət kwòd yúwzəs æprəbéyvət/. The law dispenses what use has approved.

Jus vitæ necisque /jə́s váydiy nəsískwiy/. In Roman law, the right of life and death. Originally a father, or his *pater-familias* if he was himself in domestic subjection, could decide—not arbitrarily, but judicially—whether or not to rear his child; and while this right became subject to certain restrictions, yet when the child had grown up, the father, in the exercise of his domestic jurisdiction, might visit his son's misconduct, both in private and public life, with such punishment as he thought fit, even banishment, slavery, or death. In the early Empire these rights became relaxed, and they disappeared in the Justinian law.

Juvenile. A young person who has not yet attained the age at which he or she should be treated as an adult for purposes of criminal law. In some states, this age is seventeen. Under the federal Juvenile Delinquency Act, a "juvenile" is a person who has not attained his eighteenth birthday. 18 U.S.C.A. § 5031. A term which may be, though not commonly, is applied to a person who has not reached his or her legal majority for purposes of contracting, marrying, etc. In law, the terms "juvenile" and "minor" are usually used in different contexts; the former used when referring to young criminal offenders, the latter to legal capacity or majority. See also **Minor.**

Juvenile courts. A court having special jurisdiction, of a paternal nature, over delinquent, dependent, and neglected children.

Juvenile delinquent. See **Delinquent child.**

Juvenile offenders. See **Delinquent child.**

Juxta /jə́kstə/. Lat. Near; following; according to.

Juxta conventionem /jə́kstə kənvènshiyównəm/. According to the covenant.

Juxta formam statuti /jə́kstə fórməm stət(y)úwday/. According to the form of the statute.

Juxtaposition /jə̀kstəpəzíshən/. A placing or being placed in nearness or contiguity; or side by side; as a juxtaposition of words. Brown v. State, 126 Tex. Cr.R. 449, 72 S.W.2d 269, 270.

In patent law, "juxtaposition" is the English equivalent of "aggregation." Mesta Mach. Co. v. Federal Machine & Welder Co., C.C.A.Pa., 110 F.2d 479, 481.

Juxta ratam /jə́kstə réydəm/. At or after the rate.

Juxta tenorem sequentem /jə́kstə tənórəm səkwéntəm/. According to the tenor following. A phrase used in the old books when the very words themselves referred to were set forth.

Juzgado /huwsgáðow/. In Spanish law, the judiciary; the body of judges; the judges who concur in a decree.

K

Kahawai /kàhaváyiy/. Hawaiian. The flowing stream. It may include the bed or channel of the stream and may, also, include the portion of such channel covered only in times of high water or of freshets.

Kaiage, or **kaiagium** /kéyəj/keyéyj(iy)əm/. A wharfage-due.

Kalendar /kælləndər/. An account of time, exhibiting the days of the week and month, the seasons, etc. More commonly spelled "calendar."

Kalendarium /kælləndériyəm/. In the civil law, a calendar; a book of accounts, memorandum-book, or debt-book; a book in which accounts were kept of moneys loaned out on interest. So called because the Romans used to let out their money and receive the interest on the calends of each month.

Kalends /kælləndz/. See **Calends.**

Kangaroo court. Term descriptive of a sham legal proceeding in which a person's rights are totally disregarded and in which the result is a foregone conclusion because of the bias of the court or other tribunal.

Kast-geld. Contribution for a jettison; average.

Katatonia /kædətówn(i)yə/. See **Insanity.**

Kay. A quay, or key.

Kayage. See **Cayagium.**

K.B. Abbreviation for "King's Bench".

K.C. Abbreviation for "King's Counsel".

Keelage /kíyləj/. The right to demand money for the privilege of anchoring a vessel in a harbor; also the money so paid.

Keep, v. To continue. People v. Roseberry, 23 Cal. App.2d 13, 71 P.2d 944; Briggs v. U. S., C.C.A.Mich., 45 F.2d 479, 480. To have or retain in one's power or possession; not to lose or part with; to preserve or retain. To maintain, carry on, conduct, or manage; as, to "keep" a bawdy house, gaming table, nuisance, or the like. To maintain, tend, harbor, feed, and shelter; as, to "keep" a dangerous animal.

To maintain continuously and methodically for the purposes of a record; as, to "keep" books. Thus to "keep" records of court means, not only to preserve the manual possession of the records, books, and papers, but to correctly transcribe therein the proceedings of the court.

To maintain continuously and without stoppage or variation; as, when a vessel is said to "keep her course," that is, continue in motion in the same general direction in which she was previously sailing. The Britannia, 153 U.S. 130, 14 S.Ct. 795, 38 L.Ed. 660. To maintain, to cause to continue without essential change of condition. To take care of and to preserve from danger, harm, or loss.

Keeper. A custodian, manager, or superintendent; one who has the care, custody, or management of any thing or place; one who has or holds possession of anything. See **Bailment; Custodian; Depository.**

Keeper of a bawdy house or house of ill fame. A person who has control, proprietorship, or management of the house in question. State v. Weston, 235 Iowa 148, 15 N.W.2d 922, 923.

Keeper of dog. A harborer of a dog. Elender v. White, La.App., 14 So.2d 280, 282. Any person, other than owner, harboring or having in his possession any dog. Hancock v. Finch, 126 Conn. 121, 9 A.2d 811. One who, either with or without owner's permission, undertakes to manage, control, or care for it as dog owners in general are accustomed to do.

Keeper of the forest. In old English law, an officer (called also chief warden of the forest) who had the principal government of all things relating to the forest, and the control of all officers belonging to the same.

Keeper of the great seal. In English law, a high officer of state, through whose hands pass all charters, grants, and commissions of the king under the great seal.

Keeper of the king's conscience. A name sometimes applied to the chancellor of England, as being formerly an ecclesiastic and presiding over the royal chapel.

Keeper of the privy seal. In English law, an officer through whose hands pass all charters signed by the king before they come to the great seal. He is a privy councillor, and was anciently called "clerk of the privy seal," but is now generally called the "lord privy seal."

Keeper of the touch. The master of the assay in the English mint.

Keeping a gambling house or **place.** A proprietor is guilty if with his knowledge, acquiescence, and consent, express or implied, gambling is carried on upon premises in his possession as owner or lessee, or under his management or control, by his associates or subordinates who are likewise guilty if they are present aiding and assisting in carrying on such gambling operations for him. Commonwealth v. Pinkenson, 138 Pa.Super. 485, 11 A.2d 176, 179. A proprietor of a place not kept for the purpose of gambling is guilty if he allows gambling to be carried on and participates in it or receives a benefit from it in some way. People v. Dubinsky, Sp.Sess., 31 N.Y.S.2d 234, 238. See **Gambling.**

Keeping a gambling table or **bank.** If one has possession or custody of a gaming table, and authority over its use, and supervises the gaming, he is guilty of such crime.

Keeping a lookout. Being watchful of movements of driver's own vehicle, as well as other vehicles and pedestrians. See **Lookout.**

Keeping books. Preserving an intelligent record of a merchant's or tradesman's affairs with such reasonable accuracy and care as may properly be expected from a man in that business. See **Accounting.**

Keeping the peace. Avoiding a breach of the peace; dissuading or preventing others from breaking the peace.

Keep in repair. When a lessee is bound to keep the premises in repair, he must have them in repair at all times during the term; and, if they are at any time out of repair, he is guilty of a breach of the covenant. See **Habitability.**

Kefauver-Cellar Act. Federal anti-merger statute enacted in 1950 prohibiting the acquisition of assets of one company by another (generally in the same line of business) when the effect is to lessen competition. 15 U.S.C.A. §§ 18, 21.

Keiki /kéykiy/. Hawaiian. Popular meaning is child, but the meaning of that word in any particular instance depends on context in which it is used, and it can mean "descendant of any generation." In re Kanoa's Trust Estate, 47 Hawaii 160, 393 P.2d 753, 760; Kalakaua v. Parke, 8 Hawaii 620, 621.

Kelp-shore. The land between high and low water mark.

Kentucky Resolutions. A series of resolutions drawn up by Jefferson, and adopted by the legislature of Kentucky in 1799, protesting against the "alien and sedition laws," declaring their illegality, announcing the strict constructionist theory of the federal government, and declaring "nullification" to be "the rightful remedy."

Kentucky Rule. In the allocation of dividends by trustees as between income and principal, all dividends whether paid in cash or stock are regarded as income though in most jurisdictions accepting this rule a dividend paid in the stock of the issuing corporation is considered principal and brings about an adjustment in the basis of such stock in the portfolio.

Keogh Plan. A designation for retirement plans available to self-employed taxpayers (also referred to as H.R.10 plans). Such plans extend to the self-employed tax benefits similar to those available to employees under qualified pension and profit sharing plans. Yearly contributions to the plan (up to a certain amount) are tax deductible. See also **Individual retirement account.**

Kerhere. A customary cart-way; also a commutation for a customary carriage-duty.

Kernellatus /kàrnəléydəs/. Fortified or embattled.

Kernes /kárnz/. In English law, idlers; vagabonds.

Key. A wharf for the lading and unlading of merchandise from vessels. More commonly spelled "quay."

An instrument for fastening and opening a lock.

Any descriptive words in a land contract which lead unerringly to the land. Blumberg v. Nathan, 190 Ga. 64, 8 S.E.2d 374, 375. Reference to something more definite by which an indefinite description of property is made certain.

Keyage. A toll paid for loading and unloading merchandise at a key or wharf.

Key man insurance. Type of insurance coverage purchased by companies to protect them on the death or disability of a valued employee or by partnership to provide for funds with which to buy out the interest of such partner on his death or disability.

Keyus /kíyəs/. A guardian, warden, or keeper.

Kibei /kìybéy/. Jap. A person born in the United States of Japanese parents and who has returned to Japan for education and training.

Kickback. Payment back of a portion of the purchase price to buyer or public official by seller to induce purchase or to influence improperly future purchases or leases. Such payments are not tax deductible as ordinary and necessary expenses. I.R.C. § 162.

A federal statute makes kickbacks a criminal offense in connection with a contract for construction or repair of a public building or a building financed by loans from the government. 18 U.S.C.A. § 874.

Kidnapping. At common law, the forcible abduction or stealing and carrying away of a person from own country to another. 4 Bl.Comm. 219; Collier v. Vaccaro, C.C.A.Md., 51 F.2d 17, 19; State v. Berry, 200 Wash. 495, 93 P.2d 782, 787, 792. The unlawful seizure and removal of a person from own country or state against his will. In American law, the intent to send the victim out of the country does not constitute a necessary part of the offense; the unlawful taking and carrying away of a human being by force and against his will being the essential elements. State v. Barbour, 278 N.C. 449, 180 S.E.2d 115, 118. At common law kidnapping was a misdemeanor, but under modern statutes such crime is a felony.

A person is guilty of kidnapping if he unlawfully removes another from his place of residence or business, or a substantial distance from the vicinity where he is found, or if he unlawfully confines another for a substantial period in a place of isolation, with any of the following purposes: (a) to hold for ransom or reward, or as a shield or hostage; or (b) to facilitate commission of any felony or flight thereafter; or (c) to inflict bodily injury on or to terrorize the victim or another; or (d) to interfere with the performance of any governmental or political function. Model Penal Code, § 212.1.

With respect to federal kidnapping act, see **Lindbergh Act.** See also **Abduction; Ransom.**

Child-stealing. Child-stealing statutes commonly provide a penalty for any one who shall lead, take, entice or detain a child under a specified age with intent to keep or conceal it from its parent, guardian, or other person having lawful care or control thereof.

Kidnapping for ransom. One who detains another for the purpose of extorting money from him or from another person as the price of his release is guilty of the felony of kidnapping for ransom.

Simple kidnapping. Kidnapping which is not in some aggravated form, such as holding for ransom, is commonly referred to as "simple kidnapping."

Kilberg doctrine. In conflicts of law, a rule to the effect that the forum is not bound by the law of the place of the death as to the limitations on damages for wrongful death because such law is procedural and hence the law of the forum governs on this issue. Kilberg v. Northeast Airlines, Inc., 9 N.Y.2d 34, 211 N.Y.S.2d 133, 172 N.E.2d 526.

Kilketh. An ancient servile payment made by tenants in husbandry.

Kill, *v.* To deprive of life; to destroy the life of an animal or person. The word "homicide" expresses the killing of a human being. See also **Homicide; Manslaughter; Murder.**

Killed instantly. In collision, may mean that death was instantaneous but not precisely coincidental with the impact. Cash v. Addington, 46 N.M. 451, 131 P.2d 265, 266.

Killing by misadventure. Accidental killing of a person where the slayer is doing a lawful act, unaccompanied by any criminal carelessness or reckless conduct. Excusable homicide occurring where one engaged in doing lawful act, without intention to do harm and, with proper precaution to avoid danger, unfortunately kills another.

Kind. Class, grade, or sort. City of St. Louis v. James Braudis Coal Co., Mo.App., 137 S.W.2d 668, 670. Genus; generic class; description. See **In kind; Likekind exchange; Sample.**

Kindred. See **Kin or kindred; Next of kin.**

King. The sovereign, ruler, or chief executive magistrate of a state or nation whose constitution is of the kind called "monarchical" is thus named if a man; if it be a woman, she is called "queen."

The word expresses the idea of one who rules singly over a whole people or has the highest executive power; but the office may be either hereditary or elective, and the sovereignty of the king may or may not be absolute, according to the constitution of the country.

See **Emperor.**

King can do no wrong. This maxim means that the king is not responsible legally for aught he may please to do, or for any omission. It does not mean that everything done by the government is just and lawful, but that whatever is exceptionable in the conduct of public affairs is not to be imputed to the king. See **Sovereign immunity; Sovereignty.**

King-craft. The art of governing.

Kingdom. A country where an officer called a "king" exercises the powers of government, whether the same be absolute or limited. In some kingdoms, the executive officer may be a woman, who is called a "queen."

King-geld. A royal aid; an escuage *(q.v.).*

King's (Queen's) advocate. An English advocate who holds, in the courts in which the rules of the canon and civil law prevail, a similar position to that which the attorney general holds in the ordinary courts, *i.e.,* he acts as counsel for the crown in ecclesiastical, admiralty, and probate cases, and advises the crown on questions of international law. In order of precedence, he ranks after the attorney general.

King's (Queen's) Bench. One of the superior courts of common law in England, being so called because the king (or queen) used formerly to sit there in person, the style of the court being *"coram ipso rege."*

It was called the "queen's bench" in the reign of a queen, and during the protectorate of Cromwell it was styled the "upper bench." It consisted of a chief justice and three puisne justices, who were by their office the sovereign conservators of the peace and supreme coroners of the land. It was a remnant of the *aula regis,* and was not originally fixed to any certain place, but might follow the king's person, though for some centuries past it usually sat at Westminster. It had a very extended jurisdiction both in criminal and civil causes; the former in what was called the "crown side" or "crown office," the latter in the "plea side," of the court. Its civil jurisdiction was gradually enlarged until it embraced all species of personal actions. By the Judicature Act of 1873 the jurisdiction of this court was assigned to the Queens Bench Division of the High Court of Justice.

King's (Queen's) coroner and attorney. In England, an officer of the court of king's (or queen's) bench, usually called "the master of the crown office," whose duty it was to file informations at the suit of a private subject by direction of the court. 4 Bl.Comm. 308, 309. The office is now merged in that of Master of the Crown Office.

King's (Queen's) counsel. Barristers or serjeants who have been called within the bar and selected to be the king's (or queen's) counsel. They answer in some measure to the *advocati fisci,* or advocates of the revenue, among the Romans. They could not formerly be employed in any cause against the Crown (*e.g.* in defending a prisoner) without special license. Now, however, by a general dispensation granted in 1920, they can appear against the Crown without such license. Called "Queen's" counsel when a queen holds the crown.

King's (Queen's) evidence. When several persons are charged with a crime, and one of them gives evidence against his accomplices, on the promise of being granted a pardon, he is said to be admitted king's or (in America) state's evidence. Called "Queen's" evidence when a queen holds the crown. See also **State's evidence.**

King's (Queen's) proctor. A proctor or solicitor representing the crown in the Family Division. In petitions for dissolution of marriage, or for declarations of nullity of marriage, the king's (or queen's) proctor may, under the direction of the attorney general, and by leave of the court, intervene in the suit for the purpose of proving collusion between the parties. Called "Queen's" proctor when a queen holds the crown.

King's (Queen's) remembrancer. An officer of the central office of the English supreme court. Formerly he was an officer of the exchequer, and had important duties to perform in protecting the rights of the crown; *e.g.,* by instituting proceedings for the recovery of land by writs of intrusion *(q.v.),* and for the recovery of legacy and succession duties; but of late years administrative changes have lessened the duties of the office. He was at the head of the department which had charge of all revenue suits, and of matters pertaining to the office of sheriff. He attended as the officer of the king's (queen's) bench when the lord mayor made his appearance on November 9th, and was representing the old court of exchequer when the city of London did suit and service in discharge of quit-rents for certain lands anciently held under the crown. Called a "Queen's" remembrancer when a queen holds the crown.

King's silver. In old English practice, a fine due the king *pro licentia concordandi* (for leave to agree), in the process of levying a fine.

King's widow. In feudal law, a widow of the king's tenant in chief, who was obliged to take oath in chancery that she would not marry without the king's leave.

Kin or kindred. Relation or relationship by blood or consanguinity. Relatives by blood; by birth. May be either lineal (ascending or descending) or collateral. Poff v. Pennsylvania R. Co., D.C.N.Y., 57 F.Supp. 625, 626. As to "next to kin," see **Next.** See also **Blood relations; Heirs; Next of kin.**

Kinsfolk. Relations; those who are of the same family.

Kinsman /kínzmən/. A man of the same race or family.

Kinswoman. A female relation.

Kintal, or **kintle** /k(w)íntəl/. A hundred pounds in weight. See **Quintal.**

Kissing the book. The ceremony of touching the lips to a copy of the Bible, used in administering oaths. It is the external symbol of the witness' acknowledgment of the obligation of the oath.

Kist. In Hindu law, a stated payment; installment of rent.

Kiting. The wrongful practice of taking advantage of the float, the time that elapses between the deposit of a check in one bank and its collection at another. Method of drawing checks by which the drawer uses funds which are not his by drawing checks against

deposits which have not yet cleared through the banks. "Kiting" consists of writing checks against bank account where funds are insufficient to cover them, hoping that before they are presented the necessary funds will be deposited. Sutro Bros. & Co. v. Indemnity Ins. Co. of North America, D.C.N.Y., 264 F.Supp. 273, 283.

Kleptomania /klèptəméyn(i)yə/. In medical jurisprudence, a species (or symptom) of mania, consisting of an irresistible propensity to steal.

Knave /néyv/. A rascal; a false, tricky, or deceitful person. The word originally meant a boy, attendant, or servant, but long-continued usage has given it its present signification.

Knight. In English law, the next personal dignity after the nobility. Of knights there are several orders and degrees. The first in rank are knights of the Garter, instituted by Richard I and improved by Edward III in 1344; next follows a knight banneret; then come knights of the Bath, instituted by Henry IV, and revived by George I; and they were so called from a ceremony of bathing the night before their creation. The last order are knights bachelors, who, though the lowest, are yet the most ancient, order of knighthood; for we find that King Alfred conferred this order upon his son Athelstan. Other degrees of knights include Knight of the Order of St. Michael and St. George, Knight of the Thistle, and Knight of the Most Excellent Order of the British Empire. 1 Bl.Comm. 403.

Knighthood. The rank, order, character, or dignity of a knight.

Knight-marshal. In English law, an officer in the royal household who has jurisdiction and cognizance of offenses committed within the household and verge, and of all contracts made therein, a member of the household being one of the parties.

Knights bachelors. In English law, the most ancient, though lowest, order of knighthood. See **Knight.**

Knights banneret. In English law, those created by the sovereign in person on the field of battle. They rank, generally, after knights of the Garter. See **Knight.**

Knights fee. The determinate quantity of land (held by an estate of inheritance), or of annual income therefrom, which was sufficient to maintain a knight.

Knights of the Garter. See **Garter; Knight.**

Knights of the post. A term for hireling witnesses.

Knights of the shire. In English law, members of parliament representing counties or shires, in contradistinction to citizens or burgesses, who represent boroughs or corporations.

Knight's service. Upon the Norman conquest, all the lands in England were divided into knight's fees, in number above sixty thousand. For every knight's fee, a knight was bound to attend the king in his wars forty days in a year, in which space of time a campaign was generally finished. If a man only held half a knight's fee, he was only bound to attend twenty days; and so in proportion. But this personal service, in process of time, grew into pecuniary commutations, or aids; until at last, with the military part of the feudal system, it was abolished by the Tenures Abolition Act of 1660. 1 Bl.Comm. 410.

Knock and announce rule. A peace officer, whether he arrests by virtue of warrant or by virtue of his authority to arrest without warrant on probable cause, can break door of house to effect arrest only after first stating his authority and purpose for demanding admission. Miller v. U. S., 357 U.S. 301, 78 S.Ct. 1190, 2 L.Ed.2d 1332. The officer may break open any outer or inner door or window of a house, or any part of a house, or anything therein, to execute a search warrant, if, after notice of his authority and purpose, he is refused admittance or when necessary to liberate himself or a person aiding him in the execution of the warrant. 18 U.S.C.A. § 3109.

Knock down. To assign to a bidder at an auction by a knock or blow of the hammer. Property is said to be "knocked down" when the auctioneer, by the fall of his hammer, or by any other audible or visible announcement, signifies to the bidder that he is entitled to the property on paying the amount of his bid, according to the terms of the sale. "Knocked down" and "struck off" are synonymous terms.

Knot. In seamen's language, a "knot" is a division of the log-line serving to measure the rate of the vessel's motion. The number of knots which run off from the reel in half a minute shows the number of miles the vessel sails in an hour. Hence when a ship goes 8 nautical miles an hour she is said to go "8 knots."

Know. To have knowledge; to possess information, instruction, or wisdom. To perceive or apprehend; to understand. International-Great Northern R. Co. v. Pence, Tex.Civ.App., 113 S.W.2d 206, 210. The word "familiar" is equivalent. See **Knowingly; Knowledge; Notice.**

Know all men. A form of public address, of great antiquity, and with which many written instruments, such as bonds, letters of attorney, etc., still commence.

Knowingly. With knowledge; consciously; intelligently; willfully; intentionally.

A person acts knowingly with respect to a material element of an offense when: (i) if the element involves the nature of his conduct or the attendant circumstances, he is aware that his conduct is of that nature or that such circumstances exist; and (ii) if the element involves a result of his conduct, he is aware that it is practically certain that his conduct will cause such a result. Model Penal Code, § 2.202.

The use of the word in an indictment is equivalent to an averment that the defendant knew what he was about to do, and, with such knowledge, proceeded to do the act charged.

See also **Intent; Knowledge.**

Knowingly and willfully. This phrase, in reference to violation of a statute, means consciously and intentionally.

Knowledge. Acquaintance with fact or truth. People v. Henry, 23 Cal.App.2d 155, 72 P.2d 915, 921.

It has also been defined as act or state of knowing or understanding, Witters v. U. S., 70 App.D.C. 316, 106 F.2d 837, 840; People v. Henry, 23 Cal.App.2d 155, 72 P.2d 915, 921; actual knowledge, notice or information, New York Underwriters Ins. Co. v. Central Union Bank of South Carolina, C.C.A.S.C., 65 F.2d 738, 739; Howard v. Whittaker, 250 Ky. 836, 64 S.W.2d 173; Cooper v. Independent Transfer & Storage Co., 52 Idaho 747, 19 P.2d 1057, 1058; assurance of fact or proposition founded on perception by senses, or intuition; clear perception of that which exists, or of truth, fact or duty; firm belief, Witters v. U. S., 70 App.D.C. 316, 106 F.2d 837, 840; guilty knowledge, Goldsworthy v. Anderson, 92 Colo. 446, 21 P.2d 718; information of fact, Green v. Stewart, 106 Cal.App. 518, 289 P. 940, 944; means of mental impression, Howard v. Whittaker, 250 Ky. 836, 64 S.W.2d 173; miscellaneous information and circumstances which engender belief to moral certainty or induce state of mind that one considers that he knows, Wise v. Curdes, 219 Ind. 606, 40 N.E.2d 122, 126; notice or knowledge sufficient to excite attention and put person on guard and call for inquiry, Iberville Land Co. v. Amerada Petroleum Corporation, C.C.A.La., 141 F.2d 384, 389; Hayward Lumber & Investment Co. v. Orondo Mines, 34 Cal.App.2d 697, 94 P.2d 380, 382, 383; Reynolds v. Moseley, C.C.A.Ark., 32 F.2d 979, 981; personal cognizance or knowledge or means of knowledge, The Chickie, D.C. Pa., 54 F.Supp. 19, 20; Taylor v. Moore, 87 Utah 493, 51 P.2d 222, 229; In re Eastern Transp. Co., D.C.Md., 37 F.2d 355, 363; state of being or having become aware of fact or truth, Howard v. Whittaker, 250 Ky. 836, 64 S.W.2d 173.

When knowledge of the existence of a particular fact is an element of an offense, such knowledge is established if a person is aware of a high probability of its existence, unless he actually believes that it does not exist. Model Penal Code, § 2.202.

Knowledge consists in the perception of the truth of affirmative or negative propositions, while "belief" admits of all degrees, from the slightest suspicion to the fullest assurance. The difference between them is ordinarily merely in the degree, to be judged of by the court, when addressed to the court; by the jury, when addressed to the jury.

See also **Constructive knowledge; Imputed knowledge; Knowingly; Notice.**

Agency relationship. Unless the parties have otherwise agreed, a principal or agent, with respect to the other, should know what a person of ordinary experience and intelligence would know, and in addition, what he would know if, having the knowledge and intelligence which he has or which he purports to have, he were to use due care in the performance of his duties to the other. Restatement, Second, Agency, § 10.

Carnal knowledge. See **Carnal knowledge.**

Knowledge of another's peril. One has "knowledge of peril of another," within doctrine of discovered peril, whenever it reasonably appears from the known facts and circumstances that the latter is pursuing a course which will probably terminate in serious bodily injury to him, and that he probably will pursue it to the end.

Personal knowledge. Knowledge of the truth in regard to a particular fact or allegation, which is original, and does not depend on information or hearsay.

Personal knowledge of an allegation in an answer is personal knowledge of its truth or falsity; and if the allegation is a negative one, this necessarily includes a knowledge of the truth or falsity of the allegation denied.

Reason to know. The words "reason to know" are used throughout the Restatement of Torts to denote the fact that the actor has information from which a person of reasonable intelligence or of the superior intelligence of the actor would infer that the fact in question exists, or that such person would govern his conduct upon the assumption that such fact exists. Restatement, Second, Torts, § 12.

Should know. The words "should know" are used throughout the Restatement of Torts to denote the fact that a person of reasonable prudence and intelligence or of the superior intelligence of the actor would ascertain the fact in question in the performance of his duty to another, or would govern his conduct upon the assumption that such fact exists. Restatement, Second, Torts, § 12.

Known. Familiar; perceived; recognized; understood; especially, when used absolutely, familiar to all; generally understood or perceived. Term may, according to context, refer to both actual and constructive knowledge.

Known heirs. In a statute relating to the sale of property of unknown heirs, it has been held to mean those persons who are known, and whose right to inherit, or the extent of whose right, to inherit, is dependent on the non-existence of other persons nearer or as near as the ancestor in the line of descent.

Koshuba /kòshuwvá/. The Jewish "Koshuba" is a marriage contract or marriage settlement. Hurwitz v. Hurwitz, 216 App.Div. 362, 215 N.Y.S. 184, 185.

Ku Klux Act. Federal statute which creates civil liability for interfering with a person's civil rights. 42 U.S.C.A. § 1985(3).

Kuleana /kùwleyánə/. The Hawaiian term "kuleana" means a small area of land, such as were awarded in fee by the Hawaiian monarch, about the year 1850, to all Hawaiians who made application therefor.

Kyth /kíθ/. Sax. Kin or kindred.

L

L. This letter, as a Roman numeral, stands for the number "fifty." It is also used as an abbreviation for "law," "*liber*," (a book) "lord," and some other words of which it is the initial.

La. Fr. The. The definite article in the feminine gender. Occurs in some legal terms and phrases.

Label. Anything appended to a larger writing, as a codicil.

A narrow slip of paper or parchment affixed to a deed or writ, in order to hold the appending seal.

An affixation to or marking on a manufactured article, giving information as to its nature or quality, or the contents of a material, package or container, or the name of the maker, etc. Higgins v. Keuffel, 140 U.S. 428, 11 S.Ct. 731, 35 L.Ed. 470. The informational content of such labels is often governed by federal and state laws; *e.g.* Fair Packaging and Labeling Act. 15 U.S.C.A. § 1457.

In English law, a copy of a writ in the exchequer.

Labina /ləbáynə/. In old records, water land.

Labor. Work; toil; service; mental or physical exertion. Term normally refers to work for wages as opposed to work for profits; though the word is sometimes construed to mean service rendered or part played in production of wealth. Britt v. Cotter Butte Mines, 108 Mont. 174, 89 P.2d 266, 267. Includes superintendence or supervision of work. Wandling v. Broaddus, Mo., 10 S.W.2d 651, 655; United States for Use and Benefit of Farwell, Ozmun, Kirk & Co. v. Shea-Adamson Co., D.C.Minn., 21 F.Supp. 831, 837.

Term "labor" as used in the Clayton Act is not limited to the work of manual laborers or of mechanics, but comprises intellectual labor as well. U. S. v. National Ass'n of Real Estate Boards, D.C.D.C., 84 F.Supp. 802, 803.

A Spanish land measure, in use in Mexico and formerly in Texas, equivalent to 177½ acres.

See also **Agricultural labor; Farm labor or laborer; Laborer.**

Labor a jury. To tamper with a jury; to endeavor to influence them in their verdict, or their verdict generally. Jury tampering is a crime. See *e.g.* 18 U.S.C.A. §§ 1503, 1504.

Laborariis /lèybərériyəs/. An ancient writ against persons who refused to serve and do labor, and who had no means of living; or against such as, having served in the winter, refused to serve in the summer.

Labor contract. Contract between employer and employees (*i.e.* union) which governs working conditions, wages, fringe benefits, and grievances. See **Collective bargaining agreement; Master agreement; More favorable terms clause.**

Labor dispute. Term generally includes any controversy concerning terms, tenure, hours, wages, fringe benefits, or conditions of employment, or concerning the association or representation of persons in negotiating, fixing, maintaining, changing, or seeking to arrange terms or conditions or employment. National Labor Relations Act, § 2(9). However, not every activity of labor organization and not even every controversy in which it may become involved is "labor dispute" within National Labor Relations Act. N. L. R. B. v. International Longshoremen's Ass'n, Md., 332 F.2d 992, 995, 996.

Laborer. The word ordinarily denotes one who subsists by physical labor. American Surety Co. of New York v. Stuart, Tex.Civ.App., 151 S.W.2d 886, 888. One who, as a means of livelihood, performs work and labor for another. See **Farm labor or laborer; Labor; Work.**

Laborers' lien. Species of non-possessory lien which gives preference to laborer who works on job for payment of his wages ahead of general creditors. Such liens are generally governed by state statutes. See **Mechanic's lien.**

Labor-management relations. Term used to describe broad spectrum of activities which concern relationship of employees to employers both union and non-union. See **Fair Labor Standards Act; Labor-Management Relations Act; National Labor Relations Act; National Labor Relations Board.**

Labor-Management Relations Act. Federal statute (Taft-Hartley Act) which regulates certain union activities, permits suits against unions for proscribed acts, prohibits certain strikes and boycotts and provides machinery for settling strikes which involve national emergencies. 29 U.S.C.A. § 141 et seq.

Labor organization. Means a labor organization engaged in an industry affecting commerce and includes any organization of any kind, any agency, or employee representation committee, group, association, or plan so engaged in which employees participate and which exists for the purpose, in whole or in part, or dealing with employers concerning grievances, labor disputes, wages, rates of pay, hours, or other terms or conditions of employment, and any conference, general committee, joint or system board, or joint council so engaged which is subordinate to a national or international labor organization, other than a State or local central body. National Labor Relations Act, § 2(5).

A combination of workers usually, but not necessarily, of the same trade or of several allied trades, for securing by united action, the most favorable conditions as regards wages, hours of labor, etc., for its members.

See also **Labor union.**

Labor picketing. The act of patrolling in motion at or near employer or customer entrances; usually carrying placards with a terse legend communicating the gist of the union's claims. Certain forms are prohibited. Landrum-Griffin Act, § 8(b)(7). See also **Picketing.**

Labor Relations Board. See **National Labor Relations Board.**

Labor standards. See **Fair Labor Standards Act.**

Labor union. A combination or association of workers organized for purpose of securing favorable wages, improved labor conditions, better hours of labor, etc., and righting grievances against employers. Such unions normally represent trades, crafts, and other skilled workers (*e.g.* plumbers, truck drivers. See also **Labor organization; Union.**

Lacey Act. An act of Congress, May 25, 1900, under which the states may enforce game laws against animals, birds, etc., imported from other states or countries. See 16 U.S.C.A. § 661 et seq. See also **Game laws.**

La chambre des esteilles. The star-chamber.

Laches /lǽchəz/léychəz/lǽshəz/. "Doctrine of laches," is based upon maxim that equity aids the vigilant and not those who slumber on their rights. It is defined as neglect to assert right or claim which, taken together with lapse of time and other circumstances causing prejudice to adverse party, operates as bar in court of equity. Wooded Shores Property Owners Ass'n, Inc. v. Mathews, 37 Ill.App.3d 334, 345 N.E.2d 186, 189. The neglect for an unreasonable and unexplained length of time under circumstances permitting diligence, to do what in law, should have been done. Lake Development Enterprises, Inc. v. Kojetinsky, Mo.App., 410 S.W.2d 361, 367.

Neglect or omission to assert right as, taken in conjunction with lapse of time and other circumstances, causes prejudice to adverse party, People ex rel. Mulvey v. City of Chicago, 292 Ill.App. 589, 12 N.E.2d 13, 16; neglect or omission to do what one should do as warrants presumption that one has abandoned right or claim, Eldridge v. Idaho State Penitentiary, 54 Idaho 213, 30 P.2d 781, 784; negligence by which another has been led into changing his condition with respect to property or right, Heyburn Bldg. Co. v. Highland Motor Transfer Co., 245 Ky. 514, 53 S.W.2d 944, 946; negligence or omission seasonably to assert a right, Davidson v. Grady, C.C. A.Fla., 105 F.2d 405, 408; omission of something which a party might do and might reasonably be expected to do towards vindication or enforcement of

his rights, McCauley v. Northern Texas Traction Co., Tex.Civ.App., 21 S.W.2d 309, 313; omission to do what law requires to protect one's rights under circumstances misleading or prejudicing adverse party; unconscionable, undue, unexcused, unexplained or unreasonable delay in assertion of right, Loveland Camp No. 83, W. O. W., v. Woodmen Bldg. & Benev. Ass'n, 108 Colo. 297, 116 P.2d 195, 199; Calkin v. Hudson, 156 Kan. 308, 133 P.2d 177, 184, 185; City of Paducah v. Gillispie, 273 Ky. 101, 115 S.W.2d 574, 575; unreasonable or unexplained delay in asserting right which works disadvantage to another, Kennedy v. Denny, 237 Ky. 649, 36 S.W.2d 41, 42.

Conduct of party which has placed other party in a situation where his rights will be imperiled and his defenses embarrassed is a basis of laches. State v. Abernathy, 159 Tenn. 175, 17 S.W.2d 17, 19. Knowledge, unreasonable delay, and change of position are essential elements. Shanik v. White Sewing Mach. Corporation, 25 Del.Ch. 371, 19 A.2d 831, 837. Laches requires an element of estoppel or neglect which has operated to prejudice of defendant. Scarbrough v. Pickens, 26 Tenn.App. 213, 170 S.W.2d 585, 588; Mattison-Greenlee Service Corporation v. Culhane, D.C.Ill., 20 F.Supp. 882, 884.

Laches, estoppel by /əstópəl bày lǽchəz/. A failure to do something which should be done or to claim or enforce a right at a proper time. Hutchinson v. Kenney, C.C.A.N.C., 27 F.2d 254, 256. A neglect to do something which one should do, or to seek to enforce a right at a proper time. A species of "equitable estoppel" or "estoppel by matter in pais." See **Equitable estoppel; In pais, estoppel.**

An element of the doctrine is that the defendant's alleged change of position for the worse must have been induced by or resulted from the conduct, misrepresentation, or silence of the plaintiff. Croyle v. Croyle, 184 Md. 126, 40 A.2d 374, 379. Delay in enforcement of rights until condition of other party has become so changed that he cannot be restored to his former state. Wisdom's Adm'r v. Sims, 284 Ky. 258, 144 S.W.2d 232, 235, 236. Essence of "laches" is estoppel. Burke v. Gunther, 128 N.J.Eq. 565, 17 A.2d 481, 487. To create "estoppel by laches" party sought to be estopped must with knowledge of transaction have done something to mislead other party to his prejudice. Wisdom's Adm'r v. Sims, 284 Ky. 258, 144 S.W.2d 232, 235, 236. See also **Laches.**

Lack of jurisdiction. The phrase may mean lack of power of a court to act in a particular manner or to give certain kinds of relief. In re Rowe's Estate, 66 Cal.App.2d 594, 152 P.2d 765, 770. It may consist in court's total want of power to act at all, or lack of power to act in particular case because conditions essential to exercise of jurisdiction have not been complied with, or may consist of lack of jurisdiction over subject matter or over person.

La conscience est la plus changeante des règles /la kònsiyóns ey la plyúw shonzhónt dèy réyglə/. Conscience is the most changeable of rules.

Lacta /lǽktə/. L. Lat. In old English law, defect in the weight of money; *lack* of weight. This word and the verb "*lactare*" are used in an assise or statute of the sixth year of King John.

Lada /léydə/. In old English law, a court of justice; a lade or lath.

In Saxon law, a purgation, or mode of trial by which one purged himself of an accusation; as by oath or ordeal. A watercourse; a trench or canal for draining marshy grounds. In old English, a *lade* or *lode.*

Lade, or **lode.** The mouth of a river.

Laden in bulk. A term of maritime law, applied to a vessel which is freighted with a cargo which is neither in casks, boxes, bales, nor cases, but lies loose in the hold, being defended from wet or moisture by a number of mats and a quantity of dunnage. Cargoes of corn, salt, etc., are usually so shipped.

Lading, bill of. See **Bill of lading.**

Lady. In English law, the title belonging to the wife of a peer, and (by courtesy) the wife of a baronet or knight, and also to any woman, married or sole, whose father was a nobleman of a rank not lower than that of earl.

Lady-court. In old English law, the court of a lady of the manor.

Lady's friend. The style of an officer of the English house of commons, whose duty was to secure a suitable provision for the wife, when her husband sought a divorce by special act of parliament. The act of 1857 abolished parliamentary divorces, and this office with them.

Læn (Anglo-Saxon). A loan. See **Beneficium.**

Lænland /léynlænd/. Land held of a superior whether much or little. Land given to the lessee and to two or three successive heirs of his; synonymous with loan land. This species of tenure seems to have been replaced by that of holding by book or bocland. See **Folcland.**

Læsa majestas /líyzə məjéstæs/. Lat. Leze-majesty, or injured majesty; high treason. It is a phrase taken from the civil law, and anciently meant any offense against the king's person or dignity.

Læsione fidei, suits pro /s(y)úwts pròw lìyz(h)iyówniy fáydiyay/. Suits in the ecclesiastical courts for spiritual offenses against conscience, for non-payment of debts, or breaches of civil contracts. This attempt to turn the ecclesiastical courts into courts of equity was checked by the constitutions of Clarendon, A.D. 1164. 3 Bl.Comm. 52.

Læsio ultra dimidium vel enormis /líyz(h)(i)yow óltrə dəmídiyəm vál ənórməs/. In Roman law, the injury sustained by one of the parties to an onerous contract when he had been overreached by the other to the extent of more than one-half of the value of the subject-matter; *e.g.,* when a vendor had not received half the value of property sold, or the purchaser had paid more than double value.

Læsiwerp. A thing surrendered into the hands or power of another; a thing given or delivered.

Læt. In old English law, one of a class between servile and free.

Lafordswic. In Saxon law, a betraying of one's lord or master.

Laga /léygə/. L. Lat., from the Saxon "*lag.*" Law; a law.

Lagan /lǽgən/. See **Ligan.**

Lage /léy/ló/. Laws in early Saxon times; *e.g.,* "Dane-Lage," "Mercen-Lage," and "West Saxon Lage" (see those titles).

Lage day. In old English law, a law day; a time of open court; the day of the county court; a juridical day.

Lage-man /léymən/. A lawful man; a good and lawful man. A juror.

Laghday or **lahdy** /lódèy/. A day of open court; a day of the county court.

Lagu /léy/ló/. In old English law; law; also used to express the territory or district in which a particular law was in force, as *Dena lagu, Mercna lagu,* etc. See **Lage.**

Lahlslit. A breach of law. A mulct for an offense, viz., twelve "ores."

Lahman, or **lagemannus** /lómən/léymən/lǽjəmǽnəs/. An old word for a lawyer.

Laicus /léyəkəs/. Lat. A layman. One who is not in holy orders, or not engaged in the ministry of religion.

Lairwite, or **lairesite** /lérwàyt/. A fine for adultery or fornication, anciently paid to the lords of some manors.

Lais gents /léy zhòn(ts)/. L. Fr. Lay people; a jury.

Laissez-faire /lésey fér/. Expresses a political-economic philosophy of the government of allowing the marketplace to operate relatively free of restrictions and intervention.

Laity. Those persons who do not make a part of the clergy.

Laiz, leez (O. Fr.). A legate.

Lake. A considerable body of standing water in a depression of land or expanded part of a river. An inland body of water or naturally enclosed basin serving to drain surrounding country; or a body of water of considerable size surrounded by land; a widened portion of a river or a lagoon. Wood v. Maitland, 169 Misc. 484, 8 N.Y.S.2d 146, 150. Body of water, more or less, stagnant, in which the water is supplied from drainage. Amerada Petroleum Corporation v. State Mineral Board, 203 La. 473, 14 So.2d 61, 68, 69. An inland body of water of considerable size occupying natural basin or depression in earth's surface below ordinary drainage level of region. Keener v. Sharp, Mo.App., 95 S.W.2d 648, 652. A large body of water, contained in a depression of the earth's surface, and supplied from the drainage of a more or less extended area.

La ley favour la vie d'un home /là léy favúr là víy dənóm/. The law favors the life of a man.

La ley favour l'enheritance d'un home /là léy favúr lonerətón(t)s dənóm/. The law favors the inheritance of a man.

La ley voit plus tost suffer un mischeife que un inconvenience /là léy vwá plyùwtówst suféy ən mìschíyf kən ǽŋkənvèyn(i)yón(t)s/. The law will sooner suffer a mischief than an inconvenience. It is holden for an inconvenience that any of the maxims of the law should be broken, though a private man suffer loss.

Lambard's Archaion /lǽmbàrdz arkáyən/. A discourse upon the high court of justice in England, by William Lambard, published in 1635.

Lambard's Archaionomia /lǽmbàrdz àrkiyənówmiyə/. A work printed in 1568, containing the Anglo-Saxon laws, those of William the Conqueror, and of Henry I.

Lambard's Eirenarcha /lǽmbàrdz àyrənárkə/. A work upon the office of a justice of the peace, which, having gone through two editions, one in 1579, the other in 1581, was reprinted in English in 1599.

Lambeth degree /lǽmbəθ dəgríy/. In English law, a degree conferred by the Archbishop of Canterbury, in prejudice of the universities.

Lame duck. An elected officeholder who is to be succeeded by another, between the time of the election and the date that his successor is to take office. A speculator in stock who has overbought and cannot meet his commitments.

Lame Duck Amendment. Twentieth Amendment to U. S. Constitution, abolishing the short congressional term.

Lame duck session. Legislative session conducted after election of new members but before they are installed and hence one in which some participants are voting for the last time as elected officials because of failure to become reelected or voluntary retirement.

Lammas lands /lǽməs lǽndz/. Lands over which there is a right of pasturage by persons other than the owner from about Lammas, or reaping time, until sowing time.

Land. In the most general sense, comprehends any ground, soil, or earth whatsoever; including fields, meadows, pastures, woods, moors, waters, marshes, and rock. Reynard v. City of Caldwell, 55 Idaho 342, 42 P.2d 292, 296; Holmes v. U. S., C.C.A.Okl., 53 F.2d 960, 963. In its more limited sense, "land" denotes the quantity and character of the interest or estate which a person may own in land. Holmes v. U. S., C.C.A.Okl., 53 F.2d 960, 963. "Land" may include any estate or interest in lands, either legal or equitable, as well as easements and incorporeal hereditaments. Reynard v. City of Caldwell, 55 Idaho 342, 42 P.2d 292, 297; Jones v. Magruder, D.C.Md., 42 F.Supp. 193, 198; Lynch v. Cunningham, 131 Cal. App. 164, 21 P.2d 154; Petition of Burnquist, 220 Minn. 48, 19 N.W.2d 394, 401; Cuff v. Koslosky, 165 Okl. 135, 25 P.2d 290. The land is one thing, and the estate in land is another thing, for an estate in land is a time in land or land for a time.

Technically land signifies everything which may be holden; and the term is defined as comprehending all things of a permanent and substantial nature, and even of an unsubstantial, provided they be permanent. Reynard v. City of Caldwell, 55 Idaho 342, 42 P.2d 292, 296. Ordinarily, the term is used as descriptive of the subject of ownership and not the ownership. Southern Pac. Co. v. Riverside County, 35 Cal.App.2d 380, 95 P.2d 688, 692.

Land is the material of the earth, whatever may be the ingredients of which it is composed, whether soil, rock, or other substance, and includes free or occupied space for an indefinite distance upwards as well as downwards, subject to limitations upon the use of airspace imposed, and rights in the use of airspace granted, by law. Calif.Civil Code, § 659. See **Air rights.**

The term "land" may be used interchangeably with "property"; it may include anything that may be classed as real estate or real property. Reynard v. City of Caldwell, 55 Idaho 342, 42 P.2d 292, 297.

See also Lands; Ownership; Parcel; Partition; Property *(Real);* Real estate.

Accommodation lands. See **Accommodation lands.**

Bounty lands. See **Bounty.**

Certificate lands. See **Certificate lands.**

Crown lands. See **Crown lands.**

Demesne lands. See **Demesne.**

Donation lands. See **Donation lands.**

Fabric lands. See **Fabric lands.**

General land office. See **General Land Office.**

Land patent. See **Patent.**

Mineral lands. See **Mineral lands.**

Place lands. See **Place lands.**

Public lands. See **Public lands.**

School lands. See **School.**

Seated land. See **Seated land.**

Swamp and overflowed lands. See **Swamp and overflowed lands.**

Tide lands. See **Tide.**

Landa. An open field without wood; a lawnd or lawn.

Landagende, landhlaford, or **landrica** /lǽndèyjənd/lǽndlòrd/lǽndrəkə/. In Saxon law, a proprietor of land; lord of the soil.

Land bank. A federally created bank under the Federal Farm Loan Act and organized to make loans on farm security at low interest rates. May also describe program in which land is retired from agricultural production for use in conservation or in tree cultivation and as such is sometimes called a Soil Bank.

Landboc /lǽndbùk/. In Saxon law, a charter or deed by which lands or tenements were given or held.

Land boundaries. Limits of land holdings described by linear measurements of the borders, or by points of the compass, or by stationary markers. See Boundaries; Forty; Landmark; Land measure; Legal description; Metes and bounds; Plat map; Section.

Land certificate. An obligation of government entitling owner to secure designated quantity of land by following the requirements of law. State v. Balli, Tex. Civ.App., 173 S.W.2d 522, 538. It contains a description of the land as it appears on the register and the name and address of the proprietor, and is *prima facie* evidence of the truth of the matters therein set forth. See also **Land warrant.**

Landcheap. In old English law, an ancient customary fine, paid either in money or cattle, at every alienation of land lying within some manor, or within the liberty of some borough.

Land contract. Contract for the purchase and sale of land upon execution of which title is transferred. Term commonly refers to an installment contract for the sale of land whereby purchaser (vendee) receives the deed from the owner (vendor) upon payment of final installment. The vendor retains legal title to the property as security for payment of contract price. May also be called "contract for deed", or "installment land contract".

Land cop. The sale of land which was evidenced in early English law by the transfer of a rod or festuca *(q.v.)* as a symbol of possession which was handed by the seller to the reeve and by the reeve to the purchaser. The conveyance was made in court, it is supposed, for securing better evidence of it, and barring the claims of expectant heirs.

Land court. In Massachusetts such court has exclusive original jurisdiction of all applications for registration of title to land within Commonwealth, and power to hear and determine all questions arising upon such applications. It has exclusive original jurisdiction over writs of entry and various petitions for clearing title to real estate; of petitions for determining validity and extent of municipal zoning ordinances, by-laws and regulations; original concurrent general equity jurisdiction in matters relating to land except in cases of specific performance of contracts relating to same; exclusive original jurisdiction of proceedings for foreclosure of and redemption from tax titles; and it has original jurisdiction, concurrent with Supreme Judicial, superior and probate courts, of declaratory judgment proceedings.

Land damages. See **Damages.**

Land department. See **Bureau of Land Management; Interior Department.**

Land descriptions. See **Land boundaries.**

Land district. A division of a state or territory, created by federal authority, in which is located a United States land office, with a "register of the land office" and a "receiver of public money," for the disposition of the public lands within the district.

Landed. Consisting in real estate or land; having an estate in land.

Landed estate or **property.** A colloquial or popular phrase to denote real property. Landed estate ordinarily means an interest in and pertaining to lands. Real estate in general, or sometimes, by local usage, suburban or rural land, as distinguished from real estate situated in a city.

Landed estates court. In English law, tribunals established by statute for the purpose of disposing more promptly and easily than could be done through the ordinary judicial machinery, of incumbered real estate. These courts were first established in Ireland by the act of 11 & 12 Vict., c. 48, which being defective was followed by 12 & 13 Vict., c. 77. The purpose of these was to enable the owner, or a lessee for any less than 63 years unexpired, of land subject to incumbrance, to apply to commissioners who constituted a court of record to direct a sale. This court was called the Incumbered Estates Court. A new tribunal called the Landed Estates Court was created by 21 & 22 Vict., c. 72, which abolished the former court and established a permanent tribunal.

Landed securities. Mortgages or other encumbrances affecting land.

Landefricus /lændəfráykəs/. A landlord; a lord of the soil.

Landegandman. In old English law, a kind of customary tenant or inferior tenant of a manor.

Land gabel. A tax or rent issuing out of land.

Land grant. A donation of public lands to a subordinate government, a corporation, or an individual; as, from the United States to a state, or to a railroad company to aid in the construction of its road. See also *Land patent* under **Patent.**

Landhlaford /lǽndlòrd/. In old English law, a proprietor of land; lord of the soil.

Landing. A place on a river or other navigable water for loading and unloading of goods, or for the reception and delivery of passengers or pleasure boats. The terminus of a road on a river or other navigable water for these purposes. Act or process of coming back to land after voyage or flight. See also **Port.**

Landirecta /lændərèktə/. In Saxon law, services and duties laid upon all that held land, including the three obligations called *"trinoda necessitas,"* *(q.v.)* quasi land rights.

Land, law of. See **Law of the land.**

Landlocked. An expression applied to a piece of land belonging to one person and surrounded by land belonging to other persons, so that it cannot be approached except over their land. Access to such land will normally be via an easement from surrounding landowner.

Landlord. He of whom lands or tenements are holden. He who, being the owner of an estate in land, or a rental property, has leased it to another person, called the "tenant." Also called "lessor."

Landlord and tenant relationship. A phrase used to denote the familiar legal relation existing between lessor and lessee of real estate. The relation is contractual. Renshaw v. Sullivan, Tex.Civ.App., 14 S.W.2d 919, 921; Story v. Lyon Realty Corp., 308 Mass. 66, 30 N.E.2d 845, 847; Smith v. Royal Ins. Co., C.C.A.Cal., 111 F.2d 667, 670, 671. A lease (or agreement therefor) of lands for a term of years, from year to year, for life, or at will creates the relation. The relation exists where one person occupies premises of another in subordination to other's title or rights and with his permission or consent. Marden v. Radford, 229 Mo.App. 789, 84 S.W.2d 947, 954; Coggins v. Gregorio, C.C.A.N.M., 97 F.2d 948, 950, 951. There must be reversion in landlord, an estate in tenant, transfer of possession and control of premises, and, generally, a contract, express or implied. Marden v. Radford, 229 Mo.App. 789, 84 S.W.2d 947, 954, 955; Coggins v. Gregorio, C.C.A.N.M., 97 F.2d 948, 950, 951. See also **Lease.**

Landlord's warrant. A distress warrant; a warrant from a landlord to levy upon the tenant's goods and chattels, and sell the same at public sale, to compel payment of the rent or the observance of some other stipulation in the lease.

Land management. See **Bureau of Land Management.**

Landmark. A feature of the land, monument, marker, or other erection set up on the boundary line of two adjoining estates, to fix such boundary. The removing of a landmark is a wrong for which an action lies. Building or site having historical significance. See also **Monument.**

Land measure.

1 mile—80 chains, 320 rods, 1,760 yards or 5,280 feet.

16½ feet—1 rod, perch or pole.

1 chain—66 feet, 100 links or 4 rods.

1 link—7.92 inches.

25 links—1 rod.

4 rods—1 chain.

144 square inches—1 square foot.

9 square feet—1 square yard.

30¼ square yards—1 square rod.

160 square rods—1 acre.

10,000 square links—1 square chain.

10 square chains—1 acre.

1 acre—208.708 feet by 208.708 feet.

1 acre—43,560 square feet.

1 acre—4,840 square yards.

1 acre—160 square rods.

640 acres—1 square mile or section.

36 square miles or sections—1 township.

See also **Land boundaries; Survey.**

Land offices. Government offices, administered by Bureau of Land Management, established principally in the Western States, for the transaction of local business relating to the survey, location, settlement, preemption, and sale of the public lands. A former primary function of these offices was to administer land grants.

Land patent. An instrument conveying a grant of public land; also, the land so conveyed. See also **Patent.**

Land-poor. The term generally means that a man has a great deal of unproductive land, and perhaps is obliged to borrow money to pay taxes; but a man "land-poor" may be largely responsible.

Land-reeve. In old English law, a person whose business it was to overlook certain parts of a farm or estate; to attend not only to the woods and hedge-timber, but also to the state of the fences, gates, buildings, private roads, driftways, and watercourses; and likewise to the stocking of commons, and encroachments of every kind, as well as to prevent or detect waste and spoil in general, whether by the tenants or others; and to report the same to the manager or land steward.

Land revenues. This term denotes income derived from crown lands in Great Britain. These lands have been so largely granted away to subjects that they are now contracted within very narrow limits.

Landrum-Griffin Act. Federal statute enacted in 1959, known as the Labor-Management Reporting and Disclosure Act, designed to curb corruption in union leadership and undemocratic conduct of internal union affairs as well as to outlaw certain types of secondary boycotts and "hot cargo" provisions in collective bargaining agreements.

Lands. This term, the plural of "land," is said, at common law, to be a word of less extensive signification than either "tenements" or "hereditaments." But in some of the states it has been provided by statute that it shall include both those terms. See also **Land.**

Land sale contract. See **Land contract.**

Lands, public. See **Public lands.**

Lands, tenements, and hereditaments. The technical and most comprehensive description of real property, as "goods and chattels" is of personalty. The term refers to property in land. Denver Joint Stock Land Bank of Denver v. Dixon, 57 Wyo. 523, 122 P.2d 842, 846. Under ancient law, the words comprehended only freehold estate and did not apply to easements or other incorporeal hereditaments. Hester v. Sawyers, 41 N.M. 497, 71 P.2d 646, 649.

Land tax. Property tax. A tax laid upon the legal or beneficial owner of real property, and apportioned upon the assessed value of his land. A tax on land. Texas Co. v. Moynier, 129 Cal.App. 738, 19 P.2d 280, 282. See **Property tax.**

Land tenant. The person actually in possession of land.

Land Titles and Transfer Act. An English statute (38 & 39 Vict., c. 87) providing for the establishment of a registry for titles to real property, and making sundry provisions for the transfer of lands and the recording of the evidences thereof. It presents some analogies to the recording laws of the American states; *e.g.* Registry of Deeds office in many states.

Land trust. A land trust (as used in Illinois) is a trust in which corpus consists of real estate and in which deed to trustee appears to confer upon him full powers to deal with real estate and complete legal and equitable title to trust property. So far as public records are concerned, trustee's powers are complete. Such powers, however, are in fact restricted by a trust agreement mentioned in the deed in trust. Such trust agreements typically vest in beneficiary full powers of management and control. However, beneficiary cannot deal with property as if no trust existed. Such trusts generally continue for a definite term.

Land use planning. Generic term used to describe activities such as zoning, control of real estate developments and use, environmental impact studies and the like. Many states have land use planning laws which are implemented by local zoning and land use laws and ordinances. See also **Master plan; Planned unit development (PUD); Zoning.**

Land waiter. In English law, an officer of the customhouse, whose duty is, upon landing any merchandise, to examine, taste, weigh, or measure it, and to take an account thereof.

Land warrant. A warrant issued at the local land offices of the United States to purchasers of public lands, on the surrender of which at the general land office at Washington, they receive a conveyance from the general government. See **Land certificate.**

The evidence which the state, on good consideration, gives that the person therein named is entitled to the quantity of land therein specified, the bounds and description of which the owner of the warrant may fix by entry and survey, in the section of country set apart for its location and satisfaction.

Langeman. A lord of a manor.

Langemanni. The lords of manors.

Language. Any means of conveying or communicating ideas; specifically, human speech, or the expression of ideas by written characters or by means of sign language. The letter, or grammatical import, of a document or instrument, as distinguished from its spirit; as "the language of the statute." As to "offensive language," see **Offensive language.**

Languidus /læŋgwədəs/. (Lat., sick.) In common law practice, the name of a return made by the sheriff when a defendant, whom he had taken by virtue of process, was so dangerously sick that to remove him would endanger his life or health.

Lanham Act. Federal statute enacted in 1947 which revised trademark law.

Lanns manus. (Old Fr.) A lord of the manor.

Lapidation /læpədéyshən/. The act of stoning a person to death.

Lappage /lǽpəj/. A term synonymous with "interference," "conflict," "interlock," "lap" and "overlap" as regards adverse possession. It applies to a situation existing when a deed under which one party claims and grant under which another claims cover in large part the same land. Turk v. Wilson's Heirs, 265 Ky. 78, 98 S.W.2d 4, 8.

Lapse, v. To glide; to pass slowly, silently, or by degrees. To slip; to deviate from the proper path. To fall or fail. Life & Casualty Ins. Co. of Tennessee v. Wheeler, 265 Ky. 269, 96 S.W.2d 753, 755. See also **Expiration; Termination.**

Lapse, n. The termination or failure of a right or privilege through neglect to exercise it within some limit of time, or through failure of some contingency.

Failure to vest a bequest or devise by reason of death of devisee of legatee prior to death of testator. Farmers and Merchants State Bank v. Feltis, 150 Ind.App. 284, 276 N.E.2d 204, 206. The death of a legatee before the testator causes the legacy to lapse and to fall into the residue unless there is a statute which provides for its disposition as, for example, if the legatee is a child or relation of the testator, the legacy passes to the issue of the legatee.

The expiration of a right either by the death of the holder or upon the expiration of a period of time. Thus, a power of appointment lapses upon the death of the holder if such holder has not exercised the power during life or at death (i.e., through a will).

Termination of insurance policy because of failure to pay the premium.

In the law of wills, the failure of a testamentary gift. Wilmington Trust Co. v. Wilmington Trust Co., 25 Del.Ch. 204, 15 A.2d 830, 834; Gredig v. Sterling, C.C.A.Tex., 47 F.2d 832, 834.

Lapsed devise. See **Devise.**

Lapsed legacy. See **Legacy.**

Lapsed policy. Insurance policy on which there has been default in payment of premiums. Policy remaining in force according to statutory provisions after such default (normally a 30 or 31 day grace period on non-payment of premiums is provided).

Lapse patent. A patent for land issued in substitution for an earlier patent to the same land, which was issued to another party, but has lapsed in consequence of his neglect to avail himself of it.

Lapse statutes. Those state statutory enactments which prevent the lapse or passing into the residue or by intestacy of legacies and devises when the legatee or devisee predeceases the testator, and which commonly provide that, if the legatee or devisee is a child or other relation of the testator, the legacy or devise passes to the issue of such legatee or devisee.

Larcenous /lársənəs/. Having the character of larceny; as a "larcenous taking." Contemplating or intending larceny; as a "larcenous purpose."

Larcenous intent. A larcenous intent exists where a man knowingly takes and carries away the goods of another without any claim or pretense of right, with intent wholly to deprive the owner of them or convert them to his own use.

Larceny /lársəniy/. Felonious stealing, taking and carrying, leading, riding, or driving away another's personal property, with intent to convert it or to deprive owner thereof. The unlawful taking and carrying away of property of another with intent to appropriate it to use inconsistent with latter's rights. U. S. v. Johnson, 140 U.S.App.D.C. 54, 433 F.2d 1160, 1163. The essential elements of a "larceny" are an actual or constructive taking away of the goods or property of another without the consent and against the will of the owner and with a felonious intent. People v. Goodchild, 68 Mich.App. 226, 242 N.W.2d 465, 468.

Obtaining possession of property by fraud, trick or device with preconceived design or intent to appropriate, convert or steal is "larceny." John v. United

States, 65 U.S.App.D.C. 11, 79 F.2d 136; People v. Cook, 10 Cal.App.2d 54, 51 P.2d 169, 170.

Common-law distinctions between obtaining money under false pretenses, embezzlement, and larceny no longer exist in many states; all such crimes being embraced within general definition of "larceny."

See also **Shoplifting; Stolen.**

Compound larceny. Larceny or theft accomplished by taking the thing stolen either from one's person or from his house; otherwise called "mixed" larceny, and distinguished from "simple" or "plain" larceny, in which the theft is not aggravated by such an intrusion either upon the person or the dwelling. Sometimes referred to as larceny from the person.

Constructive larceny. One where the felonious intent to appropriate the goods to his own use, at the time of the asportation, is made out by construction from the defendant's conduct, although, originally, the taking was not apparently felonious.

False pretenses and larceny distinguished. See **False pretenses.**

Grand larceny. Taking and carrying away the personal property of another to a value in excess of $100.00 (or whatever the cut-off amount may be in a given jurisdiction) with the intent to feloniously deprive the owner or possessor of it permanently. Distinguished from *petit larceny (q.v.)* only by the value of the property stolen.

In England, simple larceny, was originally divided into two sorts,—*grand* larceny, where the value of the goods stolen was above twelve pence, and *petit* larceny, where their value was equal to or below that sum. 4 Bl.Comm. 229. The distinction was abolished in England by St. 7 & 8 Geo. IV, c. 29, and is not generally recognized in the United States, although in a few states there is a statutory offense of grand larceny, one essential element of which is the value of the goods stolen, which value varies.

Larceny by bailee. The crime of larceny committed where any person, being a bailee of any property, shall fraudulently take or convert the same to his own use, or to the use of any other person except the owner thereof, although he shall not break bulk or otherwise determine the bailment.

Larceny by extortion. A person is guilty of theft if he purposely obtains property of another by threatening to: (1) inflict bodily injury on anyone or commit any other criminal offense; or (2) accuse anyone of a criminal offense; or (3) expose any secret tending to subject any person to hatred, contempt or ridicule, or to impair his credit or business repute; or (4) take or withhold action as an official, or cause an official to take or withhold action; or (5) bring about or continue a strike, boycott or other collective unofficial action, if the property is not demanded or received for the benefit of the group in whose interest the actor purports to act; or (6) testify or provide information or withhold testimony or information with respect to another's legal claim or defense; or (7) inflict any other harm which would not benefit the actor. Model Penal Code, § 223.4.

Larceny by fraud or deception. A person is guilty of theft if he purposely obtains property of another by deception. A person deceives if he purposely: (1) creates or reinforces a false impression, including false impressions as to law, value, intention or other state of mind; but deception as to a person's intention from the act alone that he did not subsequently perform the promise; or (2) prevents another from acquiring information which would affect his judgment of a transaction; or (3) fails to correct a false impression which the deceiver previously created or reinforced, or which the deceiver knows to be influencing another to whom he stands in a fiduciary or confidential relationship; or (4) fails to disclose a known lien, adverse claim or other legal impediment to the enjoyment of property which he transfers or encumbers in consideration for the property obtained, whether such impediment is or is not valid, or is or is not a matter of official record. Model Penal Code, § 223.3.

Larceny by trick. See *Larceny by fraud or deception, supra.*

Larceny from the person. Act of taking property from the person by merely lifting it from the person or pocket. State v. Stanton, Mo., 68 S.W.2d 811, 812. Larceny committed where the property stolen is on the person or in the immediate charge or custody of the person from whom the theft is made, but without such circumstances of force or violence as would constitute robbery, including pocket-picking and such like crimes.

Larceny of auto. See **Auto theft.**

Larceny of property lost, mislaid, or delivered by mistake. A person who comes into control of property of another that he knows to have been lost, mislaid, or delivered under a mistake as to the nature or amount of the property or the identity of the recipient is guilty of theft if, with purpose to deprive the owner thereof, he fails to take reasonable measures to restore the property to a person entitled to have it. Model Penal Code, § 223.5.

Mixed larceny. Otherwise called "compound" or "complicated larceny;" that which is attended with circumstances of aggravation or violence to the person, or taking from a house.

Petit larceny. Larceny of things or goods whose value is below a statutorily set amount (*e.g.* $100). The value at common law was twelve pence. Compare *Grand larceny, supra.*

Simple larceny. Felonious or wrongful taking and carrying away of personal goods of another with intent to steal, unattended by acts of violence. Larceny which is not complicated or aggravated with acts of violence. Larceny from the person, or with force and violence, is called "compound" larceny.

Larger parcel. A term used in eminent domain proceedings, signifying that the parcel taken is not a complete parcel but part of a "larger parcel"; the owner, therefore is entitled to damages from the severance as well as the value of the parcel taken. Unity of ownership, use, and contiguity must be present, although federal courts and some states do not require contiguity where there is a strong unity of use.

Larons /lérən(d)z/. In old English law, thieves.

Lascivious /ləsíviyəs/. Tending to excite lust; lewd; indecent; obscene; sexual impurity; tending to deprave the morals in respect to sexual relations; licentious. See Swearingen v. U. S., 161 U.S. 446, 16 S.Ct. 562, 40 L.Ed. 765; People on Complaint of Sumner v. Dial Press, 182 Misc. 416, 48 N.Y.S.2d 480, 481; Dunlop v. U. S., 165 U.S. 486, 17 S.Ct. 375, 41 L.Ed. 799. Conduct which is wanton, lewd, and lustful, and tending to produce voluptuous or lewd emotions. See **Lewd; Obscene.**

Lascivious cohabitation. The offense committed by two persons (not married to each other) who live together in one habitation as man and wife and practice sexual intercourse. Such offense, where it still exists, is seldom enforced.

Last, *n.* In old English law, signifies a burden; also a measure of weight used for certain commodities of the bulkier sort.

Last, *adj.* Latest; ultimate; final; most recent.

Last antecedent rule. A canon of statutory construction that relative or qualifying words or phrases are to be applied to the words or phrases immediately preceding, and as not extending to or including other words, phrases, or clauses more remote, unless such extension or inclusion is clearly required by the intent and meaning of the context, or disclosed by an examination of the entire act.

Last clear chance doctrine. Under the doctrine of last clear chance, as applied in automobile law, a plaintiff may recover from a defendant motorist for injuries or damages suffered, notwithstanding his own contributory negligence, where, as stated in terms of the essential elements of the doctrine, plaintiff was in a place of peril of which he was unaware or from which he was unable to extricate himself, the motorist discovered or had the opportunity to discover plaintiff's peril, and the motorist had the opportunity to avoid the accident through the exercise of reasonable care. The last clear chance doctrine is not recognized in every jurisdiction and is subject to limitations in others. There are many variant forms and applications of this doctrine in the jurisdictions which apply it.

Doctrine of "last clear chance" imposes upon person duty to exercise ordinary care to avoid injury to another who has negligently put himself in position of peril, and who he can reasonably apprehend is unconscious of or inattentive to peril or unable to avoid imminent harm. Vernon v. Crist, 28 N.C.App. 631, 222 S.E.2d 445, 447. Necessary elements of doctrine of "last clear chance" are: (1) plaintiff was contributorily negligent by placing herself in a position of immediate peril, (2) plaintiff was unable to remove herself from such peril by the exercise of reasonable care, (3) defendant discovered or should have discovered plaintiff's dangerous situation in time so that by exercising reasonable care defendant could have prevented the accident, (4) defendant failed to exercise any reasonable care, and (5) defendant had the last clear chance to prevent the accident. Shanahan v. Patterson, Colo.App., 539 P.2d 1289, 1290.

Last heir. In English law, he to whom lands come by escheat for want of lawful heirs; that is, in some cases, the lord of whom the lands were held; in others, the sovereign.

Last illness. The illness terminating in person's death. Proto v. Chenoweth, 40 Ariz. 312, 11 P.2d 950, 951.

Last-in, first-out (LIFO). Under the last in, first out method of inventory accounting items of inventory used are priced out at the latest purchase prices of the goods. Inventory value is thus computed by assuming that goods on hand are those remotely purchased and are valued at the successively most remote purchase prices.

A method of identifying and valuing inventories which assumes that last goods purchased are the first ones sold and therefore the goods left in inventory at the end of the year are assumed to be those first purchased. L. S. Ayres & Co. v. U. S., C.A.Ind., 285 F.2d 113, 114. Compare **FIFO.**

Last resort. A court from which there is no further appeal is called the "court of last resort."

Last sickness. See **Last illness.**

Last will. Term used alone or with "and testament" to designate the instrument which ultimately fixes the disposition of real and personal property at death.

Lata culpa /léydə kálpə/. Lat. In the law of bailment, gross fault or neglect; extreme negligence or carelessness *(nimia negligentia).*

Lata culpa dolo æquiparatur /léydə kálpə dówlo iykwəpəréydər/. Gross negligence is equivalent to fraud.

Latching. An under-ground survey.

Late. Defunct; existing recently, but now dead. Formerly; recently; lately.

Latens /léytèn(d)z/. Lat. Latent; hidden; not apparent. See **Ambiguitas.**

Latent. Hidden; concealed; dormant; that which does not appear upon the face of a thing; as, a latent ambiguity or defect.

Latent ambiguity. A defect which does not appear on the face of language used or an instrument being considered. It arises when language is clear and intelligible and suggests but a single meaning, but some intrinsic fact or some extraneous evidence creates a necessity for interpretation or a choice between two or more possible meanings. Conkle v. Conkle, 31 Ohio App.2d 44, 285 N.E.2d 883, 887.

That species of uncertainty or ambiguity in an instrument which is not apparent from a reading of it but which is revealed when the terms of the instrument are applied or made operative; *e.g.* in a bill of lading goods are to be delivered at "Essex Railroad Wharf", and there are two such wharfs with the same name. Parol evidence is admissible to prove the intention of the party drawing the instrument.

Latent deed. A deed kept for twenty years or more in a strongbox or other secret place.

Latent defect. A hidden or concealed defect. One which could not be discovered by reasonable and customary inspection; one not apparent on face of goods, product, document, etc.

Defect of which owner has no knowledge, or which, in exercise of reasonable care, he should have had no knowledge. Bichl v. Poinier, 71 Wash.2d 492, 429 P.2d 228, 231. A latent defect in the title of a vendor of land is one not discoverable by inspection made with ordinary care, even though a matter of public record.

Latent equity. See **Equity.**

Lateral railroad. A lateral road is one which proceeds from some point on the main trunk between its terminal. It is but another name for a branch road, both being a part of the main road. An offshoot from main line of railroad. Union Pac. R. Co. v. Anderson, 167 Or. 687, 120 P.2d 578, 588.

Lateral support. The right of lateral and subjacent support is the right to have land supported by the adjoining land or the soil beneath. The right of a landowner to the natural support of his land by adjoining land. The adjoining owner has the duty not to change his land (such as lowering it) so as to cause this support to be weakened or removed.

Laterare /lædərériy/. To lie sideways, in opposition to lying endways; used in descriptions of lands.

Latifundium /lædəfə́ndiyəm/. Lat. In the civil law, great or large possessions; a great or large field; a common. A great estate made up of smaller ones *(fundis),* which began to be common in the latter times of the empire.

Latifundus /lædəfə́ndəs/. A possessor of a large estate made up of smaller ones.

Latin. The language of the ancient Romans. There are three sorts of law Latin: (1) Good Latin, allowed by the grammarians and lawyers; (2) false or incongruous Latin, which in times past would make abate original writs, though it would not make void any judicial writ, declaration, or plea, etc.; (3) words of art, known only to the sages of the law, and not to grammarians, called "Lawyers' Latin."

Latinarius /lædənériyəs/. An interpreter of Latin.

Latini juniani /lətáynay jùwniyéynay/. Lat. In Roman law, a class of freedmen *(libertini)* intermediate between the two other classes of freedmen called, respectively, *"Cives Romani"* and *"Dediticii."*

Latitat /lǽdədət/. In old English practice, a writ which issued in personal actions, on the return of *non est inventus* to a bill of Middlesex; so called from the emphatic word in its recital, in which it was "testified that the defendant *lurks [latitat]* and wanders about" in the county. 3 Bl.Comm. 286. Abolished by St. 2, Wm. IV, c. 39.

Latitatio /lædətéysh(iy)ow/. Lat. In the civil law and old English practice, a lying hid; lurking; or concealment of the person.

Lator /léydər/. Lat. In the civil law, a bearer; a messenger. Also a maker or giver of laws.

Latro /lǽtrow/. Lat. In the civil and old English law, a robber; a thief.

Latrocination /lætrəsənéyshən/. The act of robbing; a depredation.

Latrocinium /lætrəsíniyəm/. The prerogative of adjudging and executing thieves; also larceny; theft; a thing stolen.

Latrociny /lǽtrəsəniy/. Larceny.

Laudare /lòdériy/. Lat. In Civil law, to name; to cite or quote; to show one's title or authority.

In Feudal law, to determine or pass upon judicially. *Laudamentum,* the finding or award of a jury. 2 Bl.Comm. 285.

Laudatio /lòdéysh(iy)ow/. Lat. In Roman law, testimony delivered in court concerning an accused person's good behavior and integrity of life. It resembled the practice which prevails in our trials of calling persons to speak to a prisoner's character. The least number of the *laudatores* among the Romans was ten.

Laudator /lòdéydər/. Lat. An arbitrator; a witness to character.

Laudemium /lòdíymiyəm/. Lat. In the civil law, a sum paid by a new *emphyteuta (q.v.)* who acquires the *emphyteusis,* not as heir, but as a singular successor, whether by gift, devise, exchange, or sale. It was a sum equal to the fiftieth part of the purchase money, paid to the *dominus* or proprietor for his acceptance of the new *emphyteuta.* Called, in old English law, "acknowledgment money."

Laudum /lódəm/. Lat. An arbitrament or award.

Laughe. Frank-pledge.

Launch. The act of launching a vessel; the movement of a vessel from the land into the water, especially the sliding on ways from the stocks on which it is built. An open boat of large size used in any service; a lighter.

Laureate /lóhriyət/. In old English law, an officer of the household of the sovereign, whose business formerly consisted only in composing an ode annually, on the sovereign's birthday, and on the new year; sometimes also, though rarely, on occasion of any remarkable victory.

Laurels /lóhrəlz/. Pieces of gold, coined in 1619, with the king's head laureated; hence the name. See **Jacobus.**

Laus Deo /lós díyow/. Lat. Praise be to God. An old heading to bills of exchange.

Law. That which is laid down, ordained, or established. A rule or method according to which phenomena or actions co-exist or follow each other. Law, in its generic sense, is a body of rules of action or conduct prescribed by controlling authority, and having binding legal force. United States Fidelity and Guaranty Co. v. Guenther, 281 U.S. 34, 50 S.Ct. 165, 74 L.Ed. 683. That which must be obeyed and followed by citizens subject to sanctions or legal consequences is a law. Law is a solemn expression of the will of the supreme power of the State. Calif. Civil Code, § 22.1.

In old English jurisprudence, "law" is used to signify an oath, or the privilege of being sworn; as in the phrases "to wage one's law," "to lose one's law."

The term is also used in opposition to "fact." Thus questions of law are to be decided by the court, while it is the province of the jury to resolve questions of fact.

The word may mean or embrace: body of principles, standards and rules promulgated by government, State ex rel. Conway v. Superior Court within and for Greenlee County, 60 Ariz. 69, 131 P.2d 983, 986; command which obliges a person or persons and obliges generally to acts or forbearances of a class; constitution or constitutional provision, Boston Elevated Ry. Co. v. Commonwealth, 310 Mass. 528, 39 N.E.2d 87, 109; Wickham v. Grand River Dam Authority, 189 Okl. 540, 118 P.2d 640, 643; county ordinance, People v. Ziady, 8 Cal.2d 149, 64 P.2d 425, 430; distinct and complete act of positive law; doctrine or procedure of the common law, from which equity is a departure; enrolled bill attested by presiding officers of two branches of General Assembly, Shannon v. Dean, 279 Ky. 279, 130 S.W.2d 812, 815; general rule of human action, taking cognizance only of external acts, enforced by a determinate authority, which authority is human, and among human authorities is that which is paramount in a political society; grant by Legislature, City of Los Angeles v. Pacific Land Corporation, 41 Cal.App.2d 223, 106 P.2d 242, 244; administrative agency rules and regulations, Columbia Broadcasting System v. United States, 316 U.S. 407, 62 S.Ct. 1194, 1200, 86 L.Ed. 1563; judicial decisions, judgments or decrees, West v. American Telephone & Telegraph Co., 311 U.S. 223, 61 S.Ct. 179, 183, 85 L.Ed. 139; Miller v. Huntington & Ohio Bridge Co., 123 W.Va. 320, 15 S.E.2d 687, 692; U. S. v. Pendergast, D.C.Mo., 35 F.Supp. 593, 599; Monteith Bros. Co. v. U. S., D.C.Ind., 48 F.Supp. 210, 211; law of the state; legislation by initiative method, Opinion of the Justices, 309 Mass. 676, 35 N.E.2d 676, 680; local rules of decision, National Fruit Product Co. v. Dwinell-Wright Co., D.C.Mass., 47 F.Supp. 499, 502; long-established local custom which has the force of law, Dubois v. Hepburn, 35 U.S. (10 Pet.) 1, 9 L.Ed. 325; Bush v. Brenner, D.C.Minn., 29 F.2d 844, 845; municipal ordinance; prescribed rules of action or conduct, U. S. Fidelity & Guaranty Co. v. Guenther, 281 U.S. 34, 50 S.Ct. 165, 166, 74 L.Ed. 683; proclamation of Governor, Williams v. State, 146 Tex. Cr.R. 430, 176 S.W.2d 177, 184; resolution passed by Legislature and approved by Governor, City of Bangor v. Inhabitants of Etna, 140 Me. 85, 34 A.2d 205, 208; revised statutes, W. R. McCullough Life Ins. Co. v. Armstrong, Tex.Civ.App., 158 S.W.2d 585, 586; rule of civil conduct commanding what is right and prohibiting what is wrong, Rich Hill Coal Co. v. Bashore, 334 Pa. 449, 7 A.2d 302, 312; City of Bangor v. Inhabitants of Etna, 140 Me. 85, 34 A.2d 205, 208; rule of civil conduct prescribed by the supreme power in a state, City of Bangor v. Inhabitants of Etna, 140 Me. 85, 34 A.2d 205, 208; rule of conduct prescribed by lawmaking power of state, Board of Education of Union Free School Dist. No. Six of Town of Greenburgh v. Town of Greenburgh, 277 N.Y. 193, 13 N.E.2d 768, 770; rules of court, Department of Finance v. Sheldon, 381 Ill. 256, 44 N.E.2d 863, 864; Goldston v. Karukas, 180 Md. 232, 23 A.2d 691, 692; State ex rel. Conway v. Superior Court within and for Greenlee County, 60 Ariz. 69, 131 P.2d 983, 986; rules of decision commonly accepted and acted upon by bar and inferior courts, West v. American Telephone

& Telegraph Co., Ohio, 311 U.S. 223, 61 S.Ct. 179, 183, 85 L.Ed. 139; rules promulgated by government, State ex rel. Conway v. Superior Court within and for Greenlee County, 60 Ariz. 69, 131 P.2d 983, 986; science or system of principles or rules of human conduct; Secretary of the Treasury regulations, In re Deyo's Estate, 180 Misc. 32, 42 N.Y.S.2d 379, 386; statute laws as construed by highest courts of state, National City Bank v. National Sec. Co., C.C.A.Tenn., 58 F.2d 7, 9; statute or enactment of legislative body, Shute v. Frohmiller, 53 Ariz. 483, 90 P.2d 998, 1001; State ex rel. McKittrick v. Missouri Public Service Commission, 252 Mo. 29, 175 S.W.2d 857, 861; United States law, U. S. v. Wagner, C.C.A.Cal., 93 F.2d 77, 79; War Department regulations, Standard Oil Co. of California v. Johnson, Cal., 316 U.S. 481, 62 S.Ct. 1168, 1169, 86 L.Ed. 1611.

A concurrent or joint resolution of legislature is not "a law", Koenig v. Flynn, 258 N.Y. 292, 179 N.E. 705, 707; Ward v. State, 176 Okl. 368, 56 P.2d 136, 137; a resolution of the house of representatives is not a "law", State ex rel. Todd v. Yelle, 7 Wash.2d 443, 110 P.2d 162, 165; an unconstitutional statute is not a "law", Flournoy v. First Nat. Bank of Shreveport, 197 La. 1067, 3 So.2d 244, 248.

With reference to its origin, "law" is derived either from judicial precedents, from legislation, or from custom.

As to the different kinds of law, or law regarded in its different aspects, see Absolute law; Adjective law; Administrative law; Arms, law of; Bankruptcy Act; Canon (*Canon law*); Case law; Citations, law of; Civil law; Commercial law; Common law; Conclusion of law; Conflicts of laws; Constitutional law; Criminal law; Custom and usage; Ecclesiastical law; Edict; Enabling statute; Equity; Evidence, law of; Flag, law of; Foreign laws; Forest law; General law; International law; Local law; Maritime; Maritime law; Marque, law of; Martial law; Mercantile law; Military law; Moral law; Municipal law; Natural law; Oleron, laws of; Ordinance; Organic law; Parliamentary law; Penal laws; Positive law; Private law; Probate; Procedural law; Prospective law; Public law; Remedial laws and statutes; Retrospective law; Revenue law or measure; Road (*Law of the road*); Roman law; Special law; Staple (*Law of the staple*); Statute; Substantive law; Unwritten law; War; Written law.

For "facts" and "law" as distinguishable, see **Fact.** For practice of law, see **Practice.**

Law arbitrary. Opposed to *immutable,* a law not founded in the nature of things, but imposed by the mere will of the legislature.

Law court of appeals. An appellate tribunal, formerly existing in the state of South Carolina, for hearing appeals from the courts of law.

Law day. See **Day.**

Law department. Department having charge of law business of government. See **Judicial branch.**

Law enforcement officer. Those whose duty it is to preserve the peace. Frazier v. Elmore, 180 Tenn. 232, 173 S.W.2d 563, 565. See also **Police officer; sheriff.**

Law French. The Norman French language, introduced into England by William the Conqueror. For several centuries, it was, in an emphatic sense, the language of the English law. It is called by Blackstone a "barbarous dialect," and the later specimens of it fully warrant the appellation, but at the time of its introduction it was, as has been observed, the best form of the language spoken in Normandy.

Lawful. Legal; warranted or authorized by the law; having the qualifications prescribed by law; not contrary to nor forbidden by the law.

The principal distinction between the terms "lawful" and "legal" is that the former contemplates the substance of law, the latter the form of law. To say of an act that it is "lawful" implies that it is authorized, sanctioned, or at any rate not forbidden, by law. To say that it is "legal" implies that it is done or performed in accordance with the forms and usages of law, or in a technical manner. In this sense "illegal" approaches the meaning of "invalid." For example, a contract or will, executed without the required formalities, might be said to be invalid or illegal, but could not be described as unlawful. Further, the word "lawful" more clearly implies an ethical content than does "legal." The latter goes no further than to denote compliance, with positive, technical, or formal rules; while the former usually imports a moral substance or ethical permissibility. A further distinction is that the word "legal" is used as the synonym of "constructive," which "lawful" is not. Thus "legal fraud" is fraud implied or inferred by law, or made out by construction. "Lawful fraud" would be a contradiction of terms. Again, "legal" is used as the antithesis of "equitable." Thus, we speak of "legal assets," "legal estate," etc., but not of "lawful assets," "legal assets," or "lawful estate." But there are some connections in which the two words are used as exact equivalents. Thus, a "lawful" writ, warrant, or process is the same as a "legal" writ, warrant, or process.

See also **Legal; Legitimate; Valid.**

Lawful age. Full age, legal age, majority; generally 18 years of age, though the "lawful age" for certain acts (*e.g.* drinking, driving motor vehicle, etc.) may vary from state to state. See also **Capacity.**

Lawful arrest. The taking of a person into legal custody either under a valid warrant or on probable cause for believing that he has committed a crime or under civil process which permits his arrest; *e.g.* capias for arrest of debtor. Term is used in connection with right to search a person and his immediate surroundings without a warrant as an incident of the arrest. Chimel v. California, 395 U.S. 752, 89 S.Ct. 2034, 23 L.Ed.2d 685. See **Arrest; Probable cause; Search; Search-warrant.**

Lawful authorities. Those persons who have right to exercise public power, to require obedience to their lawful commands, to command or act in the public name; *e.g.* police.

Lawful cause. Legitimate reason for acting, based on the law or on the evidence in a particular case as contrasted with acting on a whim or out of prejudice, or for a reason not recognized by the law. See also **Cause of action.**

Lawful damages. Such damages as the law fixes and are ascertainable in a court of law. Carr v. U. S., D.C.Ky., 28 F.Supp. 236, 241. See **Damages.**

Lawful dependents. Term generally associated with allowances or benefits from public (*e.g.* Social Security benefits) or private funds to those who qualify as dependents and whose dependency is within the terms of the law which govern the distribution. See also **Dependent; Legal dependent.**

Lawful discharge. Such a discharge in insolvency as exonerates the debtor from his debts; *e.g.* discharge pursuant to bankruptcy proceeding.

Lawful entry. An entry on real estate, by one out of possession, under claim or color of right and without force or fraud. An entry of premises pursuant to a search warrant. See **Ejection; Eviction; Process** (*Summary process*).

Lawful goods. Property which may be legally held, sold, or exported; non-contraband property.

Lawful heirs. See **Heirs.**

Lawful issue. As used in will the words primarily and generally mean descendants, In re Marsh's Will, 143 Misc. 609, 257 N.Y.S. 514, 521; including descendants more remote than children. In re Woodcock's Will, Sur., 55 N.Y.S.2d 656, 658. At common law, the term includes only those who were children of legally recognized subsisting marriage. In re Sheffer's Will, 139 Misc. 519, 249 N.Y.S. 102, 105. Lawful descendants; lineal descendants by blood; heirs. In re Sheffer's Will, 139 Misc. 519, 249 N.Y.S. 102, 104. See **Descendent; Heirs; Issue.**

Lawful man. A freeman, unattainted, and capable of bearing oath; a *legalis homo.*

Lawful money. Money which is a legal tender in payment of debts. See **Legal tender.**

Lawful representatives. Where real property is involved as subject-matter, term "lawful representatives" includes or means legal heirs. Where personal property is involved the term, when not qualified by context, is limited to executors and administrators.

Law latin. The corrupt form of the Latin language employed in the old English lawbooks and legal proceedings.

Lawless. Not subject to law; not controlled by law; not authorized by law; not observing the rules and forms of law.

Law list. A publication compiling the names and addresses of those engaged in the practice of law and information of interest to the legal profession often including the courts, court calendars, lawyers engaged in specialized fields (as admiralty or patent law), public officers, stenographers, handwriting experts, private investigators, or abstracts of law; a legal directory. The "Law Directory", as published by Martindale-Hubbell, is the most comprehensive national listing of attorneys. There are also available listings or directories for the individual states and also for many of the larger cities.

Law lords. Peers in the British parliament who have held high judicial office, or have been distinguished in the legal profession; *i.e.* a puisne judge of the High Court or higher office.

Law martial. See **Martial law.**

Law merchant. See **Commercial law; Mercantile law; Uniform Commercial Code.**

Law of a general nature. One which relates to a subject that may exist throughout the state; one whose subject-matter is common to all the people. Panhandle Eastern Pipe Line Co. v. Board of Com'rs of Miami County, 151 Kan. 533, 99 P.2d 828, 829.

Law of arms. See **Arms, law of.**

Law of capture. Under "law of capture," landowner does not own migratory substances underlying his land, but has exclusive right to drill for, produce, or otherwise gain possession of such substances, subject only to restrictions and regulations pursuant to police power. Frost v. Ponca City, Okl., 541 P.2d 1321, 1323.

Law of citations. See **Citations, law of.**

Law of evidence. See **Evidence, law of.**

Law of marque. See **Marque, law of.**

Law of nations. See **International law.**

Law of nature. See **Natural law.**

Law of the case. Term "law of the case," as generally used, designates the principle that if an appellate court has passed on a legal question and remanded the cause to the court below for further proceedings, the legal question thus determined by the appellate court will not be differently determined on a subsequent appeal in the same case where the facts remain the same. Allen v. Michigan Bell Tel. Co., 61 Mich. App. 62, 232 N.W.2d 302, 303. Doctrine of "law of the case" provides that when appellate court has rendered a decision and states in its opinion a rule of law necessary to decision, that rule is to be followed in all subsequent proceedings in the same action. People v. Scott, 16 Cal.3d 242, 128 Cal.Rptr. 39, 44, 546 P.2d 327. Doctrine is that principle under which determination of questions of law will generally be held to govern case throughout all its subsequent stages where such determination has already been made on a prior appeal to a court of last resort. Transport Ins. Co. v. Employers Cas. Co., Tex.Civ. App., 470 S.W.2d 757, 762. The doctrine expresses practice of courts generally to refuse to reopen what has been decided. White v. Higgins, C.C.A.Mass., 116 F.2d 312, 317, 318; Fleming v. Campbell, 148 Kan. 516, 83 P.2d 708, 709. It expresses the rule that final judgment of highest court is final determination of parties' rights.

Doctrine of "law of the case" is one of policy only and will be disregarded when compelling circumstances call for a redetermination of the determination of point of law on prior appeal, and this is particularly true where intervening or contemporaneous change in law has occurred by overruling former decisions or establishment of new precedent by controlling authority. Ryan v. Mike-Ron Corp., Cal.

App., 63 Cal.Rptr. 601, 605. Doctrine is merely a rule of procedure and does not go to the power of the court, and will not be adhered to where its application will result in an unjust decision. People v. Medina, Cal., 99 Cal.Rptr. 630, 635, 492 P.2d 686.

Instructions. It has been held that instructions are the "law of the case" where appealing defendant accepted instructions as correct, Ætna Life Ins. Co. v. McAdoo, C.C.A.Ark., 115 F.2d 369, 370; where such were approved on former appeal and given at second trial, Whitehead v. Stith, 279 Ky. 556, 131 S.W.2d 455, 460; where instructions were not challenged in any manner or in any particular, New York Life Ins. Co. v. Stone, C.C.A.Mass., 80 F.2d 614, 616; Codd v. New York Underwriters Ins. Co., 19 Wash.2d 671, 144 P.2d 234, 237; where no objections or exceptions taken, Miller v. Mohr, 198 Wash. 619, 89 P.2d 807, 814; Chancellor v. Hines Motor Supply Co., 104 Mont. 603, 69 P.2d 764, 769.

Law of the flag. See **Flag, law of.**

Law of the land. Due process of law (*q.v.*). By the law of the land is most clearly intended the general law which hears before it condemns, which proceeds upon inquiry, and renders judgment only after trial. Dupuy v. Tedora, 204 La. 560, 15 So.2d 886, 891. The meaning is that every citizen shall hold his life, liberty, property, and immunities under the protection of general rules which govern society. See **Due process of law.**

Law of the road. See **Road** (*Law of the road*).

Law of the staple. See **Staple** (*Law of the staple*).

Law questions. Issues or questions in a case which do not require findings of fact but are addressed to the judge for application of the law. In those instances wherein the law depends on the facts, the factual questions are first decided and then the law is applied to the facts as found by the judge or jury.

Law reporters or **reports.** Published volumes containing the decisions and opinions of state and federal courts; *e.g.* National Reporter System. Commonly such decisions are first published in advance sheets and thereafter in bound reports or reporter volumes. Law reports or reporters may be either official (published by the state or federal government) or unofficial (published by private publisher).

Law review. A publication of most law schools containing lead articles on topical subjects by law professors, judges or attorneys, and case summaries by law review member-students. Normally only honor or top law students are members of the law review staff.

Laws. Rules promulgated by government as a means to an ordered society. Strictly speaking, session laws or statutes and not decisions of court; though in common usage refers to both legislative and court made law, as well as to administrative rules, regulations and ordinances. See also **Law.**

Law School Admissions Test. See **LSAT.**

Laws of oleron. See **Oleron, laws of.**

Laws of the several states. As used in statute requiring federal courts to apply laws of the several states, includes not only state statutory law, but also state decisions on questions of general law. Erie R. Co. v. Tompkins, 304 U.S. 64, 58 S.Ct. 817, 822, 82 L.Ed. 1188.

Laws of war. See **War.**

Law spiritual. The ecclesiastical law, or law Christian. See also **Ecclesiastical law.**

Lawsuit. A vernacular term for a suit, action, or cause instituted or depending between two private persons in the courts of law. A suit at law or in equity; an action or proceeding in a civil court; a process in law instituted by one party to compel another to do him justice. Shepherd v. Standard Motor Co., 263 Ky. 329, 92 S.W.2d 337. See also **Action; Cause of action.**

Law worthy. Being entitled to, or having the benefit and protection of, the law.

Lawyer. A person learned in the law; as an attorney, counsel, or solicitor; a person licensed to practice law. Any person who prosecutes or defends causes in courts of record or other judicial tribunals of the United States, or of any of the states, or whose business it is to give legal advice or assistance in relation to any cause or matter whatever. See also **Attorney; House counsel.** For right to attorney, see **Counsel, right to.**

Lay, n. A share of the profits of a fishing or whaling voyage, allotted to the officers and seamen, in the nature of wages. See also **Lay system.**

Lay, adj. Relating to persons or things not clerical or ecclesiastical; a person not in ecclesiastical orders. Also non-professional. See also **Layman.**

Lay, v. To state or allege in pleading.

Layaway. To hold goods for future sale. An agreement by a retail seller with a consumer to retain specified consumer goods for sale to the consumer at a specified price, in earnest of which sale the consumer has deposited with the retail seller an agreed upon sum of money, and any other terms and conditions not contrary to law which are mutually agreed upon.

Lay corporation. See **Corporation.**

Lay damages. To state at the conclusion of the complaint declaration the amount of damages which the plaintiff claims. See **Ad damnum.**

Lay days. In the law of shipping, days allowed to charter-parties for loading and unloading the cargo.

Laye /léy/. Fr. Law.

Lay fee. A fee held by ordinary feudal tenure, as distinguished from the ecclesiastical tenure of *frank-almoign,* by which an ecclesiastical corporation held of the donor. The tenure of *frankalmoign* is reserved by St. 12, Car. II, which abolished military tenures. 2 Bl.Comm. 101.

Lay impropriator. In English ecclesiastical law, a lay person holding a spiritual appropriation.

Laying foundation. In law of evidence, the practice or requirement of introducing evidence of things necessary to make further evidence relevant, material or competent; *e.g.* the hypothetical question propounded before an expert is permitted to render his opinion. See Fed.Evid.R. 104.

Laying the venue. Stating in the complaint or declaration the district or county in which the plaintiff proposes that the trial of the action shall take place.

Lay investiture. In Ecclesiastical law, the ceremony of putting a bishop in possession of the temporalities of his diocese.

Lay judge. A judge who is not learned in the law, *i.e.,* not a lawyer; employed in some of the states as assessors or assistants to the presiding judges in the *nisi prius* courts or courts of first instance. Many justices of the peace are, or were, not lawyers.

Layman. One of the people, and not one of the clergy; one who is not of a particular profession (*i.e.* non-lawyer).

Layoff. A termination of employment at the will of employer. Such may be temporary (*e.g.* caused by seasonal or adverse economic conditions) or permanent.

Lay people. Jurymen.

Lay system. As applied to fishing vessels, exists where the fish caught are sold at auction and from the proceeds is deducted charges for supplies furnished and balance distributed to the master and the crew.

Lay witness. Person called to give testimony who does not possess any expertise in the matters about which he testifies. Used in contrast to expert witness who may render an opinion based on his expert knowledge if proper foundation is laid. Generally, such non-expert testimony in the form of opinions or inferences is limited to those opinions or inferences which are (a) rationally based on the perception of the witness (*i.e.* first-hand knowledge or observation) and (b) helpful to a clear understanding of his testimony or the determination of a fact at issue. Fed.Evid.R. 701. See **Opinion evidence or testimony.**

Lazzi. A Saxon term for persons of a servile condition.

L.C. An abbreviation which may stand either for "Lord Chancellor," "Lower Canada," or "Leading Cases."

LEAA. Law Enforcement Assistance Act.

Lead counsel. The counsel on either side of a litigated action who is charged with the principal management and direction of the party's case, as distinguished from his juniors or subordinates, is said to "lead in the cause," and is termed the "leading counsel" on that side. May also refer to chief or primary attorney in class action or multi-district litigation.

Leading a use. In common law, where a deed was executed before the levy of a fine of land, for the purpose of specifying to whose use the fine should inure, it was said to "lead" the use. If executed after the fine, it was said to "declare" the use. 2 Bl.Comm. 363.

Leading case. Among the various cases that are argued and determined in the courts, some, from their important character, have demanded more than usual attention from the judges, and from this circumstance are frequently looked upon as having settled or determined the law upon all points involved in such cases, and as guides for subsequent decisions, and from the importance they thus acquire are familiarly termed "leading cases."

Leading object rule. If the leading object or main purpose of a person's promise to answer for the debt of another is the promisor's own benefit, such promise need not be in writing as required by the statute of frauds; sometimes known as the "main purpose" doctrine.

Leading question. One which instructs witness how to answer or puts into his mouth words to be echoed back, People v. Hamilton, Gen.Sess., 30 N.Y.S.2d 155, 158; one which suggests to witness answer desired. Little v. State, 79 Okl.Cr. 285, 154 P.2d 772, 777; State v. Scott, 20 Wash.2d 696, 149 P.2d 152, 153, 154; Landers v. State, 118 Tex.Cr.R. 608, 39 S.W.2d 43, 44.

Leading questions should not be used on the direct examination of a witness except as may be necessary to develop his testimony. Ordinarily leading questions should be permitted on cross-examination. When a party calls a hostile witness, an adverse party, or a witness identified with an adverse party, interrogation may be by leading questions. Fed. Evid.R. 611(c).

League. An association or treaty of alliance between different nations, states, organizations, sports teams, or parties. See also **Compact; Treaty.**

A measure of distance, varying in different countries (equal to about three statute miles).

Leakage. The waste or diminution of a liquid caused by its leaking from the cask, barrel, or other vessel in which it was placed. Also an allowance made to an importer of liquids, at the custom-house, in the collection of duties, for his loss sustained by the leaking of the liquid from its cask or vessel.

Leal /l(w)eyál/. L. Fr. Loyal; that which belongs to the law.

Lealte /líy(ə)ltiy/. L. Fr. Legality; the condition of a *legalis homo,* or lawful man.

Lean. To incline in opinion or preference. A court is sometimes said to "lean against" a doctrine, construction, or view contended for, whereby it is meant that the court regards it with disfavor or repugnance, because of its inexpedience, injustice, or inconsistency.

Leap-year. See **Bissextile.**

Learn. To gain knowledge or information of; to ascertain by inquiry, study, or investigation.

Learned. Possessing learning; erudite; versed in the law; informed. In statutes prescribing the qualifications of judges, "learned in the law" designates one who has received a regular legal education, the almost invariable evidence of which is the fact of his admission to the bar.

Learning. Legal doctrine.

Lease. Any agreement which gives rise to relationship of landlord and tenant (real property) or lessor and lessee (real or personal property). Smith v. Royal Ins. Co., C.C.A.Cal., 111 F.2d 667, 671. Contract for exclusive possession of lands or tenements for determinate period. Contract for possession and profits of lands and tenements either for life, or for certain period of time, or during the pleasure of the parties. Intermountain Realty Co. v. Allen, 60 Idaho 228, 90 P.2d 704, 706. Conveyance, grant or devise of realty for designated period with reversion to grantor. Conveyance of interest in real property for specified period or at will. Conveyance or grant of estate in real property for limited term with conditions attached. State ex rel. St. Louis County v. Evans, 346 Mo. 209, 139 S.W.2d 967, 969; Holcombe v. Lorino, 124 Tex. 446, 79 S.W.2d 307, 310. Conveyance, usually in consideration of rent or other recompense, for life, years, or at will, Smith v. Royal Ins. Co., C.C.A.Cal., 111 F.2d 667, 671; Clark v. Harry, 182 Va. 410, 29 S.E.2d 231, 233; but always for a less time than lessor has in the premises. Leonard v. Autocar Sales & Service Co., 325 Ill.App. 375, 60 N.E.2d 457, 462.

When used with reference to tangible personal property, word "lease" means a contract by which one owning such property grants to another the right to possess, use and enjoy it for specified period of time in exchange for periodic payment of a stipulated price, referred to as rent. Undercofler v. Whiteway Neon Ad, Inc., 114 Ga.App. 644, 152 S.E.2d 616, 618.

The Federal Consumer Leasing Act provides for certain disclosure requirements in consumer leases. 15 U.S.C.A. § 1667 et seq. In addition, certain states require that consumer (*e.g.* residential) leases be written in "plain language." See McKinney's (N.Y.) Consol.Laws, Gen Obl, § 5–702.

The person who conveys is termed the "lessor," and the person to whom conveyed, the "lessee;" and when the lessor conveys lands or tenements to a lessee, he is said to lease, demise, or let them. The word when used as verb, means to transfer for term specified therein from lessor to lessee property therein demised, also to let, to farm out, to rent.

See also Assignable lease; Building lease; Community lease; Demise; Graduated lease; Ground lease; Mining lease; Net lease; Percentage lease; Sale and leaseback; Sandwich lease; Under lease. For "Extension of lease," see **Extension.**

Concurrent lease. One granted for a term which is to commence before the expiration or other determination of a previous lease of the same premises made to another person; or, in other words, an assignment of a part of the reversion, entitling the lessee to all the rents accruing on the previous lease after the date of his lease and to appropriate remedies against the holding tenant.

Gross lease. Lease in which lessee pays a flat sum for rent out of which the lessor is required to pay all expenses such as taxes, water, utilities, insurance, etc.

Lease and release. A species of conveyance much used in England, said to have been invented by Serjeant Moore, soon after the enactment of the Statute of Uses. It is thus contrived: A lease, or rather bargain and sale upon some pecuniary consideration for one year, is made by the tenant of the freehold to the lessee or bargainee. This, without any enrolment, makes the bargainor stand seised to the use of the bargainee, and vests in the bargainee the use of the term for one year, and then the statute immediately annexes the possession. Being thus in possession, he is capable of receiving a release of the freehold and reversion, which must be made to the tenant in possession, and accordingly the next day a release is granted to him. The lease and release, when used as a conveyance of the fee, have the joint operation of a single conveyance. 2 Bl.Comm. 339. By the Law of Property Act of 1925 all lands and all interests therein now lie in grant only.

Long term lease. See **Ground rent.**

Master lease. A lease controlling subsequent leases.

Mineral lease. Lease in which the lessee acquires the right to work a mine of oil or gas, etc. The rent is commonly based on the amount or value of the mineral withdrawn.

Mining lease. See **Mining.**

Month to month lease. Tenancy where no lease is involved, rent being paid monthly. Statutes often require one month's notice to landlord of intent to terminate such tenancy.

Net lease. Lease which requires the tenant to pay, in addition to rent, the expenses of the leased property, *e.g.* taxes, insurance, maintenance, etc.

Net-net-net lease. Lease in which the lessee pays all the expenses including mortgage interest and amortization leaving the lessor with an amount free of all claims.

Parol lease. A lease of real estate not evidenced by writing, but resting in an oral agreement.

Percentage lease. A percentage lease is one in which the amount of rent is based upon a percentage of the gross or net profits of the lessee's business, or of his gross sales, with a stipulated minimum rent. Such leases are mainly used where location of the property is an important part of its value (*e.g.* in shopping center).

Perpetual lease. A lease of lands which may last without limitation as to time; a grant of lands in fee with the reservation of a rent in fee; a fee-farm.

Sublease, or underlease. One executed by the lessee of an estate to a third person, conveying the same estate for a shorter term than that for which the lessee holds it.

Leaseback. Transaction whereby transferor sells property and later leases it back. In a sale-leaseback situation, for example, R would sell property to S and subsequently lease such property from S. Thus, R becomes the lessee and S the lessor.

Leasehold. An estate in realty held under a lease. The four principal types of leasehold estates are the estate for years, periodic tenancy, tenancy at will, and tenancy at sufferance. The asset representing the right of the lessee to use leased property.

Leasehold improvements. Improvements made by lessee. The term is used in condemnation proceedings to determine the portion of the award to which the lessee is entitled. See also **Tenant improvements.**

Leasehold interest. The interest which the lessee has in the value of the lease itself in condemnation award determination. The difference between the total remaining rent under the lease, and the rent lessee would currently pay for similar space for the same time period. See also **Leasehold value; No bonus clause.**

Leasehold mortgage. See **Mortgage.**

Leasehold mortgage bond. See **Bond.**

Leasehold value. The value of a leasehold interest. Usually applies to a long term lease when market rental for similar space is higher than rent paid under the lease. Some states allow the lessee to claim the leasehold value against the landlord in eminent domain proceedings, unless specifically prohibited by the lease itself. Other states, by statute, do not allow for such a claim. See also **No bonus clause.**

Lease with option to purchase. A lease under which the lessee has the right to purchase the property. The price and terms of the purchase must be set forth for the option to be valid. The option may run for the length of the lease period.

Leaute /l(w)èyowtéy/. L. Fr. Legality; sufficiency in law.

Leave, *v.* To give. To allow or cause to remain; to let remain, unmoved or undone; to refrain from or neglect taking, doing, or changing; to let stay or continue; to let be without interference; to suffer to remain subject to another's action, control, or the like; to suffer to be undisturbed in action. To give or dispose of by will; to bequeath or devise. To put, place, deposit, deliver, or the like.

Leave, *n.* Permission or authorization to do something.

Willful departure with intent to remain away, and not temporary absence with intention of returning. See also **Desertion.**

Leave and license. A defense to an action in trespass setting up the consent of the plaintiff to the trespass complained of.

Leave no issue. Not survived by a child or children or their descendants. A spouse of a deceased child is not "issue" (*q.v.*). In re Vigil's Estate, 38 N.M. 383, 34 P.2d 667, 668.

Leave of absence. Temporary absence from employment or duty with intention to return during which time remuneration and seniority may or may not be suspended. State ex rel. McGaughey v. Grayston, 349 Mo. 700, 163 S.W.2d 335, 341. See also **Furlough; Sick leave.**

Leave of court. Permission obtained from a court to take some action which, without such permission, would not be allowable; as, to receive an extension of time to answer complaint. Fed.R.Civil P. 6.

Leccator /ləkéydər/. A debauched person.

Lecherwite, lairwite, or **legerwite** /lécherwàyt/ lérwayt/léjərwàyt/. At common law, a fine for adultery or fornication, anciently paid to the lords of certain manors.

Le congrès /lə koŋgrés/. A species of proof on charges of impotency in France, *coitus coram testibus.* Abolished in 1677.

Le contrat fait la loi /lə kontrá féy la lwá/. The contract makes the law.

Ledger /léjər/. A book of accounts in which a merchant records transactions; there being two parallel columns in each account, one for the entries to the debit of the person charged, the other for his credits. Into this book are posted the items from the books of original entry or journals. A "ledger" is the principal book of accounts of a business establishment in which all the transactions of each day are entered under appropriate heads so as to show at a glance the debits and credits of each account. Foothill Ditch Co. v. Wallace Ranch Water Co., 25 Cal.App.2d 555, 78 P.2d 215, 220.

Ledo /líydow/. The rising water or increase of the sea.

Leet. In English law, the name of a court of criminal jurisdiction, formerly of much importance, but latterly fallen into disuse. See **Court-Leet.**

Left. To let remain or have remaining at death; to transmit, bequeath or give by will. Grimes v. Crouch, 175 Va. 126, 7 S.E.2d 115, 117. See also **Bequest; Devise; Leave; Legacy.**

Legabilis /ləgéybələs/. In old English law, that which may be bequeathed.

Legacy. A disposition of personalty by will. A bequest.

In a technical sense and strictly construed, "legacy" is a gift or bequest by will of personal property, whereas a "devise" is a testamentary disposition of real estate, but such distinction will not be permitted to defeat the intent of a testator, and such terms may be construed interchangeably or applied indifferently to either personalty or real estate if the context of the will shows that such was the intention of the testator. Festorazzi v. First Nat. Bank of Mobile, 288 Ala. 645, 264 So.2d 496, 505.

See also Ademption; Bequest; Cumulative legacies; Devise; Legatee; Vested legacy.

Absolute legacy. One given without condition and intended to vest immediately.

Accumulative legacy. A second, double, or additional legacy; a legacy given in addition to another given by the same instrument, or by another instrument.

Additional legacy. One given to the same legatee in addition to (and not in lieu of) another legacy given before by the same will or in a codicil thereto.

Alternate legacy. One by which the testator gives one of two or more things without designating which.

Conditional legacy. One which is liable to take effect or to be defeated according to the occurrence or non-occurrence of some uncertain event.

Contingent legacy. A legacy given to a person at a future uncertain time, that may or may not arrive; as "at his age of twenty-one," or "if" or "when he attains twenty-one." A legacy made dependent upon some uncertain event. A legacy which has not vested.

Cumulative legacies. These are legacies so called to distinguish them from legacies which are merely repeated. In the construction of testamentary instruments, the question often arises whether, where a testator has twice bequeathed a legacy to the same person, the legatee is entitled to both, or only to one of them; in other words, whether the second legacy must be considered as a mere repetition of the first, or as cumulative, *i.e.,* additional. In determining this question, the intention of the testator, if it appears on the face of the instrument, prevails.

Demonstrative legacy. A bequest of a certain sum of money, with a direction that it shall be paid out of a particular fund. It differs from a specific legacy in this respect: that, if the fund out of which it is payable fails for any cause, it is nevertheless entitled to come on the estate as a general legacy. And it differs from a general legacy in this: that it does not abate in that class, but in the class of specific legacies. Kenaday v. Sinnott, 179 U.S. 606, 21 S.Ct. 233, 45 L.Ed. 339. A bequest of a certain sum of money, stock, or other property, payable out of a particular fund of property or security, but it can neither amount to a gift of the corpus nor serve the purpose of releasing the estate from liability in event particular fund or property should fail. In re Jeffcott's Estate, Fla.App., 186 So.2d 80, 83. A legacy of quantity is ordinarily a general legacy; but there are legacies of quantity in the nature of specific legacies, as of so much money, with reference to a particular fund for payment. This kind of legacy is called by the civilians a "demonstrative legacy," and it is so far general and differs so much in effect from one properly specific that, if the fund be called in or fail, the legatee will not be deprived of his legacy, but be permitted to receive it out of the general assets; yet the legacy is so far specific that it will not be liable to abate with general legacies upon a deficiency of assets.

General legacy. A pecuniary legacy, payable out of the general assets of a testator. One so given as not to amount to a bequest of a particular thing or particular money of the testator, distinguished from others of the same kind; one of quantity merely, not specific.

Indefinite legacy. One which passes property by a general or collective term, without enumeration of number or quantity; as, a bequest of "all" the testator's "goods," or his "bank stock."

Lapsed legacy. Where the legatee dies before the testator, or before the legacy is payable, the bequest is said to *lapse.* Such legacy then falls into residue unless there is an anti-lapse statute in which case the legacy passes to the issue of the legatee. See **Lapse statutes.**

Modal legacy. A bequest accompanied by directions as to the mode or manner in which it shall be applied for the legatee's benefit, *e.g.,* a legacy to A. to buy him a house.

Pecuniary legacy. A bequest of a sum of money, or of an annuity. It may or may not specify the fund from which it is to be drawn. It is none the less a pecuniary legacy if it comprises the specific pieces of money in a designated receptacle, as a purse or chest.

Residuary legacy. A bequest of all the testator's personal estate not otherwise effectually disposed of by his will. A bequest of "all the rest, residue, and remainder" of the personal property after payment of debts and satisfaction of the particular legacies. Legacy containing assets after other legacies and estate debts and costs of administration have been paid. Alston v. U. S., C.A.Ga., 349 F.2d 87, 89.

Special legacy. A "specific legacy" *(q.v.)* is sometimes so called.

Specific legacy. One which operates on property particularly designated. A legacy or gift by will of a particular specified thing, as of a horse, a piece of furniture, a term of years, and the like. In a strict sense, a legacy of a particular chattel, which is specified and distinguished from all other chattels of the testator of the same kind; as of a horse of a certain color. A legacy of a quantity of chattels described collectively; as a gift of all the testator's pictures. A legacy is specific, when it is limited to a particular thing, subject, or chose in action, so identified as to render the bequest inapplicable to any other; as the bequest of a horse, a picture, or jewel, or a debt due from a person named, and, in special cases, even of a sum of money.

Trust legacy. A bequest of personal property to trustees to be held upon trust; as, to pay the annual income to a beneficiary for life.

Universal legacy. In the civil law, a testamentary disposition by which the testator gives to one or several persons the whole of the property which he leaves at his decease.

Void legacy. Term formerly used to describe legacy given to one who died before execution of will. Now, such legacy is considered a lapsed legacy and is treated as such. See **Legacy** (*Lapsed legacy*).

Legacy duty. A duty formerly imposed in England upon personal property (other than leaseholds) devolving under any will or intestacy.

Legacy or **succession tax.** An excise on privilege of taking property by will or inheritance or by succession on death of owner. In re Rosing's Estate, 337 Mo. 544, 85 S.W.2d 495, 496; State Tax Commission v. Backman, 88 Utah 424, 55 P.2d 171, 174. See also **Inheritance tax.**

Legal. 1. Conforming to the law; according to law; required or permitted by law; not forbidden or discountenanced by law; good and effectual in law. Freeman v. Fowler Packing Co., 135 Kan. 378, 11 P.2d 276, 277. See **Lawful; Valid.**

2. Proper or sufficient to be recognized by the law; cognizable in the courts; competent or adequate to fulfill the requirements of the law.

3. Cognizable in courts of law, as distinguished from courts of equity; construed or governed by the rules and principles of law, in contradistinction to rules of equity. With the merger in most states of law and equity courts, this distinction generally no longer exists. Rule of Civil Proc. 2.

4. Posited by the courts as the inference or imputation of the law, as a matter of construction, rather than established by actual proof; *e.g.,* legal malice.

5. Created by law.

6. Lawful; of or pertaining to law. Kinsley v. Herald & Globe Ass'n, 113 Vt. 272, 34 A.2d 99, 101.

As to legal Consideration; Damages; Day; Debt; Defense; Demand; Disability; Discretion; Estate; Incapacity; Irregularity; Memory; Mortgage; Process; Relevancy; Remedy; Reversion, and Tender, see those titles.

Legal acumen /líygəl əkyúwmən/. The doctrine of legal acumen is that if a defect in, or invalidity of, a claim to land is such as to require legal acumen to discover it, whether it appears upon the face of the record or proceedings, or is to be proved aliunde, then the powers or jurisdiction of a court of equity may be invoked to remove the cloud created by such defect or invalidity.

Legal age. The age at which the person acquires full capacity to make his own contracts and deeds and transact business generally (age of majority) or to enter into some particular contract or relation, as the "legal age of consent" to marriage. The age at which a person may enter into binding contracts or commit other legal acts. In most states a minor reaches legal age or majority (*i.e.,* becomes of age) at age 18; though for certain acts (*e.g.* drinking) it may be higher, and for others (*e.g.* driving) it may be lower. See also **Capacity; Majority.**

Legal aid. Country-wide system administered locally by which legal services are rendered to those in financial need and who cannot afford private counsel. See **Counsel, right to; Legal Services Corporation; Public defender.**

Legal assets. That portion of the assets of a deceased party which by law is directly liable, in the hands of his executor or administrator, to the payment of debts and legacies. Such assets as can be reached in the hands of an executor or administrator, by a suit at law against him.

Legal brief. Document containing brief statement of facts of case, issues and arguments; used most commonly on appeal, but also used at trial level (trial brief) when requested by trial judge. Content of appellate briefs is usually governed by court rules; *e.g.* Fed.R.App.P. 28–32. See also **Brief.**

Legal capacity to sue. Right to come into court. Mac-Affer v. Boston & M.R.R., 242 App.Div. 140, 273 N.Y.S. 679; American Home Benefit Ass'n v. United American Benefit Ass'n, 63 Idaho 754, 125 P.2d 1010, 1016. It is not necessary in pleadings to aver the capacity of a party to sue or be sued, except to the extent required to show the jurisdiction of the court. A party desiring to raise the issue of lack of capacity shall do so by specific negative averment. Fed.R.Civil P. 9(a). See also **Capacity; Standing to sue doctrine.**

Legal capital. Par or stated value of issued capital stock. The amount of contributed capital that, according to state law, must remain permanently in the firm as protection for creditors. Property sufficient to balance capital stock liability. Crocker v. Waltham Watch Co., 315 Mass. 397, 53 N.E.2d 230, 238.

Legal cause. Proximate cause *(q.v.)*. Substantial factor in bringing about harm. Krauss v. Greenbarg, C.C.A.Pa., 137 F.2d 569, 572; Giles v. Moundridge Milling Co., 351 Mo. 568, 173 S.W.2d 745, 750. In conflicts, denotes fact that the manner in which the actor's tortious conduct has resulted in another's injury is such that the law holds the actor responsible unless there is some defense to liability. Restatement, Second, Conflicts, § 160, Comment a.

The words "legal cause" are used throughout the Restatement of Torts to denote the fact that the causal sequence by which the actor's tortious conduct has resulted in an invasion of some legally protected interest of another is such that the law holds the actor responsible for such harm unless there is some defense to liability. Restatement, Second, Torts, § 9.

See also **Cause.**

Legal conclusion. A statement of legal duty without stating fact from which duty arises. Burton-Lingo Co. v. Morton, Tex.Civ.App., 126 S.W.2d 727, 733. A particular statement which would be considered a statement of fact in everyday conversation might, nevertheless, be considered a "legal conclusion" when used in connection with a legal proceeding if the truth of the fact stated is one of the ultimate issues to be determined in such proceeding. Cortner v. National Cash Register Co., 25 Ohio Misc. 156, 262 N.E.2d 586, 588.

Legal cruelty. Such as will warrant the granting of a divorce to the injured party, as distinguished from such kinds or degrees of cruelty as do not. Such conduct on the part of a spouse as will endanger the life, person, or health (bodily or mental) of his or her spouse, or create a reasonable apprehension of bodily or mental hurt; such acts as render cohabitation unsafe, or are likely to be attended with injury to the person or to the health of the spouse. See also **Cruelty; Mental cruelty.**

Legal custody. Restraint of or responsibility for a person according to law, such as a guardian's authority over the person or property, or both, of his ward. See also **Commitment; Custody; Guardian; Ward.**

Legal death. See **Brain death; Civil death.**

Legal dependent. Dependent according to law. The term imports right to invoke aid of law to require support. See **Dependent; Lawful dependents; Support; Ward.**

Legal description. A description of real property by government survey, metes and bounds, or lot numbers of a recorded plat including a description of any portion thereof subject to an easement or reservation, if any. Such must be complete enough that a particular parcel of land can be located and identified. See **Land boundaries; Metes and bounds.**

Legal detriment. Legal detriment to promisee means that promisee changed his legal position, or assumed duties or liabilities not theretofore imposed on him on reliance of actions of promisor. State ex rel. Kansas City v. State Highway Commission, 349 Mo. 865, 163 S.W.2d 948, 953. Term refers to giving up something which immediately prior thereto the promisee was privileged to retain, or doing or refraining from doing something which he was then privileged not to do, or not to refrain from doing. See also **Consideration; Detriment.**

Legal discretion. See **Discretion.**

Legal distributees. As used in will, term is construed to mean persons who would be entitled to take under the law.

Legal duty. An obligation arising from contract of the parties or the operation of the law; *e.g.* legal duty of husband to support wife and children. Ferrell v. Hass, 136 Ga.App. 274, 220 S.E.2d 771, 773. That which the law requires to be done or forborne to a determinate person or the public at large, correlative to a vested and coextensive right in such person or the public, and the breach of which constitutes negligence. See also **Legal obligation; Support.**

Legal entity. Legal existence. An entity, other than a natural person, who has sufficient existence in legal contemplation that it can function legally, be sued or sue and make decisions through agents as in the case of corporations.

Legal estoppel. Estoppel by deed or record, as distinguished from estoppel by matter in pais. It excludes evidence of the truth and the equity of the particular case to support a strict rule of law on grounds of public policy. See also **Estoppel.**

Legal ethics. Usages and customs among members of the legal profession, involving their moral and professional duties toward one another, toward clients, and toward the courts. That branch of moral science which treats of the duties which a member of the legal profession owes to the public, to the court, to his professional brethren, and to his client. Most states have adopted the Code of Professional Responsibility of the American Bar Association. See also **Canon.**

Legal evidence. A broad general term meaning all admissible evidence, including both oral and documentary, but with a further implication that it must be of such a character as tends reasonably and substantially to prove the point, not to raise a mere suspicion or conjecture. See also **Evidence; Relevant evidence.**

Legal excuse. Doctrine by which one seeks to avoid the consequences of his own conduct by showing justification for acts which would otherwise be considered negligent or criminal; *e.g.* killing of another in self defense. Gibbs v. Wilmeth, 261 Iowa 1015, 157 N.W.2d 93, 96. See also **Excusable; Justification; Legal impossibility.**

Legal fiction. Assumption of fact made by court as basis for deciding a legal question. A situation contrived by the law to permit a court to dispose of a matter, though it need not be created improperly; *e.g.* fiction of lost grant as basis for title by adverse possession.

Legal fraud. Contracts or acts as, though not originating in actual evil design to perpetrate fraud, yet by their tendency to mislead others or to violate confidence, are prohibited by law. Ruedy v. Toledo Factories Co., 61 Ohio App. 21, 22 N.E.2d 293, 297, 15 O.O.

56. Breach of duty which has tendency to deceive others and operates to their injury, even though there be no vicious intent. Charleroi Lumber Co. v. School Dist. of Borough of Bentleyville, 334 Pa. 424, 6 A.2d 88, 91. Misrepresentation of a material fact made wilfully to deceive, or recklessly without knowledge, and acted on by the opposite party to his damages constitutes "legal fraud." Coffey v. Wininger, 156 Ind.App. 233, 296 N.E.2d 154, 160.

Synonymous with "constructive fraud". Purcell v. Robertson, 122 W.Va. 287, 8 S.E.2d 881, 883; Tom Reed Gold Mines Co. v. United Eastern Mining Co., 39 Ariz. 533, 8 P.2d 449, 451. For definition of "Constructive fraud," see **Fraud.**

Legal heirs. As used in will, term means decedent's next of kin. In re Farkouh's Will, 134 Misc. 285, 235 N.Y.S. 165, 167. Persons entitled under laws of descent and distribution. Person to whom law would give decedent's property if decedent died intestate. In re Wagar's Estate, 302 Mich. 243, 4 N.W.2d 535, 536. "Heirs at law," "lawful heirs," "legal heirs," and similar expressions are synonymous. Corwin v. Rheims, 390 Ill. 205, 61 N.E.2d 40, 48; In re Fahnestock's Estate, 384 Ill. 26, 50 N.E.2d 733, 736. See also **Heirs; Legal issue.**

Legal holiday. A day designated by law as exempt from judicial proceedings, service of process, demand and protest of commercial paper, etc. A day designated by legislative enactment for purpose within meaning of term "holiday." Vidal v. Backs, 218 Cal. 99, 21 P.2d 952. Fed.R.Civil P. 77.

The legal or practical effect of a day being a "legal holiday" varies from state to state. A "holiday" may in some states be a day on which service of process is invalid, on which all or only some businesses are closed, on which state offices may or may not be closed. The statutes should be consulted in individual cases, as well as local custom, to determine if a "holiday" affects some particular contemplated action. See also **Holiday.**

Legal impossibility. Defense of "legal impossibility" may be established only where a defendant's actions, if fully performed would not constitute a crime, while "factual impossibility" can serve as a defense only where circumstances unknown to the actor prevent his commission of an offense. U. S. v. Johnston, C.A.Ark., 543 F.2d 55, 58. As defense to criminal charge, occurs when actions which defendant performs, or sets in motion, even if fully carried out as he desires, would not constitute crime. U. S. v. Conway, C.A.Tex., 507 F.2d 1047, 1050. See also **Impossibility.**

Legal injury. Violation or invasion of legal right. Combs v. Hargis Bank & Trust Co., 234 Ky. 202, 27 S.W.2d 955, 956; American Indemnity Co. v. Ernst & Ernst, Tex.Civ.App., 106 S.W.2d 763, 765. See **Injury.**

Legal insanity. See **Insanity.**

Legal interest. That rate of interest prescribed by law as the highest which may be lawfully contracted for or exacted. Term may also be used to distinguish interest in property or in claim cognizable at law in contrast to equitable interest. See also **Legal owner; Usury.**

Legal investments. Those investments sometimes called "legal lists" in which banks and other financial institutions may invest. State statutes often provide that trust funds be invested only in high grade, "legal list," securities. See also **Legal list; Prudent Man Rule.**

Legalis homo /ləgéyləs hówmow/. Lat. A lawful man; a person who stands *rectus in curia;* a person not outlawed, excommunicated, or infamous. It occurs in the phrase, *"probi et legales homines"* (good and lawful men, competent jurors), and "legality" designates the condition of such a man.

Legalis moneta angliæ /ləgéyləs mənéydə æŋgliyiy/. Lawful money of England.

Legal issue. When used in will and unexplained by context, means descendants. In proper context, may refer to legal question which is at the foundation of a case and which requires decision by court. See **Issue; Legal heirs.**

Legality, or **legalness.** Lawfulness.

Legalization. The act of legalizing or making legal or lawful.

Legalize. To make legal or lawful. Wight v. New Jersey Racing Commission, 128 N.J.L. 517, 26 A.2d 709, 712. To confirm or validate what was before void or unlawful. To add the sanction and authority of law to that which before was without or against law. See also **Legitimate, v.**

Legalized nuisance. A structure, erection, or other thing which would constitute a nuisance at common law, but which cannot be objected to by private persons because constructed or maintained under direct and sufficient legislative authority. Such, for example, are hospitals or recreational areas maintained by cities.

Legal jeopardy. A person is in "legal jeopardy" when he is put upon trial before a court of competent jurisdiction upon an indictment or information which is sufficient in form and substance to sustain a conviction, and a jury has been "charged with his deliverance," and a jury is thus charged when they have been impaneled and sworn. State v. Whitman, 93 Utah 557, 74 P.2d 696, 697. See also **Jeopardy.**

Legal liability. A liability which courts recognize and enforce as between parties litigant. See also **Legally liable; Liability; Strict liability.**

Legal life estate. Interest in real or personal property for the life of the holder and enforceable at law in contrast to equitable life estate.

Legal list. A list of investments selected by various states in which certain institutions and fiduciaries, such as insurance companies and banks, may invest. Legal lists are often restricted to high quality securities meeting certain specifications. See also **Legal investments; Prudent Man Rule.**

Legally. Lawfully; according to law.

Legally adopted. Adopted in accordance with laws of state.

Legally committed. Refers to accused who has been committed by magistrate who has jurisdiction to hold examination and who has actually heard evidence and determined probable cause exists for holding defendant. People v. Dal Porto, 17 Cal.App.2d 755, 63 P.2d 1199, 1200. See also **Commitment.**

Legally competent. Words "legally competent" in statute prescribing qualifications of executor mean fit or qualified to act according to judicial standards essential to proper course of justice. In re Haeffele's Estate, 145 Neb. 809, 18 N.W.2d 228, 231. See also **Capacity.**

Legally constituted court. One known to and recognized by law. See **Constitutional court.**

Legally contributing cause of injury. Substantial factor in bringing about injury. Farmer v. Central Mut. Ins. Co. of Chicago, Ill., 145 Kan. 951, 67 P.2d 511, 514. See also **Cause; Proximate cause.**

Legally determined. Determined by process of law. Black Diamond S. S. Corporation v. Fidelity & Deposit Co. of Maryland, D.C.Md., 33 F.2d 767, 769.

Legally liable. Liable under law as interpreted by courts. Beck v. Kansas City Public Service Co., Mo. App., 48 S.W.2d 213, 215. Liability imposed by law or liability which law fixes by contract. Home Ins. Co. of New York v. Moore & Rawls, 151 Miss. 189, 117 So. 524, 526. See **Liability; Strict liability.**

Legally operating automobile. As used in liability policy, means operating automobile by right or by lawful authority. Universal Automobile Ins. Co. v. Benoit, C.C.A.Ariz., 67 F.2d 52, 53; Zurich General Accident & Liability Ins. Co. v. Thompson, C.C.A.Cal., 49 F.2d 860, 861.

Legally reside. Domicile. Mitchell v. Kinney, 242 Ala. 196, 5 So.2d 788, 793. See **Domicile; Legal residence; Residence.**

Legally sufficient evidence. Competent, pertinent evidence coming from a legal source. Evidence is "legally sufficient to sustain finding", if supported by substantial evidence, and record as whole does not clearly, convincingly, or even, possibly, indisputably require contrary conclusion. Tracey v. Commissioner of Internal Revenue, C.C.A.6, 53 F.2d 575, 579. See **Evidence; Relevant evidence.**

Legally sufficient tender. A tender made under circumstances that fulfill obligations assumed by vendors. Kolling v. Martin, 109 Ind.App. 184, 33 N.E.2d 808, 815. See **Legal tender.**

Legally using automobile. See **Legally operating automobile**, *supra.*

Legal malice. Such consists of either an express intent to kill or inflict great bodily harm, or of a wickedness of disposition, hardness of heart, cruelty, recklessness of consequences and a mind regardless of social duty which indicates an unjustified disregard for the likelihood of death or great bodily harm and an extreme indifference to the value of human life. Cmwlth. v. Coleman, 455 Pa. 508, 318 A.2d 716, 717.

An expression used as the equivalent of "constructive malice," or "malice in law." Inference of malice which can be reasonably drawn from wrongful act. Chrisman v. Terminal R. Ass'n of St. Louis, 237 Mo.App. 181, 157 S.W.2d 230, 235. Intentional doing of a wrongful act without just cause. State ex rel. United Factories v. Hostetter, 344 Mo. 386, 126 S.W.2d 1173, 1176; Hatton v. Carder Wholesale Grocery Co., 235 Mo.App. 1198, 150 S.W.2d 1096, 1101.

Legal malpractice. See **Malpractice.**

Legal name. Under common law consists of one Christian name and one surname, and the insertion, omission, or mistake in middle name or initial is immaterial. The "legal name" of an individual consists of a given or baptismal name, usually assumed at birth, and a surname deriving from the common name of the parents. Application of Green, 54 Misc.2d 606, 283 N.Y.S.2d 242, 245.

Legal negligence. Negligence per se; the omission of such care as ordinarily prudent persons exercise and deem adequate to the circumstances of the case. In cases where the common experience of mankind and the common judgment of prudent persons have recognized that to do or omit certain acts is productive of danger, the doing or omission of them is "legal negligence." Failure to perform duty law imposes on one person for benefit of another. See also **Strict liability.**

Legal newspaper. Newspapers published nationally and in major cities containing summaries of important court decisions, recently enacted or pending legislation or regulatory changes, and, locally, notices of bankruptcy, probate, foreclosure, divorce, etc. proceedings, and also news of general interest to the legal profession.

Legal notice. Such notice as is adequate in point of law; notice as the law requires to be given for the specific purpose or in the particular case. Such legal notice is typically required to be published a specified number of times in a legal and/or general circulation newspaper; may also be required to be posted in designated area in court house. See also **Notice.**

Legal obligation. A legal obligation against state is an obligation which would form basis of judgment against state in court of competent jurisdiction should Legislature permit state to be sued. Fort Worth Cavalry Club, Inc. v. Sheppard, 125 Tex. 339, 83 S.W.2d 660, 663. In its broadest sense, any duty imposed by law; *e.g.* duty of parent to support children. See also **Legal duty; Support.**

Legal owner. The term has come to be used in technical contrast to the equitable owner, and not as opposed to an illegal owner. The legal owner has title to the property, although the title may actually carry no rights to the property other than a lien.

Legal personal representative. Generally, when applied by testator to personalty, signifies "executors and administrators" and when applied to realty those upon whom law casts real estate immediately upon death of ancestor. Hogate v. Hogate, 132 N.J.Eq. 480, 28 A.2d 769, 771. As respects delivery of deposit on behalf of deceased seaman, means the public administrator, or executor or administrator appointed in state where seaman resided. See **Legal representative.**

Legal possessor. One who, but for the reservation of strict legal title in conditional vendor, or the giving of a strict legal title in a conditional vendor, or the giving of a strict legal title to a chattel mortgagee, would have the status of a full and unqualified owner. One who has the legal right to possession of property as contrasted with the owner of such property who has legal title. See **Legal owner.**

Legal prejudice. Legal prejudice which will defeat plaintiff's motion to dismiss is such as deprives defendant of substantive rights of property, or concerns his defense, which will not be available or may be endangered in a second suit. General Motors Acceptance Corporation v. Baker, 161 Misc. 238, 291 N.Y.S. 1015.

Legal presumption. For "presumption of law," see **Presumption.**

Legal privity. "Legal privity", within rule that defense of usury is personal to debtor and those in legal privity with him, means those upon whom title or interest is cast by law. An agent and his principal are in legal privity to each other. See also **Privity.**

Legal proceedings. Term includes all proceedings authorized or sanctioned by law, and brought or instituted in a court or legal tribunal, for the acquiring of a right or the enforcement of a remedy.

Legal rate of interest. See **Legal interest; Usury.**

Legal representative. The term in its broadest sense, means one who stands in place of, and represents the interests of, another. A person who oversees the legal affairs of another. Examples include the executor or administrator of an estate and a court appointed guardian of a minor or incompetent person.

Term "legal representative," which is almost always held to be synonymous with term "personal representative," means, in accident cases, member of family entitled to benefits under wrongful death statute. Unsatisfied Claim and Judgment Fund v. Hamilton, 256 Md. 56, 259 A.2d 303, 306.

Legal rescission. Rescission by act of parties. Aron v. Mid-Continent Co., 141 Neb. 806, 4 N.W.2d 884, 886. See also **Rescind; Recission of contract; Void; Voidable.**

Legal reserve. Liquid assets which life insurance companies are required by statute to set aside and maintain to assure payment of claims and benefits. Lubin v. Equitable Life Assur. Soc. of U. S., 326 Ill.App. 358, 61 N.E.2d 753, 754; Old Surety Life Ins. Co. of Alva, Okl., v. Morrow, 195 Okl. 442, 158 P.2d 715, 717. In banking, that amount of percentage of bank deposits which must by law be maintained in cash or equally liquid assets to meet the demands of depositors.

Legal residence. The place of domicile or permanent abode, as distinguished from temporary residence. Permanent fixed place of abode which person intends to be his residence and to which he intends to return despite temporary residences elsewhere or despite temporary absences. U. S. v. Calhoun, C.A.Fla., 566 F.2d 969, 973. Place recognized by law as residence of person. See also **Domicile; Residence.**

Legal right. Natural rights, rights existing as result of contract, and rights created or recognized by law. Fine v. Pratt, Tex.Civ.App., 150 S.W.2d 308, 311.

Legal separation. A court order arranging the terms (custody, support, etc.) under which a married couple will live separately. See also **Separation of spouses.**

Legal Services Corporation. The Legal Services Corporation was established by the Legal Services Corporation Act of 1974 (42 U.S.C.A. § 2996) to provide financial support for legal assistance in noncriminal proceedings to persons financially unable to afford legal services. The Corporation provides financial assistance to qualified programs furnishing legal assistance to eligible clients and makes grants to and contracts with individuals, firms, corporations, organizations, and State and local governments for the purpose of providing legal assistance to these clients. The Corporation establishes maximum income levels for clients based on family size, urban and rural differences, and cost-of-living variations. Using these maximum income levels and other financial factors, the Corporation establishes guidelines to be used by the organizations it funds to determine the eligibility of clients. The Corporation also conducts research, training, and technical assistance activities and serves as a clearinghouse for information relating to the delivery of legal assistance.

Legal subdivisions. Divisions of land which result from application of ordinary methods used in making of a government survey.

Legal subrogation. A right arising by operation of law. Federal Land Bank of Baltimore v. Joynes, 179 Va. 394, 18 S.E.2d 917, 920. Where one having liability, right, or fiduciary relation pays another's debt under circumstances equitably entitling former to rights, remedies or securities held by creditor. Where person pays in performance of legal duty imposed by contract, statute, or rule of law or where payment is favored by public policy. Where person secondarily liable pays debt and becomes subrogated to creditor's rights. Where person who pays stands in situation of a surety or is compelled to pay to protect his own right or property. Martin v. Hickenlooper, 90 Utah 150, 59 P.2d 1139, 1141; Lervold v. Republic Mut. Fire Ins. Co., 142 Kan. 43, 45 P.2d 839, 842. See **Subrogation.**

Legal tender. All coins and currencies of the United States (including Federal Reserve notes and circulating notes of Federal Reserve banks and national banking associations), regardless of when coined or issued, are legal tender for all debts, public and private, public charges, taxes, duties, and dues. 31 U.S.C.A. § 392.

Legal tender cases. Two cases upholding the constitutionality of the Acts of Congress in 1862 and 1863 calling for the issuance of paper money. Knox v. Lee, 79 U.S. (12 Wall.) 457, 20 L.Ed. 287, Juilliard v. Greenman, 110 U.S. 421, 4 S.Ct. 122, 28 L.Ed. 204.

Legal title. One cognizable or enforceable in a court of law, or one which is complete and perfect so far as regards the apparent right of ownership and possession, but which carries no beneficial interest in the property, another person being equitably entitled thereto; in either case, the antithesis of "equitable title." It may also mean appearance of title as distinguished from complete title, Southern Carbon Co. v. State, 171 Misc. 566, 13 N.Y.S.2d 7, 9; full and absolute title or apparent right of ownership with beneficial or equitable title in another; not necessarily record title. Barnes v. Boyd, D.C.W.Va., 8 F.Supp. 584, 597. A tax title, which is prima facie valid, is a "legal title". Murray v. Holland, 108 Ind.App. 236, 27 N.E.2d 126, 128.

Legal usufruct /líygəl yúwzəfrəkt/. Usufructs established by operation of law are legal usufructs, Hartford Accident & Indemnity Co. v. Abdalla, 203 La. 999, 14 So.2d 815; e.g., the usufruct collated for surviving spouse in necessitous circumstances.

Legal voter. A person having constitutional requirements and who is registered. A person invested by law with right to vote. Wright v. Lee, 125 N.J.L. 256, 15 A.2d 610, 611. A person qualified by Constitution and laws of state to vote. Lefler v. City of Dallas, Tex.Civ.App., 177 S.W.2d 231, 235.

Legal willfulness. Intentional disregard of known duty necessary to safety of person or property of another and entire absence of care for life, person or property of others. Bartolucci v. Falleti, 314 Ill.App. 551, 41 N.E.2d 777, 780.

Legantine constitutions /légəntən kònstət(y)úwshən(d)z/. The name of a code of ecclesiastical laws, enacted in national synods, held under legates from Pope Gregory IX, and Clement IV, in the reign of Henry III, about the years 1220 and 1268.

Legare /ləgériy/. Lat. In the civil and old English law, to bequeath; to leave or give by will; to give in anticipation of death.

Legatarius /lègətériyəs/. Lat. In the civil law, one to whom a thing is bequeathed; a legatee or legatary. In old European law, a legate, messenger, or envoy.

Legatary /légətəriy/. One to whom anything is bequeathed; a legatee. This word is sometimes, though seldom, used to designate a legate or nuncio.

Legatee /lègətíy/. The person to whom a legacy in a will is given. The term may be used to denominate those who take under will without any distinction between realty and personalty, Brooker v. Brooker, Tex.Civ.App., 76 S.W.2d 180, 183; though commonly it refers to one who takes *personal* property under a will. See **Legacy.**

Residuary legatee. The person to whom a testator bequeaths the residue of his personal estate, after the payment of such other legacies as are specifically mentioned in the will.

Legates /légəts/. Nuncios, deputies, or extraordinary ambassadors sent by the pope to be his representatives and to exercise his jurisdiction in countries where the Roman Catholic Church is established by law.

Legation. An embassy; a diplomatic minister and his suite. The persons commissioned by one government to exercise diplomatic functions at the court of another, including the minister, secretaries, attachés, interpreters, etc., are collectively styled the "legation" of

their government. The word also denotes the official residence of a foreign minister.

Legator /ləgéydər/. One who makes a will, and leaves legacies.

Legatory /légətəriy/. In old English law, the third part of a freeman's personal estate, which by the custom of London, in case he had a wife and children, the freeman might always have disposed of by will.

Legatos violare contra jus gentium est /ləgéydows vàyəlériy kòntrə jás jénsh(iy)əm èst/. It is contrary to the law of nations to injure ambassadors.

Legatum /ləgéydəm/. Lat. In old English law, a legacy given to the church, or an accustomed mortuary. In the civil law, a legacy; a gift left by a deceased person, to be executed by the heir.

Legatum morte testatoris tantum confirmatur, sicut donatio inter vivos traditione sola /ləgéydəm mórdiy tèstətóris tǽntəm kònfərméydər síkət dənéysh(iy)ow íntər váyvows trədìshiyówniy sówlə/. A legacy is confirmed by the death of a testator, in the same manner as a gift from a living person is by delivery alone.

Legatum optionis /ləgéydəm òpshiyównəs/. In Roman law, a legacy to A. B. of any article or articles that A. B. liked to choose or select out of the testator's estate. If A. B. died after the testator, but before making the choice or selection, his representative *(hæres)* could not, prior to Justinian, make the selection for him, but the legacy failed altogether. Justinian, however, made the legacy good, and enabled the representative to chose.

Legatus regis vice fungitur a quo destinatur et honorandus est sicut ille cujus vicem gerit /ləgéydəs ríyjəs váysiy fánjədər èy kwów dèstənéydər èd ònərǽndəs èst síkəd íliy kyúwjəs váysəm jéhrət/. An ambassador fills the place of the king by whom he is sent, and is to be honored as he is whose place he fills.

Legem /líyjəm/. Lat. Accusative of *lex,* law. Occurring in various legal phrases, as follows:

Legem amittere /líyjəm əmídəriy/. To lose one's law; that is, to lose one's privilege of being admitted to take an oath.

Legem facere /líyjəm féysəriy/. In old English law, to make law or oath.

Legem ferre /líyjəm féhriy/. In Roman law, to propose a law to the people for their adoption.

Legem habere /líyjəm həbíriy/. To be capable of giving evidence upon oath. Witnesses who had been convicted of crime were incapable of giving evidence, until 6 & 7 Vict., c. 85.

Legem jubere /líyjəm jəbíriy/. In Roman law, to give consent and authority to a proposed law; to make or pass it.

Legem pone /líyjəm pówniy/. To propound or lay down the law. By an extremely obscure derivation or analogy, this term was formerly used as a slang equivalent for payment in cash or in ready money.

Legem sciscere /líyjəm sísəriy/. To give consent and authority to a proposed law; applied to the consent of the people.

Legem terræ amittentes, perpetuam infamiæ notam inde merito incurrunt /líyjəm téhriy æməténtiyz pərpéchuwəm inféymiyiy nówdəm índiy méhrədow iŋkə́hrənt/. Those who lose the law of the land, then justly incur the ineffaceable brand of infamy.

Legem vadiare /líyjəm vædiyériy/. In old English law, to wage law; to offer or to give pledge to make defense, by oath, with compurgators.

Legenita. A fine for criminal conversation with a woman. See **Legruita.**

Leges /líyjiyz/. Lat. Laws. At Rome, the *leges* (the decrees of the people in a strict sense) were laws which were proposed by a magistrate presiding in the senate, and adopted by the Roman people in the *comitia centuriata.*

Leges Angliæ /líyjiyz æŋgliyiy/. The laws of England, as distinguished from the civil law and other foreign systems.

Leges Angliæ sunt tripartitæ,—jus commune, consuetudines, ac decreta comitiorum /líyjiyz æŋgliyiy sánt tràypárdədiy, jás kəmyúwniy, kònswət(y)úwdəniyz, æk dəkríydə kəmìshiyórəm/. The laws of England are threefold,—common law, customs, and decrees of parliament.

Leges barbarorum /líyjiyz bàrbarórəm/. A class name for the codes of mediæval European law.

Leges Edwardi confessoris /líyjiyz èdwárday kònfəsórəs/. A name used for a legal treatise written from 1130 to 1135, which presents the law in force toward the end of Henry I. Its authority is said to be undeserved.

Leges et consuetudini regni /líyjiyz èt kònswət(y)úwdənay régnay/. The accepted name for the common law from an early time; since the latter half of the 12th century at least.

Leges figendi et refigendi consuetudo est periculosissima /líyjiyz fəjénday èt rèfəjénday kònswət(y)úwdow èst pərìk(y)əlowsísəmə/. The practice of fixing and refixing [making and remaking] the laws is a most dangerous one.

Leges Henrici /líyjiyz hènráysay/. A book written between 1114 and 1118 containing Anglo-Saxon and Norman law. It is said to be an invaluable source of knowledge of the period preceding the full development of the Norman law.

Leges humanæ nascuntur, vivunt, et moriuntur /líyjiyz hyəméyniy nəskántər, váyvənt, èt mòriyántər/. Human laws are born, live, and die.

Leges Juliæ /líyjiyz júwliyiy/. Laws enacted during the reign of Augustus or of Julius Cæsar which, with the *lex abutia,* effectually abolished the *legis actiones.*

Leges naturæ perfectissimæ sunt et immutabiles; humani vero juris conditio semper in infinitum decurrit, et nihil est in eo quod perpetuo stare possit. Leges humanæ nascuntur, vivunt, moriuntur /líyjiyz nətyúriy pàrfektísəmiy sánt èt ìmyuwtéybəliyz; hyuwméyniy vírow júrəs kəndísh(iy)ow sémpər ìn ìnfənáydəm dəkə́hrət, èt náy(h)əl èst ìn íyow kwòd pərpét(y)uwow stériy pósət. líyjiyz hyuméyniy nəskántər, váyvənt, mòriyántər/. The laws of nature are most perfect and immutable; but the condition of human law is an unending succession, and there is nothing in it which can continue perpetually. Human laws are born, live, and die.

Leges non scriptæ /líyjiyz nòn skríptiy/. In English law, unwritten or customary laws, including those ancient acts of parliament which were made before time of memory.

Leges non verbis, sed rebus, sunt impositæ /líyjiyz nòn várbəs sèd ríybəs sànt əmpózədiy/. Laws are imposed, not on words, but things.

Leges posteriores priores contrarias abrogant /líyjiyz pəstìriyoriyz prayóriyz kəntrériyəs æbrəgənt/. Later laws abrogate prior laws that are contrary to them.

Leges sacratæ /líyjiyz səkréydiy/. All solemn compacts between the plebeians and patricians were so called.

Leges scriptæ /líyjiyz skríptiy/. In English law, written laws; statute laws, or acts of parliament which are originally reduced into writing before they are enacted, or receive any binding power.

Leges sub graviori lege /líyjiyz sàb græviyóray líyjiy/. Laws under a weightier law.

Leges suum ligent latorem /líyjiyz s(y)úwəm líjənt lətórəm/. Laws should bind their own maker.

Leges tabellariæ /líyjiyz tæbəlériyiy/. Roman laws regulating the mode of voting by ballot (*tabella*).

Leges vigilantibus, non dormientibus, subveniunt /líyjiyz vìjəlǽntəbəs nón dormiyéntəbəs səbvíyn(i)yənt/. The laws aid the vigilant, not the negligent.

Legibus solutus /líyjəbəs səl(y)úwdəs/. Lat. Released from the laws; not bound by the laws. An expression applied in the Roman civil law to the emperor.

Legibus sumptis desinentibus, lege natureae, utendum est /líyjəbəs sə́m(p)təs dèsənéntəbəs líyjiy nət(y)úriy yuwténdəm èst/. When laws imposed by the state fail, we must act by the law of nature.

Legiosus /lìyjiyówsəs/. In old records, litigious, and so subjected to a course of law.

Legis constructio non facit injuriam /líyjəs kənstrə́ksh(iy)ow nòn féysəd ənjúriyəm/. The construction of law does no injury.

Legis interpretatio legis vim obtinet /líyjəs əntàrprətéysh(iy)ow líyjəs vím óbtənət/. The interpretation of law obtains the force of law.

Legislate. To enact laws or pass resolutions via legislation, in contrast to court-made law. State ex rel. Nunez v. Baynard, La.App., 15 So.2d 649, 655.

Legislation. The act of giving or enacting laws; the power to make laws; the act of legislating; preparation and enactment of laws; the making of laws via legislation, in contrast to court-made laws. Formulation of rule for the future. Eastern Oil Refining Co. v. Court of Burgesses of Wallingford, 130 Conn. 606, 36 A.2d 586, 589; Oklahoma City, Okl. v. Dolese, C.C.A. Okl., 48 F.2d 734, 738. See also **Act** *(Legislative act);* **Bill; Class legislation; Statute.**

Legislative. Making or giving laws; pertaining to the function of law-making or to the process of enactment of laws. Actions which relate to subjects of permanent or general character are "legislative". Keigley v. Bench, 97 Utah 69, 89 P.2d 480, 484, 485. Making or having the power to make a law or laws.

Legislative act. Enactment of laws. Law *(i.e.* statute) passed by legislature in contrast to court-made law. One which prescribes what the law shall be in future cases arising under it. Nider v. Homan, 32 Cal. App.2d 21, 89 P.2d 136, 139. See **Statute.**

Legislative apportionment. Amend. XIV, § 2, of U.S. Const. provides that representatives to congress "shall be apportioned among the several states according to their respective numbers, counting the whole number of persons in each state." Equal protection under the Fourteenth Amendment of the U.S. Constitution requires the allocation of representatives on a population basis and a justiciable issue is presented when a claim is made that states are denying right of representation to its citizens. Baker v. Carr, 369 U.S. 186, 82 S.Ct. 691, 7 L.Ed.2d 663. See also **Apportionment; Reapportionment.**

Legislative council. A legislative agency used in some states which is composed of legislators and other selected officials who study legislative problems and plan legislative strategy between regular legislative sessions.

Legislative counsel. A person or agency specially charged with assisting legislators in fulfilling their legislative tasks. Legislative counsel handles problems of research, drafting bills, legislative hearings, and other technical legislative details.

Legislative courts. Courts created by legislature in contrast to those created by constitution *(e.g.* Art. III of U.S.Const.). Examples are Court of Claims and Court of Customs and Patent Appeals. Compare **Constitutional court.**

Legislative department. That department of government *(i.e.* Congress, consisting of Senate and House of Representatives; Art. I of U.S.Const.) whose appropriate function is the making or enactment of laws, as distinguished from the judicial department (Article III), which interprets and applies the laws, and the executive department (Article II), which carries them into execution and effect. See also **Legislature.**

Legislative districting. The apportionment or division of a legislative body into territorial districts. See **Apportionment; Legislative apportionment; Reapportionment.**

Legislative divorce. A divorce decreed by an act of the legislature as to one particular couple and not by judicial decree. While legislative divorces once existed in New England states, and parliamentary divorces once were granted in England, such have long been superseded by judicial divorces.

Legislative functions. The determination of legislative policy and its formation as rule of conduct. Yakus v. United States, 321 U.S. 414, 64 S.Ct. 660, 667, 88 L.Ed. 834. The formation and determination of future rights and duties. Dal Maso v. Board of Com'rs of Prince George's County, 182 Md. 200, 34 A.2d 464, 466. See also **Legislative power.**

Legislative history. The background and events, including committee reports, hearings, and floor debates, leading up to enactment of a law. Such history is important to courts when they are required to determine the legislative intent of a particular statute. Legislative histories of major statutes are published in U.S.Code, Congressional and Administrative News.

Legislative immunity. The Constitution grants two immunities to Congressmen, first, that except for treason, felony, and a breach of the peace, they are "privileged from Arrest during their Attendance" at sessions of their body, and, second, that "for any Speech or Debate in either House, they shall not be questioned in any other Place." (Art. I, § 6, cl. 1). The first immunity is of little practical value, for its exceptions withdraw all criminal offenses and arrests therefor from the privilege, and it does not apply to the service of any process in a civil or criminal matter. The second immunity is liberally construed and includes not only opinion, speeches, debates, or other oral matter, but also voting, making a written report or presenting a resolution, and in general to whatever a congressman feels necessary to transact the legislative functions and business. Even a claim of a bad motive does not destroy the immunity, for it is the public good which is thereby served. *E.g.,* United States v. Ballin, 144 U.S. 1, 12 S.Ct. 507, 36 L.Ed. 321; United States v. Smith, 286 U.S. 6, 52 S.Ct. 475, 76 L.Ed. 954.

Legislative intent. Such is looked to when court attempts to construe or interpret a statute which is ambiguous or inconsistent. See also **Legislative history.**

Legislative investigations. Legislatures are empowered to make investigations as an incident of their legislative authority; included are powers of subpoena, cross examination, etc. Quinn v. United States, 349 U.S. 155, 161, 75 S.Ct. 668, 99 L.Ed. 964.

Legislative jurisdiction. The sphere of authority of a legislative body to enact laws and to conduct all business incidental to its law-making function. Art. I of U.S. Constitution.

Legislative officer. A member of the legislative body or department of a state or municipal corporation. One of those whose duties relate mainly to the enactment of laws, such as members of congress and of the several state legislatures. These officers are confined in their duties by the constitution generally to make laws, though sometimes, in cases of impeachment, one of the houses of the legislature exercises judicial functions somewhat similar to those of a grand jury, by presenting to the other articles of impeachment, and the other house acts as a court in trying such impeachment.

Legislative power. The lawmaking powers of a legislative body, whose functions include the power to make, alter, amend and repeal laws. In essence, the legislature has the power to make laws and such power is reposed exclusively in such body though it may delegate rule making and regulatory powers to departments in the executive branch. It may not, however, delegate its law making powers nor is the judicial branch permitted to obtrude into its legislative powers. The enumerated powers of Congress are provided for in Article I of the U.S. Constitution.

Legislator. One who makes laws; a member of a legislative body; a senator, representative, assemblyman.

Legislatorum est viva vox, rebus et non verbis legem imponere /lèjəslətórəm èst váyvə vóks, ríybəs èt nòn várbəs líyjəm impównəriy/. The voice of legislators is a living voice, to impose laws on things, and not on words.

Legislature. The department, assembly, or body of persons that makes statutory laws for a state or nation. At the federal level, and in most states, the legislature is bicameral in structure, usually consisting of two branches; *i.e.* upper house (Senate) and lower house (House of Representatives or Assembly). Legislative bodies at the local levels are variously called city councils, boards of aldermen, etc. See **Chamber; Congress; Legislative department; Legislative districting.**

Legis minister non tenetur in executione officii sui, fugere aut retrocedere /líyjəs mənístər nòn təníydər in èksəkyùwshiyówniy əfís(h)iyay s(y)úway fyúwjəriy òt rètrəsíydəriy/. The minister of the law is bound, in the execution of his office, not to fly nor to retreat.

Legisperitus /lìyjəspəráydəs/. Lat. A person skilled or learned in the law; a lawyer or advocate.

Legitimacy. Lawful birth; the condition of being born in wedlock; the opposite of illegitimacy or bastardy.

Legitimate, *v.* To make lawful; to confer legitimacy; *e.g.,* to place a child born before marriage on the legal footing of those born in lawful wedlock.

Legitimate, *adj.* That which is lawful, legal, recognized by law, or according to law; as, legitimate children, legitimate authority, lawful power, legitimate sport or amusement. People v. Commons, 64 Cal.App.2d Supp. 925, 148 P.2d 724, 731. Real, valid, or genuine. United States v. Schenck, C.C.A.N.Y., 126 F.2d 702, 705, 707. See **Presumption of legitimacy.**

Legitimation. The making legitimate or lawful that which was not originally so; especially the statutory procedure of legalizing (legitimating) the status of an illegitimate child. Such is usually necessary to assure inheritance rights to child.

Legitimation per subsequens matrimonium /ləjídəméyshən pàr səbsəkwèn(d)z mætrəmówn(i)yəm/. The legitimation of a bastard by the subsequent marriage of his parents.

Legitime /ləjídəmiy/. Lat. In the civil law, that portion of a parent's estate of which he cannot disinherit his children without a legal cause. That interest in a succession of which forced heirs may not be deprived. It may also apply to father or mother.

Legitime imperanti parere necesse est /ləjídəmiy impərǽntay pəríriy nəsésiy èst/. One lawfully commanding must be obeyed.

Legitimi hæredes /ləjídəmay həríydiyz/. Lat. In Roman law, legitimate heirs; the agnate relations of the estate-leaver; so called because the inheritance was given to them by a law of the Twelve Tables.

Legitimus /ləjídəməs/. Lawful; legitimate. *Legitimus hæres et filius est quem nuptiæ demonstrant,* a lawful son and heir is he whom the marriage points out to be lawful.

Legit vel non? /líyjət vèl nón/. In old English practice, this was the formal question propounded to the ordinary when a prisoner claimed the benefit of clergy,—does he read or not? If the ordinary found that the prisoner was entitled to clergy, his formal answer was, *"Legit ut clericus,"* he reads like a clerk.

Lego /líygow/. Lat. In Roman law, I bequeath. A common term in wills.

Legruita. In old records, a fine for criminal conversation with a woman. See **Legenita.**

Le guidon de la mer /lə gìydówn də la mér/. The title of a French work on marine insurance, by an unknown author, dating back, probably, to the sixteenth century, and said to have been prepared for the merchants of Rouen. It is noteworthy as being the earliest treatise on that subject now extant.

Leguleius /lègyəlíyəs/. A person skilled in law *(in legibus versatus);* one versed in the forms of law.

Lehurecht. The German feudal law.

Leidgrave /léyðgrèyv/. An officer under the Saxon government, who had jurisdiction over a lath.

Leipa /líypə/. In old English law, a fugitive or runaway.

Le ley de dieu et ley de terre sont tout un; et l'un et l'autre preferre et favour le common et publique bien del terre. The law of God and the law of the land are all one; and both preserve and favor the common and public good of the land.

Le ley est le plus haut enheritance que le roy ad, car per le ley il mesme et touts ses sujets sont rules; et, si le ley ne fuit, nul roy ne nul enheritance serra. The law is the highest inheritance that the king possesses, for by the law both he and all his subjects are ruled; and, if there were no law, there would be neither king nor inheritance.

Lend. To give or put out for hire or compensation. To part with a thing of value to another for a time fixed or indefinite, yet to have some time in ending, to be used or enjoyed by that other; the thing itself or the equivalent of it to be given back at the time fixed, or when lawfully asked for, with or without compensation for the use as may be agreed upon. Term "lend" when used in a will means to "give" or "devise." To provide money to another for a period of time, usually with interest charge to be incurred by borrower.

Lender. He from whom a thing or money is borrowed. The bailor of an article loaned. A bank or other lending institution.

Lending or loaning money or credit. Transactions creating customary relation of borrower and lender, in which money is borrowed for fixed time on borrower's promise to repay amount borrowed at stated time in future with interest at fixed rate. Bannock County v. Citizens' Bank & Trust Co., 53 Idaho 159, 22 P.2d 674.

Lent. In Ecclesiastical law, the quadragesimal fast; a time of abstinence; the time from Ash Wednesday to Easter.

Leod. People; a people; a nation.

Leodes /liyówdiyz/. In old European law, a vassal, or leige man; service; a *were* or *weregild*.

Leonina societas /liyənáynə səsáyətæs/. Lat. An attempted partnership, in which one party was to bear all the losses, and have no share in the profits. This was a void partnership in Roman law; and, apparently, it would also be void as a partnership in English law, as being inherently inconsistent with the notion of partnership.

Leproso amovendo /leprówsow èymǝvéndow/. An ancient writ that lay to remove a leper or lazar, who thrust himself into the company of his neighbors in any parish, either in the church or at other public meetings, to their annoyance.

Le roi, or **roy** /lǝ róy/lǝ r(w)éy/. The old law-French words for "the king".

Le roi veut en deliberer. The king will deliberate on it. This is the formula which the king of the French used when he intended to veto an act of the legislative assembly.

Le roy (or la reine) le veut. The king (or the queen) wills it. The form of the royal assent to public bills in parliament.

Le roy (or la reine) remercie ses loyal sujets, accepte leur benevolence, et ainsi le veut. The king (or the queen) thanks his (or her) loyal subjects, accepts their benevolence, and therefore wills it to be so. The form of the royal assent to a bill of supply.

Le roy (or la reine) s'avisera. The king (or queen) will advise upon it. The form of words used to express the refusal of the royal assent to public bills in parliament. 1 Bl.Comm. 184. This is supposed to correspond to the judicial phrase *"curia advisari vult"* (q.v.).

Le salut du peuple est la supreme loi. The safety of the people is the highest law.

Leschewes. Trees fallen by chance or windfalls.

Lese majesty /líyz mæjəstiy/. The old English and Scotch translation of *"læsa majestas,"* or high treason.

Les fictions naissent de la loi, et non la loi des fictions /ley fiksyówn nés dǝ la lwá, ey nówn la lwá dey fiksyówn/. Fictions arise from the law, and not law from fictions.

Lesing or **leasing.** Gleaning.

Lesion /líyzhən/. Damage; injury; detriment; sore; wound. Gasperino v. Prudential Ins. Co. of America, Mo.App., 107 S.W.2d 819, 827. Hurt, loss, or injury. Gasperino v. Prudential Ins. Co. of América, Mo.App., 107 S.W.2d 819, 827; Warbende v. Prudential Ins. Co. of America, C.C.A.Ill., 97 F.2d 749, 753; Order of United Commercial Travelers of America v. Sevier, C.C.A.Mo., 121 F.2d 650, 654. Any change in the structure of an organ due to injury or disease, whether apparent or diagnosed as the cause of a functional irregularity or disturbance.

In the civil law, the injury suffered by one who does not receive a full equivalent for what he gives in a commutative contract. Inequality in contracts.

Les lois ne se chargent de punir que les actions exterieures /ley lwá nǝ sǝ shárzh dǝ pyunír kǝ leyzàksyównz ekstèriyúr/. Laws do not undertake to punish other than outward actions.

Lessee. One who rents property from another. In the case of real estate, the lessee is also known as the tenant. He to whom a lease is made. He who holds an estate by virtue of a lease. One who has been given possession of land which is exclusive even of the landlord, except as the lease permits his entry, and except right to enter to demand rent or to make repairs. Seabloom v. Krier, 219 Minn. 362, 18 N.W.2d 88, 91. See also **Tenant.**

Lessee's interest. In appraising the value of a potential sublease or assignment (sale) of the lease, the value is the market value of the property, less the interest of the lessor. The lessor's interest would be largely determined by the ratio of the return on the lease to the market value without the lease.

Lesser included offense. One composed of some, but not all, of the elements of the greater crime, and which does not have any element not included in the greater offense. State v. Steward, La., 292 So.2d 677, 679. One which includes some of the elements of the crime charged in the information without the addition of any element irrelevant to the original charge. State v. Johnsen, 197 Neb. 216, 247 N.W.2d 638, 640. When it is impossible to commit a particular crime without concomitantly committing, by the same conduct, another offense of lesser grade or degree, the latter is, with respect to the former, a "lesser included offense". In any case in which it is legally possible to attempt to commit a crime, such attempt constitutes a lesser included offense with respect thereto.

Lessor. He who grants a lease. One who rents property to another. In the case of real estate, the lessor is also known as the landlord. One who has leased land for a definite or indefinite period, by a written or parol lease, irrespective of whether a statute of fraud requires the lease to be in writing. City of Tyler v. Ingram, 139 Tex. 600, 164 S.W.2d 516, 520. See also **Landlord.**

Lessor of the plaintiff. In the common law action of ejectment, this was the party who really and in effect prosecuted the action and was interested in its result. The reason of his having been so called arose from the circumstance of the action having been carried on in the name of a nominal plaintiff (John Doe), to whom the real plaintiff had granted a fictitious lease, and thus had become his lessor.

Lessor's interest. The present value of the future income under the lease, plus the present value of the property after the lease expires (reversion).

Let, v. *Contracts.* To award to one of several persons, who have submitted proposals (bids) therefor, the contract for erecting public works or doing some part of the work connected therewith, or rendering some other service to government for a stipulated compensation. Letting the contract is the choosing one from among the number of bidders, and the formal making of the contract with him. The letting, or putting out, is a different thing from the invitation to make proposals; the letting is subsequent to the invitation. It is the act of awarding the contract to the proposer, after the proposals have been received and considered.

Conveyancing. To demise or lease a certain property. See **Lease.**

Judicial orders and decrees. The word "let" (in the imperative) imports a positive direction or command. Thus the phrase "let the writ issue as prayed" is equivalent to "it is hereby ordered that the writ issue," etc.

Practice. To deliver. "To *let* to bail" is to deliver to bail on arrest.

Let, n. In old conveyancing, hindrance; obstruction; interruption.

Lethal. Deadly, mortal, fatal. Vaughn v. Kansas City Gas Co., 236 Mo.App. 669, 159 S.W.2d 690, 698.

Lethal weapon. A deadly weapon *(q.v.).*

Letter. One of the arbitrary marks or characters constituting the alphabet, and used in written language as the representatives of sounds or articulations of the human organs of speech.

A dispatch or epistle; a written or printed message; a communication in writing from one person to another at a distance. In the imperial law of Rome, "letter" or "epistle" was the name of the answer returned by the emperor to a question of law submitted to him by the magistrates.

A communication inclosed, sealed, stamped, carried and delivered by private or U.S. Postal service. Hyney v. U. S., C.C.A.Mich., 44 F.2d 134, 136; Wolpa v. U. S., C.C.A.Neb., 86 F.2d 35, 39.

A commission, patent, or written instrument containing or attesting the grant of some power, authority, or right.

The word appears in this generic sense in many compound phrases known to commercial law and jurisprudence; *e.g.,* letter of attorney, letter missive, letter of credit, letters patent. The plural is frequently used.

Metaphorically, the verbal expression; the strict literal meaning. The *letter* of a statute, as distinguished from its *spirit,* means the strict and exact force of the language employed, as distinguished from the general purpose and policy of the law.

As to letters of Administration; Advice; Attorney; Credit; Recommendation; see those titles. As to Letters patent; see **Patent.**

Letter-book. A book in which a merchant or trader keeps copies of letters sent by him to his correspondents.

Letter contract. In federal contract law, a written contractual instrument with sufficient provisions to permit contractor to begin performance. Boeing Co. v. Omdahl, N.D., 169 N.W.2d 696, 702.

Letter missive. In old English law, a letter from the king or queen to a dean and chapter, containing the name of the person whom he would have them elect as bishop. A request addressed to a peer, peeress, or lord of parliament against whom a bill has been filed desiring the defendant to appear and answer to the bill. In civil-law practice, the phrase "letters missive," or "letters dimissory," is sometimes used to denote the papers sent up on an appeal by the judge or court below to the superior tribunal, otherwise called the "apostles" *(q.v.).*

Letter of administration. See **Letters of administration.**

Letter of advice. Drawer's communication to the drawee that a described draft has been drawn. U.C.C. § 3–701(1).

Letter of attornment. A letter from a grantor to a tenant, stating that the property has been sold, and directing rent to be paid to the grantee (new owner).

Letter of comment. Letters of comment are sent out by the S.E.C. in most cases as a means of informing registrants of securities offerings of the respects in which a registration statement is deemed not to meet the disclosure and other requirements of the Securities Exchange Act and the forms and regulations thereunder. A letter of comment may not be sent out, however, where the circumstances are such that an investigatory or stop order proceeding is deemed more appropriate.

Letter of credence. In international law, the document which accredits an ambassador, minister, or envoy to the courts or government to which he is sent; *i.e.,* certifies to his appointment and qualification, and bespeaks credit for his official actions and representations.

Letter of credit. A written instrument, addressed by one person to another, requesting the latter to give credit to the person in whose favor it is drawn. A letter of credit is in the nature of a negotiable instrument, and is a letter whereby a person requests another to advance money or give credit to a third person, and promises to repay person making advancement. A letter authorizing one person to pay money or extend credit to another on the credit of the writer. Mead Corp. v. Farmers and Citizens Bank, 14 Ohio Misc. 163, 232 N.E.2d 431, 432, 43 O.O.2d 404.

An engagement by a bank or other person made at the request of a customer that the issuer will honor drafts or other demands for payment upon compliance with the conditions specified in the credit. A credit may be either revocable or irrevocable. The engagement may be either an agreement to honor or a statement that the bank or other person is authorized to honor. U.C.C. § 5–103.

Commercial letter. Type of letter of credit used by buyer of merchandise who sends it to bank in district in which he is to buy and seller then presents his bill of sale, etc. to obtain payment.

Confirmed letter. Type of letter of credit in which local bank gives its guarantee that seller's draft will be honored if the bank which issued letter fails to honor it.

Export letter. Type of letter of credit forwarded to seller or exporter advising him that a credit has been established in his favor by a foreign bank and further consenting to honor the seller's or exporter's draft for the goods.

General and special. A general letter of credit is one addressed to any and all persons, without naming any one in particular, while a special letter of credit is addressed to a particular individual, firm, or corporation by name.

Import letter. Type of letter of credit issued by a foreign bank to a local seller permitting him to draw draft on the foreign bank against shipment of the merchandise.

Irrevocable letter. Type of letter of credit in which issuing bank guarantees that it will not withdraw the credit or cancel the letter before the expiration date.

Open credit. See **Open letter of credit.**

Revocable letter. Letter of credit in which the issuing bank reserves the right to cancel and withdraw from the transaction upon appropriate notice.

Revolving credit. See **Revolving credit.**

Traveler's letter. Type of letter of credit used by one traveling abroad in which the issuing bank authorizes payment of funds to holder in the local currency by a local bank. The holder signs a check on the issuing bank and the local bank forwards it to the issuing bank for its credit.

Letter of exchange. A bill of exchange *(q.v.).*

Letter of intent. A letter of intent is customarily employed to reduce to writing a preliminary understanding of parties who intend to enter into contract. Garner v. Boyd, D.C.Tex., 330 F.Supp. 22, 25.

Letter of license. In English law, a written instrument in the nature of an agreement, signed by all the creditors of a failing or embarrassed debtor in trade, granting him an extension of time for the payment of the debts, allowing him in the meantime to carry on the business in the hope of recuperation, and protecting him from arrest, suit, or other interference pending the agreement. A similar arrangement with creditors is provided for in United States under the federal Bankruptcy Act. See **Arrangement with creditors.**

Letter of marque and reprisal. An authorization formerly granted in time of war by a government to the owner of a private vessel to capture enemy vessels and goods on the high seas. Art. I, Sec. 8 of U.S. Const. The signatory powers to the Declaration of Paris in 1856 agreed to stop issuing such authorizations.

Letter of recall. A document addressed by the executive of one nation to that of another, informing the latter that a minister sent by the former has been recalled. May also refer to letter sent by manufactur-

er of product to purchasers requesting that they bring product, automobile, etc. into dealer to repair or replace item.

Letter of recredentials /lédər əv rìykrədénshəlz/. A document embodying the formal action of a government upon a letter of recall of a foreign minister. It, in effect, accredits him back to his own government. It is addressed to the latter government, and is delivered to the minister by the diplomatic secretary of the state from which he is recalled.

Letter patent. See **Letters patent.**

Letter ruling. A written statement which is issued to a taxpayer by Office of Assistant Commissioner of I.R.S. in which interpretations of tax laws are made and applied to a specific set of facts. Tax Analysts and Advocates v. Internal Revenue Service, D.C.D.C., 362 F.Supp. 1298, 1301. Issued in response to request for ruling by a private party of tax implications of a particular transaction.

Letters. In probate practice, includes letters testamentary, letters of guardianship, letters of administration, and letters of conservatorship. Uniform Probate Code, § 1–201(23). See **Letters of administration.**

Letters ad colligendum bona defuncti /lédərz æd kòlʌjéndəm bównʌ dʌfʌ́ŋ(k)tay/. In default of the representatives and creditors to administer to the estate of an intestate, the officer entitled to grant letters of administration may grant to such person as he approves, *letters to collect the goods of the deceased,* which neither make him executor nor administrator; his only business being to collect the goods and keep them in his safe custody. 2 Bl.Comm. 505.

Letters close. In English law, close letters are grants of the king, and, being of private concern, they are thus distinguished from letters patent.

Letters of absolution. Absolvatory letters, used in former times, when an abbot released any of his brethren *ab omnia subjectione et obedientia,* etc., and made them capable of entering into some other order of religion.

Letters of administration. Formal document issued by probate court appointing one an administrator of an estate.

Letters of administration C.T.A. Document issued by probate court appointing one administrator cum testamento annexo (with the will annexed) by reason of the failure of the named executor to qualify.

Letters of administration D.B.N. Document issued by probate court appointing one administrator de bonis non (concerning goods—not already administered) because of failure of named executor to complete the probate of the estate.

Letters of administration D.B.N. C.T.A. Document issued by probate court to one who is thereby authorized to administer estate in place of named executor in accordance with will of testator. See **Letters of Administration C.T.A.; Letters of Administration D.B.N.**

Letters of guardianship. A commission placing ward's property in the care of officer of court as custodian. Walker v. Graves, 174 Tenn. 336, 125 S.W.2d 154, 157.

Letters of safe conduct. No subject of a nation at war with England can, by the law of nations, come into the realm, nor can travel himself upon the high seas, or send his goods and merchandise from one place to another, without danger of being seized, unless he has *letters of safe conduct.* By divers old statutes these must be granted under the great seal, and enrolled in chancery, or else are of no effect; the sovereign being the best judge of such emergencies as may deserve exemption from the general law of arms. But passports or licenses from the ambassadors abroad are now more usually obtained, and are allowed to be of equal validity.

Letters of slains, or **slanes.** In England, letters subscribed by the relatives of a person who had been slain, declaring that they had received an assythment, and concurring in an application to the crown for a pardon to the offender. These or other evidences of their concurrence were necessary to found the application.

Letters patent /lédərz péytənt/°pǽt°/. An instrument issued by a government to the patentee, granting or confirming a right to the exclusive possession and enjoyment of land, or of a new invention or discovery. See also **Land patent; Patent.**

Letters rogatory /lédərz rógət(ə)riy/. A request by one court of another court in an independent jurisdiction, that a witness be examined upon interrogatories sent with the request. The medium whereby one country, speaking through one of its courts, requests another country, acting through its own courts and by methods of court procedure peculiar thereto and entirely within the latter's control, to assist the administration of justice in the former country. The Signe, D.C.La., 37 F.Supp. 819, 820.

A formal communication in writing, sent by a court in which an action is pending to a court or judge of a foreign country, requesting that the testimony of a witness resident within the jurisdiction of the latter court may be there formally taken under its direction and transmitted to the first court for use in the pending action. Fed.R.Civil P. 28.

This process was also in use, at an early period, between the several states of the Union. The request rests entirely upon the comity of courts towards each other.

Letters testamentary. The formal instrument of authority and appointment given to an executor by the proper court, empowering him to enter upon the discharge of his office as executor. It corresponds to letters of administration granted to an administrator.

Letter stock. Stock not registered under the Securities Act of 1933, where the buyer gives the seller a letter stating the buyer intends to hold for investment purposes and does not contemplate reoffering the stock to others. Securities and Exchange Commission v. Continental Tobacco Co. of S.C., C.A.Fla., 463 F.2d 137, 150.

Letting. Leasing or awarding. City and County of San Francisco v. United States, C.C.A.Cal., 106 F.2d 569, 576. See also **Lease; Let.**

Letting out. The act of leasing property or awarding a contract. See **Let.**

Lettre /létrə/. Fr. In French law, a letter. It is used, like our English "letter," for a formal instrument giving authority.

Lettres de cachet /létrə də kàshéy/. Letters issued and signed by the kings of France, and countersigned by a secretary of state, authorizing the imprisonment of a person. Under them, persons were imprisoned for life or for a long period on the most frivolous pretexts, for the gratification of private pique or revenge, and without any reason being assigned for such punishment. They were also granted by the king for the purpose of shielding his favorites or their friends from the consequences of their crimes; and thus were as pernicious in their operation as the protection afforded by the church to criminals in a former age. Abolished during the Revolution of 1789.

Leuca /l(y)úwkə/. In old French law. A league, consisting of fifteen hundred paces.

In old English law, a league or mile of a thousand paces. A privileged space around a monastery of a league or mile in circuit.

Levandæ navis causa /ləvǽndiy néyvəs kózə/. Lat. For the sake of lightening the ship; denotes a purpose of throwing overboard goods, which renders them subjects of general average.

Levant et couchant /lévənt èy káwchənt/. L. Fr. Rising up and lying down. A term applied to trespassing cattle which have remained long enough upon land to have lain down to rest and ri. n up to feed; generally the space of a night and a day, or, at least, one night.

Levari facias /ləvéray féys(h)(i)yəs/. Lat. A writ of execution directing the sheriff to cause to be made of the lands and chattels of the judgment debtor the sum recovered by the judgment. Also a writ to the bishop of the diocese, commanding him to enter into the benefice of a judgment debtor, and take and sequester the same into his possession, and hold the same until he shall have levied the amount of the judgment out of the rents, tithes, and profits thereof.

Levari facias damna de disseisitoribus /ləvéray féys(h)(i)yəs dǽmnə dìy dəsìyzətórəbəs/. A writ formerly directed to the sheriff for the levying of damages, which a disseisor had been condemned to pay to the disseisee.

Levari facias quando vicecomes returnavit quod non habuit emptores /ləvéray féys(h)(i)yəs kwóndow vàysiykówmiyz rətàrnéyvət kwòd nòn hǽbyuwət èm(p)tóriyz/. An old writ commanding the sheriff to sell the goods of a debtor which he had already taken, and had returned that he could not sell them; and as much more of the debtor's goods as would satisfy the whole debt.

Levari facias residuum debiti /ləvéray féys(h)(i)yəs rəsídyuwəm débəday/. An old writ directed to the sheriff for levying the remnant of a partly-satisfied debt upon the lands and tenements or chattels of the debtor.

Levato velo /ləvéydow víylow/. Lat. An expression used in the Roman law, and applied to the trial of wreck and salvage. Commentators disagree about the origin of the expression; but all agree that its general meaning is that these causes were to be heard summarily. The most probable solution is that it refers to the place where causes were heard. A sail was spread before the door and officers employed to keep strangers from the tribunal. When these causes were heard, this sail was raised, and suitors came directly to the court, and their causes were heard immediately. As applied to maritime courts, its meaning is that causes should be heard without delay. These causes require dispatch, and a delay amounts practically to a denial of justice.

Levee /léviy/. An embankment or artificial mound of earth constructed along the margin of a river, to confine the stream to its natural channel or prevent inundation or overflow. Also, a landing place on a river or lake; a place on a river or other navigable water for lading and unlading goods and for the reception and discharge of passengers to and from vessels lying in the contiguous waters, which may be either a wharf or pier or the natural bank.

Levee district. A municipal subdivision of a state (which may or may not be a public corporation) organized for the purpose, and charged with the duty, of constructing and maintaining such levees within its territorial limits as are to be built and kept up at public expense and for the general public benefit.

Level rate, legal reserve policy. Insurance which seeks to build up a reserve which will equal face value of policy at the end of insured's life.

Leverage. The ability to control an investment by a small amount of outlay such as a down payment. The use of a smaller investment to generate a larger rate of return through borrowing. The effect on common stockholders of the requirements to pay bond interest and preferred stock dividends before payment of common stock dividends.

Leviable /léviyəbəl/. That which may be levied. That which is a proper or permissible subject for a levy; as, a "leviable interest" in land.

Levir /líyvər/lévər/. In Roman law, a husband's brother; a wife's brother-in-law.

Levis /líyvəs/. Lat. Light; slight; trifling. *Levis culpa*, slight fault or neglect. *Levissima culpa*, the slightest neglect. *Levis nota*, a slight mark or brand.

Levitical degrees /ləvídəkəl dəgriyz/. Degrees of kindred within which persons are prohibited to marry. They are set forth in the eighteenth chapter of Leviticus.

Levy, *v.* To assess; raise; execute; exact; tax; collect; gather; take up; seize. Thus, to levy (assess, exact, raise, or collect) a tax; to levy (raise or set up) a nuisance; to levy (acknowledge) a fine; to levy (inaugurate) war; to levy an execution, *i.e.*, to levy or collect a sum of money on an execution.

Levy, *n.* A seizure. The obtaining of money by legal process through seizure and sale of property; the raising of the money for which an execution has been issued.

In reference to taxation, the word may mean the legislative function and declaration of the subject and rate or amount of taxation, People v. Mahoney, 13 Cal.2d 729, 91 P.2d 1029; Atlantic Coast Line R. Co. v. Amos, 94 Fla. 588, 115 So. 315, 320; City of Richmond v. Eubank, 179 Va. 70, 18 S.E.2d 397, 403; or the rate of taxation rather than the physical act of applying the rate to the property, Lowden v. Texas County Excise Board, 187 Okl. 365, 103 P.2d 98, 100; or the formal order, by proper authority declaring property subject to taxation at fixed rate at its assessed valuation, State v. Davis, 335 Mo. 159, 73 S.W.2d 406, 407; or the ministerial function of assessing, listing and extending taxes, City of Plankinton v. Kieffer, 70 S.D. 329, 17 N.W.2d 494, 495, 496; or the extension of the tax, Syracuse Trust Co. v. Board of Sup'rs of Oneida County, 13 N.Y.S.2d 390, 394; People ex rel. Oswego Falls Corporation v. Foster, 251 App.Div. 65, 295 N.Y.S. 891, 895. Day v. Inland Steel Co., 185 Minn. 53, 239 N.W. 776, 777; or the doing of whatever is necessary in order to authorize the collector to collect the tax, Syracuse Trust Co. v. Board of Sup'rs of Oneida County, 13 N.Y.S.2d 390, 394. "Levy," when used in connection with authority to tax, denotes exercise of legislative function, whether state or local, determining that a tax shall be imposed and fixing amount, purpose and subject of the exaction. Carkonen v. Williams, 76 Wash.2d 617, 458 P.2d 280, 286. The qualified electors "levy" a tax when they vote to impose it.

See also **Assess; Assessment.**

Equitable levy. The lien in equity created by the filing of a creditor's bill to subject real property of the debtor, and of a lis pendens, is sometimes so called. The right to an equitable lien is sometimes called an "equitable levy."

Levy court. A court formerly existing in the District of Columbia. It was a body charged with the administration of the ministerial and financial duties of Washington county. It was charged with the duty of laying out and repairing roads, building bridges, providing poor-houses, laying and collecting the taxes necessary to enable it to discharge these and other duties, and to pay the other expenses of the county. It had capacity to make contracts in reference to any of these matters, and to raise money to meet such contracts. It had perpetual succession, and its functions were those which, in the several states, are performed by "county commissioners," "overseers of the poor," "county supervisors," and similar bodies with other designations. Levy Court v. Coroner, 69 U.S. 501 (2 Wall.) 507, 17 L.Ed. 851.

Levying war. In criminal law, the assembling of a body of men for the purpose of effecting by force a treasonable object; and all who perform any part, however minute, or however remote from the scene of action, and who are leagued in the general conspiracy, are considered as engaged in levying war, within the meaning of the constitution. Art. III, § 3, U.S. Constitution. See also **Insurrection.**

The words include forcible opposition, as the result of a combination of individuals, to the execution of any public law of the United States; and to constitute treason within the Federal Constitution, there must be a combination of individuals united for the common purpose of forcibly preventing the execution of some public law and the actual or threatened use of force by the combination to prevent its execution. Kegerreis v. Van Zile, 180 App.Div. 414, 167 N.Y.S. 874, 876.

Lewd /l(y)uwd/. Obscene, lustful, indecent, lascivious, lecherous. The term imports a lascivious intent. It signifies that form of immorality which has relation to moral impurity, United States v. Barlow, D.C.Utah, 56 F.Supp. 795–797; or that which is carried on in a wanton manner. Rebhuhn v. Cahill, D.C.N.Y., 31 F.Supp. 47, 49. See also **Indecent** (*Indecent exposure*); **Lascivious; Lewdness; Obscene; Obscenity.**

Lewd and lascivious cohabitation. Within criminal statutes, the living together of a man and woman not married to each other as husband and wife. Also called "illicit cohabitation". Where existing, such statutes are seldom enforced. See also **Lewdness.**

Lewd house. See **Bawdy-house.**

Lewdness. Gross and wanton indecency in sexual relations. State v. Brenner, 132 N.J.L. 607, 41 A.2d 532, 534, 535. Gross indecency so notorious as to tend to corrupt community's morals. Abbott v. State, 163 Tenn. 384, 43 S.W.2d 211, 212. Licentiousness; that form of immorality which has relation to sexual impurity. Moral turpitude. Lane ex rel. Cronin v. Tillinghast, C.C.A.Mass., 38 F.2d 231, 232. Open and public indecency. State v. Brenner, 132 N.J.L. 607, 41 A.2d 532, 534, 535. Sensuality; debauchery.

Any act which the actor knows is likely to be observed by others who would be affronted or alarmed and hence it is a criminal offense. Model Penal Code, § 251.1. Lewdness is specifically made an offense under some state statutes, and is included under more general clauses in others.

See also **Indecent** (*Indecent exposure*); **Lascivious; Obscene; Obscenity.**

Lewd person. One who is lawless, bad, vicious, unchaste, indecent, obscene, lascivious. State v. Harlowe, 174 Wash. 227, 24 P.2d 601.

Lex /léks/. Lat. In medieval jurisprudence, a body or collection of various laws peculiar to a given nation or people; not a code in the modern sense, but an aggregation or collection of laws not codified or systematized. Also, a similar collection of laws relating to a general subject, and not peculiar to any one people.

In modern American and English jurisprudence, a system or body of laws, written or unwritten, or so much thereof as may be applicable to a particular case or question, considered as being local or peculiar to a given state, country, or jurisdiction, or as being different from the laws or rules relating to the same subject-matter which prevail in some other place.

In old English law, a body or collection of laws, and particularly the Roman or civil law. Also a form or mode of trial or process of law, as the ordeal or battel, or the oath of a party with compurgators, as in the phrases *legem facere, legem vadiare,* etc. Also used in the sense of legal rights or civil rights or the protection of the law, as in the phrase *legem amittere.*

In Roman law, a law; the law.

This term was often used as the synonym of *jus*, in the sense of a rule of civil conduct authoritatively prescribed for the government of the actions of the members of an organized jural society.

Lex is used in a purely juridical sense, law, and not also right; while *jus* has an ethical as well as a juridical meaning, not only law, but right. *Lex* is usually concrete, while *jus* is abstract. In English we have no term which combines the legal and ethical meanings, as do *jus* and its French equivalent, *droit*.

In a more limited and particular sense, it was a resolution adopted by the whole Roman *"populus"* (patricians and plebeians) in the *comitia*, on the motion of a magistrate of senatorial rank, as a consul, a prætor, or a dictator. Such a statute frequently took the name of the proposer; as the *lex Falcidia, lex Cornelia,* etc.

A rule of law which magistrates and people had agreed upon by means of a solemn declaration of consensus.

In a somewhat wider and more generic sense, a law (whatever its origin) or the aggregate of laws, relating to a particular subject-matter, thus corresponding to the meaning of the word "law" in some modern phrases, such as the "law of evidence," "law of wills," etc.

Other specific meanings of the word in Roman jurisprudence were as follows: Positive law, as opposed to natural. That system of law which descended from the Twelve Tables, and formed the basis of all the Roman law. The terms of a private covenant; the condition of an obligation. A form of words prescribed to be used upon particular occasions.

Lex actus /léks ǽktəs/. In conflicts, the law of the transaction; this governs in choice of law situation.

Lex Æbutia /léks əbyúwsh(iy)ə/. A statute which introduced and authorized new and more simple methods of instituting actions at law.

Lex æquitate gaudet /léks ìykwətéydiy gódət/. Law delights in equity.

Lex æquitate gaudet; appetit perfectum; est norma recti /léks ìykwətéydiy gódət, əpédət pərféktəm, èst nórmə réktay/. The law delights in equity; it covets perfection; it is a rule of right.

Lex aliquando sequitur æquitatem /léks æləkwǽndow síykwədər ìykwətéydəm/. Law sometimes follows equity.

Lex amissa /léks əmísə/. One who is an infamous, perjured, or outlawed person.

Lex Anastasiana /léks ænəstèyzhiyǽnə/. The law admitting as agnati the children of emancipated brothers and sisters. A law which provided that a third person who purchased a claim or debt for less than its true or nominal value should not be permitted to recover from the debtor more than the price paid with lawful interest.

Lex Angliæ /léks ǽngliyiy/. The law of England. The common law; or, the curtesy of England.

Lex Angliæ est lex misericordiæ /léks ǽngliyiy èst léks mìzərəkórdiyiy/. The law of England is a law of mercy.

Lex Angliæ non patitur absurdum /léks ǽngliyiy nòn pǽdədər əbsə́rdəm/. The law of England does not suffer an absurdity.

Lex Angliæ nunquam matris sed semper patris conditionem imitari partum judicat /léks ǽngliyiy nə́ŋkwəm méytrəs sèd sémpər pǽtrəs kəndìshiyownəm imətéray pə́rdəm júwdəkət/. The law of England rules that the offspring shall always follow the condition of the father, never that of the mother.

Lex Angliæ nunquam sine parliamento mutari potest /léks ǽngliyiy nə́ŋkwəm sáyniy pàrl(y)əméntow myuwtéray pówdəst/. The law of England cannot be changed but by parliament.

Lex apostata /léks ǽpəstéydə/. A thing contrary to law.

Lex apparens /léks əpǽrən(d)z/. In old English and Norman law, apparent or manifest law. A term used to denote the trial by battel or duel, and the trial by ordeal, *"lex"* having the sense of process of law. Called "apparent" because the plaintiff was obliged to make his right *clear* by the testimony of witnesses, before he could obtain an order from the court to summon the defendant.

Lex Apuleja, or **Apuleia** /léks ǽpyəlíyə/. A law giving to one of several joint sureties or guarantors, who had paid more than his proportion of the debt secured, a right of action for reimbursement against his co-sureties as if a partnership existed between them.

Lex Aquilia /léks əkwíliyə/. The Aquilian law; a celebrated law passed on the proposition of the tribune C. Aquilius Gallus, A.U.C. 672, superseding the earlier portions of the Twelve Tables, and regulating the compensation to be made for that kind of damage called "injurious," in the cases of killing or wounding the slave or beast of another.

Lex Atilia /léks ətíliyə/. The Atilian law. A law of Rome proposed by the tribune L. Atilius Regulus, A.U.C. 443, which conferred upon the magistrate the right of appointing guardians. It applied only to the city of Rome.

Lex Atinia /léks ətíniyə/. The Atinian law. A law declaring that the property in things stolen should not be acquired by prescription *(usucapione).*

Lex baiuvariorum, (baioriorum, or **boiorum)** /léks beyəvèriyórəm/°bey(oriy)órəm/. The law of the Bavarians, a barbarous nation of Europe, first collected (together with the law of the Franks and Alemanni) by Theodoric I, and finally completed and promulgated by Dagobert.

Lex barbara /léks bárbərə/. The barbarian law. The laws of those nations that were not subject to the Roman empire were so called.

Lex beneficialis rei consimili remedium præstat /léks bènəfis(h)iyéyləs ríyay kənsíməlay rəmíyd(i)yəm príystət/. A beneficial law affords a remedy for a similar case.

Lex brehonia /léks brəhówn(i)yə/. The Brehon or Irish law, overthrown by King John.

Lex bretoise /léks brètóyz/. The law of the ancient Britons, or Marches of Wales.

Lex burgundionum /léks bərgàndiyórəm/. The law of the Burgundians, a barbarous nation of Europe, first compiled and published by Gundebald, one of the last of their kings, about A.D. 500.

Lex Calpurnia /léks kælpə́rn(i)yə/. A law relating to the form and prosecution of actions for the recovery of specific chattels other than money. The law which extended the scope of the action allowed by the *lex Silia* to all obligations for any certain definite thing.

Lex Canuleia /léks kən(y)úwliyə/. The law which conferred upon the plebeians the *connubium,* or the right of intermarriage with Roman citizens.

Lex celebrationis. In conflicts, the law of the place where a marriage was celebrated will govern in most cases when the court is determining the validity of the marriage. Restatement of Conflicts, Second, § 283(2).

Lex Cincia /léks sínsh(iy)ə/. A law which prohibited certain kinds of gifts and all gifts or donations of property beyond a certain measure, except in the case of near kinsmen.

Lex citius tolerare vult privatum damnum quam publicum malum /léks sísh(iy)əs tòlərériy və́lt prəvéydəm dǽmnəm kwòd pábləkəm mǽləm/. The law will more readily tolerate a private loss than a public evil.

Lex Claudia /léks klód(i)yə/. A law which abolished the ancient guardianship of adult women by their male agnate relations.

Lex comitatus /léks kòmətéydəs/. The law of the county, or that administered in the county court before the earl or his deputy.

Lex commercii. The law of business transactions or commerce.

Lex communis /léks kəmyúwnəs/. The common law. See **Jus commune.**

Lex contractus /léks kəntrǽktəs/. In conflicts, the law of the place where the contract was formed, though the term today has undergone changes from the time that substantive questions of law were decided by the law of the place of the making while procedural questions were decided by the law of the forum.

Lex contra id quod præsumit, probationem non recipit /léks kóntrə íd kwòd prəz(y)úwmət prəbèyshiyównəm nón résəpət/. The law admits no proof against that which it presumes.

Lex Cornelia /léks korníyl(i)yə/. The Cornelian law; a law passed by the dictator L. Cornelius Sylla, providing remedies for certain injuries, as for battery, forcible entry of another's house, etc.

Lex Cornelia de ædictis /léks korníyl(i)yə dìy ədíktəs/. The law forbidding a prætor to depart during his term of office from the edict he had promulgated at its commencement.

Lex Cornelia de falso (or falsis) /léks korníyl(i)yə dìy fólsow/°fólsəs/. The Cornelian law respecting forgery or counterfeiting. Passed by the dictator Sylla.

The law which provided that the same penalty should attach to the forgery of a testament of a person dying in captivity as to that of a testament made by a person dying in his own country.

Lex Cornelia de injuriis /léks korníyl(i)yə dìy ənjúriyəs/. The law providing a civil action for the recovery of a penalty in certain cases of bodily injury.

Lex Cornelia de sicariis et veneficis /léks korníyl(i)yə dìy səkériyəs èt vəníyfəsəs/. The Cornelian law respecting assassins and poisoners, passed by the dictator Sylla, and containing provisions against other deeds of violence. It made the killing of the slave of another person punishable by death or exile, and the provisions of this law were extended by the Emperor Antoninus Pius to the case of a master killing his own slave.

Lex Cornelia de sponsu /léks korníyl(i)yə dìy spóns(y)uw/. A law prohibiting one from binding himself for the same debtor to the same creditor in the same year for more than a specified amount.

Lex Danorum /léks dənórəm/. The law of the Danes; Dane-law or Dane-lage.

Lex deficere non potest in justitia exhibenda /léks dəfísəriy nòn pówdəst in jəstísh(iy)ə ègzəbéndə/. The law cannot be defective [or ought not to fail] in dispensing justice.

Lex de futuro, judex de præterito /léks dìy f(y)əchúrow, júwdeks dìy prətérədow/. The law provides for the future, the judge for the past.

Lex deraisnia /léks dəréy(z)n(i)yə/. The proof of a thing which one denies to be done by him, where another affirms it; defeating the assertion of his adversary, and showing it to be against reason or probability. This was used among the old Romans, as well as the Normans.

Lex de responsis prudentum /léks dìy rəspónsəs prədéntəm/. The law of citations.

Lex dilationes semper exhorret /léks dəlèyshiyówniyz sémpər egzóhrəd/. The law always abhors delays.

Lex domicilii /léks dòməsíliyay/. The law of the domicile. In conflicts, the law of one's domicile applied in choice of law questions.

Lex est ab æterno /léks èst æb ətárnow/. Law is from everlasting. A strong expression to denote the remote antiquity of the law.

Lex est dictamen rationis /léks èst díktəmən rèyshiyównəs/. Law is the dictate of reason. The common law will judge according to the law of nature and the public good.

Lex est norma recti /léks èst nórmə réktay/. Law is a rule of right.

Lex est ratio summa, quæ jubet quæ sunt utilia et necessaria, et contraria prohibet /léks èst réysh(iy)ow səmə kwìy júwbət kwíy sənt yuwtíl(i)yə èt kəntrériyə prów(h)əbət/. Law is the perfection of reason, which commands what is useful and necessary, and forbids the contrary.

Lex est sanctio sancta, jubens honesta, et prohibens contraria /léks èst sæŋ(k)sh(iy)ow sæŋ(k)tə, júwbən(d)z ənéstə èt prów(h)əbən(d)z kəntrériyə/. Law is a sacred sanction, commanding what is right, and prohibiting the contrary.

Lex est tutissima cassis; sub clypeo legis nemo decipitur /léks èst t(y)uwtísəmə kǽsəs; sèb klípiyow líyjəs níymow dəsípədər/. Law is the safest helmet; under the shield of the law no one is deceived.

Lex et consuetudo parliamenti /léks èt kònswət(y)úwdow párl(y)əméntay/. The law and custom (or usage) of parliament. The houses of parliament constitute a court not only of legislation, but also of justice, and have their own rules, by which the court itself and the suitors therein are governed.

Lex et consuetudo regni /léks èt kònswət(y)úwdow régnay/. The law and custom of the realm. One of the names of the common law. It was bad pleading to apply the term to law made by a statute.

Lex fabia de plagiariis /léks féybiyə dìy plæjiyériyəs/. The law providing for the infliction of capital punishment in certain cases.

Lex falcidia /léks folsídiyə/. See **Falcidian law.**

Lex favet doti /léks féyvət dówday/. The law favors dower.

Lex fingit ubi subsistit æquitas /léks fínjət yúwbay səbsístəd íykwətæs/. The law makes use of a fiction where equity subsists.

Lex fori /léks fóray/. The law of the forum, or court; that is, the positive law of the state, country, or jurisdiction of whose judicial system the court where the suit is brought or remedy sought is an integral part. The lex fori, or law of jurisdiction in which relief is sought controls as to all matters pertaining to remedial (*i.e.* procedural) as distinguished from substantive rights. Shimonek v. Tillman, 150 Okl. 177, 1 P.2d 154, 156; Sullivan v. McFetridge, Sup., 55 N.Y. S.2d 511, 516. See **Lex loci contractus.**

Lex Francorum /léks fræŋkórəm/. The law of the Franks, promulgated by Theodoric I, son of Clovis I, at the same time with the law of the Alemanni and Bavarians. This was a different collection from the Salic law.

Lex Frisionum /léks friz(h)(i)yównəm/. The law of the Frisians, promulgated about the middle of the eighth century.

Lex Furia Caninia /léks fyúriyə kəníniyə/. The Furian Caninian law. A law passed in the consulship of P. Furius Camillus and C. Caninius Gallus, A.U.C. 752, prohibiting masters from manumitting by will more than a certain number or proportion of their slaves. This law was abrogated by Justinian.

Lex Furia testamentaria /léks fyúriyə tèstəmèntériyə/. A law enacting that a testator might not bequeath as a legacy more than one thousand asses.

Lex Gabinia /léks gəbíniyə/. A law introducing the ballot in elections.

Lex Genucia /léks jən(y)úws(h)(i)yə/. A law which entirely forbade the charging or taking of interest for the use of money among Roman citizens, but which was usually and easily evaded, as it did not declare an agreement for interest to be a nullity.

Lex Gothica /léks góθəkə/. The Gothic law, or law of the Goths. First promulgated in writing A.D. 466.

Lex Horatia Vaieria /léks həréysh(iy)ə vəlíriyə/. A law which assured to the tribal assembly its privilege of independent existence. See **Lex horatii**.

Lex Horatii /léks həréyshiyay/. An important constitutional statute, taking its name from the consul who secured its enactment, to the effect that all decrees passed in the meetings of the plebeians should be laws for the whole people; formerly they were binding only on the plebeians.

Lex Hortensia /léks hòrténs(h)(i)yə/°horténz(h)(i)yə/. The law giving the plebeians a full share in the *jus publicum* and the *jus sacrum*.

Lex hostilia de iurtis /léks hostíl(i)yə dìy fárdəs/. A Roman law, which provided that a prosecution for theft might be carried on without the owner's intervention.

Lex imperatoria /léks ìmpərətóriyə/. The Imperial or Roman law.

Lex intendit vicinum vicini facta scire /léks əntándət vəsáynəm vəsáynay fǽktə sáyriy/. The law intends [or presumes] that one neighbor knows what another neighbor does.

Lex judicat de rebus necessario faciendis quasi re ipsa factis /léks júwʒəkət dìy ríybəs nèsəsériyow fǽs(h)iyéndəs kwéysay ríy ípsə fǽktəs/. The law judges of things which must necessarily be done as if actually done.

Lex judicialis /léks jədìs(h)iyéyləs/. An ordeal.

Lex Julia /léks júwl(i)yə/. Several statutes bore this name, being distinguished by the addition of words descriptive of their subject matter.

The *"lex Julia de adulteriis"* related to marriage, dower, and kindred subjects. The *lex Julia de ambitu* was a law to repress illegal methods of seeking office. The *lex Julia de annona* was designed to repress combinations for heightening the price of provisions. The *"lex Julia de cessione bonorum"* related to bankruptcies. The *lex Julia de majestate* inflicted the punishment of death on all who attempted anything against the emperor or state. The *lex Julia de maritandis ordinibus* forbade senators and their children to intermarry with freedmen or infames, and freedmen to intermarry infames. The *lex Julia de residuis* was a law punishing those who gave an incomplete account of public money committed to their charge. The *lex Julia de peculatu* punished those who had stolen public money or property or anything sacred or religious. Magistrates and those who had aided them in stealing public money during their administration were punished capitally; other persons were deported. As to *lex Julia et Papia Poppæa*, see **Lex Papia Poppæa.**

Lex Julia majestatis /léks júwl(i)yə mǽjəstéydəs/. The Julian law of majesty. A law promulgated by Julius Cæsar, and again published with additions by Augustus, comprehending all the laws before enacted to punish transgressors against the state.

Lex Junia Norbana /léks júwn(i)yə norbéynə/. The law conferring legal freedom on all such freedmen as were *tuitione prætoris*. See **Latini juniani.**

Lex Junia velleja conferred the same right on posthumous children born in the lifetime of the testator, but after the execution of the will, as were enjoyed by those born after the death of the testator.

Lex Junia Velleja /léks júwn(i)yə vəlíyə/. A law providing that descendants who became *sui heredes* of the testator otherwise than by birth, as by the death of their father, must be disinherited or instituted heirs in the same way as posthumous children.

Lex Kantiæ /léks kǽnshiyiy/. The body of customs prevailing in Kent during the time of Edward I. A written statement of these customs was sanctioned by the king's justices *in eyre*. They were mainly concerned with the maintenance of a form of land tenure known as gavelkind *(q.v.).*

Lex loci /léks lówsay/. The law of the place. This may be of several descriptions but, in general, *lex loci* is only used for *lex loci contractus (q.v.).*

The *"lex loci"* furnishes the standard of conduct, Russ v. Atlantic Coast Line R. Co., 220 N.C. 715, 18 S.E.2d 130, 131; it governs as to all matters going to the basis of the right of action itself, State of Maryland, for Use of Joynes, v. Coard, 175 Va. 571, 9 S.E.2d 454, 458. The substantive rights of parties to action are governed by "lex loci" or law of place where rights were acquired or liabilities incurred. Sullivan v. McFetridge, Sup., 55 N.Y.S.2d 511, 516; Gray v. Blight, C.C.A.Colo., 112 F.2d 696, 699.

Lex loci actus /léks lówsay ǽktəs/. The law of the place where the act was done.

Lex loci celebrationis /léks lówsay sèləbrèyshiyównəs/. The law of the place where a contract is made.

Lex loci contractus /léks lówsay kəntrǽktəs/. Used sometimes to denote the law of the place where the contract was made, and at other times to denote the law by which the contract is to be governed (*i.e.* place of its performance), which may or may not be the same as that of the place where it was made. The earlier cases do not regard this distinction. Pritchard v. Norton, 106 U.S. 124, 1 S.Ct. 102, 27 L.Ed. 104; Hayward v. LeBaron, 4 Fla. 404; Scudder v. Bank, 91 U.S. 406, 23 L.Ed. 245.

Lex loci delictus /léks lówsay dəlíktəs/. The law of the place where the crime or wrong took place. The "lex loci delicti", or "place of the wrong", is the state where the last event necessary to make an actor liable for an alleged tort takes place. Sestito v. Knop, C.A.Wis., 297 F.2d 33, 34. More fully expressed by the words *lex loci delicti commissi* (law of the place where a tort is committed), usually written more briefly as *lex loci delicti*, or, sometimes, simply *lex delicti.*

Lex loci domicilii /léks lówsay dòməsíliyay/. The law of the place of domicile.

Lex loci rei sitæ /léks lówsay ríyay sáydiy/. The law of the place where a thing or subject-matter is situated. The title to realty or question of real estate law can be affected only by the law of the place where the realty is situated. Colden v. Alexander, 141 Tex. 134, 171 S.W.2d 328, 335; United States v. Becktold Co., C.C.A.Mo., 129 F.2d 473, 477.

Lex loci solutionis /léks lówsay səl(y)ùwshiyównəs/. The law of the place of solution; the law of the place where payment or performance of a contract is to be made.

Lex longobardorum /léks læ̀ŋəbardórəm/. The law of the Lombards. The name of an ancient code of laws among that people, framed, probably, between the fifth and eighth centuries. It continued in force after the incorporation of Lombardy into the empire of Charlemagne, and traces of its laws and institutions are said to be still discoverable in some parts of Italy.

Lex manifesta /léks mænəféstə/. Manifest or open law; the trial by duel or ordeal.

Lex mercatoria /léks mə̀rkətóriyə/. The law-merchant; commercial law. That system of laws which is adopted by all commercial nations, and constitutes a part of the law of the land. It is part of the common law.

Lex naturale /léks næchəréyliy/. Natural law. See **Jus naturale.**

Lex necessitatis est lex temporis; i.e., instantis /léks nəsèsətéydəs èst léks témpərəs, ìd èst ənstǽntəs/. The law of necessity is the law of the time; that is, of the instant, or present moment.

Lex neminem cogit ad vana seu inutilia peragenda /léks némənəm kówjəd æd véynə s(y)ùw ìn(y)uwtíliyə pərəjéndə/léks níym°/. The law compels no one to do vain or useless things.

Lex neminem cogit ostendere quod nescire præsumitur /léks némənəm kówjəd əsténdəriy kwòd nəsáyriy prəz(y)úmədər/. The law compels no one to show that which he is presumed not to know.

Lex nemini facit injuriam /léks némənay féysəd ənjúriyəm/. The law does injury to no one.

Lex nemini operatur iniquum /léks némənay òpəréydər ənáykwəm/. The law works injustice to no one.

Lex nemini operatur iniquum, nemini facit injuriam /léks némənay opəréydər ənáykwəm, némənay féysəd ənjúriyəm/. The law never works an injury, or does a wrong.

Lex nil facit frustra /léks níl féysət frə́strə/. The law does nothing in vain.

Lex nil facit frustra, nil jubet frustra /léks níl féysət frə́strə, nìl júwbət frə́strə/. The law does nothing and commands nothing in vain.

Lex nil frustra jubet /léks níl frə́strə júwbət/. The law commands nothing vainly.

Lex non a rege est violanda /léks nón èy ríyjiy èst vayəlǽndə/. The law is not to be violated by the king.

Lex non cogit ad impossibilia /léks nòn kówjəd æd əmpòsəbíl(i)yə/. The law does not compel the doing of impossibilities.

Lex non curat de minimis /léks nòn kyúrət dìy mínəməs/. The law cares not about trifles. The law does not regard small matters.

Lex non deficit in justitia exhibenda /léks nòn défəsəd ìn jəstísh(iy)ə ègzəbéndə/. The law does not fail in showing justice.

Lex non exacte definit, sed arbitrio boni viri permittit /léks nòn əgzǽktiy dəfáynət, sèd arbítriyow bównay víray pərmídət/. The law does not define exactly, but trusts in the judgment of a good man.

Lex non favet delicatorum votis /léks nòn féyvət dèləkətórəm vówdəs/. The law favors not the wishes of the dainty.

Lex non intendit aliquid impossibile /léks nòn ənténdəd ǽləkwəd ìmposíbəliy/. The law does not intend anything impossible. For otherwise the law should not be of any effect.

Lex non patitur fractiones et divisiones statuum /léks nòn péydədər frǽkshiówniys èt dəvìz(h)iyówniyz stǽchuwəm/. The law does not suffer fractions and divisions of estates.

Lex non præcipit inutilia, quia inutilis labor stultus /léks nòn présəpəd ìnyuwtíl(i)yə, kwáyə inyúwdələs léybər stáltəs/. The law commands not useless things, because useless labor is foolish.

Lex non requirit verificari quod apparet curiæ /léks nòn rəkwírət vèhrəfəkéray kwòd əpǽrət kyúriyiy/. The law does not require that to be verified [or proved] which is apparent to the court.

Lex non scripta /léks nòn skríptə/. The unwritten or common law, which includes general and particular customs, and particular local laws.

Lex ordinandi /léks òrdənǽnday/. The same as *lex fori* *(q.v.).*

Lex Papia Poppæa /léks péypiyə popíyə/. The Papian Poppæan law. A law proposed by the consuls Papius and Poppæus at the desire of Augustus A.U.C. 762, enlarging the *Lex Prœtoria (q.v.).* The law which exempted from tutelage women who had three children. It is usually considered with the *Lex Julia de maritandis ordinibus* as one law.

Lex patriæ /léks pǽtriyiy/. National law.

Lex Petronia /léks pətrówniyə/. The law forbidding masters to expose their slaves to contests with wild beasts.

Lex Plætoria /léks plətóriyə/. A law designed for the protection of minors against frauds and allowing them in certain cases to apply for the appointment of a guardian.

Lex plus laudatur quando ratione probatur /léks plə́s lòdéydər kwóndow rèyshiyówniy prəbéydər/. The law is the more praised when it is approved by reason.

Lex Poetelia /léks p(òw)ətíyliyə/. The law abolishing the right of a creditor to sell or kill his debtor.

Lex Pompeia de parricidiis /léks pòmpíyə dìy pærəsáy diyəs/. The law which inflicted a punishment on one who had caused the death of a parent or child. The offender was by this law to be sewn up in a sack with a dog, a cock, a viper, and an ape, and thrown into the sea or a river, so that even in his lifetime he might begin to be deprived of the use of the elements; that the air might be denied him whilst he lived and the earth when he died.

Lex posterior derogat priori /léks pəstíriyər dérəwgət priyóray/. A later statute takes away the effect of a prior one. But the later statute must either expressly repeal, or be manifestly repugnant to, the earlier one.

Lex prætoria /léks prətóriyə/. The prætorian law. A law by which every freedman who made a will was commanded to leave a moiety to his patron. The term has been applied to the rules that govern in a court of equity.

Lex prospicit, non respicit /léks pró(w)spəsət, nón réspəsət/. The law looks forward, not backward.

Lex Publilia /léks pəblíliyə/. The law providing that the *plebiscita* should bind the whole people. The *lex Publilia de sponsu* allowed sponsores, unless reimbursed within six months, to recover from their principal by a special *actio* what they had paid.

Lex punit mendacium /léks pyúwnət məndéys(h)-(i)yəm/. The law punishes falsehood.

Lex regia /léks ríyjiyə/. The royal or imperial law. A law enacted (or supposed or claimed to have been enacted) by the Roman people, constituting the emperor a source of law, conferring the legislative power upon him, and according the force and obligation of law to the expression of his mere will or pleasure.

Lex rei sitæ /léks ríyay sáydiy/. The law of the place of situation of the thing. It is said to be an inexact mode of expression; *lex situs,* or *lex loci rei sitæ* are better.

Lex rejicit superflua, pugnantia, incongrua /léks ríyjəsət səpárfluwə, pəgnǽnsh(iy)ə, iŋkóŋgruwə/. The law rejects superfluous, contradictory, and incongruous things.

Lex reprobat moram /léks rəprówbət mórəm/. The law dislikes delay.

Lex respicit æquitatem /léks réspəsəd ìykwətéydəm/. The law pays regard to equity.

Lex Rhodia /léks rówd(i)yə/. See **Rhodian laws.**

Lex romana /léks rəméynə/. See **Civil Law; Roman law.**

Lex sacramentalis /léks sækrəməntéyləs/. Purgation by oath.

Lex Scribonia /léks skrəbówniyə/. The law abolishing the *usucapio servitutis.*

Lex scripta /léks skríptə/. Written law; law deriving its force, not from usage, but from express legislative enactment; statute law.

Lex scripta si cesset, id custodiri oportet quod moribus et consuetudine inductum est; et, si qua in re hoc defecerit, tunc id quod proximum et consequens ei est; et, si id non appareat, tunc jus quo urbs romana utitur servari oportet. If the written law be silent, that which is drawn from manners and custom ought to be observed; and, if that is in any manner defective, then that which is next and analogous to it; and, if that does not appear, then the law which Rome uses should be followed.

Lex semper dabit remedium /léks sémpər déybət rəmíyd(i)yəm/. The law will always give a remedy.

Lex semper intendit quod convenit rationi /léks sémpər ənténdət kwód kənvíynət ræshiyównay/. The law always intends what is agreeable to reason.

Lex Sempronia /léks semprówniyə/. The law preventing senators from being judges and allowing the office to the knights.

Lex Silia /léks síliyə/. A law concerning personal actions.

Lex situs /léks sáydəs/. Modern law Latin for "the law of the place where property is situated." The general rule is that lands and other immovables are governed by the *lex situs; i.e.,* by the law of the country in which they are situated.

Lex solutionis. The law of the place in which a contract is to be performed or payment is to be made.

Lex spectat naturæ ordinem /léks spéktət nəchúriy órdənəm/. The law regards the order of nature.

Lex succurrit ignoranti /léks səkáhrət ìgnərǽntay/. The law assists the ignorant.

Lex succurrit minoribus /léks səkáhrət mənórəbəs/. The law aids minors.

Lex talionis /léks tæliyównəs/. The law of retaliation; which requires the infliction upon a wrongdoer of the same injury which he has caused to another. Expressed in the Mosaic law by the formula, "an eye for an eye; a tooth for a tooth," etc. In modern international law, the term describes the rule by which one state may inflict upon the citizens of another state death, imprisonment, or other hardship, in retaliation for similar injuries imposed upon its own citizens.

Lex terræ /léks téhriy/. The law of the land. The common law, or the due course of the common law; the general law of the land. Equivalent to "due process of law". In the strictest sense, trial by oath; the privilege of making oath.

Lex uno ore omnes alloquitur /léks yúwnow óriy ómniyz əlówkwədər/. The law addresses all with one [the same] mouth or voice.

Lex validitatis /léks vəlìdətéydəs/. In conflicts, refers to presumptions of validity in marriages, contracts, etc.

Lex vigilantibus, non dormientibus, subvenit /léks vijəlǽntəbəs nón dormiyéntəbəs sə́bvənət/. Law assists the wakeful, not the sleeping.

Lex Voconia /léks vəkówniyə/. A *plebiscitum* forbidding a legatee to receive more than each heir had.

Lex Wallensica /léks wòlénzəkə/. The Welsh law; the law of Wales.

Lex Wisigothorum /léks vìzəgəθórəm/. The law of the Visigoths, or Western Goths who settled in Spain; first reduced to writing A.D. 466. A revision of these laws was made by Egigas.

Ley /léy/. L. Fr. (A corruption of *loi*.) Law; the law. For example, *Termes de la Ley*, Terms of the Law. In another, and an old technical, sense, ley signifies an oath, or the oath with compurgators; as, il tend sa *ley* aiu pleyntiffe. See also **Lex.**

In Spanish law, a law; the law; law in the abstract.

Ley civile /léy səvíyl/. In old English law, the civil or Roman law. Otherwise termed *"ley escripte,"* the written law. See also **Civil law.**

Ley gager /léy géyjər/. Law wager; wager of law; the giving of gage or security by a defendant that he would make or perfect his law at a certain day.

An offer to make an oath denying the cause of action of the plaintiff, confirmed by compurgators, which oath was allowed in certain cases. When it was accomplished, it was called the "doing of the law," *"fesans de ley."*

Leze majesty, or **lese majesty** /líyz mǽjəstiy/. An offense against sovereign power; treason; rebellion.

L.H.W.C.A. Longshoremen's and Harbor Workers' Compensation Act.

Liability. The word is a broad legal term. Mayfield v. First Nat. Bank of Chattanooga, Tenn., C.C.A.Tenn., 137 F.2d 1013, 1019. It has been referred to as of the most comprehensive significance, including almost every character of hazard or responsibility, absolute, contingent, or likely. It has been defined to mean: all character of debts and obligations, Public Market Co. of Portland v. City of Portland, 171 Or. 522, 130 P.2d 624, 643, 646; amenability or responsibility, Eberhard v. Ætna Ins. Co., 134 Misc. 386, 235 N.Y.S. 445, 447; an obligation one is bound in law or justice to perform, State ex rel. Diederichs v. Board of Trustees of Missoula County High School, 91 Mont. 300, 7 P.2d 543, 545; an obligation which may or may not ripen into a debt; any kind of debt or liability, either absolute or contingent, express or implied, Public Market Co. of Portland v. City of Portland, 171 Or. 522, 130 P.2d 624, 643, 646; condition of being actually or potentially subject to an obligation; condition of being responsible for a possible or actual loss, penalty, evil, expense, or burden; condition which creates a duty to perform an act immediately or in the future, Union Oil Co. of California v. Basalt Rock Co., 30 Cal.App.2d 317, 86 P.2d 139, 141; duty to pay money or perform some other service, Dehne v. Hillman Inv. Co., C.C.A.Pa., 110 F.2d 456, 458; duty which must at least eventually be performed, Vandegrift v. Riley, Cal.Sup., 16 P.2d 734, 736; estate tax, Lyeth v. Hoey, C.C.A.N.Y., 112 F.2d 4, 6; every kind of legal obligation, responsibility, or duty, Mayfield v. First Nat. Bank of Chattanooga, Tenn., C.C.A.Tenn., 137 F.2d 1013, 1019; fixed liability, Vandegrift v. Riley, Cal. Sup., 16 P.2d 734, 736; Ivester v. State ex rel. Gillum, 183 Okl. 519, 83 P.2d 193, 196; legal responsibility, Clark v. Lowden, D.C.Minn., 43 F.Supp. 261, 263; penalty for failure to pay tax when due, State v.

Fischl, 94 Mont. 92, 20 P.2d 1057, 1059; present, current, future, fixed or contingent debts, Erickson v. Grande Ronde Lumber Co., 162 Or. 556, 92 P.2d 170, 174; punishment, Holliman v. Cole, 168 Okl. 473, 34 P.2d 597, 599; responsibility for torts, Italiani v. Metro-Goldwyn-Mayer Corporation, 45 Cal.App.2d 464, 114 P.2d 370, 372; tax, State ex rel. DuFresne v. Leslie, 100 Mont. 449, 50 P.2d 959, 963; Thompson v. Smith, 189 Okl. 217, 114 P.2d 922, 924; that which one is under obligation to pay, or for which one is liable, Reconstruction Finance Corporation v. Gossett, Tex., 111 S.W.2d 1066; the state of being bound or obliged in law or justice to do, pay, or make good something; the state of one who is bound in law and justice to do something which may be enforced by action, Fidelity Coal Co. v. Diamond, 310 Ill.App. 387, 34 N.E.2d 123; Clark v. Lowden, D.C.Minn., 48 F.Supp. 261, 263; unliquidated claim.

All the claims against a corporation. Liabilities include accounts and wages and salaries payable, dividends declared payable, accrued taxes payable, fixed or long-term liabilities such as mortgage bonds, debentures and bank loans.

See also Current liabilities; Employer's liability acts; Legal liability; Liable; Limitation of Liability Act; Malpractice; Parental liability; Personal liability; Product liability; Several liability; Strict liability; Vicarious liability.

Accrued liability. Obligation which has been incurred but not yet paid; *e.g.* taxes, rent.

Children. See **Parental liability.**

Contingent liability. A liability not yet fixed but dependent on events to occur in the future (*e.g.* a pending law suit).

Fixed liability. One fixed as to time, amount, etc.; *e.g.* mortgage.

Joint and several liability. Responsible together and individually. The person who has been harmed can sue and recover from both wrongdoers or from either one of the wrongdoers (if he goes after both of them, he does not, however, receive double compensation). See **Joint tort-feasors.**

Joint liability. Liability for which more than one person is responsible. See also **Contribution; Joint tort-feasors.**

Liability bond. See **Bond.**

Primary liability. A liability for which a person is directly responsible as contrasted with own which is contingent or secondary.

Secondary liability. A liability in the nature of a contigent claim such as the liability of a guarantor as contrasted with that of a strict surety or comaker. A guarantor's liability does not arise until the principal debtor has failed to pay the creditor.

Liability created by statute. One depending for its existence on the enactment of a statute, and not on the contract of the parties. One which would not exist but for the statute. Cannon v. Miller, 22 Wash.2d 227, 155 P.2d 500, 507, 508.

Liability for damages. Liability for an amount to be ascertained by trial of the facts in particular cases.

Liability imposed by law. Liability imposed in a definite sum by a final judgment against assured. Girard v. Commercial Standard Ins. Co., 66 Cal.App.2d 483, 152 P.2d 509, 513. Total liability imposed by law upon a person. Schwartz v. Merola Bros. Const. Corporation, 290 N.Y. 145, 48 N.E.2d 299, 303.

Liability in solido. Liability in solido, whether emanating from tort or contract, means that either of the debtors may be required to discharge obligation in full at creditor's election. Cunningham v. Hardware Mut. Cas. Co., La.App., 228 So.2d 700, 705.

Liability insurance. Contract by which one party promises on consideration to compensate or reimburse other if he shall suffer loss from specified cause or to guaranty or indemnify or secure him against loss from that cause. Fidelity General Ins. Co. v. Nelsen Steel & Wire Co., 132 Ill.App.2d 635, 270 N.E.2d 616, 620. That type of insurance protection which indemnifies one from liability to third persons as contrasted with insurance coverage for losses sustained by the insured. See also **Insurance.**

Liable. Bound or obliged in law or equity; responsible; chargeable; answerable; compellable to make satisfaction, compensation, or restitution. Homan v. Employers Reinsurance Corporation, 345 Mo. 650, 136 S.W.2d 289, 298. Obligated; accountable for or chargeable with. Condition of being bound to respond because a wrong has occurred. Condition out of which a legal liability might arise. Pacific Fire Ins. Co. v. Murdoch Cotton Co., 193 Ark. 327, 99 S.W.2d 233, 235. Justly or legally responsible or answerable.

Exposed or subject to a given contingency, risk, or casualty, which is more or less probable. Pacific Fire Ins. Co. v. Murdoch Cotton Co., 193 Ark. 327, 99 S.W.2d 233, 235. Exposed, as to damage, penalty, expense, burden, or anything unpleasant or dangerous. See also **Liability.**

Future possible or probable happening which may not actually occur, and relates to an occurrence within the range of possibility. Alabama Great Southern R. Co. v. Smith, 209 Ala. 301, 96 So. 239, 240; Pacific Fire Ins. Co. v. Murdoch Cotton Co., 193 Ark. 327, 99 S.W.2d 233, 235. In all probability. Neely v. Chicago Great Western R. Co., Mo.App., 14 S.W.2d 972, 978. See also **Contingency; Contingent.**

Liable to action. Liable to judgment in given action. Haas v. New York Post Graduate Medical School and Hospital, 131 Misc. 395, 226 N.Y.S. 617, 620.

Liable to penalty. Subject to penalty. The Motorboat, D.C.N.J., 53 F.2d 239, 241.

Libel /láybəl/. A method of defamation expressed by print, writing, pictures, or signs. In its most general sense, any publication that is injurious to the reputation of another. A false and unprivileged publication in writing of defamatory material. Bright v. Los Angeles Unified School Dist., 51 Cal.App.3d 852, 124 Cal.Rptr. 598, 604. A maliciously written or printed publication which tends to blacken a person's reputation or to expose him to public hatred, contempt, or ridicule, or to injure him in his business or profession. Corabi v. Curtis Pub. Co., 441 Pa. 432, 273 A.2d 899, 904.

Accusation in writing or printing against the character of a person which affects his reputation, in that it tends to hold him up to ridicule, contempt, shame, disgrace, or obloquy, to degrade him in the estimation of the community, to induce an evil opinion of him in the minds of rightthinking persons, to make him an object of reproach, to diminish his respectability or abridge his comforts, to change his position in society for the worse, to dishonor or discredit him in the estimation of the public, or his friends and acquaintances, or to deprive him of friendly intercourse in society, or cause him to be shunned or avoided, or where it is charged that one has violated his public duty as a public officer. Almost any language which upon its face has a natural tendency to injure a man's reputation, either generally or with respect to his occupation. Washer v. Bank of America Nat. Trust & Savings Ass'n, 21 Cal.2d 822, 136 P.2d 297, 300.

There can be no presumption of malice or bad faith consistent with freedom of the press under First Amend., U.S.Const. if plaintiff is a public figure. Malice must be proved on a showing that defendant published material either knowing it to be false or recklessly without regard as to whether it is true or false. N. Y. Times v. Sullivan, 376 U.S. 254, 84 S.Ct. 710, 11 L.Ed.2d 686.

See also Actionable per quod; Actionable per se; Criminal (Criminal libel); Innuendo; Libelous per quod; Libelous per se; Malice; Obscene libel; Privilege; Publication; Seditious libel; Single publication rule.

Constitutional privilege. Prior to New York Times v. Sullivan, 376 U.S. 254, 84 S.Ct. 710, 11 L.Ed.2d 686 (1964), media comment on the conduct of public officials or public figures was free from liability for libel only in certain limited circumstances, usually difficult to prove at trial. If a statement of fact was involved, it had to be substantially true; if a comment or opinion was involved, it had to be based on true facts which fully and fairly justified the comment or opinion. The United States Supreme Court, however, in a series of decisions beginning with New York Times Co. v. Sullivan, imposed constitutional limitations on State libel laws, based upon the First Amendment guarantees of freedom of speech and press. In New York Times, the Supreme Court eroded the prior common law libel standard of strict liability, holding that misstatements of fact or unjustified comments or opinions published by the media about the conduct of public officials were constitutionally privileged, unless the false or unjustified material was published with "actual malice," i.e., with actual knowledge of falsity or with reckless disregard of probable falsity. By requiring a public official plaintiff to prove actual malice on the part of defendant, the burden of proving that the material was false was shifted to plaintiff, contrary to the common law rule which presumed falsity.

Group libel. The holding up of a group to ridicule, scorn or contempt to a respectable and considerable part of the community. The plaintiff must prove that he is a member of the group.

Pleadings. Formerly, the initiatory pleading in an admiralty action, corresponding to the declaration, bill or complaint. Since 1966 the Federal Rules of Civil Procedure and Supp. Admiralty Rules have governed admiralty actions and as such, admiralty actions are now commenced by complaint.

Libelant /láybələnt/. Formerly, the complainant or party who files a libel in an ecclesiastical or admiralty case, corresponding to the plaintiff in actions at law. See **Libel** (*Pleadings*).

Libelee /làybəlíy/. Formerly, a party against whom a libel has been filed in an ecclesiastical court or in admiralty, corresponding to the defendant in actions at law. See **Libel** (*Pleadings*).

Libellus /ləbéləs/. Lat. In the civil law, a little book.

Feudal law. An instrument of alienation or conveyance, as of a fief, or a part of it.

Libellus supplex. A petition, especially to the emperor, all petitions to whom must be in writing. *Libellum rescribere*, to mark on such petition the answer to it. *Libellum agere*, to assist or counsel the emperor in regard to such petitions. *Libellus accusatorius*, an information and accusation of a crime. *Libellus divortii*, a writing of divorcement. *Libellus rerum*, an inventory. *Libellus* or *oratio consultoria*, a message by which emperors laid matters before the senate. *Libellus appellatorius*, an appeal.

Libellus conventionis /ləbéləs kənvènshiyównəs/. In the civil law, the statement of a plaintiff's claim in a petition presented to the magistrate, who directed an officer to deliver it to the defendant.

Libellus famosus /ləbéləs fəmówsəs/. In the civil law, a defamatory publication; a publication injuriously affecting character; a libel.

Libel of review. New proceeding instituted to attack final decree after expiration of term and right to appeal. The Astorian, C.C.A.Cal., 57 F.2d 85, 87.

Libelous /láyb(ə)ləs/. Defamatory; of the nature of a libel; constituting or involving libel. See also **Libel.**

Libelous per quod /láyb(ə)ləs pər kwód/. Expressions "libelous per quod" are such as require that their injurious character or effect be established by allegation and proof. They are those expressions which are not actionable upon their face, but which become so by reason of the peculiar situation or occasion upon which the words are written. Publications which are susceptible of two reasonable interpretations, one of which is defamatory and the other is not, or publications which are not obviously defamatory, but which become so when considered in connection with innuendo, colloquium, and explanatory circumstances. See **Actionable per quod.**

Libelous per se /láyb(ə)ləs pər síy/. A publication is libelous *per se* when the words are of such a character that an action may be brought upon them without the necessity of showing any special damage, the imputation being such that the law will presume that any one so slandered must have suffered damage. Robinson v. Nationwide Ins. Co., 273 N.C. 391, 159 S.E.2d 896, 898. To render words "libelous per se," the words must be of such character that a presumption of law will arise therefrom that the plaintiff has been degraded in the estimation of his friends or of the public or has suffered some other loss either in his property, character, reputation, or business or in his domestic or social relations. When a publication is "libelous per se", that is, defamatory on its face, it is actionable per se; *i.e.* one need not prove that he received any injury as a result of the publication in order to recover damages, and in such a case general damages for loss of personal or business reputation are recoverable and no averments or proof of special damages are necessary. Rosenbloom v. Metromedia, Inc., D.C.Pa., 289 F.Supp. 737, 743. See **Actionable per se.**

Liber, *adj.* /láybər/. Lat. Free; open and accessible, as applied to courts, places, etc.; of the state or condition of a freeman, as applied to persons. Exempt from the service or jurisdiction of another.

Liber, *n.* /láybər/. Lat. A book, of whatever material composed; a main division or unit of a literary or professional work.

Libera /líb(ə)rə/. Lat. (Feminine of *liber, adj.*) Free; at liberty; exempt; not subject to toll or charge.

Libera batella /líb(ə)rə bətélə/. In old records, a free boat; the right of having a boat to fish in a certain water; a species of free fishery.

Libera chasea habenda /líb(ə)rə chéys(h)(i)yə həbéndə/. In old English law, a judicial writ granted to a person for a free chase belonging to his manor after proof made by inquiry of a jury that the same of right belongs to him.

Libera eleemosyna /líb(ə)rə ìyləmósənə/. In old English law, free alms, frankalmoigne.

Libera falda /líb(ə)rə fóldə/. In old English law, frank fold; free fold; free foldage.

Liberal /líb(ə)rəl/. Free in giving; generous; not restrained or narrow-minded; not literal or strict.

Liberal construction or **interpretation** /líb(ə)rəl kənstrákshən/°əntàrprətéyshən/. See **Construction.**

Libera lex /líb(ə)rə léks/. In old English law, free law; frank law; the law of the land. The law enjoyed by free and lawful men, as distinguished from such men as have lost the benefit and protection of the law in consequence of crime. Hence this term denoted the *status* of a man who stood guiltless before the law, and was *free*, in the sense of being entitled to its full protection and benefit. *Amittere liberam legem* (to lose one's free law) was to fall from that *status* by crime or infamy.

Liberam legem amittere /líbərəm líyjəm əmídəriy/. To lose one's free law (called the villainous judgment), to become discredited or disabled as juror and witness, to forfeit goods and chattels and lands for life, to have those lands wasted, houses razed, trees rooted up, and one's body committed to prison. It was anciently pronounced against conspirators but is now disused, the punishment substituted being fine and imprisonment.

Libera piscaria /líb(ə)rə pəskériyə/. In old English law, a free fishery.

Liberare /lìbərériy/. Lat. In old English law, to deliver, transfer, or hand over. Applied to writs, panels of jurors, etc.

In the civil law, to free or set free; to liberate; to give one his liberty.

Liber assisarum /láybər əsàyzérəm/. The Book of Assizes or pleas of the crown. A collection of cases that arose on assizes and other trials in the country. It was the fourth volume of the reports of the reign of Edward III.

Liberata pecunia non liberat offerentem /lìbəréydə pəkyúwn(iy)ə nón líbərəd òfəréntəm/. Money being restored does not set free the party offering.

Liberate /lìbəréydiy/. In old English practice, an original writ issuing out of chancery to the treasurer, chamberlains, and barons of the exchequer, for the payment of any annual pension, or other sum.

A writ issued to a sheriff, for the delivery of any lands or goods taken upon forfeits of recognizance. A writ issued to a gaoler for the delivery of a prisoner that had put in bail for his appearance. A writ which issues on lands, tenements, and chattels, being returned under an extent on a statute staple, commanding the sheriff to deliver them to the plaintiff, by the extent and appraisement mentioned in the writ of extent and in the sheriff's return thereto.

To set free, as from bondage, slavery, oppression, or enemy control.

Liberatio /lìbəréysh(iy)ow/. In old English law, livery; money paid for the delivery or use of a thing.

Liberation /lìbəréyshən/. In civil law, the extinguishment of a contract, by which he who was bound becomes free or liberated. Synonymous with payment.

Liber authenticorum /láybər əθèntəkórəm/. The authentic collection of the novels of Justinian, so called to distinguish them from the Epitome Juliani.

Libera warrena /líb(ə)rə wóhrənə/. In old English law, free warren (q.v.).

Liber bancus /láybər bǽŋkəs/. In old English law, free bench.

Liber et legalis homo /láybər èt ləgéyləs hówmow/. In old English law, a free and lawful man. A term applied to a juror, or to one worthy of being a juryman, from the earliest period.

Liber feudorum /láybər fyuwdórəm/. See **Feudorum liber.**

Liber homo /láybər hówmow/. See **Homo liber.**

Liberi /líbəray/. In Saxon law, freemen; the possessors of allodial lands.

In the civil law, children. The term included "grandchildren."

Liber judicialis of Alfred /láybər jədìs(h)iyéyləs əv ǽlfrəd/. Alfred's dome-book. See **Dombec; Domebook.**

Liber judiciarum /láybər jədìs(h)iyérəm/. The book of judgment, or doom-book. The Saxon Domboc. Conjectured to be a book of statutes of ancient Saxon kings.

Liber niger /láybər náyjər/. Black book or register in the exchequer. Chartularies of abbeys, cathedrals, etc. A name given to several ancient records.

Liber niger domus regis /láybər náyjər dówməs ríyjəs/. The black book of the king's household.

Liber ruber scaccarii /láybər rúwbər skəkériyay/. The red book of the exchequer.

Libertas /líbərtæs/. Lat. Liberty; freedom; a privilege; a franchise.

Libertas ecclesiastica /líbərtæs əklìyziyǽstəkə/. Church liberty, or ecclesiastical immunity.

Libertas est naturalis facultas ejus quod cuique facere libet, nisi quod de jure aut vi prohibetur /líbərtæs èst næchəréyləs fəkáltæs íyjəs kwòd k(yuw)áykwiy féysəriy láybət, náysay kwòd dìy júriy òt váy pròw(h)əbíydər/. Liberty is that natural faculty which permits every one to do [or the natural power of doing] anything he pleases except that which is restrained by law or force.

Libertas inestimabilis res est /líbərtæs inèstəméybələs ríyz èst/. Liberty is an inestimable thing; a thing above price.

Libertas non recipit æstimationem /líbərtæs nòn résəpət èstəmèyshiyównəm/. Freedom does not admit of valuation.

Libertas omnibus rebus favorabilior est /líbərtæs ómnəbəs ríybəs fèyvərəbíliyər èst/. Liberty is more favored than all things [anything].

Libertates regales ad coronam spectantes ex concessione regum à coronâ exierunt /lìbərtéydiyz rəgéyliyz æd kərównəm spektæntiyz èks kənsèshiyówniy ríygəm èy kərównə ègziyírənt/. Royal franchises relating to the crown have emanated from the crown by grant of kings.

Libertatibus allocandis /lìbərtéydəbəs æləkǽndəs/. A writ lying for a citizen or burgess, impleaded contrary to his liberty, to have his privilege allowed.

Libertatibus exigendis in itinere /lìbərtéydəbəs egzəjéndəs ìn ətínəriy/. An ancient writ whereby the king commanded the justices in eyre to admit an attorney for the defense of another's liberty.

Liberti /ləbárday/, **libertini** /lìbərtáynay/. Lat. In Roman law, freedmen. The condition of those who, having been slaves, had been made free. There seems to have been some difference in the use of these two words; the former denoting the manumitted slaves considered in their relations with their former master, who was now called their "patron;" the latter term applying to them in their *status* in the general social economy of Rome subsequent to manumission.

Liberticide /ləbárdəsayd/líbər°/. A destroyer of liberty.

Liberties /líbərdiyz/. Privileged districts exempt from the sheriff's jurisdiction; as, "gaol liberties." See **Gaol.**

In colonial times, laws, or legal rights resting upon them. The early colonial ordinances in Massachusetts were termed laws and liberties, and the code of 1641 the "Body of Liberties."

Formerly, political subdivisions of Philadelphia; as, Northern Liberties.

Libertinum ingratum leges civiles in pristinam servitutem redigunt; sed leges Angliæ semel manumissum semper liberum judicant /lìbərtáynəm ingréydəm líyjiyz sívəliyz in prístənəm sərvət(y)úwdəm rédəgənt, sèd líyjiyz ǽ ŋgliyiy sémǝl mǽ nyuwmísǝm sémpǝr líbǝrǝm júwdǝkǽ nt/. The civil laws reduce an ungrateful freedman to his original slavery; but the laws of England regard a man once manumitted as ever after free.

Liberty. Freedom; exemption from extraneous control. Freedom from all restraints except such as are justly imposed by law. Freedom from restraint, under conditions essential to the equal enjoyment of the same right by others; freedom regulated by law. The absence of arbitrary restraint, not immunity from reasonable regulations and prohibitions imposed in the interests of the community. Arnold v. Board of Barber Examiners, 45 N.M. 57, 109 P.2d 779, 785.

The power of the will to follow the dictates of its unrestricted choice, and to direct the external acts of the individual without restraint, coercion, or control from other persons. See Booth v. Illinois, 184 U.S. 425, 22 S.Ct. 425, 46 L.Ed. 623; Munn v. Illinois, 94 U.S. 113, 24 L.Ed. 77.

The word "liberty" includes and comprehends all personal rights and their enjoyment. Rosenblum v. Rosenblum, 181 Misc. 78, 42 N.Y.S.2d 626, 630. It embraces freedom from duress; freedom from governmental interference in exercise of intellect, in formation of opinions, in the expression of them, and in action or inaction dictated by judgment, Zavilla v. Masse, 112 Colo. 183, 147 P.2d 823, 827; freedom from servitude, imprisonment or restraint, Committee for Industrial Organization v. Hague, D.C.N.J., 25 F.Supp. 127, 131, 141; People v. Wood, 151 Misc. 66, 272 N.Y.S. 258; freedom in enjoyment and use of all of one's powers, faculties and property, Grosjean v. American Press Co., 297 U.S. 233, 56 S.Ct. 444, 446, 80 L.Ed. 660; City of Mt. Vernon v. Julian, 369 Ill. 447, 17 N.E.2d 52, 55; freedom of assembly, Rosenblum v. Rosenblum, 181 Misc. 78, 42 N.Y.S.2d 626, 630; freedom of citizen from banishment, Committee for Industrial Organization v. Hague, D.C.N.J., 25 F.Supp. 127, 141; freedom of conscience, Gobitis v. Minersville School Dist., D.C.Pa., 21 F.Supp. 581, 584, 587; freedom of contract, State ex rel. Hamby v. Cummings, 166 Tenn. 460, 63 S.W.2d 515; State v. Henry, 37 N.M. 536, 25 P.2d 204; freedom of locomotion or movement, Committee for Industrial Organization v. Hague, D.C.N.J., 25 F.Supp. 127, 131, 141; freedom of occupation, Koos v. Saunders, 349 Ill. 442, 182 N.E. 415, 418; freedom of press, Commonwealth v. Nichols, 301 Mass. 584, 18 N.E.2d 166, 167; Near v. State of Minnesota ex rel. Olson, 283 U.S. 697, 51 S.Ct. 625, 628, 75 L.Ed. 1357; freedom of religion, Gabrielli v. Knickerbocker, 12 Cal.2d 85, 82 P.2d 391, 393; Hamilton v. City of Montrose, 109 Colo. 228, 124 P.2d 757, 759; Cantwell v. State of Connecticut, 310 U.S. 296, 60 S.Ct. 900, 903, 84 L.Ed. 1213; freedom of speech, Ghadiali v. Delaware State Medical Soc., D.C. Del., 28 F.Supp. 841, 844; Carpenters and Joiners Union of America, Local No. 213, v. Ritter's Cafe, 315 U.S. 722, 62 S.Ct. 807, 86 L.Ed. 1143. It also embraces right of self-defense against unlawful violence; right to acquire and enjoy property; right to acquire useful knowledge; right to carry on business, Mlle. Reif, Inc., v. Randau, 166 Misc. 247, 1 N.Y.S.2d 515,

518; right to earn livelihood in any lawful calling; right to emigrate, and if a citizen, to return, Committee for Industrial Organization v. Hague, D.C.N.J., 25 F.Supp. 127, 141; right to engage in a lawful business, to determine the price of one's labor, and to fix the hours when one's place of business shall be kept open, State Board of Barber Examiners v. Cloud, 220 Ind. 552, 44 N.E.2d 972, 980; right to enjoy to the fullest extent the privileges and immunities given or assured by law to people living within the country, McGrew v. Industrial Commission, 96 Utah 203, 85 P.2d 608, 611; right to forswear allegiance and expatriate oneself, Committee for Industrial Organization v. Hague, D.C.N.J., 25 F.Supp. 127, 141; right to freely buy and sell as others may; right to live and work where one will, People v. Wood, 151 Misc. 66, 272 N.Y.S. 258; right to marry and have a family, Committee for Industrial Organization v. Hague, D.C. N.J., 25 F.Supp. 127, 141; Rosenblum v. Rosenblum, 181 Misc. 78, 42 N.Y.S.2d 626, 630; right to pursue chosen calling, People v. Cohen, 255 App.Div. 485, 8 N.Y.S.2d 70, 72; right to use property according to owner's will.

Liberty, on its positive side, denotes the fullness of individual existence; on its negative side it denotes the necessary restraint on all, which is needed to promote the greatest possible amount of liberty for each.

The word "liberty" as used in the state and federal constitutions means, in a negative sense, freedom from restraint, but in a positive sense, it involves the idea of freedom secured by the imposition of restraint, and it is in this positive sense that the state, in the exercise of its police powers, promotes the freedom of all by the imposition upon particular persons of restraints which are deemed necessary for the general welfare. Fitzsimmons v. New York State Athletic Commission, Sup., 146 N.Y.S. 117, 121.

Term "liberty" as used in Constitution means more than freedom from arrest or restraint and includes freedom of action, freedom to own, control, and use property, freedom to pursue any lawful trade, business or calling, and freedom to make all proper contracts in relation thereto. State v. Nuss, 79 S.D. 522, 114 N.W.2d 633, 635.

The "personal liberty" guaranteed by Thirteenth Amend., U.S.Const., consists in the power of locomotion without imprisonment or restraint unless by due course of law, except those restraints imposed to prevent commission of threatened crime or in punishment of crime committed, those in punishment of contempts of courts or legislative bodies or to render their jurisdiction effectual, and those necessary to enforce the duty citizens owe in defense of the state to protect community against acts of those who by reason of mental infirmity are incapable of self-control.

The "liberty" safeguarded by Fourteenth Amendment is liberty in a social organization which requires the protection of law against the evils which menace the health, safety, morals, and welfare of the people. West Coast Hotel Co. v. Parrish, 300 US 379, 57 S.Ct. 578, 581, 582, 81 L.Ed. 703.

Also, a franchise or personal privilege, being some part of the sovereign power, vested in an individual, either by grant or prescription.

The term is used in the expression, rights, liberties, and franchises, as a word of the same general class and meaning with those words and privileges. This use of the term is said to have been strictly conformable to its sense as used in Magna Charta and in English declarations of rights, statutes, grants, etc.

In a derivative sense, the place, district, or boundaries within which a special franchise is enjoyed, an immunity claimed, or a jurisdiction exercised. In this sense, the term is commonly used in the plural; as the "liberties of the city."

Civil liberty. The liberty of a member of society, being a man's natural liberty, so far restrained by human laws (and no further) as is necessary and expedient for the general advantage of the public. 1 Bl.Comm. 125. The power of doing whatever the laws permit. 1 Bl.Comm. 6. The greatest amount of absolute liberty which can, in the nature of things, be equally possessed by every citizen in a state. Guaranteed protection against interference with the interests and rights held dear and important by large classes of civilized men, or by all the members of a state, together with an effectual share in the making and administration of the laws, as the best apparatus to secure that protection. See **Civil rights.**

Liberty of a port. In marine insurance, a license or permission incorporated in a marine policy allowing the vessel to touch and trade at a designated port other than the principal port of destination.

Liberty of conscience. Liberty for each individual to decide for himself what is to him religious. Gobitis v. Minersville School Dist., D.C.Pa., 21 F.Supp. 581, 584. See, also, *Religious liberty,* as defined below.

Liberty of contract. The ability at will, to make or abstain from making, a binding obligation enforced by the sanctions at the law. The right to contract about one's affairs, including the right to make contracts of employment, and to obtain the best terms one can as the result of private bargaining. Adkins v. Children's Hospital of District of Columbia, 261 U.S. 525, 43 S.Ct. 394, 396, 67 L.Ed. 785. It includes the corresponding right to accept a contract proposed. There is, however, no absolute freedom of contract. The government may regulate or forbid any contract reasonably calculated to affect injuriously public interest. Atlantic Coast Line R. Co. v. Riverside Mills, 219 U.S. 186, 31 S.Ct. 164, 55 L.Ed. 167; Carleton Screw Products Co. v. Fleming, C.C.A.Minn., 126 F.2d 537, 541. It means freedom from arbitrary or unreasonable restraint, not immunity from reasonable regulation to safeguard public interest; or the right to make contracts with competent persons on a plane of relative parity or freedom of choice and within the limits allowed or not forbidden by law. McGrew v. Industrial Commission, 96 Utah 203, 85 P.2d 608, 612. See Art. I, § 10, U.S. Constitution.

Liberty of speech. Freedom accorded by the Constitution (First Amendment of U.S.Const.) or laws to express opinions and facts by word of mouth, uncontrolled by any censorship or restrictions of government. As used in Constitution, "freedom of speech" means freedom of speech as it was understood by the common law when the Constitution was adopted. State v. Boloff, 138 Or. 568, 7 P.2d 775, 781. See however **Clear and present danger doctrine.** See also **Symbolic speech.**

Liberty of the globe. In marine insurance, a license or permission incorporated in a marine policy authorizing the vessel to go to any part of the world, instead of being confined to a particular port of destination.

Liberty of the press. The right to print and publish the truth, from good motives and for justifiable ends, as guaranteed by First Amendment of U.S. Constitution. Kline v. Robert M. McBride & Co., 170 Misc. 974, 11 N.Y.S.2d 674, 679. The right to print without any previous license, subject to the consequences of the law. The right to publish whatever one may please, Knapp v. Post Printing & Publishing Co., 111 Colo. 492, 144 P.2d 981, 985; Howard Sports Daily v. Weller, 179 Md. 355, 18 A.2d 210, 215; and to be protected against any responsibility for so doing except so far as such publications, from their blasphemy, obscenity, or scandalous character, may be a public offense, or as by their falsehood and malice they may injuriously affect the standing, reputation, or pecuniary interests of individuals. Immunity from previous restraints or [from] censorship. Grosjean v. American Press Co., 297 U.S. 233, 56 S.Ct. 444, 449, 80 L.Ed. 660; Near v. Minnesota, 283 U.S. 697, 51 S.Ct. 625, 75 L.Ed. 1357. See **Censor; Censorship; Prior restraint.**

Liberty to hold pleas. The liberty of having a court of one's own. Thus certain lords had the privilege of holding pleas within their own manors.

Natural liberty. The power of acting as one thinks fit, without any restraint or control, unless by the law of nature. The right which nature gives to all mankind of disposing of their persons and property after the manner they judge most consistent with their happiness, on condition of their acting within the limits of the law of nature, and so as not to interfere with an equal exercise of the same rights by other men. 1 Bl.Comm. 125.

Personal liberty. The right or power of locomotion; of changing situation, or moving one's person to whatsoever place one's own inclination may direct, without imprisonment or restraint, unless by due course of law. Civil Rights Cases, 109 U.S. 3, 3 S.Ct. 42, 27 L.Ed. 835.

Political liberty. Liberty of the citizen to participate in the operations of government, and particularly in the making and administration of the laws.

Religious liberty. Freedom, as guaranteed by First Amendment of U.S. Constitution, from dictation, constraint, or control in matters affecting the conscience, religious beliefs, and the practice of religion. Freedom to entertain and express any or no system of religious opinions, and to engage in or refrain from any form of religious observance or public or private religious worship, not inconsistent with the peace and good order of society and the general welfare. See also **Religion; Religious freedom.**

Liberum corpus nullam recipit æstimationem /líbərəm kórpəs nóləm résəpəd èstəmèyshiyównəm/. The body of a freeman does not admit of valuation.

Liberum est cuique apud se explorare an expediat sibi consilium /líbərəm èst k(yuw)áykwiy ǽpəd sìy èksplərériy æn əkspíydiyət síbay kənsíl(i)yəm/. Every one is free to ascertain for himself whether a recommendation is advantageous to his interest.

Liberum maritagium /líbərəm mærətéyj(iy)əm/. In old English law, frank-marriage.

Liberum servitium /líbərəm sərvísh(iy)əm/. Free service. Service of a warlike sort by a feudatory tenant; sometimes called *"servitium liberum armorum."* See also **Servitium liberum.** Service not unbecoming the character of a freeman and a soldier to perform; as to serve under the lord in his wars, to pay a sum of money, and the like. 2 Bl.Comm. 60.

Liberum socagium /líbərəm səkéyj(iy)əm/. In old English law, free socage.

Liberum tenementum /líbərəm tènəméntəm/. In common law pleading, a plea of freehold. A plea by the defendant in an action of trespass to real property that the *locus in quo* is his freehold, or that of a third person, under whom he acted.

In realty law, freehold. Frank-tenement.

Liblac /líblæk/. In Saxon law, witchcraft, particularly that kind which consisted in the compounding and administering of drugs and philters. Sometimes occurring in the Latinized form *liblacum* /ləbléykəm/.

Libra /láybrə/. In old English law, a pound; also a sum of money equal to a pound sterling.

Libra arsa /láybrə ársə/. A pound burned; that is, melted, or assayed by melting, to test its purity. *Libræ arsæ et pensatæ,* pounds burned and weighed. A frequent expression in Domesday, to denote the purer coin in which rents were paid.

Libra numerata /láybrə n(y)ùwməréydə/. A pound of money counted instead of being weighed.

Libra pensa /láybrə pén(t)sə/. A pound of money by weight.

Libripens /líbrəpen(d)z/. In Roman law, a weigher or balance-holder. The person who held a brazen balance in the ceremony of emancipation, *per æs et libram.* A neutral person or balance holder, who was present at a conveyance of real property. He held in his hand the symbolic balance, which was struck by the purchaser with a piece of bronze as a sign of the completion of the conveyance. The bronze was then transferred to the seller as a sign of the purchase money.

License. The permission by competent authority to do an act which, without such permission, would be illegal, a trespass, or a tort. People v. Henderson, 391 Mich. 612, 218 N.W.2d 2, 4. Certificate or the document itself which gives permission. Leave to do thing which licensor could prevent. Western Electric Co. v. Pacent Reproducer Corporation, C.C.A.N.Y., 42 F.2d 116, 118. Permission to do a particular thing, to exercise a certain privilege or to carry on a particular business or to pursue a certain occupation. Blatz Brewing Co. v. Collins, 88 Cal.App.2d 438, 160 P.2d 37, 39, 40. Permission to do something which without the license would not be allowable. Great Atlantic & Pacific Tea Co. v. City of Lexington, 256 Ky. 595, 76 S.W.2d 894, 896. Privilege from state or sovereign. M. Itzkowitz & Sons v. Geraghty, 139 Misc. 163, 247 N.Y.S. 703, 704; Alabama Power Co. v. Federal Power Commission, 75 U.S.App.D.C. 315, 128 F.2d 280, 289.

A permit, granted by an appropriate governmental body, generally for a consideration, to a person, firm, or corporation to pursue some occupation or to carry on some business subject to regulation under the police power. A license is not a contract between the state and the licensee, but is a mere personal permit. Rosenblatt v. California State Board of Pharmacy, 69 Cal.App.2d 69, 158 P.2d 199, 203. Neither is it property or a property right. American States Water Service Co. of California v. Johnson, 31 Cal.App.2d 606, 88 P.2d 770, 774; Asbury Hospital v. Cass County, 72 N.D. 359, 7 N.W.2d 438, 452.

License with respect to real property is a privilege to go on premises for a certain purpose, but does not operate to confer on, or vest in, licensee any title, interest, or estate in such property. Timmons v. Cropper, 40 Del.Ch. 29, 172 A.2d 757, 759.

See also Certificate; Exclusive license; Letter of license; Licensee; Marriage license; Permit.

Executed license. That which exists when the licensed act has been done.

Executory license. That which exists where the licensed act has not been performed.

Express license. One which is granted in direct terms.

Implied license. One which is presumed to have been given from the acts of the party authorized to give it.

License bond. See **Bond.**

Patents. A written authority granted by the owner of a patent to another person empowering the latter to make or use the patented article for a limited period or in a limited territory. A permission to make, use or sell articles embodying invention. De Forest Radio Telephone & Telegraph Co. v. Radio Corporation of America, D.C.Del., 9 F.2d 150, 151. A transfer which does not affect the monopoly, except by estopping licensor from exercising his prohibitory powers in derogation of privileges conferred upon licensee. L. L. Brown Paper Co. v. Hydroiloid, Inc., D.C.N.Y., 32 F.Supp. 857, 867, 868; De Forest Radio Telephone & Telegraph Co. v. Radio Corporation of America, D.C.Del., 9 F.2d 150, 151. An assignment by the patentee to another of rights less in degree than the patent itself. Any right to make, use, or sell the patented invention, which is less than an undivided part interest in the patent itself. Any transfer of patent rights short of assignment. Language used by owner of patent, or any conduct on his part exhibited to another, from which that other may properly infer that owner consents to his use of patent, on which the other acts, constitutes a license. General Motors Corporation v. Dailey, C.C.A.Mich., 93 F.2d 938, 941; Finley v. Asphalt Paving Co. of St. Louis, C.C.A.Mo., 69 F.2d 498, 504. Transfer of exclusive right to do merely two of the three rights under patent to make, use, and vend invention. Overman Cushion Tire Co. v. Goodyear Tire & Rubber Co., C.C.A.N.Y., 59 F.2d 998, 1000.

Pleading. The defense of justification to an action of trespass that the defendant was authorized by the owner of the land to commit the trespass complained of. License is an affirmative defense which must be pleaded by defendant. Fed.R.Civil P. 8(c).

Real property. A license is ordinarily considered to be a mere personal or revocable privilege to perform an act or series of acts on the land of another. Hennebont Co. v. Kroger Co., 221 Pa.Super. 65, 289 A.2d 229, 231. A privilege to go on premises for a certain purpose, but does not operate to confer on, or vest in, licensee any title, interest, or estate in such property. Timmons v. Cropper, 40 Del.Ch. 29, 172 A.2d 757, 759. Such privilege is unassignable.

A license is distinguished from an "easement," which implies an interest in the land, and a "lease," or right to take the profits of land. It may be, however, and often, is, coupled with a grant of some interest in the land itself, or right to take the profits. National Memorial Park v. C. I. R., C.C.A.4, 145 F.2d 1008, 1015.

Simple license. One revocable at the will of the grantor; *i.e.,* one not coupled with a grant.

Streets and highways. A permit to use street is a mere license revocable at pleasure. City of Boston v. A. W. Perry, Inc., 304 Mass. 18, 22 N.E.2d 627, 630; Lanham v. Forney, 196 Wash. 62, 81 P.2d 777, 779. The privilege of using the streets and highways by the operation thereon of motor carriers for hire can be acquired only by permission or license from the state or its political subdivisions.

Trade, business or calling. Authority or permission to do or carry on some trade or business which would otherwise be unlawful. Standard Oil Co. (Indiana) v. State Board of Equalization, 110 Mont. 5, 99 P.2d 229, 234. Permission conferred by proper authority to pursue certain trade, profession, or calling. Lloyds of Texas v. Bobbitt, Tex.Civ.App., 40 S.W.2d 897, 901. A license confers upon licensee neither contractual nor vested rights. Rosenblatt v. California State Board of Pharmacy, 69 Cal.App.2d 69, 158 P.2d 199, 203; Asbury Hospital v. Cass County, 72 N.D. 359, 7 N.W.2d 438, 452. Nor does it create a property right.

Trade-mark. Permission to use a trade-mark in an area where the purported owner's goods have not become known and identified by his use of mark is a naked "license". E. F. Prichard Co. v. Consumers Brewing Co., C.C.A.Ky., 136 F.2d 512, 521.

License cases. The name given to the group of cases including Peirce v. New Hampshire, 46 U.S. (5 How.) 504, 12 L.Ed. 256, decided by the United States Supreme Court in 1847, to the effect that state laws requiring a license or the payment of a tax for the privilege of selling intoxicating liquors were not in conflict with the constitutional provision giving to Congress the power to regulate interstate commerce, even as applied to liquors imported from another state and remaining in the original and unbroken packages. This decision was overruled in Leisy v. Hardin, 135 U.S. 100, 10 S.Ct. 681, 34 L.Ed. 128, which in turn was counteracted by the act of Congress of August 8, 1890, commonly called the "Wilson law."

Licensee. A person who has a privilege to enter upon land arising from the permission or consent, express or implied, of the possessor of land but who goes on the land for his own purpose rather than for any purpose or interest of the possessor. Reddington v. Beefeaters Tables, Inc., 72 Wis.2d 119, 240 N.W.2d 363, 366. One who is privileged to enter or remain upon land by virtue of possessor's consent, whether given by invitation or permission. Backman v. Vickers Petroleum Co., 187 Kan. 448, 357 P.2d 748, 751.

One who comes on to the premises for his own purpose but with the occupier's consent. Formerly, the duty owed to a licensee was that of refraining from wilful, wanton and reckless conduct. This rule has been changed and now, in most jurisdictions, the occupier of land owes the licensee the duty of reasonable or due care. Mounsey v. Ellard, 363 Mass. 693, 297 N.E.2d 43.

See also **Exclusive licensee; Invitee.**

Licensee by invitation. A person who goes upon the lands of another with express or implied invitation to transact business with the owner or occupant or do some act to his advantage or to the mutual advantage of both the licensee and the owner or occupant. Samuel E. Pentecost Const. Co. v. O'Donnell, 112 Ind.App. 47, 39 N.E.2d 812. An invitee.

Licensee by permission. One who, for his own convenience, curiosity, or entertainment, goes upon the premises of another by the owner's or occupant's permission or sufferance. Samuel E. Pentecost Const. Co. v. O'Donnell, 112 Ind.App. 47, 39 N.E.2d 812, 817.

License fee or **tax.** Charge imposed by sovereign for a privilege. Pennsylvania Liquor Control Board v. Publicker Commercial Alcohol Co., 347 Pa. 555, 32 A.2d 914, 917. Charge or fee imposed primarily for the discouragement of dangerous employments, the protection of the safety of the public, or the regulation of relative rights, privileges, or duties as between individuals. Conard v. State, Del.Super., 2 Terry 107, 16 A.2d 121, 125. Price paid to governmental or municipal authority for a license to engage in and pursue a particular calling or occupation. Tax on privilege of exercising corporate franchise. City Investments v. Johnson, 6 Cal.2d 150, 56 P.2d 939, 940. The term "license tax" includes both charge imposed under police power for privilege of obtaining license to conduct particular business, and tax imposed upon business for sole purpose of raising revenue; "license tax" being defined as sum exacted fr privilege of carrying on particular occupation. Where a fee is exacted and something is required or permitted in addition to the payment of the sum, either to be done by the licensee, or by some regulation or restriction imposed on him, then the fee is a "license fee". Conard v. State, Del.Super., 2 Terry 107, 16 A.2d 121, 125. A license fee is charge made primarily for regulation, with the fee to cover cost and expenses of supervision or regulation. State v. Jackman, 60 Wis.2d 700, 211 N.W.2d 480, 487.

License in amortization. A license authorizing a conveyance of property which, without it, would be invalid under the statutes of mortmain.

License tax. See **License fee or tax.**

Licensing. The sale of a license permitting the use of patents, trademarks, or other technology to another firm. See also **Cross-licensing.**

Licensing power. The authority in a governmental body to grant a license to pursue a particular activity; *e.g.* license to sell liquor.

Licensor /láysən(t)sər/. The person who gives or grants a license.

Licentia /ləsénsh(iy)ə/. Lat. License; leave; permission.

Licentia concordandi /ləsénsh(iy)ə koŋkərdǽnday/. In old practice and conveyancing, license or leave to agree; one of the proceedings on levying a fine of lands. 2 Bl.Comm. 350.

Licentia loquendi /ləsénsh(iy)ə ləkwénday/. In old practice, leave to speak (*i.e.,* with the plaintiff); an imparlance; or rather leave to imparl. 3 Bl.Comm. 299.

Licentia surgendi /ləsénsh(iy)ə sərjénday/. In old English practice, license to arise; permission given by the court to a tenant in a real action, who had cast an essoin *de malo lecti,* to *arise* out of his bed. Also, the writ thereupon. If the demandant can show that the tenant was seen abroad before leave of court, and before being viewed by the knights appointed by the court for that purpose, such tenant shall be taken to be deceitfully essoined, and to have made default.

Licentiate /ləsénshət/laysénshiyèyt/. One who has license to practice any art or faculty.

Licentiousness /ləsénshəsnəs/. The indulgence of the arbitrary will of the individual, without regard to ethics or law, or respect for the rights of others. Also, lewdness or lasciviousness.

Licere /ləsíriy/. Lat. To be lawful; to be allowed or permitted by law.

Licere, liceri /ləsíriy/ləsíray/. Lat. In Roman law, to offer a price for a thing; to bid for it.

Licet /láysət/lísət/. Lat. From the verb *"licere"* (*q.v.*). It is allowed; it is permissible; it is lawful; not forbidden by law.

Licet dispositio de interesse futuro sit inutilis, tamen potest fieri declaratio præcedens quæ sortiatur effectum, interveniente novo actu /láysət dìspəzísh(iy)ow dìy ìntərésiy fyuwt(y)úrow sìd inyúwdələs, téymən pówdəst fáyəray dèkləréysh(iy)ow prəsíydèn(d)z kwìy sòrshiyéydər əféktəm, ìntərvìyniyéntiy nówvow ǽkt(y)uw/. Although the grant of a future interest be inoperative, yet a declaration precedent may be made, which may take effect provided a new act intervene.

Licita bene miscentur, formula nisi juris obstet /lísədə bíyniy məséntər, fórmyələ náysay júrəs óbstət/. Lawful acts [done by several authorities] are well mingled [*i.e.,* become united or consolidated into one good act], unless some form of law forbid. (*E.g.,* Two having a right to convey, each a moiety, may unite and convey the whole.)

Licitare /lìsətériy/. Lat. In Roman law, to offer a price at a sale; to bid; to bid often; to make several bids, one above another.

Licitation /lìsətéyshən/. In the civil law, an offering for sale to the highest bidder, or to him who will give most for a thing. An act by which co-heirs or other co-proprietors of a thing in common and undivided between them put it to bid between them, to be adjudged and to belong to the highest and last bidder, upon condition that he pay to each of his co-proprietors a part in the price equal to the undivided part which each of the said co-proprietors had in the estate *licited,* before the adjudication.

Licitator /lìsətéydər/. In Roman law, a bidder at a sale.

Licking of thumbs /líkiŋ əv θəmz/. An ancient formality by which bargains were completed.

Lidford law /lídfərd ló/. A sort of lynch law, whereby a person was first punished and then tried.

Lie, *n.* An untruth deliberately told; the uttering or acting of that which is false for the purpose of deceiving; intentional misstatement. See **Perjury.**

Lie, *v.* To subsist; to exist; to be sustainable; to be proper or available. Thus the phrase "an action will not *lie*" means that an action cannot be sustained, or that there is no ground upon which to found the action.

Lie detector. A machine which records by a needle on a graph varying emotional disturbances when answering questions truly or falsely, as indicated by fluctuations in blood pressure, respiration or perspiration. State v. Cole, 354 Mo. 181, 188 S.W.2d 43, 51. A pathometer; also called "polygraph". In general, the results of lie detector tests are not admissible as evidence; though such have been held admissible on stipulation of the parties by certain courts. Herman v. Eagle Star Ins. Co., 283 F.Supp. 33, affd. 396 F.2d 427. See **Polygraph.**

Liege. In feudal law, bound by a feudal tenure; bound in allegiance to the lord paramount, who owned no superior. The term was applied to the lord, or liege lord, to whom allegiance was due, since he was *bound* to protection and a just government, and also to the feudatory, liegeman, or subject bound to allegiance, for he was *bound* to tribute and due subjection. So *lieges* are the king's subjects.

In old records, full; absolute; perfect; pure. *Liege* widowhood was pure widowhood. *Ligius* was also used; *e.g. ligia potestas,* full and free power of disposal.

Liege homage /líyzh (h)óməj/líyj°/. Homage which, when performed by one sovereign prince to another, included fealty and services, as opposed to *simple homage,* which was a mere acknowledgment of tenure.

Liege lord /líyzh lórd/líyj°/. A sovereign; a superior lord.

Liegeman /líyjmən/. He that oweth allegiance.

Lieger, or **leger** /léjər/líyjər/. A resident ambassador.

Lieges, or **liege people** /líyzhəz/líyzh píypəl/líyj°/. Subjects.

Lie in franchise. Property is said to "lie in franchise" when it is of such a nature that the persons entitled thereto may seize it without the aid of a court; *e.g.,* wrecks, waifs, estrays.

Lie in grant. Incorporeal hereditaments are said to "lie in grant;" that is, they pass by force of the grant (deed or charter) without livery.

Lie in livery. A common law term applied to corporeal hereditaments, freeholds, etc., signifying that they pass by livery, not by the mere force of the grant.

Lie in wait. See **Lying in wait.**

Lien /líy(ə)n/. A charge or security or encumbrance upon property. Theatre Realty Co. v. Aronberg-Fried Co., C.C.A.Mo., 85 F.2d 383, 388; Springer v. J. R. Clark Co., C.C.A.Minn., 138 F.2d 722, 726. A claim or charge on property for payment of some debt, obligation or duty. Sullins v. Sullins, 65 Wash.2d 283, 396 P.2d 886, 888. Qualified right of property which a creditor has in or over specific property of his debtor, as security for the debt or charge or for performance of some act. Right or claim against some interest in property created by law as an incident of contract. Right to enforce charge upon property of another for payment or satisfaction of debt or claim. Vaughan v. John Hancock Mut. Life Ins. Co., Tex.Civ.App., 61 S.W.2d 189, 190; Day v. Ostergard, 146 Pa.Super. 27, 21 A.2d 586, 588. Right to retain property for payment of debt or demand. Samuels v. Public Nat. Bank & Trust Co. of New York, 140 Misc. 744, 251 N.Y.S. 671, 674; Bell v. Dennis, 43 N.M. 350, 93 P.2d 1003, 1006; Huie v. Soo Hoo, 132 Cal.App. Supp. 787, 22 P.2d 808. Security for a debt, duty or other obligation, Hurley v. Boston R. Holding Co., 315 Mass. 591, 54 N.E.2d 183, 193. Tie that binds property to a debt or claim for its satisfaction. United States v. 1364.76875 Wine Gallons, More or Less, of Spirituous Liquors, D.C.Mo., 60 F.Supp. 389, 392. Liens are "property rights". In re Pennsylvania Central Brewing Co., C.C.A.Pa., 114 F.2d 1010, 1013. The word "lien" is a generic term and, standing alone, includes liens acquired by contract or by operation of law. Egyptian Supply Co. v. Boyd, C.C.A.Ky., 117 F.2d 608, 612.

A change against or interest in property to secure payment of a debt or performance of an obligation. Bankruptcy Act, § 101(28).

Lien *by operation of law.* Where the law itself, without the stipulation of the parties, raises a lien, as an implication or legal consequence from the relation of the parties or the circumstances of their dealings. Liens of this species may arise either under the rules of common law or of equity or under a statute. In the first case they are called "common-law liens;" in the second, "equitable liens;" in the third, "statutory liens."

Roman or Civil law. The peculiar securities which, in the common and maritime law and equity, are termed "liens," are embraced under the head of "mortgage and privilege."

See also Architect's lien; Artisan's lien; Attorney's lien; Banker's lien; Charging Lien; Chattel lien; Common-law lien; Concurrent liens; Deferred lien; Equitable lien; Execution lien; Factor's lien; First lien; Floating lien; General lien; Inchoate lien; Invol-untary lien; Judgment lien; Judicial lien; Laborers' lien; Maritime lien; Marshalling liens; Materialman's lien; Mechanic's lien; Municipal lien; Retaining lien; Second lien; Secret lien; Special lien; Statutory lien; Tax lien; Vendor's lien.

Lien account. Such statement of claims as fairly apprises property owner and public of nature and amount of demand asserted as lien. Hanenkamp v. Hagedorn, Mo.App., 110 S.W.2d 826, 829.

Lien creditor. One whose debt or claim is secured by a lien on particular property, as distinguished from a "general" creditor, who has no such security. A creditor who has acquired a lien on the property involved, by attachment, levy or the like, and includes an assignee for benefit of creditors from the time of assignment, and a trustee in bankruptcy from the date of the filing of the petition, or a receiver in equity from the time of appointment. U.C.C. § 9–301(3). See also **Creditor.**

Lienee /lìyníy/. One whose property is subject to a lien.

Lien of a covenant. The commencement of a covenant stating the names of the covenantors and convenantees, and the character of the covenant, whether joint or several.

Lien of factor at common law. Lien not created through statutory enactment, but lien of ordinary factor as known to common law.

Lienor /líy(ə)nər/. The person having or owning a lien; one who has a right of lien upon property of another.

Lien waiver. A waiver of mechanic's lien rights, signed by subcontractors so that the owner or general contractor can receive a draw on a construction loan.

Lie to. To adjoin.

Lieu conus /l(y)úw kónyuw/. L. Fr. In old pleading, a known place; a place well known and generally taken notice of by those who dwell about it, as a castle, a manor, etc.

Lieu lands. A term used to indicate public lands within the indemnity limits granted in *lieu* of those lost within place limits. Weyerhaeuser v. Hoyt, 219 U.S. 380, 31 S.Ct. 300, 55 L.Ed. 258.

Lieu tax. A lieu tax means instead of or a substitute for, and it is not an additional tax. Lebeck v. State, 62 Ariz. 171, 156 P.2d 720, 721.

Lieutenancy, commission of. See **Commission of array.**

Lieutenant /l(y)uwténənt/lefténənt/. A deputy; substitute; an officer who supplies the place of another; one acting by vicarious authority. Etymologically, one who holds the post or office of another, in the place and stead of the latter.

The word is used in composition as part of the title of several civil and military officers, who are subordinate to others, and especially where the duties and powers of the higher officer may, in certain contingencies, devolve upon the lower; as lieutenant governor, lieutenant colonel, etc. See *infra.*

In the army, a lieutenant is a commissioned officer, ranking next below a captain. In the United States navy, he is an officer whose rank is intermediate between that of an ensign and that of a lieutenant commander. In the British navy, his rank is next below that of a commander.

Lieutenant colonel. An officer of the army whose rank is above that of a major and below that of a colonel.

Lieutenant commander. A commissioned officer of the United States navy, whose rank is above that of lieutenant and below that of commander.

Lieutenant general. An officer in the army, whose rank is above that of Major General and below that of a Full General or Four Star General which is below a General of the Army or Five Star General.

Lieutenant governor. An elected officer of a state, sometimes charged with special duties, but chiefly important as the deputy or substitute of the governor, acting in the place of the governor upon the latter's death, resignation, or disability.

Life. That state of animals, humans, and plants or of an organized being, in which its natural functions and motions are performed, or in which its organs are capable of performing their functions. The interval between birth and death. The sum of the forces by which death is resisted.

Human life begins at conception but the stage of pregnancy of a woman determines the conditions under which she may be entitled to an abortion free of state interference. Roe v. Wade, 410 U.S. 113, 93 S.Ct. 705, 35 L.Ed.2d 147. See also **Abortion; Viable child.**

"Life" protected by the Federal Constitution includes all personal rights and their enjoyment of the faculties, acquiring useful knowledge, the right to marry, establish a home, and bring up children, freedom of worship, conscience, contract, occupation, speech, assembly and press.

See also **Natural life; Useful life; Wrongful life action.**

Life annuity. An engagement to pay an income yearly during the life of some person; also the sum thus promised. An annuity, depending on the continuance of an assigned life or lives, is sometimes called a life annuity. Bodine v. Commissioner of Internal Revenue, C.C.A.3, 103 F.2d 982, 985. See also **Annuity.**

Life beneficiary. One who receives payments or other rights from a trust for his or her lifetime.

Life care contract. An agreement in which one party is assured of care and maintenance for his natural life in consideration of a transfer of property to the other party. Such contracts exist primarily between elderly persons and nursing homes.

Life estate. An estate whose duration is limited to the life of the party holding it, or some other person. See also **Life interest.**

A legal arrangement whereby the beneficiary (*i.e.,* the life tenant) is entitled to the income from the property for his or her life. Upon the death of the life tenant, the property will go to the holder of the remainder interest or to the grantor by reversion.

Life expectancy. The period of time in which a person of a given age and sex is expected to live according to

statistical (*i.e.* actuarial) tables. See also **Actuarial table; Life tables.**

Life in being. A phrase used in the common-law and statutory rules against perpetuities, meaning the remaining duration of the life of a person who is in existence at the time when the deed or will takes effect. McArthur v. Scott, 113 U.S. 340, 5 S.Ct. 652, 28 L.Ed. 1015.

Life insurance. See **Insurance.**

Life insurance proceeds. Generally, life insurance proceeds paid to a beneficiary upon the death of the insured are exempt from Federal income tax. An exception is provided where a life insurance contract has been transferred for valuable consideration to another individual who assumes ownership rights. In such case the proceeds are income to the assignee to the extent that the proceeds exceed the amount paid for the policy plus any subsequent premiums paid. Insurance proceeds may be subject to the Federal estate tax if the decedent retained any incidents of ownership in the policy prior to death or if the proceeds are payable to his estate. I.R.C. §§ 101 and 2042.

Life insurance reserves. Fund which, together with future premiums and interest, will be sufficient to pay future claims. Jefferson Standard Life Ins. Co. v. U. S., C.A.N.C., 408 F.2d 842, 845.

Life insurance trust. Type of trust, the res of which consists in whole or in part of life insurance policies owned by the trustees and payable to the trust on the death of the insured. A device commonly used in estate planning.

Life interest. A claim or interest in real or personal property, not amounting to ownership, and limited by a term of life, either that of the person in whom the right is vested or that of another. See also **Life estate.**

Life-land, or **life-hold.** Land held on a lease for lives.

Life of a writ. The period during which a writ (execution, etc.) remains effective and can lawfully be served or levied, terminating with the day on which, by law or by its own terms, it is to be returned into court.

Life or limb. The phrase "life or limb" within constitutional provision that no person shall be subject for the same offense to be twice put in jeopardy of life or limb is not construed strictly but applies to any criminal penalty. Fifth Amend., U.S.Const. Clawans v. Rives, 70 U.S.App.D.C. 107, 104 F.2d 240, 242.

Life peerage. Letters patent, conferring the dignity of baron for life only, do not enable the grantee to sit and vote in the house of lords, not even with the usual writ of summons to the house.

Life policy. See **Insurance** (*Life insurance*).

Life sentence. See **Sentence.**

Life tables. Statistical (*i.e.* actuarial) tables exhibiting the probable proration of persons who will live to reach different ages. Such tables are used for many purposes, such as the computation of the present value of annuities, dower rights, etc.; and for the computation of damages resulting from injuries which destroy the earning capacity of a person, or those resulting from the death of a person to those who are dependent upon him. See also **Actuarial tables.**

Life tenancy. An estate in real property in which the tenant has a freehold interest for his life or for the life of another *(pur autre vie)*.

Life tenant. One who holds an estate in lands for the period of his own life or that of another certain person.

LIFO. See last-in, first-out.

Lift. To raise; to take up. To "lift" a promissory note is to discharge its obligation by paying its amount or substituting another evidence of debt. To "lift the bar" of the statute of limitations, or of an estoppel, is to remove the obstruction which it interposes, by some sufficient act or acknowledgment.

Liga /líygə/. In old European law, a league or confederation.

Ligan, lagan /láygən/léygən/. Goods cast into the sea tied to a buoy, so that they may be found again by the owners, are so denominated. When goods are cast into the sea in storms or shipwrecks, and remain there, without coming to land, they are distinguished by the barbarous names of "jetsam," "flotsam," and "ligan."

Ligare /ləgériy/. To tie or bind. To enter into a league or treaty.

Ligea /líyj(iy)ə/. In old English law, a liege-woman; a female subject.

Ligeance /líyjən(t)s/. Allegiance; the faithful obedience of a subject to his sovereign, of a citizen to his government. Also, derivatively, the territory of a state or sovereignty.

Ligeantia /lìjiyǽnsh(iy)ə/. Lat. Ligeance; allegiance.

Ligeantia est quasi legis essentia; est vinculum fidei /lìjiyǽnsh(iy)ə èst kwéyzay líyjəs əsénsh(iy)ə, èst vínk(y)ələm fáydiyay/. Allegiance is, as it were, the essence of law; it is the chain of faith.

Ligeantia naturalis nullis claustris coercetur, nullis metis refrænatur, nullis finibus premitur /lìjiyǽnsh(iy)ə næchəréyləs nə́ləs klóstrəs kowə́rsədər, nə́ləs médəs rèfrənéydər, nə́ləs fínəbəs prémədər/. Natural allegiance is restrained by no barriers, reined by no bounds, compressed by no limits.

Ligeas /líyj(iy)əs/. In old records, a liege.

Light. A window, or opening in the wall for the admission of light. Also a privilege or easement to have light admitted into one's building by the openings made for that purpose, without obstruction or obscuration by the walls of adjacent or neighboring structures. Also an instrument through which illumination is projected. Santos v. Dondero, 11 Cal.App.2d 720, 54 P.2d 764, 766.

Lighterage. The business of transferring, loading, and unloading, merchandise to and from vessels by means of lighters; also the compensation or price demanded for such service. The loading, unloading and transfer of freight between a car and a ship's side. Hoboken Manufacturers' R. Co. v. United States, D.C.N.J., 47 F.Supp. 779, 782.

Lighterman /láydərmən/. The master or owner of a lighter. He is liable as a common carrier.

Ligius /líyj(iy)əs/. A person bound to another by a solemn tie or engagement; used to express the relation of a subject to a sovereign. See also **Liege.**

Ligna et lapides sub "armorum" appellatione non continentur /lígnə èt lǽpədiyz sə̀b armórəm ǽpəlèy-shiyówniy nòn kòntənéntər/. Sticks and stones are not contained under the name of "arms".

Lignagium /lignéyj(iy)əm/. A right of cutting fuel in woods; also a tribute or payment due for the same.

Ligula /lígyələ/. In old English law, a copy, exemplification, or transcript of a court roll or deed.

Like. Equal in quantity, quality, or degree or exactly corresponding. Bader v. Coale, 48 Cal.App.2d 276, 119 P.2d 763, 765; Braren v. Horner, Cust. & Pat. App., 47 F.2d 358, 365. Also means having the same, or nearly the same, appearance, qualities, or characteristics, Japan Import Co. v. United States, Cust. & Pat.App., 86 F.2d 124, 131; Clarke v. Johnson, 199 Ga. 163, 33 S.E.2d 425, 427; resembling another; same manner, Seilaz v. Seilaz, 24 Tenn.App. 611, 148 S.W.2d 23, 25; similar, Castell v. United States, D.C. N.Y., 20 F.Supp. 175, 179; or, substantially similar, Jones v. H. D. & J. K. Crosswell, C.C.A.S.C., 60 F.2d 827, 829.

Like a shot. Quickly, instantaneously.

Like benefits. Similar in salient features.

Like character. Similarity. Bader v. Coale, 48 Cal. App.2d 276, 119 P.2d 763, 765.

Like-kind exchange. An exchange of property held for productive use in trade or business or for investment (except inventory and stocks and bonds) for property of the same type. Unless different property is received (*i.e.*, "boot") the exchange will be nontaxable. I.R.C. § 1031(a).

Likelihood. Probability. Clark v. Welch, C.C.A.Mass., 140 F.2d 271, 273. The word imports something less than reasonably certain.

Likely. Probable. Horning v. Gerlach, 139 Cal.App. 470, 34 P.2d 504, 505. In all probability. Neely v. Chicago Great Western R. Co., Mo.App., 14 S.W.2d 972, 978.

Limenarcha /lìmənárkə/. In Roman law, an officer who had charge of a harbor or port.

Limine. See **Motion in limine.**

Limit, *v.* To abridge, confine, restrain, and restrict. To mark out; to define; to fix the extent of. Thus, to limit an estate means to mark out or to define the period of its duration, and the words employed in deeds for this purpose are thence termed "words of limitation," and the act itself is termed "limiting the estate."

Limit, *n.* A bound; a restriction; a restraint; a circumscription. Boundary, border, or outer line of thing. Extent of power, right or authority conferred.

Limitation. Restriction or circumspection; settling an estate or property. A certain time allowed by a statute for bringing litigation (see *Statute of limitation, infra*). The provisions of state constitution are not a "grant" but a "limitation" of legislative power. Ellerbe v. David, 193 S.C. 332, 8 S.E.2d 518, 520; Mulholland v. Ayers, 109 Mont. 558, 99 P.2d 234, 239. See also **Proviso.**

Corporations. Under statute providing that all corporations expiring by their own "limitation" shall for certain purposes be continued as bodies corporate for a term of three years, the word "limitation" is an act of limiting, a restriction of power, a qualification. Porter v. Tempa Min. & Mill. Co., 59 Nev. 332, 93 P.2d 741, 743.

Estates. The restriction or circumscription of an estate, in the conveyance by which it is granted, in respect to the interest of the grantee or its duration. The specific curtailment or confinement of an estate, by the terms of the grant, so that it cannot endure beyond a certain period or a designated contingency. A "limitation" on a grant determines an estate upon the happening of the event itself without the necessity of doing any act to regain the estate, such as re-entry. Gulf Production Co. v. Continental Oil Co., Tex., 132 S.W.2d 553, 563. A limitation, whether made by the express words of the party or existing in intendment of law, circumscribes the continuance of time for which the property is to be enjoyed, and by positive and certain terms, or by reference to some event which possibly may happen, marks the period at which the time of enjoyment shall end.

Collateral limitation. One which gives an interest in an estate for a specified period, but makes the right of enjoyment to depend on some collateral event, as an estate to A. till B. shall go to Rome.

Conditional limitation. A condition followed by a limitation over to a third person in case the condition be not fulfilled or there be a breach of it. A conditional limitation is where an estate is so expressly defined and limited by the words of its creation that it cannot endure for any longer time than till the contingency happens upon which the estate is to fail. Between conditional limitations and estates depending on conditions subsequent there is this difference: that in the former the estate determines as soon as the contingency happens; but in the latter it endures until the grantor or his heirs take advantage of the breach.

Contingent limitation. When a remainder in fee is limited upon any estate which would by the common law be adjudged a fee tail, such a remainder is valid as a contingent limitation upon a fee, and vests in possession on the death of the first taker without issue living at the time of his death.

Limitation in law. A limitation in law, or an estate limited, is an estate to be holden only during the continuance of the condition under which it was granted, upon the determination of which the estate vests immediately in him in expectancy.

Limitation over. This term includes any estate in the same property created or contemplated by the conveyance, to be enjoyed after the first estate granted expires or is exhausted. Lane v. Citizens & Southern Nat. Bank, 195 Ga. 828, 25 S.E.2d 800, 802, 803. Thus, in a gift to A. for life, with remainder to the heirs of his body, the remainder is a "limitation over" to such heirs.

Limitation title. Full title, precluding all claims. Free v. Owen, 131 Tex. 281, 113 S.W.2d 1221, 1224.

Special limitation. A qualification serving to mark out the bounds of an estate, so as to determine it *ipso facto* in a given event, without action, entry, or claim, before it would, or might, otherwise expire by force of, or according to, the general limitation.

Title by limitation. A prescriptive title; one which is indefeasible because of the expiration of the time prescribed by the statute of limitations for the bringing of actions to test or defeat it.

Words of limitation. In a conveyance or will, words which have the effect of marking the duration of an estate are termed "words of limitation." Thus, in a grant to A. and his heirs, the words "and his heirs" are words of limitation, because they show that A. is to take an estate in fee-simple and do not give his heirs anything. Summit v. Yount, 109 Ind. 506, 9 N.E. 582.

Limitation of actions. See *Statute of limitations*, below.

Limitation of assize. In old practice, a certain time prescribed by statute, within which a man was required to allege himself or his ancestor to have been seized of lands sued for by a writ of assize.

Statute of limitations. A statute prescribing limitations to the right of action on certain described causes of action or criminal prosecutions; that is, declaring that no suit shall be maintained on such causes of action, nor any criminal charge be made, unless brought within a specified period of time after the right accrued. Statutes of limitation are statutes of repose, and are such legislative enactments as prescribe the periods within which actions may be brought upon certain claims or within which certain rights may be enforced. In criminal cases, however, a statute of limitation is an act of grace, a surrendering by sovereign of its right to prosecute.

Limitation of Liability Act. Federal statute which permits shipowner to restrict his liability to cargo, passengers, employees to some other ship, or harbor workers, to whatever value the ship has after an event such as a sinking or collision. 46 U.S.C.A. §§ 181–189.

Limitation of prosecutions. See **Limitation** (*Statute of limitations*).

Limitations, statute of. See **Limitation** (*Statute of limitations*).

Limited. Restricted; bounded; prescribed. Confined within positive bounds; restricted in duration, extent, or scope.

As to limited Company; Divorce; Fee; and Partnership, see those titles.

Ltd. A designation following a corporate business name and indicating its corporate and limited liability status. It is found most commonly after British and Canadian corporate names, though it is sometimes used in the United States.

Limited administration. An administration of a temporary character, granted for a particular period, or for a special or particular purpose.

Limited admissibility. In law of evidence, testimony or things may be admitted into evidence for a restricted purpose, and the trial judge should so instruct the jury at the time of its admission; *e.g.* prior contradictory statements are admissible to impeach but not admissible for the truth of the statements. However, if the evidence has multiple purposes, one being in violation of a constitutional protection for a criminal defendant, such evidence should not be admitted. Bruton v. United States, 391 U.S. 123, 88 S.Ct. 1620, 20 L.Ed.2d 476.

Similarly, evidence may frequently be competent as against one party, but not as against another, in which event the practice is to admit the evidence, with an instruction, if requested, that the jury are to consider it only as to the party against whom it is competent. Fed.Evid.R. 105.

Limited appeal. An appeal from only adverse portions of a decree; such is limited to the particular portions of the decree appealed from. Fox v. River Heights, 22 Tenn.App. 166, 118 S.W.2d 1104, 1114. See also **Interlocutory appeal; Interlocutory Appeals Act.**

Limited court. Where special authority, in derogation of common law, is conferred by statute on a court of general jurisdiction, it becomes an "inferior or limited court". For example, a probate court is a court of limited jurisdiction. Partlow v. Partlow, 246 Ala. 259, 20 So.2d 517, 518. See **Limited or special jurisdiction.**

Limited divorce. A divorce decree or judgment may be restricted to a dissolution of the marriage with no provision for support. In another sense, term refers to a divorce a mensa et thoro (from bed and board) with no right to remarry.

Limited executor. An executor whose appointment is qualified by limitations as to the time or place wherein, or the subject-matter whereon, the office is to be exercised; as distinguished from one whose appointment is absolute, *i.e.*, certain and immediate, without any restriction in regard to the testator's effects or limitation in point of time.

Limited guaranty. A limited guaranty is ordinarily one restricted in its application to a single transaction. Cooling v. Springer, 3 Terry 228, 30 A.2d 466, 469.

Limited or special jurisdiction. Jurisdiction which is confined to particular causes, or which can be exercised only under the limitations and circumstances prescribed by the statute. A court's power over an action is governed generally by statute and some courts have limited authority or power and the limita-

tion is in terms of the nature of the case (*e.g.* probate courts), or the amount in controversy, or the type of crime with which the defendant is charged or the age of the accused (*e.g.* juvenile courts). See also **Limited court.**

Limited owner. A tenant for life, or by the curtesy, or other person not having absolute ownership.

Limited partner. A partner whose liability to third party creditors of the partnership is limited to the amount invested by such partner in the partnership. See **Limited partnership.**

Limited partnership. An unincorporated association, or firm, in which one or more of the partners are, on compliance with the provisions of various state statutes regulating such partnerships, relieved from liability beyond the amount of the capital contributed by them. A partnership formed by two or more persons under the provisions of the Uniform Limited Partnership Act, having as members one or more general partners and one or more limited partners. The limited partners, as such, are not bound by the obligations of the partnership. Uniform Limited Partnership Act § 1. Most all states have adopted the Uniform Limited Partnership Act.

Limited partnership is type of partnership comprised of one or more general partners who manage business and who are personally liable for partnership debts, and one or more limited partners who contribute capital and share in profits but who take no part in running business and incur no liability with respect to partnership obligations beyond contribution. Evans v. Galardi, 16 Cal.3d 300, 128 Cal.Rptr. 25, 30, 546 P.2d 313.

See also **General partner; Limited partner.**

Limited payment plan. A policy upon a "limited payment plan" is a paid-up policy, and insurance upon which no further premium is to be paid. Bankers Life & Loan Ass'n v. Chase, Tex.Civ.App., 114 S.W.2d 374, 376.

Limited policy. Insurance policy specifically excluding certain classes or types of loss. State Compensation Ins. Fund v. Industrial Accident Commission, 56 Cal. App.2d 443, 132 P.2d 890, 894.

Limited power of appointment. Power of appointment is limited when it is exercisable only in favor of persons or a class of persons designated in the instrument creating the power. Johnstone v. Commissioner of Internal Revenue, C.C.A.9, 76 F.2d 55, 57.

Limited publication. Communication to a select number on condition, express or implied, that it is not intended to be thereafter common property. A limited publication is one which is restricted both as to persons and as to purpose and is a publication which communicates a knowledge of its contents under conditions expressly or impliedly precluding its dedication to the public. Masterson v. McCroskie, Colo. App., 556 P.2d 1231, 1233.

Limit order. A restriction on the sale or purchase of a security placed by a customer with a broker, limiting the price at which the customer is willing to buy or sell.

Lincoln's Inn /líŋkənz ín/. An inn of court. See **Inns of Court.**

Lindbergh Act. Federal law which punishes kidnapping for ransom or reward when the victim is transported from one state to another or to a foreign country. The failure to release the victim within 24 hours creates a rebuttable presumption that such person has been transported in interstate or foreign commerce. 18 U.S.C.A. § 1201.

Line. A demarcation, border, or limit. The boundary or line of division between two estates. Person's trade, occupation or business. Carrier's route.

Building line. See **Building line.**

Collateral line. See **Descent.**

Descent. See **Descent.**

Direct line. See **Descent.**

Line by line budget. A detailed itemization of all expenditures by budget line. Block v. Sprague, Sup., 24 N.Y.S.2d 245, 247.

Line of an intersection. A straight line substantially at right angles to bounds of highway at a point where, to the reasonable perception of a driver, the highway starts to widen as the result of the outcurving of its bounds to form the junction. Beck v. Sosnowitz, 125 Conn. 553, 7 A.2d 389, 391.

Line of credit. A margin or fixed limit of credit granted by one to another, to the full extent of which the latter may avail himself in his dealings with the former, but which he must not exceed; usually intended to cover a series of transactions, in which case, when the customer's line of credit is nearly or quite exhausted, he is expected to reduce his indebtedness by payments before drawing upon it further. Pittinger v. Southwestern Paper Co. of Fort Worth, Tex.Civ.App., 151 S.W.2d 922, 925. The maximum borrowing power (*i.e.* credit limit) of a person from a financial institution. Agreement with bank or number of banks for short-term borrowings on demand.

Line of credit signifies a limit of credit extended by bank to its customer, to the full extent of which the customer may avail itself in its dealing with the bank, but which the customer may not exceed. It most frequently covers a series of transactions, in which case, when the customer's line of credit is nearly exhausted or not replenished, the customer is expected to reduce its indebtedness by payments to the bank before making additional use thereof. Modoc Meat & Cattle Co. v. First State Bank of Oregon, 271 Or. 276, 532 P.2d 21, 25.

Line of duty. In military law and usage, an act is said to be done, or an injury sustained, "in the line of duty," when done or suffered in the performance or discharge of a duty incumbent upon the individual in his character as a member of the military or naval forces. An injury suffered or disease contracted by a sailor is considered to have been in "line of duty" unless actually caused by something for which sailor is responsible which intervenes between his performance of duty and the injury or disease. Meyer v. Dollar S. S. Line, C.C.A.Wash., 49 F.2d 1002, 1003.

Line of ordinary high tide. Ordinary high tide may, for practical purposes, within a restricted area, be conceived as a level plane; the "line of ordinary high tide" is the intersection of said plane with the surface of the land. Swarzwald v. Cooley, 39 Cal.App.2d 306, 103 P.2d 580, 584.

Maternal line. See **Maternal line.**

Paternal line. See **Paternal line.**

Public utilities. See **Public utility.**

Linea /líniyə/. Lat. A line; line of descent. See **Descent.**

Lineage /lín(i)yəj/. Race; progeny; family, ascending or descending. Line of descent from an ancestor, hence, family, race, stock. See also **Descent.**

Lineal /líniyəl/. That which comes in a line; especially a direct line, as from father to son. Collateral relationship is not called "lineal," though the expression "collateral line," is not unusual. Proceeding in direct or unbroken line, hereditary, unbroken in course; distinguished from collateral, as lineal descent, lineal succession, having an ancestral basis or right. See also **Descent.**

Lineal consanguinity /líniyəl kònsæŋgwínədiy/. That kind of consanguinity which subsists between persons of whom one is descended in a *direct line* from the other; as between a particular person and his father, grandfather, great-grandfather, and so upward, in the direct ascending line; or between the same person and his son, grandson, great-grandson, and so downwards in the direct descending line.

Lineal descendant. A person in the direct line of descent such as a child or grandchild as contrasted with a collateral descendant such as a niece.

Lineal descent. See **Descent.**

Lineal heir /líniyəl é(yə)r/. One who inherits in a line either ascending or descending from a common source as distinguished from a collateral heir. Ferraro v. Augustine, 45 Ill.App.2d 295, 196 N.E.2d 16, 19. The words "lineal heirs" like "heirs of the body" mean all lineal descendants to the remotest posterity and are words of "inheritance" and not of "purchase", unless the instrument clearly shows that they were used in a restricted sense to denote "children". Sims v. Clayton, 193 S.C. 98, 7 S.E.2d 724, 727. See also **Heirs.**

Lineals. Blood relatives of decedent.

Lineal warranty. A warranty by an ancestor from whom the title did or might have come to the heir.

Linea obliqua /líniyə əbláykwə/°əblíykwə/. In the civil law, the oblique line. More commonly termed *"linea transversalis."*

Linea recta /líniyə réktə/. The direct line; the vertical line. In computing degrees of kindred and the succession to estates, this term denotes the direct line of ascendants and descendants. Where a person springs from another immediately, or mediately through a third person, they are said to be in the direct line *(linea recta)*, and are called "ascendants" and "descendants."

Linea recta est index sui et obliqui; lex est linea recti /líniyə réktə èst índeks s(y)úway èd əbláykway; léks èst líniyə réktə/. A right line is a test of itself, and of an oblique; law is a line of right.

Linea recta semper præfertur transversali /líniyə réktə sémpər prəfə́rdər trænzvərséylay/. The right line is always preferred to the collateral.

Linea transversalis /líniyə trænzvərséyləs/. A collateral, transverse, or oblique line. Where two persons are descended from a third, they are called "collaterals," and are said to be related in the collateral line (*linea transversa* or *obliqua*).

Line of credit. See Line (*Line of credit*).

Lines and corners. In deeds and surveys, boundary-lines and their angles with each other.

Lineup. A police identification procedure by which the suspect in a crime is exhibited before the victim or witness to determine if he committed the offense. To be accepted as valid, the lineup must meet certain standards and be free of undue suggestiveness. U. S. v. Wade, 388 U.S. 218, 87 S.Ct. 1926, 18 L.Ed.2d 1149. If the standards are met, the person who has identified the defendant may so testify at trial. "Lineup" involves and requires lining up of a number of individuals from which one of those lined up may or may not be identified as committer of a crime and there cannot be a one-man lineup. Dozie v. State, 49 Wis.2d 209, 181 N.W.2d 369, 371.

Post-indictment lineups are considered to be a "critical stage" of criminal proceedings at which the accused has the constitutional right to be represented by counsel. United States v. Wade, 388 U.S. 218, 87 S.Ct. 1926, 18 L.Ed.2d 1149; Gilbert v. California, 388 U.S. 263, 87 S.Ct. 1951, 18 L.Ed. 1178.

Link. A unit in a connected series; anything which serves to connect or bind together the things which precede and follow it. Thus, we speak of a "link in the chain of title." Something which binds together, or connects, separate things; a part of a connected series; a tie, a bond. City of Independence v. Board of Com'rs of Montgomery County, 140 Kan. 661, 38 P.2d 105, 106.

As a unit of land measurement, see **Land measure.**

Link-in-chain. The 5th Amendment (U.S.Const.) privilege against self incrimination protects a witness not only from the requirement of answering questions which might call for directly incriminating answers but also from answers which might tie or link the defendant to criminal activity in the chain of evidence. Estes v. Potter, C.A.Tex., 183 F.2d 865. Immunity also protects one from such result. State v. Buchanan, Fla.App., 207 So.2d 711, 717.

Liquere /ləkwíriy/. Lat. In the civil law, to be clear, evident, or satisfactory. When a *judex* was in doubt how to decide a case, he represented to the prætor, under oath, *sibi non liquere* (that it was not clear to him), and was thereupon discharged.

Liquet /líkwət/. It is clear or apparent; it appears. *Satis liquet,* it sufficiently appears.

Liquid. Said of a business with a substantial amount (the amount is unspecified) of working capital, especially quick assets. See also **Liquidity.**

Liquid assets. Cash, or assets immediately convertible to cash.

Liquidate. To pay and settle. Farmers State Bank & Trust Co. v. Brady, 137 Tex. 39, 152 S.W.2d 729, 732; Fleckner v. Bank of U. S., 21 U.S. (8 Wheat.) 338, 362, 5 L.Ed. 631. To adjust, State ex rel. Banister v. Cantley, 330 Mo. 943, 52 S.W.2d 397, 399; Belden v. Modern Finance Co., Ohio App., 61 N.E.2d 801, 804, 44 O.L.A. 163. To ascertain the amount, or the several amounts, of the liabilities of insolvent and apportion the assets toward discharge of the indebtedness, Farmers State Bank & Trust Co. v. Brady, 137 Tex. 39, 152 S.W.2d 729, 732; to ascertain the balance due and to whom payable, State ex rel. Banister v. Cantley, 330 Mo. 943, 52 S.W.2d 397, 399; to assemble and mobilize the assets, settle with the creditors and the debtors and apportion the remaining assets, if any, among the stockholders or owners, United States v. Metcalf, C.C.A.Cal., 131 F.2d 677, 679; to clear up, State ex rel. Banister v. Cantley, 330 Mo. 943, 52 S.W.2d 397, 399; Fleckner v. Bank of U. S., La., 21 U.S. (8 Wheat.) 338, 362, 5 L.Ed. 631; to determine by agreement or litigation precise amount of indebtedness, Continental Ins. Co. v. Harris, 190 Ark. 1110, 82 S.W.2d 841, 843; to discharge, Continental Ins. Co. v. Harris, 190 Ark. 1110, 82 S.W.2d 841, 843; to extinguish an indebtedness, Gibson v. American Ry. Express Co., 195 Iowa 1126, 193 N.W. 274, 278; Belden v. Modern Finance Co., Ohio App., 61 N.E.2d 801, 804, 44 O.L.A. 163; to gather in the assets, convert them into cash and distribute them according to the legal rights of the parties interested; to lessen, Fleckner v. Bank of U. S., La., 21 U.S. (8 Wheat.) 338, 362, 5 L.Ed. 631; to make amount of indebtedness clear and certain, Continental Ins. Co. v. Harris, 190 Ark. 1110, 82 S.W.2d 841, 843; to reduce to precision in amount and to satisfy, State ex rel. Banister v. Cantley, 330 Mo. 943, 52 S.W.2d 397, 399; to sell, Esser v. Chimel, 27 Del.Ch. 69, 30 A.2d 685, 687; to "wind up" affairs of a business. See also **Bankruptcy proceedings; Liquidation; Settle; Settlement.**

Liquidated. Ascertained; determined; fixed; settled; made clear or manifest. Cleared away; paid; discharged. Adjusted, certain, or settled. Murchison v. Levy Plumbing Co., Tex.Civ.App., 73 S.W.2d 967, 968. Declared by the parties as to amount, U. S. v. Skinner & Eddy Corporation, D.C.Wash., 28 F.2d 373, 386; made certain as to what and how much is due, Gasper v. Mayer, 171 Okl. 457, 43 P.2d 467, 471; Electrical Products Corporation of Oregon v. Ziegler Drug Stores, 157 Or. 267, 71 P.2d 583, 584. Made certain or fixed by agreement of parties or by operation of law, Miller v. Prince Street Elevator Co., 41 N.M. 330, 68 P.2d 663, 666. Settled, paid, discharged. Trenton Banking Co. v. Kennedy, 17 N.J.Misc. 222, 8 A.2d 232, 234. See also **Liquidation; Settle; Settlement.**

Liquidated account. An account whereof the amount is certain and fixed, either by the act and agreement of the parties or by operation of law; a sum which cannot be changed by the proof. It is so much or nothing; but the term does not necessarily refer to a writing. Gasper v. Mayer, 171 Okl. 457, 43 P.2d 467, 471; Williamson v. City of Eastland, Tex.Civ.App., 65 S.W.2d 774, 775.

Liquidated claim. Claim, amount of which has been agreed on by parties to action or is fixed by operation of law. Tapp v. Tapp's Trustee, 299 Ky. 345, 185 S.W.2d 534, 535; United States Fidelity & Guaranty Co. v. American Bldg. Maintenance Co. of Los Angeles, 7 Cal.App.2d 683, 46 P.2d 984, 988. A claim which can be determined with exactness from parties' agreement or by arithmetical process or application of definite rules of law. Huo Chin Yin v. Amino Products Co., 141 Ohio St. 21, 46 N.E.2d 610, 614; Petersen v. Graham, 7 Wash.2d 464, 110 P.2d 149, 154. Claim for debt or damages is "liquidated" in character if amount thereof is fixed, has been agreed upon, or is capable of ascertainment by mathematical computation or operation of law. Robinson v. Loyola Foundation, Inc., Fla.App., 236 So.2d 154, 157.

Liquidated damages. See **Damages.**

Liquidated debt. A debt is liquidated when it is certain what is due and how much is due. That which has been made certain as to amount due by agreement of parties or by operation of law. Gasper v. Mayer, 171 Okl. 457, 43 P.2d 467, 471.

Liquidated demand. A demand the amount of which has been ascertained or settled by agreement of the parties, or otherwise. Williamson v. City of Eastland, Tex.Civ.App., 65 S.W.2d 774, 775. Amount claimed is a "liquidated demand" if it is susceptible of being made certain in amount by mathematical calculations from factors which are or ought to be in possession or knowledge of party to be charged. Rifkin v. Safenovitz, 131 Conn. 411, 40 A.2d 188, 189.

Liquidating distribution. A distribution of stock pursuant to reorganization plan. Dworsky v. Buzza Co., 215 Minn. 282, 9 N.W.2d 767, 769. See **Liquidation.**

Liquidating partner. The partner who upon the dissolution or insolvency of the firm, is appointed to settle its accounts, collect assets, adjust claims, and pay debts.

Liquidating trust. A trust, the object of which is liquidation as soon as possible. Helvering v. Washburn, C.C.A.Minn., 99 F.2d 478.

Liquidation. The act or process of settling or making clear, fixed, and determinate that which before was uncertain or unascertained. Payment, satisfaction, or collection; realization on assets and discharge of liabilities. To clear away (to lessen) a debt. Craddock-Terry Co. v. Powell, 180 Va. 242, 22 S.E.2d 30, 34. To pay or settle. In re Klink's Estate, 310 Ill.App. 609, 35 N.E.2d 684, 687. To take over for collection. Belden v. Modern Finance Co., Ohio App., 61 N.E.2d 801, 804, 44 O.L.A. 163. Winding up or settling with creditors and debtors. Wilson v. Superior Court in and for Santa Clara County, 2 Cal.2d 632, 43 P.2d 286, 288. Winding up of corporation so that assets are distributed to those entitled to receive them. Process of reducing assets to cash, discharging liabilities and dividing surplus or loss.

The settling of financial affairs of a business or individual, usually by liquidating (turning to cash) all assets for distribution to creditors, heirs, etc. It is to be distinguished from dissolution which is the end of the legal existence of a corporation. Liquidation may precede or follow dissolution, depending upon statutes.

See also Bankruptcy proceedings; Distressed sale; Distribution in liquidation; Liquidate; Liquidated; Receivership.

One month liquidation. A special election available to certain shareholders of a corporation which determines how the distributions received in liquidation by the electing shareholders will be treated for Federal income tax purposes. In order to qualify for the election, the corporation must be completely liquidated within the time span of any one calendar month.

Partial liquidation. A partial liquidation occurs when some of the corporation's assets are distributed to its shareholders (usually on a pro rata basis) and the corporation continues doing business in a contracted form. Distributions of cash or property beyond the amount of earned surplus of a corporation is a partial liquidation.

Tax implications. In a complete or partial liquidation of a corporation, amounts received by the shareholders in exchange for their stock are usually treated as a sale or exchange of the stock resulting in capital gain or loss treatment. Special rules apply to one month liquidations, twelve month liquidations, and the liquidation of a subsidiary.

Twelve-month liquidation. A provision of the Internal Revenue Code that requires a corporation selling property within the 12-month period from the adoption of a plan of liquidation to its complete liquidation to recognize no gain or loss on such sales. Generally, inventory is not included within the definition unless a bulk sale occurs. See I.R.C. § 337.

Liquidation dividend. Act or operation in winding up affairs of firm or corporation, a settling with its debtors and creditors, and an appropriation and distribution to its stockholders ratably of the amount of profit and loss. Hellman v. Helvering, 63 App.D.C. 18, 68 F.2d 763, 765.

Liquidation price. A price paid for property sold to liquidate a debt. Usually less than market value since there is pressure to sell or a forced sale, either of which does not usually bring the highest price.

Liquidator. A person appointed to carry out the winding up of a company. In England and Canada, a receiver who liquidates a corporation on dissolution.

Liquid debt /líkwəd dét/. A debt immediately and unconditionally due.

Liquidity. The status or condition of a person or a business in terms of his or its ability to convert assets into cash. In relationship to markets, the capacity of the market in a particular security to withstand an amount of buying and selling at reasonable prices.

Liquor. Alcoholic beverage made by distillation; to be contrasted with wines which are made by fermentation. See also **Alcoholic liquors; Intoxicating liquor.**

Liquor offenses. Generic term describing crimes connected with the use, sale or abuse of intoxicating liquor or the absence of a license to sell liquor. See **Dram Shop Acts; Driving while intoxicated.**

Lis /lís/. Lat. A controversy or dispute; a suit or action at law.

Lis alibi pendens /lís ǽləbay péndèn(d)z/. A suit pending elsewhere. The fact that proceedings are pending between a plaintiff and defendant in one court in respect to a given matter is a ground for preventing the plaintiff from taking proceedings in another court against the same defendant for the same object arising out of the same cause of action.

Lis mota /lís mówdə/. A controversy moved or begun. By this term is meant a dispute which has arisen upon a point or question which afterwards forms the issue upon which legal proceedings are instituted. After such controversy has arisen *(post litem motam),* it is held, declarations as to pedigree, made by members of the family since deceased, are not admissible.

Lis pendens /lís péndèn(d)z/. A pending suit. Jurisdiction, power, or control which courts acquire over property in suit pending action and until final judgment.

Notice of lis pendens. A notice filed on public records for the purpose of warning all persons that the title to certain property is in litigation, and that they are in danger of being bound by an adverse judgment. The notice is for the purpose of preserving rights pending litigation. Mitchell v. Federal Land Bank of St. Louis, 206 Ark. 253, 174 S.W.2d 671, 674. Purpose of "lis pendens" is to notify prospective purchasers and encumbrancers that any interest acquired by them in property in litigation is subject to decision of court and while it is simply a notice of pending litigation the effect thereof on the owner of property is constraining. Beefy King Intern., Inc. v. Veigle, C.A.Fla., 464 F.2d 1102, 1104.

List. A docket or calendar of causes ready for trial or argument, or of motions ready for hearing. Entering in an official list or schedule; as, to list property for taxation, to put into a list or catalogue, to register, to list a property with a real estate broker. Official registry of voters. See also **Docket; Listing.**

Listed. Included in a list; put on a list; *e.g.* on a list of taxable persons or property. See **Listing.**

Listed security. A security that has met the requirements of a stock exchange for listing. Such requirements include submitting financial reports, consenting to certain supervision, and so on. See also **Listing** *(Securities);* **Offering.**

Listers. This word is used in some of the states to designate the persons appointed to make lists of taxables.

Listing. *Real estate.* An agreement between an owner of real property and a real estate agent, whereby the agent agrees to secure a buyer or tenant for specific property at a certain price and terms in return for a fee or commission. The various types of real estate listings are as follows:

An *open* or *general listing* is the right to sell that may be given to more than one agent at a time. An *exclusive agency listing* is the right of one agent to be the only one other than the owner who may sell the property during a period of time. An *exclusive authorization to sell listing* is a written contract that gives one agent the sole right to sell the prop-

erty during a time period. This means that even if the owner finds the buyer, the agent will get a commission. *Multiple listing* occurs when an agent with an exclusive listing shares information about the property sale with many members of a real estate association and shares the sale commission with an agent who finds the buyer. A *net listing* is an arrangement in which the seller sets a minimum price he or she will take for the property and the agent's commission is the amount the property sells for over that minimum selling price.

See also **Brokerage listing; Multiple listing; Open listing.**

Securities. In securities, the contract between a firm and a stock exchange covering the trading of that firm's securities on the stock exchange. See also **Listed security; Offering.**

Taxation. "Listing property for taxation" is the making of a schedule or inventory of such property, whereby owner makes statement of property in response to assessor's inquiries. Templing v. Bennett, 156 Kan. 68, 131 P.2d 904, 907. The word listing ordinarily implies an official listing of the persons and property to be taxed, and a valuation of the property of each person as a basis of apportionment.

List of creditors. Documentation in the form of a list with names and addresses and amounts owed to creditors, required as a schedule in bankruptcy proceedings.

List price. The published or advertised price of goods which may change after negotiation and be reduced by a discount or rebate for prompt payment or volume purchase.

Litem denunciare /láydəm dənənsiyériy/. Lat. In the civil law, to cast the burden of a suit upon another; particularly used with reference to a purchaser of property who, being sued in respect to it by a third person, gives notice to his vendor and demands his aid in its defense.

Litem suam facere /láydəm s(y)úwəm fǽsəriy/. Lat. To make a suit his own. Where a *judex,* from partiality or enmity, evidently favored either of the parties, he was said *litem suam facere.*

Lite pendente /láydiy pəndéntiy/. Lat. Pending the suit.

Litera /lídərə/. Lat. A letter. The letter of a law, as distinguished from its spirit. See **Letter.**

Literacy. Literacy means ability to read and write. Bazemore v. Bertie County Bd. of Elections, 254 N.C. 398, 119 S.E.2d 637, 642.

Literacy test. Test required in certain states as a precondition to right to vote. Such tests are unconstitutional if invidiously discriminatory. Lassiter v. Northhampton Election Bd., 360 U.S. 45, 79 S.Ct. 985, 3 L.Ed.2d 1072. The Voting Rights Act of 1965 suspended such tests in states where less than half the adult population were registered or had voted in the previous election.

Literæ /lídəriy/. Letters. A term applied in old English law to various instruments in writing, public and private.

Literæ dimissoriæ /lídəriy dìməsóriyiy/. Dimissory letters (q.v.).

Literæ mortuæ /lídəriy mórchuwiy/. Dead letters; fulfilling words of a statute.

Literæ patentes /lídəriy pəténtiyz/. Letters patent; literally, open letters.

Literæ patentes regis non erunt vacuæ /lídəriy pəténtiyz ríyjəs nòn érənt vǽkyuwiy/. The king's letters patent shall not be void.

Literæ procuratoriæ /lídəriy pròkyərətóriyiy/. In old English law, letters procuratory; letters of procuration; letters of attorney.

Literæ recognitionis /lídəriy rèkəgnìshiyównəs/. In maritime law, a bill of lading.

Literæ scriptæ manent /lídəriy skríptiy mǽnənt/. Written words last.

Literæ sigillatæ /lídəriy sìjəléydiy/. In old English law, sealed letters. The return of a sheriff was so called.

Literal /lídərəl/. According to language; following expression in words. A literal construction of a document adheres closely to its words, without making differences for extrinsic circumstances; a literal performance of a condition is one which complies exactly with its terms.

Literal construction. The interpretation of a document according to its words alone without any consideration of the intent of the parties who drafted or signed it beyond the fact that they used such language.

Literal contract. In Roman law, a species of written contract, in which the formal act by which an obligation was superinduced on the convention was an entry of the sum due, where it should be specifically ascertained, on the debit side of a ledger. A contract, the whole of the evidence of which is reduced to writing, and binds the party who subscribed it, although he has received no consideration.

Literal proof. In the civil law, written evidence.

Literary /lídərehriy/. Pertaining to literature; connected with authors and the study or use of books and writings.

Literary composition. An original result of mental production, developed in a series of written or printed words, arranged for an intelligent purpose, in an orderly succession of expressive combinations. See also **Literary work.**

Literary property. May be described as the right which entitles an author and his assigns to all the use and profit of his composition, to which no independent right is, through any act or omission on his or their part, vested in another person. Literary property is the exclusive right of owner to possess, use and dispose of intellectual productions, the term denotes the corporal property in which an intellectual production is embodied; and it may consist of letters, lectures, sermons or addresses. Carpenter Foundation v. Oakes, 26 Cal.App.3d 784, 103 Cal.Rptr. 368, 375. See also **Copyright; Literary work.**

Literary work. Under Copyright Act, "literary works" are works, other than audiovisual works, expressed in words, numbers, or other verbal or numerical symbols or indicia, regardless of the nature of the material objects, such as books, periodicals, manuscripts, phonorecords, film, tapes, disks, or cards in which they are embodied. 17 U.S.C.A. § 101.

Literate. A person is literate if he can read and write a language. Knowledgable and educated.

Literatura /lìdərət(y)úrə/. "Ad literaturam ponere" means to put children to school. This liberty was anciently denied to those parents who were servile tenants, without the lord's consent. The prohibition against the education of sons arose from the fear that the son, being bred to letters, might enter into holy orders, and so stop or divert the services which he might otherwise do as heir to his father.

Literis obligatio /lídərəs òbləgéysh(iy)ow/. In Roman law, the contract of *nomen,* which was constituted by writing *(scripturâ).* It was of two kinds, viz.: (1) *A re in personam,* when a transaction was transferred from the daybook *(adversaria)* into the ledger *(codex)* in the form of a debt under the name or heading of the purchaser or debtor *(nomen);* and (2) *a personâ in personam,* where a debt already standing under one *nomen* or heading was transferred in the usual course of *novatio* from that *nomen* to another and substituted *nomen.* By reason of this transferring, these obligations were called *"nomina transcriptia."* No money was, in fact, paid to constitute the contract. If ever money was paid, then the *nomen* was *arcarium (i.e.,* a real contract, *re contractus),* and not a *nomen proprium.*

Litigant. A party to a lawsuit; one engaged in litigation; usually spoken of active parties, not of nominal ones.

Litigare /lìdəgériy/. Lat. To litigate; to carry on a suit *(litem agere),* either as plaintiff or defendant; to claim or dispute by action; to test or try the validity of a claim by action.

Litigate /lídəgeyt/. To dispute or contend in form of law; to settle a dispute or seek relief in a court of law; to carry on a suit. To bring into or engage in litigation; the act of carrying on a suit in a law court; a judicial contest; hence, any controversy that must be decided upon evidence. To make the subject of a lawsuit; to contest in law, to prosecute or defend by pleadings, evidence, and debate in a court. Valley Exp., Inc. v. U. S., D.C.Wis., 264 F.Supp. 1006, 1009. See also **Adjudge; Adjudication.**

Litigation /lìdəgéyshən/. A lawsuit. Legal action, including all proceedings therein. Contest in a court of law for the purpose of enforcing a right or seeking a remedy. A judicial contest, a judicial controversy, a suit at law.

Litigious /lətíjəs/. That which is the subject of a lawsuit or action; that which is contested in a court of law. In another sense, "litigious" signifies fond of litigation; prone to engage in suits.

Litigious right /lətíjəs ráyt/. In the civil law, a right which cannot be exercised without undergoing a lawsuit. Civil Code La. art. 3556, par. 18.

A right, to be considered "litigious" under Louisiana law, must be in litigation at time of the sale thereof, and ceases to be litigious if at time of the sale judgment has become final. Saucier v. Crichton, C.C. A.La., 147 F.2d 430, 435.

Litis æstimatio /láydəs èstəméysh(iy)ow/. Lat. The measure of damages.

Litis contestatio /láydəs kòntəstéysh(iy)ow/. Lat.

Civil and Canon Law. Contestation of suit; the process of contesting a suit by the opposing statements of the respective parties; the process of coming to an issue; the attainment of an issue; the issue itself.

Ecclesiastical Courts. The general answer made by the defendant, in which he denied the matter charged against him in the libel.

Litis denunciatio /láydəs dənènsiyéysh(iy)ow/. Lat. In old civil law, the process by which a purchaser of property, who is sued for its possession or recovery by a third person, falls back upon his vendor's covenant of warranty, by giving the latter notice of the action and demanding his aid in defending it.

Litis dominium /láydəs dəmíniyəm/. Lat. In old civil law, ownership, control, or direction of a suit. A fiction of law by which the employment of an attorney or proctor (*procurator*) in a suit was authorized or justified, he being supposed to become, by the appointment of his principal (*dominus*) or client, the *dominus litis*.

Litis nomen omnem actionem significat, sive in rem, sive in personam sit /láydəs nówmən ómnəm èkshiyównəm səgnífəkət, sáyviy in rém, sáyviy in pərsównəm sít/. A lawsuit signifies every action, whether it be *in rem* or *in personam*.

Litispendence /làydəspéndən(t)s/. An obsolete term for the time during which a lawsuit is going on.

Litre /líydər/. Fr. A measure of capacity in the metric system, being a cubic decimetre, equal to 61.022 cubic inches, or 2.113 American pints, or 1.76 English pints.

Littering. Littering is dumping, throwing, placing, depositing or leaving, or causing to be dumped, thrown, deposited or left any refuse of any kind or any object or substance which tends to pollute, mar or deface, into, upon or about: (a) Any public street, highway, alley, road, right-of-way, park or other public place, or any lake, stream, watercourse, or other body of water, except by direction of some public officer or employee authorized by law to direct or permit such acts; or (b) Any private property without the consent of the owner or occupant of such property.

Littoral. Belonging to shore, as of seas and great lakes. Wernberg v. State, Alaska, 516 P.2d 1191, 1195.

Littoral land. Land boardering ocean, sea, or lake.

Littoral rights. Rights concerning properties abutting an ocean, sea or lake rather than a river or stream (riparian). Littoral rights are usually concerned with the use and enjoyment of the shore. See **Water rights** (*Water rights*).

Litura /lət(y)úrə/. Lat. In the civil law, an obliteration or blot in a will or other instrument.

Litus /láydəs/. In civil law, the bank of a stream or shore of the sea; the coast.

In old European law, a kind of servant; one who surrendered himself into another's power.

Litus est quousque maximus fluctus a mari pervenit /láydəs èst kwowóskwiy mæksəməs flóktəs èy mæray pərvíynət/. The shore is where the highest wave from the sea has reached.

Litus maris /láydəs mæras/. The sea-shore.

Live, *adj.* Having or possessing life. See also **Alive; Life.**

Live, *v.* To live in a place, is to reside there, to abide there, to occupy as one's home. Leroux v. Industrial Accident Commission of California, 140 Cal.App. 569, 35 P.2d 624, 626. See also **Domicile; Living; Residence.**

Live and cohabit together as husband and wife. As applied to common-law marriages, means a living together, claiming to be married, in the relationship of husband and wife. Drummond v. Benson, Tex.Civ. App., 133 S.W.2d 154, 159.

Livelihood. Means of support or subsistence.

Livelode. Maintenance; support.

Livery /lív(ə)riy/. In old English law, delivery of possession of their lands to the king's tenants *in capite* or tenants by knight's service. A writ which could be sued out by a ward in chivalry, on reaching his majority, to obtain delivery of the possession of his lands out of the hands of the guardian.

Act of delivering legal possession of property. See **Livery of seisin.**

A particular dress or garb appropriate or peculiar to certain persons, as the members of a guild, or, more particularly, the servants of a nobleman or gentleman.

The privilege of a particular guild or company of persons, the members thereof being called "liverymen."

A contract of hiring out of work-beasts, particularly horses, to the use of the hirer. It is commonly used in the compound, "livery-stable." Feeding, stabling, and care of horses for pay. Rental of vehicles, boats, etc. Word "livery" as used in automobile policy excluding coverage for automobile while being used as a livery conveyance means the hiring out of horses and carriages or a concern offering vehicles of various kinds for rent. Gagnard v. Thibodeaux, La.App., 336 So.2d 1069, 1070.

Livery conveyance. A vehicle used indiscriminately in conveying the public, without limitation to certain persons or particular occasions or without being governed by special terms. Elliott v. Behner, 150 Kan. 876, 96 P.2d 852, 857.

Livery in chivalry. In feudal law, the delivery of the lands of a ward in chivalry out of the guardian's hands, upon the heir's attaining the requisite age,— twenty-one for males, sixteen for females. 2 Bl. Comm. 68.

Livery office. An office appointed for the delivery of lands.

Livery of seisin /lív(ə)riy əv síyzən/. The appropriate ceremony, at common law, for transferring the corporal possession of lands or tenements by a grantor to his grantee. It was livery *in deed* where the parties went together upon the land, and there a twig, clod, key, or other symbol was delivered in the name of the whole. Livery *in law* was where the same ceremony was performed, not upon the land itself, but in sight of it. 2 Bl.Comm. 315, 316.

Lives in being. As used in rule against perpetuities, means any lives in being at any time future interest is created, regardless of personal interest therein.

Livestock. Domestic animals used or raised on a farm. Boland v. Cecil, 65 Cal.App.2d 832, 150 P.2d 819, 822. The term in its generic sense includes all domestic animals. Meader v. Unemployment Compensation Division of Industrial Accident Board, 64 Idaho 716, 136 P.2d 984, 987. It includes fur bearing animals raised in captivity. Fromm Bros. v. United States, D.C.Wis., 35 F.Supp. 145, 147.

Livestock insurance. See **Insurance.**

Live storage. As applied to storage of automobiles in garages, "dead storage" is where cars not in use are deposited or put away, sometimes for the season, and "live storage" is the storage of cars in active daily use. Hogan v. O'Brien, 123 Misc. 865, 206 N.Y.S. 831, 832, affirmed 212 App.Div. 193, 208 N.Y.S. 477. The extent of responsibility of a garage keeper for cars put in his garage sometimes depends on whether they are in "dead storage" or "live storage."

Living. Existing, surviving, or continuing in operation. Also means to abide, to dwell, to reside and literally signifies the pecuniary resources by means of which one exists. Leroux v. Industrial Accident Commission of California, 140 Cal.App. 569, 35 P.2d 624, 626. See also **Alive; Domicile; Life; Residence.**

Living apart. To live in a separate abode. McDaniel v. McDaniel, 292 Ky. 56, 165 S.W.2d 966, 967. See also **Living separate and apart.**

Living at time of another's death. Remaining in life after such other person's death. Sabit v. Safe Deposit & Trust Co. of Baltimore, 184 Md. 24, 40 A.2d 231, 238.

Living in open and notorious adultery. To constitute, parties must dwell together openly and notoriously as if conjugal relation existed between them. People v. Potter, 319 Ill.App. 409, 49 N.E.2d 307, 309. The parties must reside together in face of society as if conjugal relations existed between them, and fact of their so living and that they are not husband and wife must be known in community in which they reside. Mathis v. State, 60 Okl.Cr. 58, 61 P.2d 261, 267.

Living issue. Living children.

Living separate and apart. Exists where the spouses have come to a parting of the ways and have no present intention of resuming marital relations and taking up life together under the same roof, not where they are residing temporarily in different places for economic or social reasons. Woodall v. Commissioner of Internal Revenue, C.C.A.9, 105 F.2d 474, 477. This is a no-fault ground for divorce in many states when the spouses have lived apart for the statutorily prescribed period.

Living together. As respects court's right to allow suit money to wife in divorce action, means dwelling together in same house, eating at same table, the two parties holding themselves out to world and conducting themselves toward each other as husband and wife. Lipp v. Lipp, Mo.App., 117 S.W.2d 364–366.

Living trust. Trust which is operative during life of settlor; an active or inter vivos trust.

Living with husband. Means to dwell, to reside, to make one's abiding place or home with him, and may also mean to cohabit. Living together as husband and wife in ordinary acceptation of words in common understanding; maintaining a home and living together in same household or actually cohabiting under conditions which would be regarded as constituting a family relation. McPadden v. Morris, 126 Conn. 654, 13 A.2d 679, 680.

L.J. An abbreviation for "Law Judge;" also for "Law Journal."

LL. The reduplicated form of the abbreviation "L." for "law," used as a plural. It is generally used in citing old collections of statute law; as "LL. Hen. I."

L.L. (Also L.Lat.) and **L.F.** (also L.Fr.) are used as abbreviations of the terms "Law Latin" and "Law French."

LL.B., LL.M., and LL.D. Abbreviations used to denote, respectively, the three academic degrees in law,— bachelor, master, and doctor of laws; the latter commonly being an honorary degree. See also **J.D.**

Lloyd's bonds. The name of a class of evidences of debt, used in England; being acknowledgments, by a borrowing company made under its seal, of a debt incurred and actually due by the company to a contractor or other person for work done, goods supplied, or otherwise, as the case may be, with a covenant for payment of the principal and interest at a future time.

Lloyd's insurance. Under this type of insurance, insurers are such as individuals and not as a corporate insurance company and the liability for loss is several and not joint. Jones v. Hollywood Style Shop, Tex. Civ.App., 62 S.W.2d 167. The "Lloyds' Plan," contemplates individual liability of the several underwriters. Harris v. Prince, 132 Tex. 231, 121 S.W.2d 983, 986. See also **Lloyd's of London; Lloyds underwriters; London Lloyds.**

Lloyd's of London. An association in the city of London, originally for the transaction of marine insurance, the members of which underwrite one another's policies. An insurance mart in London at which individual underwriters gather to quote rates and write insurance on the widest variety of risks. See also **London Lloyds.**

Lloyds underwriters. Any aggregation of individuals, who under a common name engage in the business of insurance for profit through an attorney-in-fact having authority to obligate the underwriters severally, within such limits as may be lawfully specified in the power of attorney, on contracts of insurance made or issued by such attorney-in-fact, in the name of such aggregation of individuals, to and with any person or persons insured. N.Y.Consol. Laws, Insurance § 425.

Loading. The act of putting a load on or in; as to load a car or a vessel.

The difference between gross and net premiums on insurance policies. Commissioner of Insurance v. Massachusetts Accident Co., 314 Mass. 558, 50 N.E.2d 801, 809; Metropolitan Life Ins. Co. v. Rouillard, 92 N.H. 16, 24 A.2d 264, 266; Magers v. Northwestern Mut. Life Ins. Co., 348 Mo. 96, 152 S.W.2d 148, 150. In insurance, that portion of the premium used for meeting selling and administrative expenses beyond that portion required to meet the liability reserve. In an open-end investment company, that portion of the price of the share added to cover selling expenses.

Load line. The depth to which a ship will sink in salt water when loaded. A design, painted on each side of vessel, intended as a guide to determine safe loading depth under various conditions. The Indien, C.C. A.Cal., 71 F.2d 752, 759.

Loadmanage. The pay to loadsmen; that is, persons who sail before ships, in barks or small vessels, with instruments for towing the ship and directing her course, in order that she may escape the dangers in her way.

Loaf. To spend time in idleness, to lounge or loiter about or along. City of Olathe v. Lauck, 156 Kan. 637, 135 P.2d 549, 551. See also **Malinger.**

Loan. A lending. Delivery by one party to and receipt by another party of sum of money upon agreement, express or implied, to repay it with or without interest. Isaacson v. House, 216 Ga. 698, 119 S.E.2d 113, 116. Anything furnished for temporary use to a person at his request, on condition that it shall be returned, or its equivalent in kind, with or without compensation for its use. Liberty Nat. Bank & Trust Co. v. Travelers Indem. Co., 58 Misc.2d 443, 295 N.Y.S.2d 983, 986.

Bailment without reward, consisting of the delivery of an article by the owner to another person, to be used by the latter gratuitously, and returned either *in specie* or in kind. A borrowing of money or other personal property by a person who promises to return it.

"Loan" includes: (1) the creation of debt by the lender's payment of or agreement to pay money to the debtor or to a third party for the account of the debtor; (2) the creation of debt by a credit to an account with the lender upon which the debtor is entitled to draw immediately; (3) the creation of debt pursuant to a lender credit card or similar arrangement; and (4) the forbearance of debt arising from a loan. Uniform Consumer Credit Code, § 3–106.

See also **Morning loan; Participation loan.** For term loan, see **Term.**

Amortized loan. One which calls for periodic payments which are applied first to interest and then to principal as provided by the terms of the note.

Call loan. One which is payable on demand or call by the lender.

Collateral loan. One which is secured by property or securities.

Commercial loan. Generally a short term loan for 30 to 90 days given by financial institutions.

Commodity loan. One which is secured by a commodity such as cotton or wool in the form of a warehouse receipt or other negotiable instrument.

Consumer loan. One which is made or extended to a natural person for family, household, personal or agricultural purposes and generally governed by truth-in-lending statutes and regulations.

Day loan. One made to a broker on a day to day basis to finance his daily transactions.

Demand loan. One on which the lender may make demand or call at any time for repayment. See also *Call loan.*

Installment loan. One which is repaid according to its terms over a period of time in installments.

Non-recourse loan. Loans made to farmers by a government organization in exchange for a particular commodity; *e.g.* wheat or corn. They are called nonrecourse because the government can never demand payment for the loan.

Personal loan. One which is generally for a short period of time for personal as contrasted with commercial purposes. It may be secured or unsecured. See also *Consumer loan.*

Secured loan. One which is secured by property or securities. See also *Collateral loan.*

Short-term loan. One which runs for a period of less than a year and which is commonly evidenced by a note or other negotiable instrument.

Time loan. One which is made for a fixed period of time and which generally may not be repaid before the expiration of such time (without penalty) as distinguished from a call or demand loan.

Loan association. See **Building and loan association.**

Loan certificates. Certificates issued by a clearinghouse to the associated banks to a specified per cent. of the value of the collaterals deposited by the borrowing banks with the loan committee of the clearing-house. Documents issued by a borrower to evidence participation in a loan for an extended term; formerly used by municipalities. These have been replaced, in the main, by coupon bonds. See also **Certificate of indebtedness.**

Loan commitment. Commitment to borrower by lending institution that it will loan a specific amount at a certain rate on a particular piece of real estate. Such commitment is limited to a specified time period (*e.g.* four months), which is commonly based on the estimated time that it will take the borrower to construct or purchase the home contemplated by the loan.

Loaned employee or **servant.** Whether an employee should be regarded as a "loaned employee" in the service of a special employer, or whether he should be regarded as remaining in the service of his general employer, depends upon in whose work the employee was engaged at the time of injury. Owen v. St. Louis Spring Co., 175 Tenn. 543, 136 S.W.2d 498–500.

Loaned servant is an employee who is loaned or hired out to another master for some specific service or particular transaction and who is under exclusive control of that employer who may then be held vicariously liable for acts of employee under ordinary principles of respondeat superior. Kiefer Concrete, Inc. v. Hoffman, Colo., 562 P.2d 745, 746.

Loaned servant doctrine. Under the "loaned servant doctrine", when one lends his servant to another for a particular employment, servant, for anything done in that employment, must be dealt with as servant of one to whom he is lent. Blair v. Durham, C.C.A. Tenn., 134 F.2d 729, 732. Loaned-servant doctrine provides that if employer loans employee to another for performance of some special service, then that employee, with respect to that special service, may become employee of party to whom his services have been loaned. Danek v. Meldrum Mfg. and Engineering Co., Inc., Minn., 252 N.W.2d 255, 258. In order for employee to be a "loaned servant", it is not essential that general employer relinquish full control over his employee, or that special employee be completely subservient to borrower. U. S. v. N. A. Degerstrom, Inc., C.A.Wash., 408 F.2d 1130, 1138.

Loan for consumption. An agreement by which one person delivers to another a certain quantity of things which are consumed by the borrower, with the obligation to return as much of the same kind and quality. See also **Loan for use.**

Loan for exchange. A loan for exchange is a contract by which one delivers personal property to another, and the latter agrees to return to the lender a similar thing at a future time, without reward for its use. Cal.Civil Code § 1902.

Loan for use. The loan for use is an agreement by which a person delivers a thing to another, to use it according to its natural destination, or according to the agreement, under the obligation on the part of the borrower, to return it after he shall be done using it. Civ.Code La. art. 2893. A loan for use is a contract by which one gives to another the temporary possession and use of personal property, and the latter agrees to return the same thing to him at a future time, without reward for its use. Slack v. Bryam, 299 Ky. 132, 184 S.W.2d 873, 876. Cal.Civil Code, § 1884. A loan for use is the gratuitous grant of an article to another for use, to be returned *in specie,* and may be either for a certain time or indefinitely, and at the will of the grantor.

Loan for use (called *"commodatum"* in th civil law) differs from a loan for consumption (called *"mutuum"* in the civil law), in this: that the *commodatum* must be specifically returned; the *mutuum* is to be returned in kind. In the case of a *commodatum*, the property in the thing remains in the lender; in a *mutuum*, the property passes to the borrower.

Loan ratio. The ratio, expressed as a percentage, of the amount of a loan to the value or selling price of real property. Usually, the higher the percentage, the greater the interest charged. Maximum percentages for banks, savings and loan, or government insured loans, is set by statute.

Loan sharking. Practice of lending money at excessive and usurious interest rates, with the threat or em-

ployment of extortionate means to enforce repayment of the loan. Such activities are termed "extortionate credit transactions" under Federal Criminal Code. 18 U.S.C.A. § 891 *et seq.*

Loan societies. In English law, a kind of club formed for the purpose of advancing money on loan to the industrial classes.

Loan value. The maximum amount which can be safely lent on property or life insurance consistent with the lender's rights to protection in the event of the borrower's default.

Lobbying. All attempts including personal solicitation to induce legislators to vote in a certain way or to introduce legislation. It includes scrutiny of all pending bills which affect one's interest or the interests of one's clients, with a view towards influencing the passage or defeat of such legislation. Thiles v. County Board of Sarpy County, 189 Neb. 1, 200 N.W.2d 13, 18. Federal, and most state statutes, require that lobbyists be registered. See **Lobbying acts.**

Lobbying acts. Federal and state statutes governing conduct of lobbyists; *e.g.* Federal Regulation of Lobbying Act requires that lobbyists register with House and Senate and file quarterly reports of amount and source of payments received for lobbying activities. See 12 U.S.C.A. § 261 et seq.

Lobbyist. One who makes it a business to procure the passage or defeat of bills pending before a legislative body. See also **Lobbying.**

L'obligation sans cause, ou sur une fausse cause, ou sur cause illicite, ne peut avoir aucun effet /lòwbligasyówn sòn kówz, ùw sár (y)ùwn fóws kówz, ùw sár kówz ìlisíyt nə pyúwt əvwár owkyúwn əféy/. An obligation without consideration, or upon a false consideration (which fails), or upon unlawful consideration, cannot have any effect.

Local. Relating to place, expressive of place; belonging or confined to a particular place. Distinguished from "general," "personal," and "transitory."

As to local Allegiance; Customs; Government; Tax and Venue, see those titles.

Local act. See **Local law.**

Local actions. Term embraces all actions in which the subject or thing sought to be recovered is in its nature local. Action which must be brought in jurisdiction of act or subject matter, as opposed to transitory action. Actions are "local" when the transactions on which they are based could not occur except in some particular place. One wherein all principal facts on which it is founded are of a local nature; as where possession of land is to be recovered, or damages for an actual trespass, or for waste affecting land, because in such case the cause of action relates to some particular locality, which usually also constitutes the venue of the action. A "transitory action" may be brought in any court of general jurisdiction in any district wherein defendant can be found and served with process, whereas in a "local action" the plaintiff must bring suit in the court designated, if not statutorily required to do otherwise. Moreland v. Rucker Pharmacal Co., D.C.La., 59 F.R.D. 537, 540. Compare **Transitory action.**

Local affairs. The "local affairs" over which regulation, management and control are delegated to cities are affairs within the jurisdiction of the city by the law of its being. Robia Holding Corporation v. Walker, 136 Misc. 358, 239 N.Y.S. 659, 662.

Local agent. An agent at a given place or within a definite district. Sharp & Dohme v. Waybourne, Tex. Civ.App., 74 S.W.2d 413. An agent may be a general agent as to his powers, although he represents the company only in a particular locality or within a limited territory, and in the latter aspect is called a "local agent". Prudential Ins. Co. of America v. Jenkins, 290 Ky. 802, 162 S.W.2d 791, 795. An agent placed in charge of corporation's local business for purpose of winding it up. National Hardware & Stove Co. v. Walters, Tex.Civ.App., 58 S.W.2d 146, 147. One appointed to act as the representative of a corporation and transact its business generally (or business of a particular character) at a given place or within a defined district. One who represents corporation in promotion of business for which it was incorporated, in county in which suit is filed. National Hardware & Stove Co. v. Walters, Tex.Civ.App., 58 S.W.2d 146. One who stands in shoes of corporation in relation to particular matters committed to his care and represents corporation in its business in either a general or limited capacity. McDonald Service Co. v. Peoples Nat. Bank of Rock Hill, S.C., 218 N.C. 533, 11 S.E.2d 556, 558, 559. A "local agent" to receive and collect money means an agent residing either permanently or temporarily within the state for purpose of his agency. McDonald Service Co. v. Peoples Nat. Bank of Rock Hill, S.C., 218 N.C. 533, 11 S.E.2d 556, 558. By statute or court rule in most states, service of process on a foreign corporation may be made on a local agent of such corporation. See Fed.R.Civil P. 4; New York C.P.L.R. §§ 308, 318.

Local and special legislation. Term applies to special or particular places or special and particular person, and is distinguished from general statute in operation and relation to classes of persons or subjects. Madison County Board of Education v. Smith, 250 Ky. 495, 63 S.W.2d 620.

Local assessment. A charge in the nature of tax, levied to pay the whole or part of the cost of local improvements (*e.g.* sewers, sidewalks) and assessed upon the various parcels of property specially benefited thereby. See also **Local improvement assessment.**

Local chattel. A thing is local that is fixed to the freehold.

Local concern. An activity is of "local concern" if it is exercised by the municipality in its proprietary capacity. Luhrs v. City of Phoenix, 52 Ariz. 438, 83 P.2d 283, 285.

Local courts. Courts whose jurisdiction is limited to a particular territory or district. The expression often signifies the courts of the state, in opposition to the United States courts, or to municipal or county courts in contrast to courts with state-wide jurisdiction.

Local government. City, county, or other governing body at a level smaller than a state. Local government has the greatest control over real property, zoning, and other local matters.

Local improvement. A public improvement made in a particular locality, by which the real property adjoining or near such locality is specially benefited. Floyd v. Parker Water & Sewer Sub-District, 203 S.C. 276, 17 S.E.2d 223, 227.

Local improvement assessment. A charge placed upon lands within a given district to pay the benefits which the respective parcels of land derive from the improvement. Wells v. Union Oil Co. of California, 25 Cal.App.2d 165, 76 P.2d 696, 697. An assessment for construction of improvement; *e.g.* sewers. University Nat. Co. v. Grays Harbor County, 12 Wash.2d 549, 122 P.2d 501, 502.

Locality. A definite region in any part of space; geographical position. Warnock v. Kraft, 30 Cal.App.2d 1, 85 P.2d 505, 506. Place; vicinity; neighborhood; community. Conley v. Valley Motor Transit Co., C.C. A.Ohio, 139 F.2d 692, 693; Lukens Steel Co. v. Perkins, 70 App.D.C. 354, 107 F.2d 627, 631. See also **Situs.**

Word "localities" in act prohibiting carrier from giving undue preference to any locality or subjecting it to undue prejudice denotes origin or destination of traffic and shipping, producing, and consuming areas affected by carrier's rates and practices. Texas & P. Ry. Co. v. U. S., Tex., 289 U.S. 627, 53 S.Ct. 768, 77 L.Ed. 1410.

Locality of a lawsuit. Place where judicial authority may be exercised. Graver Tank & Manufacturing Corporation v. New England Terminal Co., C.C.A.R.I., 125 F.2d 71, 73; Neirbo Co. v. Bethlehem Shipbuilding Corporation, 308 U.S. 165, 60 S.Ct. 153, 154, 84 L.Ed. 167. See also **Venue.**

Localization. The doctrine that concerns the amount and nature of local activity of a foreign corporation sufficient to subject it to the laws of the state in which it operates. National Mutual Building and Loan Assoc. v. Brahan, 193 U.S. 635, 24 S.Ct. 532, 48 L.Ed. 823.

Local law. A local law is one which operates over a particular locality instead of over the whole territory of the state. Ulrich v. Beatty, 139 Ind.App. 174, 216 N.E.2d 737, 746. One which relates to particular persons or things or to particular persons or things of a class or which operates on or over a portion of a class instead of all of the class. In re Annexation of Reno Quartermaster Depot Military Reservation to Independent School Dist. No. 34, Canadian County, Okl., 180 Okl. 274, 69 P.2d 659, 662. One whose operation is confined within territorial limits, other than those of the whole state or any properly constituted class or locality therein. State v. Kallas, 97 Utah 492, 94 P.2d 414, 420; Ravitz v. Steurele, 257 Ky. 108, 77 S.W.2d 360, 364.

The law of a particular jurisdiction as contrasted with the law of a foreign state. Term is used in conflicts to describe the power of the forum to determine questions of procedure while acknowledging the law of the situs to govern substantive questions. As used in the Restatement of this subject, the "local law" of a state is the body of standards, principles and rules, exclusive of its rules of conflict of laws, which the courts of that state apply in the decision of controversies brought before them. Restatement, Second, Conflicts, § 4(1).

Local option. An option of self-determination available to a municipality or other governmental unit to determine a particular course of action without specific approval from state officials. Local option is often used in local elections to determine whether the selling and consumption of alcoholic beverages will be permitted in local areas. Such is also used in many states to permit home rule elections for determining the structures of local governmental units. See also **Home rule.**

Local rules. Those promulgated in view of local physical conditions in the state, the character of the people, their peculiar customs, usages, and beliefs. Term may also refer to court rules adopted by individual U.S. district courts which supplement Federal Rules of Civil Procedure. See Fed.R.Civil P. 83.

Local statute. See **Local law.**

Local usage. A practice or method of dealing regularly observed in a particular place and such that it may be considered by the court under certain circumstances in interpreting a document. See U.C.C. § 1–205(2), (3). See also **Custom and usage.**

Locare /ləkériy/. To let for hire; to deliver or bail a thing for a certain reward or compensation.

Locarium /ləkériyəm/. In old European law, the price of letting; money paid for the hire of a thing; rent.

Locataire /lòwkətér/. In French law, a lessee, tenant, or renter.

Locatarius /lòwkətériyəs/. Lat. A depositee.

Locate. To find. To discover by survey. Guardian Trust Co. of Houston, Tex. v. Jefferson Lake Oil Co., C.C.A.La., 85 F.2d 465, 467. Also means to ascertain place in which something belongs. To ascertain and fix the position of something, the place of which was before uncertain or not manifest, as to locate the calls in a deed. To decide upon the place or direction to be occupied by something not yet in being, as to locate a road. To define location or limits, Delaware, L. & W. R. Co. v. Chiara, C.C.A.N.J., 95 F.2d 663, 668; or designate site or place, Union Pac. R. Co. v. City of Los Angeles, 53 Cal.App.2d 825, 128 P.2d 408, 410. To settle or become situated or established.

Located. Having a physical presence or existence in a place.

Locatio /lowkéysh(iy)ow/. Lat. In the civil law, letting for hire.

Locatio-conductio /lowkéysh(iy)ow-kəndáksh(iy)ow/. In the civil law a compound word used to denote the contract of bailment for hire, expressing the action of *both* parties, viz., a letting by the one and a hiring by the other.

Locatio custodiæ /lowkéysh(iy)ow kəstówdiyiy/. A letting to keep; a bailment or deposit of goods for hire. According to the classification of bailments at civil law, a "locatio custodiæ" is the hiring of care and services to be bestowed on the thing delivered.

Location. Site or place where something is or may be located. Act of locating. See also **Situs.**

Mining law. The act of appropriating a mining claim (parcel of land containing precious metal in its soil or rock) according to certain established rules. It usually consists in placing on the ground, in a conspicuous position, a notice setting forth the name of the locator, the fact that it is thus taken or located, with the requisite description of the extent and boundaries of the parcel. St. Louis Smelting, etc., Co. v. Kemp, 104 U.S. 649, 26 L.Ed. 875; Producers' Oil Co. v. Hanszen, 132 La. 691, 61 So. 754, 759; Cole v. Ralph, 252 U.S. 286, 40 S.Ct. 321, 326, 64 L.Ed. 567. In a secondary sense, the mining claim covered by a single act of appropriation or location. The act or series of acts whereby the boundaries of the claim are marked, etc., but it confers no right in the absence of discovery, both being essential to a valid claim. United States v. Mobley, D.C.Cal., 45 F.Supp. 407, 410. See also **Mining claim; Mining location.**

Real property. The designation of the boundaries of a particular piece of land, either upon record or on the land itself. The finding, surveying and marking out the bounds of a particular tract of land or mining claims. See **Locative calls.**

Locatio operis /lowkéysh(iy)ow ó(w)pərəs/. In the civil law, the contract of hiring work, *i.e.*, labor and services. It is a contract by which one of the parties gives a certain work to be performed by the other, who binds himself to do it for the price agreed between them, which he who gives the work to be done promises to pay to the other for doing it.

Locatio operis faciendi /lowkéysh(iy)ow ó(w)pərəs fæshiyénday/. A letting out of work to be done; a bailment of a thing for the purpose of having some work and labor or care and pains bestowed on it for a pecuniary recompense.

Locatio operis mercium vehendarum /lowkéysh(iy)ow ó(w)pərəs márs(h)(i)yəm vìy(h)əndérəm/. A letting of work to be done in the carrying of goods; a contract of bailment by which goods are delivered to a person to carry for hire.

Locatio rei /lowkéysh(iy)ow ríyay/. A letting of a thing to hire. The bailment or letting of a thing to be used by the bailee for a compensation to be paid by him.

Locative calls. In a deed, patent, or other instrument containing a description of land, locative calls are specific calls, descriptions, or marks of location, referring to landmarks, physical objects, or other points by which the land can be exactly located and identified.

In harmonizing conflicting calls in a deed or survey of public lands, courts will ascertain which calls are locative and which are merely directory, and conform the lines to the locative calls; "directory calls" being those which merely direct the neighborhood where the different calls may be found, whereas "locative calls" are those which serve to fix boundaries.

Locator /lówkèydər/ləkéydər/. One who locates land, or sets the boundaries of a mining claim, or intends or is entitled to locate. See **Finder; Location.**

Locatum /ləkéydəm/. A hiring. See **Bailment.**

Locked in. A predicament of one who has profits on securities which he owns but which he is unwilling to sell because of the liability for capital gains.

Lockout. Cessation of furnishing of work to employees or withholding work from them in effort to get for employer more desirable terms. Zura v. Marblehead Stone Division, Standard Slag Corp., 13 Ohio Misc. 317, 224 N.E.2d 176, 178, 42 O.O.2d 15. Counterpart of employee's strike.

Lockup. A place of detention in a police station, court or other facility used for persons awaiting trial.

Lococession. The act of giving place.

Loco parentis /lówkow pəréntəs/. See In loco parentis.

Locum tenens /lówkəm tíynən(d)z/. Lat. Holding the place, a deputy, substitute, lieutenant, or representative.

Locuples /lókyəplìyz/. Lat. In the civil law, able to respond in an action; good for the amount which the plaintiff might recover.

Locus /lówkəs/. A place; the place where a thing is done.

Locus contractus /lówkəs kəntrǽktəs/. The place of a contract; the place where a contract is made. The place where the last act is performed which makes an agreement a binding contract. Grain Dealers Mut. Ins. Co. v. Van Buskirk, 241 Md. 58, 215 A.2d 467, 471.

Locus contractus regit actum /lówkəs kəntrǽktəs ríyjəd ǽktəm/. The place of the contract governs the act. Scudder v. Union Nat. Bank, 91 U.S. 406, 23 L.Ed. 245. See **Lex loci.**

Locus criminis /lówkəs krímənəs/. The locality of a crime; the place where a crime was committed.

Locus delicti /lówkəs dəlíktay/. The place of the offense; the place where an offense was committed. State where last event necessary to make actor liable occurs. Hunter v. Derby Foods, C.C.A.N.Y., 110 F.2d 970, 972.

Locus in quo /lówkəs ìn kwów/. The place in which. The place in which the cause of action arose, or where anything is alleged, in pleadings, to have been done. The phrase is most frequently used in actions of trespass *quare clausum fregit.*

Locus partitus /lówkəs partáydəs/. In old English law, a place divided. A division made between two towns or counties to make out in which the land or place in question lies.

Locus pœnitentiae /lówkəs pènəténshiyiy/. A place for repentance; an opportunity for changing one's mind; an opportunity to undo what one has done; a chance to withdraw from a contemplated bargain or contract before it results in a definite contractual liability; a right to withdraw from an incompleted transaction. Morris v. Johnson, 219 Ga. 81, 132 S.E.2d 45, 51. Also, used of a chance afforded to a person, by the circumstances, of relinquishing the intention which he has formed to commit a crime, before the perpetration thereof.

Locus pro solutione reditus aut pecuniæ secundum conditionem dimissionis aut obligationis est stricte observandus /lówkəs pròw səl(y)ùwshiyówniy rédədəs òt pəkyúwniyiy səkándəm kəndìshiyównəm dəmis(h)iyównəs òd òblɘgèyshiyównəs èst stríktiy òbsərvǽndəs/. The place for the payment of rent or money, according to the condition of a lease or bond, is to be strictly observed.

Locus publicus /lówkəs pə́bləkəs/. In the civil law, a public place.

Locus regit actum /lówkəs ríyjəd ǽktəm/. In private international law, the rule that, when a legal transaction complies with the formalities required by the law of the country where it is done, it is also valid in the country where it is to be given effect, although by the law of that country other formalities are required.

Locus rei sitæ /lówkəs ríyay sáydiy/. The place where a thing is situated. In proceedings *in rem,* or the real actions of the civil law, the proper forum is the *locus rei sitœ.*

Locus sigilli /lówkəs səjílay/. In place of the seal; the place occupied by the seal of written instruments. Usually abbreviated to "L.S." on documents in place of a seal.

Locus standi /lówkəs stǽnday/. A place of standing; standing in court. A right of appearance in a court of justice, or before a legislative body, on a given question.

Lodemanage /lówdmǽnəj/. The hire of a pilot for conducting a vessel from one place to another.

Lodger. An occupant who has mere use without actual or exclusive possession. Roberts v. Casey, 36 Cal. App.2d, Supp. 767, 93 P.2d 654, 657, 658, 659; Coggins v. Gregorio, C.C.A.N.M., 97 F.2d 948, 951; Marden v. Radford, 229 Mo.App. 789, 84 S.W.2d 947, 955, 957, 959. Person who rents a furnished room or rooms.

Lodger has been defined as a tenant of part of another's house, one who for time being has his home at his lodging place, one who has leave to inhabit another man's house, one who inhabits portion of a house of which another has general possession and custody, one who lives at board or in a hired room or who has a bed in another's house, one who lives in a hired room or rooms in house of another, one who occupies hired apartments in another's house. The term is also defined as a person who lives and sleeps in a place, a person whose occupancy is a part of a house and subordinate to and in some degree under the control of a landlord or his representative. The term is used to indicate a personal relationship of some one lodging somewhere with somebody. Marden v. Radford, 229 Mo.App. 789, 84 S.W.2d 947, 955, 957, 959.

Lodging house. A house where lodgings are let; houses containing furnished apartments which are let out by the week or by the month, without meals, or with limited meals. Marden v. Radford, 229 Mo.App. 789, 84 S.W.2d 947, 955.

Lodging place. A place of rest for a night or a residence for a time; a temporary habitation.

Lodgings. Habitation in another's house; apartments in another's house, furnished or unfurnished, occupied for habitation; the occupier being termed a "lodger."

Lods et ventes /lów èy vón/. In old French and Canadian law, a fine payable by a *roturier* on every change of ownership of his land; a mutation or alienation fine.

Logbook. A ship's or aircraft's journal containing a detailed account of the ship's course, with a short history of every occurrence during the voyage.

Logia /lój(iy)ə/. A small house, lodge, or cottage.

Logic. The science of reasoning, or of the operations of the understanding which are subservient to the estimation of evidence. The term includes both the process itself of proceeding from known truths to unknown, and all other intellectual operations, in so far as auxiliary to this.

Logical relevancy. Existence of such a relationship in logic between the fact of which evidence is offered and a fact in issue that the existence of the former renders probable or improbable the existence of the latter.

Logium /lój(iy)əm/. In old records, a lodge, hovel, or outhouse.

Logographus /lògəgréfəs/. In Roman law, a public clerk, register, or book-keeper; one who wrote or kept books of accounts.

Log rolling. A legislative practice of embracing in one bill several distinct matters, none of which, perhaps, could singly obtain the assent of the legislature, and then procuring its passage by a combination of the minorities in favor of each of the measures into a majority that will adopt them all.

Practice of including in one statute or constitutional amendment more than one proposition, inducing voters to vote for all, notwithstanding they might not have voted for all if amendments or statutes had been submitted separately.

Loiter /lóydər/. To be dilatory; to be slow in movement; to stand around or move slowly about; to stand idly around; to spend time idly; to saunter; to delay; to idle; to linger; to lag behind. City of Columbus v. Aldrich, 69 Ohio App. 396, 42 N.E.2d 915, 917, 24 O.O. 142; People v. Morris, Mich.App., 239 N.W.2d 649, 652; State v. Caez, 81 N.J.Super. 315, 195 A.2d 496, 498.

Term as used in statute prohibiting loitering or prowling upon the private property of another, means to be slow in moving, to delay, to linger, to saunter, to lag behind. State ex rel. Purcell v. Superior Court In and For Maricopa County, 111 Ariz. 582, 535 P.2d 1299, 1301.

Lombardian law. See **Lex longobardorum.**

Lombards. A name given to the merchants of Italy, numbers of whom, during the twelfth and thirteenth centuries, were established as merchants and bankers in the principal cities of Europe.

London Lloyds. Voluntary association of merchants, shipowners, underwriters, and brokers, which writes no policies, but, when broker for one wishing insurance posts particulars of risk, underwriting members wishing to so subscribe name and share of total that each wishes to take, and policy is issued when total is reached containing names of underwriters bound thereby and name of attorney in fact who handles insurance affairs of the group. See **Lloyd's of London.**

Long. In various compound legal terms (see *infra*) this word carries a meaning not essentially different from its signification in the vernacular.

Long account. An account involving numerous separate items or charges, on one side or both, or the statement of various complex transactions, such as a court of equity will refer to a master, referee or commissioner.

For "Examination of a long account," see **Examination.**

Long and short haul clause. Without special permission of the I.C.C., a carrier may not charge more for a shorter haul than a longer haul over the same route. 49 U.S.C.A. § 4(1).

Longa patientia trahitur ad consensum /lóŋgə pæshiyénsh(iy)ə træhədər æd kənsénsəm/. Long sufferance is construed as consent.

Longa possessio est pacis jus /lóŋgə pəzésh(iy)ow èst péysəs jás/. Long possession is the law of peace.

Longa possessio jus parit /lóŋgə pəzésh(iy)ow jós pærət/. Long possession begets right.

Longa possessio parit jus possidendi, et tollit actionem vero domino /lóŋgə pəzésh(iy)ow pærət jós pəsìdiyénday, èt tóləd ækshiyównəm vírow dómənow/. Long possession produces the right of possession, and takes away from the true owner his action.

Long arm statutes. Various state legislative acts which provide for personal jurisdiction, via substituted service of process, over persons or corporations which are nonresidents of the state and which voluntarily go into the state, directly or by agent, or communicate with persons in the state, for limited purposes, in actions which concern claims relating to the performance or execution of those purposes, *e.g.* transacting business in the state, contracting to supply services or goods in the state, or selling goods outside the state when the seller knows that the goods will be used or consumed in the state. In New York, as to cause of action arising from any of following acts, court may exercise personal jurisdiction over any nondomiciliary, or his executor or administrator, who in person or through agent: (1) Transacts any business within state; (2) commits tortious act other than defamation within state; (3) commits tortious act, other than defamation, outside state causing injury to person or property within state, if such nondomiciliary regularly does or solicits business, or engages in any other persistent course of conduct, or derives substantial revenue from goods used or consumed or services rendered within state; or (4) owns, uses, or possesses real property within state. N.Y.Consol. Laws, CPLR § 302. See also Mass.G.L.A. c. 223A. See also **Minimal contacts.**

Longevity pay. Extra compensation for longevity in actual service in the army or navy. Thornley v. U. S., 18 Ct.Cl. 111, 113 U.S. 310, 5 S.Ct. 491, 28 L.Ed. 999; Barton v. U. S., 129 U.S. 249, 9 S.Ct. 285, 32 L.Ed. 663; U. S. v. Alger, 151 U.S. 362, 14 S.Ct. 346, 38 L.Ed. 192; U. S. v. Stahl, 151 U.S. 366, 14 S.Ct. 347, 38 L.Ed. 194.

Long parliament. The name usually given to the parliament which met in November, 1640, under Charles I., and was dissolved by Cromwell on the 10th of April, 1653. The name "Long Parliament" is, however, also given to the parliament which met in 1661, after the restoration of the monarchy, and was dissolved on the 30th of December, 1678. This latter parliament is sometimes called, by way of distinction, the "long parliament of Charles II."

Long position. The status of one who owns securities which he holds in expectation of a rise in the market or for income as contrasted with one who goes in and out of the market on a short point spread.

In the language of the stock exchange, a broker or speculator is said to be "long" on stock, or as to a particular security, when he has in his possession or control an abundant supply of it, or a supply exceeding the amount which he has contracted to deliver, or, more particularly, when he has bought a supply of such stock or other security for future delivery, speculating on a considerable future advance in the market price. A trader is said to be "long" on the market when he takes the full price risk; *i.e.* gains if the market price goes up, and loses if it goes down. Valley Waste Mills v. Page, C.C.A.Ga., 115 F.2d 466, 467.

Long robe. A metaphorical expression designating the practice of profession of the law; as, in the phrase "gentlemen of the long robe."

Longshoreman. A maritime laborer, such as a stevedore or loader, who works about wharves of a port. Duke v. Helena-Glendale Ferry Co., 203 Ark. 865, 159 S.W.2d 74, 77. Person who loads and unloads ships.

Longshoremen's and Harbor Workers' Compensation Act. The Longshoremen's and Harbor Workers' Compensation Act (33 U.S.C.A. § 901 *et seq.*) is designed to provide the benefit of workmen's compensation to employees, other than seamen, of private employers any of whose employees work in maritime employment upon the navigable waters of the United States (including any adjoining pier, wharf, dry dock, terminal, building way, marine railway, or other adjoining area customarily used by an employer in loading, unloading, repairing, or building a vessel). The principal employments subject to the Longshoremen's Act are stevedoring and ship service operations. The Act is administered by the Office of Workmen's Compensation Programs.

For federal compensation act covering seamen, see **Jones Act.**

Long term capital gain. See **Capital** (*Capital gains*).

Long term capital loss. See **Capital** (*Capital loss*).

Long term financing. A mortgage or deed of trust for a term of ten years or more, as distinguished from construction, interim, or other short term loans.

Long ton. A measure of weight equivalent to 20 hundred-weight of 112 pounds each, or 2,240 pounds, as distinguished from the "short" ton of 2,000 pounds.

Longum tempus et longus usus qui excedit memoria hominum sufficit pro jure /lóŋgəm témpəs èt lóŋgəs yúwsəs kwày əksíydət məmóriyə hómənəm sə́fəsət pròw júriy/. Long time and long use, exceeding the memory of men, suffices for right.

Look and listen. The requirement that a man shall "look and listen" before crossing street railroad track means only that he shall observe and estimate with reasonable accuracy his distance from the car and the speed of its oncoming, and then make calculation and comparison of the time it will take the car to come and the time it will take to cross the track. Kansas City Public Service Co. v. Knight, C.C.A.Kan., 116 F.2d 233, 234.

Lookout. The exercise of ordinary diligence requires that the driver of a motor vehicle be on the lookout for other travelers so that he may avoid placing himself or them in peril. As variously expressed, the rule requires that a motorist maintain a reasonable and proper lookout, which implies being watchful of the movements of the driver's own vehicle as well as of the movements of other traffic; a careful lookout; an efficient lookout; a vigilant watch ahead. A lookout must be made from the most effective place reasonably possible. The failure of a motorist to exercise ordinary care with respect to lookout, proximately resulting in injury or damage, may constitute negligence. Pickett v. Travelers Indem. Co., C.A. Wis., 283 F.2d 835. That watchfulness which prudent and reasonable person must maintain for his own safety and safety of others taking into consideration circumstances with which he is immediately concerned or confronted. Cobb v. Atkins, 239 Ark. 151, 388 S.W.2d 8, 11.

Generally, a "lookout" is a person, other than pilot, who has duty of observing sounds, lights, echoes and obstructions to navigation and he is generally stationed on the bow of the vessel. Clary Towing Co., Inc. v. Port Arthur Towing Co., D.C.Tex., 367 F.Supp. 6, 12.

See also **Proper lookout.**

Loquela /ləkwíylə/. Lat. A colloquy; talk. In old English law, this term denoted the oral altercations of the parties to a suit, which led to the issue, now called the "pleadings." It also designated an "imparlance" (*q.v.*), both names evidently referring to the talking together of the parties. *Loquela sine die,* a postponement to an indefinite time.

Loquendum ut vulgus; sentiendum ut docti /ləkwéndəm ət válgəs, sènshiyéndəm ət dóktay/. We must speak as the common people; we must think as the learned. This maxim expresses the rule that, when words are used in a technical sense, they must be understood technically; otherwise, when they may be supposed to be used in their ordinary acceptation.

Lord. A feudal superior or proprietor; one of whom a fee or estate is held.

A title of honor or nobility belonging properly to the degree of baron, but applied also to the whole peerage, as in the expression "the House of Lords." 1 Bl.Comm. 396–400.

A title of office, as lord mayor, lord commissioner, etc.

Law lords. See **Law.**

Lord and vassal. In the feudal system, the grantor, who retained the dominion or ultimate property, was called the "lord," and the grantee, who had only the use or possession, was called the "vassal" or "feudatory."

Lord chief baron. The chief judge of the English court of exchequer, prior to the judicature acts.

Lord chief justice. See **Justice.**

Lord high chancellor. See **Chancellor.**

Lord high steward. In England, when a person was impeached, or when a peer was tried on indictment for treason or felony before the house of lords, one of the lords was appointed lord high steward, and acted as speaker *pro tempore.* The privilege of peerage in criminal proceedings was abolished in 1948.

Lord high treasurer. An officer formerly existing in England, who had the charge of the royal revenues and customs duties, and of leasing the crown lands. His functions are now vested in the lords commissioners of the treasury.

Lord in gross. In feudal law, he who is lord, not by reason of any manor, but as the king in respect of his crown, etc. "Very lord" is he who is immediate lord to his tenant; and "very tenant," he who holds immediately of that lord. So that, where there is lord paramount, lord mesne, and tenant, the lord paramount is not very lord to the tenant.

Lord keeper. Originally another name for the lord chancellor. After Henry II's reign they were sometimes divided, but now there cannot be a lord chancellor and lord keeper at the same time, for by St. 5 Eliz. c. 18, they are declared to be the same office.

Lord lieutenant. In English law, the viceroy of the crown in Ireland. The principal military officer of a county, originally appointed for the purpose of mustering the inhabitants for the defense of the country.

Lord mayor. The chief officer of the corporation of the city of London was formerly so called. The origin of the appellation of "lord," which the mayor of London enjoyed was attributed to the fourth charter of Edward III, which conferred on that officer the honor of having maces, the same as royalty, carried before him by the sergeants.

Lord mayor's court. In English law, this was a court of record, of law and equity, and was the chief court of justice within the corporation of London. Such was abolished by the Courts Act of 1971.

Lord of a manor. The grantee or owner of a manor.

Lord paramount. A term applied to the King of England as the chief feudal proprietor, the theory of the feudal system being that all lands in the realm were held mediately or immediately from him.

Lord's day. A name sometimes given to Sunday.

Lords justices of appeal. In English law, the title of the ordinary judges of the court of appeal, by Jud.Act 1877, § 4. Prior to the judicature acts, there were two "lords justices of appeal in chancery," to whom an appeal lay from a vice-chancellor, by 14 & 15 Vict., c. 83.

Black's Law Dictionary 5th Ed.—19

Lords of appeal. Those members of the house of lords of whom at least three must be present for the hearing and determination of appeals. They are the lord chancellor, the lords of appeal in ordinary, and such peers of parliament as hold, or have held, high judicial offices, such as ex-chancellors and judges of the superior courts in Great Britain and Ireland.

Lords of appeal in ordinary. These are appointed to aid the house of lords in the hearing of appeals. They rank as barons for life, but sit and vote in the house of lords during the tenure of their office only.

Lords of parliament. Those who have seats in the house of lords.

Lords ordainers. Lords appointed in 1312, in the reign of Edward II, for the control of the sovereign and the court party, and for the general reform and better government of the country.

Lords spiritual. The archbishops and bishops who have seats in the house of lords.

Lords temporal. Those lay peers who have seats in the house of lords.

Lord Campbell Act. An act which fixes the maximum amount recoverable for wrongful death. Most states have such statutes. See **Wrongful death statutes.**

In England, also refers to the Libel Act of 1843 which permits the defendant in a libel action to assert the defense of truth and that the publication was made for the benefit of the public.

Lord Mansfield's Rule. Such Rule renders inadmissible testimony by either spouse on the question of whether the husband had access to the wife at time of conception. This Rule has been abandoned by several states as having outlived its original policy foundations. Serafin v. Serafin, 401 Mich. 629, 258 N.W.2d 461.

Lordship. In English law, dominion, manor, seigniory, domain; also a title of honor used to a nobleman not being a duke. It is also the customary titulary appellation of the judges, and some other persons in authority and office.

Lose. To bring to destruction; to ruin; to destroy; to suffer the loss of; to be deprived of; to part with, especially in an accidental or unforeseen manner; as to lose an eye. Logan v. Johnson, 218 N.C. 200, 10 S.E.2d 653, 655. See also **Mislay.**

Loss. Loss is a generic and relative term. It signifies the act of losing or the thing lost; it is not a word of limited, hard and fast meaning and has been held synonymous with, or equivalent to, "damage", "damages", "deprivation", "detriment", "injury", and "privation". Mason v. City of Albertville, 276 Ala. 68, 158 So.2d 924, 927.

It may mean act of losing, or the thing lost, Fidelity Union Casualty Co. v. Wilkinson, Tex.Civ.App., 94 S.W.2d 763, 766; United States v. City Nat. Bank of Duluth, D.C.Minn., 31 F.Supp. 530, 534, 535; actual losses, Cheney v. National Surety Corporation, 256 App.Div. 1041, 10 N.Y.S.2d 706; N. L. R. B. v. Cowell Portland Cement Co., C.C.A.9, 148 F.2d 237, 246; bad and uncollectible accounts, Duke v. Cregan, 91 Colo.

120, 12 P.2d 354, 355; damage, Wilbur v. U. S. ex rel. C. L. Wold Co., 58 App.D.C. 347, 30 F.2d 871, 872; a decrease in value of resources or increase in liabilities; depletion or depreciation or destruction of value; deprivation; destruction, Wells v. Thomas W. Garland, Inc., Mo.App., 39 S.W.2d 409, 411; detriment, Fidelity Union Casualty Co. v. Wilkinson, Tex. Civ.App., 94 S.W.2d 763, 766; United States v. City Nat. Bank of Duluth, D.C.Minn., 31 F.Supp. 530, 534, 535; failure to keep that which one has or thinks he has; injury, United Service Automobile Ass'n v. Miles, 139 Tex. 138, 161 S.W.2d 1048; United States v. City Nat. Bank of Duluth, D.C.Minn., 31 F.Supp. 530, 534, 535; privation, United States v. City Nat. Bank of Duluth, D.C.Minn., 31 F.Supp. 530, 534, 535; ruin, Logan v. Johnson, 218 N.C. 200, 10 S.E.2d 653, 655; shrinkage in value of estate or property; state or fact of being lost or destroyed, Logan v. Johnson, 218 N.C. 200, 10 S.E.2d 653, 655; that which is gone and cannot be recovered or that which is withheld or that of which a party is dispossessed, Walker v. Thomas, 64 App.D.C. 148, 75 F.2d 667, 669; Surety Co., 60 S.D. 100, 243 N.W. 664, 666; unintentional parting with something of value, Providence Journal Co. v. Broderick, C.C.A.R.I., 104 F.2d 614, 616.

See also Actual loss; Capital *(Capital loss)*; Casualty loss; Constructive loss; Constructive total loss; Damages; Direct loss; Disaster loss; General average loss; Hobby loss; Net operating loss; Pain and suffering; Partial loss; Pecuniary injury; Pecuniary loss; Reasonable certainty, rule of; Total loss. As to loss of consortium, see **Consortium**; salvage loss, see **Salvage**; proof of loss, see **Proof**.

Disability benefits. State workers' compensation laws, social security, and disability insurance contracts provide disability benefits for partial or permanent loss of use of limbs, eyes, etc.

Insurance. Ascertained liability of insurer, Michel v. American Fire & Casualty Co., C.C.A.Fla., 82 F.2d 583, 586; decrease in value of resources or increase in liabilities; depletion or depreciation or destruction or shrinkage of value; injury, damage, etc., to property or persons injured; Miles v. United Services Automobile Ass'n, Tex.Civ.App., 149 S.W.2d 233, 235, 236; injury or damage sustained by insured in consequence of happening of one or more of the accidents or misfortunes against which insurer has undertaken to indemnify the insured; pecuniary injury resulting from the occurrence of the contingency insured against, Ocean Accident & Guarantee Corporation v. Southwestern Bell Telephone Co., C.C.A.Mo., 100 F.2d 441, 446. Word "loss" implies that property is no longer in existence. Littrell v. Allemannia Fire Ins. Co. of Pittsburgh, Pa., 222 App.Div. 302, 226 N.Y.S. 243, 244.

"Loss of eye" means loss of use for any practical purpose, Order of United Commercial Travelers of America v. Knorr, C.C.A.Kan., 112 F.2d 679, 682. Loss of member or loss of an entire member means destruction of usefulness of member or entire member for purposes to which in its normal condition it is susceptible of application, in absence of more specific definition. Loss of use of hand means substantial and material impairment of use in practical performance of its function. Loss of use of member is equivalent to loss of member, Continental Casualty Co. v.

Linn, 226 Ky. 328, 10 S.W.2d 1079, 1082, Noel v. Continental Casualty Co., 138 Kan. 136, 23 P.2d 610. Loss of vision to extent that one cannot perceive and distinguish objects is "loss of sight".

To constitute "loss or damage by fire" existence of actual fire, which becomes uncontrollable or breaks out from where it was intended to be and becomes a hostile element, is sufficient. Princess Garment Co. v. Fireman's Fund Ins. Co. of San Francisco, Cal., C.C.A.Ohio, 115 F.2d 380, 382.

The word "loss" in insurance policy in its common usage means a state of fact of being lost or destroyed, ruin or destruction. Sitzman v. National Life & Acc. Ins. Co., 133 Ind.App. 578, 182 N.E.2d 448, 450.

Loss leader. Item sold by a merchant at very low price and sometimes below cost in order to attract people to store with the hope that they will buy additional items on which a profit will be made.

Loss of consortium. See **Consortium**.

Loss of earning capacity. Damage to one's ability to earn wages in the future and recoverable as element of damage in tort actions. It is not the same as loss of earnings though loss of actual earnings is competent evidence of loss of earning capacity. A person unemployed at the time of the accident has an earning capacity though he has no earnings.

Loss payable clause. A clause in a fire insurance policy, listing the priority of claims in the event of destruction of the property insured. Generally, a mortgagee, or beneficiary under a deed of trust, is the party appearing in the clause, being paid to the amount owing under the mortgage or deed of trust before the owner is paid. A provision in property insurance contracts that authorizes payments to persons other than the insured to the extent that they have an insurable interest in the property.

Loss payee. Person named in insurance policy to be paid in event of loss or damage to property insured.

Loss ratio. In insurance, the proportion between premiums collected and loss payments made.

Loss reserve. That portion of insurance company's assets set aside for payment of losses which will probably arise or which have arisen but have not been paid.

Lost. An article is "lost" when the owner has lost the possession or custody of it, involuntarily and by any means, but more particularly by accident or his own negligence or forgetfulness, and when he is ignorant of its whereabouts or cannot recover it by an ordinarily diligent search. See also **Lost property**.

As applied to ships and vessels, the term means "lost at sea," and a vessel lost is one that has totally gone from the owners against their will, so that they know nothing of it, whether it still exists or not, or one which they know is no longer within their use and control, either in consequence of capture by enemies or pirates, or an unknown foundering, or sinking by a known storm, or collision, or destruction by shipwreck.

Lost corner. See **Corner**.

Lost or not lost. A phrase sometimes inserted in policies of marine insurance. It signifies that the contract is meant to relate back to the beginning of a voyage now in progress, or to some other antecedent time, and to be valid and effectual even if, at the moment of executing the policy, the vessel should have already perished by some of the perils insured against, provided that neither party has knowledge of that fact or any advantage over the other in the way of superior means of information. Hooper v. Robinson, 98 U.S. 528, 25 L.Ed. 219; Insurance Co. v. Folsom, 85 U.S. (18 Wall.) 237, 21 L.Ed. 827.

Lost papers. Papers which have been so mislaid that they cannot be found after diligent search.

Lost property. Property which the owner has involuntarily parted with and does not know where to find or recover it, not including property which he has intentionally concealed or deposited in a secret place for safe-keeping. Distinguishable from mislaid property which has been deliberately placed somewhere and forgotten. The majority of the states have adopted the Uniform Disposition of Unclaimed Property Act.

Lost will. A will which was once executed but cannot be found at death of testator. The contents can be proved by parol in many jurisdictions, though in some states there is a rebuttable presumption that a will once in existence has been revoked if it cannot be found at testator's death.

Lot. A number of associated persons or things taken collectively. Hitchcock v. United States, D.C.Mich., 36 F.Supp. 507, 510.

Real estate. A share; one of several parcels into which property is divided. Any portion, piece, division or parcel of land. Fractional part or subdivision of block, according to plat or survey, Mawson-Peterson Lumber Co. v. Sprinkle, 59 Wyo. 334, 140 P.2d 588, 591; portion of platted territory measured and set apart for individual and private use and occupancy, Hunter v. Roman Catholic Bishop of Los Angeles and San Diego Corporation Sole, 128 Cal.App. 90, 16 P.2d 1048, 1049.

A lot is commonly one of several other contiguous parcels of land making up a block. Real property is typically described by reference to lot and block numbers on recorded maps and plats.

Local zoning laws commonly require minimum lot sizes for residential and commercial building.

See also **Nonconforming lot; Parcel.**

Sales. In sales, a parcel or single article which is the subject matter of a separate sale or delivery whether or not it is sufficient to perform the contract. U.C.C. § 2–105(5).

Securities. In securities and commodities market, a specified number of shares or specific quantity of a commodity designated for trading. See **Odd lot; Odd lot doctrine.**

Lot and scot. In English law, certain duties which formerly had to be paid by those who claimed to exercise the elective franchise within certain cities and boroughs, before they were entitled to vote.

Lot book. Plat book.

Lotherwite, or **leyerwit.** In old English law, a liberty or privilege to take amends for lying with a bondwoman without license.

Lottery /lódəriy/. A chance for a prize for a price. Essential elements of a lottery are consideration, prize and chance and any scheme or device by which a person for a consideration is permitted to receive a prize or nothing as may be determined predominantly by chance. State v. Wassick, W.Va., 191 S.E.2d 283, 288.

An unlawful gambling scheme in which (a) the players pay or agree to pay something of value for chances, represented and differentiated by numbers or by combinations of numbers or by some other media, one or more of which chances are to be designated the winning ones; and (b) the winning chances are to be determined by a drawing or by some other method based upon the element of chance; and (c) the holders of the willing chances are to receive something of value. New Jersey Criminal Code, § 2C:37–1.

Also defined as device whereby anything of value is for a consideration allotted by lot or chance. State ex Inf. McKittrick v. Globe-Democrat Pub. Co., 341 Mo. 862, 110 S.W.2d 705, 713, 714, 717, 718. Game by which a person paying money becomes entitled to money or other thing of value on certain contingencies, determinable by lot cast in a particular way by the manager of the game; game of hazard in which small sums of money are ventured for chance of obtaining a larger value in money or other articles; State v. Jones, 44 N.M. 623, 107 P.2d 324, 326; gaming contract by which for a valuable consideration one may by favor of the lot obtain a prize of value superior to the amount or value of that which he risks, Troy Amusement Co. v. Attenweiler, 64 Ohio App. 105, 28 N.E.2d 207, 212, 17 O.O. 443; hazard in which sums are ventured for a chance of obtaining a greater value, People v. Hines, 284 N.Y. 93, 29 N.E.2d 483, 488. Scheme by which result is reached by some action or means taken, and in which result man's choice or will has no part nor can human reason, foresight, sagacity, or design enable him to know or determine such result until the same has been accomplished, State v. Schwemler, 154 Or. 533, 60 P.2d 938, 940; scheme for distribution of prizes or things of value by lot or chance, Engle v. State, 593 Ariz. 458, 90 P.2d 988, 992, 993; scheme for raising money by selling chances to share in distribution of prizes. Scheme where money is paid for chance of receiving money or a prize in return. People v. Psallis, Mag.Ct.N.Y., 12 N.Y.S.2d 796, 797, 798, 799. Scheme whereby one on paying money or other valuable thing to another becomes entitled to receive from him such a return in value or nothing as some formula of chance may determine. Scheme which, played or operated once, destroys the value of ticket provided as the prizes are distributed. Scheme which tends to induce one to pay or agree to pay a valuable consideration for a chance to draw a prize.

The sending of lottery tickets through the mails and by other instrumentalities of interstate commerce is prohibited by federal law. 18 U.S.C.A. §§ 1301 et seq., 1953.

See also **Dutch lottery; Gambling; Game of chance.**

Louage /luwázh/. Fr. This is the contract of hiring and letting in French law, and may be either of things or of labor. The varieties of each are the following: 1. Letting of things,—*bail à loyer* being the letting of houses; *bail à ferme* being the letting of lands. 2. Letting of labor, *em loger* being the letting of personal services; *bail à cheptel* being the letting of animals.

L'ou le ley done chose, la ceo done remedie a vener a ceo /lúw lə léy dówn shówz, là sów dówn rèmədíy à vənéy à sów/. Where the law gives a right, it gives a remedy to recover.

Love and affection. Such is a sufficient consideration when a gift is contemplated, but is not considered "valuable" consideration where such is required. See **Nudum pactum.**

Love-day. In old English law, the day on which any dispute was amicably settled between neighbors; or a day on which one neighbor helps another without hire.

Lowbote. In old English law, a recompense for the death of a man killed in a tumult.

Lower of cost or **market.** A basis for inventory valuation where the inventory value is set at the lower of acquisition cost or current replacement cost (market).

Lowers. Fr. In French maritime law, wages.

Lowest responsible bidder. Bidder who not only has lowest price, but also is financially able and competent to complete work as evidenced by prior performance.

Low justice. In old European law, jurisdiction of petty offenses, as distinguished from *"high justice" (q.v.).*

Low-water mark. Line on the shore marking the lowest ebb of the tide. See also **Water mark.**

Loyal. Legal; authorized by or conforming to law. Also faithful in one's political relations; giving faithful support and allegiance to one's prince or sovereign or to the existing government. Faithful support to cause, ideal, office, or person.

Loyalty. Adherence to law. Faithfulness to one's office or sovereign or to the existing government.

Loyalty oath. An oath whereby an individual declares his allegiance to his government and its institutions and disclaims any support of foreign ideologies or associations. Such oaths as are required of various classifications of public officials and persons working in "sensitive" government positions. See *e.g.* Art. II, § 1, cl. 7; Art. VI, cl. 3, U.S.Const. However, oaths too vague to specify clearly what constitutes seditious acts and utterances have been declared unconstitutional. Communist Party of Indiana v. Whitcomb, 414 U.S. 441, 94 S.Ct. 656, 38 L.Ed.2d 635. See also **Oath.**

L.R. An abbreviation for "Law Reports."

L.S. An abbreviation for *"Locus sigilli,"* the place of the seal; *i.e.,* the place where a seal is to be affixed, or a scroll which stands instead of a seal. See **Locus sigilli.**

LSAT. Law School Admission Test. This test is given to law school applicants. The LSAT is a half-day multiple choice test designed to measure certain basic reasoning abilities important in the study of law, general academic ability and command of written English. It provides two scores: an LSAT score and a writing ability (WA) score. The LSAT portion measures the ability to understand and reason with a variety of verbal, quantitative, and symbolic materials. The writing ability portion measures the use of standard English to express ideas clearly and precisely. The test is intended to supplement the undergraduate record and other information about the student in the assessment of potential for law school work. It covers a broad range of disciplines, measures skills acquired over a long period of time, and gives no advantage to students with particular specializations.

Ltd. Limited.

Lubricum linguæ non facile trahendum est in pœnam /lúwbrəkəm líŋgwiy nòn fǽsəliy trəhéndəm èst in píynəm/. A slip of the tongue ought not lightly to be subjected to punishment.

Lucid. Easily understood; clear; rational; sane.

Lucid interval. A temporary cure; temporary restoration to sanity. Intervals occurring in the mental life of an insane person during which he is completely restored to the use of his reason, or so far restored that he has sufficient intelligence, judgment, and will to enter into contractual relations, or perform other legal acts, without disqualification by reason of his disease. Oklahoma Natural Gas Corporation v. Lay, 175 Okl. 75, 51 P.2d 580, 583. With respect to marriage, refers to period of time during which person had sufficient mental capacity to know and understand nature and consequence of marriage relation, and the reciprocal and mutual duties and obligations thereof. Carter v. Bacle, Tex.Civ.App., 94 S.W.2d 817, 819. In connection with wills, a period of time within which an insane person enjoys the restoration of his faculties sufficiently to enable him to judge his act. In re Cook's Estate, 231 Or. 133, 372 P.2d 520, 522.

Lucra nuptialia /l(y)úwkrə nəpshiyéyl(i)yə/. Lat. In Roman law, a term including everything which a husband or wife, as such, acquires from the estate of the other, either before the marriage, or on agreeing to it, or during its continuance, or after its dissolution, and whether the acquisition is by pure gift, or by virtue of the marriage contract, or against the will of the other party by law or statute.

Lucrativa causa /l(y)ùwkrətáyvə kózə/. Lat. In Roman law, a consideration which is voluntary; that is to say, a gratuitous gift, or such like. It was opposed to *onerosa causa,* which denoted a valuable consideration. It was a principle of the Roman law that two lucrative causes could not concur in the same person as regarded the same thing; that is to say, that, when the same thing was bequeathed to a person by two different testators, he could not have the thing (or its value) twice over.

Lucrativa usucapio /l(y)ùwkrətáyvə yùwzhuwkǽpiyow/. Lat. This species of *usucapio* was permitted in Roman law only in the case of persons taking possession of property upon the decease of its late owner, and in exclusion or deforcement of the heir, whence it was called *"usucapio pro hœrede."* The adjective *"lucrativa"* denoted that property was acquired by this *usucapio* without any consideration or payment for it by way of purchase; and, as the possessor who so acquired the property was a *malâ fide* possessor, his acquisition, or *usucapio,* was called also *"improba"* (*i.e.,* dishonest); but this dishonesty was tolerated (until abolished by Hadrian) as an incentive to force the *hæres* to take possession, in order that the debts might be paid and the sacrifices performed; and, as a further incentive to the *hæres,* this *usucapio* was complete in one year.

Lucrative. Yielding gain or profit; profitable; bearing or yielding a revenue or salary.

Lucrative bailment. See **Bailment.**

Lucrative office. One which yields a revenue (in the form of fees or otherwise) or a fixed salary to the incumbent. According to some authorities, one which yields a compensation supposed to be adequate to the services rendered and in excess of the expenses incidental to the office. One the pay of which is affixed to performance of duties of office.

Lucre /l(y)úwkər/. Gain in money or goods; profit; usually in an ill sense, or with the sense of something base or unworthy.

Lucri causa /l(y)úwkray kózə/. Lat. In criminal law, a term descriptive of the intent with which property is taken in cases of larceny, the phrase meaning "for the sake of lucre" or gain.

Lucrum /l(y)úwkrəm/. A small slip or parcel of land.

Lucrum cessans /l(y)úwkrəm sésæn(d)z/. Lat. A ceasing gain, as distinguished from *damnum datum,* an actual loss. That element of contract damages which accounts for lost profits.

Lucrum facere ex pupilli tutela tutor non debet /l(y)úwkrəm féysəriy èks p(y)əpílay t(y)ətíylə tyúdər nòn débət/. A guardian ought not to make money out of the guardianship of his ward.

Luctuosa hæreditas /ləkchuwówsə həríydətæs/. A mournful inheritance. See **Hæreditas luctuosa.**

Luctus /ləktəs/. In Roman law, mourning. See **Annus luctus.**

Luminare /l(y)ùwmənériy/. A lamp or candle set burning on the altar of any church or chapel, for the maintenance whereof lands and rent-charges were frequently given to parish churches, etc.

Lumping sale. As applied to judicial sales, this term means a sale in mass, as where several distinct parcels of real estate, or several articles of personal property, are sold together for a "lump" or single gross sum. See **Bulk sale.**

Lump-sum alimony. Settlement or payment of money or property in divorce action made in single payment instead of installments. Sometimes called "alimony in gross." See **Alimony.**

Lump-sum distribution. Payment of the entire amount due at one time rather than in installments. Such distributions often occur from qualified pension or profit-sharing plans upon the retirement or death of a covered employee.

Lump-sum payment. A single amount in contrast to installments; *e.g.* single premium payment for life insurance; a single lump sum divorce settlement; or single worker's compensation payment in lieu of future monthly installment payments. See also **Alimony.**

Lunacy. Lunacy is that condition or habit in which the mind is directed by the will, but is wholly or partially misguided or erroneously governed by it; or it is the impairment of any one or more of the faculties of the mind, accompanied with or inducing a defect in the comparing faculty. This general legal term for a major mental disorder or illness is seldom used in medical terminology; the reference now being to the specific mental illness involved. See also **Insanity.**

Lunar. Belonging to or measured by the revolutions of the moon.

Lunar month. See **Month.**

Lunatic. See **Lunacy.**

Lushborow /lə́shbərow/lə́shbə̀rg/. In old English law, a base sort of money, coined beyond sea in the likeness of English coin, and introduced into England in the reign of Edward III. Prohibited by St. 25 Edw. III, c. 4.

Luxury tax. Generic term for excise imposed on purchase of items which are not necessaries; *e.g.* tax on liquor or cigarettes.

Lying by. A person who, by his presence and silence at a transaction which affects his interests, may be fairly supposed to acquiesce in it, if he afterwards propose to disturb the arrangement, is said to be prevented from doing so by reason that he has been lying by. See also **Estoppel.**

Lying in franchise. A term descriptive of waifs, wrecks, estrays, and the like, which may be seized without suit or action.

Lying in grant. A phrase applied to incorporeal rights, incapable of manual tradition, and which must pass by mere delivery of a deed.

Lying in wait. Lying in ambush; lying hidden or concealed for the purpose of making a sudden and unexpected attack upon a person when he shall arrive at the scene. In some jurisdictions, where there are several degrees of murder, lying in wait is made evidence of that deliberation and premeditated intent which is necessary to characterize murder in the first degree.

Lynch law. A term descriptive of the action of unofficial persons, organized bands, or mobs, who seize persons charged with or suspected of crimes, or take them out of the custody of the law, and inflict summary punishment upon them, without legal trial, and without the warrant or authority of law.

Lyndhurst's (Lord) Act /lòrd línd(h)ərsts ǽkt/. This English statute (5 & 6 Wm. IV, c. 54) renders marriages within the prohibited degrees absolutely null and void. Theretofore such marriages were voidable merely.

Lytæ /láydiy/. In old Roman law, a name given to students of the civil law in the fourth year of their course, from their being supposed capable of *solving* any difficulty in law.

M

M. This letter, used as a Roman numeral, stands for one thousand.

It was also, in old English law, a brand or stigma impressed upon the brawn of the thumb of a person convicted of manslaughter and admitted to the benefit of clergy.

This letter was sometimes put on the face of treasury notes of the United States, and signified that the treasury note bears interest at the rate of one mill per centum, and not one per centum interest. U. S. v. Hardyman, 38 U.S. (13 Pet.) 176, 10 L.Ed. 113.

Mace. A large staff, made of the precious metals, and highly ornamented. It is used as an emblem of authority, and carried before certain public functionaries by a mace-bearer. In many legislative bodies, the mace is employed as a visible symbol of the dignity and collective authority of the house. In the house of lords and house of commons of the British parliament, it is laid upon the table when the house is in session. In the United States House of Representatives, it is borne upright by the sergeant-at-arms on extraordinary occasions, as when it is necessary to quell a disturbance or bring refractory members to order.

Chemical liquid which, when sprayed in face of person, causes dizziness and immobilization.

Macedonian decree /mæsədówniyən dəkríy/. In Roman law, this was the *Senatus-consultum Macedonianum,* a decree of the Roman senate, first given under Claudius, and renewed under Vespasian by which it was declared that no action should be maintained to recover a loan of money made to a child who was under the *patria potestas.* It was intended to strike at the practice of usurers in making loans, on unconscionable terms, to family heirs who would mortgage their future expectations from the paternal estate. The law is said to have derived its name from that of a notorious usurer.

Mace-greff /méysgrèf/. In old English law, one who buys stolen goods, particularly food, knowing it to have been stolen.

Mace-proof. Secure against arrest.

Machination /mækənéyshən/mæsh°/. The act of planning or contriving a scheme for executing some purpose, particularly an evil purpose; an artful design formed with deliberation.

Mactator /mæktéydər/. L. Lat. In old European law, a murderer.

Maculare /mækyəlériy/. In old European law, to wound.

Made. Filed. St. Louis Law Printing Co. v. Aufderheide, 226 Mo.App. 680, 45 S.W.2d 543, 545. Produced or manufactured artificially. United States v. Anderson, D.C.Cal., 45 F.Supp. 943, 946. To have required or compelled. Dickinson v. Mingea, 191 Ark. 946, 88 S.W.2d 807, 809. Executed. Lone Star Gas Co. v. Coastal States Gas Producing Co., 388 S.W.2d 251, 255.

Made known. Where a process or other legal paper has been actually served upon a defendant, the proper return is that its contents have been "made known" to him. A crime is "made known" to an officer when facts which come to knowledge of the officer are such as to indicate to him that it is his official duty to act or to see that an investigation of the alleged crime is instituted within his jurisdiction. See also **Notice**.

Madman. This is not a technical term either of medicine or of the law, and because of this it is incapable of being applied with scientific precision; as such, is no longer in use. See **Insanity**.

Mad Parliament. Henry III, in 1258, at the desire of the Great Council in Parliament, consented to the appointment of a committee of twenty-four, of whom twelve were appointed by the Barons and twelve by the King, in a parliament which was stigmatized as the "Mad Parliament." Unlimited power was given to it to carry out all necessary reforms. It drew up the Provisions of Oxford.

Mæc-burgh /mǽkbὸrg/. In Saxon law, kindred; family.

Mæg /mǽg/. A kinsman.

Mægbote /mǽgbòwt/. In Saxon law, a recompense or satisfaction for the slaying or murder of a kinsman.

Magic. In English statutes, witch-craft and sorcery.

Magis de bono quam de malo lex intendit /méyjəs dìy bównow kwæm díy mǽlow lèks əntέndət/. The law favors a good rather than a bad construction. Where the words used in an agreement are susceptible of two meanings, the one agreeable to, the other against, the law, the former is adopted. Thus, a bond conditioned "to assign all offices" will be construed to apply to such offices only as are assignable.

Magis dignum trahit ad se minus dignum /méyjəs dígnəm tréy(h)ət ǽd síy máynəs dígnəm/. The more worthy draws to itself the less worthy.

857

Magister. Lat. *Civil law.* A title of several offices under the Roman Empire.

English law. A master or ruler; a person who has attained to some eminent degree in science.

Magister ad facultates /məjístər æd fækəltéydiyz/. In English ecclesiastical law, the title of an officer who grants dispensations; as to marry, to eat meat on days prohibited and the like.

Magister bonorum vendendorum /məjístər bənórəm vèndəndórəm/. In Roman law, a person appointed by judicial authority to inventory, collect, and sell the property of an absent or absconding debtor for the benefit of his creditors. He was generally one of the creditors, and his functions corresponded generally to those of a receiver or an assignee for the benefit of creditors under modern bankruptcy practice.

Magister cancellariæ /məjístər kæn(t)səlériyiy/. In old English law, master of the chancery; master in chancery. These officers were said to be called "*magistri*," because they were priests.

Magisterial /mæjəstíriyəl/. Relating or pertaining to the character, office, powers, or duties of a magistrate or of the magistracy.

Magisterial precinct. In some American states, a local subdivision of a county, defining the territorial jurisdiction of justices of the peace and constables; also called magisterial district.

Magister libellorum /məjístər làybəlórəm/. Master of requests. A title of office under the Roman Empire.

Magister litis /məjístər láydəs/. Master of the suit; the person who controls the suit or its prosecution, or has the right to do so.

Magister navis /məjístər néyvəs/. In the civil law, the master of a ship or vessel. He to whom the care of the whole vessel is committed.

Magister palatii /məjístər pəléyshiyay/. Master of the palace or of the offices. An officer under the Roman Empire bearing some resemblance to the modern lord chamberlain.

Magister rerum usus /məjístər rírəm yúwsəs/. Use is the master of things. Usage is a principal guide in practice.

Magister rerum usus; magistra rerum experientia /məjístər rírəm yúwsəs, məjístrə rírəm əkspiriyènsh(iy)ə/. Use is the master of things; experience is the mistress of things.

Magister societatis /məjístər səsàyətéydəs/. In the civil law, the master or manager of a partnership; a managing partner or general agent; a manager specially chosen by a firm to administer the affairs of the partnership.

Magistracy /mæjəstrəsiy/. This term may have a more or less extensive signification according to the use and connection in which it occurs. In its widest sense it includes the whole body of public functionaries, whether their offices be legislative, judicial, executive, or administrative. In a more restricted (and more usual) meaning, it denotes the class of officers who are charged with the application and execution of the laws. In a still more confined use, it designates the body of judicial officers of the lowest rank, and more especially those who have jurisdiction for the trial and punishment of petty misdemeanors or the preliminary steps of a criminal prosecution, such as police judges and justices of the peace. The term also denotes the office of a magistrate. Golden v. Golden, 41 N.M. 356, 68 P.2d 928, 930. See also **Magistrate.**

Magistralia brevia /mæjəstréyl(i)yə bríyv(i)yə/. In old English practice, magisterial writs; writs adapted to special cases, and so called from being framed by the masters or principal clerks of the chancery.

Magistrate. The term in its generic sense refers to a person clothed with power as a public civil officer, or a public civil officer invested with executive or judicial power. Ex parte Noel, Ky., 338 S.W.2d 903, 907. Minor officials or officers with limited judicial authority; *e.g.* justices of the peace, judges of police courts, mayor's courts, or magistrate's courts. In a general sense, a "magistrate" is a public officer, possessing such power, legislative, executive, or judicial, as government appointing him may ordain, although in a narrow sense he is regarded as an inferior judicial officer. Shadwick v. City of Tampa, Fla., 250 So.2d 4, 5.

U.S. Magistrates. A judicial officer, appointed by judges of federal district courts, having some but not all of the powers of a judge. In the federal district courts magistrates may conduct many of the preliminary or pre-trial proceedings in both civil and criminal cases. In addition, U.S. Magistrates have jurisdiction to try minor offenses. The procedure in such trials is governed by the "Rules for Minor Offenses Before U.S. Magistrates." 18 U.S.C.A. §§ 3401, 3402; 28 U.S.C.A. § 631 *et seq.* United States Magistrates have generally taken over the duties formerly performed by U.S. Commissioners.

For Chief magistrate; Committing magistrate; Police magistrate; and Stipendiary magistrates, see those titles.

Magistrate's courts. The jurisdiction of these courts of limited jurisdiction differs from state to state. Such may be divisions of courts of general jurisdiction, and, may have concurrent jurisdiction with other courts. Commonly their jurisdiction is restricted to the handling of minor offenses or preliminary hearings.

Magistratus /mæjəstréydəs/. Lat. In the civil law, a magistrate. A judicial officer who had the power of hearing and determining causes, but whose office properly was to inquire into matters of law, as distinguished from fact.

Magna assisa /mægnə əsáyzə/. In old English law, the grand assize.

Magna assisa eligenda /mægnə əsáyzə éləjéndə/. An ancient writ to summon four lawful knights before the justices of assize, there to choose twelve others, with themselves to constitute the *grand assize* or great jury, to try the matter of right. The trial by grand assize was instituted by Henry II, in parliament, as an alternative to the dual in a writ of right. Abolished by 3 & 4 Wm. IV, c. 27.

Magna centum /mǽgnə séntəm/. The great hundred, or six score.

Magna Charta /mǽgnə kárdə/. The great charter. The name of a charter (or constitutional enactment) granted by King John of England to the barons, at Runnymede, on June 15, 1215, and afterwards, with some alterations, confirmed in parliament by Henry III and Edward I. This charter is justly regarded as the foundation of English constitutional liberty. Among its thirty-eight chapters are found provisions for regulating the administration of justice, defining the temporal and ecclesiastical jurisdictions, securing the personal liberty of the subject and his rights of property, and the limits of taxation, and for preserving the liberties and privileges of the church. *Magna Charta* is so called, partly to distinguish it from the *Charta de Foresta,* which was granted about the same time, and partly by reason of its own transcendent importance.

Magna Charta et Charta de Foresta sont appelés les "deux grandes charters" /mǽgnə kárdə èy kárdə dìy fəréstə sówn əpéley lèy dyúw gránd chárdərz/. *Magna Charta* and the Charter of the Forest are called the "two great charters."

Magna componere parvis /mǽgnə kəmpównəriy párvəs/. To compare great things with small things.

Magna culpa /mǽgnə kə́lpə/. Great fault; gross negligence.

Magna negligentia /mǽgnə nèglə jénsh(iy)ə/. In the civil law, great or gross negligence.

Magna negligentia culpa est; magna culpa dolus est /mǽgnə nèglə jénsh(iy)ə kə́lpə èst; mǽgnə kə́lpə dówləs èst/. Gross negligence is fault; gross fault is fraud.

Magnuson-Moss Warranty Act. Federal statute (15 U.S.C.A. § 2301 *et seq.*) requiring that written warranties as to consumer products must fully and conspicuously disclose in simple and readily understood language the terms and conditions of such warranty, including whether the warranty is a full or limited warranty according to standards set forth in the Act.

Magnus rotulus statutorum /mǽgnəs rót(y)ələs stǽtyuwtórəm/. The great statute roll. The first of the English statute rolls, beginning with *Magna Charta,* and ending with Edward III.

Maiden. A young unmarried woman. In an indictment for adultery, not necessarily a virgin.

Maiden assize /méydən əsáyz/. In English law, originally an assize at which no person was condemned to die; later a session of a criminal court at which there were no prisoners to be tried.

Maiden rents. In old English law, a fine paid to lords of some manors, on the marriage of tenants, originally given in consideration of the lord's relinquishing his customary right of lying the first night with the bride of a tenant.

Maihem /méy(h)əm/. See **Mayhem; Maim.**

Maihematus /mèy(h)əméydəs/. Maimed or wounded.

Maihemium /mèyhíym(i)yəm/. In old English law, mayhem (*q.v.*).

Maihemium est homicidium inchoatum /mèyhíym(i)yəm èst hòməsáyd(i)yəm ìnkowéydəm/. Mayhem is incipient homicide.

Maihemium est inter crimina majora minimum, et inter minora maximum /mèyhíym(i)yəm èst íntər krímənə məjórə mínəməm, èd íntər mənórə mǽksəməm/. Mayhem is the least of great crimes, and the greatest of small.

Maihemium est membri mutilatio, et dici poterit, ubi aliquis in aliqua parte sui corporis effectus sit inutilis ad pugnandum /mèyhíym(i)yəm èst mémbray myùwdəléysh(iy)ow, èt dáysay pódərət, yúwbay ǽləkwis in ǽləkwə párdiy syúway kórpərəs əféktəs sìd inyúwdələs æd pəgnǽndəm/. Mayhem is the mutilation of a member, and can be said to take place when a man is injured in any part of his body so as to be useless in fight.

Mail. See **Mailed; Registered mail.**

Mailable. Suitable or admissible for transmission by the mail; belonging to the classes of articles which, by the laws and postal regulations, may be sent by mail.

Mailed. A letter, package, or other mailable matter is "mailed" when it is properly addressed, stamped with the proper postage, and deposited in a proper place for receipt of mail. Texas Cas. Ins. Co. v. McDonald, Tex.Civ.App., 269 S.W.2d 456, 457.

Under rules practice in some jurisdictions, an action is deemed commenced when the complaint and appropriate entry fee is deposited in the mails under either certified or registered mail procedure; *e.g.* Mass.R.Civ.P. 3.

Mail fraud. The use of the mails to defraud is a federal offense requiring the government to prove a knowing use of the mails to execute the fraudulent scheme. U. S. v. Dondich (C.A.Cal.), 506 F.2d 1009. Elements of "mail fraud" are a scheme to defraud and the mailing of a letter for the purpose of executing the scheme. U. S. v. Scoblick, D.C.Pa., 124 F.Supp. 881, 887. See 18 U.S.C.A. §§ 1341, 1342. See **Using mail to defraud.**

Mail order divorce. Divorce obtained by parties who are not physically present nor domiciled in the jurisdiction which purports to grant divorce (*e.g.* Mexican divorce). Such divorces are not recognized because of the complete absence of the usual bases for divorce jurisdiction. Unruh v. Industrial Commission, 81 Ariz. 118, 301 P.2d 1029.

Maim. To cripple or mutilate in any way. To inflict upon a person any injury which deprives him of the use of any limb or member of the body, or renders him lame or defective in bodily vigor. To inflict bodily injury; to seriously wound or disfigure; disable. State v. Thomas, 157 Kan. 526, 142 P.2d 692, 693; Phillips v. State, 140 Tex.Cr.R. 84, 143 S.W.2d 591, 592. See also **Mayhem.**

At common law, to deprive a person of a member or part of the body, the loss of which renders him less capable of fighting, or of defending himself; to commit mayhem (*q.v.*).

Main. Principal, leading, primary, chief. Most important in size, extent, rank, importance, strength or utility.

Mainad /méynəd/. In old English law, a false oath; perjury. Probably from Sax. *"manath"* or *"mainath"* a false or deceitful oath.

Main-a-main. Immediately.

Main channel. The main channel of a river is that bed over which the principal volume of water flows. The deeper or more navigable channel of river.

Maine-port. In old English law, a small tribute, commonly of loaves of bread, which in some places the parishioners paid to the rector in lieu of small tithes.

Mainly. Principally, chiefly, in the main.

Mainour /méynər/. An article stolen, when found in the hands of the thief. A thief caught with the stolen goods in his possession is said to be taken "with the mainour," that is, with the property *in manu*, in his hands. 4 Bl.Comm. 307.

Mainovre, or **mainœuvre** /mənúwvər/. A trespass committed by hand.

Mainpernable /méynpərnəbəl/. Capable of being bailed; bailable; admissible to bail on giving surety by mainpernors.

Mainpernor /méynpə̀rnər/. In old practice, a surety for the appearance of a person under arrest, who is delivered out of custody into the hands of his bail.

Mainprise. In old English law, the delivery of a person into the custody of *mainpernors (q.v.)*. Also the name of a writ (now obsolete) commanding the sheriff to take the security of mainpernors and set the party at liberty. "Mainpernors" differ from "bail" in that a man's bail may imprison or surrender him up before the stipulated day of appearance; mainpernors can do neither, but are barely sureties for his appearance at the day. Bail are only sureties that the party be answerable for the special matter for which they stipulate; mainpernors are bound to produce him to answer all charges whatsoever. 3 Bl.Comm. 128. Other distinctions are made in the old books.

Main purpose doctrine. The Statute of Frauds requires contracts to answer for the debt, default or misdoing of another to be in writing to be enforceable. However, if the main purpose of the promisor's undertaking is his own benefit or protection, such promise need not be in writing. MacDonald v. Stack, 345 Mass. 709, 189 N.E.2d 221. The "main purpose rule" is that whenever the main purpose and object of promisor is not to answer for another but to subserve some purpose of his own, his promise is not within statute of frauds, although it may be in form a promise to pay debt of another and although performance of promise may incidentally have effect of extinguishing liability of another. Cooper Petroleum v. La Gloria Oil & Gas Co., Tex.Civ.App., 423 S.W.2d 645, 655.

Main-rent. Vassalage.

Main sea. See **Sea**.

Mainsworn /méynswòrn/. Forsworn, by making false oath with *hand (main)* on book. Used in the north of England.

Maintain. The term is variously defined as acts of repairs and other acts to prevent a decline, lapse or cessation from existing state or condition; bear the expense of; carry on; commence; continue; furnish means for subsistence or existence of; hold; hold or keep in an existing state or condition; hold or preserve in any particular state or condition; keep from change; keep from falling, declining, or ceasing; keep in existence or continuance; keep in force; keep in good order; keep in proper condition; keep in repair; keep up; preserve; preserve from lapse, decline, failure, or cessation; provide for; rebuild; repair; replace; supply with means of support; supply with what is needed; support; sustain; uphold. Negatively stated, it is defined as not to lose or surrender; not to suffer or fail or decline. El Paso County Water Imp. Dist. No. 1 v. City of El Paso, D.C.Tex., 243 F.2d 927, 931.

To "maintain" an action is to uphold, continue on foot, and keep from collapse a suit already begun, or to prosecute a suit with effect. George Moore Ice Cream Co. v. Rose, Ga., 289 U.S. 373, 53 S.Ct. 620, 77 L.Ed. 1265. To maintain an action or suit may mean to commence or institute it; the term imports the existence of a cause of action. Maintain, however, is applied to actions already brought, but not yet reduced to judgment. Smallwood v. Gallardo, 275 U.S. 56, 48 S.Ct. 23, 72 L.Ed. 152. In this connection it means to continue or preserve in or with; to carry on.

The words "maintains" and "maintaining" in statutes prohibiting maintenance of a liquor nuisance denote continuous or recurrent acts approaching permanence. The term "maintaining government" means providing money to enable government to perform duties which it is required by law to perform.

See also **Maintenance; Repair**.

Maintained. Carried on; kept possession and care of; kept effectively; commenced and continued.

Maintainor. In criminal law, one that maintains or seconds a cause pending in suit between others, either by disbursing money or otherwise giving assistance. One who is guilty of *maintenance (q.v.)*.

Maintenance. Act of maintaining, keeping up, supporting; livelihood; means of sustenance. Federal Land Bank of St. Louis v. Miller, 184 Ark. 415, 42 S.W.2d 564, 566. The upkeep, or preserving the condition of property to be operated. See also **Maintain**.

Sustenance; support; assistance; aid. The furnishing by one person to another, for his support, of the means of living, or food, clothing, shelter, etc., particularly where the legal relation of the parties is such that one is bound to support the other, as between father and child, or husband and wife. State ex rel. Blume v. State Board of Education of Montana, 97 Mont. 371, 34 P.2d 515, 519. The supplying of the necessaries of life. Federal Land Bank of St. Louis v. Miller, 184 Ark. 415, 42 S.W.2d 564, 566. Term "maintenance" means primarily food, clothing and shelter, but it does include such items as reasonable and necessary transportation or automobile expenses, medical and drug expenses, utilities and household expenses. Hughes v. Hughes, La.App., 303 So.2d 766, 769. See also **Support**.

Assets. Expenditures undertaken to preserve an asset's service potential for its originally-intended life; these expenditures are treated as period expenses or product costs. Contrast with **Improvement.** See also **Maintain; Repair.**

Roads. "Maintenance" of public roads and highways includes all necessary powers to provide and keep up a system of highways. Handy v. Johnson, D.C.Tex., 51 F.2d 809, 813.

Seamen. See **Maintenance and cure.**

Suits. An officious intermeddling in a suit which in no way belongs to one, by maintaining or assisting either party, with money or otherwise, to prosecute or defend it. Schnabel v. Taft Broadcasting Co., Inc., Mo.App., 525 S.W.2d 819, 823. See also **Champerty.**

Maintenance and cure. Contractual form of compensation given by general maritime law to seaman who falls ill while in service of his vessel. McCorpen v. Central Gulf S. S. Corp., C.A.Tex., 396 F.2d 547, 548. A shipowner is liable to a seaman under articles for illness and injury whether or not they arise out of his shipboard duties, and to this extent such benefits are broader than workmen's compensation. The seaman who accepts such benefits is not deemed to have waived his right to sue the shipowner for negligence under the Jones Act. Pacific S.S. Co. v. Peterson, 278 U.S. 130, 49 S.Ct. 75, 73 L.Ed. 220.

Maintenance assessment. One for purpose of keeping an improvement in working order. University Nat. Co. v. Grays Harbor County, 12 Wash.2d 549, 122 P.2d 501, 502.

Maior /mé(yə)r/. An old form of "mayor."

Maister /méystər/. An old form of "master."

Maître /méytrə/. Fr. In French maritime law, master; the master or captain of a vessel.

Majestas /məjéstæs/. Lat. In Roman law, the majesty, sovereign authority, or supreme prerogative of the state or prince. Also a shorter form of the expression *"crimen majestatis,"* or *"crimen læsæ majestatis,"* an offense against sovereignty, or against the safety or organic life of the Roman people; *i.e.,* high treason.

Majesty. Royal dignity. A term used of kings and emperors as a title of honor.

Major. A person of full age; one who is no longer a minor; one who has attained the management of his own concerns and the enjoyment of his civic rights. See also **Adult; Legal age; Majority.**

   Greater or larger. Zenith Radio Distributing Corporation v. Mateer, 311 Ill.App. 263, 35 N.E.2d 815, 816.

   Military law. The officer next in rank above a captain.

Major and minor fault rule. Vessel guilty of gross fault has burden of showing that other vessel committed a plain fault. General Seafoods Corporation v. J. S. Packard Dredging Co., C.C.A.Mass., 120 F.2d 117, 119, 120. Where fault on part of one vessel is established by uncontradicted testimony and such fault is, of itself, sufficient to account for the disaster, it is not enough for such vessel to raise a doubt with regard to

management of other vessel and any reasonable doubt with regard to propriety of conduct of such other vessel should be resolved in its favor. Intagliata v. Shipowners & Merchants Towboat Co., 26 Cal.2d 365, 159 P.2d 1, 10; General Seafoods Corporation v. J. S. Packard Dredging Co., C.C.A.Mass., 120 F.2d 117, 119, 120.

Major annus /méyjər ǽnəs/. The greater year; the bissextile year, consisting of 366 days.

Majora regalia /məjórə rəgéyl(i)yə/. The king's dignity, power, and royal prerogative, as opposed to his revenue, which is comprised in the *minora* regalia.

Major crimes. A loose classification of serious crimes such as murder, rape, armed robbery, etc.

Major dispute. Major disputes within Railway Labor Act are those concerned with formation of collective bargaining agreements or with efforts to secure such agreements and look to acquisition of rights of future rather than to rights which vested in past and "minor disputes" are those arising where there is existing agreement and there has been no effort to bring about formal change in terms or to create new agreement but dispute relates to application of particular provision. Railway Exp. Agency, Inc. v. Gulf Dept., Dist. Bd. of Adjustment, Broth. of Ry., Airline and S. S. Clerks, Freight Handlers, Exp. and Station Emp., D.C.Ga., 306 F.Supp. 1243, 1246. See also **Minor dispute.**

Majore pœna affectus quam legibus statuta est, non est infamis /məjóriy píynə əféktəs kwæm líyjəbəs stətyúwdə èst, nón èst ənféyməs/. One affected with a greater punishment than is provided by law is not infamous.

Majores /məjóriyz/. In old English law, greater persons; persons of higher condition or estate.

   In Roman law and genealogical tables, the male ascendants beyond the sixth degree.

Major general. An officer next in rank above a brigadier general, and next below a lieutenant general, and who usually commands a division or an army corps.

Major hæreditas venit unicuique nostrum a jure et legibus quam a parentibus /méyjər hərédətæs víynət yùwnək(yuw)áykwiy nóstrəm èy júriy èt líyjəbəs kwæm éy pəréntəbəs/. A greater inheritance comes to every one of us from right and the laws than from parents.

Majority. Full age; legal age; the age at which, by law, a person is entitled to the management of his own affairs and to the enjoyment of civic rights. The opposite of minority. Also the *status* of a person who is a major in age. See **Adult; Capacity; Legal age.**

   The greater number. The number greater than half of any total.

Majority of qualified electors. Refers to those who actually vote on election day. Harris v. Baden, 154 Fla. 373, 17 So.2d 608, 609. See **Majority rule; Majority vote.**

Majority opinion. The opinion of an appellate court in which the majority of its members join. May also refer to a view of a legal principle in which most jurisdictions concur. See also **Opinion.**

Majority rule. Rule by the choice of the majority of those who actually vote, irrespective of whether a majority of those entitled participate. N. L. R. B. v. Standard Lime & Stone Co., C.C.A.Va., 149 F.2d 435, 437. See also **Majority vote.**

Majority vote. Vote by more than half of voters for candidate or other matter on ballot. When there are only two candidates, he who receives the greater number of the votes cast is said to have a majority; when there are more than two competitors for the same office, the person who receives the greatest number of votes has a *plurality,* but he has not a majority unless he receives a greater number of votes than those cast for all his competitors combined.

As regards voting by stockholders, means majority per capita when the right to vote is per capita, and a majority of stock when each share of stock is entitled to a vote, each particular case being determined by provisions of charter regulating voting. Simon Borg & Co. v. New Orleans City R. Co., D.C.La., 244 F. 617, 619.

Major numerus in se continet minorem /méyjər n(y)úwmərəs ìn síy kóntənət mənórəm/. The greater number contains in itself the less.

Majus dignum trahit ad se minus dignum /méyjəs dígnəm tréy(h)əd æd síy máynəs dígnəm/. The more worthy draws to itself the less worthy.

Majus est delictum seipsum occidere quam alium /méyjəs èst dəlíktəm sìyípsəm oksídəriy kwæm éyliyəm/. It is a greater crime to kill one's self than another. See **Suicide.**

Majus jus /méyjəs jə́s/. In old practice, greater right or more right. A plea in the old real actions. *Majus jus merum,* more mere right.

A writ proceeding in some customary manors to try a right to land.

Majus Latium /méyjəs léysh(iy)əm/. See **Jus Latium.**

Make. To cause to exist. United States v. Giles, 300 U.S. 41, 57 S.Ct. 340, 344, 81 L.Ed. 493. To form, fashion, or produce. To do, perform, or execute; as to make an issue, to make oath, to make a presentment. To do in form of law; to perform with due formalities; to execute in legal form; as to make answer, to make a return or report.

To execute as one's act or obligation; to prepare and sign; to issue; to sign, execute, and deliver; as to make a conveyance, to make a note. To conclude, determine upon, agree to, or execute; as to make a contract.

To cause to happen by one's neglect or omission; as to make default. To make acquisition of; to procure; to collect; as to make the money on an execution or to make a loan. To have authority or influence; to support or sustain; as in the phrase, "This precedent makes for the plaintiff."

Make a contract. To agree upon, and conclude or adopt, a contract. In case of a written contract, to reduce it to writing, execute it in due form, and deliver it as binding.

Make an award. To form and publish a judgment on the facts.

Make default. To fail or be wanting in some legal duty; particularly to omit the entering of an appearance when duly summoned in an action at law or other judicial proceeding. To neglect to obey the command of a subpœna, etc. See also **Default.**

Maker. One who makes, frames, or ordains; as a "law-maker." One who makes or executes; as the maker of a promissory note. One who signs a note to borrow. One who signs a check; in this context, synonymous with drawer. See **Draft.**

Accommodation maker. See **Accommodation.**

Making law. In old practice, the formality of denying a plaintiff's charge under oath, in open court, with compurgators. One of the ancient methods of trial, frequently, though inaccurately, termed "waging law," or "wager of law." 3 Bl.Comm. 341.

Term may also refer to a court decision that establishes new law on a particular matter or subject.

Making record. The preparation of an appellate record. May also refer to the process of trying a case with a view towards an eventual appeal in which the record of the trial is important. In the later instance care is taken during trial to make all appropriate objections so that such become part of the record on appeal.

Mal. A prefix meaning bad, wrong, fraudulent; as maladministration, malpractice, malversation, etc.

Mala /mǽlə/. Lat. Bad; evil; wrongful.

Maladministration /mælədmìnəstréyshən/. This term is used interchangeably with *misadministration,* and both words mean "wrong administration."

Mala fides /mǽlə fáydiyz/. Bad faith. The opposite of *bona fides (q.v.). Malâ fide,* in bad faith. *Malæ fidei possessor,* a possessor in bad faith.

Mala grammatica non vitiat chartam. Sed in expositione instrumentorum mala grammatica quoad fieri possit evitanda est /mǽlə grəmǽdəkə nòn víshiyət kárdəm sèd ìn èkspəzìshiyówniy ìnstrəmèntórəm mǽlə grəmǽdəkə kwówæd fáyəray pósəd èvətǽndə sít/. Bad grammar does not vitiate a deed. But in the exposition of instruments, bad grammar, as far as it can be done, is to be avoided.

Mala in se /mǽlə in siy/. Wrongs in themselves; acts morally wrong; offenses against conscience.

Malandrinus /mæləndráynəs/. In old English law, a thief or pirate.

Malapportionment. An improper or unconstitutional apportionment of legislative districts. See **Gerrymander; Legislative apportionment.**

Mala praxis /mǽlə prǽksəs/. Malpractice; unskillful management or treatment. Particularly applied to the neglect or unskillful management of a physician, surgeon, or apothecary. See **Malpractice.**

Mala prohibita /mǽlə prəhíbədə/. Prohibited wrongs or offenses; acts which are made *offenses* by positive laws, and *prohibited* as such. Acts or omissions which are made criminal by statute but which, of themselves, are not criminal. Generally, no criminal intent or mens rea is required and the mere accomplishment of the act or omission is sufficient for criminal liability. Term is used in contrast to mala in se which are acts which are wrongs in themselves such as robbery.

Malconduct /mælkóndèkt/. Ill conduct, especially dishonest conduct, maladministration, or, as applied to officers, official misconduct. See **Malfeasance; Misfeasance.**

Male /méyl/. Of the masculine sex.

Male creditus /mǽliy krédədəs/. In old English law, unfavorably thought of; in bad repute or credit.

Maledicta est expositio quæ corrumpit textum /mæ̀lədíktə èst èkspəzísh(iy)ow kwìy kərʌ́mpət tékstəm/. That is a cursed interpretation which corrupts the text.

Malediction /mæ̀lədíkshən/. A curse, which was anciently annexed to donations of lands made to churches or religious houses, against those who should violate thier rights.

Malefaction /mæ̀ləfǽkshən/. A crime; an offense.

Malefactor /mǽləfæ̀ktər/. He who is guilty, or has been convicted, of some crime or offense.

Maleficia non debent remanere impunita; et impunitas continuum affectum tribuit delinquenti /mæ̀ləfísh(iy)ə nòn débənt rìyməníriy ìmpyúwnədə; èd ìmpyúwnətæ̀s kəntínyuwəm əféktəm tríbyuwət dèlənkwéntay/. Evil deeds ought not to remain unpunished; and impunity affords continual incitement to the delinquent.

Maleficia propositis distinguuntur /mæ̀ləfísh(iy)ə prəpózədəs dìstingwə́ntər/. Evil deeds are distinguished from evil purposes, or *by* their purposes.

Maleficium /mæ̀ləfísh(iy)əm/. In the civil law, waste; damage; tort; injury.

Maleson, or **malison** /mǽləsən/°zən/. A curse.

Malesworn, or **malsworn** /méylswòrn/. Forsworn.

Malfeasance /mælfíyzən(t)s/. Evil doing; ill conduct. The commission of some act which is positively unlawful; the doing of an act which is wholly wrongful and unlawful; the doing of an act which person ought not to do at all or the unjust performance of some act which the party had no right or which he had contracted not to do. Comprehensive term including any wrongful conduct that affects, interrupts or interferes with the performance of official duties. State ex rel. Knabb v. Frater, 198 Wash. 675, 89 P.2d 1046, 1048. Malfeasance is a wrongful act which the actor has no legal right to do, or any wrongful conduct which affects, interrupts, or interferes with performance of official duty, or an act for which there is no authority or warrant of law or which a person ought not to do at all, or the unjust performance of some act, which party performing it has no right, or has contracted not, to do. Daugherty v. Ellis, 142 W.Va. 340, 97 S.E.2d 33, 42. It differs from "misfeasance" and "non-feasance" *(q.v.).*

Mal gree /mæl gríy/. L. Fr. Against the will; without the consent. Hence the single word *"malgre,"* and more modern *"maugre" (q.v.).*

Malice. The intentional doing of a wrongful act without just cause or excuse, with an intent to inflict an injury or under circumstances that the law will imply an evil intent. A condition of mind which prompts a person to do a wrongful act willfully, that is, on purpose, to the injury of another, or to do intentionally a wrongful act toward another without justification or excuse. A conscious violation of the law (or the prompting of the mind to commit it) which operates to the prejudice of another person. A condition of the mind showing a heart regardless of social duty and fatally bent on mischief. Cockrell v. State, 135 Tex.Cr.R. 218, 117 S.W.2d 1105, 1109, 1110.

In murder, that condition of mind which prompts one to take the life of another without just cause or provocation. A willful or corrupt intention of the mind. It includes not only anger, hatred and revenge, but also every other unlawful and unjustifiable motive. State v. Scherr, 243 Wis. 65, 9 N.W.2d 117, 119.

Malice in law is not necessarily personal hate or ill will, but it is that state of mind which is reckless of law and of the legal rights of the citizen.

In libel and slander, as to privileged communications, "malice" involves an evil intent or motive arising from spite or ill will; personal hatred or ill will; or culpable recklessness or a willful and wanton disregard of the rights and interests of the person defamed. In a libel case it consists in intentionally publishing, without justifiable cause, any written or printed matter which is injurious to the character of another. Becker v. Brinkop, 230 Mo.App. 871, 78 S.W.2d 538, 541. Malice may be defined, insofar as defamation is concerned, as acting in bad faith and with knowledge of falsity of statements. Rice v. Winkelman Bros. Apparel, Inc., 13 Mich.App. 281, 164 N.W.2d 417, 420. In the context of a libel suit brought by a public figure, it consists in publishing the false defamation knowing it to be false or with a reckless disregard of whether it is true or false. New York Times Co. v. Sullivan, 376 U.S. 254, 84 S.Ct. 710, 11 L.Ed.2d 686. See also **Libel; Slander.**

In the law of malicious prosecution, it means that the prosecution was instituted primarily because of a purpose other than that of bringing an offender to justice. Brown v. Kisner, 192 Miss. 746, 6 So.2d 611, 617. See also **Malicious prosecution.**

Actual malice. Express malice, or malice in fact. Eteenpain Co-op. Soc. v. Lillback, C.C.A.Mass., 18 F.2d 912, 917.

Constructive malice. Implied malice; malice inferred from acts; malice imputed by law; malice which is not shown by direct proof of an intention to do injury (express malice), but which is inferentially established by the necessarily injurious results of the acts shown to have been committed. See also *Implied malice, infra.*

Express malice. Actual malice; malice in fact; ill will or wrongful motive. A deliberate intention to commit an injury, evidenced by external circumstances. Sparf v. U. S., 156 U.S. 51, 15 S.Ct. 273, 39 L.Ed. 343. See also **Express malice.**

Implied malice. Malice inferred by legal reasoning and necessary deduction from the *res gestæ* or the conduct of the party. Malice inferred from any deliberate cruel act committed by one person against another, however sudden. What is called "general malice" is often thus inferred. Sparf v. U. S., 156 U.S. 51, 15 S.Ct. 273, 39 L.Ed. 343. See also *Constructive malice, supra.*

Legal malice. See **Legal malice.**

Particular malice. Malice directed against a particular individual. Ill will; a grudge; a desire to be revenged on a particular person. See also *Special malice,* below.

Preconceived malice. Malice prepense or aforethought. See **Malice aforethought; Premeditation.**

Premeditated malice. An intention to kill unlawfully, deliberately formed in the mind as the result of a determination meditated upon and fixed before the act. See **Malice aforethought; Premeditation.**

Special malice. Particular or personal malice; that is, hatred, ill will, or a vindictive disposition against a particular individual.

Universal malice. By this term is not meant a malicious purpose to take the life of all persons, but it is that depravity of the human heart which determines to take life upon slight or insufficient provocation, without knowing or caring who may be the victim.

Malice aforethought. A predetermination to commit an act without legal justification or excuse. Harrison v. Commonwealth, 279 Ky. 510, 131 S.W.2d 454, 455. A malicious design to injure. State v. Thomas, 157 Kan. 526, 142 P.2d 692, 693. The intentional doing of an unlawful act which was determined upon before it was executed. State v. Lane, Mo., 371 S.W.2d 261, 263. An intent, at the time of a killing, willfully to take the life of a human being, or an intent willfully to act in callous and wanton disregard of the consequences to human life; but "malice aforethought" does not necessarily imply any ill will, spite or hatred towards the individual killed. See also **Premeditation.**

Malice in fact. Express or actual malice. It implies desire or intent to injure, while "malice in law," or "implied malice," means wrongful act done intentionally, without just cause or excuse, and jury may infer it as a deduction from want of probable cause.

Malice in law. The intentional doing of a wrongful act without just cause or excuse. Lyons v. St. Joseph Belt Ry. Co., 232 Mo.App. 575, 84 S.W.2d 933, 944. Implied, inferred, or legal malice. As distinguished from malice in fact, it is presumed from tortious acts, deliberately done without just cause, excuse, or justification, which are reasonably calculated to injure another or others.

Malice prepense. Malice aforethought; deliberate, predetermined malice.

Malicious /məlíshəs/. Characterized by, or involving, malice; having, or done with, wicked or mischievous intentions or motives; wrongful and done intentionally without just cause or excuse. See also **Malice; Willful.**

Malicious abandonment. In criminal law, the desertion of a wife or husband without just cause.

Malicious abuse of legal process. Wilfully misapplying court process to obtain object not intended by law. The wilful misuse or misapplication of process to accomplish a purpose not warranted or commanded by the writ; the malicious perversion of a regularly issued process, whereby a result not lawfully or properly obtained on a writ is secured; not including cases where the process was procured maliciously but not abused or misused after its issuance. The tort of "malicious abuse of process" requires a perversion of court process to accomplish some end which the process was not designed to accomplish, and does not arise from a regular use of process, even with ulterior motives. Capital Elec. Co. v. Cristaldi, D.C.Md., 157 F.Supp. 646, 648. See also **Abuse (Process); Malicious use of process.**

Malicious accusation. Procuring accusation or prosecution of another from improper motive and without probable cause. See **Malicious prosecution.**

Malicious act. A wrongful act intentionally done without legal justification or excuse; an unlawful act done willfully or purposely to injure another.

Malicious assault with deadly weapon. Form of aggravated assault in which the victim is threatened with death or serious bodily injury from the defendant's use of a deadly weapon. The element of malice can be inferred from the nature of the assault and the selection of the weapon.

Malicious injury. An injury committed against a person at the prompting of malice or hatred towards him, or done spitefully or wantonly. The willful doing of an act with knowledge it is liable to injure another and regardless of consequences. Injury involving element of fraud, violence, wantonness and willfulness, or criminality. An injury that is intentional, wrongful and without just cause or excuse, even in the absence of hatred, spite or ill will. Panchula v. Kaya, 59 Ohio App. 556, 18 N.E.2d 1003, 1005, 13 O.O. 301. Punitive damages may be awarded to plaintiff for such injury.

Malicious killing. Any intentional killing without a legal justification or excuse and not within the realm of voluntary manslaughter. State v. Cope, 78 Ohio App. 429, 67 N.E.2d 912, 920, 34 O.O. 171.

Maliciously. Imports a wish to vex, annoy, or injure another, or an intent to do a wrongful act, and may consist in direct intention to injure, or in reckless disregard of another's rights. See also **Malice; Malicious.**

Malicious mischief. Willful destruction of personal property, from actual ill will or resentment towards its owner or possessor. Though only a trespass at the common law, it is now, by most statutes, made severely penal.

Malicious motive. Any motive for instituting a prosecution, other than a desire to bring an offender to justice. Lounder v. Jacobs, 119 Colo. 511, 205 P.2d 236, 238. See **Malicious prosecution.**

Malicious prosecution. One begun in malice without probable cause to believe the charges can be sustained. An action for damages brought by person, against whom civil suit or criminal prosecution has been instituted maliciously and without probable cause, after termination of prosecution of such suit in favor of person claiming damages. Beaurline v. Smith, Tex.Civ.App., 426 S.W.2d 295, 298.

One who takes an active part in the initiation, continuation or procurement of civil proceedings against another is subject to liability to the other for wrongful civil proceedings if: (a) he acts without probable cause, and primarily for a purpose other than that of securing the proper adjudication of the claim in which the proceedings are based, and (b) except when they are ex parte, the proceedings have terminated in favor of the person against whom they are brought. Restatement, Second, Torts, § 674.

Elements of a cause of action for malicious prosecution are: (1) commencement of prosecution of proceedings against present plaintiff; (2) its legal causation by present defendant; (3) its termination in favor of present plaintiff; (4) absence of probable cause for such proceedings; (5) presence of malice therein; and (6) damage to plaintiff by reason thereof. Palermo v. Cottom, Mo.App., 525 S.W.2d 758, 764.

In addition to the tort remedy for malicious criminal proceedings, the majority of states also permit tort actions for malicious institution of civil actions.

See also **Advice of counsel.**

Malicious trespass. The act of one who maliciously or mischievously injures or causes to be injured any property of another or any public property.

Malicious use of process. Exists where plaintiff proceeds maliciously and without probable cause to execute object which law intends process to subserve. See also **Abuse** *(Process)*; **Malicious abuse of legal process.**

Malignare /mæləgnériy/. To malign or slander; also to maim.

Malinger /məlíŋgər/. To feign sickness or any physical disablement or mental lapse or derangement, especially for the purpose of escaping the performance of a task, duty, or work. Person who consciously feigns or simulates mental or physical illness for gain.

Malitia /məlísh(iy)ə/. Lat. Actual evil design; express malice.

Malitia est acida; est mali animi affectus /məlísh(iy)ə èst ǽsədə, èst mǽlay ǽnəmay əféktəs/. Malice is sour; it is the quality of a bad mind.

Malitia præcogitata /məlísh(iy)ə prìykojətéydə/. Malice aforethought.

Malitia supplet ætatem /məlísh(iy)ə sə́pləd ətéydəm/. Malice supplies [the want of] age.

Malitiis hominum est obviandum /məlíshiyəs hómənəm èst òbviyǽndəm/. The wicked or malicious designs of men must be thwarted.

Malleable /mǽliyəbəl/. Capable of being drawn out and extended by beating; capable of extension by hammering; reducible to laminated form by beating.

Mallory Rule. Rule derived from case of the same name in which the court held that a confession given by one who had been detained an unreasonable time before being brought before magistrate was inadmissible though it was otherwise voluntary and trustworthy. Mallory v. U. S., 354 U.S. 449, 77 S.Ct. 1356, 1 L.Ed.2d 1479. Also known as McNabb-Mallory Rule.

Mallum. In old European law, a court of the higher kind in which the more important business of the county was dispatched by the count or earl. A public national assembly.

Malo animo /mǽlow ǽnəmow/. Lat. With an evil mind; with a bad purpose or wrongful intention; with malice.

Malo grato /mǽlow gréydow/. Lat. In spite; unwillingly.

Maloney Act. Amendment passed in 1938 to Securities Exchange Act requiring registration of brokers in over-the-counter securities.

Malpractice. Professional misconduct or unreasonable lack of skill. This term is usually applied to such conduct by doctors, lawyers, and accountants. Failure of one rendering professional services to exercise that degree of skill and learning commonly applied under all the circumstances in the community by the average prudent reputable member of the profession with the result of injury, loss or damage to the recipient of those services or to those entitled to rely upon them. It is any professional misconduct, unreasonable lack of skill or fidelity in professional or fiduciary duties, evil practice, or illegal or immoral conduct. Matthews v. Walker, 34 Ohio App.2d 128, 296 N.E.2d 569, 571, 63 O.O.2d 208. See also **Discovery rule; Standard of care.**

Legal malpractice. Consists of failure of an attorney to use such skill, prudence, and diligence as lawyers of ordinary skill and capacity commonly possess and exercise in performance of tasks which they undertake, and when such failure proximately causes damage it gives rise to an action in tort. Neel v. Magana, Olney, Levy, Cathcart and Gelfand, 6 Cal.3d 176, 98 Cal.Rptr. 837, 838, 491 P.2d 421.

Medical malpractice. In medical malpractice litigation, negligence is the predominant theory of liability. In order to recover for negligent malpractice, the plaintiff must establish the following elements: (1) the existence of the physician's duty to the plaintiff, usually based upon the existence of the physician-patient relationship; (2) the applicable standard of care and its violation; (3) a compensable injury; and, (4) a causal connection between the violation of the standard of care and the harm complained of. Kosberg v. Washington Hospital Center, Inc., 129 U.S.App.D.C. 322, 394 F.2d 947, 949. See also **Captain of ship doctrine; Discovery rule; Maltreatment.**

Maltreatment. In reference to the treatment of his patient by a surgeon, this term signifies improper or unskillful treatment; it may result either from ignorance, neglect, or willfulness; but the word does not necessarily imply that the conduct of the surgeon, in his treatment of the patient, is either willfully or grossly careless. See also **Malpractice** *(Medical).*

Malum /mǽləm/, *adj.* Lat. Wrong; evil; wicked; reprehensible.

Malum in se /mǽləm in síy/. A wrong in itself; an act or case involving illegality from the very nature of the transaction, upon principles of natural, moral, and public law. Grindstaff v. State, 214 Tenn. 58, 377 S.W.2d 921, 926; State v. Shedoudy, 45 N.M. 516, 118 P.2d 280, 287. An act is said to be *malum in se* when it is inherently and essentially evil, that is, immoral in its nature and injurious in its consequences, without any regard to the fact of its being noticed or punished by the law of the state. Such are most or all of the offenses cognizable at common law (without the denouncement of a statute); as murder, larceny, etc.

Malum non habet efficientem, sed deficientem, causam /mǽləm nòn hǽbəd əfis(h)iyéntəm sèd dəfis(h)iyéntəm kózəm/. Evil has not an efficient, but a deficient, cause.

Malum non præsumitur /mǽləm nòn prəz(y)úwmədər/. Wickedness is not presumed.

Malum prohibitum /mǽləm prəhíbədəm/. A wrong prohibited; a thing which is wrong *because* prohibited; an act which is not inherently immoral, but becomes so because its commission is expressly forbidden by positive law; an act involving an illegality resulting from positive law. Contrasted with *malum in se.*

Malum quo communius eo pejus /mǽləm kwòw kəmyúwn(i)yəs íyow píyjəs/. The more common an evil is, the worse it is.

Malus usus abolendus est /mǽləs yúwsəs æbəléndəs èst/. A bad or invalid custom is [ought] to be abolished.

Malveilles. In old English law, ill will; crimes and misdemeanors; malicious practices.

Malveis procurors /mǽlvey prəkyúrərz/. L. Fr. Such as used to pack juries, by the nomination of either party in a cause, or other practice.

Malversation /mælvərséyshən/. In French law, this word is applied to all grave and punishable faults committed in the exercise of a charge or commission (office), such as corruption, exaction, concussion, larceny.

Man. A human being. A person of the male sex. A male of the human species above the age of puberty.

In its most extended sense the term includes not only the adult male sex of the human species, but women and children. See **Mankind.**

In feudal law, a vassal; a tenant or feudatory. The Anglo-Saxon relation of *lord and man* was originally purely personal, and founded on mutual contract.

Manacles. Chain for the hands; shackles.

Manage. To control and direct, to administer, to take charge of. To conduct; to carry on the concerns of a business or establishment. Generally applied to affairs that are somewhat complicated and that involve skill and judgment.

Management. Government, control, superintendence, physical or manual handling or guidance; act of managing by direction or regulation, or administration, as management of family, or of household, or of servants, or of great enterprises, or of great affairs. Branch v. Veterans' Administration, 189 Ark. 662, 74 S.W.2d 800, 804. Discretionary power of direction.

Manager. One who has charge of corporation and control of its business, or of its branch establishments, divisions, or departments, and who is vested with a certain amount of discretion and independent judgment. Braniff v. McPherren, 177 Okl. 292, 58 P.2d 871, 872. A person chosen or appointed to manage, direct, or administer the affairs of another person or of a corporation or company. The designation of "manager" implies general power and permits reasonable inferences that the employee so designated is invested with the general conduct and control of his employer's business. U. S. Auto Ass'n v. Alexander Film Co., D.C.Mun.App., 93 A.2d 770, 771. See also **General manager.**

Also one of the persons appointed on the part of the House of Representatives to prosecute impeachments before the Senate.

Managers of a conference. In England, members of the houses of parliament appointed to represent each house at a conference between the two houses. It is an ancient rule that the number of commons named for a conference should be double those of the lords.

Managing agent. See **Agent.**

Managium /mənéyj(iy)əm/. A mansion-house or dwelling-place.

Manas mediæ /mǽnəs míydiyiy/. Men of a mean condition, or of the lowest degree.

Manbote /mǽnbòwt/. In Saxon law, a compensation or recompense for homicide, particularly due to the lord for killing his man or vassal, the amount of which was regulated by that of the *were.*

Manca, mancus, or **mancusa** /mǽŋkə/mǽŋkəs(ə)/. A square piece of gold coin, commonly valued at thirty pence.

Manceps /mǽn(t)sèps/. Lat. In Roman law, a purchaser; one who took the article sold in his hand; a formality observed in certain sales. A farmer of the public taxes.

Manche-present /mónsh prèyzón/. A bribe; a present from the donor's own hand.

Mancipare /mænsəpériy/. Lat. In Roman law, to sell, alienate, or make over to another; to sell with certain formalities; to sell a person; one of the forms observed in the process of emancipation.

Mancipate /mǽn(t)səpèyt/. To enslave; to bind; to tie.

Mancipatio /mǽn(t)səpéysh(iy)ow/. Lat. In Roman law, a certain ceremony or formal process anciently required to be performed, to perfect the sale or conveyance of *res mancipi* (land, houses, slaves, horses, or cattle).

The parties were present (vendor and vendee), with five witnesses and a person called *"libripens,"* who held a balance or scales. A set form of words was repeated on either side, indicative of transfer of ownership, and certain prescribed gestures made, and the vendee then struck the scales with a piece of copper, thereby symbolizing the payment, or weighing out, of the stipulated price.

The ceremony of *mancipatio* was used, in later times, in one of the forms of making a will. The testator acted as vendor, and the heir (or *familiæ emptor*) as purchaser, the latter symbolically *buying* the whole estate or succession, of the former. The ceremony was also used by a father in making a fictitious sale of his son, which sale, when three times repeated, effectuated the emancipation of the son.

Mancipi res /mǽn(t)səpay ríyz/. Lat. In Roman law, certain classes of things which could not be aliened or transferred except by means of a certain formal ceremony of conveyance called *"mancipatio"* (q.v.). These included land, houses, slaves, horses, and cattle. All other things were called *"res nec mancipi."*

The distinction was abolished by Justinian. The distinction corresponded as nearly as may be to the early distinction of English law into real and personal property; *res mancipi* being objects of a military or agricultural character, and *res nec mancipi* being all other subjects of property. Like personal estate, *res nec mancipi* were not originally either valuable *in se* or valued.

Mancipium /mænsípiyəm/. Lat. In Roman law, the momentary condition in which a *filius*, etc., might be when in course of emancipation from the *potestas*, and before that emancipation was absolutely complete. The condition was not like the *dominica potestas* over slaves, but slaves are frequently called *"mancipia"* in the non-legal Roman authors.

To form a clear conception of the true import of the word in the Roman jurisprudence, it is necessary to advert to the four distinct powers which were exercised by the *pater familias*, viz.; the *manus*, or martial power; the *mancipium*, resulting from the *mancipatio*, or *alienatio per æs et libram*, of a freeman; the *dominica potestas*, the power of the master over his slaves, and the *patria potestas*, the paternal power. When the *pater familias* sold his son, *venum dare, mancipare*, the paternal power was succeeded by the *mancipium*, or the power acquired by the purchaser over the person whom he held *in mancipio*, and whose condition was assimilated to that of a slave. What is most remarkable is, that on the emancipation from the *mancipium* he fell back into the paternal power, which was not entirely exhausted until he had been sold three times by the *pater familias*. *Si pater filium ter venum dat, filius a patre liber esto.* Gaius speaks of the *mancipatio* as *imaginaria quædam venditio*, because in his times it was only resorted to for the purpose of adoption or emancipation.

Mancomunal /mànkomuwnál/. In Spanish law, an obligation is said to be *mancomunal* when one person assumes the contract or debt of another, and makes himself liable to pay or fulfill it.

Mancus /mǽŋkəs/. See **Manca.**

Mandamiento /màndamyéntow/. In Spanish law, commission; authority or power of attorney. A contract of good faith, by which one person commits to the gratuitous charge of another his affairs, and the latter accepts the charge.

Mandamus /mændéyməs/. Lat. We command. This is the name of a writ (formerly a high prerogative writ) which issues from a court of superior jurisdiction, and is directed to a private or municipal corporation, or any of its officers, or to an executive, administrative or judicial officer, or to an inferior court, commanding the performance of a particular act therein specified, and belonging to his or their public, official, or ministerial duty, or directing the restoration of the complainant to rights or privileges of which he has been illegally deprived. A writ issuing from a court of competent jurisdiction, commanding an inferior tribunal, board, corporation, or person to perform a purely ministerial duty imposed by law. Nebel v. Nebel, 241 N.C. 491, 85 S.E.2d 876, 882. Extraordinary writ which lies to compel performance of ministerial act or mandatory duty where there is a clear legal right in plaintiff, a corresponding duty in defendant, and a want of any other appropriate and adequate remedy. Cohen v. Ford, 19 Pa. Cmwlth. 417, 339 A.2d 175, 177.

The U.S. District Courts have original jurisdiction of any action in the nature of mandamus to compel an officer or employee of the United States or any agency thereof to perform a duty owed to the plaintiff. 28 U.S.C.A. § 1361.

Mandamus has traditionally issued in response to abuses of judicial power. Thus, where a district judge refuses to take some action he is required to take or takes some action he is not empowered to take, mandamus will lie. Bankers Life & Cas. Co. v. Holland, 346 U.S. 379, 384, 74 S.Ct. 145, 98 L.Ed. 106. The Supreme Court may issue a writ of mandamus in aid of the appellate jurisdiction that might otherwise be defeated by the unauthorized action of the court below. McClellan v. Carland, 217 U.S. 268, 30 S.Ct. 501, 503, 54 L.Ed. 762.

The remedy of mandamus is a drastic one, to be invoked only in extraordinary situations. Will v. United States, 389 U.S. 90, 95, 88 S.Ct. 269, 273, 19 L.Ed.2d 305; Banker's Life & Cas. Co. v. Holland, 346 U.S. 379, 382–385, 74 S.Ct. 145, 147–149, 98 L.Ed. 106; Ex parte Fahey, 332 U.S. 258, 259, 67 S.Ct. 1558, 1559, 91 L.Ed. 2041. The writ has traditionally been used in the federal courts only "to confine an inferior court to a lawful exercise of its prescribed jurisdiction or to compel it to exercise its authority when it is its duty to do so." Will v. United States, 389 U.S., at 95, 88 S.Ct., at 273, quoting Roche v. Evaporated Milk Assn., 319 U.S. 21, 26, 63 S.Ct. 938, 941, 87 L.Ed. 1185.

Pleading. Like most of the extraordinary writs, the *writ* of mandamus has been abolished under rules practice in favor of a complaint in the nature of mandamus which accomplishes the same object; *e.g.* Mass.R.Civ.P. 81(b).

Mandans /mǽndænz/. Lat. In the civil law, the employing party in a contract of mandate. One who gives a thing in charge to another; one who requires, requests, or employs another to do some act for him.

Mandant /mǽndənt/. In French and Scotch law, the employing party in the contract of *mandatum*, or mandate.

Mandataire /mændətér/. Fr. In French law, a person employed by another to do some act for him; a mandatary.

Mandata licita recipiunt strictam interpretationem, sed illicita latam et extensam /məndéydə lísədə rəsípiyənt stríktəm intàrprətèyshiyównəm, sèd əlísədə léydəm èd əkstén(t)səm/. Lawful commands receive a strict interpretation, but unlawful commands a broad and extended one.

Mandatarius terminos sibi positos transgredi non potest /mændətériyəs tármənəs síbay pózədows træn(d)zgríyday nòn pówdèst/. A mandatary cannot exceed the limits assigned him.

Mandatary /mændətèriy/. He to whom a mandate, charge, or commandment is given; also, he that obtains a benefice by *mandamus.* Briggs v. Spaulding, 141 U.S. 132, 11 S.Ct. 924, 35 L.Ed. 662.

Mandate. A command, order, or direction, written or oral, which court is authorized to give and person is bound to obey. Silverman v. Seneca Realty Co., 154 Misc. 35, 276 N.Y.S. 466. A judicial command or precept proceeding from a court or judicial officer, directing the proper officer to enforce a judgment, sentence, or decree. A precept or order issued upon the decision of an appeal or writ of error, directing action to be taken, or disposition to be made of case, by inferior court. Official mode of communicating judgment of appellate court to lower court, directing action to be taken or disposition to be made of cause by trial court. Tierney v. Tierney, Fla.App., 290 So.2d 136, 137. See also **Decree; Order.**

A bailment of property in regard to which the bailee engages to do some act without payment. Agreement to perform services for another without pay.

A contract by which a lawful business is committed to the management of another, and by him undertaken to be performed gratuitously. The mandatary is bound to the exercise of slight diligence, and is responsible for gross neglect. Williams v. Conger, 125 U.S. 397, 8 S.Ct. 933, 31 L.Ed. 778.

A mandate, procuration, or letter of attorney is an act by which one person gives power to another to transact for him and in his name one or several affairs. See also **Power of attorney.**

Mandato /mandátow/. In Spanish law, the contract of mandate.

Mandator /mændéydər/. The person employing another to perform a mandate.

Mandatory /mændət(ə)riy/. *adj.* Containing a command; preceptive; imperative; peremptory; obligatory.

Mandatory injunction /mændət(ə)riy ìnjén(k)shən/. See **Injunction.**

Mandatory instructions. See **Jury instructions.**

Mandatory sentencing. See **Sentence.**

Mandatory statutes. Generic term describing statutes which require and not merely permit a course of action. They are characterized by such directives as "shall" and not "may."

A "mandatory" provision in a statute is one the omission to follow which renders the proceedings to which it relates void, while a "directory" provision is

one the observance of which is not necessary to validity of the proceeding. It is also said that when the provision of a statute is the essence of the thing required to be done, it is mandatory, Kavanaugh v. Fash, C.C.A.Okl., 74 F.2d 435, 437; otherwise, when it relates to form and manner, and where an act is incident, or after jurisdiction acquired, it is directory merely.

Mandatory statutory provision is one which must be observed, as distinguished from "directory" provision, which leaves it optional with department or officer to which addressed to obey it or not. State ex rel. Dworken v. Court of Common Pleas of Cuyahoga County, 131 Ohio St. 23, 1 N.E.2d 138, 139, 5 O.O. 291.

Mandatum /mændéydəm/. Lat. In the civil law, the contract of mandate *(q.v.).*

Mandatum nisi gratuitum nullum est /mændéydəm náysay grəchúwədəm nə́ləm èst/. Unless a mandate is gratuitous, it is not a mandate.

Mandavi ballivo /məndéyvay bǽləvow/. (I have commanded or made my mandate to the bailiff.) In English practice, the return made by a sheriff, where the bailiff of a liberty has the execution of a writ, that he has commanded the bailiff to execute it.

Manerium /məníriyəm/. In old English law, a manor.

Manerium dicitur a manendo, secundum excellentiam, sedes magna, fixa, et stabilis /məníriyəm dísədər èy mənéndow, səkə́ndəm èksəlénsh(iy)əm, síydiyz mǽgnə, fíksəm, èt stéybələs/. A manor is so called from *manendo,* according to its excellence, a seat, great, fixed, and firm.

Mangonare /mæ̀ŋgənériy/. In old English law, to buy in a market.

Manhood. The status of one who has reached his legal majority which in most jurisdictions is 18. Formerly, it was the age of 21. When this status is achieved, a person may act sui juris. See also **Legal age; Majority.**

In feudal law, a term denoting the ceremony of doing homage by the vassal to his lord. The formula used was, *"Devenio vester homo",* I become your man. 2 Bl.Comm. 54.

Mania /méyniyə/. See **Insanity.**

Manic. Phase of manic-depressive psychosis in which the mood of the patient is overactive and expansive; characterized by excessive ego valuation and over-estimation of personal importance. Manic mood may include boisterousness, joviality, anger, joyousness.

Manifest. Evident to the senses, especially to the sight, obvious to the understanding, evident to the mind, not obscure or hidden, and is synonymous with open, clear, visible, unmistakable, indubitable, indisputable, evident, and self-evident. In evidence, that which is clear and requires no proof; that which is notorious. Houston v. Leyden Motor Coach Co., 102 Ill.App.2d 348, 243 N.E.2d 293, 296; Graf v. Ford Motor Co., 102 Ill.App.2d 390, 243 N.E.2d 337, 341; Little v. Scheu, 99 Ill.App.2d 421, 241 N.E.2d 702, 706.

The word "manifest", in rule that appellate court cannot substitute its opinion for that of trial court as to facts unless trial court's finding is manifestly against the weight of the evidence, means clearly evidence, clear, plain, or indisputable, and requires that an opposite conclusion be clearly evident. Levin v. Siver, 27 Ill.App.2d 134, 169 N.E.2d 156.

Document used in shipping and warehousing containing a list of the contents, value, origin, carrier and destination of the goods to be shipped or warehoused. A written document required to be carried by merchant vessels, containing an account of the cargo, with other particulars, for the facility of the customs officers. The Sylvia II, D.C.Mass., 28 F.2d 215, 216. List of passengers and cargo kept by vessel and aircraft.

Manifesta probatione non indigent /mænəféstə prəbèyshiyówniy nòn índəjənt/. Things manifest do not require proof.

Manifestation of intention. In trusts and wills, the external expression of intention as distinguished from the undisclosed internal intention. Restatement of Trusts, Second, § 2, comment g.

Manifest law. See Lex manifesta, *s. v.* Lex.

Manifest necessity. Doctrine of "manifest necessity" which will authorize granting of mistrial in criminal case, and preclude defendant from successfully raising plea of former jeopardy, contemplates a sudden and overwhelming emergency beyond control of court and unforeseeable, and it does not mean expediency. Fonseca v. Judges of Family Court of Kings County, 59 Misc.2d 492, 299 N.Y.S.2d 493, 498.

Manifesto /mænəféstow/. A formal written declaration, promulgated by a sovereign, or by the executive authority of a state or nation, proclaiming its reasons and motives for declaring a war, or for any other important international action. Public declaration or proclamation of political or social principals.

Manipulation. Series of transactions involving the buying or selling of a security for the purpose of creating a false or misleading appearance of active trading or to raise or depress the price to induce the purchase or sale by others.

Mankind. The race or species of human beings. In law, females, as well as males, are included under this term.

Mann Act. Federal statute (White Slave Traffic Act, 18 U.S.C.A. § 2421) making it a crime to transport a woman or girl in interstate or foreign commerce for the purpose of prostitution or debauchery, or for any other immoral purpose.

Manner. A way, mode, method of doing anything, or mode of proceeding in any case or situation. See also **Custom.**

Manner and form; modo et forma. In common law pleading, formal words introduced at the conclusion of a traverse. Their object is to put the party whose pleading is traversed not only to the proof that the matter of fact denied is, in its general effect, true as alleged, but also that the manner and form in which

the fact or facts are set forth are also capable of proof.

Manning. A day's work of a man. A summoning to court.

Mannire /mənáyriy/. To cite any person to appear in court and stand in judgment there. It is different from *bannire;* for, though both of them are citations, this is by the adverse party, and that is by the judge.

Mannopus /mænówpəs/. In old English law, goods taken in the hands of an apprehended thief. The same as *"mainour"* (q.v.).

Man of straw. See **Men of Straw.**

Manor. A house, dwelling, seat, or residence.

In English law, the manor was originally a tract of land granted out by the king to a lord or other great person, in fee. It was otherwise called a "barony" or "lordship," and appendant to it was the right to hold a court, called the "court-baron." The lands comprised in the manor were divided into *terræ tenementales* (tenemental lands or bocland) and *terræ dominicales*, or demesne lands. The former were given by the lord of the manor to his followers or retainers in freehold. The latter were such as he reserved for his own use; but of these part were held by tenants in copyhold, *i.e.*, those holding by a copy of the record in the lord's court; and part, under the name of the "lord's waste," served for public roads and commons of pasture for the lord and tenants. The tenants, considered in their relation to the court-baron and to each other, were called *"pares curiæ".* The word also signified the franchise of having a manor, with jurisdiction for a court-baron and the right to the rents and services of copyholders.

Reputed manor. Whenever the demesne lands and the services become absolutely separated, the manor ceases to be a manor in reality, although it may (and usually does) continue to be a manor in reputation, and is then called a "reputed manor," and it is also sometimes called a "seigniory in gross."

Manorial extent /mənóriyəl əkstént/. In old English law, a survey of a manor made by a jury of tenants, often of unfree men sworn to sit for the particulars of each tenancy, and containing the smallest details as to the nature of the service due. These manorial extents were made in the interest of the lords, who were anxious that all due services should be done; but they imply that other and greater services were not due, that the customary tenants, even though they be unfree men, owed these services for their tenements, no less and no more. Statements that the tenants were not bound to do services of a particular kind were not very uncommon. The "extents" of manors are descriptions that give the numbers and names of the tenants, the size of their holdings, the legal kind of their tenure and the kind and amount of their service.

Manorial system. A medieval system of land ownership by lords of the manor for whom serfs and some freemen toiled in the soil in return for protection from the lord. See also **Manor.**

Manqueller /mænkwèlər/°kìlər/. In Saxon law, a murderer.

Manse /mǽn(t)s/. In old English law, a habitation or dwelling, generally with land attached. A residence or dwelling-house for the parish priest; a parsonage or vicarage house.

Manser /mǽn(t)sər/. A bastard.

Mansio /mǽnsh(iy)ow/. In Anglo-Saxon times the amount of land which would support a man and his family, called by various names.

Mansion-house. In the law of burglary, etc., any species of dwelling-house.

Manslaughter. The unlawful killing of another without malice, either express or implied. Such may be either voluntarily, upon a sudden heat, or involuntarily, but in the commission of some unlawful act. The unlawful killing of a human without any deliberation, which may be involuntary, in the commission of a lawful act without due caution and circumspection. Wallace v. U. S., 162 U.S. 466, 16 S.Ct. 859, 40 L.Ed. 1039.

The unlawful killing of a human without malice and without premeditation and deliberation. State v. Wingler, 238 N.C. 485, 78 S.E.2d 303, 307. It is of two kinds: voluntary—upon a sudden quarrel or heat of passion; and, involuntary—in the commission in an unlawful manner, or without due caution and circumspection, of a lawful act which might produce death. 18 U.S.C.A. § 1112.

Criminal homicide constitutes manslaughter when: (a) it is committed recklessly; or (b) a homicide which would otherwise be murder is committed under the influence of extreme mental or emotional disturbance for which there is reasonable explanation or excuse. The reasonableness of such explanation or excuse shall be determined from the viewpoint of a person in the actor's situation under the circumstances as he believes them to be. Model Penal Code, § 210.3.

The heat of passion, which will reduce a murder to manslaughter, must be such passion as would be aroused naturally in the mind of the ordinary reasonable person under the same or similar circumstances, as shown by the evidence in the case.

See also Adequate cause; Assault with intent to commit manslaughter; Hot blood; Negligent manslaughter; Sudden heat of passion.

There are various degrees of manslaughter recognized by different states:

Involuntary manslaughter. Such exists where a person in committing an unlawful act not felonious or tending to great bodily harm, or in committing a lawful act without proper caution or requisite skill, unguardedly or undesignedly kills another. Model Penal Code, § 210.3(1)(a).

Voluntary manslaughter. Manslaughter committed voluntarily upon a sudden heat of the passions; as if, upon a sudden quarrel, two persons fight, and one of them kills the other. Model Penal Code, § 210.-3(1)(b). It is the unlawful taking of human life under circumstances falling short of willful or deliberate intent to kill and approaching too near thereto to be justifiable homicide.

The absence of intention to kill or to commit any unlawful act which might reasonably produce death or great bodily harm is the distinguishing feature between voluntary and involuntary homicide.

Manstealing. A word sometimes used synonymously with "kidnapping" (q.v.).

Mansuetae naturae /mænswíydiy nətyúriy/. Tamed and domesticated animals.

Mansuetus /mænswíydəs/. Lat. Tame; as though accustomed to come to the hand.

Mantheoff /mǽnθìyf/. In Saxon law, a horse-stealer.

Manticulate /mæntíkyəlèyt/. To pick pockets.

Mantle children /mǽntəl chíldrən/. See **Pallio cooperire.**

Manual. Of, or pertaining to, the hand or hands; done, made, or operated by or used with the hand or hands; or as manual labor. Performed by the hand; used or employed by the hand; held in the hand. See also **Manual labor.**

Manual delivery. Delivery of personal property sold, donated, mortgaged, etc., by passing it into the "hand" of the purchaser or transferee, that is, by an actual and corporeal change of possession.

Manual gift. The manual gift, that is, the giving of corporeal movable effects, accompanied by a real delivery; such is not subject to any formality.

Manualis obedientia /mænyuwéyləs əbìydiyénsh(iy)ə/. Sworn obedience or submission upon oath.

Manual labor. Work done with the hand. State v. Ash, 53 Ariz. 197, 87 P.2d 270, 272. Labor performed by hand or by the exercise of physical force, with or without the aid of tools, machinery or equipment, but depending for its effectiveness chiefly upon personal muscular exertion rather than upon skill, intelligence or adroitness.

Manu brevi /mǽn(y)uw bríyvay/. Lat. With a short hand. A term used in the civil law, signifying shortly; directly; by the shortest course; without circuity.

Manucaptio /mænyuwkǽpsh(iy)ow/. In old English practice, a writ which lay for a man taken on suspicion of felony, and the like, who could not be admitted to bail by the sheriff, or others having power to let to mainprise.

Manucaptors /mænyuwkǽptərz/. Same as mainpernors (q.v.).

Manufacture, v. From Latin words manus and factura, literally, put together by hand. Now it means the process of making products by hand or machinery. United States v. Anderson, D.C.Cal., 45 F.Supp. 943, 946. Meaning of word "manufacture," which is defined as the making of goods or wares by manual labor or by machinery, especially on a large scale, has expanded as workmanship and art have advanced, so that now nearly all artificial products of human industry, nearly all such materials as have acquired changed conditions or new and specific combinations, whether from the direct action of the human hand, from chemical processes devised and directed by human skill, or by the employment of machinery, are commonly designated as "manufactured."

Manufacture, *n.* The process or operation of making goods or any material produced by hand, by machinery or by other agency; anything made from raw materials by the hand, by machinery, or by art. The production of articles for use from raw or prepared materials by giving such materials new forms, qualities, properties or combinations, whether by hand labor or machine. Cain's Coffee Co. v. City of Muskogee, 171 Okl. 635, 44 P.2d 50, 52.

In patent law, any useful product made directly by human labor, or by the aid of machinery directed and controlled by human power, and either from raw materials, or from materials worked up into a new form. Also the process by which such products are made or fashioned.

Manufacturer. One who by labor, art, or skill transforms raw material into some kind of a finished product or article of trade. Henry v. Markesan State Bank, C.C.A.Minn., 68 F.2d 554, 557. Any individual, partnership, corporation, association, or other legal relationship which manufactures, assembles, or produces goods.

Manufacturers liability doctrine. The foundation for the liability under this doctrine is knowledge of the danger attending use of manufactured or assembled product and negligence in failing to give appropriate warning, or negligence in failing to discover and appreciate the danger, and the probable consequences that injury will proximately result from the use of such product for the purposes for which it was intended. See **Strict liability.**

Manufacturing corporation. A corporation engaged in the production of some article, thing, or object, by skill or labor, out of raw material, or from matter which has already been subjected to artificial forces, or to which something has been added to change its natural condition.

Manufacturing establishment. Any place where machinery is used for manufacturing purposes. Lilley v. Eberhardt, Mo., 37 S.W.2d 599, 601.

Manu forti /mǽn(y)uw fórday/. Lat. With strong hand. A term used in old writs of trespass. *Manu forti et cum multitudine gentium,* with strong hand and multitude of people.

Manu longa /mǽn(y)uw lóŋgə/. Lat. With a long hand. A term used in the civil law, signifying indirectly or circuitously.

Manumission /mænyəmíshən/. The act of liberating a slave from bondage and giving him freedom. In a wider sense, releasing or delivering one person from the power or control of another. Enfranchisement.

Manumittere idem est quod extra manum vel postestatem ponere /mænyəmídəriy áydəm èst kwód ékstrə mǽnəm vèl pòwdəstéydəm pównəriy/. To manumit is the same as to place beyond hand and power.

Manung, or **monung.** In old English law, the district within the jurisdiction of a reeve, apparently so called from his power to exercise therein one of his chief functions, viz., to exact *(amanian)* all fines.

Manu opera /mǽn(y)uw ópərə/. Lat. Cattle or implements of husbandry; also stolen goods taken from a thief caught in the fact.

Manupes /mǽnyəpìyz/. In old English law, a foot of full and legal measure.

Manupretium /mænyəpríysh(iy)əm/. Lat. In Roman law, the hire or wages of labor; compensation for labor or services performed.

Manurable /mən(y)úrəbəl/. In old English law, capable of being had or held in hand; capable of manual occupation; capable of being cultivated; capable of being touched; tangible; corporeal.

Manure. In old English law, to occupy; to use or cultivate; to have in manual occupation; to bestow manual labor upon.

Manus /mǽnəs/. Lat. A hand.

In the civil law, this word signified power, control, authority, the right of physical coercion, and was often used as synonymous with *"potestas."*

In old English law, it signified an oath or the person taking an oath; a compurgator.

Manuscript. An author's work product which is submitted to the publisher either in his own hand or typewritten. Lit., written by hand. A writing; a paper written with the hand; a writing that has not been printed.

Manus mortua /mǽnəs mórchuwə/. A dead hand; mortmain.

Manutenentia /mænyətənénsh(iy)ə/. The old writ of maintenance.

Manworth. In old English law, the price of value of a man's life or head.

Many. The word "many" is defined as consisting of a great number, numerous, not few. Many is a word of very indefinite meaning, and, though it is defined to be numerous and multitudinous, it is also recognized as synonymous with "several", "sundry", "various" and "divers". Goslin v. Kurn, 351 Mo. 395, 173 S.W.2d 79, 87.

Map. A representation of the earth's surface, or of some portion of it, showing the relative position of the parts represented, usually on a flat surface. See also **Plat map.**

Mapp v. Ohio. Landmark Supreme Court case decided in 1961 in which it was ruled that evidence illegally obtained by state officers is not admissible in a state trial if appropriate motions are filed to suppress. The rationale for the rule is that the 4th Amendment (U.S.Const.) protection against unreasonable search and seizure is applicable to the states under and through the 14th Amendment. Mapp v. Ohio, 367 U.S. 643, 81 S.Ct. 1684, 6 L.Ed.2d 1081.

Mar. To make defective; to damage greatly; to impair, spoil, ruin; to do physical injury to, especially by cutting off or defacing a part; to mutilate; mangle; disfigure; deface.

Mara /mérə/. In old records, a mere or moor; a lake, pool, or pond; a bog or marsh that cannot be drained.

Marajuana. See **Marihuana.**

Maraud. To rove about in search of booty; to pillage or plunder. To invade another's domain to pillage or to loot.

Marbury v. Madison. Landmark case decided in 1803 in which the Supreme Court established the right of the judicial branch to pass on the constitutionality of an act of Congress, thereby establishing the functions and prerogatives of the judiciary in its relation to the legislative branch. Marbury v. Madison, 5 U.S. (1 Cranch) 137, 2 L.Ed. 60.

Marcatus /markéydəs/. The rent of a mark by the year anciently reserved in leases, etc.

Marchandises avariees. In French mercantile law, damaged goods.

Marchers. In old English law, noblemen who lived on the marches of Wales or Scotland, and who, according to Camden, had their private laws, as if they had been petty kings; which were abolished by the statute 27 Hen. VIII, c. 26. Called also "lords marchers."

Marches. An old English term for boundaries or frontiers, particularly the boundaries and limits between England and Wales, or between England and Scotland, or the borders of the dominions of the crown, or the boundaries of properties in Scotland.

Marcheta /markéydə/. In old English law, a fine paid for leave to marry, or to bestow a daughter in marriage.

Marchioness /márshənès/. A dignity in a woman answerable to that of marquis in a man, conferred either by creation or by marriage with a marquis.

Mare /mériy/. Lat. The sea.

Marescallus /mærəskǽləs/. In old English law, a marshal; a master of the stables; an officer of the exchequer; a military officer of high rank, having powers and duties similar to those of a constable. See also **Marshal.**

Mareschal /mærəshǽl/. L. Fr. Marshal; a high officer of the royal household.

Marettum /mərédəm/. Marshy ground overflowed by the sea or great rivers.

Margin. The edge or border; the edge of a body of water where it meets the land. As applied to a boundary line of land, the "margin" of a river, creek, or other watercourse means the center of the stream. But in the case of a lake, bay, or natural pond, the "margin" means the line where land and water meet.

A sum of money, or its equivalent, placed in the hands of a stockbroker by the principal or person on whose account a purchase or sale is to be made, as a security to the former against losses to which he may be exposed by subsequent fluctuations in the market value of the stock. The amount paid by the customer when he uses his broker's credit to buy a security. See also **Margin account; Margin transaction.**

In commercial transactions the difference between the purchase price paid by a middleman or retailer and his selling price. Also called gross margin. See also **Profit.**

Margin account. Securities industry's method of extending credit to customers. Under such practice customer purchases specified amount of stock from securities firm by advancing only portion of purchase price, with brokerage firm extending credit or making loan for balance due, and firm maintains such stock as collateral for loan and charges interest on balance of purchase price. Stephens v. Reynolds Securities, Inc., D.C.Ala., 413 F.Supp. 50.

Marginal street. Dock or wharf used in conjunction with and in furtherance of commerce and navigation. In re Triborough Bridge Approach, City of New York, 159 Misc. 617, 288 N.Y.S. 697, 711, 716.

Margin call. A demand by a broker to put up money or securities upon purchase of a stock, or, if the stock is already owned on margin, to increase the money or securities in the event the price of the stock has fallen since purchase. The last process is remargining.

Margin list. List of Federal Reserve Board which limits the loan value of a bank's stock to a certain per cent (*e.g.* 50%) of its market value. When a bank is not on the margin list, no limit is placed on the value of its stock for use as collateral.

Margin profit. See **Margin; Profit.**

Margin trading. See **Margin; Margin account; Margin transaction.**

Margin transaction. The purchase of a stock or commodity with payment in part in cash (called the margin) and in part by a loan. Usually the loan is made by the broker effecting the purchase. See also **Margin account.**

Marihuana, mariguana, marijuana /mærə(h)wónə/. An annual herb, cannabis sativa, having angular rough stem and deeply lobed leaves. The bast fibres of cannabis are the hemp of commerce. A drug prepared from "cannabis sativa," designated in technical dictionaries as "cannabis" and commonly known as marijuana, marihuana, marajuana, maraguana, or marihuana. State v. Navaro, 83 Utah 6, 26 P.2d 955.

"Marihuana" means all parts of the plant Cannabis sativa L., whether growing or not; the seeds thereof; the resin extracted from any part of the plant; and every compound, manufacture, salt, derivative, mixture, or preparation of the plant, its seeds or resin. It does not include the mature stalks of the plant, fiber produced from the stalks, oil or cake made from the seeds of the plant, any other compound, manufacture, salt, derivative, mixture, or preparation of the mature stalks (except the resin extracted therefrom), fiber, oil, or cake, or the sterilized seed of the plant which is incapable of germination. Uniform Controlled Substances Act, § 101(n). See also **Cannabis.**

Marihuana is also commonly referred to as "pot", "grass", "tea", "weed" or "Mary-Jane"; and in cigarette form as a "joint" or "reefer".

Marinarius /mærənériyəs/. An ancient word which signified a mariner or seaman. In England, *marinarius capitaneus* was the admiral or warden of the ports.

Marine. Naval; relating or pertaining to the sea; native to or formed by the sea, such as marine life; transacted at sea; doing duty or service on the sea.

The mercantile and naval shipping of a country. Concerned with navigation and commerce of the sea; *i.e.* maritime matters. Member of U.S. Marine Corps. See also **Maritime.**

Marine belt. That portion of the main or open sea, adjacent to the shores of a given country, over which the jurisdiction of its municipal laws and local authorities extends. Territorial waters, defined by international law as extending out three miles from the shore. See also **Territorial waters.**

Marine carrier. By statutes of several states this term is applied to carriers plying upon the ocean, arms of the sea, the Great Lakes, and other navigable waters within the jurisdiction of the United States.

Marine contract. One relating to maritime affairs, shipping, navigation, marine insurance, affreightment, maritime loans, or other business to be done upon the sea or in connection with navigation.

Marine court in the city of New York. Formerly, a local court of New York City, originally created as a tribunal for the settlement of causes between seamen. It was the predecessor of the City Court of the city of New York.

Marine insurance. See **Insurance.**

Marine interest. Interest, allowed to be stipulated for at an extraordinary rate, for the use and risk of money loaned on *respondentia* and bottomry bonds.

Marine league /mǝríyn líyg/. A measure of distance commonly employed at sea, being equal to one-twentieth part of a degree of latitude, or three geographical or nautical miles.

Mariner. A seaman or sailor; one engaged in navigating vessels upon the sea; persons employed aboard ships or vessels.

Marine risk. The perils of the sea; the perils necessarily incident to navigation.

Mariner's will. A nuncupative or oral will permitted in some jurisdictions for the sailor who is actually at sea at the time of making the will. Generally, such will affects personal property only.

Maris et fœminæ conjunctio est de jure naturæ /mǽrǝs èt fémǝniy kǝnjóŋksh(iy)ow èst dìy júriy nǝchúriy/. The connection of male and female is by the law of nature.

Maritagio amisso per defaltam /mæ̀rǝtéyj(iy)ow ǝmísow pǝ̀r dǝfóltǝm/. An obsolete writ for the tenant in frank-marriage to recover lands, etc., of which he was deforced.

Maritagium /mæ̀rǝtéyj(iy)ǝm/. The portion which is given with a daughter in marriage. Also the power which the lord or guardian in chivalry had of disposing of his infant ward in matrimony.

Maritagium est aut liberum aut servitio obligatum; liberum maritagium dicitur ubi donator vult quod terra sic data quieta sit et libera ab omni seculari servitio. A marriage portion is either free or bound to service; it is called "frank-marriage" when the giver wills that land thus given be exempt from all secular service.

Maritagium habere /mæ̀rǝtéyj(iy)ǝm hǝbíriy/. To have the free disposal of an heiress in marriage.

Marital /mǽrǝdǝl/mǝráydǝl/. Relating to, or connected with, the *status* of marriage; pertaining to a husband; incident to a husband.

Marital agreements. Contracts between parties who are either on the threshold of marriage or on the verge of separation, though, in general, the term refers to all agreements between married people. Such agreements are primarily concerned with the division and ownership of marital property. In some jurisdictions, the contract must be made through a third person if the law does not permit the spouses to contract directly with each other. See also **Antenuptial settlements; Equitable distribution; Marriage settlement; Postnuptial agreement.**

Marital communications privilege. In most jurisdictions private communications between the spouses during the marriage are privileged at the option of the witness spouse and hence inadmissible in a trial. In some jurisdictions the communications are disqualified, and hence not admissible, even with the consent of the witness spouse. This privilege is subject to certain limitations; *e.g.* prosecutions for crimes committed by one spouse against the other or against the children of either. See also **Husband-wife privilege.**

Marital deduction. A deduction allowed upon the transfer of property from one spouse to another. The deduction is allowed under the Federal gift tax for lifetime (*i.e.,* inter vivos) transfers and also under the Federal estate tax for testamentary transfers. I.R.C. §§ 2056, 2523. See also **Pecuniary formulas.**

Minimum deduction. Under the Tax Reform Act of 1976, a minimum marital deduction of $250,000 is allowed for death tax purposes if this amount of qualifying property passes to the surviving spouse. The previous limitation of 50% of the deceased spouse's adjusted gross estate continues to be in effect when the marital deduction exceeds $250,000. The minimum marital deduction for gift tax purposes is the first $100,000 passing from one spouse to the other spouse. To the extent that the marital deduction allowed for gift tax purposes exceeds one-half of the value of the property transferred, there is a dollar-for-dollar offset to the estate's allowable minimum marital deduction (or the marital deduction computed in accordance with the 50% of the adjusted gross estate rule).

Marital deduction trust. In estate planning, a device in the form of a trust utilized to gain the maximum benefit of the marital deduction by dividing the property in half. Commonly, one half of the property is transferred to the marital deduction trust and the other half is disposed of in a trust or like arrangement with a view towards having it escape taxation in the estate of the surviving spouse.

Marital portion. In Louisiana, the name given to that part of a deceased husband's estate to which the widow is entitled.

Marital privileges. Those rights, immunities and advantages which attach to the state of marriage such as the right to connubial relations and the right to hold property as husband and wife. See also **Marital communications privilege.**

Marital property. Property purchased by persons while married to each other and which, in some jurisdictions, on dissolution of the marriage is divided in proportions as the court deems fit. Claunch v. Claunch, Mo.App., 525 S.W.2d 788, 790. See **Community property; Equitable distribution.**

Marital rights and duties. Those arising from marriage contract and constituting its object, and therefore embracing what the parties agree to perform towards each other and to society. Rights of husband and wife to a specified share of other's personal estate upon death of other. In re Dean's Estate, 350 Mo. 494, 166 S.W.2d 529, 534, 535.

Maritima Angliae /mərídəmə ǽngliyiy/. In old English law, the emolument or revenue coming to the king from the sea, which the sheriffs anciently collected, but which was afterwards granted to the admiral.

Maritima incrementa /mərídəmə iŋkrəméntə/. In old English law, marine increases. Lands gained from the sea.

Maritime. Pertaining to navigable waters, *i.e.* to the sea, ocean, great lakes, navigable rivers, or the navigation or commerce thereof.

All work occurring on navigable waters is "maritime" within meaning of Longshoremen's and Harbor Workers' Compensation Act. St. Julien v. Diamond M Drilling, D.C.La., 403 F.Supp. 1256, 1259.

See also **Federal Maritime Commission; Maritime court; Navigable waters.**

Maritime Administration. An agency within the Department of Commerce which promotes and regulates the activities of the U.S. merchant marine, directs emergency operations related to merchant marine activities, establishes specifications for shipbuilding and design, determines routes, and manages other areas of merchant operations. See also **Maritime Commission.**

Maritime belt. That part of the sea which, in contradistinction to the open sea, is under the sway of the riparian states. Louisiana v. Mississippi, 202 U.S. 1, 26 S.Ct. 408, 50 L.Ed. 913. See also **Marine belt; Territorial waters.**

Maritime bills. See **Bill** (*Maritime Law*).

Maritime cause. A case arising on the sea, ocean, great lakes, or navigable rivers, or from some act or contract concerning the commerce and navigation thereof. The Thomas Jefferson, 23 U.S. (10 Wheat.) 428, 6 L.Ed. 358; and Peyroux v. Howard, 32 U.S. (7 Pet.) 324, 8 L.Ed. 700. An action based upon an injury to a passenger of a vessel while on navigable waters and caused by negligence comes within scope of "maritime cause of action" within original jurisdiction of federal District Court. Cuozzo v. Italian Line, Italia-Societa Per Azioni Di Navigazione–Genoa, D.C.N.Y., 168 F.Supp. 304, 306. See also **Maritime law; Maritime tort; Navigable waters.**

Maritime Commission. The Federal Maritime Commission regulates the waterborne foreign and domestic offshore commerce of the United States, assures that United States international trade is open to all nations on fair and equitable terms, and guards against unauthorized monopoly in the waterborne commerce of the United States. This is accomplished through maintaining surveillance over steamship conferences and common carriers by water; assuring that only the rates on file with the Commission are charged; approving agreements between persons subject to the Shipping Act; guaranteeing equal treatment to shippers and carriers by terminal operators, freight forwarders, and other persons subject to the shipping statutes; and ensuring that adequate levels of financial responsibility are maintained for indemnification of passengers or oil spill cleanup. See also **Maritime Administration.**

Maritime contract. A contract relating to business of navigation. Massman Const. Co. v. Bassett, D.C.Mo., 30 F.Supp. 813, 815. A contract whose subject-matter has relation to the navigation of the seas or to trade or commerce to be conducted by navigation or to be done upon the sea or in ports. One having reference to maritime services or maritime transactions. Marubeni-Iida (America), Inc. v. Nippon Yusen Kaisha, D.C.N.Y., 207 F.Supp. 418, 419.

Maritime court. A court exercising jurisdiction in maritime causes; one which possesses the powers and jurisdiction of a court of admiralty. See **Admiralty Court; Maritime jurisdiction.**

Maritime interest. An expression equivalent to marine interest (*q.v.*).

Maritime jurisdiction. Jurisdiction over maritime causes is granted to Federal district courts. 28 U.S.C.A. § 1333. Procedure in maritime actions is governed by the Fed.R.Civil P. and Supp. Admiralty Rules. See **Admiralty Court.**

Maritime law. That which the Congress has enacted or the Federal courts, sitting in admiralty, or in the exercise of their maritime jurisdiction, have declared and would apply. J. B. Effenson Co. v. Three Bays Corp., C.A.Fla., 238 F.2d 611, 615. That system of law which particularly relates to marine commerce and navigation, to business transacted at sea or relating to navigation, to ships and shipping, to seamen, to the transportation of persons and property by sea, and to marine affairs generally. The law relating to harbors, ships, and seamen, divided into a variety of subject areas, such as those concerning harbors, property of ships, duties and rights of masters and seamen, contracts of affreightment, average, salvage, etc. It extends to civil marine torts and injuries, illegal dispossession or withholding of possession from the owners of ships, municipal seizures of ships, etc.

Substantively, in the United States, it is federal law, and jurisdiction to administer it is vested in the federal courts, though not to the entire exclusion of the courts of the states. O'Donnell v. Great Lakes Dredge & Dock Co., 318 U.S. 36, 63 S.Ct. 488, 87 L.Ed. 596. See **Maritime jurisdiction.**

Maritime lien. A privileged claim on a vessel for some service rendered to it to facilitate its use in navigation, or an injury caused by it in navigable waters, to be carried into effect by legal process in the admiralty court. The Westmoor, D.C.Or., 27 F.2d 886, 887. A special property right in a ship given to a creditor by law as security for a debt or claim subsisting from the moment the debt arises with right to have the ship sold and debt paid out of proceeds. Such a lien is a proprietary interest or right of property in the vessel itself, and not a cause of action or demand for personal judgment against the owner. The lien is enforced by a direct proceeding against the vessel or other property in which it exists.

Any person furnishing repairs, supplies, towage, use of dry dock or marine railway, or other necessaries, to any vessel, whether foreign or domestic, upon the order of the owner of such vessel, or of a person authorized by the owner, shall have a maritime lien on the vessel, which may be enforced by suit in rem, and it shall not be necessary to allege or prove that credit was given to the vessel. Federal Maritime Lien Act, § 971.

Maritime loan. A contract or agreement by which one, who is the lender, lends to another, who is the borrower, a certain sum of money, upon condition that if the thing upon which the loan has been made should be lost by any peril of the sea, or *vis major*, the lender shall not be repaid unless what remains shall be equal to the sum borrowed; and if the thing arrive in safety, or in case it shall not have been injured but by its own defects or the fault of the master or mariners, the borrower shall be bound to return the sum borrowed, together with a certain sum agreed upon as the price of the hazard incurred.

Maritime prize. See **Prize.**

Maritime service. In admiralty law, a service rendered upon the seas, ocean, great lakes, or a navigable river, and which has some relation to commerce or navigation,—some connection with a vessel employed in trade, with her equipment, her preservation, or the preservation of her cargo or crew.

Maritime state. In English law, consists of the officers and mariners of the British navy, who are governed by express and permanent laws, or the articles of the navy, established by act of parliament.

Maritime tort. Civil wrongs committed on navigable waters. Pierside Terminal Operators, Inc. v. M/V Floridian, D.C.Va., 374 F.Supp. 27, 30.

See **Jones Act; Longshoremen's and Harbor Workers' Compensation Act.**

Maritus /mɜráydəs/mǽrədəs/. Lat. A husband; a married man.

Mark. A character, usually in the form of a cross, made as a substitute for his signature by a person who cannot write, in executing a conveyance, will or other legal document.

It is commonly made as follows: A third person writes the name of the marksman, leaving a blank space between the Christian name and surname; in this space the latter traces the mark, or crossed lines, and above the mark is written "his" (or "her"), and below it, "mark."

The sign, writing, or ticket put upon manufactured goods to distinguish them from others, appearing thus in the compound, "trade-mark."

A token, evidence, or proof; as in the phrase "a mark of fraud."

A weight used in several parts of Europe, and for several commodities, especially gold and silver.

Monetary unit, *e.g.* German Deutsche mark.

The word is sometimes used as another form of "*marque,*" a license of reprisals.

In early Teutonic and English law, a species of village community, being the lowest unit in the political system; one of the forms of the *gens* or clan, variously known as the "*mark,*" "*gemeinde,*" "*commune,*" or "*parish.*" Also the land held in common by such a community. The union of several such village communities and their *marks*, or common lands, forms the next higher political union, the hundred.

See also **Bench mark; Certification mark; Collective mark.**

Demi-mark. Half a mark; a sum of money which was anciently required to be tendered in a writ of right, the effect of such tender being to put the demandant, in the first instance, upon proof of the seisin as stated in his count; that is, to prove that the seisin was in the king's reign there stated.

High and low water-mark. See **Water-mark.**

Trademark. See **Trade-mark.**

Marked money. Term used to describe money given by undercover agent who buys contraband or gives bribe in money, or ransom money given to kidnapper, or money given to bank robber, which bears a tell-tale mark for use in identifying and connecting the money to the perpetrator of the crime.

Market. Place of commercial activity in which articles are bought and sold. Zemel v. Commercial Warehouses, 132 N.J.L. 341, 40 A.2d 642, 643. The region in which any commodity can be sold; the geographical or economic extent of commercial demand. A public time and appointed place of buying and selling; also purchase and sale. It differs from the *forum*, or market of antiquity, which was a public marketplace on one side only, or during one part of the day only, the other sides being occupied by temples, theaters, courts of justice, and other public buildings.

In a limited sense, "market" is the range of bid and asked prices reported by brokers making the market in over-the-counter securities. Opper v. Hancock Securities Corp., D.C.N.Y., 250 F.Supp. 668, 675.

By the term "market" is also understood the demand there is for any particular article; as, "the cotton market is depressed." Is also an abbreviated term for "stock" or "commodity" markets.

See also **Common market; Current market value.**

Clerk of the market. See **Clerk of the market.**

Geographic market. In antitrust context, that geographic area in which a product is sold and in which there is or is not competition. It generally implies agreement allocating different areas to each competitor with the understanding that the other competitors will not sell in those areas. Timken Roller Bearing Co. v. U. S., 341 U.S. 593, 71 S.Ct. 971, 95 L.Ed. 1199. A relevant "geographic market" for purposes of assessing monopoly power is the territorial area in which businessmen effectively compete. Telex Corp. v. International Business Machines Corp., D.C.Okl., 367 F.Supp. 258, 336. Within broad geographic market, well-defined submarkets may exist which, in themselves, constitute "geographic markets" for antitrust purposes. U. S. Steel Corp. v. F. T. C., C.A. Ohio, 426 F.2d 592, 596. See also *Product market; Relevant market, infra.*

Listed market securities. The market value of a security as reflected by transactions of that security on the floor of an exchange.

Open market. A market wherein supply and demand are expressed in terms of a price.

Product market. In antitrust context, a market in which competitors agree among themselves to limit the manufacture or sales of products so as to prevent competition among themselves. Hartford Empire Co. v. U. S., 323 U.S. 386, 65 S.Ct. 373, 89 L.Ed. 322.

Public market. A market which is not only open to the resort of the general public as purchasers, but also available to all who wish to offer their wares for sale, stalls, stands, or places being allotted to those who apply, to the limits of the capacity of the market, on payment of fixed rents or fees.

Relevant market. In antitrust context, it may refer to geographic area in which competitors agree to respect the rights of others to sell a product. It may also refer to product markets in which competitors agree among themselves to limit the manufacture or sales of products so as to prevent or limit competition among themselves. Hartford Empire Co. v. U. S., 323 U.S. 386, 65 S.Ct. 373, 89 L.Ed. 322. See also **Relevant market.**

Marketability. Salability. The probability of selling property at a specific time, price, and terms.

Marketable. Salable. Such things as may be sold in the market; those for which a buyer may be found; merchantable.

Marketable securities. Stocks and bonds held of other companies that can be readily sold on stock exchanges or over-the-counter markets and that the company plans to sell as cash is needed. Classified as current liquid assets and as part of working capital.

Marketable title. A title which is free from encumbrances and any reasonable doubt as to its validity, and such as a reasonably intelligent person, who is well informed as to facts and their legal bearings, and ready and willing to perform his contract, would be willing to accept in exercise of ordinary business prudence. Sinclair v. Weber, 204 Md. 324, 104 A.2d 561, 565. Such a title as is free from reasonable doubt in law and in fact; not merely a title valid in fact, but one which readily can be sold or mortgaged to a reasonably prudent purchaser or mortgagee; one acceptable to a reasonable purchaser, informed as to the facts and their legal meaning, willing to perform his contract, in the exercise of that prudence which businessmen usually bring to bear on such transactions; one under which a purchaser may have quiet and peaceful enjoyment of the property; one that is free from material defects, or grave doubts, and reasonably free from litigation. Myrick v. Austin, 141 Kan. 778, 44 P.2d 266, 268.

Marketable title is one which is free from reasonable doubt and will not expose party who holds it to hazards of litigation. Tri-State Hotel Co. v. Sphinx Investment Co., 212 Kan. 234, 510 P.2d 1223, 1230.

One that may be freely made the subject of resale. Krulee v. F. C. Huyck & Sons, 121 Vt. 299, 156 A.2d 74, 77.

A marketable title to land is such a title as a court, when asked to decree specific performance of the contract of sale, will compel the vendee to accept as sufficient. It is said to be not merely a defensible title, but a title which is free from plausible or reasonable objections.

See also **Merchantable title.**

Marketable Title Acts. Many states have adopted Marketable Title Acts the purpose of which is to simplify land title transactions through making it possible to determine marketability by limited title searches over some reasonable period of the immediate past (*e.g.* 40 yrs.) and thus avoid the necessity of examining the record back into distant time for each new transaction.

Market geld. The toll of a market.

Marketing contract. An agreement between a cooperative and its members in which the members agree to sell their products through the cooperative and the cooperative agrees to obtain their price. Hiroshi Kaneko v. Jones, 192 Or. 523, 235 P.2d 768.

Market making. Regarding securities in over the counter trading, the process consisting of bid and ask quotations which results in the establishment of a market for such securities. Opper v. Hancock Securities Corp., D.C.N.Y., 250 F.Supp. 668, 671.

Market order. An order to buy or sell on a stock or commodity exchange at the current price when the order reaches the floor of the exchange.

Market overt. In English law, an open and public market. The market-place or spot of ground set apart by custom for the sale of particular goods is, in the country, the only market *overt;* but in London every shop in which goods are exposed publicly to sale is market overt, for such things only as the owner professes to trade in.

Market price. The price at which a seller is ready and willing to sell and a buyer ready and willing to buy in the ordinary course of trade. The price actually given in current market dealings; the actual price at which given stock or commodity is currently sold, or has recently been sold in open market, that is, not at forced sale, but in the usual and ordinary course of trade and competition between sellers and buyers equally free to bargain, as established by records of late sales. In the case of a security, market price is usually considered the last reported price at which the stock or bond sold.

Market price is synonymous with market value, and means the price actually given in current market dealings, or the price at which the supply and demand are equal. Public Service Commission of State v. Montana-Dakota Utilities Co., N.D., 100 N.W.2d 140, 146. The point of intersection of supply and demand in the market.

See also **Market value.**

Market quotations. The latest (most current) prices at which securities or commodities have been bought and sold on an exchange or other market. Board of

Trade of Chicago v. L. A. Kinsey Co., C.A.Ind., 130 F. 507, aff'd 198 U.S. 236, 25 S.Ct. 637, 49 L.Ed. 1031.

Market share. The percentage of a market that is controlled by a firm. A 20 percent share of market means that the firm has captured 20 percent of the actual sales in the market.

Market structure. Refers to the broad organizational characteristics of a market. The major characteristics are seller concentration, product differentiation, and barriers to entry.

Market value. The price property would command in the market. The highest price a willing buyer would pay and a willing seller accept, both being fully informed, and the property being exposed for a reasonable period of time. The market value may be different from the price a property can actually be sold for at a given time (market price). The market value of an article or piece of property is the price which it might be expected to bring if offered for sale in a fair market; not the price which might be obtained on a sale at public auction or a sale forced by the necessities of the owner, but such a price as would be fixed by negotiation and mutual agreement, after ample time to find a purchaser, as between a vendor who is willing (but not compelled) to sell and a purchaser who desires to buy but is not compelled to take the particular article or piece of property. U. S. v. Certain Property in Borough of Manhattan, City, County and State of New York, C.A.N.Y., 403 F.2d 800, 802. See also Actual market value; Clear market value; Fair cash market value; Fair market value.

Marking up. The process wherein a legislative committee goes through a bill section by section, revising its language and amending the bill as desired. Extensive revision may lead to the introduction of a clean bill under a new number. May also refer to procedure by which a case is placed on the trial calendar; *e.g.* "marking up for trial."

Markon. An amount originally added to cost to obtain list price. Usually expressed as a percentage of cost. Further increases in list price are called markups; decreases are called markdowns. See also **Markup.**

Marksman. In practice and conveyancing, one who makes his mark; a person who cannot write, and only makes his mark in executing instruments.

Markup. An amount originally added to cost. Usually expressed as a percentage of selling price. Also refers to an increase above an originally-established retail price. See **Markon.**

Markush doctrine /márkəsh dóktrən/. The doctrine permits an applicant for a patent where there is no known subgeneric term which would include elements which applicant found useful and exclude those which are not, to employ a generic term limited to the elements found to be operative and recognizes as unobjectionable as to form, claims containing a coined subgeneric expression. In re Swenson, C.C. P.A., 132 F.2d 336.

Marque and reprisal, letters of /lédərz əv márk ən rəprάyzəl/. These words, "marque" and "reprisal," are frequently used as synonymous, but, taken in their strict etymological sense, the latter signifies "taking in return;" the former, the passing the frontiers (*marches*) in order to such taking. Letters of marque and reprisal are grantable, by the law of nations, whenever the subjects of one state are oppressed and injured by those of another, and justice is denied by that state to which the oppressor belongs; and the party to whom these letters are granted may then seize the bodies or the goods of the subjects of the state to which the offender belongs, until satisfaction be made, wherever they happen to be found. Reprisals are to be granted only in case of a clear and open denial of justice. At the present day, in consequence partly of treaties and partly of the practice of nations, the making of reprisals is confined to the seizure of commercial property on the high seas by public cruisers, or by private cruisers specially authorized thereto. Article I, Sec. 8, of U.S.Const. grants Congress the power to grant Letters of Marque and Reprisal.

Marque, law of /ló əv márk/. A sort of law of reprisal, which entitles him who has received any wrong from another and cannot get ordinary justice to take the shipping or goods of the wrongdoer, where he can find them within his own bounds or precincts, in satisfaction of the wrong.

Marquis, or **marquess** /màrkíy/márkwəs/. In English law, one of the second order of nobility; next in order to a duke.

Marquisate /márkwəsət/°zət/. The seigniory of a marquis.

Marriage. Legal union of one man and one woman as husband and wife. Singer v. Hara, 11 Wash.App. 247, 522 P.2d 1187, 1193. Marriage, as distinguished from the agreement to marry and from the act of becoming married, is the legal status, condition, or relation of one man and one woman united in law for life, or until divorced, for the discharge to each other and the community of the duties legally incumbent on those whose association is founded on the distinction of sex. A contract, according to the form prescribed by law, by which a man and woman capable of entering into such contract, mutually engage with each other to live their whole lives (or until divorced) together in state of union which ought to exist between a husband and wife. The word also signifies the act, ceremony, or formal proceeding by which persons take each other for husband and wife.

In old English law, marriage is used in the sense of "*maritagium*" (q.v.), or the feudal right enjoyed by the lord or guardian in chivalry of disposing of his ward in marriage.

See also Avail of marriage; Banns of matrimony; Common-law marriage; Consensual marriage; Restraint of marriage; Voidable marriage; Void marriage.

Ceremonial marriage. Marriage which follows all the statutory requirements of blood tests, license, waiting period, and which has been solemnized before an official (religious or civil) capable of presiding at the marriage.

Informal marriage. A marriage in which promises are exchanged between the parties without an official ecclesiastical representative present. In most cases, the law requires consummation of the marriage to consider such valid. See **Consensual marriage.**

Jactitation of marriage. See **Jactitation.**

Manus marriage. A form of marriage in early Rome; it formed a relation called *manus* (hand) and brought the wife into the husband's power, placing her as to legal rights in the position of a daughter.

Marriage in jest. A marriage in jest is subject to annulment for lack of requisite consent and intention to marry.

Mixed marriage. A marriage between persons of different nationalities or religions; or, more particularly, between persons of different racial origin; as between a white person and a negro or an Indian. See **Miscegenation.**

Morganatic marriage. The lawful and inseparable conjunction of a man, of noble or illustrious birth, with a woman of inferior station, upon condition that neither the wife nor her children shall partake of the titles, arms, or dignity of the husband, or succeed to his inheritance, but be contented with a certain allowed rank assigned to them by the morganatic contract. But since these restrictions relate only to the rank of the parties and succession to property, without affecting the nature of a matrimonial engagement, it must be considered as a just marriage. The marriage ceremony is regularly performed; the union is indissoluble; the children legitimate.

Plural marriage. In general, any bigamous or polygamous union, but particularly, a second or subsequent marriage of a man who already has one wife living under system of polygamy. Such marriages are prohibited.

Proxy marriage. Marriage contracted or celebrated by one or more agents rather than by the parties themselves.

Putative marriage. One contracted in good faith and in ignorance of some existing impediment on the part of at least one of the contracting parties. U. S. Fidelity & Guaranty Co. v. Henderson, Tex.Civ.App., 53 S.W.2d 811. Such marriages are recognized in very few jurisdictions.

Marriage Act, Royal. An English act of 12 Geo. III, c. 1 (1772), by which members of the royal family are forbidden to marry without the king's (or queen's) consent, or except on certain onerous conditions.

Marriage articles. Articles of agreement between parties contemplating marriage, intended as preliminary to a formal marriage settlement, to be drawn after marriage.

Marriage broker. One who for a consideration brings a woman and man together in marriage. Such activity is void and illegal as against public policy.

Marriage ceremony. The form, religious or civil, for the solemnization of a marriage.

Marriage certificate. An instrument which certifies a marriage, and is executed by the person officiating at the marriage; it is not intended to be signed by the parties, but is evidence of the marriage.

Marriage license. A license or permission granted by public authority to persons who intend to intermarry, usually addressed to the minister or magistrate who is to perform the ceremony, or, in general terms, to any one authorized to solemnize marriages. By statute in most jurisdictions, it is made an essential prerequisite to the lawful solemnization of the marriage.

Marriage-notice book. A book kept, in England, by the registrar, in which applications for and issue of registrar's licenses to marry are recorded.

Marriage per verba de praesenti /mǽrəj pər vərbə dìy prəzéntay/. To constitute such a marriage, there must be an agreement to become husband and wife immediately from the time when the mutual consent is given. Pitney v. Pitney, 151 Kan. 848, 101 P.2d 933, 935.

Marriage portion. Dowry; a sum of money or other property which is given to or settled on a woman on her marriage.

Marriage promise. Betrothal; engagement to intermarry with another.

Marriage records. Those documents kept by a state, city or town official which are permanent records of marriages and which include the names of the spouses, the maiden name of the wife, their addresses and the date of the marriage. From these documents certificates of marriages are prepared.

Marriage settlement. An agreement in contemplation of marriage in which each party agrees to release or modify property rights which would otherwise arise from the marriage. A written agreement in the nature of a conveyance, called a "settlement," which is made in contemplation of a proposed marriage and in consideration thereof, either by the parties about to marry, or one of them, or by a parent or relation on their behalf, by which the title to certain property is settled, *i.e.,* fixed or limited to a prescribed course of succession; the object being, usually, to provide for the wife and children. Thus, the estate might be limited to the husband and issue, or to the wife and issue, or to husband and wife for their joint lives, remainder to the survivor for life, remainder over to the issue, or otherwise. Such settlements may also be made after marriage, in which case they are called "postnuptial." See also; **Antenuptial agreement; Marital agreements; Palimony; Postnuptial agreement.**

Married woman. A woman who has a husband living and not divorced; a *feme covert.*

Marshal. The President is required to appoint a U.S. Marshal to each judicial district. It is the responsibility of U.S. marshals to execute all lawful writs, process and orders issued under authority of the United States. In executing the laws of the United States within a state, the marshal may exercise the same powers which a sheriff of the State may exercise in executing the laws thereof. 28 U.S.C.A. §§ 561, 569, 570.

Also, in some of the states, this is the name of a law officer in certain cities having powers and duties corresponding generally to those of a constable or sheriff. Administrative head of city police or fire department.

See also **Provost-Marshall.**

In old English law, the title borne by several officers of state and of the law, of whom the most important were the following: (1) The earl-marshal, who presided in the court of chivalry; (2) the marshal of the king's house, or knight-marshal, whose special authority was in the king's palace, to hear causes between members of the household, and punish faults committed within the verge; (3) the marshal of the king's bench prison, who had the custody of that jail; (4) the marshal of the exchequer, who had the custody of the king's debtors; (5) the marshal of the judge of assize, whose duty was to swear in the grand jury.

Marshaling. Arranging, ranking, or disposing in order; particularly, in the case of a group or series of conflicting claims or interests, arranging them in such an order of sequence, or so directing the manner of their satisfaction, as shall secure justice to all persons concerned and the largest possible measure of satisfaction to each. Equitable doctrine of "marshaling" rests upon principle that creditor having two funds to satisfy his debt may not, by his application of them to his demand, defeat another creditor, who may resort to only one of the funds. Columbia Bank for Cooperatives v. Lee, C.A.N.C., 368 F.2d 934, 939. Under the doctrine of "marshaling", one claiming a lien against two or more classes of property, one of which is also subject to a junior lien, is required to exact satisfaction from the property not subject to the junior lien; thus, the junior lien is preserved where other assets exist sufficient to satisfy the senior lien. In re Einhorn Bros., Inc., D.C.Pa., 171 F.Supp. 655, 660. See sub-titles *infra.*

Marshaling assets. In equity, the arranging or ranking of assets in the due order of administration. Such an arrangement of the different funds under administration as shall enable all the parties having equities therein to receive their due proportions, notwithstanding any intervening interests, liens, or other claims of particular persons to prior satisfaction out of a portion of these funds. In re Van Zandt's Estate, 142 Misc. 663, 255 N.Y.S. 359, 366. The arrangement or ranking of assets in a certain order towards the payment of debts. The arrangement of assets or claims so as to secure the proper application of the assets to the various claims; especially when there are two classes of assets, and some creditors can enforce their claims against both, and others against only one, and the creditors of the former class are compelled to exhaust the assets against which they alone have a claim before having recourse to other assets, thus providing for the settlement of as many claims as possible. Equitable rule of "marshaling assets" is that where one claimant has two funds to which he may resort to answer his demand, and another claimant has interest in only one of such funds, he can compel former to take satisfaction out of fund in which latter has no lien. In re Creem's Will, Sur., 147 N.Y.S.2d 634, 636.

Marshaling liens. The ranking or ordering of several estates or parcels of land, for the satisfaction of a judgment or mortgage to which they are all liable, though successively conveyed away by the debtor. The rule is that, where lands subject to the lien of a judgment or mortgage have been sold or incumbered by the owner at different times to different purchasers, the various tracts are liable to the satisfaction of the lien in the inverse order of their alienation or incumbrance, the land last sold being first chargeable.

Marshaling remedies. The basis for "marshaling of remedies" is that where one creditor has security on two funds of common debtor and another creditor has security on only one of such funds, second creditor has right in equity to compel first creditor to resort to the other fund, if it is necessary for satisfaction of both creditors and will not prejudice rights or interests of party entitled to double fund, do injustice to debtor, or operate inequitably on other persons' interests. Greenwich Trust Co. v. Tyson, 129 Conn. 211, 27 A.2d 166, 174.

Marshaling securities. An equitable practice, which consists in so ranking or arranging classes of creditors, with respect to the assets of the common debtor, as to provide for satisfaction of the greatest number of claims. The process is this: where one class of creditors have liens or securities on *two* funds, while another class of creditors can resort to only *one* of those funds, equity will compel the doubly-secured creditors to first exhaust that fund which will leave the single security of the other creditors intact.

Marshal of the queen's bench. An officer who had the custody of the queen's bench prison. The St. 5 & 6 Vict., c. 22, abolished this office, and substituted an officer called "keeper of the queen's prison."

Marshalsea /márshəlsìy/. In English law, a prison belonging to the king's bench. It was subsequently consolidated with others, under the name of the "King's Prison."

Marshalsea, court of /kórd əv márshəlsìy/. In English law, the court or seat of the marshal. A court originally held before the steward and marshal of the king's house, instituted to administer justice between the king's domestic servants. It had jurisdiction of all trespasses committed within the verge of the king's court, where one of the parties was of the royal household; and of all debts and contracts, when both parties were of that establishment. It was abolished by 12 & 13 Vict., c. 101, § 13.

Mart. A place of public traffic or sale. See also **Market.**

Marte suo decurrere /márdiy s(y)úwow dəkə́hrəriy/. Lat. To run by its own force. A term applied in the civil law to a suit when it ran its course to the end without any impediment.

Martial law /márshəl ló/. Exists when military authorities carry on government or exercise various degrees of control over civilians or civilian authorities in domestic territory. Ochikubo v. Bonesteel, D.C.Cal., 60 F.Supp. 916, 928, 929, 930. Such may exist either in time of war or when civil authority has ceased to function or has become ineffective. A system of law, obtaining only in time of actual war and growing out of the exigencies thereof, arbitrary in its character, and depending only on the will of the commander of an army, which is established and administered in a place or district of hostile territory held in belligerent possession, or, sometimes, in places occupied or pervaded by insurgents or mobs, and which suspends all existing civil laws, as well as the civil authority and the ordinary administration of justice. See also **Military government; Military law.**

Mary Carter agreement. A settlement device used in multiparty litigation. Under the typical Mary Carter agreement the plaintiff releases his cause of action against a joint tortfeasor in return for the settling joint tortfeasor's continued participation in the trial. The plaintiff also promises to pay the settling tortfeasor a portion of the recovery received from the nonsettling tortfeasor. The settling tortfeasor thus represents himself to be a defendant whose financial interest is adverse to the plaintiff, while in fact he has a vested financial interest in the success of the plaintiff's cause of action against the nonsettling defendant. Daniel v. Penrod Drilling Co., D.C.La., 393 F.Supp. 1056.

Mashgiach /mashgíyək/. A qualified supervisor designated by rabbinical authority to supervise the receipt and handling of kosher meat. People on Complaint of Waller v. Jacob Branfman & Son, 147 Misc. 290, 263 N.Y.S. 629.

Masochism /mǽsəkizəm/. [From Leopold von Sacher-Masoch, a nineteenth-century Austrian novelist and historian.] A form of perversion in which sexual pleasure is heightened when one is beaten and maltreated at the hands of the other party; the opposite of sadism. Sexual perversion, in which a member of one sex takes delight in being dominated, even to the extent of violence or cruelty, by one of the other sex.

Mason and Dixon Line. The boundary line between Pennsylvania on the north and Maryland on the south, celebrated before the extinction of slavery as the line of demarcation between the slave and the free states. It was run by Charles Mason and Jeremiah Dixon, commissioners in a dispute between the Penn Proprietors and Lord Baltimore. The line was carried 244 miles from the Delaware river where it was stopped by Indians. A resurvey was made in 1849, and in 1900 a new survey was authorized by the two states.

Massa /mǽsə/. In the civil law, a mass; an unwrought substance, such as gold or silver, before it is wrought into cups or other articles.

Massachism. See **Masochism.**

Massachusetts ballot. The office-block type of Australian ballot in which, under each office, the names of candidates, with party designations, are printed in alphabetical order.

Massachusetts rule. As regards sending out checks through banks for collection, the "Massachusetts rule" is that each bank that receives the item acts as an agent for the depositor; but in some other states, the "New York rule" prevails, under which only the bank first receiving the item is responsible to, or is the agent of, the depositor, the other banks being the agent of the bank, in the process of the collection.

Massachusetts trust. A business organization wherein property is conveyed to trustees and managed for benefit of holders of certificates like corporate stock certificates. A "Massachusetts business trust" is an unincorporated association organized under Massachusetts law for purpose of investing in real estate in much the same manner as a mutual fund invests in corporate securities. Kusner v. First Pa. Corp., D.C. Pa., 395 F.Supp. 276, 281.

Masses. Religious ceremonials or observances of the Roman Catholic Church.

Master. A principal who employs another to perform service in his affairs and who controls or has right to control physical conduct of other in performance of the service. Restatement, Second, Agency, § 2. A "master" is one standing to another in such a relation that he not only controls the results of the work of that other but also may direct the manner in which such work shall be done. Matonti v. Research-Cottrell, Inc., D.C.Pa., 202 F.Supp. 527, 532.

One having authority; one who rules, directs, instructs, or superintends; a head or chief; an instructor; an employer. Applied to several judicial officers. See *infra.*

One who has reached the summit of his trade and who has the right to hire apprentices and journeymen.

Fed.R.Civil P. 53, and analogous state rules, provide for the appointment by the court of a master to assist it in specific judicial duties as may arise in a case. The master's powers and duties depend upon the terms of the order of reference and the controlling court rule, and may include taking of testimony, discovery of evidence and other acts or measures necessary for the performance of his duties specified in the order of reference. The master is required to prepare a report of his proceedings for the court. In the federal courts the appointment of a master is the "exception rather than the rule", while under money state rules, the court has more liberal powers to appoint such. See also **Reference.**

Special master. A master appointed to act as the representative of the court in some particular act or transaction, as, to make a sale of property under a decree. Pewabic Min. Co. v. Mason, 145 U.S. 349, 12 S.Ct. 887, 36 L.Ed. 732.

Master agreement. The omnibus labor agreement reached between a union and the leaders of the industry or a trade association. It becomes the pattern for labor agreements between the union and individual employers.

Master and servant. The relation of master and servant exists where one person, for pay or other valuable consideration, enters into the service of another and devotes to him his personal labor for an agreed period. The relation exists where the employer has the right to select the employee, the power to remove and discharge him and the right to direct both what work shall be done and the manner in which it shall be done. Matonti v. Research-Cottrell, Inc., D.C.Pa., 202 F.Supp. 527, 532. Such term has generally been replaced by "employer and employee".

Master at common law. The title of officers of the English superior courts of common law appointed to record the proceedings of the court to which they belong; to superintend the issue of writs and the formal proceedings in an action; to receive and account for the fees charged on legal proceedings, and moneys paid into court.

Master deed or **lease.** Conveyancing document used by owners or lessees of condominiums.

Master in chancery. An officer of a court of chancery who acts as an assistant to the judge or chancellor. His duties are to inquire into such matters as may be referred to him by the court, examine causes, take testimony, take accounts, compute damages, etc., reporting his findings to the court in such shape that a decree may be made; also to take oaths and affidavits and acknowledgments of deeds. In modern practice, many of the functions of a master are performed by clerks, commissioners, auditors, and referees, and in those states that have merged law and equity courts in adopting Rules of Civil Procedure the office has been superseded. See **Master.**

Master in lunacy. In old English law, the masters in lunacy were judicial officers appointed by the lord chancellor for the purpose of conducting inquiries into the state of mind of persons alleged to have been lunatics. Such inquiries usually took place before a jury.

Master of a ship. In maritime law, the commander of a merchant vessel, who has the chief charge of her government and navigation and the command of the crew, as well as the general care and control of the vessel and cargo, as the representative and confidential agent of the owner. He is commonly called the "captain."

Master of the Crown Office. In England, the Queen's coroner and attorney in the criminal department of the court of Queen's bench, who prosecutes at the complaint or relation of some private person or common informer, the crown being the nominal prosecutor. He is an officer of the Supreme Court.

Master of the Faculties. In English law, an officer under the archbishop, who grants licenses and dispensations, etc.

Master of the Horse. In English law, the third great officer of the royal household, being next to the lord steward and lord chamberlain. He has the privilege of making use of any horses, footmen, or pages belonging to the royal stables.

Master of the Mint. In English law, an officer who receives bullion for coinage, and pays for it, and superintends everything belonging to the mint. He is usually called the "warden of the mint." It is provided by St. 33 Vict., c. 10, § 14, that the chancellor of the exchequer for the time being shall be the master of the mint.

Master of the Ordnance. In English law, a great officer, to whose care all the royal ordnance and artillery were committed.

Master of the rolls. In English law, an assistant judge of the court of chancery, who held a separate court ranking next to that of the lord chancellor, and had the keeping of the rolls and grants which passed the great seal, and the records of the chancery. He was originally appointed only for the superintendence of the writs and records appertaining to the common-law department of the court, and is still properly the chief of the masters in chancery. Under the act constituting the Supreme Court of Judicature, the master of the rolls became a judge of the high court of justice and *ex officio* a member of the court of appeal. The same act, however, provided for the abolition of this office, under certain conditions when the next vacancy occurs.

Master plan. Term used in land use control law, zoning and urban redevelopment to describe the omnibus plan of a city or town for housing, industry and recreational facilities and their impact on environmental factors. See also **Planned unit development.**

Master policy. An insurance policy which covers a group of persons as in health or life insurance written as group insurance. Generally, there is only one master policy and the participants have only certificates evidencing their participation.

Masters of the supreme court. In English law, officials deriving their title from Jud. (Officers') Act 1879, and being, or filling the places of, the sixteen masters of the common-law courts, the queen's coroner and attorney, the master of the crown office, the two record and writ clerks, and the three associates.

Master's report. The formal report or statement made by a master in chancery of his decision on any question referred to him, or of any facts or action he has been directed to ascertain or take.

The document filed with the court after a master has heard the evidence and made his findings. The report should contain his findings and conclusions of law where necessary. Fed.R.Civil P. 53(e).

Mast-selling. In old English law, the practice of selling the goods of dead seamen at the mast.

Mate. A spouse. The officer second in command on a merchant vessel. In Navy, petty officer who is assistant to warranty officer.

Matelotage /mǽtlowtázh/. In French law, the hire of a ship or boat.

Seamanship; seaman's wages, pay.

Mater-familias /méydər fəmíl(i)yəs/. Lat. In civil law, the mother or mistress of a family. A chaste woman, married or single.

Materia /mətír(i)yə/. Lat. In Civil law, materials; as distinguished from *species,* or the *form* given by labor and skill.

In English law, matter; substance; subject-matter. 3 Bl.Comm. 322.

Material. Important; more or less necessary; having influence or effect; going to the merits; having to do with matter, as distinguished from form. Representation relating to matter which is so substantial and important as to influence party to whom made is "material." See **Material fact.**

Material allegation. An allegation is said to be material when it forms a substantive part of the case presented by the pleading. A material allegation in a pleading is one essential to the claim or defense, and which could not be stricken from the pleading without leaving it insufficient.

Material alteration. A material alteration in any written instrument is one which changes its tenor, or its legal meaning and effect; one which causes it to speak a language different in effect from that which it originally spoke. A material alteration of a deed is one which effects a change in its legal effect. Boys v. Long, Okl., 268 P.2d 890, 893.

Any alteration of an instrument is material which changes the contract of any party thereto in any respect, including any such change in: (a) the number or relations of the parties; or (b) an incomplete instrument, by completing it otherwise than as authorized; or (c) the writing as signed, by adding to it or by removing any part of it. U.C.C. § 3–407(1).

Material evidence. That quality of evidence which tends to influence the trier of fact because of its logical connection with the issue. Evidence which has an effective influence or bearing on question in issue is "material". Barr v. Dolphin Holding Corp., Sup., 141 N.Y.S.2d 906, 908. "Materiality" of evidence refers to pertinency of the offered evidence to the issue in dispute. Vine Street Corp. v. City of Council Bluffs, Iowa, 220 N.W.2d 860, 863.

Material evidence is evidence which is material to question in controversy, and which must necessarily enter into the consideration of the controversy, and which by itself or in connection with other evidence is determinative of the case. Camurati v. Sutton, 48 Tenn.App. 54, 342 S.W.2d 732, 739.

See also **Evidence; Relevancy; Relevant evidence.**

Material fact. *Contracts.* One which constitutes substantially the consideration of the contract, or without which it would not have been made. See also **Reliance.**

Insurance. A fact which, if communicated to the agent or insurer, would induce him either to decline the insurance altogether, or not accept it unless a higher premium is paid. One which necessarily has some bearing on the subject-matter. A fact which increases the risk, or which, if disclosed, would have been a fair reason for demanding a higher premium. Any fact the knowledge or ignorance of which would naturally influence the insurer in making or refusing the contract, or in estimating the degree and character of the risk, or in fixing the rate.

Pleading and practice. One which is essential to the case, defense, application, etc., and without which it could not be supported. One which tends to establish any of issues raised. The "material facts" of an issue of fact are such as are necessary to determine the issue. Material fact is one upon which outcome of litigation depends. Amant v. Pacific Power & Light Co., 10 Wash.App. 785, 520 P.2d 481, 484.

Securities. To be a "material" fact within the Securities Act of 1933, it must concern information about which an average prudent investor ought reasonably be informed before purchasing a security. Gridley v. Sayre & Fisher Co., D.C.S.D., 409 F.Supp. 1266, 1270. With respect to securities fraud violations, a material fact is one that a reasonable man would attach importance to in determining his choice of action in the transaction in question. List v. Fashion Park, Inc., C.A.N.Y., 340 F.2d 457; Gilbert v. Nixon, C.A.Kan., 429 F.2d 348. An omitted fact is material if there is a substantial likelihood that a reasonable shareholder would consider it important in deciding how to vote.

TSC Industries, Inc. v. Northway Inc., 426 U.S. 438, 96 S.Ct. 2126, 48 L.Ed.2d 757. See also **Reliance; Rule 10b–5.**

Summary judgment. In determining what constitutes a genuine issue as to any material fact for purposes of summary judgment, an issue is "material" if the facts alleged are such as to constitute a legal defense or are of such nature as to affect the result of the action. Austin v. Wilder, 26 N.C.App. 229, 215 S.E.2d 794, 796. See Fed.R.Civil P. 56(c).

A fact is "material" and precludes grant of summary judgment if proof of that fact would have effect of establishing or refuting one of essential elements of a cause of action or defense asserted by the parties, and would necessarily affect application of appropriate principle of law to the rights and obligations of the parties. Johnson v. Soulis, Wyo., 542 P.2d 867, 872.

Materialman. A person who has furnished materials or supplies used in the construction or repair of a building, structure, etc.

Materialman's lien. By statute in most states, a person who furnishes material for the construction, improvement or alteration of a building or other structure has a priority for payment of his claim based on his lien as a supplier of such materials. See also **Mechanic's lien.**

Material representation. In law of deceit, a statement or undertaking of sufficient substance and importance as to be the foundation of an action if such representation is false. See also **Material fact; Representation.**

Material witness. A person who can give testimony no one else, or at least very few, can give. In an important criminal case, a material witness may sometimes be held by the government against his or her will. He may be the victim or an eye witness. See also **Witness.**

Maternal. That which belongs to, or comes from, the mother; as maternal authority, maternal relation, maternal estate, maternal line.

Maternal line. A line of descent or relationship between two persons which is traced through the mother of the younger.

Maternal property. That which comes from the mother of the party, and other ascendants of the maternal stock.

Materna maternis /mətárnə mətárnəs/. Lat. A maxim of the French law, signifying that property of a decedent acquired by him through his mother descends to the relations on the mother's side.

Maternity. The character, relation, state, or condition of a mother.

Matertera /mətártərə/. Lat. In civil law, a maternal aunt; a mother's sister.

Matertera magna /mətártərə mǽgnə/. A great aunt; a grandmother's sister (*aviæ soror*).

Matertera major /mətártərə méyjər/. A greater aunt; a great-grandmother's sister (*proaviæ soror*); a father's or mother's great-aunt *(patris vel matris matertera magna).*

Matertera maxima /mətə́rdərə mǽksəmə/. A greatest aunt; a great-great-grandmother's sister *(abaviæ soror);* a father's or mother's greater aunt *(patris vel matris matertera major).*

Mathematical evidence. Demonstrative evidence; such as establishes its conclusions with absolute necessity and certainty. It is used in contradistinction to *moral* evidence.

Matima. A godmother.

Matricide /mǽtrəsàyd/. The murder of a mother; or one who has slain his mother.

Matricula /mətríkyələ/. In civil and old English law, a register of the admission of officers and persons entered into any body or society, whereof a list was made. Hence those who are admitted to a college or university are said to be "matriculated." Also a kind of almshouse, which had revenues appropriated to it, and was usually built near the church, whence the name was given to the church itself.

Matriculate /mətríkyəleyt/. To enroll; to enter in a register; specifically, to enter or admit to membership in a body or society, particularly in a college or university, by enrolling the name in a register; to go through the process of admission to membership, as by examination and enrollment, in a society or college.

Matrimonia debent esse libera /mǽtrəmówn(i)yə débənt ésiy líbərə/. Marriages ought to be free. A maxim of the civil law.

Matrimonial. Of or pertaining to matrimony or the estate of marriage.

Matrimonial action. The term "matrimonial action" includes actions for a separation, for an annulment or dissolution of a marriage, for a divorce, for a declaration of the nullity of a void marriage, for a declaration of the validity or nullity of a foreign judgment of divorce and for a declaration of the validity or nullity of a marriage. New York C.P.L.R. § 105. See also **Annulment; Custody; Divorce; Equitable distribution; Separation of Spouses.**

Matrimonial cohabitation. The living together of a man and woman ostensibly as husband and wife. Also the living together of those who are legally husband and wife, the term carrying with it, in this sense, an implication of mutual rights and duties as to sharing the same habitation.

Matrimonial domicile. Place where parties live together as husband and wife either actually or constructively.

Matrimonial res /mǽtrəmówn(i)yəl ríyz/. The marriage state. Usen v. Usen, 136 Me. 480, 13 A.2d 738, 749.

Matrimonium /mǽtrəmówn(i)yəm/. Lat. In Roman law, a legal marriage, contracted in strict accordance with the forms of the older Roman law, *i.e.,* either with the *farreum,* the *coemptio,* or by *usus.* This was allowed only to Roman citizens and to those neighboring peoples to whom the right of *connubium* had been conceded. The effect of such a marriage was to bring the wife into the *manus,* or marital power, of the husband, and to create the *patria potestas* over the children.

Matrimonium subsequens tollit peccatum præcedens /mǽtrəmówn(i)yəm sə́bsəkwən(d)z tólət pəkéydəm prəsíydèn(d)z/. Subsequent marriage cures preceding criminality.

Matrimony. Marriage *(q.v.),* in the sense of the relation or *status,* not of the ceremony.

Matrix /méytrəks/. In civil law, the protocol or first draft of a legal instrument, from which all copies must be taken.

Matrix ecclesia /méytrəks əklíyziyə/. Lat. A mother church. This term was anciently applied to a cathedral, in relation to the other churches in the same see, or to a parochial church, in relation to the chapels or minor churches attached to it or depending on it.

Matron. A married woman; an elderly woman. The female superintendent of an establishment or institution, such as a hospital, an orphan asylum, etc., is often so called.

Matrons, jury of. Jury impaneled to determine if a woman condemned to death is pregnant. In common-law practice, a jury of twelve matrons or discreet women, impaneled upon a writ *de ventre inspiciendo,* or where a female prisoner, being under sentence of death, pleaded her pregnancy as a ground for staying execution. In the latter case, such jury inquired into the truth of the plea.

Matter. Substantial facts forming basis of claim or defense; facts material to issue; substance as distinguished from form; transaction, event, occurrence; subject-matter of controversy. See **Issue; Material fact; Matter in issue; Subject-matter.**

Matter in controversy, or **in dispute.** Subject of litigation; matter on which action is brought and issue is joined and in relation to which, if issue be one of fact, testimony is taken. Golden v. Sixth Judicial Dist. Ct. in and for Pershing County, 57 Nev. 114, 58 P.2d 1042, 1044. Rights which plaintiffs assert and seek to have protected and enforced. Gavica v. Donaugh, C.C.A.Or., 93 F.2d 173, 175. See also **Cause of action; Issue; Matter in issue; Subject-matter.**

Matter in deed. In English law, such matter as may be proved or established by a deed or specialty. Matter of fact, in contradistinction to matter of law. See also **Matter of record.**

Matter in issue. That matter on which plaintiff proceeds by his action, and which defendant controverts by his pleadings. MacKenzie v. Union Guardian Trust Co., 262 Mich. 563, 247 N.W. 914. Not including facts offered in evidence to establish the matters in issue. That ultimate fact or state of facts in dispute upon which the verdict or finding is predicated. See also **Matter in controversy,** or **in dispute.**

Matter in ley ne serra mise in boutche del jurors /mǽdər ìn léy nə sərá míyz ìn búsh dèl júrərz/. Matter of law shall not be put into the mouth of the jurors.

Matter in pais /mǽdər ìn péy/. Matter of fact that is not in writing; thus distinguished from matter in deed and matter of record; matter that must be proved by parol evidence.

Matter of course. Anything done or taken in the course of routine or usual procedure, which is permissible and valid without being specially applied for and allowed.

Matter of fact. That which is to be ascertained by the senses, or by the testimony of witnesses describing what they have perceived. Distinguished from matter of law and matter of opinion. See also **Fact**.

Matter of form. See **Form**.

Matter of law. Whatever is to be ascertained or decided by the application of statutory rules or the principles and determinations of the law, as distinguished from the investigation of particular facts, is called "matter of law."

Matter of record. Any judicial matter or proceeding entered on the records of a court, and to be proved by the production of such record. It differs from matter in deed, which consists of facts which may be proved by specialty.

Matter of record, estoppel by. See **Record, estoppel by**.

Matter of substance. That which goes to the merits. The opposite of matter of form.

Matters of subsistence for man. This phrase comprehends all articles or things, whether animal or vegetable, living or dead, which are used for food, and whether they are consumed in the form in which they are bought from the producer or are only consumed after undergoing a process of preparation, which is greater or less, according to the character of the article.

Matured claim. Claim which is unconditionally due and owing. See **Liquidated claim**.

Maturity. The date at which an obligation, such as the principal of a bond or a note, becomes due.

Maturity value. The amount which is due and payable on the maturity date of an obligation.

Maugre /mógɔr/. L. Fr. In spite of; against the will of.

Maxim /mǽksɔm/. Maxims are but attempted general statements of rules of law and are law only to extent of application in adjudicated cases. Swetland v. Curtiss Airports Corporation, D.C.Ohio, 41 F.2d 929, 936. An established principle or proposition. A principle of law universally admitted as being a correct statement of the law, or as agreeable to reason. Principles invoked in equity jurisdiction; *e.g.* "equity treats as done what ought to be done."

The various maxims of law appear in alphabetical order throughout this dictionary.

Maxime paci sunt contraria vis et injuria /mǽksɔmiy péysay sɔnt kɔntréeriyɔ vís èd ɔnjúriyɔ/. The greatest enemies to peace are force and wrong.

Maximum. The highest or greatest amount, quality, value, or degree.

Maximus erroris populus magister /mǽksɔmɔs ɔróerɔs pópyɔlɔs mɔjístɔr/. The people is the greatest master of error.

May. An auxiliary verb qualifying the meaning of another verb by expressing ability, competency, liberty, permission, possibility, probability or contingency. U. S. v. Lexington Mill & E. Co., 232 U.S. 399, 34 S.Ct. 337, 340, 58 L.Ed. 658. Regardless of the instrument, however, whether constitution, statute, deed, contract or whatever, courts not infrequently construe "may" as "shall" or "must" to the end that justice may not be the slave of grammar. However, as a general rule, the word "may" will not be treated as a word of command unless there is something in context or subject matter of act to indicate that it was used in such sense. Bloom v. Texas State Bd. of Examiners of Psychologists, Tex.Civ.App., 475 S.W.2d 374, 377. In construction of statutes and presumably also in construction of federal rules word "may" as opposed to "shall" is indicative of discretion or choice between two or more alternatives, but context in which word appears must be controlling factor. U. S. v. Cook, C.A.Ill., 432 F.2d 1093, 1098.

Mayhem /méy(h)ɔm/. Mayhem at common law required a type of injury which permanently rendered the victim less able to fight offensively or defensively; it might be accomplished either by the removal of (dismemberment), or by the disablement of, some bodily member useful in fighting. Today, by statute, permanent disfigurement has been added; and as to dismemberment and disablement, there is no longer a requirement that the member have military significance. See also **Maim**.

Mayn /méyn/. L. Fr. A hand; handwriting.

Maynover /mèynówvɔr/mɔnúwvɔr/. L. Fr. A work of the hand; a thing produced by manual labor.

Mayor. A governmental figure who is generally the principal administrative officer of a city or other municipal area. The position of mayor varies from city to city. In some cities the mayor is essentially a ceremonial figure, while in others he is a major executive official. In some instances he is popularly elected and in others, such as in the commission plan, he is selected from within the administrative council to serve as a presiding officer and ceremonial figure. Duties of mayor are usually prescribed by statute or municipal charter.

Mayoralty /méy(ɔ)rɔltiy/. The office or dignity of a mayor.

Mayorazgo /màyorásgow/. In Spanish law, the right to the enjoyment of certain aggregate property, left with the condition thereon imposed that they are to pass in their integrity, perpetually, successively to the eldest son.

Mayor's court. A court established in some cities, in which the mayor sits with the powers of a police judge or committing magistrate in respect to offenses committed within the city (*e.g.* traffic or ordinance violations) and sometimes with civil jurisdiction in small causes, or other special statutory powers.

McCarran Act. A federal statute which permits a state to regulate and to tax foreign insurance companies which do business within the state. 15 U.S.C.A. § 1011 *et seq.* See also **Internal security acts.**

McNabb-Mallory Rule. The rule which requires that a suspect be promptly brought before a magistrate or else incriminating statements made by him during the illegal detention will be suppressed. McNabb v. U. S., 318 U.S. 332, 63 S.Ct. 608, 87 L.Ed. 819, and Mallory v. U. S., 354 U.S. 449, 77 S.Ct. 1356, 1 L.Ed.2d 1479. "McNabb Rule" is that there must be reasonable promptness in taking prisoner before committing magistrate, or confession obtained during period between arrest and commitment is inadmissible in prosecution of party arrested, and that rule applies to voluntary as well as involuntary confessions. Muldrow v. U. S., C.A.Cal., 281 F.2d 903, 906.

McNaghten Rule. See **M'Naghten Rule.**

M.D. An abbreviation for "Middle District," in reference to the division of the United States into judicial districts; *e.g.* U.S. District Court for middle district of Ohio. Also an abbreviation for "Doctor of Medicine" or "Medical Doctor."

Meadow. A tract of low or level land producing grass which is mown for hay. A tract which lies above the shore, and is overflowed by spring and extraordinary tides only, and yields grasses which are good for hay.

Mean, or **mesne.** A middle between two extremes, whether applied to persons, things, or time. Average, having an intermediate value between two extremes or between the several successive values of variable quantity during one cycle of variation. Western & Southern Life Ins. Co. v. Huwe, C.C.A. Ohio, 116 F.2d 1008, 1009.

Meander /miyǽndər/. To meander means to follow a winding or flexuous course; and when it it said, in a description of land, "thence with the meander of the river," it must mean a meandered line,—a line which follows the sinuosities of the river,—or, in other words, that the river is the boundary between the points indicated.

This term is used in some jurisdictions with the meaning of surveying and mapping a stream according to its meanderings, or windings and turnings. See **Meander lines.**

Meander lines. Lines run in surveying particular portions of the public lands which border on navigable rivers, not as boundaries of the tract, but for the purpose of defining the sinuosities of the banks of the stream, and as the means of ascertaining the quantity of land in the fraction subject to sale, and which is to be paid for by the purchaser. In preparing the official plat from the field notes, the meander line is represented as the border line of the stream, and shows that the watercourse, and not the meander line as naturally run on the ground, is the boundary. Niles v. Cedar Point Club, 175 U.S. 300, 20 S.Ct. 124, 44 L.Ed. 171.

Mean high tide. The "mean high tide" or "ordinary high tide" is a mean of all the high tides, and the average to be used should be, if possible, the average of all the high tides over a period of 18.6 years. O'Neill v. State Highway Dept., N.J., 50 N.J. 307, 235 A.2d 1, 9.

Meaning. That which is, or is intended to be, signified or denoted by act or language; signification; sense; import. See also **Construction.**

Mean lower low tide. The average of lower low tides over a fixed period of time. State v. Edwards, 188 Wash. 467, 62 P.2d 1094, 1095.

Mean low tide. The average of all low tides both low and lower low over a fixed period of time. State v. Edwards, 188 Wash. 467, 62 P.2d 1094, 1095.

Mean reserve. The mean of the reserve at the beginning of the policy year, after the premium for such year is paid, and the terminal reserve at end of such policy year. Kentucky Home Life Ins. Co. v. Leisman, 268 Ky. 825, 105 S.W.2d 1046, 1047.

Means. That through which, or by the help of which, an end is attained; something tending to an object desired; intermediate agency or measure; necessary condition or co-agent; instrument. Under insurance policy, equivalent to cause. Pope v. Business Men's Assur. Co. of America, 235 Mo.App. 263, 131 S.W.2d 887, 892.

Enactments and initiative and referendum measures. State ex rel. Bylander v. Hoss, 143 Or. 383, 22 P.2d 883.

Resources; available property; money or property, as an available instrumentality for effecting a purpose, furnishing a livelihood, paying a debt, or the like.

Measure. That by which extent or dimension is ascertained, either length, breadth, thickness, capacity, or amount. The rule by which anything is adjusted or proportioned. See **Land measure; Metes and bounds; Survey.**

Measure of damages. The rule, or rather the system of rules, governing the adjustment or apportionment of damages as a compensation for injuries in actions at law. See **Damages.**

Measure of value. In the ordinary sense of the word, "measure" would mean something by comparison with which we may ascertain what is the value of anything. When we consider, further, that value itself is relative, and that two things are necessary to constitute it, independently of the third thing, which is to measure it, we may define a "measure of value" to be something by comparing with which any two other things we may infer their value in relation to one another. See **Value.**

Measuring money. In old English law, a duty which some persons exacted, by letters patent, for every piece of cloth made, besides alnage. Now abolished.

Mechanical equivalent. If two devices do the same work in substantially the same way, and accomplish substantially the same result, they are "mechanical equivalents." Wire Tie Machinery Co. v. Pacific Box Corporation, C.C.A.Cal., 107 F.2d 54, 56. A device which may be substituted or adopted, instead of another, by any person skilled in the particular art from his knowledge of the art, and which is competent to perform the same functions or produce the same result, without introducing an original idea or changing the general idea of means. The test of equivalency is whether the substituted element operates in substantially the same way to produce substantially the same result.　See also **Equivalent**.

Mechanical process.　See **Process**.

Mechanic's lien.　A claim created by state statutes for the purpose of securing priority of payment of the price or value of work performed and materials furnished in erecting or repairing a building or other structure, and as such attaches to the land as well as buildings and improvements erected thereon.　In re Louisville Daily News & Enquirer, D.C.Ky., 20 F.Supp. 465, 466.　Such lien covers materialmen, tradesmen, suppliers, and the like, who furnish services, labor, or materials on construction or improvement of property.　See also **Commence** (*Commencement of building improvement*); **Lien waiver**.

Mechanic's lienor.　The term "mechanic's lienor" means any person who under local law has a lien on real property (or on the proceeds of a contract relating to real property) for services, labor, or materials furnished in connection with the construction or improvement of such property.　I.R.C. § 6323(h).

Medfee /médfiy/.　In old English law, a bribe or reward; a compensation given in exchange, where the things exchanged were not of equal value.

Media annata /méyðiya anáta/míydiyə ənéydə/.　In Spanish law, half-yearly profits of land.

Media concludendi /míydiyə kòŋkluwdénday/.　The steps of an argument.　Thus "a judgment is conclusive as to all the *media concludendi*."　Fauntleroy v. Lum, 210 U.S. 230, 28 S.Ct. 641, 52 L.Ed. 1039.　The theory or basis of facts upon which a legal conclusion is reached, per Holmes, C. J., in Hoseason v. Keegen, 178 Mass. 247, 59 N.E. 627.　Grounds for asserting the right known when the suit was brought.　Mendez v. Baetjer, C.C.A.Puerto Rico, 106 F.2d 163, 166.

Mediæ et infirmæ manus homines /míydiyiy èd infərmiy mænəs hóməniyz/.　Men of a middle and base condition.

Media nox /míydiyə nòks/.　In old English law, midnight.　*Ad mediam noctem*, at midnight.

Medianus homo /mìydiyéynəs hówmow/.　A man of middle fortune.

Mediate datum /mìydiyéydiy déydəm/.　A fact from whose existence may be rationally inferred the existence of ultimate facts.　The Evergreens v. Nunan, C.C.A.N.Y., 141 F.2d 927, 928.

Mediate descent.　See **Descent**.

Mediate powers.　Those incident to primary powers given by a principal to his agent.　For example, the general authority given to collect, receive, and pay debts by or to the principal is a primary power.　In order to accomplish this, it is frequently required to settle accounts, adjust disputed claims, resist those which are unjust, and answer and defend suits.　These subordinate powers are sometimes called "mediate powers."

Mediate testimony.　Secondary evidence (*q.v.*).

Mediation.　Intervention; interposition; the act of a third person in intermediating between two contending parties with a view to persuading them to adjust or settle their dispute.　Settlement of dispute by action of intermediary (neutral party).　See also **Arbitration; Conciliation**.

Also, the friendly interference of a neutral nation in the controversies of others, for the purpose, by its influence and by adjusting their difficulties, of keeping the peace in the family of nations.

Mediation and Conciliation Service.　An independent department of the federal government charged with trying to settle labor disputes by conciliation and mediation.　29 U.S.C.A. § 172 *et seq.*

The Federal Mediation and Conciliation Service represents the public interest by promoting the development of sound and stable labor-management relationships; preventing or minimizing work stoppages by assisting labor and management to settle their disputes through mediation; advocating collective bargaining, mediation, and voluntary arbitration as the preferred processes for settling issues between employers and representatives of employees; developing the art, science, and practice of dispute resolution; and fostering constructive joint relationships of labor and management leaders to increase their mutual understanding and solution of common problems.　See also **National Mediation Board**.

Mediator.　One who interposes between parties at variance for purpose of reconciling them.

Mediators of questions.　In old English law, six persons authorized by statute (27 Edw. III, St. 2, c. 24), who, upon any question arising among merchants relating to unmerchantable wool, or undue packing, etc., might, before the mayor and officers of the staple upon their oath certify and settle the same; to whose determination therein the parties concerned were to submit.

Medicaid.　A form of public assistance sponsored jointly by the federal and state governments providing medical aid for people whose income falls below a certain level.　See also **Medicare**.

Medical.　Pertaining, relating or belonging to the study and practice of medicine, or the science and art of the investigation, prevention, cure, and alleviation of disease.

Medical care.　The term "medical care" is defined broadly in the Internal Revenue Code (I.R.C. § 213) and more comprehensively in the regulations.　It includes expenses for doctors, nurses and other medical services, as well as payments for operations, hospitals, institutional care and transportation necessary to obtain medical care.　The basic test for the allowance of medical deductions is whether the expense was incurred and paid primarily for the prevention or alleviation of a physical or mental defect or illness.　Edward A. Harvey, 12 T.C. 409 (1949).　See also **Medical expenses**.

Medical deduction.　See **Medical care**.

Medical evidence.　Evidence furnished by doctors, nurses, and other medical personnel testifying in their professional capacity as experts, or by standard treatises on medicine or surgery. Fed.Evid.R. 702, 703. See **Expert witness.**

Medical examiner. Public officer charged with responsibility of investigating all sudden, unexplained, unnatural or suspicious deaths reported to him, including the performance of autopsies and assisting the state in criminal homicide cases. Term may also include a physician who conducts examinations for insurance companies and other institutions. The medical examiner has replaced the coroner in many states. See also **Coroner.**

Medical expenses. Medical expenses of an individual and his dependents are allowed as an itemized deduction to the extent that such amounts (less insurance reimbursements) exceed 3 percent of adjusted gross income. Special rules are provided for medicines and drugs and health insurance premiums. I.R.C. § 213.

Medical jurisprudence. The science which applies the principles and practice of the different branches of medicine to the elucidation of doubtful questions in a court of justice. Otherwise called "forensic medicine" (q.v.). A sort of mixed science, which may be considered as common ground to the practitioners both of law and medicine.

Medical malpractice. See **Malpractice.**

Medicare. Federal Act to provide hospital and medical insurance for aged under Social Security Act. See also **Medicaid** (state provided medical assistance).

Medicine. The science and art dealing with the prevention, cure and alleviation of diseases; in a narrower sense that part of the science and art of restoring and preserving health which is the province of the physician as distinguished from the surgeon and obstetrician. Burke v. Kansas State Osteopathic Ass'n, C.C. A.Kan., 111 F.2d 250, 253. The term is not limited to substances supposed to possess curative or remedial properties. People v. Kabana, 321 Ill.App. 158, 52 N.E.2d 320.

Forensic medicine. Another name for medical jurisprudence. See **Forensic medicine.**

Schools of medicine. See **Osteopathy; Psychotherapy.**

Medico-legal. Relating to the law concerning medical questions. See **Forensic medicine.**

Medietas linguæ /mədáyətæs língwiy/. In old practice, moiety of tongue; half-tongue. Applied to a jury impaneled in a cause consisting the one half of natives, and the other half of foreigners. See **De medietate linguæ.**

Medio acquietando /míydiyow əkwàyətǽndow/. A judicial writ to distrain a lord for the acquitting of a mesne lord from a rent, which he had acknowledged in court not to belong to him.

Mediterranean passport. A pass issued by the admiralty of Great Britain under various treaties with the Barbary States in the eighteenth century. They were granted to British built ships and were respected by the Barbary pirates. They were also issued by the United States.

Medium of exchange. Anything which serves to facilitate the exchange of things by providing a common basis of measurement such as money, checks, drafts etc. See **Legal tender.**

Medium tempus /míydiyəm témpəs/. In old English law, meantime; mesne profits.

Medletum /medlíydəm/. In old English law, a mixing together; a medley or *mêlée;* an affray or sudden encounter. An offense suddenly committed in an affray. The English word "medley" is preserved in the term "chance-medley." An intermeddling, without violence, in any matter of business.

Medley /médliy/. An affray; a sudden or casual fighting; a hand to hand battle; a *mêlée.* See **Chance-medley; Chaud-medley.**

Medsceat /médzchìyt/. In old English law, a bribe; hush money.

Meeting. A coming together of persons; an assembly. Particularly, in law, an assembling of a number of persons for the purpose of discussing and acting upon some matter or matters in which they have a common interest; *e.g.* in corporate law, a meeting of the Board of Directors or of the stockholders.

Called meeting. In the law of corporations, a meeting not held at a time specially appointed for it by the charter or by-laws, but assembled in pursuance of a "call" or summons proceeding from some officer, committee or group of stockholders, or other persons having authority in that behalf.

Family meeting. See **Family.**

General meeting. A meeting of all the stockholders of a corporation, all the creditors of a bankrupt, etc.

Regular meeting. In the law of public and private corporations, a meeting (of directors, trustees, stockholders, etc.) held at the time and place appointed for it by statute, by-law, charter or other positive direction.

Special meeting. In the law of corporations, a meeting called for special purposes; one limited to particular business; a meeting for those purposes of which the parties have had special notice.

Stated meeting. A meeting held at a stated or duly appointed time and place; a regular meeting (q.v.).

Town meeting. See **Town.**

Meeting of creditors. Under federal bankruptcy law, at the first meeting of creditors the bankrupt is examined, claims may be allowed or disallowed and a trustee appointed. There may also be interim meetings of creditors to consider the affairs of the bankrupt and a final meeting when the affairs are to be closed. 11 U.S.C.A. § 341.

Meeting of minds. Mutual agreement and assent of parties to contract to substance and terms. The "meeting of the minds" required to make a contract is not based on secret purpose or intention on the part of one of the parties, stored away in his mind and not brought to the attention of the other party, but must be based on purpose and intention which has been made known or which from all the circumstances should be known. McClintock v. Skelly Oil Co., 232 Mo.App. 1204, 114 S.W.2d 181, 189.

Megalomania /mègələméyniyə/. See **Insanity.**

Megalopolis. Heavily populated continuous urban area including many cities.

Megbote /mégbòwt/. In Saxon law, a recompense for the murder of a relation.

Meigne, or **maisnader** /míyn/. In old English law, a family.

Meilicke system. Consists of computing fractions on the basis of a 30-day month, and does not charge interest for the 31st day of any month. Swistak v. Personal Finance Co., 175 Misc. 791, 24 N.Y.S.2d 80, 81.

Meindre age /míndər éyj/°ázh/. L. Fr. Minority; lesser age.

Meiny, meine, or **meinie** /míyn(iy)/. In old English law, a household; staff or suite of attendants; a retinue; particularly, the royal household.

Melancholia /mèlənkówliyə/. A kind of mental unsoundness characterized by extreme depression of spirits, ill-grounded fears, delusions, and brooding over one particular subject or train of ideas. Depressed phase of manic-depressive psychosis, the intensity and duration of which is out of proportion to any apparent precipitating factors. See **Insanity.**

Meldfeoh /méldfiy/. In Saxon law, the recompense due and given to him who made discovery of any breach of penal laws committed by another person, called the "promoter's [i.e., informer's] fee."

Melior /míyl(i)yər/. Lat. Better; the better. *Melior res,* the better (best) thing or chattel.

Meliorations /mìyl(i)yəréyshən(d)z/. In Scotch law, improvements of an estate, other than mere repairs; betterments. Occasionally used in English and American law in the sense of valuable and lasting improvements or betterments.

Meliorem conditionem ecclesiæ suæ facere potest prælatus, deteriorem nequaquam /mìyl(i)yórəm kəndìshiyównəm əklíyziyiy s(y)úwiy fǽysəriy pówdəst prəléydəs, dətìriyórəm nəkwéykwəm/. A bishop can make the condition of his own church better, but by no means worse.

Meliorem conditionem suam facere potest minor, deteriorem nequaquam /mìyl(i)yórəm kəndìshiyównəm s(y)úwəm fǽsəriy pówdəst máynər, dətìriyórəm nəkwéykwəm/. A minor can make his own condition better, but by no means worse.

Melior est causa possidentis /míyl(i)yər èst kózə pòsədéntəs/. The cause of the possessor is preferable.

Melior est conditio defendentis /míyl(i)yər èst kəndísh(iy)ow dəfèndéntəs/. The condition of the party in possession is the better one, i.e., where the right of the parties is equal.

Melior est conditio possidentis, et rei quam actoris míyl(i)yər èst kəndísh(iy)ow pòsədéntəs èt ríyay kwæm æktórəs/. The condition of the possessor is the better, and the condition of the defendant is better than that of the plaintiff.

Melior est conditio possidentis ubi neuter jus habet /míyl(i)yər èst kəndísh(iy)ow pòsədéntəs yúwbay n(y)úwdər jás héybət/. The condition of the possessor is the better where neither of the two has a right.

Melior est justitia vere præveniens quam severe puniens /míyl(i)yər èst jəstísh(iy)ə víriy prəvíyn(i)yən(d)z kwæm səvíriy pyúwniyən(d)z/. That justice which absolutely prevents [a crime] is better than that which severely punishes it.

Melius est in tempore occurrere, quam post causam vulneratum remedium quærere /míyl(i)yəs èst in témpəriy əkáhrəriy, kwæm pòst kózəm vəlnəréydəm rəmíyd(i)yəm kwírəriy/. It is better to meet a thing in time than after an injury inflicted to seek a remedy.

Melius est jus deficiens quam jus incertum /míyl(i)yəs èst jás dəfíshiyən(d)z kwæm jás ənsárdəm/. Law that is deficient is better than law that is uncertain.

Melius est omnia mala pati quam malo consentire /míyl(i)yəs èst ómniyə mǽlə pǽday kwæm mǽlow kònsentáyriy/. It is better to suffer every ill than to consent to ill.

Melius est petere fontes quam sectari rivulos /míyl(i)yəs èst pédəriy fóntiyz kwæm sèktéray rívyələws/. It is better to go to the fountain head than to follow little streamlets.

Melius est recurrere quam malo currere /míyl(i)yəs èst rəkáhrəriy kwæm mǽlow káhrəriy/. It is better to run back than to run badly; it is better to retrace one's steps than to proceed improperly.

Melius inquirendum /míyl(i)yəs ìnkwəréndəm/. To be better inquired into.

In old English law, the name of a writ commanding a further inquiry respecting a matter; as, after an imperfect inquisition in proceedings in outlawry, to have a new inquest as to the value of lands.

Member. One of the persons constituting a family, partnership, association, corporation, guild, court, legislature, or the like.

A part or organ of the body; especially a limb or other separate part. California Casualty Indemnity Exchange v. Industrial Accident Commission, Cal. App., 82 P.2d 1115, 1116.

Member bank. A bank which has become affiliated with (i.e. purchased stock in) one of the Federal Reserve banks. See **Federal Reserve System.**

Member firm. In securities and commodities trading, a brokerage firm that is a member of a particular exchange (e.g. member of New York Stock Exchange).

Member of Congress. A member of the Senate or House of Representatives of the United States. In popular usage, particularly the latter.

Member of Parliament. One having the right to sit in either house of the British parliament.

Membrana /membréynə/. Lat. In old Civil and English law, a skin of parchment. The ancient rolls usually consist of several of these skins, and the word *"membrana"* is used, in citations to them, in the same way as "page" or "folio," to distinguish the particular skin referred to.

Membrum /mémbrəm/. A slip or small piece of land.

Mémoire /mèmwóhr/mémwòhr/. In French law, a document in the form of a petition, by which appeals to the court of cassation are initiated.

Memorandum /mèmərǽndəm/. Lat. To be remembered; be it remembered. A formal word with which the body of a record in the Court of King's Bench anciently commenced.

An informal note or instrument embodying something that the parties desire to fix in memory by the aid of written evidence, or that is to serve as the basis of a future formal contract or deed. A brief written statement outlining the terms of an agreement or transaction. Informal interoffice communication.

Under portion of statute of frauds providing that a contract not to be performed within a year is invalid unless the contract, or some memorandum of the contract, is in writing and subscribed by the party to be charged or his agent, the word "memorandum" implies something less than a complete contract, and the "memorandum" functions only as evidence of the contract and need not contain every term, so that a letter may be a sufficient "memorandum" to take a case out of the statute of frauds. Kerner v. Hughes Tool Co., 128 Cal.Rptr. 839, 845, 56 C.A.3d 924.

This word is used in the statute of frauds as the designation of the written agreement, or note or evidence thereof, which must exist in order to bind the parties in the cases provided. The memorandum must be such as to disclose the parties, the nature and substance of the contract, the consideration and promise, and be signed by the party to be bound or his authorized agent. See U.C.C. § 2–201. See also **Contract.**

Memorandum articles. In the law of marine insurance, this phrase designates the articles of merchandise which are usually mentioned in the memorandum clause (q.v.), and for which the underwriter's liability is thereby limited.

Memorandum check. See **Check.**

Memorandum clause. In a policy of marine insurance the memorandum clause is a clause inserted to prevent the underwriters from being liable for injury to goods of a peculiarly perishable nature, and for minor damages. It might begin, for example, as follows: "N. B. Corn, fish, salt, fruit, flour, and seed are warranted free from average, unless general, or the ship be stranded,"—meaning that the underwriters are not to be liable for damage to these articles caused by seawater or the like.

Memorandum decision. A court's decision that gives the ruling (what it decides and orders done), but no opinion (reasons for the decision). Memorandum decision is not judgment nor decision of court but merely announcement of court's intended decision and is not appealable order. In re Pieper's Estate, 224 C.A.2d 670, 37 Cal.Rptr. 46, 50.

Memorandum in error. A document alleging error in fact, accompanied by an affidavit of such matter of fact.

Memorandum of alteration. Formerly, in England, where a patent was granted for two inventions, one of which was not new or not useful, the whole patent was bad, and the same rule applied when a material part of a patent for a single invention had either of those defects. To remedy this the statute 5 & 6 Wm. IV, c. 83, empowers a patentee (with the fiat of the attorney general) to enter a disclaimer (q.v.) or memorandum of an alteration in the title or specification of the patent, not being of such a nature as to extend the exclusive right granted by the patent, and thereupon the memorandum is deemed to be part of the letters patent or the specification.

Memorandum of association. In England, a document to be subscribed by seven or more persons associated for a lawful purpose, by subscribing which, and otherwise complying with the requisitions of the companies' acts in respect of registration, they may form themselves into an incorporated company, with or without limited liability. See also **Articles of association; Articles of incorporation.**

Memorandum sale. See **Sale.**

Memorial. A document presented to a legislative body, or to the executive, by one or more individuals, containing a petition or a representation of facts.

In practice, a short note, abstract, memorandum, or rough draft of the orders of the court, from which the records thereof may at any time be fully made up.

In English law, that which contains the particulars of a deed, etc., and is the instrument registered, as in the case of an annuity which must be registered.

Memoriter /məmórədər/. Lat. From memory; by or from recollection. Thus, *memoriter* proof of a written instrument is such as is furnished by the recollection of a witness who had seen and known it.

Memory. The word as used in Blackstone and other ancient authorities, appeared to be synonymous with "mind", whereas the word "memory" in modern times is used in a more restricted sense of recollection of past events rather than the general state of one's mental power.

Mental capacity; the mental power to review and recognize the successive states of consciousness in their consecutive order.

This word, as used in jurisprudence to denote one of the psychological elements necessary in the making of a valid will or contract or the commission of a crime, implies the mental power to conduct a consecutive train of thought, or an orderly planning of affairs, by recalling correctly the past states of the mind and past events, and arranging them in their due order of sequence and in their logical relations with the events and mental states of the present. See also **Mind and memory.**

The phrase "sound and disposing mind and memory" means not merely distinct recollection of the items of one's property and the persons among whom it may be given, but entire power of mind to dispose of property by will. See **Capacity.**

The reputation and name, good or bad, which a man leaves at his death.

Legal memory. An ancient usage, custom, supposed grant (as a foundation for prescription) and the like are said to be immemorial when they are really or fictitiously of such an ancient date that "the memory of man runneth not to the contrary," or, in other words, "beyond legal memory." And legal memory or "time out of mind," according to the rule of the common law, commenced from the reign of Richard I, A.D. 1189. But under the statute of limitation of 32 Hen. VIII this was reduced to 60 years, and again by that of 2 & 3 Wm. IV, c. 71, to 20 years. In the American states, by statute, the time of legal memory is generally fixed at a period corresponding to that prescribed for actions for the recovery of real property, usually about 20 years.

Menace. A threat; the declaration or show of a disposition or determination to inflict an evil or injury upon another.

Men of straw. Men who used in former days to ply about courts of law, so called from their manner of making known their occupation (*i.e.*, by a straw in one of their shoes), recognized by the name of "straw-shoes." An advocate or lawyer who wanted a convenient witness knew by these signs where to meet with one, and the colloquy between the parties was brief. "Don't you remember?" said the advocate; to which the ready answer was, "To be sure I do." "Then come into court and swear it." And straw-shoes went into court and swore. Athens abounded in straw-shoes. See also **Straw man.**

Mens /mén(d)z/. Lat. Mind; intention; meaning; understanding; will.

Mensa et thoro /mén(t)sə èt θórow/. From bed and board. See **Divorce.**

Mensalia /mèn(t)séyl(i)yə/. Parsonages or spiritual livings united to the tables of religious houses, and called "mensal benefices" amongst the canonists.

Mensis /men(t)səs/. Lat. In the civil and old English law, a month. *Mensis vetitus,* the prohibited month; fence-month (*q.v.*).

Mens legis /mén(d)z líyjəs/. The mind of the law; that is, the purpose, spirit, or intention of a law or the law generally.

Mens legislatoris /mén(d)z lèjəslətórəs/. The intention of the law-maker.

Mensor /mén(t)sòr/. In civil law, a measurer of land; a surveyor.

Mens rea /mén(d)z ríyə/. A guilty mind; a guilty or wrongful purpose; a criminal intent. Guilty knowledge and wilfulness. United States v. Greenbaum, C.C.A.N.J., 138 F.2d 437, 438. See also **Knowledge.**

Mens testatoris in testamentis spectanda est /mén(d)z tèstətórəs in tèstəméntəs spektændə èst/. The intention of the testator is to be regarded in wills.

Mensularius /mèn(t)səlériyəs/. In civil law, a money-changer or dealer in money.

Mensura /mens(y)úrə/. In old English law, a measure.

Mensura domini regis /mens(y)úrə dómənay ríyjəs/. "The measure of our lord the king," being the weights and measures established under King Richard I, in his parliament at Westminster, 1197.

Mental. Relating to or existing in the mind; intellectual, emotional, or psychic, as distinguished from bodily or physical.

Mental alienation. A phrase sometimes used to describe insanity (*q.v.*).

Mental anguish. When connected with a physicial injury, this term includes both the resultant mental sensation of pain and also the accompanying feelings of distress, fright, and anxiety. In other connections, and as a ground for divorce or for damages or an element of damages, it includes the mental suffering resulting from the excitation of the more poignant and painful emotions, such as grief, severe disappointment, indignation, wounded pride, shame, public humiliation, despair, etc. See also **Mental cruelty.**

Mental capacity or **competence.** Term contemplates the ability to understand the nature and effect of the act in which a person is engaged and the business he or she is transacting. Jones v. Traders & General Ins. Co., Tex.Civ.App., 144 S.W.2d 689, 694. Such a measure of intelligence, understanding, memory, and judgment relative to the particular transaction (*e.g.* making of will) as will enable the person to understand the nature of his act. Conley v. Nailor, 118 U.S. 127, 6 S.Ct. 1001, 30 L.Ed. 112. See also **Capacity; Insanity.**

Mental cruelty. A course of conduct on the part of one spouse toward the other spouse which can endanger the mental and physical health and efficiency of the other spouse to such an extent as to render continuance of the marital relation intolerable. Such conduct is normally a ground for divorce. Steele v. Steele, Fla.App., 177 So.2d 873. See also **Indignity; Mental anguish.**

Mental disease or **defect.** See **Insanity.**

Mental incapacity; mental incompetency. Such is established when there is found to exist an essential privation of reasoning faculties, or when a person is incapable of understanding and acting with discretion in the ordinary affairs of life. See **Incapacity; Insanity.**

Mental reservation. A silent exception to the general words of a promise or agreement not expressed, on account of a general understanding on the subject. But the word has been applied to an exception existing in the mind of the one party only, and has been degraded to signify a dishonest excuse for evading or infringing a promise.

Mental state. Capacity or condition of one's mind in terms of ability to do or not do a certain act. See **Mental capacity.**

Mental suffering. See **Mental anguish; Mental cruelty.**

Mente captus /méntiy kǽptəs/. Persons who are habitually insane. Clanton v. Shattuck, 211 La. 750, 30 So.2d 823, 824.

Mentiri /mèntáyray/. Lat. To lie; to assert a falsehood.

Mentition /mèntíshən/. The act of lying; a falsehood.

Mera noctis /mírə nóktəs/. Midnight.

Mercable /márkəbəl/. Merchantable; to be sold or bought.

Mercantant /márkəntænt/mǝr°/. A foreign trader.

Mercantile /márkəntàyl/°əl/. Of, pertaining to, or characteristic of, merchants, or the business of merchants; having to do with trade or commerce or the business of buying and selling merchandise; trading; commercial; conducted or acting on business principles.

Mercantile agencies. See **Credit bureau.**

Mercantile law. An expression substantially equivalent to commercial law. It designates the system of rules, customs, and usages generally recognized and adopted by merchants and traders, and which, either in its simplicity or as modified by common law or statutes, constitutes the law for the regulation of their transactions and the solution of their controversies. The Uniform Commercial Code is the general body of law governing commercial or mercantile transactions.

Mercantile Law Amendment Acts. The statutes 19 & 20 Vict., cc. 60, 97, passed mainly for the purpose of assimilating the mercantile law of England, Scotland, and Ireland.

Mercantile paper. See **Commercial paper; Negotiable instruments.**

Mercative /márkədəv/. Belonging to trade.

Mercatum /mərkéydəm/. Lat. A market. A contract of sale. Supplies for an army (*commeatus*).

Mercature /márkəchər/. The practice of buying and selling.

Mercedary /mársədèry/. A hirer; one that hires.

Mercenarius /màrsənériyəs/. A hireling or servant.

Mercen-lage /mársənlò/. The law of the Mercians. One of the three principal systems of laws which prevailed in England about the beginning of the eleventh century. It was observed in many of the midland counties, and those bordering on the principality of Wales. 1 Bl.Comm. 65.

Merces /mársiyz/. Lat. In the civil law, reward of labor in money or other things. As distinguished from *"pensio,"* it means the rent of farms (*prædia rustici*).

Merchandise. All goods which merchants usually buy and sell, whether at wholesale or retail; wares and commodities such as are ordinarily the objects of trade and commerce. But the term is generally not understood as including real estate, and is rarely applied to provisions such as are purchased day by day for immediate consumption (*e.g.* food).

Stock of merchandise. See **Stock.**

Merchandise broker. One who negotiates the sale of merchandise without having it in his possession or control, being simply an agent with very limited powers. Hughes v. Young, 17 Tenn.App. 24, 65 S.W.2d 858. See **Broker.**

Merchandise Marks Act, 1862. The statute 25 & 26 Vict., c. 88, designed to prevent the fraudulent marking of merchandise and the fraudulent sale of merchandise falsely marked.

Merchant. One who is engaged in the purchase and sale of goods; a trafficker; a retailer; a trader. Term commonly refers to person who purchases goods at wholesale for resale at retail; *i.e.* person who operates a retail business (retailer).

A person who deals in goods of the kind or otherwise by his occupation holds himself out as having knowledge or skill peculiar to the practices or goods involved in the transaction or to whom such knowledge or skill may be attributed by his employment of an agent or broker or other intermediary who by his occupation holds himself out as having such knowledge or skill. U.C.C. § 2–104(1).

A man who traffics or carries on trade with foreign countries, or who exports and imports goods and sells them by wholesale. Merchants of this description are commonly known by the name of "shipping merchants."

Commission merchant. See **Commission merchant.**

Law merchant. See **Commercial law; Mercantile law.**

Statute merchant. See **Statute.**

Merchantability /mèrchəntəbílədiy/. Means that the article sold shall be of the general kind described and reasonably fit for the general purpose for which it shall have been sold, and where the article sold is ordinarily used in but one way, its fitness for use in that particular way is impliedly warranted unless there is evidence to the contrary. See also **Fitness for particular purpose; Merchantable; Warranty.**

Merchantable /márchəntəbəl/. Goods to be merchantable must be at least such as: pass without objection in the trade under the contract description; and in the case of fungible goods, are of fair average quality within the description; and are fit for the ordinary purposes for which such goods are used; and run, within the variations permitted by the agreement, of even kind, quality and quantity within each unit and among all units involved; and are adequately contained, packaged, and labeled as the agreement may require; and conform to the promises or affirmations of fact made on the container or label if any. U.C.C. § 2–314(2).

Goods, to be "merchantable," must be fit for the ordinary purposes for which such goods are to be used. Consolidated Supply Co. v. Babbitt, 96 Idaho 636, 534 P.2d 466, 468. Within § 2–314 of the U.C.C. creating implied warranty of merchantability, term "merchantable" implies that the goods sold conform to ordinary standards of care and that they are of average grade, quality and value of similar goods sold under similar circumstances. Woodruff v. Clark County Farm Bureau Co-op Ass'n, 153 Ind.App. 31, 286 N.E.2d 188, 194.

Merchantable title. A good and marketable title in fee simple, free from litigation, palpable defects, and grave doubts, a title which will enable the owner not only to hold it in peace but to sell it to a person of reasonable prudence. Overboe v. Overboe, N.D., 160 N.W.2d 650, 654. Good record title acceptable to a knowledgeable buyer not being under duress to purchase. One that can be held without reasonable apprehension of being assailed and readily transferable in market. Crow Creek Gravel & Sand Co. v. Dooley, 182 Ark. 1009, 33 S.W.2d 369, 370. See also **Marketable title; Warranty** (*Warranty of title*).

Merchant appraiser. See **Appraiser.**

Merchantman /mə́rchəntmən/. A ship or vessel employed in foreign or domestic commerce or in the merchant service.

Merchants' accounts. Accounts between merchant and merchant, which must be current, mutual, and unsettled, consisting of debts and credits for merchandise.

Merchant seaman. A sailor employed in a private vessel, as distinguished from one employed in the navy or public ships.

Merchant Shipping Acts. Certain English statutes, beginning with the St. 16 & 17 Vict., c. 131, whereby a general superintendence of merchant shipping is vested in the board of trade. See **Maritime Commission.**

Merchet /mə́rchət/mär°/. In feudal law, a fine or composition paid by inferior tenants to the lord for liberty to dispose of their daughters in marriage. The same as *marcheta* (*q.v.*).

Merciament /mə́rs(h)yəmənt/. An amerciament, penalty, or fine (*q.v.*).

Mercimoniatus Angliæ /mərsəmòwniyéydəs æ̀ngliyiy/. In old records, the impost of England upon merchandise.

Mercis appellatio ad res mobiles tantum pertinet /mə́rsəs æpəléysh(iy)ow æd ríyz mówbəliyz tǽntəm pə́rdənət/. The term "merchandise" belongs to movable things only.

Mercis appellatione homines non contineri /mə́rsəs æpəlèyshiyówniy hóməniyz nòn kòntəníray/. Men are not included under the denomination of "merchandise."

Mercna lagu /mə́rknə láguw/. See **Lagu; Mercen-lage.**

Mercy. In old English practice, the arbitrament of the king or judge in punishing offenses not directly censured by law. So, "to be in mercy" signifies to be amerced or fined for bringing or defending an unjust suit, or to be liable to punishment in the discretion of the court.

In criminal law, the discretion of a judge, within the limits prescribed by law, to remit altogether the punishment to which a convicted person is liable, or to mitigate the severity of his sentence; as when a jury recommends the prisoner to the *mercy* of the court.

Mercy killing. Euthanasia. The affirmative act of bringing about immediate death allegedly in a painless way and generally administered by one who thinks that the dying person wishes to die because of a terminal or hopeless disease or condition. See also **Brain death; Death** (*Natural Death Acts*).

Mere /mér/. L. Fr. Mother. *Æle, mere, fille*, grandmother, mother, daughter. *En ventre sa mere*, in its mother's womb.

Mere evidence rule. In search and seizure, it was once the rule that in a lawful search the officer had a right to seize instrumentalities and fruits of the crime but no right to seize other items (*e.g.* clothing of the suspect) which are mere evidence. This rule no longer prevails. Warden, Md. Penitentiary v. Hayden, 387 U.S. 294, 87 S.Ct. 1642, 18 L.Ed.2d 782.

Mere licensee. One who enters upon the land or property of another without objection, or by the mere permission, sufferance, or acquiescence of the owner or occupier. Mann v. Des Moines Ry. Co., 232 Iowa 1049, 7 N.W.2d 45, 50. See **License.**

Merely. Without including anything else; purely; only; solely; absolute; wholly. In re Plymouth Motor Corporation, Cust. & Pat.App., 46 F.2d 211, 212.

Mere motion. The free and voluntary act of a party himself, done without the suggestion or influence of another person, is said to be done of his mere motion, *ex mero motu* (*q.v.*).

The phrase is used of an interference of the courts of law, who will, under some circumstances, of their own motion, object to an irregularity in the proceedings, though no objection has been taken to the informality by the plaintiff or defendant in the suit.

Mere right. The mere right of property in land; the *jus proprietatis,* without either possession or even the right of possession. The abstract right of property.

Mere-stone. In old English law, a stone for bounding or dividing lands.

Meretricious /mèhrətríshəs/. Of the nature of unlawful sexual connection. The term is descriptive of the relation sustained by persons who contract a marriage that is void by reason of legal incapacity.

Merger. The fusion or absorption of one thing or right into another; generally spoken of a case where one of the subjects is of less dignity or importance than the other. Here the less important ceases to have an independent existence.

Contract law. The extinguishment of one contract by its absorption into another, and is largely a matter of intention of the parties. Caranas v. Jones, Tex.Civ. App., 437 S.W.2d 905, 910.

Corporations. The absorption of one company by another, latter retaining its own name and identity and acquiring assets, liabilities, franchises, and powers of former, and absorbed company ceasing to exist as separate business entity. Morris v. Investment Life Ins. Co., 27 Ohio St.2d 26, 272 N.E.2d 105, 108, 109, 56 O.O.2d 14. It differs from a consolidation wherein all the corporations terminate their existence and become parties to a new one.

The antitrust laws seek not only to control existing monopolies but also to discourage the acquisition of market power. Historically, mergers have provided an important route to positions of market dominance. Therefore, Congress has required all mergers, whether vertical, horizontal, or conglomerate, to be scrutinized under the provisions of section 7 of the Clayton Act. 15 U.S.C.A. § 18. See also **Kefauver-Celler Act.**

Accounting methods. See **Pooling of interests; Purchase method of accounting.**

Conglomerate merger. Merger of corporations which are neither competitors nor potential or actual customers or suppliers of each other. U. S. v. General Dynamics Corp., D.C.N.Y., 258 F.Supp. 36, 56. One in which there are no economic relationships between the acquiring and the acquired firm. Kennecott Copper Corp. v. F. T. C., C.A.Colo., 467 F.2d 67, 75. A *conglomerate* merger is one that is neither vertical nor horizontal and can be any of three types. A *geographic extension* merger occurs when the acquiring firm, by merger, extends its dominance to an adjacent geographic market. See, *e.g.*, United States v. Marine Bancorporation, 418 U.S. 602, 94 S.Ct. 2856, 41 L.Ed.2d 978. A *product extension* merger occurs when the merger joins firms in related product markets. See, *e.g.*, FTC v. Procter & Gamble Co. (Clorox), 386 U.S. 568, 87 S.Ct. 1224, 18 L.Ed.2d 303. A "pure" conglomerate merger occurs when the two merging firms operate in unrelated markets having no functional economic relationship. See, *e.g.*, United States v. International Tel. & Tel. Corp., 324 F.Supp. 19. These categories are not mutually exclusive: for example, a merger may have both horizontal and vertical aspects. See, *e.g.*, Brown Shoe Co. v. United States, 370 U.S. 294, 82 S.Ct. 1502, 8 L.Ed.2d 510.

Horizontal merger. Merger between business competitors, such as manufacturers of the same type products or distributors selling competing products in the same market area. See also **Vertical merger.**

Short form merger. A number of states provide special rules for the merger of a subsidiary corporation into its parent where the parent owns substantially all of the shares of the subsidiary. This is known as a "short-form" merger. Short-form mergers under such special statutes may generally be effected by: (a) adoption of a resolution of merger by the parent corporation, (b) mailing a copy of the plan of merger to all shareholders of record of the subsidiary, and (c) filing the executed articles of merger with the secretary of state and his issuance of a certificate of merger. This type of merger is less expensive and time consuming than the normal type merger.

Vertical merger. Union with corporate customer or supplier. U. S. v. General Dynamics Corp., D.C. N.Y., 258 F.Supp. 36, 56.

Criminal law. When a man commits a major crime which includes a lesser offense, or commits a felony which includes a tort against a private person, the latter is merged in the former.

Divorce law. Substitution of rights and duties under judgment or decree for those under property settlement agreement. Roesbery v. Roesbery, 88 Idaho 514, 401 P.2d 805, 807.

Judgments. A valid and personal judgment merges the original claim in the judgment and thereafter suit is brought on the judgment and not on the original claim. Restatement of Judgments § 45, comment a.

Law and equity. Under Rules of Civil Procedure, there is now only one form of action, the "civil action," in which the parties may be given both legal and equitable relief. Fed.R.Civil P. 2.

Property interests. It is a general principle of law that where a greater estate and a less coincide and meet in one and the same person, without any intermediate estate, the less is immediately annihilated, or, in the law phrase, is said to be *merged;* that is, sunk or drowned, in the greater. Thus, if there be tenant for years, and the reversion in fee-simple descends to or is purchased by him, the term of years is *merged* in the inheritance, and shall never exist any more. Similarly, a lesser interest in real estate merges into a greater interest when lessee purchases leased property.

Rights. This term, as applied to rights, is equivalent to *"confusio"* in the Roman law, and indicates that where the qualities of debtor and creditor become united in the same individual, there arises a confusion of rights which extinguishes both qualities; whence, also, merger is often called "extinguishment."

Rights of action. In the law relating to rights of action, when a person takes or acquires a remedy or security of a higher nature, in legal estimation, than the one which he already possesses for the same right, then his remedies in respect of the minor right or security merge in those attaching to the higher one; as, for example, where a claim is merged in the judgment recovered upon it.

Sentences. If a defendant is charged in two duplicitous indictments with commission of two crimes, he may be sentenced on conviction of the more serious crime but not on both indictments, *e.g.* possession of marihuana and possession of the same marihuana at the same time and place with intent to sell. Kuklis v. Com., 361 Mass. 302, 280 N.E.2d 155.

Merger clause. A provision in a contract to the effect that the written terms may not be varied by prior or oral agreements because all such agreements have been merged into the written document. See U.C.C. § 2–202.

Meridians. These are imaginary north and south lines which are used in the Governmental Survey System. These intersect the base line to form a starting point for the measurement of land under that system.

Meritorious /mèhrətór(i)yəs/. Possessing or characterized by "merit" in the legal sense of the word. See **Merits.**

Meritorious cause of action. This description is sometimes applied to a person with whom the ground of action, or the consideration, originated or from whom it moved. For example, where a cause of action accrues to a woman while single, and is sued for, after her marriage, by her husband and herself jointly, she is called the "meritorious cause of action."

Meritorious consideration. One founded upon some moral obligation; a valuable consideration in the second degree.

Meritorious defense. See **Defense.**

Merits. The word "merit" as a legal term is to be regarded as referring to the strict legal rights of the parties. Mink v. Keim, 266 App.Div. 184, 41 N.Y. S.2d 769, 771.

Merit system. System used by federal and state governments for hiring and promoting governmental employees to civil service positions on basis of competence. See also **Civil service.**

Mero motu /mírow mówduw/. See **Ex mero motu; Mere motion.**

Merton, statute of /stǽchuwd əv mə́rtən/. An old English statute, relating to dower, legitimacy, wardships, procedure, inclosure of common, and usury. It was passed in 1235 (20 Hen. III), and was named from Merton, in Surrey, where parliament sat that year.

Merum /mírəm/. In old English law, mere; naked or abstract. *Merum jus,* mere right.

Merx /mə́rks/. Lat. Merchandise; movable articles that are bought and sold; articles of trade.

Merx est quicquid vendi potest /mə́rks èst kwí(d)kwìd vénday pówdəst/. Merchandise is whatever can be sold.

Mescreauntes /méskriyònts/mískriyənts/. L. Fr. Apostates; unbelievers.

Mescroyant /méskriyònt/mískriyənt/. A term used in the ancient books to designate an infidel or unbeliever.

Mese /míys/. A house and its appurtenance.

Mesnalty, or **mesnality** /míynəltiy/mìynǽlədiy/. A manor held under a superior lord. The estate of a mesne.

Mesne /míyn/. Intermediate; intervening; the middle between two extremes, especially of rank or time.

In feudal law, an intermediate lord; a lord who stood between a tenant and the chief lord; a lord who was also a tenant.

As to mesne "Conveyance" and "Process," see those titles.

Mesne assignment. If A. grant a lease of land to B., and B. assign his interest to C., and C. in his turn assign his interest therein to D., in this case the assignments so made by B. and C. would be termed "mesne assignments;" that is, they would be assignments intervening between A.'s original grant and the vesting of D.'s interest in the land under the last assignment.

Mesne incumbrance. An intermediate charge, burden, or liability; an incumbrance which has been created or has attached to property between two given periods.

Mesne lord. In old English law, a middle or intermediate lord; a lord who held of a superior lord. 2 Bl.Comm. 59. More commonly termed a "mesne" *(q.v.).*

Mesne process. See **Process.**

Mesne profits. Intermediate profits; *i.e.,* profits which have been accruing between two given periods. Dumas v. Ropp, 98 Idaho 61, 558 P.2d 632, 633. Value of use or occupation of land during time it was held by one in wrongful possession and is commonly measured in terms of rents and profits. See also **Profit.**

Mesne, writ of. An ancient and abolished writ, which lay when the lord paramount distrained on the tenant paravail. The latter had a writ of mesne against the mesne lord.

Message. Any notice, word, or communication, no matter the mode and no matter how sent, from one person to another.

President's message. An annual communication from the president of the United States to Congress, made at or near the beginning of each session, embodying his views on the state and exigencies of national affairs, suggestions and recommendations for legislation, and other matters. U.S.Const. art. 2, § 3.

Message from the crown. In old English law, the method of communicating between the sovereign and the house of parliament. A written message under the royal sign-manual was brought by a member of the house, being a minister of the crown or one of the royal household. Verbal messages were also sometimes delivered.

Messarius /məsériyəs/. In old English law, a chief servant in husbandry; a bailiff.

Messenger. One who bears messages or errands; a ministerial officer employed by executive officers, legislative bodies, and courts of justice, whose service consists principally in carrying verbal or written communications or executing other orders.

Messuage. Dwelling-house with the adjacent buildings and curtilage. Term formerly had a more extended signification.

Meta /míydə/. Lat. A goal, bound, or turning-point. In old English law, the term was used to denote a bound or boundary line of land; a landmark; a material object, as a tree or a pillar, marking the position or beginning of a boundary line.

Metabolism. The sum total of all processes of the human body by which food is transformed into chemicals which are absorbed into blood stream and lymphatic system for purpose of so nourishing body that it can continue to function. United States v. 62 Packages, More or Less, of Marmola Prescription Tablets, C.C.A.Wis., 142 F.2d 107, 109.

Metachronism /mətǽkrənizəm/. An error in computation of time.

Metallum /mətǽləm/. Lat. In Roman law, metal; a mine. Labor in mines, as a punishment for crime.

Metatus /mətéydəs/. In old European law, a dwelling; a seat; a station; quarters; the place where one lives or stays.

Metayer system /mətéyər°/mèdəyéy°/mətéyèy sístəm/. A system of agricultural holdings, under which the land is divided, in small farms, among single families, the landlord generally supplying the stock which the agricultural system of the country is considered to require, and receiving, in lieu of rent and profit, a fixed proportion of the produce. This proportion, which is generally paid in kind, is usually one-half. The system prevails in some parts of France and Italy.

Metecorn. A measure or portion of corn, given by a lord to customary tenants as a reward and encouragement for labor.

Metegavel /míytgǽvəl/. A tribute or rent paid in victuals.

Meter. An instrument of measurement; as a coal-meter, a gas-meter, a land-meter.

The basic metric unit of length; equivalent to 39.37 inches. See also **Metric system.**

Meter rate. Rate applied to charge for utility services based upon quantity used; *e.g.* kilowatt hours of electricity.

Metes and bounds /míyts ən báwndz/. The boundary lines of land, with their terminal points and angles. A way of describing land by listing the compass directions and distances of the boundaries. It is often used in connection with the Government Survey System. See also **Land measure.**

Metewand, or meteyard /míytwònd/míytyàrd/. A staff of a certain length wherewith measures are taken.

Methadone. A synthetic opiate of approximately the same strength as morphine.

Methamphetamine. A synthetic drug, closely related to amphetamines and producing prominent central stimulant reactions without peripheral effects.

Methel /méθəl/. Sax. Speech; discourse. *Mathlian,* to speak; to harangue.

Method. The mode of operating, or the means of attaining an object. In patent law, "engine" and "method" mean the same thing, and may be the subject of a patent. Method, properly speaking, is only placing several things, or performing several operations, in the most convenient order, but it may signify a contrivance or device.

Metric system. A decimal system of weights and measures based on the meter as a unit length and the kilogram as a unit mass. Derived units include the liter for liquid volume, the stere for solid volume, and the are for area.

Metropolitan /mètrəpóləd ən/. Of or pertaining to a city or metropolis and the cluster of towns surrounding it.

Metropolitan council. Official or quasi-official body appointed or elected by voters in the city and towns which comprise the metropolitan area. The powers and duties of such council are set by statute. Created to provide unified administration of functions and services common to cities and towns within metropolitan area; *e.g.* sewage disposal, public transportation, water supply.

Metropolitan district. A special district embracing parts or the whole of several contiguous cities or other areas, created by a State to provide unified administration of one or more functions; *e.g.,* sewage disposal, water supply, metropolitan transit.

Metteshep, or mettenschep /míytshəp/. In old English law, an acknowledgment paid in a certain measure of corn; or a fine or penalty imposed on tenants for default in not doing their customary service in cutting the lord's corn.

Metus /míydəs/. Lat. Fear; terror. In a technical sense, a reasonable and well-grounded apprehension of some great evil, such as death or mayhem, and no arising out of mere timidity, but such as might fa upon a man of courage. Fear must be of this description in order to amount to duress avoiding a contract

Meubles /myúwblə/. In French law, the movables o English law. Things are *meubles* from either of two causes: (1) From their own nature, *e.g.,* tables chairs; or (2) from the determination of the law, *e.g.* obligations.

Meum est promittere, non dimittere /míyəm ès prəmídəriy nòn dəmídəriy/. It is mine to promise, no to discharge.

Mexican divorce. Term used to describe divorce decre in Mexico either by mail order or by the appearanc of one spouse who never acquires a Mexican domi cile. In both cases, the divorce is not entitled to recognition in the United States. Bethune v. Beth une, 192 Ark. 811, 94 S.W.2d 1043.

M.F.B.M. An abbreviation meaning 1,000 feet board measure. T. L. James & Co. v. Galveston County Tex., C.C.A.Tex., 74 F.2d 313.

Miche, or mich /mích/. O. Eng. To practice crime requiring concealment or secrecy; to pilfer articles secretly. *Micher,* one who practices secret crime

Michel-gemot /míkəlgəmòwt/. One of the names of the general council immemorially held in England. The *Witenagemote.*

One of the great councils of king and noblemen i Saxon times.

Michel-synoth /míkəlsìnəd/. Great council. One of the names of the general council of the kingdom in the times of the Saxons.

Michery /míchəriy/. In old English law, theft; cheat ing.

Mid-channel. In international law and by the usage of European nations, the terms "middle of the stream" and "mid-channel" of a navigable river are synony mous and interchangeably used.

Middle line of main channel. The equidistant point in the main channel of the river between the well-defined banks on either shore.

Middleman. One who merely brings parties together in order to enable them to make their own contracts

An agent between two parties; an intermediary who performs the office of a broker or factor between seller and buyer, producer and consumer, land-owner and tenant, etc. One who has been employed as an agent by a principal, and who has employed a sub-agent under him by authority of the principal, either express or implied.

A person who is employed both by the seller and purchaser of goods, or by the purchaser alone, to receive them into his possession, for the purpose of doing something in or about them. One who buys at one price from a manufacturer for resale at a higher price. Distribu-Dor, Inc. v. Karadanis, 11 Cal.App.3d 463, 90 Cal.Rptr. 231, 235.

See also **Broker; Finder; Jobber.**

Middle of the river. The phrases "middle of the river" and "middle of the main channel" are equivalent expressions, and both mean the main line of the channel or the middle thread of the current.

Middle term. A phrase used in logic to denote the term which occurs in both of the premises in the syllogism, being the means of bringing together the two terms in the conclusion.

Middle thread. The middle thread of a stream is an imaginary line drawn lengthwise through the middle of its current.

Midnight deadline. Midnight deadline with respect to a bank is midnight on its next banking day following the banking day on which it receives the relevant item or notice or from which the time for taking action commences to run, whichever is later. U.C.C. § 4–104(h).

Midshipman. A kind of naval cadet, whose business is to second or transmit the orders of the superior officers and assist in the necessary business of the vessel, but understood to be in training for a commission. A *passed* midshipman is one who has passed an examination and is a candidate for promotion to the rank of lieutenant. U. S. v. Cook, 128 U.S. 254, 9 S.Ct. 108, 32 L.Ed. 464. Cadet at U.S. Naval Academy.

Midsummer-day. The summer solstice, which is about June Twenty-Second, and the feast of St. John the Baptist, a festival first mentioned by Maximus Tauricensis, A.D. 400. It was generally a quarter-day for the payment of rents, etc.

Midway. See **Thalweg.**

Midwife. A woman who assists at childbirth; an *accoucheuse.*

Might, *v.* The past tense of the word "may". Equivalent to "had power" or "was possible" or "have the physical or moral opportunity to be contingently possible." In re Weidberg's Estate, 172 Misc. 524, 15 N.Y.S.2d 252, 257.

Migrans jura amittat ac privilegia et immunitates domicilii prioris /máygræn(d)z júrə əmídət æk prívəlíyj(iy)ə èd əmyùwnətéydiyz dòməsíliyay prayórəs/. One who emigrates will lose the rights, privileges, and immunities of his former domicile.

Migration. Movement from one place to another; from one country or region to another country or region.

Migratory divorce. Term used to describe a divorce secured by a spouse who leaves his domicile and moves to, or resides temporarily in, another state or country for purpose of securing the divorce. See also **Mexican divorce.**

Migratory game. Generally applied to birds which move from one place to another in season.

Mile. A measure of length or distance, containing 8 furlongs, or 1,760 yards, or 5,280 feet; or 1,609 kilometers. This is the measure of an ordinary or statute mile; but the nautical or geographical mile contains 6,080 feet. See **Land measure.**

Mileage. Allowance for traveling expenses at certain rate per mile. Especially to members of legislative bodies, witnesses, sheriffs, and bailiffs.

Mileage tax. License tax imposed upon intrastate business of transportation for compensation on public roads of state.

Miles /máyliyz/. Lat. In civil law, a soldier.

In old English law, a knight, because military service was part of the feudal tenure. Also a tenant by military service, not a knight. 1 Bl.Comm. 404.

Milestones. Stones set up to mark the miles on a road or railway.

Militare /mìlətériy/. To be knighted.

Military. Pertaining to war or to the army; concerned with war. Also the whole of military forces, staff, etc. under the Department of Defense.

Military appeals. See **Court of Military Appeals.**

Military base. See **Base.**

Military boards. A military board is a body of persons appointed to act as a fact finding agency or as an advisory body to the appointing authority. A military board may be appointed to investigate, advise, administer or adjudicate. Military boards may act as investigating committees to determine the cause of property damage, injury, or death, or to inquire into loss or misappropriation of property or funds. Boards may also act as administrative tribunals to examine the applicable facts, hear evidence, and make determination concerning personnel matters such as promotion, separation, and retirement.

Military bounty land. See **Bounty.**

Military commissions. Courts whose procedure and composition are modeled upon courts-martial, being the tribunals by which alleged violations of martial law are tried and determined. The membership of such commissions is commonly made up of civilians and army officers. They are probably not known outside of the United States, and were first used by General Scott during the Mexican war.

Military courts. Courts convened subject to the Code of Military Justice (10 U.S.C.A. § 801 *et seq.*); *e.g.* Courts-martial, Court of Military Review, U.S. Court of Military Appeals.

Military feuds. See **Feud.**

Military government. Exercised by military commander under direction of President in time of foreign war without the boundaries of the United States, or in time of rebellion and civil war within states or districts occupied by rebels. Hammond v. Squier, D.C. Wash., 51 F.Supp. 227, 230. See **Martial law.**

Military jurisdiction. There are under the Constitution, three kinds of military jurisdiction: one to be exercised both in peace and war; another to be exercised in time of foreign war without the boundaries of the United States or in time of rebellion and civil war within states or districts occupied by rebels treated as belligerents; and a third to be exercised in time of invasion or insurrection within the limits of the United States or during rebellion within the limits of states maintaining adhesion to the National Government, when the public danger requires its exercise. The first of these may be called jurisdiction under "military law" and is found in acts of Congress prescribing rules and articles of war, or otherwise providing for the government of the national forces; the second may be distinguished as "military government" superseding, as far as may be deemed expedient the local law, and exercised by the military commander under the direction of the President, with the express or implied sanction of Congress; while the third may be denominated "martial law", and is called into action by Congress, or temporarily when the action of Congress cannot be invited, and in the face of justifying or excusing peril, by the President in times of insurrection or invasion, or of civil or foreign war, within districts or localities where ordinary law no longer adequately secures public safety and private rights. United States v. Minoru Yasui, D.C.Or., 48 F.Supp. 40, 46, 47.

Military justice. See **Code of Military Justice; Court Martial; Court of Military Appeals.**

Military law. A system of regulations for the government of armed forces. That branch of the laws which respects military discipline and the government of persons employed in the military service. Military law is distinct from martial law, in that it applies only to persons in the military or naval service of the government; whereas, martial law, when once established, applies alike to citizens and soldiers and supersedes civil law. See **Code of Military Justice.**

Military offenses. Those offenses which are cognizable by the military courts, as insubordination, sleeping on guard, desertion, etc. See **Code of Military Justice.**

Military office. See **Office.**

Military officer. See **Officer.**

Military Review, Courts of. Each armed service has a Court of Military Review which reviews courts-martial decisions. Further appeal is to the U.S. Court of Military Appeals.

Military tenures. The various tenures by knight-service, grand-serjeanty, cornage, etc., were frequently called "military tenures," from the nature of the services which they involved.

Military testament. See **Testament.**

Milites /mílədiyz/. Lat. Knights.

Militia /məlíshə/. The body of citizens in a state, enrolled for discipline as a military force, but not engaged in actual service except in emergencies, as distinguished from regular troops or a standing army.

Militiamen /məlíshəmən/. Comprehends every temporary citizen-soldier who in time of war or emergency enters active military service of the country. Critchlow v. Monson, 102 Utah 378, 131 P.2d 794, 798.

Mill. One-tenth of one cent. Many states use a mill rate to compute property taxes.

Milled money. This term means merely coined money; and it is not necessary that it should be marked or rolled on the edges.

Miller Act. Federal statute which requires the posting of performance and payment bonds before an award may be made for a contract beyond a certain amount for construction, alteration or repair of a public building or public work of the U.S. government. 40 U.S.C.A. §§ 270a–270f.

Miller-Tydings Act. Federal Act (15 U.S.C. § 1) granting anti-trust exemption to State laws which permitted resale price maintenance agreements (fair trade laws). This exemption was repealed in 1975.

Milling in transit. A special privilege allowable at certain designated points, whereby the carrier, having transported grain to a shipper's mill, agrees that the shipper may reship the meal without charge and for which extra compensation is usually exacted by interstate carriers under control of the Interstate Commerce Commission.

Mill power. An expression designating a unit of water power. It is the descriptive term used to rate water power for the purpose of renting it. It indicates the amount of power due to a stated quantity of water used on the particular fall. It is a term of practical convenience in defining the quantity and weight of water available for use by the lessee. The actual amount of horse power developed may vary with the efficiency of the water wheels and other appliances supplied by the lessee.

Mill privilege. The right of a riparian proprietor to erect a mill on his land and to use the power furnished by the stream for the purpose of operating the mill, with due regard to the rights of other owners above and below him on the stream.

Millrate. See **Mill.**

Mill site. A parcel of land on or contiguous to a water-course, suitable for the erection and operation of a mill operated by the power furnished by the stream. Specifically, in mining law, a parcel of land constituting a portion of the public domain, located and claimed by the owner of a mining claim under the laws of the United States (or purchased by him from the government and patented), not exceeding five acres in extent, not including any mineral land, not contiguous to the vein or lode, and occupied and used for the purpose of a mill or for other uses directly connected with the operation of the mine; or a similar parcel of land located and actually used for the purpose of a mill or reduction plant, but not by the owner of an existing mine nor in connection with any particular mining claim. See 30 U.S.C.A. § 42.

Mina /máynə/. In old English law, a measure of corn or grain.

Minage /máynəj/. A toll or duty paid for selling corn by the mina.

Minare /mənériy/. In old records, to mine or dig mines. *Minator,* a miner.

Minatur innocentibus qui parcit nocentibus /mənéydər ìnəséntəbəs kwày pársət nəséntəbəs/. He threatens the innocent who spares the guilty.

Mind. In its legal sense, "mind" means only the ability to will, to direct, to permit, or to assent.

Mind and memory. A phrase applied to testators, denoting the possession of mental capacity to make a will. In other words, one ought to be capable of making his will, with an understanding of the nature of the business in which he is engaged, a recollection of the property he means to dispose of, of the persons who are the objects of his bounty, and the manner in which it is to be distributed between them. See also **Capacity.**

Mind, state of. Evidence is admissible to show a person's state of mind when this issue is material and relevant to the case; *e.g.* statements indicating despair may be admissible on issue of suicide. Fed. Evid.R. 803(3). See also **Mental state.**

Mine. An excavation in the earth from which ores, coal, or other mineral substances are removed by digging or other mining methods, and in its broader sense it denotes the vein, lode, or deposit of minerals. Atlas Milling Co. v. Jones, C.C.A.Okl., 115 F.2d 61, 63. It may include open cut, strip, or hydraulic methods of mining. Rudd v. Hayden, 265 Ky. 495, 97 S.W.2d 35, 37.

Mineral, *adj.* Relating to minerals or the process and business of mining; bearing or producing valuable minerals.

Mineral, *n.* Any valuable inert or lifeless substance formed or deposited in its present position through natural agencies alone, and which is found either in or upon the soil of the earth or in the rocks beneath the soil.

Any natural constituent of the crust of the earth, inorganic or fossil, homogeneous in structure, having a definite chemical composition and known crystallization. The term includes all fossil bodies or matters dug out of mines or quarries, whence anything may be dug, such as beds of stone which may be quarried.

The word is not a definite term and is susceptible of limitations or extensions according to intention with which it is used. Standing alone it might by itself embrace the soil, hence include sand and gravel, or, under a strict definition, it might be limited to metallic substances. Puget Mill Co. v. Duecy, 1 Wash.2d 421, 96 P.2d 571, 573, 574. The term "mineral" as it is used in the public land laws is more restricted than it is when used in some other respects. Its definition has presented many difficulties. It has been held that for purposes of mining laws, a mineral is whatever is recognized as mineral by the standard authorities on the subject. United States v. Toole, D.C.Mont., 224 F.Supp. 440, 444.

Mineral deed. A realty conveyance involving a severance from fee of present title to minerals in place, either effecting such severance in first instance or conveying part of such mineral ownership previously severed from the fee. Hickey v. Dirks, 156 Kan. 326, 133 P.2d 107, 109, 110.

Mineral district. A term occasionally used in acts of congress, designating in a general way those portions or regions of the country where valuable minerals are mostly found, or where the business of mining is chiefly carried on, but carrying no very precise meaning and not a known term of the law.

Mineral land entry. See **Entry.**

Mineral lands. Lands containing deposits of valuable, useful, or precious minerals in such quantities as to justify expenditures in the effort to extract them, and which are more valuable for the minerals they contain than for agricultural or other uses. Northern Pac. R. Co. v. Soderberg, 188 U.S. 526, 23 S.Ct. 365, 47 L.Ed. 575; Deffeback v. Hawke, 115 U.S. 392, 6 S.Ct. 95, 29 L.Ed. 423. Lands on which metals or minerals have been discovered in rock in place. Such lands include not merely metaliferous lands, but all such as are chiefly valuable for their deposits of mineral character, which are useful in arts or valuable for purposes of manufacture, Dunbar Lime Co. v. Utah-Idaho Sugar Co., C.C.A.Utah, 17 F.2d 351, 354; and embrace not only those which the lexicon defines as "mineral", but, in addition, such as are valuable for deposits of marble, slate, petroleum, asphaltum, and even guano. United States v. Northern Pac. R. Co., 311 U.S. 317, 61 S.Ct. 264, 284, 85 L.Ed. 210.

Mineral lease. An agreement permitting use of land to explore, and then, if mineral is discovered, giving right to take mineral either for definite term or so long as it can be produced in paying quantities upon reserved royalty. Gordon v. Empire Gas & Fuel Co., C.C.A.Tex., 63 F.2d 487, 488. A mineral lease so characterized as a real right, is merely a contract which permits the lessee to explore for minerals on the land of the lessor in consideration of the payment of a rental and/or bonuses. Prestridge v. Humble Oil & Refining Co., La.App., 131 So.2d 810, 820. See also **Mining lease.**

Mineral lode. A mineral bed of rock with definite boundaries in a general mass of the mountain and also any zone or belt of mineralized rock lying within boundaries clearly separating it from the neighboring rock.

Mineral right. An interest in minerals in land. A right to take minerals or a right to receive a royalty. Missouri Pac. R. Co. v. Strohacker, 202 Ark. 645, 152 S.W.2d 557, 561; Sheppard v. Stanolind Oil & Gas Co., Tex.Civ.App., 125 S.W.2d 643, 648.

Mineral royalty. Income received from lessees of mineral land. Logan Coal & Timber Ass'n v. Helvering, C.C.A.Pa., 122 F.2d 848, 850. The term is distinguished from mineral interest. Maddox v. Butchee, 203 La. 299, 14 So.2d 4, 9. See also **Mineral lease; Royalty.**

Mineral servitude. The right to exploit or develop. Frost Lumber Industries v. Republic Production Co., C.C.A.La., 112 F.2d 462, 466.

Minerator /mínərèydər/. In old records, a miner.

Miner's inch. See **Inch.**

Minimal contacts. That doctrine of jurisdiction which provides that before a foreign corporation is subject to suit in a state such corporation's activity within the state must meet basic activity requirements. International Shoe Co. v. State of Wash., 326 U.S. 310, 66 S.Ct. 154, 90 L.Ed. 95. For nonresident to be subject to state's personal jurisdiction, he must have certain minimum contacts with state such that maintenance of suit does not offend traditional notions of fair play and substantial justice, and this is the "minimum contacts principle." Lichina v. Futura, Inc., D.C.Colo., 260 F.Supp. 252, 254. See also **Doing business.**

Minima pœna corporalis est major qualibet pecuniaria /mínəmə píynə kòrpəréyləs ést méyjər kwéyləbət pəkyùwniyériyə/. The smallest corporal punishment is greater than any pecuniary one.

Mini-maxi. An underwriting arrangement with a broker requiring the broker to sell the minimum on an all-or-none basis and the balance on a best-efforts basis.

Minimum. The least quantity assignable, admissible or possible in given case and is opposed to maximum. Board of Ed. of City of Rockford v. Page, 33 Ill.2d 372, 211 N.E.2d 361, 363.

Minimum contacts. See **Minimal contacts.**

Minime mutanda sunt quæ certam habuerunt interpretationem /mínəmiy myuwtǽndə sənt kwìy sə́rdəm hæbyuwírənt əntə̀rprətèyshiyównəm/. Things which had had a certain interpretation [whose interpretation has been settled, as by common opinion] are not to be altered.

Miniment /mínəmənt/. An old form of muniment (q.v.).

Minimum charge. The lowest tariff which may be charged to a customer of a public utility or common carrier regardless of the amount of service rendered.

Minimum est nihilo proximum /mínəməm èst náy-(h)əlow próksəməm/. The smallest is next to nothing.

Minimum fee schedules. Schedules of fees which may be charged by lawyers and published generally by bar associations for guidance of the members of the local bar. The trend has been to abolish such schedules as being in violation of the anti-trust laws. Goldfarb v. Virginia State Bar Ass'n, 421 U.S. 773, 95 S.Ct. 2004, 44 L.Ed.2d 572.

Minimum royalty clause. Provision in royalty agreement which prescribes a fixed obligation of the licensee regardless of whether the invention is used or not.

Minimum sentence. The least severe sentence which a judge may impose.

Minimum wage. Such an amount as will maintain a normal standard of living, including the preservation of the health and efficiency of the worker. The least wage on which an ordinary individual can be self-sustaining and obtain the ordinary requirements of life. Associated Industries of Oklahoma v. Industrial Welfare Commission, 185 Okl. 177, 90 P.2d 899, 913. Such minimum wages are set and required by federal statutes of employers engaged in businesses which affect interstate commerce. See **Fair Labor Standards Act.**

Mining. The process or business of extracting from the earth the precious or valuable metals, either in their native state or in their ores.

Mining claim. A parcel of land, containing precious metal in its soil or rock, and appropriated by an individual, according to established rules, by the process of "location." St. Louis Smelting & Refining Co. v. Kemp, 104 U.S. 636, 26 L.Ed. 875. 30 U.S.C.A. § 21 et seq.

A mining claim on public lands is a possessory interest in land that is mineral in character and a respects which discovery within the limits of the claim has been made. Best v. Humboldt Placer Min Co., 371 U.S. 334, 83 S.Ct. 379, 382, 9 L.Ed.2d 350 See also **Mining location; Placer claim.**

Mining district. A section of country usually designated by name and described or understood as being confined within certain natural boundaries, in which the precious metals (or their ores) are found in paying quantities, and which is worked therefor, under rules and regulations prescribed or agreed upon by the miners therein. See also **Mining location.**

Mining lease. A lease of a mine or mining claim or a portion thereof, to be worked by the lessee, usually under conditions as to the amount and character of work to be done, and reserving compensation to the lessor either in the form of a fixed rent or a royalty on the tonnage of ore mined, and which (as distinguished from a license) conveys to the lessee an interest or estate in the land, and (as distinguished from an ordinary lease) conveys not merely the temporary use and occupation of the land, but a portion of the land itself, that is, the ore in place and unsevered and to be extracted by the lessee. See also **Mineral lease.**

Mining location. The act of appropriating and claiming, according to certain established rules and local customs, a parcel of land of defined area, upon or in which one or more of the precious metals or their ores have been discovered, and which constitutes a portion of the public domain, with the declared intention to occupy and work it for mining purposes under the implied license of the United States. Also the parcel of land so occupied and appropriated. St. Louis Smelting & Refining Co. v. Kemp, 104 U.S. 636, 26 L.Ed. 875. Essential to any valid location is the discovery of a valuable mineral deposit. Upon making a valid location the locator has vested rights in the land which are property in the true sense of the word. Cole v. Ralph, 252 U.S. 286, 295, 40 S.Ct. 321, 325, 64 L.Ed. 567. Once the land is patented, the land is private property. See also **Location** (Mining law).

Mining partnership. An association of several owners of a mine for co-operation in working the mine. Kahn v. Central Smelting Co., 102 U.S. 645, 26 L.Ed. 266; Kimberly v. Arms, 129 U.S. 512, 9 S.Ct. 355, 32 L.Ed. 764. Generally, where the parties co-operate in developing a lease for oil and gas, each agreeing to pay his part of the expenses and to share in the profits or losses, a "mining partnership" exists. Continental Supply Co. v. Dickson Oil Co., 194 Okl. 660, 153 P.2d 1017, 1019. A special type of partnership different in many respects from ordinary or trading partnerships. Meister v. Farrow, 109 Mont. 1, 92 P.2d 753, 757, 758, 760, 761.

Mining rent. Consideration given for a mining lease, whether such lease creates a tenancy, conveys a fee, or grants an incorporeal right or a mere license.

Minister. Person acting as agent for another in performance of specified duties or orders. A person ordained according to the usages of some church or associated body of Christians for the preaching of the gospel and filling the pastoral office. In England, holder of government office; *e.g.* Prime Minister.

Foreign minister. An ambassador, minister, or envoy from a foreign government.

International law. An officer appointed by the government of one nation as a mediator or arbitrator between two other nations who are engaged in a controversy, with their consent, with a view to effecting an amicable adjustment of the dispute.

A general name given to the diplomatic representatives sent by one state to another, including ambassadors, envoys, and residents.

Public law. One of the highest functionaries in the organization of civil government, standing next to the sovereign or executive head, acting as his immediate auxiliary, and being generally charged with the administration of one of the great bureaus or departments of the executive branch of government. In England, otherwise called a "cabinet minister," "secretary of state," or "secretary of a department". See also **Ministry.**

Public minister. A general term comprehending all the higher classes of diplomatic representatives,—as ambassadors, envoys, residents,—but not including the commercial representatives, such as consuls.

Ministerial /minəstír(i)yəl/. That which is done under the authority of a superior; opposed to *judicial.* That which involves obedience to instructions, but demands no special discretion, judgment, or skill. State Tax Commission of Utah v. Katsis, 90 Utah 406, 62 P.2d 120, 123; Arrow Exp. Forwarding Co. v. Iowa State Commerce Commission, Iowa, 130 N.W.2d 451, 453. Official's duty is "ministerial" when it is absolute, certain and imperative, involving merely execution of a specific duty arising from fixed and designated facts. Long v. Seabrook, 260 S.C. 562, 197 S.E.2d 659, 662.

Ministerial act. One which a person or board performs in a given state of facts in a prescribed manner in obedience to the mandate of legal authority without regard to or the exercise of his or their own judgment upon the propriety of the act being done. State Tax Commission of Utah v. Katsis, 90 Utah 406, 62 P.2d 120, 123; Gibson v. Winterset Community School Dist., 258 Iowa 440, 138 N.W.2d 112, 115.

Ministerial duty. One regarding which nothing is left to discretion—a simple and definite duty, imposed by law, and arising under conditions admitted or proved to exist.

Ministerial function. A function as to which there is no occasion to use judgment or discretion. Hood Motor Co., Inc. v. Lawrence, La., 320 So.2d 111, 115.

Ministerial office. See **Office.**

Ministerial officer. One whose duties are purely ministerial, as distinguished from executive, legislative, or judicial functions, requiring obedience to the mandates of superiors and not involving the exercise of judgment or discretion.

Ministerial power. See **Power.**

Ministerial trust. See **Trust.**

Ministers plenipotentiary /mínəstərz plènəpətén(t)-shəriy/°shiyèhriy/. *Ministers plenipotentiary* possess full powers, and are of much greater distinction than simple ministers. These are without any particular attribution of rank and character, but by custom are now placed immediately below the ambassador, or on a level with the envoy extraordinary.

Ministrant /mínəstrənt/. The party cross-examining a witness was so called, under the old system of the ecclesiastical courts.

Ministri regis /mənístray ríyjəs/. Lat. In old English law, ministers of the king, applied to the judges of the realm, and to all those who hold ministerial offices in the government.

Ministry. The term as used in England is wider than Cabinet and includes all the holders of public office who come in and go out with the Prime Minister. In this respect it may be contrasted with the Permanent Civil Service, whose tenure is independent of public changes. The first English Ministry as now understood was formed after the general election of 1696.

"Ecclesiastical functions," or "duties." Rector, etc., of St. George's Church in City of New York v. Morgan, 88 Misc. 702, 152 N.Y.S. 497, 498.

Minor. An infant or person who is under the age of legal competence. A term derived from the civil law, which described a person under a certain age as *less than* so many years. In most states, a person is no longer a minor after reaching the age of 18. See also **Delinquent child; Infancy; Juvenile; Legal age; Majority.**

Also, less; of less consideration; lower; a person of inferior condition.

Minor ætas /máynər íytæs/. Lat. Minority or infancy. Literally, lesser age.

Minor ante tempus agere non potest in casu proprietatis nec etiam convenire; differetur usque ætatem; sed non cadit breve /máynər æntiy témpəs æjəriy nòn pówdəst ìn kéys(y)uw prəpràyətéydəs nék éshiyəm kònvənáyriy; dìfəríydər ə́skwiy ətéydəm; sèd nòn kéydət bríyviy/. A minor before majority cannot act in a case of property, nor even agree; it should be deferred until majority; but the writ does not fail.

Minora regalia /mənórə rəgéyl(i)yə/. In English law, the lesser prerogatives of the crown, including the rights of the revenue.

Minor deviation rule. Under "minor deviation rule" for determining when the deviation from purpose and use for which permission to drive insured vehicle is granted will preclude coverage under omnibus clause of policy, if bailee's use is not gross, substantial, or major violation, even though it may have amounted to deviation, protection is still afforded to bailee under omnibus clause. James v. Aetna Life & Cas., 1148, 26 Ariz.App. 137, 546 P.2d 1146.

Minor dispute. A "major dispute" is one which arises over the formation of collective agreements or where there is no such agreement while a "minor dispute" contemplates the existence of collective agreement, no effort is made to bring about a new agreement and the dispute arises over the meaning of the agreement or the proper application of the agreement. Piedmont Aviation, Inc. v. Air Line Pilots Ass'n, Intern., D.C.N.C., 347 F.Supp. 363, 365, 367. See also **Major dispute**.

Minor fact. In the law of evidence, a relative, collateral, or subordinate fact; a circumstance.

Minority. The state or condition of a minor; infancy. Opposite of "majority." See **Minor**.

The smaller number of votes of a deliberative assembly; opposed to majority (q.v.).

Minority opinion. See **Opinion**.

Minority stockholder. Those stockholders of a corporation who hold so few shares in relation to the total outstanding that they are unable to control the management of the corporation or to elect directors.

Minor jurare non potest /máynər jəréríy nòn pówdəst/. A minor cannot make oath. An infant cannot be sworn on a jury.

Minor minorem custodire non debet, alios enim præsumitur male regere qui seipsum regere nescit /máynər mənórəm kɔ̀stədáyriy nòn débət, éyliyows íynəm prəz(y)úwmədər mǽliy réjəriy kwày siyípsəm réjəriy nésət/. A minor ought not to be guardian to a minor, for he who knows not how to govern himself is presumed to be unfit to govern others.

Minor non tenetur respondere durante minori ætate, nisi in causa dotis, propter favorem /máynər nòn təníydər rəspóndəriy d(y)ərǽntiy mənóray ətéydiy, náysay in dówdəs, próptər fəvórəm/. A minor is not bound to reply during his minority, except as a matter of favor in a cause of dower.

Minor offenses. See **Petty offense**.

Minor qui infra ætatem 12 annorum fuerit uteagari non potest, nec extra legem poni, quia ante talem ætatem, non est sub lege aliqua, nec in decenna /máynər kwày ínfrə ətéydəm d(y)uwódəsəm ənórəm fyúwərəd ətləgéray nòn pówdəst, nèk ékstrə líyjəm pównay, kwáyə ǽntiy téyləm ətéydəm, nón èst sɔ̀b líyjiy ǽləkwə nék in dəsénə/. A minor who is under twelve years of age cannot be outlawed, nor placed without the law, because before such age he is not under any law, nor in a decennary.

Minor septemdecim annis non admittitur fore executorem /máynər sèptəmdésəm ǽnəs nòn ədmídədər fóriy əgzèkyətórəm/. A person under seventeen years is not admitted to be an executor. A rule of ecclesiastical law.

Minors' estates. Property of those who have not reached their legal majority and which must be administered after their death or during their lives under a court appointed fiduciary.

Mint. The place designated by law where bullion is coined into money under authority of the government.

Mintage /míntəj/. The charge or commission taken by the mint as a consideration for coining into money

the bullion which is brought to it for that purpose; the same as "seigniorage."

Also that which is coined or stamped as money; the product of the mint.

Mint-mark. The masters and workers of the English mint, in the indentures made with them, agreed "to make a privy mark in the money they make, of gold and silver, so that they may know which moneys were of their own making." After every trial of the pix, having proved their moneys to be lawful, they were entitled to their *quietus* under the great seal, and to be discharged from all suits or actions.

Mint-master. One who manages the coinage.

Minus /máynəs/. Lat. In the civil law, less; less than. The word had also, in some connections, the sense of "not at all." For example, a debt remaining wholly unpaid was described as *"minus solutum."*

Minus Latium /máynəs léyshəm/. See **Jus Latium**.

Minus solvit, qui tardius solvit /máynəs sólvət kwày tárdiyəs sólvət/. He does not pay who pays too late.

Minute. In measures of time or circumference, a minute is the sixtieth part of an hour or degree.

Minutes. Memoranda or notes of a transaction or proceeding. Thus, the record of the proceedings at a meeting of directors or shareholders of a company is called the "minutes."

A memorandum of what takes place in court, made by authority of the court.

Minutes book. A book kept by the clerk or prothonotary of a court for entering memoranda of its proceedings. A record of all actions authorized at corporate board of directors' or stockholders' meeting.

Minutio /mən(y)úwsh(iy)ow/. Lat. In the civil law, a lessening; diminution or reduction.

Miranda hearing. A pre-trial proceeding to determine whether there has been compliance with the requirements of the Miranda Rule (q.v.). The outcome will decide whether the prosecution will be permitted to introduce into evidence statements of the defendant made during custodial interrogation. See **Miranda Rule**.

Miranda Rule /mərǽndə rúwl/. Prior to any custodial interrogation (that is, questioning initiated by law enforcement officers after a person is taken into custody or otherwise deprived of his freedom in any significant way) the person must be warned: 1. That he has a right to remain silent; 2. That any statement he does make may be used as evidence against him; 3. That he has a right to the presence of an attorney; 4. That if he cannot afford an attorney, one will be appointed for him prior to any questioning if he so desires.

Unless and until these warnings or a waiver of these rights are demonstrated at the trial, no evidence obtained in the interrogation may be used against the accused. Miranda v. Arizona, 384 U.S. 436, 444, 478, 479, 86 S.Ct. 1602, 1612, 1630, 16 L.Ed.2d 694.

Mis. An inseparable particle used in composition, to mark an ill sense or depravation of the meaning; as "miscomputation" or "misaccompting," *i.e.,* false reckoning.

Misa /máyzə/. In old English law, the mise or issue in a writ of right; a compact or agreement; a form of compromise.

Misadventure. A mischance or accident; a casualty caused by the act of one person inflicting injury upon another. Homicide "by misadventure" occurs where a man, doing a lawful act, without any intention of hurt, unfortunately kills another.

Misallege /mìsəléj/. To cite falsely as a proof or argument.

Misapplication. Improper, illegal, wrongful, or corrupt use of application of funds, property, etc. See also **Misappropriation.**

Misappropriation. The act of misappropriating or turning to a wrong purpose; wrong appropriation; a term which does not necessarily mean peculation, although it may mean that. Term may also embrace the taking and use of another's property for sole purpose of capitalizing unfairly on good will and reputation of property owner. Pocket Books, Inc. v. Dell Pub. Co., 49 Misc.2d 252, 267 N.Y.S.2d 269, 272.

Misbehavior. Ill conduct; improper or unlawful behavior. So as to support contempt conviction is conduct inappropriate to particular role of actor, be he judge, juror, party, witness, counsel or spectator. U. S. v. Seale, C.A.Ill., 461 F.2d 345, 366.

Misbranding. False or misleading labeling. People v. Rosenbloom, 119 Cal.App. 759, 2 P.2d 228, 231. Such practices are prohibited by federal and state statutes; *e.g.* Fair Packaging and Labeling Act.

Miscarriage /məskǽrəj/mískæ̀rəj/. Poor management or administration; mismanagement.

Miscarriage of justice. Decision or outcome of legal proceeding that is prejudicial or inconsistent with substantial rights of party.

As used in constitutional standard of reversible error, "miscarriage of justice" means a reasonable probability of more favorable outcome for the defendant. People v. Lopez, 251 Cal.App.2d 918, 60 Cal. Rptr. 72, 76. A miscarriage of justice, warranting reversal, should be declared only when the court, after examination of entire cause, including the evidence, is of the opinion that it is reasonably probable that a result more favorable to appealing party would have been reached in absence of the error. People v. Bernhardt, 222 C.A.2d 567, 35 Cal.Rptr. 401, 419.

Miscarriage of justice from erroneous charge to jury, under statute declaring that no judgment shall be set aside or new trial granted on basis of error which does not result in such miscarriage, results only when an erroneous charge is reasonably calculated to confuse or mislead. Marley v. Saunders, Fla., 249 So.2d 30, 35.

Miscegenation /məsèjənéyshən/mísəjə°/. Mixture of races; marriage between persons of different races, as between a white person and a Negro.

Mischarge. An erroneous charge; a charge, given by a court to a jury, which involves errors for which the judgment may be reversed.

Mischief. In legislative parlance, the word is sometimes used to signify the evil or danger which a statute is intended to cure or avoid.

In the phrase "malicious mischief," *(q.v.)* it imports a wanton or reckless injury to persons or property.

A person is guilty of criminal mischief if he: (a) damages tangible property of another purposely, recklessly, or by negligence in the employment of fire, explosives, or other dangerous means, or (b) purposely or recklessly tampers with tangible property of another so as to endanger person or property; or (c) purposely or recklessly causes another to suffer pecuniary loss by deception or threat. Model Penal Code, § 220.3.

Misconduct. A transgression of some established and definite rule of action, a forbidden act, a dereliction from duty, unlawful behavior, willful in character, improper or wrong behavior; its synonyms are misdemeanor, misdeed, misbehavior, delinquency, impropriety, mismanagement, offense, but not negligence or carelessness. Term "misconduct" when applied to act of attorney, implies dishonest act or attempt to persuade court or jury by use of deceptive or reprehensible methods. People v. Sigal, 249 C.A.2d 299, 57 Cal.Rptr. 541, 549. Misconduct, which renders discharged employee ineligible for unemployment compensation, occurs when conduct of employee evinces willful or wanton disregard of employer's interest, as in deliberate violations, or disregard of standards of behavior which employer has right to expect of his employees, or in carelessness or negligence of such degree or recurrence as to manifest wrongful intent or evil design. Wilson v. Brown, La.App., 147 So.2d 27, 29. See also **Wanton misconduct.**

Misconduct in office. Any unlawful behavior by a public officer in relation to the duties of his office, willful in character. Term embraces acts which the office holder had no right to perform, acts performed improperly, and failure to act in the face of an affirmative duty to act. See also **Malfeasance; Misfeasance.**

Miscontinuance. In practice, an improper continuance; want of proper form in a continuance; the same with "discontinuance."

Miscreant /mískriyənt/. In old English law, an apostate; an unbeliever; one who totally renounced Christianity. 4 Bl.Comm. 44.

Misdate. A false or erroneous date affixed to a paper or document.

Misdelivery. Delivery of mail, freight, goods, or the like, to person other than authorized or specified recipient. The delivery of property by a carrier or warehouseman to a person not authorized by the owner or person to whom the carrier or warehouseman is bound by his contract to deliver it.

Misdemeanant /mìsdəmíynənt/. A person guilty of a misdemeanor; one sentenced to punishment upon conviction of a misdemeanor.

Misdemeanor /mìsdəmíynər/. Offenses lower than felonies and generally those punishable by fine or imprisonment otherwise than in penitentiary. Under federal law, and most state laws, any offense other than a felony is classified as a misdemeanor. 18 U.S.C.A. § 1. Certain states also have various classes of misdemeanors (*e.g.* Class A, B, etc.). See also **Infraction; Petty offense.**

Misdescription. An error or falsity in the description of the subject-matter of a contract which deceives one of the parties to his injury, or is misleading in a material or substantial point. See also **Misrepresentation.**

Misdirection. An error made by a judge in instructing the jury upon the trial of a cause.

Mise /máyz/míyz/. In common law pleading, the issue in a writ of right. When the tenant in a writ of right pleads that his title is better than the demandant's, he is said to join the *mise* on the mere right.

Also expenses; costs; disbursements in an action.

Mise-money. In old English law, money paid by way of contract or composition to purchase any liberty, etc.

Miserabile depositum /mìzəréybəliy dəpózədəm/. Lat. In the civil law, the name of an involuntary deposit, made under pressing necessity; as, for instance, shipwreck, fire, or other inevitable calamity.

Misera est servitus, ubi jus est vagum aut incertum /mízərə èst sárvədəs yúwbay jás èst véygəm òd ənsárdəm/. It is a wretched state of slavery which subsists where the law is vague or uncertain.

Miserere /mìzəríriy/. The name and first word of one of the penitential psalms, being that which was commonly used to be given by the ordinary to such condemned malefactors as were allowed the benefit of clergy; whence it is also called the "psalm of mercy."

Misericordia /mìzərəkórd(i)yə/. Lat. Mercy; a fine or amerciament; an arbitrary or discretionary amercement.

Misericordia communis /mìzərəkórd(i)yə kəmyúwnəs/. In old English law, a fine set on a whole county or hundred.

Misfeasance /mìsfíyzən(t)s/. The improper performance of some act which a man may lawfully do. "Nonfeasance" means the omission of an act which a person ought to do; "misfeasance" is the improper doing of an act which a person might lawfully do; and "malfeasance" is the doing of an act which a person ought not to do at all.

Misfeazance. See **Misfeasance.**

Misfortune. An adverse event, calamity, or evil fortune, arising by accident (or without the will or concurrence of him who suffers from it), and not to be foreseen or guarded against by care or prudence. In its application to the law of homicide, this term always involves the further idea that the person causing the death is not at the time engaged in any unlawful act. See also **Accident.**

Misjoinder. See **Joinder.**

Miskenning /mìskéniŋ/. In Saxon and old English law, an unjust or irregular summoning to court; to speak unsteadily in court; to vary in one's plea.

Mislaid property. See **Property.**

Mislay. To deposit in a place not afterwards recollected; to lose anything by forgetfulness of the place where it was laid.

Misleading. Delusive; calculated to lead astray or to lead into error. A Judge's instructions which are of such a nature as to be misunderstood by the jury, or to give them a wrong impression, are said to be "misleading." See also **Misrepresentation.**

Misnomer. Mistake in name; giving incorrect name to person in accusation, indictment, pleading, deed or other instrument. Under rules practice in some states, such is ground for dismissal by motion. In most states, however, as well as in the federal courts, such misnomer can be corrected by amendment of the pleadings.

When a misnomer occurs in a deed, the normal procedure is to prepare and record a correction deed. Commonly, a quit claim deed is used for this purpose.

Mispleading. Pleading incorrectly, or omitting anything in pleading which is essential to the support or defense of an action, is so called; as in the case of a plaintiff not merely stating his title in a defective manner, but setting forth a title which is essentially defective in itself; or if, to an action of debt, the defendant pleads "not guilty" instead of *nil debet.* Rules of Civil Procedure (in effect in the federal and many state courts) permit liberal amendment of incorrect or deficient pleadings. See Fed.R.Civil P. 15.

Misprision. A word used to describe an offense which does not possess a specific name. United States v. Perlstein, C.C.A.N.J., 126 F.2d 789, 798. But more particularly and properly the term denotes either: (1) a contempt against the sovereign, the government, or the courts of justice, including not only contempts of court, properly so called, but also all forms of seditious or disloyal conduct and leze-majesty; (2) maladministration of public office; neglect or improper performance of official duty, including peculation of public funds; (3) neglect of light account made of a crime, that is, failure in the duty of a citizen to endeavor to prevent the commission of a crime, or, having knowledge of its commission, to fail to reveal it to the proper authorities.

Concealment of crime. See **Misprision of felony.**

Negative misprision. The concealment of something which ought to be revealed; that is, misprision in the third of the specific meanings given above.

Positive misprision. The commission of something which ought not to be done; that is, misprision in the first and second of the specific meanings given above.

Misprision of felony. The offense of concealing a felony committed by another, but without such previous concert with or subsequent assistance to the felon as would make the party concealing an accessory before or after the fact. United States v. Perlstein, C.C.A. N.J., 126 F.2d 789, 798.

Whoever, having knowledge of the actual commission of a felony cognizable by a court of the United States, conceals and does not as soon as possible make known the same to some judge or other person in civil or military authority under the United States, is guilty of the federal crime of misprision of felony. 18 U.S.C.A. § 4.

Misprision of treason. The bare knowledge and concealment of an act of treason or treasonable plot by failing to disclose it to the appropriate officials; that is, without any assent or participation therein, for if the latter elements be present the party becomes a principal. 18 U.S.C.A. § 2382.

Misreading. Reading a deed or other instrument to an illiterate or blind man (who is a party to it) in a false or deceitful manner, so that he conceives a wrong idea of its tenor or contents.

Misrecital /mìsrəsáydəl/. The erroneous or incorrect recital of a matter of fact, either in an agreement, deed, or pleading.

Misrepresentation. Any manifestation by words or other conduct by one person to another that, under the circumstances, amounts to an assertion not in accordance with the facts. An untrue statement of fact. An incorrect or false representation. That which, if accepted, leads the mind to an apprehension of a condition other and different from that which exists. Colloquially it is understood to mean a statement made to deceive or mislead.

In a limited sense, an intentional false statement respecting a matter of fact, made by one of the parties to a contract, which is material to the contract and influential in producing it. A "misrepresentation," which justifies the rescission of a contract, is a false statement of a substantive fact, or any conduct which leads to a belief of a substantive fact material to proper understanding of the matter in hand, made with intent to deceive or mislead.

See also **Deceit; Fraud; Material fact; Reliance.**

Insurance law. A statement of something as a fact which is untrue and material to the risk, and which assured states knowing it to be untrue and with intent to deceive, or which insured states positively as true, not knowing it to be true, and which has a tendency to mislead. One that would influence a prudent insurer in determining whether or not to accept the risk, or in fixing the amount of the premium in the event of such acceptance. See also **Material fact.**

Missilia /məsáyl(i)yə/. In Roman law, gifts or liberalities, which the prætors and consuls were in the habit of throwing among the people.

Missing ship. In maritime law, a vessel is so called when, computed from her known day of sailing, the time that has elapsed exceeds the average duration of similar voyages at the same season of the year.

Missions. In church parlance, the establishment of churches and schools and relief depots through which are taught the principles of Christianity, the afflicted cared for, and the needy supplied.

Missura /mìs(y)úrə/. The ceremonies used in a Roman Catholic church to recommend and dismiss a dying person.

Mistake. Some unintentional act, omission, or error arising from ignorance, surprise, imposition, or misplaced confidence. A mistake exists when a person,

under some erroneous conviction of law or fact, does, or omits to do, some act which, but for the erroneous conviction, he would not have done or omitted. It may arise either from unconsciousness, ignorance, forgetfulness, imposition, or misplaced confidence. Salazar v. Steelman, 22 Cal.App.2d 402, 71 P.2d 79, 82. See also **Error; Ignorance.**

Mistake of fact is a mistake not caused by the neglect of a legal duty on the part of the person making the mistake, and consisting in (1) an unconscious ignorance or forgetfulness of a fact, past or present, material to the contract; or (2) belief in the present existence of a thing material to the contract which does not exist, or in the past existence of such a thing which has not existed.

A *mistake of law* happens when a party, having full knowledge of the facts, comes to an erroneous conclusion as to their legal effect. It is a mistaken opinion or inference, arising from an imperfect or incorrect exercise of the judgment, upon facts, Page v. Provines, 179 Okl. 391, 66 P.2d 7, 10; and necessarily presupposes that the person forming it is in full possession of the facts. The facts precede the law, and the true and false opinion alike imply an acquaintance with them. The one is the result of a correct application of legal principles, which every man is presumed to know, and is called "law;" the other, the result of a faulty application, and is called a "mistake of law."

Mutual mistake is where the parties have a common intention, but it is induced by a common or mutual mistake. "Mutual" as used in the expression mutual mistake of fact expresses a thought of reciprocity and distinguishes it from a mistake which is a common mistake of both parties. There is something of the thought of a common mistake because it must affect both parties. Mistake of fact as ground for relief may be neither "mutual" nor common in the strict sense because it may be wholly the mistake of one of the parties, the other being wholly ignorant both of the fact upon the faith of which the other has mistakenly acted and that the other has acted upon such an understanding of the fact situation.

Mister. A title of courtesy. A trade, craft, occupation, employment, office.

Mistery. A trade or calling.

Mistrial. An erroneous, invalid, or nugatory trial. A trial of an action which cannot stand in law because of want of jurisdiction, or a wrong drawing of jurors, or disregard of some other fundamental requisite before or during trial. Trial which has been terminated prior to its normal conclusion. The judge may declare a mistrial because of some extraordinary event (*e.g.* death of juror, or attorney), for prejudicial error that cannot be corrected at trial, or because of a deadlocked jury.

Misuser /mìsyúwzər/. An unlawful use of a right. Abuse of an office or franchise. 2 Bl.Comm. 153.

Mitigating circumstances. Such as do not constitute a justification or excuse of the offense in question, but which, in fairness and mercy, may be considered as extenuating or reducing the degree of moral culpability. Mitigating circumstances which will reduce degree of homicide to manslaughter are the commission of the killing in a sudden heat of passion caused by adequate legal provocation. People v. Morrin, 31 Mich.App. 301, 187 N.W.2d 434, 438.

Those that affect basis for award of exemplary damages, or reduce actual damages by showing, not that they were never suffered, but that they have been partially extinguished.

In actions for libel and slander, circumstances bearing on defendant's liability for exemplary damages by reducing moral culpability, or on liability for actual damages by showing partial extinguishment thereof. The "mitigating circumstances" which the statute allows defendant in libel action to prove are those which tend to show that defendant in speaking the slanderous words acted in good faith, with honesty of purpose, and not maliciously. Roemer v. Retail Credit Co., 44 C.A.3d 926, 119 Cal.Rptr. 82, 91.

Mitigation. Alleviation, reduction, abatement or diminution of a penalty or punishment imposed by law.

Mitigation of damages. Doctrine of "mitigation of damages," sometimes called doctrine of avoidable consequences, imposes on injured party duty to exercise reasonable diligence and ordinary care in attempting to minimize his damages after injury has been inflicted and care and diligence required of him is the same as that which would be used by man of ordinary prudence under like circumstances. Darnell v. Taylor, La.App., 236 So.2d 57, 61. Mitigation of damages is an affirmative defense and applies when plaintiff fails to take reasonable actions that would tend to mitigate his injuries. Mott v. Persichetti, Colo.App., 534 P.2d 823, 825. See Restatement, Contracts § 336(1); U.C.C. § 2–603. See also **Avoidable consequences, doctrine of.**

Mitigation of punishment. A judge may reduce or order a lesser sentence in consideration of such factors as the defendant's past good behavior, his family situation, his cooperation with the police and kindred factors.

Mitior sensus /míshiyər sén(t)səs/. Lat. The more favorable acceptation.

Mitius imperanti melius paretur /míshiyəs impərǽntay míyl(i)yəs pəríydər/. The more mildly one commands, the better is he obeyed.

Mitter. L. Fr. To put, to send, or to pass; as, *mitter l'estate*, to pass the estate; *mitter le droit*, to pass a right. These words are used to distinguish different kinds of releases.

Mitter avant /mídər əvǽnt/. L. Fr. In old practice, to put before; to present before a court; to produce in court.

Mittimus /mídəməs/. The name of a precept in writing, issuing from a court or magistrate, directed to the sheriff or other officer, commanding him to convey to the prison the person named therein, and to the jailer, commanding him to receive and safely keep such person until he shall be delivered by due course of law. State v. Lenihan, 151 Conn. 552, 200 A.2d 476, 478. Transcript of minutes of conviction and sentence duly certified by court clerk. United States ex rel. Chasteen v. Denmark, C.C.A.Ill., 138 F.2d 289, 291.

Old English law. A writ enclosing a record sent to be tried in a county palatine; it derives its name from the Latin word *mittimus*, "we send." It is the jury process of these counties, and commands the proper officer of the county palatine to command the sheriff to summon the jury for the trial of the cause, and to return the record, etc.

Mixed. Formed by admixture or commingling; partaking of the nature, character, or legal attributes of two or more distinct kinds or classes.

As to mixed Action; Blood relations *(Mixed blood)*; Contract; Government; Jury; Larceny; Marriage; Nuisance; Policy; Presumption; Property; Tithes; and War, see those titles.

Mixed insurance company. One which has, at least in part, the nature of both stock and mutual companies, and in which a certain portion of the profits is divided among the stockholders and distribution of other funds is made among the insured. Ohio Farmers Indemnity Co. v. Commissioner of Internal Revenue, C.C.A.Ohio, 108 F.2d 665, 667; Pink v. Town Taxi Co., 138 Me. 44, 21 A.2d 656, 658, 659.

Mixed laws. A name sometimes given to those which concern both persons and property.

Mixed question of law and fact. A question depending for solution on questions of both law and fact, but is really a question of either law or fact to be decided by either judge or jury.

Mixed questions. This phrase may mean either those which arise from the conflict of foreign and domestic laws, or questions arising on a trial involving both law and fact.

Mixed subjects of property. Such as fall within the definition of things real, but which are attended, nevertheless, with some of the legal qualities of things personal, as emblements, fixtures, and shares in public undertakings, connected with land. Besides these, there are others which, though things personal in point of definition, are, in respect of some of their legal qualities, of the nature of things real; such are animals *feræ naturæ*, charters and deeds, court rolls, and other evidences of the land, together with the chests in which they are contained, ancient family pictures, ornaments, tombstones, coats of armor, with pennons and other ensigns, and especially heirlooms.

Mixtion /míks(h)chən/. The mixture or confusion of goods or chattels belonging severally to different owners, in such a way that they can no longer be separated or distinguished; as where two measures of wine belonging to different persons are poured together into the same cask. See also **Commingle; Fungibles.**

Mixtum imperium /míkstəm impíriyəm/. Lat. In old English law, mixed authority; a kind of civil power. A term applied by Lord Hale to the "power" of certain subordinate civil magistrates as distinct from "jurisdiction."

M'Naghten Rule. In the majority of jurisdictions in this country, what is most often referred to as the M'Naghten Rule has long been accepted as the test to be applied for the defense of insanity. Under

M'Naghten test or rule, an accused is not criminally responsible if, at the time of committing the act, he was laboring under such a defect of reason from disease of the mind as not to know the nature and quality of the act he was doing, or if he did know it that he did not know he was doing what was wrong. M'Naghten's Case, 8 Eng.Rep. 718 (1843).

The standard under the "M'Naghten insanity" test to determine whether a person is sane is did the defendant have sufficient mental capacity to know and understand what he was doing, and did he know and understand that it was wrong and a violation of the rights of another; to be "sane" and thus responsible to the law for the act committed, the defendant must be able to both know and understand the nature and quality of his act and to distinguish between right and wrong at the time of the commission of the offense. People v. Crosier, 41 Cal.App.3d 712, 116 Cal.Rptr. 467, 471.

See also **Insanity,** *supra,* regarding other tests used by courts in determining criminal responsibility.

Mob. An assemblage of many people, acting in a violent and disorderly manner, defying the law, and committing, or threatening to commit, depredations upon property or violence to persons.

The word, in legal use, is practically synonymous with "riot," but the latter is the more correct term.

Mobilia /mowbíliyə/. Lat. Movables; movable things; otherwise called *"res mobiles."*

Mobilia non habent situm /mowbíliyə nòn héybənt sáydəm/. Movables have no *situs* or local habitation.

Mobilia sequuntur personam /mowbíliyə səkwántər pərsównəm/. Movables follow the [law of the] person.

Mock. To deride, to laugh at, to ridicule, to treat with scorn and contempt.

Modal legacy. See **Legacy.**

Mode. The manner in which a thing is done; as the mode of proceeding, the mode of process.

Model. A preliminary pattern or representation of something to be made or something already made. A *facsimile* of something invented, made on a reduced scale, in compliance with the patent laws. Style or design of product or item. See also **Sample.**

Model act. Statute proposed by the National Conference of Commissioners of Uniform State Laws for adoption by state legislatures, *e.g.* Model Business Corporation Act; Model Penal Code; Model Probate Code. Frequently, the state adopting the model act will modify it to some extent to meet its own needs or may adopt only a portion of such.

Model Jury Instructions. See **Jury instructions.**

Moderamen inculpatæ tutelæ /modəréymən ìnkəlpéydiy tyuwtíyliy/. Lat. In Roman law, the regulation of justifiable defense. A term used to express that degree of force in defense of the person or property which a person might safely use, although it should occasion the death of the aggressor.

Moderata misericordia /mòdəréydə mìzərəkórd(i)yə/. A writ founded on *Magna Charta,* which lies for him who is amerced in a court, not of record, for any transgression beyond the quality or quantity of the offense. It is addressed to the lord of the court, or his bailiff, commanding him to take a moderate amerciament of the parties.

Moderate castigavit /mòdəréydiy kæstəgéyvət/. Lat. In old pleading, be moderately chastised. The name of a plea in trespass which justifies an alleged battery on the ground that it consisted in a moderate chastisement of the plaintiff by the defendant, which, from their relations, the latter had a legal right to inflict.

Moderator. A chairman or president of an assembly. A person appointed to preside at a popular meeting. The presiding officer of town meetings in New England is so called.

Modiatio /mòwdiyéysh(iy)ow/. In old English law, a certain duty paid for every tierce of wine.

Modica circumstantia facti jus mutat /mówdəkə sàrkəmstǽnsh(iy)əm fǽktay jə́s myúwdət/. A small circumstance attending an act may change the law.

Modification. A change; an alteration or amendment which introduces new elements into the details, or cancels some of them, but leaves the general purpose and effect of the subject-matter intact.

Modify. To alter; to change in incidental or subordinate features; enlarge, extend; amend; limit, reduce. Such alteration or change may be characterized, in quantitative sense, as either an increase or decrease. Johnson v. Three Bays Properties No. 2, Inc., Fla. App., 159 So.2d 924, 926. See **Modification.**

Modius /mówd(i)yəs/. Lat. A measure. Specifically, a Roman dry measure having a capacity of about 550 cubic inches; but in medieval English law used as an approximate translation of the word "bushel."

Modius terræ vel agri /mówd(i)yə téhriy vèl ǽgray/. In old English law, a quantity of ground containing in length and breadth 100 feet.

Modo et forma /mówdow èt fórmə/. Lat. In manner and form. Words used in the old Latin forms of pleadings by way of traverse, and literally translated in the modern precedents, importing that the party traversing denies the allegation of the other party, not only in its general effect, but in the exact *manner and form* in which it is made.

Modus /mówdəs/. Lat. In Civil law, manner; means; way.

Criminal pleading. The *modus* of an indictment is that part of it which contains the narrative of the commission of the crime; the statement of the mode or manner in which the offense was committed.

Ecclesiastical law. A peculiar manner of tithing, growing out of custom.

Old conveyancing. Mode; manner; the arrangement or expression of the terms of a contract or conveyance.

Also a consideration; the consideration of a conveyance, technically expressed by the word *"ut".*

A qualification, involving the idea of variance or departure from some general rule or form, either by way of restriction or enlargement, according to the circumstances of a particular case, the will of a donor, the particular agreement of parties, and the like.

Rank modus. One that is too large. Rankness is a mere rule of evidence, drawn from the improbability of the fact, rather than a rule of law.

Modus decimandi /mówdəs dèsəmǽnday/. In Ecclesiastical law, a manner of tithing; a partial exemption from tithes, or a pecuniary composition prescribed by immemorial usage, and of reasonable amount; for it will be invalid as a *rank modus* if greater than the value of the tithes in the time of Richard I.

Modus de non decimando /mówdəs dìy nòn dèsəmǽndow/. In Ecclesiastical law, a custom or prescription of entire exemption from the payment of tithes; this is not valid, unless in the case of abbeylands.

Modus de non decimando non valet /mówdəs dìy nòn desəmǽndow nòn vǽlət/. A *modus* (prescription) not to pay tithes is void.

Modus et conventio vincunt legem /mówdəs èt kənvénsh(iy)ow vínkənt líyjəm/. Custom and agreement overrule law. This maxim forms one of the first principles relative to the law of contracts. The exceptions to the rule here laid down are in cases against public policy, morality, etc.

Modus habilis /mówdəs hǽbələs/. A valid manner.

Modus legem dat donationi /mówdəs líyjəm dæt dənèyshiyównay/. Custom gives law to the gift.

Modus operandi /mówdəs òpərǽnday/. Method of operating or doing things (M.O.). Term used by police and criminal investigators to describe the particular method of a criminal's activity.

Modus tenendi /mówdəs tənénday/. The manner of holding; *i.e.,* the different species of tenures by which estates are held.

Modus transferrendi /mówdəs trænsfərénday/. The manner of transferring.

Modus vacandi /mówdəs vəkǽnday/. The manner of vacating. How and why an estate has been relinquished or surrendered by a vassal to his lord might well be referred to by this phrase.

Moeble /myuwbəl/. L. Fr. Movable. *Biens moebles,* movable goods.

Moerda /mə́rdə/. The secret killing of another; murder.

Mohatra. In French law, a transaction covering a fraudulent device to evade the laws against usury. It takes place where an individual buys merchandise from another on a credit at a high price, to sell it immediately to the first seller, or to a third person who acts as his agent, at a much less price for cash.

Moiety /móyədiy/. The half of anything. Joint tenants are said to hold by moieties. See also **Community property**.

Moiety acts. A name sometimes applied to penal and criminal statutes which provide that half the penalty or fine shall inure to the benefit of the informer.

Molliter manus imposuit /mólədər mǽnəs impóz(h)uwət/. Lat. He gently laid hands upon. Formal words in the old Latin pleas in actions of trespass and assault where a defendant justified laying hands upon the plaintiff, as where it was done to keep the peace, etc. The phrase is literally translated in the modern precedents, and the original is retained as the name of the plea in such cases.

Monarchial. Of or pertaining to a monarchy or government by royalty. See **Monarchy**.

Monarchy /mónərkiy/. A government in which the supreme power is vested in a single person. Where a monarch is invested with absolute power, the monarchy is termed "despotic;" where the supreme power is virtually in the laws, though the majesty of government and the administration are vested in a single person, it is a "limited" or "constitutional" monarchy. It is hereditary where the regal power descends immediately from the possessor to the next heir by blood, as in England; or elective, as was formerly the case in Poland.

Moneta /məníydə/. Lat. Money (*q.v.*).

Moneta est justum medium et mensura rerum commutabilium, nam per medium monetæ fit omnium rerum conveniens et justa æstimatio /məníydə èst jə́stəm míydiyəm èt mens(y)úrə rírəm kòmyuwdəbíl(i)yəm, nǽm pər míydiyəm məníydiy fid ómniyəm rírəm kənvíyn(i)yən(d)z èt jə́stə èstəméysh(iy)ow/. Money is the just medium and measure of commutable things, for by the medium of money a convenient and just estimation of all things is made.

Monetagium /mònətéyj(iy)əm/. Mintage, or the right of coining money. Hence, anciently, a tribute payable to a lord who had the prerogative of coining money, by his tenants, in consideration of his refraining from changing the coinage.

Monetandi jus comprehenditur in regalibus quæ nunquam a regio sceptro abdicantur /mònətǽnday jə́s kòmprəhéndədər in rəgéyləbəs kwíy nə́ŋkwæm èy ríyj(iy)ow séptrow æbdəkǽntər/. The right of coining money is comprehended among those royal prerogatives which are never relinquished by the royal scepter.

Monetary. The usual meaning is "pertaining to coinage or currency or having to do with money", but it has been held to include personal property. In re Kipp's Will, Sur., 37 N.Y.S.2d 541, 543.

Monetary bequest. A transfer by will of cash. It is often designated as a pecuniary bequest.

Money. In usual and ordinary acceptation it means coins and paper currency used as circulating medium of exchange, and does not embrace notes, bonds, evidences of debt, or other personal or real estate. Lane v. Railey, 280 Ky. 319, 133 S.W.2d 74, 79, 81. See also Currency; Current money; Flat money; Legal tender; Near money; Scrip; Wampum.

A medium of exchange authorized or adopted by a domestic or foreign government as a part of its currency. U.C.C. § 1–201(24).

Public money. Revenue received from federal, state, and local governments from taxes, fees, fines, etc. See **Revenue.**

Money-bill. An act by which revenue is directed to be raised, for any purpose or in any shape whatsoever, either for governmental purposes, and collected from the whole people generally, or for the benefit of a particular district, and collected in that district, or for making appropriations. All federal revenue bills must arise in the House of Representatives, but the Senate may propose or concur with amendments as on other bills. Art. I, Sec. 7, U.S.Const.

Money changers. A money changer is one whose occupation is the exchanging of kinds or denominations of currency, and the common meaning of the term pertained to those persons who, in early history, engaged in the business of foreign exchange and it includes the business of a banker and buying and selling of uncurrent funds and the exchanging of one kind of money for another. Arnold v. City of Chicago, 387 Ill. 532, 56 N.E.2d 795, 799. Such functions are today handled by the international departments of banks.

Money claims. In English practice, under the Judicature Act of 1875, claims for the price of goods sold, for money lent, for arrears of rent, etc., and other claims where money is directly payable on a contract express or implied, as opposed to the cases where money is claimed by way of damages for some independent wrong, whether by breach of contract or otherwise. These "money claims" correspond very nearly to the "money counts" or "common counts" formerly in use.

Money demand. A claim for a fixed and liquidated amount of money, or for a sum which can be ascertained by mere calculation; in this sense, distinguished from a claim which must be passed upon and liquidated by a jury, called "damages."

Moneyed corporation. See **Corporation.**

Money had and received. In common law pleading, the technical designation of a form of declaration in *assumpsit,* wherein the plaintiff declares that the defendant *had and received* certain money, etc.

Gist of action for "money had and received" is that defendant has received money which, in equity and good conscience, should have been paid to plaintiff and under such circumstances that he ought to pay it over.

Money judgment. A final order, decree or judgment of a court by which a defendant is required to pay a sum of money in contrast to a decree or judgment of equity in which the court orders some other type of relief; *e.g.* injunction or specific performance. See also **Judgment.** For enforcement of money judgments, see **Execution.**

Money land. A phrase descriptive of money which is held upon a trust to convert it into land.

Money lent. In common law pleading, the technical name of a declaration in an action of *assumpsit* for which the defendant promised to pay the plaintiff for money lent.

Money made. The return made by a sheriff to a writ of execution, signifying that he has collected the sum of money required by the writ.

Money market. The financial machinery for dealing in short term paper such as notes and loans in contrast to the capital market which furnishes long term financing.

Money of adieu. In French law, earnest money; so called because given at parting in completion of the bargain. *Arrhes* is the usual French word for earnest money; "money of adieu" is a provincialism found in the province of Orleans.

Money order. A type of negotiable draft issued by banks, post offices, telegraph companies and express companies and used by the purchaser as a substitute for a check. Form of credit instrument calling for payment of money to named payee, and involving three parties: remitter, payee, and drawee. Fidelity Bank & Trust Co. v. Fitzimons, Minn., 261 N.W.2d 586, 589. Money order may encompass nonnegotiable as well as negotiable instruments and may be issued by a governmental agency, a bank, or private person or entity authorized to issue it, but essential characteristic is that it is purchased for purpose of paying a debt or to transmit funds upon credit of the issuer of the money order. People v. Norwood, 26 C.A.3d 148, 103 Cal.Rptr. 7, 12.

Money-order office. One of the post-offices authorized to draw or pay money orders.

Money paid. In common law pleading, the technical name of a declaration in *assumpsit,* in which the plaintiff declares for money paid for the use of the defendant. See also **Money had and received.**

Money-purchase plan. A pension plan where the employer contributes a specified amount of cash each year to each employee's pension fund. Benefits ultimately received by the employee are not specifically defined but depend on the rate of return on the cash invested.

Monger /móngər/. A dealer or seller. It is seldom or never used alone, or otherwise than after the name of any commodity, to express a seller of such commodity; *e.g.* fishmonger, moneymonger.

Moniers, or **moneyers** /mówniyərz/mə́niyərz/. Ministers of the mint; also bankers.

Moniment /mónəmənt/. A memorial, superscription, or record.

Monition /məníshən/. In admiralty, formerly the summons to appear and answer, issued on filing the libel; which was either a simple monition *in personam* or an attachment and monition *in rem.* With the unification of the Admiralty Rules and Federal Rules of Civil Procedure in 1966, the monition was abolished.

General monition. In civil law practice, a monition or summons to all parties in interest to appear and show cause against the decree prayed for.

Practice. A monition is a formal order of the court commanding something to be done by the person to whom it is directed, and who is called the "person monished." Thus, when money is decreed to be paid, a monition may be obtained commanding its payment. In ecclesiastical procedure, a monition is an order monishing or warning the party complained against to do or not to do a certain act "under pain of the law and contempt thereof." A monition may also be appended to a sentence inflicting a punishment for a past offense; in that case the monition forbids the repetition of the offense.

Monitory letters /mónət(ə)riy lédərz/. Communications of warning and admonition sent from an ecclesiastical judge, upon information of scandal and abuses within the cognizance of his court.

Monocracy /mənókrəsiy/. A government by one person.

Monocrat /mónəkræt/. A monarch who governs alone; an absolute governor.

Monogamy /mənógəmiy/. The marriage of one wife only, or the state of such as are restrained to a single wife. The term is used in opposition to "bigamy" and "polygamy."

Monomachy /mənóməkiy/. A duel; a single combat. It was anciently allowed by law for the trial or proof of crimes. It was even permitted in pecuniary causes, but it is now forbidden both by the civil law and canon laws.

Monopolia dicitur, cum unus solus aliquod genus mercaturæ universum emit, pretium ad suum libitum statuens. It is said to be a monopoly when one person alone buys up the whole of one kind of commodity, fixing a price at his own pleasure.

Monopolium /mònəpówl(i)yəm/. The sole power, right, or privilege of sale; monopoly; a monopoly.

Monopoly /mənóp(ə)ly/. A privilege or peculiar advantage vested in one or more persons or companies, consisting in the exclusive right (or power) to carry on a particular business or trade, manufacture a particular article, or control the sale of the whole supply of a particular commodity. A form of market structure in which one or only a few firms dominate the total sales of a product or service.

"Monopoly", as prohibited by Section 2 of the Sherman Antitrust Act, has two elements: possession of monopoly power in relevant market and willful acquisition or maintenance of that power, as distinguished from growth or development as a consequence of a superior product, business acumen, or historic accident. U. S. v. Grinnell Corp., 384 U.S. 563, 86 S.Ct. 1698, 1704, 16 L.Ed.2d 778. A monopoly condemned by the Sherman Act is the power to fix prices or exclude competition, coupled with policies designed to use or preserve that power. U. S. v. Otter Tail Power Co., D.C.Minn., 331 F.Supp. 54, 58.

It is "monopolization" in violation of Sherman Antitrust Act for persons to combine or conspire to acquire or maintain power to exclude competitors from any part of trade or commerce, provided they also have such power that they are able, as group, to exclude actual or potential competition and provided that they have intent and purpose to exercise that power. Davidson v. Kansas City Star Co., D.C.Mo., 202 F.Supp. 613, 617.

See also **Market; Relevant market.**

Natural monopoly. A natural monopoly is one resulting where one firm of efficient size can produce all or more than market can take at remunerative price. Ovitron Corp. v. General Motors Corp., D.C.N.Y., 295 F.Supp. 373, 377. One which is created from circumstances over which the monopolist has no power. For example, a market for a particular product may be so limited that it is impossible to profitably produce such except by a single plant large enough to supply the whole demand. U. S. v. Aluminum Co. of America, C.C.A.N.Y., 148 F.2d 416, 430.

Monopoly power. The "monopoly power" which must exist in order to establish a violation of Sherman Antitrust Act may be defined as the power to fix prices, to exclude competitors, or to control the market in the relevant geographical area in question. H. F. & S. Co. v. American Standard, Inc., D.C.Kan., 336 F.Supp. 110, 123. See also **Market; Relevant market.**

Monopsony. A condition of the market in which there is but one buyer for a particular commodity.

Monstrans de droit /mónstrən(d)z də dróyt/. L. Fr. In English law, a showing or manifestation of right; one of the common law methods of obtaining possession or restitution from the crown, of either real or personal property. It is the proper proceeding when the right of the party, as well as the right of the crown, appears upon record, and consists in putting in a claim of right grounded on facts already acknowledged and established, and praying the judgment of the court whether upon these facts the king or the subject has the right. 3 Bl.Comm. 256.

Monstrans de faits /mónstrən(d)z də féy(ts)/. L. Fr. In old English practice, a showing of deeds; a species of profert.

Monstraverunt, writ of /ríd əv mònstrəvírənt/. In English law, a writ which lies for the tenants of ancient demesne who hold by free charter, and not for those tenants who hold by copy of court roll, or by the rod, according to the custom of the manor.

Montes pietatis /móntiyz pàyətéydəs/. Public pawnbroking establishments; institutions established by government, in some European countries, for lending small sums of money on pledges of personal property. In France they are called *"monts de piété."*

Month. Word "month," unless otherwise defined, means "calendar month," or time from any day of any of the months as adjudged in the calendar to corresponding day, if any, if not any, to last day, of next month.

The space of time denoted by this term varies according as one or another of the following varieties of months is intended:

Astronomical, containing one-twelfth of the time occupied by the sum in passing through the entire zodiac.

Calendar, civil, or *solar,* which is one of the months in the Gregorian calendar,—January, February, March, etc.,—which are of unequal length.

Lunar, being the period of one revolution of the moon, or twenty-eight days.

The word "month," when used in a statute or contract without qualification, meant at common law a lunar month of 28 days. State v. White, 73 Fla. 426, 74 So. 486, 487.

Monument. Anything by which the memory of a person, thing, idea, art, science or event is preserved or perpetuated. A tomb where a dead body has been deposited.

In real-property law and surveying, monuments are visible marks or indications left on natural or other objects indicating the lines and boundaries of a survey. In this sense the term includes not only posts, pillars, stone markers, cairns, and the like, but also fixed natural objects, blazed trees, and even a watercourse. Any physical object on ground which helps to establish location of line called for; it may be either natural or artificial, and may be a tree, stone, stake, pipe, or the like. Delphey v. Savage, 227 Md. 373, 177 A.2d 249, 251. See also **Natural monument.**

Monumenta quæ nos recorda vocamus sunt veritatis et vetustatis vestigia /mónyəmentə kwìy nóws rəkórdə vowkéyməs sènt vèhrətéydəs èt vèdəstéydəs vəstíj(iy)ə/. Monuments, which we call "records," are the vestiges of truth and antiquity.

Monung. See **Manung.**

Moonshine. Intoxicating liquor illicitly produced or smuggled into community for beverage purposes, or spirituous liquor, illegally distilled or manufactured. State v. King, 331 Mo. 268, 53 S.W.2d 252, 254.

Moorage. A sum charged for use of mooring facilities. Act of mooring vessel.

Mooring. Anchoring or making fast to the shore or dock. The securing or confining a vessel in a particular station, as by cables and anchors or by a line or chain run to the wharf.

Moot. A subject for argument; unsettled; undecided. A moot point is one not settled by judicial decisions.

A case is "moot" when a determination is sought on a matter which, when rendered, cannot have any practical effect on the existing controversy. Leonhart v. McCormick, D.C.Pa., 395 F.Supp. 1073, 1076. Question is "moot" when it presents no actual controversy or where the issues have ceased to exist. Matter of Lawson's Estate, 41 Ill.App.3d 37, 353 N.E.2d 345, 347.

Generally, an action is considered "moot" when it no longer presents a justiciable controversy because issues involved have become academic or dead. Sigma Chi Fraternity v. Regents of University of Colo., D.C.Colo., 258 F.Supp. 515, 523. Case in which the matter in dispute has already been resolved and hence, one not entitled to judicial intervention unless the issue is a recurring one and likely to be raised again between the parties, Super Tire Engineering Co. v. McCorkle, 416 U.S. 115, 94 S.Ct. 1694, 40 L.Ed.2d 1.

Moot court. A court held (normally in law schools) for the arguing of moot or hypothetical cases.

Moot hill. Hill of meeting (gemot), on which the Britons used to hold their courts, the judge sitting on the eminence; the parties, etc., on an elevated platform below.

Mooting. The exercise of arguing questions of law or equity, raised for the purpose. See **Moot court.**

Moot man. One of those who used to argue the reader's cases in the inns of court.

Mora /mórə/. Lat. In the civil law, delay; default; neglect; culpable delay or default.

Moral. Pertains to character, conduct, intention, social relations, etc.

1. Pertaining or relating to the conscience or moral sense or to the general principles of right conduct.

2. Cognizable or enforceable only by the conscience or by the principles of right conduct, as distinguished from positive law.

3. Depending upon or resulting from probability; raising a belief or conviction in the mind independent of strict or logical proof.

4. Involving or affecting the moral sense; as in the phrase "moral insanity."

Moral actions. Those only in which men have knowledge to guide them, and a will to choose for themselves.

Moral certainty. That degree of assurance which induces a man of sound mind to act, without doubt, upon the conclusions to which it leads. A high degree of impression of the truth of a fact, falling short of absolute certainty, but sufficient to justify a verdict of guilty, even in a capital case. Such signifies a probability sufficiently strong to justify action on it; a very high degree of probability, although not demonstrable, as a certainty. It has also been used as indicating a conclusion of the mind established beyond a reasonable doubt. Gray v. State, 56 Okl.Cr. 208, 38 P.2d 967.

Moral consideration. See **Consideration.**

Moral duress. Consists in imposition, oppression, undue influence, or the taking of undue advantage of the business or financial stress or extreme necessity or weakness of another. Lafayette Dramatic Productions v. Ferentz, 305 Mich. 193, 9 N.W.2d 57, 66. See also **Coercion; Duress.**

Moral evidence. As opposed to "mathematical" or "demonstrative" evidence, this term denotes that kind of evidence which, without developing an absolute and necessary certainty, generates a high degree of probability or persuasive force. It is founded upon analogy or induction, experience of the ordinary course of nature or the sequence of events, and the testimony of men.

Moral fraud. This phrase is one of the less usual designations of "actual" or "positive" fraud or "fraud in fact," as distinguished from "constructive fraud" or "fraud in law." It means fraud which involves actual guilt, a wrongful purpose, or moral obliquity.

Moral hazard. See **Hazard.**

Moral law. The law of conscience; the aggregate of those rules and principles of ethics which relate to right and wrong conduct and prescribe the standards to which the actions of men should conform in their dealings with each other. See also **Natural law.**

Moral obligation. See **Obligation.**

Moral turpitude. The act of baseness, vileness, or the depravity in private and social duties which man owes to his fellow man, or to society in general, contrary to accepted and customary rule of right and duty between man and man. State v. Adkins, 40 Ohio App.2d 473, 320 N.E.2d 308, 311, 69 O.O.2d 416. Act or behavior that gravely violates moral sentiment or accepted moral standards of community and is a morally culpable quality held to be present in some criminal offenses as distinguished from others. Lee v. Wisconsin State Bd. of Dental Examiners, 29 Wis.2d 330, 139 N.W.2d 61, 65. The quality of a crime involving grave infringement of the moral sentiment of the community as distinguished from statutory mala prohibita. People v. Ferguson, 55 Misc.2d 711, 286 N.Y.S.2d 976, 981. See also **Turpitude.**

Morandæ solutionis causa /mərǽndiy səl(y)ùwshiyównəs kózə/. Lat. For the purpose of delaying or postponing payment or performance.

Mora reprobatur in lege /mórə rèprəbéydər in líyjiy/. Delay is reprobated in law.

Moratorium /mòhrətór(i)yəm/. A term designating suspension of all or of certain legal remedies against debtors, sometimes authorized by law during financial distress. A period of permissive or obligatory delay; specifically, a period during which an obligor has a legal right to delay meeting an obligation. State ex rel. Jensen Livestock Co. v. Hyslop, 111 Mont. 122, 107 P.2d 1088, 1092. Delay or postponement of an action or proceeding. See **Injunction; Restraining order.**

More favorable terms clause. A provision in a labor-management contract by which the union agrees not to make more favorable agreements with other and competing employers.

More or less. About; substantially; or approximately; implying that both parties assume the risk of any ordinary discrepancy. The words are intended to cover slight or unimportant inaccuracies in quantity, Carter v. Finch, 186 Ark. 954, 57 S.W.2d 408; and are ordinarily to be interpreted as taking care of unsubstantial differences or differences of small importance compared to the whole number of items transferred.

Moreover. In addition thereto, also, furthermore, likewise, beyond this, besides this.

Morganatic-marriage. See **Marriage.**

Morgangina, or **morgangiva** /morgǽnjənə/°jəvə/. A gift on the morning after the wedding; dowry; the husband's gift to his wife on the day after the wedding.

Morgue /mórg/. A place where the bodies of persons found dead are kept for a limited time and exposed to view, to the end that their relatives or friends may identify them.

Mormon. A member of the Church of Jesus Christ of Latter-day Saints. The Church was organized in 1830 at Seneca, New York, by Joseph Smith, and today its headquarters are in Salt Lake City, Utah.

Morning loan. An unsecured loan to permit the borrower, generally a stockbroker, to carry on his business for the day.

Moron. A term indicating a mentally defective person usually having a mental age of eight to twelve years and an I.Q. of 50 to 70.

Morphinomania, or **morphinism** /mòrfənəméyn(i)yə /mórfənìzəm/. The opium habit. An excessive desire for morphia.

Morris Plan Company. An industrial bank which accepts money from the public for investment in investment certificates which draw interest periodically payable to the investor, and which bank lends money principally to steadily employed salaried people who are required to secure repayment with the endorsement of two other employed salaried people, the contract calling for installment payments over a one year period. Other secured loans are also made. Board of Com'rs of Tulsa County v. Remedial Finance Corporation, 186 Okl. 648, 100 P.2d 240, 242.

Mors /mórz/. Lat. Death. State v. Logan, 344 Mo. 351, 126 S.W.2d 256, 259.

Mors dicitur ultimum supplicium /mórz dísədər ə́ltəməm səplísh(iy)əm/. Death is called the "last punishment," the "extremity of punishment."

Morsellum, or **morsellus, terræ** /morséləm téhriy /°ləs°/. In old English law, a small parcel or bit of land.

Mors omnia solvit /mórz ómniyə sólvət/. Death dissolves all things. Applied to the case of the death of a party to an action.

Mortal. Destructive to life; causing or occasioning death; exposing to or deserving death, especially spiritual death; deadly; fatal, as, a mortal wound, or mortal sin; of or pertaining to time of death.

Mortality. The relative incidence of death.

Mortality tables. A means of ascertaining the probable number of years any man or woman of a given age and of ordinary health will live. A mortality table expresses, on the basis of the group studied, the probability that, of a number of persons of equal expectations of life who are living at the beginning of any year, a certain number of deaths will occur within that year. National Life & Acc. Ins. Co. v. U. S., D.C.Tenn., 381 F.Supp. 1034, 1037.

Such tables are used by insurance companies to determine the premium to be charged for those in the respective age groups.

Mort civile /mór(t) səvíyl/. In French law, civil death, as upon conviction for felony. It was nominally abolished in 1854, but something very similar to it, in effect at least, still remains. Thus, the property of the condemned, possessed by him at the date of his conviction, goes and belongs to his successors (*héritiers*), as in case of an intestacy; and his future acquired property goes to the state by right of its prerogative (*par droit de déshérence*), but the state may, as a matter of grace, make it over in whole or in part to the widow and children.

Mort d'ancestor /mórt dǽnsəstər/. An ancient and now almost obsolete remedy in the English law. An assize of *mort d'ancestor* was a writ which lay for a person whose ancestor died seised of lands in fee-simple, and after his death a stranger abated; and this writ directed the sheriff to summon a jury or assize, who should view the land in question and recognize whether such ancestor were seised thereof on the day of his death, and whether the demandant were the next heir.

Mortgage /mórgəj/. A mortgage is an interest in land created by a written instrument providing security for the performance of a duty or the payment of a debt.

At common law, an estate created by a conveyance absolute in its form, but intended to secure the performance of some act, such as the payment of money, and the like, by the grantor or some other person, and to become void if the act is performed agreeably to the terms prescribed at the time of making such conveyance. The mortgage operates as a conveyance of the legal title to the mortgagee, but such title is subject to defeasance on payment of the debt or performance of the duty by the mortgagor.

The above definitions are applicable to the common-law (*i.e.* estate or title) conception of a mortgage. Such conception is still applicable in certain states. But in many other states, a mortgage is regarded as a mere lien, and not as creating a title or estate. Zeigler v. Sawyer, Tex.Civ.App., 16 S.W.2d 894, 896. It is a pledge or security of particular property for the payment of a debt or the performance of some other obligation, whatever form the transaction may take, but is not now regarded as a conveyance in effect, though it may be cast in the form of a conveyance. Still other states have adopted a hybrid or intermediate theory or category of mortgage.

See also Assumption of mortgage; Balloon mortgage; Bulk mortgage; Chattel mortgage; Collateral mortgage; Corporate mortgage trust; Deed *(Deed of trust)*; In rem mortgage; Potomac mortgages; Release *(Release of mortgage)*; Ship Mortgage Act; Submortgage; Tacit mortgage; Trust *(Trust deed)*; Union mortgage clause. For "bona fide mortgage," see **Bona fide.**

Amortized mortgage. One in which the mortgagor pays the current interest charge as well as a portion of principal in his periodic payment.

Blanket mortgage. One which conveys title to or creates a lien on all the borrower's assets or a substantial portion of them rather than on a specific asset.

Closed-end mortgage. One in which neither the property mortgaged nor the amount borrowed may be altered during the term of the mortgage.

Consolidated mortgage. A single mortgage given to replace or to combine several outstanding mortgages.

Construction draw mortgage. Type of mortgage used to finance building construction.

Conventional mortgage. The conventional mortgage is a contract by which a person binds the whole of his property, or a portion of it only, in favor of another, to secure the execution of some engagement, but without divesting himself of possession. It is distinguished from the "legal" mortgage, which is a privilege which the law alone in certain cases gives to a creditor over the property of his debtor, without stipulation of the parties. This last is very much like a general lien at common law, created by the law rather than by the act of the parties, such as a judgment lien.

Conventional home mortgage. The common security device used by those who wish to purchase a home by transferring to the bank or other financial institution a lien or defeasible legal title in return for the price or part of the price of the home. A non-FHA or VA home loan; *i.e.* not backed by government insurance or security. The mortgage is conventional in that the lender looks only to the credit of the borrower and the security of the property, and not to the additional backing of another such as would be the case with an FHA insured mortgage.

Equitable mortgage. A specific lien upon real property to secure the payment of money or the performance of some other obligation, which a court of equity will recognize and enforce, in accordance with the clearly ascertained intent of the parties to that effect, but which lacks the essential features of a legal mortgage, either because it grows out of the transactions of the parties without any deed or express contract to give a lien, or because the instrument used for that purpose is wanting in some of the characteristics of a common-law mortgage, or, being absolute in form, is accompanied by a collateral reservation of a right to redeem, or because an explicit agreement to give a mortgage has not been carried into effect.

FHA mortgage. One in which the loan has been insured in whole or in part by the Federal Housing Administration.

First mortgage. The first (in time or right) of a series of two or more mortgages covering the same property and successively attaching as liens upon it. Also, in a more particular sense, a mortgage which is a first lien on the property, not only as against other mortgages, but as against any other charges or incumbrances. Also called "senior" mortgage.

First mortgage bonds. Bonds the payment of which is secured by a first mortgage on property.

General mortgage. Mortgages are sometimes classified as general and special, a mortgage of the former class being one which binds all property, present and future, of the debtor (sometimes called a "blanket" mortgage); while a special mortgage is limited to certain particular and specified property.

Graduated payment mortgage (GPM). Type of mortgage financing, offered primarily to aid first time home buyers, wherein the monthly payments gradually increase over a number of years as the income of the mortgagee increases.

Joint mortgage. One which is given to or by two or more mortgagees jointly.

Judicial mortgage. In the law of Louisiana, the lien resulting from judgments, whether rendered on contested cases or by default, whether final or provisional, in favor of the person obtaining them. Civ.Code La. art. 3321.

Junior mortgage. One which ranks below another mortgage of the name property in the value of the security, and is subordinate to senior mortgages in its rights.

Leasehold mortgage. Mortgage secured by lessee's interest in leased property.

Legal mortgage. A term used in Louisiana. The law alone in certain cases gives to the creditor a mortgage on the property of his debtor, without it being requisite that the parties should stipulate it. That is called "legal mortgage." It is also called a *tacit* mortgage, because it is established by the law without the aid of any agreement. Civ.Code La. art. 3311.

Mortgage of goods. See **Chattel mortgage.**

Open-end mortgage. A mortgage permitting the mortgagor to borrow additional money under the same mortgage, with certain conditions, usually as to the assets of the mortgagor.

Package mortgage. A package mortgage is used to include not only the real property but many items of personal property incident to the real property, such as stoves, refrigerators, and the like.

Purchase money mortgage. Generally, any mortgage given to secure a loan made for the purpose of acquiring the land on which the mortgage is given; more particularly, a mortgage given to the seller of land to secure payment of a portion of the purchase price. A mortgage given, concurrently with a conveyance of land, by the vendee to the vendor, on the same land, to secure the unpaid balance of the purchase price.

Second mortgage. One which takes rank immediately after a first mortgage on the same property, without any intervening liens, and is next entitled to satisfaction out of the proceeds of the property. Properly speaking, however, the term designates the second of a series of mortgages, not necessarily the second lien. For instance, the lien of a judgment might intervene between the first and second mortgages; in which case, the second mortgage would be the third lien. Also called "junior" mortgage. See also *Wrap-around mortgage,* below.

Senior mortgage. One which ranks ahead of another mortgage in terms of rights in the security. See also *First mortgage, supra.*

Straight mortgage. One in which the mortgagor is obligated to pay interest during the term of the mortgage and a final payment of principal at the end of the term in contrast to an amortized mortgage.

Tacit mortgage. See *Legal mortgage, supra.*

Variable rate mortgage. A long-term mortgage contract which includes a provision permitting the lending institution to adjust, upward and downward, the contract's interest rate in response to changes in money market rates and the conditions of demand for mortgages.

Wrap around mortgage. Method of refinancing whereby a new mortgage to cover a new loan is placed in a secondary position to the existing mortgage on the original loan. The entire loan is treated as a single obligation.

Mortgage banker. A person or firm engaged in the business of dealing in mortgages including their placement and refinancing. Normally such banker uses its own funds as opposed to a commercial or savings and loan bank which uses primarily funds of depositors. While some mortgage bankers do provide long term (permanent) financing, the majority specialize in short term and interim financing.

Mortgage bond. Bonds for which real estate or personal property is pledged as security that the bond will be paid as stated in its terms. May be first, second, refunding, and so on.

Mortgage broker. Person or firm who functions as intermediary between borrower and lender in securing loan.

Mortgage certificate. Document evidencing participation in a large mortgage held by the mortgagee for the benefit of the certificate holders.

Mortgage clause. Provision in fire insurance policies protecting the mortgagee as his interest may appear.

Mortgage commitment. A formal written communication by a lender, agreeing to make a mortgage loan on specific property, specifying the loan's amount, length of time, and conditions.

Mortgage company. A firm engaged in the business of originating and closing mortgages which are then assigned or sold to investors.

Mortgage contingency clause. Clause in an agreement for sale of real estate conditioning the purchaser's performance on his obtaining a mortgage from a third party.

Mortgagee /mòrgəjíy/. He that takes or receives a mortgage.

Mortgagee in possession. A mortgagee of real property who is in possession of it with the agreement or assent of the mortgagor, express or implied, and in recognition of his mortgage and because of it, and under such circumstances as to make the satisfaction of his lien an equitable prerequisite to his being dispossessed.

Mortgage foreclosure. See **Foreclosure.**

Mortgage guarantee insurance. A type of insurance which guarantees to the mortgagee a given portion of the loss if the mortgagee suffers a loss due to nonpayment on the loan. See **Federal Housing Administration; Insurance.**

Mortgage insurance. See **Insurance.**

Mortgage lien. Lien on property of mortgagor which secures debt obligation. In some states, the mortgagor retains legal title until foreclosure and the mortgagee has a security interest called a lien which is recognized ahead of other claims to the property.

Mortgage loan. A loan secured by a mortgage on real estate in which the borrower is the mortgagor and the lender the mortgagee. See **Mortgage.**

Mortgaging out. The process by which a mortgagor secures one hundred percent financing of his purchase. He purchases property with no money of his own but entirely with mortgage money.

Mortgagor /mórgəjər/. One who, having all or some part of title to property, by written instrument pledges that property for some particular purpose such as security for a debt. That party to a mortgage who gives legal title or a lien to the mortgagee to secure the mortgage loan.

Morth. Sax. Murder, answering exactly to the French *"assassinat"* or *"muertre de guet-apens"*.

Morthlaga /mórθlèygə/. A murderer.

Morthlage /mórθlèyj/. Murder.

Mortis causa /mórdəs kózə/. Lat. By reason of death; in contemplation of death. Thus used in the phrase *"Donatio mortis causa" (q.v.)*.

Mortis momentum est ultimum vitæ momentum /mórdəs məméntəm èst óltəməm váydiy məméntəm/. The last moment of life is the moment of death.

Mortmain /mórtmèyn/. A term applied to denote the alienation of lands or tenements to any corporation, sole or aggregate, ecclesiastical or temporal. These purchases having been chiefly made by religious houses, in consequence of which lands became perpetually inherent in one dead hand, this has occasioned the general appellation of "mortmain" to be applied to such alienations. 2 Bl.Comm. 268; Perin v. Carey, 65 U.S. (24 How.) 465, 16 L.Ed. 701.

Mortmain acts. These acts had for their object to prevent lands getting into the possession or control of religious corporations, or, as the name indicates, *in mortua manu*. After numerous prior acts dating from the reign of Edward I, it was enacted by the statute 9 Geo. II, c. 36 (called the "Mortmain Act" *par excellence*), that no lands should be given to charities unless certain requisites should be observed.

Mortuary. A burial-place. Term applied to undertaking and embalming establishments.

A kind of ecclesiastical heriot, being a customary gift of the second best living animal belonging to the deceased, claimed by and due to the minister in many parishes, on the death of his parishioners, whether buried in the church-yard or not. 2 Bl.Comm. 425.

Term has been sometimes used in a civil as well as in an ecclesiastical sense, and applied to a payment to the lord of the fee.

Mortuary tables. See **Actuarial table; Mortality tables.**

Mortuum vadium /mórchuwəm véydiyəm/. A dead pledge; a mortgage *(q.v.);* a pledge where the profits or rents of the thing pledged are not applied to the payment of the debt.

Mortuus /mórchuwəs/. Lat. Dead. So in sheriff's return. *Mortuus est*, he is dead.

Mortuus civiliter /mórchuwəs səvílədər/. Civil death *(q.v.)*.

Mortuus exitus non est exitus /mórchuwəs égzədəs nón èst égzədəs/. A dead issue is no issue. A child born dead is not considered as issue.

Mortuus sine prole /mórchuwəs sáyniy prówliy/. Dead without issue. In genealogical tables often abbreviated to *"m.s.p."*

Moslem Law. One of the two great systems of customary law which the English found in India. It regulated the life and relations of all Moslems, and parts of it, especially its penal provisions, were applied to both Moslems and Hindus.

Mos retinendus est fidelissimæ vetustatis /móws rètənéndəs èst fàydəlísəmiy vèdəstéydəs/. A custom of the truest antiquity is to be retained.

Most favored nation clause. A clause found in most treaties providing that the citizens or subjects of the contracting nations may enjoy the privileges accorded by either party to those of the most favored nations. The general design of such clauses is to establish the principle of equality of international treatment. The test of whether this principle is violated by the concession of advantages to a particular nation is not the form in which such concession is made, but the condition on which it is granted; whether it is given for a price, or whether this price is in the nature of a substantial equivalent, and not of a mere evasion. The United States has generally taken the stand that reciprocal commercial concessions are given for a valuable consideration and are not within the scope of this clause. Whitney v. Robertson, 124 U.S. 190, 8 S.Ct. 456, 31 L.Ed. 386. See also **Reciprocal trade agreements.**

A primary effect of "most favored nation" status is lower import tariffs or duties.

Most suitable use valuation. For gift and death tax purposes, property that is transferred normally is valued in accordance with its most suitable or highest and best use. Thus, if a farm is worth more as a potential shopping center, this value will control even though the transferee (*i.e.*, the donee or heir) continues to use the property as a farm. For an exception to this rule concerning the valuation of certain kinds of real estate transferred by death, see **Special use valuation.**

Mote /mówt/. Sax. A meeting; an assembly. Used in composition, as *burgmote, folkmote*, etc.

Moteer. A customary service or payment at the mote or court of the lord, from which some were exempted by charter or privilege.

Mother. A woman who has borne a child. A female parent. The term includes maternity during prebirth period.

Mother-in-law. The mother of one's wife or of one's husband.

Motion. In parliamentary law, the formal mode in which a member submits a proposed measure or resolve for the consideration and action of the meeting.

An application made to a court or judge for purpose of obtaining a rule or order directing some act to be done in favor of the applicant. State v. James, Mo., 347 S.W.2d 211, 216. It is usually made within the framework of an existing action or proceeding and is ordinarily made on notice, but some motions may be made without notice. One without notice is called an ex parte motion. Written or oral application to court for ruling or order, made before (*e.g.* motion to dismiss) during (*e.g.* motion for directed verdict), or after (*e.g.* motion for new trial) trial. For requisite form of motions, see Fed.R.Civil P. 7(b).

See also **Speaking motion.**

Motion for judgment notwithstanding verdict. A motion that judgment be entered in accordance with the movant's earlier motion for a directed verdict and notwithstanding the contrary verdict actually returned by the jury. Huff v. Thornton, 287 N.C. 1, 213 S.E.2d 198, 204. See Fed.R.Civil P. 50(b).

Motion for judgment on pleadings. Under Fed.R.Civil P. 12(c) any party may move after the pleadings are closed for judgment thereon. It is a device for disposing of cases when the material facts are not in dispute and only questions of law remain. See also **Summary judgment.**

Motion for more definite statement. If a pleading is so vague or ambiguous that a party cannot reasonably be required to frame a responsive pleading, he may move for a more definite statement. Fed.R.Civil P. 12(e).

Motion for new trial. A request that the judge set aside the judgment and order a new trial on the basis that the trial was improper or unfair due to specified prejudicial errors that occurred. Fed.R.Civil P. 59.

Motion in bar. One which, if allowed, will absolutely bar the action; *e.g.* plea of double jeopardy. U. S. v. Jorn, 400 U.S. 470, 91 S.Ct. 547, 27 L.Ed.2d 543.

Motion in limine. A written motion which is usually made before or after the beginning of a jury trial for a protective order against prejudicial questions and statements. Robinson v. State, Ind.App., 309 N.E.2d 833, 854. Purpose of such motion is to avoid injection into trial of matters which are irrelevant, inadmissible and prejudicial and granting of motion is not a ruling on evidence and, where properly drawn, granting of motion cannot be error. Redding v. Ferguson, Tex.Civ.App., 501 S.W.2d 717, 724.

Motion to dismiss. One which is generally interposed before trial to attack the action on the basis of insufficiency of the pleading, of process, venue, joinder, etc. Fed.R.Civil P. 12(b).

Motion to strike. On motion of either party, the court may order stricken from any pleading any insufficient defense, or any redundant, immaterial, impertinent or scandalous matter. Fed.R.Civil P. 12(f).

Motion to suppress. Device used to eliminate from the trial of a criminal case evidence which has been secured illegally, generally in violation of the Fourth Amendment (search and seizure), the Fifth Amendment (privilege against self incrimination), or the Sixth Amendment (right to assistance of counsel, right of confrontation etc.), of U.S. Constitution. See Fed.R.Crim.P. 12(b) and 41(f); also **Suppression hearing.**

Motive. Cause or reason that moves the will and induces action. An inducement, or that which leads or tempts the mind to indulge a criminal act. People v. Lewis, 275 N.Y. 33, 9 N.E.2d 765, 768.

In common usage intent and "motive" are not infrequently regarded as one and the same thing. In law there is a distinction between them. "Motive" is the moving power which impels to action for a definite result. Intent is the purpose to use a particular means to effect such result. "Motive" is that which incites or stimulates a person to do an act. People v. Weiss, 252 App.Div. 463, 300 N.Y.S. 249, 255.

As to criminal motive, see **Criminal.** See also **Intent.**

Motor Carrier Act. Federal statute (administered by ICC) which regulates (routes, rates, etc.) motor carriers of freight and passengers in interstate commerce. 49 U.S.C.A. § 301 *et seq.*

Mouth of river. By statute in some states, the mouth of a river or creek, which empties into another river or creek, is defined as the point where the middle of the channel of each intersects the other.

Movable. That which can be changed in place, as movable property; or in time, as movable feasts or terms of court. Compare **Fixture.**

Movable estate. A term equivalent to "personal estate" or "personal property."

Movable freehold. A term applied by Lord Coke to real property which is capable of being increased or diminished by natural causes; as where the owner of seashore acquires or loses land as the waters recede or approach.

Movables. Things movable; movable or personal chattels which may be annexed to or attendant on the person of the owner, and carried about with him from one place to another. Things which may be carried from one place to another whether they move by themselves or whether they are inanimate objects capable of being moved by extraneous power. Succession of Young, La.App., 205 So.2d 791, 796.

Movant. One who moves; one who makes a motion before a court; the applicant for a rule or order.

Move. To make an application to a court for a rule or order, or to take action in any matter. The term comprehends all things necessary to be done by a litigant to obtain an order of the court directing the relief sought. See **Motion.**

To propose a resolution, or recommend action in a deliberate body.

To pass over; to be transferred, as when the consideration of a contract is said to "move" from one party to the other.

To occasion; to contribute to; to tend or lead to.

Movent. An alternative spelling of *movant.*

Move out. To vacate; to yield up possession.

Moving papers. Such papers as are made the basis of some motion in court proceedings, *e.g.* a motion for summary judgment with supporting affidavits.

Mrs. Title of courtesy prefixed to name of woman to indicate that she is or has been married. Guide Pub. Co. v. Futrell, 175 Va. 77, 7 S.E.2d 133, 138.

Muciana cautio /m(y)ùwsiyéynə kósh(iy)ow/. See **Cautio.**

Mug book. Collection of pictures or "mug shots" of suspects in criminal cases kept by police and FBI and displayed to victim or witnesses in order to obtain identification of criminal offender.

Mugshot. Pictures taken when person is booked; usually used as an official photograph by police officers.

Mulatto /məládow/m(y)uw°/°də/. A person that is the offspring of a negress by a white man, or of a white woman by a negro. In a more general sense, a person of mixed Caucasian and negro blood, or Indian and negro blood.

Mulct /málkt/. A penalty or punishment imposed on a person guilty of some offense, tort, or misdemeanor, usually a pecuniary fine or condemnation in damages. A forfeit, fine, or penalty. To sentence to a pecuniary penalty or forfeiture as a punishment; fine; hence to fine unjustly; to punish. Gorton v. Doty, 57 Idaho 792, 69 P.2d 136, 142.

Formerly, an imposition laid on ships or goods by a company of trade for the maintenance of consuls and the like.

Mulcta damnum famæ non irrogat /málktə dǽmnəm féymiy nòn íhrəgət/. A fine does not involve loss of character.

Mulier /myúwl(i)yər/. Lat. A woman; a wife; a widow; a virgin; a legitimate child.

The term is used always in contradistinction to a bastard, *mulier* being always legitimate.

Mulieratus /myùwl(i)yəréydəs/. A legitimate son.

Mulier puisné /myúwl(i)yər pyúwniy/°pwíynèy/. L. Fr. When a man has a bastard son, and afterwards marries the mother, and by her has also a legitimate son, the elder son is *bastard eigné*, and the younger son is *mulier puisné*.

Mulierty /myúwliyərdiy/. In old English law, the state or condition of a *mulier*, or lawful issue. The opposite of bastardy.

Multa /máltə/. A fine or final satisfaction, anciently given to the king by the bishops, that they might have power to make their wills, and that they might have the probate of other men's wills, and the granting of administration. Called, also, *multura episcopi*.

A fine imposed *ex arbitrio* by magistrates on the *præsides probinciarum*.

Multa conceduntur per obliquum quæ non conceduntur de directo /máltə kònsədántər pər əbláykwəm kwìy nón kònsədántər dìy dəréktow/. Many things are allowed indirectly which are not allowed directly.

Multa fidem promissa levant /máltə fáydəm prəmísə lévənt/. Many promises lessen confidence.

Multa ignoramus quæ nobis non laterent si veterum lectio nobis fuit familiaris /máltə ìgnəréyməs kwìy nówbəs nòn lǽdərənt sày védərəm léksh(iy)ow nówbəs fyúwət fəmiliyérəs/. We are ignorant of many things which would not be hidden from us if the reading of old authors was familiar to us.

Multa in jure communi contra rationem disputandi, pro communi utilitate introducta sunt /máltə in júriy kəmyúwnay kòntrə rǽshiyównəm dìspyuwtǽnday, pròw kəmyúwnay yuwtìlətéydiy ìntrədáktə sánt/. Many things have been introduced into the common law, with a view to the public good, which are inconsistent with sound reason.

Multa multo exercitatione facilius quam regulis percipies /máltə máltow egzərsətèyshiyówniy fəsíliyəs kwǽm régyələs pərsípiyiyz/. You will perceive many things much more easily by practice than by rules.

Multa non vetat lex, quæ tamen tacite damnavit /máltə nòn víydət léks, kwìy téymən tǽsədiy dæmnéyvət/. The law forbids not many things which yet it has silently condemned.

Multa transeunt cum universitate quæ non per se transeunt /máltə trǽnziyənt kàm yùwnəvərsətéydiy kwìy nón pàr síy trǽnziyənt/. Many things pass with the whole which do not pass separately.

Multicraft union. A labor union which craftsmen in different trades may join.

Multidistrict litigation. When civil actions involving one or more common (and often complex) questions of fact are pending in several different federal district courts, such actions may be transferred to one district for coordinated and consolidated management and trial under a single judge. 28 U.S.C.A. § 1407. The types of cases in which massive filings of multidistrict litigation are reasonably certain to occur include not only civil antitrust actions but also, common disaster (air crash) actions, patent and trademark suits, products liability actions and securities law violation actions, among others. Such cases are assigned and transferred by a Judicial Panel on Multidistrict Litigation, and are governed by the "Manual for Complex Litigation" and "Rules of Procedure of the Judicial Panel on Multidistrict Litigation."

Multifarious issue. A multifarious issue is one that inquires about several different facts when each fact should be inquired about in a separate issue. District Trustees of Campbellton Consol. Common School Dist. No. 16 v. Pleasanton Independent School Dist., Tex.Civ.App., 362 S.W.2d 122, 127. See **Multifariousness.**

Multifariousness /màltəfér(i)yəsnəs/. In equity pleading, the misjoinder of causes of action in a bill. The fault of improperly joining in one bill distinct and independent matters, and thereby confounding them; as, for example, the uniting in one bill of several matters perfectly distinct and unconnected against one defendant (more commonly called misjoinder of claims), or the demand of several matters of a distinct and independent nature against several defendants, in the same bill. Essen v. Adams, 342 Mo. 1196, 119 S.W.2d 773, 777.

This problem does not generally arise in the federal courts or in the majority of state courts, for Rule of Civil Procedure 8(e) permits pleading of inconsistent claims or defenses and Rule 18(a) permits liberal joinder of independent or alternative claims. Civil Rule 18 permits a party to join, either as independent or as alternate claims, as many claims, legal, equitable, or maritime, as he has against an opposing party.

Legislation. The joining, in a single legislative act, of dissimilar and discordant subjects, which, by no fair intendment, can be considered as having a legitimate connection or relation to the subject of the act.

Multilateral agreement. An agreement among more than two persons, firms, or governments.

Multi multa, nemo omnia novit /máltay máltə, níymow ómniyə nówvət/. Many men have known many things; no one has known everything.

Multinational. In a strict sense this term is descriptive of a firm which has centers of operation in many countries in contrast to an "international" firm which does business in many countries but is based in only one country, though the terms are often used interchangeably.

Multipartite /mə̀ltiypártayt/. Divided into many or several parts.

Multiple access. The defense of several lovers in paternity actions. Yarmark v. Strickland, Fla.App., 193 So.2d 212.

Multiple counts. A civil pleading (*e.g.* complaint) or a criminal indictment which contains several separate causes of action or crimes within the framework of one pleading. Joinder of multiple claims against opposing party is permitted under Fed.R.Civil P. 18.

Multiple evidence. That which is admissible for a specific purpose to which it must be confined and inadmissible to prove a different fact.

Multiple listing. An agreement between the owner of real estate and a broker in which the broker will permit other brokers to sell property for a percentage of his commission or on some other basis satisfactory to the brokers. Device used by real estate brokers to give wide exposure to properties listed for sale whereby each cooperating broker informs all other participating brokers of properties listed with him. Grempler v. Multiple Listing Bureau of Harford County, Inc., 258 Md. 419, 266 A.2d 1, 3. See also **Listing**.

Multiple offenses. A single act may be an offense against two statutes, and if each statute requires proof of an additional fact which the other does not, an acquittal or conviction under either statute does not exempt the defendant from prosecution and punishment under the other. If there is identity between the two charges, the defendant may not be punished for both, though he may be punished for the more serious. Com. v. Kuklis, 361 Mass. 302, 280 N.E.2d 155.

Multiple-party accounts. A multiple-party account is any of the following types of account: (i) a joint account, (ii) a P.O.D. account, or (iii) a trust account. It does not include accounts established for deposit of funds of a partnership, joint venture, or other association for business purposes, or accounts controlled by one or more persons as the duly authorized agent or trustee for a corporation, unincorporated association, charitable or civic organization or a regular fiduciary or trust account where the relationship is established other than by deposit agreement. Uniform Probate Code, § 6–101(5).

Multiple sentences. If a defendant has been found guilty of more than one offense, he may be given consecutive ("on and after") sentences.

Multiplex et indistinctum parit confusionem; et quæstiones, quo simpliciores, eo lucidiores /mə́l-təpleks èd ìndəstíŋktəm pǽrət kənfyùz(h)iyównəm èt kwès(h)chiyówniyz, kwòw simplìsiyóriyz íyow l(y)uwsìdiyóriyz/. Multiplicity and indistinctness produce confusion; and questions, the more simple they are, the more lucid.

Multiplicata transgressione crescat pœnæ inflictio /mə̀ltəpləkéydə trænzgrèshiyówniy kréskət píyniy inflíksh(iy)ow/. As transgression is multiplied, the infliction of punishment should increase.

Multiplicity /mə̀ltəplísədiy/. A state of being many. That quality of a pleading which involves a variety of matters or particulars. A multiplying or increasing.

Multiplicity of actions, or **suits.** Numerous and unnecessary attempts to litigate the same right. A phrase descriptive of the situation where several different suits or actions are brought upon the same issue. The actions must be against a single defendant. Prospect Park & C. I. R. Co. v. Morey, 155 App.Div. 347, 140 N.Y.S. 380, 385. Under Civil Rules practice such claims should properly be joined or maintained as a single class action. Fed.R.Civil P. 23.

Term "multiplicity" refers to the practice of charging the commission of a single offense in several counts. Federal Rules of Criminal Procedure have been drafted to discourage this practice. U. S. v. Allied Chemical Corp., D.C.Va., 420 F.Supp. 122, 123.

See **Collateral estoppel doctrine; Final decision rule; Res** (*Res judicata*).

Multitude. An assemblage of many people.

Multitudinem decem faciunt /mə̀ltət(y)úwdənəm díysəm féyshiyənt/. Ten makes a multitude.

Multitudo errantium non parit errori patrocinium /mə̀ltətyúwdow ərǽnsh(iy)əm nòn pǽrəd əróray pætrəsíniyəm/. The multitude of those who err furnishes no countenance or excuse for error. It is no excuse for error that it is entertained by numbers.

Multitudo imperitorum perdit curiam /mə̀ltətyúwdow ìmpərətórəm pə́rdət kyúriyəm/. A great number of unskillful practitioners ruins a court.

Multo utilius est pauca idonea effundere quam multis inutilibus homines gravari /mə́ltow yuwtíliyəs èst pókə idówniyə əfə́ndəriy kwǽm mə́ltəs ìnyuwtíləbəs hóməniyz grəvéray/. It is more useful to pour forth a few useful things than to oppress men with many useless things.

Multura episcopi /məlt(y)úrə əpískəpay/. See **Multa.**

Mummification /mə̀məfəkéyshən/. The complete drying up of the body as the result of burial in a dry, hot soil, or the exposure of the body to a dry, cold atmosphere.

Mund. In old English law, peace; whence *mundbryc*, a breach of the peace.

Mundbyrd, mundeburde /mə́ndbə̀rd/. A receiving into favor and protection.

Mundium /mə́ndiyəm/. In old French law, a tribute paid by a church or monastery to their seignorial *avoués* and *vidames*, as the price of protecting them.

Munera /myúwnərə/. In the early ages of the feudal law, the name given to the grants of land made by a king or chieftain to his followers, which were held by no certain tenure, but merely at the will of the lord. Afterwards they became life-estates, and then hereditary, and were called first "benefices," and then "feuds."

Municeps /myúwnəsèps/. Lat. In Roman law, eligible to office. A provincial person; a countryman. This was the designation of one born in the provinces or in a city politically connected with Rome, who had come to Rome, and though a Roman citizen, yet was looked down upon as a provincial, and not allowed to hold the higher offices.

In the provinces the term seems to have been applied to the freemen of any city who were eligible to the municipal offices.

Municipal. In narrower, more common, sense, it means pertaining to a local governmental unit, commonly, a city or town or other governmental unit. In its broader sense, it means pertaining to the public or governmental affairs of a state or nation or of a people. Chadwick v. City of Crawfordsville, 216 Ind. 399, 24 N.E.2d 937, 941, 942. Relating to a state or nation, particularly when considered as an entity independent of other states or nations. Hammel v. Little, 66 App.D.C. 356, 87 F.2d 907, 910.

Municipal action. Exercise of governmental power by a municipal board, agency, or other body, or by a municipal officer. Orme v. Atlas Gas & Oil Co., 217 Minn. 27, 13 N.W.2d 757, 761.

Municipal affairs. A term referring to the internal business affairs of a municipality. Griffin v. City of Los Angeles, 134 Cal.App. 763, 26 P.2d 655. The term is frequently used in constitutional and statutory provisions concerning the power to legislate as to the concerns of municipalities. And it has come to include public service activities, such as supplying water to the inhabitants, the construction of a reservoir for their benefit, the sale and distribution of electrical energy, and the establishment and operation of transportation service, which were once regarded as being of a strictly private nature. See also **Municipal function.**

Municipal aid. A contribution or assistance granted by a municipal corporation towards the execution or progress of some enterprise, undertaken by private parties, but likely to be of benefit to the municipality; *e.g.*, urban redevelopment projects.

Municipal authorities. As used in statutes contemplating the consent of such authorities, the term means the consent by the legislative authorities of the city acting by ordinance; for example, in a town, the members of the town board.

Municipal bonds. Evidences of indebtedness issued by cities or other corporate public body, negotiable in form, payable at designated future time, and intended for sale in market with object of raising money for municipal expense, which is beyond immediate resources of reasonable taxation, as distinguished from temporary evidences of debt, such as vouchers, certificates of indebtedness, orders, or drafts drawn by one officer on another and similar devices for liquidating current obligations in anticipation of collection of taxes. A bond issued by a village, town, city, county, state, or other public body. Interest on such bonds is generally exempt from federal income taxes and from some state income taxes. Sometimes referred to as "tax exempts."

Municipal charter. A legislative enactment conferring governmental powers of the state upon its local agencies.

Municipal corporation. A legal institution formed by charter from sovereign (*i.e.* state) power erecting a populous community of prescribed area into a body politic and corporate with corporate name and continuous succession and for the purpose and with the authority of subordinate self-government and improvement and local administration of affairs of state. A body corporate consisting of the inhabitants of a designated area created by the legislature with or without the consent of such inhabitants for governmental purposes, possessing local legislative and administrative power, also power to exercise within such area so much of the administrative power of the state as may be delegated to it and possessing limited capacity to own and hold property and to act in purveyance of public conveniences.

Municipal corporation is a body politic and corporate, created to administer the internal concerns of the district embraced with its corporate limits, in matters peculiar to such place and not common to the state at large. Tribe v. Salt Lake City Corp., Utah, 540 P.2d 499, 502. A municipal corporation has a dual character, the one public and the other private, and exercises correspondingly twofold functions and duties—one class consisting of those acts performed by it in exercise of delegated sovereign powers for benefit of people generally, as arm of state, enforcing general laws made in pursuance of general policy of the state, and the other consisting of acts done in exercise of power of the municipal corporation for its own benefit, or for benefit of its citizens alone, or citizens of the municipal corporation and its immediate locality. Associated Enterprises, Inc. v. Toltec Watershed Imp. Dist., Wyo., 490 P.2d 1069, 1070.

Quasi municipal corporations. Bodies politic and corporate, created for the sole purpose of performing one or more municipal functions. Public corporations organized for governmental purposes and having for most purposes the status and powers of municipal corporations (such as counties, townships, school districts, drainage districts, irrigation districts, etc.), but not municipal corporations proper, such as cities and incorporated towns.

Municipal corporation de facto. One which exists when there is (1) some law under which a corporation with the powers assumed might lawfully have been created; (2) a colorable and bona fide attempt to perfect an organization under such a law; (3) user of the rights claimed to have been conferred by the law.

Municipal courts. In the judicial organization of several states, courts are established under this name with territorial authority confined to the city or community in which they are established. Such courts usually have a criminal jurisdiction corresponding to that of a police court, and, in some cases, possess civil jurisdiction in small causes. In certain cities, small claims or traffic courts are under the jurisdiction of the municipal court.

Municipal domicile. Sometimes used in contradistinction to "national domicile" and "quasi national domicile" to refer to residence in a county, township, or municipality; called also "domestic domicile."

Municipal election. One at which municipal officers are chosen.

Municipal function. One created or granted for the special benefit and advantage of the urban community embraced within the corporate boundaries. State ex rel. Gebhardt v. City Council of Helena, 102 Mont. 27, 55 P.2d 671, 673.

Municipal functions are those which specially and peculiarly promote the comfort, convenience, safety and happiness of the citizens of the municipality, rather than the welfare of the general public. Under this class of functions are included, in most jurisdictions, the proper care of streets and alleys, parks and other public places, and the erection and maintenance of public utilities and improvements generally.

Municipal government. Instrumentalities of state for purpose of local government. Moore v. State, 159 Tenn. 468, 19 S.W.2d 233. This term, in certain state constitutions, embraces the governmental affairs of counties, and includes all forms of representative municipal government—towns, cities, villages, etc. See also **Municipality.**

Municipality. A legally incorporated or duly authorized association of inhabitants of limited area for local governmental or other public purposes. A body politic created by the incorporation of the people of a prescribed locality invested with subordinate powers of legislation to assist in the civil government of the state and to regulate and administer local and internal affairs of the community. State ex rel. McIntire v. City Council of City of Libby, 107 Mont. 216, 82 P.2d 587, 588. A city, borough, town, township or village. Also, the body of officers taken collectively, belonging to a city, who are appointed to manage its affairs and defend its interests.

Political subdivision or public agency or instrumentality of a State. Bankruptcy Act, § 101(29).

See also **Person.**

Municipal law. That which pertains solely to the citizens and inhabitants of a state, and is thus distinguished from political law, commercial law, and international law. City of Louisville v. Babb, C.C.A.Ind., 75 F.2d 162, 165. In its more common and narrower connotation however it means those laws which pertain to towns, cities and villages and their local government. People ex rel. Ray v. Martin, 294 N.Y. 61, 60 N.E.2d 541, 547, 548.

Municipal lien. A lien or claim existing in favor of a municipal corporation against a property owner for his proportionate share of a public improvement, made by the municipality, whereby his property is specially and individually benefited.

Municipal officer. One who holds an office of a municipality; e.g. mayor, city manager.

Municipal ordinance. A law, rule, or ordinance enacted or adopted by a municipal corporation for the proper conduct of its affairs or the government of its inhabitants; e.g. zoning or traffic ordinances, building codes. Particularly a regulation under a delegation of power from the state.

Municipal purposes. Public or governmental purposes as distinguished from private purposes. It may comprehend all activities essential to the health, morals, protection, and welfare of the municipality.

Municipal securities. The evidences of indebtedness issued by cities, towns, counties, townships, school-districts, and other such territorial divisions of a state. They are of two general classes: (1) Municipal warrants, orders, or certificates; (2) municipal bonds.

The term "municipal securities" means securities which are direct obligations of, or obligations guaranteed as to principal or interest by, a State or any political subdivision thereof, or any agency or instrumentality of a State or any political subdivision thereof, or any municipal corporate instrumentality of one or more States, or any security which is an industrial development bond (as defined in § 103(c)(2) of the Internal Revenue Code of 1954) the interest on which is excludable from gross income. Securities Exchange Act of 1934, § 3.

See **Municipal bonds; Municipal warrants.**

Municipal warrants. A municipal warrant or order is an instrument drawn by an officer of a municipality upon its treasurer, directing him to pay an amount of money specified therein to the person named or his order, or to bearer.

Municipium /myùwnəsípiyəm/. In Roman law, a foreign town to which the freedom of the city of Rome was granted, and whose inhabitants had the privilege of enjoying offices and honors there. A free town which retained its original right of self-government, but whose inhabitants also acquired certain rights of Roman citizens.

Muniment-house, or **muniment-room.** A house or room of strength, in cathedrals, collegiate churches, castles, colleges, public buildings, etc., purposely made for keeping deeds, charters, writings, etc.

Muniments of title /myúwnəmənts əv táydəl/. Documentary evidence of title. The instruments of writing and written evidences which the owner of lands, possessions, or inheritances has, by which he is enabled to defend the title of his estate. See **Deed.**

The records of title transactions in the chain of title of a person purporting to create the interest in land claimed by such person and upon which he relies as a basis for the marketability of his title, commencing with the root of title and including all subsequent transactions.

Under "muniment of title doctrine" when ownership of property has been litigated between individuals and title has been adjudicated in one of the parties, the losing party cannot relitigate the matter with those who rely upon the title of the winning party. Purdes v. Carvel Hall, Inc., D.C.Iowa, 301 F.Supp. 1256, 1264.

Murder. The unlawful killing of a human being by another with malice aforethought, either express or implied. State v. Hutter, 145 Neb. 798, 18 N.W.2d 203, 206. Murder is the unlawful killing of a human being, or fetus, with malice aforethought. Cal.Penal Code, § 187. The crime is defined by statute in most states. The Model Penal Code definition is as follows:

Criminal homicide constitutes murder when: (a) it is committed purposely or knowingly; or (b) it is committed recklessly under circumstances manifesting extreme indifference th the value of human life. Such recklessness and indifference are presumed if the actor is engaged or is an accomplice in the commission of, or an attempt to commit, or flight after committing or attempting to commit robbery, rape or deviate sexual intercourse by force or threat of force, arson, burglary, kidnapping or felonious escape. Model Penal Code, § 210.2.

See also **Assassination; Assault with intent to commit murder; Felony murder doctrine; Homicide; Manslaughter.**

Degrees of murder. In most states murder is divided into two degrees, for the purpose of awarding a more severe penalty for some murders than for others. All murder which shall be perpetrated by means of poison, or by lying in wait, or by any other kind of wilful, deliberate and premeditated killing, or which shall be committed in the perpetration of, or attempt to perpetrate any arson, rape, robbery or burglary, are commonly deemed murder of the first degree; and all other kinds of murder are deemed murder of the second degree. This general pattern has been followed in most of the states although slight changes have been made in a few of these. Some, for example, have omitted any reference to "poison", while a few have added "torture" to "poison". To the felony-murder clause of the statute several have added "mayhem" and sometimes the inclusion of some other felony may be found, such as kidnapping, sodomy or larceny. In certain states there is also the crime of murder in the third degree.

Depraved heart murder. Killing of a human being accomplished by extreme atrocity; malice is inferred from the act of atrocity. Extremely negligent conduct, which creates what a reasonable man would realize to be not only an unjustifiable but also a very high degree of risk of death or serious bodily injury to another or to others—though unaccompanied by any intent to kill or do serious bodily injury—and which actually causes the death of another, may constitute murder.

Murdrum /márdrəm/. In old English law, the killing of a man in a secret manner.

The fine formerly imposed in England upon a person who had committed homicide *per infortunium* or *se defendendo.*

Murorum operatio /myuróːrəm òpəréysh(iy)ow/. Lat. The service of work and labor done by inhabitants and adjoining tenants in building or repairing the walls of a city or castle; their personal service was commuted into *murage (q.v.).*

Must. This word, like the word "shall," is primarily of mandatory effect, State ex rel. McCabe v. District Court of Third Judicial Dist. in and for Deer Lodge County, 106 Mont. 272, 76 P.2d 634, 637; and in that sense is used in antithesis to "may". But this meaning of the word is not the only one, and it is often used in a merely directory sense, and consequently is a synonym for the word "may" not only in the permissive sense of that word, but also in the mandatory sense which it sometimes has.

Muster. To assemble together troops and their arms, whether for inspection, drill, or service in the field.

To take recruits into the service in the army and inscribe their names on the muster-roll or official record. To summon together; to enroll in service. In the latter sense the term implies that the persons mustered are not already in the service.

Muster-roll. In maritime law, a list or account of a ship's company, required to be kept by the master or other person having care of the ship, containing the name, age, national character, and quality of every person employed in the ship. At time of war it is of great use in ascertaining the ship's neutrality.

Mustizo /məstíyzow/. A name given in a South Carolina Act of 1740 to the issue of an Indian and a negro.

Mutatio nominis /myuwtéysh(iy)ow nómənəs/. Lat. In the civil law, change of name.

Mutatis mutandis /myuwtéydəs myuwtǽndəs/. Lat. With the necessary changes in points of detail, meaning that matters or things are generally the same, but to be altered when necessary, as to names, offices, and the like. Housman v. Waterhouse, 191 App.Div. 850, 182 N.Y.S. 249, 251.

Mute. Speechless; dumb; that cannot or will not speak.

Mutilation. As applied to written documents, such as wills, court records, and the like, this term means rendering the document imperfect by the subtraction from it of some essential part, as, by cutting, tearing, burning, or erasure, but without totally destroying it. See U.C.C. § 3–407. Also, the alteration in the writing, as in a negotiable instrument, so as to make it another and different instrument and no longer evidence of the contract which the parties made. Clem v. Chapman, Tex.Civ.App., 262 S.W. 168, 171. See also **Alteration; Deface; Spoliation.**

In criminal law, the depriving a man of the use of any of those limbs which may be useful to him in fight, the loss of which amounts to *mayhem.* People v. Bullington, 27 Cal.App.2d 396, 80 P.2d 1030, 1032. See **Maim; Mayhem.**

Mutinous. Insubordinate; disposed to mutiny; tending to incite or encourage mutiny.

Mutiny, *v.* To rise against lawful or constituted authority, particularly in the naval or military service.

Mutiny, *n.* In criminal law, an insurrection of soldiers or seamen against the authority of their commanders; a sedition or revolt in the army or navy. One is guilty of mutiny who with intent to usurp or override lawful military authority refuses in concert with any other person or persons to obey orders or otherwise do his duty or creates any violence or disturbance. 10 U.S.C.A. § 894. (Uniform Code of Military Justice, Art 94.) See also **Desertion.**

Mutiny Act. In English law, an act of parliament annually passed to punish mutiny and desertion, and for the better payment of the army and their quarters. It was first passed April 12, 1689, and was the only provision for the payment of the army. 1 Bl.Comm. 415.

Mutual. Common to both parties. Interchangeable; reciprocal; each acting in return or correspondence to the other; given and received;—spoken of an engagement or relation in which like duties and obligations are exchanged; *e.g.*, the marital relation.

As to mutual Account; Assent; Combat; Condition; Contract; Covenant; Credits; Debt; Insurance; Insurance *(Mutual insurance)*; Mistake; Promise; and Testament, see those titles. See also **Mutuality.**

Mutual affray. A fight in which both parties willingly enter and is similar to a duel. Taylor v. Commonwealth, 281 Ky. 442, 136 S.W.2d 544.

Mutual agreement. A meeting of the minds on a specific subject, and a manifestation of intent of the parties to do or refrain from doing some specific act or acts. See **Agreement; Contract; Treaty.**

Mutual benefit association. One based on reciprocal contracts and requires that a member receive benefits as a matter of right. In re Henderson's Estate, 17 Cal.2d 853, 112 P.2d 605, 609. Commonly a fraternal or social organization which provides insurance for its members on an assessment basis.

Mutual benefit insurance. Type of insurance offered to members of a mutual benefit association commonly characterized by assessment of members to meet claims. See **Mutual benefit association.**

Mutual company. A corporation in which shares are held exclusively by members to whom profits are distributed as dividends in proportion to the business which the members did with the company. One in which the members are both the insurers and the insured. Pink v. Town Taxi Co., 138 Me. 44, 21 A.2d 656, 659.

Mutual demands. Those between the same parties and due in the same capacity or right. Thompson v. Prince, Tex.Civ.App., 126 S.W.2d 574, 576.

Mutual fund. An investment company that raises money by selling its own stock to the public and investing the proceeds in other securities, with the value of its stock fluctuating with its experience with the securities in its portfolio. Mutual funds are of two types: "open-end," in which capitalization is not fixed and more shares may be sold at any time, and "closed-end," in which capitalization is fixed and only the number of shares originally authorized may be sold.

See also **Investment company; Open-end investment company.**

Load fund. Type of open-end investment trust in which a charge is made at time of purchase of shares to cover administrative and commission expenses.

No-load fund. A mutual fund that has no service charge for buying its shares.

Mutual insurance company. Type of insurance company in which there is no capital stock and in which the policyholders are the owners. See also **Insurance** *(Mutual insurance).*

Mutuality. Reciprocation; interchange. An acting by each of two parties; an acting in return. "Mutuality of contract" means that obligation rests on each party to do or permit doing of something in consideration of other party's act or promise; neither party being bound unless both are bound. Aden v. Dalton,

341 Mo. 454, 107 S.W.2d 1070, 1073. Called, also, mutuality of obligation. United Appliance Corporation v. Boyd, Tex.Civ.App., 108 S.W.2d 760, 764.

As to mutuality of "Assent," "Mistake," etc., see those titles.

Mutuality doctrine. Doctrine in equity to the effect that equitable relief will be denied a party to a contract on a showing that the plaintiff is not bound to the same extent as the defendant in fulfilling the contract. In another context, it refers to the obligation of a meeting of the minds before a contract can be found.

Mutuality of obligation. Mutuality of obligation requires that unless both parties to a contract are bound, neither is bound. Sala & Ruthe Realty, Inc. v. Campbell, 89 Nev. 483, 515 P.2d 394, 396. Mutuality of obligation as pertains to executory contract requires that each party to agreement be bound to perform, and if it appears that one party was never bound to do the acts which formed the consideration for promise of the other, there is lack of mutuality of obligation and other party is not bound. McCandles v. Schick, 85 Idaho 509, 380 P.2d 893, 898.

Mutuality of remedy. In equity, one party to a contract may not have equitable relief if he is not bound by the contract to the same extent as the other party, or if his remedy is not co-extensive. Generally, specific performance will be granted only where there is "mutuality of remedy", which means that right to performance must be mutual. Burr v. Greenland, Tex. Civ.App., 356 S.W.2d 370, 375.

Mutual mistake. One common to both contracting parties, wherein each labors under same misconception as to past or existing material fact. Artman v. O'Brien, Mo.App., 398 S.W.2d 24, 27. Mutual mistake with regard to contract exists where there has been a meeting of the minds of the parties and an agreement actually entered into but the agreement in its written form does not express what was really intended by the parties. Sierra Blanca Sales Co., Inc. v. Newco Industries, Inc., App., 84 N.M. 524, 505 P.2d 867, 873.

Mutual relief association. An insurer, chartered under a designated statute, having no capital stock, having relief funds created and sustained by assessments made upon the members, which files reports with insurance commissioner evidencing that it is not conducted for profit of its officers. State v. Texas Mut. Life Ins. Co. of Texas, Tex.Civ.App., 51 S.W.2d 405, 412.

Mutual reserve company. A company issuing "benefit thrift certificates" containing both savings features and renewable term insurance features, paid for by a single premium, with cash and loan values and limitation upon the expense liable for cost of supervision and management, was a "mutual reserve company".

Mutual savings bank. A bank organized by depositors, whose interest is shown by certificates of deposit, for the purpose of furnishing a safe depositary for money of members. It need not be incorporated or under supervision unless state law so requires. A–C Investment Ass'n v. Helvering, 62 App.D.C. 339, 68 F.2d 386, 387. A banking institution in which the depositors are the owners and which has no capital stock. See also **Savings and Loan Association.**

Mutual wills. Those made as the separate wills of two people which are reciprocal in provision. Or those executed pursuant to agreement or compact between two or more persons to dispose of their property in particular manner, each in consideration of the other. See **Reciprocal wills.**

Mutuant. The person who lends chattels in the contract of *mutuum (q.v.).*

Mutuari /myùwchuwéray/. To borrow; *mutuatus*, a borrowing.

Mutuary /myúwchuwèhriy/. A person who borrows personal chattels to be consumed by him and returned to the lender in kind and quantity; the borrower in a contract of *mutuum.*

Mutuatus /myúwchuwéydəs/. A loan of money.

Mutus et surdus /myúwdəs èt sə́rdəs/. Lat. In civil and old English law, dumb and deaf.

Mutuum /myùwchuwəm/. Lat. A loan for consumption; a loan of chattels, upon an agreement that the borrower may consume them, returning to the lender an equivalent in kind and quantity; as, a loan of corn, wine, or money which is to be used or consumed, and is to be replaced by other corn, wine, or money. In re Ellis' Estate, 24 Del.Ch. 393, 6 A.2d 602, 611. At common law, such a transaction is regarded as a sale or exchange, and not a bailment. See also **Loan for exchange; Loan for use.**

Mysterious disappearance. Term refers to theft insurance policy provision covering any disappearance or loss under unknown, puzzling or baffling circumstances which arouse wonder, curiosity or speculation, or circumstances which are difficult to understand or explain. Claiborne v. U. S. Fire Ins. Co., La.App., 193 So.2d 315, 317.

Mystery. A trade, art, or occupation. Masters frequently bind themselves in the indentures with their apprentices to teach them their art, trade, and *mystery.*

N

N.A. An abbreviation for *"non allocatur";* it is not allowed. Also sometimes used as abbreviation for "not available" or "not applicable".

Naam /næm/. Sax. The attaching or taking of movable goods and chattels, called *"vif"* or *"mort"* according as the chattels were living or dead.

Naif /nayíyf/. L. Fr. A villein; a born slave; a bondwoman.

Nail. A lineal measure of two inches and a quarter.

Naked. Bare; wanting in necessary conditions; incomplete, as a naked contract *(nudum pactum), i.e.,* a contract devoid of consideration, and therefore invalid; or, simple, unilateral, comprising but a single element, as a naked authority, *i.e.,* one which is not coupled with any interest in the agent, but subsists for the benefit of the principal alone.

As to naked Confession; Deposit; Possession; Possibility; Power; Promise; and Trust, see those titles.

Nam /næm/. In old English law, a distress or seizure of chattels.

As a Latin conjunction, for; because. Often used by the old writers in introducing the quotation of a Latin maxim.

Namare /nəmériy/. L. Lat. In old English law, to take, seize or distrain.

Namatio /nəméysh(iy)ow/. L. Lat. In old English and Scotch law, a distraining or taking of a distress; an impounding.

Name. The designation of an individual person, or of a firm or corporation.

A person's "name" consists of one or more Christian or given names and one surname or family name. It is the distinctive characterization in words by which one is known and distinguished from others, and description, or abbreviation, is not the equivalent of a "name."

See also Alias; Christian name; Corporate name; Fictitious name; Full name; Generic *(Generic name)*; Legal name; Nickname; Street name; Surname; Tradename.

Corporate name. Most states require corporations doing business under an assumed or fictitious name to register, record, or register and record, the name with state, county, or state and county officials.

Distinctive name. As used in regulation of United States Department of Agriculture, a trade, arbitrary, or fancy name which clearly distinguishes a food product, mixture, or compound from any other food product, mixture, or compound. U. S. v. Forty Barrels and Twenty Kegs of Coca Cola, 241 U.S. 265, 36 S.Ct. 573, 580, 60 L.Ed. 995.

Generic name. The general or nontrademark name of a product. For example, the trade names of a particular type of fiber may be Antron, Cantrece, Qiana; but the generic name of that fiber is nylon.

Name and arms clause. The popular name in English law for the clause, sometimes inserted in a will or settlement by which property is given to a person, for the purpose of imposing on him the condition that he shall assume the surname and arms of the testator or settlor, with a direction that, if he neglects to assume or discontinues the use of them, the estate shall devolve on the next person in remainder, and a provision for preserving contingent remainders.

Named insured. In insurance, the person specifically designated in the policy as the one protected and, commonly, it is the person with whom the contract of insurance has been made.

Namely. A difference, in grammatical sense, in strictness exists between the words namely and including. Namely imports interpretation, *i.e.,* indicates what is included in the previous term; but including imports addition, *i.e.,* indicates something not included.

Namium /néymiyəm/. L. Lat. In old English law, a taking; a distress. Things, goods, or animals taken by way of distress. *Simplex namium,* a simple taking or pledge.

Namium vetitum /néymiyəm védədəm/. An unjust taking of the cattle of another and driving them to an unlawful place, pretending damage done by them.

Nantissement /nòntismón/. In French law, the contract of pledge; if of a movable, it is called *"gage;"* and if of an immovable, it is called *"antichrèse."*

Narcoanalysis. Process whereby a subject is put to sleep, or into a semi-somnolent state by means of chemical injections and then interrogated while in this dreamlike state.

Narcotic. Generic term for any drug which dulls the senses or induces sleep and which commonly becomes addictive after prolonged use.

NAR. National Association of Realtors.

Narr. A common abbreviation of *"narratio" (q.v.)*. A declaration in an action.

Narr and cognovit law. Law providing that judgment may be had for plaintiff on notes by confession of any attorney that amount shown on notes, together with interest and costs, constitutes legal and just claim; word "narr" being an abbreviation of Latin word "narratio," meaning complaint or petition, and word "cognovit" meaning that defendant has confessed judgment and justice of claim. Dyer v. Johnson, Tex.Civ.App., 19 S.W.2d 421, 422. See **Judgment** *(Confession of judgment)*.

Narratio /nəréysh(iy)ow/. Lat. One of the common law names for a plaintiff's count or declaration, as being a narrative of the facts on which he relies.

Narrative evidence. Testimony from a witness which he is permitted to give without the customary questions and answers; *e.g.* when witness explains in detail what happened without interruption.

Narrator. A countor; a pleader who draws *narrs*. *Serviens narrator,* a serjeant at law.

Narrow seas. Those seas which run between two coasts not far apart. The term is sometimes applied to the English channel.

NASA. National Aeronautics and Space Administration.

Nasciturus /næsət(y)úrəs/. Lat. That shall hereafter be born. A term used in marriage settlements to designate the future issue of the marriage, as distinguished from *"natus,"* a child already born.

NASD. The National Association of Securities Dealers, Inc. An association of brokers and dealers in the over-the-counter securities business. The Association has the power to expel members who have been declared guilty of unethical practices.

Natale /nətéyliy/. The state and condition of a man acquired by birth.

Nati et nascituri /néyday èt næsət(y)úray/. Born and to be born. All heirs, near and remote.

Natio /néysh(iy)ow/. In old records, a native place.

Nation. A people, or aggregation of men, existing in the form of an organized jural society, usually inhabiting a distinct portion of the earth, speaking the same language, using the same customs, possessing historic continuity, and distinguished from other like groups by their racial origin and characteristics, and generally, but not necessarily, living under the same government and sovereignty. Montoya v. U. S., 180 U.S. 261, 21 S.Ct. 358, 45 L.Ed. 521; Worcester v. Georgia, 31 U.S. (6 Pet.) 515, 8 L.Ed. 483.

In American constitutional law the word "state" is applied to the several members of the American Union, while the word "nation" is applied to the whole body of the people embraced within the jurisdiction of the federal government.

National. Pertaining or relating to a nation as a whole. Commonly applied in American law to institutions, laws, or affairs of the United States or its government, as opposed to those of the several states. "National" contemplates an activity with a nationwide scope. In re National Foundation for Diarrheal Diseases, 8 Misc.2d 12, 164 N.Y.S.2d 177, 178. See also **Federal.**

The term "national" as used in the phrase "national of the United States" is broader than the term "citizen". Brassert v. Biddle, D.C.Conn., 59 F.Supp. 457, 462.

National bank. A bank incorporated and doing business under the laws of the United States, as distinguished from a *state* bank, which derives its powers from the authority of a particular state. Most such banks are members of the Federal Reserve System and the Federal Deposit Insurance Corporation.

National currency. Legal tender; that which circulates as money. Notes issued by national banks, and by the United States government. See **Currency; Federal Reserve notes; Legal tender.**

National debt. The money owing by government to some of the public or to financial institutions, the interest of which is paid out of the taxes raised by the whole of the public (*i.e.* out of general revenues).

National defense. A generic concept and refers to the military and naval establishments and the related activities of national preparedness and includes all matters directly and reasonably connected with the defense of the nation against its enemies. Gorin v. United States, 312 U.S. 19, 61 S.Ct. 429, 434, 436, 85 L.Ed. 488.

National domain. See **Domain.**

National domicile. See **Domicile.**

National emergency. A state of national crisis; a situation demanding immediate and extraordinary national or federal action. Congress has made little or no distinction between a "state of national emergency" and a "state of war". Brown v. Bernstein, D.C.Pa., 49 F.Supp. 728, 732.

National Environmental Policy Act. Federal Act setting forth declaration of national environmental policy and goals. Major provision requires that every federal agency submit an environmental impact statement with every legislative recommendation or program affecting the quality of the environment. See **Environmental impact statements.**

National government. The government of a whole nation, as distinguished from that of a state, local or territorial division of the nation, and also as distinguished from that of a league or confederation. Commonly referred to as the "federal government".

National Guard. Organization of men maintained as a reserve for the U.S. Army and Air Force. Members serve on a state-wide basis but are subject to being activated for federal service as well as for state emergencies.

Nationality. That quality or character which arises from the fact of a person's belonging to a nation or state. Nationality determines the political *status* of the individual, especially with reference to allegiance;

while domicile determines his civil *status*. Nationality arises either by birth or by naturalization. See also **Naturalization**.

Nationality Act. Shortened name for Immigration and Nationality Act which is a comprehensive federal statute embracing such matters as immigration, naturalization and admission of aliens. 8 U.S.C.A. § 1101 *et seq.*

Nationalization. The acquisition and control of privately owned business by government. See also **Denationalization**.

National Labor Relations Act. A federal statute known as the Wagner Act of 1935 and amended by the Taft-Hartley Act of 1947; it is comprehensive legislation regulating the relations between employers and employees, and establishing National Labor Relations Board. 29 U.S.C.A.

National Labor Relations Board. The National Labor Relations Board is an independent agency created by the National Labor Relations Act of 1935 (Wagner Act), as amended by the acts of 1947 (Taft-Hartley Act) and 1959 (Landrum-Griffin Act).

The Board has two principal functions under the act: preventing and remedying unfair labor practices by employers and labor organizations or their agents, and conducting secret ballot elections among employees in appropriate collective-bargaining units to determine whether or not they desire to be represented by a labor organization. The Board also conducts secret ballot elections among employees who have been covered by a union-shop agreement to determine whether or not they wish to revoke their union's authority to make such agreements; in jurisdictional disputes, decides and determines which competing group of workers is entitled to perform the work involved; and conducts secret ballot elections among employees concerning employers' final settlement offers in national emergency labor disputes.

National Mediation Board. The National Mediation Board was created on June 21, 1934, by an act of Congress amending the Railway Labor Act (48 Stat. 1185, 45 U.S.C.A. §§ 151–58, 160–62).

The Board's major responsibilities are: (1) the mediation of disputes over wages, hours, and working conditions which arise between rail and air carriers and organizations representing their employees, and (2) the investigation of representation disputes and certification of employee organizations as representatives of crafts or classes of carrier employees.

National origin. Term "national origin," within equal employment provision prohibiting discrimination based upon national origin, refers not to alienage, but to country where a person was born, or, more broadly, country from which his or her ancestors came. Jones v. United Gas Imp. Corp., D.C.Pa., 68 F.R.D. 1, 20.

National Service Life Insurance. Special type of life insurance for military and naval personnel during and after their service created by the National Service Life Insurance Act of 1940 and containing highly favorable rates and terms.

Nations, law of. See **International law**.

Native. A natural-born subject or citizen; a citizen by birth; one who owes his domicile or citizenship to the fact of his birth within the country referred to. The term may also include one born abroad, if his parents were then citizens of the country, and not permanently residing in foreign parts. U. S. v. Wong Kim Ark, 169 U.S. 649, 18 S.Ct. 456, 42 L.Ed. 890.

The word "natives", as used in Alien Enemy Act, refers to person's place of birth, so that a person remains a native of country of his birth, though he has moved away therefrom. United States ex rel. D'Esquiva v. Uhl, C.C.A.N.Y., 137 F.2d 903, 905.

Native born. See **Native**.

Nativi conventionarii /nətáyvay kənvènsh(iy)ənériyay/. Villeins or bondmen by contract or agreement.

Nativi de stipite /nətáyvay dìy stípədiy/. Villeins or bondmen by birth or stock.

Nativitas /nətívətæs/. Villenage; that state in which men were born slaves.

Nativo habendo /nətáyvow həbéndow/. In old English law, a writ which lay for a lord when his villein had run away from him. It was directed to the sheriff, and commanded him to apprehend the villein, and to restore him together with his goods to the lord.

Nativus /nətáyvəs/. Lat. In old English law, a native; specifically, one born into a condition of servitude; a born serf or villein.

Natura appetit perfectum; ita et lex /nəchúrə əpédət pərféktəm; áydə èst léks/. Nature covets perfection; so does law also.

Naturæ vis maxima; natura bis maxima /nəchúriy vís mǽksəmə; nəchúrə bís mǽksəmə/. The force of nature is greatest; nature is doubly great.

Natura fide jussionis sit strictissimi juris et non durat vel extendatur de re ad rem, de persona ad personam, de tempore ad tempus /nətyúrə fáydiy jə̀siyównəs sìt striktísəmay júrəs èt nòn dyúrət vèl èkstendéydər dìy ríy æd rém, dìy pərsównə æd pərsównəm, dìy témpəriy æd témpəs/. The nature of the contract of suretyship is *strictissimi juris*, and cannot endure nor be extended from thing to thing, from person to person, or from time to time.

Natural. The juristic meaning of this term does not differ from the vernacular, except in the cases where it is used in opposition to the term "legal;" and then it means proceeding from or determined by physical causes or conditions, as distinguished from positive enactments of law, or attributable to the nature of man rather than to the commands of law, or based upon moral rather than legal considerations or sanctions.

As to natural Allegiance; Boundary; Channel; Child; Day; Death; Domicile; Equity; Fruit; Guardian; Heirs; Infancy; Liberty; Obligation; Person; Possession; Presumption; Rights; Succession; Watercourse, and Year, see those titles.

Natural affection. Such as naturally subsists between near relatives, as a father and child, brother and sister, husband and wife. This is regarded in law as a good consideration.

Natural and probable consequences. Those consequences that a person by prudent human foresight can anticipate as likely to result from an act, because they happen so frequently from the commission of such an act that in the field of human experience they may be expected to happen again. Pope v. Pinkerton-Hays Lumber Co., Fla.App., 120 So.2d 227, 230.

Natural-born subject. In English law, one born within the dominions, or rather within the allegiance, of the king of England.

Naturale est quidlibet dissolvi eo modo quo ligatur /nÆchəréyliy èst kwídləbət dəzólvay íyow mówdow kwów ləgéydər/. It is natural for a thing to be unbound in the same way in which it was bound.

Natural flood channel. A channel beginning at some point on banks of stream and ending at some other point lower down stream, through which flood waters naturally flow at times of high water. C. M. Bott Furniture Co. v. City of Buffalo, 131 Misc. 624, 227 N.Y.S. 660, 665.

Naturalization. The process by which a person acquires nationality after birth and becomes entitled to the privileges of citizenship. 8 U.S.C.A. § 1101 *et seq.*

In the United States collective naturalization occurs when designated groups are made citizens by treaty (as Louisiana Purchase), or by a law of Congress (as in annexation of Texas and Hawaii). Individual naturalization must follow certain steps: (a) petition for naturalization by a person of lawful age who has been a lawful resident of the United States for 5 years; (b) investigation by the Immigration and Naturalization Service to determine whether the applicant can speak and write the English language, has a knowledge of the fundamentals of American government and history, is attached to the principles of the Constitution and is of good moral character; (c) hearing before a U.S. District Court or certain State courts of record; and (d) after a lapse of at least 30 days a second appearance in court when the oath of allegiance is administered.

Naturalization clause. The Fourteenth Amendment to the U.S. Constitution, Section 1, provides that all persons born or naturalized in the United States, and subject to the jurisdiction thereof, are citizens of the United States, and of the State wherein they reside.

Naturalization courts. Both federal and state courts of record have jurisdiction over naturalization matters. 8 U.S.C.A. § 1421.

Naturalized citizen. One who, being an alien by birth, has received citizenship under naturalization laws.

Natural law. This expression, "natural law," or *jus naturale,* was largely used in the philosophical speculations of the Roman jurists of the Antonine age, and was intended to denote a system of rules and principles for the guidance of human conduct which, independently of enacted law or of the systems peculiar to any one people, might be discovered by the rational intelligence of man, and would be found to grow out of and conform to his *nature,* meaning by that word his whole mental, moral, and physical constitution. The point of departure for this conception was

the Stoic doctrine of a life ordered "according to nature," which in its turn rested upon the purely supposititious existence, in primitive times, of a "state of nature;" that is, a condition of society in which men universally were governed solely by a rational and consistent obedience to the needs, impulses, and promptings of their true nature, such nature being as yet undefaced by dishonesty, falsehood, or indulgence of the baser passions. In ethics, it consists in practical universal judgments which man himself elicits. These express necessary and obligatory rules of human conduct which have been established by the author of human nature as essential to the divine purposes in the universe and have been promulgated by God solely through human reason.

Natural life. The period of a person's existence considered as continuing until terminated by physical dissolution or death occurring in the course of nature; used in contradistinction to that juristic and artificial conception of life as an aggregate of legal rights or the possession of a legal personality, which could be terminated by "civil death" *(q.v.),* that is, that extinction of personality which resulted from entering a monastery or being attainted of treason or felony.

Natural monument. Objects permanent in character which are found on the land as they were placed by nature, such as streams, lakes, ponds, shores, and beaches; sometimes including highways and streets, walls, fences, trees, hedges, springs, and rocks, and the like.

Natural object of testator's bounty. In testamentary law, term comprises whoever would take, in the absence of a will, because they are the persons whom the law has so designated, and in the ordinary case the law follows the normal condition of near relationship.

Natural objects. In interpretation of boundaries term includes mountains, lakes, rivers, etc. See also **Natural monument.**

Natural premium. Actual sum necessary to meet maturing death claims each year and is necessarily exceeded by the "net premium". Fox v. Mutual Ben. Life Ins. Co., C.C.A.Mo., 107 F.2d 715, 718.

Natural resources. Any material in its native state which when extracted has economic value. Timberland, oil and gas wells, ore deposits, and other products of nature that have economic value. The cost of natural resources is subject to depletion. Often called "wasting assets."

The term includes not only timber, gas, oil, coal, minerals, lakes, and submerged lands, but also, features which supply a human need and contribute to the health, welfare, and benefit of a community, and are essential to the well-being thereof and proper enjoyment of property devoted to park and recreational purposes.

Natural rights. Those which grow out of nature of man and depend upon his personality and are distinguished from those which are created by positive laws enacted by a duly constituted government to create an orderly civilized society. In re Gogabashvele's Estate, 195 Cal.App.2d 503, 16 Cal.Rptr. 77, 91.

Natura non facit saltum; ita nec lex /nəchúrə nòn féysət sóltəm; aýdə nèk léks/. Nature makes no leap [no sudden or irregular movement]; so neither does law. Applied in old practice to the regular observance of the degrees in writs of entry, which could not be passed over *per saltum.*

Natura non facit vacuum, nec lex supervacuum /nəchúrə nòn féysət vǽkyuwəm, nèk léks s(y)úwpər-vǽkyuwəm/. Nature makes no vacuum, the law nothing purposeless.

Natus /néydəs/. Lat. Born, as distinguished from *nasciturus,* about to be born. *Ante natus,* one born before a particular person or event, *e.g.,* before the death of his father, before a political revolution, etc. *Post natus,* one born after a particular person or event.

Nauclerus /nòklírəs/. Lat. In the civil law, the master or owner of a merchant vessel.

Naulage /nóləyj/. The freight of passengers in a ship.

Naulum /nóləm/. In the civil law, the freight or fare paid for the transportation of cargo or passengers over the sea in a vessel. This is a Latinized form of a Greek word.

Nauta /nódə/. Lat. In the civil and maritime law, a sailor; one who works a ship. Any one who is on board a ship for the purpose of navigating her. The employer of a ship.

Nautical. Pertaining to ships or to the art of navigation or the business of carriage by sea. See also **Marine.**

Nautical assessors. Experienced shipmasters, or other persons having special knowledge of navigation or nautical affairs, who are called to the assistance of a court of admiralty, in difficult cases involving questions of negligence, and who sit with the judge during the argument, and give their advice upon questions of seamanship or the weight of testimony.

Nautical mile. See **Mile.**

Nautica pecunia /nódəkə pəkyúwn(i)yə/. A loan to a shipowner, to be repaid only upon the successful termination of the voyage, and therefore allowed to be made at an extraordinary rate of interest *(nauticum fœnus).*

Nauticum fœnus /nódəkəm fíynəs/. Lat. In the civil law, nautical or maritime interest; an extraordinary rate of interest agreed to be paid for the loan of money on the hazard of a voyage; corresponding to interest on contracts of bottomry or respondentia in English and American maritime law.

Navagium /nævéyj(iy)əm/. In old English law, a duty on certain tenants to carry their lord's goods in a ship.

Naval. Appertaining to the navy (*q.v.*).

Naval base. See **Base.**

Naval law. The system of regulations and principles for the government of the navy. See also **Code of Military Justice.**

Navarchus /nævárkəs/. In the civil law, the master or commander of a ship; the captain of a man-of-war.

Navicularius /nəvìkyəlériyəs/. In the civil law, the master or captain of a ship.

Navigable. Capable of being navigated; that which may be navigated or passed over by ships or vessels. Natcher v. City of Bowling Green, 264 Ky. 584, 95 S.W.2d 255, 259. The term at common law was understood in a more restricted sense, viz., subject to the ebb and flow of the tide. Luscher v. Reynolds, 153 Or. 625, 56 P.2d 1158, 1162. See also **Navigable waters.**

Navigable in fact. Streams or lakes are navigable in fact when they are used or are susceptible of being used in their natural and ordinary condition as highways for commerce over which trade and travel are or may be conducted in the customary modes of trade and travel on water. Taylor Fishing Club v. Hammett, Tex.Civ.App., 88 S.W.2d 127, 129. See also **Navigable waters.**

Navigable river or **stream.** At common law, a river or stream in which the tide ebbs and flows, or as far as the tide ebbs and flows. But as to the definition in American law, see **Navigable,** *supra.*

Navigable waters. Those waters which afford a channel for useful commerce.

Any body of water, navigable in fact, which by itself or by uniting with other waters forms a continued highway over which commerce may be carried on with other states or countries. United States v. Appalachian Electric Power Co., 311 U.S. 377, 61 S.Ct. 291, 85 L.Ed. 243, rehearing denied 312 U.S. 712, 61 S.Ct. 548, 85 L.Ed. 1143, petition denied 317 U.S. 594, 63 S.Ct. 67, 87 L.Ed. 487. Waters are navigable in fact when used or susceptible of use in their ordinary condition as highways for commerce. United States v. Oregon, 295 U.S. 1, 55 S.Ct. 610, 79 L.Ed. 1663.

A water is "navigable," for purposes of admiralty jurisdiction, provided that it is used or susceptible of being used as an artery of commerce. Adams v. Montana Power Co., C.A.Mont., 528 F.2d 437, 440. Rivers are "navigable" in fact when they are used, or are susceptible of being used, in their ordinary condition as highways for commerce over which trade and travel are or may be conducted in the customary modes of trade and travel on water. Madole v. Johnson, D.C.La., 241 F.Supp. 379, 381.

Navigable waters of the United States. Waters are "navigable waters of the United States" when they form in their ordinary condition by themselves, or by uniting with other waters, a continued highway over which commerce is or may be carried on with other states or foreign countries in the customary modes in which such commerce is conducted by water. United States v. Appalachian Electric Power Co., D.C.Va., 23 F.Supp. 83. Navigable waters of the United States are only those waters in or adjacent to states and territories and the District of Columbia. 33 U.S.C.A. § 902(9).

Navigate. To journey by water; to go in a vessel; to sail or manage a vessel; to use the waters as a highway for commerce or communication; to ply. To direct one's course through any medium; to steer, especially to operate an airplane or airship. United States v. Monstad, C.C.A.Cal., 134 F.2d 986, 987, 988.

Navigation. The act or the science or the business of traversing the sea or other navigable waters in ships or vessels. The Silvia, 171 U.S. 462, 19 S.Ct. 7, 43 L.Ed. 241.

Regular navigation. In this phrase, the word "regular" may be used in contradistinction to "occasional," rather than to "unlawful," and refer to vessels that, alone or with others, constitute lines, and not merely to such as are regular in the sense of being properly documented under the laws of the country to which they belong.

Rules of navigation. Rules and regulations adopted by commercial nations to govern the steering and management of vessels approaching each other at sea so as to avoid the danger of collision or fouling.

Navigational visibility. Visibility as affecting speed with reference to distance within which boat in fog could be brought to stop, before any course of any vessel emerging from fog on either side would cross her projected course alongside the fog bank at its nearest point. The Silver Palm, C.C.A.Cal., 94 F.2d 754, 767.

Navigation servitude. Public right of navigation for the use of the people at large. United States v. 412.715 Acres of Land, Contra Costa County, Cal., D.C.Cal., 53 F.Supp. 143, 148, 149.

Navis /néyvəs/. Lat. A ship; a vessel.

Navy. A fleet of ships; the aggregate of vessels of war belonging to a nation. In a broader sense, and as equivalent to "naval forces," the entire corps of officers and men enlisted in the naval service and who man the public ships of war, including in this sense, in the United States, the officers and men of the Marine Corps. Wilkes v. Dinsman, 48 U.S. (7 How.) 89, 12 L.Ed. 618; U. S. v. Dunn, 120 U.S. 249, 7 S.Ct. 507, 30 L.Ed. 667. One of the Armed Forces of the United States.

Navy Department. Part of the Department of Defense, presided over by the Secretary of the Navy, who is responsible to the Secretary of Defense for the operation and efficiency of the Navy. (10 U.S.C.A. § 5031). The primary mission of the Navy is to protect the United States, as directed by the President or the Secretary of Defense, by the effective prosecution of war at sea including, with its Marine Corps component, the seizure or defense of advanced naval bases; to support, as required, the forces of all military departments of the United States; and maintain freedom of the seas.

Nazeranna /næzərǽnə/. In old English law, a sum paid to government as an acknowledgment for a grant of lands, or any public office.

N.B. An abbreviation for *"nota bene,"* mark well, observe; also *"nulla bona,"* no goods.

N.C.D. *Nemine contra dicente.* No one dissenting.

N.D. An abbreviation for "Northern District," *e.g.* U.S. District Court for Northern District of N.Y.

Ne admittas /níy ədmídəs/. Lat. In ecclesiastical law, the name of a prohibitory writ, directed to the bishop, at the request of the plaintiff or defendant, where a *quare impedit* is pending, when either party fears that the bishop will admit the other's clerk pending the suit between them.

Neap tide /níyp táyd/. When the moon is in its first and third quarters, the tides do not rise as high, nor fall as low, as on the average; at such times the tides are known as "neap tides." Borax Consolidated v. City of Los Angeles, Cal., 296 U.S. 10, 56 S.Ct. 23, 80 L.Ed. 9.

Near. Proximate; close-by; about; adjacent; contiguous; abutting. The word as applied to space is a relative term without positive or precise meaning, depending for its signification on the subject-matter in relation to which it is used and the circumstances under which it becomes necessary to apply it to surrounding objects. Closely akin or related by blood; as, a near relative. Close to one's interests and affections, etc.; touching or affecting intimately, as one's near affairs, friends. Not far distant in time, place or degree; not remote; adjoining. Zeigenfus v. Snelbaker, 38 N.J.Super. 304, 118 A.2d 876, 879.

Near money. Liquid assets which are readily convertible into money.

Neat, net. The clear weight or quantity of an article, without the bag, box, keg, or other thing in which it may be enveloped.

Ne baila pas /nə béylə pá/. L. Fr. He did not deliver. A plea in detinue, denying the delivery to the defendant of the thing sued for.

Necation. The act of killing.

Nec curia deficeret in justitia exhibenda /nék kyúriyə dəfísərət in jəstísh(iy)ə ègzəbéndə/. Nor should the court be deficient in showing justice.

Necessaries. An article which a party actually needs. State v. Earnest, Mo.App., 162 S.W.2d 338, 341. Things indispensable, or things proper and useful, for the sustenance of human life.

The word has no hard and fast meaning, but varies with the accustomed manner of living of the parties. Smitti v. Roth Cadillac Co., 145 Pa.Super. 292, 21 A.2d 127, 130. Word includes not only those services which are proper and required to sustain life but also those suitable for the individual involved according to his circumstances and condition in life. Trask v. Davis, Mo.App., 297 S.W.2d 792.

Necessaries consist of food, drink, clothing, medical attention, and a suitable place of residence, and they are regarded as necessaries in the absolute sense of the word. However, liability for necessaries is not limited to articles required to sustain life; it extends to articles which would ordinarily be necessary and suitable, in view of the rank, position, fortune, earning capacity, and mode of living of the husband or father.

Whether attorney's services are to be considered "necessaries" depends on whether there is necessity therefor. Fenn v. Hart Dairy Co., 231 Mo.App. 1005, 83 S.W.2d 120, 124. But such services are usually "necessaries." Leonard v. Alexander, 50 Cal.App.2d 385, 122 P.2d 984, 986.

What constitutes "necessaries" for which an admiralty lien will attach depends upon what is reasonably needed in the ship's business, regard being had to the character of the voyage and the employment in which the vessel is being used. Walker Skageth Food Stores v. The Bavois, D.C.N.Y., 43 F.Supp. 109, 110, 111.

See also **Necessary; Necessitous circumstances; Support.**

Necessaries, doctrine of. One who sells goods to a wife or child may charge the husband or father if the goods are required for their sustenance or support.

Necessarily included offense. For a lesser offense to be "necessarily included" in offense charged, within lesser included offense rule, it must be such that the greater offense cannot be committed without also committing the lesser. Kelly v. U. S., 125 U.S.App. D.C. 205, 370 F.2d 227, 228. Necessarily included offense is that which occurs when offense cannot be committed without necessarily committing another offense. People v. Doolittle, 23 C.A.3d 14, 99 Cal. Rptr. 810, 814.

Necessarium est quod non potest aliter se habere /nèsəsériyəm èst kwòd nòn pówdəst ǽlədər síy həbíriy/. That is necessary which cannot be otherwise.

Necessarius /nèsəsériyəs/. Lat. Necessary; unavoidable; indispensable; not admitting of choice or the action of the will; needful.

Necessary. This word must be considered in the connection in which it is used, as it is a word susceptible of various meanings. It may import absolute physical necessity or inevitability, or it may import that which is only convenient, useful, appropriate, suitable, proper, or conducive to the end sought. It is an adjective expressing degrees, and may express mere convenience or that which is indispensable or an absolute physical necessity. It may mean something which in the accomplishment of a given object cannot be dispensed with, or it may mean something reasonably useful and proper, and of greater or lesser benefit or convenience, and its force and meaning must be determined with relation to the particular object sought. Kay County Excise Board v. Atchison, T. & S. F. R. Co., 185 Okl. 327, 91 P.2d 1087, 1088.

In eminent domain proceedings, it means land reasonably requisite and proper for accomplishment of end in view, not absolute necessity of particular location. State v. Whitcomb, 94 Mont. 415, 22 P.2d 823.

With respect to taxation, means appropriate and helpful in furthering the taxpayer's business or income producing activity. I.R.C. §§ 162(a) and 212. See also **Ordinary.**

As to necessary Damages; Deposit; Domicile; Implication; Intromission; Repairs; and Way, see those titles. See also **Necessaries; Necessity.**

Necessary and proper. Words "necessary and proper" mean appropriate and adapted to carrying into effect given object. Petition of Public Service Coordinated Transport, 103 N.J.Super. 505, 247 A.2d 888, 891.

Necessary and proper clause. Art. I, § 8, par. 18 of U.S. Constitution, which authorizes Congress to make all laws necessary and proper to carry out the enumerated powers of Congress and all other powers vested in the government of the United States or any department or officer thereof. See **Penumbra doctrine.**

Necessary inference. One which is inescapable or unavoidable from the standpoint of reason. Taylor v. Twiner, 193 Miss. 410, 9 So.2d 644, 646.

Necessary parties. In pleading and practice, those persons who must be joined in an action because, *inter alia,* complete relief cannot be given to those already parties without their joinder. Fed.R.Civil P. 19(a).

Necessary parties are those who must be included in action either as plaintiffs or defendants, unless there is a valid excuse for their nonjoinder. City of Hutchinson for Human Relations Commission of Hutchinson v. Hutchinson, Kansas Office of Kansas State Employment Service, 213 Kan. 399, 517 P.2d 117, 122. Those persons who have such an interest in controversy that a final judgment or decree cannot be made without either affecting their interests or leaving the controversy in such a condition that its final adjudication may be wholly inconsistent with equity and good conscience. Royal Petroleum Corp. v. Dennis, 160 Tex. 392, 332 S.W.2d 313, 314. A "necessary party" is one whose joinder is required in order to afford the plaintiff the complete relief to which he is entitled against the defendant who is properly suable in that county. Orange Associates, Inc. v. Albright, Tex.Civ.App., 548 S.W.2d 806, 807.

See also **Indispensable parties; Joinder; Parties.**

Necessitas /nəsésətæs/. Lat. Necessity; a force, power, or influence which compels one to act against his will.

Necessitas culpabilis /nəsésətæs kə̀lpéybələs/. Culpable necessity; unfortunate necessity; necessity which, while it excuses the act done under its compulsion, does not leave the doer entirely free from blame. The necessity which compels a man to kill another in self-defense is thus distinguished from that which requires the killing of a felon.

Necessitas est lex temporis et loci /nəsésətæs èst léks témpərəs èt lówsay/. Necessity is the law of time and of place.

Necessitas excusat aut extenuat delictum in capitalibus, quod non operatur idem in civilibus /nəsésətæs əkskyúwzət òd əkstényuwət dəlíktəm in kæpətéylabəs kwòd nón opəréydər áydəm ən səvíləbəs/. Necessity excuses or extenuates a delinquency in capital cases, which has not the same operation in civil cases.

Necessitas facit licitum quod alias non est licitum /nəsésətæs féysət lísədəm kwòd éyliyəs nón èst lísədəm/. Necessity makes that lawful which otherwise is not lawful.

Necessitas inducit privilegium quoad jura privata /nəsésətæs ənd(y)úwsət privəlíyj(i)yəm kwówæd júrə prəvéydə/. Necessity gives a privilege with reference to private rights. The necessity involved in this maxim is of three kinds, viz.: (1) Necessity of self-preservation; (2) of obedience; and (3) necessity resulting from the act of God, or of a stranger.

Necessitas non habet legem /nəsésətæs nòn héybət líyjəm/. Necessity has no law.

Necessitas publica major est quam privata /nəsésətæs pə́bləkə méyjər èst kwǽm prəvéydə/. Public necessity is greater than private. "Death," it has been observed, "is the last and furthest point of particular necessity, and the law imposes it upon every subject that he prefer the urgent service of his king and country before the safety of his life."

Necessitas quod cogit, defendit /nəsésətæs kwòd kówjət dəféndət/. Necessity defends or justifies what it compels. Applied to the acts of a sheriff, or ministerial officer, in the execution of his office.

Necessitas sub lege non continetur, quia quod alias non est licitum necessitas facit licitum /nəsésətæs sə̀b líyjiy nòn kòntəníydər, kwáyə kwòd éyliyəs nón èst lísədəm nəsésətæs féysət lísədəm/. Necessity is not restrained by law, since what otherwise is not lawful, necessity makes lawful.

Necessitas vincet legem; legum vincula irridet /nəsésətæs vínsət líyjəm; líygəm víŋkyələ írədet/. Necessity overcomes law; it derides the fetters of laws.

Necessitas vincit legem /nəsésətæs vínsət líyjəm/. Necessity overrules the law.

Necessities. See **Necessaries.**

Necessitous /nəsésədəs/. Indigent or pressed by poverty. See **Indigent.**

Necessitous circumstances /nəsésədəs sárkəmstæn(t)səz/. Needing the necessaries of life, which cover not only primitive physical needs, things absolutely indispensable to human existence and decency, but those things, also, which are in fact necessary to the particular person left without support. In the civil code of Louisiana the words are used relative to the fortune of the deceased and to the condition in which the claimant lived during the marriage. See also **Necessaries; Non-support.**

Necessitudo /nəsèsət(y)úwdow/. Lat. In the civil law, an obligation; a close connection; relationship by blood.

Necessity. Controlling force; irresistible compulsion; a power or impulse so great that it admits no choice of conduct. That which makes the contrary of a thing impossible. The quality or state of being necessary, in its primary sense signifying that which makes an act or event unavoidable. Quality or state of fact of being in difficulties or in need, a condition arising out of circumstances that compels a certain course of action. Bykofsky v. Borough of Middletown, D.C.Pa., 401 F.Supp. 1242, 1250. See **Irresistible impulse.**

A person is excused from criminal liability if he acts under a duress of circumstances to protect life or limb or health in a reasonable manner and with no other acceptable choice. See **Self-defense.**

The word "necessity", within certificate of public convenience and necessity, is not used in the sense of being essential or absolutely indispensable but merely that certificate is reasonably necessary for public good. Alabama Public Service Commission v. Crow, 247 Ala. 120, 22 So.2d 721, 724. To fulfill requirements for easement of right of way of necessity, the necessity must be actual, real, and reasonable, as distinguished from inconvenience, but it need not be absolute and irresistible necessity. When used in relation to power of eminent domain does not mean absolute necessity, but only reasonable necessity.

The "necessity" of and appurtenance for the beneficial use of leased premises, which will entitle the lessee thereto, is not an absolute necessity in the sense that it must be completely indispensable, but is a real necessity and not a mere convenience or advantage.

See also **Necessaries; Necessary.**

Neck-verse. The Latin sentence, *"Miserere mei, Deus,"* was so called, because the reading of it was made a test for those who claimed benefit of clergy.

Necrophilism /nəkrófəlìzəm/. See **Insanity.**

Necropsy /nékròpsiy/. An autopsy, or *post-mortem* examination of a human body.

Nec tempus nec locus occurrit regi /nèk témpəs nèk lówkəs əkáhrət ríyjay/. Neither time nor place affects the king.

Nec veniam effuso sanguine casus habet /nèk víyniyəm, əfyúwzow sǽŋgwəniy, kéysəs héybət/. Where blood is spilled, the case is unpardonable.

Nec veniam, læso numine, casus habet /nèk víyniyəm, líyzow n(y)úwməniy, kéysəs héybət/. Where the Divinity is insulted the case is unpardonable.

Ne disturba pas /nə dəstárbə pá/. L. Fr. (Does or did not disturb.) In old English practice, the general issue or general plea in *quare impedit.*

Ne dona pas, or **non dedit** /nə dównə pá/nòn díydət/. The general issue in a formedon, now abolished. It denied the gift in tail to have been made in manner and form as alleged; and was therefore the proper plea, if the tenant meant to dispute the fact of the gift, but did not apply to any other case.

Need. A relative term, the conception of which must, within reasonable limits, vary with the personal situation of the individual employing it. Term means to have an urgent or essential use for (something lacking); to want, require. City of Dayton v. Borchers, 13 Ohio Misc. 273, 232 N.E.2d 437, 440. See **Necessaries.**

Needful. Necessary, requisite, essential, indispensable. See **Necessaries.**

Needless. In a statute against "needless" killing or mutilation of any animal, this term denotes an act done without any useful motive, in a spirit of wanton cruelty, or for the mere pleasure of destruction.

Needy. Indigent, necessitous, very poor. Moore v. State Social Security Commission, 233 Mo.App. 536, 122 S.W.2d 391, 393; Nichols v. State Social Security Commission of Missouri, 349 Mo. 1148, 164 S.W.2d 278, 280. See **Indigent.**

Ne exeat /níy éksiyət/. A writ which forbids the person to whom it is addressed to leave the country, the state, or the jurisdiction of the court. Available in some cases to keep a defendant within the reach of the court's process, where the ends of justice would be frustrated if he should escape from the jurisdiction. Sometimes a ne exeat writ is issued only to restrain a person from leaving the jurisdiction, and sometimes it is issued against a person who is removing or attempting to remove property beyond the jurisdiction. August v. August, 65 Ga.App. 883, 16 S.E.2d 784, 785.

Ne exeat regno /níy éksiyət régnow/. Lat. In English practice, a writ which issues to restrain a person from leaving the kingdom. It was formerly used for political purposes, but is now only resorted to in equity when the defendant is about to leave the kingdom; it is only in cases where the intention of the party to leave can be shown that the writ is granted.

Ne exeat republica /níy éksiyət rəpábləkə/. Lat. In American practice, a writ similar to that of *ne exeat regno (q.v.)*, available to the plaintiff in a civil suit, under some circumstances, when the defendant is about to leave the state.

Nefas /níyfæs/. Lat. That which is against right or the divine law. A wicked or impious thing or act.

Nefastus /nəfæstəs/. Lat. Inauspicious. Applied, in the Roman law, to a day on which it was unlawful to open the courts or administer justice.

Negatio conclusionis est error in lege /nəgéysh(iy)ow kənklùwz(h)iyównəs èst éhrər ìn líyjiy/. The denial of a conclusion is error in law.

Negatio destruit negationem, et ambæ faciunt affirmationem /nəgéysh(iy)ow déstruwət nəgèyshiyównəm èd æmbiy féyshiyənt æfərmèyshiyównəm/. A negative destroys a negative, and both make an affirmative.

Negatio duplex est affirmatio /nəgéysh(iy)ow d(y)úwplèks èst æfərméysh(iy)ow/. A double negative is an affirmative.

Negative. A denial; a proposition by which something is denied; a statement in the form of denial. Two negatives do not make a good issue.

As to negative Covenant; Easement; Servitude; Statute; and Testimony, see those titles.

Negative averment. As opposed to the traverse or simple denial of an affirmative allegation, a negative averment is an allegation of some substantive fact, *e.g.*, that premises are not in repair, which, although negative in form, is really affirmative in substance, and the party alleging the fact of non-repair must prove it. An averment in some of the pleadings in a case in which a negative is asserted. U. S. v. Eisenminger, D.C.Del., 16 F.2d 816, 819.

Negative condition. One by which it is stipulated that a given thing shall not happen.

Negative covenant. A provision in an employment agreement or a contract of sale of a business which prohibits the employee or seller from competing in the same area or market. Such restriction must be reasonable in scope and duration.

Negative easement. A right in owner of dominant tenement to restrict owner of servient tenement in exercise of general and natural rights of property. Fort Dodge, D. M. & S. Ry. v. American Community Stores Corp., 256 Iowa 1344, 131 N.W.2d 515, 521. A negative easement is one effect of which is not to authorize doing of act by person entitled to easement, but merely to preclude owner of land subject to easement from doing of an act which, if no easement existed, he would be entitled to do. McLaughlin v. Neiger, Mo.App., 286 S.W.2d 380, 383.

Negative evidence. Testimony that an alleged fact did not exist. See **Rebuttal evidence.**

Negative pregnant. In pleading, a negative implying also an affirmative. Such a form of negative expression as may imply or carry within it an affirmative. A denial in such form as to imply or express an admission of the substantial fact which apparently is controverted; or a denial which, although in the form of a traverse, really admits the important facts contained in the allegations to which it relates. Cramer v. Aiken, 63 App.D.C. 16, 68 F.2d 761, 762.

Neggildare. To claim kindred.

Neglect. May mean to omit, fail, or forbear to do a thing that can be done, or that is required to be done, but it may also import an absence of care or attention in the doing or omission of a given act. And it may mean a designed refusal or unwillingness to perform one's duty. In re Perkins, 234 Mo.App. 716, 117 S.W.2d 686, 692.

The term is used in the law of bailment as synonymous with "negligence." But the latter word is the closer translation of the Latin *"negligentia."*

Failure to pay money which the party is bound to pay without demand. An omission to do or perform some work, duty, or act. Failure to perform or discharge a duty, covering positive official misdoing or official misconduct as well as negligence.

See also **Excusable neglect; Negligence.**

Culpable neglect. Such neglect which exists where the loss can fairly be ascribed to the party's own carelessness, improvidence, or folly. State ex rel. Fulton v. Coburn, 133 Ohio St. 192, 12 N.E.2d 471, 477, 10 O.O. 249.

Willful neglect. The neglect of the husband to provide for his wife the common necessaries of life, he having the ability to do so; or it is the failure to do so by reason of idleness, profligacy, or dissipation.

Neglected child. A child is "neglected" when his parent or custodian, by reason of cruelty, mental incapacity, immorality or depravity, is unfit properly to care for him, or neglects or refuses to provide necessary physical, affectional, medical, surgical, or institutional or hospital care for him, or he is in such condition of want or suffering, or is under such improper care or control as to endanger his morals or health. In re DuMond, 196 Misc. 16, 17, 92 N.Y.S.2d 805.

Neglected minor. One suffering from neglect and in state of want. People v. De Pue, 217 App.Div. 321, 217 N.Y.S. 205, 206. See **Neglected child.**

Negligence. The omission to do something which a reasonable man, guided by those ordinary considerations which ordinarily regulate human affairs, would do, or the doing of something which a reasonable and prudent man would not do.

Negligence is the failure to use such care as a reasonably prudent and careful person would use under similar circumstances; it is the doing of some act which a person of ordinary prudence would not have done under similar circumstances or failure to do what a person of ordinary prudence would have done under similar circumstances. Amoco Chemical Corp. v. Hill, Del.Super., 318 A.2d 614, 617. Conduct which falls below the standard established by law for the protection of others against unreasonable risk of harm; it is a departure from the conduct expectable of a reasonably prudent person under like circumstances. Pence v. Ketchum, La., 326 So.2d 831, 836.

The term refers only to that legal delinquency which results whenever a man fails to exhibit the care which he ought to exhibit, whether it be slight, ordinary, or great. It is characterized chiefly by inadvertence, thoughtlessness, inattention, and the like, while "wantonness" or "recklessness" is characterized by willfulness. The law of negligence is founded on reasonable conduct or reasonable care under all circumstances of particular case. Doctrine of negligence rests on duty of every person to exercise due care in his conduct toward others from which injury may result.

See also Actionable negligence; Active negligence; Cause; Comparative negligence; Concurrent negligence; Fault; Imputed negligence; Invitation; Joint negligence; Laches; Legal negligence; Palsgraph doctrine; Parental liability; Product liability; Reasonable man doctrine; Reckless; Simple negligence; Standard of care; Strict liability; Supervening negligence.

Actionable negligence. See **Actionable negligence.**

Active negligence. See **Active negligence.**

Collateral negligence. In the law relating to the responsibility of an employer or principal for the negligent acts or omissions of his employee, the term "collateral" negligence is sometimes used to describe negligence attributable to a contractor employed by the principal and for which the latter is not responsible, though he would be responsible for the same thing if done by his servant. Weber v. Buffalo Railway Co., 20 App.Div. 292, 47 N.Y.S. 7.

Comparative negligence. See **Comparative negligence.**

Concurrent negligence. Arises where the injury is proximately caused by the concurrent wrongful acts or omissions of two or more persons acting independently. See also **Concurrent negligence.**

Contributory negligence. The act or omission amounting to want of ordinary care on part of complaining party, which, concurring with defendant's negligence, is proximate cause of injury. Honaker v. Crutchfield, 247 Ky. 495, 57 S.W.2d 502. Conduct by a plaintiff which is below the standard to which he is legally required to conform for his own protection and which is a contributing cause which cooperates with the negligence of the defendant in causing the plaintiff's harm. Li v. Yellow Cab Co. of California, 13 Cal.3d 804, 119 Cal.Rptr. 858, 864, 532 P.2d 1226.

Conduct for which plaintiff is responsible amounting to a breach of duty which law imposes on persons to protect themselves from injury, and which, concurring and cooperating with actionable negligence for which defendant is responsible, contributes to injury complained of as a proximate cause. Cowan v. Dean, 81 S.D. 486, 137 N.W.2d 337, 341.

The defense of contributory negligence has been replaced by the doctrine of comparative negligence *(q.v.)* in many states. See also *Exceptions and limitations, infra.*

An affirmative defense which must be pleaded and proved by defendant. Fed.R.Civil P., Rule 8(c).

Doctrine is also applicable to one who through his own negligence has contributed to material alteration of a negotiable instrument. U.C.C. § 3–406.

Criminal negligence. Criminal negligence which will render killing a person manslaughter is the omission on the part of the person to do some act which an ordinarily careful and prudent man would do under like circumstances, or the doing of some act which an ordinarily careful, prudent man under like circumstances would not do by reason of which another person is endangered in life or bodily safety; the word "ordinary" being synonymous with "reasonable" in this connection.

Negligence of such a character, or occurring under such circumstances, as to be punishable as a crime by statute; or (at common law) such a flagrant and reckless disregard of the safety of others, or wilful indifference to the injury liable to follow, as to convert an act otherwise lawful into a crime when it results in personal injury or death.

That species of want of care by which a person may be criminally liable. It varies from jurisdiction to jurisdiction and is called culpable negligence in some. However, it generally refers to conduct which is not intentional and ordinarily not wilful, wanton and reckless.

See **Negligent homicide; Negligently; Negligent manslaughter.**

Culpable negligence. Failure to exercise that degree of care rendered appropriate by the particular circumstances, and which a man of ordinary prudence in the same situation and with equal experience would not have omitted.

Degrees of negligence. While there are degrees of care, and failure to exercise proper degree of care is "negligence," most courts hold that there are no degrees (e.g. slight, ordinary, gross) of negligence, except in bailment cases or under automobile guest statutes. Murray v. De Luxe Motor Stages of Illinois, Mo.App., 133 S.W.2d 1074, 1078. The prevailing view is that there are no "degrees" of care in negligence, as a matter of law; there are only different amounts of care as a matter of fact. To the extent that the degrees of negligence survive, they are described below.

Exceptions and limitations. The general rule in automobile accident cases that contributory negligence bars recovery for the injuries sustained is subject to various exceptions and limitations. Thus the defense of contributory negligence may be inapplicable where defendant's negligence is of a gross or willful character. Moreover, application of the doctrine of contributory negligence is limited by the last clear chance doctrine or similar doctrines, or by comparative negligence statutes.

Gross negligence. The intentional failure to perform a manifest duty in reckless disregard of the consequences as affecting the life or property of another.

It is materially more want of care than constitutes simple inadvertence. It is an act or omission respecting legal duty of an aggravated character as distinguished from a mere failure to exercise ordinary care. It is very great negligence, or the absence of slight diligence, or the want of even scant care. It amounts to indifference to present legal duty and to utter forgetfulness of legal obligations so far as other persons may be affected. It is a heedless and palpable violation of legal duty respecting the rights of others. The element of culpability which characterizes all negligence is in gross negligence magnified to a high degree as compared with that present in ordinary negligence. Gross negligence is a manifestly smaller amount of watchfulness and circumspection than the circumstances require of a person of ordinary prudence. But it is something less than the wilful, wanton and reckless conduct which renders a defendant who has injured another liable to the latter even though guilty of contributory negligence, or which renders a defendant in rightful possession of real estate liable to a trespasser whom he has injured. It falls short of being such reckless disregard of probable consequences as is equivalent to a wilful and intentional wrong. Ordinary and gross negligence differ in degree of inattention, while both differ in kind from wilful and intentional conduct which is or ought to be known to have a tendency to injure.

Gross negligence consists of conscious and voluntary act or omission which is likely to result in grave injury when in face of clear and present danger of which alleged tortfeasor is aware. Glaab v. Caudill, Fla.App., 236 So.2d 180, 182, 183, 185. That entire want of care which would raise belief that act or omission complained of was result of conscious indifference to rights and welfare of persons affected by it. Claunch v. Bennett, Tex.Civ.App., 395 S.W.2d 719, 724; Snyder v. Jones, Tex.Civ.App., 392 S.W.2d 504, 505, 507. Indifference to present legal duty and utter forgetfulness of legal obligations, so far as other persons may be affected, and a manifestly smaller amount of watchfulness and circumspection than the circumstances require of a person of ordinary prudence.

Hazardous negligence. Such careless or reckless conduct as exposes one to very great danger of injury or to imminent peril.

Imputed negligence. Refers to doctrine that places upon one person responsibility for the negligence of another; such responsibility or liability is imputed by reason of some special relationship of the parties, such as parent and child, husband and wife, driver and passenger, owner of vehicle and driver, bailor and bailee, master and servant, joint enterprise, and parent and custodian of a child. Schmidt v. Martin, 212 Kan. 373, 510 P.2d 1244, 1246.

Generally the doctrine of imputed negligence, as applied to automobile accidents, visits on one person legal responsibility for the negligent conduct of another. The doctrine applies only in limited classes of cases, as where there is a right to control in the relationship of master and servant, principal and agent, or a joint enterprise. The independent negligence of one person ordinarily is not imputable to another person except where the relation between the persons gives rise to an express or implied agency in the person committing the act of negligence.

Legal negligence. See **Legal negligence.**

Ordinary negligence. The omission of that care which a man of common prudence usually takes of his own concerns. Briggs v. Spaulding, 141 U.S. 132, 11 S.Ct. 924, 35 L.Ed. 662. Failure to exercise care of an ordinarily prudent person in same situation. A want of that care and prudence that the great majority of mankind exercise under the same or similar circumstances. Wherever distinctions between gross, ordinary and slight negligence are observed, "ordinary negligence" is said to be the want of ordinary care.

Ordinary negligence is based on fact that one ought to have known results of his acts, while "gross negligence" rests on assumption that one knew results of his acts, but was recklessly or wantonly indifferent to results. The distinction between "ordinary negligence" and "gross negligence" is that the former lies in the field of inadvertence and the latter in the field of actual or constructive intent to injure.

Passive negligence. Failure to do something that should have been done. It is negligence which permits defects, obstacles, or pitfalls to exist on premises; that is, negligence which causes dangers arising from physical condition of land. Pachowitz v. Milwaukee & Suburban Transport Corp., 56 Wis.2d 383, 202 N.W.2d 268, 275.

Difference between "active" and "passive" negligence is that one is only passively negligent if he merely fails to act in fulfillment of duty of care which law imposes upon him, while one is actively negligent if he participates in some manner in conduct or omission which caused injury. King v. Timber Structures, Inc. of Cal., 240 Cal.App.2d 178, 49 Cal.Rptr. 414, 417.

Per se negligence. The unexcused violation of a statute which is applicable is per se or automatic negligence in some states. See also **Negligence per se.**

Slight negligence. A failure to exercise great care. Slight negligence is defined to be only an absence of that degree of care and vigilance which persons of extraordinary prudence and foresight are accustomed to use. Briggs v. Spaulding, 141 U.S. 132, 11 S.Ct. 924, 35 L.Ed. 662.

Subsequent negligence. Exists where defendant sees plaintiff in a position of danger and fails to exercise due and proper precaution to prevent injury to plaintiff. Holman v. Brady, 241 Ala. 487, 3 So.2d 30, 33.

Wilful, wanton or reckless negligence. These terms are customarily treated as meaning essentially the same thing. The usual meaning assigned to "wilful," "wanton" or "reckless," according to taste as to the word used, is that the actor has intentionally done an act of an unreasonable character in disregard of a risk known to him or so obvious that he must be taken to have been aware of it, and so great as to make it highly probable that harm would follow. It usually is accompanied by a conscious indifference to the consequences, amounting almost to a willingness that they shall follow; and it has been said that this is indispensable. See for example Tyndall v. Rippon, 5 Del.Super. 458, 61 A.2d 422; Wolters v. Venhaus, 350 Ill.App. 322, 112 N.E.2d 747; Clarke v. Storchak, 384 Ill. 564, 52 N.E.2d 229, appeal dismissed 322 U.S. 713, 64 S.Ct. 1270, 88 L.Ed. 1555; Tighe v. Diamond, 149

Ohio St. 520, 80 N.E.2d 122, 37 O.O. 243. The result is that "wilful," "wanton" or "reckless" conduct tends to take on the aspect of highly unreasonable conduct, or an extreme departure from ordinary care, in a situation where a high degree of danger is apparent. As a result there is often no clear distinction at all between such conduct and "gross" negligence, and the two have tended to merge and take on the same meaning, of an aggravated form of negligence, differing in quality rather than in degree from ordinary lack of care. It is at least clear, however, that such aggravated negligence must be more than any mere mistake resulting from inexperience, excitement, or confusion, and more than mere thoughtlessness or inadvertence, or simple inattention.

"Wantonness" constituting gross and wanton negligence within automobile guest statute indicates a realization of imminence of danger and a reckless disregard, complete indifference, and unconcern of probable consequences of the wrongful act. Mann v. Good, 202 Kan. 631, 451 P.2d 233, 236.

Negligence, estoppel by. An estoppel which occurs when one who is under a legal duty, either to the person injured or to the public, to act with due care, fails to do so, and such failure is the natural and proximate cause of misleading that person to alter his position. An estoppel arises when one by acts, representations, intentionally or negligently, induces another to change his position for the worse. Smith v. Vara, 136 Misc. 500, 241 N.Y.S. 202, 209.

An estoppel arises when one by acts, representations, or admissions, or by silence when he ought to speak, intentionally or through culpable negligence, induces another to believe certain facts to exist and such other rightfully relies and acts on such belief so that he will be prejudiced if the former is permitted to deny the existence of such facts.

Estoppel may exist where a party has led another into the belief of a certain state of facts by conduct of culpable negligence, calculated to have that result, and the other party has acted upon such belief to his prejudice. Scott v. First Nat. Bank, 343 Mo. 77, 119 S.W.2d 929, 938.

Negligence in law. "Actionable negligence" or "negligence in law" grows out of nonobservance of a duty prescribed by law. See also **Negligence per se.**

Negligence per se. Conduct, whether of action or omission, which may be declared and treated as negligence without any argument or proof as to the particular surrounding circumstances, either because it is in violation of a statute or valid municipal ordinance, or because it is so palpably opposed to the dictates of common prudence that it can be said without hesitation or doubt that no careful person would have been guilty of it. As a general rule, the violation of a public duty, enjoined by law for the protection of person or property, so constitutes. See also **Strict liability.**

Negligent. See **Negligence.**

Negligent escape. Where prisoner escapes through officer's negligence. Hershey v. People, 91 Colo. 113, 12 P.2d 345, 347.

Negligent homicide. The criminal offense committed by one whose negligence is the direct and proximate cause of another's death. The crime of negligent homicide consists of three component elements: (1) death of human being (2) by instrumentality of motor vehicle (3) operated on highway in negligent manner. State v. Colombo, 4 Conn.Cir. 671, 238 A.2d 806, 808. See also **Homicide** (*Vehicular homicide*).

Negligentia /nèglǝjénsh(iy)ǝ/. Lat. In the civil law, carelessness; inattention; the omission of proper care or forethought. The term is not exactly equivalent to our "negligence," inasmuch as it was not any *negligentia,* but only a high or gross degree of it, that amounted to *culpa* (actionable or punishable fault).

Negligentia semper habet infortunium comitem /nèglǝjénsh(iy)ǝ sémpǝr héybǝd ìnforchúwn(i)yǝm kómǝdǝm/. Negligence always has misfortune for a companion.

Negligently. A person acts negligently with respect to a material element of an offense when he should be aware of a substantial and unjustifiable risk that the material element exists or will result from his conduct. The risk must be of such a nature and degree that the actor's failure to perceive it, considering the nature and purpose of his conduct and the circumstances known to him, involves a gross deviation from the standard of care that a reasonable person would observe in the actor's situation. Model Penal Code, § 2.02. See also **Negligence.**

Negligently done. The doing of an act where ordinary care required that it should not have been done at all, or that it should have been done in some other way, and where the doing of the act was not consistent with the exercise of ordinary care under the circumstances. See **Negligence.**

Negligent manslaughter. A statutory crime in some jurisdictions consisting of an unlawful and unjustified killing of a person by negligence but without malice.

Negligent offense. One which ensues from a defective discharge of a duty, which defect could have been avoided by the exercise of that care which is usual, under similar circumstances, with prudent persons of the same class. People v. Gaydica, 122 Misc. 31, 203 N.Y.S. 243, 258.

Negligent violation of statute. One occasioned by or accompanied with negligent conduct.

Negoce /nǝgóws/. Fr. Business; trade; management of affairs.

Negotiability /nǝgòwsh(iy)ǝbílǝdiy/. Legal character of being negotiable (*q.v.*).

Negotiable /nǝgówsh(iy)ǝbǝl/. Legally capable of being transferred by endorsement or delivery. Usually said of checks and notes and sometimes of stocks and bearer bonds. See **Commercial paper; Negotiable instruments; Non-negotiable.**

Negotiable bond. Type of bond which may be transferred by negotiation from original holder to another.

Negotiable document of title. A document is negotiable if by its terms the goods are to be delivered to "bearer", or to the order of a named party, or, where recognized in overseas trade, to a named person "or assigns". U.C.C. § 7–104(1).

Negotiable instruments. To be negotiable within the meaning of U.C.C. Article 3, an instrument must meet the requirements set out in Section 3–104: (1) it must be a writing signed by the maker or drawer; it must contain an (2) unconditional (3) promise (example: note) or order (example: check) (4) to pay a sum certain in money; (5) it must be payable on demand or at a definite time; (6) it must be payable to the bearer or to order (examples of instruments payable to order are (a) "Pay to the order of Daniel Dealer," and (b) "Pay Daniel Dealer or order"); and (7) it must not contain any other promise, order, obligation, or power given by the maker or drawer except as authorized by Article 3. See also **Commercial paper; Negotiation.**

Negotiable words. Words and phrases which impart the character of negotiability to bills, notes, checks, etc., in which they are inserted; for instance, a direction to pay to A. "or order" or "bearer". See **Negotiable instruments.**

Negotiate /nəgówshiyèyt/. To transact business; to bargain with another respecting a purchase and sale; to conduct communications or conferences with a view to reaching a settlement or agreement. It is that which passes between parties or their agents in the course of or incident to the making of a contract and is also conversation in arranging terms of contract.

To communicate or confer with another so as to arrive at the settlement of some matter. To meet with another so as to arrive through discussion at some kind of agreement or compromise about something. Al Herd, Inc. v. Isaac, 271 Cal.App.2d 749, 76 Cal.Rptr. 697, 699. To discuss or arrange a sale of bargain; to arrange the preliminaries of a business transaction. Also to sell or discount negotiable paper, or assign or transfer it by indorsement and delivery. To conclude by bargain, treaty, or agreement. See also **Negotiation.**

Negotiated plea. The effect of plea bargaining in which the criminal defendant agrees to plead guilty to the charge or to a reduced charge in return for a recommendation from the prosecutor of a disposition less severe than possible under the particular statute. See **Plea bargaining.**

Negotiation /nəgòws(h)iyéyshən/. The transfer of an instrument in such form that the transferee becomes a holder. If the instrument is payable to order it is negotiated by delivery with any necessary indorsement; if payable to bearer it is negotiated by delivery. U.C.C. § 3–202(1). The act by which a check or promissory note is put into circulation by being passed by one of the original parties to another person.

Negotiation is process of submission and consideration of offers until acceptable offer is made and accepted. Gainey v. Brotherhood of Ry. and S. S. Clerks, Freight Handlers, Exp. & Station Emp., D.C. Pa., 275 F.Supp. 292, 300. The deliberation, discussion, or conference upon the terms of a proposed agreement; the act of settling or arranging the terms and conditions of a bargain, sale, or other business transaction.

See also **Negotiate.**

Negotiorum gestio /nəgòwshiyórəm jés(h)ch(iy)òw/. Lat. In the civil law, literally, a doing of business or businesses. A species of spontaneous agency, or an interference by one in the affairs of another, in his absence, from benevolence or friendship, and without authority.

Negotiorum gestor /nəgòwshiyórəm jéstòr/. Lat. In the civil law, a transactor or manager of business; a person voluntarily constituting himself agent for another; one who, without any mandate or authority, assumes to take charge of an affair or concern for another person, in the latter's absence, but for his interest.

One who spontaneously, and without the knowledge or consent of the owner, intermeddles with his property, as to do work on it, or to carry it to another place, etc.

N.E.I. An abbreviation for *"non est inventus,"* he is not found.

Neife, naif, nativus /níyf/nayíyf/nətáyvəs/. In old English law, a woman who was born a villein, or a bond-woman.

Neighbor. One who lives in close proximity to another.

Neighborhood. A place near; an adjoining or surrounding district; a more immediate vicinity; vicinage. Connally v. General Const. Co., 269 U.S. 385, 46 S.Ct. 126, 129, 70 L.Ed. 322.

It is not synonymous with territory or district, but is a collective noun, with the suggestion of proximity, and refers to the units which make up its whole, as well as to the region which comprehends those units. A district or locality, especially when considered with relation to its inhabitants or their interests. In ordinary and common usage "locality" is synonymous in meaning with "neighborhood," and neither connote large geographical areas with widely diverse interests. Lukens Steel Co. v. Perkins, 70 App.D.C. 354, 107 F.2d 627, 631.

As used with reference to a person's reputation, "neighborhood" means in general any community or society where person is well known and has established a reputation.

Ne injuste vexes /níy ənjəstiy véksiyz/. Lat. In old English practice, a prohibitory writ, commanding a lord not to demand from the tenant more services than were justly due by the tenure under which his ancestors held.

Neither party. An abbreviated form of docket entry, meaning that, by agreement, neither of the parties will further appear in court in that suit used as a form of judgment in some states where a case has been settled.

Ne luminibus officiatur /níy l(y)uwmínəbəs əfishiyéydər/. Lat. In the civil law, the name of a servitude which restrains the owner of a house from making such erections as obstruct the light of the adjoining house.

Nemine contradicente /néməniy kòntrədəséntiy/. Lat. No one dissenting; no one voting in the negative. A phrase used to indicate the unanimous consent of a court or legislative body to a judgment, resolution, vote, or motion. Commonly abbreviated *"nem. con."*

Neminem lædit qui jure suo utitur /némənəm líydət kwày júriy s(y)úwow yúwdədər/. He who stands on his own rights injures no one.

Neminem oportet esse sapientiorem legibus /némənəm əpórdəd ésiy sæpiyènshiyórəm líyjəbəs/. No man ought to be wiser than the laws.

Nemo /níymow/. Lat. No one; no man. The initial word of many Latin phrases and maxims, among which are the following:

Nemo admittendus est inhabilitare seipsum /níymow ædməténdəs èst inhəbìlətériy siyípsəm/. No man is to be admitted to incapacitate himself.

Nemo agit in seipsum /níymow éyjəd ən siyípsəm/. No man acts against himself. A man cannot be a judge and a party in his own cause.

Nemo alienæ rei, sine satisdatione, defensor idoneus intelligitur /níymow æliyíyniy ríyay, sáyniy sædəsdèyshiyówniy, dəfén(t)sòr ədówniyəs intəlíjədər/. No man is considered a competent defender of another's property, without security. A rule of the Roman law, applied in part in admiralty cases.

Nemo alieno nomine lege agere potest /níymow æliyíynow nóməniy líyjiy æjəriy pówdəst/. No one can sue in the name of another.

Nemo aliquam partem recte intelligere potest, antequam totum iterum atque iterum perlegerit /níymow æləkwəm párdəm réktiy intəlíjəriy pówdəst, æntəkwəm tówdəm ídərəm pərlíyjərət/. No one can properly understand any part of a thing till he has read through the whole again and again.

Nemo allegans suam turpitudinem audiendus est /níymow æləgæn(d)z s(y)úwəm tərpət(y)úwdənəm òdiyéndəs ést/. No one alleging his own turpitude is to be heard as a witness. This is not a rule of evidence, but applies to a party seeking to enforce a right founded on an illegal consideration.

Nemo bis punitur pro eodem delicto /níymow bís pyúwnədər pròw iyówdəm dəlíktow/. No man is punished twice for the same offense.

Nemo cogitationis pœnam patitur /níymow kòjətèyshiyównəs píynəm pædədər/. No one suffers punishment on account of his thoughts.

Nemo cogitur rem suam vendere, etiam justo pretio /níymow kó(w)jədər rém s(y)úwəm véndəriy, íysh(iy)əm jástow présh(iy)ow/. No man is compelled to sell his own property, even for a just price.

Nemo contra factum suam venire potest /níymow kóntrə fæktəm s(y)úwəm vənáyriy pówdəst/. No man can contravene or contradict his own deed. The principle of estoppel by deed.

Nemo damnum facit, nisi qui id fecit quod facere jus non habet /níymow dæmnow féysət, náysay kwày íd fíysət kwòd fæsəriy jás nòn héybət/. No one is considered as doing damage, unless he who is doing what he has no right to do.

Nemo dare potest quod non habet /níymow dériy pówdəst kwód nòn héybət/. No man can give that which he has not.

Nemo dat qui non habet /níymow dæt kwày nòn héybət/. He who hath not cannot give.

Nemo debet aliena jactura locupletari /níymow débəd æliyíynə jækt(y)úrə lòk(y)əplétəray/. No one ought to gain by another's loss.

Nemo debet bis puniri pro uno delicto /níymow débət bís pyənáyray pròw yúwnow dəlíktow/. No man ought to be punished twice for one offense. No man shall be placed in peril of legal penalties more than once upon the same accusation.

Nemo debet bis vexari pro eadem causa /níymow débət bís vekséray pròw iyéydəm kózə/. No one should be twice harassed for the same cause.

Nemo debet bis vexari [si constet curiæ quod sit] pro una et eadem causa /níymow débət bis vekséray (sáy kónstət kyúriyiy kwòd sít) pròw yúwnə èd iyéydəm kózə/. No man ought to be twice troubled or harassed [if it appear to the court that it is] for one and the same cause. No man can be sued a second time for the same cause of action, if once judgment has been rendered. No man can be held to bail a second time at the suit of the same plaintiff for the same cause of action.

Nemo debet esse judex in propria causa /níymow débəd ésiy júwdeks ìn prówpriyə kózə/. No man ought to be a judge in his own cause. A maxim derived from the civil law.

Nemo debet immiscere se rei ad se nihil pertinenti /níymow débəd əmísəriy síy ríyay æd sìy náy(h)əl pərdənéntay/. No one should intermeddle with a thing that in no respect concerns him.

Nemo debet in communione invitus teneri /níymow débəd ìn kəmyùwniyówniy ənváydəs təníray/. No one should be retained in a partnership against his will.

Nemo debet locupletari aliena jactura /níymow débət lòk(y)əplétéray æliyíynə jækt(y)úrə/. No one ought to be enriched by another's loss.

Nemo debet locupletari ex alterius incommodo /níymow débət lòk(y)əplétéray èks oltíriyəs ìnkóməwdow/. No one ought to be made rich out of another's loss.

Nemo debet rem suam sine facto aut defectu suo amittere /níymow débət rém s(y)úwəm sáyniy fæktow òt dəfékt(y)uw əmídəriy/. No man ought to lose his property without his own act or default.

Nemo de domo sua extrahi potest /níymow dìy dówmow s(y)úwə ekstréyhay pówdəst/. No one can be dragged out of his own house. In other words, every man's house is his castle.

Nemo duobus utatur officiis /níymow d(y)uwówbəs yuwtéydər əfís(h)iyəs/. No one should hold two offices, *i.e.*, at the same time.

Nemo ejusdem tenementi simul potest esse hæres et dominus /níymow əjásdəm tènəméntay sáyməl pówdəst ésiy híriyz èt dómənəs/. No one can at the same time be the heir and the owner of the same tenement.

Nemo enim aliquam partem recte intelligere possit antequam totum iterum atque iterum perlegerit /níymow íynəm ǽləkwəm párdəm réktiy ìntəlíjəriy pósət ǽntəkwəm tówdəm ídərəm ǽtkwiy ídərəm pərlíyjərət/. No one is able rightly to understand one part before he has again and again read through the whole.

Nemo est hæres viventis /níymow èst híriyz vəvéntəs/. No one is the heir of a living person. No one can be heir during the life of his ancestor. No person can be the actual complete heir of another till the ancestor is previously dead.

Nemo est supra leges /níymow èst s(y)úwprə líyjiyz/. No one is above the law.

Nemo ex alterius facto prægravari debet /níymow èks oltíriyəs fǽktow prìygrəvéray débət/. No man ought to be burdened in consequence of another's act.

Nemo ex consilio obligatur /níymow èks kənsíl(i)yow òbləgéydər/. No man is bound in consequence of his advice. Mere advice will not create the obligation of a mandate.

Nemo ex dolo suo proprio relevetur, aut auxilium capiat /níymow èks dówlow s(y)úwow prówpriyow rèləvíydər, òd ògzíl(i)yəm kǽpiyət/. Let no one be relieved or gain an advantage by his own fraud. A civil law maxim.

Nemo ex proprio dolo consequitur actionem /níymow èks prówpriyow dówlow kənsékwədər ǽkshiyównəm/. No one maintains an action arising out of his own wrong.

Nemo ex suo delicto meliorem suam conditionem facere potest /níymow èks s(y)úwow dəlíktow mìyliyórəm s(y)úwəm kəndishiyównəm fǽsəriy pówdəst/. No one can make his condition better by his own misdeed.

Nemo inauditus condemnari debet si non sit contumax /níymow inódədəs kòndəmnéray débət sáy nòn sìt kóntyuwmæks/. No man ought to be condemned without being heard unless he be contumacious.

Nemo in propria causa testis esse debet /níymow ìn prówpriyə kózə téstəs ésiy débət/. No one ought to be a witness in his own cause.

Nemo jus sibi dicere potest /níymow jás síbay dísəriy pówdəst/. No one can declare the law for himself. No one is entitled to take the law into his own hands.

Nemo militans deo implicetur secularibus negotiis /níymow mílətæn(d)z díyow ìmpləsíydər sèkyəlérəbəs nəgówshiyəs/. No man who is warring for [in the service of] God should be involved in secular matters. A principle of the old law that men of religion were not bound to go in person with the king to war.

Nemo nascitur artifex /níymow nǽsədər árdəfèks/. No one is born an artificer.

Nemo patriam in qua natus est exuere, nec ligeantiæ debitum ejurare possit /níymow pǽtriyəm ìn kwéy néydəs èst əgz(y)úwəriy, nèk lìjiyǽnshiyiy débədəm ìyjərériy pósət/. No man can renounce the country in which he was born, nor abjure the obligation of his allegiance.

Nemo plus commodi hæredi suo relinquit quam ipse habuit /níymow plás kómədway həríyday s(y)úwow rəlíŋkwət kwǽm ípsiy hǽbyuwət/. No one leaves a greater benefit to his heir than he had himself.

Nemo plus juris ad alium transferre potest quam ipse habet /níymow plás júrəs ǽd éyliyəm trænsfáriy pówdəst kwǽm ípsiy héybət/. No one can transfer more right to another than he has himself.

Nemo potest contra recordum verificare per patriam /níymow pówdəst kóntrə rəkórdəm vèhrəfəkériy pər pǽtriyəm/. No one can verify by the country against a record. The issue upon matter of record cannot be to the jury. A maxim of old practice.

Nemo potest esse dominus et hæres /níymow pówdəst ésiy dómənəs èt híriyz/. No man can be both owner and heir.

Nemo potest esse simul actor et judex /níymow pówdəst ésiy sáyməl ǽktər èt júwdèks/. No one can be at once suitor and judge.

Nemo potest esse tenens et dominus /níymow pówdəst ésiy ténen(d)z èt dómənəs/. No man can be both tenant and lord [of the same tenement].

Nemo potest exuere patriam /níymow pówdest əgz(y)úwəriy pǽtriyəm/. No man can renounce his own country.

Nemo potest facere per alium quod per se non potest /níymow pówdəst fǽsəriy pár ǽliyəm kwód pàr síy nòn pówdəst/. No one can do that by another which he cannot do of himself. A rule said to hold in original grants, but not in descents; as where an office descended to a woman, in which case, though she could not exercise the office in person, she might by deputy.

Nemo potest facere per obliquum quod non potest facere per directum /níymow pówdəst fǽsəriy pàr əbláykwəm kwód nòn pówdəst fǽsəriy pàr dəréktəm/. No man can do that indirectly which he cannot do directly.

Nemo potest mutare consilium suum in alterius injuriam /níymow pówdəst myuwtériy kənsíl(i)yəm s(y)úwəm ìn oltíriyəs ənjúriyəm/. No man can change his purpose to another's injury.

Nemo potest nisi quod de jure potest /níymow pówdəst náysay kwód dìy júriy pówdəst/. No one is able to do a thing, unless he can do it lawfully.

Nemo potest plus juris ad alium transferre quam ipse habet /níymow pówdəst plás júrəs ǽd ǽliyəm trænsfáriy kwǽm ípsəm héybət/. No one can transfer a greater right to another than he himself has.

Nemo potest sibi debere /níymow pówdəst síbay dəbíriy/. No one can owe to himself.

Nemo præsens nisi intelligat /níymow príyzən(d)z náysay əntéləgət/. One is not present unless he understands.

Nemo præsumitur alienam posteritatem suæ prætulisse /níymow prəz(y)úwmədər ǽliyíynəm pəstèrətéydəm s(y)úwiy prìydəlísiy/. No man is presumed to have preferred another's posterity to his own.

Nemo præsumitur donare /níymow prəz(y)úwmədər dənériy/. No one is presumed to give.

Nemo præsumitur esse immemor suæ æternæ salutis, et maxime in articulo mortis /níymow prəz(y)úwmədər ésiy ímamòr s(y)úwiy atárniy sal(y)úwdas, èt mǽksamiy ìn artíkyalow mórdas/. No one is presumed to be forgetful of his own eternal welfare, and particularly at the point of death.

Nemo præsumitur ludere in extremis /níymow praz(y)úwmadar l(y)úwdariy in akstríymas/. No one is presumed to trifle at the point of death.

Nemo præsumitur malus /níymow praz(y)úwmadar mǽlas/. No one is presumed to be bad.

Nemo prohibetur plures negotiationes sive artes exercere /níymow pròw(h)abíydar pl(y)úriyz nagòwshiyèyshiyówniyz sáyviy árdiyz ègzarsíriy/. No one is prohibited from following several kinds of business or several arts. The common law doth not prohibit any person from using several arts or mysteries at his pleasure.

Nemo prohibetur pluribus defensionibus uti /níymow pròw(h)abíydar pl(y)úrabas dafènsiyównabas yúwtay/. No one is prohibited from making use of several defenses.

Nemo prudens punit ut præterita revocentur, sed ut futura præveniantur /níymow prúdèn(d)z pyúwnad àt pratéhrada rìyvaséntar, séd àt f(y)achúra pravìyniyǽntar/. No wise man punishes in order that past things may be recalled, but that future wrongs may be prevented.

Nemo punitur pro alieno delicto /níymow pyúwnadar pròw æliyíynow dalíktow/. No one is punished for another's wrong.

Nemo punitur sine injuria, facto, seu defalta /níymow pyúwnadar sáyniy anjúriya, fǽktow, syúw dafólta/. No one is punished unless for some wrong, act, or default.

Nemo qui condemnare potest, absolvere non potest /níymow kwày kòndamnériy pówdast, abzólvariy nòn pówdast/. No one who may condemn is unable to acquit.

Nemo sibi esse judex vel suis jus dicere debet /níymow síbay ésiy júwdèks vèl s(y)úwas jás dísariy débat/. No man ought to be his own judge, or to administer justice in cases where his relations are concerned.

Nemo sine actione experitur, et hoc non sine breve sive libello conventionali /níymow sáyniy ǽkshiyówniy akspéradar, èt hók nòn sáyniy bríyviy sáyviy labélow kanvénshanéylay/. No one goes to law without an action, and no one can bring an action without a writ or bill.

Nemo tenetur ad impossibile /níymow taníydar ǽd impossíbaliy/. No one is bound to an impossibility.

Nemo tenetur armare adversarium contra se /níymow taníydar armériy ǽdvarsériyam kóntra síy/. No one is bound to arm his adversary against himself.

Nemo tenetur divinare /níymow taníydar dìvanériy/. No man is bound to divine, or to have foreknowledge of, a future event.

Nemo tenetur edere instrumenta contra se /níymow taníydar íydariy ìnstraménta kóntra síy/. No man is bound to produce writings against himself. A rule of

the Roman law, adhered to in criminal prosecutions, but departed from in civil questions.

Nemo tenetur informare qui nescit, sed quisquis scire quod informat /níymow taníydar ìnfarmériy kwày nésat, séd kwískwis sáyriy kwód infórmat/. No one is bound to give information about things he is ignorant of, but every one is bound to know that which he gives information about.

Nemo tenetur jurare in suam turpitudinem /níymow taníydar jurériy in s(y)úwam tarpat(y)úwdanam/. No one is bound to swear to the fact of his own criminality; no one can be forced to give his own oath in evidence of his guilt.

Nemo tenetur prodere seipsum /níymow taníydar prówdariy siyípsam/. No one is bound to betray himself. In other words, no one can be compelled to criminate himself.

Nemo tenetur seipsum accusare /níymow taníydar siyípsam ǽkyazériy/. No one is bound to accuse himself.

Nemo tenetur seipsum infortuniis et periculis exponere /níymow taníydar siyípsam ìnforchúwniyas èt paríkyalas ekspównariy/. No one is bound to expose himself to misfortunes and dangers.

Nemo tenetur seipsum prodere /níymow taníydar siyípsam prówdariy/. No one is bound to betray himself.

Nemo unquam judicet in se /níymow ángkwam júwdasat in síy/. No one can ever be a judge in his own cause.

Nemo unquam vir magnus fuit, sine aliquo divino afflatu /níymow ángkwam vír mǽgnas f(y)úwat, sáyniy ǽlakwow daváynow afléyt(y)uw/. No one was ever a great man without some divine inspiration.

Nemo videtur fraudare eos qui sciunt et consentiunt /níymow vadíydar frodíriy íyows kwày sáyant èt kansénshiyant/. No one seems [is supposed] to defraud those who know and assent [to his acts].

Nephew. The son of one's brother or sister, or one's brother-in-law or sister-in-law.

Nepos /népos/níypòws/. Lat. A grandson.

Nepotism /népadizam/. Bestowal of patronage by public officers in appointing others to positions by reason of blood or marital relationship to appointing authority.

Neptis /néptas/. Lat. A granddaughter; sometimes great-granddaughter.

Neque leges neque senatus consulta ita scribi possunt ut omnis casus qui quandoque in sediriunt comprehendatur; sed sufficit ea quae placrumque accidunt contineri /nékwiy líyjiyz nékwiy sanéydas kansálta áyda skráybay pósant àt ómnas kéysas kwày kwondówkwiy in sadíriyant kòmprahendéydar; sèd sáfasad íya kwiy plarámkwiy ǽksadant kòntaníray/. Means that neither laws nor acts of a parliament can be so written as to include all actual or possible cases; it is sufficient if they provide for those things which frequently or ordinarily may happen.

Ne quid in loco publico vel itinere fiat /níy kwíd in lówkow páblǝkow vèl aytínǝriy fáyǝt/. Lat. That nothing shall be done (put or erected) in a public place or way. The title of an interdict in the Roman law.

Ne recipiatur /níy rǝsìpiyéydǝr/. Lat. That it be not received. A *caveat* or warning given to a law officer, by a party in a cause, not to receive the next proceedings of his opponent.

Ne relessa pas /nǝ rǝlésǝ pá/. L. Fr. Did not release. Where the defendant had pleaded a release, this was the proper replication by way of traverse.

Net. That which remains after all allowable deductions, such as charges, expenses, discounts, commissions, taxes, etc., are made.

Net assets. A bookkeeping balance obtained by subtracting company's liabilities from its gross assets. Commonwealth v. Union Trust Co. of Pittsburgh, 345 Pa. 298, 27 A.2d 15, 17. Model Bus. Corp. Act § 2(i).

Net asset value. Term used in evaluating stock of investment company and arrived at by deducting total liabilities from total market value of all assets of company. Net asset value of corporation, for stock appraisal purpose, is share which stock represents in value of net assets of corporation, including every kind of property and value, whether realty or personalty, tangible or intangible, good will, and corporation's value as going concern. In re Watt & Shand, 452 Pa. 287, 304 A.2d 694, 698.

Net balance. The proceeds of sale, after deducting expenses.

Net cost. The actual cost of an item after deductions of all income and financial gain from the gross cost. As used in insurance, it represents the total premiums paid less the dividends paid and cash surrender value.

Net earnings. See **Earnings.**

Net estate. Under estate tax statute the term means that which is left of the gross estate after the deduction of proper and lawful items in the course of settlement. United States Tust Co. of New York v. Sears, D.C.Conn., 29 F.Supp. 643, 649. In general, the net estate is the gross estate less the following allowable deductions: (a) funeral expenses; (b) claims against the estate; and (c) unpaid mortgages or indebtedness on property which is included in the gross estate.

Nether house of Parliament. A name given to the English house of commons in the time of Henry VIII.

Net income. Income subject to taxation after allowable deductions and exemptions have been subtracted from gross or total income. The excess of all revenues and gains for a period over all expenses and losses of the period.

Net income for income tax purposes is what remains out of gross income after subtracting ordinary and necessary expenses incurred in efforts to obtain or to keep it. Walling's Estate v. C. I. R., C.A.Pa., 373 F.2d 190, 193.

See also **Distributable net income.**

Net interest. Pure interest which is theoretical and excludes overhead and risks from cost of capital.

Net lease. Lease in which provision is made for the lessee to pay, in addition to rent, the taxes, insurance and maintenance charges. See also **Escalator clause; Net rent.**

Net level annual premium. An amount which, if exacted from a group of policyholders and increased by interest, will yield a sum sufficient to satisfy all death claims. The result is generally referred to as the "net" or "net level premium" of the policy. Fox v. Mutual Ben. Life Ins. Co., C.C.A.Mo., 107 F.2d 715, 718.

Net listing. A type of listing contract whereby the broker is only entitled to a commission to the extent that sales price exceeds the given amount. For example, a net listing of $15,000 where the property sold for $18,000 would result in a $3,000 commission. See also **Listing; Multiple listing; Net sale contract.**

Net loss. Any deficit from operations, plus any shrinkage in value of plant investment. Ickes v. U. S. ex rel. Chestatee Pyrites & Chemical Corporation, D.C., 289 U.S. 510, 53 S.Ct. 700, 77 L.Ed. 1352. The excess of all expenses and losses for a period over all revenues and gains of the period. Negative net income.

Net national product. In a given period of time, the gross national product less allowance for capital consumption. See also **Gross National Product.**

Net operating assets. The assets, net of depreciation and bad debts, employed in the ordinary course of business. Hence excludes investments in stocks and bonds owned by a manufacturing company, for example.

Net operating income. Income before interest and income taxes but after depreciation produced by operating assets.

Net operating loss. Loss before interest and income taxes but after depreciation produced by operating assets. In income taxation term means the excess of the deductions allowed over the gross income. I.R.C. § 172(c).

Net position. In securities and commodity trading, the difference between contracts long and contracts short held by a trader.

Net premium. In life insurance, this term is used to designate that portion of the premium which is intended to meet the cost of the insurance, both current and future. Its amount is calculated upon the basis of the mortality tables and upon the assumption that the company will receive a certain rate of interest upon all its assets; it does not include the entire premium paid by the assured, but does include a certain sum for expenses.

Net price. The lowest price, after deducting all deductions, discounts, etc.

Net proceeds. Gross proceeds, less charges which may be rightly deducted. Pflueger v. United States, 73 App.D.C. 364, 121 F.2d 732, 736.

Net profits. Profits after deduction of all expenses; may be classified as net before or after taxes. Deducting the cost of goods sold from sales gives the *gross profit*. Deducting the operating expenses (overhead) from gross profit gives the *operating profit*. Deducting income taxes from operating profits gives the *net profit*. See also **Net income**.

Net rent. Basic rent charge plus additional monthly charges for taxes, utilities and maintenance. See also **Net lease**.

Net return. See **Net income; Net profits**.

Net revenues. See **Net income; Net profits**.

Net sale contract. One in which the principal agrees to accept a specified net price for property to be sold, and the agent's compensation for negotiating a sale is to be any amount received in excess of the specified figure. Loughlin v. Idora Realty Co., 259 Cal.App.2d 619, 66 Cal.Rptr. 747, 751, 752. See also **Net listing**.

Net sales. Gross sales minus returns, allowances, rebates, and discounts.

Net single premium. Aggregate of future yearly costs of insurance, severally discounted to age from which computation is made. Magers v. Northwestern Mut. Life Ins. Co., 348 Mo. 96, 152 S.W.2d 148, 152.

Premium which, if exacted from a group of policyholders and immediately invested at the assumed rate of interest, will yield in the aggregate a sum exactly sufficient to pay all death claims as they mature providing the mortality rate is in accord with the table used. Fox v. Mutual Ben. Life Ins. Co., C.C.A. Mo., 107 F.2d 715, 718.

Net tonnage. The cubic contents of the interior of a vessel, when the spaces occupied by the crew and by propelling machinery are deducted, numbered in tons. Kiessig v. San Diego County, 51 Cal.App.2d 47, 124 P.2d 163, 165.

Net value. In insurance, accumulation of balances of past net premiums not absorbed in carrying risk. Fox v. Mutual Ben. Life Ins. Co., C.C.A.Mo., 107 F.2d 715, 718, 719. Policy "reserve". Magers v. Northwestern Mut. Life Ins. Co., 348 Mo. 96, 152 S.W.2d 148, 152, 153.

Net weight. The weight of an article or collection of articles, after deducting from the gross weight the weight of the boxes, coverings, casks, etc., containing the same. The weight of an animal dressed for sale, after rejecting hide, offal, etc.

Net worth. Remainder after deduction of liabilities from assets. W. H. Miner, Inc. v. Peerless Equipment Co., C.C.A.Ill., 115 F.2d 650, 655. Difference between total assets and liabilities of individual, corporation, etc.

The total assets of a person or business less the total liabilities (amounts due to creditors). In the case of a corporation net worth includes both capital stock and surplus; in the case of a partnership or single proprietorship it is the original investment plus accumulated and reinvested profits.

Net worth of corporation may be determined by subtracting liabilities from assets or by adding the capital account and surplus account as reflected in general ledger of corporation. Eastern Capital Corp. v. Freeman, 10 Misc.2d 412, 168 N.Y.S.2d 834, 838.

Net worth method. An approach used by the Internal Revenue Service to reconstruct the income of a taxpayer who fails to maintain adequate records. Under this approach, the gross income for the year is the increase in net worth of the taxpayer (*i.e.*, assets in excess of liabilities) with appropriate adjustment for nontaxable receipts and nondeductible expenditures. The net worth method often is used when tax fraud is suspected.

Net yield. The return on an investment after deducting all costs, losses and charges for management.

Ne unques accouple /niyə́ŋkwiyz əkápəl/. L. Fr. Never married. More fully, *ne unques accouple en loiall matrimonie*, never joined in lawful marriage. The name of a plea in the action of dower *unde nihil habet*, by which the tenant denied that the dowress was ever lawfully married to the decedent.

Ne unques executor /niyə́ŋkwiyz əgzékyədər/. L. Fr. Never executor. The name of a plea by which the defendant denies that he is an executor, as he is alleged to be; or that the plaintiff is an executor, as he claims to be.

Ne unques seise que dower /niyə́ŋkwiyz síyziy kə dáwər/. L. Fr. (Never seised of a dowable estate.) In pleading, the general issue in the action of dower *unde nil habet*, by which the tenant denies that the demandant's husband was *ever seised* of an estate of which dower might be had.

Ne unques son receiver /niyə́ŋkwiyz sòn rəsíyvər/. L. Fr. In old pleading, the name of a plea in an action of account-render, by which the defendant denies that he ever was receiver of the plaintiff.

Neurasthenia /n(y)ùrəsθíyniyə/. Neurosis manifested chiefly by exhaustion, mental and physical fatigue, irritability and poorly localized symptoms without any underlying physical disorder.

Neurology. Branch of medicine dealing with nervous system and its disorders.

Neutral. Indifferent; unbiased; impartial; not engaged on either side; not taking an active part with either of the contending sides. In an international war, the principal hostile powers are called "belligerents;" those actively co-operating with and assisting them, their "allies;" and those taking no part whatever, "neutrals."

Neutrality. The state of a nation which takes no part between two or more other nations at war. U. S. v. The Three Friends, 166 U.S. 1, 17 S.Ct. 495, 41 L.Ed. 897.

Neutrality laws. Acts of Congress which forbid the fitting out and equipping of armed vessels, or the enlisting of troops, for the aid of either of two belligerent powers with which the United States is at peace.

Neutrality proclamation. A proclamation by the President of the United States, issued on the outbreak of a war between two powers with both of which the

United States is at peace, announcing the neutrality of the United States and warning all citizens to refrain from any breach of the neutrality laws.

Neutralization. Erasure or cancellation of unexpected harmful testimony by showing either by cross-examination or other witnesses that the witness has made a statement in conflict with his testimony. State v. Gallicchio, 44 N.J. 540, 210 A.2d 409, 412. See also **Impeachment.**

Neutral property. Property which belongs to citizens of neutral powers, and is used, treated, and accompanied by proper *insignia* as such.

Ne varietur /níy vèriyíydər/. Lat. It must not be altered. A phrase sometimes written by a notary upon a bill or note, for the purpose of establishing its identity, which, however, does not affect its negotiability.

Never indebted, plea of. In common law pleading, a species of traverse which occurs in actions of debt on simple contract, and is resorted to when the defendant means to deny in point of fact the existence of any express contract to the effect alleged in the declaration, or to deny the matters of fact from which such contract would by law be implied.

New. As an element in numerous compound terms and phrases of the law, this word may denote novelty, or the condition of being previously unknown or of recent or fresh origin, but ordinarily it is a purely relative term and is employed in contrasting the date, origin, or character of one thing with the corresponding attributes of another thing of the same kind or class.

In order to be "new", as that word is used in the patent laws, the achievement must be either one that produces an unusual or improved or advanced result, which was unknown to the same prior art at the time of the claimed invention; or the achievement must be one that produces an old result in an unusual and substantially more efficient, or more economical way.

New acquisition. An estate derived from any source other than descent, devise, or gift from father or mother or any relative in the paternal or maternal line. Webb v. Caldwell, 198 Ark. 331, 128 S.W.2d 691, 694.

New and useful. The phrase used in the patent laws to describe the two qualities of an invention or discovery which are essential to make it patentable, viz., novelty, or the condition of having been previously unknown, and practical utility. To accomplish a new and useful result it is not necessary that result before unknown should be brought about, but it is sufficient if an old result is accomplished in a new and more effective way. Hirschy v. Wisconsin-Minnesota Gas & Electric Household Appliances Co., D.C.Minn., 18 F.2d 347, 354. An invention achieves a new result, where a function which had been performed by other means was performed to an efficient degree by an association of means never before combined, though all of them were old, and some of the changes seemed to be only in degree.

New assets. In the law governing the administration of estates, this term denotes assets coming into the hands of an executor or administrator after the expiration of the time when, by statute, claims against the estate are barred so far as regards recourse against the assets with which he was originally charged.

New assignment. Under common law practice, where the declaration in an action is ambiguous, and the defendant pleads facts which are literally an answer to it, but not to the real claim set up by the plaintiff, the plaintiff's course is to reply by way of new assignment; *i.e.,* allege that he brought his action not for the cause supposed by the defendant, but for some other cause to which the plea has no application.

New cause of action. With reference to the amendment of pleadings, this term may refer to a new state of facts out of which liability is claimed to arise, or it may refer to parties who are alleged to be entitled under the same state of facts, or it may embrace both features. Amended and supplemental pleadings are permitted under Fed.R.Civil P. 15.

New for old. In making an adjustment of a partial loss under a policy of marine insurance, the rule is to apply the old materials towards the payment of the new, by deducting the value of them from the gross amount of the expenses for repairs, and to allow the deduction of one-third *new for old* upon the balance.

New inn. An inn of chancery. See **Inns of Chancery.**

Newly-discovered evidence. Evidence of a new and material fact, or new evidence in relation to a fact in issue, discovered by a party to a cause after the rendition of a verdict or judgment therein. Testimony discovered after trial, not discoverable before trial by exercise of due diligence. Kash N'Karry Wholesale Supermarkets, Inc. v. Garcia, Fla.App., 221 So.2d 786, 788.

Newly discovered evidence such as will support motion for new trial or to reopen for amended findings refers to evidence of facts existing at the time of trial of which the aggrieved party was excusably ignorant. Chromalloy Am. Corp. v. Alloy Surfaces Co., D.C.Del., 55 F.R.D. 406, 409. To constitute newly discovered evidence for which new trial may be granted, evidence must pertain to facts in existence at time of trial, and not to facts that have occurred subsequently. U. S. v. DePugh, D.C.Mo., 266 F.Supp. 417, 434.

Motions for new trial based on newly discovered evidence must generally be made within a specified time period; see *e.g.* Fed.R.Crim.P. 33.

New matter. In pleading, matter of fact not previously alleged by either party in the pleadings. Amended and supplemental pleadings are permitted under Fed. R.Civil P. 15.

New promise. See **Promise.**

Newsman's privilege. The alleged constitutional right (freedom of speech and press) of a newsman to refuse to disclose the sources of his information. See **Shield law.**

Newspaper. A publication, usually in sheet form, intended for general circulation, and published regularly at short intervals, containing information and editorials on current events and news of general interest.

Official newspaper. One designated by a state or municipal legislative body, or agents empowered by them, in which the public acts, resolves, advertisements, and notices are required to be published. See also **Legal newspaper.**

New trial. See **Motion for new trial; Plain error rule; Trial.**

New York interest. System of computing interest by using the exact number of days in a month and not 30 days uniformly.

New York Stock Exchange. An unincorporated association of member firms which handle the purchase and sale of securities for themselves and customers. It is the largest stock exchange in the country.

New York Times v. Sullivan. Landmark case in which the U.S. Supreme Court held that the constitutional guarantee of a free press and free speech require a public official who sues for defamation to prove malice on the part of the defendant in the publication of the matter. Malice in this context is the publishing of the material knowing it to be false or with a reckless disregard of its falsity. 376 U.S. 254, 279–280, 84 S.Ct. 710–726, 11 L.Ed.2d 686. See also **Libel.**

Nexi /néksay/. Lat. In Roman law, bound; bound persons. A term applied to such insolvent debtors as were delivered up to their creditors, by whom they might be held in bondage until their debts were discharged.

Next. Nearest; closest; immediately following.

Next devisee /nékst dəvàyzíy/°dèvəzíy/. Person to whom remainder is given by will.

Next eventual estate. Estate taking effect upon happening of the event terminating accumulation. In re Shupack's Estate, 158 Misc. 873, 287 N.Y.S. 184, 196.

Next friend. One acting for benefit of infant, married woman, or other person not sui juris, without being regularly appointed guardian. In re Boulware's Will, 144 Misc. 235, 258 N.Y.S. 522. A "next friend" is not a party to an action, but is an officer of the court, especially appearing to look after the interests of the minor whom he represents. Youngblood v. Taylor, Fla., 89 So.2d 503, 505. See also **Parens Patriæ.**

"Next friend" or "prochein ami" is one admitted to court to prosecute for infant. Crawford v. Amusement Syndicate Co., Mo., 37 S.W.2d 581, 584.

Next of kin. In the law of descent and distribution, this term properly denotes the persons nearest of kindred to the decedent, that is, those who are most nearly related to him by blood; but it is sometimes construed to mean only those who are entitled to take under the statute of distributions, and sometimes to include other persons. The term "next of kin" is used with two meanings: (1) nearest blood relations according to law of consanguinity and (2) those entitled to take under statutory distribution of intestate's estates, and term is not necessarily confined to relatives by blood, but may include a relationship existing by reason of marriage, and may well embrace persons, who in natural sense of word, and in contemplation of Roman law, bear no relation of kinship at all. In re Kyle's Autopsy, Okl., 309 P.2d 1070, 1073.

Within wrongful death statutes, means those who inherit from decedent under law of descents and distributions. Ellis v. Sill, 190 Kan. 300, 374 P.2d 213, 215.

Next presentation. In the law of advowsons, the right of next presentation is the right to present to the first vacancy of a benefice.

Nexum /néksəm/. Lat. In Roman law, in ancient times the *nexum* seems to have been a species of formal contract, involving a loan of money, and attended with peculiar consequences, solemnized with the "copper and balance." Later, it appears to have been used as a general term for any contract struck with those ceremonies, and hence to have included the special form of conveyance called *"mancipatio."* In a general sense it means the obligation or *bond* between contracting parties.

In Roman law, this word expressed the tie or obligation involved in the old conveyance by *mancipatio;* and came latterly to be used interchangeably with (but less frequently than) the word *"obligatio"* itself.

Nichills /níkəlz/. In old English practice, debts due to the exchequer which the sheriff could not levy, and as to which he returned *nil.* These sums were transcribed once a year by the clerk of the nichills, and sent to the treasurer's remembrancer's office, whence process was issued to recover the "nichill" debts. Both of these offices were abolished in 1833.

Nickname. A short name; one *nicked* or cut off for the sake of brevity, without conveying an idea of opprobrium, and frequently evincing the strongest affection or the most perfect familiarity.

Niece. The daughter of one's brother or sister, or of one's brother-in-law or sister-in-law.

Niefe /níyf/. In old English law, a woman born in vassalage; a bondwoman.

Nient /niy(ént)/. L. Fr. Nothing; not.

Nient comprise /niy(ént) kəmpríyz/. Not comprised; not included. An exception taken to a petition because the thing desired is not contained in that deed or proceeding whereon the petition is founded.

Nient culpable /niy(ént) kálpəbəl/. Not guilty. The name in French law of the general issue in tort or in a criminal action.

Nient dedire /niy(ént) dədír/. To say nothing; to deny nothing; to suffer judgment by default.

Nient le fait /niy(ént) ləféy(t)/. In pleading, not the deed; not his deed. The same as the plea of *non est factum.*

Nient seisi /niy(ént) síyziy/. In old pleading, not seised. The general plea in the writ of annuity.

NIFO. "Next-in, first-out" inventory valuation. See also **Last-in, First-out (LIFO),** and **First-in, First-out (FIFO).**

Nighttime. At common-law, that period between sunset and sunrise during which there is not daylight enough to discern a man's face. State v. Perkins, 342

Mo. 560, 116 S.W.2d 80, 81, 82. The rule is often followed that "nighttime" begins thirty minutes after sunset and ends thirty minutes before sunrise, Model Penal Code, § 221.01(2); State v. Perkins, 342 Mo. 560, 116 S.W.2d 80, 82; or, that period of time from one hour after sunset to one hour before sunrise, Com. v. Lavery, 255 Mass. 327, 333–334, 151 N.E. 466, 468.

The common-law definition is still adhered to in some states, but in others "night" has been defined by statute (see *e.g.* Model Penal Code definition above).

Night walkers. Described in the statute 5 Edw. III, c. 14, as persons who sleep by day and walk by night. Persons who prowl about at night, and are of a suspicious appearance and behavior. Persons whose habit is to be abroad at night for the purpose of committing some crime or nuisance or mischief or disturbing the peace; not now generally subject to the criminal laws except in respect to misdemeanors actually committed, or in the character of vagrants or suspicious persons. In a narrower or more popular sense, a night walker is a prostitute who walks the streets at night for the purpose of soliciting men for lewd purposes.

Nigrum nunquam excedere debet rubrum /náygrəm náŋkwəm əksíydəriy débət rúwbrəm/. The black should never go beyond the red [*i.e.*, the text of a statute should never be read in a sense more comprehensive than the rubric, or title].

Nihil /náy(h)əl/. Lat. Nothing. Often contracted to "*nil.*" The word standing alone is the name of an abbreviated form of return to a writ made by a sheriff or constable, the fuller form of which would be "*nihil est*" or "*nihil habet,*" according to circumstances.

Nihil aliud potest rex quam quod de jure potest /náy(h)əl æl(i)yəd pówdəst réks kwæm kwód dìy júriy pówdəst/. The king can do nothing except what he can by law do.

Nihil capiat per breve /náy(h)əl kæpiyət pər bríyviy/. In practice, that he take nothing by his writ. The form of judgment against the plaintiff in an action, either in bar or in abatement. When the plaintiff has commenced his proceedings by bill, the judgment is *nihil capiat per billam.*

Nihil consensui tam contrarium est quam vis atque metus /náy(h)əl kənsénshuwày tæm kəntrériyəm ést kwæm vís ætkwiy míydəs/. Nothing is so opposed to consent as force and fear.

Nihil dat qui non habet /náy(h)əl dæt kwày nòn héybət/. He gives nothing who has nothing.

Nihil de re accrescit ei qui nihil in re quando jus accresceret habet /náy(h)əl dìy ríy əkrésəd íyay kwày náy(h)əl ìn ríy kwóndow jás əkrésərət héybət/. Nothing of a matter accrues to him who, when the right accrues, has nothing in that matter.

Nihil dicit /náy(h)əl dísət/°dáy°/. He says nothing. The name of the judgment which may be taken as of course against a defendant who omits to plead or answer the plaintiff's declaration or complaint within the time limited. In some jurisdictions it is otherwise known as judgment "for want of a plea."

Judgment taken against party who withdraws his answer is *judgment nihil dicit,* which amounts to confession of cause of action stated, and carries with it, more strongly than judgment by default, admission of justice of plaintiff's case. See also **Nil dicit judgment.**

Nihil dictum quod non dictum prius /náy(h)əl díktəm kwòd nón díktəm práyəs/. Nothing is said which was not said before. Said of a case where former arguments were repeated.

Nihil est /náy(h)əl èst/. There is nothing. A form of return made by a sheriff when he has been unable to serve the writ.

Nihil est enim liberale quod non idem justum /náy(h)əl èst íynəm lìbəréyliy kwód nòn áydəm jástəm/. For there is nothing generous which is not at the same time just.

Nihil est magis rationi consentaneum quam eodem modo quodque dissolvere quo conflatum est /náy(h)əl èst méyjəs ræshiyównay kònsəntéyniyəm kwæm iyówdəm mówdow kwódkwiy dəzólvəriy kwòw kənfléydəm èst/. Nothing is more consonant to reason than that a thing should be dissolved or discharged in the same way in which it was created.

Nihil facit error nominis cum de corpore constat /náy(h)əl féysəd éhrər nómənəs kàm dìy kórpəriy kón(t)stæt/. An error as to a name is nothing when there is certainty as to the person.

Nihil habet /náy(h)əl héybət/. He has nothing. The name of a return made by a sheriff to a *scire facias* or other writ which he has been unable to serve on the defendant.

Nihil habet forum ex scena /náy(h)əl héybət fórəm èks síynə/. The court has nothing to do with what is not before it.

Nihil infra regnum subditos magis conservat in tranquilitate et concordia quam debita legum administratio /náy(h)əl ínfrə régnəm sábdədows méyjəs kənsárvəd in træŋkwìlətéytiy èt kənkórd(i)yə kwæm débədə líygəm ədmìnəstréysh(iy)ow/. Nothing preserves in tranquillity and concord those who are subjected to the same government better than a due administration of the laws.

Nihil iniquius quam æquitatem nimis intendere /náy(h)əl əníkwiyəs èst kwæm ìykwətéydəm níməs ənténdəriy/. Nothing is more unjust than to extend equity too far.

Nihil in lege intolerabilius est [quam] eandem rem diverso jure censeri /náy(h)əl in líyjiy ìntolərəbíliyəs èst kwæm iyændəm rém dəvársow júriy sən(t)síray/. Nothing is more intolerable in law than that the same matter, thing, or case should be subject to different views of law. Applied to the difference of opinion entertained by different courts, as to the law of a particular case.

Nihilist /níy(h)ələst/náy°/. One advocating doctrine of nihilism. One devoted to the destruction of the present political, religious, and social institutions.

Nihil magis justum est quam quod necessarium est /náy(h)əl méyjəs jástəm èst kwæm kwód nèsəsériyəm èst/. Nothing is more just than that which is necessary.

Nihil nequam est præsumendum /náy(h)əl nékwəm èst prìyz(y)əméndəm/. Nothing wicked is to be presumed.

Nihil perfectum est dum aliquid restat agendum /náy(h)əl pərféktəm èst dàm ǽləkwid réstəd əjéndəm/. Nothing is perfect while anything remains to be done.

Nihil peti potest ante id tempus quo per rerum naturam persolvi possit /náy(h)əl péday pówdəst ǽntiy íd témpəs kwòw pər rírəm nəchúrəm pərsólvay pósət/. Nothing can be demanded before the time when, by the nature of things, it can be paid.

Nihil possumus contra veritatem /náy(h)əl pósəməs kóntrə vèhrətéydəm/. We can do nothing against truth.

Nihil præscribitur nisi quod possidetur /náy(h)əl prəskríbədər náysay kwòd pòsədíydər/. There is no prescription for that which is not possessed.

Nihil quod est contra rationem est licitum /náy(h)əl kwód èst kóntrə rǽshiyównəm èst lísədəm/. Nothing that is against reason is lawful.

Nihil quod est inconveniens est licitum /náy(h)əl kwód èst ìnkənvíyn(i)yən(d)z èst lísədəm/. Nothing that is inconvenient is lawful. A maxim very frequently quoted by Lord Coke, but to be taken in modern law with some qualification.

Nihil simul inventum est et perfectum /náy(h)əl sáyməl ənvéntəm ést èt pərféktəm/. Nothing is invented and perfected at the same moment.

Nihil tam conveniens est naturali æquitati quam unumquodque dissolvi eo ligamine quo ligatum est /náy(h)əl tæm kənvíyn(i)yən(d)z èst nǽchəréylay ìykwətéyday kwæm yùwnəmkwódkwiy dəzólvay íyow ləgéyməniy kwòw ləgéydəm èst/. Nothing is so consonant to natural equity as that a thing should be dissolved by the same means by which it was bound.

Nihil tam conveniens est naturali æquitati quam voluntatem domini rem suam in alium transferre ratam habere /náy(h)əl tæm kənvíyn(i)yən(d)z èst nǽtyuréylay èkwətéyday kwæm vòləntéydəm dòmənay rém s(y)úwəm ìn éyl(i)yəm trænsfəriy réydəm həbíriy/. Nothing is so consonant to natural equity as to regard the intention of the owner in transferring his own property to another.

Nihil tam naturale est, quam eo genere quidque dissolvere, quo colligatum est; ideo verborum obligatio verbis tollitur; nudi consensus obligatio contrario consensu dissolvitur /náy(h)əl tæm nǽtyuréyliy èst, kwæm íyow jénəriy kwídkwiy dəzólvəriy, kwòw kòləgéydəm èst; ídiyow vərbórəm òbləgéysh(iy)ow várbəs tóldər; n(y)úwday kən(t)sén(t)səs òbləgéysh(iy)ow kəntrériyow kən(t)sén(t)s(y)uw dəzólvədər/. Nothing is so natural as to dissolve anything in the way in which it was bound together; therefore the obligation of words is taken away by words; the obligation of mere consent is dissolved by the contrary consent.

Nihil tam proprium imperio quam legibus vivere /náy(h)əl tæm prówpriyəm impíriyow kwæm líyjəbəs váyvəriy/. Nothing is so becoming to authority as to live in accordance with the laws.

Nil /níl/. Lat. Nothing. A contracted form of "nihil," which see.

Nil agit exemplum litem quod lite resolvit /níl éyjəd əgzémpləm láydəm kwòd láydiy rəzólvət/. An example does no good which settles one question by another.

Nil consensui tam contrarium est quam vis atque metus /níl kənsénshuway tæm kəntrériyəm èst kwæm vís ǽtkwiy míydəs/. Nothing is so opposed to consent as force and fear.

Nil debet /níl débət/. He owes nothing. The form of the general issue in all actions of debt on simple contract.

Nil dicit judgment. Judgment entered against defendant, in proceeding in which he is in court but has not filed an answer, is a "nil dicit judgment"; all error of pleading being waived, court examines petition only to determine if it attempts to state cause of action within court's jurisdiction. Gonzalez v. Regalado, Tex.Civ.App., 542 S.W.2d 689, 691. See also **Nihil dicit.**

Nil facit error nominis cum de corpore vel persona constat /níl féysəd éhrər nómənəs kàm dìy kórpəriy vél pərsównə kónstæt/. A mistake in the name does not matter when the body or person is manifest.

Nil habuit in tenementis /níl hǽbyuwəd ən tènəméntəs/. He had nothing [no interest] in the tenements. A plea in debt on a lease indented, by which the defendant sets up that the person claiming to be landlord had no title or interest.

Nil ligatum /níl ləgéydəm/. Nothing bound; that is, no obligation has been incurred.

Nil sine prudenti fecit ratione vetustas /níl sáyniy pruwdéntay féysət rǽshiyówniy vətástæs/. Antiquity did nothing without a good reason.

Nil temere novandum /níl téməriy nəvǽndəm/. Nothing should be rashly changed.

Nimia certitudo certitudinem ipsam destruit /nímiyə sàrdət(y)úwdow sàrdət(y)úwdənəm ípsəm dəstrúwət/. Too great certainty destroys certainty itself.

Nimia subtilitas in jure reprobatur /nímiyə sà(b)tílətæs ìn júriy rèprəbéydər/. Too much subtlety in law is discountenanced.

Nimium altercando veritas amittitur /nímiyəm òltərkǽndow véhrətæs əmídədər/. By too much altercation truth is lost.

Nimmer /nímər/. A thief; a pilferer.

Nineteenth Amendment. Known as the women's suffrage amendment to the U.S. Const., it provides that the right of citizens of the U.S. to vote shall not be denied or abridged by the U.S. or by any state on account of sex. The 19th Amendment was ratified in 1920.

Ninety (90) day letter. Statutory notice sent by I.R.S. to taxpayer of tax deficiency. During the 90 day period after the mailing of such notice the taxpayer may either pay the tax and seek a refund or not pay the tax and challenge such alleged deficiency on petition to the Tax Court. I.R.C. §§ 6212, 6213. Notice of Commissioner's determination of tax liability must, absent jeopardy, precede assessment. Bromberg v. Ingling, C.A.Guam, 300 F.2d 859, 861. See also **Thirty-day letter.**

Ninth Amendment. This amendment to the U.S. Const. provides that the enumeration in the Constitution of certain rights, shall not be construed to deny or disparage others retained by the people.

Nisei /níysèy/. Jap. Second generation. Particularly a person born in the United States of Japanese parents. See also **Kibei.**

Nisi /náysay/. Lat. Unless. The word is often affixed, as a kind of elliptical expression, to the words "rule," "order," "decree," "judgment," or "confirmation," to indicate that the adjudication spoken of is one which is to stand as valid and operative *unless* the party affected by it shall appear and show cause against it, or take some other appropriate step to avoid it or procure its revocation. Thus a "decree *nisi*" is one which will definitely conclude the defendant's rights unless, within the prescribed time, he shows cause to set it aside or successfully appeals. The word, in this sense, is opposed to "absolute." And when a rule *nisi* is finally confirmed, for the defendant's failure to show cause against it, it is said to be "made absolute." See also **Show cause order.**

Nisi decree. An interim decree or order which will ripen into a final decree unless something changes, or some event takes place. See also **Nisi.**

Nisi feceris /náysay fíysərəs/. The name of a clause commonly occurring in the old manorial writs, commanding that, if the lords failed to do justice, the king's court or officer should do it. By virtue of this clause, the king's court usurped the jurisdiction of the private, manorial, or local courts.

Nisi prius /náysay práyəs/. The *nisi prius* courts are such as are held for the trial of issues of fact before a jury and one presiding judge. In America the phrase was formerly used to denote the forum (whatever may be its statutory name) in which the cause was tried to a jury, as distinguished from the appellate court.

Nisi prius clause /nàysay práyəs klóz/. In practice, a clause entered on the record in an action at law, authorizing the trial of the cause at *nisi prius* in the particular county designated. It was first used by way of continuance.

Nisi prius roll /nàysay práyəs rówl/. In practice, the roll or record containing the pleadings, issue, and jury process of an action, made up for use in the *nisi prius* court.

NKA. Now known as.

N.L. An abbreviation of *"non liquet"* (which see).

N.L.R.A. National Labor Relations Act.

N.L.R.B. National Labor Relations Board.

No-action clause. Provision commonly found in liability insurance policies to the effect that the insurer is not liable to the insured and that no action may be brought against the insurer by the insured until an action has been brought and the insured has either paid the amount to the third person or until a judgment has been rendered fixing the amount due or until an agreement has been reached.

No-action letter. Letter written by attorney for governmental agency (*e.g.* S.E.C.) to effect that, if facts are as represented in request for ruling, he will advise agency not to take action because the facts do not warrant prosecution.

No arrival, no sale. Provision in sales contract that if goods do not arrive at destination buyer acquires no property therein and does not become liable for price.

No award. The name of a plea in an action on an award, by which the defendant traverses the allegation that an award was made.

Nobiles magis plectuntur pecunia; plebes vero in corpore /nówbəliyz méyjəs plèktántər pəkyúwn(i)yə, plíybiyz vírow in kórpəriy/. The higher classes are more punished in money; but the lower in person.

Nobiles sunt, qui arma gentilitia antecessorum suorum proferre possunt /nówbəliyz sànt kwày ármə jèntəlísh(iy)ə æntiysesórəm s(y)uwórəm prowféhriy pósənt/. The gentry are those who are able to produce amorial bearings derived by descent from their own ancestors.

Nobiliores et benigniores præsumptiones in dubiis sunt præferendæ /nəbiliyóriyz èt bənigniyóriyz prəzàm(p)shiyówniz in d(y)úwbiyəs sànt prèfərǽndæ/. In cases of doubt, the more generous and more benign presumptions are to be preferred. A civil-law maxim.

Nobilitas est duplex, superior et inferior /nowbílətæs èst d(y)úwpleks, səpíriyər èd infíriyər/. There are two sorts of nobility, the higher and the lower.

Nobility. In English law, a division of the people, comprehending dukes, marquises, earls, viscounts, and barons. These had anciently duties annexed to their respective honors. They are created either by writ, *i.e.*, by royal summons to attend the house of peers, or by letters patent, *i.e.*, by royal grant of any dignity and degree of peerage; and they enjoy many privileges, exclusive of their senatorial capacity.

No bill. This phrase, endorsed by a grand jury on the indictment, is equivalent to "not found", "no indictment", or "not a true bill". It means that, in the opinion of the jury, evidence was insufficient to warrant the return of a formal charge. See **Indictment.**

No bonus clause. In states where applicable, a clause under the eminent domain section of a lease, giving the lessee the right to recover only the value of his physical improvements in the event of a taking, and not the value of his leasehold interest (the difference between the fixed rent of the lease and current market rental value).

Nocent /nówsənt/. From Latin *"nocere,"* guilty. "The *nocent* person."

No contest clause. Provision in a will to the effect that the legacy or devise is given on condition that no action is taken to contest the will; and if such action is initiated, the legacy or devise is forfeited.

Noctanter /noktǽntər/. By night; an abolished writ which issued out of chancery, and returned to the queen's bench, for the prostration of inclosures, etc.

Noctes and **noctem de firma** /nóktiyz dìy fə́rmə /nóktəm°/. Entertainment of meat and drink for so many nights.

Nocumentum /nòkyəméntəm/. Lat. In old English law, a nuisance. *Nocumentum damnosum,* a nuisance occasioning loss or damage. *Nocumentum injuriosum,* an injurious nuisance. For the latter only a remedy was given.

No evidence. Under the rule that the court may render judgment non obstante veredicto if directed verdict would have been proper, the term "no evidence" does not mean literally no evidence at all; "no evidence" comprehends those situations wherein by the application of established principles of law the evidence is deemed legally insufficient to establish an asserted proposition of fact. Fields v. Burlison Packing Co., Tex.Civ.App., 405 S.W.2d 105, 106. "No evidence" points may be sustained only when (1) evidence of a vital fact is completely absent; (2) rules of law or evidence bar court from giving weight to only evidence offered to prove a vital fact; (3) no more than a mere scintilla of evidence is offered to prove a vital fact; and (4) the evidence conclusively establishes the opposite of the vital fact. State v. Vargas, Tex. Civ.App., 419 S.W.2d 926, 927.

No eyewitness rule. The "no eyewitness rule" is that where there is no obtainable direct evidence of what decedent did or failed to do immediately before injury, trier of facts may infer that decedent was in exercise of ordinary care for his own safety. Marean v. Petersen, 259 Iowa 557, 144 N.W.2d 906, 913.

No fault. A type of automobile insurance, in force in many states, in which each person's own insurance company pays for injury or damage up to a certain limit irregardless of whether its insured was actually at fault. See **Insurance.** Also, popular name for a type of divorce in which a marriage can be ended on a mere allegation that it has "irretrievably" broken down or because of "irreconcilable" differences between the spouses. Under such statutory ground for dissolution of marriage, fault on the part of either spouse need not be shown or proved.

No fault insurance. See **Insurance; No fault.**

No funds. Endorsement marked on check when a check is drawn on bank in which the drawer has no funds with which to cover check. See also **Fund.**

No goods. This is the English equivalent of the Latin term *"nulla bona,"* being the form of the return made by a sheriff or constable, charged with an execution, when he has found no property of the debtor on which to levy.

N.O.I.B.N. Abbreviation, used under terms of tariffs, filed with Interstate Commerce Commission, meaning not otherwise indexed by name. Pennsylvania R. Co. v. U. S., Ct.Cl., 42 F.2d 600, 602.

Nolens volens /nówlèn(d)z vówlèn(d)z/. Lat. Whether willing or unwilling; consenting or not.

No limit order. An order to buy or sell securities in which there is no stipulation as to price.

Nolissement /nòlismón/. Fr. In French marine law, affreightment.

Nolle prosequi /nóliy prósəkwày/. Lat. A formal entry upon the record, by the plaintiff in a civil suit, or, more commonly, by the prosecuting officer in a criminal action, by which he declares that he "will no further prosecute" the case, either as to some of the defendants, or altogether. A nolle prosequi is a formal entry on the record by the prosecuting officer by which he declares that he will not prosecute the case further. State v. Gaskins, 263 S.C. 343, 210 S.E.2d 590, 592. Commonly called "nol pros".

No-load fund. A type of mutual fund which charges little or nothing for administrative and selling expenses in the sale of its shares. See **Mutual fund.**

Nolo contendere /nówlow kənténdəriy/. Latin phrase meaning "I will not contest it"; a plea in a criminal case which has a similar legal effect as pleading guilty. Hudson v. U. S., 272 U.S. 451, 455, 47 S.Ct. 127, 129, 71 L.Ed. 347. Type of plea which may be entered with leave of court to a criminal complaint or indictment by which the defendant does not admit or deny the charges, though a fine or sentence may be imposed pursuant to it. The principal difference between a plea of guilty and a plea of nolo contendere is that the latter may not be used against the defendant in a civil action based upon the same acts. As such, this plea is particularly popular in antitrust actions (*e.g.* price fixing) where the likelihood of civil actions following in the wake of a successful antitrust prosecution is very great.

A defendant may plead nolo contendere only with the consent of the court. Such a plea shall be accepted by the court only after due consideration of the views of the parties and the interest of the public in the effective administration of justice. Fed.R.Crim.P. 11(b).

Nomen /nówmən/. Lat. In the civil law, a name; the name, style, or designation of a person. Properly, the name showing to what *gens* or tribe he belonged, as distinguished from his own individual name *(the prœnomen),* from his surname or family name *(cognomen),* and from any name added by way of a descriptive title *(agnomen).* The name or style of a class or genus of persons or objects. A debt or a debtor.

Nomen collectivum /nówmən kòləktáyvəm/. A collective name or term; a term expressive of a class; a term including several of the same kind; a term expressive of the plural, as well as singular, number.

Nomen est quasi rei notamen /nówmən èst kwéysay ríyay nowtéymən/. A name is, as it were, the note of a thing.

Nomen generale /nówmən jènəréyliy/. A general name; the name of a *genus.*

Nomen generalissimum /nówmən jènərəlísəməm/. A name of the most general kind; a name or term of the most general meaning. By the name of "land," which is *nomen generalissimum,* everything terrestrial will pass.

Nomen juris /nówmən júrəs/. A name of the law; a technical legal term.

Nomen non sufficit, si res non sit de jure aut de facto /nówmən nòn səfəsət sày ríy nòn sít dìy júriy ót dìy fæktow/. A name is not sufficient if there be not a thing [or subject for it] *de jure* or *de facto*.

Nomen transcriptitium /nówmən trænskriptíshiyəm/. See **Nomina transcriptitia**.

Nominal. Titular; existing in name only; not real or substantial; connected with the transaction or proceeding in name only, not in interest. Park Amusement Co. v. McCaughn, D.C.Pa., 14 F.2d 553, 556. Not real or actual; merely named, stated, or given, without reference to actual conditions; often with the implication that the thing named is so small, slight, or the like, in comparison to what might properly be expected, as scarcely to be entitled to the name; *e.g.,* a nominal price. Lehman v. Tait, C.C.A.Md., 58 F.2d 20, 23.

Nominal account. In accounting, a ledger account of expenses and income, closed into surplus when the books are balanced.

Nominal capital. Very small or negligible capital, whose use in particular business is incidental. Strayer's Business College v. Commissioner of Internal Revenue, C.C.A.Md., 35 F.2d 426, 429. Capital in name only and which is not substantial; not real or actual; merely named, stated, or given, without reference to actual conditions. Feeders' Supply Co. v. Commissioner of Internal Revenue, C.C.A.Mo., 31 F.2d 274, 276.

Nominal consideration. See **Consideration**.

Nominal damages. See **Damages**.

Nominal defendant. A person who is joined as defendant in an action, not because he is immediately liable in damages or because any specific relief is demanded as against him, but because his connection with the subject-matter is such that the plaintiff's action would be defective, under the technical rules of practice, if he were not joined. See also **Parties**.

Nominal interest rate. The rate of interest stated in a security as opposed to the actual interest yield that is based upon the price at which the interest-bearing property is purchased and the length of time to maturity of the obligation.

Nominal partner. A person who appears to be a partner in a firm, or is so represented to persons dealing with the firm, or who allows his name to appear in the style of the firm or to be used in its business, in the character of a partner, but who has no actual interest in the firm or business.

Nominal party. See **Nominal defendant; Parties**.

Nominal trust. A dry or passive trust in which the duties of the trustee are minimal and in which the beneficiary has virtual control.

Nomina mutabilia sunt, res autem immobiles /nómənə myùwdəbíl(i)yə sənt, ríyz ódəm əmówbəliyz/. Names are mutable, but things are immovable [immutable]. A name may be true or false, or may change, but the thing itself always maintains its identity.

Nomina si nescis perit cognitio rerum; et nomina si perdas, certe distinctio rerum perditur /nómənə sày nésəs pérət kògnísh(iy)ow rírəm èt nómənə sáy pérdæs sárdiy dəstínksh(iy)ow rírəm pérdədər/. If you know not the names of things, the knowledge of things themselves perishes; and, if you lose the names, the distinction of the things is certainly lost.

Nomina sunt notæ rerum /nómənə sənt nówtiy rírəm/. Names are the notes of things.

Nomina sunt symbola rerum /nómənə sənt símbələ rírəm/. Names are the symbols of things.

Nominate. To name, designate by name, appoint, or propose for election or appointment.

Nominate contracts. In the civil law, contracts having a proper or peculiar name and form, and which were divided into four kinds, expressive of the ways in which they were formed, viz.: (1) Real, which arose *ex re,* from something done; (2) verbal, *ex verbis,* from something said; (3) literal, *ex literis,* from something written; and (4) consensual, *ex consensu,* from something agreed to.

Nominatim /nòmənéydəm/. Lat. By name; expressed one by one.

Nominating and reducing. A mode of obtaining a panel of special jurors in England, from which to select the jury to try a particular action.

Nominatio auctoris /nòmənéyshow òktórəs/. Lat. In Roman law, a form of plea or defense in an action for the recovery of real estate, by which the defendant, sued as the person apparently in possession, alleges that he holds only in the name or for the benefit of another, whose name he discloses by the plea, in order that the plaintiff may bring his action against such other.

Nomination. An appointment or designation of a person to fill an office or discharge a duty. The act of suggesting or proposing a person by name as a candidate for an office.

Nomination paper. A paper used for selection of candidates by a political body which is not a political party and is not entitled to use a "nomination petition". Commonwealth v. Antico, 146 Pa.Super. 293, 22 A.2d 204, 209.

Nomination to a living. In English ecclesiastical law, the rights of nominating and of presenting to a living are distinct, and may reside in different persons. Presentation is the offering a clerk to the bishop. Nomination is the offering a clerk to the person who has the right of presentation.

Nominativus pendens /nòmənətáyvəs péndèn(d)z/. Lat. A nominative case grammatically unconnected with the rest of the sentence in which it stands. The opening words in the ordinary form of a deed *inter partes,* "This indenture," etc., down to "whereas," though an intelligible and convenient part of the deed, are of this kind.

Nomina transcriptitia /nómənə trænskrəptísh(iy)ə/. In Roman law, obligations contracted by *literæ* (i.e., *literis obligationes*) were so called because they arose from a peculiar *transfer (transcriptio)* from the creditor's day-book *(adversaria)* into his ledger *(codex)*.

Nomina villarum /nómənə vəlérəm/. In English law, an account of the names of all the villages and the possessors thereof, in each county, drawn up by several sheriffs (9 Edw. II), and returned by them into the exchequer, where it is still preserved.

Nomine /nóməniy/. Lat. By name; by the name of; under the name or designation of.

Nominee /nòməníy/. One who has been nominated or proposed for an office. One designated to act for another in his or her place.

One designated to act for another as his representative in a rather limited sense. It is used sometimes to signify an agent or trustee. It has no connotation, however, other than that of acting for another, in representation of another, or as the grantee of another. Schuh Trading Co. v. Commissioner of Internal Revenue, C.C.A.Ill., 95 F.2d 404, 411.

Nominee trust. An arrangement for holding title to real property under which one or more persons or corporations, pursuant to a written declaration of trust, declare that they will hold any property that they acquire as trustees for the benefit of one or more undisclosed beneficiaries.

Nomine pœnæ /nóməniy píyniy/. In the name of a penalty.

In the civil law, a legacy was said to be left *nomine pœnæ* where it was left for the purpose of coercing the heir to do or not to do something.

The term has also been applied, in English law, to some kinds of covenants, such as a covenant inserted in a lease that the lessee shall forfeit a certain sum on non-payment of rent, or on doing certain things, as plowing up ancient meadow, and the like.

Nomocanon /nòwmokǽnən/. (1) A collection of canons and imperial laws relative or conformable thereto. The first nomocanon was made by Johannes Scholasticus in 554. Photius, patriarch of Constantinople, in 883, compiled another nomocanon, or collation of the civil laws with the canons; this is the most celebrated. Balsamon wrote a commentary upon it in 1180. (2) A collection of the ancient canons of the apostles, councils, and fathers, without regard to imperial constitutions.

Nomographer /nəmógrəfər/. One who writes on the subject of laws.

Nomography /nəmógrəfiy/. A treatise or description of laws.

Nomotheta /nòwməthíydə/. A lawgiver; such as Solon and Lycurgus among the Greeks, and Cæsar, Pompey, and Sylla among the Romans.

Non. Lat. Not. The common prefix of negation.

Non-ability. Want of ability to do an act in law, as to sue. A plea founded upon such cause.

Non-acceptance. A buyer's right under a contract of sale to reject the goods because of non-conformance with the contract. U.C.C. § 3–601(a). Failure or refusal of a drawee to accept a draft or bill. The refusal to accept anything.

Non acceptavit /nón ækseptéyvət/. In common law pleading, the name of a plea to an action of assumpsit brought against the drawee of a bill of exchange by which he denies that he *accepted* the same.

Non-access. Absence of opportunities for sexual intercourse between husband and wife; or the absence of such intercourse. Defense interposed by alleged father in paternity cases.

Non accipi debent verba in demonstrationem falsam, quæ competunt in limitationem veram /nòn ǽksəpay débənt várbə in dèmənstrèyshiyównəm fól(t)səm, kwìy kómpədənt in lìmətèyshiyównəm vírəm/. Words ought not to be taken to import a false demonstration which may have effect by way of true limitation.

Non accrevit infra sex annos /nón əkríyvət ínfrə séks ǽnows/. It did not accrue within six years. The name of a plea by which the defendant sets up the statute of limitations against a cause of action which is barred after six years.

Nonacquiescence. Disagreement by the I.R.S. on the result reached by the U.S. Tax Court in a regular decision. Sometimes abbreviated as non-acqu. or NA.

Non-admission. The refusal of admission.

Nonæ et decimæ /nówniy ét désəmiy/. In old European law, payments made to the church, by those who were tenants of churchfarms. The first was a rent or duty for things belonging to husbandry; the second was claimed in right of the church.

Non-age. Lack of requisite legal age. A minor. In general, the legal status of a person who is under eighteen years of age.

Nonagium or **nonage** /nownéyj(iy)əm/nównəj/. In old European law, a ninth part of movables which was paid to the clergy on the death of persons in their parish, and claimed on pretense of being distributed to pious uses.

Non alio modo puniatur aliquis quam secundum quod se habet condemnatio /nòn éyliyow mówdow pyùwniyéydər ǽləkwis kwǽm səkándəm kwòd siy héybət kòndemnéysh(iy)ow/. A person may not be punished differently than according to what the sentence enjoins.

Non aliter a significatione verborum recedi oportet quam cum manifestum est, aliud sensisse testatorem /nòn éylədər èy sìgnəfəkèyshiyówniy vərbórəm rəsíyday əpórtət kwǽm kàm mǽnəféstəm èst, éyliyəd sèn(t)sísiy tèstətórəm/. We must never depart from the signification of words, unless it is evident that they are not conformable to the will of the testator.

Non-ancestral estate. Realty coming to deceased in any way other than by descent or devise from a now dead ancestor, or by deed of actual gift from a living one, there being no other consideration than that of blood. One acquired by purchase or by act or agreement of the parties, as distinguished from one acquired by descent or by operation of law.

Non-apparent easement. A non-continuous or discontinuous easement. See **Easement.**

Non-appearance. A failure of appearance; the omission of the defendant to appear within the time limited.

Non-assessable. This word, placed upon a certificate of stock, does not cancel or impair the obligation to pay the amount due upon the shares created by the acceptance and holding of such certificate. At most its legal effect is a stipulation against liability from further assessment or taxation after the entire subscription of one hundred per cent. shall have been paid. Upton v. Tribilcock, 91 U.S. 45, 23 L.Ed. 203.

Non assumpsit /nón əsə́m(p)sət/. The general issue in the action of *assumpsit;* being a plea by which the defendant avers that "he did not undertake" or promise as alleged.

Non assumpsit infra sex annos /nón əsə́m(p)səd ínfrə séks ǽnows/. He did not undertake within six years. The name of the plea of the statute of limitations, in the action of *assumpsit.*

Non auditur perire volens /nón ódədər pəráyriy vówlèn(d)z/. He who is desirous to perish is not heard. He who confesses himself guilty of a crime, with the view of meeting death, will not be heard. A maxim of the foreign law of evidence.

Non-bailable. Not admitting of bail; not requiring bail.

Non bis in idem /nón bís ìn áydəm/. Not twice for the same; that is, a man shall not be twice tried for the same crime. This maxim of the civil law expresses the same principle as the familiar rule of our law that a man shall not be twice "put in jeopardy" for the same offense.

Non-cancellable /nón kǽn(t)sələbəl/. Such provision in insurance policy precludes insurer from cancelling policy after an illness or accident, so long as the premium has been paid. Dudgeon v. Mutual Ben. Health & Accident Ass'n, C.C.A.W.Va., 70 F.2d 49, 52.

Non cepit /nón síypət/. He did not take. The general issue in replevin, where the action is for the wrongful *taking* of the property; putting in issue not only the taking, but the *place* in which the taking is stated to have been made.

Non-claim. The omission or neglect of person who ought to claim his right within the time limited by law.

Covenant of non-claim. See **Covenant.**

Non-combatant. A person connected with an army or navy, but for purposes other than fighting; such as the surgeons and chaplains or conscientious objectors. Also a neutral.

Non-commissioned. A non-commissioned officer of the armed services is an officer who holds his rank, not by commission from the executive authority, but by appointment by a superior officer.

Non compos mentis /nón kómpəs méntəs/. Lat. Not sound of mind; insane. This is a very general term, embracing all varieties of mental derangement. See **Insanity.**

Non concedantur citationes priusquam exprimatur super qua re fieri debet citatio /nón kònsədǽntər sətèyshiyówniyz prayə́skwəm èksprəméydər s(y)úwpər kwèy ríy fáyəray débət saytéysh(iy)ow/. Summonses should not be granted before it is expressed on what matter the summons ought to be made.

Non concessit /nón kənsésət/. Lat. He did not grant. The name of a common law plea denying a grant, which could be made only by a stranger.

Nonconforming lot. A lot the area, dimension or location of which was lawful prior to the adoption, revision or amendment of a zoning ordinance, but now fails to conform to the requirements of the zoning district in which it is located by reason of such adoption, revision, or amendment.

Nonconforming use. A structure the size, dimension or location of which was lawful prior to the adoption, revision or amendment of a zoning ordinance, but which fails to conform to the requirements of the zoning district in which it is located by reasons of such adoption, revision or amendment. A use which does not comply with present zoning provisions but which existed lawfully and was created in good faith prior to the enactment of the zoning provision. Camaron Apartments, Inc. v. Zoning Bd. of Adjustment of City of Philadelphia, 14 Pa.Cmwlth. 571, 324 A.2d 805, 807.

Uses permitted by zoning statutes or ordinances to continue notwithstanding that similar uses are not permitted in area in which they are located. Beyer v. Mayor and Council of Baltimore City, 182 Md. 444, 34 A.2d 765, 766.

See also **Variance.**

Non-conformist. One who refuses to comply with others; one who refuses to join in the established forms of custom, belief, styles, usages, rules, etc.

Non consentit qui errat /nón kənséntət‛kwày éhrət/. He who mistakes does not consent.

Non constat /nón kónstət/. Lat. It does not appear; it is not clear or evident. A phrase used in general to state some conclusion as not necessarily following although it may appear on its face to follow.

Non-contestable clause. A non-contestable clause secures to insured indemnity by way of short limitations by contract against belated charges of fraud and mistake and rescission therefor, when he has acted thereon to his detriment by payment of premiums and foregoing other insurance.

Non-continuous easement. "Continuous easement" is one which may be enjoyed without any act by party claiming it, while "noncontinuous easement," such as right of way, is one to enjoyment of which party's act is essential. A non-apparent or discontinuous easement. See **Easement.**

Noncontribution clause. In fire insurance policies, a provision that only the interests of the owner and first mortgagee are protected under the policy.

Non culpabilis /nón kə̀lpéybələs/. Lat. In pleading, not guilty. It is usually abbreviated *"non cul."*

Noncumulative dividends. Commonly incident to preferred stock if a dividend is "passed" (not paid) in a particular year or period; such passed dividends are gone forever and there is no obligation to pay such when the next dividend is paid.

Non damnificatus /nón dæmnəfəkéydəs/. Lat. Not injured.

A common law plea in an action of debt on an indemnity bond, or bond conditioned "to keep the plaintiff harmless and indemnified," etc. It is in the nature of a plea of performance, being used where the defendant means to allege that the plaintiff has been kept harmless and indemnified, according to the tenor of the condition.

Non dat qui non habet /nón dǽt kwáy nòn héybət/. He who has not does not give.

Non debeo melioris conditionis esse, quam auctor meus a quo jus in me transit /nón débiyow mìyliyórəs kəndìshiyównəs ésiy kwǽm óktər míyəs èy kwòw jǽs in míy trǽn(d)zət/. I ought not to be in better condition than he to whose rights I succeed.

Non deberet alii nocere quod inter alios actum esset /nón débərət éyliyay nósəriy kwòd íntər éyliyows ǽktəm ésət/. No one ought to be injured by that which has taken place between other parties.

Non debet actori licere quod reo non permittitur /nón débəd æktóray ləsíriy kwòd ríyow nòn pərmídədər/. A plaintiff ought not to be allowed what is not permitted to a defendant. A rule of the civil law.

Non debet adduci exceptio ejus rei cujus petitur dissolutio /nón débəd əd(y)úwsay əksépsh(iy)ow íyjəs ríyəs k(y)úwjəs pédədər dìsəl(y)úwsh(iy)ow/. A plea of the same matter the dissolution of which is sought [by the action] ought not to be brought forward.

Non debet alii nocere, quod inter alios actum est /nón débəd éyliyay nəsíriy, kwód íntər éyliyows ǽktəm èst/. A person ought not to be prejudiced by what has been done between others.

Non debet alteri per alterum iniqua conditio inferri /nón débəd óltəray pàr óltərəm ənáykwə kəndísh(iy)ow inféhray/. A burdensome condition ought not to be brought upon one man by the act of another.

Non debet cui plus licet, quod minus est non licere /nón débət kwúway plás lísət, kwòd máynəs èst nón ləsíriy/. He to whom the greater is lawful ought not to be debarred from the less as unlawful.

Non debet dici tendere in præjudicium ecclesiasticæ liberatatis quod pro rege et republica necessarium videtur /nón débət dáysay téndəriy in prèjuwdísh(iy)əm əklìyziyǽstəsiy lìbər(ə)téydəs kwòd pròw ríyjiy èt rəpáhləkə nèsəsériyəm vodíydər/. That which seems necessary for the king and the state ought not to be said to tend to the prejudice of spiritual liberty.

Non decet homines dedere causa non cognita /nón désət hóməniyz dédəriy kózə nòn kógnədə/. It is unbecoming to surrender men when no cause is shown.

Non decimando /nón dèsəmǽndow/. See **De non decimando.**

Non decipitur qui scit se decipi /nón dəsípədər kwày sít síy désəpay/. He is not deceived who knows himself to be deceived.

Non dedit /nón díydət/. Lat. In old pleading, he did not grant. The general issue in formedon.

Non definitur in jure quid sit conatus /nón dəfínədər in júriy kwíd sìt kənéydəs/. What an attempt is, is not defined in law. See **Attempt.**

Non-delivery. Neglect, failure, or refusal to deliver goods, on the part of a carrier, vendor, bailee, etc.

Non demisit /nón dəmáyzət/. Lat. He did not demise.

Non-detachable facilities. Facilities which may not be put back into channels of commerce. Briggs Mfg. Co. v. U. S., D.C.Conn., 30 F.2d 962, 967.

Non detinet /nón dédənət/. Lat. He does not detain.

The name of the general issue in the action of detinue. The general issue in the action of replevin, where the action is for the wrongful detention only.

Non differunt quæ concordant re, tametsi non in verbis iisdem /nón dífərənt kwíy kənkórdænt riy, tæmétsay nón in várbəs iyáysdəm/. Those things do not differ which agree in substance, though not in the same words.

Non dimisit /nón dəmáyzət/. L. Lat. He did not demise. A common law plea resorted to where a plaintiff declared upon a demise without stating the indenture in an action of debt for rent. Also, a plea in bar, in replevin, to an avowry for arrears of rent, that the avowant did not demise.

Non-direction. Omission on the part of a judge to properly instruct the jury upon a necessary conclusion of law.

Non-disclosure. A failure to reveal facts, which may exist when there is no "concealment." State v. Watson, 145 Kan. 792, 67 P.2d 515, 517. See **Fraud; Material fact; Misrepresentation.**

Non distringendo /nón dìstrinjéndow/. A writ not to distrain.

Non dubitatur, etsi specialiter venditor evictionem non promiserit, re evicta, ex empto competere actionem /nón d(y)ùwbətéydər, étsay spèshiyéylədər véndədər əvikshiyównəm nòn prəmísərət, ríy əvíktə, èks émptow kəmpédəriy ǽkshiyównəm/. It is certain that, although the vendor has not given a special guaranty, an action *ex empto* lies against him, if the purchaser is evicted.

Non efficit affectus nisi sequatur effectus /nón èfəsəd əféktəs náysay səkwéydər əféktəs/. The intention amounts to nothing unless the effect follow.

Non erit alia lex Romæ, alia Athænis; alia nunc, alia posthac; sed et omnes gentes, et omni tempore, una lex, et sempiterna, et immortalis continebit /nón éhrət éyliyə léks rówmiy, éyliyə əθíynəs, éyliyə nánk, éyliyə pówsthæk; séd èt ómniyz jéntiyz èd ómnay témpəriy yúwnə léks, èt sèmpətárnə èt imortéyləs, kòntəníybət/. There will not be one law at Rome, another at Athens; one law now, another hereafter; but one eternal and immortal law shall bind together all nations throughout all time.

Nones /nówn(d)z/. In the Roman calendar, the fifth, and, in March, May, July, and October, the seventh, day of the month. So called because, counting inclusively, they were *nine* days from the ides.

Non est arctius vinculum inter homines quam jusjurandum /nón èst árkshiyəs víŋk(y)ələm íntər hómǝniyz kwæm jə̀sjərǽndǝm/. There is no closer [or firmer] bond between men than an oath.

Non est certandum de regulis juris /nón èst sərtǽndǝm dìy régyələs júrǝs/. There is no disputing about rules of law.

Non est consonum rationi, quod cognitio accessorii in curia christianitatis impediatur, ubi cognitio causæ principalis ad forum ecclesiasticum noscitur pertinere /nón èst kónsǝnǝm ræ̀shiyównay kwòd kognísh(iy)ow ǽksǝsóriyay in kyúriyǝ krìs(h)chiyæ̀nǝtéydǝs impìydiyéydǝr, yúwbay kognísh(iy)ow kóziy prìn(t)sǝpéyləs æd fórǝm ǝklìyziyǽstǝkǝm nósǝdǝr pǝrdǝníriy/. It is unreasonable that the cognizance of an accessory matter should be impeded in an ecclesiastical court, when the cognizance of the principal cause is admitted to appertain to an ecclesiastical court.

Non est disputandum contra principia negantem /nón èst díspyǝtǽndǝm kóntrǝ prìnsípiyǝ nǝgǽntǝm/. We cannot dispute against a man who denies first principles.

Non est factum /nón èst fǽktǝm/. Lat. A plea denying execution of instrument sued on. Blair v. Lockwood, 226 Ky. 412, 11 S.W.2d 107, 109.

Non est inventus /nón èst ìnvéntǝs/. Lat. He is not found. The sheriff's return to process requiring him to arrest the body of the defendant, when the latter is not found within his jurisdiction. It is often abbreviated, *"n. e. i.,"* or written, in English, "not found."

Non est justum aliquem antenatum post mortem facere bastardum qui toto tempore vitæ suæ pro legitimo habebatur /nón èst jóstǝm ǽlǝkwǝm æ̀ntiynéydǝm pòwst mórdǝm féysǝriy bǽstárdǝm kwày tówdow témpǝriy váydiy s(y)úwiy pròw lǝjídǝmow hæ̀bǝbéydǝr/. It is not just to make an elderborn a bastard after his death, who during his lifetime was accounted legitimate.

Non est novum ut priores leges ad posteriores trahantur /nón èst nówvǝm ə̀t prayóriyz líyjiyz æd pǝstìriyóriyz trǝhǽntǝr/. It is no new thing that prior statutes should give place to later ones.

Non est recedendum a communi observantia /nón èst rèsǝdéndǝm éy kǝmyúwnay òbzǝrvǽnsh(iy)ǝ/. There should be no departure from a common observance.

Non est regula quin fallet /nón èst régyǝlǝ kwìn fólǝt/. There is no rule but what may fail.

Non est reus nisi mens sit rea /nón èst ríyǝs náysay mén(d)z sít ríyǝ/. One is not guilty unless his intention be guilty. This maxim is much criticized and is only applicable when the absence of intent reduces the seriousness of the crime. See **Actus non facit reum, etc.; Mens rea.**

Non est singulis concedendum, quod per magistratum publice possit fieri, ne occasio sit majoris tumultus faciendi /nón èst síŋgyǝlǝs kòn(t)sǝdéndǝm kwòd pàr mæ̀jǝstréydǝm pə́blǝsiy pósǝt fáyǝray, níy ǝkéyzh(iy)ow sìt mǝjórǝs tǝmáltǝs fǽshiyénday/. That is not to be conceded to private persons which can be publicly done by the magistrate, lest it be the occasion of greater tumults.

Non exemplis sed legibus judicandum est /nón ǝgzémplǝs sèd líyjǝbǝs jùwdǝkǽndǝm èst/. Not by the facts of the case, but by the law must judgment be made.

Non ex opinionibus singulorum, sed ex communi usi, nomina exaudiri debent /nón èks ǝpìniyównǝbǝs síŋgyǝlórǝm sèd èks kǝmyúwnay yúws(y)uw nómǝnǝ èksodáyray débǝnt/. The names of things ought to be understood, not according to the opinions of individuals, but according to common usage.

Non facias malum, ut inde fiat bonum /nón féysh(iy)ǝs mǽlǝm ə̀d índiy fáyǝt bównǝm/. You are not to do evil, that good may be or result therefrom.

Nonfeasance /nónfíyzǝn(t)s/. Nonperformance of some act which ought to be performed, omission to perform a required duty at all, or total neglect of duty. Desmarais v. Wachusett Regional School Dist., 360 Mass. 591, 276 N.E.2d 691, 693.

There is a distinction between "nonfeasance" and "misfeasance" or "malfeasance"; and this distinction is often of great importance in determining an agent's liability to third persons. "Nonfeasance" means the total omission or failure of an agent to enter upon the performance of some distinct duty or undertaking which he has agreed with his principal to do; "misfeasance" means the improper doing of an act which the agent might lawfully do, or, in other words, it is the performing of his duty to his principal in such a manner as to infringe upon the rights and privileges of third persons; and "malfeasance" is a doing of an act which he ought not to do at all.

See also **Malfeasance.**

Non fecit /nón fíysǝt/. Lat. He did not make it. A plea in an action of *assumpsit* on a promissory note.

Non fecit vastum contra prohibitionem /nón fíysǝt vǽstǝm kóntrǝ pròw(h)ǝbíshiyównǝm/. He did not commit waste against the prohibition. A plea to an action founded on a writ of estrepement for waste.

Non-forfeitable. Not subject to forfeiture. Columbian Nat. Life Ins. Co. v. Griffith, C.C.A.Mo., 73 F.2d 244, 246. See also **Non-leviable.**

Non-freehold estates. All estates in real property without seisin; hence, all estates except the fee simple, fee tail and life estates are non-freehold.

Non-functional. A feature of goods is "non-functional" if it does not affect their purpose, action or performance, or the facility or economy of processing, handling or using them. In effect a mere form of merchandising or a business method. J. C. Penney Co. v. H. D. Lee Mercantile Co., C.C.A.Mo., 120 F.2d 949, 954. A feature if, when omitted, nothing of substantial value in the goods is lost. Ainsworth v. Gill Glass & Fixture Co., D.C.Pa., 26 F.Supp. 183, 187.

Non hæc in fœdera veni /nón híyk ìn fédǝrǝ víynay/. I did not agree to these terms.

Non impedit clausula derogatoria quo minus ad eadem potestate res dissolvantur a qua constituuntur /nón impíydət klóz(y)ələ dərògətóriyə kwòw máynəs æd iyéydəm pòwdəstéydiy ríyz dəzòlvæntər èy kwèy kənstit(y)uwæntər/. A derogatory clause does not impede things from being dissolved by the same power by which they are created.

Non impedivit /nón impədáyvət/. Lat. He did not impede. The plea of the general issue in *quare impedit*. The Latin form of the law French *"ne disturba pas."*

Non implacitando aliquem de libero tenemento sine brevi /nón implǽsətǽndow ǽləkwem dìy líbərow tènəméntow sáyniy briyvay/. A writ to prohibit bailiffs, etc., from distraining or impleading any man touching his freehold without the king's writ.

Non infregit conventionem /nón infríyjət kənvènshiyównəm/. Lat. He did not break the contract. The name of a plea sometimes pleaded in the action of covenant, and intended as a general issue, but held to be a bad plea; there being, properly speaking, no general issue in that action.

Non in legendo sed in intelligendo legis consistunt /nón in ləjéndow sèd in intèləjéndow líyjiyz kənsístənt/. The laws consist not in being read, but in being understood.

Noninsurable risk. A hazard or risk for which insurance will not be written because not subject to evaluation by actuarial computations; such risk being too uncertain.

Non-intercourse. The refusal of one state or nation to have commercial dealings with another; similar to an embargo (*q.v.*).

The absence of access, communication, or sexual relations between husband and wife. See **Non-access.**

Non interfui /nón intərf(y)uwày/. I was not present. A reporter's note.

Non-intervention will. A term sometimes applied to a will which authorizes the executor to settle and distribute the estate without the intervention of the court and without giving bond.

Non intromittant clause /nón intrəmídənt klóz/. In English law, a clause of a charter of a municipal borough, whereby the borough is exempted from the jurisdiction of the justices of the peace for the county.

Non intromittendo, quando breve præcipe in capite subdole impetratur /nón intrəməténdow, kwóndow bríyviy présəpiy in kǽpədiy sə́bdəliy impətréydər/. In old English law, a writ addressed to the justices of the bench, or in eyre, commanding them not to give one, who, under color of entitling the king to land, etc., as holding of him *in capite*, had deceitfully obtained the writ called *"præcipe in capite,"* any benefit thereof, but to put him to his writ of right.

Non-issuable pleas. Those upon which a decision would not determine the action upon the merits, as a plea in abatement.

Non-joinder. See **Joinder.**

Non-judicial day. Day on which process cannot ordinarily issue or be executed or returned, and on which courts do not usually sit. Vidal v. Backs, 218 Cal. 99, 21 P.2d 952.

Non juridicus /nón jərídəkəs/. Not judicial; not legal. *Dies non juridicus* is a day on which legal proceedings cannot be had.

Non-jurors. In English law, persons who refuse to take the oaths, required by law, to support the government.

Non jus ex regula, sed regula ex jure /nón jás èks régyələ séd régyələ èks júriy/. The law does not arise from the rule (or maxim), but the rule from the law.

Non jus, sed seisina, facit stipitem /nón jás sèd síyzənə féysət stípədəm/. Not right, but seisin, makes a stock. It is not a mere *right* to enter on lands, but actual *seisin*, which makes a person the root or *stock* from which all future inheritance by right of blood must be derived.

Non-leviable /nón léviyəbəl/. Not subject to be levied upon. Property exempt from seizure, forfeiture or sale in bankruptcy, attachment, garnishment, etc. Non-leviable assets are assets upon which an execution cannot be levied. See also **Exemption; Homestead.**

Non licet quod dispendio licet /nón lísət kwód dəspéndiyow lísət/. That which may be [done only] at a loss is not allowed [to be done]. The law does not permit or require the doing of an act which will result only in loss. The law forbids such recoveries whose ends are vain, changeable, and unprofitable.

Non liquet /nón líkwət/°láykwət/. Lat. It is not clear.

In the Roman courts, when any of the judges, after the hearing of a cause, were not satisfied that the case was made clear enough for them to pronounce a verdict, they were privileged to signify this opinion by casting a ballot inscribed with the letters "N. L.," the abbreviated form of the phrase *"non liquet."*

Non-mailable. A term applied to all letters and parcels which are by law excluded from transportation in the United States mails, whether on account of the size of the package, the nature of its contents, its obscene character, or for other reasons.

Non-medical policy. Insurance policy issued without medical examination of an applicant. Reserve Loan Life Ins. Co. of Texas v. Brown, Tex.Civ.App., 159 S.W.2d 179, 180.

Non merchandizanda victualia /nón mèrchəndəzǽndə vìkchuwéyl(i)yə/. An ancient writ addressed to justices of assize, to inquire whether the magistrates of a town sold victuals in gross or by retail during the time of their being in office, which was contrary to an obsolete statute; and to punish them if they did.

Non-merchantable title. The title to realty need not be bad in fact to render it "non-merchantable", but it is sufficient, if an ordinarily prudent man with knowledge of facts and aware of legal questions involved would not accept it in ordinary course of business. Ghormley v. Kleeden, 155 Kan. 319, 124 P.2d 467, 470. See **Merchantable title.**

Non molestando /nón mòwləstǽndow/. A writ that lay for a person who was molested contrary to the king's protection granted to him.

Non nasci, et natum mori, paria sunt /nón nǽsay èt néydəm móray pǽriyə sánt/. Not to be born, and to be dead-born, are the same.

Non-navigable. At common law, streams or bodies of water not affected by tide were "non-navigable". Luscher v. Reynolds, 153 Or. 625, 56 P.2d 1158, 1162. Bodies of water other than navigable waters (q.v.).

Non-negotiable. Not negotiable; not capable of passing title or property by indorsement and delivery. An instrument which may not be transferred by indorsement and delivery or by delivery alone, though it may be assigned. The transferee does not become a holder unless it is negotiated.

Non obligat lex nisi promulgata /nón óbləgət léks náysay prómálgéydə/. A law is not obligatory unless it be promulgated.

Non obstante /nón əbstǽntiy/. Lat. Notwithstanding.

Words anciently used in public and private instruments, intended to preclude, in advance, any interpretation contrary to certain declared objects or purposes.

A clause frequent in old English statutes and letters patent (so termed from its initial words), importing a license from the crown to do a thing which otherwise a person would be restrained by act of parliament from doing. A power in the crown to dispense with the laws in any particular case. This was abolished by the bill of rights at the Revolution.

Non obstante veredicto /nón əbstǽntiy vèhrədíktow/. Notwithstanding the verdict. A judgment entered by order of court for the plaintiff (or defendant) although there has been a verdict for the defendant (or plaintiff). Judgment *non obstante veredicto* in its broadest sense is a judgment rendered in favor of one party notwithstanding the finding of a verdict in favor of the other party. A motion for a directed verdict is a prerequisite to a subsequent grant of judgment notwithstanding the verdict. Fed.R. Civil P. 50.

Judgment *non obstante veredicto* originally, at common law, was a judgment entered for plaintiff "notwithstanding the verdict" for defendant; which could be done only, after verdict and before judgment, where it appeared that defendant's plea confessed the cause of action and set up matters in avoidance which, although verified by the verdict, were insufficient to constitute a defense or bar to the action. But either by statutory enactment or because of relaxation of the early common-law rule, the generally prevailing rule now is that either plaintiff or defendant may have a judgment *non obstante veredicto* in proper cases.

Non-occupational. Not of or pertaining to an occupation, trade, or work. Morgan v. Equitable Life Assur. Soc. of U. S., La.App., 22 So.2d 595, 597.

Non officit conatus nisi sequatur effectus /nón ófəsət kənéydəs náysay səkwéydər əféktəs/. An attempt does not harm unless a consequence follow.

Non omittas /nón əmídəs/. A clause usually inserted in writs of execution, in England, directing the sheriff "not to omit" to execute the writ by reason of any liberty, because there are many liberties or districts in which the sheriff has no power to execute process unless he has special authority.

Non omne damnum inducit injuriam /nón ómniy dǽmnəm ənd(y)úwsəd ənjúriyəm/. It is not every loss that produces an injury.

Non omne quod licet honestum est /nón ómniy kwòd lísəd (h)ənéstəm èst/. It is not everything which is permitted that is honorable.

Non omnium quæ a majoribus nostris constituta sunt ratio reddi potest /nón ómniyəm kwìy èy məjórəbəs nóstrə kònstət(y)úwdə sànt rǽsh(iy)ow réday pówdəst/. There cannot be given a reason for all the things which have been established by our ancestors.

Nonpayment. The neglect, failure, or refusal of payment of a debt or evidence of debt when due.

Non-performance. Neglect, failure, or refusal to do or perform an act stipulated to be done. Failure to keep the terms of a contract or covenant, in respect to acts or doings agreed upon. The failure or neglect to render performance called for in a contract, rendering the non-performer liable in damages or subject to a decree or judgment of specific performance.

Non pertinet ad judicem secularem cognoscere de iis quæ sunt mere spiritualia annexa /nón pə́rdənət ǽd júwdəsəm sèkyələrəm kə(g)nósəriy dìy áyəs kwìy sànt míriy spìrət(y)uwéyl(i)yə ənéksə/. It belongs not to the secular judge to take cognizance of things which are merely spiritual.

Non plevin /nón plévən/. In old English law, default in not replevying land in due time, when the same was taken by the king upon a default. The consequence thereof (loss of seisin) was abrogated by St. 9 Edw. III, c. 2.

Non ponendis in assisis et juratis /nón pənéndəs ìn əsáyzəs et jəréydəs/. A writ formerly granted for freeing and discharging persons from serving on assizes and juries.

Non possessori incumbit necessitas probandi possessiones ad se pertinere /nón pòwzəsóray inkámbət nəsésətǽs prəbǽnday pəzèshiyówniyz ǽd síy pərdəníriy/. A person in possession is not bound to prove that the possessions belong to him.

Non potest adduci exceptio ejus rei cujus petitur dissolutio /nón pówdəst əd(y)úwsay əksépsh(iy)ow íyjəs ríyay kyúwjəs pédədər dìsəl(y)úwsh(iy)ow/. An exception of the same thing whose avoidance is sought cannot be made.

Non potest probari quod probatum non relevat /nón pówdəst prəbéray kwòd prəbéydəm nòn réləvət/. That cannot be proved which, if proved, is immaterial.

Non potest quis sine brevi agere /nón pówdəst kwís sáyniy bríyvay ǽjəriy/. No one can sue without a writ. A fundamental rule of old practice.

Non potest rex gratiam facere cum injuria et damno aliorum /nón pówdəst réks gréysh(iy)əm féysəriy kəm injúriyə èt dǽmnow èyliyórəm/. The king cannot confer a favor on one subject which occasions injury and loss to others.

Non potest rex subditum renitentem onerare impositionibus /nón pówdəst réks sə́bdədəm rènəténtəm òwnərériy impəzìshiyównəbəs/. The king cannot load a subject with imposition against his consent.

Non potest videri desisse habere qui nunquam habuit /nón pówdəst vədíray dəsáyziy həbíriy kwày nə́ŋkwæm hǽbyuwət/. He cannot be considered as having ceased to have a thing who never had it.

Non præstat impedimentum quod de jure non sortitur effectum /nón príystət əmpèdəméntəm kwòd dìy júriy nòn sórdədər əféktəm/. A thing which has no effect in law is not an impediment.

Non procedendo ad assissam rege inconsulto /nón pròwsədéndəm æd əsáyzəm ríyjiy ìnkənsáltow/. A writ to put a stop to the trial of a cause appertaining unto one who is in the king's service, etc., until the king's pleasure respecting the same be known.

Non-profit association. A group organized for purposes other than generating profit, such as a charitable, scientific, or literary organization. See also **Non-profit corporation.**

Non-profit corporation. A corporation no part of the income of which is distributable to its members, directors or officers. Corporations may be organized under the Model Non-Profit Corporation Act "for any lawful purpose or purposes, including, without being limited to, any one or more of the following purposes: charitable; benevolent; eleemosynary; educational; civic; patriotic; political; religious; social; fraternal; literary; cultural; athletic; scientific; agricultural; horticultural; animal husbandry, and professional, commercial, industrial or trade association; but labor unions, cooperative organizations, and organizations subject to any of the provisions of the insurance laws of this State may not be organized under this Act." Id. § 4. For purposes of federal income taxation, an organization may be exempt as an "exempt organization" if it is organized and operated exclusively for one or more of the following purposes: (a) religious, (b) charitable, (c) scientific, (d) testing for public safety, (e) literary, (f) educational, (g) prevention of cruelty to children or animals, or (h) to foster national or international sports. See I.R.C. § 501(c) for a list of exempt organizations.

Non pros /nón prós/. Abbreviation of non prosequitur (q.v.).

Non prosequitur /nón prəsékwədər/. Lat. He does not follow up, or pursue. If, in the proceedings in an action at law, the plaintiff neglects to take any of those steps which he ought to take within the time prescribed by the practice of the court for that purpose, the defendant may enter judgment of non pros. against him, whereby it is adjudged that the plaintiff does not follow up (non prosequitur) his suit as he ought to do, and therefore the defendant ought to have judgment against him. Under current rules practice, such failure would result in a dismissal of

the action or in a default judgment for defendant. Fed.R. Civil P. 41, 55.

Non quieta movere /nón kwayíydə məvíriy/. Lat. Not to disturb what is settled. A rule expressing the same principle as that of stare decisis (q.v.).

Non quod dictum est, sed quod factum est inspicitur /nón kwòd díktəm èst séd kwòd fǽktəm èst inspísədər/. Not what is said, but what is done, is regarded.

Nonrecourse. Status of person who holds an instrument which gives him no legal right against prior endorsers or the drawer to compel payment if the instrument is dishonored.

Nonrecourse loan. Type of security loan which bars the lender from action against the borrower if the security value falls below the amount required to repay the loan. It is used by the U.S. in loans to farmers on surplus crops.

Non refert an quis assensum suum præfert verbis, aut rebus ipsis et factis /nón réfərt æn kwís əsén(t)səm s(y)úwəm príyfərt várbəs òt ríybəs ípsəs èt fǽktəs/. It matters not whether a man gives his assent by his words or by his acts and deeds.

Non refert quid ex æquipollentibus fiat /nón réfərt kwíd èks èkwəpəléntəbəs fáyət/. It matters not which of [two] equivalents happen.

Non refert quid notum sit judici, si notum non sit in forma judicii /nón réfərt kwìd nówdəm sít júwdəsay, sáy nówdəm nón sìd in fórmə júwdəsay/. It matters not what is known to a judge, if it be not known in judicial form.

Non refert verbis an factis fit revocatio /nón réfərt várbəs æn fǽktəs fít rèvəkéysh(iy)ow/. It matters not whether a revocation is made by words or deeds.

Non-residence. Residence beyond the limits of the particular jurisdiction.

In ecclesiastical law, the absence of spiritual persons from their benefices.

Non-resident. One who does not reside within jurisdiction in question; not an inhabitant of the state of the forum. Special rules govern service of process on non-residents; e.g. Fed.R. Civil P. 4(e). See **Long arm statutes.**

For the distinction between "residence" and "domicile," see **Domicile.**

Non-resident alien. One who is neither a resident nor a citizen of this country.

Non-resident decedent. Decedent domiciled in another jurisdiction at the time of his death. Uniform Probate Code, § 1–201(26).

Non-resident motorist statutes. State laws governing the liability and obligations of non-residents who use the state's highways.

Non residentio pro clerico regis /nón rèzədénsh(iy)ow pròw kléhrəkow ríyjəs/. A writ, addressed to a bishop, charging him not to molest a clerk employed in the royal service, by reason of his nonresidence; in which case he is to be discharged.

Non respondebit minor nisi in causa dotis, et hoc pro favore doti /nón rəspòndíybət máynər náysay ìn kózə dówdəs èt hók prów fəvóriy dówday/. A minor shall not answer unless in a case of dower, and this in favor of dower.

Non sanæ mentis /nón séyniy méntəs/. Lat. Of unsound mind.

Non-sane. As "sane," when applied to the mind, means whole, sound, in a healthful state, "non-sane" means not whole, not sound, not in a healthful state; that is, broken, impaired, shattered, infirm, weak, diseased, unable, either from nature or accident, to perform the rational functions common to man upon the objects presented to it. See also **Insanity.**

Non sequitur /nón sékwədər/. Lat. It does not follow.

Non solent quæ abundant vitiare scripturas /nón sówlənt kwìy əbándænt vìshiyériy skrìpt(y)úrəs/. Superfluities [things which abound] do not usually vitiate writings.

Non solum quid licet, sed quid est conveniens, est considerandum; quia nihil quod est inconveniens est licitum /nón sówləm kwíd láysət sèd kwíd èst kənvíyn(i)yən(d)z, ést kən(t)sìdərǽndəm, kwáyə náy(h)əl kwód èst ìnkənvíyn(i)yən(d)z èst lísədəm/. Not only what is lawful, but what is proper or convenient, is to be considered; because nothing that is inconvenient is lawful.

Non solvendo pecuniam ad quam clericus mulctatur pro non-residentia /nón solvéndow pəkyún(i)yəm ǽd kwæm kléhrəkəs mòlktéydər pròw nónrezədénsh(iy)ə/. A writ prohibiting an ordinary to take a pecuniary mulct imposed on a clerk of the sovereign for nonresidence.

Non-stock corporation. Species of non-profit corporation in which the members hold no shares of stock as in the cases of religious and charitable corporations.

Non submissit /nón səbmísət/. Lat. He did not submit. A plea to an action of debt, on a bond to perform an award, to the effect that the defendant did not submit to the arbitration.

Non sui juris /nón s(y)úway júrəs/. Lat. Not his own master. The opposite of *sui juris (q.v.).* Lacking legal capacity to act for oneself as in the case of a minor or mentally incompetent person.

Nonsuit. A term broadly applied to a variety of terminations of an action which do not adjudicate issues on the merits. McColgan v. Jones, Hubbard & Donnell, 11 Cal.2d 243, 78 P.2d 1010, 1011. Name of a judgment given against the plaintiff when he is unable to prove a case, or when he refuses or neglects to proceed to trial and leaves the issue undetermined. Generally speaking, "nonsuit" is name of judgment rendered against party in legal proceeding on his inability to maintain his cause in court, or when he is in default in prosecuting his suit or in complying with orders of court. Jaquith v. Revson, 159 Conn. 427, 270 A.2d 559, 561.

Action in form of a judgment taken against a plaintiff who has failed to appear to prosecute his action or failed to prove his case. Under rules practice, the applicable term is "dismissal", not nonsuit. Fed.R. Civil P. 41.

See also **Default-judgment; Directed verdict.**

Judgment of nonsuit (*i.e.* "dismissal") is of two kinds,—*voluntary* and *involuntary.* When plaintiff abandons his case, and consents that judgment go against him for costs, it is *voluntary.* Fed.R. Civil P. 41(a). But when he, being called, neglects to appear, or when he has given no evidence on which a jury could find a verdict, or when his case is put out of court by some adverse ruling precluding a recovery, it is *involuntary.* Rule 41(b).

A *peremptory* nonsuit is a compulsory or involuntary nonsuit, ordered by the court upon a total failure of the plaintiff to substantiate his claim by evidence.

Non sum informatus /nón səm ìnfərméydəs/. Lat. I am not informed; I have not been instructed.

Non-summons, wager of law of. In common law pleading, the mode in which a tenant or defendant in a real action pleaded, when the summons which followed the original was not served within the proper time.

Non sunt longa ubi nihil est quod demere possis /nón sənt lóngə yúwbay náy(h)əl èst kwòd déməriy pósəs/. There is no prolixity where there is nothing that can be omitted.

Non-support. The failure or neglect unreasonably to support those to whom an obligation of support is due; *e.g.* duty of parents to support children; duty to support spouse. Such failure to support is a criminal offense in most states.

Nonsupport of a child is a parent's failure, neglect or refusal without lawful excuse to provide for the support and maintenance of his or her child in necessitous circumstances. Nonsupport of a spouse is an individual's failure without just cause to provide for the support of his or her spouse in necessitous circumstances.

See also **Necessitous circumstances; Reciprocal Enforcement of Support Act; Support.**

Non temere credere est nervus sapientiæ /nón téməriy krédəriy èst nárvəs sæpiyénshiyiy/. Not to believe rashly is the nerve of wisdom.

Non tenent insimul /nón ténənt ínsaməl/. Lat. In old pleading, a plea to an action in partition, by which the defendant denied that he and the plaintiff were joint tenants of the estate in question.

Non tenuit /nón tényuwət/. Lat. He did not hold. A plea in bar in replevin, by which the plaintiff alleges that he did not hold in manner and form as averred, being given in answer to an avowry for rent in arrear.

Non-tenure. A common law plea in a real action, by which the defendant asserts, either as to the whole or as to some part of the land mentioned in the plaintiff's declaration, that he does not hold it.

Non-term. The vacation between two terms of a court.

Non-terminus /nón tármənəs/. The vacation between term and term, formerly called the time of days of the king's peace.

Non-user. Neglect to use. Neglect to use a franchise; neglect to exercise an office. Neglect or omission to use an easement or other right. A right acquired by use may be lost by non-user.

Non usurpavit /nón yùwsərpéyvət/. Lat. He has not usurped. A form of traverse, in an action or proceeding against one alleged to have usurped an office or franchise, denying the usurpation charged.

Non valebit felonis generatio, nec ad hæreditatem paternam vel maternam; si autem ante feloniam generationem fecerit, talis generatio succedit in hæreditate patris vel matris a quo non fuerit felonia perpetrata /nón vəlíybət fəlównəs jènəréysh(iy)ow nèk æd hərèdətéydəm pətárnəm vèl mətárnəm; sáy òdəm æntiy fəlówniyəm jènəréysh(iy)ównəm fésərət téyləs jènəréysh(iy)ow səksíydəd in hərèdətéydiy pætrəs vèl méytrəs èy kwòw nón fyúwərət fəlówniyə pèrpətréydə/. The offspring of a felon cannot succeed either to a maternal or paternal inheritance; but, if he had offspring before the felony, such offspring may succeed as to the inheritance of the father or mother by whom the felony was not committed.

Non valentia agere /nón vəlénsh(iy)ə æjəriy/. Inability to sue.

Non valet confirmatio, nisi ille, qui confirmat, sit in possessione rei vel juris unde fieri debet confirmatio; et eodem modo, nisi ille cui confirmatio fit sit in possessione /nón vælət kònfərméysh(iy)ow, náysay íliy, kwày kənfármət, sìd in pəzèshiyówniy ríyay vèl júrəs ándiy fáyəray débət kònfərméysh(iy)ow; èd iyówdəm mówdow, náysay íliy k(yúw)ay kònfərméysh(iy)ow fit síd in pəzèshiyówniy/. Confirmation is not valid unless he who confirms is either in possession of the thing itself or of the right of which confirmation is to be made, and, in like manner, unless he to whom confirmation is made is in possession.

Non valet donatio nisi subsequatur traditio /nón vælət dənéysh(iy)ow náysay sèbsəkwéydər trədísh(iy)ow/. A gift is not valid unless accompanied by possession.

Non valet exceptio ejusdem rei cujus petitur dissolutio /nón væləd əksépsh(iy)ow iyjásdəm ríyay kyúwjəs pédədər dísəl(y)úwsh(iy)ow/. A plea of the same matter the dissolution of which is sought, is not valid. Called a "maxim of law and common sense."

Non valet impedimentum quod de jure non sortitur effectum /nón væləd əmpèdəméntəm kwód dìy júriy nón sórdədər əféktəm/. An impediment which does not derive its effect from law is of no force.

Non verbis, sed ipsis rebus, leges imponimus /nón várbəs, sèd ípsəs ríybəs, líyjiyz impównəməs/. We impose laws, not upon words, but upon things themselves.

Non videntur qui errant consentire /nón vədéntər kwày éhrænt kònsəntáyriy/. They are not considered to consent who commit a mistake.

Non videntur rem amittere quibus propria non fuit /nón vədéntər rém əmídəriy kwíbəs prówpriyə nòn f(y)úwət/. They are not considered as losing a thing whose own it was not.

Non videtur consensum retinuisse si quis ex præscripto minantis aliquid immutavit. He does not appear to have retained consent, who has changed anything through menaces.

Non videtur perfecte cujusque id esse, quod ex casu auferri potest /nón vədíytər pərféktiy kyuwjáskwiy íd ésiy, kwòd èks kéysyuw oféhray pówdəst/. That does not seem to be completely one's own which can be taken from him on occasion.

Non videtur quisquam id capere quod ei necesse est alii restitutere /nòn vədíydər kwískwæm íd kæpəriy kwòd íyay nəsésiy èst éyliyay rèstətyúwəriy/. No one is considered entitled to recover that which he must give up to another.

Non videtur vim facere, qui jure suo utitur et ordinaria actione experitur /nón vədíydər vím féysəriy kwày júriy s(y)úwow yúwdədər èd òrdənériyə ækshiyówniy ekspírədər/. He is not deemed to use force who exercises his own right, and proceeds by ordinary action.

Non vult /nón vált/. Lit. He does not wish (to contend). A plea similar to nolo contendere *(q.v.)* and carrying the implications of a plea of guilty.

Non vult contendere /nòn vált kəntÉndəriy/. Lat. He (the defendant in a criminal case) will not contest it. A plea legally equivalent to that of guilty, being a variation of the form *"nolo contendere" (q.v.)*, and sometimes abbreviated *"non vult."*

Non-waiver agreement. Such agreement reserves to insurer every right under fire policy not previously waived, and to the insured every right which had not been forfeited. Ætna Ins. Co. of Hartford, Conn., v. Powers, 190 Okl. 116, 121 P.2d 599, 602.

Nook of land. In English law, twelve acres and a half.

No par. Said of stock without a par value.

No protest. Term used to describe the waiver of any right of protest when an instrument is not paid. Protest of dishonor is necessary, unless excused, to charge a drawer and endorser on any draft payable outside the United States. U.C.C. §§ 3–501(3), 509, 511.

No recourse. No access to; no return; no coming back upon; no assumption of any liability whatsoever; no looking to the party using the term for any reimbursement in case of loss or damage or failure of consideration in that which was the cause, the motive, or the object, of the undertaking or contract.

Normal. According to, constituting, or not deviating from an established norm, rule, or principle; conformed to a type, standard or regular form; performing the proper functions; regular; average; natural. Railroad Commission v. Konowa Operating Co., Tex. Civ.App., 174 S.W.2d 605, 609.

Normal law. A term employed by modern writers on jurisprudence to denote the law as it affects persons who are in a normal condition; *i.e., sui juris* and sound in mind.

Normally. As a rule; regularly; according to rule, general custom, etc.

Normal mind. One which in strength and capacity ranks reasonably well with the average of the great body of men and women who make up organized human society in general and are by common consent recognized as sane and competent to perform the ordinary duties and assume the ordinary responsibilities of life.

Normal school. See **School.**

Norman French. The tongue in which several formal proceedings of state in England are still carried on. The language, having remained the same since the date of the Conquest, at which it was introduced into England, is very different from the French of this day, retaining all the peculiarities which at that time distinguished every province from the rest. A peculiar mode of pronunciation (considered authentic) is handed down and preserved by the officials who have, on particular occasions, to speak the tongue. Norman French was the language of English legal procedure till the 36 Edw. III (A.D. 1362).

Norris-La Guardia Act. Federal statute restricting the use of injunctions by federal courts in labor disputes.

Norroy. In English law, the title of the third of the three kings-at-arms, or provincial heralds.

North. Means due north; opposite direction of south. Same with word *northerly.*

Northwest territory. A name formerly applied to the territory northwest of the Ohio river.

Noscitur a sociis /nósədər èy sówsiyəs/. It is known from its associates. The meaning of a word is or may be known from the accompanying words. Under the doctrine of "noscitur a sociis", the meaning of questionable words or phrases in a statute may be ascertained by reference to the meaning of words or phrases associated with it. Wong Kam Wo v. Dulles, C.A.Hawaii, 236 F.2d 622, 626.

Noscitur ex socio, qui non cognoscitur ex se /nósədər èks sówsh(iy)ow kwày nón kəgnósədər èks síy/. He who cannot be known from himself may be known from his associate.

Nosocomi /nòsəkówmay/. In the civil law, persons who have the management and care of hospitals for paupers.

No-strike clause. Provision commonly found in public service labor-management agreements to the effect that the employees will not strike for any reason.

Nota /nówdə/. Lat. In the civil law, a mark or brand put upon a person by the law.

Notæ /nówdiy/. In civil and old European law, shorthand characters or marks of contraction, in which the emperors' secretaries took down what they dictated.

Notarial /nòwtériyəl/. Taken by a notary; performed by a notary in his official capacity; belonging to a notary and evidencing his official character, as, a notarial seal.

Notarial acts. Official acts of notary public *(q.v.).*

Notarial will. A will executed by the testator in the presence of a Notary Public and two witnesses.

Notarius /nòwtériyəs/. Lat. In old English law, a scribe or scrivener who made short draughts of writings and other instruments; a notary.

In Roman law, a draughtsman; an amanuensis; a shorthand writer; one who took notes of the proceedings in the senate or a court, or of what was dictated to him by another; one who prepared draughts of wills, conveyances, etc.

Notary public. A public officer whose function it is to administer oaths; to attest and certify, by his hand and official seal, certain classes of documents, in order to give them credit and authenticity in foreign jurisdictions; to take acknowledgments of deeds and other conveyances, and certify the same; and to perform certain official acts, chiefly in commercial matters, such as the protesting of notes and bills, the noting of foreign drafts, and marine protests in cases of loss or damage. One who is authorized by the state or federal government to administer oaths, and to attest to the authenticity of signatures.

Notation credit. A credit which specifies that any person purchasing or paying drafts drawn or demands for payment made under it must note the amount of the draft or demand on the letter or advise of credit. U.C.C. § 5–108(1).

Note, *v.* To make a brief written statement; to enter a memorandum, as to note an exception.

Note, *n.* An instrument containing an express and absolute promise of signer (*i.e.* maker) to pay to a specified person or order, or bearer, a definite sum of money at a specified time. Two party instrument made by the maker and payable to payee which is negotiable if signed by the maker and contains an unconditional promise to pay sum certain in money, on demand or at a definite time, to order or bearer. U.C.C. § 3–104(1). A note not meeting these requirements may be assignable but not negotiable.

An abstract; a memorandum; an informal statement in writing.

See also Balloon note; Coal note; Judgment note; Promissory note; Sold note; Treasury note.

Circular note. See **Letter of credit.**

Collateral note. Two party instrument containing promise to pay and secured by pledge of property such as securities, real estate, etc.

Demand note. Note payable on demand as contrasted with a time note which is payable at a definite time in the future.

Installment note. One of a series of notes payable at regular intervals or a single note calling for payment in installments at fixed periods of time.

Joint and several note. A note signed by persons as makers who agree to be bound both jointly and severally; *i.e.* they may be joined in a suit or they may be sued separately.

Joint note. Note evidencing an indebtedness in which two or more persons agree to be liable jointly and for payment of which all such persons must be joined in an action to recover.

Mortgage note. A note evidencing a loan for which real estate has been offered as security.

Negotiable note. To qualify as negotiable, the note must be signed by the maker, contain an unconditional promise to pay a sum certain in money and be payable on demand or at a definite time to order or bearer. U.C.C. § 3–104(1).

Secured note. A note for which security in the form of either real or personal property has been pledged or mortgaged. See also *Collateral note, supra.*

Time note. Note payable at a definite future time as contrasted with a demand note.

Unsecured note. Note evidencing an indebtedness for which no security has been pledged or mortgaged.

Note of a fine. In old English conveyancing, one of the parts of a fine of lands, being an abstract of the writ of covenant, and the concord; naming the parties, the parcels of land, and the agreement.

Note of allowance. In English practice, a note delivered by a master to a party to a cause, who alleged that there was error in law in the record and proceedings, allowing him to bring error.

Note of hand. A popular name (now obsolete) for a promissory note.

Note of protest. A memorandum of the fact of protest, indorsed by the notary upon the bill, at the time, to be afterwards written out at length.

Note or **memorandum.** Under statute of frauds, an informal minute or memorandum made on the spot. It must contain all the essential elements and substantial parts of the contract. Stanley v. A. Levy & J. Zentner Co., 60 Nev. 432, 112 P.2d 1047, 1053.

Notes payable. In bookkeeping, an account reflecting the aggregate indebtedness evidenced by promissory notes; the notes themselves are liabilities.

Notes receivable. In bookkeeping, an account containing evidence of indebtedness for which promissory notes have been given to the account of the party making the entry; the notes themselves are assets.

Not exceeding. Usually a term of limitation only, denoting uncertainty of amount. Stuyvesant Ins. Co. v. Jacksonville Oil Mill, C.C.A.Tenn., 10 F.2d 54, 56.

Not found. These words, indorsed on a bill of indictment by a grand jury, have the same effect as the indorsement "Not a true bill", "No bill," or *"Ignoramus."* See also **Non est inventus.**

Not guilty. A plea of the general issue in the actions of trespass and case.

Plea entered by the accused to criminal charge. See *e.g.* Fed.R.Crim.P. 11. The form of the verdict in criminal cases, where the jury acquits the defendant; *i.e.* finds him "not guilty".

Not guilty by statute. In old English practice, a plea of the general issue by a defendant in a civil action, when he intends to give special matter in evidence by virtue of some act or acts of parliament, in which case he must add the reference to such act or acts, and state whether such acts are public or otherwise. But, if a defendant so plead, he will not be allowed to plead any other defense, without the leave of the court or a judge.

Nothus /nówθəs/. Lat. In Roman law, a natural child or a person of spurious birth.

Notice. Information; the result of observation, whether by the senses or the mind; knowledge of the existence of a fact or state of affairs; the means of knowledge. Intelligence by whatever means communicated. Koehn v. Central Nat. Ins. Co. of Omaha, Neb., 187 Kan. 192, 354 P.2d 352, 358.

Notice is knowledge of facts which would naturally lead an honest and prudent person to make inquiry, and does not necessarily mean knowledge of all the facts. Wayne Bldg. & Loan Co. of Wooster v. Yarborough, 11 Ohio St.2d 195, 228 N.E.2d 841, 847, 40 O.O.2d 182. In another sense, "notice" means information, an advice, or written warning, in more or less formal shape, intended to apprise a person of some proceeding in which his interests are involved, or informing him of some fact which it is his right to know and the duty of the notifying party to communicate.

Fed.R. Civil P. 5(a) requires that every written notice be served upon each of the parties.

A person has notice of a fact if he knows the fact, has reason to know it, should know it, or has been given notification of it. Restatement, Second, Agency § 9.

Notice may be either (1) statutory, *i.e.*, made so by legislative enactment; (2) actual, which brings the knowledge of a fact directly home to the party; or (3) constructive. Constructive notice may be subdivided into: *(a)* Where there exists actual notice of matter, to which equity has added constructive notice of facts, which an inquiry after such matter would have elicited; and *(b)* where there has been a designed abstinence from inquiry for the very purpose of escaping notice.

See also Adequate notice; Charged; Due notice; Immediate notice; Imputed notice; Judicial notice; Knowledge; Legal notice; Reasonable notice.

Actual notice. Actual notice has been defined as notice expressly and actually given, and brought home to the party directly. The term "actual notice," however, is generally given a wider meaning as embracing two classes, express and implied; the former includes all knowledge of a degree above that which depends upon collateral inference, or which imposes upon the party the further duty of inquiry; the latter imputes knowledge to the party because he is shown to be conscious of having the means of knowledge. In this sense actual notice is such notice as is positively proved to have been given to a party directly and personally, or such as he is presumed to have received personally because the evidence within his knowledge was sufficient to put him upon inquiry.

Averment of notice. The statement in a pleading that notice has been given.

Commercial law. A person has "notice" of a fact when: (a) he has actual knowledge of it; or (b) he has received a notice or notification of it; or (c) from all the facts and circumstances known to him at the time in question he has reason to know that it exists. A person "knows" or has "knowledge" of a fact when he has actual knowledge of it. "Discover" or "learn" or a word or phrase of similar import refers to knowledge rather than to reason to know. The time and circumstances under which a notice or notification may cease to be effective are not determined by this Act. U.C.C. § 1–201(25).

A person "notifies" or "gives" a notice or notification to another by taking such steps as may be reasonably required to inform the other in ordinary course whether or not such other actually comes to know of it. A person "receives" a notice or notification when: (a) it comes to his attention; or (b) it is duly delivered at the place of business through which the contract was made or at any other place held out by him as the place for receipt of such communications. U.C.C. § 1–201(26).

Under the Uniform Commercial Code, the law on "notice," actual or inferable, is precisely the same whether the instrument is issued to a holder or negotiated to a holder. Eldon's Super Fresh Stores, Inc. v. Merrill Lynch, Pierce, Fenner & Smith, Inc., 296 Minn. 130, 207 N.W.2d 282, 287.

Constructive notice. Constructive notice is information or knowledge of a fact imputed by law to a person (although he may not actually have it), because he could have discovered the fact by proper diligence, and his situation was such as to cast upon him the duty of inquiring into it. Every person who has actual notice of circumstances sufficient to put a prudent man upon inquiry as to a particular fact, has constructive notice of the fact itself in all cases in which, by prosecuting such inquiry, he might have learned such fact.

Constructive "notice" includes implied actual notice and inquiry notice. F. P. Baugh, Inc. v. Little Lake Lumber Co., C.A.Cal., 297 F.2d 692, 696.

Express notice. Express notice embraces not only knowledge, but also that which is communicated by direct information, either written or oral, from those who are cognizant of the fact communicated. See also *Actual notice.*

Implied notice. Implied notice is one of the varieties of actual notice (not constructive) and is distinguished from "express" actual notice. It is notice inferred or imputed to a party by reason of his knowledge of facts or circumstances collateral to the main fact, of such a character as to put him upon inquiry, and which, if the inquiry were followed up with due diligence, would lead him definitely to the knowledge of the main fact. "Implied notice" is a presumption of fact, relating to what one can learn by reasonable inquiry, and arises from actual notice of circumstances, and not from constructive notice. Or as otherwise defined, implied notice may be said to exist where the fact in question lies open to the knowledge of the party, so that the exercise of reasonable observation and watchfulness would not fall to apprise him of it, although no one has told him of it in so many words.

Personal notice. Communication of notice orally or in writing (according to the circumstances) directly to the person affected or to be charged, as distinguished from constructive or implied notice, and also from notice imputed to him because given to his agent or representative. See *Actual notice; Express notice, supra.*

Public notice. Notice given to the public generally, or to the entire community, or to all whom it may concern. Such must commonly be published in a newspaper of general circulation.

Reasonable notice. Such notice or information of a fact as may fairly and properly be expected or required in the particular circumstances.

Notice of action. See **Lis pendens.**

Notice of appeal. A document giving notice of an intention to appeal filed with the appellate court and served on the opposing party. Fed.R.App.P. 3.

Notice of appearance. See **Appearance.**

Notice of dishonor. Notice of dishonor may be given to any person who may be liable on the instrument by or on behalf of the holder or any party who has himself received notice, or any other party who can be compelled to pay the instrument. In addition an agent or bank in whose hands the instrument is dishonored may give notice to his principal or customer or to another agent or bank from which the instrument was received. U.C.C. § 3–508(1). See also **Dishonor.**

Notice of lis pendens /nówdəs əv lís péndən(d)z/. See **Lis pendens.**

Notice of motion. A notice in writing, entitled in a cause, stating that on a certain day designated, a motion will be made to the court for the purpose or object stated. Such notice is required to be served upon all parties. Fed.R. Civil P. 5(a).

Notice of orders or **judgments.** Immediately upon the entry of an order or judgment the clerk shall serve notice of the entry by mail upon each party who is not in default for failure to appear, and shall make a note in the docket of the mailing. Fed.R. Civil P. 77(d).

Notice of protest. See **Protest.**

Notice of trial. A notice given by one of the parties in an action to the other, after an issue has been reached, that he intends to bring the cause forward for trial at the next term of the court.

Notice race statutes. In some jurisdictions, in recording of documents of title to real estate, the first grantee or mortgagee to record in the chain of title without actual notice of a prior unrecorded deed or mortgage prevails. Also known as Race-Notice Statute. See also **Notice recording statutes; Recording acts.**

Notice recording statutes. An unrecorded conveyance or other instrument is invalid as against a subsequent bona fide purchaser (creditor or mortgagee if the statute so provides) for value and without notice. Under this type of statute the subsequent bona fide purchaser prevails over the prior interest whether the subsequent purchaser records or not. Insofar as the subsequent purchaser is concerned, there is no premium on his race to the recorder's office. His priority is determined upon his status at the time he acquires his deed or mortgage. See also **Recording acts.**

Notice to appear. Shorthand expression for the form of summons or order of notice in which the defendant is ordered to appear and show cause why judgment should not be entered against him. Fed.R. Civil P. 4(b). See also **Show cause order; Summons.**

Notice to creditors. Formal notification in bankruptcy proceeding to creditors of the bankrupt that a meeting will be held, or that proof of claims must be filed on or before a certain date, or that an order for relief has been granted. See Bankruptcy Act, § 342.

Notice to plead. A notice which, in the practice of the federal courts, and most state courts, is prerequisite to the taking judgment by default. It proceeds from the plaintiff, and warns the defendant that he must plead to the declaration or complaint within a prescribed time. Such notice is required in the summons. Fed.R. Civil P. 4(b).

Notice to quit. A written notice given by a landlord to his tenant, stating that the former desires to repossess himself of the demised premises, and that the latter is required to quit and remove from the same at a time designated, either at the expiration of the term, if the tenant is in under a lease, or immediately, if the tenancy is at will or by sufferance. The term is also sometimes applied to a written notice given by the tenant to the landlord, to the effect that he intends to quit the demised premises and deliver possession of the same on a day named.

Notification. See **Notice.**

Notify. To give notice to; to inform by words or writing, in person or by message, or by any signs which are understood; to make known. To "notify" one of a fact is to make it known to him; to inform him by notice. Fast v. Scruggs, 164 Okl. 196, 23 P.2d 383. See **Notice.**

Notio /nówsh(iy)ow/. Lat. In the civil law, the power of hearing and trying a matter of fact; the power or authority of a *judex;* the power of hearing causes and of pronouncing sentence, without any degree of jurisdiction.

Notitia /nowtísh(iy)ə/. Lat. Knowledge; information; intelligence; notice.

Notitia dicitur a noscendo; et notitia non debet claudicare /nowtísh(iy)ə dísədər èy nòséndow èt nowtísh(iy)ə nòn débət klòdəkériy/. Notice is named from a knowledge being had; and notice ought not to halt (*i.e.,* be imperfect).

Not later than. "Within" or "not beyond" time specified.

Not less than. The words "not less than" signify in the smallest or lowest degree, at the lowest estimate; at least.

Notoriety /nòwdəráyədiy/. The state of being notorious or universally well known.

Notorious /nowtóriyəs/. Generally known and talked of; well or widely known; forming a part of common knowledge, or universally recognized. Mathis v. State, 60 Okl.Cr. 58, 61 P.2d 261, 267. Open; generally or commonly known and spoken of.

Notorious cohabitation. The statutory offense in some jurisdictions committed by two persons who live together openly while not being married to each other. Such laws are seldom enforced.

Notorious insolvency. A condition of insolvency which is generally known throughout the community or known to the general class of persons with whom the insolvent has business relations.

Notorious possession. As a requisite of adverse possession, such possession that is so conspicuous that it is generally known and talked of by the public or the people in the neighborhood. Possession or character of holding in its nature having such elements of notoriety that the owner may be presumed to have notice of it and of its extent. See also **Adverse possession.**

Not possessed. A special traverse used in an action of trover, alleging that defendant was not possessed, at the time of action brought, of the chattels alleged to have been converted by him.

Not satisfied. A return sometimes made by sheriffs or constables to a writ of execution; but it is not a technical formula, and has been criticised by the courts as ambiguous and insufficient. See **Nulla bona.**

Not to be performed within one year. The clause "not to be performed within one year" includes any agreement which by a reasonable interpretation in view of all the circumstances does not admit of its performance, according to its language and intention, within one year from the time of its making.

N.O.V. See **Non obstante veredicto.**

Nova constitutio futuris formam imponere debet non præteritis /nówvə kònstət(y)úwsh(iy)ow fyuwtyúrəs fórməm ìmpównəriy débət nòn prətérədəs/. A new state of the law ought to affect the future, not the past.

Nova custuma /nówvə kástəmə/. The name of an imposition or duty. See **Antiqua custuma.**

Novæ narrationes /nówviy nərèyshiyówniyz/. New counts. The collection called *"Novæ Narrationes"* contains pleadings in actions during the reign of Edward III. It consists principally of declarations, as the title imports; but there are sometimes pleas and subsequent pleadings. The *Articuli ad Novas Narrationes* is usually subjoined to this little book, and is a small treatise on the method of pleading. It first treats of actions and courts, and then goes through each particular writ, and the declaration upon it, accompanied with directions, and illustrated by precedents.

Nova statuta /nówvə stət(y)úwdə/. New statutes. An appellation sometimes given to the statutes which have been passed since the beginning of the reign of Edward III.

Novation. Substitution of a new contract, debt, or obligation for an existing one, between the same or different parties. The substitution by mutual agreement of one debtor for another or of one creditor for another, whereby the old debt is extinguished. The requisites of a novation are a previous valid obligation, an agreement of all the parties to a new contract, the extinguishment of the old obligation, and the validity of the new one. Blyther v. Pentagon Federal Credit Union, D.C.Mun.App., 182 A.2d 892, 894.

A novation substitutes a new party and discharges one of the original parties to a contract by agreement of all three parties. A new contract is created with the same terms as the original one but only the parties are changed. Restatement of Contracts, §§ 423, 430.

In the civil law, there are three kinds of novation: where the debtor and creditor remain the same, but a new debt takes the place of the old one; where the debt remains the same, but a new debtor is substituted; where the debt and debtor remain, but a new creditor is substituted. Wheeler v. Wardell, 173 Va. 168, 3 S.E.2d 377, 380.

Novatio non præsumitur /nowvéysh(iy)ow nòn prəz(y)úwmədər/. Novation is not presumed.

Novel assignment. See **New assignment**.

Novel disseisin. See **Assise** (*Assise of novel disseisin*).

Novellæ (or novellæ constitutiones) /nowvéliy (kònstət(y)ùwshiyówniyz)/. New constitutions; generally translated in English, "Novels." The Latin name of those constitutions which were issued by Justinian after the publication of his Code; most of them being originally written in Greek. After his death, a collection of 168 Novels was made, 154 of which had been issued by Justinian, and the rest by his successors. These were afterwards included in the *Corpus Juris Civilis* (*q.v.*), and now constitute one of its four principal divisions.

Novellæ leonis /nowvéliy liyównəs/. The ordinances of the Emperor Leo, which were made from the year 887 till the year 893, are so called. These Novels changed many rules of the Justinian law. This collection contains 113 Novels, written originally in Greek, and afterwards, in 1560, translated into Latin by Agilæus.

Novels /nóvəlz/. The title given in English to the New Constitutions (*Novellæ Constitutiones*) of Justinian and his successors, now forming a part of the *Corpus Juris Civilis*. See **Novellæ**.

Novelty. In order that there may be "novelty" so as to sustain a patent, the thing must not have been known to any one before, mere novelty of form being insufficient. Seaver v. Wm. Filene's Sons Co., D.C.Mass., 37 F.Supp. 762, 765. An objection to a patent or claim for a patent on the ground that the invention is not new or original is called an objection "for want of novelty."

Noverca /nəvárkə/. Lat. In the civil law, a stepmother.

Noverint universi per præsentes /nówvərənt yùwnəvársay pàr prəzéntiyz/. Know all men by these presents. Formal words used at the commencement of deeds of release in the Latin forms.

Novigild /nówvəgìld/. In Saxon law, a pecuniary satisfaction for an injury, amounting to nine times the value of the thing for which it was paid.

Novi operis nunciatio /nówvay ópərəs nànshiyéysh(iy)ow/. Lat. Denunciation of, or protest against, a new work. This was a species of remedy in the civil law, available to a person who thought his rights or his property were threatened with injury by the act of his neighbor in erecting or demolishing any structure, which was called a "new work." In such case, he might go upon the ground, while the work was in progress, and publicly protest against or forbid its completion, in the presence of the workmen or of the owner or his representative.

Noviter perventa, or **noviter ad notitiam perventa** /nówvədər (ǽd nowtísh(iy)əm) pərvéntə/. In ecclesiastical procedure, facts "newly come" to the knowledge of a party to a cause. Leave to plead facts *noviter perventa* is generally given, in a proper case, even after the pleadings are closed.

Novum judicium non dat novum jus, sed declarat antiquum; quia judicium est juris dictum et per judicium jus est noviter revelatum quod diu fuit velatum /nówvəm juwdísh(iy)əm nón dæt nówvəm jás, sèd dəklérəd æntáykwəm; kwáy juwdísh(iy)əm èst júrəs díktəm èt pàr juwdísh(iy)əm jás èst nówvədər rèvəléydəm kwòd dáyuw f(y)úwət vəléydəm/. A new adjudication does not make a new law, but declares the old; because adjudication is the utterance of the law, and by adjudication the law is newly revealed which was for a long time hidden.

Novus homo /nówvəs hówmow/. Lat. A new man. This term is applied to a man who has been pardoned of a crime, and so made, as it were, a "new man."

Now. At this time, or at the present moment; or at a time contemporaneous with something done. At the present time.

"Now" as used in a statute ordinarily refers to the date of its taking effect, but the word is sometimes used, not with reference to the moment of speaking but to a time contemporaneous with something done, and may mean at the time spoken of or referred to as well as at the time of speaking.

Word "now" used in will normally refers to time of testator's death; but, in light of context, may apply to date of will.

N.O.W. Negotiable Order of Withdrawal. Form of interest bearing checking account; permitted only in certain states.

Noxa /nóksə/. Lat. In the civil law, any damage or injury done to persons or property by an unlawful act committed by a man's slave or animal. An action for damages lay against the master or owner, who, however, might escape further responsibility by delivering up the offending agent to the party injured. *"Noxa"* was also used as the designation of the offense committed, and of its punishment, and sometimes of the slave or animal doing the damage.

Noxalis actio /nokséyləs ǽksh(iy)ow/. Lat. In the civil law, an action which lay against the master of a slave, for some offense (as theft or robbery) committed or damage or injury done by the slave, which was called *"noxa."* Usually translated "noxal action."

Noxia /nóks(i)yə/. Lat. In the civil law, an offense committed or damage done by a slave.

Noxious. Hurtful; offensive; offensive to the smell. The word "noxious" includes the complex idea both of insalubrity and offensiveness. That which causes or tends to cause injury, especially to health or morals.

N.P. An abbreviation for "notary public."

N.R. An abbreviation for "New Reports;" also for "not reported," and for "nonresident."

N.S. An abbreviation for "New Series;" also for "New Style."

N.T.S.B. National Traffic Safety Board.

Nubilis /n(y)úwbələs/. Lat. In the civil law, marriageable; one who is of a proper age to be married.

Nuda pactio obligationem non parit /n(y)úwdə pǽksh(iy)ow òbləgèyshiyównəm nòn pǽrət/. A naked agreement [*i.e.*, without consideration] does not beget an obligation.

Nuda patientia /n(y)úwdə pǽshiyénsh(iy)ə/. Lat. Mere sufferance.

Nuda possessio /n(y)úwdə pəzésh(iy)ow/. Lat. Bare or mere possession.

Nuda ratio et nuda pactio non ligant aliquem debitorem /n(y)úwdə rǽsh(iy)ow èt n(y)úwdə pǽksh(iy)ow nòn lígənt ǽləkwəm dèbətórəm/. Naked reason and naked promise do not bind any debtor.

Nude. Naked. This word is applied metaphorically to a variety of subjects to indicate that they are lacking in some essential legal requisite.

Nude contract. One made without any consideration; upon which no action will lie, in conformity with the maxim *"ex nudo pacto non oritur actio."* 2 Bl. Comm. 445.

Nude matter. A bare allegation of a thing done, unsupported by evidence.

Nude pact. One without consideration; an executory contract without a consideration; a naked promise.

Nudum pactum /n(y)úwdəm pǽktəm/. A voluntary promise, without any other consideration than mere goodwill, or natural affection.

A naked pact; a bare agreement; a promise or undertaking made without any consideration for it.

Roman law. Informal agreements not coming within any of the privileged classes. They could not be sued on. The term was sometimes used with a special and rather different meaning to express the rule that a contract without delivery will not pass property.

Nudum pactum est ubi nulla subest causa præter conventionem; sed ubi subest causa, fit obligatio, et parit actionem /n(y)úwdəm pǽktəm èst yúwbay nálə sə́best kózə príydər kənvènshiyównəm, sèd yúwbay sə́bèst kózə fít òbləgéysh(iy)ow èt pǽrət ǽkshiyównəm/. A naked contract is where there is no consideration except the agreement; but, where there is a consideration, it becomes an obligation and gives a right of action.

Nudum pactum ex quo non oritur actio /n(y)úwdəm pǽktəm èks kwów nòn órədər ǽksh(iy)ow/. *Nudum pactum* is that upon which no action arises.

Nugatory /n(y)úwgətəriy/. Futile; ineffectual; invalid; destitute of constraining force or vitality. A legislative act may be "nugatory" because unconstitutional. Avery & Co. v. Sorrell, 157 Ga. 476, 121 S.E. 828, 829.

Nuisance. Nuisance is that activity which arises from unreasonable, unwarranted or unlawful use by a person of his own property, working obstruction or injury to right of another, or to the public, and producing such material annoyance, inconvenience and discomfort that law will presume resulting damage. State ex rel. Herman v. Cardon, 23 Ariz.App. 78, 530 P.2d 1115, 1118. That which annoys and disturbs one in possession of his property, rendering its ordinary use or occupation physically uncomfortable to him. Patton v. Westwood Country Club Co., 18 Ohio App.2d 137, 247 N.E.2d 761, 763, 47 O.O.2d 247. Everything that endangers life or health, gives offense to senses, violates the laws of decency, or obstructs reasonable and comfortable use of property. Annoyance; anything which essentially interferes with enjoyment of life or property. That class of wrongs that arise from the unreasonable, unwarrantable, or unlawful use by a person of his own property, either real or personal, or from his own improper, indecent, or unlawful personal conduct, working an obstruction of or injury to the right of another or of the public, and producing such material annoyance, inconvenience, discomfort, or hurt, that the law will presume resulting damage. City of Phoenix v. Johnson, 51 Ariz. 115, 75 P.2d 30. An offensive, annoying, unpleasant, or obnoxious thing or practice; a cause or source of annoyance, especially a continuing or repeated invasion or disturbance of another's right, or anything that works a hurt, inconvenience or damage. Renken v. Harvey Aluminum (Inc.), D.C.Or., 226 F.Supp. 169, 175.

Nuisance comprehends interference with an owner's reasonable use and enjoyment of his property by means of smoke, odors, noise, or vibration, obstruction of private easements and rights of support, interference with public rights, such as free passage along streams and highways, enjoyment of public parks and places of recreation, and, in addition, activities and structures prohibited as statutory nuisances. Awad v. McColgan, 357 Mich. 386, 98 N.W.2d 571, 573.

Nuisances are commonly classed as *public, private,* and *mixed.* A *public* nuisance is one which affects an indefinite number of persons, or all the residents of a particular locality, or all people coming within the extent of its range or operation, although the extent of the annoyance or damage inflicted upon individuals may be unequal. Maintaining a *public* nuisance is by act, or by failure to perform a legal duty, intentionally causing or permitting a condition to exist which injures or endangers the public health, safety or welfare. An invasion of a person's interest in the private use and enjoyment of land by any type of liability-forming conduct is termed a *private* nuisance. It is a tort against a private person, and actionable by him as such. As distinguished from public nuisance, a *private* nuisance includes any wrongful act which destroys or deteriorates the property of an individual or of a few persons or interferes with their lawful use or enjoyment thereof, or any act which unlawfully hinders them in the enjoyment of a common or public right and causes them a special injury different from that sustained by the general public. Therefore, although the ground of distinction between public and private nuisances is still the injury to the community at large or, on the other hand, to a single individual, it is evident that the same thing or act may constitute a public nuisance and at the same time a private nuisance. A *mixed* nuisance is of the kind last described; that is, it is one which is both public and private in its effects,—public because it injures many persons or all the community, and private in that it also produces special injuries to private rights. Kelley v. New York, 6 Misc. 516, 27 N.Y.S. 164.

See also Attractive nuisance; Common nuisance; Legalized nuisance; Offenseve; Private nuisance; Public nuisance.

Abatement of a nuisance. The removal, stoppage, prostration, or destruction of that which causes a nuisance, whether by breaking or pulling it down, or otherwise removing, destroying, or effacing it. See also **Abatable nuisance.**

Actionable nuisance. See **Actionable.**

Assize of nuisance. In old English practice, this was a judicial writ directed to the sheriff of the county in which a nuisance existed, in which it was stated that the party injured complained of some particular fact done *ad nocumentum liberi tenementi sui* (to the nuisance of his freehold), and commanding the sheriff to summon an assize (that is, a jury) to view the premises, and have them at the next commission of assizes, that justice might be done, etc. 3 Bl.Comm. 221.

Common nuisance. One which affects the public in general, and not merely some particular person; a public nuisance.

Continuing nuisance. An uninterrupted or periodically recurring nuisance; not necessarily a constant or unceasing injury, but a nuisance which occurs so often and is so necessarily an incident of the use of property complained of that it can fairly be said to be continuous.

Permanent nuisance. A nuisance of such a character that its continuance is necessarily an injury which will continue without change. One that cannot be readily abated at small expense.

Nuisance at law. See **Nuisance per se** *(q.v.).*

Nuisance in fact. Acts, occupations or structures which are not nuisances per se but may become nuisances by reason of the circumstances of the location and surroundings or manner in which it is performed or operated. Robichaux v. Happunbauer, 258 La. 139, 245 So.2d 385, 389.

Nuisance per accidens /n(y)úwsən(t)s pər æksədèn(t)s/. See **Nuisance in fact** *(q.v.).*

Nuisance per se /n(y)úwsən(t)s pər síy/. An act, occupation, or structure which is a nuisance at all times and under all circumstances, regardless of location or surroundings, Bluemer v. Saginaw Central Oil & Gas Service, Inc., 356 Mich. 399, 97 N.W.2d 90, 96; Koeber v. Apex-Albuq Phoenix Exp., 72 N.M. 4, 380 P.2d 14, 15, 16; as, things prejudicial to public morals or dangerous to life or injurious to public rights; distinguished from things declared to be nuisances by statute, and also from things which constitute nuisances only when considered with reference to their particular location or other individual circumstances. The difference between a "nuisance per se" and a "nuisance per accidens" is that in the former, injury in some form is certain to be inflicted, while in the latter, the injury is uncertain or contingent until it actually occurs. State ex rel. Cunningham v. Feezell, 218 Tenn. 17, 400 S.W.2d 716, 719.

Nul. No; none. A law French negative particle commencing many phrases.

Nul agard /nə́l əgárd/. No award. The name of a plea in an action on an arbitration bond, by which the defendant traverses the making of any legal award.

Nul charter, nul vente, ne nul done vault perpetualment, si le donor n'est seise al temps de contracts de deux droits, sc. del droit de possession et del droit de properite. No grant, no sale, no gift, is valid forever unless the donor, at the time of the contract, is seised of two rights, namely, the right of possession, and the right of property.

Nul disseisin /nə́l dəsíyzən/. In pleading, means no disseisin. A plea of the general issue in a real action, by which the defendant denies that there was any desseisin.

Null. Naught; of no validity or effect. Usually coupled with the word "void;" as "null and void." The words "null and void," when used in a contract or statute are often construed as meaning "voidable." Burns Mortg. Co. v. Schwartz, C.C.A.N.J., 72 F.2d 991, 992; Metropolitan Life Ins. Co. v. Hall, 191 Ga. 294, 12 S.E.2d 53, 61. "Null and void" means that which binds no one or is incapable of giving rise to any rights or obligations under any circumstances, or that which is of no effect. Zogby v. State, 53 Misc.2d 740, 279 N.Y.S.2d 665, 668. See also **Void; Voidable.**

Nulla bona /nə́lə bównə/. Lat. No goods. The name of the return made by the sheriff to a writ of execution, when he has not found any goods of the defendant within his jurisdiction on which he could levy. Walter J. Klein Co. v. Kneece, 239 S.C. 478, 123 S.E.2d 870, 874.

Nulla curia quæ recordum non habet potest imponere finem neque aliquem mandare carceri; quia ista spectant tantummodo ad curias de recordo /nə́lə kyúriyə kwìy rəkórdəm nòn héybət pówdəst impównəriy fáynəm nékwiy æləkwəm mændériy karsíray, kwáyə ìstə spéktænt tæntəmówdow æd kyúriyəs dìy rəkórdow/. No court which has not a record can impose a fine or commit any person to prison; because those powers belong only to courts of record.

Nulla emptio sine pretio esse potest /nə́lə émpsh(iy)ow sáyniy présh(iy)ow ésiy pówdəst/. There can be no sale without a price.

Nulla impossibilia aut inhonesta sunt præsumenda; vera autem et honesta et possibilia /nə́lə impòsəbíl(i)yə òd in(h)onéstə sònt prìyz(y)əméndə, vírə ódəm èd (h)onéstə èt pòsəbíl(i)yə/. No things that are impossible or dishonorable are to be presumed; but things that are true and honorable and possible.

Nulla pactione effici potest ut dolus præstetur /nə́lə pækshiyówniy éfəsay pówdəst àt dówləs prəstíydər/. By no agreement can it be effected that a fraud shall be practiced. Fraud will not be upheld, though it may seem to be authorized by express agreement.

Nulla virtus, nulla scientia, locum suum et dignitatem conservare potest sine modestia. Without modesty, no virtue, no knowledge, can preserve its place and dignity.

Nulle règle sans faute /nyúl réyglə sòn fówt/. There is no rule without a fault.

Nulle terre sans seigneur /nyúl tér sòn sèynyúr/. No land without a lord. A maxim of feudal law.

Nulli enim res sua servit jure servitutis /nálay íynəm ríyz s(y)úwə sárvət júriy sərvət(y)úwdəs/. No one can have a servitude over his own property.

Nullification. The state or condition of being void; without legal effect or status. Also, the act which produces such effect.

Nullity. Nothing; no proceeding; an act or proceeding in a cause which the opposite party may treat as though it had not taken place, or which has absolutely no legal force or effect.

Nullity of marriage. The entire invalidity of a supposed, pretended, or attempted marriage, by reason of relationship or incapacity of the parties or other diriment impediments. An action seeking a decree declaring such an assumed marriage to be null and void is called a suit of "nullity of marriage." It differs from an action for divorce, because the latter supposes the existence of a valid and lawful marriage. See **Annulment.**

Nullius filius /nəláyəs fíl(i)yəs/. Lat. The son of nobody; a bastard. A bastard is considered *nullius filius* as far as regards his right to inherit. But the rule of *nullius filius* does not apply in other respects, and has been changed by statute in most states so as to make him the child of his mother, in respect of inheritance. State v. Chavez, 42 N.M. 569, 82 P.2d 900, 902.

Nullius hominis auctoritas apud nos valere debet, ut meliora non sequeremur si quis attulerit /nəláyəs hómənəs októrətæs æpəd nóws vəlíriy débət, àt mìyliyórə non sèkwəríymər sày kwís ətálərət/. The authority of no man ought to prevail with us, so far as to prevent our following better [opinions] if any one should present them.

Nullius in bonis /nəláyəs ìn bównəs/. Lat. Among the property of no person.

Nullius juris /nəláyəs júrəs/. Lat. In old English law, of no legal force.

Nulli vendemus, nulli negabimus, aut differemus rectum vel justitiam /nálay vendíyməs, nálay nəgéybəməs, ot difəríyməs réktəm vèl jəstísh(iy)əm/. We neither sell nor deny, nor delay, to any person, equity or justice. State ex rel. Macri v. City of Bremerton, 8 Wash.2d 93, 111 P.2d 612, 619.

Nullo est erratum plea /nálow èst əréydəm pliy/. Pleading interposed in a writ or assignment of error to the effect that there was no error and such a plea does not admit facts not well pleaded. Silverton v. Com., 314 Mass. 52, 49 N.E.2d 439.

Nullum arbitrium /náləm àrbítriyəm/. L. Lat. No award. The name of a plea in an action on an arbitration bond, for not fulfilling the award, by which the defendant traverses the allegation that there was an award made.

Nullum crimen majus est inobedientia /náləm krímən méyjəs èst ìnowbìydiyénsh(iy)ə/. No crime is greater than disobedience. Applied to the refusal of an officer to return a writ.

Nullum exemplum est idem omnibus /náləm əgzémpləm èst áydəm ómnəbəs/. No example is the same for all purposes. No one precedent is adapted to all cases. A maxim in conveyancing.

Nullum fecerunt arbitrium /náləm fəsírənt àrbítriyəm/. L. Lat. The name of a plea to an action of debt upon an obligation for the performance of an award, by which the defendant denies that he submitted to arbitration, etc.

Nullum iniquum est præsumendum in jure /náləm əníkwəm èst prìyz(y)əméndəm ənjúriy/. No iniquity is to be presumed in law.

Nullum matrimonium, ibi nulla dos /náləm mætrəmówn(i)yəm, áybay nálə dóws/. No marriage, no dower. Wait v. Wait, 4 Barb. N.Y., 192, 194.

Nullum simile est idem nisi quatuor pedibus currit /náləm síməliy èst áydəm náysay kwóduwər pédəbəs káhrət/. No like is identical, unless it run on all fours.

Nullum simile quatour pedibus currit /náləm síməliy kwóduwər pédəbəs káhrət/. No simile runs upon four feet (or *all fours,* as it is otherwise expressed). No simile holds in everything.

Nullum Tempus Act /náləm témpəs ǽkt/. A name given to the statute 3 Geo. III, c. 16, because that act, in contravention of the maxim "*Nullum tempus occurrit regi*" (no lapse of time bars the king), limited the crown's right to sue, etc., to the period of sixty years.

Nullum tempus aut locus occurit regi /náləm témpəs òt lówkəs əkáhrət ríyjay/. No time or place affects the king.

Nullum tempus occurrit regi /náləm témpəs əkáhrət ríyjay/. Time does not run against the king. The rule refers to the king in his official capacity as representing the sovereignty of the nation and not to the king as an individual. City of Bisbee v. Cochise County, 52 Ariz. 1, 78 P.2d 982, 984.

Nullum tempus occurrit reipublicæ /náləm témpəs əkáhrət rìyaypábləsiy/. No time runs [time does not run] against the commonwealth or state. State v. Mudd, 273 Ala. 579, 143 So.2d 171, 174.

Nullus alius quam rex possit episcopo demandare inquisitionem faciendam /náləs éyliyəs kwǽm réks pósəd əpískəpow dìymændériy ìnkwəzìshiyównəm fǽ shiyéndəm/. No other than the king can command the bishop to make an inquisition.

Nullus commodum capere potest de injuria sua propria /náləs kómədəm kǽpəriy pówdəst dìy ənjúriyə s(y)úwə prówpriyə/. No one can obtain an advantage by his own wrong. De Zotell v. Mutual Life Ins. Co. of New York, 60 S.D. 532, 245 N.W. 58, 59.

Nullus debet agere de dolo, ubi alia actio subest /náləs débəd ǽjəriy dìy dówlow, yúwbay éyliyə ǽksh(iy)ow sábèst/. Where another form of action is given, no one ought to sue in the action *de dolo.*

Nullus dicitur accessorius post feloniam, sed ille qui novit principalem feloniam fecisse, et illum receptavit et comfortavit /náləs dísədər ǽksəsóriyəs pòwst fəlówniyəm, sèd íliy kwày nówvət prìn(t)səpéyləm fəlówniyəm fəsísiy, èd íləm rèseptéyvət èt kàmfərtéyvət/. No one is called an "accessory" after the fact but he who knew the principal to have committed a felony, and received and comforted him.

Nullus dicitur felo principalis nisi actor, aut qui præsens est, abettans aut auxilians ad feloniam faciendam /nálǝs dísǝdǝr fíylow prìn(t)sǝpéylǝs náysay ǽktǝr òt kwày príyzǝnz èst, ǝbétænz òd ogzíl(i)yænz æd fǝlówniyǝm fæshiyéndǝm/. No one is called a "principal felon" except the party actually committing the felony, or the party present aiding and abetting in its commission.

Nullus idoneus testis in re sua intelligitur /nálǝs ǝdówniyǝs téstǝs ìn ríy s(y)úwǝ ìntǝlíjǝdǝr/. No person is understood to be a competent witness in his own cause.

Nullus jus alienum forisfacere potest /nálǝs jás æliyíynǝm fòrǝsfǽsǝriy pówdǝst/. No man can forfeit another's right.

Nullus recedat e curia cancellaria sine remedio /nálǝs rǝsíydǝd ìy kyúriyǝ kæn(t)sǝlériyǝ sáyniy rǝmíydiyow/. No person should depart from the court of chancery without a remedy.

Nullus simile est idem, nisi quatuor pedibus currit /nálǝs símǝliy èst áydem, náysay kwáduwor pédǝbǝs kə́hrǝt/. No like is exactly identical unless it runs on all fours.

Nullus videtur dolo facere qui suo jure utitur /nálǝs vǝdíydǝr dówlo fǽsǝriy kwày s(y)úwow júriy yúw.dǝdǝr/. No one is considered to act with guile who uses his own right.

Nul ne doit s'enrichir aux depens des autres /nál nǝ dwá sònriyshéy òwdǝpón deyzówtrǝ/. No one ought to enrich himself at the expense of others.

Nul prendra advantage de son tort demesne /nál pròndrá àdvantázh dǝ sówn tór dǝmén/. No one shall take advantage of his own wrong.

Nul sans damage avera error ou attaint /nál són dàmázh àvehrá ehrór uw àtǽn/. No one shall have error or attaint unless he has sustained damage.

Nul tiel corporation /nál tíyl kòrpǝréyshǝn/. No such corporation [exists]. The form of a plea denying the existence of an alleged corporation.

Nul tiel record /nál tíyl rékǝrd/. No such record. A plea denying the existence of any such record as that alleged by the plaintiff. It is the general plea in an action of debt on a judgment.

Judgment of *nul tiel record* occurs when some pleading denies the existence of a record and issue is joined thereon; the record being produced is compared by the court with the statement in the pleading which alleges it; and if they correspond, the party asserting its existence obtains judgment; if they do not correspond, the other party obtains judgment of *nul tiel record* (no such record).

Nul tort. In pleading, a plea of the general issue to a real action, by which the defendant denies that he committed any wrong.

Nul waste. No waste. The name of a plea in an action of waste, denying the committing of waste, and forming the general issue.

Numbers game. "Numbers" or the numbers game is that game wherein the player wagers or plays that on a certain day a certain series of digits will appear or "come out" in a series such as the United States Treasury balance or parimutuel payoff totals of particular races at a certain racetrack for the day used as a reference, and though number of digits is fixed, usually at three, any player is free to select any number or quantity of numbers within the range of those digits, and designate amount of his wager upon each, and in such game neither number of players nor amount of money wagered nor total amount of payoffs can be predicted in any one day. U. S. v. Baker, C.A.Pa., 364 F.2d 107, 111. See also **Lottery.**

Numerata pecunia /n(y)ùwmǝréydǝ pǝkyúwn(i)yǝ/. Lat. In the civil law, money told or counted; money paid by tale.

Numerical lottery. See **Genoese lottery.**

Nummata /nǝméydǝ/. The price of anything in money, as *denariata* is the price of a thing by computation of pence, and *librata* of pounds.

Nummata terræ /nǝméydǝ téhriy/. An acre of land.

Nunciatio /nǝnshiyéysh(iy)ow/. Lat. In the civil law, a solemn declaration, usually in prohibition of a thing; a protest.

Nuncio /nǝnsh(iy)ow/. The permanent official representative of the Pope at a foreign court or seat of government. They are called "ordinary" or "extraordinary," according as they are sent for general purposes or on a special mission.

Nuncius /nǝnsh(iy)ǝs/. In international law, a messenger; a minister; the pope's legate, commonly called a "nuncio."

Nunc pro tunc /nǝnk pròw tǝ́nk/. Lat. Now for then. In re Peter's Estate, 175 Okl. 90, 51 P.2d 272, 274. A phrase applied to acts allowed to be done after the time when they should be done, with a retroactive effect, *i.e.*, with the same effect as if regularly done. Nunc pro tunc entry is an entry made now of something actually previously done to have effect of former date; office being not to supply omitted action, but to supply omission in record of action really had but omitted through inadvertence or mistake. Seabolt v. State, Okl.Cr., 357 P.2d 1014.

Nunc pro tunc merely describes inherent power of court to make its records speak the truth, *i.e.*, to record that which is actually but is not recorded. Simmons v. Atlantic Coast Line R. Co., D.C.S.C., 235 F.Supp. 325, 330. Nunc pro tunc signifies now for them, or, in other words, a thing is done now, which shall have same legal force and effect as if done at time when it ought to have been done. State v. Hatley, 72 N.M. 377, 384 P.2d 252, 254.

Nuncupare /nàŋk(y)ǝpériy/. Lat. In the civil law, to name; to pronounce orally or in words without writing.

Nuncupate /nǝ́ŋkyǝpèyt/. To declare publicly and solemnly.

Nuncupative will. An oral will declared or dictated by the testator in his last sickness before a sufficient number of witnesses, and afterwards reduced to writing. A will made by the verbal declaration of the testator, and usually dependent merely on oral testimony for proof. Such wills are invalid in certain states, and in others are valid only under certain circumstances.

Nundinæ /nándəniy/. Lat. In the civil and old English law, a fair. *In nundinis et mercatis* /ìn nándənəs èt mərkéydəs/, in fairs and markets.

Nundination /nàndənéyshən/. Traffic at fairs and markets; any buying and selling.

Nunquam crescit ex post facto præteriti delicti æstimatio /nə́ŋkwæm krésəd èks pòwst fǽktow prətéhrəday dəlíktay èstəméysh(iy)ow/. The character of a past offense is never aggravated by a subsequent act or matter.

Nunquam decurritur ad extraordinarium sed ubi deficit ordinarium /nə́ŋkwæm dəkáhrədər ǽd èkstr(ə)òrdə nériyəm sèd yúwbay défəsəd òrdənériyəm/. We are never to resort to what is extraordinary, but [until] what is ordinary fails.

Nunquam fictio sine lege /nə́ŋkwæm fíksh(iy)ow sáyniy líyjiy/. There is no fiction without law.

Nunquam indebitatus /nə́ŋkwæm indèbətéydəs/. Lat. Never indebted. The name of a plea in an action of *indebitatus assumpsit*, by which the defendant alleges that he is not indebted to the plaintiff.

Nunquam nimis dicitur quod nunquam satis dicitur /nə́ŋkwæm níməs dísədər kwòd nə́ŋkwæm séydəs dísədər/. What is never sufficiently said is never said too much.

Nunquam res humanæ prospere succedunt ubi negliguntur divinæ /nə́ŋkwæm ríyz hyuwméyniy próspəriy

səksíydənt yúwbay nèglə gántər dəváyniy/. Human things never prosper where divine things are neglected.

Nuntius /nánshiyəs/. In old English practice, a messenger. One who was sent to make an excuse for a party summoned, or one who explained as for a friend the reason of a party's absence. An officer of a court; a summoner, apparitor, or beadle.

Nuper obiit /n(y)úwpər óbiyət/. Lat. In practice, the name of a writ (now abolished) which, in the English law, lay for a sister coheiress dispossessed by her coparcener of lands and tenements whereof their father, brother, or any common ancestor died seised of an estate in fee-simple.

Nuptiæ secundæ /nápshiyiy səkándiy/. Lat. A second marriage. In the canon law, this term included any marriage subsequent to the first.

Nuptial /nápshəl/. Pertaining to marriage; constituting marriage; used or done in marriage.

Nuptias non concubitus sed consensus facit /nápshiyəs nòn kənkyúwbədəs sèd kən(t)sén(t)səs féysət/. Not cohabitation but consent makes the marriage.

Nurture. To give nourishment to, to feed; to bring up, or train; to educate. The act of taking care of children, bringing them up, and educating them.

Nurus /n(y)úrəs/. Lat. In the civil law, a son's wife; a daughter-in-law.

Nycthemeron /nìkθəméron/. The whole natural day, or day and night, consisting of twenty-four hours.

Nymphomania /nìmfəméyn(i)yə/. See **Insanity.**

N.Y.S.E. New York Stock Exchange.

O

OASDI. Old Age, Survivors' and Disability Insurance. See **Social Security Administration.**

Oath. Any form of attestation by which a person signifies that he is bound in conscience to perform an act faithfully and truthfully, *e.g.* President's oath on entering office, Art. II, Sec. 1, U.S.Const. Vaughn v. State, 146 Tex.Cr.R. 586, 177 S.W.2d 59, 60. An affirmation of truth of a statement, which renders one willfully asserting untrue statements punishable for perjury. An outward pledge by the person taking it that his attestation or promise is made under an immediate sense of responsibility to God. A solemn appeal to the Supreme Being in attestation of the truth of some statement. An external pledge or asseveration, made in verification of statements made, or to be made, coupled with an appeal to a sacred or venerated object, in evidence of the serious and reverent state of mind of the party, or with an invocation to a supreme being to witness the words of the party, and to visit him with punishment if they be false. In its broadest sense, the term is used to include all forms of attestation by which a party signifies that he is bound in conscience to perform the act faithfully and truly. In a more restricted sense, it excludes all those forms of attestation or promise which are not accompanied by an imprecation.

See also Affirmation; Attestation; False swearing; Jurat; Loyalty oath; Pauper's oath; Verification.

Affirmation in lieu of oath. Fed.R.Civil P. 43 provides that whenever an oath is required under the rules, a solemn affirmation may be accepted in lieu thereof. See also Art. II, Sec. 1, and Art. VI, U.S. Const.

Assertory oath. One relating to a past or present fact or state of facts, as distinguished from a "promissory" oath which relates to future conduct; particularly, any oath required by law other than in judicial proceedings and upon induction to office, such, for example, as an oath to be made at the custom-house relative to goods imported.

Corporal oath. See **Corporal oath.**

Decisive or decisory oath. In the civil law, where one of the parties to a suit, not being able to prove his charge, offered to refer the decision of the cause to the oath of his adversary, which the adversary was bound to accept, to tender the same proposal back again, otherwise the whole was taken as confessed by him.

Extrajudicial oath. One not taken in any judicial proceeding, or without any authority or requirement of law, though taken formally before a proper person.

False oath. See **False swearing; Perjury.**

Judicial oath. One taken in some judicial proceeding or in relation to some matter connected with judicial proceedings. One taken before an officer in open court, as distinguished from a "non-judicial" oath, which is taken before an officer ex parte or out of court. See also *Witnesses, below.*

Loyalty oath. An oath requiring one to swear his loyalty to the state and country generally as a condition of public employment. Such oaths which are not overbroad have been upheld. Elfbrandt v. Russell, 384 U.S. 11, 86 S.Ct. 1238, 16 L.Ed.2d 321; Cole v. Richardson, 405 U.S. 676, 92 S.Ct. 1332, 31 L.Ed.2d 593. See also **Oath of allegiance.**

Official oath. One taken by an officer when he assumes charge of his office, whereby he declares that he will faithfully discharge the duties of the same, or whatever else may be required by statute in the particular case. See Art. VI, U.S. Const.

Poor debtor's oath. See **Pauper's oath.**

Promissory oaths. Oaths which bind the party to observe a certain course of conduct, or to fulfill certain duties, in the future, or to demean himself thereafter in a stated manner with reference to specified objects or obligations; such, for example, as the oath taken by a high executive officer, a legislator, a judge, a person seeking naturalization, an attorney at law. A solemn appeal to God, or, in a wider sense, to some superior sanction or a sacred or revered person in witness of the inviolability of a promise or undertaking.

Purgatory oath. An oath by which a person *purges* or clears himself from presumptions, charges or suspicions standing against him, or from a contempt.

Solemn oath. A corporal oath.

Suppletory oath. In the civil and ecclesiastical law, the testimony of a single witness to a fact is called "half-proof," on which no sentence can be founded; in order to supply the other half of proof, the party himself (plaintiff or defendant) is admitted to be examined in his own behalf, and the oath administered to him for that purpose is called the "suppletory oath," because it supplies the necessary *quantum* of proof on which to found the sentence. This term, although without application in American law in its original sense, is sometimes used as a designation of a party's oath required to be taken in authentication or support of some piece of documentary evidence which he offers, for example, his books of account.

Voluntary oath. Such as a person may take in extra-judicial matters, and not regularly in a court of justice, or before an officer invested with authority to administer the same.

Witnesses. Before testifying, every witness shall be required to declare that he will testify, truthfully, by oath or affirmation administered in a form calculated to awaken his conscience and impress his mind with his duty to do so. Fed.Evid.R. 603. See also *Affirmation in lieu of oath,* above.

Oath against bribery. In England, one which could have been administered to a voter at an election for members of parliament. Abolished in 1854.

Oath ex officio /ówθ èks əfísh(iy)ow/. In old English law, the oath by which a clergyman charged with a criminal offense was formerly allowed to swear himself to be innocent; also the oath by which the compurgators swore that they believed in his innocence.

Oath in litem /ówθ in láydəm/. In the civil law, an oath permitted to be taken by the plaintiff, for the purpose of proving the value of the subject-matter in controversy, when there was no other evidence on that point, or when the defendant fraudulently suppressed evidence which might have been available.

Oath of allegiance. An oath by which a person promises and binds himself to bear true allegiance to a particular sovereign or government (*e.g.,* the United States), administered generally to high public officers and to soldiers and sailors, also to aliens applying for naturalization, and, occasionally, to citizens generally as a prerequisite to their suing in the courts or prosecuting claims before government bureaus. 31 U.S. C.A. § 204. As to oath of allegiance to Constitution, see Art. II, Sec. 1, and Art. VI, U.S. Const. See also **Oath** *(Loyalty oath).*

Oath of calumny /ówθ əv kǽləmniy/. In the civil law, an oath which a plaintiff was obliged to take that he was not prompted by malice or trickery in commencing his action, but that he had *bona fide* a good cause of action.

Oath-rite. The form used at the taking of an oath.

Ob. Lat. On account of; for. Several Latin phrases and maxims, commencing with this word, are more commonly introduced by *"in" (q.v.).*

Obæratus /òbəréydəs/. Lat. In Roman law, a debtor who was obliged to serve his creditor until his debt was discharged.

Ob continentiam delicti /òb kòntənénsh(iy)əm dəlíktay/. On account of contiguity to the offense, *i.e.,* being contaminated by conjunction with something illegal.

Ob contingentiam /òb kòntinjénsh(iy)əm/. On account of connection; by reason of similarity.

Obedience. Compliance with a command, prohibition, or known law and rule of duty prescribed. The performance of what is required or enjoined by au-

thority, or the abstaining from what is prohibited, in compliance with the command or prohibition.

Obedientia /əbìydiyénsh(iy)ə/. An office, or the administration of it; a kind of rent; submission; obedience.

Obedientia est legis essentia /əbìydiyénsh(iy)ə èst líyjəs əsénsh(iy)ə/. Obedience is the essence of the law.

Obediential obligation /əbìydiyénshəl òbləgéyshən/. See **Obligation.**

Obedientiarius; obedientiary /əbìydiyènshiyériyəs; əbìydiyénshəriy/. A monastic officer.

Ob favorem mercatorum /òb fəvórəm màrkətórəm/. In favor of merchants.

Ob infamiam non solet juxta legem terræ aliquis per legem apparentem se purgare, nisi prius convictus fuerit vel confessus in curia /òb inféym(i)yəm nòn sówlət jə́kstə líyjəm téhriy ǽləkwəs pər líyjəm ǽpəréntəm siy pərgériy, náysay práyəs kənvíktəs vèl kənfésəs in kyúr(i)yə/. On account of evil report, it is not usual, according to the law of the land, for any person to purge himself, unless he have been previously convicted, or confessed in court.

Obit /ówbət/. A funeral solemnity, or office for the dead. The anniversary of a person's death; the anniversary office.

Obiter /ó(w)bədər/. Lat. By the way; in passing; incidentally; collaterally.

Obiter dictum /ó(w)bədər díktəm/. Words of an opinion entirely unnecessary for the decision of the case. Noel v. Olds, 78 U.S.App.D.C. 155, 138 F.2d 581, 586. A remark made, or opinion expressed, by a judge, in his decision upon a cause, "by the way," that is, incidentally or collaterally, and not directly upon the question before him, or upon a point not necessarily involved in the determination of the cause, or introduced by way of illustration, or analogy or argument. Such are not binding as precedent. See **Dicta; Dictum.**

Obit sine prole /ówbət sáyniy prówliy/. Lat. [He] died without issue.

Object, *v.* In legal proceedings, to object (*e.g.,* to the admission of evidence) is to interpose a declaration to the effect that the particular matter or thing under consideration is not done or admitted with the consent of the party objecting, but is by him considered improper or illegal, and referring the question of its propriety or legality to the court. See also **Objection.**

Object, *n.* End aimed at, the thing sought to be accomplished; the aim or purpose, the thing sought to be attained.

Anything which comes within the cognizance or scrutiny of the senses, especially anything tangible or visible. Moore v. Union Mut. Fire Ins. Co., 112 Vt. 218, 22 A.2d 503, 505. That which is perceived, known, thought of, or signified; that toward which a cognitive act is directed. The term includes whatever may be presented to the mind as well as to the senses; whatever, also, is acted upon or operated upon affirmatively, or intentionally influenced by anything done, moved, or applied thereto. It may be used as having the sense of effect.

See also **Intent; Motive.**

Objection. Act of objecting; that which is, or may be, presented in opposition; an adverse reason or argument; a reason for objecting or opposing; a feeling of disapproval.

The act of a party who objects to some matter or proceeding in the course of a trial, or an argument or reason urged by him in support of his contention that the matter or proceeding objected to is improper or illegal. Used to call the court's attention to improper evidence or procedure. Such objections in open court are important so that such will appear on the record for purposes of appeal. See Fed.Evid.R. 103(a)(1); Fed.R.Civil P. 46, and Fed.R.Crim.P. 51. See also **Object** *(v)*.

Objection to jury. See **Challenge.**

Objective symptom. Those which a surgeon or physician discovers from an examination of his patient; "subjective symptoms" being those which he learns from what his patient tells him. Schroeder v. Western Union Telegraph Co., Mo.App., 129 S.W.2d 917, 922.

Object of an action. Legal relief to prevent or redress the wrong. The thing sought to be obtained by the action; the remedy demanded or the relief or recovery sought or prayed for; not the same thing as the cause of action or the subject of the action.

Object of a statute. Aim, intent or purpose of its enactment. End or design which it is meant to accomplish, while the "subject" is the matter to which it relates and with which it deals. Matter or thing forming groundwork of statute.

Objects of a power. Those among whom donee is given power to appoint.

Objurgatrix /òbjərgéytrəks/. In old English law, scolds or unquiet women were referred to as objurgatrices and were punished with the cucking-stool *(q.v.).*

Oblata /əbléydə/. Gifts or offerings made to the king by any of his subjects; old debts, brought, as it were, together from preceding years, and put on the present sheriff's charge.

Oblata terræ /əbléydə téhriy/. Half an acre, or, as some say, half a perch, of land.

Oblate. See **Oblati.**

Oblate Rolls. Chancery Rolls (1199–1641), called also Fine Rolls, containing records of payments to the king by way of oblate or fine for the grant of privileges, or by way of amercement for breach of duty.

Oblati /əbléyday/. In old European law, voluntary slaves of churches or monasteries.

Oblati actio /əbléyday ǽksh(iy)ow/. In the civil law, an action given to a party against another who had *offered* to him a stolen thing, which was found in his possession.

Oblatio /əbléysh(iy)ow/. Lat. In the civil law, a tender of money in payment of a debt made by debtor to creditor. Whatever is offered to the church by the pious.

Oblation. Oblations, or obventions, are offerings or customary payments made, in England, to the minister of a church, including fees on marriages, burials, mortuaries, etc. *(q.v.),* and Easter offerings. They may be commuted by agreement.

Oblationes dicuntur quæcunque a piis fidelibusque christianis offeruntur deo et ecclesiæ, sive res solidæ sive mobiles /əblèyshiyówniyz dəkántər kwiykáŋkwiy èy páyəs fədìyləbáskwiy krìstiyéynəs òfərántər díyow èd əklíyziyiy, sáyviy ríyz sólədiy sáyviy mówbəliyz/. Those things are called "oblations" which are offered to God and to the Church by pious and faithful Christians, whether they are movable or immovable.

Obligate. To bind or constrain; to bind to the observance or performance of a duty; to place under an obligation. To bind one's self by an obligation or promise; to assume a duty; to execute a written promise or covenant; to make a writing obligatory.

Obligatio /òbləgéysh(iy)ow/. Lat. In Roman law, a legal bond which obliges the performance of something in accordance with the law of the land. It corresponded nearly to our word contract. The legal relation existing between two certain persons whereby one (the creditor) is authorized to demand of the other (the debtor) a certain performance which has a money value. In this sense *obligatio* signifies not only the duty of the debtor, but also the right of the creditor. The fact establishing such claim and debt, as also the instrument evidencing it, is termed "obligation."

Obligatio civilis /òbləgéysh(iy)ow sívələs/. An obligation enforceable by action, whether it derives its origin from the *jus civile,* as the obligation engendered by formal contracts or the obligation enforceable by bilaterally penal suits, or from such portion of the *jus gentium* as had been completely naturalized in the civil law and protected by all its remedies, such as the obligation engendered by formless contracts.

Obligatio ex contractu /òbləgéysh(iy)ow èks kəntrǽktuw/. An obligation arising from contract, or an antecedent *jus in personam.* In this there are two stages,—first, a primary or sanctioned personal right antecedent to wrong, and, afterwards, a secondary or sanctioning personal right consequent on a wrong.

Obligatio ex delicto, or **obligatio ex maleficio** /òbləgéysh(iy)ow èks dəlíktow/°mǽləfísh(iy)ow/. An obligation founded on wrong or tort, or arising from the invasion of a *jus in rem.* In this there is the second stage, a secondary or sanctioning personal right consequent on a wrong, but the first stage is not a personal right *(jus in personam),* but a real right *(jus in rem),* whether a primordial right, right of *status,* or of property.

Obligation. A generic word, derived from the Latin substantive "obligatio," having many, wide, and varied meanings, according to the context in which it is used. That which a person is bound to do or forbear; any duty imposed by law, promise, contract, relations of society, courtesy, kindness, etc. Rucks-Brandt Const. Co. v. Price, 165 Okl. 178, 23 P.2d 690; Helvering v. British-American Tobacco Co., C.C.A., 69 F.2d 528, 530. Law or duty binding parties to perform their agreement. An undertaking to perform. That which constitutes a legal or moral duty and which renders a person liable to coercion and punishment for neglecting it; a word of broad meaning, and the particular meaning intended is to be gained by consideration of its context. An obligation or debt may exist by reason of a judgment as well as an express contract, in either case there being a legal duty on the part of the one bound to comply with the promise. Schwartz v. California Claim Service, 52 Cal.App.2d 47, 125 P.2d 883, 888. Liabilities created by contract or law (*i.e.* judgments). Rose v. W. B. Worthen Co., 186 Ark. 205, 53 S.W.2d 15, 16. As legal term word originally meant a sealed bond, but it now extends to any certain written promise to pay money or do a specific thing. Lee v. Kenan, C.C.A.Fla., 78 F.2d 425. A formal and binding agreement or acknowledgment of a liability to pay a certain sum or do a certain thing. United States v. One Zumstein Briefmarken Katalog 1938, D.C.Pa., 24 F.Supp. 516, 519. The binding power of a vow, promise, oath, or contract, or of law, civil, political, or moral, independent of a promise; that which constitutes legal or moral duty.

See also **Contract; Duty; Liability.**

Absolute obligation. One which gives no alternative to the obligor, but requires fulfillment according to the engagement.

Conjunctive or alternative obligation. The former is one in which the several objects in it are connected by a copulative, or in any other manner which shows that all of them are severally comprised in the contract. This contract creates as many different obligations as there are different objects; and the debtor, when he wishes to discharge himself, may force the creditor to receive them separately. But where the things which form the object of the contract are separated by a disjunctive, then the obligation is alternative, and the performance of either of such things will discharge the obligor. The choice of performing one of the obligations belongs to the obligor, unless it is expressly agreed that it shall belong to the creditor. A promise to deliver a certain thing or to pay a specified sum of money is an example of an alternative obligation. Civ.Code La. arts. 2063, 2066, 2067.

Contractual obligation. One which arises from a contract or agreement. See **Contract.**

Current obligation. See **Current obligations.**

Determinate or indeterminate obligation. A determinate obligation is one which has for its object a certain thing: as, an obligation to deliver a certain horse named Bucephalus, in which case the obligation can be discharged only by delivering the identical horse. An indeterminate obligation is one where the obligor binds himself to deliver one of a certain species: as, to deliver a horse, where the delivery of any horse will discharge the obligation.

Divisible or indivisible obligation. A divisible obligation is one which, being a unit, may nevertheless be lawfully divided, with or without the consent of the parties. An indivisible obligation is one which is not susceptible of division: as, for example, if I promise to pay you one hundred dollars, you cannot assign one-half of this to another, so as to give him a right of action against me for his share.

Express or implied obligation. Express or conventional obligations are those by which the obligor binds himself in express terms to perform his obliga-

tion, while implied obligations are such as are raised by the implication or inference of the law from the nature of the transaction.

Failure to meet obligations. See **Failure to meet obligations.**

Joint or several obligation. A joint obligation is one by which two or more obligors bind themselves jointly for the performance of the obligation. A several obligation is one where the obligors promise, each for himself, to fulfill the engagement.

Moral obligation. A duty which is valid and binding in conscience and according to natural justice, but is not recognized by the law as adequate to set in motion the machinery of justice; that is, one which rests upon ethical considerations alone, and is not imposed or enforced by positive law. A duty which would be enforceable by law, were it not for some positive rule, which, with a view to general benefit, exempts the party in that particular instance from legal liability. See also **Love and affection.**

Natural or civil obligation. A natural obligation is one which cannot be enforced by action, but which is binding on the party who makes it in conscience and according to natural justice. As, for instance, when the action is barred by the act of limitation, a natural obligation still subsists, although the civil obligation is extinguished. Ogden v. Saunders, 25 U.S. 213, 337, (12 Wheat.) 6 L.Ed. 606. A civil obligation is a legal tie, which gives the party with whom it is contracted the right of enforcing its performance by law.

Obediential obligation. One incumbent on parties in consequence of the situation or relationship in which they are placed.

Perfect or imperfect obligation. A perfect obligation is one recognized and sanctioned by positive law; one of which the fulfillment can be enforced by the aid of the law. But if the duty created by the obligation operates only on the moral sense, without being enforced by any positive law, it is called an "imperfect obligation," and creates no right of action, nor has it any legal operation. The duty of exercising gratitude, charity, and the other merely moral duties are examples of this kind of obligation. Edwards v. Kearzey, 96 U.S. 595, 600, 24 L.Ed. 793.

Personal or heritable obligation. An obligation is heritable when the heirs and assigns of one party may enforce the performance against the heirs of the other. It is personal when the obligor binds himself only, not his heirs or representatives. An obligation is strictly personal when none but the obligee can enforce the performance, or when it can be enforced only against the obligor. An obligation may be personal as to the obligee, and heritable as to the obligor, and it may in like manner be heritable as to the obligee, and personal as to the obligor. For the term *personal obligation,* as used in a different sense, see the next paragraph.

Personal or real obligation. A personal obligation is one by which the obligor binds himself to perform an act, without directly binding his property for its performance. A real obligation is one by which real estate, and not the person, is liable to the obligee for the performance.

Primary or secondary obligation. An obligation which is the principal object of the contract. For example, the primary obligation of the seller is to deliver the thing sold, and to transfer the title to it. It is distinguished from the accessory or secondary obligation to pay damages for not doing so. The words "primary" and "direct," contrasted with "secondary," when spoken with reference to an obligation, refer to the remedy provided by law for enforcing the obligation, rather than to the character and limits of the obligation itself.

A primary obligation, which in one sense may also be called a principal obligation, is one which is contracted with a design that it should itself be the first fulfilled. A secondary obligation is one which is contracted and is to be performed in case the primitive cannot be. For example, if one sells his house, he binds himself to give a title; but if he finds he cannot as when the title is in another, then his secondary obligation is to pay damages for nonperformance of the obligation.

Principal or accessory obligation. A principal obligation is one which arises from the principal object of the engagement of the contracting parties; while an accessory obligation depends upon or is collateral to the principal. For example, in the case of the sale of a house and lot of ground, the principal obligation on the part of the vendor is to make title for it; the accessory obligation is to deliver all the title-papers which the vendor has relating to it, to take care of the estate until it is delivered, and the like. See, further, the title **Accessory obligation.**

Pure obligation. One which is not suspended by any condition, whether it has been contracted without any condition, or, when thus contracted, the condition has been accomplished. See *Simple or conditional obligation.*

Simple or conditional obligation. Simple obligations are such as are not dependent for their execution on any event provided for by the parties, and which are not agreed to become void on the happening of any such event. Conditional obligations are such as are made to depend on an uncertain event. If the obligation is not to take effect until the event happens, it is a suspensive condition; if the obligation takes effect immediately, but is liable to be defeated when the event happens, it is then a resolutory condition. A simple obligation is also defined as one which is not suspended by any condition, either because it has been contracted without condition, or, having been contracted with one, the condition has been fulfilled; and a conditional obligation is also defined as one the execution of which is suspended by a condition which has not been accomplished, and subject to which it has been contracted.

Single or penal obligation. A penal obligation is one to which is attached a penal clause, which is to be enforced if the principal obligation be not performed. A single obligation is one without any penalty, as where one simply promises to pay another one hundred dollars. This is called a single bill, when it is under seal.

Solidary obligation. In the law of Louisiana, one which binds each of the obligors for the whole debt, as distinguished from a "joint" obligation, which binds the parties each for his separate proportion of the debt. Groves v. Sentell, 153 U.S. 465, 14 S.Ct. 898, 38 L.Ed. 785. See **Solidary.**

Obligatio naturalis /òblǝgéysh(iy)ow nǽchǝréylǝs/. An obligation not immediately enforceable by action; one deriving its validity from the law of nature, or one imposed by that portion of the *jus gentium* which is only imperfectly recognized by civil law.

Obligationes ex delicto or **ex maleficio** /òblǝgèyshiyów niyz èks dǝlíktow/°mǽlǝfísh(iy)ow/. Obligations arising from the commission of a wrongful injury to the person or property of another.

"*Delictum*" is not exactly synonymous with "tort," for, while it includes most of the wrongs known to the common law as torts, it is also wide enough to cover some offenses (such as theft and robbery) primarily injurious to the individual, but now only punished as crimes. Such acts gave rise to an *obligatio,* which consisted in the liability to pay damages.

Obligationes ex variis causarum figuris /òblǝgèyshiyówniyz èks vériyǝs kozérǝm fǝgúrǝs/. Although Justinian confined the divisions of obligations to four classes, namely *obligationes ex contractu, quasi ex contractu, ex maleficio* and *quasi ex maleficio,* there are many species of obligations which cannot properly be reduced within any of these classes. Some authorities, consequently, established a fifth class, to receive the odds and ends which belonged nowhere else, and gave to this class the above designation.

Obligationes quasi ex contractu /òblǝgèyshiyówniyz kwéyzay èks kǝntrǽkt(y)uw/. Often persons who have not contracted with each other, under a certain state of facts, are regarded by the Roman law as if they had actually concluded a convention between themselves. The legal relation which then takes place between these persons, which has always a similarity to a contract obligation, is therefore termed *obligatio quasi ex contractu.* Obligations in the nature of a contract called quasi contract or implied in law contract. See **Contract.**

Such a relation arises from the conducting of affairs without authority (*negotiorum gestio*) or unauthorized agency; from the management of property that is in common when the community arose from casualty (*communio incidens*); from the payment of what was not due (*solutio indebiti*); from tutorship and curatorship (*tutela* and *cura*), resembling the relation of guardian and ward; from taking possession of an inheritance (*additio hereditatis* and *agnitio bonorum possessionis*); and in many other cases.

Obligationes quasi ex delicto, or **obligationes quasi ex maleficio** /òblǝgèyshiyówniyz kwéyzay èks dǝlíktow/°mǽlǝfísh(iy)ow/. This class embraces all torts not coming under the denomination of *delicta* and not having a special form of action provided for them by law. They differed widely in character, and at common law would in some cases give rise to an action on the case, in others to an action on an implied contract.

Obligation of a contract. That which the law in force when contract is made obliges parties to do or not to do, and the remedy and legal means to carry it into effect. The "obligation of a contract" is the duty of performance. The term includes everything within the obligatory scope of the contract, and it includes the means of enforcement.

Obligation solidaire /òbligasyówn sòlidér/. This, in French law, corresponds to joint and several liability in English law, but is applied also to the joint and several rights of the creditors and parties to the obligation.

Obligatio Prætoriæ /òbləgéysh(iy)ow prətóriyiy/. The Romans considered that obligations derived their validity solely from positive law. At first the only ones recognized were those established in special cases in accordance with the forms prescribed by the strict *jus civile*. In the course of time, however, the prætorian jurisdiction, in mitigation of the primitive rigor of the law, introduced new modes of contracting obligations and provided the means of enforcing them; hence the twofold division made by Justinian of *obligationes civiles* and *obligationes prætoriæ.*

Obligatory pact. See **Pact.**

Obligatory rights. See **Right.**

Obligatory writing. See **Writing obligatory.**

Obligee /òbləjíy/. A promisee. The person in favor of whom some obligation is contracted, whether such obligation be to pay money or to do or not to do something. The party to whom someone else is obligated under a contract. The party to whom a bond is given.

Obligor /óbləgər/òbləgór/. A promisor. The person who has engaged to perform some obligation. Person obligated under a contract or bond.

Obliquus /əbláykwəs/. Lat. In the old law of descents, oblique; cross; transverse; collateral. The opposite of *rectus,* right, or upright.

In the law of evidence, indirect; circumstantial.

Obliterated corner. See **Corner.**

Obliteration. To destroy; wipe or rub out; erase. Erasure or blotting out of written words. A method of revoking a will or a clause therein if accompanied by the required intent to revoke. See also **Alteration; Deface; Spoliation.**

Oblivion. Act of forgetting, or fact of having forgotten; forgetfulness. Official ignoring of offenses. Amnesty, or general pardon, as, an act of oblivion. State or fact of being forgotten. See **Amnesty; Pardon.**

Oblivious. Evincing oblivion; forgetful; forgetting. Where thing is extinguished from mind.

Obloquy /óbləkwiy/. Censure and reproach. Blame, reprehension, being under censure, a cause or object of reproach, a disgrace.

Obnoxious. "Obnoxious" and "offensive" in ordinary use are synonymous, and mean highly objectionable, disagreeable, displeasing, and distasteful.

Obreptio /òbrépsh(iy)ow/. Lat. The obtaining a thing by fraud or surprise.

Obreption /òbrépshən/. Obtaining anything by fraud or surprise. Acquisition of escheats, etc., from the sovereign, by making false representations. See also **Subreption.**

Obrogare /òbrəgériy/. Lat. In the civil law, to pass a law contrary to a former law, or to some clause of it; to change a former law in some part of it.

Obrogation. In the civil law, the annulling a law, in whole or in part, by passing a law contrary to it. The alteration of a law. See also **Abrogation.**

Obscene. Objectionable or offensive to accepted standards of decency. Basic guidelines for trier of fact in determining whether a work which depicts or describes sexual conduct is obscene is whether the average person, applying contemporary community standards would find that the work, taken as a whole, appeals to the prurient interest, whether the work depicts or describes, in a patently offensive way, sexual conduct specifically defined by the applicable state law, and whether the work, taken as a whole, lacks serious literary, artistic, political, or scientific value. Miller v. California, 413 U.S. 15, 24, 93 S.Ct. 2607, 2615, 37 L.Ed.2d 419. See also Censor; Censorship; Dominant theme; Lewd; Obscenity; Pornographic; Prurient interest.

Obscene libel. That type of defamation which holds up a person to ridicule, scorn or contempt to a considerable and respectable class in the community by printed words or configurations of a lewd and lascivious nature.

Obscenity. The character or quality of being obscene; conduct tending to corrupt the public morals by its indecency or lewdness.

Material is obscene if, considered as a whole, its predominant appeal is to prurient interest, that is, a shameful or morbid interest, in nudity, sex or excretion, and if in addition it goes substantially beyond customary limits of candor in describing or representing such matters. Predominant appeal shall be judged with reference to ordinary adults unless it appears from the character of the material or the circumstances of its dissemination to be designed for children or other specially susceptible audience. Undeveloped photographs, molds, printing plates, and the like, shall be deemed obscene notwithstanding that processing or other acts may be required to make the obscenity patent or to disseminate it. Model Penal Code, § 251.4.

Federal laws prohibit the mailing, transportation for sale or distribution, importation, and broadcasting of obscene matters. 18 U.S.C.A. § 1461 et seq.

See also Censor; Censorship; Lewd; Obscene; Pander *(Pandering of obscenity);* Profanity.

Obscure. When applied to words, statements or meanings, it signifies not perspicuous, not clearly expressed, vague, hard to understand.

Observe. To perform that which has been prescribed by some law or usage. To adhere to or abide by.

Obses /óbsiyz/. Lat. In time of war, a hostage. *Obsides,* hostages.

Obsignare /òbsignériy/. Lat. In the civil law, to seal up; as money that had been tendered and refused.

Obsignatory /òbsígnət(ə)riy/. Ratifying and confirming.

Obsolescence. Condition or process of falling into disuse. The diminution in value of property caused by changes in technology, public taste, and new inventions rendering the property less desirable on the market. A decline in market value of an asset caused by improved alternatives becoming available that will be more cost-effective; such decline in market value is unrelated to physical changes in the asset itself. See also **Economic obsolescence; Functional obsolescence.**

Obsolescent. Becoming obsolete; going out of use; not entirely disused, but gradually becoming so. See **Obsolescence.**

Obsolete. That which is no longer used. Becker v. Anheuser-Busch, Inc., C.C.A.Mo., 120 F.2d 403, 416. Disused; neglected; not observed. See also **Obsolescence.**

The term is applied to statutes which have become inoperative by lapse of time, either because the reason for their enactment has passed away, or their subject-matter no longer exists, or they are not applicable to changed circumstances, or are tacitly disregarded by all men, yet without being expressly abrogated or repealed.

Obstante /əbstǽntiy/. Withstanding; hindering. See **Non obstante.**

Obsta principiis /óbstə prìnsípiyəs/. Lat. Withstand beginnings; resist the first approaches or encroachments. Bradley v. U. S., 116 U.S. 616, 635, 6 S.Ct. 524, 535, 29 L.Ed. 746.

Obstinate desertion. "Obstinate" as used of desertion, which is a ground for divorce, means determined, fixed, persistent. Persisted in against the willingness of the injured party to have it concluded.

Obstriction. Obligation; bond.

Obstruct. To hinder or prevent from progress, check, stop, also to retard the progress of, make accomplishment of difficult and slow. Conley v. United States, C.C.A.Minn., 59 F.2d 929, 936. To be or come in the way of or to cut off the sight of an object. To block up; to interpose obstacles; to render impassable; to fill with barriers or impediments, as to obstruct a road or way. To impede; to interpose impediments to the hindrance or frustration of some act or service, as to obstruct an officer in the execution of his duty. As applied to navigable waters, to "obstruct" them is to interpose such impediments in the way of free and open navigation that vessels are thereby prevented from going where ordinarily they have a right to go or where they may find it necessary to go in their maneuvers.

Obstructing justice. Impeding or obstructing those who seek justice in a court, or those who have duties or powers of administering justice therein. The act by which one or more persons attempt to prevent, or do prevent, the execution of lawful process. The term applies also to obstructing the administration of justice in any way—as by hindering witnesses from appearing, assaulting process server, influencing jurors, obstructing court orders or criminal investigations. Any act, conduct, or directing agency pertaining to pending proceedings, intended to play on human frailty and to deflect and deter court from performance of its duty and drive it into compromise with its own unfettered judgment by placing it, through medium of knowingly false assertion, in wrong position before public, constitutes an obstruction to administration of justice. Toledo Newspaper Co. v. U. S., 247 U.S. 402, 38 S.Ct. 560, 564, 62 L.Ed. 1186. See 18 U.S.C.A. § 1501 et seq. See also **Withholding of evidence.**

Obstructing mails. Federal offense consisting of interfering with the mails. 18 U.S.C.A. § 324.

Obstructing proceedings of legislature. The term embraces not only things done in the presence of the legislature, but those done in disobedience of a committee.

Obstructing process. In criminal law, the act by which one or more persons attempt to prevent or do prevent the execution of lawful process. Obstructing legal process or official duty is knowingly and willfully obstructing, resisting or opposing any person authorized by law to serve process or order of a court, or in the discharge of any official duty.

Obstruction. A hindrance, obstacle, or barrier. Delay, impeding or hindering. See also **Obstruct.**

Obstruction to navigation. Any unnecessary interference with the free movements of vessels.

Obtain. To get hold of by effort; to get possession of; to procure; to acquire, in any way. State v. Bowdry, 346 Mo. 1090, 145 S.W.2d 127, 129. See also **False pretenses.**

Obtaining money or property by false pretenses. See **False pretenses.**

Obtemperandum est consuetudini rationabili tanquam legi /əbtèmpərǽndəm èst kònswət(y)úwdənay ræsh(iy)ənéybəlay tǽnkwəm líyjay/. A reasonable custom is to be obeyed as a law.

Obtest /əbtést/. To protest.

Obtulit se /óbtələt síy/. Offered himself. In old English practice, the emphatic words of entry on the record where one party *offered himself* in court against the other, and the latter did not appear.

Ob turpem causam /òb tə́rpəm kózəm/. For an immoral consideration.

Obventio /əbvénsh(iy)ow/. Lat. (From *obvenire*, to fall in.) In the civil law, rent; profits; income; the return from an investment or thing owned; as the earnings of a vessel. Generally used in the plural.

In old English law, the revenue of a spiritual living, so called. Also, in the plural, "offerings."

Obvention /əbvénshən/. See **Oblation; Obventio.**

Obvious. Easily discovered, seen, or understood; readily perceived by the eye or the intellect; plain; patent; apparent; evident; clear; manifest.

Obvious danger. Apparent in exercise of ordinary observation and disclosed by use of eyes and other senses. Plain and apparent to a reasonably observant person.

Obvious risk. One so plain that it would be instantly recognized by a person of ordinary intelligence. Within an accident policy, one which would be plain and apparent to a reasonably prudent and cautious person in the use of his faculties. It does not mean an unnecessary risk.

O.C. An abbreviation, in the civil law, for *"ope consilio" (q.v.)*. In American law, these letters are used as an abbreviation for "Orphans' Court."

Ocasion /òkasyówn/. In Spanish law, accident.

Occasio /əkéyzh(iy)ow/. In feudal law, a tribute which the lord imposed on his vassals or tenants for his necessity. Hindrance; trouble; vexation by suit.

Occasion, n. That which provides an opportunity for the causal agency to act. Meaning not only particular time but carrying idea of opportunity, necessity, or need, or even cause in a limited sense. Condition of affairs; juncture entailing need; exigency; or juncture affording ground or reason for something.

Occasion, v. To cause or bring about by furnishing the condition or opportunity for the action of some other cause. Smart v. Raymond, Mo.App., 142 S.W.2d 100, 104. To give occasion to, to produce; to cause incidentally or indirectly; bring about or be the means of bringing about or producing.

Occasionari /əkèyzh(iy)ənéray/. To be charged or loaded with payments or occasional penalties.

Occupancy. Taking possession of property and use of the same; said *e.g.* of a tenant's use of leased premises. Period during which person owns, rents, or otherwise occupies real property or premises. Occupancy is a mode of acquiring property by which a thing which belongs to nobody becomes the property of the person who took possession of it with the intention of acquiring a right of ownership in it. The taking possession of things which before belonged to nobody, with an intention of appropriating them to one's own use. To constitute occupancy, there must be a taking of a thing corporeal, belonging to nobody, with an intention to becoming the owner of it. See also **Occupant; Occupation; Possession.**

Term also refers to the constitutional concept of "occupancy of the field" when the federal government has so claimed for its jurisdiction a particular sphere that state action is no longer allowed; *e.g.* sedition and espionage laws. See **Pre-emption.**

In International law, the taking possession of a newly discovered or conquered country with the intention of holding and ruling it.

See also Adverse possession; Certificate of occupancy; Occupant; Occupation; Occupy; Possession.

Occupant. Person in possession. Person having possessory rights, who can control what goes on on premises. One who has actual use, possession or control of a thing. Redevelopment Authority of Allegheny County v. Stepanik, 25 Pa.Cmwlth. 180, 360 A.2d 300, 302. One who takes the first possession of a thing of which there is no owner. One who occupies and takes possession. Person who acquires title by occupancy. See also **Occupancy; Occupation; Possession.**

Common occupant. See *General occupant,* below.

General occupant. At common law where a man was tenant *pur autre vie,* or had an estate granted to himself only (without mentioning his heirs) for the life of another man, and died without alienation during the life of *cestui que vie,* or him by whose life it was holden, he that could first enter on the land might lawfully retain the possession, so long as *cestui que vie* lived, by right of occupancy, and was hence termed a "general" or common "occupant."

Special occupant. A person having a special right to enter upon and occupy lands granted pur autre vie, on the death of the tenant, and during the life of cestui que vie.

Occupantis fiunt derelicta /òkyəpǽntəs fáyənt dèhrəlíktə/. Things abandoned become the property of the (first) occupant.

Occupare /òkyəpériy/. Lat. In the civil law, to seize or take possession of; to enter upon a vacant possession; to take possession before another.

Occupatile /ókyəpətàyl/. That which has been left by the right owner, and is now possessed by another.

Occupation. Possession; control; tenure; use. The act or process by which real property is possessed and enjoyed. Where a person exercises physical control over land.

That which principally takes up one's time, thought, and energies, especially, one's regular business or employment; also, whatever one follows as the means of making a livelihood. Particular business, profession, trade, or calling which engages individual's time and efforts; employment in which one regularly engages or vocation of his life.

Actual occupation. An open, visible occupancy as distinguished from the constructive one which follows the legal title. See also **Adverse possession.**

Occupational. Of or pertaining to an occupation, trade or work.

Occupational disease. A disease (as black lung disease incurred by miners) resulting from exposure during employment to conditions or substances detrimental to health. Compensation for such is provided by state worker's compensation acts and such federal acts as the Black Lung Benefits Act. Impairment of health not caused by accident but by exposure to conditions arising out of or in the course of one's employment.

A disease is compensable under worker's compensation statute as being an "occupational" disease where: (1) the disease is contracted in the course of employment; (2) the disease is peculiar to the claimant's employment by its causes and the characteristics of its manifestation or the conditions of employment result in a hazard which distinguishes the employment in character from employment generally, and (3) the employment creates a risk of contracting the disease in a greater degree and in a different manner than in the public generally. State ex rel. Ohio Bell Tel. Co. v. Krise, 42 Ohio St.2d 247, 327 N.E.2d 756, 758, 71 O.O.2d 226.

Occupational hazard. A risk of accident or disease which is peculiar to a particular calling or occupation.

Occupational Safety and Health Act. The federal law which is administered by the Occupational Safety and Health Administration.

Occupational Safety and Health Administration. The Occupational Safety and Health Administration, established pursuant to the Occupational Safety and Health Act of 1970 (84 Stat. 1590), develops and promulgates occupational safety and health standards; develops and issues regulations; conducts investigations and inspections to determine the status of compliance with safety and health standards and regulations; and issues citations and proposes penalties for noncompliance with safety and health standards and regulations.

Occupational Safety and Health Review Commission. The Occupational Safety and Health Review Commission is an independent adjudicatory agency established by the Occupational Safety and Health Act of 1970 (84 Stat. 1590; 29 U.S.C.A. § 651). The act, enforced by the Secretary of Labor, is an effort to reduce the incidence of personal injuries, illnesses, and deaths among working men and women in the United States which result from their employment. The Review Commission was created to adjudicate enforcement actions initiated under the act when they are contested by employers, employees, or representatives of employees.

Occupation tax. A tax imposed upon an occupation or the prosecution of a business, trade, or profession; not a tax on property, or even the capital employed in the business, but an excise tax on the business itself; to be distinguished from a "license tax," which is a fee or exaction for the privilege of engaging in the business, not for its prosecution. An occupation tax is form of excise tax imposed upon persons for privilege of carrying on business, trade or occupation.

Occupative. Pertaining to or involving occupation or the right of occupation.

Occupavit /òkyǝpéyvǝt/. Lat. In old English law, a writ that lay for one who was ejected out of his land or tenement in time of war.

Occupier. An occupant; one who is in the enjoyment of a thing.

Occupy. To take or enter upon possession of; to hold possession of; to hold or keep for use; to possess; to tenant; to do business in; to take or hold possession. Actual use, possession, and cultivation. See **Occupancy; Occupant; Occupation; Possession.**

Occupying claimant. An occupant claiming right under statute to recover for improvements he has placed on the land subsequently found not to be his. See **Occupying Claimant Acts.**

Occupying Claimant Acts. Statutes providing for the reimbursement of a *bona fide* occupant and claimant of land, on its recovery by the true owner, to the extent to which lasting improvements made by him have increased the value of the land, and generally giving him a lien therefor.

Occur. To happen; to meet one's eye; to be found or met with; to present itself; to appear; hence, to befall in due course; to take place; to arise.

Occurrence. A coming or happening. Any incident or event, especially one that happens without being designed or expected. Farmers & Merchants Nat. Bank v. Arrington, Tex.Civ.App., 98 S.W.2d 378, 382. See also **Accident; Act of God; Event.**

Ocean. The main or open sea; the high sea; that portion of the sea which does not lie within the body of any country and is not subject to the territorial jurisdiction or control of any country, but is open, free, and common to the use of all nations. U. S. v. Rodgers, 150 U.S. 249, 14 S.Ct. 109, 37 L.Ed. 1071. Body of salt water that covers over 70% of earth's surface.

Ochlocracy /oklókrǝsiy/. Government by the multitude. A form of government wherein the populace has the whole power and administration in its own hands. The abuse of a democracy.

Octo tales /óktow téyl(iy)z/. Lat. Eight such; eight such men; eight such jurors. The name of a writ, at common law, which issues when upon a trial at bar, *eight* more jurors are necessary to fill the panel, commanding the sheriff to summon the requisite number.

Octroi /óktroy/òktrwá/. Fr. In French law, originally, a toll or duty, which, by the permission of the *seigneur*, any city was accustomed to collect on liquors and some other goods, brought within its precincts, for the consumption of the inhabitants. Afterwards appropriated to the use of the king.

Oculist /ókyǝlǝst/. A duly licensed physician specializing in the diseases of the eye. See **Ophthalmologist.**

Odal /ówdǝl/. Complete property, as opposed to feudal tenure. Blackstone notes the relation of this word to "allodial".

Odal right /ówdǝl ráyt/. An allodial right.

Odd lot. An amount of stock less than the established 100-share unit or 10-share unit of trading: from 1 to 99 shares for the great majority of issues, 1 to 9 for so-called inactive stocks.

Odd lot doctrine. Doctrine which permits finding of total disability where claimant is not altogether incapacitated for any kind of work but is nevertheless so handicapped that he will not be able to obtain regular employment in any well-known branch of the competitive labor market absent superhuman efforts, sympathetic friends or employers, a business boom, or temporary good luck. Vester v. Diamond Lumber Co., 21 Or.App. 587, 535 P.2d 1373, 1376. Under the "odd-lot doctrine", worker's compensation claimant will be considered to be totally disabled if it appears probable that claimant cannot sell his services in a competitive labor market. Hill v. U. S. Plywood-Champion Co., 12 Or.App. 1, 503 P.2d 728, 730.

Odd lot order. Order for less than 100 shares of stock.

Oderunt peccare boni, virtutis amore; oderunt peccare mali, formidine pœnæ /owdírǝnt pǝkériy bównay vǝrt(y)úwdǝs ǝmóriy; owdírǝnt pǝkériy mǽlay formídǝniy píyniy/. Good men hate to sin through love of virtue; bad men, through fear of punishment.

•dio et atia /ówd(i)yow èd éysh(iy)ə/. See **De odio et atia.**

•diosa et inhonesta non sunt in lege præsumenda /òwdiyówsə èd ìn(h)ənéstə nón sə̀nt ìn líyjiy prèz(y)əméndə/. Odius and dishonest acts are not presumed in law.

•diosa non præsumuntur /òwdiyówsə nòn prèz(y)əmántər/. Odius things are not presumed.

•dious /ówd(i)yəs/. Synonymous with infamous; hateful; repugnant.

•dium /ówdiyəm/. Condition or fact of being subjected to hatred and dislike. In venue statute, it implies such a general ill-feeling toward a party to an action as will render it uncertain whether the cause can be tried by impartial triers, free from an atmosphere impregnated with malice or corrupting prejudices.

Economicus /ìykənóməkəs/. L. Lat. In old English law, the executor of a last will and testament.

Economus /iykónəməs/. Lat. In the civil law, a manager or administrator.

)f. A term denoting that from which anything proceeds; indicating origin, source, descent, and the like; as, he is of noble blood. Associated with or connected with, usually in some causal relation, efficient, material, formal, or final. The word has been held equivalent to after; at, or belonging to; in possession of; manufactured by; residing at; from.

)f age. See **Legal age; Majority.**

)f counsel. A phrase commonly applied in practice to the counsel employed by a party in a cause, and particularly to one employed to assist in the preparation or management of an action, or its presentation on appeal, but who is not the principal attorney of record for the party.

)f course. As a matter of right. Jones v. McGonigle, 327 Mo. 457, 37 S.W.2d 892. Any action or step taken in the course of judicial proceedings which will be allowed by the court upon mere application, without any request or contest, or which may be effectually taken without having to apply to the court for leave to take such action; e.g. Fed.R. Civil P. 15(a) permits a party to amend his pleadings once as a matter of course at any time before a responsive pleading is served.

)ff-board. This term may refer to transactions over-the-counter in unlisted securities, or to a transaction involving listed shares which was not executed on a national securities exchange.

)ffender. Commonly used in statutes to indicate person implicated in the commission of a crime and includes person guilty of a misdemeanor or traffic offense. State ex rel. Smith v. Jameson, 70 S.D. 503, 19 N.W.2d 505, 508.

)ffense. A felony or misdemeanor; a breach of the criminal laws. The word "offense," while sometimes used in various senses, generally implies a felony or a misdemeanor infringing public as distinguished from mere private rights, and punishable under the criminal laws, though it may also include the violation of a criminal statute for which the remedy is merely a civil suit to recover the penalty.

Offenses may be classified into general categories as offenses against the person (e.g. murder, manslaughter), against habitation and occupancy (e.g. burglary, arson), against property (e.g. larceny), against morality and decency (e.g. adultery), against public peace, against government (e.g. treason).

See also Anticipatory offense; Civil offense; Continuing offense; Crime; Degrees of crime; Delict; Felony; Graded offense; Included offense; Index offenses; Joint offense; Lesser included offense; Misdemeanor; Multiple offenses; Petty offense; Same offense; Tort.

Continuing offense. A transaction or a series of acts set on foot by a single impulse, and operated by an unintermittent force, no matter how long a time it may occupy. Conspiracy is an example of a continuing offense.

Criminal offense. Includes misdemeanors as well as felonies. It is an offense which subjects the offender to imprisonment, and/or fine. See **Crime; Degrees of crime; Felony; Misdemeanor.**

Joinder of offenses. See **Joinder.**

Same offense. As used in a provision against double jeopardy, the term means the same crime, not the same transaction, acts, circumstances, or situation.

Second offense. One committed after conviction for a first offense. It is the previous conviction, and not the indictment, which is the basis of the charge of a second offense. People v. Boardman, 172 App.Div. 733, 159 N.Y.S. 577.

Offensive. In the law relating to nuisances and similar matters, this term means noxious, causing annoyance, discomfort, or painful or disagreeable sensations. In ordinary use, the term is synonymous with "obnoxious" and means objectionable, disagreeable, displeasing and distasteful.

Offensive and defensive league. In international law, a league binding the contracting powers not only to aid each other in case of aggression upon either of them by a third power, but also to support and aid each other in active and aggressive measures against a power with which either of them may engage in war.

Offensive language. Language adapted to give offense; displeasing or annoying language. See **Defamation; Libel; Slander.**

Offensive weapon. . As occasionally used in criminal law and statutes, a weapon primarily meant and adapted for attack and the infliction of injury, but practically the term includes anything that would come within the description of a "deadly" or "dangerous" weapon (q.v.).

Offer, *v.* To bring to or before; to present for acceptance or rejection; to hold out or proffer; to make a proposal to; to exhibit something that may be taken or received or not. To attempt or endeavor; to make an effort to effect some object, as, to offer to bribe; in this sense used principally in criminal law.

In trial practice, to "offer" evidence is to state its nature and purport, or to recite what is expected to be proved by a given witness or document, and demand its admission. See **Offer of proof.**

Offer, *n.* A proposal to do a thing or pay an amount, usually accompanied by an expected acceptance, counter-offer, return promise or act. A manifestation of willingness to enter into a bargain, so made as to justify another person in understanding that his assent to that bargain is invited and will conclude it. Restatement, Second, Contracts, § 24. A promise; a commitment to do or refrain from doing some specified thing in the future. The offer creates a power of acceptance permitting the offeree by accepting the offer to transform the offeror's promise into a contractual obligation. See also **Offer and acceptance.**

An attempt; endeavor.

With respect to securities, the price at which a person is ready to sell. Opposed to bid, the price at which one is ready to buy. See also **Offering.**

See also Bid; Counter offer; Firm offer; Issue; Offer and acceptance; Offer of proof; Promise; Proposal; Tender; Utter.

Irrevocable offer. One which may not be withdrawn after it has been communicated without the consent of the offeree.

Offer and acceptance. In a bilateral contract, the two elements which constitute mutual assent, a requirement of the contract. In a unilateral contract, the acceptance is generally the act or performance of the offeree, though, in most jurisdictions, a promise to perform is inferred if the offeree commences the undertaking and the offeror attempts to revoke before the offeree has had an opportunity to complete the act. See also **Offer; Parol evidence rule.**

Offeree. In contracts, the person to whom an offer is made by the offeror.

Offering. An issue of securities offered for sale to the public or private group. Securities offerings are generally of two types: primary (proceeds going to the company for some lawful purpose) and secondary (where the funds go to a person other than the company; *i.e.,* selling stockholders). Primary offerings are also termed "new issues" as they involve the issuance of securities not previously offered and sold. See also Issue; Letter of comment; Prospectus; Red herring; Registration statement; Secondary distribution; Secondary offering; Tombstone ad; Underwrite.

Interstate offerings. A public securities offering made or which may be made to residents of more than one state. Such offerings are regulated by federal securities laws and regulations.

Intrastate offerings. A restricted public securities offering which is made by an issuer organized under the laws of a state, doing its principal business in such state, and offered solely to bona fide residents of such state with substantially all of the proceeds of the offering remaining in the state.

Private offerings. An offering made to a limited number of persons, who are so well-informed concerning the affairs of a company, through the possession of information which would be found in a registration statement, that they do not require the protection afforded by the disclosure provisions of the Securities Act of 1933. Sale of unregistered stock which is exempt from securities laws. U. S. v. Custer Channel Wing Corp., D.C.Md., 247 F.Supp. 481, 487.

Public offerings. The offering of securities at random and in general to anyone who will buy, and whether solicited or unsolicited. Sale of stock to the public in contrast to a "private" offering or placement. Public offerings are generally regulated by federal and state laws and regulations.

Offering circular. An offering circular is required to be filed with the S.E.C. and distributed with any securities offerings. The content of such is similar to the prospectus *(q.v.)* and is governed by S.E.C. rules and regulations.

Offerings. In English ecclesiastical law, personal tithes payable by custom to the parson or vicar of a parish, either occasionally, as at sacraments, marriages, churching of women, burials, etc., or at constant times, as at Easter, Christmas, etc. See Oblation; Obventio.

Offering statement. See **Offering circular.**

Offer of compromise. An offer to settle a dispute or difference amicably for the purpose of avoiding a lawsuit and without admitting liability. A tender or offer to settle or compromise a claim. The fact that such offer has been made is generally not admissible at the trial of the action as an admission of liability but any admissions made during the negotiations leading up to the offer and compromise are admissible. See Fed.Evid. Rule 408.

Offer of judgment. See **Judgment.**

Offer of proof. At a trial or hearing, when an objection to a question has been sustained, the party aggrieved by the ruling may indicate for the record (out of the presence of the jury) the answer which would have been given if the question had not been excluded. The appellate court is then in a position to determine from the record the correctness of the ruling and the prejudice in its exclusion, if any. See Fed.Evid.Rule 103(a)(2).

Offeror. In contracts, the party who makes the offer and looks for acceptance from the offeree.

Offertorium /òfərtór(i)yəm/. In English ecclesiastical law, the offerings of the faithful, or the place where they are made or kept; the service at the time of the Communion.

Office. A right, and correspondent duty, to exercise a public trust. A public charge or employment. An employment on behalf of the government in any station or public trust, not merely transient, occasional, or incidental. The most frequent occasions to use the word arise with reference to a duty and power conferred on an individual by the government; and when this is the connection, "public office" is a usual and more discriminating expression. But a power and duty may exist without immediate grant from government, and may be properly called an "office;" as the office of executor. Here the individual acts towards legatees in performance of a duty, and in exercise of a power not derived from their consent, but devolved on him by an authority which *quoad hoc* is superior.

An "assigned duty" or "function." Synonyms are "post", "appointment", "situation", "place", "position", and "office" commonly suggests a position of (especially public) trust or authority. Also right to exercise a public function or employment, and to take the fees and emoluments belonging to it. A public charge or employment, and he who performs the duties of the office is an officer. Although an office is an employment, it does not follow that every employment is an office. A man may be employed under a contract, express or implied, to do an act, or to perform a service, without becoming an officer. But, if the duty be a continuing one, which is defined by rule prescribed by the government, which an individual is appointed by the government to perform, who enters upon the duties appertain to his status, without any contract defining them, it seems very difficult to distinguish such a charge or employment from an office, or the person who performs the duty from an officer. In the constitutional sense, the term implies an authority to exercise some portion of the sovereign power, either in making, executing, or administering the laws.

A place for the regular transaction of business or performance of a particular service.

As to various particular offices, see **Home office; Land offices; Public office,** etc.

County office. Public office filled by the electorate of the entire county.

Judicial office. See **Judicial.**

Lucrative office. See **Lucrative.**

Ministerial office. One which gives the officer little or no discretion as to the matter to be done, and requires him to obey mandates of a superior. It is a general rule that a judicial office cannot be exercised by a deputy, while a ministerial office may. See **Ministerial.**

Office audit. An audit by the Internal Revenue Service of a taxpayer's return which is conducted in the agent's office. It may be distinguished from a correspondence audit or a field audit.

Office copy. A copy or transcript of a deed or record or any filed document, made by the officer having it in custody or under his sanction, and by him sealed or certified.

Office grant. A designation of a conveyance made by some officer of the law to effect certain purposes, where the owner is either unwilling or unable to execute the requisite deeds to pass the title; such, for example, as a tax-deed.

Office hours. That portion of the day during which offices are usually open for the transaction of business.

Office of honor. See **Honor.**

Office of judge. In old English law, a criminal suit in an ecclesiastical court, not being directed to the reparation of a private injury, was regarded as a proceeding emanating from the *office of the judge,* and could be instituted by the mere motion of the judge. But, in practice, these suits were instituted by private individuals, with the permission of the judge or his surrogate; and the private prosecutor in any such case was, accordingly, said to "promote the office of the judge."

Principal office. The principal office of a corporation is its headquarters, or the place where the chief or principal affairs and business of the corporation are transacted. Usually it is the office where the company's books are kept, where its meetings of stockholders are held, and where the directors, trustees, or managers assemble to discuss and transact the important general business of the company; but no one of these circumstances is a controlling test. Synonymous with "principal place of business," being the place where the principal affairs of a corporation are transacted.

Public office. The right, authority, and duty created and conferred by law, by which for a given period, either fixed by law or enduring at the pleasure of the creating power, an individual is invested with some portion of the sovereign functions of government for the benefit of the public. An agency for the state, the duties of which involve in their performance the exercise of some portion of the sovereign power, either great or small.

State office. Public offices to be filled by the electorate of the entire state.

Office-block ballot. A form of ballot in which the names of candidates, with or without party designations, are grouped under the offices for which they are contesting; also called "Massachusetts" ballot.

Officer. Person holding office of trust, command or authority in corporation, government, armed services, or other institution or organization.

In corporations, a person charged with important functions of management such as president, vice president, treasurer, etc.

In determining whether one is an "officer" or "employee," important tests are the tenure by which a position is held, whether its duration is defined by the statute or ordinance creating it, or whether it is temporary or transient or for a time fixed only by agreement; whether it is created by an appointment or election, or merely by a contract of employment by which the rights of the parties are regulated; whether the compensation is by a salary or fees fixed by law, or by a sum agreed upon by the contract of hiring.

For definitions of the various classes and kinds of officers, see the titles Commissioned; Constitutional; Corporate; Executive; Fiscal; Judicial; Legislative; Ministerial; Municipal; Naval; Non-commissioned; Peace; Public; State; Subordinate.

Civil officer. The word "civil," as regards civil officers, is commonly used to distinguish those officers who are in public service but not of the military. Hence, any officer of the United States who holds his appointment under the national government, whether his duties are executive or judicial, in the highest or the lowest departments of the government, with the exception of officers of the armed services.

Military officer. Commissioned officer in armed services. Officer who has command in armed forces.

Officer de facto. As distinguished from an officer *de jure;* this is the designation of one who is in the actual possession and administration of the office, under some colorable or apparent authority, although his title to the same, whether by election or appointment, is in reality invalid or at least formally questioned. Norton v. Shelby County, 118 U.S. 425, 6 S.Ct. 1121, 30 L.Ed. 178. "Officer de facto" includes one whose duties of office are exercised under color of election or appointment by or pursuant to public, unconstitutional law, before same is adjudged to be such. Platte v. Dortch, 255 Ind. 157, 263 N.E.2d 266, 268.

Officer de jure. One who is in all respects legally appointed and qualified to exercise the office. One who is clothed with the full legal right and title to the office; he is one who has been legally elected or appointed to an office, and who has qualified himself to exercise the duties thereof according to the mode prescribed by law. Trost v. Tynatishon, 12 Ill.App.3d 406, 299 N.E.2d 14, 17.

Officer of justice. A general name applicable to all persons connected with the administration of the judicial department of government, but commonly used only of the class of officers whose duty is to serve the process of the courts, such as sheriffs, constables, bailiffs, marshals, sequestrators, etc.

Officer of the United States. An officer nominated by the President and confirmed by the senate or one who is appointed under an act of congress, by the President alone, a court of law, or a head of a department. U. S. v. Germaine, 99 U.S. 508, 25 L.Ed. 482; U. S. v. Mouat, 124 U.S. 303, 8 S.Ct. 505, 31 L.Ed. 463. See also **United States officer.**

Public officer. An officer of a public corporation; that is, one holding office under the government of a municipality, state, or nation. One occupying a public office created by law. One of necessary characteristics of "public officer" is that he performs public function for public benefit and in so doing he be vested with exercise of some sovereign power of state.

Warrant officer. Officer of armed forces, with rank between commissioned and non-commissioned officer, holding rank by virtue of warrant.

Officia judicialia non concedantur antequam vacent /əfísh(iy)ə jədìshiyéyl(i)yə nòn kònsədǽntər ǽntək-wəm véysənt/. Judicial offices should not be granted before they are vacant.

Official, *n.* An officer; a person invested with the authority of an office. See also **Officer.**

In *Canon law,* a person to whom a bishop commits the charge of his spiritual jurisdiction.

In *Civil law,* the minister or apparitor of a magistrate or judge.

Official, *adj.* Pertaining to an office; invested with the character of an officer; proceeding from, sanctioned by, or done by, an officer. Authorized act.

As to official Bond; Liquidator; Log Book; Newspaper; Oath; Use, see those titles.

Demi-official. Partly official or authorized. Having color of official right.

Official act. One done by an officer in his official capacity under color and by virtue of his office. Authorized act.

Official misconduct. Any unlawful behavior by a public officer in relation to the duties of his office, willful in its character, including any willful or corrupt failure, refusal, or neglect of an officer to perform any duty enjoined on him by law. See **Malfeasance; Misfeasance.**

Official bond. Type of fidelity bond required to be posted by certain public officials to indemnify the government, municipality or court in the event of defalcation by the officer.

Official Gazette. Weekly publication of U.S. Patent and Trademark Office containing patent and trademark notices and applications, as well as mark registrations.

Official immunity doctrine. Doctrine of "official immunity" provides that government officials enjoy an absolute privilege from civil liability should the activity in question fall within the scope of their authority and if the action undertaken requires the exercise of discretion, and this rule of immunity is not limited to the highest executive officers of the government. Watson v. Barker, D.C.Pa., 428 F.Supp. 590, 592.

Official map. In zoning and land use, the authorized map for the determination of proper land use in the city or town, showing the zones and areas and their authorized uses.

Official record. Fed.Evid.R. 803(8) provides, without regard to availability of the declarant, a hearsay exception for: "Records, reports, statements, or data compilations, in any form, of public offices or agencies . . . ." Proof of official records at trial is governed by Fed.R.Civil P. 44. Admissibility of official records at administrative proceedings is governed by the Official Records Act *(q.v.).* Official records are those kept in the performance of duty by an officer even if not specifically required by statute. State v. Biscoe, 112 Ariz. 98, 537 P.2d 968, 969.

Official Records Act. Federal statute applicable to cases in which the Federal Rules of Evidence do not apply *(i.e.* administrative proceedings) providing that books and records of account and minutes of any department or agency of the U.S. shall be admissible to prove the act or transaction as a memorandum of which it was made or kept. Properly authenticated copies are equally admissible with the originals. 28 U.S.C.A. § 1733(a).

Official reports or reporters. Publication of court decisions as directed by statute; *e.g.* United States Supreme Court Reports. See **Reports or reporters.**

Officialty. The court or jurisdiction of which an official is head.

Officia magistratus non debent esse vennalia /əfísh(iy)ə mǽjəstréydəs nòn débənt ésiy vənéyl(i)yə/. The offices of magistrates ought not to be sold.

Officiariis non faciendis vel amovendis /əfishiyériyəs nón fǽs(h)iyéndəs vèl èyməvéndəs/. A writ addressed to the magistrates of a corporation, requiring them not to make such a man an officer, or to put one out of the office he has, until inquiry is made of his manners, etc.

Officina justitiæ /òfəsáynə jə̀stíshiyiy/. The workshop or office of justice. The chancery was formerly so called. 3 Bl.Comm. 273.

Officio, ex, oath /ówθ éks əfísh(iy)ow/. An oath whereby a person may be obliged to make any presentment of any crime or offense, or to confess or accuse himself of any criminal matter or thing whereby he may be liable to any censure, penalty, or punishment. 3 Bl.Comm. 447.

Officious will /əfíshəs wíl/. A testament by which a testator leaves his property to his family. Inofficious testament.

Officit conatus si effectus sequatur /ófəsət kənéydəs sày əféktəs səkwéydər/. The attempt becomes of consequence, if the effect follows.

Of force. In force; extant; not obsolete; existing as a binding or obligatory power.

Offset. A deduction; a counterclaim; a contrary claim or demand by which a given claim may be lessened or canceled. An "offset" may be defined as a claim that serves to counterbalance or to compensate for another claim. Steinmeyer v. Warner Consolidated Corp., 42 Cal.App.3d 515, 116 Cal.Rptr. 57. See also **Counterclaim; Recoupment; Set-off.**

Type of entry in bookkeeping which counters the effect of a prior entry. See **Offset account.**

Offset account. In bookkeeping, a ledger account which has a corresponding account to be washed against it when the books are closed.

Offspring. Children; issue.

Of grace. This phrase had its origin in an age when kings dispensed their royal favors at the hands of chancellors. A term applied to any permission or license granted to a party in the course of a judicial proceeding which is not claimable as a matter of course or of right, but is allowed by the favor or indulgence of the court. See **Act of grace.**

Of record. Recorded; entered on the records; existing and remaining in or upon the appropriate records; *e.g.* a mortgage to be "of record" must normally be recorded in the county in which it is properly and legally recordable for purpose of constructive notice. Riley v. Commonwealth, 275 Ky. 370, 121 S.W.2d 921. See also **Attorney** (*Attorney of record*); **Court** (*Court of record*); **Record.**

Of right. As a matter of course. See **Of course; Right.**

Of the blood. A technical legal phrase meaning to be descended from the person referred to or from the same common stock and from a common ancestor. In re Easter's Estate, 24 Cal.2d 191, 148 P.2d 601.

Oil and gas lease. Grant of right to extract oil and/or gas from land.

O.K. A conventional symbol, of obscure origin much used in commercial practice and occasionally in indorsements on legal documents, signifying "correct," "approved," "accepted," "satisfactory," or "assented to."

Okay. The colloquial expression means correct, all right, to approve, and is of such common usage that it immediately conveys to the mind of person to whom it is addressed that a proposition submitted is agreed to. Muegler v. Crosthwait, 239 Mo.App. 801, 179 S.W.2d 761, 763. See also **O. K.**

Old Age, Survivors' and Disability Insurance. A system established under the Federal Social Security Act providing for retirement, disability, widows', widowers', and dependent benefits. Such program is funded by employer, employee and self-employed contributions. See **Social Security Administration.**

Old natura brevium /ówld nəchúrə bríyviyəm/. The title of a treatise written in the reign of Edward III, containing the writs which were then most in use, annexing to each a short comment concerning their nature and the application of them, with their various properties and effects.

Old tenures. A treatise, so called to distinguish it from Littleton's book on the same subject, which gives an account of the various tenures by which land was holden, the nature of estates, and some other incidents to landed property in the reign of Edward III. It is a very scanty tract, but has the merit of having led the way to Littleton's famous work.

Oleron, Laws of /lóz əv ówləròn/. A code of maritime laws published at the island of Oleron in the twelfth century by Eleanor of Guienne. They were adopted in England successively under Richard I, Henry III, and Edward III, and are often cited before the admiralty courts.

Oligarchy /óləgàrkiy/. A form of government wherein the administration of affairs is lodged in the hands of a few persons.

Oligopoly /òləgópəliy/. Economic climate existing where a few sellers sell only a standardized product. U. S. v. E. I. DuPont de Nemours & Co., D.C.Del., 118 F.Supp. 41, 49.

Olograph /óləgræf/. An instrument (*e.g.*, a will) wholly written by the person from whom it emanates. See **Holograph.**

Ombudsman /ómbədzmən/. An official or semi official office to which people may come with grievances connected with the government. The ombudsman stands between, and represents, the citizen before the government.

Ome bueno /ówmey bwéynow/. In Spanish law, a good man; a substantial person.

Omissio eorum quæ tacite insunt nihil operatur /əmísh(iy)ow iyórəm kwìy tǽsədiy ínsənt náy(h)əl òpərèydər/. The omission of those things which are tacitly implied is of no consequence.

Omission. The neglect to perform what the law requires. The intentional or unintentional failure to act which may or may not impose criminal liability depending upon the existence, vel non, of a duty to act under the circumstances. See also **Neglect.**

Omissis omnibus aliis negotiis /əmísəs ómnəbəs ǽliyəs nəgówshiyəs/. Lat. Laying aside all other businesses.

Omittance /əmítən(t)s/. Forbearance; omission.

Omne actum ab intentione agentis est judicandum /ómniy ǽktəm æb intènshiyówniy əjéntəs èst jùwdəkǽndəm/. Every act is to be judged by the intention of the doer.

Omne crimen ebrietas et incendit et detegit. Drunkenness both inflames (or aggravates) and reveals every crime.

Omne jus aut consensus fecit, aut necessitas constituit aut firmavit consuetudo /ómniy jós òt kənsén(t)səs fíysəd, òd nəsésətæs kənstíchuwət òt fərméyvət kònswət(y)úwdow/. Every right is either made by consent, or is constituted by necessity, or is established by custom.

Omne magis dignum trahit ad se minus dignum, quamvis minus dignum sit antiquius /ómniy méyjəs dígnəm træhəd æd síy máynəs dígnəm, kwǽmvis máynəs dígnəm sìd æntíkwiyəs/. Every worthier thing draws to it the less worthy, though the less worthy be the more ancient.

Omne magnum exemplum habet aliquid ex iniquo, quod publica utilitate compensatur /ómniy mǽgnəm əgzémpləm héybəd ǽləkwid èks ənáykwow, kwòd pə́bləkə yuwtìlətéydiy kòmpənséydər/. Every great example has some portion of evil, which is compensated by the public utility.

Omne majus continet in se minus /ómniy méyjəs kóntənəd in síy máynəs/. Every greater contains in itself the less. The greater always contains the less.

Omne majus dignum continet in se minus dignum /ómniy méyjəs dígnəm kóntənəd in síy máynəs dígnəm/. The more worthy contains in itself the less worthy.

Omne majus minus in se complectitur /ómniy méyjəs máynəs in síy kəmpléktədər/. Every greater embraces in itself the less.

Omne principale trahit ad se accessorium /ómniy prìn(t)səpéyliy trǽhəd æd síy ǽksesóriyəm/. Every principal thing draws to itself the accessory.

Omne quod solo inædificatur solo cedit /ómniy kwòd sówlow inèdəfəkéydər sówlow síydət/. Everything which is built upon the soil belongs to the soil.

Omne sacramentum debet esse de certa scientia /ómniy sǽkrəméntəm débəd ésiy dìy sə́rdə sayénsh(iy)ə/. Every oath ought to be of certain knowledge.

Omnes actiones in mundo infra certa tempora habent limitationem /ómniyz ækshiyówniyz ìn mándow ínfra sə́rdə témpərə héybənt lìmətèyshiyównəm/. All actions in the world are limited within certain periods.

Omnes homines aut liberi sunt aut servi /ómniyz hóməniyz òt líbəray sə́nt òt sə́rvay/. All men are freemen or slaves.

Omnes licentiam habere his quæ pro se indulta sunt, renunciare /ómniyz ləsénsh(iy)əm həbíriy hís kwìy pròw síy indáltə sònt rənənshiyériy/. [It is a rule of the ancient law that] all persons shall have liberty to renounce those privileges which have been conferred for their benefit.

Omnes prudentes illa admittere solent quæ probantur iis qui arte sua bene versati sunt /ómniyz pruwdéntiyz íla ədmídəriy sówlənt kwìy prəbǽntər áyəs kwày árdiy s(y)úwə bíyniy vərséyday sònt/. All prudent men are accustomed to admit those things which are approved by those who are well versed in the art.

Omnes sorores sunt quasi unus hæres de una hæreditate /ómniyz səróriyz sònt kwéysay yúwnəs híriyz dìy yùwnə hərèdətéydiy/. All sisters are, as it were, one heir to one inheritance.

Omne testamentum morte consummatum est /ómniy tèstəméntəm mórdiy kòn(t)səméydəm èst/. Every will is completed by death.

Omnia delicta in aperto leviora sunt /ómniyə dəlíktə in əpə́rdow lèviyórə sònt/. All crimes that are committed openly are lighter [or have a less odious appearance than those committed secretly].

Omnia performavit /ómniyə pə̀rforméyvət/. He has done all. In pleading. A good plea in bar where all the covenants are in the affirmative.

Omnia præsumuntur contra spoliatorem /ómniyə prìyz(y)əmántər kóntrə spòwl(i)yətórəm/. All things are presumed against a despoiler or wrongdoer.

Omnia præsumuntur legitime facta donec probetur in contrarium /ómniyə prìyz(y)əmántər ləjídəmiy fǽktə dównèk prowbíydər ìn kəntrériyəm/. All things are presumed to be lawfully done, until proof be made to the contrary.

Omnia præsumuntur rite et solemniter esse acta donec probetur in contrarium /ómniyə prìyz(y)əmántər ráydiy èt səlémnədər ésiy ǽktə dównək prəbíydər in kəntrériyəm/. All things are presumed to have been rightly and duly performed until it is proved to the contrary.

Omnia præsumuntur solemniter esse acta /ómniyə prìyz(y)əmántər səlémnədər ésiy ǽktə/. All things are presumed to have been done rightly.

Omnia presumuntur rite esse acta /ómniyə prìyz(y)əmántər ráydiy ésiy ǽktə/. A prima facie presumption of the regularity of the acts of public officers exists until the contrary appears.

Omnia quæ jure contrahuntur contrario jure pereunt /ómniyə kwìy júriy kòntrəhántər kəntrériyow júriy péhriyənt/. All things which are contracted by law perish by a contrary law.

Omnia quæ sunt uxoris sunt ipsius viri /ómniyə kwìy sònt əksórəs sònt ipsáyəs víray/. All things which are the wife's are the husband's.

Omnia rite acta præsumuntur /ómniyə ráydiy ǽktə prìyz(y)əmántər/. All things are presumed to have been rightly done.

Omnibus /ómnəbəs/. For all; containing two or more independent matters. Applied most commonly to a legislative bill which comprises more than one general subject. See **Omnibus bill.**

Omnibus ad quos præsentes literæ pervenerint, salutem /ómnəbəs æd kwóws prəzéntiyz lídəriy pərvénərənt səl(y)úwdəm/. To all to whom the present letters shall come, greeting. A form of address with which charters and deeds were anciently commenced.

Omnibus bill /ómnəbəs bíl/. A legislative bill including in one act various separate and distinct matters, and frequently one joining a number of different subjects in one measure in such a way as to compel the executive authority to accept provisions which he does not approve or else defeat the whole enactment.

In equity pleading, a bill embracing the whole of a complex subject-matter by uniting all parties in interest having adverse or conflicting claims, thereby avoiding circuity or multiplicity of action.

mnibus clause. Clause in a will or decree of distribution passing all property not specifically mentioned or known of at the time.

"Omnibus clause" in automotive liability policy extends coverage thereunder to person using automobile owned by named insured with express or implied permission of the latter. Uber v. Ohio Cas. Ins. Co., 247 Cal.App.2d 611, 55 Cal.Rptr. 720, 724.

mnibus hearing. Hearing at which there are many unrelated matters on the agenda for discussion and consideration.

mni exceptione majus /ómnay əksèpshiyównay méyjəs/. Above all exception.

mnis actio est loquela /ómnəs ǽksh(iy)ow èst lowkwíylə/. Every action is a plaint or complaint.

mnis conclusio boni et veri judicii sequitur ex bonis et veris præmissis et dictis juratorum /ómnəs kənklúwzh(iy)ow bównay èt víray jədíshiyay sékwədər èks bównəs èt vírəs prəmísəs èt díktəs jùrətórəm/. Every conclusion of a good and true judgment follows from good and true premises, and the verdicts of jurors.

mnis consensus tollit errorem /ómnəs kənsén(t)səs tóləd ehrórəm/. Every consent removes error. Consent always removes the effect of error.

mnis definitio in jure civili periculosa est, parum est enim ut non subverti possit /ómnəs dèfənísh(iy)ow ìn júriy sívəlay pərìkyəlówsə èst, pǽrəm èst énəm ət nòn səbvárday pósət/. Every definition in the civil law is dangerous, for there is very little that cannot be overthrown. (There is no rule in the civil law which is not liable to some exception; and the least difference in the facts of the case renders its application useless.)

mnis definitio in lege periculosa /ómnəs dèfənísh(iy)ow ìn líyjiy pərìkyəlówsə/. All definition in law is hazardous.

mnis exceptio est ipsa quoque regula /ómnəs əksépsh(iy)ow èst ípsə kwówkwiy régyələ/. Every exception is itself also a rule.

mnis indemnatus pro innoxis legibus habetur /ómnəs ìndemnéydəs pròw ənóksəs líyjəbəs həbíydər/. Every uncondemned person is held by the law as innocent.

mnis innovatio plus novitate perturbat quam ultilitate prodest /ómnəs ìnəvéysh(iy)ow plás nòvvətéydiy pərtárbət kwǽm yuwtilətéydiy prówdest/. Every innovation occasions more harm by its novelty than benefit by its utility.

mnis interpretatio si fieri potest ita fienda est in instrumentis, ut omnes contrarietates amoveantur /ómnəs əntàrprətéysh(iy)ow, sáy fáyəray pówdəst áydə fayéndə èst ìn instrəméntəs, əd ómniyz kəntrèriyətéydiyz əmòwviyǽntər/. Every interpretation, if it can be done, is to be so made in instruments that all contradictions may be removed.

Omnis interpretatio vel declarat, vel extendit, vel restringit /ómnəs əntàrprətéysh(iy)ow vél dəklérət, vél əksténdət, vél rəstrínjət/. Every interpretation either declares, extends, or restrains.

Omnis nova constitutio futuris formam imponere debet, non præteritis /ómnəs nówvə kònstət(y)úwsh(iy)ow fyəchúrəs fórməm impównəriy débət, nòn prətéhrədəs/. Every new statute ought to prescribe a form to future, not to past, acts.

Omnis persona est homo, sed non vicissim /ómnəs pərsównə èst hówmow sèd nón vəsísəm/. Every person is a man, but not every man a person.

Omnis privatio præsupponit habitum /ómnəs prəvéysh(iy)ow prìysəpównət hǽbədəm/. Every privation presupposes a former enjoyment. A "rule of philosophie" quoted by Lord Coke, and applied to the discontinuance of an estate.

Omnis quereia et omnis actio injuriarum limita est infra certa tempora /ómnəs kwəríylə èd ómnəs ǽksh(iy)ow ənjùriyérəm límədə èst ínfrə sárdə témpərə/. Every plaint and every action for injuries is limited within certain times.

Omnis ratihabitio retrotrahitur et mandato priori æquiparatur /ómnəs rædəhæbísh(iy)ow rètrowtrǽhədər èt mændéydow prayóray èkwəpəréydər/. Every ratification relates back and is equivalent to a prior authority.

Omnis regula suas patitur exceptiones /ómnəs régyələ s(y)úwəs pǽdədər əksèpshiyówniyz/. Every rule is liable to its own exceptions.

Omnium /ómniyəm/. In mercantile law, a term used to express the aggregate value of the different stock in which a loan is usually funded.

Omnium contributione sarciatur quod pro omnibus datum est /ómniyəm kòntrəbyùwshiyówniy sàrshiyéydər kwòd pròw ómnəbəs déydəm èst/. That which is given for, all is recompensed by the contribution of all. A principle of the law of general average.

Omnium rerum quarum usus est, potest esse abusus, virtute solo excepta /ómniyəm rírəm kwérəm yúwsəs èst, powdəst esɪy əbyuwsəs, vərtyùwdiy sówlow əksepsha/. There may be an abuse of everything of which there is a use, virtue only excepted.

On. Upon; as soon as; near to; along; along side of; adjacent to; contiguous to; at the time of; following upon; in; during; at or in contact with upper surface of a thing.

On account. In part payment; in partial satisfaction of an account. The phrase is usually contrasted with "in full."

On account of whom it may concern. When a policy of insurance expresses that the insurance is made "on account of whom it may concern," it will cover all persons having an insurable interest in the subject-matter at the date of the policy and who were then contemplated by the party procuring the insurance.

On all fours. A phrase used to express the idea that a case at bar is in all points similar to another. The one is said to be on all fours with the other when the facts are similar and the same questions of law are involved.

O.N.B. An abbreviation for "Old Natura Brevium."

On call. There is no legal difference between an obligation payable "when demanded" or "on demand" and one payable "on call" or "at any time called for." In each case the debt is payable on demand. See **On demand.**

Once a mortgage, always a mortgage. This rule or maxim signifies that an instrument originally intended as a mortgage, and not a deed, cannot be converted into anything else than a mortgage by any subsequent clause or agreement.

Once in jeopardy. A phrase used to express the condition of a person charged with crime, who has once already, by legal proceedings, been put in danger of conviction and punishment for the same offense. See also **Jeopardy.**

Oncunne. L. Fr. Accused.

On default. In case of default; upon failure of stipulated action or performance; upon the occurrence of a failure, omission, or neglect of duty.

On demand. Note payable on request. If no due date is stated in note, such is payable on demand. Instruments payable "on demand" include those payable at sight or on presentation and those in which no time for payment is stated. U.C.C. § 3–108.

One person, one vote. State legislative districting which gives equal legislative representation to all citizens of all places. The rule was established in Reynolds v. Sims, 377 U.S. 533, 568, 84 S.Ct. 1362, 1385, 12 L.Ed.2d 506, which required that the seats in both houses of a bicameral state legislature be apportioned on a population basis. Gray v. Sanders, 372 U.S. 368, 83 S.Ct. 801, 9 L.Ed.2d 821; Wesberry v. Sanders, 376 U.S. 1, 84 S.Ct. 526, 11 L.Ed.2d 481; Baker v. Carr, 369 U.S. 186, 82 S.Ct. 691, 7 L.Ed.2d 663. See also **Reapportionment.**

Onerando pro rata portionis /ownərǽndow pròw réydə pòrshiyównəs/. A writ that lay for a joint tenant or tenant in common who was distrained for more rent than his proportion of the land comes to.

Onerari non /ównəréray nòn/. In pleading, the name of a plea, in an action of debt, by which the defendant says that he ought not to be charged.

Oneratio /ównəréysh(iy)ow/. Lat. A lading; a cargo.

Oneratur nisi /ównəréydər náysay/. See **O. Ni.**

Oneris ferendi /ównərəs fərénday/. Lat. In the civil law, the servitude of support; a servitude by which the wall of a house is required to sustain the wall or beams of the adjoining house.

Onerous /ównərəs/. A contract, lease, share, or other right is said to be "onerous" when the obligations attaching to it unreasonably counterbalance or ex-

ceed the advantage to be derived from it, either absolutely or with reference to the particular possessor Unreasonably burdensome or one-sided. See **Unconscionability.**

As used in the civil law and in the systems derived from it (French, Scotch, Spanish, Mexican), the term also means based upon, supported by, or relating to a good and valuable consideration, i.e., one which imposes a burden or charge in return for the benefit conferred.

Onerous contract. See **Contract.**

Onerous gift. A gift made subject to certain charges imposed by the donor on the donee.

Onerous title. A title acquired by the giving of a valuable consideration, as the payment of money or rendition of services or the performance of conditions or assumption or discharge of liens or charges.

One sided. See **Unconscionability.**

One year. A calendar year, regardless of whether it be a leap year or otherwise. Douglas v. Acacia Mut Life Ins. Co., Tex.Civ.App., 118 S.W.2d 643.

On file. Filed; entered or placed upon the files; existing and remaining upon or among the proper files

O.Ni. In old English practice it was the course of the exchequer, as soon as the sheriff entered into and made up his account for issues, amerciaments, etc., to mark upon each head "O. Ni.," which denoted *oneratur, nisi habeat sufficientem exonerationem,* and presently he became the king's debtor, and a *debet* was set upon his head; whereupon the parties *paravaile* became debtors to the sheriff, and were discharged against the king, etc.

Only. Solely; merely; for no other purpose; at no other time; in no otherwise; along; of or by itself; without anything more; exclusive; nothing else or more.

Onomastic /ònəmǽstək/. A term applied to the signature of an instrument, the body of which is in a different handwriting from that of the signature.

On or about. A phrase used in reciting the date of an occurrence or conveyance, or the location of it to escape the necessity of being bound by the statement of an exact date, or place; approximately; about; without substantial variance from; near.

As used in statutes making it an offense to carry a weapon "on or about" the person, it is generally held that the word "on" means connected with or attached to, and that "about" is a comprehensive term having a broader meaning than "on," and conveying the idea of being nearby, in close proximity, within immediate reach, or conveniently accessible.

On or before. These words, inserted in a stipulation to do an act or pay money, entitle the party stipulating to perform at any time before the day; and upon performance, or tender and refusal, he is immediately vested with all the rights which would have attached if performance were made on the day.

Onset date. A term of art used by the Social Security Administration that marks the commencement of a period of disability for purposes of disability payments. Michalak v. Weinberger, D.C.Tex., 416 F.Supp. 1213, 1214.

On the person. In common parlance, when it is said that someone has an article on his person, it means that it is either in contact with his person or is carried in his clothing. See also **On or about.**

Onus /ównəs/. Lat. A burden or load; a weight. Burden of responsibility or proof. The lading, burden, or cargo of a vessel. A charge; an incumbrance. *Cum onere (q.v.),* with the incumbrance.

Onus episcopale /ównəs əpìskəpéyliy/. Ancient customary payments from the clergy to their diocesan bishop, of synodals, pentecostals, etc.

Onus probandi /ównəs prəbǽnday/. Burden of proving; the burden of proof. The strict meaning of the term *"onus probandi"* is that, if no evidence is adduced by the party on whom the burden is cast, the issue must be found against him.

OPEC. Organization of Petroleum Exporting Countries.

Ope consilio /ówpiy (èt) kənsíl(i)yow/. Lat. By aid and counsel. A civil law term applied to accessaries, similar in import to the "aiding and abetting" of the common law. Often written *"ope et consilio."*

Open, *v.* To render accessible, visible, or available; to submit or subject to examination, inquiry, or review, by the removal of restrictions or impediments.

Open a case. In practice, to open a case is to begin it; to make an initiatory explanation (*i.e.* opening statement) of its features to the court, jury, referee, etc., by outlining the nature of the occurrence or transaction on which it is founded, the questions involved, and the character and general course of the evidence to be adduced. See also **Opening statement of counsel.**

Open a commission. To enter upon the duties under a commission, or commence to act under a commission. Thus, in England the judges of assize and *nisi prius* derived their authority to act under or by virtue of commissions directed to them for that purpose; and, when they commenced acting under the powers so committed to them, they were said to open the commissions; and the day on which they so commenced their proceedings was as such termed the "commission day of the assizes".

Open a court. To open a court is to make a formal announcement, usually by the crier or bailiff, that its session has now begun and that the business before the court will be proceeded with.

Open a judgment. To lift or relax the bar of finality and conclusiveness which it imposes so as to permit a re-examination of the merits of the action in which it was rendered. This is done at the instance of a party showing good cause why the execution of the judgment would be inequitable. It so far annuls the judgment as to prevent its enforcement until the final determination upon it. Fed.R.Civil P. 60 governs relief from judgment because of mistakes, inadvertence, excusable neglect, newly discovered evidence, fraud, etc.

Open a rule. To restore or recall a rule which has been made absolute to its conditional state, as a rule *nisi,* so as to readmit of cause being shown against the rule. Thus, when a rule to show cause has been made absolute under a mistaken impression that no counsel had been instructed to show cause against it, it is usual for the party at whose instance the rule was obtained to consent to have the rule opened, by which all the proceedings subsequent to the day when cause ought to have been shown against it are in effect nullified, and the rule is then argued in the ordinary way.

Open a street or highway. To establish it by law and make it passable and available for public travel.

Open the door. If one party to litigation puts in evidence part of document or correspondence or conversation which is detrimental to the opposing party, the latter may introduce balance of document, correspondence or conversation in order to explain or rebut adverse inferences which might arise from the fragmentary or incomplete character of evidence introduced by his adversary. This is known as Rule of Completeness. U. S. v. Corrigan, C.C.A.N.Y., 168 F.2d 641, 645. See also Fed.Evid. R. 106.

Open, *adj.* Patent; visible; apparent; notorious; not clandestine; not closed, settled, fixed, or terminated.

As to open Corporation; Entry; Insolvency; Lewdness; Policy; Possession; Verdict, see those titles.

Open account. Type of credit extended by a seller to buyer which permits buyer to make purchases without a note or security and it is based on an evaluation of the buyer's credit. A contractual obligation which may be modified by subsequent agreement of the parties, either by expressed assent or implied from the conduct of the parties, provided the agreement changing the contractual obligation is based upon independent consideration. Bloch v. Fedak, 210 Kan. 63, 499 P.2d 1052, 1054. See also **Open credit; Open-end credit.**

Open and notorious. Acts on the land of another sufficient to alert the owner of a claim to his land which may ripen into title under adverse possession. See also **Adverse possession.**

Behavior which is "open and notorious" for purposes of statute prohibiting adultery is behavior which is prominent, conspicuous and generally known and recognized by the public. The prohibition of open and notorious adultery is meant to protect the public from conduct which disturbs the peace, tends to promote breaches of the peace, and openly flouts accepted standards of morality in the community. People v. Cessna, 1 Ill.Dec. 433, 42 Ill.App.3d 746, 356 N.E.2d 621, 623.

Open bid. An offer to perform a contract, generally of a construction nature, in which the bidder reserves the right to reduce his bid to compete with a lower bid.

Open bulk. In the mass; exposed to view; not tied or sealed up.

Open court. This term may mean either a court which has been formally convened and declared open for the transaction of its proper judicial business, or a court which is freely open to spectators.

Open credit. Line of credit extended up to a certain amount by a merchant, bank or supplier so as to permit borrowings or purchases to such amount without posting security or reestablishing credit limit. See also **Open account; Open-end credit.**

Open-end contract. Contract which permits buyer to make purchases over a period of time without change in the price or terms by the seller.

Open-end credit. Credit cards and "revolving charges" where one can pay a part of what he owes each month on several different purchases. For purposes of Truth in Lending Act, "open end credit plan" is one in which credit terms are initially established with the opening of the account, but no fixed amount of debt is incurred at that time with purchases made from time to time instead being added to the outstanding balance in the account; each new purchase represents an additional extension of credit. Goldman v. First Nat. Bank of Chicago, C.A.Ill., 532 F.2d 10, 17.

Open-end investment company. A mutual fund which will buy back its shares at net asset value and which is continuously offering to sell new shares to the public. See **Mutual fund.**

Open-end investment trust. Type of trust in which the trustees are permitted to make on-going investments for its portfolio.

Open-end mortgage. A mortgage that allows the borrowing of additional sums, usually providing that at least the stated ratio of assets to the debt must be maintained. A mortgage which provides for future advances on the given mortgage and increases the amount of the existing mortgage.

Open-end transaction. Generic term to describe a loose transaction in which the parties may add to or amend the original bargain or agreement. It may include an open-end mortgage or open-end credit arrangement.

Opening statement of counsel. Outline or summary of nature of case and of anticipated proof presented by counsel to jury at start of trial. Speer v. Shipley, 149 Kan. 15, 85 P.2d 999, 1001. Its purpose is to advise the jury of facts relied upon and of issues involved, and to give jury a general picture of the facts and the situations so that jury will be able to understand the evidence. State v. Erwin, 101 Utah 365, 120 P.2d 285, 313.

Open letter of credit. An unrestricted letter of credit which will be paid on a simple draft without the need of documentary title. See also **Letter of credit.**

Open listing. A type of listing contract whereby any agent who has a right to participate in the open listing is entitled to a commission if he produces the sale.

Open mortgage clause. See **Union mortgage clause.**

Open order. An order to buy securities or commodities at or below or above a certain price and such order remains viable until canceled by the customer.

Open price term. The parties if they so intend can conclude a contract for sale even though the price is not settled. In such a case the price is a reasonable price at the time for delivery if: (a) nothing is said as to price; or (b) the price is left to be agreed by the parties and they fail to agree; or (c) the price is to be fixed in terms of some agreed market or other standard as set or recorded by a third person or agency and it is not so set or recorded. U.C.C. § 2-305.

Open sea. The expanse and mass of any great body of water, as distinguished from its margin or coast, its harbors, bays, creeks, inlets.

Open season. That portion of the year wherein the laws for the preservation of game and fish permit the killing of a particular species of game or the taking of a particular variety of fish.

Open shop. A business in which union and non-union workers are employed indiscriminately. Business in which union membership is not a condition of securing or maintaining employment. See **Right-to-work laws.**

Open space. Any parcel or area of land or water essentially unimproved and set aside, dedicated, designated or reserved for public or private use or enjoyment or for the use and enjoyment of owners and occupants of land adjoining or neighboring such open spaces.

Common open space. An open space area within or related to a site designated as a development and designed and intended for the use or enjoyment of residents and owners of the development. Common open space may contain such complementary structures and improvements as are necessary and appropriate for the use or enjoyment of residents and owners of the development.

Open union. A labor union without restrictive membership provisions. See also **Open shop.**

Operarii /òpərériyay/. Such tenants, under feudal tenures, as held some little portions of land by the duty of performing bodily labor and servile works for their lord.

Operate. To perform a function, or operation, or produce an effect. See **Operation.**

Operating expenses. Those expenses required to keep the business running, e.g. rent, electricity, heat. Expenses incurred in the course of ordinary activities of an entity.

Operating margin. Net operating income divided by sales for the period.

Operating profit. Deducting the cost of goods sold from sales gives gross profit. Deducting the operating expense (overhead) from the gross profit gives the operating profit.

Operatio /òpəréysh(iy)ow/. One day's work performed by a tenant for his lord.

Operation. Exertion of power; the process of operating or mode of action; an effect brought about in accordance with a definite plan; action; activity. In surgical practice, the term may be defined as an act or succession of acts performed upon the body of a patient, for his relief or restoration to normal conditions, by the use of surgical instruments as distinguished from therapeutic treatment by the administration of drugs or other remedial agencies.

Operation of law. This term expresses the manner in which rights, and sometimes liabilities, devolve upon a person by the mere application to the particular transaction of the established rules of law, without the act or co-operation of the party himself.

Operative. A workman; a laboring man; an artisan; particularly one employed in factories. Secret agent or detective.

Operative part. That part of a conveyance, or of any instrument intended for the creation or transference of rights, by which the main object of the instrument is carried into effect. It is distinguished from introductory matter, recitals, formal conclusion, etc.

Operative words. In a deed or lease, such are the words which effect the transaction intended to be consummated by the instrument.

Operis novi nuntiatio /ópərəs nówvay nənshiyéysh(iy)ow/. Lat. In the civil law, a protest or warning against [of] a new work.

Opetide /ówptàyd/. The ancient time of marriage, from Epiphany to Ash-Wednesday.

Ophthalmologist /òfθælmóləjəst/. One who is skilled in, or practices, ophthalmology. Practice of "oculists" and "ophthalmologists" has relation to practice of medicine and surgery in treatment of diseases of eye, while practice of "optometry" relates to measurement of powers of vision and adaptation of lenses for aid thereof. See **Oculist.**

Opiate. Any substance having an addiction-forming or addiction-sustaining liability similar to morphine or being capable of conversion into a drug having addiction-forming or addiction-sustaining liability.

OPIC. Overseas Private Investment Corporation.

Opinio est duplex, scilicet, opinio vulgaris, orta inter graves et discretos, et quæ vultum veritatis habet; et opinio tantum orta inter leves et vulgares homines, absque specie veritatis /əpín(i)yow èst d(y)úwpleks síləsət əpín(i)yow vəlgérəs, órdə íntər gréyviyz èt dəskríydows, èt kwìy vóltəm vèhrətéydəs héybət; èd əpín(i)yow tǽntəm, órdə íntər líyviyz èt vəlgériyz hóməniyz, ǽbskwiy spíyshiy(iy) vèhrətéydəs/. Opinion is of two kinds, namely, common opinion, which springs up among grave and discreet men, and which has the appearance of truth, and opinion which springs up only among light and foolish men, without the semblance of truth.

Opinion. A document prepared by an attorney for his client, embodying his understanding of the law as applicable to a state of facts submitted to him for that purpose; *e.g.* an opinion of an attorney as to the marketability of a land title as determined from a review of the abstract of title and other public records.

The statement by a judge or court of the decision reached in regard to a cause tried or argued before them, expounding the law as applied to the case, and detailing the reasons upon which the judgment is based.

An expression of the reasons why a certain decision (the judgment) was reached in a case. A *majority* opinion is usually written by one judge and repre-

sents the principles of law which a majority of his colleagues on the court deem operative in a given decision; it has more precedential value than any of the following. A *separate opinion* may be written by one or more judges in which he or they concur in or dissent from the majority opinion. A *concurring opinion* agrees with the result reached by the majority, but disagrees with the precise reasoning leading to that result. A *dissenting or minority opinion* disagrees with the result reached by the majority and thus disagrees with the reasoning and/or the principles of law used by the majority in deciding the case. A *plurality opinion* is agreed to by less than a majority as to the reasoning of the decision, but is agreed to by a majority as to the result. A *per curiam opinion* is an opinion "by the court" which expresses its decision in the case but whose author is not identified. A *memorandum opinion* is a holding of the whole court in which the opinion is very concise.

See also **Advisory opinion; Letter ruling; Majority opinion; Plurality; Slip opinion.**

Opinion evidence or testimony. Evidence of what the witness thinks, believes, or infers in regard to facts in dispute, as distinguished from his personal knowledge of the facts themselves. The rules of evidence ordinarily do not permit witnesses to testify as to opinions or conclusions. An exception to this rule exists as to "expert witnesses". Witnesses who, by education and experience, have become expert in some art, science, profession, or calling, may state their opinions as to relevant and material matter, in which they profess to be expert, and may also state their reasons for the opinion.

By expert witness. If scientific, technical, or other specialized knowledge will assist the trier of fact to understand the evidence or to determine a fact in issue, a witness qualified as an expert by knowledge, skill, experience, training, or education, may testify thereto in the form of an opinion or otherwise. Fed. Evid. Rule 702. See also **Expert witness.**

By lay witness. If the witness is not testifying as an expert, his testimony in the form of opinions or inferences is limited to those opinions or inferences which are (a) rationally based on the perception of the witness and (b) helpful to a clear understanding of his testimony or the determination of a fact in issue. Fed.Evid. Rule 701.

Opinio quæ favet testamento est tenenda /əpín(i)yow kwìy féyvət tèstəméntow èst tənéndə/. The opinion which favors a will is to be followed.

Opium /ówpiyəm/. Drug consisting of inspissated juice of opium poppy.

Oportet quod certæ personæ, terræ, et certi status comprehendantur in declaratione usuum /əpórdət kwòd sárdiy pərsówniy, téhriy èt sárday stéydəs kòmprəhendǽntər in dèklərèyshiyówniy yúwsyuwəm/. It is necessary that given persons, lands, and estates should be comprehended in a declaration of uses.

Oportet quod certa res deducatur in donationem /əpórdət kwòd sárdə ríyz dìyd(y)əkéydər in dənèyshiyównəm/. It is necessary that a certain thing be brought into the gift, or made the subject of the conveyance.

Oportet quod certa res deducatur in judicium /əpórdət kwòd sə́rdə ríyz dìyd(y)əkéydər in jədísh(iy)əm/. A thing certain must be brought to judgment.

Oportet quod certa sit res quæ venditur /əpórdət kwòd sə́rdə sit rí‌yz kwìy véndədər/. It is necessary that there should be a certain thing which is sold. To make a valid sale, there must be certainty as to the thing which is sold.

Oppignerare /əpìgnərériy/. Lat. In the civil law, to pledge.

Opposer /əpówzər/. An officer formerly belonging to the green-wax in the exchequer.

Opposite. An old word for "opponent."

Opposite party. Within statutes providing that opposite party shall be incompetent to testify as to matters equally within knowledge of deceased is one whose personal and financial interests, either immediate or remote, are antagonistic to like interests of protected party.

Opposition. Act of opposing or resisting; antagonism; state of being opposite or opposed; antithesis. Also, a position confronting another or placing in contrast; that which is or furnishes an obstacle to some result. Political party opposed to ministry or administration; or might be construed to include peaceful and orderly opposition to government.

Oppression. The misdemeanor committed by a public officer, who under color of his office, wrongfully inflicts upon any person any bodily harm, imprisonment, or other injury. An act of cruelty, severity, unlawful exaction, or excessive use of authority. An act of subjecting to cruel and unjust hardship; an act of domination. See **Coercion; Cruelty; Threat.**

Oppressor. A public officer who unlawfully uses his authority by way of oppression (q.v.).

Opprobrium /əprówbriyəm/. In the civil law, ignominy; infamy; shame.

Optimacy /óptəməsiy/. Nobility; men of the highest rank.

Optima est legis interpres consuetudo /óptəmə èst líyjəs əntárpriyz kònswət(y)úwdow/. Custom is the best interpreter of the law.

Optima est lex quæ minimum relinquit arbitrio judicis; optimus judex qui minimum sibi /óptəmə èst léks kwày mínəməm rəlíŋkwəd arbítriyow júwdəsəs; óptəməs júwdeks kwày mínəməm síbay/. That law is the best which leaves least to the discretion of the judge; that judge is the best who leaves least to his own. That system of law is best which confides as little as possible to the discretion of the judge; that judge the best who relies as little as possible on his own opinion.

Optimam esse legem, quæ minimum relinquit arbitrio judicis; id quod certitudo ejus præstat /óptəməm ésiy líyjəm kwày mínəməm rəlíŋkwəd arbítriyow júwdəsəs; id kwòd sə́rdət(y)úwdow íyjəs préstæt/. That law is the best which leaves the least discretion to the judge; and this is an advantage which results from its certainty.

Optima statuti interpretatrix est (omnibus particuli ejusdem inspectis) ipsum statutum /óptəmə stətyúw‌day intàrprətéytræks èst (ómnəbəs partíkyələs iyjásdəm inspéktəs) ípsəm stətyúwdəm/. The best interpreter of a statute is (all its parts being considered) the statute itself.

Optimus interpres rerum usus /óptəməs əntárpriyz rírəm yúwsəs/. Use or usage is the best interpreter of things.

Optimus interpretandi modus est sic leges interpretar ut leges legibus concordant /óptəməs intàrprətǽnday mówdəs èst sík líyjiyz intàrprətéray àt líyjiyz líyjəbəs kəŋkórdənt/. The best mode of interpretation is so to interpret laws that they may accord with each other.

Optimus judex, qui minimum sibi /óptəməs júwdeks, kwày mínəməm síbay/. He is the best judge who relies as little as possible on his own discretion.

Optimus legum interpres consuetudo /óptəməs líygəm əntárpriyz kònswət(y)úwdow/. Custom is the best interpreter of the laws.

Option. A right, which acts as a continuing offer, given for consideration, to purchase or lease property at an agreed upon price and terms, within a specified time. An option is an agreement which gives the optionee the power to accept an offer for a limited time. Kelman v. Bohi, 27 Ariz.App. 24, 550 P.2d 671, 675. An option to purchase or to sell is not a contract to purchase or sell, as optionee has the right to accept or to reject the offer, in accordance with its terms, and is not bound. Catmull v. Johnson, Utah, 541 P.2d 793, 795. Right of election to exercise a privilege.

A privilege existing in one person, for which he has paid money, which gives him the right to *buy* certain commodities or certain specified securities from another person, if he chooses, at any time within an agreed period, at a fixed price, or to *sell* such commodities or securities to such other person at an agreed price and time. If the option gives the choice of buying or not buying, it is denominated a "call." If it gives the choice of selling or not, it is called a "put." If it is a combination of both these, and gives the privilege of *either* buying or selling or not, it is called a "straddle" or a "spread eagle."

The sale or exchange of an option to buy or sell property results in capital gain or loss if the property is a capital asset.

See also **Call; Cash value option; Local option; Put.**

Commodity futures option. The right—but not the obligation—to buy or sell a futures contract at a specified price within a fixed period, say, three, six, nine months or longer. The option buyer pays a premium to the dealer for this right, plus the usual commission and nothing else. The option buyer does not have to be concerned about margin calls. All he can lose is the premium paid and commission.

Commodity option. The commodity option is, in theory, no different from the more familiar types of option contracts relating to real estate, securities or personal services. Essentially, an option is a right that is purchased by the option holder entitling him either to buy from or to sell to the grantor of the option the subject of the option at a stated price and within a stated time. In the case of a commodity option, the right pertains to an underlying physical commodity (such as a specific quantity of gold, a train carload of coffee, etc.) or to a commodity futures contract relating to that commodity. The price paid for the option right is referred to as the "premium," and the price at which the option purchaser is entitled to buy or sell the underlying commodity for futures contract is referred to as the "striking price." "Exercise" is the decision of an option holder to require performance by the grantor of his obligation with respect to the underlying commodity or futures contract. The period during which an option may be exercised is specified in the contract and may range from one day to as long as 18 months. The "exercise date" or "expiration date" is the final day on which the option holder may exercise the option.

Naked options. Options sold by investors granting others the right to buy stock from them even though they own no stock to back up those commitments.

Stock option. The right to buy stock in the future at a price fixed in advance. See also **Stock.**

> *Non-qualified stock option.* Stock option which does not meet the qualifications of a restricted stock option. See *Restricted stock option,* below.

> *Restricted stock option.* The right to buy stock in the future at a fixed price established in advance but restricted as to the percentage of market price, time within which it may be exercised, the amount of stock owned by the optionee, non-transferability and minimum holding time. I.R.C. § 424.

Optional writ. In old English practice, that species of original writ, otherwise called a *"præcipe,"* which was framed in the alternative, commanding the defendant to do the thing required, *or* show the reason wherefore he had not done it.

Optionee. One who receives an option.

Option to purchase. A bilateral contract in which one party is given the right to buy the property within a period of time for a consideration paid to the seller. A right acquired by contract to accept or reject a present offer within a limited or reasonable time and is simply a contract by which the owner of property agrees with another person that he shall have the right to buy his property at a fixed price within a certain time. Crockett v. Lowther, Wyo., 549 P.2d 303, 308. See also **Option.**

Opus /ówpəs/. Lat. Work; labor; the product of work or labor.

Opus locatum /ówpəs lowkéydəm/. The product of work let for use to another; or the hiring out of work or labor to be done upon a thing.

Opus manificum /ówpəs mænəfísh(iy)əm/. In old English law, labor done by the hands; manual labor; such as making a hedge, digging a ditch.

Opus novum /ówpəs nówvəm/. In the civil law, a new work. By this term was meant something newly built upon land, or taken from a work already erected. He was said *opus novum facere* (to make a new work) who, either by building or by taking anything away, changed the former appearance of a work.

Or, *n.* A term used in heraldry, and signifying gold; called "sol" by some heralds when it occurs in the arms of princes, and "topaz" or "carbuncle" when borne by peers. Engravers represent it by an indefinite number of small points.

Or, *conj.* A disjunctive particle used to express an alternative or to give a choice of one among two or more things. It is also used to clarify what has already been said, and in such cases, means "in other words," "to-wit," or "that is to say." The word "or" is to be used as a function word to indicate an alternative between different or unlike things. City of Toledo v. Lucas County Budget Commission, 33 Ohio St.2d 62, 294 N.E.2d 661, 663. In some usages, the word "or" creates a multiple rather than an alternative obligation; where necessary in interpreting an instrument, "or" may be construed to mean "and." Atchison v. City of Englewood, Colo., 568 P.2d 13, 18.

Oraculum /ərækyələm/. In the civil law, the name of a kind of response or sentence given by the Roman emperors.

Oral. Uttered by the mouth or in words; spoken, not written.

Oral argument. Presentation of reasons for affirmance, reversal, modification, etc. by appellee and appellant before appellate court; generally limited in time by court rule; *e.g.* Fed.R.App.P. 34.

Oral confession. Statement given orally by defendant in which he admits the commission of the crime. Its admissibility in evidence is dependent upon its voluntariness, the condition of the defendant at the time of the confession, the length of time during which the defendant was held by the police before being brought before a magistrate and other factors. Federal courts generally hold that the burden of establishing the constitutional admissibility of a confession rests upon the prosecution. Pea v. United States, 130 U.S.App.D.C. 66, 397 F.2d 627. See also **Confession; Miranda Rule.**

Oral contract. One which is partly in writing and partly depends on spoken words, or none of which is in writing; one which, so far as it has been reduced to writing, is incomplete or expresses only a part of what is intended, but is completed by spoken words; or one which, originally written, has afterwards been changed orally.

Oral evidence. Evidence given by word of mouth; the oral testimony of a witness. See **Parol evidence.**

Oral pleading. Pleading by word of mouth, in the actual presence of the court. This was the ancient mode of pleading in England, and continued to the reign of Edward III.

Oral trust. The transfer of property in trust informally through an oral declaration in contrast to a formal trust which is in writing. Real estate trusts may not be created orally.

Oral will. See **Nuncupative will.**

Orando pro rege et regno /ərændow pròw ríyjiy èt régnow/. An ancient writ which issued, while there was no standing collect for a sitting parliament, to pray for the peace and good government of the realm.

Orator. The plaintiff in a cause or matter in chancery, when addressing or petitioning the court, used to style himself "orator," and, when a woman, "oratrix." But these terms have long gone into disuse, and the customary phrases now are "plaintiff" or "petitioner."

In Roman law, the term denoted an advocate.

Oratrix /əréytrəks/. A female petitioner; a female plaintiff in a bill of chancery was formerly so called. This term is obsolete.

Orbation /orbéyshən/. Deprivation of one's parents or children, or privation in general.

Orcinus libertus /órsənəs ləbárdəs/. Lat. In Roman law, a freedman who obtained his liberty by the direct operation of the will or testament of his deceased master was so called, being the freedman of the deceased (*orcinus*), not of the *hæres*.

Ordain. To institute or establish; to make an ordinance; to enact a constitution or law. To confer on a person the holy orders of priest or deacon.

Ordeal. The most ancient species of trial, in Saxon and old English law, being peculiarly distinguished by the appellation of *"judicium Dei,"* or "judgment of God," it being supposed that supernatural intervention would rescue an innocent person from the danger of physical harm to which he was exposed in this species of trial. The ordeal was of two sorts,—either fire ordeal or water ordeal; the former being confined to persons of higher rank, the latter to the common people.

Fire ordeal. The ordeal by fire or red-hot iron, which was performed either by taking up in the hand a piece of red-hot iron, of one, two, or three pounds weight, or by walking barefoot and blindfolded over nine red-hot plowshares, laid lengthwise at unequal distances.

Water ordeal. In Saxon and old English law, the ordeal or trial by water. The *hot-water* ordeal was performed by plunging the bare arm up to the elbow in boiling water, and escaping unhurt thereby. The *cold-water* ordeal was performed by casting the person suspected into a river or pond of cold water, when, if he floated therein, without any action of swimming it was deemed an evidence of his guilt; but, if he sunk, he was acquitted. 4 Bl.Comm. 343.

Ordeffe, or **ordelfe** /órdelf/. A liberty whereby a man claims the ore found in his own land; also, the ore lying under land.

Ordels /ordíylz/. In old English law, the right of administering oaths and adjudging trials by ordeal within a precinct or liberty.

Order. A mandate; precept; command or direction authoritatively given; rule or regulation. Brady v. Interstate Commerce Commission, D.C.W.Va., 43 F.2d 847, 850. Direction of a court or judge made or entered in writing, and not included in a judgment. An application for an order is a motion.

A designation of the person to whom a bill of exchange or negotiable promissory note is to be paid. An "order" is a direction to pay and must be more than an authorization or request. It must identify the person to pay with reasonable certainty. It may be addressed to one or more such persons jointly or in the alternative but not in succession. U.C.C. § 3–102(b).

Term is also used to designate a rank, class, or division of men; as the order of nobles, order of knights, order of priests, etc.

See also Appealable order; Decree; Decision; Executive order; Intermediate order; Judgment; Limit order; Payable to order; Percentage order; Restraining order.

Agreed order. See **Appeal.**

Day order. Order from a customer to a broker to buy or sell a security on the particular day and such order is automatically cancelled at the end of that day.

Decretal order. In chancery practice, an order made by the court of chancery, in the nature of a decree, upon a motion or petition. An order in a chancery suit made on motion or otherwise not at the regular hearing of a cause, and yet not of an interlocutory nature, but finally disposing of the cause, so far as a decree could then have disposed of it.

Discretionary order. An order from a customer to a broker to sell a security at a price deemed acceptable by the broker.

Final order. One which either terminates the action itself, or finally decides some matter litigated by the parties, or operates to divest some right; or one which completely disposes of the subject-matter and the rights of the parties. See also **Final decision rule.**

General orders. Orders or rules of court, promulgated for the guidance of practitioners and the regulation of procedure in general, or in some general branch of its jurisdiction; as opposed to a rule or an order made in an individual case. General orders have generally been replaced by rules of court.

Interlocutory order. An order which decides not the cause, but only settles some intervening matter relating to it or affords some temporary relief (*e.g.* temporary restraining order).

Limit order. An order from a customer to a broker in which the customer places a lower limit on the price at which the security may be sold and a ceiling on the price at which the security may be bought.

Market order. An order from a customer to a broker to buy or to sell a security at the market price then prevailing and hence the order must be executed promptly.

Money order. See **Money.**

Open order. An order from a customer to a broker to buy or to sell a security and the order remains in force until it is either executed or cancelled by the customer.

Percentage order. See that title.

Restraining order. An order which may issue upon the filing of an application for an injunction forbidding the defendant to do the threatened act until a hearing on the application can be had. Though the term is sometimes used as a synonym of "injunction," a restraining order is properly distinguishable from an injunction, in that the former is intended only as a restraint upon the defendant until the propriety of granting an injunction, temporary or perpetual, can be determined, and it does no more than restrain the proceedings until such determination. Fed.R. Civil P. 65.

Speaking order. An order which contains matter which is explanatory or illustrative of the mere direction which is given by it is sometimes thus called.

Stop order. Order to stockbroker to wait until the market price of the particular security reaches a specified figure, and then to "stop" the transaction by either selling or buying, as the case may be, as well as possible.

Stop payment order. Order from the drawer of a check to the drawee bank to stop payment on a check which has been drawn and given to the payee or lost.

Order bill of lading. A negotiable bill of lading directing that the goods be delivered to the person named or his order upon indorsement.

Order nisi. A provisional or conditional order, allowing a certain time within which to do some required act, on failure of which the order will be made absolute.

Order of coif. See **Coif.**

Order of filiation. An order made by a court or judge having jurisdiction, fixing the paternity of a bastard child upon a given man, and requiring him to provide for its support.

Orders. The directions as to the course and purpose of a voyage given by the owner of the vessel to the captain or master. For other meanings, see **Order.**

Order to show cause. See **Show cause order.**

Ordinance. A rule established by authority; a permanent rule of action; a law or statute. In its most common meaning, the term is used to designate the enactments of the legislative body of a municipal corporation. An ordinance is the equivalent of a municipal statute, passed by the city council, or equivalent body, and governing matters not already covered by federal or state law. Ordinances commonly govern zoning, building, safety, etc. matters of municipality.

The name has also been given to certain enactments, more general in their character than ordinary statutes, and serving as organic laws, yet not exactly to be called "constitutions." Such was the "Ordinance for the government of the North-West Territory," enacted by congress in 1787.

See also **Municipal ordinance.**

Ordinance of 1647. A law passed by the Colony of Massachusetts, still in force, in a modified form, whereby the state owns the great ponds within its confines, which are held in trust for public uses. Watuppa Reservoir Co. v. Fall River, 147 Mass. 548, 18 N.E. 465.

Ordinance of 1787. A statute for the government of the Northwest Territory. Religious and legal freedom, encouragement of education, just treatment of the Indians, the future division into States, and the exclusion of slavery were ordained.

Ordinandi lex /ɔ̀rdənǽnday léks/. Lat. The law of procedure, as distinguished from the substantial part of the law.

Ordinarius ita dicitur quia habet ordinariam jurisdictionem, in jure proprio, et non propter deputationem /ɔ̀rdənériyəs áydə dísədər kwáyə héybət ɔ̀rdənériyəm jùrəsdìkshiyównəm ìn júriy prówpriyow èt nón próptər dèpyətèyshiyównəm/. The ordinary is so called because he has an ordinary jurisdiction in his own right, and not a deputed one.

Ordinary, n. At common law, one who had exempt and immediate jurisdiction in causes ecclesiastical. Also a bishop; and an archbishop is the ordinary of the whole province, to visit and receive appeals from inferior jurisdictions. Also a commissary or official of a bishop or other ecclesiastical judge having judicial power; an archdeacon; officer of the royal household.

In American law, a judicial officer, in several of the states, clothed by statute with powers in regard to wills, probate, administration, guardianship, etc. See also **Court of Ordinary.**

Former term for a public house where food and lodging were furnished to the traveler and his beast, at fixed rates, open to whoever may apply for accommodation, and where intoxicating liquor was sold at retail.

In the civil law, a judge who has authority to take cognizance of causes in his own right, and not by deputation.

Ordinary, adj. Regular; usual; normal; common; often recurring; according to established order; settled; customary; reasonable; not characterized by peculiar or unusual circumstances; belonging to, exercised by, or characteristic of, the normal or average individual.

As to ordinary Care; Diligence; Negligence, see those titles.

Ordinary calling. Those things which are repeated daily or weekly in the course of business.

Ordinary care. That degree of care which ordinarily prudent and competent person engaged in same line of business or endeavor should exercise under similar circumstances, and in law means same as "due care" and "reasonable care." Warner v. Kiowa County Hospital Authority, Okl.App., 551 P.2d 1179, 1188. That care which reasonably prudent persons exercise in the management of their own affairs, in order to avoid injury to themselves or their property, or the persons or property of others. Ordinary care is not an absolute term, but a relative one. That is to say, in deciding whether ordinary care was exercised in a given case, the conduct in question must be viewed in the light of all the surrounding circumstances, as shown by the evidence in the case. See also **Care.**

Ordinary course of business. The transaction of business according to the usages and customs of the commercial world generally or of the particular community or (in some cases) of the particular individual whose acts are under consideration. Term used in connection with sales made by a merchant as part of his regular business and in contrast with a sale in bulk which is regulated by statute, *e.g.* U.C.C. § 6–102(1). In general, any matter which transpires as a matter of daily custom in business.

Ordinary dangers incident to employment. Those commonly and usually pertaining to and incident to it, which a reasonably prudent person might anticipate, and do not include danger by acts of negligence, unless habitual and known to the servant.

Ordinary expenses. Common and accepted in the general industry or type of activity in which the taxpayer is engaged. It comprises one of the tests for the deductibility of expenses incurred or paid in connection with a trade or business; for the production or collection of income; for the management, conservation, or maintenance of property held for the production of income; or in connection with the determination, collection, or refund of any tax. I.R.C. §§ 162(a) and 212. See also **Necessary.**

Ordinary income. For income tax purposes, reportable income not qualifying as capital gains. Term used to describe income taxed at ordinary rates in contrast to income taxed at the more advantageous rates of capital gains. Term embraces income from regular sources such as wages, commissions, interest, dividends and the like.

Ordinary loss. In taxation, a loss which does not qualify as a capital loss.

Ordinary negligence. The failure to use that degree of care which the ordinary or reasonably prudent person would have used under the circumstances and for which the negligent person is liable. Term is used in contradistinction to gross negligence which is more serious and a more flagrant lack of care. See also **Negligence,** and *Ordinary care, supra.*

Ordinary persons. Men of ordinary care and diligence in relation to any particular thing.

Ordinary proceeding. Such a proceeding as was known to the common law and was formerly conducted in accordance with the proceedings of the common-law courts, and as is generally known under the current Rules of Civil Procedure and Codes to be such a proceeding as is started by the issuance of a summons, and results in a judgment enforceable by execution.

Ordinary repairs. Such as are necessary to make good the usual wear and tear or natural and unavoidable decay and keep the property in good condition. Compare **Improvements.**

Ordinary risks. Those incident to the business, and do not imply the result of the employer's negligence. The expression "extraordinary risks" is generally used to describe risks arising from the negligence of the employer, and they are generally held not to be assumed unless known or obvious.

Ordinary seaman. A sailor who is capable of performing the ordinary or routine duties of a seaman, but who is not yet so proficient in the knowledge and practice of all the various duties of a sailor at sea as to be rated as an "able" seaman.

Ordinary services of administrators include all the services incident to the closing and distribution of an estate, and not merely the receiving and disbursing of the funds and to justify an allowance of further compensation the administrator must have rendered services of an extraordinary character necessary to the protection of the estate, and, if he employs another to perform services which he is required to perform under the law, he cannot charge such services as an expense of administration.

Ordinary skill in an art. That degree of skill which men engaged in that particular art usually employ; not that which belongs to a few men only, of extraordinary endowments and capacities.

Ordinary written law. Law made, within constitutional restrictions, by the Legislature; *i.e.* statutes

Ordination. Ceremony by which a bishop confers on a person the privileges and powers necessary for the execution of sacerdotal functions in the church.

Ordinatum est /òrdənéydəm èst/. In old practice, it is ordered. The initial words of rules of court when entered in Latin.

Ordine placitandi servato, servatur et jus /órdəniy plæsətǽnday sərvéydow, sərvéydər èt jús/. When the order of pleading is observed, the law also is observed.

Ordines /órdəniyz/. A general chapter or other solemn convention of the religious of a particular order.

Ordinis beneficium /órdənəs bènəfísh(iy)əm/. Lat. In the civil law, the benefit or privilege of order; the privilege which a surety for a debtor had of requiring that his principal should be discussed, or thoroughly prosecuted, before the creditor could resort to him.

Ordo attachiamentorum /órdow ətæch(iy)əmèntórəm/. In old English practice, the order of attachments.

Ordo judiciorum /órdow jədìshiyórəm/. In the canon law, the order of judgments; the rule by which the due course of hearing each cause was prescribed.

Ordonnance /òrdownón(t)s/órdənən(t)s/. Fr. In French law, an ordinance; an order of a court; a compilation or systematized body of law relating to a particular subject-matter, as, commercial law or maritime law. Particularly, a compilation of the law relating to prizes and captures at sea.

Ore-leave. A license or right to dig and take ore from land.

Ore tenus /óriy tíynəs/. Lat. By word of mouth; orally. Pleading was anciently carried on *ore tenus,* at the bar of the court. 3 Bl.Comm. 293.

Ore tenus rule. Under the "ore tenus rule," reviewing court must affirm the trial court unless its findings are plainly and palpably erroneous. Hamaker v. Hamaker, 57 Ala.App. 333, 328 So.2d 588, 592.

Orfgild /órfgìld/. In Saxon law, the price or value of a beast. A payment for a beast. The payment or forfeiture of a beast. A penalty for taking away cattle.

Organic Act. An act of Congress conferring powers of government upon a territory. In re Lane, 135 U.S. 443, 10 S.Ct. 760, 34 L.Ed. 219.

A statute by which a municipal corporation is organized and created is its "organic act" and the limit of its power, so that all acts beyond the scope of the powers there granted are void.

Organic law. The fundamental law, or constitution, of a state or nation, written or unwritten. That law or system of laws or principles which defines and establishes the organization of its government.

Organization. Organization includes a corporation, government or governmental subdivision or agency, business trust, estate, trust, partnership or association, two or more persons having a joint or common interest, or any other legal or commercial entity. U.C.C. § 1–201(28). See also **Charitable organizations.**

Organize. To establish or furnish with organs; to systematize; to put into working order; to arrange in order for the normal exercise of its appropriate functions. City of Beaumont v. City of Beaumont Independent School Dist., Tex.Civ.App., 164 S.W.2d 753, 756.

Organized county. A county which has its lawful officers, legal machinery, and means for carrying out the powers and performing the duties pertaining to it as a quasi municipal corporation. City of Beaumont v. City of Beaumont Independent School Dist., Tex.Civ. App., 164 S.W.2d 753, 757.

Organized labor. Segments of labor force represented by unions.

Orgild /órgìld/. In Saxon law, without recompense; as where no satisfaction was to be made for the death of a man killed, so that he was judged lawfully slain.

Original. Primitive; first in order; bearing its own authority, and not deriving authority from an outside source; as *original* jurisdiction, *original* writ, etc. As applied to documents, the original is the first copy or archetype; that from which another instrument is transcribed, copied, or imitated. See also *Original evidence, infra.*

In copyright law means that the work owes its creation or origin to the author and this in turn means that the work must not consist in actual copying. L. Batlin & Son Inc. v. Jeffrey Snyder and Etna Products Co. Inc., C.A.N.Y., 536 F.2d 486, 489.

Original bill. In equity pleading, a bill which relates to some matter not before litigated in the court by the same persons standing in the same interests. The ancient mode of commencing actions in the English court of King's bench. See **Bill.**

Original contractor. One who for a fixed price agrees with owner to perform certain work or furnish certain material.

Original conveyances. Those conveyances at common law, otherwise termed "primary," by which a benefit or estate is created or first arises; comprising feoffments, gifts, grants, leases, exchanges, and partitions. 2 Bl.Comm. 309.

Original entry. The first entry of an item of an account made by a merchant or other person in his account-books, as distinguished from entries posted into the ledger or copied from other books.

Original estates. See **Estate.**

Original evidence. An original document, writing, or other material object introduced in evidence as distinguished from a copy of it or from extraneous evidence of its content or purport.

An "original" of a writing or recording is the writing or recording itself or any counterpart intended to have the same effect by a person executing or issuing it. An "original" or a photograph includes the negative or any print therefrom. If data are stored in a computer or similar device, any printout or other output readable by sight shown to reflect the data accurately, is an "original". Fed.Evid.R. 1001. See also **Copy; Duplicate.**

Original inventor. In patent law, a pioneer in the art; one who evolves the original idea and brings it to some successful, useful and tangible result; as distinguished from an improver.

Original jurisdiction. Jurisdiction in the first instance. Jurisdiction to take cognizance of a cause at its inception, try it, and pass judgment upon the law and facts. Distinguished from *appellate* jurisdiction.

Original package. A package prepared for interstate or foreign transportation, and remaining in the same condition as when it left the shipper, that is, unbroken and undivided. A package of such form and size as is used by producers or shippers for the purpose of securing both convenience in handling and security in transportation of merchandise between dealers in the ordinary course of actual commerce. Austin v. Tennessee, 179 U.S. 343, 21 S.Ct. 132, 45 L.Ed. 224. See also **Original package doctrine.**

Original plat. The first plat of a town from the subsequent additions, and "original town" is employed in the same way.

Original process. See **Process.**

Original promise. An original promise, without the statute of frauds, is one in which the direct and leading object of the promisor is to further or promote some purpose or interest of his own, although the incidental effect may be the payment of the debt of another.

Original writ. See **Writ.**

Single original. An original instrument which is executed singly, and not in duplicate.

Original document rule. The best evidence of the contents of a document is the original of that document. The party bearing the burden of proving the contents of a document is required to introduce the original unless he is excused from its production because of its nonavailability and in this instance, secondary evidence is admissible. There are no degrees of secondary evidence. See also **Best evidence.**

Original grade doctrine. The "original-grade doctrine" relieves public body from any liability for property damaged in the reduction of the surface of the street to the grade line for the first time established. Dickson v. City of Pullman, 11 Wash.App. 813, 525 P.2d 838–841.

Originalia /ərìjənéyl(i)yə/. In old English law, transcripts sent to the remembrancer's office in the exchequer out of the chancery, distinguished from *recorda,* which contain the judgments and pleadings in actions tried before the barons. The treasurer-remembrancer's office was abolished in 1833.

Original issue. The first issue of stocks or bonds of a particular kind or series.

Original package doctrine. In Brown v. Maryland, 25 U.S. (12 Wheat.) 419, 6 L.Ed. 678, a landmark case under the commerce clause of the U.S.Const., the Supreme Court held that a state was free to levy a tax or license fee on imports only after the original package had been broken because at this juncture the goods no longer were in the flow of interstate commerce and therefore no longer subject to federal regulation.

Origine propria neminem posse voluntate sua eximi manifestum est /əríjəniy prówpriyə némənəm pósiy vòləntéydiy s(y)úwə mǽnəféstəm èst/. It is evident that no one is able of his own pleasure, to do away with his proper origin.

Origo rei inspici debet /óhrəgow ríyay ínspəsay débət/. The origin of a thing ought to be regarded.

Ornest. In old English law, the trial by battle, which does not seem to have been usual in England before the time of the Conqueror, though originating in the kingdoms of the north, where it was practiced under the name of *"holmgang,"* from the custom of fighting duels on a small island or *holm.*

ORP. Ordinary, reasonable and prudent (man). See "negligence". The standard of care on which negligence cases are based.

Orphan /órfən/. Any person (but particularly a minor or infant) who has lost both (or, sometimes, one) of his or her parents.

Orphanotrophi /òrfənətrówfay/. In the civil law, managers of houses for orphans.

Orphan's courts. Courts in several New England states with probate jurisdiction.

Orphan's deduction. Deduction from the taxable estate of the decedent permitted if the decedent does not have a surviving spouse, and is survived by a minor child who, immediately after the death of the decedent, has no known parent. The amount of the deduction is governed by I.R.C. § 2057.

Orwige, sine witâ. In old English law, without war or feud, such security being provided by the laws, for homicides under certain circumstances, against the *foehth,* or deadly feud, on the part of the family of the slain.

O.S. An abbreviation for "Old Style," or "Old Series."

OSHA. Occupational Safety and Health Act.

Ostendit vobis /osténdət vówbəs/. Lat. In old pleading, "shows to you." Formal words with which a demandant began his count.

Ostensible agency. An implied or presumptive agency, which exists where one, either intentionally or from want of ordinary care, induces another to believe that a third person is his agent, though he never in fact employed him. It is, strictly speaking, no agency at all, but is in reality based entirely upon estoppel.

Ostensible authority. Such authority as a principal, intentionally or by want of ordinary care, causes or allows a third person to believe that the agent possesses. National Cash Register Co. v. Wichita Frozen Food Lockers, Tex.Civ.App., 172 S.W.2d 781, 787.

Ostensible ownership. Apparent ownership derived from conduct or words. Theory of "ostensible ownership" estops an owner of property who clothes another with apparent title from later asserting his title against an innocent third party who has been induced to deal with apparent owner. Domarad v. Fisher & Burke, Inc., 270 Cal.App.2d 543, 76 Cal.Rptr. 529, 535.

Ostensible partner. One whose name appears to the world as such, though he have no interest in the firm.

Ostensio /osténsh(iy)ow/. A tax anciently paid by merchants, etc., for leave to show or expose their goods for sale in markets.

Osteopath /óstiyəpæθ/. One who practices osteopathy.

Osteopathy /òstiyópəθiy/. A system of complete medical practice based on the maintenance of proper relationships among the various parts of the body. Osteopathic physicians, licensed in all 50 states, employ manipulative therapy, drugs, surgery, x-ray, and all other accepted therapeutic methods in the treatment of disease and injury.

Osteopathic medicine focuses special attention on the biological mechanisms by which the musculoskeletal system, through the nervous and circulatory systems, interacts with all body organs and systems in both health and disease. D.O.S., or Doctors of Osteopathy, diagnose and treat disorders of the musculoskeletal system through palpation and appropriately applied manipulative procedures. See Holt v. College of Osteopathic Physicians and Surgeons, 61 Cal.2d 750, 40 Cal.Rptr. 244, 394 P.2d 932; Falcone v. Middlesex County Medical Society, 34 N.J. 582, 170 A.2d 791.

O.T.C. See **Over-the-counter market.**

Other. Different or distinct from that already mentioned; additional, or further. Following an enumeration of particular classes "other" must be read as "other such like," and includes only others of like kind and character.

Otherwise. In a different manner; in another way, or in other ways.

Othesworthe /ówθ(ə)swèrθ/. In Saxon law, oathsworth; oathworthy; worthy or entitled to make oath.

Ought. This word, though generally directory only, will be taken as mandatory if the context requires it.

Ounce. The twelfth part; the twelfth part of a pound troy or the sixteenth part of a pound avoirdupois.

Ourlop. The lierwite or fine paid to the lord by the inferior tenant when his daughter was debauched.

Oust. To put out; to eject; to remove or deprive; to deprive of the possession or enjoyment of an estate or franchise.

Ouster. A putting out; dispossession; amotion of possession. A species of injuries to things real, by which the wrong-doer gains actual occupation of the land, and compels the rightful owner to seek his legal remedy in order to gain possession. An "ouster" is a wrongful dispossession or exclusion of a party from real property and involves a question of intent. Hamilton v. MacDonald, C.A.Ariz., 503 F.2d 1138, 1146. Notorious and unequivocal act by which one cotenant deprives another of right to common and equal possession and enjoyment of property. Young v. Young, 37 Md.App. 211, 376 A.2d 1151, 1158.

Ouster le main /áwstər ləméyn/. L. Fr. Literally, out of the hand.

Ouster le mer /áwstər ləmér/. L. Fr. Beyond the sea; a cause of excuse if a person, being summoned, did not appear in court. Spurious form for "Oulter le mer".

Ouster of jurisdiction. A condition which exists when a court which once had jurisdiction over a matter ceases to retain its jurisdiction.

Outage. A tax or charge formerly imposed by the state of Maryland for the inspection and marking of hogsheads of tobacco intended for export. Turner v. Maryland, 107 U.S. 38, 2 S.Ct. 44, 27 L.Ed. 370.

Outbuilding. Something used in connection with a main building. A small building appurtenant to a main building, and generally separated from it; e.g. outhouse; storage shed. See also **Outhouse.**

Outcome test. In a diversity of citizenship action in the federal court, the result should be the same as if the action had been commenced in the state court. Guaranty Trust Co. of N. Y. v. York, 326 U.S. 99, 109, 65 S.Ct. 1464, 1470, 89 L.Ed. 2079.

Outer bar. In the English courts, barristers at law have been divided into two classes, viz., king's counsel, who are admitted within the bar of the courts, in seats specially reserved for themselves, and junior counsel, who sit without the bar; and the latter are thence frequently termed barristers of the "outer bar," or "utter bar," in contradistinction to the former class.

Outer continental shelf. All lands lying submerged seaward and not including lands beneath navigable waters. The subsoil and sea bed of such lands are subject to the jurisdiction and control of the United States. 43 U.S.C.A. § 1331.

Outer door. In connection with the rule, statutory or otherwise, forbidding an officer to break open the outer door to serve civil process, this term designates the door of each separate apartment, where there are different apartments having a common outer door.

Outfangthef /áwtfæŋθìyf/. A liberty or privilege in the ancient common law, whereby a lord was enabled to call any man dwelling in his manor, and taken for felony in another place out of his fee, to judgment in his own court. See **Infangenthef.**

Outgo. Expenditures.

Outhouse. A building subservient to, yet distinct from, the principal dwelling, located either within or without the curtilage. A smaller or subordinate building connected with a dwelling, usually detached from it and standing at a little distance from it, not intended for persons to live in, but to serve some purpose of convenience or necessity; as a barn, outside privy, a dairy, a toolhouse, and the like. Under statutes, such a building may be subservient to and adjoin a busi-

ness building as well as a dwelling house. See also **Outbuilding.**

Outland. The Saxon thanes divided their hereditary lands into inland, such as lay nearest their dwelling, which they kept to their own use, and outland, which lay beyond the demesnes, and was granted out to tenants, at the will of the lord, like copyhold estates. This outland they subdivided into two parts. One part they disposed among those who attended their persons, called "theodans," or lesser thanes; the other part they allotted to their husbandmen, or churls.

Outlaw. In English law, one who is put out of the protection or aid of the law. 3 Bl.Comm. 283, 284. Popularly, a person violating the law; a fugitive.

Outlawed. With reference to a debt means barred by the statute of limitations. Brady v. Tarr, 145 Pa.Super. 316, 21 A.2d 131, 133.

Outlawry. In old English law, a process by which a defendant or person in contempt on a civil or criminal process was declared an outlaw. If for treason or felony, it amounted to conviction and attainder.

In the United States, the process of outlawry seems to be unknown, at least in civil cases. Hall v. Lanning, 91 U.S. 160, 23 L.Ed. 271.

Outline. The line which marks the outer limits of an object or figure; an exterior line or edge; contour.

Outlot. In early American land law (particularly in Missouri), a lot or parcel of land lying outside the corporate limits of a town or village but subject to its municipal jurisdiction or control. Term now generally refers to an area of land on a plat which is to be used for a purpose other than a building site.

Out of benefit. A term descriptive of insurance policyholders who have been suspended for nonpayment of premiums.

Out-of-court settlement. The phrase is used with reference to agreements and transactions in regard to a pending suit which are arranged or take place between parties or their counsel privately and without being referred to the judge or court for authorization or approval. Thus, a case which is compromised, settled, and withdrawn by private agreement of the parties, after its institution, is said to be settled "out of court."

Out-of-pocket expenses. Said of an expenditure usually paid for with cash. An incremental cost.

Out-of-pocket loss. The difference between the value of what the purchaser parted with (i.e., the purchase price paid by him) and the value of what he has received (i.e., the actual market value of the goods). Otte v. Ron Tonkin Chevrolet Co., 264 Or. 265, 503 P.2d 716, 720.

Out-of-pocket rule. Determination for damages for fraudulent misrepresentations which permits recovery of difference between price paid and actual value of property acquired. Also called "out-of-pocket loss rule."

Out of term. At a time when no term of the court is being held; in the vacation or interval which elapses between terms of the court.

Out of the state. In reference to rights, liabilities, or jurisdictions arising out of the common law, this phrase is equivalent to "beyond sea" *(q.v.)*. In other connections, it means physically beyond the territorial limits of the particular state in question, or constructively so, as in the case of a foreign corporation. But a foreign corporation maintaining an agent within the state is not deemed to be "out of the state," within various statutes dealing with jurisdiction over foreign corporations "doing business" within state.

Out of time. A mercantile phrase applied to a ship or vessel that has been so long at sea as to justify the belief of her total loss. In another sense, a vessel is said to be *out of time* when, computed from her known day of sailing, the time that has elapsed exceeds the average duration of similar voyages at the same season of the year. The phrase is identical with "missing ship."

Outparters /áwtpàrtərz/. Stealers of cattle. A spurious form for "outputters".

Output contract. See **Contract; Entire output contract.**

Outrage. A grave injury; injurious violence. In general, any species of serious wrong offered to the person, feelings, or rights of another. Synonyms are affront, insult, and abuse. State ex rel. and to Use of Donelon v. Deuser, 345 Mo. 628, 134 S.W.2d 132, 133.

Outriders. In old English law, bailiffs-errant employed by sheriffs or their deputies to ride to the extremities of their counties or hundreds to summon men to the county or hundred court.

Outright. Free from reserve or restraint; direct; positive; down-right; altogether; entirely; openly.

Outroper /áwtròwpər/. A person to whom the business of selling by auction was confined by statute.

Outs. In banking parlance, are conditions or warranties, failure to comply with which by the prospect give the banker a right to escape from a contract and to terminate negotiations. Cray, McFawn & Co. v. Hegarty, Conroy & Co., D.C.N.Y., 27 F.Supp. 93, 100.

Outside. To the exterior of; without; outward from.

Outside director. A member of a corporate board of directors who is not a company officer and does not participate in the corporation's day-to-day management.

Outside salesmen. An outside salesman is one who solicits business away from the employer's place of business on a full-time basis. If an employee qualifies as an outside salesman, all employment related expenses are deductible.

Outstanding. Remaining undischarged; unpaid; uncollected; as an outstanding debt. Constituting an effective obligation. When said of stock, the shares issued less treasury stock. When said of checks, it means a check issued that did not clear the drawer's bank prior to the bank statement date.

Existing as an adverse claim or pretension; not united with, or merged in, the title or claim of the party; as an outstanding title.

Outstanding and open account. In legal and commercial transactions it is an unsettled debt arising from items of work and labor, goods sold and delivered, and other open transactions, not reduced to writing, and subject to future settlement and adjustment and usually disclosed by account books of the owner of the demand and does not include express contracts or obligations which have been reduced to writing such as bonds, bills of exchange, or notes. Lee v. De Forest, 22 Cal.App.2d 351, 71 P.2d 285, 291; Checotah Hardware Co. v. Housel, 169 Okl. 112, 35 P.2d 966, 967.

Outstroke. To mine by outstroke is to take out mineral from adjoining property through the tunnels and shafts of the demised premises.

Ouverture des successions /ùwvertyúr dey səksèsyówn/. In French law, the right of succession which arises to one upon the death, whether natural or civil, of another.

Ovell /ow(v)él/. L. Fr. Equal.

Ovelty /ów(v)əltiy/. In old English law, equality.

Over. Above; overhead; more than; in excess of.

Continued;—sometimes written on one page or sheet to indicate a continuation of matter on a separate page or sheet.

In conveyancing, the word is used to denote a contingent limitation intended to take effect on the failure of a prior estate. Thus, in what is commonly called the "name and arms clause" in a will or settlement there is generally a proviso that if the devisee fails to comply with the condition the estate is to go to some one else. This is a limitation or gift over.

Overawe /òwvəró/. To subjugate or restrain by awe, or profound reverence.

Overbreadth doctrine. Requirement that a statute be invalidated if it is fairly capable of being applied to punish people for constitutionally protected speech or conduct. A law is void on its face if it "does not aim specifically at evils within the allowable area of [government] control, but . . . sweeps within its ambit other activities that constitute an exercise" of protected expressive or associational rights. Thornhill v. Alabama, 310 U.S. 88, 97, 60 S.Ct. 296, 84 L.Ed. 460. A plausible challenge to a law as *void for overbreadth* can be made only when (1) the protected activity is a significant part of the law's target, and (2) there exists no satisfactory way of severing the law's constitutional from its unconstitutional applications so as to excise the latter clearly in a single step from the law's reach.

Overcharge. With respect to public carriers or public utilities, a charge collected above a lawful tariff rate; a charge of more than is permitted by law. As regards interest rates, see **Usury.**

Overcome. As used in a statute providing that a presumption may be overcome by other evidence, this term is not synonymous with overbalance or outweigh, but requires merely that such evidence counterbalance the presumption, where the party relying on it has the burden of proof.

Overcyted, or **overcyhsed.** Proved guilty or convicted.

Overdraft. A check written on a checking account containing less funds than the amount of the check. Term may also refer to the condition which exists when vouchers or purchase orders are drawn in amounts in excess of budgeted or appropriated amount. See also **Kiting.**

Overdraw. To draw upon a person or a bank in an amount in excess of the funds remaining to the drawer's credit with the drawee, or to an amount greater than what is due. See also **Overdraft.**

Overdue. Due and more than due; delayed or unpaid. Bliss v. California Co-op Producers, Cal.App., 156 P.2d 259, 260. A negotiable instrument or other evidence of debt is overdue when the day of its maturity is past and it remains unpaid.

A vessel is said to be overdue when she has not reached her destination at the time when she might ordinarily have been expected to arrive.

Overflowed lands. Those that are covered by nonnavigable waters (not including lands between high and low water mark of navigable streams or bodies of water, nor lands covered and uncovered by ordinary daily ebb and flow of normal tides of navigable waters).

Overhaul. To inquire into; to review; to disturb. To examine thoroughly, as machinery, with a view to repairs.

Overhead. All administrative or executive costs incident to the management, supervision, or conduct of the capital outlay, or business; distinguished from "operating charges," or those items that are inseparably connected with the productive end and may be seen as the work progresses, and are the subject of knowledge from observation. Continuous expenses of a business; the expenses and obligations incurred in connection with operation; expenses necessarily incurred in organization, office expenses, engineering, inspection, supervision, and management during construction; and general expenditures in financial or industrial enterprise which cannot be attributed to any one department or product, excluding cost of materials, labor, and selling. Guillot v. State Highway Commission of Montana, 102 Mont. 149, 56 P.2d 1072, 1075.

Any cost not specifically or directly associated with the production of identifiable goods and services. Sometimes called "burden" or "indirect costs" and, in Britain, "oncosts." Frequently limited to manufacturing overhead.

Overhernissa /òwvərhə́rnisə/. In Saxon law, contumacy or contempt of court.

Over-insurance. See **Double insurance.**

Overissue. To issue in excessive quantity; to issue in excess of fixed legal limits. Thus, "overissued stock" of a corporation is capital stock issued in excess of the amount limited and prescribed by the charter or certificate of incorporation. U.C.C. § 8–104(2). See also **Oversubscription.**

Overload. To cause to bear too heavy a burden; to load too heavily.

Overlying right. Right of owner of land to take water from ground underneath for use on his land within basin or watershed. Right is based on ownership of land and is appurtenant thereto. City of Pasadena v. City of Alhambra, 33 Cal.2d 908, 207 P.2d 17, 28.

Overplus. What is left beyond a certain amount; the residue; the surplus; the remainder of a thing.

Overrate. In its strictest signification, a rating by way of excess and not one which ought not to have been made at all.

Overreaching clause. In a resettlement, a clause which saves the powers of sale and leasing annexed to the estate for life created by the original settlement, when it is desired to give the tenant for life the same estate and powers under the resettlement. The clause is so called because it provides that the resettlement shall be overreached by the exercise of the old powers. If the resettlement were executed without a provision to this effect, the estate of the tenant for life and the annexed powers would be subject to any charges for portions, etc., created under the original settlement.

Override. An estate carved out of working interest under an oil or gas lease. Commissions paid to managers on sales made by subordinates. Provision in real estate brokers listing agreement giving him right to certain commission for a reasonable period of time after expiration of listing in event owner sells to purchaser with whom broker negotiated during term of listing.

Overriding royalty. As applied to an existing oil and gas lease is a given percentage of the gross production payable to some person other than the lessor or persons claiming under him. Royalty interest carved out of working interest created by oil and gas lease, and is interest in oil and gas produced at surface free of expense of production and its outstanding characteristic is that its duration is limited by duration of lease under which it is created. Cline v. Angle, 216 Kan. 328, 532 P.2d 1093, 1097.

Overrule. To supersede; annul; reverse; make void; reject by subsequent action or decision. A judicial decision is said to be overruled when a later decision, rendered by the same court or by a superior court in the same system, expresses a judgment upon the same question of law directly opposite to that which was before given, thereby depriving the earlier opinion of all authority as a precedent. The term is not properly applied to conflicting decisions on the same point by co-ordinate or independent tribunals. It also signifies that a majority of the judges of a court have decided against the opinion of the minority, in which case the minority judges are said to be overruled. See **Reverse; Vacate.**

To refuse to sustain, or recognize as sufficient, an objection made in the course of a trial, as to the introduction of particular evidence, etc.

Overs. In the meat packing business, the increase in the weight of meat resulting from salt put on it.

Oversamessa. In old English law, a forfeiture for contempt or neglect in not pursuing a malefactor.

Over sea. Beyond the sea; outside the limits of the state or country. See **Beyond the seas.**

Overseer /ówvərsì(yə)r/òwvərsíyər/. A superintendent or supervisor; a public officer whose duties involve general superintendence of routine affairs. Member of a University board. See also **Regent.**

Overseers of highways. The name given, in some of the states, to a board of officers of a city, township, or county, whose special function is the construction and repair of the public roads or highways.

Oversubscription. Condition which exists when there are more orders or subscriptions for corporate stock than can be issued. See also **Overissue.**

Overt. Open; manifest; public; issuing in action, as distinguished from that which rests merely in intention or design.

Market overt. See **Market.**

Overt act. An open, manifest act from which criminality may be implied. An outward act done in pursuance and manifestation of an intent or design. An open act, which must be manifestly proved.

An overt act essential to establish an attempt to commit a crime is an act done to carry out the intention, and it must be such as would naturally effect that result unless prevented by some extraneous cause. It must be something done that directly moves toward the crime, and brings the accused nearer to its commission than mere acts of preparation or of planning, and will apparently result, in the usual and natural course of events, if not hindered by extraneous causes, in the commission of the crime itself.

In reference to the crime of treason, and the provision of the federal Constitution that a person shall not be convicted thereof unless on the testimony of two witnesses to the same "overt act," the term means a step, motion, or action really taken in the execution of a treasonable purpose, as distinguished from mere words, and also from a treasonable sentiment, design, or purpose not issuing in action. It is an act in furtherance of the crime. One which manifests the intention of the traitor to commit treason.

An overt act which will justify the exercise of the right of self-defense is such as would manifest to the mind of a reasonable person a present intention to kill him or do him great bodily harm.

An overt act which completes crime of conspiracy to violate federal law is something apart from conspiracy and is an act to effect the object of the conspiracy, and need be neither a criminal act, nor crime that is object of conspiracy, but must accompany or follow agreement and must be done in furtherance of object of agreement. Marino v. United States, C.C.A.Cal., 91 F.2d 691, 694, 695.

Overtake. To come or catch up with in a course of motion. Ringwald v. Beene, 170 Tenn. 116, 92 S.W.2d 411, 413. To catch up with and pass.

Over-the-counter market. Purchases and sales of securities by brokers for themselves, between themselves, and for their customers rather than on an exchange. The over-the-counter market is the principal market for U.S. Government and municipal bonds.

Overtime. After regular working hours; beyond the regular fixed hours.

Overtime wage. Portion of wages paid employee for services rendered beyond regularly fixed working hours.

Overture. An opening; a proposal.

Overt word. An open, plain word, not to be misunderstood.

Owe. To be bound to do or omit something, especially to pay a debt. May also refer to a moral or social obligation.

Owelty /ówəltiy/. Equality; an equalization charge. This word is used in law in several compound phrases, as follows:

Owelty of exchange. A sum of money given, when two persons have exchanged lands, by the owner of the less valuable estate to the owner of the more valuable, to equalize the exchange.

Owelty of partition. A sum of money paid by one of two coparceners or co-tenants to the other, when a partition has been effected between them, but, the land not being susceptible of division into exactly equal shares, such payment is required to make the portions respectively assigned to them of equal value. The power to grant owelty has been exercised from the courts of equity from time immemorial.

Owelty of services. In the feudal law, the condition obtaining when there is lord, mesne, and tenant, and the tenant holds the mesne by the same service that the mesne holds over the lord above him.

Owing. Unpaid. A debt, for example, is owing while it is unpaid, and whether it be due or not.

Owling /áw(ə)liŋ/. In English law, the offense of transporting wool or sheep out of the kingdom; so called from its being usually carried on in the night. 4 Bl.Comm. 154.

Own. To have a good legal title; to hold as property; to have a legal or rightful title to; to have; to possess.

Owner. The person in whom is vested the ownership, dominion, or title of property; proprietor. He who has dominion of a thing, real or personal, corporeal or incorporeal, which he has a right to enjoy and do with as he pleases, even to spoil or destroy it, as far as the law permits, unless he be prevented by some agreement or covenant which restrains his right.

The term is, however, a nomen generalissimum, and its meaning is to be gathered from the connection in which it is used, and from the subject-matter to which it is applied. The primary meaning of the word as applied to land is one who owns the fee and who has the right to dispose of the property, but the term also includes one having a possessory right to land or the person occupying or cultivating it.

The term "owner" is used to indicate a person in whom one or more interests are vested for his own benefit. The person in whom the interests are vested has "title" to the interests whether he holds them for his own benefit or for the benefit of another. Thus the term "title," unlike "ownership," is a colorless word; to say without more that a person has title to certain property does not indicate whether he holds such property for his own benefit or as trustee. Restatement, Second, Trusts, § 2, Comment (d); Restatement of Property, § 10.

See also **Ownership.**

Beneficial owner. See **Beneficial owner;** also *Equitable owner,* below.

Equitable owner. One who is recognized in equity as the owner of property, because the real and beneficial use and title belong to him, although the bare legal title is vested in another, *e.g.,* a trustee for his benefit. One who has a present title in land which will ripen into legal ownership upon the performance of conditions subsequent. There may therefore be two "owners" in respect of the same property, one the nominal or legal owner, the other the beneficial or equitable owner. See also **Beneficial owner.**

General and beneficial owner. The person whose interest is primarily one of possession and enjoyment in contemplation of an ultimate absolute ownership; —not the person whose interest is primarily in the enforcement of a collateral pecuniary claim, and does not contemplate the use or enjoyment of the property as such. See also **Beneficial owner.**

General owner. He who has the primary or residuary title to it; as distinguished from a *special* owner, who has a special interest in the same thing, amounting to a qualified ownership, such, for example, as a bailee's lien. One who has both the right of property and of possession.

Joint owners. Two or more persons who jointly own and hold title to property, *e.g.,* joint tenants, and also partners and tenants in common. In its most comprehensive sense, the term embraces all cases where the property in question is owned by two or more persons regardless of the special nature of their relationship or how it came into being. An estate by entirety is a "joint ownership" of a husband and wife as at common law notwithstanding legislative enactments touching joint tenancy. Cullum v. Rice, 236 Mo.App. 1113, 162 S.W.2d 342, 344. See also **Joint estate; Tenancy.**

Legal owner. One who is recognized and held responsible by the law as the owner of property. In a more particular sense, one in whom the legal title to real estate is vested, but who holds it in trust for the benefit of another, the latter being called the "equitable" owner.

Part owners. Joint owners; co-owners; those who have shares of ownership in the same thing. See *Joint owners, supra.*

Record owner. This term, particularly used in statutes requiring notice of tax delinquency or sale, means the owner of record, not the owner described in the tax roll; the owner of the title at time of notice.

Reputed owner. One who has to all appearances the title to, and possession of, property; one who, from all appearances, or from supposition, is the owner of a thing. He who has the general credit or reputation of being the owner or proprietor of goods.

Riparian owner. See **Riparian.**

Sole and unconditional owner. An expression commonly used in fire insurance policies, in which the word "sole" means that no one else has any interest in the property as owner, and "unconditional" means that the quality of the estate is not limited or affected by any condition. To be "unconditional and sole," the interest or ownership of the insured must be completely vested, not contingent or conditional, nor in common or jointly with others, but of such nature that the insured must alone sustain the entire loss if the property is destroyed; and this is so whether the title is legal or equitable. It is sufficient to satisfy the requirements of "sole and unconditional ownership" that the insured is the sole equitable owner and has the full equitable title. It is enough that the insured is equitably entitled to immediate and absolute legal ownership. The term contemplates beneficial and practical proprietorship and not necessarily technical title.

Special owner. One who has a special interest in an article of property, amounting to a qualified ownership of it, such, for example, as a bailee's lien; as distinguished from the *general* owner, who has the primary or residuary title to the same thing. Some person holding property with the consent of, and as representative of, the actual owner.

Ownership. Collection of rights to use and enjoy property, including right to transmit it to others. Trustees of Phillips Exeter Academy v. Exeter, 92 N.H. 473, 33 A.2d 665, 673. The complete dominion, title, or proprietary right in a thing or claim. The entirety of the powers of use and disposal allowed by law.

The right of one or more persons to possess and use a thing to the exclusion of others. The right by which a thing belongs to some one in particular, to the exclusion of all other persons. The exclusive right of possession, enjoyment, and disposal; involving as an essential attribute the right to control, handle, and dispose.

Ownership of property is either absolute or qualified. The ownership of property is absolute when a single person has the absolute dominion over it, and may use it or dispose of it according to his pleasure, subject only to general laws. The ownership is qualified when it is shared with one or more persons, when the time of enjoyment is deferred or limited, or when the use is restricted. Calif.Civil Code, §§ 678–680.

There may be ownership of all inanimate things which are capable of appropriation or of manual delivery; of all domestic animals; of all obligations; of such products of labor or skill as the composition of an author, the goodwill of a business, trademarks and signs, and of rights created or granted by statute. Calif.Civil Code, § 655.

In the civil law, ownership is divided into *perfect* and *imperfect.* Ownership is perfect when it is perpetual, and when the thing is unincumbered with any real right towards any other person than the owner. On the contrary, ownership is imperfect when it is to terminate at a certain time or on a condition, or if the thing which is the object of it, being an immovable, is charged with any real right towards a third person; as a usufruct, use, or servitude. When an immovable is subject to a usufruct, the owner of it is said to possess the naked ownership. Civ.Code La. art. 490.

In connection with burglary, "ownership" means any possession which is rightful as against the burglar.

See also Equitable ownership; Exclusive ownership; Hold; Incident of ownership; Interest; Interval ownership; Ostensible ownership; Owner; Possession; Title.

Oxfild /óksfild/. In old English law, a restitution anciently made by a hundred or county for any wrong done by one that was within the same.

Oxgang. In old English law, as much land as an ox could till. A measure of land of uncertain quantity. In the north of England a division of a carucate. According to some, fifteen acres.

Oyer /óyər/. In old English practice, hearing; the hearing a deed read, which a party sued on a bond, etc., might pray or demand, and it was then *read* to him by the other party; the entry on the record being, *"et ei legitur in hœc verba"* (and it is read to him in these words). 3 Bl.Comm. 299.

A *copy* of a bond or specialty sued upon, given to the opposite party, in lieu of the old practice of reading it.

Oyer and terminer /óyər ən tə́rmənər/. A half French phrase applied in England to the assizes, which are so called from the commission of *oyer and terminer* directed to the judges, empowering them to "inquire, hear, and determine" all treasons, felonies, and misdemeanors. This commission is now issued regularly, but was formerly used only on particular occasions, as upon sudden outrage or insurrection in any place. In the United States, certain higher criminal courts were called "courts of oyer and terminer."

Oyer de record /óyər də rékərd/. A petition made in court that the judges, for better proof's sake, will hear or look upon any record.

Oyez /óyeyz/ °(t)s/. Hear ye. A word used in courts by the public crier to command attention when a proclamation is about to be made. Usually pronounced "O yes." 4 Bl.Comm. 340.

P

P.A. Professional Association.

Paage /péyəj/ In old English law, a toll for passage through another's land. The same as "pedage."

Pacare /pəkériy/. L. Lat. To pay.

Pacatio /pəkéysh(iy)ow/. Payment.

Pace. A measure of length containing two feet and a half, being the ordinary length of a step. The geometrical pace is five feet long, being the length of two steps, or the whole space passed over by the same foot from one step to another.

Paceatur /pèysiyéydər/. Lat. Let him be freed or discharged.

Pacification. The act of making peace between two hostile or belligerent states; reestablishment of public tranquillity.

Pacifist. One who seeks to maintain peace and to abolish war; one who refuses or is unwilling for any purpose to bear arms because of conscientious considerations, and who is disposed to encourage others in such refusal. U. S. v. Schwimmer, Ill., 279 U.S. 644, 49 S.Ct. 448, 451, 73 L.Ed. 889. A conscientious objector.

Paci sunt maxime contraria vis et injuria /péysay sənt mǽksəmiy kəntrériyə vís ed ənjúriyə/. Violence and injury are the things chiefly hostile to peace.

Pack. To decide by false appearances; to counterfeit; to delude; to put together in sorts with a fraudulent design. To pack a jury is to use unlawful, improper, or deceitful means to have the jury made up of persons favorably disposed to the party so contriving, or who have been or can be improperly influenced to give the verdict he seeks. The term imports the improper and corrupt selection of a jury sworn and impaneled for the trial of a cause.

Package. A bundle put up for transportation or commercial handling; a thing in form to become, as such, an article of merchandise or delivery from hand to hand. A parcel is a small package; "parcel" being the diminutive of "package." Each of the words denotes a thing in form suitable for transportation or handling, or sale from hand to hand. As ordinarily understood in the commercial world, it means a shipping package. See also **Parcel**.

Original package. See **Original**.

Packed parcels. The name for a consignment of goods, consisting of one large parcel made up of several small ones (each bearing a different address), collected from different persons by the immediate consignor (a carrier), who unites them into one for his own profit, at the expense of the railway by which they are sent, since the railway company would have been paid more for the carriage of the parcels singly than together.

Packing list. Document which contains the contents, weight and other information concerning the package to be shipped. It accompanies the package and is available for inspection.

Pact. A bargain; compact; agreement. An agreement between two or more nations or states usually less elaborate than a treaty but nearly equivalent thereto. See also **Compact; Pactum; Treaty**.

Nude pact. A translation of the Latin *"nudum pactum,"* a bare or naked pact, that is, a promise or agreement made without any consideration on the other side, which is therefore not enforceable.

Obligatory pact. In civil law, an informal obligatory declaration of consensus, which the Roman law refused to acknowledge.

Pact de non alienando /pǽkt dìy nón èyliyənǽndow/. An agreement not to alienate incumbered (particularly mortgaged) property. This stipulation, sometimes found in mortgages made in Louisiana, and derived from the Spanish law, binds the mortgagor not to sell or incumber the mortgaged premises to the prejudice of the mortgagee; it does not avoid a sale made to a third person, but enables the mortgagee to proceed directly against the mortgaged property in a proceeding against the mortgagor alone and without notice to the purchaser.

Pacta conventa quæ neque contra leges neque dolo malo inita sunt omni modo observanda sunt /pǽktə kənvéntə kwìy nékwiy kóntrə líyjiyz nékwiy dówlow mǽlow ínədə sònt ómnay mówdow òbzərvǽndə sònt/. Agreements which are not contrary to the laws nor entered into with a fraudulent design are in all respects to be observed.

Pacta dant legem contractui /pǽktə dǽnt líyjəm kəntrǽkchuway/. The stipulations of parties constitute the law of the contract. Agreements give the law to the contract.

998

Pacta privata juri publico derogare non possunt /pǽktə prayvéydə júray pə́bləkow dìyrəgériy non pósənt/. Private compacts cannot derogate from public right.

Pacta quæ contra leges constitutionesque, vel contra bonos mores fiunt, nullam vim habere, indubitati juris est /pǽktə kwìy kóntrə líyjiyz kònstət(y)ùwshiyəníyzkwiy, vèl kóntrə bównows móriyz fáyənt, nə́ləm vím həbíriy, indyùwbətéyday júrəs èst/. That contracts which are made against law or against good morals have no force is a principle of undoubted law.

Pacta quæ turpem causam continent non sunt observanda /pǽktə kwìy tə́rpəm kózəm kóntənənt nón sə̀nt òbzərvǽndə/. Agreements founded upon an immoral consideration are not to be observed.

Pacta sunt servanda /pǽktə sə̀nt sə̀rvǽndə/. Agreements (and stipulations) of the parties (to a contract) must be observed.

Pactio /pǽksh(iy)ow/. Lat. In the civil law, a bargaining or agreeing of which *pactum* (the agreement itself) was the result. It is used, however, as the synonym of *"pactum."*

Pactional /pǽkshənəl/. Relating to or generating an agreement; by way of bargain or covenant.

Pactions /pǽkshənz/. In international law, contracts between nations which are to be performed by a single act, and of which execution is at an end at once.

Pactis privatorum juri publico non derogatur /pǽktəs pràyvətórəm júray pə́bləkow nòn dìyrəgéydər/. Private contracts do not derogate from public law.

Pactitious /pǽktíshəs/. Settled by covenant.

Pacto aliquod licitum est, quod sine pacto non admittitur /pǽktow ǽləkwod lísədəm èst kwòd sáyniy pǽktow nòn ədmídədər/. By special agreement things are allowed which are not otherwise permitted.

Pactum /pǽktəm/. Lat. *Civil law.* A pact. An agreement or convention without specific name, and without consideration, which, however, might, in its nature, produce a civil obligation.

Roman law. With some exceptions, those agreements that the law does not directly enforce, but which it recognizes only as a valid ground of defense, were called *"pacta."* Those agreements that are enforced, in other words, are supported by actions, are called *"contractus."* The exceptions are few, and belong to a late period.

Nudum pactum. A bare or naked pact or agreement; a promise or undertaking made without any consideration for it, and therefore not enforceable.

Pactum commissorium /pǽktəm kòməsóriyəm/. An agreement of forfeiture.

Pactum constitutæ pecuniæ /pǽktəm kònstət(y)úwdiy pəkyúwniyiy/. In the Civil law, an agreement by which a person appointed to his creditor a certain day, or a certain time, at which he promised to pay; or term may be defined as simply an agreement by which a person promises a creditor to pay him. There is a striking conformity between the *pactum constitutæ pecuniæ,* as above defined, and our *indebitatus assumpsit.*

Pactum de non alienando /pǽktəm dìy nón èyliyənǽndow/. A pact or agreement binding the owner of property not to alienate it, intended to protect the interests of another; particularly an agreement by the mortgagor of real estate that he will not transfer the title to a third person until after satisfaction of the mortgage. A clause inserted in mortgages in Louisiana to secure to the mortgage creditor the right to foreclose his mortgage by executory process directed solely against the mortgagor, and to give him the right to seize and sell the mortgaged property, regardless of any subsequent alienations. Shields v. Schiff, 124 U.S. 351, 355, 8 S.Ct. 510, 31 L.Ed. 445.

Pactum de non petendo /pǽktəm dìy nón pəténdow/. In the civil law, an agreement not to sue. A simple convention whereby a creditor promises the debtor that he will not enforce his claim.

Pactum de quota litis /pǽktəm dìy kwówdə láydəs/. In the civil law, an agreement by which a creditor promised to pay a portion of a debt difficult to recover to a person who undertook to recover it.

Padder. A robber; a foot highwayman; a foot-pad.

Pagarchus /pəgárkəs/. A petty magistrate of a pagus or little district in the country.

Pagoda /pəgówdə/. A gold or silver coin, of several kinds and values, formerly current in India. It was valued at the United States custom-house, at $1.94.

Pagus /péygəs/. A county.

Paid-in-capital. Money or property paid to a corporation for its capital stock.

Paid-in-surplus. That portion of the surplus of a corporation not generated by profits but contributed by the stockholders. See also **Capital** *(Capital surplus).*

Paid-up insurance. Insurance coverage for which no additional premiums are due.

Paid-up stock. Shares of stock for which full payment has been received by the corporation.

Pain and suffering. Term used to describe not only physical discomfort and distress but also mental and emotional trauma which are recoverable as elements of damage in torts.

Paine forte et dure /péyn fórt ey dyúr/. See **Peine fort et dure.**

Pains and penalties, bills of. The name given to acts of parliament to attaint particular persons of treason or felony, or to inflict pains and penalties beyond or contrary to the common law, to serve a special purpose. They are in fact new laws, made *pro re nata.* See also **Bill of pains and penalties.**

Pairing-off. In the practice of legislative bodies, a species of negative proxies, by which two members, who belong to opposite parties or are on opposite sides with regard to a given question, mutually agree that they will both be absent from voting, either for a specified period or when a division is had on the particular question. By this mutual agreement a vote is neutralized on each side of the question, and the relative numbers on the division are precisely the same as if both members were present. It is said to have originated in the house of commons in Cromwell's time.

Pais, pays /pey(s)/. Fr. The country; the neighborhood.

A trial *per pais* signifies a trial by the country; that is, by jury.

An assurance by matter *in pais* is an assurance transacted between two or more private persons "in the country;" that is, upon the very spot to be transferred.

Matter *in pais* signifies matter of fact, probably because matters of fact are triable by the country; *i.e.*, by jury.

Estoppels *in pais* are estoppels by conduct, as distinguished from estoppels by deed or by record.

Conveyances *in pais* are ordinary conveyances between two or more persons *in the country; i.e.*, upon the land to be transferred.

See also **In pais; Matter in pais.**

Palace court. See **Court of the Steward and Marshal.**

Palam /pǽləm/. Lat. In the civil law, openly; in the presence of many.

Palimony. Term has meaning similar to "alimony" except that award, settlement or agreement arises out of nonmarital relationship of parties (*i.e.* nonmarital partners). It has been held that courts should enforce express contracts between nonmarital partners except to the extent the contract is explicitly founded on the consideration of meretricious sexual services, despite contention that such contracts violate public policy; that in the absence of express contract, the court should inquire into the conduct of the parties to determine whether that conduct demonstrates implied contract, agreement of partnership or joint venture, or some other tacit understanding between the parties, and may also employ the doctrine of quantum meruit or equitable remedies such as constructive or resulting trust, when warranted by the facts of the case. Marvin v. Marvin, 557 P.2d 106, 18 Cal.3d 660, 134 Cal.Rptr. 815.

Pallio cooperire /pǽliyow kowò(w)pəráyriy/. In old English law, an ancient custom, where children were born out of wedlock, and their parents afterwards intermarried. The children, together with the father and mother, stood under a cloth extended while the marriage was solemnized. It was in the nature of adoption. The children were legitimate by the civil, but not by the common, law. They were called "mantle children" in Germany, France, and Normandy. The custom also existed in Scotland.

Palmarium /pælmériyəm/. In civil law, a conditional fee for professional services in addition to the lawful charge.

Palmer Act. A name given to the English statute 19 & 20 Vict., c. 16, enabling a person accused of a crime committed out of the jurisdiction of the central criminal court, to be tried in that court.

Palming off doctrine. Rule of law itself by which it is determined whether a given state of facts constitutes "unfair competition." Soft-Lite Lens Co. v. Ritholz,

301 Ill.App. 100, 21 N.E.2d 835, 838. See also **Palm off.**

Palmistry /pámǝstriy/. The practice of telling fortunes by a feigned interpretation of the lines and marks on the hand. Also, a trick with the hand.

Palm off. To impose by fraud; to put off by unfair means. "Palming off" is conduct, the nature and probable effect of which is to deceive public so as to pass off goods of one person as and for goods of another. Surgical Supply Service, Inc. v. Adler, D.C. Pa., 206 F.Supp. 564, 570.

Palm prints. The impression made by a person's palm on a smooth surface. They may be used for purpose of identification in criminal cases.

Palpable. Easily perceptible, plain, obvious, readily visible, noticeable, patent, distinct, manifest. People v. Hughey, 382 Ill. 136, 47 N.E.2d 77, 80.

Palsgraf doctrine. The rule derived from the case of Palsgraf v. Long Island R. Co., 248 N.Y. 339, 162 N.E. 99, to the effect that one who is negligent is liable only for the harm or injury which is within the orbit of foreseeability and not for every injury which follows from his negligence.

Pandects /pǽndekts/. A compilation of Roman law, consisting of selected passages from the writings of the most authoritative of the older jurists, methodically arranged, prepared by Tribonian with the assistance of sixteen associates, under a commission from the emperor Justinian. This work, which is otherwise called the "Digest," because in his compilation the writings of the jurists were reduced to order and condensed *quasi digestiœ,* comprises fifty books, and is one of the four great works composing the *Corpus Juris Civilis.* It was first published in A.D. 533, when Justinian gave to it the force of law.

Pander, *n.* One who caters to the lust of others; a male bawd, a pimp, or procurer.

Pander, *v.* To pimp; to cater to the gratification of the lust of another. To entice or procure a female, by promises, threats, fraud, or artifice, to enter any place in which prostitution is practiced, for the purpose of prostitution. Pandering is established when evidence shows that accused has succeeded in inducing his victim to become an inmate of a house of prostitution. People v. Charles, 218 Cal.App.2d 812, 32 Cal. Rptr. 653, 658.

Pandering of obscenity. Business of purveying pictorial or graphic matter openly advertised to appeal to erotic interest of customers, or potential customers, by either blatant and explicit advertising or subtle and sophisticated advertising. State v. Albini, 29 Ohio App.2d 227, 281 N.E.2d 26, 31, 58 O.O.2d 416.

Panderer. One who solicits for prostitute. A pimp.

P & L. See **Profit** (*Profit and loss*); **Profit and loss statement.**

Panel. A list of jurors to serve in a particular court, or for the trial of a particular action. Group of judges (smaller than the entire court) which decides a case; *e.g.* a nine member appellate court might be divided into three, three member panels with each panel hearing and deciding cases.

Prepaid legal services. "Open panel" legal services is a plan in which legal services are paid for in advance (usually by a type of insurance) and members can choose their own lawyer. Under a "closed panel", however, all legal services are performed by a group of attorneys previously selected by the insurer, union, etc. See **Prepaid legal services.**

See also **Jury panel.**

Pannellation /pænəléyshən/. The act of impaneling a jury.

Papal supremacy. The supremacy which the Pope claimed not only over the Emperor of the Holy Roman Empire, but over all other Christian princes. The theory was that they stood to the Pope as feudal vassals to a supreme lord; as such, the Pope claimed the right to enforce the duties due to him from his feudal subordinates through an ascending scale of penalties culminating in the absolution of the prince's subjects from the bonds of allegiance, and in the disposition of the sovereign himself. The papal supremacy was overthrown in England by acts of the Parliament which met in 1529 and was dissolved in 1536, ending in the Act of Supremacy which substituted the King for the Pope.

Paper. A written or printed document or instrument. A document filed or introduced in evidence in a suit at law, as, in the phrase "papers in the case" and in "papers on appeal." Any writing or printed document, including letters, memoranda, legal or business documents, and books of account, as in the constitutional provision which protects the people from unreasonable searches and seizures in respect to their "papers" as well as their houses and persons. A written or printed evidence of debt, particularly a promissory note or a bill of exchange, as in the phrases "accommodation paper" and "commercial paper" (*q.v.*). See also **Document.**

Paper money. Bills drawn by a government against its own credit, engaging to pay money, but which do not profess to be immediately convertible into specie, and which are put into compulsory circulation as a substitute for coined money. See **Federal reserve notes; Legal tender.**

Paper patent. Term used derisively to refer to a discovery or invention which has never been put to commercial use nor recognized in the trade. Coltman v. Colgate-Palmolive-Peet Co., C.C.A.Ind., 104 F.2d 508.

Paper profit. An unrealized profit on a security or other investment still held. Paper profits become realized profits only when the security or other investment is sold.

Paper standard. A money system based on pure paper which is not convertible into gold or other metal of intrinsic value.

Papian poppæan law. See **Lex Papia Poppæa.**

Par. In commercial law, equal; equality. An equality subsisting between the nominal or face value of a bill of exchange, share of stock, etc., and its actual selling value. When the values are thus equal, the instrument or share is said to be "at par;" if it can be sold for more than its nominal worth, it is "above par;" if

for less, it is "below par." See also **Par of exchange; Par value.**

Any standard or norm of conduct which is expected of people.

Parachronism /pərækrənizəm/. Error in the computation of time.

Paracium /pəréysh(iy)əm/. In old English law, the tenure between parceners, viz., that which the youngest owes to the eldest without homage or service.

Parage /pǽrəj/ or **paragium** /pəréyj(iy)əm/. In old English law, an equality of blood or dignity, but more especially of land, in the partition of an inheritance between co-heirs. More properly, however, an equality of condition among nobles, or persons holding by a noble tenure. Thus, when a fief is divided among brothers, the younger hold their part of the elder by parage; *i.e.*, without any homage or service. Also the portion which a woman may obtain on her marriage.

Paragraph. A distinct part of a discourse or writing; any section or subdivision of writing or chapter which relates to particular point, whether consisting of one or many sentences.

A part or section of a statute, pleading, affidavit, will, trust, etc., which contains one article, the sense of which is complete.

Fed.R.Civil P. 10(a) provides that: "All averments of claim or defense shall be made in numbered paragraphs, the contents of each of which shall be limited as far as practicable to a statement or of a single set of circumstances; and a paragraph may be referred to by number in all succeeding pleadings."

Paralegal. A person with legal skills, but who is not an attorney, and who works under the supervision of a lawyer or who is otherwise authorized by law to use those legal skills. Paralegal courses leading to degrees in such specialty are now afforded by many schools.

Parallel citation. A citation reference to the same case printed in two or more different reports. See *e.g.* the case citation to the definition directly below.

Paramount. Above; upwards. Higher; superior; pre-eminent; of the highest rank or nature. Board of Com'rs of Big Horn County v. Bench Canal Drainage Dist., 56 Wyo. 285, 108 P.2d 590, 594.

Paramount equity. An equitable right or claim which is prior, superior, or preferable to that with which it is compared.

Paramount title. In the law of real property, properly one which is superior to the title with which it is compared, in the sense that the former is the source or origin of the latter. It is, however, frequently used to denote a title which is simply better or stronger than another, or will prevail over it. But this use is scarcely correct, unless the superiority consists in the seniority of the title spoken of as "paramount."

Paramour. In general, a lover; but term is used commonly in connection with a person of either sex in an adulterous alliance.

Paranoia /pǽrənóyə/. See **Insanity.**

Parapherna /pæ̀rəfə́rnə/. In the civil law, goods brought by wife to husband over and above her dowry *(dos)*.

Paraphernalia /pæ̀rəfərnéyl(i)yə/. The separate property of a married woman, other than that which is included in her dowry, or dos. Those goods which a woman is allowed to have, after the death of her husband, besides her dower, consisting of her apparel and ornaments, suitable to her rank and degree. Those goods which a wife could bequeath by her testament.

In the civil law, the separate property of the wife is divided into dotal and extradotal. Total property is that which the wife brings to the husband to assist him in bearing the expenses of the marriage establishment. Extradotal property, otherwise called "paraphernal property," is that which forms no part of the dowry. It is property brought to the marriage by one of the spouses.

Paraphernal property /pæ̀rəfə́rnəl própərdiy/. See **Paraphernalia.**

Paraprofessional. One who assists a professional person though not a member of the profession himself; *e.g.* a paralegal *(q.v.)* who assists a lawyer.

Parasynexis /pæ̀rəsənéksəs/. In the civil law, a conventicle, or unlawful meeting.

Paratitla /pæ̀rətáytlə/. In the civil law, notes or abstracts prefixed to titles of law, giving a summary of their contents. An abbreviated explanation of some titles or books of the Code or Digest.

Paratum habeo /pəréydəm hǽbiyow/. Lat. I have him in readiness. The return by the sheriff to a *capias ad respondendum,* signifying that he has the defendant in readiness to be brought into court. This was a fiction, where the defendant was at large. Afterwards he was required, by statute, to take bail from the defendant, and he returned *cepi corpus* and bail-bond. But still he might be ruled to bring in the body.

Paratus est verificare /pəréydəs èst vèhrəfəkériy/. Lat. He is ready to verify. The Latin form for concluding a pleading with a *verification (q.v.).*

Paravail /pǽrəvèyl/pæ̀rəvéyl/. Inferior; subordinate. In old English law, tenant paravail signified the lowest tenant of land, being the tenant of a mesne lord. He was so called because he was supposed to make "avail" or profit of the land for another.

Parcel, *v.* To divide an estate.

Parcel, *n.* A small package or bundle. See **Package.**

A part or portion of land. A part of an estate. "Parcel" as used with reference to land generally means a contiguous quantity of land in the possession of an owner. United States ex rel. and for Use of Tennessee Val. Authority v. Easements and Rights over Certain Land in Hamilton County, D.C.Tenn., 259 F.Supp. 377, 382. A contiguous quantity of land in possession of, owned by, or recorded as property of the same claimant person or company. Adams Tree Service, Inc. v. Transamerica Title Ins. Co., 20 Ariz.App. 214, 511 P.2d 658, 662. Term may be synonymous with "lot."

Parcella terræ /parsélə téhriy/. A parcel of land.

Parcel makers /pársəl mèykərz/. In old English law, two officers in the exchequer who formerly made the parcels or items of the escheators' accounts, wherein they charged them with everything they had levied for the king during the term of their office.

Parcels. A description of property, formally set forth in a conveyance, together with the boundaries thereof, in order to its easy identification.

Parcels, bill of. An account of the items composing a parcel or package of goods, transmitted with them to the purchaser. See, *Bill of parcels* under **"Bill."**

Parcenary /pársənèhriy/. The state or condition of holding title to lands jointly by parceners, before the common inheritance has been divided.

Parcener /pársənər/. A joint heir; one who, with others, holds an estate in co-parcenary *(q.v.).* Gibson v. Johnson, 331 Mo. 1198, 56 S.W.2d 783.

Parchment. Sheep-skins dressed for writing, so called from *Pergamus,* Asia Minor, where they were invented. Used for deeds, and used for writs of summons in England previous to the Judicature Act of 1875. The skin of a lamb, sheep, goat, young calf, or other animal, prepared for writing on; also, any of various papers made in imitation thereof.

Parco fracto /párkow frǽktow/. Pound-breach; also the name of an old English writ against one who violently breaks a pound and takes beasts which, for some trespass done, or some other just cause, were lawfully impounded.

Par delictum /pár dəlíktəm/. (In pari delicto.) Equal guilt.

Pardon. An act of grace, proceeding from the power intrusted with the execution of the laws, which exempts the individual on whom it is bestowed from the punishment the law inflicts for a crime he has committed. An act of grace from governing power which mitigates the punishment the law demands for the offense and restores the rights and privileges forfeited on account of the offense. Verneco, Inc. v. Fidelity & Cas. Co. of New York, 253 La. 721, 219 So.2d 508, 511.

The power to pardon for non-federal crimes is generally invested in state governors, while the President has the power to pardon for federal offenses (Art. II, Sec. 2, U.S.Const.).

See also Amnesty; Board of pardons; Clemency; Commutation; Condonation; Parole; Reprieve.

Distinguished from amnesty. The distinction between amnesty and pardon is one rather of philological interest than of legal importance. Knote v. U. S., 95 U.S. 149, 153, 24 L.Ed. 442, 443. This is so as to their ultimate effect, but there are incidental differences of importance. They are of different character and have different purposes. The one overlooks offense; the other remits punishment. The first is usually addressed to crimes against the sovereignty of the state, to political offenses, forgiveness being deemed more expedient for the public welfare than prosecution and punishment. The second condones infractions of the peace of the state. Amnesty is usually general, addressed to classes or even communities—a legislative act, or under legislation, constitutional or statutory—the act of the supreme magistrate. There may or may not be distinct acts of acceptance. If other rights are dependent upon it and are asserted, there is affirmative evidence of acceptance. Burdick v. U. S., 236 U.S. 79, 271, 35 S.Ct. 267, 59 L.Ed. 476. "Pardon" applies only to the individual, releases him from the punishment fixed by law for his specific offense, but does not affect the criminality of the same or similar acts when performed by other persons or repeated by the same person.

Distinguished from commutation. A pardon, to be effective, must be accepted, Burdick v. U. S., 236 U.S. 79, 35 S.Ct. 267, 268, 59 L.Ed. 476; but a commutation is merely a cessation of the exercise of sovereign authority, and does not obliterate guilt nor restore civil rights, and need not be accepted by the convict to be operative. A commutation is simply a remission of a part of the punishment, a substitution of a less penalty for the one originally imposed; while a "pardon" avoids or terminates punishment for crime. U. S. v. Commissioner of Immigration at Port of New York, C.C.A.N.Y., 5 F.2d 162, 165.

Distinguished from parole. A "pardon" releases the offender from the entire punishment prescribed for the offense, and from all the disabilities consequent on his conviction, while by a "parole" a convict is merely released before the expiration of his term, to remain subject during the remainder thereof to supervision by the public authority, and to return to imprisonment on violation of the condition of the parole.

Types of Pardons

Absolute or unconditional pardon. One which frees the criminal without any condition whatever. That which reaches both the punishment prescribed for the offense and the guilt of the offender. It obliterates in legal contemplation the offense itself. It goes no further than to restore the accused to his civil rights and remit the penalty imposed for the particular offense of which he was convicted in so far as it remains unpaid. State v. Cullen, 14 Wash.2d 105, 127 P.2d 257, 259.

Conditional pardon. One to which a condition is annexed, performance of which is necessary to the validity of the pardon. A pardon which does not become operative until the grantee has performed some specific act, or where it becomes void when some specific event transpires. One granted on the condition that it shall only endure until the voluntary doing of some act by the person pardoned, or that it shall be revoked by a subsequent act on his part, as that he shall leave the state and never return.

Executive pardon. See **Executive pardon.**

Full pardon. One freely and unconditionally absolving party from all legal consequences, direct and collateral, of crime and conviction. Warren v. State, 127 Tex.Cr.R. 71, 74 S.W.2d 1006, 1008.

General pardon. One granted to all the persons participating in a given criminal or treasonable offense (generally political), or to all offenders of a given class or against a certain statute or within certain limits of time. But "amnesty" is the more appropriate term for this. It may be express, as when a general declaration is made that all offenders of a certain class shall be pardoned, or implied, as in case of the repeal of a penal statute.

Partial pardon. That which remits only portion of punishment or absolves from only portion of legal consequences of crime. Warren v. State, 127 Tex. Cr.R. 71, 74 S.W.2d 1006, 1008.

Pardon attorney. Official of Justice Department who considers applications for federal pardons and makes recommendations for the exercise of Presidential clemency.

Pardoners /párdənərz/. In old English law, persons who carried about the pope's indulgences, and sold them to any who would buy them.

Parens /pǽrèn(d)z/pér°/. Lat. In Roman law, a parent; originally and properly only the father or mother of the person spoken of; but also, by an extension of its meaning, any relative, male or female, in the line of direct ascent.

"Parens" est nomen generale ad omne genus cognationis /pǽrèn(d)z èst nówmən jènəréyliy æd ómniy jíynəs kəgnèyshiyównəs/. "Parent" is a name general for every kind of relationship.

Parens patriæ /pǽrèn(d)z pǽtriyiy/pérèn(d)z péytriyiy/. "Parens patriæ," literally "parent of the country," refers traditionally to role of state as sovereign and guardian of persons under legal disability. State of W. Va. v. Chas. Pfizer & Co., C.A.N.Y., 440 F.2d 1079, 1089. It is a concept of standing utilized to protect those quasi-sovereign interests such as health, comfort and welfare of the people, interstate water rights, general economy of the state, etc. Gibbs v. Titelman, D.C.Pa., 369 F.Supp. 38, 54.

Parens patriæ originates from the English common law where the King had a royal prerogative to act as guardian to persons with legal disabilities such as infants, idiots and lunatics. In the United States, the *parens patriæ* function belongs with the states.

State attorney generals have *parens patriæ* authority to bring actions on behalf of state residents for anti-trust offenses and to recover on their behalf. 15 U.S.C.A. § 15c.

The use of this power to deprive a person of freedom has been limited by recent laws and decisions; *e.g.* Kent v. U. S., 383 U.S. 541, 554–555, 86 S.Ct. 1045, 1054, 16 L.Ed.2d 84.

See also **Surrogate parent.**

Parent. The lawful father or mother of a person. One who procreates, begets, or brings forth offspring.

By statute, "parent" has been defined to include (1) either the natural father or the natural mother of a child born of their valid marriage to each other, if no subsequent judicial decree has divested one or both of them of their statutory coguardianship as created by their marriage; (2) either the adoptive father or the adoptive mother of a child jointly adopted by them, if no subsequent judicial decree has divested one or both of them of their statutory coguardianship as created by the adoption; (3) the natural mother of an illegitimate child, if her position as sole guardian of such a child has not been divested by a subsequent judicial decree; (4) a child's putative blood parent who has expressly acknowledged paternity and contributed meaningfully to the child's support; (5) any individual or agency whose status as guardian of the person of the child has been established by judicial decree.

Includes any person entitled to take, or who would be entitled to take if the child died without a will, as a parent under the Uniform Probate Code by intestate succession from the child whose relationship is in question and excludes any person who is only a stepparent, foster parent, or grandparent. Uniform Probate Code, § 1–201(28).

See also **Adoption; Loco parentis; Parens patriæ; Surrogate parent.**

Parentage. Kindred in the direct ascending line. The state or condition of being a parent.

Parental liability. By statute in certain states, the parents may be held liable up to a specified amount for damages caused to property of others by their children if such damage is found to have resulted from negligent control of parent over acts of child.

Parental rights. The sum total of the rights of the parent or parents in and to the child as well as the rights of the child in and to the parent or parents. Anguis v. Superior Court In and For Maricopa County, 6 Ariz.App. 68, 429 P.2d 702, 705. The following are "parental rights" protected to varying degrees by constitution: physical possession of child, which, in case of custodial parent, includes day-to-day care and companionship of child; right to discipline child, which includes right to inculcate in child parent's moral and ethical standards; right to control and manage minor child's earnings; right to control and manage minor child's property; right to be supported by adult child; right to have child bear parent's name; and right to prevent adoption of child without parents' consent. L. A. M. v. State, Alaska, 547 P.2d 827, 835.

Parent-child immunity. In some jurisdictions a parent is immune from liability for negligence in an action brought by his or her child, though the trend has been to abolish or restrict such immunity.

Parent company. Company owning more than 50 percent of the voting shares of another company, called the subsidiary. A corporation which has working control through stock ownership of its subsidiary corporations. Culcal Stylco, Inc. v. Vornado, Inc., 26 Cal.App.3d 879, 103 Cal.Rptr. 419, 421. A "parent corporation" is one which has working control through stock ownership of its subsidiary corporations. Culcal Stylco, Inc. v. Vornado, Inc., 26 C.A.3d 879, 103 Cal.Rptr. 419, 421.

Parentela /pæ̀rəntíylə/. The sum of those persons who trace descent from one ancestor.

In old English law, parentela, or *de parentela se tollere*, signified a renunciation of one's kindred and family. This was, according to ancient custom, done in open court, before the judge, and in the presence of twelve men, who made oath that they believed it was done for a just cause. After such abjuration, the person was incapable of inheriting anything from any of his relations, etc.

Parenticide /pəréntəsàyd/. One who murders a parent; also the crime so committed.

Parentum est liberos alere etiam nothos /pəréntəm èst líbərows əlíriy íyshiyəm nówθows/. It is the duty of parents to support their children even when illegitimate.

Pares /pǽriyz/pér°/. Lat. In old English law, a person's peers or equals; as the jury for the trial of causes, who were originally the vassals or tenants of the lord, being the equals or peers of the parties litigant; and, as the lord's vassals judged each other in the lord's courts, so the sovereign's vassals, or the lords themselves, judged each other in the sovereign's courts.

Pares curiæ /pǽriyz kyúriyiy/. In old English law, peers of the court. Vassals who were bound to attend the lord's court.

Paresis /pəríysəs/pǽrəsəs/. Progressive general paralysis, involving or leading to the form of insanity known as *"dementia paralytica."* Popularly, but not very correctly, called "softening of the brain." See **Insanity.**

Pares regni /pǽriyz régnay/. Peers of the realm.

Paria copulantur paribus /pǽriyə kòpyəlǽntər pǽrəbəs/. Like things unite with like.

Paribus sententiis reus absolvitur /pǽrəbəs senténshiyəs ríyəs əbzólvədər/. Where the opinions are equal [where the court is equally divided], the defendant is acquitted.

Pari causa /pǽray kózə/. Lat. With equal right; upon an equal footing; equivalent in rights or claims.

Pari delicto /pǽray dəlíktow/. Lat. In equal fault; in a similar offense or crime; equal in guilt or in legal fault. "Pari delicto" doctrine rests on rule that courts will not enforce an invalid contract and that no party can recover in any action where it is necessary for him to prove an illegal contract in order to make out his case. Neal v. Pennsylvania Life Ins. Co., Okl., 480 P.2d 923, 925. See **In pari delicto.**

Paries communis /pǽriyiyz kəmyúwnəs/. A common wall; a party-wall.

Pari materia /pǽray mətíriyə/. Lat. Of the same matter; on the same subject; as, laws *pari materia* must be construed with reference to each other.

Pari mutuel betting /pæ̀riy myúwch(u)wəl bédiŋ/. A mutual stake or wager; a betting pool. A form of betting on horses or dogs in which those who bet on winner share total stakes less a small percent to the management. Donovan v. Eastern Racing Ass'n, 324 Mass. 393, 86 N.E.2d 903, 906. Such betting is illegal in a number of states.

Par in parem imperium non habet /pár ìn pérəm əmpíriyəm nòn héybət/. An equal has no dominion over an equal.

Pari passu /pǽray pǽs(y)uw/péray péys(y)uw/. Lat. By an equal progress; equably; ratably; without preference. Used especially of creditors who, in marshalling assets, are entitled to receive out of the same fund without any precedence over each other.

Pari ratione /pǽray rèshiyówniy/. Lat. For the like reason; by like mode of reasoning.

Paris, declaration of /dekləréyshən əv pǽrəs/. See **Declaration.**

Parish. In English ecclesiastical law a circuit of ground, committed to the charge of one parson or vicar, or other minister having cure of souls therein. 1 Bl.Comm. 111. The precinct of a parish church, and the particular charge of a secular priest. An ecclesiastical division of a town, city or district, subject to the ministry of one pastor.

In Louisiana, a territorial governmental division of the state corresponding to what is elsewhere called a "county."

Parish apprentice. In old English law, the children of parents unable to maintain them could, by law, be apprenticed, by the guardians or overseers of their parish, to such persons as may be willing to receive them as apprentices. Such children were called "parish apprentices."

Parish church. This expression has various significations. It is applied sometimes to a select body of Christians, forming a local spiritual association, and sometimes to the building in which the public worship of the inhabitants of a parish is celebrated; but the true legal notion of a parochial church is a consecrated place, having attached to it the rights of burial and the administration of the sacraments.

Parish court. The name of a court established in each parish in Louisiana, and corresponding to the county courts or common pleas courts in the other states. It has a limited civil jurisdiction, besides general probate powers.

Parishioners. Members of a parish. In England, for many purposes they form a body politic.

Par items. Items which a drawee bank will remit to another bank without charge.

Parity. Equality in amount or value. Equivalence of prices of farm products in relation to those existing at some former date (base period) or to the general cost of living. Equivalence of prices of goods or services in two different markets.

The relationship between two currencies such that they are exchangeable for each other at the par or official rate of exchange. See **Exchange rate.**

Parity ratio. A relationship developed between the index of prices received by farmers for their crops and the index of costs of the farmers for the items which they buy.

Parium eadem est ratio, idem jus /pǽriyəm iyéydəm èst réysh(iy)ow, áydəm jós/. Of things equal, the reason is the same, and the same is the law.

Parium judicium /pǽriyəm jədíshiyəm/. The judgment of peers; trial by a jury of one's peers or equals.

Park, *n.* An inclosed pleasure-ground in or near a city, set apart for the recreation of the public.

Park, *v.* Term "park" as used in statutes or ordinances regulating parking, does not comprehend or include merely temporary or momentary stoppage but rather connotes a stoppage with intent of permitting vehicle to remain standing for an appreciable length of time. Ford v. Stevens, 280 Minn. 16, 157 N.W.2d 510, 513.

Parliament. The supreme legislative assembly of Great Britain and Ireland, consisting of the king or queen and the three estates of the realm, viz., the lords spiritual, the lords temporal, and the commons.

High Court of Parliament. In English law, the English parliament, as composed of the house of peers and house of commons; or the house of lords sitting in its judicial capacity.

Parliamentary. Relating or belonging to, connected with, enacted by or proceeding from, or characteristic of, the English parliament in particular, or any legislative body in general.

Parliamentary agents. Persons who act as solicitors in promoting and carrying private bills through parliament. They are usually attorneys or solicitors, but they do not usually confine their practice to this particular department.

Parliamentary committee. A committee of members of the house of peers or of the house of commons, appointed by either house for the purpose of making inquiries, by the examination of witnesses or otherwise, into matters which could not be conveniently inquired into by the whole house.

Parliamentary law. The general body of enacted rules (*e.g.* Roberts Rules of Order) and recognized usages which governs the procedure of legislative assemblies and other deliberative bodies such as meetings of stockholders and directors of corporations, town meetings, boards, clubs, and the like.

Parliamentary taxes. See **Tax.**

Parliamentum /pàrl(iy)əméntəm/. L. Lat. A legislative body in general or the English parliament in particular.

Parliamentum religiosorum /pàrl(iy)əméntəm rəlij-iyowsórəm/. In most convents there has been a common room into which the brethren withdrew for conversation; conferences there being termed "*parliamentum.*" Likewise, the societies of the two temples, or inns of court, call that assembly of the benchers or governors wherein they confer upon the common affairs of their several houses a "parliament."

Parochial. Relating or belonging to a parish.

Par of exchange. The precise equality or equivalency of any given sum or quantity of money of one country, and the like sum or quantity of money of any other foreign country into which it is to be exchanged. The par of the currencies of any two countries means the equivalence of a certain amount of the currency of the one in the currency of the other. See **Exchange rate.**

Parol. A word; speech; hence, oral or verbal. Expressed or evidenced by speech only; as opposed to by writing or by sealed instrument.

As to parol Agreement; Arrest; Demurrer; Lease; and Promise; see those titles.

Parol contract. An oral contract as distinguished from a written or formal contract.

Parole /pərówl/. Release from jail, prison or other confinement after actually serving part of sentence. State v. Ludwig, 218 Or. 483, 344 P.2d 764, 766. A conditional release of prisoner, generally under supervision of a parole officer, who has served part of the term for which he was sentenced to prison. Such may be revoked if he fails to observe the conditions provided in parole order.

"Parolee" gains his conditional freedom as result of exercise of discretion by parole board which may grant parole when it is of opinion there is reasonable probability that prisoner will live and remain at liberty without violating laws. Birch v. Anderson, C.A. D.C., 358 F.2d 520, 524, 123 U.S.App.D.C. 153.

The granting, denying, revocation, and supervision of parole for federal prisoners rests in the U.S. Parole Commission. Most states have similar boards or commissions. See **Parole board.**

In military law, a promise given by a prisoner of war, when he has leave to depart from custody, that he will return at the time appointed, unless discharged. An engagement by a prisoner of war, upon being set at liberty, that he will not again take up arms against the government by whose forces he was captured, either for a limited period or while hostilities continue.

See also **Amnesty; Pardon.**

Probation distinguished. "Probation" relates to judicial action taken before the prison door is closed, whereas "parole" relates to executive action taken after the door has closed on a convict. State v. Hewett, 270 N.C. 348, 154 S.E.2d 476, 479.

Revocation hearing. Parole revocation hearing is in the nature of an administrative proceeding for the purpose of determining whether a parolee has violated the conditions of his parole. State ex rel. McNeil v. New York State Bd. of Parole, 87 Misc.2d 497, 385 N.Y.S.2d 731, 734.

Parole board. The state and federal administrative bodies empowered to decide whether inmates shall be conditionally released from prison before completion of their sentences. Called "Correctional Boards" in some states.

The federal Board of Parole consists of eight members, appointed by the President by and with the advice and consent of the Senate. It has sole authority to grant, modify, or revoke paroles of all U.S. prisoners. It is responsible for the supervision of parolees and prisoners released upon the expiration of their sentences with allowances for statutory good time. U.S. probation officers supervise parolees and mandatory releases.

Parolee. Ex-prisoner who has been placed on parole.

Parole officers. Parole system is administered by parole officers whose duties include supervision of parolees. Normally, parolees must periodically report to such officers.

Parol evidence. Oral or verbal evidence; that which is given by word of mouth; the ordinary kind of evidence given by witnesses in court. In a particular sense, and with reference to contracts, deeds, wills, and other writings, parol evidence is the same as extraneous evidence or evidence *aliunde.* See also **Aliunde; Extraneous evidence; Oral evidence.**

Parol evidence rule. This evidence rule seeks to preserve integrity of written agreements by refusing to permit contracting parties to attempt to alter import of their contract through use of contemporaneous oral declarations. Rose v. Food Fair Stores, Inc., 437 Pa. 117, 262 A.2d 851. Under this rule, when parties put their agreement in writing, all previous oral agreements merge in the writing and a contract as written cannot be modified or changed by parol evidence, in the absence of a plea of mistake or fraud in the preparation of the writing. Russell v. Halteman's Adm'x, 287 Ky. 404, 153 S.W.2d 899, 904. But rule does not forbid a resort to parol evidence not inconsistent with the matters stated in the writing. Elkins v. Super-Cold Southwest Co., Tex.Civ.App., 157 S.W.2d 946, 947. Also, as regards sales of goods, such written agreement may be explained or supplemented by course of dealing or usage of trade or by course of conduct, and by evidence of consistent additional terms unless the court finds the writing to have been intended also as a complete and exclusive statement of the terms of the agreement. U.C.C. § 2–202.

This rule is also applicable to wills and trusts.

Parols de ley /pərówlz də léy/. L. Fr. Words of law; technical words.

Parols font plea /pərówls fónt plíy/. Words make the plea.

Parricide /pǽrəsayd/. The crime of killing one's father; also a person guilty of killing his father.

Parricidium /pæ̀rəsáyd(i)yəm/. Lat. In the civil law, parricide; the murder of a parent.

Pars /parz/. Lat. A part; a party to a deed, action, or legal proceeding.

Pars enitia /párz ənáysh(iy)ə/. In old English law, the privilege or portion of the eldest child in the partition of lands by lot.

Pars gravata /párz grəvéydə/. A party aggrieved; the party aggrieved.

Parson. The rector of a church; one that has full possession of all the rights of a parochial church.

Parson mortal. In old English law, a rector instituted and inducted for his own life. But any collegiate or conventional body, to whom a church was forever appropriated, was termed *"persona immortalis."*

Pars rationabilis /párz ræshənéybələs/. That part of a man's goods which the law gave to his widow and children.

Pars rea /párz ríyə/. A party defendant.

Pars viscerum matris /párz vísərəm méytrəs/. Part of the bowels of the mother; *i.e.,* an unborn child.

Part. An integral portion, something essentially belonging to a larger whole; that which together with another or others makes up a whole. First-Mechanics Nat. Bank of Trenton v. Norris, 134 N.J.Eq. 229, 34 A.2d 746, 749. A portion, share, or purpart. One of two duplicate originals of a conveyance or covenant, the other being called "counterpart." Also, in composition, partial or incomplete; as part payment, part performance.

Partage /pàrtázh/. In French law, a division made between co-proprietors of a particular estate held by them in common. It is the operation by means of which the goods of a succession are divided among the co-heirs; while licitation *(q.v.)* is an adjudication to the highest bidder of objects which are not divisible.

Parte inaudita /párdiy inódədə/. Lat. One side being unheard. Spoken of any action which is taken *ex parte.*

Partem aliquam recte intelligere nemo potest, antequam totum, iterum atque iterum, perlegerit /párdəm ǽləkwəm réktiy intəléjəriy níymow pówdəst ǽntəkwəm tówdəm ídərəm ǽtkwiy ídərəm pərlíyjərət/. No one can rightly understand any part until he has read the whole again and again.

Parte non comparente /párdiy nón kòmpəréntiy/. Lat. The party not having appeared. The condition of a cause called "default."

Parte quacumque integrante sublata, tollitur totum /párdiy kwəkə́mkwiy ìntəgrǽntiy səbléydə tóladər tówdəm/. An integral part being taken away, the whole is taken away.

Partes finis nihil habuerunt /párdiyz fáynəs náy(h)əl hæbyuwírənt/. In old pleading, the parties to the fine had nothing; that is, had no estate which could be conveyed by it. A plea to a fine which had been levied by a stranger.

Partial. Relating to or constituting a part; not complete; not entire or universal; not general or total. United States Fidelity & Guaranty Co. v. Baker, Tex. Civ.App., 65 S.W.2d 344, 346.

Partial account. An account of an executor, administrator, guardian, etc., not exhibiting his entire dealings with the estate or fund from his appointment to final settlement, but covering only a portion of the time or of the estate.

Partial average. Another name for particular average. See **Average.**

Partial dependency. Test as to existence of such dependency for purpose of worker's compensation is whether contributions were relied on by claimants to aid and maintain them in present position in life and whether they were to substantial degree depending on support or aid of employee at time of death. Federal Underwriters Exchange v. Hinkle, Tex.Civ. App., 187 S.W.2d 122, 124.

Partial eviction. That which takes place when the possessor is deprived of only a portion of his rights in the premises. Such may result in constructive eviction.

Partial evidence. That which goes to establish a detached fact, in a series tending to the fact in dispute. It may be received, subject to be rejected as incompetent, unless connected with the fact in dispute by proof of other facts; for example, on an issue of title to real property, evidence of the continued possession of a remote occupant is partial, for it is of a detached fact, which may or may not be afterwards connected with the fact in dispute.

Partial incapacity. Such occurs when injury disables a workman to perform part of the usual tasks of his job, though such disablement does not prevent him from procuring and retaining employment reasonably suitable to his physical condition and ability to work, or when because of his injury he is only able to perform labor of a less remunerative class than he performed before the injury, and as a consequence he suffers a depression or reduction in his earning capacity. Commercial Ins. Co. of Newark, New Jersey v. Puente, Tex.Civ.App., 535 S.W.2d 948, 957.

Partial limitation. Provision found in some insurance policies in which the insurer agrees to pay a total loss if the actual loss exceeds a certain amount.

Partial loss. A loss of a part of a thing or of its value, or any damage not amounting (actually or constructively) to its entire destruction; as contrasted with *total* loss. Partial loss is one in which the damage done to the thing insured is not so complete as to amount to a total loss, either actual or constructive. In every such case the underwriter is liable to pay such proportion of the sum which would be payable on total loss as the damage sustained by the subject of insurance bears to the whole value at the time of insurance. Partial loss implies a damage sustained by the ship or cargo, which falls upon the respective owners of the property so damaged; and, when happening from any peril insured against by the policy, the owners are to be indemnified by the underwriters, unless in cases excepted by the express terms of the policy.

Partial payment. See **Payment.**

Partial release. Clause in blanket mortgage directing mortgagee to release specified parcels from lien upon payment of certain sum.

Partial taking. See **Eminent domain.**

Partial verdict. See **Verdict.**

Partiarius /pàrshiyériyəs/. Lat. In Roman law, a legatee who was entitled, by the directions of the will, to receive a share or portion of the inheritance left to the heir.

Partible lands. Lands which might be divided; lands held in gavelkind.

Particeps /párdəsèps/. Lat. A participant; a sharer; anciently, a part owner, or parcener.

Particeps criminis /párdəsèps krímənəs/. A participant in a crime; an accomplice. One who shares or co-operates in a criminal offense, tort or fraud.

Participate /pərtísəpèyt/. To receive or have a part or share of; to partake of; experience in common with others; to have or enjoy a part or share in common with others. To partake, as to "participate" in a discussion, or in a pension or profit sharing plan. To take equal shares and proportions; to share or divide, as to participate in an estate. To take as tenants in common.

Participation. Provision in insurance policies by which the insured shares or participates in each loss incurred and covered by the policy on a specified percentage basis. Sometimes loosely referred to as coinsurance but latter term is not strictly applicable.

Participation loan. Because of statutory and regulatory limitations on the amount which a bank may lend to a single borrower, in some large loan arrangements two or more banks join in a loan with each bank lending a portion of the amount to the borrower.

Participation mortgage. Type of mortgage where lender participates in profits of venture beyond or in addition to normal interest rate.

Participes plures sunt quasi unum corpus in eo quod unum jus habent, et oportet quod corpus sit integrum, et quod in nulla parte sit defectus /partísəpiyz plúriyz sènt kwéyzay yúwnəm kórpəs ìn íyow kwòd yúwnəm jás héybənt, èd əpórtət kwòd kórpəs sìd íntəgrəm èt kwòd ìn nálə párdiy sìt dəféktəs/. Many parceners are as one body, inasmuch as they have one right, and it is necessary that the body be perfect, and that there be a defect in no part.

Particula /partíkyələ/. A small piece of land.

Particular. Relating to a part or portion of anything; separate; sole; single; individual; specific; local; comprising a part only; partial in extent; not universal. Opposed to general. State v. Patterson, 60 Idaho 67, 88 P.2d 493, 497. Of, or pertaining to, a single person, class or thing. Albin v. Hughes, Tex.Civ. App., 304 S.W.2d 371, 372.

As to particular Average; Customs; Estate; Malice; and Partnership; see those titles.

Particularity. In a pleading, affidavit, or the like, is the detailed statement of particulars.

Particular lien. A particular lien is a right to retain a thing for some charge or claim growing out of, or connected with, the identical thing. Right to retain property of another on account of labor employed or money expended on that specific property, and such lien may arise by implication of law, usages of a trade, or by express contract.

Particulars. The details of a claim, or the separate items of an account. When these are stated in an orderly form, for the information of a defendant, the statement is called a "bill of particulars". See **Particulars of criminal charges.**

Particulars, bill of. See **Particulars of criminal charges.**

Particulars of breaches and objections. In an action brought, in England, for the infringement of letters patent, the plaintiff is bound to deliver with his declaration (now with his statement of claim) particulars (*i.e.*, details) of the breaches which he complains of.

Particulars of criminal charges. A prosecutor, when a charge is general, is frequently ordered to give the defendant a statement of the specific acts charged (bill of particulars). Fed.R.Crim.P. 7. See **Bill.**

Particulars of sale. When property such as land, houses, shares, reversions, etc., is to be sold by auction, it is usually described in a document called the "particulars," copies of which are distributed among intending bidders. They should fairly and accurately describe the property.

Particular tenant. The tenant of a particular estate. See **Estate.**

Parties. The persons who take part in the performance of any act, or who are directly interested in any affair, contract, or conveyance, or who are actively concerned in the prosecution and defense of any legal proceeding. Green v. Bogue, 158 U.S. 478, 15 S.Ct. 975, 39 L.Ed. 1061. See also **Party.**

In the Roman civil law, the parties were designated as *"actor" and "reus".* In civil actions they are called "plaintiff" and "defendant"; in equity, "complainant", or "plaintiff", and "defendant"; in admiralty practice, "libelant" and "respondent" or "libelee"; in appeals, "appellant" and "respondent" or "appellee", or sometimes, "plaintiff in error" and "defendant in error"; in criminal proceedings, "State of ____," or "United States of America", and "defendant".

See also Coparties; Identity of parties; Indispensable parties; Interpleader; Intervention; Joinder; Necessary parties; Party; Proper party; Real party in interest; Substitution of parties; Third-party practice.

Indispensible parties. See **Joinder.**

Joinder of parties. See **Joinder.**

Necessary parties. See **Joinder.**

Parties to crime. See **Accessory; Accomplice; Principal.**

Proper parties. See **Joinder.**

Real party in interest. See **Party.**

Parties and privies. Parties to a deed or contract are those with whom the deed or contract is actually made or entered into. By the term "privies," as applied to contracts, is frequently meant those between whom the contract is mutually binding, although not literally parties to such contract. Thus, in the case of a lease, the lessor and lessee are both parties and privies, the contract being literally made between the two, and also being mutually binding; but, if the lessee assign his interest to a third party, then a privity arises between the assignee and the original lessor, although such assignee is not literally a party to the original lease.

Parties in interest. See **Party** (*Real party in interest).*

Partisan. An adherent to a particular party or cause as opposed to the public interest at large.

Partitio /pərtísh(iy)ow/. Lat. In the civil law, partition; division. This word did not always signify *dimidium*, a dividing into halves.

Partitio legata /pərtísh(iy)ow ləgéydə/. In the civil law, a testamentary partition. This took place where the testator, in his will, directed the heir to divide the inheritance and deliver a designated portion thereof to a named legatee.

Partition. The dividing of lands held by joint tenants, coparceners, or tenants in common, into distinct portions, so that they may hold them in severalty. And, in a less technical sense, any division of real or personal property between co-owners, resulting in individual ownership of the interests of each. Division between several persons of property which belongs to them as co-owners; it may be compulsory (judicial) or voluntary. O'Brien v. O'Brien, 89 Misc.2d 433, 391 N.Y.S.2d 502, 503.

Commonly, the court will order the property sold and the proceeds divided instead of ordering a physical partition of the property.

Owelty of partition. See **Owelty.**

Partition, deed of. In conveyancing, a species of primary or original conveyance between two or more joint tenants, coparceners, or tenants in common, by which they divide the lands so held among them in severalty, each taking a distinct part.

Partition of a succession. The partition of a succession is the division of the effects of which the succession is composed, among all the co-heirs, according to their respective rights. Partition is voluntary or judicial. It is voluntary when it is made among all the co-heirs present and of age, and by their mutual consent. It is judicial when it is made by the authority of the court, and according to the formalities prescribed by law. Every partition is either definitive or provisional. Definitive partition is that which is made in a permanent and irrevocable manner. Provisional partition is that which is made provisionally, either of certain things before the rest can be divided, or even of everything that is to be divided, when the parties are not in a situation to make an irrevocable partition.

Partner. A member of partnership or firm; one who has united with others to form a partnership in business. See also **General partner; Partnership.**

Dormant partners. Those whose names are not known or do not appear as partners, but who nevertheless are silent partners, and partake of the profits, and thereby become partners, either absolutely to all intents and purposes, or at all events in respect to third parties. Dormant partners, in strictness of language, mean those who are merely passive in the firm, whether known or unknown, in contradistinction to those who are active and conduct the business of the firm, as principals. See also **Silent partner.**

Full or general partner. A partner who participates fully in the profits, losses and management of the partnership and who is personally liable for its debts.

Junior partner. A partner whose participation in the firm is limited as to both profits and management. See also *Limited partner, infra.*

Limited partner. A partner whose participation in the profits is limited by the agreement and who is not liable for the debts of the partnership beyond his capital contribution. See also **Partnership** *(Limited partnership).*

Liquidating partner. The partner who, upon the dissolution or insolvency of the firm, is appointed to settle its accounts, collect assets, adjust claims, and pay debts.

Nominal partner. One whose name appears in connection with the business as a member of the firm, but who has no real interest in it.

Ostensible partner. One whose name appears to the world as such, or who is held out to all persons having dealings with the firm in the character of a partner, whether or not he has any real interest in the firm.

Quasi partner. One who has joined with others in a business which appears to be a partnership but who is not actually a partner, *e.g.* joint adventurer.

Secret partner. See *Dormant partners, supra.*

Silent partner. See *Dormant partners, supra.*

Special partner. A member of a limited partnership, who furnishes certain funds, and whose liability extends no further than the fund furnished. A partner whose responsibility is restricted to the amount of his investment.

Surviving partner. The partner who, on the dissolution of the firm by the death of his copartner, occupies the position of a trustee to settle up its affairs.

Partnership. A voluntary contract between two or more competent persons to place their money, effects, labor, and skill, or some or all of them, in lawful commerce or business, with the understanding that there shall be a proportional sharing of the profits and losses between them. Burr v. Greenland, Tex.Civ.App., 356 S.W.2d 370, 376; Preston v. State Industrial Accident Commission, 174 Or. 553, 149 P.2d 957, 961, 962. An association of two or more persons to carry on, as co-owners, a business for profit. Uniform Partnership Act, § 6(1). A synallagmatic and commutative contract made between two or more persons for the mutual participation in the profits which may accrue from property, credit, skill, or industry, furnished in determined proportions by the parties. Nearly all states have adopted the Uniform Partnership Act.

Partnerships are treated as a conduit and are, therefore, not subject to taxation. The various items of partnership income, gains and losses, etc. flow through to the individual partners and are reported on their personal income tax returns.

Collapsible partnership. See that title.

Commercial partnership. See **Trading partnership.**

Family partnership. One which family members control by being partners. Children may be partners but for tax purposes they should be given complete control over their interests; otherwise, the entire profits will be considered income of the active adult partners. See also **Family partnership.**

General partnership. A partnership in which the parties carry on all their trade and business, whatever it may be, for the joint benefit and profit of all the parties concerned, whether the capital stock be limited or not, or the contributions thereto be equal or unequal. One in which all the partners share the profits and losses as well as the management equally, though their capital contributions may vary.

Implied partnership. One which is not a real partnership but which is recognized by the court as such because of the conduct of the parties; in effect, the parties are estopped from denying the existence of a partnership.

Limited partnership. A partnership consisting of one or more general partners, jointly and severally responsible as ordinary partners, and by whom the business is conducted, and one or more special partners, contributing in cash payments a specific sum as capital to the common stock, and who are not liable for the debts of the partnership beyond the fund so contributed. See also **Limited partnership.**

Mining partnership. See that title.

Particular partnership. One existing where the parties have united to share the benefits of a single individual transaction or enterprise.

Partnership assets. Property of any kind belonging to the firm as such (not the separate property of the individual partners) and available to the recourse of the creditors of the firm in the first instance.

Partnership at will. One designed to continue for no fixed period of time, but only during the pleasure of the parties, and which may be dissolved by any partner without previous notice.

Partnership debt. One due from the partnership or firm as such and not (primarily) from one of the individual partners.

Partnership in commendam. A partnership formed by a contract by which one person or partnership agrees to furnish another person or partnership a certain amount, either in property or money, to be employed by the person or partnership to whom it is furnished, in his or their own name or firm, on condition of receiving a share in the profits, in the proportion determined by the contract, and of being liable to losses and expenses to the amount furnished and no more.

Secret partnership. One where the existence of certain persons as partners is not avowed to the public by any of the partners. See **Partner** *(Dormant partners).*

Special partnership. At common law, one formed for the prosecution of a special branch of business, as distinguished from the general business of the parties, or for one particular venture or subject. A joint adventure under state statutes; such are usually considered "limited partnerships".

Subpartnership. One formed where one partner in a firm makes a stranger a partner with him in his share of the profits of that firm. It is not a partnership but an arrangement in which the subpartner shares in the profits and losses of a partner.

Statutory partnership association. A statutory creation in some states *(e.g.* Michigan, New Jersey, Ohio) which resembles a corporation more than a partnership, but which has many attributes of the limited partnership.

Trading partnership. See that title.

Universal partnership. One in which the partners jointly agree to contribute to the common fund of the partnership the whole of their property, of whatever character, and future, as well as present.

Partnership agreement. The document embodying the terms and conditions of a partnership and sometimes referred to as the articles of partnership.

Partnership articles. See **Articles of partnership.**

Partnership association. Type of business association which resembles in part a partnership and a joint stock company. Its salient feature is the limited liability of the members and is seldom used today.

Partnership certificate. A document evidencing the participation of the partners in a partnership and commonly furnished to financial institutions when the partnership borrows money.

Partnership insurance. See **Insurance.**

Part performance. A plaintiff who renders partial performance of a contract relying on the promised performance of the other party may successfully resist the defense of the statute of frauds under certain conditions. In order to establish part performance taking an oral contract for the sale of realty out of the statute of frauds, the acts relied upon as part performance must be of such a character that they can reasonably be naturally accounted for in no other way than that they were performed in pursuance of the contract, and they must be in conformity with its provisions. Camerota v. Wisniewski, 21 Conn.Sup. 88, 145 A.2d 139, 141. See U.C.C. § 2–201(3). See also **Performance.**

Partus /párdəs/. Lat. Child; offspring; the child just before it is born, or immediately after its birth.

Partus ex legitimo thoro non certius noscit matrem quam genitorem suum /párdəs èks ləjídəmow θórow nòn sə́rsh(iy)əs nósət méytrəm kwǽm jènətórəm s(y)úwəm/. The offspring of a legitimate bed knows not his mother more certainly than his father.

Partus sequitur ventrem /párdəs sékwədər véntrəm/. The offspring follows the mother; the brood of an animal belongs to the owner of the dam; the offspring of a slave belongs to the owner of the mother, or follows the condition of the mother. A maxim of the civil law, which has been adopted in the law of England in regard to animals, though never allowed in the case of human beings.

Party, *n.* A person concerned or having or taking part in any affair, matter, transaction, or proceeding, considered individually. A "party" to an action is a person whose name is designated on record as plaintiff or defendant. M & A Elec. Power Co-op. v. True, Mo.App., 480 S.W.2d 310, 314. Term, in general, means one having right to control proceedings, to make defense, to adduce and cross-examine witnesses, and to appeal from judgment. City of Chattanooga v. Swift, 223 Tenn. 46, 442 S.W.2d 257, 258.

"Party" is a technical word having a precise meaning in legal parlance; it refers to those by or against whom a legal suit is brought, whether in law or in equity, the party plaintiff or defendant, whether composed of one or more individuals and whether natural or legal persons; all others who may be affected by the suit, indirectly or consequently, are persons interested but not parties. Golatte v. Mathews, D.C.Ala., 394 F.Supp. 1203, 1207.

See also **Nominal defendant; Parties; Prevailing party.**

Party aggrieved. Under statutes permitting any party aggrieved to appeal, one whose right has been directly and injuriously affected by action of court. Freeman v. Thompson, 216 N.C. 484, 5 S.E.2d 434, 436; Singer v. Allied Factors, 216 Minn. 443, 13 N.W.2d 378, 380. Any person having an interest recognized by law in the subject matter of the judgment, which interest is injuriously affected by the judgment, is a "party aggrieved" and entitled to be heard on appeal. Mize v. Crail, 29 C.A.3d 797, 106 Cal.Rptr. 34, 38. To be "party aggrieved" by judgment, appellant's interest must be immediate, pecuniary and substantial and not nominal or remote consequence of judgment. Leoke v. San Bernardino County, 249 C.A.2d 767, 57 Cal.Rptr. 770, 772, 773. See also **Aggrieved party.**

Party to be charged. A phrase used in the statute of frauds, meaning the party against whom the contract is sought to be enforced. The party to be charged in the action—that is, the defendant.

Political party. A body of voters organized for the purpose of influencing or controlling the policies and conduct of government through the nomination and election of its candidates to office.

Real party in interest. Fed.R. Civil P. 17(a) provides that every action shall be prosecuted by the "real party in interest." The adoption of this rule was intended to change the common law rule which permitted suit to be brought only in the name of the person having the legal title to the right of action, and thus precluded suit by persons who had only equitable or beneficial interests. Under the rule the "real party in interest" is the party who, by the substantive law, possesses the right sought to be enforced, and not necessarily the person who will ultimately benefit from the recovery. This is illustrated by the further language of the rule stating that executors, administrators, and other named representatives may sue in their own name without joining with them the party for whose benefit the action is brought.

Third parties. A term used to include all persons who are not parties to the contract, agreement, or instrument of writing by which their interest in the thing conveyed is sought to be affected. See also **Beneficiary.**

In civil actions, a defendant, as a third-party plaintiff, may cause a summons and complaint to be served upon a person not a party to the action who is or may be liable to him for all or part of the plaintiffs' claim against him. A similar right is afforded to the plaintiff when a counterclaim is asserted against him. Fed.R. Civil P. 14. See **Third party complaint; Third-party practice.**

Party wall. A wall erected on a property boundary as a common support to structures on both sides, which are under different ownerships. A wall built partly on the land of one owner, and partly on the land of another, for the common benefit of both in supporting the construction of contiguous buildings. A division wall between two adjacent properties belonging to different persons and used for mutual benefit of both parties, but it is not necessary that the wall should stand part upon each of two adjoining lots, and it may stand wholly upon one lot. Soma Realty Co. v. Romeo, 31 Misc.2d 20, 220 N.Y.S.2d 752, 755.

In the primary and most ordinary meaning of the term, a party-wall is (1) a wall of which the two adjoining owners are tenants in common. But it may also mean (2) a wall divided longitudinally into two strips, one belonging to each of the neighboring owners; (3) a wall which belongs entirely to one of the adjoining owners, but is subject to an easement or right in the other to have it maintained as a dividing wall between the two tenements (the term is so used in some of the English building acts); or (4) a wall divided longitudinally into two moieties, each moiety being subject to a cross-easement in favor of the owner of the other moiety.

Parum /pǽrəm/. Lat. Little; but little.

Parum cavisse videtur /pǽrəm kəvísiy vədíydər/. Lat. Roman law. He seems to have taken too little care; he seems to have been incautious, or not sufficiently upon his guard. A form of expression used by the judge or magistrate in pronouncing sentence of death upon a criminal.

Parum differunt quæ re concordant /pǽrəm dífərənt kwìy ríy kənkórdənt/. Things which agree in substance differ but little.

Parum est latam esse sententiam nisi mandetur executioni /pǽrəm èst léydəm ésiy sənténsh(iy)əm náysay mændéydər èksəkyùwshiyównay/. It is little [or to little purpose] that judgment be given unless it be committed to execution.

Parum proficit scire quid fieri debet, si non cognoscas quomodo sit facturum /pǽrəm prófəsət sáyriy kwìd fáyəray débət, sày nón kəgnóskəs kwówmədow sìt fækt(y)úrəm/. It profits little to know what ought to be done, if you do not know how it is to be done.

Par value. As regards stock, the face value of a share of stock. With reference to mortgages or trust deeds, the value of the mortgage based on the balance owing, without discount.

In the case of a common share, par means a dollar amount assigned to the share by the company's charter. Par value may also be used to compute the dollar amount of the common shares on the balance sheet. Par value has little significance so far as market value of common stock is concerned. Many companies today issue no-par stock but give a stated per share value on the balance sheet. In the case of preferred shares and bonds, however, par is important. It often signifies the dollar value upon which dividends on preferred stocks, and interest on bonds, are figured. In the case of bonds and stock, the face value appearing on the certificate is the par value. Those stocks not containing such a statement have no par value.

Parva serjeantia /párvə sərjiyǽnsh(iy)ə/. Petty serjeanty (*q.v.*).

Parvum cape /párvəm kéyp(iy)/. See **Petit cape.**

Pas /pá/. In French. Precedence; right of going foremost.

Pass, *v.* To utter or pronounce, as when the court *passes* sentence upon a prisoner. Also to proceed; to be rendered or given, as when judgment is said to *pass* for the plaintiff in a suit.

In legislative parlance, a bill or resolution is said to *pass* when it is agreed to or enacted by the house, or when the body has sanctioned its adoption by the requisite majority of votes; in the same circumstances, the body is said to *pass* the bill or motion. See also **Passage.**

When an auditor appointed to examine into any accounts certifies to their correctness, he is said to *pass* them; *i.e.*, they pass through the examination without being detained or sent back for inaccuracy or imperfection.

The term also means to examine into anything and then authoritatively determine the disputed questions which it involves. In this sense a jury is said to *pass upon* the rights or issues in litigation before them.

In the language of conveyancing, the term means to move from one person to another; *i.e.* to be transferred or conveyed from one owner to another.

To publish; utter; transfer; circulate; impose fraudulently. This is the meaning of the word when the offense of *passing* counterfeit money or a forged paper is spoken of.

"Pass," "utter," "publish," and "sell" are in some respects convertible terms, and, in a given case, "pass" may include utter, publish, and sell. The words "uttering" and "passing," used of notes, do not necessarily import that they are transferred as genuine. The words include any delivery of a note to another for value, with intent that it shall be put into circulation as money. Word "pass" when used in connection with negotiable instrument means to deliver, to circulate, to hand from one person to another. State v. Beaver, 266 N.C. 115, 145 S.E.2d 330, 331. See **Delivery; Negotiation; Transfer; Utter.**

Pass, n. Permission to pass; a license to go or come; a certificate, emanating from authority, wherein it is declared that a designated person is permitted to go beyond certain boundaries which, without such authority, he could not lawfully pass. Also a ticket issued by a railroad or other transportation company, authorizing a designated person to travel free on its lines, between certain points or for a limited time.

Passage. Act of passing; transit; transition. A way over water or land or through the air. An easement giving the right to pass over a piece of private water. Travel by sea; a voyage over water; the carriage of passengers by water; price paid for such carriage.

Enactment; the act of carrying a bill or resolution through a legislative or deliberative body in accordance with the prescribed forms and requisites. The emergence of the bill in the form of a law, or the motion in the form of a resolution. Passage may mean when bill has passed either or both houses of legislature or when it is signed by President or Governor.

Passagio /pæséyj(iy)ow/. An ancient writ addressed to the keepers of the ports to permit a man who had the king's leave to pass over sea.

Passator /pæséydər/. In old English law, he who has the interest or command of the passage of a river; or a lord to whom a duty is paid for passage.

Passbook. Document issued by a bank in which the customer's transactions (*i.e.* savings deposits and withdrawals) are recorded.

Passenger. In general, a passenger is one who gives compensation for a ride. Shapiro v. Bookspan, 155 Cal.App.2d 353, 318 P.2d 123, 126. The word passenger has however various meanings, depending upon the circumstances under which and the context in which the word is used; sometimes it is construed in a restricted legal sense as referring to one who is being carried by another for hire; on other occasions, the word is interpreted as meaning any occupant of a vehicle other than the person operating it. American Mercury Ins. Co. v. Bifulco, 74 N.J.Super. 191, 181 A.2d 20, 22.

The essential elements of "passenger" as opposed to "guest" under guest statute are that driver must receive some benefit sufficiently real, tangible, and substantial to serve as the inducing cause of the transportation so as to completely overshadow mere hospitality or friendship; it may be easier to find compensation where the trip has commercial or business flavor. Friedhoff v. Engberg, 82 S.D. 522, 149 N.W.2d 759, 761, 762, 763.

A person whom a common carrier has contracted to carry from one place to another, and has, in the course of the performance of that contract, received under his care either upon the means of conveyance, or at the point of departure of that means of conveyance.

Passenger mile. In statistics of transportation, a unit of measure equal to the transport of one passenger over one mile of route.

Passim /pǽsəm/. Lat. Everywhere. Often used to indicate a very general reference to a book or legal authority.

Passion. In the definition of manslaughter as homicide committed without premeditation but under the influence of sudden "passion" or "heat of passion", this term means any of the emotions of the mind known as rage, anger, hatred, furious resentment, or terror, rendering the mind incapable of cool reflection.

Passive. As used in law, this term means inactive; permissive; consisting in endurance or submission, rather than action; and in some connections it carries the implication of being subjected to a burden or charge.

As to passive Debt; Negligence; Title; Trust; and Use; see those titles.

Passport. A document identifying a citizen, in effect requesting foreign powers to allow the bearer to enter and to pass freely and safely, recognizing the right of the bearer to the protection and good offices of American diplomatic and consular offices. U. S. v. Laub, U.S.N.Y., 385 U.S. 475, 87 S.Ct. 574, 578, 17 L.Ed.2d 526. A passport is evidence of permission from sovereign to its citizen to travel to foreign countries and to return to land of his allegiance, as well as request to foreign powers that such citizen be allowed to pass freely and safely. Worthy v. U. S., C.A.Fla., 328 F.2d 386, 391.

In international law. A license or safe-conduct, issued during the progress of a war, authorizing a person to remove himself or his effects from the territory of one of the belligerent nations to another country, or to travel from country to country without arrest or detention on account of the war.

Maritime. A document issued to a neutral merchant vessel, by her own government, during the progress of a war, to be carried on the voyage, to evidence her nationality and protect her against the cruisers of the belligerent powers. This paper is otherwise called a "pass," "sea-pass," "sea-letter," "sea-brief." It usually contains the captain's or master's name and residence, the name, property, description, tonnage, and destination of the ship, the nature and quantity of the cargo, the place from whence it comes, and its destination, with such other matters as the practice of the place requires.

Past consideration. In contracts, a detriment suffered by a contracting party at a time antecedent to the formation of a contract and hence, except in unusual cases, is not legally sufficient consideration to support a contract. In law of negotiable instruments, past consideration is sufficient to support a note or other negotiable instrument.

Past recollection recorded. A memorandum or record concerning a matter about which a witness once had knowledge but now has insufficient recollection to enable him to testify fully and accurately, shown to have been made or adopted by the witness when the matter was fresh in his memory and to reflect that knowledge correctly, is not excluded by the hearsay rule, even though the declarant is available as a witness. If admitted, the memorandum or record may be read into evidence but may not itself be received as an exhibit unless offered by an adverse party. Fed.Evid.R. 803(5).

Under the "past recollection recorded" doctrine, written report is properly admissible into evidence if witness has testified that on examination of the report he had no independent recollection of the matters contained therein. Lawson v. Belt Ry. Co. of Chicago, 34 Ill.App.3d 7, 339 N.E.2d 381, 394. Past recollection recorded is where a witness, who is either devoid of a present recollection or possessed of an imperfect present recollection, desires to use a past recollection by employing some record of such recollection. Askins v. State, 13 Md.App. 702, 284 A.2d 626, 630.

Pastus /pǽstəs/. In feudal law, the procuration or provision which tenants were bound to make for their lords at certain times, or as often as they made a progress to their lands. It was often converted into money.

Pateat universis per præsentes /pǽdiyət yùwnəvɔ́rsəs pər prəzéntiyz/. Know all men by these presents. Words with which letters of attorney anciently commenced.

Patent, *adj.* Open; manifest; evident; unsealed. Used in this sense in such phrases as "patent ambiguity," "patent writ," "letters patent."

Letters patent. Open letters, as distinguished from letters close. An instrument proceeding from the government, and conveying a right, authority, or grant to an individual, as a patent for a tract of land, or for the exclusive right to make and sell a new invention. See **Letters patent; Patent and Trademark Office.**

Patent ambiguity. See **Ambiguity.**

Patent defect. In sales of personal property, one which is plainly visible or which can be discovered by such an inspection as would be made in the exercise of ordinary care and prudence. U.C.C. § 2–605(1).

A patent defect in a legal description is one which cannot be corrected on its face, and a new description must be used. *Compare* **Latent defect.**

Patent, *n.* A grant of some privilege, property, or authority, made by the government or sovereign of a country to one or more individuals.

The instrument by which a state or government grants public lands to an individual. A grant made by the government to an inventor, conveying and securing to him the exclusive right to make, use and sell his invention for a term of years. See **Patent and Trademark Office.**

See also Combination patent; File wrapper estoppel; Identity; Invent; Invention; Lapse patent; Letter patent; License; Official Gazette; Paper patent; Patent license; Process patent; Public use; Scope of patent; Shop right rule.

Design patent. Granted for giving a new and pleasing appearance to an article of manufacture whereby its sale is enhanced. Viehmann v. D. F. H. Novelty Furniture Co., D.C.N.Y., 27 F.Supp. 566, 567; 35 U.S.C.A. § 171 et seq.

Land patent. A muniment of title issued by a government or state for the conveyance of some portion of the public domain.

Patent ambiguity. A patent ambiguity is an ambiguity which appears on the face of an instrument and arises from defective, obscure or insensible language used. Paliotto v. Town of Islip, 31 Misc.2d 447, 224 N.Y.S.2d 466, 474.

Patent-right. A right secured by patent; usually meaning a right to the exclusive manufacture and sale of an invention or patented article.

Patent-right dealer. Any one whose business it is to sell, or offer for sale, patent-rights.

Patent suit. A suit with issues affecting the legality or infringement of a patent. Rubens v. Bowers, C.C. A.Cal., 136 F.2d 887, 889.

Pioneer patent. A patent for an invention covering a function never before performed, or a wholly novel device, or one of such novelty and importance as to mark a distinct step in the progress of the art, as distinguished from a mere improvement or perfecting of what has gone before. Westinghouse v. Boyden Power-Brake Co., 170 U.S. 537, 18 S.Ct. 707, 42 L.Ed. 1136.

Plant patent. Granted to person who invents or discovers and asexually reproduces a distinct and new variety of plant; word "plant" being used in the popular sense. Kim Bros. v. Hagler, D.C.Cal., 167 F.Supp. 665, 667; 35 U.S.C.A. § 161 *et seq.*

Reissued patent. A patent securing rights of an inventor more definitely in some particular wherein the original patent was defective.

Tax treatment. A patent is an identifiable intangible asset which may be amortized over the remaining life of the patent. The sale of a patent usually results in favorable long-term capital gain treatment. I.R.C. § 1235. If developed internally by a company, the development costs are expenses when incurred under generally accepted accounting principles.

Patentable. Suitable to be patented; entitled by law to be protected by the issuance of a patent. And to be patentable, a device must embody some new idea or principle not before known, and it must be a discovery as distinguished from mere mechanical skill or knowledge. Hobart Mfg. Co. v. Landers, Frary & Clark, D.C.Conn., 26 F.Supp. 198, 202; In re Herthel, Cust. & Pat.App., 104 F.2d 824, 826.

Patent and copyright clause. Art. I, Sec. 8, cl. 8, U.S. Constitution, which provides for promoting the progress of science and useful arts, by securing for limited times to authors and inventors the exclusive right to their respective writings and discoveries.

Patent and Trademark Office. Federal agency in the Department of Commerce headed by the Commissioner of Patents and Trademarks. In addition to the examination of patent and trademark applications, issuance of patents, and registration of trademarks, the Patent and Trademark Office (PTO) sells printed copies of issued documents; records and indexes documents transferring ownership; maintains a scientific library and search files containing over 20 million documents, including U.S. and foreign patents and U.S. trademarks; provides search rooms for the public to research their applications; hears and decides appeals from prospective inventors and trademark applicants; participates in legal proceedings involving the issue of patents or trademark registrations; helps represent the United States in international efforts to cooperate on patent and trademark policy; compiles the Official Gazettes—a weekly list of all patents and trademarks issued by the PTO; and maintains a roster of agents and attorneys qualified to practice before the PTO.

Patent appeals. See **Board of Patent Appeals.**

Patentee. He to whom a patent has been granted. The term is usually applied to one who has obtained letters patent for a new invention.

Patent infringement. The act of using or selling any patented invention without authority during the term of the patent and this includes one who induces the infringement. 35 U.S.C.A. § 271. See also **Infringement.**

Patent medicine. Patent medicine means a packaged remedy for public use, protected by letters patent and sold without a physician's prescription. Board of Pharmacy v. Sherman, 74 N.J.Super. 417, 181 A.2d 418, 419.

Patent pooling. An arrangement in which a number of manufacturers agree to an interchange of patent licenses among the members of the pooling group.

Pater /péydər/. Lat. A father; the father. In the civil law, this word sometimes included *avus* (grandfather).

Paterfamilias /pèydərfəmíl(i)yəs/. The father of a family.

In Roman law, the head or master of a family. This word is sometimes employed, in a wide sense, as equivalent to *sui juris*. A person *sui juris* is called *"paterfamilias"* even when under the age of puberty. In the narrower and more common use, a *paterfamilias* is any one invested with *potestas* over any person. It is thus as applicable to a grandfather as to a father.

Pater is est quem nuptiæ demonstrant /péydər ís èst kwèm nápshiyiy dəmónstrænt/. The father is he whom the marriage points out.

Paternal. That which belongs to the father or comes from him.

Paternal line. A line of descent or relationship between two persons which is traced through the father.

Paternal power. The authority lawfully exercised by parents over their children. This phrase is also used to translate the Latin *"patria potestas"* (q.v.).

Paternal property. That which descends or comes to one from his father, grandfather, or other ascendant or collateral on the paternal side of the house.

Paternity. The state or condition of a father; the relationship of a father.

Paternity suit. A court action to prove that a person is the father of an illegitimate child and to enforce support obligations. See also **Multiple access.**

Pater patriæ /péydər pætriyiy/. Father of the country. See **Parens patriæ.**

Pathologist. One trained in the scientific study of disease, its causes, development and consequences.

Pathology. The science or doctrine of diseases. That part of medicine which explains the nature of diseases, their causes, and their symptoms.

Patiens /pǽshiyèn(d)z/. Lat. One who suffers or permits; one to whom an act is done; the passive party in a transaction.

Patient. Person under medical or psychiatric treatment and care.

Patient-physician privilege. The right of one who is a patient to refuse to divulge, or have divulged by his physician, the communications made between he and his physician. This privilege is provided for by statute in most states, and, where recognized, it belongs to the patient and not to the physician and hence, it may be waived by the patient.

Patria /pǽtriyə/péytriyə/. Lat. The country, neighborhood, or vicinage; the men of the neighborhood; a jury of the vicinage. Synonymous, in this sense, with *"pais."*

Patria laboribus et expensis non debet fatigari /pǽtriyə ləbórəbəs èd əkspénsəs nòn débət fǽtəgéray/. A jury ought not to be harassed by labors and expenses.

Patria potestas /pǽtriyə pətéstǽs/. Lat. In Roman law, paternal authority; the paternal power. This term denotes the aggregate of those peculiar powers and rights which, by the civil law of Rome, belonged to the head of a family in respect to his wife, children (natural or adopted), and any more remote descendants who sprang from him through males only. Anciently, it was of very extensive reach, embracing even the power of life and death, but was gradually curtailed, until finally it amounted to little more than a right in the *paterfamilias* to hold as his own any property or acquisitions of one under his power.

Patria potestas in pietate debet, non in atrocitate, consistere /pǽtriyə pətéstǽs ìn pàyətéydiy débət, nón ìn ətròsətéydiy kənsístəriy/. Paternal power should consist [or be exercised] in affection, not in atrocity.

Patricide /pǽtrəsàyd/. One who has killed his father.

Patrimonial /pæ̀trəmówn(i)yəl/. Pertaining to a patrimony; inherited from ancestors, but strictly from the direct male ancestors.

Patrimonium /pæ̀trəmówn(i)yəm/. In civil law, that which is capable of being inherited. The private and exclusive ownership or dominion of an individual. Things capable of being possessed by a single person to the exclusion of all others (or which are actually so possessed) are said to be *in patrimonio;* if not capable of being so possessed (or not actually so possessed), they are said to be *extra patrimonium.*

Patrimony /pǽtrəməniy/. Such estate as has descended in the same family. Estates which have descended or been devised in a direct line from the father, and, by extension, from the mother or other ancestor. It has been held that the word is not necessarily restricted to property inherited directly from the father.

Patrimony is the total mass of existing or potential rights and liabilities attached to a person for the satisfaction of his economic needs and patrimony is always attached to a natural or juridical person. Creech v. Capitol Mack, Inc., La., 287 So.2d 497, 503.

Patrimony of a debtor is totality of assets and liabilities susceptible of pecuniary evaluation; as practical matter, debtor's patrimony consists of assets which are subject to execution for benefit of creditor. Hastings v. Dinning, La.App., 314 So.2d 744, 746.

Patrocinium /pæ̀trəsíniyəm/. In Roman law, patronage; protection; defense. The business or duty of a patron or advocate.

Patrolman. A policeman assigned to duty in patrolling a certain beat or district; also the designation of a grade or rank in the organized police force of large cities, a patrolman being generally a private in the ranks, as distinguished from sergeants, lieutenants, etc.

Patron. In ordinary usage one who protects, countenances, or supports some person or thing; one who habitually extends material assistance; a regular customer; a protector or benefactor.

Patronage /pǽtrənəj/péytr°/. Collective term to describe the customers of a business. Also, the practice of a public official in making appointments to public (non-civil service) offices and to confer honors. The right of appointing to office, considered as a perquisite, or personal right; not in the aspect of a public trust.

Patronize /péytrənayz/pǽtr°/. To act as a patron, extend patronage, countenance, encourage, favor.

Patronum faciunt dos, ædificatio, fundus /pətrównəm féysh(iy)ənt dóws, iydəfəkéysh(iy)ow, fándəs/ Endowment, building, and land make a patron.

Patruelis /pæ̀truwíyləs/. Lat. In the civil law, a cousin-in-german by the father's side; the son or daughter of a father's brother.

Patruus /pǽtruwəs/. Lat. An uncle by the father's side; a father's brother.

Patruus magnus /pǽtruwəs mǽgnəs/. A grandfather's brother; granduncle.

Patruus major /pǽtruwəs méyjər/. A great-grandfather's brother.

Patruus maximus /pǽtruwəs mǽksəməs/. A great-grandfather's father's brother.

Pattern. A reliable sample of traits, acts or other observable features characterizing an individual. Richerson v. Superior Court In and For Sacramento County, App., 70 Cal.Rptr. 350, 352.

The words "pattern or practice" within the Civil Rights Act provision which permits the Attorney General to seek relief when there is a pattern or practice of resistance to the Act is more than isolated or accidental instance of conduct in violation of the Act; it means an intentional, regular or repeated violation of the right granted by the Act. U. S. v. Hunter, C.A.Md., 459 F.2d 205, 217.

Pauper /pópər/. A person so poor that he must be supported at public expense. A suitor who, on account of poverty, is allowed to sue or defend without being chargeable with costs; also, an indigent criminal defendant who has a right to assigned defense counsel. Fed.R.Crim.P. 44; Fed.R.App.P. 24. See **Counsel, right to; Indigent; Pauper's oath.**

Dispauper. To deprive one of the status of a pauper and of any benefits incidental thereto: particularly, to take away the right to sue *in forma pauperis* because the person so suing, during the progress of the suit, has acquired money or property which would enable him to sustain the costs of the action.

Pauperies /pópəriyz/. Lat. In Roman law, damage or injury done by an irrational animal, without active fault on the part of the owner, but for which the latter was bound to make compensation.

Pauper's oath. Affidavit, verification, or oath by person seeking public assistance, appointment of counsel, waiver of court fees, or other free services or benefits, that he or she is in fact impoverished and as such unable to pay for such. See also **Poverty affidavit.**

Pawn, *v.* To deliver personal property to another in pledge, or as security for a debt or sum borrowed.

Pawn, *n.* A bailment of goods to a creditor, as security for some debt or engagement; a pledge. In common usage pawn means a pledge of chattels as distinguished from pledges of choses in action, and in more limited sense means a deposit of personal property made to a pawnbroker as security for a loan; that sort of bailment when goods or chattels are delivered to another as security to him for money borrowed of him by the bailor.

Also the specific chattel delivered to the creditor as a pledge.

See **Bailment; Pledge.**

Pawnbroker. A person whose business is to lend money, usually in small sums, on security of personal property deposited with him or left in pawn.

Pawnee. The person receiving a pawn, or to whom a pawn is made; the person to whom goods are delivered by another in pledge.

Pawnor. The person pawning goods or delivering goods to another in pledge.

Pax regis /pǽks ríyjəs/. Lat. The peace of the king; that is, the peace, good order, and security for life and property which it is one of the objects of government to maintain, and which the king, as the personification of the power of the state, is supposed to guaranty to all persons within the protection of the law.

This name was also given, in ancient times, to a certain privileged district or sanctuary. The *pax regis,* or verge of the court, as it was afterwards called, extended from the palace-gate to the distance of three miles, three furlongs, three acres, nine feet, nine palms, and nine barleycorns.

Pay, *n.* Compensation; wages; salary; commissions; fees. The act or fact of paying or being paid. See **Discharge; Payment.**

Pay, *v.* To discharge a debt by tender of payment due; to deliver to a creditor the value of a debt, either in money or in goods, for his acceptance. U.C.C. §§ 2–511, 3–604. To compensate for goods, services or labor. See also **Discharge; Payment.**

Payable. Capable of being paid; suitable to be paid; admitting or demanding payment; justly due; legally enforceable. A sum of money is said to be payable when a person is under an obligation to pay it. Payable may therefore signify an obligation to pay at a future time, but, when used without qualification, term normally means that the debt is payable at once, as opposed to "owing."

Payable after sight. Payable after acceptance of bill or protest for nonacceptance.

Payable on demand. Instruments payable on demand include those payable at sight or on presentation and those in which no time for payment is stated. U.C.C. § 3–108.

Payable to bearer. A negotiable instrument is payable to bearer when by its terms it is payable to (a) bearer or the order of bearer; or (b) a specified person or bearer; or (c) "cash" or the order of "cash", or any other indication which does not purport to designate a specific payee. U.C.C. § 3–111. See also **Negotiation.**

Payable to order. A negotiable instrument is payable to order when by its terms it is payable to the order or assigns of any person therein specified with reasonable certainty, or to him or his order, or when it is conspicuously designated on its face as "exchange" or the like and names a payee. U.C.C. § 3–110. See also **Negotiation.**

Pay any bank. After an item has been indorsed with the words "pay any bank" or the like, only a bank may acquire the rights of a holder: (a) until the item has been returned to the customer initiating collection; or (b) until the item has been specially indorsed by a bank to a person who is not a bank. U.C.C. § 4–201(2).

Payee. The person in whose favor a bill of exchange, promissory note, or check is made or drawn; the person to whom or to whose order a bill, note, or check is made payable. The entity to whom a cash payment is made or who will receive the stated amount of money on a check. One to whom money is paid or is to be paid. See **Draft; Fictitious payee.**

Payer, or **payor.** One who pays, or who is to make a payment; particularly the person who is to make payment of a check, bill or note. Correlative to "payee."

Paying quantities. This phrase, as used in oil and gas leases, when applied to the production of oil, means such a quantity as will pay a profit on the cost of operating the well. Sufficient quantities to pay a reasonable profit on the whole sum required to be expended, including the cost of drilling, equipping, and operating the well. If the well pays a profit, even small, over operating expenses, it produces in paying quantities, though it may never repay its cost, and the operation as a whole may prove unprofitable.

Payment. The fulfilment of a promise, or the performance of an agreement. A discharge of an obligation or debt, and part payment, if accepted, is a discharge pro tanto.

In a more restricted legal sense payment is the performance of a duty, promise, or obligation, or discharge of a debt or liability, by the delivery of money or other value by a debtor to a creditor, where the money or other valuable thing is tendered and accepted as extinguishing debt or obligation in whole or in part. Also the money or other thing so delivered. U.C.C. §§ 2–511, 3–604.

Payment is a delivery of money or its equivalent in either specific property or services by one person from whom it is due to another person to whom it is due. Sizemore v. E. T. Barwick Industries, Inc., 225 Tenn. 226, 465 S.W.2d 873, 875. A discharge in money or its equivalent of an obligation or debt owing by one person to another, and is made by debtor's delivery to creditor of money or some other valuable thing, and creditor's receipt thereof, for purpose of extinguishing debt. Allmon v. Allmon, Mo. App., 306 S.W.2d 651, 655.

Under Internal Revenue Code provision allowing deduction for charitable contribution of which payment is made within taxable year, "payment" need not be in money, but subject matter must have been placed beyond dominion and control of donor. Pauley v. U. S., C.A.Cal., 459 F.2d 624, 626.

The execution and delivery of negotiable papers is not payment unless it is accepted by the parties in that sense. U.C.C. § 3–410.

See also **Compulsory payment; Conditional payment; Constructive payment; Down payment; Installment credit; Installment loan; Installment sale; Involuntary payment; Liquidation; Lump-sum payment; Pay.**

Affirmative defense. Payment is an affirmative defense which must be pleaded under Fed.R. Civil P. 8(c).

Payment is a plea in avoidance. Harrison v. Leasing Associates, Inc., Tex.Civ.App., 454 S.W.2d 808, 809.

Balloon payment. See **Balloon payment.**

Part payment. The reduction of any debt or demand by the payment of a sum less than the whole amount originally due.

The rule of partial payments is to apply the payment, in the first place, to the discharge of the interest then due. If the payment exceeds the interest, the surplus goes toward discharging the principal, and the subsequent interest is to be computed on the balance of principal remaining due. If the payment be less than the interest, the surplus of the interest must not be taken to augment the principal; but interest continues on the former principal until the period of time when the payments, taken together, exceed the interest then due, to discharge which they are applied, and the surplus, if any, is to be applied towards the discharge of the principal, and the interest is to be computed on the balance as aforesaid, and this process continues until final settlement.

Payment into court. The act of a defendant in depositing the amount which he admits to be due, with the proper officer of the court, for the benefit of the plaintiff and in answer to his claim. Fed.R. Civil P. 67.

Voluntary payment. A payment made by a debtor of his own will and choice, as distinguished from one exacted from him by process of execution or other compulsion.

Payment guaranteed. "Payment guaranteed" or equivalent words added to a signature mean that the signer engages that if the instrument is not paid when due he will pay it according to its tenor without resort by the holder to any other party. U.C.C. § 4–416.

Payor. The person by whom a bill or note has been or should have been paid.

Payroll tax. Tax based on and deducted from payroll. A "payroll tax" is a government or state tax on employers as a percentage of wages and salaries paid to employees. City of Richmond v. Fary, 210 Va. 338, 171 S.E.2d 257, 260.

PBGC. Pension Benefit Guaranty Corporation.

P.C. An abbreviation for "Pleas of the Crown;" sometimes also for "Privy Council," "Parliamentary Cases," "Patent Cases," "Practice Cases," "Penal Code," "Political Code," or "Professional Corporation."

Peace. For purposes of breach of the peace statute, peace is that state and sense of safety which is necessary to the comfort and happiness of every citizen, and which government is instituted to secure. State v. Boles, 5 Conn.Cir. 22, 240 A.2d 920, 927. Term, within law of breach of the peace, means tranquility enjoyed by citizens of the municipality or community where good order reigns among its members. State v. Edwards, 239 S.C. 339, 123 S.E.2d 247, 249.

The tranquility enjoyed by a political society internally, by the good order which reigns among its members, and externally by the good understanding it has with all other nations. Applied to the internal regulations of a nation, peace imports, in a technical sense, not merely a state of repose and security as opposed to one of violence or warfare, but likewise a state of public order and decorum. Catlette v. U. S., C.C.A.W.Va., 132 F.2d 902, 906.

Articles of the peace. See **Articles.**

Bill of peace. See **Bill.**

Breach of peace. See **Breach.**

Conservator of the peace. See **Conservator.**

Justice of the peace. See that title.

Peace and quietude. Public tranquility and obedience to law, and that public order and security which is commanded by the laws of a particular sovereign.

Peace officers. This term is variously defined by statute in the different states; but generally it includes sheriffs and their deputies, constables, marshals, members of the police force of cities, and other officers whose duty is to enforce and preserve the public peace. In general, any person who has been given general authority to make arrests. Generally a "peace officer" is a person designated by public authority to keep the peace and arrest persons guilty or suspected of crime and he is a conservator of the peace, which term is synonymous with the term "peace officer". Vandiver v. Manning, 215 Ga. 874, 114 S.E.2d 121, 124.

Peace of God and the church. In old English law, that rest and cessation which the king's subjects had from trouble and suit of law between the terms and on Sundays and holidays.

Public peace. The peace or tranquility of the community in general; the good order and repose of the people composing a state or municipality. That invisible sense of security which every man feels so necessary to his comfort, and for which all governments are instituted.

Public peace and quiet. Peace, tranquility, and order and freedom from agitation or disturbance; the security, good order, and decorum guaranteed by civil society and by the law.

Peaceable. Free from the character of force, violence, or trespass; as, a "peaceable entry" on lands. "Peaceable possession" of real estate is such as is acquiesced in by all other persons, including rival claimants, and not disturbed by any forcible attempt at ouster nor by adverse suits to recover the possession or the estate. Stanley v. Schwalby, 147 U.S. 508, 13 S.Ct. 418, 37 L.Ed. 259.

Peace bond. Type of surety bond required by a judge or magistrate of one who has threatened to breach the peace.

Peccata contra naturam sunt gravissima /pəkéydə kóntrə nət(y)úrəm sənt grəvísəmə/. Crimes against nature are the most heinous.

Peccatum peccato addit qui culpæ quam facit patrocinia defensionis adjungit /pəkéydəm pəkéydow ǽdɪt kwày kálpiy kwæm féysət pætrəsín(i)yə dəfènshiyównəs əjə́njət/. He adds fault to fault who sets up a defense of a wrong committed by him.

Peck. A measure of two gallons; a dry measure.

Peculation. The unlawful appropriation, by a depositary of public funds, of the property of the government intrusted to his care, to his own use, or that of others. The fraudulent misappropriation by one to his own use of money or goods intrusted to his care.

Peculatus /pèkyəléydəs/. Lat. In the civil law, the offense of stealing or embezzling the public money.

Peculiar, *adj.* /pəkyúwl(i)yər/. Particular or special. Wolf v. Mallinckrodt Chemical Works, 336 Mo. 746, 81 S.W.2d 323, 330.

Peculium /pəkyúwl(i)yəm/. Lat. In Roman law, such private property as might be held by a slave, wife, or son who was under the *patria potestas,* separate from the property of the father or master, and in the personal disposal of the owner.

Pecunia /pəkyúwn(i)yə/. In old English law, goods and chattels.

In the civil law, property in general, real or personal; anything that is actually the subject of private property. In a narrower sense, personal property; fungible things. In the strictest sense, money. This has become the prevalent, and almost the exclusive, meaning of the word.

Pecunia constituta /pəkyúwn(i)yə kònstət(y)úwdə/. In Roman law, money owing (even upon a moral obligation) upon a day being fixed *(constituta)* for its payment, became recoverable upon the implied promise to pay on that day, in an action called *"de pecunia constituta,"* the implied promise not amounting (of course) to a *stipulatio.*

Pecunia non numerata /pəkyúwn(i)yə nòn n(y)ùwməréydə/. In the civil law, money not paid. The subject of an exception or plea in certain cases.

Pecunia numerata /pəkyúwn(i)yə n(y)ùwməréydə/. Money numbered or counted out; *i.e.,* given in payment of a debt.

Pecuniary /pəkyúwn(i)yəriy/. Monetary; relating to money; financial; consisting of money or that which can be valued in money.

As to pecuniary Consideration; Damages; and Legacy; see those titles.

Pecuniary benefits. Benefits that can be valued in money. Dallas Ry. & Terminal Co. v. Moore, Tex.Civ. App., 52 S.W.2d 104. Pecuniary benefits available to parents by reason of death of an adult child encompass those benefits, including money, that can be reasonably estimated in money, such as labor, services, kindness and attention of child to parents. Borak v. Bridge, Tex.Civ.App., 524 S.W.2d 773, 776.

Pecuniary bequest. A bequest of money to a legatee by a testator. Also known as a monetary bequest. See **Bequest.**

Pecuniary causes. In English ecclesiastical practice, causes arising from the withholding of ecclesiastical dues, or the doing or neglecting some act relating to the church whereby some damage accrues to the plaintiff. 3 Bl.Comm. 88.

Pecuniary condition. Within statute relative to obtaining goods by false pretenses, comprehends, not only money in hand, but property and all other assets of value constituting an existing fact that go to make up financial responsibility as a basis of credit.

Pecuniary consideration. See **Consideration.**

Pecuniary damages. See **Damages; Pecuniary loss.**

Pecuniary formulas. In federal estate taxation, a gift to a surviving spouse of an amount equal to the maximum marital deduction to which the estate is entitled, less the value of any other interests passing to the surviving spouse that qualify for the marital deduction. See also **Marital deduction.**

Pecuniary injury. The words "pecuniary injuries" within wrongful death statute mean the deprivation of a reasonable expectation of a pecuniary advantage, which would have resulted by continuance of life of deceased. Gluckauf v. Pine Lake Beach Club, Inc., 78 N.J.Super. 8, 187 A.2d 357, 363. Such compensation includes damages for deprivation of support, of companionship, guidance, advice, love and affection of deceased. Hall v. Gillins, 13 Ill.2d 26, 147 N.E.2d 352, 355. See also **Consortium; Damages** *(Pecuniary damages);* **Loss; Pecuniary loss.**

Pecuniary interest. A direct interest related to money in an action or case as would, for example, require a judge to disqualify himself from sitting on a case if he owned stock in corporate party.

Pecuniary legacy. See **Legacy.**

Pecuniary loss. A loss of money, or of something by which money or something of money value may be acquired. As applied to a dependent's loss from death pecuniary loss means the reasonable expectation of pecuniary benefit from the continued life of the deceased; such includes loss of services, training, nurture, education, guidance, and society. Sea Land Services, Inc. v. Gaudet, 414 U.S. 573, 94 S.Ct. 806, 39 L.Ed.2d 9.

Pecuniary loss within Wrongful Death Act means what the life of decedent was worth, in a pecuniary sense, to the survivors. Flynn v. Vancil, 89 Ill.App. 368, 232 N.E.2d 473, 474.

See also **Pecuniary injury.**

Pecunia sepulchralis /pəkyúwn(i)yə sèpəlkréyləs/. Money anciently paid to the priest at the opening of a grave for the good of the deceased's soul.

Pecunia trajectitia /pəkyúwn(i)yə træjektísh(iy)ə/. In the civil law, a loan in money, or in wares which the debtor purchases with the money to be sent by sea, and whereby the creditor, according to the contract, assumes the risk of the loss from the day of the departure of the vessel until the day of her arrival at her port of destination. Interest does not necessarily arise from this loan, but when it is stipulated for, it is termed *"nauticum fœnus"* (maritime interest), and, because of the risk which the creditor assumes, he is permitted to receive a higher interest than usual.

Pedage /pédəj/. In old English law, a toll or tax paid by travelers for the privilege of passing, on foot or mounted, through a forest or other protected place.

Pedagium /pədéyj(iy)əm/. L. Lat. Pedage *(q.v.).*

Pedaulus /pədóləs/. (Lat. *Pes* foot). In civil law, a judge who sat at the foot of the tribunal, *i.e.* on the lowest seats, ready to try matters of little moment at command of the prætor.

Peddler. An itinerant trader; a person who sells small wares which he carries with him in traveling about from place to place, and whose activities generally require that he be licensed by the city or town within which he peddles. Distinguished from "trader" who has goods for sale and sells them in a fixed place of business. Commonwealth v. Bergeron, 296 Mass. 60, 5 N.E.2d 31, 32. See also **Hawker.**

Pederasty /pédəræstiy/. In criminal law, the unnatural carnal copulation of male with male, particularly of a man with a boy; a form of sodomy (q.v.).

Pedestrian. A person traveling on foot. The statutory definition of "pedestrian" is broad enough to include persons standing upon the highway as well as those traversing it. See v. Willett, 58 Wash.2d 39, 360 P.2d 592, 593. Person on foot does not cease to be "pedestrian" within policy covering injuries sustained while a pedestrian merely because he is not in motion. Peterson v. Continental Cas. Co., 25 Utah 2d 408, 483 P.2d 445, 446.

Pedigree /pédəgriy/. Lineage, descent, and succession of families; line of ancestors from which a person descends; genealogy. An account or register of a line of ancestors. Family relationship.

Evidence. Statements of fact concerning genealogy are not excluded by the hearsay rule, even though the declarant is available as a witness. Fed.Evid.R. 803.

Pedis abscissio /píydəs æbsísh(iy)ow/. Lat. In old feudal criminal law, the cutting off a foot; a punishment anciently inflicted instead of death.

Pedis positio /píydəs pəzísh(iy)ow/. Lat. In the civil and old English law, a putting or placing of the foot. A term used to denote the possession of lands by actual corporal entry upon them.

Pedis possessio /píydəs pəzésh(iy)ow/. Lat. A foot-hold; an actual possession. To constitute adverse possession there must be *pedis possessio,* or a substantial inclosure.

Peeping tom. A person who makes it a habit of sneaking up to windows and peeping in, for the purpose generally of seeing the women of the household in the nude. Browder v. Cook, D.C.Idaho, 59 F.Supp. 225, 231.

Peerage /pírəj/. The rank or dignity of a peer or nobleman. Also the body of nobles taken collectively.

Peeress /pírəs/. A woman who belongs to the nobility, which may be either in her own right or by right of marriage.

Peers /pírz/. In feudal law, the vassals of a lord who sat in his court as judges of their co-vassals, and were called "peers," as being each other's equals, or of the same condition. The nobility of Great Britain, being the lords temporal having seats in parliament, and including dukes, marquises, earls, viscounts, and barons.

Equals; those who are a man's equals in rank and station; thus "trial by a jury of his peers" means trial by jury of citizens. For "judgment of his peers," see **Judgment.**

Peers of fees. Vassals or tenants of the same lord, who were obliged to serve and attend him in his courts, being equal in function. These were termed "peers of fees," because holding fees of the lord, or because their business in court was to sit and judge, under their lords, of disputes arising upon fees; but, if there were too many in one lordship, the lord usually chose twelve, who had the title of peers, by way of distinction; whence, it is said, we derive our common juries and other peers.

Peg. To fix the price of something, as the government may stabilize the price of gold by offering to buy all the gold offered at a stated price. Speculators in stocks may peg the price of securities by frequent buying and selling at the pegged price, though today such manipulation is illegal.

Peine fort et dure /péyn fórt èy dyúr/. L. Fr. In old English law, a special form of punishment for those who, being arraigned for felony, obstinately "stood mute," that is, refused to plead or to put themselves upon trial. It is described as a combination of solitary confinement, slow starvation, and crushing the naked body with a great load of iron. This atrocious punishment was vulgarly called "pressing to death."

Peles /píylz/. Issues arising from or out of a thing.

Pelfe, or **pelfre** /pélf(ər)/. Booty; also the personal effects of a felon convict.

Pellage /péləj/. The custom or duty paid for skins of leather.

Pellex /pélèks/. Lat. In Roman law, a concubine.

Pells, clerk (or master) of the /klárk əv ðə pélz/mástər°/. Formerly, an officer in the English exchequer, who entered every teller's bill on the parchment rolls, *i.e.,* "pells," commonly two in number, one being the pell or roll of receipts, and the other the pell or roll of disbursements.

Penal. Punishable; inflicting a punishment; containing a penalty, or relating to a penalty.

Penal action. In its broadest context, it refers to criminal prosecution. More particularly, it refers to a civil action in which a wrongdoer is subject to a fine or penalty payable to the aggrieved party.

The word "penal" is inherently a much broader term than "criminal" since it pertains to any punishment or penalty and relates to acts which are not necessarily delineated as criminal. State v. Lowry, 95 N.J.Super. 307, 230 A.2d 907, 913. Action is essentially "penal" if amount sought to be recovered is arbitrarily exacted for some act or omission of the defendant. Tasner v. U. S. Industries, Inc., D.C.Ill., 379 F.Supp. 803, 806.

An action upon a penal statute; an action for the recovery of a penalty given by statute. Smith Engineering Works v. Custer, 194 Okl. 318, 151 P.2d 404, 407, 408. In a broad sense, the term has been made to include all actions in which there may be a recovery of exemplary or vindictive damages, as suits for libel and slander, or in which special, double, or treble damages are given by statute, such as actions to recover money paid as usury or for violation of antitrust laws. But in a more particular sense it means (1) an action on a statute which gives a certain penalty to be recovered by any person who will sue for it, or (2) an action in which the judgment against the defendant is in the nature of a fine or is intended as a punishment, actions in which the recovery is to be compensatory in its purpose and effect not being penal actions but civil suits, though they may carry special damages by statute.

Penal bill. An instrument formerly in use, by which a party bound himself to pay a certain sum or sums of money, or to do certain acts, or, in default thereof, to pay a certain specified sum by way of penalty; thence termed a "penal sum." These instruments have been superseded by the use of a bond in a penal sum, with conditions.

Penal bond. A promise to pay a named sum of money, the penalty, in the event of nonperformance, with a condition underwritten that, if a stipulated collateral thing, other than the payment of money, be done or forborne, the obligation shall be void. Maryland Casualty Co. v. Kansas City, Mo., C.C.A.Mo., 128 F.2d 998, 1004. Bond conditioned upon forfeiture of penalty for its breach. See **Penalty**.

Penal clause. A secondary obligation entered into for purpose of enforcing performance of a primary obligation, and nature of penalty is by way of compensation for damages and not as punishment for failure to perform obligation. Also a clause in a statute declaring a penalty for a violation of the preceding clauses.

Penal code. Bringing together and codification of substantive criminal laws of state or federal government; e.g. California Penal Code; Title 18 of U.S. Code. Several state Penal or Criminal Codes are patterned on the A.L.I. Model Penal Code.

Penal institutions. Generic term to describe all places of confinement for those convicted of crime such as jails, prisons, and houses of correction.

Penal laws. Term, in general, refers to state and federal statutes that define criminal offenses and specify corresponding fines and punishment. Statutes imposing a penalty, fine, or punishment for certain offenses of a public nature or wrongs committed against the state.

Strictly speaking, statutes giving a private action against a wrongdoer are not penal in their nature, neither the liability imposed nor the remedy given being penal. If the wrong done is to the individual, the law giving him a right of action is remedial, rather than penal, though the sum to be recovered may be called a "penalty" or may consist in double or treble damages. Huntington v. Attrill, 146 U.S. 657, 13 S.Ct. 224, 36 L.Ed. 1123.

Where a statute is both penal and remedial, as where it is penal in one part and remedial in the other, it should be considered as a "penal statute" when it is sought to enforce the penalty, and as a "remedial statute" when it is sought to enforce the remedy. Collins v. Kidd, D.C.Tex., 38 F.Supp. 634, 637.

See also **Penal code**.

Penal servitude. In English criminal law, is a punishment which consists in keeping an offender in confinement, and compelling him to labor.

Penal statutes. See **Penal code; Penal laws**.

Penal sum. A sum agreed upon in a bond, to be forfeited if the condition of the bond is not fulfilled. See also **Penal bond; Penalty**.

Penalty. An elastic term with many different shades of meaning; it involves idea of punishment, corporeal or pecuniary, or civil or criminal, although its meaning is generally confined to pecuniary punishment. Allied v. Graves, 261 N.C. 31, 134 S.E.2d 186, 192.

The sum of money which the obligor of a bond undertakes to pay in the event of his omitting to perform or carry out the terms imposed upon him by the conditions of the bond. A penalty is a sum inserted in a contract, not as a measure of compensation for its breach, but rather as punishment for default, or by way of security for actual damages which might be sustained by reason of nonperformance. Stein v. Bruce, Mo.App., 366 S.W.2d 732, 735. The sum a party agrees to pay in the event of a contract breach, but which is fixed, not as a pre-estimate of probable actual damages, but as a punishment, the threat of which is designed to prevent the breach. Westmount Country Club v. Kameny, 82 N.J.Super. 200, 197 A.2d 379, 382.

A penalty provision operates to compel performance of act and usually becomes effective only in event of default on which a forfeiture is compelled without regard to actual damages sustained by party aggrieved by breach. Garrett v. Coast and Southern Federal Sav. and Loan Ass'n, 9 C.3d 731, 108 Cal. Rptr. 845, 850.

A penalty is a sum of money which the law exacts payment of by way of punishment for doing some act which is prohibited or for not doing some act which is required to be done. Hidden Hollow Ranch v. Collins, 146 Mont. 321, 406 P.2d 365, 368. A punishment imposed by statute as a consequence of the commission of an offense. Also money recoverable by virtue of a statute imposing a payment by way of punishment.

See also **Fine; Forfeiture; Penal action; Statutory penalty**.

Penalty clause. Any provision in a contract or a law which calls for the exaction of a penalty instead of actual damages; e.g. in a mortgage, a clause requiring the mortgagor to pay a flat sum or a percentage of the mortgage debt if he exercises his right to pay off the mortgage before the due date or within a short time after the mortgage has been given.

Penance. An ecclesiastical punishment inflicted by an ecclesiastical court for some spiritual offense.

Pendency. Suspense; the state of being pendent or undecided; the state of an action, etc., after it has been begun, and before the final disposition of it.

Pendens /péndèn(d)z/. Lat. Pending; as lis pendens, a pending suit.

Pendente lite /pendéntiy láydiy/. Lat. Pending the suit; during the actual progress of a suit; during litigation.

Pendente lite nihil innovetur /pendéntiy láydiy náy(h)əl ìnəvíydər/. During a litigation nothing new should be introduced.

Pendent jurisdiction. Pendent jurisdiction is discretionary matter whereby court may allow assertion of nonfederal claim for which no independent jurisdictional ground exists along with recognized federal claim between same parties who are properly before the court, provided relationship between federal claim and state claim permits conclusion that entire action before court comprises but one constitutional case. Schwab v. Erie Lackawanna R. Co., D.C.Pa., 303 F.Supp. 1398, 1399. Original jurisdiction resting under federal claim extends to any nonfederal claim against same defendant if the federal question is substantial and the federal and nonfederal claims constitute a single cause of action. Fullerton v. Monongahela Connecting R. Co., D.C.Pa., 242 F.Supp. 622, 626. Such jurisdiction exists, even though it is determined that no cause of action is made out under federal grounds. Taussig v. Wellington Fund, Inc., D.C.Del., 187 F.Supp. 179, 191. The test is whether substantially the same evidence will prove both the federal and nonfederal claims. Wagner v. World Wide Automobiles Corp., D.C.N.Y., 201 F.Supp. 22, 24.

Pendent jurisdiction pertains to the concept whereby a federal district court, in the exercise of jurisdiction over a federal law claim properly before it, may also, in its discretion, proceed to extend jurisdiction over a related state law claim where both claims arise from a common nucleus of operative facts. Barnes v. Childs, D.C.Miss., 63 F.R.D. 628, 630.

Pending. Begun, but not yet completed; during; before the conclusion of; prior to the completion of; unsettled; undetermined; in process of settlement or adjustment. Thus, an action or suit is "pending" from its inception until the rendition of final judgment.

Pending means awaiting an occurrence or conclusion of action, period of continuance or indeterminacy. Schull Const. Co. v. Board of Regents of Ed., 79 S.D. 487, 113 N.W.2d 663, 665.

See also **Pendente lite.**

Penetration. A term used in criminal law, and denoting (in cases of alleged rape) the insertion of the male part into the female parts to however slight an extent; and by which insertion the offense is complete without proof of emission.

Penitentiary. A prison or place of confinement where convicted felons are sent to serve out the term of their sentence.

Pennoyer Rule. A rule to the effect that a court which has no personal jurisdiction over a defendant may not issue an in personam judgment or decree against him. Pennoyer v. Neff, 95 U.S. 714, 24 L.Ed. 565.

Pennsylvania Rule. Under the "Pennsylvania Rule," when one party has committed a statutory violation that is claimed to have caused a collision, the rule requires the alleged violator to show, if he is to be freed from fault, that the violation could not have been a cause of the collision. Crown, Zellerbach Corp. v. Willamette-Western Corp., C.A.Or., 519 F.2d 1327, 1329.

Penny stocks. Low-priced issues often highly speculative, selling at less than $1 a share.

Pennyweight. A Troy weight, equal to twenty-four grains, or one-twentieth part of an ounce.

Penology. The science of prison management and rehabilitation of criminals.

Pen register. A pen register is a mechanical device that records the numbers dialed on a telephone by monitoring the electrical impulses caused when the dial on the telephone is released. It does not overhear oral communications and does not indicate whether calls are actually completed.

Pensam /pénsəm/. The full weight of twenty ounces.

Pensio /pénsh(iy)ow/. Lat. In the civil law, a payment, properly, for the use of a thing. A rent; a payment for the use and occupation of another's house.

Pension. Retirement benefit paid regularly (normally, monthly), with the amount of such based generally on length of employment and amount of wages or salary of pensioner. Deferred compensation for services rendered. State ex rel. Bolen v. City of Seattle, Wash., 377 P.2d 454; Waite v. Waite, 6 C.3d 461, 99 Cal.Rptr. 325, 330, 492 P.2d 13. See also **Pension plan; Vested pension.**

Pension Benefit Guaranty Corporation. Title IV of the Employee Retirement Income Security Act of 1974 (ERISA), approved September 2, 1974 (88 Stat. 1004; 29 U.S.C.A. § 1302), established the Pension Benefit Guaranty Corporation (PBGC) to guarantee payment of insured benefits if covered employee retirement plans terminate without sufficient assets to pay such benefits.

Pensioner. Recipient or beneficiary of a pension plan.

Pension plan. A plan established and maintained by an employer primarily to provide systematically for the payment of definitely determinable benefits to his employees, or their beneficiaries, over a period of years (usually for life) after retirement. Retirement benefits are measured by, and based on, such factors as years of service and compensation received by the employees. The Employees Retirement Income Security Act (ERISA) governs plan qualification, operation, and administration, and specifically such matters as participation requirements, funding, vesting and filing and reporting with the Internal Revenue Service and Labor Department. Pension benefits under qualified plans are guaranteed by the Pension Benefit Guaranty Corporation.

A stated allowance out of the public treasury granted by government to an individual, or to his representatives, for his valuable services to the country, or in compensation for loss or damage sustained by him in the public service. Frisbie v. U. S., 157 U.S. 160, 15 S.Ct. 586, 39 L.Ed. 657.

See also **Individual retirement account; Keogh Plan; Money-purchase plan; Pension trust.**

Defined pension plan. A pension plan where the employer promises specific benefits to each employee. The employer's cash contributions and pension expense are adjusted in relation to investment performance of the pension fund. Sometimes called a "fixed-benefit" pension plan.

Funded pension plan. See **Funded.**

Noncontributory plan. A pension plan where only the employer makes payments to a pension fund.

Qualified pension plan. An employer-sponsored plan that meets the requirements of I.R.C. § 401. If these requirements are met, none of the employer's contributions to the plan will be taxed to the employee until distributed to him or her [§ 402]. The employer will be allowed a deduction in the year the contributions are made [§ 404].

Pension trust. Type of funded pension plan in which the employer transfers to trustees an amount sufficient to cover cost of pensions to employees who are the beneficiaries of the trust.

Penumbra doctrine. The implied powers of the federal government predicated on the Necessary and Proper Clause of the U.S.Const., Art. I, Sec. 8(18), permits one implied power to be engrafted on another implied power. Kohl v. U. S., 91 U.S. 367, 23 L.Ed. 449.

Peonage /píyǝnǝj/. A condition of servitude (prohibited by 13th Amendment) compelling persons to perform labor in order to pay off a debt.

People. A state; as the people of the state of New York. A nation in its collective and political capacity. The aggregate or mass of the individuals who constitute the state. Loi Hoa v. Nagle, C.C.A.Cal., 13 F.2d 80, 81. In a more restricted sense, and as generally used in constitutional law, the entire body of those citizens of a state or nation who are invested with political power for political purposes. See also **Citizen; Person.**

Peppercorn. A dried berry of the black pepper. In English law, the reservation of a merely nominal rent, on a lease, was sometimes expressed by a stipulation for the payment of a peppercorn.

Per /pǝr/. Lat. By, through, or by means of.

Perambulation /pǝræmbyǝléyshǝn/. The act or custom of walking over the boundaries of a district or piece of land, either for the purpose of determining them or of preserving evidence of them. Thus, in many parishes in England, it is the custom for the parishioners to perambulate the boundaries of the parish in rogation week in every year. Such a custom entitles them to enter any man's land and abate nuisances in their way. The custom has now largely fallen into disuse.

Perambulatione facienda, writ de /rít dìy pǝræmbyǝlèy-shiyówniy fæshiyéndǝ/. In old English law, the name of a writ which was sued by consent of both parties when they were in doubt as to the bounds of their respective estates. It was directed to the sheriff to make perambulation, and to set the bounds and limits between them in certainty.

Per and post /pǝr ǝnd pówst/. In old English law, to come in in the *per* is to claim by or through the person last entitled to an estate; as the heirs or assigns of the grantee. To come in in the *post* is to claim by a paramount and prior title; as the lord by escheat.

Per annum /pǝr ǽnǝm/. By the year; annually; yearly.

Per autre vie /pǝr ówtrǝ víy/°váy/. L. Fr. For or during another's life; for such period as another person shall live.

Per aversionem /pǝr ǝvǝrz(h)iyównǝm/. Lat. In the civil law, by turning away. A term applied to that kind of sale where the goods are taken in bulk, and not by weight or measure, and for a single price; or where a piece of land is sold as containing in gross, by estimation, a certain number of acres. So called because the buyer acts without particular examination or discrimination, *turning* his face, as it were, *away.*

Per bouche /pǝr bú(w)sh/. L. Fr. By the mouth; orally.

Perca /pǝrkǝ/. A perch of land; sixteen and one-half feet. See **Perch.**

Per capita /pǝr kǽpǝdǝ/. Lat. By the heads or polls; according to the number of individuals; share and share alike. This term, derived from the civil law, is much used in the law of descent and distribution, and denotes that method of dividing an intestate estate by which an equal share is given to each of a number of persons, all of whom stand in equal degree to the decedent, without reference to their stocks or the right of representation. It is the antithesis of *per stirpes (q.v.).* Buxton v. Noble, 146 Kan. 671, 73 P.2d 43, 47; MacGregor v. Roux, 198 Ga. 520, 32 S.E.2d 289, 291. A division "per capita" means by a number of individuals equally or share and share alike. Gilbert v. Wenzel, 247 Iowa 1279, 78 N.W.2d 793, 794.

Per cent. An abbreviation of the Latin *"per centum,"* meaning by the hundred, or so many parts in the hundred, or so many hundredths.

Percentage lease. A lease, usually on a retail business property, using a percentage of the gross or net sales to determine the rent. There is usually a minimum or "base" rental, in the event of poor sales.

Percentage of completion method. A method of reporting gain or loss on certain long-term contracts. Under this method of accounting, the gross contract price is included in income as the contract is completed.

Percentage order. A market or limited price order to buy (or sell) a stated amount of a certain stock after a fixed number of shares of such stock have traded.

Perception. Taking into possession. Thus, perception of crops or of profits is reducing them to possession. As used with respect to money, it means the counting out and payment of a debt. Seeing, noticing or otherwise comprehending.

Perch. A measure of land containing five yards and a half, or sixteen feet and a half in length; otherwise called a "rod" or "pole."

Percolate /pǝrkǝleyt/. As used in the cases relating to the right of land-owners to use water on their premises, designates any flowage of sub-surface water other than that of a running stream, open, visible, clearly to be traced.

Percolating waters /pǝrkǝlèydiŋ wódǝrz/. See **Water.**

Percolation test. The test to determine the capability of the soil to absorb and drain water, both for construction and septic systems.

Per consequens /pər kón(t)səkwənz/. Lat. By consequence; consequently.

Per considerationem curiæ /pər kən(t)sìdərèyshiyównəm kyúriyiy/. Lat. In old practice, by the consideration (judgment) of the court.

Per curiam /pər kyúriyəm/. Lat. By the court. A phrase used to distinguish an opinion of the whole court from an opinion written by any one judge. Sometimes it denotes an opinion written by the chief justice or presiding judge, or to a brief announcement of the disposition of a case by court not accompanied by a written opinion.

Perdida /pərdíyðə/. A synonym of damages. Ponce De Leon v. Coca Cola Bottling Co., D.C.Puerto Rico, 75 F.Supp. 966.

Per diem /pər dáyəm/°díyəm/. By the day; an allowance or amount of so much per day. For example, state legislators are often given a per diem allowance to cover expenses while attending legislature sessions. Generally, as used in connection with compensation, wages or salary, means pay for a day's service.

Perdonatio utlagariæ /pərdənéysh(iy)ow ətləgériyiy/. L. Lat. A pardon for a man who, for contempt in not yielding obedience to the process of a court, is outlawed, and afterwards of his own accord surrenders.

Perduellio /pərd(y)uwél(i)yow/. Lat. In Roman law, hostility or enmity towards the Roman republic; traitorous conduct on the part of a citizen, subversive of the authority of the laws or tending to overthrow the government.

Perdurable /pərd(y)úrəbəl/párjərəbəl/. In old English law, as applied to an estate, perdurable signifies lasting long or forever. Thus, a disseisor or tenant in fee upon condition has as high and great an estate as the rightful owner or tenant in fee-simple absolute, but not so perdurable. The term is chiefly used with reference to the extinguishment of rights by unity of seisin, which does not take place unless both the right and the land out of which it issues are held for equally high and perdurable estates.

Perempt /pərém(p)t/. In old ecclesiastical procedure, to waive or bar an appeal by one's own act so as partially to comply with or acquiesce in a sentence of a court.

Peremption /pərém(p)shən/. A nonsuit; also a quashing or killing.

Peremptorius /pàrem(p)tóriyəs/. Lat. In the civil law, that which takes away or destroys forever; hence, *exceptio peremptoria,* a plea which is a perpetual bar.

Peremptory /pərém(p)təriy/. Imperative; final; decisive; absolute; conclusive; positive; not admitting of question, delay, reconsideration or of any alternative. Self-determined; arbitrary; not requiring any cause to be shown. Wolfe v. State, 147 Tex.Cr.R. 62, 178 S.W.2d 274, 279.

As to peremptory Defense; Mandamus; Nonsuit; Plea; and Writ, see those titles.

Peremptory challenge. The right to challenge a juror without assigning a reason for the challenge. In most jurisdictions each party to an action, both civil and criminal, has a specified number of such challenges and after using all his peremptory challenges he is required to furnish a reason for subsequent challenges. Fed.R.Crim.P. 24. See also **Challenge; Jury challenge.**

Peremptory day. A day assigned for trial or hearing in court, absolutely and without further opportunity for postponement.

Peremptory exceptions. In the civil law, any defense which denies entirely the ground of action. Those exceptions which tend to the dismissal of the action.

Peremptory rule. In practice, an absolute rule; a rule without any condition or alternative of showing cause. Ruling made by a trial judge or hearing magistrate "on the spot" and without taking the matter under advisement.

Peremptory undertaking. In English law, an undertaking by a plaintiff to bring on a cause for trial at the next sittings or assizes.

Per eundem /pər iyéndəm/. Lat. By the same. This phrase is commonly used to express "by, or from the mouth of, the same judge." So *"per eundem in eadem"* means "by the same judge in the same case."

Perfect or **perfected.** Complete; finished; executed; enforceable; without defect; merchantable; marketable.

As to perfect Equity; Obligation; Ownership; Title; and Usufruct; see those titles.

Perfect attestation clause. One that asserts performance of all acts required to be done to make valid testamentary disposition.

Perfected. Brought to a state of perfection, completed. See **Perfect; Perfection of security interest.**

Perfecting bail. Certain qualifications of a property character being required of persons who tender themselves as bail, when such persons have justified, *i.e.,* established their sufficiency by satisfying the court that they possess the requisite qualifications; a rule or order of court is made for their allowance, and the bail is then said to be perfected, *i.e.,* the process of giving bail is finished or completed.

Perfect instrument. An instrument such as a deed or mortgage is said to become perfect or perfected when recorded (or registered) or filed for record, because it then becomes good as to all the world.

Perfection of security interest. Perfection of a security interest deals with those steps legally required to give a secured party an interest in subject property against debtor's creditors. Bramble Transp., Inc. v. Sam Senter Sales, Inc., Del.Super., 294 A.2d 97, 102.

The minimum meaning of this term in connection with a security interest is that the secured party has done whatever is necessary in the way of giving notice to make his security interest effective at least against lien creditors of the debtor. Depending upon the type of collateral and the method of perfection, it may mean more: it may mean that the interest is good even against all purchasers. The methods for attaining perfection are stated in U.C.C. Sections 9–302 through 9–306. In most cases the secured party may obtain perfection either by filing (*i.e.* with Secretary of State) or by taking possession of the collateral. When the collateral is held by a bailee who has not issued a negotiable document of title, perfection by notification is possible: the secured party may obtain perfection by notifying the bailee of the secured party's interest. For a few special situations the Code provides that a security interest is perfected without any of the above actions on the part of the secured party. Such perfection is called automatic perfection, or perfection by attachment.

Perfect trust. An executed trust (*q.v.*).

Perfectum est cui nihil deest secundum suæ perfectionis vel naturæ modum /pərféktəm èst k(yúw)ày náy(h)əl díyèst səkándəm s(y)úwiy pərfèkshiyównəs vèl nəchúriy mówdəm/. That is perfect to which nothing is wanting, according to the measure of its perfection or nature.

Perfidy /pə́rfədiy/. The act of one who has engaged his faith to do a thing, and does not do it, but does the contrary. Faithlessness, treachery, violation of a promise or vow or a trust reposed.

Perform. To perform an obligation or contract is to execute, fulfill, or accomplish it according to its terms. This may consist either in action on the part of the person bound by the contract or in omission to act, according to the nature of the subject-matter; but the term is usually applied to any action in discharge of a contract other than payment.

Per formam doni /pə̀r fórməm dównay/. L. Lat. In English law, by the form of the gift; by the designation of the giver, and not by the operation of law.

Performance. The fulfillment or accomplishment of a promise, contract, or other obligation according to its terms. See also **Execute; Execution; Part performance; Payment; Substantial performance.**

Non performance. See **Commercial frustration; Default; Impossibility.**

Part performance. The doing some portion, yet not the whole, of what either party to a contract has agreed to do.

Part performance of an obligation, either before or after a breach thereof, when expressly accepted by the creditor in writing, in satisfaction, or rendered in pursuance of an agreement in writing for that purpose, though without any new consideration, extinguishes the obligation.

As regards the sale of goods, the statute of frauds requirement is dispensed with by partial performance for the goods which have been accepted or for which payment has been made and accepted. U.C.C. § 2–201(3). See also **Part performance.**

Specific performance. The remedy of performance of a contract in the specific form in which it was made, or according to the precise terms agreed upon. The actual accomplishment of a contract by a party bound to fulfill it. The doctrine of specific performance is that, where damages would be an inadequate compensation for the breach of an agreement, the contractor or vendor will be compelled to perform specifically what he has agreed to do; *e.g.* ordered to execute a specific conveyance of land. See Fed.R. Civil P. 70.

With respect to sale of goods, specific performance may be decreed where the goods are unique or in other proper circumstances. The decree for specific performance may include such terms and conditions as to payment of the price, damages, or other relief as the court may deem just. U.C.C. §§ 2–711(2)(b), 2–716.

As the exact fulfillment of an agreement is not always practicable, the phrase may mean, in a given case, not literal, but substantial performance.

Performance bond. A performance bond or, as it is sometimes referred to, "completion bond", is given to insure public authority that contract once awarded will be completed as awarded within fixed period of time. Extruded Louver Corp. v. McNulty, 34 Misc.2d 566, 226 N.Y.S.2d 220, 224. Bond which guarantees that contractor will perform contract and guarantees against breach of contract. Isaac v. Reliance Ins. Co., 201 Kan. 288, 440 P.2d 600, 605.

Per fraudem /pə̀r fródəm/. Lat. By fraud. In common law pleading, where a plea alleges matter of discharge, and the replication avers that the discharge was fraudulently obtained and is therefore invalid, it is called a "replication *per fraudem.*"

Periculosum existimo quod bonorum virorum non comprobatur exemplo /pərìkyəlówsəm əgzístəmow kwòd bənórəm vərórəm nòn kòmprəbéydər əgzémplow/. I consider that dangerous which is not approved by the example of good men.

Periculosus /pərìkyəlówsəs/. Lat. Dangerous; perilous.

Periculum /pəríkyələm/. Lat. In the civil law, peril; danger; hazard; risk.

Peril. The risk, hazard, or contingency insured against by a policy of insurance. In general, the cause of any loss such as may be caused by fire, hail, etc. See also **Imminent peril.**

Perils of the lakes. As applied to navigation of the Great Lakes, this term has the same meaning as "perils of the sea." See *infra.*

Perils of the sea. In maritime and insurance law, natural accidents peculiar to the sea, which do not happen by the intervention of man, nor are to be prevented by human prudence. Hence to recover on marine policy insuring against loss by perils of sea, vessel must be seaworthy when it is sent to sea. Perils of the sea are from (1) storms and waves; (2) rocks, shoals, and rapids; (3) other obstacles, though of human origin; (4) changes of climate; (5) the confinement necessary at sea; (6) animals peculiar to the sea; (7) all other dangers peculiar to the sea. All losses caused by the action of wind and water acting on the property insured under extraordinary circumstances, either directly or mediately, without the intervention of other independent active external causes, are losses by "perils of the sea or other perils and dangers," within the meaning of the usual clause in a policy of marine insurance. In an enlarged sense, all losses which occur from maritime adventure may be said to arise from the perils of the sea; but underwriters are not bound to this extent. They insure against losses from extraordinary occurrences only; such as stress of weather, winds and waves, lightning, tempests, etc. These are understood to be meant by the phrase "the perils of the sea," in a marine policy, and not those ordinary perils which every vessel must encounter.

Peril of the sea within a marine policy envisions extraordinary and unusual perils which vessel may not reasonably expect to encounter; circumstances which are ordinarily encountered such as predictable winds, tides, wave actions and conditions of the water do not fall within such classification. Vining v. Security Ins. Co. of New Haven, La.App., 252 So.2d 754, 757. Under Carriage of Goods by Sea Act, "perils of the sea" are understood to mean those perils which are peculiar to sea and which are of extraordinary nature or arise from irresistible force or overwhelming power, and which cannot be guarded against by ordinary exertions of human skill and prudence. New Rotterdam Ins. Co. v. S. S. Loppersum, D.C.N.Y., 215 F.Supp. 563, 566, 567.

Per incuriam /pèr ink(y)úriyəm/. Lat. Through inadvertence.

Per industriam hominis /pèr indástriyəm hómənəs/. Lat. In old English law, by human industry. A term applied to the reclaiming or taming of wild animals by art, industry, and education.

Per infortunium /pèr ìnforchúwn(i)yəm/. Lat. By misadventure. In criminal law, homicide *per infortunium* is committed where a man, doing a lawful act, without any intention of hurt, unfortunately kills another. See **Homicide**.

Period. Any point, space, or division of time.

Periodic. Recurring at fixed intervals; to be made or done, or to happen, at successive periods separated by determined intervals of time, as periodic payments of interest on a bond, or periodic alimony payments.

Periodic alimony. An allowance payable at intermittent times, usually by the week or by the month, in a definite amount over a definite or indefinite period of time. An award of periodic alimony is appropriate according to the needs of the spouse requesting alimony and the corresponding ability of the other spouse to pay. Cann v. Cann, Fla.App., 334 So.2d 325, 328. State statutes which provide for alimony payments only from husbands, and not wives, have been held unconstitutional. Orr v. Orr, 99 S.Ct. 1102. See also **Alimony; Permanent alimony**.

Periodic tenancy. Generic term descriptive of a tenancy from week to week, month to month, or year to year.

Periodic tenancy is one continuing tenancy subject to termination at various rental periods rather than a series of individual and new tenancies. Rossow Oil Co., Inc. v. Heiman, 72 Wis.2d 696, 242 N.W.2d 176, 180. An estate that continues for successive periods unless terminated at end of a period by notice. State v. Fin & Feather Club, Me., 316 A.2d 351, 357.

Peripheral rights. Those rights which surround or spring from other rights.

Periphrasis. Circumlocution; use of many words to express the sense of one.

Perish. To come to an end; to cease to be; to die.

Perishable. Subject to speedy and natural decay (*e.g.* fruits, vegetables, dairy products, meat). But, where the time contemplated is necessarily long, the term may embrace property liable merely to material depreciation in value from other causes than such decay.

Perishable commodity. A relative term used to describe a product, like fruit or fresh vegetables, which quickly deteriorates in quality and value. In re Rosenbaum Grain Corporation, C.C.A.Ill., 83 F.2d 391, 393.

Perishable goods. Goods which quickly decay and lose their value if not put to their intended use within a short period of time.

Perjuri sunt qui servatis verbis juramenti decipiunt aures eorum qui accipiunt /pərjúray sánt kwày sərvətéydəs várbəs jurəméntay dəsípiyənt óriyz iyórəm kwày əksípiyənt/. They are perjured, who, preserving the words of an oath, deceive the ears of those who receive it.

Perjury. In criminal law, the willful assertion as to a matter of fact, opinion, belief, or knowledge, made by a witness in a judicial proceeding as part of his evidence, either upon oath or in any form allowed by law to be substituted for an oath, whether such evidence is given in open court, or in an affidavit, or otherwise, such assertion being material to the issue or point of inquiry and known to such witness to be false. Perjury is a crime committed when a lawful oath is administered, in some judicial proceeding, to a person who swears wilfully, absolutely, and falsely, in a matter material to the issue or point in question. Gatewood v. State, 15 Md.App. 314, 290 A.2d 551, 553.

A person is guilty of perjury if in any official proceeding he makes a false statement under oath or equivalent affirmation, or swears or affirms the truth of a statement previously made, when the statement is material and he does not believe it to be true. Model Penal Code, § 241.1. See also 18 U.S.C.A. § 1621.

Subornation of perjury is procuring another to commit perjury. See 18 U.S.C.A. § 1622.

See also **False swearing**.

Perks. See **Perquisites**.

Per legem terræ /pèr líyjəm téhriy/. Lat. By the law of the land; by due process of law.

Permanent. Continuing or enduring in the same state, status, place, or the like, without fundamental or marked change, not subject to fluctuation, or alteration, fixed or intended to be fixed; lasting; abiding; stable; not temporary or transient. Hiatt v. Department of Labor and Industries, 48 Wash.2d 843, 297 P.2d 244, 246. Generally opposed in law to "temporary," but not always meaning "perpetual."

As to permanent "Injunction"; and "Trespass"; see those titles.

Permanent abode. A domicile or fixed home, which the party may leave as his interest or whim may dictate, but which he has no present intention of abandoning. See also **Domicile; Residence.**

Permanent alimony. An allowance for the support and maintenance of a spouse during his or her lifetime, and its purpose is to provide nourishment, sustenance and the necessities of life to a former spouse who has neither the resources nor ability to be self-sustaining. Cann v. Cann, Fla.App., 334 So.2d 325, 329. See also **Alimony; Periodic alimony.**

Permanent disability. Generally, permanent disability is one which will remain substantially the same during remainder of workers' compensation claimant's life. Subsequent Injuries Fund v. Industrial Acc. Commission, 226 Cal.App.2d 136, 37 Cal.Rptr. 844, 849. A permanent disability is one which causes impairment of earning capacity, impairment of normal use of member, or competitive handicap in open labor market. State Compensation Ins. Fund v. Industrial Acc. Commission, 59 Cal.2d 45, 27 Cal.Rptr. 702, 707, 377 P.2d 902.

Within insurance policies does not mean that disability must continue throughout life of insured, but it connotes idea that disability must be something more than temporary, and at least presumably permanent.

Permanent employment. As provided for by contract, means only that employment is to continue indefinitely and until either party wishes to sever relation for some good reason. Speegle v. Board of Fire Underwriters of Pacific, Cal.App., 158 P.2d 426, 429.

Permanent injury. A permanent injury is one which will last during lifetime of injured person. Russell v. Mount Hood R. Co., 267 Or. 335, 517 P.2d 276, 278. Those reasonably certain to be followed by permanent impairment of earning power or producing permanent, irremedial pain. Messer v. Beighley, 409 Pa. 551, 187 A.2d 168, 170. See also **Permanent disability.**

Permanent law. An act which continues in force for an indefinite time.

Per metas et bundas /pàr míydəs ət bə́ndəs/. L. Lat. In old English law, by metes and bounds.

Per minas /pàr máynəs/. Lat. By threats. See **Duress.**

Per misadventure /pàr mìsədvénchər/. In old English law, by mischance. The same with *per infortunium* (q.v.).

Permission. A license to do a thing; an authority to do an act which, without such authority, would have been unlawful. An act of permitting, formal consent, authorization, leave, license or liberty granted, and it has a flexible meaning depending upon the sense in which it is used. Winterton v. Van Zandt, Mo., 351 S.W.2d 696, 700. See also **Authority; Certificate; License; Permit.**

Permissions. Negations of law, arising either from the law's silence or its express declaration.

Permissive. Allowed; allowable; that which may be done. Lenient; tolerant.

Permissive counterclaim. Federal Rule of Civil Procedure 13(b) grants defendant unqualified right to interpose "permissive counterclaim"; one that does not arise out of same transaction or occurrence furnishing subject matter of plaintiff's claim, and court possesses no discretion to reject it. U. S. for Use and Benefit of Kashulines v. Thermo Contracting Corp., D.C.N.J., 437 F.Supp. 195, 198. See also **Counterclaim.**

Permissive use. See **Use.**

Permissive waste. See **Waste.**

Permit, *v.* To suffer, allow, consent, let; to give leave or license; to acquiesce, by failure to prevent, or to expressly assent or agree to the doing of an act.

Permit, *n.* In general, any document which grants a person the right to do something. A license or grant of authority to do a thing. Matter of Building Permit and Zoning, 29 N.C.App. 749, 225 S.E.2d 647, 649. A written license or warrant, issued by a person in authority, empowering the grantee to do some act not forbidden by law, but not allowable without such authority.

A license or instrument granted by the officers of excise (or customs), certifying that the duties on certain goods have been paid, or secured, and permitting their removal from some specified place to another.

See also **Building permit; Certificate; License; Special permit.**

Permit card. A document given by a union to a non-union member which allows an employer to hire him for a job for which the union is unable to supply sufficient members.

Per mitter le droit /pàr mídər lə dróyt/. L. Fr. By passing the right. One of the modes by which releases at common law were said to inure was *"per mitter le droit,"* as where a person who had been disseised released to the disseisor or his heir or feoffee. In such case, by the release, the right which was in the releasor was added to the possession of the releasee, and the two combined perfected the estate.

Per mitter l'estate /pàr mídər ləstéyt/. L. Fr. By passing the estate. At common law, if two or more are seised, either by deed, devise, or descent, as joint tenants or coparceners of the same estate, and one of them releases to the other, this is said to inure by way of *"per mitter l'estate."*

Permutatio /pàrmyətéysh(iy)ow/. Lat. In the civil law, exchange; barter.

Permutation /pàrmyətéyshən/. The exchange of one movable subject for another; barter.

Per my et per tout /pàr míy ey pàr túw(t)/. L. Fr. By the half and by the whole. A phrase descriptive of the mode in which joint tenants hold the joint estate, the effect of which, technically considered, is that for purposes of tenure and survivorship each is the holder of the whole, but for purposes of alienation each has only his own share, which is presumed in law to be equal.

Pernancy. Taking; a taking or receiving; as of the profits of an estate. Actual pernancy of the profits of an estate is the taking, perception, or receipt of the rents and other advantages arising therefrom.

Pernor of profits /pə́rnər əv prófəts/. He who receives the profits of lands, etc.; he who has the actual pernancy of the profits.

Pernour /pə́rnər/. L. Fr. A taker. *Le pernour ou le detenour*, the taker or the detainer.

Per pais, trial /tráy(ə)l pə̀r péy(s)/. Trial by the country; *i.e.*, by jury.

Perpars /pərpárz/. L. Lat. A purpart; a part of the inheritance.

Perpetration. The act of one committing a crime either with his own hands, or by some means or instrument or through some innocent agent.

Perpetrator /pə́rpətrèydər/. Generally, this term denotes the person who actually commits a crime or delict, or by whose immediate agency it occurs.

Perpetual /pərpéchuwəl/. Never ceasing; continuous; enduring; lasting; unlimited in respect of time; continuing without intermission or interval.

As to perpetual Injunction; Lease; and Statute, see those titles.

Perpetual edict. In Roman law, originally the term "perpetual" was merely opposed to "occasional" and was used to distinguish the general edicts of the prætors from the special edicts or orders which they issued in their judicial capacity. But under Hadrian the edict was revised by the jurist Julianus, and was republished as a permanent act of legislation. It was then styled "perpetual," in the sense of being calculated to endure *in perpetuum,* or until abrogated by competent authority.

Perpetua lex est nullam legem humanam ac positivam perpetuam esse, et clausula quæ abrogationem excludit ab initio non valet /pərpéchuwə léks èst nə́ləm líyjəm hyuwméynəm æ̀k pòzətáyvəm pərpéchuwəm ésiy, èt klóz(y)ələ kwiy æ̀brəgèyshiyównəm əkskl(y)úwdət æ̀b ənísh(iy)ow nòn vǽlət/. It is a perpetual law that no human and positive law can be perpetual, and a clause [in a law] which precludes the power of abrogation is void *ab initio.*

Perpetual succession. That continuous existence which enables a corporation to manage its affairs, and hold property without the necessity of perpetual conveyances, for the purpose of transmitting it. By reason of this quality, this ideal and artificial person remains, in its legal entity and personality, the same, though frequent changes may be made of its members.

Perpetuating testimony. Means or procedure permitted by federal and state discovery rules for preserving the testimony of witness, which might otherwise be lost before the trial in which it is intended to be used. Fed.R. Civil P. 27(a) (depositions before trial).

Perpetuities, rule against. See **Perpetuity; Rule** (*Rule against perpetuities*).

Perpetuity /pə̀rpəchúwədiy/. Continuing forever. Legally, pertaining to real property, any condition extending the inalienability or property beyond the time of a life or lives in being plus twenty one years. A perpetuity is a limitation which takes the subject-matter of the perpetuity out of commerce for a period greater than a life or lives in being and 21 years thereafter, plus ordinary period of gestation. Zahn v. National Bank of Commerce of Dallas, Tex.Civ.App., 328 S.W.2d 783, 789. See also **Rule** (*Rule against perpetuities*).

Perpetuity of the king. That fiction of the English law which for certain political purposes ascribes to the king in his political capacity the attribute of immortality; for, though the reigning monarch may die, yet by this fiction the king never dies, *i.e.,* the office is supposed to be reoccupied for all political purposes immediately on his death.

Per procuration /pə̀r pròkyəréyshən/. By proxy; by one acting as an agent with special powers, as under a letter of attorney. These words give notice to all persons that the agent is acting under a special and limited authority. The phrase is commonly abbreviated to *"per proc.,"* or *"p. p.,"* and is more used in the civil law and in England than in American law. A proxy or signature of a principal executed by an agent who discloses his role as agent on the document.

Per quæ servitia /pə̀r kwíy sərvísh(iy)ə/. Lat. In old English law, a real action by which the grantee of a seigniory could compel the tenants of the grantor to attorn to himself. It was abolished by St. 3 & 4 Wm. IV, c. 27, § 35.

Perquisites /pə́rkwəzəts/. Emoluments, fringe benefits, or other incidental profits or benefits attaching to an office or position. Shortened term "Perks" is used with reference to such extraordinary benefits afforded to business executives (*e.g.* free cars, club memberships, insurance, etc.).

Perquisitio /pə̀rkwəzísh(iy)ow/. Purchase. Acquisition by one's own act or agreement, and not by descent.

Perquisitor /pərkwízədər/. In old English law, a purchaser; one who first acquired an estate to his family; one who acquired an estate by sale, by gift, or by any other method, except only that of descent.

Per quod /pə̀r kwód/. Lat. Whereby. When the declaration in an action of tort, after stating the acts complained of, goes on to allege the consequences of those acts as a ground of special damage to the plaintiff, the recital of such consequences is prefaced by these words, *"per quod,"* whereby; and sometimes the phrase is used as the name of that clause of the declaration or complaint.

At the common law, "per quod" acquired two meanings in the law of defamation: when used in the frame of reference of slander it meant proof of special damages was required and when used in the frame of reference of libel it meant that proof of extrinsic circumstances was required. General Motors Corp. v. Piskor, 27 Md.App. 95, 340 A.2d 767, 783.

Words "actionable per quod" are those not actionable per se upon their face, but are only actionable in consequence of extrinsic facts showing circumstances under which they were said or the damages resulting to slandered party therefrom.

See also **Actionable per quod.**

Per quod consortium amisit /pàr kwód kənsórsh(iy)əm əmáyzət/. Lat. In old pleading, whereby he lost the company [of his wife]. A phrase used in the old declarations in actions of trespass by a husband for beating or ill using his wife, descriptive of the special damage he had sustained. Crocker v. Crocker, C.C. Mass., 98 F. 702, 703. See **Consortium.**

Per quod servitium amisit /pàr kwód sərvísh(iy)əm əmáyzət/. Lat. In old pleading, whereby he lost the service [of his servant]. A phrase used in the old declarations in actions of trespass by a master, for beating or ill using his servant, descriptive of the special damage he had himself sustained. This action was commonly brought by the father for the seduction of his daughter, in which case very slight evidence of the relation of master and servant was necessary; but still some loss of service, or some expense, had to be shown.

Per rationes pervenitur ad legitimam rationem /pàr ræshiyówniyz pərvíynədər æd ləjídəməm ræshiyównəm/. By reasoning we come to true reason.

Per rerum naturam factum negantis nulla probatio est /pàr rírəm nəchúrəm fæktəm nəgæntəs nə́lə prəbéysh(iy)ow èst/. It is in the nature of things that he who denies a fact is not bound to give proof.

Per saltum /pàr sóltəm/. Lat. By a leap or bound; by a sudden movement; passing over certain proceedings.

Per sample /pàr sǽmpəl/. By sample. A purchase so made is a collateral engagement that the goods shall be of a particular quality. U.C.C. § 2–313(1)(c).

Per se /pàr síy/°séy/. Lat. By himself or itself; in itself; taken alone; inherently; in isolation; unconnected with other matters. The term "per se" means by itself; simply as such; in its own nature without reference to its relation; and, in connection with libel, the term is applied to words which are actionable because they of themselves, without anything more, are opprobrious. McGaw v. Webster, 79 N.M. 104, 440 P.2d 296, 298.

In law of defamation, certain words and phrases are actionable as slander in and of themselves without proof of special damages, *e.g.* accusation of crime. Used in contrast to defamation per quod which requires proof of special damage. See **Actionable per se.**

Persecutio /pàrsəkyúwsh(iy)ow/. Lat. In the civil law, a following after; a pursuing at law; a suit or prosecution. Properly that kind of judicial proceeding before the prætor which was called "extraordinary." In a general sense, any judicial proceeding, including not only "actions" *(actiones),* properly so called, but other proceedings also.

Per se doctrine. Under the "per se doctrine," if an activity is blatant in its intent and pernicious in its effect, a court need not inquire into the reasonableness of the same before determining that it is a violation of the antitrust laws. Connecticut Ass'n of Clinical Laboratories v. Connecticut Blue Cross, Inc., 31 Conn.Sup. 10, 324 A.2d 288, 291. See **Per se violations.**

Persequi /pàrsəkwày/. Lat. In the civil law, to follow after; to pursue or claim in form of law. An action is called a *"jus persequendi."*

Per se violations. A term that implies that certain types of business agreements, such as price-fixing, are considered inherently anti-competitive and injurious to the public without any need to determine if the agreement has actually injured market competition. See **Per se doctrine.**

Person. In general usage, a human being (*i.e.* natural person), though by statute term may include a firm, labor organizations, partnerships, associations, corporations, legal representatives, trustees, trustees in bankruptcy, or receivers. National Labor Relations Act, § 2(1).

Bankruptcy Act. "Person" includes individual, partnership, and corporation, but not governmental unit. Sec. 101(30).

Corporation. A corporation is a "person" within meaning of equal protection and due process provisions of United States Constitution. Allen v. Pavach, Ind., 335 N.E.2d 219, 221; Borreca v. Fasi, D.C.Hawaii, 369 F.Supp. 906, 911. The term "persons" in statute relating to conspiracy to commit offense against United States, or to defraud United States, or any agency, includes corporation. Alamo Fence Co. of Houston v. U. S., C.A.Tex., 240 F.2d 179, 181.

Foreign government. Foreign governments otherwise eligible to sue in U.S. courts are "persons" entitled to bring treble-damage suit for alleged antitrust violations under Clayton Act, Section 4. Pfizer, Inc. v. Government of India, C.A.Minn., 550 F.2d 396.

Illegitimate child. Illegitimate children are "persons" within meaning of the Equal Protection Clause of the Fourteenth Amendment, Levy v. Louisiana, 391 U.S. 68, 88 S.Ct. 1509, 1511, 20 L.Ed.2d 436; and scope of wrongful death statute, Jordan v. Delta Drilling Co., Wyo., 541 P.2d 39, 48.

Interested person. Includes heirs, devisees, children, spouses, creditors, beneficiaries and any others having a property right in or claim against a trust estate or the estate of a decedent, ward or protected person which may be affected by the proceeding. It also includes persons having priority for appointment as personal representative, and other fiduciaries representing interested persons. The meaning as it relates to particular persons may vary from time to time and must be determined according to the particular purposes of, and matter involved in, any proceeding. Uniform Probate Code, § 1–201(20).

Municipalities. Municipalities and other government units are "persons" within meaning of 42 U.S.C.A. § 1983. Local government officials sued in their official capacities are "persons" for purposes of Section 1983 in those cases in which a local government would be suable in its own name. Monell v. N. Y. City Department of Social Services, 436 U.S. 658, 98 S.Ct. 2018, 56 L.Ed.2d 611. See **Color of law.**

Protected person. One for whom a conservator has been appointed or other protective order has been made. Uniform Probate Code, § 5–101(3).

Resident alien. A resident alien is a "person" within the meaning of the due process and equal protection clauses of the Fourteenth Amendment. C. D. R. Enterprises, Ltd. v. Board of Ed. of City of New York, D.C.N.Y., 412 F.Supp. 1164, 1168.

Unborn child. Word "person" as used in the Fourteenth Amendment does not include the unborn. Roe v. Wade, 410 U.S. 113, 93 S.Ct. 705, 729, 35 L.Ed.2d 147. A fetus is not a "person" and is not entitled to protection under the equal protection clause. Murrow v. Clifford, C.A.N.J., 502 F.2d 1066, 1068.

A viable unborn child, which would have been born alive but for the negligence of defendant, is a "person" within meaning of Wrongful Death Statute. Simmons v. Howard University, D.C.D.C., 323 F.Supp. 529. Unborn child is a "person" for purpose of remedies given for personal injuries, and child may sue after his birth. Weaks v. Mounter, 88 Nev. 118, 493 P.2d 1307, 1309.

Persona /pərsównə/. Lat. In the civil law, character in virtue of which certain rights belong to a man and certain duties are imposed upon him. Thus one man may unite many characters *(personæ)*, as, for example, the characters of father and son, of master and servant.

Personable /pərsənəbəl/. Having the rights and powers of a person; able to hold or maintain a plea in court; also capacity to take anything granted or given.

Persona conjuncta æquiparatur interesse proprio /pərsównə kənjə́ŋktə èkwəpəréydər intərésiy prów-priyow/. A personal connection [literally, a united person, union with a person] is equivalent to one's own interest; nearness of blood is as good a consideration as one's own interest.

Persona designata /pərsównə dèzəgnéydə/. A person pointed out or described as an individual, as opposed to a person ascertained as a member of a class, or as filling a particular character.

Persona ecclesiæ /pərsównə əklíyziyiy/. The parson or personation of the church.

Persona est homo cum statu quodam consideratus /pərsównə èst hówmow kə̀m stǽchuw kwówdəm kənsìdəréydəs/. A person is a man considered with reference to a certain *status.*

Person aggrieved. To have standing as a "person aggrieved" under equal employment opportunities provisions of Civil Rights Act, or to assert rights under any federal regulatory statute, a plaintiff must show (1) that he has actually suffered an injury, and (2) that the interest sought to be protected by the complainant is arguably within the zone of interests to be protected or regulated by the statute in question. Foust v. Transamerica Corp., D.C.Cal., 391 F.Supp. 312, 314.

A "person aggrieved" as contemplated by federal rule governing standing to object to alleged illegal search and seizure is one who is the victim of the search and seizure, as distinguished from one who claims prejudice only through the use of evidence gathered in a search directed at someone else. U. S. ex rel. Mann v. Mazurkiewicz, D.C.Pa., 316 F.Supp. 1041, 1043.

See also **Aggrieved party; Standing to sue doctrine.**

Personal. Appertaining to the person; belonging to an individual; limited to the person; having the nature or partaking of the qualities of human beings, or of movable property. In re Steimes' Estate, 150 Misc. 279, 270 N.Y.S. 339.

As to personal Action; Assets; Chattel; Contract; Covenant; Credit; Demand; Disability; Franchise; Injury; Judgment; Knowledge; Liberty; Notice; Obligation; Property; Replevin; Representative; Right; Security; Service; Servitude; Statute; Tax; Tithes; Tort; and Warranty, see those titles.

Personal effects. Articles associated with person, as property having more or less intimate relation to person of possessor; "effects" meaning movable or chattel property of any kind. Usual reference is to the following items owned by a decedent at the time of death: clothing, furniture, jewelry, stamp and coin collections, silverware, china, crystal, cooking utensils, books, cars, televisions, radios, etc. Term when used in will, includes only such tangible property as attended the person, or such tangible property as is worn or carried about the person. In re Sorensen's Estate, 46 Cal.App.2d 35, 115 P.2d 241, 243. Term "personal effects" when employed in a will enjoys no settled technical meaning and, when used in its primary sense, without any qualifying words, ordinarily embraces such tangible property as is worn or carried about the person, or tangible property having some intimate relation to the person of the testator or testatrix; where it is required by the context within which the term appears, it may enjoy a broader meaning. In re Stengel's Estate, Mo.App., 557 S.W.2d 255, 260.

Personal holding company. Type of corporation subject to special Personal Holding Company Tax (I.R.C. § 541 et seq.) on undistributed income so as to preclude use of such organization by individuals in high tax brackets to avoid taxes. Typically, the major sources of income of such corporations include dividends, interest, annuities, royalties, rent, and the like.

Personal holding company tax. Federal tax imposed on personal holding companies and designed to force the distribution of corporate earnings through the threat of a penalty tax on the corporation. I.R.C. § 541.

Personalia personam sequuntur /pèrsənéyl(i)yə pərsównəm səkwántər/. Personal things follow the person.

Personal income. The income which an individual earns or receives. National income minus corporate profits and social security contributions, plus dividends, government transfer payments to individuals, net interest paid by government, money and imputed income received by individuals, unincorporated businesses, and nonprofit institutions.

Personalis actio /pèrsənéyləs ǽksh(iy)ow/. Lat. *Civil law.* A personal action; an action against the person *(in personam).*

Old English law. A personal action. In this sense, the term was borrowed from the civil law by Bracton. The English form is used as the designation of one of the chief divisions of civil actions.

Personaliter /pèrsənéylədər/. In old English law, personally; in person.

Personal jurisdiction. The power of a court over the person of a defendant in contrast to the jurisdiction of a court over a defendant's property or his interest therein; *in personam* as opposed to *in rem* jurisdiction.

Personal liability. A kind of responsibility for the payment or performance of an obligation which exposes the personal assets of the responsible person to payment of the obligation.

The liability of the stockholders in corporations, under certain statutes, by which they may be held individually responsible for the debts of the corporation, either to the extent of the par value of their respective holdings of stock, or to twice that amount, or without limit, or otherwise, as the particular statute directs. This may be required by state statute of stockholders of a new corporation that is undercapitalized.

Personal property. See **Property.**

Personal property tax. Tax on such items of personal property as household furniture, jewelry, etc. levied by local or state governments.

Personal recognizance. Pre-trial release based on the person's own promise that he will show up for trial (no bond required). A species of bail in which the defendant acknowledges personally without sureties his obligation to appear in court at the next hearing or trial date of his case. It is used in place of a bail bond when the judge or magistrate is satisfied that the defendant will appear without the need of a surety bond or other form of security. Also referred to as "release on own recognizance" or "ROR".

Personalty. Personal property; movable property; chattels.

Quasi personalty. Things which are movable in point of law, though fixed to things real, either actually, as emblements *(fructus industriales),* fixtures, etc.; or fictitiously, as chattels-real, leases for years, etc.

Persona non grata /pərsównə nòn grǽdə/°gréydə/. Person not wanted; an undesirable person. In international law and diplomatic usage, a person not acceptable (for reasons peculiar to himself) to the court or government to which it is proposed to accredit him in the character of an ambassador or minister.

Persona standi in judicio /pərsównə stǽnday in juwdísh(iy)ow/. Capacity of standing in court or in judgment; capacity to be a party to an action; capacity or ability to sue.

Personate /pársənèyt/. To assume the person (character) of another, without his consent or knowledge, in order to deceive others, and, in such feigned character, to fraudulently do some act or gain some advantage, to the harm or prejudice of the person counterfeited. To pass one's self off as another having a certain identity. Lane v. U. S., C.C.A.Ohio, 17 F.2d 923. See also **Impersonation.**

Personero /pèrsownérow/. In Spanish law, an attorney. So called because he represents the *person* of another, either in or out of court.

Person in loco parentis /pársən in lówkow pəréntəs/. One who has assumed status and obligations of parent without formal adoption. Workman v. Workman, Okl., 498 P.2d 1384, 1386. See **In loco parentis.**

Personne /pèrsón/. Fr. A person. This term is applicable to men and women, or to either.

Person under disability. Any person who is impaired by reason of mental illness, mental deficiency, physical illness or disability, advanced age, chronic use of drugs, chronic intoxication, or other cause (except minority) to the extent that he lacks sufficient understanding or capacity to make or communicate responsible decisions concerning his person. Uniform Probate Code, § 5–101(1).

Perspicua vera non sunt probanda /pərspíkyuwə vírə nón sənt pròwbǽndə/. Plain truths need not be proved.

Per stirpes /pàr stárpiyz/. Lat. By roots or stocks; by representation. This term, derived from the civil law, is much used in the law of descents and distribution, and denotes that method of dividing an intestate estate where a class or group of distributees take the share which their deceased would have been entitled to, taking thus by their right of representing such ancestor, and not as so many individuals. It is the antithesis of *per capita (q.v.).* Buxton v. Noble, 146 Kan. 671, 73 P.2d 43, 47.

Persuade. To induce one by argument, entreaty, or expostulation into a determination, decision, conclusion, belief, or the like; to win over by an appeal to one's reason and feelings, as into doing or believing something; to bring oneself or another to belief, certainty or conviction; to argue into an opinion or procedure. La Page v. U. S., C.C.A.Minn., 146 F.2d 536, 538.

Persuasion. The act of persuading; the act of influencing the mind by arguments or reasons offered, or by anything that moves the mind or passions, or inclines the will to a determination. For **Fair persuasion,** see that title.

Pertain. To belong or relate to, whether by nature, appointment, or custom.

Pertenencia /pèrtenénsiya/. In Spanish law, the claim or right which one has to the property in anything; the territory which belongs to any one by way of jurisdiction or property; that which is accessory or consequent to a principal thing, and goes with the ownership of it.

Perticata terræ /pàrdəkéydə téhriy/. The fourth part of an acre.

Pertinent /párdənənt/. Applicable; relevant. Evidence is called "pertinent" when it is directed to the issue or matters in dispute, and legitimately tends to prove the allegations of the party offering it; otherwise it is called "impertinent." A pertinent hypothesis is one which, if sustained, would logically influence the issue. Vaughn v. State, 136 Tex.Cr.R. 455, 125 S.W.2d 568, 570. See **Material; Relevant.**

Per totam curiam /pàr tówdəm kyúriyəm/. L. Lat. By the whole court. A common phrase in the old reports.

Per tout et non per my /pər túw(t) ey nón pər míy/. L. Fr. By the whole, and not by the moiety. Where an estate in fee is given to a man and his wife, they cannot take the estate by moieties, but both are seised of the entirety, *per tout et non per my.*

Perturbation /pərdərbéyshən/. In old English ecclesiastical courts, a "suit for perturbation of seat" is the technical name for an action growing out of a disturbance or infringement of one's right to a pew or seat in a church.

Perturbatrix /pərdərbéytrəks/. A woman who breaks the peace.

Per universitatem /pər yùwnəvə̀rsətéydəm/. Lat. In the civil law, by an aggregate or whole; as an entirety. The term described the acquisition of an entire estate by one act or fact, as distinguished from the acquisition of single or detached things.

Per varios actus legem experientia facit /pər vériyows ǽktəs líyjəm əkspìriyénsh(iy)ə fǽsət/. By various acts experience frames the law.

Per verba de futuro /pər vérbə dìy fyəchúrow/. Lat. By words of the future [tense]. A phrase applied to contracts of marriage.

Per verba de præsenti /pər vérbə dìy prəzéntay/. Lat. By words of the present [tense]. A phrase applied to contracts of marriage.

Perverse verdict. A verdict whereby the jury refuse to follow the direction of the judge on a point of law.

Per vivam vocem /pər váyvəm vówsəm/. Lat. In old English law, by the living voice; the same with *viva voce.*

Per year. In a contract, is equivalent to the word "annually."

Pesa /píyzə/. A weight of two hundred and fifty-six pounds.

Pessimi exempli /pésəmay əgzémplay/. Lat. Of the worst example.

Pessurable wares /píyzhərəbəl wérz/. Merchandise which takes up a good deal of room in a ship.

Petens /pédənz/. Lat. In old English law, a demandant; the plaintiff in a real action.

Peter-pence. An ancient levy or tax of a penny on each house throughout England, paid to the Pope. It was called "Peter-pence," because collected on the day of St. Peter, *ad vincula;* by the Saxons it was called "Romefeoh," "Romescot," and "Rome-pennying," because collected and sent to Rome; and, lastly, it was called "hearth money," because every dwelling-house was liable to it, and every religious house, the abbey of St. Albans alone excepted.

Petit /pédiy/pətíy(t)/. Fr. Small; minor; inconsiderable. Used in several compounds, and sometimes written "petty." As to petit Jury; Larceny; Sergeanty; and Treason, see those titles.

Petit cape /pédiy kéyp(iy)/. A judicial writ, issued in the old actions for the recovery of land, requiring the sheriff to take possession of the estate, where the tenant, after having appeared in answer to the summons, made default in a subsequent stage of the proceedings.

Petite assize /pətíyd əsáyz/pédiy°/. Used in contradistinction from the *grand assize,* which was a jury to decide on questions of property. *Petite assize,* a jury to decide on questions of possession.

Petitio /pətísh(iy)ow/. Lat. *Civil law.* The plaintiff's statement of his cause of action in an action *in rem.*

Old English law. Petition or demand; the count in a real action; the form of words in which a title to land was stated by the demandant, and which commenced with the word *"peto."*

Petition. A written address, embodying an application or prayer from the person or persons preferring it, to the power, body, or person to whom it is presented, for the exercise of his or their authority in the redress of some wrong, or the grant of some favor, privilege, or license. A formal written request addressed to some governmental authority. The right of the people to petition for redress of grievances is guaranteed by the First Amendment, U.S. Constitution.

A formal paper filed with the N.L.R.B. seeking a secret ballot election among a certain group of employees (bargaining unit).

A formal, written application to a court requesting judicial action on a certain matter. An application made to a court *ex parte,* or where there are no parties in opposition, praying for the exercise of the judicial powers of the court in relation to some matter which is not the subject for a suit or action, or for authority to do some act which requires the sanction of the court; as for the appointment of a guardian, for leave to sell trust property, etc. A written request to a board for action on some matter therein laid before it. McKillop v. County Bd. of Ed. of Sanborn County, 78 S.D. 587, 105 N.W.2d 671, 675.

Written request to the court after notice. Uniform Probate Code, § 1–201(31).

Petition de droit /pətíshən də dróyt/. L. Fr. In old English practice, a petition of right; a form of proceeding to obtain restitution from the crown of either real or personal property, being of use where the crown is in possession of any hereditaments or chattels, and the petitioner suggests such a right as controverts the title of the crown, grounded on facts disclosed in the petition itself. 3 Bl.Comm. 256.

Petitioner. One who presents a petition to a court, officer, or legislative body. In legal proceedings begun by petition, the person against whom action or relief is prayed, or who opposes the prayer of the petition, is called the "respondent." The one who starts an equity proceeding or the one who takes an appeal from a judgment.

Petition in bankruptcy. A paper filed in a court of bankruptcy, or with the clerk, by a debtor seeking the benefits of the bankruptcy act, or by creditors alleging the commission of an act of bankruptcy by their debtor and seeking an adjudication of bankruptcy against him. See Bankruptcy Act, § 301 et seq.

Petitioning creditor. The creditor at whose instance an adjudication of bankruptcy is made against a bankrupt.

Petition of right. In old English law, a proceeding in chancery by which a subject may recover property in the possession of the king. See **Petition de droit.**

Petition of rights. A parliamentary declaration of the liberties of the people, assented to by King Charles I, in 1629. It is to be distinguished from the bill of rights, (1689), which has passed into a permanent constitutional statute.

Petit jury. See **Jury.**

Petitory action /pédət(ə)riy ǽkshən/. A droitural action; that is, one in which the plaintiff seeks to establish and enforce, by an appropriate legal proceeding, his right of property, or his title, to the subject-matter in dispute; as distinguished from a *possessory* action, where the right to the possession is the point in litigation, and not the mere right of property. In admiralty, suits to try title to property independent of questions concerning possession are referred to as "petitory suits," which suits must be based on a claim of legal title; the assertion of a mere equitable interest is not sufficient. Hunt v. A Cargo of Petroleum Products Laden on Steam Tanker Hilda, D.C.Pa., 378 F.Supp. 701, 703.

In Louisiana, an action brought by an alleged owner out of possession against one having possession to determine ownership, in which plaintiff must recover on strength of his own title, not on weakness of defendant's title. Saucier v. Crichton, C.C.A.La., 147 F.2d 430, 433.

Petronian law. See **Lex Petronia.**

Pettifogger /pédəfògər/. A lawyer who is employed in a small or mean business, or who carries on a disreputable business by unprincipled or dishonorable means.

Petty. Small, minor, of less or inconsiderable importance. The English form of *"petit,"* and sometimes used instead of that word in such compounds as "petty jury," "petty larceny," and "petty treason." See **Misdemeanor; Petit.** As to petty Average; Constable; Larceny; and Session, see those titles.

Petty cash. Currency maintained for expenditures that are conveniently made with cash on hand. A fund used by business to pay small expenses for such items as travel, stationery, etc. Sometimes called imprest fund, it is operated by a voucher system in which the person desiring the money submits a voucher properly authorized and receives the cash.

Petty larceny. See **Larceny.**

Petty offense. A crime, the maximum punishment for which is generally a fine or short term in jail or house of correction. In some states, it is a classification in addition to misdemeanor and felony.

Any misdemeanor, the penalty for which does not exceed imprisonment for a period of six months or a fine of not more than $500, or both, is a petty offense. 18 U.S.C.A. § 1. State v. Holliday, 109 R.I. 93, 280 A.2d 333, 336. For purpose of determining right to jury trial, crimes carrying more than six-month sentences are "serious crimes" and those carrying less are "petty crimes." Maita v. Whitmore, C.A.Cal., 508 F.2d 143, 145.

See also **Infraction; Misdemeanor.**

Petty officers. Inferior officers in the naval service, of various ranks and kinds, corresponding to the non-commissioned officers in the army. U. S. v. Fuller, 160 U.S. 593, 16 S.Ct. 386, 40 L.Ed. 549.

Peyote. A type of cactus called mescal, found in Mexico and southwestern U.S. It contains button-like tubercles that are dried and chewed as an hallucinatory drug. Mescaline is an alkaloid of it.

P.H.V. An abbreviation for *"pro hac vice,"* for this turn, for this purpose or occasion.

Phylasist. A jailer.

Physical. Relating or pertaining to the body, as distinguished from the mind or soul or the emotions. Material, substantive, having an objective existence, as distinguished from imaginary or fictitious; real, having relation to facts, as distinguished from moral or constructive.

Physical cruelty. As used in divorce law means actual personal violence, or such a course of physical treatment as endangers life, limb or health, and renders cohabitation unsafe. Godwin v. Godwin, 140 S.E.2d 593, 595, 245 S.C. 370.

Physical depreciation. Reduction in value of structure due to actual wear and tear or physical deterioration. People ex rel. Union Bag & Paper Corporation v. Fitzgerald, 166 Misc. 237, 2 N.Y.S.2d 290, 295.

Physical disability. See **Disability.**

Physical fact. In the law of evidence, a fact having a physical existence, as distinguished from a mere conception of the mind; one which is visible, audible, or palpable, such as the sound of a pistol shot, a man running, impressions of human feet on the ground. See **Demonstrative evidence.**

Physical fact rule. In evidence, a judge is required to take case from jury if plaintiff's evidence as to physical facts leads to an impossibility in the light of undisputed physical laws. An appellate court is not bound by findings which violate physical laws. Zollman v. Symington Wayne Corp., 438 F.2d 28, 31.

The physical fact rule is that if a driver does not see that which he could or should have seen, he is guilty of negligence as a matter of law. Pennsylvania Nat. Mut. Cas. Ins. Co. v. Dennis, 195 Kan. 594, 408 P.2d 575, 579.

Physical force. Force applied to the body; actual violence.

Physical harm. The words "physical harm" are used throughout the Restatement of Torts to denote the physical impairment of the human body, or of land or chattels. Restatement, Second, Torts, § 7. See also **Physical injury.**

Physical impossibility. Practical impossibility according to the knowledge of the day. State v. Hillis, 79 Ind.App. 599, 124 N.E. 515, 516.

Physical incapacity. In the law of marriage and divorce, impotence, inability to accomplish sexual coition, arising from physical imperfection or malformation.

Physical injury. Bodily harm or hurt, excluding mental distress, fright, or emotional disturbance. See also **Physical harm.**

Physical necessity. A condition in which a person is absolutely compelled to act in a particular way by overwhelming superior force; as distinguished from *moral* necessity, which arises where there is a duty incumbent upon a rational being to perform, which he ought at the time to perform.

Physician. A practitioner of medicine; a person duly authorized or licensed to treat diseases; one lawfully engaged in the practice of medicine.

Physician-patient privilege. See **Patient-physician privilege.**

Physiotherapy /fìziyowθéhrəpiy/. Treatment of disease by physical remedies rather than drugs. Physical therapy.

Piacle /páyəkəl/. An obsolete term for a serious crime.

Pia fraus /páyə frós/. Lat. A pious fraud; a subterfuge or evasion considered morally justifiable on account of the ends sought to be promoted. Particularly applied to an evasion or disregard of the laws in the interests of religion or religious institutions, such as circumventing the statutes of mortmain.

Picaroon /pìkərúwn/. A robber; a plunderer.

Picketing. Term refers to presence at an employer's business by one or more employees and/or other persons to publicize labor dispute, influence employees or customers to withhold their work or business, respectively, or show union's desire to represent employees; picketing is usually accompanied by patrolling with signs. C. Comella, Inc. v. United Farm Workers Organizing Committee, 33 Ohio App.2d 61, 292 N.E.2d 647, 655, 62 O.O.2d 128. Patrolling the entrance of a business by members of a labor union in order to inform other employees and the public of the existence of a strike and to influence or deter them from entering. See also **Labor picketing; Secondary picketing; Unlawful picketing.** Compare **Boycott.**

Peaceable picketing, in which laboring men and women have right to participate during labor dispute, means tranquil conduct, conduct devoid of noise or tumult, the absence of a quarrelsome demeanor, and a course of conduct that does not violate or disturb the public peace. Lilly Dache, Inc., v. Rose, Sup., 28 N.Y.S.2d 303, 305; Ex parte Bell, 37 Cal.App.2d 582, 100 P.2d 339, 340. It connotes peaceable methods of presenting a cause to the public in the vicinity of the employer's premises. Music Hall Theatre v. Moving Picture Mach. Operators Local No. 165, 249 Ky. 639, 61 S.W.2d 283.

Pick of land. A narrow slip of land running into a corner.

Pickpocket. A thief who secretly steals money or other property from the person of another.

Piecework. Work done or paid for by the piece or quantity. Calascibett v. Highway Freight Co., 18 N.J.Misc. 144, 11 A.2d 408, 409.

Piepoudre. See **Court of Piepoudre.**

Pierage /píraj/. The duty for maintaining piers and harbors.

Piercing corporate veil. Judicial process whereby court will disregard usual immunity of corporate officers or entities from liability for corporate activities; *e.g.* when incorporation was for sole purpose of perpetrating fraud. The doctrine which holds that the corporate structure with its attendant limited liability of stockholders may be disregarded and personal liability imposed on stockholders, officers and directors in the case of fraud. The court, however, may look beyond the corporate form only for the defeat of fraud or wrong or the remedying of injustice. Hanson v. Bradley, 298 Mass. 371, 381, 10 N.E.2d 259, 264. See also **Instrumentality rule.**

Pignoratio /pìgnəréysh(iy)ow/. Lat. In the civil law, the contract of pledge; and also the obligation of such contract. Sealing up *(obsignatio).* A shutting up of an animal caught in one's field and keeping it till the expenses and damage have been paid by its master.

Pignoratitia actio /pìgnərətísh(iy)ə ǽksh(iy)ow/. Lat. In the civil law, an action of pledge, or founded on a pledge, which was either *directa,* for the debtor, after payment of the debt, or *contraria,* for the creditor.

Pignorative contract /pìgnəréydəv kóntrækt/. In the civil law, a contract of pledge, hypothecation, or mortgage of realty.

Pignoris capio /pignórəs kǽpiyow/. Lat. In Roman law, this was the name of one of the *legis actiones.* It was employed only in certain particular kinds of pecuniary cases, and consisted in that the creditor, without preliminary suit and without the co-operation of the magistrate, by reciting a prescribed formula, took an article of property from the debtor to be treated as a pledge or security. The proceeding bears a marked analogy to distress at common law.

Pignus /pígnəs/. Lat. In the civil law, a pledge or pawn; a delivery of a thing to a creditor, as security for a debt. Also a thing delivered to a creditor as security for a debt.

Pilfer /pílfər/. To pilfer, in the plain and popular sense, means to steal.

Pilferage /pílf(ə)rəj/. Petty larceny; stealing of small items, generally of stored goods.

Pilferer /pílfərər/. One who steals petty things, or a small part of a thing.

Pillage /píləj/. Plunder; the forcible taking of private property by an invading or conquering army from the enemy's subjects.

Pillory /píləriy/. A frame erected on a pillar, and made with holes and movable boards, through which the heads and hands of criminals were put.

Pimp. One who obtains customers ("tricks") for a whore or prostitute. See also **Pander.**

Pin-money. A small allowance set apart by a husband for the personal expenses of his wife; for her dress and pocket money.

Pint. A liquid measure of half a quart, or the eighth part of a gallon.

Pioneer patent. See **Patent.**

Pious uses /páyəs yúwsəz/. See **Charitable use.**

Piracy. Those acts of robbery and depredation upon the high seas which, if committed on land, would have amounted to a felony. Brigandage committed on the sea or from the sea. Whoever, on the high seas, commits the crime of piracy as defined by the law of nations, and is afterwards brought into or found in the United States, shall be imprisoned for life. 18 U.S.C.A. § 1651. See also **Air piracy.**

The term is also applied to the illicit reprinting or reproduction of a copyrighted book or print or to unlawful plagiarism from it.

Pirata est hostis humani generis /pəréydə èst hóstəs hyuwméynay jénərəs/. A pirate is an enemy of the human race.

Pirate. One guilty of the crime of piracy.

Piscary /pískəriy/. The right of fishing. Thus, common of piscary is the right of fishing in waters belonging to another person.

Pistol. A short firearm, intended to be aimed and fired from one hand. Campbell v. Commonwealth, 295 Ky. 511, 174 S.W.2d 778, 779.

P.J. An abbreviation for "president" (or presiding) "judge" (or justice).

P.L. An abbreviation for "Pamphlet Laws" or "Public Laws."

Placard. An edict; a declaration; a manifesto. Also an advertisement or public notification.

Place. An old form of the word "pleas." Thus the "Court of Common Pleas" was sometimes called the "Court of Common Place."

Place, n. This word is a very indefinite term. It is applied to any locality, limited by boundaries, however large or however small. It may be used to designate a country, state, county, town, or a very small portion of a town. The extent of the locality designated by it must generally be determined by the connection in which it is used. In its primary and most general sense means locality, situation, or site, and it is also used to designate an occupied situation or building. See also **Site; Situs.**

Place, v. To arrange for something as to place a mortgage or to place an order. See also **Placement.**

Place lands. Lands granted which were within certain limits on each side of the road, and which became instantly fixed by the adoption of the line of the road. There is a well-defined difference between place lands and "indemnity lands." See **Indemnity.**

Placement. The act of selling a new issue of securities or arranging a loan or mortgage. The act of finding employment for a person as in the case of an employment agency. See also **Finder; Offering.**

Place of abode. One's residence or domicile (q.v.).

Place of business. The location at which one carries on his business or employment. Under many state statutes, service of process may be made at one's place of business and jurisdiction may be acquired by a court whose territorial district includes one's place of business. See also **Domicile.**

Place of contract. The place (country or state) in which a contract is made, and whose law must determine questions affecting the execution, validity, and construction of the contract. Scudder v. Union Nat. Bank, 91 U.S. 406, 412, 23 L.Ed. 245.

Place of delivery. The place where delivery is to be made of goods sold. If no place is specified in the contract, the articles sold must, in general, be delivered at the place where they are at the time of the sale. Hatch v. Standard Oil Co., 100 U.S. 124, 25 L.Ed. 554. See U.C.C. §§ 2–503, 2–504.

Place of employment. Within the safe place statutes, a place where active work, either temporary or permanent, is being conducted in connection with a business for profit; that is, where some process or operation related to such industry, trade or business is carried on and where any person is directly or indirectly employed by another.

Placer /pléysər/. In mining law, a superficial deposit of sand, gravel, or disintegrated rock, carrying one or more of the precious metals, along the course or under the bed of a watercourse, ancient or current, or along the shore of the sea. Under the acts of congress, the term includes all forms of mineral deposits, except veins of quartz or other rock in place. 30 U.S.C.A. § 35.

Placer claim. A mining claim located on the public domain for the purpose of placer mining, that is, ground within the defined boundaries which contains mineral in its earth, sand, or gravel; ground which includes valuable deposits not "in place," that is, not fixed in rock, or which are in a loose state. U. S. v. Iron Silver Min. Co., 128 U.S. 673, 9 S.Ct. 195, 32 L.Ed. 571; Clipper Min. Co. v. Eli Min. Co., 194 U.S. 220, 24 S.Ct. 632, 48 L.Ed. 944.

Placer location. A placer claim located and occupied on the public domain.

Place where. A phrase used in the older reports, being a literal translation of *locus in quo* (q.v.).

Placit /plǽsət/, or **placitum** /plǽsət(əm)/. Decree; determination.

Placita /plǽsədə/. See **Placitum.**

Placitabile /plǽsətéybəliy/. In old English law, pleadable.

Placita communia /plǽsədə kəmyúwn(i)yə/. Common pleas. All civil actions between subject and subject.

Placita coronæ /plǽsədə kərówniy/. Pleas of the crown. All trials for crimes and misdemeanors, wherein the king is plaintiff, on behalf of the people.

Placita de transgressione contra pacem regis, in regno Angliæ vi et armis facta, secundum legem et consuetudinem Angliæ sine brevi regis placitari non debent /plǽsədə dìy trænzgrèshiyówniy kóntrə péysəm ríyjəs, ìn régnow ǽngliyiy váy èd árməs fǽktə, səkándəm líyjəm èt kònswət(y)úwdənəm ǽngliyiy sáyniy bríyvay ríyjəs plǽsətéray nòn débənt/. Pleas of trespass against the peace of the king in the kingdom of England, made with force and arms, ought not, by the law and custom of England, to be pleaded without the king's writ.

Placita juris /plǽsədə júrəs/. Pleas or rules of law; particular and positive learnings of laws; grounds and positive learnings received with the law and set down; as distinguished from maxims or the formulated conclusions of legal reason.

Placita negativa duo exitum non faciunt /plǽsədə nègətáyvə d(y)úwow égzədəm nòn fǽsh(iy)ənt/. Two negative pleas do not form an issue.

Placitare /plǽsətériy/. To plead.

Placitory /plǽsət(ò)riy/. Relating to pleas or pleading.

Placitum /plǽsədəm/. In civil law, an agreement of parties; that which is their *pleasure* to arrange between them.

An imperial ordinance or constitution; literally, the prince's pleasure.

A judicial decision; the judgment, decree, or sentence of a court.

In old English law, a public assembly at which the king presided, and which comprised men of all degrees, met for consultation about the great affairs of the kingdom.

A court; a judicial tribunal; a lord's court. *Placita* was the style or title of the courts at the beginning of the old *nisi prius* record.

A suit or cause in court; a judicial proceeding; a trial. *Placita* were divided into *placita coronœ* (crown cases or pleas of the crown, *i.e.*, criminal actions) and *placita communia* (common cases or common pleas, *i.e.*, private civil actions).

A fine, mulct, or pecuniary punishment.

A pleading or plea. In this sense, the term was not confined to the defendant's answer to the declaration, but included all the pleadings in the cause, being *nomen generalissimum.*

In the old reports and abridgments, *"placitum"* was the name of a paragraph or subdivision of a title or page where the point decided in a cause was set out separately. It is commonly abbreviated "pl."

Placitum aliud personale, aliud reale, aliud mixtum /plǽsədəm ǽliyəd pərsənéyliy, ǽliyəd riyéyliy, ǽliyəd míkstəm/. Pleas [*i.e.*, actions] are personal, real, and mixed.

Placitum fractum /plǽsədəm frǽktəm/. A day past or lost to the defendant.

Placitum nominatum /plǽsədəm nòmənéydəm/. The day appointed for a criminal to appear and plead and make his defense.

Plagiarism /pléyjərìzəm/. The act of appropriating the literary composition of another, or parts or passages of his writings, or the ideas or language of the same, and passing them off as the product of one's own mind.

To be liable for plagiarism it is not necessary to exactly duplicate another's literary work, it being sufficient if unfair use of such work is made by lifting of substantial portion thereof, but even an exact counterpart of another's work does not constitute plagiarism if such counterpart was arrived at independently. O'Rourke v. RKO Radio Pictures, D.C. Mass., 44 F.Supp. 480, 482, 483.

See also **Fair use doctrine.**

Plagiarist /pléyjərəst/, or **plagiary** /pléyjiyèhriy/. One who publishes the thoughts and writings of another as his own.

Plagiarius /plèyjiyériyəs/. Lat. In the civil law, a kidnapper.

Plagium /pléyj(iy)əm/. Lat. In the civil law, kidnapping. The offense of enticing away and stealing men, children, and slaves. The persuading a slave to escape from his master, or the concealing or harboring him without the knowledge of his master.

Plaideur /plèydɚ́r/. Fr. An obsolete term for an attorney who pleaded the cause of his client; an advocate.

Plain error rule. Doctrine of "plain error" encompasses those errors which are obvious, which affect the substantial rights of the accused, and which, if uncorrected, would be an affront to the integrity and reputation of judicial proceedings. U. S. v. McCord, 166 U.S.App.D.C. 1, 501 F.2d 334, 341. The principle that an appeals court can reverse a judgment because of an error in the proceedings even if the error was not objected to at the time. "Plain error" doctrine applies where evidence is extremely damaging, the need for a limiting instruction is obvious, and failure to give it is so prejudicial that it affects defendant's substantial rights. U. S. v. Cox, C.A.Tex., 536 F.2d 65, 69. Doctrine encompasses those errors which are obvious, which affect the substantial rights of the accused, and which, if uncorrected, would be an affront to the integrity and reputation of judicial proceedings. U. S. v. McCord, 166 U.S.App.D.C. 1, 501 F.2d 334, 341.

Plain error, requiring an award of a new trial although no objection was made at time error occurred, is error possessing a clear capacity to bring about an unjust result and which substantially prejudiced defendant's fundamental rights to have jury fairly evaluate merits of defendant's defense. State v. Thornton, 38 N.J. 380, 185 A.2d 9, 18.

Plaint /pléynt/. In civil law, a complaint; a form of action, particularly one for setting aside a testament alleged to be invalid. This word is the English equivalent of the Latin *"querela."*

In English practice, a private memorial tendered in open court to the judge, wherein the party injured sets forth his cause of action. A proceeding in inferior courts by which an action is commenced without original writ. This mode of proceeding is commonly adopted in cases of replevin.

Plaintiff. A person who brings an action; the party who complains or sues in a civil action and is so named on the record. A person who seeks remedial relief for an injury to rights; it designates a complainant. City of Vancouver v. Jarvis, 76 Wash.2d 110, 455 P.2d 591, 593. The prosecution (*i. e.* State or United States) in a criminal case.

Plaintiff in error. The party who sues out a writ of error to review a judgment or other proceeding at law.

Plain view doctrine. In search and seizure context, objects falling in plain view of officer who has the right to be in position to have that view are subject to seizure without a warrant and may be introduced in evidence. Harris v. U. S., 390 U.S. 234, 236, 88 S.Ct. 992, 993, 19 L.Ed.2d 1069. Under "plain view doctrine," warrantless seizure of incriminating evidence may be permitted when police are lawfully searching specified area if it can be established that police had prior justification for intrusion into area searched, that police inadvertently came across item seized, and that it was immediately apparent to the police that the item seized was evidence. Smith v. State, 33 Md.App. 407, 365 A.2d 53, 55.

Plan. A delineation; a design; a draft, form or representation. The representation of anything drawn on a plane, as a map or chart; a scheme; a sketch. Also, a method of design or action, procedure, or arrangement for accomplishment of a particular act or object. Shainwald v. City of Portland, 153 Or. 167, 55 P.2d 1151, 1156. Method of putting into effect an intention or proposal.

Planned unit development (PUD). An area with a specified minimum contiguous acreage to be developed as a single entity according to a plan, containing one or more residential clusters or planned unit residential developments and one or more public, quasi-public, commercial or industrial areas in such ranges of ratios of nonresidential uses to residential uses as shall be specified in the zoning ordinance.

Area of land controlled by landowner to be developed as a single entity for a number of dwelling units, and commercial and industrial uses, if any, the plan for which does not correspond in lot size, bulk or type of dwelling or commercial or industrial use, density, lot coverage and required open space to the regulations established in any one or more districts, created from time to time, under the provisions of a municipal zoning ordinance enacted pursuant to the conventional zoning enabling act of the state.

Plantation. In English law, a colony; an original settlement in a new country.

In American law, a farm; a large cultivated estate. Term used chiefly in the southern states to refer to large farms on which cotton, tobacco, sugar, and like crops are grown.

Plat, or plot. A map of a town, section, or subdivision showing the location and boundaries of individual parcels of land subdivided into lots, with streets, alleys, easements, etc., usually drawn to a scale. See also **Plat map.**

Platform. A statement of principles and of policies adopted by a party convention as a basis for the party's appeal for public support.

Plat map. A plat map is generally drawn after the property has been described by some other means, such as a Government Survey System. Once a plat map is set, legal descriptions are defined by referring to the given map, in a lot and block description.

Play-debt. Debt contracted by gaming.

Plea. In common law pleading (now obsolete with adoption of Rules of Civil Procedure) a pleading; any one in the series of pleadings. More particularly, the first pleading on the part of the defendant. In the strictest sense, the answer which the defendant in an action at law made to the plaintiff's declaration, and in which he set up matter of *fact* as defense, thus distinguished from a demurrer, which interposed objections on grounds of *law*.

In equity pleading (now obsolete with adoption of Rules of Civil Procedure) a special answer showing or relying upon one or more things as a cause why the suit should be either dismissed or delayed or barred. A short statement, in response to a bill in equity, of facts which, if inserted in the bill, would render it demurrable.

Affirmative plea. In equity pleading, one which sets up a single fact, not appearing in the bill, or sets up a number of circumstances all tending to establish a single fact, which fact, if existing, destroys the complainant's case. Such is obsolete under Rules of Civil Procedure. See **Affirmative defense.**

Anomalous plea. One which is partly affirmative and partly negative. Obsolete under Rules of Civil Procedure.

Common pleas. In common law pleading, common causes or suits; civil actions brought and prosecuted between subjects or citizens, as distinguished from criminal cases. Such are obsolete under Rules of Civil Procedure.

Criminal pleas. The defendant's response to a criminal charge (guilty, not guilty, or nolo contendere). If a defendant refuses to plead or if a defendant corporation fails to appear, the court shall enter a plea of not guilty. Fed.R.Crim.P. 11(a). See also **Arraignment; Guilty plea; Nolo contendere; Not guilty; Plea bargaining.**

Dilatory pleas. See **Dilatory.**

Double plea. In common law pleading, one having the technical fault of duplicity; one consisting of several distinct and independent matters alleged to the same point and requiring different answers. This does not present any problem under Rules of Civil Procedure which permits party to plead as many separate claims or defenses, regardless of consistency. Fed.R.Civil P. 8(e)(2).

False plea. A sham plea (q.v. infra).

Negative plea. In equity pleading, one which does not undertake to answer the various allegations of the bill, but specifically denies some particular fact or matter the existence of which is essential to entitle the complainant to any relief. Abolished under Rules of Civil Procedure. See **Denial.**

Peremptory pleas. In common law pleading, "pleas in bar" are so termed in contradistinction to that class of pleas called "dilatory pleas." The former, viz., peremptory pleas, are usually pleaded to the merits of the action, with the view of raising a material issue between the parties; while the latter class, viz., dilatory pleas, are generally pleaded with a view of retarding the plaintiff's proceedings, and not for the purpose of raising an issue upon which the parties may go to trial and settle the point in dispute. Peremptory pleas are also called "pleas in bar," while dilatory pleas are said to be in abatement only. Abolished under Rules of Civil Procedure.

Plea agreements. See **Plea bargaining.**

Plea in abatement. In common law pleading, a plea which, without disputing justice of plaintiff's claim, objects to place, mode, or time of asserting it. It allows plaintiff to renew suit in another place or form, or at another time, and does not assume to answer action on its merits, or deny existence of particular cause of action on which plaintiff relies. Abolished under Rules of Civil Procedure. See **Abatement of action.**

Plea in bar. A plea which goes to *bar* the plaintiff's action; that is, to defeat it absolutely and entirely. A plea in bar sets forth matters which per se destroy right of action and bar its prosecution absolutely, such as bar of statute of limitations or constitutional guarantee against self-incrimination. U. S. v. Brodson, C.A.Wis., 234 F.2d 97, 99. A plea in bar is one that denies a plaintiff's right to maintain the action and which, if established, will destroy the action. Gillikin v. Gillikin, 248 N.C. 710, 104 S.E.2d 861, 862.

Plea in discharge. In common law pleading, one which admits that the plaintiff had a cause of action, but shows that it was discharged by some subsequent or collateral matter, as, payment or accord and satisfaction. Abolished under Rules of Civil Procedure. See **Affirmative defense.**

Plea in reconvention. In the civil law, a plea which sets up new matter, not in defense to the action, but by way of cross-complaint, set-off, or counterclaim.

Plea of confession and avoidance. In common law pleading, one which admits that plaintiff had a cause of action, but which avers that it has been discharged by some subsequent or collateral matter. Abolished under Rules of Civil Procedure. See **Affirmative defense.**

Plea of guilty. A confession of guilt in open court. See also *Criminal pleas, supra.*

Plea of nolo contendere /plíy əv nówlow kənténdəriy/. One which has the same effect as a "plea of guilty" in so far as regards the proceedings on the indictment, and it is a confession only for the purposes of the criminal prosecution and does not bind the defendant in a civil suit for the same wrong. Schireson v. State Board of Medical Examiners of New Jersey, 129 N.J.L. 203, 28 A.2d 879, 881. See also **Nolo contendere.**

Plea of release. In common law pleading, one which admits the cause of action, but sets forth a release subsequently executed by the party authorized to release the claim. Abolished by Rules of Civil Procedure. See **Affirmative defense.**

Sham plea. A false plea; a plea of false or fictitious matter, subtly drawn so as to entrap an opponent, or create delay. A vexatious or false defense, resorted to under the old system of pleading for purposes of delay and annoyance. Such a plea may be ordered stricken on motion under Rules of Civil P. 12(f).

Special plea. In common law pleading, a special kind of plea in bar, distinguished by this name from the general issue, and consisting usually of some new affirmative matter, though it may also be in the form of a traverse or denial. Abolished under Rules of Civil Procedure.

Special plea in bar. In common law pleading, one which advances new matter. It differs from the general, in this: that the latter denies some material allegation, but never advances new matter. Abolished under Rules of Civil Procedure.

Plea agreement. See **Plea bargaining.**

Plea bargaining. The process whereby the accused and the prosecutor in a criminal case work out a mutually satisfactory disposition of the case subject to court approval. It usually involves the defendant's pleading guilty to a lesser offense or to only one or some of the counts of a multi-count indictment in return for a lighter sentence than that possible for the graver charge. Plea bargaining procedures in the federal courts are governed by Fed.R.Crim.P. 11(e).

Plead. To make, deliver, or file any pleading; to conduct the pleadings in a cause. To interpose any pleading in a civil action. More particularly, to deliver in a formal manner the defendant's answer to the plaintiff's declaration, complaint or to the indictment, as the case may be. See **Pleadings.**

Pleader. A person whose business it was to draw pleadings. Formerly, when pleading at common law was a highly technical and difficult art, there was a class of men known as "special pleaders not at the bar," who held a position intermediate between counsel and attorneys. In current usage, the pleader is the party asserting a particular pleading.

Pleadings. The formal allegations by the parties of their respective claims and defenses.

Rules or Codes of Civil Procedure. Unlike the rigid technical system of common law pleading, pleadings under federal and state rules or codes of civil procedure have a far more limited function, with determination and narrowing of facts and issues being left to discovery devices and pre-trial conferences. In addition, the rules and codes permit liberal amendment and supplementation of pleadings.

Under rules of civil procedure the pleadings consist of a complaint, an answer, a reply to a counterclaim, an answer to a cross-claim, a third party complaint, and a third party answer. Fed.R.Civil P. 7(a).

For amendment of pleadings, see **Amendment.** For judgment on pleadings, see **Judgment.** See also Alternative pleading; Responsive pleading; Sham (Sham pleading); Supplemental pleading; Variance

Common law pleading. The system of rules and principles, established in the common law, according to which the pleadings or responsive allegations of litigating parties were framed with a view to preserve technical propriety and to produce a proper issue.

The process performed by the parties to a suit or action, in alternately presenting written statements of their contention, each responsive to that which precedes, and each serving to narrow the field of controversy, until there evolves a single point, affirmed on one side and denied on the other, called the "issue," upon which they then go to trial.

The individual allegations of the respective parties to an action at common law, proceeding from them alternately, in the order and under the distinctive names following: The plaintiff's *declaration,* the defendant's *plea,* the plaintiff's *replication,* the defendant's *rejoinder,* the plaintiff's *surrejoinder,* the defendant's *rebutter,* the plaintiff's *surrebutter;* after which they have no distinctive names.

Plead over. To pass over, or omit to notice, a material allegation in the last pleading of the opposite party; to pass by a defect in the pleading of the other party without taking advantage of it. In another sense, to plead the general issue, after one has interposed a demurrer or special plea which has been dismissed by a judgment of *respondeat ouster.* Obsolete under Rules of Civil Procedure.

Plea in abatement. A plea in abatement is one which, without disputing the jurisdiction of plaintiff's claim, objects to the place, mode or time of asserting it, and it allows plaintiff to renew his suit in another place or form, or at another time, and does not assume to answer the action on its merits, or deny the existence of the particular cause of action on which plaintiff relies. A plea in abatement sets forth facts extrinsic to merits which affect only manner in which action is framed or circumstances under which it is sought to be prosecuted, and does not destroy the right of action but merely suspends or postpones its prosecution. U. S. v. Brodson, C.A.Wis., 234 F.2d 97, 99. See also **Abatement of action.**

Plea negotiations. See **Plea bargaining.**

Plea of privilege. In Texas, objection to venue is raised by a plea of privilege to be sued in the county of one's residence, and such plea if filed in due time, must be sustained unless the case falls within one of the exceptions in the venue statute.

Plebeity /pləbíyədiy/ or **plebity** /plébədiy/. The common or meaner sort of people; the plebeians.

Plebeyos /plebéyows/. In Spanish law, commons; those who exercise any trade, or who cultivate the soil.

Plebiscite /plébəsàyt/ °sət/ °sìyt/. A vote of the people expressing their choice for or against a proposed law or enactment, submitted to them, and which, if adopted, will work a change in the constitution, or which is beyond the powers of the regular legislative body. See also **Referendum.**

Plebiscitum /plèbəsáydəm/. Lat. In Roman law, a law enacted by the *plebs* or commonalty (that is, the citizens, with the exception of the patricians and senators), at the request or on the proposition of a plebeian magistrate, such as a "tribune."

Plebs /plébz/. Lat. In Roman law, the commonalty or citizens, exclusive of the patricians and senators.

Pledge. A bailment of goods to a creditor as security for some debt or engagement. A pledge, considered as a transaction, is a bailment or delivery of goods or property by way of security for a debt or engagement, or as security for the performance of an act. Another definition is that a pledge is a security interest in a chattel or in an intangible represented by an indispensable instrument (such as formal, written evidence of an interest in an intangible so representing the intangible that the enjoyment, transfer, or enforcement of the intangible depends upon possession of the instrument), the interest being created by a

bailment for the purpose of securing the payment of a debt or the performance of some other duty. A pledge is a promise or agreement by which one binds himself to do or forbear something. Elmquist v. Lock, 194 Cal.App.2d 372, 15 Cal.Rptr. 447, 450.

Much of the law of pledges has been replaced by the provisions for secured transactions in Article 9 of the U.C.C.

See also **Collateral; Hypothecate; Secured transaction; Security.**

Pledgee. The party to whom goods are pledged, or delivered in pledge.

Pledgery. Suretyship, or an undertaking or answering for another.

Pledges. In common law pleading, those persons who became sureties for the prosecution of the suit. Their names were anciently appended at the foot of the declaration. In time it became purely a formal matter, because the plaintiff was no longer liable to be amerced for a false claim, and the fictitious persons John Doe and Richard Roe became the universal pledges, or they might be omitted altogether; or inserted at any time before judgment; they are now omitted.

Pledgor /pléjər/. The party delivering goods in pledge; the party pledging.

Plegii de retorno habendo /pléjiyay dìy rətórnow həbéndow/. In common law, pledges to return the subject of distress, should the right be determined against the party bringing the action of replevin.

Plegiis acquietandis /pléjiyəs əkwàyətǽndəs/. A writ that anciently lay for a surety against him for whom he was surety, if he paid not the money at the day.

Plena ætas /plíynə íytǽs/. Lat. In old English law, full age.

Plena et celeris justitia fiat partibus /plíynə èt sélərəs jəstísh(iy)ə fáyət párdəbəs/. Let full and speedy justice be done to the parties.

Plena forisfactura /plíynə fòrəsfǽkchúrə/. A forfeiture of all that one possesses.

Plena probatio /plíynə prowbéysh(iy)ow/. In the civil law, a term used to signify full proof (that is, proof by two witnesses), in contradistinction to *semi-plena probatio,* which is only a presumption.

Plenarty /plíynərdiy/plén°/. In old English law, fullness; a state of being full. A term applied to a benefice when full, or possessed by an incumbent. The opposite state to a *vacation,* or vacancy.

Plenary. Full, entire, complete, absolute, perfect, unqualified. Mashunkashey v. Mashunkashey, 191 Okl. 501, 134 P.2d 976, 979.

Plenary action. A complete and formal hearing or trial on the merits as distinguished from a summary hearing which is commonly less strict and more informal. May v. Henderson, 268 U.S. 111, 45 S.Ct. 456, 69 L.Ed. 870.

Plenary confession. A full and complete confession. An admission or confession, whether in civil or criminal law, is said to be "plenary" when it is, if believed, conclusive against the person making it.

Plenary jurisdiction. Full and complete jurisdiction or power of a court over the subject matter as well as the parties to a controversy. See also **Jurisdiction.**

Plenary powers. Authority and power as broad as is required in a given case.

Plenary session. A meeting of all members of a deliberative body, as distinguished from a meeting of a committee of the same body.

Plenary suit. One that proceeds on formal pleadings. Central Republic Bank and Trust Co. v. Caldwell, C.C.A.Mo., 58 F.2d 721. See also **Plenary action.**

Plene /plíyniy/. Lat. Completely; fully; sufficiently.

Plene administravit /plíyniy ədmìnəstréyvət/. A plea by an executor or administrator that he has fully administered all the assets that have come to his hands, and that no assets remain out of which the plaintiff's claim could be satisfied.

Plene administravit præter /plíyniy ədmìnəstréyvət príydər/. A plea by an executor or administrator that he has "fully administered" all the assets that have come to his hands, "except" assets to a certain amount, which are not sufficient to satisfy the plaintiff.

Plene computavit /plíyniy kòmpyətéyvət/. He has fully accounted. A plea in an action of account render, alleging that the defendant has fully accounted.

Plenipotentiary /plènəpəténsh(iy)əriy/. One who has full power to do a thing; a person fully commissioned to act for another. A term applied in international law to ministers and envoys of the second rank of public ministers.

Plenum dominium /plíynəm dəmíniyəm/. Lat. In the civil law, full ownership; the property in a thing united with the usufruct.

Plevin /plévən/. A warrant, or assurance.

Pleyto /pléytow/. In Spanish law, the pleadings in a cause.

Plight. In old English law, an estate, with the habit and quality of the land; extending to a rent charge and to a possibility of dower.

Plot. See **Plat.**

Plottage. A term used in appraising land values and particularly in eminent domain proceedings to designate the additional value given to city lots by the fact that they are contiguous, which enables the owner to utilize them as large blocks of land. Plottage is a recognized concept in the field of eminent domain, referring to an added increment of value which may accrue to two or more vacant and unimproved contiguous parcels of land held in one ownership because of their potentially enhanced marketability by reason of their greater use adaptability as a single unit; simplistically stated, an assemblage of vacant and unimproved contiguous parcels held in one ownership may have a greater value as a whole than the sum of their values as separate constituent parcels and, hence,

plottage value may be considered in determining fair market value. State ex rel. State Highway Commission of Missouri v. Armacost Motors, Inc., Mo.App., 552 S.W.2d 360, 364.

Plow back. To retain earnings for continued investment in the business. To reinvest the earnings and profits into the business instead of paying them out as dividends or withdrawals by partners or proprietor.

Plunder, v. To pillage or loot. To take property from persons or places by open force, and this may be in course of a war, or by unlawful hostility, as in the case of pirates or robbers. The term is also used to express the idea of taking property from a person or place, without just right, but not expressing the nature or quality of the wrong done.

Plunder, n. Personal property belonging to an enemy, captured and appropriated on land; booty. Also the act of seizing such property. See **Booty; Prize.**

Plunderage. In maritime law, the embezzlement of goods on board of a ship is so called.

Plural. Containing more than one; consisting of or designating two or more.

Plurality /plurǽlədiy/. The excess of the votes cast for one candidate over those cast for any other. Where there are only two candidates, he who receives the greater number of the votes cast is said to have a *majority;* when there are more than two competitors for the same office, the person who receives the greatest number of votes has a *plurality,* but he has not a majority unless he receives a greater number of votes than those cast for all his competitors combined, or, in other words, more than one-half of the total number of votes cast.

A plurality normally refers to the state of being numerous; a large number or quantity; while it may perhaps mean two, it embraces any number in excess of two. Technograph Printed Circuits, Limited v. Bendix Aviation Corp., D.C.Md., 218 F.Supp. 1, 52.

An opinion of an appellate court in which more justices join than in any concurring opinion (though not a majority of the court) is a plurality opinion as distinguished from a majority opinion in which a larger number of the justices on the panel join than not.

Plural marriage. See **Marriage; Polygamy.**

Pluries fi. fa. /pl(y)úriyiyz fáy(əray) féy(shiyəs)/. A writ issued where other commands of the court have proved ineffectual.

Plus exempla quam peccata nocent /plə́s əgzémplə kwǽm pəkéydə nósənt/. Examples hurt more than crimes.

Plus peccat author quam actor /plə́s pékəd óθər kwǽm ǽktər/°pékəd óktər°/. The originator or instigator of a crime is a worse offender than the actual perpetrator of it. Applied to the crime of subornation of perjury.

Plus petitio /plə́s pətísh(iy)ow/. In Roman law, a phrase denoting the offense of claiming more than was just in one's pleadings. Prior to Justinian's time, this offense was in general fatal to the action; but, under the legislation of the emperors Zeno and Justinian, the offense (if *re, loco,* or *causa*) exposed the party to the payment of three times the damage, if any, sustained by the other side, and (if *tempore*) obliged him to postpone his action for double the time, and to pay the costs of his first action before commencing a second.

Plus valet consuetudo quam concessio /plás vǽlət kònswətyúwdow kwǽm kənsésh(iy)ow/. Custom is more powerful than grant.

Plus valet unus oculatus testis quam auriti decem /plás vǽlət yúwnəs òkyəléydəs téstəs kwǽm órəday désəm/. One eye-witness is of more weight than ten ear-witnesses [or those who speak from hearsay].

Plus vident oculi quam oculus /plás vídənt ókyəlay kwǽm ókyələs/. Several eyes see more than one.

P.M. An abbreviation for "postmaster;" also for *"post-meridiem,"* afternoon.

Pneumoconiosis /nùwmowkòwniyówsəs/. A generic term including all lung diseases caused by dust particles of any sort. Genesco, Inc. v. Greeson, 105 Ga. App. 798, 125 S.E.2d 786, 789. See **Black Lung Benefits Act.**

P.O. An abbreviation of "public officer;" also of "post-office."

Poach. To steal or destroy game on another's land. See **Poaching.**

Poaching. In criminal law, the unlawful entry upon land for the purpose of taking or destroying fish or game. The illegal taking or killing of fish or game.

Pocket veto. The act of the President in retaining a legislative bill without approving or rejecting it at the end of the legislative session and, in effect, vetoing it by such inactivity.

P.O.D. account. An account payable on request to one person during lifetime and on his death to one or more P.O.D. payees, or to one or more persons during their lifetimes and on the death of all of them to one or more P.O.D. payees. Uniform Probate Code, § 5–101.

Pœna /píynə/. Lat. Punishment; a penalty.

Pœna ad paucos, metus ad omnes perveniat /píynə ǽd pókows, míydəs ǽd ómniyz pərvíyn(i)yət/. If punishment be inflicted on a few, a dread comes to all.

Pœna corporalis /píynə kòrpəréyləs/. Corporal punishment.

Pœnæ potius molliendæ quam exasparandæ sunt /píyniy pówsh(iy)əs mòliyéndiy kwǽm əgzǽspərǽndiy sə́nt/. Punishments should rather be softened than aggravated.

Pœnæ sint restringendæ /píyniy sìnt rèstrinjéndiy/. Punishments should be restrained.

Pœnæ suos tenere debet actores et non alios /píynə súwows təníriy débəd æktóriyz èt nón ǽliyows/. Pun-

ishment ought to be inflicted upon the guilty, and not upon others.

Pœna ex delicto defuncti hæres teneri non debet /píynə èks dəlíktow dəfə́ŋktay híriyz təníray nòn débət/. The heir ought not to be bound by a penalty arising out of the wrongful act of the deceased.

Pœnalis /pənéyləs/. Lat. In the civil law, penal; imposing a penalty; claiming or enforcing a penalty. *Actiones pœnales,* penal actions.

Pœna non potest, culpa perennis erit /píynə nòn pówdəst, kə́lpə pərénəs éhrət/. Punishment cannot be, crime will be, perpetual.

Pœna pilloralis /píynə pìləréyləs/. In old English law, punishment of the pillory.

Pœna suos tenere debet actores et non alios /píynə s(y)úwows təníriy débəd æktóriyz èt nón ǽliyows/. Punishment ought to bind the guilty, and not others.

Pœna tolli potest, culpa perennis erit /píynə tólay pówdəst, kə́lpə pərénəs éhrət/. The punishment can be removed, but the crime remains.

Pœnitentia /pènəténsh(iy)ə/píyn°/. Lat. In the civil law, repentance; reconsideration; changing one's mind; drawing back from an agreement already made, or rescinding it.

Locus pœnitentiæ. Room or place for repentance or reconsideration; an opportunity to withdraw from a negotiation before finally concluding the contract or agreement. Also, in criminal law, an opportunity afforded by the circumstances to a person who has formed an intention to kill or to commit another crime, giving him a chance to reconsider and relinquish his purpose.

Point. A distinct proposition or question of law arising or propounded in a case. See also **Issue.**

In the case of shares of stock, a point means $1. In the case of bonds a point means $10, since a bond is quoted as a percentage of $1,000. In the case of market averages, the word point means merely that and no more. If, for example, the Dow-Jones Industrial Average rises from 870.25 to 871.25, it has risen a point. A point in this average, however, is not equivalent to $1.

Real estate financing. The word "point" as used in home mortgage finance industry denotes a fee or charge equal to one percent of principal amount of loan which is collected by lender at time the loan is made. It is a fee or charge which is collected only once, at inception of loan, and is in addition to constant long-term stated interest rate on face of loan. V. F. Saul Co. v. West End Park North, Inc., 250 Md. 707, 246 A.2d 591, 595, 597.

Point reserved. When, in the progress of the trial of a cause, an important or difficult point of law is presented to the court, and the court is not certain of the decision that should be given, it may *reserve* the point, that is, decide it provisionally as it is asked by the party, but reserve its more mature consideration for the hearing on a motion for a new trial, when, if it shall appear that the first ruling was wrong, the verdict will be set aside. The point thus treated is technically called a "point reserved."

Points. See **Point.**

Point system. In some states points are assessed against motor vehicle law violators and when a pre-established number of points has been assessed against a driver during a given period, his license to operate is suspended.

Poison. A substance having an inherent deleterious property which renders it, when taken into the system, capable of destroying life. A substance which, on being applied to the human body, internally or externally, is capable of destroying the action of the vital functions, or of placing the solids and fluids in such a state as to prevent the continuance of life.

Poisonous tree doctrine. Doctrine refers to an illegal arrest or search which leads officers to evidence seized in a proper manner that may be inadmissible because of the taint of the original illegality. Com. v. Spofford, 343 Mass. 703, 180 N.E.2d 673. Sometimes also referred to as "fruit of poisonous tree" doctrine (q.v.).

Polar star rule. The rule that the intent of the maker of a written document, as gathered from its four corners, shall prevail unless such intent conflicts with some statutory provision within the jurisdiction, or is against public policy. Hanks v. McDanell, 307 Ky. 243, 210 S.W.2d 784, 786.

Pole. A measure of length, equal to five yards and a half.

Police. Branch of the government which is charged with the preservation of public order and tranquillity, the promotion of the public health, safety, and morals, and the prevention, detection, and punishment of crimes. See also **Internal police; Peace** (Peace officers); **Sheriff.**

Police court. The name of an inferior court in several of the states, which has jurisdiction over minor offenses and city ordinances, concurrent jurisdiction in certain matters with justices of the peace, and the powers of a committing magistrate in respect to more serious crimes, and, in some states, a limited jurisdiction for the trial of civil causes.

Police jury. In Louisiana, the governing bodies of the parishes, which are political subdivisions of the state, comparable to counties in other states. National Liberty Ins. Co. of America v. Police Jury of Natchitoches Parish, C.C.A.La., 96 F.2d 261, 262.

Police justice. A magistrate charged exclusively with the duties incident to the common-law office of a conservator or justice of the peace; the prefix "police" serving merely to distinguish them from justices having also civil jurisdiction.

Police magistrate. An inferior judicial officer having jurisdiction of minor criminal offenses, breaches of police regulations, and the like; so called to distinguish them from magistrates who have jurisdiction in civil cases also, as justices of the peace.

Police officer. One of the staff of men employed in cities and towns to enforce the municipal laws and ordinances for preserving the peace, safety, and good order of the community. Also called "policeman"; "patrolman."

Police power. An authority conferred by the American constitutional system in the Tenth Amendment, U.S. Const., upon the individual states, and, in turn, delegated to local governments, through which they are enabled to establish a special department of police; adopt such laws and regulations as tend to prevent the commission of fraud and crime, and secure generally the comfort, safety, morals, health, and prosperity of its citizens by preserving the public order, preventing a conflict of rights in the common intercourse of the citizens, and insuring to each an uninterrupted enjoyment of all the privileges conferred upon him or her by the general laws.

The power of the State to place restraints on the personal freedom and property rights of persons for the protection of the public safety, health, and morals or the promotion of the public convenience and general prosperity. The police power is subject to limitations of the federal and State constitutions, and especially to the requirement of due process. Police power is the exercise of the sovereign right of a government to promote order, safety, health, morals and general welfare within constitutional limits and is an essential attribute of government. Marshall v. Kansas City, Mo., 355 S.W.2d 877, 883.

Policy. The general principles by which a government is guided in its management of public affairs, or the legislature in its measures.

A general term used to describe all contracts of insurance. See **Policy of insurance.**

This term, as applied to a law, ordinance, or rule of law, denotes its general purpose or tendency considered as directed to the welfare or prosperity of the state or community.

A species of "lottery" whereby the chance is determined by numbers; "numbers game" also being a lottery. People v. Hines, 258 App.Div. 466, 17 N.Y. S.2d 141, 142. Policy is a lottery or game of chance where bettors select numbers to bet on and place the bet with a policy writer. State v. Harris, Mo.App., 325 S.W.2d 352, 354. See **Lottery.**

Public policy. That principle of the law which holds that no subject can lawfully do that which has a tendency to be injurious to the public or against the public good. The principles under which the freedom of contract or private dealings is restricted by law for the good of the community. The term "policy," as applied to a statute, regulation, rule of law, course of action, or the like, refers to its probable effect, tendency, or object, considered with reference to the social or political well-being of the state. Thus, certain classes of acts are said to be "against public policy," when the law refuses to enforce or recognize them, on the ground that they have a mischievous tendency, so as to be injurious to the interests of the state, apart from illegality or immorality.

Policyholder. The person who owns the policy of insurance whether he is the insured or not. In most states, any person with an insurable interest may be a policyholder.

Policy of insurance. An instrument in writing, by which one party (insurer), in consideration of a premium, engages to indemnify another (insured) against a contingent loss, by making him a payment in compensation, whenever the event shall happen by which the loss is to accrue. Contract whereby insurer, in return for premiums, engages, on happening of designated event, to pay certain sum as provided. In re O'Neill's Estate, 143 Misc. 69, 255 N.Y.S. 767, 771.

The written instrument in which a contract of insurance is set forth.

See also **Face of policy; Floater policy; Homeowner's policy; Master policy.**

Assessable policy. A policy under which a policyholder may be held liable for losses of the insurance company beyond its reserves.

Blanket policy. A policy of fire insurance which contemplates that the risk is shifting, fluctuating, or varying, and is applied to a class of property rather than to any particular article or thing.

The term "specific" as applied in insurance phraseology is frequently used in contrast with "blanket insurance" and denotes coverage of a particular piece of property or property at a specific location, as contrasted with blanket insurance which covers the same and other property in several different locations.

Class of life insurance policies. Those policies issued in the same calendar year, upon the lives of persons of the same age, and on the same plan of insurance.

Endowment policy. In life insurance, a policy the amount of which is payable to the assured himself at the end of a fixed term of years, if he is then living, or to his heirs or a named beneficiary if he shall die sooner.

Extended policy. A policy which provides protection beyond the time when premiums are no longer paid.

Floater policy. A policy of fire insurance not applicable to any specific described goods, but to any and all goods which may at the time of the fire be in a certain building.

Incontestable policy. A policy which contains a provision to the effect that the company after the policy has been in force cannot contest, challenge or cancel the policy on the basis of statements made in the application. The period of contestability may be one, two or three years.

Interest policy. One where the assured has a real, substantial, and assignable interest in the thing insured; as opposed to a wager policy.

Master policy. In group life, medical, etc. insurance, the single policy under which the participants are covered. The individuals covered by the master policy receive a certificate indicating their participation.

Mixed policy. A policy of marine insurance in which not only the time is specified for which the risk is limited, but the voyage also is described by its local termini; as opposed to policies of insurance for a particular voyage, without any limits as to time, and also to purely time policies, in which there is no designation of local termini at all.

Open policy. One in which the value of the subject insured is not fixed or agreed upon in the policy as between the assured and the underwriter, but is left to be estimated in case of loss. The term is opposed to "valued policy," in which the value of the subject insured is fixed for the purpose of the insurance, and expressed on the face of the policy. But this term is also sometimes used to describe a policy in which an aggregate amount is expressed in the body of the policy, and the specific amounts and subjects are to be indorsed from time to time.

Paid-up policy. In life insurance, a policy on which no further payments are to be made in the way of annual premiums.

Participating policy. A policy commonly found in mutual insurance companies and in some stock companies in which the insured participates in the profits by receiving dividends or rebates from future premiums.

Policy loan. An advancement on life policy without a personal obligation on the part of the policyholder as to repayment. Board of Assessors of the Parish of Orleans v. New York Life Ins. Co., 216 U.S. 517, 30 S.Ct. 385, 54 L.Ed. 597. A loan made by an insurance company which takes the policy's cash reserve as security for the loan.

Term policy. In life insurance, a policy which gives protection for a specified period of time but no cash or reserve value is created in the policy. See **Insurance.**

Time policy. In fire insurance, one made for a defined and limited time, as, one year. In marine insurance, one made for a particular period of time, irrespective of the voyage or voyages upon which the vessel may be engaged during that period.

Valued policy. One in which the value of the thing insured, and also the amount to be paid thereon in the event of loss, is settled by agreement between the parties and inserted in the policy.

Voyage policy. A policy of marine insurance effected for a particular voyage or voyages of the vessel, and not otherwise limited as to time.

Wager policy. An insurance upon a subject-matter in which the party assured has no real, valuable, or insurable interest. A mere wager policy is that in which the party assured has no interest in the thing assured, and could sustain no possible loss by the event insured against, if he had not made such wager. Such policies are generally illegal, or not otherwise written, because the insured does not have an insurable interest.

Policy value. The amount of cash available to the policyholder on the surrender or cancellation of the insurance policy.

Policy year. In insurance, the year which commences with the date of the commencement or anniversary of the policy.

Politiæ legibus non leges politiis adaptandæ /pəlíshiy(iy) líyjəbəs nòn líyjiyz pəlíshiyəs ædəptǽndiy/. Politics are to be adapted to the laws, and not the laws to politics.

Political. Pertaining or relating to the policy or the administration of government, state or national. Pertaining to, or incidental to, the exercise of the functions vested in those charged with the conduct of government; relating to the management of affairs of state, as political theories; of or pertaining to exercise of rights and privileges or the influence by which individuals of a state seek to determine or control its public policy; having to do with organization or action of individuals, parties, or interests that seek to control appointment or action of those who manage affairs of a state. State ex rel. Maley v. Civic Action Committee, 238 Iowa 851, 28 N.W.2d 467, 470.

Political corporation. A public or municipal corporation; one created for political purposes, and having for its object the administration of governmental powers of a subordinate or local nature.

Political crime. In general, any crime directly against the government; *e.g.* treason; sedition. It includes any violent political disturbance without reference to a specific crime. See also **Political offenses.**

Political law. That branch of jurisprudence which treats of the science of politics, or the organization and administration of government. More commonly called "Political science."

Political liberty. See **Liberty.**

Political offenses. As a designation of a class of crimes usually excepted from extradition treaties, this term denotes crimes which are incidental to and form a part of political disturbances; but it might also be understood to include offenses consisting in an attack upon the political order of things established in the country where committed, and even to include offenses committed to obtain any political object. Under extradition treaties, such offense must involve uprising of some other violent political disturbance and act in question must have been incidental to occurrence; status of offense is to be determined by circumstances attending it and not by motives of those who subsequently handle prosecution. Garcia-Guillern v. U. S., C.A.Fla., 450 F.2d 1189, 1192. See also **Political crime.**

Political office. See **Office.**

Political party. A number of persons united in opinion and organized in the manner usual to the then existing political parties. Swindall v. State Election Board, 168 Okl. 97, 32 P.2d 691, 695. An unincorporated, voluntary association of persons sponsoring certain ideas of government or maintaining certain political principles or beliefs in public policies of government, not a governmental agency or instrumentality. Robinson v. Holman, 181 Ark. 428, 26 S.W.2d 66, 68.

Political questions. Questions of which courts will refuse to take cognizance, or to decide, on account of their purely political character, or because their determination would involve an encroachment upon the executive or legislative powers.

A matter of dispute which can be handled more appropriately by another branch of the government is not a "justiciable" matter for the courts. However, a state apportionment statute is not such a political question as to render it nonjusticiable. Baker v. Carr, 369 U.S. 186, 208–210, 82 S.Ct. 691, 705–706, 7 L.Ed.2d 663.

Political rights. Those which may be exercised in the formation or administration of the government. Rights of citizens established or recognized by constitutions which give them the power to participate directly or indirectly in the establishment or administration of government.

Political subdivision. A division of the state made by proper authorities thereof, acting within their constitutional powers, for purpose of carrying out a portion of those functions of state which by long usage and inherent necessities of government have always been regarded as public. State ex rel. Maisano v. Mitchell, 155 Conn. 256, 231 A.2d 539, 542.

Political trial. Term loosely applied to trials in which the parties represent fundamentally different political convictions and in which the parties or one of them attempts to litigate their political beliefs.

Politics. The science of government; the art or practice of administering public affairs.

Polity. The form of government; civil constitution.

Poll, v. To single out, one by one, of a number of persons. To examine each juror separately, after a verdict has been given, as to his concurrence in the verdict. See **Polling the jury.**

Poll, n. A head; an individual person; a register of persons. In the law of elections, a list or register of heads or individuals who may vote in an election; the aggregate of those who actually cast their votes at the election, excluding those who stay away.

Polling the jury. A practice whereby the jurors are asked individually whether they assented, and still assent, to the verdict. To poll a jury is to call the names of the persons who compose a jury and require each juror to declare what his verdict is before it is recorded. This may be accomplished by questioning them individually or by ascertaining fact of unanimous concurrence by general question, and once concurrence has been determined, the polling is at an end. Fortenberry v. New York Life Ins. Co., C.A.Tenn., 459 F.2d 114, 115.

If upon the poll there is not unanimous concurrence, the jury may be directed to retire for further deliberations or may be discharged. Fed.R.Crim.P. 31.

Polls. The place where electors cast in their votes.

Poll-tax. A capitation tax; a tax of a specific sum levied upon each person within the jurisdiction of the taxing power and within a certain class (as, all males of a certain age, etc.) without reference to his property or lack of it.

Poll taxes as a prerequisite to voting in federal elections are prohibited by the 24th Amendment and as to state elections such were held to be unconstitutional in Harper v. Virginia Bd. of Elections, 383 U.S. 663, 86 S.Ct. 1079, 16 L.Ed.2d 169.

Po. lo. suo. An old abbreviation for the words *"ponit loco suo"* (puts in his place), used in warrants of attorney.

Pollute. To corrupt or defile. The contamination of soil, air and water by noxious substances and noises.

Polyandry /póliyændriy/. The civil condition of having more husbands than one to the same woman; a social order permitting plurality of husbands.

Polygamia est plurium simul virorum uxorumve connubium /pòləgéymiyə èst pl(y)úriyəm sáyməl vərórəm əksərə́mviy kən(y)úwbiyəm/. Polygamy is the marriage with many husbands or wives at one time.

Polygamy /pəlígəmiy/. The offense of having several wives or husbands at the same time, or more than one wife or husband at the same time. Bigamy literally means a second marriage distinguished from a third or other; while polygamy means many marriages,—implies more than two. Polygamy is a crime in all states.

A person is guilty of polygamy, a felony of the third degree, if he marries or cohabits with more than one spouse at a time in purported exercise of the right of plural marriage. The offense is a continuing one until all cohabitation and claim of marriage with more than one spouse terminates. This section does not apply to parties to a polygamous marriage, lawful in the country of which they are residents or nationals, while they are in transit through or temporarily visiting this State. Model Penal Code, § 230.1.

Polygarchy /póləgàrkiy/. A term sometimes used to denote a government of many or several; a government where the sovereignty is shared by several persons; a collegiate or divided executive.

Polygraph. Lie detector test and the apparatus for conducting the test. The "polygraph" is an electro-mechanical instrument which simultaneously measures and records certain physiological changes in the human body which it is believed are involuntarily caused by an examinee's conscious attempts to deceive an interrogator while responding to a carefully prepared set of questions. U. S. v. DeBetham, D.C. Cal., 348 F.Supp. 1377, 1384. While the general rule is that the results of such tests are not admissible as evidence (United States v. Tremont, C.A.Tenn., 351 F.2d 144), a minority of courts permit such if the parties have entered into an adequate stipulation to that effect. Herman v. Eagle Star Ins. Co., D.C.Cal., 283 F.Supp. 33. See also **Lie detector.**

Polyopsony. The condition of a market characterized by the fewness of buyers. The fewness has an effect on the price of the materials or products.

Polypoly. A market condition characterized by the fewness of sellers and this has a direct effect on prices.

Pomerene Act. Federal Bills of Lading Act, 49 U.S.C.A. §§ 81–124. See also **Bill of lading acts.**

Pond. A body of stagnant water without an outlet, larger than a puddle and smaller than a lake; or a like body of water with a small outlet.

Great ponds. In Maine and Massachusetts, natural ponds having a superficial area of more than ten acres, and not appropriated by the proprietors to their private use prior to a certain date.

Public pond. In New England, a great pond; a pond covering a superficial area of more than ten acres.

Private pond. A body of water wholly on the lands of a single owner, or of a single group of joint owners or tenants in common, which did not have any such connection with any public waters that fish could pass from one to the other. At common law, if pond was so connected with public waters that at time of high water, fish could go in and out, it was not "private pond" from which defendants could seine fish whether fish might go out same day or next season.

Ponderantur testes, non numerantur /pòndərǽntər téstiyz nón n(y)ùwmərǽntər/. Witnesses are weighed, not counted.

Pondus /póndəs/. In old English law, poundage; *i.e.,* a duty paid to the crown according to the weight of merchandise.

Pondus regis /póndəs ríyjəs/. The king's weight; the standard weight appointed by the king.

Pone /pówniy/. In old English practice, an original writ formerly used for the purpose of removing suits from the court-baron or county court into the superior courts of common law. It was also the proper writ to remove all suits which were before the sheriff by writ of justices. But this writ is now in disuse, the writ of *certiorari* being the ordinary process by which at the present day a cause is removed from a county court into any superior court.

Ponendis in assisis /pənéndəs in əsáyzəs/. An old writ directing a sheriff to impanel a jury for an assize or real action.

Ponendum in ballium /pənéndəm in bǽliyəm/. An old writ commanding that a prisoner be bailed in cases bailable.

Ponendum sigillum ad exceptionem /pənéndəm səjíləm æd əksèpshiyównəm/. A writ by which justices were required to put their seals to exceptions exhibited by a defendant against a plaintiff's evidence, verdict, or other proceedings, before them.

Pone per vadium /pówniy pàr véydiyəm/. In English practice, an obsolete writ to the sheriff to summon the defendant to appear and answer the plaintiff's suit, on his putting in sureties to prosecute. It was so called from the words of the writ, *"pone per vadium et salvos plegios,"* "put by gage and safe pledges, A. B., the defendant."

Ponit se super patriam /pównət sìy s(y)úwpər pǽtriyəm/. Lat. He puts himself upon the country. The defendant's plea of not guilty in a criminal action was recorded, in old English practice, in these words, or in the abbreviated form *"po. se."*

Pool. A combination of persons or corporations engaged in the same business, or for the purpose of engaging in a particular business or commercial or speculative venture, where all contribute to a common fund, or place their holdings of a given stock or other security in the hands and control of a managing member or committee, with the object of eliminating competition as between the several members of the pool, or of establishing a monopoly or controlling prices or rates by the weight and power of their combined capital, or of raising or depressing prices on the stock market, or simply with a view to the successful conduct of an enterprise too great for the capital of any member individually, and on an agreement for the division of profits or losses among the members, either equally or pro rata. Also, a similar combination not embracing the idea of a pooled or contributed capital, but simply the elimination of destructive competition between the members by an agreement to share or divide the profits of a given business or venture, as, for example, a contract between two or more competing railroads to abstain from "rate wars" and (usually) to maintain fixed rates, and to divide their earnings from the transportation of freight in fixed proportions. Such type pooling arrangements are illegal under the Sherman Antitrust Act. See also **Cartel; Trust.**

In various methods of gambling, a "pool" is a sum of money made up of the stakes contributed by various persons, the whole of which is then wagered as a stake on the event of a race, game, or other contest, and the winnings (if any) are divided among the contributors to the pool pro rata. Or it is a sum similarly made up by the contributions of several persons, each of whom then makes his guess or prediction as to the event of a future contest or hazard, the successful bettor taking the entire pool. Such pools are distinct from the practice of bookmaking. U. S. v. Berent, C.A.Nev., 523 F.2d 1360, 1361.

A body of standing water, without a current or issue, accumulated in a natural basin or depression in the earth, and not artificially formed. See **Pond.**

Pooling of interests. In accounting for a merger, the asset and liability accounts of the merging companies are combined with any difference between book values of the net worth of the combined companies in the capital surplus accounts and the merger terms.

Pope. The bishop of Rome, and supreme head of the Roman Catholic Church.

Popular sense. In reference to the construction of a statute, this term means that sense which people conversant with the subject-matter with which the statute is dealing would attribute to it.

Populiscitum /pòpyələsáydəm/. Lat. In Roman law, a law enacted by the people; a law passed by an assembly of the Roman people, in the *comitia centuriata,* on the motion of a senator; differing from a *plebiscitum,* in that the latter was always proposed by one of the tribunes.

Populus /póp(y)ələs/. Lat. In Roman law, the people; the whole body of Roman citizens, including as well the patricians as the plebeians.

Porcion /pòrθ(i)yówn/. In Spanish law, a part or portion; a lot or parcel; an allotment of land.

Pornographic. That which is of or pertaining to obscene literature; obscene; licentious. Material is pornographic or obscene if the average person, applying contemporary community standards, would find that the work taken as a whole appeals to the prurient interest and if it depicts in a patently offensive way sexual conduct and if the work taken as a whole lacks serious literary, artistic, political or scientific value. Miller v. California, 413 U.S. 15, 24–25, 93 S.Ct. 2607, 2615, 37 L.Ed.2d 419. See also **Dominant theme; Obscene; Prurient interest.**

Port. A place for the loading and unloading of the cargoes of vessels, and the collection of duties or customs upon imports and exports. A place, either on the seacoast or on a river, where ships stop for the purpose of loading and unloading cargo, or for purpose of taking on or letting off passengers, from whence they depart, and where they finish their voyage. A port is a place intended for loading or unloading goods; hence includes the natural shelter surrounding water, as also sheltered water produced by artificial jetties, etc. The Baldhill, C.C.A.N.Y., 42 F.2d 123, 125.

Foreign port. One exclusively within the jurisdiction of a foreign nation, hence one without the United States. But the term is also applied to a port in any state other than the state where the vessel belongs or her owner resides. Port other than home port.

Home port. The port at which a vessel is registered or enrolled or where the owner resides.

Port charges, dues, or tolls. Pecuniary exactions upon vessels availing themselves of the commercial conveniences and privileges of a port. Wilkens v. Trafikaktiebolaget Grangesberg Okelosund, C.C.A., 10 F.2d 129, 131; Christianssand Shipping Co. v. Marshall, D.C.Pa., 22 F.2d 192, 194.

Port of call. Port at which ships usually stop on a route or voyage.

Port of delivery. The port which is to be the terminus of any particular voyage, and where the vessel is to unlade or deliver her cargo, as distinguished from any port at which she may touch, during the voyage, for other purposes.

Port of departure. The port from which vessel clears and departs upon start of voyage. As used in the United States statutes requiring a ship to procure a bill of health from the consular officer at the place of departure, is not the last port at which the ship stops while bound for the United States, but the port from which she cleared.

Port of destination. The port at which a voyage is to end. In maritime law and marine insurance, the term includes both ports which constitute the termini of the voyage; the home port and the foreign port to which the vessel is consigned as well as any usual stopping places for the receipt or discharge of cargo.

Port of discharge. In a policy of marine insurance, means the place where the substantial part of the cargo is discharged, although there is an intent to complete the discharge at another basin.

Port of entry. One of the ports designated by law, at which a custom-house or revenue office is established for the execution of the laws imposing duties on vessels and importations of goods. Port where immigrants arrive. 8 U.S.C.A. § 1221.

Port-reeve, or port-warden. An officer maintained in some ports to oversee the administration of the local regulations; a sort of harbor-master.

Port-risk. In marine insurance, a risk upon a vessel while lying in port, and before she has taken her departure upon another voyage. See also **Port risk insurance.**

Port toll. The toll paid for bringing goods into a port.

Portal-to-Portal Act. Federal statute regulating pay for non-productive time required of employee to reach place of employment and to return in some instances.

Port authority. Governmental agency authorized by a state or the federal government to regulate and plan traffic through a port, and also commonly charged with responsibility of encouraging or securing businesses to locate on land or areas served by port. Sometimes such authorities also have responsibility over establishment and maintenance of airports, bridges, tollways, and surface transportation in metropolitan area of port; *e.g.* New York Port Authority, which is operated jointly by New York and New Jersey under an interstate compact.

Portfolio. In investments, the collective term for all the securities held by one person or institution.

Portio legitima /pórsh(iy)ow ləjídəmə/. Lat. In the civil law, the birthright portion; that portion of an inheritance to which a given heir is entitled, and of which he cannot be deprived by the will of the decedent, without special cause, by virtue merely of his relationship to the testator.

Portion. An allotted part; a share, a parcel; a division in a distribution; a share of an estate or the like, received by gift or inheritance. Lecompte v. Davis' Ex'r, 285 Ky. 433, 148 S.W.2d 292, 295. See **Per capita; Per stirpes.**

Portion disponible. Fr. In French law, that part of a man's estate which he may bequeath to other persons than his natural heirs. A parent leaving one legitimate child may dispose of one-half only of his property; one leaving two, one-third only; and one leaving three or more, one-fourth only; and it matters not whether the disposition is *inter vivos* or by will.

Portoria /portóriyə/. In the civil law, duties paid in ports on merchandise. Taxes levied in old times at city gates. Tolls for passing over bridges.

Port risk insurance. Under New York law, "port risk insurance," in contradistinction to voyage or time insurance, means a risk upon a vessel while lying in port, and before she has taken her departure on another voyage. Bristol S.S. Corp. v. London Assur., D.C.N.Y., 404 F.Supp. 749, 752.

Portsale. In old English law, an auction; a public sale of goods to the highest bidder; also a sale of fish as soon as it is brought into the haven.

Portus est locus in quo exportantur et importantur merces /pórdəs èst lówkəs in kwów èksportǽntər èd importǽntər mársiyz/. A port is a place where goods are exported or imported.

Positive. Laid down, enacted, or prescribed. Express or affirmative. Direct, absolute, explicit. As to positive Condition; Fraud; Proof; and Servitude, see those titles.

Positive evidence. Direct evidence. Direct proof of the fact or point in issue; evidence which, if believed, establishes the truth or falsehood of a fact in issue, and does not arise from any presumption. It is distinguished from circumstantial evidence. See also **Evidence.**

Positive law. Law actually and specifically enacted or adopted by proper authority for the government of an organized jural society.

Positive wrong. A wrongful act, wilfully committed. Padgett v. Missouri Motor Distributing Corporation, Mo., 177 S.W.2d 490, 492.

Positivi juris /pòzətáyvay júrəs/. Lat. Of positive law.

Posito uno oppositorum, negatur alterum /pəzísh(iy)ow yúwnow əpòzətórəm nəgéydər oltərəm/. One of two opposite positions being affirmed, the other is denied.

Posse /pósiy/. Lat. A possibility. A thing is said to be *in posse* when it may possibly be; *in esse* when it actually is. Group of people acting under authority of police or sheriff and engaged in searching for a criminal or in making an arrest. Same as **Posse comitatus** (*q.v.*).

Posse comitatus /pósiy kòmətéydəs/. Lat. The power or force of the county. The entire population of a county above the age of fifteen, which a sheriff may summon to his assistance in certain cases, as to aid him in keeping the peace, in pursuing and arresting felons, etc. Williams v. State, 253 Ark. 973, 490 S.W.2d 117, 121.

Possess. To occupy in person; to have in one's actual and physical control; to have the exclusive detention and control of; to have and hold as property; to have a just right to; to be master of; to own or be entitled to.

Term "possess," under narcotic drug laws, means actual control, care and management of the drug. Collini v. State, Tex.Cr.App., 487 S.W.2d 132, 135. See also **Hold; Possession.**

Possessio /pəzésh(iy)ow/. Lat. *Civil law.* That condition of fact under which one can exercise his power over a corporeal thing at his pleasure, to the exclusion of all others. This condition of fact is called "detention," and it forms the substance of possession in all its varieties.

Old English law. Possession; seisin. The detention of a corporeal thing by means of a physical act and mental intent, aided by some support of right.

General Classification

Pedis possessio /píydəs pəzésh(iy)ow/. A foothold; an actual possession of real property, implying either actual occupancy or enclosure and use.

Possessio bona fide /pəzésh(iy)ow bównə fáydiy/. Possession in good faith. *Possessio mala fide,* possession in bad faith. A possessor *bona fide* is one who believes that no other person has a better right to the possession than himself. A possessor *mala fide* is one who knows that he is not entitled to the possession.

Possessio bonorum /pəzésh(iy)ow bownórəm/. In the civil law, the possession of goods. More commonly termed "*bonorum possessio*" (*q.v.*).

Possessio civilis /pəzésh(iy)ow sívələs/. In Roman law, a legal possession, *i.e.,* a possessing accompanied with the intention to be or to thereby become owner; and, as so understood, it was distinguished from "*possessio naturalis,*" otherwise called "*nuda detentio,*" which was a possessing without any such intention. *Possessio civilis* was the basis of *usucapio* or of *longi temporis possessio,* and was usually (but not necessarily) adverse possession.

Possessio fratris /pəzésh(iy)ow frǽtrəs/. The possession or seisin of a brother; that is, such possession of an estate by a brother as would entitle his sister of the whole blood to succeed him as heir, to the exclusion of a half-brother. Hence, derivatively, that doctrine of the older English law of descent which shut out the half-blood from the succession to estates; a doctrine which was abolished by the descent act, 3 & 4 Wm. IV, c. 106.

Possessio longi temporis /pəzésh(iy)ow lónjay témpərəs/. See **Usucapio.**

Possessio naturalis /pəzésh(iy)ow nèchəréyləs/. See *Possessio civilis, supra.*

Possessio est quasi pedis positio /pəzésh(iy)ow èst kwéysay píydəs pəzísh(iy)ow/. Possession is, as it were, the position of the foot.

Possessio fratris de feodo simplici facit sororem esse hæredem /pəzésh(iy)ow frǽtrəs dìy fyúwdow símpləsay féysət sərórəm ésiy həríydəm/. The brother's possession of an estate in fee-simple makes the sister to be heir.

Possession. The detention and control, or the manual or ideal custody, of anything which may be the subject of property, for one's use and enjoyment, either as owner or as the proprietor of a qualified right in it, and either held personally or by another who exercises it in one's place and name. Act or state of possessing. That condition of facts under which one can exercise his power over a corporeal thing at his pleasure to the exclusion of all other persons.

The law, in general, recognizes two kinds of possession: actual possession and constructive possession. A person who knowingly has direct physical control over a thing, at a given time, is then in actual possession of it. A person who, although not in actual possession, knowingly has both the power and the intention at a given time to exercise dominion or control over a thing, either directly or through another person or persons, is then in constructive possession of it. The law recognizes also that possession may be sole or joint. If one person alone has actual or constructive possession of a thing, possession is sole. If two or more persons share actual or constructive possession of a thing, possession is joint.

Generally, "possession" within context of title insurance policies refers to open, visible and exclusive use. Happy Canyon Inv. Co. v. Title Ins. Co. of Minnesota, Colo.App., 560 P.2d 839, 842.

See also Adverse possession; Constructive possession; Contentious possession; Exclusive possession; Hold; Notorious possession; Occupancy; Repossession.

Actual possession. Exists where the thing is in the immediate occupancy and control of the party. Field Furniture Co. v. Community Loan Co., 257 Ky. 825, 79 S.W.2d 211, 215. See also general definition above.

Adverse possession. See **Adverse possession.**

Chose in possession. A thing (subject of personal property) in actual possession, as distinguished from a "chose in action," which is not presently in the owner's possession, but which he has a right to demand, receive, or recover by suit.

Civil possession. In modern civil law and in the law of Louisiana, that possession which exists when a person ceases to reside in a house or on the land which he occupied, or to detain the movable which he possessed, but without intending to abandon the possession. It is the detention of a thing by virtue of a just title and under the conviction of possessing as owner. A fiction resulting from the registry of the title of the original owner.

Constructive possession. Possession not actual but assumed to exist, where one claims to hold by virtue of some title, without having the actual occupancy, as, where the owner of a tract of land, regularly laid out, is in possession of a part, he is constructively in possession of the whole. See also general definition above.

Corporeal possession. The continuing exercise of a claim to the exclusive use of a material thing. The elements of this possession are first, the mental attitude of the claimant, the intent to possess, to appropriate to oneself; and second, the effective realization of this attitude. All the authorities agree that an intent to exclude others must coexist with the external facts, and must be fulfilled in the external physical facts in order to constitute possession.

Criminal law. Possession as necessary for conviction of offense of possession of controlled substances with intent to distribute may be constructive as well as actual. U. S. v. Craig, C.A.Tenn., 522 F.2d 29, 31. The defendants must have had dominion and control over the contraband. U. S. v. Morando-Alvarez, C.A. Ariz., 520 F.2d 882, 884. See also **Possess.**

Possession, as an element of offense of stolen goods, is not limited to actual manual control upon or about the person, but extends to things under ne's power and dominion. McConnell v. State, 48 Ala. App. 523, 266 So.2d 328, 333.

Possession as used in indictment charging possession of stolen mail may mean actual possession or constructive possession. U. S. v. Ellison, C.A.Cal., 469 F.2d 413, 415.

To constitute "possession" of a concealable weapon under statute proscribing possession of a concealable weapon by a felon, it is sufficient that defendant have constructive possession and immediate access to the weapon. State v. Kelley, 12 Or.App. 496, 507 P.2d 837, 839.

Derivative possession. The kind of possession of one who is in the lawful occupation or custody of the property, but not under a claim of title of his own, but under a right derived from another, as, for example, a tenant, bailee, licensee, etc.

Dispossession. The act of ousting or removing one from the possession of property previously held by him, which may be tortious and unlawful, as in the case of a forcible amotion, or in pursuance of law, as where a landlord "dispossesses" his tenant at the expiration of the term or for other cause by the aid of judicial process. See **Dispossess proceedings; Ejectment; Eviction.**

Estate in possession. An estate whereby a present interest passes to and resides in the tenant, not depending on any subsequent circumstance or contingency. An estate where the tenant is in actual pernancy, or receipt of the rents and other advantages arising therefrom.

Exclusive possession. See **Exclusive possession.**

Hostile possession. This term, as applied to an occupant of real estate holding adversely, is not construed as implying actual emnity or ill will, but merely means that he claims to hold the possession in the character of an owner, and therefore denies all validity to claims set up by any and all other persons. See **Adverse possession.**

Naked possession. The actual occupation of real estate, but without any apparent or colorable right to hold and continue such possession; spoken of as the lowest and most imperfect degree of title.

Natural possession. That by which a man detains a thing corporeally, as, by occupying a house, cultivating ground, or retaining a movable in possession; natural possession is also defined to be the corporeal detention of a thing which we possess as belonging to us, without any title to that possession or with a title which is void.

Open possession. Possession of real property is said to be "open" when held without concealment or attempt at secrecy, or without being covered up in the name of a third person, or otherwise attempted to be withdrawn from sight, but in such a manner that any person interested can ascertain who is actually in possession by proper observation and inquiry. See **Adverse possession.**

Peaceable possession. See **Peaceable.**

Pedal possession. In establishing title by adverse possession this means actual possession; that is, living upon or actually occupying the land, or placing improvements directly upon it.

Possession, writ of. Where the judgment in an action of ejectment is for the delivery of the land claimed, or its possession, this writ is used to put the plaintiff in possession. It is in the nature of execution.

Quasi possession. Is to a right what possession is to a thing, it is the exercise or enjoyment of the right, not necessarily the continuous exercise, but such an exercise as shows an intention to exercise it at any time when desired.

Scrambling possession. By this term is meant a struggle for possession on the land itself, not such a contest as is waged in the courts, or possession gained by an act of trespass, such as building a fence.

Unity of possession. Joint possession of two rights by several titles, as where a lessee of land acquires the title in fee-simple, which extinguishes the lease. The term also describes one of the essential properties of a joint estate, each of the tenants having the entire possession as well of every parcel as of the whole.

Vacant possession. An estate which has been abandoned, vacated, or forsaken by the tenant. The abandonment must be complete in order to make the possession vacant, and, therefore, if the tenant have goods on the premises it will not be so considered.

Possession is nine-tenths of the law. This adage is not to be taken as true to the full extent, so as to mean that the person in possession can only be ousted by one whose title is nine times better than his, but it places in a strong light the legal truth that every claimant must succeed by the strength of his own title, and not by the weakness of his antagonist's.

Possession vaut titre /pəzéshən vów tíytr(ə)/. Fr. In English law, as in most systems of jurisprudence, the fact of possession raises a *prima facie* title or a presumption of the right of property in the thing possessed. In other words, the possession is as good as the title (about).

Possessio pacifica per annos 60 facit jus /pəzésh(iy)ow pəsífəkə pàr ǽnows sèksəjíntə féysət jə́s/. Peaceable possession for sixty years gives a right.

Possessor. One who possesses; one who has possession. See also **Occupant.**

Possessor bona fide /pəzésər bównə fáydiy/. He is a *bona fide* possessor who possesses as owner by virtue of an act sufficient in terms to transfer property, the defects of which he was ignorant of. He ceases to be a *bona fide* possessor from the moment these defects are made known to him, or are declared to him by a suit instituted for the recovery of the thing by the owner.

Possessor mala fide /pəzésər mǽlə fáydiy/. The possessor in bad faith is he who possesses as master, but who assumes this quality, when he well knows that he has no title to the thing, or that his title is vicious and defective.

Possessory. Relating to possession; founded on possession; contemplating or claiming possession.

Possessory action. See next title.

Possessory claim. The title of a pre-emptor of public lands who has filed his declaratory statement but has not paid for the land.

Possessory lien. A lien is possessory where the creditor has the right to hold possession of the specific property until satisfaction of the debt or performance of an obligation.

Possessory action. An action which has for its immediate object to obtain or recover the actual *possession* of the subject-matter; as distinguished from an action which merely seeks to vindicate the plaintiff's *title,* or which involves the bare right only; the latter being called a "petitory" action; *e.g.* summary process action to dispossess tenant for non-payment of rent. A "possessory action" is one brought by a possessor of immovable property to be maintained in his possession when his possession has been disturbed or to be restored to possession from which he has been evicted. Mott v. Smith, La.App., 273 So.2d 675, 677.

An action founded on possession. Trespass for injuries to personal property is called a "possessory" action, because it lies only for a plaintiff who, at the moment of the injury complained of, was in actual or constructive, immediate, and exclusive possession.

Admiralty practice. One which is brought to recover the possession of a vessel, had under a claim of title.

Old English law. A real action which had for its object the regaining possession of the freehold, of which the demandant or his ancestors had been unjustly deprived by the present tenant or possessor thereof.

Possessory interest. Right to exert control over specific land to exclusion of others. Right to possess property by virtue of an interest created in the property though it need not be accompanied by title; *e.g.* right of a tenant for years.

A possessory interest in land exists in a person who has (a) a physical relation to the land of a kind which gives a certain degree of physical control over the land, and an intent so to exercise such control as to exclude other members of society in general from any present occupation of the land; or (b) interests in the land which are substantially identical with those arising when the elements stated in Clause (a) exist. Restatement, Property, § 7.

Possessory warrant. The proceeding by possessory warrant is a summary remedy for the recovery of a personal chattel which has been taken by fraud, violence, enticement, or seduction from the possession of the party complaining or which, having been in his recent possession, has disappeared and is believed to be in the possession of the party complained against. The purpose of the proceeding is to protect and quiet the possession of personalty, but only as against acts which are inhibited by statute.

Possibilitas /pòsəbílətæs/. Lat. Possibility; a possibility. *Possibilitas post dissolutionem executionis nunquam reviviscatur,* a possibility will never be revived after the dissolution of its execution. *Post executionem status, lex non patitur possibilitatem,* after the execution of an estate the law does not suffer a possibility.

Possibility. An uncertain thing which may happen. A contingent interest in real or personal estate.

It is either *near* (or *ordinary*), as where an estate is limited to one after the death of another, or *remote* (or *extraordinary*), as where it is limited to a man, provided he marries a certain woman, and that she shall die and he shall marry another.

See also **Impossibility; Probability.**

Bare possibility. The same as a "naked" possibility. See *infra.*

Naked possibility. A bare chance or expectation of acquiring a property or succeeding to an estate in the future, but without any present right in or to it which the law would recognize as an estate or interest.

Possibility coupled with an interest. An expectation recognized in law as an estate or interest, such as occurs in executory devises and shifting or springing uses. Such a possibility may be sold or assigned.

Possibility of reverter. Future estate left in creator or in his successors in interest upon simultaneous creation of estate that will terminate automatically within in a period of time defined by occurrence of specified event. United Methodist Church in West Sand Lake v. Kunz, 78 Misc.2d 565, 357 N.Y.S.2d 637, 640. The interest which remains in a grantor or testator after the conveyance or devise of a fee simple determinable and which permits the grantor to be revested automatically of his estate on breach of the condition.

Possibility on a possibility. A remote possibility, as if a remainder be limited in particular to A.'s son John, or Edward, it is bad if he have no son of that name, for it is too remote a possibility that he should not only have a son, but a son of that particular name.

Possible. Capable of existing, happening, being, becoming or coming to pass; feasible, not contrary to nature of things; neither necessitated nor precluded; free to happen or not; contrasted with impossible. In another sense, the word denotes improbability, without excluding the idea of feasibility. It is also sometimes equivalent to "practicable" or "reasonable," as in some cases where action is required to be taken "as soon as possible." See also **Potential.**

Post. Lat. After; as occurring in a report or a textbook, term is used to send the reader to a subsequent part of the book. Same as "infra."

Post, *n.* Military establishment where body of troops is stationed; also place where soldier is stationed.

Post, *v.* To bring to the notice or attention of the public by affixing to a post or wall, or putting up in some public place; to announce, publish or advertise by use of placard. To place in mails. In accounting, to transfer an entry from an original record to a ledger. As regards posting of bail, see **Bail.** See also **Posting.**

Post-act. An after-act; an act done afterwards.

Postage. Charges for postal service.

Postal. Relating to the mails; pertaining to the post-office.

Postal currency. During a brief period following soon after the commencement of the civil war in the United States, when specie change was scarce, postage stamps were popularly used as a substitute; and the first issues of paper representatives of parts of a dollar, issued by authority of congress, were called "postal currency." This issue was soon merged in others of a more permanent character, for which the later and more appropriate name is "fractional currency."

Postal order. A money order. A letter of credit furnished by the government, at a small charge, to facilitate the transmission of money.

Postal Service. The United States Postal Service replaced the Post Office Department in 1971. It is administered by a governing board whose members are appointed by the President. The head of the Service is the Postmaster General.

Post-conviction remedies. *Federal.* A federal prisoner, attacking the constitutionality of his sentence, may move the court which imposed the sentence to vacate, set aside or correct the same. This motion, under 28 U.S.C.A. § 2255, must normally be made before the prisoner can seek habeas corpus relief.

State. Almost every state has one or more post-conviction procedures that permit prisoners to challenge at least some constitutional violations. A substantial group of states have adopted special post-conviction statutes or court rules, roughly similar to section 2255 of 28 U.S.C.A., that encompass all constitutional claims. Case v. Neb., 381 U.S. 336, 338, 85 S.Ct. 1486, 14 L.Ed.2d 422. Others, following the federal habeas corpus statute, have held that at least some constitutional violations are jurisdictional defects cognizable under a common law or statutory writ of habeas corpus. Ex Parte Story, 88 Okl.Cr. 358, 203 P.2d 474. The writ of coram nobis is also viewed in several states as an appropriate remedy for presenting certain types of constitutional claims. People v. Cooper, 307 N.Y. 253, 120 N.E.2d 813. In addition, several states have adopted the Uniform Post Conviction Procedure Act.

Post-date. To date an instrument as of a time later than that at which it is really made. The negotiability of an instrument is not affected by the fact that it is post-dated. U.C.C. § 3–114.

Post-dated check. One delivered prior to its date, generally payable at sight or on presentation on or after day of its date. See **Post-date.**

Post diem /pówst dáyəm/. After the day; as, a plea of payment *post diem,* after the day when the money became due.

Post disseisin /pówst dəsíyzən/. In old English law, the name of a writ, which lies for him who, having recovered lands and tenements by force of a novel disseisin, is again disseised by a former disseisor.

Postea /pówstiyə/. In the common-law practice, a formal statement, indorsed on the *nisi prius* record, which gives an account of the proceedings at the trial of the action.

Posted waters. Waters flowing through or lying upon inclosed or cultivated lands, which are preserved for the exclusive use of the owner or occupant by his posting notices (according to the statute) prohibiting all persons from shooting, trapping, or fishing thereon, under a prescribed penalty.

Posteriora derogant prioribus /pəstìriyórə dérəgənt prayórəbəs/. Posterior things derogate from things prior.

Posteriores /pəstèriyóriyz/. Lat. This term was used by the Romans to denote the descendants in a direct line beyond the sixth degree.

Posteriority /pəstèhriyóhrədiy/. This is a word of comparison and relation in tenure, the correlative of which is the word "priority." Thus, a man who held lands or tenements of two lords was said to hold of his more ancient lord by priority, and of his less ancient lord by posteriority. It has also a general application in law consistent with its etymological meaning, and, as so used, it is likewise opposed to priority.

Posterity /postéhrədiy/. All the descendants of a person in a direct line to the remotest generation.

Post executionem status lex non patitur possibilitatem /pòwst èksəkyùwshiyównəm stéydəs léks nòn pǽdədər pòsəbilətéydəm/. After the execution of the estate the law suffers not a possibility.

Post facto /pòwst fǽktow/. After the fact. See **Ex post facto.**

Post-factum, or **postfactum** /pòwstfǽktəm/. An after-act; an act done afterwards; a post-act.

Post-fine. In old conveyancing, a fine or sum of money, (otherwise called the "king's silver") formerly due on granting the *licentia concordandi,* or leave to agree, in levying a fine of lands. It amounted to three-twentieths of the supposed annual value of the land, or ten shillings for every five marks of land.

Post hac /pòwst hǽk/. Lat. After this; after this time; hereafter.

Posthumous. That which is done after the death of a person as the publication of a book after the death of the author, or the birth of a child after the death of its father.

Posthumous child /póstyəməs cháyld/. Child born after the death of his or her father. See **Unborn child.**

Posthumous work /póstyəməs wə́rk/. Work on which original copyright has been taken out by someone to whom literary property passed before publication. Shapiro, Bernstein & Co. v. Bryan, C.C.A.N.Y., 123 F.2d 697, 699.

Posthumus pro nato habetur /póstyəməs pròw néydow həbéydər/. A posthumous child is considered as though born [at the parent's death].

Posting. The act of transferring an original entry to a ledger. The act of mailing a document. Form of service of process consisting of displaying the process in a prominent place when other forms of service are unavailing.

Postliminium /pòwstləmíniyəm/. Lat. In the civil law, a doctrine or fiction of the law by which the restoration of a person to any *status* or right formerly possessed by him was considered as relating back to the time of his original loss or deprivation; particularly in the case of one who, having been taken prisoner in war, and having escaped and returned to Rome, was regarded, by the aid of this fiction, as having never been abroad, and was thereby reinstated in all his rights.

The term is also applied, in international law, to the recapture of property taken by an enemy, and its consequent restoration to its original owner.

Postliminium fingit eum qui captos est in civitate semper fuisse /pòwstləmíniyəm fínjəd íyəm kwày kǽptows èst ìn sìvətéydiy sémpər fyuwísiy/. Postliminy feigns that he who has been captured has never left the state.

Postliminy /pòwstlíməniy/. See **Postliminium.**

Post litem motam /pòwst láydəm mówdəm/. Lat. After suit moved or commenced. Depositions in relation to the subject of a suit, made after litigation had commenced, were formerly sometimes so termed.

Postman. A letter-carrier; mailman. In England, a senior barrister in the court of exchequer, who has precedence in motions, so called from the place where he sits.

Postmark. A stamp or mark put on letters or other mailable matter received at the post-office for transmission through the mails.

Postmaster. An officer of the United States Postal Service appointed to take charge of a local post-office and transact the business of receiving and forwarding the mails at that point, and such other business as is committed to him under the postal laws.

Postmaster general. The head of the U.S. Postal Service.

Post-mortem /pòwstmórdəm/. After death; pertaining to matters occurring after death. A term generally applied to an autopsy or examination of a dead body, to ascertain the cause of death, or to the inquisition for that purpose by the coroner.

Postnati /pòwstnéyday/. Those born after. See **Post natus.**

Post natus /pòwst néydəs/. Born afterwards. A term once used in private international law to designate a person who was born *after* some historic event (such as the American Revolution or the act of union between England and Scotland), and whose rights or *status* will be governed or affected by the question of his birth before or after such event.

Post-notes /pówstnòwts/. A species of bank-notes payable at a future time, and not on demand.

Post-nuptial /pòwstnápshəl/. After marriage.

Post-nuptial agreement. Post-nuptial agreements or settlements are made after marriage between couples still married; they take the form of separation agreements, property settlements in contemplation of a separation or divorce, or property settlements where there is no intention of the parties to separate. Friedlander v. Friedlander, 80 Wash.2d 293, 494 P.2d 208, 212.

Post-nuptial settlement. See **Post-nuptial agreement.**

Post-obit. Lat. An agreement by which the obligor borrows a certain sum of money and promises to pay a larger sum, exceeding the lawful rate of interest, upon the death of a person from whom he has some expectation, if the obligor be then living.

Post-obit bond. A bond given by an expectant, to become due on the death of a person from whom he will have property. A bond or agreement given by a borrower of money, by which he undertakes to pay a larger sum, exceeding the legal rate of interest, on or *after the death* of a person from whom he has expectations, in case of surviving him. Such are common in England.

Postpone. To put off; defer; delay; continue; adjourn; as when a hearing is *postponed.* Also to place after; to set below something else; as when an earlier lien is for some reason *postponed* to a later lien. The word "postpone" carries with it the idea of deferring the doing of something or the taking effect of something until a future or later time. Gartner v. Roth, 26 Cal.2d 184, 157 P.2d 361, 363.

Post prolem suscitatam /pòwst prówləm səsətéydəm/. After issue born (raised).

Post-terminal sittings. Sittings after term. See **Sitting.**

Post terminum /pòwst tármənəm/. After term, or post-term. The return of a writ not only after the day assigned for its return, but after the term also, for which a fee was due.

Post-trial discovery. Under rules procedure, a party may take depositions pending appeal to perpetuate the testimony of witness for use in the event of further proceedings in the trial court. Fed.R.Civil P. 27(b).

Post-trial motions. Generic term to describe those motions which are permitted after trial such as motion for new trial (Fed.R.Civil P. 59), and motion for relief from judgment (Rule 60).

Post-trial remedies. See **Post-conviction remedies; Post-trial motions.**

Postulatio /pòs(h)chəléysh(iy)ow/. Lat. In old English ecclesiastical law, a species of petition for transfer of a bishop.

In Roman law, a request or petition. This was the name of the first step in a criminal prosecution, corresponding somewhat to "swearing out a warrant" in modern criminal law. The accuser appeared before the prætor, and stated his desire to institute criminal proceedings against a designated person, and prayed the authority of the magistrate therefor.

Postulatio actionis /pòs(h)chəléysh(iy)ow ǽkshiyównəs/. In Roman law, the demand of an action; the request made to the prætor by an *actor* or plaintiff for an action or formula of suit; corresponding with the application for a writ in old English practice. Or, as otherwise explained, the *actor's* asking of leave to institute his action, on appearance of the parties before the prætor.

Pot. Jargon name for marihuana.

Potable. Suitable for drinking; drinkable.

Pot-de-vin /pòwd(ə)vǽn/. In French law, a sum of money frequently paid, at the moment of entering into a contract, beyond the price agreed upon. It differs from *arrha,* in this: that it is no part of the price of the thing sold, and that the person who has received it cannot, by returning double the amount, or the other party by losing what he has paid, rescind the contract.

Potentate /pówtəntèyt/. A person who possesses great power or sway; a prince, sovereign, or monarch.

By the naturalization law of the United States, an alien is required to renounce all allegiance to any foreign "prince, potentate, or sovereign whatever."

Potentia /pəténsh(iy)ə/. Lat. Possibility; power.

Potentia debet sequi justitiam, non antecedere /pəténsh(iy)ə débət sékway jəstísh(iy)əm, nòn ǽntəsíydəriy/. Power ought to follow justice, not go before it.

Potentia est duplex, remota et propinqua; et potentia remotissima et vana est quæ nunquam venit in actum /pəténsh(iy)ə èst d(y)úwpleks, rəmówdə èt prəpíŋkwə; èt pəténsh(iy)ə rəmowtísəmə èt véynə èst kwìy nóŋkwəm víynəd in ǽktəm/. Possibility is of two kinds, remote and near; that which never comes into action is a power the most remote and vain.

Potentia inutilis frustra est /pəténsh(iy)ə ìnyúwdələs frástrə èst/. Useless power is to no purpose.

Potential. Existing in possibility but not in act. Naturally and probably expected to come into existence at some future time, though not now existing; for example, the future product of grain or trees already planted, or the successive future installments or payments on a contract or engagement already made. Things having a "potential existence" may be the subject of mortgage, assignment, or sale. See **Possible.**

Potentia non est nisi ad bonum /pəténsh(iy)ə nòn ést náysay æd bównəm/. Power is not conferred but for the public good.

Potentia propinqua /pəténsh(iy)ə prəpíŋkwə/. Common possibility. See **Possibility.**

Potestas /pətéstæs/. Lat. In the civil law, power; authority, domination; empire. *Imperium,* or the jurisdiction of magistrates. The power of the father over his children, *patria potestas.* The authority of masters over their slaves.

Potestas stricte interpretatur /pətéstæs stríktiy intàrprətéydər/. A power is strictly interpreted.

Potestas suprema seipsum dissolvere potest, ligare non potest /pətéstæs səpríymə siyípsəm dəzólvəriy pówdəst ləgériy nòn pówdəst/. Supreme power can dissolve [unloose] but cannot bind itself.

Potest quis renunciare pro se et suis juri quod pro se introductum est /pówdəst kwís rənənshiyériy pròw síy èt syúwəs júray kwòd pàr síy intrədáktəm èst/. One may relinquish for himself and his heirs a right which was introduced for his own benefit.

Potior est conditio defendentis /pówsh(iy)ər èst kəndísh(iy)ow dəfèndéntəs/. Better is the condition of the defendant [than that of the plaintiff].

Potior est conditio possidentis /pówsh(iy)ər èst kəndísh(iy)ow pəsìdiyéntəs/. Better is the condition of the possessor.

Potomac mortgages. "Deeds of trust", sometimes called "Potomac mortgages", are utilized interchangeably with mortgages in the Maryland counties which are adjacent to the District of Columbia. Tolzman v. Gwynn, 267 Md. 96, 296 A.2d 594, 595.

Potts' fracture /póts frækchər/. A fracture of the lower part of the fibula, accompanied with injury to the ankle joint, so that the foot is dislocated outward. Stockham v. Hall, 145 Kan. 291, 65 P.2d 348.

Pound. A place, inclosed by public authority, for the detention of stray animals; *e.g.* dog pound. Place where impounded property is held until redeemed.

A pound-*overt* is said to be one that is open overhead; a pound-*covert* is one that is close, or covered over, such as a stable or other building.

A measure of weight, equal to 16 avoirdupois ounces or 7,000 grains; the pound troy 12 ounces or 5,760 grains.

Basic monetary unit of United Kingdom; also called pound sterling.

Poundage fees. An allowance to the sheriff, commissioner, or the like, of so much upon the amount levied under an execution. The money which an owner of animals (or other property) impounded must pay to obtain their release.

In old English law, a subsidy to the value of twelve pence in the *pound,* granted to the king, of all manner of merchandise of every merchant, as well denizen as alien, either exported or imported.

Pound breach. The common law offense of breaking a pound, for the purpose of taking out the cattle or goods impounded.

Pour acquit. Fr. In French law, the formula which a creditor prefixes to his signature when he gives a receipt.

Pour appuyer. For the support of, or "in the support of."

Pour appuyer nouvelle demande. In support of his new action.

Pour autrui. For others.

Pour compte de qui il appartient. Fr. For account of whom it may concern.

Pour faire proclaimer. L. Fr. An ancient writ addressed to the mayor or bailiff of a city or town, requiring him to make proclamation concerning nuisances, etc.

Pour-over. Provision in a will which directs the distribution of property into a trust. Also, a similar provision in a trust which directs property into a will.

Pour-over trust. See **Pour-over; Trust.**

Pour-over will. See **Pour-over.**

Pourparler. Fr. In French law, the preliminary negotiations or bargainings which lead to a contract between the parties. As in English law, these form no part of the contract when completed. The term is also used in this sense in international law and the practice of diplomacy.

Pourparty /púrpàrdiy/pár°/. To make *pourparty* is to divide and sever the lands that fall to parceners, which, before partition, they held jointly and *pro indiviso.*

Pourpresture /pùrpréshchər/pàr°/. In old English law, an inclosure. Anything done to the nuisance or hurt of the public demesnes, or the highways, etc., by inclosure or building, endeavoring to make that private which ought to be public. The difference between a *pourpresture* and a public nuisance is that *pourpresture* is an invasion of the *jus privatum* of the crown; but where the *jus publicum* is violated it is a nuisance.

Pour seisir terres /pùr síyzər téhriyz/. L. Fr. An ancient writ whereby the crown seized the land which the wife of its deceased tenant, who held *in capite,* had for her dower, if she married without leave.

Poursuivant /pérswəvənt/. The king's messenger; a royal or state messenger. In the heralds' college, a functionary of lower rank than a herald, but discharging similar duties, called also "poursuivant at arms."

Pourveyance /púrvéyənts/pər°/. In old English law, the providing corn, fuel, victuals, and other necessaries for the king's house.

Pourveyor, or **purveyor** /pərvéyər/. A buyer; one who provided for the royal household.

Poverty. The state or condition of being poor. See also **Indigent.**

Poverty affidavit. An affidavit, made and filed by person seeking public assistance, appointment of counsel, waiver of court fees, or other free services or benefits, that he or she is in fact, financially unable to pay for such.

Document signed under oath which may be the basis of a court's permitting one to proceed in forma pauperis. Leave to proceed on appeal in forma pauperis from district court to court of appeals is governed by Fed.R.App.P. 24.

See also **Pauper's oath.**

Power. The right, ability, authority, or faculty of doing something. Authority to do any act which the grantor might himself lawfully perform. Porter v. Household Finance Corp. of Columbus, D.C.Ohio, 385 F.Supp. 336, 341.

A power is an ability on the part of a person to produce a change in a given legal relation by doing or not doing a given act. Restatement, Second, Agency, § 6; Restatement, Property, § 3.

In a restricted sense a "power" is a liberty or authority reserved by, or limited to, a person to dispose of real or personal property, for his own benefit, or benefit of others, or enabling one person to dispose of interest which is vested in another.

See also Authority; Beneficial power; Capacity; Concurrent power; Control; Delegation of powers; Donee of power; Enumerated powers; Executive powers; Governmental powers; Judicial power; Legislative power; Police power; Right.

Appendant or appurtenant powers. Those existing where the donee of the power has an estate in the land and the power is to take effect wholly or in part out of that estate, and the estate created by its exercise affects the estate and interest of the donee of the power.

Collateral powers. Those in which the donee of the power has no interest or estate in the land which is the subject of the power. Also called "naked powers."

Constitutional powers. The right to take action in respect to a particular subject-matter or class of matters, involving more or less of discretion, granted by the constitution to the several departments or branches of the government, or reserved to the people. Powers in this sense are generally classified as legislative, executive, and judicial (*q.v.*); and further classified as enumerated (or express), implied, inherent, resulting, or sovereign powers.

Commerce powers. Power of Congress to regulate commerce with foreign nations, and among the several states. Art. I, § 8, Cl. 3, U.S.Const.

Enforcement powers. The 13th, 14th, 15th, 19th, 23rd, 24th, and 26th Amendments each contain a section providing, in these or equivalent words,

that "Congress shall have the power to enforce by appropriate legislation, the provisions of this article."

Enumerated or express powers. Powers expressly provided for in Constitution; *e.g.,* U.S.Const. Art. I, § 8.

Implied powers. Such as are necessary to make available and carry into effect those powers which are expressly granted or conferred, and which must therefore be presumed to have been within the intention of the constitutional or legislative grant. See *Enforcement powers,* above; also *Necessary and proper powers,* below. See also **Penumbra doctrine.**

Inherent powers. Powers which necessarily inhere in the government by reason of its role as a government; *e.g.* conducting of foreign affairs. United States v. Curtiss-Wright Export Corp., 299 U.S. 304, 315, 316, 57 S.Ct. 216, 81 L.Ed. 255. See also **Supremacy clause.**

Necessary and proper powers. Art. I, § 8, Cl. 18 gives Congress power "To make all laws which shall be necessary and proper for carrying into execution the foregoing powers (*i.e.* those enumerated in clauses 1–17), and all other powers vested by this Constitution in the Government of the United States, or in any Department or Officer thereof." See also **Penumbra doctrine.**

Preemptive powers. See **Pre-emption; Supremacy clause.**

Reserved or residual state powers. The powers not delegated to the United States by the Constitution, nor prohibited by it to the States, are reserved to the States respectively, or to the people. 10th Amend., U.S.Const.

Resulting powers. Those powers which "result from the whole mass of the powers of the National Government and from the nature of political society." American Ins. Co. v. Canter, 26 U.S. (1 Pet.) 516, 7 L.Ed. 242.

Spending power. Power of Congress "to pay the debts and provide for the common defense and general welfare of the United States." Art. I, § 8, Cl. 1, U.S.Const.

Taxing power. Power of Congress "to lay and collect taxes, duties, imports and excises." Art. I, § 8, Cl. 1.

Corporate powers. The right or capacity to act or be acted upon in a particular manner or in respect to a particular subject; as, the power to have a corporate seal, to sue and be sued, to make by-laws, to carry on a particular business or construct a given work.

General and special powers. A power is general when it authorizes the alienation in fee, by means of a conveyance, will, or charge, of the lands embraced in the power to any alienee whatsoever. It is special (1) when the persons or class of persons to whom the disposition of the lands under the power is to be made are designated, or (2) when the power authorizes the alienation, by means of a conveyance, will, or charge, of a particular estate or interest less than a fee.

General and special powers in trust. A general power is in trust when any person or class of persons other than the grantee of such power is designated as entitled to the proceeds or any portion of the proceeds or other benefits to result from the alienation. A special power is in trust (1) when the disposition or charge which it authorizes is limited to be made to any person or class of persons other than the holder of the power, or (2) when any person or class of persons other than the holder is designated as entitled to any benefit from the disposition or charge authorized by the power.

Implied powers. Powers not granted in express terms but existing because they are necessary and proper to carry into effect some expressly granted power. See also *Constitutional powers, supra.*

Inherent powers. Those which are enjoyed by the possessors of natural right, without having been received from another. Such are the powers of a people to establish a form of government, of a father to control his children. Some of these are regulated and restricted in their exercise by law, but are not technically considered in the law as powers.

Inherent agency power is a term used in the Restatement of Agency to indicate the power of an agent which is derived not from authority, apparent authority or estoppel, but solely from the agency relation and exists for the protection of persons harmed by or dealing with a servant or other agent. Restatement, Second, Agency § 8A.

Ministerial powers. See **Ministerial.**

Naked power. One which is simply collateral and without interest in the donee, which arises when, to a mere stranger, authority is given of disposing of an interest, in which he had not before, nor has by the instrument creating the power, any estate whatsoever.

Power of revocation. A power which is to divest or abridge an existing estate.

Powers in gross. Those which give a donee of the power, who has an estate in the land, authority to create such estates only as will not attach on the interest limited to him or take effect out of his interest, but will take effect after donee's estate has terminated.

Real property law. An authority to do some act in relation to real property, or to the creation or revocation of an estate therein, or a charge thereon, which the owner granting or reserving such power might himself perform for any purpose. An authority expressly reserved to a grantor, or expressly given to another, to be exercised over lands, etc., granted or conveyed at the time of the creation of such power. See **Power of alienation.**

For other compound terms, such as Power of appointment; Power of sale; etc., see the following titles.

Power coupled with an interest. A right or power to do some act, together with an interest in the subject-matter on which the power is to be exercised. It is distinguished from a *naked* power, which is a mere authority to act, not accompanied by any interest of the donee in the subject-matter of the power. Arcweld Mfg. Co. v. Burney, 12 Wash.2d 212, 121 P.2d 350, 355.

Power of alienation. The power to sell, transfer, assign or otherwise dispose of property.

Power of appointment. A power or authority conferred by one person by deed or will upon another (called the "donee") to appoint, that is, to select and nominate, the person or persons who are to receive and enjoy an estate or an income therefrom or from a fund, after the testator's death, or the donee's death, or after the termination of an existing right or interest.

A power of appointment may be exercisable by deed or by will depending upon the terms established by the donor of the power, and is defined, generally, as power or authority given to person to dispose of property, or interest therein, which is vested in person other than donee of the power. In re Conroy's Estate, 67 C.A.3d 734, 136 Cal.Rptr. 807, 809.

Powers are either: *Collateral,* which are given to strangers; *i.e.,* to persons who have neither a present nor future estate or interest in the land. These are also called simply "collateral," or powers not coupled with an interest, or powers not being interests. Or they are powers relating to the land. These are called *"appendant"* or *"appurtenant,"* because they strictly depend upon the estate limited to the person to whom they are given. Thus, where an estate for life is limited to a man, with a power to grant leases in possession, a lease granted under the power may operate wholly out of the life-estate of the party executing it, and must in every case have its operation out of his estate during his life. Such an estate must be created, which will attach on an interest actually vested in himself. Or they are called *"in gross,"* if given to a person who had an interest in the estate at the execution of the deed creating the power, or to whom an estate is given by the deed, but which enabled him to create such estates only as will not attach on the interest limited to him. Of necessity, therefore, where a man seised in fee settles his estate on others, reserving to himself only a particular power, the power is in gross.

An important distinction is established between *general* and *particular* powers. By a general power we understand a right to appoint to whomsoever the donee pleases including himself or his estate. By a particular power it is meant that the donee is restricted to some objects designated in the deed or will creating the power.

A general power is *beneficial* when no person other than the grantee has, by the terms of its creation, any interest in its execution. A general power is *in trust* when any person or class of persons, other than the grantee of such power, is designated as entitled to the proceeds, or any portion of the proceeds, or other benefits to result from the alienation.

When a power of appointment among a class requires that each shall have a share, it is called a "distributive" or "non-exclusive" power; when it authorizes, but does not direct, a selection of one or more to the exclusion of the others, it is called "exclusive" power, and is also distributive; when it gives the power of appointing to a certain number of the class, but not to all, it is exclusive only, and not distributive. A power authorizing the donee either to give the whole to one of a class or to give it equally among such of them as he may select (but not to give one a larger share than the others) is called a "mixed" power.

See also General power of appointment; Illusory appointment; Limited power of appointment.

Testamentary power. A power of appointment that can only be exercised through a will (*i.e.,* upon the death of the holder).

Power of attorney. An instrument authorizing another to act as one's agent or attorney. The agent is attorney in fact and his power is revoked on the death of the principal by operation of law. Such power may be either general or special.

Power of disposition. Every power of disposition is deemed absolute, by means of which the donee of such power is enabled in his life-time to dispose of the entire fee for his own benefit; and, where a general and beneficial power to devise the inheritance is given to a tenant for life or years, it is absolute, within the meaning of the statutes of some of the states. See **Power of appointment.**

Power of sale. A clause commonly inserted in mortgages and deeds of trust, giving the mortgagee (or trustee) the right and power, on default in the payment of the debt secured, to advertise and sell the mortgaged property at public auction (but without resorting to a court for authority), satisfy the creditor out of the net proceeds, convey by deed to the purchaser, return the surplus, if any, to the mortgagor, and thereby divest the latter's estate entirely and without any subsequent right of redemption.

Power of termination. The interest left in the grantor or testator after the conveyance or devise of a fee simple on condition subsequent or conditional fee, *e.g.* "to A on condition that the property be used for church purposes." When such property is no longer used for church purposes, the grantor may enter or commence an action for entry based on the breach of the condition. However, he is not automatically revested. He must enter or commence an action.

P.P. An abbreviation for *"propria persona,"* in his proper person, in his own person, and for *per procuration (q.v.).*

P.P.I. Policy proof of interest, *i.e.,* in the event of loss, the insurance policy is to be deemed sufficient proof of interest.

Practicable, practicably. Practicable is that which may be done, practiced, or accomplished; that which is performable, feasible, possible; and the adverb practicably means in a practicable manner. Within liability policy providing that when accident occurred, written notice should be given by or on behalf of insured to insurer or any of its authorized agents as soon as practicable, "practicable" was held to mean feasible in the circumstances. Frey v. Security Ins. Co. of Hartford, D.C.Pa., 331 F.Supp. 140, 143.

Practice. Repeated or customary action; habitual performance; a succession of acts of similar kind; custom; usage. Application of science to the wants of men. The exercise of any profession.

The form or mode or proceeding in courts of justice for the enforcement of rights or the redress of wrongs, as distinguished from the substantive law which gives the right or denounces the wrong. The form, manner, or order of instituting and conducting an action or other judicial proceeding, through its successive stages to its end, in accordance with the rules and principles laid down by law or by the regulations and precedents of the courts. The term applies as well to the conduct of criminal as to civil actions, to proceedings in equity as well as at law, and to the defense as well as the prosecution of any proceeding. Wells Lamont Corp. v. Bowles, Em. App., 149 F.2d 364, 366.

Practice of law. The rendition of services requiring the knowledge and the application of legal principles and technique to serve the interests of another with his consent. R. J. Edwards, Inc. v. R. L. Hert, Okl., 504 P.2d 407, 416. It is not limited to appearing in court, or advising and assisting in the conduct of litigation, but embraces the preparation of pleadings, and other papers incident to actions and special proceedings, conveyancing, the preparation of legal instruments of all kinds, and the giving of all legal advice to clients. It embraces all advice to clients and all actions taken for them in matters connected with the law. Rhode Island Bar Ass'n v. Lesser, 68 R.I. 14, 26 A.2d 6, 7. An attorney engages in the "practice of law" by maintaining an office where he is held out to be an attorney, using a letterhead describing himself as an attorney, counseling clients in legal matters, negotiating with opposing counsel about pending litigation, and fixing and collecting fees for services rendered by his associate. State v. Schumacher, 214 Kan. 1, 519 P.2d 1116, 1127.

Practice of medicine. The treatment of injuries as well as the discovery of the cause and nature of disease, and the administration of remedies, or the prescribing of treatment therefor.

Practice court. In English law, a court attached to the court of king's bench, which heard and determined common matters of business and ordinary motions for writs of *mandamus,* prohibition, etc. It was usually called the "bail court." It was held by one of the puisne justices of the king's bench. See also **Moot court.**

Practices. A succession of acts of a similar kind or in a like employment.

Practitioner. He who is engaged in the exercise or employment of any art or profession as contrasted with one who teaches such.

Præceptores /priyseptóriyz/. Lat. In old English law, masters. The chief clerks in chancery were formerly so called, because they had the direction of making out remedial writs.

Præceptories /praséptariyz/. In feudal law, a kind of benefices, so called because they were possessed by the more eminent templars whom the chief master by his authority created and called *"Præceptores Templi."*

Præcipe /présapiy/. Lat. In practice, an original writ drawn up in the alternative, commanding the defendant to do the thing required, or show the reason why he had not done it. It includes an order to the clerk of court to issue an execution on a judgment already rendered. Yazoo & M.V.R. Co. v. Clarksdale, 257 U.S. 10, 42 S.Ct. 27, 66 L.Ed. 104.

A paper upon which the particulars of a writ are written. It is filed in the office out of which the required writ is to issue. Also an order, written out and signed, addressed to the clerk of a court, and requesting him to issue a particular writ.

Præcipe quod reddat /présəpiy kwòd rédət/. Command that he render. A writ directing the defendant to restore the possession of land, employed at the beginning of a common recovery.

Præcipe, tenant to the /ténənt tə ðə présəpiy/. A person having an estate of freehold in possession, against whom the *præcipe* was brought by a tenant in tail, seeking to bar his estate by a recovery.

Præcipitium /prèsəpísh(iy)əm/. The punishment of casting headlong from some high place.

Præco /príykow/. Lat. In Roman law, a herald or crier.

Præcognita /prìykógnədə/. Things to be previously known in order to the understanding of something which follows.

Prædia /príyd(i)yə/. In the civil law, lands; estates; tenements; properties. See **Prædium.**

Prædia bellica /príyd(i)yə béləkə/. Booty. Property seized in war.

Prædial /príydiyəl/. That which arises immediately from the ground: as, grain of all sorts, hay, wood, fruits, herbs, and the like.

Prædial servitude /príydiyəl sárvət(y)uwd/. A right which is granted for the advantage of one piece of land over another, and which may be exercised by every possessor of the land entitled against every possessor of the servient land. It always presupposes two pieces of land (*prædia*) belonging to different proprietors; one burdened with the servitude, called "*prædium serviens,*" and one for the advantage of which the servitude is conferred, called "*prædium dominans.*"

Prædial tithes /príydiyəl táyðz/. Such as arise merely and immediately from the ground; as grain of all sorts, hops, hay, wood, fruit, herbs.

Prædia stipendiaria /príyd(i)yə stàypèndiyériyə/. In the civil law, provincial lands belonging to the people.

Prædia tributaria /príydiyə trìbyətériyə/. In the civil law, provincial lands belonging to the emperor.

Prædictus /prədíktəs/. Lat. Aforesaid. In civil law pleading, of the three words, "*idem,*" "*prædictus,*" and "*præfatus,*" "*idem*" was most usually applied to plaintiffs or demandants; "*prædictus,*" to defendants or tenants, places, towns, or lands; and "*præfatus,*" to persons named, not being *actors* or parties. These words may all be rendered in English by "said" or "aforesaid."

Prædium /príydiyəm/. Lat. In the civil law, land; an estate; a tenement; a piece of landed property.

Prædium dominans /príydiyəm dómənæn(d)z/. In the civil law, the name given to an estate to which a servitude is due; the dominant tenement.

Prædium serviens /príydiyəm sárviyèn(d)z/. In the civil law, the name of an estate which suffers a servitude or easement to another estate; the servient tenement.

Prædium servit prædio /príydiyəm sárvət príydiyow/. Land is under servitude to land [*i.e.,* servitudes are not personal rights, but attach to the dominant tenement].

Prædium urbanum /príydiyəm àrbéynəm/. In the civil law, a building or edifice intended for the habitation and use of man, whether built in cities or in the country.

Prædo /príydow/. Lat. In Roman law, a robber.

Præfatus /prəféydəs/. Lat. Aforesaid. Sometimes abbreviated to "*præfat,*" and "*p. fat.*"

Præfecturæ /príyfekt(y)úriy/. In Roman law, conquered towns, governed by an officer called a "prefect," who was chosen in some instances by the people, in others by the prætors.

Præfectus vigilum /prəféktəs vəjíliyəm/. Lat. In Roman law, the chief officer of the night watch. His jurisdiction extended to certain offenses affecting the public peace, and even to larcenies; but he could inflict only slight punishments.

Præfectus villæ /prəféktəs víliy/. The mayor of a town.

Præfine /príyfàyn/. The fee paid on suing out the writ of covenant, on levying fines, before the fine was passed.

Præjuramentum /prìyjurəméntəm/. In old English law, a preparatory oath.

Prælegatum /prìyləgéydəm/. Lat. In Roman law, a payment in advance of the whole or part of the share which a given heir would be entitled to receive out of an inheritance; corresponding generally to "advancement" in English and American law.

Præmium /príymiyəm/. Lat. Reward; compensation. *Præmium assecurationis,* compensation for insurance; premium of insurance.

Præmium emancipationis /príymiyəm əmæn(t)səpèy-shiyównəs/. In Roman law, a reward or compensation anciently allowed to a father on emancipating his child, consisting of one-third of the child's separate and individual property, not derived from the father himself.

Præmium pudicitiæ /príymiyəm pyùwdəsíshiyiy/. The price of chastity; or compensation for loss of chastity. A term applied to bonds and other engagements given for the benefit of a seduced female. Sometimes called "*præmium pudoris.*"

Præmunire /prìymyuwnáyriy/. In old English law, an offense against the king and his government, though not subject to capital punishment. So called from the words of the writ which issued preparatory to the prosecution: "*Præmunire facias A. B. quod sit coram nobis,*" etc.; "Cause A. B. to be forewarned that he appear before us to answer the contempt with which he stands charged." The statutes establishing this offense, the first of which was made in the thirty-first year of the reign of Edward I, were framed to encounter the papal usurpations in England; the original meaning of the offense called *"præmunire"* being the introduction of a foreign power into the kingdom, and creating *imperium in imperio,* by paying that obedience to papal process which constitutionally belonged to the king alone. The penalties of *præmunire* were afterwards applied to other heinous offenses. 4 Bl. Comm. 103–117.

Prænomen /prìynówmən/. Lat. Forename, or first name. The first of the three names by which the Romans were commonly distinguished. It marked the individual, and was commonly written with one letter; as "A." for "Aulus;" "C." for "Caius," etc.

Præpositus /prìypózədəs/. In old English law, an officer next in authority to the alderman of a hundred, called *"præpositus regius;"* or a steward or bailiff of an estate, answering to the *"wicnere."*

Also the person from whom descents are traced under the old canons.

Præpositus villæ /prìypózədəs víliy/. A constable of a town, or petty constable.

Præpropera consilia raro sunt prospera /prìyprówpərə kən(t)síl(i)yə rérow sànt próspərə/. Hasty counsels are rarely prosperous.

Præscriptio /prəskrípsh(iy)ow/. Lat. In the civil law, that mode of acquisition whereby one becomes proprietor of a thing on the ground that he has for a long time possessed it as his own; prescription. It was anciently distinguished from *"usucapio" (q.v.),* but was blended with it by Justinian.

Præscriptio est titulus ex usu et tempore substantiam capiens ab auctoritate legis /prəskrípsh(iy)ow èst tít(y)ələs èks yúws(y)uw èt témpəriy səbstǽnshiyəm kǽpiyèn(d)z æb oktòhrətéydiy líyjəs/. Prescription is a title by authority of law, deriving its force from use and time.

Præscriptio et executio non pertinent ad valorem contractus, set ad tempus et modum actionis instituendæ /prəskrípsh(iy)ow ed èksəkyúwsh(iy)ow nòn pə́rdənənt æd vəlórəm kəntrǽktəs, séd æd témpəs èt mówdəm ǽkshiyównəs instìt(y)uwéndiy/. Prescription and execution do not affect the validity of the contract, but the time and manner of bringing an action.

Præscriptiones /prəskrìpshiyówniyz/. Lat. In Roman law, forms of words (of a qualifying character) inserted in the *formulæ* in which the claims in actions were expressed; and, as they occupied an early place in the *formulæ,* they were called by this name, *i.e.,* qualifications *preceding* the claim. For example, in an action to recover the arrears of an annuity, the claim was preceded by the words "so far as the annuity is due and unpaid," or words to the like effect (*"cujus rei dies fuit"*).

Præsentare nihil aliud est quam præsto dare seu offere /prèzəntériy náy(h)əl ǽliyəd èst kwæm príystow dériy syùw oféhriy/. To present is no more than to give or offer on the spot.

Præsentia corporis tollit errorem nominis; et veritas nominis tollit errorem demonstrationis /prəzénsh(iy)ə kórpərəs tóləd ərórəm nómənəs, èt véhrətæs nómənəs tóləd ərórəm dèmənstrèyshiyównəs/. The presence of the body cures error in the name; the truth of the name cures an error of description.

Præses /príysiyz/. Lat. In Roman law, a president or governor. Called a *"nomen generale,"* including proconsuls, legates, and all who governed provinces.

Præstare /prìystériy/. Lat. In Roman law, *"præstare"* meant to make good, and, when used in conjunction with the words *"dare," "facere," "oportere,"* denoted obligations of a personal character, as opposed to real rights.

Præstat cautela quam medela /príystæt kotíylə kwæm mədíylə/. Prevention is better than cure.

Præsumatur pro justitia sententiæ /prìyz(y)əméydər pròw jəstísh(iy)ə senténshiyiy/. The presumption should be in favor of the justice of a sentence.

Præsumitur pro legitimatione /prəz(y)úwmədər pròw ləjìdəmèyshiyówniy/. The presumption is in favor of legitimacy.

Præsumitur pro negante /prəz(y)úwmədər prów nəgǽntiy/. It is presumed for the negative. The rule of the house of lords when the numbers are equal on a motion.

Præsumptio /prəzə́m(p)sh(iy)ow/. Lat. Presumption; a presumption. Also intrusion, or the unlawful taking of anything.

Præsumptio, ex eo quod plerumque fit /prəzə́m(p)sh(iy)ow èks íyow kwòd plərə́mkwiy fít/. Presumptions arise from what generally happens.

Præsumptio fortior /prəzə́m(p)sh(iy)ow fórsh(iy)ər/. A strong presumption; a presumption of fact entitled to great weight. One which determines the tribunal in its belief of an alleged fact, without, however, excluding the belief of the possibility of its being otherwise; the effect of which is to shift the burden of producing evidence to the opposite party, and, if this proof be not made, the presumption is held for truth. See **Presumption.**

Præsumptio hominis /prəzə́m(p)sh(iy)ow hómənəs/. The presumption of the man or individual; that is, natural presumption unfettered by strict rule.

Præsumptio juris /prəzə́m(p)sh(iy)ow júrəs/. A legal presumption or presumption of law; that is, one in which the law assumes the existence of something until it is disproved by evidence; a conditional, inconclusive, or rebuttable presumption.

Præsumptio juris et de jure /prəzə́m(p)sh(iy)ow júrəs èt dìy júriy/. A presumption of law and of right; a presumption which the law will not suffer to be contradicted; a conclusive or irrebuttable presumption.

Præsumptio muciana /prəzə́m(p)sh(iy)ow myùwshiyéynə/. In Roman law, a presumption of law that property in the hands of a wife came to her as a gift from her husband and was not acquired from other sources; available only in doubtful cases and until the contrary is shown.

Præsumptiones sunt conjecturæ ex signo verisimili ad probandum assumptæ /prəzə̀m(p)shiyówniyz sə̀nt kònjektyúriy èks sígnow vèhrəsíməlay æ̀d prəbǽndəm əsə́mptiy/. Presumptions are conjectures from probable proof, assumed for purposes of evidence.

Præsumptio violenta piena probatio /prəzə́m(p)sh(iy)ow vàyəléntə plíynə prəbéysh(iy)ow/. Strong presumption is full proof.

Præsumptio violenta valet in lege /prəzə́m(p)sh(iy)ow vàyəléntə vǽləd ìn líyjiy/. Strong presumption is of weight in law.

Præteritio /prèdərísh(iy)ow/. Lat. A passing over or omission. Used in the Roman law to describe the act of a testator in excluding a given heir from the inheritance by silently passing him by, that is, neither instituting nor formally disinheriting him.

Prætextu liciti non debet admitti illicitum /prətékst(y)uw lísəday nòn débəd ədmíday əlísədəm/. Under pretext of legality, what is illegal ought not to be admitted.

Prætextus /prətékstəs/. Lat. A pretext; a pretense or color. *Prætextu cujus,* by pretense, or under pretext whereof.

Prætor /príydər/. Lat. In Roman law, a municipal officer of the city of Rome, being the chief judicial magistrate, and possessing an extensive equitable jurisdiction.

Prætor fidei-commissarius /príydər fáydiyày kòməsériyəs/. In the civil law, a special prætor created to pronounce judgment in cases of trusts or *fidei-commissa.*

Prætorian law /prətóriyən ló/. See **Lex prætoria.**

Prævaricator /prəvǽrəkeydər/°vǽrəkéy°/. Lat. In the civil law, one who betrays his trust, or is unfaithful to his trust. An advocate who aids the opposite party by betraying his client's cause.

Pragmatica /pragmátiykə/. In Spanish colonial law, an order emanating from the sovereign, and differing from a *cedula* only in form and in the mode of promulgation.

Prairie /prériy/. An extensive tract of level or rolling land, destitute of trees, covered with coarse grass, and usually characterized by a deep, fertile soil.

Pratique /prætíyk/. A license for the master of a ship to traffic in the ports of a given country, or with the inhabitants of a given port, upon the lifting of quarantine or production of a clean bill of health.

Praxis /prǽksəs/. Lat. Use; practice.

Praxis judicum est interpres legum /prǽksəs júwdikəm èst intə́rpriyz líygəm/. The practice of the judges is the interpreter of the laws.

Prayer. The request contained in a bill in equity that the court will grant the process, aid, or relief which the complainant desires. Also, by extension, the term is applied to that part of the bill which contains this request. Under rules practice, the pleader does not pray for relief, but, rather, demands it. Fed.R. Civil P. 8(a). See **Prayer for relief.**

Prayer for relief. That portion of a complaint (more properly called "demand for relief") in a civil action which sets forth the requested relief or damages to which the pleader deems himself entitled. This is a requisite element of the complaint. Fed.R.Civil P. 8(a).

Prayer of process. A petition with which a bill in equity used to conclude, to the effect that a writ of subpœna might issue against the defendant to compel him to answer upon oath all the matters charged against him in the bill.

Pray in aid. In old English practice, to call upon for assistance. In real actions, the tenant might *pray in aid* or call for assistance of another, to help him to plead, because of the feebleness or imbecility of his own estate.

In current English practice, term refers to practice of attorney in action involving several parties to claim benefit for his client of argument used by another counsel for his client.

Preamble. A clause at the beginning of a constitution or statute explanatory of the reasons for its enactment and the objects sought to be accomplished. Generally, a preamble is a declaration by the legislature of the reasons for the passage of the statute and is helpful in the interpretation of any ambiguities within the statute to which it is prefixed. Griffith v. New Mexico Public Service Comm., 86 N.M. 113, 520 P.2d 269, 271. It has been held however to not be an essential part of act, and neither enlarges nor confers powers. Portland Van & Storage Co. v. Hoss, 139 Or. 434, 9 P.2d 122, 126.

Preappointed evidence. The kind and degree of evidence prescribed in advance (as, by statute) as requisite for the proof of certain facts or the establishment of certain instruments. It is opposed to *casual* evidence, which is left to grow naturally out of the surrounding circumstances.

Preaudience /priyódiyən(t)s/. The right of being heard before another. A privilege belonging to the English bar, the members of which are entitled to be heard in their order, according to rank, beginning with the Attorney and Solicitor General, and Queen's Counsel, and ending with barristers at large.

Prebend. In English ecclesiastical law, a stipend granted in cathedral churches; also, but improperly, a prebendary. A simple prebend is merely a revenue; a prebend with dignity has some jurisdiction attached to it. The term "prebend" is generally confounded with "canonicate;" but there is a difference between them. The former is the stipend granted to an ecclesiastic in consideration of his officiating and serving in the church; whereas the canonicate is a mere title or spiritual quality which may exist independently of any stipend.

Fixed portion of rents and profits of cathedral church used for maintenance of prebendaries.

Prebendary /prébəndèry/. An ecclesiastical person serving on the staff of a cathedral, and receiving a stated allowance or stipend from the income or endowment of the cathedral, in compensation for his services.

Precariæ /prəkériyiy/ or **preces** /príysiyz/. Day-works which the tenants of certain manors were bound to give their lords in harvest time. *Magna precaria* was a great or general reaping day.

Precarious /prəkériyəs/. Liable to be returned or rendered up at the mere demand or request of another; hence, held or retained only on sufferance or by permission; and, by an extension of meaning, doubtful, uncertain, dangerous, very liable to break, fail, or terminate.

Precarious loan. A bailment by way of loan which is not to continue for any fixed time, but may be recalled at the mere will and pleasure of the lender. A loan, the repayment of which is in doubt or uncertain.

Precarious possession. In modern civil law, possession is called "precarious" which one enjoys by the leave of another and during his pleasure.

Precarious right. The right which the owner of a thing transfers to another, to enjoy the same until it shall please the owner to revoke it.

Precarious trade. In international law, such trade as may be carried on by a neutral between two belligerent powers by the mere sufferance of the latter.

Precarium /prəkériyəm/. Lat. In the civil law, a convention whereby one allows another the use of a thing or the exercise of a right gratuitously until revocation. The bailee acquires thereby the lawful possession of the thing, except in certain cases. The bailor can redemand the thing at any time, even should he have allowed it to the bailee for a designated period.

Precatory /prékət(ə)riy/. Having the nature of prayer, request, or entreaty; conveying or embodying a recommendation or advice or the expression of a wish, but not a positive command or direction.

Precatory trust. A trust created by certain words, which are more like words of entreaty and permission than of command or certainty. Examples of such words, which the courts have held sufficient to constitute a trust, are "wish and request," "have fullest confidence," "heartily beseech," and the like.

Precatory words. Words of entreaty, request, desire, wish, or recommendation, employed in wills, as distinguished from direct and imperative terms. Mere precatory words or expressions in a trust or will are ineffective to dispose of property. There must be a command or order as to the disposition of property.

Precaution /prəkóshən/. Previous action; proven foresight; care previously employed to prevent mischief or to secure good result; or a measure taken beforehand; an active foresight designed to ward off possible problems, accidents, liability, or secure good results. Rincon v. Berg Co., Tex.Civ.App., 60 S.W.2d 811, 813.

Precedence /présədən(t)s/ or **precedency** /présədən(t)siy/. The act or state of going before; adjustment of place. The right of being first placed in a certain order. See also **Preference; Precedent; Priority.**

Precedence, patent of. In old English law, a grant from the crown to such barristers as it thinks proper to honor with that mark of distinction, whereby they are entitled to such rank and preaudience as are assigned in their respective patents.

Precedent /présədənt/. An adjudged case or decision of a court, considered as furnishing an example or authority for an identical or similar case afterwards arising or a similar question of law. Courts attempt to decide cases on the basis of principles established in prior cases. Prior cases which are close in facts or legal principles to the case under consideration are called precedents. A rule of law established for the first time by a court for a particular type of case and thereafter referred to in deciding similar cases.

A course of conduct once followed which may serve as a guide for future conduct. See **Custom and usage; Habit.**

See also **Stare decisis.**

Precedent condition. Such as must happen or be performed before an estate can vest or be enlarged. See **Condition.**

Precedents sub silentio /présədənts sàb səlénsh(iy)ow/. Silent uniform course of practice, uninterrupted though not supported by legal decisions.

Prece partium /príysiy pársh(iy)əm/. The continuance of a suit by consent of both parties.

Precept /príysept/. An order, writ, warrant, or process. An order or direction, emanating from authority, to an officer or body of officers, commanding him or them to do some act within the scope of their powers. An order in writing, sent out by a justice of the peace or other like officer, for the bringing of a person or record before him. Precept is not to be confined to civil proceedings, and is not of a more restricted meaning than "process." It includes warrants and processes in criminal as well as civil proceedings.

Rule imposing standard of conduct or action.

In English law, the direction issued by a sheriff to the proper returning officers of cities and boroughs within his jurisdiction for the election of members to serve in parliament. The direction by the judges or commissioners of assize to the sheriff for the summoning a sufficient number of jurors. The direction issued by the clerk of the peace to the overseers of parishes for making out the jury lists. Written command of justice of the peace or other like officer for the bringing of a person or record before him. In old English criminal law, instigation to commit a crime.

In old French law, a kind of letters issued by the king in subversion of the laws, being orders to the judges to do or tolerate things contrary to law.

Precept of attachment. Precept of attachment is an order to attach the goods and property of the defendant issued by a court generally after the action has been commenced when a writ of attachment has not been used.

Preces /príysiyz/. Lat. In Roman law, prayers. One of the names of an application to the emperor.

Preces primariæ /príysiyz prəmériyiy/. In English ecclesiastical law, a right of the crown to name to the first prebend that becomes vacant after the accession of the sovereign, in every church of the empire. This right was exercised by the crown of England in the reign of Edward I.

Precinct /príysiŋkt/. A constable's or police district. A small geographical unit of government. An election district created for convenient localization of polling places. A county or municipal subdivision for casting and counting votes in elections.

Precipe /présəpiy/. Another form of the name of the written instructions to the clerk of court; also spelled "præcipe" (q.v.).

Precipitation /prəsìpətéyshən/. Hastening occurrence of event or causing to happen or come to crisis suddenly, unexpectedly or too soon.

Preciput. In French law, a portion of an estate or inheritance which falls to one of the coheirs over and above his equal share with the rest, and which is to be taken out before partition is made.

Precise /prəsáys/. Having determinate limitations. To the point.

Preclude /prəkl(y)úwd/. Estop. To prohibit or prevent from doing something; e.g. injunction.

Precludi non /prəkl(y)úwday nón/. Lat. In common law pleading, the commencement of a replication to a plea in bar, by which the plaintiff "says that, by reason of anything in the said plea alleged, he *ought not to be barred* from having and maintaining his aforesaid action against him, the said defendant, because he says," etc.

Preclusion order. Under Fed.R.Civil P. 37(b)(2)(B), a party to an action who fails to comply with an order for discovery may be precluded from supporting or opposing designated claims or defenses.

Preconization /prìykənəzéyshən/. Proclamation.

Precontract. A contract or engagement made by a person, which is of such a nature as to preclude him from lawfully entering into another contract of the same nature.

Predatory intent. "Predatory intent," in purview of Robinson-Patman Act, means that alleged price discriminator must have at least sacrificed present revenues for purpose of driving competitor out of market with hope of recouping losses through subsequent higher prices. International Air Industries, Inc. v. American Excelsior Co., C.A.Tex., 517 F.2d 714, 723.

Predecessor. One who goes or has gone before; the correlative of "successor." One who has filled an office or station before the present incumbent. Applied to a body politic or corporate, in the same sense as "ancestor" is applied to a natural person.

Predial servitude /príydiyəl sárvət(y)uwd/. A charge laid on an estate for the use and utility of another estate belonging to another owner. See **Prædial servitude.**

Predominant. Something greater or superior in power and influence to others with which it is connected or compared.

Pre-emption /priyém(p)shən/. Doctrine adopted by U.S. Supreme Court holding that certain matters are of such a national, as opposed to local, character that federal laws pre-empt or take precedence over state laws. As such, a state may not pass a law inconsistent with the federal law. Examples are federal laws governing interstate commerce. See also **Federal pre-emption; Supremacy clause.**

In international law, the right of pre-emption was formerly the right of a nation to detain the merchandise of strangers passing through her territories or seas, in order to afford to her subjects the preference of purchase.

In old English law, the first buying of a thing. A privilege formerly enjoyed by the crown, of buying up provisions and other necessaries, by the intervention of the king's purveyors, for the use of his royal household, at an appraised valuation, in preference to all others, and even without consent of the owner.

Pre-emption claimant. One who has settled upon land subject to pre-emption, with the intention to acquire title to it, and has complied, or is proceeding to comply, in good faith, with the requirements of the law to perfect his right to it. Hosmer v. Wallace, 97 U.S. 575, 581, 24 L.Ed. 1130. See **Pre-emption right.**

Pre-emption doctrine. See **Pre-emption.**

Pre-emption entry. See **Entry.**

Pre-emption right. A privilege accorded by the government to the actual settler upon a certain limited portion of the public domain, to purchase such tract at a fixed price to the exclusion of all other applicants. Nix v. Allen, 112 U.S. 129, 5 S.Ct. 70, 28 L.Ed. 675. One who, by settlement upon the public land, or by cultivation of a portion of it, has obtained the right to purchase a portion of the land thus settled upon or cultivated, to the exclusion of all other persons.

Pre-emptive right. The privilege of a stockholder to maintain a proportionate share of ownership by purchasing a proportionate share of any new stock issues. An existing stockholder in most jurisdictions has the right to buy additional shares of a new issue to preserve his equity before others have a right to purchase shares of the new issue. See also **Stock.**

Prefect. In French law, the name given to the public functionary who is charged in chief with the administration of the laws, in each department of the country. Crespin v. U. S., 168 U.S. 208, 18 S.Ct. 53, 42 L.Ed. 438. The term is also used, in practically the same sense, in Mexico. But in New Mexico, a prefect is a probate judge.

Prefer. To bring before; to prosecute; to try; to proceed with. Thus, preferring an indictment signifies prosecuting or trying an indictment.

To give advantage, priority, or privilege; to select for first payment, as to prefer one creditor over others.

Preference. The paying or securing to one or more of his creditors, by an insolvent debtor, the whole or a part of their claim, to the exclusion or detriment of the rest. The act of an insolvent debtor who, in distributing his property or in assigning it for the benefit of his creditors, pays or secures to one or more creditors the full amount of their claims or a larger amount than they would be entitled to receive on a *pro rata* distribution. Jackson v. Coons, 285 Ky. 154, 147 S.W.2d 45, 47. It imports the relation of existing creditors having equal equities at the time of the transfer whereby the rights of one are advanced over those of another. Adams v. City Bank & Trust Co. of Macon, Ga., C.C.A.Ga., 115 F.2d 453, 454. The treatment of such preferential payments in bankruptcy is governed by Bankruptcy Act, § 547. See also **Voidable preference.**

Preference share. One giving its holder a preference, either as to receipt of dividends, or as to payment in case of winding up, or both. In re Schaffer Stores Co., 224 App.Div. 268, 229 N.Y.S. 735, 739.

Preferential assignment. An assignment of property for the benefit of creditors, made by an insolvent debtor, in which it is directed that a preference (right to be paid first in full) shall be given to a creditor or creditors therein named. Such assignments are controlled by statute in most states, normally requiring recording, filing of schedules of assets and liabilities, giving notice to creditors, etc. Most all state statutes prohibit preferential assignments as being fraudulent conveyances. See **Preference.**

Preferential claim. See **Preferential debts.**

Preferential debts. In bankruptcy, those debts which are payable in preference to all others; as, wages of employees and administrative costs. Such debts are classified according to priority of claim. See Bankruptcy Act § 507.

Preferential dividend. See **Preferred stock.**

Preferential shop. A place of employment in which union members are given preference over nonunion members in matters of employment by agreement with the employer. A labor situation in a business in which preference is given to union men in hiring and layoff, but nonunion men may be hired when members of the union are not available. See **Right-to-work laws.**

Preferential tariff. A tariff which imposes lower rates of duty on goods imported from some countries ("preferred countries") than on the same goods imported from other countries. See also **Most favored nation clause.**

Preferential transfer. See **Preference; Preferential assignment.**

Preferred. Possessing or accorded a priority, advantage, or privilege. Generally denoting a prior or superior claim or right of payment as against another thing of the same kind or class; *e.g.* creditor with perfected security interest.

Preferred creditor. Creditor with preferential right to payment over junior creditors; *e.g.* creditor with perfected security interest has priority over unsecured creditor. U.C.C. § 9–301.

Preferred dividend. See **Dividend.**

Preferred dockets. Lists of preference cases prepared by the clerks when the cases are set for trial. For example, because of the constitutional right to a speedy trial in criminal cases, criminal dockets are normally given preference over civil dockets.

Preferred stock. Capital stock with a claim to income or assets after bondholders but before common stock. Dividends on preferred stock are income distributions, not expenses. Type of capital stock in which stockholder is entitled to preference in payment of dividends and assets on dissolution. Such stock is generally expressed as a percentage of par; *e.g.* 7% preferred. See also **Stock.**

Callable. Preferred stock which is subject by its terms to being called in for payment at a predetermined price.

Cumulative. If a dividend is passed, it must be paid before the common stockholders receive their current dividend, and hence, the dividends accumulate in connection with this type of preferred stock.

Non-cumulative. Once a preferred dividend is passed in a particular period, the right to that dividend has passed though the preferred stockholder is entitled to his dividend in the next period before the common stockholders receive their dividend.

Participating. That type of preferred stock which is entitled to additional dividends beyond its stated dividend after the common stock dividend has been paid.

Preferred stock bailout. A procedure whereby the issuance, sale, and later redemption or a preferred stock dividend was used by a shareholder to obtain long-term capital gains without any loss of voting control over the corporation. In effect, therefore, the shareholder was able to bail-out corporate profits without suffering the consequences of dividend income treatment. This procedure led to the enactment by Congress of I.R.C. § 306 which, if applicable, converts the prior long-term capital gain on the sale of the stock to ordinary income. Under these circumstances, the amount of ordinary income is limited to the shareholder's portion of the corporation's earnings and profits existing when the preferred stock was issued as a stock dividend.

Prior. Preferred stock which takes precedence over other issues of preferred stock of the same corporation.

Pregnancy. The condition resulting from the fertilized ovum. The existence of the condition beginning at the moment of conception and terminating with delivery of the child.

Extra uterine or ectopic pregnancy is the development of the ovum outside of the uterine cavity, as in the Fallopian tubes or ovary. Extra uterine pregnancy commonly terminates by rupture of the sac, profuse internal hemorrhage, and death if not relieved promptly by a surgical operation.

Pregnancy, plea of. A plea which a woman capitally convicted may plead in stay of execution; for this, though it is no stay of judgment, yet operates as a respite of execution until she is delivered. See also **Matrons, jury of.**

Pregnant negative. See **Negative pregnant.**

Prejudice. A forejudgment; bias; preconceived opinion. A leaning towards one side of a cause for some reason other than a conviction of its justice.

See also **Average man test; Bias; Discrimination.**

Of judge. That which disqualifies judge is condition of mind, which sways judgment and renders judge unable to exercise his functions impartially in particular case. It refers to mental attitude or disposition of the judge toward a party to the litigation, and not to any views that he may entertain regarding the subject matter involved. State ex rel. Mitchell v. Sage Stores Co., 157 Kan. 622, 143 P.2d 652, 655.

Speedy trial. Prejudice with respect to right to speedy trial means actual prejudice to defendant's ability to present effective defense. U. S. v. Menke, D.C.Pa., 339 F.Supp. 1023, 1026. Prejudice as a factor in a speedy trial claim is not confined to merely an impairment of the defense but includes any threat to what has been termed an accused's significant stakes, psychological, physical and financial, in the prompt termination of a proceeding which may ultimately deprive him of life, liberty or property. U. S. v. Dreyer, C.A.N.J., 533 F.2d 112, 115.

Without prejudice. Where an offer or admission is made "without prejudice," or a motion is denied or a bill in equity dismissed "without prejudice," it is meant as a declaration that no rights or privileges of the party concerned are to be considered as thereby waived or lost, except in so far as may be expressly conceded or decided. See also **Dismissal without prejudice; Without prejudice; With prejudice.**

Prejudicial error. Error substantially affecting appellant's legal rights and obligations. Erskine v. Upham, 56 Cal.App.2d 235, 132 P.2d 219, 228; Trepanier v. Standard Min. & Mill. Co., 58 Wyo. 29, 123 P.2d 378, 380. Such may be ground for new trial and reversal of judgment. Fed.R.Civil P. 59. A prejudicial error is one which affects or presumptively affects the final results of the trial. State v. Gilcrist, 15 Wash.App. 892, 552 P.2d 690, 693. See also **Error; Plain error rule.**

Prejudicial publicity. Due process requires that all parties to an action, civil or criminal, receive a trial by an impartial jury or tribunal free from outside influences. Extensive newspaper, radio and television coverage of a criminal trial may deprive the defendant of a fair trial. Sheppard v. Maxwell, 384 U.S. 333, 86 S.Ct. 1507, 16 L.Ed.2d 600. See **Gag order; Trial** *(Trial by news media).*

Preliminary. Introductory; initiatory; preceding; temporary and provisional; as preliminary examination, injunction, articles of peace, etc.

Preliminary complaint. In some states, a court without jurisdiction to hear a criminal case on its merits may issue a preliminary complaint or process and conduct a probable cause or bind over hearing on such complaint.

Preliminary evidence. Such evidence as is necessary to commence a hearing or trial and which may be received conditionally in anticipation of other evidence linking it to issues in the case.

Preliminary examination. See **Preliminary hearing.**

Preliminary hearing. The hearing by a judge to determine whether a person charged with a crime should be held for trial. A hearing held in felony cases prior to indictment during which the state is required to produce sufficient evidence to establish that there is probable cause to believe (a) that a crime has been committed and (b) that the defendant committed it. See Fed.R.Crim.P. 5.1.

Preliminary hearing before magistrate is, basically, a first screening of the charge; its function is not to try the defendant, nor does it require the same degree of proof or quality of evidence as is necessary for an indictment or for conviction at trial. Mattioli v. Brown, 71 Misc.2d 99, 335 N.Y.S.2d 613, 615.

Indigent defendants have a right to be represented by counsel at a preliminary examination. Coleman v. Alabama, 399 U.S. 1, 90 S.Ct. 1999, 26 L.Ed.2d 387; Adams v. Illinois, 405 U.S. 278, 92 S.Ct. 916, 31 L.Ed.2d 202.

Preliminary injunction. An interlocutory injunction issued after notice and hearing which restrains a party pending trial on the merits. Pruitt v. Williams, 288 N.C. 368, 218 S.E.2d 348, 350. Fed.R.Civil P. 65. A procedural device which is interlocutory in nature and which is designed to preserve the existing status of the litigants until a determination can be made on merits of the controversy. National Pac. Corp. v. American Com. Financial Corp., La.App., 348 So.2d 735, 736.

A preliminary injunction should be granted only upon a clear showing by party seeking the extraordinary remedy of (1) probable success upon a trial on the merits, and (2) likely irreparable injury to him unless the injunction is granted, or (3) if his showing of probable success is limited but he raised substantial and difficult issues meriting further inquiry, that the harm to him outweighs the injury to others if it is denied. Cohen v. Price Commission, D.C.N.Y., 337 F.Supp. 1236, 1239.

See also **Injunction.**

Preliminary proof. In insurance, the first proof offered of a loss occurring under the policy, usually sent in to the underwriters with the notification of claim.

Preliminary warrant. In some jurisdictions, a warrant or order to bring a person to court for a preliminary hearing on probable cause.

Premeditate. To think of an act beforehand; to contrive and design; to plot or lay plans for the execution of a purpose. See **Deliberate; Premeditation.**

Premeditated design. In homicide cases, the mental purpose, the formed intent, to take human life. Premeditated murder is murder in the first degree.

Premeditatedly. Thought of beforehand, for any length of time, however short.

Premeditation. The act of meditating in advance; deliberation upon a contemplated act; plotting or contriving; a design formed to do something before it is done. Decision or plan to commit a crime, such as murder, before committing it. A prior determination to do an act, but such determination need not exist for any particular period before it is carried into effect. Term "premeditation," means "thought of beforehand for any length of time, however short." State v. Marston, Mo., 479 S.W.2d 481, 484. See also **Malice aforethought; Willful.**

Premises. That which is put before; that which precedes; the foregoing statements. Thus, in logic, the two introductory propositions of the syllogism are called the "premises," and from them the conclusion is deduced. So, in pleading, the expression "in consideration of the premises" means in consideration of the matters hereinbefore stated.

In conveyancing. That part of a deed which precedes the *habendum,* in which are set forth the names of the parties with their titles and additions, and in which are recited such deeds, agreements, or matters of fact as are necessary to explain the reasons upon which the present transaction is founded; and it is here, also, the consideration on which it is made is set down and the certainty of the thing granted.

In equity pleading. The stating part of a bill. It contains a narrative of the facts and circumstances of the plaintiff's case, and the wrongs of which he complains, and the names of the persons by whom done and against whom he seeks redress. In most states equity pleading is obsolete, having been replaced by notice pleading under Rules of Civil Procedure. See **Complaint.**

In estates and property. Lands and tenements; an estate, including land and buildings thereon; the subject-matter of a conveyance. F. F. Proctor Troy Properties Co. v. Dugan Store, 191 App.Div. 685, 181 N.Y.S. 786, 788. The area of land surrounding a house, and actually or by legal construction forming one inclosure with it. A distinct and definite locality, and may mean a room, shop, building, or other definite area, or a distinct portion of real estate. Land and its appurtenances.

In Worker's Compensation Acts. "Premises" of the employer as used in Worker's Compensation Acts is not restricted to the permanent site of the statutory employer's business nor limited to property owned or leased by him but contemplates any place under the exclusive control of statutory employer where his usual business is being carried on or conducted. Boatman v. Superior Outdoor Advertising Co., Mo. App., 482 S.W.2d 743, 745.

Premium. A reward for an act done. Brown v. Board of Police Com'rs of City of Los Angeles, 58 Cal. App.2d 473, 136 P.2d 617, 619. See also **Bonus.**

A bounty or bonus; a consideration given to invite a loan or a bargain, as the consideration paid to the assignor by the assignee of a lease, or to the transferer by the transferee of shares of stock, etc. So stock is said to be "at a premium" when its market price exceeds its nominal or face value. The excess of issue (or market) price over par value. See **Par.**

In granting a lease, part of the rent is sometimes capitalized and paid in a lump sum at the time the lease is granted. This is called a "premium."

The sum paid or agreed to be paid by an insured to the underwriter (insurer) as the consideration for the insurance. The price for insurance protection for a specified period of exposure.

See also **Earned premium; Net premium; Net single premium.**

Premium note. A promissory note given by the insured for part or all of the amount of the premium.

Securities issue. The amount by which a preferred stock or bond may sell above its par value. In the case of a new issue of bonds or stocks, premium is the amount the market price rises over the original selling price. Also refers to a charge sometimes made when a stock is borrowed to make delivery on a short sale. May refer, also, to redemption price of a bond or preferred stock if it is higher than face value.

Unearned premium. That portion which must be returned to insured on cancellation of policy. In accounting, the account which reflects that portion of a premium that has been paid for insurance coverage which has not yet been extended.

Premium loan. Loan made for purpose of paying an insurance premium and secured by the policy.

Premium pudicitiæ /príymiyəm pyùwdəsíshiyiy/. The price of chastity. A compensation for the loss of chastity, paid or promised to, or for the benefit of, a seduced female.

Premium tax. Tax paid by insurer on gross insurance premiums sold in state.

Premunire /prèmənáyriy/. See **Præmunire.**

Prenatal injuries. See **Child.**

Prenda /prénda/. In Spanish law, pledge.

Prender, prendre /préndər/próndr(ə)/. L. Fr. To take. The power or right of taking a thing without waiting for it to be offered. See **À prendre.**

Prender de baron /préndər də bǽrən/. L. Fr. In old English law, a taking of husband; marriage. An exception or plea which might be used to disable a woman from pursuing an appeal of murder against the killer of her former husband.

Prenomen /priynówmən/. Lat. The first or Christian name of a person.

Pre-nuptial agreement. One entered into by prospective spouses prior to marriage but in contemplation and in consideration thereof; by it, the property rights of one or both of the prospective spouses are determined or are secured to one or both of them or their children. Friedlander v. Friedlander, 80 Wash.2d 293, 494 P.2d 208, 212. See also **Antenuptial agreement; Post-nuptial agreement.**

Prepaid expense. An expense paid before it is currently due. In accounting, an expenditure for a benefit not yet enjoyed, *e.g.* pre-paid insurance premiums from the standpoint of the insured. Cash basis as well as accrual basis taxpayers are generally required to capitalize prepayments for rent, insurance, etc. that cover more than one year. Deductions are taken during the period the benefits are received.

Prepaid income. In accounting, income received but not yet earned.

Prepaid legal services. System by which persons may pay premiums to cover future legal services much the same as payments are made for future medical expenses. Such plan may be either open-ended whereby the person can secure legal services from the attorney of his choice, or closed-end whereby he must secure the services of a particular attorney, group of attorneys, or list of attorneys.

Preparation. With respect to criminal offense, consists in devising or arranging means or measures necessary for its commission, while attempt is direct movement toward commission after preparations are made. State v. Quick, 199 S.C. 256, 19 S.E.2d 101, 103. See also **Aid and abet.**

Prepare. To provide with necessary means; to make ready; to provide with what is appropriate or necessary.

Prepayment penalty. A penalty under a note, mortgage, or deed of trust, imposed when the loan is paid before its due date. Consideration to terminate loan at borrower's election before maturity.

Prepayments. Deferred charges. Assets representing expenditures for future benefits. Rent and insurance premiums paid in advance are usually classified as current prepayments.

Prepense. Forethought; preconceived; premeditated.

Preponderance of evidence. Evidence which is of greater weight or more convincing than the evidence which is offered in opposition to it; that is, evidence which as a whole shows that the fact sought to be proved is more probable than not. Braud v. Kinchen, La.App., 310 So.2d 657, 659. With respect to burden of proof in civil actions, means greater weight of evidence, or evidence which is more credible and convincing to the mind. That which best accords with reason and probability. The word "preponderance" means something more than "weight"; it denotes a superiority of weight, or outweighing. The words are not synonymous, but substantially different. There is generally a "weight" of evidence on each side in case of contested facts. But juries cannot properly act upon the weight of evidence, in favor of the one having the *onus*, unless it overbear, in some degree, the weight upon the other side.

That amount of evidence necessary for the plaintiff to win in a civil case. It is that degree of proof which is more probable than not.

Preponderance of evidence may not be determined by the number of witnesses, but by the greater weight of all evidence, which does not necessarily mean the greater number of witnesses, but opportunity for knowledge, information possessed, and manner of testifying determines the weight of testimony.

Prerogative /prərógədəv/. An exclusive or peculiar right or privilege. The special power, privilege, immunity, right or advantage vested in an official person, either generally, or in respect to the things of his office, or in an official body, as a court or legislature.

Prerogative court. In old English law, a court established for the trial of all testamentary causes, where the deceased left *bona notabilia* within two different dioceses; in which case the probate of wills belonged to the archbishop of the province, by way of special prerogative. And all causes relating to the wills, administrations, or legacies of such persons were originally cognizable herein, before a judge appointed by the archbishop, called the "judge of the prerogative court," from whom an appeal lay to the privy council. The jurisdiction of these courts became obsolete with the transfer of the testamentary jurisdiction of the ecclesiastical courts to the Chancery Division of the High Court.

Prerogative law. That part of the common law of England which is more particularly applicable to the king.

Prerogative writs. In English law, the name was given to certain judicial writs issued by the courts only upon proper cause shown, never as a mere matter of right, the theory being that they involved a direct interference by the government with the liberty and property of the subject, and therefore were justified only as an exercise of the extraordinary power (prerogative) of the crown. In America, issuance is now generally regulated by statute, and such are generally referred to as extraordinary writs or remedies.

Such writs have been abolished in the federal and most state courts with the adoption of Rules of Civil Procedure. The relief formerly available by such writs is now available by appropriate action or motion under the Rules of Civil Procedure. See Rule 81. These writs are the writs of mandamus, procedendo, prohibition, quo warranto, habeas corpus, and certiorari.

Pres /préy/. L. Fr. Near. *Cy pres*, so near; as near. See **Cy pres.**

Presbyter /prézbədər/. Lat. In civil and ecclesiastical law, an elder; a presbyter; a priest.

Presbyterianism. One of the principal systems of church polity known as the "Christian Protestant Church", occupying an intermediate position between episcopacy and congregationalism. A religious faith or doctrine, based on the Westminster Confession of Faith and the Larger and Shorter Catechisms.

Presbyterium. That part of the church where divine offices are performed; formerly applied to the choir or chancel, because it was the place appropriated to the bishop, priest, and other clergy, while the laity were confined to the body of the church.

Prescribable /prəskráybəbəl/. That to which a right may be acquired by prescription.

Prescribe. To assert a right or title to the enjoyment of a thing, on the ground of having hitherto had the uninterrupted and immemorial enjoyment of it.

To lay down authoritatively as a guide, direction, or rule; to impose as a peremptory order; to dictate; to point, to direct; to give as a guide, direction, or rule of action; to give law. To direct; define; mark out.

In a medical sense "prescribe" means to direct, designate, or order use of a particular remedy, therapy, medicine, or drug.

Prescription. A direction of remedy or remedies for a disease, illness, or injury and the manner of using them. Also, a formula for the preparation of a drug or medicine.

Prescription is a peremptory and perpetual bar to every species of action, real or personal, when creditor has been silent for a certain time without urging his claim. Jones v. Butler, La.App., 346 So.2d 790, 791.

Acquisition of a personal right to use a way, water, light and air by reason of continuous usage. See also **Prescriptive easement.**

International law. Acquisition of sovereignty over a territory through continuous and undisputed exercise of sovereignty over it during such a period as is necessary to create under the influence of historical development the general conviction that the present condition of things is in conformity with international order. State of Arkansas v. State of Tennessee, 310 U.S. 563, 60 S.Ct. 1026, 1030, 84 L.Ed. 1362.

Prescription in a que estate. A claim of prescription based on the immemorial enjoyment of the right claimed, by the claimant and those former owners "whose estate" he has succeeded to and holds.

Real property law. The name given to a mode of acquiring title to incorporeal hereditaments by immemorial or long-continued enjoyment. Hester v. Sawyers, 41 N.M. 497, 71 P.2d 646, 649. Prescription is the term usually applied to incorporeal hereditaments, while "adverse possession" is applied to lands.

In Louisiana, prescription is defined as a manner of acquiring the ownership of property, or discharging debts, by the effect of time, and under the conditions regulated by law. Each of these prescriptions has its special and particular definition. The prescription by which the ownership of property is acquired, is a right by which a mere possessor acquires the ownership of a thing which he possesses by the continuance of his possession during the time fixed by law. The prescription by which debts are released, is a peremptory and perpetual bar to every species of action, real or personal, when the creditor has been silent for a certain time without urging his claim. In this sense of the term it is very nearly equivalent to what is elsewhere expressed by "limitation of actions," or rather, the "bar of the statute of limitations."

See also **Adverse possession; Prescriptive easement.**

Prescriptive easement. A right to use another's property which is not inconsistent with the owner's rights and which is acquired by a use, open and notorious, adverse and continuous for the statutory period (*e.g.* twenty years). To a certain extent, it resembles title by adverse possession but differs to the extent that the adverse user acquires only an easement and not title. To create an easement by "prescription," the use must have been open, continuous, exclusive, and under claim of right for statutory period. See also **Adverse possession.**

Presence. Act, fact, or state of being in a certain place and not elsewhere, or within sight or call, at hand, or in some place that is being thought of. The existence of a person in a particular place at a given time particularly with reference to some act done there and then. Besides actual presence, the law recognizes *constructive* presence, which latter may be predicated of a person who, though not on the very spot, was near enough to be accounted present by the law, or who was actively co operating with another who was actually present.

Presence of an officer. An offense is committed in "presence" or "view" of officer, within rule authorizing arrest without warrant, when officer sees act constituting it, though at distance, or when circumstances within his observation give probable cause for belief that defendant has committed offense, or when he hears disturbance created by offense and proceeds as once to scene, or if offense is continuing, or has not been fully consummated when arrest is made.

Presence of defendant. In the trial of all felonies, the defendant or accused has the right to be present at every stage of the criminal proceeding unless he wilfully and without justification absents himself or by his conduct renders it impossible to conduct the trial. In many states, this rule does not obtain as to misdemeanors. Fed.R.Crim.P. 43 specifies when the presence of the defendant is required and not required.

Presence of the court. A contempt is in the "presence of the court," if it is committed in the ocular view of the court, or where the court has direct knowledge of the contempt.

Presence of the testator. Will is attested in presence of testator if witnesses are within range of any of testator's senses. In re Demaris' Estate, 166 Or. 36, 110 P.2d 571, 585, 586. See **Attestation.**

Present, *n.* A gift; a gratuity; anything presented or given.

Present, *adj.* Now existing; at hand; relating to the present time; considered with reference to the present time. See also **Presentment.**

Present ability. As used in describing an element of the crime of assault, it means immediate or a point near immediate as regards the defendant's capacity to inflict harm. People v. Ranson, 40 Cal.App.3d 317, 114 Cal.Rptr. 874, 877.

Present conveyance. A conveyance made with the intention that it take effect at once and not at a future time.

Present danger test. See **Clear and present danger doctrine.**

Present enjoyment. The immediate or present possession and use of an estate or property, as distinguished from such as is postponed to a future time.

Present estate. An estate in immediate possession; one now existing, or vested at the present time; as distinguished from a *future* estate, the enjoyment of which is postponed to a future time.

Present interest. One which entitles the owner to the immediate possession of the property.

A "present interest", as distinguished from a future interest for purpose of federal gift tax annual exclusion, denotes a present right to realize, enjoy or use donated property. Duffey v. U. S., D.C.Minn., 182 F.Supp. 765, 767. An interest in property is a "present interest" if the donee has the right presently to use, possess, or enjoy it. Gilmore v. C. I. R., C.A. 6th, 213 F.2d 520, 521.

Present sale. A sale which is accomplished by the making of the contract. U.C.C. § 2–106(1).

Present time. A period of appreciable and generally considerable duration within which certain transactions are to take place.

Present use. One which has an immediate existence, and is at once operated upon by the statute of uses.

Presentative advowson /prəzéntədəv ədváwzən/. See **Advowson.**

Pre-sentence hearing. Procedural step prior to sentencing at which a judge may examine the presentence report and all other relevant material before imposing sentence. Sentencing is a "critical stage" of a criminal prosecution requiring assistance of appointed counsel. Mempa v. Rhay, 389 U.S. 128, 88 S.Ct. 254, 19 L.Ed.2d 336. See **Pre-sentence investigation; Pre-sentence report.**

Pre-sentence investigation. Investigation of the relevant background of a convicted offender, usually conducted by a probation officer attached to a court, designed to act as a sentencing guide for the sentencing judge. Fed.R.Crim.P. 32(c).

Pre-sentence report. The report prepared from the presentence investigation, which is designed to assist the judge in passing sentence on a convicted defendant. Presentence reports vary in scope and focus, but should contain at least the following items: (1) complete description of the situation surrounding the criminal activity; (2) offender's educational background; (3) offender's employment background; (4) offender's social history; (5) residence history of the offender; (6) offender's medical history; (7) information about environment to which the offender will return; (8) information about any resources available to assist the offender; (9) probation officer's view of the offender's motivations and ambitions; (10) full description of the defendant's criminal record; and, (11) recommendation as to disposition.

Presenter. Any person presenting a draft or demand for payment for honor under a credit even though that person is a confirming bank or other correspondent which is acting under an issuer's authorization. U.C.C. § 5–112(3). See also **Presentment.**

Presenting bank. Any bank presenting an item except a payor bank. U.C.C. § 4–105(e).

Presently. Immediately; now; at once. A right which may be exercised "presently" as opposed to one in reversion or remainder.

Presentment. The written notice taken by a grand jury of any offense, from their own knowledge or observation, without any bill of indictment laid before them at the suit of the government. A presentment is an accusation, initiated by the grand jury itself, and in effect an instruction that an indictment be drawn. U. S. v. Briggs, C.A.Fla., 514 F.2d 794, 804. A written accusation of crime made and returned by the grand jury upon its own initiative in the exercise of its lawful inquisitorial powers, is in the form of a bill of indictment, and in practice is signed individually by all the grand jurors who return it. State v. Hudson, Tenn.Cr.App., 487 S.W.2d 672, 674. See also **Indictment; Information; Presenter.**

The production of a negotiable instrument to the drawee for his acceptance, or to the drawer or acceptor for payment; or of a promissory note to the party liable, for payment of the same. Presentment is a demand for acceptance or payment made upon the maker, acceptor, drawee or other payor by or on behalf of the holder. U.C.C. § 3–504(1).

Present recollection recorded. A witness may use any document which helps revive or "jog" his memory of a past event and such document does not thereby become evidence. His testimony is the evidence though the opponent is entitled to see and examine the document and to impeach the credibility of the witness with it. Fed.Evid.R. 612.

Present recollection revived. The use by a witness of some writing or other object to refresh his recollection so that he may testify about past events from present recollection. Askins v. State, Md.App., 284 A.2d 626, 631. See also **Present recollection recorded.**

Presents. The present instrument. The phrase "these presents" is used in any legal document to designate the instrument in which the phrase itself occurs.

Preservation. Keeping safe from harm; avoiding injury, destruction, or decay; maintenance. It is not creation, but the saving of that which already exists, and implies the continuance of what previously existed. See **Maintenance.**

Preside. To occupy the place of authority as of president, chairman, moderator, etc. To direct, control or regulate proceedings as chief officer, moderator, etc. To possess or exercise authority. To preside over a court is to "hold" it,—to direct, control, and govern it as the chief officer. A judge may "preside" whether sitting as a sole judge or as one of several judges.

President. One placed in authority over others; a chief officer; a presiding or managing officer; a governor, ruler, or director. The chairman, moderator, or presiding officer of a legislative or deliberative body, appointed to keep order, manage the proceedings, and govern the administrative details of their business.

The chief officer of a corporation, company, board, committee, etc., generally having the main direction and administration of their concerns. Roe v. Bank of Versailles, 167 Mo. 406, 67 S.W. 303. The term does not ordinarily include "vice president." First Nat. Bank v. C. H. Meyers & Co., Tex.Civ.App., 283 S.W. 265, 266.

The chief executive magistrate of a state or nation, particularly under a democratic form of government; or of a province, colony, or dependency. In the United States, the word is commonly used in reference to the private as well as public character of the nation's chief executive. U. S. v. Metzdorf, D.C. Mont., 252 F. 933, 937.

Presidential electors. A body of electors chosen in the different states, whose sole duty it is to elect a president and vice-president of the United States. Each state appoints, in such manner as the legislature thereof may direct, a number of electors equal to the whole number of senators and representatives to which the state is entitled in congress. Const.U.S. Art. 2, § 1; Amendment XII; McPherson v. Blacker, 146 U.S. 1, 13 S.Ct. 3, 36 L.Ed. 869. The usual method of appointment is by general ballot, so that each voter in a state votes for the whole number of electors to which his state is entitled. See **Electoral college.**

Presidential powers. See **Executive powers.**

President of the United States. The official title of the chief executive officer of the federal government in the United States.

Press. In old English practice, a piece or skin of parchment, several of which used to be sewed together in making up a roll or record of proceedings. 1 Bl. Comm. 183.

The aggregate of publications issuing from the press, or the giving publicity to one's sentiments and opinions through the medium of printing; as in the phrase "liberty of the press." Freedom of the press is guaranteed by the First Amendment. See **Liberty.**

Pressing seamen. See **Impressment.**

Pressing to death. See **Peine forte et dure.**

Prest. In old English law, a duty in money to be paid by the sheriff upon his account in the exchequer, or for money left or remaining in his hands.

Prestation /prəstéyshən/. In old English law, a presting or payment of money. A payment or performance; the rendering of a service.

Prestimony /préstəməniy/ or **præstimonia** /prèstəmówn-(i)yə/. In canon law, a fund or revenue appropriated by the founder for the subsistence of a priest, without being erected into any title or benefice, chapel, prebend, or priory. It is not subject to the ordinary; but of it the patron, and those who have a right from him, are the collators.

Prest money. In old English law, a payment which binds those who receive it to be ready at all times appointed, being meant especially of soldiers.

Presumably. Fit to be assumed as true in advance of conclusive evidence; credibly deduced; fair to suppose; by reasonable supposition or inference; what appears to be entitled to belief without direct evidence. See **Presumption.**

Presume. To assume beforehand. In a more technical sense, to believe or accept upon probable evidence. See **Presumption.**

Presumed intent. A person is presumed to intend the natural and probable consequences of his voluntary acts. The government is not required in crimes to prove that a defendant intended the precise consequences of his act and his criminal intent can be inferred from his act.

Presumption. A presumption is a rule of law, statutory or judicial, by which finding of a basic fact gives rise to existence of presumed fact, until presumption is rebutted. Van Wart v. Cook, Okl.App., 557 P.2d 1161, 1163.

In all civil actions and proceedings not otherwise provided for by Act of Congress or by these rules, a presumption imposes on the party against whom it is directed the burden of going forward with evidence to rebut or meet the presumption, but does not shift to such party the burden of proof in the sense of the risk of nonpersuasion, which remains throughout the trial upon the party on whom it was originally cast. Federal Evidence Rule 301.

A presumption is an assumption of fact resulting from a rule of law which requires such fact to be assumed from another fact or group of facts found or otherwise established in the action. Uniform Evidence Rule 13.

A presumption is a rebuttable assumption of fact resulting from a rule of law which requires such fact to be assumed from another fact or group of facts found or otherwise established in the action. N.J. Evidence Rule 13.

A presumption is an assumption of fact that the law requires to be made from another fact or group of facts found or otherwise established in the action. A presumption is not evidence. A presumption is either conclusive or rebuttable. Every rebuttable presumption is either (a) a presumption affecting the burden of producing evidence or (b) a presumption affecting the burden of proof. Calif.Evid.Code.

See also **Disputable presumption; Inference; Juris et de jure; Raise a presumption.**

Commercial law. A presumption means that the trier of fact must find the existence of the fact presumed unless and until evidence is introduced which would support a finding of its non-existence. U.C.C. § 1–201(31).

Conclusive presumptions. A conclusive presumption is one in which proof of basic fact renders the existence of the presumed fact conclusive and irrebuttable. Few in number and often statutory, the majority view is that a conclusive presumption is in reality a substantive rule of law, not a rule of evidence. An example of this type of presumption is the rule that a child under seven years of age is presumed to be incapable of committing a felony. The Federal Evidence Rules (301, 302) and most state rules of evidence are concerned only with rebuttable presumptions.

Conflicting presumptions. If two presumptions arise which are conflicting with each other, the judge shall apply the presumption which is founded on the weightier considerations of policy and logic. If there is no such preponderance both presumptions shall be disregarded. Maine Evidence Rule 310(c); Uniform Evidence Rule 15.

Effect of presumption. If evidence to the contrary of a presumed fact is offered, the existence or nonexistence of such fact shall be for the trier of fact, unless the evidence is such that the minds of reasonable men would not differ as to the existence or nonexistence of the presumed fact. New Jersey Evidence Rule 14.

The better rule is that once evidence tending to rebut the presumption is introduced, the presumption loses all its force.

Inconsistent presumptions. See *Conflicting presumptions, supra.*

Irrebuttable presumption. In evidence, a conclusive presumption which requires a finding of the presumed fact once the underlying evidence is introduced, e.g. incapacity of a child five years old to commit a crime. Evidence tending to rebut it is not admissible. See *Conclusive presumptions, supra.*

Presumptions of fact. Such are presumptions which do not compel a finding of the presumed fact but which warrant one when the basic fact has been proved. The trend has been to reject the classifications of presumptions of "fact" and presumptions of "law". See **Inference.**

Presumptions of law. A presumption of law is one which, once the basic fact is proved and no evidence to the contrary has been introduced, compels a finding of the existence of the presumed fact. The presumption of law is rebuttable and in most cases the adversary introduces evidence designed to overcome it. The trend has been to reject the classifications of presumptions of "law" and presumptions of "fact."

Rebuttable presumption. A presumption that can be overturned upon the showing of sufficient proof. In general, all presumptions other than conclusive presumptions are rebuttable presumptions. Once evidence tending to rebut the presumption is introduced, the force of the presumption is entirely dissipated and the party with the burden of proof must come forward with evidence to avoid a directed verdict.

Statutory presumption. A presumption, either rebuttable or conclusive, which is created by statute in contrast to a common law presumption.

Example of presumptions. Thompson v. Mecey, 101 Ariz. 125, 416 P.2d 558 (receipt of letter by addressee presumed from proper mailing); Hobart-Farrell Plumbing and Heating Co. v. Klayman, 302 Mass. 508, 19 N.E.2d 805 (same presumption: mailing is "prima facie case" of receipt in ordinary and due course of post); American-First Title & Trust Co. v. First Federal Savings & Loan Ass'n, Okl., 415 P.2d 930 (presumption that, upon receipt of mail, regular course of business regarding opening and filing was followed).

Presumption of death. A presumption which arises upon the disappearance and continued absence of a person from his customary location or home for an extended period of time, commonly 7 years, without any apparent reason for such absence. Magers v. Western & Southern Life Ins. Co., C.A.Mo., 335 S.W.2d 355.

Presumption of innocence. A hallowed principle of criminal law to the effect that the government has the burden of proving every element of a crime beyond a reasonable doubt and that the defendant has no burden to prove his innocence. It arises at the first stage of the criminal process but it is not a true presumption because the defendant is not required to come forward with proof of his innocence once evidence of guilt is introduced to avoid a directed verdict of guilty.

Presumption of innocence succinctly conveys the principle that no person may be convicted of a crime unless the Government carries the burden of proving his guilt beyond a reasonable doubt but it does not mean that no significance at all may be attached to the indictment. U. S. v. Friday, D.C.Mich., 404 F.Supp. 1343, 1346.

Presumption of legitimacy. Whenever it is established in an action that a child was born to a woman while she was the lawful wife of a specified man, the party asserting the illegitimacy of the child has the burden of producing evidence and the burden of persuading the trier of fact beyond reasonable doubt that the man was not the father of the child. Bernheimer v. First Natl. Bank, 359 Mo. 1119, 225 S.W.2d 745; Model Code of Evidence, Rule 703.

Presumption of survivorship. A presumption of fact, to the effect that one person survived another, applied for the purpose of determining a question of succession or similar matter, in a case where the two persons perished in the same catastrophe, and there are no circumstances extant to show which of them actually died first, except those on which the presumption is founded, viz., differences of age, sex, strength, or physical condition.

Presumptive. Resting on presumption; created by or arising out of presumption; inferred; assumed; supposed; as, "presumptive" damages, evidence, heir, notice, or title.

Presumptive evidence. Prima facie evidence or evidence which is not conclusive and admits of explanation or contradiction; evidence which must be received and treated as true and sufficient until and unless rebutted by other evidence, *i.e.,* evidence which a statute says shall be presumptive of another fact unless rebutted. See **Presumption; Prima facie evidence.**

Presumptive trust. Trust raised by implication of law and presumed always to have been contemplated by parties, intention as to which is to be found in nature of transaction but not expressed in deed or instrument of conveyance, and is thus distinguished from "constructive trust." Kollbaum v. K & K Chevrolet Inc., 196 Neb. 555, 244 N.W.2d 173, 174. Also called "Resulting trust."

Prêt /préy/. In French law, a loan. A contract by which one of the parties delivers an article to the other, to be used by the latter, on condition of his returning, after having used it, the same article in nature or an equivalent of the same species and quality.

Prêt à intérêt /préy à ænteréy/. Loan at interest. A contract by which one of the parties delivers to the other a sum of money, or commodities, or other movable or fungible things, to receive for their use a profit determined in favor of the lender.

Prêt à usage /préy à yuwsázh/. Loan to use. A contract by which one of the parties delivers an article to the other, to be used by the latter, the borrower agreeing to return the specific article after having used it. A contract identical with the *commodatum (q.v.)* of the civil law.

Prêt de consommation /préy də kònsomasyówn/. Loan for consumption. A contract by which one party delivers to the other a certain quantity of things, such as are consumed in the use, on the undertaking of the borrower to return to him an equal quantity of the same species and quality. A contract identical with the *mutuum (q.v.)* of the civil law.

Pretend. To feign or simulate; to hold that out as real which is false or baseless.

Prête-nom /prètnówm/. One who lends his name.

Pretense. See **False pretenses.**

Preter legal /príydər líygəl/. Not agreeable to law; exceeding the limits of law; not legal.

Pretermission. The state of one who is pretermitted, as an heir or child of the testator. The act of omitting a child or heir from a will.

Pretermission statute. Those laws of the various states which make provision for children and heirs who have been omitted from the will of the father or ancestor. Commonly the child takes the same share of the estate which he would have taken if the testator had died intestate unless the omission was intentional and not occasioned by accident or mistake. Nicholson v. Sorensen, Alaska, 517 P.2d 766, 768.

Pretermit /priydərmít/. To "pretermit" is to pass by, to omit or to disregard, *e.g.,* failure of testator to mention his children in his will.

Pretermitted heir /priydərmídəd ér/. A child or other descendant omitted by a testator. Where a testator unintentionally fails to mention in his will, or make provision for, a child, either living at the date of the execution of the will or born thereafter, a statute may provide that such child, or the issue of a deceased child, shall share in the estate as though the testator had died intestate. In re Price's Estate, 56 Cal. App.2d 335, 132 P.2d 485.

Pretext. Ostensible reason or motive assigned or assumed as a color or cover for the real reason or motive; false appearance, pretense.

In international law, a reason alleged as justificatory, but which is so only in appearance, or which is even absolutely destitute of all foundation. The name of "pretexts" may likewise be applied to reasons which are in themselves true and well-founded, but, not being of sufficient importance for undertaking a war [or other international act], are made use of only to cover ambitious views.

Pretium /príysh(iy)əm/. Lat. Price; cost; value; the price of an article sold.

Pretium affectionis /príysh(iy)əm əfèkshiyównəs/. An imaginary value put upon a thing by the fancy of the owner, and growing out of his attachment for the specific article, its associations, his sentiment for the donor, etc.

Pretium periculi /príysh(iy)əm pəríkyəlay/. The price of the risk, *e.g.,* the premium paid on a policy of insurance; also the interest paid on money advanced on bottomry or respondentia.

Pretium sepulchri /príysh(iy)əm səpélkray/. A mortuary (*q.v.*).

Pretium succedit in locum rei /príysh(iy)əm səksíydəd ən lówkəm ríyay/. The price stands in the place of the thing sold.

Pretorial court /prətóriyəl kórt/. In the colony of Maryland, formerly a court for the trial of capital crimes, consisting of the lord proprietor or his lieutenant-general, and the council. Also called *Pretorial.*

Pre-trial conference. Procedural device used prior to trial to narrow issues to be tried, to secure stipulations as to matters and evidence to be heard, and to take all other steps necessary to aid in the disposition of the case. Such conferences between opposing attorneys may be called at the discretion of the court.

The actions taken at the conference are made the subject of an order which controls the future course of the action. Fed.R.Civil P. 16. See **Pre-trial order.**

Criminal cases. At any time after the filing of the indictment or information the court upon motion of any party or upon its own motion may order one or more conferences to consider such matters as will promote a fair and expeditious trial. At the conclusion of a conference the court shall prepare and file a memorandum of the matters agreed upon. No admissions made by the defendant or his attorney at the conference shall be used against the defendant unless the admissions are reduced to writing and signed by the defendant and his attorney. Fed.R.Crim.P. 17.1.

Pre-trial discovery. Those devices which may be used by the parties to an action prior to trial such as interrogatories, depositions, requests for admission of fact, etc. provided for under rules of procedure and statutes; *e.g.* Fed.R.Civil P. 26–37. See **Discovery.**

Pre-trial diversion. A system of recent origin by which certain defendants in criminal cases are referred to community agencies prior to trial while their criminal complaints or indictments are held in abeyance. The defendant may be given job training, counselling, and education. If he responds successfully within a specified period (*e.g.* 90 days, more or less), the charges against him are commonly dismissed.

Pre-trial hearing. See **Pre-trial conference.**

Pre-trial order. An order embodying the terms and stipulations agreed upon at the pre-trial conference or hearing. This order governs the conduct of the trial and binds the parties unless, for good cause shown, the trial judge modifies it. Fed.R.Civil P. 16.

Prevail. To be or become effective or effectual, to be in force, to obtain, to be in general use or practice, to be commonly accepted or adopted; to exist. Atlantic Coast Line R. Co. v. Gamble, 155 Fla. 678, 21 So.2d 348, 350. To succeed; to win.

Prevailing party. The party to a suit who successfully prosecutes the action or successfully defends against it, prevailing on the main issue, even though not necessarily to the extent of his original contention. The one in whose favor the decision or verdict is rendered and judgment entered. Dunne v. New York Telephone Co., 107 Misc. 439, 176 N.Y.S. 519, 520; O'Hare v. Peacock Dairies, 28 Cal.App.2d 562, 82 P.2d 1112, 1113. The party ultimately prevailing when the matter is finally set at rest. Comparri v. James Readding, Inc., 121 N.J.L. 59, 3 A.2d 802, 803. May be the party prevailing in interest, and not necessarily the prevailing person. To be such does not depend upon the degree of success at different stages of the suit, but whether, at the end of the suit, or other proceeding, the party who has made a claim against the other, has successfully maintained it.

Prevarication /prəværəkéyshən/. In the civil law, the acting with unfaithfulness and want of probity; deceitful, crafty, or unfaithful conduct; particularly, such as is manifested in concealing a crime.

In English law, a collusion between an informer and a defendant, in order to a feigned prosecution. Any secret abuse committed in a public office or private commission; willful concealment or misrepresentation of truth, by giving evasive or equivocating evidence.

Prevent. To hinder, frustrate, prohibit, impede, or preclude; to obstruct; to intercept. Orme v. Atlas Gas and Oil Co., 217 Minn. 27, 13 N.W.2d 757, 761. To stop or intercept the approach, access, or performance of a thing. See **Injunction; Restraining order.**

Prevention. In the civil law, the right of a judge to take cognizance of an action over which he has concurrent jurisdiction with another judge.

In canon law, the right which a superior person or officer has to lay hold of, claim, or transact an affair prior to an inferior one, to whom otherwise it more immediately belongs.

Preventive detention. Confinement imposed generally on a defendant in criminal case who has threatened to violate the law while awaiting trial or disposition, or of a mentally ill person who may harm himself or others. The term is also used to describe the improper use of bail. See also **Commitment; Preventive justice.**

Preventive justice. The system of measures taken by government with reference to the direct prevention of crime. It generally consists in obliging those persons whom there is probable ground to suspect of future misbehavior to give full assurance to the public that such offense as is apprehended shall not happen, by requiring pledges or securities to keep the peace, or for their good behavior (*e.g.* peace bonds).

Previous. Antecedent; prior; before. Sometimes limited in meaning to "next prior to" or "next preceding".

Previously taxed income. The taxable income of a Subchapter S corporation is taxed to its shareholders whether distributed or not. To the extent such income is not distributed as dividends (known as undistributed taxable income or UTI), it later becomes previously taxed income (*i.e.,* PTI). Since such income has been taxed to the shareholders when earned by the corporation, it may later be distributed to them without further income tax consequences.

Price. Something which one ordinarily accepts voluntarily in exchange for something else. The consideration given for the purchase of a thing. Amount which a prospective seller indicates as the sum for which he is willing to sell; market value. The term may be synonymous with cost, and with value, as well as with consideration, though price is not always identical either with consideration.

See also **Asking price; Fair market value; Going price; Liquidation price; Open price term.**

Support price. A minimum price set by the government for a particular agricultural raw commodity. For example, the support price of wheat may be set at, say $2 per bushel. That means that the farmer never has to sell his or her wheat below that support price. See also **Parity.**

Target price. Prices set by the government for particular agricultural commodities such as wheat and corn. If the actual market price falls below the target price, farmers get a subsidy from the government for the difference. See **Parity.**

Unit pricing. Pricing of food products expressed in a well-known unit such as ounces or pounds.

Price current. A list or enumeration of various articles of merchandise, with their prices, the duties, if any, payable thereon, when imported or exported, with the drawbacks occasionally allowed upon their exportation, etc.

Price discrimination. Exists when a buyer pays a price that is different from the price paid by another buyer for an identical product or service. Price discrimination is prohibited if the effect of this discrimination may be to lessen substantially or injure competition, except where it was implemented to dispose of perishable or obsolete goods, was the result of differences in costs incurred, or was given in good faith to meet an equally low price of a competitor. Clayton Act, § 2. See also **Predatory intent; Robinson-Patman Act.**

Price earnings ratio. At a given time, the market value of a company's common stock, per share, divided by the earnings per common share for the past year. For example, a stock selling for $50 a share and earning $5 a share is said to be selling at a price-earnings ratio of 10 to 1.

Price-fixing. The cooperative setting of price levels or ranges by competing firms. Such agreements are in violation of the Sherman Antitrust Act. Price-fixing within intent of Sherman Act is either horizontal (dealing with arrangements among competitors) or vertical (attempting to control resale price). Knuth v. Erie-Crawford Dairy Co-op. Ass'n, D.C.Pa., 326 F.Supp. 48, 53.

Minimum fee schedules proposed and enforced by state bar associations are within orbit of prohibited price-fixing under Sherman Act. Goldfarb v. Virginia State Bar, 421 U.S. 773, 95 S.Ct. 2004, 44 L.Ed.2d 572.

See also Horizontal price-fixing contracts; Peg; Predatory intent; Resale price maintenance; Vertical price-fixing contract.

Price index. A number representing average prices as a percent of the average prevailing at some other time (called the base or base year).

Price leadership. A market condition in which a leader in the industry establishes a price and the others in the field follow suit by adopting that price as their own. Price leadership implies a set of industry practices or customs under which list price changes are normally announced by a specific firm accepted as the leader by others, who follow the leader's initiatives. Such practices have been held to not be in violation of the antitrust laws in the absence of a showing of confederated action or an intent to monopolize. United States v. United States Steel Corp., 251 U.S. 417, 40 S.Ct. 293, 64 L.Ed. 343; United States v. International Harvester Co., 274 U.S. 693, 47 S.Ct. 748, 71 L.Ed. 1302.

Price supports. A device used generally by the federal government to keep prices (normally commodity prices) from falling below a predesignated level by such means as loans, subsidies, and government purchases. See also **Parity; Price.**

Priest. A sacerdotal minister of a church. A person in the second order of the ministry, as distinguished from bishops and deacons.

Priest-penitent privilege. In evidence, the recognition of the seal of confession which bars testimony as to the contents of a communication from one to his confessor. Nearly all states provide for this privilege by statute.

Primæ impressionis /práymiy imprèshiyównəs/. A case *primæ impressionis* (of the first impression) is a case of a new kind, to which no established principle of law or precedent directly applies, and which must be decided entirely by reason as distinguished from authority. See **First impression case.**

Primæ preces /práymiy príysiyz/. Lat. In the civil law, an imperial prerogative by which the emperor exercised the right of naming to the first prebend that became vacant after his accession, in every church of the empire.

Prima facie /práymə féyshiy(iy)/. Lat. At first sight; on the first appearance; on the face of it; so far as can be judged from the first disclosure; presumably; a fact presumed to be true unless disproved by some evidence to the contrary. State ex rel. Herbert v. Whims, 68 Ohio App. 39, 38 N.E.2d 596, 599, 22 O.O. 110.

Prima facie case. Such as will prevail until contradicted and overcome by other evidence. Pacific Telephone & Telegraph Co. v. Wallace, 158 Or. 210, 75 P.2d 942, 947. A case which has proceeded upon sufficient proof to that stage where it will support finding if evidence to contrary is disregarded. In re Hoagland's Estate, 126 Neb. 377, 253 N.W. 416.

A prima facie case consists of sufficient evidence in the type of case to get plaintiff past a motion for directed verdict in a jury case or motion to dismiss in a nonjury case; it is the evidence necessary to require defendant to proceed with his case. White v. Abrams, C.A.Cal., 495 F.2d 724, 729. Courts use concept of "prima facie" case in two senses: (1) in sense of plaintiff producing evidence sufficient to render reasonable a conclusion in favor of allegation he asserts; this means plaintiff's evidence is sufficient to allow his case to go to jury, and (2) courts used "prima facie" to mean not only that plaintiff's evidence would reasonably allow conclusion plaintiff seeks, but also that plaintiff's evidence compels such a conclusion if the defendant produces no evidence to rebut it. Husbands v. Com. of Pa., D.C.Pa., 395 F.Supp. 1107, 1139.

Prima facie evidence. Evidence good and sufficient on its face; such evidence as, in the judgment of the law, is sufficient to establish a given fact, or the group or chain of facts constituting the party's claim or defense, and which if not rebutted or contradicted, will remain sufficient. Prima facie evidence is evidence which, if unexplained or uncontradicted, is sufficient to sustain a judgment in favor of the issue which it supports, but which may be contradicted by other evidence. State v. Haremza, 213 Kan. 201, 515 P.2d 1217, 1222.

Prima facie evidence is evidence that, until its effect is overcome by other evidence, will suffice as proof of fact in issue; "prima facie case" is one that will entitle party to recover if no evidence to contrary is offered by opposite party. Duncan v. Butterowe, Inc., Tex.Civ.App., 474 S.W.2d 619, 621. Evidence which suffices for the proof of a particular fact until contradicted and overcome by other evidence. Evidence which, standing alone and unexplained, would maintain the proposition and warrant the conclusion to support which it is introduced. An inference or presumption of law, affirmative or negative of a fact, in the absence of proof, or until proof can be obtained or produced to overcome the inference.

See also **Presumptive evidence.**

Prima facie tort. The infliction of intentional harm, resulting in damage, without excuse or justification, by an act or series of acts which would otherwise be lawful. Cartwright v. Golub Corp., 51 A.D.2d 407, 381 N.Y.S.2d 901, 902.

Primage /práyməj/. In old mercantile law, a small allowance or compensation payable to the master and mariners of a ship or vessel; to the former for the use of his cables and ropes to discharge the goods of the merchant; to the latter for lading and unlading in any port or haven. It is no longer, however, a gratuity to the master, unless especially stipulated; but it belongs to the owners or freighters, and is nothing but an increase of the freight rate.

Prima pars æquitatis æqualitas /práymə párz èkwətéydəs əkwólətæs/. The radical element of equity is equality.

Primary. First; principal; chief; leading. First in order of time, or development, or in intention. As to primary Conveyance; Election; Obligation; and Vein, see those titles.

Primary activity. Concerted action such as a strike or picketing directed against the employer with whom it has a dispute. Compare, secondary activity.

Primary allegation. The opening pleading in a suit in the ecclesiastical court. It is also called a "primary plea."

Primary beneficiary. In life insurance, the person named in the policy who is to receive the proceeds on the death of the insured if such person is alive. If deceased, the proceeds are payable to a secondary beneficiary also designated as such in the policy.

Primary boycott. Action by a union by which it tries to induce people not to use, handle, transport or purchase goods of an employer with which the union has a grievance. See also **Boycott.**

Primary disposal of the soil. In acts of congress admitting territories as states, and providing that no laws shall be passed interfering with the primary disposal of the soil, this means the disposal of it by the United States government when it parts with its title to private persons or corporations acquiring the right to a patent or deed in accordance with law.

Primary election. A preliminary election for the nomination of candidates for office or of delegates to a party convention, designed as a substitute for party conventions. Such elections are classified as closed or open depending on whether or not tests of party

affiliation are required. See also **Closed primary;**
Election.

Primary evidence. Primary evidence means original or
first-hand evidence; the best evidence that the nature
of the case admits of; the evidence which is required
in the first instance, and which must fail before secondary evidence can be admitted. That evidence
which the nature of the case or question suggests as
the proper means of ascertaining the truth. It is the
particular means of proof which is the most natural
and satisfactory of which the case admits, and includes the best evidence which is available to a party
and procurable under the existing situation, and all
evidence falling short of such standard, and which in
its nature suggests there is better evidence of the
same fact, is "secondary evidence." See also **Best**
evidence.

Primary jurisdiction. Under the "primary jurisdiction"
doctrine, in cases raising issues not within the conventional experience of judges or cases requiring the
exercise of administrative discretion, agencies created
by Congress for regulating the subject matter should
not be passed over. Cavanagh Communities Corp. v.
New York Stock Exchange, Inc., D.C.N.Y., 422
F.Supp. 382, 385, 386. The doctrine of "primary
jurisdiction" does not involve jurisdiction in the technical sense, but it is a doctrine predicated on an
attitude of judicial self-restraint and is applied when
the court feels that the dispute should be handled by
an administrative agency created by the legislature to
deal with such problems. Kerr v. Department of
Game, 14 Wash.App. 427, 542 P.2d 467, 469. The
doctrine of "primary jurisdiction" is properly invoked
whenever the enforcement of a claim, which is originally cognizable in the courts, requires the resolution
of issues which, under a regulatory scheme, have
been placed within the special competence of an
administrative body. W. U. Tel. Co., v. Graphic
Scanning Corp., D.C.N.Y., 360 F.Supp. 593, 595.

Primary market. In finance, the market where the
initial sale by the issuer of securities occurs.

Primary obligation. In contract law, the foundational
requirement of a contracting party from which other
obligations may spring; e.g. in a contract of sale, the
buyer's primary obligation is to purchase the goods.

Primary powers. The principal authority given by a
principal to his agent. It differs from "mediate powers."

Primary purpose. That which is first in intention;
which is fundamental. The principal or fixed intention with which an act or course of conduct is undertaken.

Primate. A chief ecclesiastic; an archbishop who has
jurisdiction over his province, or one of several met-
ropolitans presiding over others. Exarch comes nearest to it in the Greek church. Thus the archbishop of
Canterbury is styled "Primate of all England;" the
archbishop of York is "Primate of England."

Prime. To stand first or paramount; to take precedence or priority of; to outrank.

Prime contractor. The party to a building contract who
is charged with the total construction and who enters

into sub-contracts for such work as electrical, plumbing and the like. Also called "general contractor."

Prime cost. The true price paid for goods upon a *bona*
fide purchase.

Prime maker. The person who signs a negotiable instrument such as a note and becomes primarily liable
thereon.

Prime minister. The responsible head of a ministry or
executive government, especially of a monarchical
government. In England, he is the head of the cabinet, and usually holds the office of First Lord of the
Treasury. The office was unknown to the law until
1906, when the prime minister was accorded a place
in the order of precedence.

Primer. A law French word, signifying first; primary.

Prime rate. Usually defined as the lowest rate of interest from time to time charged by a specific lender to
its best customers for short term unsecured loans.
The prime rate is often used as the measuring rod for
interest rates on other loans.

Primer election /práymər əlékshən/. A term used to
signify first choice; e.g., the right of the eldest co-par-
cener to first choose a purpart.

Primer fine /práymər fáyn/. On suing out the writ or
præcipe called a "writ of covenant," there was due to
the crown, by ancient prerogative, a *primer fine,* or a
noble for every five marks of land sued for. That
was one-tenth of the annual value.

Primer seisin /práymər síyzən/. See **Seisin.**

Prime serjeant /práym sárjənt/. In English law, the
king's first serjeant at law.

Primicerius /pràyməsír(i)yəs/. In old English law, the
first of any degree of men.

Primitiæ /prəmíshiyiy/. In old English law, first fruits;
the first year's whole profits of a spiritual preferment.

Primitive obligation /prímədəv òbləgéyshən/. See **Obli-**
gation.

Primo beneficio /práymow bènəfísh(iy)ow/. Lat. A
writ directing a grant of the first benefice in the
sovereign's gift.

Primo executienda est verbi vis, ne sermonis vitio ob-
struatur oratio, sive lex sine argumentis /práymow
èksəkyùwshiyéndə èst várbay vís, niy sərmównəs
vísh(iy)ow òbstruwéydər əréysh(iy)ow, sáyviy léks
sáyniy argyəméntəs/. The full meaning of a word
should be ascertained at the outset, in order that the
sense may not be lost by defect of expression, and
that the law be not without reasons [or arguments].

Primogeniture /pràyməjénəchər/. The state of being
the first-born among several children of the same
parents; seniority by birth in the same family. The
superior or exclusive right possessed by the eldest
son, and particularly, his right to succeed to the
estate of his ancestor, in right of his seniority by
birth, to the exclusion of younger sons.

Primogenitus /pràyməjénədəs/. Lat. In old English
law, a first-born or eldest son.

Primo venienti /práymow vèniyéntay/. Lat. To the one first coming. An executor anciently paid debts as they were presented, whether the assets were sufficient to meet all debts or not.

Primum decretum /práyməm dəkríydəm/. Lat. In the canon law, the first decree; a preliminary decree granted on the non-appearance of a defendant, by which the plaintiff was put in possession of his goods, or of the thing itself which was demanded. In the courts of admiralty, this name was given to a provisional decree.

Prince. In a general sense, a sovereign; the ruler of a nation or state. More particularly, the son of a king or emperor, or the issue of a royal family; as princes of the blood. The chief of any body of men.

Princeps /prín(t)seps/. Lat. In the civil law, the prince; the emperor.

Princeps et respublica ex justa causa possunt rem meam auferre /prín(t)seps èt rəzpábləkə èks jástə kózə pósənt rém míyəm oféhriy/. The prince and the commonwealth, for a just cause, can take away my property.

Princeps legibus solutus est /prín(t)seps líyjəbəs səl(y)úwdəs èst/. The emperor is released from the laws; is not bound by the laws.

Princeps mavult domesticos milites quam stipendiarios bellicis opponere casibus /prín(t)seps méyvàlt dəméstəkows mílədiyz kwǽm stəpèndiyériyows béləsəs əpównəriy kéysəbəs/. A prince, in the chances of war, had better employ domestic than stipendiary troops.

Princess royal /prín(t)səs róyəl/. In English law, the eldest daughter of the sovereign.

Principal, *adj.* Chief; leading; most important or considerable; primary; original. Highest in rank, authority, character, importance, or degree.

As to principal Challenge; Contract; Obligation; Office; and Vein, see those titles.

Principal establishment. In the law concerning domicile, the principal domestic establishment. Mosely v. Dabezies, 142 La. 256, 76 So. 705, 706. See **Domicile; Resident.**

Principal fact. In the law of evidence, a fact sought and proposed to be proved by evidence of other facts (termed "evidentiary facts") from which it is to be deduced by inference. A fact which is the principal and ultimate object of an inquiry, and respecting the existence of which a definite belief is required to be formed.

Principal, *n.* The source of authority or right. A superintendent, as of a school.

The capital sum of a debt or obligation, as distinguished from interest or other additions to it. An amount on which interest is charged or earned. Amount of debt, not including interest. The face value of a note, mortgage, etc. Capital sum placed at interest, due as a debt, or use as a fund, as distinguished from interest or profit. Klitgaard v. Gaines, Tex.Civ.App., 479 S.W.2d 765, 770.

See also **Coprincipal; Undisclosed principal.**

Criminal law. A chief actor or perpetrator, or an aider and abettor actually or constructively present at the commission of the crime, as distinguished from an "accessory." At common law, a principal in the first degree is he that is the actor or absolute perpetrator of the crime; and, in the second degree, he who is present, aiding and abetting the principal in the first degree. The distinction between principals in the first and second degrees has been abrogated in the Model Penal Code and by many state codes.

A "principal" differs from an "accessory before the fact" only in the requirement of presence during commission of crime. Huff v. State, 23 Md.App. 211, 326 A.2d 198, 201.

Whoever commits an offense against the United States or aids, abets, counsels, commands, induces or procures its commission, is punishable as a principal. Also, whoever willfully causes an act to be done which if directly performed by him or another would be an offense against the United States, is punishable as a principal. 18 U.S.C.A. § 2.

Principal in the first degree. A principal in the first degree may simply be defined as the criminal actor. He is the one who, with the requisite mental state, engages in the act or omission concurring with the mental state which causes the criminal result.

Principal in the second degree. To be a principal in the second degree, one must be present at the commission of a criminal offense and aid, counsel, command, or encourage the principal in the first degree in the commission of that offense. This requirement of presence may be fulfilled by constructive presence. A person is constructively present when he is physically absent from the situs of the crime but aids and abets the principal in the first degree at the time of the offense from some distance.

Investments. The person for whom a broker executes an order, or a dealer buying or selling for his own account. The term "principal" may also refer to a person's capital or to the face amount of a bond.

Law of agency. The term "principal" describes one who has permitted or directed another (*i.e.* agent or servant) to act for his benefit and subject to his direction and control. Principal includes in its meaning the term "master", a species of principal who, in addition to other control, has a right to control the physical conduct of the species of agents known as servants, as to whom special rules are applicable with reference to harm caused by their physical acts.

If, at the time of a transaction conducted by an agent, the other party thereto has notice that the agent is acting for a principal and of the principal's identity, the principal is a *disclosed* principal. If the other party has notice that the agent is or may be acting for a principal but has no notice of the principal's identity, the principal for whom the agent is acting is a *partially disclosed* principal. If the other party has no notice that the agent is acting for a principal, the one for whom he acts is an *undisclosed* principal. Restatement, Second, Agency, § 4.

Law of guaranty and suretyship. The person primarily liable, for whose performance of his obligation the guarantor or surety has become bound.

Principal and surety. Relationship between accommodation maker and party accommodated on promissory note is that of "principal and surety." Putney Credit Union v. King, 130 Vt. 86, 286 A.2d 282, 284.

Trust law. Property as opposed to income. The term is often used to designate the corpus of a trust. If, for example, G places real estate in trust with income payable to A for life and the remainder to B upon A's death, the real estate is the principal or corpus of the trust. See also **Kentucky Rule.** The majority of states have adopted the Uniform Principal and Income Act.

Vice principal. A vice principal is an employee to whom the master delegates those absolute or nondelegable duties cast upon a master for protection of his employees, and who is in charge of the master's business or any department thereof, and whose duties are exclusively supervision, direction and control of the work of subordinate employees engaged therein, whose duty it is to obey him. Haynie v. Haynie, Okl., 426 P.2d 717, 724. Vice principal is servant who, in addition to his authority to direct and supervise work of those under him, has authority to hire and discharge a subordinate servant. Sartain v. Southern Nat. Life Ins. Co., Tex.Civ.App., 364 S.W.2d 245, 252.

Principalis /prìn(t)səpéyləs/. Lat. Principal; a principal debtor; a principal in a crime.

Principalis debet semper excuti antequam perveniatur ad fideijussores /prìn(t)səpéyləs débət sémpər əkskyúwday ǽntəkwəm pərvèniyéydər ǽd fàydiyayjəsóriyz/. The principal should always be exhausted before coming upon the sureties.

Principia data sequuntur concomitantia /prin(t)síp(i)yə déydə səkwántər kənkòmətǽnsh(iy)ə/. Given principles are followed by their concomitants.

Principia probant, non probantur /prin(t)síp(i)yə prówbənt, nón prəbǽntər/. Principles prove; they are not proved. Fundamental principles require no proof.

Principiis obsta /prin(t)sípiyəs óbstey/. Withstand beginnings; oppose a thing in its early stages, if you would do so with success.

Principiorum non est ratio /prin(t)sìpiyórəm nón èst réysh(iy)ow/. There is no reasoning of principles; no argument is required to prove fundamental rules.

Principium est potissima pars cujusque rei /prin(t)sípiyəm èst pətísəmə párz kəjáskwiy ríyay/. The principle of anything is its most powerful part.

Principle. A fundamental truth or doctrine, as of law; a comprehensive rule or doctrine which furnishes a basis or origin for others; a settled rule of action, procedure, or legal determination. A truth or proposition so clear that it cannot be proved or contradicted unless by a proposition which is still clearer. That which constitutes the essence of a body or its constituent parts. That which pertains to the theoretical part of a science.

Printers Ink Statute. A model statute drafted in 1911 and adopted with some variations in a number of states making it a misdemeanor to advertise a representation that is untrue, deceptive or misleading.

Prior /práyər/. Lat. The former; earlier; preceding; preferable or preferred.

Prior, *n.* The chief of a convent; next in dignity to an abbot.

Prior, *adj.* Earlier; elder; preceding; superior in rank, right, or time; as, a prior lien, mortgage, or judgment.

Prior art. Practical definition of "prior art" is anything in tangible form that may properly be relied on by patent office in patent cases in support of rejection on matter of substance, not form, of claim in pending application for patent. Borden, Inc. v. Occidental Petroleum Corp., D.C.Tex., 381 F.Supp. 1178, 1203.

Prior creditor. Generally, the creditor who is accorded priority in payment from the assets of his debtor. See **Preferential debts.**

Prior inconsistent statements. In evidence, prior statements made by the witness which contradict statements made on the witness stand may be introduced to impeach the witness after a foundation has been laid and an opportunity given to the witness to affirm or deny whether such prior statements were made. Such impeachment may be made through the witness himself or through another witness who heard the prior statements or by means of inconsistent prior depositions (Fed.R.Civil P. 32(a)). Such prior inconsistent statements are not admissible to prove the truth of the matter asserted but only to impeach the credibility of the witness.

Priori petenti /prayóray pəténtay/. To the person first applying. In probate practice, where there are several persons equally entitled to a grant of administration (*e.g.,* next of kin of the same degree), the rule of the court is to make the grant *priori petenti,* to the first applicant.

Priority. Precedence; going before. A legal preference or precedence. When two persons have similar rights in respect of the same subject-matter, but one is entitled to exercise his right to the exclusion of the other, he is said to have priority. The order in which claims may be satisfied out of the sale of real property. See also **Preferential debts.**

Priority of liens. Liens are ranked in the order in which they are perfected and those which are perfected first are said to be priority liens. For priority of security interests, see U.C.C. § 9–301 et seq.

Prior jeopardy. See **Jeopardy.**

Prior lien. This term commonly denotes a first or superior lien, and not one necessarily antecedent in time.

Prior petens /práyər pédən(d)z/. The person first applying.

Prior restraint. In constitutional law, the First Amendment, U.S.Const., prohibits the imposition of a restraint on a publication before it is published. The person defamed is left to his remedy in libel. Near v. Minnesota, 283 U.S. 697, 51 S.Ct. 625, 75 L.Ed. 1357. Three exceptions are recognized: a publication creating a "clear and present danger" to the country, Schenck v. U. S., 249 U.S. 47, 52, 39 S.Ct. 247, 249, 63 L.Ed. 470; obscene publications, and publications which invade the zone of personal privacy.

A prohibited prior restraint is not limited to the suppression of a thing before it is released to the public; rather, an invalid prior restraint is an infringement upon constitutional right to disseminate matters that are ordinarily protected by the First Amendment without there first being a judicial determination that the material does not qualify for First Amendment protection. State v. I, A Woman—Part II, 53 Wis.2d 102, 191 N.W.2d 897, 902, 903.

See also **Censor; Censorship.**

Prior tempore potior jure /práyər témpəriy pówsh(iy)ər júriy/. He who is first in time is preferred in right.

Prior use doctrine. Between two public bodies, property already devoted to a public use may not be taken for another public use in absence of express legislative authority. City of Miami v. Florida East Coast Ry. Co., Fla.App., 286 So.2d 247, 250.

Prisage /práyzəj/. An ancient hereditary revenue of the crown, consisting in the right to take a certain quantity from cargoes of wine imported into England. In Edward I's reign it was converted into a pecuniary duty called "butlerage."

Prise /príyz/. Fr. In French law, prize; captured property.

Prisel en auter lieu /príyzel òn ówtey lyúw/. L. Fr. A taking in another place. A plea in abatement in the action of replevin.

Prison. A public building or other place for the confinement of persons, whether as a punishment imposed by the law or otherwise in the course of the administration of justice. The words "prison" and "penitentiary" are used synonymously to designate institutions for the imprisonment of persons convicted of the more serious crimes, as distinguished from reformatories and county or city jails.

Prison breaking, or breach. The common-law offense of one who, being lawfully in custody, escapes from the place where he is confined, by the employment of force and violence. This offense is to be distinguished from "rescue" (q.v.), which is a deliverance of a prisoner from lawful custody by a third person, and from "escape" which is an unauthorized departure of a prisoner from legal custody without the use of force. The trend however of modern statutes is to abandon these common-law distinctions based upon the presence or absence of force, and substitute other factors to determine the grade of the offense; with "prison breaking" generally referring to escaping from prison or jail by any means.

Prisoner. One who is deprived of his liberty. One who is against his will kept in confinement or custody in a prison, penitentiary, or jail as a result of conviction of a crime.

Prisoner at the bar. An accused person, while on trial before the court, is so called. One accused of crime, who is actually on trial, is in legal effect a "prisoner at the bar," notwithstanding he has given bond for his appearance at the trial. He is a "prisoner" if held in custody either under bond or other process of law, or when physically held under arrest, and when actually on trial he is a "prisoner at the bar."

Prist /príst/. L. Fr. Ready. In the old forms of oral pleading, this term expressed a tender or joinder of issue.

Prius vitiis laboravimus, nunc legibus /práyəs víshiyəs læbəréyvəməs, nə́ŋk líyjəbəs/. We labored first with vices, now with laws.

Privacy acts. Those federal and state statutes which prohibit an invasion of a person's right to be left alone (e.g. to not be photographed in private), and also restrict access to personal information (e.g. income tax returns, credit reports); and overhearing of private communications (e.g. electronic surveillance). Some provide for equitable relief in the form of injunction to prevent the invasion of privacy while others specifically call for money damages and some provide for both legal and equitable protection. See e.g. Fair Credit Reporting Act (15 U.S.C.A. § 1681n–p).

The federal Privacy Act (5 U.S.C.A. § 552a) provides for making known to the public the existence and characteristics of all personal information systems kept by every Federal agency. The Act permits an individual to have access to records containing personal information on that individual and allows the individual to control the transfer of that information to other Federal agencies for nonroutine uses. The Act also requires all Federal agencies to keep accurate accountings of transfers of personal records to other agencies and outsiders, and to make the accountings available to the individual. The Act further provides for civil remedies for the individual whose records are kept or used in contravention of the requirements of the Act.

Breach of privacy is knowingly and without lawful authority: (a) Intercepting, without the consent of the sender or receiver, a message by telephone, telegraph, letter or other means of private communications; or (b) Divulging, without the consent of the sender or receiver, the existence or contents of such message if such person knows that the message was illegally intercepted, or if he illegally learned of the message in the course of employment with an agency in transmitting it. Kansas Criminal Code. See **Eavesdropping; Wiretapping.**

Privacy, right of. The right to be let alone; the right of a person to be free from unwarranted publicity. Term "right of privacy" is generic term encompassing various rights recognized to be inherent in concept of ordered liberty, and such right prevents governmental interference in intimate personal relationships or activities, freedoms of individual to make fundamental choices involving himself, his family, and his relationship with others. Industrial Foundation of the South v. Texas Indus. Acc. Bd., Tex., 540 S.W.2d 668, 679. The right of an individual (or corporation) to withhold himself and his property from public scrutiny, if he so chooses. It is said to exist only so far as its assertion is consistent with law or public policy, and in a proper case equity will interfere, if there is no remedy at law, to prevent an injury threatened by the invasion of, or infringement upon, this right from motives of curiosity, gain or malice. Federal Trade Commission v. American Tobacco Co., 264 U.S. 298, 44 S.Ct. 336, 68 L.Ed. 696. See also Whalen v. Roe, 429 U.S. 589, 97 S.Ct. 869, 51 L.Ed.2d 64; Warren and Brandeis, The Right to Privacy, 4 Harv.L.Rev. 193.

Tort actions for invasion of privacy fall into four general classes: *Appropriation,* consisting of appropriation, for the defendant's benefit or advantage, of the plaintiff's name or likeness, Carlisle v. Fawcett Publications, 201 Cal.App.2d 733, 20 Cal.Rptr. 405; *Intrusion,* consisting of intrusion upon the plaintiff's solitude or seclusion, as by invading his home (Ford Motor Co. v. Williams, 108 Ga.App. 21, 132 S.E.2d 206), eavesdropping (LaCrone v. Ohio Bell Tel. Co., 114 Ohio App. 299, 182 N.E.2d 15, 19 O.O.2d 236); as well as persistent and unwanted telephone calls (Housh v. Peth, 165 Ohio St. 35, 133 N.E.2d 340, 59 O.O. 60); *Public disclosure of private facts,* consisting of a cause of action in publicity, of a highly objectionable kind, given to private information about the plaintiff, even though it is true and no action would lie for defamation, Melvin v. Reid, 112 Cal.App. 285, 297 P. 91; *False light in the public eye,* consisting of publicity which places the plaintiff in a false light in the public eye, Norman v. City of Las Vegas, 64 Nev. 38, 177 P.2d 442.

See also **Invasion of privacy.**

Private. Affecting or belonging to private individuals, as distinct from the public generally. Not official; not clothed with office. People v. Powell, 280 Mich. 699, 274 N.W. 372, 373.

As to private Act; Agent; Bill; Boundary; Business; Carrier; Chapel; Corporation; Detective; Dwelling; Easement; Examination; Ferry; Nuisance; Pond; Property; Prosecutor; Rights; Road; Sale; School; Seal; Statute; Stream; Trust; Water; War; Way; Wharf; and Wrongs, see those titles.

Private bank. An unincorporated banking institution owned by an individual or partnership and, depending upon state statutes, subject to or free from state regulation.

Private bill. Legislation for the special benefit of an individual or a locality. Many State constitutions prohibit such legislation except by general law. See also **Private law.**

Privateer /pràyvətír/. A vessel owned, equipped, and armed by one or more private individuals, and duly commissioned by a belligerent power to go on cruises and make war upon the enemy, usually by preying on his commerce. A private vessel commissioned by a nation by the issue of a letter of marque to its owner to carry on all hostilities by sea, presumably according to the laws of war. Formerly a state issued letters of marque to its own subjects, and to those of neutral states as well, but a privateersman who accepted letters of marque from both belligerents was regarded as a pirate. By the Declaration of Paris (April, 1856), privateering was abolished, but the United States, Spain, Mexico, and Venezuela did not accede to this declaration. It has been thought that the constitutional provision empowering Congress to issue letters of marque deprives it of the power to join in a permanent treaty abolishing privateering. See **Piracy.**

Piracy and privateering are federal offenses. 18 U.S.C.A. § 1651 *et seq.*

Private foundations. A charitable or scientific organization which is operated privately for the advancement of charitable or educational projects.

Private international law. A name used by some writers to indicate that branch of the law which is now more commonly called "Conflict of laws" *(q.v.).*

Private law. As used in contradistinction to public law, the term means all that part of the law which is administered between citizen and citizen, or which is concerned with the definition, regulation, and enforcement of rights in cases where both the person in whom the right inheres and the person upon whom the obligation is incident are private individuals. See also **Private bill; Public law; Special law.**

Private letter ruling. A written statement issued to the taxpayer by the Internal Revenue Service in which interpretations of the tax laws are made and applied to a specific set of facts. Function of the letter ruling, usually sought by the taxpayer in advance of a contemplated transaction, is to advise the taxpayer regarding the tax treatment he can expect from the I.R.S. in the circumstances specified by the ruling. U. S. v. Wahlin, D.C.Wis., 384 F.Supp. 43, 47. See also **Letter ruling.**

Private nuisance. A private nuisance is generally anything that by its continuous use or existence works annoyance, harm, inconvenience or damage to another landowner in the enjoyment of his property. Mandell v. Pasquaretto, 76 Misc.2d 405, 350 N.Y.S.2d 561, 566. Activity which results in an unreasonable interference with the use and enjoyment of another's property. Robie v. Lillis, 112 N.H. 492, 299 A.2d 155, 158; City of Newport News v. Hertzler, 216 Va. 587, 221 S.E.2d 146, 150. A nuisance affecting a single individual or definite small number of persons in enjoyment of private rights not common to the public. Spur Industries, Inc. v. Del E. Webb Development Co., 108 Ariz. 178, 494 P.2d 700, 705. See also **Nuisance.**

Private offering. See **Offering.**

Private person. Term sometimes used to refer to persons other than those holding public office or in military services.

Private placement. *Adoption.* In adoption cases, the placement of a child for adoption by the mother or parents themselves or by an intermediary like a lawyer or doctor, rather than by an adoption agency. Also sometimes called a "direct" placement.

Securities. In securities law, the sale of corporate stock to private persons outside of a public offering. Securities Act, 1933, § 4(2).

Private ruling. In a private ruling, the Internal Revenue Service advises individual taxpayers on the tax consequences of specific transactions that are either contemplated or completed. See also **Letter ruling; Private letter ruling.**

Privation /prəvéyshən/. A taking away or withdrawing.

Privatio præsupponit habitum /prəvéysh(iy)ow priysəpównət hǽbədəm/. A deprivation presupposes a possession.

Privatis pactionibus non dubium est non lædi jus cæterorum /prəvéydəs pækshiyównəbəs nòn d(y)úwbiyəm èst nón líyday jás sèdərórəm/. There is no doubt that the rights of others [third parties] cannot be prejudiced by private agreements.

Privatorum conventio juri publico non derogat /pràyvətórəm kənvénsh(iy)ow júray pə́bləkow nòn dérəgət/. The agreement of private individuals does not derogate from the public right [law].

Privatum /prəvéydəm/. Lat. Private. *Privatum jus,* private law.

Privatum commodum publico cedit /prəvéydəm kómədəm pə́bləkow síydət/. Private good yields to public. The interest of an individual should give place to the public good.

Privatum incommodum publico bono pensatur /prəvéydəm inkómədəm pə́bləkow bównow penséydər/. Private inconvenience is made up for by public benefit.

Privies /príviyz/. Those who are partakers or have an interest in any action or thing, or any relation to another. Brown v. Fidelity Union Trust Co., 126 N.J.Eq. 406, 9 A.2d 311, 326; Hamelik v. Sypek, 152 Misc. 799, 274 N.Y.S. 875. They are of six kinds:

(1) Privies of blood; such as the heir to his ancestor.

(2) Privies in representation; as executors or administrators to their deceased testator or intestate.

(3) Privies in estate; as grantor and grantee, lessor and lessee, assignor and assignee, etc.

(4) Privies in respect to contract.

(5) Privies in respect of estate and contract; as where the lessee assigns his interest, but the contract between lessor and lessee continues, the lessor not having accepted of the assignee.

(6) Privies in law; as the lord by escheat, a tenant by the curtesy, or in dower, the incumbent of a benefice, a husband suing or defending in right of his wife, etc.

"Privies," in the sense that they are bound by the judgment, are those who acquired an interest in the subject-matter after the rendition of the judgment. "Privies" to a judgment are those whose succession to the rights of property affected occurs after the institution of the suit and form a party to it.

Privigna /prəvígnə/. Lat. In the civil law, a stepdaughter.

Privignus /prəvígnəs/. Lat. In the civil law, a son of a husband or wife by a former marriage; a stepson.

Privilege. A particular and peculiar benefit or advantage enjoyed by a person, company, or class, beyond the common advantages of other citizens. An exceptional or extraordinary power or exemption. A right, power, franchise, or immunity held by a person or class, against or beyond the course of the law.

An exemption from some burden or attendance, with which certain persons are indulged, from a supposition of law that the stations they fill, or the offices they are engaged in, are such as require all their time and care, and that, therefore, without this indulgence, it would be impracticable to execute such offices to that advantage which the public good requires. That which releases one from the performance of a duty or obligation, or exempts one from a liability which he would otherwise be required to perform, or sustain in common with all other persons.

A peculiar advantage, exemption, or immunity. See also **Exemption; Immunity.**

See also Doctor-patient privilege; Executive privilege; Husband-wife privilege; Journalist's privilege; Legislative immunity; Marital communications privilege; Newsmen's privilege; Patient-physician privilege; Priest-penitent privilege; Privileged communications; Right.

Attorney-client, doctor-patient, etc. privilege. See **Privileged communications.**

Civil law. A right which the nature of a debt gives to a creditor, and which entitles him to be preferred before other creditors. Civil Code La. art. 3186. It is merely an accessory of the debt which it secures, and falls with the extinguishment of the debt. The civil law privilege became, by adoption of the admiralty courts, the admiralty lien. The J. E. Rumbell, 148 U.S. 1, 13 S.Ct. 498, 37 L.Ed 345.

Communications. See **Privileged communications.**

Discovery. When interrogatories, depositions or other forms of discovery seek information which is otherwise privileged, the party from whom it is sought may claim his privilege. Fed.R.Civil P. 26; Fed.R. Crim.P. 16. See also **Protective order; Work product rule.**

Evidence. See **Privileged communications; Privileged evidence.**

Exclusive privilege. See **Exclusive privilege.**

Executive privilege. The protection afforded to confidential presidential communications. However, the generalized need for confidentiality of high level communications cannot sustain an absolute unqualified presidential privilege. U. S. v. Nixon, 418 U.S. 683, 94 S.Ct. 3090, 41 L.Ed.2d 1039. See also **Executive privilege.**

Journalist's privilege. See **Journalist's privilege; Newsmen's privilege; Shield laws.**

Libel and slander. An exemption from liability for the speaking or publishing of defamatory words concerning another, based on the fact that the statement was made in the performance of a political, judicial, social, or personal duty. Privilege is either *absolute* or *conditional.* The former protects the speaker or publisher without reference to his motives or the truth or falsity of the statement. This may be claimed in respect, for instance, to statements made in legislative debates, in reports of military officers to their superiors in the line of their duty, and statements made by judges, witnesses, and jurors in trials in court. Conditional privilege (called also "qualified privilege") will protect the speaker or publisher unless actual malice and knowledge of the falsity of the statement is shown. This may be claimed where the communication related to a matter of public interest, or where it was necessary to protect one's private interest and was made to a person having an interest in the same matter. Saroyan v. Burkett, 57 Cal.2d 706, 21 Cal.Rptr. 557, 558, 371 P.2d 293.

For defense of "constitutional privilege" in libel actions, see **Libel.**

Maritime law. An allowance to the master of a ship of the same general nature with primage, being compensation, or rather a gratuity, customary in certain trades, and which the law assumes to be a fair and equitable allowance, because the contract on both sides is made under the knowledge of such usage by the parties.

Parliamentary law. The right of a particular question, motion, or statement to take precedence over all other business before the house and to be considered immediately, notwithstanding any consequent interference with or setting aside the rules of procedure adopted by the house. The matter may be one of "personal privilege," where it concerns one member of the house in his capacity as a legislator, or of the "privilege of the house," where it concerns the rights, immunities, or dignity of the entire body, or of "constitutional privilege," where it relates to some action to be taken or some order of proceeding expressly enjoined by the constitution.

Privilege from arrest. A privilege extended to certain classes of persons, either by the rules of international law, the policy of the law, or the necessities of justice or of the administration of government, whereby they are exempted from arrest on civil process, and, in some cases, on criminal charges, either permanently, as in the case of a foreign minister and his suite, or temporarily, as in the case of members of the legislature, parties and witnesses engaged in a particular suit, etc. Art. I, § 6, U.S.Const. See also **Immunity.**

Privilege tax. A tax on the privilege of carrying on a business or occupation for which a license or franchise is required. Gulf & Ship Island R. Co. v. Hewes, 183 U.S. 66, 22 S.Ct. 26, 46 L.Ed. 86.

Torts. Privilege is the general term applied to certain rules of law by which particular circumstances justify conduct which otherwise would be tortious, and thereby defeat the tort liability (or defense) which, in the absence of such circumstances, ordinarily would follow from that conduct. In other words, even if all of the facts necessary to a prima facie case of tort liability can be proved, there are additional facts present sufficient to establish some privilege, and therefore defendant has committed no tort. Privileges thus differ from other defenses, such as contributory negligence, which operate to bar plaintiff's recovery but do not negate the tortious nature of defendant's conduct. Conversely, plaintiff's privilege may defeat a defense which defendant otherwise might have had. The term and concept of privilege apply primarily to the intentional torts, but also appear in other areas, such as defamation. (See *Libel and slander* above.)

A privilege may be based upon: (a) the consent of the other affected by the actor's conduct, or (b) the fact that its exercise is necessary for the protection of some interest of the actor or of the public which is of such importance as to justify the harm caused or threatened by its exercise, or (c) the fact that the actor is performing a function for the proper performance of which freedom of action is essential. Restatement, Second, Torts, § 10.

Privileges may be divided into two general categories: (1) consent, and (2) privileges created by law irrespective of consent. In general, the latter arise where there is some important and overriding social value in sanctioning defendant's conduct, despite the fact that it causes plaintiff harm.

Privilege is an affirmative defense which must be pleaded by defendant. Fed.R.Civil P. 8(c).

Writ of privilege. A common law process to enforce or maintain a privilege; particularly to secure the release of a person arrested in a civil suit contrary to his privilege.

Privilege against self-incrimination. The privilege derived from the Fifth Amendment, U.S.Const., and similar provisions in the constitutions of states. It requires the government to prove a criminal case against the defendant without the aid of the defendant as a witness against himself, though it protects only communications, not physical evidence such as handwriting and fingerprints. It is invocable by any witness who is called to the witness stand against his wishes whether the proceeding be a trial or grand jury hearing or a proceeding before an investigating body, but it is waived when the witness voluntarily takes the witness stand. See also **Immunity; Link-in-chain.**

Privileged. Possessing or enjoying a privilege; exempt from burdens; entitled to priority or precedence.

Privileged communications. Those statements made by certain persons within a protected relationship such as husband-wife, attorney-client, priest-penitent and the like which the law protects from forced disclosure on the witness stand at the option of the witness client, penitent, spouse. The extent of the privilege is governed by state statutes. Fed.Evid.Rule 501. See also **Attorney-client privilege; Communication; Conditionally privileged communication; Journalist's privilege.**

Privileged copyholds. See **Copyhold.**

Privileged debts. Those which an executor or administrator, trustee in bankruptcy, and the like, may pay in preference to others; such as funeral expenses, servants' wages, and doctors' bills during last sickness, etc. See also **Preferential debts.**

Privileged evidence. In addition to privileged communications *(q.v.)*, privileged evidence may also include governmental secrets or records, identity of informer, grand jury proceedings, certain types of accident reports, and attorney's work product.

Privileged vessel. That one of two vessels which, as against the other, ordinarily has the right or duty to hold her course and speed. Under International Rules, arts. 20, 22 (33 U.S.C.A. §§ 105, 107), a sailing vessel, except when the overtaking vessel, is always the privileged vessel, as against a steamer. But the fact that a vessel is privileged does not excuse her from failing to observe the rules, inattention to signals, or failure to answer where an answer is required, or from adopting such precautions as may be necessary to avoid a collision.

Privileges and immunities clause. There are two Privileges and Immunities Clauses in the federal Constitution and Amendments, the first being found in Art. IV, and the second in the 14th Amendment, § 1, second sentence, clause 1. The provision in Art. IV states that "The Citizens of each State shall be entitled to all Privileges and Immunities of Citizens in the several States," while the 14th Amendment provides that "No State shall make or enforce any law which shall abridge the privileges or immunities of citizens of the United States.

The purpose of these Clauses is to place the citizens of each State upon the same footing with citizens of other states, so far as the advantages resulting from citizenship in those states is concerned; to insure that a citizen of State A who ventures into State B be accorded the same privileges that the citizens of State B enjoy. Toomer v. Witsell, 334 U.S. 385, 68 S.Ct. 1156, 92 L.Ed. 1460. See also **Full faith and credit clause.**

Privilegia quæ re vera sunt in præjudicium reipublicæ, magis tamen habent speciosa frontispicia, et boni publici prætextum, quam bonæ et legales concessiones; sed prætextu liciti non debet admitti illictum /prìvəlíyj(iy)ə kwìy ríy víra sánt ìn prèjədísh(iy)əm ríyaypóblasiy, méyjəs téymən hǽbənt spìyshiyówsə fràntəspísh(iy)ə, èt bównay póblasay prətékstəm, kwǽm bówniy èt ləgéyliyz kən(t)sèshiyówniyz; sèd prətékst(y)uw lísaday nòn débənt ədmíday əlísədəm/. Privileges which are truly in prejudice of public good have, however, a more specious front and pretext of public good than good and legal grants; but, under pretext of legality, that which is illegal ought not to be admitted.

Privilegium /prìvəlíyj(iy)əm/. In Roman law, a special constitution by which the Roman emperor conferred on some single person some anomalous or irregular right, or imposed upon some single person some anomalous or irregular obligation, or inflicted on some single person some anomalous or irregular punishment. When such *privilegia* conferred anomalous rights, they were styled "favorable." When they imposed anomalous obligations, or inflicted anomalous punishments, they were styled "odious." A private law inflicting a punishment or conferring a reward.

In civil law, every peculiar right or favor granted by the law, contrary to the common rule. A species of lien or claim upon an article of property, not dependent upon possession, but continuing until either satisfied or released. Such is the lien, recognized by maritime law, of seamen upon the ship for their wages.

Privilegium clericale /prìvəlíyj(iy)əm klèhrəkéyliy/. The benefit of clergy (q.v.).

Privilegium est beneficium personale, et extinguitur cum persona /prìvəlíyj(iy)əm èst bènəfísh(iy)əm pərsənéyliy ed əkstíŋgwədər kàm pərsównə/. A privilege is a personal benefit, and dies with the person.

Privilegium est quasi privata lex /prìvəlíyj(iy)əm èst kwéysay prayvéydə léks/. Privilege is, as it were, a private law.

Privilegium non valet contra rempublicam /prìvəlíyj(iy)əm nòn vǽlət kóntrə rèmpóbləkəm/. Privilege is of no force against the commonwealth. Even necessity does not excuse, where the act to be done is against the commonwealth.

Privilegium, property propter /própərdiy próptər prìvəlíyj(iy)əm/. A qualified property in animals *feræ naturæ; i.e.,* a privilege of hunting, taking, and killing them, in exclusion of others.

Privity. Mutual or successive relationship to the same rights of property. In its broadest sense, "privity" is defined as mutual or successive relationships to the same right of property, or such an identification of interest of one person with another as to represent the same legal right. Petersen v. Fee Intern., Ltd., D.C.Okl., 435 F.Supp. 938, 942. Derivative interest founded on, or growing out of, contract, connection, or bond of union between parties; mutuality of interest. Hodgson v. Midwest Oil Co., C.C.A.Wyo., 17 F.2d 71, 75. Thus, the executor is in privity with the testator, the heir with the ancestor, the assignee with the assignor, the donee with the donor, and the lessee with the lessor. Litchfield v. Crane, 123 U.S. 549, 8 S.Ct. 210, 31 L.Ed. 199.

Concept of "privity" pertains to the relationship between a party to a suit and a person who was not a party, but whose interest in the action was such that he will be bound by the final judgment as if he were a party. Foltz v. Pullman Inc., Del.Super., 319 A.2d 38, 41.

Private knowledge; joint knowledge with another of a private concern; cognizance implying a consent or concurrence. See **Insider; Legal privity; Privy.**

Privity of blood. Such existed between an heir and his ancestor (privity in blood inheritable), and between coparceners. This privity was formerly of importance in the law of descent cast.

Privity of contract. That connection or relationship which exists between two or more contracting parties. It was traditionally essential to the maintenance of an action on any contract that there should subsist such privity between the plaintiff and defendant in respect of the matter sued on. However, the absence of privity as a defense in actions for damages in contract and tort actions is generally no longer viable with the enactment of warranty statutes (see *e.g.* U.C.C. § 2–318 below), acceptance by states of doctrine of strict liability *(q.v.),* and court decisions (*e.g.* MacPherson v. Buick Motor Co., 217 N.Y. 382, 111 N.E. 1050) which have extended the right to sue for injuries or damages to third party beneficiaries, and even innocent bystanders (Elmore v. American Motors Corp., 70 Cal.2d 578, 75 Cal.Rptr. 652, 451 P.2d 84).

U.C.C. § 2–318 provides three Alternative provisions (A–C) covering third party beneficiaries of express or implied warranties. Most states have enacted Alternative A: "A seller's warranty whether express or implied extends to any natural person who is in the family or household of his buyer or who is a guest in his home if it is reasonable to expect that such person may use, consume or be affected by the goods and who is injured in person by breach of the warranty. A seller may not exclude or limit the operation of this section." Other states have further broadened this model provision. For example Massachusetts U.C.C. § 2–318 provides: "Lack of privity between plaintiff and defendant shall be no defense in any action brought against the manufacturer, seller, lessor or supplier of goods to recover damages for breach of warranty, express or implied, or for negligence, although the plaintiff did not purchase the goods from the defendant if the plaintiff was a person whom the manufacturer, seller, lessor or supplier might reasonably have expected to use, consume or be affected by the goods. . . ."

Privity of estate. That which exists between lessor and lessee, tenant for life and remainderman or reversioner, etc., and their respective assignees, and between joint tenants and coparceners.

Privity of possession. Relationship which exists between parties in successive possession of real property. Such relationship becomes important in cases of adverse possession claims.

Privity or knowledge. Under Rev.St. §§ 4283–4286 (46 U.S.C.A. §§ 183–186) withholding the right to limit liability if the shipowner had "privity or knowledge" of the fault which occasioned damages, privity or knowledge must be actual and not merely constructive, and must involve a personal participation of the owner in some fault or act of negligence causing or contributing to the injury suffered. The words import actual knowledge of the things causing or contributing to the loss, or knowledge or means of knowledge of a condition of things likely to produce or contribute to the loss without adopting proper means to prevent it.

Privy. A person who is in privity with another. One who is a partaker or has any part or interest in any action, matter, or thing. See **Insider; Privies; Privity.**

As an adjective, the word has practically the same meaning as "private."

Privy council. In England, the principal council of the sovereign, composed of the cabinet ministers, and other persons chosen by the king or queen as privy councillors. The Judicial Committee of the Privy Council acts as a court of ultimate appeal in various cases. The importance of the Privy Council has been replaced to a great extent by the Cabinet.

Privy councillor. A member of the privy council.

Privy purse. In England, the income set apart for the sovereign's personal use.

Privy seal. In England, a seal used in making out grants or letters patent, preparatory to their passing under the great seal. A seal which the sovereign uses to such grants or things as pass the great seal. A seal of the British government which is affixed to documents not requiring the great seal.

Privy signet /prɪ́viy sɪ́gnət/. In English law, the signet or seal which is first used in making out grants and private letters and which is always in the custody of the Queen's secretaries.

Privy token /prɪ́viy tówkən/. A false mark or sign, forged object, counterfeited letter, key, ring, etc., used to deceive persons, and thereby fraudulently obtain possession of property. A false privy token is a false privy document or sign, not such as is calculated to deceive men generally, but designed to defraud one or more individuals. Cheating by such false token was not indictable at common law.

Privy verdict. A verdict given privily to the judge out of court, but which was of no force unless afterwards affirmed by a public verdict given openly in court. Now generally superseded by the "sealed verdict," *i.e.,* one written out, sealed up, and delivered to the judge or the clerk of the court.

Prize. Anything offered as a reward of contest. A reward offered to the person who, among several persons or among the public at large, shall first (or best) perform a certain undertaking or accomplish certain conditions. An award or recompense for some act done; some valuable thing offered by a person for something done by others. It is distinguished from a "bet" or "wager" in that it is known before the event who is to give either the premium or the prize, and there is but one operation until the accomplishment of the act, thing, or purpose for which it is offered.

The fair market value of a prize or award is generally includible in gross income. Certain exceptions are provided where the prize or award is made in recognition of religious, charitable, scientific, educational, artistic, literary, or civic achievement providing certain other requirements are met. I.R.C. § 74.

A vessel or cargo, belonging to one of two belligerent powers, apprehended or forcibly captured at sea by a war-vessel or privateer of the other belligerent, and claimed as enemy's property, and therefore liable to appropriation and condemnation under the laws of war. The apprehension and detention at sea of a ship or other vessel, by authority of a belligerent power, either with the design of appropriating it, with the goods and effects it contains, or with that of becoming master of the whole or a part of its cargo.

Prize courts. Courts having jurisdiction to adjudicate upon captures made at sea in time of war, and to condemn the captured property as prize if lawfully subject to that sentence. In England, the admiralty courts have jurisdiction as prize courts, distinct from the jurisdiction on the instance side. A special commission issues in time of war to the judge of the admiralty court, to enable him to hold such court. In the United States, the federal district courts have jurisdiction in cases of prize. 28 U.S.C.A. § 1333.

Prize goods. Goods which are taken on the high seas, *jure belli,* out of the hands of the enemy.

Prize law. The system of laws and rules applicable to the capture of prize at sea; its condemnation, rights of the captors, distribution of the proceeds, etc.

Prize money. A dividend from the proceeds of a captured vessel, etc., paid to the captors. U. S. v. Steever, 113 U.S. 747, 5 S.Ct. 765, 28 L.Ed. 1133.

Pro. For; in respect of; on account of; in behalf of. The introductory word of many Latin phrases.

Proamita /prowǽmədə/. Lat. In the civil law, a great paternal aunt; the sister of one's grandfather.

Proamita magna /prowǽmədə mǽgnə/. Lat. In the civil law, a great-great-aunt.

Pro and con /prów ən kón/. For and against. A phrase descriptive of the presentation of arguments or evidence on both sides of a disputed question.

Proavia /prowéyv(i)yə/. Lat. In the civil law, a great-grandmother.

Proavunculus /pròwəvə́ŋkyələs/. Lat. In the civil law, a great-grandfather's or great-grandmother's brother.

Proavus /prówəvəs/. Lat. In the civil law, a great-grandfather. Employed in making genealogical tables.

Probability. Likelihood; appearance of reality or truth; reasonable ground of presumption; verisimilitude; consonance to reason. The likelihood of a proposition or hypothesis being true, from its conformity to reason or experience, or from superior evidence or arguments adduced in its favor. A condition or state created when there is more evidence in favor of the existence of a given proposition than there is against it.

High probability rule. A rule relating to the right of insured to abandon a vessel, by virtue of which the right of abandonment does not depend upon the certainty, but upon the high probability of a total loss, either of the property, or voyage, or both. The result is to act not upon certainties, but upon probabilities; and if the facts present a case of extreme hazard, and of probable expense, exceeding half the value of the ship, the insured may abandon, though it should happen that she was afterwards recovered at a less expense.

Probable. Having the appearance of truth; having the character of probability; appearing to be founded in reason or experience. Having more evidence for than against; supported by evidence which inclines the mind to believe, but leaves some room for doubt; likely. See also **Possible.**

Probable cause. Reasonable cause; having more evidence for than against. A reasonable ground for belief in the existence of facts warranting the proceedings complained of. An apparent state of facts found to exist upon reasonable inquiry (that is, such inquiry as the given case renders convenient and proper), which would induce a reasonably intelligent and prudent man to believe, in a criminal case, that the accused person had committed the crime charged, or, in a civil case, that a cause of action existed. Cook v. Singer Sewing Mach. Co., 138 Cal.App. 418, 32 P.2d 430, 431. See also **Information and belief; Reasonable and probable cause; Reasonable belief; Reasonable grounds.**

Arrest, search and seizure. Reasonable grounds for belief that a person should be arrested or searched. Probable cause exists where the facts and circumstances would warrant a person of reasonable caution to believe that an offense was or is being committed. Com. v. Stewart, 358 Mass. 747, 267 N.E.2d 213. Probable cause is the existence of circumstances which would lead a reasonably prudent man to believe in guilt of arrested party; mere suspicion or belief, unsupported by facts or circumstances, is insufficient. State v. Jones, 248 Or. 428, 435 P.2d 317, 319. It permits an officer to arrest one for a felony without a warrant. Probable cause justifying officer's arrest without warrant has been defined as situation where officer has more evidence favoring suspicion that person is guilty of crime than evidence against such suspicion, but there is some room for doubt. Nugent v. Superior Court for San Mateo County, 254 C.A.2d 420, 62 Cal.Rptr. 217, 221.

Probable cause exists when facts and circumstances within officer's knowledge and of which he has reasonably trustworthy information are sufficient to warrant a man of reasonable caution in believing that offense has been or is being committed. State v. Kolb, N.D., 239 N.W.2d 815, 817. Probable cause for search and seizure with or without search warrant involves probabilities which are not technical but factual and practical considerations of every day life upon which reasonable and prudent men act, and essence of probable cause is reasonable ground for belief of guilt. Paula v. State, Fla.App., 188 So.2d 388, 390.

The finding of probable cause for issuance of an arrest warrant (as required by 4th Amend.) may be based upon hearsay evidence in whole or part. Fed. R.Crim.P. 4(b). See also Rule 5.1(a) (Preliminary examination), and Rule 41(c) (search and seizure).

See also **Arrest; Probable cause hearing; Search; Search-warrant.**

False imprisonment action. For arrest which must be shown as justification by defendants in action for false imprisonment is reasonable ground of suspicion supported by circumstances sufficient in themselves to warrant cautious man in believing accused to be guilty, but does not depend on actual state of case in point of fact, as it may turn out upon legal investigation, but on knowledge of facts which would be sufficient to induce reasonable belief in truth of accusation. Christ v. McDonald, 152 Or. 494, 52 P.2d 655, 658.

Probable cause hearing. That procedural step in the criminal process at which the judge or magistrate decides whether a complaint should issue or a person should be bound over to a grand jury on a showing of probable cause. See **Preliminary hearing.**

Probable consequence. One that is more likely to follow its supposed cause than it is not to follow it.

Probable evidence. Presumptive evidence is so called, from its foundation in probability.

Probably. In all probability; so far as the evidence shows; presumably; likely.

Probandi necessitas incumbit illi qui agit /prəbǽnday nəsésətæs ənkámbəd ílay kwày éyjət/. The necessity of proving lies with him who sues. In other words, the burden of proof of a proposition is upon him who advances it affirmatively.

Probate. Court procedure by which a will is proved to be valid or invalid; though in current usage this term has been expanded to generally include all matters and proceedings pertaining to administration of estates, guardianships, etc. See **Letters; Probate court; Probate jurisdiction.**

In the canon law, "probate" consisted of *probatio,* the proof of the will by the executor, and *approbatio,* the approbation given by the ecclesiastical judge to the proof.

Probate bond. One required by law to be given to the probate court or judge, as incidental to proceedings in such courts, such as the bonds of executors, administrators, and guardians.

Probate code. The body or system of law relating to all matters of which probate courts have jurisdiction; *e.g.* Uniform Probate Code.

Probate court. A court having general powers over probate of wills, administration of estates, and, in some States, empowered to appoint guardians or approve the adoption of minors. Court with similar functions is called Surrogate or Orphan's Court in certain states. See also **Court of orphan's; Probate jurisdiction.**

Probate duty. A tax laid by government on every will admitted to probate or on the gross value of the personal property of the deceased testator, and payable out of the decedent's estate. See also **Estate tax; Inheritance tax.**

Probate homestead. See **Homestead.**

Probate jurisdiction. The exercise of the ordinary, generally understood power of a probate, surrogate or orphan's court, which includes the establishment of wills, settlement of decedents' estates, supervision of guardianship of infants, control of their property, and other powers and functions pertaining to such subjects. See also **Probate court.**

Probate proceeding. A general designation of the actions and proceedings whereby the law is administered upon the various subjects within "probate jurisdiction" (q.v.).

Probatio /prəbéysh(iy)ow/. Lat. Proof; more particularly direct, as distinguished from indirect or circumstantial evidence.

Probatio mortua /prəbéysh(iy)ow mórchuwə/. Dead proof; that is proof by inanimate objects, such as deeds or other written evidence.

Probation. The evidence which proves a thing; the act of proving; proof; trial; test. Used in the latter sense when referring to the initial period of employment during which a new, transferred, or promoted employee must prove or show that he is capable of performing the required duties of the job or position before he will be considered as permanently employed in such position. As applied to teachers, term means that teacher is on trial, with his competence and suitability remaining to be finally determined. Turner v. Board of Trustees, Calexico Unified School Dist., 121 Cal.Rptr. 705, 535 P.2d 1171, 1178.

A sentence releasing the defendant into the community under the supervision of a probation officer. The status of a convicted person who is allowed his freedom after conviction subject to the condition that for a stipulated period he shall conduct himself in a manner approved by a special officer to whom he must make periodic reports. Probation is release by court before sentence has commenced. State v. Gates, 230 Or. 84, 368 P.2d 605. Compare **Parole.**

System of allowing a person convicted of some lesser offense (frequently juveniles or first offenders) to avoid imprisonment, under a suspension of sentence, during good behavior, and generally under the supervision of a probation officer. An act of grace and clemency which may be granted by the trial court to a seemingly deserving defendant whereby such defendant may escape the extreme rigors of the penalty imposed by law for the offense of which he stands convicted. People v. Leach, 22 Cal.App.2d 525, 71 P.2d 594, 595.

Probationer. A convicted offender who is allowed to go at large, under suspension of sentence, during good behavior.

Probationes debent esse evidentes, id est, perspicuæ et faciles intelligi /prəbèyshiyówniyz débənt ésiy èvədéntiyz, íd èst, pərspíkyuway èt fǽsəliyz intélǝjay/. Proofs ought to be evident, that is, perspicuous and easily understood.

Probation officer. One who supervises a person (commonly juveniles) placed on probation by a court in a criminal proceeding. He is required to report to the court the progress of the probationer and to surrender him if he violates the terms and conditions of his probation.

Probatio plena /prəbéysh(iy)ow plíynə/. In the civil law, full proof; proof by two witnesses, or a public instrument.

Probatio semi-plena /prəbéysh(iy)ow sémayplíynə/. In the civil law, half-full proof; half-proof. Proof by one witness, or a private instrument.

Probatio viva /prəbéysh(iy)ow váyvə/. Living proof; that is, proof by the mouth of living witnesses.

Probatis extremis, præsumuntur media /prəbéydəs əkstríymǝs, prìyzyəmántər míyd(i)yə/. The extremes being proved, the intermediate proceedings are presumed.

Probative evidence /prówbədəv/. In the law of evidence, having the effect of proof; tending to prove, or actually proving. Testimony carrying quality of proof and having fitness to induce conviction of truth, consisting of fact and reason co-operating as co-ordinate factors. Globe Indemnity Co. v. Daviess, 243 Ky. 356, 47 S.W.2d 990, 992.

Term "probative," as applied to evidence means that which furnishes, establishes, or contributes toward proof. Akin v. Hill's Estate, 201 Kan. 306, 440 P.2d 585, 590. Evidence has "probative value" if it tends to prove an issue. Liquor Control Commission v. Bartolas, 10 Ohio Misc. 225, 225 N.E.2d 859, 862, 39 O.O.2d 343.

See **Relevant evidence.**

Probative facts. In the law of evidence, facts which actually have effect of proving facts sought; evidentiary facts. Matters of evidence required to prove ultimate facts. Johnson v. Inter-Southern Life Ins. Co., 244 Ky. 83, 50 S.W.2d 16.

Probator /prəbéydər/. In old English law, strictly, an accomplice in felony who to save himself confessed the fact, and charged or accused any other as principal or accessory, against whom he was bound to make good his charge. It also signified an approver, or one who undertakes to prove a crime charged upon another.

Probatum est /prəbéydəm èst/. Lat. It is tried or proved.

Pro bono /prów bównow/. Lit. For the good; used to describe work or services (e.g. legal services) done or performed free of charge.

Pro bono et malo /pròw bównow èt mǽlow/. For good and ill; for advantage and detriment.

Pro bono publico /pròw bównow páblakow/. For the public good; for the welfare of the whole.

Probus et legalis homo /prówbas èt lagéylas hówmow/. Lat. A good and lawful man. A phrase particularly applied to a juror or witness who was free from all exception, and competent in point of law to serve on juries. In the plural form: *probi et legales homines.*

Procedendo /pròwsadéndow/. Action wherein court of superior jurisdiction orders court of inferior jurisdiction to proceed to judgment but has no bearing on nature of judgment to be entered. State ex rel. Jacobs v. Municipal Court of Franklin County, 26 Ohio App.2d 113, 269 N.E.2d 629, 631, 55 O.O.2d 245. A writ by which a cause which has been removed from an inferior to a superior court by *certiorari* or otherwise is sent down again to the same court, *to be proceeded in* there, where it appears to the superior court that it was removed on insufficient grounds.

More commonly, a case returned to a lower court is said to be remanded to such court.

A writ *(procedendo ad judicium)* which issued out of the common-law jurisdiction of the court of chancery, when judges of any subordinate court delayed the parties for that they would not give judgment either on the one side or on the other, when they ought so to do. In such a case, a writ of *procedendo ad judicium* was awarded, commanding the inferior court in the sovereign's name to proceed to give judgment, but without specifying any particular judgment. It was the earliest remedy for the refusal or neglect of justice on the part of the courts. In re Press Printers & Publishers, C.C.A.N.J., 12 F.2d 660, 664.

A writ by which the commission of a justice of the peace is revived, after having been suspended. 1 Bl.Comm. 353.

Procedendo on aid prayer /pròwsadéndow òn éyd pré(ya)r/. If one pray in aid of the crown in real action, and aid be granted, it shall be awarded that he sue to the sovereign in chancery, and the justices in the common pleas shall stay until this writ of *procedendo de loquela* come to them. So, also, on a personal action.

Procedural due process. Those safeguards to one's liberty and property mandated by the 14th Amend., U.S.Const., such as the right to counsel appointed for one who is indigent, the right to a copy of a transcript, the right of confrontation; all of which are specifically provided for in the 6th Amendment and made applicable to the states' procedure by the 14th Amendment.

Central meaning of procedural due process is that parties whose rights are to be affected are entitled to be heard and, in order that they may enjoy that right, they must be notified. Parham v. Cortese, 407 U.S. 67, 92 S.Ct. 1983, 1994, 32 L.Ed.2d 556. Reasonable notice and opportunity to be heard and present any claim or defense are embodied in the term "procedural due process." In re Nelson, 78 N.M. 739, 437 P.2d 1008.

Procedural law. That which prescribes method of enforcing rights or obtaining redress for their invasion; machinery for carrying on procedural aspects of civil or criminal action; *e.g.* Rules of Civil, Criminal, and Appellate Procedure, as adopted by the Federal and most state courts. Barker v. St. Louis County, 340 Mo. 986, 104 S.W.2d 371, 377, 378, 379; Schultz v. Gosselink, 260 Iowa 115, 148 N.W.2d 434, 436. As a general rule, laws which fix duties, establish rights and responsibilities among and for persons, natural or otherwise, are "substantive laws" in character, while those which merely prescribe the manner in which such rights and responsibilities may be exercised and enforced in a court are "procedural laws". State ex rel. Blood v. Gibson Circuit Court, 239 Ind. 394, 157 N.E.2d 475, 478. See also **Procedure.**

Procedure. The mode of proceeding by which a legal right is enforced, as distinguished from the substantive law which gives or defines the right, and which, by means of the proceeding, the court is to administer; the machinery, as distinguished from its product. That which regulates the formal steps in an action or other judicial proceeding; a form, manner, and order of conducting suits or prosecutions. The judicial process for enforcing rights and duties recognized by substantive law and for justly administering redress for infraction of them. Sims v. United Pacific Ins. Co., D.C.Idaho, 51 F.Supp. 433, 435.

Procedure is machinery for carrying on suit including pleading, process, evidence and practice, whether in trial court or appellate court. Brooks v. Texas Emp. Ins. Ass'n, Tex.Civ.App., 358 S.W.2d 412, 414.

The law of procedure is what is commonly termed by jurists "adjective law" *(q.v.).*

See also **Procedural law.**

Proceeding. In a general sense, the form and manner of conducting juridical business before a court or judicial officer. Regular and orderly progress in form of law, including all possible steps in an action from its commencement to the execution of judgment. Term also refers to administrative proceedings before agencies, tribunals, bureaus, or the like.

An act which is done by the authority or direction of the court, agency, or tribunal, express or implied; an act necessary to be done in order to obtain a given end; a prescribed mode of action for carrying into effect a legal right. All the steps or measures adopted in the prosecution or defense of an action. Statter v. United States, C.C.A.Alaska, 66 F.2d 819, 822. The word may be used synonymously with "action" or "suit" to describe the entire course of an action at law or suit in equity from the issuance of the writ or filing of the complaint until the entry of a final judgment, or may be used to describe any act done by authority of a court of law and every step required to be taken in any cause by either party. The proceedings of a suit embrace *all* matters that occur in its progress judicially.

Term "proceeding" may refer not only to a complete remedy but also to a mere procedural step that is part of a larger action or special proceeding. Rooney v. Vermont Investment Corp., 10 Cal.3d 351, 110 Cal.Rptr. 353, 365, 515 P.2d 297. A "proceeding" includes action and special proceedings before judicial tribunals as well as proceedings pending before quasi-judicial officers and boards. State ex rel. Johnson v. Independent School Dist. No. 810, Wabasha County, 260 Minn. 237, 109 N.W.2d 596, 602. In a more particular sense, any application to a court of justice, however made, for aid in the enforcement of rights, for relief, for redress of injuries, for damages, or for any remedial object.

"Proceeding" means any action, hearing, investigation, inquest, or inquiry (whether conducted by a court, administrative agency, hearing officer, arbitrator, legislative body, or any other person authorized by law) in which, pursuant to law, testimony can be compelled to be given. Calif.Evid.Code.

Collateral proceeding. One in which the particular question may arise or be involved incidentally, but which is not instituted for the very purpose of deciding such question; as in the rule that a judgment cannot be attacked, or a corporation's right to exist be questioned, in any collateral proceeding. See **Collateral estoppel doctrine.**

Legal proceedings. See **Legal proceedings.**

Ordinary proceedings. Those founded on the regular and usual mode of carrying on a suit by due course at common law.

Special proceeding. Generic term for remedies or proceedings which are not ordinary actions; *e.g.* condemnation (Fed.R.Civil P. 71A); vesting title (Rule 70).

A "special proceeding" has reference only to such proceedings as may be commenced independently of a pending action by petition or motion upon notice in order to obtain special relief, and, generally speaking, a special proceeding is confined to type of case which was not, under the common-law or equity practice, either an action at law or a suit in equity. Church v. Humboldt County, 248 C.A.2d 855, 57 Cal.Rptr. 79, 81.

Summary proceeding. Any proceeding by which a controversy is settled, case disposed of, or trial conducted, in a prompt and simple manner, without the aid of a jury, without presentment or indictment, or in other respects out of the regular course of the common law. In procedure, proceedings are said to be summary when they are short and simple in comparison with regular proceedings; *e.g.* conciliation or small claims court proceedings as contrasted with usual civil trial.

Supplementary proceeding. A separate proceeding in an original action, in which the court where the action is pending is called upon to exercise its jurisdiction in aid of execution of the judgment in the action. It is a statutory equivalent in actions at law of the creditor's bill in equity, and in the majority of states where law and equity are merged, is provided as a substitute therefor. See *e.g.* Fed.R.Civil P. 69. In this proceeding the judgment debtor is summoned to appear before the court (or a referee or examiner) and submit to an oral examination touching all his property and effects, and if property subject to execution and in his possession or control is thus discovered, he is ordered to deliver it up, or a receiver may be appointed. See **Execution; Supplementary proceedings.**

Proceeds. Issues; income; yield; receipts; produce; money or articles or other thing of value arising or obtained by the sale of property; the sum, amount, or value of property sold or converted into money or into other property. Proceeds does not necessarily mean only cash or money. Phelps v. Harris, 101 U.S. 370, 25 L.Ed. 855. That which results, proceeds, or accrues from some possession or transaction. State Highway Commission v. Spainhower, Mo., 504 S.W.2d 121, 125. The funds received from disposition of assets or from the issue of securities.

Proceeds includes whatever is received when collateral or proceeds is sold, exchanged, collected or otherwise disposed of. The term also includes the account arising when the right to payment is earned under a contract right. Money, checks and the like are "cash proceeds". All other proceeds are "non-cash proceeds". U.C.C. § 9–306(1).

Proceres /prósəriyz/. Nobles; lords. The house of lords in England is called, in Latin, *"Domus Procerum."* Formerly, the chief magistrates in cities.

Process. A series of actions, motions, or occurrences; progressive act or transaction; continuous operation; method, mode or operation, whereby a result or effect is produced; normal or actual course of procedure; regular proceeding, as, the process of vegetation or decomposition; a chemical process; processes of nature. Sokol v. Stein Fur Dyeing Co., 216 App.Div. 573, 216 N.Y.S. 167, 169; Kelley v. Coe, App.D.C., 99 F.2d 435, 441.

Process is mode, method or operation whereby a result is produced; and means to prepare for market or to convert into marketable form. Employment Security Commission of Ariz. v. Bruce Church, Inc., 109 Ariz. 183, 507 P.2d 108, 112.

Patent Law

An art or method by which any particular result is produced. An act or series of acts performed upon the subject-matter to be transformed or reduced to a different state or thing. A means or method employed to produce a certain result or effect, or a mode of treatment of given materials to produce a desired result, either by chemical action, by the operation or application of some element or power of nature, or of one substance to another, irrespective of any machine or mechanical device; in this sense a "process" is patentable, though, strictly speaking, it is the art and not the process which is the subject of patent. Broadly speaking, a "process" is a definite combination of new or old elements, ingredients, operations, ways, or means to produce a new, improved or old result, and any substantial change therein by omission, to the same or better result, or by modification or substitution, with different function, to the same or better result, is a new and patentable process.

Civil and Criminal Proceedings

Process is defined as any means used by court to acquire or exercise its jurisdiction over a person or over specific property. Austin Liquor Mart, Inc. v. Department of Revenue, 18 Ill.App.3d 894, 310 N.E.2d 719, 728. Means whereby court compels appearance of defendant before it or a compliance with its demands. Dansby v. Dansby, 222 Ga. 118, 149 S.E.2d 252, 254.

When actions were commenced by original writ, instead of, as at present, by summons, the method of compelling the defendant to appear was by what was termed "original process," being founded on the original writ, and so called also to distinguish it from "mesne" or "intermediate" process, which was some writ or process which issued during the progress of the suit. The word "process," however, as now commonly understood, refers to a summons, or, summons and complaint, and, less commonly, to a writ. The content of the summons, and service requirements, are provided for in Rule of Civil Proc. 4.

See also Abuse *(Process)*; Alias process; Compulsory process; Constructive service of process; Executory process; Long arm statute; Malicious abuse of legal process; Malicious use of process; Prohibition; Service *(Service of process)*; Summons.

Abuse of process. See **Abuse.**

Alias process. See that title.

Compulsory process. See **Compulsory.**

Criminal process. See **Warrant.**

Final process. The last process in an action; *i.e.* process issued to enforce execution of judgment.

Irregular process. Term is usually applied to process not issued in strict conformity with the law, whether the defect appears upon the face of the process, or by reference to extrinsic facts, and whether such defects render the process absolutely void or only voidable. Under current practice, a defective summons may be amended under Rule of Civil Proc. 15.

Judicial process. In a wide sense, this term may include all the acts of a court from the beginning to the end of its proceedings in a given cause; but more specifically it means the writ, summons, mandate, or other process which is used to inform the defendant of the institution of proceedings against him and to compel his appearance, in either civil or criminal cases.

Legal process. This term is sometimes used as equivalent to "lawful process." Thus, it is said that legal process means process not merely fair on its face, but in fact valid. But properly it means a summons, writ, warrant, mandate, or other process issuing from a court.

Mesne process. As distinguished from *final* process, this signifies any writ or process issued between the commencement of the action and the suing out of execution. "Mesne" in this connection may be defined as intermediate; intervening; the middle between two extremes. The writ of *capias ad respondendum* was called "mesne" to distinguish it, on the one hand, from the original process by which a suit was formerly commenced; and, on the other, from the final process of execution.

Original process. That by which a judicial proceeding is instituted; process to compel the appearance of the defendant. Distinguished from "mesne" process, which issues, during the progress of a suit, for some subordinate or collateral purpose; and from "final" process, which is process of execution. See **Summons.**

Process of interpleader. A means of determining the right to property claimed by each of two or more persons, which is in the possession of a third. See **Interpleader.**

Process of law. See **Due process of law.**

Regular process. Such as is issued according to rule and the prescribed practice, or which emanates, lawfully and in a proper case, from a court or magistrate possessing jurisdiction.

Service of process. See **Service.**

Summary process. Such as is immediate or instantaneous, in distinction from the ordinary course, by emanating and taking effect without intermediate applications or delays. In some jurisdictions (*e.g.* Massachusetts), term used to describe action for eviction of tenant.

Trustee process. The name given in some states (particularly in New England) to the process of garnishment or foreign attachment.

Void process. Such as was issued without power in the court to award it, or which the court had not acquired jurisdiction to issue in the particular case, or which fails in some material respect to comply with the requisite form of legal process.

Process agent. Person authorized to accept service of process in behalf of another (*e.g.* on behalf of corporation).

Processioning. Subjecting to some special treatment, to prepare for the market, to convert into marketable form, to make usable, marketable or the like. State v. Four States Drilling Co., 278 Ala. 273, 177 So.2d 828, 831.

A survey and inspection of boundaries formerly performed in some of the American colonies by the local authorities. It was analogous in part to the English perambulation *(q.v.)*, and was superseded by the introduction of the practice of accurate surveying and of recording.

Process patent. A process patent is one concerning mode of treatment of certain materials to produce certain result. Phillips Petroleum Co. v. Sid Richardson Carbon & Gasoline Co., C.A.Tex., 416 F.2d 10, 11.

"Product patent" applies to discovered article, and "process patent" applies to new method of making an article. Ethyl Corp. v. Hercules Powder Co., D.C. Del., 232 F.Supp. 453, 457.

See also **Process** *(Patent law)*.

Process server. Person authorized by law (*e.g.* sheriff) to serve process papers on defendant.

Processum continuando /prəsésəm kəntìnyuwǽndow/. In old English practice, a writ for the continuance of process after the death of the chief justice or other justices in the commission of *oyer* and *terminer*.

Processus legis est gravis vexatio; executio legis coronat opus /prəsésəm líyjəs èst gréyvəs vekséysh(iy)ow; èksəkyúwsh(iy)ow kərównəd òwpəs/. The process of the law is a grievous vexation; the execution of the law crowns the work. The proceedings in an action while in progress are burdensome and vexatious; the execution, being the end and object of the action, crowns the labor, or rewards it with success.

Procès-verbal. In French law, a true relation in writing in due form of law, of what has been done and said verbally in the presence of a public officer, and what he himself does upon the occasion. It is a species of inquisition of office, and must be signed by the officer.

Prochein ami /prəshén əmíy/. (Spelled, also, *prochein amy* and *prochain amy*.) Next friend. As an infant cannot legally sue in his own name, the action must be brought by his *prochein ami;* that is, some friend (not being his guardian) who will appear as plaintiff in his name.

Prochronism /pró(w)krənizəm/. An error in chronology, consisting in dating a thing before it happened.

Procinctus /prəsíŋ(k)təs/. Lat. In the Roman law, a girding or preparing for battle. *Testamentum in procinctu,* a will made by a soldier, while girding himself, or preparing to engage in battle.

Proclaim. To promulgate; to announce; to publish, by governmental authority, intelligence of public acts or transactions or other matters important to be known by the people. To give wide publicity to; to disclose.

Proclamation. The act of publicly proclaiming or publishing; a formal declaration; an avowal. The act of causing some governmental matters to be published or made generally known. A written or printed document in which are contained such matters, issued by proper authority, usually by a high governmental executive (President, Governor, Mayor).

The declaration made by the bailiff, by authority of the court, that something is about to be done.

In equity practice, proclamation made by a sheriff upon a writ of attachment, summoning a defendant who has failed to appear personally to appear and answer the plaintiff's bill.

Proclamation by lord of manor. In old English law, proclamation made by the lord of a manor (thrice repeated) requiring the heir or devisee of a deceased copyholder to present himself, pay the fine, and be admitted to the estate; failing which appearance, the lord might seize the lands *quousque* (provisionally).

Proclamation of a fine. The notice or proclamation at common law which was made after the engrossment of a fine of lands, and which consisted in its being openly read in court sixteen times, viz., four times in the term in which it was made, and four times in each of the three succeeding terms, which, however, was afterwards reduced to one reading in each term.

Proclamation of exigents /pròkləméyshən əv égzəjənts/. In old English law, when an *exigent* was awarded, a writ of proclamation issued, at the same time, commanding the sheriff of the county wherein the defendant dwelt to make three proclamations thereof in places the most notorious, and most likely to come to his knowledge, a month before the outlawry should take place.

Proclamation of rebellion. In old English law, a proclamation to be made by the sheriff commanding the attendance of a person who had neglected to obey a subpœna or attachment in chancery. If he did not surrender himself after this proclamation, a commission of rebellion issued.

Proclamation of recusants /pròkləméyshən əv rékyəzənts/°rəkyúwzənts/. A proclamation whereby recusants were formerly convicted, on non-appearance at the assizes.

Proclamator /prókləmeydər/. An officer of the English court of common pleas.

Pro confesso /pròw kənfésow/. For confessed; as confessed. A term applied to a bill in equity, and the decree founded upon it, where no answer is made to it by the defendant. Under rules practice, this has been replaced by a default for want of prosecution. Fed.R.Civil P. 55(a).

Pro consilio /pròw kən(t)síl(i)yow/. For counsel given. An annuity *pro consilio* amounts to a condition, but in a feoffment or lease for life, etc., it is the consideration, and does not amount to a condition; for the state of the land by the feoffment is executed, and the grant of the annuity is executory.

Pro-consul /pròwkón(t)səl/. Lat. In the Roman law, originally a consul whose command was prolonged after his office had expired. An officer with consular authority, but without the title of "consul." The governor of a province.

Pro corpore regni /pròw kórpəriy régnay/. In behalf of the body of the realm.

Procreation. The generation of children.

Proctor /próktər/. One appointed to manage the affairs of another or represent him in judgment. A procurator, proxy, or attorney. Formerly, an officer of the admiralty and ecclesiastical courts whose duties and business correspond exactly to those of an attorney at law or solicitor in chancery. See also **Power of attorney; Procuration; Proxy.**

Procuracy /prókyərəsiy/. The writing or instrument which authorizes a procurator to act.

Procurador del comun /pròkuraðór dèl komúwn/. Sp. In Spanish law, an officer appointed to make inquiry, put a petitioner in possession of land prayed for, and execute the orders of the executive in that behalf. Lecompte v. U. S., 52 U.S. (11 How.) 115, 126, 13 L.Ed. 627.

Procurare /pròkyəréry/. Lat. To take care of another's affairs for him, or in his behalf; to manage; to take care of or superintend.

Procuratio /pròkyəréysh(iy)ow/. Lat. Management of another's affairs by his direction and in his behalf; procuration; agency.

Procuratio est exhibitio sumptuum necessariorum facta prælatis, qui diœceses peragrando, ecclesias subjectas visitant /pròkyəréysh(iy)ow èst èksəbísh(iy)ow sám(p)chuwəm nèsəsèriyórəm fæktə prəléydəs, kway dàyəsíyziyz pèrəgrǽndow, əklíyziyəs səbjéktəs vízətænt/. Procuration is the providing of necessaries for the bishops, who, in traveling through their dioceses, visit the churches subject to them.

Procuration /pròkyəréyshən/. Agency; proxy; the act of constituting another one's attorney in fact. The act by which one person gives power to another to act in his place, as he could do himself. Action under a power of attorney or other constitution of agency. Indorsing a bill or note "by procuration" is doing it as proxy for another or by his authority. The use of the word procuration (usually, *per procuratione,* or abbreviated to *per proc.* or *p. p.*) on a promissory note by an agent is notice that the agent has but a limited authority to sign.

An *express* procuration is one made by the express consent of the parties. An *implied* or *tacit* procuration takes place when an individual sees another managing his affairs and does not interfere to prevent it. Procurations are also divided into those which contain absolute power, or a general authority, and those which give only a limited power.

Also, the act or offence of procuring women for lewd purposes.

See also **Proctor.**

Procurationem adversus nulla est præscriptio /pròkyərèyshiyównəm ədvársəs nálə èst prəskrípsh(iy)ow/. There is no prescription against procuration.

Procuration fee, or money /pròkyəréyshən fíy/ °mániy/. In English law, brokerage or commission allowed to scriveners and solicitors for obtaining loans of money.

Procurator /prókyərèydər/. In the civil law, a proctor; a person who acts for another by virtue of a procuration.

In old English law, an agent or attorney; a bailiff or servant. A proxy of a lord in parliament.

In ecclesiastical law, one who collected the fruits of a benefice for another. An advocate of a religious house, who was to solicit the interest and plead the causes of the society. A proxy or representative of a parish church.

See **Proctor; Procuration.**

Procuratores ecclesiæ parochialis /pròkyərətóriyz əklíyziyiy pəròwkiyéyləs/. The old name for churchwardens.

Procurator in rem suam /pròkyəréydər ìn rém s(y)úwəm/. Proctor (attorney) in his own affair, or with reference to his own property. This term is used in Scotch law to denote that a person is acting under a procuration (power of attorney) with reference to a thing which has become his own property.

Procuratorium /pròkyərətóriyəm/. In old English law, the procuratory or instrument by which any person or community constituted or delegated their *procurator* or proctors to represent them in any judicial court or cause.

Procurator litis /pròkyəréydər láydəs/. In the civil law, one who by command of another institutes and carries on for him a suit. *Procurator* is properly used of the attorney of *actor* (the plaintiff), *defensor* of the attorney of *reus* (the defendant). It is distinguished from *advocatus,* who was one who undertook the defence of persons, not things, and who was generally the patron of the person whose defence he prepared, the person himself speaking it. It is also distinguished from *cognitor* who conducted the cause in the presence of his principal, and generally in cases of citizenship; whereas the procurator conducted the cause in the absence of his principal.

Procurator negotiorum /pròkyəréydər nəgòwshiyórəm/. In the civil law, an attorney in fact; a manager of business affairs for another person.

Procurator provinciæ /pròkyəréydər prəvínshiyiy/. In Roman law, a provincial officer who managed the affairs of the revenue, and had a judicial power in matters that concerned the revenue.

Procuratrix /pròkyəréytrəks/. In old English law, a female agent or attorney in fact.

Procure. To initiate a proceeding; to cause a thing to be done; to instigate; to contrive, bring about, effect, or cause. To persuade, induce, prevail upon, or cause a person to do something. Rose v. Hunter, 155 Cal. App.2d 319, 317 P.2d 1027, 1030. To obtain, as a prostitute, for another. Procure connotes action and means to cause, acquire, gain, get, obtain, bring about, cause to be done. Ford v. City of Caldwell, 79 Idaho 499, 321 P.2d 589, 593. To find or introduce;— said of a broker who obtains a customer. To bring the seller and the buyer together so that the seller has an opportunity to sell. See also **Finder; Pander; Procurer.**

Procurement. The act of obtaining, attainment, acquisition, bringing about, effecting. Ford v. City of Caldwell, 79 Idaho 499, 321 P.2d 589, 593. See also **Procure.**

Procurement contract. A government contract with a manufacturer or supplier of goods or machinery or services under the terms of which a sale is made to the government. Such contracts are governed by government regulations, standard forms, etc.

Procurer /prəkyúrər/. One who prevails upon, induces or persuades a person to do something. One who procures for another the gratification of his lusts; a pimp; a panderer. One who solicits trade for a prostitute or lewd woman. One that procures the seduction or prostitution of girls. The offense is punishable by statute. See *e.g.* Model Penal Code, § 251.2.

One who uses means to bring anything about, especially one who does so secretly and corruptly. As regards solicitation of crime, see **Solicitation.**

Procureur /pròkyur(y)úr/. In French law, an attorney; one who has received a commission from another to act on his behalf. There were in France two classes of *procureurs: Procureurs ad negotia,* appointed by an individual to act for him in the administration of his affairs; persons invested with a power of attorney; corresponding to "attorneys in fact." *Procureurs ad lites* were persons appointed and authorized to act for a party in a court of justice. These corresponded to attorneys at law (now called, in England, "solicitors of the supreme court"). The order of *procureurs* was abolished in 1791, and that of *avoués* established in their place.

Procureur de la république /pròkyur(y)úr də la rèypublíyk/. (Formerly *procureur du roi.*) In French law, a public prosecutor, with whom rests the initiation of all criminal proceedings. In the exercise of his office (which appears to include the apprehension of offenders) he is entitled to call to his assistance the public force *(posse comitatus);* and the officers of police are auxiliary to him.

Procureur general, or imperial /pròkyur(y)úr jènərál / °impèriyál/. In French law, an officer of the imperial court, who either personally or by his deputy prosecuted every one who was accused of a crime according to the forms of French law. His functions were apparently confined to preparing the case for trial at the assizes, assisting in that trial, demanding the sentence in case of a conviction, and being present at the delivery of the sentence. He had a general superintendence over the officers of police and of the *juges d'instruction,* and he required from the *procureur du roi* a general report once in every three months.

Procuring cause. The proximate cause; the cause originating a series of events, which, without break in their continuity, result in the accomplishment of the prime object. The inducing cause; the direct or proximate cause. Substantially synonymous with "efficient cause."

A broker will be regarded as the "procuring cause" of a sale, so as to be entitled to commission, if his efforts are the foundation on which the negotiations resulting in a sale are begun. A cause originating a series of events which without break in their continuity result in accomplishment of prime objective of the employment of the broker who is producing a purchaser ready, willing and able to buy real estate on the owner's terms. Mohamed v. Robbins, 23 Ariz. App. 195, 531 P.2d 928, 930.

See also **Producing cause; Proximate cause.**

Pro defectu emptorum /pròw dəfékt(y)uw em(p)tórəm/. For want (failure) of purchasers.

Pro defectu exitus /pròw dəfékt(y)uw égzədəs/. For, or in case of, default of issue.

Pro defectu hæredis /pròw dəfékt(y)uw həríydəs/. For want of an heir.

Pro defectu justitiæ /pròw dəfékt(y)uw jəstíshiyiy/. For defect or want of justice.

Pro defendente /pròw dèfəndéntiy/. For the defendant. Commonly abbreviated *"pro def."*

Pro derelicto /pròw dèhrəlíktow/. As derelict or abandoned. A species of usucaption in the civil law.

Prodigal. Wasteful; extravagant. A spendthrift.

In civil law, a person who, though of full age, is incapable of managing his affairs, and of the obligations which attend them, in consequence of his bad conduct, and for whom a curator is therefore appointed. See **Prodigus.**

Pro dignitate regali /pròw dìgnətéydiy rəgéylay/. In consideration of the royal dignity.

Prodigus /pródəgəs/. Lat. In Roman law, a prodigal; a spendthrift; a person whose extravagant habits manifested an inability to administer his own affairs, and for whom a guardian might therefore be appointed.

Prodition /prowdíshən/. Treason; treachery.

Proditor /prówdədər/. A traitor.

Proditorie /pròwdətóriyiy/. Treasonably. This is a technical word formerly used in indictments for treason, when they were written in Latin.

Pro diviso /pròw dəváyzow/. As divided; *i.e.,* in severalty.

Pro domino /pròw dómənow/. As master or owner; in the character of master.

Pro donato /pròw dənéydow/. As a gift; as in case of gift; by title of gift. A species of usucaption in the civil law.

Pro dote /pròw dówdiy/. As a dowry; by title of dowry. A species of usucaption.

Produce /pró(w)d(y)uws/, *n.* The product of natural growth, labor, or capital. Articles produced or grown from or on the soil, or found in the soil.

Produce /prəd(y)úws/, *v.* To bring forward; to show or exhibit; to bring into view or notice; as, to present a play, including its presentation in motion pictures. To produce witnesses or documents at trial in obedience to a subpoena (Fed.R.Civil P. 45; Fed.R.Crim.P. 17); or to be compelled to produce materials subject to discovery rules (Fed.R.Civil P. 37; Fed.R.Crim.P. 16).

To make, originate, or yield, as gasoline. To bring to the surface, as oil.

To yield, as revenue. Thus, sums are "produced" by taxation, not when the tax is levied, but when the sums are collected.

Producent /prəd(y)úwsənt/. The party calling a witness under the old system of the English ecclesiastical courts.

Producer. One who produces, brings forth, or generates. Boland v. Cecil, 65 Cal.App.2d Supp. 832, 150 P.2d 819, 822. "Producer" is commonly used to denote person who raises agricultural products and puts them in condition for the market. Tennessee Burley Tobacco Growers' Ass'n v. Commodity Credit Corp., C.A.Tenn., 350 F.2d 34, 41.

Producing. Bring about; to cause to happen or take place, as an effect or result. Strong v. Aetna Casualty & Surety Co., Tex.Civ.App., 170 S.W.2d 786, 788.

Producing cause. Respecting broker's commission, is act which, continuing in unbroken chain of cause and effect, produces result. Schebesta v. Stewart, Tex. Civ.App., 37 S.W.2d 781, 786. A producing cause of an employee's death for which compensation is sought is that cause which, in a natural and continuous sequence, produces the death, and without which death would not have occurred. Jones v. Traders & General Ins. Co., 140 Tex. 599, 169 S.W.2d 160, 162. A producing cause is an efficient, existing, or contributing cause which, in natural and continuing sequence, produces the injury or damage complained of, if any. O. M. Franklin Serum Co. v. C. A. Hoover and Son, Tex.Civ.App., 437 S.W.2d 613, 619. See also **Procuring cause; Proximate cause.**

Product. With reference to property, term refers to proceeds; yield; income; receipts; return. Goods produced or manufactured, either by natural means, by hand, or with tools, machinery, chemicals, or the like. "Product" means something produced by physical labor or intellectual effort or something produced naturally or as result of natural process as by generation or growth. Minnesota Power & Light Co. v. Personal Property Tax, Taxing Dist., City of Fraser, School Dist. No. 695, 289 Minn. 64, 182 N.W.2d 685, 691.

Production. Process or act of producing. That which is produced or made; *i.e.* goods. Fruit of labor, as the productions of the earth, comprehending all vegetables and fruits; the productions of intellect, or genius, as poems and prose compositions; the productions of art, as manufactures of every kind.

Production for commerce. Within Fair Labor Standards Act, includes production of goods which, at time of production, employer, according to normal course of his business, intends or expects to move in interstate commerce immediately following initial sale. Fair Labor Standards Act of 1938, §§ 6, 7; 29 U.S.C.A. §§ 206, 207. Hill v. Janes, D.C.Ky., 59 F.Supp. 569, 572.

Production of suit. In common law pleading, the formula, "and therefore [or thereupon] he brings his suit," etc., with which declarations always conclude. This referred to the production by the plaintiff of his *secta* or suit, *i.e.* persons prepared to confirm what he had stated in the declaration.

Productio sectæ /prədǽksh(iy)ow séktiy/. In old English law, production of suit; the production by a plaintiff of his *secta* or witnesses to prove the allegations of his count.

Product liability. Refers to the legal liability of manufacturers and sellers to compensate buyers, users, and even bystanders, for damages or injuries suffered because of defects in goods purchased. A tort which makes a manufacturer liable if his product has a defective condition that makes it unreasonably dangerous to the user or consumer. Cobbins v. General Acc. Fire & Life Assur. Corp., 3 Ill.App.3d 379, 279 N.E.2d 443, 446.

Although the ultimate responsibility for injury or damage in a products liability case most frequently rests with the manufacturer, liability may also be imposed upon a retailer, occasionally upon a wholesaler or middleman, a bailor or lessor, and infrequently upon a party wholly outside the manufacturing and distributing process, such as a certifier. This ultimate responsibility may be imposed by an action by the plaintiff against the manufacturer directly, or by a claim for indemnification, asserted by way of a cross-claim or third party claim by the retailer or wholesaler, or others who might be held liable for the injury caused by a defective product. Under modern principles of products liability, and with the elimination of privity requirements in most instances, recovery is no longer limited to the purchaser of the product, or even to a user, but may extend to the non-user; the bystander who is injured or damaged by a defective product, for example. However, the term "products liability" normally contemplates injury or damage caused by a defective product, and if loss occurs as a result of a condition on the premises, or as a result of a service, as distinguished from loss occasioned by a defective product, a products liability claim does not ordinarily arise, even though a product may be involved.

See also **Intended use doctrine; Privity; Strict liability; Warranty.**

Product liability insurance. Type of insurance coverage which protects manufacturers and suppliers when claims are made for injuries and damage incurred in the use of their goods or products.

Pro emptore /pròw em(p)tóriy/. As a purchaser; by the title of a purchaser. A species of usucaption.

Pro facto /pròw fǽktow/. For the fact; as a fact; considered or held as a fact.

Pro falso clamore suo /pròw fól(t)sow kləmóriy s(y)úwow/. A nominal amercement of a plaintiff for *his false claim,* which used to be inserted in a judgment for the defendant. Obsolete.

Profane. Irreverence toward God or holy things; writing, speaking, or acting, in manifest or implied contempt of sacred things. Town of Torrington v. Taylor, 59 Wyo. 109, 137 P.2d 621, 624; Duncan v. U. S., C.C.A.Or., 48 F.2d 128, 133. That which has not been consecrated.

Profanity. Irreverence towards sacred things; particularly, an irreverent or blasphemous use of the name of God. Vulgar, irreverent, or coarse language. It is a federal offense to utter an obscene, indecent, or profane language on the radio. 18 U.S.C.A. § 1464. See also **Obscenity.**

Profectitius /pròwfektísh(iy)əs/. Lat. In the civil law, that which descends to us from our ascendants.

Profer or **Profert** /prowfór/. In old English law, an offer or proffer; an offer or endeavor to proceed in an action, by any man concerned to do so. A return made by a sheriff of his accounts into the exchequer; a payment made on such return. See **Profert in curia.**

Profert in curia /prófərd ən kyúriyə(m)/. L. Lat. (Sometimes written *profert in curiam.*) He produces in court. In old practice, these words were inserted in a declaration, as an allegation that the plaintiff was ready to produce, or did actually produce, in court, the deed or other written instrument on which his suit was founded, in order that the court might inspect the same and the defendant hear it read. The same formula was used where the defendant pleaded a written instrument.

An allegation formally made in a pleading, where a party alleged a deed, that he showed it in court, it being in fact retained in his own custody. But by virtue of the allegation, the deed was then constructively in possession of the court. The profert of any recorded instrument, as letters patent, was equivalent to annexing a copy. This result did not occur, however, in the case of other documents, such as a note.

Profess. To make open declaration of, to make public declaration or avowal.

Professio juris /prəfésh(iy)ow júrəs/. In conflicts and contract law, a recognition of the right of parties to a contract to stipulate in the document the law which will govern their contract.

Profession. A vocation or occupation requiring special, usually advanced, education and skill; *e.g.* law or medical professions. Also refers to whole body of such profession.

The labor and skill involved in a profession is predominantly mental or intellectual, rather than physical or manual.

The term originally contemplated only theology, law, and medicine, but as applications of science and learning are extended to other departments of affairs, other vocations also receive the name, which implies professed attainments in special knowledge as distinguished from mere skill.

Act of professing; a public declaration respecting something. Profession of faith in a religion.

Professional association. Any group of professional people organized to practice their profession together, though not necessarily in corporate or partnership form. A group of professionals organized for education, social activity, lobbying and the like; *e.g.* bar or medical association. See also **Corporation** (*Professional*).

Professional corporation. See **Corporation.**

Professional responsibility. See **Canon; Code of Professional Responsibility.**

Proffer. To offer or tender, as, the production of a document and offer of the same in evidence.

Proffered evidence. See **Proffer.**

Proficua /prəfíkyuwə/. L. Lat. In old English law, profits; especially the "issues and profits" of an estate in land.

Profit. Most commonly, the gross proceeds of a business transaction less the costs of the transaction; *i.e.* net proceeds. Excess of revenues over expenses for a transaction; sometimes used synonymously with net income for the period. Gain realized from business or investment over and above expenditures.

Profit means accession of good, valuable results, useful consequences, avail, gain, as an office of profit, excess of returns over expenditures or excess of income over expenditure. U. S. v. Mintzes, D.C.Md., 304 F.Supp. 1305, 1312.

The benefit, advantage, or pecuniary gain accruing to the owner or occupant of land from its actual use; as in the familiar phrase "rents, issues and profits," or in the expression "mesne profits."

A division sometimes made of incorporeal hereditaments. Profits are divided into *profits à prendre* and *profits à rendre (q.v.).*

Community of profits. See that title.

Gross profit. The difference between sales and cost of goods sold, but excluding expenses and taxes. See also **Gross income.**

Mesne profits. Intermediate profits; that is, profits which have been accruing between two given periods. Value of use or occupation of land during time it was held by one in wrongful possession and is commonly measured in terms of rents and profits. Thus, after a party has recovered the land itself in an action of ejectment, he frequently brings another action for the purpose of recovering the profits which have been accruing or arising out of the land between the time when his title to the possession accrued or was raised and the time of his recovery in the action of ejectment, and such an action is thence termed an "action for mesne profits."

Net profit. The amount arrived at by deducting from total sales the cost of goods sold and all expenses. See also **Net income; Net profits.**

Operating profit. The profit arrived at by deducting from sales all expenses attributable to operations but excluding expenses and income related to non-operating activities such as interest payments.

Paper profit. Profit not yet realized as derived from an appreciation in value of an asset not yet sold.

Profit and loss. The gain or loss arising from goods bought or sold, or from carrying on any other business, the former of which, in bookkeeping, is placed on the creditor's side; the latter on the debtor's side. See also **Profit and loss account; Profit and loss statement.**

Profit à prendre /prófəd à próndər/. Called also "right of common." A right exercised by one man in the soil of another, accompanied with participation in the profits of the soil thereof. A right to take a part of the soil or produce of the land. A right to take from the soil, such as by logging, mining, drilling, etc. The taking (profit) is the distinguishing characteristic from an easement.

Right of "profit à prendre" is a right to make some use of the soil of another, such as a right to mine metals, and it carries with it the right of entry and the right to remove and take from the land the designated products or profit and also includes right to use such of the surface as is necessary and convenient for exercise of the profit. Costa Mesa Union School Dist. of Orange County v. Security First Nat. Bank, 254 Cal.App.2d 4, 62 Cal.Rptr. 113, 118.

Profit à rendre /prófəd à róndər/. Such as is received at the hands of and rendered by another. The term comprehends rents and services.

Surplus profits. Within the meaning of a statute prohibiting the declaration of corporate dividends other than from such profits, means the excess of receipts over expenditures, or net earnings or receipts, or gross receipts, less expenses of operation. Of a corporation, the difference over and above the capital stock, debts, and liabilities.

Undistributed profits. Profits which have not been distributed to the stockholders in the form of dividends though earned by the corporation. See also **Undistributed profits tax.**

Undivided profits. See that title.

Profit and loss account. A transfer account of all income and expense accounts which is closed into the surplus account of a corporation or the capital account of a partnership.

Profit and loss statement. A statement showing the income and expenses of a business over a stated time; the difference being the profit or loss for the period. See also **Income statement.**

Profiteering. Taking advantage of unusual or exceptional circumstances to make excessive profits; *e.g.* selling of scarce or essential goods at inflated prices during time of emergency or war.

Profit margin. Sales minus all expenses as a single amount. Frequently used to mean the ratio of sales minus all operating expenses divided by sales.

Profit-sharing plan. A plan established and maintained by an employer to provide for the participation in his profits by his employees or their beneficiaries. In order to qualify for tax benefits, the plan must provide a definite predetermined formula for allocating the contributions made to the plan among the participants and for distributing the funds accumulated under the plan after a fixed number of years, the attainment of a stated age, or upon the prior occurrence of some event such as layoff, illness, disability, retirement, death, or severance of employment. Such plans are regulated by the Employee Retirement Income Security Act (ERISA).

Pro forma /pròw fórmə/. As a matter of form or for the sake of form. Used to describe accounting, financial, and other statements or conclusions based upon assumed or anticipated facts.

The phrase "pro forma," in an appealable decree or judgment, usually means that the decision was rendered, not on a conviction that it was right, but merely to facilitate further proceedings. Cramp & Sons S. & E. Bldg. Co. v. Turbine Co., 228 U.S. 645, 33 S.Ct. 722, 57 L.Ed. 1003.

Progener /prowjíynər/. Lat. In the civil law, a grandson-in-law.

Progressive tax. A type of graduated tax as in the case of the federal income tax which applies higher tax rates as the income increases.

Pro hac vice /pròw hǽk váysiy/. For this turn; for this one particular occasion. A lawyer may be admitted to practice in a jurisdiction for a particular case only.

Prohibetur ne quis faciat in suo quod nocere possit alieno /pròw(h)əbíydər nìy kwís fǽshiyəd ìn s(y)úwow kwòd nósəriy pósəd ǽliyíynow/. It is forbidden for any one to do or make on his own [land] what may injure another's.

Prohibit. To forbid by law; to prevent;—not synonymous with "regulate."

Prohibited degrees. Those degrees of relationship by consanguinity which are so close that marriage between persons related to each other in any of such degrees is forbidden by law; e.g. brother and sister.

Prohibitio de vasto, directa parti /pròw(h)əbísh(iy)ow dìy vǽstow, dəréktə párday/. A judicial writ which was formerly addressed to a tenant, prohibiting him from waste, pending suit.

Prohibition. Inhibition; interdiction. Act or law prohibiting something, as 18th Amendment to U.S.Const. (1920) prohibited the manufacture, sale, or transportation of intoxicating liquors, except for medicinal purposes (such Prohibition Amendment was repealed by 21st Amendment in 1933).

Writ or process. Prohibition is that process by which a superior court prevents an inferior court or tribunal possessing judicial or quasi-judicial powers from exceeding its jurisdiction in matters over which it has cognizance or usurping matters not within its jurisdiction to hear or determine. The Florida Bar, Fla., 329 So.2d 301, 302. A writ issued by a superior court, directed to the judge and parties of a suit in an inferior court, commanding them to cease from the prosecution of the same, upon a suggestion that the cause originally, or some collateral matter arising

therein, does not belong to that jurisdiction, but to the cognizance of some other court.

The writ of prohibition is the counterpart of the writ of mandamus.

Pro illa vice /pròw ílə váysiy/. For that turn.

Pro indefenso /pròw ìndəfén(t)sow/. As undefended; as making no defense.

Pro indiviso /pròw ìndəváyzow/. As undivided; in common. The joint occupation or possession of lands. Thus, lands held by coparceners are held *pro indiviso;* that is, they are held undividedly, neither party being entitled to any specific portions of the land so held, but both or all having a joint interest in the undivided whole.

Pro interesse suo /pròw ìntərésiy s(y)úwow/. According to his interest; to the extent of his interest. Thus, a third party may be allowed to intervene in a suit *pro interesse suo.*

Examination *pro interesse suo.* When a person claims to be entitled to an estate or other property sequestered, whether by mortgage, judgment, lease, or otherwise, or has a title paramount to the sequestration, he should apply to the court to direct an inquiry whether the applicant has any, and what, interest in the property; and this inquiry is called an "examination *pro interesse suo.*" Krippendorf v. Hyde, 110 U.S. 276, 4 S.Ct. 27, 28 L.Ed. 145; Hitz v. Jenks, 185 U.S. 155, 22 S.Ct. 598, 46 L.Ed. 851.

Projectio /prəjéksh(iy)ow/. Lat. In old English law, a throwing up of earth by the sea.

Projet. Fr. In international law, the draft of a proposed treaty or convention.

Projet de loi. A bill in a legislative body.

Pro læsione fidei /pròw lìyzhiyówniy fáydiyày/. For breach of faith.

Pro legato /pròw ləgéydow/. As a legacy; by the title of a legacy. A species of usucaption.

Prolem ante matrimonium natam, ita ut post legitimam, lex civilis succedere facit in hæreditate parentum; sed prolem, quam matrimonium non parit, succedere non sinit lex anglorum /prówləm ǽntiy mætrəmówn(i)yəm néydəm, áydə àt pówst ləjídəməm, léks sívələs səksíydəriy féysəd in hərèdətéydiy pəréntəm; sèd prówləm, kwæm mætrəmówn(i)yəm nòn pérət, səksíydəriy nòn sáynət léks æŋglórəm/. The civil law permits the offspring born before marriage, provided such offspring be afterwards legitimized, to be the heirs of their parents; but the law of the English does not suffer the offspring not produced by the marriage to succeed.

Proles /prówliyz/. Lat. Offspring; progeny; the issue of a lawful marriage. In its enlarged sense, it signifies any children.

Proles sequitur sortem paternam /prówliyz sékwədər sórdəm pətárnəm/. The offspring follows the condition of the father.

Proletariat, proletariate /pròwlətériyət/°tǽr°/. The class or body of proletarians. The class of unskilled laborers, without property or capital, engaged in the lower grades of work. The class of *proletarii* (see the next title); the lowest stratum of the people of a country, consisting mainly of the waste of other classes, or of those fractions of the population who, by their isolation and their poverty, have no place in the established order of society.

Proletarius /pròwlətériyəs/. Lat. In Roman law, a proletary; a person of poor or mean condition; one among the common people whose fortunes were below a certain valuation; one of a class of citizens who were so poor that they could not serve the state with money, but only with their children *(proles)*.

Prolicide /prówləsàyd/. A word used to designate the destruction of the human offspring. Jurists divide the subject into *feticide,* or the destruction of the *fetus in utero,* and *infanticide,* or the destruction of the new-born infant. See also **Abortion.**

Prolixity /prowlíksədiy/. The unnecessary and superfluous statement of facts in pleading or in evidence.

Prolocutor /prəlók(y)ədər/prówlòk(y)ədər/. In ecclesiastical law, the president or chairman of a convocation. The speaker of the house of lords is called the prolocutor. The office belongs to the lord chancellor by prescription.

Prolongation /pròwloŋgéyshən/. Time added to the duration of something; an extension of the time limited for the performance of an agreement.

Pro majori cautela /pròw məjóray kòtíylə/. For greater caution; by way of additional security. Usually applied to some act done, or some clause inserted in an instrument, which may not be really necessary, but which will serve to put the matter beyond any question.

Promatertera /pròwmətárdərə/. Lat. In the civil law, a maternal great-aunt; the sister of one's grandmother.

Promatertera magna /pròwmətárdərə mǽgnə/. Lat. In the civil law, a great-great-aunt.

Promise. A declaration which binds the person who makes it, either in honor, conscience, or law, to do or forbear a certain specific act, and which gives to the person to whom made a right to expect or claim the performance of some particular thing. A declaration, verbal or written, made by one person to another for a good or valuable consideration, in the nature of a covenant by which the promisor binds himself to do or forbear some act, and gives to the promisee a legal right to demand and enforce a fulfillment. An express undertaking, or agreement to carry a purpose into effect. E. I. Du Pont De Nemours & Co. v. Claiborne-Reno Co., C.C.A.Iowa, 64 F.2d 224.

Promise is an undertaking, however expressed, either that something shall happen, or that something shall not happen, in the future. Plumbing Shop, Inc. v. Pitts, 67 Wash.2d 514, 408 P.2d 382, 384.

A promise is a manifestation of intention to act or refrain from acting in a specified way, so made as to justify a promisee in understanding that a commitment has been made. Restatement, Second, Contracts § 2.

While a "promise" is sometimes loosely defined as a declaration by any person of his intention to do or

forbear from anything at the request or for the use of another, it is to be distinguished, on the one hand, from a mere declaration of intention involving no engagement or assurance as to the future, and, on the other, from "agreement," which is an obligation arising upon reciprocal promises, or upon a promise founded on a consideration.

See also Aleatory promise; Conditional promise; Illusory promise; Implied promise; Offer; Raising a promise.

Commercial law. An undertaking to pay and it must be more than an acknowledgment of an obligation. U.C.C. § 3–102(1)(c).

Fictitious promise. Sometimes called "implied promises," or "promises implied in law," occur in the case of those contracts which were invented to enable persons in certain cases to take advantage of the old rules of pleading peculiar to contracts, and which are not now of practical importance.

Illusory promise. A promise in which the promisor does not bind himself to do anything and hence it furnishes no basis for a contract because of the lack of consideration; *e.g.* a promise to buy whatever goods the promisor chooses to buy.

Mutual promises. Promises simultaneously made by and between two parties; each promise being the consideration for the other.

Naked promise. One given without any consideration, equivalent, or reciprocal obligation, and for that reason not enforceable at law.

New promise. An undertaking or promise, based upon and having relation to a former promise which, for some reason, can no longer be enforced, whereby the promisor recognizes and revives such former promise and engages to fulfill it.

Parol promise. A simple contract; a verbal promise.

Promise implied in fact. Promise implied in fact is merely tacit promise, one which is inferred in whole or in part from expressions other than words by promisor. Cooke v. Adams, Miss., 183 So.2d 925, 927.

Promise implied in law. Promise implied in law is one in which neither words nor conduct of party involved are promissory in form or justify inference of promise and term is used to indicate that party is under legally enforceable duty as he would have been, if he had in fact made promise. Cooke v. Adams, Miss., 183 So.2d 925, 927.

Promise of marriage. A contract mutually entered into by a man and a woman that they will marry each other.

Promise to pay the debt of another. Within the statute of frauds, a promise to pay the debt of another is an undertaking by a person not before liable, for the purpose of securing or performing the same duty for which the party for whom the undertaking is made, continues liable.

Promisee. One to whom a promise has been made.

Promisor. One who makes a promise.

Promissor /prəmísər/. Lat. In the civil law, a promiser; properly the party who undertook to do a thing in answer to the interrogation of the other party, who was called the "stipulator."

Promissory /prómǝs(ò)riy/. Containing or consisting of a promise; in the nature of a promise; stipulating or engaging for a future act or course of conduct.

As to promissory Oath; Representation; and Warranty, see those titles.

Promissory estoppel. That which arises when there is a promise which promisor should reasonably expect to induce action or forbearance of a .definite and substantial character on part of promisee, and which does induce such action or forbearance, and such promise is binding if injustice can be avoided only by enforcement of promise. "Moore" Burger, Inc. v. Phillips Petroleum Co., Tex., 492 S.W.2d 934.

Promissory fraud. A promise to perform made at a time when the promisor has a present intention not to perform. It is a misrepresentation of the promisor's frame of mind and is, for that reason a fact which makes it the basis of an action for deceit. It is sometimes called common law fraud.

Promissory note. A promise or engagement, in writing, to pay a specified sum at a time therein limited, or on demand, or at sight, to a person therein named, or to his order, or bearer. A written promise made by one or more to pay another, or order, or bearer, at a specified time, a specific amount of money, or other articles of value. An unconditional written promise, signed by the maker, to pay absolutely and at all events a sum certain in money, either to the bearer or to a person therein designated or his order, at a time specified therein, or at a time which must certainly arrive.

A signed paper promising to pay another a certain sum of money. An unconditional written promise to pay a specified sum of money on demand or at a specified date. Such a note is negotiable if signed by the maker and containing an unconditional promise to pay a sum certain in money either on demand or at a definite time and payable to order or bearer. U.C.C. § 3–104.

Promissory warranty. In insurance law, a promissory warranty is an absolute undertaking by insured, contained in a policy or in an instrument properly incorporated by reference, that certain facts or conditions pertaining to the risk insured against shall continue, or shall be done or omitted. Reid v. Hardware Mut. Ins. Co. of Carolinas, 252 S.C. 339, 166 S.E.2d 317, 321.

Promote. To contribute to growth, enlargement, or prosperity of; to forward; to further; to encourage; to advance.

Promoter. One who promotes, urges on, encourages, incites, advances, etc. One promoting a plan by which it is hoped to insure the success of a business, entertainment, etc. venture.

The persons who, for themselves or others, take the preliminary steps to the organization of a corporation. Those persons who first associate themselves together for the purpose of organizing the company, issuing its prospectus, procuring subscriptions to the stock, securing a charter, etc. Incorporators. Dick-

erman v. Northern Trust Co., 176 U.S. 181, 20 S.Ct. 311, 44 L.Ed. 423.

Prompt. To act immediately, responding on the instant.

Prompt delivery. Delivery as promptly as possible, all things considered.

Promptly. Adverbial form of the word "prompt," which means ready and quick to act as occasion demands. The meaning of the word depends largely on the facts in each case, for what is "prompt" in one situation may not be considered such under other circumstances or conditions. To do something "promptly" is to do it without delay and with reasonable speed. Application of Beattie, 4 Storey 506, 180 A.2d 741, 744.

Prompt shipment. Shipment within a reasonable time, all things considered.

Promulgare /prò(w)mǝlgériy/. Lat. In Roman law, to make public; to make publicly known; to promulgate. To publish or make known a law after its enactment.

Promulgate /pró(w)mǝlgeyt/prǝmálgeyt/. To publish; to announce officially; to make public as important or obligatory. The formal act of announcing a statute or rule of court.

Promutuum /prǝmyúwchuwǝm/. Lat. In the civil law, a *quasi* contract, by which he who receives a certain sum of money, or a certain quantity of fungible things, which have been paid to him through mistake, contracts towards the payer the obligation of returning him as much.

Pronepos /prównepòs/. Lat. In the civil law, a great-grandson.

Proneptis /prównéptǝs/. Lat. In the civil law, a great-granddaughter; a niece's daughter.

Pro non scripto /prów nòn skríptow/. As not written; as though it had not been written; as never written.

Pronotary /pròwnówdǝriy/. First notary. See **Prothonotary.**

Pronounce. To utter formally, officially, and solemnly; to declare or affirm; to declare aloud and in a formal manner. In this sense a court is said to "pronounce" judgment or a sentence.

Pronunciation /prǝnàn(t)siyéyshǝn/. L. Fr. A sentence or decree.

Pronurus /prównǝrǝs/. Lat. In the civil law, the wife of a grandson or great-grandson.

Proof. The effect of evidence; the establishment of a fact by evidence. New England Newspaper Pub. Co. v. Bonner, C.C.A.Mass., 77 F.2d 915, 916. Any fact or circumstance which leads the mind to the affirmative or negative of any proposition. The conviction or persuasion of the mind of a judge or jury, by the exhibition of evidence, of the reality of a fact alleged. Ellis v. Wolfe-Shoemaker Motor Co., 227 Mo.App. 508, 55 S.W.2d 309.

"Proof" is the establishment by evidence of a requisite degree of belief concerning a fact in the mind of the trier of fact or the court. Calif. Evidence Code.

See also Burden of going forward; Burden of persuasion; Burden of producing evidence; Burden of proof; Clear and convincing proof; Clear evidence of proof; Degree of proof; Evidence; Failure of proof; Offer of proof; Testimony.

Evidence and proof distinguished. Proof is the logically sufficient reason for assenting to the truth of a proposition advanced. In its juridical sense it is a term of wide import, and comprehends everything that may be adduced at a trial, within the legal rules, for the purpose of producing conviction in the mind of judge or jury, aside from mere argument; that is, everything that has a probative force intrinsically, and not merely as a deduction from, or combination of, original probative facts. But "evidence" is a narrower term, and includes only such kinds of proof as may be legally presented at a trial, by the act of the parties, and through the aid of such concrete facts as witnesses, records, or other documents. Thus, to urge a presumption of law in support of one's case is adducing proof, but it is not offering evidence. "Belief" is a subjective condition resulting from proof. It is a conviction of the truth of a proposition, existing in the mind, and induced by persuasion, proof, or argument addressed to the judgment. Proof is the result or effect of evidence, while evidence is the medium or means by which a fact is proved or disproved, but the words "proof" and "evidence" may be used interchangeably. Proof is the perfection of evidence; for without evidence there is no proof, although there may be evidence which does not amount to proof; for example, if a man is found murdered at a spot where another has been seen walking but a short time before, this fact will be *evidence* to show that the latter was the murderer, but, standing alone, will be very far from *proof* of it.

Affirmative proof. Evidence establishing the fact in dispute by a preponderance of the evidence.

Burden of proof. See that title.

Degree of proof. Refers to effect of evidence rather than medium by which truth is established, and in this sense expressions "preponderance of evidence" and "proof beyond reasonable doubt" are used.

Full proof. See **Full.**

Half proof. See **Half.**

Negative proof. See *Positive proof, infra.*

Positive proof. Direct or affirmative proof. That which directly establishes the fact in question; as opposed to *negative* proof, which establishes the fact by showing that its opposite is not or cannot be true.

Preliminary proof. See **Preliminary.**

Proof beyond a reasonable doubt. Such proof as precludes every reasonable hypothesis except that which it tends to support and which is wholly consistent with defendant's guilt and inconsistent with any other rational conclusion. State v. Dubina, 164 Conn. 95, 318 A.2d 95, 97. Such is the required standard of proof in criminal cases.

Proof evident or presumption great. As used in constitutional provisions that accused shall be bailable unless for capital offenses when the "proof is evident" or "presumption great," means evidence clear and strong, and which leads well guarded, dispassion-

ate judgment to conclusion that accused committed offense and will be punished capitally. Ex parte Coward, 145 Tex.Cr.R. 593, 170 S.W.2d 754, 755; Ex parte Goode, 123 Tex.Cr.R. 492, 59 S.W.2d 841.

Proof of claim. Statement under oath filed in a bankruptcy proceeding by a creditor in which the creditor sets forth the amount owed and sufficient detail to identify the basis for the claim. Also used in probate proceedings to submit the amount owed by the decedent to the creditor and filed with the court for payment by the fiduciary.

Proof of debt. The formal establishment by a creditor of his debt or claim, in some prescribed manner (as, by his affidavit or otherwise), as a preliminary to its allowance, along with others, against an estate or property to be divided, such as the estate of a bankrupt or insolvent, a deceased person or a firm or company in liquidation. See *Proof of claim, supra.*

Proof of loss. A formal statement made by the policy-owner to the insurer regarding a loss, intended to give insurer enough information to enable it to determine the extent of its liability under a policy or bond.

Proof of service. Evidence submitted by a process server that he has made service on a defendant in an action. It is also called a return of service. Fed.R. Civil P. 4.

Proof of will. A term having the same meaning as "probate," *(q.v.),* and used interchangeably with it.

Standard of proof. A statement of how convincing the evidence must be in order for a party to comply with his/her burden of proof. The main standards of proof are proof beyond a reasonable doubt (in criminal cases only), proof by clear and convincing evidence, and proof by a preponderance of the evidence.

Pro opere et labore /pròw ópəriy èt ləbóriy/. For work and labor.

Propagate /própəgèyt/. To cause to spread.

Pro partibus liberandis /pròw párdəbəs lìbərǽndəs/. An ancient writ for partition of lands between co-heirs.

Propatruus /prowpǽtruwəs/. Lat. In the civil law, a great-grandfather's brother.

Propatruus magnus /prowpǽtruwəs mǽgnəs/. In the civil law, a great-great-uncle.

Proper. That which is fit, suitable, appropriate, adapted, correct. Reasonably sufficient. Peculiar; naturally or essentially belonging to a person or thing; not common; appropriate; one's own. See also **Reasonable.**

Proper care. That degree of care which a prudent man should use under like circumstances. Baskin v. Montgomery Ward & Co., C.C.A.N.C., 104 F.2d 531, 533.

Proper evidence. Such evidence as may be presented under the rules established by law and recognized by the courts; *i.e.* admissible evidence; material, relevant evidence.

Proper feuds. In feudal law, the original and genuine feuds held by purely military service.

Proper independent advice. As to donor means that he had preliminary benefit of conferring upon subject of intended gift with a person who was not only competent to inform him correctly of its legal effect, but who was so disassociated from interests of donee as to be in position to advise with donor impartially and confidentially as to consequences to donor of his proposed gift.

Proper lookout. Duty imposed on motorist to keep such lookout requires motorist to use care, prudence, watchfulness, and attention of an ordinarily prudent person under same or similar circumstances. Such lookout as person of ordinary care and prudence would have kept under same or similar conditions. Duncan v. Durham, Tex.Civ.App., 356 S.W.2d 377, 380. See also **Lookout.**

Proper party. As distinguished from a necessary party, is one who has an interest in the subject-matter of the litigation, which may be conveniently settled therein. One without whom a substantial decree may be made, but not a decree which shall completely settle all the questions which may be involved in the controversy and conclude the rights of all the persons who have any interest in the subject of the litigation. See Fed.R.Civil P. 19.

A proper party is one who may be joined in action but whose nonjoinder will not result in dismissal. Jones Knitting Corp. v. A. M. Pullen & Co., D.C.N.Y., 50 F.R.D. 311, 314. Those without whom cause might proceed but whose presence will allow judgment more clearly to settle controversy among all parties. Cities Service Oil Co. v. Kronewitter, 199 Kan. 228, 428 P.2d 804, 807. See also **Parties.**

Property. That which is peculiar or proper to any person; that which belongs exclusively to one. In the strict legal sense, an aggregate of rights which are guaranteed and protected by the government. Fulton Light, Heat & Power Co. v. State, 65 Misc.Rep. 263, 121 N.Y.S. 536. The term is said to extend to every species of valuable right and interest. More specifically, ownership; the unrestricted and exclusive right to a thing; the right to dispose of a thing in every legal way, to possess it, to use it, and to exclude every one else from interfering with it. That dominion or indefinite right of use or disposition which one may lawfully exercise over particular things or subjects. The exclusive right of possessing, enjoying, and disposing of a thing. The highest right a man can have to anything; being used to refer to that right which one has to lands or tenements, goods or chattels, which no way depends on another man's courtesy.

The word is also commonly used to denote everything which is the subject of ownership, corporeal or incorporeal, tangible or intangible, visible or invisible, real or personal; everything that has an exchangeable value or which goes to make up wealth or estate. It extends to every species of valuable right and interest, and includes real and personal property, easements, franchises, and incorporeal hereditaments, and includes every invasion of one's property rights by actionable wrong. Labberton v. General Cas. Co. of America, 53 Wash.2d 180, 332 P.2d 250, 252, 254.

Property embraces everything which is or may be the subject of ownership, whether a legal ownership, or whether beneficial, or a private ownership. Davis v. Davis, Tex.Civ.App., 495 S.W.2d 607, 611. Term includes not only ownership and possession but also the right of use and enjoyment for lawful purposes. Hoffmann v. Kinealy, Mo., 389 S.W.2d 745, 752.

Property, within constitutional protection, denotes group of rights inhering in citizen's relation to physical thing, as right to possess, use and dispose of it. Cereghino v. State By and Through State Highway Commission, 230 Or. 439, 370 P.2d 694, 697.

Goodwill is property, Howell v. Bowden, Tex.Civ. App., 368 S.W.2d 842, 848; as is an insurance policy and rights incident thereto, including a right to the proceeds, Harris v. Harris, 83 N.M. 441, 493 P.2d 407, 408.

Criminal code. "Property" means anything of value, including real estate, tangible and intangible personal property, contract rights, choses-in-action and other interests in or claims to wealth, admission or transportation tickets, captured or domestic animals, food and drink, electric or other power. Model Penal Code, § 223.0. See also *Property of another, infra.*

Trusts. Under definition in Restatement, Second, Trusts, § 2(c), it denotes interest in things and not the things themselves.

Classification

Property is either: real or immovable; or, personal or movable. Calif.Civil Code, § 657.

See also Chattel; Community property; Intangible property; Interest; Land; Literary property; Lost property; Marital property.

Absolute property. In respect to chattels personal property is said to be "absolute" where a man has, solely and exclusively, the right and also the possession of movable chattels. In the law of wills, a bequest or devise "to be the absolute property" of the beneficiary may pass a title in fee simple. Or it may mean that the property is to be held free from any limitation or condition or free from any control or disposition on the part of others. See **Fee simple.**

Common property. A term sometimes applied to lands owned by a municipal corporation and held in trust for the common use of the inhabitants. Also property owned jointly by husband and wife under the community system. See **Community property,** also *"Public property", infra.*

Community property. See that title.

Ganancial property. See that title.

General property. The right and property in a thing enjoyed by the *general owner.* See **Owner.**

Intangible property. Property which cannot be touched because it has no physical existence such as claims, interests, and rights. See also **Intangible asset.**

Literary property. See **Literary.**

Mislaid property. Property which an owner has put deliberately in a certain place but owner is unable to remember where he put it, as distinguished from lost property which the owner leaves unwittingly in a place, forgetting its location.

Mixed property. Property which is personal in its essential nature, but is invested by the law with certain of the characteristics and features of real property. Heirlooms, fixtures, and title-deeds to an estate are of this nature.

Movable property. Property the location of which can be changed, including things growing on, affixed to, or found in land, and documents although the rights represented thereby have no physical location. "Immovable property" is all other property. Model Penal Code, § 223.0.

Personal property. In broad and general sense, everything that is the subject of ownership, not coming under denomination of real estate. A right or interest in things personal, or right or interest less than a freehold in realty, or any right or interest which one has in things movable.

Generally, all property other than real estate. It is sometimes designated as personalty when real estate is termed realty. Personal property also can refer to property which is not used in a taxpayer's trade or business or held for the production or collection of income. When used in this sense, personal property could include both realty (*e.g.,* a personal residence) and personalty (*e.g.,* personal effects such as clothing and furniture).

The term "personal property" in its broadest legal signification includes everything the subject of ownership not being land or any interest in land, as goods, chattels, money, notes, bonds, stocks and choses in action generally, including intangible property. Bismarck Tribune Co. v. Omdahl, N.D., 147 N.W.2d 903, 906.

Personal property includes money, goods, chattels, things in action, and evidences of debt. Calif. Evid.Code.

Personal property is divisible into (1) corporeal personal property, which includes movable and tangible things, such as animals, furniture, merchandise, etc.; and (2) incorporeal personal property, which consists of such rights as personal annuities, stocks, shares, patents, and copyrights.

Private property. As protected from being taken for public uses, is such property as belongs absolutely to an individual, and of which he has the exclusive right of disposition. Property of a specific, fixed and tangible nature, capable of being in possession and transmitted to another, such as houses, lands, and chattels. Scranton v. Wheeler, 179 U.S. 141, 21 S.Ct. 48, 45 L.Ed. 126.

Property of another. Includes property in which any person other than the actor has an interest which the actor is not privileged to infringe, regardless of the fact that the actor also has an interest in the property and regardless of the fact that the other person might be precluded from civil recovery because the property was used in an unlawful transaction or was subject to forfeiture as contraband. Property in possession of the actor shall not be deemed property of another who has only a security interest therein, even if legal title is in the creditor pursuant to a conditional sales contract or other security agreement. Model Penal Code, § 223.0.

Property tax. See that title.

Public property. This term is commonly used as a designation of those things which are *publici juris* (*q.v.*), and therefore considered as being owned by "the public," the entire state or community, and not restricted to the dominion of a private person. It may also apply to any subject of property owned by a state, nation, or municipal corporation as such. See also *State property, infra.*

Qualified property. Property in chattels which is not in its nature permanent, but may at some times subsist and not at other times; such for example, as the property a man may have in wild animals which he has caught and keeps, and which are his only so long as he retains possession of them. Any ownership not absolute. See also *Special property, infra.*

Real property. Land, and generally whatever is erected or growing upon or affixed to land. Also rights issuing out of, annexed to, and exercisable within or about land. A general term for lands, tenements, and hereditaments; property which, on the death of the owner intestate, passes to his heir.

Real or immovable property consists of: Land; that which is affixed to land; that which is incidental or appurtenant to land; that which is immovable by law; except that for the purposes of sale, emblements, industrial growing crops and things attached to or forming part of the land, which are agreed to be severed before sale or under the contract of sale, shall be treated as goods and be governed by the regulating the sales of goods. Calif.Civil Code, § 658.

Separate property. See that title.

Special property. Property of a qualified, temporary, or limited nature; as distinguished from absolute, general, or unconditional property. Such is the property of a bailee in the article bailed, of a sheriff in goods temporarily in his hands under a levy, of the finder of lost goods while looking for the owner, of a person in wild animals which he has caught. See also *Qualified property, supra.*

State property. The State is the owner of all land below tide water, and below ordinary high-water mark, bordering upon tide water within the State; of all land below the water of a navigable lake or stream; of all property lawfully appropriated by it to its own use; of all property dedicated to the State; and of all property of which there is no other owner. Calif.Civil Code, § 670.

Tangible property. All property which is touchable and has real existence (physical) whether it is real or personal.

Unclaimed property. The majority of states have adopted the Uniform Disposition of Unclaimed Property Act.

Property right. A generic term which refers to any type of right to specific property whether it is personal or real property, tangible or intangible; *e.g.* professional baseball player has valuable property right in his name, photograph and image, and such right may be saleable by him. Cepeda v. Swift & Co., C.A.Mo., 415 F.2d 1205, 1206.

Property settlement. Agreement made between spouses as an incident of a divorce proceeding. Such agreement may contain provisions for division of property owned by the spouses during the marriage, periodic payments by the husband or a lump sum payment or one time conveyance of property. See **Equitable distribution.**

Property tax. A tax levied on both real and personal property; the amount of the tax being dependent on the value of the property, generally expressed as a uniform rate per thousand of valuation. See **Ad valorem.**

Property torts. Such involve injury or damage to property, real or personal, in contrast to "personal torts" which involve injuries to person, *i.e.*, the body, reputation, or feelings. Travelers Indem. Co. v. Chumbley, Mo.App., 394 S.W.2d 418, 422.

Propinqui et consanguinei /prəpíŋkway èt kònsæŋwíniyay/. Lat. The nearest of kin to a deceased person.

Propinquior excludit propinquum; propinquus remotum; et remotus remotiorem /prəpíŋkwiyər əkskl(y)úwdət prəpíŋkwəm, prəpíŋkwəs rəmówdəm, èt rəmówdəs rəmòwshiyórəm/. He who is nearer excludes him who is near; he who is near, him who is remote; he who is remote, him who is remoter.

Propinquity /prəpíŋkwədiy/. Kindred; parentage; nearness; proximity.

Propior sobrino, propior sobrina /prówpiyər səbráynow/°səbráynə/. Lat. In the civil law, the son or daughter of a great-uncle or great-aunt, paternal or maternal.

Propios, proprios /prówp(r)iyòws/. In Spanish law, certain portions of ground laid off and reserved when a town was founded in Spanish America as the unalienable property of the town, for the purpose of erecting public buildings, markets, etc., or to be used in any other way, under the direction of the municipality, for the advancement of the revenues or the prosperity of the place.

Propone /prəpówn/. In ecclesiastical and probate law, to bring forward for adjudication; to exhibit as basis of a claim; to proffer for judicial action.

Proponent /prəpównənt/. The propounder of a thing. Thus, the proponent of a will is the party who offers it for probate *(q.v.).*

Proportionate /prəpórshənət/. Adjusted to something else according to certain rate of comparative relation. See **Pro rata.**

Proposal. An offer; something proffered. An offer, by one person to another, of terms and conditions with reference to some work or undertaking, or for the transfer of property, the acceptance whereof will make a contract between them. Signification by one person to another of his willingness to enter into a contract with him on the terms specified in the offer.

The initial overture or preliminary statement for consideration by the other party to a proposed agreement. As so used, it is not an offer but it contemplates an offer and hence, its acceptance does not ripen into a contract. See also **Offer.**

Propositio indefinita æquipollet universali /pròpəzísh(iy)ow indèfənáydə èkwəpólət yùwnəvərséylay/. An indefinite proposition is equivalent to a general one.

Proposition. An offer to do a thing. See **Offer; Proposal.**

Propositus /prəpózədəs/. Lat. The person proposed; the person from whom a descent is traced.

Pro possessione præsumitur de jure /pròw pəzèshiyówniy prəz(y)úmədər dìy júriy/. From possession arises a presumption of law.

Pro possessore /pròw pòwzəsóriy/. As a possessor; by title of a possessor.

Pro possessore habetur qui dolo injuriave desiit possidere /pròw pòwzəsóriy həbíydər kwày dówlow ənjùriyéyviy désiyət pòsədíriy/. He is esteemed a possessor whose possession has been disturbed by fraud or injury.

Pro posse suo /pròw pósiy s(y)úwow/. To the extent of his power or ability.

Propound. To offer; to propose. An executor or other person is said to propound a will when he takes proceedings for obtaining probate solemn form.

Propria persona /prówpriyə pərsównə/. See **In propria persona.**

Propriedad /prowpriyeyðáð/. In Spanish law, property.

Proprietary, *n.* /prəpráyət(èh)riy/. A proprietor or owner; one who has the exclusive title to a thing; one who possesses or holds the title to a thing in his own right; one who possesses the dominion or ownership of a thing in his own right. The grantees of Pennsylvania and Maryland and their heirs were called the proprietaries of those provinces.

Proprietary, *adj.* /prəpráyət(èh)riy/. Belonging to ownership; belonging or pertaining to a proprietor; relating to a certain owner or proprietor. Made and marketed by a person or persons having the exclusive right to manufacture and sell such; as a proprietary article, medicine, or food.

Proprietary articles. Goods manufactured under some exclusive individual right to make and sell them. The term is so used in the internal revenue laws of the United States. Ferguson v. Arthur, 117 U.S. 482, 6 S.Ct. 861, 29 L.Ed. 979.

Proprietary capacity. Used to describe functions of a city or town when it engages in a business-like venture as contrasted with a governmental function. See *Proprietary functions,* below.

Proprietary capital. In accounting, that account in a sole proprietorship which represents the original investment in addition to accumulated profits.

Proprietary duties. Those duties of a municipality which are not strictly governmental duties. See also **Governmental duties.**

Proprietary functions. Functions which city, in its discretion, may perform when considered to be for best interests of citizens of city. Sarmiento v. City of Corpus Christi, Tex.Civ.App., 465 S.W.2d 813, 816, 819. Acts done by municipality for general betterment and improvement of such. Municipal corporations act in two distinct capacities: (1) governmental, legislative or public and (2) proprietary, commercial or quasi-private; the "governmental functions" of a municipal corporation are those functions exercised as arm of state, and for public good generally, whereas "proprietary functions" are those exercised for peculiar benefit and advantage of citizens of municipality. City of Pueblo v. Weed, Colo.App., 570 P.2d 15, 18. See **Governmental duties.**

Proprietary governments. This expression is used by Blackstone to denote governments granted out by the crown to individuals, in the nature of feudatory principalities, with inferior regalities and subordinate powers of legislation such as formerly belonged to the owners of counties palatine. 1 Bl.Comm. 108.

Proprietary interest. The interest of an owner of property together with all rights appurtenant thereto such as the right to vote shares of stock and right to participate in managing if the person has a proprietary interest in the shares. Stroh v. Blackhawk Holding Corp., 48 Ill.2d 471, 272 N.E.2d 1.

Proprietary lease. Type of lease in cooperative apartment between owner-cooperative and tenant-stockholder.

Proprietary rights. Those rights which an owner of property has by virtue of his ownership. Asch v. First Nat. Bank in Dallas, Tex.Civ.App., 304 S.W.2d 179, 183; Douglas v. Taylor, Tex.Civ.App., 497 S.W.2d 308, 310. See also *Proprietary interest, supra.*

Proprietas /prǝpráyǝtæs/. Lat. In the civil and old English law, property; that which is one's own; ownership.

Proprietas nuda, naked or mere property of ownership; the mere title, separate from the usufruct.

Proprietas plena, full property, including not only the title, but the usufruct, or exclusive right to the use.

Proprietas totius navis carinæ causam sequitur /prǝpráyǝtæs towshíyǝs néyvǝs kǝráyniy kózǝm sékwǝdǝr/. The property of the whole ship follows the condition of the keel. If a man builds a vessel from the very keel with the materials of another, the vessel belongs to the owner of the materials.

Proprietas verborum est salus proprietatum /prǝpráyǝtæs vǝrbórǝm èst sǽlǝs prǝpràyǝtéydǝm/. Propriety of words is the salvation of property.

Proprietate probanda, de /díy prǝpràyǝtéydǝm prowbǽndǝ/. A writ addressed to a sheriff to try by an inquest in whom certain property, previous to distress, subsisted.

Proprietates verborum servandæ sunt /prǝpràyǝtéydiyz vǝrbórǝm sǝrvǽndiy sànt/. The proprieties of words [proper meanings of words] are to be preserved or adhered to.

Propriété /prowprìyeytéy/. The French law term corresponding to our "property," or the right of enjoying and of disposing of things in the most absolute manner, subject only to the laws.

Proprietor /prǝpráyǝdǝr/. One who has the legal right or exclusive title to anything. In many instances it is synonymous with owner.

Proprietorship. Business, usually unincorporated, owned and controlled exclusively by one person. Such a business is commonly designated a "sole proprietorship" *(q.v.).*

Propriety. As used in Massachusetts colonial ordinance of 1741 term is nearly, if not precisely, equivalent to property.

In old English law, property; propriety in action; propriety in possession; mixed propriety.

Proprios /prówpriyows/. In Spanish and Mexican law, productive lands, the usufruct of which had been set apart to the several municipalities for the purpose of defraying the charges of their respective governments.

Proprio vigore /prówpriyow vǝgóriy/. Lat. By its own force; by its intrinsic meaning.

Propter /próptǝr/. For; on account of. The initial word of several Latin phrases.

Propter affectum /próptǝr ǝféktǝm/. For or on account of some affection or prejudice. The name of a species of *challenge (q.v.).*

Propter defectum /próptǝr dǝféktǝm/. On account of or for some defect. The name of a species of *challenge (q.v.).*

Propter defectum sanguinis /próptǝr dǝféktǝm sǽngwǝnǝs/. On account of failure of blood.

Propter delictum /próptǝr dǝlíktǝm/. For or on account of crime. The name of a species of *challenge (q.v.).*

Propter honoris respectum /próptǝr (h)ǝnórǝs rǝspéktǝm/. On account of respect of honor or rank. See **Challenge.**

Propter impotentiam /próptǝr ìmpǝténsh(iy)ǝm/. On account of helplessness. The term describes one of the grounds of a qualified property in wild animals, consisting in the fact of their inability to escape; as is the case with the young of such animals before they can fly or run. 2 Bl.Comm. 394.

Propter privilegium /próptǝr prìvǝlíyj(iy)ǝm/. On account of privilege. The term describes one of the grounds of a qualified property in wild animals, consisting in the special privilege of hunting, taking and killing them, in a given park or preserve, to the exclusion of other persons. 2 Bl.Comm. 394.

Pro querente /pròw kwǝréntiy/. For the plaintiff; usually abbreviated *pro quer.*

Pro rata /pròw réydǝ/. Proportionately; according to a certain rate, percentage, or proportion. According to measure, interest, or liability. According to a certain rule or proportion. For example, if a corporation has ten shareholders each of whom owns 10% of the stock, a pro-rata dividend distribution of $1,000 would mean that each shareholder would receive $100. See also **Per capita; Pro rate.**

Pro rata clause. Such clause commonly used as other insurance provision in automobile liability policy provides that when an insured has other insurance available, company will be liable only for proportion of loss represented by ratio between its policy limit and total limits of all available insurance. Putnam v. New Amsterdam Cas. Co., 48 Ill.2d 71, 269 N.E.2d 97, 99. Provision in insurance policy to the effect that the insurer will not be liable for a greater proportion of any loss than the amount of the policy bears to the total amount of insurance on the property.

Pro-rata distribution clause. In fire insurance, provision in the policy that the amount of insurance written shall apply to each parcel of property in the proportion which the value of each parcel bears to the total value of all the property insured under the policy.

Pro rate. To divide, share, or distribute proportionally; to assess or apportion pro-rata.

The act of adjusting, dividing or prorating property taxes, interest, insurance premiums, rental income, etc., between buyer and seller proportionately to time of use, or the date of closing. See also **Pro rata.**

Pro re nata /pròw ríy néydə/. For the affair immediately in hand; for the occasion as it may arise; adapted to meet the particular occasion. Thus, a course of judicial action adopted under pressure of the exigencies of the affair in hand, rather than in conformity to established precedents, is said to be taken *pro re nata.*

Prorogation /pròwrəgéyshən/. Prolonging or putting off to another day. The discontinuation or termination of a session of the legislature, parliament, or the like. In English law, a prorogation is the continuance of the parliament from one session to another, as an adjournment is a continuation of the session from day to day.

In the civil law, the giving time to do a thing beyond the term previously fixed.

Prorogue. To direct suspension of proceedings of parliament; to terminate a legislative session.

Pro salute animæ /pròw səl(y)úwdiy ǽnəmiy/. For the good of his soul. All prosecutions in the ecclesiastical courts are *pro salute animœ;* hence it will not be a temporal damage founding an action for slander that the words spoken put any one in danger of such a suit.

Proscribed /prəskráybd/. In the civil law, among the Romans, a man was said to be "proscribed" when a reward was offered for his head; but the term was more usually applied to those who were sentenced to some punishment which carried with it the consequences of civil death.

Pro se /pròw síy/. For himself; in his own behalf; in person. Appearing for oneself, as in the case of one who does not retain a lawyer and appears for himself in court.

Prosecute. To follow up; to carry on an action or other judicial proceeding; to proceed against a person criminally. To "prosecute" an action is not merely to commence it, but includes following it to an ultimate conclusion. See also **Prosecution.**

Prosecuting attorney. The name of the public officer who is appointed or elected in each judicial district, circuit, or county, to conduct criminal prosecutions on behalf of the State or people. Federal prosecutors represent the United States in prosecuting federal crimes.

A locally elected officer who represents the State in securing indictments and informations and in prosecuting criminal cases. Also called district attorney or State's attorney.

See also **Prosecutor.**

Prosecuting witness. The private person upon whose complaint or information a criminal accusation is founded and whose testimony is mainly relied on to secure a conviction at the trial. In a more particular sense, the person who was chiefly injured, in person or property, by the act constituting the alleged crime (as in case of robbery, assault, criminal negligence, bastardy, and the like), and who instigates the prosecution and gives evidence.

Prosecutio legis est gravis vexatio, executio legis coronat opus /pròsəkyúwsh(iy)ow líyjəs èst grǽvəs vekséysh(iy)ow, èksəkyúwsh(iy)ow líyjəs kərównət ówpəs/. Litigation is vexatious, but an execution crowns the work.

Prosecution. A criminal action; a proceeding instituted and carried on by due course of law, before a competent tribunal, for the purpose of determining the guilt or innocence of a person charged with crime. U. S. v. Reisinger, 128 U.S. 398, 9 S.Ct. 99, 32 L.Ed. 480. The continuous following up, through instrumentalities created by law, of a person accused of a public offense with a steady and fixed purpose of reaching a judicial determination of the guilt or innocence of the accused.

By an extension of its meaning, "prosecution" is also used to designate the government (state or federal) as the party proceeding in a criminal action, or the prosecutor, or counsel; as when we speak of "the evidence adduced by the prosecution."

The term is also used respecting civil litigation, and includes every step in action, from its commencement to its final determination. The Brazil, C.C.A.Ill., 134 F.2d 929, 930.

The Fifth Amendment, U.S.Const., requires that all prosecutions for infamous *federal* crimes (*i.e.* federal offenses carrying a term of imprisonment in excess of one year) be commenced by grand jury indictment. This requirement, however, does not apply to *state* prosecutions for such crimes, which may be prosecuted on the basis of an information. Hurtado v. California, 110 U.S. 516, 4 S.Ct. 111, 28 L.Ed.2d 232.

Malicious prosecution. See that title.

Prosecutor. One who prosecutes another for a crime in the name of the government. One who instigates a prosecution by making affidavit charging a named person with the commission of a penal offense on which a warrant is issued or an indictment or information is based. One who instigates the prosecution upon which an accused is arrested or who prefers an accusation against the party whom he suspects to be guilty. A "prosecutor" is one who takes charge of case and performs function of trial lawyer for the people, as does a district attorney. People v. Pohl, 47 Ill.App.2d 232, 197 N.E.2d 759, 764. See also **Prosecuting attorney.**

Private prosecutor. One who sets in motion the machinery of criminal justice against a person whom he suspects or believes to be guilty of a crime, by laying an accusation before the proper authorities, and who is not himself an officer of the government. Compare *Public prosecutor* below.

Prosecutor of the pleas. This name was given in New Jersey to the county officer who was charged with the prosecution of criminal actions, corresponding to the "district attorney" or "county attorney" in other states.

Public prosecutor. An officer of government (such as a state's attorney or district attorney) whose function is the prosecution of criminal actions, or suits partaking of the nature of criminal actions. See also **Prosecuting attorney.**

Prosecutrix /pròsəkyúwtrəks/. A female prosecutor.

Prosequi /prósəkway/. Lat. To follow up or pursue; to sue or prosecute. See **Nolle prosequi.**

Prosequitur /prəsékwədər/. Lat. He follows up or pursues; he prosecutes. See **Non pros.**

Prosocer /prówsəsər/. Lat. In the civil law, a father-in-law's father; a grandfather of wife.

Prosocerus /prəsósərəs/. Lat. In the civil law, a wife's grandmother.

Pro socio /pròw sówsh(iy)ow/. For a partner; the name of an action in behalf of a partner. A title of the civil law.

Pro solido /prów sóladow/. For the whole; as one; jointly; without division.

Prospective /prəspéktəv/. Looking forward; contemplating the future.

Prospective damages /prəspéktəv dǽməjəz/. See **Damages.**

Prospective law /prəspéktəv ló/. One applicable only to cases which shall arise after its enactment.

Prospectus. A document published by a company or corporation, or by persons acting as its agents or assignees, setting forth the nature and objects of an issue of shares, debentures, or other securities created by the company or corporation, and inviting the public to subscribe to the issue. The principal document of a registration statement required by law to be furnished an investor prior to any purchase. It is the document which is to contain all material facts concerning a company and its operations so that a prospective investor may make an informed decision as to the merit of an investment. The content of the prospectus is governed by federal securities laws and regulations.

The term "prospectus" means any prospectus, notice, circular, advertisement, letter, or communication, written or by radio or television, which offers any security for sale or confirms the sale of any security. Securities Act of 1933, § 1.

See also **Red herring.**

Prostitute. A woman who indiscriminately consorts with men for hire. A woman who offers herself indiscriminately for sexual intercourse for hire. People v. Schultz, 238 Cal.App.2d 804, 48 Cal.Rptr. 328, 334. A woman submitting to indiscriminate sexual intercourse, which she solicits. Trent v. Commonwealth, 181 Va. 338, 25 S.E.2d 350, 352. See also **Pander.**

The word in its most general sense means the act of setting one's self to sale, or of devoting to infamous purposes what is in one's power: as, the prostitution of talents or abilities; the prostitution of the press, etc.

Prostitution. Prostitution is performing an act of sexual intercourse for hire, or offering or agreeing to perform an act of sexual intercourse or any unlawful sexual act for hire. The act or practice of a female of prostituting or offering her body to an indiscriminate intercourse with men for money or its equivalent.

A person is guilty of prostitution, a petty misdemeanor, if he or she: (a) is an inmate of a house of prostitution or otherwise engages in sexual activity as a business; or (b) loiters in or within view of any public place for the purpose of being hired to engage in sexual activity. Model Penal Code, § 251.2.

See also **Mann Act; Pander.**

Pro tanto /pròw tǽntow/. For so much; for as much as may be; as far as it goes. Partial payment made on a claim. Commonly used in eminent domain cases to describe a partial payment made for the taking by the government without prejudice to the right of the petitioner to bring action for the full amount that he claims is due.

Protection. In old English law, a writ by which the king might, by a special prerogative, privilege a defendant from all personal and many real suits for one year at a time, and no longer, in respect of his being engaged in his service out of the realm. In former times the name "protection" was also given to a certificate given to a sailor to show that he was exempt from impressment into the royal navy.

In mercantile law, the name of a document generally given by notaries public to sailors and other persons going abroad, in which it is certified that the bearer therein named is a citizen of the United States.

In public commercial law, a system by which a government imposes customs duties upon commodities of foreign origin or manufacture when imported into the country, for the purpose of stimulating and developing the home production of the same or equivalent articles, by discouraging the importation of foreign goods, or by raising the price of foreign commodities to a point at which the home producers can successfully compete with them. See **Protective tariff.**

Protectio trahit subjectionem, et subjectio protectionem /prəjéksh(iy)ow tréy(h)ət səbjèkshiyównəm, èt səbjéksh(iy)ow prətèkshiyównəm/. Protection draws with it subjection, and subjection protection. The protection of an individual by government is on condition of his submission to the laws, and such submission on the other hand entitles the individual to the protection of the government.

Protective committee. A group of security holders or preferred stockholders appointed to protect the interest of their group at a time of liquidation or reorganization of corporation.

Protective custody. The condition of one who is held under force of law for his own protection as in the case of a material witness whose safety is in jeopardy, or one who is drunk in public though public drunkenness may not be a criminal offense, or of a person who because of mental illness may harm himself or others.

Protective order. Any order or decree of a court whose purpose is to protect a person from further harassment or service of process or discovery; *see e.g.* Fed.R.Civil P. 26(c); Fed.R.Crim.P. 16(d)(1). See also **Gag order.**

Protective tariff. A law imposing duties on imports, with the purpose and the effect of discouraging the importation of competitive products of foreign origin, and consequently of stimulating and protecting the home production of the same or equivalent articles.

Protective trust. A species of spendthrift trust *(q.v.)* containing a provision for forfeiture to protect against creditors and voluntary alienation.

Pro tem /pròw tém/. Abbreviation for "pro tempore" which means, literally, for the time being. Hence, one who acts as a substitute on a temporary basis is said to serve pro tem.

Pro tempore /pròw témpəriy/. For the time being; temporarily; provisionally.

Protest. A formal declaration made by a person interested or concerned in some act about to be done, or already performed, whereby he expresses his dissent or disapproval, or affirms the act against his will. The object of such a declaration is generally to save some right which would be lost to him if his implied assent could be made out, or to exonerate himself from some responsibility which would attach to him unless he expressly negatived his assent.

A notarial act, being a formal statement in writing made by a notary under his seal of office, at the request of the holder of a bill or note, in which it is declared that the bill or note described was on a certain day presented for payment (or acceptance), and that such payment or acceptance was refused, and stating the reasons, if any, given for such refusal, whereupon the notary *protests* against all parties to such instrument, and declares that they will be held responsible for all loss or damage arising from its dishonor. It denotes also all the steps or acts accompanying dishonor necessary to charge an indorser.

A protest is a certificate of dishonor made under the hand and seal of a United States consul or a notary public or other person authorized to certify dishonor by the law of the place where dishonor occurs. It may be made upon information satisfactory to such person. U.C.C. § 3–509. See also **Dishonor.**

A formal declaration made by a minority (or by certain individuals) in a legislative body that they dissent from some act or resolution of the body, usually adding the grounds of their dissent. The term, in this sense, refers to such a proceeding in the English House of Lords.

The formal statement, usually in writing, made by a person who is called upon by public authority to pay a sum of money, in which he declares that he does not concede the legality or justice of the claim or his duty to pay it, or that he disputes the amount demanded; the object being to save his right to recover or reclaim the amount, which right would be lost by his acquiescence. Thus, taxes may be paid under "protest."

The name of a paper served on a collector of customs by an importer of merchandise, stating that he believes the sum charged as duty to be excessive, and that, although he pays such sum for the purpose of getting his goods out of the custom-house, he reserves the right to bring an action against the collector to recover the excess.

In maritime law, a written statement by the master of a vessel, attested by a proper judicial officer or a notary, to the effect that damage suffered by the ship on her voyage was caused by storms or other perils of the sea, without any negligence or misconduct on his own part.

Notice of protest. A notice given by the holder of a bill or note to the drawer or indorser that the bill has been protested for refusal of payment or acceptance. U.C.C. § 3–509.

Waiver of protest. As applied to a note or bill, a waiver of protest implies not only dispensing with the formal act known as "protest," but also with that which ordinarily must precede it, viz., demand and notice of non-payment.

Protestando /prò(w)dəstǽndow/. L. Lat. Protesting. The emphatic word formerly used in pleading by way of protestation. See **Protestation.**

Protestants. Those who adhered to the doctrine of Luther; so called because, in 1529, they protested against a decree of the emperor Charles V and of the diet of Spires, and declared that they appealed to a general council. The name is now applied indiscriminately to all the sects, of whatever denomination, who have seceded from the Church of Rome.

Protestation. In old pleading, the indirect affirmation or denial of the truth of some matter which cannot with propriety or safety be positively affirmed, denied, or entirely passed over. The exclusion of a conclusion.

Protest fee. Fee charged by banks or other financial agencies when items (such as checks) presented for collection cannot be collected.

Prothonotary /pròwdənówdəriy/pròwθə°/. The title given (in *e.g.* Pennsylvania) to an officer who officiates as principal clerk of some courts.

Protocol /prówdəkòl/. A brief summary of the text of a document. Also, the minutes of a meeting which are generally initialed by the parties present to reflect their assent to the accuracy of the minutes.

A section of the Department of State charged with the preparation of agreements and treaties. Commonly, term refers to the etiquette of diplomacy and the ranking of officials.

Protutor /prowt(y)úwdər/. Lat. In the civil law, he who, not being the tutor of a minor, has administered his property or affairs as if he had been, whether he thought himself legally invested with the authority of a tutor or not. He who marries a woman who is tutrix becomes, by the marriage, a protutor. The protutor is equally responsible with the tutor.

Prout patet per recordum /prówət péydət pər rəkórdəm/. As appears by the record. In the Latin phraseology of pleading, this was the proper formula for making reference to a record.

Provable. Susceptible of being proved.

Prove. To establish or make certain; to establish a fact or hypothesis as true by satisfactory and sufficient evidence. Lawson v. Superior Court In and For Los Angeles County, 155 Cal.App.2d 755, 318 P.2d 812, 814. The word "prove" as used in legal matters and proceedings means to establish, to render or make certain. Texas & N. O. R. Co. v. Flowers, Tex.Civ. App., 336 S.W.2d 907, 914. See also **Proof.**

Prover. In old English law, a person who, on being indicted of treason or felony, and arraigned for the same, confessed the fact before plea pleaded, and appealed or accused others, his accomplices, in the same crime, in order to obtain his pardon.

Provide. To make, procure, or furnish for future use, prepare. To supply; to afford; to contribute.

Provided. The word used in introducing a proviso (q.v.). Ordinarily it signifies or expresses a condition; but this is not invariable, for, according to the context, it may import a covenant, or a limitation or qualification, or a restraint, modification, or exception to something which precedes.

Provided by law. This phrase when used in a constitution or statute generally means prescribed or provided by some statute.

Province. The district into which a country has been divided; as, the province of Quebec in Canada. More loosely, a sphere of activity or a profession such as medicine or law.

Provincialis /prəvìnshiyéyləs/. Lat. In the civil law, one who has his domicile in a province.

Provision. Foresight of the chance of an event happening, sufficient to indicate that any present undertaking upon which its assumed realization might exert a natural and proper influence was entered upon in full contemplation of it as a future possibility.

In commercial law, funds remitted by the drawer of a bill of exchange to the drawee in order to meet the bill, or property remaining in the drawee's hands or due from him to the drawer, and appropriated to that purpose.

Provisional. Temporary; preliminary; tentative; taken or done by way of precaution or *ad interim.*

Provisional committee. A committee appointed for a temporary occasion.

Provisional court. A federal court with jurisdiction and powers governed by the order from which it derives its authority. A provisional court established in conquered or occupied territory by military authorities, or the provisional government, is a federal court

deriving its existence and all its powers from the federal government.

Provisional government. One temporarily established in anticipation of and to exist and continue until another (more regular or more permanent) shall be organized and instituted in its stead.

Provisional injunction. Term sometimes used for interlocutory or temporary injunction.

Provisional remedy. A remedy provided for present need or for the immediate occasion; one adapted to meet a particular exigency. Particularly, a temporary process available to a plaintiff in a civil action, which secures him against loss, irreparable injury, dissipation of the property, etc., while the action is pending. Such include the remedies of injunction, appointment of a receiver, attachment, or arrest.

Provisional seizure. A remedy known under the law of Louisiana, and substantially the same in general nature as attachment of property in other states.

Proviso /prəváyzow/. A condition, stipulation, limitation, or provision which is inserted in a deed, lease, mortgage, or contract, and on the performance or nonperformance of which the validity of the instrument frequently depends; it usually begins with the word "provided."

A limitation or exception to a grant made or authority conferred, the effect of which is to declare that the one shall not operate, or the other be exercised, unless in the case provided.

A clause or part of a clause in a statute, the office of which is either to except something from the enacting clause, or to qualify or restrain its generality, or to exclude some possible ground of misinterpretation of its extent.

A "proviso" is used to limit, modify or explain the main part of section of statute to which it is appended. Saginaw County Tp. Officers Ass'n v. City of Saginaw, 373 Mich. 477, 130 N.W.2d 30, 32. The office of a "proviso" in a statute is to restrict or make clear that which has gone before. Allen v. Burkhart, Okl., 377 P.2d 821, 827. A clause engrafted on a preceding enactment for the purpose of restraining or modifying the enacting clause or of excepting something from its operation which would otherwise have been within it. Stoller v. State, 171 Neb. 93, 105 N.W.2d 852, 856. A proviso is sometimes misused to introduce independent pieces of legislation. Cox v. Hart, 260 U.S. 427, 43 S.Ct. 154, 157, 67 L.Ed. 332. Its proper use, however, is to qualify what is affirmed in the body of the act, section, or paragraph preceding it, or to except something from the act, but not to enlarge the enacting clause. And it cannot be held to enlarge the scope of the statute.

Exception and proviso distinguished. See **Exception.**

Proviso est providere præsentia et futura, non præterita /prəváyzow èst pròvədíriy prəzénsh(iy)ə èt f(y)əchúrə, nòn prətéhrədə/. A proviso is to provide for the present or future, not the past.

Provisor /prəváyzər/. In old English law, a provider, or purveyor. Also a person nominated to be the next incumbent of a benefice (not yet vacant) by the pope.

He that hath the care of providing things necessary; but more especially one who sued to the court of Rome for a provision.

Proviso, trial by. In old English practice, a trial brought on by the defendant, in cases where the plaintiff, after issue joined, neglects to proceed to trial; so called from a clause in the writ to the sheriff, which directs him, in case two writs come to his hands, to execute but one of them. The defendant may take out a *venire facias* to the sheriff, which hath in it these words, *Proviso quod,* etc., provided that if the plaintiff shall take out any writ to that purpose, the sheriff shall summon but one jury on them both.

Provocation. The act of inciting another to do a particular deed. That which arouses, moves, calls forth, causes, or occasions. Such conduct or actions on the part of one person towards another as tend to arouse rage, resentment, or fury in the latter against the former, and thereby cause him to do some illegal act against or in relation to the person offering the provocation. See also **Procurer.**

Provocation which will reduce killing to manslaughter must be of such character as will, in mind of average reasonable man, stir resentment likely to cause violence, obscure the reason, and lead to action from passion rather than judgment. There must be a state of passion without time to cool placing defendant beyond control of his reason. Provocation carries with it the idea of some physical aggression or some assault which suddenly arouses heat and passion in the person assaulted.

Provoke. To excite; to stimulate; to arouse. To irritate, or enrage.

Provost-Marshall. In military law, the officer acting as the head of the military police of any post, camp, city or other place in military occupation, or district under the reign of martial law. He or his assistants may, at any time, arrest and detain for trial, persons subject to military law committing offenses, and may carry into execution any punishments to be inflicted in pursuance of a court martial.

Proxeneta /pròksəníydə/. Lat. In the civil law, a broker; one who negotiated or arranged the terms of a contract between two parties, as between buyer and seller; one who negotiated a marriage; a match-maker.

Proximate. Immediate; nearest; direct, next in order. In its legal sense, closest in causal connection. Armijo v. World Ins. Co., 78 N.M. 204, 429 P.2d 904, 905. Next in relation to cause and effect.

Proximate cause. That which, in a natural and continuous sequence, unbroken by any efficient intervening cause, produces injury, and without which the result would not have occurred. Wisniewski v. Great Atlantic & Pac. Tea Co., 226 Pa.Super. 574, 323 A.2d 744, 748. That which is nearest in the order of responsible causation. That which stands next in causation to the effect, not necessarily in time or space but in causal relation. The proximate cause of an injury is the primary or moving cause, or that which, in a natural and continuous sequence, unbroken by any efficient intervening cause, produces the injury and without which the accident could not have happened, if the injury be one which might be reasonably anticipated or foreseen as a natural consequence of the wrongful act. An injury or damage is proximately caused by an act, or a failure to act, whenever it appears from the evidence in the case, that the act or omission played a substantial part in bringing about or actually causing the injury or damage; and that the injury or damage was either a direct result or a reasonably probable consequence of the act or omission.

The last negligent act contributory to an injury, without which such injury would not have resulted. The dominant, moving or producing cause. The efficient cause; the one that necessarily sets the other causes in operation. The causes that are merely incidental or instruments of a superior or controlling agency are not the proximate causes and the responsible ones, though they may be nearer in time to the result. It is only when the causes are independent of each other that the nearest is, of course, to be charged with the disaster. Act or omission immediately causing or failing to prevent injury; act or omission occurring or concurring with another, which, had it not happened, injury would not have been inflicted. Herron v. Smith Bros., 116 Cal.App. 518, 2 P.2d 1012, 1013.

See also **Concurrent causes; Efficient cause; Immediate cause; Legal cause.**

Proximate consequence or result. One which succeeds naturally in the ordinary course of things. A consequence which, in addition to being in the train of physical causation, is not entirely outside the range of expectation or probability, as viewed by ordinary men. The Mars, D.C.N.Y., 9 F.2d 183, 184. One ordinarily following from the negligence complained of, unbroken by any independent cause, which might have been reasonably foreseen. One which a prudent and experienced man, fully acquainted with all the circumstances which in fact existed, would, at time of the negligent act, have thought reasonably possible to follow, if it had occurred to his mind. Coast S. S. Co. v. Brady, C.C.A.Ala., 8 F.2d 16, 19. A mere possibility of the injury is not sufficient, where a reasonable man would not consider injury likely to result from the act as one of its ordinary and probable results.

Proximate damages. See **Damages.**

Proximately. Directly or immediately. Pertaining to that which in an ordinary natural sequence produces a specific result, no independent disturbing agency intervening. Weaver v. Landis, 66 Cal.App.2d 34, 151 P.2d 884, 886. See **Proximate; Proximate cause.**

Proximity. Kindred between two persons. Quality or state of being next in time, place, causation, influence, etc.; immediate nearness.

Proximus est cui nemo antecedit, supremus est quem nemo sequitur /pròksəməs èst k(yuw)ay níymow æntəsíydət, səpríyməs èst kwém níymow sékwədər/. He is next whom no one precedes; he is last whom no one follows.

Proxy. (Contracted from procuracy.) A person who is substituted or deputed by another to represent him and act for him, particularly in some meeting or public body. An agent representing and acting for principal. Also the instrument containing the appointment of such person. Cliffs Corporation v. United States, C.C.A.Ohio, 103 F.2d 77, 80.

Written authorization given by one person to another so that the second person can act for the first, such as that given by a shareholder to someone else to represent him and vote his shares at a shareholders' meeting. See also **Power of attorney; Proxy statement.**

Proxy marriage. A marriage contracted or celebrated through agents acting on behalf of one or both parties. A proxy marriage differs from the more conventional ceremony only in that one or both of the contracting parties are represented by an agent; all the other requirements having been met. State v. Anderson, 239 Or. 200, 396 P.2d 558, 561.

Proxy statement. Information required by SEC to be given stockholders as a prerequisite to solicitation of proxies for a security subject to the requirements of Securities Exchange Act.

Prudence. Carefulness, precaution, attentiveness, and good judgment, as applied to action or conduct. That degree of care required by the exigencies or circumstances under which it is to be exercised. This term, in the language of the law, is commonly associated with "care" and "diligence" and contrasted with "negligence." See those titles.

Prudent. Sagacious in adapting means to end; circumspect in action, or in determining any line of conduct. Practically wise, judicious, careful, discreet, circumspect, sensible. Tureen v. Peoples Motorbus Co. of St. Louis, Mo.App., 97 S.W.2d 847, 848. In defining negligence, practically synonymous with cautious.

Prudenter agit qui præcepto legis obtemperat /pruwdéntər éyjət kwày prəséptow líyjəs obtémpərət/. He acts prudently who obeys the command of the law.

Prudent Man Rule. An investment standard. In some states, the law requires that a fiduciary, such as a trustee, may invest the trust's or fund's money only in a list of securities designated by the state—the so-called legal list. In other states, the trustee may invest in a security if it is one which a prudent man of discretion and intelligence, who is seeking a reasonable income and preservation of capital, would buy. A federal "prudent man rule" which governs investment of pension funds is found in ERISA § 404(a)(1); 29 U.S.C.A. § 1104(a)(1).

Prurient interest. A shameful or morbid interest in nudity, sex, or excretion. Attorney General v. Book Named "John Cleland's Memoirs of a Woman of Pleasure", 349 Mass. 69, 206 N.E.2d 403, 405. "Prurient" means having lustful ideas or desires. State v. A Quantity of Copies of Books, 191 Kan. 13, 379 P.2d 254, 256. An obsessive interest in immoral and lascivious matters. One of the criteria of obscenity enunciated in Miller v. California, 413 U.S. 15, 93 S.Ct. 2607, 37 L.Ed.2d 419, is whether the material appeals to the "prurient interest" in sex. See also **Obscene; Obscenity.**

P.S. An abbreviation for "Public Statutes;" also for "postscript."

Pseudo /s(y)úwdow/. False, counterfeit, pretended, spurious.

Pseudograph /s(y)úwdəgræf/. False writing.

P.S.I.A. An abbreviation for "pounds per square inch absolute."

Psychoneurosis /sàykown(y)ərówsəs/. See **Insanity.**

Psychosis /saykówsəs/. A severe mental disorder in which the patient departs from the normal pattern of thinking, feeling, and acting. There is generally a loss of contact with reality. Progressive deterioration may occur. See also **Insanity.**

Psychotherapy /sàykowθéhrəpiy/. A method or system of alleviating or curing certain forms of disease, particularly diseases of the nervous system or such as are traceable to nervous disorders, by suggestion, persuasion, encouragement, the inspiration of hope or confidence, the discouragement of morbid memories, associations, or beliefs, and other similar means addressed to the mental state of the patient, without (or sometimes in conjunction with) the administration of drugs or other physical remedies.

PTI. Previously taxed income.

Puberty. The earliest age at which persons are capable of begetting or bearing children. In the civil and common law, the age at which one became capable of contracting marriage. It was in boys fourteen, and in girls twelve years.

Public, *n.* The whole body politic, or the aggregate of the citizens of a state, nation, or municipality. The inhabitants of a state, county, or community. In one sense, everybody, and accordingly the body of the people at large; the community at large, without reference to the geographical limits of any corporation like a city, town, or county; the people. In another sense the word does not mean all the people, nor most of the people, nor very many of the people of a place, but so many of them as contradistinguishes them from a few. Accordingly, it has been defined or employed as meaning the inhabitants of a particular place; all the inhabitants of a particular place; the people of the neighborhood. Also, a part of the inhabitants of a community.

Public, *adj.* Pertaining to a state, nation, or whole community; proceeding from, relating to, or affecting the whole body of people or an entire community. Open to all; notorious. Common to all or many; general; open to common use. Belonging to the people at large; relating to or affecting the whole people of a state, nation, or community; not limited or restricted to any particular class of the community. Peacock v. Retail Credit Co., D.C.Ga., 302 F.Supp. 418, 423.

As to public Accounts; Acknowledgment; Act; Administrator; Agent; Attorney; Auction; Breach; Blockade; Boundary; Business; Capacity; Carrier; Chapel; Charge; Charity; Company; Corporation; Debt; Document; Domain; Easement; Enemy; Ferry; Fund; Good; Grant; Health; Highway; Holiday; Hospital; House; Indecent; Institution;

Market; Minister; Money; Necessity; Notice; Nuisance; Office; Officer; Peace; Policy; Pond; Property; Prosecutor; Record; Revenue; River; Road; Sale; School; Seal; Square; Stock; Store; Tax; Things; Thoroughfare; Trial; Trust; Trustee; Verdict; Vessel; War; Works; Worship, and Wrong, see those titles.

Public advocate. One who may or may not be an attorney who purports to represent the public at large in matters of public concern such as utility rates, environmental quality, and other consumer matters. See also **Ombudsman.**

Public agency. A department or agency of government which has official or quasi official status. An administrative body.

Publican /páblǝkǝn/. In the civil law, a farmer of the public revenue; one who held a lease of some property from the public treasury; a collector of taxes and tolls.

In English law, a person authorized by license to keep a public house, and retail therein, for consumption on or off the premises where sold, all intoxicating liquors; also termed "licensed victualler." A victualer; one who serves food or drink prepared for consumption on the premises.

Publicanus /pǝblǝkéynǝs/. Lat. In Roman law, a farmer of the customs; a publican.

Public appointments. Public offices or positions which are to be filled by the appointment of individuals, under authority of law, instead of by election.

Publication. To make public; to make known to people in general; to bring before public; to exhibit, display, disclose or reveal. Tiffany Productions v. Dewing, D.C.Md., 50 F.2d 911, 914. The act of publishing anything; offering it to public notice, or rendering it accessible to public scrutiny. An advising of the public; a making known of something to them for a purpose. It implies the means of conveying knowledge or notice. See also **Notice; Proclamation; Publish.**

Term "publication" is both a business term meaning printing and distribution of written materials and a legal term meaning communication of libelous matter to a third person. Applewhite v. Memphis State University, Tenn., 495 S.W.2d 190, 192. See also *Law of libel, infra;* **Libel; Utter.**

As descriptive of the publishing of laws and ordinances, it means printing or otherwise reproducing copies of them and distributing them in such a manner as to make their contents easily accessible to the public.

Copyright law. The act of making public a book, writing, chart, map, etc.; that is, offering or communicating it to the public by the sale or distribution of copies. Publication, as used in connection with common-law copyrights, is employed to denote those acts of an author or creator which evidence a dedication of his work to public and on which depends the loss of his common-law copyright. Vic Alexander & Associates v. Cheyenne Neon Sign Co., Wyo., 417 P.2d 921, 923. See also **Common-law copyright.**

Law of libel. The act of making the defamatory matter known publicly, of disseminating it, or com-

municating it to one or more persons (*i.e.* to third person or persons). The reduction of libelous matter to writing and its delivery to any one other than the person injuriously affected thereby. Great Atlantic & Pac. Tea Co. v. Paul, 256 Md. 643, 261 A.2d 731, 734, 735. See also **Libel.**

Law of wills. The formal declaration made by a testator at the time of signing his will that it is his last will and testament. The act or acts of the testator by which he manifests that it is his intention to give effect to the paper as his last will and testament; any communication indicating to the witness that the testator intends to give effect to the paper as his will, by words, sign, motion, or conduct.

Service of process. Under Rules of Civil Procedure, publication of a summons is the process of giving it currency as an advertisement in a newspaper, under the conditions prescribed by law, as a means of giving notice of the suit to a defendant upon whom personal service cannot be made. See *e.g.* New York CPLR § 315; Florida Rule of Civil P. 1.070.

Public authority. An agency established by government though not a department thereof but subject to some governmental control, *e.g.* Mass. Port Authority. Opinion of the Justices, 334 Mass. 721, 136 N.E.2d 223, 235.

Public building. One of which the possession and use, as well as the property in it, are in the public. Any building held, used, or controlled exclusively for public purposes by any department or branch of government, state, county, or municipal, without reference to the ownership of the building or of the realty upon which it is situated. A building belonging to or used by the public for the transaction of public or quasi public business.

Public character. An individual who asks for and desires public recognition, such as a political figure, statesman, author, artist, or inventor. See also **Public figure.**

Public contract. Any contract in which there are public funds provided though private persons may perform the contract and the subject of the contract may ultimately benefit private persons. Nat'l Sur. Corp. v. Edison, 240 Ark. 641, 401 S.W.2d 754.

Public convenience and necessity. The common criterion used in public utility matters when a board or agency is faced with a petition for action at the request of the utility. In a statute requiring the issuance of a certificate of public convenience and necessity by the Public Utilities Commission for the operation of a public transportation line, "convenience" is not used in its colloquial sense as synonymous with handy or easy of access, but in accord with its regular meaning of suitable and fitting, and "public convenience" refers to something fitting or suited to the public need. See also **Convenience and necessity; Public utility.**

Public corporations. An artificial person (*e.g.* municipality or a government corporation) created for the administration of public affairs. Unlike a private corporation it has no protection against legislative acts altering or even repealing its charter. Instrumentalities created by state, formed and owned by it in public interest, supported in whole or part by public funds, and governed by managers deriving their authority from state. Sharon Realty Co. v. Westlake, Ohio Com.Pl., 188 N.E.2d 318, 323, 25 O.O.2d 322. A public corporation is an instrumentality of the state, founded and owned in the public interest, supported by public funds and governed by those deriving their authority from the state. York County Fair Ass'n v. South Carolina Tax Commission, 249 S.C. 337, 154 S.E.2d 361, 362.

Term is also commonly used to distinguish a corporation whose stock is owned and traded by the public from a corporation with closely held shares (*i.e.* close or private corporation).

Public defender. An attorney appointed by a court or employed by a government agency whose work consists primarily in defending indigent defendants in criminal cases. Federal Public Defender Organizations and Community Defender Organizations are provided for under 18 U.S.C.A. § 3006A. Most states also have public defender programs. See also **Counsel, right to; Legal aid; Legal Services Corporation.**

Public entity. Public entity includes a nation, state, county, city and county, city, district, public authority, public agency, or any other political subdivision or public corporation, whether foreign or domestic. Calif.Evid.Code.

Public figure. Term "public figure," for purposes of determining standard to be applied in defamation action, includes artists, athletes, business people, dilettantes, and anyone who is famous or infamous because of who he is or what he has done. Rosanova v. Playboy Enterprises, Inc., D.C.Ga., 411 F.Supp. 440, 444. Public figures, for libel purposes, are those who have assumed roles of special prominence in society; commonly, those classed as public figures have thrust themselves to forefront of particular public controversies in order to influence resolution of issues involved. Widener v. Pacific Gas & Elec. Co., 75 C.A.3d 415, 142 Cal.Rptr. 304, 313.

For right of privacy action purposes, includes anyone who has arrived at position where public attention is focused upon him as a person. Dietemann v. Time, Inc., D.C.Cal., 284 F.Supp. 925, 930.

Public funds. Moneys belonging to government, or any department of it, in hands of public official. Droste v. Kerner, 34 Ill.2d 495, 217 N.E.2d 73, 78.

Publici juris /pábləsay júrəs/. Lat. Of public right. The word "public" in this sense means pertaining to the people, or affecting the community at large; that which concerns a multitude of people; and the word "right," as so used, means a well-founded claim; an interest; concern; advantage; benefit. This term, as applied to a thing or right, means that it is open to or exercisable by all persons. It designates things which are owned by "the public;" that is, the entire state or community, and not by any private person. When a thing is common property, so that any one can make use of it who likes, it is said to be *publici juris;* as in the case of light, air, and public water.

Public interest. Something in which the public, the community at large, has some pecuniary interest, or some interest by which their legal rights or liabilities

are affected. It does not mean anything so narrow as mere curiosity, or as the interests of the particular localities, which may be affected by the matters in question. Interest shared by citizens generally in affairs of local, state or national government. Russell v. Wheeler, 165 Colo. 296, 439 P.2d 43, 46.

If by public permission one is making use of public property and he chances to be the only one with whom the public can deal with respect to the use of that property, his business is affected with a public interest which requires him to deal with the public on reasonable terms. The circumstances which clothe a particular kind of business with a "public interest," as to be subject to regulation, must be such as to create a peculiarly close relation between the public and those engaged in it and raise implications of an affirmative obligation on their part to be reasonable in dealing with the public. One does not devote his property or business to a public use, or clothe it with a public interest, merely because he makes commodities for and sells to the public in common callings such as those of the butcher, baker, tailor, etc. Chas. Wolff Packing Co. v. Court of Industrial Relations of State of Kansas, 262 U.S. 522, 43 S.Ct. 630, 633, 67 L.Ed. 1103. A business is not affected with a public interest merely because it is large, or because the public has concern in respect of its maintenance, or derives benefit, accommodation, ease, or enjoyment from it. Tyson & Bro.-United Theatre Ticket Offices v. Banton, 273 U.S. 418, 47 S.Ct. 426, 71 L.Ed. 718.

Public invitee. A public invitee to whom owner of property owes duty to exercise ordinary care for his safety is person who is invited to enter or remain on land as member of public for purpose for which land is held open to public. Lemon v. Busey, 204 Kan. 119, 461 P.2d 145, 149. See also **Invitee.**

Publicist /pábləsəst/. One versed in, or writing upon, public law, the science and principles of government, or international law.

Public lands. The general public domain; unappropriated lands; lands belonging to the United States and which are subject to sale or other disposal under general laws, and not reserved or held back for any special governmental or public purpose. Newhall v. Sanger, 92 U.S. 761, 763, 23 L.Ed. 769.

Public land system. Legal descriptions of land by reference to the public land survey.

Public law. A general classification of law, consisting generally of constitutional, administrative, criminal, and international law, concerned with the organization of the state, the relations between the state and the people who compose it, the responsibilities of public officers to the state, to each other, and to private persons, and the relations of states to one another. An act which relates to the public as a whole. It may be (1) general (applying to all persons within the jurisdiction), (2) local (applying to a geographical area), or (3) special (relating to an organization which is charged with a public interest).

That branch or department of law which is concerned with the state in its political or sovereign capacity, including constitutional and administrative law, and with the definition, regulation, and enforcement of rights in cases where the state is regarded as the subject of the right or object of the duty,—including criminal law and criminal procedure,—and the law of the state, considered in its *quasi* private personality, *i.e.,* as capable of holding or exercising rights, or acquiring and dealing with property, in the character of an individual. That portion of law which is concerned with political conditions; that is to say, with the powers, rights, duties, capacities, and incapacities which are peculiar to political superiors, supreme and subordinate. In one sense, a designation given to international law, as distinguished from the laws of a particular nation or state. In another sense, a law or statute that applies to the people generally of the nation or state adopting or enacting it, is denominated a public law, as contradistinguished from a private law, affecting only an individual or a small number of persons.

Public liability insurance. Type of insurance coverage which protects against claims arising from the conduct, property and agents of the insured and which idemnifies against loss arising from liability.

Publicly. Openly. In public, well known, open, notorious, common, or general, as opposed to private, secluded, or secret.

Public nuisance. A condition dangerous to health, offensive to community moral standards, or unlawfully obstructing the public in the free use of public property. Public nuisance is one affecting rights enjoyed by citizens as part of public and must affect a considerable number of people or an entire community or neighborhood. Spur Industries, Inc. v. Del E. Webb Development Co., 108 Ariz. 178, 494 P.2d 700, 705. An unreasonable interference with a right, common to the general public; it is behavior which unreasonably interferes with the health, safety, peace, comfort or convenience of the general community. Robie v. Lillis, 112 N.H. 492, 299 A.2d 155, 158. *Compare* **Private nuisance.**

Public offense. An act or omission forbidden by law, and punishable as by law provided. Term used to describe a crime as distinguished from an infringement of private rights. A public offense, the commission of which authorizes private person to arrest another, includes misdemeanors. People v. Sjosten, 262 C.A.2d 539, 68 Cal.Rptr. 832, 835. See **Crime.**

Public offering. See **Offering.**

Public office. Essential characteristics of "public office" are (1) authority conferred by law, (2) fixed tenure of office, and (3) power to exercise some portion of sovereign functions of government; key element of such test is that "officer" is carrying out sovereign function. Spring v. Constantino, 168 Conn. 563, 362 A.2d 871, 875. Essential elements to establish public position as "public office" are: position must be created by constitution, legislature, or through authority conferred by legislature, portion of sovereign power of government must be delegated to position, duties and powers must be defined, directly or impliedly, by legislature or through legislative authority, duties must be performed independently without control of superior power other than law, and position must have some permanency and continuity. State v. Taylor, 260 Iowa 634, 144 N.W.2d 289, 292.

Public official. The holder of a public office though not all persons in public employment are public officials, because public official's position requires the exercise of some portion of the sovereign power, whether great or small. Town of Arlington v. Bds. of Conciliation and Arbitration, Mass., 352 N.E.2d 914.

Public passage. A right, subsisting in the public, to pass over a body of water, whether the land under it be public or owned by a private person. This term is synonymous with public highway, with this difference: by the latter is understood a right to pass over the land of another; by the former is meant the right of going over the water which is on another's land.

Public place. A place to which the general public has a right to resort; not necessarily a place devoted solely to the uses of the public, but a place which is in point of fact public rather than private, a place visited by many persons and usually accessible to the neighboring public (*e.g.* a park or public beach). Also, a place in which the public has an interest as affecting the safety, health, morals, and welfare of the community. A place exposed to the public, and where the public gather together or pass to and fro.

Public purpose. In the law of taxation, eminent domain, etc., this is a term of classification to distinguish the objects for which, according to settled usage, the government is to provide, from those which, by the like usage, are left to private interest, inclination, or liberality. The constitutional requirement that the purpose of any tax, police regulation, or particular exertion of the power of eminent domain shall be the convenience, safety, or welfare of the entire community and not the welfare of a specific individual or class of persons.

The term is synonymous with governmental purpose. As employed to denote the objects for which taxes may be levied, it has no relation to the urgency of the public need or to the extent of the public benefit which is to follow; the essential requisite being that a public service or use shall affect the inhabitants as a community, and not merely as individuals. A public purpose or public business has for its objective the promotion of the public health, safety, morals, general welfare, security, prosperity, and contentment of all the inhabitants or residents within a given political division, as, for example, a state, the sovereign powers of which are exercised to promote such public purpose or public business.

Public record. Public records are those records which a governmental unit is required by law to keep or which it is necessary to keep in discharge of duties imposed by law. Curran v. Board of Park Com'rs, Lake County Metropolitan Park Dist., Com.Pl., 22 Ohio Misc. 197, 259 N.E.2d 757, 759, 51 O.O.2d 321. A record is a "public record" within purview of statute providing that books and records required by law to be kept by county clerk may be received in evidence in any court if it is a record which a public officer is required to keep and if it is filed in such a manner that it is subject to public inspection. In re LaSarge's Estate, Okl., 526 P.2d 930, 933. See also **Record.**

Public safety. A state may exercise its police power (derivatively, a city or town) by enacting laws for the protection of the public from injury and dangers.

Public sale. Sale at auction of property upon notice to public of such. May result from *e.g.* tax foreclosure. See also **Sheriff's sale.**

Public service. A term applied to the objects and enterprises of certain kinds of corporations, which specially serve the needs of the general public or conduce to the comfort and convenience of an entire community, such as railroad, gas, water, and electric light companies; and companies furnishing public transportation. A public service or quasi public corporation is one private in its ownership, but which has an appropriate franchise from the state to provide for a necessity or convenience of the general public, incapable of being furnished by private competitive business, and dependent for its exercise on eminent domain or governmental agency. It is one of a large class of private corporations which on account of special franchises conferred on them owe a duty to the public which they may be compelled to perform. See also **Public corporations.**

Public service commission. A board or commission created by the legislature to exercise power of supervision or regulation over public utilities or public service corporations. An administrative agency established by the State legislature to regulate rates and services of electric, gas, telephone, and other public utilities. Such a commission is a legal, administrative body, provided for the administration of certain matters within the police power, with power to make regulations as to certain matters when required for the public safety and convenience, and to determine facts on which existing laws shall operate.

Public service corporation. A utility company privately owned but regulated by the government. It may sell gas, water or electricity but its rates are established by the state. It may be a broadcasting company. See also **Public convenience and necessity; Public utility.**

Public trial. Term "public trial" contemplated by Constitution (Art. VI) is a trial which is not secret, one that the public is free to attend. To a great extent, it is a relative term and its meaning depends largely on circumstances of each particular case. Hampton v. People, 171 Colo. 153, 465 P.2d 394, 399.

Public, true, and notorious. The old form by which charges in the *allegations* in the ecclesiastical courts were described at the end of each particular.

Public trust. See **Charitable trust; Trust.**

Public trustee. County official who is appointed to act for the public in administering deeds of trust.

Publicum jus /pə́bləkəm jə́s/. Lat. In the civil law, public law; that law which regards the state of the commonwealth.

Public use. *Eminent domain.* The constitutional and statutory basis for taking by eminent domain. For condemnation purposes, "public use" is one which confers some benefit or advantage to the public; it is not confined to actual use by public. It is measured in terms of right of public to use proposed facilities for which condemnation is sought and, as long as public has right of use, whether exercised by one or many members of public, a "public advantage" or

"public benefit" accrues sufficient to constitute a public use. Montana Power Co. v. Bokma, Mont., 457 P.2d 769, 772, 773.

Public use, in constitutional provisions restricting the exercise of the right to take private property in virtue of eminent domain, means a use concerning the whole community as distinguished from particular individuals. But each and every member of society need not be equally interested in such use, or be personally and directly affected by it; if the object is to satisfy a great public want or exigency, that is sufficient. Rindge Co. v. Los Angeles County, 262 U.S. 700, 43 S.Ct. 689, 692, 67 L.Ed. 1186. The term may be said to mean public usefulness, utility, or advantage, or what is productive of general benefit. It may be limited to the inhabitants of a small or restricted locality, but must be in common, and not for a particular individual. The use must be a needful one for the public, which cannot be surrendered without obvious general loss and inconvenience. A "public use" for which land may be taken defies absolute definition for it changes with varying conditions of society, new appliances in the sciences, changing conceptions of scope and functions of government, and other differing circumstances brought about by an increase in population and new modes of communication and transportation. Katz v. Brandon, 156 Conn. 521, 245 A.2d 579, 586.

Patent law. "Public use" within statute providing that patent is invalid if invention was in public use more than one year prior to date of application for patent is defined as any nonsecret use of a completed and operative invention in its natural and intended way. Atlas Chemical Industries, Inc. v. Moraine Products, C.A.Mich., 509 F.2d 1, 4. In patent law, a public use is entirely different from a use by the public. If an inventor allows his machine to be used by other persons generally, either with or without compensation, or if it is, with his consent, put on sale for such use, then it will be in "public use" and on public sale.

Public utility. A privately owned and operated business whose services are so essential to the general public as to justify the grant of special franchises for the use of public property or of the right of eminent domain, in consideration of which the owners must serve all persons who apply, without discrimination. It is always a virtual monopoly.

A business or service which is engaged in regularly supplying the public with some commodity or service which is of public consequence and need, such as electricity, gas, water, transportation, or telephone or telegraph service. Gulf States Utilities Co. v. State, Tex.Civ.App., 46 S.W.2d 1018, 1021. Any agency, instrumentality, business industry or service which is used or conducted in such manner as to affect the community at large, that is, which is not limited or restricted to any particular class of the community. The test for determining if a concern is a public utility is whether it has held itself out as ready, able and willing to serve the public. The term implies a public use of an article, product, or service, carrying with it the duty of the producer or manufacturer, or one attempting to furnish the service, to serve the public and treat all persons alike, without discrimination. It is synonymous with "public use," and refers to persons or corporations charged with the duty to supply the public with the use of property or facilities owned or furnished by them. Buder v. First Nat. Bank in St. Louis, C.C.A.Mo., 16 F.2d 990, 992. To constitute a true "public utility," the devotion to public use must be of such character that the public generally, or that part of it which has been served and which has accepted the service, has the legal right to demand that that service shall be conducted, so long as it is continued, with reasonable efficiency under reasonable charges. The devotion to public use must be of such character that the product and service is available to the public generally and indiscriminately, or there must be the acceptance by the utility of public franchises or calling to its aid the police power of the state.

Public Utility Holding Company Act. Federal statute enacted in 1935 designed to free local operating companies from the control and domination of absentee and uneconomic holding companies. It caused the breakup of huge utility combines and sought to restrict the operations of utility holding companies to one or more systems whose operations are integrated and confined to a single state and states which are contiguous. 15 U.S.C.A. §§ 79–79Z.

Public vessel. See **Vessel.**

Public Vessels Act. Federal law which provides for libel in personam against the United States or a petition impleading the United States for damages caused by public vessels of the United States. 46 U.S.C.A. § 781–790.

Public welfare. The prosperity, well-being, or convenience of the public at large, or of a whole community, as distinguished from the advantage of an individual or limited class. It embraces the primary social interests of safety, order, morals, economic interest, and non-material and political interests. In the development of our civic life, the definition of "public welfare" has also developed until it has been held to bring within its purview regulations for the promotion of economic welfare and public convenience.

Publish. To make public; to circulate; to make known to people in general. To issue; to put into circulation. To utter; to present (*e.g.* a forged instrument) for payment. To declare or assert, directly or indirectly, by words or actions, that a forged instrument is genuine. An advising of the public or making known of something to the public for a purpose. Estill County v. Noland, 295 Ky. 753, 175 S.W.2d 341, 346. See also **Publication; Utter.**

Publisher. One who by himself or his agent makes a thing publicly known. One whose business is the manufacture and sale of books, pamphlets, magazines, newspapers, or other literary productions. One who publishes, especially one who issues, or causes to be issued, from the press, and offers for sale or circulation matter printed, engraved, or the like.

P.U.C. Public Utilities Commission.

PUD. Planned Unit Development. In zoning, a device which has as its goal a self-contained mini-community, built within a zoning district, under density and

use rules controlling the relation of private dwellings to open space, of homes to commercial establishments, and of high income dwellings to low and moderate income housing. See **Planned unit development.**

Pudicity /pyuwdísədiy/. Chastity; purity; continence; modesty; the abstaining from all unlawful carnal commerce or connection.

Pudzeld /wúdgèld/. In old English law, supposed to be a corruption of the Saxon *"wudgeld"* (woodgeld), a freedom from payment of money for taking *wood* in any forest.

Pueblo /p(yu)wé(y)blow/. In Spanish law, people; all the inhabitants of any country or place, without distinction. A town, township, or municipality. A small settlement or gathering of people, a steady community; the term applies equally whether the settlement be a small collection of Spaniards or Indians. Pueblo of Santa Rosa v. Fall, 56 App.D.C. 259, 12 F.2d 332, 335. This term *"pueblo,"* in its original signification, means "people" or "population," but is used in the sense of the English word "town." It has the indefiniteness of that term, and, like it, is sometimes applied to a mere collection of individuals residing at a particular place, a settlement or village, as well as to a regularly organized municipality. Trenouth v. San Francisco, 100 U.S. 251, 25 L.Ed. 626.

Community dwelling, constructed of stone or adobe, resided in by Indian tribes of the southwestern United States. Term may also refer to inhabitants of such dwelling or of the entire village.

Puer /pyúwər/. Lat. In the civil law, a child; one of the age from seven to fourteen, including, in this sense, a girl. But it also meant a "boy," as distinguished from a "girl;" or a servant.

Puerility /p(y)ùwərílədiy/. In the civil law, a condition intermediate between infancy and puberty, continuing in boys from the seventh to the fourteenth year of their age, and in girls from seven to twelve.

Pueri sunt de sanguine parentum, sed pater et mater non sunt de sanguine puerorum / pyúwəray sànt dìy sǽngwəniy pəréntəm, sèd péydər èt méydər nón sànt dìy sǽngwəniy pyuwərórəm/. Children are of the blood of their parents, but the father and mother are not of the blood of the children.

Pueritia /p(y)ùwərísh(iy)ə/. Lat. In the civil law, childhood; the age from seven to fourteen. The age from birth to fourteen years in the male, or twelve in the female.

Puffer. A person employed by the owner of property which is sold at auction to attend the sale and run up the price by making spurious bids. See also **Puffing.**

Puffing. An expression of opinion by seller not made as a representation of fact. Gulf Oil Corp. v. Federal Trade Commission, C.C.A.5, 150 F.2d 106, 109. Exaggeration by a salesperson concerning quality of goods (not considered a legally binding promise); usually concerns opinions rather than facts.

Term also describes secret bidding at auction by or on behalf of seller. Feaster Trucking Service, Inc. v. Parks-Davis Auctioneers, Inc., 211 Kan. 78, 505 P.2d 612, 617.

Puis /pwíy/pwís/. Fr. In law. Afterwards; since.

Puis darrein continuance /pwìs dǽrən kəntínyu-wən(t)s/. Since the last continuance. In common law pleading, the name of a plea which a defendant was allowed to put in, after having already pleaded, where some *new* matter of defense arose after issue joined; such as payment, a release by the plaintiff, the discharge of the defendant under an insolvent or bankrupt law, and the like.

Pulsare /pəlsériy/. Lat. In the civil law, to beat; to accuse or charge; to proceed against at law.

Pulsator /pəlséydər/. The plaintiff, or actor.

Punctum temporis /péŋktəm témpərəs/. Lat. A point of time; an indivisible period of time; the shortest space of time; an instant.

Pundbrech /páwndbrìych/. In old English law, pound-breach; the offense of breaking a pound. The illegal taking of cattle out of a pound by any means whatsoever.

Punishable. Deserving of or capable or liable to punishment; capable of being punished by law or right. People v. Superior Court of City and County of San Francisco, 116 Cal.App. 412, 2 P.2d 843, 844.

Punishment. Any fine, penalty, or confinement inflicted upon a person by the authority of the law and the judgment and sentence of a court, for some crime or offense committed by him, or for his omission of a duty enjoined by law. A deprivation of property or some right. But does not include a civil penalty redounding to the benefit of an individual, such as a forfeiture of interest. People v. Vanderpool, 20 Cal.2d 746, 128 P.2d 513, 515. See also **Sentence.**

Cumulative punishment. An increased punishment inflicted for a second or third conviction of the same offense, under the statutes relating to habitual criminals. To be distinguished from a "cumulative sentence," as to which see **Sentence.**

Cruel and unusual punishment. Such punishment as would amount to torture or barbarity, and any cruel and degrading punishment not known to the common law, and also any punishment so disproportionate to the offense as to shock the moral sense of the community. In re Kemmler, 136 U.S. 436, 10 S.Ct. 930, 34 L.Ed. 519. Punishment which is excessive for the crime committed is cruel and unusual. Coker v. Georgia, 433 U.S. 584, 97 S.Ct. 2861, 53 L.Ed.2d 982. The death penalty is not per se cruel and unusual punishment within the prohibition of the 8th Amendment, U.S.Const., but states must follow strict safeguards in the sentencing of one to death. Gregg v. Georgia, 428 U.S. 153, 96 S.Ct. 2909, 49 L.Ed.2d 859. See also **Capital** (*Capital punishment*); **Corporal punishment; Excessive punishment; Hard labor.**

Infamous punishment. Punishment by imprisonment, particularly in a penitentiary. Sometimes, imprisonment at hard labor regardless of the place of imprisonment. U. S. v. Moreland, 258 U.S. 433, 42 S.Ct. 368, 66 L.Ed. 700.

Punitive. Relating to punishment; having the character of punishment or penalty; inflicting punishment or a penalty.

Punitive damages. See **Damages.**

Punitive statute. One which creates forfeiture or imposes penalty.

Pupillus /pyuwpíləs/. Lat. In the civil law, a ward or infant under the age of puberty; a person under the authority of a *tutor (q.v.).*

Pupillus pati posse non intelligitur /pyuwpíləs péyday pósiy nòn intəlíjədər/. A pupil or infant is not supposed to be able to suffer, *i.e.,* to do an act to his own prejudice.

Pur /pór/púr/. L. Fr. By or for. Used both as a separable particle, and in the composition of such words as "purparty," "purlieu."

Pur autre vie /pər ó(w)tra váy/pùr ówtra víy/. For (or during) the life of another. An estate *pur autre vie* is an estate in lands which a man holds for the life of another person.

Pur cause de vicinage /pər kóz də vəsáynəj/pùr kówz də visinázh/. By reason of neighborhood. See **Common.**

Purchase. Transmission of property from one person to another by voluntary act and agreement, founded on a valuable consideration. Spur Independent School Dist. v. W. A. Holt Co., Tex.Civ.App., 88 S.W.2d 1071, 1073. In a technical and broader meaning relative to land, generally means the acquisition of real estate by any means whatever except by descent. Oklahoma City v. Board of Education of Oklahoma City, 181 Okl. 539, 75 P.2d 201.

Includes taking by sale, discount, negotiation, mortgage, pledge, lien, issue or re-issue, gift or any other voluntary transaction creating an interest in property. U.C.C. § 1–201(32). The term "purchase" includes any contract to purchase or otherwise acquire. Securities Exchange Act, § 3.

Quasi purchase. In the civil law, a purchase of property not founded on the actual agreement of the parties, but on conduct of the owner which is inconsistent with any other hypothesis than that he intended a sale.

Words of purchase. Words which denote the person who is to take the estate. Thus, if a person grants land to A. for twenty-one years, and after the determination of that term to A.'s heirs, the word "heirs" does not denote the duration of A.'s estate, but the person who is to take the remainder on the expiration of the term, and is therefore called a "word of purchase."

Purchase agreement. An agreement between a buyer and seller of property, setting forth, in general, the price and terms of the sale. A sales agreement or contract.

Purchase method of accounting. That method of accounting for a *merger* in which any difference between the merger terms and the book value of the acquired company is accounted for as goodwill on the asset side of the balance sheet and as *acquired surplus* on the liability side. The *earned surplus* of the acquired company is added to the *capital surplus* of the acquiring company.

Purchase money. The actual money paid in cash or check initially for the property while the balance may be secured by a mortgage and note calling for periodic payments. See also **Earnest money.**

As used with reference to part performance under statute of frauds, comprehends consideration, whether it be money or property or services, for which lands are to be conveyed. Hall v. Haer, 160 Okl. 118, 16 P.2d 83, 84.

Purchase money mortgage. A mortgage or security device taken back to secure the performance of an obligation incurred in the purchase of the property. A "purchase money" security interest for personal property is controlled by Article 9 of the Uniform Commercial Code. See also **Mortgage; Purchase money security interest.**

Purchase money resulting trust. When one person furnishes the money for the purchase of property title to which is to be taken in the name of another, the party furnishing the funds is the equitable owner under a purchase money resulting trust. It is not necessary that he furnish the entire purchase price, but he must intend to acquire an interest.

Purchase money security interest. A security interest is a "purchase money security interest" to the extent that it is: (a) taken or retained by the seller of the collateral to secure all or part of its price; or (b) taken by a person who by making advances or incurring an obligation gives value to enable the debtor to acquire rights in or the use of collateral if such value is in fact so used. U.C.C. § 9–107.

Purchase order. Document authorizing a seller to deliver goods with payment to be made later. A written authorization calling on a vendor or supplier to furnish goods to the person ordering such. It constitutes an offer which is accepted when the vendor supplies the quantity and quality ordered.

Purchase price. Price agreed upon as a consideration for which property or goods are sold and purchased.

Purchaser. One who acquires real property in any other mode than by descent. One who acquires either real or personal property by buying it for a price in money; a buyer; vendee. One who has contracted to purchase property or goods. Also, a successful bidder at judicial sale. In re Spokane Sav. Bank, 198 Wash. 665, 89 P.2d 802, 806. Term may be employed in broad sense to include anyone who obtains title otherwise than by descent and distribution but is more commonly used to refer to a vendee or buyer who has purchased property for valuable consideration. Smith v. Enochs, D.C.Miss., 233 F.Supp. 925, 927.

One who takes by purchase which includes taking by sale, discount, negotiation, mortgage, pledge, lien, issue or re-issue, gift, or any other voluntary transaction creating an interest in property. U.C.C. § 1–201(32)(33).

The term "purchaser" means a person who, for adequate and full consideration in money or money's worth, acquires an interest (other than a lien or security interest) in property which is valid under local law against subsequent purchasers without actual notice. I.R.C. § 6323(h).

Transferee of a voluntary transfer, and includes immediate or mediate transferee of such a transferee. Bankruptcy Act § 101(32).

Bona fide purchaser. See **Bona fide.**

First purchaser. In the law of descent, this term signifies the ancestor who first acquired (in any other manner than by inheritance) the estate which still remains in his family or descendants.

Innocent purchaser. One who acquires title to property without knowledge of any defect in the title. See also **Innocent purchaser.**

Purchaser of a note or bill. The person who buys a promissory note or bill of exchange from the holder without his indorsement.

Purchaser for value. One who pays consideration for property or goods bought.

Pure. Absolute; complete; simple; unmixed; unqualified. Free from conditions or restrictions, as in the phrases pure charity, pure debt, pure obligation, pure plea, pure villenage, as to which see the nouns. See also **Purity.**

Pure accident. Implies that accident was caused by some unforeseen and unavoidable event over which neither party to the action had control, and excludes the idea that it was caused by carelessness or negligence of defendant. Maletis v. Portland Traction Co., 160 Or. 30, 83 P.2d 141, 142. Unavoidable accident has been held to be synonymous. Brewer v. Berner, 15 Wash.2d 644, 131 P.2d 940, 942. See **Act of God.**

Pure race statute. In some states, the first purchaser of real estate to record regardless of notice has the best claim to title and hence it is described as a race to the registry of deeds or other office for the recording of deeds and instruments of conveyance of real property. See also **Recording acts.**

Pur faire proclamer /pàr fér prəkléymər/pùr fér pròklaméy/. An ancient writ addressed to the mayor or bailiff of a city or town, requiring him to make proclamation concerning nuisances, etc.

Purgation /pərgéyshən/. The act of cleansing or exonerating one's self of a crime, accusation, or suspicion of guilt, by denying the charge on oath or by ordeal.

Canonical purgation was made by the party's taking his own oath that he was innocent of the charge, which was supported by the oath of twelve compurgators, who swore they believed he spoke the truth. To this succeeded the mode of purgation by the single oath of the party himself, called the "oath *ex officio,*" of which the modern defendant's oath in chancery is a modification. 3 Bl.Comm. 447; 4 Bl.Comm. 368.

Vulgar purgation consisted in ordeals or trials by hot and cold water, by fire, by hot irons, by battel, by corsned, etc.

Purge. To cleanse; to clear. To clear or exonerate from some charge or imputation of guilt, or from a contempt.

Purge des hypothèques /pórzh deyz iypowték/. Fr. In French law, an expression used to describe the act of freeing an estate from the mortgages and privileges with which it is charged, observing the formalities prescribed by law.

Purity. Within food adulteration statute is freedom from extraneous matter or anything debasing or contaminating. People v. Enders, 38 Misc.2d 746, 237 N.Y.S.2d 879, 889. See also **Pure.**

Purpart /pə́rpart/. A share; a part in a division; that part of an estate, formerly held in common, which is by partition allotted to any one of the parties. The word was anciently applied to the shares falling separately to co-parceners upon a division or partition of the estate, and was generally spelled "purparty;" but it is now used in relation to any kind of partition proceedings.

Purparty /pə́rpərdiy/. That part of an estate which, having been held in common by parceners, is by partition allotted to any of them. To make purparty is to divide and sever the lands which fall to parceners. Formerly *pourparty.* The word *purpart* is commonly used to indicate a part of an estate in any connection.

Purport, *n.* Meaning; import; substantial meaning; substance; legal effect. The "purport" of an instrument means the substance of it as it appears on the face of the instrument, and is distinguished from "tenor," which means an exact copy.

Purport, *v.* To convey, imply, or profess outwardly; to have the appearance of being, intending, claiming, etc. United States v. 306 Cases Containing Sandford Tomato Catsup with Preservative, D.C.N.Y., 55 F.Supp. 725, 727.

Purpose. That which one sets before him to accomplish; an end, intention, or aim, object, plan, project.

Purposely. Intentionally; designedly; consciously; knowingly. A person acts purposely with respect to a material element of an offense when: (i) if the element involves the nature of his conduct or a result thereof, it is his conscious object to engage in conduct of that nature or to cause such a result; and (ii) if the element involves the attendant circumstances, he is aware of the existence of such circumstances or he believes or hopes that they exist. Model Penal Code, § 2.02.

Purpresture /pərprés(h)chər/. An encroachment upon public rights and easements by appropriation to private use of that which belongs to public. Hill Farm, Inc. v. Hill County, Tex., 436 S.W.2d 320, 321. An inclosure by a private party of a part of that which belongs to and ought to be open and free to the enjoyment of the public at large. It is not necessarily a public nuisance. A public nuisance must be something which subjects the public to some degree of inconvenience or annoyance; but a purpresture may exist without putting the public to any inconvenience whatever.

Purprise /pərpráyz/. L. Fr. A close or inclosure; as also the whole compass of a manor.

Purpure, /pə́rp(y)ər/ or **porprin** /pórprən/. A term used in heraldry; the color commonly called "purple," expressed in engravings by lines in bend sinister. In the arms of princes it was formerly called "mercury," and in those of peers "amethyst."

Purse. Some valuable thing, offered by a person for the doing of something by others; prize; premium. Sum of money available to winner(s) of contest or event.

Purser /pə́rsər/. The person on a ship or vessel in charge of financial accounts and transactions with passengers.

Pursuant. A following after or following out. To execute or carry out in accordance with or by reason of something. To do in consequence or in prosecution of anything. "Pursuant to" means "in the course of carrying out: in conformance to or agreement with: according to" and, when used in a statute, is a restrictive term. Knowles v. Holly, 82 Wash.2d 694, 513 P.2d 18, 23.

Pursue. To follow, prosecute, or enforce a matter judicially, as a complaining party. To pursue the practice of any profession or business, contemplates a course of business or professional practice, and not single isolated acts arising from unusual circumstances. Dane v. Brown, C.C.A.Mass., 70 F.2d 164, 165.

Pursuer. One who pursues; one who follows in order to overtake.

Pursuit. That which one engages in as an occupation, trade, or profession; that which is followed as a continued or at least extended and prolonged employment. Dorrell v. Norida Land & Timber Co., 53 Idaho 793, 27 P.2d 960. To follow or chase in order to apprehend or overtake. See also **Fresh pursuit.**

Pursuit of happiness. As used in constitutional law, this right includes personal freedom, freedom of contract, exemption from oppression or invidious discrimination, the right to follow one's individual preference in the choice of an occupation and the application of his energies, liberty of conscience, and the right to enjoy the domestic relations and the privileges of the family and the home. Butchers' Union, etc., Co. v. Crescent City Live Stock, etc., Co., 4 S.Ct. 652, 111 U.S. 746, 28 L.Ed. 585. The right to follow or pursue any occupation or profession without restriction and without having any burden imposed upon one that is not imposed upon others in a similar situation. Myers v. City of Defiance, 67 Ohio App. 159, 36 N.E.2d 162, 21 O.L.A. 165.

Pur tant que /pèr tǽnt kyúw/pùr tón kə/. Forasmuch as; because; to the intent that.

Purus idiota /pyúrəs ìdiyówdə/. Lat. A congenital idiot.

Purview. Enacting part of a statute, in contradistinction to the preamble. That part of a statute commencing with the words "Be it enacted," and continuing as far as the repealing clause; and hence, the design, contemplation, purpose, or scope of the act.

Pusher. Slang term for person who engages in illegal sale of drugs.

Put. An option permitting its holder to sell a certain stock or commodity at a fixed price for a stated quantity and within a stated period. Such a right is purchased for a fee paid the one who agrees to accept the stock or goods if they are offered. The buyer of this right to sell expects the price of the stock or commodity to fall so that he can deliver the stock or commodity (the put) at a profit. If the price rises, the option need not be exercised. The reverse transaction is a *call*. See **Puts and calls.**

Putagium hæreditatem non adimit /pyuwtéyjiyəm hərèdətéydəm nòn ǽdəmət/. Incontinence does not take away an inheritance.

Putative. Reputed; supposed; commonly esteemed.

Putative father. The alleged or reputed father of an illegitimate child.

Putative marriage. A marriage contracted in good faith and in ignorance (on one or both sides) that impediments exist which render it unlawful. Davis v. Davis, Tex.Civ.App., 507 S.W.2d 841, 844.

Putative spouse. One thought to be the spouse of another in a marriage in opposition to which there are impediments.

Put in. To place in due form before a court; to place among the records of a court.

Put off. To postpone. In a bargain for the sale of goods, it may mean to postpone its completion or to procure a resale of the goods to a third person.

Puts and calls. A "put" in the language of the commodity or stock market is a privilege of delivering or not delivering the subject-matter of the sale; and a "call" is a privilege of calling or not calling for it. See **Put.**

Putting in fear. These words are used in the common-law definition of a robbery from the person; *i.e.* the offense must have been committed by *putting in fear* the person robbed. 4 Bl.Comm. 243. No matter how slight the cause creating the fear may be, if transaction is attended with such circumstances of terror, such threatening by word or gesture, as in common experience is likely to create an apprehension of danger and induce a man to part with his property for sake of his person, victim is put in fear. State v. Sawyer, 224 N.C. 61, 29 S.E.2d 34, 37.

Pyramiding. In the stock market, a device for increasing holdings of a stock by financing new holdings out of the increased margin of those already owned. In corporate finance, the use of small equity and capital to finance controlling interest in more corporations. See also **Leverage.**

Pyramid sales scheme. A device, illegal in many states, in which a buyer of goods is promised a payment for each additional buyer procured by him.

Q

Q.B. An abbreviation of "Queen's Bench."

Q.B.D. An abbreviation of "Queen's Bench Division."

Q.C. An abbreviation of "Queen's Counsel."

Q.C.F. An abbreviation of *"quare clausum fregit"* (q.v.).

Q.D. An abbreviation of *"quasi dicat,"* as if he should say.

Q.E.N. An abbreviation of *"quare executionem non,"* wherefore execution [should] not [be issued].

Q.S. An abbreviation for "Quarter Sessions."

Q.T. An abbreviation of *"qui tam"* (q.v.).

Qua /kwéy/. Lat. Considered as; in the character or capacity of. For example, "the trustee *qua* trustee [that is, in his character as trustee] is not liable," etc.

Quack. A pretender to medical skill which he does not possess; one who practices as a physician or surgeon without adequate preparation or due qualification.

Quacunque via data /kweykə́ŋkwiy váyə déydə/. Lat. Whichever way you take it.

Quadragesima /kwòdrəjézəmə/. Lat. The fortieth. The first Sunday in Lent is so called because it is about the fortieth day before Easter.

Quadragesimals /kwòdrəjézəməlz/. Offerings formerly made, on Mid-Lent Sunday, to the mother church.

Quadrant /kwódrənt/. An angular measure of ninety degrees. One of the quarters created by two intersecting roads or streets.

Quadriennium /kwòdr(iy)én(i)yəm/. Lat. In the civil law, the four-year course of study required to be pursued by law-students before they were qualified to study the Code or collection of imperial constitutions.

Quadripartite /kwòdrəpártayt/. Divided into four parts. A term applied in conveyancing to an indenture executed in four parts.

Quadruplatores /kwòdrəplətóriyz/. Lat. In Roman law, informers who, if their information were followed by conviction, had the fourth part of the confiscated goods for their trouble.

Quadruplicatio /kwòdrəpləkéysh(iy)ow/. Lat. In the civil law, a pleading on the part of a defendant, corresponding to the *rebutter* at common law. The third pleading on the part of the defendant.

Quadruplication /kwòdrəpləkéyshən/. A pleading in admiralty, third in order after a replication; now obsolete. Formerly this word was used instead of surrebutter.

Quæ ab hostibus capiuntur, statim capientium fiunt /kwíy æb (h)óstəbəs kæpiyántər, stéydəm kæpiyénsh(iy)əm fáyənt/. Things which are taken from enemies immediately become the property of the captors.

Quæ ab initio inutilis fuit institutio, ex post facto convalescere non potest /kwíy æb ənísh(iy)ow inyúwdələs f(y)úwəd ìnstət(y)úwsh(iy)ow, éks pòwst fǽktow konvəlésəriy nòn pówdəst/. An institution which was at the beginning of no use or force cannot acquire force from after matter.

Quæ ab initio non valent, ex post facto convalescere non possunt /kwíy æb ənísh(iy)ow nòn vǽlənt, éks pòwst fǽktow kònvəlésəriy nòn pósənt/. Things invalid from the beginning cannot be made valid by subsequent act.

Quæ accessionum locum obtinent, extinguuntur cum principales res peremptæ fuerint /kwíy əksèsiyównəm lówkəm óbtənənt, èkstiŋwántər kə̀m prìn(t)səpéyliyz ríyz pərém(p)tiy f(y)úwərìnt/. Things which hold the place of accessories are extinguished when the principal things are destroyed.

Quæ ad unum finem loquuta sunt, non debent ad alium detorqueri /kwíy æd yúwnəm fáynəm ləkyúwdə sə̀nt, nòn débənt æd éyliyəm dìytorkwíray/. Those words which are spoken to one end ought not to be perverted to another.

Quæ cohærent personæ a persona separari nequeunt /kwíy kəhírənt pərsówniy èy pərsównə sèpəréray nékwiyənt/. Things which cohere to, or are closely connected with, the person, cannot be separated from the person.

Quæ communi lege derogant stricte interpretantur /kwíy kəmyúwnay líyjiy dérəgənt stríktiy əntàrprətǽntər/. [Statutes] which derogate from the common law are strictly interpreted.

Quæ contra rationem juris introducta sunt, non debent trahi in consequentiam /kwìy kóntrə ræshiyównəm júrəs ìntrədáktə sènt, nòn débənt tréyhay in kònsəkwénsh(iy)əm/. Things introduced contrary to the reason of law ought not to be drawn into a precedent.

Quæcunque intra rationem legis inveniuntur intra legem ipsam esse judicantur /kwiykə́ŋkwiy íntrə ræshiyównəm líyjəs invìyniyántər íntrə líyjəm ípsəm ésiy jùwdəkǽntər/. Things which are found within the reason of a law are supposed to be within the law itself.

Quæ dubitationis causa tollendæ inseruntur communem legem non lædunt /kwìy d(y)ùwbətèyshiyównəs kózə toléndiy ìnsərántər, kəmyúwnəm líyjəm nòn líydənt/. Things which are inserted for the purpose of removing doubt hurt not the common law.

Quæ dubitationis tollendæ causa contractibus inseruntur, jus commune non lædunt /kwìy d(y)ùwbətèyshiyównəs toléndiy kózə kəntrǽktəbəs ìnsərántər, jás kəmyúwniy nòn líydənt/. Particular clauses inserted in agreements to avoid doubts and ambiguity do not prejudice the general law.

Quæ est eadem /kwíy èst iyéydəm/. Lat. Which is the same. Words used for alleging that the trespass or other fact mentioned in the plea is the same as that laid in the declaration, where, from the circumstances, there is an apparent difference between the two.

Quæ incontinenti fiunt inesse videntur /kwíy inkòntənéntay fáyənt inésiy vədéntər/. Things which are done incontinently [or simultaneously with an act] are supposed to be inherent [in it; to be a constituent part of it].

Quæ in curia regis acta sunt rite agi præsumuntur /kwíy ìn kyúriyə ríyjəs ǽktə sènt ráydiy éyjay priyz(y)əmántər/. Things done in the king's court are presumed to be rightly done.

Quæ in partes dividi nequeunt solida a singulis præstantur /kwíy ìn pártiyz dəváyday nékwiyənt sólədə èy síngyələs prəstǽntər/. Services which are incapable of division are to be performed in whole by each individual.

Quæ inter alios acta sunt nemini nocere debent, sed prodesse possunt /kwìy íntər ǽliyows ǽktə sènt némənay nósəriy débənt, séd prowdésiy pósənt/. Transactions between strangers ought to hurt no man, but may benefit.

Quæ in testamento ita sunt scripta ut intelligi non possint, perinde sunt ac si scripta non essent /kwíy ìn tèstəméntow áydə sènt skríptə əd intéləjay nòn pósənt, pəríndiy sènt æk sáy skríptə nòn ésənt/. Things which are so written in a will that they cannot be understood, are the same as if they had not been written at all.

Quæ legi communi derogant non sunt trahenda in exemplum /kwìy líyjay kəmyúwnay dérəgənt nón sènt trəhéndə ìn əgzémpləm/. Things derogatory to the common law are not to be drawn into precedent.

Quæ legi communi derogant stricte interpretantur /kwìy líyjay kəmyúwnay dérəgənt stríktiy intàrprətǽntər/. Those things which are derogatory to the common law are to be strictly interpreted.

Quælibet concessio domini regis capi debet stricte contra dominum regem, quando potest intelligi duabus viis /kwíyləbət kənsésh(iy)ow dómənay ríyjəs kǽpay débət stríktiy kóntrə dómənəm ríyjəm, kwóndow pówdəst intéləjay d(y)uwéybəs váyəs/. Every grant of our lord the king ought to be taken strictly against our lord the king, when it can be understood in two ways.

Quælibet concessio fortissime contra donatorem interpretanda est /kwíyləbət kənsésh(iy)ow fortísəmiy kóntrə dòwnətórəm intàrprətǽndə èst/. Every grant is to be interpreted most strongly against the grantor.

Quælibet jurisdictio cancellos suos habet /kwíyləbət jùrəsdíksh(iy)ow kænsélows s(y)úwows héybət/. Every jurisdiction has its own bounds.

Quælibet pardonatio debet capi secundum intentionem regis, et non ad deceptionem regis /kwíyləbət pàrdənéysh(iy)ow débət kǽpay səkándəm inténshiyównəm ríyjəs èt nón æd dəsèpshiyównəm ríyjəs/. Every pardon ought to be taken according to the intention of the king, and not to the deception of the king.

Quælibet pœna corporalis, quamvis minima, major est qualibet pœna pecuniaria /kwíyləbət píynə kòrpəréyləs, kwǽmvis mínəmə, méyjər èst kwéyləbət píynə pəkyùwniyériyə/. Every corporal punishment, although the very least, is greater than any pecuniary punishment.

Quæ mala sunt inchoata in principio vix bono peraguntur exitu /kwìy mǽlə sənt ìnkowéydə in prin(t)sípiyow víks bównow pàrəgántər égzət(y)uw/. Things bad in principle at the commencement seldom achieve a good end.

Quæ nihil frustra /kwìy náy(h)əl frástrə/. Lat. Which [does or requires] nothing in vain. Which requires nothing to be done, that is, to no purpose.

Quæ non fieri debent, facta, valent /kwíy nòn fáyəray débənt, fǽktə, vǽlənt/. Things which ought not to be done are held valid when they have been done.

Quæ non valeant singula, juncta juvant /kwíy nòn vǽliyənt síngyələ, jə́ŋktə júwvènt/. Things which do not avail when separate, when joined avail.

Quæ plura /kwìy pl(y)úrə/. Lat. In old English practice, a writ which lay where an inquisition had been made by an escheator in any county of such lands or tenements as any man died seised of, and all that was in his possession was imagined not to be found by the office; the writ commanding the escheator to inquire *what more (quæ plura)* lands and tenements the party held on the day when he died, etc.

Quæ præter consuetudinem et morem majorum fiunt neque placent neque recta videntur /kwìy príydər kònswət(y)úwdənəm èt mórəm məjórəm fáyənt nékwiy plǽsənt nékwiy réktə vədéntər/. Things which are done contrary to the custom of our ancestors neither please nor appear right.

Quæ propter necessitatem recepta sunt, non debent in argumentum trahi /kwìy próptər nəsèsətéydəm rəséptə sènt, nòn débənt ìn àrgyəméntəm tréyhay/. Things which are admitted on the ground of necessity ought not to be drawn into question.

Quæras de dubiis legem bene discere si vis /kwírəs dìy d(y)úwbiyəs, líyjəm bíyniy dísəriy sày vís/. Inquire into doubtful points if you wish to understand the law well.

Quære /kwíriy/. A query; question; doubt. This word, occurring in the syllabus of a reported case or elsewhere, shows that a question is propounded as to what follows, or that the particular rule, decision, or statement is considered as open to question.

Quære de dubiis, quia per rationes pervenitur ad legitimam rationem /kwíriy dìy d(y)úwbiyǝs, kwáyǝ pǝr ræshiyówniyz pǝrvénǝdǝr æd lǝjídǝmǝm ræshiyównǝm/. Inquire into doubtful points, because by reasoning we arrive at legal reason.

Quærens /kwíren(d)z/. Lat. A plaintiff; the plaintiff.

Quærens nihil capiat per billam /kwíren(d)z náy(h)ǝl kǽpiyǝt pǝr bílǝm/. The plaintiff shall take nothing by his bill. A form of judgment for the defendant.

Quærens non invenit plegium /kwíren(d)z nòn invíynǝt pléj(iy)ǝm/. L. Lat. The plaintiff did not find a pledge. A return formerly made by a sheriff to a writ requiring him to take security of the plaintiff to prosecute his claim.

Quærere dat sapere quæ sunt legitima vere /kwírǝriy dǽt sǽpǝriy kwìy sánt lǝjídǝmǝ víriy/. To inquire into them, is the way to know what things are truly lawful.

Quæ rerum natura prohibentur nulla lege confirmata sunt /kwìy rírǝm nǝchúrǝ pròw(h)ǝbéntǝr nálǝ líyjiy kònfǝrméydǝ sànt/. Things which are forbidden by the nature of things are [can be] confirmed by no law. Positive laws are framed after the laws of nature and reason.

Quæ singula non prosunt, juncta juvant /kwìy síŋgyǝlǝ nòn prówsǝnt, jáŋktǝ júwvǝnt/. Things which taken singly are of no avail afford help when taken together.

Quæsta /kwíystǝ/. An indulgence or remission of penance, authorized by the Pope.

Quæstio /kwés(h)ch(iy)ow/. *Medieval law.* The question; the torture; inquiry or inquisition by inflicting the torture.

Roman law. Anciently a species of commission granted by the *comitia* to one or more persons for the purpose of inquiring into some crime or public offense and reporting thereon. In later times, the *quæstio* came to exercise plenary criminal jurisdiction, even to pronouncing sentence, and then was appointed periodically, and eventually became a *permanent* commission or regular criminal tribunal, and was then called *"quæstio perpetua."*

Cadit quæstio. The question falls; the discussion ends; there is no room for further argument.

Quæstio vexata. A vexed question or mooted point; a question often agitated or discussed but not determined; a question or point which has been differently decided, and so left doubtful.

Quæstionarii /kwès(h)ch(iy)ǝnériyay/. Those who carried *quæsta* about from door to door.

Quæstiones perpetuæ /kwès(h)chiyówniyz pǝrpéchuwiy/. In Roman law, were commissions (or courts)

of inquisition into crimes alleged to have been committed. They were called *"perpetuæ,"* to distinguish them from *occasional* inquisitions, and because they were permanent courts for the trial of offenders.

Quæstor /kwéstor/. Lat. A Roman magistrate, whose office it was to collect the public revenue.

Quæstores classici /kwestóriyz klǽsǝsay/. Lat. In Roman law, officers entrusted with the care of the public money. Their duties consisted in making the necessary payments from the *ærarium,* and receiving the public revenues. Of both they had to keep correct accounts in their *tabulæ publicæ.* Demands which any one might have on the *ærarium,* and outstanding debts were likewise registered by them. Fines to be paid to the public treasury were registered and exacted by them. They were likewise to provide proper accommodations for foreign ambassadors and such persons as were connected with the republic by ties of public hospitality. Lastly, they were charged with the care of the burials and monuments of distinguished men, the expenses for which had been decreed by the senate to be paid by the treasury. Their number at first was confined to two; but this was afterwards increased as the empire became extended. There were quæstors of cities and of provinces, and quæstors of the army; the latter were in fact paymasters.

Quæstores parricidii /kwestóriyz pæ̀rǝsáydiyay/. See **Questores parricidii.**

Quæstor sacri palatii /kwéstor sǽkray pǝléyshiyay/. Quæstor of the sacred palace. An officer of the imperial court at Constantinople, with powers and duties resembling those of a chancellor.

Quæstus /kwéstǝs/. L. Lat. That estate which a man has by acquisition or purchase, in contradistinction to *"hœreditas,"* which is what he has by descent.

Quæ sunt minoris culpæ sunt majoris infamiæ /kwíy sànt mǝnórǝs kálpiy sànt mǝjórǝs inféymiyiy/. [Offenses] which are of a lower grade of guilt are of a higher degree of infamy.

Quaker. In England, the statutory, as well as the popular, name of a member of a religious society, by themselves denominated "Friends."

Quale jus /kwóliy jǝs/. Lat. In old English law, a judicial writ, which lay where a man of religion had judgment to recover land before execution was made of the judgment. It went forth to the escheator between judgment and execution, to inquire what *right* the religious person had to recover, or whether the judgment was obtained by the collusion of the parties, to the intent that the lord might not be defrauded.

Qualification. The possession by an individual of the qualities, properties, or circumstances, natural or adventitious, which are inherently or legally necessary to render him eligible to fill an office or to perform a public duty or function. Thus, a "qualified voter" is one who meets the residency, age, and registration requirements.

Also, a modification or limitation of terms or language; usually intended by way of restriction of expressions which, by reason of their generality, would carry a larger meaning than was designed.

See also **Qualified.**

Qualified. Adapted; fitted; entitled; susceptible; capable; competent; fitting; possessing legal power or capacity; eligible; as a "qualified voter" (*q.v.*). Applied to one who has taken the steps to prepare himself for an appointment or office, as by taking oath, giving bond, etc. Also limited; restricted; confined; modified; imperfect, or temporary. See also **Capacity; Competency; Duly qualified.**

Qualified acceptance. See **Acceptance.**

Qualified elector. A person who is legally qualified to vote. See also **Qualified voter.**

Qualified estate. See **Estate.**

Qualified fee. See **Fee.**

Qualified indorsement. See **Indorsement.**

Qualified oath. See **Oath.**

Qualified pensions. See **Pension plan.**

Qualified privilege. In the law of libel and slander, the same as conditional privilege. "Absolute privilege" renders defendant absolutely immune from civil liability for his defamatory statements, while "qualified privilege" protects defendant from liability only if he uttered defamatory statements without actual malice. Martinez v. Cardwell, 25 Ariz.App. 253, 542 P.2d 1133, 1135. See also **Privilege.**

Qualified property. See **Property.**

Qualified voter. A legal voter. A person qualified to vote generally; *i.e.* one who meets the residency, age, and registration requirements. One having constitutional qualifications for privilege, who is duly registered pursuant to law, and has present right to vote at election being held. State ex rel. Burke v. Campbell, Mo.App., 542 S.W.2d 355, 357.

Qualify. To make one's self fit or prepared to exercise a right, office, or franchise. To take the steps necessary to prepare one's self for an office or appointment, as by taking oath, giving bond, etc. Also to limit; to modify; to restrict. Thus, it is said that one section of a statute qualifies another.

Qualitas quæ inesse debet, facile præsumitur /kwólətæs kwíy inésiy débət, fǽsəliy prəz(y)úwmədər/. A quality which ought to form a part is easily presumed.

Quality. Quality is descriptive of organic composition of substance, expressed in definite quantitative units, and definitive of character, nature and decree of excellence of an article. Dean Rubber Mfg. Co. v. U. S., C.A.Mo., 356 F.2d 161, 163. In respect to persons, this term denotes comparative rank; state or condition in relation to others; social or civil position or class. In pleading, it means an attribute or characteristic by which one thing is distinguished from another. Adoptiveness, suitableness, fitness; grade; condition. Within food adulteration statute means character or nature, as belonging to or distinguishing a thing, or character with respect to excellence, fineness, etc., or grade of excellence. People v. Enders, 38 Misc.2d 746, 237 N.Y.S.2d 879, 888, 889.

Quality of estate. The period when, and the manner in which, the right of enjoying an estate is exercised. It is of two kinds: (1) The period when the right of enjoying an estate is conferred upon the owner, whether at present or in future; and (2) the manner in which the owner's right of enjoyment of his estate is to be exercised, whether solely, jointly, in common, or in coparcenary.

Quamdiu /kwǽmdiyuw/. Lat. As long as; so long as. A word of limitation in old conveyances.

Quamdiu se bene gesserit /kwǽmdiyuw sìy bíyniy jésərət/. As long as he shall behave himself well; during good behavior; a clause frequent in letters patent or grants of certain offices, to secure them so long as the persons to whom they are granted shall not be guilty of abusing them, the opposite clause being *"durante bene placito"* (during the pleasure of the grantor).

Quam longum debet esse rationabile tempus non definitur in lege, sed pendet ex discretione justiciariorum /kwǽm lóngəm débəd ésiy ræshənéybəliy témpəs nòn dəfínədər ìn líyjiy, sèd péndəd èks dəskrèshiyówniy jəstìshiyèriyórəm/. How long *reasonable time* ought to be is not defined by law, but depends upon the discretion of the judges.

Quam rationabilis debet esse finis, non definitur, sed omnibus circumstantiis inspectis pendet ex justiciariorum discretione /kwǽm ræshənéybələs débəd ésiy fáynəs, non dəfínədər, sèd ómnəbəs sàrkəmstǽnshiyəs ənspéktəs péndəd èks jəstìshiyèriyórəm dəskrèshiyówniy/. What a reasonable fine ought to be is not defined, but is left to the discretion of the judges, all the circumstances being considered.

Quamvis aliquid per se non sit malum, tamen, si sit mali exempli, non est faciendum /kwǽmvis ǽləkwid pàr síy nón sìt mǽləm, tǽmən, sáy sìt mǽlay əgzémplay, nón sit fǽshiyéndəm/. Although a thing may not be bad in itself, yet, if it is of bad example, it is not to be done.

Quamvis lex generaliter loquitur, restringenda tamen est, ut, cessante ratione, ipsa cessat /kwǽmvis léks jènəréylədər lówkwədər, rèstrinjéndə tǽmən èst, ət, səsǽntiy ræshiyówniy ípsə sésət/. Although a law speaks generally, yet it is to be restrained, so that when its reason ceases, it should cease also.

Quando abest provisio partis, adest provisio legis /kwóndow ǽbest prəvíz(h)(i)yow párdəs, ǽdest prəvíz(h)(i)yow líyjəs/. When the provision of the party is wanting, the provision of the law is at hand.

Quando aliquid mandatur, mandatur et omne per quod pervenitur ad illud /kwóndow ǽləkwid mændéydər, mændéydər èd ómniy pàr kwód pərvénədər æd íləd/. When anything is commanded, everything by which it can be accomplished is also commanded.

Quando aliquid per se non sit malum, tamen si sit mali exemplii, non est faciendum /kwóndow ǽləkwid pàr síy nón sìt mǽləm, tǽmən sày sit mǽlay əgzémplay, nón èst fǽshiyéndəm/. When anything by itself is not evil, and yet may be an example for evil, it is not to be done.

Quando aliquid prohibetur ex directo, prohibetur et per obliquum /kwóndow ǽləkwid pròw(h)əbíydər éks dəréktow, pròw(h)əbíydər èt pár əbláykwəm/. When anything is prohibited directly, it is prohibited also indirectly.

Quando aliquid prohibetur, prohibetur et omne per quod devenitur ad illud /kwóndow ǽləkwid pròw(h)əbíydər, pròw(h)əbíydər èd ómniy pər kwód dəvénədər æd íləd/. When anything is prohibited, everything by which it is reached is prohibited also. That which cannot be done directly shall not be done indirectly.

Quando aliquis aliquid concedit, concedere videtur et id sine quo res uti non potest /kwóndow ǽləkwis ǽləkwid kənsíydət, kənsíydəriy vədíydər èd íd sáyniy kwòw ríyz yúwday nòn pówdəst/. When a person grants anything, he is supposed to grant that also without which the thing cannot be used. When the use of a thing is granted, everything is granted by which the grantee may have and enjoy such use.

Quando charta continet generalem clausulam, posteaque descendit ad verba specialia quæ clausulæ generali sunt consentanea, interpretanda est charta secundum verba specialia /kwóndow kárdə kóntinət jènəréyləm klóz(y)ələm, pòwstiyéykwiy dəséndəd æd várbə spèshiyéyl(i)yə kwìy klózyəliy jènəréylay sànt kòn(t)sentéyn(i)yə, intərprətǽndə əst kárdə səkándəm várbə spèshiyéyl(i)yə/. When a deed contains a general clause, and afterwards descends to special words which are agreeable to the general clause, the deed is to be interpreted according to the special words.

Quando de una et eadem re duo onerabiles existunt, unus, pro insufficientia alterius, de integro onerabitur /kwóndow dìy yúwnə èd iyéydəm ríy d(y)úwow òwnəréybəliyz əgzístənt, yúwnəs, pròw ìnsəfishiyénsh(iy)ə oltíriyəs, dìy íntəgrow ownəréybədər/. When there are two persons liable for one and the same thing, one of them, in case of default of the other, shall be charged with the whole.

Quando dispositio referri potest ad duas res ita quod secundum relationem unam vitietur et secundum alteram utilis sit, tum facienda est relatio ad illam ut valeat dispositio /kwóndow dìspəzísh(iy)ow rəfáray pówdəst æd d(y)úwəs ríyz áydə kwòd səkándəm rəlèyshiyównəm yúwnəm vìshiyíydər èt səkándəm óltərəm yúwdələs sìt, tàm fèyshiyéndə èst rəléysh(iy)ow æd íləm èt vǽliyət dìspəzísh(iy)ow/. When a disposition may refer to two things, so that by the former it would be vitiated, and by the latter it would be preserved, then the relation is to be made to the latter, so that the disposition may be valid.

Quando diversi desiderantur actus ad aliquem statum perficiendum, plus respicit lex actum originalem /kwóndow dəvársay dəsidərǽntər ǽktəs æd ǽləkwəm stéydəm pərfishiyéndəm, plás réspəsət léks ǽktəm ərìjənéyləm/. When different acts are required to the formation of any estate, the law chiefly regards the original act. When to the perfection of an estate or interest divers acts or things are requisite, the law has more regard to the original act, for that is the fundamental part on which all the others are founded.

Quando duo jura concurrunt in una persona, æquum est ac si essent in diversis /kwóndow d(y)úwow júrə kənkárəd in yúwnə pərsównə, íykwəm èst æk sày ésənt ìn dəvársəs/. When two rights concur in one person, it is the same as if they were in two separate persons.

Quando jus domini regis et subditi concurrunt, jus regis præferri debet /kwóndow jás dómənay ríyjəs èt sábdəday kənkárənt, jás ríyjəs prəfáray débət/. When the right of king and of subject concur, the king's right should be preferred.

Quando lex aliquid alicui concedit, concedere videtur et id sine quo res ipsæ esse non potest /kwóndow léks ǽləkwid ǽlək(w)ay kənsíydət, kənsíydəriy vədíydər èd íd sáyniy kwòw ríyz ípsiy ésiy nòn pówdəst/. When the law gives a man anything, it gives him that also without which the thing itself cannot exist.

Quando lex aliquid alicui concedit, omnia incidentia tacite conceduntur /kwóndow léks ǽləkwid ǽlək(w)ay kənsíydət, ómn(i)yə ìnsədénsh(iy)ə tǽsədiy kònsədántər/. When the law gives anything to any one, all incidents are tacitly given.

Quando lex est specialis, ratio autem generalis, generaliter lex est intelligenda /kwóndow léks èst spèshiyéyləs, réysh(iy)ow ódəm jènəréyləs, jènəréylədər léks èst intèləjéndə/. When a law is special, but its reason [or object] general, the law is to be understood generally.

Quando licet id quod majus, videtur et licere id quod minus /kwóndow láysəd íd kwòd méyjəs, vədíydər èt lísəriy íd kwòd máynəs/. When the greater is allowed, the less is to be understood as allowed also.

Quando mulier nobilis nupserit ignobili, desinit esse nobilis nisi nobilitas nativa fuerit /kwóndow myúwliyər nówbələs nápsərət ignówbəlay, désənəd ésiy nówbələs náysay nowbílətæs nətáyvə f(y)úwərət/. When a noble woman marries a man not noble, she ceases to be noble, unless her nobility was born with her.

Quando plus fit quam fieri debet, videtur etiam illud fieri quod faciendum est /kwóndow plás fít kwæm fáyəray débət, vədíydər ésh(iy)əm íləd fáyəray kwòd fæshiyéndəm èst/. When more is done than ought to be done, that at least shall be considered as performed which should have been performed [as, if a man, having a power to make a lease for ten years, make one for twenty years, it shall be void only for the surplus].

Quando quod ago non valet ut ago, valeat quantum valere potest /kwóndow kwód éygow nòn vǽləd əd éygow, vǽliyət kwóntəm vəlíriy pówdəst/. When that which I do does not have effect as I do it, let it have as much effect as it can.

Quando res non valet ut ago, valeat quantum valere potest /kwóndow ríyz nòn vǽləd əd éygow, vǽliyət kwóntəm vəlíriy pówdəst/. When a thing is of no effect as I do it, it shall have effect as far as [or in whatever way] it can.

Quando verba et mens congruunt, non est interpretationi locus /kwóndow várbə èt mén(d)z kóŋgruwənt, nón èst əntàrprətèyshiyównay lówkəs/. When the words and the mind agree, there is no place for interpretation.

Quando verba statuti sunt specialia, ratio autem generalis, generaliter statutum est intelligendum /kwóndow várbə stətyúwday sànt spèshiyéyl(i)yə, réysh(iy)ow ódəm jènəréyləs, jènəréylədər stətyúwdəm èst əntèləjéndəm/. When the words of a statute are special, but the reason or object of it general, the statute is to be construed generally.

Quanti minoris /kwóntay mənórəs/. Lat. The name of an action in the civil law (and in Louisiana), brought by the purchaser of an article, for a reduction of the agreed price on account of defects in the thing which diminish its value.

Quantum damnificatus /kwóntəm dæmnəfəkéydəs/. How much damnified? The name of an issue directed by a court of equity to be tried in a court of law, to ascertain the amount of compensation to be allowed for damage.

Quantum meruit /kwóntəm méhruwət/. Expression "quantum meruit" means "as much as he deserves" and it is an expression that describes the extent of liability on a contract implied by law. Nardi & Co., Inc. v. Allabastro, 20 Ill.App.3d 323, 314 N.E.2d 367, 370. An equitable doctrine, based on the concept that no one who benefits by the labor and materials of another should be unjustly enriched thereby; under those circumstances, the law implies a promise to pay a reasonable amount for the labor and materials furnished, even absent a specific contract therefor. Swiftships, Inc. v. Burdin, La.App., 338 So.2d 1193, 1195. Essential elements of recovery under quantum meruit are: (1) valuable services were rendered or materials furnished, (2) for person sought to be charged, (3) which services and materials were accepted by person sought to be charged, used and enjoyed by him, and (4) under such circumstances as reasonably notified person sought to be charged that plaintiff, in performing such services, was expected to be paid by person sought to be charged. Montes v. Naismith & Trevino Const. Co., Tex.Civ.App., 459 S.W.2d 691, 694.

The common count in an action of *assumpsit* for work and labor, founded on an implied *assumpsit* or promise on the part of the defendant to pay the plaintiff *as much as he* reasonably *deserved* to have for his labor. 3 Bl.Comm. 161. It refers to class of obligations imposed by law, without regard to intention or assent of parties bound, for reasons dictated by reason and justice; such obligations not being contracts though form of action is contract. Carpenter v. Josey Oil Co., C.C.A.Okl., 26 F.2d 442, 443. Amount of recovery being only the reasonable value of the services rendered regardless of any agreement as to value. Smith v. Bliss, 44 Cal.App.2d 171, 112 P.2d 30, 33.

Quantum tenens domino ex homagio, tantum dominus tenenti ex dominio debet præter solam reverentiam; mutua debet esse dominii et homagii fidelitatis connexio /kwóntəm ténən(d)z dómənow èks (h)əméyj(iy)ow, tǽntəm dómənəs tənéntay èks dəmín(i)yow débət príydər sówləm rèvərénsh(iy)əm; myúwchuwə débəd èsiy dəmíniyay èt (h)əméyjiyay fədèlətéydəs kənéksh(iy)ow/. As much as the tenant by his homage owes to his lord, so much is the lord, by his lordship, indebted to the tenant, except reverence alone; the tie of dominion and of homage ought to be mutual.

Quantum valebant /kwóntəm vəlíybænt/. As much as they were worth. The common count in an action of

assumpsit for goods sold and delivered, founded on an implied *assumpsit* or promise, on the part of the defendant, to pay the plaintiff *as much as* the goods *were* reasonably *worth.*

Quarantine. A period of time during which a vessel, coming from a place where a contagious or infectious disease is prevalent, is detained by authority in the harbor of her port of destination, or at a station near it, without being permitted to land or to discharge her crew or passengers. Quarantine is said to have been first established at Venice in 1484.

Isolation of person afflicted with contagious disease. To keep persons, when suspected of having contracted or having been exposed to an infectious disease, out of a community, or to confine them to given place therein, and to prevent intercourse between them and people generally of the community. Application of Halko, 246 Cal.App.2d 553, 54 Cal. Rptr. 661, 664.

A provision or interest given in law to the widow in her husband's estate, such as the privilege of occupying the mansion house and curtilage without charge until her dower is assigned, and technically is a dower right, or more broadly is a part of the dower estate.

Quare /kwériy/kwohriy/. Lat. Wherefore; for what reason; on what account. Used in the Latin form of several common-law writs.

Quare clausum fregit /kwériy klózəm fríyjət/. Lat. Wherefore he broke the close. That species of the action of trespass which has for its object the recovery of damages for an unlawful entry upon another's land is termed "trespass *quare clausum fregit;*" "breaking a close" being the technical expression for an unlawful entry upon land. The language of the declaration in this form of action is "that the defendant, with force and arms, broke and entered the close" of the plaintiff. The phrase is often abbreviated to *"qu. cl. fr."* or *"q.c.f."*

Quare ejecit infra terminum /kwériy əjíysəd ínfrə tə́rmənəm/. Wherefore he ejected within the term. In old practice, a writ which lay for a lessee where he was ejected before the expiration of his term, in cases where the wrong-doer or ejector was not himself in possession of the lands, but his feoffee or another claiming under him. 3 Bl.Comm. 199, 206.

Quare impedit /kwériy impíydət/. Wherefore he hinders. In old English practice, a writ or action which lay for the patron of an advowson, where he had been disturbed in his right of patronage; so called from the emphatic words of the old form, by which the disturber was summoned to answer *why he hinders* the plaintiff. 3 Bl.Comm. 246, 248.

Quare incumbravit /kwériy ìnkəmbréyvət/. In old English law, a writ which lay against a bishop who, within six months after the vacation of a benefice, conferred it on his clerk, while two others were contending at law for the right of presentation, calling upon him to show cause why he had incumbered the church. Abolished by 3 & 4 Wm. IV, c. 27.

Quare intrusit /kwériy intrúwzət/. In old English law, a writ that formerly lay where the lord proffered a suitable marriage to his ward, who rejected it, and entered into the land, and married another, the value of his marriage not being satisfied to the lord. Abolished by 12 Car. II, c. 24.

Quare non permittit /kwériy nón pərmídət/. An ancient writ, which lay for one who had a right to present to a church for a turn against the proprietary.

Quarentena terræ /kwòrəntíynə téhriy/. A furlong.

Quare obstruxit /kwériy əbstráksət/. Wherefore he obstructed. In old English practice, a writ which lay for one who, having a liberty to pass through his neighbor's ground, could not enjoy his right because the owner had so obstructed it.

Quarrel. An altercation, an angry dispute, an exchange of recriminations, taunts, threats or accusations between two persons.

Quart. A liquid measure, containing one-fourth part of a gallon.

Quarta divi pii /kwórdə dáyvay páyay/. In Roman law, that portion of a testator's estate which he was required by law to leave to a child whom he had adopted and afterwards emancipated or unjustly disinherited, being one-fourth of his property.

Quarta falcidia /kwórdə folsídiyə/. In Roman law, that portion of a testator's estate which, by the Falcidian law, was required to be left to the heir, amounting to at least one-fourth.

Quarter. The fourth part of anything, especially of a year. A quarter section (q.v.) of land. Stations, buildings, lodgings, etc., of military personnel (usually referred to as "quarters".

Quarter-day. The four days in the year upon which, by law or custom, moneys payable in quarter-yearly installments are collectible (payable).

Quarter-eagle. A gold coin of the United States, of the value of two and a half dollars.

Quartering. In old English criminal law, the dividing a criminal's body into quarters, after execution. A part of the punishment of high treason. 4 Bl.Comm. 93.

Furnishing of living quarters to military personnel.

Quarterization. Quartering of criminals.

Quarterly. Quarter yearly; once in a quarter year.

Quarter seal. See **Seal**.

Quarter section. The quarter of a section of land according to the divisions of the government survey, laid off by dividing the section into four equal parts by north-and-south and east-and-west lines, and containing 160 acres. A quarter of a square mile of land. Amount of land originally granted to homesteader.

Quarter session courts. Courts formerly established in some of the states, to be holden four times in the year, invested with criminal jurisdiction, usually of offenses less than felony, and sometimes with the charge of certain administrative matters, such as the care of public roads and bridges.

In England, all quarter session courts were abolished. The Courts Act of 1971, with the jurisdiction of such transferred to the Crown Court.

Quarters of coverage. Social Security benefits are dependent on number of quarters in which person made contributions (i.e. payments) into social security fund.

Quarto die post /kwórdow dáyiy pówst/. Lat. On the fourth day after. Appearance day, in the former English practice, the defendant being allowed four days, inclusive, from the return of the writ, to make his appearance.

Quash /kwósh/. To overthrow; to abate; to vacate; to annul; to make void; e.g. to quash an indictment.

Quasi /kwéysay/kwóziy/. Lat. As if; almost as it were; analogous to. This term is used in legal phraseology to indicate that one subject resembles another, with which it is compared, in certain characteristics, but that there are intrinsic and material differences between them. Cannon v. Miller, 22 Wash.2d 227, 155 P.2d 500, 503, 507. A term used to mark a resemblance, and supposes a difference beween two objects. It is exclusively a term of classification. It implies that conception to which it serves as index is connected with conception with which comparison is instituted by strong superficial analogy or resemblance. Moreover it negatives idea of identity, but points out that the conceptions are sufficiently similar for one to be classed as the equal of the other. South Discount Foods, Inc. v. Retail Clerks Union Local 1552, Com. Pl., 14 Ohio Misc. 188, 235 N.E.2d 143, 147. It is often prefixed to English words, implying mere appearance or want of reality.

As to quasi Affinity; Contract; Corporation; Crime; Delict; Deposit; Derelict; Easement; Entail; Fee; In rem; Municipal corporation; Offense; Partner; Personalty; Possession; Posthumous child; Purchase; Realty; Tenant; Tort; Traditio; Trustee; and Usufruct, see those titles.

Quasi admission. An act or utterance, usually extrajudicial, which creates an inconsistency with and discredits to a greater or lesser degree, present claim or other evidence of person creating the inconsistency, and person who enacted or uttered it may nevertheless disprove its correctness by introduction of other evidence. Sutherland v. Davis, 286 Ky. 743, 151 S.W.2d 1021, 1024.

Quasi contract. An obligation which law creates in absence of agreement; it is invoked by courts where there is unjust enrichment. Andrews v. O'Grady, 44 Misc.2d 28, 252 N.Y.S.2d 814, 817. Function of "quasi contract" is to raise obligation in law where in fact the parties made no promise, and it is not based on apparent intention of the parties. Fink v. Goodson-Todman Enterprises, Limited, 9 C.A.3d 996, 88 Cal. Rptr. 679, 690. See also **Contract**.

Quasi estoppel. The principle which precludes a party from asserting, to another's disadvantage, a right inconsistent with a position previously taken by him.

"Equitable estoppel" and "estoppel in pais" are convertible terms embracing "quasi estoppel" and embody doctrine that one may not repudiate an act done or position assumed by him where such course would work injustice to another rightfully relying thereon. Brown v. Corn Exchange Nat. Bank & Trust Co., 136 N.J.Eq. 430, 42 A.2d 474, 480.

See **Equitable estoppel**.

Quasi in rem. Type of jurisdiction of a court based on a person's interest in property within the jurisdiction of the court. There must be a connection involving minimum contact between the property and the subject matter of the action for a state to exercise quasi in rem jurisdiction. Shaffer v. Heitner, 433 U.S. 186, 97 S.Ct. 2569, 53 L.Ed.2d 683. "Quasi in rem proceedings" is generally defined as affecting only interest of particular persons in specific property and is distinguished from proceedings in rem which determine interests in specific property as against the whole world. Avery v. Bender, 124 Vt. 309, 204 A.2d 314, 317. See also **Jurisdiction.**

Quasi judicial. A term applied to the action, discretion, etc., of public administrative officers or bodies, who are required to investigate facts, or ascertain the existence of facts, hold hearings, and draw conclusions from them, as a basis for their official action, and to exercise discretion of a judicial nature.

Quasi judicial act. A judicial act performed by one not a judge. State Tax Commission of Utah v. Katsis, 90 Utah 406, 62 P.2d 120, 123.

Quasi-traditio /kwéysay trədísh(iy)ow/. Lat. In civil law, a term used to designate that a person is in the use of the property of another, which the latter suffers and does not oppose. It also signifies the act by which the right of property is ceded in a thing to a person who is in possession of it; as, if I loan a boat to Paul, and deliver it to him, and afterwards I sell him the boat, it is not requisite that he should deliver the boat to me to be again delivered to him: there is a *quasi*-tradition or delivery.

Quater cousin. See **Cousin.**

Quatuor pedibus currit /kwóduwor pédəbəs kə́hrət/. Lat. It runs upon four feet; it runs upon all fours. See **All-fours.**

Quean /kwíyn/. A worthless woman; a strumpet. Obsolete.

Queen. A woman who possesses the sovereignty and royal power in a country under a monarchical form of government. The wife of a king.

Queen regnant. In English law, a queen who holds the crown in her own right; as the first Queen Mary, Queen Elizabeth, Queen Anne, and Queen Victoria.

For the titles and descriptions of various officers in the English legal system, called "Queen's Advocate," "Queen's Coroner," "Queen's Counsel," "Queen's Proctor," "Queen's Remembrancer," etc., during the reign of a female sovereign, see terms under **King** and also the following titles.

Queen's bench. The English court of king's bench is so called during the reign of a queen. See **King's bench.**

Queen's counsel. See **King's counsel.**

Queen's evidence. See **King's evidence.**

Queen's prison. A jail which used to be appropriated to the debtors and criminals confined under process or by authority of the superior courts at Westminster, the high court of admiralty, and also to persons imprisoned under the bankrupt law.

Queen's proctor. See **King's proctor.**

Que estate /kwíy əstéyt/. L. Fr. Whose estate. A term used in old pleading, particularly in claiming prescription, by which it was alleged that the plaintiff and those former owners *whose estate* he had had immemorially exercised the right claimed. This was called "prescribing in a *que* estate."

Que est le mesme /kwíy èy lə mém/. L. Fr. Which is the same. A term used in actions of trespass, etc. See **Quæ est eadem.**

Quemadmodum ad quæstionem facti non respondent judices, ita ad quæstionem juris non respondent juratores /kwemǽdmədəm ǽd kwèshchiyównəm fǽktay nòn rəspóndənt júwdəsiyz, áydə ǽd kwèshchiyownəm júrəs nòn rəspóndənt jùrətóriyz/. In the same manner that judges do not answer to questions of fact, so jurors do not answer to questions of law.

Quem reditum reddit /kwém rédədəm rédət/. L. Lat. An old English writ which lay where a rent-charge or other rent which was not rent service was granted by fine holding of the grantor. If the tenant would not attorn, then the grantee might have had this writ.

Querela /kwəríylə/. Lat. An action preferred in any court of justice. The plaintiff was called *"querens,"* or complainant and his brief, complaint, or declaration was called *"querela."*

Querela coram rege a concilio discutienda et terminanda /kwəríylə kórəm ríyjiy èy kənsíl(i)yow dəskə̀shiyéndə èt tàrmənǽndə/. A writ by which one is called to justify a complaint of a trespass made to the king himself, before the king and his council.

Querela inofficiosi testamenti /kwəríylə inəfishiyówsay tèstəméntay/. Lat. In the civil law, a species of action allowed to a child who had been unjustly disinherited, to set aside the will, founded on the presumption of law, in such cases, that the parent was not in his right mind.

Querens /kwírən(d)z/. Lat. A plaintiff; complainant; inquirer.

Querulous /kwéhr(y)ələs/. Apt to find fault; habitually complaining; disposed to murmur. Expressing, or suggestive of complaint; fretful; whining.

Questa /kwéstə/. A quest; an inquest, inquisition, or inquiry, upon the oaths of an impaneled jury.

Question. A subject or point of investigation, examination or debate; theme of inquiry; problem; matter to be inquired into, as subject matter of civil or criminal discovery. A point on which the parties are not agreed, and which is submitted to the decision of a judge and jury. See also **Issue.**

An interrogation put to a witness, for the purpose of having him declare the truth of certain facts as far as he knows them; *e.g.* direct or cross examination of witness at trial. See also **Discovery; Interrogation.**

Categorical question. One inviting a distinct and positive statement of fact; one which can be answered by "yes" or "no." In the plural, a series of questions, covering a particular subject-matter, arranged in a systematic and consecutive order.

Federal question. See **Federal.**

Hypothetical question. See that title.

Judicial question. See **Judicial.**

Leading question. See that title.

Political question. See **Political.**

Question of fact. An issue involving the resolution of a factual dispute and hence within the province of the jury in contrast to a question of law.

Question of law. An issue which involves the application or interpretation of a law and hence within the province of the judge and not the jury.

Questman /kwéstmæn/, or **questmonger** /kwéstmòŋgǝr/. In old English law, a starter of lawsuits, or prosecutions; also a person chosen to inquire into abuses, especially such as relate to weights and measures; also a church-warden.

Questores parricidii /kwestóriyz pǽrǝsáydiyay/. Lat. In Roman law, certain officers, two in number, who were deputed by the *comitia,* as a kind of commission, to search out and try all cases of parricide and murder. They were probably appointed annually.

Questus est nobis /kwéstǝs èst nówbǝs/. Lat. A writ of nuisance, which, by 15 Edw. I, lay against him to whom a house or other thing that caused a nuisance descended or was alienated; whereas, before that statute the action lay only against him who first levied or caused the nuisance to the damage of his neighbor.

Quia /kwáyǝ/. Lat. Because; whereas; inasmuch as.

Qui abjurat regnum amittit regnum, sed non regem; patriam, sed non patrem patriæ /kwày ǝbjúrǝt régnǝm, eymídǝt régnam, séd nòn ríyjǝm; pǽtriyǝm, séd nòn pǽtrǝm pǽtriyiy/. He who abjures the realm leaves the realm, but not the king; the country, but not the father of the country.

Qui accusat integræ famæ sit, et non criminosus /kwày ǝkyúwzǝd íntǝgriy féymiy sìt, èt nón krìmǝnówsǝs/. Let him who accuses be of clear fame, and not criminal.

Qui acquirit sibi acquirit hæredibus /kwày ǝkwráyrǝt síbay ǝkwáyrǝt hǝríydǝbǝs/. He who acquires for himself acquires for his heirs.

Quia datum est nobis intelligi /kwáyǝ déydǝm èst nówbǝs intélǝjay/. Because it is given to us to understand. Formal words in old writs.

Qui adimit medium dirimit finem /kwày ǽdǝmǝt míyd(i)yǝm díhrǝmǝt fáynǝm/. He who takes away the mean destroys the end. He that deprives a man of the mean by which he ought to come to a thing deprives him of the thing itself.

Quia emptores /kwáyǝ em(p)tóriyz/. Lat. "Because the purchasers." The title of the statute of Westm. 3, (18 Edw. I, c. 1). This statute took from the tenants of common lords the feudal liberty they claimed of disposing of part of their lands to hold of themselves, and, instead of it, gave them a general liberty to sell all or any part, to hold of the next superior lord, which they could not have done before without con-

sent. The effect of this statute was twofold: (1) To facilitate the alienation of fee-simple estates; and (2) to put an end to the creation of any new manors, *i.e.,* tenancies in fee-simple of a subject.

Quia erronice emanavit /kwáyǝ ǝrównǝsiy èmǝnéyvǝt/. Because it issued erroneously, or through mistake. A term in old English practice.

Qui aliquid statuerit, parte inaudita altera æquum licet dixerit, haud æquum fecerit /kwày ǽlǝkwid stǝtyúwǝrǝt, párdiy inódǝdǝ óltǝrǝ íykwǝm lísǝt díksǝrǝt, hód íykwǝm fésǝrǝt/. He who determines any matter without hearing both sides, though he may have decided right, has not done justice.

Qui alterius jure utitur, eodem jure uti debet /kwáy oltíriyǝs júriy yúwdǝdǝr, iyówdǝm júriy yúwday débǝt/. He who uses the right of another ought to use the same right.

Quia non refert aut quis intentionem suam declaret, verbis, aut rebus ipsis vel factis /kwáyǝ nòn réfǝrd òt kwís intènshiyównǝm s(y)úwǝm dǝklérǝt, várbǝs, òt ríybǝs ípsǝs vèl fǽktǝs/. It is immaterial whether the intention be collected from the words used or the acts done. Tocci v. Nowfall, 220 N.C. 550, 18 S.E.2d 225, 228.

Qui approbat non reprobat /kwáy ǽprǝbǝt nòn réprǝbǝt/. He who approbates does not reprobate, [*i.e.,* he cannot both accept and reject the same thing].

Quia timet /kwáyǝ táymǝt/. Lat. Because he fears or apprehends. In equity practice, the technical name of a bill filed by a party who seeks the aid of a court of equity, *because he fears* some future probable injury to his rights or interests, and relief granted must depend upon circumstances.

Quibble. A cavilling or verbal objection. A slight difficulty raised without necessity or propriety.

Qui bene distinguit bene docet /kwày bíyniy dǝstíŋgwǝt bíyniy dósǝt/. He who distinguishes well teaches well.

Qui bene interrogat bene docet /kwày bíyniy intéhrǝgǝt bíyniy dósǝt/. He who questions well teaches well. Information or express averment may be effectually conveyed in the way of interrogation.

Qui cadit a syllaba cadit a tota causa /kwày kǽdǝd èy sílǝbǝ kǽdǝd èy tówdǝ kózǝ/. He who fails in a syllable fails in his whole cause.

Quick. Living; alive. See **Quickening.**

Quick asset ratio. Ratio of cash, accounts receivable and marketable securities to current liabilities. Also called the "acid test."

Quick assets. Liquid assets such as cash, marketable securities and accounts receivable which can be converted into cash without delay.

Quick child. One that has developed so that it moves within the mother's womb. State v. Timm, 244 Wis. 508, 12 N.W.2d 670, 671. See also **Quickening.**

Quickening. The first motion of the fetus in the womb felt by the mother, occurring usually about the middle of the term of pregnancy.

Quick with child. Having conceived.

Qui concedit aliquid, concedere videtur et id sine quo concessio est irrita, sine quo res ipsa esse non potuit /kwáy kənsíydəd ǽləkwid, kənsíydəriy vədíydər èd íd sáyniy kwòw kənsésh(iy)ow èst íhrədə, sáyniy kwòw ríyz ípsə ésiy nòn póduwət/. He who concedes anything is considered as conceding that without which his concession would be void, without which the thing itself could not exist.

Qui concedit aliquid concedit omne id sine quo concessio est irrita /kwáy kənsíydəd ǽləkwid kənsíydəd ómniy íd sáyniy kwòw kənsésh(iy)ow èst íhrədə/. He who grants anything grants everything without which the grant is fruitless.

Qui confirmat nihil dat /kwáy kənfármət náy(h)əl dǽt/. He who confirms does not give.

Qui contemnit præceptum contemnit præcipientem /kwáy kəntémnət prəséptəm kəntémnət prəsìpiyéntəm/. He who contemns [contemptuously treats] a command contemns the party who gives it.

Quicquid acquiritur servo acquiritur domino /kwíkwid əkwáyrədər sárvow əkwáyrədər dómənow/. Whatever is acquired by the servant is acquired for the master. Whatever rights are acquired by an agent are acquired for his principal.

Quicquid demonstratæ rei additur satis demonstratæ frustra est /kwíkwid dèmənstréydiy ríyay ǽdədər sǽdəs dèmənstréydiy frástrə èst/. Whatever is added to demonstrate anything already sufficiently demonstrated is surplusage.

Quicquid est contra normam recti est injuria /kwíkwid èst kóntrə nórməm réktay èst injúriyə/. Whatever is against the rule of right is a wrong.

Quicquid in excessu actum est, lege prohibetur /kwíkwid ín əksés(y)uw ǽktəm èst, líyjiy pròw(h)əbíydər/. Whatever is done in excess is prohibited by law.

Quicquid judicis auctoritati subjicitur novitati non subjicitur /kwíkwid júwdəsəs oktòrətéyday səbjísədər nòwvətéyday nòn səbjísədər/. Whatever is subject to the authority of a judge is not subject to innovation.

Quicquid plantatur solo, solo cedit /kwíkwid plǽntéydər sówlow, sówlow síydət/. Whatever is affixed to the soil belongs to the soil.

Quicquid recipitur, recipitur secundum modum recipientis /kwíkwid rəsípədər, rəsípədər səkándəm mówdəm rəsìpiyéntəs/. Whatever is received is received according to the intention of the recipient.

Quicquid solvitur, solvitur secundum modum solventis; quicquid recipitur, recipitur secundum modum recipientis /kwíkwid sólvədər, sólvədər səkándəm mówdəm solvéntəs; kwíkwid rəsípədər, rəsípədər səkándəm mówdəm rəsìpiyéntəs/. Whatever money is paid, is paid according to the direction of the payer; whatever money is received, is received according to that of the recipient.

Qui cum alio contrahit, vel est, vel esse debet non ignarus conditionis ejus /kwáy kàm éyl(i)yow kəntréy(h)ət, vèl ést, vèl ésiy débət nón ignérəs kəndìshiyównəs íyjəs/. He who contracts with another either is or ought to be not ignorant of his condition.

Quicunque habet jurisdictionem ordinariam est illius loci ordinarius /kwaykánkwiy héybət jùrəsdìkshiyównəm òrdənériyəm ést iláyəs lówsay òrdənériyəs/. Whoever has an ordinary jurisdiction is ordinary of that place.

Quicunque jussu judicis aliquid fecerit non videtur dolo malo fecisse, quia parere necesse est /kwaykánkwiy jás(y)uw júwdəsəs ǽləkwid fésərət nòn vədíydər dówlow mǽlow fəsísiy, kwáyə pəríriy nəsésiy èst/. Whoever does anything by the command of a judge is not reckoned to have done it with an evil intent, because it is necessary to obey.

Quidam /kwáydəm/. Lat. Somebody. This term is used in the French law to designate a person whose name is not known.

Qui dat finem, dat media ad finem necessaria /kwày dǽt fáynəm, dǽt míyd(i)yə ǽd fáynəm nèsəsériyə/. He who gives an end gives the means to that end.

Qui destruit medium destruit finem /kwày déstruwət míyd(i)yəm déstruwət fáynəm/. He who destroys the mean destroys the end.

Quid juris clamat /kwìd júrəs klǽmət/. In old English practice, a writ which lay for the grantee of a reversion or remainder, where the particular tenant would not attorn, for the purpose of compelling him.

Qui doit inheriter al pere doit inheriter al fitz /kwày dóyd inhérədər àel pér dóyd ənhéridər àel fíts/. He who would have been heir to the father shall be heir to the son.

Quid pro quo /kwíd pròw kwów/. What for what; something for something. Used in law for the giving one valuable thing for another. It is nothing more than the mutual consideration which passes between the parties to a contract, and which renders it valid and binding.

Quidquid enim sive dolo et culpa venditoris accidit in eo venditor securus est /kwídkwid énəm sáyviy dówlow èt kálpə vèndətórəs ǽksədəd ìn íyow véndədər səkyúrəs èst/. For concerning anything which occurs without deceit and wrong on the part of the vendor, the vendor is secure.

Quid sit jus, et in quo consistit injuria, legis est definire /kwíd sìt jás, èd in kwów kənsístəd injúriyə, líyjəs èst dèfənáyriy/. What constitutes right, and what injury, it is the business of the law to declare.

Quid turpi ex causa promissum est non valet /kwìd tárpay èks kózə prəmísəm èst nòn vǽlət/. A promise arising out of immoral circumstances is invalid.

Quiet, *v.* To pacify; to render secure or unassailable by the removal of disquieting causes or disputes.

Quiet, *adj.* Unmolested; tranquil; free from interference or disturbance.

Covenant of quiet enjoyment. A covenant, usually inserted in leases and conveyances on the part of the grantor, promising that the tenant or grantee shall enjoy the possession of the premises in peace and without disturbance.

Quieta non movere /kwayíydə nòn məvíriy/. Not to unsettle things which are established.

Quietare /kwàyətériy/. L. Lat. To quit, acquit, discharge, or save harmless. A formal word in old deeds of donation and other conveyances.

Quiete clamantia /kwayíydiy kləmǽnsh(iy)ə/. L. Lat. In old English law, quitclaim.

Quiete clamare /kwayíydiy kləmériy/. L. Lat. To quitclaim or renounce all pretensions of right and title.

Quiet title action. A proceeding to establish the plaintiff's title to land by bringing into court an adverse claimant and there compelling him either to establish his claim or be forever after estopped from asserting it. See also **Action to quiet title.**

Quietus /kwayíydəs/. In old English law, quit; acquitted; discharged. A word used by the clerk of the pipe, and auditors in the exchequer, in their acquittances or discharges given to accountants; usually concluding with an *abinde recessit quietus* (hath gone quit thereof), which was called a *"quietus est."*

    A final discharge or acquittance, as from a debt or obligation; that which silences claims. State ex rel. Jones v. Edwards, 203 La. 1039, 14 So.2d 829, 834.

Quietus redditus /kwayíydəs rédədəs/. In old English law, quitrent. See **Quitrent.**

Qui evertit causam, evertit causatum futurum /kwáy əvə́rdət kózəm, əvə́rdət kozéydəm fyuwchúrəm/. He who overthrows the cause overthrows its future effects.

Qui ex damnato coitu nascuntur inter liberos non computentur /kwáy èks dæmnéydow kówətyuw næskántər íntər líbərows nòn kòmpyuwténtər/. Those who are born of an unlawful intercourse are not reckoned among the children.

Qui facit id quod plus est, facit id quod minus est, sed non convertitur /kwày féysəd íd kwòd plás èst, féysəd íd kwòd máynəs èst, sèd nón kənvə́rdədər/. He who does that which is more does that which is less, but not *vice versa.*

Qui facit per alium facit per se /kwày féysət pàr éyl(i)yəm féysət pàr síy/. He who acts through another acts himself [*i.e.,* the acts of an agent are the acts of the principal].

Qui habet jurisdictionem absolvendi, habet jurisdictionem ligandi /kwày héybət jùrəsdìkshiyównəm æbsolvénday, hǽbət jùrəsdìkshiyównəm ləgǽnday/. He who has jurisdiction to loosen, has jurisdiction to bind. Applied to writs of prohibition and consultation, as resting on a similar foundation.

Qui hæret in litera hæret in cortice /kwày hírəd in lídərə hírəd in kórdəsiy/. He who considers merely the letter of an instrument goes but skin deep into its meaning.

Qui ignorat quantum solvere debeat, non potest improbus videre /kwáy ignórət kwóntəm sólvəriy débiyət, nòn pówdəst imprówbəs vidíriy/. He who does not know what he ought to pay, does not want probity in not paying.

Qui improvide /kwáy impróvədiy/. A *supersedeas* granted where a writ was erroneously sued out or misawarded.

Qui in jus dominiumve alterius succedit jure ejus uti debet /kwáy in jás dəmìniyə́mviy oltíriyəs səksíydət júriy íyjəs yúwday débət/. He who succeeds to the right or property of another ought to use his right, [*i.e.,* holds it subject to the same rights and liabilities as attached to it in the hands of the assignor].

Qui in utero est pro jam nato habetur, quoties de ejus commodo quæritur /kwáy in yúwdərow èst pròw jǽm néydow həbíydər, kwówshiyiyz diy íyjəs kómədow kwírədər/. He who is in the womb is held as already born, whenever a question arises for his benefit.

Qui jure suo utitur, nemini facit injuriam /kwày júriy s(y)úwow yúwdədər, némənay féysəd injúriyəm/. He who uses his legal rights harms no one.

Qui jussu judicis aliquod fecerit non videtur dolo malo fecisse, quia parere necesse est /kwày jás(y)uw júwdəsəs ǽləkwòd fésərət nòn vədíydər dówlow mǽlow fəsísiy, kwáyə pəríriy nəsésiy èst/. Where a person does an act by command of one exercising judicial authority, the law will not suppose that he acted from any wrongful or improper motive, because it was his bounden duty to obey.

Quilibet potest renunciare juri pro se introducto /kwáyləbət pówdəst rənànshiyériy júray pròw síy indáktow/. Every one may renounce or relinquish a right introduced for his own benefit.

Qui male agit odit lucem /kwày mǽliy éyjəd ówdət l(y)úwsəm/. He who acts badly hates the light.

Qui mandat ipse fecissi videtur /kwày mǽndəd ípsiy fəsísay vədíydər/. He who commands [a thing to be done] is held to have done it himself.

Qui melius probat melius habet /kwày míyl(i)yəs prówbət míyl(i)yəs héybət/. He who proves most recovers most.

Qui molitur insidias in patriam id facit quod insanus nauta perforans navem in qua vehitur /kwày mólədər insídiyəs in pǽtriyəm id féysət kwòd inséynəs nódə párfəræn(d)z néyvəm in kwéy víy(h)ədər/. He who betrays his country is like the insane sailor who bores a hole in the ship which carries him.

Qui nascitur sine legitimo matrimonio, matrem sequitur /kwày nǽsədər sáyniy ləjídəmow mætrəmówn(i)yow, mǽtrəm sékwədər/. He who is born out of lawful matrimony follows the condition of the mother.

Qui non cadunt in constantem virum vani timores sunt æstimandi /kwáy nòn kǽdənt in kənstǽntəm váyrəm véynay timóriyz sànt èstəmǽnday/. Those fears are to be esteemed vain which do not affect a firm man.

Qui non habet, ille non dat /kwáy nòn héybəd, íliy nòn dǽt/. He who has not, gives not. He who has nothing to give, gives nothing. A person cannot convey a right that is not in him. If a man grant that which is not his, the grant is void.

Qui non habet in ære, luat in corpore, ne quis peccetur impune /kwáy nòn héybəd in ériy, l(y)úwəd in kórpəriy, nìy kwís pəksíydər impyúwniy/. He who cannot pay with his purse must suffer in his person, lest he who offends should go unpunished.

Qui non habet potestatem alienandi habet necessitatem retinendi /kwáy nòn héybət pòwdəstéydəm ǽliyənǽnday héybət nəsèsətéydəm rèdənénday/. He who has not the power of alienating is obliged to retain.

Qui non improbat, approbat /kwáy nòn ímprəbət, ǽprəbət/. He who does not blame, approves.

Qui non libere veritatem pronunciat proditor est veritatis /kwáy nòn líbəriy vèhrətéydəm prənánshiyət prówdədər èst vèhrətéydəs/. He who does not freely speak the truth is a betrayer of the truth.

Qui non negat fatetur /kwáy nòn négət fætíydər/. He who does not deny, admits. A well-known rule of pleading.

Qui non obstat quod obstare potest, facere videtur /kwáy nòn óbstæt kwód obstériy pówdəst, fǽsəriy vədíydər/. He who does not prevent [a thing] which he can prevent, is considered to do [as doing] it.

Qui non prohibet id quod prohibere potest assentire videtur /kwáy nòn prów(h)əbəd íd kwòd pròw-(h)əbíriy pówdəst æsəntáyriy vədíydər/. He who does not forbid what he is able to prevent, is considered to assent.

Qui non propulsat injuriam quando potest, infert /kwáy nòn prəpálsəd ənjúr(i)yəm kwóndow pówdəst, ínfərt/. He who does not repel an injury when he can, induces it.

Quinquepartite /kwìnkwəpártayt/. Consisting of five parts; divided into five parts.

Quintal, or **kintal** /kwíntəl/. A weight of one hundred pounds.

Quinto exactus /kwíntow əgzǽktəs/. In old English practice, called or exacted the fifth time. A return made by the sheriff, after a defendant had been proclaimed, required, or exacted in five county courts successively, and failed to appear, upon which he was outlawed by the coroners of the county. 3 Bl.Comm. 283.

Qui obstruit aditum, destruit commodum /kwày óbstruwəd ǽdədəm, déstruwət kómədəm/. He who obstructs a way, passage, or entrance destroys a benefit or convenience. He who prevents another from entering upon land destroys the benefit which he has from it.

Qui omne dicit nihil excludit /kwày ómniy dísət náy(h)əl əkskl(y)úwdət/. He who says all excludes nothing.

Qui parcit nocentibus innocentes punit /kwày pársət nəséntəbəs ìnəséntiyz pyúwnət/. He who spares the guilty punishes the innocent.

Qui peccat ebrius luat sobrius /kwày pékəd íybriyəs l(y)úwət sówbriyəs/. He who sins when drunk shall be punished when sober.

Qui per alium facit per seipsum facere videtur /kwáy pər éyl(i)yəm féysət pər siyípsəm fǽsəriy vədíydər/. He who does a thing by an agent is considered as doing it himself.

Qui per fraudem agit frustra agit /kwáy pər fródəm éyjət frástrə éyjət/. What a man does fraudulently he does in vain.

Qui potest et debet vetare, jubet /kwày pówdəst èt débət vətériy, júwbət/. He who can and ought to forbid a thing [if he do not forbid it] directs it.

Qui primum peccat ilie facit rixam /kwày práyməm pékət íliy féysət ríksəm/. He who sins first makes the strife.

Qui prior est tempore potior est jure /kwày práyər èst témpəriy pówsh(iy)ər èst júriy/. He who is before in time is the better in right. Priority in time gives preference in law. A maxim of very extensive application, both at law and in equity.

Qui pro me aliquid facit mihi fecisse videtur /kwáy pròw míy ǽləkwid féysət máy(h)ay fəsísiy vədíydər/. He who does anything for me appears to do it to me.

Qui providet sibi providet hæredibus /kwày próvədət síbay próvədət hərédəbəs/. He who provides for himself provides for his heirs.

Qui rationem in omnibus quærunt rationem subvertunt /kwày ræshiyównəm ìn ómnəbəs kwírənt ræshiyównəm səbvárdənt/. They who seek a reason for everything subvert reason.

Quiritarian ownership /kwìhrətér(i)yən ównərship/. In Roman law, ownership held by a title recognized by the municipal law, in an object also recognized by that law, and in the strict character of a Roman citizen.

Qui sciens solvit indebitum donandi consilio id videtur fecisse /kwày sáyən(d)z sólvəd indébədəm dənǽnday kən(t)síl(i)yow ìd vədíydər fəsísiy/. One who knowingly pays what is not due is supposed to have done it with the intention of making a gift.

Qui semel actionem renunciaverit amplius repetere non potest /kwày sémǝl ǽkshiyównǝm rǝnànshiyéyvǝrǝt ǽmpliyǝs rǝpédǝriy nòn pówdǝst/. He who has once relinquished his action cannot bring it again. A rule descriptive of the effect of a *retraxit* and *nolle prosequi.*

Qui semel est malus, semper præsumitur esse malus in eodem genere /kwày sémǝl èst mǽlǝs, sémpǝr prəz(y)úwmǝdǝr ésiy mǽlǝs ìn iyówdǝm jénǝriy/. He who is once criminal is presumed to be always criminal in the same kind or way.

Qui sentit commodum sentire debet et onus /kwày séntǝt kómǝdǝm sentáyriy débǝd èd ównǝs/. He who receives the advantage ought also to suffer the burden.

Qui sentit onus sentire debet et commodum /kwày séntǝd ównǝs sǝntáyriy débǝd èt kómǝdǝm/. He who bears the burden of a thing ought also to experience the advantage arising from it.

Quisquis erit qui vult juris-consultus haberi continuet studium, velit a quocunque doceri /kwískwis éhrǝt kwày vált jùrǝskǝnsáltǝs hǝbíray kǝntínyuwǝt st(y)úwd(i)yǝm, vélǝd èy kwowkáŋkwiy dosíray/. Whoever wishes to be a juris-consult, let him continually study, and desire to be taught by every one.

Quisquis præsumitur bonus; et semper in dubiis pro reo respondendum /kwískwis prəz(y)úwmədər bównəs; èt sémpər in d(y)úwbiyəs pròw ríyow rəspòndéndəm/. Every one is presumed good; and in doubtful cases the resolution should be ever for the accused.

Quit, v. To leave; remove from; surrender possession of; as when a tenant "quits" the premises or receives a "notice to quit."

Notice to quit. A written notice given by a landlord to his tenant, stating that the former desires to repossess himself of the demised premises, and that the latter is required to quit and remove from the same at a time designated, either at the expiration of the term, if the tenant is in under a lease, or immediately, if the tenancy is at will or by sufferance.

Quit, adj. Clear; discharged; free; also spoken of persons absolved or acquitted of a charge.

Qui tacet, consentire videtur /kwày tǽsət, kònsentáyriy vədíydər/. He who is silent is supposed to consent. The silence of a party implies his consent.

Qui tacet consentire videtur, ubi tractatur de ejus commodo /kwày tǽsət kònsentáyriy vədíydər, yúwbay trǽktíydər dìy íyjəs kómədow/. He who is silent is considered as assenting, when his interest is at stake.

Qui tacet non utique fatetur, sed tamen verum est eum non negare /kwày tǽsət nòn yúwdəkwiy fətíydər, sèd tǽmən vírəm èst íyəm nón nəgériy/. He who is silent does not indeed confess, but yet it is true that he does not deny.

Qui tam action /kwày tǽm ǽkshən/. Lat. "Who as well _____." An action brought by an informer, under a statute which establishes a penalty for the commission or omission of a certain act, and provides that the same shall be recoverable in a civil action, part of the penalty to go to any person who will bring such action and the remainder to the state or some other institution, is called a "*qui tam* action"; because the plaintiff states that he sues *as well* for the state as for himself.

Qui tardius solvit, minus solvit /kwày tárdiyəs sólvət, máynəs sólvət/. He who pays more tardily [than he ought] pays less [than he ought].

Quitclaim, v. In conveyancing, to release or relinquish a claim; to execute a deed of quitclaim. See **Quitclaim, n.**

Quitclaim, n. A release or acquittance given to one man by another, in respect of any action that he has or might have against him. Also acquitting or giving up one's claim or title.

Quitclaim deed. A deed of conveyance operating by way of release; that is, intended to pass any title, interest, or claim which the grantor may have in the premises, but not professing that such title is valid, nor containing any warranty or covenants for title. Under the law of some states the grantor warrants in such deed that neither he nor anyone claiming under him has encumbered the property and that he will defend the title against defects arising under and through him, but as to no others.

Qui timent, cavent vitant /kwày táymənt, kǽvənt váydənt/. They who fear, take care and avoid.

Qui totum dicit nihil excipit /kwày tówdəm dísəi náy(h)əl éksəpət/. He who says all excepts nothing.

Quit rent. A rent paid by the tenant of the freehold, by which he goes quit and free,—that is, discharged from any other rent. 2 Bl.Comm. 42.

Quittance /kwítən(t)s/. An abbreviation of "acquittance;" a release (*q.v.*).

Qui vult decipi, decipiatur /kwày vált désəpay, dəsìpiyéydər/. Let him who wishes to be deceived, be deceived.

Quoad hoc /kwówæd hók/. Lat. As to this; with respect to this; so far as this in particular is concerned. A prohibition *quoad hoc* is a prohibition as to certain things among others. Thus, where a party was complained against in the ecclesiastical court for matters cognizable in the temporal courts, a prohibition *quoad* these matters issued, i.e., *as to such matters* the party was prohibited from prosecuting his suit in the ecclesiastical court.

Quoad sacra /kwówæd séykrə/. Lat. As to sacred things; for religious purposes.

Quo animo /kwòw ǽnəmow/. Lat. With what intention or motive. Used sometimes as a substantive, in lieu of the single word "*animus*," design or motive. "The *quo animo* is the real subject of inquiry."

Quocumque modo velit; quocumque modo possit /kwowkámkwiy mówdow vélət; kwowkámkwiy mówdow pósət/. In any way he wishes; in any way he can.

Quod ab initio non valet in tractu temporis non convalescet /kwód æb ənísh(iy)ow nòn vǽləd in trǽkt(y)uw témpərəs nòn kònvəlésət/. That which is bad in its commencement improves not by lapse of time.

Quod ad jus naturale attinet omnes homines æquales sunt /kwód æd jás næchəréyliy ǽtənəd ómniyz hóməniyz iykwéyliyz sànt/. All men are equal as far as the natural law is concerned.

Quod ædificatur in area legata cedit legato /kwòd èdəfəkéydər in ériyə ləgéydə síydət ləgéydow/. Whatever is built on ground given by will goes to the legatee.

Quod alias bonum et justum est, si per vim vel fraudem petatur, malum et injustum efficitur /kwòd éyliyəs bównəm èt jástəm èst, sáy pər vím vèl fródəm pətéydər, mǽləm èd injástəm əfíshədər/. What otherwise is good and just, if it be sought by force and fraud, becomes bad and unjust.

Quod alias non fuit licitum, necessitas licitum facit /kwòd éyliyəs nòn f(y)úwət lísədəm, nəsésətæs lísədəm féysət/. What otherwise was not lawful, necessity makes lawful.

Quod approbo non reprobo /kwòd ǽprəbow nòn réprəbow/. What I approve I do not reject. I cannot approve and reject at the same time. I cannot take the benefit of an instrument, and at the same time repudiate it.

Quod a quoque pœnæ nomine exactum est id eidem restituere nemo cogitur /kwód èy kwówkwiy píyniy nómaniy əgzǽktəm èst íd iyáydəm rèstət(y)úwəriy níymow kójədər/. That which has been exacted as a penalty no one is obliged to restore.

Quod attinet ad jus civile, servi pro nullis habentur, non tamen et jure naturali, quia, quod ad jus naturale attinet, omnes homines æquales sunt /kwód ǽdənəd æd jǽs sívəliy, sárvay pròw nǽləs həbéntər, nòn tǽmən èt júriy næchəréylay, kwáyə, kwód æd jǽs næchəréyliy ǽdənət, ómniyz hóməniyz iykwéyliyz sènt/. So far as the civil law is concerned, slaves are not reckoned as persons, but not so by natural law, for, so far as regards natural law, all men are equal.

Quod billa cassetur /kwòd bílə kəsíydər/. That the bill be quashed. The common-law form of a judgment sustaining a plea in abatement, where the proceeding is by bill, *i.e.*, by a *capias* instead of by original writ.

Quod clerici beneficiati de cancellaria /kwòd kléhrəsay bènəfishiyéyday dìy kæn(t)səlériyə/. A writ to exempt a clerk of the chancery from the contribution towards the proctors of the clergy in parliament, etc.

Quod clerici non eligantur in officio ballivi, etc. /kwòd kléhrəsay nòn èləgǽntər in əfísh(iy)ow bæláyvay/. A writ which lay for a clerk, who, by reason of some land he had, was made, or was about to be made, bailiff, beadle, reeve, or some such officer, to obtain exemption from serving the office.

Quod computet /kwòd kómpyədət/. That he account.

Judgment quod computet. A preliminary or interlocutory judgment given in the action of account-render (also in the case of creditors' bills against an executor or administrator), directing that accounts be taken before a master or auditor.

Quod constat clare non debet verificari /kwòd kónstæt klériy nòn débət vèhrəfəkéray/. What is clearly apparent need not be proved.

Quod constat curiæ opere testium non indiget /kwòd kónstæt kyúriyiy ówpəriy téstiyəm nòn índəjət/. That which appears to the court needs not the aid of witnesses.

Quod contra legem fit pro infecto habetur /kwòd kóntrə líyjəm fít pròw inféktow həbíydər/. That which is done against law is regarded as not done at all.

Quod contra rationem juris receptum est, non est producendum ad consequentias /kwòd kóntrə rǽshiyównəm júrəs rəséptəm èst, nón èst pròwdəséndəm æd kònsəkwénsh(iy)əs/. That which has been received against the reason of the law is not to be drawn into a precedent.

Quod cum /kwód kàm/. In common law pleading, for that whereas. A form of introducing matter of inducement in certain actions, as *assumpsit* and case.

Quodcunque aliquis ob tutelam corporis sui fecerit, jure id fecisse videtur /kwodkánkwiy ǽləkwəs òb t(y)uwtíyləm kórpərəs s(y)úway fésərət, júriy íd fəsísiy vədíydər/. Whatever any one does in defense of his person, that he is considered to have done legally.

Quod datum est ecclesiæ, datum est deo /kwòd déydəm èst əklíyziyiy, déydəm èst díyow/. What is given to the church is given to God.

Quod demonstrandi causa additur rei satis, demonstratæ, frustra fit /kwòd dèmənstrǽnday kózə ǽdədər ríyay séydəs, dèmənstréydiy, frástrə fít/. What is added to a thing sufficiently palpable, for the purpose of demonstration, is vain.

Quod dubitas, ne feceris /kwód d(y)úwbədəs, nìy fésərəs/. What you doubt of, do not do. In a case of moment, especially in cases of life, it is safest to hold that in practice which hath least doubt and danger.

Quod ei deforceat /kwòd íyay dəfórsiyət/. In old English law, the name of a writ given by St. Westm. 2, 13 Edw. I, c. 4, to the owners of a particular estate, as for life, in dower, by the curtesy, or in fee-tail, who were barred of the right of possession by a recovery had against them through their default or nonappearance in a possessory action, by which the right was restored to him who had been thus unwarily deforced by his own default. 3 Bl.Comm. 193.

Quod enim semel aut bis existit, prætereunt legislatores /kwód ènim séməl òt bís əgzístət, prətéhriyənt lèjəslətóriyz/. That which never happens but once or twice, legislators pass by.

Quod est ex necessitate nunquam introducitur, nisi quando necessarium /kwód èst éks nəsèsətéydiy nánkwəm intrəd(y)úwsədər, náysay kwóndow nèsəsériyəm/. That which is of necessity is never introduced, unless when necessary.

Quod est inconveniens aut contra rationem non permissum est in lege /kwód èst ìnkənvíyn(iy)en(d)z ót kóntrə rǽshiyównəm nón pərmísəm èst ìn líyjiy/. That which is inconvenient or against reason is not permissible in law.

Quod est necessarium est licitum /kwód èst nèsəsériyəm èst lísədəm/. What is necessary is lawful.

Quod factum est, cum in obscuro sit, ex affectione cujusque capit interpretationem /kwòd fǽktəm èst, kám in obsk(y)úrow sìt, èks əfèkshiyówniy k(y)uwjáskwiy kǽpəd əntàrprətèyshiyównəm/. When there is doubt about an act, it receives interpretation from the (known) feelings of the actor.

Quod fieri debet facile præsumitur /kwòd fáyəray débət fǽsəliy prəz(y)úwmədər/. That which ought to be done is easily presumed.

Quod fieri non debet, factum valet /kwòd fáyəray nòn débət, fǽktəm vǽlət/. That which ought not to be done, when done, is valid.

Quod fuit concessum /kwòd f(y)úwət kənsésəm/. Which was granted. A phrase in the reports, signifying that an argument or point made was conceded or acquiesced in by the court.

Quod inconsulto fecimus, consultius revocemus /kwòd ìnkənsóltow fésəməs, kənsólsh(iy)əs rèvəsíyməs/. What we have done without due consideration, upon better consideration we may revoke.

Quod initio non valet, tractu temporis non valet /kwòd ənísh(iy)ow nòn vǽlət, trǽkt(y)uw témpərəs nòn vǽlət/. A thing void in the beginning does not become valid by lapse of time.

Quod initio vitiosum est non potest tractu temporis convalescere /kwòd ənísh(iy)ow vìshiyówsəm èst nòn pówdəst trǽkt(y)uw témpərəs kònvəlésəriy/. That which is void from the beginning cannot become valid by lapse of time.

Quod in jure scripto "jus" appellatur, id in lege angliæ "rectum" esse dicitur /kwód ìn júriy skríptow jə́s æpəléydər, íd ìn líyjiy ǽŋgliyiy réktəm ésiy dísədər/. What in the civil law is called "jus," in the law of England is said to be "rectum" (right).

Quod in minori valet valebit in majori; et quod in majori non valet nec valebit in minori /kwód ìn mənóray vǽlət vəlíybəd ìn məjóray; èt kwód ìn məjóray nòn vǽlət nèk vəlíybəd ìn mənóray/. That which is valid in the less shall be valid in the greater; and that which is not valid in the greater shall neither be valid in the less.

Quod in uno similium valet valebit in altero /kwód ìn yúwnow səmíliyəm vǽlət vəlíybəd ìn óltərow/. That which is effectual in one of two like things shall be effectual in the other.

Quod ipsis qui contraxerunt obstat, et successoribus eorum obstabit /kwòd ípsəs kwày kòntræksírənt óbstæt, èt səksesórəbəs iyórəm obstéybət/. That which bars those who have made a contract will bar their successors also.

Quod jussu /kwòd jə́s(y)uw/. Lat. In the civil law, the name of an action given to one who had contracted with a son or slave, *by order* of the father or master, to compel such father or master to stand to the agreement.

Quod jussu alterius solvitur pro eo est quasi ipsi solutum esset /kwòd jə́s(y)uw oltíriyəs sólvədər pròw íyow èst kwéysay ípsay səl(y)úwdəm ésət/. That which is paid by the order of another is the same as though it were paid to himself.

Quod meum est sine facto meo vel defectu meo amitti vel in alium transferri non potest /kwòd míyəm èst sáyniy fǽktow míyow vèl dəfékt(y)uw míyow əmíday vèl ìn éyl(i)yəm trænsfáray nòn pówdəst/. That which is mine cannot be lost or transferred to another without my alienation or forfeiture.

Quod meum est sine me auferri non potest /kwòd míyəm èst sáyniy míy òféhray nòn pówdəst/. That which is mine cannot be taken away without me [without my assent].

Quod minus est in obligationem videtur deductum /kwòd máynəs èst ìn òbləgèyshiyównəm vədíydər dədə́ktəm/. That which is the less is held to be imported into the contract; (*e.g.*, A. offers to hire B.'s house at six hundred dollars, at the same time B. offers to let it for five hundred dollars; the contract is for five hundred dollars).

Quod naturalis ratio inter omnes homines constituit, vocatur jus gentium /kwòd nǽchəréyləs réysh(iy)ow íntər ómniyz hóməniyz kənstíchuwət, vowkéydər jə́s jénsh(iy)əm/. That which natural reason has established among all men is called the "law of nations."

Quod necessarie intelligitur non deest /kwòd nèsəsériyiy ìntəlíjədər nòn díyèst/. That which is necessarily understood is not wanting.

Quod necessitas cogit, defendit /kwòd nəsésətæ: kó(w)jət, dəféndət/. That which necessity compels, i justifies.

Quod non apparet non est; et non apparet judicialite: ante judicium /kwòd nón əpǽrət nòn ést èt nón əpǽrə juwdìshiyéylədər ǽntiy juwdísh(iy)əm/. That which appears not is not; and nothing appears judicially before judgment.

Quod non capit christus, capit fiscus /kwód nón kǽpə· krístəs kǽpət fískəs/. What Christ [the church] doe; not take the treasury takes. Goods of a *felo de se* gc to the king. A maxim in old English law.

Quod non fuit negatum /kwód nòn f(y)úwət nəgéydəm/. Which was not denied. A phrase found in the olc reports, signifying that an argument or propositior was not denied or controverted by the court.

Quod non habet principium non habet finem /kwód nòr héybət prənsíp(i)yəm nòn héybət fáynəm/. That which has not beginning has not end.

Quod non legitur, non creditur /kwód nòn léjədər nòr krédədər/. What is not read is not believed.

Quod non valet in principali, in accessorio seu consequenti non valebit; et quod non valet in magis propinquo non valebit in magis remoto /kwód nòn vǽləd ìn prìn(t)səpéylay, ìn ǽksəsóriyow syùw kòn(t)səkwén tay nòn vəlíybət; èt kwód nòn vǽləd ìn méyjəs prəpíŋkwow nòn vəlíybəd ìn méyjəs rəmówdow/. That which is not good against the principal will not be good as to accessories or consequences; and that which is not of force in regard to things near it will not be of force in regard to things remote from it.

Quod nota /kwòd nówdə/. Which note; which mark. A reporter's note in the old books, directing attention to a point or rule.

Quod nullius esse potest id ut alicujus fieret nulla obligatio valet efficere /kwód nə̀láyəs ésiy pówdəst íd əd æləkyúwjəs fáyərət nə́lə òbləgéysh(iy)ow vǽləd əfísəriy/. No agreement can avail to make that the property of any one which cannot be acquired as property.

Quod nullius est, est domini regis /kwód nə̀láyəs èst, èst dómənay ríyjəs/. That which is the property of nobody belongs to our lord the king.

Quod nullius est, id ratione naturali occupanti conceditur /kwód nə̀láyəs èst, ìd ræshiyówniy næchəréylay òkyəpǽntay kənsíydədər/. That which is the property of no one is, by natural reason, given to the [first] occupant. Adopted in the common law.

Quod nullum est, nullum producit effectum /kwód nə́ləm èst, nə́ləm prəd(y)úwsəd əféktəm/. That which is null produces no effect.

Quod omnes tangit ab omnibus debet supportari /kwòd ómniyz tǽnjəd æb ómnəbəs débət səpòrtéray/. That which touches or concerns all ought to be supported by all.

Quod partes replacitent /kwód párdiyz rəplǽsədənt/. That the parties do replead.

Judgment quod partes replacitent. A judgment for repleader which is given if an issue is formed on so immaterial a point that the court cannot know for whom to give judgment. The parties must then reconstruct their pleadings.

Quod partitio fiat /kwód partísh(iy)ow fáyət/. That partition be made. The name of the judgment in a suit for partition, directing that a partition be effected.

Quod pendet non est pro eo quasi sit /kwód péndət nón èst pròw íyow kwéysay sìt/. What is in suspense is considered as not existing during such suspense.

Quod per me non possum, nec per alium /kwód pər míy nòn pósəm, nék pər éyl(i)yəm/. What I cannot do by myself, I cannot by another.

Quod permittat /kwód pərmídət/. That he permit. In old English law, a writ which lay for the heir of him that was disseised of his common of pasture, against the heir of the disseisor.

Quod permittat prosternere /kwód pərmídəriy prəs-tárnəriy/. That he permit to abate. In old practice, a writ, in the nature of a writ of right, which lay to abate a nuisance. 3 Bl.Comm. 221.

Quod per recordum probatum, non debet esse negatum /kwòd pàr rəkórdəm prəbéydəm, nón débəd ésiy nəgéydəm/. What is proved by record ought not to be denied.

Quod persona nec prebendarii, etc. /kwód pərsównə nèk prèbəndériyay/. A writ which lay for spiritual persons, distrained in their spiritual possessions, for payment of a fifteenth with the rest of the parish.

Quod populus postremum jussit, id jus ratum esto /kwòd póp(y)ələs pəstríyməm jásəd, íd jás réydəm éstow/. What the people have last enacted, let that be the established law. A law of the Twelve Tables, the principle of which is still recognized. 1 Bl.Comm. 89.

Quod primum est intentione ultimum est in operatione /kwòd práyməm èst intènshiyówniy áltəməm ést in òpərèyshiyówniy/. That which is first in intention is last in operation.

Quod principi placuit, legis habet vigorem; ut pote cum lege regia, quæ de imperio ejus lata est, populus ei et in eum omne suum imperium et potestatem conferat. The will of the emperor has the force of law; for, by the royal law which has been made concerning his authority, the people have conferred upon him all its sovereignty and power.

Quod prius est verius est; et quod prius est tempore potius est jure /kwòd práyəs èst véhriyəs èst; èt kwód práyəs èst témpəriy pówsh(iy)əs èst júriy/. What is first is true; and what is first in time is better in law.

Quod pro minore licitum est et pro majore licitum est /kwód pròw mənóriy lísədəm èst ét pròw məjóriy lísədəm èst/. That which is lawful as to the minor is lawful as to the major.

Quod prostravit /kwód prostréyvət/. That he do abate. The name of a judgment upon an indictment for a nuisance, that the defendant abate such nuisance.

Quod pure debetur præsenti die debetur /kwòd pyúriy dəbíydər prəzéntay dáyiy dəbíydər/. That which is due unconditionally is due now.

Quodque dissolvitur eodem modo quo ligatur /kwód-kwiy dəzólvədər iyówdəm mówdow kwòw ləgéydər/. In the same manner that a thing is bound, in the same manner it is unbound.

Quod quis ex culpa sua damnum sentit non intelligitur damnum sentire /kwòd kwís èks kálpə s(y)úwə dæmnəm séntət nòn intəlíjədər dæmnəm sentáyriy/. The damage which one experiences from his own fault is not considered as his damage.

Quod quisquis norit in hoc se exerceat /kwòd kwískwis nórəd ìn hók síy əgzársiyət/. Let every one employ himself in what he knows.

Quod quis sciens indebitum debit hac mente, ut postea repeteret, repetere non potest /kwòd kwís sáyən(d)z ìndébədəm débət hæk méntiy, àt pówstiyə rəpédərət, rèpətíriy nòn pówdəst/. That which one has given, knowing it not to be due, with the intention of redemanding it, he cannot recover back.

Quod recuperet /kwód rək(y)úwpərət/. That he recover. The ordinary form of judgments for the plaintiff in actions at law.

Judgment of quod recuperet. When an issue in fact, or an issue in law arising on a peremptory plea, is determined for the plaintiff, the judgment is "that the plaintiff do recover," etc., which is called a judgment quod recuperet. It is either final or interlocutory, according as the quantum of damages is or is not ascertained at the rendition of the judgment.

Quod remedio destituitur ipsa re valet si culpa absit /kwód rəmíyd(i)yow dèstət(y)úwədər ípsə ríy vælət sày kálpə æbsit/. That which is without remedy avails of itself, if there be no fault in the party seeking to enforce it.

Quod semel meum est amplius meum esse non potest /kwòd séməl míyəm èst æmpliyəs míyəm ésiy nòn pówdəst/. What is once mine cannot be more fully mine.

Quod semel placuit in electione, amplius displicere non potest /kwòd séməl plæk(y)uwəd ìn əlèkshiyówniy, æmpliyəs displísəriy nòn pówdəst/. What a party has once determined, in a case where he has an election, cannot afterwards be disavowed.

Quod si contingat /kwòd sáy kontəŋgət/. That if it happen. Words by which a condition might formerly be created in a deed.

Quod solo inædificatur solo cedit /kwòd sówlow inèdəfəkéydər sówlow síydət/. Whatever is built on the soil is an accessory of the soil.

Quod sub certa forma concessum vel reservatum est non trahitur ad valorem vel compensationem /kwód sàb sárdə fórmə kənsésəm vèl rèzərvéydəm èst nòn tréy(h)ədər æd vəlórəm vèl kòmpənsèyshiyównəm/. That which is granted or reserved under a certain form is not [permitted to be] drawn into valuation or compensation. That which is granted or reserved in a certain specified form must be taken as it is granted, and will not be permitted to be made the subject of any adjustment or compensation on the part of the grantee.

Quod subintelligitur non deest /kwòd sàbintəlíjədər nòn díyest/. What is understood is not wanting.

Quod tacite intelligitur deesse non videtur /kwòd tǽsədiy intəlíjədər dìyésiy nòn vədíydər/. What is tacitly understood is not considered to be wanting.

Quod vanum et inutile est, lex non requirit /kwòd véynəm èd inyúwdəliy èst, léks nòn rəkwáyrət/. The law requires not what is vain and useless.

Quod vero contra rationem juris receptum est, non est producendum ad consequentias /kwòd vírow kóntrə rǽshiyównəm júrəs rəséptəm èst, nón èst pròwdəséndəm ǽd kòn(t)səkwénsh(iy)əs/. But that which has been admitted contrary to the reason of the law, ought not to be drawn into precedents.

Quod vide /kwód váydiy/. Which see. A direction to the reader to look to another part of the book, or to another book, there named, for further related information. Usually abbreviated "*q.v.*"

Quod voluit non dixit /kwòd vól(y)uwət nòn díksət/. What he intended he did not say, or express. An answer sometimes made in overruling an argument that the lawmaker or testator *meant* so and so.

Quo jure /kwòw júriy/. Lat. In old English practice, a writ which lay for one that had land in which another claimed common, to compel the latter to show *by what title* he claimed it.

Quo ligatur, eo dissolvitur /kwów ləgéydər, íyow dəzólvədər/. By the same mode by which a thing is bound, by that is it released.

Quo minus /kwów máynəs/. Lat. A writ upon which all proceedings in the court of exchequer were formerly grounded. In it the plaintiff suggests that he is the king's debtor, and that the defendant has done him the injury or damage complained of, *quo minus sufficiens existit*, by which *he is less able* to pay the king's debt. This was originally requisite in order to give jurisdiction to the court of exchequer; but now this suggestion is a mere form. 3 Bl.Comm. 46.

Quo modo quid constituitur eodem modo dissolvitur /kwów mówdow kwíd kònstət(y)úwdər iyówdəm mówdow dəzólvədər/. In the same manner by which anything is constituted by that it is dissolved.

Quorum /kwórəm/. A majority of the entire body; *e.g.,* a quorum of a state supreme court. The number of members who must be present in a deliberative body before business may be transacted. In both houses of Congress a quorum consists of a majority of those chosen and sworn.

Such a number of the members of a body as is competent to transact business in the absence of the other members. The idea of a quorum is that, when that required number of persons goes into a session as a body, such as directors of a corporation, the votes of a majority thereof are sufficient for binding action. Benintendi v. Kenton Hotel, 294 N.Y. 112, 60 N.E.2d 829, 831. When a committee, board of directors, meeting of shareholders, legislature or other body of persons cannot act unless a certain number

at least of them are present, that number is called a "quorum." In the absence of any law or rule fixing the quorum, it consists of a majority of those entitled to act.

Quorum prætextu nec auget nec minuit sententiam, sed tantum confirmat præmissa /kwórəm prətékst(y)uw nèk ógənt nèk mín(y)uwət sənténsh(iy)əm, sèd tǽntəm kənfármət prəmísə/. "*Quorum prætextu*" neither increases nor diminishes a sentence, but only confirms that which went before.

Quota /kwówdə/. A proportional part or share, the proportional part of a demand or liability, falling upon each of those who are collectively responsible for the whole.

An assigned goal, as a sales quota; a limiting number or percentage such as the quota of immigrants from a particular country.

See also **Export quotas; Import quota.**

Quotation. The production to a court or judge of the exact language of a statute, precedent, or other authority, in support of an argument or proposition advanced.

The verbatim transcription of part of a literary composition into another book or writing.

A statement of the market price of one or more securities or commodities; or the price specified to a correspondent. Often shortened to "quote." The highest bid to buy and the lowest offer to sell a security or commodity in a given market at a given time.

Quotiens dubia interpretatio libertatis est, secundum libertatem respondendum erit /kwówsh(iy)en(d)z d(y)úwbiyə intàrprətéysh(iy)ow lìbərtéydəs èst, səkándəm lìbərtéydəm rèspondéndəm éhrət/. Whenever there is a doubt between liberty and slavery, the decision must be in favor of liberty.

Quotiens idem sermo duas sententias exprimit, ea potissimum accipiatur, quæ rei gerendæ aptior est /kwówsh(iy)en(d)z áydəm sármow d(y)úwəs sənténsh(iy)əs éksprəmət, íyə pətísəməm əksìpiyéydər, kwìy ríyay jərénday ǽpshiyər èst/. Whenever the same words express two meanings, that is to be taken which is the better fitted for carrying out the proposed end.

Quotient verdict /kwówshənt várdikt/. A "quotient verdict" is one resulting from agreement whereby each juror writes down amount of damages to which he thinks party is entitled and such amounts are then added together and divided by number of jurors. Index Drilling Co. v. Williams, 242 Miss. 775, 137 So.2d 525, 530. A verdict arrived at by agreement by jurors to be bound by quotient in advance of figuring amount of quotient; using quotient merely as a point for discussion is not improper. Womble v. J. C. Penney Co., D.C.Tenn., 47 F.R.D. 350, 355. A chance verdict such that no juror knows what the verdict will be when he submits his vote on damages because the final amount is calculated by a preagreed formula. Freight Terminals, Inc. v. Ryder System, Inc., C.A.Tex., 461 F.2d 1046, 1053.

Quoties dubia interpretatio libertatis est, secundum libertatem respondendum erit /kwówshiy(iy)z d(y)úwbiyə intàrprətéysh(iy)ow lìbərtéydəs èst, səkándəm lìbərtéydəm rəspòndéndəm èst/. Whenever the interpretation of liberty is doubtful, the answer should be on the side of liberty.

Quoties idem sermo duas sententias exprimit, ea potissimum excipiatur, quæ rei gerendæ aptior est /kwówshiy(iy)z áydəm sə́rmow d(y)úwəs sənténsh(i)yəs éksprəmət, íyə pətísəməm éksprəmət, kwìy ríyay jərénday ǽpshiyər èst/. Whenever the same language expresses two meanings that should be adopted which is the better fitted for carrying out the subject-matter.

Quoties in stipulationibus ambigua oratio est, commodissimum est id accipi quo res de qua agitur in tuto sit /kwówshiy(iy)z ìn stìpyəlèyshiyównəbəs æmbíg(y)uwə oréysh(iy)ow èst, kòmədísəməm èst íd ǽksəpay kwòw ríyz dìy kwéy éyjədər ìn t(y)úwdow sít/. Whenever the language of stipulations is ambiguous, it is most fitting that that [sense] should be taken by which the subject-matter may be protected.

Quoties in verbis nulla est ambiguitas, ibi nulla expositio contra verba fienda est /kwówshiy(iy)z ìn várbəs nə́lə èst æmbəgyúwətæs, áybay nə́lə èkspəzísh(iy)ow kóntrə várbə fayéndə èst/. When in the words there is no ambiguity, then no exposition contrary to the words is to be made.

Quousque /kwowə́skwiy/. Lat. How long; how far; until. In old conveyances it is used as a word of limitation.

Quovis modo /kwówvis mówdow/. Lat. In whatever manner.

Quo warranto /kwów wərǽntow/. In old English practice, a writ in the nature of a writ of right for the king, against him who claimed or usurped any office, franchise, or liberty, to inquire *by what authority* he supported his claim, in order to determine the right. It lay also in case of non-user, or long neglect of a franchise, or misuser or abuse of it; being a writ commanding the defendant to show *by what warrant* he exercises such a franchise, having never had any grant of it, or having forfeited it by neglect or abuse. 3 Bl.Comm. 262.

An extraordinary proceeding, prerogative in nature, addressed to preventing a continued exercise of authority unlawfully asserted. Johnson v. Manhattan Ry. Co., N.Y., 289 U.S. 479, 53 S.Ct. 721, 77 L.Ed. 1331. It is intended to prevent exercise of powers that are not conferred by law, and is not ordinarily available to regulate the manner of exercising such powers.

The remedy of "quo warranto" belongs to the state, in its sovereign capacity, to protect the interests of the people as a whole and guard the public welfare, and it is a preventative remedy addressed to preventing a continuing exercise of an authority unlawfully asserted, rather than to correcting what has already been done under that authority. Citizens Utilities Co. of Cal. v. Superior Court, Alameda County, 56 Cal. App.3d 399, 128 Cal.Rptr. 582, 588. "Quo warranto" is legal action whereby legality of exercise of powers by municipal corporation may be placed in issue. People ex rel. City of Des Plaines v. Village of Mount Prospect, 29 Ill.App.3d 807, 331 N.E.2d 373, 377.

The federal rules are applicable to proceedings for quo warranto "to the extent that the practice in such proceedings is not set forth in statutes of the United States and has heretofore conformed to the practice in civil actions." Fed.R. Civil P. 81(a)(2). Any remedy that could have been obtained under the historic writ of quo warranto may be obtained by a civil action of that nature. U. S. v. Nussbaum, D.C.Cal., 306 F.Supp. 66.

Quum de lucro duorum quæratur, melior est causa possidentis /kə́m dìy l(y)úwkrow d(y)uwórəm kwəréydər, míyl(i)yər èst kózə pəsìdiyéntəs/. When the question is as to the gain of two persons, the title of the party in possession is the better one.

Quum in testamento ambigue aut etiam perperam scriptum est, benigne interpretari et secundum id quod credible et cogitatum, credendum est /kə́m ìn tèstəméntow æmbígyuwiy òt ésh(iy)əm pə́rpərəm skríptəm èst, bənígniy intàrprətéray èt səkándəm íd kwòd krədíbəliy èt kòjətéydəm, krədéndəm èst/. When in a will an ambiguous or even an erroneous expression occurs, it should be construed liberally and in accordance with what is thought the probable meaning of the testator.

Quum principalis causa non consistit ne ea quidem quæ sequuntur locum habent /kə̀m prìn(t)səpéyləs kózə nón kənsístət nìy íyə kwáydəm kwìy səkwántər lówkəm héybənt/. When the principal does not hold, the incidents thereof ought not to obtain.

Quum quod ago non valet ut ago, valeat quantum valere potest /kə́m kwòd éygow nòn vǽləd əd éygow, vǽliyət kwóntəm vəlíriy pówdəst/. When what I do is of no force as to the purpose for which I do it, let it be of force to as great a degree as it can.

Q.V. An abbreviation of *"quod vide,"* meaning "which see".

R

R. In the signatures of royal persons, "R." is an abbreviation for *"rex"* (king) or *"regina"* (queen). In descriptions of land, according to the divisions of the governmental survey, it stands for "range." Simms v. Rolfe, 177 Ark. 52, 5 S.W.2d 718, 719.

Rabbinical divorce. Divorce granted under authority of rabbis.

Race. An ethnical stock; a great division of mankind having in common certain distinguishing physical peculiarities constituting a comprehensive class appearing to be derived from a distinct primitive source. A tribal or national stock, a division or subdivision of one of the great racial stocks of mankind distinguished by minor peculiarities.

Race-notice recording statutes. State laws which provide that an unrecorded conveyance is invalid as against a subsequent purchaser for value who records without knowledge of the prior unrecorded instrument. The recording of the later instrument, however, must generally be in the chain of title. Such laws combine the features of both notice and race statute. See also **Pure race statute; Recording acts.**

Race recording statutes. In a state with a race recording statute, the party who records an instrument of conveyance has the better claim regardless of notice of prior unrecorded instruments. See **Pure race statutes; Recording acts.**

Rachat /ràshá/. In French law, the right of repurchase which, in English and American law, the vendor may reserve to himself. It is also called *"réméré."*

Rachater /ràshatéy/. L. Fr. To redeem; to repurchase, (or buy back).

Rack. An engine of torture anciently used in the inquisitorial method of examining persons charged with crime, the office of which was to break the limbs or dislocate the joints.

Racket. Engaging in an operation to make money illegitimately, implying continuity of behavior.

Racketeer. A person who makes money by violations of racketeering laws.

Racketeering. An organized conspiracy to commit the crimes of extortion or coercion, or attempts to commit extortion or coercion. From the standpoint of extortion, it is the obtaining of money or property from another, without his consent, induced by the wrongful use of force or fear. The fear which constitutes the legally necessary element in extortion is induced by oral or written threats to do an unlawful injury to the property of the threatened person by means of explosives, fire, or otherwise; or to kill, kidnap, or injure him or a relative of his or some member of his family. See **Extortion.**

Activities of organized criminals who extort money from legitimate businesses by violence or other forms of threats or intimidation or conduct of illegal enterprises such as gambling, narcotics traffic, or prostitution.

Racketeering is demanding, soliciting or receiving anything of value from the owner, proprietor, or other person having a financial interest in a business, by means of either a threat, express or implied, or a promise, express or implied, that the person so demanding, soliciting or receiving such thing of value will: (a) Cause the competition of the person from whom the payment is demanded, solicited or received to be diminished or eliminated; or (b) Cause the price of goods or services purchased or sold in the business to be increased, decreased or maintained at a stated level; or (c) Protect the property used in the business or the person or family of the owner, proprietor or other interested person from injury by violence or other unlawful means.

See also **Extortion; Hobbs Act.**

Rack-rent. A rent of the full value of the tenement, or near it. Exorbitant rent which equals or exceeds the economic value of the property.

Raffle. A kind of lottery in which several persons pay, in shares, the value of something put up as a stake or prize, and then determine by chance (as by casting dice or drawing a number) which one of them shall become the sole possessor of it.

Railroad. With respect to legislation, to force through legislation over the objection of a minority.

Railway Labor Act. An act of Congress (1962) designed to secure the prompt settlement of disputes between interstate railroad companies and their employees. A 1934 amendment created the National Mediation Board. 45 U.S.C.A. § 151 et seq.

Raise. To create; to infer; to create or bring to light by construction or interpretation. To cause or procure to be produced, bred or propagated. To bring together; to get together or obtain for use or service; to gather; to collect; to levy, as to raise money by levying taxes; to increase income by increasing salary, wages, or commissions. To solicit, secure or otherwise obtain funds for a given purpose, organization, charity, etc.

To alter the amount of an instrument such as a negotiable instrument by changing the face value to a higher amount. See also **Raised check; Rasure.**

Raise an issue. To bring pleadings to an issue; to have the effect of producing an issue between the parties pleading in an action.

Raise a presumption. To give occasion or ground for a presumption; to be of such a character, or to be attended with such circumstances, as to justify an inference or presumption of law. Thus, a person's silence, in some instances, will "raise a presumption" of his consent to what is done. See also **Presumption.**

Raised check. A demand negotiable instrument, the face amount of which has been increased, generally without authority of the drawer and hence fraudulently. See also **Rasure.**

Raise revenue. To levy a tax, as a means of collecting revenue; to bring together, collect, or levy revenue.

Raising a promise. The act of the law in extracting from the facts and circumstances of a particular transaction a promise which was implicit therein, and postulating it as a ground of legal liability.

Raising a use. Creating, establishing, or calling into existence a use. Thus, if a man conveyed land to another in fee, without any consideration, equity would presume that he meant it to be to the use of himself, and would, therefore, raise an implied use for his benefit.

Raising portions. In old English law, when a landed estate was settled on an eldest son, it was generally burdened with the payment of specific sums of money in favor of his brothers and sisters. A direction to this effect was called a direction for "raising portions for younger children;" and, for this purpose, it was usual to demise or lease the estate to the required portions by a sale or mortgage of the same.

Rake-off. Share of profits of transaction or business, demanded, paid, or otherwise taken illegally. Illegal pay-off or bribe, or skimming of profits.

Ran. Sax. In Saxon and old English law, open theft, or robbery.

Rancho /rǽnchow/. Sp. A small collection of men or their dwellings; a hamlet. As used, however, in Mexico and in the Spanish law formerly prevailing in California, the term signifies a ranch or large tract of land suitable for grazing purposes where horses or cattle are raised, and is distinguished from *hacienda*, a cultivated farm or plantation.

Range, *v.* To have or extend in certain direction, to correspond in direction or line, or to trend or run.

Range, *n.* In the government survey of the United States, one of the divisions of a state, consisting of a row or tier of townships as they appear on the map. A division of a state in the government survey, being a six mile wide row of townships, running North and South, and used in legal descriptions.

A tract or district of land within which domestic animals in large numbers range for subsistence; an extensive grazing ground. The term is used on the great plains of the United States to designate a tract commonly of many square miles occupied by one or different proprietors and distinctively called a cattle range, stock range, or sheep range. The animals on a range are usually left to take care of themselves during the whole year without shelter, except when periodically gathered in a round-up for counting and selection, and for branding, when the herds of several proprietors run together.

Ranger. In old English law, a sworn officer of the forest, whose office chiefly consisted in three points: To walk daily through his charge to see, hear, and inquire as well of trespasses as trespassers in his bailiwick; to drive the beasts of the forest, both of venery and chace, out of the deafforested into the forested lands; and to present all trespassers of the forest at the next courts holden for the forest.

Person responsible for maintaining and patrolling forests. Member of police force in Texas.

Rank, *n.* Position in society. Grade of quality or value. Grade of official standing. The order or place in which certain officers are placed in the army and navy, in relation to others. *Rank* is often used to express something different from *office*. It then becomes a designation or title of honor, dignity, or distinction conferred upon an officer in order to fix his relative position in reference to other officers in matters of privilege, precedence, and sometimes of command, or by which to determine his pay and emoluments. This is the case with the staff officers of the army. Wood v. U. S., 15 Ct.Cl. 151, 159.

Rank, *adj.* Excessive; too large in amount. Indecent. Absolute; complete.

Ranking of creditors. See **Preference; Priority.**

Ransom. The money, price, or consideration paid or demanded for redemption of a kidnapped person or persons; a payment that releases from captivity. Whoever knowingly receives, possesses, or disposes of such commits a crime. 18 U.S.C.A. § 1202. See **Kidnapping.**

In international law, the redemption of captured property from the hands of an enemy, particularly of property captured at sea. A sum paid or agreed to be paid for the redemption of captured property.

In old English law, a sum of money paid for the pardoning of some great offense. The distinction between ransom and amerciament is said to be that ransom was the redemption of a corporal punishment, while amerciament was a fine or penalty directly imposed, and not in lieu of another punishment. 4 Bl.Comm. 380. A sum of money paid for the redemption of a person from captivity or imprisonment. Thus one of the feudal "aids" was to ransom the lord's person if taken prisoner. 2 Bl.Comm. 63.

Ransom bill. A contract by which a captured vessel, in consideration of her release and of safe-conduct for a stipulated course and time, agrees to pay a certain sum as ransom.

Rap. Slang for criminal conviction.

Rape. Unlawful sexual intercourse with a female without her consent. The unlawful carnal knowledge of a woman by a man forcibly and against her will. The act of sexual intercourse committed by a man with a woman not his wife and without her consent, committed when the woman's resistance is overcome by force or fear, or under other prohibitive conditions. State v. Lora, 213 Kan. 184, 515 P.2d 1086, 1093.

A male who has sexual intercourse with a female not his wife is guilty of rape if: (a) he compels her to submit by force or by threat of imminent death, serious bodily injury, extreme pain or kidnapping, to be inflicted on anyone; or (b) he has substantially impaired her power to appraise or control her conduct by administering or employing without her knowledge drugs, intoxicants or other means for the purpose of preventing resistance; or (c) the female is unconscious; or (d) the female is less than 10 years old. Model Penal Code, § 213.1.

Under some statutes, crime embraces unnatural as well as natural sexual intercourse; *e.g.* M.G.L.A. (Mass.) c. 277, § 39.

See also **Assault with intent to commit rape; Carnal abuse; Carnal knowledge; Fresh complaint rule.**

Statutory rape. Under modern statutes which often materially change the common-law definition and create an offense commonly known as "statutory rape," where the offense consists in having sexual intercourse with a female under statutory age, the offense may be either with or without the female's consent. See also **Statutory rape.**

In old English law, an intermediate division between a shire and a hundred; or a division of a county, containing several hundreds. Apparently peculiar to the county of Sussex.

Rape of the forest. In old English law, trespass committed in a forest by violence.

Rape-reeve. In old English law, the chief officer of a rape *(q.v.).*

Rapine /réypayn/. The felonious taking of another man's personal property, openly and by violence, against his will.

In the civil law, *rapina* is defined as the forcible and violent taking of another man's movable property with the criminal intent to appropriate it to the robber's own use. A prætorian action lay for this offense, in which quadruple damages were recoverable.

Rapport à succession. In French law and in Louisiana, a proceeding similar to hotchpot; the restoration to the succession of such property as the heir may have received by way of advancement from the decedent, in order that an even division may be made among all the co-heirs.

Raptor /ræptər/. In old English law, a ravisher.

Raptu hæredis /ræpt(y)uw həríydəs/. In old English law, a writ for taking away an heir holding in socage, of which there were two sorts: One when the heir was married; the other when he was not.

Rapuit /ræp(y)uwət/. Lat. In old English law, ravished. A technical word in old indictments.

RAR. A revenue agent's report which reflects any adjustments made by the agent as a result of an audit of the taxpayer. The RAR is mailed to the taxpayer along with the 30-day letter which outlines the appellate procedures available to the taxpayer.

Rasure /réyzhər/. The act of scraping, scratching, or shaving the surface of a written instrument, for the purpose of removing certain letters or words from it. It is to be distinguished from "obliteration," as the latter word properly denotes the crossing out of a word or letter by drawing a line through it with ink. But the two expressions are often used interchangeably. See also **Raise; Raised check.**

Rasus /réysəs/. In old English law, a rase; a measure of onions, containing twenty flones, and each flon is twenty-five heads.

Ratable. Proportional; proportionately rated upon a constant ratio adjusted to due relation. According to a measure which fixes proportions. It has no meaning unless referable to some rule or standard, and never means equality or equal division but implies unequal division as between different persons. Chenoweth v. Nordan & Morris, Tex.Civ.App., 171 S.W.2d 386, 387.

Ratable estate or property. Property in its quality and nature capable of being rated, *i.e.* appraised, assessed. Taxable estate; the real and personal property which the legislature designates as "taxable."

Ratam rem habere /réydəm rém həbíriy/. Lat. In the civil law, to hold a thing ratified; to ratify or confirm it.

Rate. Proportional or relative value, measure, or degree. The proportion or standard by which quantity or value is adjusted. Thus, the *rate* of interest is the proportion or ratio between the principal and interest; the buildings in a town are *rated* for insurance purposes; *i.e.,* classified and individually estimated with reference to their insurable qualities. In this sense also we speak of articles as being in "first-rate" or "second-rate" condition.

A fixed relation of quantity, amount or degree; also, a charge, valuation, payment or price fixed according to ratio, scale or standard; comparative price or amount of demands. E. C. Miller Cedar Lumber Co. v. United States, Cust. & Pat.App., 86 F.2d 429, 434. Cost per unit of a commodity or service.

In connection with public utilities, a charge to the public for a service open to all and upon the same terms. The unit cost of a service supplied to the public by a utility. When used in connection with public utilities, such as a telephone company, generally means price stated or fixed for some commodity or service of general need or utility supplied to the public measured by specific unit or standard. Bird v. Chesapeake & Potomac Tel. Co., D.C.Mun.App., 185 A.2d 917, 918.

As used in the interstate commerce law, it means the net cost to the shipper of the transportation of his property; that is to say, the net amount the carrier receives from the shipper and retains. Great Northern Ry. Co. v. Armour & Co., D.C.Ill., 26 F.Supp. 964, 967.

See also Commodity rate; Confiscatory rates; Discount rate; Flat rate; Freight rate; Interest rate; Joint through rate; Meter rate; Prime rate.

Class rate. A single rate applying to the transportation of a number of articles of the same general character.

Commodity rate. A rate which applies to the transportation of a specific commodity alone.

Joint rate. As applied to railroads, a rate prescribed to be charged for the transportation of goods or passengers over the connecting lines of two or more railroads, and to be divided among them for the service rendered by each respectively.

Rate of exchange. In commercial law, the actual price at which a bill, drawn in one country upon another country, can be bought or obtained in the former country at any given time. Also, the price at which the money of one country may be exchanged for money of another country (*e.g.* dollars for marks).

Rate of interest. The charge imposed by a lender of money for the use of the money; the borrowing charge.

    Discount rate. Rate charged to member banks by Federal Reserve Board for borrowing money from Federal Reserve.

    Legal rate. The statutory maximum rate of interest which may be charged for loans. See also **Usury.**

    Prime rate. The rate of interest charged for high quality commercial loans (*i.e.* rate charged by bank to its most credit worthy customers) which is pegged to the discount rate established by the Federal Reserve Board. This rate tends to establish the rate of interest charged for various types of personal and commercial loans.

Rate of return. The annual percentage of return on investment, usually of income property. The percentage by which the rate base is multiplied to provide a figure that allows a utility to collect revenues sufficient to pay operating expenses and attract investment. Providence Gas. Co. v. Burman, R.I., 376 A.2d 687, 695.

Rate tariff. Statement by carrier to possible shippers that it will furnish certain services under certain conditions for certain price. Union Wire Rope Corporation v. Atchison T. & S. F. Ry. Co., C.C.A.Mo., 66 F.2d 965, 966. See **Tariff.**

Ratification. In a broad sense, the confirmation of a previous act done either by the party himself or by another; as, confirmation of a voidable act. The affirmance by a person of a prior act which did not bind him, but which was done or professedly done on his account, whereby the act, as to some or all persons, is given effect as if originally authorized by him. Askew v. Joachim Memorial Home, N.D., 234 N.W.2d 226, 237. The adoption by one, as binding upon himself, of an act done in such relations that he may claim it as done for his benefit, although done under such circumstances as would not bind him except for his subsequent assent. It is equivalent to a previous authorization and relates back to time when act ratified was done, except where intervening rights of third persons are concerned. Voluntary election by person to adopt in some manner as his own an act which was purportedly done on his behalf by another person, the effect of ratification, as to some or all persons, is to treat the act as if originally authorized by him. Rakestraw v. Rodrigues, 8 Cal.3d 67, 104 Cal.Rptr. 57, 500 P.2d 1401, 1404.

Approval, as by legislatures or conventions, of a constitutional amendment proposed by two-thirds of both houses of Congress. Approval by the electorate of a proposed State constitutional amendment.

In the law of principal and agent, the adoption and confirmation by one person with knowledge of all material facts, of an act or contract performed or entered into in his behalf by another who at the time assumed without authority to act as his agent. Essence of "ratification" by principal of act of agent is manifestation of mental determination by principal to affirm the act, and this may be manifested by written word or by spoken word or by conduct, or may be inferred from known circumstances and principal's acts in relation thereto.

Express ratifications are those made in express and direct terms of assent. *Implied* ratifications are such as the law presumes from the acts of the principal.

Estoppel and ratification distinguished, see **Estoppel.** See also **Acknowledgment; Approval; Confirmation.**

Ratify. To approve and sanction; to make valid; to confirm; to give sanction to. See **Approval; Confirm; Ratification.**

Ratihabitio /ræ̀dəhəbísh(iy)ow/. Lat. Confirmation, agreement, consent, approbation of a contract.

Ratihabitio mandato æquiparatur /ræ̀dəhəbísh(iy)ow mændéydow èkwəpəréydər/. Ratification is equivalent to express command.

Rating. See **Credit rating.**

Ratio. Rate; proportion; degree. Reason, or understanding. Also a cause, or giving judgment therein. The number resulting when one number is divided by another.

Ratio decidendi /réysh(iy)ow dèsədénday/. The ground or reason of decision. The point in a case which determines the judgment.

Ratio est formalis causa consuetudinis /réysh(iy)ow èst forméyləs kózə kònswət(y)úwdənəs/. Reason is the formal cause of custom.

Ratio est legis anima; mutata legis ratione mutatur et lex /réysh(iy)ow èst líyjəs ǽnəmə; myuwtéydə líyjəs ræshiyówniy myuwtéydə èt léks/. Reason is the soul of law; the reason of law being changed the law is also changed.

Ratio est radius divini luminis /réysh(iy)ow èst rćyd(i)yəs dəváynay l(y)úwmənəs/. Reason is a ray of the divine light.

Ratio et auctoritas, duo clarissima mundi lumina /réysh(iy)ow èd októrətæs, d(y)úwow klærísəmə mánday l(y)úwmənə/. Reason and authority, the two brightest lights of the world.

Ratio in jure æquitas integra /réysh(iy)ow in júriy ékwətæs íntəgrə/. Reason in law is perfect equity.

Ratio legis /réysh(iy)ow líyjəs/. The reason or occasion of a law; the occasion of making a law.

Ratio legis est anima legis /réysh(iy)ow líyjəs èst ǽnəmə líyjəs/. The reason of law is the soul of law.

Rationabile estoverium /rǽshənéybəliy èstəvíriyəm/. A Latin phrase equivalent to "alimony."

Rationabili parte bonorum /rǽshənéybəlay párdiy bənórəm/. A writ that lay for the wife against the executors of her husband, to have the third part of his goods after his just debts and funeral expenses had been paid.

Rational basis test. An appellate court will not second-guess the legislature as to the wisdom or rationality of a particular statute if there is a rational basis for its enactment. The same test may be applied when a court is reviewing a decision of an administrative body because of the expertise of such body. It has been said that the protection of the public from unwise or improvident statutes is to be found at the voting polls or by referendum, not in court. Munn v. Illinois, 94 U.S. 113, 134, 24 L.Ed. 77. This test does not apply, of course, if the statute or decision is unconstitutional.

Rational doubt. A doubt based upon reasonable inferences such as are ordinarily drawn by ordinary men in the light of their experiences in ordinary life. Hicks v. State, 66 Ga.App. 577, 18 S.E.2d 637, 640. See also **Reasonable doubt.**

Rationalibus divisis /rǽsh(iy)ənéyləbəs dəváyzəs/. An abolished writ which lay where two lords, in divers towns, had seigniories adjoining for him who found his waste by little and little to have been encroached upon, against the other, who had encroached, thereby to rectify their bounds.

Rational purpose test. See **Rational basis test.**

Ratione impotentiæ /rǽshiyówniy ìmpəténshiyiy/. Lat. On account of inability. A ground of qualified property in some animals *feræ naturæ;* as in the young ones, while they are unable to fly or run.

Ratione materiæ /rǽshiyówniy mətíriyiy/. Lat. By reason of the matter involved; in consequence of, or from the nature of, the subject-matter.

Ratione personæ /rǽshiyówniy pərsówniy/. Lat. By reason of the person concerned; from the character of the person.

Ratione privilegii /rǽshiyówniy prìvəlíyjiyay/. Lat. This term describes a species of property in wild animals, which consists in the right which, by a peculiar franchise anciently granted by the English crown, by virtue of its prerogative, one man may have of killing and taking such animals on the land of another.

Rationes /rǽshiyówniyz/. In old law, the pleadings in a suit. *Rationes exercere,* or *ad rationes stare,* to plead.

Ratione soli /rǽshiyówniy sówlay/. Lat. On account of the soil; with reference to the soil. Said to be the ground of ownership in bees.

Ratione tenuræ /rǽshiyówniy tényəriy/. L. Lat. By reason of tenure; as a consequence of tenure.

Ratio non clauditur loco /réysh(iy)ow nòn klódədər lówkow/. Reason is not confined to any place.

Ratio potest allegari deficiente lege; sed ratio vera et legalis, et non apparens /réysh(iy)ow pówdəst æləgéray dəfishiyéntiy líyjiy, sèd réysh(iy)ow vírə èt ləgéyləs, èt nón əpǽrən(d)z/. Reason may be alleged when law is defective; but it must be true and legal reason, and not merely apparent.

Rattening /rǽt(ə)niŋ/. The offense on the part of members of a trade union, of causing the tools, clothes, or other property of a workman to be taken away or hidden, in order to compel him to join the union or cease working. It is, in England, an offense punishable by fine or imprisonment.

Ravine. A long, deep, and narrow hollow, worn by a stream or torrent of water; a long, deep, and narrow hollow or pass through the mountains.

Ravish. To have carnal knowledge of a woman by force and against her will; to rape. State v. Harvey, Mo.App., 544 S.W.2d 593, 595.

Ravisher. One who has carnal knowledge of a woman by force and against her consent. Hart v. State, 144 Tex.Cr.R. 161, 161 S.W.2d 791, 793.

Ravishment. See **Rape; Ravish.**

Ravishment de gard /rǽvəshmənt də gárd/. L. Fr. An abolished writ which lay for a guardian by knight's service or in socage, against a person who took from him the body of his ward.

Ravishment of ward. In old English law, the marriage of an infant ward without the consent of the guardian.

Raw land. Unimproved land.

Raw materials. Goods purchased for use in manufacturing a product; *e.g.* wood, steel.

Raze /réyz/. To erase.

Razon /raθówn/rasówn/. In Spanish law, cause *(causa).*

Re /ríy/. Lat. In the matter of; in the case of. A term of frequent use in designating judicial proceedings, in which there is only one party. Thus, "*Re* Vivian" signifies "In the matter of Vivian," or in "Vivian's Case."

R.E.A. Rural Electrification Administration.

Reacquired stock. See **Treasury stock.**

Readjustment. A voluntary reorganization of a corporation which is in financial difficulties by the stockholders themselves without the intervention of a receiver or a court appointed fiduciary.

Ready. Prepared for what one is about to do or experience; equipped or supplied with what is needed for some act or event; prepared for immediate movement or action. Fitted, arranged, or placed for immediate use; causing no delay for lack of being prepared or furnished.

Ready and willing. Implies capacity to act as well as disposition; *e.g.* ready, willing and able buyer.

Real. In civil law, relating to a *thing* (whether movable or immovable), as distinguished from a person.

Relating to *land,* as distinguished from personal property. This term is applied to lands, tenements, and hereditaments.

As to real Action; Asset; Chattel; Contract; Covenant; Estate; Issue; Obligation; Party; Privilege; Property; Representative; Right; Security; Servitude; Statute, and Wrong, see those titles.

Real estate. Land and anything permanently affixed to the land, such as buildings, fences, and those things attached to the buildings, such as light fixtures, plumbing and heating fixtures, or other such items which would be personal property if not attached. The term is generally synonymous with real property. See also **Property** *(Real property).*

Real estate broker. See **Broker.**

Real estate investment trust (REIT). Financial device in which investors purchase shares in a trust the res of which is invested in real estate ventures. See also **Trust.**

Real estate listing. See **Listing.**

Real Estate Settlement Procedures Act. See **RESPA.**

Real estate syndicate. A loose aggregation of persons who invest in real estate for common profits and gains. Kilbourn v. Thompson, 103 U.S. 168, 26 L.Ed. 377.

Real evidence. Evidence furnished by things themselves, on view or inspection, as distinguished from a description of them by the mouth of a witness; *e.g.,* the physical appearance of a person when exhibited to the jury, marks, scars, wounds, fingerprints, etc.; also, the weapons or implements used in the commission of a crime, and other inanimate objects, and evidence of the physical appearance of a place (the scene of an accident or of the commission of a crime or of property to be taken under condemnation proceedings) as obtained by a jury when they are taken to view it. See also **Demonstrative evidence.**

Real injury. In the civil law, an injury arising from an unlawful *act,* as distinguished from a verbal injury, which was done by words. See **Injury.**

Realize. To convert any kind of property into money; but especially to receive the returns from an investment.

Realized gain or loss. The difference between the amount realized upon the sale or other disposition of property and the adjusted basis of such property. I.R.C. § 1001.

Real law. Real estate law. The body of laws relating to real property. This use of the term is popular rather than technical.

In the civil law, a law which relates to specific property, whether movable or immovable.

Realm /rélm/. A kingdom; a country.

Real money. Money which has real metalic, intrinsic value as distinguished from paper currency, checks and drafts.

Real party in interest. Under the traditional test, party is a "real party in interest" if it has the legal right under the applicable substantive law to enforce the claim in question. White Hall Bldg. Corp. v. Profexray Division of Litton Industries, Inc., D.C.Pa., 387 F.Supp. 1202, 1204. Real party in interest within rule that every civil action in federal courts must be prosecuted in name of real party in interest is the one, who, under applicable substantive law, has legal right to bring suit, Boeing Airplane Co. v. Perry, C.A.Kan., 322 F.2d 589, 591; and not necessarily person who will ultimately benefit from the recovery. First Nat. Bank of Chicago v. Mottola, D.C.Ill., 302 F.Supp. 785, 791, 792. See Fed.R.Civil P. 17.

Under Fed.R.Civil P. 17(a), a guardian, executor, bailee, and the like, may sue in his own name without joining the party for whom the action is brought.

See also **Parties.**

Real property. See **Property** *(Real property).*

Real things (or things real). In common law, such things as are permanent, fixed, and immovable, which cannot be carried out of their place; as lands and tenements. Things substantial and immovable, and the rights and profits annexed to or issuing out of them. See also **Real estate.**

Realtor. "Realtor" is a federally registered collective membership mark owned by the National Association of Realtors and properly used only in reference to members of the association.

Realty. A brief term for real property or real estate; also for anything which partakes of the nature of real property. See **Property** *(Real property).*

Reapportionment. A realignment or change in legislative districts brought about by changes in population and mandated by the constitutional requirement of equality of representation. A new apportionment of seats in the House of Representatives among States "according to their respective numbers", is required by Art. 1, § 2 of the U.S. Constitution after every decennial census. A similar requirement as to State legislative seats is found in many State constitutions.

A state statute which violates the rights of persons to vote on a one man-one vote apportionment is contrary to the equal protection clause of the 14th Amend., U.S.Const. Baker v. Carr, 369 U.S. 186, 82 S.Ct. 691, 7 L.Ed.2d 663.

Reappraiser. A person who, in certain cases, is appointed to make a revaluation or second appraisement of imported goods at the customhouse.

Reargument. Purpose of reargument is to demonstrate to court that there is some decision or principle of law which would have a controlling effect and which has been overlooked, or that there has been a misapprehension of facts. In re Hooker's Estate, 173 Misc. 515, 18 N.Y.S.2d 107, 110. See also **Rehearing; Retrial.**

Reason. A faculty of the mind by which it distinguishes truth from falsehood, good from evil, and which enables the possessor to deduce inferences from facts or from propositions. Also an inducement, motive, or ground for action, as in the phrase "reasons for an appeal."

Reasonable. Fair, proper, just, moderate, suitable under the circumstances. Fit and appropriate to the end in view. Having the faculty of reason; rational; governed by reason; under the influence of reason; agreeable to reason. Thinking, speaking, or acting according to the dictates of reason. Not immoderate or excessive, being synonymous with rational, honest, equitable, fair, suitable, moderate, tolerable. Cass v. State, 124 Tex.Cr.R. 208, 61 S.W.2d 500.

As to reasonable Aids; Care; Diligence; Doubt; Notice; Skill, and Time, see those titles. See also **Fair.**

Reasonable act. Such as may fairly, justly, and reasonably be required of a party.

Reasonable and probable cause. Such grounds as justify any one in suspecting another of a crime, and placing him in custody thereon. It is a suspicion founded upon circumstances sufficiently strong to warrant reasonable man in belief that charge is true. Henry v. U. S., 361 U.S. 98, 80 S.Ct. 168, 4 L.Ed.2d 134; Com. v. Stewart, 358 Mass. 747, 267 N.E.2d 213. See also **Probable cause.**

Reasonable belief. "Reasonable belief" or "probable cause" to make an arrest without a warrant exists when facts and circumstances within arresting officer's knowledge, and of which he had reasonably trustworthy information, are sufficient in themselves to justify a man of average caution in belief that a felony has been or is being committed. State v. Johnson, 249 La. 950, 192 So.2d 135, 141. See also **Probable cause; Reasonable and probable cause.**

The words "reasonably believes" are used throughout the Restatement, Second, Torts to denote the fact that the actor believes that a given fact or combination of facts exists, and that the circumstances which he knows, or should know, are such as to cause a reasonable man so to believe. Sec. 11.

Reasonable care. That degree of care which a person of ordinary prudence would exercise in the same or similar circumstances. Pampas v. Cambridge Mut. Fire Ins. Co., La.App., 169 So.2d 200, 201; Pierce v. Horvath, 142 Ind.App. 278, 233 N.E.2d 811, 815. Due care under all the circumstances. Failure to exercise such care is ordinary negligence. See also **Care.**

Reasonable cause. As basis for arrest without warrant, is such state of facts as would lead man of ordinary care and prudence to believe and conscientiously entertain honest and strong suspicion that person sought to be arrested is guilty of crime. People v. Newell, 272 Cal.App.2d 638, 77 Cal.Rptr. 771, 773. See also **Probable cause; Reasonable and probable cause; Reasonable belief.**

Reasonable certainty, rule of. Permits recovery of damages only for such future pain and suffering as is reasonably certain to result from the injury received.

Prettyman v. Topkis, Del., 3 A.2d 708, 710. To authorize recovery under such rule for permanent injury, permanency of injury must be shown with reasonable certainty, which is not mere conjecture or likelihood or ever a probability of such injury. State ex rel. Kansas City Public Service Co. v. Shain, 350 Mo. 316, 165 S.W.2d 428, 430.

Reasonable doubt. Reasonable doubt which will justify acquittal is doubt based on reason and arising from evidence or lack of evidence, and it is doubt which reasonable man or woman might entertain, and it is not fanciful doubt, is not imagined doubt, and is not doubt that juror might conjure up to avoid performing unpleasant task or duty. U. S. v. Johnson, C.A. N.Y., 343 F.2d 5, 6. Reasonable doubt is such a doubt as would cause prudent men to hesitate before acting in matters of importance to themselves. U. S. v. Chas. Pfizer & Co., Inc., D.C.N.Y., 367 F.Supp. 91, 101. See also **Beyond a reasonable doubt; Doubt.**

Reasonable force. That degree of force which is not excessive and is appropriate in protecting oneself or one's property. When such force is used, a person is justified and is not criminally liable, nor is he liable in tort.

Reasonable grounds. Reasonable grounds within statute authorizing arrest without warrant by officer who has reasonable grounds for believing that person to be arrested has committed criminal offense means substantially probable cause. Beyer v. Young, 32 Colo.App. 273, 513 P.2d 1086, 1088. See also **Probable cause; Reasonable and probable cause; Reasonable cause.**

Reasonable inference rule. The trier of fact may consider as evidence not only the testimony and real evidence presented at trial but also all inferences which may be reasonably drawn, though they are not necessary inferences.

Reasonable man doctrine or standard. The standard which one must observe to avoid liability for negligence is the standard of the reasonable man under all the circumstances, including the foreseeability of harm to one such as the plaintiff.

Reasonable notice. While the term is relative, State v. Boles, 5 Conn.Cir. 22, 240 A.2d 920, it is notice which is plainly calculated to apprise the appropriate person of its contents. See also **Notice.**

Reasonable part. In old English law, that share of a man's goods which the law gave to his wife and children after his decease. 2 Bl.Comm. 492.

Reasonable suspicion. Reasonable suspicion which will justify officer in stopping defendant in public place is quantum of knowledge sufficient to induce ordinarily prudent and cautious man under circumstances to believe criminal activity is at hand. People v. Johnson, 56 A.D.2d 766, 392 N.Y.S.2d 294, 295. See also **Probable cause; Reasonable cause.**

Reasonable time. Any time which is not manifestly unreasonable may be fixed by agreement of the parties, and what is reasonable depends on the nature, purpose and circumstances of each case. U.C.C. § 1–204(1)(2). Acceptance of an offer must be made within a reasonable time if no time is specified. U.C.C. §§ 2–206(2), 207.

Where contract does not fix a time for performance, the law allows "reasonable time" for performance, defined as such time as is necessary, conveniently, to do what the contract requires to be done, as soon as circumstances will permit. Houston County v. Leo L. Landauer & Associates, Inc., Tex. Civ.App., 424 S.W.2d 458, 463.

See also **Time.**

Reasonable use theory. A riparian owner may make reasonable use of his water for either natural or artificial wants. However, he may not so use his rights so as to affect the quantity or quality of water available to a lower riparian owner.

Reassessment. Re-estimating the value of a specific property or all property in a given area for tax assessment purposes.

Reassurance. Exists where an insurer procures the whole or a part of the sum which he has insured (*i.e.,* contracted to pay in case of loss, death, etc.) to be insured again to him by another insurer. See also **Reinsurance.**

Rebate. Discount; deduction or refund of money in consideration of prompt payment. A deduction from a stipulated premium on a policy of insurance, in pursuance of an antecedent contract. A deduction or drawback from a stipulated payment, charge, or rate (as, a rate for the transportation of freight by a railroad), not taken out in advance of payment, but handed back to the payer after he has paid the full stipulated sum. See also **Discount.**

Portion of a transportation charge refunded to a shipper. Rebates are forbidden by the Interstate Commerce Act.

Tax rebate is an amount returned (*i.e.* refunded) to the taxpayer after he has made full payment of the tax.

See also **Elkins Act; Kickback; Refund.**

Rebellion. Deliberate, organized resistance, by force and arms, to the laws or operations of the government, committed by a subject. Crashley v. Press Pub. Co., 74 App.Div. 118, 77 N.Y.S. 711. It is a federal crime to incite, assist, or engage in any rebellion or insurrection against the authority of the United States or the laws thereof. 18 U.S.C.A. § 2383.

In old English law, also a contempt of a court manifested by disobedience to its process, particularly of the court of chancery. If a defendant refused to appear, after attachment and proclamation, a "commission of rebellion" issued against him. 3 Bl.Comm. 444.

Rebellious assembly. In old English law, a gathering of twelve persons or more, intending, going about, or practicing unlawfully and of their own authority to change any laws of the realm; or to destroy the inclosure of any park or ground inclosed, banks of fish-ponds, pools, conduits, etc., to the intent the same shall remain void; or that they shall have way in any of the said grounds; or to destroy the deer in any park, fish in ponds, coneys in any warren, dovehouses, etc.; or to burn sacks of corn; or to abate rents or prices of victuals, etc. See also **Unlawful assembly.**

Rebus sic stantibus /ríybəs sik stǽntəbəs/. Lat. At this point of affairs; in these circumstances. A name given to a tacit condition, said to attach to all treaties, that they shall cease to be obligatory so soon as the state of facts and conditions upon which they were founded has substantially changed.

Rebut. In pleading and evidence, to defeat, refute, or take away the effect of something. When a plaintiff in an action produces evidence which raises a presumption of the defendant's liability, and the defendant adduces evidence which shows that the presumption is ill-founded, he is said to "rebut it." See **Rebuttable presumption; Rebuttal evidence.**

Rebuttable presumption. In the law of evidence, a presumption which may be rebutted by evidence. Otherwise called a "disputable" presumption. A species of legal presumption which holds good until evidence contrary to it is introduced. Beck v. Kansas City Public Service Co., Mo.App., 48 S.W.2d 213, 215. It shifts burden of proof. Heiner v. Donnan, 285 U.S. 312, 52 S.Ct. 358, 362, 76 L.Ed. 772. And which standing alone will support a finding against contradictory evidence. Lieber v. Rigby, 34 Cal.App.2d 582, 94 P.2d 49, 50. See also **Presumption.**

Rebuttal evidence. Evidence given to explain, repel, counteract, or disprove facts given in evidence by the adverse party. That which tends to explain or contradict or disprove evidence offered by the adverse party. Layton v. State, 261 Ind. 251, 301 N.E.2d 633, 636. Evidence which is offered by a party after he has rested his case and after the opponent has rested in order to contradict the opponent's evidence.

Also evidence given in opposition to a presumption of fact or a *prima facie* case; in this sense, it may be not only counteracting evidence, but evidence sufficient to counteract, that is, conclusive. See **Rebuttable presumption.**

Rebutter. In common law pleading, a defendant's answer of fact to a plaintiff's surrejoinder; the third pleading in the series on the part of the defendant.

Recall. A method of removal of official in which power of removal is either granted to or reserved by the people. Jones v. Harlan, Tex.Civ.App., 109 S.W.2d 251, 254. Right or procedure by which a public official may be removed from office before the end of his term of office by a vote of the people to be taken on the filing of a petition signed by required number of qualified voters. Wallace v. Tripp, 358 Mich. 668, 101 N.W.2d 312, 314. Recall may also be applicable to judges.

To summon a diplomatic minister back to his home court, at the same time depriving him of his office and functions.

Recall a judgment. To revoke, cancel, vacate, or reverse a judgment for matters of fact; when it is annulled by reason of errors of law, it is said to be "reversed."

Recant. To withdraw or repudiate formally and publicly. Pradlik v. State, 131 Conn. 682, 41 A.2d 906, 907.

Recapitalization. An arrangement whereby stock, bonds or other securities of a corporation are adjusted as to type, amount, income or priority. United

Gas Improvement Co. v. Commissioner of Internal Revenue, C.C.A.3, 142 F.2d 216, 218, 219. Reshuffling of capital structure within framework of existing corporation. Helvering v. Southwest Consol. Corporation, La., 315 U.S. 194, 62 S.Ct. 546, 552, 86 L.Ed. 789. See also **Reorganization.**

Recaption. At common law, a retaking, or taking back. A species of remedy by the mere act of the party injured (otherwise termed "reprisal"), which happens when any one has deprived another of his property in goods or chattels personal, or wrongfully detains one's wife, child, or servant. In this case, the owner of the goods, and the husband, parent, or master may lawfully claim and retake them, wherever he happens to find them, so it be not in a riotous manner, or attended with a breach of the peace. Prigg v. Pennsylvania, 41 U.S. (16 Pet.) 539, 612, 10 L.Ed. 1060. It also signifies the taking a second distress of one formerly distrained during the plea grounded on the former distress. See also **Distraint; Distress; Ejectment; Repossession.**

Also, formerly, a writ to recover damages for him whose goods, being distrained for rent in service, etc., are distrained again for the same cause, pending the plea in the county court, or before the justice.

Recapture. To recover the tax benefit of a deduction or a credit previously taken. The taking from an enemy, by a force friendly to the former owner, of a vessel previously taken for prize by such enemy. See **Recapture of depreciation.**

Recapture clause. In contracts, a provision for determining rates in the event that the contract rate is more favorable than anticipated. Also, a provision in a contract for recovering possession of goods. As used in leases, a clause giving the lessor a percentage of profits above a fixed amount of rent; or, in a percentage lease, a clause granting landlord right to terminate lease if tenant fails to realize minimum sales.

Recapture of depreciation. Upon the disposition of depreciable property used in a trade or business, gain or loss is determined as measured by the difference between the consideration received (*i.e.*, the amount realized) and the adjusted basis of the property. I.R.C. §§ 1245 and 1250 generally require that gain be reported as ordinary income to the extent of the depreciation previously taken as a deduction under I.R.C. § 167. The recapture of depreciation rules do not apply when the property is disposed of at a loss.

Recapture of investment tax credit. When investment credit property is disposed of or ceases to be used in the trade or business of the taxpayer, some of the investment tax credit claimed on such property may be recaptured as additional tax liability. The amount of the recapture is the difference between the amount of the credit originally claimed and what should have been claimed in light of the length of time the property was actually held or used for qualifying purposes. See **Investment tax credit.**

Receditur a placitis juris, potius quam injuriæ et delicta maneant impunita /rəsíydədər èy plǽsədəs júrəs pówsh(iy)əs kwǽm injúriyiy èt dəlíktə mǽniyənt impyúwnədə/. Positive rules of law (as distinguished from maxims or conclusions of reason) will be reced-

ed from (given up or dispensed with), rather than that crimes and wrongs should remain unpunished.

Receipt. Written acknowledgment of the receipt of money, or a thing of value, without containing any affirmative obligation upon either party to it; a mere admission of a fact, in writing. And, being a mere acknowledgment of payment, is subject to parol explanation or contradiction.

Receipt is a writing which acknowledges taking or receiving either money or goods which have been paid or have been delivered. Manley v. Nelson, 50 Hawaii 484, 524, 443 P.2d 155, 158. Act of receiving; also, the fact of receiving or being received; that which is received. That which comes in, in distinction from what is expended, paid out, sent away, and the like. State v. Texas Co., 173 Tenn. 154, 116 S.W.2d 583, 584.

Receipt of goods. Taking physical possession of goods. U.C.C. § 2–103(1)(c).

Warehouse receipt. See that title.

Receiptor. A name formerly given in some of the states to a person who received from the sheriff goods which the latter had seized under process of garnishment, on giving to the sheriff a bond conditioned to have the property forthcoming when demanded, or when execution issues.

Receivable. Any collectible whether or not it is currently due. That which is due and owing a person or company (*e.g.* account receivable). In bookkeeping, the name of an account which reflects a debt due.

Receive. To take into possession and control; accept custody of; collect.

To "receive" stolen property, means acquisition of control in sense of physical dominion or apparent legal power to dispose of property and envisages possession or control as an essential element. U. S. v. Walker, D.C.Tenn., 384 F.Supp. 262, 263. See also **Receiving stolen goods or property.**

Receiver. A ministerial officer, agent, creature, hand, or arm of, and a temporary occupant and caretaker of the property for, the court, and he represents the court appointing him, and he is the medium through which the court acts. Pacific Indem. Co. v. Workmen's Compensation Appeals Bd., 258 Cal.App.2d 35, 65 Cal.Rptr. 429, 432. An indifferent person between the parties to a cause, appointed by the court to receive and preserve the property or fund in litigation, and receive its rents, issues, and profits, and apply or dispose of them at the direction of the court when it does not seem reasonable that either party should hold them. A fiduciary of the court, appointed as an incident to other proceedings wherein certain ultimate relief is prayed. He is a trustee or ministerial officer representing court, and all parties in interest in litigation, and property or fund intrusted to him.

A person appointed by a court to manage property in litigation or the affairs of a bankrupt. In bankruptcy or state court proceeding, one who is empowered to take charge of the assets of an insolvent person or business and preserve them for sale and distribution to creditors.

A custodian of assets involved in litigation and title to assets remain in owner or owners who are parties in proceedings which lead to appointment of receiver who is managing agent of property for benefit of parties. A. S. S. Wrecking Co. v. Guaranty Bank & Trust Co., 2 Ill.App.3d 66, 275 N.E.2d 724, 728.

As to receivers appointed by federal courts, see Fed.R.Civil P. 66.

See also **Receivership; Trustee.**

Receiver pendente lite /rəsíyvər pəndéntiy láydiy/. A person appointed to take charge of the fund or property to which the receivership extends while the case remains undecided. The title to the property is not changed by the appointment. The receiver acquires no title, but only the right of possession as the officer of the court. The title remains in those in whom it was vested when the appointment was made. The object of the appointment is to secure the property pending the litigation, so that it may be appropriated in accordance with the rights of the parties, as they may be determined by the judgment in the action. Title Guarantee & Trust Co. v. 457 Schenectady Ave., 235 App.Div. 509, 257 N.Y.S. 413, 417.

Receiver's certificate. A non-negotiable evidence of debt, or debenture, issued by authority of a court of chancery, as a first lien upon the property of a debtor corporation in the hands of a receiver.

Receivership. Legal or equitable proceeding in which a receiver is appointed for an insolvent corporation, partnership or individual. The state or condition of a corporation, partnership or individual over whom a receiver has been appointed for protection of its assets and for ultimate sale and distribution to creditors. See also **Receiver; Trustee.**

Receiving stolen goods or property. Offense of receiving any property with the knowledge that it has been feloniously, or unlawfully stolen, taken, extorted, obtained, embezzled, or disposed of.

Receiving stolen property—a statutory crime separate from the crime involved in the stealing of the property—is defined in the typical statute as the receiving of stolen property knowing that it is stolen. Although most statutes do not specifically mention it, the receiver must, in addition to knowing the property is stolen, intend to deprive the owner of his property. Four elements are necessary to constitute crime of "receiving stolen goods": (1) the property must be received; (2) it must, at time of its receipt, be stolen property; (3) the receiver must have guilty knowledge that it is stolen property; and (4) his intent in receiving it must be fraudulent. Fletcher v. State, 231 Md. 190, 189 A.2d 641, 643.

A person is guilty of theft if he purposely receives, retains, or disposes of movable property of another knowing that it has been stolen, or believing that it has probably been stolen, unless the property is received, retained, or disposed with purpose to restore it to the owner. "Receiving" means acquiring possession, control or title, or lending on the security of the property. Model Penal Code, § 223.6.

Recens insecutio /ríysen(d)z insəkyúwsh(iy)ow/. In old English law, fresh suit; fresh pursuit. Pursuit of a thief immediately after the discovery of the robbery. See **Fresh pursuit.**

Receptus /rəséptəs/. Lat. In the civil law, the name sometimes given to an arbitrator, because he had been received or chosen to settle the differences between the parties.

Recess. In the practice of the courts, a short interval or period of time during which the court suspends business, but without adjourning. The period between sessions of court. A temporary ajournment of a trial or a hearing that occurs after a trial or hearing has commenced. State v. Charles, La., 350 So.2d 595, 598.

In legislative practice, the interval, occurring in consequence of an adjournment, between the sessions of the same continuous legislative body; not the interval between the final adjournment of one body and the convening of another at the next regular session.

Recession. The act of ceding or falling back. Term is commonly used with reference to a temporary setback or slow-down in the economic growth of a nation, but less severe than a depression.

Recessus maris /rəsésəs mérəs/. Lat. In old English law, a going back; reliction or retreat of the sea.

Recht /rékt/. Ger. Right; justice; equity; the whole body of law; unwritten law; law; also a right.

Recidivist /rəsídəvəst/. A habitual criminal; a criminal repeater. An incorrigible criminal. One who makes a trade of crime.

Reciprocal. Given or owed mutually as between two persons; interchanged. Reciprocal obligations are those due from one person to another and vice versa. See also **Reciprocity.**

Reciprocal contract. A contract, the parties to which enter into mutual engagements. A mutual or bilateral contract.

Reciprocal Enforcement of Support Act. Uniform law, adopted in most all states, by which a court in the jurisdiction of a wife or mother can commence proceedings for support against the husband or father residing in another state. The court in the jurisdiction where he lives issues process for his appearance and an order of support is made. This is transmitted to the court of the initiating state.

Reciprocal laws. Laws of one state which extend rights and privileges to citizens of another state if such state grants similar privileges to citizens of the first state; e.g. Reciprocal Enforcement of Support Act.

Reciprocal or interinsurance exchange. Group or association of persons cooperating through an attorney in fact for purpose of insuring themselves and each other. In re Minnesota Ins. Underwriters, D.C.Minn., 36 F.2d 371, 372.

Reciprocal promises. Mutual promises exchanged between two parties. See also **Reciprocal contract.**

Reciprocal trade agreements. Agreement between two countries providing for interchange of goods between them at lower tariffs and better terms than exist between one such country and other countries; e.g. U.S. Reciprocal Trade Agreements Act of 1934.

Reciprocal trusts. Mutual trusts in one of which A is beneficiary of trust established by B and B is beneficiary of trust settled by A. Commonly these trusts are established by husband and wife.

Reciprocal wills. Wills made by two or more persons in which they make reciprocal testamentary provisions in favor of each other, whether they unite in one will or each executes a separate one. This may be done by one will, in which case the will is both joint and reciprocal, or it may be done by separate wills. Father Flanagan's Boys' Home v. Turpin, 252 Iowa 603, 106 N.W.2d 637, 639.

Reciprocity. Mutuality. The term is used to denote the relation existing between two states when each of them gives the subjects of the other certain privileges, on condition that its own subjects shall enjoy similar privileges at the hands of the latter state. Term may also refer to practice, prohibited by Sherman Antitrust Act, whereby a company, overtly or tacitly, agrees to conduct one or more aspects of its business so as to confer a benefit on the other party to the agreement, the consideration being the return promise in kind by the other party, and it is basically a policy of favoring one's customers in purchasing commodities sold by them. Stavrides v. Mellon Nat. Bank & Trust Co., D.C.Pa., 353 F.Supp. 1072, 1077. See also **Reciprocal.**

Recision. The right of recision is the right to cancel (rescind) a contract upon the occurrence of certain kinds of default by the other contracting party. Not every default in a contract will give rise to a right of recission. See also **Cancellation; Rescission of contract.**

Recital. The formal statement or setting forth of some matter of fact, in any deed or writing, in order to explain the reasons upon which the transaction is founded. The recitals are situated in the premises of a deed, that is, in that part of a deed between the date and the *habendum,* and they usually commence with the formal word "whereas."

In pleading, the statement of matter as introductory to some positive allegation, beginning in declarations with the words, "For that *whereas.*"

Recite. To state in a written instrument facts connected with its inception, or reasons for its being made. Also to quote or set forth the words or the contents of some other instrument or document; as, to "recite" a statute.

Reck. To take heed; have a care, mind, heed.

Reckless. Not recking; careless, heedless, inattentive; indifferent to consequences. According to circumstances it may mean desperately heedless, wanton or willful, or it may mean only careless, inattentive, or negligent. For conduct to be "reckless" it must be such as to evince disregard of, or indifference to, consequences, under circumstances involving danger to life or safety to others, although no harm was intended. Duckers v. Lynch, 204 Kan. 649, 465 P.2d 945, 948. See also **Recklessly; Recklessness.**

Reckless disregard of rights of others. As used in automobile guest law, means the voluntary doing by motorist of an improper or wrongful act, or with

knowledge of existing conditions, the voluntary refraining from doing a proper or prudent act when such act or failure to act evinces an entire abandonment of any care, and heedless indifference to results which may follow and the reckless taking of chance of accident happening without intent that any occur. Albert McGann Securities Co. v. Coen, 114 Ind.App. 60, 48 N.E.2d 58, 60; Gill v. Hayes, 188 Okl. 434, 108 P.2d 117, 120; Boswell v. State, 250 Ind. 607, 238 N.E.2d 283, 286.

"Reckless disregard" so as to show actual malice in publication may be shown to exist where there exists sufficient evidence to permit conclusion that defendant in fact entertained serious doubts as to truth of his publication or where there are obvious reasons to doubt veracity of informant or accuracy of his reports. Pape v. Time, Inc., D.C.Ill., 294 F.Supp. 1087, 1088.

Reckless driving. Operation of automobile manifesting reckless disregard of possible consequences and indifference to others' rights. To establish statutory offense of reckless driving requires proof that defendant in management of automobile intentionally did something with knowledge that injury to another was probable or acted with wanton and reckless disregard for safety of others and in reckless disregard of consequences of acts. People v. Schumacher, 194 C.A.2d 335, 14 Cal.Rptr. 924, 926.

Reckless homicide. A species of statutory homicide in some states characterized by a wilful and wanton disregard of consequences and resulting in death. In some states, it may amount to manslaughter. See **Homicide** (*Vehicular homicide*).

Recklessly. A person acts recklessly with respect to a material element of an offense when he consciously disregards a substantial and unjustifiable risk that the material element exists or will result from his conduct. The risk must be of such a nature and degree that, considering the nature and purpose of the actor's conduct and the circumstances known to him, its disregard involves a gross deviation from the standard of conduct that a law-abiding person would observe in the actor's situation. Model Penal Code, § 2.02.

As used in statute proscribing driving recklessly imparts a disregard by a driver for consequences of his act and an indifference to safety of life, limb or property. Powers v. Com., 211 Va. 386, 177 So.2d 628, 630.

Reckless misconduct. A person is guilty of reckless misconduct when he intentionally does an act, or fails to do an act in violation of his duty, with knowledge of serious danger to others involved in it or of facts which would disclose such danger to a reasonable man. State v. Vertefeuille, 3 Conn.Cir. 508, 217 A.2d 725, 726.

Recklessness. Rashness; heedlessness; wanton conduct. The state of mind accompanying an act, which either pays no regard to its probably or possibly injurious consequences, or which, though foreseeing such consequences, persists in spite of such knowledge. Recklessness is a stronger term than mere or ordinary negligence, and to be reckless, the conduct must be such as to evince disregard of or indifference to consequences, under circumstances involving danger to life or safety of others, although no harm was intended. Blackburn v. Colvin, 191 Kan. 239; 380 P.2d 432, 437.

Reclaim. To claim or demand back; to ask for the return or restoration of a thing; to insist upon one's right to recover that which was one's own, but was parted with conditionally or mistakenly; as, to *reclaim* goods which were obtained from one under false pretenses.

Reclaimed animals. Those that are made tame by art, industry, or education, whereby a qualified property may be acquired in them.

Reclamation. The process of bringing economically unusable land to a higher dollar value by physically changing it; *e.g.* draining a swamp, irrigating desert, replanting a forest.

A banking term used to describe a draft or check set aside because of an error in the listing of the check in clearing house balance.

Reclamation Act. The Reclamation Act of 1902 (43 U.S.C.A. § 391 et seq.), authorized the Secretary of the Interior to locate, construct, operate, and maintain works for the storage, diversion, and development of waters for the reclamation of arid and semiarid lands in the Western States. To perform these functions, the Secretary in July 1902 established a Reclamation Service in the Geological Survey. In March 1907 the Reclamation Service was separated from the Survey, and in June 1923 the name was changed to Bureau of Reclamation. The basic objectives of the Federal Reclamation program, as administered by the Bureau of Reclamation, are to assist the States, local governments, and other Federal agencies to stabilize and stimulate local and regional economies, enhance and protect the environment, and improve the quality of life through development of water and related land resources throughout the 17 contiguous Western States and Hawaii.

Reclamation Bureau. See **Reclamation Act.**

Reclamation district. A subdivision of a state created by legislative authority, for the purpose of reclaiming swamp, marshy, or desert lands within its boundaries and rendering them fit for habitation or cultivation, generally with funds raised by local taxation or the issue of bonds, and sometimes with authority to make rules or ordinances for the regulation of the work in hand.

Reclusion /rəkl(y)úwzhən/. In French law and in Louisiana, incarceration as a punishment for crime; a temporary, afflictive, and infamous punishment, consisting in being confined at hard labor in a penal institution, and carrying civil degradation. Solitary confinement in prison.

Recognition. Ratification; confirmation; an acknowledgment that something done by another person in one's name had one's authority.

Recognitione adnullanda per vim et duritiem facta /rèkəgnìshiyówniy ædnəlǽndə pàr vím èt d(y)ərísh(iy)əm fǽktə/. A writ to the justices of the common bench for sending a record touching a recognizance, which the recognizor suggests was acknowl-

edged by force and duress; that if it so appears the recognizance may be annulled.

Recognitors /rəkógnədərz/. In English law, the name by which the jurors impaneled on an assize are known. See **Recognition.**

The word is sometimes used as meaning the person who enters into a recognizance, being thus another form of recognizor.

Recognizance /rəkógnəzən(t)s/. An obligation entered into before a court or magistrate duly authorized for that purpose whereby the recognizor acknowledges that he will do some act required by law which is specified therein. The act of recognizing is performed by the recognizor's assenting to the words of the magistrate and acknowledging himself to be indebted to a certain party in a specific amount to be paid if he fails to perform the requisite act. State v. Vinal, 113 R.I. 426, 325 A.2d 81, 83.

An obligation undertaken by a person, generally a defendant in a criminal case, to appear in court on a particular day or to keep the peace. It runs to the court and may not require a bond. In this case it is called personal recognizance. See **Personal recognizance; Release on own recognizance.**

Recognize /rékəgnàyz/. To try; to examine in order to determine the truth of a matter. Also to enter into a recognizance.

Recognized. Actual and publicly known.

Recognized gain or loss. The portion of realized gain or loss that is subject to income taxation.

Recognizee. He to whom one is bound in a recognizance.

Recognizor. He who enters into a recognizance.

Recollection. The act of recalling something to mind. In evidence, a person may use almost anything to refresh his recollection of an event in order to testify and the evidence then is his testimony not the document which has refreshed his recollection.

A memorandum or record concerning a matter about which a witness once had knowledge but now has insufficient recollection to enable him to testify fully and accurately, shown to have been made or adopted by the witness when the matter was fresh in his memory and to reflect that knowledge correctly is not excluded by the hearsay rule. If admitted, the memorandum or record may be read into evidence but may not itself be received as an exhibit unless offered by an adverse party. See Fed.Evid.Rules 612 and 803(5).

See also **Recorded past recollection; Refreshing the memory.**

Recommend. To advise or counsel. Kirby v. Nolte, 351 Mo. 525, 173 S.W.2d 391. See **Counsel.**

Recommendation. In feudal law, a method of converting allodial land into feudal property. The owner of the allod surrendered it to the king or a lord, doing homage, and received it back as a benefice or feud, to hold to himself and such of his heirs as he had previously nominated to the superior.

The act of one person in giving to another a favorable account of the character, responsibility, or skill of a third.

Recommendation refers to an action which is advisory in nature rather than one having any binding effect. People v. Gates, 41 C.A.3d 590, 116 Cal.Rptr. 172, 178.

Letter of recommendation. A writing whereby one person certifies concerning another that he is of good character, solvent, possessed of commercial credit, skilled in his trade or profession, or otherwise worthy of trust, aid, or employment. It may be addressed to an individual or to whom it may concern, and is designed to aid the person commended in obtaining credit, employment, etc. See **Letter of credit.**

Recommendatory. Precatory, advisory, or directory. Recommendatory words in a will are such as do not express the testator's command in a peremptory form, but advise, counsel, or suggest that a certain course be pursued or disposition made.

Recompense /rékǝmpèn(t)s/. A reward for services; remuneration for goods or other property.

Recompense or recovery in value. That part of the judgment in a "common recovery" by which the tenant is declared entitled to recover lands of equal value with those which were warranted to him and lost by the default of the vouchee. 2 Bl.Comm. 358–359.

Reconciliation /rèkǝn(t)sìliyéyshǝn/. The renewal of amicable relations between two persons who had been at emnity or variance; usually implying forgiveness of injuries on one or both sides. In law of domestic relations, a voluntary resumption of marital relations in the fullest sense. Keller v. Keller, 122 Cal.App. 712, 10 P.2d 541. In bookkeeping, it is the practice of adjusting the bank statement with the depositor's books. Also, a statement showing the consistency of two or more other financial statements. See also **Reconciliation statement.**

Reconciliation statement. In accounting, a statement prepared to bring two or more accounts which show a discrepancy into agreement.

Reconduction. In the civil law, a renewing of a former lease; relocation.

Reconsignment. A change in the terms of a consignment after the goods are in transit. Privilege extended by carriers to shippers under which goods may be forwarded to a point other than their original destination, without removal from the car and at the through rate from initial point to that of final delivery. Southern Pac. Co. v. Brown, Alcantar & Brown, Inc., C.A. Tex., 409 F.2d 1331, 1332.

Reconstruct. To construct again, to rebuild, either in fact or idea, or to remodel. To form again or anew as in the imagination or to restore again as an entity the thing which was lost or destroyed. City of Seattle v. Northern Pac. Ry. Co., 12 Wash.2d 247, 121 P.2d 382, 386. See also **Recollection.**

Reconstruction. Act of constructing again. It presupposes the nonexistence of the thing to be reconstructed, as an entity; that the thing before existing has

lost its entity. Miller Hatcheries v. Buckeye Incubator Co., C.C.A.Mo., 41 F.2d 619.

Also the name commonly given to the process of reorganizing, by acts of congress and executive action, the governments of the states which had passed ordinances of secession, and of re-establishing their constitutional relations to the national government, restoring their representation in congress, and effecting the necessary changes in their internal government, after the close of the civil war.

Recontinuance. Used to signify that a person has recovered an incorporeal hereditament of which he had been wrongfully deprived.

Reconvenire /rìykonvǝnáyriy/. Lat. In the canon and civil law, to make a cross-demand upon the actor, or plaintiff.

Reconvention. In the civil law, an action by a defendant against a plaintiff in a former action; a cross-bill or litigation.

The term is used in practice in the states of Louisiana and Texas, derived from the *reconventio* of the civil law. Reconvention is not identical with set-off, but more extensive. Pacific Exp. Co. v. Malin, 132 U.S. 531, 10 S.Ct. 166, 33 L.Ed. 450.

Reconventional demand. Any plea by a defendant which constitutes more than mere defense and amounts to counterclaim. Alfonso v. Ruiz, La.App., 2 So.2d 480, 483, 484.

Reconversion. That imaginary process by which a prior constructive conversion is annulled and the property restored in contemplation of equity to its original actual quality.

Record, v. To commit to writing, to printing, to inscription, or the like. To make an official note of; to write, transcribe, or enter in a book, file, docket, register, computer tape or disc, or the like, for the purpose of preserving authentic evidence of. To transcribe a document, or enter the history of an act or series of acts, in an official volume, for the purpose of giving notice of the same, of furnishing authentic evidence, and for preservation. Shimmel v. People, 108 Colo. 592, 121 P.2d 491, 493.

Record, n. A written account of some act, court proceeding, transaction, or instrument, drawn up, under authority of law, by a proper officer, and designed to remain as a memorial or permanent evidence of the matters to which it relates. People ex rel. Simons v. Dowling, 84 Misc. 201, 146 N.Y.S. 919, 920. A memorandum public or private, of what has been done, ordinarily applied to public records, in which sense it is a written memorial made by a public officer. Nogueira v. State, 123 Tex.Cr.R. 449, 59 S.W.2d 831.

The act or fact of recording or being recorded; reduction to writing as evidence, also, the writing so made. A register, a family record, official contemporaneous writing; an authentic official copy of document entered in book or deposited in keeping of officer designated by law; an official contemporaneous memorandum stating the proceedings of a court or official copy of legal papers used in a case. Shimmel v. People, 108 Colo. 592, 121 P.2d 491, 493.

Records are generally admissable under Fed.Evid.R. 803. See also Rules 901 and 902 (authentication), and Rule 1005 (public records).

The term "records" means accounts, correspondence, memorandums, tapes, discs, papers, books, and other documents or transcribed information of any type, whether expressed in ordinary or machine language. Securities Exchange Act of 1934, § 3.

See also Congressional record; Court (Court of record); Defective record; Docket; File; Freedom of Information Act; Judgment book; Making record; Minutes book; Official record; Official Records Act; Of record; Public record; Sealing of records; Shop-book rule.

Arrest record. See **Arrest record.**

Court proceedings. The official collection of all the trial pleadings, exhibits, orders and word-for-word testimony that took place during the trial. The "record" includes pleadings, the process, the verdict, the judgment and such other matters as by some statutory or other recognized method have been made a part of it. C. J. Tower & Sons of Buffalo, Inc. v. U. S., Cust.Ct., 347 F.Supp. 1388, 1389.

A written memorial of all the acts and proceedings in an action or suit, in a court of record. The official and authentic history of the cause, consisting in entries of each successive step in the proceedings, chronicling the various acts of the parties and of the court, couched in the formal language established by usage, terminating with the judgment rendered in the cause, and intended to remain as a perpetual and unimpeachable memorial of the proceedings and judgment. Such record in civil cases consists primarily of the "civil docket" (Fed.R.Civil P. 79); and in criminal cases of the "criminal docket" (Fed.R. Crim.P. 55). See also **Docket; Transcript,** and *Record on appeal,* below.

Courts of record. A court whose proceedings are recorded. Also a court of general jurisdiction. States vary as to the requirements and strata of courts qualifying as courts of record. See also **Court (Court of record).**

Debts of record. Those which appear to be due by the evidence of a court of record; such as a judgment, recognizance, etc.

Diminution of record. Incompleteness of the record sent up on appeal. See **Diminution.**

Face of record. See **Face of record.**

Judicial record. A precise history of civil or criminal proceeding from commencement to termination. See **Docket.**

Matter of record. See that title.

Nul tiel record. See **Nul.**

Of record. See that title.

Public record. A record, memorial of some act or transaction, written evidence of something done, or document, considered as either concerning or interesting the public, affording notice or information to the public, or open to public inspection. Any writing prepared, owned, used or retained by any agency in pursuance of law or in connection with the transac-

tion of public business. "Writings" means all documents, papers, letters, maps, books, photographs, films, sound recordings, magnetic or other tapes, electronic date-processing records, artifacts or other documentary material, regardless of physical form or characteristics.

Record commission. The name of a board of commissioners appointed for the purpose of searching out, classifying, indexing, or publishing the public records of a state or county.

Record date. Dividends are paid on payment date to those who own the stock on the record date. The date on which a person must be registered as a shareholder on the stock book of a company in order to receive a declared dividend or, among other things, to vote on company affairs.

Record of nisi prius. In England, formerly an official copy or transcript of the proceedings in an action, entered on parchment and "sealed and passed" as it is termed, at the proper office. It served as a warrant to the judge to try the cause, and was the only document at which he could judicially look for information as to the nature of the proceedings and the issues joined.

Record on appeal. In the practice of appellate tribunals, the history of the proceedings on the trial of the action below (with the pleadings, offers, objections to evidence, rulings of the court, exceptions, charge, etc.), in so far as the same appears in the record furnished to the appellate court in the paperbooks or other transcripts. Hence, derivatively, it means the aggregate of the various judicial steps taken on the trial below, in so far as they were taken, presented, or allowed in the formal and proper manner necessary to put them upon the record of the court. This is the meaning in such phrases as "no error in the record," "contents of the record," "outside the record," etc.

The official documentation of all the proceedings in court in a particular case, including the pleadings, exhibits and commonly the transcript of the examination of witnesses; may also include docket entries. Fed.R.App.P. 10(a).

Records of a corporation. Such records include the transcript of its charter and by-laws, the minutes of its meetings—the books containing the accounts of its official doings and the written evidence of its contracts and business transactions. U. S. v. Louisville & N. R. Co., 236 U.S. 318, 35 S.Ct. 363, 368, 59 L.Ed. 598.

Trial by record. In old English law, a species of trial adopted for determining the existence or non-existence of a record. When a record was asserted by one party to exist, and the opposite party denied its existence under the form of a traverse that there was no such record remaining in court as alleged, and issue was joined thereon, this was called an "issue of *nul tiel record,*" and in such case the court awarded a trial by inspection and examination of the record. Upon this the party affirming its existence was bound to produce it in court on a day given for the purpose, and, if he failed to do so, judgment was given for his adversary.

Title of record. A title to real estate, evidenced and provable by one or more conveyances or other instruments all of which are duly entered on the public land records. See also **Abstract of title.**

Recordare /rìkordériy/. A writ to bring up judgments of justices of the peace.

Recordari facias loquelam /rìykordéray féysh(iy)əs ləkwíyləm/. In old English practice, a writ by which a suit or plaint in replevin could be removed from a county court to one of the courts of Westminster Hall. So termed from the emphatic words of the old writ, by which the sheriff was commanded to *cause the plaint to be recorded,* and to have the record before the superior court.

Recorda sunt vestigia vetustatis et veritatis /rəkórdə sənt vestíj(iy)ə vèdəstéydəs èt vèhrətéydəs/. Records are vestiges of antiquity and truth.

Recordation. The act or process of recording an instrument such as a deed or mortgage in a public registry. Also, the system of recording court proceedings by stenography, voice-writing or tapes.

Recordatur /rìykordéydər/. In old English practice, an entry made upon a record, in order to prevent any alteration of it. An order or allowance that the verdict returned on the *nisi prius* roll be recorded.

Recorded past recollection. In evidence, a document which was prepared at a time when the events recorded were fresh in the mind and memory of the person preparing it may be admissible as an exception to the hearsay rule if, as a preliminary matter, the judge is satisfied that it is the work of the witness and that it is the original unless such is excused under the best evidence rule. See Fed.Evid.R. 612 and 803(5); see also **Recollection.**

Recorder, *v.* L. Fr. In Norman law, to recite or testify on recollection what had previously passed in court. This was the duty of the judges and other principal persons who presided at the *placitum;* thence called *"recordeurs."*

Recorder, *n.* A magistrate, in the judicial systems of some of the states, who has a criminal jurisdiction analogous to that of a police judge or other committing magistrate, and usually a limited civil jurisdiction, and sometimes authority conferred by statute in special classes of proceedings. An officer appointed to make record or enrolment of deeds and other legal instruments authorized by law to be recorded. A local government officer in whose office deeds, mortgages, liens, and other instruments are registered.

Record, estoppel by. An "estoppel by record" is the preclusion to deny the truth of a matter set forth in a record, whether judicial or legislative, also to deny the facts adjudicated by a court of competent jurisdiction. An estoppel by record cannot be invoked where allegations or recitals did not conclude pleader in prior proceeding. Blackburn v. Blackburn, Tex. Civ.App., 163 S.W.2d 251, 255. It bars a second action between the same parties on an issue necessarily raised and decided in the first action. Woods v. Duval, 151 Kan. 472, 99 P.2d 804, 808. It exists only as between the same parties, or those in privity with them, in same case on same issues. Smith v. Maine, 145 Misc. 521, 260 N.Y.S. 425. The doctrine prevents a party not only from litigating again what was actu-

ally litigated in the former case, but litigating what might have been litigated therein.

Recording acts. Statutes enacted in the several states relative to the official recording of deeds, mortgages, bills of sale, chattel mortgages, etc., and the effect of such records as notice to creditors, purchasers, encumbrancers, and others interested.

Notice acts. That type of recording statute provides that a person with notice of an unrecorded instrument is barred from claiming priority as of the date on which he received the instrument. See also **Notice race statutes; Notice recording statutes.**

Race acts. The first to record regardless of notice of an unrecorded deed earlier in time has the better rights under a race type recording statute. See **Pure race statute.**

Race-notice acts. The first to record in the chain of title without notice of a prior unrecorded deed or mortgage has the better rights under a race-notice type statute. See **Race-notice recording statutes.**

Record notice. When an instrument of conveyance or a mortgage is recorded in the appropriate public office, it is constructive notice of its contents to the whole world.

Recordum /rəkórdəm/. A record; a judicial record. It is used in the phrase *prout patet per recordum,* which is a formula employed, in pleading, for reference to a record, signifying as it appears from the record.

Recoup, or **recoupe** /rəkúwp/. To deduct, defalk, discount, set off, or keep back; to withhold part of a demand. See **Recoupment.**

Recoupment /rəkúwpmənt/. To recover a loss by a subsequent gain. In pleading, to set forth a claim against the plaintiff when an action is brought against one as a defendant. A keeping back something which is due, because there is an equitable reason to withhold it. A right of the defendant to have a deduction from the amount of the plaintiff's damages, for the reason that the plaintiff has not complied with the cross-obligations or independent covenants arising under the same contract. It implies that plaintiff has cause of action, but asserts that defendant has counter cause of action growing out of breach of some other part of same contract on which plaintiff's action is founded, or for some cause connected with contract.

It is keeping back something which is due because there is an equitable reason to withhold it; and is applied where a man brings an action for breach of a contract between him and the defendant; and where the latter can show that some stipulation in the same contract was made by the plaintiff, which he has violated, the defendant may, if he choose, instead of suing in his turn, *recoupe* his damages arising from the breach committed by the plaintiff, whether they be liquidated or not.

Recoupment is a purely defensive matter growing out of transaction constituting plaintiff's cause of action and is available only to reduce or satisfy plaintiff's claim and permits of no affirmative judgment. Schroeder v. Prince Charles, Inc., Mo., 427 S.W.2d 414, 419.

Recoupment is the equivalent of the old counter-claim in which a defendant sets up a claim owed to him by the plaintiff though it need not arise out of the same transaction as the plaintiff's claim and the defendant may not recover more than the amount claimed by the plaintiff against him. Under rules practice, recoupment has been replaced by the modern counterclaim.

Set-off distinguished. A "set-off" is a demand which the defendant has against the plaintiff, arising out of a transaction extrinsic to the plaintiff's cause of action, whereas a "recoupment" is a reduction or rebate by the defendant of part of the plaintiff's claim because of a right in the defendant arising out of the same transaction. Zweck v. D P Way Corp., 70 Wis.2d 426, 234 N.W.2d 921, 924.

Recourse. To recur. The right of a holder of a negotiable instrument to recover against a party secondarily liable, *e.g.* prior endorser. Therefore, if a prior endorser signs *without recourse*, he exempts himself from liability for payment. U.C.C. § 3–414(1). See also **Without recourse; With recourse.**

Recover. To get or obtain again, to collect, to get renewed possession of; to win back. To regain, as lost property, territory, appetite, health, courage. In a narrower sense, to be successful in a suit, to collect or obtain amount, to have judgment, to obtain a favorable or final judgment, to obtain in any legal manner in contrast to voluntary payment. Covert v. Randles, 53 Ariz. 225, 87 P.2d 488, 490; Olds v. General Acc. Fire and Life Assur. Corp., 67 Cal. App.2d 812, 155 P.2d 676, 680. See also **Recovery.**

Recoveree. In old conveyancing, the party who suffered a common recovery.

Recoverer. The demandant in a common recovery, after judgment has been given in his favor.

Recovery. In its most extensive sense, the restoration or vindication of a right existing in a person, by the formal judgment or decree of a competent court, at his instance and suit, or the obtaining, by such judgment, of some right or property which has been taken or withheld from him. St. Paul Fire & Marine Ins. Co. v. Wood, 242 Ark. 879, 416 S.W.2d 322, 327. This is also called a "true" recovery, to distinguish it from a "feigned" or "common" recovery.

The obtaining of a thing by the judgment of a court, as the result of an action brought for that purpose. The amount finally collected, or the amount of judgment. In re Lahm, 179 App.Div. 757, 167 N.Y.S. 217, 219.

See **Common recovery; Recoupment; Repossession; Restitution.**

Final recovery. The final judgment or verdict in an action.

Recreant /rékriyənt/. Coward or craven. The word pronounced by a combatant in the trial by battel, when he acknowledged himself beaten. 3 Bl.Comm. 340.

Recrimination /rəkrìmənéyshən/. A charge made by an accused person against the accuser; in particular a counter-charge of adultery or cruelty made by one charged with the same offense in a suit for divorce, against the person who has charged him or her. Under doctrine of "recrimination", if conduct of both husband and wife has been such as to furnish grounds for divorce neither is entitled to relief. Mason v. Mason, 276 Ala. 265, 160 So.2d 881, 882. A showing by the defendant of any cause of divorce against the plaintiff, in bar of the plaintiff's cause of divorce. And to bar divorce, complainant's misconduct need not be of equal degree with that of defendant, but must be of same general character. The defense of recrimination has been abolished in many states with the enactment of "no-fault" divorce statutes.

Recross examination. An examination of a witness by a cross-examiner subsequent to a redirect examination of the witness.

Rectification. The act or process by which something is made right or by which a wrong is adjusted. See also **Restitution.**

Rectification of boundaries. In old English law, the action to rectify or ascertain the boundaries of two adjoining pieces of land.

Rectification of register. In old English law, the process by which a person whose name is wrongly entered on (or omitted from) a register may compel the keeper of the register to remove (or enter) his name.

Rectify. To correct or define something which is erroneous or doubtful. Thus, where the parties to an agreement have determined to embody its terms in the appropriate and conclusive form, but the instrument meant to effect this purpose (*e.g.*, a conveyance, settlement, etc.) is, by mutual mistake, so framed as not to express the real intention of the parties, an action may be brought to have it rectified.

Rectitudo /rèktət(y)úwdow/. Lat. Right or justice; legal dues; tribute or payment.

Recto, breve de /bríyviy dìy réktow/. A common law writ of right, which was of so high a nature that as other writs in real actions were only to recover the possession of the land, etc., in question, this aimed to recover the seisin and the property, and thereby both the rights of possession and property were tried together.

Recto de advocatione ecclesiæ /réktow dìy ædvəkèy-shiyówniy əklíyziyiy/. A writ which lay at common law, where a man had right of advowson of a church, and, the parson dying, a stranger had presented.

Recto de custodia terræ et hæredis /réktow dìy kəstówd(i)yə téhriy èt həríydəs/. A writ of right of ward of the land and heir. Abolished.

Recto de dote /réktow dìy dówdiy/. A writ of right of dower, which lay for a widow who had received part of her dower, and demanded the residue, against the heir of the husband or his guardian. Abolished.

Recto de dote unde nihil habet /réktow dìy dówdiy ə́ndiy náy(h)əl héybət/. A writ of right of dower whereof the widow had nothing, which lay where her deceased husband, having divers lands or tenements, had assured no dower to his wife, and she thereby was driven to sue for her thirds against the heirs or his guardian. Abolished.

Recto de rationabili parte /réktow dìy ræshənéybəlay párdiy/. A writ of right, of the reasonable part, which lay between privies in blood; as brothers in gavelkind, sisters, and other coparceners, for land in fee-simple.

Recto quando (or quia) dominus remisit curiam /réktow kwóndow dómənəs rəmáyzət kyúriyəm/°kwáyə°/. A writ of right, when or because the lord had remitted his court, which lay where lands or tenements in the seignory of any lord were in demand by a writ of right.

Rector. In ecclesiastical law, one who rules or governs. A name given to certain officers of the Roman Catholic Church.

The spiritual head and presiding officer of church. A clergyman elected by the members of the parish to have permanent charge of it. He is the official head of the parish and ex officio head of all parochial organizations.

In English law, he that has full possession of a parochial church. A rector (or parson) has, for the most part, the whole right to all the ecclesiastical dues in his parish; while a *vicar* has an appropriator over him, entitled to the best part of the profits, to whom the vicar is, in effect, perpetual curate, with a standing salary. 1 Bl.Comm. 384, 388.

Rectorial tithes /rektóriyəl táyðz/. Great or predial tithes.

Rector provinciæ /réktər prəvínshiyiy/. Lat. In Roman law, the governor of a province.

Rector sinecure /réktər sàyniykyúriy/. A rector of a parish who has not the cure of souls.

Recto sur disclaimer /réktow sər dəskléymər/. An abolished writ on disclaimer.

Rectum /réktəm/. Lat. Right; also a trial or accusation.

Rectum esse /réktəm ésiy/. To be right in court.

Rectum rogare /réktəm rəgériy/. To ask for right; to petition the judge to do right.

Rectum, stare ad /stériy æd réktəm/. To stand trial or abide by the sentence of the court.

Rectus /réktəs/. In the old law of descents, right; upright; the opposite of obliquus *(q.v.)*.

Rectus in curia /réktəs ìn kyúriə/. Lat. Right in court. The condition of one who stands at the bar, against whom no one objects any offense. When a person outlawed has reversed his outlawry, so that he can have the benefit of the law, he is said to be *"rectus in curia."*

Recuperatio /rək(y)ùwpəréysh(iy)ow/. Lat. In old English law, recovery; restitution by the sentence of a judge of a thing that has been wrongfully taken or detained.

Recuperatio, i.e., ad rem, per injuriam extortam sive detentam, per sententiam judicis restitutio /rək(y)ùwpəréysh(iy)ow, íd èst, pər ənjúriyəm əkstórdəm sáyviy dəténtəm pàr senténsh(iy)əm júwdəsəs rèstət(y)úwsh(iy)ow/. Recovery, *i.e.,* restitution by sen-

tence of a judge of a thing wrongfully extorted or detained.

Recuperatio est alicujus rei in causam, alterius adductæ per judicem acquisitio /rək(y)ùwpəréysh(iy)ow èst ǽlək(y)úwjəs ríyay ìn kózəm, oltíriyəs ədáktiy pèr júwdəsəm ǽkwəzísh(iy)ow/. Recovery is the acquisition by sentence of a judge of anything brought into the cause of another.

Recuperatores /rək(y)ùwpərətóriyz/. In Roman law, a species of judges first appointed to decide controversies between Roman citizens and strangers concerning rights requiring speedy remedy, but whose jurisdiction was gradually extended to questions which might be brought before ordinary judges.

Recurrendum est ad extraordinarium quando non valet ordinarium /rèkəhréndəm èst æd èkstrəòrdənér(i)yəm kwóndow nòn vǽləd òrdənér(i)yəm/. We must have recourse to what is extraordinary, when what is ordinary fails.

Recusal. See **Recusation.**

Recusants /rékyəzənts/rəkyúwzənts/. In old English law, persons who willfully absented themselves from their parish church, and on whom penalties were imposed by various statutes passed during the reigns of Elizabeth and James I. Those persons who separate from the church established by law. The term was practically restricted to Roman Catholics.

Recusation /rèkyəzéyshən/. The process by which a judge is disqualified (or disqualifies himself or herself) from hearing a lawsuit because of interest or prejudice.

In the civil law, a species of exception or plea to the jurisdiction, to the effect that the particular judge is disqualified from hearing the cause by reason of interest or prejudice. The challenge of jurors. An act, of what nature soever it may be, by which a strange heir, by deeds or words, declares he will not be heir.

Recusatio testis /rèkyuwzéysh(iy)ow téstəs/. Lat. In the civil law, rejection of a witness, on the ground of incompetency.

Red, raed, or **rede** /réd/ríyd/. Sax. Advice; counsel.

Red book of the exchequer. An ancient record, wherein are registered the holders of lands *per baroniam* in the time of Henry II, the number of hides of land in certain counties before the Conquest, and the ceremonies on the coronation of Eleanor, wife of Henry III.

Reddendo singula singulis /rədéndow síŋgyələ síŋgyələs/. Lat. By referring each to each; referring each phrase or expression to its appropriate object. A rule of construction.

Reddendum /rədéndəm/. Lat. In old English conveyancing, rendering; yielding. The technical name of that clause in a conveyance by which the grantor creates or reserves some new thing to himself, out of what he had before granted; as *"rendering* therefor yearly the sum of ten shillings, or a pepper-corn," etc. That clause in a lease in which a rent is reserved to the lessor, and which commences with the word *"yielding."* 2 Bl.Comm. 299.

Reddens causam scientiæ /réden(d)z kózəm sayénshiyiy/. Lat. Giving the reason of his knowledge.

Reddere, nil aliud est quam acceptum restituere; seu, reddere est quasi retro dare, et redditur dicitur a redeundo, quia retro it /rédəriy níl ǽliyəd èst kwǽm əkséptəm rèstət(y)úwəriy; syúw rédəriy èst kwéyzay rétrow dériy, èt rédədər dísədər èy rèdiyǽndow kwáyə rétrow ít/. To render is nothing more than to restore that which has been received; or, to render is as it were to give back, and it is called "rendering" from "returning," because it goes back again.

Reddidit se /rédədət síy/. Lat. He has rendered himself.

In old English practice, a term applied to a principal who had rendered himself in discharge of his bail.

Reddition /rədíshən/. A surrendering or restoring; also a judicial acknowledgment that the thing in demand belongs to the demandant, and not to the person surrendering.

Redeem /rədíym/. To buy back. To free property or article from mortgage or pledge by paying the debt for which it stood as security. To repurchase in a literal sense; as, to redeem one's land from a tax-sale. It implies the existence of a debt and means to rid property of that incumbrance. Talley v. Eastland, 259 Ky. 241, 82 S.W.2d 368, 372. See also **Redemption.**

Redeemable /rədíyməbəl/. Subject to redemption; admitting of redemption or repurchase; given or held under conditions admitting of reacquisition by purchase; as, a "redeemable pledge."

Redeemable bond. A bond which the issuer may call for payment pursuant to the terms of the bond and indenture; a callable bond.

Redeemable rights. Rights which return to the conveyor or disposer of land, etc., upon payment of the sum for which such rights are granted.

Redeemable stock. Capital stock, generally preferred, which, by its terms, may be called by the issuing corporation and paid.

Redelivery. A yielding and delivering back of a thing.

Redelivery bond. A bond given to a sheriff or other officer, who has attached or levied on personal property, to obtain the release and repossession of the property, conditioned to redeliver the property to the officer or pay him its value in case the levy or attachment is adjudged good.

Redemise /rìydəmáyz/. A regranting of land demised or leased.

Redemption. The realization of a right to have the title of property restored free and clear of the mortgage; performance of the mortgage obligation being essential for that purpose.

A repurchase; a buying back. The act of a vendor of property in buying it back again from the purchaser at the same or an enhanced price. The process of annulling and revoking a conditional sale of property, by performance of the conditions on which it was stipulated to be revocable.

The process of cancelling and annulling a defeasible title to land, such as is created by a mortgage or a tax-sale, by paying the debt or fulfilling the other conditions. The liberation of an estate from a mortgage. Webb v. Williamson, 202 Ark. 763, 152 S.W.2d 312, 314. The liberation of a chattel from pledge or pawn, by paying the debt for which it stood as security.

Repurchase of notes, bonds, stock, bills, or other evidences of debt, by paying their value to their holders. The payment of principal and unpaid interest on bonds or other debt obligations.

Repurchase by corporation of its shares at a price equal to the net asset value of the shares on date a redemption request is received by the corporation. Kreis v. Mates Inv. Fund, Inc., D.C.Mo., 335 F.Supp. 1299, 1302. See also **Stock** (*Stock redemption*).

See also **Equitable redemption; Equity of redemption; Tax redemption.**

Redemptiones /rədèm(p)shiyówniyz/. In old English law, heavy fines. Distinguished from *misericordia* (which see).

Redemption period. A time period during which a defaulted mortgage, land contract, deed of trust, etc., can be redeemed. Such period is commonly provided for by state statute.

Redemption price. The price at which a bond may be redeemed before maturity, at the option of the issuing company. Such term also applies to the price the company must pay to call in certain types of preferred stock.

Redemptio operis /rədém(p)sh(iy)ow ówpərəs/. Lat. In Roman law, a contract for the hiring or letting of services, or for the performance of a certain work in consideration of the payment of a stipulated price. It is the same contract as *"locatio operis,"* but regarded from the standpoint of the one who is to do the work, and who is called *"redemptor operis,"* while the hirer is called *"locator operis."*

Redeundo /rìydiyǽndow/. Lat. Returning; in returning; while returning.

Redevance. In old French and Canadian law, dues payable by a tenant to his lord, not necessarily in money.

Red handed. With the marks of crime fresh on him.

Red herring. In finance, an advance copy of the statement (prospectus) to be filed with the SEC preceding an issue of securities. The copy is marked in red ink, "not a solicitation, for information only."

Redhibere /rèd(h)əbíriy/. Lat. In the civil law, to have again; to have back; to cause a seller to have again what he had before.

Redhibition /rèd(h)əbíshən/. Avoidance of sale on account of vice or defect in thing sold which renders it either absolutely useless or its use so inconvenient and imperfect that it may be presumed that buyer would not have purchased it had he known of defects. LaFleur v. Boyce Machinery Corp., La.App., 282 So.2d 819, 821.

Redhibitory action /rəd(h)íbət(ə)riy ǽkshən/. In the civil law, an action for redhibition. An action to avoid a sale on account of some vice or defect in the thing sold, which renders its use impossible, or so inconvenient and imperfect that it must be supposed the buyer would not have purchased it had he known of the vice. Civ.Code La. art. 2520. An action in which buyer, alleging seller's breach of express or implied warranty, seeks to return thing sold or part thereof and to recover back all or part of price paid. Hermanos v. Matos, C.C.A.Puerto Rico, 81 F.2d 930, 931.

Redhibitory defect or **vice** /rəd(h)íbət(ə)riy dəfékt /°váys/. In the civil law, a defect in an article sold, for which the seller may be compelled to take it back; a defect against which the seller is bound to warrant.

Redimere /rədíməriy/. Lat. In Roman law, to buy back. Talley v. Eastland, 259 Ky. 241, 82 S.W.2d 368, 372.

Redirect examination. An examination of a witness by the direct examiner subsequent to the cross-examination of the witness. See also **Rehabilitation.**

Rediscount. The act of discounting an instrument which has already been discounted as in the case of a bank which has already discounted a note and then discounts or sells it again.

Rediscount rate. The rate, fixed by the Federal Reserve Board, at which a Federal Reserve Bank can make loans to member banks on the security of commercial paper already discounted by such banks.

Redisseisin /rìydəsíyzən/. In old English law, a second disseisin of a person of the same tenements, and by the same disseisor, by whom he was before disseised. 3 Bl.Comm. 188.

Redistribution /rìydistrəbyúwshən/. In gambling, payoff to holders of winning tickets. Delaware Steeplechase & Race Ass'n v. Wise, 2 Terry (Del.) 587, 27 A.2d 357, 361.

Reditus /rédədəs/. Lat. A revenue or return; income or profit; specifically, rent.

Reditus albi /rédədəs ǽlbay/. White rent; blanche farm; rent payable in silver or other money.

Reditus assisus /rédədəs əsáyzəs/. A set or standing rent.

Reditus capitales /rédədəs kæpətéyliyz/. Chief rent paid by freeholders to go quit of all other services.

Reditus nigri /rédədəs nígray/. Black rent; black mail; rent payable in provisions, corn, labor, etc.; as distinguished from "money rent," called *"reditus albi."*

Reditus quieti /rédədəs kwayíyday/. Quitrents (q.v.).

Reditus siccus /rédədəs síkəs/. Rent seck (q.v.).

Red lights ahead doctrine. Under this doctrine, third party obtaining securities is required to investigate only under exceptional circumstances which arise when a party to a transaction has knowledge that some fact or facts exist with respect to transaction which would prevent action by commercially honest men for whom law is made. Thomes v. Atkins, D.C.Minn., 52 F.Supp. 405, 410.

Redlining. Redlining is a pattern of discrimination in which financial institutions refuse to make mortgage loans, regardless of credit record of the applicant, on properties in specified areas because of alleged deteriorating conditions. At one time, lenders actually outlined these areas with a red pencil. Such practice violates federal laws.

Redmans. In feudal law, men who, by the tenure or custom of their lands, were to ride with or for the lord of the manor, about his business.

Redobatores /rədòwbətóriyz/. In old English law, those that bought stolen cloth and turned it into some other color or fashion that it may not be recognized. Redubbers (q.v.).

Redraft. A second or cross bill drafted by the original drawer after the first draft has been dishonored and protested. The amount includes the additional costs as well as the original face amount.

Redress. Satisfaction for an injury or damages sustained. Damages or equitable relief. See **Recovery; Restitution.**

Red tape. In a derivative sense, order carried to fastidious excess; system run out into trivial extremes. Term commonly refers to excessive bureaucracy.

Redubbers /riydə́bərz/. In old English law, those who bought stolen cloth and dyed it of another color to prevent its being identified were anciently so called.

Reductio ad absurdum /rədə́ksh(iy)ow ǽd əbsə́rdəm/. Lat. In logic, the method of disproving an argument by showing that it leads to an absurd consequence.

Reduction into possession. The act of exercising the right conferred by a chose in action, so as to convert it into a chose in possession; thus, a debt is reduced into possession by payment.

Reduction of capital. Voluntary liquidation of retired corporate capital. Jay Ronald Co. v. Marshall Mortg. Corporation, 265 App.Div. 622, 40 N.Y.S.2d 391, 399.

Reduction to possession. Conversion of a right existing as a claim into actual custody and enjoyment. Newell v. McLaughlin, 126 Conn. 138, 9 A.2d 815, 819.

Reduction to practice. As respects priority of invention for purposes of patentability is accomplished when inventor's conception is embodied in such form as to render it capable of practical and successful use. Pyrene-Minimax Corporation v. Palmer, 67 App.D.C. 33, 89 F.2d 505, 510. But device need not be perfect or commercial success. Pierson v. Beck, Cust. & Pat.App., 40 F.2d 769, 770.

Redundancy. Introducing superfluous matter into a legal instrument; particularly the insertion in a pleading of matters foreign, extraneous, and irrelevant to that which it is intended to answer. In re Wise's Estate, 144 Neb. 273, 13 N.W.2d 146, 151. Redundant matter in pleadings may be ordered stricken on motion. Fed.R. Civil P. 12(f).

Re-enact. To enact again; to revive.

Re-enactment rule. If the legislature enacts again a statute which had long continued executive construction by an agency, it can be said that the legislature has adopted that construction.

Re-entry. The act of resuming the possession of lands or tenements in pursuance of a right which party exercising it reserved to himself when he quit his former possession. The right reserved by a grantor to enter the premises on breach of a condition of the conveyance. See also **Repossession.**

Re-establish. To restore to its former position. Baron v. Prudence Life Ins. Co., 315 Ill.App. 129, 42 N.E.2d 137, 138.

Reeve /ríyv/. An ancient English officer of justice inferior in rank to an alderman. He was a ministerial officer appointed to execute process, keep the King's peace, and put the laws in execution. He witnessed all contracts and bargains, brought offenders to justice and delivered them to punishment, took bail for such as were to appear at the county court, and presided at the court or folcmote. He was also called *gerefa.*

There were several kinds of reeves, as, the *shire-gerefa,* shire-reeve or sheriff; the *heh-gerefa,* or high-sheriff; *tithing-reeve,* burghor or borough-reeve.

Land reeve. See **Land.**

Re-examination. An examination of a witness after a cross-examination, upon matters arising out of such cross-examination.

Re-exchange. The damages or expenses caused by the dishonor and protest of a bill of exchange in a foreign country, where it was payable, and by its return to the place where it was drawn or indorsed, and its being there taken up.

Re-export. The act of exporting a product which has been imported and left relatively unchanged in form before exporting again.

Re-extent. In old English practice, a second extent made upon lands or tenements, upon complaint made that the former extent was partially performed.

Re. fa. lo. /ríy féy lów/. The abbreviation of *"recordari facias loquelam,"* (q.v.).

Refare /rəfériy/. To bereave, take away, rob.

Refection /rəfékshən/. In the civil law, reparation; re-establishment of a building.

Refer. When a case or action involves matters of account or other intricate details which require minute examination, and for that reason are not fit to be brought before a jury, it is common to *refer* the whole case, or some part of it, to the decision of an auditor, master, or referee, and the case is then said to be referred. See **Referee; Reference.**

Taking this word in its strict, technical use, it relates to a mode of determining questions which is distinguished from "arbitration," in that the latter word imports submission of a controversy without any lawsuit having been brought, while "reference" imports a lawsuit pending, and an issue framed or question raised which (and not the controversy itself) is sent out. Thus, arbitration is resorted to instead of any judicial proceeding; while reference is one mode of decision employed in the course of a judicial proceeding.

To point, allude, direct, or make reference to. This is the use of the word in conveyancing and in literature, where a word or sign introduced for the purpose of directing the reader's attention to another place in the deed, book, document, etc., is said to "refer" him to such other connection.

Referee. A person to whom a cause pending in a court is referred by the court, to take testimony, hear the parties, and report thereon to the court. Person who is appointed to exercise judicial powers, to take testimony, to hear parties, and report his findings. Department of Motor Vehicles v. Superior Court for Los Angeles County, 271 Cal.App.2d 770, 76 Cal.Rptr. 804, 806. He is an officer exercising judicial powers, and is an arm of the court for a specific purpose. Segal v. Jackson, 183 Misc. 460, 48 N.Y.S.2d 877, 879. Similar functions are performed by auditors or masters *(q.v.).* See also **Master; Reference.**

Referee in bankruptcy. An officer appointed by the courts of bankruptcy under the act of 1898 (11 U.S. C.A. § 1) corresponding to the "registers in bankruptcy" under earlier statutes having administrative and quasi-judicial functions under the bankruptcy law, and whose functions and powers were to administer proceedings under the federal Bankruptcy Act *(q.v.).* Such referees (called "bankruptcy judges" after 1973) were abolished by the 1978 Bankruptcy Act; their functions now being performed by Bankruptcy Court judges.

Reference. The act of referring a case to a referee, auditor, or master to find facts and submit report to the court. The document by which the reference is made. Fed.R.Civil P. 53. See also **Master; Referee.**

In contracts, an agreement to submit to arbitration; the act of parties in submitting their controversy to chosen referees or arbitrators.

A person who will provide information for you about your character, credit, etc. The act of sending or directing one person to another, for information or advice as to the character, solvency, standing, etc., of a third person, who desires to open business relations with the first, or to obtain credit with him.

Reference in case of need. When a person draws or indorses a bill of exchange, he sometimes adds the name of a person to whom it may be presented "in case of need;" *i.e.,* in case it is dishonored by the original drawee or acceptor.

Reference statutes. Statutes which refer to other statutes and make them applicable to the subject of legislation. Their object is to incorporate into the act of which they are a part the provisions of other statutes by reference and adoption. State ex rel. School Dist. of Kansas City v. Lee, 334 Mo. 513, 66 S.W.2d 521.

Referendarius /rèfərendér(i)yəs/. An officer by whom the order of causes was laid before the Roman emperor, the desires or petitioners made known, and answers returned to them.

Referendary /rèfərénd(ə)riy/. In Saxon law, a master of requests; an officer to whom petitions to the king were referred.

Referendo singula singulis /rèfəréndow síng(y)ələ síng(y)ələs/. Lat. Referring individual or separate words to separate subjects; making a distributive reference of words in an instrument; a rule of construction.

Referendum /rèfəréndəm/. The process of referring to the electorate for approval a proposed new State constitution or amendment (constitutional referendum) or of a law passed by the legislature (statutory referendum). Reservation by people of state, or local subdivision thereof, of right to have submitted for their approval or rejection, under prescribed conditions, any law or part of law passed by lawmaking body. Anne Arundel County v. McDonough, 277 Md. 271, 354 A.2d 788, 796. Not all state constitutions make provision for referendum. See also **Initiative; Plebiscite; Proposition.**

In international law, a communication sent by a diplomatic representative to his home government, in regard to matters presented to him which he is unable or unwilling to decide without further instructions.

Refinance. To finance again or anew; to pay off existing debts with funds secured from new debt. The discharge of an obligation with funds acquired through the creation of a new debt. See also **Debt adjustment; Recapitalization.**

Reform. To correct, rectify, amend, remodel. Instruments *inter partes* may be *reformed,* when defective, by a court. By this is meant that the court, after ascertaining the real and original intention of the parties to a deed or other instrument (which intention they failed to sufficiently express, through some error, mistake of fact, or inadvertence), will decree that the instrument be held and construed as if it fully and technically expressed that intention. See also **Reformation.**

Reformation. Equitable remedy used to reframe written contracts to reflect accurately real agreement between contracting parties when, either through mutual mistake or unilateral mistake coupled with actual or equitable fraud by other party, the writing does not embody contract as actually made. Mutual of Omaha Ins. Co. v. Russell, C.A.Kan., 402 F.2d 339, 344.

If by mistake of fact as to the contents of a written agreement or conveyance, or by mistake of law as to its legal effect, the writing does not conform to the agreement of the parties to it, the writing can be reformed to accord with the agreement. Restatement, Second, Agency, § 8D.

Reformation means doing over to bring about a better result, correction or rectification. Tuel v. Gladden, 234 Or. 1, 379 P.2d 553, 555.

See also **Reform.**

Reformatory. A penal institution for youthful offenders where the emphasis is on reformation of the juvenile's behavior.

Refreshing recollection. See **Recollection; Recorded past recollection; Refreshing the memory.**

Refreshing the memory. The act of a witness who consults his documents, memoranda, or books, to bring more distinctly to his recollection the details of past events or transactions, concerning which he is testifying. See also **Recollection; Recorded past recollection; Refreshing the memory.**

Refund, *n.* That which is refunded. United States v. Wurts, 303 U.S. 414, 58 S.Ct. 637, 639, 82 L.Ed. 932.

Refund, *v.* To repay or restore; to return money in restitution or repayment; *e.g.* to refund overpaid taxes; to refund purchase price of returned goods. See also **Rebate; Refund claim; Refunds.**

To fund again or anew; specifically, finance, to borrow, usually by the sale of bonds, in order to pay off an existing loan with the proceeds. Street Improvement Dist. No. 315 v. Arkansas Highway Commission, 190 Ark. 1045, 83 S.W.2d 81, 82. See also **Recapitalization; Refinance.**

Refund annuity contract. A contract by which an insurance company agrees to repay to the annuitant, in installments during his life, amount paid in by him to company, and if at his death there be a balance unpaid, to pay that balance to person designated by annuitant. In re Atkins' Estate, 129 N.J.Eq. 186, 18 A.2d 45, 49.

Refund claim. A request directed to the Internal Revenue Service for repayment (*i.e.* refund) of taxes overpaid.

Refunding. Type of refinancing (*q.v.*) in which the issuer of bonds replaces outstanding bonds with a new issue. In general, any act of repayment of a loan or money advanced. See also **Recapitalization; Refinance.**

Refunding bond. A bond which replaces or pays off outstanding bond which holder surrenders in exchange for new security. Fore v. Alabama State Bridge Corporation, 242 Ala. 455, 6 So.2d 508, 512. Also a bond given to an executor by a legatee, upon receiving payment of the legacy, conditioned to *refund* the same, or so much of it as may be necessary, if the assets prove deficient.

Refunds. Money received by the government or its officers which, for any cause, are to be refunded or restored to the parties paying them; such as excessive duties or taxes, duties paid on goods destroyed by accident, duties received on goods which are re-exported, etc. See also **Rebate; Refund.**

Refusal. The act of one who has, by law, a right and power of having or doing something of advantage, and declines it. Also, the declination of a request or demand, or the omission to comply with some requirement of law, as the result of a positive intention to disobey. In the latter sense, the word is often coupled with "neglect," as if a party shall "neglect or refuse" to pay a tax, file an official bond, obey an order of court, etc. But "neglect" signifies a. mere omission of a duty, which may happen through inattention, dilatoriness, mistake, or inability to perform, while "refusal" implies the positive denial of an application or command, or at least a mental determination not to comply. A rejection, a denial of what is asked. Board of Public Instruction of Palm Beach County, Fla. v. Cohen, C.A.Fla., 413 F.2d 1201, 1203. See also **Renunciation; Repudiation; Rescind.**

Refuse, *v.* /rəfyúwz/. To deny, decline, reject. "Fail" is distinguished from "refuse" in that "refuse" involves an act of the will, while "fail" may be an act of inevitable necessity. Maestas v. American Metal Co. of New Mexico, 37 N.M. 203, 20 P.2d 924, 928.

Refuse, *n.* /réfyuws/. That which is refused or rejected as useless or worthless. Worthless matter, rubbish, scum, leavings. In statute prohibiting discharge into navigable waters of refuse, "refuse" includes all foreign suabstances and pollutants other than liquid sewage. U. S. v. Kennebec Log-Driving Co., D.C.Me., 399 F.Supp. 754, 757.

Refutantia /rèfyuwtǽnsh(iy)ə/. In old English law, an acquittance or acknowledgment of renouncing all future claim.

Regale episcoporum /rəgéyliy əpìskəpórəm/. The temporal rights and privileges of a bishop.

Regalia /rəgéyl(i)yə/. An abbreviation of *"jura regalia,"* royal rights, or those rights which a King or Queen has by virtue of his or her prerogative, comprising: power of judicature; power of life and death; power of war and peace; masterless goods; assessments; minting of money. Owners of counties palatine were formerly said to have *"jura regalia"* in their counties as fully as the king in his palace. 1 Bl. Comm. 117. The term is sometimes used in the same sense in the Spanish law.

Regalia facere /rəgéyl(i)yə fǽsəriy/. To do homage or fealty to the sovereign by a bishop when he is invested with the regalia.

Regard. In old English law, inspection; supervision. Also a reward, fee, or perquisite.

Regardant /rəgárdənt/. A term which was applied, in feudal law, to a villein annexed to a manor, and having charge to do all base services within the same, and to see the same freed from all things that might annoy his lord. Such a villein *regardant* was thus opposed to a villein *en gros*, who was transferable by deed from one owner to another.

Regarder of a forest. An ancient officer of the forest, whose duty it was to take a view of the forest hunts, and to inquire concerning trespasses, offenses, etc.

Regard of the forest. In old English law, the oversight or inspection of it, or the office and province of the regarder, who is to go through the whole forest, and every bailiwick in it, before the holding of the sessions of the forest, or justice-seat, to see and inquire after trespassers, and for the survey of dogs.

Rege inconsulto /ríyjiy ìnkən(t)sóltow/. Lat. In old English law, a writ issued from the sovereign to the judges, not to proceed in a cause which may prejudice the crown, until advised.

Regency. Rule; government; kingship; office or government of regent, or body of regents, during rule of regent. The man or body of men intrusted with the vicarious government of a kingdom during the minority, absence, insanity, or other disability of the King.

Regent. A governor or ruler. One who vicariously administers the government of a kingdom, in the name of the king, during the latter's minority or other disability.

A master, governor, director, or superintendent of a public institution, particularly a college or university. Board of Regents is the governing body of a state university or college system.

In the canon law, it signifies a master or professor of a college.

Reg. gen. An abbreviation of *"Regula Generalis,"* a general rule (of court).

Regia dignitas est indivisibilis, et quælibet alia derivativa dignitas est similiter indivisibilis /ríyj(iy)ə dígnətæs èst ìndəvəzíbələs èt kwíyləbəd éyl(i)yə dərìvətáyvə dígnətæs èst səmílədər ìndəvəzíbələs/. The kingly power is indivisible, and every other derivative power is similarly indivisible.

Regicide /réjəsàyd/ríy°/. The murder of a sovereign; also the person who commits such murder.

Regidor /rèyhiydór/. In Spanish law, one of a body, never exceeding twelve, who formed a part of the *ayuntamiento*. The office of regidor was held for life; that is to say, during the pleasure of the supreme authority. In most places the office was purchased; in some cities, however, they were elected by persons of the district, called *"capitulares."*

Régime /reyzhíym/. In French law, a system of rules or regulations.

Régime dotal /reyzhíym dowtál/. The *dot*, being the property which the wife brings to the husband as her contribution to the support of the burdens of the marriage, and which may either extend as well to future as to present property, or be expressly confined to the present property of the wife, is subject to certain regulations which are summarized in the phrase *"régime dotal."* The husband has the entire administration during the marriage; but, as a rule, where the *dot* consists of immovables, neither the husband nor the wife, nor both of them together, can either sell or mortgage it. The *dot* is returnable upon the dissolution of the marriage, whether by death or otherwise.

Régime en communauté /reyzhíym on komyùwnowtéy/. The community of interests between husband and wife which arises upon their marriage. It is either (1) legal or (2) conventional, the former existing in the absence of any "agreement" properly so called, and arising from a mere declaration of community; the latter arising from an "agreement," properly so called.

Regimiento /rèyhiymyéntow/. In Spanish law, the body of regidores, who never exceeded twelve, forming a part of the municipal council, or *ayuntamiento*, in every capital of a jurisdiction.

Regina /rəjáynə/. Lat. The Queen.

Regio assensu /ríyj(iy)ow əsén(t)s(y)uw/. A writ whereby the sovereign gives his assent to the election of a bishop.

Register, *v.* To record formally and exactly; to enroll; to enter precisely in a list or the like. Los Angeles County v. Craig, 38 Cal.App.2d 58, 100 P.2d 818, 820.

To make correspond exactly one with another; to fit correctly in a relative position; to be in correct alignment one with another. Cover v. Schwartz, Cust. & Pat.App., 28 C.C.P.A. 831, 116 F.2d 512, 515. See also **Record.**

Register, n. An officer authorized by law to keep a record called a "register" or "registry."

A book of public facts such as births, deaths and marriages (also called a registry), or the public official who keeps such book. Other examples of public record books are the register of patents (a list of all patents granted) and the register of ships (kept by customs). Other examples of public record keeping officials are the register of copyrights, register of deeds (land records) and the register of wills (clerk of probate court). They are often called "Recorder" or "Registrar."

See also **Federal Register.**

Registered. Entered or recorded in some official register or record or list.

Registered bond. A bond entered on the books of the issuing corporation or of its transfer agent in the name of the purchaser, whose name also appears on the face of the bonds. Either principal alone or both principal and interest may be registered.

A bond the number of which is recorded by the seller in the name of the purchaser and which only the latter, or one legally authorized to act for him, can redeem. Principal of such a bond and interest, if registered as to interest, is paid to the owner listed on the books of the issuer, as opposed to a bearer bond where the possessor of the bond is entitled to interest and principal.

The bonds of the United States government (and of many municipal and private corporations) are either registered or "coupon bonds." In the case of a registered bond, the name of the owner or lawful holder is entered in a register or record, and it is not negotiable or transferable except by an entry on the register, and checks or warrants are sent to the registered holder for the successive installments of interest as they fall due. A bond with interest coupons attached is transferable by mere delivery, and the coupons are payable, as due, to the person who shall present them for payment. But the bond issues of many private corporations now provide that the individual bonds "may be registered as to principal," leaving the interest coupons payable to bearer, or that they may be registered as to both principal and interest, at the option of the holder.

Registered check. A check purchased by a person at a bank and drawn on funds of the bank, though not certified by the bank.

Registered mail. Type of special mailing privilege given by the U.S. Postal Service for an extra fee and which provides insurance of its delivery up to certain amount.

Registered representative. A person who has met the qualifications set by law or regulation to sell securities to the public.

Registered tonnage. The registered tonnage of a vessel is the capacity or cubical contents of the ship, or the amount of weight which she will carry, as ascertained in some proper manner and entered on an official register or record.

Registered trade-mark. A trade-mark filed in the United States Patent and Trademark office, with the necessary description and other statements required by the act of congress, and there duly recorded, securing its exclusive use to the person causing it to be registered. 18 U.S.C.A. § 1051.

Registered voters. Persons whose names are placed upon the registration books provided by law as the record or memorial of the duly qualified voters of the state or county. See also **Qualified voter.**

Register in bankruptcy. An officer of the courts of bankruptcy, under the earlier acts of congress in that behalf, having substantially the same powers and duties as the "referees in bankruptcy" under the Act of 1898 (11 U.S.C.A.). See **Referee in bankruptcy.**

Register of deeds. The name given in some states to the officer whose duty is to record deeds, mortgages, and other instruments affecting realty in the official books provided and kept for that purpose; also commonly called "registrar" or "recorder" of deeds.

Register of land office. Formerly, a federal officer appointed for each federal land district, to take charge of the local records and attend to the preliminary matters connected with the sale, preemption, or other disposal of the public lands within the district.

Register of ships. A register kept by the collectors of customs, in which the names, ownership, and other facts relative to merchant vessels are required by law to be entered. This register is evidence of the nationality and privileges of an American ship. The certificate of such registration, given by the collector to the owner or master of the ship, is also called the ship's register.

Register of the Treasury. An officer of the United States Treasury, whose duty is to keep all accounts of the receipt and expenditure of public money and of debts due to or from the United States, to preserve adjusted accounts with vouchers and certificates, to record warrants drawn upon the treasury, to sign and issue government securities, and take charge of the registry of vessels under United States laws. 31 U.S.C.A. § 161.

Register of wills. An officer in some of the states, whose function is to record and preserve all wills admitted to probate, to issue letters testamentary or of administration, to receive and file accounts of executors, etc., and generally to act as the clerk of the probate court.

Register's court. A court, formerly in the state of Pennsylvania which had jurisdiction in matters of probate. See **Orphan's Courts.**

Registrant. One who registers; particularly, one who registers anything (*e.g.*, a trademark) for the purpose of securing a right or privilege granted by law on condition of such registration.

Registrar /réjəstràr/. An officer who has the custody and charge of keeping of a registry or register. Person in educational institution in charge of registering students for enrollment. Person in hospital responsible for admitting of patients.

An agent, usually a bank or trust company, appointed by a corporation to keep track of the names of stockholders and distributions of earnings.

Registrarius /rèjəstrér(i)yəs/. In old English law, a notary; a registrar or register.

Registrar of deeds. A term used in some states to describe the person in charge of recorded instruments affecting land title. Also commonly called a recorder or register (q.v.).

Registration. Recording; enrolling; inserting in an official register. Enrollment, as registration of voters, registration for school, etc. The act of making a list, catalogue, schedule, or register, particularly of an official character, or of making entries therein.

Any schedule containing a list of voters, the being upon which constitutes a prerequisite to vote.

Securities. Statutory procedure requiring the filing with the S.E.C. of various documents including a prospectus in order for securities to be publicly offered. Clearance must be obtained from the S.E.C. before the securities may be sold. There is no ceiling relative to the number of shares or dollar amount that may be registered. See also **Registration statement.**

Registration of stock. Recording in the official books of the company of the name and address of the holder of each certificate of stock, with the date of its issue, and, in the case of a transfer of stock from one holder to another, the names of both parties and such other details as will identify the transaction and preserve an official record of its essential facts. Such information is required for paying of dividends; mailing of proxies, annual reports, etc.

Registration statement. Statement required by the Securities Act of 1933 of most companies wishing to issue securities to the public or by the Securities Exchange Act of 1934 of a company wishing to have its securities traded in public markets. The statement discloses financial data and other items of interest to potential investors. See **Letter of comment.**

Registrum brevium /rəjístrəm bríyv(i)yəm/. The register of writs (q.v.).

Registry. A register, or book authorized or recognized by law, kept for the recording or registration of facts or documents.

The list or record of ships subject to the maritime regulations of a particular country. The listing of a vessel at a custom house under the name of the country whose flag it flies, though such flag is not necessarily indicative of the nationality of the owner. Generally, "registry" applies to vessels in foreign commerce, whereas "enrollment" refers to coastwise navigation. R. C. Craig Limited v. Ships of Sea Inc., D.C.Ga., 345 F.Supp. 1066, 1070.

Registry of deeds. See **Register of deeds; Registrar of deeds.**

Reg. Jud. An abbreviation of *"Registrum Judiciale,"* the register of judicial writs.

Reg. Lib. An abbreviation of *"Registrarii Liber,"* the register's book in chancery, containing all decrees.

Regnal years /régnəl yírz/. Statutes of the British parliament are usually cited by the name and year of the sovereign in whose reign they were enacted, and the successive years of the reign of any king or queen are denominated the "regnal years."

Regnant /régnənt/. One having authority as a king; one in the exercise of royal authority.

Reg. Orig. An abbreviation of *"Registrum Originale,"* the register of original writs.

Reg. Pl. An abbreviation of *"Regula Placitandi,"* rule of pleading.

Regrant /rìygrǽnt/. In the English law of real property, when, after a person has made a grant, the property granted comes back to him (*e.g.,* by escheat or forfeiture), and he grants it again, he is said to regrant it. The phrase is chiefly used in the law of copyholds.

Regrating. In old English law, the offense of buying or getting into one's hands at a fair or market any provisions, corn, or other dead victual, with the intention of selling the same again in the same fair or market, or in some other within four miles thereof, at a higher price. The offender was termed a "regrator."

Regress. To return, go back or re-enter. Used principally in the phrase "free entry, egress, and regress" but it is also used to signify the reentry of a person who has been disseised of land.

Regressive tax. A tax levied at rates which increase less rapidly than the increase of the tax base, thus bearing more heavily on poorer taxpayers. Tax for which the rate decreases as the taxed base, such as income, increases. Contrast with progressive tax.

Regs. An abbreviation for U.S. Treasury Department Regulations. See **Regulations.**

Regula /régyələ/. Lat. A rule. *Regula generalis,* a general rule; a standing rule or order of a court. Frequently abbreviated *"Reg. Gen."*

Regulæ generales /régyəliy jènəréyliyz/. Lat. General rules, which the courts promulgate from time to time for the regulation of their practice.

Regula est, juris quidem ignorantiam cuique nocere, facti vero ignorantiam non nocere /régyələ èst, júrəs kwáydəm ìgnərǽnshiyəm k(yuw)áykwiy nəsériy, fǽktay vírow ìgnərǽnsh(iy)əm nòn nəsériy/. It is a rule, that every one is prejudiced by his ignorance of law, but not by his ignorance of fact.

Regula pro lege, si deficit lex /régyələ pròw líyjiy, sày défəsət léks/. In default of the law, the maxim rules.

Regular. Conformable to law. Steady or uniform in course, practice, or occurrence; not subject to unexplained or irrational variation. Usual, customary or general. Gerald v. American Cas. Co. of Reading, Pa., D.C.N.C., 249 F.Supp. 355, 357. Made according to rule, duly authorized, formed after uniform type; built or arranged according to established plan, law, or principle. Antonyn of "casual" or "occasional." Palle v. Industrial Commission, 79 Utah 47, 7 P.2d 284, 290.

As to regular Clergy; Deposit; Election; Indorsement; Meeting; Navigation; Process; Session, and Term, see those titles.

Regular and established place of business. Under Judicial Code, § 48 (28 U.S.C.A. §§ 1400, 1694), permitting patent infringement suits to be brought in the district in which defendant committed acts of infringement and has a regular and established place of business, a "regular" place of business is one where business is carried on regularly, and not temporarily, or for some special work or particular transaction, while an "established" place of business must be a permanent place of business, and a "regular and established place of business" is one where the same business in kind, if not in degree, as that done at the home office or principal place of business, is carried on. A foreign corporation may have a "regular and established place of business" although business therein is merely securing orders and forwarding them to the home office. Shelton v. Schwartz, C.C.A. Ill., 131 F.2d 805, 808.

Regular course of business. This phrase within worker's compensation acts excluding from their benefits person whose employment is not in regular course of business of employer, refers to habitual or regular occupation that party is engaged in with view of winning livelihood or some gain, excluding incidental or occasional operations arising out of transaction of that business; to normal operations which constitute business.

Term used in connection with books and records kept by a business and which are admissible in evidence if the court finds as a preliminary matter that the entries therein were made in good faith, before the action was commenced, and that such records are part of the customary operation of the business.

A memorandum, report, record, or data compilation, in any form, of acts, events, conditions, opinions, or diagnoses, made at or near the time by, or from information transmitted by, a person with knowledge, if kept in the course of a regularly conducted business activity, and if it was the regular practice of that business activity to make the memorandum, report, record, or data compilation, all as shown by the testimony of the custodian or other qualified witness, is not excluded by the hearsay rule, unless the source of information or the method or circumstances of preparation indicate lack of trustworthiness. Fed.Evid.R. 803(6).

Term is also descriptive of sales which are ordinarily made by a business in contrast to a bulk sale.

Regular entries. Entries made in books of account in regular course of business. See also **Regular course of business.**

Regulariter non valet pactum de re mea non alienanda /règyəlérədər nòn vǽlət pǽktəm dìy ríy míyə nòn èyliyənǽndə/. It is a rule that a compact not to alienate my property is not binding.

Regularly /régyələrliy/. At fixed and certain intervals, regular in point of time. In accordance with some consistent or periodical rule or practice.

Regular on its face. Process is "regular on its face" when it proceeds from a court, officer, or body having authority of law to issue process of that nature, and is legal in form and contains nothing to notify or fairly apprise any one that it is issued without authority.

Regulate. To fix, establish, or control; to adjust by rule, method, or established mode; to direct by rule or restriction; to subject to governing principles or laws. The power of Congress to regulate commerce is the power to enact all appropriate legislation for its protection or advancement; to adopt measures to promote its growth and insure its safety; to foster, protect, control, and restrain. Virginian Ry. Co. v. System Federation No. 40, Railway Employees Department of American Federation of Labor, C.C.A. Va., 84 F.2d 641, 650. It is also power to prescribe rule by which commerce is to be governed, and embraces prohibitory regulations. United States v. Darby, 312 U.S. 100, 657, 61 S.Ct. 451, 456, 85 L.Ed. 609. Regulate means to govern or direct according to rule or to bring under control of constituted authority, to limit and prohibit, to arrange in proper order, and to control that which already exists. Farmington River Co. v. Town Plan and Zoning Commission of Town of Farmington, 25 Conn.Sup. 125, 197 A.2d 653, 660.

Regulation. The act of regulating; a rule or order prescribed for management or government; a regulating principle; a precept. Rule of order prescribed by superior or competent authority relating to action of those under its control. Regulation is rule or order having force of law issued by executive authority of government. State ex rel. Villines v. Freeman, Okl., 370 P.2d 307, 309. See **Regulations.**

Regulation A. This SEC regulation covers exemption from registration filing requirements for certain securities offerings under a stated amount. Securities Act of 1933, 15 U.S.C.A. § 77c(b).

Regulation Z. Regulations of Federal Reserve Board which implement provisions of Federal Truth-in-Lending Act. See **Truth-in-Lending Act.**

Regulation charge. Charge exacted for privilege or as condition precedent to carrying on business. See also **Privilege** (*Privilege tax*).

Regulation of an executive department. The general rules relating to the subject on which a department acts, made by the head of the department under some act of Congress conferring power to make such regulations, and thereby give to them the force of law. State ex rel. Kaser v. Leonard, 164 Or. 579, 102 P.2d 197.

Regulations. Such are issued by various governmental departments to carry out the intent of the law. Agencies issue regulations to guide the activity of those regulated by the agency and of their own employees and to ensure uniform application of the law. Regulations are not the work of the legislature and do not have the effect of law in theory. In practice, however, because of the intricacies of judicial review of administrative action, regulations can have an important effect in determining the outcome of cases involving regulatory activity. United States Government regulations appear first in the *Federal Register*, published five days a week, and are subsequently arranged by subject in the *Code of Federal Regulations.*

Treasury Regulations. Treasury Department Regulations represent the position of the Internal Revenue Service as to how the Internal Revenue Code is to be interpreted. Their purpose is to provide taxpayers and I.R.S. personnel with rules of general and specific application to the various provisions of the tax law. Regulations are published in the Federal Register and in tax services.

Truth-in-Lending Act. See **Regulation Z.**

Rehabilitation. Investing or clothing again with some right, authority, or dignity. Restoring to a former capacity; reinstating; qualifying again. In re Coleman, D.C.Ky., 21 F.Supp. 923, 924, 925. For rehabilitation of debtor, see **Wage earner's plan.**

Alimony. Term "rehabilitative alimony" contemplates sums necessary to assist a divorced person in regaining a useful and constructive role in society through vocational or therapeutic training or retraining and for the further purpose of preventing financial hardship on society or individual during the rehabilitative process. Mertz v. Mertz, Fla.App., 287 So.2d 691, 692.

Corporation. Attempt to conserve and administer assets of insolvent corporation in hope of its eventual return from financial stress to solvency. In re Title & Mortgage Guarantee Co. of Buffalo, 152 Misc. 428, 274 N.Y.S. 270. Contemplates continuance of corporate life and activities, and its effort to restore and reinstate corporation to former condition of successful operation and solvency. New York Title & Mortgage Co. v. Friedman, 153 Misc. 697, 276 N.Y.S. 72. See Bankruptcy Act, Ch. 11 (11 U.S.C.A.). See also **Reorganization.**

Witness. After cross examination, a witness whose credibility has suffered may be examined again (redirect examination) to improve his standing with the trier of fact in matters covered on cross examination. See Fed.Evid.R. 608(a).

Rehearing. Second consideration of cause for purpose of calling to court's or administrative board's attention any error, omission, or oversight in first consideration. A retrial of issues and presumes notice to parties entitled thereto and opportunity for them to be heard. Yee v. State Board of Equalization of California, 16 Cal.App.2d 417, 60 P.2d 322, 323. Administrative decisions and determinations in social security cases may be reopened for "good cause" and other specified grounds. See also **Retrial.**

Rehypothecation. To pledge to another or to transfer to another a note or goods which have been pledged; *e.g.* a broker may pledge securities pledged to him by a customer to finance his borrowings from a bank.

Reif /ríyf/. A robbery.

Rei interventus /ríyay ìntərvéntəs/. Lat. Things intervening; that is, things done by one of the parties to a contract, in the faith of its validity, and with the assent of the other party, and which have so affected his situation that the other will not be allowed to repudiate his obligation, although originally it was imperfect.

Reimburse. To pay back, to make restoration, to repay that expended; to indemnify, or make whole. Los Angeles County v. Frisbie, 19 Cal.2d 634, 122 P.2d 526. See also **Restitution.**

Reincorporation. A new incorporation of a business which had already been incorporated. Also, a new incorporation of a document by reference which had previously been incorporated by reference but subsequently disassociated.

Reinstate. To reinstall; to reestablish; to place again in a former state, condition, or office; to restore to a state or position from which the object or person had been removed. Lowry v. Aetna Life Ins. Co., Tex.Civ. App., 120 S.W.2d 505, 507.

Reinstate a case. To place case again in same position as before dismissal. United States v. Green, C.C.A. Mont., 107 F.2d 19, 22.

Reinstatement. In insurance, a restoration of the insured's rights under a policy which has lapsed or been cancelled. To reinstate a policy holder or one who has allowed his policy to lapse does not mean new insurance or taking out a new policy, but does mean that the insured has been restored to all the benefits accruing to him under the policy contract, the original policy. See also **Reinstate.**

Reinsurance. A contract by which an insurer procures a third person to insure him against loss or liability by reason of original insurance. A contract that one insurer makes with another to protect the latter from a risk already assumed. It binds the reinsurer to pay to the reinsured the whole loss sustained in respect to the subject of the insurance to the extent to which he is reinsured. Also the substitution, with the consent of the insured, of a second insurer for the first, so that the original insurer is released.

An agreement to indemnify the assured, partially or altogether, against a risk assumed by it in policy issued to third party. Great American Ins. Co. v. Fireman's Fund Ins. Co., C.A.N.Y., 481 F.2d 948, 950. A contract that one insurer makes with another to protect the first insurer from a risk he has already assumed. McDonough Const. Corp. v. Pan Am. Sur. Co., Fla.App., 190 So.2d 617, 619.

Reinsured. An insurer who is insured against loss under its policies.

Reinsurer. An insurance carrier which insures insurers.

Reintegration. The restoration of a part to the whole after separation. Term may be used in connection with documents to be read or understood together.

Reipublicæ interest voluntates defunctorum effectum sortiri /rìyaypábləsiy íntərèst vòləntéydiyz diyfə̀ŋktórəm əféktəm sortáyray/. It concerns the state that the wills of the dead should have their effect.

Reissuable notes. Bank-notes which, after having been once paid, may again be put into circulation.

REIT. Real Estate Investment Trust.

Rei turpis nullum mandatum est /ríyay tə́rpəs nə́ləm mændéydəm èst/. The mandate of an immoral thing is void. A contract of mandate requiring an illegal or immoral act to be done has no legal obligation.

Rejection. See **Non-acceptance; Refusal; Repudiation; Rescind.**

Rejoin. In common-law pleading, to answer a plaintiff's replication in an action at law, by some matter of fact.

Rejoinder. In common-law pleading, the second pleading on the part of the defendant, being his answer to the plaintiff's replication.

Rejoining gratis /rəjóyniŋ gréydəs/. In common law pleading, rejoining voluntarily, or without being required to do so by a rule to rejoin. When a defendant was under terms to rejoin *gratis*, he had to deliver a rejoinder, without putting the plaintiff to the necessity and expense of obtaining a rule to rejoin.

Relate. To stand in some relation; to have bearing or concern; to pertain; refer; to bring into association with or connection with; with "to."

Related. Standing in relation; connected; allied; akin. Nowland Realty Co. v. Commissioner of Internal Revenue, C.C.A.7, 47 F.2d 1018, 1021. Goods are "related" for trademark purposes if they are used in conjunction with one another or are associated together in some way in the minds of the consuming public. Alfred Dunhill of London, Inc. v. Kasser Distillers Products Corp., D.C.Pa., 350 F.Supp. 1341, 1352. See also **Relative.**

Related claim. Within statute permitting joinder of claim for unfair competition with substantial and related claim under patent laws is claim resting on substantially identical facts. Lyon v. General Motors Corp., D.C.Ill., 200 F.Supp. 89, 91.

Related party transactions. The tax law places restrictions upon the recognition of gains and losses between related parties due to the potential for abuse. For example, restrictions are placed upon the deduction of losses from the sale or exchange of property between related parties. A related party includes a corporation which is controlled by the taxpayer. I.R.C. § 267.

Relatio est fictio juris et intenta ad unum /rəléysh(iy)ow èst fíksh(iy)ow júrəs èd əntént ǽd yúwnəm/. Relation is a fiction of law, and intended for one thing.

Relation. A relative or kinsman; a person connected by consanguinity. A person connected with another by blood or affinity. Liprie v. Michigan Millers Mut. Ins. Co., La.App., 143 So.2d 597, 600.

The words "relatives" and "relations," in their primary sense, are broad enough to include any one connected by blood or affinity, even to the remotest degree, but where used in wills, as defining and determining legal succession, are construed to include only those persons who are entitled to share in the estate as next of kin under the statute of distributions.

The connection of two persons, or their situation with respect to each other, who are associated, whether by the law, by their own agreement, or by kinship, in some social *status* or union for the purposes of domestic life; as the relation of guardian and ward, husband and wife, master and servant, parent and child; so in the phrase "domestic relations."

The doctrine of "relation" is that principle by which an act done at one time is considered by a fiction of law to have been done at some antecedent period. It is usually applied where several proceedings are essential to complete a particular transaction, such as a conveyance or deed. The last proceeding which consummates the conveyance is held for certain purposes to take effect by relation as of the day when the first proceeding was had. Knapp v. Alexander-Edgar Lumber Co., 237 U.S. 162, 35 S.Ct. 515, 517, 59 L.Ed. 894; U. S. v. Anderson, 194 U.S. 394, 24 S.Ct. 716, 48 L.Ed. 1035. See also **Relation back.**

A recital, account, narrative of facts; information given. Thus, suits by *quo warranto* are entitled "on the relation of" a private person, who is called the "relator." But in this connection the word seems also to involve the idea of the suggestion, instigation, or instance of the relator.

See also **Blood relations; Kin or kindred; Relative.**

Relation back. General rule of "relation back" is that a pleading may not be amended to allege a new or different claim or defense unless it arose out of, or is based on or related to, claim, transaction or occurrence originally set forth or attempted to be set forth. Harastej v. Reliable Car Rental, Inc., D.C.Puerto Rico, 58 F.R.D. 197, 198. See also *Amended pleadings, infra.*

A principle that an act done today is considered to have been done at an earlier time. A document held in escrow and finally delivered is deemed to have been delivered as of the time at which it was escrowed.

Amended pleadings. Whenever the claim or defense asserted in the amended pleading arose out of the conduct, transaction, or occurrence set forth or attempted to be set forth in the original pleading, the amendment relates back to the date of the original pleading. Fed.R.Civil P. 15(c).

Relations. A term which, in its widest sense, includes all the kindred of the person spoken of.

Relatio semper fiat ut valeat dispositio /rəléysh(iy)ow sémpər fáyəd ət vǽliyət dìspəzísh(iy)ow/. Reference should always be had in such a manner that a disposition in a will may avail.

Relative. A kinsman; a person connected with another by blood or affinity. When used generically, includes persons connected by ties of affinity as well as consanguinity, and, when used with a restrictive meaning, refers to those only who are connected by blood.

Individual related by affinity or consanguinity within the third degree as determined by the common law, or individual in a step or adoptive relationship within such third degree. Bankruptcy Act, § 101(34).

A person or thing having relation or connection with some other person or thing; as, relative rights, relative powers, *infra.* See also **Relation.**

Relative confession. See **Confession.**

Relative convenience doctrine. Equity may refuse an injunction or other equitable relief if the inconvenience to one party is great while to the other party there is little or no inconvenience. Duke v. Crossfield, 241 Mo.App. 579, 240 S.W.2d 180.

Relative fact. In the law of evidence, a fact having relation to another fact; a minor fact; a circumstance.

Relative powers. Those which relate to land; so called to distinguish them from those which are collateral to it.

Relative rights. Those rights of persons which are incident to them as members of society, and standing in various relations to each other. Those rights of persons in private life which arise from the civil and domestic relations.

Relativorum, cognito uno, cognoscitur et alterum /rèlədəvórəm, kógnədow yúwnow, kəgnósədər èd óltərəm/. Of relatives, one being known, the other is also known.

Relator. An informer. The person upon whose complaint, or at whose instance certain writs are issued such as information or writ of *quo warranto,* and who is *quasi* the plaintiff in the proceeding. For example if John Smith is the relator and Jones is the defendant, the citation would read, State ex rel. John Smith v. Jones. A party in interest who is permitted to institute a proceeding in the name of the People or the Attorney General when the right to sue resides solely in that official. Veterans' Industries, Inc., of Long Beach, Cal. v. Lynch, 8 Cal.App.3d 902, 88 Cal.Rptr. 303, 317. See also **Ex relatione.**

Relatrix /rəléytrəks/. A female relator or petitioner.

Relaxatio /rèlækséysh(iy)ow/. In old conveyancing, a release; an instrument by which a person relinquishes to another his right in anything.

Release, *v.* To discharge a claim one has against another, as for example in a tort case the plaintiff may discharge the liability of the defendant in return for a cash settlement. To lease again or grant new lease. See **Accord and satisfaction.**

Release, *n.* The relinquishment, concession, or giving up of a right, claim, or privilege, by the person in whom it exists or to whom it accrues, to the person against whom it might have been demanded or enforced. Abandonment of claim to party against whom it exists, and is a surrender of a cause of action and may be gratuitous or for consideration. Melo v. National Fuse & Powder Co., D.C.Colo., 267 F.Supp. 611, 612. Giving up or abandoning of claim or right to person against whom claim exists or against whom right is to be exercised. Adder v. Holman & Moody, Inc., 288 N.C. 484, 219 S.E.2d 190, 195.

A discharge of a debt by act of party, as distinguished from an extinguishment which is a discharge by operation of law, and, in distinguishing release from receipt, "receipt" is evidence that an obligation has been discharged, but "release" is itself a discharge of it. Glickman v. Weston, 140 Or. 117, 11 P.2d 281, 284.

An *express* release is one directly made in terms by deed or other suitable means. An *implied* release is one which arises from acts of the creditor or owner, without any express agreement. A *release by operation of law* is one which, though not expressly made, the law presumes in consequence of some act of the releasor; for instance, when one of several joint obli-

gors is expressly released, the others are also released by operation of law.

Liberation, discharge, or setting free from restraint or confinement. Thus, a man unlawfully imprisoned may obtain his *release* on *habeas corpus.* See also **Bail.**

The abandonment to (or by) a person called as a witness in a suit of his interest in the subject-matter of the controversy, in order to qualify him to testify, under the common-law rule.

A receipt or certificate given by a ward to the guardian, on the final settlement of the latter's accounts, or by any other beneficiary on the termination of the trust administration, relinquishing all and any further rights, claims, or demands, growing out of the trust or incident to it.

In admiralty actions, when a ship, cargo, or other property has been arrested, the owner may obtain its release by giving bail, or paying the value of the property into court.

The conveyance of a person's interest or right which he has in a thing to another that has the possession thereof or some estate therein. The relinquishment of some right or benefit to a person who has already some interest in the property, and such interest as qualifies him for receiving or availing himself of the right or benefit so relinquished.

Conditional release. See that title.

Deed of release. A deed operating by way of release; but more specifically, in those states where deeds of trust are in use instead of common-law mortgages, as a means of pledging real property as security for the payment of a debt, a "deed of release" is a conveyance in fee, executed by the trustee or trustees, to the grantor in the deed of trust, which conveys back to him the legal title to the estate, and which is to be given on satisfactory proof that he has paid the secured debt in full or otherwise complied with the terms of the deed of trust.

Release by way of enlarging an estate. A conveyance of the ulterior interest in lands to the particular tenant; as, if there be tenant for life or years, remainder to another in fee, and he in remainder releases all his right to the particular tenant and his heirs, this gives him the estate in fee. 2 Bl.Comm. 324.

Release by way of entry and feoffment. If there be two joint disseisors, and the disseisee releases to one of them, he shall be sole seised, and shall keep out his former companion; which is the same in effect as if the disseisee had entered and thereby put an end to the disseisin, and afterwards had enfeoffed one of the disseisors in fee. 2 Bl.Comm. 325.

Release by way of extinguishment. If my tenant for life makes a lease to A. for life, remainder to B. and his heirs, and I release to A., this extinguishes my right to the reversion, and shall inure to the advantage of B.'s remainder, as well as of A.'s particular estate. 2 Bl.Comm. 325.

Release by way of passing an estate. As, where one or two coparceners releases all her right to the other, this passes the fee-simple of the whole. 2 Bl.Comm. 324, 325.

Release by way of passing a right. If a man be disseised and releaseth to his disseisor all his right, hereby the disseisor acquires a new right, which changes the quality of his estate, and renders that lawful which before was tortious or wrongful. 2 Bl.Comm. 325.

Release of dower. The relinquishment by a married woman of her expectant dower interest or estate in a particular parcel of realty belonging to her husband, as, by joining with him in a conveyance of it to a third person.

Release of mortgage. A written document which discharges the obligation of a mortgage upon payment and which is given by mortgagee to mortgagor or holder of equity and recorded in the office where deeds and other instruments of conveyance are recorded.

Release to uses. The conveyance by a deed of release to one party to the use of another is so termed. Thus, when a conveyance of lands was effected, by those instruments of assurance termed a lease and release, from A. to B. and his heirs, to the use of C. and his heirs, in such case C. at once took the whole fee-simple in such lands; B. by the operation of the statute of uses, being made a mere conduit-pipe for conveying the estate to C.

Releasee. The person to whom a release is made.

Release on own recognizance. Release of a defendant on personal recognizance when, having acquired control over his person, the court permits him to be at liberty during the pendency of the criminal action or proceeding upon his written promise to appear whenever his attendance before court may be required and to render himself amenable to the orders and processes of the court. Abbreviated R.O.R.

Releaser, or **releasor.** The maker of a release.

Relegatio /rèləgéysh(iy)ow/. Lat. A kind of banishment known to the civil law, which differed from *"deportatio"* in leaving to the person his rights of citizenship.

Relegation. In old English law, banishment for a time only.

Relevancy /réləvən(t)siy/. Applicability to the issue joined. That quality of evidence which renders it properly applicable in determining the truth and falsity of the matters in issue between the parties to a suit. Two facts are said to be relevant to each other when so related that according to the common course of events, one either taken by itself or in connection with other facts, proves or renders probable the past, present, or future existence or non-existence of the other.

Relevancy is that which conduces to the proof of a pertinent hypothesis; a pertinent hypothesis being one which, if sustained, would logically influence the issue. Hampton v. State, 126 Tex.Cr.R. 211, 70 S.W.2d 1001. Relevant evidence is such evidence as relates to, or bears directly upon, the point or fact in issue, and proves or has a tendency to prove the proposition alleged; evidence which conduces to prove a pertinent theory in a case. It does not mean evidence addressed with positive directness to the point but that which according to the common course of events either taken by itself or in connection with

other facts, proves or renders probable the past, present or future existence or nonexistence of the other.

Relevancy of evidence refers to its probative value in relation to the purpose for which it is offered. Vine Street Corp. v. City of Council Bluffs, Iowa, 220 N.W.2d 860, 863. Term describes the logical relationship between a proffered item of evidence and a proposition that is material or provable in a given case. U. S. v. Allison, C.A.La., 474 F.2d 286, 289; and means a logical relation between evidence and fact to be established. State v. Whalon, 1 Wash.App. 785, 464 P.2d 730, 735.

See also **Relevant evidence.**

Relevant. Applying to the matter in question; affording something to the purpose. Fact is relevant to another fact when, according to common course of events, existence of one taken alone or in connection with the other fact renders existence of the other certain or more probable. Gulf, C. & S. F. Ry. Co. v. Downs, Tex.Civ.App., 70 S.W.2d 318, 322. See also **Material evidence; Relevancy; Relevant evidence.**

Relevant evidence. Evidence having any tendency to make the existence of any fact that is of consequence to the determination of the action more probable or less probable than it would be without the evidence. Fed.Evid.R. 401.

Basic test for admissibility of evidence is relevancy, and testimony is "relevant" if reasonable inferences can be drawn therefrom regarding or if any light is shed upon, a contested matter. State v. Smith, 5 Wash.App. 237, 487 P.2d 227, 229. Evidence is "relevant" not only when it tends to prove or disprove precise fact in issue but when it tends to establish fact from which existence or nonexistence of fact in issue can be directly inferred. People v. Warner, App., 270 C.A.2d 900, 76 Cal.Rptr. 160, 165.

Relevant market. To establish claim of monopolization or of attempt to monopolize under the Sherman Act, plaintiff must define the "relevant market" within which defendant allegedly possesses monopoly power, and such "relevant market" is the geographic market composed of products that have reasonable interchangeability for purposes for which they are produced, considering their price, use and quality. Tire Sales Corp. v. Cities Service Oil Co., D.C.Ill., 410 F.Supp. 1222, 1230; U. S. v. E. I. DuPont De Nemours & Co., 353 U.S. 586, 77 S.Ct. 872, 1 L.Ed.2d 1057. Term "relevant market", in relation to case involving alleged violation of Sherman Act, consists of both a product market and a geographic market. U. S. v. Otter Tail Power Co., D.C.Minn., 331 F.Supp. 54, 58. See also **Market.**

Reliable. Trustworthy, worthy of confidence.

Reliance. In tort for deceit, it is necessary for plaintiff to prove that he relied on misrepresentation though such misrepresentation need not be the sole or even dominant reason for acting if it was a substantial factor in the plaintiff's decision. For fraud purposes, "reliance" might be defined as a belief which motivates an act. Berry v. Robotka, 9 Ariz.App. 461, 453 P.2d 972, 979.

The test of "reliance" on misrepresentation in sale of stock as ground for recovery under Securities

Exchange Act is whether the misrepresentation is a substantial factor in determining the course of conduct which results in the recipient's loss. Where case involves primarily a failure to disclose, positive proof of reliance is not a prerequisite for recovery; all that is necessary is that the facts withheld be material in sense that reasonable investor might have considered them important in making of such decision. Gordon v. Burr, D.C.N.Y., 366 F.Supp. 156, 165.

Term "reliance" as used in rule imposing liability on one who volunteers to undertake action for the protection of another's person or things for failure to exercise reasonable care if harm is suffered because of the other's reliance upon the undertaking connotes dependence; it bespeaks a voluntary choice of conduct by the person harmed and infers that the person exercising it can decide between available alternatives. Barnum v. Rural Fire Protection Co., 24 Ariz. App. 233, 537 P.2d 618, 622.

See also **Estoppel; Fraud; Material fact; Misrepresentation.**

Reliance on promise. In promissory estoppel, the plaintiff is required to prove that he relied on promise of defendant to his damage. See also **Promissory estoppel.**

Relict /rélǝkt/rǝlíkt/. A widow or widower. The survivor of a pair of married people, whether the survivor is the husband or the wife; it means the relict of the united pair (or of the marriage union), not the relict of the deceased individual.

Relicta verificatione /rǝlíktǝ vèhrǝfǝkèyshiyówniy/. (Lat. his pleading being abandoned.) A confession of judgment made after plea pleaded; viz., a *cognovit actionem* accompanied by a withdrawal of the plea.

Reliction /rǝlíkshǝn/. An increase of the land by the permanent withdrawal or retrocession of the sea or a river. Process of gradual exposure of land by permanent recession of body of water. State Engineer v. Cowles Bros., Inc., 86 Nev. 872, 478 P.2d 159, 161.

Relief. The public or private assistance or support, pecuniary or otherwise, granted to indigent persons.

Deliverance from oppression, wrong, or injustice. In this sense it is used as a general designation of the assistance, redress, or benefit which a complainant seeks at the hands of a court, particularly in equity. It may be thus used of such remedies as specific performance, injunction, or the reformation or rescission of a contract.

See also **Cause of action; Remedy.**

Relieve. To give ease, comfort, or consolation to; to give aid, help, or succor to; alleviate, assuage, ease, mitigate; succor, assist, aid, help; support, sustain; lighten, diminish. Brollier v. Van Alstine, 236 Mo. App. 1233, 163 S.W.2d 109, 115.

To release from a post, station, or duty; to put another in place of, or to take the place of, in the bearing of any burden, or discharge of any duty. Kemp v. Stanley, 204 La. 110, 15 So.2d 1, 11.

Religion. Man's relation to Divinity, to reverence, worship, obedience, and submission to mandates and precepts of supernatural or superior beings. In its broadest sense includes all forms of belief in the existence of superior beings exercising power over human beings by volition, imposing rules of conduct, with future rewards and punishments. Bond uniting man to God, and a virtue whose purpose is to render God worship due him as source of all being and principle of all government of things. Nikulnikoff v. Archbishop, etc., of Russian Orthodox Greek Catholic Church, 142 Misc. 894, 255 N.Y.S. 653, 663.

As used in constitutional provisions of First Amendment forbidding the "establishment of religion," the term means a particular system of faith and worship recognized and practised by a particular church, sect, or denomination. Reynolds v. U. S., 98 U.S. 145, 149, 25 L.Ed. 244; Wolman v. Walter, 433 U.S. 229, 97 S.Ct. 2593, 53 L.Ed.2d 714; Roemer, et al. v. Board of Public Works of Md., 426 U.S. 736, 96 S.Ct. 2337, 49 L.Ed.2d 1.

Religion, offenses against. In old English law, they were enumerated by Blackstone as including: (1) Apostasy; (2) heresy; (3) reviling the ordinances of the church; (4) blasphemy; (5) profane swearing; (6) conjuration or witchcraft; (7) religious imposture; (8) simony; (9) profanation of the Lord's day; (10) drunkenness; (11) lewdness. 4 Bl.Comm. 43.

Religio sequitur patrem /rǝlíj(iy)ow sékwǝdǝr pǽtrǝm/. The father's religion is prima facie the infant's religion. Lit. Religion will follow the father.

Religious corporation. See **Corporation.**

Religious freedom. Within Constitution embraces not only the right to worship God according to the dictates of one's conscience, but also the right to do, or forbear to do, any act, for conscience sake, the doing or forbearing of which is not inimical to the peace, good order, and morals of society. Barnette v. West Virginia State Board of Education, D.C.W.Va., 47 F.Supp. 251, 253, 254; Jones v. City of Moultrie, 196 Ga. 526, 27 S.E.2d 39. See also **Establishment clause.**

Religious liberty. See **Liberty.**

Religious use. See **Charitable use.**

Relinquish. To abandon, to give up, to surrender, to renounce some right or thing. See **Abandonment; Release.**

Relinquishment. A forsaking, abandoning, renouncing, or giving over a right. See **Abandonment; Release.**

Reliqua /rélǝkwǝ/. The remainder or debt which a person finds himself debtor in upon the balancing or liquidation of an account. Hence *reliquary,* the debtor of a *reliqua;* as also a person who only pays piece-meal.

Relocatio /riylowkéysh(iy)ow/. Lat. In the civil law, a renewal of a lease on its determination. It may be either express or tacit; the latter is when the tenant holds over with the knowledge and without objection of the landlord.

Relocation. In mining law, a new or fresh location of an abandoned or forfeited mining claim by a stranger, or by the original locator when he wishes to change the boundaries or to correct mistakes in the original location.

Remainder. The remnant of an estate in land, depending upon a particular prior estate created at the same time and by the same instrument, and limited to arise immediately on the determination of that estate, and not in abridgement of it. A future interest created in some person other than the grantor or transferor. Folden v. Folden, Ohio App., 188 N.E.2d 193, 194.

The property that passes to a beneficiary after the expiration of an intervening income interest. If, for example, G. places real estate in trust with income to A. for life and remainder to B. upon A.'s death, B. has a remainder interest.

An estate limited to take effect and be enjoyed after another estate is determined. As, if a man seised in fee-simple grants lands to A. for twenty years, and, after the determination of the said term, then to B. and his heirs forever, here A. is tenant for years, *remainder* to B. in fee. An estate in reversion is the residue of an estate, usually the fee left in the grantor and his heirs after the determination of a particular estate which he has granted out of it. The rights of the reversioner are the same as those of a vested remainderman in fee.

In will, the terms rest, residue, and remainder of estate are usually and ordinarily understood as meaning that part of the estate which is left after all of the other provisions of the will have been satisfied.

See also **Cross remainder; Defeasibly vested remainder.** *Compare* **Reversion.**

Charitable remainder. A gift over to a charity generally after a life estate. It may be vested or contingent.

Contingent remainder. One which is either limited to a person not in being or not certain or ascertained, or so limited to a certain person that his right to the estate depends upon some contingent event in the future. Maryland Nat. Bank v. Comptroller of Treasury, 264 Md. 536, 287 A.2d 291, 294.

An estate in remainder which is limited to take effect either to a dubious and uncertain person, or upon a dubious and uncertain event, by which no present or particular interest passes to the remainderman, so that the particular estate may chance to be determined and the remainder never take effect. A remainder limited so as to depend upon an event or condition which may never happen or be performed, or which may not happen or be performed till after the determination of the preceding estate.

Cross-remainder. Where land is devised or conveyed to two or more persons as tenants in common, or where different parts of the same land are given to such persons in severalty, with such limitations that, upon the determination of the particular estate of either, his share is to pass to the other, to the entire exclusion of the ultimate remainderman or reversioner until all the particular estates shall be exhausted, the remainders so limited are called "cross-remainders." In wills, such remainders may arise by implication; but, in deeds, only by express limitation.

Executed remainder. A remainder which vests a present interest in the tenant, though the enjoyment is postponed to the future.

Executory remainder. A contingent remainder; one which exists where the estate is limited to take effect either to a dubious and uncertain person or upon a dubious and uncertain event.

Vested remainder. An estate by which a present interest passes to the party, though to be enjoyed in *futuro,* and by which the estate is invariably fixed to remain to a determinate person after the particular estate has been spent. One limited to a certain person at a certain time or upon the happening of a necessary event.

Remainderman. One who is entitled to the remainder of the estate after a particular estate carved out of it has expired. One who becomes entitled to estate after intervention of precedent estate or on termination by lapse of time of rights of precedent estate created at same time. In re Washburn's Will, 44 Misc.2d 56, 252 N.Y.S.2d 948, 952.

Remainder vested subject to being divested. A remainder given to one person, with proviso that it shall go to another under certain contingencies. In re Barnes' Estate, 155 Misc. 320, 279 N.Y.S. 117.

Remand. To send back. The sending by the appellate court of the cause back to the same court out of which it came, for purpose of having some further action taken on it there. Amalgamated Workers Union of Virgin Islands v. Hess Oil Virgin Islands Corp., C.A.Virgin Islands, 478 F.2d 540, 543. When a prisoner is brought before a judge on habeas corpus, for the purpose of obtaining liberty, the judge hears the case, and either discharges him or remands him. See also **Procedendo.**

Remanentia /rèmənénsh(iy)ə/. In old English law, a remainder. A perpetuity, or perpetual estate.

Remanent pro defectu emptorum /rəméynənt pròw dəfékt(y)uw em(p)tórəm/. The return made by the sheriff to a writ of execution when he has not been able to sell the property seized, that the same *remains unsold for want of buyers.*

Remanet /rémənət/. A remnant; that which remains. Thus the causes of which the trial is deferred from one term to another, or from one sitting to another, are termed "*remanets.*"

Remargining. The furnishing of additional security when securities which were originally purchased on margin decline in value below a certain percent of their market price at the time of purchase.

Remedial. Affording a remedy; giving means of obtaining redress; of the nature of a remedy; intended to remedy wrongs and abuses, abate faults, or supply defects; pertaining to or affecting remedy, as distinguished from that which affects or modifies the right. Schultz v. Gosselink, 260 Iowa 115, 148 N.W.2d 434, 436.

Remedial action. One which is brought to obtain compensation or indemnity. Cummings v. Board of Education of Oklahoma City, 190 Okl. 533, 125 P.2d 989, 994.

Remedial laws or statutes. Legislation providing means or method whereby causes of action may be effectuated, wrongs redressed and relief obtained is "remedial". Schmitt v. Jenkins Truck Lines, Inc., 260 Iowa 556, 149 N.W.2d 789, 792. Those statutes which pertain to or affect a remedy, as distinguished from those which affect or modify a substantive right or duty. Perkins v. Willamette Industries, Inc., Or., 542 P.2d 473, 475.

Those designed to correct imperfections in the prior law and to cure a wrong where an aggrieved party had an ineffective remedy under existing statutes. Application of City of New York, 71 Misc.2d 1019, 337 N.Y.S.2d 753, 756. One that intends to afford a private remedy to a person injured by the wrongful act. That which is designed to correct an existing law, redress an existing grievance, or introduce regulations conducive to the public good. A statute giving a party a mode of remedy for a wrong, where he had none, or a different one, before. One which furnishes new remedy to claimant who has suffered injustice due to technical requirements of general statute. In re McCracken's Estate, 9 Ohio Misc. 195, 224 N.E.2d 181, 182.

The underlying test to be applied in determining whether a statute is penal or remedial is whether it primarily seeks to impose an arbitrary, deterring punishment upon any who might commit a wrong against the public by a violation of the requirements of the statute, or whether the purpose is to measure and define the damages which may accrue to an individual or class of individuals, as just and reasonable compensation for a possible loss having a causal connection with the breach of the legal obligation owing under the statute to such individual or class.

See also **Curative** (*Curative statute*).

Remedy. The means by which a right is enforced or the violation of a right is prevented, redressed, or compensated. Long Leaf Lumber, Inc. v. Svolos, La.App., 258 So.2d 121, 124. The means employed to enforce a right or redress an injury, as distinguished from right, which is a well founded or acknowledged claim. Chelentis v. Luckenbach S. S. Co., 247 U.S. 372, 38 S.Ct. 501, 503, 62 L.Ed. 1171.

The rights given to a party by law or by contract which that party may exercise upon a default by the other contracting party, or upon the commission of a wrong (a tort) by another party.

Remedy means any remedial right to which an aggrieved party is entitled with or without resort to a tribunal. "Rights" includes remedies. U.C.C. § 1–201.

That which relieves or cures a disease, including a medicine or remedial treatment.

See also Adequate remedy; Administrative remedy; Alternative relief; Cause of action; Extraordinary remedies; Inadequate remedy at law; Marshaling remedies; Mutuality of remedy; Provisional remedy.

Civil remedy. The remedy afforded by law to a private person in the civil courts in so far as his private and individual rights have been injured by a delict or crime; as distinguished from the remedy by criminal prosecution for the injury to the rights of the public.

Cumulative remedy. See **Cumulative.**

Equitable remedy. See **Equity; Injunction; Performance** (*Specific performance*); **Reformation.**

Extraordinary remedy. See **Extraordinary.**

Joinder of remedies. See **Joinder.**

Legal remedy. A remedy available, under the particular circumstances of the case, in a court of law, as distinguished from a remedy available only in equity. Procedurally, this distinction is no longer generally relevant, for under Rules of Civil Procedure there is only one form of action known as a "civil action." Rule 2.

Remedy over. A person who is primarily liable or responsible, but who, in turn, can demand indemnification from another, who is responsible to him, is said to have a "remedy over." For example, a city, being compelled to pay for injuries caused by a defect in the highway, has a "remedy over" against the person whose act or negligence caused the defect, and such person is said to be "liable over" to the city. See **Subrogation.**

Remise /rəmáyz/. To remit or give up. A formal word in deeds of release and quitclaim; the usual phrase being "remise, release, and forever quitclaim."

Remise de la dette. In French law, the release of a debt.

Remission. A release or extinguishment of a debt. It is *conventional,* when it is expressly granted to the debtor by a creditor having a capacity to alienate; or *tacit,* when the creditor voluntarily surrenders to his debtor the original title, under private signature constituting the obligation.

A diminution or abatement of symptoms of a disease; also the period during which such diminution occurs. In re Meyers, 410 Pa. 455, 189 A.2d 852, 862.

Forgiveness or condonation of an offense or injury.

At common law, the act by which a forfeiture or penalty is forgiven. United States v. Morris, 23 U.S. (10 Wheat.) 246, 6 L.Ed. 314.

Remissius imperanti melius paretur. A man commanding not too strictly is better obeyed.

Remissness. The doing of the act in question in a tardy, negligent, or careless manner; but term does not apply to the entire omission or forbearance of the act.

Remit. To send or transmit; as to *remit* money. To send back, as to remit a check or refer a case back to a lower court for further consideration. To give up; to pardon or forgive; to annul; to relinquish; as to *remit* a fine, sentence, or punishment.

Remitment /rəmítmənt/. The act of sending back to custody; an annulment.

Remittance /rəmítən(t)s/. Money sent by one person to another, either in specie, bill of exchange, check, or otherwise.

Remittee. A person to whom a remittance is made.

Remitter /rəmídər/. The relation back of a later defective title to an earlier valid title. *Remitter* occurs where he who has the true property or *jus proprietatis* in lands, but is out of possession thereof, and has no right to enter without recovering possession in an action, has afterwards the freehold cast upon him by some subsequent and of course defective title. In this case he is *remitted,* or sent back by operation of law, to his ancient and more certain title.

Remitting bank. Any payor or intermediary bank remitting for an item. U.C.C. § 4–105(f).

Remittit damna /rəmídət dǽmnə/. Lat. An entry on the record, by which the plaintiff declares that he remits a part of the damages which have been awarded him.

Remittitur /rəmídədər/. The procedural process by which a verdict of the jury is diminished by subtraction. Pippen v. Denision, Division of Abex Corp., 66 Mich.App. 664, 239 N.W.2d 704, 710.

If money damages awarded by a jury are grossly excessive as a matter of law, the judge may order the plaintiff to remit a portion of the award. In the alternative, the court may order a complete new trial or a trial limited to the issue of damages. The court may also condition a denial of a motion for new trial upon the filing by the plaintiff of a remittitur in a stated amount. Fed.R.Civil P. 59(a).

Remittitur of record /rəmídədər əv rékərd/. The returning or sending back by a court of appeal of the record and proceedings in a cause, after its decision thereon, to the court whence the appeal came, in order that the cause may be tried anew (where it is so ordered), or that judgment may be entered in accordance with the decision on appeal, or execution be issued, or any other necessary action be taken in the court below.

Remittor /rəmídər/. A person who makes a remittance to another.

Remnant rule. The rule that width of lot, frontage of which is not specified on plat specifying frontage of all other lots in same block, is length of block, minus total width of other lots.

Remodel. To model anew; reconstruct, recast, reform, reshape, reconstruct, to make over in a somewhat different way. Board of Com'rs of Guadalupe County v. State, 43 N.M. 409, 94 P.2d 515, 520.

Remonitization. Removal of one type of money from a country's legal tender list. Also, the reestablishment of a currency system which has not functioned for a time.

Remonstrance /rəmónstrən(t)s/. Expostulation; showing of reasons against something proposed; a representation made to a court or legislative body wherein certain persons unite in urging that a contemplated measure be not adopted or passed. A formal protest against the policy or conduct of the government or of certain officials drawn up and presented by aggrieved citizens.

Remote. At a distance; afar off; inconsiderable; slight.

Remote cause. In the law of negligence with respect to injury or accident, a cause which would not according to experience of mankind, lead to the event which happened. Riley v. Burgess, Ky., 410 S.W.2d 712, 713. One where the effect is uncertain, vague, or indeterminate, and where the effect does not necessarily follow. Jaggers v. Southeastern Greyhound Lines, D.C.Tenn., 34 F.Supp. 667, 669. A cause operating mediately through other causes to produce effect. Improbable cause. Nashville, C. & St. L. Ry. v.

Harrell, 21 Tenn.App. 353, 110 S.W.2d 1032, 1038. See also **Cause.**

Proximate cause distinguished. "Proximate cause" is cause in which is involved idea of necessity, and one from which effect must follow, while "remote cause", though necessary for existence of effect, is one not necessarily implying existence of effect. Hebert v. United Gas Pipe Line Co., La.App., 210 So.2d 71, 74.

To determine whether a given cause is a "proximate cause" or a "remote cause," it must be determined whether the facts constitute a succession of events, so linked together that they become a natural whole, or whether chain of events is so broken that they become independent, and final result cannot be said to be the natural and probable consequence of the primary cause, the negligence of defendants.

Remote damage. See **Damages.**

Remoteness. Want of close connection between a wrong and the injury which prevents the party injured from claiming compensation from the wrongdoer.

Remoteness of evidence. When the fact or facts proposed to be established as a foundation from which indirect evidence may be drawn, by way of inference, have not a visible, plain, or necessary connection with the proposition eventually to be proved, such evidence is rejected for "remoteness."

Remote possibility. In the law of estates, a double possibility, or a limitation dependent on two or more facts or events both or all of which are contingent and uncertain; as, for example, the limitation of an estate to a given man provided that he shall marry a certain woman and that she shall then die and he shall marry another.

Remoto impedimento, emergit actio /rəmówdow impèdəméntow əmárjəd ǽksh(iy)ow/. The impediment being removed, the action rises. When a bar to an action is removed, the action rises up into its original efficacy.

Removal. In a broad sense, the transfer of a person or thing from one place to another. See also **Asportation.**

As used in statutes relative to removal from state is often limited to such absence from state as amounts to a change of residence.

See also **Recall.**

Removal bond. In customs law, a bond furnished for possible duties by one who removes imported goods from a warehouse for export. Also, bond required in some states when a party to pending action in one court desires to remove action to another court.

Removal from office. Deprivation of office by act of competent superior officer acting within scope of authority. "Suspension" is the temporary forced removal from the exercise of office; "removal" is the dismissal from office. See **Election** *(Recall election);* **Impeachment.**

Removal of causes. The transfer of a cause from one court to another; *e.g.* from one state court to another, or from state court to federal court. Commonly used of the transfer of the jurisdiction and cognizance of an action commenced but not finally determined, with all further proceedings therein, from one trial court to another trial court. More particularly, the transfer of a cause, before trial or final hearing thereof, from a state court to the United States District Court, under 28 U.S.C.A. § 1441.

Removal to avoid tax. Within a statute relating to forfeiture, some transfer of the thing involved from some definite place of manufacture, production, origin, or the like to some other place, whereat or wherefrom collection of tax on it might be less easily effected.

Removing cloud from title. Acts or proceedings necessary to render title marketable. See **Action to quiet title.**

Remuneration /rəmyùwnəréyshən/. Reward; recompense; salary; compensation.

Renant, or **reniant** /rənáyənt/. In old English law, denying.

Rencounter /renkáwntər/. A sudden hostile collision, as with an enemy; an unexpected encounter or meeting, as of travelers; a contest or debate; a sudden meeting as opposed to a duel which is deliberate.

Render, *v.* To give up; to yield; to return; to surrender. Also to pay or perform; used of rents, services, and the like.

Render judgment. To pronounce, state, declare, or announce the judgment of the court in a given case or on a given state of facts; not used with reference to judgments by confession, and not synonymous with "entering," "docketing," or "recording" the judgment. Judgment is "rendered" when decision is officially announced, either orally in open court or by memorandum filed with clerk. Comet Aluminum Co. v. Dibrell, Tex., 450 S.W.2d 56, 58. See **Rendition of judgment.**

Render verdict. To agree on and to report the verdict in due form. To return the written verdict into court and hand it to the trial judge who announces it in open court.

Render, *n.* In feudal law, used in connection with rents and heriots. Goods subject to rent or heriot-service were said to lie in *render,* when the lord might not only seize the identical goods, but might also distrain for them.

Rendezvous /ròndeyvúw/°diy°/. Fr. A place appointed for meeting. Especially used of places appointed for the assembling of troops, the coming together of the ships of a fleet, or the meeting of vessels and their convoy.

Rendition. The return of a fugitive to the State in which he is accused of having committed a crime, by the order of the governor of the State to which the fugitive has gone. See also **Extradition; Interstate rendition.**

Rendition of judgment. Rendition of a judgment is effected when trial court in open court declares the decision of the law upon the matters at issue, and it is distinguishable from "entry of judgment," which is a purely ministerial act by which the judgment is made

of record and preserved. Ex parte Gnesoulis, Tex. Civ.App., 525 S.W.2d 205, 209. A judgment is rendered as of date on which trial judge declares in open court his decision on matters submitted to him for adjudication, and oral pronouncement by the court of its decision is sufficient for "rendition of judgment". Farr v. McKinzie, Tex.Civ.App., 477 S.W.2d 672, 676.

The rendition of judgment is the pronouncement of the court of its conclusions and decision upon the matter submitted to it for adjudication; a judgment may be rendered either orally in open court or by memorandum filed with the clerk. Travelers Express Co., Inc. v. Winters, Tex.Civ.App., 488 S.W.2d 890, 892. "Rendition" of judgment is distinguishable from its "entry" in the records. Rehm v. Fishman, Mo. App., 395 S.W.2d 251, 255. See **Entering judgment.**

Rendition of verdict. See **Render.**

Renegotiation. Lit. To negotiate again. As to government contracts, it consists of a review of a contract after its performance to determine whether excess profits have been made. If they were made, the government can recapture them.

Renegotiation Act. Federal law which provides for reexamination of government contracts to determine whether excess profits were made which can be recaptured by the government. 50 U.S.C.A.App. 1191 et seq. See **Renegotiation Board.**

Renegotiation Board. The Renegotiation Board was created as an independent establishment in the executive branch by the Renegotiation Act of 1951 (65 Stat. 7; 50 U.S.C.A.App. § 1211) and was organized on October 8, 1951. The Board seeks the elimination of excessive profits on defense and space contracts and related subcontracts. This is accomplished through informal and nonadversary proceedings before the Board and its regional boards. Contractors not agreeing with Board determinations may petition the Court of Claims for redetermination.

Renew. To make new again; to restore to freshness; to make new spiritually; to regenerate; to begin again; to recommence; to resume; to restore to existence; to revive; to reestablish; to recreate; to replace; to grant or obtain an extension of. To "renew" a contract means to begin again or continue in force the old contract. East Bay Union of Machinists, Local 1304, United Steelworkers of America, AFL–CIO v. Fibreboard Paper Products Corp., D.C. Cal., 285 F.Supp. 282, 287.

Renewal. The act of renewing or reviving. A revival or rehabilitation of an expiring subject; that which is made anew or re-established. The substitution of a new right or obligation for another of the same nature. A change of something old to something new. To grant or obtain extension of; to continue in force for a fresh period, as commonly used with reference to notes and bonds importing a postponement of maturity of obligations dealt with. An extension of time in which that obligation may be discharged; an obligation being "renewed" when the same obligation is carried forward by the new paper or undertaking, whatever it may be. Campbell River Timber Co. v. Vierhus, C.C.A.Wash., 86 F.2d 673, 675.

Renounce. To make an affirmative declaration of abandonment. To reject; cast off; repudiate; disclaim; forsake; abandon; divest one's self of a right, power, or privilege. Usually it implies an affirmative act of disclaimer or disavowal. See also **Renunciation; Repudiation.**

Will. Under law of many states, a widow may waive or relinquish her rights under the will of her husband and claim her statutory rights.

Renovare /rènəvériy/. Lat. In old English law, to renew. *Annuatim renovare,* to renew annually. A phrase applied to profits which are taken and the product renewed again.

Rent. Consideration paid for use or occupation of property. In a broader sense, it is the compensation or fee paid, usually periodically, for the use of any property, land, buildings, equipment, etc.

At common law, term referred to compensation or return of value given at stated times for the possession of lands and tenements corporeal. A sum of money or other consideration, issuing yearly out of lands and tenements corporeal; something which a tenant renders out of the profits of the land which he enjoys; a compensation or return, being in the nature of an acknowledgment or recompense given for the possession of some corporeal inheritance. 2 Bl. Comm. 41. In re Perlmutter's Will, 156 Misc. 571, 282 N.Y.S. 282.

The payment of royalty under a mineral lease. Robinson v. Horton, 197 La. 919, 2 So.2d 647, 649.

In Louisiana, the contract of *rent of lands* is a contract by which one of the parties conveys and cedes to the other a tract of land, or any other immovable property, and stipulates that the latter shall hold it as owner, but reserving to the former an annual rent of a certain sum of money, or of a certain quantity of fruits, which the other party binds himself to pay him. It is of the essence of this conveyance that it be made in perpetuity. If it be made for a limited time, it is a lease. Civ.Code La. arts. 2779, 2780.

Fair rent. See **Fair rent.**

Fee farm rent. A rent charge issuing out of an estate in fee; a perpetual rent reserved on a conveyance of land in fee simple.

Ground rent. See that title.

Net rent. Rent after all expenses.

Quit rent. Certain established rents of the freeholders and ancient copyholders of manors were so called, because by their payment the tenant was free and "quit" of all other services.

Rack rent. A rent of the full annual value of the tenement or near it.

Rental-rights. In old English law, a species of lease usually granted at a low rent and for life. Tenants under such leases were called "rentalers" or "kindly tenants."

Rent-charge. This arises where the owner of the rent has no future interest or reversion in the land. It is usually created by deed or will, and is accompanied with powers of distress and entry.

Rent-roll. A list of rents payable to a particular person or public body.

Rent seck. Barren rent; a rent reserved by deed, but without any clause of distress.

Rent-service. This consisted at common law of fealty, together with a certain rent, and was the only kind of rent originally known to the common law. It was so called because it was given as a compensation for the services to which the land was originally liable.

Rents of assize. The certain and determined rents of the freeholders and ancient copyholders of manors. Apparently so called because they were assized or made certain, and so distinguished from a *redditus mobilis,* which was a variable or fluctuating rent.

Rents resolute. Rents anciently payable to the crown from the lands of abbeys and religious houses; and after their dissolution, notwithstanding that the lands were demised to others, yet the rents were still reserved and made payable again to the crown.

Rentage. Rent.

Rental. See **Rent.**

Rent control. A restriction or limitation imposed in certain cities upon the maximum rent that may be charged on rental property.

Rente /rónt/. In French law, the annual return which represents the revenue of a capital or of an immovable alienated. The constitution of *rente* is a contract by which one of the parties lends to the other a capital which he agrees not to recall, in consideration of the borrower's paying an annual interest. It is this interest which is called *"rente."* The word is therefore nearly synonymous with "annuity."

Rente foncière /rónt fonsyér/. A rent which issues out of land, and it is of its essence that it be perpetual, for, if it be made but for a limited time, it is a lease. It may, however, be extinguished.

Rente viagère /rónt v(i)yajér/. That species of *rente,* the duration of which depends upon the contingency of the death of one or more persons indicated in the contract. The uncertainty of the time at which such death may happen causes the *rente viagère* to be included in the number of aleatory contracts. Defines the contract of annuity as that by which one party delivers to another a sum of money, and agrees not to reclaim it so long as the receiver pays the rent agreed upon.

Rentier /rontyéy/. In French law, a fundholder, a person having an income from personal property.

Rents, issues and profits. The profits arising from property generally. Rents collected by party in possession; the net profits. Phrase does not apply to rental value or value of use and occupation. People v. Gustafson, 53 Cal.App.2d 230, 127 P.2d 627, 632.

Rent strike. An organized undertaking by tenants in which rent is withheld until grievances between landlord and tenants are settled.

Renunciation. The act by which a person abandons a right acquired without transferring it to another.

Under the Uniform Commercial Code the unilateral act of the holder, usually, without consideration, whereby he expresses the intention of abandoning his rights on the instrument or against one or more parties thereto. U.C.C. § 1–107. Within Uniform Commercial Code it is a gratuitous abandonment or giving up of right, and does not require a consideration. Miller v. Gayman, Mo., 482 S.W.2d 414 or 419.

In connection with wills, the act of waiving a will and claiming a statutory share as in the case of a spouse whose share under a will is less than her statutory share.

See also **Disclaimer; Repudiation.**

Renvoi /renvóy/. The "doctrine of renvoi" is a doctrine under which court in resorting to foreign law adopts rules of foreign law as to conflict of laws, which rules may in turn refer court back to law of forum. Green v. Robertshaw-Fulton Controls Co., D.C.Ind., 29 F.R.D. 490, 500; Cooper v. Cherokee Village Development Co., 236 Ark. 37, 364 S.W.2d 158, 162.

Reo absente /ríyow əbséntiy/. Lat. The defendant being absent; in the absence of the defendant.

Reopening a case. Is to permit the introduction of new evidence and, practically to permit a new trial.

Reorganization. Act or process of organizing again or anew. People ex rel. Barrett v. Halsted Street State Bank, 295 Ill.App. 193, 14 N.E.2d 872, 876.

In corporate law, the total adjustment made in the capital structure of the corporation in which old securities and indebtedness are retired and new securities and bonds are issued. Commonly accomplished when a corporation is bankrupt or near the point of insolvency (see Chapter 11 of Bankruptcy Act). A major change in the capital structure of a corporation that leads to changes in the rights, interests, and implied ownership of the various security owners. Such usually results from a merger or agreement by senior security holders to take action to forestall bankruptcy.

Reorganization of a corporation contemplates the preparation of a plan of reorganization by the trustee, the submission thereof to the court, and, after a hearing, the determination of the feasibility of such plan by the court, followed by the court's approval thereof if it finds such plan is feasible and proper.

Tax free reorganization. Under the Internal Revenue Code, a corporate reorganization wherein a corporation which is a party thereto exchanges property, pursuant to a plan of reorganization, solely for stock or securities of a second corporate party, without recognition of gain or loss. I.R.C. § 361.

Type "A" reorganization. Under the Internal Revenue Code, a corporate merger or consolidation. I.R.C. § 368(a)(1)(A).

Type "B" reorganization. Under the Internal Revenue Code, a corporate reorganization involving the acquisition by one corporation, in exchange solely for all or a part of its voting stock, of stock of another corporation if, immediately after the acquisition, the acquiring corporation has control of such other corporation. I.R.C. § 368(a)(1)(B).

Type "C" reorganization. Under the Internal Revenue Code, a corporate reorganization involving the acquisition by one corporation, in exchange solely for all or a part of its voting stock, or in exchange solely for all or a part of the voting stock of a corporation which controls the acquiring corporation, of substantially all of the property of another corporation. I.R.C. § 368(a)(1)(C).

Repair. To mend, remedy, restore, renovate. To restore to a sound or good state after decay, injury, dilapidation, or partial destruction. Weiss v. Mitchell, Tex.Civ.App., 58 S.W.2d 165, 166. The word "repair" contemplates an existing structure or thing which has become imperfect, and means to supply in the original existing structure that which is lost or destroyed, and thereby restore it to the condition in which it originally existed, as near as may be. Childers v. Speer, 63 Ga.App. 848, 12 S.E.2d 439, 440.

Repairs are chargeable to current income whereas an improvement is a capital expenditure which requires depreciation over the life of the improvement. See also **Extraordinary repairs.**

Landlord has obligation to keep premises in such repair as to meet local building and sanitary code requirements. Boston Housing Authority v. Hemingway, 363 Mass. 184, 293 N.E.2d 831. See **Habitability.**

Reparation /rèpəréyshən/. Payment for an injury; redress for a wrong done. Several states have adopted the Uniform Crime Victims Reparation Act. Certain federal statutes also provide for reparations for violation of Act; *e.g.* persons suffering losses because of violations of Commodity Futures Trading Act may seek reparation under the Act against violator. 7 U.S.C.A. § 18.

Payment made by one country to another for damages during war.

See also **Restitution.**

Repartiamento /reypàrtiyaméntow/. In Spanish law, a judicial proceeding for the partition of property held in common.

Repatriation /rìypeytriyéyshən/°pæt°/. The regaining nationality after expatriation. The return to one's own country of investments held by foreigners.

Repay. To pay back; refund; restore; return.

Repeal. The abrogation or annulling of a previously existing law by the enactment of a subsequent statute which declares that the former law shall be revoked and abrogated (which is called "express" repeal), or which contains provisions so contrary to or irreconcilable with those of the earlier law that only one of the two statutes can stand in force (called "implied" repeal). To revoke, to rescind or abrogate by authority. Golconda Lead Mines v. Neill, 82 Idaho 96, 350 P.2d 221, 223. See also **Abrogation; Express repeal.**

Amendment distinguished. "Repeal" of a law means its complete abrogation by the enactment of a subsequent statute, whereas the "amendment" of a statute means an alteration in the law already existing, leaving some part of the original still standing.

Repeaters. Persons who commit crime and are sentenced, and then commit another and are sentenced again. See **Habitual criminal; Recidivist.**

Repellitur a sacramento infamis /rəpélədər èy sækrəméntow inféyməs/. An infamous person is repelled or prevented from taking an oath.

Repellitur exceptione cedendarum actionum /rəpélədər əksèpshiyówniy sìydendérəm ǽkshiyównəm/. He is defeated by the plea that the actions have been assigned.

Repertory /répərt(ò)riy/. In French law, the inventory or minutes which notaries make of all contracts which take place before them.

Repetition. In the civil law, a demand or action for the restoration of money paid under mistake, or goods delivered by mistake or on an unperformed condition. See **Solutio indebiti.**

Repetitum namium /rəpédədəm néymiyəm/. A repeated, second, or reciprocal distress; witherham.

Repetundæ, or **pecuniæ repetundæ** /(pəkyúwniyiy) rèpətándiy/. In Roman law, the terms used to designate such sums of money as the *socii* of the Roman state, or individuals, claimed to recover from *magistratus, judices,* or *publici curatores,* which they had improperly taken or received in the *provinciæ,* or in the *urbs Roma,* either in the discharge of their *jurisdictio,* or in their capacity of *judices,* or in respect of any other public function. Sometimes the word "*repetundæ*" was used to express the illegal act for which compensation as sought.

Repetundarum crimen /rèpətàndérəm kráymən/. In Roman law, the crime of bribery or extortion in a magistrate, or person in any public office.

Replace. To place again, to restore to a former condition. Illinois Cent. R. Co. v. Franklin County, 387 Ill. 301, 56 N.E.2d 775, 779. Term, given its plain, ordinary meaning, means to supplant with substitute or equivalent. Olenick v. Government Employees Ins. Co., 42 A.D.2d 760, 346 N.Y.S.2d 320, 321. To take the place of.

Replacement insurance. Insurance coverage which provides that the loss will be measured by replacement of the property new. If the property is actually replaced, the measure is the difference between the depreciated value and the replacement cost.

Replead. To plead anew; to file new pleadings.

Repleader. In common law pleading, when, after issue has been joined in an action, and a verdict given thereon, the pleading is found (on examination) to have miscarried and failed to effect its proper object, viz., of raising an apt and material question between the parties, the court will, on motion of the unsuccessful party, award a *repleader;* that is, will order the parties to plead *de novo* for the purpose of obtaining a better issue. Under modern rules practice, amendments to pleadings are liberally allowed. Fed. R.Civil P. 15.

Replegiare /rəplèjiyériy/. To replevy; to redeem a thing detained or taken by another by putting in legal sureties.

Repleviable, or **replevisable** /rəpléviyəbəl/rəplévəzəbəl/. Property is said to be repleviable or replevisable when proceedings in replevin may be resorted to for the purpose of trying the right to such property.

Replevin /rəplévən/. An action whereby the owner or person entitled to repossession of goods or chattels may recover those goods or chattels from one who has wrongfully distrained or taken or who wrongfully detains such goods or chattels. Jim's Furniture Mart, Inc. v. Harris, 42 Ill.App.3d 488, 1 Ill.Dec. 175, 176, 356 N.E.2d 175, 176. Replevin is designed to permit one having right to possession to recover property in specie from one who has either wrongfully taken or detained property. Epps v. Cortese, D.C.Pa., 326 F.Supp. 127, 132.

Under the following conditions a buyer of goods may have the right of replevin: "The buyer has a right of replevin for goods identified to the contract if after reasonable effort he is unable to effect cover for such goods or the circumstances reasonably indicate that such effort will be unavailing or if the goods have been shipped under reservation and satisfaction of the security interest in them has been made or tendered." See U.C.C. § 2–711(2)(b); § 2–716(3).

See also **Replevy.**

Personal replevin. At common law, a species of action to replevy a man out of prison or out of the custody of any private person. It took the place of the old writ *de homine replegiando;* but, as a means of examining into the legality of an imprisonment, it is now superseded by the writ of *habeas corpus.*

Replevin bond. A bond executed to indemnify the officer who executed a writ of replevin and to indemnify the defendant or person from whose custody the property was taken for such damages as he may sustain. Such bond guarantees that the replevisor will have the property in the same condition to abide the decision of the court. Kelso v. Hanson, Tex.Civ. App., 388 S.W.2d 396, 399.

Replevish /rəplévəsh/. In old English law, to let one to mainprise upon surety.

Replevisor /rəplévəzər/. The plaintiff in an action of replevin.

Replevy /rəpléviy/. In reference to the action of replevin, to redeliver goods which have been distrained, to the original possessor of them, on his pledging or giving security to prosecute an action against the distrainor for the purpose of trying the legality of the distress. Also the bailing or liberating a man from prison on his finding bail to answer for his forthcoming at a future time. See also **Replevin.**

Replevy bond. Such bond guarantees that the replevisor will have the property in the same condition to abide the decision of the court. Kelso v. Hanson, Tex., 388 S.W.2d 396, 399.

Repliant, or **replicant** /rəpláyənt/répləkənt/. A litigant who replies or files or delivers a replication.

Replicare /rèpləkériy/. Lat. In the civil law and old English pleading, to reply; to answer a defendant's plea.

Replicatio /rèpləkéysh(iy)ow/. Lat. In the civil law and old English pleading, the plaintiff's answer to the defendant's exception or plea; corresponding with and giving name to the *replication* in modern pleading.

Replication. In common law pleading, a reply made by the plaintiff in an action to the defendant's plea, or in a suit in chancery to the defendant's answer. See **Reply.**

In equity practice (now obsolete in the federal and most state courts), a general replication is a general denial of the truth of defendant's plea or answer, and of the sufficiency of the matter alleged in it to bar the plaintiff's suit, and an assertion of the truth and sufficiency of the bill. A special replication is occasioned by the defendant's introducing new matter into his plea or answer, which makes it necessary for the plaintiff to put in issue some additional fact on his part in avoidance of such new matter.

Reply. In its general sense, the plaintiff's answer to the defendant's set-off or counterclaim. Under Fed.R. Civil P. 7(a), a reply is only allowed in two situations: to a counterclaim denominated as such, or, on order of court to an answer or a third-party answer.

Report. An official or formal statement of facts or proceedings. To give an account of, to relate, to tell, to convey or disseminate information. State v. Fenster, 2 Conn.Cir. 184, 199 A.2d 177, 181. See also **Annual report; Consumer report; Credit report.**

The formal statement in writing made to a court by a master, clerk, or referee, as the result of his inquiries into some matter referred to him by the court. Fed.R.Civil P. 53.

A "report" of a public official is distinguished from a "return" of such official, in that "return" is typically concerned with something done or observed by officer, while "report" embodies result of officer's investigation not originally occurring within his personal knowledge. E. K. Hardison Seed Co. v. Jones, C.C.A.6, 149 F.2d 252, 257.

The name is also applied (usually in the plural) to the published volumes, appearing periodically, containing accounts of the various cases argued and determined in the various courts of record with the decisions and opinions thereon. See **Reporter; Reports.**

Reporter. A person who reports the decisions of a court of record; also, published volumes of decisions by a court or group of courts. The "court reporter" is the person who records court proceedings in court and later transcribes such. See also **Court reporter; Reports or reporters.**

Report of legislative committee. That communication which the chairman of the committee makes to the house at the close of the investigation upon which it has been engaged.

Reports or **reporters.** Published volumes of case decisions by a particular court or group of courts; e.g. Supreme Court Reporter, Federal Reporter, Federal Supplement.

Term includes: (1) (court reports) published judicial cases arranged according to some grouping, such as jurisdiction, court, period of time, subject matter or case significance, (2) (administrative reports or decisions) published decisions of an administrative agency, (3) annual statements of progress, activities or policy issued by an administrative agency or an association.

See also **Law reporters or reports; Reporter; United States Reports.**

Reports, The. The name given, *par excellence,* to Lord Coke's Reports, from 14 Eliz. to 13 Jac. I, which are cited as "Rep." or "Coke." They are divided into thirteen parts, and the modern editions are in six volumes, including the index.

Repositorium /rəpòzətór(i)yəm/. A storehouse or place wherein things are kept; a warehouse.

Repossession. To take back—as when a seller repossesses or takes back an item if the buyer misses an installment payment. To recover goods sold on credit or in installments when the buyer fails to pay for them. The conditions for repossession are entirely statutory and due process standards must be met as to notice, manner, etc.

Term is commonly understood as act of resuming possession of property when purchaser fails to keep up payments on it. Greer v. Zurich Ins. Co., Mo., 441 S.W.2d 15, 27. The act or process by which goods are recovered by a seller or finance company on the buyer's failure to pay.

Self-help (*i.e.* without legal process) repossession of collateral is permitted under U.C.C. § 9–503. See **Self-help.**

Represent. To appear in the character of; personate; to exhibit; to expose before the eyes. To represent a thing is to produce it publicly. To represent a person is to stand in his place; to speak or act with authority on behalf of such person; to supply his place; to act as his substitute or agent. See also **Agent; Power of appointment; Representative.**

Representation. Any conduct capable of being turned into a statement of fact. Scandrett v. Greenhouse, 244 Wis. 108, 11 N.W.2d 510, 512. Statement of fact made to induce another to enter into contract. As element of actionable fraud includes deeds, acts or artifices calculated to mislead another, as well as words or positive assertions. Kestner v. Jakobe, Mo. App. 446 S.W.2d 188, 193. See also **Material fact; Misrepresentation; Reliance.**

Act of representing another. See **Represent; Representation.**

Contracts. A statement express or implied made by one of two contracting parties to the other, before or at the time of making the contract, in regard to some past or existing fact, circumstance, or state of facts pertinent to the contract, which is influential in bringing about the agreement.

False representation. See **False representation; Fraud; Material fact; Misrepresentation.**

Insurance. A collateral statement, either by writing not inserted in the policy or by parol, of such facts or circumstances, relative to the proposed adventure, as are necessary to be communicated to the underwriters, to enable them to form a just estimate of the risks. The allegation of any facts, by the applicant to the insurer, or *vice versa*, preliminary to making the contract, and directly bearing upon it, having a plain and evident tendency to induce the making of the policy. The statements may or may not be in writing, and may be either express or by obvious implication.

Law of distribution and descent. The principle upon which the issue of a deceased person take or inherit the share of an estate which their immediate ancestor would have taken or inherited, if living; the taking or inheriting *per stirpes.* In re Paterson's Estate, Cal. App., 76 P.2d 138, 143.

Material representation. One having been a real moving cause inducing the making of a contract. A representation is "material" if it relates directly to matter in controversy and is of such nature that ultimate result would not have followed if there had been no representation or if one who acted upon it had been aware of its falsity. Schoen v. Lange, Mo.App., 256 S.W.2d 277, 281. To be "material", a representation must be of such character that if it had not been made, the contract or transaction would not have been entered into. Zinn v. Ex-Cell-O Corp., Cal.App., 141 P.2d 948, 958.

In life insurance, one that would influence a prudent insurer in determining whether or not to accept the risk, or in fixing the amount of the premium in the event of such acceptance.

See **Material fact; Misrepresentation.**

Misrepresentation. An intentional false statement respecting a matter of fact, made by one of the parties to a contract, which is material to the contract and influential in producing it. See **False representation; Material fact; Misrepresentation.**

Promissory representation. A term used chiefly in insurance, and meaning a representation made by the assured concerning what is to happen during the term of the insurance, stated as a matter of expectation or even of contract, and amounting to a promise to be performed after the contract has come into existence.

Representation, estoppel by. It arises when one by acts, representations, admissions, or silence when he ought to speak out, intentionally or through culpable negligence induces another to believe certain facts to exist and such other rightfully relies and acts on such belief, so that he will be prejudiced if the former is permitted to deny the existence of such facts. Carter v. Curlew Creamery Co., 16 Wash.2d 476, 134 P.2d 66, 73. It differs from estoppel by record, deed, or contract, in that it is not based on agreement of parties or finding of fact which may not be disputed, and is not mutual, but applies to only one party.

It is the effect of voluntary conduct of a party whereby he is absolutely precluded from asserting rights which might perhaps have otherwise existed. Strand v. State, 16 Wash.2d 107, 132 P.2d 1011, 1015. It is species of "equitable estoppel" or estoppel by matter in pais. Elements or essentials of such estoppel include change of position for the worse, Carter v. Curlew Creamery Co., 16 Wash.2d 476, 134 P.2d 66, 73; Campbell v. Salyer, 290 Ky. 493, 161 S.W.2d 596, 599; detriment or injury or prejudice to party claiming estoppel, Abbott v. Bean, 295 Mass. 268, 3 N.E.2d 762, 768; express or implied representations; false representation, Chicago, R. I. & P. Ry. Co. v. Sawyer, 176 Okl. 446, 56 P.2d 418, 420; Cushing v. United States, D.C.Mass., 18 F.Supp. 83, 85; ignorance of facts by party claiming estoppel, United States v. Dickinson, C.C.A.Mass., 95 F.2d 65, 68; inducement to action by party claiming estoppel, Rhoads v.

Rhoads, 342 Mo. 934, 119 S.W.2d 247, 252; intent that other party should act on representation or gross and culpable negligence of party sought to be estopped; knowledge, actual or constructive, of facts by person estopped, Rhoads v. Rhoads, 342 Mo. 934, 119 S.W.2d 247, 252; misleading of person claiming estoppel, Campbell v. Salyer, 290 Ky. 493, 161 S.W.2d 596, 599; reliance of one party on conduct of other party, Mosley v. Magnolia Petroleum Co., 45 N.M. 230, 114 P.2d 740, 751. The doctrine ordinarily applies only to representations as to past or present facts. In re Watson's Estate, 177 Misc. 308, 30 N.Y. S.2d 577, 586.

See also **Equitable estoppel; In pais, estoppel.**

Representation of persons. A fiction of the law, the effect of which is to put the representative in the place, degree, or right of the person represented. Civ.Code La. art. 894.

Representative. One who represents or stands in the place of another. One who represents others or another in a special capacity, as an agent, and term is interchangeable with "agent". Sunset Mill & Grain Co. v. Anderson, 39 Cal.2d 773, 249 P.2d 24, 27.

A person chosen by the people to represent their several interests in a legislative body; *e.g.* representative elected to serve in Congress from a state congressional district.

"Representative" includes an agent, an officer of a corporation or association, and a trustee, executor or administrator of an estate, or any other person empowered to act for another. U.C.C. § 1–201(35).

See also **Agent; Class or representative action; Legal representative.**

Personal representative. Executors and administrators of person deceased; but it may have a wider meaning, according to the intention of the person using it, and may include heirs, next of kin, descendants, assignees, grantees, receivers, and trustees in insolvency.

Includes executor, administrator, successor, personal representative, special administrator, and persons who perform substantially the same function under the law governing their status. "General personal representative" excludes special administrator. Uniform Probate Code, § 1–201(30).

Reprieve. Temporary relief from or postponement of execution of criminal punishment or sentence. It does no more than stay the execution of a sentence for a time, and it is ordinarily an act of clemency extended to a prisoner to afford him an opportunity to procure some amelioration of the sentence imposed. It differs from a commutation which is a reduction of a sentence and from a pardon which is a permanent cancellation of a sentence.

Reprimand /réprəmǽnd/. To reprove severely; to censure formally, especially with authority. Federal Labor Union 23393, American Federation of Labor v. American Can Co., 28 N.J.Super. 306, 100 A.2d 693, 695. A public and formal censure or severe reproof, administered to a person in fault by his superior officer or by a body or organization to which he belongs. Thus, a member of a legislative body may be reprimanded by the presiding officer, in pursuance of a vote of censure, for improper conduct in the house; similarly, an attorney might be reprimanded by the Supreme Court or Bar Association of his State for unethical or improper conduct.

Reprisal /rəpráyzəl/. In general, any action taken by one person either in spite or as a retaliation for an assumed or real wrong by another. The forcible taking by one nation of a thing that belonged to another, in return or satisfaction for an injury committed by the latter on the former.

General reprisals. Take place by virtue of commissions delivered to officers and citizens of the aggrieved nation, directing them to take the persons and property belonging to the offending nation wherever found.

Negative reprisals. Take place when a nation refuses to fulfill a perfect obligation which it has contracted, or to permit another state to enjoy a right which it justly claims.

Positive reprisals. Consist in seizing the persons and effects belonging to the other nation, in order to obtain satisfaction.

Special reprisals. Such as are granted in times of peace to particular individuals who have suffered an injury from the citizens or subjects of the other nation.

Reprobata pecunia liberat solventem /rèprəbéydə pəkyúwn(i)yə líbərət solvéntəm/. Money refused [the refusal of money tendered] releases him who pays [or tenders it].

Reprobation /rèprəbéyshən/. In ecclesiastical law, the interposition of objections or exceptions; as to the competency of witnesses, to the due execution of instruments offered in evidence and the like.

Republic. A commonwealth; that form of government in which the administration of affairs is open to all the citizens. In another sense, it signifies the state, independently of its form of government.

Republican government. A government in the republican form; a government of the people; a government by representatives chosen by the people. In re Duncan, 139 U.S. 449, 11 S.Ct. 573, 35 L.Ed. 219.

Republication. The re-execution or reestablishment by a testator of a will which he had once revoked. A second publication of a will, either expressly or by construction. A codicil duly executed is a republication of the will. For "Express republication," see that title.

Repudiate. To put away, reject, disclaim, or renounce a right, duty, obligation, or privilege.

Repudiation. Rejection; disclaimer; renunciation. The rejection or refusal of an offered or available right or privilege, or of a duty or relation. The act of a buyer or seller in rejecting a contract of sale either partially or totally. U.C.C. §§ 2–708, 2–711.

Repudiation of a contract means refusal to perform duty or obligation owed to other party. Pitcher v. Lauritzen, 18 Utah 2d 368, 423 P.2d 491, 493; Draughon's Business College v. Battles, 35 Ala.App. 587, 50 So.2d 788, 790. Such consists in such words or actions by contracting party as indicate that he is not going to perform his contract in the future. Continental Cas. Co. v. Boerger, Tex.Civ.App., 389 S.W.2d 566, 568.

Repudiation of contract is in nature of anticipatory breach before performance is due, but does not operate as anticipatory breach unless promisee elects to treat repudiation as breach, and brings suit for damages. Such repudiation is but act or declaration in advance of any actual breach and consists usually of absolute and unequivocal declaration or act amounting to declaration on part of promisor to promisee that he will not make performance on future day at which contract calls for performance. Robinson v. Raquet, 1 Cal.App.2d 533, 36 P.2d 821, 825.

In the civil law, the casting off or putting away of a woman betrothed; also, but less usually, of a wife; divorcement.

In ecclesiastical law, the refusal to accept a benefice which has been conferred upon the party repudiating.

See also **Renunciation.**

Repudium /rəpyúwd(i)yəm/. Lat. In Roman law, a breaking off of the contract of espousals, or of a marriage intended to be solemnized. Sometimes translated "divorce;" but this was not the proper sense.

Inconsistency; a condition which occurs if one part of a document is true (or correct), so that another part cannot be true (or correct).

Repugnancy. An inconsistency, opposition, or contrariety between two or more clauses of the same deed, contract, or statute, or between two or more material allegations of the same pleading, or any two writings.

Inconsistent defenses or claims are permitted under Rule of Civil Proc. 8.

Repurchase. See **Redemption.**

Reputable. Worthy of repute or distinction, held in esteem, honorable, praiseworthy.

Reputable citizen. One who is well spoken of by his neighbors and hence presumably of good character. H. L. Shaffer & Co. v. Prosser, 99 Colo. 335, 62 P.2d 1161, 1163.

Reputatio est vulgaris opinio ubi non est veritas. Et vulgaris opinio est duplex, scil.: opinio vulgaris orta inter graves et discretos homines, et quæ vultum veritatis habet; et opinio tantum orta inter leves et vulgares homines, absque specie veritatis /rèpyuwtéysh-(iy)ow èst vəlgérəs əpín(i)yow yúwbay nón èst véhrətæes. èt vəlgérəs əpín(i)yow èst d(y)úwpleks, síləsət: əpín(i)yow vəlgérəs órdə íntər gréyviyz èt dəskríydows hóməniyz, èt kwìy váltəm vèhrətéydəs héybət; èd əpín(i)yow tæntəm órdə íntər líyviyz èt vəlgériyz hóməniyz æbskwiy spíyshiyiy vehrətéydəs/. Reputation is common opinion where there is not truth. And common opinion is of two kinds, to-wit: Common reputation arising among grave and sensible men, and which has the appearance of truth; and mere opinion arising among foolish and ignorant men, without any appearance of truth.

Reputation. Estimation in which one is held; the character imputed to a person by those acquainted with him. That by which we are known and is the total sum of how we are seen by others. Taylor v. State, 28 Md.App. 560, 346 A.2d 718, 720. General opinion, good or bad, held of a person by those of the community in which he resides. State v. Kiziah, 217 N.C. 399, 8 S.E.2d 474, 477; Citizens Bank of Morehead v. Hunt, 287 Ky. 646, 154 S.W.2d 730, 731. It is necessarily based upon hearsay, Stewart v. State, 148 Tex. Cr.R. 480, 188 S.W.2d 167, 170, but may be admissible if falling within the established exceptions to the hearsay rule. See *e.g.* Fed.Evid.R. 803(19–21).

"Character" is made up of the things an individual actually is and does whereas "reputation" is what people think an individual is and what they say about him. McNaulty v. State, 138 Tex.Cr.R. 317, 135 S.W.2d 987, 989; James v. State ex rel. Loser, 24 Tenn.App. 453, 145 S.W.2d 1026, 1033.

See also **Character; General reputation.**

Repute. By "repute" essential to effect common-law marriage is meant reputation or the character and status commonly ascribed to one's actions by public. Miller v. Townsend Lumber Co., 152 Mont. 210, 448 P.2d 148, 152.

Reputed. Accepted by general, vulgar, or public opinion.

Reputed owner. See **Owner.**

Request, *v.* To ask for something or for permission or authority to do, see, hear, etc., something; to solicit. In its ordinary or natural meaning when used in a will, is precatory and not mandatory. Byars v. Byars, 143 Tex. 10, 182 S.W.2d 363, 364, 366.

Request, *n.* An asking or petition. The expression of a desire to some person for something to be granted or done, particularly for the payment of a debt or performance of a contract. Also, direction or command in law of wills. For **Express request,** see that title.

Request for admission. Written statements of facts concerning the case which are submitted to an adverse party and which that party is required to admit or deny; those statements which are admitted will be treated by the court as having been established and need not be proved at trial. Fed.R.Civil P. 36.

Request for instructions. At the close of the evidence or at such earlier time during the trial as the court reasonably directs, any party may file written requests that the court instruct the jury on the law as set forth in the requests. Fed.R.Civil P. 51.

Require. To direct, order, demand, instruct, command, claim, compel, request, need, exact. State ex rel. Frohmiller v. Hendrix, 59 Ariz. 184, 124 P.2d 768, 773. To be in need of. To ask for authoritatively or imperatively. State v. Community Distributors, Inc., 123 N.J.Super. 589, 304 A.2d 213, 217.

Requirement contract. A contract in writing whereby one agrees to buy, for a sufficient consideration, all the merchandise of a designated type which the buyer may require for use in his own established business. Such contract is not void for uncertainty nor is it illusory. Fuchs v. United Motor Stage Co., 135 Ohio St. 509, 21 N.E.2d 669, 672, 14 O.O. 399. One in which party promises to supply all specific goods or services which other party may need during a certain period at an agreed price, and in which other party

expressly or implicitly promises he will obtain his goods or services from the first party exclusively. Bank of America Nat. Trust & Sav. Ass'n v. Smith, C.A.Cal., 336 F.2d 528, 529.

Requisition. A demand in writing, or formal request or requirement. The taking or seizure of property by government.

The formal demand by one government upon another, or by the governor of one of the United States upon the governor of a sister state, of the surrender of a fugitive criminal. See **Extradition.**

Rerum ordo confunditur si unicuique jurisdictio non servetur /rírəm órdow kənfándədər sày yùwnək(yuw)áykwiy jùrəsdíksh(iy)ow nón sərvíydər/. The order of things is confounded if every one preserve not his jurisdiction.

Rerum progressus ostendunt multa, quæ in initio præcaveri seu prævideri non possunt /rírəm prəgrésəs əsténdənt máltə, kwíy in ənísh(iy)ow priykəvíray s(y)ùw priyvədíray nòn pósənt/. The progress of events shows many things which, at the beginning, could not be guarded against or foreseen.

Rerum suarum quilibet est moderator et arbiter /rírəm s(y)uwérəm kwáyləbəd èst mòdəréydər èd árbədər/. Every one is the regulator and disposer of his own property.

Res /ríyz/. Lat. The subject matter of a trust or will. In the civil law, a thing; an object. As a term of the law, this word has a very wide and extensive signification, including not only things which are objects of property, but also such as are not capable of individual ownership. And in old English law it is said to have a general import, comprehending both corporeal and incorporeal things of whatever kind, nature, or species. By *"res,"* according to the modern civilians, is meant everything that may form an *object* of rights, in opposition to *"persona,"* which is regarded as a *subject* of rights. *"Res,"* therefore, in its general meaning, comprises *actions* of all kinds; while in its restricted sense it comprehends every object of right, except actions. This has reference to the fundamental division of the Institutes, that all law relates either to *persons,* to *things,* or to *actions.*

Res is everything that may form an object of rights and includes an object, subject-matter or status. In re Riggle's Will, 11 A.D.2d 51, 205 N.Y.S.2d 19, 21, 22. The term is particularly applied to an object, subject-matter, or *status,* considered as the defendant in an action, or as the object against which, directly, proceedings are taken. Thus, in a prize case, the captured vessel is "the *res*"; and proceedings of this character are said to be *in rem.* (See In Personam; In Rem.) *"Res"* may also denote the action or proceeding, as when a cause, which is not between adversary parties, is entitled *"In re _____."*

Classification

Things (res) have been variously divided and classified in law, *e.g.,* in the following ways: (1) Corporeal and incorporeal things; (2) movables and immovables; (3) *res mancipi* and *res nec mancipi;* (4) **things** real and things personal; (5) things in possession and choses (*i.e.,* things) in action; (6) fungible things and things not fungible *(fungibles vel non fungibiles);* and (7) *res singulæ (i.e.,* individual objects) and *universitates rerum (i.e.,* aggregates of things). Also persons are for some purposes and in certain respects regarded as things.

Res accessoria /ríyz æksəsór(i)yə/. In the civil law, an accessory thing; that which belongs to a principal thing, or is in connection with it.

Res adiratæ /ríyz ædəréydiy/. The gist of the old action for *res adiratæ* was the fact that the plaintiff had lost his goods, that they had come into the hands of the defendant, and that the defendant, on request, refused to give them up.

Res adjudicata /ríyz æjùwdəkéydə/. A common misspelling of *res judicata.* The latter term designates a point or question or subject-matter which was in controversy or dispute and has been authoritatively and finally settled by the decision of a court; that issuable fact once legally determined is conclusive as between parties in same action or subsequent proceeding. Tiffany Production of California v. Superior Court of California for Los Angeles County, 131 Cal. App. 729, 22 P.2d 275. See *Res judicata, infra.*

Res caduca /ríyz kəd(y)úwkə/. In the civil law, a fallen or escheated thing; an escheat.

Res communes /ríyz kəmyúwniyz/. In the civil law, things common to all; that is, those things which are used and enjoyed by every one, even in single parts, but can never be exclusively acquired as a whole, *e.g.,* light and air.

Res controversa /ríyz kòntrəvársə/. In the civil law, a matter controverted; a matter in controversy; a point in question; a question for determination.

Res coronæ /ríyz kərówniy/. In old English law, things of the crown; such as ancient manors, homages of the king, liberties, etc.

Res corporales /ríyz kòrpəréyliyz/. In the civil law, corporeal things; things which can be touched, or are perceptible to the senses.

Res derelicta /ríyz dèhrəlíktə/. Abandoned property; property thrown away or forsaken by the owner, so as to become open to the acquisition of the first taker or occupant.

Res fungibiles /ríyz fənjíbəliyz/°fánjəbliyz/. In the civil law, fungible things, things of such a nature that they can be replaced by equal quantities and qualities when returning a loan or delivering goods purchased, for example, so many bushels of wheat or so many dollars; but a particular horse or a particular jewel would not be of this character.

Res gestæ /ríyz jéstiy/. Things done. McClory v. Schneider, Tex.Civ.App., 51 S.W.2d 738, 741. The "res gestæ" rule is that where a remark is made spontaneously and concurrently with an affray, collision or the like, it carries with it inherently a degree of credibility and will be admissible because of its spontaneous nature. Carroll v. Guffey, 20 Ill.App.2d 470, 156 N.E.2d 267, 270. "Res gestæ" means literally things or things happened and therefore, to be admissible as exception to hearsay rule, words spoken, thoughts expressed, and gestures made, must all be so closely connected to occurrence or event in both time and substance as to be a part of the happening. McCandless v. Inland Northwest Film Service, Inc., 64 Wash.2d 523, 392 P.2d 613, 618. Those circumstances which are the automatic and undesigned incidents of a particular litigated act, which may be separated from act by lapse of time more or less appreciable, and which are admissible when illustrative of such act. The whole of the transaction under investigation and every part of it. Res gestæ is considered as an exception to the hearsay rule. In its operation it renders acts and declarations which constitute a part of the things done and said admissible in evidence, even though they would otherwise come within the rule excluding hearsay evidence or self-serving declarations. The rule is extended to include, not only declarations by the parties to the suit, but includes statements made by bystanders and strangers, under certain circumstances. See Fed.Evid.Rule 803(3).

A spontaneous declaration made by a person immediately after an event and before the mind has an opportunity to conjure a falsehood. It represents an exception to the hearsay rule and should be referred to as a spontaneous exclamation rather than res gestæ.

Res habiles /ríyz hæbəliyz/. In the civil law, things which are prescriptible; things to which a lawful title may be acquired by ordinary prescription.

Res immobiles /ríyz imówbəliyz/. In the civil law, immovable things; including land and that which is connected therewith, either by nature or art, such as trees and buildings.

Res incorporales /ríyz inkòrpəréyliyz/. In the civil law, incorporeal things; things which cannot be touched; such as those things which consist in right. Such things as the mind alone can perceive.

Res integra /ríyz íntəgrə/°əntégrə/. A whole thing; a new or unopened thing. The term is applied to those points of law which have not been decided, which are untouched by *dictum* or decision.

Res inter alios acta /ríyz ìntər éyl(i)yows æktə/. See **Res inter alios acta.**

Res ipsa loquitur /ríyz ípsə lówkwədər/. The thing speaks for itself. Rebuttable presumption or inference that defendant was negligent, which arises upon proof that instrumentality causing injury was in defendant's exclusive control, and that the accident was one which ordinarily does not happen in absence of negligence. Res ipsa loquitur is rule of evidence whereby negligence of alleged wrongdoer may be inferred from mere fact that accident happened provided character of accident and circumstances attending it lead reasonably to belief that in absence of negligence it would not have occurred and that thing which caused injury is shown to have been under management and control of alleged wrongdoer. Hillen v. Hooker Const. Co., Tex.Civ.App., 484 S.W.2d 113, 115. Under doctrine of "res ipsa loquitur" the happening of an injury permits an inference of negligence where plaintiff produces substantial evidence that injury was caused by an agency or instrumentality under exclusive control and management of defendant, and that the occurrence was such that in the ordinary course of things would not happen if reasonable care had been used.

Res judicata /ríyz jùwdəkéydə/. A matter adjudged; a thing judicially acted upon or decided; a thing or matter settled by judgment. Rule that a final judgment rendered by a court of competent jurisdiction on the merits is conclusive as to the rights of the parties and their privies, and, as to them, constitutes an absolute bar to a subsequent action involving the same claim, demand or cause of action. Matchett v. Rose, 36 Ill.App.3d 638, 344 N.E.2d 770, 779. And to be applicable, requires identity in thing sued for as well as identity of cause of action, of persons and parties to action, and of quality in persons for or against whom claim is made. The sum and substance of the whole rule is that a matter once judicially decided is finally decided. Massie v. Paul, 263 Ky. 183, 92 S.W.2d 11, 14. See also *Res adjudicata, supra;* and, **Collateral estoppel doctrine; Final decision rule; Issue preclusion.**

Estoppel and res judicata distinguished, see **Estoppel.**

Res litigiosæ /ríyz lətìjiyówsay/. In Roman law, things which are in litigation; property or rights which constitute the subject-matter of a pending action.

Res mancipi /ríyz mǽn(t)səpay/. See **Mancipi res.**

Res mobiles /ríyz mówbəliyz/. In the civil law, movable things; things which may be transported from one place to another, without injury to their substance and form. Things corresponding with the chattels personal of the common law.

Res nova /ríyz nówvə/. A new matter; a new case; a question not before decided.

Res nullius /ríyz nəláyəs/. The property of nobody. A thing which has no owner, either because a former owner has finally abandoned it, or because it has never been appropriated by any person, or because (in the Roman law) it is not susceptible of private ownership.

Res periit domino /ríyz péhriyət dómənow/. A phrase used to express that, when a thing is lost or destroyed, it is lost to the person who was the owner of it at the time.

Res privatæ /ríyz prəvéydiy/. In the civil law, things the property of one or more individuals.

Res publicæ /ríyz pə́bləsiy/. Things belonging to the public; public property; such as the sea, navigable rivers, highways, etc.

Res quotidianæ /ríyz kwowtìdiyéyniy/. Every-day matters; familiar points or questions.

Res religiosæ /ríyz rəlìjiyówsiy/. Things pertaining to religion. In Roman law, especially, burial-places, which were regarded as sacred, and could not be the subjects of commerce.

Res universitatis /ríyz yùwnəvərsətéydəs/. In the civil law, things belonging to a community (as, to a municipality), the use and enjoyment of which, according to their proper purpose, is free to every member of the community, but which cannot be appropriated to the exclusive use of any individual; such as the public buildings, streets, etc.

Res accendent lumina rebus /ríyz əkséndənt l(y)úwmənə ríybəs/. One thing throws light upon others.

Res accessoria sequitur rem principalem /ríyz æk-səsór(i)yə sékwədər prìn(t)səpéyləm/. The accessory follows the principal.

Resale. Exists where a person who has sold goods or other property to a purchaser sells them again to someone else. Sometimes a vendor reserves the right of reselling if the purchaser commits default in payment of the purchase money, and in some cases (*e.g.,* on a sale of perishable articles) the vendor may do so without having reserved the right. U.C.C. § 2–706 provides the conditions under which a seller has a right of resale on breach by the buyer of the sales contract.

Term may also refer to act of retailer who purchases goods from manufacturer or wholesaler for purpose of selling such goods in normal course of business. See also **Retail; Retailer.**

Resale price maintenance. An agreement between a manufacturer and retailer that the latter should not resell below a specified minimum price. Until 1976, federal statutes exempted such state-permitted agreements from antitrust actions.

Resceit /rəsíyt/. In old English practice, an admission or receiving a third person to plead his right in a cause formerly commenced between two others; as, in an action by tenant for life or years, he in the reversion might come in and pray to be received to defend the land, and to plead with the demandant.

Resceit of homage /rəsíyd əv (h)óməj/. In old English law, the lord's receiving homage of his tenant at his admission to the land.

Rescind. To abrogate, annul, avoid, or cancel a contract; particularly, nullifying a contract by the act of a party. To declare a contract void in its inception and to put an end to it as though it never were. Russell v. Stephens, 191 Wash. 314, 71 P.2d 30, 31. Not merely to terminate it and release parties from further obligations to each other but to abrogate it from the beginning and restore parties to relative positions which they would have occupied had no contract ever been made. Sylvania Industrial Corporation v. Lilienfeld's Estate, C.C.A.Va., 132 F.2d 887, 892. See also **Rescission of contract.**

Rescissio /rəsísh(iy)ow/. Lat. In the civil law, an annulling; avoiding, or making void; abrogation; rescission.

Rescission of contract. A "rescission" amounts to the unmaking of a contract, or an undoing of it from the beginning, and not merely a termination, and it may be effected by mutual agreement of parties, or by one of the parties declaring rescission of contract without consent of other if a legally sufficient ground therefor exists, or by applying to courts for a decree of rescission. Abdallah, Inc. v. Martin, 242 Minn. 416, 65 N.W.2d 641, 644. Annulling, abrogation or unmaking of contract and the placing of the parties to it in status quo. Sessions v. Meadows, 13 Cal.App.2d 748, 57 P.2d 548, 549. It necessarily involves a repudiation of the contract and a refusal of the moving party to be further bound by it. See also **Renunciation; Repudiation.**

An action of an equitable nature in which a party seeks to be relieved of his obligations under a contract on the grounds of mutual mistake, fraud, impossibility, etc.

Rescous /réskyuw/. Rescue. The taking back by force goods which had been taken under a distress, or the violently taking away a man who is under arrest, and setting him at liberty, or otherwise procuring his escape, are both so denominated. This was also the name of a writ which lay in cases of rescue.

Rescript /ríyskript/. In canon law, a term including any form of apostolical letter emanating from the Pope. The answer of the Pope in writing.

At common law, a counterpart, duplicate, or copy.

In American law, a written order from the court to the clerk, giving directions concerning the further disposition of a case. The written statement by an appellate court of its decision in a case, with the reasons therefor, sent down to the trial court. A short appellate opinion which does not bear the name of any justice.

In the civil law, a species of imperial constitutions, being the answers of the prince in individual cases, chiefly given in response to inquiries by parties in relation to litigated suits, or to inquiries by the judges, and which became rules for future litigated or doubtful legal questions.

Rescriptum /rəskríptəm/. Lat. In the civil law, a species of imperial constitution, in the form of an answer to some application or petition; a rescript.

Rescue. Act of saving or freeing. At common law, forcibly and knowingly freeing another from arrest, imprisonment or legal custody without any effort by prisoner to free himself. Merrill v. State, 42 Ariz. 341, 26 P.2d 110. The unlawfully or forcibly taking back goods which have been taken under a distress for rent, damage feasant, etc. See also **Repossession**.

In admiralty and maritime law, the deliverance of property taken as prize, out of the hands of the captors, either when the captured party retake it by their own efforts, or when, pending the pursuit or struggle, the party about to be overpowered receive reinforcements, and so escape capture.

Rescue doctrine. Rescue doctrine is that one who has, through his negligence, endangered safety of another may be held liable for injuries sustained by third person who attempts to save other from injury. National Dairy Products Corp. v. Freschi, Mo.App., 393 S.W.2d 48, 57. Danger invites rescue.

"Rescue", "humanitarian" or "good samaritan" doctrine is that one who sees a person in imminent and serious peril through negligence of another cannot be charged with contributory negligence, as a matter of law, in risking his own life or serious injury in attempting to effect a rescue, provided the attempt is not recklessly or rashly made. Jobst v. Butler Well Servicing, Inc., 190 Kan. 86, 372 P.2d 55, 59.

Rescyt /rəsíyt/. L. Fr. Resceit; receipt; the receiving or harboring a felon, after the commission of a crime.

Res denominatur a principali parte /ríyz dənòmənéydər èy prìn(t)səpéylay párdiy/. The thing is named from its principal part.

Resealing writ. In English law, the second sealing of a writ by a master so as to continue it, or to cure it of an irregularity.

Reservation. A clause in a deed or other instrument of conveyance by which the grantor creates, and reserves to himself, some right, interest, or profit in the estate granted, which had no previous existence as such, but is first called into being by the instrument reserving it; such as rent, or an easement. Reservation occurs where granting clause of the deed operates to exclude a portion of that which would otherwise pass to the grantee by the description in the deed and "reserves" that portion unto the grantor. Board of County Com'rs of Weld County v. Anderson, 34 Colo.App. 37, 525 P.2d 478, 482.

A right created and retained by a grantor. The reservation may be temporary (such as a life estate) or permanent (such as an easement running with the land).

The reservation of a point of law is the act of the trial court in setting it aside for future consideration, allowing the trial to proceed meanwhile as if the question had been settled one way, but subject to alteration of the judgment in case the court *in banc* should decide it differently.

For exception and reservation distinguished, see **Exception**.

A reservation is a tract of land, more or less considerable in extent, which is by public authority withdrawn from sale or settlement, and appropriated to specific public uses; such as parks, military posts, Indian lands, etc. A tract of land (under control of the Bureau of Indian Affairs) to which an American Indian tribe retains its original title to ownership or which has been set aside for its use out of the public domain.

Reservation of claim. A draft or demand presented under a letter of credit is non-complying if there is an explicit reservation of claim. U.C.C. § 5–110.

Reservatio non debet esse de proficuis ipsis, quia ea conceduntur, sed de reditu novo extra proficua /rèzərvéysh(iy)ow nòn débəd ésiy dìy prəfíkyuwəs ípsəs, kwáyə íyə kòn(t)sədántər sèd dìy rédət(y)uw nówvow ékstrə prəfíkyuwə/. A reservation ought not to be of the profits themselves, because they are granted, but from the new rent, apart from the profits.

Reserve, *v.* To keep back, to retain, to keep in store for future or special use, and to retain or hold over to a future time. Commissioner of Internal Revenue v. Strong Mfg. Co., C.C.A.6, 124 F.2d 360, 363. To set aside funds, usually for indefinite contingencies, such as future maintenance of a structure, or to pay future claims.

Reserve, *n.* Funds set aside to cover future expenses, losses, or claims. In insurance law, a sum of money, variously computed or estimated, which, with accretions from interest, is set aside as a fund with which to mature or liquidate by payment or reinsurance with other companies future unaccrued and contingent claims, and claims accrued but contingent and indefinite as to amount or time of payment. Royal Highlanders v. Commissioner of Internal Revenue, C.C.A.8, 138 F.2d 240, 242, 244. Reserves of insurance company are amount treated as liability on balance sheet which company estimates will be sufficient to meet its policy obligations. United Life & Acc. Ins. Co. v. U. S., D.C.N.H., 329 F.Supp. 765, 768.

"With reserve" in an auction means that the thing will not be sold if the highest bid is not high enough. To "reserve title" is to keep an ownership right as security that the thing will be fully paid for.

Bad debt reserve. In accounting, a reserve set aside for losses on accounts and notes receivable. An account for bad debts is offset by an account or reserve for bad debts. When accounts become uncollectible they are washed against the reserve.

Contingency reserve. See that title.

Depletion reserve. An account used in connection with diminishing assets such as mines, timber, etc. to reflect the depletion of the asset.

Depreciation reserve. An account used to recover the cost of an asset by writing off a portion of the cost over the life of the asset or by some other acceptable method.

Legal reserve. A reserve account required by law for insurance companies and banks as protection against losses.

Replacement reserve. An account set up for the actual replacement of machinery and equipment.

Sinking fund reserve. An account set up for the redemption of long term debt. It is commonly required by a bond indenture.

Reserve banks. Member banks of Federal Reserve System.

Reserve Board. See **Federal Reserve Board of Governors.**

Reserve clause. A clause inserted in contracts of professional athletes whereby the athlete's service is reserved for the team holding his contract. It represents a hold on the player by the team which has contracted with him, and such team has the exclusive right to trade the player to another team without his consent. Such reserve clauses in professional baseball contracts have long since been held to be exempt from federal antitrust laws. See Toolson v. New York Yankees, Inc., 346 U.S. 356, 74 S.Ct. 78, 98 L.Ed. 64; Flood v. Kuhn, 407 U.S. 258, 92 S.Ct. 2099, 32 L.Ed.2d 728.

Reserved. Retained, kept or set apart, for a purpose or a person.

Reserved land. Public land that has been withheld or kept back from sale or disposition. See **Reservation.**

Reserved power. A power specifically withheld because not mentioned or reasonably implied in other powers conferred by a constitution or statute. See also **Power** (*Constitutional powers*).

Reserve fund. See **Reserve.**

Reserve ratio. In banking, the primary reserve ratio is the ratio of the balance of Federal Reserve balance of the bank plus cash in vault to the demand deposits of the bank. The secondary ratio is the ratio between the government securities of the bank and its demand deposits. There is also a ratio between time deposits and Federal Reserve balances plus cash in vault.

Res est misera ubi jus est vagum et incertum /ríyz èst mízərə yúwbay jás èst véygəm èd ənsárdəm/. It is a wretched state of things when law is vague and mutable.

Reset. In old English law, the receiving or harboring an outlawed person.

Resettlement. The reopening of an order or decree for the purpose of including therein some recital or provision which should have been included and was initially omitted through inadvertence. In re Bartlett's Will, 164 Misc. 524, 299 N.Y.S. 316, 317.

Res generalem habet significationem quia tam corporea quam incorporea cujuscunque sunt generis, naturæ, sive speciei, comprehendit /ríyz jènəréyləm héybət sìgnəfəkèyshiyównəm kwáyə tæm korpóriyə kwæm ìnkorpóriyə k(y)ùwjáskáŋkwiy sànt jénərəs, nətyúriy sáyviy spíyshiyay, kòmprəhéndət/. The word "thing" has a general signification, because it comprehends corporeal and incorporeal objects, of whatever nature, sort, or species.

Res gestæ. See **Res.**

Resiance /réziyən(t)s/. Residence, abode, or continuance.

Resiant /réziyənt/. In old English law, continually dwelling or abiding in a place; resident; a resident.

Reside. Live, dwell, abide, sojourn, stay, remain, lodge. Western-Knapp Engineering Co. v. Gilbank, C.C.A. Cal., 129 F.2d 135, 136. To settle oneself or a thing in a place, to be stationed, to remain or stay, to dwell permanently or continuously, to have a settled abode for a time, to have one's residence or domicile; specifically, to be in residence, to have an abiding place, to be present as an element, to inhere as a quality, to be vested as a right. State ex rel. Bowden v. Jensen, Mo., 359 S.W.2d 343, 349.

Residence. Personal presence at some place of abode with no present intention of definite and early removal and with purpose to remain for undetermined period, not infrequently, but not necessarily combined with design to stay permanently. T. P. Laboratories, Inc. v. Huge, D.C.Md., 197 F.Supp. 860, 865. Bodily presence and the intention of remaining in a place, to sit down, to stay in a place, to settle, to remain, and is made up of fact and intention, the fact of abode and the intention of remaining, and is a combination of acts and intention. Application of People ex rel. Croen, 2 Misc.2d 141, 155 N.Y.S.2d 393, 398. Residence implies something more than mere physical presence and something less than domicile. Petition of Castrinakis, D.C.Md., 179 F.Supp. 444, 445. See also **Abode; Domicile; Legal residence.**

"Domicile" compared and distinguished. As "domicile" and "residence" are usually in the same place, they are frequently used as if they had the same meaning, but they are not identical terms, for a person may have two places of residence, as in the city and country, but only one domicile. Residence means living in a particular locality, but domicile means living in that locality with intent to make it a fixed and permanent home. Residence simply requires bodily presence as an inhabitant in a given place, while domicile requires bodily presence in that

place and also an intention to make it one's domicile. Fuller v. Hofferbert, C.A.Ohio, 204 F.2d 592, 597. "Residence" is not synonymous with "domicile," though the two terms are closely related; a person may have only one legal domicile at one time, but he may have more than one residence. Fielding v. Casualty Reciprocal Exchange, La.App., 331 So.2d 186, 188.

In certain contexts the courts consider "residence" and "domicile" to be synonymous (*e.g.* divorce action, Cooper v. Cooper, 269 Cal.App.2d 6, 74 Cal. Rptr. 439, 441); while in others the two terms are distinguished (*e.g.* venue, Fromkin v. Loehmann's Hewlett, Inc., 16 Misc.2d 117, 184 N.Y.S.2d 63, 65).

Legal residence. See that title.

Residency requirements. Broad term to describe terms of residence required by states for such things as welfare benefits, admission to the bar, divorce, etc. As regards divorce and welfare prerequisites, the requirements must not be so stringent as to violate due process or equal protection. See **Right to travel.**

Resident. Any person who occupies a dwelling within the State, has a present intent to remain within the State for a period of time, and manifests the genuineness of that intent by establishing an ongoing physical presence within the State together with indicia that his presence within the State is something other than merely transitory in nature. The word "resident" when used as a noun, means a dweller, habitant or occupant; one who resides or dwells in a place for a period of more, or less, duration; it signifies one having a residence, or one who resides or abides. Hanson v. P. A. Peterson Home Ass'n, 35 Ill.App.2d 134, 182 N.E.2d 237, 240. Word "resident" has many meanings in law, largely determined by statutory context in which it is used. Kelm v. Carlson, C.A.Ohio, 473 F.2d 1267, 1271. See also **Residence.**

Resident agent. Person in a jurisdiction authorized to accept service of process for another, especially a corporation.

Resident alien. One, not yet a citizen of this country, who has come into the country from another with the intent to abandon his former citizenship and to reside here.

Resident freeholder. A person who resides in the particular place (town, city, county, etc.) and who owns an estate in lands therein amounting at least to a freehold interest.

Residential cluster. An area to be developed as a single entity according to a plan containing residential housing units which have a common or public open space area as an appurtenance. See also **Planned unit development.**

Residential density. The number of dwelling units per gross acre of residential land area including streets, easements and open space portions of a development.

Residual /rəzídyuwəl/rəzíj(uw)əl/. Relating to the residue; relating to the part remaining; that which is left over. Term may also refer to deferred commissions.

Residuary /rəzídyuwəriy/. Pertaining to the residue; constituting the residue; giving or bequeathing the residue; receiving or entitled to the residue. See **Residue.**

Residuary account. In English practice, the account which every executor and administrator, after paying the debts and particular legacies of the deceased, and before paying over the residuum, must pass before the board of inland revenue.

Residuary bequest. A bequest of all of testator's estate not otherwise effectually disposed of.

Residuary clause. Clause in will by which that part of property is disposed of which remains after satisfying bequests and devises. Any part of the will which disposes of property not expressly disposed of by other provisions of the will. Jackson v. Jackson, 217 Kan. 448, 536 P.2d 1400, 1406.

Residuary devise and devisee. See **Devise.**

Residuary estate. That which remains after debts and expenses of administration, legacies, and devises have been satisfied. It consists of all that has not been legally disposed of by will, other than by residuary clause. Gross estate less all charges, debts, costs, and all other legacies. In re Miller's Estate, Fla.App., 301 So.2d 137, 139.

Residuary gift. See **Legacy.**

Residuary legacy. See **Legacy.**

Residuary legatee. See **Legatee.**

Residue. The surplus of a testator's estate remaining after all the debts and particular legacies have been discharged. See also **Residuary estate.**

Residuum /rəzídyuwəm/. That which remains after any process of separation or deduction; a residue or balance. That which remains of a decedent's estate, after debts have been paid and legacies deducted.

Residuum rule. While a decision of an administrative board may be based partly on hearsay evidence introduced at the hearing, it will be upheld on judicial review only if there is a residuum of competent evidence on which it is founded. The residuum rule has generally been rejected by the federal courts. See Richardson v. Perales, 402 U.S. 389, 91 S.Ct. 1420, 28 L.Ed.2d 842.

Resignatio est juris proprii spontanea refutatio /rèzəgnéysh(iy)ow èst júrəs prówpriyay spontéyn(i)yə rèfyuwtéysh(iy)ow/. Resignation is a spontaneous relinquishment of one's own right.

Resignation. Formal renouncement or relinquishment of an office. It must be made with intention of relinquishing the office accompanied by act of relinquishment.

Resilire /rezəláyriy/. Lat. In old English law, to draw back from a contract before it is made binding.

Res inter alios acta /ríyz íntər éyliyows ǽktə/. The rule "res inter alios acta" forbids the introduction of collateral facts which by their nature are incapable of affording any reasonable presumption or inference as to the principal matter in dispute, and thus evidence

1178

as to acts, transactions or occurrences to which accused is not a party or is not connected is inadmissible. State v. McCarty, Iowa, 179 N.W.2d 548, 550.

In law of evidence, a thing or event which occurs at a time different from the time in issue is generally not admissible to prove what occurred at the time in issue. Also events which involve those not parties to an action are generally not admissible because they are immaterial and commonly not relevant.

Res inter alios acta alteri nocere non debet /ríyz íntər éyl(i)yows ǽktə óltəray nəsíriy nòn débət/. Things done between strangers ought not to injure those who are not parties to them.

Res inter alios judicatæ nullum aliis præjudicium faciunt /ríyz íntər éyl(i)yows jùwdəkéydiy nóləm éyliyəs prèjuwdísh(iy)əm fǽshiyənt/. Matters adjudged in a cause do not prejudice those who were not parties to it.

Res ipsa loquitur. See **Res.**

Resist. To oppose. This word properly describes an opposition by direct action and *quasi* forcible means.

Resistance. The act of resisting opposition. The employment of forcible means to prevent the execution of an endeavor in which force is employed; standing against; obstructing. Withstanding the force or effect of or the exertion of oneself to counteract or defeat. Landry v. Daley, D.C.Ill., 280 F.Supp. 938, 959. See **Self defense.**

Resisting an officer. In criminal law, the offense of obstructing, opposing, and endeavoring to prevent (with or without actual force) a peace officer in the execution of a writ or in the lawful discharge of his duty while making an arrest or otherwise enforcing the peace.

Res judicata. See **Res.**

Res judicata facit ex albo nigrum; ex nigro, album; ex curvo, rectum; ex recto, curvum /ríyz jùwdəkéydə féyshəd èks ǽlbow náygrəm, èks náygrow ǽlbəm, èks kárvow réktəm, èks réktow kárvəm/. A thing adjudged [the solemn judgment of a court] makes white, black; black, white; the crooked, straight; the straight, crooked.

Res judicata pro veritate accipitur /ríyz jùwdəkéydə pròw vèhrətéytiy əksípədər/. A matter adjudged is taken for truth. A matter decided or passed upon by a court of competent jurisdiction is received as evidence of truth.

Res nullius naturaliter fit primi occupantis /ríyz nəláyəs nǽchəréylədər fit práymay òkyəpǽntəs/. A thing which has no owner naturally belongs to the first finder.

Resolution. A formal expression of the opinion or will of an official body or a public assembly, adopted by vote; as a legislative resolution. Such may be either a simple, joint or concurrent resolution.

The term is usually employed to denote the adoption of a motion, the subject-matter of which would not properly constitute a statute, such as a mere expression of opinion; an alteration of the rules; a vote of thanks or of censure, etc. Such is

not law but merely a form in which a legislative body expresses an opinion. Baker v. City of Milwaukee, 271 Or. 500, 533 P.2d 772, 775.

The chief distinction between a "resolution" and a "law" is that the former is used whenever the legislative body passing it wishes merely to express an opinion as to some given matter or thing and is only to have a temporary effect on such particular thing, while by a "law" it is intended to permanently direct and control matters applying to persons or things in general.

Concurrent resolution. An action of Congress passed in the form of a resolution of one house, the other concurring, which expresses the sense of Congress on a particular subject.

Joint resolution. A resolution adopted by both houses of congress or a legislature. When such a resolution has been approved by the president or passed with his approval, it has the effect of a law.

The distinction between a joint resolution and a concurrent resolution of congress, is that the former requires the approval of the president while the latter does not.

Ordinance distinguished. "Resolution" denotes something less formal than "ordinance"; generally, it is mere expression of opinion or mind of council concerning some matter of administration, within its official cognizance, and provides for disposition of particular item of administrative business of a municipality; it is not a law, and in substance there is no difference between resolution, order and motion. City of Salisbury v. Nagel, Mo.App., 420 S.W.2d 37, 43.

Resoluto jure concedentis resolvitur jus concessum /rèzəl(y)úwdow júriy kòn(t)sədéntəs rəzólvədər jás kən(t)sésəm/. The right of the grantor being extinguished, the right granted is extinguished.

Resolutory condition /rəzólyət(ə)riy kəndíshən/. See **Condition.**

Resort, *v.* To frequent; to go, especially to go frequently, customarily, or usually. To have recourse; to look to for relief or help.

Resort, *n.* Recourse; a person or thing that is looked to for help. A place of frequent assembly; a haunt. U. S. ex rel. Dobra v. Lindsey, D.C.Tex., 51 F.2d 141, 142.

Court of last resort. A court whose decision is final and without further appeal in reference to the particular case; *e.g.* Supreme Court of the United States.

Resources. Money or any property that can be converted to meet needs; means of raising money or supplies; capabilities of raising wealth or to supply necessary wants; available means or capability of any kind. Cerenzia v. Department of Social Security of Washington, 18 Wash.2d 230, 138 P.2d 868, 871. See also **Natural resources.**

RESPA (Real Estate Settlement Procedures Act). A federal statute governing disclosure of settlement costs in the sale of residential (one to four family) improved property which is to be financed by a federally insured lender. 12 U.S.C.A. § 2601 et seq. See also **Closing.**

Respective. Relating to particular persons or things, each to each; particular; several; as, their respective homes.

Respectu computi vicecomitis habendo /rəspékt(y)uw kómpyəday vàysiykómədəs həbéndow/. A writ for respiting a sheriff's account addressed to the treasurer and barons of the exchequer.

Res per pecuniam æstimatur, et non pecunia per rem /ríyz pòr pəkyúwn(i)yəm èstəméydər èt nón pəkyúwn(i)yə pòr rém/. The value of a thing is estimated according to its worth in money, but the value of money is not estimated by reference to a thing.

Respiciendum est judicanti ne quid aut durius aut remissius constituatur quam causa deposcit; nec enim aut severitatis aut clementiæ gloria affectanda est /rəspìshiyéndəm èst jùwdəkǽntay nìy kwíd òt dyúriyəs òt rəmís(i)yəs kən(t)stìt(y)uwéydər kwǽm kózə dəpósət, nèk íynəm òt səvèhrətéydəs òt kləménshiyiy glóriyə ǽfektǽndə èst/. The judge must see that no order be made or judgment given or sentence passed either more harshly or more mildly than the case requires; he must not seek renown, either as a severe or as a tender-hearted judge.

Respite /réspət/rəspáyt/. The temporary suspension of the execution of a sentence; a reprieve; a delay, forbearance, or continuation of time.

In the civil law, an act by which a debtor, who is unable to satisfy his debts at the moment, transacts (compromises) with his creditors, and obtains from them time or delay for the payment of the sums which he owes to them. The respite is either voluntary or forced. It is *voluntary* when all the creditors consent to the proposal, which the debtor makes, to pay in a limited time the whole or a part of the debt. It is *forced* when a part of the creditors refuse to accept the debtor's proposal, and when the latter is obliged to compel them by judicial authority to consent to what the others have determined, in the cases directed by law.

Respite of appeal. Adjourning an appeal to some future time.

Respite of homage. To dispense with the performance of homage by tenants who held their lands in consideration of performing homage to their lords.

Respondeat ouster /rəspóndiyət áwstər/. Upon an issue in law arising upon a dilatory plea, the form of judgment for the plaintiff is that the defendant answer over, which is thence called a judgment of *"respondeat ouster."* This not being a final judgment, the pleading is resumed, and the action proceeds.

Respondeat raptor, qui ignorare non potuit quod pupillum alienum abduxit /rəspóndiyət rǽptər kwày ignərériy nòn póduwət kwòd p(y)əpíləm ǽliyíynəm æbdə́ksət/. Let the ravisher answer, for he cannot be ignorant that he has taken away another's ward.

Respondeat superior /rəspóndiyət s(y)əpíriyər/. Let the master answer. This maxim means that a master is liable in certain cases for the wrongful acts of his servant, and a principal for those of his agent. Burger Chef Systems, Inc. v. Govro, C.A.Mo., 407 F.2d 921, 925. Under this doctrine master is responsible for want of care on servant's part toward those to whom master owes duty to use care, provided failure of servant to use such care occurred in course of his employment. Shell Petroleum Corporation v. Magnolia Pipe Line Co., Tex.Civ.App., 85 S.W.2d 829, 832. Doctrine applies only when relation of master and servant existed between defendant and wrongdoer at time of injury sued for, in respect to very transaction from which it arose. Hence doctrine is inapplicable where injury occurs while servant is acting outside legitimate scope of authority. Rogers v. Town of Black Mountain, 224 N.C. 119, 29 S.E.2d 203, 205. But if deviation be only slight or incidental, employer may still be liable. Klotsch v. P. F. Collier & Son Corporation, 349 Mo. 40, 159 S.W.2d 589, 593, 595; Adams v. South Carolina Power Co., 200 S.C. 438, 21 S.E.2d 17, 19, 20.

Respondent /rəspóndənt/. In equity practice, the party who makes an answer to a bill or other proceeding in equity. In appellate practice, the party who contends against an appeal; *i.e.* the appellee.

In the civil law, one who answers or is security for another; a fidejussor.

Respondentia /rèspondénsh(iy)ə/. The hypothecation of the cargo or goods on board a ship as security for the repayment of a loan, the term "bottomry" being confined to hypothecations of the ship herself; but now the term "respondentia" is seldom used, and the expression "bottomry" is generally employed, whether the vessel or her cargo or both be the security.

A contract by which a cargo, or some part thereof, is hypothecated as security for a loan, the repayment of which is dependent on maritime risks.

Respondera son soveraigne /rə(s)póndərə sòn sóv(ə)r-ən/°sòvərén/. His superior or master shall answer.

Respondere non debet /rəspóndəriy nòn débət/. Lat. In common law pleading, the prayer of a plea where the defendant insists that he ought not to answer, as when he claims a privilege; for example, as being a member of congress or a foreign ambassador.

Responsalis /rèspon(t)séyləs/. In old English law, one who appeared for another.

In ecclesiastical law, a proctor.

Responsalis ad lucrandum vel petendum /rèspon(t)-séyləs æd l(y)uwkrǽndəm vèl pəténdəm/. He who appears and answers for another in court at a day assigned; a proctor, attorney, or deputy.

Responsa prudentium /rəspón(t)sə pruwdénsh(iy)əm/. Lat. Answers of jurists; responses given upon cases or questions of law referred to them, by certain learned Roman jurists, who, though not magistrates, were authorized to render such opinions. These *responsa* constituted one of the most important sources of the earlier Roman law, and were of great value in developing its scientific accuracy. They held much the same place of authority as our modern precedents and reports.

Responsibility. The state of being answerable for an obligation, and includes judgment, skill, ability and capacity. McFarland v. George, Mo.App., 316 S.W.2d 662, 671. The obligation to answer for an act done, and to repair or otherwise make restitution for any injury it may have caused. See also **Responsible.**

Responsibility of eviction. In a lease the burden of expelling by legal process those in possession, if they wrongfully withhold it.

Responsible. Liable; legally accountable or answerable. Able to pay a sum for which he is or may become liable, or to discharge an obligation which he may be under.

Responsible bidder. One who is capable financially and competent to complete the job for which he is bidding. A responsible bidder is one who is not only financially responsible, but who is possessed of a judgment, skill, ability, capacity and integrity requisite and necessary to perform a public contract according to its terms. Federal Elec. Corp. v. Fasi, 56 Haw. 57, 527 P.2d 1284, 1291.

Responsible cause. So as to relieve defendant from liability for injuries, a cause which is the culpable act of a human being who is legally responsible for such act.

Responsible government. This term generally designates that species of governmental system in which the responsibility for public measures or acts of state rests upon the ministry or executive council, who are under an obligation to resign when disapprobation of their course is expressed by a vote of want of confidence, in the legislative assembly, or by the defeat of an important measure advocated by them.

Responsio unius non omnino audiatur /rəsponsh(iy)ow yuwnáyəs nòn omnáynow odiyéydər/. The answer of one witness shall not be heard at all. A maxim of the Roman law of evidence.

Responsive. Answering; constituting or comprising a complete answer. A "responsive allegation" is one which directly answers the allegation it is intended to meet.

Responsive pleading. A pleading which joins issue and replies to a prior pleading of an opponent in contrast to a dilatory plea or motion which seeks to dismiss on some ground other than the merits of the action.

Res propria est quæ communis non est /ríyz prówpriyə èst kwìy kəmyúwnəs nón èst/. A thing is private which is not common.

Res quæ intra præsidia perductæ nondum sunt, quanquam ab hostibus occupatæ, ideo postliminii non egent, quia dominium nondum mutarunt ex gentium jure /ríyz kwìy íntrə prəsídiyə pərdə́ktiy nóndəm sə́nt, kwǽŋkwəm æ̀b (h)óstəbəs okyəpéydiy, ídiyow powstlímənay nòn íyjənt kwàyə dəmíniyəm nóndəm myuwtérənt èks jénsh(iy)əm júriy/. Things which have not yet been introduced within the enemy's lines, although held by the enemy, do not need the fiction of postliminy on this account, because their ownership by the law of nations has not yet changed.

Res sacra non recipit æstimationem /ríyz sǽkrə nòn résəpəd èstəmèyshiyównəm/. A sacred thing does not admit of valuation.

Resseiser /rəsíyzər/. The taking of lands into the hands of the crown, where a general livery or *ouster le main* was formerly misused.

Res sua nemini servit /ríyz s(y)úwə némənay sə́rvət/. No one can have a servitude over his own property.

Rest, *v.* In the trial of an action, a party is said to "rest," or "rest his case," when he advises the court or intimates that he has produced all the evidence he intends to offer at that stage, and submits the case, either finally, or subject to his right to afterwards offer rebutting evidence.

Rest, *n.* Repose; cessation or intermission of motion, exertion or labor; freedom from activity; quiet. Corrugating Machinery Corporation v. Progressive Corrugated Paper Machinery Co., D.C.N.Y., 47 F.2d 273, 275. Also residue (which title see).

Restatement of Law. A series of volumes authored by the American Law Institute that tell what the law in a general area is, how it is changing, and what direction the authors think this change should take; for example, Restatement of the Law of Contracts; Restatement of the Law of Torts.

Restaur, or **restor** /rəstór/. In old English law, the remedy or recourse which marine underwriters have against each other, according to the date of their assurances, or against the master, if the loss arise through his default, as through ill loading, want of caulking, or want of having the vessel tight; also the remedy or recourse a person has against his guarantor or other person who is to indemnify him from any damage sustained.

Restitutio in integrum /rèstət(y)úwsh(iy)ow in íntəgrəm /°intégrəm/. Lat. In the civil law, restoration or restitution to the previous condition. This was effected by the prætor on equitable grounds, at the prayer of an injured party, by rescinding or annulling a contract or transaction valid by the strict law, or annulling a change in the legal condition produced by an omission, and restoring the parties to their previous situation or legal relations. The restoration of a cause to its first state, on petition of the party who was cast, in order to have a second hearing.

Maximum measure of damages awarded in event of a marine collision is "restitutio in integrum" which strictly construed limits damages to the difference in value of vessel before and after collision, but measure is equated with the cost of necessary repairs and loss of earnings while they are being made. Delta Marine Drilling Co. v. M/V Baroid Ranger, C.A.La., 454 F.2d 128, 129.

Restitution. Act of restoring; restoration; restoration of anything to its rightful owner; the act of making good or giving equivalent for any loss, damage or injury; and indemnification. State v. Barnett, 110 Vt. 221, 3 A.2d 521, 525, 526. Restoration of status quo and is amount which would put plaintiff in as good a position as he would have been if no contract had been made and restores to plaintiff value of what he parted with in performing contract. Explorers Motor Home Corp. v. Aldridge, Tex.Civ.App., 541 S.W.2d 851, 852. A person who has been unjustly enriched at the expense of another is required to make restitution to the other. Restatement of the Law, Restitution, § 1.

In torts, restitution is essentially the measure of damages, while in contracts a person aggrieved by a breach is entitled to be placed in the position in which he would have been if the defendant had not breached.

In the law of commercial sales, the buyer's rights to restitution are governed by U.C.C. § 2–718.

See also **Unjust enrichment, doctrine of.**

Criminal law. Many states have restitution programs under which the criminal offender is required to repay, as a condition of his sentence, the victim or society in money or services.

Maritime law. The placing back or restoring articles which have been lost by jettison: This is done, when remainder of the cargo has been saved, at the general charge of the owners of the cargo.

Restitution of conjugal rights. In English ecclesiastical law, a species of matrimonial cause or suit which was brought whenever either a husband or wife was guilty of the injury of subtraction, or lived separate from the other without any sufficient reason; in which case the ecclesiastical jurisdiction compelled them to come together again, if either be weak enough to desire it, contrary to the inclination of the other. 3 Bl.Comm. 94.

Writ of restitution. See that title.

Restitutione extracti ab ecclesia /rèstət(y)ùwshiyówniy ekstrǽktay ǽb əklíyz(i)yə/. In ecclesiastical law, a writ to restore a man to the church, which he had recovered for his sanctuary, being suspected of felony.

Restitutione temporalium /rèstət(y)ùwshiyówniy tèmpəréyl(i)yəm/. In ecclesiastical law, a writ addressed to the sheriff, to restore the temporalities of a bishopric to the bishop elected and confirmed.

Restrain. To limit, confine, abridge, narrow down, restrict, obstruct, impede, hinder, stay, destroy. To prohibit from action; to put compulsion upon; to restrict; to hold or press back. To keep in check; to hold back from acting, proceeding, or advancing, either by physical or moral force, or by interposing obstacle; to repress or suppress; to curb. N. L. R. B. v. Exchange Parts Co., C.A.5, 304 F.2d 368, 374.

To enjoin. See **Injunction; Restraining order.**

Restraining order. An order in the nature of an injunction. An order which may issue upon filing of an application for an injunction forbidding the defendant to do the threatened act until a hearing on the application can be had, and is distinguishable from an injunction, in that the former is intended only as a restraint until the propriety of granting an injunction can be determined and it does no more than restrain the proceeding until such determination. Laundry, Dry Cleaning, Dye House Workers Union, Local 3008, AFL–CIO v. Laundry Workers Intern. Union, 4 Wis.2d 542, 91 N.W.2d 320, 326. See also **Injunction; Order; Temporary restraining order.**

Restraining powers. Restrictions or limitations imposed upon the exercise of a power by the donor thereof.

Restraint. Confinement, abridgment, or limitation. Prohibition of action; holding or pressing back from action. Hindrance, confinement, or restriction of liberty. Obstruction, hindrance or destruction of trade or commerce. See **Restraint of trade; Stop.**

Unlawful restraint. Unlawful restraint is knowingly and without legal authority restraining another so as to interfere substantially with his liberty.

Person is guilty of "unlawful restraint" if he knowingly: (1) restrains another unlawfully in circumstances exposing him to risk of serious bodily injury; or (2) holds another in a condition of involuntary servitude. 18 Pa.C.S.A. § 2902. See also **Imprisonment.** *(False imprisonment);* **Kidnapping.**

Restraint of marriage. The law will not enforce a general restraint of marriage which bars the donee or legatee from ever marrying as a condition of receiving the gift or legacy; but limitations on a gift which conditions it on the donee's or legatee's marrying within a certain religion or nationality have been upheld.

Restraint of princes and rulers. In marine and war risk policies, refers to operation of sovereign power by exercise of vis major, in its sovereign capacity, controlling and divesting for the time, the authority of owner over ship, and clause applies only to acts done in exercise of sovereign power. Baker Castor Oil Co. v. Ins. Co. of North America, 157 F.2d 13. Where the "restraint of princes" clause or similar language is found in the contract, a reasonable apprehension of capture or destruction of the ship or cargo will justify nonperformance of the agreement to carry. The George J. Goulandris, D.C.Me., 36 F.Supp. 827, 830, 834. A "restraint of princes" may be an act performed for purposes connected with the prosecution of war, or some other act, such as quarantines or prohibition of entry into port for sanitary reasons.

Restraint of trade. Contracts or combinations which tend or are designed to eliminate or stifle competition, effect a monopoly, artificially maintain prices, or otherwise hamper or obstruct the course of trade and commerce as it would be carried on if left to the control of natural economic forces. U. S. v. Reading Co., 253 U.S. 26, 40 S.Ct. 425, 429, 64 L.Ed. 760; U. S. v. Patten, 226 U.S. 525, 33 S.Ct. 141, 144, 145, 57 L.Ed. 333. Term as used in Sherman Act means "unreasonable restraints of trade" which are illegal per se restraints interfering with free competition in business and commercial transactions which tend to restrict production, affect prices, or otherwise control market to detriment of purchasers or consumers of goods and services, or those restraints of trade, ordinarily reasonable, but made unreasonable because accompanied with specific intent to accomplish equivalent of a forbidden restraint. Klor's Inc. v. Broadway-Hale Stores, Inc., C.A.Cal., 255 F.2d 214, 230. To restrain interstate trade and commerce means to interfere unreasonably with the ordinary, usual and freely-competitive pricing or distribution system of the open market in interstate trade and commerce. A conspiracy may restrain interstate commerce even though some or all of the defendants are not engaged in interstate commerce, and even though some or all of the means employed may be acts wholly within a state, if there is a substantial and direct effect on interstate commerce. Sherman Antitrust Act, § 1. See also **Rule** *(Rule of reason);* **Sherman Antitrust Act.**

Restraint on alienation. A provision in an instrument of conveyance which prohibits the grantee from selling or transferring the property which is the subject of the conveyance. Many such restraints are unenforceable as against public policy and the law's policy of free alienability of land. A "restraint on alienation" is any provision in a trust or other instrument which, either by express terms or by implication, purports to prohibit or penalize the use of the power of alienation; the trusts usually involved are spendthrift, discretionary and support trusts. Philp v. Trainor, Fla.App., 100 So.2d 181, 183. See also **Perpetuity.**

Res transit cum suo onere /ríyz trǽnzət kòm s(y)úwow ównəriy/. The thing passes with its burden. Where a thing has been incumbered by mortgage, the incumbrance follows it wherever it goes.

Restrict. To restrain within bounds; to limit; to confine. See also **Restraint.**

Restriction. A limitation, often imposed in a deed or lease respecting the use to which the property may be put. See *e.g.* **Restrictive covenant.**

Restrictive covenant. Provision in a deed limiting the use of the property and prohibiting certain uses. Also, clauses in contracts of partnership and employment which limit a contracting party after termination of the contract in performing similar work for a period of time and within a certain geographical area. If reasonable as to time and area, such clauses are enforceable.

Restrictive indorsement. An indorsement so worded as to restrict the further negotiability of the instrument. Thus, "Pay the contents to J. S. only," or "to J. S. for my use," are restrictive indorsements, and put an end to the negotiability of the paper.

An indorsement is restrictive which either (a) is conditional; or (b) purports to prohibit further transfer of the instrument; or (c) includes the words "for collection", "for deposit", "pay any bank", or like terms signifying a purpose of deposit or collection; or (d) otherwise states that it is for the benefit or use of the indorser or of another person. U.C.C. § 3–205.

Resulting powers. Powers of the federal government derived from a combination of several grants or the aggregate of power granted to the federal government. See **Power** (*Constitutional powers*).

Resulting trust. Trust implied in law from intentions of parties to a given transaction. Diel v. Beekman, 1 Wash.App. 874, 465 P.2d 212, 214.

One in which a party, through no actual or constructive fraud, becomes invested with legal title, but holds that title for the benefit of another, although without expressed intent to do so, because of a presumption of such intent arising by operation of law. First Nat. Bank of Denver v. Harry W. Rabb Foundation, 29 Colo.App. 34, 479 P.2d 986, 988, 989. A "resulting trust" arises where a person makes or causes to be made a disposition of property under circumstances which raise an inference that he does not intend that person taking or holding the property should have the beneficial interest therein, unless inference is rebutted or the beneficial interest is otherwise effectively disposed of. Long v. Kyte, Mo., 340 S.W.2d 623, 627. Restatement, Second, Trusts, § 404.

Resulting use. See **Use.**

Resummons. A second summons. The calling a person a second time to answer an action, where the first summons is defeated upon any occasion; as the death of a party, or the like.

Resumption. In old English law, the taking again into the king's hands such lands or tenements as before, upon false suggestion, or other error, he had delivered to the heir, or granted by letters patent to any man.

Resurrender. Where copyhold land has been mortgaged by surrender, and the mortgagee has been admitted, then, on the mortgage debt being paid off, the mortgagor is entitled to have the land reconveyed to him, by the mortgagee surrendering it to the lord to his use. This is called a resurrender.

Retail, *v.* To sell by small quantities, in broken lots or parcels, not in bulk, directly to consumer. In general, wholesalers sell to retailers who in turn sell to consumers.

Retail, *n.* A sale for final consumption in contrast to a sale for further sale or processing (*i.e.* wholesale). A sale to the ultimate consumer.

Retailer. A person engaged in making sales to ultimate consumers. One who sells personal or household goods for use or consumption.

The essential distinction between a "wholesaler" and "retailer" as respects application of the Fair Labor Standards Act is that the person buying from the retailer is the ultimate user or consumer of the article or commodity or does not sell it again whereas the one buying from a wholesaler buys only for the purpose of selling the article again. Haynie v. Hogue Lumber & Supply Co. of Gulfport, 96 F.Supp. 214, 216.

Retail installment account. An account established by an agreement entered into pursuant to which the buyer promises to pay, in installments, to a retail seller his outstanding balance incurred in retail installment sales, whether or not a security interest in the goods sold is retained by the seller, and which provides for a finance charge which is expressed as a percent of the periodic balances to accrue thereafter providing such charge is not capitalized or stated as a dollar amount in such agreement. Calif.Civil Code, § 1802.7.

Retail installment contract. Any contract for a retail installment sale between a buyer and seller, entered into or performed which provides for (a) repayment in installments, whether or not such contract contains a title retention provision, and in which a finance charge is computed upon and added to the unpaid balance at the time of sale or where no finance charge is added but the goods or services are available at a lesser price if paid by cash or where the buyer, if he had paid cash, would have received any additional goods or services or any higher quality goods or services at no added cost over the total amount he pays in installments, or (b) which provides for payment in four or more installments. Calif.Civil Code, § 1802.6.

Retail sale. A sale in small quantities or direct to consumer, as distinguished from sale at "wholesale" in large quantity to one who intends to resell. Mitchell v. Sorvas, D.C.Pa., 182 F.Supp. 800, 802. The ordinary meaning of term "retail sale" within sales tax statutes is a sale to an ultimate consumer. Standard Oil Co. of Cal. v. State, 57 Wash.2d 56, 355 P.2d 349, 352. See also **Retail.**

Retain. To continue to hold, have, use, recognize, etc., and to keep.

To engage the services of an attorney or counsellor to manage a specific matter or action or all legal matters in general. See **Retainer.**

Retained earnings. Net income over the life of a corporation less all income distributions (including capitalization through stock dividends); owner's equity less contributed capital. That portion of profits which has not been paid out as dividends. See also **Surplus.**

Retainer. The act of withholding what one has in one's own hands by virtue of some right. Act of the client in employing his attorney or counsel, and also denotes the fee which the client pays when he retains the attorney to act for him, and thereby prevents him from acting for his adversary. Term can mean a fee not only for the rendition of professional services when requested, but also for the attorney taking the case, making himself available to handle it, and refusing employment by plaintiff's adversary; or it can mean solely the compensation for services to be performed in a specific case. Chippenham Manor, Inc. v. Dervishian, 214 Va. 448, 201 S.E.2d 794, 796.

A contract between attorney and client stating the nature of the services to be rendered and the cost of the services. When a client retains an attorney to act for him, he thereby prevents him from acting for his adversary. In re Hawkins, 81 Wash.2d 504, 503 P.2d 95, 98.

Right to retainer. The right which the executor or administrator of a deceased person has to retain out of the assets sufficient to pay any debt due to him from the deceased in priority to the other creditors whose debts are of equal degree. 3 Steph.Comm. 263. In re Smith's Estate, 179 Wash. 417, 38 P.2d 244, 245.

Retainer pay. Compensation paid to enlisted men retained in the service but not rendering active service. French v. French, Cal., 105 P.2d 155, 157.

Retaining fee. A fee given to counsel on engaging his services. See **Retainer.**

Retaining lien. Attorney's right to retain possession of property belonging to his client which comes into his hands within the scope of his employment until his charges are paid. Jovan v. Starr, 87 Ill.App.2d 350, 231 N.E.2d 637, 639. See also **Attorney's lien.**

Retaking. The taking one's goods, from another, who without right has taken possession thereof. See **Recaption.**

Retaliation. See *lex talionis (q.v.).*

Retaliatory eviction. Act of landlord in commencing eviction proceedings against tenant because of tenant's complaints, participation in tenant's union, or like activities with which the landlord is not in agreement. In some states, such retaliation will bar the landlord from enforcing his normal remedies against tenant.

Retaliatory law. Restraints placed by state law on foreign companies equal to the restraints placed by such foreign jurisdictions on companies doing business in such states. Many states have such laws. For example, in Pennsylvania if by laws of any other state or foreign government any taxes, fines, penalties, license fees or other obligations or prohibitions additional to or in excess of those imposed by Pennsylvania laws on insurance companies, associations and exchanges of other states, are imposed on insurance companies, associations and exchanges of Pennsylvania doing business in such state, like obligations and prohibitions are imposed on insurance companies, associations and exchanges of such state doing business in Pennsylvania.

Retallia /rətǽliyə/. In old English law, retail; the cutting up again, or division of a commodity into smaller parts.

Retenementum /rətènəméntəm/. In old English law, restraint; detainment; withholding.

Retinentia /rèdənénsh(iy)ə/. A retinue, or persons retained by a prince or nobleman.

Retire. To terminate employment or service upon reaching retirement age.

Retirement annuity. Type of pension plan paid through annuities to those who have retired. Plans differ as to the rights of survivors of the annuitant.

Retorna brevium /rətórnə bríyv(i)yəm/. The return of writs. The indorsement by a sheriff or other officer of his doings upon a writ.

Retorno habendo /rətórnow həbéndow/. A writ that layed for the distrainor of goods (when, on replevin brought, he had proved his distress to be a lawful one) against him who was so distrained, to have them returned to him according to law, together with damages and costs.

Retorsion /rətórshən/. In international law, a species of retaliation, which takes place where a government, whose citizens are subjected to severe and stringent regulation or harsh treatment by a foreign government, employs measures of equal severity and harshness upon the subjects of the latter government found within its dominions.

Retraction. To take back. To retract an offer is to withdraw it before acceptance. In law of defamation, a formal recanting of the defamatory material. Retraction is not a defense but, under certain circumstances, it is admissible in mitigation of damages.

In probate practice, a withdrawal of a renunciation, *(q.v.).*

Retraxit /rətrǽksət/. Lat. He has withdrawn.

A retraxit is a voluntary renunciation by plaintiff in open court of his suit and cause thereof, and by it plaintiff forever loses his action. Virginia Concrete Co. v. Board of Sup'rs of Fairfax County, 197 Va. 821, 91 S.E.2d 415, 419. It is equivalent to a verdict and judgment on the merits of the case and bars another suit for the same cause between the same parties. Datta v. Staab, 343 P.2d 977, 982, 173 C.A.2d 613. Under rules practice, this is accomplished by a voluntary dismissal. Fed.R.Civil P. 41(a).

Retreat, n. A place for contemplation especially of a religious nature. The totality of exercises in a religious house where a person may "take stock" of himself.

Retreat, v. To withdraw from the world or from an encounter.

Retreat to the wall. In the law relating to homicide in self-defense, this phrase means that the party must avail himself of any apparent and reasonable avenues of escape by which his danger might be averted, and the necessity of slaying his assailant avoided.

Retrial. A new trial of an action which has already been once tried. See also **Rehearing.**

Retribution. Something given or demanded in payment. In criminal law, it is punishment based on the theory which bears its name and based strictly on the fact that every crime demands payment in the form of punishment. See also **Restitution.**

Retro /rétrow/. Lat. Back; backward; behind. *Retrofeodum,* a rerefief, or *arriere* fief.

Retroactive. Retrospective *(q.v.).*

Retroactive inference. The inferring of a previous fact from present conditions by a trier of facts. Gray v. Kurn, 345 Mo. 1027, 137 S.W.2d 558, 568.

Retroactive law. "Retroactive" or "retrospective" laws are generally defined from a legal viewpoint as those which take away or impair vested rights acquired under existing laws, create new obligations, impose a new duty, or attach a new disability in respect to the transactions or considerations already past. Barbieri v. Morris, Mo., 315 S.W.2d 711, 714. One which is intended to act on things that are past. Aetna Ins. Co. v. Richardelle, Tex.Civ.App., 528 S.W.2d 280, 284. A statute which creates a new obligation on transactions or considerations already past or destroys or impairs vested rights. London Guarantee & Accident Co. v. Pittman, 69 Ga.App. 146, 25 S.E.2d 60, 65, 66. Such laws may be unenforceable because violative of the ex post facto clause of the U.S.Const., Art. I, Sec. 9, Cl. 3. See also **Retrospective law.**

Retrocession /rètrəséshən/. In the civil law, when the assignee of heritable rights conveys his rights back to the cedent.

Retrospective. Looking backward; contemplating what is past; having reference to a state of things existing before the act in question.

Retrospective law. A law which looks backward or contemplates the past; one which is made to affect acts or facts occurring, or rights accruing, before it came into force. Every statute which takes away or impairs vested rights acquired under existing laws, or creates a new obligation, imposes a new duty, or attaches a new disability in respect to transactions or considerations already past. One that relates back to a previous transaction and gives it a different legal

effect from that which it had under the law when it occurred. Bear Val. Mut. Water Co. v. San Bernardino County, 242 Cal.App.2d 68, 51 Cal.Rptr. 53, 56. See also **Ex post facto; Retroactive law.**

Return. To bring, carry, or send back; to place in the custody of; to restore; to re-deliver.

The act of a sheriff, constable, marshall, or other ministerial officer, in delivering back to the court a writ, notice, process or other paper, which he was required to serve or execute, with a brief account of his doings under the mandate, the time and mode of service or execution, or his failure to accomplish it, as the case may be. Also the indorsement made by the officer upon the writ or other paper, stating what he has done under it, the time and mode of service, etc. Such return (proof of service) is required under Rule of Civil Procedure 4. See *False return; Return day, below.*

A schedule of information required by governmental bodies, such as the tax return required by the Internal Revenue Service. See **Joint tax return; Tax return.**

Merchandise which is brought back to the seller for credit or refund.

Profit on sale, or income from investments. See **Income; Profit; Revenue.**

The report made by the court, body of magistrates, returning board, or other authority charged with the official counting of the votes cast at an election.

In English practice, the election of a member of parliament.

Fair return. See **Fair return on investment.**

False return. A return of a writ or process in which the officer charged with it falsely reports that he served it, when he did not, or makes some other false or incorrect statement, whereby injury results to a person interested. In taxation, a return that is incorrect. To constitute civil or criminal fraud under the Internal Revenue laws, such falsity must have been intentional. Mitchell v. C. I. R., C.C.A.Ga., 118 F.2d 308.

Return day. The day named in a writ or process, upon which the officer is required to return it. Under Fed.R.Civil P. 4 the person serving the process shall make proof of service (return) to the court promptly and in any event within the time during which the person served must respond to the process.

Day on which votes cast are counted and the official result is declared. Landrum v. Centennial Rural High School Dist. No. 2, Tex.Civ.App., 134 S.W.2d 353, 354.

Return of premium. The repayment of the whole or a ratable part of the premium paid for a policy of insurance, upon the cancellation of the contract before the time fixed for its expiration. Equitable Life Assur. Soc. of United States v. Johnson, 53 Cal. App.2d 49, 127 P.2d 95.

Returnable. To be returned; requiring a return. When a writ or process is said to be "returnable" on a certain day, it is meant that on that day the officer must return it.

Return day. See **Return.**

Returning board. This is the official title in some of the states of the board of canvassers of elections.

Return of process. See **Return.**

Reus /ríyəs/. Lat. In the civil and canon law, the defendant in an action or suit. A person judicially accused of a crime; a person criminally proceeded against.

A party to a suit, whether plaintiff or defendant; a litigant. This was the ancient sense of the word.

A party to a contract. *Reus stipulandi,* a party stipulating; the party who asked the question in the form prescribed for stipulations. *Reus promittendi,* a party promising; the party who answered the question.

Revaluation. The restoration of purchasing power to an inflated currency. Also, the resetting of the tax base by recomputing the value of real estate subject to taxation.

Reve /ríyv/. In old English law, the bailiff of a franchise or manor; an officer in parishes within forests, who marks the commonable cattle.

Revel /révəl/. To behave in a noisy, boisterous manner.

Reve mote /ríyv mòwt/. In Saxon law, the court of the *reve, reeve,* or *shire reeve.*

Revendication /rìyvendəkéyshən/. In civil law, to reclaim or to demand the restoration of; to "reclaim" being to claim something back, which is in the possession of another, but which belongs to the claimant. The right of a vendor to reclaim goods sold out of the possession of the purchaser, where the price was not paid. Ellis v. Davis, 109 U.S. 485, 3 S.Ct. 327, 27 L.Ed. 1006.

Revendication action /rìyvendəkéyshən ǽkshən/. In civil law, one by which a man demands a restoration of a thing of which he claims to be the owner.

Revenue. Return or yield, as of land; profit, as that which returns or comes back from an investment; the annual or periodical rents, profits, interest or issues of any species of property, real or personal; income of individual, corporation, government, etc. Willoughby v. Willoughby, 66 R.I. 430, 19 A.2d 857, 860.

As applied to the income of a government, a broad and general term, including all public moneys which the state collects and receives, from whatever source and in whatever manner. See *Public revenues,* below.

Land revenues. See **Land revenues.**

Public revenues. The income which a government collects and receives into its treasury, and is appropriated for the payment of its expenses. Public Market Co. of Portland v. City of Portland, 171 Or. 522, 130 P.2d 624, 644. Annual or periodical yield of taxes, excise, custom, dues, rents, etc., which a nation, state or a municipality collects and receives into treasury for public use; public income of whatever kind. City of Phoenix v. Arizona Sash, Door & Glass Co., 80 Ariz. 100, 293 P.2d 438, 440. Current income of nation, state, or local government from whatever source derived which is subject to appropriation for public uses. Spink v. Kemp, 365 Mo. 368, 283 S.W.2d 502, 513.

Revenue bills. Legislative bills that levy or raise taxes. Bills for raising federal revenue must arise in the House of Representatives. Art. I, Sec. 7, U.S.Const. See also **Revenue law or measure.**

Revenue bonds. Type of bond issued by a state or local government repayable by the particular unit of government which issues it. Also, a bond issued for a specific public purpose such as the construction or maintenance of a bridge and repayable from income generated by such project. Term is a descriptive qualification which indicates that the instruments are payable solely from a revenue producing public project. Dalton v. State Property and Buildings Commission, Ky., 304 S.W.2d 342, 352.

Revenue law or measure. Any law which provides for the assessment and collection of a tax to defray the expenses of the government. Such legislation is commonly referred to under the general term "revenue measures," and those measures include all the laws by which the government provides means for meeting its expenditures. Western Heights Land Corp. v. City of Fort Collins, 146 Colo. 464, 362 P.2d 155, 158. See also **Revenue bills.**

Revenue Procedure. A matter of procedural importance to both taxpayers and the I.R.S. concerning the administration of the tax laws is issued as a Revenue Procedure (abbreviated as "Rev.Proc."). A Revenue Procedure is first published in an Internal Revenue Bulletin (I.R.B.) and later transferred to the appropriate Cumulative Bulletin (C.B.). Both the Internal Revenue Bulletins and the Cumulative Bulletins are published by the U.S. Government.

Revenue Ruling. A Revenue Ruling (abbreviated "Rev. Rul.") is issued by the National Office of the I.R.S. to express an official interpretation of the tax law as applied to specific transactions. Unlike a Regulation, it is more limited in application. A Revenue Ruling is first published in an Internal Revenue Bulletin (I.R.B.) and later transferred to the appropriate Cumulative Bulletin (C.B.). Both the Internal Revenue Bulletins and the Cumulative Bulletins are published by the U.S. Government.

Revenue stamps. Formerly, a federal tax on sale of real property; since replaced by state tax stamps. The stamps are affixed to the conveyancing instrument (deed), or a rubber stamp is used to show the amount of the tax.

Re, verbis, scripto, consensu, traditione, junctura vestes sumere pacta solent /ríy, várbəs, skríptow, kən(t)-sén(t)s(y)uw, trədìshiyówniy, jeŋkt(y)úrə véstiyz s(y)úwməriy pǽktə sówlənt/. Compacts usually take their clothing from the thing itself, from words, from writing, from consent, from delivery.

Reversal. The annulling or setting aside by an appellate court of a decision of a lower court. See also **Remand; Vacate.**

Reverse. To overthrow, vacate, set aside, make void, annul, repeal, or revoke; as, to reverse a judgment, sentence or decree, or to change to the contrary or to a former condition. Department of Water and Power of City of Los Angeles v. Inyo Chemical Co., Cal. App., 100 P.2d 822, 826; Securities and Exchange Comm. v. C. M. Joiner Leasing Corp., D.C.Tex., 53 F.Supp. 714, 715. To reverse a judgment means to overthrow it by contrary decision, make it void, undo or annul it for error. Atlantic Coast Line R. Co. v. St. Joe Paper Co., C.A.Fla., 216 F.2d 832, 833.

Reverse discrimination. Prejudice or bias exercised against a person or class for purpose of correcting a pattern of discrimination against another person or class. Also called "benign" discrimination, such may be defined as classifications that are designed to assist selected groups of persons presumed to be shown to be disadvantaged. Alevy v. Downstate Medical Center, 39 N.Y.2d 326, 384 N.Y.S.2d 82, 348 N.E.2d 537, 540; Regents of University of California v. Bakke, 438 U.S. 265, 98 S.Ct. 2733, 57 L.Ed. 2d 750. See also **Affirmative action programs.**

Reverse stock split. The reduction in the number of corporate shares outstanding by calling in all shares and issuing a smaller number, though the capital of the corporation remains the same. It is the opposite of a stock split. Its effect is to increase the value of each share.

Reversible error. See **Error.**

Reversio /rəvárzh(iy)ow/. L. Lat. In old English law, the returning of land to the donor.

Reversion, or **estate in reversion** /(əstéyd ən) rəvárzhən/. The residue of an estate left by operation of law in the grantor or his heirs, or in the heirs of a testator, commencing in possession on the determination of a particular estate granted or devised. Any future interest left in a transferor or his successor. Miller v. Dierken, 153 Pa.Super. 389, 33 A.2d 804, 805. It is a vested interest or estate, in as much as person entitled to it has a fixed right to future enjoyment. Any reversionary interest which is not subject to condition precedent; it arises when the owner of real estate devises or conveys an interest in it less than his own. Mayor and City Council of Ocean City v. Tabor, 279 Md. 115, 367 A.2d 1233, 1240.

The term reversion has two meanings, first, as designating the estate left in the grantor during the continuance of a particular estate and also the residue left in grantor or his heirs after termination of particular estate. Davidson v. Davidson, 350 Mo. 639, 167 S.W.2d 641, 642; Miller v. C. I. R., C.C.A.6, 147 F.2d 189, 193. It differs from a remainder in that it arises by act of the law, whereas a remainder is by act of the parties. A reversion, moreover, is the remnant left in the grantor, while a remainder is the remnant of the whole estate disposed of, after a preceding part of the same has been given away.

See also **Escheat; Possibility** (*Possibility of reverter*); **Reversionary interest.** *Compare* **Remainder.**

Reversionary /rəvárzhənehriy/. That which is to be enjoyed in reversion.

Reversionary interest. The interest which a person has in the reversion of lands or other property. A right to the future enjoyment of property, at present in the possession or occupation of another. The property that reverts to the grantor after the expiration of an intervening income interest. Assume, for example, G places real estate in trust with income to A for eleven years and, upon the expiration of this term, the property returns to G. Under these circumstances, G has retained a reversionary interest in the property. A reversionary interest is the same as a remainder interest except that in the latter case the property passes to someone other than the original owner (*e.g.,* the grantor of a trust) upon the expiration of the intervening interest. See **Remainder; Reversion.**

Reversionary lease. One to take effect *in futuro.* A second lease, to commence after the expiration of a former lease.

Reversioner /rəvárzhənər/. A person who is entitled to an estate in reversion. By an extension of its meaning, one who is entitled to any future estate or any property in expectancy.

Reversio terræ est tanquam terra revertens in possessione donatori, sive hæredibus suis post donum finitum /rəvárzh(iy)ow téhriy èst tǽŋkwəm téhrə rəvárten(d)z in pəzèshiyówniy dòwnətóray, sáyviy hərédəbəs s(y)úwəs pòwst dównəm fənáydəm/. A reversion of land is, as it were, the return of the land to the possession of the donor or his heirs after the termination of the estate granted.

Revert /rəvárt/. To turn back, to return to. With respect to property to go back to and lodge in former owner, who parted with it by creating estate in another which has expired, or to his heirs. As used in a deed connotes an undisposed of residue and imports that property is to return to a person who formerly owned it, but who parted with the possession or title by creating an estate in another person which has terminated by his act or by operation of law. Thurman v. Hudson, Ky., 280 S.W.2d 507, 508. See also **Reversion; Reversionary interest.**

Reverter /rəvárdər/. Reversion. A possibility of reverter is that species of reversionary interest which exists when the grant is so limited that it may possibly terminate. See **Formedon in the reverter.**

Revest. To vest again. A seisin is said to *revest,* where it is acquired a second time by the party out of whom it has been divested. Opposed to "divest." The words "revest" and "divest" are also applicable to the mere right or title, as opposed to the possession.

Revestire /rìyvestáyriy/. In old European law, to return or resign an investiture, seisin, or possession that has been received; to reinvest; to re-enfeoff.

Review. To re-examine judicially or administratively. A reconsideration; second view or examination; revision; consideration for purposes of correction. Used especially of the examination of a cause by an appellate court or appellate administrative body (*e.g.* Appeals Council in social security cases). See **Appeal; Board of review; Rehearing; Retrial.**

Bill of review. In equity practice, a bill, in the nature of a writ of error, filed to procure an examination and alteration or reversal of a decree made upon a former bill, which decree has been signed and enrolled. See also **Bill.**

Revise. To review and re-examine for correction. To go over a thing for the purpose of amending, correcting, rearranging, or otherwise improving it; as, to revise statutes, or a judgment. State ex rel. Taylor v. Scofield, 184 Wash. 250, 50 P.2d 896, 897.

Revised statutes. A body of statutes which have been revised, collected, arranged in order, and re-enacted as a whole. This is the legal title of the collections of compiled laws of several of the states, and also of the United States. Such a volume is usually cited as "Rev.Stat.," "Rev.St.," or "R.S." See also **Code.**

Revision. A re-examination or careful reading over for correction or improvement.

Revision of statutes. Such is more than a restatement of the substance thereof in different language, but implies a reexamination of them, and may constitute a restatement of the law in a corrected or improved form, in which case the statement may be with or without material change, and is substituted for and displaces and repeals the former law as it stood relating to the subjects within its purview. Elite Laundry Co. v. Dunn, 126 W.Va. 858, 30 S.E.2d 454, 458. See also **Codification; Revised statutes.**

Revisor of statutes. Person or body charged with revising statutes.

Revival. The process of renewing the operative force of a judgment which has remained dormant or unexecuted for so long a time that execution cannot be issued upon it without new process to reanimate it.

The act of renewing the legal force of a contract or obligation, which had ceased to be sufficient foundation for an action, on account of the running of the statute of limitations, by giving a new promise or acknowledgment of it.

A will may be revived under certain conditions if the testator revokes an instrument which purported to revoke his will.

Revival of action. Under certain conditions, a cause of action barred by the statute of limitations may be brought to life again.

The substitution of the personal representative of a deceased party will revive an action and make it prosecutable by the substituted party. Fed.R.Civ.P. 17(a). Grant v. McAuliffe, 41 Cal.2d 859, 264 P.2d 944.

Revival of will. See **Revival.**

Revival statutes. State and federal laws which provide for the renewal of actions, wills and the legal effect of documents.

Revive. To renew, revivify; to make one's self liable for a debt barred by the statute of limitations by acknowledging it; or for a matrimonial offense, once condoned, by committing another.

Revivor, bill of. In equity practice, a bill filed for the purpose of reviving or calling into operation the proceedings in a suit when, from some circumstance (as the death of the plaintiff), the suit had abated.

Revivor, writ of. In English practice, where it became necessary to revive a judgment, by lapse of time, or change by death, etc., of the parties entitled or liable to execution, the party alleging himself to be entitled to execution might sue out a writ of revivor in the form given in the act, or apply to the court for leave to enter a suggestion upon the roll that it appeared that he was entitled to have and issue execution of the judgment, such leave to be granted by the court or a judge upon a rule to show cause, or a summons, to be served according to the then present practice.

Revocable. Susceptible of being revoked, withdrawn or cancelled; _e.g._ revocable letter of credit.

Revocable credit. A credit which can be withdrawn or cancelled before its expiration date and without the consent of the person in whose favor it was drawn. Used in foreign trade. U.C.C. § 5-103(a).

Revocable letter of credit. Letter of credit which can be cancelled or withdrawn at any time. U.C.C. § 5-103(a).

Revocable transfer. A transfer of property whereby the transferor retains the right to recover the property. The creation of a revocable trust is an example of a revocable transfer.

Revocable trust. A trust in which the settlor reserves to himself the right to revoke. Such provision may have tax implications depending upon the time following its creation within which he may revoke.

Revocation /rèvəkéyshən/. The recall of some power, authority, or thing granted, or a destroying or making void of some deed that had existence until the act of revocation made it void. It may be either _general,_ of all acts and things done before; or _special,_ revoking a particular thing.

Revocation by act of the party is an intentional or voluntary revocation. The principal instances occur in the case of authorities and powers of attorney and wills. In contract law, an offer may generally be revoked before acceptance.

A revocation in law, or constructive revocation, is produced by a rule of law, irrespectively of the intention of the parties. Thus, a power of attorney is in general revoked by the death of the principal.

See also **Abrogation; Cancel; Cancellation; Rescind.**

Revocatione parliamenti /rèvəkèyshiyówniy pàrl(iy)əméntay/. An ancient writ for recalling a parliament.

Revocation of probate. Exists where probate of a will, having been granted, is afterwards recalled by the court of probate, on proof of a subsequent will, or other sufficient cause.

Revocation of will. The recalling, annulling or rendering inoperative an existing will, by some subsequent act of the testator, which may be by the making of a new will inconsistent with the terms of the first, or by destroying the old will, or by disposing of the property to which it related, or otherwise.

Revocatur /rìyvowkéydər/. Lat. It is recalled. This is the term, in English practice, appropriate to signify that a judgment is annulled or set aside for error in fact; if for error in law, it is then said to be *reversed.*

Revoke. To annul or make void by recalling or taking back; to cancel, rescind, repeal, or reverse. See also **Revocation.**

Revolt. A revolt goes beyond insurrection in aim, being an attempt actually to overthrow the government itself, whereas insurrection has as its objective some forcible change within the government. A large-scale revolt is called a rebellion and if it is successful it becomes a revolution. See also **Insurrection; Rebellion.**

The endeavor of the crew of a vessel, or any one or more of them, to overthrow the legitimate authority of her commander, with intent to remove him from his command, or against his will to take possession of the vessel by assuming the government and navigation of her, or by transferring their obedience from the lawful commander to some other person. See 18 U.S.C.A. §§ 2192, 2193. See also **Mutiny.**

Revolution. A complete overthrow of the established government in any country or state by those who were previously subject to it. Gitlow v. Kiely, D.C. N.Y., 44 F.2d 227, 232. See **Insurrection; Rebellion.**

Revolutionary, *adj.* Pertaining to or connected with, characterized by, or of nature of, revolution. Gitlow v. Kiely, D.C.N.Y., 44 F.2d 227, 233.

Revolutionary, *n.* One who instigates or favors revolution or one taking part therein. Gitlow v. Kiely, D.C.N.Y., 44 F.2d 227, 233.

Revolving charge account. See **Revolving credit.**

Revolving credit. Type of credit arrangement which permits a buyer or a borrower to purchase goods or secure loans on a continuing basis so long as the outstanding balance of the account does not exceed a certain limit. Loans are repaid and new loans granted in a cycle. See also **Charge account.**

Revolving fund. A fund from which withdrawals are made either as loans or as disbursements, with the obligation of repaying the fund (with or without interest) to keep the fund intact. A fund whose amounts are continually expended and then replenished; for example, a petty cash fund.

Revolving letter of credit. A self-renewing letter of credit. The unused portion of the credit is cumulative.

Revolving loan. A loan which is expected to be renewed (*i.e.* turned over) at maturity.

Rev. Proc. See **Revenue Procedure.**

Rev. Rul. See **Revenue Ruling.**

Reward. A recompense or premium offered or bestowed by government or an individual in return for special or extraordinary services to be performed, or for special attainments or achievements, or for some act resulting to the benefit of the public; as, a reward for useful inventions, for the discovery and apprehension of criminals, for the restoration of lost property. That which is offered or given for some service or attainment; sum of money paid or taken for doing, or forbearing to do, some act. See also **Award; Prize.**

Rex /réks/. Lat. The king. The king regarded as the party prosecuting in a criminal action; as in the form of entitling such actions, "Rex v. Doe."

Rex debet esse sub lege quia lex facit regem /réks débəd ésiy sə̀b líyjiy kwàyə léks féysət ríyjəm/. The king ought to be under the law, because the law makes the king. 1 Bl.Comm. 239.

Rex est legalis et politicus /réks èst ləgéyləs èt pəlídəkəs/. The king is both a legal and political person.

Rex est lex vivens /réks èst léks váyven(d)z/. The king is the living law.

Rex est major singulis, minor universis /réks èst méyjər síŋ(y)ələs, máynər yùwnəvársəs/. The king is greater than any single person, less than all.

Rex hoc solum non potest facere quod non potest injuste agere /réks hòk sówləm nòn pówdəst fǽsəriy kwód nòn pówdəst injə́stiy ǽjəriy/. The king can do everything but an injustice.

Rex non debit esse sub homine, sed sub deo et sut lege, quia lex facit regem /réks nòn débəd ésiy sə̀b hómərniy séd səb díyo èt sə̀b líyjiy, kwáyə léks féysət ríyjəm/. The king ought to be under no man, but under God and ʼhe law, because the law makes a king.

Rex non potest fallere nec falli /réks nòn pówdəst fǽləriy nèk fǽlay/. The king cannot deceive or be deceived.

Rex non potest peccare /réks nòn pówdəst pəkériy/. The king cannot do wrong; the king can do no wrong. An ancient and fundamental principle of the English constitution.

Rex nunquam moritur /réks nə́ŋkwəm mórədər/. The king never dies.

R.F.C.A. Reconstruction Finance Corporation Act.

R.G. An abbreviation for *Regula Generalis,* a general rule or order of court; or for the plural of the same.

Rhandir. A part in the division of Wales before the Conquest. Every township comprehended four gavels, and every gavel had four rhandirs, and four houses or tenements constituted every rhandir.

Rhodian laws /rówdiyən lóz/. The earliest code or collection of maritime laws. It was formulated by the people of the island of Rhodes, who, by their commercial prosperity and the superiority of their navies, had acquired the sovereignty of the seas. Its date is very uncertain, but is supposed (by Kent and others) to be about 900 B.C. Nothing of it is now extant except the article on jettison, which has been preserved in the Roman collections or Pandects (Dig. 14, 2; 3 Kent, Comm. 232, 233 *"Lex Rhodia de Jactu."*) The Lex Rhodia de Jactu provided that when the goods of an owner are thrown overboard for the safety of the ship or of the property of other owners, he becomes entitled to a ratable contribution. It has been adopted into the law of all civilized nations. Another code, under the same name, was published in more modern times, but is generally considered, by the best authorities, to be spurious.

Rial /riyál/. A piece of gold coin current for 10s., in the reign of Henry VI, at which time there were half-rials and quarter-rials or rial-farthings. In the beginning of Queen Elizabeth's reign, golden rials were coined at 15s. a piece; and in the time of James I there were rose-rials of gold at 30s. and spur-rials at 15s.

Ribaud /riybów/. A rogue; vagrant; whoremonger; a person given to all manner of wickedness.

Rider. A schedule or small piece of paper reflecting an amendment, addition or endorsement annexed to some part of a roll, document, or record. Any kind of a schedule or writing annexed to a document which cannot well be incorporated in the body of such document. Such are deemed to be incorporated into the terms of the document. Thus, in passing bills through a legislature, when a new clause or law is added after the bill has passed through committee, such new law or clause is termed a "rider." Another common example of a rider is an attachment to an insurance policy that modifies the conditions of the policy by expanding or restricting its benefits or excluding certain conditions from coverage. With the use of the rider the entire document does not have to be rewritten or redrafted again.

Rien culp. In old pleading, not guilty.

Rien dit. In old pleading, says nothing (nil dicit).

Rien luy doit. In old pleading, owes him nothing. The plea of nil debet.

Riens en arrière. Nothing in arrear. A plea in an action of debt for arrearages of account.

Riens passa per le fait. Nothing passed by the deed. A plea by which a party might avoid the operation of a deed, which had been enrolled or acknowledged in court; the plea of non est factum not being allowed in such case.

Riens per descent. Nothing by descent. The plea of an heir, where he is sued for his ancestor's debt, and has no land from him by descent, or assets in his hands.

Rier county /rír káwntiy/. In old English law, after-county; i.e., after the end of the county court. A time and place appointed by the sheriff for the receipt of the king's money after the end of his county, or county court.

Rifflare /riflériy/. To take away anything by force.

Rigging the market. A term of the stock-exchange, denoting the practice of inflating the price of given stocks, or enhancing their quoted value, by a system of pretended purchases, designed to give the air of an unusual demand for such stocks.

Right. As a noun, and taken in an abstract sense, means justice, ethical correctness, or consonance with the rules of law or the principles of morals. In this signification it answers to one meaning of the Latin "jus," and serves to indicate law in the abstract, considered as the foundation of all rights, or the complex of underlying moral principles which impart the character of justice to all positive law, or give it an ethical content. As a noun, and taken in a concrete sense, a power, privilege, faculty, or de-

mand, inherent in one person and incident upon another. Rights are defined generally as "powers of free action." And the primal rights pertaining to men are enjoyed by human beings purely as such, being grounded in personality, and existing antecedently to their recognition by positive law. But leaving the abstract moral sphere, and giving to the term a juristic content, a "right" is well defined as "a capacity residing in one man of controlling, with the assent and assistance of the state, the actions of others."

As an adjective, the term "right" means just, morally correct, consonant with ethical principles or rules of positive law. It is the opposite of wrong, unjust, illegal.

A power, privilege, or immunity guaranteed under a constitution, statutes or decisional laws, or claimed as a result of long usage. See **Bill of rights; Civil liberties; Civil Rights Acts; Natural rights.**

In a narrower signification, an interest or title in an object of property; a just and legal claim to hold, use, or enjoy it, or to convey or donate it, as he may please.

A legally enforceable claim of one person against another, that the other shall do a given act, or shall not do a given act. Restatement of the Law of Property, § 1.

That which one person ought to have or receive from another, it being withheld from him, or not in his possession. In this sense "right" has the force of "claim," and is properly expressed by the Latin "jus."

See also Conditional right; Correlative rights; Droit; Jus; Natural rights; Power; Recht; Vested rights.

General Classification

Rights may be described as perfect or imperfect, according as their action or scope is clear, settled, and determinate, or is vague and unfixed.

Rights are also either in personam or in rem. A right in personam is one which imposes an obligation on a definite person. A right in rem is one which imposes an obligation on persons generally; i.e., either on all the world or on all the world except certain determinate persons. Thus, if I am entitled to exclude all persons from a given piece of land, I have a right in rem in respect of that land; and, if there are one or more persons, A., B., and C., whom I am not entitled to exclude from it, my right is still a right in rem.

Rights may also be described as either primary or secondary. Primary rights are those which can be created without reference to rights already existing. Secondary rights can only arise for the purpose of protecting or enforcing primary rights. They are either preventive (protective) or remedial (reparative).

Preventive or protective secondary rights exist in order to prevent the infringement or loss of primary rights. They are judicial when they require the assistance of a court of law for their enforcement, and extrajudicial when they are capable of being exercised by the party himself. Remedial or reparative secondary rights are also either judicial or extrajudicial. They may further be divided into (1) rights of restitution or restoration, which entitle the person injured to be replaced in his original position; (2) rights of enforcement, which entitle the person injured to the performance of an act by the person bound; and (3) rights of satisfaction or compensation.

With respect to the ownership of external objects of property, rights may be classed as *absolute* and *qualified.* An absolute right gives to the person in whom it inheres the uncontrolled dominion over the object at all times and for all purposes. A qualified right gives the possessor a right to the object for certain purposes or under certain circumstances only. Such is the right of a bailee to recover the article bailed when it has been unlawfully taken from him by a stranger.

Rights are also either *legal* or *equitable.* The former is the case where the person seeking to enforce the right for his own benefit has the legal title and a remedy at law. The latter are such as are enforceable only in equity; as, at the suit of *cestui que trust.* Procedurally, under Rules of Civil Procedure, both legal and equitable rights are enforced in the same court under a single cause of action.

Constitutional Rights

There is also a classification of rights, with respect to the constitution of civil society. Thus, according to Blackstone, "the rights of persons, considered in their natural capacities, are of two sorts,—*absolute* and *relative;* absolute, which are such as appertain and belong to particular men, merely as individuals or single persons; relative, which are incident to them as members of society, and standing in various relations to each other." 1 Bl.Comm. 123.

Rights are also classified in constitutional law as natural, civil, and political, to which there is sometimes added the class of "personal rights."

Natural rights are those which grow out of the nature of man and depend upon personality, as distinguished from such as are created by law and depend upon civilized society; or they are those which are plainly assured by natural law; or those which, by fair deduction from the present physical, moral, social, and religious characteristics of man, he must be invested with, and which he ought to have realized for him in a jural society, in order to fulfill the ends to which his nature calls him. Such are the rights of life, liberty, privacy, and good reputation.

Civil rights are such as belong to every citizen of the state or country, or, in a wider sense, to all its inhabitants, and are not connected with the organization or administration of government. They include the rights of property, marriage, equal protection of the laws, freedom of contract, trial by jury, etc. Or, as otherwise defined, civil rights are rights appertaining to a person by virtue of his citizenship in a state or community. Such term may also refer, in its very general sense, to rights capable of being enforced or redressed in a civil action. Also, a term applied to certain rights secured to citizens of the United States by the Thirteenth and Fourteenth amendments to the Constitution, and by various acts of Congress (*e.g.* Civil Rights Acts) made in pursuance thereof. See **Bill of Rights; Civil liberties; Civil Rights Acts.**

Political rights consist in the power to participate, directly or indirectly, in the establishment or adminis-

tration of government, such as the right of citizenship, that of suffrage, the right to hold public office, and the right of petition.

Personal rights is a term of rather vague import, but generally it may be said to mean the right of personal security, comprising those of life, limb, body, health, reputation, and the right of pesonal liberty.

Other Compound and Descriptive Terms

Bill of rights. See that title.

Common right. See **Common.**

Declaration of rights. See **Bill of Rights.**

Exclusive right. See that title.

Marital rights. See **Marital.**

Mere right. In the law of real estate, the mere right of property in land; the right of a proprietor, but without possession or even the right of possession; the abstract right of property.

Patent right. See **Patent.**

Petition of right. See **Petition.**

Private rights. Those rights which appertain to a particular individual or individuals, and relate either to the person, or to personal or real property.

Right heir. See **Heir.**

Riparian rights. See **Riparian.**

Stock rights. See **Stock.**

Vested rights. See **Vested.**

Right and wrong test. Under this test of criminal responsibility, if, at the time of committing an act, the party was laboring under such a defect of reason from disease of the mind as not to know the nature and quality thereof, that he did not know that he was doing what was wrong, he should not be held criminally responsible for his act. State v. Wallace, 170 Or. 60, 131 P.2d 222, 229, 230. See **Insanity** with respect to other criminal responsibility defenses. See also **M'Naghten Rule.**

Right in action. This is a phrase frequently used in place of *chose in action,* and having an identical meaning.

Right in court. See **Rectus in curia.**

Right of action. The right to bring suit; a legal right to maintain an action, growing out of a given transaction or state of facts and based thereon. Right of action pertains to remedy and relief through judicial procedure. Landry v. Acme Flour Mills Co., 202 Okl. 170, 211 P.2d 512, 515. Right of injured one to secure redress for violation of his rights. Fields v. Synthetic Ropes, Inc., 9 Storey 135, 215 A.2d 427, 432. A right presently to enforce a cause of action by suit. McMahon v. U. S., C.A.Pa., 186 F.2d 227, 230. See also **Cause of action.**

Right of entry. The right of taking or resuming possession of land by entering on it in a peaceable manner.

Right of first refusal. Right to have first opportunity to purchase real estate when such becomes available, or right to meet any other offer.

Right of local self-government. Power of citizens to govern themselves, as to matters purely local in nature, through officers of their own selection. City of Ardmore v. Excise Board of Carter County, 155 Okl. 126, 8 P.2d 2, 11. See **Home rule.**

Right of possession. Right which may reside in one man while another has the actual possession, being the right to enter and turn out such actual occupant; e.g., the right of a disseisee; right of ejectment or eviction. An apparent right of possession is one which may be defeated by a better right; an actual right of possession is one which will stand the test against all opponents. See also **Repossession.**

Right of privacy. See **Privacy, right of.**

Right of property. The mere right of property in land; the abstract right which remains to the owner after he has lost the right of possession, and to recover which the writ of right was given. United with possession, and the right of possession, this right constitutes a complete title to lands, tenements, and hereditaments.

Right of redemption. The right to disencumber property or to free it from a claim or lien; specifically, the right (granted by statute only) to free property from the encumbrance of a foreclosure or other judicial sale, or to recover the title passing thereby, by paying what is due, with interest, costs, etc. Not to be confounded with the "equity of redemption," which exists independently of statute but must be exercised before sale. See also **Redemption.**

Right of survivorship. The right of a survivor of a deceased person, to the property of said deceased. A distinguishing characteristic of a joint tenancy relationship. See also **Tenancy** (Joint tenancy).

Right of way. Term "right of way" sometimes is used to describe a right belonging to a party to pass over land of another, but it is also used to describe that strip of land upon which railroad companies construct their road bed, and, when so used, the term refers to the land itself, not the right of passage over it. Bouche v. Wagner, 206 Or. 621, 293 P.2d 203, 209.

As used with reference to right to pass over another's land, it is only an easement; and grantee acquires only right to a reasonable and usual enjoyment thereof with owner of soil retaining rights and benefits of ownership consistent with the easement. Minneapolis Athletic Club v. Cohler, 287 Minn. 254, 177 N.W.2d 786, 789. See also **Easement.**

"Right of way" is also used to refer to a preference of one of two vehicles, or as between a vehicle and a pedestrian, asserting right of passage at the same place and time, but it is not an absolute right in the sense that possessor thereof is relieved from duty of exercising due care for his own safety and that of others. Cheramie v. Scott, Tex.Civ.App., 324 S.W.2d 87, 90. With respect to intersections, the term has been described as the right of one driver to cross before the other; and it has been defined by statute as the right of a vehicle to proceed uninterruptedly in a lawful manner in the direction in which it is moving in preference to another vehicle approaching from a different direction into its path. The "right-of-way rule" is simply a rule of precedence as to which of two users of intersecting highways shall have the immediate right of crossing first at an intersection where the users simultaneously approach the intersection on the intersecting streets so nearly at the same time and at such rates of speed that, if they proceed without regard to each other, a collision or interference between them is reasonably to be apprehended.

Right patent. An old English writ, which was brought for lands and tenements, and not for an advowson, or common, and lay only for an estate in fee-simple, and not for him who had a lesser estate; as tenant in tail, tenant in frank marriage, or tenant for life.

Rights, petition of. See **Petition.**

Rights, stock. See **Stock** (Stock rights).

Right to attorney. See **Counsel, right to.**

Right to redeem. See **Right of redemption.**

Right to travel. Basic constitutional right exemplified in case of persons applying for welfare assistance in a state in which they have not resided for a prescribed period of time. It is said that to deny such a right to such persons is to inhibit their right to travel and hence to deny them equal protection of the law. Shapiro v. Thompson, 394 U.S. 618, 89 S.Ct. 1322, 22 L.Ed.2d 600.

Right to work laws. Such state laws (as permitted by Sec. 14(b) of the National Labor Relations Act) provide in general that employees are not to be required to join a union as a condition of receiving or retaining a job. The wording of these state statutes (existing in about 20 states) vary, with some states generally barring discrimination in employment so as to encourage union membership, others more vaguely barring an employment "monopoly" by a labor union, but most expressly barring the requirement of union membership (or paying dues to a union) as a condition of employment. See also **Open shop.**

Rigor juris /rígər júrəs/. Lat. Strictness of law. Distinguished from gratia curiæ, favor of the court.

Rigor mortis /rígər mórdəs/. Cadaveric rigidity; a rigidity or stiffening of the muscular tissue and joints of the body, which sets in at a greater or less interval after death, but usually within a few hours, and which is one of the recognized tests of death.

Ring. A clique; an exclusive combination of persons for illegitimate or selfish purposes; as to control elections or political affairs, distribute offices, obtain contracts, control the market or the stock-exchange, etc.

Ringing the changes. A larceny effected by tendering a large bill or coin in payment of a small purchase and after correct change has been given, asking for other change and repeating the request until in the confusion of mind created by so many operations, more money is obtained than the thief is entitled to.

Ringing up. A custom among commission merchants and brokers (not unlike the clearing-house system) by which they exchange contracts for sale against contracts for purchase, or reciprocally cancel such contracts, adjust differences of price between themselves, and surrender margins. U. S. v. New York Coffee & Sugar Exchange, 263 U.S. 611, 44 S.Ct. 225, 226, 68 L.Ed. 475.

Riot. The term "riot" means a public disturbance involving (1) an act or acts of violence by one or more persons part of an assemblage of three or more persons, which act or acts shall constitute a clear and present danger of, or shall result in, damage or injury to the property of any other person or to the person of any other individual or (2) a threat or threats of the commission of an act or acts of violence by one or more persons part of an assemblage of three or more persons having, individually or collectively, the ability of immediate execution of such threat or threats, where the performance of the threatened acts or acts of violence would constitute a clear and present danger of, or would result in, damage or injury to the property of any other person or to the person of any other individual. 18 U.S.C.A. § 2102(a).

A person is guilty of riot if he participates with two or more others in a course of disorderly conduct: (a) with purpose to commit or facilitate the commission of a felony or misdemeanor; (b) with purpose to prevent or coerce official action; or (c) when the actor or any other participant to the knowledge of the actor uses or plans to use a firearm or other deadly weapon. Model Penal Code, § 250.1.

Incitement to riot. Incitement to riot is by words or conduct urging others to commit acts of force or violence against persons or property or to resist the lawful authority of law enforcement officers under circumstances which produce a clear and present danger of injury to persons or property or a breach of the public peace.

The term "to incite a riot," or "to organize, promote, encourage, participate in, or carry on a riot", includes, but is not limited to urging or instigating other persons to riot, but shall not be deemed to mean the mere oral or written (1) advocacy of ideas or (2) expression of belief, not involving advocacy of any act or acts of violence or assertion of the rightness of, or the right to commit, any such act or acts. 18 U.S.C.A. § 2102(b).

See also **Unlawful assembly.**

Rioter. One who encourages, promotes, or takes part in riots. Symonds v. State, 66 Okl.Cr. 49, 89 P.2d 970, 974.

Riotous assembly. In old English criminal law, the unlawful assembling of twelve persons or more, to the disturbance of the peace, and not dispersing upon proclamation. 4 Bl.Comm. 142. See also **Unlawful assembly.**

Riparian /rəpériyən/. Belonging or relating to the bank of a river or stream; of or on the bank. Land lying beyond the natural watershed of a stream is not "riparian." The term is sometimes used as relating to the shore of the sea or other tidal water, or of a lake or other considerable body of water not having the character of a watercourse. But this is not accurate. The proper word to be employed in such connections is "littoral."

Riparian owner. One who owns land on bank of river, or one who is owner of land along, bordering upon, bounded by, fronting upon, abutting or adjacent and contiguous to and in contact with river. State ex rel. Buckson v. Pennsylvania R. Co., Del.Super., 228 A.2d 587, 594.

Riparian proprietor. An owner of land, bounded generally upon a stream or river of water, and as such having a qualified property in the soil to the thread of the stream or river with the privileges annexed thereto by law. Potomac Steamboat Co. v. Upper Potomac Steamboat Co., 109 U.S. 672, 3 S.Ct. 445, 27 L.Ed. 1070.

Riparian rights. The rights of the owners of lands on the banks of watercourses, relating to the water, its use, ownership of soil under the stream, accretions, etc. Term is generally defined as the right which every person through whose land a natural watercourse runs has to benefit of stream as it passes through his land for all useful purposes to which it may be applied. People ex rel. State Water Resources Control Bd. v. Forni, 54 Cal.App.3d 743, 126 Cal.Rptr. 851, 857. See also **Water** (*Water rights*).

Riparian water. Water which is below the highest line of normal flow of the river or stream, as distinguished from flood water. See also **Water** (*Water rights*).

Riparum usus publicus est jure gentium, sicut ipsius fluminis /rəpérəm yúwzəs pə́bləkəs èst júriy jénsh(iy)əm, síkəd ipsáyəs flúwmənəs/. The use of river-banks is by the law of nations public, like that of the stream itself.

Ripe for judgment. An action that is so far advanced, by verdict, default, confession, the determination of all pending motions, or other disposition of preliminary or disputed matters, that nothing remains for the court but to render the appropriate judgment. A case is ripe for decision by an appellate court if the legal issues involved are clear enough and well enough evolved and presented so that a clear decision can come out of the case. See also **Ripeness doctrine.**

Ripeness doctrine. The constitutional mandate of case or controversy, U.S.Const. Art. III, requires an appellate court to consider whether a case has matured or ripened into a controversy worthy of adjudication before it will determine the same.

The question in each case is whether there is a substantial controversy, between parties having adverse legal interests, of sufficient immediacy and reality to warrant the issuance of a declaratory judgment. Lake Carriers' Ass'n v. MacMullan, 406 U.S. 498, 92 S.Ct. 1749, 32 L.Ed.2d 257.

Basic rationale of "ripeness doctrine" arising out of courts' reluctance to apply declaratory judgment and injunctive remedies unless administrative determinations arise in context of a controversy ripe for judicial resolution, is to prevent courts, through avoidance of premature adjudication, from entangling themselves in abstract disagreements over administrative policies, and also to protect the agencies from judicial interference until an administrative decision has been formalized and its effects felt in a concrete way by the challenging parties, and court is required to evaluate both fitness of issues for judicial decision and hardship to parties of withholding court consideration. Abbott Laboratories v. Gardner, 387 U.S. 136, 87 S.Ct. 1507, 1515, 18 L.Ed.2d 681.

See **Case** *(Cases and controversies);* **Final decision rule; Justiciable controversy.**

Rising of court. Properly the final adjournment of the court for the term, though the term is also sometimes used to express the cessation of judicial business for the day or for a recess; it is the opposite of "sitting" or "session." This term is generally obsolete.

Risk. In insurance law, the danger or hazard of a loss of the property insured; the casualty contemplated in a contract of insurance; the degree of hazard; a specified contingency or peril; and, colloquially, the specific house, factory, ship, etc., covered by the policy. Hazard, danger, peril, exposure to loss, injury, disadvantage or destruction, and comprises all elements of danger. Knox Jewelry Co., Inc. v. Cincinnati Ins. Co., 130 Ga.App. 519, 203 S.E.2d 739, 740.

In general, the element of uncertainty in an undertaking. Risk may be moral, physical or economic.

Risk of loss in commercial sales contracts as between buyer and seller is governed by U.C.C. § 2–509.

Assumption of risk. See that title.

Obvious risk. See **Obvious.**

Ordinary risk. See **Ordinary.**

Risk capital. Money or property invested in a business venture and commonly represented by common stock, or capital in a partnership, as distinguished from loans or bonded indebtedness.

Risk incident to employment. Within worker's compensation acts, one growing out of or connected with what worker must do in fulfilling his or her contract of service, and may be either ordinary risk, directly connected with employment, or extraordinary risk indirectly connected with employment because of its special nature.

Risk premium. Extra compensation paid to an employee or extra interest paid to a lender, over amounts usually considered normal, in return for their undertaking to engage in activities more risky than normal.

River. A natural stream of water, of greater volume than a creek or rivulet, flowing in a more or less permanent bed or channel, between defined banks or walls, with a current which may either be continuous in one direction or affected by the ebb and flow of the tide.

Public river. A river capable in its natural state of some useful service to the public because of its existence as such, navigability being not the sole test. St. Regis Paper Co. v. New Hampshire Water Resources Board, 92 N.H. 164, 26 A.2d 832, 838.

River banks. The boundaries which confine the water to its channel throughout the entire width when stream is carrying its maximum quantity of water. Mammoth Gold Dredging Co. v. Forbes, 39 Cal. App.2d 739, 104 P.2d 131, 137.

R.L. This abbreviation may stand either for "Revised Laws" or "Roman law."

Road. A highway; an open way or public passage; a line of travel or communication extending from one town or place to another; a strip of land appropriated and used for purposes of travel and communication between different places. See also **Highway.**

In maritime law, an open passage of the sea that receives its denomination commonly from some part adjacent, which, though it lie out at sea, yet, in respect of the situation of the land adjacent, and the depth and wideness of the place, is a safe place for the common riding or anchoring of ships.

Law of the road. Custom or practice which has become crystallized into accepted system of rules regulating travel on highways. Short v. Robinson, 280 Ky. 707, 134 S.W.2d 594, 596. It relates to safety of travel, and is adjustment of rights of travelers using highway at same time. For example, "law of the road" refers to the rule which requires that vehicles meeting shall keep to the right of the middle of the highway. See also **Right of way.**

Public road. A highway; a road or way established and adopted (or accepted as a dedication) by the proper authorities for the use of the general public, and over which every person has a right to pass and to use it for all purposes of travel or transportation to which it is adapted and devoted. The proper test in determining whether road is a "public" or "private road" is use to which such roadway is put, and fact that road has been constructed at public expense is not conclusive. Kitchens v. Duffield, 83 Ohio App. 41, 76 N.E.2d 101, 105, 38 O.O. 142.

Road districts. Public or *quasi* municipal corporations organized or authorized by statutory authority in many of the states for the special purpose of establishing, maintaining, and caring for public roads and highways within their limits, sometimes invested with powers of local taxation, and generally having elective officers styled "overseers" or "commissioners" of roads.

Rob. To take personalty in possession of another from his person or his presence, feloniously and against his will, by violence or by putting him in fear. People v. Flohr, 30 Cal.App.2d 576, 86 P.2d 862, 864. See **Robbery.**

Robbery. Felonious taking of money, personal property, or any other article of value, in the possession of another, from his person or immediate presence, and against his will, accomplished by means of force or fear. Hatcher v. State, Ala.Cr.App., 335 So.2d 415; People v. Eddy, 123 Cal.App.2d 826, 268 P.2d 47, 51.

A person is guilty of robbery if, in the course of committing a theft, he: (a) inflicts serious bodily injury upon another; or (b) threatens another with or purposely puts him in fear of immediate serious bodily injury; or (c) commits or threatens immediately to commit any felony of the first or second degree. An act shall be deemed "in the course of committing a theft" if it occurs in an attempt to commit theft or in flight after the attempt or commission. Model Penal Code, § 222.1.

Most jurisdictions today divide robbery, for purposes of punishment, into simple robbery and aggravated robbery, the principal example of the latter being "armed" robbery.

See also **Armed robbery; Hobbs Act.**

Aggravated robbery. A robbery committed by a person who is armed with a dangerous weapon or who inflicts bodily harm upon any person in the course of such robbery.

Highway robbery. The crime of robbery committed upon or near a public highway. The felonious and forcible taking of property from the person of another on a highway. It differs from robbery in general only in the place where it is committed. Robbery by hold-up originally applied to the stopping and robbery of traveling parties, but the term has acquired a broader meaning. It has come to be applied to robbery in general, by the use of force or putting in fear. See **Hijacking.**

Robinson-Patman Act. Section 2(a) of the Clayton Act, as amended in 1936 by the Robinson-Patman Act (15 U.S.C.A. § 13) makes it unlawful for any seller engaged in commerce to directly or indirectly discriminate in the price charged purchasers on the sale of commodities of like grade and quality where the effect may be to injure, destroy or prevent competition with any person who grants or knowingly receives a discrimination, or the customer of either. See also **Price discrimination.**

Rod. A lineal measure of 5½ yards or 16½ feet; otherwise called a "perch." See also **Land measure.**

Rogationes, quæstiones, et positiones debent esse simplices /rəgèyshiyówniyz kwès(h)chiyówniyz èt pəzì-shiyówniyz débənt ésiy símpləsiyz/. Demands, questions, and claims ought to be simple.

Rogatio testium /rəgéysh(iy)ow tés(h)ch(iy)əm/. This in making a nuncupative will, is where the testator formally calls upon the persons present to bear witness that he has declared his will.

Rogator /rəgéydər/. Lat. In Roman law, the proposer of a law or rogation.

Rogatory letters /rógətoriy lédərz/. A commission from one judge to another requesting him to examine a witness. See also **Letters rogatory.**

Rogo /rówgow/. Lat. In Roman law, I ask; I request. A precatory expression often used in wills.

Rogue /rówg/. An idle and disorderly person; a trickster; a wandering beggar; a vagrant or vagabond; a scoundrel. 4 Bl.Comm. 169.

Roll, n. Record of the proceedings of a court or public office. See *Judgment roll,* below.

A register; list of persons belonging to particular group. See also **Roster.**

In taxation, the list or record of taxable persons and property, as compiled by assessors. See *Tax roll,* below.

Judgment roll. Such is required to be filed in certain states by the clerk when he enters judgment. It normally contains the summons, pleadings, admissions, and each judgment and each order involving the merits or necessarily affecting the final judgment. New York C.P.L.R. § 5017. In the federal and most state courts, judgments are recorded in the "civil docket" (Fed.R.Civil P. 79) or "criminal docket" (Fed. R.Crim.P. 55).

In old English practice, a roll of parchment containing the entries of the proceedings in an action at law to the entry of judgment inclusive, and which was filed in the treasury of the court.

Tax roll. A schedule or list of the persons and property subject to the payment of a particular tax, with the amounts severally due, prepared and authenticated in proper form to warrant the collecting officers to proceed with the enforcement of the tax.

Roll, v. To rob by force.

Rolling over. Banking term for extension or renewal of short term loan from one period (*e.g.* 90 day) to another. See also **Roll-over paper.**

Roll-over paper. Short term notes which may be extended (rolled over) or converted to installment payments, after the initial due date.

Roman Catholic Church. The juristic personality of the Roman Catholic Church, with the right to sue and to take and hold property has been recognized by all systems of European law from the fourth century. It was formally recognized between Spain and the Papacy and by Spanish laws from the beginning of the settlements in the Indies, also by our treaty with Spain in 1898, whereby its property rights were solemnly safeguarded. Municipality of Ponce v. Roman Catholic Church in Porto Rico, 210 U.S. 296, 28 S.Ct. 737, 52 L.Ed. 1068; Santos v. Roman Catholic Church, 212 U.S. 463, 29 S.Ct. 338, 53 L.Ed. 599.

Roman law. In a general sense, comprehends all the laws which prevailed among the Romans, without regard to the time of their origin, including the collections of Justinian. In a more restricted sense, the Germans understand by this term merely the law of Justinian, as adopted by them.

In England and America, it appears to be customary to use the phrase, indifferently with "the civil law," to designate the whole system of Roman jurisprudence, including the *Corpus Juris Civilis;* or, if any distinction is drawn, the expression "civil law" denotes the system of jurisprudence obtaining in those countries of continental Europe which have derived their juridical notions and principles from the Justinian collection, while "Roman law" is reserved as the proper appellation of the body of law developed under the government of Rome from the earliest times to the fall of the empire. See **Civil law.**

Rood of land /rúwd əv lǽnd/. The fourth part of an acre in square measure, or one thousand two hundred and ten square yards.

Roomer. A lodger; one who rents a room or rooms.

Root of descent. The same as "stock of descent."

Root of title. The document with which an abstract of title properly commences.

ROR. Release on Own Recognizance.

Rorschach test /rórshæk tèst/. Projective method of determining the structure of personality by noting the patient's reaction to a set of ten cards containing standardized ink blots; used in detecting neurotic and psychotic traits.

Roster /róstər/. A roll or list of persons. A list of persons who are to perform certain duties when called upon in their turn.

Rota /rówdə/. L. Lat. Succession; rotation; *e.g.* "*Rota* of presentations;" "*rota* of the terms."

Rotten clause. A clause sometimes inserted in policies of marine insurance to the effect that "if, on a regular survey, the ship shall be declared unseaworthy by reason of being *rotten* or unsound," the insurers shall be discharged.

Round lot. Unit of trading on N.Y. Stock Exchange. For stocks, it is 100 shares; for bonds, $1000 par value.

Route. Course, or line of travel from one place to another. Cities or towns between which common carriers or airlines are permitted by I.C.C., C.A.B., etc. to carry goods or passengers.

In railroad parlance, a designated course over a way or right of way, irrespective of the singleness or multiplicity of operation thereon. Regenhardt Const. Co. v. Southern Ry. in Kentucky, 297 Ky. 840, 181 S.W.2d 441, 444.

Routously. In old pleading, a technical word in indictments, generally coupled with the word "riotously."

Roy /róy/réy/rwa/. L. Fr. The king.

Royal. Of or pertaining to or proceeding from the king or sovereign in a monarchical government.

Royal prerogative. Those rights and capacities which the king enjoys alone in contradistinction to others and not to those which he enjoys in common with any of his subjects. It is that special pre-eminence which the sovereign has over all other persons, and out of the course of the common law by right of regal dignity. Ætna Casualty & Surety Co. v. Bramwell, D.C.Or., 12 F.2d 307, 309.

Royalty. Compensation for the use of property, usually copyrighted material or natural resources, expressed as a percentage of receipts from using the property or as an account per unit produced. A payment which is made to an author or composer by an assignee, licensee or copyright holder in respect of each copy of his work which is sold, or to an inventor in respect of each article sold under the patent. Royalty is share of product or profit reserved by owner for permitting another to use the property. In its broadest aspect, it is share of profit reserved by owner for permitting another the use of property. Alamo Nat. Bank of San Antonio v. Hurd, Tex.Civ.App., 485 S.W.2d 335, 338.

In mining and oil operations, a share of the product or profit paid to the owner of the property. Marias River Syndicate v. Big West Oil Co., 98 Mont. 254, 38 P.2d 599, 601.

See also **Minimum royalty clause; Overriding royalty; Shut-in royalty.**

Overriding royalty. A retained royalty by a lessee when the property is subleased. Common in oil and gas leases.

Royalty acres. That part of the oil that goes to landowner, whether it be in place or after production. Dickens v. Tisdale, 204 Ark. 838, 164 S.W.2d 990, 992.

Royalty bonus. The consideration for oil and gas lease over and above the usual royalty. Sheppard v. Stanolind Oil & Gas Co., Tex.Civ.App., 125 S.W.2d 643, 648.

Roy est l'original de touts franchises. The king is the origin of all franchises.

Roy n'est lie per ascun statute si il ne soit expressment nosme. The king is not bound by any statute, unless expressly named.

Roy poet dispenser ove malum prohibitum, mais non malum per se. The king can grant a dispensation for a *malum prohibitum,* but not for a *malum per se.*

R.S. An abbreviation for "Revised Statutes."

Rubber check. Slang for a check which has been returned by the drawee bank because of insufficient funds in the account of the drawer.

Rudeness. Roughness; incivility; violence. Touching another with rudeness may constitute a battery.

Rule, *v.* To command or require by a rule of court; as, to rule the sheriff to return the writ, to rule the defendant to plead, to rule against an objection to evidence. To settle or decide a point of law arising upon a trial, and, when it is said of a judge presiding at such a trial that he "ruled" so and so, it is meant that he laid down, settled, or decided such and such to be the law.

Rule, *n.* An established standard, guide, or regulation. A principle or regulation set up by authority, prescribing or directing action or forbearance; as, the rules of a legislative body, of a company, court, public office, of the law, of ethics. Precept attaching a definite detailed legal consequence to a definite detailed state of facts.

An order made by a court, at the instance of one of the parties to a suit, commanding a ministerial officer, or the opposite party, to do some act, or to show cause why some act should not be done. It is usually upon some interlocutory matter. See also **Decree; Order.**

A rule of law. Thus, we speak of the rule against perpetuities; the Rule in Shelley's Case, etc. See also *Rule of law, infra.*

Rule absolute. One which commands the subject-matter of the rule to be forthwith enforced. It is common, for example, when the party has failed to show sufficient cause against a rule *nisi,* to "make the rule absolute," *i.e.,* imperative and final.

Rule against perpetuities. Principle that no interest in property is good unless it must vest, if at all, not later than 21 years, plus period of gestation, after some life or lives in being at time of creation of interest. Perkins v. Iglehart, 183 Md. 520, 39 A.2d 672, 676. St. Louis Union Trust Co. v. Bassett, 337 Mo. 604, 85 S.W.2d 569, 575. The "rule against perpetuities" prohibits the granting of an estate which will not necessarily vest within a time limited by a life or lives then in being and 21 years thereafter together with the period of gestation necessary to cover cases of posthumous birth. Nelson v. Mercantile Trust Co., Mo., 335 S.W.2d 167, 172.

This common law rule or principle has been modified by statute in certain states; *e.g.* under some statutes an inquiry may be made as to whether the gift *did* vest in fact within the period. If it actually vested, it will be upheld. Under original rule, the inquiry was whether it *must* vest by its terms. See *e.g.* M.G.L.A. c. 184A (Mass.).

See also **Perpetuity.**

Rule in Shelley's Case. See **Shelley's Case, Rule in.**

Rule nisi. A rule which will become imperative and final *unless* cause be shown against it. This rule commands the party to show cause why he should not be compelled to do the act required, or why the object of the rule should not be enforced. An ex parte order directing the other party to show cause why such a temporary order should not become permanent.

Rule of apportionment. Rule that, where subdivided tract contains more or less than aggregate amount called for, excess or deficiency is apportioned among several tracts.

Rule of four. Working rule devised by Supreme Court for determining if a case is deserving of review; the theory being that if four justices find that a legal question of general importance is raised, that is ample proof that the question has such importance. Rogers v. Missouri Pac. R. Co., Ill., 352 U.S. 521, 77 S.Ct. 459, 478, 1 L.Ed.2d 515.

Rule of law. A legal principle, of general application, sanctioned by the recognition of authorities, and usually expressed in the form of a maxim or logical proposition. Called a "rule," because in doubtful or unforeseen cases it is a guide or norm for their decision. The rule of law, sometimes called "the supremacy of law", provides that decisions should be made by the application of known principles or laws without the intervention of discretion in their application. See *e.g. Rule against perpetuities, supra;* also, **Shelley's Case, Rule in.**

Rule of lenity. Where the intention of Congress is not clear from the act itself and reasonable minds might differ as to its intention, the court will adopt the less harsh meaning. U. S. v. Callanan, D.C.Mo., 173 F.Supp. 98, 100. Under "rule of lenity," when it is unclear whether legislature intended multiple sentences for single act involving multiple victims, doubt will be resolved in favor of defendant. Davenport v. State, Alaska, 543 P.2d 1204, 1209.

Rule of necessity. While a judge should disqualify himself when called upon to decide a matter in which he has a direct interest, if he is the only judge with power to hear and determine the matter, the rule of necessity requires that he hear it. Evans v. Gore, 253 U.S. 245, 40 S.Ct. 550, 64 L.Ed. 887.

Rule of presumption. Rule changes one of burdens of proof, that is, it declares that main fact will be inferred or assumed from some other fact until evidence to contrary is introduced. Barrett v. U. S., C.A.Ga., 322 F.2d 292, 294. See **Presumption.**

Rule of reason. Under the "rule of reason" the legality of restraints on trade is determined by weighing all the factors of the case such as the history of the restraint, the evil believed to exist, the reason for adopting the particular remedy and the purpose or end sought to be attained. U. S. v. National Soc. of Professional Engineers, D.C.D.C., 404 F.Supp. 457, 463.

To constitute a crime under § 1 of the Sherman Antitrust Act, the defendant's conduct must result in an unreasonable restraint of interstate commerce. It is for the jury to determine from a consideration of all the facts and circumstances, including the economic conditions of the industry and the effect on competition, whether defendants' conduct creates an unreasonable restraint on interstate commerce. Standard Oil Co. v. United States, 221 U.S. 1, 31 S.Ct. 502, 55 L.Ed. 619; Best Advertising Corp. v. Illinois Bell Tel. Co., C.A.Ill., 339 F.2d 1009; Walker Process Equipment, Inc. v. Food Machinery & Chemical Corp., 382 U.S. 172, 86 S.Ct. 347, 15 L.Ed.2d 247. The "rule of reason" test is not however applied in instances of per se antitrust violations; *e.g.* price-fixing.

Rule of road. See **Right of way; Road.**

Rule to show cause. A rule commanding the party to appear and show cause why he should not be compelled to do the act required, or why the object of the rule should not be enforced; a rule *nisi (q.v.).* See **Show cause order.**

Rulemaking power. Congress has from time to time conferred upon the Supreme Court power to prescribe rules of procedure to be followed by the lower courts of the United States. Pursuant to these statutes (28 U.S.C.A. §§ 2071–2076, re Civil, Appellate, Bankruptcy, Evidence Rules; 18 U.S.C.A. §§ 3771, 3772, re Criminal Rules) there are now in force rules promulgated by the Court to govern civil and criminal cases in the district courts, bankruptcy proceedings, admiralty cases, copyright cases, appellate proceedings, and minor criminal offense proceedings before U.S. magistrates.

Rule of 78. Method of computing refunds of unearned finance charges on early payment of loan so that refund is proportional to the monthly unpaid balance. 78 is the sum of the digits of one to twelve, *i.e.,* the number of months in a one-year installment contract.

Rules of Appellate Procedure. Federal Rules of Appellate Procedure govern procedure in appeals from the U.S. district courts and Tax Court to the U.S. Courts of Appeal. Fed.R.App.P. 1(a). In states which have adopted similar rules, they govern procedure from the trial court to appellate courts. See **Federal Rules of Appellate Procedure.**

Rules of Civil Procedure. Federal Rules of Civil Procedure govern procedure in the U.S. district courts in all suits of a civil nature whether cognizable as cases at law or in equity or in admiralty with some exceptions. Fed.R.Civil P. 1. Many states have adopted similar rules which track the Federal Rules. See **Federal Rules of Civil Procedure.**

Rules of court. Such regulate practice and procedure before the various courts; *e.g.* Rules of Civil, Criminal, or Appellate Procedure; Rules of Evidence. In most jurisdictions, these rules are issued by the court itself, or by the highest court in that jurisdiction, while in others, such are adopted or enacted by the legislature. See also **Court rule; Rulemaking power.**

Rules of Criminal Procedure. Federal Rules of Criminal Procedure govern the procedure in all criminal proceedings in the courts of the United States, including preliminary, supplementary, and special proceedings before U.S. magistrates. Fed.R.Crim.P. 1. Many states have adopted similar rules which track the Federal Rules. See **Federal Rules of Criminal Procedure.**

Rules of Decision Act. Section 34 of the Judiciary Act of 1789—the famous Rules of Decision Act—provided that "the laws of the several states, except where the constitution, treaties, or statutes of the United States shall otherwise require or provide, shall be regarded as rules of decision in trials at common law in the courts of the United States in cases where they apply." The statute has remained substantially unchanged to this day.

Rules of Evidence. Rules of court which govern the admissibility of evidence at trials and hearings; *e.g.* Federal Rules of Evidence; Uniform Rules of Evidence; Maine Rules of Evidence; California Evidence Code. See **Federal Rules of Evidence.**

Rules of navigation. See **Navigation.**

Rule 10b–5. Rule 10b–5 of the Securities and Exchange Commission makes it unlawful, in connection with the purchase or sale of any security, to make any untrue statement of a material fact or to omit to state a material fact necessary in order to make the statements made, in the light of circumstances under which they were made, not misleading. See also Sec. 10(b) of the Securities Exchange Act, 15 U.S.C.A. § 78(j)(b). See also **Insider; Material fact.**

Ruling. A judicial or administrative interpretation of a provision of a statute, order, regulation, or ordinance; *e.g.* Revenue Rulings. May also refer to judicial determination of admissibility of evidence, allowance of motion, etc. See also **Decree; Order; Rule.**

Rumor. A current story passing from one person to another without any known authority for the truth of it. Such are not generally admissible in evidence.

Run, *v.* To have currency or legal validity in a prescribed territory; as, the writ *runs* throughout the county.

    To have applicability or legal effect during a prescribed period of time; as, the statute of limitations has *run* against the claim.

    To follow or accompany; to be attached to another thing in pursuing a prescribed course or direction; as, the covenant *runs* with the land.

    To conduct, manage, carry on.

Run, *n.* A watercourse of small size. In business, a continuous round of manufacturing. In banking, a widespread and sudden withdrawal of deposits from a bank because of fear of the bank's collapse.

Runaway shop. An employer who moves his business to another location or temporarily closes his business for anti-union purposes.

Runner. Person who solicits business for attorney from accident victims. Also means a person employed by a bail bondsman for the purpose of assisting the bail bondsman in presenting the defendant in court when required, or to assist in apprehension and surrender of defendant to the court, or keeping defendant under necessary surveillance, or to execute bonds on behalf of the licensed bondsman when the power of attorney has been duly recorded. See also **Ambulance chaser.**

Running account. An open unsettled account, as distinguished from a stated and liquidated account. Running accounts mean mutual accounts and reciprocal demands between the parties, which accounts and demands remain open and unsettled. See also **Charge account; Revolving credit.**

Running at large. This term is applied to wandering or straying animals.

Running days. Days counted in their regular succession on the calendar, including Sundays and holidays.

Running of the statute of limitations. A metaphorical expression, by which is meant that the time mentioned in the statute of limitations is considered as having passed and hence the action is barred. United States v. Markowitz, D.C.Cal., 34 F.Supp. 827, 829.

Running policy. One which contemplates successive insurances, and which provides that the object of the policy may be from time to time defined, especially as to the subjects of insurance, by additional statements or indorsements.

Running with the land. Passing with transfer of the land. A covenant is said to run with the land when either the liability to perform it or the right to take advantage of it passes to the assignee of that land. Usually concerned with easements and covenants.

Running with the reversion. A covenant is said to run with the reversion when either the liability to perform it or the right to take advantage of it passes to the assignee of that reversion.

Rural. Concerning the country, as opposed to urban (concerning the city).

Rusticum judicium /rástəkəm juwdísh(iy)əm/. Lat. In maritime law, a rough or rude judgment or decision. A judgment in admiralty dividing the damages caused by a collision between the two ships.

Rustler. Cattle thief.

Rustling. Larceny of cattle.

Ruta /rúwdə/. Lat. In the civil law, things extracted from land; as sand, chalk, coal, and such other matters.

Ruta et cæsa /rúwdə èt síyzə/. In the civil law, things dug (as sand and lime), and things cut (as wood, coal, etc.).

Rylands v. Fletcher case. The early English case which is the progenitor of the doctrine of absolute liability for abnormally dangerous things and activities. 3 H.L. 330.

S

S. As an abbreviation, this letter stands for "section," "statute," and various other words of which it is the initial.

Sabbath. One of the names of the first day of the week; more properly called "Sunday" (*q.v.*).

Sabbath-breaking. The offense of violating the laws prescribed for the observance of Sunday; *i.e.* violation of Sunday closing laws (Blue-laws).

Sabotage /sǽbətázh/. Term has reference to the wilful destruction or injury of, or defective production of, war material or national-defense material, or harm to war premises or war utilities. 18 U.S.C.A. § 2151 et seq. Term also refers to wilful and malicious destruction of employer's property during a labor dispute or interference with his normal operations. Burns v. U. S., 274 U.S. 328, 47 S.Ct. 650, 71 L.Ed. 1077.

Sac /sæk/. In old English law, a liberty of holding pleas; the jurisdiction of a manor court; the privilege claimed by a lord of trying actions of trespass between his tenants, in his manor court, and imposing fines and amerciaments in the same.

Sacaburth, sacabere, sakabere /sǽkəbə̀r(θ)/. In old English law, he that was robbed, or by theft deprived of his money or goods, and put in surety to prosecute the felon with fresh suit.

Saccabor /sǽkəbər/. In old English law, the person from whom a thing had been stolen, and by whom the thief was freshly pursued.

Sacramentales /sǽkrəməntéyliyz/. L. Lat. In feudal law, compurgators; persons who came to purge a defendant by their oath that they believed him innocent.

Sacramentum /sǽkrəméntəm/. Lat. *Common law.* An oath.

Roman law. An oath, as being a very sacred thing; more particularly, the oath taken by soldiers to be true to their general and their country.

In one of the formal methods of beginning an action at law (*legis actiones*) known to the early Roman jurisprudence, the *sacramentum* was a sum of money deposited in court by each of the litigating parties, as a kind of wager or forfeit, to abide the result of the suit. The successful party received back his stake; the losing party forfeited his, and it was paid into the public treasury, to be expended for sacred objects (*in sacris rebus*), whence the name.

Sacramentum decisionis /sǽkrəméntəm dəsìzhiyównəs/. The voluntary or decisive oath of the civil law, where one of the parties to a suit, not being able to prove his case, offers to refer the decision of the cause to the oath of his adversary, who is bound to accept or make the same offer on his part, or the whole is considered as confessed by him.

Sacramentum fidelitatis /sǽkrəméntəm fədèlətéydəs/. In old English law, the oath of fealty.

Sacramentum habet in se tres comites,—veritatem, justitiam, et judicium; veritas habenda est in jurato; justitia et justicium in judice. An oath has in it three component parts,—truth, justice, and judgment; truth in the party swearing; justice and judgment in the judge administering the oath.

Sacramentum si fatuum fuerit, licet falsum, tamen non committit perjurium /sǽkrəméntəm sày fǽchuwəm f(y)úwərət, láysət fól(t)səm, tǽmən nòn kəmídət pərjúriyəm/. A foolish oath, though false, makes not perjury.

Sacrilege /sǽkrələj/. In old English criminal law, larceny from a church. The crime of breaking a church or chapel, and stealing therein. The desecration of anything considered holy; the alienation to lay-men or to profane or common purposes of what was given to religious persons and to pious uses.

Sacrilegium /sǽkrəlíyj(iy)əm/. Lat. In the civil law, the stealing of sacred things, or things dedicated to sacred uses; the taking of things out of a holy place.

Sacrilegus /səkríləgəs/. Lat. In the civil and common law, a sacrilegious person; one guilty of sacrilege.

Sacrilegus omnium prædonum cupiditatem et scelera superat /səkríləgəs ómn(i)yəm prədównəm kyuwpìdətéydəm èt sélərə s(y)úwpərət/. A sacrilegious person transcends the cupidity and wickedness of all other robbers.

Sacristan /sǽkrəstən/. A sexton, anciently called "*sagerson*", or "*sagiston*", the keeper of things belonging to divine worship.

Sadism /séydizəm/sǽd°/. A form of satisfaction, commonly sexual, derived from inflicting harm on another. It is a type of insanity or mental disease. The opposite of *masochism* (*q.v.*).

Sæmend. In old English law, an umpire, or arbitrator.

Sæpe constitutum est, res inter alios judicatas aliis non præjudicare /síypiy kòn(t)stət(y)úwdəm èst ríyz íntər éyl(i)yows jùwdəkéydəs éyliyəs nòn prəjùwdəkériy/. It has often been settled that matters adjudged between others ought not to prejudice those who were not parties.

Sæpenumero ubi proprietas verborum attenditur, sensus veritatis amittitur /sìypiynámərow yúwbay prəpráyətæs vərbórəm əténdədər sén(t)səs vèhrətéydəs əmídədər/. Oftentimes where the propriety of words is attended to, the true sense is lost.

Sævitia /səvísh(iy)ə/. Lat. In the law of divorce, cruelty; anything which tends to bodily harm, and in that manner renders cohabitation unsafe.

Safe. A metal receptacle for the preservation of valuables. Untouched by danger; not exposed to danger; secure from danger, harm or loss.

One of the papers usually carried by vessels in time of war, and necessary to the safety of neutral merchantmen. It is in the nature of a license to the vessel to proceed on a designated voyage, and commonly contains the name of the master, the name, description, and nationality of the ship, the voyage intended, and other matters. A distinction is sometimes made between a *passport,* conferring a general permission to travel in the territory belonging to, or occupied by, the belligerent, and a *safe-conduct,* conferring permission upon an enemy subject or others to proceed to a particular place for a defined object.

Safe deposit box. A metal container kept by a customer in a bank in which he deposits papers, securities and other valuable items. Generally, there are two keys required to open, one retained by the bank and the other by the customer.

Safe deposit company. A company which maintains vaults for the deposit and safe-keeping of valuables in which compartments or boxes are rented to customers who have exclusive access thereto, subject to the oversight and under the rules and regulations of the company. See **Depository; Safe deposit box.**

Safe limit of speed. As regards limitation on speed of automobiles at crossings, the limit at which one may discern an approaching train and stop before he is in the danger zone. Horton v. New York Cent. R. Co., 205 App.Div. 763, 200 N.Y.S. 365, 366.

Safe place to work. In the law of master and servant, a place in which the master has eliminated all danger which in the exercise of reasonable care the master should remove or guard against. Master's duty to provide a "safe place" to work includes places to and from which the employee might be required or expected to go. High Splint Coal Co. v. Ramey's Adm'x., 271 Ky. 532, 112 S.W.2d 1007, 1008.

It is the master's duty to exercise a reasonable care to provide his servant a "safe place to work," by which is meant not the absolute elimination of all danger, but of all danger which the exercise of reasonable care by the master would remove or guard against; and such duty is as applicable to a railroad switch yard as to a machine shop. Melody v. Des Moines Union Ry. Co., 141 N.W. 438, 439, 161 Iowa 695.

Federal, state, and local regulations and regulatory bodies require health and safety standards for workers. See *e.g.* **Occupational Safety and Health Act.**

Safety Appliance Act. Federal Act regulating safety of equipment used by common carriers engaged in interstate commerce. 45 U.S.C.A. § 1 *et seq.*

Sagibaro /ságəbærow/. In old European law, a judge or justice; literally, a man of causes, or having charge or supervision of causes. One who administered justice and decided causes in the *mallum,* or public assembly.

Said. Before mentioned. This word is frequently used in contracts, pleadings, and other legal papers, with the same force as "aforesaid." Greeley Nat. Bank v. Wolf, C.C.A.Colo., 4 F.2d 67, 69.

Sail. To put to sea; to begin a voyage. To get ship under way in complete readiness for voyage, with purpose of proceeding without further delay.

Sailors. Seamen; mariners.

Sailors' Relief Act. See **Soldiers' and Sailors' Civil Relief Act.**

Sailors' will. A nuncupative or oral will which the law allows in the case of a sailor at sea. It has the power to pass personal property at death but not real estate. See also **Nuncupative will.**

Saisie /sèyzíy/. Fr. In French law, a judicial seizure or sequestration of property, of which there are several varieties. See *infra.*

Saisie-arrêt. An attachment of property in the possession of a third person.

Saisie-exécution. A writ resembling that of *fieri facias;* defined as that species of execution by which a creditor places under the hand of justice (custody of the law) his debtor's movable property liable to seizure, in order to have it sold, so that he may obtain payment of his debt out of the proceeds.

Saisie-foraine. A permission given by the proper judicial officer to authorize a creditor to seize the property of his debtor in the district which the former inhabits. It has the effect of an attachment of property, which is applied to the payment of the debt due.

Saisie-gagerie. A conservatory act of execution, by which the owner or principal lessor of a house or farm causes the furniture of the house or farm leased, and on which he has a lien, to be seized; similar to the *distress* of the common law.

Saisie-immobilière. The proceeding by which a creditor places under the hand of justice (custody of the law) the immovable property of his debtor, in order that the same may be sold, and that he may obtain payment of his debt out of the proceeds.

Sake. In old English law, a lord's right of amercing his tenants in his court.

Acquittance of suit at county courts and hundred courts.

Salable. Merchantable; fit for sale in usual course of trade, at usual selling prices. See **Marketable title; Merchantability.**

Salable value. Usual selling price at place where property is situated when its value is to be ascertained. Fort Worth & D. N. Ry. Co. v. Sugg, Tex.Civ.App., 68 S.W.2d 570, 572. See also **Value.**

Salarium /səlériyəm/. Lat. In the civil law, an allowance of provisions. A stipend, wages, or compensation for services. An annual allowance or compensation.

Salary. A reward or recompense for services performed. In a more limited sense, a fixed periodical compensation paid for services rendered. A stated compensation paid periodically as by the year, month, or other fixed period, in contrast to wages which are normally based on an hourly rate. See also **Fixed salary; Wages.**

Sale. A contract between two parties, called, respectively, the "seller" (or vendor) and the "buyer" (or purchaser), by which the former, in consideration of the payment or promise of payment of a certain price in money, transfers to the latter the title and the possession of property. Transfer of property for consideration either in money or its equivalent. Wade-Corry Co. v. Moseley, 223 Ga. 474, 156 S.E.2d 64, 65. Passing of title from seller to buyer for a price. U.C.C. § 2–106(1).

The general law governing the sale of goods is the Uniform Commercial Code (Art. 2).

A contract whereby property is transferred from one person to another for a consideration of value, implying the passing of the general and absolute title, as distinguished from a special interest falling short of complete ownership.

An agreement by which one gives a thing for a price in current money, and the other gives the price in order to have the thing itself. Three circumstances concur to the perfection of the contract, to-wit, the thing sold, the price, and the consent. Civ.Code La. art. 2439.

To constitute a "sale," there must be parties standing to each other in the relation of buyer and seller, their minds must assent to the same proposition, and a consideration must pass. Commissioner of Internal Revenue v. Freihofer, C.C.A.3, 102 F.2d 787, 789, 790.

A revenue transaction where goods or services are delivered to a customer in return for cash or a contractual obligation to pay. Term comprehends transfer of property from one party to another for valuable recompense. Herskovitz v. Vespico, 238 Pa.Super. 529, 362 A.2d 394, 396.

The term "sale" includes any contract to sell or otherwise dispose of. Securities Exchange Act, § 3.

"Sale", "sell", "offer to sell", or "offer for sale" includes every contract of sale or disposition of, attempt or offer to dispose of, or solicitation of an offer to buy, a security or interest in a security, for value. Any security given or delivered with, or as a bonus on account of, any purchase of securities or any other thing, shall be conclusively presumed to constitute a part of the subject of such purchase and to have been sold for value. Investment Company Act, § 2.

Sale, as applied to relation between landowner and real estate broker working to secure purchaser of land, means procuring purchaser able, ready and willing to buy on terms fixed by seller.

See also Approval sale; Bargain and sale; Bargain sale or purchase; Bootstrap sale; Bulk sale; Buy and sell agreement; Cash sale; Casual sale; Consignment; Contract of sale; Credit sale; Fire sale; Forced sale; Installment sale; Isolated sale; Judicial sale; Scalper; Sheriff's sale; Simulated sale; Symbolic delivery; Tax sale; Wash sale.

Other Terms Distinguished

The contract of "sale" is distinguished from "barter" (which applies only to goods) and "exchange" (which is used of both land and goods), in that both the latter terms denote a commutation of property for property; i.e., the price or consideration is always paid in money if the transaction is a sale, but, if it is a barter or exchange, it is paid in specific property susceptible of valuation. "Sale" differs from "gift" in that the latter transaction involves no return or recompense for the thing transferred. But an onerous gift sometimes approaches the nature of a sale, at least where the charge it imposes is a payment of money. "Sale" is also to be distinguished from "bailment;" and the difference is to be found in the fact that the contract of bailment always contemplates the return to the bailor of the specific article delivered, either in its original form or in a modified or altered form, or the return of an article which, though not identical, is of the same class, and is equivalent. But sale never involves the return of the article itself, but only a consideration in money. This contract differs also from "accord and satisfaction;" because in the latter the object of transferring the property is to compromise and settle a claim, while the object of a sale is the price given.

The cardinal difference between the relation of seller and buyer and that of principal and factor is that in a "sale" title passes to the buyer, while in a "consignment" by principal to factor title remains in principal, and only possession passes to factor. Also, a "sale" is distinguished from a mortgage, in that the former is a transfer of the absolute property in the goods for a price, whereas a mortgage is at most a conditional sale of property as security for the payment of a debt or performance of some other obligation, subject to the condition that on performance title shall revest in the mortgagor.

An abandonment must be made without any desire that any other person shall acquire the thing abandoned, since if it is made for a consideration it is a "sale" or "barter," and if made without consideration, but with an intention that some other person shall become the possessor, it is a "gift." Del Giorgio v. Powers, 27 Cal.App.2d 668, 81 P.2d 1006, 1014.

General Classification

Absolute and conditional sales. An absolute sale is one where the property in chattels passes to the buyer upon the completion of the bargain. A conditional sale is one in which the transfer of title is made to depend on the performance of a condition, usually the payment of the price; it is a purchase for a price paid or to be paid, to become absolute on a particular event, or a purchase accompanied by an agreement to resell upon particular terms. Under a conditional sale the seller reserves title as security for payment for goods. See also **Secured transaction.**

Bill of sale. See **Bill.**

Bulk sale. The sale of all or a substantial part of the seller's materials, supplies, merchandise, other inventory or in some cases equipment not in the ordinary course of business. U.C.C. § 6–102. Statutes prescribe the procedure for such sales because of the danger of fraud on the creditors of the seller.

Cash sale. A transaction whereby payment is to be in full on receipt of the goods. A sale where title is not to pass until the price is paid, or where title has passed, but possession is not to be delivered until payment is made. Compare *Sale on credit, infra.*

Conditional sale. See *Absolute and conditional sales,* above.

Credit sale. See *Sale on credit, infra.*

Consignment sale. See **Consignment.**

Exclusive sale. With respect to a real estate broker, an agreement by the owner that he will not sell the property during the life of the contract to any purchaser not procured by the broker in question. See **Exclusive agency listing; Listing.**

Executed and executory sales. An executed sale is one which is final and complete in all its particulars and details, nothing remaining to be done by either party to effect an absolute transfer of the subject-matter of the sale. An executory sale is one which has been definitely agreed on as to terms and conditions, but which has not yet been carried into full effect in respect to some of its terms or details, as where it remains to determine the price, quantity, or identity of the thing sold, or to pay installments of purchase-money, or to effect a delivery.

Execution sale. See **Execution sale.**

Fair sale. See **Fair sale.**

Forced sale. A sale made without the consent or concurrence of the owner of the property, but by virtue of judicial process, such as resulting from a writ of execution or an order under a decree of foreclosure. See *Judicial sale; Sheriff's sale; Tax-sale, infra.*

Foreclosure sale. See **Foreclosure.**

Fraudulent sale. One made for the purpose of defrauding the creditors of the owner of the property, by covering up or removing from their reach and converting into cash property which would be subject to the satisfaction of their claims. Such sales may be voided by Bankruptcy Court.

Gross sale. In accounting, the total sales before deduction for return sales and allowances.

Installment sale. A sale in which the buyer makes periodic payments and generally the seller reserves title until full payment has been made. See *Retail installment sale; Sale on credit, infra.*

Judicial sale. One made under the process of a court having competent authority to order it, by an officer duly appointed and commissioned to sell, as distinguished from a sale by an owner in virtue of his right of property. See also *Sheriff's sale; Tax sale, infra.*

Memorandum sale. That form of conditional sale in which the goods are placed in the possession of the vendee subject to his approval; the title remaining in the seller until they are either accepted or rejected by the vendee.

Net sale. Gross sales *(q.v.)* less returns and allowances.

Private sale. One negotiated and concluded privately between buyer and seller, and not made by advertisement and public notice or auction or through a broker or agent.

Public sale. A sale made in pursuance of a notice, by auction or sheriff. See also *Judicial sale; Sheriff's sale; Tax sale.*

Retail installment sale. Sale of goods or the furnishing of services by a retail seller to a retail buyer for a deferred payment price payable in installments.

Sale and return. A species of contract by which the seller (usually a manufacturer or wholesaler) delivers a quantity of goods to the buyer, on the understanding that, if the latter should desire to retain or use or resell any portion of such goods, he will consider such part as having been sold to him, and will pay their price, and the balance he will return to the seller, or hold them, as bailee, subject to his order. Sturm v. Boker, 150 U.S. 312, 14 S.Ct. 99, 37 L.Ed. 1093. Under "contract of sale and return" title vests immediately in buyer, who has privilege of rescinding sale, and until privilege is exercised title remains in him. See U.C.C. § 2–326.

Sale by sample. A sales contract in which it is the understanding of both parties that the goods exhibited constitute the standard with which the goods not exhibited correspond and to which deliveries should conform. Any sample which is made part of the basis of the bargain creates an express warranty that the whole of the goods shall conform to the sample or model. U.C.C. § 2–313. See also **Sample, sale by.**

Sale in gross. A sale by the tract, without regard to quantity; it is in that sense a contract of hazard. See also *Gross sale, supra.*

Sale-note. A memorandum of the subject and terms of a sale, given by a broker or factor to the seller, who bailed him the goods for that purpose, and to the buyer, who dealt with him. Also called "bought and sold notes."

Sale on approval. A species of conditional sale, which is to become absolute only in case the buyer, on trial, approves or is satisfied with the article sold. The approval, however, need not be express; it may be inferred from his keeping the goods beyond a reasonable time.

A sale is a sale on approval if the goods may be returned by the buyer though they conform to the contract and if they are primarily delivered for use. Generally, such goods are not subject to the claims of the creditors of the buyer until acceptance. U.C.C. § 2–326.

Sale on credit. A sale of property accompanied by delivery of possession, but where payment of the price is deferred to a future day. See **Credit;** *also, Installment sale, supra.*

Sale or return. A type of sale wherein the goods may be returned to the seller though they conform to the contract if the goods are delivered primarily for resale. U.C.C. § 2–326(1), (3). A contract for sale of goods whereby title passes immediately to buyer subject to his option to rescind or return goods if he does not resell them. American Nat. Bank of Denver v. Christensen, 28 Colo.App. 501, 476 P.2d 281, 285.

Sale per aversionem. In the civil law, a sale where the goods are taken in bulk, or not by weight or measure, and for a single price, or where a piece of land is sold for a gross sum, to be paid for the whole premises, and not at a fixed price by the acre or foot. A sale per aversionem is sale of either distinct or separate immovable, such as a field enclosed or island in a river, or an immovable property sold by certain bounds or limits. Cornish v. Kinder Canal Co., La.App., 267 So.2d 625, 629.

Sale with all faults. Under what is called a "sale with all faults," or "sale as is", unless the seller fraudulently and inconsistently represents the article sold to be faultless, or contrives to conceal any fault from the purchaser, the latter must take the article for better or worse.

Sale with right of redemption. A sale in which vendor reserves right to take back property by returning price paid. See also *Sale on approval; Sale or return, supra.*

Sheriff's sale. A sale of property, conducted by a sheriff, or sheriff's deputy by virtue of his authority as an officer holding process. See *Forced sale; Judicial sale, supra,* also, **Foreclosure; Sheriff's sale.**

Short sale. See **Short sale.**

Tax-sale. A sale of land for unpaid taxes; a sale of property, by authority of law, for the collection of a tax assessed upon it, or upon its owner, which remains unpaid.

Voluntary sale. One made freely, without constraint, by the owner of the thing sold. Contrast *Forced sale, supra.*

Wash sale. In security trading, a spurious transaction in which the same stock is sold and bought by the same person to create the impression of market activity or to establish a market for the stock. Such transactions are forbidden.

Sale against the box. A species of short sale *(q.v.)* at a time when the taxpayer owns substantially identical shares.

Sale and leaseback. A sale of an asset to a vendee who immediately leases back to the vendor. The usual objectives are (1) to free cash in the amount of the purchase price for other uses by the vendor, (2) for benefits not otherwise available such a deduction by the vendor of the full value of the property for income tax purposes as rental payments over a period of time shorter than would be in depreciation where the base period is the allowable depreciable life. The rental payments total the purchase price plus interest less an estimated salvage value. Although the lease actually follows the sale, both are agreed to as part of the same transaction.

Sale of land. See **Conveyance; Conveyancing.**

Sale or exchange. Term used in taxation to qualify a disposition of property for capital gain or loss treatment. I.R.C. § 1222.

Sales agreement. A contract to sell goods. It may refer to a contract for sale which includes both a present sale and a contract to sell goods at a future time. U.C.C. § 2–106(1). Also, term used to describe a contract for the sale of real estate, including a contract for deed. See also **Conditional sale contract.**

Sales finance company. A business engaged primarily in the purchase of accounts receivable at a discount. The company then undertakes to collect them.

Sales invoice. See **Invoice.**

Salesman. See **Commercial traveler; Dealer; Drummer; Hawker; Peddler.**

Sales tax. Tax imposed by many states on sales of goods with certain statutory exceptions (*e.g.* food, drugs). It is a percentage of the purchase price and the seller is required to remit such tax to the state. State and local sales taxes are deductible for federal income tax purposes.

Saloon. A place of refreshment. Hinton v. State, 137 Tex.Cr.R. 352, 129 S.W.2d 670, 673. In common parlance, a place where intoxicating liquors are sold and consumed.

Salus /sǽləs/. Lat. Health; prosperity; safety.

Salus populi suprema lex /sǽləs póp(y)əlay səpríymə léks/. The welfare of the people is the supreme law. Lingo Lumber Co. v. Hayes, Tex.Civ.App., 64 S.W.2d 835, 839.

Salvage. In general, that portion of goods or property which has been saved or remains after a casualty such as fire or other loss.

In business, any property which is no longer useful (*e.g.* obsolete equipment) but which has scrap value.

In insurance, that portion of property which is taken over by the insurance company after payment of a claim for the loss. The insurance company may deduct the salvage value from the amount of the claim paid and leave the property with the insured.

In maritime law, a compensation allowed to persons by whose assistance a ship or its cargo has been saved, in whole or in part, from impending danger, or recovered from actual loss, in cases of shipwreck, derelict, or recapture. Cope v. Vallette Dry-Dock Co., 119 U.S. 625, 7 S.Ct. 336, 30 L.Ed. 501. Elements necessary to valid "salvage" are marine peril, with service voluntarily rendered, when not required as existing duty, or from a special contract, and success in whole or in part, and that service rendered contributed to such success. Robert R. Sizer & Co. v. Chiarello Bros., D.C.N.Y., 32 F.2d 333, 335.

Equitable salvage. By analogy, the term "salvage" is sometimes also used in cases which have nothing to do with maritime perils, but in which property has been preserved from loss by the last of several advances by different persons. In such a case, the person making the last advance is frequently entitled to priority over the others, on the ground that, without his advance, the property would have been lost altogether. This right, which is sometimes called that of "equitable salvage," and is in the nature of a lien, is chiefly of importance with reference to payments made to prevent leases or policies of insurance from being forfeited, or to prevent mines and similar undertakings from being stopped or injured.

Salvage charges. This term includes all the expenses and costs incurred in the work of saving and preserving the property which was in danger. The salvage charges ultimately fall upon the insurers.

Salvage loss. That kind of loss which it is presumed would, but for certain services rendered and exertions made, have become a total loss. In the language of marine underwriters, this term means the difference between the amount of salvage, after deducting the charges, and the original value of the property insured.

Salvage service. A service voluntarily rendered to a vessel in need of assistance, and is designed to relieve her from distress or danger, either present or to be reasonably apprehended and for which a salvage reward is allowed by the maritime law. It is distinguished from "towage service," in that the latter is rendered for the mere purpose of expediting a vessel's voyage, without reference to any circumstances of danger, though the service in each case may be rendered in the same way. The Emanuel Stavroudis, D.C.Md., 23 F.2d 214, 216.

Salvage value. That value of an asset which remains after the useful life of the asset has expired. It is commonly equivalent to scrap value and must be deducted in computing depreciation. Actual or estimated selling price, net of removal or disposal costs, of a used plant asset to be sold or otherwise retired.

The value of a building or portion of a building to be moved from one location for use at another site. Occurs in condemnation, especially for highway purposes, where large tracts of land must be cleared.

Salvo /sǽlvow/. Lat. Saving; excepting; without prejudice to. *Salvo me et hœredibus meis*, except me and my heirs. *Salvo jure cujuslibet*, without prejudice to the rights of any one.

Salvor /sǽlvər/. A person who, without any particular relation to a ship in distress, proffers useful service, and gives it as a volunteer adventurer, without any pre-existing covenant that connected him with the duty of employing himself for the preservation of that ship.

Salvus plegius /sǽlvəs plíyj(iy)əs/. L. Lat. A safe pledge; called, also, *"certus plegius,"* a sure pledge.

Same. Identical, equal, equivalent. The word "same", however, does not always mean "identical." It frequently means of the kind or species, not the specific thing. When preceded by the definite article, means the one just referred to.

Two offenses are "the same" under the double jeopardy clause of the Federal Constitution unless each requires proof of an additional fact that the other does not. Ex parte Joseph, Tex.Cr.App., 558 S.W.2d 891, 893. See also **Jeopardy; Same offense.**

Same evidence test. The "same-evidence test" used in determining issue of double jeopardy is whether facts alleged in second indictment, if given in evidence, would have sustained a conviction under the first indictment or whether the same evidence would support a conviction in each case. State v. Ballard, 280 N.C. 479, 186 S.E.2d 372, 375.

Same invention. Within reissue statute, refers to whatever invention was described in original letters patent, and appears therein to have been intended to be secured thereby. Morgan v. Drake, Cust. & Pat.App., 36 F.2d 511, 512. It is not to be determined by the claims of the original patent but from the description and such other evidence as the commissioner may deem relevant. Detrola Radio & Television Corporation v. Hazeltine Corporation, C.C.A.Mich., 117 F.2d 238, 241.

Same offense. As used in Constitution, providing that no person shall be twice put in jeopardy for the same offense, does not signify the same offense eo nomine, but the same criminal act, transaction, or omission. Term "same offense" as used in statute relating to enhancement of punishment for subsequent conviction of same offense means a similar offense, one of the same character or nature. Cherry v. State, Tex. Cr.App., 447 S.W.2d 154, 158. See also **Jeopardy; Same.**

Sample. A specimen; a small quantity of any commodity, presented for inspection or examination as evidence of the quality of the whole; as a sample of cloth or of wheat.

Sample, sale by. A sale at which only a sample of the goods sold is exhibited to the buyer. Any sample or model which is made part of the basis of the bargain creates an express warranty that the whole of the goods shall conform to the sample or model. U.C.C. § 2–313(1)(c). See also **Sale.**

Sanæ mentis /séyniy méntəs/. Lat. In old English law, of sound mind.

Sanctio /sǽŋksh(iy)ow/. Lat. In the civil law, that part of a law by which a penalty was ordained against those who should violate it.

Sanction, *v.* To assent, concur, confirm, reprimand, or ratify. U. S. v. Tillinghast, D.C.R.I., 55 F.2d 279, 283. Approval or ratification.

Sanction, *n.* That part of a law which is designed to secure enforcement by imposing a penalty for its violation or offering a reward for its observance. For example, Fed.R.Civil P. 37 provides for sanctions for failure to comply with discovery orders. See also **Contempt.**

A punitive act taken by one nation against another nation which has violated a treaty or international law.

See **Criminal sanctions.**

Sanctuary. In old English law, a consecrated place which had certain privileges annexed to it, and to which offenders were accustomed to resort for refuge, because they could not be arrested there, nor the laws be executed. In general, any holy or consecrated place.

Sandwich lease. The first lease of land from lessor to lessee who releases to another.

Sane. Of natural and normal mental condition; healthy in mind. One who knows the difference between right and wrong, and appreciates the consequences of his acts. Stout v. State, 142 Tex.Civ.R. 537, 155 S.W.2d 374, 377. Compare **Insanity.**

Sanguis /sǽŋgwəs/. Lat. In the civil and old English law, blood; consanguinity. The right or power which the chief lord of the fee had to judge and determine cases where blood was shed.

Sanipractic /sǽnəprǽktək/. A method of drugless healing. Martin v. Department of Social Security, 12 Wash.2d 329, 121 P.2d 394, 395.

Sanipractors /sǽnəprǽktərz/. Drugless healers. State v. Lydon, 170 Wash. 354, 16 P.2d 848, 851.

Sanitary. That which pertains to health, with especial reference to cleanliness and freedom from infective and deleterious influences.

Sanitary code. Municipal ordinances regulating sanitary conditions of establishments which produce, distribute or serve food, or provide medical services.

Sanitation. Devising and applying of measures for preserving and promoting public health; removal or neutralization of elements injurious to health; practical application of sanitary science. See **Sanitary code.**

Sanity. Sound understanding; the normal condition of the human mind; the reverse of insanity (q.v.).

Sanity hearing. A preliminary inquiry into the mental competency of a person to stand trial, though it may be held at any time within the criminal proceeding. See Fed.R.Crim.P. 12.2.

A proceeding to determine whether one should be confined under a civil commitment to an institution.

Sanity trial. In some states the issues of sanity and guilt may be tried separately in a bifurcated trial.

Sans ceo que /sǽn(d)z síy kə/. L. Fr. Without this. See **Absque hoc.**

Sans frais /sòn fréy/. Fr. Without expense.

Sans impeachment de wast /sǽn(d)z əmpíychmənt də wéyst/. L. Fr. Without impeachment of waste. See **Absque impetitione vasti.**

Sans jour /sòn zhúr/sǽn(d)z júr/. Fr. Without day; *sine die.*

Sans recours /sòn rəkúr/sǽn(d)z°/. Fr. Without recourse. See **Indorsement.**

Sap. A general term which, as applied to weapons, includes a "blackjack," "slung shot," "billy," "sandbag," or "brass knuckles" (see those terms). People v. Mulherin, 140 Cal.App. 212, 35 P.2d 174, 175, 176.

Sapiens incipit a fine, et quod primum est in intentione, ultimum est in executione /séyp(i)yen(d)z ən(t)sípəd èy fáyniy, èt kwód práyməm èst in intènshiyówniy ə́ltəməm èst in èksəkyùwshiyówniy/. A wise man begins with the last, and what is first in intention is last in execution.

Sapiens omnia agit cum consilio /séyp(i)yen(d)z ómn(i)yə éyjət kə̀m kən(t)síl(i)yow/. A wise man does everything advisedly.

Sapientia legis nummario pretio non est æstimanda /sæpiyénsh(iy)ə líyjəs nəmér(i)yow présh(iy)ow nón èst èstəmǽndə/. The wisdom of the law cannot be valued by money.

Sapientis judicis est cogitare tantum sibi esse permissum, quantum commissum et creditum /sæpiyéntəs júwdəsəs èst kòjətériy tǽntəm síbay ésiy pərmísəm kwóntəm kəmísəm èt krédədəm/. It is the part of a wise judge to think that a thing is permitted to him, only so far as it is committed and intrusted to him. That is, he should keep his jurisdiction within the limits of his commission.

Satisdare /sǽdəsdériy/. Lat. In the civil law, to guaranty the obligation of a principal.

Satisdatio /sǽdəsdéysh(iy)ow/. Lat. In the civil law, security given by a party to an action, as by a defendant, to pay what might be adjudged against him.

Satisfaction. Act of satisfying; the state of being satisfied. Seago v. New York Cent. R. Co., 349 Mo. 1249, 164 S.W.2d 336, 341. The discharge of an obligation by paying a party what is due to him (as on a mortgage, lien, or contract), or what is awarded to him, by the judgment of a court or otherwise. Thus, a judgment is satisfied by the payment of the amount due to the party who has recovered such judgment, or by his levying the amount. The execution or carrying into effect of an accord. Barber v. Mallon, Mo.App., 168 S.W.2d 177, 179; R. J. Bearings Corporation v. Warr, 192 Okl. 133, 134 P.2d 355, 357.

A legacy is deemed satisfied if the testator makes an inter vivos gift to the legatee with the intent that it be in lieu of the legacy.

An entry made on the record, by which a party in whose favor a judgment was rendered declares that he has been satisfied and paid.

See also **Payment; Performance.**

Accord and satisfaction. An "accord" is an agreement whereby one of parties undertakes to give or perform, and other to accept in satisfaction of liquidated or disputed claim arising in either contract or tort something different from what he is or considers himself entitled to; and "satisfaction" is execution or performance of agreement. Harris, Upham & Co., Inc. v. Ballantyne, Tex.Civ.App., 538 S.W.2d 153, 158.

Equity. The doctrine of satisfaction in equity is somewhat analogous to performance in equity, but differs from it in this respect: that satisfaction is always something given either in whole or in part as a substitute or equivalent for something else, and not (as in performance) something that may be construed as the identical thing covenanted to be done.

Satisfaction, contracts to. A class of contracts in which one party agrees to perform his promise to the satisfaction of the other. A contract for construction work "to the entire satisfaction of the owners" imports that the construction be to the satisfaction of a reasonable man and not to the personal satisfaction of owners.

Satisfaction of judgment. A document such as an execution enforced by the judgment creditor and indicating that the judgment has been paid. See **Execution.**

Satisfaction of lien. Document signed by a lien holder in which he releases the property subject to the lien.

Satisfaction of mortgage. A discharge signed by the mortgagee or holder of the mortgage indicating that the property subject to the mortgage is released or that the mortgage debt has been paid and that all terms and conditions of the mortgage have been satisfied. See also **Redemption.**

Satisfaction piece. A memorandum in writing, entitled in a cause, stating that satisfaction is acknowledged between the parties, plaintiff and defendant. Upon this being duly acknowledged and filed in the office where the record of the judgment is, the judgment becomes satisfied, and the defendant discharged from it. See New York CPLR § 5020.

Satisfactory. Where a contract provides that it is to be performed in a manner "satisfactory" to one of the parties, the provision must be construed as meaning that the performance must be such that the party, as a reasonable person, should be satisfied with it.

Satisfactory evidence. Such evidence as is sufficient to produce a belief that the thing is true; credible evidence. Such evidence as, in respect to its amount or weight, is adequate or sufficient to justify the court or jury in adopting the conclusion in support of which it is adduced. Sometimes called "sufficient evidence," means that amount of proof which ordinarily satisfies an unprejudiced mind beyond a reasonable doubt. See **Relevant evidence; Sufficient evidence.**

Satisfied term. A term of years in land is thus called when the purpose for which it was created has been satisfied or executed before the expiration of the set period.

Satisfy. To answer or discharge, as a claim, debt, legal demand or the like. Swaner v. Union Mortg. Co., 99 Utah 298, 105 P.2d 342, 345. To comply actually and fully with a demand; to extinguish, by payment or performance. To convince, as to satisfy a jury. See also **Satisfaction.**

Satius est petere fontes quam sectari rivulos /séysh(iy)əs èst pédəriy fóntiyz kwæm sektéray rívyələws/. It is better to seek the source than to follow the streamlets.

Saunkefin /sǽnfæn/. L. Fr. End of blood; failure of the direct line in successions.

Sauvagine /sóvəjiyn/. L. Fr. Wild animals.

Save. To except, reserve, or exempt; as where a statute "saves" vested rights. To toll, or suspend the running or operation of; as to "save" the statute of limitations. See **Saving clause.**

Save harmless clause. A provision in a document by which one party agrees to indemnify and hold harmless another party as to claims and suits which may be asserted against him. In some states, such clauses in leases are deemed against public policy and, hence, void. See also **Hold harmless agreement.**

Saver default. L. Fr. In old English practice, to excuse a default.

Saving. Preservation from danger or loss; economy in outlay; prevention of waste; something laid up or kept from becoming expended or lost; a reservation. Oklahoma Tax Commission v. Sisters of the Sorrowful Mother, 186 Okl. 339, 97 P.2d 888, 892.

Saving clause. In a statute, an exception of a special thing out of the general things mentioned in the statute. Ordinarily a restriction in a repealing act, which is intended to save rights, pending proceedings, penalties, etc., from the annihilation which would result from an unrestricted repeal. That provision in a statute which rescues the balance of the statute from a declaration of unconstitutionality if one or more clauses or parts are invalidated. It is sometimes referred to as the severability clause. Such clause continues in force the law repealed as to existing rights. Dade County v. Wiseheart, Fla.App., 198 So.2d 94, 97. See also **Separability clause; Severable statute.**

Savings account. Accounts maintained in commercial and savings banks for purpose of accumulating money, in contrast to a checking account. Savings accounts generally yield interest on the deposited funds, though the trend is to also pay interest on checking account balances.

Savings account trust. An account opened in the name of one person in trust for another; e.g. A in trust for B. See also **Trust** (Totten Trust).

Savings and loan association. One of a number of types of mutually-owned, cooperative, savings associations, originally established for the primary purpose of making loans to members and others, usually for the purchase of real estate or homes. Such may be chartered by the state, or by the federal government, in which case it is known as a "Federal Savings and Loan Association". The deposits are insured by the Federal Savings and Loan Insurance Corporation. Such associations are also known as "Building and Loan Associations", etc.

A bank chartered by the Federal Home Loan Bank Board and engaged primarily in making home loan mortgages from the savings accounts of the depositors. Associations at the federal level are regulated by the Federal Home Loan Bank System.

Savings bank. See **Bank.**

Savings bank trust. See **Trust.**

Savings bond. See **Bond.**

Savings notes. Short term paper issued by a bank and bearing interest. The U.S. government issues such notes on a 90 day basis and for other periods of time.

Saving to suitors clause. That provision in 28 U.S.C.A. § 1333(1) which gives the U.S. District Courts original jurisdiction, "exclusive of the courts of the state" of any civil case of admiralty or maritime jurisdiction, "saving to suitors in all cases all other remedies to which they are otherwise entitled." The "saving to suitors" clause of the section of the Judiciary Act implementing constitutional provision extending federal judicial powers to cases of admiralty and maritime jurisdiction means that a suitor asserting an in personam admiralty claim may elect to sue in a "common law" state court through an ordinary civil action, and in such actions, the state courts must apply the same substantive law as would be applied had the suit been instituted in admiralty in a federal court. Shannon v. City of Anchorage, Alaska, 478 P.2d 815, 818.

Savour /séyvǝr/. To partake the nature of; to bear affinity to.

Say about. This phrase, like "more or less," is frequently introduced into conveyances or contracts of sale, to indicate that the quantity of the subject-matter is uncertain, and is only estimated, and to guard the vendor against the implication of having warranted the quantity.

S.B. Abbreviation for "Senate Bill."

S.B.A. Small Business Administration.

S.B.I.C. Small Business Investment Company.

S.C. Abbreviation for "same case." Inserted between two citations, it indicates that the same case is reported in both places. Also an abbreviation for "supreme court."

Sc. An abbreviation for "scilicet"; that is to say.

Scab. Person who works for lower wages than or under conditions contrary to those prescribed by a trade union; also one who takes the place of a workingman on a strike. Non-union workers who pass through a union picket line. A worker who works under non-union conditions.

Scabini /skǝbáyay/. In old European law, the judges or assessors of the judges in the court held by the count. Assistants or associates of the count; officers under the count. The permanent selected judges of the Franks. Judges among the Germans, Franks, and Lombards, who were held in peculiar esteem.

Scalam /skéylǝm/. At the scale; the old way of paying money into the exchequer.

Scale order. An order to buy (or sell) a security which specifies the total amount to be bought (or sold) and the amount to be bought (or sold) at specified price variations.

Scale tolerance. Nominal variation between different scales in respect of the mass or weight of the same goods.

Scaling laws. A term used to signify statutes establishing the process of adjusting the difference in value between depreciated paper money and specie. Such statutes were rendered necessary by the depreciation of paper money necessarily following the establishment of American independence. And, thereafter, to discharge those debts which were made payable in Confederate money. The statutes are now obsolete.

Scalper. In securities business, a small operator who takes his profits on slight fluctuations in the market. A small scale speculator. One who sells tickets to sporting, theatre and other entertainment events at prices in excess of face price (*i.e.* box office price) of ticket.

Scandal. Defamatory reports or rumors; aspersion or slanderous talk, uttered recklessly or maliciously. Scandalous matter may be ordered stricken from the pleadings by a motion to strike. Fed.R.Civ.P. 12(f). See also **Defamation.**

Scandalum magnatum /skǽndǝlǝm mǽgnéydǝm/. In English law, scandal or slander of great men or nobles. Words spoken in derogation of a peer, a judge, or other great officer of the realm, for which an action lies, though it is now rarely resorted to. 3 Bl.Comm. 123. This offense has not existed in America since the formation of the United States.

Schedule. A sheet of paper annexed to a statute, deed, deposition, or other instrument, exhibiting in detail the matters mentioned or referred to in the principal document; *e.g.* schedule of assets and liabilities (debts) in bankruptcy proceeding.

Any list of planned events to take place on a regular basis such as a train schedule or a schedule of work to be performed in a factory.

Scheduled injuries. In worker's compensation law, an injury for which a specific sum is payable by statute.

Scheduled property. In insurance, a list of property and the value of each piece of such property for which the insurer will pay in the event of loss or damage.

Scheme. A design or plan formed to accomplish some purpose; a system. Snider v. Leatherwood, Tex.Civ. App., 49 S.W.2d 1107, 1110. When used in a bad sense, term corresponds with "trick" or "fraud". "Scheme to defraud" within meaning of mail fraud statute is the intentional use of false or fraudulent representations for the purpose of gaining a valuable undue advantage or working some injury to something of value held by another. U. S. v. Mandel, D.C.Md., 415 F.Supp. 997, 1005. Plan reasonably calculated to deceive persons of ordinary prudence and comprehension. U. S. v. Goldman, 439 F.Supp. 337, 343. See also **Artifice.**

Schism /sízǝm/. A division of a union into two factions resulting in one group leaving the union. In ecclesiastical law, a division or separation in a church or denomination of Christians, occasioned by a diversity of faith, creed, or religious opinions.

School. An institution or place for instruction or education.

Common schools. Schools maintained at the public expense and administered by a bureau of the state, district, or municipal government, for the gratuitous education of the children of all citizens without distinction. See also *Public schools, infra.*

Consolidated school district. A common school district where two or more existing schools have consolidated into one single district.

District school. A common or public school for the education at public expense of the children residing within a given district; a public school maintained by a "school district." See *infra.*

Private school. One maintained by private individuals, religious organizations, or corporations, not at public expense, and open only to pupils selected and admitted by the proprietors or governors, or to pupils of a certain religion or possessing certain qualifications, and generally supported, in part at least, by tuition fees or charges.

Public schools. Schools established under the laws of the state (and usually regulated in matters of detail by the local authorities), in the various districts, counties, or towns, maintained at the public expense by taxation, and open, usually without charge, to the children of all the residents of the city, town or other district. Schools belonging to the public and established and conducted under public authority.

School board or committee. A board of municipal officers charged with the administration of the affairs of the public schools. They are commonly organized under the general laws of the state, and fall within the class of *quasi* corporations, sometimes coterminous with a county or district, but not necessarily so. The members of the school board or committee are usually elected by the voters of the school district. The circuit of their territorial jurisdiction is called a "school district," and each school district is commonly a separate taxing district for school purposes.

School directors. See *School board.*

School district. A public and quasi municipal corporation, organized by legislative authority or direction, comprising a defined territory, for the erection, maintenance, government, and support of the public schools within its territory in accordance with and in subordination to the general school laws of the state, invested, for these purposes only, with powers of local self-government and generally of local taxation, and administered by a board of officers, usually elected by the voters of the district, who are variously styled "school directors", "school boards", "school committees", "trustees", "commissioners", or "supervisors" of schools.

School lands. Public lands of a state set apart by the state (or by congress in a territory) to create, by the proceeds of their sale, a fund for the establishment and maintenance of public schools.

Sciendum est /sayéndəm èst/. Lat. It is to be known; be it remarked. In the books of the civil law, this phrase is often found at the beginning of a chapter or paragraph, by way of introduction to some explanation, or directing attention to some particular rule.

Scienter /sayéntər/. Lat. Knowingly. The term is used in pleading to signify an allegation (or that part of the declaration or indictment which contains it) setting out the defendant's previous knowledge of the cause which led to the injury complained of, or rather his previous knowledge of a state of facts which it was his duty to guard against, and his omission to do which has led to the injury complained of. The term is frequently used to signify the defendant's guilty knowledge.

The term "scienter," as applied to conduct necessary to give rise to an action for civil damges under Securities Exchange Act of 1934 and rule 10b–5 refers to a mental state embracing intent to deceive, manipulate or defraud. Ernst and Ernst v. Hochfelder, Ill., 425 U.S. 185, 96 S.Ct. 1375, 1381, 47 L.Ed.2d 668.

Scientia sciolorum est mixta ignorantia /sayénsh(iy)ə sàyəlórəm èst míkstə ìgnərǽnsh(iy)ə/. The knowledge of smatterers is diluted ignorance.

Scientia utrimque par pares contrahentes facit /sayénsh(iy)ə yuwtrímkwiy pár périyz kòntrəhéntiyz féysət/. Equal knowledge on both sides makes contracting parties equal. An insured need not mention what the underwriter knows, or what he ought to know.

Scienti et volenti non fit injuria /sayéntay èt vəléntay nón fid ənjúriyə/. An injury is not done to one who knows and wills it.

Sci. fa. /sáy féy/. An abbreviation for *"scire facias" (q.v.).*

Scilicet /síləsət/sáyləsət/. Lat. To-wit; that is to say. A word used in pleadings and other instruments, as introductory to a more particular statement of matters previously mentioned in general terms.

Scintilla /sintílə/. Lat. A spark; a remaining particle; a trifle; the least particle.

Scintilla juris /sintílə júrəs/. In real property law, a spark of right or interest. By this figurative expression was denoted the small particle of interest, which, by a fiction of law, was supposed to remain in a feoffee to uses, sufficient to support contingent uses afterwards coming into existence, and thereby enable the statute of uses (27 Hen. VIII, c. 10) to execute them.

Scintilla of evidence /sintílə əv évədən(t)s/. A spark of evidence. A metaphorical expression to describe a very insignificant or trifling item or particle of evidence; used in the statement of the common-law rule that if there is any evidence at all in a case, even a mere *scintilla*, tending to support a material issue, the case cannot be taken from the jury, but must be left to their decision.

Any material evidence that, if true, would tend to establish issue in mind of reasonable juror. Something of substance and relevant consequence and not vague, uncertain, or irrelevant matter not carrying quality of proof or having fitness to induce conviction. City of Houston v. Scanlan, 120 Tex. 264, 37 S.W.2d 718; Wigginton's Adm'r v. Louisville Ry. Co., 256 Ky. 287, 75 S.W.2d 1046, 1051. Courts differ as to what constitutes a "scintilla," and some courts do not accept the rule. For example, it has been held that while the cogency of evidence is not dependent on its quantity, if the party with the burden of proof has introduced only a *scintilla* of evidence on an essential element of his case, a judge may direct a verdict against him. Such evidence is inadequate as a matter of law. It has also been held that it is the duty of trial court to instruct a verdict, though there is slight testimony, if its probative force is so weak that it only raises suspicion of existence of facts sought to be established, since such testimony falls short of being "evidence". Texas Pacific Coal & Oil Co. v. Wells, Tex.Civ.App., 151 S.W.2d 927, 929.

Scire debes cum quo contrahis /sáyriy díybiyz kàm kwów kəntréy(h)əs/. You ought to know with whom you deal.

Scire et scire debere æquiparantur in jure /sáyriy èt sáyriy dəbíriy èkwəpərǽntər ìn júriy/. To know a thing, and to be bound to know it, are regarded in law as equivalent.

Scire facias /sáyriy féysh(iy)əs/. Lat. A judicial writ, founded upon some matter of record, such as a judgment or recognizance and requiring the person against whom it is brought to show cause why the party bringing it should not have advᵃntage of such record, or (in the case of a *scire facias* to repeal letters patent) why the record should not be annulled and vacated. The name is used to designate both the writ and the whole proceeding. City of St. Louis v. Miller, 235 Mo.App. 987, 145 S.W.2d 504, 505. The most common application of this writ is as a process to revive a judgment, after the lapse of a certain time, or on a change of parties, or otherwise to have execution of the judgment, in which cases it is merely a continuation of the original action. It is used more rarely as a mode of proceeding against special bail on their recognizance, and as a means of repealing letters patent, in which cases it is an original proceeding. Under current rules practice in most states, this writ has been abolished; *e.g.* Mass.R.Civil P. 81.

Scire facias ad audiendum errores /sáyriy féysh(iy)əs ǽd òdiyéndəm əróriyz/. The name of a writ which is sued out after the plaintiff in error has assigned his errors.

Scire facias ad disprobandum debitum /sáyriy féysh(iy)əs ǽd dìsprəbǽndəm débədəm/. The name of a writ which lies by a defendant in foreign attachment against the plaintiff, in order to enable him, within a year and a day next ensuing the time of payment to the plaintiff in the attachment, to disprove or avoid the debt recovered against him.

Scire facias ad rehabendam terram /sáyriy féysh(iy)əs ǽd rìyhəbéndəm téhrəm/. Lies to enable a judgment debtor to recover back his lands taken under an *elegit* when the judgment creditor has satisfied or been paid the amount of his judgment.

Scire facias quare restitutionem non /sáyriy féysh(iy)əs kwériy rèstət(y)ùwshiyównəm nón/. This writ lies where execution on a judgment has been levied, but the money has not been paid over to the plaintiff, and the judgment is afterwards reversed in error or on appeal; in such a case a *scire facias* is necessary before a writ of restitution can issue.

Scire facias sur mortgage /sáyriy féysh(iy)əs sòr mórgəj/. A writ issued upon the default of a mortgagor to make payments or observe conditions, requiring him to show cause why the mortgage should not be foreclosed, and the mortgaged property taken and sold in execution.

Scire facias sur municipal claim /sáyriy féysh(iy)əs sòr myuwnísəpəl kléym/. A writ authorized to be issued as a means of enforcing payment of a municipal claim (*q.v.*) out of the real estate upon which such claim is a lien.

Scire feci /sáyriy fíysay/. Lat. The name given to the sheriff's return to a writ of *scire facias* that he has caused notice to be given to the party or parties against whom the writ was issued.

Scire fieri inquiry /sáyriy fáyərày ənkwáyriy/°ínkwəriy/. In old English law, the name of a writ formerly used to recover the amount of a judgment from an executor.

Scire leges non hoc est verba earum tenere, sed vim ac potestatem /sáyriy líyjiyz nòn hók èst várbə iyérəm təníriy sèd vím ǽk pòwdəstéydəm/. To know the laws is not to observe their mere words, but their force and power [that is, the essential meaning in which their efficacy resides].

Scire proprie est rem ratione et per causam cognoscere /sáyriy prówpriyiy èst rém rǽshiyówniy èt pòr kózəm kəgnósəriy/. To know properly is to know a thing in its reason, and by its cause. We are truly said to know anything, where we know the true cause thereof.

Scirewyte /sháyrwàyt/. In old English law, a tax or prestation paid to the sheriff for holding the assizes or county courts.

Scite, or **site** /sáyt/. The sitting or standing on any place; the seat or situation of a capital messuage, or the ground whereon it stands.

Scold. At common law, a troublesome and angry person who, by brawling and wrangling among his or her neighbors, breaks the public peace, increases discord, and becomes a public nuisance to the neighborhood. A quarrelsome, brawling, vituperative person.

Scope of a patent. The boundaries or limits of the invention protected by the patent, which are not matters of metes and bounds and can never be defined in the definite sense employed in thinking of physical things, but must be determined by methods based upon established principles of patent law. Smith v. Mid-Continent Inv. Co., C.C.A.Mo., 106 F.2d 622, 624.

Scope of authority. Includes not only actual authorization conferred upon agent by his principal, but also that which has apparently or impliedly been delegated to agent. Angerosa v. White Co., 248 App.Div. 425, 290 N.Y.S. 204, 208. Under doctrine of respondeat superior (*q.v.*) a principal is liable for the contracts of his agent if the agent contracted within the scope of his actual or apparent authority. See also **Authority; Scope of employment.**

Scope of employment. Under doctrine of respondeat superior (*q.v.*), a principal is liable for the torts of his agent committed within the scope, actual or apparent, of his employment.

An employee acts in scope of his employment, for purpose of invoking a doctrine of respondeat superior, when he is doing something in furtherance of duties he owes to his employer and where employer is, or could be, exercising some control, directly or indirectly, over employee's activities. Lundberg v. State, 255 N.E.2d 177, 179, 25 N.Y.2d 467, 306 N.Y. S.2d 947. Employee is in "scope of employment," such that corporate employer is liable to third party for his torts, whenever he is engaged in activities that fairly and reasonably may be said to be incident of the employment or logically and naturally connected with it. Daughdrill v. Diamond M. Drilling Co., C.A. La., 447 F.2d 781, 785.

Scorn. To hold in extreme contempt; to reject as unworthy of regard; to despise, to contemn, to disdain.

Scot. In old English law, a tax, or tribute; one's *share* of a contribution.

Scotal /skódèyl/. In old English law, an extortionate practice by officers of the forest who kept alehouses, and compelled the people to drink at their houses for fear of their displeasure. Prohibited by the Charter of the Forest, c. 7. See **Charta** (*Charta de foresta*).

Scot and lot. In old English law, the name of a customary contribution, laid upon all subjects according to their ability.

Scottare /skətériy/. To pay scot, tax, or customary dues.

Scoundrel /skáwndrəl/. An opprobrious epithet, implying rascality, villainy, or a want of honor or integrity. In slander, this word is not actionable *per se*.

Scrambling possession. See **Possession.**

Scratching the ticket. Exists where partisan voters support and vote for one or more of nominees of opposite political party. Swindall v. State Election Board, 168 Okl. 97, 32 P.2d 691, 696.

Scrawl. Scroll, which title see.

Scriba /skráybə/. Lat. A scribe; a secretary. *Scriba regis* /skráybə ríyjəs/, a king's secretary; a chancellor.

Scribere est agere /skráybəriy èst ǽjəriy/. To write is to act. Treasonable words set down in writing amount to overt acts of treason.

Scrip. A document which entitles the holder to receive something of value. It is ultimately exchanged for money or some privilege. In corporations, when a stock dividend is declared, scrip is issued in place of fractional shares and when the holder has sufficient scrip he may exchange the scrip for a share.

Paper money issued for temporary use.

The term has also formerly been applied to warrants, certificates, or other like orders drawn on a municipal treasury showing the holder to be entitled to a certain portion or allotment of public or state lands, and also to the fractional paper currency issued by the United States during the period of the Civil War.

Scrip dividend. Type of deferred dividend commonly in the form of a promissory note which is redeemable in stock or cash at a future time. See also **Dividend.**

Script. Something written (*e.g.* manuscript). The original of an instrument or document. Where instruments are executed in part and counterpart, the original or principal is so called.

Scriptæ obligationes scriptis tolluntur, et nudi consensus obligatio contrario consensu dissolvitur /skríptiy oblǝgèyshiyówniyz skríptǝs tolántǝr, èt n(y)úwday kǝn(t)sén(t)sǝs òblǝgéysh(iy)ow kǝntrériyow kǝn(t)sén(t)s(y)uw dǝzólvǝdǝr/. Written obligations are su-

perseded by writings, and an obligation of naked assent is dissolved by assent to the contrary.

Scriptum /skríptǝm/. Lat. A writing; something written.

Scriptum indentatum /skríptǝm ìndentéydǝm/. A writing indented; an indenture or deed.

Scriptum obligatorium /skríptǝm òblǝgǝtóriyǝm/. A writing obligatory. The technical name of a bond in old pleadings. Any writing under seal.

Scrivener /skrív(ǝ)nǝr/. A writer; scribe; conveyancer. One whose occupation is to draw contracts, write deeds and mortgages, and prepare other species of written instruments. Also an agent to whom property is intrusted by others for the purpose of lending it out at an interest payable to his principal, and for a commission or bonus for himself, whereby he gains his livelihood.

Money scrivener. A money broker. The name was also formerly applied in England to a person (generally an attorney or solicitor) whose business was to find investments for the money of his clients, and see to perfecting the securities, and who was often intrusted with the custody of the securities and the collection of the interest and principal.

Scroll. A mark intended to supply the place of a seal, made with a pen or other instrument of writing.

A paper or parchment containing some writing, and rolled up so as to conceal it.

Scruet-roll /skrúwǝt rówl/. In old practice, a species of roll or record, on which the bail on *habeas corpus* was entered.

Scrutator /skruwtéydǝr/. Lat. In old English law, a searcher or bailiff of a river; a water-bailiff, whose business was to look to the king's rights, as to his wrecks, his flotsam, jetsam, water-strays, royal fishes.

Scurrilous /skárǝlǝs/. Low and indecent language; low indecency or abuse; mean; foul; vile. Synonymous with vulgar, foul or foul-mouthed.

Scutage /sk(y)úwdǝj/. In feudal law, a tax or contribution raised by those that held lands by knight's service, towards furnishing the king's army, at the rate of one, two or three marks for every knight's fee.

A pecuniary composition or commutation made by a tenant by knight-service in lieu of actual service.

A pecuniary aid or tribute originally reserved by particular lords, instead or in lieu of personal service, varying in amount according to the expenditure which the lord had to incur in his personal attendance upon the king in his wars.

Scutagio habendo /sk(y)ǝtéyj(iy)ow hǝbéndow/. A writ that anciently lay against tenants by knight's service to serve in the wars, or send sufficient persons, or pay a certain sum.

Scyra /sháyrǝ/. In old English law, shire; county; the inhabitants of a county.

Scyregemote /sháyrgǝmòwt/. In Saxon law, the meeting or court of the shire. This was the most important court in the Saxon polity, having jurisdiction of both ecclesiastical and secular causes. Its meetings were held twice in the year. Its Latin name was "curia comitatis".

S.D. Southern District; *e.g.* U.S. District Court for Southern District of New York.

S/D B/L. The abbreviation "S/D B/L" in a contract of sale means sight draft—bill of lading attached.

Sea. The ocean; the great mass of water which surrounds the land. In marine insurance "sea" includes not only the high seas but the bays, inlets, and rivers as high up as the tide ebbs and flows. The "navigable sea" is divided into three zones: (1) nearest to the nation's shores are its internal or "inland waters"; (2) beyond the inland waters, and measured from their seaward edge, is a belt known as the marginal or "territorial sea"; and (3) outside the territorial sea are the "high seas". U. S. v. State of La., 89 S.Ct. 773, 781. See also **Seaworthy**.

High seas. The ocean; public waters. According to the English doctrine, the high sea begins at the distance of three miles from the coast of any country; according to the American view, at low-water mark, except in the case of small harbors and roadsteads inclosed within the *fauces terræ.* U. S. v. Rodgers, 150 U.S. 249, 14 S.Ct. 109, 37 L.Ed. 1071. The open ocean outside of the *fauces terræ,* as distinguished from arms of the sea; the waters of the ocean without the boundary of any country. Any waters on the sea-coast which are without the boundaries of low-water mark. Waters outside of territorial jurisdiction of nation.

Main sea. The open, uninclosed ocean; or that portion of the sea which is without the *fauces terræ* on the sea-coast, in contradistinction to that which is surrounded or inclosed between narrow headlands or promontories. U. S. v. Rodgers, 150 U.S. 249, 14 S.Ct. 109, 37 L.Ed. 1071.

Sea bed. All that portion of land under the sea that lies beyond the sea-shore.

Sea-brief. See *Sea letter, infra.*

Sea laws. Laws relating to the sea, as the laws of Oleron, etc.

Sea letter. A species of manifest, containing a description of the ship's cargo, with the port from which it comes and the port of destination. This is one of the documents necessary to be carried by all neutral vessels, in the merchant service, in time of war, as an evidence of their nationality. The last sea letter was issued at the Port of New York in 1806, and the use of sea letters was discontinued by proclamation of President Madison in 1815. 46 U.S.C.A. §§ 61, 62, note.

Sea-reeve. An officer in maritime towns and places who took care of the maritime rights of the lord of the manor, and watched the shore, and collected wrecks for the lord.

Sea-rovers. Pirates and robbers at sea.

Sea-shore. The margin of the sea in its usual and ordinary state. When the tide is out, low-water mark is the margin of the sea; and, when the sea is full, the margin is high-water mark. The sea-shore is therefore all the ground between the ordinary high-water

mark and low-water mark. It cannot be considered as including any ground always covered by the sea, for then it would have no definite limit on the seaboard. Neither can it include any part of the upland, for the same reason. Commonwealth of Massachusetts v. State of New York, 271 U.S. 65, 46 S.Ct. 357, 362, 70 L.Ed. 838. That space of land over which the waters of the sea are spread in the highest water during the winter season.

Seal. An impression upon wax, wafer, or some other tenacious substance capable of being impressed. In current practice, a particular sign (*e.g.* L.S.) or the word "seal" is made in lieu of an actual seal to attest the execution of the instrument.

As regards sealing of records, means to close by any kind of fastening that must be broken before access can be obtained. See **Sealing of records**.

See also **Contract under seal**.

Corporate seal. A seal adopted and used by a corporation for authenticating its corporate acts and executing legal instruments.

Great seal. The United States and also each of the states has and uses a seal, always carefully described by law, and sometimes officially called the "great" seal, though in some instances known simply as "the seal of the United States," or "the seal of the state."

Private seal. The seal (however made) of a private person or corporation, as distinguished from a seal employed by a state or government or any of its bureaus or departments.

Public seal. A seal belonging to and used by one of the bureaus or departments of government, for authenticating or attesting documents, process, or records. An impression made of some device, by means of a piece of metal or other hard substance, kept and used by public authority. See also **State seal**.

Sealed. Authenticated by a seal; executed by the affixing of a seal.

Sealed and delivered. These words, followed by the signatures of the witnesses, constitute the usual formula for the attestation of conveyances.

Sealed bid. A method for submitting a bid to buy or to perform work on a proposed contract. In general, each party interested submits a bid in a sealed envelope, and all such bids are opened at the same time and the most favorable responsible bid is accepted.

Sealed instrument. An instrument of writing to which the party to be bound has affixed not only his name, but also his seal. See also **Seal**.

The affixing of a seal to a contract for sale or an offer to buy or sell goods does not make the writing a sealed instrument and the law of sealed instruments does not apply to such contract. U.C.C. § 2–203.

Sealed verdict. When the jury have agreed upon a verdict, if the court is not in session at the time, they are permitted (usually) to put their written finding in a sealed envelope, and then separate. This verdict they return when the court again convenes. The verdict thus returned has the same effect, and must be treated in the same manner, as if returned in open court before any separation of the jury had taken place.

Sealing. In matters of succession, the placing, by the proper officer, of seals on the effects of a succession for the purpose of preserving them, and for the interest of third persons. The seals are affixed by order of the judge having jurisdiction.

Sealing of records. Statutes in some states permit a person's criminal record to be sealed and thereafter such records cannot be examined except by order of the court or by designated officials. Such statutes commonly pertain to juvenile offenders.

Seaman's will. See **Sailors' will.**

Seamen. Sailors; mariners; persons whose business is navigating ships, or who are connected with the ship as such and in some capacity assist in its conduct, maintenance or service. Commonly exclusive of the officers of a ship. City of Los Angeles v. United Dredging Co., C.C.A.Cal., 14 F.2d 364, 366; The Lillian, D.C.Me., 16 F.2d 146, 148. One whose occupation is to navigate vessels upon the sea including all those on board whose labor contributes to the accomplishment of the main object in which the vessel is engaged. Osland v. Star Fish & Oyster Co., C.C.A.Ala., 107 F.2d 113, 114. One whose duties are maritime in character and are rendered on a vessel in navigable waters. Helena Glendale Ferry Co. v. Walling, C.C.A. Ark., 132 F.2d 616, 619, 620. Term "seamen" includes anyone who, in course of his work about a ship, exposes himself to risks traditionally associated with maritime duties of a member of ship's crew. Garrett v. Gutzeit, C.A.Va., 491 F.2d 228, 233.

To determine whether injured workman is a seaman with Jones Act rights, vessel he is on must be in navigation, there must be a more or less permanent connection with vessel, and he must be aboard primarily to aid in navigation. Sandoval v. Mitsui Sempaku K. K. Tokyo, D.C.Canal Zone, 313 F.Supp. 719, 725. See also **Longshoreman.**

Seance /seyón(t)s/séyon(t)s/. In French law, a session; as of some public body.

Search. An examination of a man's house or other buildings or premises, or of his person, or of his vehicle, aircraft, etc., with a view to the discovery of contraband or illicit or stolen property, or some evidence of guilt to be used in the prosecution of a criminal action for some crime or offense with which he is charged. State v. Woodall, 16 Ohio Misc. 226, 241 N.E.2d 755, 757. A prying into hidden places for that which is concealed and it is not a search to observe that which is open to view. Probing or exploration for something that is concealed or hidden from searcher; an invasion, a quest with some sort of force, either actual or constructive. People v. Carroll, 12 Ill.App.3d 869, 299 N.E.2d 134, 140. Visual observation which infringes upon a person's reasonable expectation of privacy constitutes a "search" in the constitutional sense. People v. Harfmann, Colo. App., 555 P.2d 187, 189.

A "search" to which the exclusionary rule may apply is one in which there is a quest for, a looking for, or a seeking out of that which offends against the law by law enforcement personnel or their agents. Vargas v. State, Tex.Cr.App., 542 S.W.2d 151, 153.

Unreasonable searches and seizures are prohibited by the Fourth Amendment.

See also Border search; Consent search; Exclusionary rule; Fruit of poisonous tree doctrine; Illegally obtained evidence; Incidental to arrest; Inspection searches; Knock and announce rule; Mapp v. Ohio; McNabb-Mallory Rule; Mere evidence rule; Plain view doctrine; Poisonous tree doctrine; Probable cause; Search-warrant; Seizure; Stop and frisk; Warrant.

International law. The right of search is the right on the part of ships of war to visit and search merchant vessels during war, in order to ascertain whether the ship or cargo is liable to seizure. Resistance to visitation and search by a neutral vessel makes the vessel and cargo liable to confiscation. Numerous treaties regulate the manner in which the right of search must be exercised.

Title search. An examination of the official books, records and dockets, made in the process of investigating a title to land, for the purpose of discovering if there are any mortgages, judgments, tax-liens, or other incumbrances upon it. See also **Abstract of title.**

Unlawful or unreasonable search. Within constitutional immunity (Fourth Amendment) from unreasonable searches and seizures, an examination or inspection without authority of law of premises or person with view to discovery of stolen, contraband, or illicit property, or for some evidence of guilt to be used in prosecution of criminal action. Bush v. State, 64 Okl.Cr. 161, 77 P.2d 1184, 1187. See **Exclusionary rule; Fruit of poisonous tree doctrine; Probable cause; Search-warrant.**

Search incident to arrest. A police officer who has the right to arrest a person either with or without a warrant may search his person and the immediate area of the arrest for weapons. Chimel v. California, 395 U.S. 752, 89 S.Ct. 2034, 23 L.Ed.2d 685.

Search-warrant. An order in writing, issued by a justice or other magistrate, in the name of the state, directed to a sheriff, constable, or other officer, authorizing him to search for and seize any property that constitutes evidence of the commission of a crime, contraband, the fruits of crime, or things otherwise criminally possessed; or, property designed or intended for use or which is or has been used as the means of committing a crime. A warrant may be issued upon an affidavit or sworn oral testimony. Fed.R.Crim.P. 41.

The Fourth Amendment to U.S. Constitution provides that "no warrants shall issue, but upon probable cause, supported by oath or affirmation, and particularly describing the place to be searched, and the persons or things to be seized."

See also **Blanket search warrant; Exclusionary rule; Exigent circumstances; Probable cause.**

Search without warrant. A search without a warrant but incidental to an arrest is permitted if it does not extend beyond the person of the accused and the area into which the accused might reach in order to grab a weapon or other evidentiary items. Chimel v. California, 395 U.S. 752, 89 S.Ct. 2034, 23 L.Ed.2d 685. See also **Frisk; Search incident to arrest.**

Seashore. That portion of land adjacent to the sea which is alternately covered and left dry by the ordinary flux and reflux of the tides.

Seasonable. An action is seasonable when taken within the time agreed or if no time is agreed within a reasonable time. U.C.C. § 1–204.

Seasonal employment. As used in compensation laws, as basis for determining amount of compensation, refers to occupations which can be carried on only at certain seasons or fairly definite portions of the year, and does not include such occupations as may be carried on throughout entire year.

Seated land. Land that is occupied, cultivated, improved, reclaimed, farmed, or used as a place of residence. Residence without cultivation, or cultivation without residence, or both together, impart to land the character of being seated.

Seat of government. The state capitol or the town within a district or county where the principal government offices and officers are located; e.g. "county seat."

Seawan. The name used by the Algonquin Indians for the shell beads (or wampum) which passed among the Indians as money.

Seaworthy. This adjective, applied to a vessel, signifies that she is properly constructed, prepared, manned, equipped, and provided, for the voyage intended. A seaworthy vessel must, in general, be sufficiently strong and staunch and equipped with appropriate appurtenances to allow it to safely engage in trade for which it was intended. Texaco v. Universal Marine, Inc., D.C.La., 400 F.Supp. 311, 320. Reasonable fitness to perform or do the work at hand. In re Brown & Root Marine Operators, Inc., D.C.Tex., 267 F.Supp. 588, 592. Test of whether vessel or its equipment is seaworthy is whether ship or its appurtenances are reasonably fit for her intended service. Melancon v. I. M. C. Drilling Mud, La.App., 282 So.2d 532, 536.

In marine insurance, a warranty of seaworthiness means that the vessel is competent to resist the ordinary attacks of wind and weather, and is competently equipped and manned for the voyage, with a sufficient crew, and with sufficient means to sustain them, and with a captain of general good character and nautical skill.

A warranty of seaworthiness extends not only to the condition of the structure of the ship itself, but requires that it be properly laden, and provided with a competent master, a sufficient number of competent officers and seamen, and the requisite appurtenances and equipments, such as ballast, cables and anchors, cordage and sails, food, water, fuel, and lights, and other necessary or proper stores and implements for the voyage.

See, also **Unseaworthy.**

S.E.C. Securities and Exchange Commission.

Secession. The act of withdrawing from membership in a group. Certain states attempted unsuccessfully to secede from the United States at the time of the Civil War.

Seck. A want of remedy by distress. Want of present fruit or profit, as in the case of the reversion without rent or other service, except fealty. See **Rent.**

Second. This term, as used in law, may denote either sequence in point of time or inferiority or postponement in respect to rank, lien, order, or privilege.

As to second Cousin; Deliverance; Distress; Mortgage; and Surcharge, see those titles.

Second Amendment. The Second Amendment to the U.S. Constitution provides that a well regulated militia, being necessary to the security of a free state, the right of the people to keep and bear arms shall not be infringed. State and federal laws however regulate the sale, transportation and possession of firearms.

Secondary, n. In English practice, an officer of the courts of king's bench and common pleas; so called because he was *second* or next to the chief officer. In the king's bench he was called "Master of the King's Bench Office," and was a deputy of the prothonotary or chief clerk. By St. 7 Wm. IV, and 1 Vict., c. 30, the office of secondary was abolished.

Secondary, adj. Of a subsequent, subordinate, or inferior kind or class; generally opposed to "primary."

As to secondary Conveyance; Easement; Evidence; Franchise; Meaning; Use; and Vein, see those titles.

Secondary boycott. Any combination if its purpose and effect are to coerce customers or patrons, or suppliers through fear of loss or bodily harm, to withhold or withdraw their business relations from employer who is under attack. Wright v. Teamsters' Union Local No. 690, 33 Wash.2d 905, 207 P.2d 662, 665. Term refers to refusal to work for, purchase from or handle products of secondary employer with whom union has no dispute, with object of forcing such employer to stop doing business with primary employer with whom union has dispute. C. Comella, Inc. v. United Farm Workers Organizing Committee, 33 Ohio App.2d 61, 292 N.E.2d 647, 656. See also **Boycott; Secondary picketing.**

Secondary distribution. In securities, the new distribution of stock after it has been sold by the issuing corporation. Also, the sale of a large block of stock after the close of business of the exchange. See also **Offering; Secondary offering.**

Secondary easement. An easement to accomplish the intended purposes of the primary easement. One which is appurtenant to the primary or actual easement.

Secondary evidence. That which is inferior to primary or best evidence. Thus, a copy of an instrument, or oral evidence of its contents, is secondary evidence of the instrument and contents. It is that species of evidence which becomes admissible, when the primary or best evidence of the fact in question is lost or inaccessible; as when a witness details orally the contents of an instrument which is lost or destroyed. See also **Best evidence; Second-hand evidence.**

Secondary liability. A liability which does not attach until or except upon the fulfillment of certain conditions; as that of a surety, or that of an accommodation indorser.

Secondary meaning. Doctrine of "secondary meaning," for purposes of trademark laws, refers to protection afforded geographic or descriptive terms that producer has used to such an extent as to lead general public to identify producer or the product with the mark, and thus establishment of "secondary meaning" permits users to protect an otherwise unprotectable mark. Mushroom Makers, Inc. v. R. G. Barry Corp., D.C.N.Y., 441 F.Supp. 1220, 1226. Secondary meaning exists when a party through advertising or massive exposure has established its trademark in minds of consumers as an indication of origin from one particular source. FS Services, Inc. v. Custom Farm Services, Inc., C.A.Ill., 471 F.2d 671, 674. For purposes of unfair competition, term refers to association formed in the mind of the consumer which links an individual product with its manufacturer or distributor. J. Josephson, Inc. v. General Tire & Rubber Co., D.C.N.Y., 357 F.Supp. 1047, 1048.

Secondary offering. In securities, the offering for sale of a large block of stock by an investment underwriter. It is not a new issue but one which has been held by the corporation or by a large stockholder. See also **Offering; Secondary distribution.**

Secondary parties. In negotiable instruments, a drawer or endorser. U.C.C. § 3–102(1)(d).

Secondary picketing. A form of picketing in which pressure is put on one business establishment with which there is no dispute in order to induce such business to put pressure on the business establishment with which the employees have a primary dispute. See also **Secondary boycott; Secondary strike.**

Secondary strike. A strike against firms which supply goods and materials to the firm with which there is a primary dispute. See also **Secondary boycott.**

Second degree crime. A crime of lesser gravity than a first degree crime. Some states have first, second and third degree crimes and the punishment for each varies according to the degree. See *e.g.* **Second degree murder.**

Second degree murder. The unlawful taking of human life with malice but without the other aggravating elements of first degree murder; *i.e.* without deliberation or premeditation.

Second-hand evidence. Evidence which has passed through one or more media before reaching the witness; hearsay evidence. See also **Secondary evidence.**

Second lien. One which takes rank immediately after a first lien on the same property and is next entitled to satisfaction out of the proceeds.

Second mortgage. A mortgage of property which ranks in priority below a first mortgage. In title states, it is the transfer of the mortgagor's equity of redemption to secure a debt.

Secrecy. The quality or condition of being concealed or secret, as the proceedings of a grand jury are to be held in secrecy.

Secret. Concealed; hidden; not made public; particularly, in law, kept from the knowledge or notice of persons liable to be affected by the act, transaction, deed, or other thing spoken of. Something known only to one or a few and kept from others.

As to secret Committee; Equity; Partnership, and Trust, see those titles. See also **Secrete; Trade secret.**

Secretary. In reference to a corporation or association, refers to an officer charged with the direction and management of that part of the business of the company which is concerned with keeping the records, the official correspondence, with giving and receiving notices, countersigning documents, etc.

Also a name given to several of the heads of executive departments in the government of the United States; as the "Secretary of State", "Secretary of the Interior," etc.

Secretary General. The chief administrative officer of the United Nations, who is nominated by the Security Council and elected by the General Assembly.

Secretary of Embassy. A diplomatic officer appointed as secretary or assistant to an ambassador or minister plenipotentiary.

Secretary of Legation. An officer employed to attend a foreign mission and to perform certain duties as clerk.

Secretary of State. The Secretary of State, as principal foreign policy adviser to the President, is responsible for the overall direction, coordination, and supervision of U.S. foreign relations and for the interdepartmental activities of the U.S. Government overseas. The Secretary is the first-ranking member of the Cabinet, a member of the National Security Council, and is in charge of the operations of the Department, including the Foreign Service.

In most state governments, the official who is responsible for many types of formal state business, such as the licensing of corporations, filing of security agreements, etc.

Secrete. To conceal or hide away. Particularly, to put property out of the reach of creditors, either by corporally hiding it, or putting the title in another's name, or otherwise hindering creditors from levying on it or attaching it.

Secret lien. A lien reserved by the vendor of chattels, who has delivered them to the vendee, to secure the payment of the price, which is concealed from all third persons.

Secret Service. The major responsibilities of the U.S. Secret Service are defined in section 3056, Title 18, United States Code. The investigative responsibilities are to detect and arrest persons committing any offense against the laws of the United States relating to coins obligations, and securities of the United States and of foreign governments; and to detect and arrest persons violating certain laws relating to the Federal Deposit Insurance Corporation, Federal land banks, joint-stock land banks, and Federal land bank associations. The protective responsibilities include protection of the President of the United States and the members of his immediate family; the President-elect and the members of his immediate family unless the members decline such protection; the Vice President or other officer next in the order of succession to the Office of the President, and the members of his immediate family unless the members decline such protection; the Vice President-elect, and the members of his immediate family unless the members decline such protection; a former President and his wife during his lifetime; the widow of a former President until her death or remarriage; the minor children of a former President until they reach 16 years of age, unless such protection is declined; a visiting head of a foreign state or foreign government and, at the direction of the President, other distinguished foreign visitors to the United States and official representatives of the United States performing special missions abroad. In addition, Pub.L. 90–331 authorizes the Secret Service to protect major Presidential and Vice Presidential candidates, unless such protection is declined; the spouse of a major Presidential or Vice Presidential nominee, except that such protection shall not commence more than sixty days prior to the general Presidential election.

Sect. As applied to religious bodies, a party or body of persons who unite in holding certain special doctrines or opinions concerning religion, which distinguish them from others holding the same general religious belief.

Secta /séktə/. In old English law, suit; attendance at court; the plaintiff's suit or following, *i.e.,* the witnesses whom he was required, in the ancient practice, to bring with him and produce in court, for the purpose of confirming his claim, before the defendant was put to the necessity of answering the declaration. A survival from this proceeding is seen in the formula still used at the end of declarations, "and therefore he brings his suit" *(et inde producit sectam).* This word, in its secondary meaning, signifies suit in the courts; lawsuit.

Secta curiæ /séktə kyúriyiy/. In old English law, suit of court; attendance at court. The service, incumbent upon feudal tenants, of attending the lord at his court, both to form a jury when required, and also to answer for their own actions when complained of.

Secta est pugna civilis; sicut actores armantur actionibus, et, quasi, gladiis accinguntur, ita rei muniuntur exceptionibus, et defenduntur, quasi, clypeis /séktə èst pə́gnə sívələs; síkəd æktóriyz armǽntər ǽkshiyównəbəs, èt, kwéyzay, glǽdiyəs æksiŋgə́ntər, áydə ríyay myùwniyǽntər əksèpshiyównəbəs, et dèfendǽntər, kwéyzay clípiyəs/. A suit is a civil warfare; for as the plaintiffs are armed with actions, and, as it were, girded with swords, so the defendants are fortified with pleas, and are defended, as it were, by shields.

Secta facienda per illam quæ habet eniciam partem /séktə fæshiyéndə pèr íləm kwìy héybəd ənísh(iy)əm párdəm/. A writ to compel the heir, who has the elder's part of the co-heirs, to perform suit and services for all the coparceners.

Secta quæ scripto nititur a scripto variari non debet /séktə kwìy skríptow nídədər èy skríptow væriyéray nòn débət/. A suit which is based upon a writing ought not to vary from the writing.

Secta regalis /séktə rəgéyləs/. In old English law, a suit so called by which all persons were bound twice in the year to attend in the sheriff's tourn, in order that they might be informed of things relating to the public peace. It was so called because the sheriff's tourn was the king's leet, and it was held in order that the people might be bound by oath to bear true allegiance to the king.

Sectarian. Denominational; devoted to, peculiar to, pertaining to, or promotive of, the interest of a sect, or sects. In a broader sense, used to describe the activities of the followers of one faith as related to those of adherents of another. The term is most comprehensive in scope. See also **Sect.**

Sectatores /sèktətóriyz/. Suitors of court who, among the Saxons, gave their judgment or verdict in civil suits upon the matter of fact and law.

Secta unica tantum facienda pro pluribus hæreditatibus /séktə yúwnəkə tǽntəm fæshiyéndə prów pl(y)úrəbəs hərèdətéydəbəs/. In old English law, a writ for an heir who was distrained by the lord to do more suits than one, that he should be allowed to do one suit only in respect of the land of divers heirs descended to him.

Section. In text-books, codes, statutes, and other juridical writings, the smallest distinct and numbered subdivisions are commonly called "sections," sometimes "articles," and occasionally "paragraphs."

Section of land. A division or parcel of land, on the government survey, comprising one square mile or 640 acres. Each "township" (six miles square) is divided by straight lines into thirty-six sections, and these are again divided into half-sections and quarter-sections. See also **Quarter section.**

Sectis non faciendis /séktəs nòn fæshiyéndəs/. In old English law, a writ which lay for a dowress, or one in wardship, to be free from suit of court.

Sectores /sektóriyz/. Lat. In Roman law, purchasers at auction, or public sales.

Secular. Not spiritual; not ecclesiastical; relating to affairs of the present (temporal) world.

Secular business. As used in Sunday closing laws, this term includes all forms of activity in the business affairs of life, the prosecution of a trade or employment, and commercial dealings, such as the making of promissory notes, lending money, and the like.

Secular clergy. In ecclesiastical law, the parochial clergy, who perform their ministry *in seculo* (in the world), and who are thus distinguished from the monastic or "regular" clergy.

Secundum /səkándəm/. Lat. In the civil and common law, according to. Occurring in many phrases of familiar use, as follows:

Secundum æquum et bonum /səkándəm íykwəm ət bównəm/. According to what is just and right.

Secundum allegata et probata /səkándəm æləgéydə èt prəbéydə/. According to what is alleged and proved; according to the allegations and proofs.

Secundum artem /səkándəm árdəm/. According to the art, trade, business, or science.

Secundum bonos mores /səkándəm bównows móriyz/. According to good usages; according to established custom; regularly; orderly.

Secundum consuetudinem manerii /səkándəm kònswət(y)úwdənəm məníriyay/. According to the custom of the manor.

Secundum formam chartæ /səkándəm fórməm kárdiy/. According to the form of the charter (deed).

Secundum formam doni /səkándəm fórməm dównay/. According to the form of the gift or grant. See **Formedon.**

Secundum formam statuti /səkándəm fórməm statyúwday/. According to the form of the statute.

Secundum legem communem /səkándəm líyjəm kəmyúwnəm/. According to the common law.

Secundum naturam est commoda cujusque rei eum sequi, quem sequuntur incommoda /səkándəm nət(y)úrəm èst kómədə k(y)uwjəskwiy ríyay íyəm sékway kwém səkwántər ínkòmədə/. It is according to nature that the advantages of anything should attach to him to whom the disadvantages attach.

Secundum normam legis /səkándəm nórməm líyjəs/. According to the rule of law; by the intendment and rule of law.

Secundum regulam /səkándəm régyələm/. According to the rule; by rule.

Secundum subjectam materiam /səkándəm səbjéktəm mətíriyəm/. According to the subject-matter. All agreements must be construed *secundum subjectam materiam* if the matter will bear it.

Secure. To give security; to assure of payment, performance, or indemnity; to guaranty or make certain the payment of a debt or discharge of an obligation. One "secures" his creditor by giving him a lien, mortgage, pledge, or other security, to be used in case the debtor fails to make payment.

Also, not exposed to danger; safe; so strong, stable or firm as to insure safety and financial security. See also **Security.**

Secured. Supported or backed by security or collateral such as a secured debt for which property has been pledged or mortgaged. See **Security.**

Secured creditor. A creditor who holds some special pecuniary assurance of payment of his debt, such as a mortgage, collateral, or lien. See **Secured party; Security interest.**

Secured loan. A loan for which some form of property has been pledged or mortgaged, as in the case of an automobile loan in which title to the vehicle is held as security by lender. See **Collateral.**

Secured party. A lender, seller or other person in whose favor there is a security interest, including a person to whom accounts or chattel paper have been sold. When the holders of obligations issued under an indenture of trust, equipment trust agreement or the like are represented by a trustee or other person, the representative is the secured party. Section 9–105(1)(m) of the 1972 U.C.C. Code; § 9–105(1)(i) of the 1962 U.C.C. Code.

Secured transaction. A transaction which is founded on a security agreement. Such agreement creates or provides for a security interest. U.C.C. § 9–105(h).

Securitas /səkyúrətæs/. In old English law, security; surety. In the civil law, an acquittance or release.

Securitatem inveniendi /səkyùrətéydəm ənvìyniyénday/. An ancient writ, lying for the sovereign, against any of his subjects, to stay them from going out of the kingdom to foreign parts; the ground whereof is that every man is bound to serve and defend the commonwealth as the crown shall think fit.

Securitatis pacis /səkyùrəteydəs péysəs/. In old English law, security of the peace. A writ that lay for one who was threatened with death or bodily harm by another, against him who so threatened.

Securities. Evidences of debts or of property. State v. Allen, 216 N.C. 621, 5 S.E.2d 844, 845, 847. Evidences of obligations to pay money or of rights to participate in earnings and distribution of corporate, trust, and other property. Oklahoma-Texas Trust v. Securities and Exchange Commission, C.C.A.10, 100 F.2d 888, 890. Stocks, bonds, notes, convertible debentures, warrants, or other documents that represent a share in a company or a debt owed by a company.

See also Bond; Consolidated securities; Convertible securities; Debenture; Distribution; Letter stock; Marketable securities; Municipal securities; Security; Stock. For marshalling of securities, see **Marshalling.**

Coupon securities. See **Coupons.**

Exempt securities. Those securities which need not be registered under provisions of Securities Act of 1933, §§ 4(2), 5.

Securities Act of 1933. Federal law which provides for registration of securities which are to be sold to the public and for complete information as to the issuer and the stock offering. 15 U.S.C.A. § 77a *et seq.* See also **Securities Exchange Act of 1934.**

Securities Acts. Federal and state statutes governing the registration, offering, sale, etc. of securities. Major federal acts include the Securities Act of 1933 and the Securities Exchange Act of 1934 (*q.v.*). The majority of the states have adopted the Uniform Securities Act.

Securities and Exchange Commission. The federal agency which administers such laws as the Securities Act of 1933, the Securities Exchange Act of 1934, the Trust Indenture Act of 1939, the Public Utility Holding Company Act of 1935, the Investment Adviser's Act of 1940 and the Investment Company Act of 1940.

Securities broker. See **Broker.**

Securities Exchange Act of 1934. A federal law which governs the operation of stock exchanges and over the counter trading. It requires, among other things, publication of information concerning stocks which are listed on these exchanges. 15 U.S.C.A. § 78 *et seq.* See also **Securities Act of 1933.**

Securities Investor Protection Act. Federal law which established Securities Investor Protection Corp., which, though not an agency of the U.S. Government, is designed to help brokers and dealers in financial trouble. 15 U.S.C.A. §§ 78aaa *et seq.*

Securities offering. See **Issue** *(Securities);* **Offering; Underwrite.**

Security. Protection; assurance; indemnification. The term is usually applied to an obligation, pledge, mortgage, deposit, lien, etc., given by a debtor in order to assure the payment or performance of his debt, by furnishing the creditor with a resource to be used in case of failure in the principal obligation. Document that indicates evidence of indebtedness. The name is also sometimes given to one who becomes surety or guarantor for another.

Test for a "security" is whether the scheme involves an investment of money in a common enterprise with profits to come solely from the efforts of others so that whenever an investor relinquishes control over his funds and submits their control to another for the purpose and hopeful expectation of deriving profits therefrom he is in fact investing his funds in a security. Investment Co. Institute v. Camp, D.C.D.C., 274 F.Supp. 624, 642. "Security" under Securities Act of 1933, means investment in common enterprise in which investors are purchasing interest and where growth of that investment is to result from efforts of promoter, Neuwirth Inv. Fund, Ltd., v. Swanton, D.C.N.Y., 422 F.Supp. 1187, 1194; and the label attached to the transaction is not determinative. McGovern Plaza Joint Venture v. First of Denver Mortg. Investors, 562 F.2d 645, 646.

A "security" is an instrument which: (i) is issued in bearer or registered form; and (ii) is of a type commonly dealt in upon securities exchanges or markets or commonly recognized in any area in which it is issued or dealt in as a medium for investment; and (iii) is either one of a class or series or by its terms is divisible into a class or series of instruments; and (iv) evidences a share, participation or other interest in property or in an enterprise or evidences an obligation of the issuer. U.C.C. § 8–102(1)(a).

"Security" includes any note, stock, treasury stock, bond, debenture, evidence of indebtedness, certificate of interest or participation in an oil, gas or mining title or lease or in payments out of production under such a title or lease, collateral trust certificate, transferable share, voting trust certificate or, in general, any interest or instrument commonly known as a security, or any certificate of interest or participation, any temporary or interim certificate, receipt or certificate of deposit for, or any warrant or right to subscribe to or purchase, any of the foregoing. Uniform Probate Code, § 1–201.

The term "security" means any note, stock, treasury stock, bond, debenture, certificate of interest or participation in any profit-sharing agreement or in any oil, gas, or other mineral royalty or lease, any collateral-trust certificate, preorganization certificate or subscription, transferable share, investment contract, voting-trust certificate, certificate of deposit, for a security, or in general, any instrument commonly known as a "security"; or any certificate of interest or participation in, temporary or interim certificate for, receipt for, or warrant or right to subscribe

to or purchase, any of the foregoing; but shall not include currency or any note, draft, bill of exchange, or banker's acceptance which has a maturity at the time of issuance of not exceeding nine months, exclusive of days of grace, or any renewal thereof the maturity of which is likewise limited. Securities Exchange Act, § 3.

The term "security" means any bond, debenture, note or certificate or other evidence of indebtedness, issued by a corporation or a government or political subdivision thereof, with interest coupons or in registered form, share of stock, voting trust certificate, or any certificate of interest or participation in, certificate of deposit or receipt for, temporary or interim certificate for, or warrant or right to subscribe to or purchase, any of the foregoing; negotiable instrument; or money. I.R.C. § 6323(h).

As defined in the Bankruptcy Act (§ 101(35)), "security" includes: note, stock, treasury stock, bond, debenture, collateral trust certificate, preorganization certificate or subscription, transferable share, voting-trust certificate, certificate of deposit, investment contract or certificate of interest, etc.

See also Collateral; Equity security; Hybrid security; Internal security acts; Investment security; Lien; Listed security; Pledge; Securities; Stock.

Assessable security. A security on which a charge or assessment for the obligations of the issuing company may be made. In many instances, bank and insurance company stocks are assessable.

Collateral security. Property which has been pledged or mortgaged to secure a loan or a sale.

Convertible security. See **Convertible securities.**

Equity security. The term "equity security" means any stock or similar security; or any security convertible, with or without consideration, into such a security; or carrying any warrant or right to subscribe to or purchase such a security; or any such warrant or right; or any other security which the Securities and Exchange Commission shall deem to be of similar nature and consider necessary or appropriate, by such rules and regulations as it may prescribe in the public interest or for the protection of investors, to treat as an equity security. Securities Exchange Act, § 3.

(A) share in a corporation, whether or not transferable or denominated "stock", or similar security; (B) interest of a limited partner in a limited partnership; or (C) warrant or right, other than a right to convert, to purchase, sell, or subscribe to a share, security, or interest of a kind specified in subparagraph (A) or (B) of this paragraph. Bankruptcy Act, § 101(15).

Exempted security. A security which is not required to be registered under the provisions of the Securities Exchange Act.

Government security. Any security issued or guaranteed as to principal or interest by the United States, or by a person controlled or supervised by and acting as an instrumentality of the Government of the United States pursuant to authority granted by the Congress of the United States; or any certificate of deposit for any of the foregoing. Investment Company Act, § 2.

Hybrid security. A security which combines features of both debt and equity; *i.e.* of both bond and stock. See also **Hybrid security.**

Listed security. A security which has been listed for trading on one of the stock exchanges or which has been listed with the Securities and Exchange Commission.

Marketable security. A security which is of reasonable investment caliber and which can be easily sold on the market.

Non-marketable security. A security which cannot be sold on the market such as certain government bonds and notes. It can only be redeemed by the holder. Also, a security which is not of investment quality.

Outstanding security. A security which is held by an investor and which has not been redeemed or purchased back by the issuing corporation.

Personal security. An obligation to repay a debt evidenced by a pledge, note or bond in contrast to collateral security. Evidences of debt which bind the person of the debtor, not real property. Merrill v. National Bank, 173 U.S. 131, 19 S.Ct. 360, 43 L.Ed. 640.

A person's legal and uninterrupted enjoyment of his life, his limbs, his body, his health, and his reputation. 1 Bl.Comm. 129.

Public security. Bonds, notes, certificates of indebtedness, and other negotiable or transferable instruments evidencing the public debt of a state or government.

Real security. The security of mortgages or other liens or encumbrances upon land. See Merrill v. National Bank, 173 U.S. 131, 19 S.Ct. 360, 43 L.Ed. 640. See also **Collateral.**

Redeemable security. Any security, other than short-term paper, under the terms of which the holder upon its presentation to the issuer or to a person designated by the issuer, is entitled (whether absolutely or only out of surplus) to receive approximately his proportionate share of the issuer's current net assets, or the cash equivalent thereof. Investment Company Act, § 2.

Security for costs. See **Security for costs.**

Security for good behavior. A bond or recognizance which the magistrate exacts from a defendant brought before him on a charge of disorderly conduct or threatening violence, conditioned upon his being of good behavior, or keeping the peace, for a prescribed period, towards all people in general and the complainant in particular. A peace bond.

Short term security. A bond or note which matures in and is payable within a short span of time. Such securities are purchased by institutional investors for income rather than for growth potential.

Treasury securities. See **Treasury securities.**

Unlisted security. An over the counter security which is not listed on a stock exchange.

Voting security. Any security presently entitling the owner or holder thereof to vote for the election of directors of a company. Investment Company Act, § 2.

Security agreement. An agreement which creates or provides for a security interest. U.C.C. § 9–105(h); Bankruptcy Act § 101(36). An agreement granting a creditor a security interest in personal property, which security interest is normally perfected either by the creditor taking possession of the collateral or by filing financing statements in the proper public records. See **Perfection of security interest; Purchase money security interest.**

Security council. The executive body of the United Nations, charged with the duty of preventing or stopping wars by diplomatic, economic or military action. It is composed of five permanent members and six additional members elected at stated intervals.

Security deposit. Money deposited by tenant with landlord as security for full and faithful performance by tenant of terms of lease, including damages to premises. It is refundable unless the tenant has caused damage or injury to the property or has breached the terms of the tenancy or the laws governing the tenancy. Certain states also require the landlord to make a security deposit to cover essential repairs required on rental property.

Security for costs. Payment into court in the form of cash, property or bond by a plaintiff or an appellant to secure the payment of costs if such person does not prevail; *e.g.* Fed.R.Civ.P. 65(c) provides for security when restraining order or preliminary injunction is issued. See also **Costs.**

Security fund. See **Client security fund.**

Security interest. A form of interest in property which provides that the property may be sold on default in order to satisfy the obligation for which the security interest is given. A mortgage is used to grant a security interest in real property. An interest in personal property or fixtures which secures payment or performance of an obligation. U.C.C. §§ 1–201(37), 9–102. Lien created by an agreement. Bankruptcy Act § 101(37).

The term "security interest" means any interest in property acquired by contract for the purpose of securing payment or performance of an obligation or indemnifying against loss or liability. A security interest exists at any time, (A) if, at such time, the property is in existence and the interest has become protected under local law against a subsequent judgment lien arising out of an unsecured obligation, and (B) to the extent that, at such time, the holder has parted with money or money's worth. I.R.C. § 6323(h).

Purchase money security interest. A secured interest which is created when a buyer uses the money of the lender to make the purchase and immediately gives to the lender a security interest. See **Mortgage** (*Purchase money mortgage*).

Securius expediuntur negotia commissa pluribus, et plus vident oculi quam oculus /səkyúriyəs əkspìydiyántər nəgówsh(iy)ə kəmísə pl(y)úrəbəs, èt plás váydənt ók(y)əlay kwæm ókyələs/. Matters intrusted to several are more securely dispatched, and eyes see more than eye [*i.e.,* "two heads are better than one"].

Secus /síykəs/. Lat. Otherwise; to the contrary. This word is used in the books to indicate the converse of a foregoing proposition, or the rule applicable to a different state of facts, or an exception to a rule before stated.

Sedato animo /sədéydow ǽnəmow/. Lat. With settled purpose.

Se defendendo /síy dəfèndéndow/. Lat. In defending himself; in self-defense. Homicide committed *se defendendo* is excusable.

Sedente curia /sədéntiy kyúr(i)yə/. Lat. The court sitting; during the sitting of the court.

Sede plena /síydiy plíynə/. Lat. The see being filled. A phrase used when a bishop's see is not vacant.

Sedes /síydiyz/. Lat. A see; the dignity of a bishop.

Sedge flat /séj flǽt/. A tract of land below high-water mark.

Sedimentation. The deposition of soil that has been transported from its site of origin by water, ice, wind, gravity or other natural means as a product of erosion.

Sedition. Communication or agreement which has as its objective the stirring up of treason or certain lesser commotions, or the defammation of the government. Sedition is advocating, or with knowledge of its contents knowingly publishing, selling or distributing any document which advocates, or, with knowledge of its purpose, knowingly becoming a member of any organization which advocates the overthrow or reformation of the existing form of government of this state by violence or unlawful means. An insurrectionary movement tending towards treason, but wanting an overt act; attempts made by meetings or speeches, or by publications, to disturb the tranquillity of the state. See 18 U.S.C.A. § 2383 *et seq.;* see also **Alien and sedition laws; Smith Act.**

Seditious libel. A communication written with the intent to incite the people to change the government otherwise than by lawful means, or to advocate the overthrow of the government by force or violence. Smith Act, 18 U.S.C.A. § 2385. See **Alien and sedition laws.**

Seditious speech. Oral advocacy of the overthrow of the government by force or violence.

Sed non allocatur /sèd nón ǽləkéydər/. Lat. But it is not allowed. A phrase used in the old reports, to signify that the court disagreed with the arguments of counsel.

Sed per curiam /séd pər kyúriyəm/. Lat. But by the court. This phrase is used in the reports to introduce a statement made by the court, on the argument, at variance with the propositions advanced by counsel, or the opinion of the whole court, where that is different from the opinion of a single judge immediately before quoted.

Sed quære /sèd kwíriy/. Lat. But inquire; examine this further. A remark indicating, briefly, that the particular statement or rule laid down is doubted or challenged in respect to its correctness.

Seduce. To induce to surrender chastity. To lead away or astray. See also **Seduction.**

Seduction. The act of seducing. Act of man enticing woman to have unlawful intercourse with him by means of persuasion, solicitation, promises, bribes, or other means without employment of force. A male is guilty of seduction if he induces a female of previously chaste character to indulge in sexual intercourse with him. Many statutes provide that a subsequent marriage is a bar to prosecution. Also, by statute in some states, actions for seduction of a person over age of legal consent are prohibited. See **Heart Balm statutes.**

Sed vide /sèd váydiy/. Lat. But see. This remark, followed by a citation, directs the reader's attention to an authority or a statement which conflicts with or contradicts the statement or principle laid down.

See. The circuit of a bishop's jurisdiction; or his office or dignity, as being bishop of a given diocese.

Segregation. The act or process of separation. The unconstitutional policy and practice of separating people on the basis of color, nationality, religion, etc. in housing and schooling.

Seignior /séyn(i)yər/. In its general signification, means "lord," but in law it is particularly applied to the lord of a fee or of a manor; and the fee, dominions, or manor of a seignior is thence termed a "seigniory," *i.e.,* a lordship. He who is a lord, but of no manor, and therefore unable to keep a court, is termed a "seignior in gross."

Seigniorage /séynyərəj/. A royalty or prerogative of the sovereign, whereby an allowance of gold and silver, brought in the mass to be exchanged for coin, is claimed. Mintage; the charge for coining bullion into money at the mint.

A sum equivalent to the difference between interest payable upon a mortgage held by a title insurance and mortgage company at the rate named therein for any period and the interest payable for such period on securities issued by the company with respect to such mortgage, at the rate named in such securities. Commissioner of Insurance v. Conveyancers Title Ins. & Mortg. Co., 300 Mass. 457, 15 N.E.2d 820, 822.

Seignioress /séynyərəs/. A female superior.

Seigniory /séynyəray/. In English law, a lordship; a manor. The rights of a lord, as such, in lands.

Seisi /síyzay/. In old English law, seised; possessed.

Seisin /síyzən/. Possession of real property under claim of freehold estate. The completion of the feudal investiture, by which the tenant was admitted into the feud, and performed the rights of homage and fealty. Possession with an intent on the part of him who holds it to claim a freehold interest. Right to immediate possession according to the nature of the estate. Williams v. Swango, 365 Ill. 549, 7 N.E.2d 306, 309.

Actual seisin. Possession of the freehold by the *pedis positio* of one's self or one's tenant or agent, or by construction of law, as in the case of a state grant or a conveyance under the statutes of uses, or (probably) of grant or devise where there is no actual adverse possession; it means actual possession as distinguished from constructive possession or possession in law.

Constructive seisin. Seisin in law where there is no seisin in fact; as where the state issues a patent to a person who never takes any sort of possession of the lands granted, he has constructive seisin of all the land in his grant, though another person is at the time in actual possession.

Covenant of seisin. See **Covenant.**

Equitable seisin. A seisin which is analogous to legal seisin; that is, seisin of an equitable estate in land. Thus a mortgagor is said to have equitable seisin of the land by receipt of the rents.

Livery of seisin. Delivery of possession; called, by the feudists, "investiture."

Primer seisin. In old English law, the right which the king had, when any of his tenants died seised of a knight's fee, to receive of the heir, provided he were of full age, one whole year's profits of the lands, if they were in immediate possession; and half a year's profits, if the lands were in reversion, expectant on an estate for life. 2 Bl.Comm. 66.

Quasi seisin. A term applied to the possession which a copyholder has of the land to which he has been admitted. The freehold in copyhold lands being in the lord, the copyholder cannot have seisin of them in the proper sense of the word, but he has a customary or *quasi* seisin analogous to that of a freeholder.

Seisin in deed. Actual possession of the freehold; the same as actual seisin or seisin in fact. Roetzel v. Beal, 196 Ark. 5, 116 S.W.2d 591, 593.

Seisin in fact. Possession with intent on the part of him who holds it to claim a freehold interest; the same as actual seisin.

Seisin in law. A right of immediate possession according to the nature of the estate. As the old doctrine of corporeal investiture is no longer in force, the delivery of a deed gives seisin in law.

Seisina /síyzənə/. L. Lat. Seisin.

Seisina facit stipitem /síyzənə féysət stípədəm/. Seisin makes the stock. 2 Bl.Comm. 209.

Seisina habenda /síyzənə həbéndə/. A writ for delivery of seisin to the lord, of lands and tenements, after the sovereign, in right of his prerogative, had had the year, day, and waste on a felony committed, etc.

Seize /síyz/. To put in possession, invest with fee simple, be seized of or in, be legal possessor of, or be holder in fee simple. Hanley v. Stewart, 155 Pa.Super. 535, 39 A.2d 323, 326. To "seize" means to take possession of forcibly, to grasp, to snatch or to put in possession. State v. Dees, Fla.App., 280 So.2d 51, 52.

Seized. A person is "seized" within Fourth Amendment when he is accosted by a police officer who restrains his freedom to walk away. State v. Ochoa, 112 Ariz. 582, 544 P.2d 1097, 1099.

Seizin /síyzən/. See **Seisin.**

Seizure. The act of taking possession of property, *e.g.,* for a violation of law or by virtue of an execution. Term implies a taking or removal of something from the possession, actual or constructive, of another person or persons. Molina v. State, 53 Wis.2d 662, 193 N.W.2d 874, 877.

The act performed by an officer of the law, under the authority and exigence of a writ, in taking into the custody of the law the property, real or personal, of a person against whom the judgment of a competent court has passed, condemning him to pay a certain sum of money, in order that such property may be sold, by authority and due course of law, to satisfy the judgment. Or the act of taking possession of goods in consequence of a violation of public law.

Seizure of an individual, within the Fourth Amendment, connotes the taking of one physically or constructively into custody and detaining him, thus causing a deprivation of his freedom in a significant way, with real interruption of his liberty of movement. People v. P. A. J. Theater Corp., 72 Misc.2d 354, 339 N.Y.S.2d 152, 155.

See also **Capture; Confiscate; Forfeiture; Impound; Levy.**

"Search" distinguished. A "search" is a probing or exploration for something that is concealed or hidden from the searcher, whereas a "seizure" is a forcible or secretive dispossession of something against the will of the possessor or owner. U. S. v. Marti, D.C. N.Y., 321 F.Supp. 59, 63. See also **Search.**

Select. To take by preference from among others; to pick out; to cull.

Select council. The name given, in some states, to the upper house or branch of the council of a city.

Selecti judices /səléktay júwdəsiyz/. Lat. In Roman law, judges who were selected very much like our juries. They were returned by the prætor, drawn by lot, subject to be challenged, and sworn. 3 Bl.Comm. 366.

Selectmen. The name of certain municipal officers, in the New England states, elected by the towns to transact their general public business, and possessing certain executive powers.

Self-dealing. Relates to transactions wherein a trustee, acting for himself and also as "trustee," a relation which demands strict fidelity to others, seeks to consummate a deal wherein self-interest is opposed to duty. *Cestui que* trust has in such case the election to affirm or disaffirm, unless countervailing equities have intervened.

Self-defense. The protection of one's person or property against some injury attempted by another. The right of such protection. An excuse for the use of force in resisting an attack on the person, and especially for killing an assailant. The right of a man to repel force by force even to the taking of life in defense of his person, property or habitation, or of a member of his family, against any one who manifests, intends, attempts or endeavors by violence or surprise, to commit a forcible felony. Essential elements of "self-defense" are that defendant does not provoke difficulty and that there must be impending peril without convenient or reasonable mode of escape. The law of "self-defense" justifies an act done in the reasonable belief of immediate danger, and, if an injury was done by defendant in justifiable self-defense, he can never be punished criminally nor held responsible for damages in a civil action. Baltimore Transit Co. v. Faulkner, 179 Md. 598, 20 A.2d 485, 487.

A person is justified in the use of force against an aggressor when and to the extent it appears to him and he reasonably believes that such conduct is necessary to defend himself or another against such aggressor's imminent use of unlawful force. One who is not the aggressor in an encounter is justified in using a reasonable amount of force against his adversary when he reasonably believes: (a) that he is in immediate danger of unlawful bodily harm from his adversary and (b) that the use of such force is necessary to avoid this danger. It may be reasonable to use nondeadly force against the adversary's nondeadly attack (*i.e.*, one threatening only bodily harm), and to use deadly force against his deadly attack (an attack threatening death or serious bodily harm), but it is never reasonable to use deadly force against his nondeadly attack.

See also **Imminent danger; Reasonable force.**

Self-employment tax. Social security tax imposed on earnings of self-employed.

Self-executing constitutional provision. Term has reference to provisions which are immediately effective without the necessity of ancillary legislation. Constitutional provision is "self-executing" if it supplies sufficient rule by which right given may be enjoyed or duty imposed enforced; constitutional provision is not "self-executing" when it merely indicates principles without laying down rules giving them force of law.

Self-executing judgments. Those requiring no affirmative action of the court or action under process issued by the court to execute them.

Self-help. Taking an action in person or by a representative with legal consequences, whether the action is legal or not; for example, a "self-help eviction" may be a landlord's removing the tenant's property from an apartment and locking the door against the tenant. Self-help repossession (*i.e.* without judicial process) of goods by creditor is permitted under U.C.C. § 9–503, if such can be done "without breach of the peace."

Self-incrimination. Acts or declarations either as testimony at trial or prior to trial by which one implicates himself in a crime. The Fifth Amendment, U.S. Const., as well as provisions in many state constitutions and laws, prohibit the government from requiring a person to be a witness against himself involuntarily or to furnish evidence against himself. It is the burden of the government to accuse and to carry the burden of proof of guilt. The defendant cannot be compelled to aid the government in this regard. See also **Compulsory self-incrimination; Link-in-chain; Privilege against self-incrimination.**

Self-insurance. The practice of setting aside a fund to meet losses instead of insuring against such through insurance. A common practice of business is to self-insure up to a certain amount, and then to cover any excess with insurance. Worker's compensation obligations may also be met through this method if statutory requirements are met.

Self-murder, self-destruction, or **self-slaughter.** See **Felo de se; Suicide.**

Self serving declaration. A species of hearsay evidence consisting of an extrajudicial declaration by a party to an action, the import of which is to prove an essential element of his case. Such statements are inadmissible unless they fall under a recognized category of exception to the hearsay rule such as a business entry, declaration of a deceased party, etc., or unless they are offered for a non-hearsay purpose such as the fact that the party made the statement and not for the truth of the statement. Statement, oral or written, or equivalent act, by or on behalf of a party which if admitted would constitute evidence in his favor. Werdell v. Turzynski, 128 Ill.App.2d 139, 262 N.E.2d 833, 838.

Sell. To dispose of by sale (*q.v.*).

Seller. Vendor; one who has contracted to sell property. A person who sells or contracts to sell goods. U.C.C. § 2–103(d).

One who sells anything; the party who transfers property in the contract of sale. The correlative is "buyer," or "purchaser." These terms are, however, generally not inapplicable to the persons concerned in a transfer of real estate, it being more customary to use "vendor" and "purchaser," or "vendee" in that case.

Test of whether a person is a "seller" of unregistered securities, so as to be liable to the buyer under the Securities Act, is whether such person is the "proximate cause" of the sale. Lewis v. Walston & Co., Inc., C.A.Fla., 487 F.2d 617, 621.

Selling stocks short. Term refers to selling stocks customer does not possess, customer borrowing the number of shares he has sold from some third person to deliver to his vendee expecting to be able to buy the stocks later at a lower figure and return them to the person from whom he borrowed them. The agreement to deliver at a future date a security or commodity the seller does not own but which he hopes to buy later at a lower price.

Semble. L. Fr. It seems; it would appear. This expression is often used in the reports to preface a statement by the court upon a point of law which is not directly decided, when such statement is intended as an intimation of what the decision would be if the point were necessary to be passed upon. It is also used to introduce a suggestion by the reporter, or his understanding of the point decided when it is not free from obscurity.

Semel civis semper civis /sémǝl sívǝs sémpǝr sívǝs/. Once a citizen always a citizen.

Semel malus semper præsumitur esse malus in eodem genere /sémǝl mǽlǝs sémpǝr prǝz(y)úwmǝdǝr ésiy mǽlǝs in iyówdǝm jénǝriy/. Whoever is once bad is presumed to be so always in the same kind of affairs.

Semestria /sǝméstriyǝ/. Lat. In the civil law, the collected decisions of the emperors in their councils.

Semi-matrimonium /sèmiymǽtrəmówn(i)yəm/. Lat. In Roman law, half-marriage. Concubinage was so called.

Seminary. A place of training; an institution of education. A school, academy, college, or university in which young persons are instructed in the several branches of learning which may qualify them for their future employment, and the origin of the word seems to imply a place where the seeds of education are sown and implanted.

Seminaufragium /sèmiynofréyj(iy)əm/. Lat. In maritime law, half-shipwreck, as where goods are cast overboard in a storm; also where a ship has been so much damaged that her repair costs more than her worth.

Semi-plena probatio /sèmiyplíynə prəbéysh(iy)ow/. Lat. In the civil law, half-full proof; half-proof. See **Half-proof.**

Semper /sémpər/. Lat. Always. A word which introduces several Latin maxims, of which some are also used without this prefix.

Semper in dubiis benigniora præferenda sunt /sémpər in d(y)úwbiyəs bənìgniyórə prèfəréndə sánt/. In doubtful cases, the more favorable constructions are always to be preferred.

Semper in dubiis id agendum est, ut quam tutissimo loco res sit bona fide contracta, nisi quum aperte contra leges scriptum est /sémpər in d(y)úwbiyəs íd əjéndəm èst, ət kwǽm t(y)uwtísəmow lówkow ríyz sit bównə fáydiy kəntrǽktə, náysay k(w)əm əpərdiy kóntrə líyjiyz skríptəm èst/. In doubtful cases, such a course should always be taken that a thing contracted *bona fide* should be in the safest condition, unless when it has been openly made against law.

Semper in obscuris, quod minimum est sequimur /sémpər in əbskyúrəs kwòd mínəməm èst sékwəmər/. In obscure constructions we always apply that which is the last obscure.

Semper in stipulationibus, et in ceteris contractibus, id sequimur quod actum est /sémpər in stìpyəlèyshiyównəbəs, èd in sédərəs kəntrǽktəbəs, íd sékwəmər kwòd ǽktəm èst/. In stipulations and in other contracts we follow that which was done [we are governed by the actual state of the facts].

Semper ita fiat relatio ut valeat dispositio /sémpər áydə fáyət rəléysh(iy)ow ət vǽliyət dìspəzísh(iy)ow/. Reference [of a disposition in a will] should always be so made that the disposition may have effect.

Semper necessitas probandi incumbit ei qui agit /sémpər nəsésətæs prəbǽnday inkámbəd íyay kwày éyjət/. The claimant is always bound to prove [the burden of proof lies on the actor].

Semper paratus /sémpər pəréydəs/. Lat. Always ready. The name of a plea by which the defendant alleges that he has always been ready to perform what is demanded of him.

Semper præsumitur pro legitimatione puerorum /sémpər prəz(y)úwmədər pròw ləjìdəmèyshiyówniy p(y)ùwərórəm/. The presumption always is in favor of the legitimacy of children.

Semper præsumitur pro matrimonio /sémpər prəz(y)úwmədər pròw mætrəmówn(i)yow/. The presumption is always in favor of the validity of a marriage.

Semper præsumitur pro negante /sémpər prəz(y)úwmədər pròw nəgǽntiy/. The presumption is always in favor of the one who denies.

Semper præsumitur pro sententia /sémpər prəz(y)úwmədər pròw senténsh(iy)ə/. The presumption always is in favor of a sentence.

Semper qui non prohibet pro se intervenire, mandare creditur /sémpər kwày nòn prów(h)əbət pròw síy ìntərvənáyriy, mændériy krédədər/. He who does not prohibit the intervention of another in his behalf is supposed to authorize it.

Semper sexus masculinus etiam femininum sexum continet /sémpər séksəs mæskyəláynəs íysh(iy)əm fèmənáynəm séksəm kóntənət/. The masculine sex always includes the feminine.

Semper specialia generalibus insunt /sémpər spèshiyéyl(i)yə jènəréyləbəs ínsənt/. Specials are always included in generals.

Senage /síynəj/. Money paid for synodals.

Senate. The name of the upper chamber, or less numerous branch, of the Congress of the United States. Also the name of a similar body in the legislatures of most of the states.

The U.S. Senate is composed of 100 Members, 2 from each State, who are elected to serve for a term of 6 years. Senators were originally chosen by the State legislatures. This procedure was changed by the Seventeenth Amendment to the Constitution, adopted in 1913, which made the election of Senators a function of the people. One-third of the Senate is elected every 2 years.

Senator. One who is a member of a senate, either of the United States or of a state. See **Seventeenth Amendment.**

Senatus /sənéydəs/. Lat. In Roman law, the senate; the great national council of the Roman people. The place where the senate met.

Senatus consultum /sənéydəs kən(t)sáltəm/. In Roman law, a decision or decree of the Roman senate, having the force of law, made without the concurrence of the people. These enactments began to take the place of laws enacted by popular vote, when the commons had grown so great in number that they could no longer be assembled for legislative purposes.

Senatus consultum ultimæ necessitatis /sənéydəs kən(t)sáltəm nəsèsətéydəs/. A decree of the senate of the last necessity. The name given to the decree which usually preceded the nomination of a dictator. 1 Bl.Comm. 136.

Senatus decreta /sənéydəs dəkríydə/. Lat. In the civil law, decisions of the senate. Private acts concerning particular persons merely.

Send. Term in connection with any writing or notice means to deposit in the mail or deliver for transmission by any other usual means of communication with postage or cost of transmission provided for and properly addressed and in the case of an instrument to an address specified thereon or otherwise agreed, or if there be none, to any address reasonable under the circumstances. The receipt of any writing or notice within the time at which it would have arrived if properly sent has the effect of a proper sending. U.C.C. § 1–201(38).

Senescallus /sènəskǽləs/. In old English law, a sene schal; a steward; the steward of a manor.

Seneschal /sénəshəl/. In old European law, a title of office and dignity, derived from the middle ages, answering to that of steward or high steward in England. Seneschals were originally the lieutenants of the dukes and other great feudatories of the kingdom, and sometimes had the dispensing of justice and high military commands.

Senility /sənílədiy/. Quality of being senile; an infirmity resulting from deterioration of mind and body experienced in old age. Feebleness of body and mind incident to old age; and an incapacity to contract arising from the impairment of the intellectual faculties by old age.

Senior. The elder. An addition to the name of the elder of two persons in the same family having the same name.

Senior counsel. Of two or more counsel retained on the same side of a cause, he is the "senior" who is the elder, or more important in rank or estimation, or who is charged with the more difficult or important parts of the management of the case. May also refer to "lead" counsel in a class or multi-district action.

Senior interest. An interest or right that takes effect or has preference over that of others; _e.g._ a person with a perfected security interest has a senior interest over other security holders in same property.

Seniority. Precedence or preference in position over others similarly situated. As used with reference to job seniority, worker with most years of service is first promoted within range of jobs subject to seniority, and is the last laid off, proceeding so on down the line to the youngest in point of service. Dooley v. Lehigh Valley R. Co. of Pennsylvania, 130 N.J.Eq. 75, 21 A.2d 334, 338, 339. Term may also refer to the priority of a lien or encumbrance. See also **Dovetail seniority; Priority.**

Senior judge. Of several judges composing a court, the one who holds the oldest commission, or who has served the longest time under his present commission; _e.g._ senior judge of U.S. District Court or Court of Appeals.

Senior lien. A prior lien which has precedence as to the property under the lien over another lien or encumbrance.

Senior mortgage. A mortgage which is of superior priority; above those which are often referred to as junior mortgages.

Sensus /sén(t)səs/. Lat. Sense, meaning, signification. _Malo sensu_, in an evil or derogatory sense. _Mitiori sensu_, in a milder, less severe, or less stringent sense. _Sensu honesto_, in an honest sense; to interpret words

sensu honesto is to take them so as not to impute impropriety to the persons concerned.

Sensus verborum est anima legis /sén(t)səs vərbórəm èst ǽnəmə líyjəs/. The meaning of the words is the spirit of the law.

Sensus verborum est duplex—mitis et asper; et verba semper accipienda sunt in mitiori sensu /sén(t)səs vərbórəm èst d(y)úwpleks—máydəs èd ǽspər, èt várbə sémpər əksipiyéndə sànt in mìshiyóray sén(t)s(y)uw/. The meaning of words is twofold,—mild and harsh; and words are always to be received in their milder sense.

Sensus verborum ex causa dicendi accipiendus est; et sermones semper accipiendi sunt secundum subjectam materiam /sén(t)səs vərbórəm èks kózə dəsénday əksìpiyéndəs èst; èt sərmówniyz sémpər əksìpiyénday sànt səkándəm səbjéktəm mətíriyəm/. The sense of words is to be taken from the occasion of speaking them; and discourses are always to be interpreted according to the subject-matter.

Sentence. The judgment formally pronounced by the court or judge upon the defendant after his conviction in a criminal prosecution, imposing the punishment to be inflicted. Judgment formally declaring to accused legal consequences of guilt which he has confessed or of which he has been convicted. The word is properly confined to this meaning. In _civil_ cases, the terms "judgment," "decision," "award," "finding," etc., are used. Archer v. Snook, D.C.Ga., 10 F.2d 567, 569.

For review of sentence of federal prisoner, see **Post-conviction review.**

See also Accumulative sentence; Commutation; Concurrent sentences; Consecutive sentences; Cumulative sentence; Definite sentence; Diversion program; Pardon; Pre-sentence hearing; Pre-sentence investigation; Pre-sentence report; Probation; Punishment; Reprieve; Sentencing; Split sentence; Suspended sentence.

Concurrent sentence. A sentence imposed which is to be served at the same time as another sentence imposed earlier or at the same proceeding.

Consecutive sentence. See _Cumulative sentences, infra._

Cumulative sentences. Separate sentences (each additional to the others) imposed upon a defendant who has been convicted upon an indictment containing several counts, each of such counts charging a distinct offense, or who is under conviction at the same time for several distinct offenses; one of such sentences being made to begin at the expiration of another. Carter v. McClaughry, 183 U.S. 365, 22 S.Ct. 181, 46 L.Ed. 236.

Deferred sentence. A sentence, the execution of which is postponed until a future time.

Determinate sentence. A sentence for a fixed period of time. See _Fixed sentence._

Ecclesiastical sentence. In ecclesiastical procedure, analogous to "judgment" _(q.v.)_ in an ordinary action.

Final sentence. One which puts an end to a case. Distinguished from interlocutory.

A definite sentence is one which puts an end to the suit, and regards the principal matter in question as concluded. An interlocutory sentence determines only some incidental matter in the proceedings.

Fixed sentence. Fixed sentencing statutes specify the exact penalty that will follow conviction of each offense. See *Mandatory sentence, infra.*

Indeterminate sentence. A form of sentence to imprisonment upon conviction of crime, authorized by statute in several states, which, instead of fixing rigidly the duration of the imprisonment, declares that it shall be for a period "not less than" so many years "nor more than" so many years, or not less than the minimum period prescribed by statute as the punishment for the particular offense nor more than the maximum period, the exact length of the term being afterwards fixed, within the limits assigned by the court or the statute, by an executive authority (the governor, board of pardons, etc.), on consideration of the previous record of the convict, his behavior while in prison or while out on parole, the apparent prospect of reformation and other such considerations. See also *Presumptive sentence, infra.*

A sentence to incarceration with a spread of time between a minimum date of parole eligibility and a maximum discharge date. A completely indeterminate sentence has a minimum of one day and a maximum of natural life.

Interlocutory sentence. In the civil law, a sentence on some indirect question arising from the principal cause.

Life sentence. The disposition of a serious criminal case (*e.g.* capital offenses) by which the convicted defendant is sentenced to spend the rest of his natural life in prison.

Mandatory sentence. Statutes in some jurisdictions require a judge to sentence a convicted defendant to a penal institution and furnish no room for discretion. These statutes generally provide that the sentence may not be suspended and that no probation may be imposed, leaving the judge with no alternative but commitment. See *Fixed sentence, supra.*

Maximum sentence. A maximum sentence sets the outer limit beyond which a prisoner cannot be held in custody.

Merger of sentences. See **Merger.**

Minimum sentence. The minimum time which an offender must spend in prison before becoming eligible for parole or release.

Presumptive sentence. Presumptive sentencing statutes specify a "normal" sentence for each offense but permit limited departures from the norm in atypical cases. See also *Indeterminate sentence, supra.*

Sentence in abstentia. Sentencing of defendant in his absence.

Straight or flat sentence. Fixed sentence without a maximum or minimum.

Suspension of sentence. This term may mean either a withholding or postponing the sentencing of a prisoner after the conviction, or a postponing of the execution of the sentence after it has been pronounced. In the latter case, it may, for reasons addressing themselves to the discretion of the court, be indefinite as to time, or during the good behavior of the prisoner. See **Suspended sentence.**

Withheld sentence. Sentence not imposed.

Sentencing. The postconviction stage of the criminal justice process in which the defendant is brought before the court for imposition of sentence. Usually a trial judge imposes sentence, but in some jurisdictions sentencing is performed by jury or by sentencing councils.

Sentencing has been held to be a "critical stage" of a criminal proceeding requiring assistance of appointed counsel. Mempa v. Rhay, 389 U.S. 128, 88 S.Ct. 254, 19 L.Ed.2d 336.

Imposition of sentence. Sentence shall be imposed without unreasonable delay. Before imposing sentence, the court shall afford counsel an opportunity to speak on behalf of the defendant and shall address the defendant personally and ask him if he wishes to make a statement in his own behalf and to present any information in mitigation of punishment. The attorney for the government shall have an equivalent opportunity to speak to the court. Fed.R.Crim.P. 32(a).

Sentencing council. A panel of three or more judges which confers to determine a criminal sentence. Sentencing councils are not as commonly used as sentencing by a trial judge.

Sententia /senténsh(iy)ə/. Lat. In the civil law, sense; import; as distinguished from mere words. The deliberate expression of one's will or intention. The sentence of a judge or court.

Sententia a non judice lata nemini debet nocere /senténsh(iy)ə èy nòn júwdəsiy léydə némənay débət nəsíriy/. A sentence pronounced by one who is not a judge should not harm any one.

Sententia contra matrimonium numquam transit in rem judicatam /senténsh(iy)ə kóntrə mætrəmówn(i)yəm námkwæm træn(d)zət ìn rém jùwdəkéydəm/. A sentence against marriage never becomes a matter finally adjudged, *i.e., res judicata.*

Sententia facit jus, et legis interpretatio legis vim obtinet /senténsh(iy)ə féysət jás, èt líyjəs intərprətéysh(iy)ow líyjəs vím óbtənət/. Judgment creates right, and the interpretation of the law has the force of law.

Sententia facit jus, et res judicata pro veritate accipitur /senténsh(iy)ə féysət jás, èt ríyz jùwdəkéydə pròw vèhrətéydiy əksípədər/. Judgment creates right, and what is adjudicated is taken for truth.

Sententia interlocutoria revocari potest, definitiva non potest /senténsh(iy)ə interlòk(y)ətór(i)yə rìyvəkéray pówdəst, dəfinətáyvə nòn pówdəst/. An interlocutory judgment may be recalled, but not a final.

Sententia non fertur de rebus non liquidis /senténsh(iy)ə nòn fárdər dìy ríybəs nòn líkwədəs/. Sentence is not given upon matters that are not clear.

Separability clause. A clause commonly found in contracts which provides that in the event that one or more provisions are declared void the balance of the contract remains in force. Such a provision is also commonly found in legislation.   See also **Saving clause.**

Separable.   Capable of being separated, disjoined, or divided.   In re Babcock, 27 C.C.P.A. 1097, 110 F.2d 665, 667.

Separable controversy.   With respect to removal of case from state to federal court, 28 U.S.C.A. § 1441(c) provides: "Whenever a separate and independent claim or cause of action, which would be removable if sued upon alone, is joined with one or more otherwise non-removable claims or causes of action, the entire case may be removed and the district court may determine all issues therein, or, in its discretion, may remand all matters not otherwise within its original jurisdiction."   See American Fire & Casualty Company v. Finn, 341 U.S. 6, 71 S.Ct. 534, 95 L.Ed. 702.

Separaliter /sèpəréylədər/.   Lat.   Separately.   Used in indictments to indicate that two or more defendants were charged separately, and not jointly, with the commission of the offense in question.

Separate, *v.*   To disunite, divide, disconnect, or sever.   See **Sever.**

Separate.   Individual; distinct; particular; disconnected.   Generally used in law as opposed to "joint," though the more usual antithesis of the latter term is "several."   Either of these words implies division, distribution, disconnection, or aloofness.   As to separate Acknowledgment and Covenant, see those titles.

Separate action.   As opposed to a *joint* action, an action brought for himself alone by each of several complainants who are all concerned in the same transaction, but cannot legally join in the suit.   See also **Joinder; Separate trial.**

Separate but equal doctrine.   The doctrine first enunciated in Plessy v. Ferguson, 163 U.S. 537, 16 S.Ct. 1138, 41 L.Ed. 256, to the effect that equality of treatment is accorded when the races are provided substantially equal facilities even though these facilities be separate.   This rule was declared to be unconstitutional with respect to educational facilities in Brown v. Board of Education, etc., 347 U.S. 483, 74 S.Ct. 686, 98 L.Ed. 873, and as to other public facilities by other Supreme Court decisions and Civil Rights Acts.

Separate demise in ejectment.   A demise in a declaration in ejectment used to be termed a "separate demise" when made by the lessor separately or individually, as distinguished from a demise made jointly by two or more persons, which was termed a "joint demise."   No such demise, either separate or joint, is now necessary in this action.

Separate estate.   The individual property of one of two persons who stand in a marital or business relation, as distinguished from that which they own jointly or are jointly interested in.   See also **Community property; Separate property.**

Separate examination.   The interrogation of a married woman, who appears before an officer for the purpose of acknowledging a deed or other instrument, conducted by such officer in private or out of the hearing of her husband in order to ascertain if she acts of her own will and without compulsion or constraint of the husband.   Also the examination of a witness in private or apart from, and out of the hearing of, the other witnesses in the same cause.

Separate maintenance.   Allowance granted to a wife for support of herself and children while she is living apart from her husband.   Cohn v. Cohn, 4 Wash.2d 322, 103 P.2d 366, 367.   Money paid by one married person to the other for support if they are no longer living as husband and wife.   See also **Alimony; Support.**

Separate offenses.   A person may be tried, convicted and sentenced for offenses which, though sharing many elements, are distinct.   A particular act may offend more than one law and hence a person may be subjected to more than one punishment for acts arising out of the same event.

Separate property.   Property owned by married person in his or her own right during marriage.   The real and personal property, including wages and earnings, of a woman which she owns at the time of her marriage, and the real and personal property, and the rents, issues and profits thereof, of a married woman, which she receives or obtains in any manner whatever after her marriage, shall be her separate property as if she were a *feme sole.*   N.J.S.A. 37:2–12, 37:2–13.

Community property.   In a community property jurisdiction, separate property is that property which belongs entirely to one of the spouses.   Generally, it is property acquired before marriage or acquired after marriage by gift or inheritance.   For purposes of community property settlement, "separate property" is that which either party brings into the marriage, acquires during the marriage with separate funds, or receives by inheritance or particular donation.   Langlinais v. David, La.App., 289 So.2d 343, 345.   See also **Community property.**

Separate return.   See **Tax return.**

Separate trial.   The separate and individual trial of each of several persons jointly accused of a crime.   Court may also order separate trials in civil actions (*e.g.* Fed.R.Civil P. 42) in furtherance of convenience or to avoid prejudice, or when separate trials will be conducive to expedition and economy.

Separatim /sèpəréydəm/.   Lat.   In old conveyancing, severally.   A word which made a several covenant.

Separation agreement.   Written arrangements concerning custody, child support, alimony and property division made by a married couple who are usually about to get a divorce or legal separation.

Separation a mensa et thoro /sèpəréyshən èy mén(t)sə èt θórow/.   A partial dissolution of the marriage relation.

Separation from bed and board.   A species of separation not amounting to a dissolution of the marriage.   Same as separation a mensa et thoro (*q.v.*).

Separation of jury.   After a case has been given to the jury for deliberation, they are not permitted to separate until a verdict is reached except under the control of the court through officers and sheriffs.   In civil cases in some jurisdictions this rule is relaxed generally with admonition from the judge not to discuss the case with anybody. See also **Sequester.**

Separation of patrimony. In Louisiana probate law, the creditors of the succession may demand, in every case and against every creditor of the heir, a separation of the property of the succession from that of the heir. This is what is called the "separation of patrimony." The object of a separation of patrimony is to prevent property out of which a particular class of creditors have a right to be paid from being confounded with other property, and by that means made liable to the debts of another class of creditors.

Separation of powers. The governments of states and the United States are divided into three departments or branches: the legislative, which is empowered to make laws, the executive which is required to carry out the laws, and the judicial which is charged with interpreting the laws and adjudicating disputes under the laws. One branch is not permitted to encroach on the domain of another. See also **Power** *(Constitutional).*

Separation of spouses. A cessation of cohabitation of husband and wife by mutual agreement, or, in the case of "judicial separation," under the decree of a court. Separation of spouses for a statutorily prescribed period is a prerequisite to "no-fault" divorce in many states. See also **Living separate and apart; Separation order.**

Separation of witnesses. An order of the court requiring all witnesses, except the plaintiff and defendant, to remain outside the courtroom until each is called to testify.

Separation order. A decree or judgment of a court authorizing spouses to separate and generally included is an order respecting custody of children and support.

Sequamur vestigia patrum nostrorum /səkwéymər vestíj(iy)ə pǽtrəm nostrórəm/. Let us follow the footsteps of our fathers.

Sequatur sub suo periculo /səkwéydər sə̀b s(y)úwow pərík(y)əlow/. In old English practice, a writ which issued where a sheriff had returned *nihil,* upon a *summoneas ad warrantizandum,* and after an *alias* and *pluries* had been issued. So called because the tenant lost his lands without any recovery in value, unless upon that writ he brought the vouchee into court.

Sequela /səkwíylə/. L. Lat. In old English law, suit; process or prosecution. *Sequela causœ,* the process of a cause.

Sequela curiæ /səkwíylə kyúriyiy/. Suit of court.

Sequela villanorum /səkwíylə vìlənórəm/. The family retinue and appurtenances to the goods and chattels of villeins, which were at the absolute disposal of the lord.

Sequester, *v.* To separate or isolate; *e.g.* to sequester jurors is to isolate them from contact with the public during the course of a sensational trial. See **Jury.**

Civil law. To renounce or disclaim, etc.; as, for example, when a widow came into court and disclaimed having anything to do with her deceased husband's estate, she was said to sequester. The word more commonly signifies the act of taking in execution under a writ of sequestration.

To deposit a thing which is the subject of a controversy in the hands of a third person, to hold for the contending parties.

To take a thing which is the subject of a controversy out of the possession of the contending parties, and deposit it in the hands of a third person.

Equity practice. To take possession of the property of a defendant, and hold it in the custody of the court, until he purges himself of a contempt.

International law. To confiscate; to appropriate private property to public use; to seize the property of the private citizens of a hostile power, as when a belligerent nation sequesters debts due from its own subjects to the enemy.

Sequester, *n.* /səkwéstər/. Lat. In the civil law, a person with whom two or more contending parties deposited the subject-matter of the controversy.

Sequestered account. In accounting, an account which has been ordered separated and impounded by order of the court. No disbursements may be made from this account without order of the court.

Sequestrari facias /sèkwəstréray féysh(iy)əs/. In English ecclesiastical practice, a process in the nature of a *levari facias,* commanding the bishop to enter into the rectory and parish church, and to take and sequester the same, and hold them until, of the rents, tithes, and profits thereof, and of the other ecclesiastical goods of a defendant, he having levied the plaintiff's debt. 3 Bl.Comm. 418.

Sequestratio /sèkwəstréysh(iy)ow/. Lat. In the civil law, the separating or setting aside of a thing in controversy, from the possession of both parties that contend for it. It is two-fold,—*voluntary,* done by consent of all parties; and *necessary,* when a judge orders it.

Sequestration /sèkwəstréyshən/siỳ°/. In general, the process by which property or funds are attached pending the outcome of litigation. See also **Sequester.**

Contracts. A species of deposit which two or more persons, engaged in litigation about anything, make of the thing in contest with an indifferent person who binds himself to restore it, when the issue is decided, to the party to whom it is adjudged to belong. Civ. Code La. art. 2973.

English ecclesiastical law. The act of the ordinary in disposing of the goods and chattels of one deceased, whose estate no one claims.

Equity practice. A writ authorizing the taking into the custody of the law of the real and personal estate (or rents, issues, and profits) of a defendant who is in contempt, and holding the same until he shall comply.

International law. The seizure of the property of an individual, and the appropriation of it to the use of the government. Expropriation.

Sequestrator /sékwəstrèydər/síy°/. One to whom a sequestration is made. One appointed or chosen to perform a sequestration, or execute a writ of sequestration.

Sequestro habendo /səkwéstrow həbéndow/. In English ecclesiastical law, a judicial writ for discharging of a sequestration of the profits of a church benefice, granted by the bishop at the sovereign's command, thereby to compel the parson to appear at the suit of another. Upon his appearance, the parson may have this writ for the release of the sequestration.

Sequi debet potentia justitiam non præcedere /síykway débət pəténsh(iy)ə jəstísh(iy)əm nòn prəsíydəriy/. Power should follow justice, not precede it.

Serf. In the feudal polity, a class of persons whose social condition was servile, and who were bound to labor and perform onerous duties at the will of their lords. They differed from slaves only in that they were bound to their native soil, instead of being the absolute property of a master.

Sergeant. Noncommissioned officer in armed forces. Officer in police force with rank below captain or lieutenant.

Sergeant-at-arms. Officer appointed by, and attending on, a legislative body or court, whose principal duties are to preserve order during the sessions of such body.

Serial bonds. A serial bond issue consists of a number of bonds issued at the same time but with different maturity dates (serially due), usually with interest rates varying for the different maturity dates. To be distinguished from the *series bonds (q.v.)*. An issue of bonds that mature in part on one date, another part on another date, and so on; the various maturity dates usually are equally spaced.

Serial note. A promissory note payable in installments.

Serial right. A right reserved in a publishing contract between author and publisher giving the author or publisher the right to have the manuscript published in installments in a magazine or periodical before or after the publication of the book.

Seriately /síhriyətliy/. In series, or following one after another. In re Flint, 32 C.C.P.A. 1116, 150 F.2d 126, 131.

Seriatim /sìriyéydəm/. Lat. Severally; separately; individually; one by one.

Series bonds. Groups of bonds (for example, series A, series B) usually issued at different times and with different maturities but under the authority of the same indenture. To be distinguished from *serial bonds (q.v.)*.

Serious. Important; weighty; momentous, grave, great, as in the phrases "serious bodily harm," "serious personal injury," etc.

Serious and wilful misconduct. In worker's compensation law, the intentional doing of something with the knowledge that it is likely to result in a serious injury, or with a wanton and reckless disregard of its probable consequences.

Serious crime. For purpose of determining right to jury trial, crimes carrying more than six-month sentences are "serious crimes" and those carrying less are "petty crimes." Maita v. Whitmore, C.A.Cal., 508 F.2d 143, 145.

Serious illness. In life insurance, an illness that permanently or materially impairs, or is likely to permanently or materially impair, the health of the applicant. Not every illness is serious. An illness may be alarming at the time, or thought to be serious by the one afflicted, and yet not be serious in the sense of that term as used in insurance contracts. An illness that is temporary in its duration, and entirely passes away, and is not attended, nor likely to be attended, by a permanent or material impairment of the health or constitution, is not a serious illness. It is not sufficient that the illness was thought serious at the time it occurred, or that it might have resulted in permanently impairing the health.

Serjeant-at-arms. See **Sergeant-at-arms.**

Serjeanty /sárjəntiy/. A species of tenure by knight service, which was due to the king only, and was distinguished into grand and petit serjeanty. The tenant holding by *grand* serjeanty was bound, instead of attending the king generally in his wars, to do some honorary service to the king in person, as to carry his banner or sword, or to be his butler, champion, or other officer at his coronation. *Petit* serjeanty differed from grand serjeanty, in that the service rendered to the king was not of a personal nature, but consisted in rendering him annually some small implement of war, as a bow, sword, arrow, lance, or the like.

Serment /sármənt/. In old English law, oath; an oath.

Sermo index animi /sármow índeks ǽnəmay/. Speech is an index of the mind.

Sermones semper accipiendi sunt secundum subjectam materiam, et conditionem personarum /sərmówniyz sémpər əksìpiyénday sànt səkándəm səbjéktəm mətíriyəm/. Language is always to be understood according to its subject-matter, and the condition of the persons.

Sermo relatus ad personam intelligi debet de conditione personæ /sármow rəléydəs æd pərsównəm intéləjay débət dìy kəndìshiyówniy pərsówniy/. Language which is referred to a person ought to be understood of the condition of the person.

Serological test. A laboratory test required in many states to determine the presence of venereal disease prior to marriage.

Serrated. Notched on the edge; cut in notches like the teeth of a saw. This was anciently the method of trimming the top or edge of a deed of indenture. See **Indent, v.**

Servage /sárvəj/. In feudal law, where a tenant, besides payment of a certain rent, found one or more workmen for his lord's service.

Servanda est consuetudo loci ubi causa agitur /sərvǽndə èst kònswət(y)úwdow lówsay yúwbay kózə ǽjədər/. The custom of the place where the action is brought is to be observed.

Servant. One employed to perform service in master's affairs, whose physical conduct in performance of the service is controlled or is subject to right to control by the master. Brenner v. Socony Vacuum Oil Co., 236 Mo.App. 524, 158 S.W.2d 171, 174, 175; Reiling v. Missouri Ins. Co., 236 Mo.App. 164, 153 S.W.2d 79; Restatement, Second, Agency, § 2. A person in the employ of another and subject to his control as to what work shall be done and the means by which it shall be accomplished. Pantell v. Shriver Allison Co., 61 Ohio App. 119, 22 N.E.2d 497, 499. One who is employed to render personal service to another otherwise than in the pursuit of an independent calling, and who, in such service, remains entirely under control and direction of employer. Henley v. State, 59 Ga.App. 595, 2 S.E.2d 139, 142. A person of whatever rank or position in employ and subject to direction or control of another in any department of labor or business. A servant, for purposes of doctrine of vicarious liability, is one who is employed to perform services for another, and who is subject to such other's "control" or "right to control" as regards his physical conduct in the performance of such services. Gifford-Hill & Co. v. Moore, Tex.Civ.App., 479 S.W.2d 711, 714.

The term is often given special meanings by statutes and like other words is greatly influenced by context in wills and other documents.

See also **Agent; Employee; Fellow servant; Subservant.**

Servi /sɔ́rvay/. Lat. Slaves. In old English law, bondmen; servile tenants; persons over whom their masters had absolute dominion.

Service. This term has a variety of meanings, dependent upon the context or the sense in which used. Central Power & Light Co. v. State, Tex.Civ.App., 165 S.W.2d 920, 925.

Contracts. Duty or labor to be rendered by one person to another, the former being bound to submit his will to the direction and control of the latter. The act of serving the labor performed or the duties required. Occupation, condition, or status of a servant, etc. Performance of labor for benefit of another, or at another's command; attendance of an inferior, hired helper, etc. Claxton v. Johnson County, 194 Ga. 43, 20 S.E.2d 606, 610. "Service" and "employment" generally imply that the employer, or person to whom the service is due, both selects and compensates the employee, or person rendering the service.

The term is used also for employment in one of the offices, departments, or agencies of the government; as in the phrases "civil service," "public service," "military service," etc.

Domestic relations. The "services" of a wife, for the loss of which occasioned by an injury to the wife, the husband may recover in an action against the tortfeasor include whatever of aid, assistance, comfort, and society the wife would be expected to render to bestow upon her husband in the circumstances in which they were situated. See **Consortium.**

Feudal law. The consideration which the feudal tenants were bound to render to the lord in recompense for the lands they held of him. The services, in respect of their quality, were either free or base

services, and, in respect of their quantity and the time of exacting them, were either certain or uncertain. 2 Bl.Comm. 60.

Practice. The exhibition or delivery of a writ, summons and complaint, criminal summons, notice, order, etc., by an authorized person, to a person who is thereby officially notified of some action or proceeding in which he is concerned, and is thereby advised or warned of some action or step which he is commanded to take or to forbear. Fed.R.Civil Proc. 4 and 5; Fed.R.Crim.P. 4 and 49. Pleadings, motions, orders, etc., after the initial summons are normally served on the party's attorney unless otherwise ordered by court. See *Service of process,* below.

General Classification

Civil service. See that title.

Public utilities. The furnishing of water, heat, light and power, etc., by utility. Claxton v. Johnson County, 194 Ga. 43, 20 S.E.2d 606, 610.

Salvage service. See **Salvage.**

Secular service. Worldly employment or service, as contrasted with spiritual or ecclesiastical.

Service of process. The service of writs, summonses, etc., signifies the delivering to or leaving them with the party to whom or with whom they ought to be delivered or left; and, when they are so delivered, they are then said to have been served. Usually a copy only is served and the original is shown. The service must furnish reasonable notice to defendant of proceedings to afford him opportunity to appear and be heard. Chemical Specialties Sales Corp. Industrial Div. v. Basic Inc., D.C.Conn., 296 F.Supp. 1106, 1107. Fed.R.Civil P. 4; Fed.R.Crim.P. 4. The various types of service of process are as follows:

Constructive service of process. Any form of service other than actual personal service. Notification of an action or of some proceeding therein, given to a person affected by sending it to him in the mails or causing it to be published in a newspaper. Fed.R.Civil P. 4(e). See also *Service by publication; Substituted service,* below.

Long arm statutes. Laws enacted in most states which permit courts to acquire personal jurisdiction of non-residents by virtue of activity within the state. See **Foreign service; Long arm statutes; Minimal contacts.**

Personal service. Actual delivery of process to person to whom it is directed or to someone authorized to receive it in his behalf. Green Mountain College v. Levine, 120 Vt. 332, 139 A.2d 822, 824. Personal service is made by delivering a copy of the summons and complaint to the person named or by leaving copies thereof at his dwelling or usual place of abode with some responsible person or by delivering a copy to an agent authorized to receive such. Special rules are also provided for service on infants, incompetents, corporations, the United States or officers or agencies thereof, etc. Fed.R.Civil P. 4(d); Fed.R.Crim.P. 4(d).

Proof of service. See **Proof.**

Service by publication. Service of a summons or other process upon an absent or nonresident defendant, by publishing the same as an advertisement in a designated newspaper, with such other efforts to give him actual notice as the particular statute may prescribe. See also *Substituted service,* below.

Substituted service. Any form of service of process other than personal service, such as service by mail or by publication in a newspaper; service of a writ or notice on some person other than the one directly concerned, for example, his attorney of record, who has authority to represent him or to accept service for him. See also **Long arm statutes.**

Service charge. That charge assessed by bank against the expense of maintaining a customer's demand deposit or checking account, and is calculated on basis of a formula whereby bank's cost of maintaining account for customer is determined. U. S. v. First Nat. Bank of Jackson, D.C.Miss., 301 F.Supp. 1161, 1207.

"Credit service charge" means the sum of (1) all charges payable directly or indirectly by the buyer and imposed directly or indirectly by the seller as an incident to the extension of credit, including any of the following types of charges which are applicable: time price differential, service, carrying or other charge, however denominated, premium or other charge for any guarantee or insurance protecting the seller against the buyer's default or other credit loss; and (2) charges incurred for investigating the collateral or credit-worthiness of the buyer or for commissions or brokerage for obtaining the credit, irrespective of the person to whom the charges are paid or payable, unless the seller had no notice of the charges when the credit was granted. Uniform Consumer Credit Code, § 2.109.

Service contract. A written agreement to perform maintenance or repair service on a consumer product for a specified duration. 15 U.S.C.A. § 2301.

Service establishment. Within Fair Labor Standards Act, an establishment which has ordinary characteristics of retail establishments except that services instead of goods are sold. An establishment the principal activity of which is to furnish service to the consuming public, and includes barber shops, beauty parlors, shoe shining parlors, clothes pressing clubs, laundries and automobile repair shops. Fleming v. A. B. Kirschbaum Co., C.C.A.Pa., 124 F.2d 567, 572.

Service life. Period of expected usefulness of an asset; such may not necessarily coincide with depreciable life for income tax purposes.

Service mark. A mark used in the sale or advertising of services to identify the services of one person and distinguish them from the services of others. Titles, character names and other distinctive features of radio or television programs may be registered as service marks notwithstanding that they, or the programs, may advertise the goods of the sponsor. 15 U.S.C.A. § 1127.

Service occupation tax. Tax imposed on persons making sales of service and is computed as a percentage of net cost to servicemen of tangible personal property transferred as an incident to such sale. Hagerty v. General Motors Corp., 14 Ill.App.3d 33, 302 N.E.2d 678, 681.

Service of process. See **Service.**

Servicing. See **Service charge.**

Serviens narrator /sə́rv(i)yen(d)z nəréydər/. A serjeant-at-law *(q.v.).*

Servient /sə́rv(i)yənt/. Serving; subject to a service or servitude. A *servient* estate is one which is burdened with a servitude.

Servient tenement /sə́rv(i)yənt ténəmənt/. An estate in respect of which a service is owing, as the *dominant tenement* is that to which the service is due. Northwestern Improvement Co. v. Lowry, 104 Mont. 289, 66 P.2d 792, 795. An estate burdened with a servitude. Most commonly a parcel of land burdened by an easement for the benefit of another parcel (dominant tenement).

Servitia personalia sequuntur personam /sərvísh(iy)ə pə̀rsənéyl(i)yə səkwə́ntər pərsównəm/. Personal services follow the person.

Servitiis acquietandis /sərvísh(iy)əs əkwàyətǽndəs/. A judicial writ for a man distrained for services to one, when he owes and performs them to another, for the acquittal of such services.

Servitium /sərvísh(iy)əm/. Lat. In feudal and old English law, the duty of obedience and performance which a tenant was bound to render to his lord, by reason of his fee.

Servitium feodale et prædiale /sərvísh(iy)əm fyuwdéyliy èt prediyéyliy/. A personal service, but due only by reason of lands which were held in fee.

Servitium forinsecum /sərvísh(iy)əm fərín(d)zəkəm/. Forinsec, foreign, or extra service; a kind of service that was due to the king, over and above *(foris)* the service due to the lord.

Servitium, in lege Angilæ, regulariter accipitur pro servitio quod per tenentes dominis suis debetur ratione feodi sui /sərvísh(iy)əm, ìn líyjiy ǽngliyiy, règyəlérədər əksípədər pròw sərvísh(iy)ow kwòd pə̀r tənéntiyz dómənəs s(y)úwəs dəbíydər ræ̀shiyówniy fyúwday s(y)úway/. Service, by the law of England, means the service which is due from the tenants to the lords, by reason of their fee.

Servitium intrinsecum /sərvísh(iy)əm intrín(d)zəkəm/. Intrainsic or ordinary service; the ordinary service due the chief lord, from tenants within the fee.

Servitium liberum /sərvísh(iy)əm líbərəm/. A service to be done by feudatory tenants, who were called *"liberi homines,"* and distinguished from vassals, as was their service, for they were not bound to any of the base services of plowing the lord's land, etc., but were to find a man and horse, or go with the lord into the army, or to attend the court, etc. See also **Liberum servitium.**

Servitium regale /sərvísh(iy)əm rəgéyliy/. Royal service, or the rights and prerogatives of manors which belong to the king as lord of the same, and which were generally reckoned to be six, viz.: Power of judicature, in matters of property; power of life and death, in felonies and murder; a right to waifs and strays; assessments; minting of money; and assise of bread, beer, weights, and measures.

Servitium scuti /sərvísh(iy)əm sk(y)úwday/. Service of the shield; that is, knight-service.

Servitium socæ /sərvísh(iy)əm sówsiy/. Service of the plow; that is, socage.

Servitors of bills /sárvədərz əv bílz/. In old English practice, servants or messengers of the marshal of the king's bench, sent out with bills or writs to summon persons to that court. Thereafter commonly called "tipstaves."

Servitude. The state of a person who is subjected, voluntarily or otherwise, to another person as his servant. A charge or burden resting upon one estate for the benefit or advantage of another; a species of incorporeal right derived from the civil law (see Servitus) and closely corresponding to the "easement" of the common-law, except that "servitude" rather has relation to the burden or the estate burdened, while "easement" refers to the benefit or advantage or the estate to which it accrues.

Classification

All servitudes which affect lands may be divided into two kinds,—*personal* and *real*. Personal servitudes are those attached to the person for whose benefit they are established, and terminate with his life. This kind of servitude is of three sorts,—usufruct, use, and habitation. Real servitudes, which are also called "predial" or "landed" servitudes, are those which the owner of an estate enjoys on a neighboring estate for the benefit of his own estate. They are called "predial" or "landed" servitudes because, being established for the benefit of an estate, they are rather due to the estate than to the owner personally. Frost-Johnson Lumber Co. v. Salling's Heirs, 150 La. 756, 91 So. 207, 245; Tide-Water Pipe Co. v. Bell, 280 Pa. 104, 124 A. 351, 354.

Real servitudes are divided, in the civil law, into *rural* and *urban* servitudes. Rural servitudes are such as are established for the benefit of a landed estate; such, for example, as a right of way over the servient tenement, or of access to a spring, a coalmine, a sand-pit, or a wood that is upon it. Urban servitudes are such as are established for the benefit of one building over another. (But the buildings need not be in the city, as the name would apparently imply.) They are such as the right of support, or of view, sewer, or the like.

Servitudes are also classed as *positive* and *negative*. A positive servitude is one which obliges the owner of the servient estate to permit or suffer something to be done on his property by another. A negative servitude is one which does not bind the servient proprietor to permit something to be done upon his property by another, but merely restrains him from making a certain use of his property which would impair the easement enjoyed by the dominant tenement. Rowe v. Nally, 81 Md. 367, 32 A. 198.

Involuntary servitude. See that title.

Servitus /sárvədəs/. Lat. In the civil law, slavery; bondage; the state of service. An institution of the conventional law of nations, by which one person is subjected to the dominion of another, contrary to natural right.

Also a service or servitude; an easement.

Servitus actus /sárvədəs ǽktəs/. The servitude or right of walking, riding, or driving over another's ground. A species of right of way.

Servitus altius non tollendi /sárvədəs ǽlsh(iy)əs nòn tolénday/. The servitude of not building higher. A right attached to a house, by which its proprietor can prevent his neighbor from building his own house higher.

Servitus aquæ ducendæ /sárvədəs ǽkwiy d(y)uwséndiy/. The servitude of leading water; the right of leading water to one's own premises through another's land.

Servitus aquæ educendæ /sárvədəs ǽkwiy iyd(y)uwséndiy/. The servitude of leading off water; the right of leading off the water from one's own onto another's ground.

Servitus aquæ hauriendæ /sárvədəs ǽkwiy hòhriyéndiy/. The servitude or right of draining water from another's spring or well.

Servitus fumi immittendi /sárvədəs fyúwmay ìmaténday/. The servitude or right of leading off smoke or vapor through the chimney or over the ground of one's neighbor.

Servitus itineris /sárvədəs aytínərəs/. The servitude or privilege of walking, riding, and being carried over another's ground. A species of right of way.

Servitus luminum /sárvədəs l(y)úwmənəm/. The servitude of lights; the right of making or having windows or other openings in a wall belonging to another, or in a common wall, in order to obtain light for one's building.

Servitus ne luminibus officiatur /sárvədəs nìy l(y)umínəbəs əfishiyéydər/. A servitude not to hinder lights; the right of having one's lights or windows unobstructed or darkened by a neighbor's building, etc.

Servitus ne prospectus offendatur /sárvədəs níy prəspéktəs òfendéydər/. A servitude not to obstruct one's prospect, *i.e.*, not to intercept the view from one's house.

Servitus oneris ferendi /sárvədəs ównərəs fərénday/. The servitude of bearing weight; the right to let one's building rest upon the building, wall, or pillars of one's neighbor.

Servitus pascendi /sárvədəs pæsénday/. The servitude of pasturing; the right of pasturing one's cattle on another's ground; otherwise called *"jus pascendi."*

Servitus pecoris ad aquam adpulsam /sərvədəs pèkərəs æd ǽkwəm ædpálsəm/. A right of driving one's cattle on a neighbor's land to water.

Servitus prædii rustici /sárvədəs príydiyay rástəsay/. The servitude of a rural or country estate; a rural servitude.

Servitus prædii urbani /sárvədəs príydiyay ərbéynay/. The servitude of an urban or city estate; an urban servitude.

Servitus prædiorum /sárvədəs prìydiyórəm/. A prædial servitude; a service, burden, or charge upon one estate for the benefit of another.

Servitus projiciendi /sárvədəs prəjìshiyénday/. The servitude of projecting; the right of building a projection from one's house in the open space belonging to one's neighbor.

Servitus prospectus /sárvədəs prəspéktəs/. A right of prospect. This may be either to give one a free prospect over his neighbor's land or to prevent a neighbor from having a prospect over one's own land.

Servitus stillicidii /sárvədəs stiləsídiyay/. The right of drip; the right of having the water drip from the eaves of one's house upon the house or ground of one's neighbor.

Servitus tigni immittendi /sárvədəs tígnay iməténday/. The servitude of letting in a beam; the right of inserting beams in a neighbor's wall.

Servitus viæ /sárvədəs váyiy/. The servitude or right of way; the right of walking, riding, and driving over another's land.

Servus /sárvəs/. Lat. In the civil and old English law, a slave; a bondman.

Sess /sés/. In English law, a tax, rate, or assessment.

Sessio /sésh(iy)ow/. Lat. In old English law, a sitting; a session. *Sessio parliamenti,* the sitting of parliament.

Session. The sitting of a court, legislature, council, commission, etc., for the transaction of its proper business. Hence, the period of time, within any one day, during which such body is assembled in form, and engaged in the transaction of business, or, in a more extended sense, the whole space of time from its first assembling to its prorogation or adjournment *sine die.* Either a day or a period of days in which a court, legislature, etc. carries on its business.

Strictly speaking, the word "session," as applied to a court of justice, is not synonymous with the word "term." The "session" of a court is the time during which it actually sits for the transaction of judicial business, and hence terminates each day with the rising of the court. A "term" of court is the period fixed by law, usually embracing many days or weeks, during which it shall be open for the transaction of judicial business and during which it may hold sessions from day to day. But this distinction is not always observed, many authorities using the two words interchangeably.

See also **Extra session; Extraordinary session; Lame duck session; Term.**

Biennial session. See that title.

Joint session. Meeting together and commingling of the two houses of a legislative body, sitting and acting together as one body, instead of separately in their respective houses.

Quarter sessions. See **Quarter session courts.**

Regular session. An ordinary, general, or stated session (as of a legislative body), as distinguished from a special or extra session.

Session laws. The name commonly given to the body of laws enacted by a state legislature at one of its annual or biennial sessions. So called to distinguish them from the "compiled laws" or "revised statutes" of the state. Published laws of a state enacted by each assembly and separately bound for the session and for extra sessions. The session laws are normally published on a periodic basis, in a pamphlet format, throughout the legislative session and then at the end of the session are bound into a more permanent form.

Set aside. To reverse, vacate, cancel, annul, or revoke a judgment, order, etc.

Setback. A distance from a curb, property line, or structure, within which building is prohibited. Setback requirements are normally provided for by ordinances or building codes. Provision in zoning ordinance regulating the distance from the lot line to the point where improvements may be constructed.

Set down. To "set down" a cause for trial or hearing at a given term is to enter its title in the calendar, list, or docket of causes which are to be brought on at that term.

Seti. As used in mining laws, a lease.

Set of exchange. In commercial law, foreign bills are usually drawn in duplicate or triplicate, the several parts being called respectively "first of exchange," "second of exchange," etc., and these parts together constitute a "set of exchange." Any one of them being paid, the others become void.

Set-off. A counter-claim demand which defendant holds against plaintiff, arising out of a transaction extrinsic of plaintiff's cause of action. Remedy employed by defendant to discharge or reduce plaintiff's demand by an opposite one arising from transaction which is extrinsic to plaintiff's cause of action. Edmonds v. Stratton, Mo.App., 457 S.W.2d 228, 232.

A claim filed by a defendant against the plaintiff when sued and in which he seeks to cancel the amount due from him or to recover an amount in excess of the plaintiff's claim against him. In equity practice it is commenced by a declaration in set-off, though under rules practice (which merged law and equity) it has been displaced by the counterclaim. Fed.R.Civil P. 13.

For the distinction between set-off and recoupment, see **Recoupment.** See also **Counterclaim; Offset.**

Set out. To recite or narrate facts or circumstances; to allege or aver; to describe or to incorporate; as, to set out a deed or contract.

Settle. A word of equivocal meaning; meaning different things in different connections, and the particular sense in which it is used may be explained by the context or the surrounding circumstances. Accordingly, the term may be employed as meaning to agree, to approve, to arrange, to ascertain, to liquidate, to come to or reach an agreement, to determine, to establish, to fix, to free from uncertainty, to place, or to regulate.

Parties are said to *settle* an account when they go over its items and ascertain and agree upon the balance due from one to the other. And, when the party indebted pays such balance, he is also said to settle it.

Under U.C.C. § 4–104(j), "settle" means to pay in cash, by clearing house settlement, in a charge or credit or by remittance, or otherwise as instructed. A settlement may be either provisional or final.

See also **Adjust; Liquidate; Settlement.**

Settled estate. See **Estate.**

Settle up. A term, colloquial rather than legal, which is applied to the final collection, adjustment, and distribution of the estate of a decedent, a bankrupt, or an insolvent corporation. It includes the processes of collecting the property, paying debts and charges, and turning over the balance to those entitled to receive it.

Settlement. Act or process of adjusting or determining; an adjusting; an adjustment between persons concerning their dealings or difficulties; an agreement by which parties having disputed matters between them reach or ascertain what is coming from one to the other; arrangement of difficulties; composure of doubts or differences; determination by agreement; and liquidation. Sowers v. Robertson, 144 Kan. 273, 58 P.2d 1105, 1107. Payment or satisfaction. Ledbetter v. Hall, 191 Ark. 791, 87 S.W.2d 996, 999. In legal parlance, implies meeting of minds of parties to transaction or controversy. Ezmirlian v. Otto, 139 Cal.App. 486, 34 P.2d 774, 778. To fix or resolve conclusively; to make or arrange for final disposition. Wager v. Burlington Elevators, Inc., 116 N.J.Super. 390, 282 A.2d 437, 441.

Closing; the culmination of a particular transaction involving real property, such as the purchase and sale of the property, the execution of a lease or the making of a mortgage loan. See also **Closing.**

See also Adjust; Closing; Liquidate; Mary Carter agreement; Out-of-court settlement; Settle.

Contracts. Adjustment or liquidation of mutual accounts; the act by which parties who have been dealing together arrange their accounts and strike a balance. Also full and final payment or discharge of an account.

Equity of settlement. The equitable right of a wife, when her husband sues in equity for the reduction of her equitable estate to his own possession, to have the whole or a portion of such estate settled upon herself and her children. Also a similar right now recognized by the equity courts as directly to be asserted against the husband. Also called the "wife's equity."

Estates. The settlement of an estate consists in its administration by the executor or administrator carried so far that all debts and legacies have been paid and the individual shares of distributees in the corpus of the estate, or the residuary portion, as the case may be, definitely ascertained and determined, and accounts filed and passed, so that nothing remains but to make final distribution. "Settlement," in reference to a decedent's estate, includes the full process of administration, distribution and closing. Uniform Probate Code, § 1–201. See also *Final settlement,* below.

Family settlement. See **Family settlement.**

Final settlement. This term, as applied to the administration of an estate, is usually understood to have reference to the order of court approving the account which closes the business of the estate, and which finally discharges the executor or administrator from the duties of his trust.

Voluntary settlement. A settlement of property upon a wife or other beneficiary, made gratuitously or without valuable consideration.

Settlement option. In life insurance, a provision for payment made by the insurer with the beneficiary or insured such as for lump sum, periodic payments, and the like.

Settlement statement. A statement prepared by an escrow agent or lender, giving a complete breakdown of costs involved in a real estate sale. A separate statement is prepared for the seller and buyer. Such statements are regulated by the federal Real Estate Settlement Procedures Act. See also **Closing; RESPA.**

Settler. A person who, for the purpose of acquiring a pre-emption right, has gone upon the land in question, and is actually resident there.

Settlor. The grantor or donor in a deed of settlement. Also one who creates trust. Restatement, Second, Trusts § 3(1).

One who furnishes the consideration for the creation of a trust, though in form the trust is created by another. Lehman v. Commissioner of Internal Revenue, C.C.A.2, 109 F.2d 99, 100.

Set up. To bring forward or allege, as something relied upon or deemed sufficient. To propose or interpose, by way of defense, explanation, or justification; as, to set up the statute of limitations, *i.e.,* offer and rely upon it as a defense to a claim.

Seventeenth Amendment. An Amendment of 1913 to the U.S. Constitution which transferred the election of U.S. Senators from the State legislature to the voters of the State, but provided that the legislature may impower the governor to make a temporary appointment to fill a vacancy until an election can be held.

Seventh Amendment. In suits at common law, where the value in controversy shall exceed twenty dollars, the right of trial by jury shall be preserved, and no fact tried by a jury, shall be otherwise reexamined in any Court of the United States, than according to the rules of the common law. This constitutional right of trial by jury is preserved by Fed.R.Civil P. 38. See also **Trial** *(Trial by jury).*

Sever. To separate, as one from another; to cut off from something; to divide. To part in any way, especially by violence, as by cutting, rending, etc.; as, to sever the head from the body. To cut or break open or apart; to divide into parts. To cut through; to disjoin. In practice, to insist upon a plea distinct from that of other codefendants. To separate the cases of multiple defendants in such a way as to allow separate trials for each or for fewer than all.

Relief from prejudicial joinder. If it appears that a defendant or the government is prejudiced by a joinder of offenses or of defendants in an indictment or information or by such joinder for trial together, the court may order an election or separate trials of counts, grant a severance of defendants or provide whatever other relief justice requires. In ruling on a motion by a defendant for severance the court may order the attorney for the government to deliver to the court for inspection *in camera* any statements or confessions made by the defendants which the government intends to introduce in evidence at the trial. Fed.R.Crim.P. 14.

Severability clause. See **Saving clause; Severable statute.**

Severability doctrine. If promise sued on is related to an illegal transaction, but is not illegal in and of itself, "severability doctrine" applies, and recovery should not be denied, if aid of illegal transaction is not relied on or required, or if promise sued on is remote from or collateral to illegal transaction, or is supported by independent consideration. Sherwood & Roberts-Yakima, Inc. v. Cohan, 2 Wash.App. 703, 469 P.2d 574, 578, 582.

Severable. Admitting of severance or separation; capable of being divided; separable; capable of being severed from other things to which it was joined, and yet maintaining a complete and independent existence. Capable of carrying on an independent existence; for example, a severable statute is one that can still be valid even if one part of it is struck down as invalid by a court. It is common for statutes to have a severability or savings clause (q.v.).

Severable contract. A contract, the nature and purpose of which is susceptible of division and apportionment, having two or more parts, in respect to matters and things contemplated and embraced by it, not necessarily dependent upon each other, or intended by parties as being dependent. Gross v. Maytex Knitting Mills of Cal., 116 C.A.2d 705, 254 P.2d 163, 167.

The usual test of "severability" of a contract is whether the consideration is so segregated that it may be severally applied to each independent covenant in the contract. Hospelhorn v. Circle City Coal Co., C.C.A.Ky., 117 F.2d 166, 168. One of the tests of "severability" of a contract is whether the consideration is expressly or by necessary implication apportionable. Read v. Gibson & Johnson, Tex.Civ., 12 S.W.2d 620, 623.

Severable statute. A statute if after an invalid portion of it has been stricken out, that which remains is self-sustaining and capable of separate enforcement without regard to the stricken portion, in which case that which remains should be sustained. See **Saving clause; Separability clause.**

Several. More than two, often used to designate a number greater than one. First Nat. Trust & Savings Bank of San Diego v. Industrial Accident Commission, 213 Cal. 322, 2 P.2d 347, 351. Each particular, or a small number singly taken. Nashville, C. & St. L. Ry. v. Marshall County, 161 Tenn. 236, 30 S.W.2d 268. Separate; individual; independent; severable. In this sense the word is distinguished from "joint." Also exclusive; individual; appropriated. In this sense it is opposed to "common."

As to several Count; Covenant; Demise; Fishery; Tail, and Tenancy, see those titles.

Several actions. Where a separate and distinct action is brought against each of two or more persons who are all liable to the plaintiff in respect to the same subject-matter, the actions are said to be "several." If all the persons are joined as defendants in one and the same action, it is called a "joint" action.

Several inheritance. An inheritance conveyed so as to descend to two persons severally, by moieties, etc.

Several liability. Liability separate and distinct from liability of another to the extent that an independent action may be brought without joinder of others.

Severally. Distinctly, separately, apart from others. When applied to a number of persons the expression *severally liable* usually implies that each one is liable alone.

Severalty. A state of separation. An estate in *severalty* is one that is held by a person in his own right only, without any other person being joined or connected with him, in point of interest therein. 2 Bl.Comm. 179.

Severalty, estate in. An estate which is held by the tenant in his own right only, without any other being joined or connected with him in point of interest during the continuance of his estate. 2 Bl.Comm. 179.

Severance. Act of severing, or state of being severed; partition; separation; *e.g.* a claim against a party may be severed and proceeded with separately. Fed. R.Civil P. 21. Severance divides lawsuit into two or more independent causes, each of which terminates in separate, final and enforceable judgment. Kansas University Endowment Ass'n v. King, 162 Tex. 599, 350 S.W.2d 11, 19. See also **Severance of actions.**

The destruction of any one of the unities of a joint tenancy. It is so called because the estate is no longer a joint tenancy, but is severed. Term may also refer to cutting of the crops, such as corn, wheat, etc., or the separating of anything from the realty.

Severance damage. Essence of severance damages is the loss in value to the remainder tract by reason of a partial taking of land and this is predicated on the enhanced value of the remainder tract because of its relationship to whole prior to the taking. U. S. v. 105.40 Acres of Land, More or Less in Porter County, State of Indiana, C.A.Ind., 471 F.2d 207, 211. If only part of single tract is taken, owner's compensation for taking includes any and all elements of value arising out of relation of part taken to entire tract and such damages are often called severance damages. U. S. v. 26.81 Acres of Land, More or Less, in Benton County, Ark., D.C.Ark., 244 F.Supp. 831, 839.

Expropriation. The difference between the market value of the remainder immediately before and immediately after taking. State through Dept. of Highways v. Denham Springs Development Co., Inc., La. App., 294 So.2d 281, 283.

Severance of actions. An action of a court in separating the claims of multiple parties and permitting separate actions on each claim or on fewer than all claims at one time. Fed.R.Civ.P. 21. "Severance" divides lawsuit into two or more independent causes, each of which terminates in separate, final and enforceable judgment. Kansas University Endowment Ass'n v. King, 162 Tex. 599, 350 S.W.2d 11, 19.

Severance pay. Payment by an employer to employee beyond his wages on termination of his employment. Generally, it is paid when the termination is not due to employee's fault and many union contracts provide for it.

Severance tax. A tax on mineral or forest products at the time they are removed or severed from the soil and usually regarded as a form of property taxation.

Severe. Sharp, grave, distressing, violent, extreme, torture, rigorous, difficult to be endured. Traders & General Ins. Co. v. Crouch, Tex.Civ.App., 113 S.W.2d 650, 652.

Seward, or **seaward** /s(y)úwərd/síywòrd/. One who guards the sea-coast; *custos maris.*

Sex. The sum of the peculiarities of structure and function that distinguish a male from a female organism; the character of being male or female.

S.F.S. An abbreviation in the civil law for *"sine fraude sua"* (without fraud on his part).

Shack. In old English law, the straying and escaping of cattle out of the lands of their owners into other uninclosed land; an intercommoning of cattle.

Shakedown. Extortion of money with threats of physical harm or, in case of police officer, threat of arrest. See also **Blackmail; Extortion.**

Shall. As used in statutes, contracts, or the like, this word is generally imperative or mandatory. In common or ordinary parlance, and in its ordinary signification, the term "shall" is a word of command, and one which has always or which must be given a compulsory meaning; as denoting obligation. It has a peremptory meaning, and it is generally imperative or mandatory. It has the invariable significance of excluding the idea of discretion, and has the significance of operating to impose a duty which may be enforced, particularly if public policy is in favor of this meaning, or when addressed to public officials, or where a public interest is involved, or where the public or persons have rights which ought to be exercised or enforced, unless a contrary intent appears. People v. O'Rourke, 124 Cal.App. 752, 13 P.2d 989, 992.

But it may be construed as merely permissive or directory (as equivalent to "may"), to carry out the legislative intention and in cases where no right or benefit to any one depends on its being taken in the imperative sense, and where no public or private right is impaired by its interpretation in the other sense. Wisdom v. Board of Sup'rs of Polk County, 236 Iowa 669, 19 N.W.2d 602, 607, 608.

Sham. False. A transaction without substance that will be disregarded for tax purposes. See also **Dummy.**

Sham pleading. Those which are inherently false and must have been known by interposing party to be untrue. Pentecostal Holiness Church, Inc. v. Mauney, Fla.App., 270 So.2d 762, 769. A "sham pleading", subject to motion to strike (Fed.R.Civil P. 12(f)), is one that is good in form, but false in fact, and not pleaded in good faith. Scott v. Meek, 228 S.C. 29, 88 S.E.2d 768, 769. A pleading is "sham" only when it is so clearly false that it does not raise any bona fide issue. Fontana v. Town of Hempstead, 219 N.Y.S.2d 383, 384.

Shanghai /shæŋháy/. Practice of drugging, tricking, intoxicating or otherwise forcing persons to become sailors—usually to secure advance money or a premium.

Under federal law, the offense of procuring or inducing, or attempting to do so, by force, or threats, or by representations which one knows or believes to be untrue, or while the person is intoxicated or under the influence of any drug, to go on board of any vessel, or agree to do so, to perform service or labor thereon, such vessel being engaged in interstate or foreign commerce, on the high seas or any navigable water of the United States, or knowingly to detain on board such vessel such person, so procured or induced, or knowingly aiding or abetting such things. 18 U.S.C.A. § 2194.

Share, *v.* To partake; enjoy with others; have a portion of.

Share, *n.* A part or definite portion of a thing owned by a number of persons in common and contemplates something owned in common by two or more persons and has reference to that part of the undivided interest which belongs to some one of them. A unit of stock representing ownership in a corporation. See also **Distributive share; Share of corporate stock; Stock.**

Share and share alike. In equal shares or proportions. The words commonly indicate per capita division; and they may be applied to a division between classes as well as to a division among individuals. See **Per capita.**

Share certificate. An instrument of a corporation certifying that the person therein named is entitled to a certain number of shares; it is prima facie evidence of his title thereto. Document which evidences participation in a voting trust of shares of a corporation.

Sharecropper. Type of tenant farmer who lives on and works the land of another, his compensation being a portion of the crops minus any advances for seed, food, tools, etc.

Sharecropping. Type of agricultural arrangement in which the landowner leases land and equipment to tenant or sharecropper who, in turn, gives to the landlord a percentage of the crops as rent.

Shareholder. See **Stockholder.**

Share of corporate stock. A proportional part of certain rights in a corporation during its existence, and in the assets upon dissolution, and evidence of the stockholder's ratable share in the distribution of the assets on the winding up of the corporation's business. Department of Treasury of Indiana v. Crowder, 214 Ind. 252, 15 N.E.2d 89, 91. See **Share certificate; Stock.**

Share split. See **Stock** *(Stock split).*

Share-warrant to bearer. A warrant or certificate of a corporation, stating that the bearer of the warrant is entitled to a certain number or amount of fully paid up shares or stock. Coupons for payment of dividends may be annexed to it. Delivery of the share-warrant operates as a transfer of the shares or stock.

Sharp. A "sharp" clause in a mortgage or other security (or the whole instrument described as "sharp") is one which empowers the creditor to take prompt and summary action upon default in payment or breach of other conditions.

Shave. Sometimes used to denote the act of obtaining the property of another by oppression and extortion. Also used in an innocent sense to denote the buying of existing notes and other securities for money, at a discount. Hence to charge a man with using money for shaving is not libelous *per se.*

Shelley's Case, Rule in. "When the ancestor, by any gift or conveyance, taketh an estate of freehold, and in the same gift or conveyance an estate is limited, either mediately or immediately, to his heirs in fee or in tail, 'the heirs' are words of limitation of the estate, and not words of purchase." 1 Co.Rep. 93b (1581). This rule has also been expressed as follows: "Where a person takes an estate of freehold, legally, or equitably, under a deed, will, or other writing, and in the same instrument there is a limitation by way of remainder, either with or without the interposition of another estate, of any interest of the same legal or equitable quality to his heirs, or heirs of his body, as a class of persons to take in succession from generation to generation, the limitation to the heirs entitles the ancestor to the whole estate." In re Thorne's Estate, 344 Pa. 503, 25 A.2d 811, 819.

Intimately connected with the quantity of estate which a tenant may hold in realty is the antique feudal doctrine generally known as the "Rule in Shelley's Case," which is reported by Lord Coke in 1 Coke, 93*b* (23 Eliz. in C.B.). This rule was not first laid down or established in that case, but was then simply admitted in argument as a well-founded and settled rule of law, and has always since been quoted as the "Rule in Shelley's Case." The rule was adopted as a part of the common law of this country, though it has long since been abolished by most states.

Shelter. In statutes relating to the provision of food, clothing, and shelter for one's children, term generally refers to a home with proper environments, as well as protection from the weather.

Sheriff. The chief executive and administrative officer of a county, being chosen by popular election. His principal duties are in aid of the criminal courts and civil courts of record; such as serving process, summoning juries, executing judgments, holding judicial sales and the like. He is also the chief conservator of the peace within his territorial jurisdiction. When used in statutes, the term may include a deputy sheriff. He is in general charge of the county jail in most states. See also **Constable; Marshall.**

Deputy sheriff. See **Deputy.**

Sheriff's deed. A document giving ownership rights in property to a buyer at a sheriff's sale (*i.e.* a sale held by a sheriff to pay a court judgment against the owner of the property). Deed given at sheriff's sale in foreclosure of a mortgage. The giving of said deed begins a statutory redemption period.

Sheriff's sale. A sale, commonly by auction, conducted by a sheriff or other court officer to carry out a decree of execution or foreclosure issued by a court. Examples include sales pursuant to attachments, liens and mortgages. See also **Judicial sale.**

Sherman Antitrust Act. Such Act (15 U.S.C.A. §§ 1–7) prohibits any unreasonable interference, by contract, or combination, or conspiracy, with the ordinary, usual and freely-competitive pricing or distribution system of the open market in interstate trade. See also **Clayton Acts; Restraint of trade; Robinson-Patman Act; Rule** *(Rule of reason).*

Shield laws. State statutes which afford privilege to journalists to not disclose information (*i.e.* notes and other materials) obtained during course of their newsgathering.

Shifting. Changing; varying; passing from one person to another by substitution.

Shifting clause. In a settlement at common law, a clause by which some other mode of devolution is substituted for that primarily prescribed. Examples of shifting clauses are: The ordinary name and arms clause, and the clause of less frequent occurrence by which a settled estate is destined as the foundation of a second family, in the event of the elder branch becoming otherwise enriched. These shifting clauses take effect under the statute of uses.

Shifting income. Device used by taxpayers in high tax brackets to move income from themselves to their children and others who are in a lower bracket. Short term or Clifford trusts, as well as gifts to minors, are among the devices used to accomplish this purpose.

Shifting risk. In insurance, a risk created by a contract of insurance on a stock of merchandise, or other similar property, which is kept for sale, or is subject to change in items by purchase and sale; the policy being conditioned to cover the goods in the stock at any and all times and not to be affected by changes in its composition.

Shifting severalty. See **Severalty.**

Shifting stock of merchandise. A stock of merchandise subject to change from time to time, in the course of trade by purchases, sales, or other transactions.

Shifting the burden of proof. Transferring it from one party to the other, or from one side of the case to the other, when he upon whom it rested originally has made out a *prima facie* case or defense by evidence, of such a character that it then becomes incumbent upon the other to rebut it by contradictory or defensive evidence.

Shifting use. See **Use.**

Shilling. Slang term for the act of posing as an innocent bystander at a confidence game but giving aid and assistance to the perpetrators of the scheme as a decoy.

Shinney /shíniy/. A local name for a homemade whisky. Moonshine.

Shin-plaster. Formerly, a jocose term for a bank-note greatly depreciated in value; also for paper money of a denomination less than a dollar.

Ship, v. To put on board a ship; to send by ship. Harrison v. Fortlage, 161 U.S. 57, 16 S.Ct. 488, 490, 40 L.Ed. 616. To place (goods) on board a vessel for the purchaser or consignee, to be transported at his risk. In a broader sense, to transport; to deliver to a carrier (public or private) for transportation. To send away, to get rid of. To send by established mode of transportation, as to "carry," "convey," or "transport," which are synonymous and defined, respectively, as "to bear or cause to be borne as from one place to another," and "to carry or convey from one place to another." Chicago, R. I. & P. Ry. Co. v. Petroleum Refining Co., D.C.Ky., 39 F.2d 629, 630. See also **Send; Shipment; Shipping.**

Ship, *n.* A vessel of any kind employed in navigation.

General ship. Where a ship is not chartered wholly to one person, but the owner offers her generally to carry the goods of all comers, or where, if chartered to one person, he offers her to several subfreighters for the conveyance of their goods, she is called a "general" ship, as opposed to a "chartered" one. One which is employed by the charterer or owner on a particular voyage, and is hired to a number of persons, unconnected with each other to convey their respective goods to the place of destination. Alexander Eccles & Co. v. Strachan Shipping Co., D.C.Ga., 21 F.2d 653, 655.

Ship broker. An agent for the transaction of business between shipowners and charterers or those who ship cargoes.

Ship-master. The captain or master of a merchant ship, appointed and put in command by the owner, and having general control of the vessel and cargo, with power to bind the owner by his lawful acts and engagements in the management of the ship.

Ship's husband. In old maritime law, a person appointed by the several part-owners of a ship, and usually one of their number, to manage the concerns of the ship for the common benefit. Generally understood to be the general agent of the owners in regard to all the affairs of the ship in the home port.

Ship's papers. The papers which must be carried by a vessel on a voyage, in order to furnish evidence of her national character, the nature and destination of the cargo, and of compliance with the navigation laws. The ship's papers are of two sorts: Those required by the law of a particular country; such as the certificate of registry, license, charter-party, bills of lading and of health and the like. Those required by the law of nations to be on board neutral ships, to vindicate their title to that character; these are the pass-port, sea-brief, or sea-letter, proofs of property, the muster roll or *rôle d'equipage*, the charter-party, the bills of lading and invoices, the log-book or ship's journal, and the bill of health.

Shipment. The delivery of goods to a carrier and his issuance of a bill of lading therefor. The transportation of goods. Pennsylvania R. Co. v. Carolina Portland Cement Co., C.C.A.S.C., 16 F.2d 760, 761. Also, the property which is the subject of transportation. Pennsylvania R. Co. v. Carolina Portland Cement Co., C.C.A.S.C., 16 F.2d 760, 761. An order. A consignment of goods as delivered by the carrier. See also **Ship; Shipping.**

Ship Mortgage Act. Federal statute regulating mortgages on ships registered as U.S. vessels. It provides for enforcement of maritime liens in favor of those who furnish supplies or maintenance to such vessels. 46 U.S.C.A. § 911 *et seq.*

Shipper. One who transports goods for a charge; a common carrier; *e.g.* motor carrier, railroad, air freight carrier, freight forwarder.

Shipping. Ships in general; ships or vessels of any kind intended for navigation. Relating to ships; as, shipping interests, shipping affairs, shipping business, shipping concerns. Putting on board a ship or vessel, or receiving on board a ship or vessel.

Law of shipping. A comprehensive term for all that part of the maritime law which relates to ships and the persons employed in or about them. It embraces such subjects as the building and equipment of vessels, their registration and nationality, their ownership and inspection, their employment (including charter-parties, freight, demurrage, towage, and salvage), and their sale, transfer, and mortgage; also, the employment, rights, powers, and duties of masters and mariners; and the law relating to ship-brokers, ship-agents, pilots, etc. See **Maritime; Jones Act; Longshoremen's and Harbor Workers' Compensation Act; Maritime.**

Shipping articles. A written agreement between the master of a vessel and the mariners, specifying the voyage or term for which the latter are shipped, and the rate of wages. 46 U.S.C.A. § 564.

Shipping document. Generic term to describe all papers which cover a shipment in foreign or inland trade such as bill of lading, letter of credit, certificate of insurance and the like. See also **Ship** (*Ship's papers*).

Shipping order. Copy of bill of lading which carries shipper's instructions to carrier as to the disposition of the goods.

Shipping papers. See **Shipping document.**

Shipwreck. The demolition or shattering of a vessel, caused by her driving ashore or on rocks and shoals in the midseas, or by the violence of winds and waves in tempests.

Shire /shay(ə)r/. A Saxon word which signified a division; it was made up of an indefinite number of hundreds—later called a county (*Comitatus*).

In England, a county. So called because every county or shire is divided and parted by certain metes and bounds from another.

Knights of the shire. See that title.

Shire-clerk. He that keeps the county court.

Shire-gemot, scire-gemote, scir-gemot. (From the Saxon *scir* or *scyre*, county, shire, and *gemote*, a court, an assembly.) Variants of *scyregemote (q.v.).* See, also, Shire-mote, *infra.*

Shire-man, or scyre-man. Before the Conquest, the judge of the county, by whom trials for land, etc., were determined.

Shire-mote. The assize of the shire, or the assembly of the people, was so called by the Saxons. It was nearly if not exactly, the same as the *scyregemote,* and in most respects corresponded with what were afterwards called the "county courts."

Shire-reeve (spelled, also, Shire rieve, or Shire reve). In Saxon law, the reeve or bailiff of the shire. The *viscount* of the Anglo-Normans, and the *sheriff* of later times.

Shock. A sudden agitation of the physical or mental sensibilities. A sudden depression of the vital forces of the entire body, or a part of it, marking some profound impression produced upon the nervous system, as by severe injury, a surgical operation, profound emotion, or the like, or a prostration of the bodily functions, as from sudden injury or mental disturbance. Provident Life & Accident Ins. Co. v. Campbell, 18 Tenn.App. 452, 79 S.W.2d 292, 295. See also **Trauma.**

Mental shock. A sudden agitation of the mind; startling emotion, as the shock of a painful discovery, a shock of grief or joy. Provident Life and Accident Ins. Co. v. Campbell, 18 Tenn.App. 452, 79 S.W.2d 292, 295.

Physical shock. A blow, impact, collision, concussion, or violent shake or jar, or a violent collision of bodies, or the concussion caused by it; a sudden striking or dashing together or against something. Provident Life and Accident Ins. Co. v. Campbell, 18 Tenn.App. 452, 79 S.W.2d 292, 295.

Shoot. To strike with something shot; to hit, wound, or kill, with a missile discharged from a weapon. The term generally implies the use of firearms.

Shop-book rule. An exception to the hearsay evidence rule, permitting the introduction in evidence of books of original entry made in the usual course of business, and introduced by one with custody of them, and upon general authentication. Clayton v. Metropolitan Life Ins. Co., 96 Utah 331, 85 P.2d 819, 822; Fed.Evid.R. 803(6), (7).

Shop-books. Books of original entry kept by tradesmen, shop-keepers, mechanics, and the like, in which are entered their accounts and charges for goods sold, work done, etc., commonly called "account-books," or "books of account."

Shoplifting. Larceny of merchandise from a store or business establishment. Essential constituents of "shoplifting" are (1) willfully taking possession of merchandise offered for sale in mercantile establishment, (2) with intention of converting merchandise to taker's own use without paying purchase price thereof. Yearwood v. State, 2 Tenn.Cr.App. 552, 455 S.W.2d 612, 617.

Shop right rule. In patent law, the right of an employer to use employee's invention in employer's business without payment of royalty. The "shop right" doctrine is that, where an employee during his hours of employment working with his employer's materials and appliances conceives and perfects an invention for which he obtains a patent, he must accord his employer a nonexclusive right to practice the invention. The employer, however, is not entitled to a conveyance of the invention, this remains the right of the employee-inventor. U. S. v. Dubilier Condenser Corp., 289 U.S. 178, 189, 53 S.Ct. 554, 558, 77 L.Ed. 1114.

Shop steward. A union official elected to represent members in a particular department. His duties include collection of dues, recruitment of new members and initial negotiations for settlement of grievances.

Shore. Strictly and technically, lands adjacent to the sea or other tidal waters. The lands adjoining navigable waters, where the tide flows and reflows, which at high tides are submerged, and at low tides are bare. Shively v. Bowlby, 152 U.S. 1, 14 S.Ct. 548, 38 L.Ed. 331. The space bounded by the high and low water marks. Borax Consolidated v. City of Los Angeles, Cal., 296 U.S. 10, 56 S.Ct. 23, 80 L.Ed. 9. And this is also true even though the lands may lie along nonnavigable bodies of water.

Under the civil law the "shore line" boundary of lands adjoining navigable waters is the line marked by the highest tide.

In connection with salvage, "shore" means the land on which the waters have deposited things which are the subject of salvage, whether below or above ordinary high-water mark.

Shore lands. Those lands lying between the lines of high and low water mark. Lands bordering on the shores of navigable lakes and rivers below the line of ordinary high water.

Short. Not long; of brief length or duration; not coming up to a measure, standard, requirement, or the like.

A term of common use in the stock and commodity markets. To say that one is "short," in the vernacular of the exchanges, implies only that one has less of a commodity than may be necessary to meet demands and obligations. It does not imply that commodity cannot or will not be supplied upon demand.

In finance and commodity futures, a person is short when he has sold securities or commodities which he does not own at the time of the sale, though he expects to buy them back at a lower price than that at which he sold them. See also **Short sale.**

Short covering. Buying stock to return stock previously borrowed to make delivery on a short sale.

Short interest. A short sale is the sale of borrowed stock. The seller expects a price decline that would enable him to purchase an equal number of shares later at a lower price for return to the lender. The "short interest" is the number of shares that haven't been purchased for return to lenders. See also **Short sale.**

Short lease. A term applied colloquially, but without much precision, to a lease for a short term (as a month or a year), as distinguished from one running for a long period.

Shortly after. In point of time, a relative term, meaning in a short or brief time or manner; soon; presently; quickly.

Short position. A short position maybe created when an investor borrows a stock in order to sell it, figuring the price of the stock will decline. The investor is in a "short position" until he purchases stock to repay the lender. See **Short sale.**

Short sale. A contract for sale of shares of stock which the seller does not own, or certificates for which are not within his control, so as to be available for delivery at the time when, under rules of the exchange, delivery must be made. Provost v. U. S., 269 U.S. 443, 46 S.Ct. 152, 153, 70 L.Ed. 352. A short sale occurs where a taxpayer sells borrowed property (usually stock) and repays the lender with substantially identical property either held on the date of the short sale or purchased after the sale. No gain or loss is recognized until the short sale is closed and such gain or loss is generally short term. I.R.C. § 1233. See also **Short interest; Short position.**

Short summons. A process, authorized in some of the states, to be issued against an absconding, fraudulent, or nonresident debtor, which is returnable within a less number of days than an ordinary writ of summons.

Short swing profits. Profits made by insider through sale or other disposition of the corporate stock within six months after purchase. See **Insider.**

Short-term. Current; ordinarily, due within one year.

Capital gains or losses. See **Capital** *(Capital gains);* **Capital** *(Capital loss).*

Short-term debt. Debt evidenced by notes or drafts which are payable on demand or within a year of issuance.

Short term paper. Any note, draft, bill of exchange, or banker's acceptance payable on demand or having a maturity at the time of issuance of not exceeding nine months, exclusive of days of grace, or any renewal thereof payable on demand or having a maturity likewise limited. Investment Company Act, § 2.

Should. The past tense of shall; ordinarily implying duty or obligation; although usually no more than an obligation of propriety or expediency, or a moral obligation, thereby distinguishing it from "ought." It is not normally synonymous with "may," and although often interchangeable with the word "would," it does not ordinarily express certainty as "will" sometimes does.

Show, n. Something that one views or at which one looks and at the same time hears.

Show, v. To make apparent or clear by evidence, to prove.

Show cause order. An order decree, execution, etc., to appear as directed, and present to the court such reasons and considerations as one has to offer why a particular order, decree, etc., should not be confirmed, take effect, be executed, or as the case may be.

An order to a person or corporation to appear in court and explain why the court should not take a proposed action. If the person or corporation fails to appear or to give sufficient reasons why the court should take no action, the court will take the action.

Shower. One who accompanies a jury to the scene to call the attention of the jurors to specific objects to be noted. Snyder v. Mass., 291 U.S. 97, 54 S.Ct. 330, 78 L.Ed. 674. See also **View.**

Show-up. One-to-one confrontation between suspect and witness to crime. A type of pre-trial identification procedure in which a suspect is confronted by or exposed to the victim of or witness to a crime. It is less formal than a lineup but its purpose is the same. Commonly, it occurs within a short time after the crime or under circumstances which would make a lineup impracticable or impossible. Due process standards must be met if evidence of such identification is to be admissible in court. Stovall v. Denno, 388 U.S. 293, 87 S.Ct. 1967, 18 L.Ed.2d 1199; Neil v. Biggers, 409 U.S. 188, 93 S.Ct. 375, 34 L.Ed.2d 401.

Shut down. To stop work; usually said of a factory, etc.

Shut-in royalty. In oil and gas leases, a royalty payment made to keep the lease in force though there is no production.

Shyster. A trickish knave; one who carries on any business or profession in a deceitful, tricky or dishonest way.

Si actio /sày ǽksh(iy)ow/. Lat. The conclusion of a plea to an action when the defendant demands judgment, if the plaintiff ought to have his action, etc. Obsolete.

Si a jure discedas, vagus eris, et erunt omnia omnibus incerta /sáy èy júriy dəsíydəs, véygəs éhrəs, èd éhrənt ómn(i)yə ómnəbəs insárdə/. If you depart from the law, you will go astray, and all things will be uncertain to everybody.

Si alicujus rei societas sit et finis negotio impositus est, finitur societas /sáy ǽləkyúwjəs ríyay səsáyətæs síd èt fáynəs nəgówsh(iy)ow impózədəs èst, fínədər səsáyətæs/. If there is a partnership in any matter, and the business is ended, the partnership ceases.

Si aliquid ex solemnibus deficiat, cum æquitas poscit, subveniendum est /sáy ǽləkwəd èks səlémnəbəs dəfíshiyət, kàm ékwətæs pósət, səbvèniyéndəm èst/. If any one of certain required forms be wanting, where equity requires, it will be aided. The want of some of a neutral vessel's papers is strong presumptive evidence against the ship's neutrality, yet the want of any one of them is not absolutely conclusive.

Si aliquid sapit /sáy ǽləkwəd séypət/. Lat. If he knows anything; if he is not altogether devoid of reason.

Si assuetis mederi possis, nova non sunt tentanda /sáy əswíydəs mədíray pósəs, nówvə nón sànt tentǽndə/. If you can be relieved by accustomed remedies, new ones should not be tried. If an old wall can be repaired, a new one should not be made.

Si a tutela removendus est /sày éy t(y)uwtíylə rìymowvéndəs èst/. If a guardian do fraud to his ward, he shall be removed from his guardianship.

Sib /síb/. Sax. A relative or kinsman. Used in the Scotch tongue, but not now in English.

Sic /sík/. Lat. Thus; so; in such manner.

Sic enim debere quem meliorem agrum suum facere ne vicini deteriorem faciat /sík énəm dəbíriy kwèm mìyl(i)yórəm ǽgrəm s(y)úwəm fǽsəriy níy vəsáynay dətìriyórəm féysh(iy)ət/. Every one ought so to improve his land as not to injure his neighbor's. A rule of the Roman law.

Sic interpretandum est ut verba accipiantur cum effectu /sík əntàrprətǽndəm èst ət várbə əksipiyǽntər kàm əfékt(y)uw/. [A statute] is to be so interpreted that the words may be taken with effect.

Sick. Affected with disease, ill, indisposed.

Sick leave. Period allowed by an employer to an employee for the employee's sickness either with or without pay but with no loss of seniority or other benefits.

Sickness. Illness; disease. An ailment of such a character as to affect the general soundness and health; not a mere temporary indisposition, which does not tend to undermine and weaken the constitution.

Si constet de persona /sày kón(t)stət dìy pərsównə/. Lat. If it be certain who is the person meant.

Si contingat /sáy kəntíngət/. Lat. If it happen. Words of condition in old conveyances.

Sicut alias /síkəd éyl(i)yəs/. Lat. As at another time, or heretofore. This was a second writ sent out when the first was not executed.

Sic utere tuo ut alienum non lædas /sík yúwdəriy t(y)úwow əd æliyíynəm nòn líydəs/. Use your own property in such a manner as not to injure that of another. 1 Bl.Comm. 306. Chapman v. Barnett, 131 Ind.App. 30, 169 N.E.2d 212, 214.

Sicut me deus adjuvet /síkət míy díyəs ǽjəvət/. Lat. So help me God.

Sicut natura nil facit per saltum, ita nec lex /síkət nətyúrə níl féysət pàr sóltəm, áydə nék léks/. In the same way as nature does nothing by a bound, so neither does the law.

Side. The margin, edge, verge, or border of a surface; any one of the bounding lines of the surface.

The party or parties collectively to a lawsuit considered in relation to his or their opponents, *i.e.,* the plaintiff side, or the defendant side.

A province or field of jurisdiction of courts. Thus, the same court is sometimes said to have different *sides,* as an "equity side" and a "law side"; though with the procedural merger of law and equity in most states such side distinctions have been abolished.

Side-bar rules. In English practice, there are some rules which the courts authorize their officers to grant as a matter of course without formal application being made to them in open court, and these are technically termed "side-bar rules," because formerly they were moved for by the attorneys at the side bar in court; such, for instance, was the rule to plead, which was an order or command of the court requiring a defendant to plead within a specified number of days. Such also were the rules to reply, to rejoin, and many others, the granting of which depended upon settled rules of practice rather than upon the discretion of the courts, all of which have been rendered unnecessary by statutory changes.

Side lines. In commercial usage, lines of goods sold or businesses followed in addition to one's principal articles or occupation.

In mining law, the side lines of a mining claim are those which measure the extent of the claim on each side of the middle of the vein at the surface. They are not necessarily the side lines as laid down on the ground or on a map or plat; for if the claim, in its longer dimension, crosses the vein, instead of following it, the platted side lines will be treated in law as the end lines, and vice versa. Argentine Min. Co. v. Terrible Min. Co., 122 U.S. 478, 7 S.Ct. 1356, 30 L.Ed. 1140; Del Monte Min. Co. v. Last Chance Min. Co., 171 U.S. 55, 18 S.Ct. 895, 43 L.Ed. 72.

Side reports. A term sometimes applied to unofficial volumes or series of reports, as contrasted with those prepared by the official reporter of the court, or to collections of cases omitted from the official reports.

Sidesmen. In ecclesiastical law, these were originally persons whom, in the ancient episcopal synods, the bishops were wont to summon out of each parish to give information of the disorders of the clergy and people, and to report heretics. In process of time they became standing officers, under the title of "synodsmen," "sidesmen," or "questmen." The whole of their duties devolved by custom upon the churchwardens of a parish.

Sidewalk. That part of a public street or highway designed for the use of pedestrians, being exclusively reserved for them, and constructed somewhat differently than other portions of the street.

Si duo in testamento pugnantia reperientur, ultimum est ratum /sáy d(y)úwow ìn tèstəméntow pəgnǽnsh(iy)ə rəpèhriyéntər, áltəməm èst réydəm/. If two conflicting provisions are found in a will, the last is observed.

Si fecerit te securum /sáy fésərət tìy səkyúrəm/. Lat. If he makes you secure. In practice. The initial and emphatic words of that description of original writ which directs the sheriff to cause the defendant to appear in court, without any option given him, provided the plaintiff gives the sheriff security effectually to prosecute his claim. 3 Bl.Comm. 274.

Sight. The power of seeing; the faculty of vision or of perceiving objects; or the act of seeing, and perception of objects through the eyes.

Sight draft. An instrument payable on presentment. A bill of exchange for the immediate collection of money. United Ben. Fire Ins. Co. v. First Nat. Bank of Ariz., Phoenix, 1 Ariz.App. 550, 405 P.2d 488, 490.

Bills of exchange are frequently drawn payable at sight or certain number of days or months after sight. U.C.C. § 3–109(1)(b).

A demand for payment drawn by a person to whom money is owed. The draft is presented to the borrower's (the debtor's) bank in expectation that the borrower will authorize its bank to disburse the funds.

Sigil /síjəl/. In old English law, a seal, or a contracted or abbreviated signature used as a seal.

Sigillum /səjíləm/. Lat. In old English law, a seal; originally and properly a seal impressed upon wax.

Sigla /síglə/. Lat. In Roman law, marks or signs of abbreviation used in writing.

Sign. To affix one's name to a writing or instrument, for the purpose of authenticating or executing it, or to give it effect as one's act. To attach a name or cause it to be attached to a writing by any of the known methods of impressing a name on paper. To affix a signature to; to ratify by hand or seal; to subscribe in one's own handwriting. To make any mark, as upon a document, in token of knowledge, approval acceptance, or obligation. See also **Execution; Mark; Signature.**

Signa /sígnə/. The plural of *signum (q.v.)*.

Signal. A means of communication, as between vessels at sea or between a vessel and the shore. The international code of signals for the use of all nations assigns arbitrary meanings to different arrangements of flags or displays of lights.

Signatorius annulus /sìgnətóriyəs ǽnyələs/. Lat. In the civil law, a signet-ring; a seal-ring.

Signatory /sígnət(o)riy/. A term used in diplomacy to indicate a nation which is a party to a treaty. In general, a person who signs a document personally or through his agent and who becomes a party thereto.

Signature. The act of putting one's name at the end of an instrument to attest its validity; the name thus written. A signature may be written by hand, printed, stamped, typewritten, engraved, photographed, or cut from one instrument and attached to another, and a signature lithographed on an instrument by a party is sufficient for the purpose of signing it; it being immaterial with what kind of instrument a signature is made. Maricopa County v. Osborn, 60 Ariz. 290, 136 P.2d 270, 274. And whatever mark, symbol, or device one may choose to employ as representative of himself is sufficient.

A signature is made by use of any name, including any trade or assumed name, upon an instrument, or by any word or mark used in lieu of a written signature. U.C.C. § 3–401.

The signature to a deed may be made either by the grantor affixing his own signature, or by adopting one written for him, or by making his mark, or impressing some other sign or symbol on the paper by which the signature, though written by another for him, may be identified.

Public Officials. Many states have adopted the Uniform Facsimile Signatures of Public Officials Act.

Unauthorized signature. One made without actual, implied or apparent authority and includes a forgery. U.C.C. § 1 201(43).

Signature card. A card which a bank or other financial institution requires of its customers and on which the customer puts his signature and other information. It becomes a permanent file and permits the bank to compare the signature on the card with a signature on checks, withdrawal slips and other documents.

Signed. Includes any symbol executed or adopted by a party with present intention to authenticate a writing. U.C.C. § 1–201(39). See also **Signature.**

Signify. To make known by signs or words; express; communicate; announce; declare.

Signing judgment. See **Sign.**

Signum /sígnəm/. Lat. *Roman and civil law.* A sign; a mark; a seal. The seal of an instrument.

A species of proof. By *"signa"* were meant those species of *indicia* which come more immediately under the cognizance of the senses; such as stains of blood on the person of one accused of murder, indications of terror at being charged with the offense, and the like.

Saxon law. The sign of a cross prefixed as a sign of assent and approbation to a charter or deed.

Si ingratum dixeris, omnia dixeris /sáy ingréydəm díksərəs, ómn(i)yə díksərəs/. If you affirm that one is ungrateful, in that you include every charge. A Roman maxim.

Si ita est /sáy áydə èst/. Lat. If it be so. Emphatic words in the old writ of mandamus to a judge, commanding him, if the fact alleged be truly stated (*si ita est*), to affix his seal to a bill of exceptions.

Si judicas, cognosce /sày júwdəkəs kognósiy/. If you judge, understand.

Silence. The state of a person who does not speak, or of one who refrains from speaking. In the law of estoppel, "silence" implies knowledge and an opportunity to act upon it. Pence v. Langdon, 99 U.S. 578, 581, 25 L.Ed. 420; Stewart v. Wyoming Cattle Ranch Co., 128 U.S. 383, 9 S.Ct. 101, 32 L.Ed. 439.

Silence, estoppel by. Such estoppel arises where person is under duty to another to speak or failure to speak is inconsistent with honest dealings.

An agreement inferred from silence rests upon principle of "estoppel." Letres v. Washington Co-op. Chick Ass'n, 8 Wash.2d 64, 111 P.2d 594, 596. Silence, to work "estoppel", must amount to bad faith, Wise v. United States, D.C.Ky., 38 F.Supp. 130, 134; and, elements or essentials of such estoppel include: change of position to prejudice of person claiming estoppel, Sherlock v. Greaves, 106 Mont. 206, 76 P.2d 87, 91; damages if the estoppel is denied, James v. Nelson, C.C.A.Alaska, 90 F.2d 910, 917; duty and opportunity to speak, Codd v. Westchester Fire Ins. Co., 14 Wash.2d 600, 128 P.2d 968, 971; Merry v. Garibaldi, 48 Cal.App.2d 397, 119 P.2d 768, 771; ignorance of facts by person claiming estoppel, Nelson v. Chicago Mill & Lumber Corporation, C.C.A.Ark., 76 F.2d 17; inducing person claiming estoppel to alter his position; knowledge of facts and of rights by person estopped, Harvey v. Richard, 200 La. 97, 7 So.2d 674, 677; Consolidated Freight Lines v. Groenen, 10 Wash.2d 672, 117 P.2d 966, 968; misleading of party claiming estoppel, Ridgill v. Clarendon County, 192 S.C. 321, 6 S.E.2d 766, 768; Lincoln v. Bennett, Tex.Civ.App., 135 S.W.2d 632, 636; reliance upon silence of party sought to be estopped, Mosley v. Magnolia Petroleum Co., 45 N.M. 230, 114 P.2d 740, 751; New York Life Ins. Co. v. Talley, C.C.A. Iowa, 72 F.2d 715, 718.

Silence of accused. A person under arrest may maintain silence as to all matters connected with the arrest and crime except that he must furnish his correct name, permit fingerprinting, as well as voice and writing exemplars. His silence may not be commented upon at trial nor may any inference be drawn from the fact of his silence. If a defendant refuses to plead, the court will enter a plea of not guilty. Fed.R. Crim.P. 11(a).

Silentiarius /sələnshiyériyəs/. In English law, one of the privy council; also an usher who keeps good order in court.

Silent leges inter arma /sáylənt líyjiyz íntər ármə/. The power of law is suspended during war.

Silent partner. An investor in a firm who takes no active part in its management but who shares in its profits and losses. A dormant partner; one whose name does not appear in the firm, and who takes no active part in the business, but who has an interest in the concern, and shares the profits, and thereby becomes a partner, either absolutely, or as respects third persons.

Silicosis. A condition of massive fibrosis of the lungs, marked by shortness of breath and resulting from prolonged inhalation of silica dust. Froust v. Coating Specialists, Inc., D.C.La., 364 F.Supp. 1154, 1156.

Silver certificates. Species of paper money formerly in circulation in this country and which was redeemable in silver. Silver certificates have been replaced by federal reserve notes.

Silver platter doctrine. Evidence obtained illegally by state officials was formerly admissible in federal prosecutions because no federal official had participated in the violation of the defendant's rights. However, this rule no longer obtains. Elkins v. U. S., 364 U.S. 206, 80 S.Ct. 1437, 4 L.Ed.2d 1669.

Si meliores sunt quos ducit amor, plures sunt quos corrigit timor /sày mìyliyóriyz sént kwòws d(y)úwsəd éymor, pl(y)úriyz sènt kwòw kórəjət táymor/. If those are better who are led by love, those are the greater number who are corrected by fear.

Similar. Nearly corresponding; resembling in many respects; somewhat like; having a general likeness, although allowing for some degree of difference. Gangi v. Sears, Roebuck & Co., 33 Conn.Sup. 81, 360 A.2d 907, 908. Word "similar" is generally interpreted to mean that one thing has a resemblance in many respects, nearly corresponds, is somewhat like, or has a general likeness to some other thing but is not identical in form and substance, although in some cases "similar" may mean identical or exactly alike. It is a word with different meanings depending on context in which it is used. Guarantee Mut. Life Ins. Co. v. Harrison, Tex.Civ.App., 358 S.W.2d 404, 406.

Similar happenings. In law of evidence, generally things that happened at a time different from the time in dispute in the suit are not admissible because they are not material or relevant to what occurred at the disputed time. Where such happenings are admissible, the proof is limited to such issues as control of premises, or conditions which may have persisted.

Similar sales. In law of evidence, when market value is in issue, sales of similar property is admissible to prove value.

There is no specific rule to determine the degree of similarity necessary for evidence of a sale of other property to be admissible in a condemnation action. "Similar" does not mean "identical," and other sales need be only sufficiently similar in character and locality to provide the jury some reasonable basis for comparison. Lake County Forest Preserve Dist. v. Reliance Standard Life Ins. Co., 29 Ill.App.3d 145, 329 N.E.2d 344, 349. "Similarity" necessary to permit evidence of sale of one property to establish market value of another does not mean identical, but does require reasonable resemblance taking into consideration such factors as location, size and sale price; conditions surrounding sale, such as date and character of sale; business and residential advantages or disadvantages; and unimproved, improved or developed nature of land. Arkansas State Highway Commission v. Witkowski, 236 Ark. 66, 364 S.W.2d 309, 311.

Similiter /səmílədər/. Lat. In common law pleading, means likewise; the like. The name of the short formula used either at the end of pleadings or by itself, expressly of the acceptance of an issue of fact tendered by the opposite party; otherwise termed a "joinder in issue." The plaintiff's reply, that, as the defendant has put himself upon the country, he, the plaintiff, does the like. It occurs only when the plea has the conclusion to the country, and its effect is to join the plaintiff in the issue thus tendered by the defendant.

Similitudo legalis est casuum diversorum inter se collatorum similis ratio; quod in uno similium valet, valebit in altero. Dissimilium, dissimilis est ratio /səmìlətyúwdow ləgéyləs èst kéysyuwəm dəvərsórəm íntər síy kòlətórəm símələs réysh(iy)ow; kwód ìn yúnow səmíliyəm vælət, vəlíybəd ìn óltərow. dìsəmíliyəm dísímələs èst réysh(iy)ow/. Legal similarity is a similar reason which governs various cases when compared with each other; for what avails in one similar case will avail in the other. Of things dissimilar, the reason is dissimilar.

Simonia est voluntas sive desiderium emendi vel vendendi spiritualia vel spiritualibus adhærentia. Contractus ex turpi causa et contra bonos mores /səmówniyə èst vəlántæs sáyviy dèzədíriyəm əménday vèl vendénday spìhrətyuwéyl(i)yə vèl spìhrətyuwéyləbəs ædhərénsh(iy)ə. kəntræktəs èks tárpay kózə èt kóntrə bównows móriyz/. Simony is the will or desire of buying or selling spiritualities, or things pertaining thereto. It is a contract founded on a bad cause, and against morality.

Simony /síməniy/. In English ecclesiastical law, the corrupt presentation of any one to an ecclesiastical benefice for money, gift, or reward. 2 Bl.Comm. 278. An unlawful contract for presenting a clergyman to a benefice. The buying or selling of ecclesiastical preferments or of things pertaining to the ecclesiastical order. An unlawful agreement to receive a temporal reward for something holy or spiritual. Giving or receiving any material advantage in return for spiritual promotion, whether such advantage be actually received or only stipulated for.

Simpla /símplə/. Lat. In the civil law, the single value of a thing.

Simple. Pure; unmixed; not compounded; not aggravated; not evidenced by sealed writing or record.

As to simple Assault; Average; Battery; Blockade; Bond; Confession; Contract; Deposit; Imprisonment; Interest; Larceny; Obligation; and Trust, see those titles.

Simple kidnapping. A statutory form of unlawful imprisonment of a person which is not aggravated as in the case of child stealing or kidnapping for ransom.

Simple negligence. Such consists of failure to exercise for protection of others that degree of care and caution that would, under prevailing circumstances, be exercised by ordinarily prudent person. Pettingell v. Moede, 129 Colo. 484, 271 P.2d 1038, 1042, 1043. See **Negligence.**

Simple robbery. Gist of crime is the putting in fear and taking of property of another by force or intimidation. People v. Small, 177 Colo. 118, 493 P.2d 15, 19.

Simplex /símplèks/. Lat. Simple; single; pure; unqualified.

Simplex et pura donatio dici poterit, ubi nulla est adjecta conditio nec modus /símplèks èt pyúrə dənéysh(iy)ow dáysay pódərət, yúwbay nálə èst æjéktə kəndísh(iy)ow nèk mówdəs/. A gift is said to be pure and simple when no condition or qualification is annexed.

Simplicita est legibus amica; et nimia subtilitas in jure reprobatur /simplísədə èst líyjəbəs əmáykə, èt nímiyə səbtílətæs ìn júriy rèprəbéydər/. Simplicity is favorable to the laws; and too much subtlety in law is to be reprobated.

Simpliciter /simplísədər/. Lat. Simply; without ceremony; in a summary manner.

Directly; immediately; as distinguished from inferentially or indirectly.

By itself; by its own force; *per se.*

Simulate. To assume the mere appearance of, without the reality; to assume the signs or indications of, falsely; to counterfeit; feign; imitate; pretend. To engage, usually with the co-operation or connivance of another person, in an act or series of acts, which are apparently transacted in good faith, and intended to be followed by their ordinary legal consequences, but which in reality conceal a fraudulent purpose of the party to gain thereby some advantage to which he is not entitled, or to injure, delay, or defraud others.

Simulated contract. One which, though clothed in concrete form, has no existence in fact. It may at any time and at the demand of any person in interest be declared a sham and may be ignored by creditors of the apparent vendor.

Simulated fact. In the law of evidence, a fabricated fact; an appearance given to things by human device, with a view to deceive and mislead.

Simulated judgment. One which is apparently rendered in good faith, upon an actual debt, and intended to be collected by the usual process of law, but which in reality is entered by the fraudulent contrivance of the parties, for the purpose of giving to one of them an advantage to which he is not entitled, or of defrauding or delaying third persons.

Simulated sale. One which has all the appearance of an actual sale in good faith, intended to transfer the ownership of property for a consideration, but which in reality covers a collusive design of the parties to put the property beyond the reach of creditors, or proceeds from some other fraudulent purpose. It results when parties execute a formal act of sale of a thing for which no price is paid or is intended to be paid, and such sale has no legal effect and no title is transferred thereby. If there exists an actual consideration for transfer evidenced by alleged act of sale, no matter how inadequate it be, the transaction is not a "simulated sale", and, even though it be charged to be in fraud of vendor's creditors, such transfer cannot be set aside as a simulation although it may be subject to annulment on the ground of fraud or the giving of undue preference.

Simulatio latens /sìm(y)əléysh(iy)ow léyten(d)z/. Lat. A species of feigned disease, in which disease is actually present, but where the symptoms are falsely aggravated, and greater sickness is pretended than really exists.

Simulation. Assumption of appearance which was feigned, false, deceptive, or counterfeit. United States v. Peppa, D.C.Cal., 13 F.Supp. 669, 670.

In the civil law, misrepresentation or concealment of the truth; as where parties pretend to perform a transaction different from that in which they really are engaged. A feigned, pretended act; one which assumes the appearance without the reality and, being entirely without effect, it is held not to have existed, and, for that reason, it may be disregarded or attacked collaterally by any interested person. Freeman v. Woods, La.App., 1 So.2d 134, 136.

See also **Simulate.**

Simul cum /sáyməl kám/. Lat. Together with. In actions of tort and in prosecutions, where several persons united in committing the act complained of, some of whom were known and others not, it was usual to allege in the declaration or indictment that the persons therein named did the injury in question, "together with *(simul cum)* other persons unknown." In cases of riots, it was usual to charge that A B, together with others unknown, did the act complained of.

Simul et semel /sáyməl èt síyməl/. Lat. Together and at one time.

Simultaneous. A word of comparison meaning that two or more occurrences or happenings are identical in time.

Simultaneous Death Act. A Uniform State Law (adopted by most states) which provides that where passage of title to property depends upon the time of one's death, if there is insufficient evidence that persons have died otherwise than simultaneously, the property of each person shall be disposed of as if he had survived unless the Act provides otherwise. See also Uniform Probate Code, § 2–104.

Simultaneous death clause. A clause in a will which provides for the disposition of property in the event that there is no evidence as to the priority of time of death of the testator and another, commonly the testator's spouse. See Uniform Probate Code, § 2–104.

Since. This word's proper signification is "after," and in its apparent sense it includes the whole period between the event and the present time. "Since" a day named, does not necessarily include that day.

Sine /sáyniy/. Lat. Without.

Sine animo revertendi /sáyniy ǽnəmow rìyvərténday/. Without the intention of returning.

Sine assensu capituli /sáyniy əsén(t)s(y)uw kəpíchəlay/. Without the conssent of the chapter. In old English practice, a writ which lay where a dean, bishop, prebendary, abbot, prior, or master of a hospital aliened the lands holden in the right of his house, abbey, or priory, without the consent of the chapter; in which cases his successor might have this writ.

Sine consideratione curiæ /sáyniy kən(t)sìdərèyshiyówniy kyúriyiy/. Without the judgment of the court.

Sinecure /sáynəkyùr/sín°/. An office which yields a revenue to the incumbent, but makes little or no demand upon his time or attention.

Sine decreto /sáyniy dəkríydow/. Without authority of a judge.

Sine die /sáyniy dáy(iy)/. Without day; without assigning a day for a further meeting or hearing. Hence, a legislative body adjourns sine die when it adjourns without appointing a day on which to appear or assemble again. State ex rel. Jones v. Atterbury, Mo., 300 S.W.2d 806, 811.

A final adjournment; final dismissal of a cause. *Quod eat sine die,* that he go without day; the old form of a judgment for the defendant, *i.e.,* a judgment discharging the defendant from any further appearance in court.

Sine hoc quod /sáyniy hòk kwód/. Without this, that. A technical phrase in old pleading, of the same import with the phrase *"absque hoc quod."*

Sine numero /sáyniy n(y)úwmərow/. Without stint or limit. A term applied to common.

Sine possessione usucapio procedere non potest /sáyniy pəzèshiyówniy yùwsyuwkéyp(i)yow prəsíydəriy nòn pówdəst/. There can be no prescription without possession.

Sine prole /sáyniy prówliy/. Without issue. Used in genealogical tables, and often abbreviated into *"s.p."*

Sine qua non /sáyniy kwèy nón/. Without which not. That without which the thing cannot be. An indispensable requisite or condition.

Single. One only, being an individual unit; alone; one which is abstracted from others. State ex rel. Nelson v. Board of Com'rs of Yellowstone County, 111 Mont. 395, 109 P.2d 1106, 1107. Unitary; detached; individual; affecting only one person; containing only one part, article, condition, or covenant. Unmarried; the term being also applicable to a widow, and occasionally even to a married woman living apart from her husband. Sometimes, principal; dominating.

As to single Adultery; Bill; Bond; Combat; Demise; Entry; Escheat; Obligation; Original; and Tract, see those titles.

Single creditor. One having a lien only on a single fund;—distinguished from double creditor, who is one having a lien on two funds.

Single juror charge. The charge that, if there is any juror who is not reasonably satisfied from the evidence that plaintiff should recover a verdict against the defendant, jury cannot find against defendant.

Single publication rule. Under the "single publication rule," where an issue of a newspaper or magazine, or an edition of a book, contains a libelous statement, plaintiff has a single cause of action and the number of copies distributed is considered as relevant for damages but not as a basis for a new cause of action. Barres v. Holt, Rinehart and Winston, Inc., 131 N.J. Super. 371, 330 A.2d 38.

Singular. Each; as in the expression "all and singular." Also, individual. In grammar, the singular is used to express only one. In law, the singular frequently includes the plural. As to singular Successor; and Title, see those titles.

Singuli in solidum tenentur /síŋgyəlay in solədəm tənéntər/. Each is bound for the whole.

Sinking fund. Assets and their earnings earmarked for the retirement of bonds or other long-term obligations. A fund (usually invested), which will be used to replace improvements as needed. Most commonly set aside from the income of income producing property.

A fund arising from particular taxes, imposts or duties, which is appropriated toward the payment of the interest due on a public loan, and for the payment of the principal. Talbott v. City of Lyons, 171 Neb. 186, 105 N.W.2d 918, 925.

In general accounting, segregated assets that are being accumulated for a specific purpose. In governmental accounting, a fund established to accumulate resources for the retirement of bonds but not for the payment of interest, which is handled through the general fund or a special revenue fund.

Sinking fund debenture. A type of debenture which is backed by a provision for sinking fund (*q.v.*).

Sinking fund method of depreciation. The periodic charge is an amount so that when the charges are considered to be an annuity, the value of the annuity at the end of depreciable life is equal to the acquisition cost of the asset. In theory, the charge for a period ought also to include interest on the accumulated depreciation at the start of the period as well. A fund of cash is not necessarily, or even usually, accumulated.

Si non appareat quid actum est, erit consequens ut id sequamur quod in regione in qua actum est frequentatur /sáy nòn əpǽriyət kwìd ǽktəm èst, éhrət kənsíykwən(d)z əd íd səkwéymər kwòd in rìyjiyówniy in kwéy ǽktəm èst frìykwəntéydər/. If it does not appear what was agreed upon, the consequence will be that we must follow that which is the usage of the place where the agreement was made.

Si non omnes /sáy nòn ómniyz/. Lat. In English practice, a writ of association of justices whereby, if all in commission cannot meet at the day assigned, it is allowed that two or more may proceed with the business.

Si nulla sit conjectura quæ ducat alio, verba intelligenda sunt ex proprietate, non grammatica sed populari ex usu /sáy nálə sìt kònjekt(y)úrə kwìy d(y)úwkəd éyl(i)yow, várbə intèləjéndə sànt èks prəpràyətéydiy, nón grəmǽdəkə sèd popyəléray èks yúwsyuw/. If there be no inference which leads to a different result, words are to be understood according to their proper meaning, not in a grammatical, but in a popular and ordinary, sense.

Si paret /sáy pǽrət/. Lat. If it appears. In Roman law, words used in the formula by which the prætor appointed a judge, and instructed him how to decide the cause.

SIPC. Securities Investor Protection Act.

Sipessocua. In old English law, a franchise, liberty, or hundred.

Si plures conditiones ascriptæ fuerunt donationi conjunctim, omnibus est parendum; et ad veritatem copulative requiritur quod utraque pars sit vera, si divisim, quilibet vel alteri forum satis est obtemperare; et in disjunctivis, sufficit alteram partem esse veram /sày pl(y)úriyz kəndìshiyówniyz əskríptiy fyuwírənt dənèyshiyównay kənjáŋktəm, ómnəbəs èst pəréndəm, èd ǽd vèhrətéydəm kòpyələtáyviy rəkwíhrədər kwòd yuwtréykwiy párz sìt vírə, sày dəváyzəm, kwáyləbət vèl óltəray fórəm séydəs èst obtèmpərériy, èd ìn dìsjàŋktáyvəs, səfəsəd óltərəm párdəm ésiy vírəm/. If several conditions are conjunctively written in a gift, the whole of them must be complied with; and with respect to their truth, it is necessary that every part be true, taken jointly; if the conditions are separate, it is sufficient to comply with either one or other of them; and being disjunctive, that one or the other be true.

Si plures sint fidejussores, quotquot erunt numero, singuli in solidum tenentur /sáy pl(y)úriyz sìnt fàydəjəsóriyz kwótkwot éhrənt n(y)úwmərow, síŋgyəlay ìn sóladəm tənéntər/. If there are more sureties than one, how many soever they shall be, they shall each be held for the whole.

Si prius /sáy práyəs/. Lat. In old practice, if before. Formal words in the old writs for summoning juries.

Si quidem in nomine, cognomine, prænomine legatarii testator erraverit, cum de persona constat, nihilominus valet legatum /sày kwáydəm ìn nóməniy, kognóməniy, priynóməniy legətériyay testéydər ehrǽvərət, kàm díy pərsównə kón(t)stət, nay(h)ələmáynəs vǽlət ləgéydəm/. Although a testator may have mistaken the *nomen, cognomen,* or *prænomen* of a legatee, yet, if it be certain who is the person meant, the legacy is valid.

Si quid universitati debetur singulis non debetur, nec quod debet universitas singuli debent /sáy kwìd yùwnəvərsətéyday dəbíydər, síŋgyələs nòn dəbíydər, nék kwòd débət yùwnəvársətæs síŋgyəlay débənt/. If anything be owing to an entire body [or to a corporation], it is not owing to the individual members; nor do the individuals owe that which is owing by the entire body. 1 Bl.Comm. 484.

Si quis /sày kwís/. Lat. In the civil law, if any one. Formal words in the prætorian edicts. The word *"quis,"* though masculine in form was held to include women.

Si quis cum totum petiisset partem petat, exceptio rei judicatæ vocet /sày kwís kàm tówdəm pèdiyísət párdəm pédət, əksépsh(iy)ow ríyay jùwdəkéydiy vówsət/. If a party, when he should have sued for an entire claim, sues only for a part, the judgment is res judicata against another suit.

Si quis custos fraudem pupillo fecerit, a tutela removendus est /sày kwís kástəs fródəm pyuwpílow fíysərəd, èy tyuwtíylə rèmowvendus èst/. If any guardian should perform a fraudulent act against a ward, he must be removed from his charge.

Si quis prægnantem uxorem reliquit, non videtur sine liberis decessisse /sày kwís pregnǽntəm əksórəm rəlíkwət, nòn vədíydər sáyniy líbərəs dəsìysísiy/. If a man dies, leaving his wife pregnant, he shall not be considered to have died without children. A rule of the civil law.

Si quis, unum percusserit, cum alium percutere vellet, in felonia tenetur /sày kwís, yúwnəm pərkásərət, kàm éyl(i)yəm pərkyúwdəriy vélə d, ìn fəlówn(i)yə təníydər/. If a man kill one, meaning to kill another, he is held guilty of felony.

Si recognoscat /sáy rèkəgnóskət/. Lat. If he acknowledge. In old practice. A writ which lay for a creditor against his debtor for money numbered (*pecunia numerata*) or counted; that is, a specific sum of money, which the debtor had acknowledged in the county court, to owe him, as received *in pecuniis numeratis.*

Sister. A woman who has the same father and mother with another, or has one of them only. In the first case, she is called sister, simply; in the second, half-sister. The word is the correlative of "brother."

Sister corporation. Two corporations having common or substantially common ownership by same shareholders. Battelstein Inv. Co. v. U. S., D.C.Tex., 302 F.Supp. 320, 322.

Sister-in-law. Sister of one's spouse; wife of one's brother.

Si suggestio non sit vera, literæ patentes vacuæ sunt /sáy səgjés(h)ch(iy)ow nón sìt vírə, lídəriy pəténtiyz vǽkyuwiy sànt/. If the suggestion be not true, the letters patent are void.

Sit. To hold court; to do any act of a judicial nature. To hold a session, as of a court, grand jury, legislative body, etc. To be formally organized and proceeding with the transaction of business.

Sit-down strike. A strike in which the workers stay in the plant but refuse to work.

Site /sáyt/. A plot of ground suitable or set apart for some specific use. A seat or ground plot. The term does not of itself necessarily mean a place or tract of land fixed by definite boundaries. See also **Place; Scite; Situs.**

Si te fecerit securum /sáy tíy fésərət səkyúrəm/. If he make you secure. See **Si fecerit te securum.**

Sithcundmam. In Saxon law, the high constable of a hundred.

Sitting. The part of the year in which judicial business is transacted. A session or term of court; usually plural. See **Session.**

Sitting in bank or banc. A session of the court in which all judges or at least a quorum of judges sit and hear cases. Under current practice, the term is reserved almost exclusively for appellate courts and in this connection it is contrasted with single justice sitting.

Sittings in camera. See **Chamber.**

Situate. To give a specific position to; fix a site for; to place in certain position.

Situation. State of being placed; posture. Position as regards conditions and circumstances; state; condition. Bellomy v. Bruce, 303 Ill.App. 349, 25 N.E.2d 428, 433.

Situation of danger. Within the meaning of the last clear chance rule as applicable to a plaintiff operating a moving vehicle, is reached only when plaintiff, in moving toward path of an on-coming train or vehicle has reached a position from which he cannot escape by ordinary care, and it is not enough that plaintiff was merely approaching a position of danger.

Situs /sáydəs/. Lat. Situation; location; *e.g.* location or place of crime or business. Site; position; the place where a thing is considered, for example, with reference to jurisdiction over it, or the right or power to tax it. It imports fixedness of location. Situs of property, for tax purposes, is determined by whether the taxing state has sufficient contact with the personal property sought to be taxed to justify in fairness the particular tax. Town of Cady v. Alexander Const. Co., 12 Wis.2d 236, 107 N.W.2d 267, 270.

Generally, personal property has its taxable "situs" in that state where owner of it is domiciled. Smith v. Lummus, 149 Fla. 660, 6 So.2d 625, 627, 628. Situs of a trust means place of performance of active duties of trustee. Campbell v. Albers, 313 Ill.App. 152, 39 N.E.2d 672, 676.

For business situs, see **Business.** See also **Place.**

Sive tota res evincatur, sive pars, habet regressum emptor in venditorem /sáyviy tówdə ríyz ìyviŋkéydər, sáyviy párz, héybət rəgrésəm ém(p)tər in vèndətórəm/. The purchaser who has been evicted in whole or in part has an action against the vendor.

Sixteenth Amendment. An amendment of 1913 to the U.S. Constitution which permits Congress to tax incomes "from whatever source derived," thus nullifying the Supreme Court's decisions in Pollock v. Farmers' Loan and Trust Co., which had declared that an income tax was a direct tax, which would be constitutionally valid only if apportioned among the States according to population.

Sixth Amendment. The Sixth Amendment of the U.S. Constitution includes such rights as the right to speedy and public trial by an impartial jury, right to be informed of the nature of the accusation, the right to confront witnesses, the right to assistance of counsel and compulsory process.

Sixty-day notice. Under Taft-Hartley Act, notice which must be given by either party to a collective bargaining agreement for reopening or terminating the contract. During such period, strikes and lockouts are prohibited. See 29 U.S.C.A. § 158(d).

Skeleton bill. One drawn, indorsed, or accepted in blank.

Skill. Practical and familiar knowledge of the principles and processes of an art, science, or trade, combined with the ability to apply them in practice in a proper and approved manner and with readiness and dexterity.

Skilled witnesses. One possessing knowledge and experience as to particular subject which are not acquired by ordinary persons. Such witness is allowed to give evidence on matters of opinion and abstract fact. See also **Expert witness.**

Skinpop. An intramuscular injection of narcotic drug.

Skiptracing. Service which assists creditors in locating delinquent debtors. Also, such services may include location of missing heirs, witnesses, stockholders, bondholders, assets, bank accounts, or the like.

S.L. Abbreviation for "session [or statute] laws."

Slains. See **Letters of slains.**

Slander. The speaking of base and defamatory words tending to prejudice another in his reputation, office, trade, business, or means of livelihood. Little Stores v. Isenberg, 26 Tenn.App. 357, 172 S.W.2d 13, 16; Harbison v. Chicago, R. I. & P. Ry. Co., 327 Mo. 440, 37 S.W.2d 609, 616. Oral defamation; the speaking of false and malicious words concerning another, whereby injury results to his reputation. Johnston v. Savings Trust Co. of St. Louis, Mo., 66 S.W.2d 113, 114; Lloyd v. Commissioner of Internal Revenue, C.C.A.7, 55 F.2d 842, 844. The essential elements of slander are: (a) a false and defamatory statement concerning another; (b) an unprivileged communication; (c) fault amounting at least to negligence on the part of the publisher; and (d) either actionability of the statement irrespective of harm or the existence of special harm. Restatement, Second, Torts § 558.

"Libel" and "slander" are both methods of defamation; the former being expressed by print, writing, pictures, or signs; the latter by oral expressions or transitory gestures. Restatement, Second, Torts, § 568.

See also **Actionable per quod; Actionable per se; Per quod; Per se; Slanderous per se.**

Slanderer. One who commits slander. See **Slander.**

Slander of title. A false and malicious statement, oral or written, made in disparagement of a person's title to real or personal property, or of some right of his causing him special damage. Reliable Mfg. Co. v. Vaughan Novelty Mfg. Co., 294 Ill.App. 601, 13 N.E.2d 518; Cawrse v. Signal Oil Co., 164 Or. 666, 103 P.2d 729, 730. "Malice" as essential element of "slander of title" purports an intention to vex, injure or annoy another person. Cawrse v. Signal Oil Co., 164 Or. 666, 103 P.2d 729, 730. See also **Jactitation.**

Slanderous per se. Slanderous in itself; such words as are deemed slanderous without proof of special damages. Generally an utterance is deemed "slanderous per se" when publication (a) charges the commission of a crime; (b) imputes some offensive or loathsome disease which would tend to deprive a person of society; (c) charges a woman is not chaste; or (d) tends to injure a party in his trade, business, office or occupation. Munafo v. Helfand, D.C.N.Y., 140 F.Supp. 234, 238. See Restatement, Second, Torts, § 570.

Slate. List of candidates for public office or for positions on board of directors.

Slave. A person who is wholly subject to the will of another; one who has no freedom of action, but whose person and services are wholly under the control of another. One who is under the power of a master, and who belongs to him; so that the master may sell and dispose of his person, of his industry, and of his labor, without his being able to do anything, have anything, or acquire anything, but what must belong to his master. The 13th Amendment abolished slavery.

Slavery. The condition of a slave; that civil relation in which one man has absolute power over the life, fortune, and liberty of another. The 13th Amendment abolished slavery.

Slave-trade. The traffic in slaves, or the buying and selling of slaves for profit.

Slay. This word, in an indictment, adds nothing to the force and effect of the word "kill," when used with reference to the taking of human life. It is particularly applicable to the taking of human life in battle; and, when it is not used in this sense, it is synonymous with "kill."

Sleeping or silent partner. See **Silent partner.**

Slight. A word of indeterminate meaning, variously defined as inconsiderable; unimportant; trifle; remote; insignificant. Moxley v. Hertz, 216 U.S. 344, 356, 30 S.Ct. 305, 308, 54 L.Ed. 510.

As to slight Care; Evidence; Fault and Negligence, see those titles.

Slip law. A legislative enactment which is separately and promptly published in pamphlet or in single sheet format after its passage.

Slip law print. An annotated pamphlet print (called a slip law print) of each public and private law enacted by Congress is issued shortly after being signed by the President. Slip laws are cumulated into the U.S. Statutes at Large. See **Statutes** (*Statutes at large*).

Slip opinion. An individual court decision published separately soon after it is rendered.

Slot machine. Within statute prohibiting operation of slot machines or similar gambling device, an apparatus by which a person depositing money therein may, by chance, get directly or indirectly money or articles of value worth either more or less than the money deposited. Elder v. Camp, 193 Ga. 320, 18 S.E.2d 622, 624.

Slough. An arm of a river, flowing between islands and the main-land, and separating the islands from one another. Sloughs have not the breadth of the main river, nor does the main body of water of the stream flow through them.

Slowdown. An organized effort by workers in a plant by which production is slowed to bring pressure on the employer for better terms and conditions of working.

Sluiceway. An artificial channel into which water is let by a sluice. Specifically, a trench constructed over the bed of a stream, so that logs or lumber can be floated down to a convenient place of delivery.

Slum. A squalid, run-down section of a city, town or village, ordinarily inhabited by the very poor and destitute classes; overcrowding is usually a prevailing characteristic.

Slush fund. Money collected or spent for corrupt purposes such as illegal lobbying or the like. Boehm v. United States, C.C.A.Mo., 123 F.2d 791, 812.

Small Business Administration. The fundamental purposes of the Small Business Administration (SBA) are to: aid, counsel, assist, and protect the interests of small business; insure that small business concerns receive a fair proportion of Government purchases, contracts, and subcontracts, as well as of the sales of Government property; make loans to small business concerns, State and local development companies, and the victims of floods or other catastrophes, or of certain types of economic injury; license, regulate, and make loans to small business investment companies; improve the management skills of small business owners, potential owners, and managers; conduct studies of the economic environment; and guarantee leases entered into by small business concerns as well as surety bonds issued to them.

Small business corporation. A corporation which satisfies the definition of I.R.C. § 1371(a), § 1244(c)(2) or both. Satisfaction of I.R.C. § 1371(a) permits a Subchapter S election, while satisfaction of § 1244 enables the shareholders of the corporation to claim an ordinary loss on the worthlessness of the stock.

Small Business Investment Act. Federal legislation enacted in 1958 under which investment companies may be organized for supplying long term equity capital to small businesses.

Small Claims Court. A special court (sometimes also called "Conciliation Court") which provides expeditious, informal, and inexpensive adjudication of small claims. Jurisdiction of such courts is usually limited to collection of small debts and accounts. Proceedings are very informal with parties normally representing themselves. These courts are often divisions or departments of courts of general jurisdiction.

Small estate probate. See **Estate.**

Small loan acts. Statutes in effect in nearly all the States fixing the maximum legal rate of interest and other terms on short-term loans by banks and finance companies.

Smart-money. Vindictive, punitive or exemplary damages given by way of punishment and example, in cases of gross misconduct of defendant. See **Damages.**

Smith Act. Federal law which punishes, among other activities, the advocacy of the overthrow of the government by force or violence. An anti-sedition law. 18 U.S.C.A. § 2385.

Smuggling. The offense of importing or exporting prohibited articles without paying the duties chargeable upon them. The fraudulent taking into a country, or out of it, merchandise which is lawfully prohibited. Quoted and approved by Brewer, J., in Dunbar v. U. S., 156 U.S. 185, 15 S.Ct. 325, 39 L.Ed. 390.

"Smuggle" has well-understood meaning at common law, signifying bringing on shore, or carrying from shore, of goods, wares, and merchandise for which duty has not been paid, or goods the importation or exportation whereof is prohibited. Williamson v. U. S., C.A.Cal., 310 F.2d 192, 195. See also **Contraband.**

Smut. See **Obscene.**

So. In the same manner as has been stated; under this circumstance; in this way, referring to something which is asserted. Sometimes the equivalent of "hence," or "therefore," and it is thus understood whenever what follows is an illustration of, or conclusion from, what has gone before.

In connection with time, it suggests a period of indefinite duration. Thus, an agreement to pay rent "within a week or so".

Soakage /sówkəj/. As used in the laws and regulations relating to withdrawal of liquors from bonded warehouses, the spirits which in course of time in the warehouse had been absorbed by the staves of the barrel containing it.

Sober. Moderate in, or abstinent from, the use of intoxicating liquors.

Sobrini and **sobrinæ** /səbráynay/səbráyniy/. Lat. In the civil law, the children of cousins, german in general.

Soc, sok, or **soka.** In Saxon law, jurisdiction; a power or privilege to administer justice and execute the laws; also a shire, circuit, or territory.

Soca /só(w)kə/. A seigniory or lordship, enfranchised by the king, with liberty of holding a court of his *socmen* or *socagers; i.e.,* his tenants.

Socage /sówkəj/. A species of tenure, in England, whereby the tenant held certain lands in consideration of certain inferior services of husbandry to be performed by him to the lord of the fee. In its most general and extensive signification, a tenure by any certain and determinate service. And in this sense it is by the ancient writers constantly put in opposition to tenure by chivalry or knight-service, where the render was precarious and uncertain. Socage is of two sorts,—free socage, where the services are not only certain, but honorable; and villein socage, where the services, though certain, are of baser nature. Such as hold by the former tenure are also called in Glanvil and other authors by the name of "*liberi*

sokemanni," or tenants in free socage. By the statute 12 Car. 2, c. 24, all the tenures by knight-service were, with one or two immaterial exceptions, converted into free and common socage.

Socager /só(w)kəjər/. A tenant by socage.

Socagium idem est quod servitum socæ; et soca, idem est quod caruca /səkéyj(iy)əm áydəm èst sərvísh(iy)əm sówsiy, èt sówkə, áydəm èst kwòd kəhrúwkə/. Socage is the same as service of the soc; and soc is the same thing as a plow.

Socer /sówsər/. Lat. In the civil law, a wife's father; a father-in-law.

Social contract, or compact. In political philosophy, a term applied to the theory of the origin of society associated chiefly with the names of Hobbes, Locke and Rousseau, though it can be traced back to the Greek Sophists. Rousseau (Contract Social) held that in the pre-social state man was unwarlike and timid. Laws resulted from the combination of men who agreed, for mutual protection, to surrender individual freedom of action. Government must therefore rest on the consent of the governed.

Social guest. A person who goes onto the property of another for companionship, diversion and enjoyment of hospitality. Fugate v. Sears, Roebuck & Co., 12 Ill.App.3d 656, 299 N.E.2d 108, 121. See also **Guest.**

Social insurance. See **Insurance.**

Social Security Act. Federal legislation creating the Social Security Administration *(q.v.).* 42 U.S.C.A. § 301 *et seq.* See also **Federal Insurance Contributions Act.**

Social Security Administration. The Social Security Administration, under the direction of the Commissioner of Social Security, administers a national program of contributory social insurance whereby employees, employers, and the self-employed pay contributions which are pooled in special trust funds. When earnings stop or are reduced because the worker retires, dies, or becomes disabled, monthly cash benefits are paid to replace part of the earnings the person or family has lost. In addition to making social security payments, the SSA also administers cash assistance programs such as Aid to Families with Dependent Children (AFDC), and Supplementary Security Income (SSI).

Socida /səsáydə/. In civil law, the name of a contract by which one man delivers to another, either for a small recompense or for a part of the profits, certain animals on condition that if any of them perish they shall be replaced by the bailee or he shall pay their value.

A contract of hiring, with the condition that the bailee takes upon him the risk of the loss of the thing hired.

Sociedad /sowsìyeyðáð/. In Spanish law, partnership.

Sociedad anonima /sowsìyeyðáð anónima/. In Spanish and Mexican law, a business corporation.

Societas /səsáyətæs/. Lat. In the civil law, partnership; a partnership; the contract of partnership. A contract by which the goods or labor of two or more are united in a common stock, for the sake of sharing in the gain.

Societas leonina /səsáyətæs líyənáynə/. That kind of society or partnership by which the entire profits belong to some of the partners, in exclusion of the rest. So called in allusion to the fable of the lion, who, having entered into partnership with other animals for the purpose of hunting, appropriated all the prey to himself.

Societas navalis /səsáyətæs nævéyləs/. A naval partnership; an association of vessels; a number of ships pursuing their voyage in company, for purposes of mutual protection.

Société /sowsìyeytéy/. Fr. In French law, partnership. See **Commendam.**

Société anonyme /sowsìyeytéy ànowníym/. In French law originally a partnership conducted in the name of one of the members; the others were strictly secret partners. To creditors of the firm they came into no relation and under no liability. An association where the liability of all the partners is limited. It had in England until lately no other name than that of "chartered company," meaning thereby a joint-stock company whose shareholders, by a charter from the crown, or a special enactment of the legislature, stood exempted from any liability for the debts of the concern, beyond the amount of their subscriptions.

Société d'acquets. A written contract between husband and wife to regard as community property only those things which are acquired during the marriage.

Société en commandite /sowsìyeytéy òn kòmondíyt/. In Louisiana, a partnership formed by a contract by which one person or partnership agrees to furnish another person or partnership a certain amount, either in property or money, to be employed by the person or partnership to whom it is furnished, in his or their own name or firm, on condition of receiving a share in the profits, in the proportion determined by the contract, and of being liable to losses and expenses to the amount furnished and no more.

Société en nom collectif /sowsìyeytéy òn nówm kolektíyf/. A partnership in which all the members are jointly and severally liable.

Société en participation /sowsìyeytéy òn partìsiypasyówn/. A joint adventure.

Société par actions /sowsìyeytéy pàr àks(i)yówn/. A joint stock company.

Society. An association or company of persons (generally unincorporated) united together by mutual consent, in order to deliberate, determine, and act jointly for some common purpose. In a wider sense, the community or public; the people in general. Gilmer v. Stone, 120 U.S. 586, 7 S.Ct. 689, 30 L.Ed. 734.

Term "society," loss of which is recoverable element in death action under general maritime law, embraces broad range of mutual benefits each family member receives from other's continued existence, including love, affection, care, attention, companionship, comfort and protection; thus, widow, parent, brother, sister, or child may be compensated for loss of society. Consolidated Machines, Inc. v. Protein Products Corp., D.C.Fla., 428 F.Supp. 209, 228.

Within rule that husband is entitled to damages for loss of wife's "society" through wrongful injury, means such capacities for usefulness, aid, and comfort as a wife as she possessed at the time of the injuries. Homan v. Missouri Pac. R. Co., 335 Mo. 30, 70 S.W.2d 869. See also **Consortium.**

Civil society—usually, a state, nation, or body politic.

Socii mei socius meus socius non est /sówshiyay míyay sówsh(iy)əs míyəs sówsh(iy)əs nón èst/. The partner of my partner is not my partner.

Socius /sówsh(iy)əs/. Lat. In the civil law, a partner.

Socman /sókmən/. A socager.

Free socmen. In old English law, tenants in free socage.

Socmanry /sókmənriy/. Free tenure by socage.

Socna /sóknə/. A privilege, liberty, or franchise.

Sodomite /sódəmayt/. One who has been guilty of sodomy.

Sodomy. A carnal copulation by human beings with each other against nature, or with a beast. State v. Young, 140 Or. 228, 13 P.2d 604, 607. Sodomy is oral or anal copulation between persons who are not husband and wife or consenting adult members of the opposite sex, or between a person and an animal, or coitus with an animal. Kansas Criminal Code.

So help you God. The words commonly at the end of a common oath.

Soil bank. A federal program of conservation, under which farmers are paid for not growing crops, or growing noncommercial vegetation, in order to preserve the quality of the soil, as well as to avoid surpluses.

Soit /swá/swéy/. Fr. Let it be; be it so. A term used in several law; French phrases employed in English law, particularly as expressive of the will or assent of the sovereign in formal communications with parliament or with private suitors.

Soit baile aux commons /swà béyl ów kómən(d)z/. Let it be delivered to the commons. The form of indorsement on a bill when sent to the house of commons.

Soit baile aux seigneurs /swà béyl ów seynyúrz/. Let it be delivered to the lords. The form of indorsement on a bill in parliament when sent to the house of lords.

Soit droit fait al partie /swà dróyt féyt àl partíy/. In English law, let right be done to the party. A phrase written on a petition of right, and subscribed by the king.

Soit fait comme il est desire /swà féyt kòm íyl dezíréy/. Let it be as it is desired. The royal assent to private acts of parliament.

Sojourning /səjə́rniŋ/. This term means something more than "traveling," and applies to a temporary, as contradistinguished from a permanent, residence. In re Gahn's Will, 110 Misc. 96, 180 N.Y.S. 262, 266.

Sokemanries /só(w)kmənriyz/. Lands and tenements which were not held by knight-service, nor by grand serjeanty, nor by petit, but by simple services; being, as it were, lands enfranchised by the king or his predecessors from their ancient demesne. Their tenants were *sokemans.*

Sokemans /só(w)kmən(d)z/. In old English law, those who held their lands in socage.

Soke-reeve /só(w)kriyv/. The lord's rent gatherer in the soca.

Sola ac per se senectus donationem testamentum aut transactionem non vitiat /sówlə æk pàr síy sənéktəs dəneyshiyównəm tèstəméntəm òt trænzækshiyównəm nòn víshiyət/. Old age does not alone and of itself vitiate a will or gift.

Solar /sowlár/. In Spanish law, land; the demesne, with a house, situate in a strong or fortified place.

Solar day. That period of time which begins at sunrise and ends at sunset.

Solares /sowláreys/. In Spanish law, lots of ground. This term is frequently found in grants from the Spanish government of lands in America.

Solarium /səlériyəm/. Lat. In the civil law, a rent paid for the ground, where a person built on the public land. A ground rent.

Solar month. A calendar month. See **Month.**

Solatium /səléysh(iy)əm/. Compensation. Damages allowed for injury to the feelings.

Sold. See **Sale.**

Soldiers' and Sailors' Civil Relief Act. A Federal law that suspends or modifies a military person's civil liabilities and requires persons who want to enforce their claims against persons in the service to follow certain procedures. 50 U.S.C.A. App. § 501 et seq.

Soldier's will. Similar to a seaman's will which is informal in nature and may dispose only of the personal property of the testator. A nuncupative will *(q.v.).*

Sold note. A note given by a broker, who has effected a sale of merchandise, to the buyer, stating the fact of sale, quantity, price, etc. Also called "confirmation" notice.

Sole. Single; individual; separate; the opposite of joint; as a *sole tenant.* Comprising only one person; the opposite of aggregate; as a *sole corporation.* Without another or others.

Unmarried; as a *feme sole.*

Sole actor doctrine. Under this doctrine a principal is charged with the knowledge of his agent. It contemplates that agent must have ostensibly endeavored to benefit his principal, and even though he did not do so and his acts were for his personal benefit, possibly through defalcation, the third party who obligated himself must have been under the impression that he was dealing with the principal. General American

Life Ins. Co. v. Anderson, D.C.Ky., 46 F.Supp. 189, 195, 196, 198. It is based on the presumption that by reason of the relationship between an agent and his principal the principal is presumed to have been told everything the agent has done and presumed to have known of his actions and promises. Federal Deposit Ins. Corporation v. Pendleton, D.C.Ky., 29 F.Supp. 779, 782, 783.

Sole and unconditional owner. See **Owner.**

Sole cause. As respects negligence of plaintiff or third party as the sole cause of injury so as to relieve defendant from liability, means the act or negligence of plaintiff or a third party directly causing the injury without any concurring or contributory negligence of defendant. Dixon v. Wabash R. Co., Mo.App., 198 S.W.2d 395, 398. Term means the act or negligence of the plaintiff or a third party directly causing the injury without any concurring or contributory negligence of defendant. Jurgens v. Thompson, 350 Mo. 914, 169 S.W.2d 353, 357. See also **Proximate cause.**

Solemn /sóləm/. Formal; in regular form; with all the forms of a proceeding. As to solemn "Form," see Probate. As to solemn oath, see **Corporal oath;** as to solemn war, see **War.**

Solemnes legum formulæ /səlémniyz líygəm fórmyəliy/. Lat. In the civil law, solemn forms of laws; forms of forensic proceedings and of transacting legal acts. One of the sources of the unwritten law of Rome.

Solemnitas attachiamentorum /səlémnətæs ətæch(iy)-əmentórəm/. In old English practice, solemnity or formality of attachments. The issuing of attachments in a certain formal and regular order.

Solemnitates juris sunt observandæ /səlèmnətéydiyz júrəs sànt òbsərvændiy/. The solemnities of law are to be observed.

Solemnity /səlémnədiy/. A rite or ceremony; the formality established by law to render a contract, agreement, or other act valid.

Solemnize /sóləmnayz/. To enter marriage publicly before witnesses in contrast to a clandestine or common law marriage.

Solemn occasion. Within constitutional provision empowering the Legislature to require the opinion of the Justices on important questions of law means occasion when such questions of law are necessary to be determined by the body making the inquiry in the exercise of the power intrusted to it by the Constitution or laws.

Sole proprietorship. A form of business in which one person owns all the assets of the business in contrast to a partnership and corporation. The sole proprietor is solely liable for all the debts of the business.

Solicit. To appeal for something; to apply to for obtaining something; to ask earnestly; to ask for the purpose of receiving; to endeavor to obtain by asking or pleading; to entreat, implore, or importune; to make petition to; to plead for; to try to obtain; and though the word implies a serious request, it requires no particular degree of importunity, entreaty, imploration, or supplication. People v. Phillips, 70 Cal.

App.2d 449, 160 P.2d 872, 874. To awake or excite to action, or to invite. The term implies personal petition and importunity addressed to a particular individual to do some particular thing.

As used in context of solicitation to commit a crime, term means to command, authorize, urge, incite, request, or advise another to commit a crime. See also **Solicitation.**

Solicitation. Asking; enticing; urgent request. Any action which the relation of the parties justifies in construing into a serious request. Thus "solicitation of chastity" is the asking or urging a woman to surrender her chastity. The word is also used in such phrases as "solicitation to larceny," to bribery, etc.

For the crime of solicitation to be completed, it is only necessary that the actor, with intent that another person commit a crime, have enticed, advised, incited, ordered or otherwise encouraged that person to commit a crime. The crime solicited need not be committed.

A person is guilty of solicitation to commit a crime if with the purpose of promoting or facilitating its commission he commands, encourages or requests another person to engage in specific conduct which would constitute such crime or an attempt to commit such crime or which would establish his complicity in its commission or attempted commission. Model Penal Code, § 5.02.

Under Model Penal Code, § 5.05, solicitation of a crime is of the same grade and degree as the most serious offense solicited.

Solicitation of bribe. Asking, or enticing, or requesting of another to commit crime of bribery. State v. Wallace, Del.Super., 9 Storey 123, 214 A.2d 886, 889.

Solicitor. Chief law officer of city, town, or other governmental body or department; see *e.g.* **Solicitor General.**

In England, to become a solicitor a person must be articled to a practicing solicitor, pass the necessary examinations conducted by the Law Society, and be admitted by the Master of the Rolls. A solicitor may practice in the Bankruptcy Court, county courts, petty sessions, certain proceedings in the Crown Court, most inferior courts, and also in chambers of the Supreme Court. See also **Barrister.**

Solicitor General. The Solicitor General of the United States is in charge of representing the Government in the Supreme Court. He decides what cases the Government should ask the Supreme Court to review and what position the Government should take in cases before the Court. He supervises the preparation of the Government's Supreme Court briefs and other legal documents and the conduct of the oral arguments in the Court and argues most of the important cases himself. The Solicitor General's duties also include deciding whether the United States should appeal in all cases it loses before the lower courts.

Solidarity. In the civil law, when several persons bind themselves towards another for the same sum, at the same time, and in the same contract; and so obligate themselves that each may be compelled to pay the whole debt, and that payment made by one of them

exonerates the others towards the creditor; and the obligation thus contracted is one, in solido, although one of the debtors be obliged differently from the others to the payment of one and the same thing; as if the one be but conditionally bound, while the engagement of the others is pure and simple, or if the one is allowed a term which is not granted to the others.

Solidary. A term of civil-law origin, signifying that the right or interest spoken of is joint or common. A "solidary obligation" corresponds to a "joint and several" obligation in the common law; that is, one for which several debtors are bound in such wise that each is liable for the entire amount, and not merely for his proportionate share. But in the civil law the term also includes the case where there are several creditors, as against a common debtor, each of whom is entitled to receive the entire debt and give an acquittance for it.

Solidum /sólədəm/. Lat. In the civil law, a whole; an entire or undivided thing.

Solinum /səláynəm/. In old English law, two plowlands, and somewhat less than a half.

Solitary confinement. In a general sense, the separate confinement of a prisoner, with only occasional access of any other person, and that only at the discretion of the jailer. In a stricter sense, the complete isolation of a prisoner from all human society, and his confinement in a cell so arranged that he has no direct intercourse with or sight of any human being, and no employment or instruction. Medley, Petitioner, 134 U.S. 160, 10 S.Ct. 384, 33 L.Ed. 835.

Solo cedit quod solo implantatur /sówlow síydət kwòd sówlow implæntéytər/. That which is planted in the soil belongs to the soil. The proprietor of the soil becomes also the proprietor of the seed, the plant, and the tree, as soon as these have taken root.

Solo cedit quod solo inædificatur /sówlow síydət kwòd sówlow inèdəfəkéydər/. That which is built upon the soil belongs to the soil. The proprietor of the soil becomes also proprietor of the building erected upon it.

Solum provinciale /sówləm prəvìnshiyéyliy/. Lat. In Roman law, the *solum italicum* (an extension of the old *Ager Romanus*) admitted full ownership, and of the application to it of *usucapio;* whereas the *solum provinciale* (an extension of the old *Ager Publicus*) admitted of a possessory title only, and of *longi temporis possessio* only. Justinian abolished all distinctions between the two, sinking the *italicum* to the level of the *provinciale.*

Solum rex hoc non facere potest, quod non potest injuste agere /sówləm réks hók nòn fǽsəriy pówdəst, kwód nòn pówdəst injóstiy ǽjəriy/. This alone the king cannot do, he cannot act unjustly.

Solus deus facit hæredem, non homo /sówləs díyəs féysət həríydəm, nòn hówmow/. God alone makes the heir, not man.

Solutio /səl(y)úwsh(iy)ow/. Lat. In civil law, payment, satisfaction, or release; any species of discharge of an obligation accepted as satisfactory by the creditor. The term refers not so much to the counting out of money as to the substance of the obligation.

Solutio indebiti /səl(y)úwsh(iy)ow indébəday/. In the civil law, payment of what was not due. From the payment of what was not due arises an obligation *quasi ex contractu.* When one has erroneously given or performed something to or for another, for which he was in no wise bound, he may redemand it, as if he had only lent it. The term *"solutio indebiti"* is here used in a very wide sense, and includes also the case where one performed labor for another, or assumed to pay a debt for which he was not bound, or relinquished a right or released a debt, under the impression that he was legally bound to do so.

Solutione feodi militis parliamenti, or **feodi burgensis parliamenti** /səl(y)ùwshiyówniy fyúwday mílədəs pàrl(iy)əméntay/°bərjén(t)səs pàrl(iy)əméntay/. Old writs whereby knights of the shire and burgesses might have recovered their wages or allowance if it had been refused.

Solutio pretii emptionis loco habetur /səl(y)úwsh(iy)ow préshiyay èm(p)shiyównəs lówkow həbíydər/. The payment of the price [of a thing] is held to be in place of a purchase [operates as a purchase].

Solutus /səl(y)úwdəs/. In the civil law, loosed; freed from confinement; set at liberty.

Solvabilité /solvabìliytéy/. Fr. In French law, ability to pay; solvency.

Solvency. Ability to pay debts as they mature. Ability to pay debts in the usual and ordinary course of business. Jeck v. O'Meara, 343 Mo. 559, 122 S.W.2d 897, 903. Present ability of debtor to pay out of his estate all his debts. Excess of assets over liabilities. Akin v. Hull, 222 Mo.App. 1022, 9 S.W.2d 688, 690. Also such status of a person's property as that it may be reached and subjected by process of law, without his consent, to the payment of such debts. Graf v. Allen, 230 Mo.App. 721, 74 S.W.2d 61, 66. "Solvency" within Bankruptcy Act presupposes ability to make ultimate payment of obligations then owed from assets then owned. Mossler Acceptance Co. v. Martin, C.A.Fla., 322 F.2d 183, 186. The opposite of *insolvency (q.v.).* Kennedy v. Burr, 101 Wash. 61, 171 P.2d 1022, 1024.

Solvendo esse /solvéndow ésiy/. Lat. To be in a state of solvency; *i.e.,* able to pay.

Solvendo esse nemo intelligitur nisi qui solldum potest solvere /solvéndow ésiy níymow ìntəlíjədər náysay kwày sóladəm pówdəst sólvəriy/. No one is considered to be solvent unless he can pay all that he owes.

Solvendum in futuro /solvéndəm ìn fyuwtyúrow/. Lat. To be paid in the future. Used of an indebtedness which is said to be *debitum in presenti* (due now) and *solvendum in futuro* (payable in the future). An interest in an estate may be rested *in presenti,* though it be *solvendum in futuro,* enjoyable in the future.

Solvent. See **Solvency.**

For "solvent debt" and "solvent partner" see **Debt** and **Partner.**

Solvere /sólvəriy/. Lat. To pay; to comply with one's engagement; to do what one has undertaken to do; to release one's self from obligation, as by payment of a debt.

Solvere pœnas /sólvəriy píynəs/. To pay the penalty.

Solvit /sólvət/. Lat. He paid; paid.

Solvit ad diem /sólvəd æd dáyəm/. He paid at the day. The technical name of the plea, in an action of debt on bond, that the defendant paid the money *on the day* mentioned in the condition.

Solvit ante diem /sólvəd æntiy dáyəm/. A plea that the money was paid before the day appointed.

Solvit post diem /sólvət pòwst dáyəm/. He paid after the day. The plea in an action of debt on bond that the defendant paid the money *after the day* named for the payment, and before the commencement of the suit.

Solvitur adhuc societas etiam morte socii /sólvədər ǽdhək səsáyətæs ésh(iy)əm mórdiy sówshiyay/. A partnership is moreover dissolved by the death of a partner.

Solvitur eo ligamine quo ligatur /sólvədər íyow ləgéymaniy kwòw ləgéydər/. In the same manner that a thing is bound it is unloosed.

Somersett's Case. A celebrated decision of the English king's bench, in 1771 (20 How.St.Tr. 1), that slavery no longer existed in England in any form, and could not for the future exist on English soil, and that any person brought into England as a slave could not be thence removed except by the legal means applicable in the case of any free-born person.

Somnambulism /so(m)nǽmbyəlìzəm/. Sleep-walking. Whether this condition is anything more than a co-operation of the voluntary muscles with the thoughts which occupy the mind during sleep is not settled by physiologists. Such condition may be a defense to a crime committed while in such state. Fain v. Com., 78 Ky. 183. See also **Somnolentia.**

Somnolentia /sòmnəlénsh(iy)ə/. A condition of incomplete sleep resembling in its effects drunkenness and in which part of the faculties are abnormally excited while the others are in repose. It destroys moral agency and is therefore a defense to a crime. Fain v. Com., 78 Ky. 183.

Sompnour /sómnər/. In ecclesiastical law, an officer of the ecclesiastical courts whose duty was to serve citations or process.

Son. Male offspring. An immediate male descendant. The word may be applied also to a distant male descendent. In a broad use, term may be employed as designating any young male person, as a pupil, a ward, an adopted male child or dependent. The description son in wills, means prima facie legitimate son. In re Flood's Estate, 217 Cal. 763, 21 P.2d 579.

Son /sówn/. Fr. His. Civ.Code La. art. 3556.

Son assault demesne. His own assault. A plea which occurs in the actions of trespass and trespass on the case, by which the defendant alleges that it was the plaintiff's own original assault that occasioned the trespass for which he has brought the action, and that what the defendant did was merely in his own defense.

Son-in-law. The husband of one's daughter. Diebold v. Diebold, 235 Mo.App. 83, 141 S.W.2d 119, 125.

Sonticus /sóntəkəs/. Lat. In the civil law, hurtful; injurious; hindering; excusing or justifying delay. *Morbus sonticus* is any illness of so serious a nature as to prevent a defendant from appearing in court and to give him a valid excuse.

Soon. Within a reasonable time; as soon as practicable; as soon as; as soon as may be. Phrase "soon as practicable" means within a reasonable time. Miller v. Zurich General Acc. & Liability Ins. Co., 36 N.J.Super. 288, 115 A.2d 597, 600.

Soror /sóror/. Lat. Sister.

Sororicide /sərórəsàyd/. The killing or murder of a sister; one who murders his sister. This is not a technical term of the law.

Sors /sórs/. Lat. In old English law, a principal lent on interest, as distinguished from the interest itself.

A thing recovered in action, as distinguished from the costs of the action.

In the civil law, lot; chance; fortune; hazard; a lot, made of wood, gold, or other material. Money borrowed, or put out at interest. A principal sum or fund, such as the capital of a partnership.

Sortitio /sortísh(iy)ow/. Lat. In the civil law, a drawing of lots. *Sortitio judicum* was the process of selecting a number of judges, for a criminal trial, by drawing lots.

Sound, *v.* To have reference or relation to; to aim at. An action is technically said to *sound in tort or damages* where it is brought not for the specific recovery of a thing, but for damages only. See **Sounding in damages.**

Sound, *adj.* Whole; in good condition; marketable. See **Warranty.**

Free from disease; healthy; physically and mentally fit. The term may also mean free from danger to the life, safety, and welfare.

Sound and disposing mind and memory. Testamentary capacity. Such mind and memory as enables testator to know and understand business in which he is engaged at time of making will. Farmers' Union Bank of Henning v. Johnson, 27 Tenn.App. 342, 181 S.W.2d 369, 374. See also **Capacity,** and *Sound mind,* infra.

Sound health. In insurance law, means that the applicant has no grave impairment or serious disease, and is free from any ailment that seriously affects the general soundness and healthfulness of the system. A state of health unimpaired by any serious malady of which the person himself is conscious. National Life & Accident Ins. Co. v. Ware, 169 Okl. 618, 37 P.2d 905.

Sound judicial discretion. Discretion exercised on full and fair consideration of the facts presented to the judge by the well-known and established mode of procedure. Caldwell v. State, 164 Tenn. 325, 48

S.W.2d 1087, 1089. Discretion exercised not arbitrarily or willfully but with regard to what is right and equitable under the circumstances. Cornwell v. Cornwell, 73 App.D.C. 233, 118 F.2d 396, 398.

Sound mind. The normal condition of the human mind,—that state in which its faculties of perception and judgment are ordinarily well developed, and not impaired by mania, insanity, or other mental disorder. In the law of wills means that testator must have been able to understand and carry in mind, in a general way, nature and situation of his property, his relations to those having claim to his remembrance, and nature of his act. The "sound mind" necessary to execute a will means ability of testator to mentally understand in a general way nature and extent of property to be disposed of, and testator's relation to those who would naturally claim a substantial benefit from will, as well as general understanding of practical effect of will as executed. Skelton v. Davis, Fla.App., 133 So.2d 432, 435. See also **Capacity.**

Sound value. As used with reference to value of property within fire policy is the cash value of property, making an allowance for depreciation due to use at and immediately preceding the time of the fire. Reliance Ins. Co. v. Bowen, Tex.Civ.App., 54 S.W.2d 597, 598.

Sounding in damages. When an action is brought, not for the recovery of lands, goods, or sums of money (as is the case in real or mixed actions or the personal action of debt or detinue), but for damages only, as in covenant, trespass, etc., the action is said to be "sounding in damages."

Soundness. General good health; freedom from any permanent disease or illness. See **Sound.**

Source. That from which any act, movement, information, or effect proceeds. A person or thing that originates, sets in motion, or is a primary agency in producing any course of action or result. An originator; creator; origin. A place where something is found or whence it is taken or derived. Jackling v. State Tax Comm., 40 N.M. 241, 58 P.2d 1167, 1171.

The source of income. Place where, or circumstances from which, it is produced. Union Electric Co. v. Coale, 347 Mo. 175, 146 S.W.2d 631, 635.

Sources of the law. The origins from which particular positive laws derive their authority and coercive force. Such are constitutions, treaties, statutes, usages, and customs.

In another sense, the authoritative or reliable works, records, documents, edicts, etc., to which we are to look for an understanding of what constitutes the law. Such, for example, with reference to the Roman law, are the compilations of Justinian and the treatise of Gaius; and such, with reference to the common law, are especially the ancient reports and the works of such writers as Bracton, Littleton, Coke, Fleta, Blackstone, and others.

Sous /súw/. Fr. Under.

Sous seing privé /sùw sǽŋ privéy/. Fr. In French law, under private signature; under the private signature of the parties. A contract or instrument thus signed is distinguished from an "authentic act," which is formally concluded before a notary or judge.

Sovereign. A person, body, or state in which independent and supreme authority is vested; a chief ruler with supreme power; a king or other ruler with limited power. See also **Clipped sovereignty; Sovereignty.**

Sovereign immunity. Doctrine precludes litigant from asserting an otherwise meritorious cause of action against a sovereign or a party with sovereign attributes unless sovereign consents to suit. Principe Compania Naviera, S. A. v. Board of Com'rs of Port of New Orleans, D.C.La., 333 F.Supp. 353, 355. Historically, the federal and state governments, and derivatively cities and towns, were immune from tort liability arising from activities which were governmental in nature. Most jurisdictions, however, have abandoned this doctrine in favor of permitting tort actions with certain limitations and restrictions. See **Federal Tort Claims Act; Governmental immunity; Tort Claims Acts.**

Sovereign people. The political body, consisting of the entire number of citizens and qualified electors, who, in their collective capacity, possess the powers of sovereignty and exercise them through their chosen representatives. See Scott v. Sandford, 19 How. 404, 15 L.Ed. 691.

Sovereign power or **sovereign prerogative.** That power in a state to which none other is superior or equal, and which includes all the specific powers necessary to accomplish the legitimate ends and purposes of government. Ætna Casualty & Surety Co. v. Bramwell, D.C.Or., 12 F.2d 307, 309.

Sovereign right. A right which the state alone, or some of its governmental agencies, can possess, and which it possesses in the character of a sovereign, for the common benefit, and to enable it to carry out its proper functions; distinguished from such "proprietary" rights as a state, like any private person, may have in property or demands which it owns.

Sovereign states. States whose subjects or citizens are in the habit of obedience to them, and which are not themselves subject to any other (or paramount) state in any respect. The state is said to be semi-sovereign only, and not sovereign, when in any respect or respects it is liable to be controlled (like certain of the states in India) by a paramount government (e.g., by the British empire). In the intercourse of nations, certain states have a position of entire independence of others, and can perform all those acts which it is possible for any state to perform in this particular sphere. These same states have also entire power of self-government; that is, of independence upon all other states as far as their own territory and citizens not living abroad are concerned. No foreign power or law can have control except by convention. This power of independent action in external and internal relations constitutes complete sovereignty.

Sovereignty. The supreme, absolute, and uncontrollable power by which any independent state is governed; supreme political authority; paramount control of the constitution and frame of government and its administration; the self-sufficient source of political power, from which all specific political powers are derived; the international independence of a state, combined with the right and power of regulat-

ing its internal affairs without foreign dictation; also a political society, or state, which is sovereign and independent.

The power to do everything in a state without accountability,—to make laws, to execute and to apply them, to impose and collect taxes and levy contributions, to make war or peace, to form treaties of alliance or of commerce with foreign nations, and the like.

Sovereignty in government is that public authority which directs or orders what is to be done by each member associated in relation to the end of the association. It is the supreme power by which any citizen is governed and is the person or body of persons in the state to whom there is politically no superior. The necessary existence of the state and that right and power which necessarily follow is "sovereignty." By "sovereignty" in its largest sense is meant supreme, absolute, uncontrollable power, the absolute right to govern. The word which by itself comes nearest to being the definition of "sovereignty" is will or volition as applied to political affairs. City of Bisbee v. Cochise County, 52 Ariz. 1, 78 P.2d 982, 986.

Sowne. In old English law, to be leviable. An old exchequer term applied to sheriff's returns.

S.P. Abbreviation of *"sine prole,"* without issue. Also an abbreviation of "same principle," or "same point," indicating, when inserted between two citations, that the second involves the same doctrine as the first.

Spadones /spədównìyz/. Lat. In the civil law, impotent persons. Those who, on account of their temperament or some accident they have suffered, are unable to procreate.

Sparsim /spársəm/. Lat. Here and there; scattered; at intervals. For instance, trespass to realty by cutting timber *sparsim* (here and there) through a tract.

Spatæ placitum /spéydiy plǽsədəm/. In old English law, a court for the speedy execution of justice upon military delinquents.

Speaker. The official designation of the president or chairman of certain legislative bodies, particularly of the House of Representatives in the Congress of the United States, and of one or both branches of several of the state legislatures, *i.e.* Speaker of the House.

Speaking demurrer. A demurrer which introduces a new fact that does not appear from face of bill is a "speaking demurrer," and cannot be sustained. Allpress v. Lawyers Title Ins. Corp., 218 Tenn. 673, 405 S.W.2d 572, 573. A speaking demurrer is a special exception which, instead of limiting itself to the allegations of the petition and pointing out defects therein, states factual propositions not appearing in the petition and, in reliance upon such facts, seeks to challenge the plaintiff's right to recovery. Ragsdale v. Ragsdale, Tex.Civ.App., 520 S.W.2d 839, 842. See also **Demurrer.**

Speaking motion. A motion which requires consideration of matters outside the pleadings. Formerly, such motions were prohibited but under Fed.R.Civ.P. 12(b) such motions are now entertained.

Special. Relating to or designating a species, kind, individual, thing, or sort; designed for a particular purpose; confined to a particular purpose, object, person, or class. Unusual, extraordinary.

As to special Acceptance; Administration; Agent; Allocatur; Allowance; Appearance; Assessment; Assumpsit; Bail; Bailiff; Bastard; Benefit; Calendar; Charge; Constable; Contract; Count; Covenant; Customs; Damage; Demurrer; Deposit; Deputy; Election; Finding; Guaranty; Guardian; Imparlance; Indorsement; Injunction; Insurance; Issue; Jury; Legacy; Letter of credit; License; Limitation; Malice; Master; Meeting; Mortgage; Motion; Non est factum; Occupant; Owner; Partner; Partnership; Plea; Pleader; Pleadings; Power; Privilege; Proceeding; Property; Replication; Request; Restraint of trade; Retainer; Rule; Service; Session; Statute; Stock; Tail; Term; Traverse; Trust; Verdict, and Warranty, see those titles.

Special act. A private statute; an act which operates only upon particular persons or private concerns. Unity v. Burrage, 103 U.S. 447, 454, 26 L.Ed. 405. See **Special law.**

Special district. A limited governmental structure created to bypass normal borrowing limitations, to insulate certain activities from traditional political influence, to allocate functions to entities reflecting particular expertise, to provide services in otherwise unincorporated areas, or to accomplish a primarily local benefit or improvement, *e.g.* parks and planning, mosquito control, sewage removal.

Special errors. In common law pleading, special pleas in error are such as, instead of joining in error, allege some extraneous matter as a ground of defeating the writ of error, *e.g.,* a release of errors, expiration of the time within which error might be brought, or the like. To these, the plaintiff in error may either reply or demur.

Special exception. An objection to the form in which a cause of action is stated.

Special exception to municipal zoning ordinance refers to special uses which are permissive in particular zone under ordinance and are neither nonconforming uses nor akin to a variance and refers to special use which is considered by local legislative body to be essential or desirable for welfare of community and its citizenry and which is entirely appropriate and not essentially incompatible with basic uses in zone involved, but not at every or any location therein or without restriction or conditions being imposed on such use. Piscitelli v. Township Committee of Scotch Plains Tp., 103 N.J.Super. 589, 248 A.2d 274, 277. A special exception allows property owner to put his property to use which regulations expressly permit under conditions specified in zoning regulations themselves. W A T R, Inc. v. Zoning Bd. of Appeals of Town of Bethany, 158 Conn. 196, 257 A.2d 818, 821.

Special execution. A copy of a judgment with a direction to the sheriff indorsed thereon to execute it. One that directs a levy upon some special property.

Special executor. One whose power and office are limited, either in respect to the time or place of their exercise, or restricted to a particular portion of the decedent's estate. One only empowered by will to take charge of a limited portion of the estate, or such part as may lie in one place, or to carry on the administration only to a prescribed point.

Special facts rule. In corporation law, as respects director's duty of disclosure when dealing with stockholders, is that where special circumstances or facts are present which make it inequitable for the director to withhold information from the stockholder, the duty to disclose arises, and concealment is fraud. Taylor v. Wright, 69 Cal.App.2d 371, 159 P.2d 980, 985.

Special grand jury. A grand jury convened to hear a particular case or series of cases involving similar crimes. 18 U.S.C.A. § 3331 *et seq.*

Special interest groups. Groups in society that have a special interest in common. Special interest groups generally attempt to influence government legislation to benefit their own particular group interests. See **Lobbying.**

Special interrogatories. Written questions on one or more issues of fact submitted to a jury. The answers to these are necessary to a verdict. Fed.R.Civ.P. 49(b).

Specialist. Stock broker who remains at one post of exchange where particular stocks are dealt in and executes orders of other brokers, for which he receives commission; one who specializes in limited group of stocks.

Special jurisdiction. A court authorized to take cognizance of only some few kinds of causes or proceedings expressly designated by statute is called a court of special or limited jurisdiction. Power of a court over only a limited type of case (*e.g.* Probate court) or over only property and not the person or the defendant.

Special law. One relating to particular persons or things; one made for individual cases or for particular places or districts; one operating upon a selected class, rather than upon the public generally. A private law. A law is "special" when it is different from others of the same general kind or designed for a particular purpose, or limited in range or confined to a prescribed field of action or operation. A special law is one which relates to particular persons or things or to particular persons or things of a class, or which operates on or over a portion of a class instead of all of the class. Ulrich v. Beatty, 139 Ind.App. 174, 216 N.E.2d 737, 746. A special law applies only to an individual or a number of individuals out of a single class similarly situated and affected, or to a special locality. Board of County Com'rs of Lemhi County v. Swensen, Idaho, 80 Idaho 198, 327 P.2d 361, 362.

Special lien. A special lien is in the nature of a particular lien, being a lien upon particular property. A lien which the holder can enforce only as security for the performance of a particular act or obligation and of obligations incidental thereto.

Special matter. In common law pleading, under a plea of the general issue, the defendant is allowed to give special matter in evidence, usually after notice to the plaintiff of the nature of such matter, thus sparing him the necessity of pleading it specially. 3 Bl. Comm. 306.

Special permit. A special permit allows property owner to use his property in a way which the zoning regulations expressly permit under the conditions specified in the regulations themselves. Shell Oil Co. v. Zoning Bd. of Appeals of Town of Bloomfield, 156 Conn. 66, 238 A.2d 426, 428. "Special permit" and "special exception" have the same meaning and can be used interchangeably. Beckish v. Planning and Zoning Comm. of Town of Columbia, 162 Conn. 11, 291 A.2d 208, 210.

Special registration. In election laws, registration for particular election only which does not entitle elector to vote at any succeeding election.

Special session. An extraordinary session. See **Session.**

Specialty. A contract under seal. Furst v. Brady, 375 Ill. 425, 31 N.E.2d 606, 609. A writing sealed and delivered, containing some agreement. A writing sealed and delivered, which is given as a security for the payment of a debt, in which such debt is particularly specified.

For assessment purposes, a "specialty" is a building or buildings, constructed or peculiarly adapted to conduct of owner's business, which cannot be converted to general industrial use without the loss or expenditure of very substantial amounts of money. Great Atlantic & Pac. Tea Co., Inc. v. Kiernan, 49 A.D.2d 99, 371 N.Y.S.2d 173, 175.

Specialty debt. A debt due or acknowledged to be due by deed or instrument under seal. 2 Bl.Comm. 465.

Special use permit. Permitted exception to zoning ordinance; e.g. church, hospital, etc. Compare **Variance.**

Special use valuation. An option which permits the executor of an estate to value, for death tax purposes, real estate used in a farming activity or in connection with a closely-held business at its current use value rather than at its most suitable or highest and best use value. Under this option, a farm would be valued at its value for farming purposes even though, for example, the property might have a higher value as a potential shopping center. In order for the executor of an estate to elect special use valuation, the conditions of I.R.C. § 2032A must be satisfied.

Special warranty. A covenant of "special warranty" is one the operation of which is limited to certain persons or claims. Central Life Assur. Soc. v. Impelmans, 13 Wash.2d 632, 126 P.2d 757, 763. A "covenant to warrant" in the habendum clause is not a general but at most a "special warranty". New Orleans & N. E. R. R. v. Morrison, 203 Miss. 791, 35 So.2d 68, 70. See also **Warranty.**

Special warranty deed. A deed in which the grantor only covenants to warrant and defend the title against claims and demands of the grantor and all persons claiming by, through and under him. In some jurisdictions, such deed is called a quitclaim deed.

Specie /spíyshiy(iy)/. Coin of the precious metals, of a certain weight and fineness, and bearing the stamp of the government, denoting its value as currency. Metallic money; e.g. gold or silver coins.

When spoken of a contract, the expression "performance in specie" means strictly, or according to the exact terms. As applied to things, it signifies individuality or identity. Thus, on a bequest of a specific picture, the legatee would be said to be entitled to the delivery of the picture in specie; i.e., of the very thing. Whether a thing is due in genere or in specie depends, in each case, on the will of the transacting parties.

Species /spíyshiy(iy)z/. Lat. In the civil law, form; figure; fashion or shape. A form or shape given to materials.

Specific. Precisely formulated or restricted; definite; explicit; of an exact or particular nature. People v. Thomas, 25 Cal.2d 880, 156 P.2d 7, 17. Having a certain form or designation; observing a certain form; particular; precise; tending to specify, or to make particular, definite, limited or precise.

As to specific Denial; Devise; Legacy, and Performance, see those titles.

Specifically. In a specific manner; explicitly, particularly, definitely.

Specificatio /spèsəfəkéysh(iy)ow/. Lat. In the civil law, literally, a making of form; a giving of form to materials. That mode of acquiring property through which a person, by transforming a thing belonging to another, especially by working up his materials into a new species, becomes proprietor of the same.

Specification. As used in the law relating to patents, manufacturing, and construction contracts, a particular or detailed statement, account, or listing of the various elements, materials, dimensions, etc. involved.

Law of personal property. The acquisition of title to a thing by working it into new forms or species from the raw material; corresponding to the specificatio of the Roman law. Right by "specification" can only be acquired when, without the accession of any other material that of another person, which has been used by the operator innocently, has been converted by him into something specifically different in the inherent and characteristic qualities, which identify it. Such is the conversion of corn into meal, of grapes into wine, etc. Bozeman Mortuary Ass'n v. Fairchild, 253 Ky. 74, 68 S.W.2d 756.

Military law. The clear and particular description of the charges preferred against a person accused of a military offense. Carter v. McClaughry, 183 U.S. 365, 22 S.Ct. 181, 46 L.Ed. 236.

Practice. A detailed and particular enumeration of several points or matters urged or relied on by a party to a suit or proceeding; as, a "specification of errors," or a "specification of grounds of opposition to a bankrupt's discharge."

Specific bequest. A testamentary gift of specific personal property; e.g. "my old rocking chair". A specific bequest is a gift by will of a specific article or part of testator's estate, which is identified and distinguished from all things of same kind and which may be satisfied only by delivery of particular things. In re Soles Estate, 451 Pa. 568, 304 A.2d 97, 100.

Specific intent. The most common usage of "specific intent" is to designate a special mental element which is required above and beyond any mental state required with respect to the *actus reus* of the crime. Common law larceny, for example, requires the taking and carrying away of the property of another, and the defendant's mental state as to this act must be established, but in addition it must be shown that there was an "intent to steal" the property. Similarly, common law burglary requires a breaking and entry into the dwelling of another, but in addition to the mental state connected with these acts it must also be established that the defendant acted "with intent to commit a felony therein."

Specify. To mention specifically; to state in full and explicit terms; to point out; to tell or state precisely or in detail; to particularize, or to distinguish by words one thing from another. Aleksich v. Industrial Accident Fund, 116 Mont. 127, 151 P.2d 1016, 1021.

Specimen. A sample; a part of something intended to exhibit the kind and quality of the whole.

Spectrograph. Voice print analysis is a method of identification based on the comparison of graphic representations or "spectrograms" made of human voices. Such method utilizes a machine known as a "spectrograph" which separates the sound of human voices into the three component elements of time, frequency and intensity. Using a series of lines or bars, the machine plots the variables across electronically sensitive paper and the result is a "spectrogram" of the acoustical signal of the speaker, with the horizontal axis representing the time lapse, the vertical axis indicating frequency, and the thickness of the lines disclosing the intensity of the voice. People v. Kelly, 17 Cal.3d 24, 130 Cal.Rptr. 144, 147, 549 P.2d 1240. An increasing number of courts are permitting the admissibility of spectrograph results into evidence. United States v. Baller, C.A.W.Va., 519 F.2d 463; United States v. Williams, D.C.N.Y., 443 F.Supp. 269. See also **Voice exemplars.**

Speculation. Buying or selling with expectation of profiting by a rise or fall in price. Also, engaging in hazardous business transactions, or investing in risky securities or commodities, with the hope of an unusually large profit.

Speculation, upon which neither court in nonjury case nor jurors in jury case may base verdict, is the art of theorizing about a matter as to which evidence is not sufficient for certain knowledge. Jaramillo v. U. S., D.C.N.Y., 357 F.Supp. 172, 175.

Speculative damages. See **Damages.**

Speculum /spékyələm/. Lat. Mirror or lookingglass. The title of several of the most ancient lawbooks or compilations. One of the ancient Icelandic books is styled *"Speculum Regale."*

Speech. Freedom of speech is right guaranteed by First Amendment, U.S.Const. See also **Commercial speech doctrine; Freedom of speech; Liberty; Symbolic speech.**

Speech or debate clause. Art. 1, § 6, cl. 1 of U.S. Constitution grants congressmen immunity "for any speech or debate in either House." The courts have extended this privilege to matters beyond pure speech and debate in either House, but only when necessary to prevent indirect impairment of such deliberations. Gravel v. U. S., 408 U.S. 606, 92 S.Ct. 2614, 33 L.Ed.2d 583. See also **Legislative immunity.**

Speed. See **Amphetamine; Methamphetamine.**

Speedy execution. An execution which, by the direction of the judge at *nisi prius,* issues forthwith, or on some early day fixed upon by the judge for that purpose after the trial of the action.

Speedy remedy. One which, having in mind the subject-matter involved, can be pursued with expedition and without essential detriment to the party aggrieved; *e.g.* **Restraining order.**

Speedy trial. The right of the accused to a speedy trial is guaranteed by the 6th Amendment of the Constitution and such right is implemented by 18 U.S.C.A. § 3161 et seq. and Fed.R.Crim.P. 50. Barker v. Wingo, 407 U.S. 514, 92 S.Ct. 2182, 33 L.Ed.2d 101, lists four factors to be considered in determining whether delay was unreasonable: (1) Length of delay; (2) the government's justification for the delay; (3) whether and how the defendant asserted his right to a speedy trial; and (4) prejudice caused by the delay, such as lengthened pretrial incarceration. A trial as soon after indictment as prosecution can with reasonable diligence prepare for it. People v. Molinari, 23 Cal. App.2d Supp. 761, 67 P.2d 767, 770. Trial, had as soon as prosecution, with reasonable diligence, can prepare for it; a trial according to fixed rules, free from capricious and oppressive delays, but the time within which it must be had to satisfy the guaranty depends on the circumstances. Bryant v. State, 4 Md.App. 572, 244 A.2d 446, 448. See **Speedy Trial Act.**

Speedy Trial Act. Federal Act of 1974 establishing a set of time limits for carrying out the major events (*e.g.* information, indictment, arraignment) in the prosecution of federal criminal cases. 18 U.S.C.A. § 3161 et seq.

In any case involving a defendant charged with an offense, the appropriate judicial officer, at the earliest practicable time, shall, after consultation with the counsel for the defendant and the attorney for the Government, set the case for trial on a day certain, or list it for trial on a weekly or other short-term trial calendar at a place within the judicial district, so as to assure a speedy trial. 18 U.S.C.A. § 3161(a).

Spend. To consume by using in any manner; to use up, to exhaust, distribute, as to expend money or any other possession.

Spendthrift. One who spends money profusely and improvidently; a prodigal; one who lavishes or wastes his estate. By statute, a person who by excessive drinking, gaming, idleness, or debauchery of any kind shall so spend, waste, or lessen his estate as to expose himself or his family to want or suffering, or expose the government to charge or expense for the support of himself or family, or is liable to be put under guardianship on account of such excesses. See **Spendthrift trust.**

Spendthrift trust. A trust created to provide a fund for the maintenance of a beneficiary, and at the same time to secure it against his improvidence or incapacity. In re Nicholson's Estate, 104 Colo. 561, 93 P.2d 880, 883. One which provides a fund for benefit of another than settlor, secures it against beneficiary's own improvidence, and places it beyond his creditors' reach. A trust set up to protect a beneficiary from spending all of the money that he is entitled to. Only a certain portion of the total amount is given to him at any one time. Most states permit spendthrift trust provisions that prohibit creditors from attaching a spendthrift trust.

Sperate. That of which there is hope. Thus a debt which one may hope to recover may be called "sperate," in opposition to "desperate."

Spes accrescendi /spíyz ǽkrəsénday/. Lat. Hope of surviving.

Spes est vigilantis somnium /spíyz èst vìjəlǽntəs sómn(i)yəm/. Hope is the dream of the vigilant.

Spes impunitatis continuum affectum tribuit delinquendi /spíyz impyùwnətéydəs kəntínyuwəm əféktəm tríbyuwət dèliŋkwénday/. The hope of impunity holds out a continual temptation to crime.

Spes recuperandi /spíyz rək(y)ùwpərǽnday/. Lat. The hope of recovery or recapture; the chance of retaking property captured at sea, which prevents the captors from acquiring complete ownership of the property until they have definitely precluded it by effectual measures.

Spigurnel /spìgərnél/. The sealer of the royal writs.

Spin-off. A spin-off exists when a parent corporation organizes a subsidiary, to which is transferred part of parent's assets in exchange for all of capital stock of subsidiary and stock of subsidiary is transferred to parent's shareholders without surrender of their stock in parent, and if distribution of stock to parent's shareholders constitutes a dividend, then it is a taxable one. Holz v. U. S., D.C.Minn., 176 F.Supp. 330, 336. Spin-off occurs where part of assets of corporation is transferred to a new corporation and stock of transferee is distributed to shareholders of transferor without surrender by them of stock in transferor. C. I. R. v. Baan, C.A.Cal., 382 F.2d 485, 491. See also **Split-off; Split-up.**

Spinster. A woman who never has been married.

Spiritual. Relating to religious or ecclesiastical persons or affairs, as distinguished from "secular" or lay, worldly, or business matters.

As to spiritual Corporation; Courts, and Lords, see those titles.

Spital, or **spittle** /spítəl/. A charitable foundation; a hospital for diseased people; a hospital.

Spite fence. A fence of no beneficial use to person erecting and maintaining it on his land and maintained solely for purpose of annoying owner of adjoining land. Burris v. Creech, 220 N.C. 302, 17 S.E.2d 123. A high and unsightly fence erected to annoy a neighbor or adjoining landowner by obstructing his air, light or view.

Split gift. See **Gift.**

Split income. Congress, in 1948, enacted new joint tax return legislation and a new set of rates to remove the considerable disparity between tax treatment of married couples in community property and common-law states, and thereby to remove the considerable pressure on the common-law states to adopt community-property systems. By law enacted that year, married couples in all states were given the privilege to split their income, that is to have it taxed on a joint return at a rate equal to that which would apply if each had earned one-half the amount and were taxed on a separate return. In 1969, however, Congress retained but reduced the disparity between rates imposed on single persons and married couples with the same incomes. This reduction took the form of a new and lower rate schedule for single persons, which took effect beginning in 1971. See I.R.C. § 1(c). See also **Gift splitting.**

Split-off. When a corporation sets up and funds a new corporation and gives the shares of this new corporation to the old corporation's stockholders in exchange for some of their shares in the old company, this new company is a "split-off" and the process is a split-off. A type of reorganization whereby, for example, A Corporation transfers assets to B Corporation in exchange for enough B stock to represent control. A Corporation then distributes the B stock to its shareholders in exchange for some of their A stock. See also **Spin-off; Split-up.**

Split order. An order to a broker directing him to buy or sell some stock at one price and some at another.

Split sentence. One where penalty of fine and imprisonment, as provided by statute, is imposed and imprisonment part is suspended and fine part enforced. It is also exemplified in a sentence by which the defendant serves some time and the balance of the sentence is suspended.

Splitting cause of action. Dividing a single or indivisible cause of action into several parts or claims and bringing several actions thereon. Coniglio v. Wyoming Valley Fire Ins. Co., 337 Mich. 38, 59 N.W.2d 74, 78; Van Brode Mill. Co. v. Kellogg Co., D.C.Del., 113 F.Supp. 845, 852. Commencement of action for only part of the cause of action. Wood v. Baker, 217 Or. 279, 341 P.2d 134, 136. Rule against "splitting cause of action" applies only when several actions are brought as result of dividing single or indivisible cause of action. Beizer v. Dictograph Products, Inc., 6 Conn.Cir. 28, 263 A.2d 93, 97.

There is no "splitting of causes" where demand which is subject of second action was not due at time of the first action. Glavich v. Industrial Accident Commission of California, 44 Cal.App.2d 517, 112 P.2d 774, 778. The rule against "splitting causes of action" does not mean that plaintiff cannot sue for less than is his due but means merely that if he does so he may be precluded from maintaining another action for the remainder of the same demand. Scientific & Hospital Supply Corporation v. Board of Education of City of New York, 172 Misc. 770, 16 N.Y. S.2d 91, 93.

Split-up. When a corporation divides into two or more separate new corporations, gives its shareholders the shares of these new corporations, and goes out of business, this process is termed a "split-up." A type of reorganization whereby, for example, A Corporation transfers some assets to B Corporation and the remainder to Z Corporation in return for which it receives enough B and Z stock to represent control of each corporation. The B and Z stock is then distributed by A Corporation to its shareholders in return for all of their A stock. The result of the split-up is that A Corporation is liquidated and its shareholders now have control of B and Z Corporations.

Spoliation /spòwliyéyshən/. The destruction of evidence. It constitutes an obstruction of justice. The destruction, or the significant and meaningful alteration of a document or instrument. Application of Bodkin, D.C.N.Y., 165 F.Supp. 25, 30.

Any change made on a written instrument by a person *not* a party to the instrument. Such a change will have no effect, provided that the original tenor of the instrument can still be ascertained.

Spoliator /spòwliyéydər/. Lat. A spoiler or destroyer. It is a maxim of law, bearing chiefly on evidence, but also upon the value generally of the thing destroyed, that everything most to his disadvantage is to be presumed against the destroyer *(spoliator), contra spoliatorem omnia præsumuntur.*

Spoliatus debet ante omnia restitui /spòwliyéydər débəd æntiy ómn(i)yə rəstítyuway/. A party despoiled [forcibly deprived of possession] ought first of all to be restored.

Spoliatus episcopus ante omnia debet restitui /spòwliyéydəs əpískəpəs æntiy ómn(i)yə débət rəstítyuway/. A bishop despoiled of his see ought, above all, to be restored.

Spolium /spówl(i)yəm/. Lat. In the civil and common law, a thing violently or unlawfully taken from another.

Spondeo /spóndiyow/. Lat. In the civil law, I undertake; I engage.

Spondes? spondeo /spóndiyz? spóndiyow/. Lat. Do you undertake? I do undertake. The most common form of verbal stipulation in the Roman law.

Spondet peritiam artis /spóndət pərísh(iy)əm árdəs/. He promises the skill of his art; he engages to do the work in a skillful or workmanlike manner. Applied to the engagements of workman for hire.

Sponsalia per verba de futuro /spon(t)séyl(i)yə pər várbə dìy fyuwtyúrow/. An engagement or betrothal through words concerning the future.

Sponsalia, or **stipulatio sponsalitia** /spòn(t)séyl(i)yə /stìpyəléysh(iy)ow spòn(t)səlísh(iy)ə/. Lat. In the civil law, espousal; betrothal; a reciprocal promise of future marriage.

Sponsio /spónsh(iy)ow/. Lat. In the civil law, an engagement or undertaking; particularly such as was made in the form of an answer to a formal interrogatory by the other party.

An engagement to pay a certain sum of money to the successful party in a cause.

Sponsio judicialis /spónsh(iy)ow juwdìshiyéyləs/. In Roman law, a judicial wager corresponding in some respects to the "feigned issue" of modern practice.

Sponsio ludicra /spónsh(iy)ow l(y)úwdəkrə/. A trifling or ludicrous engagement, such as a court will not sustain an action for. An informal undertaking, or one made without the usual formula of interrogation.

Sponsions /spónshən(d)z/. In international law, agreements or engagements made by certain public officers (as generals or admirals in time of war) in behalf of their governments, either without authority or in excess of the authority under which they purport to be made, and which therefore require an express or tacit ratification.

Sponsor. A surety; one who makes a promise or gives security for another, particularly a godfather in baptism.

In the civil law, one who intervenes for another voluntarily and without being requested.

Spontaneous combustion. The ignition of a body by the internal development of heat without the action of an external agent.

Spontaneous declarations. A statement is admissible as a "spontaneous declaration" if there was an occurrence sufficiently startling to produce a spontaneous and unreflecting statement, if there was an absence of time to fabricate, and if the statement related to the circumstances of the occurrence. People v. Was, 22 Ill.App.3d 859, 318 N.E.2d 309, 313. See **Spontaneous exclamation.**

Spontaneous exclamation. Within res gestae rule, a statement or exclamation made immediately after some exciting occasion by a participant or spectator and asserting the circumstances of that occasion as it is observed by him, is admissible as a spontaneous and sincere response to actual perceptions produced by shock. State v. Kendrick, 239 Or. 512, 398 P.2d 471, 473. One exception to the Hearsay Rule is the exclamation made by one under the stress of excitement or at the very moment of an event before the mind has an opportunity to contrive a false statement; *cf.* Fed.Evid. Rule 803(2). Sometimes called the *res gestæ* exception to Hearsay Rule. See **Res** *(Res gestæ).*

Sponte oblata /spóntiy əbléydə/. Lat. A free gift or present to the crown.

Sponte virum mulier fugiens et adultera facta, dote sua careat, nisi sponsi sponte retracta /spóntiy víhrəm myúwl(i)yər fyúwj(i)yèn(d)z èd ədáltərə fæktə dówdiy s(y)úwə kæriyət, náysay spón(t)say rətræktə/. Let a woman leaving her husband of her own accord, and committing adultery, lose her dower, unless taken back by her husband of his own accord.

Sporting house. A house of ill-fame. A house frequented by sportsmen, betting men, gamblers, and the like, but not necessarily a house kept for unlawful sports or practices.

Sportula /spórchələ/. Lat. In Roman law, a largess, dole, or present; a pecuniary donation; an official perquisite; something over and above the ordinary fee allowed by law.

Spot. In commodity trading and in foreign exchange, immediate delivery in contrast to a future delivery.

Spot price. The selling price of commodities or goods.

Spot trading. Cash sales for immediate delivery in contrast to trading in futures.

Spot zoning. Granting of a zoning classification to a piece of land that differs from that of the other land in the immediate area. Term refers to zoning which singles out an area for treatment different from that of similar surrounding land and which cannot be justified on the bases of health, safety, morals or general welfare of the community and which is not in accordance with a comprehensive plan. Schadlick v. City of Concord, 108 N.H. 319, 234 A.2d 523, 526.

Spousals /spáwzəlz/. In old English law, mutual promises to marry.

Spouse. One's wife or husband.

Spouse-breach. In old English law, adultery.

Spread. In general, a difference between two amounts. In stock and commodity trading, the difference between the bid and asked price. In arbitrage (*q.v.*), the difference between two markets in the price or value of a currency.

Spring-branch. A branch of a stream, flowing from a spring.

Springing use. See **Use.**

Sprinkling trust. See **Trust.**

Spurious. False, counterfeit, not genuine.

Spurious bank-bill. A bill which may be a legitimate impression from the genuine plate, but it must have the signatures of persons not the officers of the bank whence it purports to have issued, or else the names of fictitious persons. It may also be an illegitimate impression from a genuine plate, or an impression from a counterfeit plate, but it must have such signatures or names as indicated. A bill, therefore, may be both counterfeit and forged, or both counterfeit and spurious, but it cannot be both forged and spurious.

Spurious class action. A spurious class action within Federal Rules of Civil Procedure is merely a permissive joinder device where there is a common question of law or fact and common relief is sought, involves separate causes of action, is a matter of efficiency to avoid multiplicity of actions, and each plaintiff must be able to avoid bar of statute of limitations without reference to the other causes of action. Athas v. Day, D.C.Colo., 161 F.Supp. 916, 919. One in which interests of members of class are several and not interdependent, and where joinder is a matter of efficiency to avoid multiplicity of suits. Slack v. Stiner, C.A.Tex., 358 F.2d 65, 69. See also **Class or representative action.**

Spurius /sp(y)úr(i)yəs/spár°/. Lat. In the civil law, a bastard; the offspring of promiscuous cohabitation.

Spy. A person sent into an enemy's camp to inspect their works, ascertain their strength and their intentions, watch their movements, and secretly communicate intelligence to the proper officer. By the laws of war among all civilized nations, a spy is punished with death. Ex parte Milligan, 71 U.S. (4 Wall.) 2, 44, 18 L.Ed. 281 (argument of counsel). Gathering, transmitting, or losing defense information with intent or reason to believe such information will be used to the injury of the United States is a federal crime. 18 U.S.C.A. § 793 *et seq.* See **Espionage.**

To watch or listen to secretly. See **Eavesdropping; Wiretapping.**

Square. As used to designate a certain portion of land within the limits of a city or town, this term may be synonymous with "block," that is, the smallest subdivision which is bounded on all sides by principal streets, or it may denote a space (more or less rectangular) not built upon, and set apart for public passage, use, recreation, or ornamentation, in the nature of a "park" but smaller.

Under government survey system, an area measuring 24 × 24 miles.

Just; settled; fair.

Public square. In its popular import, the phrase refers to ground occupied by a courthouse and other public buildings, normally at a point where two streets meet, but it may be used as synonymous with park.

Square block. Territory bounded by four streets. People ex rel. Beinert v. Miller, 100 Misc. 318, 165 N.Y.S. 602, 607; Bernfeld v. Freedenberg, 125 Misc. 645, 211 N.Y.S. 692.

Squatter. One who settles on another's land, without legal title or authority. A person entering upon lands, not claiming in good faith the right to do so by virtue of any title of his own or by virtue of some agreement with another whom he believes to hold the title. Under former laws, one who settled on public land in order to acquire title to the land.

Squatter's right. See **Adverse possession.**

Squeeze-out. A merger effected for no valid business purpose and resulting in the elimination of a minority shareholder is commonly referred to as a "freeze-out" or a "squeeze-out". It may be defined as the use of corporate control vested in the statutory majority of shareholders or the board of directors to eliminate minority shareholders from the enterprise or to reduce to relevant insignificance their voting power or claims on corporate assets. Furthermore, it implies a purpose to force upon the minority shareholder a change which is not incident to any other business goal of the corporation. Gabhart v. Gabhart, Ind., 370 N.E.2d 345, 353.

Squire. A contraction of "esquire."

SS. An abbreviation used in that part of a record, pleading, or affidavit, called the "statement of the venue." Commonly translated or read, "to-wit," and supposed to be a contraction of *"scilicet."*

S.S.A. Social Security Administration.

S.S.I. Supplemental Security Income.

S.S.S. Selective Service System.

Stabilia /stəbíl(i)yə/. A writ called by that name, founded on a custom in Normandy, that where a man in power claimed lands in the possession of an inferior, he petitioned the prince that it might be put into his hands till the right was decided, whereupon he had this writ.

Stabilize. To keep steady, fixed, as distinguished from fluctuating, shifting. McCanless v. Klein, 182 Tenn. 631, 188 S.W.2d 745, 748.

Stabilize prices. Holding prices steady against any and all increases. Philadelphia Coke Co. v. Bowles, Em. App., 139 F.2d 349, 353.

Stabit præsumptio donec probetur in contrarium /stéybət prəzám(p)sh(iy)ow dównək prəbíydər in kəntrér(i)yəm/. A presumption will stand good till the contrary is proved.

Stable-stand. In forest law, one of the four evidences or presumptions whereby a man was convicted of an intent to steal the king's deer in the forest. This was when a man was found at his *standing* in the forest with a cross-bow or long-bow bent, ready to shoot at any deer, or else standing close by a tree with greyhounds in a leash, ready to slip.

Stagiarius /stèyj(iy)ér(i)yəs/. A resident.

Stake. A deposit made to answer an event, as on a wager. Something deposited by two persons with the third on condition that it is to be delivered to the one who shall become entitled to it by the happening of a specified contingency. See also **Stakeholder**.

A boundary marker used for land survey purposes.

Stakeholder. Generally, a stakeholder is a third party chosen by two or more persons to keep on deposit property or money the right or possession of which is contested between them, and to be delivered to one who shall establish his right to it; and it is one who is entitled to interplead rival or contesting claimants to property or funds in his hands. Cochran v. Bank of Hancock County, 118 Ga.App. 100, 162 S.E.2d 765, 770. A person who is or may be exposed to multiple liability as the result of adverse claims. A stakeholder may commence an action of interpleader against two or more claimants. New York C.P.L.R. § 1006. See also **Interpleader**.

A person with whom money is deposited pending the decision of a bet or wager *(q.v.)*. His function is to receive the sums wagered and hold them against the determining event, whether that event be a horse race or otherwise, and then pay them over to the winner. Also a third person chosen by two or more persons to keep in deposit property the right or possession of which is contested between them, and to be delivered to the one who shall establish his right to it. State v. Dudley, 127 N.J.L. 127, 21 A.2d 209, 210.

Staking. Identification of boundaries of parcel of land by placing stakes in ground at boundary points.

Stale, *n.* In Saxon law, larceny.

Stale check. A check which bears a date of issue very much earlier than the date of its presentation or negotiation. A check which has been outstanding too long.

Stale demand, or **claim.** A demand or claim that has long remained unasserted, one that is first asserted after an unexplained delay which is so long as to render it difficult or impossible for the court to ascertain the truth of the matters in controversy and do justice between the parties, or as to create a presumption against the existence or validity of the claim, or a presumption that the claim has been abandoned or satisfied. Luschen v. Stanton, 192 Okl. 454, 137 P.2d 567, 572. It implies a greater lapse of time than is necessary to "laches." Bell v. Mackey, 191 S.C. 105, 3 S.E.2d 816, 824, 830. The doctrine is purely an equitable one, and arises only when, from lapse of time and laches of plaintiff, it would be inequitable to allow a party to enforce his legal rights. Wood v. City Board of Plumbing Examiners, 192 Ga. 415, 15 S.E.2d 486, 488.

Stallage /stóləj/. In old English law, the liberty of right of pitching or erecting stalls in fairs or markets, or the money paid for the same.

Stallarius /stolér(i)yəs/. In Saxon law, the *præfectus stabuli*, now master of the horse. Sometimes one who has a stall in a fair or market.

Stamp. Stamped or printed paper affixed to official or legal documents, stock certificates, etc. as evidence that tax has been paid as required by law. A small label or strip of paper, printed and sold by the government, and required to be attached to mail-matter, and to certain other documents and articles (*e.g.* liquor, cigarettes) subject to duty or excise. See **Documentary stamp; Revenue stamps; Stamp tax**.

A mark, design, seal, etc., which indicates ownership, approval, etc. An identifying or characterizing mark or impression.

Stamp acts. In English law, acts regulating the stamps upon deeds, contracts, agreements, papers in law proceedings, bills and notes, letters, receipts, and other papers. English Act of 1765 requiring that revenue stamps be affixed to all official documents in American colonies.

Stamp duties. In old English law, duties imposed upon and raised from stamps upon parchment and paper, and forming a branch of the perpetual revenue of the kingdom. 1 Bl.Comm. 323. See also **Documentary stamp; Revenue stamps; Stamp; Stamp tax**.

Stamp tax. The cost of stamps which are required to be affixed to legal documents such as deeds, certificates, and the like. See **Documentary stamp; Revenue stamp; Stamp**.

Stand. To cease from movement or progress; to pause, remain stationary or inactive. Jaggers v. Southeastern Greyhound Lines, D.C.Tenn., 34 F.Supp. 667, 668.

To abide; to submit to; as "to *stand* a trial." To appear in court.

To remain as a thing is; to remain in force. Pleadings objected to and held good are allowed to *stand*.

Standard. Stability, general recognition, and conformity to established practice. Standard Accident Ins. Co. v. Standard Surety & Casualty Co., D.C.N.Y., 53 F.2d 119, 120. A type, model, or combination of elements accepted as correct or perfect. A measure or rule applicable in legal cases such as the "standard of care" in tort actions. **Double standard; Reasonable man doctrine or standard; Standard of care**.

An ensign or flag used in war.

Standard deduction. A fixed deduction from taxable income used by a taxpayer who does not wish to itemize his deductions. I.R.C. §§ 141–145. Also referred to as the zero bracket amount. The standard deduction is built into the rate tables and rate schedules. Therefore, if an individual itemizes his or her deductions, only the amounts in excess of the standard deduction are deducted.

Standard established by law. That of a reasonable man under like circumstances. Gulf, C. & S. F. Ry. Co. v. Bell, Tex.Civ.App., 101 S.W.2d 363, 364. See **Reasonable man doctrine or standard; Standard of care.**

Standard mortgage clause. In fire policy, clause providing that in case of loss policy shall be payable to mortgagee, and that his interest as payee shall not be invalidated by act of mortgagor. Rhode Island Ins. Co. v. Wurtman, 265 Ky. 835, 98 S.W.2d 29, 31.

Standard of care. In law of negligence, that degree of care which a reasonably prudent person should exercise under same or similar circumstances. If a person's conduct falls below such standard, he may be liable in damages for injuries or damages resulting from his conduct. See **Negligence; Reasonable man doctrine or standard.**

In medical, legal, etc., malpractice cases a standard of care is applied to measure the competence of the professional. The traditional standard for doctors is that he exercise the "average degree of skill, care, and diligence exercised by members of the same profession, practicing in the same or a similar locality in light of the present state of medical and surgical science." Gillette v. Tucker, 67 Ohio St. 106, 65 N.E. 865. With increased specialization, however, certain courts have disregarded geographical considerations holding that in the practice of a board-certified medical or surgical specialty, the standard should be that of a reasonable specialist practicing medicine or surgery in the same special field. Bruni v. Tatsumi, 46 Ohio St.2d 127, 129, 346 N.E.2d 673, 676, 75 O.O.2d 184. See also **Malpractice.**

Standard of need. In public assistance law, total needs of an individual or family stipulated by the state, which, when unsatisfied by relevant resources makes the individual or family in need for public assistance purposes.

Standard of proof. The burden of proof required in a particular type of case, as in a criminal case where the prosecution has the standard (*i.e.* burden) of proof beyond a reasonable doubt, and in most civil cases where proof by a fair preponderance of the evidence is required. See **Burden of proof.**

Standard of weight, or measure. A weight or measure fixed and prescribed by law, to which all other weights and measures are required to correspond.

Standing. One's place in the community in the estimation of others; his relative position in social, commercial, or moral relations; his repute, grade, or rank. See **Reputation; Standing to sue doctrine; Status.**

Standing aside jurors. A practice by which, on the drawing of a jury for a criminal trial, the prosecuting officer puts aside a juror, provisionally, until the panel is exhausted, without disclosing his reasons, instead of being required to challenge him and show cause. The English statute 33 Edw. I deprived the crown of the power to challenge jurors without showing cause, and the practice of standing aside jurors was adopted, in England, as a method of evading its provisions. A similar practice was in use in Pennsylvania.

Standing by. Used in law as implying knowledge, under such circumstances as rendered it the duty of the possessor to communicate it; and it is such knowledge, and not the mere fact of "standing by," that lays the foundation of responsibility. The phrase does not import an actual presence, "but implies knowledge under such circumstances as to render it the duty of the possessor to communicate it." See also **Estoppel.**

Standing master. An officer of the court appointed on a regular basis to hear and determine matters within his jurisdiction for which a master may be appointed, as a master in chancery.

Standing mute. Exists in criminal case when defendant refuses to plead to the charge against him. If a defendant refuses to plead, the court shall enter a plea of not guilty. Fed.R.Crim.P. 11(a).

Standing orders. Rules adopted by particular courts for governing practice before them. In some states, the presiding judge has authority to adopt standing orders for his court alone. They may include rules as to the time at which court commences each day, a procedure for requesting continuances of cases and a method by which cases are placed on the trial list of the particular court. They may be system wide or affect only a particular court in the system.

Standing seised to uses. A covenant to stand seised to uses is one by which the owner of an estate covenants to hold the same to the use of another person, usually a relative, and usually in consideration of blood or marriage. It is a species of conveyance depending for its effect on the statute of uses.

Standing to be sued. Capacity of a person or sovereign to be a party defendant in an action. A state as sovereign has no capacity to be sued except in cases in which it has consented to suit. See **Sovereign immunity.**

Standing to sue doctrine. "Standing to sue" means that party has sufficient stake in an otherwise justiciable controversy to obtain judicial resolution of that controversy. Sierra Club v. Morton, 405 U.S. 727, 92 S.Ct. 1361, 1364, 31 L.Ed.2d 636. Standing is a concept utilized to determine if a party is sufficiently affected so as to insure that a justiciable controversy is presented to the court. The requirement of "standing" is satisfied if it can be said that the plaintiff has a legally protectible and tangible interest at stake in the litigation. Guidry v. Roberts, La.App., 331 So.2d 44, 50. Standing is a jurisdictional issue which concerns power of federal courts to hear and decide cases and does not concern ultimate merits of substantive claims involved in the action. Weiner v. Bank of King of Prussia, D.C.Pa., 358 F.Supp. 684, 695.

Standing is a requirement that the plaintiffs have been injured or been threatened with injury by governmental action complained of, and focuses on the question of whether the litigant is the proper party to fight the lawsuit, not whether the issue itself is justiciable. Carolina Environmental Study Group, Inc. v. U. S. Atomic Energy Comm., D.C.N.C., 431 F.Supp. 203, 218. Essence of standing is that no person is entitled to assail the constitutionality of an ordinance or statute except as he himself is adversely affected by it. Sandoval v. Ryan, Colo.App., 535 P.2d 244, 247. See also **Case** (*Cases and controversies*); **Justiciable controversy; Ripeness doctrine.**

Administrative Procedure Act. Such Act authorizes actions against federal officers by "any person suffering legal wrong because of agency action, or adversely affected or aggrieved by agency action within the meaning of a relevant statute." 5 U.S.C.A. § 702.

Staple. A major commodity grown, traded and demanded; *e.g.* grain, salt, flour. Such commodity is usually very important to the local economy where it is grown or produced. Raw material.

In English law, a mart or market. A place where the buying and selling of wool, lead, leather, and other articles were put under certain terms.

In International law, the right of staple, as exercised by a people upon foreign merchants, is defined to be that they may not allow them to set their merchandise and wares to sale but in a certain place. This practice is not in use in the United States.

Law of the staple. In England, law administered in the court of the mayor of the staple; the law-merchant.

Staple inn. An inn of chancery. See **Inns of Chancery.**

Statute staple. The English statute of the staple, 27 Ed. III, stat. 2, confined the sale of all commodities to be exported to certain towns in England, called *estaple* or *staple,* where foreigners might resort. It authorized a security for money, commonly called statute staple, to be taken by traders for the benefit of commerce; the mayor of the place is entitled to take recognizance of a debt in proper form, which had the effect to convey the lands of the debtor to the creditor till out of the rents and profits of them he should be satisfied. A security for a debt acknowledged to be due, so called from its being entered into before the mayor of the *staple,* that is to say, the grand mart for the principal commodities or manufactures of the kingdom, formerly held by act of parliament in certain trading towns. In other respects it resembled the *statute-merchant (q.v.),* but like that has now fallen into disuse.

Starboard. In maritime law, the righthand side of a vessel when the observer faces forward. "Starboard tack," refers to the course of vessel when she has the wind on her starboard bow.

Star-chamber. A court which originally had jurisdiction in cases where the ordinary course of justice was so much obstructed by one party, through writs, combination of maintenance, or overawing influence that no inferior court would find its process obeyed. The court consisted of the privy council, the common-law judges, and (it seems) all peers of parliament. In the reign of Henry VIII and his successors, the jurisdiction of the court was illegally extended to such a degree (especially in punishing disobedience to the king's arbitrary proclamations) that it became odious to the nation, and was abolished.

Stare decisis /stériy dəsáysəs/. Lat. To abide by, or adhere to, decided cases.

Policy of courts to stand by precedent and not to disturb settled point. Neff v. George, 364 Ill. 306, 4 N.E.2d 388, 390, 391. Doctrine that, when court has once laid down a principle of law as applicable to a certain state of facts, it will adhere to that principle, and apply it to all future cases, where facts are substantially the same; regardless of whether the parties and property are the same. Horne v. Moody, Tex.Civ.App., 146 S.W.2d 505, 509, 510. Under doctrine a deliberate or solemn decision of court made after argument on question of law fairly arising in the case, and necessary to its determination, is an authority, or binding precedent in the same court, or in other courts of equal or lower rank in subsequent cases where the very point is again in controversy. State v. Mellenberger, 163 Or. 233, 95 P.2d 709, 719, 720. Doctrine is one of policy, grounded on theory that security and certainty require that accepted and established legal principle, under which rights may accrue, be recognized and followed, though later found to be not legally sound, but whether previous holding of court shall be adhered to, modified, or overruled is within court's discretion under circumstances of case before it. Otter Tail Power Co. v. Von Bank, 72 N.D. 497, 8 N.W.2d 599, 607. Under doctrine, when point of law has been settled by decision, it forms precedent which is not afterwards to be departed from, and, while it should ordinarily be strictly adhered to, there are occasions when departure is rendered necessary to vindicate plain, obvious principles of law and remedy continued injustice. The doctrine is a salutary one, and should not ordinarily be departed from where decision is of long-standing and rights have been acquired under it, unless considerations of public policy demand it. Colonial Trust Co. v. Flanagan, 344 Pa. 556, 25 A.2d 728, 729. The doctrine is limited to actual determinations in respect to litigated and necessarily decided questions, and is not applicable to dicta or obiter dicta.

See also **Res** (*Res judicata*).

Stare decisis et non quieta movere /stériy dəsáysəs èt nón kwayíydə mowvíriy/. To adhere to precedents, and not to unsettle things which are established. Ballard County v. Kentucky County Debt Commission, 290 Ky. 770, 162 S.W.2d 771, 773. See **Stare decisis.**

Stare in judicio /stériy ìn juwdísh(iy)ow/. Lat. To appear before a tribunal, either as plaintiff or defendant.

Star page. The line and word at which the pages of the first edition of a law book began are frequently marked by a star in later editions, and always should be.

Starr, or **starra** /stár(ə)/. The old term for contract or obligation among the Jews, being a corruption from the Hebrew word *"shetar,"* a covenant, by an ordinance of Richard I, no starr was allowed to be valid, unless deposited in one of certain repositories established by law, the most considerable of which was in the king's exchequer at Westminster; and Blackstone conjectures that the room in which these chests were kept was thence called the "starr-chamber." 4 Bl. Comm. 266, 267, note *a.*

Stash. To secrete away; to hide or conceal money or property, commonly used in reference to ill-gotten gain or property.

State, *n.* A people permanently occupying a fixed territory bound together by common-law habits and custom into one body politic exercising, through the medium of an organized government, independent sovereignty and control over all persons and things within its boundaries capable of making war and peace and of entering into international relations with other communities of the globe. United States v. Kusche, D.C.Cal., 56 F.Supp. 201, 207, 208. The organization of social life which exercises sovereign power in behalf of the people. Delany v. Moraitis, C.C.A.Md., 136 F.2d 129, 130. In its largest sense, a "state" is a body politic or a society of men. Beagle v. Motor Vehicle Acc. Indemnification Corp., 44 Misc.2d 636, 254 N.Y.S.2d 763, 765. A body of people occupying a definite territory and politically organized under one government. State ex rel. Maisano v. Mitchell, 155 Conn. 256, 231 A.2d 539, 542. A territorial unit with a distinct general body of law. Restatement, Second, Conflicts, § 3. Term may refer either to body politic of a nation (*e.g.* United States) or to an individual governmental unit of such nation (*e.g.* California).

The section of territory occupied by one of the United States. One of the component commonwealths or states of the United States of America. The term is sometimes applied also to governmental agencies authorized by state, such as municipal corporations. Any state of the United States, the District of Columbia, the Commonwealth of Puerto Rico, and any territory or possession subject to the legislative authority of the United States. Uniform Probate Code, § 1–201(40).

The people of a state, in their collective capacity, considered as the party wronged by a criminal deed; the public; as in the title of a cause, "The State vs. A. B."

Term "state" as used in rules providing when a state may appeal in a criminal case is all inclusive and intended to include not only the state but its political subdivisions, counties and cities. Spokane County v. Gifford, 9 Wash.App. 541, 513 P.2d 301, 302. Federal Government is a "state" bound by all of provisions of the Interstate Agreement on Detainers. Enright v. U. S., D.C.N.Y., 437 F.Supp. 580, 581.

The circumstances or condition of a being or thing at a given time.

Foreign state. A foreign country or nation. The several United States are considered "foreign" to each other except as regards their relations as common members of the Union.

State officers. Those whose duties concern the state at large or the general public, or who are authorized to exercise their official functions throughout the entire state, without limitation to any political subdivision of the state. In another sense, officers belonging to or exercising authority under one of the states of the Union, as distinguished from the officers of the United States.

State offices. See **Office.**

State paper. A document prepared by, or relating to, the political department of the government of a state or nation, and concerning or affecting the administration of its government or its political or international relations. Also, a newspaper, designated by public authority, as the organ for the publication of public statutes, resolutions, notices, and advertisements.

State revenue. Current income of state from whatever source derived that is subject to appropriation for public uses.

State's evidence. See that title.

State tax. A tax the proceeds of which are to be devoted to the expenses of the state, as distinguished from taxation for federal, local or municipal purposes; *e.g.* state income or sales tax.

State, *v.* To express the particulars of a thing in writing or in words; to set down or set forth in detail; to aver, allege, or declare. To set down in gross; to mention in general terms, or by way of reference; to refer.

State action. In general, term used in connection with claims under due process clause and Civil Rights Act for which a private citizen is seeking damages or redress because of improper governmental intrusion into his life. In determining whether an action complained of constitutes "state action" within purview of Fourteenth Amendment, court must examine whether sufficiently close nexus exists between state and challenged action so that the action may fairly be treated as that of the state itself. Denver Welfare Rights Organization v. Public Utilities Comm., Colo., 547 P.2d 239, 243. There is no practical distinction between what constitutes "state action" for purposes of Fourteenth Amendment and what is required to fulfill "under color of state law" provision of Civil Rights Act of 1871. Weiss v. J. C. Penney Co., Inc., D.C.Ill., 414 F.Supp. 52, 54. See **Color of law.**

State auditor. The elected or appointed official in a state who is responsible for auditing the accounts of state agencies.

State banks. Those banks chartered by a state in contrast to federally chartered banks. Banks under the supervision and jurisdiction of state agencies. See also **Bank.**

State courts. Those courts which constitute the state judicial system in contrast to federal courts. City and county courts may or may not be part of the state system of courts, depending upon the jurisdiction.

Stated. Determined, fixed, or settled.

Stated meeting. A meeting of a board of directors, board of officers, etc., held at the time appointed therefor by law, ordinance, by-law, or other regulation; as distinguished from "special" meetings, which are held on call as the occasion may arise, rather than at a regularly appointed time, and from adjourned meetings.

Stated term. A regular or ordinary term or session of a court for the dispatch of its general business, held at the time fixed by law or rule; as distinguished from a *special* term, held out of the due order or for the transaction of particular business.

Stated times. Occurring at regular intervals or given regularly; fixed, regular in operation or occurrence, not occasional or fluctuating.

Stated account. Term signifies an agreed balance between the parties to a settlement; that is, that they have agreed after an investigation of their accounts that a certain balance is due from one to the other. Holt v. Western Farm Services, Inc., 19 Ariz.App. 335, 507 P.2d 674, 677.

Stated capital. Amount of capital contributed by stockholders. Sometimes used to mean legal capital.

The capital or equity of a corporation as it appears in the balance sheet. The sum of the par value of all par value shares issued, the entire amount received for no-par shares, and any amounts transferred by a stock dividend or other corporate action from surplus to stated capital. In some jurisdictions, only a portion of the amount received for no-par shares need be included in stated capital and the remainder may be credited to paid-in surplus and be distributed as a dividend.

State Department. That department in the executive branch of the federal government, headed by the Secretary of State, which is principally responsible for foreign affairs and foreign trade. The Department determines and analyzes the facts relating to our overseas interests, makes recommendations on policy and future action, and takes the necessary steps to carry out established policy. In so doing, the Department engages in continuous consultations with other states; negotiates treaties and agreements with foreign nations; speaks for the United States in the United Nations and in numerous major international organizations in which the United States participates; and represents the United States at numerous major international organizations in which the United States participates; and represents the United States at numerous international conferences annually.

Statement. In a general sense, an allegation; a declaration of matters of fact. The term has come to be used of a variety of formal narratives of facts, required by law in various jurisdictions as the foundation of judicial or official proceedings and in a limited sense is a formal, exact, detailed presentation.

An oral or written assertion, or nonverbal conduct of a person, if it is intended by him as an assertion. Fed.R.Evid. 801(a). Oral or written verbal expression, or nonverbal conduct of a person intended by him as a substitute for oral or written verbal expression. Calif.Evid.Code.

Report sent monthly or periodically by a bank to its customer or by a creditor to a debtor, setting forth amounts credited and balance due. See **Statement of account.**

For False and misleading statement; and, Opening statement of counsel, see those titles.

Statement of account. A report issued monthly or periodically by a bank or creditor to a customer setting forth the amounts billed, credits given and balance due. A bank statement includes the checks drawn and cleared, the deposits made, and the charges debited.

Statement of affairs. Document which must be filed in bankruptcy, setting forth answers to questions about the past and present financial situation of the debtor. A balance sheet showing immediate liquidation amounts, rather than historical costs, usually prepared when insolvency or bankruptcy is imminent.

Statement of claim. See **Claim; Complaint.**

Statement of condition. A balance sheet which shows the assets, liabilities, reserves and capital of a business as of a given date. See also **Statement of affairs.**

Statement of confession. Oftentimes referred to as a "power of attorney", "cognovit note", or "confession of judgment", is written authority of debtor and his direction to enter judgment against debtor as stated therein. See **Confession of judgment.**

Statement of defense. See **Answer; Reply.**

Statement of income. See **Income statement.**

Statement of particulars. See **Bill.**

State of facts. Formerly, when a master in chancery was directed by the court of chancery to make an inquiry or investigation into any matter arising out of a suit, and which could not conveniently be brought before the court itself, each party in the suit carried in before the master a statement showing how the party bringing it in represented the matter in question to be; and this statement was technically termed a "state of facts," and formed the ground upon which the evidence was received, the evidence being, in fact, brought by one party or the other, to prove his own or disprove his opponent's state of facts. And so now, a state of facts means the statement made by any one of his version of the facts.

State of mind. A person's reasons and motives for acting as he did. Term used in connection with evidence. See **State of mind exception.**

State of mind exception. Under the "state of mind exception" to the hearsay rule, an out of court declaration of a present existing motive or reason for acting is admissible even though the declarant is available to testify. Oberman v. Dun & Bradstreet, Inc., C.A.Ill., 507 F.2d 349, 351. See Fed.Evid.R. 803(3).

State of the case. In general, the posture of litigation at a given point in time. It may be ready for trial, in the process of trial, or pending appeal.

State paper office. An office established in London in 1578 for the custody of state papers. The head of it was the "Clerk of the Papers."

State police. A department or agency of a state government empowered with authority of police throughout a state and commonly trained and governed in a quasi-military fashion.

State police power. Every state has power to enact laws for the protection of its citizens' health, welfare, morals and safety and such power is derived from the 10th Amendment, U.S.Const. This power is upheld if exercised in a manner consistent with its ends and if the means used are reasonably calculated to protect one of these legitimate ends. See also **Police power.**

State's attorney. An officer who represents the State in securing indictments and in prosecuting criminal cases. Also called District Attorney or Prosecuting Attorney. Commonly he is elected in a county election and his authority is county wide.

State seal. The official die or signet having a raised emblem and used by state officials on documents of importance. Every state has its own such seal.

State's evidence. A popular term for testimony given by an accomplice or joint participant in the commission of a crime tending to criminate or convict the others, and given under an actual or implied promise of immunity or lesser sentence for himself.

State sovereignty. The right of a state to self-government. The role of supreme authority or rule exercised by every state within the Union.

State's rights. Rights not conferred on the federal government or forbidden to the States according to the 10th Amendment, U.S. Constitution.

Statim /stéydəm/. Lat. Forthwith; immediately. In old English law, this term meant either "at once," or "within a legal time," *i.e.*, such time as permitted the legal and regular performance of the act in question.

Stating an account. Exhibiting, or listing in their order, the items which make up an account.

Stating part of a bill. That part of a bill in chancery in which the plaintiff states the facts of his case; it is distinguished from the *charging* part of the bill and from the *prayer.*

Station. Social position or status. See **Standing; Status.**

A place where military duty is performed or stores are kept or something connected with war is done.

A place at which both freight and passengers are received for transportation or delivered after transportation.

In the civil law, a place where ships may ride in safety.

Stationers' company. A body formed in 1557 in London of 97 London stationers and their successors, to whom was entrusted, in the first instance, and, under Orders in Council, the censorship of the press.

Stationers' hall. In old English law, the hall of the stationers' company, at which every person claiming copyright in a book must register his title, in order to be able to bring actions against persons infringing it.

Stationery office. In old English law, a government office established as a department of the treasury, for the purpose of supplying government offices with stationery and books, and of printing and publishing government papers.

Station house. Police station or precinct.

Statist /stéydəst/. A statesman; a politician; one skilled in government.

Stat pro ratione voluntas /stǽt pròw ræshiyówniy vəlǽntæs/. The will stands in place of a reason.

Stat pro ratione voluntas populi /stǽt pròw ræshiyówniy vəlǽntæs póp(y)əlay/. The will of the people stands in place of a reason.

Statu liber /stǽchuw láybər/. Lat. In Roman law, one who is made free by will under a condition; one who has his liberty fixed and appointed at a certain time or on a certain condition.

Statu liberi /stǽchuw líbəray/. Lat. In Louisiana, slaves for a time, who had acquired the right of being free at a time to come, or on a condition which was not fulfilled, or in a certain event which had not happened, but who in the meantime remained in a state of slavery. Civ.Code La.1838.

Status. Standing; state or condition; social position. The legal relation of individual to rest of the community. The rights, duties, capacities and incapacities which determine a person to a given class. A legal personal relationship, not temporary in its nature nor terminable at the mere will of the parties, with which third persons and the state are concerned. Holzer v. Deutsche Reichsbahn Gesellschaft, 159 Misc. 830, 290 N.Y.S. 181, 191. While term implies relation it is not a mere relation.

Status crime. A class of crime which consists not in proscribed action or inaction, but in the accused's having a certain personal condition or being a person of a specified character. An example of a status crime is vagrancy.

Status de manerio /stéydəs dìy məníriyow/. In old English law, the assembly of the tenants in the court of the lord of a manor, in order to do their customary suit.

Status of irremovability. In old English law, the right acquired by a pauper, after one year's residence in any parish, not to be removed therefrom.

Status quo /stéydəs kwów/. The existing state of things at any given date. *Status quo ante bellum,* the state of things before the war. "Status quo" to be preserved by a preliminary injunction is the last actual, peaceable, uncontested status which preceded the pending controversy. Edgewater Constr. Co., Inc. v. Percy Wilson Mortg. & Finance Corp., 2 Ill.Dec. 864, 357 N.E.2d 1307, 1314.

Statutable, or statutory /stǽchədəbəl/stǽchət(ò)riy/. That which is introduced or governed by statutory law, as opposed to the common law or equity. Thus, a court is said to have statutory jurisdiction when jurisdiction is given to it in certain matters by act of the legislature.

Statuta pro publico commodo late interpretantur /stətyúwdə pròw pə́bləkow kómədow léydiy intərprətǽntər/. Statutes made for the public good ought to be liberally construed.

Statuta suo clauduntur territorio nec ultra territorium disponunt /stəchúwdə s(y)úwow klodántər tèhrətóriyow nèk ə́ltrə tèhrətóriyəm dəspównənt/. Statutes are confined to their own territory, and have no extraterritorial effect.

Statute, *n.* An act of the legislature declaring, commanding, or prohibiting something; a particular law enacted and established by the will of the legislative department of government; the written will of the legislature, solemnly expressed according to the forms necessary to constitute it the law of the state. Such may be public or private, declaratory, mandatory, directory, or enabling, in nature. For mandatory and directory statutes, see **Directory** and **Mandatory statutes.**

Depending upon its context in usage, a statute may mean a single act of a legislature or a body of acts which are collected and arranged according to a scheme or for a session of a legislature or parliament.

This word is used to designate the legislatively created laws in contradistinction to court decided or unwritten laws. See **Common law.**

See also Codification; Mandatory statutes; Revised statutes; Slip law; Slip law print; Special law.

Affirmative statute. See **Affirmative.**

Criminal statute. An act of the Legislature as an organized body relating to crime or its punishment. See **Crime; Criminal law; Penal code; Penal laws.**

Declaratory statute. See **Declaratory.**

Enabling statute. See that title.

Expository statute. See that title.

General statute. A statute relating to the whole community, or concerning all persons generally, as distinguished from a private or special statute.

Local statute. See **Local law.**

Negative statute. A statute expressed in negative terms; a statute which prohibits a thing from being done, or declares what shall *not* be done.

Penal statute. See **Crime; Criminal law; Penal code; Penal laws; Punitive statute.**

Perpetual statute. One which is to remain in force without limitation as to time; one which contains no provision for its repeal, abrogation, or expiration at any future time.

Personal statutes. In foreign and modern civil law, those statutes which have principally for their object the *person,* and treat of property only incidentally. A personal statute, in this sense of the term, is a law, ordinance, regulation, or custom, the disposition of which affects the person and clothes him with a capacity or incapacity, which he does not change with every change of abode, but which, upon principles of justice and policy, he is assumed to carry with him wherever he goes. The term is also applied to statutes which, instead of being general, are confined in their operation to one person or group of persons.

Private statute. A statute which operates only upon particular persons, and private concerns. An act which relates to certain individuals, or to particular classes of men. See **Special law.**

Public statute. A statute enacting a universal rule which regards the whole community, as distinguished from one which concerns only particular individuals and affects only their private rights. See also *General statute,* supra.

Punitive statute. See that title.

Real statutes. In the civil law, statutes which have principally for their object property, and which do not speak of persons, except in relation to property.

Reference statutes. See that title.

Remedial statute. See **Remedial.**

Revised statutes. See that title.

Special statute. One which operates only upon particular persons and private concerns. A private statute. Distinguished from a general or public statute. See **Special law.**

Statute fair. In old English law, a fair at which laborers of both sexes stood and offered themselves for hire; sometimes called also "Mop."

Statute-merchant. In old English law, a security for a debt acknowledged to be due, entered into before the chief magistrate of some trading town, pursuant to the statute 13 Edw. I, *De Mercatoribus,* by which not only the body of the debtor might be imprisoned, and his goods seized in satisfaction of the debt, but also his lands might be delivered to the creditor till out of the rents and profits of them the debt be satisfied. Now fallen into disuse.

Statute of accumulations. In old English law, the statute 39 & 40 Geo. III, c. 98, forbidding the accumulation, beyond a certain period, of property settled by deed or will.

Statute of allegiance de facto. An act of 11 Hen. VII, c. 1, requiring subjects to give their allegiance to the actual king for the time being, and protecting them in so doing.

Statute of distributions. See **Distribution.**

Statute of Elizabeth. In old English law, the statute 13 Eliz., c. 5, against conveyances made in fraud of creditors.

Statute of frauds. See **Frauds, Statute of.**

Statute of Gloucester. In old English law, the statute 6 Edw. I, c. 1, A.D. 1278. It takes its name from the place of its enactment, and was the first statute giving costs in actions. 3 Bl.Comm. 399.

Statute of laborers. See **Laborer.**

Statute of limitations. See **Limitation.**

Statute of uses. See **Use.**

Statute of wills. In old English law, the statute 32 Hen. VIII, c. 1, which enacted that all persons being seised in fee-simple (except *femes covert,* infants, idiots, and persons of non-sane memory) might, by will and testament in writing, devise to any other person, except to bodies corporate, two-thirds of their lands, tenements, and hereditaments, held in chivalry, and the whole of those held in socage. 2 Bl.Comm. 375.

Statute roll. A roll upon which an English statute, after receiving the royal assent, was formerly entered.

Statutes at large. An official compilation of the acts and resolutions of each session of Congress published by the Office of the Federal Register in the National Archives and Records Service. It consists of two parts, the first comprising public acts and joint resolutions, the second, private acts and joint resolutions, concurrent resolutions, treatises, proposed and ratified amendments to Constitution, and Presidential proclamations. The arrangement is currently by Public Law number, and by chapter number in pre-1951 volumes. This is the official print of the law for citation purposes where titles of the United States Code have not been enacted into positive law.

Statutes of amendments and jeofailes. Formerly, statutes whereby a pleader who perceived any slip in the form of his proceedings, and acknowledged the error (jeofaile), was permitted to amend.

Statute staple. See **Staple.**

Temporary statute. One which is limited in its duration at the time of its enactment. It continues in force until the time of its limitation has expired, unless sooner repealed. A statute which by reason of its nature has only a single and temporary operation—*e.g.* an appropriation bill—is also called a temporary statute.

Validating statute. See that title.

Statutes at large. See **Statute.**

Statuti /stət(y)úwday/. Lat. In Roman law, licensed or registered advocates; members of the college of advocates. The number of these was limited, and they enjoyed special privileges from the time of Constantine to that of Justinian.

Statutory. Relating to a statute; created or defined by a statute; required by a statute; conforming to a statute.

Statutory bond. One that either literally or substantially meets requirements of statute. Southern Surety Co. v. United States Cast Iron Pipe & Foundry Co., C.C.A.Mo., 13 F.2d 833, 835.

Statutory construction. That branch of the law dealing with the interpretation of laws enacted by a legislature. A judicial function required when a statute is invoked and different interpretations are in contention. Where legislature attempts to do several things one of which is invalid, it may be discarded if remainder of the act is workable and in no way depends upon invalid portion, but if that portion is an integral part of the act, and its excision changes the manifest intent of the act by broadening its scope to include subject matter or territory which was not included therein as enacted, such excision is "judicial legislation" and not "statutory construction". Ettinger v. Studevent, 219 Ind. 406, 38 N.E.2d 1000, 1007.

Statutory crime. See **Crime.**

Statutory dedication. See **Dedication.**

Statutory exception. A provision in a statute exempting certain conduct or persons from the thrust of the law enacted.

Statutory exposition. When the language of a statute is ambiguous, and any subsequent enactment involves a particular interpretation of the former act, it is said to contain a *statutory* exposition of the former act.

Statutory extortion. The unlawful extraction of money or other value by means of a threat not sufficient for robbery, or a communication for the purpose of such extraction. See also **Extortion.**

Statutory foreclosure. See **Foreclosure.**

Statutory instruments. English administrative regulations and orders. The term applies especially to the administrative rules published since 1939, supplementing the English administrative code, Statutory Rules and Orders.

Statutory law. That body of law created by acts of the legislature in contrast to law generated by judicial opinions and administrative bodies. See **Statute.**

Statutory lien. A lien arising solely by force of statute upon specified circumstances or conditions, but does not include any lien provided by or dependent upon an agreement to give security, whether or not such lien is also provided by or is also dependent upon statute and whether or not the agreement or lien is made fully effective by statute. Bankruptcy Act, § 101(38).

Statutory obligation. An obligation—whether to pay money, perform certain acts, or discharge certain duties—which is created by or arises out of a statute, as distinguished from one founded upon acts between parties or jural relationships.

Statutory partnership association. See **Partnership.**

Statutory penalty. One imposed against the offender for some statutory violation by him. People v. Corcillo, 195 Misc. 198, 88 N.Y.S.2d 534, 536. One which an individual is allowed to recover against a wrongdoer as satisfaction for wrong or injury suffered, without reference to actual damage sustained. Nording v. Johnston, 205 Or. 315, 283 P.2d 994, 998. In a civil sense, a "statutory penalty" is a pecuniary punition, imposed for doing some act which is prohibited or for omitting to do some act which is required to be done; *e.g.* Copyright Act provides statutory damages for copyright infringement. § 504(c). See also **Penalty.**

Statutory rape. The unlawful sexual intercourse with a female under the age of consent which may be 16, 17 or 18 years of age, depending upon the state. The government is not required to prove that intercourse was without the consent of the female because she is conclusively presumed to be incapable of consent by reason of her tender age. See also **Rape.**

Statutory release. In England, a conveyance which superseded the old compound assurance by lease and release. It was created by St. 4 & 5 Vict., c. 21, which abolished the lease for a year.

Statutory staple. An ancient writ that lay to take the body of a person and seize the lands and goods of one who had forfeited a bond called statute staple. See **Staple.**

Statutory successor. A statutory successor is the person to whom all assets of a corporation pass upon its dissolution under the provisions of a statute of the state of incorporation which is in force at the time of the dissolution. See Restatement, Second, Conflicts, § 388.

Statutum /stət(y)úwdəm/. Lat. Established; determined.

In the civil law, a term applied to judicial action. In old English law, a statute; an act of parliament.

Statutum affirmativum non derogat communi legi /stət(y)úwdəm əfərmətáyvəm nòn dérəgət kəmyúwnay líyjay/. An affirmative statute does not derogate from the common law.

Statutum ex gratia regis dicitur, quando rex dignatur cedere de jure suo regio, pro commodo et quiete populi sui /stət(y)úwdəm èks gréysh(iy)ə ríyjəs dísədər, kwóndow reks dignéydər síydəriy dìy s(y)úwow ríyj(iy)ow, pròw kómədow èt kwayíydiy póp(y)əlay s(y)úway/. A statute is said to be by the grace of the king, when the king deigns to yield some portion of his royal rights for the good and quiet of his people.

Statutum generaliter est intelligendum quando verba statuti sunt specialia, ratio ·autem generalis /stət(y)úwdəm jènəréylədər èst intèləjéndəm kwóndow várbə stət(y)úwday sànt spèshiyéyl(i)yə réysh(iy)ow ódəm jènəréyləs/. When the words of a statute are special, but the reason of it general, the statute is to be understood generally.

Statutum sessionum /stət(y)úwdəm sès(h)iyównəm/. In old English law, the statute session; a meeting in every hundred of constables and householders, by custom, for the ordering of servants, and debating of differences between masters and servants, rating of wages, etc.

Statutum speciale statuto speciali non derogat /stət(y)úwdəm speshiyéyliy stət(y)úwdow speshiyéylay nòn déhrəgət/. One special statute does not take from another special statute.

Stay, v. To stop, arrest, or forbear. To "stay" an order or decree means to hold it in abeyance, or refrain from enforcing it.

Stay, n. A stopping; the act of arresting a judicial proceeding by the order of a court. Also that which holds, restrains, or supports.

A stay is a suspension of the case or some designated proceedings within it. It is a kind of injunction with which a court freezes its proceedings at a particular point. It can be used to stop the prosecution of the action altogether, or to hold up only some phase of it, such as an execution about to be levied on a judgment.

Stay laws. Acts of the legislature prescribing a stay of execution in certain cases, or a stay of foreclosure of mortgages, or closing the courts for a limited period, or providing that suits shall not be instituted until a certain time after the cause of action arose, or otherwise suspending legal remedies; designed for the relief of debtors, in times of general distress or financial trouble.

Stay of execution. The stopping or arresting of execution on a judgment, that is, of the judgment-creditor's right to issue execution, for a limited period. This is given by statute in many jurisdictions, as a privilege to the debtor, usually on his furnishing bail for the debt, costs, and interest. Or it may take place by agreement of the parties. Term may also refer to the stopping of the execution of capital punishment, commonly to permit further appeals by defendant.

Stay of proceedings. The temporary suspension of the regular order of proceedings in a cause, by direction or order of the court, usually to await the action of one of the parties in regard to some omitted step or some act which the court has required him to perform as incidental to the suit; as where a nonresident plaintiff has been ruled to give security for costs.

Stay order. A stopping; the act of arresting a judicial proceeding by the order of a court or the temporary suspension of the regular order of proceedings in a cause by direction or order of the court. In re Koome, 82 Wash.2d 816, 514 P.2d 520, 522.

Steady course. A ship is on a "steady course," not only when her heading does not change, but whenever her future positions are certainly ascertainable from her present position and movements. Commonwealth & Dominion Line v. U. S., C.C.A.N.Y., 20 F.2d 729, 731.

Steal. This term is commonly used in indictments for larceny ("take, *steal,* and carry away"), and denotes the commission of theft, that is, the felonious taking and carrying away of the personal property of another, and without right and without leave or consent of owner, and with intent to keep or make use wrongfully. State v. Hillis, 145 Kan. 456, 65 P.2d 251, 252. Or, it may denote the criminal taking of personal property either by larceny, embezzlement, or false pretenses. But, in popular usage "stealing" may include the unlawful appropriation of things which are not technically the subject of larceny, *e.g.,* immovables. See also **Larceny; Robbery; Shoplifting; Theft.**

Stealing children. See **Kidnapping.**

Stealth /stélθ/. The quality or condition of being secret or furtive. The act of stealing when the victim is unaware of the theft is stealing by stealth. Any secret, sly or clandestine act to avoid discovery and to gain entrance into or to remain within residence of another without permission. State v. Lane, 50 Ohio App.2d 41, 361 N.E.2d 535, 540, 4 O.O.3d 24.

Steerer. One who gains the confidence of the person intended to be fleeced and who may be said to steer or lead the victim to the place where the latter is to be robbed or swindled.

Stellionataire. Fr. In French law, a party who fraudulently mortgages property to which he has no title.

Stellionate /stélyəneyt/. In civil law, a name given generally to all species of frauds committed in making contracts but particularly to the crime of aliening the same subject to different persons.

Stellionatus /stèlyənéydəs/. Lat. In the civil law, a general name for any kind of fraud not falling under any specific class. But the term is chiefly applied to fraud practiced in the sale or pledging of property; as, selling the same property to two different persons, selling another's property as one's own, placing a second mortgage on property without disclosing the existence of the first, etc.

Step. When used as prefix in conjunction with a degree of kinship, is repugnant to blood relationship, and is indicative of a relationship by affinity.

Step-child. The child of one of the spouses by a former marriage. A child who has a parent by his natural parent's second marriage and has not been adopted by that parent.

Step-down in basis. A reduction in the income tax basis of property. See also **Step-up in basis.**

Step-father. The husband of one's mother by virtue of a marriage subsequent to that of which the person spoken of is the offspring.

Step-in-the-dark rule. Such rule of contributory negligence is that one who enters a totally unfamiliar area in the darkness is not justified, in the absence of any special stress, in proceeding without first ascertaining whether there are any obstacles to his safe progress. Yoder v. Greenwald, Fla.App., 246 So.2d 148, 150.

Step-mother. The wife of one's father by virtue of a marriage subsequent to that of which the person spoken of is the offspring.

Step-parent. The mother or father of a child born during a previous marriage of the other parent and hence, not the natural parent of such child.

Step-son. The son of one's wife by a former husband, or of one's husband by a former wife.

Step-up in basis. An increase in the income tax basis of property.

Sterbreche, or **strebrich.** The breaking, obstructing, or straitening of a way.

Stère /stír/stéhr/. A French measure of solidity, used in measuring wood. It is a cubic meter.

Sterility /stərílədiy/. Barrenness; unfruitfulness; incapacity to germinate or reproduce.

Sterilization. The act or process by which one is rendered incapable of procreation as, for example, the act of tying the female Fallopian tubes or a vasectomy. Also, the act or process by which an article or instrument is rendered free of germs.

Sterling. In English law, current or standard coin, especially silver coin; a standard of coinage.

Stet processus /stét prəsésəs/. An entry on the roll in the nature of a judgment of a direction that all further proceedings shall be stayed (*i.e.,* that the process may stand), and it is one of the ways by which a suit may be terminated by an act of the party, as distinguished from a termination of it by judgment, which is the act of the court. It was used by the plaintiff when he wished to suspend the action without suffering a nonsuit.

Stevedore. A person employed in loading and unloading vessels.

Steward. A man appointed in the place or stead of another. A union official who represents other union employees in grievances with management and who oversees the carrying out of the union contract.

Steward of all England. In old English law, an officer who was invested with various powers; among others, to preside on the trial of peers.

Steward of a Manor. In old English law, an important officer who had the general management of all forensic matters connected with the manor of which he was steward. He stood in much the same relation to the lord of the manor as an under-sheriff did to the sheriff.

Stews. Certain brothels anciently permitted in England, suppressed by Henry VIII. Also, breeding places for tame pheasants.

Stickler. An arbitrator. An obstinate contender about anything.

Stick up. Rob at the point of a gun.

Stifling a prosecution. Agreeing, in consideration of receiving a pecuniary or other advantage, to abstain from prosecuting a person for an offense not giving rise to a civil remedy.

Still. Any device used for separating alcoholic spirits from fermented substances. The word is sometimes applied to the whole apparatus for evaporation and condensation used in the manufacture of ardent spirits, but in the description of the parts of the apparatus it is applied merely to the vessel or retort used for boiling and evaporation of the liquid.

Stillborn child. A child born dead or in such an early stage of pregnancy as to be incapable of living, though not actually dead at the time of birth.

Stillicidium /stìləsíd(i)yəm/. Lat. In the civil law, the drip of water from the eaves of a house. The servitude *stillicidii* consists in the right to have the water drip from one's eaves upon the house or ground of another. The term *"flumen"* designated the rainwater collected from the roof, and carried off by the gutters, and there is a similar easement of having it discharged upon the adjoining estate.

Stint. In English law, limit; a limited number. Used as descriptive of a species of common. See Common sans nombre.

Stipend /stáypənd/. A salary; settled pay; fixed or regular payment. Offering made to clergyman.

Stipendiary estates /stəpénd(i)yèhriy/. Estates granted in return for services, generally of a military kind.

Stipendiary magistrates. In English law, paid magistrates; appointed in London and some other cities and boroughs, and having in general the powers and jurisdiction of justices of the peace.

Stipendium /stəpénd(i)yəm/. Lat. In the civil law, the pay of a soldier; wages; stipend.

Stipes /stáypiyz/. Lat. In old English law, stock; a stock; a source of descent or title. *Communis stipes,* the common stock.

Stipital /stípədəl/. Relating to *stirpes,* roots, or stocks. "Stipital distribution" of property is distribution *per stirpes;* that is, by right of representation.

Stipulate. Arrange or settle definitely, as an agreement or covenant. See **Stipulation.**

Stipulated damage. Liquidated damage (*q.v.*).

Stipulatio /stìpyəléysh(iy)ow/. Lat. In the Roman law, *stipulatio* was the verbal contract (*verbis obliga-*

tio), and was the most solemn and formal of all the contracts in that system of jurisprudence. It was entered into by question and corresponding answer thereto, by the parties, both being present at the same time, and usually by such words as *"spondes? spondeo,"* *"promittis? promitto,"* and the like.

Stipulatio aquiliana /stìpyǝléysh(iy)ow ǝkwìliyéynǝ/. A particular application of the *stipulatio,* which was used to collect together into one verbal contract all the liabilities of every kind and quality of the debtor, with a view to their being released or discharged by an *acceptilatio,* that mode of discharge being applicable only to the verbal contract.

Stipulatio juris /stìpyǝléysh(iy)ow júrǝs/. A stipulation or agreement beforehand of a question of law or its applicability, though a court is not bound by a stipulation of erroneous law. However, the parties to a contract may stipulate as to the applicability of the law of a particular state or jurisdiction.

Stipulation. A material condition, requirement, or article in an agreement.

The name given to any agreement made by the attorneys engaged on opposite sides of a cause (especially if in writing), regulating any matter incidental to the proceedings or trial, which falls within their jurisdiction. Voluntary agreement between opposing counsel concerning disposition of some relevant point so as to obviate need for proof or to narrow range of litigable issues. Arrington v. State, Fla., 233 So.2d 634, 636. An agreement, admission or confession made in a judicial proceeding by the parties thereto or their attorneys. Bourne v. Atchison, T. & S. F. Ry. Co., 209 Kan. 511, 497 P.2d 110, 114.

Stipulations made during the course of trial may involve jury of less than twelve (Fed.R.Civil P. 48), master's findings (Rule 53(e)(4)), dismissal of action (Rule 41(a)), or discovery (see below).

A recognizance of certain persons (called in the old law *"fide jussors"*) in the nature of bail for the appearance of a defendant. 3 Bl.Comm. 108.

See also **Admission; Proviso.**

Discovery. Unless the court orders otherwise, the parties may by written stipulation (1) provide that depositions may be taken before any person, at any time or place, upon any notice, and in any manner and when so taken may be used like other depositions, and (2) modify the procedures provided by these rules for other methods of discovery, except that stipulations extending the time provided in Rules 33, 34, and 36 for responses to discovery may be made only with the approval of the court. Fed.R.Civil P. 29.

Stipulator. In the civil law, the party who asked the question in the contract of stipulation; the other party, or he who answered, being called the "promissor." But, in a more general sense, the term was applied to both the parties.

Stirpes /stárpiyz/. Lat. Descents. The root-stem, or stock of a tree. Figuratively, it signifies in law that person from whom a family is descended, and also the kindred or family. Taking property by right of representation is called "succession *per stirpes,*" in opposition to taking in one's own right, or as a

principal, which is termed "taking *per capita.*" See also **Per stirpes** and **Representation.**

Stock. The goods and wares of a merchant or tradesman, kept for sale and traffic. In a larger sense, the capital of a merchant or other person, including his merchandise, money, and credits, or, in other words, the entire property employed in business. See **Inventory.**

Corporation Law

The term is used in various senses. It may mean the capital or principal fund of a corporation or joint-stock company, formed by the contributions of subscribers or the sale of shares; the aggregate of a certain number of shares severally owned by the members or stockholders of the corporation or the proportional share of an individual stockholder; also the incorporeal property which is represented by the holding of a certificate of stock; and in a wider and more remote sense, the right of a shareholder to participate in the general management of the company and to share proportionally in its net profits or earnings or in the distribution of assets on dissolution. The term "stock" has also been held to embrace not only capital stock of a corporation but all corporate wealth and resources, subject to all corporate liabilities and obligations.

"Stock" is distinguished from "bonds" and, ordinarily, from "debentures," in that it gives right of ownership in part of assets of corporation and right to interest in any surplus after payment of debt. "Stock" in a corporation is an equity, and it represents an ownership interest, and it is to be distinguished from obligations such as notes or bonds which are not equities and represent no ownership interest. U. S. v. Evans, C.A.Or., 375 F.2d 730, 731.

See also **Discount shares; Equity security; Par value; Registration of stock; Securities; Security; Share of corporate stock.**

Classes and Types of Corporate Stock

Preferred stock is a separate portion or class of the stock of a corporation, which is accorded, by the charter or by-laws, a preference or priority in respect to dividends, over the remainder of the stock of the corporation, which in that case is called *common stock.* That is, holders of the preferred stock are entitled to receive dividends at a fixed annual rate, out of the net earnings or profits of the corporation, before any distribution of earnings is made to the common stock. If the earnings applicable to the payment of dividends are not more than sufficient for such fixed annual dividend, they will be entirely absorbed by the preferred stock. If they are more than sufficient for the purpose, the remainder may be given entirely to the common stock (which is the more usual custom) or such remainder may be distributed pro rata to both classes of the stock, in which case the preferred stock is said to "participate" with the common. The fixed dividend on preferred stock may be "cumulative" or "non-cumulative." In the former case, if the stipulated dividend on preferred stock is not earned or paid in any one year, it becomes a charge upon the surplus earnings of the next and succeeding years, and all such accumulated and unpaid dividends on the preferred stock must be paid off before the common stock is entitled to receive dividends. In the case of "non-cumulative" preferred stock, its preference for any given year is extinguished by the failure to earn or pay its dividend in that year. If a corporation has no class of preferred stock, all its stock is common stock. The word "common" in this connection signifies that all the holders of such stock are entitled to an equal pro rata division of profits or net earnings, if any there be, without any preference or priority among themselves. *Deferred stock* is rarely issued by American corporations, though it is not uncommon in England. This kind of stock is distinguished by the fact that the payment of dividends upon it is expressly postponed until some other class of stock has received a dividend, or until some certain liability or obligation of the corporation is discharged. If there is a class of "preferred" stock, the common stock may in this sense be said to be "deferred," and the term is sometimes used as equivalent to "common" stock. But it is not impossible that a corporation should have three classes of stock: (1) Preferred, (2) common, and (3) deferred; the latter class being postponed, in respect to participation in profits, until both the preferred and the common stock had received dividends at a fixed rate.

Assented stock. Stock which an owner deposits with a third person in accordance with an agreement by which the owner voluntarily accepts a change in the securities of the corporation.

Assessable stock. Stock which requires the owner to pay more than its cost if the needs of the corporation require.

Authorized stock. That amount of stock which the corporate charter permits the corporation to issue.

Blue-chip stock. Stock of a listed company which has a high grade financial record.

Bonus stock. Stock given to an underwriter as compensation for services. Stock given to purchasers as an inducement. See also **Bonus stock.**

Callable preferred stock. Preferred stock which may be called by the issuing corporation at a prestated price.

Capital stock. See **Capital** (*Capital stock*).

Common stock. Securities which represent an ownership interest in a corporation. If the company has also issued preferred stock, both common and preferred have ownership rights. The preferred normally is limited to a fixed dividend but has prior claim on dividends and, in the event of liquidation, assets. Claims of both common and preferred stockholders are junior to claims of bondholders or other creditors of the company. Common stockholders assume the greater risk, but generally exercise the greater control and may gain the greater reward in the form of dividends and capital appreciation. The terms common stock and capital stock are often used interchangeably when the company has no preferred stock. See also **Common stock.**

Control stock. That amount of capital stock which permits the owner to control the corporation. It is not necessarily a majority of the shares.

Convertible stock. Stock which may be changed or converted into common stock.

Cumulative preferred. A stock having a provision that if one or more dividends are omitted, the omitted dividends must be paid before dividends may be paid on the company's common stock.

Cumulative stock. A type of stock on which unpaid dividends accumulate until paid. They must be paid totally before the common stockholders receive their dividends. See *Cumulative preferred, supra.*

Donated stock. Stock transferred to the corporation by the stockholders for resale.

Floating stock. That part of a corporation's stock which is on the open market for speculation. Stock not yet bought by public holders.

Growth stock. Stock purchased with a view towards appreciation in value rather than dividend income.

Guaranteed stock. Usually preferred stock on which dividends are guaranteed by another company, under much the same circumstances as a bond is guaranteed.

Guaranty stock. Stock in a savings and loan association in some states which yields all dividends to the holders after dividends to depositors or savers.

Issued stock. Stock which has been authorized and actually sold to subscribers. It may include treasury stock.

Letter stock. Stock received by a buyer who gives the seller a letter stating that he will hold such stock and not reoffer it to others. Such stock need not be registered under the Securities Act of 1933. See also **Letter stock.**

Listed stock. The stock of a company which is traded on a securities exchange, and for which a listing application and a registration statement, giving detailed information about the company and its operations, have been filed with the Securities and Exchange Commission, unless otherwise exempted, and with the exchange itself. The various stock exchanges have different standards for listing.

Nonassessable stock. Stock which cannot be assessed (*i.e.* holder cannot be assessed) in the event of failure or insolvency of the corporation. Most all stock is nonassessable.

Noncumulative preferred stock. Type of preferred stock which yields no dividend once the dividend is passed. Contrast *Cumulative preferred,* above.

Noncumulative stock. A preferred stock on which unpaid dividends do not accrue. Omitted dividends are, as a rule, gone forever.

Nonvoting stock. Stock to which no rights to vote attach.

No par stock. Stock without par value but which represents a proportionate share of the ownership of a corporation based on the number of shares. A corporation may have both par and no par value stock.

Outstanding stock. Stock issued and in the hands of stockholders and such does not include treasury stock.

Paid up stock. Stock for which full payment has been made to the corporation.

Participation preferred stock. A preferred stock which is entitled to its stated dividend and, also, to additional dividends on a specified basis upon payment of dividends on the common stock.

Participation stock. In general, stock which permits the holder to participate in the profits and surplus.

Par value stock. Stock which originally had a fixed value arrived at by dividing the total value of capital stock by the number of shares to be issued. The par value does not bear a necessary relation to the actual value of the stock because of the part which surplus plays in valuation. See also **Par value.**

Penny stock. Generally, highly speculative stock which can be purchased for under a dollar a share.

Preferred stock. A class of stock with a claim on the company's earnings before payment may be made on the common stock and usually entitled to priority over common stock if company liquidates. Usually entitled to dividends at a specified rate—when declared by the Board of Directors and before payment of a dividend on the common stock—depending upon the terms of the issue.

Premium stock. Stock which carries a premium for trading as in the case of short selling.

Redeemable stock. Generally preferred stock which can be called in and retired. It is redeemable at par. See also **Redeemable stock.**

Registered stock. Stock registered under federal Securities Act. See also *Listed stock, supra.*

Restricted stock. Stock to which is attached restrictions as to transferability.

Stock options. See *Stock option, infra.*

Stock redemption. See *Stock redemption, infra.*

Stock rights. See *Stock rights, infra.*

Stock split. See *Stock split, infra.*

Subscribed stock. See that title.

Treasury stock. Stock issued by a company but later re-acquired. It may be held in the company's treasury indefinitely, reissued to the public, or retired. Treasury stock receives no dividends and has no vote while held by the company.

Unissued stock. Stock authorized by the corporate charter but not yet distributed to stockholders and subscribers.

Unlisted stock. Stock not listed on one of the stock exchanges but traded over the counter or privately.

Voting stock. Stock which carries the right to vote for directors, etc. See also **Voting stock.**

Watered stock. Stock issued for inadequate consideration. See also **Watered stock.**

Law of Descent

The term is used, metaphorically, to denote the original progenitor of a family, or the ancestor from whom the persons in question are all descended; such descendants being called "branches." Matter of Samson's Estate, 139 Misc. 490, 249 N.Y.S. 79, 83.

General

Capital stock. See **Capital** *(Capital stock).*

Certificate of stock. See **Certificate; Share certificate.**

Exchange of stock. See **Exchange.**

Public stocks. The funded or bonded debt of a government or state.

Stock association. A joint-stock company *(q.v.).*

Stock attribution. See **Attribution.**

Stock bailout. A species of stock redemption in the form of a preferred stock dividend formerly tax free, but now governed by I.R.C. § 306.

Stockbroker. One who buys or sells stock as agent of another. Allen v. Todd, 12 Cal.App.2d 654, 90 Cal.Rptr. 807, 810.

Stock certificate. See **Certificate of stock; Share certificate.**

Stock control. Type of inventory management by which a business maintains perpetual records of its inventory.

Stock corporation. A corporation having a capital stock divided into shares, and which is authorized by law to distribute to the holders thereof dividends or shares of the surplus profits of the corporation.

Stock dividend. Distributing stock as a dividend. If the dividend is common stock declared on common stock, the only result other than to reduce the value of each share of common and to maintain the proportionate interest of each stockholder is to transfer part of surplus to the stock account. To be distinguished from *stock split.*

Stock exchange. The place at which shares of stock are bought and sold. See *Stock market,* below.

Stock insurance company. An insurance company whose shares are held by the public and which pays dividends in contrast to a mutual insurance company whose assets are owned by the policyholders who receive dividends when available.

Stock in trade. The inventory carried by a retail business for sale in the ordinary course of business. Also, the tools and equipment owned and used by a tradesman.

Stock jobber. A dealer in stock; one who buys and sells stock on his own account on speculation.

Stock law district. A district in which stock is by law prohibited from running at large.

Stock life insurance company. One in which capital stock investment is made by subscribers to stock, and business is thereafter conducted by board of directors elected by its stockholders, and, subject to statutes, distribution of earnings or profits, as between stockholders and policyholders, is determined by board of directors. Atlantic Life Ins. Co. v. Moncure, D.C.Va., 35 F.2d 360, 362.

Stock market. An organized market or exchange where shares (stocks) are traded. The largest stock market in the United States is the New York Stock Exchange. See also **Over-the-counter market.**

Stock note. The term has no technical meaning, and may as well apply to a note given on the sale of stock which the bank had purchased or taken in the payment of doubtful debts as to a note given on account of an original subscription to stock.

Stock option. The right to purchase a specified number of shares of stock for a specified price at specified times, usually granted to management and key employees. The term "stock option" is used when the right is issued other than pro rata to all existing shareholders. When so issued to all existing stockholders, the option is called a "stock right." See also **Warrant.**

Stock option contract. A negotiable instrument which gives the holder the right to buy or sell a certain number of shares of the corporation's stock within a fixed period of time for a certain price.

Stock purchase plan. A plan by which employees of a corporation are allowed to purchase shares of corporate stock.

Stock redemption. A partial or complete liquidation of corporate stock by the corporation with varying tax consequences depending upon the type of redemption. It generally consists in the purchase by the corporation of its own stock. The redemption of the stock of a shareholder by the issuing corporation is generally treated as a sale or exchange of the stock unless the redemption is a dividend. I.R.C. §§ 301 and 302. A public corporation might redeem its stock for the purpose of "going private". See also *Stock bailout, supra.*

Stock rights. The privilege to subscribe to new stock issues or to purchase stock. Usually, rights are contained in securities called warrants and the warrants can be sold to others. A right to purchase stock issued pro rata to existing shareholders. Sometimes issued on a "when, as, and if" basis, that is, the holder can buy the stock when it is issued, on such basis or of such kind as is issued, and if it is issued.

A document (*i.e.* negotiable certificate) which gives an existing stockholder the privilege of buying additional stock of a corporation. The right has a value of its own because generally the holder may buy such additional stock at a price less than the market quotation. Rights are traded in the market. A stock right differs from a warrant to the extent that a right gives a privilege of buying additional stock of the same kind whereas a warrant may permit a preferred stockholder to buy common stock.

See also **Preemptive right.**

Stock split. Share splits, or stock splits, may be (a) split-ups, where one share is split into a larger number of shares, or (b) reverse splits, or split-downs, where a number of shares are combined to form a smaller number of shares. Share splits involve no transfer from surplus to stated capital or any changes except adjustments in par value or stated value per share, when applicable, so that the same stated capital which represented the issued shares before the split properly represents the changed number of shares after the split. A split-up requires not only board of directors action, but often requires advance shareholder approval as well when the articles of incorporation must be amended to change the par value or stated value of shares and also, when necessary, to authorize additional shares. The usual accounting treatment for a share split is to do nothing except to reflect the different number of issued shares and any changes in par or stated value.

A common purpose of a stock split is to reduce the per share market price in order to make for wider trading and a resulting higher per share value (*i.e.* price).

See also **Reverse stock split.**

Stock subscription. An agreement with the corporation to purchase its stock. See *Stock rights, supra.* See also **Subscribed stock; Subscriber; Subscription.**

Stock swap. In corporate reorganization, an exchange of stock in one corporation for the stock of another corporation.

Stock transfer tax. A tax imposed on the transfer of stock and based on the market value of the stock.

Stock warrant. A certificate evidencing the right to buy shares of stock and commonly attached to preferred stock and bonds. It generally has an expiration date before which the warrant must be exercised. See also **Warrant.**

Watered stock. See that title.

Stockholder. A person who owns shares of stock in a corporation or joint-stock company. See also **Minority stockholder.**

Stockholder's derivative action. An action by a stockholder for purpose of sustaining in his own name a right of action existing in corporation itself, where corporation would be an appropriate plaintiff. It is based upon two distinct wrongs: The act whereby corporation was caused to suffer damage, and act of corporation itself in refusing to redress such act. Procedure in such actions is governed by Fed.R.Civil P. 23.1.

Stockholder's equity. A stockholder's proportionate share in the corporation's capital stock and surplus.

Stockholder's liability. Phrase is frequently employed to denote stockholder's statutory, added or double liability for corporation's debts, notwithstanding full payment for stock, but is often employed where stockholder, agreeing to pay full par value of stock, obtained stock certificate before complete payment or where stock, only partly paid for, is intentionally issued by corporation as fully paid up and all or part of purported consideration therefor is entirely fictitious.

Stockholders' representative action. An action brought or maintained by a stockholder in behalf of himself and all others similarly situated. See also **Stockholder's derivative action.**

Stocks. A machine consisting of two pieces of timber, arranged to be fastened together, and holding fast the legs and/or arms of a person placed in it. This was an ancient method of punishment. See also **Stock.**

Stolen. Acquired, or possessed, as a result of some wrongful or dishonest act or taking, whereby a person willfully obtains or retains possession of property which belongs to another, without or beyond any permission given, and with the intent to deprive the owner of the benefit of ownership (or possession) permanently.

The word "stolen" as used in the crime of interstate transportation of stolen motor vehicles includes all wrongful and dishonest takings of motor vehicles with the intent to deprive the owner of the rights and benefits of ownership, regardless of whether theft constitutes common-law larceny; and felonious taking may be effected by diverse means known to both common and statutory law, such as larceny, embezzlement, false pretenses, larceny by trick and other types of wrongful acquisition. Lake v. U. S., C.A. Colo., 338 F.2d 787, 788. It is not necessary that the taking of the vehicle be unlawful. Even if possession of the vehicle is lawfully acquired, the vehicle will be deemed "stolen" if the defendant thereafter forms the intent to deprive the owner of the rights and benefits of ownership, and converts the vehicle to his own use. United States v. Turley, 352 U.S. 407, 417, 77 S.Ct. 397, 402, 1 L.Ed.2d 430.

See also **Receiving stolen goods or property.**

Stop. Within statutes requiring a motorist striking a person with automobile to stop, requires a definite cessation of movement for a sufficient length of time for a person of ordinary powers of observation to fully understand the surroundings of the accident. Moore v. State, 140 Tex.Cr.R. 482, 145 S.W.2d 887, 888.

"Stop," within term stop and frisk, is temporary restraint of person's freedom to walk away and is a permissible seizure within Fourth Amendment dimensions when such person is suspected of being involved in past, present or pending criminal activity. Terry v. Ohio, 392 U.S. 1, 88 S.Ct. 1868, 20 L.Ed.2d 889; State v. Anonymous (1971–20), 6 Conn.Cir. 583, 280 A.2d 816, 818. See also **Stop and frisk.**

Stop and frisk. The temporary seizure and "patting down" of a person who behaves suspiciously and appears to be armed. A police officer has the right to stop and pat down a person suspected of contemplating the commission of a crime. He need not have full blown probable cause but he must have more than a hunch. The scope of the search must be strictly tied to and justified by the circumstances which rendered the initiation of the stop justified. Terry v. Ohio, 392 U.S. 1, 88 S.Ct. 1868, 20 L.Ed.2d 889. See also **Frisk.**

Stop-limit order. In securities trading, a stop order in which a specific price is set below which the stock may not be sold and above which it may not be purchased.

Stop-loss order. An order given to a stockbroker to buy or sell certain securities when the market reaches a particular price.

Stop order. An order to buy securities at a price above or sell at a price below the current market. Stop buy orders are generally used to limit loss or protect unrealized profits on a short sale. Stop sell orders are generally used to protect unrealized profits or limit loss on a holding. A stop order becomes a market order when the stock sells at or beyond the specified price and, thus, may not necessarily be executed at that price.

Stoppage. In the civil law, compensation or set-off.

Stoppage in transitu /stópəj in trǽnzət(y)uw/. The act by which the unpaid vendor of goods stops their progress and resumes possession of them, while they are in course of transit from him to the purchaser, and not yet actually delivered to the latter. The right of stoppage *in transitu* is that which the vendor has, when he sells goods on credit to another, of resuming the possession of the goods while they are in the possession of a carrier or middle-man, in the transit to the consignee or vendee, and before they arrive into their actual possession, or the destination he has appointed for them on their becoming bankrupt and insolvent. The right which arises to an unpaid vendor to resume the possession, with which he has parted, of goods sold upon credit, before they come into the possession of a buyer who has become insolvent, bankrupt, or pecuniarily embarrassed. See U.C.C. § 2–705(1).

Stop payment order. An order by the drawer of a draft (check) ordering the drawee not to make payment on such.

Stop sign. A legally erected and maintained traffic signal requiring all traffic to stop before entering into or crossing an intersection. Sweet v. Awtrey, 70 Ga.App. 334, 28 S.E.2d 154, 161.

Storage. Safekeeping of goods in a warehouse or other depository. Lincoln Sav. Bank of Brooklyn v. Brown, Em.App., 137 F.2d 228, 230, 231. See also **Bailment; Warehouse; Warehouseman; Warehouse system.**

Store, *v.* To keep merchandise for safe custody, to be delivered in the same condition as when received, where the safe-keeping is the principal object of deposit, and not the consumption or sale.

Store, *n.* Any place where goods are deposited and sold by one engaged in buying and selling them.

Public store. A government warehouse, maintained for certain administrative purposes, such as the keeping of military supplies, the storing of imported goods under bonds to pay duty, etc.

Stores. The supplies of different articles provided for the subsistence and accommodation of a ship's crew and passengers.

Storehouse. A structure in which things are stored; *e.g.* a building for the storing of grain, foodstuffs, or goods of any kind. A magazine; a repository; a warehouse; a store.

Stowage. In maritime law, the storing, packing, or arranging of the cargo in a ship, in such a manner as to protect the goods from friction, bruising, or damage from leakage.

Money paid for a room where goods are laid; housage.

Stowaway. One who conceals himself aboard an outgoing vessel or aircraft for the purpose of obtaining free passage.

Stowe. In old English law, a valley.

Straddle. In stock-brokers' parlance the term means the double privilege of a "put" and a "call," and secures to the holder the right to demand of the seller at a certain price within a certain time a certain number of shares of specified stock, or to require him to take, at the same price within the same time, the same shares of stock. It is not per se a gaming contract, unless intended as a mere cover for a bet or wager on the future price of the stock or commodity. Palmer v. Love, 18 Tenn.App. 579, 80 S.W.2d 100, 106. See **Option.**

The sale of loss-property prior to the adoption of a plan of liquidation. The objective of this approach is to avoid the disallowance of the loss that would result under I.R.C. § 337 (*i.e.*, "12-month liquidation") if the property were sold after the adoption of the plan.

Straight-line depreciation. See **Depreciation.**

Stramineus homo /strəmíniyəs hówmow/. L. Lat. A man of straw, one of no substance, put forward as bail or surety.

Strand. A shore or bank of the sea or a river.

Stranding. In maritime law, the drifting, driving, or running aground of a ship on a shore or strand. *Accidental* stranding takes place where the ship is driven on shore by the winds and waves. *Voluntary* stranding takes place where the ship is run on shore either to preserve her from a worse fate or for some fraudulent purpose.

Stranger. As used with reference to the subject of subrogation, one who, in no event resulting from the existing state of affairs, can become liable for the debt, and whose property is not charged with the payment thereof and cannot be sold therefor. See also **Strangers.**

Stranger in blood. Any person not within the consideration of natural love and affection arising from relationship.

Strangers. By this term is intended third persons generally. Thus the persons bound by a fine are parties, privies, and strangers; the parties are either the cognizors or cognizees; the privies are such as are in any way related to those who levy the fine, and claim under them by any right of blood, or other right of representation; the strangers are all other persons in the world, except only the parties and privies. In its general legal signification the term is opposed to the word "privy." Those who are in no way parties to a covenant, nor bound by it, are also said to be strangers to the covenant. See also **Stranger.**

Stratagem /strǽdəjəm/. A deception either by words or actions, in times of war, in order to obtain an advantage over an enemy.

Stratocracy /strətókrəsiy/. A military government; government by military chiefs of an army.

Strator /stréydər/. In old English law, a surveyor of the highways.

Straw bail. See **Bail.**

Straw man or **party.** A "front"; a person who is put up in name only to take part in a deal. Nominal party to a transaction; one who acts as an agent for another for the purpose of taking title to real property and executing whatever documents and instruments the principal may direct respecting the property. Person who purchases property for another to conceal identity of real purchaser.

Stray. See **Estray.**

Stream. A watercourse having a source and terminus, banks, and channel, through which waters flow at least periodically, and it usually empties into other streams, lakes, or the ocean, but it does not lose its character as a watercourse even though it may break up and disappear. Mogle v. Moore, 16 Cal.2d 1, 104 P.2d 785, 789; Everett v. Davis, Cal.App., 107 P.2d 650, 655; Southern Pac. Co. v. Proebstel, 61 Ariz. 412, 150 P.2d 81, 83. A river, brook, or rivulet; anything in fact that is liquid and flows in a line or course. A current of water. A body of water having a continuous flow in one direction. It consists of a bed, banks, and watercourse. St. Paul Fire & Marine Ins. Co. v. Carroll, Tex.Civ.App., 106 S.W.2d 757, 758. See also **Water course.**

Private stream. A non-navigable creek or watercourse, the bed or channel of which is exclusively owned by a private individual.

Stream of commerce. Term used to describe goods which remain in interstate commerce though held within a state for a short period of time. If such goods remain in the stream of commerce, they are not subject to local taxation.

Street. An urban way or thoroughfare; a road or public way in a city, town, or village, generally paved, and lined or intended to be lined by houses on each side. It includes all urban ways which can be and are generally used for travel, but does not normally include service entrances or driveways leading off from the street onto adjoining premises. Hill & Combs v. First Nat. Bank of San Angelo, Tex., C.C.A.Tex., 139 F.2d 740, 743.

Any street, avenue, boulevard, road, parkway, drive or other way (1) which is an existing state, county or municipal roadway, or (2) which is shown upon a plat heretofore approved pursuant to law, or (3) which is approved by official action or (4) which is shown on a plat duly filed and recorded in the office of the county recording officer prior to the appointment of a planning board and the grant to such board of the power to review plats; and includes the land between the street lines, whether improved or unimproved, and may comprise pavement, shoulders, gutters, curbs, sidewalks, parking areas and other areas within the street lines.

See also **Ancient street.**

Street name. Securities held in the name of a broker instead of his customer's name are said to be carried in a "street name." This occurs when the securities have been bought on margin or when the customer wishes the security to be held by the broker. The name of a broker or bank appearing on a corporate security with *blank endorsement* by the broker or bank. The security can then be transferred merely by delivery since the endorsement is well known. Street name is used for convenience or to shield identity of the true owner.

Strepitus judicialis /strépədəs juwdìshiyéyləs/. Turbulent conduct in a court of justice.

Stria /stráyə/. Curved, crooked and intermittent gouges, of irregular depth and width and rough definition, of certain rock surface, sometimes due to abrasions by icebergs. A furrow, channel or hollow; depression, rut, wrinkle, concave, cup, pocket, dimple.

Strict. Exact; accurate; precise; undeviating; governed or governing by exact rules.

As to strict "Settlement," see that title.

Strict construction. A close or rigid reading and interpretation of a law. It is said that criminal statutes must be strictly construed. Rule of "strict construction" has no definite or precise meaning, has only relative application, is not opposite of liberal construction, and does not require such strained or narrow interpretation of language as to defeat object of statute. Southwestern Bell Tel. Co. v. Newingham, Mo.App., 386 S.W.2d 663, 665.

Rule of "strict construction" means that criminal statute will not be enlarged by implication or intendment beyond fair meaning of language used, or what their terms reasonably justify, and will not be held to include offenses and persons other than those which are clearly described and provided for, although court in interpreting and employing particular statutes may think legislature should have made them more comprehensive. Matthews v. Powers, Okl.Cr., 425 P.2d 479, 482. "Strict construction of a statute" is that which refuses to expand the law by implications or equitable considerations, but confines its operation to cases which are clearly within the letter of the statute as well as within its spirit or reason, resolving all reasonable doubts against applicability of statute to particular case. Kyritsis v. Fenny, 66 Misc.2d 329, 320 N.Y.S.2d 702, 704.

See also **Construction.**

Strict foreclosure. See **Foreclosure.**

Stricti juris /stríktay júrəs/. Lat. Of strict right or law; according to strict law. A license is a thing *stricti juris;* a privilege which a man does not possess by his own right, but it is conceded to him as an indulgence, and therefore it is to be strictly observed.

Strictissimi juris /striktísəmay júrəs/. Lat. Of the strictest right or law. Licenses being matter of special indulgence, the application of them was formerly *strictissimi juris.*

Strict liability. A concept applied by the courts in product liability cases in which a seller is liable for any and all defective or hazardous products which unduly threaten a consumer's personal safety. This concept applies to all members involved in the manufacturing and selling of any facet of the product. Doctrine of "strict liability" poses strict liability on one who sells product in defective condition unreasonably dangerous to user or consumer for harm caused to ultimate user or consumer if seller is engaged in business of selling such product, and product is expected to and does reach user or consumer without substantial change in condition in which it is sold. Davis v. Gibson Products Co., Tex.Civ.App., 505 S.W.2d 682, 688.

Concept of strict liability in tort is founded on the premise that when manufacturer presents his goods to the public for sale, he represents they are suitable for their intended use, and to invoke such doctrine it is essential to prove that the product was defective when placed in the stream of commerce. Herbstman v. Eastman Kodak Co., 68 N.J. 1, 342 A.2d 181, 184.

(1) One who sells any product in a defective condition unreasonably dangerous to the user or consumer or to his property is subject to liability for physical harm thereby caused to the ultimate user or consumer, or to his property, if (a) the seller is engaged in the business of selling such a product, and (b) it is expected to and does reach the user or consumer without substantial change in the condition in which it is sold. (2) The rule stated in Subsection (1) applies although (a) the seller has exercised all possible care in the preparation and sale of his product, and (b) the user or consumer has not bought the product from or entered into any contractual relation with the seller. Restatement, Second, Torts, § 402A.

See also **Warranty.**

Strict liability statute. One which imposes criminal sanction for an unlawful act without requiring a showing of criminal intent. State v. Lucero, 87 N.M. 242, 531 P.2d 1215, 1218.

Strictly /stríktliy/. A strict manner; closely, precisely, rigorously; stringently; positively.

Strictly construed. Requirement that a penal statute be strictly construed means that the court will not extend punishment to cases not plainly within the language used, but at the same time such statutes are to be fairly and reasonably construed, and will not be given such a narrow and strained construction as to exclude from their operation cases plainly within their scope and meaning. See also **Strict construction.**

Strictly ministerial duty. One that is absolute and imperative, requiring neither the exercise of official discretion nor judgment.

Stricto jure /stríktow júriy/. Lat. In strict law.

Strictum jus /stríktəm jás/. Lat. Strict right or law; the rigor of the law as distinguished from equity.

Strike. The act of quitting work by a body of workers for the purpose of coercing their employer to accede to some demand they have made upon him, and which he has refused. Jeffery-De Witt Insulator Co. v. N. L. R. B., C.C.A.4, 91 F.2d 134, 138. A combination to obtain higher wages, shorter hours of employment, better working conditions or some other concession from employer by the employees stopping work at a preconcerted time, and it involves a combination of persons and not a single individual. Moreland Theatres Corp. v. Portland Moving Picture Mach. Operators' Protective Union, 140 Or. 35, 12 P.2d 333, 338. A cessation of work as a means of enforcing compliance with some demand upon the employer. People v. Tepel, Mag.Ct., 3 N.Y.S.2d 779, 781. A combined effort among workers to compel their employer to the concession of a certain demand, by preventing the conduct of his business until compliance with the demand.

The term "strike" includes any strike or other concerted stoppage of work by employees (including a stoppage by reason of the expiration of a collective-bargaining agreement) and any concerted slow-down or other concerted interruption of operations by employees. Labor Management Relations Act, § 501(2).

See also **No-strike clause; Rent strike; Wildcat strike.** *Compare* **Lockout.**

Economic strike. A cessation of work by employees to enforce economic demands upon the employer in contrast to a strike caused by an unfair labor charge.

General strike. Cessation of work by employees effective throughout an entire industry or country.

Jurisdictional strike. Cessation of work as result of dispute by members of one union or craft against members of another union or craft as to assignment of work.

Secondary strike. Cessation of work by union members of one employer who has business dealings with another employer whose employees are on strike.

Sit-down strike. Cessation of work by employees who do not leave employer's premises but who refuse to work.

Sympathy strike. A sympathy strike involves two unions; one is striking to force some concession from the employer; the other strikes in sympathy with the first's objectives. Sympathy strikes are a common manifestation of traditional union solidarity.

Wildcat strike. Cessation of work by group of employees without authorization of union officials.

Strikebreaker. One who takes the place of workman who has left his work in an effort to force the striking employee to agree to demands of employer. See also **Scab.**

Strike off. In common parlance, and in the language of the auction-room, property is understood to be "struck off" or "knocked down," when the auctioneer, by the fall of his hammer, or by any other audible or visible announcement, signifies to the bidder that he is entitled to the property on paying the amount of his bid, according to the terms of the sale.

A court is said to "strike off" a case when it directs the removal of the case from the record or docket, as being one over which it has no jurisdiction and no power to hear and determine it.

Strike suits. Shareholder derivative action begun with hope of winning large attorney fees or private settlements, and with no intention of benefiting corporation on behalf of which suit is theoretically brought.

Striking a jury. The selecting or nominating a jury out of the whole number returned as jurors on the panel. It is especially used of the selection of a *special* jury, where a panel is prepared by the proper officer, and the parties, in turn, strike off a certain number of names, until the list is reduced to twelve. A jury thus chosen is called a "struck jury."

Striking off the roll. The disbarring of an attorney.

Striking price. The price at which named stock can be put or called is ordinarily the market price when option is written and is termed the "striking price". Reinach v. C. I. R., C.A.N.Y., 373 F.2d 900, 901.

Strip. The act of spoiling or unlawfully taking away anything from the land, by the tenant for life or years, or by one holding an estate in the land less than the entire fee.

Strong. Cogent, powerful, forcible, forceful. Wright v. Austin, Tex.Civ.App., 175 S.W.2d 281, 283. See also **Sound.**

Strong hand. The words "with strong hand" imply a degree of criminal force, whereas the words *vi et armis* ("with force and arms") are mere formal words in the action of trespass, and the plaintiff is not bound to prove any force. The statutes relating to forcible entries use the words "with a strong hand" as describing that degree of force which makes an entry or detainer of lands criminal.

Strongly corroborated. A degree of corroboration amounting to corroboration from independent facts and circumstances which is clear and satisfactory to the court and jury. Wright v. Austin, Tex.Civ.App., 175 S.W.2d 281, 283.

Struck. In common law pleading, a word essential in an indictment for murder, when the death arose from any wounding, beating, or bruising.

Struck jury. A special jury. See also **Striking a jury.**

Structural alteration or change. One that affects a vital and substantial portion of a thing; that changes its characteristic appearance, the fundamental purpose of its erection, and the uses contemplated. One that is extraordinary in scope and effect, or unusual in expenditure.

Structure. Any construction, or any production or piece of work artificially built up or composed of parts joined together in some definite manner. That which is built or constructed; an edifice or building of any kind.

A combination of materials to form a construction for occupancy, use or ornamentation whether installed on, above, or below the surface of a parcel of land.

Strumpet /strámpət/. A whore, harlot, or courtesan. This word was anciently used for an addition. It occurs as an addition to the name of a woman in a return made by a jury in the sixth year of Henry V.

Stuff gown. In England, the professional robe worn by barristers of the outer bar; viz., those who have not been admitted to the rank of king's counsel.

Stultify /stɔ́ltəfay/. To make one out mentally incapacitated for the performance of an act.

Stultiloquium /stɔ̀ltəlówkwiyəm/. Lat. In old English law, vicious pleading, for which a fine was imposed by King John, supposed to be the origin of the fines for *beau-pleader.*

Stumpage. The sum agreed to be paid to an owner of land for trees standing (or lying) upon his land, the purchaser being permitted to enter upon the land and to cut down and remove the trees; in other words, it is the price paid for a license to cut.

Stuprum /st(y)úwprəm/. Lat. In the Roman and civil law, unlawful sexual intercourse between a man and an unmarried woman;—distinguished from adultery by being committed with a virgin or widow.

Any sexual intercourse between a man and an unmarried woman (not a slave), otherwise than in concubinage; illicit intercourse.

Any union of the sexes forbidden by morality.

Sturgeon /stə́rjən/. In old English law, a royal fish which, when either thrown ashore or caught near the coast, is the property of the sovereign.

Style. As a verb, to call, name, or entitle one. As a noun, the title or appellation of a person.

Suable /s(y)úwəbəl/. Capable of being, or liable to be, sued. A suable cause of action is the matured cause of action.

Suapte natura /s(y)uwǽptiy nət(y)úrə/. Lat. In its own nature. *Suapte natura sterilis,* barren in its own nature and quality; intrinsically barren.

Sua sponte /s(y)úwə spóntiy/. Lat. Of his or its own will or motion; voluntarily; without prompting or suggestion.

Sub /sə́b/. Lat. Under; upon. For example: "sub judice" means "under judicial consideration" or in court and not yet decided, and "sublet" means to rent out something you yourself are renting.

Subagent /sə́bèyjənt/. An under-agent; a substituted agent; an agent appointed by one who is himself an agent. A person appointed by an agent to perform some duty, or the whole of the business, relating to his agency. A person employed by an agent to assist him in transacting the affairs of his principal. But a mere servant of an agent is not a "subagent." Gulf Refining Co. v. Shirley, Tex.Civ.App., 99 S.W.2d 613, 615. A subagent is a person appointed by an agent empowered to do so, to perform functions undertaken by the agent for the principal, but for whose conduct the agent agrees with the principal to be primarily responsible. Restatement, Second, Agency, § 5. See also **Agent.**

Subaltern /səbóltərn/sə́bəltərn/. An inferior or subordinate officer. An officer who exercises his authority under the superintendence and control of a superior.

Sub-ballivus /sə̀b-bəláyvəs/. In old English law, an underbailiff; a sheriff's deputy.

Subchapter S corporation. A small business corporation permitted to be taxed as if it were an individual proprietorship. I.R.C. § 1371 *et seq.* An elective provision permitting certain small business corporations and their shareholders to elect to be treated for income tax purposes in accordance with the operating rules of §§ 1373–1379. Of major significance is the fact that Subchapter S status usually avoids the corporate income tax, and corporate losses can be claimed by the shareholders.

Sub colore juris /sə̀b kəlóriy júrəs/. Under color of right; under a show or appearance of right or rightful power.

Sub conditione /sə̀b kəndìshiyówniy/. Upon condition. The proper words to express a condition in a conveyance, and to create an estate upon condition.

Subcontract. See **Contract.**

Subcontractor. One who takes portion of a contract from principal contractor or another subcontractor. Hardware Mut. Casualty Co. v. Hilderbrandt, C.C.A. Okl., 119 F.2d 291, 297, 299. One who has entered into a contract, express or implied, for the performance of an act with the person who has already contracted for its performance. One who takes from the principal or prime contractor a specific part of the work undertaken by the principal contractor. Royal

Indemnity Co. v. Kenny Constr. Co., C.A.Ill., 528 F.2d 184, 191.

Sub curia /sə̀b kyúriyə/. Lat. Under law.

Sub disjunctione /sə̀b disjə̀ŋkshiyówniy/. In the alternative.

Subditus /sə́bdədəs/. Lat. In old English law, a vassal; a dependent; any one under the power of another.

Subdivide. To divide a part into smaller parts; to separate into smaller divisions. As, where an estate is to be taken by some of the heirs *per stirpes,* it is divided and subdivided according to the number of takers in the nearest degree and those in the more remote degree respectively.

Subdivision. Division into smaller parts of the same thing or subject-matter. The division of a lot, tract or parcel of land into two or more lots, tracts, parcels or other divisions of land for sale or development.

Resubdivision. The further division or relocation of lot lines of any lot or lots within a subdivision previously made and approved or recorded according to law; or, the alteration of any streets or the establishment of any new streets within any subdivision previously made and approved or recorded according to law, but does not include conveyances so as to combine existing lots by deed or other instrument.

Subflow. Those waters which slowly find their way through sand and gravel constituting bed of a stream, or lands under or immediately adjacent to stream. Maricopa County Municipal Water Conservation Dist. No. 1 v. Southwest Cotton Co., 39 Ariz. 65, 4 P.2d 369, 380.

Subhastare /sə̀bhæstériy/. Lat. In the civil law, to sell at public auction, which was done *sub hasta,* under a spear; to put or sell under the spear.

Subhastatio /sə̀bhæstéysh(iy)ow/. Lat. In the civil law, a sale by public auction, which was done *under a spear,* fixed up at the place of sale as a public sign of it.

Subinfeudation /sə̀binfyuwdéyshən/. The system which the feudal tenants introduced of granting smaller estates out of those which they held of their lord, to be held of themselves as inferior lords. As this system was proceeding downward *ad infinitum,* and depriving the lords of their feudal profits, it was entirely suppressed by the statute *Quia Emptores,* 18 Edw. I, c. 1, and instead of it alienation in the modern sense was introduced, so that thenceforth the alienee held of the same chief lord and by the same services that his alienor before him held.

Subirrigate /sə̀bíhrəgèyt/. To irrigate below the surface, as by a system of underground porous pipes, or by natural percolation through the soil.

Subjacent support /səbjéysənt səpórt/. The right of land to be supported by the land which lies under it; distinguished from lateral (side) support. See also **Support.**

Subject. *Constitutional law.* One that owes allegiance to a sovereign and is governed by his laws. The natives of Great Britain are *subjects* of the British government. Men in free governments are subjects as well as *citizens;* as citizens they enjoy rights and franchises; as subjects they are bound to obey the laws. The term is little used, in this sense, in countries enjoying a republican form of government. Swiss Nat. Ins. Co. v. Miller, 267 U.S. 42, 45 S.Ct. 213, 214, 69 L.Ed. 504.

Legislation. The matter of public or private concern for which law is enacted. Thing legislated about or matters on which legislature operates to accomplish a definite object or objects reasonably related one to the other. Crouch v. Benet, 198 S.C. 185, 17 S.E.2d 320, 322. The matter or thing forming the groundwork of the act. McCombs v. Dallas County, Tex. Civ.App., 136 S.W.2d 975, 982.

The constitutions of several of the states require that every act of the legislature shall relate to but one *subject,* which shall be expressed in the title of the statute. But term "subject" within such constitutional provisions is to be given a broad and extensive meaning so as to allow legislature full scope to include in one act all matters having a logical or natural connection. Jaffee v. State, 76 Okl.Cr. 95, 134 P.2d 1027, 1032.

Subjection. The obligation of one or more persons to act at the discretion or according to the judgment and will of others.

Subject-matter. The subject, or matter presented for consideration; the thing in dispute; the right which one party claims as against the other, as the right to divorce; of ejectment; to recover money; to have foreclosure. Flower Hospital v. Hart, 178 Okl. 447, 62 P.2d 1248, 1252. Nature of cause of action, and of relief sought. In trusts, the *res* or the things themselves which are held in trust. Restatement, Second, Trusts, § 2.

Subject matter jurisdiction. Term refers to court's competence to hear and determine cases of the general class to which proceedings in question belong; the power to deal with the general subject involved in the action. Standard Oil Co. v. Montecatini Edison S. p. A., D.C.Del., 342 F.Supp. 125, 129. Subject matter jurisdiction deals with court's competence to hear a particular category of cases. Japan Gas Lighter Ass'n v. Ronson Corp., D.C.N.J., 257 F.Supp. 219, 224. See also **Jurisdiction of the subject matter.**

Subject to. Liable, subordinate, subservient, inferior, obedient to; governed or affected by; provided that; provided; answerable for. Homan v. Employers Reinsurance Corp., 345 Mo. 650, 136 S.W.2d 289, 302.

Sub judice /sàb júwdəsiy/. Under or before a judge or court; under judicial consideration; undetermined.

Sublata causa tollitur effectus /səbléydə kózə tólədər əféktəs/. The cause being removed the effect ceases.

Sublata veneratione magistratuum, res publica ruit /səbléydə vènərèyshiyówniy mæjəstréytyuwəm, ríyz pábləkə rúwət/. When respect for magistrates is taken away, the commonwealth falls.

Sublato fundamento cadit opus /səbléydə fəndəméntow kéydəd ówpəs/. The foundation being removed, the superstructure falls.

Sublato principali, tollitur adjunctum /səbléydow prin(t)səpéylay, tólədər əjə́ŋktəm/. When the principal is taken away, the incident is taken also.

Sublease. Transaction whereby tenant grants interests in leased premises less than his own, or reserves to himself reversionary interest in term. Ernst v. Conditt, 54 Tenn.App. 328, 390 S.W.2d 703, 707. See also **Lease.**

Subletting. A leasing by lessee of a whole or part of premises during a portion of unexpired balance of his term. See also **Sublease.**

Submerged lands. Land lying under water. Land lying oceanside of the tideland. People v. Hecker, 179 Cal.App.2d 823, 4 Cal.Rptr. 334, 341.

Submergence. As it concerns the proprietorship of land, consists in the disappearance of land under water and the formation of a more or less navigable body over it. Michelsen v. Leskowicz, 269 App.Div. 693, 55 N.Y.S.2d 831, 838.

Submission. A yielding to authority; *e.g.* a citizen is bound to submit to the laws; a child to his parents.

A contract between two or more parties whereby they agree to refer the subject in dispute to others and to be bound by their award. District of Columbia v. Bailey, 171 U.S. 161, 18 S.Ct. 868, 872, 43 L.Ed. 118. See also **Arbitration; Mediation.**

Submission bond. The bond by which the parties agree to submit their matters to arbitration, and by which they bind themselves to abide by the award of the arbitrator.

Submission to jury. The act or process by which a judge gives to the jury the case on trial for their consideration and verdict.

Submit. To commit to the discretion of another. To yield to the will of another. To propound; to present for determination; as an advocate *submits* a proposition for the approval of the court. See also **Submission.**

Sub modo /sàb mówdow/. Under a qualification; subject to a restriction or condition.

Submortgage. When a person who holds a mortgage as security for a loan which he has made, procures a loan to himself from a third person, and pledges his mortgage as security, he effects what is called a "submortgage."

Sub nomine /sàb nóməniy/. Under the name; in the name of; under the title of.

Subnotations /sàbnowtéyshənz/. In the civil law, the answers of the prince to questions which had been put to him respecting some obscure or doubtful point of law.

Subordinate. Placed in a lower order, class, or rank; occupying a lower position in a regular descending series; inferior in order, nature, dignity, power, importance, or the like; belonging to an inferior order in classification, and having a lower position in a recognized scale; secondary, minor.

Subordinated bonds or debentures. Bonds or debentures which yield priority in liquidation to other (senior) debt of a corporation. Usually such bonds or debentures are not subordinate to general creditors but only to debt owed to a financial institution.

Subordinate officer. One who performs duties imposed on him under direction of a principal or superior officer or he may be an independent officer subject only to such directions as the statute lays on him.

Subordination. The act or process by which a person's rights are ranked below the rights of others. A second mortgagee's rights are subordinate to those of the first mortgagee. A lessor may be asked to subordinate his lease to a subsequent mortgage.

Subordination agreement. An agreement by which the subordinating party agrees that its interest in real property should have a lower priority than the interest to which it is being subordinated.

Suborn. To prepare, provide, or procure especially in a secret or underhand manner. United States v. Silverman, C.C.A.Pa., 106 F.2d 750, 751.

In criminal law, to procure another to commit perjury.

Subornation of perjury. The offense of procuring another to take such a false oath as would constitute perjury in the principal.

Suborner. One who suborns or procures another to commit any crime, particularly to commit perjury.

Subpartner. See **Partner.**

Sub pede sigilli /sə̀b píydiy səjílay/. Under the foot of the seal; under seal.

Subpoena /sə(b)píynə/. A subpoena is a command to appear at a certain time and place to give testimony upon a certain matter. A subpoena duces tecum requires production of books, papers and other things. Subpoenas in federal criminal cases are governed by Fed.R.Crim.P. 17, and in civil cases by Fed.R.Civil P. 45. See also **Alias subpoena.**

Subpoena ad testificandum /sə(b)píynə æd tèstəfəkǽndəm/. Lat. Subpoena to testify. A technical and descriptive term for the ordinary subpoena. See **Subpoena.**

Subpoena duces tecum /sə(b)píynə d(y)úwsiyz tíykəm/. A process by which the court, at the instances of a party, commands a witness who has in his possession or control some document or paper that is pertinent to the issues of a pending controversy, to produce it at the trial. See Fed.R.Civil P. 45, and Fed.R.Crim.P. 17.

Sub potestate /sə̀b powdəstéydiy/. Under, or subject to, the power of another; used of a wife, child, slave, or other person not *sui juris.*

Subreptio /səbrépsh(iy)ow/. Lat. In the civil law, obtaining gifts of escheat, etc., from the king by concealing the truth.

Subreption /sùbrepsyówn/. In French law, the fraud committed to obtain a pardon, title, or grant, by alleging facts contrary to truth.

Subrogation. The substitution of one person in the place of another with reference to a lawful claim, demand or right, so that he who is substituted succeeds to the rights of the other in relation to the debt or claim, and its rights, remedies, or securities. Home Owners' Loan Corp. v. Baker, 299 Mass. 158, 12 N.E.2d 199, 201; Gerken v. Davidson Grocery Co., 57 Idaho 670, 69 P.2d 122, 126. The lawful substitution of a third party in place of a party having a claim against another party. Insurance companies, guarantors and bonding companies generally have the right to step into the shoes of the party whom they compensate and sue any party whom the compensated party could have sued.

The right of one who has paid an obligation which another should have paid to be indemnified by the other. Olin Corp. (Plastics Division) v. Workmen's Compensation Appeal Bd., 14 Pa.Cmwlth. 603, 324 A.2d 813, 816. A device adopted by equity to compel ultimate discharge of an obligation by him who in good conscience ought to pay it. Jenks Hatchery, Inc. v. Elliott, 252 Or. 25, 448 P.2d 370, 373.

Subrogation is of two kinds, either conventional or legal; the former being where the subrogation is express, by the acts of the creditor and the third person; the latter being (as in the case of sureties) where the subrogation is effected or implied by the operation of the law. See also **Legal subrogation.**

Subrogee /sə̀browjíy/°gíy/. A person who is subrogated; one who succeeds to the rights of another by subrogation.

Sub rosa /sə̀b rówzə/. Confidential, secret, not for publication.

Sub salvo et securo conductu /sə̀b sǽlvow èt səkyúrow kəndə́kt(y)uw/. Under safe and secure conduct. 1 Strange, 430. Words in the old writ of *habeas corpus.*

Subscribe. Literally to write underneath, as one's name. To sign at the end of a document. Also, to agree in writing to furnish money or its equivalent, or to agree to purchase some initial stock in a corporation. See also **Attest; Subscriber; Subscription.**

Subscribed capital. The total amount of stock or capital for which there are contracts of purchase or subscriptions.

Subscribed stock. A stockholders' equity account showing the capital that will be contributed as the subscription price is collected. A subscription is a legal contract so that an entry is made debiting a receivable and crediting subscribed stock as soon as the stock is subscribed. See also **Subscriber; Subscription.**

Subscriber. One who writes his name under a written instrument; one who affixes his signature to any document, whether for the purpose of authenticating or attesting it, of adopting its terms as his own expressions, or of binding himself by an engagement which it contains.

One who becomes bound by a subscription to the capital stock of a corporation. One who has agreed to purchase stock from the corporation on the original issue of such stock. One who agrees to buy securities of a corporation, either bonds or stocks.

Subscribing witness. He who witnesses or attests the signature of a party to an instrument, and in testimony thereof subscribes his own name to the document. One who sees a writing executed, or hears it acknowledged, and at the request of the party thereupon signs his name as a witness. See **Attestation.**

Subscriptio /səbskrípsh(iy)ow/. Lat. In the civil law, a writing under, or under-writing; a writing of the name under or at the bottom of an instrument by way of attestation or ratification; subscription.

Subscription. The act of writing one's name under a written instrument; the affixing one's signature to any document, whether for the purpose of authenticating or attesting it, of adopting its terms as one's own expressions, or of binding one's self by an engagement which it contains.

A written contract by which one engages to take and pay for capital stock of a corporation, or to contribute a sum of money for a designated purpose, either gratuitously, as in the case of subscribing to a charity, or in consideration of an equivalent to be rendered, as a subscription to a periodical, a forthcoming book, a series of entertainments, or the like. See also **Subscribed stock; Subscriber,** and compound terms below.

Subscription contract. In general, any contract by which one becomes bound to buy. In particular, a contract for the purchase of securities. See **Subscription.**

Subscription list. A list of subscribers to some agreement with each other or a third person. A list of subscribers to a periodical or series of publications or to some type of service.

Subscription rights. Rights of existing stockholders to purchase additional stock, generally at a price under market and in an amount proportionate to their existing holdings. Also, the certificates evidencing such rights. See also **Stock** *(Stock rights).*

Subsellia /səbsél(i)yə/. Lat. In Roman law, lower seats or benches, occupied by the *judices* and by inferior magistrates when they sat in judgment, as distinguished from the *tribunal* of the prætor.

Subsequens matrimonium tollit peccatum præcedens /səbsíykwən(d)z mætrəmówn(i)yəm tólət pəkéydəm priysíydən(d)z/. A subsequent marriage [of the parties] removes a previous fault, *i.e.,* previous illicit intercourse, and legitimates the offspring. A rule of Roman law.

Subsequent. Following in time; coming or being later than something else; succeeding.

Subsequent condition. See **Condition.**

Subsequent creditor. One who becomes a creditor after a transfer sought to be impeached as fraudulent is made. Edwards v. Monning, 63 Ohio App. 449, 27 N.E.2d 156, 158, 17 O.O. 174.

Subservant. In law of agency, the servant or agent of another servant or agent. Generally, such agent or servant is principal as to the subservant. See also **Subagent.**

Subsidiary. Under another's control. Term is often short for "subsidiary corporation"; *i.e.* one that is run and owned by another company which is called the "parent." See **Subsidiary corporation.**

Of secondary importance.

Subsidiary corporation. One in which another corporation (*i.e.* parent) owns at least a majority of the shares, and thus has control. Said of a company more than 50 percent of whose voting stock is owned by another.

Subsidy. A grant of money made by government in aid of the promoters of any enterprise, work, or improvement in which the government desires to participate, or which is considered a proper subject for government aid, because such purpose is likely to be of benefit to the public.

Sub silentio /sə́b səlénsh(iy)ow/. Under silence; without any notice being taken. Passing a thing *sub silentio* may be evidence of consent.

Subsistence. Support. Means of support, provisions, or that which procures provisions or livelihood. See **Necessaries; Support.**

Sub spe reconciliationis /sə̀b spíy rekən(t)sìliyèyshiyównəs/. Under the hope of reconcilement.

Substance. Essence; the material or essential part of a thing, as distinguished from "form." That which is essential.

Substantial. Of real worth and importance; of considerable value; valuable. Belonging to substance; actually existing; real; not seeming or imaginary; not illusive; solid; true; veritable. Seglem v. Skelly Oil Co., 145 Kan. 216, 65 P.2d 553, 554. Something worthwhile as distinguished from something without value or merely nominal. In re Krause's Estate, 173 Wash. 1, 21 P.2d 268. Synonymous with material. Lewandoski v. Finkel, 129 Conn. 526, 29 A.2d 762, 764.

Substantial capacity. Term used in the definition of legal insanity proposed by the Model Penal Code (§ 4.01) to the effect that a person is not responsible for criminal conduct if at the time of such conduct as a result of mental disease or defect he lacks substantial capacity either to appreciate the criminality (wrongfulness) of his conduct or to conform his conduct to the requirements of law. See also **Insanity.**

Substantial compliance rule. Compliance with the essential requirements, whether of a contract or of a statute. Wentworth v. Medellin, Tex.Civ.App., 529 S.W.2d 125, 128. In life insurance law is that where insured has done substantially all he is required to do under policy to effect change in beneficiary and mere ministerial acts of insurer's officers and agents only remain to be done, change will take effect. Inter-Southern Life Ins. Co. v. Cochran, 259 Ky. 677, 83 S.W.2d 11, 14.

Substantial damages. See **Damages.**

Substantial equivalent of patented device. Same as thing itself, so that if two devices do same work in substantially same way, and accomplish substantially same results, they are equivalent, even though differing in name, form, or shape. Bedell v. Dictograph Products Co., 251 App.Div. 243, 296 N.Y.S. 25, 32; Freeman v. Altvater, C.C.A.Mo., 66 F.2d 506, 511.

Substantial evidence. Such evidence that a reasonable mind might accept as adequate to support a conclusion. It is that quality of evidence necessary for a court to affirm a decision of an administrative board. Under the "substantial evidence rule," reviewing courts will defer to an agency determination so long as, upon an examination of the whole record, there is substantial evidence upon which the agency could reasonably base its decision. Marshall v. Consumers Power Co., 65 Mich.App. 237, 237 N.W.2d 266, 280.

Substantial evidence is evidence possessing something of substance and relevant consequence and which furnishes substantial basis of fact from which issues tendered can be reasonably resolved. State v. Green, 218 Kan. 438, 544 P.2d 356, 362. Evidence which a reasoning mind would accept as sufficient to support a particular conclusion and consists of more than a mere scintilla of evidence but may be somewhat less than a preponderance. Marker v. Finch, D.C.Del., 322 F.Supp. 905, 910. For purposes of considering sufficiency of evidence in criminal case, "substantial evidence" means evidence from which trier of fact reasonably could find issue in harmony therewith. Kansas City v. Stamper, Mo.App., 528 S.W.2d 767, 768.

Under the substantial evidence rule, as applied in administrative proceedings, all evidence is competent and may be considered, regardless of its source and nature, if it is the kind of evidence that "a reasonable mind might accept as adequate to support a conclusion." In other words, the competency of evidence for purposes of administrative agency adjudicatory proceedings is made to rest upon the logical persuasiveness of such evidence to the reasonable mind in using it to support a conclusion.

Substantial justice. Justice administered according to the rules of substantive law, notwithstanding errors of procedure. Interstate Bankers Corporation v. Kennedy, D.C.Mun.App., 33 A.2d 165, 166.

Substantially. Essentially; without material qualification; in the main; in substance; materially; in a substantial manner. About, actually, competently, and essentially. Gilmore v. Red Top Cab Co. of Washington, 171 Wash. 346, 17 P.2d 886, 887.

Substantial performance. Exists where there has been no willful departure from the terms of the contract, and no omission in essential points, and the contract has been honestly and faithfully performed in its material and substantial particulars, and the only variance from the strict and literal performance consists of technical or unimportant omissions or defects. Substantial performance of a contract is shown when party alleging substantial performance has made an honest endeavor in good faith to perform his part of the contract, when results of his endeavor are beneficial to other party, and when such benefits are retained by the other party; if any one of these circumstances is not established the performance is not substantial, and the party has no right of recovery. Alliance Tractor & Implement Co. v. Lukens Tool & Die Co., 194 Neb. 473, 233 N.W.2d 299, 301. Equitable doctrine of "substantial performance"

protects against forfeiture for technical inadvertence or trivial variations or omissions in performance. Sgarlat v. Griffith, 349 Pa. 42, 36 A.2d 330, 332.

Substantiate /səbstǽnshiyèyt/. To establish the existence or truth of, by true or competent evidence, or to verify. State v. Lock, 302 Mo. 400, 259 S.W. 116, 120; Graves v. School Committee of Wellesley, 299 Mass. 80, 12 N.E.2d 176, 179.

Substantive. An essential part or constituent or relating to what is essential. Stewart-Warner Corporation v. Le Vally, D.C.Ill., 15 F.Supp. 571, 576.

Substantive due process. Such may be broadly defined as the constitutional guarantee that no person shall be arbitrarily deprived of his life, liberty or property; the essence of substantive due process is protection from arbitrary and unreasonable action. Babineaux v. Judiciary Commission, La., 341 So.2d 396, 400. See **Due process of law.**

Substantive evidence. That adduced for the purpose of proving a fact in issue, as opposed to evidence given for the purpose of discrediting a witness (*i.e.*, showing that he is unworthy of belief), or of corroborating his testimony. See also **Substantial evidence.**

Substantive felony. An independent felony; one not dependent upon the conviction of another person for another crime.

Substantive law. That part of law which creates, defines, and regulates rights, as opposed to "adjective or remedial law," which prescribes method of enforcing the rights or obtaining redress for their invasion. That which creates duties, rights and obligations, while "procedural or remedial law" prescribes methods of enforcement of rights or obtaining redress. Kilbreath v. Rudy, 16 Ohio St.2d 70, 242 N.E.2d 658, 660, 45 O.O.2d 370. The basic law of rights and duties (contract law, criminal law, tort law, law of wills, etc.) as opposed to procedural law (law of pleading, law of evidence, law of jurisdiction, etc.).

Substantive offense. One which is complete of itself and not dependent upon another. U. S. v. Martinez-Gonzales, D.C.Cal., 89 F.Supp. 62, 64.

Substantive rights. A right to the equal enjoyment of fundamental rights, privileges and immunities; distinguished from procedural right.

Substitute, *n.* /sə́bstət(y)ùwt/. One who or that which stands in the place of another; that which stands in lieu of something else. A person hired by one who has been drafted into the military service of the country, to go to the front and serve in the army in his stead.

Substitute, *v.* To put in the place of another person or thing; to exchange. Toledo Edison Co. v. McMaken, C.C.A.Ohio, 103 F.2d 72, 75.

Substituted basis. In taxation, the basis of the value of an asset determined by reference to the basis in the hands of a transferor, donor or grantor or by reference to other property held at any time by the person for whom the basis is to be determined. I.R.C. § 1016(b).

Substitute defendant. One who takes the place of another in the same suit or controversy and not one who is sued upon an entirely different cause of action. McCann v. Bentley Stores Corp., D.C.Mo., 34 F.Supp. 231, 233. See **Substitution of parties.**

Substituted executor. One appointed to act in the place of another executor upon the happening of a certain event; *e.g.*, if the latter should refuse the office.

Substituted service. Service of process upon a defendant in any manner, authorized by statute or rule, other than personal service within the jurisdiction; as by publication, by mailing a copy to his last known address, or by personal service in another state. See Fed.R.Civil P. 4. See also **Service.**

Substitute father. A man who cohabits with the mother of children not being married to her. King v. Smith, 392 U.S. 309, 88 S.Ct. 2128, 20 L.Ed.2d 1118.

Substitutio hæredis /sàbstət(y)úwsh(iy)ow həríydəs/. Lat. In Roman law, is was competent for a testator after instituting a *hæres* (called the *"hæres institutus"*) to substitute another (called the *"hæres substitutus"*) in his place in a certain event. If the event upon which the substitution was to take effect was the refusal of the instituted heir to accept the inheritance at all, then the substitution was called *"vulgaris"* (or common); but if the event was the death of the infant *(pupillus)* after acceptance, and before attaining his majority (of fourteen years if a male, and of twelve years if a female), then the substitution was called *"pupillaris"* (or for minors).

Substitution. Putting in place of another thing; change of one thing for another; serving in lieu of another; having some of its parts replaced. See also **Subrogation.**

In the civil law, the putting one person in place of another; particularly, the act of a testator in naming a second devisee or legatee who is to take the bequest either on failure of the original devisee or legatee or after him.

Substitutional, substitutionary. Where a will contains a gift of property to a class of persons, with a clause providing that on the death of a member of the class before the period of distribution his share is to go to his issue (if any), so as to substitute them for him, the gift to the issue is said to be substitutional or substitutionary. A bequest to such of the children of A. as shall be living at the testator's death, with a direction that the issue of such as shall have died shall take the shares which their parents would have taken, if living at the testator's death, is an example.

Substitutionary evidence. Such as is admitted as a substitute for what would be the original or primary instrument of evidence; as where a witness is permitted to testify to the contents of a lost document.

Substitutionary executor /sàbstət(y)úwshənèhriy əgzékyədər/. See **Executor.**

Substitution of judgment doctrine. Such doctrine, where permitted, allows the court, upon petition of an incompetent's guardian, to approve an estate plan designed to produce tax savings. Uniform Probate Code, § 5–408. Strange v. Powers, 358 Mass. 126, 260 N.E.2d 704.

Substitution of parties. In pleading, the replacement of one party to an action by another party because of death, incompetency, transfer of interest, or in case of a public official who is a party to an action, his death or separation from office. Fed.R.Civ.P. 25.

Subtraction /sùbstraksyówn/. In French law, the fraudulent appropriation of any property, but particularly of the goods of a decedent's estate.

Sub suo periculo /sàb s(y)úwow pərík(y)əlow/. At his own risk.

Subtenant /sàbténənt/. An under-tenant; one who leases all or a part of the rented premises from the original lessee for a term less than that held by the latter. Peak v. Gaddy, 152 Okl. 138, 3 P.2d 1042, 1043.

Subterfuge /sábtəfyùwj/. That to which one resorts for escape or concealment. Los Angeles Fisheries v. Crook, C.C.A.Cal., 47 F.2d 1031, 1035.

Subterranean waters /sàbtəréyn(i)yən wódərz/. See **Water.**

Subtraction. The offense of withholding or withdrawing from another man what by law he is entitled to. There are various descriptions of this offense, of which the principal are as follows: (1) Subtraction of suit and services, which is a species of injury affecting a man's real property, and consists of a withdrawal of (or a neglect to perform or pay) the fealty, suit of court, rent, or services reserved by the lessor of the land. (2) Subtraction of tithes is the withholding from the parson or vicar the tithes to which he is entitled, and this is cognizable in the ecclesiastical courts. (3) Subtraction of conjugal rights is the withdrawing or withholding by a husband or wife of those rights and privileges which the law allows to either party. (4) Subtraction of legacies is the withholding or detaining of legacies by an executor. (5) Subtraction of church rates, in English law, consists in the refusal to pay the amount of rate at which any individual parishioner has been assessed for the necessary repairs of the parish church.

Subtraction of conjugal rights. The act of a husband or wife living separately from the other without a lawful cause. 3 Bl.Comm. 94. See also **Subtraction.**

Suburbani /sàbərbéynay/. Lat. In old English law, husbandmen.

Subversion. The act or process of overthrowing, destroying, or corrupting. Used in connection with activities designed to undermine and overthrow the government, state and federal. See **Subversive activities.**

Subversive activities. Acts directed toward the overthrow of the government, including treason, sedition and sabotage. Such acts are federal crimes. 18 U.S.C.A. § 2381 *et seq.*; 50 U.S.C.A. § 781 *et seq.* See **Espionage; Smith Act.**

Successio /səksésh(iy)ow/. Lat. In the civil law, a coming in place of another, on his decease; a coming into the estate which a deceased person had at the time of his death. This was either by virtue of an express appointment of the deceased person by his will (*ex testamento*), or by the general appointment of law in case of *intestacy* (*ab intestato*).

Succession. The devolution of title to property under the law of descent and distribution. The act or right of legal or official investment with a predecessor's office, dignity, possession, or functions; also the legal or actual order of so succeeding from that which is or is to be vested or taken. The word when applied to realty denotes persons who take by will or inheritance and excludes those who take by deed, grant, gift, or any form of purchase or contract. Olsan Bros. v. Miller, Tex.Civ.App., 108 S.W.2d 856, 857.

Although "succession" is defined in statute as the acquisition of title to the property of one who dies without disposing of it by will, the word frequently possesses the somewhat broader meaning of the acquisition of rights upon the death of another. In re Russell's Estate, 17 C.A.3d 758, 95 Cal.Rptr. 88, 95.

The right by which one set of men may, by succeeding another set, acquire a property in all the goods, movables, and other chattels of a corporation. The power of perpetual *succession* is one of the peculiar properties of a corporation. See **Perpetual.**

See also **Descent; Devise; Inheritance; Intestate; Testamentary.**

Civil Law and Louisiana

The *fact* of the transmission of the rights, estate, obligations, and charges of a deceased person to his heir or heirs. The *right* by which the heir can take possession of the decedent's estate. The right of the heir to step into the place of the deceased, with respect to the possession, control, enjoyment, administration, and settlement of all the latter's property, rights, obligations, charges, etc.

The *estate* of a deceased person, comprising all kinds of property owned or claimed by him, as well as his debts and obligations, and considered as a legal entity (according to the notion of the Roman law) for certain purposes, such as collecting assets and paying debts.

The transmission of the rights and obligations of the deceased to the heirs, also the estates, rights, and charges which a person leaves after his death, whether the property exceeds the charges or the charges exceed the property, or whether he has only left charges without any property. The succession not only includes the rights and obligations of the deceased as they exist at the time of his death, but all that has accrued thereto since the opening of the succession, as also the new charges to which it becomes subject. The coming in of another to take the property of one who dies without disposing of it by will.

General

Artificial succession. That attribute of a corporation by which, in contemplation of law, the company itself remains always the same though its constituent members or stockholders may change from time to time.

Hereditary succession. Descent or title, by descent at common law; the title whereby a man on the death of his ancestor acquires his estate by right of representation as his heir at law.

Intestate succession. The succession of an heir at law to the property and estate of his ancestor when the latter has died intestate, or leaving a will which has been annulled or set aside. See also **Descent; Devise; Inheritance; Intestate.**

Irregular succession. That which is established by law in favor of certain persons, or of the state, in default of heirs, either legal or instituted by testament.

Legal succession. That which the law establishes in favor of the nearest relation of a deceased person. See **Descent.**

Natural succession. Succession taking place between natural persons, for example, in descent on the death of an ancestor.

Testamentary succession. In the civil law, that which results from the institution of an heir in a testament executed in the form prescribed by law. See **Testamentary.**

Testate succession. Passing of property to another by will.

Vacant succession. Such exists when no one claims it, or when all the heirs are unknown, or when all the known heirs to it have renounced it. Civ.Code La. art. 1095. Simmons v. Saul, 138 U.S. 439, 11 S.Ct. 369, 34 L.Ed. 1054.

Succession duty or tax. A tax placed on the gratuitous acquisition of property passing on the death of any person by transfer from one person to another. Wachovia Bank & Trust Co. v. Maxwell, 221 N.C. 528, 20 S.E.2d 840, 842. A tax imposed upon the privilege of receiving property from a decedent by devise or inheritance. See **Inheritance tax.**

Successive. Following one after another in a line or series. In re Buchholtz, Cust. & Pat.App., 54 F.2d 965, 966.

Successor. One that succeeds or follows; one who takes the place that another has left, and sustains the like part or character; one who takes the place of another by succession. Thompson v. North Texas Nat. Bank, Tex.Com.App., 37 S.W.2d 735, 740; Wawak Co. v. Kaiser, C.C.A.Ill., 90 F.2d 694, 697. One who has been appointed or elected to hold an office after the term of the present incumbent.

Term with reference to corporations, generally means another corporation which, through amalgamation, consolidation, or other legal succession, becomes invested with rights and assumes burdens of first corporation.

Singular successor. A term borrowed from the civil law, denoting a person who succeeds to the rights of a former owner in a single article of property (as by purchase), as distinguished from a *universal* successor, who succeeds to all the rights and powers of a former owner, as in the case of a bankrupt or intestate estate.

Successor in interest. One who follows another in ownership or control of property. In order to be a "successor in interest", a party must continue to retain the same rights as original owner without change in ownership and there must be change in form only and not in substance, and transferee is not a "successor in interest." City of New York v. Turnpike Development Corp., 36 Misc.2d 704, 233 N.Y. S.2d 887, 890. In case of corporations, the term "successor in interest" ordinarily indicates statutory succession as, for instance, when corporation changes its name but retains same property. City of New York v. Turnpike Development Corp., 36 Misc.2d 704, 233 N.Y.S.2d 887, 890.

Successors. Those persons, other than creditors, who are entitled to property of a decedent under his will or this Code. Uniform Probate Code, § 1–201(42).

Successor trustee. A trustee who follows or succeeds an earlier trustee and who generally has all the powers of the earlier trustee. Trusts generally make provisions for appointment of successor trustees.

Succinct /səksíŋkt/. Brief, precise, exact.

Succurritur minori; facilis est lapsus juventutis /səkə́hrədər mənóray, fǽsələs èst lǽpsəs jùwvən-t(y)úwdəs/. A minor is [to be] aided; a mistake of youth is easy [youth is liable to err].

Such. Of that kind, having particular quality or character specified. Identical with, being the same as what has been mentioned. Alike, similar, of the like kind. "Such" represents the object as already particularized in terms which are not mentioned, and is a descriptive and relative word, referring to the last antecedent.

Sudden. Happening without previous notice or with very brief notice; coming or occurring unexpectedly; unforeseen; unprepared for. Hagaman v. Manley, 141 Kan. 647, 42 P.2d 946, 949.

Sudden emergency doctrine. When a person finds himself confronted with a sudden emergency, which was not brought about by his own negligence or want of care, such person has the legal right to do what appears to him at the time he should do, so long as he acts in a reasonably prudent manner as any other person would have done under like or similar circumstances, to avoid any injury, and if he does so act, he will not be deemed to have been negligent even though it might afterwards be apparent that some other course of action would have been safer. Swann v. Huttig Sash & Door Co., C.A.Tex., 436 F.2d 60, 62. Under sudden emergency doctrine, one placed in position of sudden emergency or peril other than by his own negligence, is not held to same degree of care and prudence as one who has time for thought and reflection. Dadds v. Pennsylvania R. Co., Del., 251 A.2d 559, 560.

Sudden heat of passion. In the common-law definition of manslaughter, this phrase means an excess of rage or anger, suddenly arising from a contemporary provocation. It means that the provocation must arise at the time of the killing, and that the passion is not the result of a former provocation, and the act must be directly caused by the passion arising out of the provocation at the time of the homicide.

Sudden or violent injury. Injury occurring unexpectedly and not naturally or in the ordinary course of events.

Sudden peril rule. Under this rule, a defendant who is guilty of primary negligence is not liable in case of sudden peril where the peril or alarm was caused by the negligence of the opposite party, apprehension of peril from the standpoint of defendant seeking to excuse his primary negligence was reasonable, and appearance of danger was so imminent as to leave no time for deliberation. White v. Munson, Tex.Civ. App., 162 S.W.2d 429, 432. But rule cannot be invoked by one bringing emergency on or not using due care, to avoid it. McClelland v. Interstate Transit Lines, 142 Neb. 439, 6 N.W.2d 384, 391. See also **Sudden emergency doctrine.**

Sudder /sádər/. In Hindu law, the best; the forecourt of a house; the chief seat of government, contradistinguished from *"mofussil,"* or interior of the country; the presidency.

Sue. To commence or to continue legal proceedings for recovery of a right; to proceed with as an action, and follow it up to its proper termination; to gain by legal process. Lervold v. Republic Mut. Fire Ins. Co., 142 Kan. 43, 45 P.2d 839, 843. To commence and carry out legal action against another. Word includes a proceeding instituted by confession of judgment. Commonwealth ex rel. Bradford County v. Lynch, 146 Pa.Super. 469, 23 A.2d 77, 78. See also **Suit.**

Sue out. To obtain by application; to petition for and take out. Properly the term is applied only to the obtaining and issuing of such process as is only accorded upon an application first made; but conventionally it is also used of the taking out of process which issues of course. The term is occasionally used of instruments other than writs.

Suerte /s(u)wértey/. In Spanish law, a small lot of ground. Particularly, such a lot within the limits of a city or town used for cultivation or planting as a garden, vineyard or orchard. Building lots in towns and cities are called "solares."

Suffer. To allow, to admit, or to permit. Osborne v. Winter, 133 Cal.App. 664, 24 P.2d 892. It includes knowledge of what is to be done under sufferance. First Nat. Bank & Trust Co. of Port Chester v. New York Title Ins. Co., 171 Misc. 854, 12 N.Y.S.2d 703, 709. To suffer an act to be done or a condition to exist is to permit or consent to it; to approve of it, and not to hinder it. It implies knowledge, a willingness of the mind and responsible control or ability to prevent. Wilson v. Nelson, 183 U.S. 191, 22 S.Ct. 74, 46 L.Ed. 147.

Also to have the feeling or sensation that arises from the action of something painful, distressing or the like; to feel or endure pain; to endure or undergo without sinking; to support; to bear up under; to be affected by; to sustain; to experience; to feel pain, physical or mental. The customary use of the word indicates some experience of conscious pain. New York Life Ins. Co. v. Calhoun, C.C.A.Mo., 97 F.2d 896, 898.

Sufferance /sáf(ə)rən(t)s/. Toleration; negative permission by not forbidding; passive consent; license implied from the omission or neglect to enforce an adverse right.

Sufferance wharves. In old English law, wharves in which goods may be landed before any duty is paid. They are appointed for the purpose by the commissioners of the customs.

Sufferentia pacis /sə̀fərénsh(iy)ə péysəs/. Lat. A grant or sufferance of peace or truce.

Suffering a recovery. A recovery was effected by the party wishing to convey the land *suffering* a fictitious action to be brought against him by the party to whom the land was to be conveyed (the demandant), and allowing the demandant to recover a judgment against him for the land in question. The vendor, or conveying party, in thus assisting or permitting the demandant so to recover a judgment against him, was thence technically said to "suffer a recovery."

Sufficiency of evidence. Term refers to test prescribed by rule providing that grand jury ought to find an indictment when all the evidence taken together, if unexplained or uncontradicted, would warrant a conviction by the trier of the offense. State v. Parks, Alaska, 437 P.2d 642, 644.

Barring plain error, an appellate court may not grant a directed verdict or a judgment n. o. v. absent an appropriate motion in the trial court; that is to say, it may not review the "sufficiency of the evidence" and grant a final judgment in favor of a party who failed to so move; and "sufficiency" is a term of art meaning that legal standard which is applied to determine whether the case may go to the jury or whether the evidence is legally sufficient to support the jury verdict as a matter of law. Urti v. Transport Commercial Corp., C.A.La., 479 F.2d 766, 769.

See also **Substantial evidence; Sufficient evidence.**

Sufficient. Adequate, enough, as much as may be necessary, equal or fit for end proposed, and that which may be necessary to accomplish an object. Of such quality, number, force, or value as to serve a need or purpose. Nissen v. Miller, 44 N.M. 487, 105 P.2d 324, 326. As to sufficient Consideration see that title.

Sufficient cause. With respect to right to remove officers does not mean any cause which removing officer may deem sufficient, but means legal cause, specifically relating to and affecting administration of office, of substantial nature directly affecting public's rights and interests, touching officer's qualifications or his performance of duties, and showing that he is not fit or proper to hold office. Zurich General Accident & Liability Ins. Co. v. Kinsler, 12 Cal.2d 98, 81 P.2d 913, 915. Sufficient cause to hold defendant to answer charges is reasonable or probable cause or that state of facts as would lead a man of ordinary caution to conscientiously entertain strong suspicion of defendant's guilt. People v. Upton, 257 Cal.App.2d 677, 65 Cal.Rptr. 103, 109. See also **Probable cause.**

Sufficient evidence. Adequate evidence; such evidence, in character, weight, or amount, as will legally justify the judicial or official action demanded; according to circumstances, it may be "prima facie" or "satisfactory" evidence. Sufficient evidence is that which is satisfactory for the purpose; that amount of proof which ordinarily satisfies an unprejudiced mind, beyond a reasonable doubt. The term is not synonymous with "conclusive;" but it may be used interchangeably with the term "weight of evidence." See also **Burden of proof; Evidence; Satisfactory evidence; Substantial evidence; Sufficiency of evidence.**

Suffocate. To kill by stopping respiration, as by strangling or asphyxiation.

Suffragan /sə́frəgən/. Bishops who in former times were appointed to supply the place of others during their absence on embassies or other business were so termed. They were consecrated as other bishops were, and were anciently called *"chorepiscopi,"* or "bishops of the county," in contradistinction to the regular bishops of the city or see. The practice of creating *suffragan* bishops, after having long been discontinued, was recently revived; and such bishops are now permanently "assistant" to the bishops.

A suffragan is a titular bishop ordained to aid and assist the bishop of the diocese in his spiritual function; or one who supplieth the place instead of the bishop, by whose suffrage ecclesiastical causes or matters committed to him are to be adjudged, acted on, or determined.

Suffrage /sə́frəj/. A vote; the act of voting; the right or privilege of casting a vote at public elections. The last is the meaning of the term in such phrases as "the extension of the suffrage," "universal suffrage," etc. Right of "suffrage" is right of a man to vote for whom he pleases. Waterbury Homeowners Ass'n v. City of Waterbury, 28 Conn.Sup. 295, 259 A.2d 650, 654.

Suffragium /sə̀fréyj(iy)əm/. Lat. In Roman law, a vote; the right of voting in the assemblies of the people.

Aid or influence used or promised to obtain some honor or office; the purchase of office.

Suggest. To introduce indirectly to the thought; to propose with diffidence or modesty; to hint; to intimate.

Suggestio falsi /səgjés(h)ch(iy)ow fólsay/. Lat. Suggestion or representation of that which is false; false representation. To recite in a deed that a will was duly executed, when it was not, is *suggestio falsi;* and to conceal from the heir that the will was not duly executed is *suppressio veri.*

Suggestion. A suggesting; presentation of an idea especially indirectly, as through association of ideas, bringing before the mind for consideration, action, solution, or the like. It is in the nature of a hint or insinuation, and lacks the element of probability. Facts which merely suggest do not raise an inference of the existence of the fact suggested, and therefore a suggestion is much less than an inference or presumption. See **Leading question.**

In practice, a statement, formally entered on the record, of some fact or circumstance which will materially affect the further proceedings in the cause, or which is necessary to be brought to the knowledge of the court in order to its right disposition of the action, but which, for some reason, cannot be pleaded. Thus, if one of the parties dies after issue and before trial, his death may be *suggested* on the record.

Suggestion of error. Request for rehearing. See also **Objection.**

Suggestive interrogation. A phrase used by some writers to signify "leading question." It is so used in the French law. See **Leading question.**

Suicide. Self-destruction; the deliberate termination of one's existence.

　　Attempted suicide is a crime in some jurisdictions, not in others. Some jurisdictions hold an attempted suicide which kills an innocent bystander or would-be rescuer to be murder, others manslaughter, others no crime. Some jurisdictions hold it to be murder for one person to persuade or aid another to commit suicide; some (by statute) make it manslaughter or a separate crime.

Sui generis /s(y)úway jénərəs/. Lat. Of its own kind or class; *i.e.,* the *only one* of its own kind; peculiar.

Sui hæredes /s(y)úway həríydiyz/. Lat. In the civil law, one's own heirs; proper heirs.

Sui juris /s(y)úway júrəs/. Lat. Of his own right; possessing full social and civil rights; not under any legal disability, or the power of another, or guardianship.

　　Having capacity to manage one's own affairs; not under legal disability to act for one's self.

Suing and laboring clause. A clause in an English policy of marine insurance, generally in the following form: "In case of any loss or misfortune, it shall be lawful for the assured, their factors, servants and assigns, to sue, labor, and travel for, in, and about the defense, safeguard, and recovery of the" property insured, "without prejudice to this insurance; to the charges whereof we, the assurers, will contribute." The object of the clause is to encourage the assured to exert themselves in preserving the property from loss.

Suit. A generic term, of comprehensive signification, referring to any proceeding by one person or persons against another or others in a court of justice in which the plaintiff pursues, in such court, the remedy which the law affords him for the redress of an injury or the enforcement of a right, whether at law or in equity. Kohl v. U. S., 91 U.S. 367, 375, 23 L.Ed. 449; Weston v. Charleston, 27 U.S. (2 Pet.) 449, 464, 7 L.Ed. 481; Syracuse Plaster Co. v. Agostini Bros. Bldg. Corporation, 169 Misc. 564, 7 N.Y.S.2d 897. It is, however, seldom applied to a criminal prosecution. And it was formerly sometimes restricted to the designation of a proceeding in equity, to distinguish such proceeding from an action at law. Term "suit" has generally been replaced by term "action"; which includes both actions at law and in equity. Fed.R.Civil P. 2. For "Ancillary" suit and suit "In Rem" see those titles. See also **Action; Proceeding.**

Old English law. The witnesses or followers of the plaintiff. 3 Bl.Comm. 295. See **Secta.**

　　Old books mention the word in many connections which are now disused,—at least, in the United States. Thus, "suit" was used of following any one, or in the sense of pursuit; as in the phrase "making fresh suit." It was also used of a petition to the king or lord. "Suit of court" was the attendance which a tenant owed at the court of his lord. "Suit covenant" and "suit custom" seem to have signified a right to one's attendance, or one's obligation to attend, at the

lord's court, founded upon a known covenant, or an immemorial usage or practice of ancestors. "Suit regal" was attendance at the sheriff's tourn or leet (his court). "Suit of the king's peace" was pursuing an offender,—one charged with breach of the peace, while *"suithold"* was a tenure in consideration of certain services to the superior lord.

Class suits. See **Class or representative action.**

Derivative suit. See **Stockholder's derivative action.**

Suit against state. Suit in which relief against the state is sought. See **Sovereign immunity; Tort claims acts.**

Suit money. Counsel fees allowed or awarded by court to party. An allowance, in the nature of temporary alimony, authorized by statute in some states to be made to a wife on the institution of her suit for divorce, intended to cover the reasonable expenses of the suit and to provide her with means for the efficient preparation and trial of her case. Many federal statutes provide for allowance of attorney fees for actions brought under respective statutes; *e.g.,* actions to recover social security disability benefits.

Suit of a civil nature. A suit for the remedy of a private wrong, called a "civil action". Fed.R.Civil P. 2. See **Action.**

Suits or proceedings at law or in chancery. Suits instituted and carried or in substantial conformity with the forms and modes prescribed by the common law or by the rules in chancery excluding cases instituted and carried on solely in accordance with statutory provisions. Under current rules practice in the federal and most state courts, there is now only one form of action called a "civil action", which embraces both actions at law and in equity. Fed.R.Civil P. 2.

Suitable. Fit and appropriate for the end in view.

Suitas. Lat. In the civil law, the condition or quality of a *suus hæres,* or proper heir.

Suite. Those persons who by his authority *follow* or attend an ambassador or other public minister.

Suitor. A party to a suit or action in court; a litigant. In its ancient sense, "suitor" meant one who was bound to attend the county court; also one who formed part of the *secta.*

Suitors' deposit account. Formerly suitors in the English court of chancery derived no income from their cash paid into court, unless it was invested at their request and risk. Now, however, it is provided by the court of chancery (funds) act, 1872, that all money paid into court, and not required by the suitor to be invested, shall be placed on deposit and shall bear interest at two per cent. per annum for the benefit of the suitor entiteld to it.

Suitors' fee fund. A fund in the English court of chancery into which the fees of suitors in that court were paid, and out of which the salaries of various officers of the court were defrayed.

Suits in Admiralty Act. Federal statute giving injured parties the right to sue the government in admiralty. 46 U.S.C.A. §§ 741–752. Donily v. U. S., D.C.Or., 381 F.Supp. 901.

Sulcus /sálkəs/. In old English law, a small brook or stream of water.

Sullery /sáləriy/. In old English law, a plowland.

Sum. In English law, a summary or abstract; a compendium; a collection. Several of the old law treatises are called "sums." Lord Hale applies the term to summaries of statute law.

The sense in which the term is most commonly used is "money"; a quantity of money or currency; any amount indefinitely, a sum of money, a small sum, or a large sum. U. S. v. Van Auken, 96 U.S. 366, 368, 24 L.Ed. 852.

Sumage /sáməj/. Toll for carriage on horseback.

Sum certain. In law of negotiable instruments, the sum payable is a sum certain even though it is to be paid (a) with stated interest or by stated installments; or (b) with stated different rates of interest before and after default or a specified date; or (c) with a stated discount or addition if paid before or after the date fixed for payment; or (d) with exchange or less exchange, whether at a fixed rate or at the current rate; or (e) with costs of collection or an attorney's fee or both upon default. U.C.C. § 3–106(1).

Sum in gross. See **In gross.**

Summa caritas est facere justitiam singulis, et omni tempore quando necesse fuerit /sámə kǽrətæs èst fǽsəriy jəstísh(iy)əm síŋgyələs, èd ómnay témpəriy kwóndow nəsésiy fyúwərət/. The greatest charity is to do justice to every one, and at any time whenever it may be necessary.

Summa est lex quæ pro religione facit /sámə èst léks kwìy pròw rəlìjiyówniy féysət/. That is the highest law which favors religion.

Summa ratio est quæ pro religione facit /sámə réysh(iy)ow èst kwìy prów rəlìjiyówniy féysət/. That consideration is strongest which determines in favor of religion.

Summarily. Without ceremony or delay, short or concise.

Summary, *n.* An abridgment; brief; compendium; digest; also a short application to a court or judge, without the formality of a full proceeding.

Summary, *adj.* Short; concise; immediate; peremptory; off-hand; without a jury; provisional; statutory. The term as used in connection with legal proceedings means a short, concise, and immediate proceeding.

Summary conviction. See **Conviction.**

Summary courts martial. See **Court-Martial.**

Summary ejectment. See **Process** (*Summary process*).

Summary eviction. See **Process** (*Summary process*).

Summary jurisdiction. The jurisdiction of a court to give a judgment or make an order itself forthwith; *e.g.,* to commit to prison for contempt. In the case of justices of the peace, a jurisdiction to convict an offender themselves instead of committing him for trial by a jury.

Summary proceeding. See **Proceeding** (*Summary*).

Summary trial. See **Proceeding** (*Summary*).

Summary process. See **Process.**

Summary judgment. Rule of Civil Procedure 56 permits any party to a civil action to move for a summary judgment on a claim, counterclaim, or cross-claim when he believes that there is no genuine issue of material fact and that he is entitled to prevail as a matter of law. The motion may be directed toward all or part of a claim or defense and it may be made on the basis of the pleadings or other portions of the record in the case or it may be supported by affidavits and a variety of outside material. See also **Genuine issue; Material fact.**

Summation. See **Summing up.**

Summing up. On the trial of an action by a jury, a recapitulation of the evidence adduced, in order to draw the attention of the jury to the salient points. The counsel for each party has the right of summing up his evidence, if he has adduced any, and the judge sometimes sums up the whole in his charge to the jury. See **Closing argument.**

Summon. To serve a summons; to cite a defendant to appear in court to answer a suit which has been begun against him; to notify the defendant that an action has been instituted against him, and that he is required to answer to it at a time and place named. See **Summons.**

Summoneas /səmówniyeys/. L. Lat. In old practice, a writ of summons; a writ by which a party was summoned to appear in court.

Summoners /sámənərz/. Petty officers, who cite and warn persons to appear in any court.

Summonitio /səmənísh(iy)ow/. L. Lat. In old English practice, a summoning or summons; a writ by which a party was summoned to appear in court, of which there were various kinds.

Summonitiones aut citationes nullæ liceant fieri intra palatium regis /səmənìshiyówniyz òt saytèyshiyówniyz nǽliy lisiyænt fayəray íntrə pəléysh(iy)əm ríyjəs/. Let no summonses or citations be served within the king's palace.

Summonitores scaccarii /səmənətóriyz skəkériyay/. Officers who assisted in collecting the revenues by citing the defaulters therein into the court of exchequer.

Summons. Instrument used to commence a civil action or special proceeding and is a means of acquiring jurisdiction over a party. In re Dell, 56 Misc.2d 1017, 290 N.Y.S.2d 287, 289. Writ or process directed to the sheriff or other proper officer, requiring him to notify the person named that an action has been commenced against him in the court from where the process issues, and that he is required to appear, on a day named, and answer the complaint in such action. Upon the filing of the complaint the clerk is required to issue a summons and deliver it for service to the marshall or to a person specially appointed to serve it. Fed.R.Civil P. 4(a). See also **Alias summons.**

Form and content of summons. The summons shall be signed by the clerk, be under the seal of the court, contain the name of the court and the names of the parties, be directed to the defendant, state the name and address of the plaintiff's attorney, if any, otherwise the plaintiff's address, and the time within which these rules require the defendant to appear and defend, and shall notify him that in case of his failure to do so judgment by default will be rendered against him for the relief demanded in the complaint. When service is made pursuant to a statute or rule of court of a state, the summons, or notice, or order in lieu of summons shall correspond as nearly as may be to that required by the statute or rule. Fed.R.Civil P. 4(b).

Summons ad respondendum /sámən(d)z æd rèspon-déndəm/. Process issuing in a civil case at law notifying defendant therein named that he must appear on day designated and thereupon make answer to plaintiff's statement of his cause of action.

Summons and order. In English practice, the summons is the application to a common-law judge at chambers in reference to a pending action, and upon it the judge or master makes the order.

Summum jus /sáməm jás/. Lat. Strict right; extreme right. The extremity or rigor of the law. See **Apex juris.**

Summum jus, summa injuria; summa lex, summa crux /sáməm jás, sámə injúriyə; sámə léks, sámə kráks/. Extreme law (rigor of law) is the greatest injury; strict law is great punishment. That is, insistence upon the full measure of a man's strict legal rights may work the greatest injury to others, unless equity can aid.

Sumner. See **Sompnour.**

Sum payable. As used within negotiable instruments law is the amount for which, by the terms of the instrument, the maker becomes liable, and which he might tender and pay in full satisfaction of his obligation.

Sumptuary laws /sám(p)chuwəriy lóz/. Laws made for the purpose of restraining luxury or extravagance, particularly against inordinate expenditures in the matter of apparel, food, furniture, etc.

Sunday. The first day of the week is designated by this name; also as the "Lord's Day," and as the "Sabbath."

For Work of necessity, see **Necessity.**

Sunday closing laws. Those laws and ordinances in many jurisdictions which prohibit businesses from operating on Sunday. Also called "blue laws."

Sundries. Miscellaneous or various items which may be considered together, without being separately specified or identified.

Sundry. Separate, divers, or various.

Sunset law. Statute which requires administrative bodies to justify periodically their existence to legislature.

Sunshine law. Law which requires open meetings of governmental agencies and departments. See also **Freedom of Information Act.**

Suo nomine /s(y)úwow nóməniy/. Lat. In his own name.

Suo periculo /s(y)úwow pərík(y)əlow/. Lat. At his own peril or risk.

Super /s(y)úwpər/. Lat. Upon; above; over; higher, as in quantity, quality and degree; more than; as in super-essential, super-natural or super-standard.

Super altum mare /s(y)úwpər æltəm mériy/. On the high sea.

Supercargo /s(y)ùwpərkárgow/. In maritime law, a person specially employed by the owner of a cargo to take charge of and sell to the best advantage merchandise which has been shipped, and to purchase returning cargoes and to receive freight, as he may be authorized.

Superficiarius /s(y)ùwpərfishiyériyəs/. Lat. In the civil law, he who has built upon the soil of another, which he has hired for a number of years or forever, yielding a yearly rent. In other words, a tenant on ground-rent.

Superficies /s(y)ùwpərfíshiyiyz/. Lat. In the civil law, the alienation by the owner of the surface of the soil of all rights necessary for building on the surface, a yearly rent being generally reserved; also a building or erection.

Superficies solo cedit /s(y)ùwpərfíshiyiyz sówlow síydət/. Whatever is attached to the land forms part of it.

Super fidem chartarum, mortuis testibus, erit ad patriam de necessitate recurrendum /s(y)úwpər fáydəm kartérəm, mórchuwəs téstəbəs, éhrəd æd pǽtriyəm dìy nəsèsətéydiy rèkəhréndəm/. The truth of charters is necessarily to be referred to a jury, when the witnesses are dead.

Superflua non nocent /s(y)uwpárfl(y)uwə nòn nósənt/. Superfluities do not prejudice. Surplusage does not vitiate.

Superinductio /s(y)ùwpərində́ksh(iy)ow/. Lat. In the civil law, a species of obliteration.

Superinstitution. The institution of one in an office to which another has been previously instituted; as where A. is admitted and instituted to a benefice upon one title, and B. is admitted and instituted on the title or presentment of another.

A church being full by institution, if a second institution is granted to the same church this is a super-institution.

Superintend. To have charge and direction of; to direct the course and oversee the details; to regulate with authority; to manage; to oversee with the power of direction; to take care of with authority.

Superintendent. One who superintends or has the oversight and charge of something with the power of direction; a manager.

Superior, *n.* One who has a right to command; one who holds a superior rank.

Superior, *adj.* Higher; belonging to a higher grade. People ex rel. McCoy v. McCahey, 296 Ill.App. 310,

15 N.E.2d 988, 993. More elevated in rank or office. Possessing larger power. Entitled to command, influence, or control over another.

In estates, some are superior to others. An estate entitled to a servitude or easement over another estate is called the "superior" or "dominant," and the other, the "inferior" or "servient," estate.

In the feudal law, until the statute *quia emptores* precluded subinfeudations *(q.v.),* the tenant who granted part of his estate to be held of and from himself as lord was called a "superior."

Superior courts. Courts of general or extensive jurisdiction, as distinguished from the inferior courts. As the official style of a tribunal, the term "superior court" bears a different meaning in different states. In some it is a court of intermediate jurisdiction between the trial courts and the chief appellate court; elsewhere it is the designation of the trial courts. See also **Court.**

Superior fellow servant. A term introduced into the law of negligence, and meaning one higher in authority than another, and whose commands and directions his inferiors are bound to respect and obey, though engaged at the same line of work.

Superior force. In the law of bailments and of negligence, an uncontrollable and irresistible force, of human agency, producing results which the person in question could not avoid; equivalent to the Latin phrase *"vis major."* See **Vis.**

Superjurare /s(y)ùwpərjurériy/. Over-swearing. A term anciently used when a criminal endeavored to excuse himself by his own oath or the oath of one or two witnesses, and the crime objected against him was so plain and notorious that he was convicted on the oaths of many more witnesses.

Supernumerarii /s(y)ùwpərnàmərériyay/. Lat. In Roman law, advocates who were not registered or enrolled and did not belong to the college of advocates. They were not attached to any local jurisdiction. See **Statuti.**

Superoneratio /s(y)ùwpəronəréysh(iy)ow/. Lat. Surcharging a common; *i.e.,* putting in beasts of a number or kind other than the right of common allows.

Superoneratione pasturæ /s(y)ùwpəronərèyshiyówniy pæschúriy/. A judicial writ that lay against him who was impleaded in the county court for the surcharge of a common with his cattle, in a case where he was formerly impleaded for it in the same court, and the cause was removed into one of the superior courts.

Superplusagium /s(y)ùwpərpləséyj(iy)əm/. In old English law, overplus; surplus; residue or balance.

Super prærogativa regis /s(y)úwpər prərògətáyvə ríyjəs/. A writ which formerly lay against the king's tenant's widow for marrying without the royal license.

Supersede /s(y)ùwpərsíyd/. Obliterate, set aside, annul, replace, make void, inefficacious or useless, repeal. To set aside, render unnecessary, suspend, or stay.

Supersedeas /s(y)ùwpərsíydiyəs/. The name of a writ containing a command to stay the proceedings at law. A suspension of the power of a trial court to issue an execution on judgment appealed from, or, if writ of execution has issued, it is a prohibition emanating from court of appeal against execution of writ. Stewart v. Hurt, 9 Cal.2d 39, 68 P.2d 726, 727. An auxiliary process designed to supersede enforcement of trial court's judgment brought up for review, and its application is limited to the judgment from which an appeal is taken. Mascot Pictures Corp. v. Municipal Court of City of Los Angeles, 3 Cal.App.2d 559, 40 P.2d 272.

Originally it was a writ directed to an officer, commanding him to desist from enforcing the execution of another writ which he was about to execute, or which might come in his hands. In modern times the term is often used synonymously with a "stay of proceedings," and is employed to designate the effect of an act or proceeding which of itself suspends the enforcement of a judgment.

Supersedeas bond. A bond required of one who petitions to set aside a judgment or execution and from which the other party may be made whole if the action is unsuccessful. See Fed.R.Civil P. 62; Fed. R.App.P. 7 and 8.

Superseding cause. An act of a third person or other force which by its intervention prevents the actor from being liable for harm to another which his antecedent negligence is a substantial factor in bringing about. An intervening act or acts of negligence which operate to insulate an antecedent tort-feasor from liability for negligently causing a dangerous condition which results in injury. Hargrove v. Frommeyer & Co., 229 Pa.Super. 298, 323 A.2d 300, 304. See also **Intervening cause; Supervening negligence.**

Super statuto /s(y)úwpər stət(y)úwdow/. A writ, upon the statute 1 Edw. III, c. 12, that lay against the king's tenant holding in chief, who aliened the king's land without his license.

Super statuto de articulis cleri /s(y)úwpər stət(y)úwdow dìy artíkyələs klíray/. A writ which lay against a sheriff or other officer who distrained in the king's highway, or on lands anciently belonging to the church.

Super statuto facto pour seneschal et marshal de roy, etc. /s(y)úwpər stət(y)úwdow fǽktow pùr sènəshál ey màr(ə)shál də róy, etsédərə/. A writ which lay against a steward or marshal for holding plea in his court, or for trespass or contracts not made or arising within the king's household.

Super statuto versus servantes et laboratores /s(y)úwpər stət(y)úwdow vársəs sərvǽntiyz èt lǽbərətóriyz/. A writ which lay against him who kept any servants who had left the service of another contrary to law.

Superstitious use. In English law, when lands, tenements, rents, goods, or chattels are given, secured, or appointed for and towards the maintenance of a priest or chaplain to say mass, for the maintenance of a priest or other man to pray for the soul of any dead man in such a church or elsewhere, to have and maintain perpetual obits, lamps, torches, etc., to be used at certain times to help to save the souls of men out of purgatory,—in such cases the king, by force of several statutes, is authorized to direct and appoint all such uses to such purposes as are truly charitable.

The doctrine has no recognition in this country; and a bequest to support a Catholic priest, and perhaps other uses void in England, would not be considered as superstitious uses.

Supervening cause. A new effective cause which, operating independently of anything else, becomes proximate cause of accident. See also **Intervening cause; Superseding cause.**

Supervening negligence. To come within the doctrine of last clear chance or supervening negligence, four conditions must coexist, to wit: (1) the injured party has already come into a position of peril; (2) the injuring party then or thereafter becomes, or in the exercise of ordinary prudence ought to have become, aware, not only of that fact, but also that the party in peril either reasonably cannot escape from it or apparently will not avail himself of opportunities open to him for doing so; (3) the injuring party subsequently has the opportunity by the exercise of reasonable care to save the other from harm; and (4) he fails to exercise such care. See also **Intervening cause; Last clear chance doctrine; Superseding cause.**

Supervise. To have general oversight over, to superintend or to inspect. See **Supervisor.**

Supervision. An act of occupation of supervising; inspection.

Supervisor. A surveyor or overseer. Also, in some states, the chief officer of a town; one of a board of county officers.

In a broad sense, one having authority over others, to superintend and direct.

The term "supervisor" means any individual having authority, in the interest of the employer, to hire, transfer, suspend, lay off, recall, promote, discharge, assign, reward, or discipline other employees, or responsibly to direct them, or to adjust their grievances, or effectively to recommend such action, if in connection with the foregoing the exercise of such authority is not of a merely routine or clerical nature, but requires the use of independent judgment. National Labor Relations Act, § 2(11).

Supervisory control. Control exercised by courts to compel inferior tribunals to act within their jurisdiction, to prohibit them from acting outside their jurisdiction, and to reverse their extrajurisdictional acts.

Supplemental. That which is added to a thing to complete it. See also **Amendment.**

Supplemental act. That which supplies a deficiency, adds to or completes, or extends that which is already in existence without changing or modifying the original. Act designed to improve an existing statute by adding something thereto without changing the original text.

Supplemental affidavit. An affidavit made in addition to a previous one, in order to supply some deficiency in it.

Supplemental answer. One which was filed for the purpose of correcting, adding to, and explaining an answer already filed. See **Supplemental pleading.**

Supplemental bill. In equity pleading, a bill filed in addition to an original bill, in order to supply some defect in its original frame or structure which cannot be supplied by amendment; or, for purpose of bringing into controversy matter occurring after original bill was filed.

Supplemental bill in nature of bill of review. A type of bill employed to invoke jurisdiction of court of chancery to recall one of its adjudications made while some fact existed which, if before court, would have prevented rendition of final decree, and which, without negligence of party presenting it, was not earlier presented to chancellor.

Supplemental claim. A further claim which was filed when further relief was sought after the bringing of a claim. See **Supplemental complaint.**

Supplemental complaint. Under the Rules of Civil Procedure in the federal and most state courts, a complaint filed in an action to bring to the notice of the court and the opposite party matters occurring after the commencement of action and which may affect the rights asserted. Fed.R.Civil P. 15(d).

It is distinguished from an "amended complaint," in that an "amended complaint" is one which corrects merely faults and errors of a pleading.

Supplemental pleading. One consisting of facts arising since filing of the original. Supplemental pleadings relate to occurrences, transactions and events which may have happened since the date of the pleadings sought to be supplemented. Fed.R.Civil P. 15(d); McKnight v. McKnight, 25 N.C.App. 246, 212 S.E.2d 902, 904.

Supplementary. Added as a supplement; additional; being, or serving as, a supplement.

Supplementary proceedings. Proceedings supplementary to an execution, directed to the discovery of the debtor's property and its application to the debt for which the execution is issued. They are purely statutory, are in the nature of a creditor's bill for the collection of a judgment or tax, and are proceedings in personam and not in rem. See also **Proceeding.**

After an execution on a judgment has issued, the judgment creditor may commence new proceedings to collect the debt. This process includes a summons to the judgment debtor to appear and to submit to an examination as to his property and the court is empowered under statutes to enter an order for payment, for violation of which the debtor may be cited for contempt and imprisoned; e.g. M.G.L.A. (Mass.) c. 246, § 6; Mass.R.Civil P. 4.3(b).

Suppletory oath. See **Oath.**

Suppliant /sǽpl(i)yənt/. The actor in, or party preferring, a petition of right.

Supplicatio /sə̀pləkéysh(iy)ow/. Lat. In the civil law, a petition for pardon of a first offense; also a petition for reversal of judgment; also equivalent to *"duplicatio,"* which corresponds to the common law rejoinder.

Supplicavit /sə̀pləkéyvət/. In English law, a writ issuing out of the king's bench or chancery for taking sureties of the peace. It is commonly directed to the justices of the peace, when they are averse to acting in the affair in their judicial capacity.   4 Bl.Comm. 253.

Supplicium /səplísh(iy)əm/.   Lat.   In the civil law, punishment; corporal punishment for crime.   Death was called *"ultimum supplicium,"* the last or extreme penalty.

Supplier.   Any person engaged in the business of making a consumer product directly or indirectly available to consumers; includes all persons in the chain of production and distribution of a consumer product including the producer or manufacturer, component supplier, wholesaler, distributor, and retailer.   15 U.S. C.A. § 2301.

Supplies.   Means of provision or relief; stores; available aggregate of things needed or demanded in amount sufficient for a given use or purpose; accumulated stores reserved for distribution; sufficiency for use or need; a quantity of something supplied or on hand.

In English law, in parliamentary proceedings the sums of money which are annually voted by the house of commons for the maintenance of the crown and the various public services.

Supply.   To furnish with what is wanted; available aggregate of things needed or demanded; anything yielded or afforded to meet a want; and the act of furnishing with what is wanted.   Clayton v. Bridgeport Mach. Co., Tex.Civ.App., 33 S.W.2d 787, 789.

Support, *v.*   Furnishing funds or means for maintenance; to maintain; to provide for; to enable to continue; to carry on.   To provide a means of livelihood.   To vindicate, to maintain, to defend, to uphold with aid or countenance.

Support, *n.*   That which furnishes a livelihood; a source or means of living; subsistence, sustenance, or living.   In a broad sense the term includes all such means of living as would enable one to live in the degree of comfort suitable and becoming to his station of life.   It is said to include anything requisite to housing, feeding, clothing, health, proper recreation, vacation, traveling expense, or other proper cognate purposes; also, proper care, nursing, and medical attendance in sickness, and suitable burial at death.   See also **Maintenance.**

Support also signifies the right to have one's ground supported so that it will not cave in, when an adjoining owner makes an excavation.   This support is of two kinds, *lateral* and *subjacent*.   Lateral support is the right of land to be supported by the land which lies next to it.   Subjacent support is the right of land to be supported by the land which lies under it.

See also Family expense statutes; Legal duty; Legal obligation; Maintenance; Necessaries; Reciprocal Enforcement of Support Act; Separate maintenance; Nonsupport.

Crime of non-support.   A person commits a misdemeanor if he persistently fails to provide support which he can provide and which he knows he is legally obliged to provide to a spouse, child or other dependent.   Model Penal Code, Section 230.5.

Ground for divorce.   Non-support of spouse, if able to so provide, is a ground for divorce under many state statutes.

Legal duty.   Most all states have statutes which impose obligation to support spouse and children; *e.g.* "Every individual shall support his or her spouse and child, and shall support his or her parent when in need."   Calif.Civil Code, § 242.

Interstate enforcement.   The majority of states have adopted the "Uniform Reciprocal Enforcement of Support Act" as a means of interstate enforcement of support obligations.

Supposition.   A conjecture based upon possibility or probability that a thing could or may have occurred, without proof that it did occur.

Suppress.   To put a stop to a thing actually existing; to prohibit, put down; to prevent, subdue, or end by force.   To "suppress evidence" is to keep it from being used in a trial by showing that it was either gathered illegally or that it is irrelevant.   See **Suppression hearing; Suppression of evidence.**

Suppression.   Conscious effort to control and conceal unacceptable impulses, thoughts, feelings or acts.

Suppression hearing.   A pretrial proceeding in criminal cases in which a defendant seeks to prevent the introduction of evidence alleged to have been seized illegally.   The ruling of the court then prevails at the trial.

Suppression of evidence.   The ruling of a trial judge to the effect that evidence sought to be admitted should be excluded because it was illegally acquired.   Motions to suppress illegally obtained evidence are governed by Fed.R.Crim.P. 12(b) and 41(f).   See also **Motion to suppress.**

The crime of compounding a felony by refusing to give evidence or to testify in a criminal proceeding.

Concept of "suppression" as that term is used in rule that suppression by the prosecution of material evidence favorable to an accused on request violates due process, implies that the government has information in its possession of which the defendant lacks knowledge and which the defendant would benefit from knowing.   U. S. v. Natale, C.A.N.Y., 526 F.2d 1160, 1170.   See also **Withholding of evidence.**

Suppressio veri /səprésh(iy)ow víray/.   Lat.   Suppression or concealment of the truth.   It is a rule of equity, as well as of law, that a *suppressio veri* is equivalent to a *suggestio falsi;* and where either the suppression of the truth or the suggestion of what is false can be proved, in a fact material to the contract, the party injured may have relief against the contract.

Suppressio veri, expressio falsi /səprésh(iy)ow víray, əksprésh(iy)ow fól(t)say/.   Suppression of the truth is [equivalent to] the expression of what is false.

Suppressio veri, suggestio falsi /səprésh(iy)ow víray, səgjésch(iy)ow fól(t)say/.   Suppression of the truth is [equivalent to] the suggestion of what is false.

Supra /s(y)úwprə/.   Lat.   Above; upon.   This word occurring by itself in a book refers the reader to a previous part of the book, like *"ante;"* it is also the initial word of several Latin phrases.

Supra protest /s(y)úwprə prówtèst/.   See **Protest.**

Supra-riparian /s(y)úwprə-rəpériyən/. Upper riparian; higher up the stream. This term is applied to the estate, rights, or duties of a riparian proprietor whose land is situated at a point nearer the source of the stream than the estate with which it is compared.

Supremacy. The state of being supreme, or in the highest station of power; paramount authority; sovereignty; sovereign power.

Act of supremacy. The English statute 1 Eliz., c. 1, whereby the supremacy and autonomy of the crown in spiritual or ecclesiastical matters was declared and established.

Oath of supremacy. An oath to uphold the supreme power of the kingdom of England in the person of the reigning sovereign.

Supremacy clause. The clause of Art. VI of the U.S. Constitution which declares that all laws made in pursuance of the Constitution and all treaties made under the authority of the United States shall be the "supreme law of the land" and shall enjoy legal superiority over any conflicting provision of a State constitution or law. See also **Preemption.**

Suprema potestas seipsam dissolvere potest /səpríymə pətéstæs siyípsəm dəzólvəriy pówdəst/. Supreme power can dissolve itself.

Supreme. Superior to all other things.

Supreme court. An appellate court existing in most of the states. In the federal court system, and in most states, it is the highest appellate court or court of last resort. In others (such as New York) the supreme court is a court of general original jurisdiction, possessing also (in New York) some appellate jurisdiction, but not the court of last resort. See also **Court of Appeals.**

Supreme court of errors. Formerly, the court of last resort in Connecticut, now called "Supreme Court".

Supreme Court of the United States. The U.S. Supreme Court comprises the Chief Justice of the United States and such number of Associate Justices as may be fixed by Congress. Under that authority, and by virtue of the act of June 25, 1948 (62 Stat. 869; 28 U.S.C.A. 1), the number of Associate Justices is eight. Power to nominate the Justices is vested in the President of the United States, and appointments are made by and with the advice and consent of the Senate. Article III, section 1, of the Constitution further provides that "the Judges, both of the supreme and inferior Courts, shall hold their Offices during good Behaviour, and shall, at stated Times, receive for their Services, a Compensation, which shall not be diminished during their Continuance in Office."

Supreme Judicial Court. Highest appellate court in Maine and Massachusetts.

Supreme law of the land. See **Supremacy clause.**

Supreme power. The highest authority in a state, all other powers in it being inferior thereto.

Supremus /səpríyməs/. Lat. Last; the last.

Supremus est quem nemo sequitur /səpríyməs èst kwém níymow sékwədər/. He is last whom no one follows.

Sur /sər/syúr/. Fr. On; upon; over. In the titles of real actions *"sur"* was used to point out what the writ was founded upon. Thus, a real action brought by the owner of a reversion or seigniory, in certain cases where his tenant repudiated his tenure, was called "a writ of right *sur disclaimer";* So, a writ of entry *sur disseisin* was a real action to recover the possession of land from a disseisor.

Surcharge, *n.* An overcharge; an exaction, impost, or encumbrance beyond what is just and right, or beyond one's authority or power. Term may also refer to a second or further mortgage.

The amount with which a court may charge a fiduciary who has breached his trust through intentional or negligent conduct. The imposition of personal liability on a fiduciary for such conduct.

An additional tax or cost. Overprint on a stamp that changes the denomination. See **Surtax.**

Surcharge, *v.* The imposition of personal liability on a fiduciary for wilful or negligent misconduct in the administration of his fiduciary duties.

In equity practice, to show that a particular item, in favor of the party surcharging, ought to have been included, but was not, in an account which is alleged to be settled or complete. To prove the omission of an item from an account which is before the court as complete, which should be inserted to the credit of the party surcharging. Perkins v. Hart, 24 U.S. 237, 6 L.Ed. 463.

The imposition of an additional tax, impost, or cost. See **Surtax.**

In old English law, to put more cattle upon a common than the herbage will sustain or than the party has a right to do. 3 Bl.Comm. 237.

Second surcharge. In old English law, the surcharge of a common a second time, by the same defendant against whom the common was before admeasured, and for which the *writ of second surcharge* was given by the statute of Westminster, 2. 3 Bl.Comm. 239.

Surcharge and falsify. This phrase, as used in the courts of chancery, denotes the liberty which these courts will occasionally grant to a plaintiff, who disputes an account which the defendant alleges to be settled, to scrutinize particular items therein without opening the entire account. The showing an item for which credit ought to have been given, but was not, is to surcharge the account; the proving an item to have been inserted wrongly is to falsity the account.

Sur cui ante divortium /sàr k(yuw)ay æntiy dəvórsh(iy)əm/. See **Cui ante divortium.**

Sur cui in vita /sàr k(yuw)ay ìn váydə/. A writ that lay for the heir of a woman whose husband had aliened her land in fee, and she had omitted to bring the writ of *cui in vita* for the recovery thereof; in which case her heir might have this writ against the tenant after her decease. See **Cui in vita.**

Sur disclaimer /sàr dəskléymər/. A writ in the nature of a writ of right brought by the lord against a tenant who had disclaimed his tenure, to recover the land.

Surdus /sə́rdəs/. Lat. In the civil law, deaf; a deaf person. *Surdus et mutus,* a deaf and dumb person.

Surenchère /syurònshéhr/. In French law, a party desirous of repurchasing property at auction before the court, can, by offering one-tenth or one-sixth, according to the case, in addition to the price realized at the sale, oblige the property to be put up once more at auction. This bid upon a bid is called a *"surenchère."*

Surety. One who undertakes to pay money or to do any other act in event that his principal fails therein. One bound with his principal for the payment of a sum of money or for the performance of some duty or promise and who is entitled to be indemnified by some one who ought to have paid or performed if payment or performance be enforced against him. Everyone who incurs a liability in person or estate, for the benefit of another, without sharing in the consideration, stands in the position of a "surety," whatever may be the form of his obligation. Howell v. War Finance Corp., C.C.A.Ariz., 71 F.2d 237, 243. Term includes a guarantor. U.C.C. § 1–201(40). See also **Suretyship, contract of.**

Guarantor and surety compared. A surety and guarantor have this in common, that they are both bound for another person; yet there are points of difference between them. A surety is usually bound with his principal by the same instrument, executed at the same time and on the same consideration. He is an original promisor and debtor from the beginning, and is held ordinarily to every known default of his principal. On the other hand, the contract of guarantor is his own separate undertaking, in which the principal does not join. It is usually entered into before or after that of the principal, and is often founded on a separate consideration from that supporting the contract of the principal. The original contract of the principal is not the guarantor's contract, and the guarantor is not bound to take notice of its nonperformance. The surety joins in the same promise as his principal and is primarily liable; the guarantor makes a separate and individual promise and is only secondarily liable. His liability is contingent on the default of his principal, and he only becomes absolutely liable when such default takes place and he is notified thereof. "Surety" and "guarantor" are both answerable for debt, default, or miscarriage of another; but liability of guarantor is, strictly speaking, secondary and collateral, while that of surety is original, primary, and direct. In case of suretyship there is but one contract, and surety is bound by the same agreement which binds his principal, while in case of guaranty there are two contracts, and guarantor is bound by independent undertaking. Howell v. Commissioner of Internal Revenue, C.C.A.8, 69 F.2d 447, 450. A surety is an insurer of the debt or obligation; a guarantor is an insurer of the solvency of the principal debtor or of his ability to pay. Under U.C.C., term "surety" includes a guarantor. § 1–201(40). See also **Guarantor.**

Surety bond. See **Bond.**

Surety company. A company, usually incorporated, whose business is to assume the responsibility of a surety on the bonds of officers, trustees, executors, guardians, etc., in consideration of a fee proportioned to the amount of the security required.

Surety insurance. This phrase is generally used as synonymous with "guaranty insurance."

Surety of the peace. A species of preventive justice, and consists in obliging those persons whom there is a probable ground to suspect of future misbehavior, to stipulate with, and to give full assurance to, the public that such offense as is apprehended shall not take place, by finding pledges or securities for keeping the peace, or for their good behavior.

Suretyship, contract of. Contract whereby one party engages to be answerable for debt, default, or miscarriage of another and arises when one is liable to pay debt or discharge obligation, and party is entitled to indemnity from person who should have made the payment in the first instance before surety was so compelled. A contract whereby one person engages to be answerable for the debt, default, or miscarriage of another. An accessory promise by which a person binds himself for another already bound, and agrees with the creditor to satisfy the obligation, if the debtor does not. A lending of credit to aid a principal having insufficient credit of his own; the one expected to pay, having the primary obligation, being the "principal," and the one bound to pay, if the principal does not, being the "surety." See also **Surety.**

Surface. This term, when used in law, is seldom, if ever, limited to mere geometrical superficies, although when used without any qualifying phrase in a deed, it ordinarily signifies only the superficial part of land. And when employed in connection with mining, it usually means that part of the earth or geologic section lying over the minerals in question, unless the contract or conveyance otherwise defines it. Thus, where the surface is granted to one and the underlying coal to another, the "surface" includes the soil and waters which lie above and are superincumbent on the coal. Nevertheless, a conveyance of the "surface," except the oil and gas rights in the land, may be deemed, under certain circumstances, to constitute a conveyance of all the land (including coal deposits), except only the oil and gas rights specifically reserved.

The term "surface," when used as the subject of a conveyance, is not a definite one capable of a definition of universal application, but is susceptible of limitation according to the intention of the parties using it; and in determining its meaning, regard may be had, not only to the language of the deed in which it occurs, but, also to the situation of the parties, the business in which they were engaged, and to the substance of the transaction.

Surface waters. See **Water.**

Surgeon. One whose profession or occupation is to cure diseases, defects, or injuries of the body by manual operation; one who practices surgery.

Surgeon General. The chief medical officer of the United States Public Health Service.

Surgery. Greek words signifying the hand and work. Originally, it was part of the profession of barbers, but later was taken up by physicians and now is recognized as that branch of medical science which treats of mechanical or operative measures for healing diseases, deformities, or injuries. State ex rel. Beck v. Gleason, 148 Kan. 1, 79 P.2d 911.

The practice of *medicine,* in contradistinction to the practice of *surgery,* denotes the treatment of disease by the administration of drugs or other sanative substances. There cannot however be a complete separation between the practice of medicine and surgery; the principles of both are the same throughout, and no one is qualified to practice either who does not properly understand the fundamental principles of both.

Surmise. Idea based on weak evidence, conjecture.

Formerly where a defendant pleaded a local custom, for instance, a custom of the city of London, it was necessary for him to "surmise," that is, to suggest that such custom should be certified to the court by the mouth of the recorder, and without such a surmise the issue was to be tried by the country as other issues of fact are.

Something offered to a court to move it to grant a prohibition, *audita querela,* or other writ grantable thereon.

In ecclesiastical law, an allegation in a libel. A collateral surmise is a surmise of some fact not appearing in the libel.

Sur mortgage /sə̀r mɔ́rgəj/. Upon a mortgage. In some states the method of enforcing the security of a mortgage, upon default, is by a writ of *"scire facias sur mortgage,"* which requires the defendant (mortgagor) to show cause why it should not be foreclosed.

Surname. The family name; the name over and above the Christian name. The part of a name which is not given in baptism. The name of a person which is derived from the common name of his parents. In re Faith's Application, 22 N.J.Misc. 412, 39 A.2d 638, 640. The last name; the name common to all members of a family.

Surplice fees /sə́rpləs fíyz/. In English ecclesiastical law, fees payable on ministerial offices of the church; such as baptisms, funerals, marriages, etc.

Surplus. That which remains of a fund appropriated for a particular purpose; the remainder of a thing; the overplus; the residue. Ordinarily, surplus means residue of assets after liabilities, including capital, have been deducted. American Life & Acc. Ins. Co. v. Love, Mo., 431 S.W.2d 177, 180.

The surplus of a corporation may mean either the net assets of the corporation in excess of all liabilities including capital stock, Winkelman v. General Motors Corp., D.C.N.Y., 44 F.Supp. 960, 996; or what remains after making provisions for all liabilities of every kind, except capital stock. The term is also defined as the residue of assets after defraying liabilities, the excess of net assets over the face value of the stock, the excess of gross assets over the outstanding capital stock, without deducting debts or liabilities; and as the accumulation of moneys or property in excess of the par value of the stock.

As to surplus Earnings; Profit, and Water, see those titles.

Accumulated surplus. That surplus which results from the accumulation of profits.

Acquired surplus. Surplus acquired by the purchase of one business by another.

Appreciation surplus. Surplus which results from the revaluation of the assets of a business.

Appropriated surplus. That portion of surplus which is earmarked or set aside for a specific purpose.

Capital surplus. All surplus which does not arise from the accumulation of profits. It may be created by a financial reorganization or by gifts to the corporation. The entire surplus of a corporation other than its earned surplus. Model Bus.Corp. Act, § 2.

Earned surplus. The portion of the surplus of a corporation equal to the balance of its net profits, income, gains and losses from the date of incorporation, or from the latest date when a deficit was eliminated by an application of its capital surplus or stated capital or otherwise, after deducting subsequent distributions to shareholders and transfers to stated capital and capital surplus to the extent such distributions and transfers are made out of earned surplus. Earned surplus shall include also any portion of surplus allocated to earned surplus in mergers, consolidations or acquisitions of all or substantially all of the outstanding shares or of the property and assets of another corporation, domestic or foreign. Model Bus.Corp. Act, § 2. See also **Earned surplus.**

Initial surplus. That surplus which appears on the financial statement at the commencement of an accounting period and which does not reflect the operations for the period covered by the statement.

Operating surplus. That surplus transferred to earned surplus at the end of an accounting period.

Paid-in surplus. Surplus paid in by stockholders as contrasted to earned surplus that arises from profits.

Reserved surplus. See *Appropriated surplus,* above.

Revaluation surplus. Surplus arising from a revaluation of assets above cost, usually in connection with a recapitalization (sometimes called "recapitalization surplus") or quasi-reorganization (sometimes called "reorganization surplus").

Unearned surplus. Includes paid-in surplus, revaluation surplus, and donated surplus.

Surplusage. Extraneous, impertinent, superfluous, or unnecessary matter. The remainder or surplus of money left. See also **Surplus.**

Pleading. Allegations of matter wholly foreign and impertinent to the cause. All matter beyond the circumstances necessary to constitute the action. Any allegation without which the pleading would yet be adequate. On motion, the court may order stricken from the pleadings any insufficient defense, redundant, immaterial, or scandalous matter. Fed.R.Civil P. 12(f).

Surplusagium non nocet /sə̀rpləséyj(iy)əm nòn nósət/. Surplusage does no harm.

Surprise. Act of taking unawares; sudden confusion or perplexity. In its legal acceptation, denotes an unforeseen disappointment against which ordinary prudence would not have afforded protection.

On motion and upon such terms as are just, the court may relieve a party or his legal representative from a final judgment, order, or proceeding because of surprise. Fed.R.Civil P. 60(b).

Equitable relief. The act by which a party who is entering into a contract is taken unawares, by which sudden confusion or perplexity is created, which renders it proper that a court of equity should relieve the party so surprised. The situation in which a party is placed without any default of his own, which will be injurious to his interests.

Anything which happens without the agency or fault of the party affected by it, tending to disturb and confuse the judgment, or to mislead him, of which the opposite party takes an undue advantage, is in equity a surprise, and one species of fraud for which relief is granted. There does not seem anything technical or peculiar in the word "surprise". Where a court relieves on the ground of surprise, it does so upon the ground that the party has been taken unawares, and that he has acted without due deliberation, and under confused and sudden impressions.

Ground for new trial. As a ground for a new trial, that situation in which a party is unexpectedly placed without fault on his part, which will work injury to his interests. He must show himself to have been diligent at every stage of the proceedings, and that the event was one which ordinary prudence could not have guarded against. A situation or result produced, having a substantive basis of fact and reason, from which the court may justly deduce, as a legal conclusion, that the party will suffer a judicial wrong if not relieved from his mistake. The general rule is that when a party or his counsel is "taken by surprise," in a material point or circumstance which could not have been anticipated, and when want of skill, care, or attention cannot be justly imputed, and injustice has been done, a new trial should be granted.

Surrebutter /sὲrəbádər/. In common law pleading, the plaintiff's answer of fact to the defendant's rebutter. It is governed by the same rules as the replication. It is no longer required under modern pleading.

Surrejoinder /sὲrəjóyndər/. In common law pleading, the plaintiff's answer of fact to the defendant's rejoinder. It is governed in every respect by the same rules as the replication.

Surrender. To give back; yield; render up; restore; and in law, the giving up of an estate to the person who has it in reversion or remainder, so as to merge it in the larger estate. A yielding up of an estate for life or years to him who has an immediate estate in reversion or remainder, wherein the estate for life or years may drown by mutual agreement between them. Roberts Inv. Co. v. Hardie Mfg. Co., 142 Or. 179, 19 P.2d 429, 431; Kimberlin v. Hicks, 150 Kan. 449, 94 P.2d 335, 339. The giving up of a lease before its expiration. In old English law, yielding up a tenancy in a copyhold estate to the lord of the manor for a specified purpose. The giving up by a bankrupt of his property to his creditors or their assignees; also, his due appearance in the bankruptcy court for examination as formerly required by the bankruptcy acts.

Surrender is contractual act and occurs only through consent of both parties. Motch's Adm'r v. Portner, 237 Ky. 25, 34 S.W.2d 744, 745. Surrender differs from "abandonment," as applied to leased premises, inasmuch as the latter is simply an act on the part of the lessee alone; but to show a surrender, a mutual agreement between lessor and lessee that the lease is terminated must be clearly proved. See **Surrender by operation of law.**

Surrender by bail. The act, by bail or sureties in a recognizance, of giving up their principal again into custody, in their own discharge.

Surrender by operation of law. This phrase is properly applied to cases where the tenant for life or years has been a party to some act the validity of which he is by law afterwards estopped from disputing, and which would not be valid if his particular estate continued to exist. An implied surrender occurs when an estate incompatible with the existing estate is accepted, or the lessee takes a new lease of the same lands.

Any acts which are equivalent to an agreement on the part of the tenant to abandon, and on the part of the landlord to resume the possession of the demised premises, amount to a "surrender by operation of law." The rule may be said to be that a surrender is created by operation of law, when the parties to a lease do some act so inconsistent with the subsisting relation of landlord and tenant as to imply that they have both agreed to consider the surrender as made.

Surrenderee. The person to whom a surrender is made.

Surrender of a preference. In bankruptcy practice, the surrender to the assignee in bankruptcy, by a preferred creditor, of anything he may have received under his preference and any advantage it gives him, which he must do before he can share in the dividend. The word as generally defined may denote either compelled or voluntary action. Keppel v. Bank, 197 U.S. 356, 25 S.Ct. 443, 49 L.Ed. 790; Bankruptcy Act, § 547.

Surrender of charter. A corporation created by charter may give up or "surrender" its charter to the people, unless the charter was granted under a statute, imposing indefeasible duties on the bodies to which it applies.

Surrender of copyhold. The mode of conveying or transferring copyhold property from one person to another by means of a surrender, which consisted in the yielding up of the estate by the tenant into the hands of the lord for such purposes as were expressed in the surrender. The process in most manors was for the tenant to come to the steward, either in court or out of court, or else to two customary tenants of the same manor, provided there was a custom to warrant it, and there, by delivering up a rod, a glove, or other symbol, as the custom directs, to resign into the hands of the lord, by the hands and acceptance of his steward, or of the said two tenants, all his interest and title to the estate, in trust, to be again granted out by the lord to such persons and for such uses as were named in the surrender, and as the custom of the manor would warrant. See **Copyhold.**

Surrender of criminals. The act by which the public authorities deliver a person accused of a crime, and who is found in their jurisdiction, to the authorities within whose jurisdiction it is alleged the crime has been committed. See **Extradition; Rendition.**

Surrenderor. One who makes a surrender. One who yielded up a copyhold estate for the purpose of conveying it.

Surrender to uses of will. Formerly a copyhold interest would not pass by will unless it had been surrendered to the use of the will. By English St. 55 Geo. III, c. 192, this was no longer necessary.

Surrender value. In insurance, the current value of a policy which will be paid to the policyholder when he elects to surrender the policy.

Surreptitious /sə̀hrəptíshəs/. Stealthily or fraudulently done, taken away, or introduced.

Surrogate /sə́hrəgət/. The name given in some of the states to the judge or judicial officer who has jurisdiction over the administration of probate matters, guardianships, etc. In other states he is called judge of probate, register, judge of the orphans' court, etc. He is ordinarily a county officer, with a local jurisdiction limited to his county. See **Surrogate court.**

In English law, one that is substituted or appointed in the room of another, as by a bishop, chancellor, judge, etc.; especially an officer appointed to dispense licenses to marry without banns.

Surrogate court. Name of court in certain states with jurisdiction similar to that of probate court.

In New York the Surrogate's Court has jurisdiction over all actions and proceedings relating to the affairs of decedents, probate of wills, administration of estates and actions and proceedings arising thereunder or pertaining thereto, guardianship of the property of minors, and such other actions and proceedings, not within the exclusive jurisdiction of the supreme court, as may be provided by law.

Surrogate parent. A person other than a parent who stands in loco parentis to the child by virtue of his or her voluntary assumption of parental rights and responsibilities. The person appointed by a juvenile court as a child's advocate in the educational decision-making process in place of the child's natural parents or guardian.

Surround. To inclose on all sides; to encompass.

Surrounding circumstances. Such as may permit inference of culpability on part of defendant under res ipsa loquitur rule, refers not to circumstances directly tending to show lack of care, but only to mere neutral circumstances of control and management by defendant, which may, when explained, appear to be entirely consistent with due care. Hepp v. Quickel Auto & Supply Co., 37 N.M. 525, 25 P.2d 197.

Sursise /sərsáyz/. L. Fr. In old English law, neglect; omission; default; cessation.

Sursum reddere /sə́rsəm rédəriy/. Lat. In old conveyancing, to render up; to surrender.

Sursumredditio /sə̀rsəmrədísh(iy)ow/. Lat. A surrender.

Surtax. An additional tax on what has already been taxed. A tax on a tax; for example: if person must pay a hundred dollar tax on a one thousand dollar income (ten percent), a ten percent surtax would be

an additional ten dollars, not an additional hundred dollars.

Surtax exemption. The portion of taxable income not subject to the surtax.

Surveillance /sərvéy(l)ən(t)s/. Oversight, superintendence, supervision. Police investigative technique involving visual or electronic observation or listening directed at a person or place (*e.g.,* stakeout, tailing suspects, wiretapping, and so on). Its objective is to gather evidence of a crime or merely to accumulate intelligence about suspected criminal activity. See also **Eavesdropping; Wiretapping.**

Survey, *v.* To survey land is to ascertain corners, boundaries, and divisions, with distances and directions, and not necessarily to compute areas included within defined boundaries. To appraise as to value or condition.

Survey, *n.* The process by which a parcel of land is measured and its boundaries and contents ascertained; also a map, plat, or statement of the result of such survey, with the courses and distances and the quantity of the land. See also **Government survey system; Meander lines.**

An investigation or examination. In insurance law, the term has acquired a general meaning, inclusive of what is commonly called the "application," which contains the questions propounded on behalf of the company, and the answers of the assured.

Polling or questioning of public regarding their views on issues, candidates, etc.

Survey of a vessel. A statement of its present condition. Chicago S. S. Lines v. U. S. Lloyds, C.C.A.Ill., 12 F.2d 733, 737. A public document, looked to both by underwriters and owners, as affording the means of ascertaining, at the time and place, the state and condition of the ship and other property at hazard.

Surveyor. One who makes surveys, determines area of portion of earth's surface, length and direction of boundary lines, and contour of surface.

Surveyor of the port. Formerly, a revenue officer of the United States appointed for each of the principal ports of entry, whose duties chiefly concerned the importations at his station and the determination of their amount and valuation. Rev.St.U.S. § 2627 (19 U.S.C.A. § 40).

Survival actions. Term refers to actions for personal injuries which by statute survives death of injured person. Britt v. Sears, 150 Ind.App. 487, 277 N.E.2d 20, 23. An action or cause of action which does not become extinguished with the death of the party claiming the action. See **Survival statutes; Wrongful death statutes.**

Survival statutes. Statutory provision for the survival, after death of the injured person, of certain causes of action for injury to the person whether death results from the injury or from some other cause. The cause of action which survives is for the wrong to the injured person. A type of wrongful death statute, that allows an action to continue, notwithstanding the death of the one who originally had a right to bring the action. Such a right usually may be enforced by or against the estate of the decedent. See also **Wrongful death statutes.**

Survive. To continue to live or exist beyond the life, or existence of; to live through in spite of; live on after passing through; to remain alive; exist in force or operation beyond any period or event specified.

Surviving. Remaining alive. Living beyond the life of another or beyond the happening of some event so as to be entitled to a distribution of property or income. See **Survival actions.**

Surviving spouse. The spouse who outlives the other spouse. Term commonly found in statutes dealing with probate, administration of estates and estate and inheritance taxes.

Survivor. One who survives another; one who outlives another; one who lives beyond some happening; one of two or more persons who lives after the death of the other or others. The word "survivor," however, in connection with the power of one of two trustees to act, is used not only with reference to a condition arising where one of such trustees dies, but also as indicating a trustee who continues to administer the trust after his cotrustee is disqualified, has been removed, renounces, or refuses to act.

Survivorship. The living of one of two or more persons after the death of the other or others. Survivorship is where a person becomes entitled to property by reason of his having survived another person who had an interest in it. United States v. Jacobs, 306 U.S. 363, 59 S.Ct. 551, 555, 83 L.Ed. 763. See also **Presumption of survivorship; Tenancy** (*Joint tenancy*).

Survivorship annuity. Type of annuity contract which provides for payments beyond the life of the annuitant, as for example, to a widow of the annuitant.

Susceptible. Capable.

Suspect. To have a slight or even vague idea concerning;—not necessarily involving knowledge or belief or likelihood. "Suspect" with reference to probable cause as grounds for arrest without warrant is commonly used in place of the word believe. A person reputed or suspected to be involved in a crime. See also **Probable cause; Suspicion.**

Suspect classifications. With regard to test to be used in determining whether statutory classification constitutes a denial of equal protection, "suspect classifications" are those based on race, alienage, national origin and sex. Anderson v. City of Detroit, 54 Mich. App. 496, 221 N.W.2d 168, 169.

Suspend. To interrupt; to cause to cease for a time; to postpone; to stay, delay, or hinder; to discontinue temporarily, but with an expectation or purpose of resumption. As a form of censure or discipline, to forbid a public officer, attorney, employee, or ecclesiastical person from performing his duties or exercising his functions for a more or less definite interval of time.

To postpone, as a judicial sentence. To cause a temporary cessation, as of work by an employee; to lay off.

See also **Suspension.**

Suspended sentence. A conviction of a crime followed by a sentence that is given formally, but not actually served. A suspended sentence in criminal law means in effect that defendant is not required at the time sentence is imposed to serve the sentence. Richards v. Crump, 260 S.C. 133, 194 S.E.2d 575, 576. See also **Sentence** (*Suspension of sentence*).

Suspense. When a rent, profit *à prendre,* and the like, are, in consequence of the unity of possession of the rent, etc., of the land out of which they issue, not *in esse* for a time, they are said to be in suspense, *tunc dormiunt;* but they may be revived or awakened.

Suspension. A temporary stop, a temporary delay, interruption, or cessation. Thus, we speak of a *suspension* of the writ of *habeas corpus,* of a statute, of the power of alienating an estate, of a person in office, etc.

A temporary cutting off or debarring one, as from the privileges of one's profession.

Temporary withdrawal or cessation from employment as distinguished from permanent severance accomplished by removal; "removal" being, however, the broader term, which may on occasion include suspension.

Ecclesiastical law. An ecclesiastical censure, by which a spiritual person is either interdicted the exercise of his ecclesiastical function or hindered from receiving the profits of his benefice. It may be partial or total, for a limited time, or forever, when it is called "deprivation" or "amotion."

Suspension of a right. The act by which a party is deprived of the exercise of his right for a time. A temporary stop of a right, a partial extinguishment for a time, as contrasted with a complete extinguishment, where the right is absolutely dead. Suspension of a right in an estate is a temporary or partial withholding of it from use or exercise. It differs from extinguishment, because a suspended right is susceptible of being revived, which is not the case where the right was extinguished.

Suspension of arms. An agreement between belligerents, made for a short time or for a particular place, to cease hostilities between them. See also **Armistice.**

Suspension of a statute. A temporary termination of its power of law. The suspension of a statute for a limited time operates so as to prevent its operation for the time; but it has not the effect of a repeal.

Suspension of business. These words in a statute contemplate an interruption of ordinary business operations, evidenced by some objective features. An interruption of the ordinary course of business, other than a mere failure to meet maturing obligations.

Suspensive condition. See **Condition.**

Suspensory condition. See **Condition.**

Sus. per coll /sás. pàr kól/. An abbreviation of "*suspendatur per collum*" /sàspendéydər pàr kóləm/, let him be hanged by the neck. Words formerly used in England in signing judgment against a prisoner who was to be executed; being written by the judge in the margin of the sheriff's calendar or list, opposite the prisoner's name. 4 Bl.Comm. 403.

Suspicion. The act of suspecting, or the state of being suspected; imagination, generally of something ill; distrust; mistrust; doubt. The apprehension of something without proof or upon slight evidence. Suspicion implies a belief or opinion based upon facts or circumstances which do not amount to proof.

Suspicious character. In the criminal laws of some of the states, a person who is known or strongly suspected to be an habitual criminal, or against whom there is reasonable cause to believe that he has committed a crime or is planning or intending to commit one, or whose actions and behavior give good account of himself, and who may therefore be arrested or required to give security for good behavior.

Sustain. To carry on; to maintain. To affirm or approve, as when an appellate court sustains the decision of a lower court. To grant, as when a judge sustains an objection to testimony or evidence, he or she agrees with the objection and gives it effect.

To support; to warrant;—said of evidence in connection with a verdict, decision, etc.

To suffer; bear; undergo. To endure or undergo without failing or yielding; to bear up under.

Suthdure. The south door of a church, where canonical purgation was performed, and plaints, etc., were heard and determined.

Sutler /sátlər/. A person who, as a business, follows an army and sells provisions and liquor to the troops. A small trader who follows an army and who is licensed to sell goods, especially edibles, to the soldiers.

Suum cuique tribuere /s(y)úwəm k(yuw)áykwiy trəbyúwəriy/. Lat. To render to everyone his own. One of the three fundamental maxims of the law laid down by Justinian.

Suus hæres /s(y)úwəs híriyz/. See **Hæres.**

Suus judex /s(y)úwəs júwdeks/. Lat. In old English law, a proper judge; a judge having cognizance of a cause. Literally, one's own judge.

Suzerain /s(y)úwz(ə)rən/. In French and feudal law, the immediate vassal of the king; a crown vassal; a tenant *in capite.* A lord who possesses a fief whence other fiefs issue. Also spelled "suzereign."

A nation that exercises political control over another nation in relation to which it is sovereign.

Term is used as descriptive of relations, ill-defined and vague, which exist between powerful and dependent states; its very indefiniteness being its recommendation. While protecting and protected states tend to draw nearer, the reverse is true of suzerain and vassal states; a protectorate is generally the preliminary to incorporation; suzerainty, to separation.

It is said that suzerainty is title without corresponding power; protectorate is power without corresponding title.

Swain; swainmote /swéyn(mowt)/. See **Swein; Sweinmote.**

Swamp. Wet, spongy land; soft, low ground saturated with water, but not usually covered by it; marshy ground away from seashore. Campbell v. Walker, 137 Or. 375, 2 P.2d 912, 914.

Swamp and overflowed lands. Lands unfit for cultivation by reason of their swampy character and requiring drainage or reclamation to render them available for beneficial use.

Swanimote. See **Sweinmote.**

Swarf-money. Warth-money; or guard-money paid in lieu of the service of castleward.

Swatch. Commercially, a small sample of cloth from which suits, etc., are to be ordered.

Swear. To put on oath; to administer an oath to a person. To take an oath; to become bound by an oath duly administered. To declare on oath the truth (of a pleading, etc.). See also **Affirmation; False swearing; Oath.**

To use obscene or profane language. Its use in public places is an offense in many states.

Swearing in. The administration of an oath as to a trial witness or to a public official or one about to become a public official, as in the case of a person who becomes a judge. See **Oath.**

Swearing the peace. Showing to a magistrate that one has just cause to be afraid of another in consequence of his menaces, in order to have him bound over to keep the peace.

Sweat equity. Equity created in property through labor of owner in making improvements to property.

Sweating. The questioning of a person in custody charged with crime with intent to obtain information concerning his connection therewith or knowledge thereof by plying him with questions, or by threats or other wrongful means, extorting information to be used against him. Such interrogation is unconstitutional. See **Interrogation; Miranda Rule.**

Sweat shop. A plant whose employees are overworked and paid low wages, or a place where employees are required to work to an extent hardly endurable, and in the public mind the term imputes unsavory and illegal business practices. Masters v. Sun Mfg. Co., 237 Mo.App. 240, 165 S.W.2d 701, 703. Sweat shops resulted in the enactment of wage and hour laws, child labor laws, minimum wage laws, etc.

Sweeping. Comprehensive; including in its scope many persons or objects; as, a sweeping objection.

Sweepstakes. In horse racing, the sum of the stakes for which the subscribers agree to pay for each horse nominated.

Sweeteners. Inducement to a brokerage firm to enter into an underwriting arrangement with an issuer.

Sweetheart contract. Derogatory term used to describe a contract between a union and an employer in which concessions are granted to one or to the other for purpose of keeping a rival union out.

Swein /swéyn/. In old English law, a freeman or freeholder within the forest.

Sweinmote /swéynmòwt/. In forest law, a court holden before the verderors, as judges, by the stewart of the sweinmote, thrice in every year, the *sweins* or freeholders within the forest composing the jury. Its principal jurisdiction was—*First,* to inquire into the oppressions and grievances committed by the officers of the forest; and, *secondly,* to receive and try presentments certified from the court of attachments in offenses against vert and venison. 3 Bl.Comm. 72.

Swell. To enlarge or increase. In an action of tort, circumstances of aggravation may "swell" the damages.

Swift v. Tyson Case. An early case decided in 1842 by the U.S. Supreme Court, 41 (16 Pet.) U.S. 1, 10 L.Ed. 865, which held that federal courts in suits founded on diversity of citizenship were free to exercise an independent judgment in matters of "general" law; *i.e.* matters not at all dependent upon local statutes or local usages of a fixed and permanent operation. Swift v. Tyson was overruled by Erie R.R. Co. v. Tompkins, 304 U.S. 64, 58 S.Ct. 817, 82 L.Ed. 1188 which requires the application of state law in diversity actions under most circumstances. See **Erie v. Tompkins; Federal common law.**

Swift witness. A term colloquially applied to a witness who is unduly zealous or partial for the side which calls him, and who betrays his bias by his extreme readiness to answer questions or volunteer information.

Swindle. A scheme for cheating or defrauding.

Swindler. A cheat; one guilty of defrauding divers persons.

Swindling. Cheating and defrauding with deliberate artifice. Usually applied to a transaction where the guilty party procures the delivery to him, under a pretended contract, of the personal property of another, with the felonious design of appropriating it to his own use. The acquisition of any personal or movable property, money, or instrument of writing conveying or securing a valuable right, by means of some false or deceitful pretense or device, or fraudulent representation, with intent to appropriate the same to the use of the party so acquiring, or of destroying or impairing the rights of the party justly entitled to the same.

To make out offense of "cheating" and "swindling" by false representations, state must prove that representations were made, that representations were knowingly and designedly false, that such were made with intent to defraud, that such did defraud, that representations related to existing fact or past event, and that party to whom representations were made, relying on their truth, was thereby induced to part with his property.

See **False pretenses; Fraud.**

Switch-yard doctrine. The doctrine that there can be no implied license to the public to use the track of a railroad company within the limits of its switch-yard.

Swoling of land. Term in old English law, meaning so much land as one's plow can till in a year; a hide of land.

Sworn. Frequently used interchangeably with "verified." See **Affirmation; Oath; Swear; Verify.**

Sworn brothers. In old English law, persons who, by mutual oaths, covenant to share in each other's fortunes.

Sworn clerks in chancery. Certain officers in the English court of chancery, whose duties were to keep the records, make copies of pleadings, etc. Their offices were abolished by St. 5 & 6 Vict., c. 103.

Sworn statement. Listing by contractor-builder of all of his suppliers and sub-contractors and their respective bids. Such is required by lending institution for interim construction financing.

Syb and som /síb ǽnd sówm/. A Saxon form of greeting, meaning peace and safety.

Syllabus. An abstract; a headnote; a note prefixed to the report or opinion of an adjudged case, containing an epitome or brief statement of the rulings of the court upon the point or points decided in the case. The syllabus constitutes no part of the opinion of the Court but is prepared by the Reporter of Decisions for the convenience of the reader. See United States v. Detroit Timber & Lumber Co., 200 U.S. 321, 337, 26 S.Ct. 282, 287, 50 L.Ed. 499. Ordinarily, where a headnote, even though prepared by the court, is given no special force by statute or rule of court, the opinion is to be looked to for the original and authentic statement of the grounds of decision. Burbank v. Ernst, 232 U.S. 162, 34 S.Ct. 299, 58 L.Ed. 551. See also **Digest; Headnote.**

Syllogism. In logic, the full logical form of a single argument. It consists of three propositions (two premises and the conclusion), and these contain three terms, of which the two occurring in the conclusion are brought together in the premises by being referred to a common class.

Sylva cædua /sílvə síyjuwə/. Lat. In ecclesiastical law, wood of any kind which was kept on purpose to be cut, and which, being cut, grew again from the stump or root.

Symbolæography /sìmbəliyógrəfiy/. The art or cunning rightly to form and make written instruments. It is either judicial or extrajudicial; the latter being wholly occupied with such instruments as concern matters not yet judicially in controversy, such as instruments of agreements or contracts, and testaments or last wills.

Symbolic delivery. The constructive delivery of the subject-matter of a sale or gift, where it is cumbersome or inaccessible, by the actual delivery of some article which is conventionally accepted as the symbol or representative of it, or which renders access to it possible, or which is evidence of the purchaser's or donee's title to it. Thus, a present gift of the contents of a box in a bank vault, accompanied by a transfer of the key thereto, is valid as a symbolical delivery.

Symbolic speech. A person's conduct which expresses opinions or thoughts about a subject and which may or may not be protected by the First Amendment. Actions which have as their primary purpose the expression of ideas as in the case of students who wore black arm bands to protest the war in Viet Nam. Such conduct is generally protected under the First Amendment as "pure speech" because very little conduct is involved. Tinker v. Des Moines School Dist., 393 U.S. 503, 89 S.Ct. 733, 21 L.Ed.2d 731. However, not all such conduct is protected. The burning of a draft card was not protected speech because of the government's substantial interest. U. S. v. O'Brien, 391 U.S. 367, 88 S.Ct. 1673, 20 L.Ed.2d 672.

Symbolum animæ /símbələm ǽnəmiy/. Lat. A mortuary, or soul scot.

Symmetry. Due proportion of several parts of a body to each other; adaptation of the form or dimensions of the several parts of a thing to each other; harmonious relation of parts; conformance; consistency; congruity; correspondence or similarity of form, dimensions, or parts on opposite sides of an axis, center, or a dividing plane.

Symond's inn. Formerly an inn of chancery.

Sympathetic strike. A boycott. See **Boycott; Strike.**

Synallagmatic contract /sìnəlægmǽdək kóntrækt/. In the civil law, a bilateral or reciprocal contract, in which the parties expressly enter into mutual engagements, each binding himself to the other. Such are the contracts of sale, hiring, etc.

Syncopare. To cut short, or pronounce things so as not to be understood.

Syndic /síndək/. In the civil law, an advocate or patron; a burgess or recorder; an agent or attorney who acts for a corporation or university; an actor or procurator; an assignee. The term corresponds very nearly with that of assignee under the common law.

In English common law, an agent appointed by a corporation for the purpose of obtaining letters of guardianship and the like, to whom such letters were issued.

In French law, the person who is commissioned by the courts to administer a bankruptcy. He fulfills the same functions as the trustee or assignee. Also, one who is chosen to conduct the affairs and attend to the concerns of a body corporate or community. In this sense the word corresponds to director or manager.

In Louisiana, the assignee of a bankrupt. Also, one of several persons to be elected by the creditors of a succession, for the purpose of administering thereon, whenever a succession has been renounced by the heirs, or has been accepted under the benefit of an inventory, and neither the beneficiary heirs, their attorney in fact, nor tutor will accept the administration and give the security required.

Syndicalism /síndəkəlìzəm/. The theory, plan, or practice of trade-union action which aims by the general strike and direct action to establish control by local organizations of workers over the means and processes of production.

A form or development of trade-unionism, originating in France, which aims at the possession of the means of production and distribution, and ultimately at the control of society and government, by the federated bodies of industrial workers, and which seeks to realize its purposes through the agency of general strikes and of terrorism, sabotage, violence, or other criminal means.

Criminal syndicalism. Any doctrine or precept advocating, teaching, or aiding and abetting the commission of crime, sabotage (defined in the act as willful and malicious physical damage or injury to physical property), or unlawful acts of force and violence or unlawful methods of terrorism, as a means of accomplishing a change in industrial ownership, or control, or effecting any political change. Gitlow v. New York, 268 U.S. 652, 45 S.Ct. 625, 69 L.Ed. 1138; Whitney v. California, 274 U.S. 357, 47 S.Ct. 641, 71 L.Ed. 1095. See also **Criminal.**

Syndicate /síndəkət/. An association of individuals, formed for the purpose of conducting and carrying out some particular business transaction, ordinarily of a financial character, in which the members are mutually interested. An organization formed for some temporary purpose, such as the organization of a real estate trust and the sale of shares to the public. Syndicates may exist as corporations or partnerships (either general or limited).

A group of investment bankers who together underwrite and distribute a new issue of securities or a large block of an outstanding issue. An association of securities broker-dealers, usually in writing, who assist the principal underwriter in the controlled distribution of the securities of an issuer.

Syndicating. Gathering materials suitable for newspaper publication from writers and artists and distributing the same at regular intervals to newspapers throughout the country for publication on the same day.

Syndication. Act or process of forming a syndicate.

Syndicos, or **syndicus** /síndəkòs/síndəkəs/. One chosen by a college, municipality, etc., to defend its cause. See **Syndic.**

Syngraph /síŋgræf/. The name given by the canonists to deeds or other written instruments of which both parts were written on the same piece of parchment, with some word or letters of the alphabet written between them, through which the parchment was cut in such a manner as to leave half the word on one part and half on the other. It thus corresponded to the chirograph or indenture of the common law. 2 Bl.Comm. 295, 296.

Formerly such writings were attested by the subscription and crosses of the witnesses; afterwards, to prevent frauds and concealments, they made deeds of mutual covenant in a script and rescript, or in a *part* and *counterpart,* and in the middle between the two copies they wrote the word *syngraphus* in large letters, which, being cut through the parchment and one being delivered to each party, on being afterwards put together proved their authenticity.

A deed, bond, or other written instrument under the hand and seal of all the parties. It was so called because the parties *wrote together.*

Synod /sínəd/. A meeting or assembly of ecclesiastical persons concerning religion; being the same thing, in Greek, as convocation in Latin. There are four kinds: (1) A general or universal synod or council, where bishops of all nations meet; (2) a national synod of the clergy of one nation only; (3) a provincial synod, where ecclesiastical persons of a province only assemble, being now what is called the "convocation;" (4) a diocesan synod, of those of one diocese. A synod in Scotland is composed of three or more presbyteries.

A convention of bishops and elders within a district including at least three presbyteries. Trustees of Pencader Presbyterian Church in Pencader Hundred v. Gibson, 26 Del.Ch. 375, 22 A.2d 782, 788. A meeting of the few adjoining presbyteries,—not the same as an ecumenical council, which is a council of all, and not of a part.

Synodal /sənódəl/. A tribute or payment in money paid to the bishop or archdeacon by the inferior clergy, at the Easter visitation.

Synodales testes /sìnədéyliyz téstiyz/. L. Lat. Synodsmen (corrupted into sidesmen) were the urban and rural deans, now the church-wardens. See **Sidesmen.**

Synonymous. Expressing the same or nearly the same idea.

Synopsis. A brief or partial statement, less than the whole; an epitome; synonymous with summary. See **Abstract; Digest; Syllabus.**

System. Orderly combination or arrangement, as of particulars, parts, or elements into a whole; especially such combination according to some rational principle. Any methodic arrangement of parts. Method; manner; mode.

T

T. As an abbreviation, this letter may stand for such terms as "term", "territory", "title", "table".

Every person who was convicted of felony, short of murder, and admitted to the benefit of clergy, was at one time marked with this letter upon the brawn of the thumb. Abolished by 7 & 8 Geo. IV, c. 27.

By a law of the Province of Pennsylvania, A.D. 1698, it was provided that a convicted thief should wear a badge in the form of the letter "T.," upon his left sleeve, which badge should be at least four inches long and of a color different from that of his outer garment.

Tabard /tǽbərd/. A short gown; a herald's coat; a surcoat.

Tabarder /tǽbərdər/. One who wears a tabard or short gown; the name is still used as the title of certain bachelors of arts on the old foundation of Queen's College, Oxford.

Tabella /təbélə/. Lat. In Roman law, a tablet. Used in voting, and in giving the verdict of juries and decision of judges; and, when written upon, commonly translated "ballot." The laws which introduced and regulated the mode of voting by ballot were called *"leges tabellariæ."*

Tabellio /təbél(i)yow/. Lat. In Roman law, an officer corresponding in some respects to a notary. His business was to draw legal instruments (contracts, wills, etc.), and witness their execution.

Tabelliones differed from notaries in many respects: they had judicial jurisdiction in some cases, and from their judgments there were no appeals. Notaries were then the clerks or aiders of the *tabelliones;* they received the agreements of the parties, which they reduced to short *notes;* and these contracts were not binding until they were written in *extenso,* which was done by the *tabelliones.*

Tabernaculum /tæ̀bərnǽk(y)ələm/. In old records, a public inn, or house of entertainment.

Tabernarius /tæ̀bərnériyəs/. Lat. In the civil law, a shopkeeper.

In old English law, a taverner or tavern keeper.

Tabes dorsalis /téybiyz dorséyləs/. In medical jurisprudence, another name for locomotor ataxia. It accompanies attacks of tabetic dementia. See **Insanity.**

Tabetic dementia /təbédək dəménsh(iy)ə/. See **Insanity.**

Table, *v.* To suspend consideration of a pending legislative bill or other measure.

Table, *n.* A synopsis, condensed statement or listing bringing together numerous items or details so as to be comprehended in a single view; as genealogical tables, exhibiting the names and relationships of all the persons composing a family; life and annuity tables, used by actuaries; interest tables, etc. Term may also refer to an alphabetical, numerical, etc. listing of cases, statutes, court rules, and the like, cited or referred to in a legal publication. See **Table of cases.**

Tableau of distribution /tǽblow əv dìstrəbyúwshən/tǽb-lów°/. In Louisiana, a list of creditors of an insolvent estate, stating what each is entitled to.

Table de marbre /táblə də márbrə/. Fr. In old French law, table of Marble; a principal seat of the admiralty, so called. These Tables de Marbre are frequently mentioned in the Ordonnance of the Marine.

Table of cases. An alphabetical list of the adjudged cases cited, referred to, or digested in a legal textbook, volume of reports, or digest, with references to the sections, pages, or paragraphs where they are respectively cited, etc., which is commonly either prefixed or appended to the volume.

Table rents. In English law, payments which used to be made to bishops, etc., reserved and appropriated to their table or housekeeping.

Tabula /tǽb(y)ələ/. Lat. In the civil law, a table or tablet; a thin sheet of wood, which, when covered with wax, was used for writing.

Tabulæ /tǽbyəliy/. Lat. In Roman law, tables. Writings of any kind used as evidences of a transaction. Contracts and written instruments of all kinds, especially wills. So called because originally written on tablets and with wax.

Tabulæ nuptiales /tǽbyəliy nəpshiyéyliyz/. In the civil law, a written record of a marriage; or the agreement as to the *dos.*

Tabula in naufragio /tǽbyələ in nofréyj(iy)ow/. Lat. A plank in a shipwreck. This phrase is used metaphorically to designate the power subsisting in a third mortgagee, who took without notice of the second mortgage, to acquire the first incumbrance, attach it to his own, and thus squeeze out and get satisfaction, before the second is admitted to the fund. It may be fairly said that the doctrine survives only in the unjust and much-criticised English rule of tacking. See **Tacking.** The use of the expression is attributed to Sir Matthew Hale.

Tabularius /tæbyəlériyəs/. Lat. A notary, or tabellio.

Tac, tak /tǽk/. In old records, a kind of customary payment by a tenant.

T–account. Account form shaped like the letter T with the title above the horizontal line. Debits are shown to the left of the vertical line; credits, to the right. In bookkeeping, an original form of account in which debits and credits may be recorded on the appropriate side of the "T".

Tac free /tǽk fríy/. In old records, free from the common duty or imposition of *tac.*

Tacit /tǽsət/. Existing, inferred, or understood without being openly expressed or stated; implied by silence or silent acquiescence, as a tacit agreement or a tacit understanding. State v. Chadwick, 150 Or. 645, 47 P.2d 232, 234. Done or made in silence, implied or indicated, but not actually expressed. Manifested by the refraining from contradiction or objection; inferred from the situation and circumstances, in the absence of express matter.

Tacit acceptance. In the civil law, a tacit acceptance of an inheritance takes place when some act is done by the heir which necessarily supposes his intention to accept and which he would have no right to do but in his capacity as heir. Civ.Code La. art. 988.

Tacit admissions. An acknowledgment or concession of a fact inferred from either silence or from the substance of what one has said.

Tacita quædam habentur pro expressis /tǽsədə kwíydəm həbéntər pròw əksprésəs/. Things unexpressed are sometimes considered as expressed.

Tacit dedication. Of property for public use is dedication arising from silence or inactivity, without express contract or agreement. Goree v. Midstates Oil Corporation, 205 La. 988, 18 So.2d 591, 596.

Tacite /tǽsədiy/. Lat. Silently; impliedly; tacitly.

Tacit hypothecation. In the civil law, a species of lien or mortgage which is created by operation of law without any express agreement of the parties. In admiralty law, this term is sometimes applied to a maritime lien, which is not, strictly speaking, an hypothecation in the Roman sense of the term, though it resembles it.

Tacit law. A law which derives its authority from the common consent of the people without any legislative enactment.

Tacit mortgage. In the law of Louisiana, the law alone in certain cases gives to the creditor a mortgage on the property of his debtor, without it being requisite that the parties should stipulate it. This is called "legal mortgage." It is called also "tacit mortgage," because it is established by the law without the aid of any agreement.

Tacit relocation. A doctrine borrowed from the Roman law. It is a presumed renovation of the contract from the period at which the former expired, and is held to arise from implied consent of parties, in consequence of their not having signified their intention that agreement should terminate at the period stipulated. Though the original contract may have been for a longer period than one year, the renewed agreement can never be for more than one year, because verbal contract of location can extend longer. Srygley v. City of Nashville, 175 Tenn. 417, 135 S.W.2d 451.

Tack. To annex some junior lien to a first lien, thereby acquiring priority over an intermediate one. See **Tacking.**

Tacking. The term is applied especially to the process of making out title to land by adverse possession, when the present occupant and claimant has not been in possession for the full statutory period, but adds or "tacks" to his own possession that of previous occupants under whom he claims. That doctrine which permits an adverse possessor to add his period of possession to that of a prior adverse possessor in order to establish a continuous possession for the statutory period. Deyrup v. Schmitt, 132 Vt. 423, 425, 321 A.2d 42, 44.

The term is also used in a number of other connections, as of possessions, disabilities, or items in accounts or other dealings. In these several cases the purpose of the proposed tacking is to avoid the bar of a statute of limitations. See Davis v. Coblens, 174 U.S. 719, 19 S.Ct. 832, 43 L.Ed. 1147.

Tacking in application by motor carriers for certificates of public convenience and necessity is joinder of two or more separate grants of authority at a point common to both. Midwest Emery Freight System, Inc. v. U. S., D.C.Ill., 295 F.Supp. 112, 115.

The uniting of securities given at different times, so as to prevent any intermediate purchaser from claiming a title to redeem or otherwise discharge one lien, which is prior, without redeeming or discharging the other liens also, which are subsequent to his own title. The term is particularly applied to the action of a third mortgagee who, by buying the first lien and uniting it to his own, gets priority over the second mortgagee.

Tactis sacrosanctis /tǽktəs sækrəsǽŋktəs/. Lat. In old English law, touching the holy evangelists. A bishop may swear *visis evangeliis* [looking at the Gospels], and not *tactis,* and it is good enough.

Tacto per se sancto evangelio /tǽktow pər síy sǽŋktow əvæŋgíyl(i)yow/. Lat. Having personally touched the holy Gospel. The description of a corporal oath.

Taft-Hartley Act. The Wagner Act was amended in 1947 by the Taft-Hartley Act to balance some of the advantages given to unions under the Wagner Act by imposing corresponding duties on unions. Principal changes imposed by the Act included the following: abolishment of the closed shop, but permitting the union shop under conditions specified in the Act; exempting supervisors from coverage of the Act; requiring the N.L.R.B. to accord equal treatment to both independent and affiliated unions; permitting the employer to file a representation petition even though only one union seeks to represent the employees; granting employees the right not only to organize and bargain collectively but also to refrain from such activities; permitting employees to file decertification petitions for elections to determine whether or not employees desire to revoke a union's designation as their bargaining agent; declaring certain activities engaged in by unions to be unfair labor practices; giving to employers, employees, and unions new guarantees of the right of free speech; providing for settlement by the N.L.R.B. of certain jurisdictional disputes; vested in the General Counsel, rather than in the Board the authority to investigate and prosecute unfair labor practices. 29 U.S.C.A. § 141 et seq.

Tail. Limited; abridged; reduced; curtailed, as a fee or estate in fee, to a certain order of succession, or to certain heirs.

Tailage. See **Tallage.**

Tail, estate in. An estate of inheritance, which, instead of descending to heirs generally, goes to the heirs of the donee's body, which means his lawful issue, his children, and through them to his grandchildren in a direct line, so long as his posterity endures in a regular order and course of descent, and upon the death of the first owner without issue, the estate determines.

Several tail. An entail severally to two; as if land is given to two men and their wives, and to the heirs of their bodies begotten; here the donees have a joint estate for their two lives, and yet they have a several inheritance, because the issue of the one shall have his moiety, and the issue of the other the other moiety.

Tail after possibility of issue extinct. A species of estate fail which arises where one is tenant in special tail, and a person from whose body the issue was to spring dies without issue, or, having left issue, that issue becomes extinct. In either of these cases the surviving tenant in special tail becomes "tenant in tail after possibility of issue extinct." 2 Bl.Comm. 124.

Tail female. When lands are given to a person and the *female* heirs of his or her body. The male heirs are not capable of inheriting it.

Tail general. An estate in tail granted to one "and the heirs of his body begotten," which is called "tail general" because, how often soever such donee in tail be married, his issue in general by all and every such marriage is, in successive order, capable of inheriting the estate tail *per formam doni.* 2 Bl.Comm. 113. This is where an estate is limited to a man and the heirs of his body, without any restriction at all; or, according to some authorities, with no other restriction than that in relation to sex. Thus, tail male general is the same thing as tail male; the word "general," in such case, implying that there is no other restriction upon the descent of the estate than that it must go in the male line. So an estate in tail female general is an estate in tail female. The word "general," in the phrase, expresses a purely negative idea, and may denote the absence of any restriction, or the absence of some given restriction which is tacitly understood.

Tail male. When certain lands are given to a person and the *male* heirs of his or her body. The female heirs are not capable of inheriting it.

Tail special. This denotes an estate in tail where the succession is restricted to certain heirs of the donee's body, and does not go to all of them in general; *e.g.,* where lands and tenements are given to a man and "the heirs of his body on Mary, his now wife, to be begotten;" here no issue can inherit but such special issue as is engendered between those two, not such as the husband may have by another wife, and therefore it is called "special tail." 2 Bl.Comm. 113. It is defined as the limitation of lands and tenements to a man and his wife and the heirs of their two bodies. But the phrase need not be thus restricted. Tail special, in its largest sense, is where the gift is restrained to certain heirs of the donor's body, and does not go to all of them in general.

Taille /táy/téyl/. Fr. In old English law, the fee which is opposed to fee-simple, because it is so minced or pared that it is not in the owner's free power to dispose of it, but it is, by the first giver, cut or divided from all other, and tied to the issue of the donee,—in short, an estate-tail.

In old French law, a tax or assessment levied by the king, or by any great lord, upon his subjects, usually taking the form of an imposition upon the owners of real estate. The equivalent of the English tallage— the typical direct tax in France of the Middle Ages, as tonlieu was the generic term for an indirect tax. See **Tallage.**

Taint. A conviction of felony, or the person so convicted.

Take. To lay hold of; to gain or receive into possession; to seize; to deprive one of the use or possession of; to assume ownership. Thus, constitutions generally provide that a man's property shall not be *taken* for public uses without just compensation. Fifth Amend., U.S.Const. Property may be deemed "taken" within the meaning of these constitutional provisions when it is totally destroyed or rendered valueless, or when it is damaged by a public use in connection with an actual taking by the exercise of eminent domain, or when there is interference with use of property to owner's prejudice, with resulting diminution in value thereof. Webster County v. Lutz, 234 Ky. 618, 28 S.W.2d 966, 967. A "taking" has occurred when the entity clothed with power of eminent domain substantially deprives owner of use and enjoyment of his property. Petition of Cornell Industrial Electric, Inc., 19 Pa.Cmwlth. 599, 338 A.2d 752, 754. "Taking" of property within Constitution is not restricted to mere change of physical possession but includes permanent or temporary deprivation of use to owner if such deprivation amounts to abridgment or destruction by reason of actions of state of lawful rights of individual to possession, use or enjoyment of his land. Hilltop Properties, Inc. v. State, 233 Cal. App.2d 349, 43 Cal.Rptr. 605, 609, 610.

The word "take" has many shades of meaning; the precise meaning which it is to bear in any case depending on the subject with respect to which it is used.

In the law of larceny, to obtain or assume possession of a chattel unlawfully, and without the owner's consent; to appropriate things to one's own use with felonious intent. Thus, an actual *taking* is essential to constitute larceny. A "taking" occurs when a person with a preconceived design to appropriate property to his own use obtains possession of it by means of fraud or trickery.

To seize or apprehend a person; to arrest the body of a person by virtue of lawful process. Thus, a *capias* commands the officer to *take* the body of the defendant.

To acquire the title to an estate; to receive or be entitled to an estate in lands from another person by virtue of some species of title. Thus one is said to "*take* by purchase," "*take* by descent," "*take* a life-interest under the devise," etc.

See also **Taking.**

Take away. This term in a statute punishing every person who shall take away any female under 18 from her father for the purpose of prostitution requires only that such person procure or cause her to go away by some persuasion, enticement, or inducement offered, exercised, or held out to the girl, or by furnishing her the means or money with which to go away.

Take back. To revoke; to retract; as, to take back one's promise.

Take by stealth. To steal; feloniously to take and carry away the personal goods of another; to take without right, secretly, and without leave or consent of the owner.

Take care of. To support; maintain; look after (a person). To pay (a debt). To attend to.

Take effect. To become operative or executed. To be in force, or go into operation.

Take-home pay. The net amount of a paycheck; gross earned wages or salary reduced by deductions for income taxes, Social Security taxes, contributions to fringe benefit plans, union dues, and so on.

Take over. To assume control or management of;—not necessarily involving the transfer of absolute title. See **Tender offer.**

Take over bid. A tender offer (*q.v.*).

Taker. One who takes or acquires; particularly, one who takes an estate by devise. When an estate is granted subject to a remainder or executory devise, the devisee of the immediate interest is called the "first taker."

Take up. To pay or discharge, as a note. Also, sometimes, to purchase a note. To retire a negotiable instrument; to discharge one's liability on it;—said particularly of an indorser or acceptor. A party to a negotiable instrument, particularly an indorser or acceptor, is said to "take up" the paper, or to "retire" it, when he pays its amount, or substitutes other security for it, and receives it again into his own hands.

Taking. In criminal law and torts, the act of laying hold upon an article, with or without removing the same. It implies a transfer of possession, dominion, or control.

Under various statutes relating to sexual offenses, such as the abduction of a girl under the age of 18 years for the purpose of carnal intercourse, to constitute a "taking" no force, actual or constructive, need

be exercised. The "taking" may be effected by persuasion, enticement, or inducement. And it is not necessary that the girl be taken from the control or against the will of those having lawful authority over her.

See also **Constructive taking; Take.**

Eminent domain. See **Take.**

Tale. The count or counting of money. Said to be derived from the same root as "tally." Whence also the modern word "teller."

In old pleading, the plaintiff's count, declaration, or narrative of his case. 3 Bl.Comm. 293.

Tales /téyliyz/. Lat. Such; such men. A number of jurors added to a deficient panel to supply the deficiency. When, by means of challenges or any other cause, a sufficient number of unexceptionable jurors does not appear at the trial, either party may request a "tales," as it is termed; that is, a supply of *such* men as are summoned on the first panel in order to make up the deficiency.

A list of such jurymen as were of the tales, kept in the king's bench office in England.

Tales de circumstantibus /téyliyz dìy sèrkəmstǽntəbəs/. So many of the by-standers. The emphatic words of the old writ awarded to the sheriff to make up a deficiency of jurors out of the persons present in court. 3 Bl.Comm. 365.

The order of the judge for taking such by-standers as jurors.

Talesman. A person summoned to act as a juror from among the by-standers in the court. A person summoned as one of the tales added to a jury.

Talio /téyl(i)yow/. Lat. In the civil law, like for like; punishment in the same kind; the punishment of an injury by an act of the same kind, as an eye for an eye, a limb for a limb, etc.

Talis interpretatio semper fienda est, ut evitetur absurdum et inconveniens, et ne judicium sit illusorium /téyləs intərprətéysh(iy)ow sémpər fayéndə èst, əd èvətíydər əbsárdəm èd ìnkənvíyn(i)yen(d)z, èt níy juwdísh(iy)əm sìd il(y)uwzóriyəm/. Interpretation is always to be made in such a manner that what is absurd and inconvenient may be avoided, and the judgment be not illusory [or nugatory].

Talis non est eadem; nam nullum simile est idem /téyləs nón èst iyéydəm; nǽm nǽləm síməliy èst áydəm/. What is like is not the same; for nothing similar is the same.

Talis res, vel tale rectum, quæ vel quod non est in homine adtunc superstite sed tantummodo est et consistit in consideratione et intelligentia legis, et quod alii dixerunt talem rem vel tale rectum fore in nubibus /téyləs ríyz, vèl téyliy réktəm, kwíy vèl kwód nón èst in hóməniy ǽdtəŋk s(y)uwpárstədiy sèd tǽntəmòwdow èst èt kən(t)sístəd in kən(t)sidəréyshiyówniy èd intèləjénsh(iy)ə líyjəs, èt kwòd éyliyay diksírənt téyləm rém vèl téyliy réktəm fóriy in nyúwbəbəs/. Such a thing or such a right as is not vested in a person then living, but merely exists in the consideration and contemplation of law [is said to be in abeyance], and others have said that such a thing or such a right is in the clouds.

Taliter processum est /tǽlədər prəsésəm èst/. So it has proceeded. Words formerly used in pleading, by which a defendant, in justifying his conduct by the process of an inferior court, alleged the proceedings in such inferior court. Upon pleading the judgment of an inferior court, the proceedings preliminary to such judgment, and on which the same was founded, must, to some extent, appear in the pleading, but the rule is that they may be alleged with a general allegation that "such proceedings were had," instead of a detailed account of the proceedings themselves, and this general allegation is called the *"taliter processum est."* A like concise mode of stating former proceedings in a suit is adopted at the present day in chancery proceedings upon petitions and in actions in the nature of bills of revivor and supplement.

Tallage, or **tailage** /tǽləj/téyləj/. A piece cut out of the whole. Used metaphorically for a share of a man's substance paid by way of tribute, toll, or tax, being derived from the French *"tailler,"* which signifies to cut a piece out of the whole. A term used to denote subsidies, taxes, customs, and, indeed, any imposition whatever by the government for the purpose of raising a revenue. A tax upon cities, townships and boroughs granted to the king as a part of the royal revenue.

Tallager /tǽləjər/. A tax or toll gatherer; mentioned by Chaucer (and spelled "talaigier").

Tallagium /təléyj(iy)əm/. L. Lat. A term including all taxes.

Tallagium facere /təléyj(iy)əm fǽsəriy/. To give up accounts in the exchequer, where the method of accounting was by tallies.

Tallatio /təléysh(iy)ow/. A keeping account by tallies.

Talley, or **tally.** A stick cut into two parts, on each whereof is marked, with notches or otherwise, what is due between debtor and creditor. It was the ancient mode of keeping accounts. One part was held by the creditor, and the other by the debtor. The use of tallies in the exchequer was abolished by St. 23 Geo. III, c. 82, and the old tallies were ordered to be destroyed by St. 4 & 5 Wm. IV, c. 15. By the custom of London, sealed tallies were effectual as a deed. They are admissible by the French and Italian Codes as evidence between traders. It is said that they were negotiable.

Tallies of loan. A term originally used in England to describe exchequer bills, which were issued by the officers of the exchequer when a temporary loan was necessary to meet the exigencies of the government, and charged on the credit of the exchequer in general, and made assignable from one person to another.

Tally trade. A system of dealing by which dealers furnish certain articles on credit, upon an agreement for the payment of the stipulated price by certain weekly or monthly installments.

Tallia /tǽl(i)yə/. L. Lat. A tax or tribute; tallage; a share taken or *cut out* of any one's income or means.

Talmud /talmúwd/tǽlməd/. A work which embodies the civil and canonical law of the Jewish people.

Taltarum's Case /toltérəmz kéys/. A case reported in Yearb. 12 Edw. IV, 19–21, which is regarded as having established the foundation of common recoveries.

Talweg /tálvèyk/. Germ. (Tal meaning valley, Weg meaning way.) Commonly used by writers on international law in definition of water boundaries between states, meaning the middle or deepest or most navigable channel, and while often styled "fairway" or "midway" or "main channel" the word has been taken over into various languages and the doctrine of Talweg is often applicable in respect of water boundaries to sounds, bays, straits, gulfs, estuaries and other arms of the sea and also applies to boundary lakes and landlocked seas whenever there is a deep water sailing channel therein. State of Louisiana v. State of Mississippi, 202 U.S. 1, 26 S.Ct. 408, 421, 50 L.Ed. 913.

Tame. Domesticated; accustomed to man; reclaimed from a natural state of wildness. In the Latin phrase, tame animals are described as *domitæ naturæ*.

Tamen /téymən/. Lat. Notwithstanding; nevertheless; yet.

Tamper. To meddle so as to alter a thing, especially to make illegal, corrupting or perverting changes; as, to tamper with a document or a text; to interfere improperly; to meddle; to busy oneself rashly; to try trifling or foolish experiments. United States v. Tomicich, D.C.Pa., 41 F.Supp. 33, 35. To illegally change as to tamper with the mileage reading on an odometer of a motor vehicle.

Tampering with jury. Embracery. The act of attempting to influence a juror corruptly by promises, threats, persuasions, entreaties, money or any other means except the production of evidence in open court. Such act is a criminal offense. See *e.g.* 18 U.S.C.A. §§ 1503, 1504.

Tam quam /tǽm kwǽm/. A phrase used as the name of a writ of error from inferior courts, when the error is supposed to be as well in giving the judgment as in awarding execution upon it. *(Tam in redditione judicii, quam in adjudicatione executionis.)*

Venire tam quam /vənáyriy tǽm kwǽm/. One by which a jury was summoned, *as well* to try an issue *as* to inquire of the damages on a default.

Tanamoshi /tànamówsh(iy)/. Japanese. An association usually consisting of from fourteen to seventeen members. Members are obligated to contribute an agreed amount per month to the association. Each month a drawing is held and the member who bids the highest amount by way of interest and who has not yet received a loan from the association is entitled to take the aggregate of contributions for that particular month, except that at the last meeting of the association no interest is paid. The interest bid each month is returned to each member of the Tanamoshi as his profit on the amount of his contribution to the association.

Tangible. Having or possessing physical form. Capable of being touched and seen; perceptible to the touch; tactile; palpable; capable of being possessed or realized; readily apprehensible by the mind; real; substantial.

Tangible evidence. Evidence which consists of something which can be seen or touched, *e.g.* gun in homicide trial. In contrast to testimonial evidence, tangible evidence is real evidence. See **Evidence.**

Tangible personal property. Property such as a chair or watch which may be touched or felt in contrast to a contract. Term commonly used in statutes which provide for taxation of personal property.

Tangible property. That which may be felt or touched, and is necessarily corporeal, although it may be either real or personal. H. D. & J. K. Crosswell, Inc. v. Jones, D.C.S.C., 52 F.2d 880, 883.

Tanistry /tǽnəstriy/θón°/. In old Irish law, a species of tenure, founded on ancient usage, which allotted the inheritance of lands, castles, etc., to the "oldest and worthiest man of the deceased's name and blood." It was abolished in the reign of James I.

Tanneria /tænír(i)yə/. In old English law, tannery; the trade or business of a tanner.

Tanteo /tantéyow/. Span. In Spanish law, pre-emption.

Tanto, right of /ráyd əv tántow/. In Mexican law, the right enjoyed by an usufructuary of property, of buying the property at the same price at which the owner offers it to any other person, or is willing to take from another.

Tantum bona valent, quantum vendi possunt /tǽntəm bównə vǽlənt, kwóntəm vénday pósənt/. Goods are worth so much as they can be sold for.

Tantum habent de lege, quantum habent de justitia /tǽntəm héybənt dìy líyjiy, kwóntəm héybənt dìy jə̀stísh(iy)ə/. (Precedents) have value in the law to the extent that they represent justice.

Tapping. The interception of a telephonic or telegraphic message by connecting a device to the lines, permitting a person to hear the message. It is regulated by federal and state statutes and normally requires prior judicial approval. See also **Eavesdropping; Surveillance; Wiretapping.**

Tarde venit /tárdiy víynət/. Lat. The name of a return made by the sheriff to a writ, when it came into his hands too late to be executed before the return-day.

Tare /tér/. A deficiency in the weight or quantity of merchandise by reason of the weight of the box, cask, bag, or other receptacle which contains it and is weighed with it. Also an allowance or abatement of a certain weight or quantity which the seller makes to the buyer, on account of the weight of such box, cask, etc. See **Tret.**

Target company. Company attempted to be taken over in tender offer. See **Tender offer.**

Target offense. In crime of conspiracy, the crime contemplated by the illegal agreement.

Target witness. A person whose testimony the investigating body is principally seeking as in the case of a grand jury which has, as its objective, the information which such a person may give. A witness called before a grand jury against whom the government is seeking an indictment. United States v. Washington, 431 U.S. 181, 97 S.Ct. 1814, 52 L.Ed.2d 238.

Tariff /tǽrəf/. The list or schedule of articles on which a duty is imposed upon their importation into the United States, with the rates at which they are severally taxed. Also the custom or duty payable on such articles. And, derivatively, the system or principle of imposing duties on the importation of foreign merchandise.

A series of schedules or rates of duties on imported goods. Tariffs are for revenue if their primary objects are fiscal; protective if designed to relieve domestic businesses from effective foreign competition; discriminatory if they apply unequally to products of different countries; and retaliatory if they are designed to compel a country to remove artificial trade barriers against the entry of another nation's products.

A public document setting forth services of common carrier being offered, rates and charges with respect to services and governing rules, regulations and practices relating to those services. International Tel. & Tel. Corp. v. United Tel. Co. of Florida, D.C.Fla., 433 F.Supp. 352, 357.

See also **GATT; Most favored nation clause.**

Antidumping tariff. A tariff calculated to prevent the dumping or unloading of imported goods below cost by fixing the tariff at the difference between the price at which the goods commonly sell in the country of origin and the price at which it is to be sold in the importing country. See also **Dumping Act.**

Autonomous tariff. Tariff set by legislation and not by commercial treaties.

Joint tariff. Schedule of rates established by two or more carriers covering shipments between places requiring the use of facilities owned by such carriers.

Preferential tariff. Tariff aimed at favoring the products of one country over those of another. See also **Most favored nation clause; Preferential tariff.**

Protective tariff. Tariff designed to protect or encourage domestic goods by imposing a high rate on imported goods of a similar nature. See also **Protective tariff.**

Revenue tariff. Tariff designed primarily to raise revenues and to support the customs service instead of encouraging production of imported goods.

Tath /táθ/téyθ/. In the counties of Norfolk and Suffolk, the lords of manors anciently claimed the privilege of having their tenants' flocks or sheep brought at night upon their own demesne lands, there to be folded for the improvement of the ground, which liberty was called by the name of the "tath."

Tauri liberi libertas /tóhray líbəray ləbártæs/°líbərtæs/. Lat. A common bull; because he was free to all the tenants within such a manor, liberty, etc.

Tautology /totóləjiy/. Describing the same thing twice in one sentence in equivalent terms; a fault in rhetoric. It differs from repetition or iteration, which is repeating the same sentence in the same or equivalent terms; the latter is *sometimes* either excusable or necessary in an argument or address; the former (tautology) never.

Taverner. In old English law, a seller of wine; one who kept a house or shop for the sale of wine.

Tavern keeper. One who owns and operates a tavern or an inn.

Tax. To impose a tax; to enact or declare that a pecuniary contribution shall be made by the persons liable, for the support of government. Spoken of an individual, to be taxed is to be included in an assessment made for purposes of taxation.

A pecuniary burden laid upon individuals or property to support the government, and is a payment exacted by legislative authority. In re Mytinger, D.C. Tex., 31 F.Supp. 977, 978, 979. Essential characteristics of a tax are that it is not a voluntary payment or donation, but an enforced contribution, exacted pursuant to legislative authority. Michigan Employment Sec. Commission v. Patt, 4 Mich.App. 228, 144 N.W.2d 663, 665. Annual compensation paid to government for annual protection and for current support of government. Alabama Power Co. v. Federal Power Commission, C.C.A.5, 134 F.2d 602, 608. A ratable portion of the produce of the property and labor of the individual citizens, taken by the nation, in the exercise of its sovereign rights, for the support of government, for the administration of the laws, and as the means for continuing in operation the various legitimate functions of the state. An enforced contribution of money or other property, assessed in accordance with some reasonable rule or apportionment by authority of a sovereign state on persons or property within its jurisdiction for the purpose of defraying the public expenses.

In a general sense, any contribution imposed by government upon individuals, for the use and service of the state, whether under the name of toll, tribute, tallage, gabel, impost, duty, custom, excise, subsidy, aid, supply, or other name. And in its essential characteristics is not a debt. City of Newark v. Jos. Hollander, Inc., 136 N.J.Eq. 539, 42 A.2d 872, 875.

See also Accumulated earnings tax; Estate tax; Estimated tax; Excess profits tax; Excise; Gift tax; Holding company tax; Import tax; Income tax; Inheritance tax; Intangibles tax; Investment tax credit; Levy; License fee or tax; Occupation tax; Payroll tax; Poll-tax; Progressive tax; Property tax; Regressive tax; Sales tax; Service occupation tax; Surtax; Taxation; Toll; Transfer tax; Undistributed profits tax; Use tax.

Synonyms

In a broad sense, *taxes* undoubtedly include *assessments,* and the right to impose assessments has its foundation in the taxing power of the government; and yet, in practice and as generally understood, there is a broad distinction between the two terms. "Taxes," as the term is generally used, are public burdens imposed generally upon the inhabitants of the whole state, or upon some civil division thereof, for governmental purposes, without reference to peculiar benefits to particular individuals or property. "Assessments" have reference to impositions for improvements which are specially beneficial to particular individuals or property, and which are imposed in proportion to the particular benefits supposed to be conferred. They are justified only because the improvements confer special benefits, and are just only when they are divided in proportion to such benefits. As distinguished from other kinds of taxation, "assessments" are those special and local impositions upon property in the immediate vicinity of municipal improvements which are necessary to pay for the improvement, and are laid with reference to the special benefit which the property is supposed to have derived therefrom.

Taxes differ from *subsidies,* in being certain and orderly, and from forced contributions, etc., in that they are levied by authority of law, and by some rule of proportion which is intended to insure uniformity of contribution, and a just apportionment of the burdens of government.

Generally

Ad valorem tax. See **Ad valorem.**

Amusement tax. See **Amusement tax.**

Capital gains tax. Provision in tax laws by which sale or exchange of capital assets are taxed at a lower rate than ordinary income.

Capital stock tax. Tax assessed as a percentage of par or assigned value of capital stock of a corporation.

Capitation tax. See that title.

Collateral inheritance tax. See that title.

Consumption tax. Tax imposed on outlay for consumption goods and services.

Direct tax. One which is demanded from the very persons who it is intended or desired should pay it. Indirect taxes are those which are demanded from one person, in the expectation and intention that he shall indemnify himself at the expense of another. Taxes are divided into "direct," under which designation would be included those which are assessed upon the property, person, business, income, etc., of those who are to pay them, and "indirect," or those which are levied on commodities before they reach the consumer, and are paid by those upon whom they ultimately fall, not as taxes, but as part of the market price of the commodity.

Estate tax. A tax upon the right to transfer property at death, while an inheritance tax is a tax upon the right to receive. See also **Estate tax; Inheritance tax.**

Excess profits tax. Tax imposed on all income beyond the normal amount calculated on either a normal return on invested capital or on the average of income of previous years. Such tax is commonly imposed in war time. See **Excess profits tax;** also, *Undistributed profits tax, infra.*

Excise tax. See **Excise.**

Floor tax. A tax on all the distilled spirits "on the floor" of a warehouse, *i.e.,* in the warehouse.

Franchise tax. See **Franchise.**

Gift tax. Tax imposed on the inter vivos transfer of property by gift. The Federal Gift Tax is imposed on the donor while some state gift taxes are imposed on the donee.

Graduated tax. A tax so structured that the rate increases as the value of the income or property increases.

Gross receipts tax. A tax based on total sales rather than on net profits.

Head tax. A flat tax imposed on a per person basis.

Income tax. See **Income tax.**

Indirect taxes. Those demanded in the first instance from one person in the expectation and intention that he shall indemnify himself at the expense of another. Ordinarily all taxes paid primarily by persons who can shift the burden upon some one else, or who are under no legal compulsion to pay them, are considered indirect taxes. Pollock v. Farmers' Loan & Trust Co., 157 U.S. 429, 15 S.Ct. 673, 39 L.Ed. 759.

Inheritance tax. See that title.

Land tax. See that title.

License tax. See **License fee or tax.**

Local taxes. Taxes imposed by municipalities such as local property taxes or city income or sales taxes.

Luxury tax. A species of property tax imposed on the manufacture, sale or purchase of luxury goods.

Normal tax. A normal tax applied to all taxable income at the same rate.

Occupation tax. See **Occupation.**

Payroll tax. A type of tax collected by deduction from a company's payroll and paid by either the employer or employee.

Personal property tax. A tax assessed against personal property by cities and towns. The tax is commonly levied against such items as furniture, motor vehicles, etc.

Personal tax. This term may mean either a tax imposed on the person without reference to property, as a capitation or poll tax, or a tax imposed on personal property, as distinguished from one laid on real property.

Poll-tax. See that title.

Property tax. Generic term describing a tax levied on the basis of the value of either personal or real property owned by the taxpayer. See also **Ad valorem.**

Proportional taxes. Taxes are "proportional" when the proportion paid by each taxpayer bears the same ratio to the amount to be raised that the value of his property bears to the total taxable value, and in the case of a special tax when that is apportioned according to the benefits received.

Public tax. A tax levied for some general public purpose or for the purposes of the general public revenue, as distinguished from local municipal taxes and assessments.

Real estate tax. Tax assessed against real property and based on the value of such property. See also **Ad valorem.**

Regressive tax. Tax whose structure is such that the revenue yield grows smaller as the value of the property taxed increases.

Sales tax. Tax levied on the sale of goods and based on their value. It may be a direct tax which is paid by the purchaser or a turnover tax paid by the seller on the gross sales of his business.

Severance tax. Tax levied on the mining or extraction of some natural resource such as oil or coal. It may be assessed on the value of the product extracted or on the volume.

Sinking fund tax. See **Fund.**

Specific tax. A tax imposed as a fixed sum on each article or item or property of a given class or kind, without regard to its value; opposed to *ad valorem* tax.

Stamp tax. Tax collected through the sale of stamps which must be affixed to certain documents such as deeds, stock certificates, etc. See **Revenue stamps.**

Stock transfer tax. Tax levied by the federal government and by certain states on the transfer or sale of shares of stock.

Succession tax. See **Succession duty or tax.**

Surtax. An additional tax imposed upon certain kinds of income, such as dividends from corporate stock, royalties, interest from money, notes, credits, bonds, and other securities. A surtax is sometimes imposed on incomes exceeding a specified amount. See also **Surtax.**

Tax certificate. A certificate of the purchase of land at a tax sale thereof, given by the officer making the sale, and which is evidence of the holder's right to receive a deed of the land if it is not redeemed within the time limited by law.

Tax-deed. The deed given upon a sale of real property made for non-payment of taxes. The deed whereby the officer of the law undertakes to convey the title of the property to the purchaser at the tax-sale. See also **Tax certificate; Tax deed;** and *Tax-title,* infra.

Taxing district. The district throughout which a particular tax or assessment is ratably apportioned and levied upon the inhabitants; it may comprise the whole state, one county, a city, a ward, or part of a street.

Tax lease. The instrument (or estate) given to the purchaser of land at a tax sale, where the law does not permit the sale of the estate in fee for non-payment of taxes, but instead thereof directs the sale of an estate for years.

Tax levy. The total sum to be raised by a tax. Also the bill, enactment, or measure of legislation by which an annual or general tax is imposed. See also **Assessment; Levy.**

Tax lien. A statutory lien, existing in favor of the state or municipality, upon the lands of a person charged with taxes, binding the same either for the taxes assessed upon the specific tract of land or (in some jurisdictions) for all the taxes due from the individual, and which may be foreclosed for non-payment, by judgment of a court or sale of the land.

Taxpayer. A person chargeable with a tax; one from whom government demands a pecuniary contribution towards its support.

Taxpayers' lists. Written exhibits required to be made out by the taxpayers resident in a district, enumerating all the property owned by them and subject to taxation, to be handed to the assessors, at a specified date or at regular periods, as a basis for assessment and valuation.

Tax purchaser. A person who buys land at a tax-sale; the person to whom land, at a tax-sale thereof, is struck down.

Tax roll. See **Roll.**

Tax sale. See **Sale.**

Tax-title. The title by which one holds land which he purchased at a tax sale. That species of title which is inaugurated by a successful bid for land at a collector's sale of the same for nonpayment of taxes, completed by the failure of those entitled to redeem within the specified time, and evidenced by the deed executed to the tax purchaser, or his assignee, by the proper officer.

Tonnage tax. See **Tonnage duty.**

Transfer tax. See *Stock transfer tax, supra.*

Undistributed profits tax. Tax imposed on the accumulation of surplus beyond a certain amount. It is designed to force corporations to pay dividends because it is assessed against that part of surplus which is not distributed as dividends and which is not reasonably necessary for the maintenance and growth of the business.

Use tax. Tax imposed on the use of certain goods which are not subject to a sales tax. It is commonly designed to discourage people from going out of state and purchasing goods which are not subject to sales tax at the point of purchase.

Withholding tax. A tax which is collected by deducting it from the wages of an employee, *e.g.* federal income taxes.

Taxa /tǽksə/. L. Lat. A tax. In old records, an allotted piece of work; a task.

Taxable. Subject to taxation; liable to be assessed, along with others, for a share in a tax. Something of value, subject to assessment, and to be levied upon and sold for taxes. Williams v. School Dist. No. 32 in County of Fremont, 56 Wyo. 1, 102 P.2d 48, 52.

As applied to costs in an action, the term means proper to be taxed or charged up; legally chargeable or assessable. See also **Taxation** (*Taxation of costs*).

Taxable estate. As defined in I.R.C. § 2051, the taxable estate is the gross estate of a decedent reduced by the deductions allowed by §§ 2053–2057 (*e.g.,* administration expenses, marital and charitable deductions). The taxable estate is the amount that is subject to the unified transfer tax at death. See also **Gross estate.**

Taxable gift. As defined in I.R.C. § 2503, a taxable gift is the gift that is subject to the unified transfer tax. Thus, a taxable gift has been adjusted by the annual exclusion and other appropriate deductions (*e.g.,* marital and charitable deductions).

Taxable income. Under Federal tax law, this is either the "gross income" of businesses or the "adjusted gross income" of individuals, minus deductions and exemptions. It is the income against which tax rates are applied to compute tax paid. Essence of "taxable income" is the accrual of some gain, profit or benefit to taxpayer. In re Goodyear Tire & Rubber Co., Corporate Income Tax 1966, 1967, 1968, 133 Vt. 132, 335 A.2d 310, 313.

Taxable year. This term in internal revenue statutes has different significations, according to its use, but when used in ordinarily accepted meaning, refers to annual accounting period of taxpayer. American-Hawaiian S. S. Co. v. U. S., Ct.Cl., 46 F.2d 592, 598. May refer to either calendar year or fiscal year upon which net taxable income is computed. New Mexico Elec. Service Co. v. Jones, 80 N.M. 791, 461 P.2d 924, 925. See also **Accounting period; Fiscal year.**

Tax anticipation warrants. A method of raising public money by the issuance of warrants payable out of tax receipts when collected.

Taxare /tæksériy/. Lat. To rate or value. To tax; to lay a tax or tribute.

In old English practice, to assess; to rate or estimate; to moderate or regulate an assessment or rate.

Tax assessment. The value given to the property which is being taxed. Multiplying the assessed valuation by the tax rate yields the tax paid. See also **Assessment.**

Tax assessor. The official responsible for tax valuation of property. See also **Assessor.**

Taxati /tækséyday/. In old European law, soldiers of a garrison or fleet, assigned to a certain station.

Taxatio /tækséysh(iy)ow/. Lat. In Roman law, taxation or assessment of damages; the assessment, by the judge, of the amount of damages to be awarded to a plaintiff, and particularly in the way of reducing the amount claimed or sworn to by the latter.

Taxatio ecclesiastica /tækséysh(iy)ow əklìyziyǽstəkə/. The value of ecclesiastical benefices made through every diocese in England, on occasion of Pope Innocent IV granting to King Henry III the tenth of all spirituals for three years. This taxation was first made by Walter, bishop of Norwich, delegated by the pope to this office in 38 Hen. III, and hence called "*Taxatio Norwicencis.*" It is also called "Pope Innocent's Valor."

Taxatio expensarum /tækséysh(iy)ow èkspen(t)sérəm/. In old English practice, taxation of costs.

Taxation. The process of taxing or imposing a tax. See **Assessment; Equalization; Tax.**

Double taxation. See **Double taxation.**

Progressive taxation. A taxing system in which the higher one's income, the higher the tax bracket one is put in.

Proportional taxation. A system of taxation in which the rate of taxation is uniform no matter what the size of income.

Regressive taxation. A system in which, unlike progressive taxation, as more and more income is earned, the tax rate falls.

Taxation of costs. The process of ascertaining and charging up the amount of costs in an action to which a party is legally entitled, or which are legally chargeable. See Fed.R.Civil P. 54(d). See also **Costs.**

Taxatio norwicensis /tækséysh(iy)ow nòrwəchén(t)səs /°nòhrəchén(t)səs/. A valuation of ecclesiastical benefices made through every diocese in England, by

Walter, bishop of Norwich, delegated by the pope to this office in 38 Hen. III.

Tax audit. See **Audit.**

Tax avoidance. The minimization of one's tax liability by taking advantage of legally available tax planning opportunities. Tax avoidance may be contrasted with tax evasion which entails the reduction of tax liability by using illegal means.

Tax benefit rule. A rule which limits the recognition of income from the recovery of an expense or loss properly deducted in a prior tax year to the amount of the deduction that generated a tax benefit. Under the "tax benefit rule" if an amount deducted from gross income in one taxable year is recovered in a later year, the recovery is income in the later year. S. E. Evans, Inc. v. U. S., D.C.Ark., 317 F.Supp. 423, 424.

Tax certificate. Instrument issued to the buyer of property at a tax sale which entitles the holder to the property thus purchased if it is not redeemed within the period provided by law.

Tax court. The United States Tax Court is a court of record under Article I of the Constitution of the United States (see I.R.C. § 7441). The Court was created originally as the United States Board of Tax Appeals by the Revenue Act of 1924 (43 Stat. 336), an independent agency in the executive branch, and continued by the Revenue Act of 1926 (44 Stat. 105), the Internal Revenue Code of 1939, and the Internal Revenue Code of 1954. A change in name to the Tax Court of the United States was made by the Revenue Act of 1942 (56 Stat. 957), and the Article I status and change in name to United States Tax Court was made by the Tax Reform Act of 1969 (83 Stat. 730).

The Tax Court tries and adjudicates controversies involving the existence of deficiencies or overpayments in income, estate, gift, and personal holding company surtaxes in cases where deficiencies have been determined by the Commissioner of Internal Revenue.

The U.S. Tax Court is one of three trial courts of original jurisdiction which decides litigation involving Federal income, death, or gift taxes. It is the only trial court where the taxpayer must not first pay the deficiency assessed by the IRS. The Tax Court will not have jurisdiction over a case unless the statutory notice of deficiency (i.e., "90-day letter") has been issued by the IRS and the taxpayer files the petition for hearing within the time prescribed.

State tax courts. Such courts exist in certain states, *e.g.* Maryland, New Jersey, Oklahoma, Oregon. Generally, court has jurisdiction to hear appeals in all tax cases and has power to modify or change any valuation, assessment, classification, tax or final order appealed from. Certain of these tax courts (*e.g.* Minnesota) have small claims sessions at which citizens can argue their own cases without attorneys.

Tax credit. Type of offset in which the taxpayer is allowed a deduction from his tax for other taxes paid. A credit differs from a deduction to the extent that the former is subtracted from the tax while the latter is subtracted from income before the tax is computed.

Foreign tax credit. If a U.S. citizen or resident incurs or pays income taxes to a foreign country on income subject to U.S. tax, the taxpayer may be able to claim some of these taxes as a deduction or as a credit against the U.S. income.

Tax deduction. A subtraction from revenues and gains to arrive at taxable income. Tax deductions are technically different from tax exemptions, but the effect of both is to reduce gross income in computing taxable income. Both are different from tax credits, which are subtracted from the computed tax itself in determining taxes payable.

Tax deed. A proof of ownership of land given to the purchaser by the government after the land has been taken from another person by the government and sold for failure to pay taxes. See also **Tax certificate.**

Taxers. Two officers yearly chosen in Cambridge, England, to see the true gauge of all the weights and measures.

Tax evasion. Illegally paying less in taxes than the law permits; committing fraud in filing or paying taxes. Such act is a crime under I.R.C. § 7201. *Compare* **Tax avoidance.**

Tax exempt. Term pertains to property used for educational, religious, or charitable purposes which is ordinarily exempted by law from assessment for taxes; or to certain bonds issued by the federal government or a State or one of its subdivisions. Interest on State and local government bonds is exempt from federal income taxation, and interest on bonds of the United States or its instrumentalities is correspondingly exempt from State income taxation. See also **Tax exempts.**

Tax exemption. Immunity from the obligation of paying taxes in whole or in part.

Tax exempts. Investments that yield income that is tax exempt. Generally, tax exempts are municipal bonds with an interest that is not taxed by the federal government. See also **Tax exempt.**

Tax ferrets. Persons engaged in the business of searching for property omitted from taxation. Their activities when permitted are usually regarded as private rather than as part of a state agency. Pickett v. United States, C.C.A.Mo., 100 F.2d 909, 913.

Tax foreclosure. Seizure and sale by public authority of property for non-payment of taxes.

Tax fraud. See **Fraud.**

Tax-free exchange. Transfers of property specifically exempted from income tax consequences by the tax law. Examples are a transfer of property to a controlled corporation and a like-kind exchange.

Tax home. Since travel expenses of an employee are deductible only if the taxpayer is away from home, the deductibility of such expenses rests upon the definition of "tax home". The IRS position is that "tax home" is the business location, post or station of the taxpayer.

Taxing master. See **Master.**

Taxing power. The power of any government to levy taxes. See **Sixteenth Amendment.**

Tax laws. See **Internal Revenue Code; Letter ruling.**

Tax levy. The order for payment of taxes. Also, the determination of the total receipts to be collected by the tax. See **Assessment; Levy.**

Tax lien. A lien on real estate in favor of a state or local government which may be foreclosed for non-payment of taxes. The majority of the states have adopted the Uniform Federal Tax Lien Registration Act. See also **Tax** *(Tax lien).*

Federal tax lien. A lien placed on property by the federal government for unpaid federal taxes.

Taxpayer. One who pays taxes; person whose income is subject to taxation.

Tax preference. Tax imposed on preference income which is commonly investment income. It is designed to bring into tax income which otherwise escapes taxation.

Tax rate. Amount of tax imposed on personal or corporate income, capital gains, gifts, estates, sales, etc.

Tax rate schedules. Rate schedules which are used by upper income taxpayers. Separate rate schedules are provided for married individuals filing jointly, unmarried individuals who maintain a household, single taxpayers, estates and trusts and married individuals filing separate returns. See also **Tax tables.**

Tax rebate. Amount of money remitted by taxing authority after payment of taxes. See **Rebate.**

Tax redemption. The act by which a taxpayer reclaims property which has been taken for nonpayment of taxes. He does so by paying the delinquent taxes in addition to interest, costs and penalties.

Tax return. The form on which a report of income, deductions and exemptions is made and which is forwarded with the tax payment. See also **Return.**

Joint return. Tax return filed jointly by both spouses; permitted even though only one had income. See **Split-income.**

Separate return. Tax return filed by only one spouse and covering only his or her income.

Tax roll. The official record maintained by cities and towns listing the names of taxpayers and the assessed property.

Tax sale. Sale of property for nonpayment of taxes. See also **Tax certificate.**

Tax shelter. A device used by taxpayers to reduce or to defer payment of taxes. Common forms of tax shelter are real estate investments where such deductions as depreciation, interest, taxes, etc. are offset against taxpayer's ordinary income.

Tax "situs". A state or jurisdiction which has a substantial relationship to assets subject to taxation.

Tax surcharge. Tax added to another tax. See also **Surcharge; Surtax.**

Tax tables. Tables established by taxing authority from which taxes may be computed. As regards federal income taxes, separate tables are provided for single taxpayers, married taxpayers filing jointly, head of household, and married taxpayers filing separately.

Tax title. Title held by one who purchases property at a tax sale. See also **Tax certificate; Tax deed.**

Tax warrant. Official process for collecting unpaid taxes and under which property may be seized and sold.

Tax year. See **Accounting period; Fiscal year.**

T.C. An abbreviation for the U.S. Tax Court. It is used to cite a Regular Decision of the U.S. Tax Court.

T.C. Memo. An abbreviation used to refer to a Memorandum Decision of the U.S. Tax Court.

Teach. To impart knowledge by means of lessons; to give instruction in; communicating knowledge; introducing into or impressing on the mind as truth or information, and may be done as well through written communications, personal direction, through the public press, or through any means by which information may be disseminated, or it may be done by the adoption of sentiment expressed or arguments made by others which are distributed to others for their adoption and guidance.

Teacher. One who teaches or instructs; especially one whose business or occupation is to teach others; an instructor; preceptor. Ortega v. Otero, 48 N.M. 588, 154 P.2d 252, 254, 255, 257; Jeu Jo Wan v. Nagle, C.C.A.Cal., 9 F.2d 309, 310.

Tea chest. A box containing a definite and prescribed amount of tea, otherwise called whole chest (a hundred weight to 140 pounds or more), now seldom shipped, the smaller package being spoken of as half chest (75 to 80 pounds, but the weight varies according to the kind of tea), and quarter chest (from 25 to 30 pounds) and thus a "tea chest" in the language of the trade is understood to be a half chest and not a whole chest.

Team or theame. In old English law, a royalty or privilege granted, by royal charter, to a lord of a manor, for the having, restraining, and judging of bondmen and villeins, with their children, goods, and chattels, etc.

Teamster. A truck driver. A member of the Teamsters' Union though not necessarily one who operates vehicles. One who drives horses and a wagon for the purpose of carrying goods for hire.

Team work. Within the meaning of an exemption law, this term means work done by a team as a substantial part of a man's business; as in farming, staging, express carrying, drawing of freight, peddling, or the transportation of material used or dealt in as a business.

Tearing of will. Under statute providing that will may be revoked by tearing, any act of tearing of paper on which will is written, however slight, constitutes an act of "tearing," if done with intent to revoke the will, but no act of tearing or cutting accomplishes such purpose unless done with intent to revoke. Fleming v. Fleming, 367 Ill. 97, 10 N.E.2d 641, 642.

Technical. Belonging or peculiar to an art or profession. Technical terms are frequently called in the books "words of art." Immaterial, not affecting substantial rights, without substance.

Technical errors. Errors committed in course of trial which have not prejudiced the party and hence are not grounds for reversal. Fed.R.Civil P. 61; Fed.R. Crim.P. 52. See also **Harmless error.**

Technical mortgage. A true and formal mortgage, as distinguished from other instruments which, in some respects, have the character of equitable mortgages.

Teding-penny. In old English law, a small tax or allowance to the sheriff from each tithing of his county towards the charge of keeping courts, etc.

Teep /tíyp/. In Hindu law, a note of hand; a promissory note given by a native banker or moneylender to *zemindars* and others, to enable them to furnish government with security for the payment of their rents.

Teind masters /tíynd mǽstərz/°ma°/. Those entitled to tithes.

Teinland /téynlǽnd/θéyn°/. Sax. In old English law, land of a thane or Saxon noble; land granted by the crown to a thane or lord.

Telegram. A telegraphic dispatch; a message sent by telegraph. Message transmitted by radio, teletype, cable, any mechanical method of transmission or the like. U.C.C. § 1–201(41).

Telegram racket. Consists in a fictitious communication such as by radiogram or telephone call authorizing a trustee to pay out money. Cordovano v. State, 61 Ga.App. 590, 7 S.E.2d 45, 47.

Teligraphum /tèləgrǽfəm/. An Anglo-Saxon charter of land.

Teller. One who numbers or counts. An officer of a bank who receives or pays out money. Also one appointed to count the votes cast in a deliberative or legislative assembly or other meeting. The name was also given to certain officers formerly attached to the English exchequer.

Tellers in parliament. In the English parliament, the members of the house selected to count the members when a division takes place.

Tellworc /télwərk/. That labor which a tenant was bound to do for his lord for a certain number of days.

Tementale, or **tenementale** /tè(nə)məntéyliy/. A tax of two shillings upon every plow-land, a decennary.

Temere /təmíriy/. Lat. In the civil law, rashly; inconsiderately. A plaintiff was said *temere litigare* who demanded a thing out of malice, or sued without just cause, and who could show no ground or cause of action.

Temperance. Habitual moderation in regard to the indulgence of the natural appetites and passions; restrained or moderate indulgence; as, temperance in eating and drinking, temperance in the indulgence of joy or mirth. Not synonymous with abstinence. Mayfield v. Fidelity Casualty Co. of New York, 16 Cal.App.2d 611, 61 P.2d 83, 89.

Tempest. A violent or furious storm; a current of wind rushing with extreme violence, and usually accompanied with rain or snow.

Templars /témplərz/. A religious order of knighthood, instituted about the year 1119, and so called because the members dwelt in a part of the temple of Jerusalem, and not far from the sepulcher of our Lord. They entertained Christian strangers and pilgrims charitably, and their profession was at first to defend travelers from highwaymen and robbers. The order was suppressed A.D. 1307, and their substance given partly to the knights of St. John of Jerusalem, and partly to other religious orders.

Temple. Two English inns of court, thus called because anciently the dwelling place of the Knights Templar. On the suppression of the order, they were purchased by some professors of the common law, and converted into *hospitia* or inns of court. They are called the "Inner" and "Middle Temple," in relation to Essex House, which was also a part of the house of the Templars, and called the "Outer Temple," because situated without Temple Bar.

Temporalis /tèmpəréyləs/. Lat. In the civil law, temporary; limited to a certain time.

Temporalis actio /tèmpəréyləs ǽksh(iy)ow/. An action which could only be brought within a certain period.

Temporalis exceptio /tèmpəréyləs əksépsh(iy)ow/. A temporary exception which barred an action for a time only.

Temporalities /tèmpərǽlədiyz/. In English law, the lay fees of bishops, with which their churches are endowed or permitted to be endowed by the liberality of the sovereign, and in virtue of which they become barons and lords of parliament. In a wider sense, the money revenues of a church, derived from pew rents, subscriptions, donations, collections, cemetery charges, and other sources.

Temporality. The laity; secular people.

Temporal lords. The peers of England; the bishops are not in strictness held to be peers, but merely lords of parliament.

Temporarily. Lasting for a time only, existing or continuing for a limited time, not of long duration, not permanent, transitory, changing, but a short time.

Temporary. That which is to last for a limited time only, as distinguished from that which is perpetual, or indefinite, in its duration. Opposite of permanent. Thus, temporary alimony is granted for the support of the wife pending the action for divorce; a temporary receiver is one appointed to take charge of property until a hearing is had and an adjudication made.

As to temporary Disability; Insanity; Injunction; and Statute, see those titles.

Temporary administration. Fiduciary appointed by court to administer the affairs of a decedent estate for a short period of time before an administrator or executor can be appointed and qualified.

Temporary alimony. Interim order of payment to spouse pending final outcome of action for divorce.

Temporary detention. Temporary exercise of custody pending final determination on merits of criminal case.

Temporary disability. Healing period during which claimant is totally or partially unable to work due to injury, and continues as long as recovery or lasting improvement of injured person's condition can reasonably be expected. Corral v. McCrory Corp., Fla., 228 So.2d 900, 903.

Temporary Emergency Court of Appeals. The Economic Stabilization Act Amendments of 1971 (85 Stat. 743) created a special court known as the Temporary Emergency Court of Appeals of the United States. The court has exclusive jurisdiction of all appeals from the district courts of the United States in cases and controversies arising under the economic stabilization laws, and consists of eight district and circuit judges appointed by the Chief Justice.

Temporary injunction. See **Injunction; Temporary restraining order.**

Temporary restraining order. An emergency remedy of brief duration which may issue only in exceptional circumstances and only until the trial court can hear arguments or evidence, as the circumstances require, on the subject matter of the controversy and otherwise determine what relief is appropriate. Paddington Corp. v. Foremost Sales Promotions, Inc., 13 Ill.App.3d 170, 300 N.E.2d 484, 487. One which is issued pending a hearing on an application for an injunction. Becker v. Becker, 66 Wis.2d 731, 225 N.W.2d 884, 886.

A temporary restraining order may be granted without written or oral notice to the adverse party or his attorney only if (1) it clearly appears from specific facts shown by affidavit or by the verified complaint that immediate and irreparable injury, loss, or damage will result to the applicant before the adverse party or his attorney can be heard in opposition, and (2) the applicant's attorney certifies to the court in writing the efforts, if any, which have been made to give the notice and the reasons supporting his claim that notice should not be required. Fed.R.Civil P. 65(b).

Temporis exceptio /témpərəs əksépsh(iy)ow/. Lat. In the civil law, a plea of time; a plea of lapse of time, in bar of an action. Corresponding to the plea of prescription, or the statute of limitations, in our law.

Tempus /témpəs/. Lat. In the civil and old English law, time in general. A time limited; a season; *e.g., tempus pessonis,* mast time in the forest.

Tempus continuum /témpəs kəntínyuwəm/. In the civil law, a continuous or absolute period of time. A term which begins to run from a certain event, even though he for whom it runs has no knowledge of the event, and in which, when it has once begun to run, all the days are reckoned as they follow one another in the calendar.

Tempus enim modus tollendi obligationes et actiones, quia tempus currit contra desides et sui juris contemptores /témpəs íynəm mówdəs tolénday òbləgèy-shiyówniyz èd ækshiyówniyz, kwáyə témpəs kə́hrət kóntrə désədiyz èt s(y)úway júrəs kòntem(p)tóriyz/. For time is a means of destroying obligations and actions, because time runs against the slothful and contemners of their own rights.

Tempus semestre /témpəs səméstriy/. In old English law, the period of six months or half a year, consisting of one hundred and eighty-two days.

Tempus utile /témpəs yúwdəliy/. In the civil law, a profitable or advantageous period of time. A term which begins to run from a certain event, only when he for whom it runs has obtained a knowledge of the event, and in which, when it has once begun to run, those days are not reckoned on which one has no *experiundi potestas; i.e.,* on which one cannot prosecute his rights before a court. A period of time which runs beneficially: *i.e.* feast-days are not included, nor does it run against one absent in a foreign country, or on business of the republic, or detained by stress of weather. But one detained by sickness is not protected from its running; for it runs where there is power to act by an agent as well as where there is power to act personally; and the sick man might have deputed his agent.

Tenancy. A tenancy involves an interest in realty which passes to the tenant, and a possession exclusive even of that of landlord, except as lease permits landlord's entry, and saving his right to enter to demand rent or to make repairs. Layton v. A. I. Namm & Sons, 275 A.D. 246, 89 N.Y.S.2d 72, 74, 75. Possession or occupancy of land or premises under lease. Period of tenant's possession or occupancy. To constitute tenancy, tenant must acquire some definite control and possession of premises. Mercantile Realty Co. v. Allen Edmonds Shoe Corporation, 263 Ky. 597, 92 S.W.2d 837, 839.

General tenancy. A tenancy which is not fixed and made certain in point of duration by the agreement of the parties.

Joint tenancy. An estate in fee-simple, fee-tail, for life, for years, or at will, arising by purchase or grant to two or more persons. Joint tenants have one and the same interest, accruing by one and the same conveyance, commencing at one and the same time, and held by one and the same undivided possession. The primary incident of joint tenancy is survivorship, by which the entire tenancy on the decease of any joint tenant remains to the survivors, and at length to the last survivor.

Type of ownership of real or personal property by two or more persons in which each owns an undivided interest in the whole and attached to which is the right of survivorship. Single estate in property owned by two or more persons under one instrument or act. D'Ercole v. D'Ercole, D.C.Mass., 407 F.Supp. 1377, 1380.

See also **Periodic Tenancy; Tenant.**

Several tenancy. A tenancy which is separate, and not held jointly with another person.

Tenancy at sufferance. See **Tenant.**

Tenancy at will. See **Tenant.**

Tenancy by the entirety. A tenancy which is created between a husband and wife and by which together they hold title to the whole with right of survivorship so that, upon death of either, other takes whole to exclusion of deceased heirs. Sams v. McDonald, 117 Ga.App. 336, 160 S.E.2d 594, 597. It is essentially a "joint tenancy," modified by the common-law theory that husband and wife are one person, and survivorship is the predominant and distinguishing feature of each. United States v. Jacobs, Ill. & N. Y., 306 U.S. 363, 59 S.Ct. 551, 555, 83 L.Ed. 763.

Tenancy for a period. A tenancy for years or for some fixed period.

Tenancy from month to month. See **Tenant** *(Tenant at will).*

Tenancy from period to period. A periodic tenancy which runs from month to month or from year to year.

Tenancy from year to year. A periodic tenancy which runs from one year to the next.

Tenancy in common. A form of ownership whereby each tenant (*i.e.,* owner) holds an undivided interest in property. Unlike a joint tenancy or a tenancy by the entirety, the interest of a tenant in common does not terminate upon his or her prior death (*i.e.,* there is no right of survivorship). Assume, for example, B and C acquire real estate as equal tenants in common, each having furnished one-half of the purchase price. Upon B's prior death, his one-half interest in the property passes to his estate or heirs.

Joint interest in which there is unity of possession, but separate and distinct titles. The relationship exists where property is held by several distinct titles by unity of possession, and is not an estate but a relation between persons, the only essential being a possessory right, as to which all are entitled to equal use and possession. De Mik v. Cargill, Okl., 485 P.2d 229, 233.

Tenancy in coparcenary. Of historical value only today; formerly it was a form of concurrent ownership in which property was acquired by intestacy by the female line of heirs and arose only by descent. Today, it is governed by the rules of tenancy in common.

Tenancy in partnership. Real estate held by partnership. See Uniform Partnership Act, § 25.

Tenant. In the broadest sense, one who holds or possesses lands or tenements by any kind of right or title, whether in fee, for life, for years, at will, or otherwise. In a more restricted sense, one who holds lands of another; one who has the temporary use and occupation of real property owned by another person (called the "landlord"), the duration and terms of his tenancy being usually fixed by an instrument called a "lease." One who occupies another's land or premises in subordination to such other's title and with his assent, express or implied. One renting land and paying for it either in money or part of crop or equivalent.

See also **Hold-over tenant; Lessee.**

Feudal law. One who holds of another (called "lord" or "superior") by some service; as fealty or rent.

Joint tenants. Two or more persons to whom are granted lands or tenements to hold in fee-simple, fee-tail, for life, for years, or at will. Persons who own lands by a joint title created expressly by one and the same deed or will. Joint tenants have one and the same interest, accruing by one and the same conveyance, commencing at one and the same time, and held by one and the same undivided possession. See also **Tenancy** *(Joint tenancy).*

Land tenant. See that title.

Quasi tenant at sufferance. An under-tenant, who is in possession at the determination of an original lease, and is permitted by the reversioner to hold over.

Sole tenant. He that holds lands by his own right only, without any other person being joined with him.

Tenant at sufferance. One who after rightfully being in possession of rented premises continues after his right has terminated. He has no estate nor title but only naked possession without right and wrongfully, and stands in no privity to landlord and is not entitled to notice to quit, and is a bare licensee to whom landlord owes merely duty not wantonly nor willfully to injure him. Welch v. Rice, 61 Wyo. 511, 159 P.2d 502, 506, 509.

Tenant at will. One who holds possession of premises by permission of owner or landlord, but without fixed term. Where lands or tenements are let by one man to another, to have and to hold to him at the will of the lessor, by force of which lease the lessee is in possession. In this case the lessee is called "tenant at will," because he has no certain nor sure estate, for the lessor may put him out at what time it pleases him.

Tenant a volunte. L. Fr. A tenant at will.

Tenant by copy of court roll (shortly, "tenant by copy") is the old-fashioned name for a copyholder.

Tenant by the curtesy. One who, on the death of his wife seised of an estate of inheritance, after having by her issue born alive and capable of inheriting her estate, holds the lands and tenements for the term of his life.

Tenant by the manner. One who has a less estate than a fee in land which remains in the reversioner. He is so called because in avowries and other pleadings it is specially shown in what manner he is tenant of the land, in contradistinction to the *veray tenant,* who is called simply "tenant."

Tenant for life. One who holds lands or tenements for the term of his own life, or for that of any other person (in which case he is called *"pur auter vie"*), or for more lives than one.

Tenant for years. One who has the temporary use and possession of lands or tenements not his own, by virtue of a lease or demise granted to him by the owner, for a determinate period of time, as for a year or a fixed number of years.

Tenant from year to year. One who holds lands or tenements under the demise of another, where no certain term has been mentioned, but an annual rent has been reserved. One who holds over, by consent given either expressly or constructively, after the determination of a lease for years. See also **Tenancy.**

Tenant in capite. In feudal and old English law, tenant in chief; one who held immediately under the king, in right of his crown and dignity. 2 Bl.Comm. 60.

Tenant in common. Tenants who hold the same land together by several and distinct titles, but by unity of possession, because none knows his own severalty, and therefore they all occupy promiscuously. Where two or more hold the same land, with interests accruing under different titles, or accruing under the same title, but at different periods, or conferred by words of limitation importing that the grantees are to take in distinct shares. See also **Tenancy** (*Tenancy in common*).

Tenant in dower. This arises where the husband of a woman is seised of an estate of inheritance and dies; in this case the wife shall have the third part of all the lands and tenements whereof he was seised at any time during the coverture, to hold to herself for life, as her dower. 2 Bl.Comm. 129.

Tenant in fee-simple (or tenant in fee). He who has lands, tenements, or hereditaments, to hold to him and his heirs forever, generally, absolutely, and simply; without mentioning *what* heirs, but referring that to his own pleasure, or to the disposition of the law.

Tenant in severalty. One who holds lands and tenements in his own right only, without any other person being joined or connected with him in point of interest during his estate therein. 2 Bl.Comm. 179.

Tenant in tail. One who holds an estate in fee-tail, that is, an estate which, by the instrument creating it, is limited to some particular heirs, exclusive of others; as to the heirs of *his body* or to the heirs, *male* or *female,* of his body.

Tenant in tail ex provisione viri. Where an owner of lands, upon or previously to marrying a wife, settled lands upon himself and his wife, and the heirs of their two bodies begotten, and then died, the wife, as survivor, became tenant in tail of the husband's lands, in consequence of the husband's provision (*ex provisione viri*). Originally, she could bar the estate-tail like any other tenant in tail; but the husband's intention having been merely to provide for her during her widowhood, and not to enable her to bar his children of their inheritance, she was early restrained from so doing, by the statute 32 Hen. VII, c. 36.

Tenant of the demesne. One who is tenant of a mesne lord; as, where A. is tenant of B., and C. of A., B. is the lord, A. the mesne lord, and C. tenant of the demesne.

Tenant paravaile. The under-tenant of land; that is, the tenant of a tenant; one who held of a mesne lord.

Tenants by the verge. The "same nature as tenants by copy of court roll [*i.e.,* copyholders]. But the reason why they be called 'tenants by the verge' is for that, when they will surrender their tenements into the hands of their lord to the use of another, they shall have a little rod (by the custome) in their hand, the which they shall deliver to the steward or to the bailife, * * * and the steward or bailife, according to the custome, shall deliver to him that taketh the land the same rod, or another rod, in the name of seisin; and for this cause they are called 'tenants by

the verge,' but they have no other evidence [title-deed] but by copy of court roll."

Tenant to the præcipe. Before the English fines and recoveries act, if land was conveyed to a person for life with remainder to another in tail, the tenant in tail in remainder was unable to bar the entail without the concurrence of the tenant for life, because a common recovery could only be suffered by the person seised of the land. In such a case, if the tenant for life wished to concur in barring the entail, he usually conveyed his life-estate to some other person, in order that the *præcipe* in the recovery might be issued against the latter, who was therefore called the "tenant to the *præcipe.*"

Tenantable repair. Such a repair as will render premises fit for present habitation.

Tenant-right. In England, the right of tenant on termination of tenancy to payment for unexhausted improvements made on his holding.

Tenant's fixtures. This phrase signifies things which are fixed to the freehold of the demised premises, but which the tenant may detach and take away, provided he does so in season.

Tencon. L. Fr. A dispute; a quarrel.

Tend. To have a leaning; serve, contribute, or conduce in some degree or way, or have a more or less direct bearing or effect; to be directed as to any end, object, or purpose; to have a tendency, conscious or unconscious, to any end, object or purpose. Rogers v. State, 122 Tex.Cr.R. 331, 54 S.W.2d 1010, 1012.

In old English law, to tender or offer.

Tender. An offer of money. The act by which one produces and offers to a person holding a claim or demand against him the amount of money which he considers and admits to be due, in satisfaction of such claim or demand, without any stipulation or condition. As used in determining whether one party may place the other in breach of contract for failure to perform, means a readiness and willingness to perform in case of concurrent performance by other party, with present ability to do so, and notice to other party of such readiness. Monroe St. Properties, Inc. v. Carpenter, C.A.Ariz., 407 F.2d 379, 380. Essential characteristics of tender are unconditional offer to perform coupled with manifested ability to carry out the offer and production of subject matter of tender. Collins v. Kingsberry Homes Corp., D.C. Ala., 243 F.Supp. 741, 744.

At a settlement under an agreement of sale the seller tenders the executed deed to the purchaser, who tenders the remainder of the purchase price to the seller.

The actual proffer of money, as distinguished from mere proposal or proposition to proffer it. Hence mere written proposal to pay money, without offer of cash, is not "tender."

Tender, though usually used in connection with an offer to pay money, is properly used in connection with offer of property other than money.

Tender, in common law pleading, is a plea by defendant that he has been always ready to pay the debt demanded, and before the commencement of the action tendered it to the plaintiff, and now brings it into court ready to be paid to him, etc.

Legal tender is that kind of coin, money, or circulating medium which the law compels a creditor to accept in payment of his debt, when tendered by the debtor in the right amount. See also **Legal tender**.

See also **Legally sufficient tender**.

Tender of issue. A form of words in common law pleading, by which a party offers to refer the question raised upon it to the appropriate mode of decision. The common tender of an issue of fact by a defendant is expressed by the words, "and of this he puts himself upon the country."

Tender offer. An offer to purchase shares made by one company direct to the stockholders of another company, sometimes subject to a minimum and/or a maximum that the offeror will accept, communicated to the shareholders by means of newspaper advertisements and (if the offeror can obtain the shareholders list, which is not often unless it is a friendly tender) by a general mailing to the entire list of shareholders, with a view to acquiring control of the second company. Used in an effort to go around the management of the second company, which is resisting acquisition. A take-over bid. Tender offers are regulated by state and federal securities laws; *e.g.* Williams Act, § 14(e), 15 U.S.C.A. § 78n(e).

Tender of performance. Offer to perform which is commonly necessary to hold the defaulting party to a contract liable for breach.

Tenement /ténəmənt/. This term, in its common acceptation, is only applied to houses and other buildings, but in its original, proper, and legal sense it signifies everything that may be *holden,* provided it be of a permanent nature, whether it be of a substantial and sensible, or of an unsubstantial, ideal, kind. Thus, *liberum tenementum,* frank tenement, or freehold, is applicable not only to lands and other solid objects, but also to offices, rents, commons, advowsons, franchises, peerages, etc. At common law, "tenements" included lands, other inheritances, capable of being held in freehold, and rents. Wood v. Galpert, Ohio Com.Pl., 199 N.E.2d 900, 901.

Dominant tenement. One for the benefit or advantage of which an easement exists or is enjoyed.

Servient tenement. One which is subject to the burden of an easement existing for or enjoyed by another tenement. See **Easement**.

Tenement house. Low rent apartment building, usually in poor condition, meeting only minimal, if even that, safety and sanitary conditions.

Tenemental land /tènəméntəl lǽnd/. Land distributed by a lord among his tenants, as opposed to the demesnes which were occupied by himself and his servants.

Tenementis legatis /tènəméntəm ləgéydəs/. An ancient writ, lying to the city of London, or any other corporation (where the old custom was that men might devise by will lands and tenements, as well as goods and chattels), for the hearing and determining any controversy touching the same.

Tenendum /tənéndəm/. Lat. To be holden. It was used to indicate the lord of whom the land was to be held and the tenure by which it was to be held, but, since all freehold tenures have been converted into socage, the *tenendum* is of no further use, and is therefore joined in the *habendum,*—"to have and to hold."

Tenens /ténèn(d)z/. A tenant; the defendant in a real action.

Tenentibus in assisâ non onerandis /tənéntəbəs ìn əsáyzə nòn ònərǽndəs/. A writ that formerly lay for him to whom a disseisor had alienated the land whereof he disseised another, that he should not be molested in assize for damages, if the disseisor had wherewith to satisfy them.

Tenere /təníriy/. Lat. In the civil law, to hold; to hold fast; to have in possession; to retain.

In relation to the doctrine of possession, this term expresses merely the fact of manual detention, or the corporal possession of any object, without involving the question of title; while *habere* (and especially *possidere*) denotes the maintenance of possession by a lawful claim; *i.e., civil* possession, as distinguished from mere·*natural* possession.

Teneri /təníray/. The Latin name for that clause in a bond in which the obligor expresses that he is "held and firmly bound" to the obligee, his heirs, etc.

Tenet; tenuit /ténət/tényuwət/. Lat. He holds; he held. In the Latin forms of the writ of waste against a tenant, these words introduced the allegation of tenure. If the tenancy still existed, and recovery of the land was sought, the former word was used (and the writ was said to be "in the *tenet*"). If the tenancy had already determined, the latter term was used (the writ being described as "in the *tenuit*"), and then damages only were sought.

Tenheded, or **tienheofed** /ténhèd(əd)/. In old English law, a dean.

10–K. The name of the annual report required by the SEC of nearly all publicly-held corporations. This report contains more information than the annual report to stockholders. Corporations must send a copy of the 10–K to those stockholders who request it.

Tenmentale /ténmantèyl/. The number of ten men, which number, in the time of the Saxons, was called a "decennary;" and ten decennaries made what was called a "hundred." Also a duty or tribute paid to the crown, consisting of two shillings for each plowland.

Tenne /téniy/. A term of heraldry, meaning orange color. In engravings it should be represented by lines in bend sinister crossed by others bar-ways. Heralds who blazon by the names of the heavenly bodies, call it "dragon's head," and those who employ jewels, "jacinth." It is one of the colors called "stainand."

Tennessee Valley Authority (TVA). A government-owned corporation that conducts a unified program of resource development for the advancement of economic growth in the Tennessee Valley region. The Authority's program of activities includes flood control, navigation development, electric power production, fertilizer development, recreation improvement, and forestry and wildlife development. While its power program is financially self-supporting, other programs are financed primarily by appropriations from Congress.

Tenor. A term used in pleading to denote that an exact copy is set out. "Tenor," in pleading a written instrument, imports that the very words are set out. "Purport" does not import this, but is equivalent only to "substance."

By the tenor of a deed, or other instrument in writing, is signified the matter contained therein, according to the true intent and meaning thereof.

In chancery pleading. A certified copy of records of other courts removed in chancery by *certiorari.*

Tenore indictamenti mittendo /tənóriy əndìktəméntay məténdow/. A writ whereby the record of an indictment, and the process thereupon, was called out of another court into the queen's bench.

Tenore præsentium /tənóriy prəzénsh(iy)əm/. By the tenor of these presents, *i.e.,* the matter contained therein, or rather the intent and meaning thereof.

Tenor est qui legem dat feudo /ténər èst kwày líyjəm dæt fyúwdow/. It is the tenor [of the feudal grant] which regulates its effect and extent.

Tenseriæ /tensíriyiy/. A sort of ancient tax or military contribution.

Tentative trust. See **Trust** *(Totten trust).*

Tenterden's Act /téntərdən(d)z ækt/. In English law, the statute 9 Geo. IV, c. 14, taking its name from Lord Tenterden, who procured its enactment, which is a species of extension of the statute of frauds, and requires the reduction of contracts to writing.

Tenth Amendment. An amendment to the U.S. Constitution (1791) which provides that the powers not delegated to the federal government are reserved to the States or to the people.

Tenths /tén(t)θs/. In English law, a temporary aid issuing out of personal property, and granted to the king by parliament; formerly the real tenth part of all the movables belonging to the subject. 1 Bl.Comm. 308.

In English ecclesiastical law, the tenth part of the annual profit of every living in the kingdom, formerly paid to the pope, but by statute 26 Hen. VIII, c. 3, transferred to the crown, and afterwards made a part of the fund called "Queen Anne's Bounty." 1 Bl. Comm. 284–286.

Tenuit /tényuwət/. A term used in stating the tenure in an action for waste done after the termination of the tenancy. See **Tenet.**

Tenura /tényərə/. In old English law, tenure.

Tenura est pactio contra communem feudi naturam ac rationem, in contractu interposita /tényərə èst pǽksh(iy)ow kóntrə kəmyúwnəm fyúwday nəchúrəm æk rǽshiyównəm, in kəntrǽkt(y)uw ìntərpózədə/. Tenure is a compact contrary to the common nature and reason of the fee, put into a contract.

Tenure /tényər/. Generally, tenure is a right, term, or mode of holding or occupying, and "tenure of an office" means the manner in which it is held, especially with regard to time. Winterberg v. University of Nevada System, 89 Nev. 358, 513 P.2d 1248, 1250.

Status afforded to teacher or professor upon completion of trial period, thus protecting him or her from summary dismissal. Tenure denotes relinquishment of the employer's unfettered power to terminate the employee's services. Zumwalt v. Trustees of California State Colleges, 31 Cal.App.3d 611, 107 Cal. Rptr. 573, 579.

Term of office. Duration of holding public or private office. The tenure of federal judges is during life and good behavior. The tenure of merit system employees is during satisfactory performance of duties until a fixed age of retirement unless the position is discontinued.

Feudal law. The mode or system of holding lands or tenements in subordination to some superior which, in feudal ages, was the leading characteristic of real property. Gibbs v. Titelman, D.C.Pa., 369 F.Supp. 38, 49.

Tenure is the direct result of feudalism, which separated the *dominium directum* (the dominion of the soil), which is placed mediately or immediately in the crown, from the *dominion utile* (the possessory title), the right to the use and profits in the soil, designated by the term "seisin," which is the highest interest a subject can acquire. Kavanaugh v. Cohoes Power & Light Corporation, 114 Misc. 590, 187 N.Y.S. 216, 231.

Wharton gives the following list of tenures which were ultimately developed:

Lay Tenures

I. Frank tenement, or freehold. (1) The military tenures (abolished, except grand serjeanty, and reduced to free socage tenures) were: Knight service proper, or tenure in chivalry; grand serjeanty; cornage. (2) Free socage, or plow-service; either petit serjeanty, tenure in burgage, or gavelkind.

II. Villeinage. (1) Pure villeinage (whence copyholds at the lord's [nominal] will, which is regulated according to custom). (2) Privileged villeinage, sometimes called "villein socage" (whence tenure in ancient demesne, which is an exalted species of copyhold, held according to custom, and not according to the lord's will), and is of three kinds: Tenure in ancient demesne; privileged copyholds, customary freeholds, or free copyholds; copyholds of base tenure.

Spiritual Tenures

I. Frankalmoigne, or free alms.

II. Tenure by divine service.

Tenure by divine service. Exists where an ecclesiastical corporation, sole or aggregate, holds land by a certain divine service; as, to say prayers on a certain day in every year, "or to distribute in almes to an hundred poore men an hundred pence at such a day."

Tenured faculty. Those members of a school's teaching staff who hold their position for life or until retirement. They may not be discharged except for cause.

Term. A word or phrase; an expression; particularly one which possesses a fixed and known meaning in some science, art, or profession.

A fixed period; period of determined or prescribed duration. A specified period of time; *e.g.* term of lease, court session, sentence. The word in a legal sense means a fixed and definite period of time which the law describes that an officer may hold an office. Sueppel v. City Council of Iowa City, 257 Iowa 1350, 136 N.W.2d 523, 527.

In civil law, a space of time granted to a debtor for discharging his obligation.

Bounds, limitation, or extent of time for which an estate is granted; as when a man holds an estate for any limited or specific number of years, which is called his "term," and he himself is called, with reference to the term he so holds, the "termor," or "tenant of the term."

Portion of agreement which relates to particular matter. U.C.C. § 1–201(42). A condition in a contract, instrument, agreement, etc. See also **Open price term.**

When used with reference to a court, signifies the space of time during which the court holds a session. A *session* signifies the time during the term when the court sits for the transaction of business, and the session commences when the court convenes for the term, and continues until final adjournment, either before or at the expiration of the term. The *term* of the court is the time prescribed by law during which it may be in *session*. The *session* of the court is the time of its actual sitting. But "term" and "session" are often used interchangeably. See also **Session;** and *Term of court,* below.

General term. A phrase used in some jurisdictions to denote the ordinary session of a court, for the trial and determination of causes, as distinguished from a *special* term, for the hearing of motions or arguments or the despatch of various kinds of formal business, or the trial of a special list or class of cases. Or it may denote a sitting of the court *in banc.*

Regular term. A term begun at the time appointed by law, and continued, in the discretion of the court, to such time as it may appoint, consistent with the law.

Special term. In court practice in certain states, that branch of the court which is held by a single judge for hearing and deciding in the first instance motions and causes of equitable nature is called the "special term," as opposed to the "general term," held by three judges (usually) to hear appeals.

Peculiar or unusual conditions imposed on a party before granting some application to the favor of the court.

Term attendant on the inheritance. See **Attendant terms.**

Term bonds. A bond issue whose component bonds all mature at the same time. Contrast with "serial bonds." See also **Bond.**

Term fee. In English practice, a certain sum which a solicitor is entitled to charge to his client, and the client to recover, if successful, from the unsuccessful party; payable for every term in which any proceedings subsequent to the summons shall take place.

Term for deliberating. The time given to the beneficiary heir, to examine if it be for his interest to accept or reject the succession which has fallen to him.

Term for years. An *estate for years* and the *time* during which such estate is to be held are each called a "term;" hence the term may expire before the time, as by a surrender.

Term in gross. A term of years is said to be either in gross (outstanding) or attendant upon the inheritance. It is outstanding, or in gross, when it is unattached or disconnected from the estate or inheritance, as where it is in the hands of some third party having no interest in the inheritance; it is attendant, when vested in some trustee in trust for the owner of the inheritance.

Term loan. A loan with a maturity date, as opposed to a demand loan which is due whenever the lender requests payment.

Term of court. Signifies the space of time prescribed by law during which a court holds session. The court's session may actually extend beyond the term. The October Term of the Supreme Court of the United States is now the only term during which the Court sits, and lasts from October to June. The U.S. district courts do not have formal terms. 28 U.S.C.A. § 138. See also *General term; Regular term; Special term, supra.*

Term of lease. The word "term," when used in connection with a lease, means the period which is granted for the lessee to occupy the premises, and does not include the time between the making of the lease and the tenant's entry. De Pauw University v. United Electric Coal Cos., 299 Ill.App. 339, 20 N.E.2d 146, 149.

Term of office. The period during which elected officer or appointee is entitled to hold office, perform its functions, and enjoy its privileges and emoluments.

Term probatory. The period of time allowed to the promoter of an ecclesiastical suit to produce his witnesses, and prove the facts on which he rests his case.

Term to conclude. In English ecclesiastical practice, an appointment by the judge of a time at which both parties are understood to renounce all further exhibits and allegations.

Term to propound all things. In English ecclesiastical practice, an appointment by the judge of a time at which both parties are to exhibit all the acts and instruments which make for their respective causes.

Under terms. A party is said to be *under terms* when an indulgence is granted to him by the court in its discretion, on certain conditions. Thus, when an injunction is granted *ex parte*, the party obtaining it is put *under terms* to abide by such order as to damages as the court may make at the hearing.

Termes de la Ley. Terms of the law. The name of a lexicon of the law French words and other technicalities of legal language in old times.

Terminable interest. An interest in property which terminates upon the death of the holder or upon the occurrence of some other specified event. The transfer of a terminable interest by one spouse to the other spouse does not qualify for the marital deduction.

Terminable property. This name is sometimes given to property of such a nature that its duration is not perpetual or indefinite, but is limited or liable to terminate upon the happening of an event or the expiration of a fixed term; *e.g.,* a leasehold, a life-annuity, etc.

Terminate. To put an end to; to make to cease; to end. Towne v. Towne, 117 Mont. 453, 159 P.2d 352, 357.

Terminating building societies. Societies, in England, where the members commence their monthly contributions on a particular day, and continue to pay them until the realization of shares to a given amount for each member, by the advance of the capital of the society to such members as required it, and the payment of interest as well as principal by them, so as to insure such realization within a given period of years. They have been superseded by permanent building societies.

Termination. End in time or existence; close; cessation; conclusion. Perruccio v. Allen, 156 Conn. 282, 240 A.2d 912, 914.

Word "termination," for purposes of insurance, refers to the expiration of a policy by lapse of the policy. Waynesville Sec. Bank v. Stuyvesant Inc. Co., Mo.App., 499 S.W.2d 218, 220.

With respect to a lease or contract, term refers to an ending, usually before the end of the anticipated term of the lease or contract, which termination may be by mutual agreement or may be by exercise of one party of one of his remedies due to the default of the other party. As regards a partnership, term refers to a winding up and cessation of the business as opposed to only a technical ending (as upon the death of a partner) which is a dissolution. A dissolved partnership may terminate or may be continued by a partnership of the remaining partners, including perhaps the estate or heirs of the deceased partner.

Under the Uniform Commercial Code, "termination" means legally ending a contract without its being broken by either side. U.C.C. § 2–106.

See also **Dissolution; Expiration; Lapse.**

Termination of conditional contract. To abrogate so much of it as remains unperformed, doing away with existing agreement under agreed terms and consequences. To put an end to all of the unperformed portions thereof. Blodgett v. Merritt Annex Oil Co., 19 Cal.App.2d 169, 65 P.2d 123, 125.

Termination of employment. Within policies providing that insurance should cease immediately upon termination of employment, means a complete severance of relationship of employer and employee. Edwards v. Equitable Life Assur. Soc. of United States, 296 Ky. 448, 177 S.W.2d 574, 577, 578.

Terminer /tə́rmənər/. L. Fr. To determine. See **Oyer and terminer.**

Termini /tə́rmənay/. Lat. Ends; bounds; limiting or terminating points.

Termino /termíynow/. In Spanish law, a common; common land. Common because of vicinage.

Term insurance. See **Insurance.**

Terminum /tə́rmənəm/. A day given to a defendant.

Terminum qui preteriit, writ of entry ad /ríd əv éntriy æd tə́rmənəm kwày prətéhriyət/. A writ which lay for the reversioner, when the possession was withheld by the lessee, or a stranger, after the determination of a lease for years.

Terminus /tə́rmənəs/. Boundary; a limit, either of space or time.

The phrases *"terminus a quo"* and *"terminus ad quem"* are used, respectively, to designate the starting point and terminating point of a private way. In the case of a street, road, or railway, either end may be, and commonly is, referred to as the "terminus."

Terminus annorum certus debet esse et determinatus /tə́rmənəs ænórəm sə́rdəs débəd ésiy èt dətə́rmənéydəs/. A term of years ought to be certain and determinate.

Terminus et feodum non possunt constare simui in una eademque persona /tə́rmənəs èt fyúwdəm nòn pósənt kon(t)stériy sáyməl ìn yúwnə iyeydémkwiy pərsównə/. A term and the fee cannot both be in one and the same person at the same time.

Terminus hominis /tə́rmənəs hómənəs/. In English ecclesiastical practice, a time for the determination of appeals, shorter than the *terminus juris*, appointed by the judge.

Terminus juris /tə́rmənəs jə́rəs/. In English ecclesiastical practice, the time of one or two years, allowed by law for the determination of appeals.

Termor /tə́rmər/. He that holds lands or tenements for a term of years or life. But we generally confine the application of the word to a person entitled for a term of years.

Terms of trust. The phrase "terms of the trust" means the manifestation of intention of the settlor with respect to the trust expressed in a manner which admits of its proof in judicial proceedings. Restatement, Second, Trusts § 4.

Terms to be under. A party is said to be *under terms*, when an indulgence is granted to him by the court in its discretion, on certain conditions. Thus, when an injunction is granted *ex parte*, the party obtaining it is put *under terms* to abide by such order as to damages as the court may make at the hearing.

Terra /téhrə/. Lat. Earth; soil; arable land.

Terra affirmata /téhrə æfərméydə/. Land let to farm.

Terra boscalis /téhrə boskéyləs/. Woody land.

Terra culta /téhrə kə́ltə/. Cultivated land.

Terra debilis /téhrə débələs/. Weak or barren land.

Terra dominica, or **indominicata** /téhrə dəmínəkə/°indəmìnəkéydə/. The demesne land of a manor.

Terræ dominicales regis /téhriy dəmìnəkéyliyz ríyjəs/. The demesne lands of the crown.

Terra excultabilis /téhrə èkskə̀ltéybələs/. Land which may be plowed.

Terra extendenda /téhrə èkstendéndə/. A writ addressed to an escheator, etc., that he inquire and find out the true yearly value of any land, etc., by the oath of twelve men, and to certify the extent into the chancery.

Terra frusca, or **frisca** /téhrə frískə/. Fresh land, not lately plowed.

Terrage /téhrəj/. In old English law, a kind of tax or charge on land; a boon or duty of plowing, reaping, etc.

Terrages /téhrəjəz/. An exemption from all uncertain services.

Terra hydata /téhrə hədéydə/. Land subject to the payment of hydage.

Terra lucrabilis /téhrə l(y)uwkréybələs/. Land gained from the sea or inclosed out of a waste.

Terra manens vacua occupanti conceditur /téhrə mǽnen(d)z vǽkyuwə òkyəpǽntay kən(t)síydədər/. Land lying unoccupied is given to the first occupant.

Terra normanorum /téhrə nòrmənórəm/. Land held by a Norman.

Terra nova /téhrə nówvə/. Land newly converted from wood ground or arable.

Terra putura /téhrə pyuwtyúrə/. Land in forests, held by the tenure of furnishing food to the keepers therein.

Terrarius /tərériyəs/. In old English law, a landholder.

Terra sabulosa /téhrə sæ̀byəlówsə/. Gravelly or sandy ground.

Terra salica /téhrə sǽləkə/. In Salic law, the land of the house; the land within that inclosure which belonged to a German house. No portion of the inheritance of Salic land passes to a woman, but this the male sex acquires; that is, the sons succeed in that inheritance.

Terra testamentalis /téhrə tèstəmentéyləs/. Gavel-kind land, being disposable by will.

Terra transit cum onere /téhrə træn(d)zət kəm ównəriy/. Land passes with the incumbrances.

Terra vestita /téhrə vəstáydə/. Land sown with corn.

Terra wainabilis /téhrə wèynéybələs/. Tillable land.

Terra warrenata /téhrə wòhrǽnéydə/. Land that has the liberty of free-warren.

Terre-tenant /tértènənt/tár°/. He who is literally in the occupation or possession of the land, as distinguished from the owner out of possession. But, in a more technical sense, the person who is seised of the land, though not in actual occupancy of it, and locally, in Pennsylvania, one who purchases and takes land subject to the existing lien of a mortgage or judgment against a former owner.

Terrier. In English law, a landroll or survey of lands, containing the quantity of acres, tenants' names, and such like; and in the exchequer there is a terrier of all the glebe lands in England, made about 1338. In general, an ecclesiastical terrier contains a detail of the temporal possessions of the church in every parish.

Terris bonis et catallis rehabendis post purgationem /téhrəs bównəs èt kətǽləs rìy(h)əbéndəs pòwst pərgèyshiyównəm/. A writ for a clerk to recover his lands, goods, and chattels, formerly seized, after he had cleared himself of the felony of which he was accused, and delivered to his ordinary to be purged.

Terris et catallis tentis ultra debitum levatum /téhrəs èt kətǽləs téntəs ə́ltrə débədəm ləvéydəm/. A judicial writ for the restoring of lands or goods to a debtor who is distrained above the amount of the debt.

Terris liberandis /téhrəs lìbərǽndəs/. A writ that lay for a man convicted by attaint, to bring the record and process before the king, and take a fine for his imprisonment, and then to deliver to him his lands and tenements again, and release him of the strip and waste. Also it was a writ for the delivery of lands to the heir, after homage and relief performed, or upon security taken that he should perform them.

Territorial. Having to do with a particular area; for example, territorial jurisdiction is the power of a court to take cases from within a particular geographical area.

Territorial courts. U.S. courts in each territory, such as the Virgin Islands. They serve as both Federal and state courts.

Territorial jurisdiction. Territory over which a government or a subdivision thereof has jurisdiction. State v. Cox, 106 Utah 253, 147 P.2d 858, 861. Jurisdiction considered as limited to cases arising or persons residing within a defined territory, as, a county, a judicial district, etc. The authority of any court is limited by the boundaries thus fixed. See also **Extraterritorial jurisdiction.**

Territorial property. The land and water over which the state has jurisdiction and control whether the legal title be in the state itself or in private individuals. Lakes and waters wholly within the state are its property and also the marginal sea within the three-mile limit, but bays and gulfs are not always recognized as state property.

Territorial; territoriality. These terms are used to signify connection with, or limitation with reference to, a particular country or territory. Thus, "territorial law" is the correct expression for the law of a particular country or state, although "municipal law" is more common.

Territorial waters. Term refers to all inland waters, all waters between line of mean high tide and line of ordinary low water, and all waters seaward to a line three geographical miles distant from the coast line. C. A. B. v. Island Airlines, Inc., D.C.Hawaii, 235 F.Supp. 990, 1002. That part of the sea adjacent to the coast of a given country which is by international law deemed to be within the sovereignty of that country, so that its courts have jurisdiction over offenses committed on those waters, even by a person on board a foreign ship. See **Three-mile limit.**

Territory. A part of a country separated from the rest, and subject to a particular jurisdiction. Geographical area under the jurisdiction of another country or sovereign power.

A portion of the United States, not within the limits of any state, which has not yet been admitted as a state of the Union, but is organized, with a separate legislature, and with executive and judicial officers appointed by the president. See **Trust territory.**

An assigned geographical area of responsibility; *e.g.* salesman's territory.

Territory of a judge. The territorial jurisdiction of a judge; the bounds, or district, within which he may lawfully exercise his judicial authority.

Terror. Alarm; fright; dread; the state of mind induced by the apprehension of hurt from some hostile or threatening event or manifestation; fear caused by the appearance of danger. In an indictment for riot at common law, it must have been charged that the acts done were "to the *terror* of the people."

Terroristic threats. A person is guilty of a felony if he threatens to commit any crime of violence with purpose to terrorize another or to cause evacuation of a building, place of assembly, or facility of public transportation, or otherwise to cause serious public inconvenience, or in reckless disregard of the risk of causing such terror or inconvenience. Model Penal Code, § 211.3.

Tertia denunciatio /tɜ́rsh(iy)ə dənə̀n(t)siyéysh(iy)ow/. Lat. In old English law, third publication or proclamation of intended marriage.

Tertius interveniens /tɜ́rsh(iy)əs ìntərvíyn(i)yèn(d)z/. Lat. In the civil law, a third person intervening; a third person who comes in between the parties to a suit; one who interpleads.

Test. To bring one to a trial and examination, or to ascertain the truth or the quality or fitness of a thing. Something by which to ascertain the truth respecting another thing; a criterion, gauge, standard, or norm.

In public law, an inquiry or examination addressed to a person appointed or elected to a public office, to ascertain his qualifications therefor, but particularly a scrutiny of his political, religious, or social views, or his attitude of past and present loyalty or disloyalty to the government under which he is to act.

See also **Competitive civil service examination; Examination.**

Discovery. Requests for permission to test tangible things in civil actions are governed by Fed.R.Civil P. 34. Requests for reports or results of examinations or tests are governed by Fed.R.Civil P. 35, and Fed.R. Crim.P. 16.

Testable. A person is said to be testable when he has capacity to make a will; a man of twenty one years of age and of sane mind is testable.

Test act. The statute 25 Car. II, c. 2, which directed all civil and military officers to take the oaths of allegiance and supremacy, and make the declaration against transubstantiation, within six months after their admission, and also within the same time receive the sacrament according to the usage of the Church of England, under penalty of £500 and disability to hold the office. This was abolished by St. 9 Geo. IV, c. 17, so far as concerns receiving the sacrament, and a new form of declaration was substituted.

Test action or case. An action selected out of a considerable number of suits, concurrently depending in the same court, brought by several plaintiffs against the same defendant, or by one plaintiff against different defendants, all similar in their circumstances, and embracing the same questions, and to be supported by the same evidence, the selected action to go first to trial (under an order of court equivalent to consolidation), and its decision to serve as a *test* of the right of recovery in the others, all parties agreeing to be bound by the result of the test action. A lawsuit brought to establish an important legal principle or right.

Testacy /téstəsiy/. The state or condition of leaving a will at one's death. Opposed to "intestacy."

Testa de nevil /téstə də névəl/. An ancient and authentic record in two volumes, in the custody of the king's remembrancer in the exchequer, said to be compiled by John de Nevil, a justice itinerant, in the eighteenth and twenty-fourth years of Henry III. These volumes were printed in 1807, under the authority of the commissioners of the public records, and contain an account of fees held either immediately of the king or of others who held of the king *in capite;* fees holden in frankalmoigne; serjeanties holden of the king; widows and heiresses of tenants *in capite*, whose marriages were in the gift of the king; churches in the gift of the king; escheats, and sums paid for scutages and aids, especially within the county of Hereford.

Testament. Under the early English law, a term that referred to the disposition of *personal* property by will; *i.e.* by "last will and testament." The words "and testament" are no longer necessary since a will now relates to both real and personal property.

Military testament. In English law, a nuncupative will, that is, one made by word of mouth, by which a soldier may dispose of his goods, pay, and other personal chattels, without the forms and solemnities which the law requires in other cases. See also **Nuncupative will; Soldier's will.**

Mutual testaments. Wills made by two persons who leave their effects reciprocally to the survivor.

Mystic testament. A form of testament made under Spanish law which prevailed in Louisiana and California. In the law of Louisiana, a sealed testament. The mystic or secret testament, otherwise called the "closed testament," is made in the following manner: The testator must sign his dispositions, whether he has written them himself or has caused them to be written by another person. The paper containing those dispositions, or the paper serving as their envelope, must be closed and sealed. The testator shall present it thus closed and sealed to the notary and to seven witnesses, or he shall cause it to be closed and sealed in their presence. Then he shall declare to the notary, in presence of the witnesses, that that paper contains his testament written by himself, or by another by his direction, and signed by him, the testator. The notary shall then draw up the act of superscription, which shall be written on that paper, or on the sheet that serves as its envelope, and that act shall be signed by the testator, and by the notary and the witnesses. Civ.Code La. art. 1584.

Testamenta cum duo inter se pugnantia reperiuntur, ultimum ratum est; sic est, cum duo inter se pugnantia reperiuntur in eodem testamento /tèstəméntə kàm d(y)úwow íntər sìy pəgnǽnsh(iy)ə rəpəriyántər, ə́ltəmə réydəm èst; sík èst, kàm d(y)úwow íntər sìy pəgnǽnsh(iy)ə rəpəriyántər ìn iyówdəm tèstəméntow/. When two conflicting wills are found, the last prevails; so it is when two conflicting clauses occur in the same will.

Testamenta latissimam interpretationem habere debent /tèstəméntə lætísəməm intàrprətèyshiyównəm həbíriy débənt/. Wills ought to have the broadest interpretation.

Testamentary. Pertaining to a will or testament; as *testamentary* causes. Derived from, founded on, or appointed by a testament or will; as a *testamentary* guardian, letters *testamentary*, etc.

A paper, instrument, document, gift, appointment, etc., is said to be "testamentary" when it is written or made so as not to take effect until after the death of the person making it, and to be revocable and retain the property under his control during his life, although he may have believed that it would operate as an instrument of a different character. See In re Murphy's Estate, 193 Wash. 400, 75 P.2d 916, 920.

Letters testamentary. The formal instrument of authority and appointment given to an executor by the proper court, upon the admission of the will to probate, empowering him to enter upon the discharge of his office as executor.

Testamentary capacity. Generally defined as ability to know and understand business in which testatrix is engaged, effect of action in making will, capacity to know objects of her bounty and claims upon her, and general nature and extent of her property. Miller v. Flyr, Tex.Civ.App., 447 S.W.2d 195, 203. That measure of mental ability which is recognized in law as sufficient for the making of a will. A testator to have such capacity must have sufficient mind and memory to intelligently understand the nature of business in which he is engaged, to comprehend generally the nature and extent of property which constitutes his estate, and which he intends to dispose of, and to recollect the objects of his bounty. See also **Capacity.**

Testamentary character. Of the nature or pertaining to a disposition of property at death.

Testamentary class. Body of persons, uncertain in number at time of gift, ascertainable in future, and each taking in equal or in other definite proportions. A "testamentary class gift" is a gift to a group whose number at the time of the gift is uncertain but which will be ascertained at some future time when all who constitute the class will take an equal or other definite portion, the amount of the share of each being dependent upon the number that ultimately constitutes the class. Lux v. Lux, 109 R.I. 592, 288 A.2d 701, 705.

Testamentary disposition. A disposition of property by way of gift, will or deed which is not to take effect unless the grantor dies or until that event.

Testamentary guardian. A guardian appointed by the last will of parent for the person and real and personal estate of child until the latter arrives of full age. In re De Saulles, 101 Misc. 447, 167 N.Y.S. 445, 453.

Testamentary paper or instrument. An instrument in the nature of a will; an unprobated will; a paper writing which is of the character of a will, though not formally such, and, if allowed as a testament, will have the effect of a will upon the devolution and distribution of property.

Testamentary power. Power to make a will. A power of appointment exercisable only by will. Restatement, Property, § 321(1).

Testamentary trust. Trust which takes effect at the death of the settlor. See also **Trust.**

Testamentary trustee. See **Trustee.**

Testamenti factio /tèstəméntay fǽksh(iy)ow/. Lat. In the civil law, the ceremony of making a testament, either as testator, heir, or witness.

Testamentum /tèstəméntəm/. Lat. In the civil law, a testament; a will, or last will.

In old English law, a testament or will; a disposition of property made in contemplation of death.

A general name for any instrument of conveyance, including deeds and charters, and so called either because it furnished written *testimony* of the conveyance, or because it was authenticated by witnesses *(testes).*

Testamentum est voluntatis nostræ justa sententia, de eo quod quis post mortem suam fieri velit /tèstəméntəm èst vòləntéydəs nóstriy jə́stə sənténsh(iy)ə, dìy íyow kwòd kwís pòwst mórdəm s(y)úwəm fàyəray víylət/. A testament is the just expression of our will concerning that which any one wishes done after his death [or, as Blackstone translates, "the legal declaration of a man's intentions which he wills to be performed after his death"].

Testamentum inofficiosum /tèstəméntəm ìnəfìshiyówsəm/. Lat. In the civil law, an inofficious testament *(q.v.).*

Testamentum omne morte consummatur /tèstəméntəm ómniy mórdiy kòn(t)səméydər/. Every will is perfected by death. A will speaks from the time of death only.

Testamentum, i.e., testatio mentis, facta nullo præsente metu periculi, sed cogitatione mortalitatis /tèstəméntəm, íd èst, testéysh(iy)ow méntəs, fǽktə nə́low prəzéntiy mét(y)uw pəríkyəlay, sèd kòjətèyshiyówniy mortǽlətéydəs/. A testament, *i.e.,* the witnessing of one's intention, made under no present fear of danger, but in expectancy of death.

Testari /testéray/. Lat. In the civil law, to testify; to attest; to declare, publish, or make known a thing before witnesses. To make a will.

Testate /tésteyt/. One who has made a will; one who dies leaving a will.

Testate succession. Acquisition of property or rights through a will.

Testation /testéyshən/. Witness; evidence.

Testator /testéydər/. One who makes or has made a testament or will; one who dies leaving a will. This term is borrowed from the civil law.

Testatoris ultima voluntas est perimplenda secundum veram intentionem suam /testətórəs ə́ltəmə vəlántæs èst pərəmpléndə səkə́ndəm vírəm intènshiyównəm s(y)úwəm/. The last will of a testator is to be thoroughly fulfilled according to his real intention.

Testatrix /testéytrəks/. A woman who makes a will; a woman who dies leaving a will; a female testator.

Testatum /testéydəm/. The name of a writ which is issued by the court of one county to the sheriff of another county in the same state, when defendant cannot be found in the county where the court is located: for example, after a judgment has been obtained, and a *ca. sa.* has been issued, which has been returned *non est inventus*, a testatum *ca. sa.* may be issued to the sheriff of the county where the defendant is.

In conveyancing, that part of a deed which commences with the words, "This indenture witnesseth."

Testatum writ /testéydəm rìt/. In practice, a writ containing a *testatum* clause; such as a *testatum capias,* a *testatum fi. fa.,* and a *testatum ca. sa.* See **Testatum.**

Testatus /testéydəs/. Lat. In the civil law, testate; one who has made a will.

Teste. To bear witness formally. See **Teste of a writ.**

Tested /téstiyd/. To be tested is to bear the teste *(q.v.).*

Teste meipso /téstiy miyípsow/. Lat. In old English law and practice, a solemn formula of attestation by the sovereign, used at the conclusion of charters, and other public instruments, and also of original writs out of chancery.

Teste of a writ /téstiy əv ə rít/. In practice, the concluding clause, commencing with the word "Witness," etc. A writ which bears the teste is sometimes said to be *tested.*

In English law, "teste" is a word commonly used in the last part of every writ, wherein the date is contained beginning with the words, *"Teste meipso,"* meaning the sovereign, if the writ be an original writ, or be issued in the name of the sovereign; but, if the writ be a judicial writ, then the word "Teste" is followed by the name of the chief judge of the court in which the action is brought, or, in case of a vacancy of such office, in the name of the senior puisne judge.

Testes /téstiyz/. Lat. Witnesses.

Testes ponderantur, non numerantur /téstiyz pòndərǽntər, nón n(y)uwmərǽntər/. Witnesses are weighed, not numbered. That is, in case of a conflict of evidence, the truth is to be sought by weighing the credibility of the respective witnesses, not by the mere numerical preponderance on one side or the other.

Testes qui postulat debet dare eis sumptus competentes /téstiyz kwày pós(h)chələt débət dériy íyəs sə́m(p)təs kòmpəténtiyz/. Whosoever demands witnesses must find them in competent provision.

Testes, trial per /tráy(ə)l pər téstiyz/. A trial had before a judge without the intervention of a jury, in which the judge is left to form in his own breast his sentence upon the credit of the witnesses examined; but this mode of trial, although it was common in the civil law, was seldom resorted to in the practice of the common law, but it is now becoming common when each party waives his right to a trial by jury.

Testibus deponentibus in pari numero, dignioribus est credendum /téstəbəs dìypənéntəbəs in péray n(y)úwmərow, dìgn(i)yórəbəs èst krədéndəm/. Where the witnesses who testify are in equal number [on both sides], the more worthy are to be believed.

Testify. To bear witness; to give evidence as a witness; to make a solemn declaration, under oath or affirmation, in a judicial inquiry, for the purpose of establishing or proving some fact.

Testimonial. In the nature of testimony. Evidence is said to be testimonial when elicited from a witness in contrast to documentary evidence or real evidence.

Besides its ordinary meaning of a written recommendation to character, "testimonial" has a special meaning, under St. 39 Eliz., c. 17, § 3, passed in 1597, under which it signified a certificate under the hand of a justice of the peace, testifying the place and time when and where a soldier or mariner landed, and the place of his dwelling or birth, unto which he was to pass, and a convenient time limited for his passage. Every idle and wandering soldier or mariner not having such a testimonial, or willfully exceeding for above fourteen days the time limited thereby, or forging or counterfeiting such testimonial, was to suffer death as a felon, without benefit of clergy. This English act was repealed, in 1812, by St. 52 Geo. III, c. 31.

Testimonial evidence. Evidence elicited from a witness in contrast to documentary or real evidence. See also **Evidence.**

Testimonial proof. In the civil law, proof by the evidence of witnesses, *i.e.,* parol evidence, as distinguished from proof by written instruments, which is called "literal" proof.

Testimonia ponderanda sunt, non numeranda /tèstəmówn(i)yə pòndərǽndə sə̀nt, nòn n(y)ùwmərǽndə/. Evidence is to be weighed, not enumerated.

Testimonio /tèstəmówn(i)yow/. In Spanish law, an authentic copy of a deed or other instrument, made by a notary and given to an interested party as evidence of his title, the original remaining in the public archives.

Testimonium clause /tèstəmówn(i)yəm klóz/. In conveyancing, that clause of a deed or instrument with which it concludes; "In witness whereof, the parties to these presents have hereunto set their hands and seals." A clause in the instrument reciting the date on which the instrument was executed and by whom.

Testimony. Evidence given by a competent witness under oath or affirmation; as distinguished from evidence derived from writings, and other sources. Testimony is particular kind of evidence that comes to tribunal through live witnesses speaking under oath or affirmation in presence of tribunal, judicial or quasi-judicial. State v. Ricci, 107 R.I. 582, 268 A.2d 692, 697.

In common parlance, "testimony" and "evidence" are synonymous. Testimony properly means only such evidence as is delivered by a witness on the trial of a cause, either orally or in the form of affidavits or depositions.

See also **Evidence; Failure to testify; Opinion evidence or testimony; Perpetuating testimony.**

Expert testimony. See **Evidence** *(Expert evidence);* **Expert witness.**

Negative testimony. Testimony not bearing directly upon the immediate fact or occurrence under consideration, but evidencing facts from which it may be inferred that the act or fact in question could not possibly have happened.

Positive testimony. Direct testimony that a thing did or did not happen.

Testis /téstəs/. Lat. A witness; one who gives evidence in court, or who witnesses a document.

Testis de visu præponderat aliis /téstəs dìy váyz(y)uw prəpóndərət éyliyəs/. An eye-witness is preferred to others.

Testis lupanaris sufficit ad factum in lupanari /téstəs l(y)ùwpənérəs səfəsəd æd fæktəm in l(y)ùwpənéray/. A lewd person is a sufficient witness to an act committed in a brothel.

Testis nemo in sua causa esse potest /téstəs níymow in s(y)úwow kózə ésiy pówdəst/. No one can be a witness in his own cause.

Testis oculatus unus plus valet quam auriti decem /téstəs òkyəléydəs yúwnəs plás vælət kwæm ohráyday désəm/. One eye-witness is worth more than ten ear-witnesses.

Testmoigne. An old law French term, denoting evidence or testimony of a witness.

Testmoignes ne poent testifier le negative, mes l'affirmative. Witnesses cannot testify to a negative; they must testify to an affirmative.

Test oath. An oath required to be taken as a criterion of the fitness of the person to fill a public or political office; but particularly an oath of fidelity and allegiance (past or present) to the established government. See also **Loyalty oath.**

Test-paper. In practice, a paper or instrument shown to a jury as evidence. A term used in the Pennsylvania courts.

Tests. See **Test.**

Textbook. A legal text or treatise which presents principles on any branch of the law. See also **Hornbook.**

Textus roffensis /tékstəs rofén(t)səs/. In old English law, the Rochester text. An ancient manuscript containing many of the Saxon laws, and the rights, customs, tenures, etc., of the church of Rochester, drawn up by Ernulph, bishop of that see from A.D. 1114 to 1124.

Thainland /θéynlænd/. In old English law, the land which was granted by the Saxon kings to their thains or thanes was so called.

Thalweg /tálvèyk/. Old German spelling of Talweg, which title see.

Thanage of the king /θéynəj əv ðə kíŋ/. A certain part of the king's land or property, of which the ruler or governor was called "thane."

Thane /θéyn/. An Anglo-Saxon nobleman; an old title of honor, perhaps equivalent to "baron." There were two orders of thanes,—the king's thanes and the ordinary thanes. Soon after the Conquest this name was disused.

Thanelands /θéynlændz/. Such lands as were granted by charter of the Saxon kings to their thanes with all immunities, except from the *trinoda necessitas*.

Thaneship /θéynship/. The office and dignity of a thane; the seigniory of a thane.

That. A relative pronoun equivalent to who or which, either singular or plural.

Thavies inn. An inn of chancery. See **Inns of chancery.**

The. An article which particularizes the subject spoken of. "Grammatical niceties should not be resorted to without necessity; but it would be extending liberality to an unwarrantable length to confound the articles 'a' and 'the'. The most unlettered persons understand that 'a' is indefinite, but 'the' refers to a certain object."

Theft. A popular name for larceny. The taking of property without the owner's consent. People v. Sims, 29 Ill.App.3d 815, 331 N.E.2d 178, 179. The fraudulent taking of personal property belonging to another, from his possession, or from the possession of some person holding the same for him, without his consent, with intent to deprive the owner of the value of the same, and to appropriate it to the use or benefit of the person taking.

It is also said that theft is a wider term than larceny and that it includes swindling and embezzlement and that generally, one who obtains possession of property by lawful means and thereafter appropriates the property to the taker's own use is guilty of a "theft". Kidwell v. Paul Revere Fire Ins. Co., 294 Ky. 833, 172 S.W.2d 639, 640; People v. Pillsbury, 59 Cal.App.2d 107, 138 P.2d 320, 322.

Theft is any of the following acts done with intent to deprive the owner permanently of the possession, use or benefit of his property: (a) Obtaining or exerting unauthorized control over property; or (b) Obtaining by deception control over property; or (c) Obtaining by threat control over property; or (d) Obtaining control over stolen property knowing the property to have been stolen by another.

See also Auto theft; Embezzlement; Extortion; Intimidation; Larceny; Robbery; Theft by false pretext.

Theft of services. Obtaining services from another by deception, threat, coercion, stealth, mechanical tampering or use of false token or device.

Theft-bote /θéftbòwt/. The offense committed by a party who, having been robbed and knowing the felon, takes back his goods again, or receives other amends, upon an agreement not to prosecute. Farmers' Nat. Bank of Somerset v. Tarter, 256 Ky. 70, 75 S.W.2d 758, 760.

Theft-bote est emenda furti capta, sine consideratione curiæ domini regis /θéftbòwt èst əméndə fə́rday kǽptə, sáyniy kən(t)sìdərèyshiyówniy kyúhriyiy dómənay ríyjəs/. Theft-bote is the paying money to have goods stolen returned, without having any respect for the court of the king.

Theft by false pretext. Obtaining property by means of false pretext with intent to deprive owner of value of property without his consent and to appropriate it to own use, followed by such appropriation. Hoovel v. State, 125 Tex.Cr.R. 545, 69 S.W.2d 104, 106.

Thegn /θéyn/. An Anglo-Saxon term meaning a retainer. Afterwards it came to designate the territorial nobility. At a later period these were king's thegns, who were persons of great importance, and inferior thegns. Military service appears to have run through it all. After the Conquest, they were merged into the class of knights.

Thegnage tenure /θéynəj tényər/. A kind of tenure in Northumbria in the 13th century and beyond, of which little is known.

Thelonio irrationabili habendo /θəlówn(i)yow ihræshənǽbəlay həbéndow/. A writ that formerly lay for him that had any part of the king's demesne in fee-farm, to recover reasonable toll of the king's tenants there, if his demesne had been accustomed to be tolled.

Thelonium /θəlówn(i)yəm/. An abolished writ for citizens or burgesses to assert their right to exemption from toll.

Thelonmannus /θèlənmǽnəs/. The toll-man or officer who receives toll.

Thelusson Act. The statute 39 & 40 Geo. III, c. 98, which restricted accumulations to a term of twenty-one years from the testator's death. It was passed in consequence of litigation over the will of one Thelusson.

Theme. In Saxon law, the power of having jurisdiction over naifs or villeins, with their suits or offspring, lands, goods, and chattels.

Themmagium /θəméyj(iy)əm/. A duty or acknowledgment paid by inferior tenants in respect of theme or team.

Then. This word, as an adverb, means "at that time," referring to a time specified, either past or future. It has no power in itself to fix a time. It simply refers to a time already fixed. It may also denote a contingency, and be equivalent to "in that event."

Then and there. At the time and place last previously mentioned or charged. Context, however, may give the phrase a more remote antecedent than the time and place *last* previously mentioned or charged.

Thence. In surveying, and in descriptions of land by courses and distances, this word, preceding each course given, imports that the following course is continuous with the one before it.

Thence down the river. This phrase as used in field notes of a surveyor of a patent, is construed to mean with the meanders of the river, unless there is positive evidence that the meander line as written was where the surveyor in fact ran it; for such lines are to show the general course of the stream and to be used in estimating acreage, and not necessarily boundary lines.

Theocracy. Government of a state by the immediate direction of God (or by the assumed direction of a supposititious divinity), or the state thus governed.

Theoden. In Saxon law, a husbandman or inferior tenant; an under-thane.

Theodosian Code /θìyədówsh(iy)ən kówd/. See **Codex Theodosianus.**

Theof. In Saxon law, offenders who joined in a body of seven to commit depredations.

Theophilus' Institutes /θiyófələsəz ínstət(y)uwts/. See **Institutes.**

Theory of case. Facts on which the right of action is claimed to exist. The basis of liability or grounds of defense. Higgins v. Fuller, 48 N.M. 218, 148 P.2d 575, 579. See **Cause of action.**

Theory of law. The legal premise or set of principles on which a case rests.

Theory of pleading doctrine. The pre-code principle that one must prove his case as pleaded. Otherwise, he fails though he has set forth facts sufficient to sustain his case on a theory different from his pleadings. The various codes and rules of civil procedure have abolished this principle; see *e.g.* Fed.R.Civil P. 15 which permits amendment of pleadings to conform to evidence.

Theowes, theowmen, or **thews** /θ(y)úwz/θ(y)úwmən/. In feudal law, slaves, captives, or bondmen.

There. In or at that place.

Thereabout. About that place.

Thereafter. After the time last mentioned; after that; after that time; afterward; subsequently; thenceforth. Dauwe v. State, 147 Tex.Cr.R. 384, 180 S.W.2d 925, 927.

Thereby. By that means; in consequence of that.

Therefor. For that thing: for it, or them.

Therein. In that place.

Thereupon. Without delay or lapse of time. Immediately where the terms thereupon and thereby are distinguished. Following on; in consequence of. Yuma County Water Users' Ass'n v. Schlecht, 262 U.S. 138, 43 S.Ct. 498, 500, 67 L.Ed. 909.

Thesaurus absconditus /θəsóhrəs əbskóndədəs/. In old English law, treasure hidden or buried.

Thesaurus competit domino regi, et non domino liberatis, nisi sit per verba specialia /θəsóhrəs kómpədət dómənow ríyjay, èt non dómənow lìbərtéydəs, náysay sít pòr várbə spèshiyéyl(i)yə/. A treasure belongs to the king, and not to the lord of a liberty, unless it be through special words.

Thesaurus inventus /θəsóhrəs ənvéntəs/. In old English law, treasure found; treasure-trove.

Thesaurus inventus est vetus dispositio pecuniæ, etc., cujus non extat modo memoria, adeo ut jam dominum non habeat /θəsóhrəs invéntəs èst víydəs dìspəzísh(iy)ow pəkyúwniyiy, etsèdərórəm, kyúwjəs nòn ékstət mówdow məmóriyə, ǽdiyow àt jæm dómənəm nòn héybiyət/. Treasure-trove is an ancient hiding of money, etc., of which no recollection exists, so that it now has no owner.

Thesaurus non competit regi, nisi quando nemo scit qui abscondit thesaurum /θəsóhrəs nòn kómpədət ríyjay, náysay kwóndow níymow sít kwáy əbskóndət θəsóhrəm/. Treasure does not belong to the king, unless no one knows who hid it.

Thesaurus regis est vinculum pacis et bellorum nervus /θəsóhrəs ríyjəs èst vínk(y)ələm péysəs èt belórəm nárvəs/. The king's treasure is the bond of peace and the sinews of war.

Thesaurus, thesaurium /θəsóhrəs/θəsóhriyəm/. The treasury; a treasure.

Thesmothete /θézməθìyt/. A law-maker; a law-giver.

Thethinga /θíyðiŋə/. A tithing.

Thia /tíyə/. Lat. In the civil and old European law, an aunt.

Thief. One who steals; one who commits theft or larceny. See also **Common thief.**

Thin capitalization. See **Thin corporation.**

Thin corporation. When debt owed by a corporation to its shareholders is large in relationship to its capital structure (*i.e.,* stock and shareholder equity), the I.R.S. may contend that the corporation is thinly capitalized. In effect, this means that some or all of the debt will be reclassified as equity. The immediate result is to disallow any interest deduction to the corporation on the reclassified debt. To the extent of the corporation's earnings and profits, interest payments and loan repayments are treated as dividends to the shareholders. I.R.C. § 385.

Things. The objects of dominion or property as contradistinguished from "persons." Western Union Telegraph Co. v. Bush, 191 Ark. 1085, 89 S.W.2d 723, 725; Gayer v. Whelan, 59 Cal.App.2d 255, 138 P.2d 763, 768. The object of a right; *i.e.,* whatever is treated by the law as the object over which one person exercises a right, and with reference to which another person lies under a duty.

The word "estate" in general is applicable to anything of which riches or fortune may consist. The word is likewise relative to the word "things," which is the second object of jurisprudence, the rules of which are applicable to persons, things, and actions. Civ.Code La. art. 448.

Such permanent objects, not being persons, as are sensible, or perceptible through the senses. Things are distributed into three kinds: (1) Things real or immovable, comprehending lands, tenements, and hereditaments; (2) things personal or movable, comprehending goods and chattels; and (3) things mixed, partaking of the characteristics of the two former, as a title-deed, a term for years. The civil law divided things into corporeal (*tangi possunt*) and incorporeal (*tangi non possunt*).

Things in action. A right to recover money or other personal property by a judicial proceeding. See **Chose in action.**

Things of value. To be the subject of gaming may refer to any thing affording the necessary lure to indulge the gambling instinct. Painter v. State, 163 Tenn. 627, 45 S.W.2d 46, 47; Heartley v. State, 178 Tenn. 254, 157 S.W.2d 1, 3.

Things personal. Goods, money, and all other movables, which may attend the owner's person wherever he may go. Things personal consist of goods, money, and all other movables, and of such rights and profits as relate to movables. Also all vegetable productions, as the fruit or other parts of a plant when severed from the body of it, or the whole plant itself, when severed from the ground. Western Union Telegraph Co. v. Bush, 191 Ark. 1085, 89 S.W.2d 723, 725. See also **Property** (*Personal property*).

Things real. Such things as are permanent, fixed, and immovable, which cannot be carried out of their place; as lands and tenements and hereditaments. 2 Bl.Comm. 16. Western Union Telegraph v. Bush, 191 Ark. 1085, 89 S.W.2d 723, 725. See also **Property** (*Real property*).

Thingus. In Saxon law, a thane or nobleman; knight or freeman.

Think. To believe, to consider, to conclude, to esteem; to recollect or call to mind.

Third. Following next after the second; also, with reference to any legal instrument or transaction or judicial proceeding, any outsider or person not a party to the affair nor immediately concerned in it.

Thirdborough, or **thirdborow** /θárdb(ə)rə/. An under-constable.

Third conviction. Before charge can be considered a "third conviction" of a felony in contemplation of Habitual Criminal Act, accused must have been convicted of a second felony subsequent to his conviction of first one and after he had paid penalty inflicted for it, and third conviction should be subsequent to second, and after he had paid penalty for it. Cobb v. Commonwealth, 267 Ky. 176, 101 S.W.2d 418, 420.

Third degree. The process of securing a confession or information from a suspect or prisoner by prolonged questioning, the use of threats, or actual violence. See also **Interrogation; Miranda Rule.**

Thirdings /θárdiŋz/. In old English law, the third part of the corn growing on the land, due to the lord for a heriot on the death of his tenant, within the manor of Turfat, in Hereford.

Third market. See **Over-the-counter market.**

Third-night-awn-hinde. By the laws of St. Edward the Confessor, if any man lay a third night in an inn, he was called a "third-night-awn-hinde," and his host was answerable for him if he committed any offense. The first night, forman-night, or uncouth (unknown), he was reckoned a stranger; the second night, twanight, a guest; and the third night, an awn-hinde, a domestic.

Third party. One not a party to an agreement or to a transaction but who may have rights therein. See also **Party; Privity.**

Third party beneficiary. One for whose benefit a promise is made in a contract but who is not a party to the contract. Chitlik v. Allstate Ins. Co., 34 Ohio App.2d 193, 299 N.E.2d 295, 297, 63 O.O.2d 364. A person not a party to an insurance contract who has legally enforceable rights thereunder. See also **Privity.**

Third party claim proceeding. A proceeding for the purpose of determining whether the debtor has any right, title or interest in the property upon which the levy has been made and the judgment of the court in such proceedings is only made conclusive as to the right of the plaintiff or other person in whose favor the writ runs to have the property taken and to subject it to payment for other satisfaction of his judgment. Deevy v. Lewis, 54 Cal.App.2d 24, 128 P.2d 577, 579. See also **Third party complaint.**

Third party complaint. A complaint filed by the defendant against a third-party (*i.e.,* a person not presently a party to the lawsuit). This complaint alleges that the third party is or may be liable for all or part of the damages which the plaintiff may win from the defendant. See Fed.R.Civil P. 14. For requisite content of third party claim under Federal Rules of Civil Procedure, see **Complaint.**

Third-party practice. Procedural device whereby defendant in an action may bring in additional party in claim against such party because of a claim that is being asserted against the defendant. Denneler v. Aubel Ditching Service, Inc., 203 Kan. 117, 453 P.2d 88, 91. See also **Third-party complaint; Vouching in.**

Thirds. The designation, in colloquial language, of that portion of a decedent's personal estate (one-third) which goes to the widow where there is also a child or children.

Thirteenth Amendment. Amendment to U.S. Constitution which abolished slavery and involuntary servitude in 1865.

Thirty-day letter. A letter which accompanies a revenue agent's report (RAR) issued as a result of an Internal Revenue Service audit of a taxpayer (or the rejection of a taxpayer's claim for refund). The letter outlines the taxpayer's appeal procedure before the Internal Revenue Service. If the taxpayer does not request any such procedures (*i.e.,* District Conference or Appellate Division Conference) within the 30-day period, the Internal Revenue Service will issue a statutory notice of deficiency (the "90-day letter"). See also **Ninety-day letter.**

Thirty-nine articles. See **Articles of faith.**

This. When "this" and "that" refer to different things before expressed, "this" refers to the thing last mentioned, and "that" to the thing first mentioned. "This" is a demonstrative adjective, used to point out with particularity a person or thing present in place or in thought.

This day six months. Fixing "this day six months," or "three months," for the next stage of a bill, is one of the modes in which the house of lords and the house of commons reject bills of which they disapprove. A bill rejected in this manner cannot be reintroduced in the same session.

Thoroughfare. The term means, according to its derivation, a street or passage *through* which one can *fare* (travel); that is, a street or highway affording an unobstructed exit at each end into another street or public passage. If the passage is closed at one end, admitting no exit there, it is called a *"cul de sac."*

Thrave. In old English law, a measure of corn or grain, consisting of twenty-four sheaves or four shocks, six sheaves to every shock.

Thread. A middle line; a line running through the middle of a stream or road. See **Filum; Filum acquæ; Filum viæ; Thalweg.**

Threat. A communicated intent to inflict physical or other harm on any person or on property. A declaration of an intention to injure another or his property by some unlawful act. State v. Schweppe, Minn., 237 N.W.2d 609, 615. A declaration of intention or determination to inflict punishment, loss, or pain on another, or to injure another by the commission of some unlawful act. U. S. v. Daulong, D.C.La., 60 F.Supp. 235, 236. A menace; especially, any menace of such a nature and extent as to unsettle the mind of the person on whom it operates, and to take away from his acts that free and voluntary action which alone constitutes consent. A declaration of one's purpose or intention to work injury to the person, property, or rights of another, with a view of restraining such person's freedom of action.

The term, "threat" means an avowed present determination or intent to injure presently or in the future. A statement may constitute a threat even though it is subject to a possible contingency in the maker's control. The prosecution must establish a "true threat," which means a serious threat as distinguished from words uttered as mere political argument, idle talk or jest. In determining whether words were uttered as a threat the context in which they were spoken must be considered.

Threats against the President and successors to the President, mailing of threatening communications, and other extortionate acts, are federal offenses. 18 U.S.C.A. § 851 *et seq.*

See also **Coercion; Duress; Extortion.**

Terroristic threat. Any threat to commit violence communicated with intent to terrorize another, or to cause the evacuation of any building, place of assembly or facility of transportation, or in wanton disregard of the risk of causing such terror or evacuation.

Threatening letters. Mailing of threatening communications is a federal offense. 18 U.S.C.A. § 876.

Three-dollar piece. A gold coin of the United States, of the value of three dollars; authorized by the seventh section of the act of February 21, 1853.

Three-judge courts. Most cases in federal district courts are heard and determined by only a single judge. For many years, however, Congress has provided for a special three-judge panel in certain categories of cases thought to require special safeguards against arbitrary action, with direct review in the Supreme Court. Three judges were first required in certain ICC and Sherman Act cases; these provisions (formerly 28 U.S.C.A. Section 2325 and 15 U.S.C.A. Section 28) were repealed by P.L. 93–584, 88 Stat. 1917 (1975), and P.L. 93–528, 88 Stat. 1706 (1974), respectively. Three judges are required in condemnation suits involving the TVA, 16 U.S.C.A. Section 831X, and in certain actions under the 1964 Civil Rights and 1965 Voting Rights Acts, 42 U.S.C.A. Sections 1971(g), 1973(a), 1973(c), 1973h(c), 2000a–5(b), 2003–6(b). Of most significance, however, were 28 U.S.C.A. Sections 2281 and 2282, which required three judges in suits to enjoin enforcement of state or federal statutes, or state administrative orders, on constitutional grounds. Sections 2281 and 2282 were however repealed in 1976 and § 2284 amended to restrict the convening of three-judge courts to when otherwise required by Congress, or to when an action is filed challenging the constitutionality of congressional apportionment.

Three-mile limit. The distance of one marine league or three miles offshore normally recognized as the limit of territorial jurisdiction. See **Territorial waters.**

Threnges. Vassals, but not of the lowest degree; those who held lands of the chief lord.

Thrithing /θráyðiŋ/. In Saxon and old English law, the third part of a county; a division of a county consisting of three or more hundreds. Gradually corrupted to "riding". 1 Bl.Comm. 116.

Through. By means of, in consequence of, by reason of; in, within; over; from end to end, or from one side to the other. By the intermediary of; in the name or as agent of; by the agency of; because of. Great Atlantic & Pacific Tea Co. v. City of Richmond, 183 Va. 931, 33 S.E.2d 795, 802. "Through" is function word capable of several meanings depending on its use; it may indicate passage from one side to another, means of communication, or movement from point to point within a broad expanse or area. State v. Smith, Mo., 431 S.W.2d 74 78.

Through bill of lading. That species of bill of lading which is used when more than one carrier is required for shipping.

Through lot. A lot that abuts upon a street at each end.

Throwback Rule. In taxation of trusts, the throwback rule requires that the amount distributed in any tax year which is in excess of that year's distributable net income must be "thrown back" to the preceding year and treated as if it had then been distributed. The beneficiary is taxed in the current year although the computation is made as if the excess had been distributed in the previous year. If the trust did not have undistributed accumulated income in the pre-

ceding year, the amount of the throwback is tested against each of the preceding years; in other words, the throwback rule may require consideration of the trust income and its distributions for all of the years preceding the tax year. I.R.C. §§ 665–668.

Thrown from automobile. This phrase within accident policy means tossed or hurled out of automobile by some force. Independence Ins. Co. v. Blanford's Adm'x, 276 Ky. 692, 125 S.W.2d 249, 251.

Throw out. To ignore (*e.g.* a bill of indictment) or dismiss a cause of action.

Thrusting. Within the meaning of a criminal statute, is not necessarily an attack with a pointed weapon; it means pushing or driving with force, whether the point of the weapon be sharp or not.

Thrymsa /θrímsə/. A Saxon coin worth fourpence.

Thude-weald /θ(y)úwdwiyld/. A woodward, or person that looks after a wood.

Thuringian Code /θərínj(iy)ən kówd/. One of the "barbarian codes," as they are termed; supposed by Montesquieu to have been given by Theodoric, king of Austrasia, to the Thuringians, who were his subjects.

Thus. In the way just indicated. Schrader v. City of Los Angeles, 19 Cal.App.2d 332, 65 P.2d 374, 375.

Thwertnick. In old English law, the custom of giving entertainments to a sheriff, etc., for three nights.

Tick. A colloquial expression for credit or trust; credit given for goods purchased.

Ticket. In contracts, a slip of paper containing a certificate that the person to whom it is issued, or the holder, is entitled to some right or privilege therein mentioned or described; such, for example, are railroad tickets, theater tickets, pawn tickets, lottery tickets, etc.

Citation or summons issued to violator of motor vehicle law.

In election law, a list of candidates for particular offices to be submitted to the voters at an election; a ballot.

See also **Citation.**

Ticket of leave. In English law, a license or permit given to a convict, as a reward for good conduct, particularly in the penal settlements, which allows him to go at large, and labor for himself, before the expiration of his sentence, subject to certain specific conditions and revocable upon subsequent misconduct. English equivalent of parole.

Ticket-of-leave man. A convict who has obtained a ticket of leave.

Ticket speculator. One who purchases and then resells tickets at a price over their face value. A scalper.

Tidal. Affected by or having tides. In order that a river may be "tidal" at a given spot, it may not be necessary that the water should be salt, but the spot must be one where the tide, in the ordinary and regular course of things, flows and reflows.

Tide. The ebb and flow of the sea. As affecting determination of upland boundary of shore, "tide" is rising and falling of water of the sea that is produced by attraction of sun and moon, uninfluenced by special winds, seasons or other circumstances, and meteorological influences should be distinguished as "meterological tides," and "atmospheric meteorological tides" should be distinguished. Humble Oil & Refining Co. v. Sun Oil Co., C.A.Tex., 190 F.2d 191, 195. See also **Mean high tide; Mean low tide.**

Neap tides. Those tides which happen between the full and change of the moon twice in every 24 hours.

Tideland. Land between the lines of the ordinary high and low tides, covered and uncovered successively by the ebb and flow thereof; land covered and uncovered by the ordinary tides; land over which the tide ebbs and flows; land which is daily covered and uncovered by water by the ordinary ebb and flow of normal tides; land usually overflowed by the neap or ordinary tides; such land as is affected by the tide, that lies between ordinary high-water mark and low-water mark, and which is alternately covered and left dry by the ordinary flux and reflux of the tides; that portion of the shore or beach covered and uncovered by the ebb and flow of ordinary tides. White v. State, 18 Cal.App.3d 729, 96 Cal.Rptr. 173, 174.

Tide-water. Water which falls and rises with the ebb and flow of the tide. The term is not usually applied to the open sea, but to coves, bays, rivers, etc.

Tideway. That land between high and low water mark. In re Inwood Hill Park in Borough of Manhattan, City of New York, 217 App.Div. 587, 217 N.Y.S. 359, 363.

Tidesmen. In English law, are certain officers of the custom-house, appointed to watch or attend upon ships until the customs are paid; and they are so called because they go aboard the ships at their arrival in the mouth of the Thames, and come up with the tide.

Tie, *v.* To bind.

Tie, *n.* When, at an election, neither candidate receives a majority of the votes cast, but each has the same number, there is said to be a "tie." Exists also when the number of votes cast in favor of any measure, in a legislative or deliberative body, is equal to the number cast against it. The Vice President of the United States has the deciding vote in the event of tie votes in the Senate. Art. I, § 3, U.S.Const.

Tied product. Tying arrangement exists when a person agrees to sell one product, the "tying product," only on the condition that the vendee also purchase another product, the "tied product." Northern v. McGraw-Edison Co., C.A.Mo., 542 F.2d 1336, 1344. See also **Tie-in arrangement; Tying arrangement.**

Tie-in arrangement. A "tie-in", which is generally illegal under the Clayton Act or the Sherman Act, is an arrangement under which vendor will sell one product only on condition that buyer also purchase another and different product. N. W. Controls, Inc. v. Outboard Marine Corp., D.C.Del., 333 F.Supp. 493, 500. See also **Tied product; Tying arrangement.**

Tiel. L. Fr. Such. *Nul tiel record,* no such record.

Tiempo inhabil /t(i)yémpow inhabíyl/. Span. A time of inability; a time when the person is not able to pay his debts (when, for instance, he may not alienate property to the prejudice of his creditors). The term is used in Louisiana.

Tierce /tírs/társ/. L. Fr. Third. *Tierce mein* /társ méyn/, third hand.

Tierce /tírs/társ/. A liquid measure, containing the third part of a pipe, or forty-two gallons.

Tigh /táy/. In old records, a close or inclosure; a croft.

Tight. As colloquially applied to a note, bond, mortgage, lease, etc., this term signifies that the clauses providing the creditor's remedy in case of default (as, by foreclosure, execution, distress, etc.) are summary and stringent.

Tigni immittendi /tígnay ìmǝténday/. Lat. In the civil law, the name of a servitude which is the right of inserting a beam or timber from the wall of one house into that of a neighboring house, in order that it may rest on the latter, and that the wall of the latter may bear this weight.

Tignum /tígnǝm/. Lat. A civil law term for building material; timber.

Tihler. In old Saxon law, an accusation.

Tillage. A place tilled or cultivated; land under cultivation, as opposed to lands lying fallow or in pasture.

Till-tapping. Theft of money from a cash register. Nash v. U. S., C.A.Mo., 405 F.2d 1047, 1049.

Timber lease. Lease of real property which contemplates that the lessee will cut timber on the demised premises.

Timberlode. A service by which tenants were bound to carry timber felled from the woods to the lord's house.

Time. The measure of duration. The word is expressive both of a precise *point* or *terminus* and of an *interval* between two points.

A point in or space of duration at or during which some fact is alleged to have been committed.

See also **Computation of time.**

Cooling time. See **Cooling-off period.**

Reasonable time. Such length of time as may fairly, properly, and reasonably be allowed or required, having regard to the nature of the act or duty, or of the subject-matter, and to the attending circumstances. It is a maxim of English law that "how long a 'reasonable time' ought to be is not defined in law, but is left to the discretion of the judges." Twin Lick Oil Co. v. Marbury, 91 U.S. 587, 591, 23 L.Ed. 328. See also **Reasonable time.**

Time-bargain. In the language of the stock exchange, an agreement to buy or sell stock at a future time, or within a fixed time, at a certain price. It is in reality nothing more than a bargain to pay differences.

Time bill. A bill of exchange which contains a definite or determinable date for payment in contrast to a demand or sight bill.

Time charter. A time charter is a specific and express contract by which the owner lets a vessel or some particular part thereof to another person for a specified time or use; the owner continues to operate the vessel, contracting to render services by his master and crew to carry goods loaded on the vessel, and the master and crew remain servants of the owner. Atlantic Banana Co. v. M. V. "Calanca", D.C.N.Y., 342 F.Supp. 447, 453.

Time deposit. Another term for a savings account in a commercial bank. It is so called because in theory (though no longer in practice) a person must wait a certain amount of time after notice of desire to withdraw part or all of his or her savings. Cash in a bank earning interest; *contrast* with demand deposit. See **Deposit.**

Time draft. See *Time bill, supra.*

Time immemorial. Time whereof the memory of a man is not to the contrary.

Time is the essence of contract. Means that performance by one party at time or within period specified in contract is essential to enable him to require performance by other party. Hayes Mfg. Corporation v. McCauley, C.C.A.Ohio, 140 F.2d 187, 189. When this phrase is in a contract, it means that a failure to do what is required by the time specified is a breach of the contract.

Time of memory. In English law, time commencing from the beginning of the reign of Richard I. 2 Bl.Comm. 31. Lord Coke defines *time of memory* to be "when no man alive hath had any proof to the contrary, nor hath any conusance to the contrary."

Time order. An order which becomes a market or limited price order at a specified time.

Time out of memory. Time beyond memory; time out of mind; time to which memory does not extend.

Time-policy. A policy of marine insurance in which the risk is limited, not to a given voyage, but to a certain fixed term or period of time.

Time-price differential. Method by which seller charges one price for immediate cash payment and a different (advance in) price when payment is made at future date or in installments and the former is the cash price and the latter the "time-price" or credit price and difference in price is the "time-price differential". State ex rel. Guste v. Council of City of New Orleans, La.App., 297 So.2d 518, 525.

Timocracy. An aristocracy of property; government by men of property who are possessed of a certain income.

Timores vani sunt æstimandi qui non cadunt constantem virum /təmóriyz véynay sènt èstəmǽnday kwày nón kéydənt kən(t)stǽntəm váyrəm/. Fears which do not assail a resolute man are to be accounted vain.

Tinel. L. Fr. A place where justice was administered.

Tineman /táynmən/. Sax. In old forest law, a petty officer of the forest who had the care of vert and venison by night, and performed other servile duties.

Tinewald /táynwòld/tín°/. The ancient parliament or annual convention in the Isle of Man, held upon Midsummer-day, at St. John's chapel.

Tinkermen /tíŋkərmən/. Fishermen who destroyed the young fry on the river Thames by nets and unlawful engines.

Tinpenny. A tribute paid for the liberty of digging in tin-mines.

Tip. A sum of money given, as to a servant, waiter, bellman, or the like, for services rendered, with the amount commonly varying upon the quality of such service. Tip income is taxable. I.R.C. § 61(a). Restaurants and Patisseries Longchamps, Inc. v. Pedrick, D.C.N.Y., 52 F.Supp. 174. A gift. Williams v. Jacksonville Terminal Co., C.C.A.Fla., 118 F.2d 324, 325.

Advance information which, if acted upon, will presumably give the actor a profit or an advantage as in the case of advance information as to likelihood of a rise or fall of the price of a security in the market. See **Tippees.**

Tippees. Persons given information by insiders in breach of trust. Ross v. Licht, D.C.N.Y., 263 F.Supp. 395, 410. The purpose of Rule 10b–5 *(q.v.)* is to prevent corporate insiders and their "tippees" from taking unfair advantage of the uninformed outsiders. Radiation Dynamics Inc. v. Goldmuntz, 464 F.2d 876. Conspiracy between corporate insiders and person to whom insiders have furnished information pertaining to corporation is not required in order for such person to be categorized as a "tippee" thus precluding him from the benefit of Securities and Exchange Commission rule prohibiting employment of any device to defraud or engagement in any act of course of business which operates as fraud or deceit. Kuehnert v. Texstar Corp., D.C.Tex., 286 F.Supp. 340, 345. See also **Insider; Tip.**

Tippling house. A place where intoxicating drinks are sold in drams or small quantities to be drunk on the premises, and where men resort for drinking purposes.

Tipstaff. An officer appointed by the court, whose duty is to wait upon the court when it is in session, preserve order, serve process, guard juries, etc. See **Bailiff.**

In English law, an officer appointed by the marshal of the king's bench to attend upon the judges with a kind of rod or staff tipped with silver, who take into their custody all prisoners, either committed or turned over by the judges at their chambers, etc.

Tithe. A tenth part of one's income, contributed for charitable or religious purposes. Broadly, any tax or assessment of one tenth. See also **Tithes; Tithing.**

Tither /táyðər/. One who gathers tithes.

Tithes /táyðz/. In English law, the *tenth* part of the increase, yearly arising and renewing from the profits of lands, the stock upon lands, and the personal industry of the inhabitants. 2 Bl.Comm. 24. A species of incorporeal hereditament, being an ecclesiastical inheritance collateral to the estate of the land, and due only to an ecclesiastical person by ecclesiastical law. See also **Tithe.**

Great tithes. In English ecclesiastical law, tithes of corn, peas and beans, hay and wood.

Minute tithes. Small tithes, such as usually belong to a vicar, as of wool, lambs, pigs, butter, cheese, herbs, seeds, eggs, honey, wax, etc.

Mixed tithes. Those which arise not immediately from the ground, but from those things which are nourished by the ground, *e.g.,* colts, chickens, calves, milk, eggs, etc.

Personal tithes. Personal tithes are tithes paid of such profits as come by the labor of a man's person; as by buying and selling, gains of merchandise and handicrafts, etc.

Predial tithes. Such as arise immediately from the ground; as, grain of all sorts, hay, wood, fruits, and herbs.

Tithe-free. Exempted from the payment of tithes.

Tithe rent-charge. A rent-charge established in lieu of tithes, under the tithes commutation act, 1836 (St. 6 § 7 Wm. IV, c. 71). As between landlord and tenant, the tenant paying the tithe rent-charge is entitled, in the absence of express agreement, to deduct it from his rent, under section 70 of the above act. And a tithe rent-charge unpaid is recoverable by distress as rent in arrear.

Tithing /táyðiŋ/. Act of paying tithes. One of the civil divisions of England, being a portion of that greater division called a "hundred." It was so called because ten freeholders with their families composed one. It is said that they were all knit together in one society, and bound to the king for the peaceable behavior of each other. In each of these societies there was one chief or principal person, who, from his office, was called "teothing-man," now "tithing-man."

Tithing-man /táyðiŋmæn/. A constable. After the introduction of justices of the peace, the offices of constable and *tithing-man* became so similar that they were regarded as precisely the same.

In New England, a parish officer annually elected to preserve good order in the church during divine service, and to make complaint of any disorderly conduct.

In Saxon law, the head or chief of a tithing or decennary of ten families; he was to decide all lesser causes between neighbors. In modern English law, he is the same as an under-constable or peace-officer.

Tithing-penny /táyðiŋpèniy/. In Saxon and old English law, money paid to the sheriff by the several tithings of his county.

Titius /tísh(iy)əs/. In Roman law, a proper name, frequently used in designating an indefinite or fictitious person, or a person referred to by way of illustration. "Titius" and "Seius," in this use, correspond to "John Doe" and "Richard Roe," or to "A.B." and "C.D."

Title. A mark, style, or designation; a distinctive appellation; the name by which anything is known. Thus, in the law of persons, a title is an appellation of dignity or distinction, a name denoting the social rank of the person bearing it; as "duke" or "count." So, in legislation, the title of a statute is the heading or preliminary part, furnishing the name by which the act is individually known. It is usually prefixed to the statute in the form of a brief summary of its contents; as "An act for the prevention of gaming."

Again, the title of a patent is the short description of the invention, which is copied in the letters patent from the inventor's petition; *e.g.,* "a new and improved method of drying and preparing malt."

The title of a book, or any literary composition, is its name; that is, the heading or caption prefixed to it, and disclosing the distinctive appellation by which it is to be known. This usually comprises a brief description of its subject-matter and the name of its author.

See also Abstract of title; Action to quiet title; Color of title; Cloud on title; Defective title; Disparagement of title; Doubtful title; Good title; Indicia of title; Just title; Legal title; Marketable title; Marketable Title Acts; Merchantable title; Muniments of title; Non-merchantable title; Onerous title; Owner; Ownership; Paramount title; Possession; Recording acts; Torrens title system; Worthier title.

Law of Trade-Marks

A title may become a subject of property; as one who has adopted a particular title for a newspaper, or other business enterprise, may, by long and prior usage, or by compliance with statutory provisions as to registration and notice, acquire a right to be protected in the exclusive use of it.

Real Property Law

Title is the means whereby the owner of lands has the just possession of his property. The union of all the elements which constitute ownership. Full independent and fee ownership. The right to or ownership in land; also, the evidence of such ownership. Such ownership may be held individually, jointly, in common, or in cooperate or partnership form.

One who holds vested rights in property is said to have title whether he holds them for his own benefit or for the benefit of another. Restatement, Second, Trusts, § 2, Comment d.

See also **Deed; Estate.**

Procedure

Every action, petition, or other proceeding has a title, which consists of the name of the court in which it is pending, the names of the parties, etc. Administration actions are further distinguished by the name of the deceased person whose estate is being administered. Every pleading, summons, affidavit, etc., commences with the title. In many cases it is sufficient to give what is called the "short title" of an action, namely, the court, the reference to the record, and the surnames of the first plaintiff and the first defendant. See also **Caption.**

Generally

Absolute title. As applied to title to land, an exclusive title, or at least a title which excludes all others not compatible with it. An absolute title to land cannot exist at the same time in different persons or in different governments. See also **Fee simple.**

Abstract of title. See that title.

Adverse title. A title set up in opposition to or defeasance of another title, or one acquired or claimed by adverse possession. See **Adverse possession.**

Bond for title. See **Bond.**

By accession. Title acquired by additions innocently acquired such as in the case of intermingling of another's property with one's own. See **Accession.**

By accretion. Title acquired by additions to one's property as in the case of deposits of soil from a stream. See **Accretion.**

By adverse possession. See **Adverse possession.**

Chain of title. See that title; also **Abstract of title.**

Clear title, good title, merchantable title, marketable title, are synonymous; "clear title" meaning that the land is free from incumbrances, "good title" being one free from litigation, palpable defects, and grave doubts, comprising both legal and equitable titles and fairly deducible of record. See **Marketable title.**

Clear title of record, or clear record title. Title free from apparent defects, grave doubts, and litigious uncertainties, and is such title as a reasonably prudent person, with full knowledge, would accept. A title dependent for its validity on extraneous evidence, ex parte affidavits, or written guaranties against the results of litigation is not a clear title of record, and is not such title as equity will require a purchaser to accept. See **Marketable title.**

Color of title. See that title.

Covenants for title. Covenants usually inserted in a conveyance of land, on the part of the grantor, and binding him for the completeness, security, and continuance of the title transferred to the grantee. They comprise "covenants for seisin, for right to convey, against incumbrances, for quiet enjoyment, sometimes for further assurance, and almost always of warranty." See **Covenant.**

Defective title. Title which has some defect or is subject to litigation and hence may not be transferred to another. See **Unmarketable title.**

Document of title. See **Document.**

Doubtful title. See that title.

Equitable title. A right in the party to whom it belongs to have the legal title transferred to him; or the beneficial interest of one person whom equity regards as the real owner, although the legal title is vested in another. See also **Equitable ownership.**

Examination of title. See **Examination; Title search.**

Good title. Title which is free of defects and litigation and hence may be transferred to another. See **Marketable title.**

Imperfect title. One which requires a further exercise of the granting power to pass the fee in land, or which does not convey full and absolute dominion.

Legal title. See that title.

Lucrative title. In the civil law, title acquired without the giving of anything in exchange for it; the title by which a person acquires anything which comes to him as a clear gain, as, for instance, by gift, descent, or devise. Opposed to "onerous title," as to which see *infra.*

Marketable title. See that title.

Onerous title. In the civil law, title to property acquired by the giving of a valuable consideration for it, such as the payment of money, the rendition of services, the performance of conditions, the assumption of obligations, or the discharge of liens on the property; opposed to "lucrative" title, or one acquired by gift or otherwise without the giving of an equivalent.

Paper title. A title to land evidenced by a conveyance or chain of conveyances; the term generally implying that such title, while it has color or plausibility, is without substantial validity.

Perfect title. Various meanings have been attached to this term: (1) One which shows the absolute right of possession and of property in a particular person. See **Fee simple.** (2) A grant of land which requires no further act from the legal authority to constitute an absolute title to the land taking effect at once. (3) A title which does not disclose a patent defect suggesting the possibility of a lawsuit to defend it; a title such as a well-informed and prudent man paying full value for the property would be willing to take. (4) A title which is good both at law and in equity. (5) One which is good and valid beyond all reasonable doubt. (6) A marketable or merchantable title. See **Marketable title.**

Presumptive title. A barely presumptive title, which is of the very lowest order, arises out of the mere occupation or simple possession of property *(jus possessionis),* without any apparent right, or any pretense of right, to hold and continue such possession.

Record title. See **Record.**

Root of title. Root of title means that conveyance or other title transaction or other link in the chain of title of a person, purporting to create the interest claimed by such person, upon which he relies as a basis for the marketability of his title, and which was the most recent to be recorded or established as of a date forty years prior to the time when marketability is being determined. The effective date of the "root of title" is the date on which it is recorded.

Singular title. The title by which a party acquires property as a singular successor.

Tax title. See **Tax.**

Title by adverse possession or prescription. The right which a possessor acquires to property by reason of his adverse possession during a period of time fixed by law. See **Adverse possession.**

The elements of title by prescription are open, visible and continuous use under a claim of right, adverse to and with knowledge of owner. Dry Gulch Ditch Co. v. Hutton, 170 Or. 656, 133 P.2d 601, 610. Such title is equivalent to a "title by deed" and cannot be lost or divested except in the same manner, and mere recognition of title in another after such acquisition will not operate to divest the adverse claimant of that which he has acquired. Maloney v. Bedford, 290 Ky. 647, 162 S.W.2d 198, 199.

Title by descent. That title which one acquires by law as heir to the deceased owner.

Title by prescription. See *Title by adverse possession, supra.*

Title deeds. Deeds which constitute or are the evidence of title to lands. See **Deed.**

Title defective in form. Title on face of which some defect appears, not one that may prove defective by circumstances or evidence dehors the instrument. Title defective in form cannot be basis of prescription.

Title insurance. See **Insurance.**

Title of a cause. The distinctive appellation by which any cause in court, or other juridical proceeding, is known and distinguished from others. See **Caption.**

Title of an act. The heading, or introductory clause, of a statute, wherein is briefly recited its purpose or nature, or the subject to which it relates.

Title of clergymen (to orders). Some certain place where they may exercise their functions; also an assurance of being preferred to some ecclesiastical benefice.

Title of declaration. That preliminary clause of a declaration which states the name of the court and the term to which the process is returnable.

Title of entry. The right to enter upon lands.

Title registration. See **Torrens title system.**

Title retention. A form of lien, in the nature of a chattel mortgage, to secure the purchase price. American Indemnity Co. v. Allen, for Use and Benefit of Commerce Union Bank, 176 Tenn. 134, 138 S.W.2d 445, 446.

Title to orders. In English ecclesiastical law, a title to orders is a certificate of preferment or provision required by the thirty-third canon, in order that a person may be admitted into holy orders, unless he be a fellow or chaplain in Oxford or Cambridge, or master of arts of five years' standing in either of the universities, and living there at his sole charges; or unless the bishop himself intends shortly to admit him to some benefice or curacy.

Unmarketable title. See that title.

Warranty of title. See **Warranty.**

Title documents. Those instruments necessary for establishing or for conveying good title; *e.g.* deed.

Title guaranty company. A business organization which searches title to determine whether any defects or encumbrances are recorded and which then gives the buyer of the property or the mortgagee a guaranty of the title.

Title insurance. See **Insurance.**

Title search. An examination of the records of the registry of deeds or other office which contains records of title documents to determine whether title to the property is good; *i.e.* whether there are any defects in the title. The examiner then prepares an abstract of the documents examined. See also **Abstract of title; Examination.**

Title standards. Criteria by which a title to real estate may be evaluated to determine whether it is defective or marketable. Many states through associations of conveyancers and real estate attorneys have adopted such standards.

Title transaction. Any transaction affecting title to any interest in land, including title by will or descent, title by tax deed, or deed by trustee, referee, guardian,

executor, administrator, master in chancery, sheriff, or any other form of deed, or decree of any court, as well as warranty deed, quitclaim deed, mortgage, or transfer or conveyance of any kind.

Titulada /tìytuwláða/. In Spanish law, title.

Titulus /tíchələs/. Lat. Title. In the civil law, the source or ground of possession; the means whereby possession of a thing is acquired, whether such possession be lawful or not.

In old ecclesiastical law, a temple or church; the material edifice. So called because the priest in charge of it derived therefrom his name and *title.*

Titulus est justa causa possidendi id quod nostrum est; dicitur a tuendo /tíchələs èst jə́stə kózə pòsədéday íd kwòd nóstrəm èst, dísədər èy t(y)uwéndow/. A title is the just right of possessing that which is our own; it is so called from *"tuendo,"* defending.

To. While this is ordinarily a word of exclusion, when used in describing premises, it has been held that the word in a statute may be interpreted as exclusionary or inclusionary depending on the legislative intent as drawn from the whole statute. Clark v. Bunnell, 172 Colo. 32, 470 P.2d 42, 44. It may be a word of inclusion, and may also mean "into."

Toft. A place or piece of ground on which a house formerly stood, which has been destroyed by accident or decay.

Toftman. In old English law, the owner of a toft.

Togati /towgéyday/. Lat. In Roman law, advocates; so called under the empire because they were required, when appearing in court to plead a cause, to wear the *toga,* which had then ceased to be the customary dress in Rome.

Together. In union with, along with. Gilmore v. Mulvihill, 109 Mont. 601, 98 P.2d 335, 341.

To have and to hold. The words in a conveyance which show the estate intended to be conveyed. Thus, in a conveyance of land in fee-simple, the grant is to "A. and his heirs, to have and to hold the said [land] unto and to the use of the said A., his heirs and assigns forever."

Strictly speaking, however, the words "to have" denote the estate to be taken, while the words "to hold" signify that it is to be held of some superior lord, *i.e.,* by way of tenure (*q.v.*). The former clause is called the *"habendum;"* the latter, the *"tenendum."*

Token. A sign or mark; a material evidence of the existence of a fact. A sign or indication of an intention to do something as in the case of one who places a small order to show good faith to a seller with a view towards placing a larger order at a future time.

Token-money. A conventional medium of exchange consisting of pieces of metal, fashioned in the shape and size of coins, and circulating among private persons, by consent, at a certain value. No longer permitted or recognized as money.

Tolerate. To allow so as not to hinder; to permit as something not wholly approved of; to suffer; to endure.

Toleration. The allowance of religious opinions and modes of worship which are contrary to, or different from, those of the established church or belief.

Toleration Act. The statute 1 W. & M. St. 1, c. 18, for exempting Protestant dissenters from the penalties of certain laws is so called.

Toll, v. To bar, defeat, or take away; thus, to toll the entry means to deny or take away the right of entry.

To suspend or stop temporarily as the statute of limitations is tolled during the defendant's absence from the jurisdiction and during the plaintiff's minority.

Toll, n. A sum of money for the use of something, generally applied to the consideration which is paid for the use of a road, bridge, or the like, of a public nature. Sands v. Manistee River Imp. Co., 123 U.S. 288, 8 S.Ct. 113, 31 L.Ed. 149; Rogge v. United States, C.C.A.Alaska, 128 F.2d 800, 802. The price of the privilege of travel over that particular highway and it is a quid pro quo and rests on principle that he who receives the toll does or has done something as an equivalent to him who pays it. State ex rel. Washington Toll Bridge Authority v. Yelle, 195 Wash. 636, 82 P.2d 120, 125. Charge for long-distance telephone calls.

Tollage. Payment of toll; money charged or paid as toll; the liberty or franchise of charging toll.

Tollbooth. A prison; a customhouse; an exchange; also the place where goods are weighed or tolls collected.

Tolldish. A vessel by which the toll of corn for grinding is measured.

Toller. One who collects tribute or taxes.

Tollere /tóləriy/. Lat. In the civil law, to lift up or raise; to elevate; to build up.

Tolle voluntatem et erit omnis actus indifferens /tóliy voləntéydəm èd éhrəd ómniy ǽktəs indífəren(d)z/. Take away the will, and every action will be indifferent.

Tolls. In a general sense, any manner of customs, subsidy, prestation, imposition, or sum of money demanded for exporting or importing of any goods or merchandise to be taken of the buyer. For Fair and reasonable tolls, see that title. See also **Toll.**

Tollsester /towlséstər/. In old English law, an excise; a duty paid by tenants of some manors to the lord for liberty to brew and sell ale.

Tolt. In old English law, a writ whereby a cause depending in a court baron was taken and removed into a county court.

Tolta /tówltə/. In old English law, wrong; rapine; extortion.

Tomb /túwm/. An excavation in earth or rock, intended to receive the dead body of a human being.

Tombstone /túwmstòwn/. Stone marking place of burial and usually inscribed with memorial of deceased.

Tombstone ad. A notice, circular or advertisement of a stock offering containing language to the effect that the announcement is neither an offer to sell nor a solicitation of an offer to buy any of the securities listed. The actual offer is made only by the prospectus.

Ton. A measure of weight; differently fixed, at two thousand pounds avoirdupois, or at twenty hundredweights, each hundred-weight being one hundred and twelve pounds avoirdupois. A short ton is 20 short hundred-weight (2000 lbs.) or 0.907 metric tons; a long ton is 20 long hundred-weight (2240 lbs.) or 1.016 metric tons. There are also various types of tons in shipping usage; e.g. freight ton and register ton.

Ton mile. In transportation, the measure equal to the transportation of one ton of freight one mile.

Tonnage. The capacity of a vessel for carrying freight or other loads, calculated in tons. But the way of estimating the tonnage varies in different countries. Per ton duty or charge on cargo. Total shipping tonnage of country or port.

Tonnage-duty. A tax laid upon vessels according to their tonnage or cubical capacity. The vital principle of a tonnage duty is that it is imposed, whatever the subject, solely according to the rule of weight, either as to the capacity to carry or the actual weight of the thing itself.

Tonnage-rent. When the rent reserved by a mining lease or the like consists of a royalty on every ton of minerals gotten in the mine, it is often called a "tonnage-rent." There is generally a dead rent in addition.

Tonnagium /tənéyj(iy)əm/. In old English law, a custom or impost upon wines and other merchandise exported or imported, according to a certain rate per ton.

Tonnetight /tántàyt/. In old English law, the quantity of a ton or tun, in a ship's freight or bulk, for which tonnage or tunnage was paid to the king.

Tonsura /tons(y)úrə/. Lat. In old English law, a shaving, or polling; the having the crown of the head shaven; tonsure. One of the peculiar badges of a clerk or clergyman.

Tontine /tontíyn/. A financial arrangement (such as an insurance policy) in which a group of participants share advantages on such terms that upon the default or death of any participant, his advantages are distributed among the remaining participants until only one remains, whereupon the whole goes to him; or on the expiration of an agreed period, the whole goes to those participants remaining at that time. Under the "Tontine" plan of insurance, no accumulation or earnings are credited to the policy unless it remains in force for the Tontine period of a specified number of years. Thus those who survive the period and keep their policies in force share in the accumulated funds and those who die or permit their policies to lapse during period do not; neither do their beneficiaries participate in such accumulation. Commercial Travelers' Ins. Co. v. Carlson, 104 Utah 41, 137 P.2d 656, 660.

In French law, a species of association or partnership formed among persons who are in receipt of perpetual or life annuities, with the agreement that the shares or annuities of those who die shall accrue to the survivors. This plan is said to be thus named from Tonti, an Italian, who invented it in the seventeenth century. The principle is used in some forms of life insurance.

Took and carried away. In criminal pleading, technical words necessary in an indictment for simple larceny.

Top lease. A subsequent oil and gas lease which covers one or more mineral interests that are subject to a valid, subsisting prior lease.

Torpedo doctrine. Attractive nuisance doctrine. Schock v. Ringling Bros. and Barnum & Bailey Combined Shows, 5 Wash.2d 599, 105 P.2d 838, 843. See **Attractive nuisance doctrine.**

Torrens title system /tóhrən(d)z táydəl sìstəm/. A system for registration of land under which, upon the landowner's application, the court may, after appropriate proceedings, direct the issuance of a certificate of title. With exceptions, this certificate is conclusive as to applicant's estate in land. System of registration of land title as distinguished from registration or recording of evidence of such title. The originator of the system was Sir Richard Torrens, 1814–1884, reformer of Australian Land Laws.

Tort (from Lat. torquere, to twist, tortus, twisted, wrested aside). A private or civil wrong or injury, other than breach of contract, for which the court will provide a remedy in the form of an action for damages. A violation of a duty imposed by general law or otherwise upon all persons occupying the relation to each other which is involved in a given transaction. Coleman v. California Yearly Meeting of Friends Church, 27 Cal.App.2d 579, 81 P.2d 469, 470. There must always be a violation of some duty owing to plaintiff, and generally such duty must arise by operation of law and not by mere agreement of the parties.

Three elements of every tort action are: Existence of legal duty from defendant to plaintiff, breach of duty, and damage as proximate result. Joseph v. Hustad Corp., 454 P.2d 916, 918.

A legal wrong committed upon the person or property independent of contract. It may be either (1) a direct invasion of some legal right of the individual; (2) the infraction of some public duty by which special damage accrues to the individual; (3) the violation of some private obligation by which like damage accrues to the individual.

See also Government tort; Husband-wife tort actions; Joint tort-feasors; Liability; Negligence; Palsgraph doctrine; Parental liability; Privilege; Privity; Privity of contract; Product liability; Strict liability; Warranty.

Children. See **Parental liability.**

Constitutional tort. Every person who under color of any statute, ordinance, regulation, custom, or usage, of any state or territory, subjects, or causes to be subjected, any citizen of the United States or any other person within the jurisdiction thereof to the deprivation of any rights, privileges, or immunities secured by the Constitution and laws, shall be liable to the party injured in an action at law, suit in equity, or other proper proceeding for redress. 42 U.S.C.A. § 1983. See also **Color of law.**

Intentional tort. Tort or wrong perpetrated by one who intends to do that which the law has declared wrong as contrasted with negligence in which the tortfeasor fails to exercise that degree of care in doing what is otherwise permissible. See also **Wilful tort.**

Maritime tort. See **Jone's Act; Longshoremen's and Harbor Workers' Compensation Act; Maritime.**

Personal tort. One involving or consisting in an injury to the person or to the reputation or feelings, as distinguished from an injury or damage to real or personal property, called a "property tort." Gray v. Blight, C.C.A.Colo., 112 F.2d 696, 699.

Prenatal injuries. See **Child.**

Quasi tort. Though not a recognized term of English law, may be conveniently used in those cases where a man who has not committed a tort is liable as if he had. Thus a master is liable for wrongful acts done by his servant in the course of his employment.

Strict tort liability. See **Strict liability.**

Wilful tort. See *Intentional tort, supra.*

Tort claims acts. See **Federal Tort Claims Act; Governmental immunity.**

Tort-feasor. A wrong-doer; one who commits or is guilty of a tort. See also **Joint tort-feasors.**

Tortious /tórshəs/. Wrongful; of the nature of a tort. The word "tortious" is used throughout the Restatement, Second, Torts, to denote the fact that conduct whether of act or omission is of such a character as to subject the actor to liability, under the principles of the law of torts. (§ 6). To establish "tortious act" plaintiff must prove not only existence of actionable wrong, but also that damages resulted therefrom. James v. Public Finance Corp., 47 C.A.3d 995, 121 Cal.Rptr. 670, 675.

Formerly certain modes of conveyance (e.g., feoffments, fines, etc.) had the effect of passing not merely the estate of the person making the conveyance, but the whole fee-simple, to the injury of the person really entitled to the fee; and they were hence called "tortious conveyances."

Tortura legum pessima /tort(y)úrə líygəm pésəmə/. The torture or wresting of laws is the worst [kind of torture].

Torture. To inflict intense pain to body or mind for purposes of punishment, or to extract a confession or information, or for sadistic pleasure. In old criminal law, the infliction of violent bodily pain upon a person, by means of the rack, wheel, or other engine, under judicial sanction and superintendence, in connection with the interrogation or examination of the person, as a means of extorting a confession of guilt, or of compelling him to disclose his accomplices.

Tory. Originally a nickname for the Irish in Ulster. Afterwards given to, and adopted by, one of the two great parliamentary parties which alternately governed Great Britain after the Revolution in 1688.

The name was also given, in America, during the struggle of the colonies for independence, to the party of those residents who favored the side of the British Crown and opposed independence.

Tot. In old English practice, a word written by the foreign opposer or other officer opposite to a debt due the king, to denote that it was a *good* debt; which was hence said to be *totted.*

Tota curia /tówdǝ kyúriyǝ/. L. Lat. In the old reports, the whole court.

Total. Whole, not divided, lacking no part, entire, full, complete, the whole amount. Utter, absolute. Glaze v. Hart, 225 Mo.App. 1205, 36 S.W.2d 684.

Total disability. Total disability, whether temporary or permanent, is that which prevents the employee from doing the substantial and material acts required of him in his usual occupation. Universal Mfg. Co. v. Barlow, Miss., 260 So.2d 827, 831. Means loss of earning power as a worker, manifested either by inability to perform work obtainable or inability to secure work, and not absolute helplessness or entire physical disability. Clark v. Gilley, Ky., 311 S.W.2d 391, 392. See also **Disability.**

Total eviction. That which occurs when the possessor is wholly deprived of his rights in the premises.

Total loss. *Fire insurance.* The complete destruction of the insured property by fire, so that nothing of value remains from it; as distinguished from a *partial* loss, where the property is damaged, but not entirely destroyed. Test whether building burned is "total loss" is whether substantial portion is left standing in condition reasonably suitable as basis on which to reconstruct building in like condition as to strength, security, and utility as it was before fire. Commerce Ins. Co. v. Sergi, Tex.Civ.App., 60 S.W.2d 1046. Total loss is such destruction of a building as that, after the fire, there remains standing in place no substantial remnant thereof which a reasonably prudent owner, uninsured, desiring to restore the building to its original condition, would utilize as a basis of such restoration. Crutchfield v. St. Paul Fire & Marine Ins. Co., Tex.Civ.App., 306 S.W.2d 948, 952.

Actual total loss. The total loss of the vessel covered by a policy of insurance, by its real and substantive destruction, by injuries which leave it no longer existing *in specie,* by its being reduced to a wreck irretrievably beyond repair, or by its being placed beyond the control of the insured and beyond his power of recovery. Distinguished from a *constructive* total loss, which occurs where the vessel, though injured by the perils insured against, remains *in specie* and capable of repair or recovery, but at such an expense, or under such other conditions, that the insured may claim the whole amount of the policy upon abandoning the vessel to the underwriters. In such cases the insured is entitled to indemnity as for a total loss.

Constructive total loss. See *Actual total loss, supra.*

Partial loss. Where an injury results to the vessel from a peril insured against, but where the loss is neither actually nor constructively total. See also *Fire insurance, supra.*

Totidem verbis /tódǝdǝm vǝ́rbǝs/. Lat. In so many words.

Toties quoties /tówshiy(iy)z kwówshiy(iy)z/. Lat. As often as occasion shall arise.

Totis viribus /tówdǝs váyrǝbǝs/. Lat. With all one's might or power; with all his might; very strenuously.

Totted /tódǝd/. A good debt to the crown, *i.e.,* a debt paid to the sheriff, to be by him paid over to the king.

Totten trust. See **Trust.**

Totum præfertur unicuique parti /tówdǝm prǝfǝ́rdǝr yùwnǝk(yuw)áykwiy párday/. The whole is preferable to any single part.

Touch. In marine insurance law, to stop at a port, usually for a brief period.

Touch and stay. Words introduced in policies of insurance, giving the party insured the right to stop and stay at certain designated points in the course of the voyage. A vessel which has the power to touch and stay at a place in the course of the voyage must confine herself strictly to the terms of the liberty so given; for any attempt to trade at such a port during such a stay, as, by shipping or landing goods, will amount to a species of deviation which will discharge the underwriters, unless the ship have also liberty to trade as well as to touch and stay at such a place.

Touching a dead body. It was an ancient superstition that the body of a murdered man would bleed freshly when touched by his murderer. Hence, in old criminal law, this was resorted to as a means of ascertaining the guilt or innocence of a person suspected of the murder.

Toujours et uncore prist /tuwzhúr ey onkór príy/. L. Fr. Always and still ready. This is the name of a plea of tender.

Tour d'echelle /túr deshél/. In French law, an easement consisting of the right to rest ladders upon the adjoining estate, when necessary in order to repair a party-wall or buildings supported by it.

Also the vacant space surrounding a building left unoccupied in order to facilitate its reparation when necessary.

Tourn /tyúrn/. In old English law, a court of record, having criminal jurisdiction, in each county, held before the sheriff, twice a year, in one place after another, following a certain circuit or rotation.

Tout /túw/. Fr. All; whole; entirely. *Tout temps prist,* always ready.

Tout ce que la loi ne defend pas est permis /túw s(ǝ) kǝ la lwá nǝ deyfon pá ey permíy/. Everything is permitted which is not forbidden by law.

Toute exception non surveillée tend à prendre la place du principe /túwt eksepsyówn non sǝrveyéy tónd a prónd la plás dyùw prænsíyp/. Every exception not watched tends to assume the place of the principle.

Tout temps prist /túw ton príy/. L. Fr. Always ready. The emphatic words of the old plea of tender; the defendant alleging that he has always been ready, and still is ready, to discharge the debt.

Tout un sound /túwd ǝn sáwnd/. L. Fr. All one sound; sounding the same; *idem sonans.*

Towage. The act or service of towing ships and vessels, usually by means of a small steamer called a "tug." That which is given for towing ships in rivers. The drawing a ship or barge along the water by another ship or boat, fastened to her, or by men or horses, etc., on land. It is also money which is given by bargemen to the owner of ground next a river, where they tow a barge or other vessel.

Towage service. In admiralty law, a service rendered to a vessel, by towing, for the mere purpose of expediting her voyage, without reference to any circumstances of danger. It is confined to vessels that have received no injury or damage.

Toward. In the direction of, or, on a course or line leading to. Coming soon; not long before.

To wit. That is to say; namely; *scilicet; videlicet.*

Town. A civil and political division of a state, varying in extent and importance, but usually one of the divisions of a county. In the New England states, the town is the political unit, and is a municipal corporation. In some other states, where the county is the unit, the town is merely one of its subdivisions, but possesses some powers of local self-government. In still other states, such subdivisions of a county are called "townships," and "town" is the name of a village, borough, or smaller city. The word "town" is quite commonly used as a generic term and as including both cities and villages.

Town-clerk. In those states where the town is the unit for local self-government, the town-clerk is a principal officer who keeps the records, issues calls for town-meetings, and performs generally the duties of a secretary to the political organization.

Town collector. One of the officers of a town charged with collecting the taxes assessed for town purposes.

Town commissioner. In some of the states where the town is the political unit the town commissioners constitute a board of administrative officers charged with the general management of the town's business.

Town-crier. An officer in a town whose business it is to make proclamations.

Town-hall. The building maintained by a town for town-meetings and the offices of the municipal authorities.

Town house. Type of dwelling unit normally having two, but sometimes three, stories; usually connected to a similar structure by a common wall, and commonly (particularly in planned unit developments) sharing and owning in common the surrounding grounds.

Town-meeting. Under the municipal organization of the New England states, the town-meeting is a legal assembly of the qualified voters of a town, held at stated intervals or on call, for the purpose of electing town officers, and of discussing and deciding on questions relating to the public business, property, and expenses of the town.

Town order or warrant. An official direction in writing by the auditing officers of a town, directing the treasurer to pay a sum of money.

Town pound. A place of confinement maintained by a town for estrays.

Town purpose. When it is said that taxation by a town, or the expenditure of the town's money, must be for town purposes, it is meant that the purposes must be public with respect to the town; *i.e.,* concern the welfare and advantage of the town as a whole.

Town-reeve. The reeve or chief officer of a town.

Township. Township, in government survey, is square tract six miles on each side containing thirty-six square miles of land. U. S. v. Weyerhaeuser Co., C.A.Or., 392 F.2d 448, 449. In some of the states, this is the name given to the civil and political subdivisions of a county.

Township trustee. One of a board of officers to whom, in some states, affairs of a township are intrusted.

Townsite. Portion of public domain segregated by proper authority and procedure as site for a town.

Town tax. Such tax as a town may levy for its peculiar expenses; as distinguished from a county or state tax.

Town treasurer. The treasurer of a town which is an organized municipal corporation.

Toxic /tóksək/. (Lat. *toxicum;* Gr. *toxikon.*) Poisonous; having the character or producing the effects of a poison; referable to a poison; produced by or resulting from a poison.

Toxical. Poisonous; containing poison.

Toxicant /tóksəkənt/. A poison; a toxic agent; any substance capable of producing toxication or poisoning.

Toxicate /tóksəkeyt/. To poison. Not used to describe the act of one who administers a poison, but the action of the drug or poison itself.

Auto-intoxication. Self-empoisonment from the absorption of the toxic products of internal metabolism, *e.g.,* ptomaine poisoning.

Intoxication. The state of being poisoned; the condition produced by the administration or introduction into the human system of a poison. This term is properly used as equivalent to "drunkenness," which, however, is more accurately described as "alcoholic intoxication." See also **Intoxication.**

Toxicology. The science of poisons; that department of medical science which treats of poisons, their effect, their recognition, their antidotes, and generally of the diagnosis and therapeutics of poisoning.

Toxin. In its widest sense, this term may denote any poison or toxicant; but as used in pathology and medical jurisprudence it signifies, in general, any diffusible alkaloidal substance (as, the ptomaines, abrin, brucin, or serpent venoms), and in particular the poisonous products of pathogenic (disease-producing) bacteria.

Tracea /tréysh(iy)ə/. In old English law, the track or trace of a felon, by which he was pursued with the hue and cry; a foot-step, hoof-print, or wheel-track.

Tracing. A tracing is a mechanical copy or *facsimile* of an original, produced by following its lines, with a pen or pencil, through a transparent medium, called tracing paper. See also **Skiptracing.**

Tract. A lot, piece or parcel of land, of greater or less size, the term not importing, in itself, any precise dimension, though term generally refers to a large piece of land. Holt v. Wichita County Water Improvement Dist. No. 2, Tex.Civ.App., 48 S.W.2d 527, 529.

Tradas in ballium /tréydəs in bæliyəm/. You deliver to bail. In old English practice, the name of a writ which might be issued in behalf of a party who, upon the writ *de odio et atia,* had been found to have been maliciously accused of a crime, commanding the sheriff that, if the prisoner found twelve good and lawful men of the county who would be mainpernors for him, he should *deliver* him *in bail* to those twelve, until the next assize.

Trade. The act or the business of buying and selling for money; traffic; barter. May v. Sloan, 101 U.S. 231, 25 L.Ed. 797. Trade is not a technical word and is ordinarily used in three senses: (1) in that of exchanging commodities by barter or by buying and selling for money; (2) in that of an occupation generally; (3) in that of a mechanical employment, in contradistinction to the learned professions, agriculture, or the liberal arts. People v. Polar Vent of America, Inc., 10 Misc.2d 378, 174 N.Y.S.2d 789, 793.

The business which a person has learned and which he carries on for procuring subsistence, or for profit; occupation or employment, particularly mechanical employment; distinguished from the liberal arts and learned professions, and from agriculture. A line of work or a form of occupation pursued as a business or calling, as for a livelihood or for profit; anything practiced as a means of getting a living, money, booty, etc.; mercantile or commercial business in general, or the buying and selling, or exchanging, of commodities, either by wholesale or retail within a country or between countries. Helvering v. Wilmington Trust Co., C.C.A.3, 124 F.2d 156, 158.

Trade acceptance. A draft or bill of exchange drawn by the seller on the purchaser of goods sold, and accepted by such purchaser, and its purpose is to make the book account liquid, and permit the seller to raise money on it before it is due under the terms of the sale, and its principal function is to take the place of selling goods on an open account and when properly drawn, it is negotiable. Gilliland & Echols Farm Supply & Hatchery v. Credit Equipment Corp., 269 Ala. 190, 112 So.2d 331, 332.

A draft drawn by a seller which is presented for signature (acceptance) to the buyer at the time goods are purchased and which then becomes the equivalent of a note receivable of the seller and the note payable of the buyer.

Trade agreement. Agreement between two countries or among many nations concerning buying and selling of each country's goods. See also **Collective bargaining agreement; Most favored nation clause; Reciprocal trade agreements.**

Trade and commerce. The words "trade" and "commerce," when used in juxtaposition impart to each other enlarged signification, so as to include practically every business occupation carried on for subsistence or profit and into which the elements of bargain and sale, barter, exchange, or traffic, enter. See **Commerce.**

Trade association. An association of business organizations having similar problems and engaged in similar fields formed for mutual protection, interchange of ideas and statistics and for maintenance of standards within their industry.

Trade commission. See **Federal Trade Commission.**

Trade discount. A discount from list price offered to all customers of a given type; *e.g.* discount offered by lumber dealer to building contractor. Contrast with a discount offered for prompt payment and quantity discount.

Trade dispute. Within Unemployment Insurance Act barring benefit payments to persons who leave work because of trade dispute, the term includes controversy over working conditions, American-Hawaiian S. S. Co. v. California Employment Commission, 24 Cal.2d 716, 151 P.2d 213, 215; and, unwillingness to cross picket lines, Mattson Terminals v. California Employment Commission, 24 Cal.2d 695, 151 P.2d 202, 206. See **Unfair labor practice.**

Trade dollar. A silver coin of the United States, of the weight of four hundred and twenty grains, troy.

Trade fixtures. Personal property used by tenants in business. Such fixtures retain the character of personal property; *e.g.* shelves used to display merchandise. See also **Fixture.**

Trade libel. Intentional disparagement of quality of property, which results in pecuniary damage to plaintiff. Erlich v. Etner, 224 C.A.2d 69, 36 Cal.Rptr. 256, 258.

Trade-mark. Generally speaking, a distinctive mark of authenticity, through which the products of particular manufacturers or the vendible commodities of particular merchants may be distinguished from those of others. It may consist in any symbol or in any form of words, but, as its office is to point out distinctively the origin or ownership of the articles to which it is affixed, it follows that no sign or form of words can be appropriated as a valid trade-mark which, from the nature of the fact conveyed by its primary meaning, others may employ with equal truth and with equal right for the same purpose. Jantzen Knitting Mills v. West Coast Knitting Mills, Cust. & Pat.App., 46 F.2d 182, 184.

A distinctive mark, motto, device, or emblem, which a manufacturer stamps, prints, or otherwise affixes to the goods he produces, so that they may be identified in the market, and their origin be vouched for. Trade-Mark Cases, 100 U.S. 82, 87, 25 L.Ed. 550. Exclusive rights to use a trade-mark are granted by the federal government for twenty-eight years.

The term "trade-mark" includes any word, name, symbol, or device or any combination thereof adopted and used by a manufacturer or merchant to identify his goods and distinguish them from those manufactured or sold by others. 15 U.S.C.A. § 1127.

See also **Common law trade-mark; Official Gazette; Patent and Trade-mark Office; Secondary meaning; Service mark.**

Trade-name distinguished. A "trade-name" is descriptive of a manufacturer or dealer and applies to business and its goodwill, whereas "trade-mark" is applicable only to vendable commodities, and different legal principles govern protection of the two. Junior Food Stores of West Florida, Inc. v. Jr. Food Stores, Inc., Fla., 226 So.2d 393, 396; American Steel Foundries v. Robertson, 269 U.S. 372, 46 S.Ct. 160, 162, 70 L.Ed. 317.

Trade-name. A "trade-name" is any designation which (a) is adopted and used by person to denominate goods which he markets, or services which he renders, or business which he conducts, or has come to be so used by others, and (b) through its association with such goods, services or business, has acquired a special significance as the name thereof, and (c) the use of which for the purpose stated in (a) is prohibited neither by legislative enactment nor by otherwise defined public policy. Walters v. Building Maintenance Service, Inc., Tex.Civ.App., 291 S.W.2d 377, 382. A "trade-name" is descriptive of the manufacturer or dealer for protection in trade, to avoid confusion in business, and to secure the advantages of a good reputation and is applied more to the goodwill of a business than as an identification of a product. Mary Muffet, Inc. v. Smelansky, Mo.App., 158 S.W.2d 168, 170.

A name used in trade to designate a particular business of certain individuals considered somewhat as an entity, or the place at which a business is located, or of a class of goods, but which is not a technical trade-mark either because not applied or affixed to goods sent into the market or because not capable of exclusive appropriation by anyone as a trade-mark. Trade-names may, or may not, be exclusive. Non-exclusive "trade-names" are names that are *publici juris* in their primary sense, but which in a secondary sense have come to be understood as indicating the goods or business of a particular trader. See **Secondary meaning.**

The terms "trade-name" and "commercial name" include individual names and surnames, firm names and trade names used by manufacturers, industrialists, merchants, agriculturists, and others to identify their businesses, vocations, or occupations; the names or titles lawfully adopted and used by persons, firms, associations, corporations, companies, unions, and any manufacturing, industrial, commercial, agricultural, or other organizations engaged in trade or commerce and capable of suing and being sued in a court of law. 15 U.S.C.A. § 1127.

See also **Certification mark; Collective mark; Service mark.** *Compare* **Trade-mark.**

Trader. A merchant; a retailer. One who makes it his business to buy merchandise, goods, or chattels to sell the same at a profit. People v. Terkanian, 27 Cal.App.2d 460, 81 P.2d 251, 253. One who sells goods substantially in the form in which they are bought; one who has not converted them into another form of property by his skill and labor. Albuquerque Lumber Co. v. Bureau of Revenue of New Mexico, 42 N.M. 58, 75 P.2d 334, 336.

In securities, one who as a member of a stock exchange buys and sells on the floor of the exchange either for brokers or on his own account. Likewise, in commodity market, one who buys and sells commodities (*e.g.* grain) and commodity futures for others and for his own account in anticipation of a speculative profit.

Trade secret. A formula, pattern, device or compilation of information which is used in one's business and which gives one opportunity to obtain advantage over competitors who do not know or use it. Rimes v. Club Corp. of America, Tex.Civ.App., 542 S.W.2d 909, 913. A plan or process, tool, mechanism, or compound known only to its owner and those of his employees to whom it is necessary to confide it. A secret formula or process not patented, but known only to certain individuals using it in compounding some article of trade having a commercial value.

Tradesman. A mechanic, craftsman, or artificer of any kind, whose livelihood depends primarily on the labor of his hands.

Trade-union. A combination of workers of the same trade or of several allied trades, for the purpose of securing by united action the most favorable conditions regarding wages, hours of labor, etc., for its members. See also **Union.**

Trade usage. The usage or customs commonly observed by persons conversant in, or connected with, a particular trade.

A usage of trade is any practice or method of dealing having such regularity of observance in a place, vocation or trade as to justify an expectation that it will be observed with respect to the transaction in question. The existence and scope of such a usage are to be proved as facts. If it is established that such a usage is embodied in a written trade code or similar writing the interpretation of the writing is for the court. U.C.C. § 1–205(2).

Tradicion /tràðiysyówn/. Span. In Spanish law, delivery.

Trading. Engaging in trade (*q.v.*); pursuing the business or occupation of trade or of a trader.

Trading corporation. See **Corporation.**

Trading partnership. A firm the nature of whose business, according to the usual modes of conducting it, imports the necessity of buying and selling. Dowling v. National Exch. Bank, 145 U.S. 512, 12 S.Ct. 928, 36 L.Ed. 795.

Trading stamps. The name for a method of conducting some kinds of retail business which consists of an agreement between a number of merchants and a corporation that the latter shall print the names of the former in its subscribers' dictionary and circulate a number of copies of the book, and that the merchants shall purchase of the corporation a number of so-called trading stamps, to be given to purchasers with their purchases, and by them preserved and pasted in the books aforesaid until a certain number have been secured, when they shall be presented to the corporation in exchange for the choice of certain articles kept in stock by the corporation.

Trading voyage. One which contemplates the touching and stopping of the vessel at various ports for the purpose of traffic or sale and purchase or exchange of commodities on account of the owners and shippers, rather than the transportation of cargo between terminal points, which is called a "freighting voyage."

Trading with the enemy. Carrying on commerce with a country or with a subject of a nation with whom the U.S. is at war. Federal laws prohibit commercial intercourse with nations and with subjects and allies of nations with whom the U.S. is at war. 50 U.S.C.A. App. § 1 et seq.

Traditio /trədísh(iy)ow/. Lat. In the civil law, delivery; transfer of possession; a derivative mode of acquiring, by which the owner of a corporeal thing, having the right and the will of aliening it, transfers it for a lawful consideration to the receiver.

Quasi traditio. A supposed or implied delivery of property from one to another. Thus, if the purchaser of an article was already in possession of it before the sale, his continuing in possession is considered as equivalent to a fresh delivery of it, delivery being one of the necessary elements of a sale; in other words, a *quasi traditio* is predicated.

Traditio brevi manu. A species of constructive or implied delivery. When he who already holds possession of a thing in another's name agrees with that other that thenceforth he shall possess it in his own name, in this case a delivery and redelivery are not necessary.

Traditio clavium. Delivery of keys; a symbolical kind of delivery, by which the ownership of merchandise in a warehouse might be transferred to a buyer.

Traditio longa manu. A species of delivery which takes place where the transferor places the article in the hands of the transferee, or, on his order, delivers it at his house.

Traditio rei. Delivery of the thing.

Traditio loqui facit chartam /trədísh(iy)ow lówkway féysət kárdəm/. Delivery makes a deed speak. Delivery gives effect to the words of a deed.

Tradition. Delivery. A close translation or formation from the Latin *"traditio."* 2 Bl.Comm. 307.

The tradition or delivery is the transferring of the thing sold into the power and possession of the buyer. Civ.Code La. art. 2477.

Past customs and usages which influence or govern present acts or practices.

Traditionary evidence. Evidence derived from tradition or reputation or the statements formerly made by persons since deceased, in regard to questions of pedigree, ancient boundaries, and the like, where no living witnesses can be produced having knowledge of the facts.

Traditio nihil amplius transferre debet vel potest, ad eum qui accipit, quam est apud eum qui tradit /trədísh(iy)ow náy(h)əl æmpliyəs træn(t)sfəriy débət vèl pówdəst, æd íyəm kwày æksəpət, kwæm èst æpəd íyəm kwày tréydət/. Delivery ought to, and can, transfer nothing more to him who receives than is with him who delivers.

Traditor /trǽdədər/tréy°/. In old English law, a traitor; one guilty of high treason.

Traditur in ballium /trǽdədər ìn bǽliyəm/. In old practice, means delivered to bail. Emphatic words of the old Latin bail-piece.

Traffic. Commerce; trade; sale or exchange of merchandise, bills, money, and the like. The passing of goods or commodities from one person to another for an equivalent in goods or money. The subjects of transportation on a route, as persons or goods; the passing to and fro of persons, animals, vehicles, or vessels, along a route of transportation, as along a street, highway, etc. See **Commerce.**

Traffic balances. Balances of moneys collected in payment for the transportation of passengers and freight.

Trafficking. Trading or dealing in certain goods and commonly used in connection with illegal narcotic sales.

Traffic regulations. Prescribed rules of conduct to promote the orderly and safe flow of traffic.

Trahens /tréy(h)en(d)z/. Lat. In French law, the drawer of a bill.

Trail-baston. Justices of trail-baston were justices appointed by King Edward I, during his absence in the Scotch and French wars, about the year 1305. They were so styled, says Hollingshed, for trailing or drawing the staff of justice. Their office was to make inquisition, throughout the kingdom, of all officers and others, touching extortion, bribery, and such like grievances, of intruders into other men's lands, barrators, robbers, breakers of the peace, and divers other offenders.

Trailer. A separate vehicle, not driven or propelled by its own power, but drawn by some independent power. A semi-trailer is a separate vehicle which is not driven or propelled by its own power, but, which, to be useful, must be attached to and become a part of another vehicle, and then loses its identity as a separate vehicle. Maryland Casualty Co. v. Cross, C.C.A. Tex., 112 F.2d 58, 60.

Trainbands. The militia; the part of a community trained to martial exercises.

Traitor. One who, being trusted, betrays; one guilty of treason *(q.v.).*

Traitorously /tréydərəsliy/. In criminal pleading at common law, an essential word in indictments for treason. The offense must be laid to have been committed *traitorously.*

Trajectitia pecunia /træjektísh(iy)ə pəkyúwn(i)yə/. A loan to a shipper to be repaid only in case of a successful voyage. The lender could charge an extraordinary rate of interest, *nauticum fœnus.*

Trajectitius /træjektísh(iy)əs/. Lat. In the civil law, sent across the sea.

Tramp. One who roams about from place to place, begging or living without labor or visible means of support; a vagrant.

Tramp steamer. A ship which is not governed by any pre-arranged ports of call but which stops at those ports for which it has cargo.

Transact. To "transact" means to prosecute negotiations; to carry on business; to have dealings; to carry through; bring about; perform; to carry on or conduct; to pass back and forth as in negotiations or trade; to bring into actuality or existence. Knoepfle v. Suko, N.D., 108 N.W.2d 456, 462. The word embraces in its meaning the carrying on or prosecution of business negotiations, but it is a broader term than the word "contract" and may involve business negotiations which have been either wholly or partly brought to a conclusion. Bozied v. Edgerton, 239 Minn. 227, 58 N.W.2d 313, 316. See also **Negotiate; Transaction.**

Transacting business. Term "transacting business," within statute providing that no foreign corporation transacting business in State without a certificate of authority shall maintain an action in State if it has not obtained a certificate of authority, is not susceptible of precise definition automatically resolving every case; each case must be dealt with on its own circumstances to determine if foreign corporation has engaged in local activity or only in interstate commerce. Materials Research Corp. v. Metron, Inc., 64 N.J. 74, 312 A.2d 147, 150.

Test of whether or not a corporation is transacting business, in a district, for purpose of section of the Clayton Act providing that an action may be brought against a corporation in any district wherein it transacts business, is the practical everyday business or commercial concept of doing business of any substantial character. Interstate Cigar Co. v. Corral Wodiska y Ca, D.C.N.Y., 30 F.R.D. 354, 355; Kolb v. Chrysler Corp., D.C.Wis., 357 F.Supp. 504, 508.

See also **Doing business; Minimal contacts.**

"Doing business" distinguished. The concept of "transacting business" under venue provisions of Investment Company Act of 1940, Securities Act of 1933, and Securities Exchange Act of 1934, requires less business activity than that necessary to sustain jurisdiction under a "doing business" or "minimum contacts" standard, and is intended to have a more flexible and broader meaning than the jurisdictional predicates. Zorn v. Anderson, D.C.N.Y., 263 F.Supp. 745, 747.

Transactio /træn(d)zǽksh(iy)ow/. Lat. In the civil law, the settlement of a suit or matter in controversy, by the litigating parties, between themselves, without referring it to arbitration. An agreement by which a suit, either pending or about to be commenced, was forborne or discontinued on certain terms.

Transaction. Act of transacting or conducting any business; negotiation; management; proceeding; that which is done; an affair. It may involve selling, leasing, borrowing, mortgaging or lending. Something which has taken place, whereby a cause of action has arisen. It must therefore consist of an act or agreement, or several acts or agreements having some connection with each other, in which more than one person is concerned, and by which the legal relations of such persons between themselves are altered. It is a broader term than "contract". Hoffman Machinery Corporation v. Ebenstein, 150 Kan. 790, 96 P.2d 661, 663. See also **Transact.**

Civil law. An agreement between two or more persons, who, for preventing or putting an end to a lawsuit, adjust their differences by mutual consent, in the manner which they agree on. This contract must be reduced into writing. Civ.Code La. art. 3071.

Evidence. A "transaction" between a witness and a decedent, within statutory provisions excluding evidence of such transactions, embraces every variety of affairs which can form the subject of negotiations, interviews, or actions between two persons, and includes every method by which one person can derive impressions or information from the conduct, condition, or language of another. An action participated in by witness and decedent and to which decedent could testify of his own personal knowledge, if alive. Nelson v. Janssen, 144 Neb. 811, 14 N.W.2d 662, 665. A personal or mutual transaction wherein deceased and witness actively participate.

Transactional immunity. See **Immunity** (*Immunity from prosecution*).

Transaction or occurrence test. Fed.R.Civil P. 13(a) provides that a claim qualifies as a *compulsory* counterclaim if it arises out of the "transaction or occurrence" that is the subject matter of the opposing party's claim. Courts generally have agreed that these words should be interpreted liberally in order to further the general policies of the federal rules which are to avoid multiple suits and to encourage the determination of the entire controversy among the parties. Thus, the "transaction" test does not require the court to differentiate between opposing legal and equitable claims or between claims in tort and those in contract. Most courts, rather than attempting to define the key terms of Rule 13(a) precisely, have preferred to suggest standards by which the compulsory or permissive nature of specific counterclaims can be determined. Four tests have been suggested: (1) Are the issues of fact and law raised by the claim and counterclaim largely the same? (2) Would res judicata bar a subsequent suit on defendant's claim absent the compulsory counterclaim rule? (3) Will substantially the same evidence support or refute plaintiff's claim as well as defendant's counterclaim? (4) Is there any logical relation between the claim and the counterclaim? Old Homestead Co. v. Continental Baking Co., 47 F.R.D. 560, 563.

Cross-claims. Most courts have held that the above standards used for dealing with the "transaction or occurrence" test for compulsory counterclaims also apply to cross-claims under Fed.R.Civil P. 13(g). Old Homestead Co. v. Continental Baking Co., 47 F.R.D. 560, 563.

Transazione /træn(d)zàtsiyówney/. An Italian term which technically refers to an instrument whereby parties agree to put an end to a dispute by means of mutual concessions and is the equivalent of "transactio" under the Roman law, the principles of which have been carried into the common law and are found in agreements of accord and satisfaction and compromise and settlement.

Transcript. That which has been transcribed. A copy of any kind, though commonly the term refers to a copy of the record of a trial, hearing or other proceeding. A writing made from or after an original. A copy of an original writing or deed and suggests the idea of an original writing. O'Quinn v. Tate, Tex.Civ. App., 187 S.W.2d 241, 243.

An official copy of the record of proceedings in a trial or hearing. Word-for-word typing of everything that was said "on the record" during the trial. The stenographer types this transcription which is paid for by the parties requesting it.

Transcript of record. Refers to the printed record as made up in each case of the proceedings and pleadings necessary for the appellate court to review the history of the case.

Transcriptio pedis finis levati mittendo in cancellarium /træn(t)skrípsh(iy)ow píydəs fáynəs ləvéyday məténdow in kæn(t)səlériyəm/. A writ which certified the foot of a fine levied before justices in eyre, etc., into the chancery.

Transcriptio recognitionis factæ coram justiciariis itinerantibus, etc. /træn(t)skrípsh(iy)ow rèkəgnìshiyównəs fæktiy kórəm jəstìshiyériyəs aytìnəræntəbəs/. An old writ to certify a cognizance taken by justices in eyre.

Transfer, *v.* To convey or remove from one place, person, etc., to another; pass or hand over from one to another; specifically, to change over the possession or control of (as, to transfer a title to land). To sell or give. Chappell v. State, 216 Ind. 666, 25 N.E.2d 999, 1001.

Transfer, *n.* An act of the parties, or of the law, by which the title to property is conveyed from one person to another. The sale and every other method, direct or indirect, of disposing of or parting with property or with an interest therein, or with the possession thereof, or of fixing a lien upon property or upon an interest therein, absolutely or conditionally, voluntarily or involuntarily, by or without judicial proceedings, as a conveyance, sale, payment, pledge, mortgage, lien, encumbrance, gift, security or otherwise. The word is one of general meaning and may include the act of giving property by will. Hayter v. Fern Lake Fishing Club, Tex.Civ.App., 318 S.W.2d 912, 915.

Transfer is the all-encompassing term used by the Uniform Commercial Code to describe the act which passes an interest in an instrument to another. Scheid v. Shields, 269 Or. 236, 524 P.2d 1209, 1210.

Transfer means every mode, direct or indirect, absolute or conditional, voluntary or involuntary, of disposing of or parting with property or with an interest in property, including retention of title as a security interest. Bankruptcy Act, § 101(40).

See **Barter; Exchange; Gift; Sale; Will.**

Transferable. A term used in a *quasi* legal sense, to indicate that the character of assignability or negotiability attaches to the particular instrument, or that it may pass from hand to hand, carrying all rights of the original holder. The words "not transferable" are sometimes printed upon a ticket, receipt, or bill of lading, to show that the same will not be good in the hands of any person other than the one to whom first issued.

Transfer agent. A transfer agent keeps a record of the name of each registered shareowner, his or her address, the number of shares owned, and sees that certificates presented to his office for transfer are properly cancelled and new certificates issued in the name of the transferee. Usually a bank or trust company designated by a corporation to make legal transfers of stock (bonds) and, perhaps, to pay dividends (coupons).

Transferee. He to whom a transfer is made.

Transferee liability. Under certain conditions, if the Internal Revenue Service is unable to collect taxes owed by a transferor of property, it may pursue its claim against the transferee of such property. The transferee's liability for taxes is limited to the extent of the value of the assets transferred. For example, the Internal Revenue Service can force a donee to pay the gift tax when such tax cannot be paid by the donor making the transfer. I.R.C. §§ 6901–6905.

Transfer in contemplation of death. A transfer made under a present apprehension on the part of the transferor, from some existing bodily or mental condition or impending peril, creating a reasonable fear that death is near at hand. See **Contemplation of death.**

Transfer of a cause. The removal of a cause from the jurisdiction of one court or judge to another by lawful authority. See **Forum non conveniens.**

Transferor. One who makes a transfer.

Transfer payments. Payments made by the government to individuals for which no services are rendered in return. A transfer payment might be a Social Security check or an unemployment check.

Transferred intent, doctrine of. If a person intentionally directs force against one person wrongfully but, instead, hits another, his intent is said to be transferred from one to the other and he is liable to the other though he did not intend it in the first instance.

Transfer tax. A tax upon the passing of the title to property or a valuable interest therein out of or from the estate of a decedent, by inheritance, devise, or bequest. See **Estate tax; Inheritance tax; Unified transfer tax.**

Tax on the transfer of property, particularly of an incorporeal nature, such as bonds or shares of stock, between living persons. A tax imposed by New York State when a security is sold or transferred from one person to another. Also, a tax imposed by states on each deed conveying real estate. The tax is paid by the seller. See also **Revenue stamps.**

Transfer ticket. An undertaking on the part of a common carrier to continue the carriage further without additional charge if the passenger, in accordance with its terms, again presents himself at the proper place for carriage. It generally designates the point at which the journey is to be renewed, but contains no contract, express or implied, for safety in making the transfer. Anton v. St. Louis Public Service Co., 335 Mo. 188, 71 S.W.2d 702, 706.

Transferuntur dominia sine titulo et traditione, per usucaptionem, scil, per longam continuam et pacificam possessionem /trænsfərántər dəmín(i)yə sáyniy tít(y)əlow èt trədìshiyówniy, pàr yúwzyuwkæpshiyównəm, síləsət, pàr lóŋgəm kəntínyuwəm èt pəsífəkəm pəzèshiyównəm/. Rights of dominion are transferred without title or delivery, by usucaption, to-wit, long and quiet possession.

Transfretatio /træn(d)zfrətéysh(iy)ow/. Lat. In old English law, a crossing of the strait [of Dover]; a passing or sailing over from England to France. The royal passages or voyages to Gascony, Brittany, and other parts of France were so called, and time was sometimes computed from them.

Transgressio /træn(d)zgrésh(iy)ow/. In old English law, a violation of law. Also trespass; the action of trespass.

Transgressio est cum modus non servatur nec mensura, debit enim quilibet in suo facto modum habere et mensuram /træn(d)zgrésh(iy)ow èst kàm mówdəs nòn sərvéydər nèk mens(y)úrə, débəd íynəm kwáyləbət ìn s(y)úwow fæktow mówdəm həbíriy èt mens(y)úrəm/. Transgression is when neither mode nor measure is preserved, for every one in his act ought to have a mode and measure.

Transgressione /træn(d)zgrèshiyówniy/. In old English law, a writ or action of trespass.

Transgressione multiplicata, crescat pœnæ inflictio /træn(d)zgrèshiyówniy màltəpləkéydə, kréskət píyniy inflíksh(iy)ow/. When transgression is multiplied, let the infliction of punishment be increased.

Transgressive trust /træn(d)zgrésəv trśst/. See **Trust**.

Transhipment. In maritime law, the act of taking the cargo out of one ship and loading it in another.

Transient, n. /trænzh(iy)ənt/. One who, or that which, is temporary. Synonymous with transitory, fugitive, fleeting, momentary.

Transient, adj. Passing across, as from one thing or person to another; passing with time of short duration; not permanent; not lasting; temporary. Tilly v. Woodham, La.App., 163 So. 771, 772.

Transient foreigner. One who visits the country, without the intention of remaining.

Transient merchant. A merchant who engages in the vending or sale of merchandise at any place in the state temporarily, and who does not intend to become, and does not become, a permanent merchant of such place.

Transient person. Within venue statute one who is found in state but who has no fixed place of residence therein. Fagg v. Benners, Tex.Civ.App., 47 S.W.2d 872, 873. Person who is in a place only temporarily.

Transire, v. /træn(d)záyriy/. Lat. To go, or pass over; to pass from one thing, person, or place to another.

Transire, n. /træn(d)záyriy/. In English law, a warrant or permit for the custom-house to let goods pass.

Transit. A stop-over privilege on a continuous journey granted by carrier by which a break de facto in continuity of carriage of goods is disregarded and two legs of a journey are treated as though covered without interruption, uniting both legs into a through route for which a joint rate can be published. Galveston Truck Line Corporation v. State, Tex.Civ.App., 123 S.W.2d 797, 802; Baltimore and O. R. Co. v. United States, D.C.N.Y., 24 F.Supp. 734, 735. Within policy covering goods in transit, term has significance of activity and of motion and direction; literally it means in course of passing from point to point, and ordinarily goods in transit would imply that foods will lawfully be picked up at given place and hauled to place designated by owner or one with authority to so designate. Simons v. Niagara Fire Ins. Co., Tex.Civ. App., 398 S.W.2d 833, 834. Term may also be applied to a check which is mailed for collection while it is still in the mails and uncollected. See also **In transitu; Stoppage in transit**.

Transportation of goods or persons from one place to another. Passage; act of passing.

Transit in rem judicatam /træn(d)zəd ən rém juwdəkéydəm/. It passes into a matter adjudged; it becomes converted into a *res judicata* or judgment. A contract upon which a judgment is obtained is said to pass *in rem judicatam*.

Transitive covenant. See **Covenant**.

Transitory. Passing from place to place; that which may pass or be changed from one place to another; the opposite of "local." See **Transitory action**.

Transitory action. A lawsuit that may be brought in any one of many places. Actions are "transitory" when transaction on which they are based might take place anywhere, and are "local" when they could not occur except in some particular place; the distinction being in nature of subject of injury and not in means used or place at which cause of action arises. Howle v. Twin States Exp., 237 N.C. 667, 75 S.E.2d 732, 736. A transitory action may be brought in any court of general jurisdiction in any district wherein defendant can be found and served with process, whereas in a "local action" the plaintiff must bring suit in the court designated, if not statutorily required to do otherwise. Moreland v. Rucker Pharmacal Co., D.C. La., 59 F.R.D. 537, 540.

Transit terra cum onere /træn(d)zət téhrə kàm ównəriy/. Land passes subject to any burden affecting it.

Transitus /træn(d)zədəs/. Lat. Passage from one place to another; transit. *In transitu*, on the passage, transit, or way.

Translado /translá∂ow/. Span. A transcript.

Translation. The reproduction in one language of a book, document, or speech in another language.

The transfer of property; but in this sense it is seldom used. 2 Bl.Comm. 294.

In ecclesiastical law, as applied to a bishop, the term denotes his removal from one diocese to another.

Translatitium edictum /træn(d)zlətísh(iy)əm ədíktəm/. Lat. In Roman law, the prætor, on his accession to office, did not usually publish an entirely new edict, but retained the whole or a part of that promulgated by his predecessor, as being of an approved or permanently useful character. The portion thus repeated or handed down from year to year was called the *"edictum translatitium."*

Translative fact. A fact by means of which a right is transferred or passes from one person to another; one, that is, which fulfills the double function of terminating the right of one person to an object, and of originating the right of another to it.

Transmission. In the civil law, the right which heirs or legatees may have of passing to their successors the inheritance or legacy to which they were entitled, if they happen to die without having exercised their rights.

Transmit. To send or transfer from one person or place to another, or to communicate. State v. Robbins, 253 N.C. 47, 116 S.E.2d 192, 193.

Transport, n. In old New York law, a conveyance of land.

Transport, v. To carry or convey from one place to another. Sacramento Nav. Co. v. Salz, 273 U.S. 326, 47 S.Ct. 368, 369, 71 L.Ed. 663; People v. One 1941 Cadillac Club Coupe, 63 Cal.2d 418, 147 P.2d 49, 51.

Transportation. The movement of goods or persons from one place to another, by a carrier. Railroad Co. v. Pratt, 22 Wall. 133, 22 L.Ed. 827; Interstate Commerce Com'n v. Brimson, 154 U.S. 447, 14 S.Ct. 1125, 38 L.Ed. 1047; Gloucester Ferry Co. v. Pennsylvania, 114 U.S. 196, 5 S.Ct. 826, 29 L.Ed. 158.

Criminal law. A species of punishment consisting in removing the criminal from his own country to another (usually a penal colony), there to remain in exile for a prescribed period. Fong Yue Ting v. U. S., 149 U.S. 698, 13 S.Ct. 1016, 37 L.Ed. 905. See **Deportation.**

Trap. A device, as a pitfall, snare, or machine that shuts suddenly as with a spring, for taking game and other animals. Hence, any device or contrivance by which one may be caught unawares, strategem; snare; gin. It imports an affirmative intent or design either malicious or mischievous, to cause injury. Gumbart v. Waterbury Club Holding Corporation, D.C.Conn., 27 F.Supp. 228, 229, 230. The doctrine of "trap" as ground for recovery by trespasser is rested upon theory that owner expected trespasser and prepared an injury. Moseley v. Alabama Power Co., 246 Ala. 416, 21 So.2d 305, 307. The "trap" or "pitfall" which would raise duty of care on part of owner or occupier of land running to a licensee must be an ultrahazardous hidden peril of which occupier has knowledge but licensee does not, and it is not necessary that such trap or pitfall be designed or intended to catch or entrap anything. Bichsel v. Blumhost, Mo.App., 429 S.W.2d 301, 306. See also **Entrapment.**

Traslado /tra(n)sláðow/. In Spanish law, a copy; a sight.

A copy of a document taken by the notary from the original, or a subsequent copy taken from the protocol, and not a copy taken directly from the matrix or protocol.

Trassans /træsǽn(d)z/. Drawing; one who draws. The drawer of a bill of exchange.

Trassatus /træséydəs/. One who is drawn, or drawn upon. The drawee of a bill of exchange.

Trauma /tráwmə/trómə/. A physical injury caused by a blow, or fall, or a psychologically damaging emotional experience. An injury, wound, shock, or the resulting condition or neurosis. Ortkiese v. Clarson & Ewell Engineering, Fla., 126 So.2d 556, 561.

Traumatic /trəmǽdək/. Caused by or resulting from a wound or any external injury; as, traumatic insanity, produced by an injury to or fracture of the skull with consequent pressure on the brain.

Traumatism /tráwmətizəm/. A diseased condition of the body or any part of it caused by a wound or external injury.

Travail /trǽveyl/trəvéyl/. The act of child-bearing. A woman is said to be in her travail from the time the pains of child-bearing commence until her delivery.

Travel. To go from one place to another at a distance; to journey. Spoken of voluntary change of place.

Travel Act. Whoever travels in interstate or foreign commerce or uses any facility in interstate or foreign commerce, including the mail, with intent to: (1) distribute the proceeds of any unlawful activity; or (2) commit any crime of violence to further any unlawful activity; or (3) otherwise promote, manage, establish, carry on, or facilitate the promotion, management, establishment, or carrying on, of any unlawful activity, and thereafter performs or attempts to perform any of the aforementioned acts, is guilty of a federal offense under 18 U.S.C.A. § 1952.

Traveled part of highway. See **Traveled way.**

Traveled place. A place where the public have, in some manner, acquired the legal right to travel.

Traveled way. The traveled path, or the path used for public travel, within located limits of the way. Also called "traveled part of highway."

Traveler. One who passes from place to place, whether for pleasure, instruction, business or health.

Traveler's check. Instrument purchased from bank, express company, or the like, in various denominations, which can be used as cash upon second signature by purchaser. It has the characteristics of a cashier's check of the issuer. Pines v. United States, C.C.A.Iowa, 123 F.2d 825, 828. It requires the signature of the purchaser at the time he buys it and also at the time when he uses it.

Traveler's letter of credit. A type of letter of credit which is addressed to a correspondent bank. When the traveler wishes to draw credit on the correspondent bank, he identifies himself as the person in whose favor the credit is drawn.

Travel expenses. Travel expenses include meals and lodging and transportation expenses while away from home in the pursuit of a trade or business (including that of an employee). See **Tax home.**

Traverse. In common law pleading, a traverse signifies a denial. Thus, where a defendant denies any material allegation of fact in the plaintiff's declaration, he is said to traverse it, and the plea itself is thence frequently termed a "traverse."

Common traverse. A simple and direct denial of the material allegations of the opposite pleading, and without inducement or *absque hoc.*

Criminal practice. To put off or delay the trial of an indictment until a succeeding term. More properly, to deny or take issue upon an indictment. 4 Bl. Comm. 351.

General traverse. One preceded by a general inducement, and denying in general terms all that is last before alleged on the opposite side, instead of pursuing the words of the allegations which it denies.

Special traverse. A peculiar form of traverse or denial, the design of which, as distinguished from a *common* traverse, is to explain or qualify the denial, instead of putting it in the direct and absolute form. It consists of an affirmative and a negative part, the first setting forth the new affirmative matter tending to explain or qualify the denial, and technically called the "inducement," and the latter constituting the direct denial itself, and technically called the *"absque hoc."*

Traverse jury. A petit jury; a trial jury; a jury impaneled to try an action or prosecution, as distinguished from a grand jury. See **Jury.**

Traverse of indictment or presentment. The taking issue upon and contradicting or denying some chief point of it.

Traverse of office. The proving that an inquisition made of lands or goods by the escheator is defective and untruly made. It is the challenging, by a subject, of an inquest of office, as being defective and untruly made.

Traverse upon a traverse. One growing out of the same point or subject-matter as is embraced in a preceding traverse on the other side.

Traverser. In pleading, one who traverses or denies. A prisoner or party indicted; so called from his traversing the indictment.

Traversing note. A pleading in chancery, consisting of a denial put in by the plaintiff on behalf of the defendant, generally denying all the statements in the plaintiff's bill. The effect of it is to put the plaintiff upon proof of the whole contents of his bill, and is only resorted to for the purpose of saving time, and in a case where the plaintiff can safely dispense with an answer. A copy of the note must be served on the defendant.

T.R.E. An abbreviation of *"Tempore Regis Edwardi"* (in the time of King Edward), of common occurrence in Domesday, when the valuation of manors, as it was in the time of Edward the Confessor, is recounted.

Treacher, trechetour, or **treachour.** A traitor.

Treachery. Deliberate and wilful betrayal of trust and confidence.

Tread-mill, or **tread-wheel.** An instrument of prison discipline, being a wheel or cylinder with an horizontal axis, having steps attached to it, up which the prisoners walk, and thus put the axis in motion. The men hold on by a fixed rail, and, as their weight presses down the step upon which they tread, they ascend the next step, and thus drive the wheel.

Treason. The offense of attempting by overt acts to overthrow the government of the state to which the offender owes allegiance; or of betraying the state into the hands of a foreign power. Treason consists of two elements: Adherence to the enemy, and rendering him aid and comfort. Cramer v. U. S., U.S. N.Y., 325 U.S. 1, 65 S.Ct. 918, 932, 89 L.Ed. 1441. See 18 U.S.C.A. § 2381. A person can be convicted of treason only on the testimony of two witnesses, or confession in open court. Art. III, Sec. 3, U.S. Constitution.

Constructive treason. Treason imputed to a person by law from his conduct or course of actions, though his deeds taken severally do not amount to actual treason. This doctrine is not known in the United States.

High treason. In English law, treason against the king or sovereign, as distinguished from petit or petty treason, which might formerly be committed against a subject.

Misprision of treason. See **Misprision of treason.**

Petit treason. In English law, the crime committed by a wife in killing her husband, or a servant his lord or master, or an ecclesiastic his lord or ordinary. 4 Bl.Comm. 75.

Treason-felony. Under the English statute 11 & 12 Vict., c. 12, passed in 1848, is the offense of compassing, devising, etc., to depose her majesty from the crown; or to levy war in order to intimidate either house of parliament, etc., or to stir up foreigners by any printing or writing to invade the kingdom. This offense is punishable with penal servitude for life, or for any term not less than five years, etc., under statutes 11 & 12 Vict., c. 12, § 3; 20 & 21 Vict., c. 3, § 2; 27 & 28 Vict., c. 47, § 2. By the statute first above mentioned, the government is enabled to treat as felony many offenses which must formerly have been treated as high treason.

Treasonable. Having the nature or guilt of treason.

Treasure. A treasure is a thing hidden or buried in the earth, on which no one can prove his property, and which is discovered by chance. See **Treasure-trove.**

Treasurer. An officer of a public or private corporation, company, or government, charged with the receipt, custody, and disbursement of its moneys or funds.

Treasurer, Lord High. Formerly the chief treasurer of England, who had charge of the moneys in the exchequer, the chancellor of the exchequer being under him. He appointed all revenue officers and escheaters, and leased crown lands. The office is obsolete, and his duties are now performed by the lords commissioners of the treasury.

Treasurer of the United States. See **Treasury Department.**

Treasurer's Remembrancer. In English law, he whose charge was to put the lord treasurer and the rest of the judges of the exchequer in remembrance of such things as were called on and dealt in for the sovereign's behalf.

Treasure-trove. Literally, treasure found. Money or coin, gold, silver, plate or bullion *found* hidden in the earth or other private place, the owner thereof being unknown. 1 Bl.Comm. 295. Called in Latin *"thesaurus inventus;"* and in Saxon *"fynderinga."* Finder of treasure trove, is entitled thereto as against owner of land where such treasure is found and all the world save the true owner, in absence of statute. Schley v. Couch, 284 S.W.2d 333, 335.

Treasury. A place or building in which stores of wealth are reposited; particularly, a place where the public revenues are deposited and kept, and where money is disbursed to defray the expenses of government.

That department of government which is charged with the receipt, custody, and disbursement (pursuant to appropriations) of the public revenues or funds.

Treasury bench. In the English house of commons, the first row of seats on the right hand of the speaker is so called, because occupied by the first lord of the treasury or principal minister of the crown.

Treasury bill. Short-term obligations of the federal government. Treasury bills are for specified terms of three, six and twelve months.

An obligation of the U.S. Treasury with a maturity date less than one year from the date of issue and bearing no interest but sold at a discount. Distinguished from a *certificate of indebtedness,* which also is of a maturity of one year or less but bears interest. See **Treasury certificate; Treasury note.**

Treasury bond. A bond issued by a corporation and then reacquired; such bonds are treated as retired when reacquired and an extraordinary gain or loss on reacquisition is recognized.

Bond issued by the federal government as evidence of long term indebtedness.

Treasury certificate. An obligation of the U.S. generally maturing in one year on which interest is paid on a coupon basis. *Compare* **Treasury bill.**

Treasury note. An obligation of the federal government, with a maturity of one to five years, on which interest is paid by coupon. *Compare* **Treasury bill.**

Treasury Department. The Treasury Department was created by act of Congress approved September 2, 1789 (1 Stat. 65; 31 U.S.C.A. § 1001). Many subsequent acts have figured in the development of the Department delegating new duties to its charge and establishing the numerous bureaus and divisions which now compose the Treasury. The Department of the Treasury performs four basic types of functions: formulating and recommending financial tax, and fiscal policies; serving as financial agent for the U.S. Government; law enforcement; and manufacturing coins and currency. See also **Internal Revenue Service.**

Treasury Regulations. See **Regulations.**

Treasury securities. Such as have been lawfully issued and thereafter have been bought by corporation for a consideration out of corporate funds or otherwise acquired from owners, and not retired but placed as an asset of the corporation in its treasury for future use as such. Miners Nat. Bank of Pottsville v. Frackville Sewerage Co., 157 Pa.Super. 167, 42 A.2d 177, 179. See also **Treasury stock.**

Treasury shares. See **Treasury stock.**

Treasury stock. Stock which has been issued as fully paid to stockholders and subsequently reacquired by the corporation to be used by it in furtherance of its corporate purposes, and stock which is merely to be held as unsubscribed for and unissued is not usually regarded as "treasury stock". In re Public Service Holding Corporation, 26 Del.Ch. 436, 24 A.2d 584, 586. Shares which have been reacquired by corporation, but not cancelled and returned to status of authorized but unissued shares, and which occupy status of issued but not outstanding shares. Fuller v. Krogh, 113 N.W.2d 25, 31, 15 Wis.2d 412. Such reacquisitions result in a reduction of stockholders' equity, and are usually shown on the balance sheet as contra to stockholders' equity.

Treasury warrant. Order in check form on U.S. Treasury on which treasury (*i.e.* government) disbursements are paid.

Treatment. A broad term covering all the steps taken to effect a cure of an injury or disease; including examination and diagnosis as well as application of remedies.

Treaty. A compact made between two or more independent nations with a view to the public welfare. Louis Wolf & Co. v. United States, Cust. & Pat.App., 107 F.2d 819, 827; United States v. Belmont, N.Y., 301 U.S. 324, 57 S.Ct. 758, 761, 81 L.Ed. 1134. An agreement, league, or contract between two or more nations or sovereigns, formally signed by commissioners properly authorized, and solemnly ratified by the several sovereigns or the supreme power of each state. Edye v. Robertson, 112 U.S. 580, 5 S.Ct. 247, 28 L.Ed. 798; Charlton v. Kelly, 229 U.S. 447, 33 S.Ct. 945, 954, 57 L.Ed. 1274, 46 L.R.A.,N.S., 397. A treaty is not only a law but also a contract between two nations and must, if possible, be so construed as to give full force and effect to all its parts. United States v. Reid, C.C.A.Or., 73 F.2d 153, 155. See also **Compact.**

United States treaties may be made by the President, by and with the advice and consent of the Senate. Art. II, Sec. 2, U.S.Const. See **Treaty clause.**

Treaty clause. The provision in the U.S. Constitution, Art. II, Sec. 2, which gives to the President the power "by and with the consent of the Senate, to make treaties, provided two thirds of the Senators present concur."

Treaty of peace. An agreement or contract made by belligerent powers, in which they agree to lay down their arms, and by which they stipulate the conditions of peace and regulate the manner in which it is to be restored and supported.

Treaty power. See **Treaty clause.**

Treble costs. See **Costs.**

Treble damages. Damages given by statute in certain cases, consisting of the single damages found by the jury, actually tripled in amount. See *e.g.* Section 4 of Clayton Act which provides for treble damages for antitrust violations. 15 U.S.C.A. § 15.

Tresael /trəséy(ə)l/. L. Fr. A great-great-grandfather. Otherwise written *"tresaiel,"* and *"tresayle."* 3 Bl. Comm. 186.

Tresayle /trəséy(ə)l/. An abolished writ sued on ouster by abatement, on the death of the grandfather's grandfather.

Tres faciunt collegium /tríyz féysh(iy)ənt kəlíyj(iy)əm/. Three make a corporation; three members are requisite to constitute a corporation. 1 Bl.Comm. 469.

Trespass. An unlawful interference with one's person, property, or rights. At common law, trespass was a form of action brought to recover damages for any injury to one's person or property or relationship with another.

Trespass comprehends any misfeasance, transgression or offense which damages another person's health, reputation or property. King v. Citizens Bank of De Kalb, 88 Ga.App. 40, 76 S.E.2d 86, 91. Doing of unlawful act or of lawful act in unlawful manner to injury of another's person or property. Waco Cotton Oil Mill of Waco v. Walker, Tex.Civ.App., 103 S.W.2d 1071, 1072. An unlawful act committed with violence, actual or implied, causing injury to the person, property, or relative rights of another. It comprehends not only forcible wrongs, but also acts the consequences of which make them tortious. Mawson v. Vess Beverage Co., Mo.App., 173 S.W.2d 606, 612, 613, 614.

See also **Forcible trespass; Intruder.**

Continuing trespass. One which is in its nature a permanent invasion of the rights of another; as, where a person builds on his own land so that a part of the building overhangs his neighbor's land or dumps rubbish on the land of another. In such a case, there is a continuing wrong so long as the offending object remains.

A trespass may be committed by the continued presence on the land of a structure, chattel, or other thing which the actor or his predecessor in legal interest has placed on the land: (a) with the consent of the person then in possession of the land, if the actor fails to remove it after the consent has been effectively terminated, or (b) pursuant to a privilege conferred on the actor irrespective of the possessor's consent, if the actor fails to remove it after the privilege has been terminated, by the accomplishment of its purpose or otherwise. Restatement, Second, Torts, § 160.

Criminal trespass. Criminal trespass is entering or remaining upon or in any land, structure, vehicle, aircraft or watercraft by one who knows he is not authorized or privileged to do so; and (a) He enters or remains therein in defiance of an order not to enter or to leave such premises or property personally communicated to him by the owner thereof or other authorized person; or (b) Such premises or property are posted in a manner reasonably likely to come to the attention of intruders, or are fenced or otherwise enclosed. See also **Criminal.**

Joint trespass. Exists where two or more persons unite in committing it, or where some actually commit the tort, the others command, encourage or direct it.

Permanent trespass. One which consists of a series of acts, done on successive days, which are of the same nature, and are renewed or continued from day to day, so that, in the aggregate, they make up one indivisible wrong. 3 Bl.Comm. 212.

Trespass ab initio. One who innocently or with a privilege enters upon land may become a trespasser "from the beginning" if his subsequent conduct constitutes trespass by an abuse of such privilege.

Trespass de bonis asportatis /tréspəs dìy bównəs æspərtéydəs/. (Trespass for goods carried away.) The technical name of that species of action of trespass for injuries to personal property which lies where the injury consists in *carrying away* the goods or property. See 3 Bl.Comm. 150, 151.

Trespass for mesne profits /tréspəs fər míyn prófəts/. A form of action supplemental to an action of ejectment, brought against the tenant in possession to recover the profits which he has wrongfully received during the time of his occupation. 3 Bl.Comm. 205.

Trespass on the case. The form of action, at common law, adapted to the recovery of damages for some injury resulting to a party from the wrongful act of another, unaccompanied by direct or immediate force, or which is the indirect or secondary consequence of defendant's act. Commonly called, by abbreviation, "Case."

Trespass quare clausum fregit /tréspəs kwóriy klózəm fríyjət/. "Trespass wherefore he broke the close." The common-law action for damages for an unlawful entry or trespass upon the plaintiff's land. In the Latin form of the writ, the defendant was called upon to show why he broke the plaintiff's close; *i.e.*, the real or imaginary structure inclosing the land, whence the name. It is commonly abbreviated to *"trespass qu. cl. fr."* See also *Trespass to try title, infra.*

Trespass to chattels. An unlawful and serious interference with the possessory rights of another to personal property.

Trespass to land. At common law, every unauthorized and direct breach of the boundaries of another's land was an actionable trespass. No intent to commit a trespass was required. All that was necessary was that the act resulting in the trespass be volitional, and that the resulting trespass be direct and immediate. Nor did actual damage need be shown. Any trespass justified at least nominal damages. The present prevailing position of the courts, and Restatement of Torts, finds liability for trespass only in the case of intentional intrusion, or negligence, or some "abnormally dangerous activity" on the part of the defendant. Restatement, Second, Torts, § 166. See Zimmer v. Stephenson, 66 Wash.2d 477, 403 P.2d 343. Compare **Nuisance.**

Extent of trespasser's liability for harm. A trespass on land subjects the trespasser to liability for physical harm to the possessor of the land at the time of the trespass, or to the land or to his things, or to members of his household or to their things, caused by any act done, activity carried on, or condition created by the trespasser, irrespective of whether his conduct is such as would subject him to liability were he not a trespasser. Restatement, Second, Torts, § 162.

Failure to remove thing tortiously placed on land. A trespass may be committed by the continued presence on the land of a structure, chattel, or other thing which the actor has tortiously placed there, whether or not the actor has the ability to remove it. A trespass may be committed by the continued presence on the land of a structure, chattel, or other thing which the actor's predecessor in legal interest therein has tortiously placed there, if the actor, having acquired his legal interest in the thing with knowledge of such tortious conduct or having thereafter learned of it, fails to remove the thing. Restatement, Second, Torts, § 161.

Intrusions upon, beneath, and above surface of land. (1) Except as stated in Subsection (2), a trespass may be committed on, beneath, or above the surface of the earth. (2) Flight by aircraft in the air space above the land of another is a trespass if, but only if, (a) it enters into the immediate reaches of the air space next to the land, and (b) it interferes substantially with the other's use and enjoyment of his land. Restatement, Second, Torts, § 159.

Liability for intentional intrusions on land. One is subject to liability to another for trespass, irrespective of whether he thereby causes harm to any legally protected interest of the other, if he intentionally (a) enters land in the possession of the other, or causes a thing or a third person to do so, or (b) remains on the land, or (c) fails to remove from the land a thing which he is under a duty to remove. Restatement, Second, Torts, § 158.

Trespass to try title. The name of the action used in several of the states for the recovery of the possession of real property, with damages for any trespass committed upon the same by the defendant. A procedure by which rival claims to title or right to possession of land may be adjudicated, and as an incident partition may also be had when the controversy concerning title or right to possession is settled. It is different from "trespass *quare clausum fregit*," in that title must be proved.

Trespass vi et armis /tréspəs váy èd árməs/. Trespass with force and arms. The common-law action for damages for any injury committed by the defendant with direct and immediate force or violence against the plaintiff or his property. See Mawson v. Vess Beverage Co., Mo.App., 173 S.W.2d 606, 613.

Trespasser. One who has committed trespass. One who intentionally and without consent or privilege enters another's property. Fitzgerald v. Montgomery County Bd. of Ed., 25 Md.App. 709, 336 A.2d 795, 797. A person who enters on the property of another without any right, lawful authority or an express or implied invitation or license. Morris v. Atchison, T. & S. F. Ry. Co., 198 Kan. 147, 422 P.2d 920, 927, 928.

Innocent trespasser. See that title.

Joint trespassers. Two or more who unite in committing a trespass.

Trespasser ab initio /tréspəsər æb ənísh(iy)ow/. Trespasser from the beginning. A term applied to a tort-feasor whose acts relate back so as to make a previous act, at the time innocent, unlawful; as if he enter peaceably, and subsequently commit a breach of the peace, his entry is considered a trespass.

Trestornare /trestərnériy/. In old English law, to turn aside; to divert a stream from its course. To turn or alter the course of a road.

Tresviri /tríyzvəray/. Lat. In Roman law, officers who had the charge of prisons, and the execution of condemned criminals.

Tret /trét/. An allowance made for the water or dust that may be mixed with any commodity. It differs from *tare* (q.v.).

Trethinga /tríyðiŋə/. In old English law, a trithing; the court of a trithing.

Treyt /tréyt/tríyt/. Withdrawn, as a juror. Written also *treat*.

Tria capita /tráyə kǽpədə/. In Roman law, were *civitas, libertas,* and *familia; i.e.,* citizenship, freedom, and family rights.

Trial. A judicial examination and determination of issues between parties to action, Gulf, C. & S. F. Ry. Co. v. Smith, Okl., 270 P.2d 629, 633; whether they be issues of law or of fact, Pulaski v. State, 23 Wis.2d 138, 126 N.W.2d 625, 628. A judicial examination, in accordance with law of the land, of a cause, either civil or criminal, of the issues between the parties, whether of law or fact, before a court that has proper jurisdiction.

See also Bifurcated trial; Civil jury trial; Examining trial; Fair and impartial trial; Fair trial; Mistrial; Speedy trial; Trifurcated trial.

New trial. A re-examination in the same court of an issue of fact, or some part or portions thereof, after the verdict by a jury, report of a referee, or a decision by the court. See Fed.R.Civil P. 59; Fed.R.Crim.P. 33. See *Trial de novo, infra.* See also **Motion for new trial; Plain error rule.**

Public trial. A trial held in public, in the presence of the public, or in a place accessible and open to the attendance of the public at large, or of persons who may properly be admitted. The Sixth Amendment, U.S.Const., affords the accused the right to a speedy and "public" trial. See, however, *Trial by news media, infra.*

Separate trial. See that title.

Speedy trial. See that title.

Trial at nisi prius /tráy(ə)l æt náysay práyəs/. The ordinary kind of trial which takes place at the sittings, assizes, or circuit, before a single judge.

Trial balance. In bookkeeping, a listing of debit and credit balances of all ledger accounts. The listing is generally taken at end of an accounting period to check as to whether all entries have been made in both debit and credit accounts, though such listing need not prove accuracy of accounts if an error has been made in both the debit and the credit entry.

A listing of account balances; all accounts with debit balances are totaled separately from accounts with credit balances. The two totals should be equal. Trial balances are taken as a partial check of the arithmetic accuracy of the entries previously made.

Trial by certificate. A form of trial formerly allowed in cases where the evidence of the person certifying was the only proper criterion of the point in dispute. Under such circumstances, the issue might be determined by the certificate alone, because, if sent to a jury, it would be conclusive upon them, and therefore their intervention was unnecessary.

Trial by court or judge. Trial before judge alone, in contrast to trial before jury and judge.

Trial by fire. See **Ordeal.**

Trial by Grand Assize. A peculiar mode of trial formerly allowed in England on writs of right. See **Assise;**

Trial by jury. A trial in which the issues of fact are to be determined by the verdict of a jury, duly selected, impaneled, and sworn. The terms "jury" and "trial by jury" were used at the adoption of the constitution, and always, it is believed, before that time, and almost always since, in a single sense. A jury for the trial of a cause was a body of twelve men, described as upright, well-qualified, and lawful men, disinterested and impartial, not of kin nor personal dependents of either of the parties, having their homes within the jurisdictional limits of the court, drawn and selected by officers free from all bias in favor of or against either party, duly impaneled under the direction of a competent court, sworn to render a true verdict according to the law and the evidence given them, who, after hearing the parties and their evidence, and receiving the instructions of the court relative to the law involved in the trial, and deliberating, when necessary, apart from all extraneous influences, must return their unanimous verdict upon the issue submitted to them. In federal court, and as well in many state courts, the parties may stipulate that the jury shall consist of less than twelve members or that a verdict of a stated majority of the jurors shall be taken as the verdict of the jury. See Fed.R.Civil P. 48; Fed.R.Crim.P. 23.

The Seventh Amendment to Federal Constitution provides that "In suits at common law, where the value in controversy shall exceed twenty dollars, the right of trial by jury shall be preserved." See also Fed.R.Civil P. 38(a). The right to a jury trial is also preserved in state constitutions. The parties, however, by stipulation may waive the right to a jury trial, and consent to trial by the court sitting without a jury. See also **Jury trial.**

Trial by news media. The process by which the news media in reporting an investigation of a person on trial leads its readers to act as judge and jury in determining guilt, liability or innocence before the person is tried in a judicial forum. Failure to protect accused from inherently prejudicial publicity may constitute deprivation of right to fair and impartial trial as guaranteed by due process clause of Fourteenth Amendment. Sheppard v. Maxwell, 384 U.S. 333, 86 S.Ct. 1507, 16 L.Ed.2d 600.

Local court rules have been widely adopted, seeking to set a proper balance between a free press and a fair trial by putting restrictions on the release of information by attorneys and courthouse personnel, making special provision for the conduct of proceedings in extensively publicized and sensational cases, and barring photography, radio, and television equipment from the courtroom and its environs.

See also **Gag order.**

Trial by proviso. A proceeding formerly allowed where the plaintiff in an action desists from prosecuting his suit, and does not bring it to trial in convenient time. The defendant, in such case, may take out the *venire facias* to the sheriff, containing these words, *"proviso quod,"* etc., *i.e.,* provided that. If plaintiff take out any writ to that purpose, the sheriff shall summon but one jury on them both. This is called "going to trial by proviso."

Trial by the record. A form of trial resorted to where issue is taken upon a plea of *nul tiel record,* in which case the party asserting the existence of a record as pleaded is bound to produce it in court on a day assigned. If the record is forthcoming, the issue is tried by inspection and examination of it. If the record is not produced, judgment is given for his adversary. 3 Bl.Comm. 330.

Trial by wager of battel. See **Wager of battel.**

Trial by wager of law. In old English law, a method of trial, where the defendant, coming into court, made oath that he did not owe the claim demanded of him, and eleven of his neighbors, as compurgators, swore that they believed him to speak the truth. 3 Bl. Comm. 343. See **Wager of law.**

Trial by witnesses. The name "trial *per testes*" was used for a trial without the intervention of a jury, was the only method of trial known to the civil law, and was adopted by depositions in chancery. The judge was thus left to form, in his own breast, his sentence upon the credit of the witnesses examined. Such type trial was very rarely used at common law.

Trial de novo. A new trial or retrial had in which the whole case is retried as if no trial whatever had been had in the first instance. Housing Authority of City of Newark v. Norfolk Realty Co., 71 N.J. 314, 334 A.2d 1052, 1058. See *New trial, supra.* See also **Motion for new trial; Plain error rule.**

Trial jury. See **Jury.**

Trial list. A list of cases marked down for trial for any one term. See **Trial calendar.**

Trial calendar. Comprehensive list of cases awaiting trial and containing the dates for trial, names of counsel, expected time required for trial, etc. In some states it is maintained by the trial judge and in others, by the clerk of court. See *e.g.* Fed.R.Civil P. 79. See also **Calendar; Docket.**

Trial court. The court of original jurisdiction; the first court to consider litigation. Used in contrast to appellate court.

Trial on merits. Trial of substantive issues in case. Ennis v. Kennedy Valve Mfg. Co., 282 A.D. 971, 125 N.Y.S.2d 535, 537. Term used in contrast to a hearing on motion or on other interlocutory matters.

Trial per pais. Historically, a trial by one's peers.

Triatio ibi semper debet fieri, ubi juratores meliorem possunt habere notitiam /trayéysh(iy)ow áybay sémpər débət fáyəray, yúwbay jurətóriyz mìyliyórəm pósənt həbíriy nowtísh(iy)əm/. Trial ought always to be had where the jurors can have the best information.

Tribal lands. Lands of Indian reservation which are not allotted to or occupied by individual Indians but rather the unallotted or common lands of the nation.

Land allotted in severalty to a restricted Indian is no longer part of the "reservation" nor is it "tribal land" but the virtual fee is in the allottee with certain restrictions on the right of alienation. United States v. Oklahoma Gas & Electric Co., C.C.A.Okl., 127 F.2d 349, 353.

See also **Indian country; Indian lands; Indian reservation; Indian tribal property.**

Tribuere /trəbyúwəriy/. Lat. In the civil law, to give; to distribute.

Tribunal. The seat of a judge; the place where he administers justice. The whole body of judges who compose a jurisdiction; a judicial court; the jurisdiction which the judges exercise.

In Roman law, an elevated seat occupied by the prætor, when he judged, or heard causes in form. Originally a kind of stage made of wood in the form of a square, and movable, but afterwards built of stone in the form of a semicircle.

Tribunaux de commerce /tribyuwnów də komérs/. In French law, certain courts composed of a president, judges, and substitutes, which take cognizance of all cases between merchants, and of disagreements among partners. Appeals lie from them to the courts of justice.

Tributary, n. /tríbyət(èh)riy/. Any stream flowing directly or indirectly into a river. Bull v. Siegrist, 169 Or. 180, 126 P.2d 832, 834.

Tributary, adj. /tríbyət(èh)riy/. Paying or yielding tribute, taxed or assessed by tribute.

Tribute /tríbyuwt/. A contribution which is raised by a prince or sovereign from his subjects to sustain the expenses of the state.

A sum of money paid by an inferior sovereign or state to a superior potentate, to secure the friendship or protection of the latter.

Acknowledgment of gratitude or respect.

Tricesima /trəsézəmə/. An ancient custom in a borough in the county of Hereford, so called because thirty burgesses paid 1d. rent for their houses to the bishop, who was lord of the manor.

Triding-mote /tráydiŋmòwt/. The court held for a triding or trithing.

Triduum /tríd(y)uwəm/. In old English law, the space of three days.

Triennial Act /trayéniyəl ǽkt/. An act of parliament of 1641, which provided that if in every third year parliament was not summoned and assembled before September 3, it should assemble on the second Monday of the next November.

Also an act of 1694, which provided that a parliament be called within three years after dissolution, and that the utmost limit of a parliament be three years. This was followed by the Septennial Act of 1716.

Triens /tráyen(d)z/. Lat. In feudal law, dower or third. 2 Bl.Comm. 129.

In Roman law, a subdivision of the *as,* containing four *unciæ;* the proportion of four-twelfths or one-third. 2 Bl.Comm. 462, note *m.* A copper coin of the value of one-third of the *as.*

Trier of fact. Term includes (a) the jury and (b) the court when the court is trying an issue of fact other than one relating to the admissibility of evidence. Calif.Evid.Code. Commonly refers to judge in jury waived trial or jury which, in either case, has the exclusive obligation to make findings of fact in contrast to rulings of law which must be made by judge.

Trifurcated trial. A trial which is divided into three stages or parts as for example, a trial on issue of liability, trial for general damages, and trial for special damages.

Trigamus /trígəməs/. In old English law, one who has been thrice married; one who, at different times and successively, has had three wives; a trigamist.

Trigild. In Saxon law, a triple gild, geld, or payment; three times the value of a thing, paid as a composition or satisfaction.

Trinepos /trínəpəs/. Lat. In Roman law, great-grandson of a grandchild.

Trineptis /trənéptəs/. Lat. Great-granddaughter of a grandchild.

Trinity House. In English law, a society at Deptford Strond, incorporated by Hen. VIII in 1515, for the promotion of commerce and navigation by licensing and regulating pilots, and ordering and erecting beacons, lighthouses, buoys, etc.

Trinity Masters. Elder brethren of the Trinity House. If a question arising in an admiralty action depends upon technical skill and experience in navigation, the judge or court is usually assisted at the hearing by two Trinity Masters who sit as assessors, and advise the court on questions of a nautical character.

Trinity sittings. Sittings of the English court of appeal and of the high court of justice in London and Middlesex, commencing on the Tuesday after Whitsun week, and terminating on the 8th of August.

Trinity term. One of the four terms of the English courts of common law, beginning on the 22d day of May, and ending on the 12th of June.

Triniumgeldum /trìniyəmgéldəm/. In old European law, an extraordinary kind of composition for an offense, consisting of *three times nine,* or twenty-seven times the single geld or payment.

Trinoda necessitas /trənówdə nəsésətæs/. Lat. In Saxon law, a threefold necessity or burden. A term used to denote the three things from contributing to the performance of which no lands were exempted, viz., *pontis reparatio* (the repair of bridges), *arcis con-*

structio (the building of castles), *et expeditio contra hostem* (military service against an enemy). 1 Bl. Comm. 263, 357.

Triors /tráyərz/. Persons who are appointed to try challenges to jurors, *i.e.*, to hear and determine whether a juror challenged for favor is or is not qualified to serve.

The lords chosen to try a peer, when indicted for felony, in the court of the lord high steward, are also called "triors."

Trip, *n.* A journey or going from one place to another.

Trip, *v.* To make a false step; to catch the foot; to stumble; to cause to stumble, or take a false step; to cause to lose the footing, as by suddenly checking the motion of a foot or leg; to throw off balance. Johnston v. City of St. Louis, Mo.App., 138 S.W.2d 666, 671.

Tripartite /tràypártayt/. In conveyancing, of three parts; a term applied to an indenture to which there are three several parties (of the first, second, and third parts), and which is executed in triplicate.

Triplicacion /trìpləkasyówn/. L. Fr. In old pleading, a rejoinder in pleading; the defendant's answer to the plaintiff's replication.

Triplicatio /trìpləkéysh(iy)ow/. Lat. In the civil law, the reply of the plaintiff to the rejoinder of the defendant. It corresponds to the surrejoinder of common law.

Tristris /trístrəs/. In old forest law, a freedom from the duty of attending the lord of a forest when engaged in the chase.

Tritavia /trətéyv(i)yə/. Lat. In the civil law, a great-grandmother's great-grandmother; the female ascendant in the sixth degree.

Tritavus /trídəvəs/. Lat. In the civil law, a great-grandfather's great-grandfather; the male ascendant in the sixth degree.

Trithing /tráyðiŋ/. In Saxon law, one of the territorial divisions of England, being the *third* part of a county, and comprising three or more hundreds. Within the trithing there was a court held (called "trithing-mote") which resembled the court-leet, but was inferior to the county court.

Trithing-mote /tráyðiŋmòwt/. The court held for a trithing or riding.

Trithing-reeve /tráyðiŋ ríyv/. The officer who superintended a trithing or riding.

Triumvir /trayə́mvər/. Lat. In old English law, a trithing man or constable of three hundred.

Triumviri capitales /trayə́mvəray kæ̀pətéyliyz/. Lat. In Roman law, officers who had charge of the prison, through whose intervention punishments were inflicted. They had eight lictors to execute their orders.

Triverbial days /trayvə́rbiyəl déyz/. In the civil law, juridical days; days allowed to the prætor for deciding causes; days on which the prætor might speak the *three* characteristic *words* of his office, viz., *do, dico, addico.* Otherwise called *"dies fasti."* 3 Bl. Comm. 424, and note *u.*

Trivial. Trifling; inconsiderable; of small worth or importance. In equity, a demurrer will lie to a bill on the ground of the *triviality* of the matter in dispute, as being below the dignity of the court.

TRO. Temporary restraining order.

Tronage /trównəj/. In English law, a customary duty or toll for weighing wool; so called because it was weighed by a common *trona,* or beam.

Tronator /trówneydər/. A weigher of wool.

Trophy. Anything taken from an enemy and shown or treasured up in proof of victory. A price or token of victory in any contest; hence, a memento of victory or success; an ornamental group of objects hung together on a wall, or any collection of objects typical of some event, art, industry, or branch of knowledge; a memento or memorial. In re Vortex Cup Co., Cust. & Pat.App., 83 F.2d 821, 822.

Trophy money. Money formerly collected and raised in London, and the several counties of England, towards providing harness and maintenance for the militia, etc.

Trover /trówvər/. In common-law practice, the action of trover (or trover and conversion) is a species of action on the case, and originally lay for the recovery of damages against a person who had *found* another's goods and wrongfully converted them to his own use. Subsequently the allegation of the loss of the goods by the plaintiff and the finding of them by the defendant was merely fictitious, and the action became the remedy for any wrongful interference with or detention of the goods of another. In form a fiction; in substance, a remedy to recover the value of personal chattels *wrongfully* converted by another to his own use. A possessory action wherein plaintiff must show that he has either a general or special property in thing converted and the right to its possession at the time of the alleged conversion. Such remedy lies only for wrongful appropriation of goods, chattels, or personal property which is specific enough to be identified. See also **Conversion.**

Troy weight. A weight of twelve ounces to the pound, having its name from Troyes, a city in Aube, France.

Truancy. Wilful and unjustified failure to attend school by one who is required to attend. It is a punishable offense within the juvenile system in some states and, in others, it is the basis of a petition for a child in need of services.

Truce. In international law, a suspension or temporary cessation of hostilities by agreement between belligerent powers; an armistice.

Truce of God. In medieval law, a truce or suspension of arms promulgated by the church, putting a stop to private hostilities at certain periods or during certain sacred seasons.

True. Conformable to fact; correct; exact; actual; genuine; honest. In one sense, that only is "true" which is conformable to the actual state of things. In that sense, a statement is "untrue" which does not express things exactly as they are. But in another and broader sense the word "true" is often used as a synonym of "honest", "sincere", not "fraudulent." Zolintakis v. Equitable Life Assur. Soc. of United States, C.C.A.Utah, 108 F.2d 902, 905; Moulor v. American Life Ins. Co., 111 U.S. 335, 4 S.Ct. 466, 28 L.Ed. 447.

True admission. A formal act done in course of judicial proceedings which waives or dispenses with production of evidence by conceding for purposes of litigation that proposition of fact alleged by opponent is true. Maltz v. Jackoway-Katz Cap Co., 336 Mo. 1000, 82 S.W.2d 909, 917. See also **Admission; Stipulation.**

True bill. The endorsement made by a grand jury upon a bill of indictment, when they find it sustained by the evidence laid before them, and are satisfied of the truth of the accusation. The endorsement made by a grand jury when they find sufficient evidence to warrant a criminal charge. An indictment.

True copy. A true copy does not mean an absolutely exact copy but means that the copy shall be so true that anybody can understand it.

True, public, and notorious. These three qualities were formally predicated in the libel in the ecclesiastical courts, of the charges which it contained, at the end of each article severally.

True value. For tax assessment purposes, term refers to the market value of the property at fair and bona fide sale at private contract, and is in essence the value property has in exchange for money. City of Newark v. West Milford Tp., Passaic County, 9 N.J. 295, 88 A.2d 211, 214. See also **Market value; Value.**

True value rule. Under this rule, one who subscribes for and receives corporate stock must pay therefor the par value thereof either in money or in money's worth, so that the real assets of the corporation shall at least square with its books, and whenever, whether by fraud, accident or mistake, the true value of property, labor or services received in payment does not equal par value, stock is deemed unpaid for to the full extent of the difference, and holders are liable to creditors for the difference, notwithstanding good faith of directors. Johansen v. St. Louis Union Trust Co., 345 Mo. 135, 131 S.W.2d 599, 603.

True verdict. The voluntary conclusion of the jury after deliberate consideration, and it is none the less a true verdict because the respective jurors may have been liberal in concessions to each other, if conscientiously and freely made. A verdict is not a "true verdict," when it is the result of any arbitrary rule or order, whether imposed by themselves, or by the court or officer in charge.

Trust. A right of property, real or personal, held by one party for the benefit of another. King v. Richardson, C.C.A.N.C., 136 F.2d 849, 856, 857. A confidence reposed in one person, who is termed trustee, for the benefit of another, who is called the cestui que trust, respecting property which is held by the trustee for the benefit of the cestui que trust. State ex rel. Wirt v. Superior Court for Spokane County, 10 Wash.2d 362, 116 P.2d 752, 755. Any arrangement whereby property is transferred with intention that it be administered by trustee for another's benefit.

A fiduciary relation with respect to property, subjecting person by whom the property is held to equitable duties to deal with the property for the benefit of another person which arises as the result of a manifestation of an intention to create it. An obligation on a person arising out of confidence reposed in him to apply property faithfully and according to such confidence; as being in nature of deposition by which proprietor transfers to another property of subject intrusted, not that it should remain with him, but that it should be applied to certain uses for the behalf of third party.

A trust can be created for any purpose which is not illegal, and which is not against public policy. Collins v. Lyon, Inc., 181 Va. 230, 24 S.E.2d 572, 579.

Essential elements of trust are designated beneficiary and trustee, fund sufficiently identified to enable title to pass to trustee, and actual delivery to trustee with intention of passing title. City Bank Farmers' Trust Co. v. Charity Organization Soc. of City of New York, 238 App.Div. 720, 265 N.Y.S. 267.

An association or organization of persons or corporations having the intention and power, or the tendency, to create a monopoly, control production, interfere with the free course of trade or transportation, or to fix and regulate the supply and the price of commodities. In the history of economic development, the "trust" was originally a device by which several corporations engaged in the same general line of business might combine for their mutual advantage, in the direction of eliminating destructive competition, controlling the output of their commodity, and regulating and maintaining its price, but at the same time preserving their separate individual existence, and without any consolidation or merger. This device was the erection of a central committee or board, composed, perhaps, of the presidents or general managers of the different corporations, and the transfer to them of a majority of the stock in each of the corporations, to be held "in trust" for the several stockholders so assigning their holdings. These stockholders received in return "trust certificates" showing that they were entitled to receive the dividends on their assigned stock, though the voting power of it had passed to the trustees. This last feature enabled the trustees or committee to elect all the directors of all the corporations, and through them the officers, and thereby to exercise an absolutely controlling influence over the policy and operations of each constituent company, to the ends and with the purposes above mentioned. Though the "trust," in this sense, is now seldom if ever resorted to as a form of corporate organization, having given place to the "holding corporation" and other devices, the word became current in statute laws as well as popular speech, to designate almost any form of combination of a monopolistic character or tendency. Northern Securities Co. v. U. S., 193 U.S. 197, 24 S.Ct. 436, 48 L.Ed. 679; Mallinckrodt Chemical Works v. State of Missouri, 238 U.S. 41, 35 S.Ct. 671, 673, 59 L.Ed. 1192.

In a looser sense the term is applied to any combination of establishments in the same line of business for securing the same ends by holding the individual interests of each subservient to a common authority for the common interests of all. Mallinckrodt Chemical Works v. State of Missouri, 238 U.S. 41, 35 S.Ct. 671, 673, 59 L.Ed. 1192.

A trust, as the term is used in the Restatement, when not qualified by the word "charitable," "resulting" or "constructive," is a fiduciary relationship with respect to property, subjecting the person by whom the title to the property is held to equitable duties to deal with the property for the benefit of another person, which arises as a result of a manifestation of an intention to create it. Restatement, Second, Trusts § 2.

See also Charitable trust; Claflin trust; Common law trust; Complex trust; Constructive trust; Equipment; Executory trust; Generation-skipping trust; Governmental trusts; Grantor trusts; Illusory trust; Indestructible trust; Investment trust; Involuntary trust; Land trust; Life insurance trust; Life interest; trust; Nominal trust; Nominee trust; Pension trust; Precatory trust; Purchase money resulting trust; Reciprocal trusts; Resulting trust; Revocable trust; Spendthrift trust; Terms of trust; Unitrust; Voting trust.

Accumulation trust. Trust in which trustees are directed to accumulate income and gains from sales of trust assets for ultimate disposition when the trust is terminated. Many states have laws governing the time over which accumulations may be made. See also **Accumulation trust.**

Active trust. One which imposes upon the trustee the duty of taking active measures in the execution of the trust, as, where property is conveyed to trustees with directions to sell and distribute the proceeds among creditors of the grantor; distinguished from a "passive" or "dry" trust.

In a "passive trust" the legal and equitable titles are merged in the beneficiaries and beneficial use is converted into legal ownership, while in an "active trust" the title remains in trustee for purpose of the trust. Johnson v. Thornton, 264 S.C. 252, 214 S.E.2d 124, 127.

Alimony trust. Device used to secure obligation of husband to pay support or alimony for wife. Transfer by husband to trustee of property from which wife as beneficiary will be supported after divorce or separation.

Annuity trust. An annuity trust is a trust from which the trustee is required to pay a sum certain annually to one or more individual beneficiaries for their respective lives or for a term of years, and thereafter either transfer the remainder to or for the use of a qualified charity or retain the remainder for such a use. The sum certain must not be less than 5% of the initial fair market value of the property transferred to the trust by the donor. A qualified annuity trust must comply with the basic statutory requirements of I.R.C. § 664. See also **Annuity trust.**

Bond trust. A trust, the *res* of which consists in bonds which yield interest income.

Business trust. See **Business; Massachusetts trust; Trust estates as business companies.**

Cestui que trust. The person for whose benefit a trust is created or who is to enjoy the income or the avails of it. See **Beneficiary.**

Charitable remainder trust. A trust which consists of assets which are paid over to the trust after the expiration of a life estate or intermediate estates and designated for charitable purposes. See also **Charitable remainder annuity trust.**

Charitable trusts. Trusts designed for the benefit of a class or the public generally. They are essentially different from private trusts in that the beneficiaries are uncertain. In general, such must be created for charitable, educational, religious or scientific purposes.

Clifford trust. Under this tax planning device, a transfer of income-producing property is made to a trust which provides that the income is either to be paid or accumulated for the benefit of a beneficiary other than the grantor for a period of more than ten years, at which time the trust is to terminate and the property reverts back to the grantor. This transfer is made at the cost of a gift tax and if the gift tax paid is less than the income tax which will be saved as the result of the shifting of the income from the high-bracket grantor to the low-bracket beneficiary, the technique has merit from a tax point of view. Helvering v. Clifford, 309 U.S. 331, 60 S.Ct. 554, 84 L.Ed. 788; I.R.C. §§ 671–678.

Community trust. An agency organized for the permanent administration of funds placed in trust for public health, educational and charitable purposes.

Complete voluntary trust. One completely created, the subject-matter being designated, the trustee and beneficiary being named, and the limitations and trusts being fully and perfectly declared.

Complex trust. A complex trust is any trust other than a simple trust. One in which the trustees have discretion as to whether to distribute and discretion as to amounts distributed. Such trusts are governed for tax purposes by I.R.C. §§ 661–663.

Constructive trust. A trust raised by construction of law, or arising by operation of law, as distinguished from an express trust. Wherever the circumstances of a transaction are such that the person who takes the legal estate in property cannot also enjoy the beneficial interest without necessarily violating some established principle of equity, the court will immediately raise a *constructive trust,* and fasten it upon the conscience of the legal owner, so as to convert him into a trustee for the parties who in equity are entitled to the beneficial enjoyment.

Constructive trusts do not arise by agreement or from intention, but by operation of law, and fraud, active or constructive, is their essential element. Actual fraud is not necessary, but such a trust will arise whenever circumstances under which property was acquired made it inequitable that it should be retained by him who holds the legal title. Constructive trusts have been said to arise through the application of the doctrine of equitable estoppel, or under the broad doctrine that equity regards and treats as done what in good conscience ought to be done, and such trusts are also known as "trusts ex maleficio" or "ex delicto" or "involuntary trusts" and their forms and varieties are practically without limit, being raised by courts of equity whenever it becomes necessary to prevent a failure of justice. See also *Involuntary trust, infra.*

Contingent trust. An express trust depending for its operation upon a future event.

Creation of trust. A trust may be created by: (a) a declaration by the owner of property that he holds it as trustee for another person; or (b) a transfer inter vivos by the owner of property to another person as trustee for the transferor or for a third person; or (c) a transfer by will by the owner of property to another person as trustee for a third person; or (d) an appointment by one person having a power of appointment to another person as trustee for the donee of the power or for a third person; or (e) a promise by one person to another person whose rights thereunder are to be held in trust for a third person. Restatement, Second, Trusts § 17.

Directory trust. One which is not completely and finally settled by the instrument creating it, but only defined in its general purpose and to be carried into detail according to later specific directions.

Direct trust. An express trust, as distinguished from a constructive or implied trust.

Discretionary trust. Trust in which trustees have discretion as to types of investment and also as to whether and when distributions may be made to beneficiaries.

Dry trust. One which merely vests the legal title in the trustee, and does not require the performance of any active duty on his part to carry out the trust.

Educational trusts. Trusts for the founding, endowing, and supporting schools for the advancement of all useful branches of learning, which are not strictly private.

Equipment trust. Financing method commonly used by railroads in which the equipment's title is transferred to trustees as security for the financing.

Estate trust. An estate trust is a trust, for all or part of the income of which is to be accumulated during the surviving spouse's life and added to corpus, with the accumulated income and corpus being paid to the estate of the surviving spouse at death. This type of trust is commonly used to qualify property for the marital deduction.

Executed trust. A trust of which the scheme has in the outset been completely declared. A trust in which the estates and interest in the subject-matter of the trust are completely limited and defined by the instrument creating the trust, and require no further instruments to complete them.

Executory trust. One which requires the execution of some further instrument, or the doing of some further act, on the part of the creator of the trust or of the trustee, towards its complete creation or full effect.

Express active trust. Where will confers upon executor authority to generally manage property of estate and pay over net income to devisees or legatees, such authority creates an "express active trust".

Express private passive trust. Such exists where land is conveyed to or held by one person in trust for another, without any power being expressly or impliedly given trustee to take actual possession of land or exercise acts of ownership over it, except by beneficiary's direction.

Express trust. A trust created or declared in express terms, and usually in writing, as distinguished from one inferred by the law from the conduct or dealings of the parties. A trust directly created for specific purposes in contrast to a constructive or resulting trust which arises by implication of law or the demands of equity. Trusts which are created by the direct and positive acts of the parties, by some writing, or deed, or will, or by words expressly or impliedly evincing an intention to create a trust. Concannon v. Concannon, 116 R.I. 323, 356 A.2d 487, 491.

Fixed trust. A non-discretionary trust in which the trustee may not exercise his own judgment.

Foreign situs trust. A trust which owes its existence to foreign law. It is treated for tax purposes as a non-resident alien individual.

Foreign trust. A trust created and administered under foreign law.

Grantor trust. A trust in which the grantor transfers or conveys property in trust for his own benefit alone or for himself and another.

Honorary trust. Trust for specific non-charitable purposes where there is no definite ascertainable beneficiary and hence unenforceable in the absence of statute.

Illusory trust. A trust arrangement which takes the form of a trust, but because of powers retained in the settlor has no real substance and in reality is not a completed trust. In re Herron's Estate, Fla.App., 237 So.2d 563, 566.

Imperfect trust. An executory trust *(q.v.);* see also *Executed trust, supra.*

Implied trust. A trust raised or created by implication of law; a trust implied or presumed from circumstances. Constructive and resulting trusts are implied trusts because they arise by implication of law or by demands of equity.

Indestructible trust. A trust which may not be terminated or revoked. See **Claflin trust.**

Instrumental trust. See *Ministerial trusts, infra.*

Insurance trust. A trust, the res of which consists of insurance policies or their proceeds. See also **Insurance.**

Inter vivos trust. Trust created by an instrument which becomes operative during the settlor's lifetime as contrasted with a testamentary trust which takes effect on the death of the settlor.

Involuntary trust. Involuntary or "constructive" trusts embrace all those instances in which a trust is raised by the doctrines of equity, for the purpose of working out justice in the most efficient manner, when there is no intention of the parties to create a trust relation. This class of trusts may usually be referred to fraud, either actual or constructive, as an essential element.

Irrevocable trust. Trust which may not be revoked after its creation as in the case of a deposit of money by one in the name of another as trustee for the benefit of a third person (beneficiary).

Land trust. See **Land trust.**

Limited trust. Trust created for a limited period of time in contrast to a perpetual trust.

Liquidation trust. Trust created for purpose of terminating a business or other undertaking and for distributing the *res.*

Living trust. An inter vivos trust created and operative during the lifetime of the settlor and commonly for benefit or support of another person.

Marital deduction trust. A testamentary trust created to take full advantage of the marital deduction *(q.v.)* provisions of the Int.Rev.Code.

Massachusetts or business trusts. See **Business; Massachusetts trust; Trust estates as business companies.**

Ministerial trusts. (Also called "instrumental trusts.") Those which demand no further exercise of reason or understanding than every intelligent agent must necessarily employ; as to convey an estate. They are a species of special trusts, distinguished from discretionary trusts, which necessarily require much exercise of the understanding.

Mixed trust. Trusts established to benefit both private individuals and charities. Green v. Austin, 222 Ga. 409, 150 S.E.2d 346.

Naked trust. A dry or passive trust; one which requires no action on the part of the trustee, beyond turning over money or property to the *cestui que trust.*

Nominee trust. An arrangement for holding title to real property under which one or more persons or corporations, pursuant to a written declaration of trust, declare that they will hold any property that they acquire as trustees for the benefit of one or more undisclosed beneficiaries.

Non-discretionary trust. A fixed trust under which the trustees may exercise no judgment or discretion at least as to distributions.

Passive trust. A trust as to which the trustee has no active duty to perform. "Passive trust," which equity court may terminate before it ends by its terms, is one in which the trustee does not have responsibilities or discretionary duties to perform. Nickson v. Filtrol Corp., Del.Ch., 262 A.2d 267, 271.

Perpetual trust. A trust which is to continue as long as the need for it continues as for the lifetime of a beneficiary or the term of a particular charity.

Personal trust. Trusts created by and for individuals and their families in contrast to business or charitable trusts.

Pour-over trust. A provision in a will in which the testator leaves the residue of his estate to a trustee of a living trust for purpose of that pour-over trust.

Power of appointment trust. Type of trust used to qualify property for the marital deduction. Property is left in trust for a surviving spouse. The trustee is required to distribute income to the spouse for life and the spouse is given an unqualified power to appoint the property to herself or to her estate.

Precatory trust. Where words employed in a will or other instrument do not amount to a positive command or to a distinct testamentary disposition, but are terms of entreaty, request, recommendation, or expectation, they are termed "precatory words," and from such words the law will raise a trust, called a "precatory trust," to carry out the wishes of the testator or grantor.

Private trust. One established or created for the benefit of a certain designated individual or individuals, or a known person or class of persons, clearly identified or capable of identification by the terms of the instrument creating the trust, as distinguished from trusts for public institutions or charitable uses.

Public trust. One constituted for the benefit either of the public at large or of some considerable portion of it answering a particular description; public trusts and charitable trusts may be considered in general as synonymous expressions.

Real estate investment trust (REIT). Type of tax shelter wherein investors purchase certificates of ownership in trust which invests such funds in real estate and then distributes profits to investors.

Reciprocal trust. Trust which one person creates for the benefit of another who in turn creates a trust for the benefit of the first party.

Resulting trust. One that arises by implication of law, or by the operation and construction of equity, and which is established as consonant to the presumed intention of the parties as gathered from the nature of the transaction. It arises where the legal estate in property is disposed of, conveyed, or transferred, but the intent appears or is inferred from the terms of the disposition, or from the accompanying facts and circumstances, that the beneficial interest is not to go or be enjoyed with the legal title.

Revocable trust. A trust in which the settlor reserves the right to revoke.

Savings bank trust. A Totten trust *(q.v.).*

Secret trusts. Where a testator gives property to a person, on a verbal promise by the legatee or devisee that he will hold it in trust for another person.

Shifting trust. An express trust which is so settled that it may operate in favor of beneficiaries additional to, or substituted for, those first named, upon specified contingencies.

Short term trust. Trust which by its terms is to be administered for a short period of time and then terminated. Such a trust, if properly drawn, may have tax advantages to those in high brackets. See also *Clifford trust, supra.*

Simple trust. A simple trust corresponds with the ancient use, and arises where property is simply vested in one person for the use of another, and the nature of the trust, not being qualified by the settlor, is left to the construction of law. A simple trust is a trust which provides that all of its income is required to be distributed currently, even if it is not in fact distributed, does not provide that any amounts are to be paid, permanently set aside, or used for charitable purposes; and does not distribute any amount other than current income.

Simple trusts are those that are not complex trusts. Such trusts may not have a charitable beneficiary, accumulate income, nor distribute corpus.

Special trust. One in which a trustee is interposed for the execution of some purpose particularly pointed out, and is not, as in case of a simple trust, a mere passive depositary of the estate, but is required to exert himself actively in the execution of the settlor's intention; as, where a conveyance is made to trustees upon trust to reconvey, or to sell for the payment of debts.

Special trusts have been divided into (1) ministerial (or instrumental) and (2) discretionary. The former, such as demand no further exercise of reason or understanding than every intelligent agent must necessarily employ; the latter, such as cannot be duly administered without the application of a certain degree of prudence and judgment.

Spendthrift trust. See **Spendthrift trust.**

Split-interest trust. Type of charitable trust commonly consisting of a life estate to an individual and a remainder to a charity. The Tax Reform Act of 1969 has placed restrictions on this type of trust.

Sprinkling trust. A trust which calls for distribution of income to various beneficiaries at different times, though provision may also be made for accumulation.

Tentative trust. See *Totten trust, infra.*

Testamentary trust. Trust created within a will and executed with the formalities required of a will in contrast to an inter vivos will. A will which does not take effect until the death of the settlor. Nearly all states have adopted the Uniform Testamentary Additions to Trust Act.

Totten trust. A trust created by the deposit by one person of his own money in his own name as a trustee for another and it is a tentative trust revocable at will until the depositor dies or completes the gift in his lifetime by some unequivocal act or declaration such as delivery of the passbook or notice to the beneficiary and if the depositor dies before the beneficiary without revocation or some decisive act or declaration of disaffirmance the presumption arises that an absolute trust was created as to the balance on hand at the death of the depositor.

Transgressive trust. A name sometimes applied to a trust which transgresses or violates the rule against perpetuities.

Trust allotments. Allotments to Indians, in which a certificate or trust patent is issued declaring that the United States will hold the land for a designated period in trust for the allottee. U. S. v. Bowling, 256 U.S. 484, 41 S.Ct. 561, 562, 65 L.Ed. 1054.

Trust certificate. An obligation issued to finance railroad equipment and by which title to the equipment is held by trustees as security for repayment of the money invested.

Trust company. A corporation formed for the purpose of taking, accepting, and executing all such trusts as may be lawfully committed to it, and acting as testamentary trustee, executor, guardian, etc. To these functions are sometimes (but not necessarily) added the business of acting as fiscal agent for corporations, attending to the registration and transfer of their stock and bonds, serving as trustee for their bond or mortgage creditors, and transacting a general banking and loan business. A bank which is authorized to serve in fiduciary capacity as executor, administrator, etc.

Trust deed. The document by which one creates a trust. An indenture by which property is transferred to a trust. May also include a deed from the trustees. In some states, a mortgage deed.

A species of mortgage given to a trustee for the purpose of securing a numerous class of creditors, as the bondholders of a railroad corporation, with power to foreclose and sell on failure of the payment of their bonds, notes, or other claims. In some of the states, a trust deed or deed of trust is a security resembling a mortgage, being a conveyance of lands to trustees to secure the payment of a debt, with a power of sale upon default, and upon a trustee to apply the net proceeds to paying the debt and to turn over the surplus to the grantor.

A trust deed on real estate as security for a bond issue is, in effect, a mortgage on property executed by the mortgagor to a third person as trustee to hold as security for the mortgage debt as evidenced by the bonds, for the benefit of the purchasers of the bonds as lenders.

See also **Deed** *(Deed of trust).*

Trust deposit. Where money or property is deposited to be kept intact and not commingled with other funds or property of bank and is to be returned in kind to depositor or devoted to particular purpose or requirement of depositor or payment of particular debts or obligations of depositor. Also called "special deposit". See also **Deposit.**

Trust estate. This term may mean either the estate of the trustee,—that is, the legal title,—or the estate of the beneficiary, or the corpus of the property which is the subject of the trust.

Trust ex delicto. See *Trust ex maleficio, infra.*

Trust ex maleficio. A species of constructive trust arising out of some fraud, misconduct, or breach of faith on the part of the person to be charged as trustee, which renders it an equitable necessity that a trust should be implied. See also *Constructive trust, supra.*

Trust fund. A fund held by a trustee for the specific purposes of the trust; in a more general sense, a fund which, legally or equitably, is subject to be devoted to a particular purpose and cannot or should not be diverted therefrom. In this sense it is often said that the assets of a corporation are a "trust fund" for the payment of its debts. See also **Trust fund.**

Trust fund doctrine. In substance, where corporation transfers all its assets with a view to going out of business and nothing is left with which to pay debts, transferee is charged with notice of the circumstances of the transaction, and takes the assets subject to an equitable lien for the unpaid debts of the transferring company; the property of a corporation being a fund subject to be first applied to the payment of debts. Meikle v. Export Lumber Co., C.C.A.Or., 67 F.2d 301, 304.

Under such doctrine, if insolvent corporation's assets are distributed among its stockholders before its debts are paid, each stockholder is liable to creditors for full amount received by him. Scott v. Commissioner of Internal Revenue, C.C.A.8, 117 F.2d 36, 39.

See **Common trust fund; Trust fund; Trust fund theory.**

Trust in invitum. A constructive trust imposed by equity, contrary to the trustee's intention and will, upon property in his hands.

Trust legacy. See **Legacy.**

Trust receipt. See **Trust receipt.**

Unitrust. A unitrust is a trust from which the trustee is required, at least annually, to pay a fixed percentage which is not less than five percent of the net fair market value of the trust assets, valued annually, to one or more beneficiaries, at least one of which is not a charity, for life or for a term of years, with an irrevocable remainder interest to be held for the benefit of, or paid over to, charity. A qualified unitrust must comply with the basic statutory requirements of I.R.C. § 664.

Vertical trust. In antitrust law, a combination which gathers together under a single ownership a number of businesses or plants engaged in successive stages of production or marketing.

Voluntary trust. An obligation arising out of a personal confidence reposed in, and voluntarily accepted by, one for the benefit of another, as distinguished from an "involuntary" trust, which is created by operation of law. According to another use of the term, "voluntary" trusts are such as are made in favor of a volunteer, that is, a person who gives nothing in exchange for the trust, but receives it as a pure gift; and in this use the term is distinguished from "trusts for value," the latter being such as are in favor of purchasers, mortgagees, etc. A "voluntary trust" is an equitable gift, and in order to be enforceable by the beneficiaries must be complete. The difference between a "gift inter vivos" and a "voluntary trust" is that, in a gift, the thing itself with title passes to the donee, while in a voluntary trust, the actual title passes to a cestui que trust while the legal title is retained by the settlor, to be held by him for the purposes of the trust or is by the settlor transferred to another to hold for the purposes of the trust.

Voting trust. A trust which holds the voting rights to stock in a corporation. It is a useful device when a majority of the shareholders in a corporation cannot agree on corporate policy. See also **Voting trust.**

Trustee. Person holding property in trust. The person appointed, or required by law, to execute a trust; one in whom an estate, interest, or power is vested, under an express or implied agreement to administer or exercise it for the benefit or to the use of another called the cestui que trust. Person who holds title to res and administers it for others' benefit. Reinecke v. Smith, Ill., 289 U.S. 172, 53 S.Ct. 570, 77 L.Ed. 1109. In a strict sense, a "trustee" is one who holds the legal title to property for the benefit of another, while, in a broad sense, the term is sometimes applied to anyone standing in a fiduciary or confidential relation to another, such as agent, attorney, bailee, etc. State ex rel. Lee v. Sartorius, 344 Mo. 912, 130 S.W.2d 547, 549, 550.

See also **Bare trustee.**

Joint trustees. Two or more persons who are intrusted with property for the benefit of one or more others.

Judicial trustee. One appointed by a decree of court to execute a trust, as distinguished from one appointed by the instrument creating the trust.

Testamentary trustee. A trustee appointed by or acting under a will; one appointed to carry out a trust created by a will. The term does not ordinarily include an executor or an administrator with the will annexed, or a guardian, except when they act in the execution of a trust created by the will and which is separable from their functions as executors, etc.

Trustee ad litem. Trustee appointed by a court in contrast to a trustee selected by a settlor or executor.

Trustee de son tort. Person who is treated as a trustee because of his wrongdoing with respect to property entrusted to him or over which he exercised authority which he lacked.

Trustee ex maleficio. A person who, being guilty of wrongful or fraudulent conduct, is held by equity to the duty and liability of a trustee, in relation to the subject-matter, to prevent him from profiting by his own wrong. Trust arising by implication of law from the wrongdoing of a person.

Trustee in bankruptcy. A person in whom the property of a bankrupt is vested in trust for the creditors. See Bankruptcy Act, § 321 *et seq.;* § 1501 *et seq.* (United States Trustees).

Trustee process. The name given, in certain New England states, to the process of garnishment or foreign attachment. See **Process.**

Trust estates as business companies. A practice originating in Massachusetts of vesting a business or certain real estate in a group of trustees, who manage it for the benefit of the beneficial owners; the ownership of the latter is evidenced by negotiable (or transferable) shares. The trustees are elected by the shareholders, or, in case of a vacancy, by the board of trustees. Provision is made in the agreement and declaration of trust to the effect that when new trustees are elected, the trust estate shall vest in them without further conveyance. The declaration of trust specifies the powers of the trustees. They have a common seal; the board is organized with the usual officers of a board of trustees; it is governed by by-laws; the officers have the usual powers of like corporate officers; so far as practicable, the trustees in their collective capacity, are to carry on the business under a specified name. The trustees may also hold shares as beneficiaries. Provision may be made for the alteration or amendment of the agreement or declaration in a specified manner. In Eliot v. Freeman, 220 U.S. 178, 31 S.Ct. 360, 55 L.Ed. 424, it was held that such a trust was not within the corporation tax provisions of the tariff act of Aug. 5, 1909. See also Zonne v. Minneapolis Syndicate, 220 U.S. 187, 31 S.Ct. 361, 55 L.Ed. 428. See also **Massachusetts trust.**

Trust fund. Money or property set aside as a trust for the benefit of another and held by a trustee. The majority of states have adopted the Uniform Common Trust Fund Act. See also **Common trust fund; Trust** *(Trust fund; Trust fund doctrine);* **Trust fund theory.**

Trust fund theory. Generic term used in many contexts to describe the imposition of fiduciary obligations on persons who control money or property of another under certain circumstances. A creature of equity which operates to treat officers, directors, or majority shareholders of a corporation as holding in trust for the benefit of creditors such corporate assets as have been improperly appropriated. Whisenhunt v. Park Lane Corp., D.C.Tex., 418 F.Supp. 1096, 1098. See also **Common trust f· nd; Trust** *(Trust fund; Trust fund doctrine).*

Trust indenture. The document which contains the terms and conditions which govern the conduct of the trustee and the rights of the beneficiaries. Commonly used when a corporation floats bonds.

Trust Indenture Act. Federal Act (1939) designed to protect investors in certain types of bonds by requiring that the trust indenture include certain protective clauses and exclude certain exculpatory clauses, and that trustees be independent of the issuing company.

Trust instrument. The formal document which creates the trust and contains the powers of the trustees and the rights of the beneficiaries. It may be a deed in trust or a formal declaration of trust. See also **Trust** *(Trust deed).*

Trustis /trástəs/. In old European law, trust; faith; confidence; fidelity.

Trust officer. The official or officer in a trust company who has direct charge of funds administered by it in its capacity as trustee.

Trustor. One who creates a trust. Also called settlor.

Trust property. The property which is the subject matter of the trust. The trust *res (q.v.).*

Trust receipt. A pre-U.C.C. security device now governed by Article 9 of the Code. A receipt stating that the wholesale buyer has possession of the goods for the benefit of the financier. Today there usually must be a security agreement coupled with the filing of a financing statement. Method of financing commercial transactions by means of which title passes directly from manufacturer or seller to banker or lender who as owner delivers goods to dealer in whose behalf he is acting secondarily, and to whom title goes ultimately when primary right of banker or lender has been satisfied. Commercial Credit Corp. v. Bosse, 76 Idaho 409, 283 P.2d 937, 938.

Trust res. The property of which the trust consists. It may be real or personal and the trustee has legal title.

Trust territory. A territory or colony placed under the administration of a country by the United Nations.

Trusty. A prisoner who, because of good conduct, is given some measure of freedom in and around the prison.

Truth. There are three conceptions as to what constitutes "truth": agreement of thought and reality; eventual verification; and consistency of thought with itself. For "Fact" and "truth" distinguished, see **Fact.**

Truth-in-Lending Act. The purpose of the Truth-in-Lending Act (15 U.S.C.A. § 1601 et seq.) is to assure that every customer who has need for consumer credit is given meaningful information with respect to the cost of that credit. In most cases the credit cost must be expressed in the dollar amount of finance charges, and as an annual percentage rate computed on the unpaid balance of the amount financed. Other relevant credit information must also be disclosed so that the customer may compare the various credit terms available to him from different sources and avoid the uninformed use of credit. The Act further provides a customer the right, in certain circumstances, to cancel a credit transaction which involves a lien on his residence. The Truth in Lending Act was amended in 1970 to regulate the issuance, holder's liability, and fraudulent use of credit cards. See also **Consumer Credit Protection Act; Regulation Z; Uniform Consumer Credit Code.**

Try. To examine judicially. To examine and investigate a controversy, by the legal method called "trial," for the purpose of determining the issues it involves.

Tsar. The less common spelling of "czar" *(q.v.).*

Tuas res tibi habeto /t(y)úwəs ríyz tíbay həbíydow/. Lat. Have or take your things to yourself. The form of words by which, according to the old Roman law, a man divorced his wife.

Tub. In mercantile law, a measure containing sixty pounds of tea, and from fifty-six to eighty-six pounds of camphor.

Tub-man. In English law, a barrister who has a preaudience in the exchequer, and also one who has a particular place in court, is so called.

Tuchas /túwchas/. In Spanish law, objections or exceptions to witnesses.

Tucker Act. The Tucker Act, which was passed in 1887, was a response by Congress to the inadequacies of the original Court of Claims legislation. By this act, the jurisdiction of the court was extended to include claims founded upon the Constitution, act of Congress, or executive department regulation, as well as claims for liquidated or unliquidated damages in cases not sounding in tort, in addition to all claims within the scope of the earlier statutes. The present provisions of the Tucker Act are embodied in 28 U.S.C.A. §§ 1346(a)(2), 1491.

Tuerto /twértow/. In Spanish law, tort.

Tullianum /tàliyéynəm/. Lat. In Roman law, that part of a prison which was under ground. Supposed to be so called from Servius Tullius, who built that part of the first prison in Rome.

Tumbrel /támbrəl/. A castigatory, trebucket, or dunking stool, anciently used as a punishment for common scolds.

Tumultuous petitioning /təmálchuwəs pətíshəniŋ/. Under English St. 13 Car. II, St. 1, c. 5, this was a misdemeanor, and consisted in more than twenty persons signing any petition to the crown or either house of parliament for the alteration of matters established by law in church or state, unless the contents thereof had been approved by three justices, or the majority of the grand jury at assizes or quarter sessions. No petition could be delivered by more than ten persons.

Tun. A measure of wine or oil, containing four hogsheads.

Tungreve /tə́ŋgriyv/. A town-reeve or bailiff.

Tunnage. A duty in England anciently due upon all wines imported, over and above the prisage and butlerage.

Turba /tə́rbə/. Lat. In the civil law, a multitude; a crowd or mob; a tumultuous assembly of persons. Said to consist of ten or fifteen, at the least.

Turbary /tə́rbəriy/. Turbary, or common of turbary, is the right or liberty of digging turf upon another man's ground.

Turf and twig. A piece of turf, or a twig or a bough, were delivered by the feoffer to the feoffee in making livery of seisin. 2 Bl.Comm. 315.

Turn, or **tourn** /tə́rn/. In English law, the great court-leet of the county, as the old county court was the court-baron. Of this the sheriff was judge, and the court was incident to his office; wherefore it was called the "sheriff's tourn;" and it had its name originally from the sheriff making a turn of circuit about his shire, and holding this court in each respective hundred.

Turncoat witness. A witness whose testimony was expected to be favorable but who turns around and becomes an adverse witness.

Turned to a right. In English law, this phrase means that a person whose estate is divested by usurpation cannot expel the possessor by mere entry, but must have recourse to an action, either possessory or droitural.

Turning State's evidence. See **State's evidence**.

Turnkey. A person, under the superintendence of a jailer, who has the charge of the keys of the prison, for the purpose of opening and fastening the doors.

Turn-key contract. Term used in building trade to designate those contracts in which builder agrees to complete work of building and installation to point of readiness for occupancy. It ordinarily means that builder will complete work to certain specified point, such as building a complete house ready for occupancy as a dwelling, and that builder agrees to assume all risk. Gantt v. Van der Hoek, 251 S.C. 307, 162 S.E.2d 267, 270.

In oil drilling industry a job wherein driller of oil well undertakes to furnish everything and does all work required to complete well, place it on production, and turn it over ready to turn the key and start oil running into tanks. Retsal Drilling Co. v. Commissioner of Internal Revenue, C.C.A.Tex., 127 F.2d 355, 357. A turn-key contract to drill a well involves the testing of the formation contemplated by the parties and completion of a producing well or its abandonment as a dry hole, all done for an agreed-upon total consideration, putting the risk of rising costs, well trouble, weather, and the like upon the

driller, but it does not, in the absence of a clear expression, require the driller to guarantee a producing well. Totah Drilling Co. v. Abraham, 64 N.M. 380, 328 P.2d 1083, 1091.

Turntable doctrine. Also termed "attractive nuisance" doctrine. This doctrine requires the owner of premises not to attract or lure children into unsuspected danger or great bodily harm, by keeping thereon attractive machinery or dangerous instrumentalities in an exposed and unguarded condition, and where injuries have been received by a child so enticed the entry is not regarded as unlawful, and does not necessarily preclude a recovery of damages; the attractiveness of the machine or structure amounting to an implied invitation to enter. It imposes a liability on a property owner for injuries to a child of tender years, resulting from something on his premises that can be operated by such a child and made dangerous by him, and which is attractive to him and calculated to induce him to use it, where he fails to protect the thing so that a child of tender years cannot be hurt by it.

Doctrine is that who maintains or creates upon his premises or upon the premises of another in any public place an instrumentality or condition which may reasonably be expected to attract children of tender years and to constitute a danger to them is under duty to take the precautions that a reasonably prudent person would take under similar circumstance, to prevent injury to such children. Schock v. Ringling Bros. and Barnum & Bailey Combined Shows, 5 Wash.2d 599, 105 P.2d 838, 843.

The dangerous and alluring qualities of a railroad turntable gave the "attractive nuisance rule" the name of "Turntable Doctrine." Louisville & N. R. Co. v. Vaughn, 292 Ky. 120, 166 S.W.2d 43, 46.

See also **Attractive nuisance doctrine**.

Turpis /tə́rpəs/. Lat. In the civil law, base; mean; vile; disgraceful; infamous; unlawful. Applied both to things and persons.

Turpis causa /tə́rpəs kózə/. A base cause; a vile or immoral consideration; a consideration which, on account of its immorality, is not allowed by law to be sufficient either to support a contract or found an action; *e.g.*, future illicit intercourse.

Turpis contractus /tə́rpəs kəntrǽktəs/. An immoral or iniquitous contract.

Turpis est pars quæ non convenit cum suo toto /tə́rpəs èst párz kwìy nón kənvíynət kə̀m s(y)úwow tówdow/. The part which does not agree with its whole is of mean account [entitled to small or no consideration].

Turpitude /tə́rpət(y)ùwd/. In its ordinary sense, inherent baseness or vileness of principle or action; shameful wickedness; depravity. In its legal sense, everything done contrary to justice, honesty, modesty, or good morals. An action showing gross depravity. Traders & General Ins. Co. v. Russell, Tex.Civ. App., 99 S.W.2d 1079, 1084.

Moral turpitude. A term of frequent occurrence in statutes, especially those providing that a witness' conviction of a crime involving moral turpitude may be shown as tending to impeach his credibility. In general, it means neither more nor less than "turpitude," *i.e.,* anything done contrary to justice, honesty, modesty, or good morals. It is also commonly defined as an act of baseness, vileness, or depravity in the private and social duties which a man owes to his fellow man or to society in general, contrary to the accepted and customary rule of right and duty between man and man.

Although a vague term, it implies something immoral in itself, regardless of its being punishable by law. Thus excluding unintentional wrong, or an improper act done without unlawful or improper intent. It is also said to be restricted to the gravest offenses, consisting of felonies, infamous crimes, and those that are *malum in se* and disclose a depraved mind. Bartos v. United States District Court for District of Nebraska, C.C.A.Neb., 19 F.2d 722, 724.

Turpitudo /tàrpət(y)úwdow/. Lat. Baseness; infamy; immorality; turpitude.

Tuta est custodia quæ sibimet creditur /t(y)úwdə èst kəstówd(i)yə kwìy síbaymet krédədər/. That guardianship is secure which is intrusted to itself alone.

Tutela /t(y)uwtíylə/. Lat. In the civil law, tutelage; that species of guardianship which continued to the age of puberty; the guardian being called *"tutor,"* and the ward, *"pupillus."* A power given by the civil law over a free person to defend him when by reason of his age he is unable to defend himself. A child under the power of his father was not subject to tutelage, because not a free person, *caput liberum.*

Tutelæ actio /t(y)uwtíyliy ǽksh(iy)ow/. Lat. In the civil law, an action of tutelage; an action which lay for a ward or pupil, on the termination of tutelage, against the *tutor* or guardian, to compel an account.

Tutelage /t(y)úwdələj/. Guardianship; state of being under a guardian. See **Tutela.**

Tutela legitima /t(y)uwtíylə ləjídəmə/. Legal tutelage; tutelage created by act of law, as where none had been created by testament.

Tutelam reddere /t(y)uwtíyləm rédəriy/. Lat. In the civil law, to render an account of tutelage. *Tutelam reposcere,* to demand an account of tutelage.

Tutela testamentaria /t(y)utíylə tèstəmentér(i)yə/. Testamentary tutelage or guardianship; that kind of tutelage which was created by will.

Tuteur. In French law, a kind of guardian.

Tuteur officieux. A person over fifty years of age may be appointed a tutor of this sort to a child over fifteen years of age, with the consent of the parents of such child, or, in their default, the *conseil de famille.* The duties which such a tutor becomes subject to are analogous to those in English law of a person who puts himself *in loco parentis* to any one.

Tuteur subrogé. The title of a second guardian appointed for an infant under guardianship. His functions are exercised in case the interests of the infant and his principal guardian conflict.

Tutius erratur ex parte mitiore /t(y)úwsh(iy)əs ehréydər èks párdiy mishiyóriy/. It is safer to err on the gentler side [or on the side of mercy].

Tutius semper est errare acquietando, quam in puniendo, ex parte misericordiæ quam ex parte justitiæ /t(y)úwsh(iy)əs sémpər èst ehrériy əkwàyətǽndow, kwǽm in pyuwniyéndow, èks párdiy mìzərəkórdiyiy kwǽm èks párdiy jàstíshiyiy/. It is always safer to err in acquitting than punishing, on the side of mercy than on the side of justice.

Tutor /t(y)úwdər/. One who teaches, usually a private instructor. State ex rel. Veeder v. State Board of Education, 97 Mont. 121, 33 P.2d 516, 522.

In the civil law, this term corresponds nearly to "guardian" (*i.e.,* a person appointed to have the care of the person of a minor and the administration of his estate), except that the guardian of a minor who has passed a certain age is called "curator," and has powers and duties differing somewhat from those of a tutor.

Tutor alienus /t(y)úwdər èyliyíynəs/. In English law, the name given to a stranger who enters upon the lands of an infant within the age of fourteen, and takes the profits. He may be called to an account by the infant and be charged as guardian in socage.

Tutor proprius /tyúwdər prówpriyəs/. The name given in old English law to one who is rightly a guardian in socage, in contradistinction to a *tutor alienus.*

Tutorship. The office and power of a tutor. The power which an individual, *sui juris,* has to take care of the person of one who is unable to take care of himself. There are four sorts of tutorships: Tutorship by nature; tutorship by will; tutorship by the effect of the law; tutorship by the appointment of the judge. Civ. Code La. art. 247.

Tutorship by nature. Upon the death of either parent, the tutorship of minor children belongs of right to the other. Upon divorce or judicial separation from bed and board of parents, the tutorship of each minor child belongs of right to the parent under whose care he or she has been placed or to whose care he or she has been entrusted. All those cases are called tutorship by nature. Civ.Code La. art. 250.

Tutorship by will. The right of appointing a tutor, whether a relation or a stranger, belongs exclusively to the father or mother dying last. This is called "tutorship by will," because generally it is given by testament; but it may likewise be given by any declaration by the surviving father or mother, or the parent who is the curator of the other spouse, executed before a notary and two witnesses. Civ.Code La. art. 257.

Tutrix /t(y)úwtriks/. A female tutor.

T.V.A. Tennessee Valley Authority.

Twa night gest /túwnayt gést/. In Saxon law, a guest on the second night. By the laws of Edward the Confessor it was provided that a man who lodged at an inn, or at the house of another, should be considered, on the first night of his being there, a stranger *(uncuth);* on the second might, a guest; on the third night, a member of the family. This had reference to the responsibility of the host or entertainer for offenses committed by the guest.

Twelfhindi. The highest rank of men in the Saxon government, who were valued at 1200s. If any injury were done to such persons, satisfaction was to be made according to their worth.

Twelfth Amendment. Amendment to the U.S. Constitution (1804) which altered the method of voting in presidential elections by requiring each elector to vote for President and Vice President on separate ballots instead of voting for two persons for President on single ballot as before.

Twelve-day writ. A writ issued under the English St. 18 & 19 Vict., c. 67, for summary procedure on bills of exchange and promissory notes, abolished by rule of court in 1880.

Twelvemonth /twélvmə̀nθ/. This term (in the singular number), includes all the year; but *twelve months* are to be computed according to twenty-eight days for every month.

Twelve-month bond. Twelve-month bond, under statute effective Jan. 20, 1837 (Hartley's Dig. art. 1277), had a double character, first as an obligation known to the Spanish civil law, and second, as a summary statutory judgment, with the force and effect of any other judgment of a court of competent jurisdiction; it being also a consent judgment.

Twelve Tables. The earliest statute or code of Roman law, framed by a commission of ten men, B.C. 450, upon the return of a commission of three who had been sent abroad to study foreign laws and institutions. The Twelve Tables consisted partly of laws transcribed from the institutions of other nations, partly of such as were altered and accommodated to the manners of the Romans, partly of new provisions, and mainly, perhaps, of laws and usages under their ancient kings. They formed the source and foundation for the whole later development of Roman jurisprudence. They exist now only in fragmentary form. See 1 Kent.Comm. 520. These laws were substantially a codification, and not merely an incorporation, of the customary law of the people. There were Greek elements in them, but still they were essentially Roman.

Twentieth Amendment. The so-called lame duck Amendment to the U.S. Constitution (1933) which changed the beginning of Presidential and Vice-Presidential terms from March 4 to January 20, and of Congressional terms from March 4 to January 3, thereby eliminating the short session of Congress which had formerly convened early in December in even-numbered years, and in which a number of Congressmen sat who had not been re-elected to office. The Amendment also provides for Presidential succession under certain circumstances.

Twenty-Fifth Amendment. Amendment to U.S. Constitution (1967) which provides for filling vacancy in offices of President and Vice-President on the death, removal, or resignation of the office holders.

Twenty-First Amendment. Amendment to the Constitution (1933) which repealed Prohibition Amendment (18th) but prohibited the importation of intoxicating beverages into any State where delivery or use of such beverages violated the State's laws.

Twenty-Fourth Amendment. Amendment to the Constitution (1964) which prohibits federal or State denial of right to vote in any primary or other election for federal elective officers because of the prospective voter's failure to pay any poll tax or other tax. See **Poll-tax.**

Twenty-Second Amendment. Amendment to the Constitution (1951) which prevents any person from being elected President more than twice, or, if he has succeeded to the Presidency before the midpoint of his predecessor's term, from being elected more than once.

Twenty-Sixth Amendment. Amendment to U.S. Constitution (1971) which established voting age at 18.

Twenty-Third Amendment. Amendment to the Constitution (1961) which allots to the District of Columbia presidential electors, to be appointed as Congress directs, equal in number to those of a State of equivalent population but never more than the number of electors allotted to the least populous State.

Twice in jeopardy. See **Jeopardy; Once in jeopardy.**

Twisting. Colloquially, in insurance, the misrepresentation or misstatements of fact or incomplete comparison of policies to induce the insured to give up a policy in one company for the purpose of taking insurance in another. Brandt v. Beha, 217 App.Div. 644, 216 N.Y.S. 178, 179.

Two issue rule. Error in charge dealing exclusively with one of two or more complete and independent issues required to be presented to jury in civil action will be disregarded, if charge in respect to another independent issue which will support verdict is free from prejudicial error, unless it is disclosed that verdict is in fact based upon issue to which erroneous instruction related. Asteri v. City of Youngstown, Ohio App., 121 N.E.2d 143, 145.

Two witness rule. This rule requires that falsity element of a perjury conviction be supported either by direct testimony of two witnesses or by direct testimony of one witness plus corroborating evidence. Com. v. Field, Pa.Super., 298 A.2d 908, 911.

Twyhindi. The lower order of Saxons, valued at 200s. in the scale of pecuniary mulcts inflicted for crimes. See **Twelfhindi.**

Tyburn ticket /táybərn tíkət/. In old English law, a certificate which was given to the prosecutor of a felon to conviction. By the 10 & 11 Will. III, c. 23, the original proprietor or first assignee of such certificate is exempted from all parish and ward offices within the parish or ward where the felony was committed.

Tyhtlan. In Saxon law, an accusation, impeachment, or charge of any offense.

Tying. A term which, as used in a contract of lease of patented machinery means that the lessee has secured only limited rights of use, and that if he exceeds such limited rights by agreeing not to use the machines of others he may lose his lease.

Tying arrangement. Such exists when a person agrees to sell one product, the "tying product," only on the condition that the vendee also purchase another product, the "tied product." Northern v. McGraw-Edison Co., C.A.Mo., 542 F.2d 1336, 1344. See also **Tie-in-arrangement; Tied product.**

Tylwith. Brit. A tribe or family branching or issuing out of another.

Tymbrella /timbrélə/. In old English law, a tumbrel, castigatory, or ducking stool, anciently used as an instrument of punishment for common scolds.

Tyranny /tíhrəniy/. Arbitrary or despotic government; the severe and autocratic exercise of sovereign power, either vested constitutionally in one ruler, or usurped by him by breaking down the division and distribution of governmental powers.

Tyrant /táyrənt/. A despot; a sovereign or ruler, legitimate or otherwise, who uses his power unjustly and arbitrarily, to the oppression of his subjects.

Tyrra, or toira /tíhrə/. A mount or hill.

Tythe /táyð/. Tithe, or tenth part.

Tything /táyðiŋ/. A company of ten; a district; a tenth part. See **Tithing.**

Tzar /tsár/zár/, **Tzarina** /tsaríynə/zəríynə/. Formerly, the emperor and empress of Russia. See **Czar.**

U

U.B. An abbreviation for "Upper Bench."

Uberrima fides /yuwbéhrəmə fáydiyz/. Lat. The most abundant good faith; absolute and perfect candor or openness and honesty; the absence of any conceal-ment or deception, however slight. A phrase used to express the perfect good faith, concealing nothing, with which a contract must be made; for example, in the case of insurance, the insured must observe the most perfect good faith towards the insurer. Contracts of life insurance are said to be "uberrimæ fidæ" when any material misrepresentation or concealment is fatal to them.

Ubi aliquid conceditur, conceditur et id sine quo res ipsa esse non potest /yúwbay ǽləkwəd kən(t)síydədər, kən(t)síydədər èd íd sáyniy kwòw ríyz ípsə ésiy nòn pówdəst/. When anything is granted, that also is granted without which the thing granted cannot exist.

Ubi aliquid impeditur propter unum, eo remoto, tollitur impedimentum /yúwbay ǽləkwəd impíydədər próptər yúwnəm, íyow rəmówdow, tóladər impèdəméntow/. Where anything is impeded by one single cause, if that be removed, the impediment is removed.

Ubi cessat remedium ordinarium, ibi decurritur ad ex-traordinarium /yúwbay sésət rəmíyd(i)yəm, òrdənériyəm, áybay dəkə́hrədər æd èkstr(ə)òrdənériy-əm/. Where the ordinary remedy fails, recourse must be had to an extraordinary one.

Ubi culpa est, ibi pœna subesse debet /yúwbay kə́lpə èst, áybay píynə səbésiy débət/. Where the crime is committed, there ought the punishment to be undergone.

Ubicunque est injuria, ibi damnum sequitur /yúwbaykə́ŋkwiy èst injúriyə, áybay dǽmnəm sék-wədər/. Wherever there is a wrong, there damage follows.

Ubi damna dantur, victus victori in expensis condem-nari debet /yúwbay dǽmnə dǽntər víktəs viktóray ìn əkspén(t)səs kondəmnéray débət/. Where damages are given, the vanquished party ought to be con-demned in costs to the victor.

Ubi eadem ratio, ibi eadem lex; et de similibus idem est judicium /yúwbay iyéydəm réysh(iy)ow, áybay iyéy-dəm léks; èt díy səmíləbəs áydəm èst juwdísh(iy)əm/. Where the same reason exists, there the same law prevails; and, of things similar, the judgment is simi-lar. Where there is the same reason, there is the same law, and the same judgment should be rendered on the same state of facts.

Ubi est forum, ibi ergo est jus /yúwbay èst fórəm, áybay ə́rgow èst jə́s/. The law of the forum governs.

Ubi est specialis, et ratio generalis generaliter accipien-da est /yúwbay èst spèshiyéyləs, èt réysh(iy)ow jènəréyləs jènəréylədər əksìpiyéndə èst/. See **Ubi lex est specialis,** etc.

Ubi et dantis et accipientis turpitudo versatur, non posse repeti dicimus; quotiens autem accipientis tur-pitudo versatur, repeti posse /yúwbay èt dǽntəs èd əksìpiyéntəs tàrpət(y)úwdow vərséydər, nòn pósiy rəpéday dísəməs; kwówshən(d)z ódəm əksìpiyéntəs tàrpət(y)úwdow vərséydər, repéday pósiy/. Where there is turpitude on the part of both giver and receiver, we say it cannot be recovered back; but as often as the turpitude is on the side of the receiver [alone] it can be recovered back.

Ubi factum nullum, ibi fortia nulla /yúwbay fǽktəm nə́ləm, áybay fórsh(iy)ə nə́lə/. Where there is no prin-cipal fact, there can be no accessory. Where there is no act, there can be no force.

Ubi jus, ibi remedium /yúwbay jə́s, áybay rəmíyd(i)yəm/. Where there is a right, there is a remedy. It is said that the rule of primitive law was the reverse: Where there is a remedy, there is a right.

Ubi jus incertum, ibi jus nullum /yúwbay jə́s in(t)sə́rdəm, áybay jə́s nə́ləm/. Where the law is un-certain, there is no law.

Ubi lex aliquem cogit ostendere causam, necesse est quod causa sit justa et legitima /yúwbay léks ǽləkwəm kó(w)jəd osténdəriy kózəm, nəsésiy èst kwòd kózə sìt jə́stə èt ləjídəmə/. Where the law compels a man to show cause, it is necessary that the cause be just and lawful.

Ubi lex est specialis, et ratio ejus generalis, generaliter accipienda est /yúwbay léks èst speshiyéyləs, èt réysh(iy)ow íyjəs, jènəréylədər əksìpiyéndə èst/. Where the law is special, and the reason of it general, it ought to be taken as being general. When the reason for a particular legislative act and acts of the same general character is the same, they should have the same effect. Guile v. La Crosse Gas & Electric Co., 145 Wis. 157, 130 N.W. 234, 241.

Ubi lex non distinguit, nec nos distinguere debemus /yúwbay léks nòn dəstíngwət, nèk nóws dəstíngwəriy dəbíyməs/. Where the law does not distinguish, nei-ther ought we to distinguish.

Ubi major pars est, ibi totum /yúwbay méyjər párz èst, áybay tówdəm/. Where the greater part is, there the whole is. That is, majorities govern.

Ubi matrimonium, ibi dos /yúwbay mætrəmówn(i)yəm, áybay dóws/. Where there is marriage, there is dower.

Ubi non adest norma legis, omnia quasi pro suspectis habenda sunt /yúwbay nòn ǽdest nórmə líyjəs, ómn(i)yə kwéysay pròw səspéktəs həbéndə sǽnt/. When the law fails to serve as a rule, almost everything ought to be suspected.

Ubi non est annua renovatio, ibi decimæ non debent solvi /yúwbay nón èst ǽnyuwə rènəvéysh(i)yow, áybay désəmiy nòn débənt sólvay/. Where there is no annual renovation, there tithes ought not to be paid.

Ubi non est condendi auctoritas, ibi non est parendi necessitas /yúwbay nón èst kənténday októhrətæs, áybay nón èst pərénday nəsésətæs/. Where there is no authority for establishing a rule, there is no necessity of obeying it.

Ubi non est directa lex, standum est arbitrio judicis, vel procedendum ad similia /yúwbay nón èst dərəktə léks, stændəm èst arbítriyow júwdəsəs, vèl pròwsədéndəm æd səmíl(i)yə/. Where there is no direct law, the opinion of the judge is to be taken, or references to be made to similar cases.

Ubi non est lex, ibi non est transgressio, quoad mundum /yúwbay nón èst léks, áybay nón èst træn(d)zgrésh(i)yow, kwówæd mándəm/. Where there is no law, there is no transgression, so far as relates to the world.

Ubi non est manifesta injustitia, judices habentur pro bonis viris, et judicatum pro veritate /yúwbay nón èst mænəféstə ìnjəstísh(i)yə, júwdəsiyz həbéntər pròw bównəs vírəs, èt jùwdəkéydəm pròw vèhrətéydiy/. Where there is no manifest injustice, the judges are to be regarded as honest men, and their judgment as truth.

Ubi non est principalis, non potest esse accessorius /yúwbay nón èst prìn(t)səpéyləs, nòn pówdest ésiy æksəsóriyəs/. Where there is no principal, there cannot be an accessory.

Ubi nulla est conjectura quæ ducat alio, verba intelligenda sunt ex proprietate, non grammatica, sed populari ex usu /yúwbay nálə èst kònjekt(y)úrə kwìy d(y)úwkəd éyl(i)yow, várbə intèləjéndə sànt èks prəpràyətéydiy, nòn grəmǽdəkə, sèd pòpyəléray èks yúwsyuw/. Where there is nothing to call for a different construction, [the] words [of an instrument] are to be understood, not according to their strict grammatical meaning, but according to their popular and ordinary sense.

Ubi nullum matrimonium, ibi nulla dos /yúwbay náləm mætrəmówn(i)yəm, áybay nálə dóws/. Where there is no marriage, there is no dower.

Ubi periculum, ibi et lucrum collocatur /yúwbay pərík(y)ələm, áybay èt l(y)úwkrəm kòləkéydər/. He at whose risk a thing is, should receive the profits arising from it.

Ubi pugnantia inter se in testamento juberentur, neutrum ratum est /yúwbay pəgnǽnsh(i)yə íntər sìy in tèstəméntow jùwbəréntər, n(y)úwtrəm réydəm èst/. Where repugnant or inconsistent directions are contained in a will, neither is valid.

Ubi quid generaliter conceditur inest hæc exceptio, si non aliquid sit contra jus fasque /yúwbay kwíd jenəréylədər kən(t)síydədər ínest híyk əksépsh(i)yow, sày nòn ǽləkwəd sìt kóntrə jás fǽskwiy/. Where a thing is conceded generally [or granted in general terms], this exception is implied: that there shall be nothing contrary to law and right.

Ubi quis delinquit, ibi punietur /yúwbay kwís dəlíŋkwət, áybay pyùwniyíydər/. Where a man offends, there he shall be punished. In cases of felony, the trial shall be always by the common law in the same place where the offense was, and shall not be supposed in any other place.

Ubiquity /yuwbíkwədiy/. Omnipresence; presence in several places, or in all places, at one time. A fiction of English law is the "legal ubiquity" of the sovereign, by which he is constructively present in all the courts. 1 Bl.Comm. 270.

Ubi re vera /yúwbay ríy vírə/. Where in reality; when in truth or in point of fact.

Ubi supra /yúwbay s(y)úwprə/. Lat. Where above mentioned.

Ubi verba conjuncta non sunt sufficit alterutrum esse factum /yúwbay várbə kənjáŋktə nón sànt səfəsəd òltər(y)úwtrəm ésiy fǽktəm/. Where words are not conjoined, it is enough if one or other be complied with. Where words are used disjunctively, it is sufficient that either one of the things enumerated be performed.

U.C. An abbreviation for "Upper Canada," used in citing the reports.

U.C.C. Uniform Commercial Code.

U.C.C.C. Uniform Consumer Credit Code.

U.C.M.J. Uniform Code of Military Justice; rules of conduct and criminal behavior for members of the Armed Forces. See **Code of Military Justice.**

Udal. A term mentioned by Blackstone as used in Finland to denote that kind of right in real property which is called, in English law, "allodial."

Ukaas, ukase /uwkás/yuwkéyz/. Originally, a law or ordinance made by the czar of Russia.

Hence, any official decree or proclamation.

ULA. Uniform Laws Annotated.

Ullage /áləj/. In commercial law, the amount wanting when a cask, on being gauged, is found not to be completely full.

Ulna ferrea /álnə féhriyə/. L. Lat. In old English law, the iron ell; the standard ell of iron, kept in the exchequer for the rule of measure.

Ulnage /álnəj/. Alnage. See **Alnager.**

Ulterior. Beyond what is manifest, seen or avowed, intentionally kept concealed. Harding v. McCullough, 236 Iowa 556, 19 N.W.2d 613, 616.

Ultima ratio /ə́ltəmə réysh(iy)ow/. Lat. The last argument; the last resort; the means last to be resorted to.

Ultimate. At last, finally, or at the end. The last in the train of progression or sequence tended toward by all that precedes; arrived at as the last result; final. Texas Employers Ins. Ass'n v. Reed, Tex.Civ.App., 150 S.W.2d 858, 862.

Ultimate facts. Issuable facts; facts essential to the right of action or matter of defense. Wichita Falls & Oklahoma Ry. Co. v. Pepper, 134 Tex. 360, 135 S.W.2d 79, 84. Facts necessary and essential for decision by court. People ex rel. Hudson & M. R. Co. v. Sexton, Sup., 44 N.Y.S.2d 884, 885. Those facts which it is expected evidence will support. McDuffie v. California Tehama Land Corporation, 138 Cal.App. 245, 32 P.2d 385, 386. The issuable, constitutive, or traversable facts essential to statement of cause of action. Johnson v. Johnson, 92 Mont. 512, 15 P.2d 842, 844. The logical conclusions deduced from certain primary evidentiary facts. Mining Securities Co. v. Wall, 99 Mont. 596, 45 P.2d 302, 306. Final facts required to establish plaintiff's cause of action or defendant's defense. Williams v. Pilot Life Ins. Co., 288 N.C. 388, 218 S.E.2d 368, 371.

Those facts found in that vaguely defined field lying between evidential facts on the one side and the primary issue or conclusion of law on the other, being but the logical results of the proofs, or, in other words, mere conclusions of fact. Christmas v. Cowden, 44 N.M. 517, 105 P.2d 484, 487.

One that is essential to the right of action or matter of defense, and the trial court is under the duty of submitting only ultimate or controlling issues. Perales v. Braslau's Furniture Co., Tex.Civ.App., 493 S.W.2d 638, 640.

Ultimate issue. That question which must finally be answered as the defendant's negligence is the ultimate issue in a personal injury action.

Ultimatum /ə̀ltəméydəm/. Lat. The last. The final and ultimate proposition made in negotiating a treaty, a contract, or the like. The word also means the result of a negotiation, and it comprises the final determination of a party concerned in the matter in dispute.

Ultima voluntas testatoris est perimplenda secundum veram intentionem suam /ə́ltəmə vələ́ntæs testətórəs èst pə̀rəmpléndə səkə́ndəm víræm intènshiyównəm s(y)úwəm/. The last will of a testator is to be fulfilled according to his true intention.

Ultimum supplicium /ə́ltəməm səplísh(iy)əm/. Lat. The last or extreme punishment; the extremity of punishment; the punishment of death. 4 Bl.Comm. 17.

Ultimum supplicium esse mortem solam interpretamur /ə́ltəməm səplísh(iy)əm ésiy mórdəm sówləm əntə̀rprətéymər/. The extremest punishment we consider to be death alone.

Ultimus hæres /ə́ltəməs híriyz/. Lat. The last or remote heir; the lord. So called in contradistinction to the *hæres proximus* and the *hæres remotior*.

Ultra /ə́ltrə/. Lat. Beyond; outside of; in excess of.

Damages ultra. Damages beyond a sum paid into court.

Ultra mare /ə́ltrə mériy/. Beyond sea. One of the old essoins or excuses for not appearing in court at the return of process.

Ultra reprises. After deduction of drawbacks; in excess of deductions or expenses.

Ultra vires /ə́ltrə váyriyz/. Acts beyond the scope of the powers of a corporation, as defined by its charter or laws of state of incorporation. State ex rel. v. Holston Trust Co., 168 Tenn. 546, 79 S.W.2d 1012, 1016. The term has a broad application and includes not only acts prohibited by the charter, but acts which are in excess of powers granted and not prohibited, and generally applied either when a corporation has no power whatever to do an act, or when the corporation has the power but exercises it irregularly. People ex rel. Barrett v. Bank of Peoria, 295 Ill.App. 543, 15 N.E.2d 333, 335. Act is ultra vires when corporation is without authority to perform it under any circumstances or for any purpose. By doctrine of ultra vires a contract made by a corporation beyond the scope of its corporate powers is unlawful. Community Federal Sav. & Loan Ass'n of Independence, Mo. v. Fields, C.C.A.Mo., 128 F.2d 705, 708. Ultra vires act of municipality is one which is beyond powers conferred upon it by law. Charles v. Town of Jeanerette, Inc., La.App., 234 So.2d 794, 798.

Ultra posse non potest esse, et vice versa /ə́ltrə pósiy nòn pówdəst ésiy, èt váysiy vársə/. What is beyond possibility cannot exist, and the reverse [what cannot exist is not possible].

Umpirage /ə́mpərəj/. The decision of an umpire. The word "Umpirage," in reference to an umpire, is the same as the word "award," in reference to arbitrators; but "award" is commonly applied to the decision of the umpire also.

Umpire /ə́mpay(ə)r/. Third party selected to arbitrate labor dispute. One clothed with authority to act alone in rendering a decision where arbitrators have disagreed. Hughes v. National Fuel Co., 121 W.Va. 392, 3 S.E.2d 621, 626. When matters in dispute are submitted to two or more arbitrators, and they do not agree in their decision, it is usual for another person to be called in as "umpire," to whose sole judgment it is then referred. An umpire, strictly speaking, makes his award independently of that of the arbitrators.

Un-. A prefix used indiscriminately, and may mean simply "not." Thus, "unlawful" means "not authorized by law."

Unable /ənéybəl/. This term, as used in a statute providing that evidence given in a former trial may be proved in a subsequent trial, where the witness is unable to testify, means mentally and physically unable.

Unaccrued /ənəkrúwd/. Not become due, as rent on a lease.

Unadjusted /ənəjə́stəd/. Uncertain; not agreed upon.

Unalienable /ənéyl(i)yənəbəl/. Inalienable; incapable of being aliened, that is, sold and transferred.

Inalienable rights. Rights which can never be abridged because they are so fundamental.

Unambiguous /ənæmbíɡyuwəs/. Susceptible of but one meaning. Lawrie v. Miller, Tex.Com.App., 45 S.W.2d 172, 173.

Unanimity /yùwnənímədiy/. Agreement of all the persons concerned, in holding one and the same opinion or determination of any matter or question; as the concurrence of a jury in deciding upon their verdict or of judges in concurring in their decision. See **Unanimous.**

Unanimous /yənǽnəməs/. To say that a proposition was adopted by a "unanimous" vote does not always mean that every one present voted for the proposition, but it may, and generally does, mean, when a *viva voce* vote is taken, that no one voted in the negative. See also **Unanimity.**

Una persona vix potest supplere vices duarum /yúwnə pərsównə vìks pówdəst səplíriy váysiyz d(y)uwérəm/. One person can scarcely supply the place of two.

Unascertained. Not certainly known or determined. Commissioner of Internal Revenue v. Owens, C.C. A.10, 78 F.2d 768, 773.

Unascertained duties. Payment in gross, on an estimate as to amount, and where the merchant, on a final liquidation, will be entitled by law to allowances or deductions which do not depend on the rate of duty charged, but on the ascertainment of the quantity of the article subject to duty.

Unauthorized. That which is done without authority, as a signature or indorsement made without actual, implied or apparent authority and this includes a forgery. U.C.C. § 1–201(43).

Unauthorized use. The criminal offense of use of a motor vehicle without authority of the owner, knowing that such use is without his permission. It differs from larceny to the extent that in the crime of unauthorized use, the government need not prove the intent to deprive permanently the owner of the vehicle.

Unavailability. In law of evidence, on a showing that a witness or his testimony is not available, prior reported testimony of that witness which can be faithfully reproduced is admissible as an exception to the hearsay rule. A witness is unavailable if he is dead, insane or beyond reach of a summons. His testimony is unavailable if he has a privilege permitting him to refuse to testify. See Fed.Evid.R. 804.

Unavailability as defined in rule providing for admission of prior testimony, requires, among other things, either that the witness be beyond the jurisdiction of the court's process to compel his appearance, or that the proponent of the prior statement be unable, despite due diligence, to obtain the attendance of the witness. Sacawa v. Polikoff, 150 N.J.Super. 172, 375 A.2d 279, 283.

Una voce /yúwnə vówsiy/. Lat. With one voice; unanimously; without dissent.

Unavoidable. Not avoidable, incapable of being shunned or prevented, inevitable, and necessary.

Unavoidable accident. An inevitable accident; one which could not have been foreseen and prevented by using ordinary diligence, and resulting without fault. Not necessarily an accident which it was physically impossible, in the nature of things, for the person to have prevented, but one not occasioned in any degree, either remotely or directly, by the want of such care or skill as the law holds every man bound to exercise. An accident which could not be prevented by the exercise of ordinary care and prudence. A casualty which occurs without negligence of either party and when all means which common prudence suggests have been used to prevent it. See also **Accident; Act of God.**

Unavoidable casualty. An event or accident which human prudence, foresight, and sagacity cannot prevent, happening against will and without negligence. Sabin v. Sunset Garden Co., 184 Okl. 106, 85 P.2d 294, 295. Within the meaning of statutes in several states relating to the vacation of judgments, means some casualty or misfortune growing out of conditions or circumstances that prevented the party or his attorney from doing something that, except therefor, would have been done, and does not include mistakes or errors of judgment growing out of misconstruction or understanding of the law, or the failure of parties or counsel through mistake to avail themselves of remedies, which if resorted to would have prevented the casualty or misfortune. If by any care, prudence, or foresight a thing could have been guarded against, it is not unavoidable. The term is not ordinarily limited to an act of God. See also **Accident; Act of God; Unavoidable accident.**

Unavoidable cause. A cause which reasonably prudent and careful men under like circumstances do not and would not ordinarily anticipate, and whose effects, under similar circumstances, they do not and would not ordinarily avoid.

Unavoidable dangers. This term in a marine policy covering unavoidable dangers of the river includes those unpreventable by persons operating the vessel, and, like the term perils of the sea, includes all kinds of marine casualties, thus including accidents in which there is human intervention.

Unborn beneficiaries. Those persons named in a general way as sharing in an estate or gift though not yet born. Commonly, a court appoints a guardian ad litem to protect and to represent their interests.

Unborn child. The individual human life in existence and developing from fertilization until birth.

A child not yet born at the happening of an event. A child not born at the time of an injury to his mother which causes the child to suffer an injury may recover in most jurisdictions after birth if the child were viable in his mother's womb at the time of the defendant's wrongdoing.

See also **Child; Viable child.**

Unbroken. Continuous, as adverse possession.

Unceasesath. In Saxon law, an oath by relations not to avenge a relation's death.

Uncertainty. The state or quality of being unknown or vague. Such vagueness, obscurity, or confusion in any written instrument, *e.g.,* a will, as to render it unintelligible to those who are called upon to execute or interpret it, so that no definite meaning can be extracted from it.

Unchastity. Impurity in mind and conduct, which may exist without actually engaging in unlawful sexual intercourse.

Uncia /ǝnshiyǝ/. Lat. In Roman law, an ounce; the twelfth of the Roman *"as,"* or pound. The twelfth part of anything; the proportion of one-twelfth. 2 Bl.Comm. 462, note *m.*

Uncia agri, uncia terræ /ǝnsh(iy)ǝ ǽgray, ǝnsh(iy)ǝ téhriy/. These phrases often occur in the charters of the British kings, and signify some measure or quantity of land. It is said to have been the quantity of twelve *modii;* each *modius* being possibly one hundred feet square.

Unciarius hæres /ǝnshiyériyǝs híriyz/. Lat. In Roman law, an heir to one-twelfth of an estate or inheritance.

Uncle. The brother of one's father or mother.

Unclean hands doctrine. Principle that one who has unclean hands is not entitled to relief in equity. Doctrine means no more than that one who has defrauded his adversary in the subject matter of the action will not be heard to assert right in equity. The doctrine has no application unless party's wrongdoing has some proximate relation to the subject matter in controversy.

Unconditional. Not limited or affected by any condition;—applied especially to the quality of an insured's estate in the property insured. See **Owner** (*Sole and unconditional owner*).

Unconditional discharge. One whose term of confinement has expired is unconditionally discharged if there are attached no parole provisions to his release.

A release from liability without any terms or delimiting conditions attached.

Unconscionability. Basic test of "unconscionability" of contract is whether under circumstances existing at time of making of contract and in light of general commercial background and commercial needs of particular trade or case, clauses involved are so one-sided as to oppress or unfairly surprise party. Division of Triple T Service, Inc. v. Mobil Oil Corp., 60 Misc.2d 720, 304 N.Y.S.2d 191, 201. Unconscionability is generally recognized to include an absence of meaningful choice on the part of one of the parties, to a contract together with contract terms which are unreasonably favorable to the other party. Gordon v. Crown Central Petroleum Corp., D.C.Ga., 423 F.Supp. 58, 61.

Typically the cases in which unconscionability is found involve gross overall one-sidedness or gross one-sidedness of a term disclaiming a warranty, limiting damages, or granting procedural advantages. In these cases one-sidedness is often coupled with the fact that the imbalance is buried in small print and often couched in language unintelligible to even a person of moderate education. Often the seller deals with a particularly susceptible clientele. Kugler v. Romain, 58 N.J. 522, 279 A.2d 640.

Uniform Commercial Code. (1) If the court as a matter of law finds the contract or any clause of the contract to have been unconscionable at the time it was made the court may refuse to enforce the contract, or it may enforce the remainder of the contract without the unconscionable clause, or it may so limit the application of any unconscionable clause as to avoid any unconscionable result. (2) When it is claimed or appears to the court that the contract or any clause thereof may be unconscionable the parties shall be afforded a reasonable opportunity to present evidence as to its commercial setting, purpose and effect to aid the court in making the determination. U.C.C. § 2–302.

Section 2–302 should be considered in conjunction with the obligation of good faith imposed at several places in the Code. See *e.g.* U.C.C. § 1–203.

Restatement of Contracts. If a contract or term thereof is unconscionable at the time the contract is made a court may refuse to enforce the contract, or may enforce the remainder of the contract without the unconscionable term, or may so limit the application of any unconscionable term as to avoid any unconscionable result. Restatement of Contracts, Second, (Tent.Draft) § 234.

Unconscionable bargain. An unconscionable bargain or contract is one which no man in his senses, not under delusion, would make, on the one hand, and which no fair and honest man would accept, on the other. Hume v. U. S., 132 U.S. 406, 10 S.Ct. 134, 33 L.Ed. 393. See also **Unconscionability.**

Unconscious. Not possessed of mind. Wilson v. Ray, 64 Ga.App. 540, 13 S.E.2d 848, 852. A state of mind of persons of sound mind suffering from some voluntary or involuntary agency rendering them unaware of their acts. Greenfield v. Com., 214 Va. 710, 204 S.E.2d 414, 417. Insensible to the reception of any stimuli and incapable of performing or experiencing any controlled functions. One who engages in what would otherwise be criminal conduct is not guilty of a crime if he does so in a state of unconsciousness. See *e.g.* Calif. Penal Code § 26(5). See also **Automatism.**

Unconstitutional. That which is contrary to the constitution. The opposite of "constitutional." Norton v. Shelby County, 118 U.S. 425, 6 S.Ct. 1121, 30 L.Ed. 178.

This word is used in two different senses. One, which may be called the English sense, is that the legislation conflicts with some recognized general principle. This is no more than to say that it is unwise, or is based upon a wrong or unsound principle, or conflicts with a generally accepted policy. The other, which may be called the American sense, is that the legislation conflicts with some provision of our written Constitution, which it is beyond the power of the Legislature to change. U. S. v. American Brewing Co., D.C.Pa., 1 F.2d 1001, 1002.

Uncontrollable. Incapable of being controlled or ungovernable.

Uncontrollable impulse. As an excuse for the commission of an act otherwise criminal, this term means an impulse towards its commission of such fixity and intensity that it cannot be resisted by the person subject to it, in the enfeebled condition of his will and moral sense resulting from derangement or mania. See **Insanity.**

Uncore prist /ə́nkor prı́st/. L. Fr. Still ready. A species of plea or replication by which the party alleges that he is still ready to pay or perform all that is justly demanded of him. In conjunction with the phrase *"tout temps prist,"* it signifies that he has always been and still is ready to do what is required, thus saving costs where the whole cause is admitted, or preventing delay where it is a replication, if the allegation is made out. 3 Bl.Comm. 303.

Uncuth /ə́nkúwθ/. In Saxon law, unknown; a stranger. A person entertained in the house of another was, on the first night of his entertainment, so called. See **Twa night gest.**

Unde nihil habet /ə́ndiy náy(h)əl héybət/. Lat. In old English law, the name of the writ of dower, which lay for a widow, where *no dower* at all had been assigned her within the time limited by law. 3 Bl.Comm. 183.

Under. Sometimes used in its literal sense of below in position, beneath, but more frequently in its secondary meaning of "inferior" or "subordinate." Also according to; as, "under the testimony."

Under and subject. Words frequently used in conveyances of land which is subject to a mortgage, to show that the grantee takes subject to such mortgage.

Under-chamberlains of the exchequer. In old English law, two officers who cleaved the tallies written by the clerk of the tallies, and read the same, that the clerk of the pell and comptrollers thereof might see their entries were true. They also made searches for records in the treasury, and had the custody of Domesday Book. The office is now abolished.

Under color of law. See **Color of law.**

Under control. This phrase does not necessarily mean the ability to stop instanter under any and all circumstances, an automobile being "under control" within the meaning of the law if it is moving at such a rate, and the mechanism and power under such control, that it can be brought to a stop with a reasonable degree of celerity. And motorist is only bound to use that degree of care, caution, and prudence that an ordinarily careful, cautious, and prudent man would have used at the time under same or similar circumstances in operation of said automobile. In general, as applied to street cars or railroad trains, the term denotes the control and preparation appropriate to probable emergencies. It is such control as will enable a train to be stopped promptly if need should arise. It implies the ability to stop within the distance the track is seen to be clear. See also **Control; Lookout.**

Undercover agent. A person who works as an agent without disclosing his role as an agent. In police work, one who makes contact with suspected criminals without disclosing his role as an agent of the police. He gathers evidence of criminal activity which may later be used at trial of the criminals. Such agents are commonly used in narcotic investigations.

Undercurrent or underflow of surface stream. Those waters which slowly find their way through sand and gravel constituting bed of a stream, or lands under or immediately adjacent to stream, and are themselves part of surface stream. Maricopa County Municipal Water Conservation Dist. No. 1 v. Southwest Cotton Co., 39 Ariz. 65, 4 P.2d 369, 380.

Underflow. See **Undercurrent.**

Underground waters. See **Water** (*Subterranean waters*).

Under herd. A term conveying the idea that a considerable number of domestic animals are gathered together and held together by herders in constant attendance and in control of their movements from place to place on a public range or within certain areas.

Under insurance. Insurance coverage in an amount less than the value of the property insured or less than the risk exposure.

Under-lease. Where lessee lets premises for less time than period of his unexpired term; a sub-lease. Also the transfer of a part only of the lands, though for the whole term.

Under protest. A payment made or an act done under compulsion while the payor or actor asserts that he waives no rights by making the payment or by doing the act. See **Protest.**

Under-sheriff. An officer who acts directly under the sheriff, and performs all the duties of the sheriff's office, a few only excepted where the personal presence of the high-sheriff is necessary. See Delfelder v. Teton Land and Investment Co., 46 Wyo. 142, 24 P.2d 702.

A sheriff's deputy, who, being designated by the sheriff as an "under sheriff," becomes his chief deputy with authority by virtue of his appointment to execute all the ordinary duties of the office of sheriff. A distinction is sometimes made between this officer and a *deputy,* the latter being appointed for a special occasion or purpose, while the former discharges, in general, all the duties required by the sheriff's office.

Undersigned, the. The person whose name is signed or the persons whose names are signed at the end of a document; the subscriber or subscribers.

Understand. To know; to apprehend the meaning; to appreciate; as, to understand the nature and effect of an act. International-Great Northern R. Co. v. Pence, Tex.Civ.App., 113 S.W.2d 206, 210. To have a full and clear knowledge of; to comprehend. Thus, to invalidate a deed on the ground that the grantor did not understand the nature of the act, the grantor must be incapable of comprehending that the effect of the act would divest him of the title to the land set forth in the deed. As used in connection with the execution of wills and other instruments, the term includes the realization of the practical effects and consequences of the proposed act. See **Capacity.**

Understanding. In the law of contracts, an agreement. An implied agreement resulting from the express terms of another agreement, whether written or oral. An informal agreement, or a concurrence as to its terms. A valid contract engagement of a somewhat informal character. This is a loose and ambiguous term, unless it be accompanied by some expression to show that it constituted a meeting of the minds of parties upon something respecting which they intended to be bound. See **Agreement; Contract.**

Understood. The phrase "it is understood," when employed as a word of contract in a written agreement, has the same general force as the words "it is agreed."

Undertake. To take on oneself; to engage in; to enter upon; to take in hand; set about; attempt; as, to undertake a task or a journey; and, specifically, to take upon oneself solemnly or expressly. To lay oneself under obligation or to enter into stipulation; to perform or to execute; to covenant; to contract. Hence, to guarantee; be surety for; promise; to accept or take over as a charge; to accept responsibility for the care of. To engage to look after or attend to, as to undertake a patient or guest. To endeavor to perform or try; to promise, engage, agree, or assume an obligation.

Undertaker. One who undertakes (to do something). In a mechanic's lien statute, the word has been held not to include a mere furnisher of material in connection with the erection of the building. One whose business is to prepare the dead for burial and to take the charge and management of funerals.

Undertaking. A promise, engagement, or stipulation. An engagement by one of the parties to a contract to the other, as distinguished from the mutual engagement of the parties to each other. It does not necessarily imply a consideration. In a somewhat special sense, a promise given in the course of legal proceedings by a party or his counsel, generally as a condition to obtaining some concession from the court or the opposite party. A promise or security in any form. See **Stipulation.**

Under-tenant. A tenant under one who is himself a tenant; one who holds by under-lease. See also **Under-lease.**

Under the influence of intoxicating liquor. Phrase as used in statutes or ordinances prohibiting the operation of motor vehicle by a party under the influence of intoxicating liquor covers not only all well-known and easily recognized conditions and degrees of intoxication, but any abnormal mental or physical condition which is the result of indulging in any degree in intoxicating liquors, and which tends to deprive one of that clearness of intellect and control of himself which he would otherwise possess. Any condition where intoxicating liquor has so far affected the nervous system, brain or muscles of the driver as to impair, to an appreciable degree, his ability to operate his automobile in the manner that an ordinary, prudent and cautious man, in full possession of his faculties, using reasonable care, would operate or drive under like conditions. Luellen v. State, 64 Okl.Cr. 382, 81 P.2d 323, 328. See also **Intoxication.**

Undertook. Agreed; promised; assumed. This is the technical word to be used in alleging the promise which forms the basis of an action of *assumpsit*.

Under-treasurer of England. He who transacted the business of the lord high treasurer.

Under-tutor. In Louisiana, in every tutorship there shall be an under-tutor, whom it shall be the duty of the judge to appoint at the time letters of tutorship are certified for the tutor. It is the duty of the under-tutor to act for the minor whenever the interest of the minor is in opposition to the interest of the tutor. Civ.Code La. Art. 273.

Underwrite. To insure life or property. To agree to sell bonds, etc., to the public, or to furnish the necessary money for such securities, and to buy those which cannot be sold. An underwriting contract, aside from its use in insurance, is an agreement, made before corporate shares are brought before the public, that in the event of the public not taking all the shares of the number mentioned in the agreement, the underwriter will take the shares which the public do not take; "underwriting" being a purchase, together with a guaranty of a sale of the bonds. In re Hackett, Hoff and Thiermann, C.C.A.Wis., 70 F.2d 815, 819. See also **Underwriter.**

Underwriter. Any person, banker, or syndicate that guarantees to furnish a definite sum of money by a definite date to a business or government in return for an issue of bonds or stock. In insurance, the one assuming a risk in return for the payment of a premium.

One who agrees to purchase an entire security issue for a specified price, usually for resale to others. A person who has acquired securities from an issuer or control person, pursuant to contract or exchange and intends to reoffer or resell said securities to the public.

Term refers to any person who has purchased from an issuer with a view to, or sells for an issuer in connection with, the distribution of any security, or participates or has a direct or indirect participation in any such undertaking, or participates or has a participation in the direct or indirect underwriting of any such undertaking; but such term shall not include a person whose interest is limited to a commission from an underwriter or dealer not in excess of the usual and customary distributor's or seller's commission. Investment Company Act, § 2.

See also **Underwrite.**

Undisclosed agency. Exists where agent deals with a third person without notifying that person of the agency.

Undisclosed principal. If, at time of transaction conducted by agent, other party thereto has no notice that agent is acting for a principal, the principal is "undisclosed principal."

Undisputed. Not questioned or challenged; uncontested.

Undisputed fact. An admitted fact, which the court has not deemed sufficiently material to add to the finding, or has inadvertently omitted from it; a fact not found by the court does not become an "undisputed fact," merely because one or more witnesses testify to it without direct contradiction.

Undistributed profits. See **Undivided profits.**

Undistributed profits tax. Tax imposed on the unreasonable accumulation of profits by a corporation which has sufficient surplus for expansion and other needs beyond the amount which it could but does not pay out in dividends. I.R.C. § 535.

Undivided profits. Profits which have not in fact been divided or distributed. Current undistributed earnings. Edwards v. Douglas, 269 U.S. 204, 46 S.Ct. 85, 89, 70 L.Ed. 235; Winkelman v. General Motors Corporation, D.C.N.Y., 44 F.Supp. 960, 966. Profits not set aside as surplus or distributed in dividends. Phillips v. U. S., D.C.Pa., 12 F.2d 598, 600.

"Surplus" and "undivided profits," as commonly employed in corporate accounting, denote an excess in the aggregate value of the assets of the corporation over the sum of liabilities, including capital stock; "surplus" describing such part of the excess in the value of the corporate assets as is treated by the corporation as part of the permanent capital, while the term "undivided profits" designates such part of the excess as consists of profits neither distributed as dividends nor carried to the surplus account. Willcuts v. Milton Dairy Co., 275 U.S. 215, 48 S.Ct. 71, 72, 72 L.Ed. 247.

Undivided right. An undivided right or title, or a title to an undivided portion of an estate, is that owned by one of two or more tenants in common or joint tenants before partition. Held by the same title by two or more persons, whether their rights are equal as to value or quantity, or unequal.

Undres /ándərz/. In old English law, minors or persons under age not capable of bearing arms.

Undue. More than necessary; not proper; illegal. It denotes something wrong, according to the standard of morals which the law enforces in relations of men, and in fact illegal, and qualifies the purpose with which influence is exercised or result which it accomplishes. Morris v. Morris, 192 Miss. 518, 6 So.2d 311, 312.

Undue influence. Any improper or wrongful constraint, machination, or urgency of persuasion whereby the will of a person is overpowered and he is induced to do or forbear an act which he would not do or would do if left to act freely. Influence which deprives person influenced of free agency or destroys freedom of his will and renders it more the will of another than his own. Misuse of position of confidence or taking advantage of a person's weakness, infirmity, or distress to change improperly that person's actions or decisions.

Term refers to conduct by which a person, through his power over mind of testator, makes the latter's desires conform to his own, thereby overmastering the volition of the testator. Parrisella v. Fotopulos, 111 Ariz. 4, 522 P.2d 1081, 1083. For purpose of executing instruments, such exists when there was such dominion and control exercised over mind of person executing such instruments, under facts and circumstances then existing, as to overcome his free agency and free will and to substitute will of another so as to cause him to do what he would not otherwise have done but for such dominion and control. Board of Regents of University of Tex. v. Yarbrough, Tex. Civ.App., 470 S.W.2d 80, 86, 92.

Undue influence consists in the use, by one in whom a confidence is reposed by another, or who holds a real or apparent authority over him, of such confidence or authority for the purpose of obtaining an unfair advantage over him; in taking an unfair advantage of another's weakness of mind; or in taking a grossly oppressive and unfair advantage of another's necessities or distress. Calif.Civil Code, § 1575.

See also **Coercion; Duress.**

Unearned income. Income that has been received but not yet earned. Normally, such income is taxed when received even in the case of accrual basis taxpayers. See also **Income.**

Unearned increment. Value due to no labor or expenditure on the part of an owner but to natural causes making an increased demand for it, such as increase of population or the general progress of society. Miller v. Huntington & Ohio Bridge Co., 123 W.Va. 320, 15 S.E.2d 687, 699.

Unearned surplus. Term "unearned surplus" of corporation suggests something other than "earned surplus" and includes: (a) "paid-in surplus"—amounts contributed for or assigned to shares in excess of stated capital applicable thereto; (b) "revaluation surplus"—surplus arising from a revaluation of assets above cost, and (c) "donated surplus"—contributions other than for shares, whether from shareholders or others. Conine v. Leikam, Okl., 570 P.2d 1156, 1160.

Uneducated. Not synonymous with illiterate. A man might be able to read and write, carry on a business correspondence, understand business transactions, and be bound by all his contracts, and yet be an "uneducated" man.

Unemployment. State of being not employed; lack of employment. A. J. Meyer & Co. v. Unemployment Compensation Commission, 348 Mo. 147, 152 S.W.2d 184, 189.

Unequal. Not uniform. Los Angeles County v. Ransohoff, 24 Cal.App.2d 238, 74 P.2d 828, 830. Ill-balanced; uneven; partial; discriminatory; prejudicial; unfair;—not synonymous with inappropriate, which means unsuitable, unfit, or improper. See **Discrimination; Separate but equal doctrine.**

Unequivocal. Clear; plain; capable of being understood in only one way, or as clearly demonstrated. Free from uncertainty, or without doubt; and, when used with reference to the burden of proof, it implies proof of the highest possible character and it imports proof of the nature of mathematical certainty. Berry v. Maywood Mut. Water Co. No. 1, 11 Cal.App.2d 479, 53 P.2d 1032; Molyneux v. Twin Falls Canal Co., 54 Idaho 619, 35 P.2d 651, 656.

Unerring. Incapable of error or failure; certain; sure; infallible.

Unethical. Not ethical; hence, colloquially, not according to business or professional standards.

Unethical conduct. See **Code of Professional Responsibility.**

Unexceptionable. Without any fault; not subject to any objection or criticism.

Unexpected. Not expected, coming without warning, sudden. See **Act of God; Accident.**

Unexpired term. Remainder of a period prescribed by law after a portion of such time has passed, and phrase is not synonymous with "vacancy." State ex rel. Sanchez v. Dixon, La.App., 4 So.2d 591, 596.

Unfair competition. A term which may be applied generally to all dishonest or fraudulent rivalry in trade and commerce, but is particularly applied to the practice of endeavoring to substitute one's own goods or products in the markets for those of another, having an established reputation and extensive sale, by means of imitating or counterfeiting the name, title, size, shape, or distinctive peculiarities of the article, or the shape, color, label, wrapper, or general appearance of the package, or other such simulations, the imitation being carried far enough to mislead the general public or deceive an unwary purchaser, and yet not amounting to an absolute counterfeit or to the infringement of a trade-mark or trade-name. Singer Mfg. Co. v. June Mfg. Co., 163 U.S. 169, 16 S.Ct. 1002, 41 L.Ed. 118. The simulation by one person of the name, materials, color scheme, symbols, patterns, or devices employed by another for purpose of deceiving the public, or substitution of goods, or wares of one person for those of another, thus falsely inducing purchase of goods and obtaining benefits belonging to competitor. Mathews Conveyor Co. v. Palmer-Bee Co., C.C.A.Mich., 135 F.2d 73, 84; American Fork & Hoe Co. v. Stampit Corporation, C.C.A.Ohio, 125 F.2d 472, 474, 475. Passing off, or attempting to pass off upon the public the goods or business of one person as the goods or business of another. Socony-Vacuum Oil Co. v. Oil City Refiners, C.C.A.Ohio, 136 F.2d 470, 474. The selling of another's product as one's own. A. L. A. Schechter Poultry Corporation v. United States, N.Y., 295 U.S. 495, 55 S.Ct. 837, 844, 79 L.Ed. 1570. Also, deceitful advertising which injures a competitor, bribery of employees, secret rebates and concessions, and other devices of unfair trade. In re Northern Pigment Co., Cust. & Pat.App., 71 F.2d 447, 453.

The equitable doctrine of "unfair competition" is not confined to cases of actual market competition between similar products of different parties, but extends to all cases in which one party fraudulently seeks to sell his goods as those of another. Wisconsin Electric Co. v. Dumore Co., C.C.A.Ohio, 35 F.2d 555, 557.

That which constitutes "unfair competition" or "unfair or fraudulent business practice" within statute providing that person performing or proposing to perform act of unfair competition within state may be enjoined in any court of competent jurisdiction is question of fact, the essential test being whether the public is likely to be deceived. Payne v. United California Bank, 23 Cal.App.3d 850, 100 Cal.Rptr. 672, 676.

Under statute providing for enjoining of unfair competition and defining the same as meaning and including "unlawful, unfair or fraudulent business practice" courts may enjoin on-going wrongful business conduct in whatever context such activity may occur; "unfair competition" within such statute is not limited to deceptive or fraudulent conduct. As used in statute prohibiting unfair competition and defining the same as meaning and including "unlawful, unfair or fraudulent business practice," "unfair competition" is not confined to practices involving competitive injury but extends to practices resulting in injury to consumers. Barquis v. Merchants Collection Ass'n of Oakland, Inc., 7 Cal.3d 94, 101 Cal.Rptr. 745, 496 P.2d 817, 828, 829.

Test of "unfair competition" is, not whether distinction between two competing products can be recognized when placed alongside each other, but whether, when the two products are not viewed together, a purchaser of ordinary prudence would be induced by reason of the marked resemblance in general effect to mistake one for the other despite differences in matters of detail. Ralston Purina Co. v. Checker Food Products Co., Mo.App., 80 S.W.2d 717, 719, 720.

See also **Unfair methods of competition.**

Unfair hearing. Where the defect, or the practice complained of, was such as might have led to a denial of justice, or where there was absent one of the elements deemed essential to due process. Ex parte Bridges, D.C.Cal., 49 F.Supp. 292, 302, 306; Bufalino v. Irvine, C.C.A.Kan., 103 F.2d 830, 832; Kielema v. Crossman, C.C.A.Tex., 103 F.2d 292, 293.

Unfair labor practice. Within National Labor Relations Act, it is an unfair labor practice for an employer: (1) To interfere with, restrain, or coerce employees in the exercise of their rights to self-organization, to form, join or assist labor organizations, to bargain collectively through representatives of their own choosing, and to engage in concerted activities, for the purpose of collective bargaining or other mutual aid or protection. (2) To dominate or interfere with the formation or administration of any labor organization or contribute financial or other support to it. (3) By discrimination in regard to hire or tenure of employment or any term or condition of employment to encourage or discourage membership in any labor organization. (4) To discharge or otherwise discriminate against an employee because he has filed charges or given testimony under the Act. (5) To refuse to bargain collectively with the representatives of his employees. National Labor Relations Act, §§ 7, 8; 29 U.S.C.A. §§ 102.1 et seq., 157, 158.

The following acts have been held to be unfair labor practices under National Labor Relations Act:

Failure to re-employ striking employees. Western Cartridge Co. v. National Labor Relations Board, C.C. A.7, 139 F.2d 855, 858. Refusal of employer to reinstate union members who were evicted from plant unless members would withdraw from union. National Labor Relations Board v. J. G. Boswell Co., C.C.A.9, 136 F.2d 585, 590, 592, 596. Refusal of employer to bargain collectively in good faith. National Labor Relations Board v. Griswold Mfg. Co., C.C.A.3, 106 F.2d 713, 724; National Labor Relations Board v. Somerset Shoe Co., C.C.A.1, 111 F.2d 681, 688, 689. Threats by employer to close if union gained a foothold in plant. National Labor Relations Board v. J. G. Boswell Co., C.C.A.9, 136 F.2d 585, 590,

592, 596. Anti-union statements made by employer's supervisory employees during and after strike, together with statement to one of the strikers that he would never get a job in that town anymore. N. L. R. B. v. Indiana Desk Co., C.C.A.7, 149 F.2d 987, 992, 996. Refusal of employer to permit posting of a notice that employer would not discriminate against employees who wished to join union. National Labor Relations Board v. J. G. Boswell Co., C.C.A.9, 136 F.2d 585, 590, 592, 596. Discharge of an employee because of membership in or activity on behalf of a labor organization. National Labor Relations Board v. Newark Morning Ledger, C.C.A.3, 120 F.2d 262, 268; National Labor Relations Board v. Bank of America Trust & Savings Ass'n, C.C.A.9, 130 F.2d 624, 628, 629. Employer's interference with and his dominating formation and administration of new labor organization. National Labor Relations Board v. Swift & Co., C.C.A.8, 116 F.2d 143, 145, 146; National Labor Relations Board v. Blossom Products Corporation, C.C.A.3, 121 F.2d 260, 262; National Labor Relations Board v. Stackpole Carbon Co., C.C.A.3, 105 F.2d 167, 173, 175. Refusal of employer which had refused to bargain with union which had been certified as the exclusive bargaining agent. National Labor Relations Board v. John Engelhorn & Sons, C.C.A.3, 134 F.2d 553, 558. Assault by persons employed by manufacturer upon union organizers or sympathizers. National Labor Relations Board v. Ford Motor Co., C.C.A.6, 114 F.2d 905, 911, 915. Discharge of employee because he would not become member of union in accordance with closed shop agreement. Virginia Electric & Power Co. v. National Labor Relations Board, C.C.A.4, 132 F.2d 390, 396.

Unfair methods of competition. This phrase within Federal Trade Commission Act has broader meaning than common-law term "unfair competition," but its scope cannot be precisely defined, and what constitutes "unfair methods of competition" must be determined in particular instances, upon evidence, in light of particular competitive conditions and of what is found to be a specific and substantial public interest. Federal Trade Commission Act § 5, 15 U.S.C.A. § 45. A. L. A. Schechter Poultry Corporation v. United States, N. Y., 295 U.S. 495, 55 S.Ct. 837, 844, 79 L.Ed. 1570.

The term though not defined by the statute is clearly inapplicable to practices never heretofore regarded as opposed to good morals because characterized by deception, bad faith, fraud, or oppression, or as against public policy because of their dangerous tendency unduly to hinder competition or create monopoly. The act was not intended to fetter free and fair competition as commonly understood and practiced by honorable opponents in trade. In re Amtorg Trading Corporation, Cust. & Pat.App., 75 F.2d 826, 830. But a method was said to be an unfair method if it does not leave to each actual or potential competitor a fair opportunity for play of his contending force engendered by an honest desire for gain. California Rice Industry v. Federal Trade Commission, C.C.A.9, 102 F.2d 716, 721.

See also **Unfair competition.**

Unfair trade practices. See **Unfair competition**; **Unfair methods of competition.**

Unfaithful. Characterized by bad faith;—not synonymous with "illegal," which means unlawful or contrary to law, nor with "improper," which, as applied to conduct, implies such conduct as a man of ordinary and reasonable prudence would not, under the circumstances, have been guilty of.

Unfinished. Not completed; not brought to an end; imperfect; the last effort, as a final touch is given to a work. Bell & Graddy v. O'Brien, Tex.Civ.App., 113 S.W.2d 560, 562.

Unfit. Unsuitable; incompetent; not adapted or qualified for a particular use or service; having no fitness. Word "unfit" means, in general, unsuitable, incompetent or not adapted for a particular use or service. In Interest of Johnson, 214 Kan. 780, 522 P.2d 330, 334. As applied to relation of rational parents to their child, word "unfit" usually, though not necessarily, imports something of moral delinquency, but, unsuitability for any reason, apart from moral defects, may render a parent unfit for custody. In Interest of Johnson, 214 Kan. 780, 522 P.2d 330, 334.

Unforeseen. Not foreseen, not expected. Pampel v. Board of Examiners, 114 Mont. 380, 136 P.2d 991, 994.

Ungeld. In Saxon law, an outlaw; a person whose murder required no composition to be made, or *were-geld* to be paid, by his slayer.

Unharmed. Within provision of Federal Kidnapping Act that death sentence shall not be imposed if kidnapped person has been liberated unharmed, means uninjured. Federal Kidnapping Act § 1 et seq., as amended, 18 U.S.C.A. § 1201 et seq. See also Robinson v. U. S., Ky., 324 U.S. 282, 65 S.Ct. 666, 668, 89 L.Ed. 944.

Unica taxatio /yúwnəkə tækséysh(iy)ow/. The obsolete language of a special award of *venire*, where, of several defendants, one pleads, and one lets judgment go by default, whereby the jury, who are to try and assess damages on the issue, are also to assess damages against the defendant suffering judgment by default.

Unifactoral obligation /yùwnəfǽktərəl òbləgéyshən/. See **Contract.**

Unified. Made one. Adams v. Salt River Valley Water Users' Ass'n, 53 Ariz. 374, 89 P.2d 1060, 1071. See **Consolidation; Joinder; Merger.**

Unified credit. A credit against the federal Unified Transfer Tax, replacing the former lifetime gift tax exemption and the estate tax exemption.

Unified transfer tax. A federal tax applicable to transfers by gift and death made after 1976.

Uniform. Conforming to one rule, mode, pattern, or unvarying standard; not different at different times or places; applicable to all places or divisions of a country. Equable; applying alike to all within a class; sameness.

A statute is general and uniform in its operation when it operates equally upon all persons who are brought within the relations and circumstances provided for; when all persons under the same conditions and in the same circumstances are treated alike, and classification is reasonable and naturally inherent in the subject-matter. The words "general" and "uniform" as applied to laws have a meaning antithetical to special or discriminatory laws.

The burdens of taxation, to be uniform, must have the essential of equality, and must bear alike upon all the property within the limits of the unit wherein it is lawful to levy taxes for a purpose, whether that unit be the state, county, or a municipality. And requirement is met when tax is equal on all persons belonging to described class on which tax is imposed. With reference to locality, a tax is "uniform" when it operates with equal force and effect in every place where the subject of it is found, and with reference to classification, it is uniform when it operates without distinction or discrimination upon all persons composing the described class. Uniformity in taxation implies equality in the burden of taxation, which cannot exist without uniformity in the mode of assessment, as well as in the rate of taxation. Further, the uniformity must be coextensive with the territory to which it applies. And it must be extended to all property subject to taxation, so that all property may be taxed alike and equally. Edye v. Robertson, 112 U.S. 580, 5 S.Ct. 247, 28 L.Ed. 798.

Uniform Code of Military Justice. The body of law which governs military persons in their conduct as military personnel. 10 U.S.C.A. §§ 801–940. See **Code of Military Justice.**

Uniform Commercial Code. One of the Uniform Laws drafted by the National Conference of Commissioners on Uniform State Laws governing commercial transactions (sales of goods, commercial paper, bank deposits and collections, letters of credit, bulk transfers, warehouse receipts, bills of lading, investment securities, and secured transactions). The U.C.C. has been adopted by all states, except Louisiana.

Uniform Consumer Credit Code. (Also called the "U.3C.") A Uniform Law, adopted by some states: (a) to simplify, clarify, and modernize the law governing consumer credit and usury; (b) to provide rate ceilings to assure an adequate supply of credit to consumers; (c) to further consumer understanding of the terms of credit transactions and to foster competition among suppliers of consumer credit so that consumers may obtain credit at reasonable cost; (d) to protect consumers against unfair practices by some suppliers of consumer credit, having due regard for the interests of legitimate and scrupulous creditors; (e) to permit and encourage the development of fair and economically sound consumer credit practices; (f) to conform the regulation of disclosure in consumer credit transactions to the Federal Truth-in-Lending Act; and (g) to make uniform the law, including administrative rules, among the various jurisdictions. See also **Consumer Credit Protection Act; Truth-in-Lending Act.**

Uniform Controlled Substances Act. A uniform and comprehensive law governing use, sale, and distribution of drugs and narcotics adopted by most states, including Puerto Rico and the Virgin Islands. See **Controlled Substance Act.**

Uniform Divorce Recognition Act. One of the Uniform Laws adopted by some states governing questions of full faith and credit and recognition of divorces of sister states.

Uniform Gifts to Minors Act. See **Gifts to Minors Act.**

Uniformity. See **Uniform.**

Uniform Laws or Acts. Laws in various subject areas, approved by the Commissioners on Uniform State Laws, that are often adopted, in whole or substantially, by individual states. Examples are the Uniform Anatomical Gifts Act, the Reciprocal Enforcement of Support Act, and the Uniform Commercial Code. See also **Model Act.**

Uniform Principal and Income Act. One of the Uniform Laws adopted by some states governing allocation of principal and income in trusts and estates.

Uniform State laws. See **Model Act; Uniform Laws or Acts.**

Unify. To cause to be one; to make into a unit; to unite; to become one; to consolidate.

Unigeniture /yùwnəjénəchər/. The state of being the only begotten.

Unilateral. One-sided; ex parte; having relation to only one of two or more persons or things.

Unilateral contract. See **Contract.**

Unilateral mistake. A mistake or misunderstanding as to the terms or effect of a contract, made or entertained by one of the parties to it but not by the other.

Unilateral record. Records are unilateral when offered to show a particular fact, as a *prima facie* case, either for or against a stranger.

Unimproved land. A statutory term which includes lands, once improved, that have reverted to a state of nature, as well as lands that have never been improved.

Uninclosed place. A place not entirely inclosed, an "inclosed" place being a place inclosed on all sides by some sort of material.

Unincorporated association. Voluntary group of persons, without a charter, formed by mutual consent for purpose of promoting common enterprise or prosecuting common objective. Local 4076, United Steelworkers of America v. United Steelworkers of America, AFL–CIO, D.C.Pa., 327 F.Supp. 1400, 1402. An organization composed of a body of persons united with a charter for the prosecution of a common enterprise. Heifetz v. Rockaway Point Volunteer Fire Dept., Sup., 124 N.Y.S.2d 257, 260.

Uninfected. Untainted or uncontaminated, not affected unfavorably, not impregnated or permeated with that which is bad or harmful. Leonardi v. A. Habermann Provision Co., 143 Ohio St. 623, 56 N.E.2d 232, 237, 28 O.O. 511.

Uninsured motorist coverage. Protection afforded an insured by first party insurance against bodily injury inflicted by an uninsured motorist, after the liability of the uninsured motorist for the injury has been established. Sturdy v. Allied Mut. Ins. Co., 203 Kan. 783, 457 P.2d 34, 36. Purpose is to guarantee that the injured insured will be in the same position in the event of injury attributable to negligence of an uninsured motorist as the insured would be if he were injured through the negligence of a motorist carrying liability insurance. Jarstad v. National Farmers Union Property & Cas. Co., Nev., 552 P.2d 49, 50.

Uninsured motorist coverage in automobile liability policies is designed to close the gaps inherent in motor vehicle financial responsibility and compulsory insurance legislation, and this insurance coverage is intended, within fixed limits, to provide financial recompense to innocent persons who receive injuries and dependents of those who are killed, through the wrongful conduct of motorists who, because they are uninsured and not financially responsible, cannot be made to respond in damages. Wright v. Fidelity & Cas. Co. of New York, 270 N.C. 577, 155 S.E.2d 100, 106.

Unintelligible. That which cannot be understood.

Unio /yúwn(i)yow/. Lat. In canon law, a consolidation of two churches into one.

Union. An organization of workers, formed for the purpose of negotiating with employers on matters of wages, seniority, working conditions and the like.

A league; a federation; an unincorporated association of persons for a common purpose; as, a trade or labor union. A joinder of separate entities. State ex rel. Dawson v. Dinwiddie, 186 Okl. 63, 95 P.2d 867, 869.

A popular term in America for the United States; also, in Great Britain, for the consolidated governments of England and Scotland, or for the political tie between Great Britain and Ireland.

See also Agency shop; Bargaining unit; Craft union; Credit union; Labor organization; Labor union; Open shop; Preferential shop; Right-to-work laws.

Closed union. Union with highly restrictive membership requirements such as high initiation fees, and long apprenticeship periods. See also **Closed shop;** compare *Open union, infra.*

Company union. Union formed or sponsored by the employer. For all practical purposes, such union is now illegal because employers are prohibited from interfering with union representation by the National Labor Relations Act.

Craft union. Union composed of members of the same trade or craft, as carpenters, plumbers, etc. regardless of the company for which they work.

Horizontal union. A craft union which cuts across employer or industry lines.

Independent union. Union formed by employees of a particular employer without affiliation with an international union.

Industrial union. Union composed of workers in a particular industry regardless of their particular trade or craft, as for example, the United Automobile Workers union.

International union. A parent union with affiliates in other countries such as Canada and Mexico.

Local union. A union of workers in one plant or location but affiliated with a parent or larger union. The local is the bargaining unit of the union.

National union. A parent union with locals in various parts of the United States, though not outside the country.

Open union. A union whose admission requirements are relatively easy to meet. See also **Open shop;** compare *Closed union, supra.*

Trade union. Generically, a labor union. Restrictively, a craft union.

Union shop. Exists where all workers are union members.

Vertical union. An industrial union organized along lines of industry and not craft.

Union certification. The process by which an official, governmental body such as the National Labor Relations Board declares that a particular union has qualified as the bargaining representative of the employees of a company or industry by reason of a majority vote of the workers.

Union contract. A written agreement between the union and employer covering such matters as wages, seniority rights and working conditions.

Union-jack. The national flag of Great Britain and Ireland, which combines the banner of St. Patrick with the crosses of St. George and St. Andrew. The word "jack" is most probably derived from the surcoat, charged with a red cross, anciently used by the English soldiery. This appears to have been called a "jacque," whence the word "jacket," anciently written "jacquit." Some, however, without a shadow of evidence, derive the word from *"Jacques,"* the first alteration having been made in the reign of King James I.

Union mortgage clause. A clause, as in a fire policy (together with the rider making the loss, if any, payable to the mortgagee), which provides that if the policy is made payable to a mortgagee of the insured real estate, no act or default of any person other than such mortgagee, or his agents or those claiming under him, shall affect his right to recover in case of loss on such real estate. Prudential Ins. Co. of America v. German Mut. Fire Ins. Ass'n of Lohman, 231 Mo.App. 699, 105 S.W.2d 1001. Such clause creates independent contract between insurer and mortgagee and is distinguished from "open mortgage clause" in that latter clause simply provides that policy is payable to mortgagee as his interest may appear. Prudential Ins. Co. of America v. German Mut. Fire Ins. Ass'n of Lohman, 231 Mo.App. 699, 105 S.W.2d 1001. And mortgagee under such latter clause is merely an appointee to receive fund recoverable in case of loss to extent of his interest. Capital Fire Ins. Co. of Cal. v. Langhorne, C.C.A.Minn., 146 F.2d 237, 241.

Union rate. The wage scale set by a union as a minimum wage to be paid and generally expressed as an hourly rate or piece-work rate.

Union security clause. Provision in union contract which establishes status of union in a plant. It provides for the relation of the union to the workers and their positions. Any contract clause requiring some or all employees represented by a union to become or remain members of the union as a condition of employment.

Unissued stock. Stock of a corporation which has been authorized but is not outstanding.

Unit. A single thing of any kind. A term sometimes used in the sense of a share, as in an oil syndicate, or as equivalent to an investment security. With respect to labor unit, see **Bargaining unit.**

Unitas personarum. Lat. The unity of persons, as that between husband and wife, or ancestor and heir.

Unite. To join in an act; to concur; to act in concert.

United in interest. A statutory term applicable to codefendants only when they are similarly interested in and will be similarly affected by the determination of the issues involved in the action; *e.g.,* joint obligors upon a guaranty.

United Kingdom of Great Britain and Ireland. The official title of the kingdom composed of England, Scotland, Ireland, and Wales, and including the colonies and possessions beyond the seas, under the act of January 1, 1801, effecting the union between Ireland and Great Britain.

United Nations. An organization started by the allied powers in World War II for the stated purposes of preventing war, providing justice and promoting welfare and human rights of peoples. Its membership is made up of nearly all nations of the world. New members may be admitted by a two-thirds vote of the General Assembly. It consists of a Security Council and a General Assembly and subordinate agencies.

United States. This term has several meanings. It may be merely the name of a sovereign occupying the position analogous to that of other sovereigns in family of nations, it may designate territory over which sovereignty of United States extends, or it may be collective name of the states which are united by and under the Constitution. Hooven & Allison Co. v. Evatt, U.S.Ohio, 324 U.S. 652, 65 S.Ct. 870, 880, 89 L.Ed. 1252.

United States Attorney. A United States Attorney is appointed by the President for each judicial district. The general duties of U.S. attorneys are to: prosecute for all offenses against the United States; prosecute or defend, for the Government, all civil actions, suits or proceedings in which the United States is concerned; appear in behalf of the defendants in all civil actions, suits or proceedings pending in his district against collectors, or other officers of the revenue or customs for any act done by them or for the recovery of any money exacted by or paid to these officers, and by them paid into the Treasury; institute and prosecute proceedings for the collection of fines, penalties, and forfeitures incurred for violation of any revenue law, unless satisfied on investigation that justice does not require the proceedings. 28 U.S.C.A. § 547.

United States Code. Prior to 1926, the positive law for federal legislation was contained in the one volume of the Revised Statutes of 1875 and then in each subsequent volume of the Statutes at Large. In 1925,

Congress authorized the preparation of the United States Code. This was prepared by a Revisor of Statutes appointed by Congress, who extracted all sections of the Revised Statutes of 1875 that had not been repealed and then all of the public and general laws from the Statutes at Large since 1873 that were still in force. These were then rearranged into fifty titles and published as the United States Code, 1926 ed., in four volumes. Each year thereafter a cumulative supplement containing the laws passed since 1926 was published. In 1932 a new edition was issued which incorporated the cumulated supplements to the 1926 edition, and this became the United States Code, 1932 ed. Every six years a new edition of the U.S. Code is published with cumulative supplement volumes being issued during the intervening years.

United States Code Annotated. This multi-volume publication includes the complete text of the United States Code, together with case notes of state and federal decisions which construe and apply specific Code sections, cross references to related sections, historical notes, and library references. U.S.C.A. is further supplemented with United States Code Congressional and Administrative News.

United States Commissioners. See **Magistrate.**

United States Courts. Except in the case of impeachments, the judicial power of the United States is vested by the Constitution in a Supreme Court and such other inferior courts as may be from time to time established by congress. All the judges are appointed by the President, with the advice and consent of the senate, to hold office during good behavior, and their compensation cannot be diminished during their term of office. Art. III, U.S.Const. Such "inferior" courts include the Courts of Appeals, District Courts, Court of Claims, Customs Court, and Court of Customs and Patent Appeals. 28 U.S.C.A. § 1 *et seq.* See also specific courts.

United States currency. Commonly understood to include every form of currency authorized by the United States government, whether issued directly by it or under its authority. See **Legal tender.**

United States Magistrates. See **Magistrate.**

United States notes. See **Treasury bill; Treasury note.**

United States officer. Usually and strictly, in United States statutes, a person appointed in the manner declared under Art. II, § 2, U.S.Const., providing for the appointment of officers, either by the President and the Senate, the President alone, the courts of law, or the heads of departments, Steele v. U. S., 267 U.S. 505, 45 S.Ct. 417, 418, 69 L.Ed. 761; Dropps v. U. S., C.C.A.Minn., 34 F.2d 15, 17.

United States Reports. The official printed record of cases heard and decided by the U.S. Supreme Court which usually includes a syllabus of each case, the opinion of the Court, concurring and dissenting opinions, if any, the disposition made of each case, and orders of the Court. Originally a series of Reports was issued during the incumbency of each successive court reporter and such were cited as Dallas (1790–

1800); Cranch (1801–1815); Wheaton (1816–1827); Peters (1828–1843); Howard (1843–1860); Black (1861–1862); and Wallace (1863–1874). By 1874, when the number of volumes totalled 90, the practice began of eliminating the reporter's name and citing them as United States Reports.

United States Supreme Court. See **Supreme Court.**

Unit of production. The "unit of production" method of determining the taxable net income or profit in the oil or gas business is accomplished by a system of accounting by which is ascertained, as nearly as science will permit, the total amount of recoverable oil in the property, and to each barrel of this oil is assigned its part of the capital investment, and from the sale price of each barrel produced and sold there is deducted the expenses of producing it, and its proportion of the capital investment, leaving the balance as profit, and thus, when the property is exhausted, the operator has received back his capital and expenses, and accounted for his net income or loss.

Unit ownership acts. State laws governing condominium ownership. See **Planned unit development.**

Unit pricing. System under which contract items are priced per unit and not on the basis of a flat contract price.

Unit rule. A method of valuing securities by multiplying the total number of shares held by the sale price of one share sold on a licensed stock exchange, ignoring all other facts regarding value. Citizens Fidelity Bank & Trust Co. v. Reeves, Ky., 259 S.W.2d 432, 434.

Unitrust. A trust from which a fixed percentage of the net fair market value of the trust's assets, valued annually, is paid each year to the beneficiary. See also **Trust.**

Unity. In the law of estates, the peculiar characteristic of an estate held by several in joint tenancy, and which is fourfold, viz., unity of interest, unity of title, unity of time, and unity of possession. In other words, joint tenants have one and the same interest, accruing by one and the same conveyance, commencing at one and the same time, and held by one and the same undivided possession. 2 Bl.Comm. 180.

Unity of interest. As required in case of joint tenancy, means that interests must accrue by one and same conveyance. Hernandez v. Becker, C.C.A.N.M., 54 F.2d 542, 547. It also signifies that no one of joint tenants can have a greater interest in the property than each of the others, while, in the case of tenants in common, one of them may have a larger share than any of the others.

Unity of possession. Joint possession of two rights by several titles. Exists for example where a person takes a lease of land from another at a certain rent, and afterwards purchases the fee-simple of such land. By this he acquires unity of possession, by which the lease is extinguished. It is also one of the essential properties of a joint estate, requiring that the joint tenants must hold the same undivided possession of the whole and enjoy same rights until death of one. Hernandez v. Becker, C.C.A.N.M., 54 F.2d 542, 547.

Unity of seisin. Where a person seised of land which is subject to an easement, *profit à prendre,* or similar right, also becomes seised of the land to which the easement or other right is annexed.

Unity of time. One of the essential properties of a joint estate; the estates of the tenants being vested at one and the same period. 2 Bl.Comm. 181; Hernandez v. Becker, C.C.A.N.M., 54 F.2d 542, 547.

Unity of title. As applied to joint tenants, signifies that they hold their property by one and the same title, while tenants in common may take property by several titles.

Uniuscujusque contractus initium spectandum est, et causa /yənàyəsk(y)əjáskwiy kəntrǽktəs ənísh(iy)əm spektǽndəm èst, ét kózə/. The commencement and cause of every contract are to be regarded.

Unius omnino testis responsio non audiatur /yuwnáyəs omnáynow téstəs rəspónsh(iy)ow nón odiyéydər/. The answer of one witness shall not be heard at all; the testimony of a single witness shall not be admitted under any circumstances. A maxim of the civil and canon law.

Universal. Having relation to the whole or an entirety; pertaining to all without exception; a term more extensive than "general," which latter may admit of exceptions.

Universal agent. One who is appointed to do all the acts which the principal can personally do, and which he may lawfully delegate the power to another to do.

Universalia sunt notiora singularibus /yùwnəvərséyl(i)yə sə̀nt nòwshiyórə sìŋgyəlérəbəs/. Things universal are better known than things particular.

Universal legacy. See **Legacy.**

Universal partnership. See **Partnership.**

Universal succession. In the civil law, succession to the entire estate of another, living or dead, though generally the latter, importing succession to the entire property of the predecessor as a juridical entirety, that is, to all his active as well as passive legal relations.

Universitas /yùwnəvársətæs/. Lat. In the civil law, a corporation aggregate. Literally, a whole formed out of many individuals. 1 Bl.Comm. 469.

Universitas facti /yùwnəvársətæs fǽktay/. In the civil law, a plurality of corporeal things of the same kind, which are regarded as a whole; *e.g.,* a herd of cattle, a stock of goods.

Universitas juris /yùwnəvársətæs júrəs/. In the civil law, a quantity of things of all sorts, corporeal as well as incorporeal, which, taken together, are regarded as a whole; *e.g.,* an inheritance, an estate.

Universitas rerum /yùwnəvársətæs rírəm/. In the civil law, literally, a whole of things. Several single things, which, though not mechanically connected with one another, are, when taken together, regarded as a whole in any legal respect.

Universitas vel corporatio non dicitur aliquid facere nisi id sit collegialiter deliberatum, etiamsi major pars id

faciat /yùwnəvársətæs vèl kòrpəréysh(iy)ow nòn dísədər ǽləkwid fǽsəriy náysay id sít kəliyjiyéylədər dəlibəréydəm, èshiyǽmsay méyjər párz id féysh(iy)ət/. A university or corporation is not said to do anything unless it be deliberated upon as a body, although the majority should do it.

University. An institution of higher learning, consisting of an assemblage of colleges united under one corporate organization and government, affording instruction in the arts and sciences and the learned professions, and conferring degrees.

Universus /yùwnəvársəs/. Lat. The whole; all together.

Unjust. Contrary to right and justice, or to the enjoyment of his rights by another, or to the standards of conduct furnished by the laws.

Unjust enrichment, doctrine of. General principle that one person should not be permitted unjustly to enrich himself at expense of another, but should be required to make restitution of or for property or benefits received, retained or appropriated, where it is just and equitable that such restitution be made, and where such action involves no violation or frustration of law or opposition to public policy, either directly or indirectly. Tulalip Shores, Inc. v. Mortland, 9 Wash. App. 271, 511 P.2d 1402, 1404. Unjust enrichment of a person occurs when he has and retains money or benefits which in justice and equity belong to another. Hummel v. Hummel, 133 Ohio St. 520, 14 N.E.2d 923, 927. Thus one who has conferred a benefit upon another solely because of a basic mistake of fact induced by a nondisclosure is entitled to restitution on above doctrine. Conkling's Estate v. Champlin, 193 Okl. 79, 141 P.2d 569, 570.

Unknown persons. Persons whose identities cannot be ascertained.

Unkouth /ənkúwθ/. Unknown. The law French form of the Saxon "uncouth."

Unlage. Sax. An unjust law.

Unlawful. That which is contrary to, prohibited, or unauthorized by law. That which is not lawful. The acting contrary to, or in defiance of the law; disobeying or disregarding the law. While necessarily not implying the element of criminality, it is broad enough to include it.

Unlawful act. Act contrary to law, and presupposes that there must be an existing law. A violation of some prohibitory law and includes all willful, actionable violations of civil rights, and is not confined to criminal acts. State v. Hailey, 350 Mo. 300, 165 S.W.2d 422, 427. The "unlawful acts" within manslaughter statutes consist of reckless conduct or conduct evincing marked disregard for safety of others. State v. Newton, 105 Utah 561, 144 P.2d 290, 293; State v. Thatcher, 108 Utah 63, 157 P.2d 258, 261.

Unlawful assembly. At common law, the meeting together of three or more persons, to the disturbance of the public peace, and with the intention of co-operat-

ing in the forcible and violent execution of some unlawful private enterprise. If they take steps towards the performance of their purpose, it becomes a *rout;* and, if they put their design into actual execution, it is a *riot.* 4 Bl.Comm. 146. An unlawful assembly is a meeting of three or more persons with a common plan in mind which, if carried out, will result in a riot. In other words, it is such a meeting with intent to (a) commit a crime by open force, or (b) execute a common design lawful or unlawful, in an unauthorized manner likely to cause courageous persons to apprehend a breach of the peace.

Unlawful assembly is the meeting or coming together of not less than five (5) persons for the purpose of engaging in conduct constituting either disorderly conduct, or a riot, or when in a lawful assembly of not less than five (5) persons, agreeing to engage in such conduct. Kansas Criminal Code.

See also **Riot.**

Unlawful belligerents. Enemies passing the boundaries of the United States for purpose of destroying war industries and supplies without a uniform or other emblem signifying their belligerent status or discarding that means of identification after entry. Ex parte Quirin, App.D.C., 317 U.S. 1, 63 S.Ct. 2, 15, 87 L.Ed. 3.

Unlawful detainer. The unjustifiable retention of the possession of lands by one whose original entry was lawful and of right, but whose right to the possession has terminated and who refuses to quit, as in the case of a tenant holding over after the termination of the lease and in spite of a demand for possession by the landlord. Brandley v. Lewis, 97 Utah 217, 92 P.2d 338, 339. Actions of "unlawful detainer" concern only right of possession of realty, and differ from ejectment in that no ultimate question of title or estate can be determined. McCracken v. Wright, 159 Kan. 615, 157 P.2d 814, 817. See also **Detainer; Forcible detainer.**

Unlawful entry. An entry upon lands effected peaceably and without force, but which is without color of title and is accomplished by means of fraud or some other willful wrong.

Unlawfully. Illegally; wrongfully. See **Unlawful; Unlawful act.**

This word is frequently used in indictments in the description of the offence; it was formerly necessary when the crime did not exist at common law, and when a statute, in describing an offence which it created, used the word; but was unnecessary whenever the crime existed at common law and was manifestly illegal.

Unlawful picketing. Picketing which is not honest or truthful. Park & Tilford Import Corporation v. International Brotherhood of Teamsters, Chauffeurs, Warehousemen and Helpers of America, Local No. 848, A. F. of L., Cal.App., 139 P.2d 963, 971; Magill Bros. v. Building Service Employees' International Union, 20 Cal.2d 506, 127 P.2d 542, 543. Picketing which involves false statements or misrepresentations of facts. Wiest v. Dirks, 215 Ind. 568, 20 N.E.2d 969, 971. Picketing when it ceases to serve the purpose it seeks to accomplish. E. M. Loew's Enterprises v. International Alliance of Theatrical Stage Employees, 125 Conn. 391, 6 A.2d 321, 323. When force or violence is used to persuade or prevent workers from continuing their employment. Ex parte Bell, 37 Cal.App.2d 582, 100 P.2d 339, 343. See also **Picketing.**

Unless. If it be not that; if it be not the case that; if not; supposing not; if it be not; except. A reservation or option to change one's mind provided a certain event happens, a conditional promise. A subordinate conjunction in common usage, connecting a dependent or subordinate clause to the main clause of a sentence. Kansas City Structural Steel Co. v. L. G. Barcus & Sons, Inc., 217 Kan. 88, 535 P.2d 419, 423.

Unless lease. An oil and gas lease which provides that lease will be rendered null and void and lessee will automatically be relieved from liability, upon failure to commence operations or to pay rent. It must be expressly stipulated in the lease that lease shall become null and void at a certain time "unless" the lessee begins operations or pays the rental stipulated. Where the word "unless" precedes the description of the act to be performed under an oil lease, no obligation to perform that act is imposed by the lease. McCrabb v. Moulton, C.C.A.Mo., 124 F.2d 689, 691.

Unlimited. Without confines, unrestricted, boundless.

Unliquidated. Not ascertained in amount; not determined; remaining unassessed or unsettled, as unliquidated damages; Davies v. Turner, 61 Ga.App. 531, 6 S.E.2d 356, 358. A debt is spoken of as "unliquidated," if the amount thereof cannot be ascertained at the trial by a mere computation, based on the terms of the obligation or on some other accepted standard. Hettrick Mfg. Co. v. Barish, 120 Misc. 673, 199 N.Y.S. 755, 767. Under the law of accord and satisfaction, a claim or debt will be regarded as unliquidated if it is in dispute as to the proper amount. Paulsen Estate v. Naches-Selah Irr. Dist., 190 Wash. 205, 67 P.2d 856, 858.

Unliquidated claim. A claim which has not been finally determined either as to liability or damages. A disputed claim. See also **Unliquidated.**

Unliquidated damages. Damages which have not been determined or calculated. See also **Damages.**

Unliquidated debt. See **Unliquidated.**

Unliquidated demand. Such exists where it is admitted that one of two specific sums is due, but there is a dispute as to which is proper amount. Perryman Burns Coal Co. v. Seaboard Coal Co. of Connecticut, 128 Conn. 70, 20 A.2d 404, 405.

Unlivery. A term used in maritime law to designate the unloading of cargo of a vessel at the place where it is properly to be delivered.

Unloading. Act of discharging a cargo; taking a load from; disburdening or removing from. American Oil & Supply Co. v. United States Casualty Co., 19 N.J. Misc. 7, 18 A.2d 257, 259.

An unloading clause in an automobile liability policy covers the entire process involved in the movement of articles by and from a motor vehicle to the place where they are turned over to the one to whom the insured is to make delivery, if the clause is con-

strued in accordance with what may be called the "complete operation" rule. Pacific Auto. Ins. Co. v. Commercial Cas. Ins. Co. of N. Y., 108 Utah 500, 161 P.2d 423. There are, however, two other rules or doctrines used by various courts in applying the unloading clause of such a policy. One is known as the "coming to rest" rule, and the other is the "continuous passage" rule. But the complete operation rule is said to be the modern doctrine, supported by the trend of the later cases. London Guarantee & Acc. Co. v. C. B. White & Bros., 188 Va. 195, 49 S.E.2d 254.

In determining whether activity constitutes "unloading" within meaning of insurance policy which provides coverage for liability arising out of loading and unloading truck, "complete operations" rule is followed under which "unloading" embraces all operations required in any specific situation to effect a complete delivery of the article; the number of temporary or intermediate stops or resting places is immaterial. Manhattan Fire & Marine Ins. Co. v. Travelers Ins. Co., 66 Cal.App.3d 794, 136 Cal.Rptr. 400, 402. "Loading or unloading" within homeowner's policy excluding personal liability coverage with respect to "loading or unloading" of automobiles has primary reference to objects transported from one place for delivery to some at least temporary final destination. Morari v. Atlantic Mut. Fire Ins. Co., 10 Ariz.App. 142, 457 P.2d 304, 306. "Unloading" as used in a motor vehicle liability policy has been completed when, following removal of the material from the vehicle, the deliverer has finished his handling of it and has placed the material in the hands of the receiver at the designated reception point, even though it is necessary for the consignee, or someone in his behalf, to transport it thereafter to another point. General Acc. Fire & Life Assur. Corp. v. Liberty Mut. Ins. Co., Fla.App., 260 So.2d 249, 255.

Unlooked for mishap or untoward event. One occurring unexpectedly and not naturally or in ordinary course of events.

Unmarketable title. Exists when for vendee to accept title proffered such would lay him open to fair probability of vexatious litigation with possibility of serious loss. It being sufficient to render it so if ordinarily prudent man with knowledge of the facts and aware of legal questions involved would not accept it in the ordinary course of business but title need not be bad in fact. Barrett v. McMannis, 153 Kan. 420, 110 P.2d 774, 777, 778; Ayers v. Graff, 153 Kan. 209, 109 P.2d 202, 203; Ghormley v. Kleeden, 155 Kan. 319, 124 P.2d 467, 470. Exists where some defect of substantial character exists and facts are known which fairly raise reasonable doubt as to title. Schul v. Clapp, 154 Kan. 372, 118 P.2d 570, 574. Title is "unmarketable" where it is of such a character as to expose the purchaser to the hazards of litigation and where there are outstanding possible interests in third persons. Boecher v. Borth, 377 N.Y.S.2d 781, 784. And mere quibbles and pecadilloes which the ingenuity of counsel can raise against a title do not alone render it an "unmarketable title". Barrett v. McMannis, 153 Kan. 420, 110 P.2d 774, 778. Compare **Marketable title.**

Unmarried. Its primary meaning is never having been married; but it is a word of flexible meaning and it may be construed as not having a husband or wife at the time in question; *e.g.* widow or widower or divorcee.

Unnatural offense. The infamous crime against nature; *i.e.,* sodomy or buggery.

Unnatural will. An expression applied to disposition of estate or large portion thereof to strangers, to exclusion of natural objects of testator's bounty without apparent reason.

Unnecessary. Not required by the circumstances of the case.

Unnecessary hardship. Unnecessary hardship, sufficient to establish basis for granting variance, is shown by establishing that: physical characteristics of property are such that it could not be used for any permitted purpose; property could be so used only at prohibitive expense; or that characteristics of area are such that property has no value or any distress value for any permitted purpose. Eighteenth & Rittenhouse Associates v. Zoning Bd. of Adjustment, 26 Pa.Cmwlth. 554, 364 A.2d 973, 975. Within zoning ordinance so as to authorize granting of variance on such ground if land cannot yield a reasonable return if used only for a purpose allowed in zone, such exists where the plight of owner is due to unique circumstances not to general conditions in the neighborhood and use to be authorized will not alter essential character of the locality. Calcagno v. Town Board of Town of Webster, 265 App.Div. 687, 41 N.Y.S.2d 140, 142. It has also been said that test whether terms of zoning ordinance impose an "unnecessary hardship" depends on whether use restriction is so unreasonable as to constitute an arbitrary interference with basic right of private property. Scaduto v. Town of Bloomfield, 127 N.J.L. 1, 20 A.2d 649, 650.

Un ne doit prise advantage de son tort demesne /ən nə dwá príyz advontázh də sòn tór dəméyn/. One ought not to take advantage of his own wrong.

Uno absurdo dato, infinita sequuntur /yúwnow əbsárdow déydow ìnfənáydə səkwántər/. One absurdity being allowed, an infinity follows.

Uno actu /yúwnow ǽkt(y)uw/. Lat. In a single act; by one and the same act.

Unoccupied. Within fire policy exempting insurer from liability in case dwelling is "unoccupied," means when it is not used as a residence, when it is no longer used for the accustomed and ordinary purposes of a dwelling or place of abode, or when it is not the place of usual return and habitual stoppage. Hence a mere temporary absence of occupants of dwelling house from such premises, with intention to return thereto does not render dwelling "unoccupied". Foley v. Sonoma County Farmers' Mut. Fire Ins. Co., 18 Cal.2d 232, 115 P.2d 1, 2, 3. See **Occupation.**

Uno flatu /yúwnow fléyt(y)uw/. Lat. In one breath. *Uno flatu, et uno intuitu,* at one breath, and in one view.

Unprecedented. Having no precedent or example, novel, new, unexampled. State v. Malone, Tex.Civ.App., 168 S.W.2d 292, 300. Unusual and extraordinary; affording no reasonable warning or expectation of recurrence.

Unprecedented rainfall. An unusual and extraordinary rainfall as has no example or parallel in the history of rainfall in the vicinity affected, or as affords no reasonable warning or expectation that it will likely occur again.

Unprofessional conduct. That which is by general opinion considered to be unprofessional because immoral, unethical or dishonorable. State Board of Dental Examiners v. Savelle, 90 Colo. 177, 8 P.2d 693, 697. That which violates ethical code of profession (*e.g.* Code of Professional Responsibility *(q.v.)*) or such conduct which is unbecoming member of profession in good standing. It involves breach of duty which professional ethics enjoin. Within statutes, rules, etc., promulgating standards of professional conduct for attorneys denotes conduct which it is recommended be made subject to disciplinary sanctions. Hawk v. Superior Court In and For Solano County, 42 C.A.3d 108, 116 Cal.Rptr. 713, 721.

Unques /áŋkwiyz/áŋkwiyz/. L. Fr. Ever; always. *Ne unques,* never.

Unques prist /áŋkwiyz príst/. L. Fr. Always ready. Another form of *tout temps prist.*

Unreasonable. Irrational; foolish; unwise; absurd; silly; preposterous; senseless; stupid. Southern Kansas State Lines Co. v. Public Service Commission, 135 Kan. 657, 11 P.2d 985, 987. Not reasonable; immoderate; exorbitant. Cass v. State, 124 Tex.Cr.R. 208, 61 S.W.2d 500. Capricious; arbitrary; confiscatory. Harris v. State Corporation Commission, 46 N.M. 352, 129 P.2d 323, 328.

Unreasonable appreciation. An unrealized holding gain; frequently used in the context of marketable securities. A paper profit *(q.v.).* See also **Equity.**

Unreasonable compensation. Under the Internal Revenue Code, a deduction is allowed for "reasonable" salaries or other compensation for personal services actually rendered. To the extent compensation is "excessive" (*i.e.,* "unreasonable"), no deduction will be allowed. The problem of unreasonable compensation usually is limited to closely-held corporations where the motivation is to pay out profits in some form deductible to the corporation. Deductible compensation, therefore, becomes an attractive substitute for nondeductible dividends when the shareholders also are employed by the corporation.

Unreasonable refusal to submit to operation. An injured employee's refusal to submit to an operation is unreasonable, so as to deprive him or her of right to workers' compensation if it appears that an operation of a simple character not involving serious suffering or danger will result in substantial physical improvement. Black Star Coal Co. v. Surgener, 297 Ky. 653, 181 S.W.2d 53, 54.

Unreasonable restraint of trade. Within Sherman Anti-Trust Act, term refers to agreements for price maintenance of articles moving in interstate commerce. Sherman Anti-Trust Act, § 1, 15 U.S.C.A. § 1. American Tobacco Co. v. U. S., C.C.A.Ky., 147 F.2d 93, 108. Any combination or conspiracy that operates directly on prices or price structure and has for its purpose the fixing of prices. United States v. Waltham

Watch Co., D.C.N.Y., 47 F.Supp. 524, 531. See **Price-fixing; Restraint of trade; Robinson-Patman Act.**

Unreasonable restraint on alienation. Such act is brought about by gift of absolute ownership in property followed by such condition as takes away incidents of such ownership.

Unreasonable search. See **Probable cause; Search.**

Unrelated offenses. Evidence of other crimes, wrongs, or acts is not admissible to prove the character of a person in order to show that he acted in conformity therewith. It may, however, be admissible for other purposes, such as proof of motive, opportunity, intent, preparation, plan, knowledge, identity, or absence of mistake or accident. Fed.Evid.R. 404(b).

Unresponsive evidence. In evidence, an answer to a question which is irrelevant to the question asked.

Unruly and dangerous animals. Within the meaning of the law, such as are likely to injure other domestic animals and persons.

Unsafe. Dangerous; not secure.

Unseaworthy. A vessel which is unable to withstand the perils of an ordinary voyage at sea. Fireman's Fund Ins. Co. v. Compania de Navegacion, Interior, S. A., C.C.A.La., 19 F.2d 493, 495. One that could not reasonably have been expected to make the voyage. Interlake Iron Corporation v. Gartland S. S. Co., C.C. A.Mich., 121 F.2d 267, 269, 270. One not manned by a competent crew; or not carrying proper navigational charts. But a ship is not unseaworthy where defect in ship is such that defect can be remedied on the spot in a short time by materials available. Middleton & Co. (Canada) Limited v. Ocean Dominion Steamship Corporation, C.C.A.N.Y., 137 F.2d 619, 622. Compare **Seaworthy.**

Unsolemn war. War denounced without a declaration; war made not upon general but special declaration; imperfect war. People v. McLeod, 1 Hill, N.Y., 409, 37 Am.Dec. 328.

Unsolemn will. In the civil law, one in which an executor is not appointed.

Unsound mind. Non-legal term referring to one who from infirmity of mind is incapable of managing himself or his affairs. The term, therefore, includes insane persons (see **Insanity**). It exists where there is an essential privation of the reasoning faculties, or where a person is incapable of understanding and acting with discretion in the ordinary affairs of life. Oklahoma Natural Gas Corporation v. Lay, 175 Okl. 75, 51 P.2d 580, 582. But eccentricity, uncleanliness, slovenliness, neglect of person and clothing, and offensive and disgusting personal habits do not constitute unsoundness of mind. See also **Capacity.**

Unthrift. A prodigal; a spendthrift. 1 Bl.Comm. 306.

Until. Up to time of. A word of limitation, used ordinarily to restrict that which precedes to what immediately follows it, and its office is to fix some point of time or some event upon the arrival or occurrence of which what precedes will cease to exist. Empire Oil and Refining Co. v. Babson, 182 Okl. 336, 77 P.2d 682, 684.

Untoward event. See **Unlooked for mishap.**

Untrue. *Prima facie* inaccurate, but not necessarily wilfully false. A statement is "untrue" which does not express things exactly as they are. Zolintakis v. Equitable Life Assur. Soc. of United States, C.C.A. Utah, 108 F.2d 902, 905. See **Misrepresentation.**

Unumquodque dissolvitur eodem ligamine quo ligatur /yùwnəmkwódkwiy dəzólvədər iyówdəm ləgéymaniy kwòw ləgéydər/. Every obligation is dissolved by the same solemnity with which it is created.

Unumquodque eodem modo quo colligatum est, dissolvitur,—quo constituitur, destruitur /yùwnəmkwódkwiy iyówdəm mówdow kwòw kolagéydəm èst, dəzólvədər, kwów kònstətyúwədər, dəstrúwədər/. Everything is dissolved by the same means by which it is put together,—destroyed by the same means by which it is established.

Unumquodque est id quod est principalius in ipso /yùwnəmkwódkwiy èst íd kwòd ést prìn(t)səpéyl(i)yəs in ípsow/. That which is the principal part of a thing is the thing itself.

Unumquodque principiorum est sibimetipsi fides; et perspicua vera non sunt probanda /yùwnəmkwódkwiy prin(t)sipiyórəm èst síbaymədípsay fáydiyz, èt pərspíkyuwə vírə nón sànt prəbǽndə/. Every general principle [or maxim of law] is its own pledge or warrant; and things that are clearly true are not to be proved.

Unus nullus rule, the /ðə yúwnəs nǽləs rúwl/. The rule of evidence which obtains in the civil law, that the testimony of *one* witness is equivalent to the testimony of *none.*

Unusual. Uncommon; not usual, rare. Thompson v. Anderson, 107 Utah 331, 153 P.2d 665, 666.

Unusual punishment. See **Corporal punishment; Punishment** (*Cruel and unusual punishment*).

Unvalued policy. One where the value of property insured is not settled in policy, and in case of loss must be agreed on or proved. Hartford Live Stock Ins. Co. v. Gibson, 256 Ky. 338, 76 S.W.2d 17, 18.

Unwholesome food. Food not fit to be eaten; food which if eaten would be injurious.

Unworthy. Unbecoming; discreditable; not having suitable qualities or value.

Unwritten law. All that portion of the law, observed and administered in the courts, which has not been enacted or promulgated in the form of a statute or ordinance, including the unenacted portions of the common law, general and particular customs having the force of law, and the rules, principles, and maxims established by judicial precedents or the successive like decisions of the courts. See also **Natural law.**

UPA. Uniform Partnership Act.

Upkeep. The act of keeping up or maintaining; maintenance, repair.

Uplands. Lands bordering on bodies of waters.

Uplifted hand. The hand raised towards the heavens, in one of the forms of taking an oath, instead of being laid upon the Gospels.

Upper bench. The court of king's bench, in England, was so called during the interval between 1649 and 1660, the period of the commonwealth, Rolle being then chief justice. See 3 Bl.Comm. 202.

Upset price. The price at which any subject, as lands or goods, is exposed to sale by auction, below which it is not to be sold. In a final decree in foreclosure, the decree should name an upset price large enough to cover costs and all allowances made by the court, receiver's certificates and interest, liens prior to the bonds, amounts diverted from the earnings, and all undetermined claims which will be settled before the confirmation and sale.

U.R. Initials of *"uti rogas,"* be it as you desire, a ballot thus inscribed, by which the Romans voted in favor of a bill or candidate.

Urban. Of or belonging to a city or town. Within city limits. Derived from the Latin "urbanis," which in that language imports the same meaning. City of South Pasadena v. City of San Gabriel, 134 Cal.App. 403, 25 P.2d 516.

Urban homestead. See **Homestead.**

Urban renewal. Comprehensive term embracing redevelopment plan indicating its relationship to such local objectives as appropriate land uses, improved traffic, public transportation, public utilities, recreation, community facilities and other public improvements. It also includes acquisition of air rights over highways and railroads which have a blighting influence if the rights are developed for low or moderate income housing.

Urban servitude. In the civil law, city servitudes, or servitudes of houses are called "urban." They are the easements appertaining to the building and construction of houses; as, for instance, the right to light and air, or the right to build a house so as to throw the rain-water on a neighbor's house.

Urbs /árbz/. Lat. In Roman law, a city, or a walled town. Sometimes it is put for *civitas,* and denotes the inhabitants, or both the city and its inhabitants; *i.e.,* the municipality or commonwealth. By way of special pre-eminence, *urbs* meant the city of Rome.

Ure /yúr/. L. Fr. Effect; practice. *Mis en ure,* put in practice; carried into effect.

U.S. An abbreviation for "United States."

Usage. A reasonable and lawful public custom in a locality concerning particular transactions which is either known to the parties, or so well established, general, and uniform that they must be presumed to have acted with reference thereto. Practice in fact. Electrical Research Products v. Gross, C.C.A.Alaska, 120 F.2d 301, 305. Uniform practice or course of conduct followed in certain lines of business or professions or some procedure or phase thereof. Turner v. Donovan, 3 Cal.App.2d 485, 39 P.2d 858, 859. Usage cannot be proved by isolated instances, but must be certain, uniform and notorious. Unkovich v.

New York Cent. R. Co., 128 N.J.Eq. 377, 16 A.2d 558, 561. Habitual or customary practice which prevails within geographical or sociological area, and is course of conduct based upon series of actual occurrences, and in order to be controlling upon parties to contract, it must be adopted by them, or be well known to parties or to persons in their circumstances. Sam Levitz Furniture Co. v. Safeway Stores, Inc., 10 Ariz.App. 225, 457 P.2d 938, 941. See also **Custom and usage; Local usage; Trade usage.**

"Custom" distinguished. "Usage" is a repetition of acts, and differs from "custom" in that the latter is the law or general rule which arises from such repetition; while there may be usage without custom, there cannot be a custom without a usage accompanying or preceding it. U. S. for Use of E & R Const. Co., Inc. v. Guy H. James Const. Co., D.C.Tenn., 390 F.Supp. 1193, 1209. It is distinguished from "custom" in that "usage" derives its efficacy from assent of parties to transaction, and hence is important only in consensual agreements, while "custom" derives its efficacy from its adoption into the law, is binding irrespective of any manifestation of assent by parties concerned, and may be of importance in any department of law. Gulf Refining Co. v. Universal Ins. Co., C.C.A.N.Y., 32 F.2d 555, 557.

Fair usage. See **Fair use doctrine.**

General usage. One which prevails generally throughout the country, or is followed generally by a given profession or trade, and is not local in its nature or observance.

Usage of trade. A course of dealing; a mode of conducting transactions of a particular kind. A mode of dealing generally observed in a particular trade. United States v. Stanolind Crude Oil Purchasing Co., C.C.A.Okl., 113 F.2d 194, 200; Codd v. Westchester Fire Ins. Co., 14 Wash.2d 600, 128 P.2d 968, 973.

A usage of trade is any practice or method of dealing having such regularity of observance in a place, vocation or trade as to justify an expectation that it will be observed with respect to the transaction in question. The existence and scope of such a usage are to be proved as facts. If it is established that such a usage is embodied in a written trade code or similar writing the interpretation of the writing is for the court. U.C.C. § 1–205(2). See also **Course of dealing.**

Usance. In mercantile law, the common period fixed by the usage or custom or habit of dealing between the country where a bill is drawn, and that where it is payable, for the payment of bills of exchange. It means, in some countries, a month, in others two or more months, and in others half a month.

U.S.C. United States Code.

U.S.C.A. United States Code Annotated.

U.S.D.C. United States District Court.

Use, *v.* To make use of, to convert to one's service, to avail one's self of, to employ. Hopkins v. Howard's Ex'x, 266 Ky. 685, 99 S.W.2d 810, 812. To leave no capacity of force or use in. Bridgeport Mach. Co. v. McKnab, 136 Kan. 781, 18 P.2d 186, 187.

Use, *n.* Act of employing everything, or state of being employed; application, as the use of a pen, or his machines are in use. Also the fact of being used or employed habitually; usage, as, the wear and tear resulting from ordinary use. Berry-Kofron Dental Laboratory Co. v. Smith, 345 Mo. 922, 137 S.W.2d 452, 454, 455, 456. The purpose served; a purpose, object or end for useful or advantageous nature. Brown v. Kennedy, Ohio App., 49 N.E.2d 417, 418. To put or bring into action or service; to employ for or apply to a given purpose. Beggs v. Texas Dept. of Mental Health and Mental Retardation, Tex.Civ.App., 496 S.W.2d 252, 254. To avail oneself of; to employ; to utilize; to carry out a purpose or action by means of; to put into action or service, especially to attain an end. State v. Howard, 221 Kan. 51, 557 P.2d 1280, 1281.

A confidence reposed in another, who was made tenant of the land, or terre-tenant, that he would dispose of the land according to the intention of the *cestui que use,* or him to whose use it was granted, and suffer him to take the profits. 2 Bl.Comm. 328.

That enjoyment of property which consists in its employment, occupation, exercise or practice. Central Sur. & Ins. Corp. v. Anderson, Tex.Civ.App., 446 S.W.2d 897, 903.

A right in one person, called the *"cestui que use,"* to take the profits of land of which another has the legal title and possession, together with the duty of defending the same, and of making estates thereof according to the direction of the *cestui que use.*

Uses and *trusts* are not so much different things as different aspects of the same subject. A use regards principally the beneficial interest; a trust regards principally the nominal ownership. The usage of the two terms is, however, widely different. The word "use" is employed to denote either an estate vested since the statute of uses, and by force of that statute, or to denote such an estate created before the statute as, had it been created since, would have become a legal estate by force of the statute. The word "trust" is employed since that statute to denote the relation between the party invested with the legal estate (whether by force of that statute or independently of it) and the party beneficially entitled, who has hitherto been said to have the equitable estate.

See also Beneficial use; Best use; Charitable use; Conforming use; Exclusive use; Highest and best use; Nonconforming use; Public use; Raising a use; Unauthorized use.

Civil law. A right of receiving so much of the natural profits of a thing as is necessary to daily sustenance. It differs from "usufruct," which is a right not only to use, but to enjoy.

Right given to any one to make a gratuitous use of a thing belonging to another, or to exact such a portion of the fruit it produces as is necessary for his personal wants and those of his family. Civ.Code La. art. 626.

Conveyancing. "Use" literally means "benefit;" thus, in an ordinary assignment of chattels, the assignor transfers the property to the assignee for his "absolute use and benefit." In the expressions "separate use," "superstitious use," and "charitable use," "use" has the same meaning.

Non-technical sense. The "use" of a thing means that one is to enjoy, hold, occupy, or have some manner of benefit thereof. Use also means usefulness, utility, advantage, productive of benefit.

Generally

Cestui que use. A person for whose use and benefit lands or tenements are held by another. The latter, before the statute of uses, was called the "feoffee to use," and held the nominal or legal title.

Charitable use. See **Charitable.**

Contingent use. A use limited to take effect upon the happening of some future contingent event; as where lands are conveyed to the use of A. and B., after a marriage shall be had between them.

Exclusive use. See **Exclusive use.**

Executed use. The first use in a conveyance upon which the statute of uses operates by bringing the possession to it, the combination of which, *i.e.,* the use and the possession, form the legal estate, and thus the statute is said to execute the use.

Executory uses. These are springing uses, which confer a legal title answering to an executory devise; as when a limitation to the use of A. in fee is defeasible by a limitation to the use of B., to arise at a future period, or on a given event.

Feoffee to uses. A person to whom (before the statute of uses) land was conveyed "for the use" of a third person. He held the nominal or legal title, while the third person, called the *"cestui que use,"* was entitled to the beneficial enjoyment of the estate.

Official use. An active use before the statute of uses, which imposed some duty on the legal owner or feoffee to uses; as a conveyance to A. with directions for him to sell the estate and distribute the proceeds among B., C., and D. To enable A. to perform this duty, he had the legal possession of the estate to be sold.

Passive use. A permissive use (*q.v.*).

Permissive use. A passive use which was resorted to before the statute of uses, in order to avoid a harsh law; as that of mortmain or a feudal forfeiture. It was a mere invention in order to evade the law by secrecy; as a conveyance to A. to the use of B. A. simply held the possession, and B. enjoyed the profits of the estate.

Resulting use. A use raised by equity for the benefit of a feoffor who has made a voluntary conveyance to uses without any declaration of the use. A resulting use arises where the legal seisin is transferred, and no use is expressly declared, nor any consideration or evidence of intent to direct the use. The use then remains in the original grantor, for it cannot be supposed that the estate was intended to be given away, and the statute immediately transfers the legal estate to such resulting use.

Secondary use. A use limited to take effect in derogation of a preceding estate, otherwise called a "shifting use," as a conveyance to the use of A. and his heirs, with a proviso that, when B. returns from India, then to the use of C. and his heirs.

Shifting use. A use which is so limited that it will be made to shift or transfer itself, from one beneficiary to another, upon the occurrence of a certain event after its creation. For example, an estate is limited to the use of A. and his heirs, provided that, upon the return of B. from Rome, it shall be to the use of C. and his heirs; this is a shifting use, which transfers itself to C. when the event happens. 2 Bl.Comm. 335. These shifting uses are common in all settlements; and, in marriage settlements, the first use is always to the owner in fee till the marriage, and then to other uses. The fee remains with the owner until the marriage, and then it *shifts* as uses arise.

Springing use. A use limited to arise on a future event where no preceding use is limited, and which does not take effect in derogation of any other interest than that which results to the grantor, or remains in him in the meantime.

Statute of uses. An English statute enacted in 1536 (27 Hen. VIII, c. 10), directed against the practice of creating uses in lands, and which converted the purely equitable title of persons entitled to a use into a legal title or absolute ownership with right of possession. The statute is said to "execute the use," that is, it abolishes the intervening estate of the feoffee to uses, and makes the beneficial interest of the *cestui que use* an absolute legal title.

Superstitious use. See that title.

Use and habitation. Within a grant does not mean the exclusive use and habitation, but the necessities of the grantee are determinative of extent of privileges to be enjoyed. Barrett v. Barrett, La.App., 5 So.2d 381, 383.

Use and occupation. This is the name of an action, being a variety of *assumpsit,* to be maintained by a landlord against one who has had the occupation and enjoyment of an estate, under a contract to pay therefor, express or implied, but not under such a lease as would support an action specifically for rent. Thackray v. Ritz, 130 Misc. 403, 223 N.Y.S. 668, 669.

Use plaintiff. In common law pleading, one for whose use (benefit) an action is brought in the name of another. Thus, where the assignee of a chose in action is not allowed to sue in his own name, the action would be entitled "A. B. (the assignor) for the Use of C. D. (the assignee) against E. F." In this case, C. D. is called the "use plaintiff."

Usee. A person for whose use a suit is brought; otherwise termed the "use plaintiff."

Useful. The term as used in the patent law, when applied to a machine, means that the machine will accomplish its purpose practically when applied in industry. By "useful" is meant such an invention as may be applied to some beneficial use in society, in contradistinction to an invention which is injurious to the morals, the health, or the good order of society.

Useful life. In accounting and taxation, the period of time for which an asset is capable of being used for the production of income.

For income tax purposes, the "useful life" of depreciable property is period over which asset may reasonably be expected to be useful to taxpayer in his trade or business or in production of income, and such is necessarily an estimate made at time when property is first put to use. Cohn v. U. S., C.A.Tenn., 259 F.2d 371, 377. Useful life for depreciation purposes is an estimate; length of the useful period must be shown by evidence that allows it to be estimated with reasonable accuracy. Richard S. Miller & Sons, Inc. v. U. S., Ct.Cl., 537 F.2d 446, 455. The term "depreciable life," as used in general excise tax law, is synonymous with the term "useful life" as used for purpose of the depreciation deduction under income tax law. Matter of 711 Motors, Inc., 56 Hawaii 644, 547 P.2d 1343, 1347.

Usefulness. Capabilities for use. The word pertains to the future as well as to the past.

Use immunity. Term generally refers to order of court which compels witness to give testimony of self-incriminating nature but provides that such testimony may not be used as evidence in subsequent prosecution of such witness. People v. Koba, 55 Ill.App.3d 298, 13 Ill.Dec. 306, 371 N.E.2d 1. See also **Immunity.**

User. The actual exercise or enjoyment of any right, property, drugs, franchise, etc.

Adverse user. Such a use of the property under claim of right as the owner himself would make, asking no permission, and disregarding all other claims to it, so far as they conflict with this use. See also **Adverse possession.**

User de action /yúwzər dǽkshən/. L. Fr. In old practice, the pursuing or bringing an action.

Use tax. An ad valorem tax on the use, consumption, or storage of tangible property, usually at the same rate as the sales tax, and levied for the purpose of preventing tax avoidance by the purchase of articles in a state or taxing jurisdiction which does not levy sales taxes.

Use variance. See **Variance.**

Usher. This word is said to be derived from *"huissier,"* and is the name of a subordinate officer in some English courts of law.

Usher of the Black Rod. In old English law, the gentleman usher of the black rod is an officer of the house of lords appointed by letters patent from the crown. His duties are, by himself or deputy, to desire the attendance of the commons in the house of peers when the royal assent is given to bills, either by the king in person or by commission, to execute orders for the commitment of persons guilty of breach of privilege, and also to assist in the introduction of peers when they take the oaths and their seats.

Using mail to defraud. The elements of this offense are the formation of a scheme or artifice to defraud, and use of mails for purpose of executing or attempting to execute such scheme or artifice; the latter element being gist of the offense. 18 U.S.C.A. § 1341. Stryker v. United States, C.C.A.Colo., 95 F.2d 601, 604, 605. The crime is complete when mails are used in such scheme, and what happened subsequently is not controlling. United States v. Ames, D.C.N.Y., 39 F.Supp. 885, 886. See **Mail fraud.**

Using the service of another for pay. This phrase as used in Compensation Act defining employer means right to control the means and manner of that service, as distinguished from results of such service, the word "service" meaning the performance of labor for the benefit of another. Rutherford v. Tobin Quarries, 336 Mo. 1171, 82 S.W.2d 918, 923.

Uso /úwsow/. In Spanish law, usage; that which arises from certain things which men say and do and practice uninterruptedly for a great length of time, without any hindrance whatever.

Usque /ə́skwiy/. Lat. Up to; until. This is a word of exclusion, and a release of all demands *usque ad* a certain day does not cover a bond made on that day. Usually applied to ownership of property. Applied to right to air it has been held that ownership extends *"usque ad coelum."* See **A coelo usque ad centrum.**

Usque ad filum aquæ, or **viæ** /ə́skwiy æd fáyləm ǽkwiy/°váyiy/. Up to the middle of the stream or road.

Usual. Habitual; ordinary; customary; according to usage or custom; commonly established, observed, or practiced. That which happens in common use or occurs in ordinary practice or course of events. Synonymous with custom, common, normal, regular. Dancy v. Abraham Bros. Packing Co., 171 Tenn. 311, 102 S.W.2d 526, 528.

Usual course. These words in statute excepting from application of Compensation Act employment not in usual course of employer's trade or business, refer to normal operations constituting regular business of employer. Longshoremen's and Harbor Workers' Compensation Act. Hoage v. Hartford Accident & Indemnity Co., 64 App.D.C. 258, 77 F.2d 381.

Usual covenants. See **Covenant.**

Usual place of abode. Within meaning of statute relating to service of process is place where defendant is actually living at time of service. See **Domicile; Residence.**

Usual terms. A phrase in the common-law practice, which meant pleading issuably, rejoining *gratis,* and taking short notice of trial. When a defendant obtained further time to plead, these were the terms usually imposed.

Usuarius /yùwsyuwériyəs/. Lat. In the civil law, one who had the mere use of a thing belonging to another for the purpose of supplying his daily wants; a usuary.

Usucapio, or **usucaptio** /yùwsyuwkéyp(i)yow/yùwsyuwkǽpsh(iy)ow/. A term of Roman law used to denote a mode of acquisition of property. It corresponds very nearly to the term "prescription." But the prescription of Roman law differed from that of the English law, in this: that no *mala fide* possessor (*i.e.,* person in possession knowingly of the property of another) could, by however long a period, acquire title by possession merely. The two essential requisites to *usucapio* were *justa causa* (*i.e.,* title) and *bona fides* (*i.e.,* ignorance). The term *"usucapio"* is sometimes, but erroneously, written *"usucaptio."* As to *"lucrativa usucapio,"* see that title.

Usucapio constituta est ut aliquis litium finis esset /yùwsyuwkéyp(i)yow kòn(t)stət(y)úwdə èst əd ǽləkwəs lísh(iy)əm fáynəs ésət/. Prescription was instituted that there might be some end to litigation.

Usufruct /yúwz(y)əfrə́kt/. In the civil law, the right of enjoying a thing, the property of which is vested in another, and to draw from the same all the profit, utility, and advantage which it may produce, provided it be without altering the substance of the thing. Civ.Code La. art. 533.

Under Greek law, a right attached to the person which may not be inherited. New England Trust Co. v. Wood, 326 Mass. 239, 93 N.E.2d 547, 549.

Imperfect usufruct. An imperfect or quasi usufruct is that which is of things which would be useless to the usufructuary if he did not consume or expend them or change the substance of them; as, money, grain, liquors. Civ.Code La. art. 534. See *Quasi usufruct, infra.*

Legal usufruct. See that title.

Perfect usufruct. An usufruct in those things which the usufructuary can enjoy without changing their substance, though their substance may be diminished or deteriorate naturally by time or by the use to which they are applied, as, a house, a piece of land, furniture, and other movable effects. Civ.Code La. art. 534.

Quasi usufruct. In the civil law, originally the usufruct gave no right to the substance of the thing, and consequently none to its consumption; hence only an inconsumable thing could be the object of it, whether movable or immovable. But in later times the right of usufruct was, by analogy, extended to consumable things, and therewith arose the distinction between true and *quasi* usufructs. Civ.Code La. art. 534. See *Imperfect usufruct, supra.*

Usufructuary /yùwz(y)əfrə́kchuwəriy/. In the civil law, one who has the usufruct or right of enjoying anything in which he has no property.

Usufruit /yúwz(y)əfrùwt/. In French law, the same as the *usufruct* of the English and Roman law.

Usura /yuwz(y)úrə/. Lat. In the civil law, money given for the use of money; interest. Commonly used in the plural, *"usuræ"* /yuwz(y)úriy/yúwzhəriy/.

Usura est commodum certum quod propter usum rei mutuatæ recipitur. Sed secundario spirare de aliqua retributione, ad voluntatem ejus qui mutuatus est, hoc non est vitiosum /yuwz(y)úrə èst kómədəm sərdəm kwòd próptər yúwsəm ríyay myùwtyuwéydiy rəsípədər. sèd sèkəndériyow spərériy diy ǽləkwə rètrəb(y)uwshiyówniy, æd vòləntéydəm íyjəs kwày myùwtyuwéydəs èst, hók nón èst vìshiyówsəm/. Usury is a certain benefit which is received for the use of a thing lent. But to have an understanding [literally, to breathe or whisper], in an incidental way, about some compensation to be made at the pleasure of the borrower, is not lawful.

Usura manifesta /yuwz(y)úrə mænəféstə/. Manifest or open usury; as distinguished from *usura velata,* veiled or concealed usury, which consists in giving a bond for the loan, in the amount of which is included the stipulated interest.

Usura maritima /yuwz(y)úrə mərídəmə/°mǽrətáymə/. Interest taken on bottomry or respondentia bonds, which is proportioned to the risk, and is not affected by the usury laws.

Usurarius /yùwzhərériyəs/. In old English law, a usurer.

Usurious /yuwzhúriyəs/. Pertaining to usury; partaking of the nature of usury; involving usury; tainted with usury; as, a usurious contract. See **Usury**.

Usurious contract. A contract where interest to be paid exceeds the rate established by statute. Commerce Farm Credit Co. v. Ramp, Tex.Civ.App., 116 S.W.2d 1144, 1149. It being sufficient when there is contingency whereby lender may get more than lawful rate of interest. Reynolds Mortg. Co. v. Thomas, Tex.Civ.App., 61 S.W.2d 1011, 1013. See also **Usury**.

Usurp /yuwsə́rp/. To seize and hold any office by force, and without right; applied to seizure of office, place, functions, powers, rights, etc. of another. State ex rel. Scanes v. Babb, 124 W.Va. 428, 20 S.E.2d 683, 686.

Usurpatio /yùwsərpéysh(iy)ow/. Lat. In the civil law, the interruption of a usucaption, by some act on the part of the real owner.

Usurpation /yùwsərpéyshən/. The unlawful encroachment or assumption of the use of property, power or authority which belongs to another. An interruption or the disturbing a man in his right and possession.

The unlawful seizure or assumption of sovereign power. The assumption of government or supreme power by force or illegally, in derogation of the constitution and of the rights of the lawful ruler.

Usurpation for which writ of prohibition may be granted involves attempted exercise of power not possessed by inferior officer.

Usurpation of advowson /yùwsərpéyshən əv ədváwzən/. An injury which consists in the absolute ouster or dispossession of the patron from the advowson or right of presentation, and which happens when a stranger who has no right presents a clerk, and the latter is thereupon admitted and instituted.

Usurpation of franchise or office /yùwsərpéyshən əv frǽnchayz ər ófəs/. The unjustly intruding upon or exercising any office, franchise, or liberty belonging to another. "Usurpation" of public office authorizing quo warranto action under statute may be with or without forcible seizure of office and prerogatives thereof, and may consist of mere unauthorized assumption and exercise of power in performing duties of office upon claim of right thereto. State ex rel. Kirk v. Wheatley, 133 Ohio St. 164, 12 N.E.2d 491, 493, 10 O.O. 236. See also **Usurpation**.

Usurped power. See **Usurp; Usurpation**.

Usurper. One who assumes the right of government by force, contrary to and in violation of the constitution of the country.

Usurper of a public office. One who either intrudes into a vacant office or ousts the incumbent without any color of title. Neal v. Parker, 200 Ark. 10, 139 S.W.2d 41, 44. One who intrudes on office and assumes to exercise its functions without legal title or color of right thereto. Alleger v. School Dist. No. 16, Newton County, Mo.App., 142 S.W.2d 660, 663; State ex rel. City of Republic v. Smith, 345 Mo. 1158, 139 S.W.2d 929, 933. Any person attempting to fill pretended office attempted to be created by an unconstitutional law. Bodcaw Lumber Co. of Louisiana v. Jordan, La.App., 14 So.2d 98, 101.

Usury. Collectively, the laws of a jurisdiction regulating the charging of interest rates. A usurious loan is one whose interest rates are determined to be in excess of those permitted by the usury laws. An illegal contract for a loan or forbearance of money, goods, or things in action, by which illegal interest is reserved, or agreed to be reserved or taken. An unconscionable and exorbitant rate or amount of interest. An unlawful contract upon the loan of money, to receive the same again with exorbitant increase. The reserving and taking, or contracting to reserve and take, either directly or by indirection, a greater sum for the use of money than the lawful interest. A profit greater than the lawful rate of interest, intentionally exacted as a bonus, for the forbearance of an existing indebtedness or a loan of money, imposed upon the necessities of the borrower in a transaction where the money is to be returned at all events. Anderson v. Beadle, 35 N.M. 654, 5 P.2d 528, 529. See also **Legal interest; Loan sharking**.

Old English law. Interest of money; increase for the loan of money; a reward for the *use* of money. 2 Bl.Comm. 454. The taking of any compensation whatever for the use of money.

Usury laws. See **Usury**.

Usus /yúwsəs/. Lat. In Roman law, a precarious enjoyment of land, corresponding with the right of *habitatio* of houses, and being closely analogous to the tenancy at sufferance or at will of English law. The *usuarius (i.e.,* tenant by *usus)* could only hold on so long as the owner found him convenient, and had to go so soon as ever he was in the owner's way *(molestus).* The *usuarius* could not have a friend to share the produce. It was scarcely permitted to him (Justinian says) to have even his wife with him on the land; and he could not let or sell, the right being strictly personal to himself.

Usus bellici /yúwsəs béləsay/. Lat. In international law, warlike uses or objects. It is the *usus bellici* which determine an article to be contraband.

Usus est dominium fiduciarium /yúwsəs èst dəmíniyəm fəd(y)ùwshiyériyəm/. Use is a fiduciary dominion.

Usus et status sive possessio potius differunt secundum rationem fori, quam secundum rationem rei /yúwsəs èt stéydəs sáyviy pəzésh(iy)ow pówsh(iy)əs difərənt səkándəm rǽshiyównəm fóray, kwǽm səkándəm rǽshiyównəm ríyay/. Use and estate, or possession, differ more in the rule of the court than in the rule of the matter.

Usus fructus /yúwsəs fráktəs/. Lat. In Roman law, usufruct; usufructuary right or possession. The temporary right of using a thing, without having the ultimate property, or full dominion, of the substance. 2 Bl.Comm. 327.

Utas /yúwdəs/. In old English practice, octave; the octave; the eighth day following any term or feast.

Ut currere solebat /ət kə́hrəriy səlíybæt/. Lat. As it was wont to run; applied to a water-course.

Ut de feodo /ət dìy fyúwdow/. L. Lat. As of fee.

Uterine /yúwdərən/. Born of the same mother. A uterine brother or sister is one born of the same mother, but by a different father.

Utero-gestation /yùwdərowjestéyshən/. Pregnancy.

Uterque /yuwtə́rkwiy/. Lat. Both; each. "The justices, being in doubt as to the meaning of this word in an indictment, demanded the opinions of grammarians, who delivered their opinions that this word doth aptly signify *one of them.*"

Utfangthef, or **utfangenethef** /áwtfæŋ(ən)θìyf/. In Saxon and old English law, the privilege of a lord of a manor to judge and punish a thief dwelling out of his liberty, and committing theft without the same, if he were caught within the lord's jurisdiction.

The right of the lord of a manor to hang a thief caught with the stolen goods, whether or not the capture was made on the manor. See **Infangenthef.**

Ut hospites /ət hóspədiyz/. Lat. As guests.

Uti /yúwday/. Lat. In the civil law, to use. Strictly, to use for necessary purposes; as distinguished from *"frui,"* to enjoy.

Uti frui /yúwday frúway/. Lat. In the civil law, to have the full use and enjoyment of a thing, without damage to its substance.

Utile per inutile non vitiatur /yúwdəliy pə̀r inyúwdəliy nón vìshiyéydər/. The useful is not vitiated by the useless. Surplusage does not spoil the remaining part if that is good in itself.

Utilidad /uwtìliyðád/. Span. In Spanish law, the profit of a thing.

Utilis /yúwdələs/. Lat. In the civil law, useful; beneficial; equitable; available. *Actio utilis,* an equitable action. *Dies utilis,* an available day.

Utility. In patent law, industrial value; the capability of being so applied in practical affairs as to prove advantageous in the ordinary pursuits of life, or add to the enjoyment of mankind. Callison v. Dean, C.C. A.Okl., 70 F.2d 55, 58. The absence of frivolity and mischievousness, and utility for some beneficial purpose. But there is no utility if the invention can be used only to commit a fraud with, Klein v. Russell, 86 U.S. (19 Wall.) 433, 22 L.Ed. 116; or for some immoral purpose, or can be used only for gambling purposes in saloons, or if the invention is dangerous in its use, Mitchell v. Tilghman, 86 U.S. (19 Wall.) 287, 22 L.Ed. 125.

Utility is established if only partial success is attained. Emery Industries v. Schumann, C.C.A.Ill., 111 F.2d 209, 211. The "utility" which an infringing defendant is estopped to deny means sufficient practical utility to make a device useful in the sense of the patent statute. The estoppel does not forbid him to deny that there is any useful function, or new result serving to give inventive character to the slight step

which a patentee has taken in differentiation from prior art. Sandy MacGregor Co. v. Vaco Grip Co., C.C.A.Ohio, 2 F.2d 655, 656.

Uti possidetis /yúwday pəsìdiyéydəs/. Lat. *Civil law.* A species of interdict for the purpose of retaining possession of a thing, granted to one who, at the time of contesting suit, was in possession of an immovable thing, in order that he might be declared the legal possessor. See **Utrubi.**

International law. A phrase used to signify that the parties to a treaty are to retain possession of what they have acquired by force during the war. A treaty which terminates a war may adopt this principle or that of the *status quo ante bellum,* or a combination of the two. In default of any treaty stipulation, the former doctrine prevails. Guillermo Alvarez y Sanches v. U. S., 42 Ct.Cl. 458.

Uti rogas /yúwday rówgəs/. Lat. In Roman law, the form of words by which a vote in favor of a proposed law was orally expressed. *Uti rogas, volo vel jubeo,* as you ask, I will or order; I vote as you propose; I am for the law. The letters "U. R." on a ballot expressed the same sentiment.

Utlagatus, or **utlagatum** /ətləgéydəs/°əm/. In old English law, an outlawed person; an outlaw.

Utlagatus est quasi extra legem positus. Caput gerit lupinum /ətləgéydəs èst kwéysay ékstrə líyjəm pózədəs. kǽpət jérət l(y)uwpáynəm/. An outlaw is, as it were, put out of the protection of the law. He bears the head of a wolf.

Utlagatus pro contumacia et fuga, non propter hoc convictus est de facto principali /ətləgéydəs pròw kòntəméysh(iy)ə èt fyúwgə, nón próptər hòk kənvíktəs èst/. One who is outlawed for contumacy and flight is not on that account convicted of the principal fact.

Utlage. L. Fr. An outlaw.

Utlesse. An escape of a felon out of prison.

Utmost care. Term is substantially synonymous with "highest care."

Utmost resistance. This term, under the rule that to constitute rape there must be utmost resistance by the woman, is a relative rather than a positive term, and means that greatest effort of which she is capable must be used to foil assailant.

Ut pœne ad paucos, metus ad omnes perveniat /ət píyniy æ̀d pókows, míydəs æ̀d ómniyz pərvíyn(i)yət/. That the punishment may reach a few, but the fear of it affect all. A maxim in criminal law, expressive of one of the principal objects of human punishment. 4 Bl.Comm. 11.

Ut res magis valeat quam pereat /ət ríyz méyjəs vǽliyət kwǽm péhriyət/. That the thing may rather have effect than be destroyed. Charitable bequests are also governed by this maxim. King v. Richardson, C.C.A.N.C., 136 F.2d 849, 858.

Utrubi /ə́trəbay/. In the civil law, the name of a species of interdict for retaining a thing, granted for the purpose of protecting the possession of a movable thing, as the *uti possidetis* was granted for an immovable.

Utrumque nostrum /yuwtrə́mkwiy nóstrəm/. Both of us. Words used formerly in bonds.

Ut summæ potestatis regis est posse quantum velit, sic magnitudinis est velle quantum possit /ət sə́miy pòwdəstéydəs ríyjəs èst pósiy kwóntəm víylət, sík mǽgnət(y)úwdənəs èst véliy kwóntəm pósət/. As the highest power of a king is to be able to do all he wishes, so the highest greatness of him is to wish all he is able to do.

Utter, *v.* To put or send (as a forged check) into circulation; to publish or put forth; to offer. To utter and publish an instrument, as a counterfeit note, is to declare or assert, directly or indirectly, by words or actions, that it is good; uttering it is a declaration that it is good, with an intention or offer to pass it. To utter, as used in a statute against forgery and counterfeiting, means to offer, whether accepted or not, a forged instrument, with the representation, by words or actions, that the same is genuine.

The phrase "utters or publishes as true", as used in federal forgery statute, means to make or attempt any use of a written or printed instrument or document, such as an attempt to place a check in circulation, whereby, or in connection with which, some assertion, representation or claim is made to another in some way or manner, directly or indirectly, expressly or impliedly, or by words or conduct, that the check or document is genuine. Carr v. United States, C.A.Tenn., 278 F.2d 702; United States v. Maybury, C.A.N.Y., 274 F.2d 899; French v. United States, C.A.La., 232 F.2d 736, cert. denied 352 U.S. 851, 77 S.Ct. 73, 1 L.Ed.2d 62; United States v. Rader, W.D. Ark., 185 F.Supp. 224, aff'd 288 F.2d 452.

Utter, *adj.* Entire; complete; absolute; total.

Utterance. See **Excited utterance; Spontaneous declarations.**

Utter bar. In English law, the bar at which those barristers, usually junior men, practice who have not yet been raised to the dignity of king's counsel. These junior barristers are said to plead without the bar; while those of the higher rank are admitted to seats within the bar, and address the court or a jury from a place reserved for them, and divided off by a bar. Also called "outer bar."

Utter barrister. In English law, those barristers who plead without the bar, and are distinguished from benchers, or those who have been readers, and who are allowed to plead within the bar, as the king's counsel are.

Uxor /ə́ksor/. Lat. In the civil law, a wife; a woman lawfully married.

Et uxor. And his wife. A term used in indexing, abstracting, and describing conveyances made by a man and his wife as grantors, or to a man and his wife as grantees. Often abbreviated *"et ux."* Thus, "John Doe *et ux.* to Richard Roe."

Jure uxoris. In right of his wife. A term used of a husband who joins in a deed, is seised of an estate, brings a suit, etc., in the right or on the behalf of his wife. 3 Bl.Comm. 210.

Uxor et filius sunt nomina naturæ /ə́ksor èt fíliyəs sə̀nt nómənə nətyúriy/. Wife and son are names of nature.

Uxoricide /əksórəsàyd/. The killing of a wife by her husband; one who murders his wife. Not a technical term of the law.

Uxor non est sui juris, sed sub potestate viri /ə́ksor nón èst s(y)úway júrəs, séd sə̀b pòwdəstéydiy víray/. A wife is not her own mistress, but is under the power of her husband.

Uxor sequitur domicilium viri /ə́ksor sékwədər dòməsíl(i)yəm víray/. A wife follows the domicile of her husband.

V

V. As an abbreviation, this letter may stand for "Victoria," "volume," or "verb;" also *"vide"* (see) and *"voce"* (word). It is also a common abbreviation of *"versus,"* in the titles of causes, and reported cases.

V.A. See **Veterans Administration.**

Vacancy. A place or position which is empty, unfilled, or unoccupied. An unoccupied or unfilled post, position, or office. An existing office, etc., without an incumbent. The state of being destitute of an incumbent, or a proper or legally qualified officer. The term is principally applied to an interruption in the incumbency of an office, or to cases where the office is not occupied by one who has a legal right to hold it and to exercise the rights and perform the duties pertaining thereto. The word "vacancy," when applied to official positions, means, in its ordinary and popular sense, that an office is unoccupied, and that there is no incumbent who has a lawful right to continue therein until the happening of a future event, though the word is sometimes used with reference to an office temporarily filled.

A strip of unsurveyed and unsold public lands. Hughes v. Rhodes, Tex.Civ.App., 137 S.W.2d 820, 821.

See also **Vacant.**

Vacant. Empty; unoccupied; as, a "vacant" office or parcel of land. Deprived of contents, without inanimate objects. It implies entire abandonment, nonoccupancy for any purpose. Foley v. Sonoma County Farmers' Mut. Fire Ins. Co. of Sonoma, Cal.App., 108 P.2d 939, 942. Absolutely free, unclaimed, and unoccupied.

"Vacant" and "unoccupied," as used together in rider to fire policy, have different meanings; term "vacant" meaning "empty," while term "unoccupied" means lack of habitual presence of human beings. Jelin v. Home Ins. Co., C.C.A.N.J., 72 F.2d 326, 327.

See also **Vacancy,** and as to vacant Possession and Succession, see those titles.

Vacantia bona /vəkǽnsh(iy)ə bównə/. Lat. In the civil law, goods without an owner, or in which no one claims a property; escheated goods.

Vacate. To annul; to set aside; to cancel or rescind. To render an act void; as, to vacate an entry of record, or a judgment. As applied to a judgment or decree it is not synonymous with "suspend" which means to stay enforcement of judgment or decree.

To put an end to; as, to vacate a street. To move out; to make vacant or empty; to leave; especially, to surrender possession by removal; to cease from occupancy.

See also **Annul; Reverse; Vacancy.**

Vacatio /vəkéysh(iy)ow/. Lat. In the civil law, exemption; immunity; privilege; dispensation; exemption from the burden of office.

Vacation. A recess or leave of absence; a respite or time of respite from active duty or employment; an intermission or rest period during which activity or work is suspended. It is a period of freedom from duty or work, but not the end of employment. In re Dauber, 151 Pa.Super. 293, 30 A.2d 214, 216. The act or result of vacating. An intermission of procedure. It is not a termination of the relation of master and servant or employer and employee. In schools, there are customary vacations at Christmas, Easter, other holidays, and during the summer.

That period of time between the end of one term of court and the beginning of another. Compare **Recess.**

Vacation of judgment. The setting aside of a judgment on grounds that it was issued by mistake, inadvertence, surprise, excusable neglect or fraud. While the term "vacate" has been replaced by Fed.R.Civil P. 60, the basis for relief from judgment is the same as formerly when one sought to vacate a judgment.

Vacatur /vəkéydər/. Lat. Let it be vacated. In practice, a rule or order by which a proceeding is vacated; a vacating.

Vacatura /vèykət(y)úrə/. An avoidance of an ecclesiastical benefice.

Vacua possessio /vǽkyuwə pəzésh(iy)ow/. Lat. The vacant possession, *i.e.,* free and unburdened possession, which (e.g.) a vendor had and has to give to a purchaser of lands.

Vacuity /vəkyúwədiy/. Emptiness; vacancy; want of reality; nihility.

Vacuus /vǽkyuwəs/. Lat. In the civil law, empty; void; vacant; unoccupied.

Vadelet /vǽlət/. See **Valec.**

Vades /véydiyz/. Lat. In the civil law, pledges; sureties; bail; security for the appearance of a defendant or accused person in court.

Vadiare duellum /væⁱdiyériy d(y)uwéləm/. L. Lat. In old English law, to wage or gage the *duellum;* to wage battel; to give pledges mutually for engaging in the trial by combat.

Vadimonium /væⁱdəmówn(i)yəm/. Lat. In Roman law, bail or security; the giving of bail for appearance in court; a recognizance. An ancient form of suretyship.

Vadium /véyd(i)yəm/. Lat. A pledge; security by pledge of property.

Vadium mortuum /véyd(i)yəm mórchuwəm/. A mortgage or *dead pledge;* a security given by the borrower of a sum of money, by which he grants to the lender an estate in fee, on condition that, if the money be not repaid at the time appointed, the estate so put in pledge shall continue to the lender as dead or gone from the mortgagor. 2 Bl.Comm. 157.

Vadium ponere /véyd(i)yəm pównəriy/. To take bail for the appearance of a person in a court of justice.

Vadium vivum /véyd(i)yəm váyvəm/. A species of security by which the borrower of a sum of money made over his estate to the lender until he had received that sum out of the issues and profits of the land. It was so called because neither the money nor the lands were lost, and were not left in dead pledge, but this was a *living* pledge, for the profits of the land were constantly paying off the debt.

Vadlet /væ̂dlət/. In old English law, the king's eldest son; hence the valet or knave follows the king and queen in a pack of cards.

Vadum /véydəm/. In old records, a ford, or wading place.

Vagabond. A vagrant or homeless wanderer without means of honest livelihood. Neering v. Illinois Cent. R. Co., 383 Ill. 366, 50 N.E.2d 497, 502. One who wanders from place to place, having no fixed dwelling, or, if he has one, not abiding in it; a wanderer, especially such a person who is lazy and generally worthless and without means of honest livelihood. See also **Vagrant.**

Vagabonds are described in old English statutes as "such as wake on the night and sleep on the day, and haunt customable taverns and ale-houses and routs about; and no man wot from whence they came, nor whither they go." 4 Bl.Comm. 169.

Vagabundum nuncupamus eum qui nullibi domicilium contraxit habitationis /væ̂gəbándəm nə̀ŋkəpéyməs íyəm kwày nǽləbày doməsíl(i)yəm kəntrǽksət hæ̀bətèyshiyównəs/. We call him a "vagabond" who has acquired nowhere a domicile of residence.

Vagrancy. At common law, the act of going about from place to place by a person without visible means of support, who is idle, and who, though able to work for his or her maintenance, refuses to do so, but lives without labor or on the charity of others.

As defined by Kansas Criminal Code, vagrancy is: (a) Engaging in an unlawful occupation; or (b) Being of the age of eighteen (18) years or over and able to work and without lawful means of support and failing or refusing to seek employment; or (c) Loitering in any community without visible means of support; or

(d) Loitering on the streets or in a place open to the public with intent to solicit for immoral purposes; or (e) Deriving support in whole or in part from begging. State vagrancy statutes, however, vary greatly, and many have been declared unconstitutional because, as drawn, they purport to punish conduct which is not criminal or are worded too vaguely to inform persons of the nature of the act declared criminal. Lanzetta v. New Jersey, 306 U.S. 451, 59 S.Ct. 618, 83 L.Ed. 888.

Vagrancy laws. See **Vagrancy; Visible means of support.**

Vagrant. At common law, wandering or going about from place to place by idle person who had no lawful or visible means of support and who subsisted on charity and did not work, though able to do so. State v. Harlowe, 174 Wash. 227, 24 P.2d 601.

A general term, including, in English law, the several classes of idle and disorderly persons, rogues, and vagabonds, and incorrigible rogues.

One who wanders from place to place; an idle wanderer, specifically, one who has no settled habitation, nor any fixed income or livelihood. A vagabond; a tramp. A person able to work who spends his time in idleness or immorality, having no property to support him and without some visible and known means of fair, honest and reputable livelihood. State v. Oldham, 224 N.C. 415, 30 S.E.2d 318, 319. One who is apt to become a public charge through his own laziness. People, on Complaint of McDonough, v. Gesino, Sp.Sess., 22 N.Y.S.2d 284, 285.

See **Vagabond; Vagrancy.**

Vagrant act. In English law, the statute 5 Geo. IV, c. 83, which is an act for the punishment of idle and disorderly persons. The act of 17 Geo. II divided vagrants into idle and disorderly persons; rogues and vagabonds; and incorrigible rogues. Other statutes were passed as late as 32 Geo. III bearing on this subject.

Vague. Indefinite. Uncertain; not susceptible of being understood.

Vagueness doctrine. Under this principle, a law which does not fairly inform a person of what is commanded or prohibited is unconstitutional as violative of due process.

Vale /váley/. In Spanish law, a promissory note.

Valeat quantum valere potest /væ̂liyət kwóntəm vəlíriy pówdəst/. It shall have effect as far as it can have effect.

Valec, valect, or **vadelet** /væ̂lət/. In old English law, a young gentleman; also a servitor or gentleman of the chamber.

Valentia /vəlénsh(iy)ə/. L. Lat. The value or price of anything.

Valesheria /væ̂ləshír(i)yə/. In old English law, the proving by the kindred of the slain, one on the father's side, and another on that of the mother, that a man was a Welshman. See **Engleshire.**

Valet /væ̂ley/væléy/. Anciently, a name denoting young gentlemen of rank and family, but afterwards applied to those of lower degree; now used for a personal servant, more particularly for hotel employee who performs personal services for guests.

Valid. Having legal strength or force, executed with proper formalities, incapable of being rightfully overthrown or set aside. Bennett v. State, 46 Ala.App. 535, 245 So.2d 570, 572. Of binding force; legally sufficient or efficacious; authorized by law. Good or sufficient in point of law; efficacious; executed with the proper formalities; incapable of being rightfully overthrown or set aside; sustainable and effective in law, as distinguished from that which exists or took place in fact or appearance, but has not the requisites to enable it to be recognized and enforced by law. A deed, will, or other instrument, which has received all the formalities required by law, is said to be valid.

Meritorious, as, a *valid* defense.

See also **Legal.**

Validate. To make valid; confirm; sanction; affirm.

Validating statute. A statute, purpose of which is to cure past errors and omissions and thus make valid what was invalid, but it grants no indulgence for the correction of future errors. Petition of Miller, 149 Pa.Super. 142, 28 A.2d 257, 258.

Validity. Legal sufficiency, in contradistinction to mere regularity.

Validity of a treaty. The term "validity," as applied to treaties, admits of two descriptions—necessary and voluntary. By the former is meant that which results from the treaties having been made by persons authorized by, and for purposes consistent with, the constitution. By voluntary validity is meant that validity which a treaty, voidable by reason of violation by the other party, still continues to retain by the silent acquiescence and will of the nation. It is voluntary, because it is at the will of the nation to let it remain or to extinguish it. The principles which govern and decide the necessary validity of a treaty are of a judicial nature, while those on which its voluntary validity depends are of a political nature.

Validity of a will. As used in will contest statute has reference only to the genuineness or legal sufficiency of will under attack. In re Elliott's Estate, 22 Wash.2d 334, 156 P.2d 427, 438.

Valid reason. These words, in a statute providing for the withdrawal of the names of petitioners for a road improvement district when valid reasons therefor are presented, mean a sound sufficient reason, such as fraud, deceit, misrepresentation, duress, etc.; a reason upon which the petitioner could support or justify his change in attitude. The word "valid" necessarily possesses an element of legal strength and force, and inconsistent positions have no such force.

Valley. As applied to a mountainous country, term refers to lowlands, in contradistinction to mountain slopes and ridges.

Valor beneficiorum /vǽlər benəfishiyórəm/. L. Lat. The value of every ecclesiastical benefice and preferment, according to which the first fruits and tenths are collected and paid. It is commonly called the "king's books," by which the clergy are at present rated.

Valor maritagii /vǽlər mæ̀rətéyjiyay/. Lat. Value of the marriage. The amount forfeited under the ancient tenures by a ward to a guardian who had offered her a marriage without disparagement, which she refused. In feudal law, the guardian in chivalry had the right of tendering to his infant ward a suitable match, without "disparagement" (inequality), which, if the infants refused, they forfeited the value of the marriage *(valor maritagii)* to their guardian; that is, so much as a jury would assess, or any one would *bona fide* give, to the guardian for such an alliance. 2 Bl.Comm. 70.

A writ which lay against the ward, on coming of full age, for that he was not married, by his guardian, for the *value of the marriage,* and this though no convenient marriage had been offered.

Valuable. Of financial or market value; commanding or worth a good price; of considerable worth in any respect, whether monetary or intrinsic.

Valuable consideration. A class of consideration upon which a promise may be founded, which entitles the promisee to enforce his claim against an unwilling promisor. Some right, interest, profit, or benefit accruing to one party, or some forbearance, detriment, loss, or responsibility given, suffered, or undertaken by the other. A gain or loss to either party is not essential, it is sufficient if the party in whose favor the contract is made parts with a right which he might otherwise exert. Miller Ice Co. v. Crim, 299 Ill.App. 615, 20 N.E.2d 347. It need not be translatable into dollars and cents, but is sufficient if it consists of performance, or promise thereof, which promisor treats and considers of value to him. It is not essential that the person to whom the consideration moves should be benefited, provided the person from whom it moves is, in a legal sense, injured. The injury may consist of a compromise of a disputed claim or forbearance to exercise a legal right, the alteration in position being regarded as a detriment that forms a consideration independent of the actual value of the right forborne. Mutual promises in contract is sufficient. For Fair and valuable consideration, see that title. See also **Consideration.**

Valuable improvements. As used in a statute relating to the specific performance of a parol contract for the purchase of real estate, improvements of such character as add permanent value to the freehold, and such as would not likely be made by one not claiming the right to the possession and enjoyment of the freehold estate. Improvements of a temporary and unsubstantial character will not amount to such part performance as, when accompanied by possession alone, will take the contract out of the operation of the statute of frauds. The valuable improvements may, however, be slight and of small value, provided they are substantial and permanent in their nature, beneficial to the freehold, and such as none but an owner would ordinarily make.

Valuable papers. This term as used in statute requiring that a holographic will devising realty be found among the "valuable papers" of decedent, in order to be effective, refers to such papers as are regarded by the testator as worthy of preservation and therefore in his estimation of some value. Fransioli v. Podesta, 21 Tenn.App. 577, 113 S.W.2d 769, 773, 777. And does not refer only to papers having money value. Pulley v. Cartwright, 23 Tenn.App. 690, 137 S.W.2d 336, 340.

Valuation. The act of ascertaining the worth of a thing. The estimated worth of a thing. See also **Appraisal; Assessed valuation; Fair value; Special use valuation; Value.**

Valuation list. In English law, a list of all the ratable hereditaments in a parish, showing the names of the occupier, the owner, the property, the extent of the property, the gross estimated rental, and the ratable value; prepared by the overseers of each parish in a union under section 14 of the union assessment committee act, 1862 (St. 25 & 26 Vict., c. 103), for the purposes of the poor rate.

Value. The utility of an object in satisfying, directly or indirectly, the needs or desires of human beings, called by economists "value in use," or its worth consisting in the power of purchasing other objects, called "value in exchange." Joint Highway Dist. No. 9 v. Ocean Shore R. Co., 128 Cal.App. 743, 18 P.2d 413, 417. Also the estimated or appraised worth of any object or property, calculated in money. To estimate the worth of; to rate at a certain price; to appraise; or to place a certain estimate of worth on in a scale of values. Hoard v. Wiley, 113 Ga.App. 328, 147 S.E.2d 782, 784.

Any consideration sufficient to support a simple contract. The term is often used as an abbreviation for "valuable consideration," especially in the phrases "purchaser for value," "holder for value," etc. See **Consideration; Valuable consideration.**

In economic consideration, the word "value," when used in reference to property, has a variety of significations, according to the connection in which the word is employed. It may mean the cost of a production or reproduction of the property in question, when it is sometimes called "sound value;" or it may mean the purchasing power of the property, or the amount of money which the property will command in exchange, if sold, this being called its "market value," which in the case of any particular property may be more or less than either the cost of its production or its value measured by its utility to the present or some other owner; or the word may mean the subjective value of property, having in view its profitableness for some particular purpose, sometimes termed its "value for use."

Salable value, actual value, market value, fair value, reasonable value, and cash value may all mean the same thing and may be designed to effect the same purpose. Cummings v. National Bank, 101 U.S. 153, 25 L.Ed. 903.

"Value," as used in Art. I, § 8, U.S.Const., giving Congress power to coin money and regulate the value thereof, is the true, inherent, and essential value, not depending upon accident, place, or person, but the same everywhere and to every one, and in this sense regulating the value of the coinage is merely determining and maintaining coinage composed of certain coins within certain limitations at a certain specific composition and weight.

Value of land for purpose of taxation is represented by price that would probably be paid therefor after fair negotiations between willing seller and buyer.

Thaw v. Town of Fairfield, 132 Conn. 173, 43 A.2d 65, 67. See **Fair market value.**

Value as it relates to stolen property is the market value at the time and place of the taking, or, in case of property without a market value, the cost of replacing it. Patterson v. State, 138 Tex.Cr.R. 551, 137 S.W.2d 1030; Givens v. State, 143 Tex.Cr.R. 277, 158 S.W.2d 535, 536. As respects whether value of stolen property equals or exceeds jurisdictional amount fixed by the National Stolen Property Act, "value" of stolen property is market value at time and place of taking, if it has a market value. National Stolen Property Act, §§ 1–7, 18 U.S.C.A. § 413 et seq. Husten v. United States, C.C.A.Minn., 95 F.2d 168.

Value as used in eminent domain proceeding means market value (q.v.). Epstein v. Boston Housing Authority, 317 Mass. 297, 58 N.E.2d 135, 137. See also **Just compensation; Market value.**

Under U.C.C. § 1–201(44), a person gives "value" for rights if he acquires them: (a) in return for a binding commitment to extend credit or for the extension of immediately available credit whether or not drawn upon and whether or not a chargeback is provided for in the event of difficulties in collection; or (b) as security for or in total or partial satisfaction of a pre-existing claim; or (c) by accepting delivery pursuant to a pre-existing contract for purchase; or (d) generally, in return for any consideration sufficient to support a simple contract.

See also Actual value; Agreed value; Annual value; Appraisal; Assess; Cash value; Commuted value; Consideration; Diminution in value; Double value; Face value; Fair cash market value; Fair cash value; Fair market value; Fair value; Going concern value; Improved value; Insurable value; Intrinsic value; Just compensation; Leasehold value; Market value; Net asset value; Par value; Policy value.

Actual cash value. In insurance, its customary meaning is replacement cost new less normal depreciation, though it may be determined by current market value of similar property or by the cost to replace or repair the property.

Book value. The value at which assets of a business are carried on the books of the company. It may also refer to the net worth of a business arrived at by subtracting liabilities from assets. See also **Book.**

Cash surrender value. In life insurance, the amount which the insurer will pay before death when the policy is cancelled. See also **Cash value.**

Intrinsic value. The value which a thing has as of itself, and not the value reflecting extrinsic factors such as market conditions.

Liquidation value. The value of a business or of an asset when it is sold other than in the ordinary course of business as in the liquidation of a business.

Market value. Fair value of property as between one who wants to purchase it and another who desires to sell it. What willing purchaser will give for property under fair market conditions. People v. F. H. Smith Co., 230 App.Div. 268, 243 N.Y.S. 446, 451. Not what the owner could realize at a forced sale, but the price he could obtain after reasonable and ample time, such as would ordinarily be taken by an owner to make a sale of like property. Wade v. Rathbun, 23 Cal. App.2d Supp. 758, 67 P.2d 765, 766. See **Fair cash market value; Fair market value; Fair value; Just compensation.**

Net value. The "reserve" or "net value" of a life insurance policy is the fund accumulated out of the net premiums during the earlier years of the policy where the premium throughout life or a term of years exceeds the actual value of the risk. The "net value" of a policy is equivalent to "reserve," and means that part of the annual premium paid by insured which, according to the American Experience Table of Mortality, must be set apart to meet or mature the company's obligations to insured, the net value of a policy on a given date being its actual value, its reserve.

No par value. Stock of a corporation which has no par value but which represents a proportionate share of the ownership of the corporation.

Par value. The nominal value of stock arrived at by dividing the total stated capital stock by the number of shares authorized.

Scrap value. The value of the constituent materials and components of a thing; not its value for the purpose for which it was made.

Stated value. The dollar value of no par stock established by the corporation as constituting the capital of the corporation.

Surrender value. See *Cash surrender value, supra.*

True value. As referring to value at which property must be assessed, is price which would be paid therefor on assessing date to willing seller, not compelled to sell, by willing purchaser, not compelled to purchase. New York Bay R. Co. v. Kelly, 22 N.J.Misc. 204, 37 A.2d 624, 628.

Use value. The value established by the usefulness of an object and not its value for sale or exchange.

Value of matter in controversy. As used in the Judicial Code, § 24 (28 U.S.C.A. § 1331 et seq.), the pecuniary result to either party which a judgment entered in the case would directly produce, either at once or in the future. Elliott v. Empire Natural Gas Co., C.C.A.Kan., 4 F.2d 493, 497. See also **Jurisdictional amount.**

Value received. A phrase usually employed in a bill of exchange or promissory note, to denote that a lawful consideration has been given for it. Clayton v. Clayton, 125 N.J.L. 537, 17 A.2d 496, 497. It is prima facie evidence of consideration, Moses v. Bank, 149 U.S. 298, 13 S.Ct. 900, 37 L.Ed. 743; although not necessarily in money.

Valued policy. One in which a definite valuation is by agreement of both parties put on the subject-matter of the insurance and written in the face of the policy and such value, in the absence of fraud or mistake, is conclusive on the parties. One in which both property insured and loss are valued. It is distinguished from an "open policy", which is one where the value of the property insured is not settled in the policy. Ellis v. Hartford Livestock Ins. Co., 293 Ky. 683, 170 S.W.2d 51, 53.

Valueless. Worthless.

Valuer /vǽlyuwər/. A person whose business is to appraise or set a value upon property; an appraiser.

Valvasors, or **vidames** /vǽvəsòrz/víydæ̀mz/. An obsolete title of dignity next to a peer.

Vana est illa potentia quæ nunquam venit in actum /véynə èst ílə pəténsh(iy)ə kwìy nə́ŋkwəm víynəd ən ǽktəm/. That power is vain [idle or useless] which never comes into action [which is never exercised].

Vandalic /vændǽlək/. Willfully or ignorantly destructive. Unkelsbee v. Homestead Fire Ins. Co. of Baltimore, D.C.Mun.App., 41 A.2d 168, 170.

Vandalism. Willful or ignorant destruction of property, especially artistic or literary treasures. Hostility to or contempt for what is beautiful or venerable. Unkelsbee v. Homestead Fire Ins. Co. of Baltimore, D.C. Mun.App., 41 A.2d 168, 170, 172. Vandalism connotes act of vandal and in ordinary usage is not limited to destruction of works of art, but has broadened its meaning to include destruction of property generally. Eis v. Hawkeye-Security Ins. Co., 192 Kan. 103, 386 P.2d 206, 210. Within dwelling policy means the willful and malicious destruction of property generally, and the destruction must have been intentional or in such reckless and wanton disregard of rights of others as to be equivalent of intent, and malice may be inferred from act of destruction. Livaditis v. American Cas. Co. of Reading, Pa., 117 Ga.App. 297, 160 S.E.2d 449, 450.

Vani timores sunt estimandi, qui non cadunt in constantem virum /véynay təmóriyz sə̀nt èstəmǽnday, kwáy nòn kéydənt ìn kən(t)stǽntəm vírəm/. Those are to be regarded as idle fears which do not affect a steady [firm or resolute] man.

Vani timoris justa excusatio non est /véynay təmórəs jə́stə èkskyuwzéysh(iy)ow nón èst/. A frivolous fear is not a legal excuse.

Vantarius /væntér(i)yəs/. L. Lat. In old records, a forefootman.

Vara /várə/. A Spanish-American measure of length, equal to 33 English inches or a trifle more or less, varying according to local usage. See U. S. v. Perot, 98 U.S. 428, 25 L.Ed. 251. A measure used in Mexican land grants equal to 32.9927 inches. Ainsa v. U. S., 161 U.S. 208, 16 S.Ct. 544, 40 L.Ed. 673.

Variable annuity. An annuity whose periodic payments depend upon some uncertain outcome, such as stock market prices. An annuity contract in which the premiums or payments are invested in securities to keep pace with inflation. The payments, therefore, which the annuitant receives vary from time to time.

Variance. *Pleading.* A discrepancy or disagreement between two instruments or two allegations in the same cause, which ought by law to be entirely consonant. Thus, if the evidence adduced by the plaintiff does not agree with the allegations of his pleadings, it is a variance. A disagreement between the allegations and the proof in some matter which, in point of law, is essential to the charge or claim. A substantial departure in the evidence adduced from the issue as made by the pleadings. The test of materiality of "variance" in an information is whether the pleading so fully and correctly informs a defendant of offense with which he is charged that, taking into account proof which is introduced against him, he is not misled in making his defense. People v. Guerrero, 22 Cal.2d 183, 137 P.2d 21, 24.

To constitute a variance, there must be a real and tangible difference between the allegations in the pleading and the proof offered in its support. The difference must be substantial and material. It must be one that actually misleads the adverse party to his prejudice in maintaining his action or defense on the merits, or, in criminal cases, one which might mislead the defense or expose a defendant to being put twice in jeopardy for the same offense. McCallister v. State, 217 Ind. 65, 26 N.E.2d 391, 393.

A variance in criminal case is an essential difference between accusation and proof, best illustrated where one crime is alleged and another proved, and test of material variance is whether offense alleged in a second indictment is the same as that alleged in the first, and accordingly, a plea of *autrefois acquit* must be upon a prosecution for the identical offense. U. S. v. Wills, C.C.A.Pa., 36 F.2d 855, 856.

Stipulations to vary discovery procedures are governed by Fed.R. Civil P. 29.

The objection or doctrine of "variance" has been essentially abolished by Fed.R. Civil P. 15(b) which permits liberal amendment of the pleadings to conform to the evidence. See also **Fatal variance.**

See also **Area variance; Departure; Irregularity.**

Zoning. Permission to depart from the literal requirements of a zoning ordinance. An authorization to a property owner to depart from literal requirements of zoning regulations in utilization of his property in cases in which strict enforcement of the zoning regulations would cause undue hardship. Daniel v. District of Columbia Bd. of Zoning Adjustment, D.C.App., 329 A.2d 773, 775. A "use variance" is a variance permitting a use other than that permitted in particular district by zoning ordinance. Anderson v. Board of Appeals, Town of Chesapeake Beach, 22 Md.App. 28, 322 A.2d 220, 225.

Various. Separate. Simmons v. Ramsbottom, 51 Wyo. 419, 68 P.2d 153, 156.

Vas /vǽs/. Lat. In the civil law, a pledge; a surety; bail or surety in a criminal proceeding or civil action.

Vasectomy. Resection of the ductus deferens. Surgical excision of part of the vas deferens, resulting in sterilization of the male.

Vassal /vǽsəl/. A feudal tenant or grantee; a feudatory; the holder of a fief on a feudal tenure, and by the obligation of performing feudal services. The correlative term was "lord." The vassal himself might have been lord of some other vassal.

In later times, this word was used to signify a species of slave who owed servitude and was in a state of dependency on a superior lord. 2 Bl.Comm. 53.

Vassalage /vǽsələj/. The state or condition of a vassal.

Vassal states. In international law, states which were supposed to possess only those rights and privileges which had been expressly granted to them, but actu-

ally they seem to have been very independent. Egypt was such; also Crete.

Vasseleria /væsəlír(i)yə/. The tenure or holding of a vassal.

Vastum /véystəm/. L. Lat. A waste or common lying open to the cattle of all tenants who have right of commoning.

Vastum forestæ vel bosci /véystəm fəréstiy vèl bósay/. Waste of a forest or wood. That part of a forest or wood wherein the trees and underwood were so destroyed that it lay in a manner waste and barren.

Vauderie /vówd(ə)riy/. In old European law, sorcery; witchcraft; the profession of the Vaudois.

Vaudeville. A species of theatrical entertainment, composed of isolated acts forming a balanced show. Hart v. B. F. Keith Vaudeville Exchange, C.C.A.N.Y., 12 F.2d 341, 342.

Vavasory /vǽvəs(ò)riy/. The lands that a vavasour held.

Vavasour /vǽvəsòr/. One who was in dignity next to a baron. One who held of a baron.

V.C. An abbreviation for "vice-chancellor."

V.C.C. An abbreviation for "vice-chancellor's court."

V.E. An abbreviation for *"venditioni exponas" (q.v.).*

Veal-money. The tenants of the manor of Bradford, in the county of Wilts, paid a yearly rent by this name to their lord, in lieu of veal paid formerly in kind.

Vecorin. In old Lombardic law, the offense of stopping one on the way; forestalling.

Vectigalia /vèktəgéyl(i)yə/. In Roman law, customsduties; taxes paid upon the importation or exportation of certain kinds of merchandise. They differed from tribute, which was a tax paid by each individual. Rent from state lands.

Vectigal judiciarium /vektáygəl juwdìshiyér(i)yəm/. Lat. Fines paid to the crown to defray the expenses of maintaining courts of justice.

Vectigal, origine ipsa, jus cæsarum et regum patrimoniale est /vektáygəl, əríjəniy ípsə, jə́s síyzərəm èt ríygəm pætrəmòwniyéyliy èst/. Tribute, in its origin, is the patrimonial right of emperors and kings.

Vectura /vekt(y)úrə/. In maritime law, freight.

Vehicle. That in or on which persons, goods, etc. may be carried from one place to another, especially along the ground. Any moving support or container fitted or used for the conveyance of bulky objects; a means of conveyance. That which is used as an instrument of conveyance, transmission or communication. Term refers to every device in, upon or by which a person or property is or may be transported upon a highway. Term has been held to include a "moped" (People v. Jordan, 75 Cal.App.3d Supp. 1, 142 Cal. Rptr. 401, 405), while a bicycle has been held by some courts to be a vehicle under traffic laws (Richards v. Goff, 26 Md.App. 344, 338 A.2d 80, 84), while others have held that it is not (Fowles v. Dakin, 160 Me. 392, 205 A.2d 169, 173).

Vehicular homicide. Homicide caused by the illegal operation of a motor vehicle. Both intentional conduct and negligence may be the basis for such charge though statutes vary from state to state as to the elements of the crime. See also **Homicide.**

Veies /víy(iy)z/. L. Fr. Distresses forbidden to be replevied; the refusing to let the owner have his cattle which were distrained.

Vein. A continuous body of mineral or mineralized rock, filling a seam or fissure in the earth's crust, within defined boundaries in the general mass of the mountain (which boundaries clearly separate it from the neighboring rock), and having a general character of continuity in the direction of its length. McMullin v. Magnuson, 102 Colo. 230, 78 P.2d 964, 968. It includes all deposits of mineral matter found through a mineralized zone or belt coming from the same source, impressed with the same forms, and appearing to have been created by the same processes. Inyo Marble Co. v. Loundagin, 120 Cal.App. 298, 7 P.2d 1067, 1072.

The terms "principal," "original," and "primary," as well as "secondary," "accidental," and "incidental," have all been employed to describe the different veins found within the same surface boundaries, but their meaning is not entirely clear in all cases. They may refer to the relative importance or value of the different veins, or the relations to each other, or to the time of discovery, but the words "secondary," "accidental," and "incidental" are most frequently used to distinguish between the discovery vein and other veins within the same surface boundaries.

Discovery vein. That vein which served as a basis of the location, in contradistinction to secondary, accidental, and incidental veins. The primary vein for the purpose of locating a mining claim and determining which are the end and which the side lines. Where the discovery vein crosses the opposite side lines of the claim as located, the side lines become end lines, not only with respect to such vein, but for determination of extralateral rights in any other vein which apexes within the claim.

Vejours. Viewers; persons sent by the court to take a view of any place in question, for the better decision of the right. It signifies, also, such as are sent to view those that *essoin* themselves *de malo lecti,* (*i.e.,* excuse themselves on ground of illness) whether they be in truth so sick as that they cannot appear, or whether they do counterfeit.

Velabrum /vəlǽbrəm/. In old English law, a tollbooth.

Velitis jubeatis quirites? /vélədəs juwbiyéydəs kwəráydiyz/. Lat. Is it your will and pleasure, Romans? The form of proposing a law to the Roman people.

Velle non creditur qui obsequitur imperio patris vel domini /véliy nòn krédədər kwáy əbsékwədər impír(i)yow pǽtrəs vèl dómənay/. He is not presumed to consent who obeys the orders of his father or his master.

Vel non /vèl nón/. Or not. These words appear in the phrase "devisavit vel non" (*q.v.*), meaning, literally, "did he devise or not." Examples of their use by the courts may be seen in the following quotations: "So the sufficiency vel non of the order of publication is important"; "the negligence vel non of the owner was * * * for the jury"; and "We come at last to the merits vel non of this appeal".

Veltraria /veltrér(i)yə/. The office of dog-leader, or courser.

Venal /víynəl/. Pertaining to something that is bought; capable of being bought; offered for sale; mercenary. Used usually in an evil sense, such purchase or sale being regarded as corrupt and illegal.

Venaria /vənér(i)yə/. Beasts caught in the woods by hunting.

Venatio /vənéysh(iy)ow/. Hunting.

Vend. To transfer to another for a pecuniary equivalent; to make an object of trade, especially by hawking or peddling; to sell. Goins v. State, 194 Ark. 598, 108 S.W.2d 1082, 1083. The term is not commonly applied to the sale of real estate, although its derivatives "vendor" and "vendee" are.

Vendee. A purchaser or buyer; one to whom anything is sold. Generally used of the purchaser of real property, one who acquires chattels by sale being called a "buyer." See also **Vendor.**

Vendens eandem rem duobus falsarius est /vénden(d)z iyǽndəm rém dyuwówbəs fol(t)sér(i)yəs èst/. He is fraudulent who sells the same thing twice.

Vendetta. A private blood feud, in which a family seeks to avenge one of its members on the offender or his family. Stephens v. Howells Sales Co., D.C.N.Y., 16 F.2d 805, 808.

Vendible /véndəbəl/. Fit or suitable to be sold; capable of transfer by sale; merchantable.

Venditæ /véndədiy/. In old European law, a tax upon things sold in markets and public fairs.

Venditio /vendísh(iy)ow/. Lat. In the civil law, in a strict sense, sale; the act of selling; the contract of sale, otherwise called *"emptio venditio."*

In a broader sense, any mode or species of alienation; any contract by which the property or ownership of a thing may be transferred.

Vendition /vendíshən/. Sale; the act of selling.

Venditioni exponas /vəndìshiyównay ekspównəs/. Lat. You expose to sale. The name of a writ of execution, requiring a sale to be made, directed to a sheriff when he has levied upon goods under a *fieri facias,* but returned that they remained unsold for want of buyers; and in some jurisdictions it is issued to cause a sale to be made of lands, seized under a former writ, after they have been condemned or passed upon by an inquisition. Frequently abbreviated to *"vend. ex."* Beeve v. U. S., 161 U.S. 104, 16 S.Ct. 532, 40 L.Ed. 633; State ex rel. First Nat. Bank v. Ogden, 173 Okl. 285, 49 P.2d 565, 567. The writ gives no new authority to the sheriff but only directs him to perform his duty under the execution. Fannin's Ex'r v. Haney, 283 Ky. 68, 140 S.W.2d 630, 632.

Venditor /véndədər/. Lat. A seller; a vendor.

Venditor regis /véndədər ríyjəs/. In old English law, the king's seller or salesman; the person who exposed to sale those goods and chattels which were seized or distrained to answer any debt due to the king.

Venditrix /véndətrəks/. Lat. A female vendor.

Vendor. The person who transfers property by sale, particularly real estate; "seller" being more commonly used for one who sells personalty. The latter may, however, with entire propriety, be termed a vendor. A merchant; a retail dealer; a supplier; one who buys to sell. See also **Vendee**.

Vendor's lien. A creature of equity, being a lien impliedly belonging to a vendor for the unpaid purchase price of land, where he has not taken any other lien or security beyond the personal obligation of the purchaser. An equitable security which arises from the fact that a vendee has received from his vendor property for which he has not paid the full consideration, and such lien exists independently of any express agreement. Sturdy v. Smith, Mo.App., 132 S.W.2d 1033, 1037; Causer v. Wilmoth, Mo.App., 142 S.W.2d 777, 779; Mollett v. Beckman, Mo.App., 78 S.W.2d 886, 890. Also, a lien existing in the unpaid vendor of chattels, the same remaining in his hands, to the extent of the purchase price, where the sale was for cash, or on a term of credit which has expired, or on an agreement by which the seller is to retain possession.

In English and American law a vendor's lien is exceptional in character, and is an importation from the civil law, which found its recognition through courts of chancery, on the equitable principle that the person who had secured the estate of another ought not in conscience to be allowed to keep it and not pay full consideration money, and that to enforce that payment it was just that the vendor should have a lien upon the property.

Vendue /vendyúw/vénd(y)uw/. A sale; generally a sale at public auction; and more particularly a sale so made under authority of law, as by a constable, sheriff, tax collector, administrator, etc.

Vendue master /vénd(y)uw mǽstər/. An auctioneer.

Venereal /vəníriyəl/. Sexual; as, *venereal* diseases.

Venereal disease /vəníriyəl dəzíyz/. One of several diseases identified with sexual intercourse. Collective term for gonorrhea, chancroid, and syphilis.

Venia /víyn(i)yə/. A kneeling or low prostration on the ground by penitents; pardon.

Venia ætatis /víyn(i)yə ətéydəs/. A privilege granted by a prince or sovereign, in virtue of which a person is entitled to act, *sui juris*, as if he were of full age.

Veniæ facilitas incentivum est delinquendi /víyniyiy fəsílətæs ìn(t)sentáyvəm èst dèliŋkwénday/. Facility of pardon is an incentive to crime.

Venire /vənáyriy/. Lat. To come; to appear in court. Sometimes used as the name of the writ for summoning a jury, more commonly called a *"venire facias"* The list of jurors summoned to serve as jurors for a particular term. A special venire is sometimes prepared for a protracted case.

Venire de novo /vənáyriy dìy nówvow/. See **Venire facias de novo**.

Venire facias /vənáyriy féysh(iy)əs/. Lat. A judicial writ, directed to the sheriff of the county in which a cause is to be tried, commanding him that he "cause to come" before the court, on a certain day therein mentioned, twelve good and lawful men of the body of his county, qualified according to law, by whom the truth of the matter may be the better known, and who are in no wise of kin either to the plaintiff or to the defendant, to make a jury of the county between the parties in the action, because as well the plaintiff as the defendant, between whom the matter in variance is, have put themselves upon that jury, and that he return the names of the jurors, etc.

Venire facias ad respondendum /vənáyriy féysh(iy)əs æd rèspondéndəm/. A writ to summon a person, against whom an indictment for a misdemeanor has been found, to appear and be arraigned for the offense. A warrant is now more commonly used.

Venire facias de novo /vənáyriy féysh(iy)əs dìy nówvow/. A fresh or new *venire*, which the court grants when there has been some impropriety or irregularity in returning the jury, or where the verdict is so imperfect or ambiguous that no judgment can be given upon it, or where a judgment is reversed on error, and a new trial awarded. The ancient common-law mode of proceeding to a new trial was by a writ of venire facias de novo. The present day relief of "new trial" is intended to mitigate the severity of the proceeding to attaint. While a venire de novo and new trial are quite different, they are alike in that a new trial takes place in both. The material difference between them is that a venire de novo must be granted upon matters appearing upon the face of the record, but a new trial may be granted for things out of the record. The terms "venire facias de novo" and "venire de novo" are used interchangeably to denote a new trial.

Venire facias juratores /vənáyriy féysh(iy)əs jùrətóriyz/. A common law judicial writ directed to the sheriff, when issue was joined in an action, commanding him to cause to come to Westminster, on such a day, twelve free and lawful men of his county by whom the truth of the matter at issue might be better known. This writ was abolished by section 104 of the common-law procedure act, 1852, and by section 105 a precept issued by the judges of assize is substituted in its place. The process so substituted is sometimes loosely spoken of as a *"venire."*

Venire facias tot matronas /vənáyriy féysh(iy)əs tòt mətrównəs/. A writ to summon a jury of matrons to execute the writ *de ventre inspiciendo*.

Venireman /vənáyriymən/. A member of a panel of jurors; a juror summoned by a writ of *venire facias*.

Venit et defendit /víynəd èt dəféndət/. L. Lat. In old pleading, comes and defends. The proper words of appearance and defense in an action.

Venit et dicit /víynəd èt dísət/. Lat. In old pleading, comes and says.

Vente /vónt/. In French law, sale; contract of sale.

Vente aleatoire /vónt àleyatwár/. A sale subject to an uncertain event.

Vente à rémére /vónt a rèymeréy/. A conditional sale, in which the seller reserves the right to redeem or repurchase at the same price. The term is used in Canada and Louisiana.

Vente aux enchères /vónt owz onshér/. An auction.

Venter /véntər/. Lat. (ventre, Fr.) The belly; the womb; the wife. Used in law as designating the maternal parentage of children. Thus, where in ordinary phraseology we should say that A. was B.'s child by his first wife, he would be described in law as "by the first *venter*." A child is said to be *en ventre sa mere* before it is born; while is it a fœtus.

Ventre inspiciendo /véntriy inspìshiyéndow/. See **De ventre inspiciendo; Venire facias tot matronas.**

Venture, v. To take (the) chances.

Venture, n. An undertaking attended with risk, especially one aiming at making money; business speculation. See also **Joint enterprise; Joint venture.**

Venue. Formerly spelled *visne.* In common law pleading and practice, a neighborhood; the neighborhood, place, or county in which an injury is declared to have been done, or fact declared to have happened. 3 Bl.Comm. 294.

The particular county, or geographical area, in which a court with jurisdiction may hear and determine a case. Venue deals with locality of suit, that is, with question of which court, or courts, of those that possess adequate personal and subject matter jurisdiction may hear the specific suit in question. Japan Gas Lighter Ass'n v. Ronson Corp., D.C.N.J., 257 F.Supp. 219, 224. It relates only to place where or territory within which either party may require case to be tried. Cushing v. Doudistal, 278 Ky. 779, 129 S.W.2d 527, 528, 530. It has relation to convenience of litigants and may be waived or laid by consent of parties. Iselin v. La Coste, C.C.A.La., 147 F.2d 791, 795.

The general venue statute governing civil actions in U.S. district courts is 28 U.S.C.A. § 1391.

In federal cases the prosecutor's discretion regarding the location of the prosecution is limited by Article III, § 2, U.S.Const., which requires trial in the state where the offense "shall have been committed," and the Sixth Amendment, which guarantees an impartial jury "of the state and district wherein the crime shall have been committed."

Venue does not refer to jurisdiction at all. Arganbright v. Good, 46 Cal.App.2d Supp. 877, 116 P.2d 186. "Jurisdiction" of the court means the inherent power to decide a case, whereas "venue" designates the particular county or city in which a court with jurisdiction may hear and determine the case. Stanton Trust and Savings Bank v. Johnson, 104 Mont. 235, 65 P.2d 1188, 1189. As such, while a defect in venue may be waived by the parties, lack of jurisdiction may not.

See also **Change of venue; Forum conveniens; Forum non conveniens.**

Federal criminal cases. Except as otherwise permitted by statute or by the rules, the prosecution shall be had in a district in which the offense was committed. The court shall fix the place of trial within the district with due regard to the convenience of the defendant and the witnesses. Fed.R.Crim.P. 18.

Venue facts. Facts to be established at hearing on plea of privilege. Central Motor Co. v. Roberson, Tex.Civ. App., 139 S.W.2d 287, 289. Facts which by statute constitute an exception to the general right of a defendant to be sued in the county of his residence. Crawford v. Sanger, Tex.Civ.App., 160 S.W.2d 115, 116.

Venue jurisdiction. Power of the particular court to function. Brand v. Pennsylvania R. Co., D.C.Pa., 22 F.Supp. 569, 571.

Veracity. Truthfulness; accuracy.

Veray /vəréy/. L. Fr. True. An old form of *vrai.* Thus, *veray*, or true *tenant*, is one who holds in fee-simple; *veray tenant by the manner*, is the same as tenant by the manner *(q.v.)*, with this difference only: that the fee-simple instead of remaining in the lord, is given by him or by the law to another.

Verba /várbə/. Lat. (Plural of *verbum.*) Words.

Verba accipienda sunt cum effectu, ut sortiantur effectum /várbə əksìpiyéndə sànt kàm əfékt(y)uw, ət sòrshiyæntər əféktəm/. Words are to be received with effect, so that they may produce effect.

Verba accipienda sunt secundum subjectam materiam /várbə əksìpiyéndə sànt səkándəm səbjéktəm mətíriyəm/. Words are to be understood with reference to the subject-matter.

Verba accipienda ut sortiantur effectum /várbə əksìpiyéndə ət sòrshiyæntər əféktəm/. Words are to be taken so that they may have some effect.

Verba æquivoca, ac in dubio sensu posita, intelliguntur digniori et potentiori sensu /várbə əkwívəkə, æk in d(y)úwbiyow pózədə, intèləgántər dìgn(i)yóray èt pətènshiyóray sén(t)s(y)uw/. Equivocal words, and such as are put in a doubtful sense, are [to be] understood in the more worthy and effectual sense [in their best and most effective sense].

Verba aliquid operari debent; debent intelligi ut aliquid operentur /várbə ǽləkwəd òpəréray débənt; débənt intélajay əd ǽləkwəd òpəréntər/. Words ought to have some operation; they ought to be interpreted in such a way as to have some operation.

Verba aliquid operari debent, verba cum effectu sunt accipienda /várbə ǽləkwid òpəréray débənt, várbə kàm əfékt(y)uw sánt əksìpiyéndə/. Words are to be taken so as to have effect.

Verba artis ex arte /várbə árdəs èks árdiy/. Terms of art should be explained from the art.

Verba cancellariæ /várbə kæn(t)səlériyiy/. Words of the chancery. The technical style of writs framed in the office of chancery.

Verba chartarum fortius accipiuntur contra proferentem /várbə kartérəm fórsh(iy)əs əksìpiyántər kóntrə pròfəréntəm/. The words of charters are to be received more strongly against the grantor [or the person offering them].

Verba cum effectu accipienda sunt /várbə kəm əfékt(y)uw əksìpiyéndə sánt/. Words ought to be used so as to give them their effect.

Verba currentis monetæ, tempus solutionis designant /várbə kəhréntəs məníydiy, témpəs səl(y)ùwshiyównəs dézəgnænt/. The words "current money" designate current at the time of payment.

Verba debent intelligi cum effectu ut res magis valeat quam pereat /várbə débənt intéləjay kəm əfékt(y)uw, ət ríyz méyjəs vǽliyət kwǽm péhriyət/. Words ought to be understood with effect, that a thing may rather be preserved than destroyed.

Verba debent intelligi ut aliquid operentur /várbə débənt intéləjay ət ǽləkwəd òpəréntər/. Words ought to be understood so as to have some operation.

Verba dicta de persona intelligi debent de conditione personæ /várbə díktə dìy pərsównə intéləjay débənt dìy kəndìshiyówniy pərsówniy/. Words spoken of a person are to be understood of the condition of the person.

Verba fortius accipiuntur contra proferentem /várbə fórsh(iy)əs əksìpiyántər kóntrə pròfəréntəm/. Words are to be taken most strongly against him who uses them.

Verba generalia generaliter sunt intelligenda /várbə jenəréyl(i)yə jenəréylədər sànt intèləjéndə/. General words are to be generally understood.

Verba generalia restringuntur ad habilitatem rei vel aptitudinem personæ /várbə jenəréyl(i)yə rèstriŋgántər ǽd həbìlətéydəm ríyay vèl ǽptət(y)úwdənəm pərsówniy/. General words must be narrowed either to the nature of the subject-matter or to the aptitude of the person.

Verba illata (relata) inesse videntur /várbə əléydə inésiy vədéntər/°rəléydə°/. Words referred to are to be considered as if incorporated.

Verba in differenti materia per prius, non per posterius, intelligenda sunt /várbə in dìfəréntay mətíriyə pər práyəs, nón pər postíriyəs, intèləjéndə sànt/. Words on a different subject are to be understood by what precedes, not by what comes after. A maxim of the civil law.

Verba intelligenda sunt in casu possibili /várbə intèləjéndə sànt in kéys(y)uw posíbələy/. Words are to be understood in [or "of," or "in reference to"] a possible case. A maxim of the civil law.

Verba intentioni, non e contra, debent inservire /várbə intènshiyównay, nón iy kóntrə, débənt ìnsərváyriy/. 8 Coke, 94. Words ought to be made subservient to the intent, not the intent to the words. Bailey v. Abington, 201 Ark. 1072, 148 S.W.2d 176, 179.

Verba ita sunt intelligenda, ut res magis valeat quam pereat /várbə áydə sànt intèləjéndə, ət ríyz méyjəs vǽliyət kwǽm péhriyət/. The words [of an instrument] are to be so understood, that the subject-matter may rather be of force than perish [rather be preserved than destroyed; or, in other words, that the instrument may have effect, if possible]. 2 Bl.Comm. 380.

Verbal. Strictly, of or pertaining to words; expressed in words, whether spoken or written, but commonly in spoken words; hence, by confusion, spoken; oral. Parol; by word of mouth; as, verbal agreement, verbal evidence; or written, but not signed, or not executed with the formalities required for a deed or prescribed by statute in particular cases.

Verbal act doctrine. Under this doctrine, utterances accompanying some act or conduct to which it is desired to give legal effect arc admissible where conduct to be characterized by words is material to issue and equivocal in its nature, and words accompany conduct and aid in giving it legal significance. Keefe v. State, 50 Ariz. 293, 295, 72 P.2d 425, 427. Under doctrine, where declarations of an individual are so connected with his acts as to derive a degree of credit from such connection, independently of the declaration, the declaration becomes part of the transaction and is admissible. The "verbal act doctrine" and the "res gestæ doctrine" coincide practically and serve equally to admit certain sorts of statements, but they are nevertheless wholly distinct in their nature and in their right to exist. American Employers Ins. Co. v. Wentworth, 90 N.H. 112, 5 A.2d 265, 269. See also **Res gestæ.**

Verbal assaults. See **Threats.**

Verbal note. A memorandum or note, in diplomacy, not signed, sent when an affair has continued a long time without any reply, in order to avoid the appearance of an urgency which perhaps is not required; and, on the other hand, to guard against the supposition that it is forgotten, or that there is an intention of not prosecuting it any further.

Verbal process. In Louisiana, *procès verbal (q.v.).*

Verba mere æquivoca, si per communem usum loquendi in intellectu certo summuntur, talis intellectus præferendus est /várbə míriy əkwìvəkéydə, sáy pər kəmyúwnəm yúwsəm lowkwénday in intəlékt(y)uw sárdow səmántər, téyləs ìntəléktəs prèfəréndəs èst/. [In the case of] words merely equivocal, if they are taken by the common usage of speech in a certain sense, such sense is to be preferred. A maxim of the civil law.

Verba nihil operari melius est quam absurde /várbə náy(h)əl òpəréray míyl(i)yəs èst kwǽm əbsárdiy/. It is better that words should have no operation at all than [that they should operate] absurdly. A maxim of the civil law.

Verba non tam intuenda, quam causa et natura rei, ut mens contrahentium ex eis potius quam ex verbis appareat /várbə nón tæm int(y)uwéndə, kwǽm kózə èt nət(y)úrə ríyay, ət mén(d)z kòntrəhénsh(iy)əm èks íyəs pówsh(iy)əs kwæm eks várbəs əpæriyət/. The words [of a contract] are not so much to be looked at as the cause and nature of the thing [which is the subject of it], in order that the intention of the contracting parties may appear rather from them than from the words.

Verba offendi possunt, imo ab eis recedere licet, ut verba ad sanum intellectum reducantur /várbə əfénday pósənt, áymow ǽb íyəs rəsíydəriy lísəd, ət várbə ǽd séynəm intəléktəm rìyd(y)uwkǽntər/. Words may be opposed [taken in a contrary sense], nay, we may disregard them altogether, in order that the [general] words [of an instrument] may be restored to a sound meaning. A maxim of the civilians.

Verba ordinationis quando verificari possunt in sua vera significatione, trahi ad extraneum intellectum non debent /várbə òrdənèyshiyównəs kwóndow vèhrəfəkéray pósənt ìn s(y)úwə vírə sìgnəfəkèyshiyówniy, tréyhay æd əkstréyn(i)yəm ìntəléktəm nòn débənt/. When the words of an ordinance can be carried into effect in their own true meaning, they ought not to be drawn to a foreign intendment. A maxim of the civilians.

Verba posteriora propter certitudinem addita, ad priora quæ certitudine indigent, sunt referenda /várbə postìriyórə próptər sərdət(y)úwdənəm ǽdədə, æd prayórə kwìy sərdət(y)úwdəniy índəjənt, sənt rèfəréndə/. Subsequent words, added for the purpose of certainty, are to be referred to the preceding words which require the certainty.

Verba precaria /várbə prəkér(i)yə/. In the civil law, precatory words; words of trust, or used to create a trust.

Verba pro re et subjecta materia accipi debent /várbə pròw ríy èt səbjéktə mətír(i)yə ǽksəpay débənt/. Words ought to be understood in favor of the thing and subject-matter. A maxim of the civilians.

Verba quæ aliquid operari possunt non debent esse superflua /várbə kwìy ǽləkwəd òpəréray pósənt nòn débənt ésiy səpárfluwə/. Words which can have any kind of operation ought not to be [considered] superfluous.

Verba, quantumvis generalia, ad aptitudinem restringantur, etiamsi nullam aliam paterentur restrictionem /várbə, kwontámvəs jènəréyl(i)yə, æd ǽptət(y)úwdənəm rèstringǽntər, èshiyǽmsay náləm éyl(i)yəm pǽdəréntər rəstríkshiyównəm/. Words, howsoever general, are restrained to fitness (i.e., to harmonize with the subject-matter), though they would bear no other restriction.

Verba relata hoc maxime operantur per referentiam, ut in eis inesse videntur /várbə rəléydə hòk mǽksəmiy opərǽntər pàr rèfərénsh(iy)əm, əd in íyəs inésiy vədéntər/. Related words [words connected with others by reference] have this particular operation by the reference, that they are considered as being inserted in those [clauses which refer to them]. Words to which reference is made in an instrument have the same effect and operation as if they were inserted in the clauses referring to them.

Verba relata inesse videntur /várbə rəléydə inésiy vədéntər/. Words to which reference is made seem to be incorporated.

Verba secundum materiam subjectam intelligi nemo est qui nesciat /várbə səkándəm mətíriyəm səbjéktəm intéləjay nýmow èst kwáy néshiyət/. There is no one who does not know that words are to be understood according to their subject-matter.

Verba semper accipienda sunt in mitiori sensu /várbə sémpər əksìpiyéndə sànt in mìshiyóray sén(t)s(y)uw/. Words are always to be taken in the milder sense.

Verba strictæ significationis ad latam extendi possunt, si subsit ratio /várbə stríktiy sìgnəfəkèyshiyównəs æd léydəm əksténday pósənt, sày sə́bsit réysh(iy)ow/. Words of a strict or narrow signification may be extended to a broad meaning, if there be ground in reason for it. A maxim of the civilians.

Verba sunt indices animi /várbə sànt índəsiyz ǽnəmay/. Words are the indices or indicators of the mind or thought.

Verbis standum ubi nulla ambiguitas /várbəs stǽndəm yúwbay nálə æmbəgyúwətæs/. One must abide by the words where there is no ambiguity.

Verbum imperfecti temporis rem adhuc imperfectam significat /várbəm ìmpərféktay témpərəs rém ǽdhàk ìmpərféktəm signífəkæt/. The imperfect tense of the verb indicates an incomplete matter.

Verderer, or verderor /várdərər/. An officer of the king's forest, who is sworn to maintain and keep the assizes of the forest, and to view, receive, and enroll the attachments and presentments of all manner of trespasses of vert and venison in the forest.

Verdict. From the Latin "veredictum," a true declaration. Clark v. State, 170 Tenn. 494, 499, 97 S.W.2d 644, 646. The formal decision or finding made by a jury, impaneled and sworn for the trial of a cause, and reported to the court (and accepted by it), upon the matters or questions duly submitted to them upon the trial. The definitive answer given by the jury to the court concerning the matters of fact committed to the jury for their deliberation and determination. Ralston v. Stump, 75 Ohio App. 375, 62 N.E.2d 293, 294, 31 O.O. 43.

The usual verdict, one where the jury decides which side wins (and how much, sometimes), is called a general verdict. When the jury is asked to answer specific questions of fact, it is called a special verdict. See *General verdict* and *Special verdict* below.

In criminal cases the verdict shall be unanimous, and shall be returned by the jury to the judge in open court. Fed.R.Crim.P. 31. In civil cases the parties may stipulate that a verdict of a stated majority of the jurors shall be taken as the verdict of the jury. Fed.R.Civil P. 48.

See also **Polling the jury.**

Chance verdict. One determined by hazard or lot, and not by the deliberate understanding and agreement of the jury. While formerly used, such are now illegal.

Compromise verdict. One which is the result, not of justifiable concession of views, but of improper compromise of the vital principles which should have controlled the decision. Although it is proper for jurors to harmonize their views and reach a verdict with proper regard for each other's opinions, it is not proper for any juror to surrender his conscientious convictions on any material issue in return for a relinquishment by others of their like settled opinions on another issue, producing a result which does not command the approval of the whole panel.

Directed verdict. Verdict ordered by the judge as a matter of law when he rules that the party with the burden of proof has failed to make out a prima facie case. The judge under these circumstances orders the jury to return a verdict for the other party. See Fed.R.Civil P. 50.

Excessive verdict. See that title.

False verdict. One obviously opposed to the principles of right and justice; an untrue verdict. Formerly, if a jury gave a false verdict, the party injured by it might sue out and prosecute a writ of attaint against them, either at common law or on the statute 11 Hen. VII, c. 24, at his election, for the purpose of reversing the judgment and punishing the jury for their verdict; but not where the jury erred merely in point of law, if they found according to the judge's direction. The practice of setting aside verdicts and granting new trials, however, so superseded the use of attaints that there is no instance of one to be found in the books or reports later than in the time of Elizabeth, and it was altogether abolished by 6 Geo. IV, c. 50, § 60.

General verdict. A verdict whereby the jury find either for the plaintiff or for the defendant in general terms; the ordinary form of a verdict. Glenn v. Sumner, 132 U.S. 152, 10 S.Ct. 41, 33 L.Ed. 301. A finding by the jury in the terms of the issue, or all the issues, referred to them. That by which they pronounce generally upon all or any of the issues, either in favor of the plaintiff or defendant;—distinguished from a special verdict, which is that by which the jury finds facts only.

General verdict with interrogatories. The court may submit to the jury, together with appropriate forms for a general verdict, written interrogatories upon one or more issues of fact the decision of which is necessary to a verdict. The court shall give such explanation or instruction as may be necessary to enable the jury both to make answers to the interrogatories and to render a general verdict, and the court shall direct the jury both to make written answers and to render a general verdict. When the general verdict and the answers are harmonious, the appropriate judgment upon the verdict and answers shall be entered. When the answers are consistent with each other but one or more is inconsistent with the general verdict, judgment may be entered in accordance with the answers, notwithstanding the general verdict, or the court may return the jury for further consideration of its answers and verdict or may order a new trial. When the answers are inconsistent with each other and one or more is likewise inconsistent with the general verdict, judgment shall not be entered, but the court shall return the jury for further consideration of its answers and verdict or shall order a new trial. Fed.R.Civil P. 49(b).

Instructed verdict. See *Directed verdict, supra.*

Joint verdict. See that title.

Open verdict. A verdict of a coroner's jury which finds that the subject "came to his death by means to the jury unknown," or "came to his death at the hands of a person or persons to the jury unknown," that is, one which leaves open either the question whether any crime was committed or the identity of the criminal.

Partial verdict. In criminal law, a verdict by which the jury acquits the defendant as to a part of the accusation and finds him guilty as to the residue.

Privy verdict. One given after the judge has left or adjourned the court, and the jury, being agreed, in order to be delivered from their confinement, obtain leave to give their verdict privily to the judge out of court. Such a verdict is of no force unless afterwards affirmed by a public verdict given openly in court. This practice is now superseded by that of rendering a sealed verdict.

Public verdict. A verdict openly delivered by the jury in court.

Quotient verdict. See that title.

Sealed verdict. See **Sealed.**

Several defendants. If there are two or more defendants, the jury at any time during its deliberations may return a verdict or verdicts with respect to a defendant or defendants as to whom it has agreed; if the jury cannot agree with respect to all, the defendant or defendants as to whom it does not agree may be tried again. Fed.R.Crim.P. 31(b).

Special verdict. The "special" verdict is a statement by the jury of the facts it has found—in essence, the jury's answers to questions submitted to it; the court determines which party, based on those answers, is to have judgment. With the advent of the apportionment rule among tortfeasors, closely followed by the adoption of a rule of comparative negligence to replace the traditional rule of contributory negligence, the need to have the jury reveal its specific findings of percentages of fault in personal injury and wrongful death cases has given rise to the increased use of the special verdict.

The court may require a jury to return only a special verdict in the form of a special written finding upon each issue of fact. In that event, the court may submit to the jury written questions susceptible of categorical or other brief answer or may submit written forms of the several special findings which might properly be made under the pleadings and evidence; or it may use such other method of submitting the issues and requiring the written findings thereon as it deems most appropriate. The court shall give to the jury such explanation and instructions concerning the matter thus submitted as may be necessary to enable the jury to make its findings upon each issue. Fed.R. Civil P. 49(a).

Stipulation on majority verdict. The parties may stipulate that a verdict of a stated majority of the jurors shall be taken as the verdict of the jury. Fed. R.Civil P. 48.

Verdict by lot. See *Chance verdict, supra.*

Verdict contrary to law. A verdict which law does not authorize jury to render on evidence because conclusion drawn is not justified thereby. One which is contrary to the principles of law as applied to the facts which the jury were called upon to try and contrary to the principles of law which should govern the cause. Piepho v. Gesse, 106 Ind.App. 450, 18 N.E.2d 468, 471. See **Non obstante veredicto.**

Verdict subject to opinion of court. A verdict returned by the jury, the entry of judgment upon which is subject to the determination of points of law reserved by the court upon the trial.

Verdict, estoppel by. Rule that where some controlling fact or question material to determination of both causes has been adjudicated in former suit by court of competent jurisdiction, and same fact or question is again an issue between the same parties, adjudication in first cause will, if properly presented, be conclusive of the same question in later suit, irrespective of whether cause of action is the same in both suits. People v. Haran, 27 Ill.2d 229, 188 N.E.2d 707, 709. "Estoppel by verdict" or "collateral estoppel" provides that prior judgment must be deemed conclusive as to all right of parties and their privies when same parties or their privies are involved with same issues actually or necessarily finally determined by court of competent jurisdiction in earlier, but different, cause of action. Riley v. Unknown Owners of 304 North Oak Park Ave. Bldg., Oak Park, 25 Ill.App.3d 895, 324 N.E.2d 78, 85. See also **Collateral estoppel doctrine; Judgment, estoppel by Res** (*Res judicata*).

Veredictum /vèhrədíktəm/. L. Lat. In old English law, a verdict; a declaration of the truth of a matter in issue, submitted to a jury for trial.

Veredictum, quasi dictum veritatis; ut judicium quasi juris dictum /vèhrədíktəm, kwéysay díktəm vèhrətéydəs; ət juwdísh(iy)əm kwéysay júrəs díktəm/. The verdict is, as it were, the *dictum* [saying] of truth; as the judgment is the *dictum* of law.

Verge, or **virge** /várj/. In old English law, the compass of the royal court, which bounds the jurisdiction of the lord steward of the household; it seems to have been twelve miles about. An uncertain quantity of land from fifteen to thirty acres. Also a stick, or rod, whereby one is admitted tenant to a copyhold estate.

Vergelt /várgèlt/. In Saxon law, a mulct or fine for a crime. See **Weregild.**

Verification. Confirmation of correctness, truth, or authenticity, by affidavit, oath, or deposition. Affidavit of truth of matter stated and object of verification is to assure good faith in averments or statements of party. Sheeley v. City of Santa Clara, 215 Cal.App.2d 83, 30 Cal.Rptr. 121, 123. In accounting, the process of substantiating entries in books of account. See also **Authentication; Certification; Confirmation; Verify.**

Verified copy. Copy of document which is shown by independent evidence to be true. A copy, if successive witnesses trace the original into the hands of a witness who made or compared the copy. Nu Car Carriers v. Traynor, 75 U.S.App.D.C. 174, 125 F.2d 47, 48.

Verified names. Names verified by county clerk in accordance with his duty to check names of signers against official registration lists. Allan v. Rasmussen, 101 Utah 33, 117 P.2d 287, 289.

Verify. To confirm or substantiate by oath or affidavit. Particularly used of making formal oath to accounts, petitions, pleadings, and other papers. The word "verified," when used in a statute, ordinarily imports

a verity attested by the sanctity of an oath. It is frequently used interchangeably with "sworn."

To prove to be true; to confirm or establish the truth or truthfulness of; to check or test the accuracy or exactness of; to confirm or establish the authenticity of; to authenticate; to maintain; to affirm; to support; second; back as a friend. MacNeill v. Maddox, 194 Ga. 802, 22 S.E.2d 653, 654.

See also **Verification.**

Verily /véhrəliy/. In very truth; beyond doubt or question; in fact; certainly; truly; confidently; really.

Veritas, a quocunque dicitur, a Deo est /véhrətæs, éy kwowkáŋkwiy dísədər, èy díyow èst/. Truth, by whomsoever pronounced, is from God.

Veritas demonstrationis tollit errorem nominis /véhrətæs dèmənstrèyshiyównəs tóləd ehrórəm nómənəs/. The truth of the description removes an error in the name.

Veritas habenda est in juratore; justitia et judicium in judice /véhrətæs həbéndə èst in jùrətóriy; jəstísh(iy)ə èt juwdísh(iy)əm in júwdəsiy/. Truth is the desideratum in a juror; justice and judgment in a judge.

Veritas nihil veretur nisi abscondi /véhrətæs náy(h)əl vəríydər náysay əbskónday/. Truth fears nothing but to be hid.

Veritas nimium altercando amittitur /véhrətæs nímiyəm òltərkǽndow əmídədər/. Truth is lost by excessive altercation.

Veritas nominis tollit errorem demonstrationis /véhrətæs nómənəs tóləd ehrórəm dèmənstrèyshiyównəs/. The truth of the name takes away the error of description.

Veritas, quæ minime defensatur opprimitur; et qui non improbat, approbat /véhrətæs, kwiy mínəmiy dèfenséydər əprímədər; èt kwáy nòn ímprəbəd ǽprəbət/. Truth which is not sufficiently defended is overpowered; and he who does not disapprove, approves.

Veritatem qui non libere pronunciat proditor est veritatis /vèhrətéydəm kwày non líbəriy prənánshiyət prówdədər èst vehrətéydəs/. He who does not freely speak the truth is a betrayer of truth.

Verity. Truth; truthfulness; conformity to fact. The records of a court "import uncontrollable verity."

Verna /várnə/. Lat. In the civil law, a slave born in his master's house.

Versari /vərséray/. Lat. In the civil law, to be employed; to be conversant. *Versari male in tutela,* to misconduct one's self in a guardianship.

Versus /vársəs/. Lat. Against. In the title of a cause, the name of the plaintiff is put first, followed by the word "*versus,*" then the defendant's name. Thus, "Fletcher *versus* Peck," or "Fletcher *against* Peck." The word is commonly abbreviated "*vs.*" or "*v.*" Vs. and *versus* have become ingrafted upon the English language; their meaning is as well understood and their use quite as appropriate as the word *against* could be.

Vert /vért/. In old English law, that power which a man had, by royal grant, to cut green wood in a forest. In heraldry, green color, called "venus" in the arms of princes, and "emerald" in those of peers, and expressed in engravings by lines in bend.

Vertical integration. Ownership or control of network of production and distribution of goods from raw materials to sale to ultimate consumer.

Vertical merger. Merger between two firms that have a buyer-seller relationship; that is, one produces a product that is then sold to the other. U. S. v. First Nat. Bank of Jackson, D.C.Miss., 301 F.Supp. 1161, 1190. Acquisition of one company which buys product sold by acquiring company or which sells product bought by acquiring company. U. S. v. International Tel. & Tel. Corp., D.C.Conn., 306 F.Supp. 766, 774. See also **Merger.**

Vertical price-fixing contract. A contract between producers and wholesalers or distributors, between producers and retailers, or between wholesalers or distributors and retailers, and not between producers themselves, between wholesalers themselves, or between retailers themselves as to sale or retail prices. Pazen v. Silver Rod Stores, 130 N.J.Eq. 407, 22 A.2d 237, 239; Seagram Distillers Corporation v. Old Dearborn Distributing Co., 363 Ill. 610, 2 N.E.2d 940, 942. See also **Price-fixing.**

Verus /víras/. Lat. True; truthful; genuine; actual; real; just.

Very. As an adjective means real, actual, or true, but as an adverb means in a high degree, exceedingly, extremely; to no small extent. Benoist v. Driveaway Co. of Missouri, Mo.App., 122 S.W.2d 86, 90.

Very high degree of care. That degree of care that would be used by a very cautious, prudent, and competent person under like or similar circumstances. Wichita Valley Ry. Co. v. Williams, Tex.Civ.App., 3 S.W.2d 141, 142.

Very lord and very tenant. They that are immediate lord and tenant one to another.

Vessel. A ship, brig, sloop, or other craft used, or capable of being used, in navigation on water.

In order to be a "vessel," for purposes of an action under Jones Act, the structure's purpose must to some reasonable degree be the transportation of passengers, cargo or equipment from place to place across navigable waters. Buna v. Pacific Far East Line, Inc., D.C.Cal., 441 F.Supp. 1360, 1364. Though, the term "vessel," in admiralty law, is not limited to ships or vessels engaged in commerce. St. Hilaire Moye v. Henderson, C.A.Ark., 496 F.2d 973, 979. Many special purpose craft, such as dredges, floating derricks and barges equipped for special purposes or operations are "vessels" within meaning of Jones Act, and persons regularly employed aboard such a vessel in aid of its purposes are "seamen." Hill v. Diamond, C.A.Va., 311 F.2d 789, 791, 792. On the other hand, however, everything that floats is not necessarily a "vessel," in purview of Jones Act. Bennett v. Perini Corp., C.A.Mass., 510 F.2d 114, 116. For example, a floating dry dock which was moored by chains and cables to shipyard dock at time of injury to shipyard employee and which was in use as a dry dock was not a "vessel" and therefore no warranty of seaworthiness arose. Keller v. Dravo Corp., C.A.La., 441 F.2d 1239, 1244.

Foreign vessel. A vessel owned by residents in, or sailing under the flag of, a foreign nation.

Public vessel. One owned and used by a nation or government for its public service, whether in its navy, its revenue service, or otherwise.

Vest. To give an immediate, fixed right of present or future enjoyment. Baldwin v. Fleck, Tex.Civ.App., 168 S.W.2d 904, 909. To accrue to; to be fixed; to take effect.

To clothe with possession; to deliver full possession of land or of an estate; to give seisin; to enfeoff. See also **Vested.**

Vesta /vésta/. The crop on the ground.

Vested. Fixed; accrued; settled; absolute. Having the character or given the rights of absolute ownership; not contingent; not subject to be defeated by a condition precedent. To be "vested," a right must be more than a mere expectation based on an anticipation of the continuance of an existing law; it must have become a title, legal or equitable, to the present or future enforcement of a demand, or a legal exemption from the demand of another. Aetna Ins. Co. v. Richardelle, Tex.Civ.App., 528 S.W.2d 280, 284. Said of pension plan benefits that are not contingent on the employee continuing to work for the employer. See also **Accrue; Vest.**

Vested devise. See **Devise.**

Vested estate. An interest clothed with a present, legal, and existing right of alienation. Chaison v. Chaison, Tex.Civ.App., 154 S.W.2d 961, 964. Any estate, whether in possession or not, which is not subject to any condition precedent and unperformed. The interest may be either a present and immediate interest, or it may be a future but uncontingent, and therefore transmissible, interest. Estate by which present interest is invariably fixed to remain to determinate person on determination of preceding freehold estate. An estate, when the person or the class which takes the remainder is in existence or is capable of being ascertained when the prior estate vests, Commissioner of Internal Revenue v. Kellogg, C.C.A.3, 119 F.2d 54, 57; or when there is an immediate right of present enjoyment or a present right of future enjoyment.

Vested gift. A gift that is absolute and not contingent or conditional. A gift is vested if it is immediate, notwithstanding that its enjoyment may be postponed. A future gift when the right to receive it is not subject to a condition precedent.

Vested in interest. A legal term applied to a present fixed right of future enjoyment; as reversions, vested remainders, such executory devises, future uses, conditional limitations, and other future interests as are not referred to, or made to depend on, a period or event that is uncertain.

Vested in possession. A legal term applied to a right of present enjoyment actually existing. See **Vest.**

Vested interest. A present right or title to a thing, which carries with it an existing right of alienation, even though the right to possession or enjoyment may be postponed to some uncertain time in the future, as distinguished from a future right, which may never materialize or ripen into title, and it matters not how long or for what length of time the future possession or right of enjoyment may be postponed, if the present right exists to alienate and pass title. Fugazzi v. Fugazzi's Committee, 275 Ky. 62, 120 S.W.2d 779, 781. A future interest not dependent on an uncertain period or event, or a fixed present right of future enjoyment. When a person has a right to immediate possession on determination of preceding or particular estate. One in which there is a present fixed right, either of present enjoyment or of future enjoyment. Painter v. Herschberger, 340 Mo. 347, 100 S.W.2d 532, 535. It is not the uncertainty of enjoyment in the future, but the uncertainty of the right of enjoyment, which makes the difference between a "vested" and a "contingent" interest. A future interest is vested when there is a person in being who would have a right, defeasible or indefeasible, to the immediate possession of the property, upon the ceasing of the intermediate or precedent interest.

Vested legacy. A legacy given in such terms that there is a fixed, indefeasible right to its payment. A legacy payable at a future time, certain to arrive, and not subject to conditions precedent, is vested, where there is a person in esse at the testator's death capable of taking when the time arrives, though his interest may be altogether defeated by his own death. A legacy is said to be vested when the words of the testator making the bequest convey a transmissible interest, whether present or future, to the legatee in the legacy. Thus a legacy to one to be paid when he attains the age of twenty-one years is a vested legacy, because it is given unconditionally and absolutely, and therefore vests an immediate interest in the legatee, of which the enjoyment only is deferred or postponed.

Vested pension. Said of a pension plan when an employee (or his or her estate) has rights to all the benefits purchased with the employer's contributions to the plan even if the employee is not employed by this employer at the time of retirement. Vesting of qualified pension plans is governed by the Employees Retirement Income Security Act (ERISA).

Vested remainder. See **Remainder**.

Vested rights. In constitutional law, rights which have so completely and definitely accrued to or settled in a person that they are not subject to be defeated or canceled by the act of any other private person, and which it is right and equitable that the government should recognize and protect, as being lawful in themselves, and settled according to the then current rules of law, and of which the individual could not be deprived arbitrarily without injustice, or of which he could not justly be deprived otherwise than by the established methods of procedure and for the public welfare. Such interests as cannot be interfered with by retrospective laws; interests which it is proper for state to recognize and protect and of which individual cannot be deprived arbitrarily without injustice.

American States Water Service Co. of California v. Johnson, 31 Cal.App.2d 606, 88 P.2d 770, 774. Immediate or fixed right to present or future enjoyment and one that does not depend on an event that is uncertain. A right complete and consummated, and of such character that it cannot be divested without the consent of the person to whom it belongs, and fixed or established, and no longer open to controversy. State ex rel. Milligan v. Ritter's Estate, Ind.App., 46 N.E.2d 736, 743.

Vestigial words /vestíjəl wə́rdz/. Those contained in a statute which by reason of a succession of statutes on the same subject-matter, amending or modifying previous provisions of the same, are rendered useless or meaningless by such amendments. They should not be permitted to defeat the fair meaning of the statute. Saltonstall v. Birtwell, 164 U.S. 54, 70, 17 S.Ct. 19, 41 L.Ed. 348.

Vestigium /vestíj(iy)əm/. Lat. In the law of evidence, a vestige, mark, or sign; a trace, track, or impression left by a physical object.

Vesting order. In English law, an order which may be granted by the chancery division of the high court of justice (and formerly by chancery), passing the legal estate in lieu of a conveyance. Commissioners also, under modern statutes, have similar powers.

Vestry. In ecclesiastical law, the place in a church where the priest's vestures are deposited. Also an assembly of the minister, church-wardens, and parishioners, usually held in the vestry of the church, or in a building called a "vestry-hall," to act upon business of the church.

Vestry-cess /véstriykès/. A rate levied in Ireland for parochial purposes, abolished by St. 27 Vict., c. 17.

Vestry-clerk /véstriyklə̀rk/°klark/. An officer appointed to attend vestries, and take an account of their proceedings, etc.

Vestry-men /véstriymən/. A select number of parishioners elected in large and populous parishes to take care of the concerns of the parish; so called because they used ordinarily to meet in the vestry of the church.

Vestura /vest(y)úrə/. A crop of grass or corn. Also a garment; metaphorically applied to a possession or seisin.

Vestura terræ /vest(y)úrə téhriy/. In old English law, the vesture of the land; that is, the corn, grass, underwood, sweepage, and the like.

Vesture /véschər/. In old English law, profit of land. "How much the *vesture* of an acre is worth."

Vesture of land /véschər əv lǽnd/. A phrase including all things, trees excepted, which grow upon the surface of the land, and clothe it externally.

Veteran. In general, any honorably discharged soldier, sailor, marine, nurse, or army field clerk, who has served in military service of the United States.

Veterans Administration. A thorough system of benefits for veterans and dependents is administered by the Veterans Administration (VA). These benefits include compensation payments for disabilities or death related to military service; pension based on financial need for totally disabled veterans or certain survivors for disabilities or death not related to military service; education and rehabilitation; home loan guaranty; burial, including cemeteries, markers, flags, etc.; and a comprehensive medical program involving a widespread system of nursing homes, clinics, and hospitals.

Vetera statuta /víydərə stət(y)úwdə/. Lat. Ancient statutes. The English statutes from *Magna Charta* to the end of the reign of Edward II are so called; those from the beginning of the reign of Edward III being contradistinguished by the appellation of *"Nova Statuta."*

Veterinarian. One who practices the art of treating diseases and injuries of domestic animals, surgically or medically.

Vetitum namium /víydədəm néym(i)yəm/. L. Lat. Where the bailiff of a lord distrains beasts or goods of another, and the lord forbids the bailiff to deliver them when the sheriff comes to make replevin, the owner of the cattle may demand satisfaction in *placitum de vetito namio.*

Veto (Lat. I forbid.) The refusal of assent by the executive officer whose assent is necessary to perfect a law which has been passed by the legislative body, and the message which is usually sent to such body by the executive, stating such refusal and the reasons therefor. A refusal by the president or a governor to sign into law a bill that has been passed by a legislature. In the case of a presidential veto, the bill can still become a law if two-thirds of each House of Congress votes to override the veto. Art. I, § 7, U.S.Const.

It is either absolute or qualified, according as the effect of its exercise is either to destroy the bill finally, or to prevent its becoming law unless again passed by a stated proportion of votes or with other formalities. Or the veto may be merely suspensive.

Item veto. The power which governors possess in most States to veto items in appropriation bills without affecting any other provisions of such bills.

Pocket veto. Non-approval of a legislative act by the president or state governor, with the result that it fails to become a law. Such is not the result of a written disapproval (a veto in the ordinary form), but rather by remaining silent until the adjournment of the legislative body, when that adjournment takes place before the expiration of the period allowed by the constitution for the examination of the bill by the executive. Art. I, § 7, U.S.Const.

Veto power. Executive's power conditionally to prevent acts passed by Legislature which have not yet become law. Fitzsimmons v. Leon, C.C.A.Puerto Rico, 141 F.2d 886, 888. See **Veto.**

Vetus jus /víydəs jə́s/. Lat. A term used in the civil law, sometimes to designate the law of the Twelve Tables, and sometimes merely a law which was in force previous to the passage of a subsequent law.

Vex. To harass, disquiet, annoy; as by repeated litigation upon the same facts.

Vexari /veksérəy/. Lat. To be harassed, vexed, or annoyed; to be prosecuted; as in the maxim, *Nemo debet bis vexari pro una et eadem causa* /níymow débət bís veksérəy pròw yúwnə èd iyéydəm kózə/, no one should be twice prosecuted for one and the same cause.

Vexata quæstio /vekséydə kwésch(iy)ow/. Lat. A vexed question; a question often agitated or discussed, but not determined or settled; a question or point which has been differently determined, and so left doubtful.

Vexation. The injury or damage which is suffered in consequence of the tricks of another.

Vexatious /veksséyshəs/. Without reasonable or probable cause or excuse. Gardner v. Queen Ins. Co. of America, 232 Mo.App. 1101, 115 S.W.2d 4, 7.

Vexatious Actions Act. An act of parliament of 1896, authorizing the High Court to make an order, on the application of the attorney-general, that a person shown to be habitually and vexatiously litigious, without reasonable ground, shall not institute legal proceedings in that or any other court, without leave of the High Court judge thereof, upon satisfactory proof that such legal proceedings are not an abuse of the process of the court and that there is a *prima facie* ground therefor. The order when made is published in the Gazette.

Vexatious delay or refusal to pay. Under statute permitting recovery of damages for "vexatious delay" of an insurer in payment of a policy, no penalty can be inflicted unless it appears to a reasonable and prudent man before the trial that refusal was willful and without reasonable cause, and penalty will not be inflicted because of adverse outcome of trial. New York Life Ins. Co. v. Calhoun, C.C.A.Mo., 114 F.2d 526, 537. An insurer is allowed an honest difference of opinion regarding its liability under a policy and so long as it acts in good faith, may contest either an issue of fact or an issue of law. Camp v. John Hancock Mut. Life Ins. Co. of Boston, Mass., Mo. App., 165 S.W.2d 277, 283.

Vexatious proceeding. Proceeding instituted maliciously and without probable cause. Paramount Pictures v. Blumenthal, 256 App.Div. 756, 11 N.Y.S.2d 768, 772. Type of malicious prosecution differing principally because based on civil action. When the party bringing proceeding is not acting *bona fide,* and merely wishes to annoy or embarrass his opponent, or when it is not calculated to lead to any practical result. Such a proceeding is often described as "frivolous and vexatious," and the court may dismiss it on that ground. See **Malicious prosecution.**

Vexatious refusal to pay. See **Vexatious delay.**

Vexed question. A question or point of law often discussed or agitated, but not determined or settled.

V.G. An abbreviation for *"verbi gratia,"* for the sake of example.

Via /váyə/. Lat. Way, road.

In the civil law, way; a road; a right of way. The right of walking, riding, and driving over another's land. A species of rural servitude, which included *iter* (a footpath) and *actus* (a driftway).

In old English law, a way; a public road; a foot, horse, and cart way.

Via antiqua via est tuta /váyə æntáykwə váyə èst t(y)úwdə/. The old way is the safe way.

Viability. Capability of living. A term used to denote the power a new-born child possesses of continuing its independent existence. That stage of fetal development when the life of the unborn child may be continued indefinitely outside the womb by natural or artificial life-supportive systems. The constitutionality of this statutory definition (V.A.M.S. (Mo.), § 188.-015) was upheld in Planned Parenthood of Central Mo. v. Danforth, 428 U.S. 52, 96 S.Ct. 2831, 49 L.Ed.2d 788.

Viable. Livable; having the appearance of being able to live; capable of life. This term is applied to a newly-born infant, and especially to one prematurely born, which is not only born alive, but in such a state of organic development as to make possible the continuance of its life. See **Viability; Viable child.**

Viable child. Viable unborn child, within protection of constitutional provision affording every man remedy for injury done to him in his person, is child which has developed in its mother's womb to point that it is capable of independent existence outside its mother's womb. Libbee v. Permanente Clinic, 268 Or. 258, 518 P.2d 636, 637. Viable means having attained such form and development of organs as to be normally capable of living outside the uterus. Wolfe v. Isbell, 291 Ala. 327, 280 So.2d 758, 759. For a child to be "viable" means that it is so far developed and formed that if then born it could exist outside its mother's womb even if only in an incubator. Sylvia v. Gobeille, 101 R.I. 76, 220 A.2d 222, 223. See also **Viability.**

Viæ servitus /váyiy sárvədəs/. Lat. A right of way over another's land.

Viagère rente /viyazhér rónt/. In French law, a rent-charge or annuity payable for the life of the annuitant.

Viander /váyəndər/. In old English law, a returning officer.

Via ordinaria; via executiva /váyə òrdənér(i)yə; váyə əgzèkyətáyvə/. In the law of Louisiana, the former phrase means in the ordinary way or by ordinary process, the latter means by executory process or in an executory proceeding. A proceeding in a civil action is "ordinary" when a citation takes place and all the delays and forms of law are observed; "executory" when seizure is obtained against the property of the debtor, without previous citation, in virtue of an act or title importing confession of judgment, or in other cases provided by law.

Via publica /váyə pábləkə/. In the civil law, a public way or road, the land itself belonging to the public.

Via regia /váyə ríyj(iy)ə/. In English law, the king's highway for all men. The highway or common road, called "the king's" highway, because authorized by him and under his protection.

Viator /viyéydər/. Lat. In Roman law, a summoner or apparitor; an officer who attended on the tribunes and ædiles.

Via trita est tutissima /váyə tráydə èst t(y)uwtísəmə/. The trodden path is the safest.

Vi aut clam /váy òt klǽm/. Lat. In the civil law, by force or covertly.

Vi bonorum raptorum /váy bownórəm ræptórəm/. Lat. In the civil law, of goods taken away by force. The name of an action given by the prætor as a remedy for the violent taking of another's property.

Vicar. One who performs the functions of another; a substitute. Also the incumbent of an appropriated or impropriated ecclesiastical benefice, as distinguished from the incumbent of a non-appropriated benefice, who is called a "rector."

Vicarage. In English ecclesiastical law, the living or benefice of a vicar, as a parsonage is of a parson. 1 Bl.Comm. 387, 388.

Vicar general. An ecclesiastical officer who assists the archbishop in the discharge of his office.

Vicarial tithes /vəkér(i)yəl táyðz/. Petty or small tithes payable to the vicar.

Vicario, etc. /vəkér(i)yow/. An ancient writ for a spiritual person imprisoned, upon forfeiture of a recognizance, etc.

Vicarious liability. Indirect legal responsibility; for example, the liability of an employer for the acts of an employee, or, a principal for torts and contracts of an agent.

Vicarius apostolicus /vəkér(i)yəs æpəstóləkəs/. An officer through whom the Pope exercises authority in parts remote, and who is sometimes sent with episcopal functions into provinces where there is no bishop resident or there has been a long vacancy in the see, or into infidel or heretical countries.

Vicarius non habet vicarium /vəkér(i)yəs nòn héybət vəkér(i)yəm/. A deputy has not [cannot have] a deputy. A delegated power cannot be again delegated.

Vice, *n.* A fault, defect, or imperfection. Immoral conduct, practice or habit; *e.g.* prostitution.

As applied to an animal, a bad habit or failing.

In the civil law, redhibitory vices are such faults or imperfections in the subject-matter of a sale as will give the purchaser the right to return the article and demand back the price.

Vice, *adj.* Lat. In the place or stead; substitution for. *Vice mea,* in my place.

Vice-admiral. An officer in the navy ranking below an admiral.

Vice-admiral of the coast. In England, a county officer formerly appointed by the admiral "to be answerable to the high admiral for all the coasts of the sea, when need and occasion shall be." He also had power to arrest ships, when found within a certain district, for the use of the king. His office was judicial as well as ministerial.

Vice-admiralty courts. In English law, courts formerly established in the king's possessions beyond the seas, with jurisdiction over maritime causes, including those relating to prize.

Vice-chamberlain. In England, formerly a great officer under the lord chamberlain, who, in the absence of the lord chamberlain, had the control and command of the officers appertaining to that part of the royal household which was called the "chamber."

Vice-chancellor. See **Chancellor.**

Vice-comes. In England, a title formerly bestowed on the sheriff of a county, when he was regarded as the deputy of the count or earl.

Vice-comitissa. In old English law, a viscountess.

Vice-commercial agent. In the consular service of the United States, this was formerly the title of a consular officer who was substituted temporarily to fill the place of a commercial agent when the latter was absent or relieved from duty. See **Commercial agent.**

Vice-constable of England. An ancient officer in the time of Edward IV.

Vice-consul. In the consular service of the United States a consular officer who is substituted temporarily to fill the place of a consul who is absent or relieved from duty. Consular officer who is subordinate to a consul or consul general. See 22 U.S.C.A. § 938. In international law generally the term designates a commercial agent who acts in the place or stead of a consul or who has charge of a portion of his territory. In old English law, it meant the deputy or substitute of an earl *(comes),* who was anciently called "consul," answering to the more modern *"vice-comes."*

Vice-dominus episcopi. The vicar general or commissary of a bishop.

Vice-gerent. A deputy or lieutenant.

Vice-judex. In old Lombardic law, a deputy judge.

Vice-marshal. An officer who was appointed to assist the earl marshal.

Vice-President of the United States. The title of the second officer, in point of rank, in the executive branch of the government of the United States. In addition to his role as President of the Senate, the Vice President is empowered to succeed to the Presidency, pursuant to Article II and the 20th and 25th Amendments to the Constitution. The executive functions of the Vice President include participation in all Cabinet meetings, and, by statute, membership in the National Security Council, the Domestic Council, and the Board of Regents of the Smithsonian Institution. By designation of the President, the Vice President is Vice Chairman of the National Security Council and the Domestic Council, and Chairman of the Commission on CIA Activities Within the United States.

Vice-principal. See **Principal.**

Vice-versa. Conversely; in inverted order; in reverse manner.

Vice crimes. Generic term applied to crimes of immorality such as prostitution, lewd and lascivious behavior and obscenity.

Viceroy /váysròy/. A person clothed with authority to act in place of the king; hence, the usual title of the governor of a dependency.

Vicinage /vísənəj/. Neighborhood; near dwelling; vicinity. In modern usage, it means the county where a trial is had, a crime committed, etc. Also a jury of the county wherein trial is had. People v. Richardson, 138 Cal.App. 404, 32 P.2d 433, 435.

Vicinetum /vìsəníydəm/. The neighborhood; vicinage; the venue.

Vicinity. Quality or state of being near, or not remote; nearness; propinquity; proximity; a region about, near or adjacent; adjoining space or country. Casper v. City and County of San Francisco, 6 Cal.2d 376, 57 P.2d 920, 922. Neighborhood; etymologically, by common understanding, it admits of a wider latitude than proximity or contiguity, and may embrace a more extended space than that lying contiguous to the place in question; and, as applied to towns and other territorial divisions, may embrace those not adjacent.

Vicini viciniora præsumuntur scire /vəsáynay vəsìniyórə prìyz(y)əmántər sáyriy/. Persons living in the neighborhood are presumed to know the neighborhood.

Vicious propensity. A propensity or tendency of animal to do any act which might endanger the safety of persons and property of others in a given situation. Hartman v. Aschaffenburg, La.App., 12 So.2d 282, 286.

Vicis et venellis mundandis /váysəs èt vənéləs məndǽndəs/. An ancient writ against the mayor or bailiff of a town, etc., for the clean keeping of their streets and lanes.

Vicountiel, or **vicontiel** /vaykáwnshəl/°kón°/. Anything that belongs to the sheriffs, as *vicontiel writs; i.e.,* such as are triable in the sheriff's court. As to vicontiel rents, see St. 3 & 4 Wm. IV, c. 99, §§ 12, 13, which places them under the management of the commissioners of the woods and forests.

Vicountiel jurisdiction /vaykáwnshəl jùrəsdíkshən/. That jurisdiction which belongs to the officers of a county; as sheriffs, coroners, etc.

Victim. The person who is the object of a crime or tort, as the victim of a robbery is the person robbed.

Victimless crimes. Term applied to a crime which generally involves only the criminal as in the crime of illegal possession of drugs.

Victualler /vít(ə)lər/. In English law, a person authorized by law to keep a house of entertainment for the public; a publican. One who serves food or drink prepared for consumption on the premises.

Victus /víktəs/. Lat. In the civil law, sustenance; support; the means of living.

Victus, victori in expensis condemnandus est /víktəs, viktóray ìn əkspén(t)səs kòndemnǽndəs èst/. The vanquished is to be condemned in costs to the conqueror, or he who loses the suit pays costs to his adversary. State ex rel. Macri v. City of Bremerton, 8 Wash.2d 93, 111 P.2d 612, 620.

Vidame /víydæm/. In French feudal law, originally, an officer who represented the bishop, as the viscount did the count. In process of time, these dignitaries erected their offices into fiefs, and became feudal nobles, such as the *vidame* of Chartres, Rheims, etc., continuing to take their titles from the seat of the bishop whom they represented, although the lands held by virtue of their fiefs might be situated elsewhere.

Vide /váydiy/. Lat. A word of reference. *Vide ante,* or *vide supra,* refers to a previous passage, *vide post,* or *vide infra,* to a subsequent passage, in a book.

Videbis ea sæpe committi quæ sæpe vindicantur /vədíybəs íyə síypiy kəmíday kwìy síypiy vìndəkǽntər/. You will see those things frequently committed which are frequently punished.

Videlicet /vədéləsət/°díy°/. Lat. The words "to-wit," or "that is to say," so frequently used in pleading, are technically called the *"videlicet"* or *"scilicet;"* and when any fact alleged in pleading is preceded by, or accompanied with these words, such fact is, in the language of the law, said to be "laid under a *videlicet."* The use of the *videlicet* is to point out, particularize, or render more specific that which has been previously stated in general language only; also to explain that which is doubtful or obscure. Its common office is to state time, place, or manner which are of the essence of the matter in issue.

Videtur qui surdus et mutus ne poet faire alienation /vədíydər kwày sárdəs èt myúwdəs nə pyúw fér èyl(i)yənéyshən/. It seems that a deaf and dumb man cannot alienate.

Vidimus /vídəməs/. An *inspeximus (q.v.).*

Vidua regis /vídyuwə ríyjəs/. Lat. In old English law, a king's widow. The widow of a tenant *in capite.* So called, because she was not allowed to marry a second time without the king's permission; obtaining her dower also from the assignment of the king, and having the king for her patron and defender.

Viduitatis professio /vədyùwətéydəs prəfésh(iy)ow/. Lat. The making a solemn profession to live a sole and chaste woman.

Viduity /vidyúwədiy/. Widowhood.

Vie. Fr. Life; occurring in the phrases *cestui que vie, pur autre vie,* etc.

Vi et armis /váy èd árməs/. Lat. With force and arms. See **Trespass.**

View. The common law right of prospect; the outlook or prospect from the windows of one's house. A species of urban servitude which prohibits the obstruction of such prospect.

The act or proceeding by which tribunal goes to an object which cannot be produced in court because it is immovable or inconvenient to remove, and there observes it. Conner v. Parker, Tex.Civ.App., 181 S.W.2d 873, 874. An inspection by the jury of property in controversy, of an accident scene, of a place where a crime has been committed, etc. An inspection by the fact finding tribunal which is a species of real evidence.

The appropriate procedures to be followed in connection with views are widely regulated by state statute. At common law, and generally in civil cases today, the presence of the trial judge at a view is not required, the more common practice being for the jury to be conducted to the scene by "showers," expressly commissioned for the purpose. Attendance at the view by the parties and their counsel is generally permitted though subject to the discretion of the trial judge. In criminal cases, the rights of the defendant to have the judge present at the view, and to be present himself, are frequently provided for by statute.

See also **Inspection; Plain view doctrine; Viewers.**

View and delivery. In old English law, when a right of common was exercisable not over the whole waste, but only in convenient places indicated from time to time by the lord of the manor or his bailiff, it was said to be exercisable after "view and delivery."

View, demand of. At common law, in real actions, the defendant was entitled to demand a *view,* that is, a sight of the thing, in order to ascertain its identity and other circumstances. As, if a real action were brought against a tenant, and such tenant did not exactly know what land it was that the demandant asked, then he might pray the view, which was that he might see the land which the demandant claimed.

Viewers. Persons appointed by a court to make an investigation of certain matters, or to examine a particular locality (as, the proposed site of a new road), and to report to the court the result of their inspection, with their opinion on the same.

View of an inquest. A view or inspection taken by a jury, summoned upon an inquisition or inquest, of the place or property to which the inquisition or inquiry refers.

View of frank-pledge. In old English law, an examination to see if every freeman above twelve years of age within the district had taken the oath of allegiance, and found nine freeman pledges for his peaceable demeanor.

Vif-gage /vífgèyj/. L. Fr. In old English law, a *vivum vadium* or living pledge, as distinguished from a *mortgage* or dead pledge. Properly, an estate given as security for a debt, the debt to be satisfied out of the rents, issues, and profits.

Vigil. In ecclesiastical law, the eve or next day before any solemn feast.

Vigilance. Watchfulness; precaution; a proper degree of activity and promptness in pursuing one's rights or guarding them from infraction, or in making or discovering opportunities for the enforcement of one's lawful claims and demands. It is the opposite of *laches.* Wynne v. Conrad, 220 N.C. 355, 17 S.E.2d 514, 518.

Vigilant. Watchful, awake, and on the alert; attentive to discover and avoid danger, or to provide for safety; circumspect; cautious; wary. City Ice & Fuel Co. v. Center, 54 Ohio App. 116, 6 N.E.2d 580, 583, 7 O.O. 434.

Vigilantibus et non dormientibus jura subveniunt /vìjəlǽntəbəs èt nón dormiyéntəbəs júrə sèbvíyn(i)yənt/. The laws aid those who are vigilant, not those who sleep upon their rights.

Vigor /vígər/. Lat. Strength; virtue; force; efficiency. *Proprio vigore* /prówpriyow vəgóriy/, by its own force.

Viis et modis /váyəs èt mówdəs/. Lat. In the ecclesiastical courts, service of a decree or citation *viis et modis, i.e.,* by all "ways and means" likely to affect the party with knowledge of its contents, is equivalent to substituted service in the temporal courts, and is opposed to personal service.

Vill. In old English law, this word was used to signify the parts into which a hundred or wapentake was divided. It also signifies a town or city.

Villa est ex pluribus mansionibus vicinata, et collata ex pluribus vicinis, et sub appellatione villarum continentur burgi et civitates /víIə èst èks pl(y)úrəbəs mǽns(h)iyównəbəs vìsənéydə, èt kəléydə èks pl(y)úrəbəs vəsáynəs, èt sèb æpəlèyshiyówniy vəlérəm kòntənéntər bárjay èt sìvətéydiyz/. Vill is a neighborhood of many mansions, a collection of many neighbors, and under the term of "vills" boroughs and cities are contained.

Village. Traditionally, word "village" has connoted an area possessed of some attributes of a community, and is not a technical word, or one having a peculiar meaning, but is a common word in general usage and is merely an assemblage or community of people, a nucleus or cluster for residential and business purposes, a collective body of inhabitants, gathered together in one group. Union Sav. Bank of Patchogue v. Saxon, 118 U.S.App.D.C. 296, 335 F.2d 718, 721. Term refers to any small assemblage of houses for dwellings or business, or both, whether they are situated on regularly laid out streets and alleys, or not. State on Information of Eagleton v. Champ, Mo., 393 S.W.2d 516, 524.

In some states, this is the legal description of a class of municipal corporations of smaller population than "cities" and having a simpler form of government, and corresponding to "towns" and "boroughs," as these terms are employed elsewhere.

Villain. An opprobrious epithet, implying great moral delinquency, and equivalent to knave, rascal, or scoundrel. The word is libelous.

Villanis regis subtractis reducendis /vəléynəs ríyjəs səbtrǽktəs rìyd(y)uwséndəs/. In old English law, a writ that lay for the bringing back of the king's bondmen, that had been carried away by others out of his manors whereto they belonged.

Villanum servitium /vəléynəm sərvísh(iy)əm/. In old English law, villein service.

Villa regia /víIə ríyj(iy)ə/. Lat. In Saxon law, a royal residence.

Villein /víIən/. In feudal law, a person attached to a manor, who was substantially in the condition of a slave, who performed the base and servile work upon the manor for the lord, and was, in most respects, a subject of property belonging to him.

Villein in gross /víIən ìn gróws/. In feudal law, a villein who was annexed to the person of the lord, and transferable by deed from one owner to another. 2 Bl.Comm. 93.

Villein regardant /víIən rəgárdənt/. In feudal law, a villein annexed to the manor of land; a serf.

Villein services /víIən sárvəsəz/. In feudal law, base services, such as villeins performed. They were not, however, exclusively confined to villeins, since they might be performed by freemen, without impairing their free condition.

Villein socage /víIən sókəj/. In feudal and old English law, a species of tenure in which the services to be rendered were certain and determinate, but were of a base or servile nature; *i.e.,* not suitable to a man of free and honorable rank. This was also called "privileged villeinage," to distinguish it from "pure villeinage," in which the services were not certain, but the tenant was obliged to do whatever he was commanded. 2 Bl.Comm. 61.

Villenage /víIənəj/. In feudal law, a servile kind of tenure belonging to lands or tenements, whereby the tenant was bound to do all such services as the lord commanded, or were fit for a villein to do. See **Villein.**

Pure villenage. A base tenure, where a man holds upon terms of doing whatsoever is commanded of him, nor knows in the evening what is to be done in the morning, and is always bound to an uncertain service.

Villenous judgment /víIənəs jójmənt/. A judgment which deprived one of his *libera lex,* whereby he was discredited and disabled as a juror or witness; forfeited his goods and chattels and lands for life; wasted the lands, razed the houses, rooted up the trees, and committed his body to prison. It has become obsolete. 4 Bl.Comm. 136.

Vim vi repellere licet, modo fiat moderamine inculpatæ tutelæ, non ad sumendam vindictam, sed ad propulsandam injuriam /vím váy rəpéləriy láysət, mowdow fáyət mòdəréyməniy ìnkəlpéydiy t(y)uwtíyliy, nón ǽd s(y)uwméndəm vindíktəm, sèd ǽd pròwpəlsǽndəm injúriyəm/. It is lawful to repel force by force, provided it be done with the moderation of blameless defense, not for the purpose of taking revenge, but to ward off injury.

Vinagium /vinéyj(iy)əm/. A payment of a certain quantity of wine instead of rent for a vineyard.

Vinculacion /vìnkuwlasyówn/. In Spanish law, an entail.

Vinculo /vínkuwlow/. In Spanish law, the bond, chain, or tie of marriage.

Vinculo matrimonii /vínk(y)əlow mǽtrəmówniyay/. See **A vinculo matrimonii; Divorce.**

Vinculum juris /vínk(y)ələm júrəs/. In the Roman law, an obligation is defined as a *vinculum juris, i.e.,* "a bond of law," whereby one party becomes or is bound to another to do something according to law.

Vindex /víndeks/. Lat. In the civil law, a defender.

Vindicare /vìndəkériy/. Lat. In the civil law, to claim, or challenge; to demand one's own; to assert a right in or to a thing; to assert or claim a property in a thing; to claim a thing as one's own.

Vindicate. To clear of suspicion, blame, or doubt.

Vindicatio /vìndəkéysh(iy)ow/. Lat. In the civil law, the claiming a thing as one's own; the asserting of a right or title in or to a thing.

Vindicatory parts of laws /víndəkətoriy párts əv lóz/. The sanction of the laws, whereby it is signified what evil or penalty shall be incurred by such as commit any public wrongs, and transgress or neglect their duty.

Vindicta /vindíktə/. In Roman law, a rod or wand; and, from the use of that instrument in their course, various legal acts came to be distinguished by the term; *e.g.,* one of the three ancient modes of manumission was by the *vindicta;* also the rod or wand intervened in the progress of the old action of *vindicatio,* whence the name of that action.

Vindictive damages /vindíktəv dǽməjəz/. See **Damages.**

Vintner /víntnər/. One who sells wine. A covenant prohibiting the trade of a vintner includes a person selling wines not to be drunk on the premises.

Viol. Fr. In French law, rape; barring.

Violation. Injury; infringement; breach of right, duty or law; ravishment; seduction.

Violence. Unjust or unwarranted exercise of force, usually with the accompaniment of vehemence, outrage or fury. People v. McIlvain, 55 Cal.App.2d 322, 130 P.2d 131, 134. Physical force unlawfully exercised; abuse of force; that force which is employed against common right, against the laws, and against public liberty. Anderson-Berney Bldg. Co. v. Lowry, Tex.Civ.App., 143 S.W.2d 401, 403. The exertion of any physical force so as to injure, damage or abuse.

Violence in labor disputes is not limited to physical contact or injury, but may include picketing conducted with misleading signs, false statements, publicity, and veiled threats by words and acts. Esco Operating Corporation v. Kaplan, 144 Misc. 646, 258 N.Y.S. 303.

Violent. Moving, acting, or characterized, by physical force, especially by extreme and sudden or by unjust or improper force. Furious, vehement; as a violent storm or wind. A violent attack marked by, or due to, strong mental excitement. Vehement, passionate; as, violent speech. Violent reproaches produced or effected by force, not spontaneous or natural; as, a violent death. Displaying or proceeding from extreme or intense force; caused by unexpected unnatural causes.

Violenta præsumptio aliquando est plena probatio /vayəlénsh(iy)ə prəzǽm(p)sh(iy)ow ǽləkwóndow èst plíynə prowbéysh(iy)ow/. Violent presumption is sometimes full proof.

Violent death. Death caused by violent external means, as distinguished from natural death as caused by disease or the wasting of the vital forces. Death is

"violent" within accident policy if it results from external agency and is not in ordinary course of nature.

Violently. By the use of force; forcibly; with violence. The term is used in indictments for certain offenses.

Violent offenses. Crimes characterized by extreme physical force such as murder, forcible rape, and assault and battery by means of a dangerous weapon.

Violent presumption. In the law of evidence, proof of a fact by the proof of circumstances which necessarily attend it. Violent presumption is many times equal to full proof. 3 Bl.Comm. 371. Something more than a mere "presumption". Hughes v. State, 212 Ind. 577, 10 N.E.2d 629, 633.

Viperina est expositio quæ corrodit viscera textus /vàypəráynə èst èkspəzísh(iy)ow kwíy kərówdət vísərə tékstəs/. It is a poisonous exposition which destroys the vitals of the text.

Vir /vár/. Lat. A man, especially as marking the sex. In the Latin phrases and maxims of the old English law, this word generally means "husband," the expression *vir et uxor* corresponding to the law French *baron et feme.*

Vires /váyriyz/. Lat. (The plural of *"vis."*) Powers; forces; capabilities; natural powers; powers granted or limited. See **Ultra** (*Ultra vires*).

Vires acquirit eundo /váyriyz əkwáyrəd iyándow/. It gains strength by continuance.

Vir et uxor censentur in lege una persona /vár èd ə́ksor sən(t)séntər in líyjiy yúwnə pərsównə/. Husband and wife are considered one person in law.

Vir et uxor sunt quasi unica persona, quia caro et sanguis unus; res licet sit propria uxoris, vir tamen ejus custos, cum sit caput mulieris /vár èd ə́ksor sə̀nt kwéyzay yúwnəkə pərsównə, kwáyə kérow èt sǽngwəs yúwnəs; ríyz láysət sìt prówpriyə əksórəs, vár téymən íyjəs kə́stəs, kə̀m sít kǽpət myuwl(i)yírəs/. Man and wife are, as it were, one person, because only one flesh and blood; although the property may be the wife's, the husband is keeper of it, since he is the head of the wife.

Virga /várgə/. In old English law, a rod or staff; a rod or ensign of office.

Virgata /vərgéydə/. A quarter of an acre of land. It might also be used to express a quarter of a hide of land.

Virgata regia /vərgéydə ríyj(iy)ə/. In old English law, the verge; the bounds of the king's household, within which the court of the steward had jurisdiction.

Virgate /várgət/. A yard-land.

Virga terræ (or **virgata terræ**) /várgə téhriy/vərgéydə téhriy/. In old English law, a yard-land; a measure of land of variable quantity, containing in some places twenty, in others twenty-four, in others thirty, and in others forty, acres.

Virge, tenant by /ténənt bày várj/. A species of copyholder, who holds by the virge or rod.

Virgo intacta /várgow intǽktə/. Lat. A pure virgin.

Viridario eligendo /virədér(i)yow èləjéndow/. A writ for choice of a verderer in the forest.

Virilia /vəríl(i)yə/. The privy members of a man, to cut off which was felony by the common law, though the party consented to it.

Vir militans deo non implicetur secularibus negotiis /vár mílətæn(d)z díyow nòn ìmpləsíydər sèkyəlérəbəs nəgówshiyəs/. A man fighting for God must not be involved in secular business.

Virtual representation, doctrine of. Under this doctrine, where parties interested are numerous and the suit is for an object common to all of them, some of the body may maintain an action on behalf of themselves and of the others. Padway v. Pacific Mut. Life Ins. Co. of California, D.C.Wis., 42 F.Supp. 569, 576; Waybright v. Columbian Mut. Life Ins. Co., D.C. Tenn., 30 F.Supp. 885, 888; Lightle v. Kirby, 194 Ark. 535, 108 S.W.2d 896, 897. Under current rules practice, such type action would proceed as a class action. See **Class or representative action.**

Virtue of office. An act by virtue of office is one in which the act is within the authority of the officer but in doing it he exercises that authority improperly or abuses the confidence which the law imposes in him. Maryland Cas. Co. v. McCormack, Ky., 488 S.W.2d 347, 349.

Virtute cujus /vərt(y)úwdiy k(y)úwjəs/. Lat. By virtue whereof. This was the clause in a pleading justifying an entry upon land, by which the party alleged that it was in virtue of an order from one entitled that he entered.

Virtute officii /vərt(y)úwdiy əfíshiyay/. Lat. By virtue of his office. By the authority vested in him as the incumbent of the particular office. An officer acts "virtute officii" when he acts by the authority vested in him as the incumbent of the particular office. Aldridge v. Wooten, 68 Ga.App. 887, 24 S.E.2d 700, 701. Where acts done are within the authority of the officer, but in doing them he exercises that authority improperly, or abuses the confidence which the law reposes in him, whilst acts done "colore officii" are where they are of such a nature that his office gives him no authority to do them. State v. Roy, 41 N.M. 308, 68 P.2d 162, 165; Yuma County v. Wisener, 45 Ariz. 475, 46 P.2d 115, 118.

Vis /vis/. Lat. Any kind of force, violence, or disturbance relating to a man's person or his property. The plural is *vires* (q.v.).

Visa /víyzə/. An official indorsement upon a document, passport, commercial book, etc., to certify that it has been examined and found correct or in due form. An endorsement made on a passport by the proper authorities denoting that it has been examined and that the bearer is permitted to proceed; a recognition by the country ad quem of the validity of the passport issued by the country a quo. U. S. v. Vargas, D.C.N.Y., 380 F.Supp. 1162, 1168. See also **Visé.**

Vis ablativa /vís ǽblətáyvə/. In the civil law, ablative force; force which is exerted in taking away a thing from another.

Vis armata /vís arméydə/. In the civil and old English law, armed force; force exerted by means of arms or weapons.

Vis à vis /vìyzavíy/. Face to face. One of two persons or things opposite or corresponding to each other. In relation to each other.

Vis clandestina /vís klǽndəstáynə/. In old English law, clandestine force; such as is used by night.

Vis compulsiva /vís kòmpəlsáyvə/. In the civil and old English law, compulsive force; that which is exerted to compel another to do an act against his will; force exerted by menaces or terror.

Viscount /váykàwnt/. A decree of English nobility, next below that of earl. An old title of the sheriff.

Vis divina /vís dəváynə/. In the civil law, divine or superhuman force; the act of God.

Visé /víyzey/. An indorsement made on a passport by the proper authorities, denoting that it has been examined, and that the person who bears it is permitted to proceed on his journey. See also **Visa.**

Vis expulsiva /vís ekspəlsáyvə/. In old English law, expulsive force; force used to expel another, or put him out of his possession. Bracton contrasts it with *"vis simplex,"* and divides it into expulsive force with arms, and expulsive force without arms.

Vis exturbativa /vís əkstàrbətáyvə/. In the civil law, exturbative force; force used to thrust out another. Force used between two contending claimants of possession, the one endeavoring to thrust out the other.

Vis fluminis /vís fl(y)úwmənəs/. In the civil law, the force of a river; the force exerted by a stream or current; water-power.

Visible. Perceptible, discernible, clear, distinct, evident, open, conspicuous.

Visible means of support. Term used in vagrancy statutes to indicate that one was without any ostensible ability to support himself, though he is able bodied.

Vis impressa /vís imprésə/. The original act of force out of which an injury arises, as distinguished from *"vis proxima,"* the proximate force, or immediate cause of the injury.

Vis inermis /vís inérməs/. In old English law, unarmed force; the opposite of *"vis armata."*

Vis injuriosa /vís injùriyówsə/. In old English law, wrongful force; otherwise called *"illicita"* (unlawful).

Vis inquietativa /vís inkwàyədətáyvə/. In the civil law, disquieting force. Bracton defines it to be where one does not permit another to use his possession quietly and in peace.

Visit. In international law, the right of visit or visitation is the right of a cruiser or war-ship to stop a vessel sailing under another flag on the high seas, and send an officer to such vessel to ascertain whether her nationality is what it purports to be. It is exercisable only when suspicious circumstances attend the vessel to be visited; as when she is suspected of a piratical character.

Visitation. Inspection; superintendence; direction; regulation. Bank of America Nat. Trust & Savings Ass'n v. Douglas, 70 App.D.C. 221, 105 F.2d 100, 105.

In England, the office of inquiring into and correcting irregularities of corporations. See also **Visitor.**

Visitation books. In old English law, books compiled by the heralds, when progresses were solemnly and regularly made into every part of the kingdom, to inquire into the state of families, and to register such marriages and descents as were verified to them upon oath; they were allowed to be good evidence of pedigree.

Visitation rights. In a dissolution or custody suit, permission granted to a parent to visit children. In domestic relations matters, the right of one parent to visit children of the marriage under order of the court.

Visitor. A visitor is, with respect to guardianship proceedings, a person who is trained in law, nursing or social work and is an officer, employee or special appointee of the Court with no personal interest in the proceedings. Uniform Probate Code (4th) § 5–308.

In England, a person appointed to visit, inspect, inquire into, and correct irregularities of corporations. Similar functions are performed by Boards of Visitors to Prisons.

Visitor of manners. The regarder's office in the forest.

Vis laica /vís léyəkə/. In old English law, lay force; an armed force used to hold possession of a church.

Vis legibus est inimica /vís líyjəbəs èst ìnəmáykə/. Violence is inimical to the laws.

Vis licita /vís lísədə/. In old English law, lawful force.

Vis major /vís méyjər/. A greater or superior force; an irresistible force. A loss that results immediately from a natural cause without the intervention of man, and could not have been prevented by the exercise of prudence, diligence, and care. National Carbon Co. v. Bankers Mortg. Co. of Topeka, C.C.A.Kan., 77 F.2d 614, 617. A natural and inevitable necessity, and one arising wholly above the control of human agencies, and which occurs independently of human action or neglect. In the civil law, this term is sometimes used as synonymous with *"vis divina,"* or the act of God. See **Act of God.**

Visne /váyniy/. L. Fr. The neighborhood; vicinage; venue. The district from which juries were drawn at common law.

Vis perturbativa /vís pərtàrbətáyvə/. In old English law, force used between parties contending for a possession.

Vis proxima /vís próksəmə/. Immediate force. See **Vis impressa.**

Vis simplex /vís símplèks/. In old English law, simple or mere force.

V.I.S.T.A. Volunteers in Service to America.

Visus /váyzəs/. Lat. In old English practice, view; inspection, either of a place or person.

Vital statistics. Public records kept by a state, city or other governmental subdivision, under a statutory provision, of births, marriages, deaths, diseases, and the like.

Vitiate. To impair; to make void or voidable; to cause to fail of force or effect. To destroy or annul, either entirely or in part, the legal efficacy and binding force of an act or instrument; as when it is said that fraud *vitiates a contract.*

Vitiligate. To litigate cavilously, vexatiously, or from merely quarrelsome motives.

Vitium clerici /vísh(iy)əm kléhrəsay/. In old English law, the mistake of a clerk; a clerical error.

Vitium clerici nocere non debet /vísh(iy)əm kléhrəsay nəsíriy nòn débət/. A clerical error ought not to hurt.

Vitium est quod fugi debet, nisi, rationem non invenias, mox legem sine ratione esse clames /vísh(iy)əm èst kwòd fyúwjay débət, náysay, ræshiyównəm nòn invíyn(iy)əs, mòks líyjəm sáyniy ræshiyówniy ésiy kléymiyz/. It is a fault which ought to be avoided, that if you cannot discover the reason you should presently exclaim that the law is without reason.

Vitium scriptoris /vísh(iy)əm skriptórəs/. In old English law, the fault or mistake of a writer or copyist; a clerical error.

Vitreous /vítriyəs/. Consisting of or resembling glass in its important characteristics.

Vitricus /vítrəkəs/. Lat. In the civil law, a stepfather; a mother's second husband.

Viva aqua /váyvə ǽkwə/. Lat. In the civil law, living water; running water; that which issues from a spring or fountain.

Viva pecunia /váyvə pək(y)úwn(i)yə/. Lat. Cattle, which obtained this name from being received during the Saxon period as money upon most occasions, at certain regulated prices.

Vivarium /vəvér(i)yəm/. Lat. In the civil law, an inclosed place, where live wild animals are kept.

Vivary /vívəriy/. In English law, a place for keeping wild animals alive, including fishes; a fish pond, park, or warren.

Viva voce /váyvə vówsiy/. Lat. With the living voice; by word of mouth. As applied to the examination of witnesses, this phrase is equivalent to "orally." It is used in contradistinction to evidence on affidavits or depositions. As descriptive of a species of voting, it signifies voting by speech or outcry, as distinguished from voting by a written or printed ballot.

Vivum vadium /váyvəm véyd(i)yəm/. See **Vadium.**

Vix ulla lex fieri potest quæ omnibus commoda sit, sed si majori parti prospiciat, utilis est /víks álə léks fáyəray pówdəst kwày ómnəbəs kómədə sìt, sèd sáy məjóray párday prəspísh(iy)ət, yúwdələs èst/. Scarcely any law can be made which is adapted to all, but, if it provide for the greater part, it is useful.

Viz /víz/. A contraction for *videlicet*, to-wit, namely, that is to say.

Vocabula artis /vowkǽbyələ árdəs/. Lat. Words of art; technical terms.

Vocabula artium explicanda sunt secundum definitiones prudentum /vowkǽbyələ ársh(iy)əm èkspləkǽndə sènt səkǽndəm dèfənìshiyówniyz pruwdéntəm/. Terms of arts are to be explained according to the definitions of the learned or skilled [in such arts].

Vocare ad curiam /vowkériy ǽd kyúriyəm/. In feudal law, to summon to court.

Vocatio in jus /vowkéysh(iy)ow ìn jə́s/. Lat. A summoning to court. In the earlier practice of the Roman law (under the *legis actiones*), the creditor orally called upon his debtor to go with him before the prætor for the purpose of determining their controversy, saying, *"In jus eamus; in jus te voco."* This was called *"vocatio in jus."*

Vocation. One's regular calling or business; one's occupation or profession. The activity on which one spends major portion of his time and out of which he makes his living. Employers' Liability Assur. Corporation v. Accident & Casualty Ins. Co. of Winterthur, Switzerland, C.C.A.Ohio, 134 F.2d 566, 568. See also **Occupation; Profession.**

Vociferatio /vòwsəfəréysh(iy)ow/. Lat. In old English law, outcry; hue and cry.

Vociferous /vowsífərəs/. Making a loud outcry; clamorous; noisy.

Voco /vówkow/. Lat. In the civil and old English law, I call; I summon; I vouch. *In jus voco te,* I summon you to court; I summon you before the prætor. The formula by which a Roman action was anciently commenced.

Voice exemplars. Type of test in which one's voice is compared to the voice heard on some particular occasion. Used in trial of cases as type of scientific evidence. An order compelling a defendant in a criminal case to furnish a sample of his voice does not violate the privilege against self-incrimination. U. S. v. Dionisio, 410 U.S. 1, 93 S.Ct. 764, 35 L.Ed.2d 67. While voiceprint identification was formerly not admissible, the trend in recent years has been towards admissibility under restricted conditions. State ex rel. Trimble v. Hedman, 291 Minn. 442, 192 N.W.2d 432; Worley v. State, Fla.App., 263 So.2d 613, United States v. Baller, C.A.W.Va., 519 F.2d 463; United States v. Franks, C.A.Tenn., 511 F.2d 25. See **Spectograph; Voiceprint.**

Voice identification. In evidence, one may testify that he heard a person's voice if he is familiar with that voice. See Fed.Evid.R. 901(5). See also **Spectograph; Voiceprint.**

Voiceprint. An instrument known as a spectograph produces "prints" of one's voice for use in comparing such readings with the actual voice of the person involved to determine whether such person uttered the material words. Used in trial of cases which require identification of voices. Com. v. Lykus, 367 Mass. 191, 327 N.E.2d 671. See **Spectograph; Voice exemplars.**

Void. Null; ineffectual; nugatory; having no legal force or binding effect; unable, in law, to support the purpose for which it was intended. Hardison v. Gledhill, 72 Ga.App. 432, 33 S.E.2d 921, 924.

There is this difference between the two words "void" and "voidable": *void* in the strict sense means that an instrument or transaction is nugatory and ineffectual so that nothing can cure it; *voidable* exists when an imperfection or defect can be cured by the act or confirmation of him who could take advantage of it. The term "void," however, as applicable to conveyances or other agreements, has not at all times been used with technical precision, nor restricted to its peculiar and limited sense, as contradistinguished from "voidable"; it being frequently introduced, even by legal writers and jurists, when the purpose is nothing further than to indicate that a contract was invalid, and not binding in law. But the distinction between the terms "void" and "voidable," in their application to contracts, is often one of great practical importance; and, whenever entire technical accuracy is required, the term "void" can only be properly applied to those contracts that are of no effect whatsoever, such as are a mere nullity, and incapable of confirmation or ratification.

The word "void," in its strictest sense, means that which has no force and effect, is without legal efficacy, is incapable of being enforced by law, or has no legal or binding force, but frequently the word is used and construed as having the more liberal meaning of "voidable."

The word "void" is used in statutes in the sense of utterly void so as to be incapable of ratification, and also in the sense of voidable and resort must be had to the rules of construction in many cases to determine in which sense the Legislature intended to use it. An act or contract neither wrong in itself nor against public policy, which has been declared void by statute for the protection or benefit of a certain party, or class of parties, is voidable only.

Void ab initio. A contract is null from the beginning if it seriously offends law or public policy in contrast to a contract which is merely voidable at the election of one of the parties to the contract. See also **Void contract; Void marriage.**

Voidable. That which may be avoided, or declared void; not absolutely void, or void in itself. That which operates to accomplish the thing sought to be accomplished, until the fatal vice in the transaction has been judicially ascertained and declared. Slaughter v. Qualls, 139 Tex. 340, 162 S.W.2d 671, 674. It imports a valid act which may be avoided rather than an invalid act which may be confirmed. Paulson v. McMillan, 8 Wash.2d 295, 111 P.2d 983, 985. See **Void.**

Voidable contract. One which is void as to wrongdoer but not void as to wronged party, unless he elects to so treat it. Depner v. Joseph Zukin Blouses, 13 Cal.App.2d 124, 56 P.2d 574, 575. For example, a contract between an infant and an adult is voidable only at the election of the infant. See also **Void contract.**

Voidable judgment. One apparently valid, but in truth wanting in some material respect. Reynolds v. Volunteer State Life Ins. Co., Tex.Civ.App., 80 S.W.2d 1087, 1092. One rendered by a court having jurisdiction but which is irregularly and erroneously rendered. Tanton v. State Nat. Bank of El Paso, Tex.Civ. App., 43 S.W.2d 957, 960; Gehret v. Hetkes, Tex. Com.App., 36 S.W.2d 700, 701; Easterline v. Bean, 121 Tex. 327, 49 S.W.2d 427, 429. See also **Void judgment.**

Voidable marriage. One which is valid when entered into and which remains valid until either party secures lawful court order dissolving the marital relationship. Darling v. Darling, 44 Ohio App.2d 5, 335 N.E.2d 708, 710, 73 O.O.2d 5. See also **Void marriage.**

Voidable preference. Under Bankruptcy Act, such exists where person while insolvent transfers property, the effect of which will be to enable one creditor to obtain greater percentage of his debt than other creditors of same class. The preference given to a creditor of a bankrupt over other creditors in the same class as the creditor given the preference and in such a situation, if other elements appear, the bankruptcy court may have the transfer set aside. See Bankruptcy Act § 547. See also **Preference.**

Void contract. One which never had any legal existence or effect, and such contract cannot in any manner have life breathed into it. National Union Indemnity Co. v. Bruce Bros., 44 Ariz. 454, 38 P.2d 648, 652. Expression denotes that the parties to the transaction have gone through the form of making a contract, but that none has been made in law because of lack of some essential element of a contract, and such contract creates no legal rights and either party thereto may ignore it at his pleasure, in so far as it is executory. Griffin v. Smith, C.C.A.Ind., 101 F.2d 348, 350. See also **Voidable contract.**

Void for vagueness. A law which is so obscure in its promulgation that a reasonable person could not determine from a reading what the law purports to command or prohibit is void as violative of due process.

Void judgment. One which has no legal force or effect, invalidity of which may be asserted by any person whose rights are affected at any time and at any place directly or collaterally. Reynolds v. Volunteer State Life Ins. Co., Tex.Civ.App., 80 S.W.2d 1087, 1092. One which, from its inception is and forever continues to be absolutely null, without legal efficacy, ineffectual to bind parties or support a right, of no legal force and effect whatever, and incapable of confirmation, ratification, or enforcement in any manner or to any degree. One that has merely semblance without some essential elements, as want of jurisdiction or failure to serve process or have party in court. See also **Voidable judgment.**

Void marriage. One not good for any legal purpose, the invalidity of which may be maintained in any proceeding between any parties, while a "voidable marriage" is one where there is an imperfection which can be inquired into only during the lives of both of the parties in a proceeding to obtain a judgment declaring it void. Such marriage is invalid from its inception, and parties thereto may simply separate without benefit of court order of divorce or annul-

ment. Darling v. Darling, 44 Ohio App.2d 5, 335 N.E.2d 708, 710, 73 O.O.2d 5. A "voidable marriage" is valid and not ipso facto void, until sentence of nullity is obtained; a "void marriage" is void ab initio. Minder v. Minder, 83 N.J.Super. 159, 199 A.2d 69, 71. See **Annulment.**

Void on its face. An instrument is void on its face when an inspection will reveal its defects and invalidity.

Void process. One which fails in some material respect to comply with the requisite form of legal process. United States v. Van Dusen, C.C.A.Minn., 78 F.2d 121, 124.

Voir dire /vwár dír/. L. Fr. To speak the truth. This phrase denotes the preliminary examination which the court may make of one presented as a witness or juror, where his competency, interest, etc., is objected to.

Voiture /vwotyúr/. Fr. Carriage; transportation by carriage.

Volens /vówlèn(d)z/. Lat. Willing. He is said to be willing who either expressly consents or tacitly makes no opposition.

Volenti non fit injuria /vowléntay nón fíd injúriyə/. The maxim "volenti non fit injuria" means that if one, knowing and comprehending the danger, voluntarily exposes himself to it, though not negligent in so doing, he is deemed to have assumed the risk and is precluded from a recovery for an injury resulting therefrom. Munson v. Bishop Clarkson Memorial Hospital, 186 Neb. 778, 186 N.W.2d 492, 494. This is an affirmative defense that should be pleaded under Fed.R.Civil P. 8. Tyler v. Dowell, Inc., C.A.N.M., 274 F.2d 890. See also **Assumption of risk.**

Volstead Act. A now repealed Federal law prohibiting the manufacture, sale, or transportation of liquor. The law was passed under the Eighteenth Amendment to the U.S. Constitution which was repealed by Twenty-First Amendment.

Voluit, sed non dixit /vól(y)uwət, sèd nòn díksət/. He willed, but he did not say. He may have intended so, but he did not say so. A maxim frequently used in the construction of wills; an answer to arguments based upon the supposed intention of a testator.

Volumen /volyúwmən/. Lat. In the civil law, a volume; so called from its form, being *rolled* up.

Volumus /vóləməs/. Lat. We will; it is our will. The first word of a clause in the royal writs of protection and letters patent.

Voluntarily. Done by design or intention, intentional, proposed, intended, or not accidental. Intentionally and without coercion. Young v. Young, 148 Kan. 876, 84 P.2d 916, 917.

Voluntariness. The quality of being voluntary or free as opposed to being forced or given under duress, as a confession of one arrested for a crime.

Voluntarius dæmon /vòləntériyəs díymən/. A voluntary madman. A term applied by Lord Coke to a drunkard, who has voluntarily contracted madness by intoxication. 4 Bl.Comm. 25.

Voluntary. Unconstrained by interference; unimpelled by another's influence; spontaneous; acting of oneself. Coker v. State, 199 Ga. 20, 33 S.E.2d 171, 174. Done by design or intention. Proceeding from the free and unrestrained will of the person. Produced in or by an act of choice. Resulting from free choice. The word, especially in statutes, often implies knowledge of essential facts. Without valuable consideration; gratuitous, as a *voluntary* conveyance. Also, having a merely nominal consideration; as, a *voluntary* deed.

As to voluntary Answer; Assignment; Bankrupt; Confession; Conveyance; Deposit; Escape; Indebtedness; Manslaughter; Nonsuit; Oath; Payment; Redemption; Sale; Settlement; Trust, and Waste, see those titles.

Voluntary abandonment. As statutory ground for divorce, exists if there is a final departure, without consent of other party, without sufficient reason and without intent to return. As used in adoption statute, the term "voluntarily abandoned" means a willful act or course of conduct such as would imply a conscious disregard or indifference to such child in respect to the parental obligation owed to the child. Elliott v. Maddox, Tex.Civ.App., 510 S.W.2d 105, 107. See also **Abandonment; Desertion.**

Voluntary courtesy. A voluntary act of kindness. An act of kindness performed by one man towards another, of the free will and inclination of the doer, without any previous request or promise of reward made by him who is the object of the courtesy; from which the law will not imply a promise of remuneration.

Voluntary discontinuance. Voluntary action on part of plaintiff, whereby his case is dismissed without decision on merits. Ferber v. Brueckl, 322 Mo. 892, 17 S.W.2d 524, 527. Fed.R.Civil P. 41(a). See **Dismissal.**

Voluntary exposure to unnecessary danger. An intentional act which reasonable and ordinary prudence would pronounce dangerous. Intentional exposure to unnecessary danger, implying a conscious knowledge of the danger. The voluntary doing of an act which is not necessary to be done, but which requires exposure to known danger to which one would not be exposed if unnecessary act is not done. The term implies a conscious, intentional exposure, something of which one is conscious but willing to take the risk. See **Assumption of risk.**

Voluntary ignorance. This exists where a party might, by taking reasonable pains, have acquired the necessary knowledge, but has neglected to do so.

Voluntary jurisdiction. In old English law, a jurisdiction exercised by certain ecclesiastical courts, in matters where there is no opposition. 3 Bl.Comm. 66. The opposite of *contentious* jurisdiction (*q.v.*).

Voluntas /vəlántæs/. Lat. Properly, volition, purpose, or intention, or a design or the feeling or impulse which prompts the commission of an act. However, in old English law the term was often used to denote a will, that is, the last will and testament of a decedent, more properly called *testamentum.*

Voluntas donatoris in charta doni sui manifeste expressa observetur /vəlántæs dòwnətórəs ìn kárdə dównay s(y)úway mænəféstiy əksprésiy òbsərvíydər/. The will of the donor manifestly expressed in his deed of gift is to be observed.

Voluntas est justa sententia de eo quod quis post mortem suam fieri velit /vəlántæs èst jástə senténsh(iy)ə dìy íyow kwòd kwís pòwst mórdəm s(y)úwəm fáyəray vélət/. A will is an exact opinion or determination concerning that which each one wishes to be done after his death.

Voluntas et propositum distinguunt maleficia /vəlántæs èt prəpózədəm distíngwənt mæləfísh(iy)ə/. The will and the proposed end distinguish crimes.

Voluntas facit quod in testamento scriptum valeat /vəlántæs féysət kwòd in tèstəméntow skríptəm væliyət/. It is intention which gives effect to the wording of a will.

Voluntas in delictis, non exitus spectatur /vəlántæs in dəlíktəs, nòn égzədəs spektéydər/. In crimes, the will, and not the consequence, is looked to.

Voluntas reputatur pro facto /vəlántæs rèpyətéydər pròw fæktow/. The intention is to be taken for the deed.

Voluntas testatoris est ambulatoria usque ad extremum vitæ exitum /vəlántæs testátórəs èst æmbyələtóriyə áskwiy æd əkstríyməm váydiy égzədəm/. The will of a testator is ambulatory until the latest moment of life.

Voluntas testatoris habet interpretationem latam et benignam /vəlántæs tèstətórəs héybəd intàrprəteyshiyównəm léydəm èt bənígnəm/. The intention of a testator has a broad and benignant interpretation.

Voluntas ultima testatoris est perimplenda secundum veram intentionem suam /vəlántæs áltəmə tèstətórəs èst pàrimpléndə səkándəm vírəm intènshiyównəm s(y)úwəm/. The last will of the testator is to be fulfilled according to his true intention.

Volunteer. A person who gives his services without any express or implied promise of remuneration. One who intrudes himself into a matter which does not concern him, or one who pays the debt of another without request, when he is not legally or morally bound to do so, and when he has no interest to protect in making such payment. One who, acting on his own initiative, pays debt of another without invitation, compulsion, or the necessity of self-protection. In re Farmers' & Merchants' State Bank of Nooksack, 175 Wash. 78, 26 P.2d 631; Trinity Universal Ins. Co. v. State Farm Mut. Auto Ins. Co., 246 Ark. 1021, 441 S.W.2d 95, 97.

Conveyancing. One who holds a title under a voluntary conveyance, *i.e.*, one made without consideration, good or valuable, to support it.

Law of master and servant. The term "Volunteer" includes one who, without the assent of the master and without justification arising from a legitimate personal interest, unnecessarily assists a servant in the performance of the master's business.

Military law. One who freely and voluntarily offers himself for service in the army or navy; as distinguished from one who is compelled to serve by draft or conscription, and also from one entered by enlistment in the standing army.

Vote. Suffrage; the expression of one's will, preference, or choice, formally manifested by a member of a legislative or deliberative body, or of a constituency or a body of qualified electors, in regard to the decision to be made by the body as a whole upon any proposed measure or proceeding or in passing laws, rules or regulations, or the selection of an officer or representative. And the aggregate of the expressions of will or choice, thus manifested by individuals, is called the "vote of the body." Commonwealth v. Baker, 237 Ky. 380, 35 S.W.2d 548, 549; Sawyer Stores v. Mitchell, 103 Mont. 148, 62 P.2d 342, 348.

See also Absentee voting; Apportionment; Ballot; Canvass; Casting vote; Cumulative voting; Fifteenth Amendment; Franchise; Gerrymander; Majority vote; Nineteenth Amendment; Twenty-Fourth Amendment; Twenty-Sixth Amendment; Twenty-Third Amendment; Voting Rights Act.

Voter. The word has two meanings—a person who performs act of voting, and a person who has the qualifications entitling him to vote. Its meaning depends on the connections in which it is used, and is not always equivalent to electors. In a limited sense a voter is a person having the legal right to vote, sometimes called a legal voter. See **Legal voter.**

Voting by ballot. The term is used to distinguish open voting from secret voting. The privilege of secrecy is of the essence of "voting by ballot." See **Ballot.**

Voting Rights Act. Federal Act (1965) which suspended all literacy and character tests for voting rights in all States and counties where less than half the adult population were registered, and which provided for federal registration of voters where the Attorney General considered it necessary to enforce rights under the 15th Amendment. See also **Poll-tax.**

Voting stock. In corporations, that type of stock which gives the holder the right to vote for directors and other matters in contrast to non-voting stock which simply entitles the holder to dividends, if any. Common stock is normally voting stock. See also **Stock.**

Voting stock rights. The stockholder's right to vote his stock in the affairs of his company. Most common shares have one vote each. Preferred stock usually has the right to vote when preferred dividends are in default for a specified period. The right to vote may be delegated by the stockholder to another person. See also **Voting stock.**

Voting tax. See **Poll-tax.**

Voting trust. One created by an agreement between a group of the stockholders of a corporation and the trustee, or by a group of identical agreements between individual stockholders and a common trustee, whereby it is provided that for a term of years, or for a period contingent upon a certain event, or until the agreement is terminated, control over the stock owned by such stockholders, either for certain purposes or for all, shall be lodged in the trustee, with or without a reservation to the owner or persons designated by them of the power to direct how such control shall be used. A device whereby two or more persons, owning stock with voting powers, divorce voting rights thereof from ownership, retaining to all intents and purposes the latter in themselves and transferring the former to trustees in whom voting rights of all depositors in the trust are pooled.

Agreement accumulating several owners' stock in hands of one or more persons in trust for voting purposes in order to control corporate business and affairs. It differs from proxy or reciprocal proxy in that it does not make either party the other's agent.

Votum /vówdəm/. Lat. A vow or promise. *Dies votorum,* the wedding day.

Vouch /váwch/. To call upon; to call in to warranty; to call upon the grantor or warrantor to defend the title to an estate; to call upon witness to give warranty of title. To substantiate with evidence; to verify.

To give personal assurance or serve as a guarantee. To call upon, rely on, or quote as an authority. Thus, formerly, to vouch a case or report was to quote it as an authority.

See also **Impleader; Third-party practice; Vouching-in.**

Vouchee /vàwchíy/. In common recoveries, the person who is called to warrant or defend the title is called the "vouchee." The person who is vouched to warranty. In this fictitious proceeding the crier of the court usually performs the office of a common vouchee. 2 Bl.Comm. 358.

Voucher /váwchər/. A receipt, acquittance, or release, which may serve as evidence of payment or discharge of a debt, or to certify the correctness of accounts. An account-book containing the acquittances or receipts showing the accountant's discharge of his obligations. When used in connection with disbursement of money, a written or printed instrument in the nature of an account, receipt, or acquittance, that shows on its face the fact, authority, and purpose of disbursement.

A document that serves to recognize a liability and authorize the disbursement of cash. Sometimes used to refer to the written evidence documenting an accounting entry, as in the term journal voucher.

In old English law, the person on whom the tenant calls to defend the title to the land, because he warranted the title to him at the time of the original purchase.

Voucher to warranty. The calling one who has warranted lands, by the party warranted, to come and defend the suit for him.

Vouching-in. Common-law device by which a defendant notifies another that suit is pending against him, that if liability is found, defendant will look to vouchee for indemnity, that the notice constitutes formal tender of right to defend the action, and that if vouchee refuses to defend, it will be bound in any subsequent litigation between them to the factual determinations necessary to the original judgment. Though largely supplanted by third-party practice, vouching-in remains marginally viable under the federal rules. Humble Oil & Refining Co. v. Philadelphia Ship Maintenance Co., C.A.Pa., 444 F.2d 727, 735. See **Impleader; Third-party practice.**

Vox emissa volat; litera scripta manet /vóks əmísə vówlət; lídərə skríptə mǽnət/. The spoken word flies; the written letter remains.

Voyage. In maritime law, the passing of a vessel by sea from one place, port, or country to another. The term is held to include the enterprise entered upon, and not merely the route.

Foreign voyage. A voyage to some port or place within the territory of a foreign nation. The *terminus* of a voyage determines its character. If it be within the limits of a foreign jurisdiction, it is a foreign voyage, and not otherwise.

Voyage charter. The document in admiralty which sets forth the arrangements and contractual engagements entered into between the charterer and the owner of the ship. Under "voyage charter," ship is engaged to carry full cargo on specific voyage, and ship is manned and navigated by owner. President of India By and Through Director of India Supply Mission v. West Coast S. S. Co., D.C.Or., 213 F.Supp. 352, 359.

Voyage policy. See **Policy of insurance.**

Voyeurism. The condition of one who derives sexual satisfaction from observing the sexual organs or acts of others, generally from a secret vantage point.

Vs. An abbreviation for *versus* (against), constantly used in legal proceedings, and especially in entitling cases.

Vulgar /vólgər/. Lack of cultivation or refinement.

Vulgaris opinio est duplex, viz., orta inter graves et discretos, quæ multum veritatis habet, et opinio orta inter leves et vulgares homines absque specie veritatis /vòlgérəs əpín(i)yow èst d(y)úwpleks, vədíyləsəd órdə íntər gréyviyz èt dəskríydows, kwìy mə́ltəm vèhrətéydəs héybət, èd əpín(i)yow órdə íntər líyviyz èt vòlgériyz hóməniyz ǽbskwiy spíyshiyiy vèhrətéydəs/. Common opinion is of two kinds, viz., that which arises among grave and discreet men, which has much truth in it, and that which arises among light and common men, without any appearance of truth.

Vulgaris purgatio /vòlgérəs pərgéysh(iy)ow/. Lat. In old English law, common purgation; a name given to the trial by *ordeal*, to distinguish it from the canonical purgation, which was by the oath of the party. 4 Bl.Comm. 342.

Vulgo concepti /vólgow kən(t)séptay/. Lat. In the civil law, spurious children; bastards.

Vulgo quæsiti /vólgow kwəzáyday/. Lat. In the civil law, spurious children; literally, gotten from the people; the offspring of promiscuous cohabitation, who are considered as having no father.

W. As an abbreviation, this letter frequently stands for "William" (king of England), "Westminster," "west," or "western."

Wacreour. L. Fr. A vagabond, or vagrant.

Wadia /wéyd(i)yə/. A pledge. See **Vadium; Fides facta.**

Waftors /wǽftərz/. Conductors of vessels at sea.

Waga /wey(g)ə/. In old English law, a weight; a measure of cheese, salt, wool, etc., containing two hundred and fifty-six pounds avoirdupois.

Wage. In old English practice, to give security for the performance of a thing. See also **Wages.**

Wage and hour laws. General term describing federal and state laws governing the maximum hours which may be worked and the minimum wage to be paid. In particular, the federal law known as Fair Labor Standards Act of 1938 which regulates wages, hours and other conditions of labor. 29 U.S.C.A. § 201 *et seq.* See also **Eight hour laws; Fair Labor Standards Act; Walsh-Healey Act.**

Wage assignments. The transfer or assignment in advance of one's wages generally in connection with a debt or judgment. Such assignments are governed by statutes in most states. See also **Assignment** *(Assignment for benefit of creditors).*

Wage earner's plan. A type of partial bankruptcy in which a person keeps his or her property and pays off a court-established proportion of debt over a period of time and under court supervision. See Bankruptcy Act Ch. 13, "Adjustment of Debts of An Individual With Regular Income".

Wage garnishment. See **Garnishment.**

Wager. A contract by which two or more parties agree that a certain sum of money or other thing shall be paid or delivered to one of them or that they shall gain or lose on the happening of an uncertain event or upon the ascertainment of a fact in dispute, where the parties have no interest in the event except that arising from the possibility of such gain or loss. The word "wagering" is practically synonymous with the words betting and gambling, and the terms are so used in common parlance and in statutory and constitutional enactments. McDonald v. Bryant, 238 Ark. 338, 381 S.W.2d 736, 738. See also **Bet; Pari-mutuel betting.**

Wagering contract. One in which the parties stipulate that they shall gain or lose, upon the happening of an uncertain event, in which they have no interest except that arising from the possibility of such gain or loss. See also **Wager.**

Wagering gain. The share of each, where individuals carrying on business in partnership make gains in wagering transactions. Jennings v. Commissioner of Internal Revenue, C.C.A.Tex., 110 F.2d 945, 946.

Wager of battel. The trial by wager of battel was a species of trial introduced into England, among other Norman customs, by William the Conqueror, in which the person accused fought with his accuser, under the apprehension that Heaven would give the victory to him who was in the right. 3 Bl.Comm. 337. It was abolished by St. 59 Geo. III, c. 46.

Wager of law. In old practice, the giving of *gage* or sureties by a defendant in an action of debt that at a certain day assigned he would *make his law;* that is, would take an oath in open court that he did not owe the debt, and at the same time bring with him eleven neighbors (called "compurgators"), who should avow upon their oaths that they believed in their consciences that he said the truth.

Wager policy. See **Policy of insurance.**

Wages. A compensation given to a hired person for his or her services. Compensation of employees based on time worked or output of production.

Every form of remuneration payable for a given period to an individual for personal services, including salaries, commissions, vacation pay, dismissal wages, bonuses and reasonable value of board, rent, housing, lodging, payments in kind, tips, and any other similar advantage received from the individual's employer or directly with respect to work for him. Ernst v. Industrial Commission, 246 Wis. 205, 16 N.W.2d 867. Term should be broadly defined and includes not only periodic monetary earnings but all compensation for services rendered without regard to manner in which such compensation is computed. Ware v. Merrill Lynch, Pierce, Fenner & Smith, Inc., 24 Cal.App.3d 35, 100 Cal.Rptr. 791, 797.

See also **Compensation; Current wages; Front wages; Minimum wage; Salary.**

Wagner Act. A Federal law, passed in 1935, that established most basic union rights. It prohibited several employer actions (such as attempting to force employees to stay out of a union) and labeled these actions "unfair labor practices." It also set up the National Labor Relations Board to help enforce the new labor laws. 29 U.S.C.A. § 151 et seq.

Wagonage /wǽgənəj/. Money paid for carriage in a wagon.

Wagonway. That part of a street ordinarily used for the passage of vehicles within the curb lines. Delaware, L. & W. R. Co. v. Chiara, C.C.A.N.J., 95 F.2d 663, 666.

Waif /wéyf/. Waifs are goods found, but claimed by nobody; that of which every one waives the claim. Also, goods stolen and waived, or thrown away by the thief in his flight, for fear of being apprehended. Waifs are to be distinguished from *bona fugitiva,* which are the goods of the felon himself, which he abandons in his flight from justice.

Wainable /wéynəbəl/. In old records, that may be plowed or manured; tillable.

Wainage /wéynəj/. In old English law, the team and instruments of husbandry belonging to a countryman, and especially to a villein who was required to perform agricultural services.

Wainagium /weynéyj(iy)əm/. What is necessary to the farmer for the cultivation of his land.

Wait and see doctrine. The "wait and see" doctrine is a rule which permits consideraton of events occurring after inception of the instruments which are relevant to the vesting of a future interest, so that if the contingency on which the interest is limited actually occurs within the period of the perpetuities rule, the interest is valid. Three Rivers Rock Co. v. Reed Crushed Stone Co., Inc., Ky., 530 S.W.2d 202, 206. In determining whether a contingent interest violates the Rule Against Perpetuities, many states have enacted laws which permit the court to look at the condition when the contingency occurs and not, as the Rule prescribes, at the creation of the interest. In some states, the doctrine is called the second look doctrine.

Waiting clerks. In old English law, officers whose duty it formerly was to wait in attendance upon the court of chancery. The office was abolished in 1842 by St. 5 & 6 Vict., c. 103.

Waiting period. The period during which an insurance policy is not in effect or for which nothing will be paid on the policy. For example, if there is a waiting period of 30 days under a particular disability policy, the insured will have to be disabled for 30 days before a payment is made for loss of earnings.

In labor law, a period following a notice of intention to strike during which a strike may not lawfully take place. See 29 U.S.C.A. § 158(d). See also **Cooling off period.**

In securities law, the period following registration of a security with Securities and Exchange Commission during which the security may not be sold to the public.

Waive, *v.* To abandon, throw away, renounce, repudiate, or surrender a claim, a privilege, a right, or the opportunity to take advantage of some defect, irregularity, or wrong. To give up right or claim voluntarily.

A person is said to waive a benefit when he renounces or disclaims it, and he is said to waive a tort or injury when he abandons the remedy which the law gives him for it.

In order for one to "waive" a right, he must do it knowingly and be possessed of the facts. Barnhill v. Rubin, D.C.Tex., 46 F.Supp. 963, 966.

Waive, *n.* In old English law, a woman outlawed. The term is, as it were, the feminine of "outlaw," the latter being always applied to a man; "waive," to a woman.

Waiver. The intentional or voluntary relinquishment of a known right, or such conduct as warrants an inference of the relinquishment of such right, or when one dispenses with the performance of something he is entitled to exact or when one in possession of any right, whether conferred by law or by contract, with full knowledge of the material facts, does or forbears to do something the doing of which or the failure of forbearance to do which is inconsistent with the right, or his intention to rely upon it. The renunciation, repudiation, abandonment, or surrender of some claim, right, privilege, or of the opportunity to take advantage of some defect, irregularity, or wrong. A doctrine resting upon an equitable principle, which courts of law will recognize. Atlas Life Ins. Co. v. Schrimsher, 179 Okl. 643, 66 P.2d 944, 948.

Waiver is essentially unilateral, resulting as legal consequence from some act or conduct of party against whom it operates, and no act of party in whose favor it is made is necessary to complete it. Coleman Production Credit Ass'n v. Mahan, Tex.Civ. App., 168 S.W.2d 903, 904. And may be shown by acts and conduct and sometimes by nonaction. Concrete Engineering Co. v. Grande Bldg. Co., 230 Mo. App. 443, 86 S.W.2d 595, 608.

Terms "estoppel" and "waiver" are not synonymous; "waiver" means the voluntary, intentional relinquishment of a known right, and "estoppel" rests upon principle that, where anyone has done an act, or made a statement, which would be a fraud on his part to controvert or impair, because other party has acted upon it in belief that what was done or said was true, conscience and honest dealing require that he not be permitted to repudiate his act or gainsay his statement. Peloso v. Hartford Fire Ins. Co., 102 N.J. Super. 357, 246 A.2d 52, 58.

See also **Abandonment; Estoppel; Forfeiture.**

Express waiver. The voluntary, intentional relinquishment of a known right.

Implied waiver. A waiver is implied where one party has pursued such a course of conduct with reference to the other party as to evidence an intention to waive his rights or the advantage to which he may be entitled, or where the conduct pursued is inconsistent with any other honest intention than an intention of such waiver, provided that the other party concerned has been induced by such conduct to act upon the belief that there has been a waiver, and has incurred trouble or expense thereby. To make out a case of implied "waiver" of a legal right, there must be a clear, unequivocal and decisive act of the party showing such purpose, or acts amounting to an estoppel on his part. Rosenthal v. New York Life Ins. Co., C.C.A.Mo., 99 F.2d 578, 579.

Insurance law. Substance of doctrine of "waiver" in insurance law is that if insurer, with knowledge of facts which would bar existing primary liability, recognizes such primary liability by treating policy as in force, it will not thereafter be allowed to plead such facts to avoid its primary liability.

Lien waiver. See that title.

Waiver by election of remedies, doctrine of. Doctrine applies if there exist two or more coexisting remedies between which there is right of election, inconsistency as to such available remedies, and actual bringing of action or doing some other decisive act, with knowledge of facts, whereby party electing indicates his choice between such inconsistent remedies. Hertz v. Mills, D.C.Md., 10 F.Supp. 979, 981.

Waiver of exemption. A clause inserted in a note, bond, lease, etc., expressly waiving the benefit of the laws exempting limited amounts of personal property from levy and sale on judicial process, so far as concerns the enforcement of the particular debt or obligation.

Waiver of immunity. A means authorized by statutes by which a witness, in advance of giving testimony or producing evidence, may renounce the fundamental right guaranteed to him by constitutions, that no person shall be compelled in any criminal case to be a witness against himself. In re Grae, 282 N.Y. 428, 26 N.E.2d 963, 966. See **Immunity.**

Waiver of premium clause. Provision in insurance policy providing for waiver of premium payments upon disability of insured. Commonly such waiver only takes effect after a certain time period of disability; *e.g.* six months.

Waiver of protest. An agreement by the indorser of a note or bill to be bound in his character of indorser without the formality of a protest in case of non-payment, or, in the case of paper which cannot or is not required to be protested, dispensing with the necessity of a demand and notice.

Waiver of tort. The election, by an injured party, for purposes of redress, to treat the facts as establishing an implied contract, which he may enforce, instead of an injury by fraud or wrong, for the committing of which he may demand damages, compensatory or exemplary.

Walapauz. In old Lombardic law, the disguising the head or face, with the intent of committing a theft.

Walensis /wəlén(t)səs/. In old English law, a Welshman.

Waleschery /wélsh(ə)riy/. The being a Welshman.

Waliscus /wəlískəs/. In Saxon law, a servant, or any ministerial officer.

Walkers. Foresters who have the care of a certain space of ground assigned to them.

Walk out. An organized withdrawal of employees from their place of employment because of a labor dispute.

Wall. An erection of stone, brick, or other material, raised to some height, and intended for purposes of privacy, security or inclosure. In law, this term occurs in such compounds as "ancient wall," "party-wall," "division-wall," etc. See also **Spite fence.**

Common wall. A party wall; one which has been built at the common expense of the two owners whose properties are contiguous, or a wall built by one party in which the other has acquired a common right.

Wallia /wól(i)yə/. In old English law, a wall; a sea-wall; a mound, bank, or wall erected in marshy districts as a protection against the sea.

Walsh-Healey Act. Federal Act (1936) which provides that government contractors should pay not less than the prevailing minimum wage, observe the eight-hour day and the forty-hour week, employ no convict labor and no female under 18 years of age or male under 16 years of age, and allow no hazardous or unsanitary working conditions in their plants. 41 U.S.C.A. §§ 35–45.

Wampum /wómpəm/. Unlike France, Britain undertook no coinage for the use of her American colonies. The earliest medium of exchange for the New England settlements was wampum ordered by The General Court of Massachusetts in 1637. The court ordered that "wampampege should passe at 6 a penny for any sum under 12d." Wampum generally consisted of shells, coon pelts and bullets and was offered in lieu of coins, which were almost non-existent. Although wampum served the purpose for average daily transactions, great confusion was experienced where larger sums were involved. With England ignoring the colonists' need for a standard medium of exchange, the General Court in 1652 ordered the first metallic currency for the English Americans.

Wander. To ramble here and there without any certain course. In its broad sense, "wander" means to ramble without a definite purpose or objective, roam, rove, or stray, and to go aimlessly, indirectly or casually. People v. Weger, 251 C.A.2d 584, 59 Cal.Rptr. 661, 667. See **Transient.**

Wanlass /wónləs/. An ancient customary tenure of lands; *i.e.,* to drive deer to a stand that the lord may have a shot.

Wantage. In marine insurance, ullage; deficiency in the contents of a cask or vessel caused by leaking.

Want of consideration. Term embraces transactions or instances where no consideration was intended to pass. Ranschenbach v. McDaniel's Estate, 122 W.Va. 632, 11 S.E.2d 852, 854. For distinction between "failure of consideration" and "want of consideration," see **Failure of consideration.**

Want of jurisdiction. Lack of jurisdiction over person or subject matter. A lack of authority to exercise in a particular manner a power which board or tribunal has; the doing of something in excess of authority possessed. Evans v. Superior Court in and for City and County of San Francisco, 14 Cal.2d 563, 96 P.2d 107, 116.

Want of repair. As to highways, anything in the state or condition of the highway which renders it unsafe or inconvenient for ordinary travel. Adams v. Town of Bolton, Mass., 297 Mass. 459, 9 N.E.2d 562, 565.

Wanton. Reckless, heedless, malicious; characterized by extreme recklessness or foolhardiness; recklessly disregardful of the rights or safety of others or of consequences. In re Wegner, C.C.A.Ill., 88 F.2d 899, 902. Means undisciplined, unruly, marked by arrogant recklessness of justice, feelings of others, or the like; willful and malicious. Lubbock Bail Bond v. Joshua, Tex.Civ.App., 416 S.W.2d 523, 525. In its ordinarily accepted sense connotes perverseness exhibited by deliberate and uncalled for conduct, recklessness, disregardful of rights and an unjustifiable course of action. Botto v. Fischesser, 174 Ohio St. 322, 189 N.E.2d 127, 130, 22 O.O.2d 380. See also **Wantonness.**

Wanton act. One done in reckless disregard of the rights of others, evincing a reckless indifference to consequences to the life, or limb, or health, or reputation or property rights of another, and is more than negligence, more than gross negligence, and is such conduct as indicates a reckless disregard of the just rights or safety of others or of the consequences of action, equivalent in its results to wilful misconduct.

Wanton acts and omissions. Those of such character or done in such manner or under such circumstances as to indicate that a person of ordinary intelligence actuated by normal and natural concern for the welfare and safety of his fellowmen who might be affected by them could not be guilty of them unless wholly indifferent to their probable injurious effect or consequences. Pupke v. Pupke, 102 Colo. 337, 79 P.2d 290, 292.

Wanton and reckless misconduct. Occurs when a person, with no intent to cause harm, intentionally performs an act so unreasonable and dangerous that he knows, or should know, that it is highly probable that harm will result. Donnelly v. Southern Pac. Co., 18 Cal.2d 863, 118 P.2d 465, 469, 470.

Wanton conduct. Occurs when a person though possessing no intent to cause harm performs an act which is so unreasonable and dangerous that imminent likelihood of harm or injury to another is reasonably apparent. Schorah v. Carey, Del.Super., 318 A.2d 610, 612.

Wanton injury. Injury produced by conscious and intentional wrongful act, or omission of known duty with reckless indifference to consequences. It must be predicated upon actual knowledge of another's peril and a failure to take available preventative action knowing that such failure will probably result in injury. Rainey v. State, 31 Ala.App. 271, 17 So.2d 683, 686.

Wanton misconduct. Act or failure to act, when there is a duty to act, in reckless disregard of rights of another, coupled with a consciousness that injury is a probable consequence of act or omission. Swain v. American Mut. Liability Ins. Co., C.C.A.La., 134 F.2d 886, 887. Term refers to intentional act of unreasonable character performed in disregard of risk known to him or so obvious that he must be taken to have been aware of it and so great as to make it highly probable that harm would follow and it is usually accompanied by conscious indifference to the consequences. Goss v. Baltimore & O. R. Co., C.A.Pa., 355 F.2d 649, 651.

Wanton negligence. Heedless and reckless disregard for another's rights with consciousness that act or omission to act may result in injury to another. Craig v. Stagner, 159 Tenn. 511, 19 S.W.2d 234, 236. See also **Negligence.**

Wantonness. Conscious doing of some act or the omission of some duty with knowledge of existing conditions and consciousness that, from the act or omission, injury will likely result to another. Bedwell v. De Bolt, 221 Ind. 600, 50 N.E.2d 875, 877. Conscious failure by one charged with a duty to exercise due care and diligence to prevent an injury after the discovery of the peril, or under circumstances where he is charged with a knowledge of such peril, and being conscious of the inevitable or probable results of such failure. Stout v. Gallemore, 138 Kan. 385, 26 P.2d 573. A reckless or intentional disregard of the property, rights, or safety of others, implying, actively, a willingness to injure and disregard of the consequences to others, and, passively, more than mere negligence, that is, a conscious and intentional disregard of duty.

Wapentake /wǽpəntèyk/. In English law, a local division of the country; the name is in use north of the Trent to denote a hundred. The derivation of the name is said to be from "weapon" and "take," and indicates that the division was originally of a military character. Also a hundred court.

War. Hostile contention by means of armed forces, carried on between nations, states, or rulers, or between citizens in the same nation or state. Gitlow v. Kiely, D.C.N.Y., 44 F.2d 227, 233. A contest by force between two or more nations, carried on for any purpose, or armed conflict of sovereign powers or declared and open hostilities, or the state of nations among whom there is an interruption of pacific relations, and a general contention by force, authorized by the sovereign. West v. Palmetto State Life Ins. Co., 202 S.C. 422, 25 S.E.2d 475, 477, 478. War does not exist merely because of an armed attack by the military forces of another nation until it is a condition recognized or accepted by political authority of government which is attacked, either through an actual declaration of war or other acts demonstrating such position. Savage v. Sun Life Assur. Co. of Canada, D.C.La., 57 F.Supp. 620, 621.

Term as used in statute proscribing any claim against United States arising out of combatant activity of Military or Naval Forces or Coast Guard during time of war includes an undeclared war as well as a formally declared war. Morrison v. U. S., D.C.Ga., 316 F.Supp. 78, 79.

Articles of war. See **Article.**

Civil war. An internecine war. A war carried on between opposing citizens of the same country or nation.

Imperfect war. See *Perfect war, infra.*

Laws of war. This term denotes a branch of public international law, and comprises the body of rules and principles observed by civilized nations for the regulation of matters inherent in, or incidental to, the conduct of a public war; such, for example, as the relations of neutrals and belligerents, blockades, captures, prizes, truces and armistices, capitulations,

prisoners, and declarations of war and peace; *e.g.*
Geneva Convention.

Mixed war. A mixed war is one which is made on
one side by public authority, and on the other by
mere private persons.

Perfect war. Where whole nation is at war with
another whole nation, but when the hostilities are
limited as respects places, persons, and things, the
war is termed "imperfect war." Bas v. Tingy, 4 U.S.
(Dall.) 37, 40, 1 L.Ed. 731.

Private war. One between private persons, lawfully
exerted by way of defense, but otherwise unknown in
civil society.

Public war. Every contention by force, between two
nations, in external matters, under the authority of
their respective governments. Prize Cases, 2 Black
666, 17 L.Ed. 459.

Solemn war. A war made in form by public declaration; a war solemnly declared by one state against
another. Bas v. Tingy, 4 U.S. (Dall.) 37, 40, 1 L.Ed.
731.

War clauses. Art. I, § 8 (Clauses 11–16) U.S.Const.,
provides, inter alia, that Congress shall have power to
declare war, and raise and support military forces.
See **War power.**

War crimes. Crimes committed by countries in violation of the international laws governing wars. At
Nuremberg after World War II, crimes committed by
the Nazis were so tried.

Ward. Guarding, caring, protecting.

A division of a city or town for elections, police,
and other purposes. A person, especially a child, or
incompetent, placed by the court under the care of a
guardian. A corridor, room, or other division of a
prison, hospital, or asylum.

See **Guardian; Guardianship.**

Wardage. Money paid and contributed to watch and
ward.

Ward-horn. In old English law, the duty of keeping
watch and *ward,* with a *horn* to blow upon any
occasion of surprise.

Ward-fegh. Sax. In old records, ward-fee; the value
of a ward, or the money paid to the lord for his
redemption from wardship.

Ward-in-chancery. An infant who is under the superintendence of the chancellor.

Ward-mote. In English law, a court kept in every
ward in London, commonly called the "ward-mote
court," or "inquest."

Ward-penny. In old English law, money paid to the
sheriff or castellains, for the duty of watching and
warding a castle.

Wardship. In military tenures, the right of the lord to
have custody, as guardian, of the body and lands of
the infant heir, without any account of profits, until
he was twenty-one or she sixteen. In socage the
guardian was accountable for profits; and he was not
the lord, but the nearest relative to whom the inheritance could not descend, and the wardship ceased at
fourteen. In copyholds, the lord was the guardian,

but was perhaps accountable for profits. See 2 Bl.
Comm. 67.

Wardship in chivalry. An incident to the tenure of
knight-service.

Wardship in copyholds. The lord is guardian of his
infant tenant by special custom.

Wards of admiralty. Seamen are sometimes thus
designated, because, in view of their general improvidence and rashness, and though they are not technically incapable of contracting, their contracts are
treated like those of fiduciaries and beneficiaries, and
if there is any inequality in terms or any disproportion in the bargain or any sacrifice of rights of seamen which are not compensated by extraordinary
benefits, the judicial interpretation of the transaction
is that the bargain is unjust and that pro tanto, the
bargain ought to be set aside as inequitable. See
Garrett v. Moore-McCormack Co., Pa., 317 U.S. 239,
63 S.Ct. 246, 251, 87 L.Ed. 239.

Wards of court. Infants and persons of unsound
mind. Davis' Committee v. Loney, 290 Ky. 644, 162
S.W.2d 189, 190. Their rights must be guarded jeal-
ously. Montgomery v. Erie R. Co., C.C.A.N.J., 97
F.2d 289, 292. See **Guardianship.**

Ward-staff. In old records, a constable's or watchman's staff.

Ward-wit. In old English law, immunity or exemption from the duty or service of ward, or from contributing to such service. Exemption from amercement for not finding a man to do ward.

Warda /wórdə/. L. Lat. In old English law, ward;
guard; protection; keeping; custody. A ward; an
infant under wardship.

Warden. A guardian; a keeper. Person in primary
charge of prison. This is the name given to various
officers.

Warden of the cinque ports /wórdən əv ðə síŋk pórts/.
In English law, the title of the governor or presiding
officer of the Cinque Ports *(q.v.).*

Wards and liveries. In English law, the title of a court
of record, established in the reign of Henry VIII. See
Court of Wards and Liveries.

Warectare /wòhrəktériy/. L. Lat. In old English law,
to fallow ground; or plow up land (designed for
wheat) in the spring, in order to let it lie fallow for
the better improvement.

Warehouse. Structure used for the reception and storage of goods and merchandise. Carter v. Bauman,
C.C.A.Cal., 19 F.2d 855, 856. The term may include
any structure used to hold goods, stores or wares
temporarily or for a length of time. In re Miller Land
& Livestock Co., D.C.Mont., 56 F.Supp. 34, 35.

Warehouse book. A book used by merchants to contain an account of the quantities of goods received,
shipped, and remaining in stock.

Warehouseman. One engaged in business of receiving
and storing goods of others for compensation or profit; person who receives goods and merchandise to be
stored in his warehouse for hire; one who, as a
business and for hire, keeps and stores goods of

others. U.C.C. § 7–102. State ex rel. and for Use and Benefit of Cawrse v. American Surety Co. of New York, 148 Or. 1, 35 P.2d 487, 491. The business is public or private as it may be conducted for storage of goods of general public or for those of certain persons. The general commercial laws governing rights and liabilities of warehousemen are provided in U.C.C. § 7–201 et seq.

Warehousemen's lien. Right of warehouseman to retain possession of goods until storage charges have been paid. See U.C.C. §§ 7–209, 7–210.

Warehouse receipt. A receipt issued by a warehouseman for goods received by him on storage in his warehouse. U.C.C. §§ 1–201(45), 7–201. It is evidence of title to goods thereby represented. Woldson v. Davenport Mill & Elevator Co., 169 Wash. 298, 13 P.2d 478, 480. For form and content of warehouse receipt, see U.C.C. § 7–202. As regards altered warehouse receipts, see U.C.C. § 7–208. See also **Field warehouse receipt.**

Warehouse system. A system of public stores or warehouses, established or authorized by law, called "bonded warehouses," in which an importer may deposit goods imported, in the custody of the revenue officers, paying storage, but not being required to pay the customs duties until the goods are finally removed for consumption in the home market, and with the privilege of withdrawing the goods from store for the purpose of re-exportation without paying any duties.

Bonded warehouse. Special type of private warehouse used to store products on which a federal tax must be paid before they can be sold.

Warning. A pointing out of danger. Also a protest against incurring it. The purpose of a "warning" is to apprise a party of the existence of danger of which he is not aware to enable him to protect himself against it, and where the party is aware of the danger, the warning will serve no useful purpose and is unnecessary, and there is no duty to warn against risks which are open and obvious. Wiseman v. Northern Pac. Ry. Co., 214 Minn. 101, 7 N.W.2d 672, 675.

Federal laws require warning labels to be affixed to potentially dangerous products, clothes, drugs, tools, and the like.

See also **Caveat; Caveat emptor.**

Under the old practice of the English court of probate, a warning was a notice given by a registrar of the principal registry to a person who had entered a *caveat,* warning him, within six days after service, to enter an appearance to the *caveat* in the principal registry, and to set forth his interest, concluding with a notice that in default of his doing so the court would proceed to do all such acts, matters, and things as should be necessary. By the rules under the judicature acts, a writ of summons has been substituted for a warning.

Warnistura /wòrnəst(y)úrə/. In old English records, garniture; furniture; provision.

Warnoth. In old English law, an ancient custom, whereby, if any tenant holding of the Castle of Dover failed in paying his rent at the day, he should forfeit double, and, for the second failure, treble, etc.

War power. Power of federal government to wage war successfully. Brown v. Wright, C.C.A.W.Va., 137 F.2d 484, 489; United States v. Maviglia, D.C.N.J., 52 F.Supp. 946, 947. It embraces every aspect of national defense, including protection of war materials as well as members of armed forces from injury and danger; but direct interference with liberty and property and abridgement of constitutional guaranties of freedom can be justified under the "war power" only where the danger to the government is real, impending and imminent. Schueller v. Drum, D.C.Pa., 51 F.Supp. 383, 387.

While Congress has power to declare war (Art. I, § 8, U.S.Const.), the President, as Commander in Chief, has ultimate power over conduct of war including tactics and strategy (Art. II, § 1).

See also **War** (*War clauses*).

Warrant, v. In contracts, to engage or promise that a certain fact or state of facts, in relation to the subject-matter, is, or shall be, as it is represented to be.

In conveyancing, to assure the title to property sold, by an express covenant to that effect in the deed of conveyance. To stipulate by an express covenant that the title of a grantee shall be good, and his possession undisturbed.

Warrant, n. An order by which the drawer authorizes one person to pay a particular sum of money.

An authority issued to a collector of taxes, empowering him to collect the taxes extended on the assessment roll, and to make distress and sale of goods or land in default of payment.

A command of a council, board, or official whose duty it is to pass upon the validity and determine the amount of a claim against the municipality, to the treasurer to pay money out of any funds in the municipal treasury, which are or may become available for the purpose specified, to a designated person whose claim therefor has been duly adjusted and allowed. Roe v. Roosevelt Water Conservation Dist., 41 Ariz. 197, 16 P.2d 967, 970; State ex rel. Toomey v. State Board of Examiners, 74 Mont. 1, 238 P. 316, 328. A "warrant" differs from a "bond" in that a bond is a "negotiable instrument", whereas a warrant is nonnegotiable and is subject at all times to the defenses it would be were it in the hands of the original payee, which is not the case with a negotiable bond. Adams v. McGill, Tex.Civ.App., 146 S.W.2d 332, 334.

See also **Land warrant; Possessory warrant; Probable cause; Search warrant; Share-warrant to bearer.**

Arrest warrant. A written order which is made on behalf of the state and is based upon a complaint issued pursuant to statute and/or court rule and which commands law enforcement officer to arrest a person and bring him before magistrate. Pillsbury v. State, 31 Wis.2d 87, 142 N.W.2d 187, 190. See Fed.R. Crim.P. 4.

Form. The warrant shall be signed by the magistrate and shall contain the name of the defendant or, if his name is unknown, any name or description by which he can be identified with reasonable certainty. It shall describe the offense charged in the complaint. It shall command that the defendant be arrested and brought before the nearest available magistrate. Fed.R.Crim.P. 4(c).

Issuance. If it appears from the complaint, or from an affidavit or affidavits filed with the complaint, that there is probable cause to believe that an offense has been committed and that the defendant has committed it, a warrant for the arrest of the defendant shall issue to any officer authorized by law to execute it. Upon the request of the attorney for the government a summons instead of a warrant shall issue. More than one warrant or summons may issue on the same complaint. If a defendant fails to appear in response to the summons, a warrant shall issue. Fed.R.Crim.P. 4(a).

See also **Arrest; Probable cause; Warrantless arrest.**

Bench warrant. See **Bench.**

Death warrant. A warrant issued generally by the chief executive authority of a state, directed to the sheriff or other proper local officer or the warden of a jail, commanding him at a certain time to proceed to carry into execution a sentence of death imposed by the court upon a convicted criminal.

Distress warrant. See **Distress.**

General warrant. A process which formerly issued from the state secretary's office in England to take up (without naming any persons) the author, printer, and publisher of such obscene and seditious libels as were specified in it. It was declared illegal and void for uncertainty by a vote of the house of commons on the 22nd April, 1766.

Interest warrant. Order drawn by a corporation on its bank directing the bank to pay a bondholder who is entitled to interest.

Landlord's warrant. See **Landlord.**

Land warrant. See that title.

Outstanding warrant. An order for arrest of a person which has not yet been executed.

Search warrant. See that title.

Stock warrant. A certificate entitling the owner to buy a specified amount of stock at a specified time(s) for a specified price. Differs from a stock option only in that options are granted to employees and warrants are sold to the public. A "warrant" is an instrument issued by a corporation giving holder right to subscribe to capital stock of corporation at fixed price either for limited period or perpetually. Miller v. General Outdoor Advertising Co., D.C.N.Y., 223 F.Supp. 790, 794.

Warrant creditor. See **Creditor.**

Warrant of arrest. See **Arrest.**

Warrant of attorney. An instrument in writing, addressed to one or more attorneys therein named, authorizing them, generally, to appear in any court, or in some specified court, on behalf of the person giving it, and to confess judgment in favor of some particular person therein named, in an action of debt. It usually contains a stipulation not to bring any action, or any writ of error, or file a bill in equity, so as to delay him; such writing usually being given as security for obligation on which judgment was authorized, and in such procedure service of process is not essential. See **Judgment** (*Confession of judgment*).

Warrant of commitment. A written authority committing a person to custody.

Warrant officers. In the United States army, navy, coast and geodetic survey, coast guard, marine corps and air force, these are a class of inferior officers who hold their rank by virtue of a written warrant instead of a commission.

Warrant of merchantability. Warranty that goods are reasonably fit for general purpose for which sold. Sperry Flour Co. v. De Moss, 141 Or. 440, 18 P.2d 242, 243. See also **Warranty.**

Warrant to sue and defend. In old English practice, a special warrant from the crown, authorizing a party to appoint an attorney to sue or defend for him. 3 Bl.Comm. 25. A special authority given by a party to his attorney, to commence a suit, or to appear and defend a suit, in his behalf. These warrants are now disused, though formal entries of them upon the record were long retained in practice.

Warrantee. A person to whom a warranty is made.

Warrantia chartæ /wohrǽnsh(iy)ə kárdiy/. In old English practice, warranty of charter. A writ which lay for one who, being enfeoffed of lands or tenements, with a clause of warranty, was afterwards impleaded in an assize or other action in which he could not vouch to warranty. In such case, it might be brought against the warrantor, to compel him to assist the tenant with a good plea or defense, or else to render damages and the value of the land, if recovered against the tenant. 3 Bl.Comm. 300.

Warrantia custodiæ /wohrǽnsh(iy)ə kəstówdiyiy/. An old English writ, which lay for him who was challenged to be a ward to another, in respect to land said to be holden by knight-service; which land, when it was bought by the ancestors of the ward, was warranted free from such thraldom. The writ lay against the warrantor and his heirs.

Warrantia diei /wohrǽnsh(iy)ə dayíyay/. A writ which lay for a man who, having had a day assigned him personally to appear in court in any action in which he was sued, was in the meantime, by commandment, employed in the king's service, so that he could not come at the day assigned. It was directed to the justices that they might not record him in default for that day.

Warrantizare /wòhrəntəzériy/. In old English law conveyancing, to warrant; to bind one's self, by covenant in a deed of conveyance, to defend the grantee in his title and possession.

Warrantizare est defendere et acquietare tenentem, qui warrantum vocavit, in seisina sua; et tenens de re warranti excambium habebit ad valentiam /wòhrəntəzériy èst dəféndəriy èd əkwayətériy tənéntəm, kwày wohrǽntəm vowkéyvəd, in síyzənə s(y)úwə; èt ténən(d)z dìy ríy wohrǽntay ekskǽmb(i)yəm həbíybəd ǽd vəlénsh(iy)əm/. To warrant is to defend and insure in peace the tenant, who calls for warranty, in his seisin; and the tenant in warranty will have an exchange in proportion to its value.

Warrantless arrest. Arrest of a person without a warrant. It is generally permissible if the arresting officer has reasonable grounds to believe that the person has committed a felony or if the person has committed a misdemeanor amounting to a breach of the peace in the officer's presence.

Warrantor. One who makes a warranty. Any supplier or other person who gives or offers to give a written warranty or who is or may be obligated under an implied warranty. 15 U.S.C.A. § 2301.

Warrantor potest excipere quod querens non tenet terram de qua petit warrantiam, et quod donum fuit insufficiens /wohrǽntor pówdǝst ǝksípǝriy kwòd kwírǝn(d)z nòn ténǝt téhrǝm dìy kwéy pédǝt wohrǽnsh(iy)ǝm, èt kwòd dównǝm fyúwǝd ìnsǝfísh-(iy)en(d)z/. A warrantor may object that the complainant does not hold the land of which he seeks the warranty, and that the gift was insufficient.

Warranty. A promise that a proposition of fact is true. The Fred Smartley, Jr., C.C.A.Va., 108 F.2d 603, 606. A promise that certain facts are truly as they are represented to be and that they will remain so, subject to any specified limitations. In certain circumstances a warranty will be presumed, known as an "implied" warranty.

Commercial Sales

A warranty is a statement or representation made by seller of goods, contemporaneously with and as a part of contract of sale, though collateral to express object of sale, having reference to character, quality, or title of goods, and by which seller promises or undertakes to insure that certain facts are or shall be as he then represents them. Bell v. Menzies, 110 Ga.App. 436, 138 S.E.2d 731, 732. A promise or agreement by seller that article sold has certain qualities or that seller has good title thereto. A statement of fact respecting the quality or character of goods sold, made by the seller to induce the sale, and relied on by the buyer.

The general statutory law governing warranties on sales of goods is provided in U.C.C. § 2–312 et seq.

See also **Magnuson-Moss Warranty Act; Privity; Promissory warranty; Special warranty.**

Express warranty. (1) Express warranties by the seller are created as follows: (a) Any affirmation of fact or promise made by the seller to the buyer which relates to the goods and becomes part of the basis of the bargain creates an express warranty that the goods shall conform to the affirmation or promise. (b) Any description of the goods which is made part of the basis of the bargain creates an express warranty that the goods shall conform to the description. (c) Any sample or model which is made part of the basis of the bargain creates an express warranty that the whole of the goods shall conform to the sample or model. (2) It is not necessary to the creation of an express warranty that the seller use formal words such as "warrant" or "guarantee" or that he have a specific intention to make a warranty, but an affirmation merely of the value of the goods or a statement purporting to be merely the seller's opinion or commendation of the goods does not create a warranty. U.C.C. § 2–313.

A written statement arising out of a sale to the consumer of a consumer good pursuant to which the manufacturer, distributor, or retailer undertakes to preserve or maintain the utility or performance of the consumer good or provide compensation if there is a failure in utility or performance; or in the event of any sample or model, that the whole of the goods conforms to such sample or model. It is not necessary to the creation of an express warranty that formal words such as "warrant" or "guarantee" be used or that a specific intention to make a warranty be present, but an affirmation merely of the value of the goods or a statement purporting to be merely an opinion or commendation of the goods does not create a warranty. Statements or representations such as expressions of general policy concerning customer satisfaction which are not subject to any limitation do not create an express warranty. Calif.Civil Code, § 1791.2.

See also *Written warranty, infra.*

Full warranty. A warranty as to full performance covering generally both labor and materials. Under a full warranty, the warrantor must remedy the consumer product within a reasonable time and without charge after notice of a defect or malfunction. 15 U.S.C.A. § 2304. Compare *Limited warranty, infra.*

Implied warranty. A promise arising by operation of law, that something which is sold shall be merchantable and fit for the purpose for which the seller has reason to know that it is required. (a) Unless excluded or modified, a warranty that the goods shall be merchantable is implied in a contract for their sale, if the seller is a merchant with respect to goods of that kind. The serving for value of food or drink to be consumed either on the premises or elsewhere is a sale for this purpose. U.C.C. § 2–314(1). (b) Where the seller, at the time of contracting, has reason to know any particular purpose for which the goods are required, and that the buyer is relying on the seller's skill or judgment to select or furnish suitable goods, there is, unless excluded or modified, an implied warranty that the goods shall be fit for such purpose. U.C.C. § 2–315.

"Implied warranty of fitness" means that when the retailer, distributor, or manufacturer has reason to know any particular purpose for which the consumer goods are required, and further, that the buyer is relying on the skill and judgment of the seller to select and furnish suitable goods, then there is an implied warranty that the goods shall be fit for such purpose. Calif.Civil Code, § 1791.1.

"Implied warranty of merchantability" or "implied warranty that goods are merchantable" means that the consumer goods meet each of the following: (1) Pass without objection in the trade under the contract description; (2) Are fit for the ordinary purposes for which such goods are used; (3) Are adequately contained, packaged, and labeled; (4) Conform to the promises or affirmations of fact made on the container or label. Calif.Civil Code, § 1791.1.

See also **Fitness for particular purpose.**

Limited warranty. A written warranty which fails to meet one or more of the minimum standards for a "full" warranty. 15 U.S.C.A. § 2303. See *Full warranty, infra.* Warranty limited to labor or to materials for a specified time, commonly given by automobile dealers in connection with sale of used cars.

Third party beneficiaries of warranties. See **Privity.**

Warranty of title. An implied promise that the seller owns the item offered for sale. (1) Subject to subsection (2) there is in a contract for sale a warranty by the seller that (a) the title conveyed shall be good, and its transfer rightful; and (b) the goods shall be delivered free from any security interest or other lien or encumbrance of which the buyer at the time of contracting has no knowledge. (2) A warranty under subsection (1) will be excluded or modified only by specified language or by circumstances which give the buyer reason to know that the person selling does not claim title in himself or that he is purporting to sell only such right or title as he or a third person may have. (3) Unless otherwise agreed a seller who is a merchant regularly dealing in goods of the kind warrants that the goods shall be delivered free of the rightful claim of any third person by way of infringement or the like but a buyer who furnishes specifications to the seller must hold the seller harmless against any such claim which arises out of compliance with the specifications. U.C.C. § 2–312.

Written warranty. Any written affirmation of fact or written promise made in connection with the sale of a consumer product by a supplier to a buyer which relates to the nature of the material or workmanship and affirms or promises that such material or workmanship is defect free or will meet a specified period of time, or any undertaking in writing in connection with the sale by a supplier of a consumer product to refund, repair, replace, or take other remedial action with respect to such product in the event that such product fails to meet with the specifications set forth in the undertaking, which written affirmation, promise, or undertaking becomes part of the basis of the bargain between a supplier and a buyer for purposes other than resale of such product. 15 U.S.C.A. § 2301. See also *Express warranty, supra.*

Insurance

A warranty in the law of insurance consists of a statement by insured upon the literal truth of which the validity of the contract depends. Statement, made in insurance contract by insured, which is susceptible of no construction other than that parties mutually intended that policy should not be binding, unless such statement be literally true. Brotherhood of Railroad Trainmen v. Wood, Tex.Civ.App., 79 S.W.2d 665, 668.

A statement, description or undertaking on the part of insured, appearing in the policy or in another instrument properly incorporated in the policy and relating contractually to the risk insured against. Reid v. Hardware Mut. Ins. Co. of Carolinas, S. C., 252 S.C. 339, 166 S.E.2d 317, 321.

Affirmative warranty. In the law of insurance, warranties may be either affirmative or promissory. Affirmative warranties may be either express or implied, but they usually consist of positive representations in the policy of the existence of some fact or state of things at the time, or previous to the time, of the making of the policy; they are, in general, conditions precedent, and if untrue, whether material to the risk or not, the policy does not attach, as it is not the contract of the insurer.

Express warranty. An agreement expressed in a policy, whereby the assured stipulates that certain facts relating to the risk are or shall be true, or certain acts relating to the same subject have been or shall be done.

Promissory warranty. In the law of insurance, a warranty which requires the performance or omission of certain things or the existence of certain facts after the beginning of the contract of insurance and during its continuance, and the breach of which will avoid the policy. See also **Promissory warranty.**

Generally

Construction warranty. An undertaking or promise made by seller or building contractor of new home that such home is fit for the purpose intended; *i.e.* free from structural, electrical, plumbing, etc. defects. Many states have statutes which provide the purchaser with such warranty protection. See **Home Owners Warranty**; also, *Warranty of habitability,* below.

Continuing warranty. One which applies to the whole period during which the contract is in force; *e.g.,* an undertaking in a charter-party that a vessel shall continue to be of the same class that she was at the time the charter-party was made.

Covenant of warranty. See **Covenant.**

Cumulation and conflict of warranties. Warranties whether express or implied shall be construed as consistent with each other and as cumulative, but if such construction is unreasonable the intention of the parties shall determine which warranty is dominant. In ascertaining that intention the following rules apply: (a) Exact or technical specifications displace an inconsistent sample or model or general language of description. (b) A sample from an existing bulk displaces inconsistent general language of description. (c) Express warranties displace inconsistent implied warranties other than an implied warranty of fitness for a particular purpose. U.C.C. § 2–317.

General warranty. The name of a covenant of warranty inserted in deeds, by which the grantor binds himself, his heirs, etc., to "warrant and forever defend" to the grantee, his heirs, etc., the title thereby conveyed, against the lawful claims of all persons whatsoever. Where the warranty is only against the claims of persons claiming "by, through, or under" the grantor or his heirs, it is called a "special warranty."

Implied warranty. Exists when the law derives it by implication or inference from the nature of the transaction or the relative situation or circumstances of the parties. Great Atlantic & Pacific Tea Co. v. Walker, Tex.Civ.App., 104 S.W.2d 627, 632. See also this topic under **Commercial Sales** above.

Lineal warranty. In old conveyancing, the kind of warranty which existed when the heir derived title to the land warranted either from or through the ancestor who made the warranty.

Personal warranty. One available in personal actions, and arising from the obligation which one has contracted to pay the whole or part of a debt due by another to a third person. Flanders v. Seelye, 105 U.S. 718, 26 L.Ed. 1217.

Special warranty. A clause of warranty inserted in a deed of lands, by which the grantor covenants, for himself and his heirs, to "warrant and forever defend" the title to the same, to the grantee and his heirs, etc., against all persons claiming "by, through, or under" the grantor or his heirs. If the warranty is against the claims of all persons whatsoever, it is called a "general" warranty. See also **Covenant.**

Warranty deed. See that title.

Warranty of fitness. Warranty by seller that goods sold are suitable for special purpose of buyer. See also *Implied warranty* under **Commercial Sales** above.

Warranty of habitability. Every landlord of dwelling unit impliedly warrants that the premises are fit for habitation at time of letting and will remain so during term of tenancy. Boston Housing Authority v. Hemingway, 363 Mass. 184, 293 N.E.2d 831.

Under "implied warranty of habitability," applicable to new housing, builder-vendor warrants that he has complied with the building code of the area in which the structure is located and that the residence was built in a workmanlike manner and is suitable for habitation. Duncan v. Schuster-Graham Homes, Inc., Colo.App., 563 P.2d 976, 977. See also **Habitability.**

Warranty deed. Deed in which grantor warrants good clear title. The usual covenants of title are warranties of seisin, quiet enjoyment, right to convey, freedom from encumbrances and defense of title as to all claims.

Warranty, voucher to. In old English practice, the calling a warrantor into court by the party warranted (when tenant in a real action brought for recovery of such lands), to defend the suit for him.

Warren. A term in English law for a place in which birds, fishes, or wild beasts are kept.

A franchise or privilege, either by prescription or grant from the king, to keep beasts and fowls of warren, which are hares, coneys, partridges, pheasants, etc. Also any place to which such privilege extends.

Free warren. A franchise for the preserving and custody of beasts and fowls of warren. 2 Bl.Comm. 39, 417. This franchise gave the grantee sole right of killing, so far as his warren extended, on condition of excluding other persons. 2 Bl.Comm. 39.

War risk insurance. See **Insurance.**

Warsaw Convention. Treaty concluded in Warsaw, Poland in 1929 consisting of rules, including limitation of liability, for international air travel. The United States is a party to such treaty.

Warscot /wórskòt/. In Saxon law, a customary or usual tribute or contribution towards armor, or the arming of the forces.

Warth. In old English law, a customary payment, supposed to be the same with *ward-penny.*

Wash. A shallow part of a river or arm of the sea. The sandy, rocky, gravelly, boulder-bestrewn part of a river bottom deposited on level land near mouth of a canyon representing rocks and gravel washed down by a mountain stream.

Wash bank. A bank composed of such substance that it is liable to be washed away by the action of the water thereon, so as to become unsafe to travelers on highway.

Washington, Treaty of. A treaty signed on May 8, 1871, between Great Britain and the United States of America, with reference to certain differences arising out of the war between the northern and southern states of the Union, the Canadian fisheries, and other matters.

Washout signal. In railroad parlance, emergency signal meaning to stop immediately. Stinson v. Aluminum Co. of America, C.C.A.Tenn., 141 F.2d 682, 684.

Wash sale. The sale and purchase of the same or similar asset within a short time period. For income tax purposes, losses on a sale of stock may not be recognized if equivalent stock is purchased within thirty days before or thirty days after the date of sale. I.R.C. § 1091.

Also a fictitious kind of sale, disallowed on stock and other exchanges, in which a broker who has received orders from one person to buy and from another person to sell a particular amount or quantity of some particular stock or commodity simply transfers the stock or commodity from one principal to the other and pockets the difference, instead of executing both orders separately to the best advantage in each case, as is required by the rules of the different exchanges. U. S. v. Keough, D.C.Nev., 48 F.2d 246, 252. Seed also **Sale.**

Wash transaction. See **Wash sale.**

Waste. An abuse or destructive use of property by one in rightful possession. Spoil or destruction, done or permitted, to lands, houses, gardens, trees, or other corporeal hereditaments, by the tenant thereof, to the prejudice of the heir, or of him in reversion or remainder. 2 Bl.Comm. 281. Camden Trust Co. v. Handle, 132 N.J.Eq. 97, 26 A.2d 865, 869. A destruction or material alteration or deterioration of the freehold, or of the improvements forming a material part thereof, by any person rightfully in possession, but who has not the fee title or the full estate. An unreasonable or improper use, abuse, mismanagement, or omission of duty touching real estate by one rightfully in possession, which results in its substantial injury. Any unlawful act or omission of duty on the part of the tenant which results in permanent injury to the inheritance. Unreasonable conduct by owner of possessory estate that results in physical damage to real estate and substantial diminution in value of estates in which others have an interest. Pleasure Time, Inc. v. Kuss, 78 Wis.2d 373, 254 N.W.2d 463, 467. The term implies neglect or misconduct resulting in material damage to or loss of property, but does not include ordinary depreciation of property due to age and normal use over a comparatively short period of time. First Ferderal Sav. & Loan Ass'n of Coffeyville v. Moulds, 202 Kan. 557, 451 P.2d 215, 220. It is the violation of an obligation to treat the premises in such manner that no harm be done to them, and that the estate may revert to those having an underlying interest, undeteriorated by any willful or negligent acts. Camden Trust Co. v. Handle, 130 N.J.Eq. 125, 21 A.2d 354, 358.

The early English doctrine was to the effect that anything which changed the character or nature of the land, notwithstanding the fact that it was an improvement thereto, constituted "waste."

The primary distinction between "waste" and "trespass" is that in waste the injury is done by one rightfully in possession. Camden Trust Co. v. Handle, 132 N.J.Eq. 97, 26 A.2d 865, 867, 869.

Old English criminal law. A prerogative or liberty, on the part of the crown, of committing *waste* on the lands of felons, by pulling down their houses, extirpating their gardens, plowing their meadows, and cutting down their woods. 4 Bl.Comm. 385.

In General

Ameliorating waste. Change in the physical characteristics of property by an unauthorized act of the tenant but an act which adds value and improves the property. A tenant is not liable for such waste.

Commissive waste. Active or positive waste; waste done by acts of spoliation or destruction, rather than by mere neglect; the same as voluntary waste. See *infra.*

Double waste. See **Double.**

Equitable waste. Injury to a reversion or remainder in real estate, which is not recognized by the courts of law as waste, but which equity will interpose to prevent or remedy. Otherwise defined as an unconscientious abuse of the privilege of non-impeachability for waste at common law, whereby a tenant for life, without impeachment of waste, will be restrained from committing willful, destructive, malicious, or extravagant waste, such as pulling down houses, cutting timber of too young a growth, or trees planted for ornament, or for shelter of premises.

Impeachment of waste. Liability for waste committed, or a demand or suit for compensation for waste committed upon lands or tenements by a tenant thereof who has no right to commit waste. On the other hand, a tenure "without impeachment of waste" signifies that the tenant cannot be called to account for waste committed.

Nul waste. "No waste." The name of a plea in an action of waste, denying the commission of waste, and forming the general issue.

Permissive waste. That kind of waste which is a matter of omission only, as by suffering a house to fall for want of necessary reparations. 2 Bl.Comm. 281.

Voluntary waste. Active or positive waste; waste done or committed, in contradistinction to that which results from mere negligence, which is called "permissive" waste. Voluntary waste is the willful destruction or carrying away of something attached to the freehold, and "permissive waste" is the failure to take reasonable care of the premises. Voluntary or commissive waste consists of injury to the demised premises or some part thereof, when occasioned by some deliberate or voluntary act, as, for instance, the pulling down of a house or removal of floors, windows, doors, furnaces, shelves, or other things affixed to and forming part of the freehold. Contrasted with "*permissive*" waste.

Writ of waste. See that title.

Waste-book. A book used by merchants, to receive rough entries or memoranda of all transactions in the order of their occurrence, previous to their being posted in the journal. Otherwise called a "blotter."

Wastel /wóstəl/. A standard of quality of bread, made of the finest white flour. *Cocket* bread was slightly inferior in quality. The statute of 1266 mentions seven kinds of bread.

Waste water. Water that is actually wasted or not needed by the claimant thereto; water which, after it has served the purpose of the lawful claimant thereto, has been permitted to run to waste or to escape; and water which from unavoidable causes escapes from the ditches, canals, or other works of the lawful claimants. Rock Creek Ditch & Flume Co. v. Miller, 93 Mont. 248, 17 P.2d 1074, 1077. But water is not "waste water" so long as it remains on the land of the original appropriator.

Wasting asset. A natural resource having a limited useful life and, hence, subject to amortization called depletion. Examples are timberland, oil and gas wells, and ore deposits. See also **Wasting property.**

Wasting property. Includes such property as leasehold interests; royalties; patent rights; interests in things the substance of which is consumed, such as mines, oil and gas wells, quarries and timberlands; interests in things which are consumed in the using or are worn out by use, such as machinery and farm implements. In re Pennock's Will, 285 N.Y. 475, 35 N.E.2d 177, 178.

Wasting trust. A trust in which the trustee may apply a part of the principal to make good a deficiency of income. Trust, the res of which consists in whole or in part of property which is gradually being consumed (*i.e.* consisting of wasting assets).

Wastors /wéystərz/. In old statutes, a kind of thieves.

Watch, v. To keep guard; to stand as sentinel; to be on guard at night, for the preservation of security, peace and good order.

Watch, n. A division of a ship's crew. At sea, the ship's company is divided into two watches, larboard and starboard, with a mate to command each. O'Hara v. Luckenbach S. S. Co., 269 U.S. 364, 46 S.Ct. 157, 160, 70 L.Ed. 313. Also the division of the day into time periods of service of the officers and crew, and, by immemorial Anglo-Saxon maritime custom, the time period of a watch never exceeded four hours. The Denali, C.C.A.Wash., 105 F.2d 413, 416. See also **Lookout.**

Watch and ward. "Watch" denotes keeping guard during the night; "ward," by day.

Watchman. One whose general duties consist of guarding, patrolling, and overseeing a building, group of buildings, or other property.

Water. As designating a commodity or a subject of ownership, this term has the same meaning in law as in common speech; but in another sense, and especially in the plural, it may designate a body of water, such as a river, a lake, or an ocean, or an aggregate of such bodies of water, as in the phrases "foreign waters," "waters of the United States," and the like.

See also Flood water; High water line or mark; Implied reservation of water doctrine; Inland waters; Intermittent stream; Low water mark; Waste water.

Backwater. See that title.

Coast waters. See that title.

Developed water. Water which is brought to the surface and made available for use by the party claiming the water.

Flood waters. Waters which escape from a water course in great volume and flow over adjoining lands in no regular channel. The fact that such errant waters make for themselves a temporary channel or follow some natural channel, gully, or depression does not affect their character as "flood waters" or give to the course which they follow the character of a natural "water course." Mogle v. Moore, Cal.App., 96 P.2d 147, 150, 151; Everett v. Davis, Cal.App., 107 P.2d 650, 654, 655. See also **Flood.**

Foreign waters. Those belonging to another nation or country or subject to another jurisdiction, as distinguished from "domestic" waters.

Inland waters. See **Inland.**

Navigable waters. See **Navigable.**

Percolating waters. Those which pass through the ground beneath the surface of the earth without any definite channel, and do not form a part of the body or flow, surface or subterranean, of any water-course. They may be either rain waters which are slowly infiltrating through the soil or waters seeping through the banks or the bed of a stream, and which have so far left the bed and the other waters as to have lost their character as a part of the flow of that stream. Those which ooze, seep, or filter, through the soil beneath the surface without a defined channel, or in a course that is unknown and not discoverable from surface indications without excavation for that purpose. C & W Coal Corp. v. Salyer, 200 Va. 18, 104 S.E.2d 50, 53.

Private waters. Non-navigable streams, or bodies of water not open to the resort and use of the general public, but entirely owned and controlled by one or more individuals.

Public waters. Such as are adapted for the purposes of navigation, or those to which the general public have a right of access, as distinguished from artificial lakes, ponds, and other bodies of water privately owned, or similar natural bodies of water owned exclusively by one or more persons.

Subterranean waters. Waters which lie wholly beneath the surface of the ground, and which either ooze and seep through the subsurface strata without pursuing any defined course or channel (percolating waters), or flow in a permanent and regular but invisible course, or lie under the earth in a more or less immovable body, as a subterranean lake.

Surface waters. As distinguished from the waters of a natural stream, lake, or pond, surface waters are such as diffuse themselves over the surface of the ground, following no defined course or channel, and not gathering into or forming any more definite body of water than a mere bog or marsh. They generally originate in rains and melting snows, but the flood waters of a river may also be considered as surface waters if they become separated from the main current, or leave it never to return, and spread out over lower ground. Water derived from rains and melting snows that is diffused over surface of the ground, and it continues to be such and may be impounded by the owner of the land until it reaches some well-defined channel in which it is accustomed to, and does, flow with other waters, or until it reaches some permanent lake or pond, whereupon it ceases to be "surface water" and becomes a "water course" or a "lake" or "pond," as the case may be. State v. Hiber, 48 Wyo. 172, 44 P.2d 1005, 1008, 1011.

Surplus water. Water running off from ground which has been irrigated; water not consumed by the process of irrigation; water which the land irrigated will not take up.

Territorial waters. See that title.

Tide waters. See **Tide.**

Water-bayley. An officer mentioned in the colony laws of New Plymouth, (A.D. 1671,) whose duty was to collect dues to the colony for fish taken in their waters. Probably another form of *water-bailiff.*

Water course. See that title, *infra.*

Water front. Land or land with buildings fronting on a body of water.

Water-gage. A sea-wall or bank to restrain the current and overflowing of the water; also an instrument to measure water.

Water-gang. A Saxon word for a trench or course to carry a stream of water, such as are commonly made to drain water out of marshes.

Water-gavel. In old records, a gavel or rent paid for fishing in or other benefit received from some river or water.

Water-logged. A vessel is "water-logged" when she becomes heavy and unmanageable on account of the leakage of water into the hold.

Water-mark. See that title, *infra.*

Water power. The water power to which a riparian owner is entitled consists of the fall in the stream when in its natural state, as it passes through his land, or along the boundary of it; or, in other words, it consists of the difference of level between the surface where the stream first touches his land, and the surface where it leaves it. The use of water for power according to common understanding means its application to a water wheel to the end that its energy under the specified head and fall may be utilized and converted into available force. Holyoke Water Power Co. v. American Writing Paper Co., D.C.Mass., 17 F.Supp. 895, 898.

Water rights. A legal right, in the nature of a corporeal hereditament, to use the water of a natural stream or water furnished through a ditch or canal, for general or specific purposes, such as irrigation, mining, power, or domestic use, either to its full capacity or to a measured extent or during a defined portion of the time. City of Los Angeles v. City of Glendale, Cal.App., 132 P.2d 574, 584. A usufruct in a stream consisting in the right to have the water flow so that some portion of it may be reduced to possession and be made private property of individual, and it is therefore the right to divert water from natural stream by artificial means and apply the same to beneficial use. Ronzio v. Denver & R. G. W. R. Co., C.C.A.Utah, 116 F.2d 604, 605. It includes right to change the place of diversion, storage, or use of water if rights of other water users will not be injured. Lindsey v. McClure, C.C.A.N.M., 136 F.2d 65, 70. It was also said to be real property which may be sold and transferred separately from land on which it has been used. Federal Land Bank of Spokane v. Union Cent. Life Ins. Co., 54 Idaho 161, 29 P.2d 1009, 1011. See also Artificially developed water; Common enemy doctrine; Drainage rights; Excess or surplus water; Implied reservation of water doctrine; Littoral rights; Mill privilege; Overlying right; Reasonable use theory; Riparian rights.

Waterscape. An aqueduct or passage for water.

Waters of the United States. All waters within the United States which are navigable for the purposes of commerce, or whose navigation successfully aids commerce, are included in this term. See also **Territorial waters.**

Water course. A running stream of water; a natural stream fed from permanent or natural sources, including rivers, creeks, runs, and rivulets. There must be a stream, usually flowing in a particular direction, though it need not flow continuously. It may sometimes be dry. It must flow in a definite channel, having a bed or banks, and usually discharges itself into some other stream or body of water. It must be something more than a mere surface drainage over the entire face of the tract of land, occasioned by unusual freshets or other extraordinary causes. Leader v. Matthews, 192 Ark. 1049, 95 S.W.2d 1138, 1139; Turner v. Big Lake Oil Co., Tex.Civ.App., 62 S.W.2d 491, 493.

A water course, in the legal meaning of the word, does not consist merely of the stream as it flows within the banks which form its channel in ordinary stages of water, but the stream still retains its character as a water course when, in times of ordinary high water, the stream extending beyond its own banks, is accustomed to flow down over the adjacent lowlands in a broader but still definable stream. Atchison, T. & S. F. Ry. Co. v. Hadley, 168 Okl. 588, 35 P.2d 463, 466.

Water flowing underground in a known and well defined channel is not "percolating water", but constitutes a "water course", and is governed by law applicable to "surface streams", rather than by law applicable to percolating waters. Bull v. Siegrist, 169 Or. 180, 126 P.2d 832, 834.

See also **Ancient water course.**

Natural water course. A natural stream flowing in a defined bed or channel; one formed by the natural flow of the water, as determined by the general superficies or conformation of the surrounding country, as distinguished from an "artificial" water course, formed by the work of man, such as a ditch or canal.

Water district. Official geographical areas which are supplied water under regulation of a body of commissioners or other officials.

Watered stock. Stock which is issued by a corporation as fully paid-up stock, when in fact the whole amount of the par value thereof has not been paid in. Stock issued as bonus or otherwise without consideration or issued for a sum of money less than par value, or issued for labor, services, or property which at a fair valuation is less than the par value.

Water-mark. A mark indicating the highest point to which water rises, or the lowest point to which it sinks.

Transparent design or symbol which can be seen when paper is held up to the light and is used to identify the manufacturer of the paper or the genuineness of the document such as a check or stamp.

High-water mark. This term is properly applicable to tidal waters, and designates the line on the shore reached by the water at the high or flood tide. With reference to the waters of artificial ponds or lakes, created by dams in unnavigable streams, it denotes the highest point on the shores to which the dams can raise the water in ordinary circumstances. The high-water mark of a river, not subject to tide, is the line which the river impresses on the soil by covering it for sufficient periods to deprive it of vegetation, and to destroy its value for agriculture.

Low-water mark. That line on the shore of the sea which marks the edge of the waters at the lowest point of the ordinary ebb tide. The "low-water mark," of a river is the point to which the water recedes at its lowest stage.

Water ordeal. See **Ordeal.**

Waterway. See **Water course.**

Waveson /wéyvsən/. In old records, such goods as, after a wreck, swim or float on the waves. See **Flotsam.**

Wax scot. A duty anciently paid twice a year towards the charge of wax candles in churches.

Way. A passage, path, road, or street. In a technical sense, a *right* of passage over land. See also **Easement.**

Private way. A right which a person has of passing over the land of another. In another sense (chiefly in New England) a private way is one laid out by the local public authorities for the accommodation of individuals and wholly or chiefly at their expense, but not restricted to their exclusive use, being subject, like highways, to the public easement of passage.

Right of way. See that title.

Way of necessity. Exists where land granted is completely environed by land of the grantor, or partially by his land and the land of strangers. The law implies from these facts that a private right of way over the grantor's land was granted to the grantee as appurtenant to the estate. It is not merely one of convenience, and never exists where person may reach highway over his own land. And it cannot legally exist where neither the party claiming the way nor owner of land over which it is claimed, nor anyone under whom either of them claim, was ever seized of both tracts of land at same time. It is not based on continuous adverse user, but arises by implication of law from necessities of case, and ceases when necessity therefor ceases. The extent of a "way of necessity" is a way such as is required for complete and beneficial use of land to which the way is impliedly attached. New York Cent. R. Co. v. Yarian, 219 Ind. 477, 39 N.E.2d 604, 606.

Way-bill. Written document made out by carrier listing point of origin and destination, consignor and consignee, and describing goods included in shipment by railroad or motor carrier. Such constitutes the written description of the shipment in the event of any claim. See also **Bill of lading.**

Way-going crop. A crop of grain sown by a tenant for a term certain, during his tenancy, but which will not ripen until after the expiration of his lease. In the absence of an express agreement to the contrary tenant is entitled thereto.

Wayleave. A right of way over or through land for the carriage of minerals from a mine or quarry. It is an easement, being a species of the class called "rights of way," and is generally created by express grant or reservation.

Waynagium /weynéyj(iy)əm/. Implements of husbandry.

Ways and means. In a legislative body, the "committee on ways and means" is a committee appointed to inquire into and consider the methods and sources for raising revenue, and to propose means for providing the funds needed by the government. Standing committee of House of Representatives responsible for supervising legislation dealing with financial matters.

W.D. An abbreviation for "Western District;" *e.g.* U.S. District Court for Western District of Kentucky.

Weald /wíyld/. Sax. A wood; the woody part of a country.

Wealreaf /wíylrìyf/. In old English law, the robbing of a dead man in his grave.

Wealth. Large quantity of possessions, assets, securities, and the like. State of having abundant financial resources and properties. All material objects, capable of satisfying human wants, desires, or tastes, having a value in exchange, and upon which human labor has been expended; *i.e.,* which have, by such labor, been either reclaimed from nature, extracted or gathered from the earth or sea, manufactured from raw materials, improved, adopted, or cultivated. The aggregate of all the things, whether material or immaterial, which contribute to comfort and enjoyment, which cannot be obtained without more or less labor, and which are objects of frequent sale.

Weapon. An instrument of offensive or defensive combat, or anything used, or designed to be used, in destroying, defeating or injuring a person. The term is chiefly used, in law, in the statutes prohibiting the carrying of "concealed" or "deadly" weapons. See also **Dangerous weapon; Deadly weapon; Offensive weapon.**

Wear, or **weir** /wér/wír/. A great dam or fence made across a river, or against water, formed of stakes interlaced by twigs of osier, and accommodated for the taking of fish, or to convey a stream to a mill.

Wear and tear. "Natural wear and tear" means deterioration or depreciation in value by ordinary and reasonable use of the subject-matter.

Wearing apparel. As generally used in statutes, refers not merely to a person's outer clothing, but covers all articles usually worn, and includes underclothing. Arnold v. U. S., 147 U.S. 494, 13 S.Ct. 406, 37 L.Ed. 253. All articles of dress generally worn by persons in the calling and condition of life and in the locality of the person in question. In re Steimes' Estate, 150 Misc. 279, 270 N.Y.S. 339.

Webb-Pomerene Act. Federal Act (1918) which provides a qualified exemption for an export association from the prohibitions of the antitrust laws. The Act is administered by the Federal Trade Commission.

Wed. Sax. A covenant or agreement. A pledge.

Wedbedrip. Sax. In old English law, a customary service which tenants paid to their lords, in cutting down their corn, or doing other harvest duties; as if a *covenant* to *reap* for the lord at the time of his *bidding* or commanding.

Wedlock. State of marriage. As used in the phrase "born out of wedlock" in Uniform Illegitimacy Act, means the ceremony or state of marriage or status of husband and wife and is equivalent to matrimony but does not include status of wife and her paramour. State v. Coliton, N.D., 73 N.D. 582, 17 N.W.2d 546, 549.

Week. A period of seven consecutive days of time; and, in some uses, the period beginning with Sunday and ending with Saturday. See Leach v. Burr, 188 U.S. 510, 23 S.Ct. 393, 47 L.Ed. 567; Progressive Building and Loan Ass'n v. McIntyre, 169 Tenn. 491, 89 S.W.2d 336, 337. Words "two weeks" mean fourteen days. Fisher v. Booher, 269 Ky. 501, 107 S.W.2d 307, 309.

Week-work. In early English times, the obligation of a tenant to work two or three days in every week for his lord, during the greater part of the year, and four or five during the summer months.

Wehading. In old European law, the judicial combat, or duel; the trial by battel.

Weighage /wéyəj/. In English law, a duty or toll paid for weighing merchandise. It is called *"tronage"* for weighing wool at the king's beam, or *"pesage"* for weighing other avoirdupois goods.

Weight. A measure of heaviness or ponderosity; and in a metaphorical sense influence, effectiveness, or power to influence judgment or conduct. The quantity of heaviness, the quality of being heavy, the **degree** or extent of downward pressure under the influence of gravity, or the quantity of matter as estimated by the balance or scale.

Gross weight. Of packaged goods, the total weight, including contents and packaging.

Net weight. Of packaged goods, includes only weight of contained goods. See also **Net weight.**

Weight of evidence. The balance or preponderance of evidence; the inclination of the greater amount of credible evidence, offered in a trial, to support one side of the issue rather than the other. It indicates clearly to the jury that the party having the burden of proof will be entitled to their verdict, if, on weighing the evidence in their minds, they shall find the greater amount of credible evidence sustains the issue which is to be established before them. Weight is not a question of mathematics, but depends on its effect in inducing belief. See also **Preponderance of evidence.**

Welfare. Well-doing or well-being in any respect; the enjoyment of health and common blessings of life; exemption from any evil or calamity; prosperity; happiness. See also **General welfare; Public welfare.**

Welfare clause. Constitutional provision (Art. I, § 8) permitting the federal government to enact laws for the overall general welfare of the people. It is the basis for the exercise of implied powers necessary to carry out the express provisions of the Constitution.

Well, *adj.* In marine insurance, a term used as descriptive of the safety and soundness of a vessel, in a warranty of her condition at a particular time and place; as, "warranted *well* at _____ on _____."

In old reports, good, sufficient, unobjectionable in law; the opposite of "ill."

Well, *n.* A hole or shaft sunk into the earth in order to obtain a fluid, such as water, oil, brine, or natural gas, from a subterranean supply. Loosely, any shaft or pit dug or bored in earth, or any space so constructed as to suggest or be likened to, a well for water; a pit or hole in the ground or a hollow cylinder built in such hole; or a shaft or excavation in mining. Seismograph Service Corporation v. Mason, 193 Okl. 623, 145 P.2d 967, 970.

Well-born men. A tribunal in New Amsterdam (New York).

Well knowing. A phrase used in pleading as the technical expression in laying a *scienter (q.v.).*

Welshing /wélshiŋ/. Receiving a sum of money or valuable thing, undertaking to return the same or the value thereof together with other money, if an event (for example, the result of a horse-race) shall be determined in a certain manner, and at the time of receiving the deposit intending to cheat and defraud the depositor. The crime is larceny at common law.

Welsh mortgage. See **Mortgage.**

Wend. In old records, a large extent of ground, comprising several *juga;* a perambulation; a circuit.

Weotuma. The purchase price of a wife among the heathen Germans.

Wera, or were /wír(ə)/. The estimation or price of a man, especially of one slain. In the criminal law of the Anglo-Saxons, every man's life had its value, called a "were," or *"capitis æstimatio."*

Weregelt thef /wírgelt-θìyf/. Sax. In old English law, a robber who might be ransomed.

Weregild, or **wergild** /wírgìld/wárgild/. This was the price of homicide, or other atrocious personal offense, paid partly to the king for the loss of a subject, partly to the lord for the loss of a vassal, and partly to the next of kin of the injured person. In the Anglo-Saxon laws, the amount of compensation varied with the degree or rank of the party slain. See **Angild; Angylde.**

Werelada. A purging from a crime by the oaths of several persons, according to the degree and quality of the accused.

Werp-geld. Belg. In European law, contribution for jettison; average.

Westminster. A city immediately adjoining London, and forming a part of the metropolis; formerly the seat of the superior courts of the kingdom.

Westminster Confession. A document containing a statement of religious doctrine, concocted at a conference of British and continental Protestant divines at Westminster, in the year 1643, which subsequently became the basis of the Scotch Presbyterian Church.

Westminster the First, Statute of. The statute 3 Edw. I, A.D. 1275. This statute, which deserves the name of a code rather than an act, is divided into fifty-one chapters. Without extending the exemption of churchmen from civil jurisdiction, it protects the property of the church from the violence and spoliation of the king and the nobles, provides for freedom of popular elections, because sheriffs, coroners, and conservators of the peace were still chosen by the freeholders in the county court, and attempts had been made to influence the election of knights of the shire, from the time when they were instituted. It contains a declaration to enforce the enactment of *Magna Charta* against excessive fines, which might operate as perpetual imprisonment; enumerates and corrects the abuses of tenures, particularly as to marriage of wards; regulates the levying of tolls, which were imposed arbitrarily by the barons and by cities and boroughs; corrects and restrains the powers of the king's escheator and other officers; amends the criminal law, putting the crime of rape on the footing to which it has been lately restored, as a most grievous, but not capital, offense; and embraces the subject of procedure in civil and criminal matters, introducing many regulations to render it cheap, simple, and expeditious. Certain parts of this act are repealed by St. 26 & 27 Vict., c. 125.

West Saxon Lage. The laws of the West Saxons, which obtained in the counties to the south and west of England, from Kent to Devonshire. Blackstone supposes these to have been much the same with the laws of Alfred, being the municipal law of the far most considerable part of his dominions, and particularly including Berkshire, the seat of his peculiar residence. 1 Bl.Comm. 65. See **Mercen-lage.**

Whack. To divide into shares, apportion, parcel out, make a division settlement, square accounts, or to pay.

Whale. A royal fish, the head being the king's property, and the tail the queen's.

Wharf. A structure on the margin or shore of navigable waters, alongside of which vessels can be brought for the sake of being conveniently loaded or unloaded, or a space of ground, artificially prepared, for the reception of merchandise from a ship or vessel, so as to promote the discharge of such vessel.

Private wharf. One whose owner or lessee has the exclusive enjoyment or use thereof. The M. L. C. No. 10, C.C.A.N.Y., 10 F.2d 699, 702.

Public wharf. One to which vessels and the public can resort, either at will or on assignment of a berth by a harbor authority. Kafline v. Brooklyn Eastern Dist. Terminal Co., 180 App.Div. 858, 168 N.Y.S. 120, 121.

Wharfage /(h)wórfəj/. The money paid for landing goods upon, or loading them from, a wharf. Manhattan Lighterage Corporation v. Moore McCormack Line, D.C.N.Y., 45 F.Supp. 271, 273. Charge for use of wharf by way of rent or compensation. Marine Lighterage Corporation v. Luckenbach S. S. Co., 139 Misc. 612, 248 N.Y.S. 71, 72.

Wharfinger /(h)wórfənjər/. The owner or occupier of a wharf; one who for hire receives merchandise on his wharf, either for the purpose of forwarding or for delivery to the consignee on such wharf.

Wharfing out, right of. A right to the exclusive use of submerged lands as by the affixing thereto or the establishment thereon of a permanent structure to some point within the navigable body of water, deep and wide enough to dock ocean-going vessels, and it presupposes exclusive use and to that extent may interfere with fishing or navigation. City of Oakland v. Hogan, 41 Cal.App.2d 333, 106 P.2d 987, 994.

Wharton Rule. In criminal law of conspiracy, the rule that an agreement by two persons to commit a particular crime cannot be prosecuted as a conspiracy when the crime is of such a nature as to require necessarily the participation of the two persons, *e.g.* adultery. It is named after the criminal law author, Francis Wharton. Iannelli v. U. S., 420 U.S. 770, 95 S.Ct. 1284, 1288, 43 L.Ed.2d 616.

Wheel. An engine of torture used in medieval Europe, on which a criminal was bound while his limbs or bones were broken one by one till he died.

Wheelage. Duty or toll paid for vehicles passing over certain ground.

Whelps /(h)wélps/. The young of certain animals of a base nature or *feræ naturæ.*

When. At what time; at the time that; at which time; at that time. Gehrung v. Collister, 52 Ohio App. 314, 3 N.E.2d 700, 701, 5 O.O. 195. At, during, or after the time that; at or just after the moment that. In re Morrow's Will, 41 N.M. 723, 73 P.2d 1360, 1364. In the event that, on condition that, in virtue of the circumstances that. Frequently employed as equivalent to the word "if" in legislative enactments and in common speech.

When and where. Technical words in pleading, formerly necessary in making *full defense* to certain actions.

Whenever. At whatever time; at what time soever. In any or every instance in which.

When issued. Abbreviated term in securities law for "when, as and if issued" in connection with a stock not yet authorized for issuance. The term refers to a conditional transaction in which one indicates a desire to buy when the security is available for sale after its authorization.

Where. At or in what place; from what place or source. As used in the statutory language, "where the prosecution is held," the word does not refer to the geographical location of the place of hearing, but rather to the tribunal or official before whom the case is tried. If; in the case of; in the event that.

Whereas. When in fact. A "whereas" clause of a contract is but an introductory or prefatory statement meaning "considering that" or "that being the case", and is not an essential part of the operating portions of the contract. Jones v. City of Paducah, 283 Ky. 628, 142 S.W.2d 365, 367.

Whereby. By or through which; by the help of which; in accordance with which.

Whereupon. Upon which; after which.

While. Pending or during the time that. Often used adversatively and to imply contrast, and in some constructions introduces a parenthetical clause. Jackson v. Texas Co., C.C.A.Okl., 75 F.2d 549, 553. "While," within provision of accidental death life policy excluding coverage for a loss as result of injury sustained by insured while committing or attempting to commit assault or felony, is word of time and not of causation. Romero v. Volunteer State Life Ins., 10 C.A.3d 571, 88 Cal.Rptr. 820, 824.

Whim. Passing fancy; an impulse or caprice. Used in jury instruction in cautioning the jurors to avoid returning a verdict based on anything but the evidence and its strength, not on the personal whim or caprice of the jurors.

Whiplash injury. A snapping of the neck when a person gets his head thrown forward or back or from side to side. Breitenberg v. Parker, 237 Ark. 261, 372 S.W.2d 828, 832. It is caused by a sudden and unexpected forced movement of the neck of an individual while he is in a relaxed position and against which he cannot protect himself. Hanover Fire Ins. Co. v. Sides, C.A.La., 320 F.2d 437, 441. It may result in several types of pathological findings, such as sprain, fracture, dislocation and so forth. Self v. Johnson, La.App., 124 So.2d 324, 325; Luquette v. Bouillion, La.App., 184 So.2d 766, 768.

Whipping. A mode of punishment, by the infliction of stripes, formerly used occasionally in England and in a few of the American states. See Act of February 28, 1839, § 5 (18 U.S.C.A. § 3564).

Whipping-post. A post or stake to which a criminal is tied to undergo the punishment of whipping.

White acre. A fictitious name given to a piece of land for purposes of illustrating real property transactions.

Whitecaps. The name of an unlawful organization against which Tennessee in 1897 enacted a statute (Acts 1897, c. 52) entitled, "An act to prevent and punish the formation or continuance of conspiracies and combinations for certain unlawful purposes," etc., commonly known as the "Law against Whitecaps." Persons guilty of any offense under the act were rendered incompetent for jury service.

White-collar crimes. Term usually signifies law violations by corporations or individuals including theft or fraud and other violations of trust committed in the course of the offender's occupation (*e.g.*, embezzlement, price fixing, antitrust violations, and the like). Non-violent crimes.

White mule. Corn whisky; contraband whisky.

White persons. As used in Rev.St.U.S. § 2169 (Naturalization Act March 26, 1790, c. 3, 1 Stat. 103, as amended by Act Feb. 18, 1875, c. 80, § 1, 18 Stat. 318 [8 U.S.C.A. § 703]), members of the white or Caucasian race, as distinct from the black, red, yellow, and brown races. Takao Ozawa v. U. S., 260 U.S. 178, 43 S.Ct. 65, 68, 67 L.Ed. 199.

In the legislation of the slave period, persons without admixture of colored blood, whatever the actual complexion might be.

White rents. In old English law, rents paid in silver, and called "white rents," or *"redditus albi,"* to distinguish them from rents payable in corn, labor, provisions, etc., called "black-rent" or "black-mail." See **Alba firma.**

White slave. A term used in the United States statutes and in common talk (though not very appropriately) to indicate a female with reference to whom an offense is committed under the so-called Mann White Slave Traffic Act of June 25, 1910 (18 U.S.C.A. §§ 2421–2424), prohibiting the transportation in interstate and foreign commerce for immoral purposes of women and girls. See **Mann Act.**

White spurs. A kind of esquires.

Whitsun farthings /(h)wítsən fárðiŋz/. Pentecostals (*q.v.*).

Whittanwarii /(h)witənwériyay/. In old English law, a class of offenders who whitened stolen ox-hides and horse-hides so that they could not be known and identified.

Whole. Hale, hearty, strong, sound; also, entire, complete.

Whole blood. See **Blood relations.**

Whole chest. In the tea trade, a chest containing 100 to 140 pounds or more.

Whole life insurance. See **Insurance** (*Life insurance*).

Wholesale. Selling to retailers or jobbers rather than to consumers. Stolze Lumber Co. v. Stratton, 386 Ill. 334, 54 N.E.2d 554, 558. A sale in large quantity to one who intends to resell.

Wholesale dealer. One whose business is the selling of goods in gross to retail dealers, and not by the small quantity or parcel to consumers thereof. Veazey Drug Co. v. Bruza, 169 Okl. 418, 37 P.2d 294.

Wholesale price. That which retailer pays in expectation of obtaining higher price by way of profit from resale to ultimate consumer. Guess v. Montague, D.C.S.C., 51 F.Supp. 61, 65.

Wholesaler. One who buys in comparatively large quantities, and then resells, usually in smaller quantities, but never to the ultimate consumer. He sells either to a "jobber," a sort of middleman, or to a "retailer," who in turn sells to the consumer. Fisch-

bach Brewing Co. v. City of St. Louis, 231 Mo.App. 793, 95 S.W.2d 335, 340. See also **Jobber.**

Wholesome. Sound, tending to promote health. Leonardi v. A. Habermann Provision Co., 143 Ohio St. 623, 56 N.E.2d 232, 237, 28 O.O. 511.

Wholly. Not partially. In a whole or complete manner; entirely; completely; perfectly. Exclusively; to the exclusion of other things. Equally. Totally; fully. Chicago & Calumet Dist. Transit Co. v. Mueller, 213 Ind. 530, 12 N.E.2d 247, 249.

Wholly and permanently disabled. Term within disability clause of life policy does not mean "partial" or "temporary," and is not to be construed literally so as to require condition of complete helplessness or utter hopelessness to be entitled to benefits. See also **Disability; Total disability; Wholly disabled.**

Wholly dependent. A person is to be regarded as "wholly dependent" upon a workman, within meaning of compensation acts, when his support is derived wholly from the workman's wages. Baker v. Western Power & Light Co., 147 Kan. 571, 78 P.2d 36, 40; Central Surety and Insurance Corporation v. Industrial Commission, 94 Colo. 341, 30 P.2d 253, 255. Person may be "wholly dependent" on workman though he may have some slight savings of his own, or some other slight property, or be able to make something by his own service. United States Coal & Coke Co. v. Sutton, 268 Ky. 405, 105 S.W.2d 173, 177.

Wholly destroyed. A building is "wholly destroyed" within the meaning of statutes permitting recovery of the full amount of a fire insurance policy, when, although some part remains standing, it can no longer be designated as a building. The words mean totally destroyed as a building, although there is not an absolute extinction of all its parts.

Wholly disabled. These words within accident policy do not mean a state of complete physical and mental incapacity or utter helplessness but mean rather inability to do all the substantial and material acts necessary to carry on a certain business or occupation or any business or occupation in a customary and usual manner and which acts the insured would be able to perform in such manner but for the disability. Total disability. See also **Disability; Total disability.**

Whore. A woman who practices illicit sexual intercourse, either for hire or to gratify a depraved passion. A woman given to promiscuous intercourse. A woman who practices unlawful commerce with men, particularly one who does so for hire; a harlot; a concubine; a prostitute.

Whoremaster. Ordinarily, one who practices lewdness; also, one who keeps or procures whores for others; a pimp; a procurer.

Wic. A place on the sea-shore or the bank of a river.

Wica. A country house or farm.

Wick. Sax. A village, town, or district. Hence, in composition, the territory over which a given jurisdiction extends. Thus, "bailiwick" is the territorial jurisdiction of a bailiff or sheriff or constable. "Sheriffwick" was also used in the old books.

Widen. To increase in width; to extend.

Widow. A woman whose husband is dead, and who has not remarried.

Widower. A man who has lost his wife by death and has not married again.

Widowhood. The state or condition of being a widow, or, sometimes, a widower. An estate is sometimes settled upon a woman "during widowhood," which is expressed in Latin, *"durante viduitate."*

Widow's allowance. The amount of money or property which a widow may claim from her husband's estate, free of all claims. State statutes govern the amount and conditions of the allowance. It is for her support and maintenance.

Widow's election. In most states, a widow may either take her share under her husband's will or waive his will and claim her statutory share which commonly is an amount equal to what she would receive if he had died intestate.

Wifa /wáyfə/. L. Lat. In old English law, a mark or sign; a mark set up on land, to denote an exclusive occupation, or to prohibit entry.

Wife. A woman united to a man by marriage; a woman who has a husband living and undivorced. The correlative term is "husband." See also **Common law wife.**

Wife's part. See **Legitime.**

Wigreve /wígrìyv/. In old English law, the overseer of a wood.

Wild animals (or animals *feræ naturæ*). Animals of an untamable disposition; animals in a state of nature.

Wildcat strike. A strike called without authorization from the union or in violation of a no-strike clause in the collective bargaining agreement.

Wild land. Land in a state of nature, as distinguished from improved or cultivated land.

Wild's case, rule in. A devise to B. and his children or issue, B. having no issue at the time of the devise, gives him an estate tail; but, if he have issue at the time, B. and his children take joint estates for life.

Will, *v.* An auxiliary verb commonly having the mandatory sense of "shall" or "must." It is a word of certainty, while the word "may" is one of speculation and uncertainty.

Will, *n.* Wish; desire; pleasure; inclination; choice; the faculty of conscious, and especially of deliberate, action. When a person expresses his "will" that a particular disposition be made of his property, his words are words of command, and the word "will" as so used is mandatory, comprehensive, and dispositive in nature.

A "will" is generally defined as an instrument by which a person makes a disposition of his property, to take effect after his death, and which by its own nature is ambulatory and revocable during his lifetime. In re Brown's Estate, Tex.Civ.App., 507 S.W.2d 801, 803. The legal declaration of a man's intentions which he wills to be performed after his death. In re Cohen's Estate, 445 Pa. 549, 284 A.2d 754, 756.

The legal expression or declaration of a person's mind or wishes as to the disposition of his property, to be performed or take effect after his death. A revocable instrument by which a person makes disposition of his property to take effect after his death. Howard's Ex'r v. Dempster, 246 Ky. 153, 54 S.W.2d 660, 661. A written instrument executed with the formalities required by statutes, whereby a person makes a disposition of his property to take effect after his death.

For competency to make will, see **Competent.**

See also Codicil; Conditional will; Duplicate will; Last will; Lost will; Mariner's will; Mutual will; No contest clause; Nuncupative will; Publication; Reciprocal will; Revocation of will; Sailor's will; Simultaneous death clause; Witness (*Witness to will*).

Ambulatory will. A changeable will (*ambulatoria voluntas*), the phrase merely denoting the power which a testator possesses of altering his will during his life-time.

Antenuptial will. See that title.

Conditional will. A conditional disposition is one which depends upon the occurrence of some uncertain event, by which it is either to take effect or to be defeated. If the happening of an event named in a will is the reason for making the will, it is "unconditional"; but, if the testator intends to dispose of his property in case the event happens, the will is "conditional."

Conjoint will. See *Joint will, infra.*

Counter wills. Another name for "double," "mutual," or "reciprocal" wills.

Double will. Called also a "counter," "mutual," or "reciprocal" will. See **Double.**

Estate at will. This estate entitles the grantee or lessee to the possession of land during the pleasure of both the grantor and himself, yet it creates no sure or durable right, and is bounded by no definite limits as to duration. It must be at the reciprocal will of both parties (for, if it be at the will of the lessor only, it is a lease for life), and the dissent of either determines it.

Holographic will. One that is entirely written, dated, and signed by the hand of the testator himself. Sometimes spelled "olographic." See **Holograph.**

Joint and mutual will. One executed jointly by two persons with reciprocal provisions, which shows on its face that the devises are made one in consideration of the other. Joint will is one in which the same paper is executed by two persons as their respective wills; mutual wills are the separate wills of two persons, more or less reciprocal in their provisions. See also *Mutual will,* below.

Joint will. One where the same instrument is made the will of two or more persons and is jointly signed by them. Such wills are usually executed to make testamentary disposition of joint property. A joint or conjoint will is a testamentary instrument executed by two or more persons, in pursuance of a common intention, for the purpose of disposing of their several interests in property owned by them in common, or of their separate property treated as a common fund, to a third person or persons.

Living will. A living will is a short document that basically states: "If the situation should arise in which there is not reasonable expectation of my recovery from physical or mental disability, I request that I be allowed to die and not be kept alive by artificial means or heroic measures." A living will is not considered a legal document in the majority of states.

Mutual and reciprocal will. See *Joint and mutual will, supra;* also *Mutual will, infra.*

Mutual will. One in which two or more persons make mutual or reciprocal provisions in favor of each other. "Mutual wills" are the separate wills of two persons which are reciprocal in their provisions, and such a will may be both joint and mutual. Sometimes called a "reciprocal," "double," or "counter" will. See also *Joint and mutual will,* above.

Mystic will. See **Testament.**

Non-intervention will. In some jurisdictions, one authorizing the executor to act without bond and to manage, control, and settle the estate without the intervention of any court whatsoever.

Nuncupative will. See that title.

Reciprocal will. One in which two or more persons make mutual or reciprocal provisions in favor of each other. Also known as a "mutual," "double," or "counter" will. See *Joint and mutual will; Mutual will, supra.*

Renunciation of will. See **Renunciation.**

Self-proved wills. A will which eliminates some of the formalities of proof by execution in compliance with statute. It is made self-proved by affidavit of attesting witnesses in the form prescribed by statute. Most statutes provide that, unless contested, such a will may be admitted to probate without testimony of subscribing witnesses. See *e.g.* Uniform Probate Code, § 2–504.

Statute of will. See **Wills Act,** *infra.*

Unofficious will. In the civil law, *testamentum inofficium.* One made in disregard of natural obligations as to inheritance. 2 Bl.Comm. 502. It has no place in the common law.

Criminal Law

The power of the mind which directs the action of a man. See **Intent; Motive; Willful and wanton act.**

Willa /wílə/. In Hindu law, the relation between a master or patron and his freedman, and the relation between two persons who had made a reciprocal testamentary contract.

Will contest. A proceeding sui generis, a suit in rem, having for its purpose determination of questions of construction of will or whether there is or is not a will. McCrary v. Michael, 233 Mo.App. 797, 109 S.W.2d 50, 51. Any kind of litigated controversy concerning the eligibility of an instrument to probate as distinguished from validity of the contents of the will. In re Hesse's Estate, 62 Ariz. 273, 157 P.2d 347, 349. Will contests are commonly governed by state statutes; *e.g.* Uniform Probate Code § 3–407, burden of proof.

Willful. Proceeding from a conscious motion of the will; voluntary. Intending the result which actually comes to pass; designed; intentional; not accidental or involuntary.

An act or omission is "willfully" done, if done voluntarily and intentionally and with the specific intent to do something the law forbids, or with the specific intent to fail to do something the law requires to be done; that is to say, with bad purpose either to disobey or to disregard the law.

Willful is a word of many meanings, its construction often influenced by its context. Screws v. United States, 325 U.S. 91, 101, 65 S.Ct. 1031, 1035, 89 L.Ed. 1495.

The word [willfully] often denotes an act which is intentional, or knowing, or voluntary, as distinguished from accidental. But when used in a criminal context it generally means an act done with a bad purpose; without justifiable excuse; stubbornly, obstinately, perversely. The word is also employed to characterize a thing done without ground for believing it is lawful or conduct marked by a careless disregard whether or not one has the right so to act. United States v. Murdock, 290 U.S. 389, 394, 395, 54 S.Ct. 223, 225, 78 L.Ed. 381.

Whatever the grade of the offense the presence of the word "willful" in the definition will carry with it the implication that for guilt the act must have been done willingly rather than under compulsion and, if something is required to be done by statute, the implication that a punishable omission must be by one having the ability and means to perform. In re Trombley, 31 Cal.2d 801, 807, 193 P.2d 734, 739.

A willful act may be described as one done intentionally, knowingly, and purposely, without justifiable excuse, as distinguished from an act done carelessly, thoughtlessly, heedlessly, or inadvertently. A willful act differs essentially from a negligent act. The one is positive and the other is negative.

Premeditated; malicious; done with evil intent, or with a bad motive or purpose, or with indifference to the natural consequences; unlawful; without legal justification.

Willful and malicious injury. For such to exist there must be an intent to commit a wrong either through actual malice or from which malice will be implied. Such an injury does not necessarily involve hatred or ill will, as a state of mind, but arises from intentional wrong committed without just cause or excuse. In re Wernecke, D.C.N.Y., 1 F.Supp. 127, 168. It may involve merely a willful disregard of what one knows to be his duty, an act which is against good morals and wrongful in and of itself, and which necessarily causes injury and is done intentionally.

Willful and wanton act. In order to constitute "willful and wanton" misconduct, act or omission must be not only negligent, but exhibit conscious disregard for safety of others. Turner v. Commonwealth Edison Co., 35 Ill.App.3d 331, 341 N.E.2d 488, 493.

Willful and wanton injury. To constitute such injury, act producing injury must have been knowingly and intentionally committed, or committed under circumstances evincing reckless disregard of safety of person injured.

Willful indifference to the safety of others. Imports an intentional lack of regard concerning the safety of others, or an intentional doing of something with knowledge that serious injury is a probable result. People v. Murray, 58 Cal.App.2d 239, 136 P.2d 389, 391.

Willfully and knowingly. An act is done willfully and knowingly when the actor intends to do it and knows the nature of the act. Deliberately. See **Willful.**

Willful misconduct of employee. Under Workers' Compensation Acts, precluding compensation, means more than mere negligence, and contemplates the intentional doing of something with knowledge that it is likely to result in serious injuries, or with reckless disregard of its probable consequences. "Wilful misconduct" disqualifying claimant for unemployment compensation involves: (1) wanton and wilful disregard of employer's interest, (2) deliberate violation of rules, (3) disregard of standards of behavior which an employer can rightfully expect from his employee, or (4) negligence which manifests culpability, wrongful intent, evil design, or intentional and substantial disregard for employer's interests or the employee's duties and obligations. Wilson v. Com. Unemployment Compensation Bd. of Review, 15 Pa.Cmwlth. 314, 325 A.2d 500, 501.

Willful murder. The unlawful and intentional killing of another without excuse or mitigating circumstances. See also **Murder; Premeditation.**

Willful neglect. The intentional disregard of a plain or manifest duty, in the performance of which the public or the person injured has an interest.

Willful neglect suggests intentional, conscious, or known negligence—a knowing or intentional mistake. Puget Sound Painters v. State, 45 Wash.2d 819, 278 P.2d 302, 303. Within adoption statutes, is neglect that is intentional, deliberate, and without just cause or excuse. In re Adoption of P. J. K., Mo.App., 359 S.W.2d 360, 363.

Willful negligence. See Negligence.

Willfulness. See Willful.

Willful or wanton misconduct. Failure to exercise ordinary care to prevent injury to a person who is actually known to be or reasonably expected to be within the range of a dangerous act being done. Georgia Power Co. v. Deese, 78 Ga.App. 704, 51 S.E.2d 724, 728. Conduct which is either intentional or committed under circumstances exhibiting a reckless disregard for the safety of others, such as a failure, after knowledge of an impending danger, to exercise ordinary care to prevent it or a failure to discover the dangers through recklessness or carelessness when it could have been discovered by the exercise of ordinary care. Lewandowski v. Bakey, 32 Ill.App.3d 26, 335 N.E.2d 572, 574. An aggravated form of negligence, differing in quality rather than degree from ordinary lack of care. Morgan v. Southern Pac.

Transp. Co., 37 Cal.App.3d 1006, 112 Cal.Rptr. 695, 698.

Willful or wanton negligence. Failure to exercise ordinary care to prevent injury to a person who is actually known to be, or reasonably is expected to be, within range of a known danger. Barall Food Stores v. Bennett, 194 Okl. 508, 153 P.2d 106, 109, 110. See also **Negligence.**

Willful tort. Term implies intent or purpose to injure. It involves elements of intent or purpose and malice or ill will, but malice or ill will may be shown by indifference to safety of others, with knowledge of their danger, or failure to use ordinary care to avoid injury after acquiring such knowledge. Hillard v. Western & Southern Life Ins. Co., 68 Ohio App. 426, 34 N.E.2d 75, 77, 23 O.O. 133.

Williams Act. See **Tender offer.**

Willingly. Voluntarily; unreluctantly; without reluctance, and of one's own free choice. See **Willful.**

As used in an instruction that one cannot invoke the doctrine of self-defense if he enters a fight willingly, it means voluntarily, aggressively, and without legal excuse.

Wills Act. In England, the statute 32 Hen. VIII, c. 1, passed in 1540, by which persons seized in fee-simple of lands holden in socage tenure were enabled to devise the same at their will and pleasure, except to bodies corporate; and those who held estates by the tenure of chivalry were enabled to devise two-third parts thereof.

Also, the statute 7 Wm. IV & 1 Vict., c. 26, passed in 1837, and also called "Lord Langdale's Act." This act permits of the disposition by will of every kind of interest in real and personal estate, and provides that all wills, whether of real or of personal estate, shall be attested by two witnesses, and that such attestation shall be sufficient. Other important alterations are effected by this statute in the law of wills.

Will substitutes. Documents which purportedly accomplish what a will is designed to accomplish, e.g. trusts, life insurance, joint ownership of property.

Winchester measure. The standard measure of England, originally kept at Winchester. 1 Bl.Comm. 274.

Winchester, Statute of. A statute passed in the thirteenth year of the reign of Edward I, by which the old Saxon law of police was enforced, with many additional provisions. It required every man to provide himself with armor to aid in keeping the peace; and if it did not create the offices of high and petty constables, it recognized and regulated them, and charged them with duties answering somewhat to those of our militia officers. The statute took its name from the ancient capital of the kingdom. It was repealed by the Statute of 7 & 8 Geo. IV, c. 27.

Winding-up acts. In English law, general acts of parliament, regulating settlement of corporate affairs on dissolution.

Window. An opening made in the wall of a building to admit light and air, and to furnish a view or prospect. The use of this word in law is chiefly in connection with the doctrine of ancient lights and other rights of adjacent owners.

Window tax. In England, a tax on windows, formerly levied on houses which contained more than six windows, and were worth more than £ 5 per annum; established by St. 7 Wm. III, c. 18. St. 14 & 15 Vict., c. 36, substituted for this tax a tax on inhabited houses.

Wind up. To settle the accounts and liquidate the assets of a partnership or corporation, for the purpose of making distribution and dissolving the concern. See **Liquidation.**

Wiretapping. A form of electronic eavesdropping where, upon court order, enforcement officials surreptitiously listen to phone calls. Federal (Crime Control and Safe Streets Act, 18 U.S.C.A. § 2510 et seq.) and state statutes govern the circumstances and procedures under which wiretaps will be permitted. See also **Eavesdropping.**

Wish. Eager desire; longing; expression of desire; a thing desired; an object of desire. As used in wills, it is sometimes merely directory or precatory; and sometimes mandatory; being equivalent to "will," to "give" or "devise."

Wista. In Saxon law, half a hide of land, or sixty acres.

Wit. To know; to learn; to be informed. Used only in the infinitive, *to wit,* which term is equivalent to "that is to say," "namely," or *"videlicet."*

Witam /wídəm/. The purgation from an offense by the oath of the requisite number of witnesses.

Witan /wídən/. In Saxon law, wise men; persons of information, especially in the laws; the king's advisers; members of the king's council; the optimates, or principal men of the kingdom.

Witchcraft. Under English Sts. 33 Hen. VIII, c. 8, and 1 Jac. I, c. 12, the offense of witchcraft, or supposed intercourse with evil spirits, was punishable with death. These acts were not repealed until 1736. 4 Bl.Comm. 60, 61. In Salem, Massachusetts in 1692, 20 persons were put to death by hanging for such offense. The last victims in England were executed in 1716, and the last in Scotland in 1722.

Wite /wáyt/. Sax. A punishment, pain, penalty, mulct, or criminal fine.

An atonement among the early Germans by a wrong-doer to the king or the community. It is said to be the germ of the idea that wrong is not simply the affair of the injured individual, and is therefore a condition precedent to the growth of a criminal law.

Witekden. A taxation of the West Saxons, imposed by the public council of the kingdom.

Witena dom /wídənə dówm/. In Saxon law, the judgment of the county court, or other court of competent jurisdiction, on the title to property, real or personal.

Witenagemote /wídənəgəmòwt/. (Spelled, also, *witenagemot, wittenagemot, witanagemote,* etc.) "The assembly of wise men." This was the great national council or parliament of the Saxons in England, comprising the noblemen, high ecclesiastics, and other great thanes of the kingdom, advising and aiding the king in the general administration of government.

It was the grand council of the kingdom, and was held, generally, in the open air, by public notice or particular summons, in or near some city or populous town. These notices or summonses were issued upon determination by the king's select council, or the body met without notice, when the throne was vacant, to elect a new king. Subsequently to the Norman Conquest it was called *commune concilium regni, curia regis* and finally *parliament;* but its character had become considerably changed. It was a court of last resort, more especially for determining disputes between the king and his thanes, and, ultimately, from all inferior tribunals. Great offenders, particularly those who were members of or might be summoned to the king's court, were here tried. The casual loss of title-deeds was supplied, and a very extensive equity jurisdiction exercised. 1 Bl.Comm. 147. It passed out of existence with the Norman Conquest, and the subsequent Parliament was a separate growth, and not a continuation of the Witenagemot.

Witens /wídən(d)z/. The chiefs of the Saxon lords or thanes, their nobles, and wise men.

With. A word denoting a relation of proximity, contiguity, or association. White v. White, 183 Va. 239, 31 S.E.2d 558, 561. Sometimes equivalent to the words, "in addition to," but not synonymous with "including," as in a complaint demanding a specified sum, "with interest." Halpern v. Langrock Bros. Co., 169 App.Div. 464, 155 N.Y.S. 167, 168.

With all faults. This phrase, used in a contract of sale, implies that the purchaser assumes the risk of all defects and imperfections, provided they do not destroy the identity of the thing sold. See also **As is.**

With consent. Phrase within a constitution providing that Governor shall appoint officers with consent of senate, requires confirmation by senate and appointment under such provision is ineffective until confirmed. State, ex rel. Nagle v. Stafford, 97 Mont. 275, 34 P.2d 372, 379. See also **Consent.**

Withdraw. To take away what has been enjoyed; to take from. To remove, as deposits from bank, or oneself from competition, candidacy, etc.

Withdrawal. Removal of money or securities from a bank or other place of deposit. Withdrawal from a conspiracy requires either making a clean breast to authorities or communicating the abandonment of the conspiracy in manner reasonably calculated to reach co-conspirators. U. S. v. Mardian, 546 F.2d 973, 978.

Withdrawal of charges. A failure to prosecute by the person preferring charges—distinguished from a dismissal, which is a determination of their invalidity by the tribunal hearing them. See **Nolle prosequi.**

Withdrawing a juror. The withdrawing of one of the twelve jurors from the box, with the result that, the jury being now found to be incomplete, no further proceedings can be had in the cause. The withdrawing of a juror is always by the agreement of the parties, and is frequently done at the recommendation of the judge, where it is doubtful whether the action will lie; and in such case the consequence is that each party pays his own costs. It is, however, no bar to a future action for the same cause. In American practice, it was formerly usually a mere method of continuing a case, for some good reason.

Withdrawing record. The withdrawing by a plaintiff of the *nisi prius* or trial record filed in a cause, just before the trial is entered upon, for the purpose of preventing the cause from being tried. This may be done before the jury are sworn, and afterwards, by consent of the defendant's counsel.

Withernam /wíðərnəm/. A taking by way of reprisal; a taking or a reprisal of other goods, in lieu of those that were formerly taken and eloigned or withholden. A reciprocal distress, in lieu of a previous one which has been eloigned. 3 Bl.Comm. 148.

The name of a writ which issues on the return of *elongata* to an alias or pluries writ of replevin, by which the sheriff is commanded to take the defendant's own goods which may be found in his bailiwick, and keep them safely, not to deliver them to the plaintiff until such time as the defendant chooses to submit himself and allow the distress, and the whole of it to be replevied; and he is thereby further commanded that he do return to the court in what manner he shall have executed the writ.

Withersake /wíðərsèyk/. An apostate, or perfidious renegade.

Withhold. To retain in one's possession that which belongs to or is claimed or sought by another. To omit to disclose upon request; as, to withhold information. To refrain from paying that which is due.

Withholding. Deductions from salaries or wages, usually for income taxes, to be remitted by the employer, in the employee's name, to the taxing authority.

Withholding of evidence. It is an obstruction of justice to stifle, suppress or destroy evidence knowing that it may be wanted in a judicial proceeding or is being sought by investigating officers, or to remove records from the jurisdiction of the court, knowing they will be called for by the grand jury in its investigation. United States v. Perlstein, 126 F.2d 799; Commonwealth v. Russo, 177 Pa.Super. 470, 111 A.2d 359.

Withholding tax. Tax collected by deductions from employee's wages as he is paid. See **Withholding.**

Within. Into. In inner or interior part of, or not longer in time than. Through. Inside the limits of; during the time of.

When used relative to time, has been defined variously as meaning any time before; at or before; at the end of; before the expiration of; not beyond; not exceeding; not later than. Glenn v. Garrett, Tex.Civ. App., 84 S.W.2d 515, 516.

Without. Outside, beyond, in excess of.

Without day. A term used to signify that an adjournment or continuance is indefinite or final, or that no subsequent time is fixed for another meeting, or for further proceedings. See **Sine die.**

Without delay. Instantly; at once. Also, within the time allowed by law.

Without giving compensation therefor. This phrase within automobile guest statute indicates an intention to exclude application of "guest" designation not only to one who has paid cash or equivalent for his transportation but also to one who pays such recompense as makes it worth the other's while to furnish the ride. Duclos v. Tashjian, 32 Cal.App.2d 444, 90 P.2d 140, 143.

Without her consent. This phrase, as used in the law of rape, is equivalent to "against the will."

Without impeachment of waste. The effect of the insertion of this clause in a lease for life is to give the tenant the right to cut timber on the estate, without making himself thereby liable to an action for waste. When a tenant for life holds the land without impeachment of waste, he is, of course, dispunishable for waste, whether wilful or otherwise. But still this right must not be wantonly abused so as to destroy the estate; and he will be enjoined from committing malicious waste.

Without notice. As used of purchasers, etc., such language is equivalent to "in good faith." To be a holder in due course, one must take a bill or note "without notice" that it is overdue or has been dishonored or of any defense against or claim to it on the part of any person. See U.C.C. §§ 3–302(1)(c), 3–304(3). See also **Good faith; Notice.**

Without prejudice. Where an offer or admission is made "without prejudice," or a motion is denied or a suit dismissed "without prejudice," it is meant as a declaration that no rights or privileges of the party concerned are to be considered as thereby waived or lost except in so far as may be expressly conceded or decided. The words "without prejudice" import into any transaction that the parties have agreed that as between themselves the receipt of money by one and its payment by the other shall not of themselves have any legal effect on the rights of the parties, but they shall be open to settlement by legal controversy as if the money had not been paid. In re Bell, 344 Pa. 223, 25 A.2d 344, 350.

A dismissal "without prejudice" allows a new suit to be brought on the same cause of action. The words "without prejudice", as used in judgment, ordinarily import the contemplation of further proceedings, and, when they appear in an order or decree, it shows that the judicial act is not intended to be res judicata of the merits of the controversy. Fiumara v. American Surety Co. of New York, 346 Pa. 584, 31 A.2d 283, 287.

Without recourse. This phrase, used in making a qualified indorsement of a negotiable instrument, signifies that the indorser means to save himself from liability to subsequent holders, and is a notification that, if payment is refused by the parties primarily liable, recourse cannot be had to him. See U.C.C. § 3–414(1).

An indorser "without recourse" specially declines to assume any responsibility for payment. He assumes no contractual liability by virtue of the indorsement itself, and becomes a mere assignor of the title to the paper, but such an indorsement does not indicate that the indorsee takes with notice of defects, or that he does not take on credit of the other parties to the note.

Without reserve. A term applied to a sale by auction, indicating that no price is reserved.

Without stint. Without limit; without any specified number.

Without this, that. In common law pleading, formal words used by way of *traverse*, particularly by way of *special* traverse, importing an express denial of some matter of fact alleged in a previous pleading, including the declaration, plea, replication, etc. The Latin term is *absque hoc.*

With prejudice. The term as applied to judgment of dismissal is as conclusive of rights of parties as if action had been prosecuted to final adjudication adverse to the plaintiff. Fenton v. Thompson, 352 Mo. 199, 176 S.W.2d 456, 460.

With recourse. Term which may be used in indorsing negotiable instrument and by which the indorser indicates that he remains liable for payment of the instrument. See also **Without recourse.**

With strong hand. In common law pleading, a technical phrase indispensable in describing a forcible entry in an indictment. No other word or circumlocution would answer the same purpose.

Witness, *v.* To subscribe one's name to a deed, will, or other document, for the purpose of attesting its authenticity, and proving its execution, if required, by bearing witness thereto. See also **Affirmation; Attest; Jurat; Verification.**

Witness, *n.* In general, one who, being present, personally sees or perceives a thing; a beholder, spectator, or eyewitness. One who testifies to what he has seen, heard, or otherwise observed. Wigginton v. Order of United Commercial Travelers of America, C.C.A.Ind., 126 F.2d 659, 666.

A person whose declaration under oath (or affirmation) is received as evidence for any purpose, whether such declaration be made on oral examination or by deposition or affidavit. Code Civ.Proc.Cal. § 1878.

A person attesting genuineness of signature to document by adding his signature. In re Gorrell's Estate, 19 N.J.Misc. 168, 19 A.2d 334, 335.

One who is called upon to be present at a transaction, or the making of a will, that he may thereafter, if necessary, testify to the transaction.

See also Accomplice witness; Competent witness; Expert witness; Hostile or adverse witness; Lay witness; Prosecuting witness; Subscribing witness; Swift witness; Target witness.

Adverse witness. A witness whose mind discloses a bias hostile to the party examining him. See also **Adverse witness.**

Attesting witness. See **Attestation.**

Credible witness. See **Credible.**

Grand jury witness. A person called to give evidence regarding matters under inquiry by the grand jury. State v. Hogervorst, 90 N.M. 580, 566 P.2d 828, 831.

Material witness. In criminal trial, a witness whose testimony is crucial to either the defense or prosecution. In most states, he may be required to furnish bond for his appearance and, for want of surety, he may be confined until he testifies. See also **Material witness.**

Witness to will. One who has attested the will by subscribing his name thereto. The trend in state statutes is to require two witnesses to attest to the signing of the will. See *e.g.* Uniform Probate Code § 2–502. See also **Attestation clause.**

Witness against himself. The federal constitutional provision that no person shall be compelled in any criminal case, to be a "witness against himself" must be applied in a broad spirit to secure to citizen immunity from self-accusation and provision applies to all proceedings wherein defendant is acting as a witness in any investigation that requires him to give testimony that might tend to show him guilty of crime. 5th Amend., U.S.Const. United States v. Goodner, D.C. Colo., 35 F.Supp. 286, 290. See also **Immunity; Self-incrimination.**

Witnessing part. In a deed or other formal instrument, is that part which comes after the recitals, or, where there are no recitals, after the parties. It usually commences with a reference to the agreement or intention to be effectuated, then states or refers to the consideration, and concludes with the operative words and parcels, if any. Where a deed effectuates two distinct objects, there are two witnessing parts.

Wittingly. With knowledge and by design, excluding only cases which are the result of accident or forgetfulness, and including cases where one does an unlawful act through an erroneous belief of his right.

Witword /wítwèrd/. A legally allowed claim, more especially the right to vindicate ownership or possession by one's affirmation under oath.

Wolf's head. In old English law, this term was used as descriptive of the condition of an outlaw. Such persons were said to carry a wolf's head (*caput lupinum*); for if caught alive they were to be brought to the king, and if they defended themselves they might be slain and their heads carried to the king, for they were no more to be accounted of than wolves. "Woolferthfod."

Wong. Sax. In old records, a field.

Wood-corn. In old records, a certain quantity of oats or other grain, paid by customary tenants to the lord, for liberty to pick up dead or broken wood.

Wood-geld. In old English law, money paid for the liberty of taking wood in a forest. Immunity from such payment.

Wood leave. A license or right to cut down, remove, and use standing timber on a given estate or tract of land.

Wood-mote. In forest law, the old name of the court of attachments; otherwise called the "Forty-Days Court." 3 Bl.Comm. 71.

Wood plea court. In old English law, a court held twice in the year in the forest of Clun, in Shropshire, for determining all matters of wood and agistments.

Woods. A forest; land covered with a large and thick collection of natural forest trees. The old books say that a grant of "all his woods" (*omnes boscos suos*) will pass the land, as well as the trees growing upon it.

Woodwards. In English law, officers of the forest, whose duty consists in looking after the wood and vert and venison, and preventing offenses relating to the same.

Words. Symbols indicating ideas and subject to contraction and expansion to meet the idea sought to be expressed. Such have been referred to as labels whose content and meaning are continually shifting with the times. Massachusetts Protective Ass'n v. Bayersdorfer, C.C.A.Ohio, 105 F.2d 595, 597.

As used in law, this term generally signifies the technical terms and phrases appropriate to particular instruments, or aptly fitted to the expression of a particular intention in legal instruments. See the subtitles following.

Words actionable in themselves. In libel and slander, refer to words which are libelous or slanderous per se. See **Actionable per se.**

Words of art. The vocabulary or terminology of a particular art or science, and especially those expressions which are idiomatic or peculiar to it.

Words of limitation. See **Limitation.**

Words of procreation. To create an estate tail by deed, it is necessary that words of procreation should be used in order to confine the estate to the descendants of the first grantee, as in the usual form of limitation, —"to A. and the heirs of his body."

Words of purchase. See **Purchase.**

Work. To exert one's self for a purpose; to put forth effort for the attainment of an object; to be engaged in the performance of a task, duty, or the like. The term covers all forms of physical or mental exertions, or both combined, for the attainment of some object other than recreation or amusement. Tennessee Coal, Iron & R. Co. v. Muscoda Local No. 123, Ala., 321 U.S. 590, 64 S.Ct. 698, 703, 705, 88 L.Ed. 949. See also **Labor.**

Work and labor. The name of one of the common counts in actions of *assumpsit*, being for work and labor done and materials furnished by the plaintiff for the defendant.

Workaway. Extra man employed on vessel as an accommodation to himself. The Tashmoo, D.C.N.Y., 48 F.2d 366, 368.

Worker. See **Workman.**

Workers' Compensation Acts. See **Workmen's Compensation Acts.**

Workhouse. Place of confinement for persons convicted of lesser offenses. Such imprisonment is usually for a relatively short duration.

Working capital. Cash and other quick assets. Crocker v. Waltham Watch Co., 315 Mass. 397, 53 N.E.2d 230, 237. In accounting the difference between current assets and current liabilities. In public utilities the amount of cash required by a business to carry on operations.

Working interest. See **Royalty.**

Working papers. By statute in certain states, such must be filed by one employing a minor.

Discovery. See **Work product rule.**

Workman. One who labors; one employed to do business for another. One employed in manual labor, skilled or unskilled; an artificer, mechanic, or artisan.

Workmen's or **Workers' Compensation Acts.** State statutes which provide for fixed awards to employees or their dependents in case of employment related accidents and diseases, dispensing with proof of negligence and legal actions. Some of the acts go beyond the simple determination of the right to compensation, and provide insurance systems, either under state supervision or otherwise. The various state acts vary as to extent of workers and employment covered, amount and duration of benefits, etc.

The effect of most workmen's or workers' compensation acts is to make the employer strictly liable to an employee for injuries sustained by the employee which arise out of and in the course of employment, without regard to the negligence of the employer or that of the employee. Where the Act applies, it has been uniformly held that this remedy is exclusive and bars any common-law remedy which the employee may have had, the compensation scheduled under the act being the sole measure of damage.

Federal employees are covered by the Federal Employees Compensation Act; seamen by the Jones Act; longshoremen and harbor workers by the Longshoremen's and Harbor Workers' Compensation Act. Additional benefits to disabled workers are provided under Title II of the Social Security Act.

Workmen's or **workers' compensation boards or courts.** Such exist in many states with jurisdiction to review cases arising under workmen's or workers' compensation acts and related rules and regulations.

Workmen's or **workers' compensation insurance.** Insurance coverage purchased by employers to cover risks under workmen's or workers' compensation laws. Such is usually mandated by state acts, unless the employer is self-insured. See also **Insurance.**

Work of national importance. Under the Selective Service Act providing that conscientious objectors should be assigned to such work means work of value to the nation for the common defense and general welfare. 50 U.S.C.A. Appendix § 305(g). United States ex rel. Zucker v. Osborne, D.C.N.Y., 54 F.Supp. 984, 986, 987.

Work of necessity. As excepted from operation of Sunday closing statutes embraces all work reasonably essential to the economic, social or moral welfare of the people, viewed in light of the habits and customs of the age in which they live and of the community in which they reside. Francisco v. Commonwealth, 180 Va. 371, 23 S.E.2d 234, 238, 239.

Work product rule. A party may obtain discovery of documents and tangible things otherwise discoverable under Rule 26(b)(1) and prepared in anticipation of litigation or for trial by or for another party or by or for that other party's representative (including his attorney, consultant, surety, indemnitor, insurer, or agent) only upon a showing that the party seeking discovery has substantial need of the materials in the preparation of his case and that he is unable without undue hardship to obtain the substantial equivalent of the materials by other means. In ordering discovery of such materials when the required showing has been made, the court shall protect against disclosure of the mental impressions, conclusions, opinions, or legal theories of an attorney or other representative of a party concerning the litigation. Fed.R.Civil P. 26(b)(3). See also Hickman v. Taylor, 329 U.S. 495, 67 S.Ct. 385, 91 L.Ed 451.

"Work product" which is protected against discovery covers material prepared by an attorney in anticipation of litigation, including private memoranda, written statements of witnesses and mental impressions of personal recollections prepared or formed by attorney in anticipation of litigation or for trial. Com. of Puerto Rico v. S S Zoe Colocotroni, D.C.Puerto Rico, 61 F.R.D. 653, 658.

Work release program. Correctional programs which allow an inmate to leave the institution for the purpose of continuing regular employment during the daytime, but reporting back to lockup nights and weekends.

Works. Sometimes, a mill, factory, or other establishment for performing industrial labor of any sort; also, a building, structure, or erection of any kind upon land, as in the civil-law phrase "new works."

New works. A term of the civil law comprehending every sort of edifice or other structure which is newly commenced on a given estate or lot. Its importance lies chiefly in the fact that a remedy is given ("denunciation of new works") to an adjacent proprietor whose property would be injured or subjected to a more onerous servitude if such a work were allowed to proceed to completion.

Public works. Works, whether of construction or adaptation, undertaken and carried out by the national, state, or municipal authorities, and designed to subserve some purpose of public necessity, use, or convenience; such as public buildings, roads, aqueducts, parks, etc. All fixed works constructed for public use. The term usually relates to the construction of public improvements and not to their maintenance or operation.

Work week. Within Fair Labor Standards Act, a week during which work is performed. 29 U.S.C.A. § 207.

World. This term sometimes denotes all persons whatsoever who may have, claim, or acquire an interest in the subject-matter; as in saying that a judgment *in rem* binds "all the world."

World Court. See **International Court of Justice.**

Worldly. Of or pertaining to the world or the present state of existence; temporal; earthly; devoted to, interested in, or connected with this present life, and its cares, advantages, or pleasures, to the exclusion of those of a future life. Concerned with enjoyment of this present existence; secular; not religious; spiritual, or holy.

Worrying cattle or sheep. Within statutes providing that any one finding a dog, not on the premises of its owner, who is worrying cattle or sheep, may kill the dog, means to run after; to chase; to bark at. Failing v. People, 105 Colo. 399, 98 P.2d 865, 867.

Worship. Any form of religious service showing reverence for Divine Being, or exhortation to obedience to or following of the mandates of such Being. Religious exercises participated in by a number of persons assembled for that purpose, the disturbance of which is a statutory offense in many states.

English law. A title of honor or dignity used in addresses to certain magistrates and other persons of rank or office.

Public worship. This term may mean the worship of God, conducted and observed under public authority; or it may mean worship in an open or public place, without privacy or concealment; or it may mean the performance of religious exercises, under a provision for an equal right in the whole public to participate in its benefits; or it may be used in contradistinction to worship in the family or the closet. In this country, what is called "public worship" is commonly conducted by voluntary societies, constituted according to their own notions of ecclesiastical authority and ritual propriety, opening their places of worship, and admitting to their religious services such persons, and upon such terms, and subject to such regulations, as they may choose to designate and establish. A church absolutely belonging to the public, and in which all persons without restriction have equal rights, such as the public enjoy in highways or public landings, is certainly a very rare institution.

Wort or **worth.** A curtilage or country farm.

Worth. The quality or value of a thing which gives it value. Although "worth" in some connections may mean more than pecuniary value, in law it means that sum of valuable qualities which renders a thing valuable and useful expressed in the current medium of the country. Furnishing an equivalent for. See also **Net worth; Value.**

Worthier title /wɔ́rðiyər táydəl/. At common law where testator undertook to devise to an heir exactly same interest in land as such heir would take by descent, descent was regarded as the "worthier title" and heir took by descent rather than by devise. Jones v. Petrie, 156 Kan. 241, 132 P.2d 396, 398. Doctrine of worthier title provides that conveyance by grantor with limitation over to grantor's heirs creates reversion in grantor, not remainder interest in heirs, and to take by descent rather than by purchase, is said to create a worthier title. Hatch v. Riggs Nat. Bank, D.C.D.C., 284 F.Supp. 396, 397. This doctrine has been abolished in many states.

Worthiest of blood. In the English law of descent, a term applied to males, expressive of the preference given to them over females. See 2 Bl.Comm. 234–240.

Worthless. Destitute of worth, of no value or use. Spring City Foundry Co. v. Commissioner of Internal Revenue, 292 U.S. 182, 54 S.Ct. 644, 78 L.Ed. 1200.

Worthless check. A check drawn on a bank account which is no longer open or on an account with funds insufficient to cover the check.

Giving a worthless check is the making, drawing, issuing or delivering or causing or directing the making, drawing, issuing or delivering of any check, order or draft on any bank or depository for the payment of money or its equivalent with intent to defraud and knowing, at the time of the making, drawing, issuing or delivering of such check, order or draft as aforesaid, that the maker or drawer has no deposit in or credits with such bank or depository or has not sufficient funds in, or credits with, such bank or depository for the payment of such check, order or draft in full upon its presentation.

Worthless securities. A loss (usually capital) is allowed for a security that becomes worthless during the year. The loss is deemed to have occurred on the last day of the year. Special rules apply to securities of affiliated companies and small business stock. See I.R.C. § 165.

Worthy. Having worth; possessing merit; valuable; deserving of honor, or the like; of high station; of high social position; deserved, merited. Woodstown Nat. Bank and Trust Co. v. Snelbaker, 136 N.J.Eq. 62, 40 A.2d 222, 227.

Would. A word sometimes expressing what might be expected or preferred or desired. Often interchangeable with the word "should," but not with "could."

Wound, n. An injury to the body of a person or animal, especially one caused by violence, by which the continuity of the covering, as skin, mucous membrane, or conjunctiva, is broken. Gasperino v. Prudential Ins. Co. of America, Mo.App., 107 S.W.2d 819, 827. Any breaking up or dispersion, or disintegration of the natural continuity of a tissue of the body. Gasperino v. Prudential Ins. Co. of America, Mo.App., 107 S.W.2d 819, 827. Also injuries of every kind which affect the body, whether they are cuts, lacerations, fractures, or bruises. Any lesion of the body.

Wound, v. To inflict a laceration, cut, fracture or bruise.

Wounded feelings. Such as result from indignities to self-respect, sensibilities, or pride of a person, as distinguished from usual mental pain and suffering consequent to physical injury. See also **Mental cruelty.**

Wounding. An aggravated species of assault and battery, consisting in one person giving another some dangerous hurt. 3 Bl.Comm. 121.

Wraparound mortgage. A second mortgage which wraps around or exists in addition to a first or other mortgages. Form of secondary financing typically used on older properties having first mortgages with low interest rates in which a lender assumes the developer's first mortgage obligation and also loans additional money, taking back from developer a junior mortgage in total amount at an intermediate interest rate. ICM Realty v. Cabot, Cabot & Forbes Land Trust, D.C.N.Y., 378 F.Supp. 918, 923.

Wrath. Not merely anger, but violent anger.

Wreccum maris significat illa bona quæ naufragio ad terram pelluntur /rékəm mǽrəs signífəkət ílə bównə kwìy nofréyj(iy)ow æ̀d téhrəm peléntər/. A wreck of the sea signifies those goods which are driven to shore from a shipwreck.

Wreck. To destroy, disable, or seriously damage. To reduce to a wreck or ruinous state by any kind of violence; to overthrow, shatter, or destroy; to cause to crash or suffer ruin, synonymous with ruin, smash, and demolish. Its antonyms are save, salvage, and preserve. Destruction, disorganization, or serious injury of anything, especially by violence. Houston Printing Co. v. Hunter, Tex.Civ.App., 105 S.W.2d 312, 317.

Goods cast ashore by the sea, and not claimed by the owner within a year, or other specified period; which, in such case, become the property of the state. The term applies to property cast upon land by the sea; to jetsam, flotsam, and ligan.

Common law. Goods cast ashore from a wrecked vessel, where no person has escaped from the wreck alive; and which are forfeited to the crown, or to persons having the franchise of wreck. But if claimed by the true owner within a year and a day the goods, or their proceeds, must be restored to him, by virtue of stat.

Maritime law. A ship becomes a wreck when, in consequence of injuries received, she is rendered absolutely unnavigable, or unable to pursue her voyage, without repairs exceeding the half of her value. A "wrecked vessel," however, in common phraseology, includes a sunken vessel. Act March 3, 1899, § 15 (33 U.S.C.A. § 409).

Wreckfree. In old English law, exempt from the forfeiture of shipwrecked goods and vessels to the king.

Wrench. Violent twist; a sprain and injury by twisting as in a joint. Traders & General Ins. Co. v. Lincecum, Tex.Civ.App., 126 S.W.2d 692, 695. See also **Whiplash injury.**

Wrinkle. A stria; furrow; channel; hollow; depression; rut; cup; pocket; dimple.

Writ. An order issued from a court requiring the performance of a specified act, or giving authority to have it done. A precept in writing, issuing from a court of justice, addressed to a sheriff or other officer of the law, or directly to the person whose action the court desires to command, either as the commencement of a suit or other proceeding or as incidental to its progress, and requiring the performance of a specified act, or giving authority and commission to have it done. See also **Order; Prerogative writs; Process.**

In old English law, an instrument in the form of a letter; a letter or letters of attorney. This is a very ancient sense of the word.

In the old books, "writ" is used as equivalent to "action;" hence writs are sometimes divided into real, personal, and mixed.

For the names and description of various particular writs, see the titles below.

Alias writ. A second writ issued in the same cause, where a former writ of the same kind has been issued without effect.

All Writs Act. Federal Act which permits federal appellate courts to "issue all writs necessary or appropriate in aid of their respective jurisdictions and agreeable to the usages and principles of law." 28 U.S.C.A. § 1651.

Close writ. In English law, a name given to certain letters of the sovereign, sealed with his great seal and directed to particular persons and for particular purposes, which, not being proper for public inspection, were closed up and sealed on the outside; also, a writ directed to the sheriff instead of to the lord. 2 Bl. Comm. 346.

Concurrent writs. In England, duplicate originals, or several writs running at the same time for the same purpose, for service on or arrest of a person, when it is not known where he is to be found; or for service on several persons, as when there are several defendants to an action.

Judicial writs. In English practice, the capias and all other writs subsequent to the original writ not issuing out of chancery, but from the court to which the original was returnable. Being grounded on what had passed in that court in consequence of the sheriff's return, they were called *judicial* writs, in contradistinction to the writs issued out of chancery, which were called *original* writs. 3 Bl.Comm. 282. Such writs as issue under the private seal of the courts, and not under the great seal of England, and are tested or witnessed, not in the king's name, but in the name of the chief judge of the court out of which they issue. The word "judicial" is used in contradistinction to "original;" original writs being such as issue out of chancery under the great seal, and are witnessed in the king's name. 3 Bl.Comm. 282.

Junior writ. One which is issued, or comes to the officer's hands, at a later time than a similar writ, at the suit of another party, or on a different claim, against the same defendant.

Original writ. In English practice, an original writ was the process formerly in use for the commencement of personal actions. It was a mandatory letter from the king, issuing out of chancery, sealed with the great seal, and directed to the sheriff of the county wherein the injury was committed, or was supposed to have been committed, requiring him to command the wrong-doer or accused party either to do justice to the plaintiff or else to appear in court and answer the accusation against him. This writ is now disused, the writ of summons being the process prescribed by the uniformity of process act for commencing personal actions; and under the judicature act, 1873, all suits, even in the court of chancery, are to be commenced by such writs of summons.

Patent writ. In old practice, an open writ; one not closed or sealed up.

Peremptory writ. An original writ, called from the words of the writ a *"si te fecerit securum"*, and which directed the sheriff to cause the defendant to appear in court without any option given him, provided the plaintiff gave the sheriff security effectually to prosecute his claim. The writ was very occasionally in use, and only where nothing was specifically demanded, but only a satisfaction in general; as in the case of writs of trespass on the case, wherein no debt or other specific thing was sued for, but only damages to be assessed by a jury.

Prerogative writs. Those issued by the exercise of the extraordinary power of the crown (the court, in modern practice) on proper cause shown; namely, the writs of *procedendo, mandamus, prohibition, quo warranto, habeas corpus,* and *certiorari.*

Writ de bono et malo /rít dìy bównow èt mǽlow/. See **Assise; De Lien et de mal.**

Writ de ejectione firmæ /rít dìy əjèkshiyówniy fə́rmiy/. See **Ejectione firmæ.**

Writ de hæretico comburendo /rít dìy hərédəkow kòmbəréndow/. See **De hæretico comburendo.**

Writ de homine replegiando /rít dìy hóməniy rəplìyjiyǽndow/. See **De homine replegiando.**

Writ de odio et atia /rít dìy ówdiyow èd éysh(iy)ə/. See **De odio et atia.**

Writ de rationabili parte bonorum /rít dìy ræ̀sh(iy)ənéybəlay párdiy bownórəm/. See **De rationabili parte bonorum.**

Write-off. To remove from books of account a debt which has become worthless. The worthless debt itself. See **Bad debt.**

Writer of the tallies /ráydər əv ðə tǽliyz/. In England, an officer of the exchequer whose duty it was to write upon the tallies the letters of tellers' bills.

Write-up. To increase the valuation of an asset in a financial statement to reflect current value.

Writing. The expression of ideas by letters visible to the eye. The giving an outward and objective form to a contract, will, etc., by means of letters or marks placed upon paper, parchment, or other material substance.

In the most general sense of the word, "writing" denotes a document, whether manuscript or printed, as opposed to mere spoken words. Writing is essential to the validity of certain contracts and other transactions. Term includes printing, typewriting or any other intentional reduction to tangible form. U.C.C. § 1–201(46).

"Writings" consist of letters, words, or numbers, or their equivalent, set down by handwriting, typewriting, printing, photostating, photographing, magnetic impulse, mechanical or electronic recording, or other form of data compilation. Fed.Evid.R. 1001(1).

"Writing" means handwriting, typewriting, printing, photostating, photographing, and every other means of recording upon any tangible thing any form of communication or representation, including letters, words, pictures, sounds, or symbols, or combinations thereof. Calif.Evid.Code.

See also **Ancient writings; Instrument.**

Writing obligatory. The technical name by which a *bond* is described in pleading.

Writ of ad quod damnum /ríd əv ǽd kwòd dǽmnəm/. See **Ad quod damnum.**

Writ of assistance. The name of a writ which issues from the court of chancery, in aid of the execution of a judgment at law, to put the complainant into possession of lands adjudged to him, when the sheriff cannot execute the judgment. A form of process issued by an equity court to transfer the possession of lands, title or possession to which it has previously adjudicated, as a means of enforcing its decree, and performs the same office in a suit in equity as an execution in an action at law. Burney v. Lee, 57 Ariz. 41, 110 P.2d 554, 556. Its office is confined to lend aid to original equity jurisdiction, and the writ cannot be employed as a substitute for other common-law or statutory actions. Patterson v. McKay, 202 Ark. 241, 150 S.W.2d 196. It is essentially a mandatory injunction, effect of which is to bring about a change in the possession of realty—it dispossesses the occupant and gives possession to one adjudged entitled thereto by the court. Dusbabek v. Local Building & Loan Ass'n, 178 Okl. 592, 63 P.2d 756, 759.

A writ of assistance is equivalent to the writ of habere facias possessionem at law, and issues as of course without notice, so far as the parties to the record are concerned, when necessary to execute a decree.

While the office of both a writ of assistance and a writ of possession is to put the party entitled thereto into the possession of property, the former issues from equity and the latter from law. In England, an ancient writ issuing out of the exchequer. A writ issuing from the court of exchequer to the sheriff commanding him to be in aid of the king's tenants by knight's service, or the king's collectors, debtors, or accountants, to enforce payment of their own dues, in order to enable them to pay their own dues to the king.

Writ of association. In English practice a writ whereby certain persons (usually the clerk of assize and his subordinate officers) are directed to associate themselves with the justices and serjeants; and they are required to admit the said persons into their society in order to take the assizes. 3 Bl.Comm. 59.

Writ of attachment. A writ employed to enforce obedience to an order or judgment of the court. It may take the form of commanding the sheriff to attach the disobedient party and to have him before the court to answer his contempt. In its generic sense, any mesne civil process in the nature of a writ on which property may be attached, including trustee process. See also **Attachment.**

Writ of capias. See **Capias.**

Writ of certiorari. An order by the appellate court which is used when the court has discretion on whether or not to hear an appeal. If the writ is denied, the court refuses to hear the appeal and, in effect, the judgment below stands unchanged. If the writ is granted, then it has the effect of ordering the lower court to certify the record and send it up to the higher court which has used its discretion to hear the appeal. See also **Certiorari.**

Writ of conspiracy. A writ which anciently lay against persons who had conspired to injure the plaintiff, under the same circumstances which would now give him an action on the case. It did not lie at common law, in any case, except when the conspiracy was to indict the party either of treason or felony; all the other cases of conspiracy in the books were but actions on the case.

Writ of covenant. A writ which lies where a party claims damages for breach of covenant; *i.e.*, of a promise under seal.

Writ of debt. A writ which lies where the party claims the recovery of a debt; *i.e.*, a liquidated or certain sum of money alleged to be due to him.

Writ of deceit. The name of a writ which lies where one man has done anything in the name of another, by which the latter is damnified and deceived.

Writ of delivery. A writ of execution employed to enforce a judgment for the delivery of chattels. It commands the sheriff to cause the chattels mentioned in the writ to be returned to the person who has obtained the judgment; and, if the chattels cannot be found, to distrain the person against whom the judgment was given until he returns them.

Writ of detinue /ríd əv détən(y)uw/. A writ which lies where a party claims the specific recovery of goods and chattels, or deeds and writings, detained from him. This is seldom used; trover is the more frequent remedy, in cases where it may be brought.

Writ of dower. This is either a writ of dower *unde nihil habet*, which lies for a widow, commanding the tenant to assign her dower, no part of which has yet been set off to her; or a writ of *right of dower*, whereby she seeks to recover the remainder of the dower to which she is entitled, part having been already received from the tenant. This latter writ is seldom used.

Writ of ejectment. The writ in an action of ejectment, for the recovery of lands. See **Ejectment.**

Writ of entry. A real action to recover the possession of land where the tenant (or owner) has been disseised or otherwise wrongfully dispossessed. If the disseisor has aliened the land, or if it has descended to his heir, the writ of entry is said to be in the *per*, because it alleges that the defendant (the alienee or heir) obtained possession *through* the original disseisor. If two alienations (or descents) have taken place, the writ is in the *per* and *cui*, because it alleges that the defendant (the second alienee) obtained possession *through* the first alienee, *to whom* the original disseisor had aliened it. If more than two alienations (or descents) have taken place, the writ is in the *post*, because it simply alleges that the defendant acquired possession *after* the original disseisin. 3 Bl.Comm. 180. The writ of entry was abolished, with other real actions, in England, by St. 3 & 4 Wm. IV, c. 27, § 36, but is still in use in a few of the states. Under rules practice, such writ has been abolished in favor of a civil action which grants similar relief, *e.g.* Mass.R. Civ.P. 81(b). See also **Entry, writ of.**

Writ of error. A writ issued from a court of appellate jurisdiction, directed to the judge or judges of a court of record, requiring them to remit to the appellate court the record of an action before them, in which a final judgment has been entered, in order that examination may be made of certain errors alleged to have been committed, and that the judgment may be reversed, corrected, or affirmed, as the case may require. It is brought for supposed error in law apparent on record and takes case to higher tribunal, which affirms or reverses. It is commencement of new suit to set aside judgment, and is not continuation of suit to which it relates. Winchester v. Winn, 225 Mo. App. 288, 29 S.W.2d 188, 190. And unless abolished by statute, is writ of right applicable to all cases in which jurisdiction is exercised according to course of common law, but is inapplicable to cases not known to or in derogation of common law, unless otherwise provided by statute. See also **Writ of error coram nobis; Writ of error coram vobis.**

Writ of error coram nobis /ríd əv éhrər kórəm nówbəs/. A common-law writ, the purpose of which is to correct a judgment in the same court in which it was rendered, on the ground of error of fact, for which the statute provides no other remedy, which fact did not appear of record, or was unknown to the court when judgment was pronounced, and which, if known, would have prevented the judgment, and which was unknown, and could not have been known to the party by the exercise of reasonable diligence in time to have been otherwise presented to the court, unless he was prevented from so presenting them by duress, fear, or other sufficient cause.

An ordinary "writ of error" is brought for a supposed error in law apparent on the record, and takes the case to a higher tribunal where the question is to be decided and the judgment, sentence or decree is to be affirmed or reversed, while the "writ of error coram nobis" is brought for an alleged error in fact not appearing on the record and lies to the same court in order that it may correct the error, which it is presumed would not have been committed had the fact been brought to the court's notice in the first instance.

At common law in England, it issued from the Court of King's Bench to a judgment of that court. Its principal aim is to afford the court in which an action was tried an opportunity to correct its own record with reference to a vital fact not known when the judgment was rendered. It is also said that at common law it lay to correct purely ministerial errors of the officers of the court.

See also **Coram nobis.**

Writ of error coram vobis /ríd əv éhrər kórəm vówbəs/. This writ, at the English common law, is distinguished from "writ of error coram nobis," in that the former issued from the Court of King's Bench to a judgment of the Court of Common Pleas, whereas the latter issued from the Court of King's Bench to a judgment of that court. See also **Coram vobis.**

Writ of execution. A writ to put in force the judgment or decree of a court. See **Execution.**

Writ of exigi facias /ríd əv égzəjay féysh(iy)əs/. See **Exigent.**

Writ of formedon /ríd əv fórmədən/. A writ which lies for the recovery of an estate by a person claiming as issue in tail, or by the remainder-man or reversioner after the termination of the entail. See **Formedon.**

Writ of habeas corpus. See **Habeas corpus.**

Writ of inquiry. In common-law practice, a writ which issued after the plaintiff in an action had obtained a judgment by default, on an unliquidated claim, directing the sheriff, with the aid of a jury, to inquire into the amount of the plaintiff's demand and assess his damages.

Writ of mainprize, or **mainprise** /ríd əv méynpràyz/. In English law, a writ directed to the sheriff (either generally, when any man is imprisoned for a bailable offense and bail has been refused, or specially, when the offense or cause of commitment is not properly bailable below), commanding him to take sureties for the prisoner's appearance, commonly called "mainpernors," and to set him at large. 3 Bl.Comm. 128. See also **Mainprise.**

Writ of mandamus. See **Mandamus.**

Writ of mesne /ríd əv míyn/. In old English law, a writ which was so called by reason of the words used in the writ, namely, *"Unde idem A. qui medius est inter C. et præfatum B.";* that is, A., who is mesne between C., the lord paramount, and B., the tenant paravail. See also **Process** *(Mesne process).*

Writ of possession. Writ of execution employed to enforce a judgment to recover the possession of land. It commands the sheriff to enter the land and give possession of it to the person entitled under the judgment. For a distinction between this writ and the "Writ of Assistance," see that title. See also **Ejectment.**

Writ of præcipe /ríd əv présəpiy/. This writ is also called a "writ of covenant," and is sued out by the party to whom lands are to be conveyed by fine, the foundation of which is a supposed agreement or covenant that the one shall convey the land to the other. 2 Bl.Comm. 349.

Writ of prevention. This name is given to certain writs which may be issued in anticipation of suits which may arise. See **Quia timet.**

Writ of probable cause. An auxiliary process designed to supersede enforcement of judgment of trial court brought up for review. Martin v. Rosen, 2 Cal. App.2d 450, 38 P.2d 855, 857.

Writ of process. See **Action; Process.**

Writ of proclamation. In English law, by the statute 31 Eliz., c. 3, § 1, when an *exigent* was sued out, a writ of proclamation issued at the same time, commanding the sheriff of the county where the defendant lived to make three proclamations thereof, in places the most notorious, and most likely to come to his knowledge, a month before the outlawry was to take place. 3 Bl.Comm. 284.

When it was not directed to the same sheriff as the *exigent* was, it was called a foreign writ of proclamation.

Writ of prohibition. See **Prohibition.**

Writ of protection. In England, the king may, by his writ of protection, privilege any person in his service from arrest in civil proceedings during a year and a day; but this prerogative is seldom, if ever, exercised.

Writ of quare impedit. See **Quare impedit.**

Writ of quo warranto. See **Quo warranto.**

Writ of recaption. If, pending an action of replevin for a distress, the defendant distrains again for the same rent or service, the owner of the goods is not driven to another action of replevin, but is allowed a writ of recaption, by which he recovers the goods and damages for the defendant's contempt of the process of the law in making a second distress while the matter is *sub judice.*

Writ of replevin. See **Replevin.**

Writ of restitution. A writ which is issued on the reversal of a judgment commanding the sheriff to restore to the defendant below the thing levied upon, if it has not been sold, and, if it has been sold, the proceeds. A writ which lies, after the reversal of a judgment, to restore a party to all that he has lost by occasion of the judgment.

Writ of review. A general designation of any form of process issuing from an appellate court and intended to bring up for review the record or decision of the court below. See **Writ of certiorari.**

Writ of right. A writ which lay for one who had the right of property, against another who had the right of possession and the actual occupation. The writ properly lay only to recover corporeal hereditaments for an estate in fee-simple; but there were other writs, said to be "in the nature of a writ of right," available for the recovery of incorporeal hereditaments or of lands for a less estate than a fee-simple. 3 Bl.Comm. 391.

In another sense, a writ which is grantable as a matter of right, as opposed to a "prerogative writ," which is issued only as a matter of grace or discretion.

In England, the writ of right was abolished in 1833.

Writ of summons. The writ by which, under the English judicature acts, all actions are commenced.

Writ of supersedeas /ríd əv s(y)ùwpərsíydiyəs/. See **Supersedeas.**

Writ of supervisory control. A writ which is issued only to correct erroneous rulings made by the lower court within its jurisdiction, where there is no appeal, or the remedy by appeal cannot afford adequate relief, and gross injustice is threatened as the result of such rulings. It is in nature of summary appeal to control course of litigation in trial court when necessary to prevent miscarriage of justice, and may be employed to prevent extended and needless litigation. State ex rel. Regis v. District Court of Second Judicial Dist. in and for Silver Bow County, 102 Mont. 74, 55 P.2d 1295.

Function of "writ of supervisory control" is to enable Supreme Court to control course of litigation in inferior courts where such courts are proceeding within their jurisdiction, but by mistake of law, or willful disregard of it, are doing gross injustice, and there is no appeal or remedy by appeal is inadequate. State ex rel. State Bank of Townsend v. District Court of First Judicial Dist. in and for Lewis and Clark County, 94 Mont. 551, 25 P.2d 396.

Writ of toit. In old English law, the name of a writ to remove proceedings on a writ of right patent from the court-baron into the county court.

Writ of trial. In English law, a writ directing an action brought in a superior court to be tried in an inferior court or before the undersheriff, under St. 3 & 4 Wm. IV, c. 42. It was superseded by the county courts act of 1867, c. 142, § 6, by which a defendant, in certain cases, became enabled to obtain an order that the action be tried in a county court.

Writ of waste. The name of a writ to be issued against a tenant who has committed waste of the premises. There were anciently several forms of this writ, adapted to the particular circumstances.

Writ pro retorno habendo /rít pròw rətórnow həbéndow/. A writ commanding the return of the goods to the defendant, upon a judgment in his favor in replevin, upon the plaintiff's default.

Written contract. See **Contract.**

Written instrument. Something reduced to writing as a means of evidence, and as the means of giving formal expression to some act or contract. See **Instrument.**

Written law. Statutory law; *i.e.* law deriving its force from express legislative enactment. See also **Common law; Statute.**

One of the two leading divisions of the Roman law, comprising the *leges, plebiscita, senatus-consulta, principum placita, magistratuum edicta,* and *responsa prudentum.*

Wrong. A violation of the legal rights of another; an invasion of right to the damage of the parties who suffer it, especially a tort. State ex rel. and to Use of Donelon v. Deuser, 345 Mo. 628, 134 S.W.2d 132, 133. It usually signifies injury to person, property or relative noncontractual rights of another than wrongdoer, with or without force, but, in more extended sense, includes violation of contract. Daurizio v. Merchants' Despatch Transp. Co., 152 Misc. 716, 274 N.Y.S. 174. See **Tort.**

The idea of *rights* naturally suggests the correlative one of *wrongs;* for every right is capable of being violated. A right to receive payment for goods sold (for example) implies a wrong on the part of him who owes, but withholds the price; a right to live in personal security, a wrong on the part of him who commits personal violence. And therefore, while, in a general point of view, the law is intended for the establishment and maintenance of *rights,* we find it, on closer examination, to be dealing both with rights and wrongs. It first fixes the character and definition of rights, and then, with a view to their effectual security, proceeds to define wrongs, and to devise the means by which the latter shall be prevented or redressed.

Private wrong. The violation of public or private rights, when considered in reference to the injury sustained by the individual, and consequently as subjects for civil redress or compensation. Huntington v. Attrill, 146 U.S. 657, 13 S.Ct. 224, 36 L.Ed. 1123. See **Tort.**

Public wrongs. Violations of public rights and duties which affect the whole community, considered as a community; crimes and misdemeanors. 3 Bl.Comm. 2; 4 Bl.Comm. 1.

Real wrong. In old English law, an injury to the freehold.

Wrongdoer. One who commits an injury; a *tort-feasor*. The term ordinarily imports an invasion of right to the damage of the party who suffers such invasion.

Wrongful. Injurious, heedless, unjust, reckless, unfair. Infringement of some right. Mathes v. Williams, Tex. Civ.App., 134 S.W.2d 853, 858. See **Tort.**

Wrongful abuse of process. See **Abuse of process; Malicious abuse of legal process.**

Wrongful act. Any act which in the ordinary course will infringe upon the rights of another to his damage, unless it is done in the exercise of an equal or superior right. Term is occasionally equated to term "negligent," but generally has been considered more comprehensive term, including criminal, wilful, wanton, reckless and all other acts which in ordinary course will infringe upon rights of another to his damage. County of DuPage v. Kussel, 12 Ill.App.3d 272, 298 N.E.2d 323, 326.

Wrongful conduct. Conduct which contravenes some duty which law attaches to relation between parties affected. Duncan v. Lumbermen's Mut. Casualty Co., 91 N.H. 349, 23 A.2d 325, 326.

Wrongful death action. Type of lawsuit brought on behalf of a deceased person's beneficiaries that alleges that death was attributable to the willful or negligent act of another. Such action is original and distinct claim for damages sustained by statutory beneficiaries and is not derivative of or continuation of claim existing in decedent. Barragan v. Superior Court of Pima County, 12 Ariz.App. 402, 470 P.2d 722, 724. See **Kilberg doctrine.**

Wrongful death statutes. Such statutes, which exist in all states, provide a cause of action in favor of the decedent's personal representative for the benefit of certain beneficiaries (*e.g.* spouse, parent, children) against person who negligently caused death of spouse, child, parent, etc. Statutory provision which operates upon the common-law rule that the death of a human being may not be complained of as an injury in a civil court. The cause of action for wrongful death permitted under such statutes is for the wrong to the beneficiaries. Most such statutes are compensatory though some states retain statutes which measure damages in terms of culpability and some statutes reflect a combination of both. See also **Death on High Seas Act; Lord Campbell Act; Survival statutes; Wrongful death action.**

Wrongful levy. Such as will entitle the owner of property levied on to damages for wrongful execution, exists where there has been done to a third person's personalty those acts that would constitute a valid and complete levy if the debtor's property had been seized. Farris v. Castor, 186 Okl. 668, 99 P.2d 900, 902, 903.

Wrongful life action. In a wrongful birth or life action the parents of an unplanned child seek to shift to the defendant various costs, including medical expenses of pregnancy and delivery, pain and suffering, and the more formidable costs of rearing and educating a child. As the history of this litigation has progressed, the damages claimed have been more extensive. The litigation arises in several contexts. Malpracticed sterilization operations, including both tubal ligations and vasectomies constitute the major number of suits. Included also are failures to diagnose pregnancy in time for abortion and failures to perform successful abortions. The suits are brought mainly on the basis of negligence. Lane v. Cohen, 201 So.2d 804. However, breach of warranty, breach of contract, and misrepresentation have also been alleged as bases of liability.

A doctor whose incorrect medical advice led a couple to have a second child who died of the same hereditary disease that killed their first baby can be sued for malpractice. Park v. Chessin, 60 A.D.2d 80, 400 N.Y.S.2d 110. Also, a doctor whose negligently performed vasectomy resulted in an unwanted child may be sued for malpractice. Sherlock v. Stillwater Clinic, 260 N.W.2d 169.

Wrongfully. In a wrong manner; unjustly; in a manner contrary to the moral law, or to justice. See also **Wrongful.**

Wrongfully intending. In the language of pleading, this phrase is appropriate to be used in alleging the malicious motive of the defendant in committing the injury which forms the cause of action.

Wurth /wə́rθ/. In Saxon law, worthy; competent; capable. *Atheswurthe*, worthy of oath; admissible or competent to be sworn.

Wye /wáy/. As applied to a street railway, a "wye" means a track with two branches, one joining the main track from one direction and the other joining the main track from another direction.

Wyte /wáyt/. In old English law, acquittance or immunity from amercement.

X. In the written terminology of various arts and trades, where two or more dimensions of the same piece or article are to be stated, this letter is a well-known symbol equivalent to the word "by." Thus, the formula "3 x 5 in." will be understood, or may be explained by parol evidence, to mean "three by five inches," that is, measuring three inches in one direction and five in another.

Xenodochium /zenədokáyəm/°dókiyəm/. In the civil and old English law, an inn allowed by public license, for the entertainment of strangers, and other guests. Also, a hospital; a place where sick and infirm persons are taken care of.

Xenodochy /zénədòkiy/. Reception of stranger; hospitality.

Xylon /záylon/. A punishment among the Greeks answering to stocks.

Y

Ya et nay. In old records, mere assertion and denial, without oath. See also **Yea and nay.**

Yard. A measure of length, containing three feet, or thirty-six inches.

A piece of land inclosed for the use and accommodation of the inhabitants of a house. Grounds of building or group of buildings.

An enclosure, with or without buildings, devoted to some work or business.

Yardland, or **virgata terræ** /vərgéydə téhriy/. A quantity of land, said by some to be twenty acres, but by Coke to be of uncertain extent.

Yea and nay. Yes and no. According to a charter of Athelstan, the people of Ripon were to be believed in all actions or suits upon their yea and nay, without the necessity of taking any oath. See also **Yeas and nays.**

Year. The period in which the revolution of the earth round the sun, and the accompanying changes in the order of nature, are completed. Generally, when a statute speaks of a year, twelve calendar, and not lunar, months are intended. The year is either astronomical, ecclesiastical, or regnal, beginning on the 1st of January, or 25th of March, or the day of the sovereign's accession.

The civil year differs from the astronomical, the latter being composed of three hundred and sixty-five days, five hours, forty-eight minutes, forty-six seconds and a fraction, while the former consists sometimes of three hundred and sixty-five days, and at others, in leap-years, of three hundred and sixty-six days.

When the period of a "year" is named, a calendar year is generally intended, but the subject-matter or context of statute or contract in which the term is found or to which it relates may alter its meaning.

See also **Current year; Fiscal year; Taxable year.**

Calendar year. See **Calendar.**

Natural year. In old English law, that period of time in which the sum was supposed to revolve in its orbit, consisting of 365 days and one-fourth of a day, or six hours.

Year and day. This period was fixed for many purposes in law. Thus, in the case of an estray, if the owner did not claim it within that time, it became the property of the lord. So the owners of wreck must claim it within a year and a day. Death must follow upon wounding within a year and a day if the wounding is to be indicted as murder. Also, a year and a day were given for prosecuting or avoiding certain legal acts; *e.g.,* for bringing actions after entry, for making claim for avoiding a fine, etc. See also **Year and a day rule.**

Year Books. Books of reports of cases in a regular series from the reign of the English King Edward I, inclusive, to the time of Henry VIII, which were taken by the prothonotaries or chief scribes of the courts, at the expense of the crown, and published annually; whence their name, "Year Books."

Year, day, and waste. In English law, an ancient prerogative of the king, whereby he was entitled to the profits, for a year and a day, of the lands of persons attainted of petty treason or felony, together with the right of wasting the tenements, afterwards restoring the property to the lord of the fee. Abrogated by St. 54 Geo. III, c. 145. See **An, jour, et waste.**

Year of Our Lord. In England the time of an offense may be alleged as that of the sovereign's reign, or as that of the year of our Lord. The former is the usual mode. Hence there "year" alone might not indicate the time intended, but as we have no other era, therefore, any particular year must mean that year in our era. The abbreviation A.D. may be omitted; and the word year is not fatal.

Year to year, tenancy from. This estate arises either expressly, as when land is let from year to year; or by a general parol demise, without any determinate interest, but reserving the payment of an annual rent; or impliedly, as when property is occupied generally under a rent payable yearly, half-yearly, or quarterly; or when a tenant holds over, after the expiration of his term, without having entered into any new contract, and pays rent (before which he is tenant on sufferance). See, also, **Tenant,** subtitle *Tenant from year to year.*

Years, estate for. See **Estate for years.**

Year and a day rule. At common law, death could not be attributed to defendant's wrongful conduct unless it occurred within a year and a day of the conduct. The rationale for this rule was the lack of medical precision in determining cause after such a long period of time, coupled with the very real probability of an intervening cause being responsible for the death. In view of the medical advances of the twentieth century, it can be argued that the year and a day rule is obsolete and should be discarded. Although some jurisdictions have done this either by legislation or judicial decision, most jurisdictions have not. See Elliott v. Mills, Okl.Cr.App., 335 P.2d 1104.

Yearly. See **Annual; Annually.**

Year of mourning. The Roman "annus luctus" *(q.v.).*

The reason for the widow's year of mourning has been stated as follows: "But if a man dies, and his widow soon after marries again, and a child is born within such a time as by the course of nature it might have been the child of either husband, in this case he is said to be more than ordinarily legitimate; for he may, when he arrives at years of discretion, choose which of the fathers he pleases. To prevent this, the civil law ordained that no widow should marry for one year, and the same constitution was probably transmitted to our ancestors from the Romans, during their stay in Britain, for we find it established under the Saxon and Danish governments." 1 Bl. Comm. 456.

Year to year tenancy. See **Tenancy.**

Yeas and nays. The affirmative and negative votes on a bill or measure before a legislative assembly. "Calling the yeas and nays" is calling for the individual and oral vote of each member, usually upon a call of the roll.

Yellow dog contract. A contract by which employer requires employee to sign an instrument promising as condition that he will not join a union during its continuance, and will be discharged if he does join. Denver Local Union No. 13 of International Brotherhood of Teamsters, Chauffeurs, Stablemen, and Helpers of America v. Perry Truck Lines, 106 Colo. 25, 101 P.2d 436, 443. Such contracts are prohibited by the National Labor Relations Act, the Norris LaGuardia Act and the Railway Labor Act.

Yellow journalism. Type of journalism which distorts and exploits the news by sensationalism in order to sell copies of the newspapers or magazines.

Yeme /yíym/. In old records, winter; a corruption of the Latin *"hiems".*

Yeoman /yówmən/. In English law, a commoner; a freeholder under the rank of gentleman. A man who has free land of forty shillings by the year; who was anciently thereby qualified to serve on juries, vote for knights of the shire, and do any other act, where the law requires one that is *probus et legalis homo.* 1 Bl.Comm. 406, 407.

This term is occasionally used in American law, but without any definite meaning, except in the United States navy, where it designates an appointive petty officer who performs clerical duties usually associated with office workers.

Yeomanry /yówmənriy/. The collected body of yeomen.

Yeomen of the guard. Properly called "yeomen of the guard of the royal household;" a body of men of the best rank under the gentry, and of a larger stature than ordinary, every one being required to be six feet high.

Yeven, or **yeoven** /yívən/. Given; dated.

Yick Wo doctrine. Doctrine which takes its name from the case of Yick Wo v. Hopkins, 118 U.S. 356, 6 S.Ct. 1064, 30 L.Ed. 220, to the effect that a law or ordinance which gives a person or body of persons absolute discretion to give or withhold permission to carry on a lawful business is in violation of the 14th Amendment, U.S.Const.

Yiddish. A Middle High German dialect, or number of dialects, spoken by Jews, containing a large number of Germanized Hebrew words, and using Hebrew characters for its literature.

Yield. To give up, relinquish, or surrender. Term also refers to a return from an investment or expenditure. The dividends or interest paid by a company expressed as a percentage of the current price. See also **Net yield; Yield upon investment.**

In old English law, to perform a service due by a tenant to his lord. Hence the usual form of reservation of a rent in a lease began with the words "yielding and paying."

Yielding and paying. In conveyancing, the initial words of that clause in leases in which the rent to be paid by the lessee is mentioned and reserved.

Yield upon investment. Proportionate rate which the income upon an investment bears to the total cost, taking into consideration the time when the investment may be outstanding before being paid off. Baltimore Mail S. S. Co. v. United States, D.C.Md., 7 F.Supp. 651, 653.

Yokelet /yówklət/. A little farm, requiring but a yoke of oxen to till it.

Yom Kippur. Day of Atonement; is the most sacred and solemn holiday in the Jewish calendar, a day on which Jews throughout the world, after a period of fasting, congregate together at their respective synagogues to worship and pray and ask divine forgiveness for sins committed during the year. Hoffman v. Graber, Mo.App., 153 S.W.2d 817, 818.

York-Antwerp rules /yórk æntwərp rùwlz/. Certain rules relating to uniform bills of lading and also governing settlement of maritime losses among the several interests such as ship owners, cargo owners, etc. These rules are commonly incorporated in contracts of affreightment. They are the result of conferences of representatives of mercantile interests from several countries, in the interest of uniformity of law. They have no statutory authority.

York, Custom of. A custom of the province of York in England, by which the effects of an intestate, after payment of his debts, were in general divided according to the ancient universal doctrine of the *pars rationabilis;* that is, one-third each to the widow, children, and administrator. 2 Bl.Comm. 518.

York, Statute of. An important English statute passed at the city of York, in the twelfth year of Edward II, containing provisions on the subject of attorneys, witnesses, the taking of inquests by *nisi prius,* etc.

Youth. This word includes children and young persons of both sexes.

Youthful offenders. Those youths who are treated as delinquents and not as criminals in the juvenile courts. The qualifying age differs from state to state.

Z

Zamindar. See **Zemindar.**

Zanja /sánha/. Span. A water ditch or artificial canal, and particularly one used for purposes of irrigation.

Zanjero /sanhérow/. Span. A water commissioner or superintendent, or supervisor of an irrigation system.

Zealous witness. An untechnical term denoting a witness, on the trial of a cause, who manifests a partiality for the side calling him, and an eager readiness to tell anything which he thinks may be of advantage to that side.

Zeir /yír/. O. Sc. Year. *"Zeir and day."*

Zemindar /zəmíyndàr/zæmən°/zémən°/. In Hindu law, landkeeper. An officer who under the Mohammedan government was charged with the financial superintendence of the lands of a district, the protection of the cultivators, and the realization of the government's share of its produce, either in money or kind.

Zetetick. Proceeding by inquiry.

Zone of employment. Within which injuries to employees are compensable under workmen's compensation acts, is the place of employment and the area thereabout, including the means of ingress thereto and egress therefrom under the control of the employer. Merz v. Industrial Commission of Ohio, 134 Ohio St. 36, 15 N.E.2d 632, 633, 11 O.O. 414. It implies reasonable proximity to place of employment. Evans v. Workmen's Compensation Commissioner, 124 W.Va. 336, 20 S.E.2d 172, 173.

Zone theory. In law of trespass and nuisance, flights above one's property may be actionable depending upon whether they are in the airspace of the lower zone or in the zone beyond the owner's "effective possession". Smith v. New England Aircraft Co., 270 Mass. 511, 170 N.E. 385.

Right of privacy is primarily restraint upon unwarranted governmental interference or intrusion into areas deemed to be within protected "zones of privacy." Industrial Foundation of the South v. Texas Indus. Acc. Bd., Tex., 540 S.W.2d 668, 679.

Zoning. The division of a city by legislative regulation into districts and the prescription and application in each district of regulations having to do with structural and architectural designs of buildings and of regulations prescribing use to which buildings within designated districts may be put.

See also Buffer-zone; Cluster zoning; Comprehensive zoning plan; Conforming use; Land use planning; Master plan; Official map; Planned unit development; Special exception; Special use permit; Spot zoning; Variance.

Aesthetic zoning. Zoning regulations designed to preserve the aesthetic features or values of an area.

Cluster zoning. Zoning regulations and laws designed to provide no greater residential density than the basic minimum lot size zoning district.

Conditional zoning. The imposition of specific restrictions upon the landowner as a condition of full realization of the benefit of rezoning.

Contract zoning. Rezoning of a property to a less restrictive zoning classification subject to an agreement by the landowner to observe certain specified limitations on the uses and physical development of the property that other properties in the zone are not required to observe. This device is used particularly in dealing with property located in a more restrictive zone but on the borderline of the less restrictive zone, for which classification the rezoning is sought.

Density zoning. Type of cluster zoning which regulates open spaces, density of population and use of land. Chrinko v. South Brunswick Township Planning Board, 77 N.J.Super. 594, 187 A.2d 221. Density zoning requires state enabling legislation. Under this device, the city council determines what percentage of a particular district must be devoted to open space and what percentage may be used for dwelling units. The task of locating in the particular district the housing and open spaces devolves upon the planning commission working in conjunction with the developer. The latter will submit a series of plans and seek approval to go forward at each stage. See also **Planned Unit Development.**

Euclidean zoning. Type of zoning based on district-and-use. It envisions the specification of determined geographic areas separated according to zoning districts with the uses permitted in each district set forth in the ordinances. Thus, a property owner could from the zoning map determine in what type of district the property was located and by reference to the district's restrictions what uses are permitted. Village of Euclid v. Ambler Realty Co., 272 U.S. 365, 47 S.Ct. 114, 71 L.Ed. 303.

Exclusionary zoning. Type of zoning which has been challenged on the grounds that it serves to erect exclusionary walls on the municipality's boundary according to local selfishness for socially improper goals which are beyond the legitimate purpose of zoning. The trend in the courts is to strike down such zoning.

Floating zone. In an attempt to avoid the inflexibility of mapped districts, some communities have created exceptional use districts to allow small tracts for such uses as shopping centers, garden type apartments or light industry. At time of ordinance approval the district is unlocated.

Spot zoning. Changing the zoning of a particular piece of land without regard to the zoning plan for the area. See also **Spot zoning.**

Zoning map. The map created by a zoning ordinance which displays the various zoning districts.

Zygocephalum /zàygowséfələm/. In the civil law, a measure or quantity of land. As much land as a yoke of oxen could plow in a day.

Zygostates /zàygowstéydiyz/. In the civil law, a weigher; an officer who held or looked to the balance in weighing money between buyer and seller; an officer appointed to determine controversies about the weight of money.

*

APPENDICES

*

TABLE OF ABBREVIATIONS

A

A.	Atlantic Reporter.
A.2d	Atlantic Reporter, Second Series.
A.B.A.J.	American Bar Association Journal.
Abb.	Abbott, U.S.
Abb.Adm.	Abbott's Admiralty, U.S.
Abb.App.Dec.	Abbott's Appeals Decisions, N.Y.
Abb.Beech.Tr.	Abbott's Reports of the Beecher Trial.
Abb.Dec.	Abbott's Decisions, N.Y.
Abb.Dig.	Abbott New York Digest.
Abb.Law Dict.	Abbott's Law Dictionary.
Abb.N.C.	Abbott's New Cases, N.Y.
Abb.Prac.	Abbott's Practice, N.Y.
Abb.Prac.N.S.	Abbott's Practice, New Series, N.Y.
A'Beck.Res.Judgm.	A'Beckett's Reserved Judgments, Vict.
Abr.	Abridgment.
1917, A.C.	1917, Appeal Cases, Can.
1918, A.C.	Law Reports, 1918, Appeal Cases, Eng.
Acton	Acton, Eng.
ADAMHA	Alcohol, Drug Abuse and Mental Health Administration.
Adams	Adams Reports, N.H.
Adams, Eq.	Adams' Equity.
Adams L.J.	Adams County Legal Journal, Pa.
A.D.2d	Appellate Division, Second Series, N.Y.
Add.	Addams' Ecclesiastical Reports.
Add.	Addison, Pa.
Add.Ecc.	Addams' Ecclesiastical Reports.
Adj.Sess.	Adjourned Session.
Ad.L.	Administrative Law.
Ad.L.B.	Administrative Law Bulletin.
Ad.L.News	Administrative Law News.
Adol. & El.	Adolphus and Ellis' English King's Bench Reports.
Adol. & El.N.S.	Adolphus and Ellis' English Queen's Bench Reports, New Series.
A. & E.Cas.	American & English Annotated Cases.
A. & E. Enc.L. & Pr.	American & English Encyclopædia of Law & Practice.
A. & E. Ency.Law	American and English Encyclopedia of Law.
A. & E.R.Cas.	American & English Railroad Cases.
AFDC	Aid to Families with Dependent Children.
Aff'd	Affirmed.
Aff'g	Affirming.
AFTR	American Federal Tax Reports.
AID	Agency for International Development.
Aik.	Aikens, Vt.
Aik.Dig.	Aikin's Digest of Laws, Ala.
Air L.Rev.	Air Law Review.
Aka	Also known as
A.K.Marsh.	A. K. Marshall, Ky.
Akron L.Rev.	Akron Law Review.
Ala.	Alabama Reports.
Ala.App.	Alabama Appellate Court.
Ala.Civ.App.	Alabama Civil Appeals.
Ala.Cr.App.	Alabama Criminal Appeals.
Ala.L.J.	Alabama Law Journal.
Ala.L.Rev.	Alabama Law Review.
Ala.Sel.Cas.	Alabama Select Cases.
Alaska	Alaska Reporter.
Alaska	Alaska Reports.
Alaska B.J.	Alaska Bar Journal.
Alb.Law J.	Albany Law Journal.
Alb.L.Rev.	Albany Law Review.
Alc. & N.	Alcott & Napier, Eng.
Alc.Reg.Cas.	Alcock's Registry Cases, Eng.
Ald.	Alden's Condensed Reports, Pa.
Aleyn	Aleyn, Eng.
ALI	American Law Institute.
Allen	Allen, Mass.
Allen N.B.	Allen, New Brunswick.
Allinson	Allinson, Pennsylvania Superior and District Court.
A.L.R.	American Law Reports.
A.L.R.2d	American Law Reports, Second Series.
A.L.R.3d	American Law Reports, Third Series.
Alta.L.	Alberta Law.
Amb.	Ambler's English Chancery Reports.

Am.Bankr.L.J.	American Bankruptcy Law Journal.
Am.Bankr.Reg.	National Bankruptcy Register, U.S.
Am.Bankr.Rep.	American Bankruptcy Reports.
Am.Bankr.Rep.N.S.	American Bankruptcy Reports, New Series.
A.M.C.	American Maritime Cases.
Am.C.L.J.	American Civil Law Journal, N.Y.
Am.Corp.Cas.	American Corporation Cases.
Am.Cr.	American Criminal.
Am.Dec.	American Decisions.
Am.Dig.	American Digest.
Am.Ed.	American Edition.
Am.Enc.Dict.	American Encyclopedic Dictionary.
Amend.	Amendment.
Am. & Eng.Corp.Cas.	American & English Corporation Cases.
Am. & Eng.Corp.Cas. N.S.	American & English Corporation Cases, New Series.
Am. & Eng.Dec.Eq.	American and English Decisions in Equity.
Am. & Eng.Enc.Law	American and English Encyclopedia of Law.
Am. & Eng.Pat.Cas.	American and English Patent Cases.
Am. & Eng.Ry.Cas.	American and English Railway Cases.
Am. & Eng.Ry.Cas. N.S.	American & English Railroad Cases, New Series.
Am.Ins.Rep.	American Insolvency Reports.
Am.J.Int.L.	American Journal of International Law.
Am.Jour.Pol.	American Journal of Politics.
Am.Jour.Soc.	American Journal of Sociology.
Am.Lab.Leg.Rev.	American Labor Legislation Review.
Am.Law Inst.	American Law Institute, Restatement of the Law.
Am.Law J.	American Law Journal.
Am.Law J.N.S.	American Law Journal, New Series.
Am.Law Mag.	American Law Magazine.
Am.Law Rec.	American Law Record, Cin.
Am.Law Reg.	American Law Register.
Am.Law Reg.N.S.	American Law Register, New Series.
Am.Law Reg.O.S.	American Law Register, Old Series.
Am.Law Rev.	American Law Review.
Am.Law T.Rep.	American Law Times Reports.
Am.Lead.Cas.	American Leading Cases, Hare & Wallace's.
Am.Leg.N.	American Legal News.

Am.L.S.Rev.	American Law School Review.
Am.L.T.Bankr.	American Law Times Bankruptcy Reports.
Am.Negl.Cas.	American Negligence Cases.
Am.Negl.R.	American Negligence Reports.
A.M. & O.	Armstrong, Macartney & Ogle, Ir.
Am.Pol.Sci.Rev.	American Political Science Review.
Am.Pr.	American Practice.
Am.Prob.	American Probate.
Am.Prob.N.S.	American Probate, New Series.
Am.R. & Corp.	American Railroad & Corporation.
Am.Rep.	American Reports.
Am.R.Rep.	American Railway Reports.
Am.St.Rep.	American State Reports.
Am.St.R.D.	American Street Railway Decisions.
Amtrak	National Railroad Passenger Corporation.
Am.Tr.M.Cas.	Cox's American Trade Mark Cases.
Am.U.L.	American University Law Review.
Anc.Charters	Ancient Charters, 1692.
And.	Anderson, Eng.
Andr.	Andrews, Eng.
Ann.	Queen Anne, as 8 Ann. c. 19; Annotated.
Ann.Cas.	American & English Annotated Cases; American Annotated Cases.
Ann.Cas.1912A	American Annotated Cases 1912A, et seq.
Ann.Code	Annotated Code.
Ann.Codes & St.	Bellinger and Cotton's Annotated Codes and Statutes, Or.
Ann.St.	Annotated Statutes.
Ann.St.Ind.T.	Annotated Statutes of Indian Territory.
Ann.Survey	Annual Survey of Massachusetts Law.
Anstr.	Anstruther's English Exchequer Reports.
Anth.N.P.	Anthon's Nisi Prius Reports, N.Y.
Antitrust L.J.	Antitrust Law Journal.
APA	Administrative Procedure Act.
App.	Appleton, Me.
App.Cas.	Appeal Cases, English Law Reports.
App.D.C.	Appeal Cases, D.C.
App.Div.	Appellate Division, N.Y.
App.Div.2d	Appellate Division, Second Series, N.Y.
Append.	Appendix.
A.R.C.	American Ruling Cases.
Archb.Cr.Law	Archbold's Pleading and Evidence in Criminal Cases.
Archb.Cr.Prac. & Pl.	Archbold's Pleading and Evidence in Criminal Cases.

Arch.Cr.Pl.	Archbold's Criminal Pleading.
Arch.N.P.	Archbold's Law of Nisi Prius.
Ariz.	Arizona Reports.
Ariz.App.	Arizona Appeals.
Ariz.B.J.	Arizona Bar Journal.
Ariz.L.Rev.	Arizona Law Review.
Ariz.State L.J.	Arizona State Law Journal.
Ark.	Arkansas Reports.
Ark.Just.	Arkley's Justiciary, Sc.
Ark.L.J.	Arkansas Law Journal, Fort Smith.
Ark.Stats.	Arkansas Statutes.
Arms.Br.P.Cas.	Armstrong's Breach of Privilege Cases, N.Y.
Arms.Con.Elec.	Armstrong's Contested Elections, N.Y.
Arn.	Arnold, Eng.
Arn. & H.	Arnold & Hodges, Eng.
A.R.S.	Arizona Revised Statutes.
AS	Alaska Statutes.
Ashm.	Ashmead, Pa.
Aspin.	Aspinall's Maritime Cases, Eng.
Assem.	Assembly, State Legislature.
Atk.	Atkyns' English Chancery Reports.
A.T.L.A.J.	American Trial Lawyers Association Journal.
Att'y Gen.	Attorney General.
Att'y Gen.Rep.	United States Attorney General's Reports.
Aust.Jur.	Austin's Jurisprudence.
Austr.C.L.R.	Commonwealth Law Reports, Australia.
Austr.Jur.	Australian Jurist.
Austr.L.T.	Australian Law Times.

B

Bac.Abr.	Bacon's Abridgment.
Bac.Law Tracts	Bacon's Law Tracts.
Bac.Max.	Bacon's Maxims of the Law.
B. & Ad.	Barnewall & Adolphus, Eng.
Bail.	Bailey, S.C.
Bailey, Dict.	Nathan Bailey's English Dictionary.
Bailey, Eq.	Bailey's Equity, S.C.
B. & Ald.	Barnewall and Alderson's English King's Bench Reports.
Baldw.	Baldwin, U.S.
Ball & B.	Ball & Beatty, Ir.
Ballinger's Ann. Codes & St.	Ballinger's Annotated Codes and Statutes, Wash.
Balt.L.Tr.	Baltimore Law Transcript.
Ban. & A.	Banning & Arden's Patent Cases, U.S.
Bank.Cas.	Banking Cases.
Bank.Ct.Rep.	Bankrupt Court Reports.
Bank. & Ins.R.	Bankruptcy and Insolvency Reports, Eng.
Bank.L.J.	Banking Law Journal.

Bankr.Act	Bankruptcy Act.
Bankr.Form	Bankruptcy Forms.
Bankr.Rule	Bankruptcy Rules.
Bann.	Bannister, Eng.
Bann. & A.	Banning & Arden, U.S.
Bar	Bar, The, West Virginia.
Barb.	Barber, Ark.
Barb.	Barbour, N.Y.
Barb.Ch.	Barbour's Chancery, N.Y.
Barb.Ch.Pr.	Barbour's Chancery Practice.
Barb. & C.Ky.St.	Barbour and Carroll's Kentucky Statutes.
Barn.	Barnardiston King's Bench, Eng.
B. & Arn.	Barron & Arnold, Eng.
Barn. & Adol.	Barnewall and Adolphus' English King's Bench Reports.
Barn. & Ald.	Barnewall and Alderson's English King's Bench Reports.
Barn. & C.	Barnewall and Cresswell's English King's Bench Reports.
Barn.Ch.	Barnardiston Chancery, Eng.
Barnes	Barnes' Practice Cases, Eng.
Barnes Notes	Barnes' Notes, Eng.
Barr	Barr, Pa.
Bates' Ann.St.	Bates' Annotated Revised Statutes, Ohio.
Bates Ch.	Bates's Chancery Reports, Del.
Bat.Rev.St.	Battle's Revisal of the Public Statutes of North Carolina.
Battle's Revisal	Battle's Revisal of the Public Statutes of North Carolina.
Batts' Rev.St.	Batts' Annotated Revised Civil Statutes, Tex.
Batty	Batty, Ir.
B. & Aust.	Barron & Austin, Eng.
Baxt.	Baxter, Tenn.
Bay	Bay, S.C.
B. & B.	Broderip & Bingham, Eng.
B.C.	British Columbia.
B. & C.	Barnewall and Cresswell's English King's Bench Reports.
B. & C.Comp.	Bellinger and Cotton's Annotated Codes and Statutes, Or.
B.C.Ind. & Com.L. Rev.	Boston College Industrial and Commercial Law Review.
B.D. & O.	Blackham, Dundas & Osborne, Ir.
Beasl.	Beasley, N.J.
Beatty	Beatty, Ir.
Beav.	Beavan's English Rolls Court Reports.
Beavan, Ch.	Beavan's English Rolls Court Reports.
Beaver	Beaver County Legal Journal, Pa.

Beav.R. & C.Cas. ___ English Railway and Canal Cases.

Beav. & Wal.Ry.Cas. Beavan & Walford's Railway and Canal Cases, Eng.

Beawes' Lex Merc. __ Beawes' Lex Mercatoria.

Bee _____ Bee, U.S.

Bell. _____ Bellewe, Eng.

Bell App.Cas. _____ Bell's Appeal Cases, Sc.

Bell Cas. _____ Bell's Cases, Sc.

Bell C.C. _____ Bell's Crown Cases, Eng.

Bell, Comm. _____ Bell's Commentaries on the Law of Scotland.

Bell Sc.Cas. _____ Bell's Scotch Court of Session Cases.

Ben. _____ Benedict, U.S.

Ben.Adm. _____ Benedict's American Admiralty Practice.

Bench & Bar _____ Bench and Bar.

Benl. _____ Benloe, Eng.

Benl. & D. _____ Benloe & Dallison, Eng.

Benn. _____ Bennett, Cal.

Benth.Jud.Ev. _____ Bentham's Judicial Evidence.

Berks _____ Berks County Law Journal, Pa.

Best & S. _____ Best and Smith's English Queen's Bench Reports.

B. & H.Cr.Cas. ____ Bennett & Heard Leading Criminal Cases, Eng.

BIA _____ Bureau of Indian Affairs.

Bibb. _____ Bibb, Ky.

Big. _____ Bignell's Reports, India.

Bi-Mo.L.Rev. _____ Bi-Monthly Law Review.

Bin. _____ Binney, Pa.

Bing. _____ Bingham's English Common Pleas Reports.

Bing.N.C. _____ Bingham's New Cases, English Common Pleas.

Biss. _____ Bissell, U.S.

Bitt.W. & P. _____ Bittleson, Wise & Parnell, Eng.

Bl. _____ Henry Blackstone's English Common Pleas Reports.

Black _____ Black, U.S.

Black.Com. _____ Blackstone's Commentaries on the Laws of England.

Black.Cond.Rep. ____ Blackwell's Condensed Reports, Ill.

Black, Const.Law ___ Black on Constitutional Law.

Black.Dict. _____ Black's Law Dictionary.

Blackf. _____ Blackford, Ind.

Black, Interp.Laws__ Black on the Construction and Interpretation of Laws.

Black, Judg. _____ Black on Judgments.

Black, Law Dict. ___ Black's Law Dictionary.

Black, St.Const. ____ Black on Construction and Interpretation of Laws.

Black, Tax Titles ___ Black's Treatise on Tax Titles.

Blackw. Tax Titles _ Blackwell's Tax Titles.

Bla.H. _____ Henry Blackstone's English Common Pleas, Eng.

Blair Co. _____ Blair County, Pa.

Bland _____ Bland, Md.

Bland's Ch. _____ Bland Chancery, Md.

Blatchf. _____ Blatchford, U.S.

Blatchf. & H. _____ Blatchford & Howland, U.S.

Blatchf.Prize Cas. __ Blatchford's Prize Cases, U.S.

Bl.Comm. _____ Blackstone's Commentaries on the Laws of England.

Bligh _____ Bligh, Eng.

Bligh N.S. _____ Bligh, New Series, Eng.

BLM _____ Bureau of Land Management.

BLS _____ Bureau of Labor Statistics.

B. & Macn. _____ Browne & Macnamara, Eng.

B.Mon. _____ B. Monroe, Ky.

BNA _____ Bureau of National Affairs.

Bond _____ Bond, U.S.

Bos. & P. _____ Bosanquet and Puller's English Common Pleas Reports.

Bos. & P.N.R. _____ Bosanquet and Puller's New Reports, English Common Pleas.

Bost.L.R. _____ Boston Law Reporter.

Boston B.J. _____ Boston Bar Journal.

Boston College L.Rev. Boston College Law Review.

Boston U.L.Rev. ___ Boston University Law Review.

Bost.Pol.Rep. _____ Boston Police Court Reports.

Bosw. _____ Bosworth, N.Y.

Bouv.Inst. _____ Bouvier's Institutes of American Law.

Bouv.Law Dict. ____ Bouvier's Law Dictionary.

Boyce _____ Boyce, Del.

B. & P. _____ Bosanquet & Puller's English Common Pleas Reports.

B. & P.N.R. _____ Bosanquet & Puller's New Reports, Eng.

Bract. _____ Bracton de Legibus et Consuetudinibus Angliæ.

Bradb. _____ Bradbury's Pleading and Practice Reports, N.Y.

Bradf.Sur. _____ Bradford's Surrogate, N.Y.

Bradw. _____ Bradwell, Ill.

Branch _____ Branch, Fla.

Brayt. _____ Brayton, Vt.

B.R.C. _____ British Ruling Cases.

Breese _____ Breese, Ill.

Brev. _____ Brevard, S.C.

Brev.Dig. _____ Brevard's Digest of the Public Statute Law, S.C.

Brewst. _____ Brewster, Pa.

Brick.Dig. _____ Brickell's Digest, Ala.

Brightly _____ Brightly, Pa.

Brightly, Dig. _____ Brightly's Analytical Digest of the Laws of the United States.

Brightly, N.P. _____ Brightly's Nisi Prius Reports, Pa.

Bro.C.C. _____ Brown's English Chancery Cases or Reports.
Bro.Ch. _____ Brown's Chancery, Eng.
Bro.Civ.Law _____ Browne's Civil and Admiralty Law.
Brock. _____ Brockenbrough, U.S.
Brock.Cas. _____ Brockenbrough's Virginia Cases.
Brock. & H. _____ Brockenbrough & Holmes, Va.
Brod. & B. _____ Broderip & Bingham's English Common Pleas Reports.
Brod. & Fr. _____ Broderick & Fremantle's Ecclesiastical Cases.
Brodix Am. & E. Pat.Cas. _____ Brodix's American & English Patent Cases.
Bro.Just. _____ Broun's Justiciary, Sc.
Brooke, Abr. _____ Brooke's Abridgment.
Brooke N.C. _____ Brooke's New Cases.
Brooklyn Daily Rec. Brooklyn Daily Record.
Brooklyn L.Rev. ____ Brooklyn Law Review.
Brook N.Cas. _____ Brook's New Cases, Eng.
Broom & H.Comm. __ Broom and Hadley's Commentaries on the Laws of England.
Broom, Leg.Max. ___ Broom's Legal Maxims.
Broom's Com.Law __ Broom's Commentaries on the Common Law.
Bro.P.C. _____ Brown's Parliament Cases, Eng.
Brown, Adm. _____ Brown's Admiralty, U.S.
Brown, C.C. _____ Brown's English Chancery Cases or Reports.
Brown, Ch. _____ Brown's English Chancery Reports.
Browne _____ Browne, Pa.
Brown Ecc. _____ Brown Ecclesiastical, Eng.
Browne, Civ.Law ___ Browne's Civil and Admiralty Law.
Browne, Jud.Interp. _ Browne's Judicial Interpretation of Common Words and Phrases.
Brown. & L. _____ Browning & Lushington, Eng.
Brownl. & G. _____ Brownlow and Goldsborough, English Common Pleas Reports.
Brown N.P. _____ Brown's Michigan Nisi Prius.
Brown, Parl.Cas. ___ Brown, Parliamentary Cases, Eng.
Brown's Roman Law_ Brown's Epitome and Analysis of Savigny's Treatise on Obligations in Roman Law.
BRTA _____ Bureau of Resources and Trade Assistance.
Bruce _____ Bruce, Sc.
Brunner, Col.Cas. __ Brunner's Collected Cases, U.S.
B. & S. _____ Best & Smith, Eng.
BTA _____ Board of Tax Appeals Reports.
Buck _____ Buck, Eng.
Bucks _____ Bucks County Law Reporter, Pa.
Buffalo L.Rev. _____ Buffalo Law Review.

Buff.Super.Ct. _____ Sheldon's Buffalo Superior Court Reports, N.Y.
B.U.L.Rev. _____ Boston University Law Review.
Bulletin Comp.L. ___ Bulletin, Comparative Law Bureau.
Bull.N.P. _____ Buller's Law of Nisi Prius.
Bulst. _____ Bulstrode's English King's Bench Reports.
Bump Fraud.Conv. __ Bump on Fraudulent Conveyances.
Bump's Int.Rev.Law_ Bump's Internal Revenue Laws.
Bunb. _____ Bunbury, Eng.
Burl.Natural & Pol. Law _____ Burlamaqui's Natural and Politic Law.
Burn. _____ Burnett, Wis.
Burn, J.P. _____ Burn's Justice of the Peace.
Burns' Ann.St. ____ Burns' Annotated Statutes, Ind.
Burns' Ecc.Law ____ Burns' Ecclesiastical Law.
Burns' Rev.St. ____ Burns' Annotated Statutes, Ind.
Burr. _____ Burrows' English King's Bench Reports.
Burr.S.Cas. _____ Burrows' Settlement Cas., Eng.
Busb. _____ Busbee, N.C.
Busb.Eq. _____ Busbee's Equity, N.C.
Bush _____ Bush, Ky.
Bus.Law _____ The Business Lawyer.
Bus.L.Rev. _____ Business Law Review.

C

C. _____ California Reports.
C.2d _____ California Reports, Second Series.
C.3d _____ California Reports, Third Series.
C.A. _____ California Appellate Reports.
C.A.2d _____ California Appellate Reports, Second Series.
C.A.3d _____ California Appellate Reports, Third Series.
C.A.Supp. _____ California Appellate Department of the Superior Court.
C.A.2d Supp. _____ California Appellate Department of the Superior Court, Second Series.
C.A.3d Supp. _____ California Appellate Department of the Superior Court, Third Series.
CAB _____ Civil Aeronautics Board.
Cab. & El. _____ Cababé and Ellis' Queen's Bench Reports.
Caines _____ Caines, N.Y.
Caines, Cas. _____ Caines' Cases, N.Y.
Cal. _____ California Reports.
Cal.2d _____ California Reports, Second Series.
Cal.3d _____ California Reports, Third Series.

Cal.App. _____ California Appellate Reports.

Cal.App.Dec. _____ California Appellate Decisions.

Cal.App.2d _____ California Appellate Reports, Second Series.

Cal.App.3d _____ California Appellate Reports, Third Series.

Calcutta L.J. _____ Calcutta Law Journal.

Cald. _____ Caldecott, Eng.

Cal.Dec. _____ California Decisions.

Cal.Jur. _____ California Jurisprudence.

Call _____ Call, Va.

Cal.Leg.Rec. _____ California Legal Record, San Francisco.

Cal.L.J. _____ California Law Journal, San Francisco.

Cal.L.Rev. _____ California Law Review.

Cal.Rptr. _____ California Reporter.

Calthr. _____ Calthrop, Eng.

Cal.Unrep. _____ California Unreported Cases.

Calvin, Lex. _____ Calvin's Lexicon Juridicum.

Cambria _____ Cambria County Legal Journal, Pa.

Cambridge L.J. _____ Cambridge Law Journal.

Cam.Cas. _____ Cameron's Cases, Can.

Cam. & N. _____ Cameron & Norwood's Conference, N.C.

Camp. _____ Campbell's English Nisi Prius Reports.

Canada L.T. _____ Canadian Law Times.

Canal Zone _____ Canal Zone Supreme Court.

Can.App.Cas. _____ Canadian Appeal Cases.

Can.Cr.Cas. _____ Canadian Criminal Cases.

Cane & L. _____ Cane & Leigh Crown Cases Reserved, Eng.

Can.Exch. _____ Canadian Exchequer.

Can.Leg.N. _____ Canada Legal News.

Can.L.J. _____ Canada Law Journal.

Can.L.J.N.S. _____ Canada Law Journal, New Series.

Can.L.T.Occ.Notes __ Canadian Law Times Occasional Notes.

Can.R.Cas. _____ Canadian Railway Cases.

Can.S.C. _____ Canada Supreme Court.

CAP _____ Civil Air Patrol.

Car. _____ Carolus, as 22 & 23 Car. II.

Car.H. & A. _____ Carrow, Hamerton & Allen, Eng.

Car. & K. _____ Carrington and Kirwan's English Nisi Prius Reports.

Car.Law Repos. ____ Carolina Law Repository, N.C.

Car. & P. _____ Carrington & Payne's English Nisi Prius Reports.

Carp.P.C. _____ Carpmael Patent Cases, Eng.

Carr. & M. _____ Carrington and Marshman's English Nisi Prius Reports.

Cart. _____ Carter, Ind.

Carter _____ Carter, Eng.

Carth. _____ Carthew's English King's Bench Reports.

Cartwr.Cas. _____ Cartwright's Cases, Can.

Carv.Carr. _____ Carver's Treatise on the Law Relating to the Carriage of Goods by Sea.

Cary _____ Cary, Eng.

Case & Com. _____ Case and Comment.

Case W.Res.L.Rev. __ Case Western Reserve Law Review.

Casey _____ Casey, Pa.

Cas.temp.Hard. _____ Cases temp. Hardwicke by Lee and Hardwicke.

Cas.t.Hardw. _____ Cases temp. Hardwicke, Eng.

Cas.t.Holt _____ Cases temp. Holt, Eng.

Cas.t.King _____ Cases temp. King, Eng.

Cas.t.Talb. _____ Cases temp. Talbot, Eng.

Cates _____ Cates Reports, Tenn.

Catholic U.L.Rev. ___ Catholic University of America Law Review.

CB _____ Cumulative Bulletin of Internal Revenue Service.

C.B. _____ English Common Bench Reports, Manning, Granger & Scott.

C.B.N.S. _____ English Common Bench Reports, New Series, by John Scott.

CBO _____ Congressional Budget Office.

C.C.A. _____ Circuit Court of Appeals U.S.

CCC _____ Commodity Credit Corporation.

CCH _____ Commerce Clearing House.

C.C.P. _____ Code of Civil Procedure, Calif.

C.C.P.A. _____ Court of Customs and Patent Appeals.

C.D. _____ Current Digest, American Digest System; Certificate of Deposit.

CDC _____ Center for Disease Control.

CEA _____ Council of Economic Advisers.

C.E.Green _____ C. E. Green, N.J.

Cent.Dict. _____ Century Dictionary.

Cent.Dict. & Ency.__ Century Dictionary and Encyclopedia.

Cent.Dig. _____ Century Digest.

Cent.Law J. _____ Central Law Journal, St. Louis, Mo.

CEQ _____ Council on Environmental Quality.

Cert. denied _____ Certiorari denied.

CFR _____ Code of Federal Regulations.

CFTC _____ Commodity Futures Trading Commission.

C.G.S.A. _____ Connecticut General Statutes Annotated.

1891 Ch. _____ Law Reports, 1891, Chancery, Eng.

Chambers' Cyclopædia _____ Ephraim Chambers' English Cyclopædia.

Chamb.Rep. _____ Chamber, Ont.

Chand. _____ Chandler, Wis.

Chan.Sentinel _____ Chancery Sentinel, N.Y.

Ch.App.	Chancery Appeal Cases, English Law Reports.	Cir.Ct.R.	Circuit Court Reports, Ohio.
Charlt., R.M.	R. M. Charlton, Ga.	Cir.Ct.Rule	Circuit Court Rule.
Charlt., T.U.P.	T. U. P. Charlton, Ga.	City Ct.R.	City Court Reports, N.Y.
Chase	Chase, U.S.	City Ct.R.Supp.	City Court Reports, Supplement, N.Y.
Chase's St.	Chase's Statutes at Large, Ohio.	City Hall Rep.	City Hall Reporter, Lomas, N.Y.
Chase, Steph.Dig.Ev.	Chase on Stephens' Digest of Evidence.	City H.Rec.	City Hall Recorder, N.Y.
Ch.Cas.	English Cases in Chancery.	Civ.Code	Civil Code.
		Civ.Code Practice	Civil Code of Practice.
Ch.Chamb.	Chancery Chambers, U.C.	Civ.Prac.Act	Civil Practice Act.
Ch.Col.Op.	Chalmers' Colonial Opinions.	Civ.Proc.R.	Civil Procedure Reports, N.Y.
Ch.D.	Law Reports Chancery Division, Eng.	C.J.	Corpus Juris.
Ch.Div.	Chancery Division, English Law Reports.	C.J.Ann.	Corpus Juris Annotations.
		C.J.S.	Corpus Juris Secundum.
Chest.Co.Rep.	Chester County Reports, Pa.	C. & K.	Carrington and Kirwan's English Nisi Prius Reports.
Cheves	Cheves, S.C.		
Cheves, Eq.	Cheves' Equity, S.C.	C.L.	English Common Law Reports, American Reprint.
Chicago Bar Rec.	Chicago Bar Record.		
Chicago-Kent L.Rev.	Chicago-Kent Law Review.	C. & L.	Connor & Lawson, Ir.
Chicago L.B.	Chicago Law Bulletin, Ill.	Cl.App.	Clark's Appeal Cases, Eng.
Chicago L.J.	Chicago Law Journal.	Clark	Clark, Pa.
Chicago L.Rec.	Chicago Law Record.	Clarke	Clarke, Iowa.
Chicago L.T.	Chicago Law Times.	Clarke, Ch.	Clarke's Chancery, N.Y.
Chi.Leg.N.	Chicago Legal News, Ill.	Clarke & S.Dr.Cas.	Clarke & Scully's Drainage Cases, Ont.
Chip., D.	D. Chipman, Vt.		
Chip., N.	N. Chipman, Vt.	Clark & F.	Clark and Finnelly's House of Lords Reports.
Chit.	Chitty, Eng.		
Chit.Bills	Chitty on Bills.		
Chit.Bl.Comm.	Chitty's Edition of Blackstone's Commentaries.	Clark's Code	Clark's Annotated Code of Civil Procedure, N.C.
Chit.Cont.	Chitty on Contracts.	Clay's Dig.	Clay's Digest of Laws of Alabama.
Chit.Cr.Law	Chitty's Criminal Law.		
Chit.Gen.Pr.	Chitty's General Practice.	Clayt.	Clayton's Reports, York Assizes, Eng.
Chit.Pl.	Chitty on Pleading.	Cl.Ch.	Clarke's Chancery, N.Y.
Chit.Pr.	Chitty's General Practice.	C.L.Chamb.	Chamber's Common Law, U.C.
Chitty	Chitty on Bills.	Cleve.Law Rec.	Cleveland Law Recorder, Ohio.
Chitty, Bl.Comm.	Chitty's Edition of Blackstone's Commentaries.	Cleve.Law Rep.	Cleveland Law Reporter, Ohio.
Chitty, Com.Law	Chitty on Commercial Law.	Clev.Insan.	Clevenger's Medical Jurisprudence of Insanity.
Choyce Cas.Ch.	Choyce Cases in Chancery, Eng.	Clev.St.L.Rev.	Cleveland State Law Review.
Ch.Pl.	Chitty on Pleading.		
Ch.Rep.	Chancery Reports, Eng.	Clev.-Mar.L.Rev.	Cleveland-Marshall Law Review.
CIA	Central Intelligence Agency.	Cl. & F.	Clark & Finnelly, Eng.
CIEP	Council on International Economic Policy.	Clif.El.Cas.	Clifford's Southwick Election Cases.
Cinc.L.Bul.	Weekly Law Bulletin, Ohio.	Cliff.	Clifford, U.S.
		C.L.R.	California Law Review.
Cin.Law Bull.	Cincinnati Law Bulletin, Ohio.	C.L.R.	Common Law Reports, Eng.
Cin.L.Rev.	Cincinatti Law Review.	C. & M.	Carrington & Marshman, Eng.
Cin.R.	Cincinnati Superior Court Reports, Ohio.	C.M.R.	Court-Martial Reports.
Cin.Super.Ct.Rep'r	Cincinnati Superior Court Reporter, Ohio.	C., M. & R.	Crompton, Meeson, and Roscoe's English Exchequer Reports.
Cir.	Circuit (Court of Appeals).	Co.	Coke's English King's Bench Reports; Company.
Cir.Ct.Dec.	Circuit Decisions, Ohio.		

Cobb, Dig.	Cobb's Digest of Statute Laws, Ga.		**Cong.**	Congress.
Cobbey, Repl.	Cobbey's Practical Treatise on the Law of Replevin.		**Cong.Rec.**	Congressional Record.
			Con. & Law.	Connor & Lawson, Ir.
			Conn.	Connecticut Reports.
			Conn.Bar J.	Connecticut Bar Journal.
Cobbey's Ann.St.	Cobbey's Annotated Statutes, Neb.		**Conn.Cir.**	Connecticut Circuit Court Reports.
Cock. & Rowe	Cockburn & Rowe's Election Cases.		**Conn.L.Rev.**	Connecticut Law Review.
Code Civ.Proc.	Code of Civil Procedure.		**Conn.Supp.**	Connecticut Supplement.
Code Cr.Proc.	Code of Criminal Procedure.		**Conn.Surr.**	Connecticut Surrogate.
			Const.	Constitution.
Code Gen.Laws	Code of General Laws.		**Con.St.**	Consolidated Statutes.
Code Prac.	Code of Practice.		**Const.Amend.**	Amendment to Constitution.
Code Proc.	Code of Procedure.			
Code Pub.Gen.Laws	Code of Public General Laws.		**Const.Rep.**	Constitutional Reports, S.C.
Code Pub.Loc.Laws	Code of Public Local Laws.		**Const.Rev.**	Constitutional Review.
			Const.U.S.Amend.	Amendment to the Constitution of the United States.
Code Rep.	Code Reporter, N.Y.			
Code R.N.S.	Code Reports, New Series, N.Y.		**Con.Sur.**	Connoly's Surrogate, N.Y.
Code Supp.	Supplement to the Code.		**Cooke**	Cooke, Eng.
Cod.St.	Codified Statutes.		**Cooke**	Cooke, Tenn.
Co.Inst.	Coke's Institutes.		**Cooke & A.**	Cooke & Alcock, Ir.
Coke	Coke's English King's Bench Reports.		**Cook Vice-Adm.**	Cook's Vice-Admiralty, L.C.
Col.C.C.	Collyer's Chancery Cases, Eng.		**Cooley, Bl.Comm.**	Cooley's Edition of Blackstone's Commentaries.
Cold.	Coldwell, Tenn.			
Colem.Cas.	Coleman's Cases, N.Y.		**Cooley, Const.Law**	Cooley's Constitutional Law.
Colem. & C.Cas.	Coleman & Caines' Cases, N.Y.		**Cooley, Const.Lim.**	Cooley's Constitutional Limitations.
Co.Litt.	Coke on Littleton.			
Coll.	Collyer, Eng.		**Coop.**	Cooper's English Chancery Reports temp. Eldon.
Col.Law Review	Columbia Law Review.			
Coll. & E.Bank	Collier and Eaton's American Bankruptcy Reports.		**Coop.Eq.Pl.**	Cooper's Equity Pleading.
			Cooper Tenn.Ch.	Cooper's Tennessee Chancery Reports.
Colles	Colles' Cases in Parliament, Eng.		**Coop.Pr.Cas.**	Cooper's Practice Cases, Eng.
Colly.	Collyer's English Chancery Cases.		**Coop.t.Brough.**	Cooper's Cases temp. Brougham, Eng.
Colo.	Colorado Reports.		**Coop.t.Cott.**	Cooper's Cases temp. Cottenham, Eng.
Colo.App.	Colorado Court of Appeals Reports.		**Coop.t.Eld.**	Cooper's Cases temp. Eldon, Eng.
Colo.Law.	Colorado Lawyer.			
Colo.Law Rep.	Colorado Law Reporter.		**Copp, Pub.Land Laws**	Copp's United States Public Land Laws.
Colq.	Colquit.			
Colq.Rom.Civ.Law	Colquhoun's Roman Civil Law.		**Copy.Bull.**	Copyright Bulletin.
			Corb. & D.	Corbett & Daniell's Election Cases, Eng.
Coltm.	Coltman, Eng.			
Colum.L.Rev.	Columbia Law Review.		**Co.Rep.**	Coke's English King's Bench Reports.
Comb.	Comberbach, Eng.			
Com.Cas.	Commercial Cases, Eng.		**Cornell L.F.**	Cornell Law Forum.
Com.Dig.	Comyns' Digest of the Laws of England.		**Cornell L.J.**	Cornell Law Journal.
Com.L.	Commercial Law, Can.		**Cornell L. Q.**	Cornell Law Quarterly.
Com.L.J.	Commercial Law Journal.		**Cornell L.Rev.**	Cornell Law Review.
Comm.	Commentaries.		**Court. & Macl.**	Courtnay & Maclean, Sc.
Comp.Gen.	Comptroller General Decisions.		**Cow.**	Cowen, N.Y.
			Cow.Cr.R.	Cowen's Criminal Reports, N.Y.
Comp.Laws	Compiled Laws.			
Comp.St.	Compiled Statutes.		**Cowell**	Cowell's Law Dictionary.
Comptr.Treas.Dec.	Comptroller Treasury Decisions.		**Cowp.**	Cowper's English King's Bench Reports.
Comst.	Comstock, N.Y.		**Cox**	Cox, Ark.
Comyn	Comyns' English King's Bench Reports.		**Cox**	Cox's English Chancery Cases.
Comyns' Dig.	Comyns' Digest, Eng.		**Cox Am.T.M.Cas.**	Cox's American Trade-Mark Cases.
Conf.R.	Conference Reports, N.C.			

Cox & Atk. _____ Cox & Atkinson, Eng.
Cox, C.C. _____ Cox's English Criminal
                      Cases.
Cox Ch. _____ Cox's Chancery, Eng.
Cox, Cr.Cas. _____ Cox's English Criminal
                      Cases.
Coxe _____ Coxe, N.J.
C. & P. _____ Carrington and Payne's
                      English Nisi Prius Re-
                      ports.
CPA _____ Certified Public Ac-
                      countant.
C.P.C. _____ C. P. Cooper's Chancery
                      Practice Cases, Eng.
C.P.D. _____ Law Reports Common
                      Pleas Division, Eng.
C.P.Div. _____ Common Pleas Division,
                      English Law Reports.
C.P.Rep. _____ Common Pleas Report-
                      er, Pa.
Crabbe _____ Crabbe, U.S.
Crabb, Eng. _____ Crabb's English Syno-
                      nyms.
Cr.Act _____ Criminal Act.
Craig, Dict. _____ Craig's Etymological,
                      Technological, and
                      Pronouncing Diction-
                      ary.
Craig & P. _____ Craig and Phillips' Eng-
                      lish Chancery Reports.
Cranch _____ Cranch, U.S.
Cranch, C.C. _____ Cranch's Circuit Court,
                      U.S.
Cranch, Pat.Dec. _____ Cranch's Patent Deci-
                      sions, U.S.
Cr.App. _____ Criminal Appeals, Eng.
Crawf. & D. _____ Crawford & Dix, Ir.
Crawf. & D. Abr.
  Cas. _____ Crawford & Dix's
                      Abridged Cases, Ir.
Cr.Cir.Comp. _____ Crown Circuit Compan-
                      ion, Irish.
Cr.Code _____ Criminal Code.
Creighton L.Rev. _____ Creighton Law Review.
Crim.L.Rptr. _____ Criminal Law Reporter.
Cripp's Ch.Cas. _____ Cripp's Church and
                      Clergy Cases.
Cr.Law Mag. _____ Criminal Law Magazine,
                      N. J.
C.Rob.Adm. _____ Charles Robinson's Eng-
                      lish Admiralty Re-
                      ports.
Cro.Car. _____ Croke's English King's
                      Bench Reports temp.
                      Charles I, 3 Cro.
Cro.Cas. _____ Croke's English King's
                      Bench Reports temp.
                      Charles I, 3 Cro.
Cro.Eliz. _____ Croke's English King's
                      Bench Reports, temp.
                      Elizabeth, 1 Cro.
Cro.Jac. _____ Croke's English King's
                      Bench Reports temp.
                      James, Jacobus, I, 2
                      Cro.
Cromp. & J. _____ Crompton & Jervis' Eng-
                      lish Exchequer Re-
                      ports.
Cromp.Just. _____ Crompton's Office of
                      Justice of the Peace.
Cromp. & M. _____ Crompton & Meeson,
                      Eng.

Cromp., M. & R. _____ Crompton, Meeson, and
                      Roscoe's English Ex-
                      chequer Reports.
Crompt. _____ Star Chamber Cases by
                      Crompton.
Crosw.Pat.Cas. _____ Croswell's Collection of
                      Patent Cases, U. S.
Cr. & Ph. _____ Craig & Phillips, Eng.
Cr.Prac.Act _____ Criminal Practice Act.
Cr.Proc.Act _____ Criminal Procedure Act.
C.R.S. _____ Colorado Revised Stat-
                      utes.
Cr.St. _____ Criminal Statutes.
Cruise's Dig. _____ Cruise's Digest of the
                      Law of Real Property.
CSC _____ Civil Service Commis-
                      sion.
Ct.Cl. _____ Court of Claims, U.S.
Cr.St. _____ Criminal Statutes.
Cruise's Dig. _____ Cruise's Digest of the
                      Law of Real Property.
Ct.Cl. _____ Court of Claims, U. S.
Ct.Cust. & Pat.App. Court of Customs and
                      Patent Appeals.
Cumb. _____ Cumberland Law Jour-
                      nal, Pa.
Cumb.L.Rev. _____ Cumberland Law Review.
Cumb.-Sam.L.Rev. _____ Cumberland-Samford
                      Law Review.
Cunn. _____ Cunningham, Eng.
Current Ct.Dec. _____ Current Court Deci-
                      sions.
Curt. _____ Curtis, U. S.
Curt.Ecc. _____ Curteis English Ecclesi-
                      astical Reports.
Cush. _____ Cushing, Mass.
Cush.Law & Prac.
  Leg.Assem. _____ Cushing's Law and
                      Practice of Legislative
                      Assemblies.
Cushm. _____ Cushman, Miss.
Cust.A. _____ United States Customs
                      Appeals.
C.W.L.R. _____ California Western Law
                      Review.
Cyc. _____ Cyclopedia of Law and
                      Procedure.
Cyc.Ann. _____ Cyclopedia of Law &
                      Procedure Annota-
                      tions.
Cyc.Law & Proc. _____ Cyclopedia of Law and
                      Procedure.
C.Z.C. _____ Canal Zone Code.

D

Daily Transc. _____ Daily Transcript.
Dak. _____ Dakota Reports (Terri-
                      torial).
Dak.L.Rev. _____ Dakota Law Review.
Dal.C.P. _____ Dalison's Common Pleas,
                      Eng.
Dall. _____ Dallas, Pa.
Dall. _____ Dallas, U. S.
Dall.Dig. _____ Dallam's Digest and
                      Opinions, Tex.
Dall.Laws _____ Dallas' Laws, Pa.
Dalr.Dec. _____ Dalrymple's Decisions,
                      Sc.
Daly _____ Daly, N. Y.
Dan. _____ Daniell, Eng.

Dana	Dana, Ky.
Dane's Abr.	Dane's Abridgment of American Law.
Daniell, Ch.Pl. & Prac.	Daniell's Chancery Pleading and Practice.
Daniell, Ch.Prac.	Daniell's Chancery Pleading and Practice.
Daniel, Neg.Inst.	Daniel's Negotiable Instruments.
Dans. & L.	Danson & Lloyd, Eng.
D'Anv.Abr.	D'Anver's Abridgment, Eng.
Dass.Ed.	Dassler's Edition, Kansas Reports.
Dauph.Co.	Dauphin County, Pa.
Davis, Cr.Law	Davis Criminal Law.
Dav. & M.	Davison & Merivale, Eng.
Davys	Davys, Ir.
Dawson's Code	Dawson's Code of Civil Procedure, Colo.
Day	Day, Conn.
Dayton	Dayton Ohio Reports.
d.b.a.	doing business as.
D.B. & M.	Dunlop, Bell & Murray, Sc.
D.C.	District of Columbia; District Court.
D. & C.	District and County, Pa.
D. & C.2d	District and County, Second Series, Pa.
DCA	Defense Communications Agency.
DCAA	Defense Contract Audit Agency.
D.C.App.	District of Columbia Appeals.
D.C.B.J.	District of Columbia Bar Journal.
D.C.C.E.	District of Columbia Code Encyclopedia.
D.Chip.	D. Chipman, Vt.
D.C.Mun.App.	Municipal Court of Appeals, D.C.
DCPA	Defense Civil Preparedness Agency.
DEA	Drug Enforcement Administration.
Deac.	Deacon, Eng.
Deac. & C.	Deacon & Chitty, Eng.
Deac.Cr.Law	Deacon on Criminal Law of England.
Deady	Deady, U. S.
Dears. & B.	Dearsley & Bell, Eng.
Dears. & B. Crown Cas.	Dearsley and Bell's English Crown Cases.
Dears.C.C.	Dearsley's Crown Cases, Eng.
Deas & A.	Deas & Anderson, Eng.
Dec.Dig.	Decennial Digest.
Defense L.J.	Defense Law Journal.
De Gex	De Gex, Eng.
De Gex, F. & J.	De Gex, Fisher & Jones' English Chancery Reports.
De Gex, J. & S.	De Gex, Jones, and Smith's English Chancery Reports.
De Gex, M. & G.	De Gex, Macnaghten, and Gordon's English Chancery Reports.
De G. & J.	De Gex & Jones, Eng.
De G. & Sm.	De Gex & Smale, Eng.
De Jure Mar.	Hale's De Jure Maris, Appendix to Hall on the Sea Shore.
Del.	Delaware Reports.
Del.Ch.	Delaware Chancery Reports.
Del.County	Delaware County Reports.
Del.Term R.	Delaware Term Reports.
Dem.Sur.	Demarest's Surrogate, N. Y.
Denio	Denio, N. Y.
Denison, Cr.Cas.	Denison's English Crown Cases.
Denver L.J.	Denver Law Journal.
Denver L.N.	Denver Legal News.
De Paul L.Rev.	De Paul Law Review.
Desaus.	Desaussure's Equity, S. C.
Detroit B.Q.	Detroit Bar Quarterly.
Det.Coll.L.Rev.	Detroit College Law Review.
Det.L.J.	Detroit Law Journal.
Detroit L.	Detroit Lawyer.
Det.L.Rev.	Detroit Law Review.
Detroit Leg.N.	Detroit Legal News, Mich.
Detroit L.Rev.	Detroit Law Review.
Dev.	Devereux, N. C.
Dev. & B.	Devereux & Battle, N. C.
Dev. & B.Eq.	Devereux & Battle's Equity, N. C.
Dev.Ct.Cl.	Devereux's Court of Claims, U. S.
Dev.Eq.	Devereux's Equity, N. C.
DIA	Defense Intelligence Agency.
Dicey, Confl.Laws	Dicey on Conflict of Laws.
Dick.	Dickens, Sc.
Dick.	Dickinson, N. J.
Dickens	Dickens' English Chancery Reports.
Dick.L.Rev.	Dickinson Law Review.
Dict.	Dictionary.
Dict.Droit Civil	Dictionnaire Droit Civil.
Dig.	Digest.
Dig.Fla.	Thompson's Digest of Laws, Fla.
Dig.St.	English's Digest of the Statutes, Ark.
Dill.	Dillon, U.S.
Dill.Laws Eng. & Am.	Dillon's Laws and Jurisprudence of England and America.
Dill.Mun.Corp.	Dillon on Municipal Corporations.
Dirl.Dec.	Dirleton's Decisions, Sc.
Disn.	Disney, Ohio.
D. & L.	Dowling & Lowndes, Eng.
DOD	Department of Defense.

Dods.	Dodson's Admiralty, Eng.
DOE	Department of Energy.
Dom.Civ.Law	Domat's Civil Law.
Dom.L.R.	Dominion Law Reports, Can.
Donnelly	Donnelly, Eng.
Dorion	Dorion, L.C.
DOT	Department of Transportation.
Doug.	Douglas' English King's Bench Reports.
Doug.	Douglas, Mich.
Dougl.El.Cas.	Douglas' Election Cases, Eng.
Dow	Dow, Eng.
Dow & C.	Dow and Clark's English House of Lord's Cases.
Dowl.	Dowling's English Bail Court Cases.
Dowl. & L.	Dowling & Lowndes' English Bail Court Reports.
Dowl.P.C.	Dowling's Practice Cases, Eng.
Dowl.P.C.N.S.	Dowling's Practice Cases, New Series, Eng.
Dowl. & R.	Dowling and Ryland's English King's Bench Reports.
Dow.N.S.	Dowling, New Series, Eng.
D. & R.	Dowling & Ryland, Eng.
Drake, Attachm.	Drake on Attachment.
Drake L.Rev.	Drake Law Review.
Draper	Draper, U.C.
Drew.	Drewry, Eng.
Drinkw.	Drinkwater, Eng.
D. & R.Mag.Cas.	Dowling & Ryland's Magistrate Cases, Eng.
D. & R.N.P.	Dowling & Ryland's Nisi Prius, Eng.
Dr. & Sm.	Drewry & Smale. Eng.
Drury	Drury, Ir.
Dr. & Wal.	Drury & Walsh, Ir.
Dr. & War.	Drury & Warren, Ir.
D. & Sw.	Deane & Swabey, Eng.
Dud.	Dudley, Ga.
Dud.Eq.	Dudley's Equity, S.C.
Dud.Law	Dudley's Law, S.C.
Duer	Duer's Superior Court, N.Y.
Duke L.J.	Duke Law Journal.
Dunl. B. & M.	Dunlop, Bell & Murray, Sc.
Dunlop	Dunlop, Sc.
Dunn.	Dunning, Eng.
Dup.Jur.	Duponceau on Jurisdiction of United States Courts.
Duquesne L.Rev.	Duquesne University Law Review.
Durie	Durie, Sc.
Durn. & E.	Durnford and East's English King's Bench Reports, Term Reports.
Dutch.	Dutcher, N.J.
Duv.	Duvall, Ky.
Dyer	Dyer's English King's Bench Reports.

E

East	East's English King's Bench Reports.
East.L.R.	Eastern Law Reporter, Can.
East, P.C.	East's Pleas of the Crown.
East.T.	Eastern Term, Eng.
E. & B.	Ellis and Blackburn's English Queen's Bench Reports.
E.B. & E.	Ellis, Blackburn & Ellis, Eng.
E.B. & S.	Ellis, Best & Smith, Eng.
Eccl.R.	English Ecclesiastical Reports.
E.C.L.	English Common Law Reports, American Reprint.
Ecology L.Q.	Ecology Law Quarterly.
Ed.	Edition.
Eden	Eden, Eng.
Eden, Pen.Law	Eden's Principles of Penal Law.
Eden's Prin.P.L.	Eden's Principles of Penal Law.
Edgar	Edgar, Sc.
Edmonds' St. at Large	Edmonds' Statutes at Large, N.Y.
Edm.Sel.Cas.	Edmonds' Select Cases, N.Y.
E.D.Smith	E.D.Smith, N.Y.
Edw.	King Edward, as 4 Edw. I.
Edw.Abr.	Edwards' Abridgment of Prerogative Court Cases.
Edw.Adm.	Edwards' Admiralty, Eng.
Edw.Bailm.	Edwards on the Law of Bailments.
Edw.Bills & N.	Edwards on Bills and Notes.
Edw.Brok. & F.	Edwards on Factors and Brokers.
Edw.Ch.	Edwards' Chancery, N.Y.
Edw.Rec.	Edwards on Receivers in Equity.
E. & E.	Ellis & Ellis, Eng.
EEOC	Equal Employment Opportunity Commission.
EHS	Environmental Health Services.
El. & Bl.	Ellis and Blackburn's English Queen's Bench Reports.
El., Bl. & El.	Ellis, Blackburn, and Ellis' English Queen's Bench Reports.
E.L. & Eq.	English Law and Equity, American Reprint.
Eliz.	Queen Elizabeth, as 13 Eliz.
Elliot, Deb.Fed. Const.	Elliot's Debates on the Federal Constitution.
Elliott, Supp.	Elliott Supplement to the Indiana Revised Statutes.

Ellis & Bl.	Ellis and Blackburn's English Queen's Bench Reports.
Elm.Dig.	Elmer's Digest of Laws, N.J.
Em.App.	Emergency Court of Appeals, U.S.
Emerig.Assur.	Emerigon, Traité des Assurances et des Contrats à la Grosse.
Emory L.J.	Emory Law Journal.
Enc.Amer.	Encyclopædia Americana.
Enc.Brit.	Encyclopædia Britannica.
Enc.Ins.U.S.	Insurance Year-Book.
Enc.Law	American and English Encyclopædia of Law.
Enc.Pl. & Prac.	Encyclopedia of Pleading and Practice.
End.Interp.St.	Endlich's Commentaries on the Interpretation of Statutes.
Eng.	English, Ark.
Eng.Ad.	English Admiralty.
Eng.C.C.	English Crown Cases.
Eng.Ch.	English Chancery.
Eng.C.L.	English Common Law Reports, American Reprint.
Eng.Ecc.R.	English Ecclesiastical Reports, American Reprint.
Eng.Exch.	English Exchequer Reports.
Eng. & Ir.App.	Law Reports, English and Irish Appeal Cases.
Eng.Law & Eq.	English Law and Equity Reports, American Reprint.
Eng.Rep.R.	English Reports, Full Reprint.
Eng.Ry. & C.Cas.	English Railway and Canal Cases.
Env.L.Rev.	Environmental Law Review.
Env.L.Rptr.	Environmental Law Reporter.
EO	Executive Order.
EPA	Environmental Protection Agency.
Eq.	Equity.
Eq.Cas.Abr.	English Equity Cases Abridged.
Eq.Rep.	Equity Reports, Eng.
E.R.C.	English Ruling Cases.
ERDA	Energy Research and Development Administration.
Erie	Erie County Legal Journal, Pa.
ERISA	Employee Retirement Income Security Act.
Ersk.Inst.	Erskine's Institutes of the Law of Scotland.
ESA	Employment Standards Administration.
Escriche, Dict.	Escriche's Dictionary of Jurisprudence.
ESA	Employment Standards Administration.
ESOP	Employee Stock Ownership Plan.
Esp.	Espinasse's English Nisi Prius Reports.
Euer	Euer, Eng.
Eur.L.Rev.	European Law Review.
Ev.	Evidence.
Ex.	English Exchequer Reports, Welsby, Hurlstone & Gordon.
Exch.	English Exchequer Reports, Welsby, Hurlstone & Gordon.
Exch.Cas.	Exchequer Cases, Sc.
Exch.Div.	Exchequer Division, English Law Reports.
Ex.D.	Law Reports, Exchequer Division, Eng.
Exec.Order	Executive Order.
Ex.Sess.	Extra Session.
Eyre	Eyre's Reports, Eng.

F

F.	Federal Reporter.
F.2d	Federal Reporter, Second Series.
FAA	Federal Aviation Administration.
Fairf.	Fairfield, Me.
Falc.	Falconer's Court of Sessions, Sc.
Falc. & F.	Falconer & Fitzherbert, Eng.
Falc.Marine Dict.	Falconer's Marine Dictionary.
Family L.Q.	Family Law Quarterly.
Far.	Farresley, Eng.
Faust	Faust's Compiled Laws, S. C.
Fay.L.J.	Fayette Legal Journal, Pa.
FBI	Federal Bureau of Investigation.
FCA	Farm Credit Administration.
FCC	Federal Communications Commission.
FCIA	Foreign Credit Insurance Association.
FCIC	Federal Crop Insurance Corporation.
FCS	Farmer Cooperative Service.
F.Ct.Sess.	Fraser's Court of Sessions Cases, Sc.
FDA	Food and Drug Administration.
FDAA	Federal Disaster Assistance Administration.
FDIC	Federal Deposit Insurance Corporation.
FDPC	Federal Data Processing Centers.
FEA	Federal Energy Administration.
FEBs	Federal Executive Boards.
Fed.B.News	Federal Bar News.
Fed.Cas.	Federal Cases, U.S.
Fed.Evid.R.	Federal Rules of Evidence.
Fed.L.Rev.	Federal Law Review.

Fed.R.App.P.	Federal Rules of Appellate Procedure.
Fed.R.Civil P.	Federal Rules of Civil Procedure.
Fed.R.Crim.P.	Federal Rules of Criminal Procedure.
Fed.Reg.	Federal Register.
Ferg.Cons.	Ferguson's Consistory, Eng.
Fernald, Eng. Synonyms	Fernald's English Synonyms.
F. & F.	Foster & Finlason, Eng.
FGIS	Federal Grain Inspection Service.
FHA	Federal Housing Administration.
FHLB	Federal Home Loan Bank.
FHLBB	Federal Home Loan Bank Board.
FHLMC	Federal Home Loan Mortgage Corporation (Freddie Mac).
FHWA	Federal Highway Administration.
FIA	Federal Insurance Administration.
FIC	Federal Information Centers.
FICA	Federal Income Contribution Act; Federal Insurance Contribution Act.
Fiduciary	Fiduciary Reporter. Pa.
Finch, Law	Finch, Sir Henry; a Discourse of Law, 1759.
Fish.Dig.	Fisher's English Common Law Digest.
Fish.Pat.Cas.	Fisher's Patent Cases, U. S.
Fish.Pat.Rep.	Fisher's Patent Reports, U. S.
Fish.Prize Cas.	Fisher's Prize Cases, U. S.
Fitz.Abridg.	Fitzherbert's Abridgment, Eng.
Fitzg.	Fitzgibbon, Eng.
Fitzh.N.Br.	Fitzherbert's Natura Brevium, Eng.
Fla.	Florida Reports.
Fla.B.J.	Florida Bar Journal.
Fla.L.J.	Florida Law Journal.
Fla.St.U.L.Rev.	Florida State University Law Review.
Flip.	Flippin, U. S.
Flipp.	Flippin, U. S.
Fl. & K.	Flanagan & Kelly, Ir.
FMC	Federal Maritime Commission.
FMCS	Federal Mediation and Conciliation Service.
FmHA	Farmers Home Administration.
FNMA	Federal National Mortgage Association (Fannie Mae).
FOIA	Freedom of Information Act.
Fonbl.	Fonblanque, Eng.
Fonbl.Eq.	Fonblanque's Equity, Eng.

Fonbl.R.	Fonblanque's English Cases.
Forbes	Forbes, Eng.
Ford.L.Rev.	Fordham Law Review.
Forr.	Forrest, Eng.
Forrester	Forrester's Cases, Eng.
Fortesc.	Fortescue, Eng.
Fost.	Foster, Eng.
Fost.	Foster, N. H.
Fost.Crown Law	Foster's English Crown Law or Crown Cases.
Foster	Legal Chronicle Reports by Foster, Pa.
Fost. & F.	Foster and Finlason's English Nisi Prius Reports.
Fount.Dec.	Fountainhall's Decisions, Sc.
Fox	Fox Reports, Eng.
Fox & S.	Fox & Smith, Ir.
FPA	Federal Preparedness Agency.
FPC	Federal Power Commission.
F.R.	Federal Register.
FRB	Federal Reserve Board.
F.R.D.	Federal Rules Decisions.
Freem.	Freeman, Ill.
Freem.Ch.	Freeman's Chancery, Eng.
Freem.Ch.	Freeman's Chancery, Miss.
Freem.K.B.	Freeman's King's Bench, Eng.
FRS	Federal Reserve System.
F.S.A.	Florida Statutes Annotated.
FSLIC	Federal Savings and Loan Insurance Corporation.
FSQS	Food Safety and Quality Service.
FSS	Federal Supply Service.
F.Supp.	Federal Supplement.
FTC	Federal Trade Commission.
FTS	Federal Telecommunications System.
FWS	Fish and Wildlife Service.

G

G.	King George, as 15 Geo. II.
Ga.	Georgia Reports.
Ga.App.	Georgia Appeals.
Ga.B.J.	Georgia Bar Journal.
Gabb.Cr.Law	Gabbett's Criminal Law.
Ga.Code Ann.	Georgia Code Annotated.
Ga.Dec.	Georgia Decisions.
Ga.L.J.	Georgia Law Journal.
Ga.L.Rev.	Georgia Law Review.
Gale	Gale, Eng.
Gale's St.	Gale's Statutes, Ill.
Gall.	Gallison, U.S.
Ga.L.Rep.	Georgia Law Reporter.
GAO	General Accounting Office.
Gard.N.Y.Rep.	Gardenier's New York Reporter.

Ga.St.B.J. _____ Georgia State Bar Journal.

GATT _____ General Agreement on Tariffs and Trade.

Gav. & H.Rev.St. ___ Gavin and Hord's Revised Statutes, Ind.

Gavel _____ Milwaukee Bar Ass'n Gavel.

G.Coop. _____ G. Cooper, Eng.

G. & D. _____ Gale & Davidson, Eng.

Gear, Landl. & T. __ Gear on Landlord and Tenant.

Geld. & M. _____ Geldart & Maddock, Eng.

Gen.Assem. _____ General Assembly.

Gen.Dig.U.S. _____ General Digest of the United States.

Gen.Laws _____ General Laws.

Gen.R.R.Act _____ General Railroad Act.

Gen.St. _____ General Statutes.

Geo. _____ King George, as 15 Geo. II.

George _____ George, Miss.

Georgetown L.J. ___ Georgetown Law Journal.

Geo.Wash.L.Rev. ____ George Washington Law Review.

Gibb.Surr. _____ Gibbon's Surrogate, N.Y.

Giffard _____ Giffard, Eng.

Giff. & H. _____ Giffard and Hemming, Eng.

Gil. _____ Gilfillan, Minn.

Gilb. _____ Gilbert's Eng.

Gilb.Cas. _____ Gilbert's Cases, Eng.

Gilb.C.P. _____ Gilbert's Common Pleas, Eng.

Gilb.Exch. _____ Gilbert's Exchequer, Eng.

Gild. _____ Gildersleeve Reports, N.M.

Gill _____ Gill, Md.

Gill & J. _____ Gill & Johnson, Md.

Gilman _____ Gilman, Ill.

Gilmer _____ Gilmer, Va.

Gilm. & Falc. _____ Gilmour & Falconer, Sc.

Gilp. _____ Gilpin, U.S.

Glasc. _____ Glascock, Ir.

Glyn & J. _____ Glyn & Jameson, Eng.

G.M.Dudl. _____ G. M. Dudley's Reports, Ga.

GNMA _____ Government National Mortgage Association.

GNP _____ Gross National Product.

Godb. _____ Godbolt, Eng.

Godo. _____ Godolphin's Abridgment of Ecclesiastical Law.

Goeb. _____ Goebel's Probate Court Cases.

Golden Gate L.Review Golden Gate Law Review.

Gonzaga L.Rev. _____ Gonzaga Law Review.

Gosf. _____ Gosford, Eng.

Gould, Pl. _____ Gould on the Principles of Pleading in Civil Actions.

Gouldsb. _____ Gouldsborough, Eng.

Gould's Dig. _____ Gould's Digest of Laws, Ark.

Gow _____ Gow, Eng.

Gow N.P. _____ Gow's English Nisi Prius Cases.

GPO _____ Government Printing Office.

Grant, Cas. _____ Grant's Cases, Pa.

Grant Ch. _____ Grant's Chancery, U.C.

Grant Err. & App. _ Grant's Error & Appeal, U.C.

Grat. _____ Grattan, Va.

Gray _____ Gray, Mass.

Green Bag _____ Green Bag, A Legal Journal, Boston.

Green, C.E. _____ C. E. Green, N.J.

Green Cr. _____ Green's Criminal Law, Eng.

Green, Cr.Law R. __ Green's Criminal Law Reports, N.Y.

Greene, G. _____ G. Greene, Iowa.

Green, H.W. _____ H. W. Green, N.J.

Green, J.S. _____ J. S. Green, N.J.

Greenl. _____ Greenleaf, Me.

Gross, St. _____ Gross' Illinois Compiled Laws, or Statutes.

Grotius _____ Grotius' Latin Law.

GSA _____ General Services Administration.

Gwill.T.Cas. _____ Gwillim's Tithe Cases, Eng.

H

Hadd. _____ Haddington, Eng.

Hagg.Adm. _____ Haggard's English Admiralty Reports.

Hagg.Cons. _____ Haggard's English Consistory Reports.

Hagg.Ecc. _____ Haggard's English Ecclesiastical Reports.

Hailes Dec. _____ Hailes' Decisions, Sc.

Hale _____ Hale's Common Law, Eng

Hale, Com.Law ____ Hale's History of the Common Law.

Hale, De Jure Mar. Hale's De Jure Maris, Appendix to Hall on the Sea Shore.

Hale Ecc. _____ Hale's Ecclesiastical, Eng.

Hale P.C. _____ Hale's Pleas of the Crown.

Hall _____ Hall's Superior Court, N.Y.

Hall, Mex.Law ____ Hall's Mexican Law.

Hall & T. _____ Hall & Twells, Eng.

Halsbury L.Eng. ___ Halsbury's Law of England.

Halst. _____ Halsted, N.J.

Halst.Ch. _____ Halsted's Chancery, N.J.

Ham. _____ Hammond, Ohio.

Hand _____ Hand, N.Y.

Handy _____ Handy, Ohio.

Han., N.B. _____ Hannay's Reports, New Brunswick.

Har. _____ Harrington, Del.

Har. _____ Harrington, Mich.

Har. _____ Harrison, N.J.

Hardin _____ Hardin, Ky.

Hardres _____ Hardres, Eng.

Hardw.Cas.temp. __ Cases temp. Hardwicke, by Lee and Hardwicke.

Hare _____ Hare's English Vice Chancellors' Reports.

Har. & G. _____ Harris & Gill, Md.

Har. & J. _____ Harris & Johnson, Md.

Har. & McH. _____ Harris & McHenry, Md.

Harg.Co.Litt. _____ Hargrave's Notes to Coke on Littleton.

Hargrave & Butler's
  Notes on Co.Litt. — Hargrave and Butler's Notes on Coke on Littleton.
Harp. — Harper, S.C.
Harp.Eq. — Harper's Equity, S.C.
Harr. — Harrison's Chancery, Mich.
Harr.Ch. — Harrison's Chancery, Eng.
Harr. & H. — Harrison & Hodgins, U.C.
Harr. & R. — Harrison & Rutherford, Eng.
Harr. & W. — Harrison & Wollaston, Eng.
Harris — Harris, Pa.
Harrison, Ch. — Harrison's Chancery Practice.
Hart.Dig. — Hartley's Digest of Laws, Tex.
Harv.Intl.L.J. — Harvard International Law Journal.
Harv.J.Legis. — Harvard Journal on Legislation.
Harv.L.Rev. — Harvard Law Review.
Hasb. — Hasbrouck's Reports, Idaho.
Hask. — Haskell, U.S.
Hastings L.J. — Hastings Law Journal.
Hats. — Hatsell's Parliamentary Precedents.
Havil. — Haviland, Pr.Edw.Isl.
Haw. — Hawaii Reports.
Hawaii B.J. — Hawaii Bar Journal.
Haw.Fed. — Hawaii Federal.
Hawes, Jur. — Hawes on Jurisdiction of Courts.
Hawk. — Hawkins' Pleas of the Crown.
Hawk.P.C. — Hawkins' Pleas of the Crown.
Hawks — Hawks, N.C.
Hawk.Wills — Hawkins' Construction of Wills.
Hay & M. — Hay & Marriott, Eng.
Hayes — Hayes' Irish Exchequer Reports.
Hayes & J. — Hayes & Jones, Ir.
Hayw. — Haywood, N.C.
Hayw. — Haywood, Tenn.
Hayw. & H. — Hayward & Hazelton, U.S.
Haz.Reg. — Hazard's Register, Pa.
H.Bl. — Henry Blackstone's English Common Pleas Reports.
H. & C. — Hurlstone & Coltman, Eng.
Head — Head, Tenn.
Heisk. — Heiskell, Tenn.
Hem. & M. — Hemming & Miller, Eng.
Hemp. — Hempstead, U.S.
Hen. — King Henry, as 8 Hen. VI.
Hen. & M. — Hening & Munford, Va.
Hen.St. — Hening's Statutes, Va.
Het. — Hetley, Eng.
Het.C.P. — Hetley's Common Pleas, Eng.

HEW — Department of Health, Education, and Welfare.
H. & H. — Horn & Hurlstone, Eng.
Hil.Abr. — Hilliard's American Law.
Hill — Hill, N.Y.
Hill — Hill, S.C.
Hill.Am.Law — Hilliard's American Law.
Hill & Den. — Hill & Denio, N.Y.
Hill & D.Supp. — Hill & Denio, Lalor's Supplement, N.Y.
Hill, Eq. — Hill's Equity, S.C.
Hill, Law — Hill's Law, S.C.
Hill's Ann.Codes & Laws — Hill's Annotated Codes and General Laws, Or.
Hill's Ann.St. & Codes — Hill's Annotated General Statutes and Codes, Wash.
Hill's Code — Hill's Annotated Codes and General Laws, Or.
Hill's Code — Hill's Annotated General Statutes and Codes, Wash.
Hilt. — Hilton, N.Y.
Hil.T. — Hilary Term, Eng.
Hil.Term 4, Will. IV. — Hilary Term 4, William IV.
Hittell's Laws — Hittell's General Laws, Cal.
H.L.Cas. — House of Lords' Cases, English.
H. & N. — Hurlstone & Norman, Eng.
Hob. — Hobart's English King's Bench Reports.
Hodg.El. — Hodgins' Election, U.C.
Hodges — Hodges, Eng.
Hoff.Ch. — Hoffman's Chancery, N.Y.
Hoff.Land Cas. — Hoffman's Land Cases, U.S.
Hoff.Mast. — Hoffman's Master in Chancery.
Hofstra L.Rev. — Hofstra Law Review.
Hog. — Hogan, Ir.
Holl.Jur. — Holland's Elements of Jurisprudence.
Holmes — Holmes, U.S.
Holt — Holt's English King's Bench Reports.
Holt Adm.Cas. — Holt's English Admiralty Cases.
Holt Eq. — Holt's Equity, Eng.
Holthouse, Law Dict. — Holthouse's Law Dictionary.
Holt K.B. — Holt's King's Bench, Eng.
Holt, N.P. — Holt's English Nisi Prius Reports.
Home — Home, Sc.
Hope Dec. — Hope's Decisions, Sc.
Hopk.Ch. — Hopkins' Chancery, N.Y.
Hopk.Dec. — Hopkins' Decisions, Pa.
Hopw. & C. — Hopwood & Coltman, Eng.
Hopw. & P. — Hopwood & Philbrick, Eng.
Horner's Ann.St. — Horner's Annotated Revised Statutes, Ind.

Horner's Rev.St.	Horner's Annotated Revised Statutes, Ind.
Hosea	Hosea, Ohio.
Houst.	Houston, Del.
Houst.Cr.Cas.	Houston's Criminal Cases, Del.
Houst.L.Rev.	Houston Law Review.
How.	Howard, Miss.
How.	Howard, U.S.
How.Ann.St.	Howell's Annotated Statutes, Mich.
How.App.Cas.	Howard's Appeal Cases, N.Y.
Howard L.J.	Howard Law Journal.
Howell, N.P.	Howell's Nisi Prius Reports, Mich.
Howell, St.Tr.	Howell's English State Trials.
How. & H.St.	Howard and Hutchinson's Statutes, Miss.
How.St.	Howell's Annotated Statutes, Mich.
HRA	Health Resources Administration.
HRS	Hawaii Revised Statutes.
HSA	Health Services Administration.
HUD	Department of Housing and Urban Development.
Hud. & B.	Hudson & Brooke, Ir.
Hughes	Hughes, Ky.
Hughes	Hughes, U.S.
Hume	Hume's Decisions, Sc.
Hume's Hist.Eng.	Hume's History of England.
Humph.	Humphrey, Tenn.
Hun	Hun, N. Y.
Hurd's Rev.St.	Hurd's Revised Statutes, Ill.
Hurl. & C.	Hurlstone & Coltman's English Exchequer Reports.
Hurl. & G.	Hurlstone and Gordon's Reports, 10, 11, English Exchequer Reports.
Hurl. & N.	Hurlstone and Norman's English Exchequer Reports.
Hurl. & W.	Hurlstone & Walmsley, Eng.
Hutch.Code	Hutchinson's Code, Miss.
Hutt.	Hutton, Eng.

I

I.C.	Idaho Code; Indiana Code; Iowa Code.
ICA	Iowa Code Annotated.
ICC	Indian Claims Commission; Interstate Commerce Commission.
I.C.C.	Interstate Commerce Commission Reports.
IDA	International Development Association.
Iddings D.R.D.	Iddings Dayton Term Reports.
Idaho	Idaho Reports.
Idaho L.J.	Idaho Law Journal.
Idaho L.Rev.	Idaho Law Review.

IFC	International Finance Corporation.
Ill.	Illinois Reports.
Ill.2d	Illinois Reports, Second Series.
Ill.App.	Illinois Appellate Court Reports.
Ill.App.2d	Illinois Appellate Court Reports, Second Series.
Ill.App.3d	Illinois Appellate Court Reports, Third Series.
Ill.Bar J.	Illinois Bar Journal.
Ill.C.C.	Illinois Circuit Court.
Ill.L.B.	Illinois Law Bulletin.
Ill.L.Q.	Illinois Law Quarterly.
Ill.L.Rev.	Illinois Law Review.
Ill.Rev.Stat.	Illinois Revised Statutes, State Bar Association Edition.
ILO	International Labor Organization.
IMF	International Monetary Fund.
Imp.Dict.	Imperial Dictionary.
Inc.	Incorporated.
Ind.	Indiana Reports.
Ind. & Lab.Rel.Rev.	Industrial and Labor Relations Review.
Ind.App.	Indiana Appellate Court Reports.
Ind.J.Int'l.	Indiana Journal of International Law.
Ind.Law J.	Indiana Law Journal.
Ind.Leg.Forum	Indiana Legal Forum.
Ind.L.Reg.	Indiana Legal Register.
Ind.L.Rep.	Indiana Law Reporter.
Ind.L.Rev.	Indiana Law Review; Indian Law Review.
Ind.Super.	Indiana Superior Court Reports (Wilson).
Ind.T.	Indian Territory.
Ind.T.Ann.St.	Indian Territory Annotated Statutes.
Indus.L.J.	Industrial Law Journal.
Indus.L.Rev.	Industrial Law Review.
INS	Immigration and Naturalization Service.
Ins.Law J.	Insurance Law Journal, Pa.
Ins.Rep.	Insurance Reporter, Phila.
Inst.	Coke's Institutes.
Int.Com.Commn.	Interstate Commerce Commission.
Int.Com.Rep.	Interstate Commerce Reports.
Internat.Dict.	Webster's International Dictionary.
INTERPOL	International Criminal Police Organization.
Interst.Com.R.	Interstate Commerce Reports.
Int.L.N.	International Law Notes.
Int.Rev.Bull.	Internal Revenue Bulletin.
Int.Rev.Code	Internal Revenue Code.
Int.Rev.Manual	Internal Revenue Manual.
Int.Rev.Rec.	Internal Revenue Record, N. Y.
Iowa	Iowa Reports.
Iowa L.B.	Iowa Law Bulletin.

Iowa L.Rev. _____ Iowa Law Review.
1891 Ir. _____ Law Reports, 1891, Irish.
IRA _____ Individual Retirement Account.
I.R.B. _____ Internal Revenue Bulletin (Weekly).
I.R.C. _____ Internal Revenue Code.
Ir.Ch. _____ Irish Chancery.
Ir.C.L. _____ Irish Common Law.
Ir.Eccl. _____ Irish Ecclesiastical Reports.
Ired. _____ Iredell's Law, N. C.
Ired.Eq. _____ Iredell's Equity, N. C.
Ir.Eq. _____ Irish Equity.
Ir.Law & Eq. _____ Irish Law and Equity Reports.
Ir.Law Rep. _____ Irish Law Reports.
Ir.R.1894 _____ Irish Law Reports for year 1894.
Ir.R.C.L. _____ Irish Reports Common Law.
Ir.R.Eq. _____ Irish Reports Equity.
I.R.S. _____ Illinois Revised Statutes; Internal Revenue Service.
Irv.Just. _____ Irvine's Justiciary Cases, Eng.
Irwin's Code _____ Clark, Cobb and Irwin's Code, Ga.
I.T. _____ Income Tax Ruling.
ITU _____ International Telecommunications Union.

J

Jac. _____ Jacob, Eng.
Jac. _____ King James, as 21 Jac. I.
Jac.Law Dict. _____ Jacob's Law Dictionary.
Jac. & W. _____ Jacob & Walker, Eng.
JAG _____ Judge Advocate General.
JAG Bull. _____ JAG Bulletin (USAF)
JAG J. _____ JAG Journal.
JAG L.Rev. _____ United States Air Force JAG Law Review.
JATLA L.J. _____ Journal of American Trial Lawyers Association.
J.Bridgm. _____ John Bridgman, Eng.
J. & C. _____ Jones & Carey, Ir.
JCS _____ Joint Chiefs of Staff.
Jebb & B. _____ Jebb & Bourke, Ir.
Jebb C.C. _____ Jebb's Crown Cases, Ir.
Jebb & S. _____ Jebb & Symes, Ir.
Jeff. _____ Jefferson, Va.
Jenk. _____ Jenkins, Eng.
Jeremy, Eq. _____ Jeremy's Equity Jurisdiction.
J.J.Marsh. _____ J. J. Marshall, Ky.
J. & L. _____ Jones & La Touche, Eng.
JOBS _____ Job Opportunities in the Business Sector.
John. _____ Johnson, N. M.
John.Dict. _____ Johnson's English Dictionary.
John.Eng.Ch. _____ Johnson's English Vice-Chancellors' Reports.
John Marshall L.J. __ John Marshall Law Journal.
John Marshall L.Q. __ John Marshall Law Quarterly.
Johns. _____ Johnson, Eng.

Johns. _____ Johnson, N. Y.
Johns.Cas. _____ Johnson's Cases, N. Y.
Johns.Ch. _____ Johnson's Chancery, N. Y.
Johns. & H. _____ Johnson & Hemming, Eng.
Johnson's Quarto
  Dict. _____ Johnson's Quarto Dictionary.
Jones _____ Jones, Pa.
Jones, Eq. _____ Jones' Equity, N. C.
Jones Exch. _____ Jones Exchequer, Ir.
Jones, Law _____ Jones' Law, N. C.
Jones & S. _____ Jones & Spencer, N. Y.
Jones T. _____ Sir Thomas Jones' English King's Bench Reports.
Jones & V.Laws ____ Jones and Varick's Laws, N. Y.
Jones W. _____ Sir William Jones' English King's Bench Reports.
Jour.Am.Jud.Soc. ___ Journal of the American Judicature Society.
Jour.Comp.Leg. ____ Journal of the Society of Comparative Legislation.
Jour.Conat.Law ____ Journal of Conational Law.
Jour.Crim.L. _____ Journal of Criminal Law and Criminology.
Jour.Juris. _____ Journal of Jurisprudence.
J.P. _____ The Justice of the Peace, London, periodical; Justice of the Peace.
J.P.Smith _____ J. P. Smith's English King's Bench Reports.
J.Scott, N.S. _____ English Common Bench Reports, New Series, by John Scott.
Jud.Pan.Mult.Lit. ___ Judicial Panel on Multidistrict Litigation.
Jud.Repos. _____ Judicial Repository, N. Y.
Jur. _____ The Jurist, London.
Jurid.Rev. _____ Juridical Review.
Jur.N.S. _____ The Jurist, New Series, London.
Just.Inst. _____ Institutes of Justinian.
Just.L.R. _____ Justices' Law Reporter, Pa.

K

Kames Dec. _____ Kames' Decisions, Sc.
Kames Elucid. _____ Kames' Elucidation, Sc.
Kames Rem.Dec. ___ Kames' Remarkable Decisions, Sc.
Kames Sel.Dec. ____ Kames' Select Decisions, Sc.
Kan. _____ Kansas Reports.
Kan.App. _____ Kansas Appeals.
Kan.C.L.Rep. _____ Kansas City Law Reporter.
Kan.Law. _____ Kansas Lawyer.
Kan.L.J. _____ Kansas Law Journal.
Kan.L.Rev. _____ University of Kansas Law Review.
Kay _____ Kay, Eng.

Kay & J.	Kay and Johnson's English Vice Chancellors' Reports.
1917 K.B.	Law Reports, 1917, King's Bench, Eng.
K.B.J.	Kansas Bar Journal.
Keane & Gr.	Keane & Grant, Eng.
Keb.	Keble's English King's Bench Reports.
Keen	Keen's English Rolls Court Reports.
Keen, Ch.	Keen's English Rolls Court Reports.
Keilway	Keilway's English King's Bench Reports.
Kel.	Sir John Kelyng's English Crown Cases.
Kelly	Kelly, Ga.
Kelyng, J.	Kelyng's English Crown Cases.
Kelynge, W.	Kelynge's Chancery, Eng.
Kent, Comm.	Kent's Commentaries on American Law.
Kent & R.St.	Kent and Radcliff's Law of New York, Revision of 1801.
Kern.	Kernan, N.Y.
Kersey, Dict.	John Kersey's English Dictionary, 1708.
Keyes	Keyes, N.Y.
Keyl.	Keilway, Eng.
K. & G.	Keane & Grant, Eng.
Kilk.	Kilkerran's Decisions, Sc.
Kinney, Law Dict. & Glos.	Kinney's Law Dictionary and Glossary.
Kirby	Kirby, Conn.
Knapp	Knapp, Eng.
Knapp & O.	Knapp & Ombler, Eng.
Kn. & Moo.	Knapp & Moore, Eng.
Knox	Knox, N.S.Wales.
Knox & F.	Knox & Fitzhardinge, N.S.Wales.
K. & R.	Kent and Radcliff's Law of New York, Revision of 1801.
KRS	Kentucky Revised Statutes.
K.S.A.	Kansas Statutes Annotated.
Kulp	Kulp, Pa.
Ky.	Kentucky Reports.
Ky.Dec.	Kentucky Decisions.
Ky.Law Rep.	Kentucky Law Reporter.
Ky.L.J.	Kentucky Law Journal.
Ky.Op.	Kentucky Opinions.
Ky.St.Law	Morehead and Brown Digest of Statute Laws, Ky.

L

La.	Louisiana.
La.A. (Orleans)	Court of Appeal, Parish of Orleans.
La.Ann.	Louisiana Annual.
La.App.	Louisiana Court of Appeals.
Lab.	Labatt's District Court, Cal.
Lack.Bar	Lackawanna Bar, Pa.
Lack.Jur.	Lackawanna Jurist, Pa.

Lack.Leg.N.	Lackawanna Legal News, Pa.
Lack.Leg.Rec.	Lackawanna Legal Record, Pa.
La.L.J.	Louisiana Law Journal, Schmidt's.
Lalor, Supp.	Lalor's Supplement to Hill & Denio's Reports, N.Y.
Lamb.Eir.	Lambard's Eiranarcha.
Lanc.Bar	Lancaster Bar.
Lanc.Law Rev.	Lancaster Law Review.
Land Dec.	Land Decisions, U.S.
Land & Water L.R.	Land & Water Law Review.
Lane	Lane, Eng.
Lans.	Lansing, N.Y.
Lans.Ch.	Lansing's Chancery, N.Y.
Latch	Latch, Eng.
Law. & Bank.	Lawyer and Banker.
Law Bull.	Law Bulletin, San Francisco.
Law Forum	University of Ill. Law Forum.
Law J.Ch.	Law Journal, New Series, Chancery.
Law J.Exch.	Law Journal, New Series, Exchequer.
Law J.Q.B.	Law Journal, New Series, Queen's Bench, Eng.
Law Lib.J.	Law Library Journal.
Law.L.J.	Lawrence Law Journal, Pa.
Law Mag. & Rev.	Law Magazine and Review.
Law Notes	Law Notes.
Law Q.Rev.	Law Quarterly Review.
Law Rep.	Monthly Law Reporter, Boston, Mass.
Law Rep.Ex.	English Law Reports, Exchequer.
Law Rep.N.S.	Law Reports, New Series, N.Y.
Law Stud.H.	Law Students' Helper.
Law T.	English Law Times Reports.
Law T., N.S.	English Law Times Reports, New Series.
L.C.	Lower Canada.
L. & C.	Leigh & Cave, Eng.
L.C.Jur.	Lower Canada Jurist.
L.C.L.J.	Lower Canada Law Journal.
L.C.Rep.S.Qu.	Lower Canada Reports Seignorial Questions.
L.D.	Law Dictionary.
Ld.Ken.	Lord Kenyon, Eng.
Ld.Raym.	Lord Raymond's English King's Bench Reports.
Lea	Lea, Tenn.
LEAA	Law Enforcement Assistance Administration.
Leach, Cr.Cas.	Leach's English Crown Cases.
Leach's C.L.	Leach's Club Cases, London.
Leam. & Spic.	Leaming and Spicer's Laws, Grants, Concessions and Original Constitutions, N.J.

Lebanon	Lebanon County Legal Journal, Pa.
L.Ed.	Lawyers' Edition Supreme Court Reports.
L.Ed.2d	Lawyers' Edition Supreme Court Reports, Second Series.
Lee	Lee, Cal.
Lee Eccl.	Lee's Ecclesiastical, Eng.
Lee t.Hardw.	Lee temp. Hardwicke, Eng.
Lef.Dec.	Lefevere's Parliamentary Decisions, Eng.
Leg.	Acts of the Legislature.
Leg.Chron.	Legal Chronicle.
Leg.Gaz.	Legal Gazette, Pa.
Leg.Gaz.R.	Legal Gazette Reports, Pa.
Leg. & Ins.Rep.	Legal & Insurance Reporter.
Leg.Int.	Legal Intelligencer, Pa.
Leg.News	Legal News, Chicago.
Leg.Op.	Legal Opinions.
Leg.Rec.	Legal Record, Pa.
Leg.Rec.Rep.	Legal Record Reports, Pa.
Leg.Rep.	Legal Reporter, Tenn.
Leh.L.J.	Lehigh Law Journal, Pa.
Lehigh Val.Law Rep.	Lehigh Valley Law Reporter.
Leigh	Leigh, Va.
Leigh & C.	Leigh and Cave's English Crown Cases.
Leon.	Leonard's English King's Bench Reports.
L. & E.Rep.	Law & Equity Reporter, N.Y.
Lev.	Levinz's English King's Bench Reports.
Lewin, Cr.Cas.	Lewin's English Crown Cases Reserved.
Lewis, Em.Dom.	Lewis on Eminent Domain.
Lewis, Perp.	Lewis' Law of Perpetuity.
Ley	Ley, Eng.
L.G.	Law Glossary.
Liberian L.	Liberian Law.
Litt.	Coke on Littleton.
Litt.	Littell, Ky.
Litt.Comp.Laws	Littell's Statute Law, Ky.
Litt. & S.St.Law	Littell and Swigert's Digest of Statute Law, Ky.
Litt.Sel.Cas.	Littell's Select Cases, Ky.
Liv.Jud.Op.	Livingston's Judicial Opinions, N.Y.
Liv.Law Mag.	Livingston's Law Magazine, N.Y.
Liv.L.Reg.	Livingston's Law Register, N.Y.
L.J.	Law Journal.
L.J.Adm.	Law Journal Admiralty, New Series, Eng.
L.J.Bankr.	Law Journal Bankruptcy, New Series, Eng.
L.J.Ch.	Law Journal, New Series, Chancery, English.
L.J.Ch.O.S.	Law Journal Chancery, Old Series, Eng.

L.J.C.P.	Law Journal Common Pleas, New Series, Eng.
L.J.C.P.O.S.	Law Journal Common Pleas, Old Series, Eng.
L.J.Eccl.	Law Journal Ecclesiastical, New Series, Eng.
L.J.Exch.	Law Journal, New Series, Exchequer.
L.J.Exch.O.S.	Law Journal Exchequer, Old Series, Eng.
L.J.K.B.	Law Journal King's Bench, New Series, Eng.
L.J.K.B.O.S.	Law Journal King's Bench, Old Series, Eng.
L.J.M.Cas.	Law Journal, New Series, Magistrates' Cases.
L.J.M.C.O.S.	Law Journal Magistrate Cases, Old Series, Eng.
L.J.P.C.	Law Journal Privy Council, New Series, Eng.
L.J.P.D. & Adm.	Law Journal Probate Divorce & Admiralty, New Series, Eng.
L.J.P. & M.	Law Journal Probate & Matrimonial, New Series, Eng.
L.J.Prob.N.S.	Law Journal Probate, Divorce and Admiralty Reports, N.Y.
L.J.Q.B.	Law Journal Queen's Bench, New Series, Eng.
L.J.Rep.	Law Journal Reports, Eng.
Ll. & G.t.Pl.	Lloyd & Goold temp. Plunket, Ir.
Ll. & G.t.S.	Lloyd & Goold temp. Sugden, Ir.
Ll. & W.	Lloyd & Welsby, Eng.
L. & M.	Lowndes & Maxwell, Eng.
L.M. & P.	Lowndes, Maxwell & Pollack, Eng.
LMSA	Labor Management Services Administration.
Loc.Acts	Local Acts.
Loc.Code	Local Code.
Loc.Gov.	Local Government, Eng.
Loc.Laws	Local Laws.
Lock.Rev.Cas.	Lockwood's Reversed Cases, N.Y.
Lofft	Lofft's English King's Bench Reports.
Lom.C.H.Rep.	Lomas's City Hall Reporter, N.Y.
Lom.Dig.	Lomax's Digest of Real Property.
Longf. & T.	Longfield & Townsend, Ir.
Los Angeles Bar Bull.	Los Angeles Bar Bulletin.
Low.	Lowell, U.S.
Low.Can.Seign.	Lower Canada Seignorial Reports.
Lower Ct.Dec.	Lower Court Decisions, Ohio.
Loyola L.Rev.	Loyola Law Review.

Loyola U.L.J. _____ Loyola University Law
Journal.
L.P.R.A. _____ Laws of Puerto Rico An-
notated.
L.R. _____ Law Reports, U.S.
L.R.A. _____ Lawyers' Reports An-
notated.
L.R.A.1915A _____ Lawyers' Reports Anno-
tated 1915A, et seq.
L.R.A. & E. _____ Law Reports Admiralty
& Ecclesiastical, Eng.
L.R.A.N.S. _____ Lawyers' Reports Anno-
tated, New Series.
L.R.App.Cas. _____ English Law Reports,
Appeal Cases, House
of Lords.
L.R.C.C. _____ Law Reports Crown Cas-
es, Eng.
L.R.Ch. _____ Law Reports Chancery
Appeal Cases, Eng.
L.R.C.P. _____ English Law Reports,
Common Pleas.
L.R.Eq. _____ English Law Reports,
Equity.
L.R.Ex.Cas. _____ English Law Reports,
Exchequer.
L.R.Exch. _____ English Law Reports,
Exchequer.
L.R.H.L. _____ English Law Reports,
English and Irish Ap-
peal Cases.
L.R.H.L.Sc. _____ English Law Reports,
Scotch and Divorce
Appeal Cases.
L.R.Indian App. ____ Law Reports Indian Ap-
peals, Eng.
L.R.Ir. _____ Law Reports Irish.
L.R.P.C. _____ English Law Reports,
Privy Council, Appeal
Cases.
L.R.Prob.Div. _____ English Law Reports,
Probate, Divorce and
Admiralty Division.
L.R.Prob. & Div. ___ English Law Reports
Probate and Divorce.
L.R.Q.B. _____ English Law Reports,
Queen's Bench.
L.R.Q.B.Div. _____ English Law Reports,
Queen's Bench Divi-
sion.
LSA _____ Louisana Statutes Anno-
tated.
R.S. ___Revised Statutes.
C.C. ___Civil Code.
C.C.P. ___Code of Civil
Procedure.
C.Cr.P. ___Code of Crim-
inal Procedure.
L.T. _____ Law Times, Pa.
Ltd. _____ Limited.
L.T.N.S. _____ Law Times, New Series,
Pa.
L.T.O.S. _____ Law Times, Old Series,
Eng.
L.T.Rep.N.S. _____ Law Times Reports,
New Series, Eng.
Lush. _____ Lushington's English Ad-
miralty Reports.
Lut. _____ Lutwyche's English Com-
mon Pleas Reports.
Lutw.Reg.Cas. _____ Lutwyche's Registration
Cases, Eng.

Luz.L.J. _____ Luzerne Law Journal.
Luz.Law T. _____ Luzerne Law Times, Pa.
Luz.Leg.Obs. _____ Luzerne Legal Observer,
Pa.
Luz.Leg.Reg. _____ Luzerne Legal Register,
Pa.
Lycoming _____ Lycoming Reporter, Pa.
Lynd.Prov. _____ Lyndwood's Provinciales.

M

MA _____ Manpower Administra-
tion; Maritime Admin-
istration.
McAll. _____ McAllister, U.S.
MacArthur _____ MacArthur, D.C.
MacArthur & M. ___ MacArthur & Mackey, D.
C.
MacArthur, Pat.Cas. MacArthur's Patent Cas-
es, U.S.
Macaulay, Hist.Eng. Macaulay's History of
England.
McCahon _____ McCahon, Kan.
McCart. _____ McCarter, N.J.
McCarty, Civ.Proc. _ McCarty's Civil Proce-
dure Reports, N.Y.
Maccl. _____ Macclesfield, Eng.
McClain's Code ____ McClain's Annotated
Code and Statutes,
Iowa.
McClain, Cr.Law ___ McClain's Criminal Law.
McClel.Dig. _____ McClellan's Digest of
Laws, Fla.
McClell. _____ McClelland, Eng.
McClell. & Y. _____ McClelland & Younge,
Eng.
McCord _____ McCord's Law, S.C.
McCord, Eq. _____ McCord's Equity, S.C.
McCrary _____ McCrary, U.S.
McCul.Dict. _____ McCulloch's Commercial
Dictionary.
MacFarl. _____ MacFarlane, Sc.
McGloin _____ McGloin, La.
McK Consol.Laws __ McKinney's Consolidated
Laws of New York.
Mackey _____ Mackey, D.C.
McLean _____ McLean, U.S.
Macl. & R. _____ Maclean & Robinson,
Eng.
McMul. _____ McMullan, S.C.
Macn. & G. _____ Macnaghten and Gor-
don's English Chancery
Reports.
Macph. _____ Macpherson, Sc.
Macph., S. & L. ___ Macpherson, Shirreff &
Lee, Sc.
Macq. _____ Macqueen's Scotch Ap-
peal Cases.
Madd. _____ Maddock's Reports, Eng-
lish Chancery.
Madd.Ch.Pr. _____ Maddock's Chancery
Practice, Eng.
Madras L.J. _____ Madras Law Journal.
Maine, Anc.Law ___ Maine's Ancient Law.
Maine Bar _____ Maine State Bar Asso-
ciation Reports.
Maine L.Rev. _____ Maine Law Review.
Malloy _____ Malloy, Ir.
Man. _____ Manitoba Law.
Man. _____ Manning, Mich.
Man.El.Cas. _____ Manning's Election Cas-
es, Eng.

Man.Exch.Pr.	Manning's Exchequer Practice, Eng.
Man. & G.	Manning & Granger's English Common Pleas Reports.
Man., G. & S.	Manning, Granger, and Scott's English Common Pleas Reports.
Man.L.J.	Manitoba Law Journal.
Man. & R.	Manning & Ryland's English Magistrates' Cases.
Man. & S.	Manning & Scott, Eng.
Mansf.Dig.	Mansfield's Digest of Statutes, Ark.
Manson	Manson, Eng.
Man.t.Wood	Manitoba temp. Wood.
Man.Unrep.Cas.	Manning's Unreported Cases, La.
March	March, Eng.
Mar.Prov.	Maritime Province Reports, Can.
Marq.L.Rev.	Marquette Law Review.
Mars.Adm.	Marsden's Admiralty, Eng.
Marsh.	Marshall's English Common Pleas Reports.
Marsh., A.K.	A. K. Marshall, Ky.
Marsh., J.J.	J. J. Marshall, Ky.
Mart.	Martin, N.C.
Martin, Dict.	Edward Martin's English Dictionary.
Mart.,N.S.	Martin's New Series, La.
Mart.,O.S.	Martin's Old Series, La.
Mart. & Y.	Martin & Yerger, Tenn.
Marv.	Marvel's Reports, Del.
Mason	Mason, U.S.
Mason's Code	Mason's United States Code Annotated.
Mass.	Massachusetts Reports.
Mass.Elec.Cas.	Massachusetts Election Cases.
Mass.L.Q.	Massachusetts Law Quarterly.
Mass.L.R.	Massachusetts Law Reporter, Boston.
Maule & S.	Maule and Selwyn's English King's Bench Reports.
Maxw.Adv.Gram.	W. H. Maxwell's Advanced Lessons in English Grammar.
Mayn.	Maynard, Eng.
M.C.A.	Mississippi Code Annotated; Montana Code Annotated.
M.C.L.A.	Michigan Compiled Laws Annotated.
M. & C.Partidas	Moreau-Lislet and Carleton's Laws of Las Sièté Partidas in force in Louisiana.
Md.	Maryland Reports.
Md.App.	Maryland Appellate Reports.
Md.B.J.	Maryland Bar Journal.
Md.Ch.	Maryland Chancery.
Md.L.Rec.	Maryland Law Record, Baltimore.
Md.L.Rep.	Maryland Law Reporter, Baltimore.

Md.L.Rev.	Maryland Law Review.
Me.	Maine Reports.
Med.Leg.J.	Medico-Legal Journal.
Med.Trial Tech.Q.	Medical Trial Technique Quarterly.
Med.-Legal J.	Medico-Legal Journal.
Mees. & Ros.	Meeson & Roscoe, Eng.
Mees. & W.	Meeson and Welsby's English Exchequer Reports.
Meg.	Megone, Eng.
Meigs	Meigs, Tenn.
Meigs, Dig.	Meigs' Digest of Decisions of the Courts of Tennessee.
Memphis L.J.	Memphis Law Journal, Tenn.
Memphis St.U.L.Rev.	Memphis State University Law Review.
Mer.	Merivale's English Chancery Reports.
Mercer L.Rev.	Mercer Law Review.
Meriv.	Merivale, Eng.
Merl.Repert.	Merlin, Répertoire de Jurisprudence.
MESA	Mining and Enforcement Administration.
MESBIC	Minority Enterprise Small Business Investment Companies.
Metc.	Metcalfe, Ky.
Metc.	Metcalf, Mass.
M. & G.	Manning & Granger, Eng.
M.F.P.D.	Modern Federal Practice Digest.
MGIC	Mortgage Guaranty Insurance Corporation.
M.G.L.A.	Massachusetts General Laws Annotated.
M. & H.	Murphy & Hurlstone, Eng.
Miami L.Q.	Miami Law Quarterly.
Mich.	Michigan Reports.
Mich.App.	Michigan Court of Appeals.
Mich.Lawyer	Michigan Lawyer.
Mich.Leg.News	Michigan Legal News.
Mich.L.J.	Michigan Law Journal.
Mich.L.Rev.	Michigan Law Review.
Mich.N.P.	Michigan Nisi Prius.
Mich.S.B.J.	Michigan State Bar Journal.
Mich.T.	Michaelmas Term, Eng.
Miles	Miles, Pa.
Mill, Const.	Mill's Constitutional Reports, S.C.
Mill.Dec.	Miller's Decisions, U.S.
Miller's Code	Miller's Revised and Annotated Code, Iowa.
Mills	Mills, N.Y.
Mills' Ann.St.	Mills' Annotated Statutes, Colo.
Mill. & V.Code	Milliken & Vertrees' Code, Tenn.
Milw.	Milward, Ir.
Minn.	Minnesota Reports.
Minn.Ct.Rep.	Minnesota Court Reporter.
Minn.L.Rev.	Minnesota Law Review.
Minor	Minor, Ala.

Minor, Inst.	Minor's Institutes of Common and Statute Law.
Misc.	Miscellaneous Reports, N.Y.
Misc.2d	Miscellaneous Reports, Second Series, N.Y.
Misc.Laws	Miscellaneous Laws, Or.
Miss.	Mississippi Reports.
Miss.Dec.	Mississippi Decisions.
Miss.L.J.	Mississippi Law Journal.
Miss.St.Cas.	Mississippi State Cases.
Mitf.Eq.Pl.	Mitford's Equity Pleading.
M.L.R.	Military Law Review.
MLS	Multiple Listing Service.
M. & M.	Moody & Malkin, Eng.
Mo.	Missouri Reports.
Moak, Eng.R.	Moak's English Reports.
Moak, Underh.Torts	Moak's Edition of Underhill on Torts.
Mo.App.	Missouri Appeal Reports.
Mo.B.J.	Missouri Bar Journal.
Mod.	Modern Reports, English King's Bench.
Mod.Am.Law	Modern American Law.
Mod.Cas.L. & Eq.	Modern Cases at Law and Equity, Eng.
Mo.L.Rev.	Missouri Law Review.
Molloy	Molloy, Ir.
Monag.	Monaghan, Pa.
Mon., B.	B. Monroe, Ky.
Monroe L.R.	Monroe Legal Reporter, Pa.
Mont.	Montagu, Eng.
Mont.	Montana Reports.
Mont. & A.	Montagu & Ayrton, Eng.
Mont. & B.	Montagu & Bligh's English Bankruptcy Reports.
Mon., T.B.	T. B. Monroe, Ky.
Mont.Bank.Rep.	Montagu's English Bankruptcy Reports.
Mont. & C.	Montagu & Chitty, Eng.
Mont.D. & DeG.	Montagu, Deacon & De-Gex, Eng.
Montg.	Montgomery County Law Reporter, Pa.
Month.Jur.	Monthly Jurist, Bloomington, Ill.
Month.Law Bul.	Monthly Law Bulletin, N.Y.
Month.Leg.Exam.	Monthly Legal Examiner, N.Y.
Month.L.J.	Monthly Journal of Law, Wash.
Month.L.Rep.	Monthly Law Reporter, Boston.
Month.L.Rev.	Monthly Law Review.
Month.West.Jur.	Monthly Western Jurist (Bloomington, Ill.)
Mont.L.R.	Montreal Law Reports, Can.
Mont. & M.	Montagu and MacArthur's English Bankruptcy Reports.
Montr.Cond.Rep.	Montreal Condensed Reports.
Montr.Leg.N.	Montreal Legal News.
Montr.Q.B.	Montreal Law Reports, Queen's Bench.
Montr.Super.	Montreal Law Reports, Superior Court.
Moody, Cr.Cas.	Moody's Crown Cases, English Courts.
Moody & M.	Moody and Malkin's English Nisi Prius Reports.
Moody & R.	Moody and Robinson's English Nisi Prius Reports.
Moore	Moore, Ark.
Moore	Sir Francis Moore's English King's Bench Reports.
Moore C.P.	Moore's Common Pleas, Eng.
Moore Indian App.	Moore's Indian Appeals, Eng.
Moore K.B.	Moore's King's Bench, Eng.
Moore P.C.	Moore's Privy Council Reports.
Moore P.C.N.S.	Moore's Privy Council New Series, Eng.
Moore & S.	Moore and Scott's English Common Pleas Reports.
Moore & W.	Moore & Walker, Tex.
Moreau & Carleton's Partidas	Moreau-Lislet and Carleton's Laws of Las Sièté Partidas in force in Louisiana.
Morrell, Bankr.Cas.	Morrell's English Bankruptcy Cases.
Morris	Morris, Iowa.
Morr.Min.Rep.	Morrison's Mining Reports.
Morr.St.Cas.	Morris' State Cases, Miss.
Morr.Trans.	Morrison's Transcript of United States Supreme Court Decisions.
Mos.	Mosely's English Chancery Reports.
Mo.St.Ann.	Missouri Statutes Annotated.
M. & P.	Moore & Payne, Eng.
M. & R.	Manning & Ryland, Eng.
M. & Rob.	Moody & Robinson, Eng.
M.R.S.A.	Maine Revised Statutes Annotated.
M. & S.	Maule & Selwyn, Eng.
M.S.A.	Minnesota Statutes Annotated.
M.T.	Miscellaneous Tax Ruling.
Mun.	Municipal Law Reporter, Pa.
Mun.Att'y	Municipal Attorney.
Mun.Code	Municipal Code.
Mun.Corp.Cas.	Municipal Corporation Cases.
Munf.	Munford, Va.
Mun.L.J.	Municipal Law Journal.
Murfree, Off.Bonds	Murfree on Official Bonds.
Murph.	Murphey, N.C.
Murr.	Murray, Sc.
Murray's Eng.Dict.	Murray's English Dictionary.

M. & W.	Meeson and Welsby's English Exchequer Reports.
Myl. & C.	Mylne & Craig's English Chancery Reports.
Myl. & K.	Mylne and Keen's English Chancery Reports.
Myr.Prob.	Myrick's Probate Court Reports, Cal.

N

NAB	National Alliance of Businessmen.
NACCA L.J.	NACCA Law Journal.
N.Am.Rev.	North American Review.
NAS	National Academy of Science.
NASA	National Aeronautics and Space Administration.
NASD	National Association of Securities Dealers.
Nat.Bankr.Law	National Bankruptcy Law.
Nat.Bankr.R.	National Bankruptcy Register, U.S.
Nat.Corp.Rep.	National Corporation Reporter.
Nat.L.Rec.	National Law Record.
Nat.L.Rep.	National Law Reporter.
Nat.L.Rev.	National Law Review, Phila.
NATO	North Atlantic Treaty Organization.
N.B.	New Brunswick.
N.Benl.	New Benloe, Eng.
N.B.Eq.	New Brunswick Equity.
N.B.N.Rep.	National Bankruptcy News and Reports.
N.B.R.	National Bankruptcy Register, U.S.
NBS	National Bureau of Standards.
N.C.	North Carolina Reports.
N.C.App.	North Carolina Appeals.
N.C.Cent.L.J.	North Carolina Central Law Journal.
N.C.L.Rev.	North Carolina Law Review.
N.C.Conf.	North Carolina Conference.
N.Chip.	N. Chipman, Vt.
N.C.L.Rev.	North Carolina Law Review.
N.C.Term R.	North Carolina Term Reports.
NCUA	National Credit Union Administration.
N.D.	North Dakota Reports.
NDCC	North Dakota Century Code.
N.D.L.Rev.	North Dakota Law Review.
N.E.	North Eastern Reporter.
N.E.2d	North Eastern Reporter, Second Series.
Neb.	Nebraska Reports.
Neb.L.B.	Nebraska Law Bulletin.
Neb.L.Rev.	Nebraska Law Review.
Neb.St.B.J.	Nebraska State Bar Journal.

Neb., Unoff.	Nebraska Unofficial.
Nels.	Nelson, Eng.
Nels.Abr.	Nelson's Abridgment of the Common Law.
Nev.	Nevada Reports.
Nev. & M.	Nevile and Manning's English King's Bench Reports.
Newb.Adm.	Newberry's Admiralty, U.S.
New Eng.L.Rev.	New England Law Review.
Newfoundl.	Newfoundland.
Newf.Sel.Cas.	Newfoundland Select Cases.
Newl.Ch.Prac.	Newland's Chancery Practice.
New Rep.	New Reports in all Courts, Eng.
New Sess.Cas.	New Session Cases, Eng.
New York City B.A. Bul.	Bulletin of Ass'n of the Bar of the City of N. Y.
New Zeal.L.	New Zealand Law.
NFPCA	National Fire Prevention and Control Administration.
N.H.	New Hampshire Reports.
N.H.B.J.	New Hampshire Bar Journal.
N.H.Judicial Council	New Hampshire Judicial Council.
N.H.R.S.	New Hampshire Revised Statutes.
NHTSA	National Highway Transportation Safety Administration.
Nisi Prius & Gen. T.Rep.	Nisi Prius & General Term Reports, Ohio.
Nix.Dig.	Nixon's Digest of Laws, N.J.
N.J.	New Jersey Supreme Court Reports.
N.J.Eq.	New Jersey Equity.
N.J.L.	New Jersey Law.
N.J.L.J.	New Jersey Law Journal.
N.J.Misc.	New Jersey Miscellaneous.
N.J.S.A.	New Jersey Statutes Annotated.
N.J.St.B.J.	New Jersey State Bar Journal.
N.J.Super.	New Jersey Superior Court Reports.
nka	Now known as.
NLRB	National Labor Relations Board.
N.M.	New Mexico Reports.
N.M.App.	New Mexico Appeals.
N.Mex.L.Rev.	New Mexico Law Review.
N. & M.	Nevile & Manning, Eng.
N. & Macn.	Neville & Macnamara, Eng.
N.M.S.	New Mexico Statutes.
NOAA	National Oceanic and Atmospheric Administration.
Nolan	Nolan, Eng.
Norris	Norris, Pa.

North.	Northington, Eng.
Northam.Law Rep.	Northampton County Law Reporter, Pa.
North.	Northampton County Reporter, Pa.
Northumb.Co.Leg.N.	Northumberland County Legal News, Pa.
Northumb.L.J.	Northumberland Legal Journal, Pa.
North.W.L.J.	Northwestern Law Journal.
Notes of Cas.	Notes of Cases, Eng.
Notre Dame L.	Notre Dame Lawyer.
Nott & McC.	Nott & McCord, S.C.
Noy	Noy, Eng.
N. & P.	Nevile & Perry, Eng.
N.P.R.	Nisi Prius Reports.
NRC	National Research Council; Nuclear Regulatory Commission.
N.R.L.	Revised Laws 1813, N.Y.
N.R.S.	Nevada Revised Statutes.
N.S.	New Series; Nova Scotia.
NSA	National Security Agency.
NSC	National Security Council.
N.S.Dec.	Nova Scotia Decisions.
NSF	National Science Foundation.
N.S.Wales	New South Wales.
N.S.Wales L.	New South Wales Law.
N.S.Wales L.R.Eq.	New South Wales Law Reports Equity.
NTSB	National Transportation Safety Board.
N.W.	Northwestern Reporter.
N.W.2d	Northwestern Reporter, Second Series.
N.W.L.Rev.	Northwestern University Law Review.
N.Y.	New York Court of Appeals Reports.
N.Y.2d	New York Court of Appeals Reports, Second Series.
N.Y.Ann.Cas.	New York Annotated Cases.
N.Y.App.Dec.	New York Appeals Decisions.
N.Y.Cas.Err.	New York Cases in Error, Caines's Cases.
N.Y.Ch.Sent.	New York Chancery Sentinel.
N.Y.City Ct.	New York City Court.
N.Y.City Ct. Suppl.	New York City Court Supplement.
N.Y.City H.Rec.	New York City Hall Recorder.
N.Y.Civ.Proc.	New York Civil Procedure.
N.Y.Civ.Proc.R., N.S.	New York Civil Procedure Reports, New Series.
N.Y.Civ.Pr.Rep.	New York Civil Procedure Reports.
N.Y.Code Rep.	New York Code Reporter.
N.Y.Code Reports, N.S.	New York Code Reports, New Series.

N.Y.Cond.	New York Condensed Reports.
N.Y.Cr.R.	New York Criminal Reports.
N.Y.Daily L.Gaz.	New York Daily Law Gazette.
N.Y.Daily Reg.	New York Daily Register.
N.Y.Elect.Cas.	New York Election Cases.
N.Y.Jur.	New York Jurist.
N.Y.Law J.	New York Law Journal.
N.Y.L.C.Ann.	New York Leading Cases Annotated.
N.Y.Leg.N.	New York Legal News.
N.Y.Leg.Obs.	New York Legal Observer.
N.Y.Leg.Reg.	New York Legal Register.
N.Y.L.Gaz.	New York Law Gazette, N. Y.
N.Y.L.J.	New York Law Journal.
N.Y.L.Rec.	New York Law Record.
N.Y.L.Rev.	New York Law Review.
N.Y.Misc.	New York Miscellaneous Reports.
N.Y.Misc.2d	New York Miscellaneous, Second Series.
N.Y.Month.L.Bul.	New York Monthly Law Bulletin.
N.Y.Month.L.R.	New York Monthly Law Reports.
N.Y.Mun.Gaz.	New York Municipal Gazette.
N.Y.Ops.Atty.Gen.	Sickel's Opinions of the Attorney-General of New York.
N.Y.Pr.Rep.	New York Practice Reports.
N.Y.Rec.	New York Record.
N.Y.S.	New York Supplement.
N.Y.S.2d	New York Supplement Reporter, Second Series.
N.Y.St.B.J.	New York State Bar Journal.
N.Y.St.Rep.	New York State Reporter.
N.Y.Super.Ct.	New York Superior Court.
N.Y.U.L.Q.Rev.	New York University Law Quarterly Review.
N.Y.U.L.Rev.	New York University Law Review.
N.Y.Wkly.Dig.	New York Weekly Digest.

O

OAS	Organization of American States.
O.Ben.	Old Benloe, Eng.
O.Bridgm.	Orlando Bridgman, Eng.
O.C.D.	Ohio Circuit Decisions.
ODAP	Office of Drug Abuse Policy.
OEDP	Office of Employment Development Programs.
OFCC	Office of Federal Contract Compliance.
Off.Gaz.	Official Gazette.

OFPP	Office of Federal Procurement Policy.
OFR	Office of the Federal Register.
Ogilvie, Dict.	Ogilvie's Imperial Dictionary of the English Language.
Ohio	Ohio Reports.
Ohio App.	Ohio Appellate Reports.
Ohio App.2d	Ohio Appellate Reports, Second Series.
Ohio Cir.Ct.R.	Ohio Circuit Court Reports.
Ohio Cir.Ct.R.N.S.	Ohio Circuit Court Reports, New Series.
Ohio Cir.Dec.	Ohio Circuit Decisions.
Ohio Dec.	Ohio Decisions.
Ohio Dec.Reprint	Ohio Decisions, Reprint.
Ohio F.Dec.	Ohio Federal Decisions.
Ohio Law Bul.	Ohio Law Bulletin.
Ohio Law J.	Ohio Law Journal.
Ohio Law Rep.	Ohio Law Reporter.
Ohio Leg.N.	Ohio Legal News.
Ohio North U.L.Rev.	Ohio Northern University Law Review.
Ohio N.P.	Ohio Nisi Prius.
Ohio N.P.N.S.	Ohio Nisi Prius New Series.
Ohio O.	Ohio Opinions.
Ohio O.2d	Ohio Opinions, Second Series.
Ohio Prob.	Ohio Probate.
Ohio S. & C.P.Dec.	Ohio Superior and Common Pleas Decisions.
Ohio St.	Ohio State Reports.
Ohio St.2d	Ohio State, Second Series.
Ohio St.L.J.	Ohio State Law Journal.
Ohio Supp.	Ohio Supplement.
Okl.	Oklahoma.
Okl.App.	Oklahoma Appeals.
Okl.Cty.U.L.Rev.	Oklahoma City University Law Review.
Okl.Cr.	Oklahoma Criminal.
Okl.Jud.	Oklahoma Court on the Judiciary.
Okl.L.J.	Oklahoma Law Journal.
Okl.L.Rev.	Oklahoma Law Review.
Okl.St.Ann.	Oklahoma Statutes Annotated.
Olcott	Olcott, U. S.
O.L.D.	Ohio Lower Court Decisions.
Oliv.B. & L.	Oliver, Beavan & Lefroy, Eng.
OMB	Office of Management and Budget.
OMBE	Office of Minority Business Enterprise.
O'M. & H.	O'Malley & Hardcastle, Ir.
ONAP	Office of Native American Programs.
Ont.	Ontario Reports.
Ont.A.	Ontario Appeals.
Ont.El.Cas.	Ontario Election Cases.
Ont.L.	Ontario Law.
Ont.L.J.	Ontario Law Journal.
Ont.L.J.N.S.	Ontario Law Journal New Series.
Ont.Pr.	Ontario Practice.
Ont.W.N.	Ontario Weekly Notes.

Ont.W.R.	Ontario Weekly Reporter.
O.O.	Ohio Opinions.
OOG	Office of Oil and Gas.
Op.Attys.Gen.	Opinions of the United States Attorneys General.
Op.Sol.Dept.Labor	Opinions of the Solicitor for the Department of Labor dealing with Workmen's Compensation.
Or.	Oregon Reports.
Or.App.	Oregon Appeals.
Or.Bar Bull.	Oregon Bar Bulletin.
ORC	Ohio Revised Code.
Ord.	Ordinance.
Orleans App.	Orleans Appeals, La.
Orleans T.R.	Orleans Term Reports, 1 and 2 Martin's Reports, La.
Or.L.Rev.	Oregon Law Review.
ORS	Oregon Revised Statutes.
O.S.	Oklahoma Statutes; Old Series.
OSHA	Occupational Safety and Health Administration.
OT	Office of Telecommunications.
OTC	Over the counter.
Outerbridge	Outerbridge, Pa.
Overt.	Overton, Tenn.
O. & W.Dig.	Oldham and White's Digest of Laws, Tex.
Owen	Owen's English King's Bench Reports.

P

P.	Pacific Reporter.
P.2d	Pacific Reporter, Second Series.
1891 P.	Law Reports, 1891, Probate, Eng.
Pa.	Pennsylvania State Reports.
Pa.B.A.Q.	Pennsylvania Bar Ass'n Quarterly.
Pa.Cas.	Pennsylvania Supreme Court Cases, Sadler.
Pacific C.L.J.	Pacific Coast Law Journal, San Francisco.
Pac.L.J.	Pacific Law Journal.
Pacific Law Mag.	Pacific Law Magazine.
Pa.Cmwlth.	Pennsylvania Commonwealth Court Reports.
Pa.Co.Ct.R.	Pennsylvania County Court Reports.
Pa.Com.Pl.	Pennsylvania Common Pleas Reporter.
Pa.Corp.	Pennsylvania Corporation Reporter.
Pa.C.S.A.	Pennsylvania Consolidated Statutes Annotated.
Pa.Dist. & Co.	Pennsylvania District and County Reports.
Pa.Dist. & Co.2d	Pennsylvania District and County Reports, Second Series.
Pa.Dist.R.	Pennsylvania District Reports.

Paige	Paige's Chancery, N. Y.
Paine	Paine, U. S.
Pa.Law J.	Pennsylvania Law Journal.
Pa.Law Ser.	Pennsylvania Law Series.
Pa.Leg.Gaz.	Legal Gazette Reports (Campbell) Pa.
Pa.L.Rec.	Pennsylvania Law Record.
Palm.	Palmer, Eng.
Pa.L.J.R.	Clark's Pennsylvania Law Journal Reports.
Pa.L.Rec.	Pennsylvania Law Record.
Pa.Misc.	Pennsylvania Miscellaneous Reports.
Pamph.Laws	Pamphlet Laws, Acts.
Par.Dec.	Parson's Decisions, Mass.
Park.	Parker, Eng.
Parker, Cr.R.	Parker's Criminal Reports, N. Y.
Park.Exch.	Parker's Exchequer, Eng.
Park.Ins.	Parker's Insurance, Eng.
Pars.Eq.Cas.	Parsons' Select Equity Cases, Pa.
Partidas	Moreau-Lislet and Carleton's Laws of Las Sièté Partidas in force in Louisiana.
Paschal's Ann.Const.	Paschal's United States Constitution, Annotated.
Pasch.Dig.	Paschal's Texas Digest of Decisions.
Pa.St.Tr.	Pennsylvania State Trials (Hogan).
Pa.Super.	Pennsylvania Superior Court Reports.
Pat.	Paterson's Laws.
Pat. & H.	Patton & Heath, Va.
Pat.Law Rev.	Patent Law Review, Washington, D. C.
Pat.Off.Gaz.	Patent Office Gazette.
Pat.Off.Rep.	Patent Office Reports.
Paton App.Cas.	Paton's Appeal Cases, Sc.
Patrick El.Cas.	Patrick's Election Cases, Can.
Patt. & H.	Patton & Heath, Va.
PBGC	Pension Benefit Guaranty Corporation.
P.C.	Penal Code.
P.D.	Law Reports Probate Division, Eng.
P. & D.	Perry & Davison, Eng.
Peake N.P.	Peake's Nisi Prius, Eng.
Pearce C.C.	Pearce's Reports in Dearsly's Eng.
Pears.	Pearson, Pa.
Peck	Peck, Ill.
Peck	Peck, Tenn.
Peck.El.Cas.	Peckwell's Election Cases, Eng.
Pen.Code	Penal Code.
Pen.Laws	Penal Laws.
Pennewill	Pennewill Reports, Del.
Penning.	Pennington, N. J.
Penny.	Pennypacker, Pa.
Pen. & W.	Penrose & Watts, Pa.

PEP	Public Employment Program.
Pepper & L.Dig. Laws	Pepper and Lewis' Digest of Laws, Pa.
Perry & Kn.	Perry & Knapp Election Cases, Eng.
Pet.	Peters, U. S.
Pet.Ab.	Peterdorff's Abridgment.
Pet.Adm.	Peters' Admiralty, U. S.
Pet.C.C.	Peters' Circuit Court, U. S.
Petersd.Ab.	Petersdorff's Abridgment.
P.F.Smith	P. F. Smith, Pa.
Phil.	Phillips, Eng.
Phil.	Phillips' Law, N. C.
Phila.	Philadelphia, Pa.
Phila.Leg.Int.	Philadelphia Legal Intelligencer, Pa.
Phil.Ch.	Phillips' English Chancery Reports.
Phil.Eq.	Phillips' Equity, N. C.
Philippine	Philippine Reports.
Philippine L.J.	Philippine Law Journal.
Phillim.	Phillimore Ecclesiastical, Eng.
Phil. & M.	Philip and Mary, as 4 & 5 Phil. & M.
PHS	Public Health Service.
P & I	Principal and interest.
Pick.	Pickering, Mass.
Pickle	Pickle, Tenn.
Pig. & R.	Pigott & Rodwell, Eng.
Pig.Rec.	Pigott's Recoveries, Eng.
Pike	Pike, Ark.
Pin.	Pinney, Wis.
Pitt.L.J.	Pittsburgh Legal Journal.
Pittsb.	Pittsburgh, Pa.
Pittsb.Leg.J.	Pittsburgh Legal Journal, Pa.
Pittsb.Leg.J., N.S.	Pittsburgh Legal Journal, New Series, Pa.
Pittsb.R.	Pittsburgh Reports, Pa.
P. & K.	Perry & Knapp, Eng.
P.L.	Public Laws.
P. & L.Dig.Laws	Pepper & Lewis' Digest of Laws, Pa.
P.L.J.	Pittsburgh Legal Journal, Pa.
P. & L.Laws	Private and Local Laws.
Plow.	Plowden's English King's Bench Reports.
Pol.Code	Political Code.
Pol.Cont.	Pollock on Principles of Contract at Law and Equity.
Pollexf.	Pollexfen, Eng.
Pol.Sci.Q.	Political Science Quarterly.
Pom.Code Rem.	Pomeroy on Code Remedies.
Pom.Eq.Jur.	Pomeroy's Equity Jurisprudence.
Pom.Rem.	Pomeroy on Civil Remedies.
Pom.Rem. & Rem. Rights	Pomeroy on Civil Remedies & Remedial Rights.

Pom.Spec.Perf.	Pomeroy on Specific Performance of Contracts.	P.Wms.	Peere Williams' English Chancery Reports.
Poph.	Popham's English King's Bench Reports.	Pyke	Pyke, Can.
Port.	Porter, Ala.		
Portia L.J.	Portia Law Journal.		**Q**
Porto Rico	Porto Rico Reports.		
Posey, Unrep.Cas.	Posey's Unreported Cases, Tex.	Q.B.	Queen's Bench Reports, Adolphus & Ellis, N.S., Eng.
Pow.App.Proc.	Powell's Law of Appellate Proceedings.	Q.B.D.	Law Reports, Queen's Bench Division, Eng.
Power's Sur.	Power's Surrogate, N.Y.	Q.B.Div.	Queen's Bench Division (English Law Reports).
Pow.Surr.	Powers' Surrogate, N.Y.		
Prac.Act	Practice Act.		
PRC	Postal Rate Commission.	Quart.L.J.	Quarterly Law Journal (Richmond, Va.).
Pr.Ch.	Precedents in Chancery, by Finch.	Quart.L.Rev.	Quarterly Law Review (Richmond, Va.).
Pr.Dec.	Printed Decisions, Sneed's, Ky.	Queensl.J.P.	Queensland Justice of the Peace.
P.R. & D.El.Cas.	Power, Rodwell & Dew's Election Cases, Eng.	Queensl.L.	Queensland Law.
Prec.Ch.	Precedents in Chancery, Eng.	Queensl.L.J.	Queensland Law Journal.
		Que.L.	Quebec Law.
Pr.Edw.Isl.	Prince Edward Island.	Que.Pr.	Quebec Practice.
Price	Price, Eng.	Que.Q.B.	Quebec Official Reports, Queen's Bench.
Price Pr.Cas.	Price's Practice Cases, Eng.	Que.Rev.Jud.	Quebec Revised Judicial.
Prid. & C.	Prideaux & Cole, Eng.	Que.Super.	Quebec Official Reports, Superior Court.
Priv.Laws	Private Laws.		
Priv.St.	Private Statutes.	Quincy	Quincy, Mass.
Prob.	English Probate and Admiralty Reports for year cited.		**R**
Prob.1917	Law Reports, Probate Division, Eng.	Railway Cas.	Railway Cases.
Prob.Ct.Rep.	Probate Court Reporter, Ohio.	Railway & Corp. Law J.	Railway and Corporation Law Journal.
Prob.Div.	Probate Division, English Law Reports.	Rand.	Randolph, Va.
Prob.Pr.Act	Probate Practice Act.	Rap. & L.Law Dict.	Rapalje and Lawrence Law Dictionary.
Prob.R.	Probate Reports, Ohio.	Rap.Jud.Q.C.S.	Rapport's Judiciaries de Quebec Cour Superieure.
Prob.Rep.	Probate Reports, Eng.		
Prov.St.	Statutes, Laws, of the Province of Massachusetts.	Rawle	Rawle, Pa.
		Raym.	Lord Raymond's English King's Bench Reports.
P.R.R.	Puerto Rico Supreme Court Reports.	R.C.	Ohio Revised Code; Revised Statutes 1855, Mo.
Pr.Rep.	Practice Reports, Eng.		
P.S.	Purdon's Pennsylvania Statutes Annotated.	R. & Can.Cas.	Railway & Canal Cases, Eng.
Psych. & M.L.J.	Psychological and Medico-Legal Journal, N.Y.	R. & Can.Tr.Cas.	Railway & Canal Traffic Cases, Eng.
PTO	Patent and Trademark Office.	R.C.L.	Ruling Case Law.
Pub.Acts	Public Acts.	R.C.M.	Revised Code of Montana.
Pub.Gen.Laws	Public General Laws.	RCWA	Revised Code of Washington.
Pub.Laws	Public Laws.		
Pub.Loc.Laws	Public Local Laws.	REA	Rural Electrification Administration.
Pub. & Loc.Laws	Public and Local Laws.		
Pub.St.	Public Statutes.	REAP	Rural Environmental Assistance Program.
PUD	Planned unit development.	Redf. & B.	Redfield & Bigelow's Leading Cases, Eng.
Puerto Rico	Puerto Rico.	Rees' Cyclopædia	Abraham Rees' English Cyclopædia.
Puerto Rico Fed.	Puerto Rico Federal.		
Puffendorf	Puffendorf's Law of Nature and Nations.	Reeve Eng.L.	Reeve's English Law.
P.U.R.	Public Utilities Reports.	REIT	Real Estate Investment Trust.
Purd.Dig.Laws	Purdon's Digest of Laws, Pa.	Rem'g	Remanding.
Purple's St.	Purple's Statutes, Scates' Compilation.	Rep.	Coke's English King's Bench Reports.

Reports _____ The Reports, English.
Rep.t.Finch _____ Cases, temp. Finch, Eng.
Rep.t.Hard. _____ Lee's Reports temp.
    Hardwicke, Eng.
Rep.t.Holt _____ Reports temp. Holt,
    English Cases of Set-
    tlement.
Reprint _____ English Reprint.
Res. & Eq.Judgm. __ Reserved & Equity Judg-
    ments, N.S.Wales.
RESPA _____ Real Estate Settlement
    Procedures Act.
Rev. _____ Revision of the Statutes
    Revised.
Rev.Civ.Code _____ Revised Civil Code.
Rev.Civ.St. _____ Revised Civil Statutes.
Rev.Code _____ Revised Code.
Rev.Code Civ.Proc. _ Revised Code Civil Pro-
    cedure.
Rev.Cr.Code _____ Revised Criminal Code.
Rev.Crit. _____ Revue Critique, Can.
Rev.Code Cr.Proc. __ Revised Code of Crim-
    inal Procedure.
Rev.de Jur. _____ Revue de Jurisprudence,
    Can.
Rev.de Legis _____ Revue de Legislation,
    Can.
Rev'g _____ Reversing.
Rev.Laws _____ Revised Laws.
Rev.Leg. _____ Revue Legale, Can.
Rev.Leg.N.S. _____ Revue Legale New Se-
    ries, Can.
Rev.Mun.Code _____ Revised Municipal Code.
Rev.Ord. _____ Revised Ordinances.
Rev.Pen.Code _____ Revised Penal Code.
Rev.Pol.Code _____ Revised Political Code.
Rev.Proc. _____ Revenue Procedure.
Rev.Rep. _____ Revised Reports, Eng.
Rev.Rul. _____ Revenue Ruling.
Rev.St. _____ Revised Statutes.
Reynolds' Land Laws Reynolds' Spanish and
    Mexican Land Laws.
R.I. _____ Rhode Island.
Rice _____ Rice's Law, S.C.
Rice's Code _____ Rice's Code of Practice,
    Colo.
Rice, Eq. _____ Rice's Equity, S.C.
Rich. _____ Richard, as 5 Rich. II.
Rich. _____ Richardson, S.C.
Rich.C.P. _____ Richardson's Practice
    Common Pleas, Eng.
Rich.Eq. _____ Richardson's Equity, S.
    C.
Rich.Eq.Cas. _____ Richardson's Equity Cas-
    es, S.C.
Rich.Law _____ Richardson's Law, S.C.
Riddle's Lex. _____ Riddle's Lexicon.
Ridg. _____ Ridgeway's Reports
    temp. Hardwicke, Eng.
Ridg.Ap. _____ Ridgeway's Appeal, Ir.
Ridg.L. & S. _____ Ridgeway, Lapp &
    Schoale, Ir.
Ridg.P.C. _____ Ridgeway's Parliament
    Cases, Ir.
Ridg.t.Hardw. _____ Ridgeway temp. Hard-
    wicke, Eng.
Riley _____ Riley's Law, S.C.
Riley, Eq. _____ Riley's Equity, S.C.
R.L. _____ Revised Laws.
R. & M. _____ Ryan & Moody, Eng.
R.M.Charlt. _____ R. M. Charlton, Ga.

Rob. _____ Christopher Robinson's
    English Admiralty Re-
    ports.
Rob. _____ Robertson, N.Y.
Rob. _____ Robinson, La.
Rob. _____ Robinson, Va.
Robb, Pat.Cas. _____ Robb's Patent Cases, U.
    S.
Rob.Eccl. _____ Robertson's Ecclesias-
    tical, Eng.
Robert.App.Cas. ____ Robertson's Appeal Cas-
    es, Sc.
Robin.App.Cas. ____ Robinson's Appeal Cas-
    es, Sc.
Rob.S.I. _____ Robertson's Sandwich Is-
    land Reports, Hawaii.
Rob.Wm.Adm. _____ William Robinson's Ad-
    miralty, Eng.
Rolle _____ Rolle's English King's
    Bench Reports.
Rolle, Abr. _____ Rolle's Abridgement of
    the Common Law.
Roll.Rep. _____ Rolle's English King's
    Bench Reports.
Rolls Ct.Rep. _____ Rolls' Court Reports.
Rom.Cas. _____ Romilly's Notes of Cas-
    es, **Eng.**
Root _____ Root, Conn.
Rose _____ Rose, Eng.
Ross Lead.Cas. _____ Ross' Leading Cases,
    Eng.
R. & R. _____ Russell & Ryan Crown
    Cases, Eng.
RRB _____ Railroad Retirement
    Board.
R. & Ry.C.C. _____ Russell and Ryan's Eng-
    lish Crown Cases.
R.S. _____ Revised Statutes.
R.S.Comp. _____ Statutes of Connecticut,
    Compilation of 1854.
R.S.N. _____ Revised Statutes of Ne-
    braska.
Russ. _____ Russell, Eng.
Russ. & C.Eq.Cas. _ Russell's & Chesley's
    Equity Cases, N.S.
Russ.Ch. _____ Russell's English Chan-
    cery Reports.
Russ.Eq.Cas. _____ Russell's Equity Cases,
    N.S.
Russ. & Geld. _____ Russell & Geldert, Nova
    Scotia.
Russ. & M. _____ Russell and Mylne's Eng-
    lish Chancery Reports.
Russ. & R.Cr.Cas. __ Russell and Ryan's Eng-
    lish Crown Cases Re-
    served.
Rutgers-Camden
  L.J. _____ Rutgers-Camden **Law**
    Journal.
Rutgers L.Rev. _____ Rutgers Law Review.
Ruth.Inst. _____ Rutherford's Institutes
    of Natural Law.
Ry. & Corp.Law J. __ Railway and Corporation
    Law Journal.
Ry. & M. _____ Ryan and Moody's Eng-
    lish Nisi Prius Reports.

S

Salk. _____ Salkeld's English King's
    Bench Reports.

SALT _____ Strategic Arms Limitation Talks.

Sanb. & B.Ann.St. ___ Sanborn and Berryman's Annotated Statutes, Wis.

Sandf. _____ Sandford, N.Y.

Sandf.Ch. _____ Sandford's Chancery, N. Y.

Sand. & H.Dig. _____ Sandels and Hill's Digest of Statutes, Ark.

San Diego L.Rev. ___ San Diego Law Review.

Sand.Inst.Just.In-
trod. _____ Sandars' Edition of Justinian's Institutes.

Sand.I.Rep. _____ Sandwich Island Reports, Hawaii.

San Fran.L.J. _____ San Francisco Law Journal.

Santa Clara L. _____ Santa Clara Lawyer.

Sask.L. _____ Saskatchewan Law.

Saund. _____ Saunders' English King's Bench Reports.

Saund. & C. _____ Saunders & Cole, Eng.

Saund.Pl. & Ev. ____ Saunders' Pleading and Evidence.

Sau. & Sc. _____ Sausse & Scully, Ir.

S.Austr.L. _____ South Australia Law.

Sav. _____ Savile, Eng.

Sawy. _____ Sawyer, U.S.

Saxt.Ch. _____ Saxton's Chancery, N.J.

Say. _____ Sayer, Eng.

Sayer _____ Sayer's English King's Bench Reports.

Sayles' Ann.Civ.St. __ Sayles' Annotated Civil Statutes, Tex.

Sayles' Civ.St. _____ Sayles' Revised Civil Statutes, Tex.

Sayles' Rev.Civ.St. __ Sayles' Revised Civil Statutes, Tex.

Sayles' St. _____ Sayles' Revised Civil Statutes, Tex.

Sayles' Supp. _____ Supplement to Sayles' Annotated Civil Statutes, Tex.

SBA _____ Small Business Administration.

S.Bar J. _____ Journal of the State Bar of California.

SBIC _____ Small Business Investment Companies.

S.Bar J. _____ Journal of the State Bar of California.

1907 S.C. _____ Court of Session Cases, Sc.

S.C. _____ South Carolina Reports.

Scam. _____ Scammon, Ill.

Scates' Comp.St. ___ Treat, Scates & Blackwell Compiled Statutes, Ill.

S.C.Eq. _____ South Carolina Equity.

Sch.L.R. _____ Schuylkill Legal Record, Pa.

Sch. & Lef. _____ Schoales & Lefroy, Ir.

S.C.L. _____ South Carolina Law.

S.C.L.R. _____ South Carolina Law Review.

Schmidt, Civ.Law ___ Schmidt on the Civil Law of Spain and Mexico.

Schoales & L. _____ Schoales and Lefroy's Irish Chancery Reports.

Schouler, U.S.Hist. _ Schouler's History of the United States under the Const.1783–1847.

Schuyl.Leg.Reg. ____ Schuylkill Legal Record, Pottsville, Pa.

1907 S.C., J. _____ Court of Justiciary Cases, Sc.

Sc.Jur. _____ Scottish Jurist.

Sc.L.Rep. _____ Scottish Law Reporter.

Scot L.T. _____ Scot Law Times.

Scott _____ Scott, Eng.

Scott N.R. _____ Scott's New Reports, Eng.

S. & C.Rev.St. _____ Swan and Critchfield's Revised Statutes, Ohio.

Scr.L.T. _____ Scranton Law Times, Pa.

SCS _____ Soil Conservation Service.

Sc.Sess.Cas. _____ Scotch Court of Session Cases.

S.Ct. _____ Supreme Court Reporter.

S.D. _____ South Dakota Reports.

SDCL _____ South Dakota Compiled Laws.

S.D.L.Rev. _____ South Dakota Law Review.

S.E. _____ South Eastern Reporter.

S.E.2d _____ South Eastern Reporter, Second Series.

Searle & Sm. _____ Searle & Smith, Eng.

SEATO _____ Southeast Asia Treaty Organization.

SEC _____ Securities and Exchange Commission.

Sel.Cas.Ch. _____ Select Cases in Chancery, Eng.

Sel.Cas.N.Y. _____ Yates's Select Cases, N. Y.

Seld. _____ Selden, N.Y.

Seld.Notes _____ Selden's Notes, N.Y.

Sell.Prac. _____ Sellon's Practice in the King's Bench.

Selw. _____ Selwyn's Nisi Prius, Eng.

Serg. & R. _____ Sergeant & Rawle, Pa.

Sess. _____ Session.

Sess.Acts _____ Session Acts.

Sess.Cas. _____ Court of Session Cases, Eng.

Sess.Laws _____ Session Laws.

Seton Hall L.Rev. ___ Seton Hall Law Review.

S.F.L.R. _____ San Francisco Law Review.

S.H.A. _____ Smith-Hurd Illinois Annotated Statutes.

Shan. _____ Shannon, Tenn.

Shan.Cas. _____ Shannon's Tennessee Cases.

Shankland's St. _____ Shankland's Public Statutes, Tenn.

Shannon's Code ____ Shannon's Annotated Code, Tenn.

Shars.Bl.Comm. ____ Sharswood's Edition of Blackstone's Commentaries.

Shars. & B.Lead.
Cas.Real Prop. ___ Sharswood and Budd's Leading Cases of Real Property.

Shaw _____ Shaw, Sc.

Shaw & D. _____ Shaw & Dunlop, Sc.

Shaw Dec.	Shaw's Digest of Decisions, Sc.
Shaw, Dunl. & B.	Shaw, Dunlop & Bell, Sc.
Shaw & M.	Shaw & MacLean, Sc.
Shear. & R.Neg.	Shearman and Redfield on Negligence.
Sheld.	Sheldon, N.Y.
Sheld.Subr.	Sheldon on Subrogation.
Shep.	Shepley, Me.
Shep.Abr.	Sheppard's Abridgement.
Sheph.Sel.Cas.	Shepherd's Select Cases, Ala.
Shep.Touch.	Sheppard's Touchstone of Common Assurances.
Shingle	The Shingle.
Show.	Shower's English King's Bench Reports.
Show.P.C.	Shower's Parliament Cases, Eng.
Sid.	Siderfin's English King's Bench Reports.
Si De Ka Quarterly	Si De Ka Quarterly.
Silv.A.	Silvernail's Appeals, N.Y.
Silvernail	Silvernail, N.Y.
Silv.Sup.	Silvernail's Supreme, N.Y.
Sim.	Simons' English Vice Chancery Reports.
Sim., N.S.,	Simon's English Vice Chancery Reports, New Series.
Sim. & S.	Simons & Stuart's English Vice Chancery Reports.
Skill.Pol.Rep.	Skillman's Police Reports, N.Y.
Skin.	Skinner's English King's Bench Reports.
S&L	Savings and Loan Association.
Slade's St.	Slade's Laws, Vt.
Smale & G.	Smale & Giffard, Eng.
Smedes & M.	Smedes & Marshall, Miss.
Smedes & M.Ch.	Smedes & Marshall's Chancery, Miss.
Smith	Smith, Ind.
Smith	Smith, N.H.
Smith	Smith, N.Y.
Smith & B.	Smith & Batty, Ir.
Smith, C.C.M.	Smith's Circuit Courts-Martial Reports, Me.
Smith Cond.Rep.	Smith's Condensed Reports, Ala.
Smith, E.D.	E. D. Smith, N.Y.
Smith-Hurd Ann.St.	Smith-Hurd Illinois Annotated Statutes.
Smith, J.P.	J. P. Smith's English King's Bench Reports.
Smith K.B.	Smith's King's Bench, Eng.
Smith L.J.	Smith's Law Journal.
Smith Man.Eq.Jur.	Smith's Manual of Equity Jurisprudence.
Smith, P.F.	P. F. Smith, Pa.
Smith Reg.	Smith's Registration, Eng.
Smith's Laws	Smith's Laws, Pa.
Smith's Lead.Cas.	Smith's Leading Cases.
Smythe	Smythe, Ir.
Sneed	Sneed, Tenn.
So.	Southern Reporter.
So.2d	Southern Reporter, Second Series.
So.Cal.L.R.	Southern California Law Review.
So.Car.L.J.	South Carolina Law Journal, Columbia.
So.Car.L.Rev.	South Carolina Law Review.
So.Dak.L.Rev.	South Dakota Law Review.
Sol.J.	Solicitors' Journal, London.
So.L.J.	Southern Law Journal & Reporter, Nashville, Tenn.
So.L.Q.	Southern Law Quarterly.
So.L.Rev.	Southern Law Review, Nashville, Tenn.
So.L.Rev.	Southern Law Review, St. Louis.
So.L.Rev.N.S.	Southern Law Review, New Series, St. Louis, Mo.
So.L.T.	Southern Law Times.
Som.	Somerset Legal Journal, Pa.
So.U.L.Rev.	Southern University Law Review.
Soule, Syn.	Soule's Dictionary of English Synonyms.
Southard	Southard, N.J.
Southwestern U.L. Rev.	Southwestern University Law Review.
Sp.Acts	Special Acts.
Speers	Speers' Law, S.C.
Speers, Eq.	Speers' Equity, S.C.
Spence, Eq.Jur.	Spence's Equitable Jurisdiction of the Court of Chancery.
Spencer	Spencer, N.J.
Spinks	Spinks' Ecclesiastical and Admiralty, Eng.
Spinks, Prize Cas.	Spinks' Admiralty Prize Cases.
Sp.Laws	Special Laws.
Spottisw.	Spottiswoode, Sc.
Spottisw.Eq.	Spottiswoode's Equity, Sc.
Spr.	Sprague, U.S.
Sp.Sess.	Special Session.
Sp.St.	Private and Special Laws.
SSA	Social Security Administration.
S. & S.	Swan and Sayler's Supplement to the Revised Statutes, Ohio.
SSS	Selective Service System.
St.	State, Statutes.
St.	Laws or Acts, in some states.
Stair	Stair, Sc.
Stand.Dict.	Standard Dictionary.
Stan.L.R.	Stanford Law Review.
Stanton's Rev.St.	Stanton's Revised Statutes, Ky.
Starkie	Starkie's English Nisi Prius Reports.

Starr & C.Ann.St.	Starr and Curtis' Annotated Statutes, Ill.
Stat.	Statutes at Large, U.S.
Stat. at L.	United States Statutes at Large.
St.Clem.	St. Clement's Church Case, Phila.
Steph.Comm.	Stephen's Commentaries on the Laws of England.
Steph.Cr.Law	Stephen's General View of the Criminal Law.
Steph.Dig.Cr.Law	Stephen's Digest of the Criminal Law.
Steph.Dig.Ev.	
Steph.Ev.	Stephen's Digest of the Law of Evidence.
Steph.Pl.	Stephen on Pleading.
Stet.L.Rev.	Stetson Law Review.
Stew.	Stewart, Ala.
Stew.	Stewart, N.J.
Stew.	Stewart's Reports, N.S.
Stew.Dig.	Stewart's Digest of Decisions of the Courts of Law and Equity, N.J.
Stew. & P.	Stewart & Porter, Ala.
Stiles	Stiles, Iowa.
St.John's L.Rev.	St. John's Law Review.
St.Law	Loughborough's Digest of Statute Law, Ky.
St.Lim.	Statute of Limitations.
St.Louis L.Rev.	St. Louis Law Review.
St.Mark	St. Mark's Church Case, Phila.
St.Mary's L.Rev.	St. Mary's Law Review.
Stockt.	Stockton's Equity, N.J.
Stockt.Vice-Adm.	Stockton's Vice-Admiralty, N.B.
Sto.Const.	Storey's Commentaries on the Constitution of the United States.
Stor.Dict.	Stormouth's Dictionary of the English Language.
Story	Story, U.S.
Story, Ag.	Story on Agency.
Story, Bailm.	Story on Bailment.
Story, Bills	Story on Bills.
Story, Comm.Const.	Story's Commentaries on the Constitution of the United States.
Story, Confl.Laws	Story on the Conflict of Laws.
Story, Const.	Story's Commentaries on the Constitution of the United States.
Story, Cont.	Story on Contracts.
Story, Eq.Jur.	Story on Equity Jurisprudence.
Story Eq.Pl.	Story on Equity Pleading.
Story, Merchants	Abbott's Merchant Ships and Seamen by Story.
Story, Partn.	Story on Partnership.
Story, Prom.Notes	Story on Promissory Notes.
Story, Sales	Story on Sales of Personal Property.
Story's Laws	Story's United States Laws.

Strange	Strange's English King's Bench Reports.
St.Rep.	State Reporter.
Strob.	Strobhart's Law, S.C.
Strob.Eq.	Strobhart's Equity, S.C.
Stuart, Vice-Adm.	Stuart's Vice-Admiralty, L.C.
Stu.M. & P.	Stuart, Milne & Peddie, Sc.
Style	Style's English King's Bench Reports.
Suffolk U.L.Rev.	Suffolk University Law Review.
Sugd.Powers	Sugden on Powers.
Suffolk U.L.Rev.	Suffolk University Law Review.
Sumn.	Sumner, U.S.
Super.Ct.	Superior Court Reports. Pa.
Supp.Code	Supplement to Code.
Supp.Gen.St.	Supplement to the General Statutes.
Supp.Rev.	Supplement to the Revision.
Supp.Rev.Code	Supplement to the Revised Code.
Supp.Rev.St.	Supplement to the Revised Statutes.
Sus.Leg.Chron.	Susquehanna Legal Chronical, Pa.
Suth.Dam.	Sutherland on Damages.
Suth.St.Const.	Sutherland on Statutes and Statutory Construction.
S.W.	South Western Reporter.
S.W.2d	South Western Reporter Second Series.
Swab.	Swabey's English Admiralty Reports.
Swab. & T.	Swabey and Tristram's English Probate and Divorce Reports.
Swan	Swan, Tenn.
Swan & C.R.St.	Swan and Critchfield's Revised Statutes, Ohio.
Swan & S.St.	Swan and Sayler's Supplement to the Revised Statutes, Ohio.
Swanst.	Swanston's English Chancery Reports.
Swan's St.	Swan's Statutes, Ohio.
Sweeny	Sweeny, N.Y.
Swift, Dig.	Swift's Digest of Laws, Conn.
S.W.L.J.	Southwestern Law Journal.
S.W.L.Rev.	Southwestern Law Review.
Syn.Ser.	Synopsis Series of Treasury Decisions, U.S.

T

Taml.	Tamlyn, Eng.
Taney	Taney, U.S
Tapp.	Tappan, Ohio.
Tariff Ind., New	New's Tariff Index.
Tate's Dig.	Tate's Digest of Laws, Va.
Taunt.	Taunton's English Common Pleas Reports.

Tayl.	Taylor, N. C.
Tayl.St.	Taylor's Revised Statutes, Wis.
Tax Law	Tax Lawyer, The.
Tax Law Rev.	Tax Law Review.
T.B.M.	Advisory Tax Board Memorandum.
T.B.Mon.	T. B. Monroe, Ky.
T.B.R.	Advisory Tax Board Recommendation.
T.C.	United States Tax Court.
T.C.A.	Tennessee Code Annotated.
T.C.M.	Tax Court Memorandum Decisions.
T.D.	Treasury Department Decision.
Temple L.Q.	Temple Law Quarterly.
Tenn.	Tennessee Reports.
Tenn.App.	Tennessee Appeals.
Tenn.Cas.	Shannon's Tennessee Cases.
Tenn.Ch.	Tennessee Chancery.
Tenn.Ch.A.	Tennessee Chancery Appeals.
Tenn.Civ.A.	Tennessee Civil Appeals.
Tenn.Cr.App.	Tennessee Criminal Appeals.
Tenn.Leg.Rep.	Tennessee Legal Reporter, Nashville, Tenn.
Tenn.L.Rev.	Tennessee Law Review.
Ter.Laws	Territorial Laws.
Termes de la Ley	Terms of the Common Laws and Statutes Expounded and Explained by John Rastell.
Term R.	Term Reports, English King's Bench, Durnford and East's Reports.
Tex.	Texas Reports.
Tex.A.Civ.Cas.	White & Wilson's Civil Cases, Tex.
Tex.App.	Texas Appeals Reports.
Tex.Civ.App.	Texas Civil Appeals Reports.
Tex.Com.App.	Texas Commission of Appeals.
Tex.Cr.R.	Texas Criminal Reports.
Tex.Ct.App.R.	Texas Court of Appeals Reports.
Tex.L.J.	Texas Law Journal, Tyler.
Tex.L.Rev.	Texas Law Review.
Tex.So.U.L.Rev.	Texas Southern University Law Review.
Tex.Supp.	Texas Supplement.
Tex.Tech.L.Rev.	Texas Tech Law Review.
Tex.Unrep.Cas.	Posey's Unreported Cases.
Thacher, Cr.Cas.	Thacher's Criminal Cases, Mass.
Thom.Co.Litt.	Thomas' Edition of Coke upon Littleton.
Thomp. & C.	Thompson & Cook, N. Y.
Thomp.Dig.	Thompson's Digest of Laws, Fla.
Thomp.Cas.	Thompson's Cases, Tenn.
Thomp. & St.Code	Thompson and Steger's Code, Tenn.
Thomp.Tenn.Cas.	Thompson's Unreported Tennessee Cases.

T. & H.Prac.	Troubat and Haly's Pennsylvania Practice.
Tiffany	Tiffany, N. Y.
Times L.Rep.	Times Law Reports.
Tinw.	Tinwald, Sc.
T.I.R.	Technical Information Bureau.
T.Jones	Thomas Jones, Eng.
T.L.R.	Times Law Reports, Eng.
T. & M.	Temple & Mew, Eng.
T.M.R.	Trade Mark Reports.
Toml.Law Dict.	Tomlins' Law Dictionary.
Toth.	Tothill, Eng.
T.R.	Term Reports, English King's Bench, Durnford and East's Reports.
Transcr.A.	Transcript Appeals, N. Y.
T.Raym.	Sir Thomas Raymond's English King's Bench Reports.
Tread.Const.	Treadway's Constitutional Reports, S. C.
Treas.Dec.	Treasury Decisions, U. S.
Treas.Reg.	Treasury Regulation.
Tr. & H.Pr.	Troubat & Haly's Practice, Pa.
Trint.T.	Trinity Term, Eng.
Troub. & H.Prac.	Troubat & Haly's Practice, Pa.
Truem.Eq.Cas.	Trueman's Equity Cases, N. B.
T.T.	Trinity Term.
Tuck.	Tucker's Surrogate, N. Y.
Tucker's Blackstone	Tucker's Blackstone's Commentaries.
Tuck.Sel.Cas.	Tucker's Select Cases, Newfoundland.
Tuck.Surr.	Tucker's Surrogate, N. Y.
Tul.L.Rev.	Tulane Law Review.
Tulsa L.J.	Tulsa Law Journal.
T.U.P.Charlt.	T. U. P. Charlton, Ga.
Turn.	Turner, Ark.
Turn. & R.	Turner and Russell's English Chancery Reports.
TVA	Tennessee Valley Authority.
Tyler	Tyler, Vt.
Tyr.	Tyrwhitt's English Exchequer Reports.
Tyr. & G.	Tyrwhitt & Granger, Eng.

U

U.C.	Upper Canada.
U.C.A.	Utah Code Annotated.
U.C.C.	Uniform Commercial Code.
U.C.Ch.	Upper Canada Chancery.
U.C.Cham.	Upper Canada Chamber.
U.C.C.L.J.	Uniform Commercial Code Law Journal.
U.C.C.P.	Upper Canada Common Pleas.

U.C.E. & A.	Upper Canada Error and Appeal.
U.Chicago L.Rev.	Univ. of Chicago Law Review.
U.C.K.B.	Upper Canada King's Bench Reports.
U.C.L.A.Law R.	Univ. of Cal. Los Angeles Law Review.
U.C.Q.B.	Upper Canada Queen's Bench.
U.C.Q.B.O.S.	Upper Canada Queen's Bench Old Series.
U.Detroit L.J.	University of Detroit Law Journal.
U.Detroit L.Rev.	University of Detroit Law Review.
U.L.A.	Uniform Laws Annotated.
U.Maine L.Rev.	University of Maine Law Review.
U.Mo.B.,Law Ser.	University of Missouri Bulletin, Law Series.
UN	United Nations.
UNESCO	United Nations Educational, Scientific and Cultural Organization.
UNICEF	United Nations International Children's Emergency Fund (now United Nations Children's Fund).
Unof.	Unofficial, Reports.
UPA	Uniform Partnership Act.
U.Pa.L.Rev.	University of Pennsylvania Law Review.
U.Pitt.L.Rev.	Univ. of Pittsburgh Law Review.
UPC	Uniform Probate Code.
Urban L.J.	University of Detroit, Urban Law Journal.
U.S.	United States Supreme Court Reports.
U.S.App.	United States Appeals.
U.S.Aviation Rep.	Aviation Reports, U. S.
USC	United States Code.
U.S.C.A.	United States Code Annotated.
U.S.Const.	United States Constitution.
USDA	United States Department of Agriculture.
USES	United States Employment Service.
USIA	United States Information Agency.
USIS	United States Information Service.
U.S.Jur.	United States Jurist, Washington, D. C.
U.S.Law Mag.	United States Law Magazine, N. Y.
U.S.L.Ed.	Lawyers' Ed. Supreme Court Reports.
U.S.L.J.	United States Law Journal, New Haven and New York.
U.S.L.W.	United States Law Week.
U.S.Month.Law Mag.	United States Monthly Law Magazine.

U.S.P.Q.	United States Patent Quarterly.
USPS	United States Postal Service.
USTC	United States Tax Cases.
USTS	United States Travel Service.
Utah	Utah Reports.
Utah 2d	Utah Reports, Second Series.

V

VA	Veterans Administration.
Va.	Virginia Reports.
Va.Cas.	Virginia Cases.
Vac'g	Vacating.
Va.Dec.	Virginia Decisions.
Va.Ch.Dec.	Chancery Decisions, Va.
Va.Law J.	Virginia Law Journal, Richmond.
Va.L.Reg.	Virginia Law Register.
Va.L.Reg.,N.S.	Virginia Law Register, New Series.
Va.L.Rev.	Virginia Law Review.
Val.U.L.Rev.	Valparaiso University Law Review.
V.A.M.S.	Vernon's Annotated Missouri Statutes.
V.A.M.R.	Vernon's Annotated Missouri Rule.
Van.L.R.	Vanderbilt Law Review.
Van Ness, Prize Cas.	Van Ness' Prize Cases, U. S.
V.A.T.S.	Vernon's Annotated Texas Statutes.
Vaugh.	Vaughan, Eng.
Vaux	Vaux's Decisions, Pa.
Vaux Rec.Dec.	Vaux's Recorder's Decisions, Phila.
Vent.	Ventris' English Common Pleas Reports.
Vern.	Vernon's English Chancery Reports.
Vernon's Ann.C.C.P.	Vernon's Annotated Texas Code of Civil Procedure.
Vernon's Ann.Civ.St.	Vernon's Annotated Texas Civil Statutes.
Vernon's Ann.P.C.	Vernon's Annotated Texas Penal Code.
Vern. & S.	Vernon & Scriven, Ir.
Ves.	Vesey, Junior, English Chancery Reports.
Ves. & B.	Vesey and Beames' English Chancery Reports.
Ves.Jr.	Vesey, Junior, English Chancery Reports.
Ves.Jr.Suppl.	Vesey Junior Supplement, Eng.
Ves.Sr.	Vesey, Senior, English Chancery Reports.
Ves.Sr.Suppl.	Vesey, Senior, Supplement, Eng.
V.I.C.	Virgin Islands Code.
Vict.	Queen Victoria, as 5 & 6 Vict.
Vict.L.	Victorian Law.
Vict.L.T.	Victorian Law Times.
Vict.Rep.	Victorian Reports.
Vict.St.Tr.	Victorian State Trials.

Vill.L.Rev. _____ Villanova Law Review.
Vin.Abr. _____ Viner's Abridgment.
Virgin Islands _____ Virgin Islands.
VISTA _____ Volunteers in Service to America.
VITA _____ Volunteers in Technical Assistance.
VOA _____ Voice of America.
Vroom _____ Vroom, N.J.
V.S. _____ Vermont Statutes.
V.S.A. _____ Vermont Statutes Annotated.
Vt. _____ Vermont Reports.
V.T.C.A. _____ Vernon's Texas Codes Annotated.

W

W. _____ William, as Wm. IV.
Wag.St. _____ Wagner's Statutes, Mo.
Wake For.L.Rev. ___ Wake Forest Law Review.
Walk. _____ Walker, Miss.
Walk. _____ Walker, Pa.
Wall. _____ Wallace, U. S.
Wall.C.C. _____ Wallace, U. S.
Wallis _____ Wallis, Ir.
Wall.Jr. _____ Wallace, Junior, U. S.
Wall.Sr. _____ Wallace, Senior, U. S.
Ware _____ Ware, U. S.
Wash. _____ Washington Reports.
Wash. _____ Washington, Va.
Wash. & Lee L.Rev. Washington and Lee Law Review.
Wash.2d _____ Washington Reports, Second Series.
Wash.App. _____ Washington Appellate Reports.
Washb.Real Prop. __ Washburn on Real Property.
Washburn L.J. _____ Washburn Law Journal.
Wash.C.C. _____ Washington Circuit Court, U.S.
Wash.Co. _____ Washington County Reports, Pa.
Wash.Law Rep. ____ Washington Law Reporter, D. C.
Wash.L.Rev. _____ Washington Law Review.
Wash.St. _____ Washington State.
Wash.T. _____ Washington Territory.
Watts _____ Watts, Pa.
Watts & S. _____ Watts & Sergeant, Pa.
Wayne L.R. _____ Wayne Law Review.
W.Bl. _____ Sir William Blackstone's English King's Bench Reports.
Webb, A'B. & W.I.
P. & M. _____ Webb, A'Beckett & Williams' Insolvency, Probate, and Matrimonial Reports, Victoria.
Webst.Dict. _____ Webster's Dictionary.
Webst.Dict.Unab. ___ Webster's Unabridged Dictionary.
Webst.Int.Dict. _____ Webster's International Dictionary.
Webst.New Int.D. __ Webster's New International Dictionary.
Web.Pat.Cas. _____ Webster's Patent Cases, Eng.

Wedgw.Dict.Eng.
Etymology _____ Wedgwood's Dictionary of English Etymology.
Week.Jur. _____ Weekly Jurist, Ill.
Week.L.Rec. _____ Weekly Law Record.
Week.L.Rev. _____ Weekly Law Review, San Francisco.
Week.Trans.Rep. ___ Weekly Transcript Reports, N.Y.
Welsb., Hurl. & G. __ Welsby, Hurlstone, and Gordon's Reports, 1–9 English Exchequer Reports.
Welsh _____ Welsh Registry Cases, Ir.
Wend. _____ Wendell, N.Y.
West _____ West, Eng.
West. _____ Western Reporter.
West Coast Rep. ___ West Coast Reporter.
West.Jur. _____ Western Jurist, Des Moines, Iowa.
West.Law J. _____ Western Law Journal, Cincinnati, Ohio.
West.Law Month. __ Western Law Monthly, Ohio.
West.L.Gaz. _____ Western Law Gazette, Cincinnati, Ohio.
West.L.M. _____ Western Law Monthly, Ohio.
West.L.R. _____ Western Law Reporter, Can.
West.L.T. _____ Western Law Times, Can.
Westm. _____ Statute of Westminster.
West. _____ Westmoreland Law Journal, Pa.
West.R. _____ Western Reporter.
West t.Hardw. _____ West temp. Hardwicke, Eng.
West.Wkly. _____ Western Weekly, Can.
1917 West.Wkly. ___ 1917 Western Weekly, Can.
Whart. _____ Wharton, Pa.
Whart.Ag. _____ Wharton on Agency.
Whart.Am.Cr.Law __ Wharton's American Criminal Law.
Whart.Confl.Laws __ Wharton's Conflict of Laws.
Whart.Cr.Ev. _____ Wharton on Criminal Evidence.
Whart.Cr.Law _____ Wharton's American Criminal Law.
Whart.Cr.Pl. &
Brace _____ Wharton's Criminal Pleading & Practice.
Whart.Ev. _____ Wharton on Evidence in Civil Issues.
Whart.Homicide ____ Wharton's Law of Homicide.
Whart.Law Dict. ___ Wharton's Law Dictionary, or Law Lexicon.
Whart.Law Lexicon _ Wharton's Law Dictionary (or Law Lexicon).
Whart.Neg. _____ Wharton on Negligence.
Whart. & S.Med.Jur. Wharton and Stille's Medical Jurisprudence.
Whart.St.Tr. _____ Wharton's State Trials, U.S.
Wheat. _____ Wheaton, U.S.
Wheeler, Am.Cr.Law Wheeler's Abridgment of American Common Law Cases.

Wheeler, Cr.Cas. ___ Wheeler's Criminal Cases, N.Y.

White & T.Lead.
Cas.Eq. _____ White and Tudor's Leading Cases in Equity.

White & W.Civ.Cas.
Ct.App. _____ White & Willson's Civil Cases Court of Appeals, Tex.

Whitm.Pat.Cas. ___ Whitman's Patent Cases, U.S.

Whitm.Pat.Law Rev. Whitman's Patent Law Review, D.C.

WHO _____ World Health Organization.

Wight. _____ Wightwicke, Eng.
Wilcox _____ Wilcox, Pa.
Will. _____ William, as 1 Will. IV.
Willamette L.J. ____ Willamette Law Journal.
Will.Eq.Jur. _____ Willard's Equity Jurisprudence.

Willes _____ Willes' English Common Pleas Reports.

William Mitchell L.
Rev. _____ William Mitchell Law Review.

Williams _____ Williams, Vt.

Willson, Civ.Cas.Ct.
App. _____ Willson's Civil Cases Court of Appeals, Tex.

Willson, Tex.Cr.Law Willson's Revised Penal Code, Code of Criminal Procedure, and Penal Laws of Texas.

Wilm. _____ Wilmot's Notes, Eng.
Wils. _____ Wilson, Ind.
Wils. _____ Wilson's English Common Pleas Reports.
Wils.Ch. _____ Wilson's Chancery, Eng.
Wils.C.P. _____ Wilson's Common Pleas, Eng.
Wils.Exch. _____ Wilson's Exchequer, Eng.

Wilson's Rev. &
Ann.St. _____ Wilson's Revised and Annotated Statutes, Okl.
Wils.P.C. _____ Wilson's Privy Council, Eng.
Wils. & S. _____ Wilson & Shaw, Sc.
WIN _____ Work Incentive Program.
Winch _____ Winch's English Common Pleas Reports.
Winst. _____ Winston, N.C.
Wis. _____ Wisconsin Reports.
Wis.2d _____ Wisconsin Reports, Second Series.
Wis.Bar Bull. _____ Wisconsin Bar Bulletin.
Wis.L.Rev. _____ Wisconsin Law Review.
Wis.L.N. _____ Wisconsin Legal News, Milwaukee.
Wkly.Dig. _____ Weekly Digest, N.Y.
Wkly.Law Bul. ____ Weekly Law Bulletin, Ohio.
Wkly.Law Gaz. ____ Weekly Law Gazette, Ohio.
Wkly.Notes Cas. __ Weekly Notes Cases, Pa.
Wkly.Rep. _____ Weekly Reporter, London, Eng.
W.Jones _____ William Jones, Eng.
W.Kel. _____ William Kelynge, Eng.

Wm. _____ William, as 9 Wm. III.
Wm.Bl. _____ Sir William Blackstone's English King's Bench Reports.
Wm. & Mary _____ William and Mary, as 2 Wm. & Mary, c. 1.
Wm. & Mary L.Rev. William and Mary Law Review.
Wms.Ann.Reg. ____ William's Annual Register, N.Y.
W.N. _____ Weekly Notes, Eng.
W.N.C. _____ Weekly Notes Cases, Pa.
Wolf. & B. _____ Wolferstan & Bristow's Election Cases, Eng.
Wolf. & D. _____ Wolferstan & Dew's Election Cases, Eng.
Woll. _____ Wollaston, Eng.
Woodb. & M. _____ Woodbury & Minot, U.S.
Wood.Lect. _____ Wooddeson's Lectures on Laws of England.
Wood, Inst. _____ Wood's Institutes of the Common Laws of England.
Woods _____ Woods, U.S.
Wood's Civ.Law ___ Wood's Institutes of the Civil Law of England.
Wood's Dig. _____ Wood's Digest of Laws, Cal.
Woodw.Dec. _____ Woodward's Decisions, Pa.
Woolw. _____ Woolworth, U.S.
Woolr.Waters _____ Woolrych's Law of Waters.
Wor.Dict. _____ Worcester's Dictionary.
Worcest.Dict. _____ Worcester's Dictionary.
W.Res.L.Rev. _____ Western Reserve Law Review.
Wright _____ Wright, Ohio.
Wright _____ Wright, Pa.
Wm.Rob.Adm. ____ William Robinson's English Admiralty Reports.
W.Rob.Adm. _____ W. Robinson's English Admiralty Reports.
Wr.Pa. _____ Wright, Pa.
W.S. _____ Wagner's Statutes, Mo.
W.S. _____ Wyoming Statutes.
W.S.A. _____ Wisconsin Statutes Annotated.
W.Va. _____ West Virginia Reports.
W.Va.L.Q. _____ West Virginia Law Quarterly.
WVC _____ West Virginia Code.
W.W. & D. _____ Willmore, Wollaston & Davidson, Eng.
W.W. & H. _____ Willmore, Wollaston & Hodges, Eng.
W.W.Harr. _____ W. W. Harrington, Del.
Wyatt, Prac.Reg. __ Wyatt's Practical Register in Chancery.
Wyo. _____ Wyoming Reports.
Wythe _____ Wythe's Chancery, Va.
Wy. & W. _____ Wyatt & Webb, Vict.
Wy.W. & A'Beck. __ Wyatt, Webb & A'Beckett, Vict.

Y

Yale L.J. _____ Yale Law Journal.
Yates Sel.Cas. ____ Yates Select Cases, N. Y.
Y.B. _____ Year Book, Eng.

Y. & C.Exch. _____ Younge & Collyer's Exchequer, Eng.

Y. & Coll. _____ Younge & Collyer's Chancery, Eng.

Yeates _____ Yeates, Pa.

Yelv. _____ Yelverton, Eng.

Yerg. _____ Yerger, Tenn.

Y. & J. _____ Younge & Jervis, Eng.

York Leg.Rec. _____ York Legal Record, Pa.

Young Adm. _____ Young's Admiralty Decisions, N.S.

Younge _____ Younge Exchequer, Eng.

Younge & C.Ch. ____ Younge & Collyer's English Chancery Reports.

Z

Zab. _____ Zabriskie, N.J.

THE CONSTITUTION OF THE UNITED STATES

We the People of the United States, in Order to form a more perfect Union, establish Justice, insure domestic Tranquility, provide for the common defence, promote the general Welfare, and secure the Blessings of Liberty to ourselves and our Posterity, do ordain and establish this Constitution for the United States of America.

ARTICLE I

Section 1.   All legislative Powers herein granted shall be vested in a Congress of the United States, which shall consist of a Senate and House of Representatives.

Section 2.   [1]   The House of Representatives shall be composed of Members chosen every second Year by the People of the several States, and the Electors in each State shall have the Qualifications requisite for Electors of the most numerous Branch of the State Legislature.

[2]   No Person shall be a Representative who shall not have attained to the Age of twenty five Years, and been seven Years a Citizen of the United States, and who shall not, when elected, be an Inhabitant of that State in which he shall be chosen.

[3]   Representatives and direct Taxes shall be apportioned among the several States which may be included within this Union, according to their respective Numbers, which shall be determined by adding to the whole Number of free Persons, including those bound to Service for a Term of Years, and excluding Indians not taxed, three fifths of all other Persons.   The actual Enumeration shall be made within three Years after the first Meeting of the Congress of the United States, and within every subsequent Term of ten Years, in such Manner as they shall by Law direct.   The Number of Representatives shall not exceed one for every thirty Thousand, but each State shall have at Least one Representative; and until such enumeration shall be made, the State of New Hampshire shall be entitled to chuse three, Massachusetts eight, Rhode Island and Providence Plantations one, Connecticut five, New York six, New Jersey four, Pennsylvania eight, Delaware one, Maryland six, Virginia ten, North Carolina five, South Carolina five, and Georgia three.

[4]   When vacancies happen in the Representation from any State, the Executive Authority thereof shall issue Writs of Election to fill such Vacancies.

[5]   The House of Representatives shall chuse their Speaker and other Officers; and shall have the sole Power of Impeachment.

Section 3.   [1]   The Senate of the United States shall be composed of two Senators from each State, chosen by the Legislature thereof, for six Years; and each Senator shall have one Vote.

[2]   Immediately after they shall be assembled in Consequence of the first Election, they shall be divided as equally as may be into three Classes.   The Seats of the Senators of the first Class shall be vacated at the Expiration of the Second Year, of the second Class at the Expiration of the fourth Year, and of the third Class at the Expiration of the sixth Year, so that one third may be chosen every second Year; and if Vacancies happen by Resignation, or otherwise, during the Recess of the Legislature of any State, the Executive thereof may make temporary Appointments until the next Meeting of the Legislature, which shall then fill such Vacancies.

[3]   No Person shall be a Senator who shall not have attained to the Age of thirty Years, and been nine Years a Citizen of the United States, and who shall not, when elected, be an Inhabitant of that State for which he shall be chosen.

[4]   The Vice President of the United States shall be President of the Senate, but shall have no Vote, unless they be equally divided.

[5]   The Senate shall chuse their other Officers, and also a President pro tempore, in the Absence of the Vice President, or when he shall exercise the Office of President of the United States.

[6]   The Senate shall have the sole Power to try all Impeachments. When sitting for that Purpose, they shall be on Oath or Affirmation. When the President of the United States is tried, the Chief Justice shall preside: And no Person shall be convicted without the Concurrence of two thirds of the Members present.

[7]   Judgment in Cases of Impeachment shall not extend further than to removal from Office, and disqualification to hold and enjoy any Office of honor, Trust, or Profit under the United States: but the Party convicted shall nevertheless be liable and subject to Indictment, Trial, Judgment, and Punishment, according to Law.

Section 4.   [1]   The Times, Places and Manner of holding Elections for Senators and Representatives, shall be prescribed in each State by the Legislature thereof; but the Congress may at any time by Law make or alter such Regulations, except as to the Places of chusing Senators.

[2]   The Congress shall assemble at least once in every Year, and such Meeting shall be on the first Monday in December, unless they shall by Law appoint a different Day.

Section 5.   [1]   Each House shall be the Judge of the Elections, Returns, and Qualifications of its own Members, and a Majority of each shall constitute a Quorum to do Business; but a smaller Number may adjourn from day to day, and may be authorized to compel the Attendance of absent Members, in such Manner, and under such Penalties as each House may provide.

[2]   Each House may determine the Rules of its Proceedings, punish its Members for disorderly Behavior, and, with the Concurrence of two thirds, expel a Member.

[3]   Each House shall keep a Journal of its Proceedings, and from time to time publish the same, excepting such Parts as may in their Judgment require Secrecy; and the Yeas and Nays of the Members of either House on any question shall, at the Desire of one fifth of those Present, be entered on the Journal.

[4]   Neither House, during the Session of Congress, shall, without the Consent of the other, adjourn for more than three days, nor to any other Place than that in which the two Houses shall be sitting.

Section 6.   [1]   The Senators and Representatives shall receive a Compensation for their Services, to be ascertained by Law, and paid out of the Treasury of the United States. They shall in all Cases, except Treason, Felony and Breach of the Peace, be privileged from Arrest during their Attendance at the Session of their respective Houses, and in going to and returning from the same; and for any Speech or Debate in either House, they shall not be questioned in any other Place.

[2]   No Senator or Representative shall, during the Time for which he was elected, be appointed to any civil Office under the Authority of the United States, which shall have been created, or the Emoluments whereof shall have been increased during such time. and no Person holding any Office under the United States, shall be a Member of either House during his Continuance in Office.

Section 7.   [1]   All Bills for raising Revenue shall originate in the House of Representatives; but the Senate may propose or concur with Amendments as on other Bills.

[2]   Every Bill which shall have passed the House of Representatives and the Senate, shall, before it become a Law, be presented to the President of the United States; If he

approve he shall sign it, but if not he shall return it, with his Objections to the House in which it shall have originated, who shall enter the Objections at large on their Journal, and proceed to reconsider it. If after such Reconsideration two thirds of that House shall agree to pass the Bill, it shall be sent together with the Objections, to the other House, by which it shall likewise be reconsidered, and if approved by two thirds of that House, it shall become a Law. But in all such Cases the Votes of both Houses shall be determined by Yeas and Nays, and the Names of the Persons voting for and against the Bill shall be entered on the Journal of each House respectively. If any Bill shall not be returned by the President within ten Days (Sundays excepted) after it shall have been presented to him, the Same shall be a Law, in like Manner as if he had signed it, unless the Congress by their Adjournment prevent its Return in which Case it shall not be a Law.

[3] Every Order, Resolution, or Vote, to Which the Concurrence of the Senate and House of Representatives may be necessary (except on a question of Adjournment) shall be presented to the President of the United States; and before the Same shall take Effect, shall be approved by him, or being disapproved by him, shall be repassed by two thirds of the Senate and House of Representatives, according to the Rules and Limitations prescribed in the Case of a Bill.

Section 8. [1] The Congress shall have Power To lay and collect Taxes, Duties, Imposts and Excises, to pay the Debts and provide for the common Defence and general Welfare of the United States; but all Duties, Imposts and Excises shall be uniform throughout the United States;

[2] To borrow money on the credit of the United States;

[3] To regulate Commerce with foreign Nations, and among the several States, and with the Indian Tribes;

[4] To establish an uniform Rule of Naturalization, and uniform Laws on the subject of Bankruptcies throughout the United States;

[5] To coin Money, regulate the Value thereof, and of foreign Coin, and fix the Standard of Weights and Measures;

[6] To provide for the Punishment of counterfeiting the Securities and current Coin of the United States;

[7] To Establish Post Offices and Post Roads;

[8] To promote the Progress of Science and useful Arts, by securing for limited Times to Authors and Inventors the exclusive Right to their respective Writings and Discoveries;

[9] To constitute Tribunals inferior to the supreme Court;

[10] To define and punish Piracies and Felonies committed on the high Seas, and Offenses against the Law of Nations;

[11] To declare War, grant Letters of Marque and Reprisal, and make Rules concerning Captures on Land and Water;

[12] To raise and support Armies, but no Appropriation of Money to that Use shall be for a longer Term than two Years;

[13] To provide and maintain a Navy;

[14] To make Rules for the Government and Regulation of the land and naval Forces;

[15] To provide for calling forth the Militia to execute the Laws of the Union, suppress Insurrections and repel Invasions;

[16] To provide for organizing, arming, and disciplining, the Militia, and for governing such Part of them as may be employed in the Service of the United States, reserving to the States respectively, the Appointment of the Officers, and the Authority of training the Militia according to the discipline prescribed by Congress;

[17] To exercise exclusive Legislation in all Cases whatsoever, over such District (not exceeding ten Miles square) as may, by Cession of particular States, and the Acceptance of Congress, become the Seat of the Government of the United States, and to exercise like Authority over all Places purchased by the Consent of the Legislature of the State in which the Same shall be, for the Erection of Forts, Magazines, Arsenals, dock-Yards, and other needful Buildings;—And

[18] To make all Laws which shall be necessary and proper for carrying into Execution the foregoing Powers, and all other Powers vested by this Constitution in the Government of the United States, or in any Department or Officer thereof.

Section 9. [1] The Migration or Importation of Such Persons as any of the States now existing shall think proper to admit, shall not be prohibited by the Congress prior to the Year one thousand eight hundred and eight, but a Tax or duty may be imposed on such Importation, not exceeding ten dollars for each Person.

[2] The privilege of the Writ of Habeas Corpus shall not be suspended, unless when in Cases of Rebellion or Invasion the public Safety may require it.

[3] No Bill of Attainder or ex post facto Law shall be passed.

[4] No Capitation, or other direct, Tax shall be laid, unless in Proportion to the Census or Enumeration herein before directed to be taken.

[5] No Tax or Duty shall be laid on Articles exported from any State.

[6] No Preference shall be given by any Regulation of Commerce or Revenue to the Ports of one State over those of another: nor shall Vessels bound to, or from, one State be obliged to enter, clear, or pay Duties in another.

[7] No money shall be drawn from the Treasury, but in Consequence of Appropriations made by Law; and a regular Statement and Account of the Receipts and Expenditures of all public Money shall be published from time to time.

[8] No Title of Nobility shall be granted by the United States: And no Person holding any Office of Profit or Trust under them, shall, without the Consent of the Congress, accept of any present, Emolument, Office, or Title, of any kind whatever, from any King, Prince, or foreign State.

Section 10. [1] No State shall enter into any Treaty, Alliance, or Confederation; grant Letters of Marque and Reprisal; coin Money; emit Bills of Credit; make any Thing but gold and silver Coin a Tender in Payment of Debts; pass any Bill of Attainder, ex post facto Law, or Law impairing the Obligation of Contracts, or grant any Title of Nobility.

[2] No State shall, without the Consent of the Congress, lay any Imposts or Duties on Imports or Exports, except what may be absolutely necessary for executing its inspection Laws: and the net Produce of all Duties and Imposts, laid by any State on Imports or Exports, shall be for the Use of the Treasury of the United States; and all such Laws shall be subject to the Revision and Controul of the Congress.

[3] No State shall, without the Consent of Congress, lay any Duty of Tonnage, keep Troops, or Ships of War in time of Peace, enter into any Agreement or Compact with another State, or with a foreign Power, or engage in War, unless actually invaded, or in such imminent Danger as will not admit of delay.

ARTICLE II

Section 1. [1] The executive Power shall be vested in a President of the United States of America. He shall hold his Office during the Term of four Years, and, together with the Vice President, chosen for the same Term, be elected, as follows:

[2] Each State shall appoint, in such Manner as the Legislature thereof may direct, a Number of Electors, equal to the whole Number of Senators and Representatives to which

the State may be entitled in the Congress; but no Senator or Representative, or Person holding an Office of Trust or Profit under the United States, shall be appointed an Elector.

[3]   The Electors shall meet in their respective States, and vote by Ballot for two Persons, of whom one at least shall not be an Inhabitant of the same State with themselves. And they shall make a List of all the Persons voted for, and of the Number of Votes for each; which List they shall sign and certify, and transmit sealed to the Seat of the Government of the United States, directed to the President of the Senate. The President of the Senate shall, in the Presence of the Senate and House of Representatives, open all the Certificates, and the Votes shall then be counted. The Person having the greatest Number of Votes shall be the President, if such Number be a Majority of the whole Number of Electors appointed; and if there be more than one who have such Majority, and have an equal Number of Votes, then the House of Representatives shall immediately chuse by Ballot one of them for President; and if no Person have a Majority, then from the five highest on the List the said House shall in like Manner chuse the President. But in chusing the President, the Votes shall be taken by States the Representation from each State having one Vote; A quorum for this Purpose shall consist of a Member or Members from two thirds of the States, and a Majority of all the States shall be necessary to a Choice. In every Case, after the Choice of the President, the Person having the greater Number of Votes of the Electors shall be the Vice President. But if there should remain two or more who have equal Votes, the Senate shall chuse from them by Ballot the Vice President.

[4]   The Congress may determine the Time of chusing the Electors, and the Day on which they shall give their Votes; which Day shall be the same throughout the United States.

[5]   No person except a natural born Citizen, or a Citizen of the United States, at the time of the Adoption of this Constitution, shall be eligible to the Office of President; neither shall any Person be eligible to that Office who shall not have attained to the Age of thirty five Years, and been fourteen Years a Resident within the United States.

[6]   In case of the removal of the President from Office, or of his Death, Resignation or Inability to discharge the Powers and Duties of the said Office, the Same shall devolve on the Vice President, and the Congress may by Law provide for the Case of Removal, Death, Resignation or Inability, both of the President and Vice President, declaring what Officer shall then act as President, and such Officer shall act accordingly, until the Dis ability be removed, or a President shall be elected.

[7]   The President shall, at stated Times, receive for his Services, a Compensation, which shall neither be increased nor diminished during the Period for which he shall have been elected, and he shall not receive within that Period any other Emolument from the United States, or any of them.

[8]   Before he enter on the Execution of his Office, he shall take the following Oath or Affirmation: "I do solemnly swear (or affirm) that I will faithfully execute the Office of President of the United States, and will to the best of my Ability, preserve, protect and defend the Constitution of the United States."

Section 2.   [1]   The President shall be Commander in Chief of the Army and Navy of the United States, and of the militia of the several States, when called into the actual Service of the United States; he may require the Opinion, in writing, of the principal Officer in each of the Executive Departments, upon any Subject relating to the Duties of their respective Offices, and he shall have Power to grant Reprieves and Pardons for Offenses against the United States, except in Cases of Impeachment.

[2]   He shall have Power, by and with the Advice and Consent of the Senate to make Treaties, provided two thirds of the Senators present concur; and he shall nominate, and by and with the Advice and Consent of the Senate, shall appoint Ambassadors, other public Ministers and Consuls, Judges of the supreme Court, and all other Officers of the United States, whose Appointments are not herein otherwise provided for, and which shall be established by Law; but the Congress may by Law vest the Appointment of such inferior

Officers, as they think proper, in the President alone, in the Courts of Law, or in the Heads of Departments.

[3] The President shall have Power to fill up all Vacancies that may happen during the Recess of the Senate, by granting Commissions which shall expire at the End of their next Session.

Section 3. He shall from time to time give to the Congress Information of the State of the Union, and recommend to their Consideration such Measures as he shall judge necessary and expedient; he may, on extraordinary Occasions, convene both Houses, or either of them, and in Case of Disagreement between them, with Respect to the Time of Adjournment, he may adjourn them to such Time as he shall think proper; he shall receive Ambassadors and other public Ministers; he shall take Care that the Laws be faithfully executed, and shall Commission all the Officers of the United States.

Section 4. The President, Vice President and all civil Officers of the United States, shall be removed from Office on Impeachment for, and Conviction of, Treason, Bribery, or other high Crimes and Misdemeanors.

ARTICLE III

Section 1. The judicial Power of the United States, shall be vested in one supreme Court, and in such inferior Courts as the Congress may from time to time ordain and establish. The Judges, both of the supreme and inferior Courts, shall hold their Offices during good Behaviour, and shall, at stated Times, receive for their Services a Compensation, which shall not be diminished during their Continuance in Office.

Section 2. [1] The judicial Power shall extend to all Cases, in Law and Equity, arising under this Constitution, the Laws of the United States, and Treaties made, or which shall be made, under their Authority;—to all Cases affecting Ambassadors, other public Ministers and Consuls;—to all Cases of admiralty and maritime Jurisdiction;—to Controversies to which the United States shall be a Party;—to Controversies between two or more States;—between a State and Citizens of another State;—between Citizens of different States;—between Citizens of the same State claiming Lands under the Grants of different States, and between a State, or the Citizens thereof, and foreign States, Citizens or Subjects.

[2] In all Cases affecting Ambassadors, other public Ministers and Consuls, and those in which a State shall be a Party, the supreme Court shall have original Jurisdiction. In all the other Cases before mentioned, the supreme Court shall have appellate Jurisdiction, both as to Law and Fact, with such Exceptions, and under such Regulations as the Congress shall make.

[3] The trial of all Crimes, except in Cases of Impeachment, shall be by Jury; and such Trial shall be held in the State where the said Crimes shall have been committed; but when not committed within any State, the Trial shall be at such Place or Places as the Congress may by Law have directed.

Section 3. [1] Treason against the United States, shall consist only in levying War against them, or, in adhering to their Enemies, giving them Aid and Comfort. No Person shall be convicted of Treason unless on the Testimony of two Witnesses to the same overt Act, or on Confession in open Court.

[2] The Congress shall have Power to declare the Punishment of Treason, but no Attainder of Treason shall work Corruption of Blood, or Forfeiture except during the Life of the Person attainted.

ARTICLE IV

Section 1. Full Faith and Credit shall be given in each State to the public Acts, Records, and judicial Proceedings of every other State. And the Congress may by general

Laws prescribe the Manner in which such Acts, Records and Proceedings shall be proved, and the Effect thereof.

Section 2. [1] The Citizens of each State shall be entitled to all Privileges and Immunities of Citizens in the several States.

[2] A Person charged in any State with Treason, Felony, or other Crime, who shall flee from Justice, and be found in another State, shall on demand of the executive Authority of the State from which he fled, be delivered up, to be removed to the State having Jurisdiction of the Crime.

[3] No Person held to Service or Labour in one State, under the Laws thereof, escaping into another, shall, in Consequence of any Law or Regulation therein, be discharged from such Service or Labour, but shall be delivered up on Claim of the Party to whom such Service or Labour may be due.

Section 3. [1] New States may be admitted by the Congress into this Union; but no new State shall be formed or erected within the Jurisdiction of any other State; nor any State be formed by the Junction of two or more States, or Parts of States, without the Consent of the Legislatures of the States concerned as well as of the Congress.

[2] The Congress shall have Power to dispose of and make all needful Rules and Regulations respecting the Territory or other Property belonging to the United States; and nothing in this Constitution shall be so construed as to Prejudice any Claims of the United States, or of any particular State.

Section 4. The United States shall guarantee to every State in this Union a Republican Form of Government, and shall protect each of them against Invasion; and on Application of the Legislature, or of the Executive (when the Legislature cannot be convened) against domestic Violence.

ARTICLE V

The Congress, whenever two thirds of both Houses shall deem it necessary, shall propose Amendments to this Constitution, or, on the Application of the Legislatures of two thirds of the several States, shall call a Convention for proposing Amendments, which, in either Case, shall be valid to all Intents and Purposes, as part of this Constitution, when ratified by the Legislatures of three fourths of the several States, or by Conventions in three fourths thereof, as the one or the other Mode of Ratification may be proposed by the Congress; Provided that no Amendment which may be made prior to the Year One thousand eight hundred and eight shall in any Manner affect the first and fourth Clauses in the Ninth Section of the first Article; and that no State, without its Consent, shall be deprived of its equal Suffrage in the Senate.

ARTICLE VI

[1] All Debts contracted and Engagements entered into, before the Adoption of this Constitution shall be as valid against the United States under this Constitution, as under the Confederation.

[2] This Constitution, and the Laws of the United States which shall be made in Pursuance thereof; and all Treaties made, or which shall be made, under the Authority of the United States, shall be the supreme Law of the Land; and the Judges in every State shall be bound thereby, any Thing in the Constitution or Laws of any State to the Contrary notwithstanding.

[3]   The Senators and Representatives before mentioned, and the Members of the several State Legislatures, and all executive and judicial Officers, both of the United States and of the several States, shall be bound by Oath or Affirmation, to support this Constitution; but no religious Test shall ever be required as a Quaification to any Office or public Trust under the United States.

ARTICLE VII

The Ratification of the Conventions of nine States shall be sufficient for the Establishment of this Constitution between the States so ratifying the Same.

ARTICLES IN ADDITION TO, AND AMENDMENT OF, THE CONSTITUTION OF THE UNITED STATES OF AMERICA, PROPOSED BY CONGRESS, AND RATIFIED BY THE LEGISLATURES OF THE SEVERAL STATES PURSUANT TO THE FIFTH ARTICLE OF THE ORIGINAL CONSTITUTION.

AMENDMENT I [1791]

Congress shall make no law respecting an establishment of religion, or prohibiting the free exercise thereof; or abridging the freedom of speech, or of the press; or the right of the people peaceably to assemble, and to petition the Government for a redress of grievances.

AMENDMENT II [1791]

A well regulated Militia, being necessary to the security of a free State, the right of the people to keep and bear Arms, shall not be infringed.

AMENDMENT III [1791]

No Soldier shall, in time of peace be quartered in any house, without the consent of the Owner, nor in time of war, but in a manner to be prescribed by law.

AMENDMENT IV [1791]

The right of the people to be secure in their persons, houses, papers, and effects, against unreasonable searches and seizures, shall not be violated, and no Warrants shall issue, but upon probable cause, supported by Oath or affirmation, and particularly describing the place to be searched, and the persons or things to be seized.

AMENDMENT V [1791]

No person shall be held to answer for a capital, or otherwise infamous crime, unless on a presentment or indictment of a Grand Jury, except in cases arising in the land or naval forces, or in the Militia, when in actual service in time of War or public danger; nor shall any person be subject for the same offence to be twice put in jeopardy of life or limb; nor shall be compelled in any criminal case to be a witness against himself, nor be deprived of life, liberty, or property, without due process of law; nor shall private property be taken for public use, without just compensation.

AMENDMENT VI [1791]

In all criminal prosecutions, the accused shall enjoy the right to a speedy and public trial, by an impartial jury of the State and district wherein the crime shall have been committed, which district shall have been previously ascertained by law, and to be informed of the nature and cause of the accusation; to be confronted with the witnesses against him;

to have compulsory process for obtaining witnesses in his favor, and to have the Assistance of Counsel for his defence.

AMENDMENT VII [1791]

In Suits at common law, where the value in controversy shall exceed twenty dollars, the right of trial by jury shall be preserved, and no fact tried by jury, shall be otherwise re-examined in any Court of the United States, than according to the rules of the common law.

AMENDMENT VIII [1791]

Excessive bail shall not be required, nor excessive fines imposed, nor cruel and unusual punishments inflicted.

AMENDMENT IX [1791]

The enumeration in the Constitution, of certain rights, shall not be construed to deny or disparage others retained by the people.

AMENDMENT X [1791]

The powers not delegated to the United States by the Constitution, nor prohibited by it to the States, are reserved to the States respectively, or to the people.

AMENDMENT XI [1798]

The Judicial power of the United States shall not be construed to extend to any suit in law or equity, commenced or prosecuted against one of the United States by Citizens of another State, or by Citizens or Subjects of any Foreign State.

AMENDMENT XII [1804]

The Electors shall meet in their respective states and vote by ballot for President and Vice-President, one of whom, at least, shall not be an inhabitant of the same state with themselves; they shall name in their ballots the person voted for as President, and in distinct ballots the person voted for as Vice-President, and they shall make distinct lists of all persons voted for as President, and of all persons voted for as Vice-President, and of the number of votes for each, which lists they shall sign and certify, and transmit sealed to the seat of the government of the United States, directed to the President of the Senate;—The President of the Senate shall, in the presence of the Senate and House of Representatives, open all the certificates and the votes shall then be counted;—The person having the greatest number of votes for President, shall be the President, if such number be a majority of the whole number of Electors appointed; and if no person have such majority, then from the persons having the highest numbers not exceeding three on the list of those voted for as President, the House of Representatives shall choose immediately, by ballot, the President. But in choosing the President, the votes shall be taken by states, the representation from each state having one vote; a quorum for this purpose shall consist of a member or members from two-thirds of the states, and a majority of all the states shall be necessary to a choice. And if the House of Representatives shall not choose a President whenever the right of choice shall devolve upon them before the fourth day of March next following, then the Vice-President shall act as President, as in the case of the death or other constitutional disability of the President.—The person having the greatest number of votes as Vice-President, shall be the Vice-President, if such number be a majority of the whole number of Electors appointed, and if no person have a majority, then from the two highest numbers on the list, the Senate shall choose the Vice-President; a quorum for the purpose shall consist of two-thirds of the whole number of Senators, and a majority of the whole number shall be necessary to a choice. But no person constitutionally ineligible to the office of President shall be eligible to that of Vice-President of the United States.

AMENDMENT XIII [1865]

Section 1. Neither slavery nor involuntary servitude, except as a punishment for crime whereof the party shall have been duly convicted, shall exist within the United States, or any place subject to their jurisdiction.

Section 2. Congress shall have power to enforce this article by appropriate legislation.

AMENDMENT XIV [1868]

Section 1. All persons born or naturalized in the United States, and subject to the jurisdiction thereof, are citizens of the United States and of the State wherein they reside. No State shall make or enforce any law which shall abridge the privileges or immunities of citizens of the United States; nor shall any State deprive any person of life, liberty, or property, without due process of law; nor deny to any person within its jurisdiction the equal protection of the laws.

Section 2. Representatives shall be apportioned among the several States according to their respective numbers, counting the whole number of persons in each State excluding Indians not taxed. But when the right to vote at any election for the choice of electors for President and Vice President of the United States, Representatives in Congress, the Executive and Judicial officers of a State, or the members of the Legislature thereof, is denied to any of the male inhabitants of such State, being twenty-one years of age, and citizens of the United States, or in any way abridged, except for participation in rebellion, or other crime, the basis of representation therein shall be reduced in the proportion which the number of such male citizens shall bear to the whole number of male citizens twenty-one years of age in such State.

Section 3. No person shall be a Senator or Representative in Congress, or elector of President and Vice President, or hold any office, civil or military, under the United States, or under any State, who having previously taken an oath, as a member of Congress, or as an officer of the United States, or as a member of any State legislature, or as an executive or judicial officer of any State, to support the Constitution of the United States, shall have engaged in insurrection or rebellion against the same, or given aid or comfort to the enemies thereof. But Congress may by a vote of two-thirds of each House, remove such disability.

Section 4. The validity of the public debt of the United States, authorized by law, including debts incurred for payment of pensions and bounties for services in suppressing insurrection or rebellion, shall not be questioned. But neither the United States nor any State shall assume or pay any debt or obligation incurred in aid of insurrection or rebellion against the United States, or any claim for the loss or emancipation of any slave; but all such debts, obligations and claims shall be held illegal and void.

Section 5. The Congress shall have power to enforce, by appropriate legislation, the provisions of this article.

AMENDMENT XV [1870]

Section 1. The right of citizens of the United States to vote shall not be denied or abridged by the United States or by any State on account of race, color, or previous condition of servitude.

Section 2. The Congress shall have power to enforce this article by appropriate legislation.

AMENDMENT XVI [1913]

The Congress shall have power to lay and collect taxes on incomes, from whatever source derived, without apportionment among the several States, and without regard to any census or enumeration.

AMENDMENT XVII [1913]

[1] The Senate of the United States shall be composed of two Senators from each State, elected by the people thereof, for six years; and each Senator shall have one vote. The electors in each State shall have the qualifications requisite for electors of the most numerous branch of the State legislatures.

[2] When vacancies happen in the representation of any State in the Senate, the executive authority of such State shall issue writs of election to fill such vacancies: *Provided,* That the legislature of any State may empower the executive thereof to make temporary appointments until the people fill the vacancies by election as the legislature may direct.

[3] This amendment shall not be so construed as to affect the election or term of any Senator chosen before it becomes valid as part of the Constitution.

AMENDMENT XVIII [1919]

Section 1. After one year from the ratification of this article the manufacture, sale, or transportation of intoxicating liquors within, the importation thereof into, or the exportation thereof from the United States and all territory subject to the jurisdiction thereof for beverage purposes is hereby prohibited.

Section 2. The Congress and the several States shall have concurrent power to enforce this article by appropriate legislation.

Section 3. This article shall be inoperative unless it shall have been ratified as an amendment to the Constitution by the legislatures of the several States, as provided in the Constitution, within seven years from the date of the submission hereof to the States by the Congress.

AMENDMENT XIX [1920]

[1] The right of citizens of the United States to vote shall not be denied or abridged by the United States or by any State on account of sex.

[2] Congress shall have power to enforce this article by appropriate legislation.

AMENDMENT XX [1933]

Section 1. The terms of the President and Vice President shall end at noon on the 20th day of January, and the terms of Senators and Representatives at noon on the 3d day of January, of the years in which such terms would have ended if this article had not been ratified; and the terms of their successors shall then begin.

Section 2. The Congress shall assemble at least once in every year, and such meeting shall begin at noon on the 3d day of January, unless they shall by law appoint a different day.

Section 3. If, at the time fixed for the beginning of the term of the President, the President elect shall have died, the Vice President elect shall become President. If the

President shall not have been chosen before the time fixed for the beginning of his term, or if the President elect shall have failed to qualify, then the Vice President elect shall act as President until a President shall have qualified; and the Congress may by law provide for the case wherein neither a President elect nor a Vice President elect shall have qualified, declaring who shall then act as President, or the manner in which one who is to act shall be selected, and such person shall act accordingly until a President or Vice President shall have qualified.

Section 4. The Congress may by law provide for the case of the death of any of the persons from whom the House of Representatives may choose a President whenever the right of choice shall have devolved upon them, and for the case of the death of any of the persons from whom the Senate may choose a Vice President whenever the right of choice shall have devolved upon them.

Section 5. Sections 1 and 2 shall take effect on the 15th day of October following the ratification of this article.

Section 6. This article shall be inoperative unless it shall have been ratified as an amendment to the Constitution by the legislatures of three-fourths of the several States within seven years from the date of its submission.

Amendment XXI [1933]

Section 1. The eighteenth article of amendment to the Constitution of the United States is hereby repealed.

Section 2. The transportation or importation into any State, Territory, or possession of the United States for delivery or use therein of intoxicating liquors, in violation of the laws thereof, is hereby prohibited.

Section 3. This article shall be inoperative unless it shall have been ratified as an amendment to the Constitution by conventions in the several States, as provided in the Constitution, within seven years from the date of the submission hereof to the States by the Congress.

Amendment XXII [1951]

Section 1. No person shall be elected to the office of the President more than twice, and no person who has held the office of President, or acted as President, for more than two years of a term to which some other person was elected President shall be elected to the office of President more than once. But this Article shall not apply to any person holding the office of President when this Article was proposed by the Congress, and shall not prevent any person who may be holding the office of President, or acting as President, during the term within which this Article becomes operative from holding the office of President or acting as President during the remainder of such term.

Section 2. This article shall be inoperative unless it shall have been ratified as an amendment to the Constitution by the legislatures of three-fourths of the several States within seven years from the date of its submission to the States by the Congress.

Amendment XXIII [1961]

Section 1. The District constituting the seat of Government of the United States shall appoint in such manner as the Congress may direct:

A number of electors of President and Vice President equal to the whole number of Senators and Representatives in Congress to which the District would be entitled if it were a State, but in no event more than the least populous state; they shall be in addition to those appointed by the states, but they shall be considered, for the purposes of the election of President and Vice President, to be electors appointed by a state; and they shall meet in the District and perform such duties as provided by the twelfth article of amendment.

Section 2.   The Congress shall have power to enforce this article by appropriate legislation.

Amendment XXIV [1964]

Section 1.   The right of citizens of the United States to vote in any primary or other election for President or Vice President, for electors for President or Vice President, or for Senator or Representative in Congress, shall not be denied or abridged by the United States, or any State by reason of failure to pay any poll tax or other tax.

Section 2.   The Congress shall have power to enforce this article by appropriate legislation.

Amendment XXV [1967]

Section 1.   In case of the removal of the President from office or of his death or resignation, the Vice President shall become President.

Section 2.   Whenever there is a vacancy in the office of the Vice President, the President shall nominate a Vice President who shall take office upon confirmation by a majority vote of both Houses of Congress.

Section 3.   Whenever the President transmits to the President pro tempore of the Senate and the Speaker of the House of Representatives his written declaration that he is unable to discharge the powers and duties of his office, and until he transmits to them a written declaration to the contrary, such powers and duties shall be discharged by the Vice President as Acting President.

Section 4.   Whenever the Vice President and a majority of either the principal officers of the executive departments or of such other body as Congress may by law provide, transmit to the President pro tempore of the Senate and the Speaker of the House of Representatives their written declaration that the President is unable to discharge the powers and duties of his office, the Vice President shall immediately assume the powers and duties of the office as Acting President.

Thereafter, when the President transmits to the President pro tempore of the Senate and the Speaker of the House of Representatives his written declaration that no inability exists, he shall resume the powers and duties of his office unless the Vice President and a majority of either the principal officers of the executive department or of such other body as Congress may by law provide, transmit within four days to the President pro tempore of the Senate and the Speaker of the House of Representatives their written declaration and the President is unable to discharge the powers and duties of his office.   Thereupon Congress shall decide the issue, assembling within forty-eight hours for that purpose if not in session.   If the Congress, within twenty-one days after receipt of the latter written declaration, or, if Congress is not in session, within twenty-one days after Congress is required to assemble, determines by two-thirds vote of both Houses that the President is unable to discharge the power and duties of his office, the Vice President shall continue to discharge the same as Acting President; otherwise, the President shall resume the powers and duties of his office.

AMENDMENT XXVI [1971]

Section 1. The right of citizens of the United States, who are eighteen years of age or older, to vote shall not be denied or abridged by the United States or by any State on account of age.

Section 2. The Congress shall have power to enforce this article by appropriate legislation.

PROPOSED CONSTITUTIONAL AMENDMENT [a]

Section 1. Equality of rights under the law shall not be denied or abridged by the United States or by any State on account of sex.

Section 2. The Congress shall have the power to enforce, by appropriate legislation, the provisions of this article.

Section 3. This amendment shall take effect two years after the date of ratification.

PROPOSED CONSTITUTIONAL AMENDMENT [b]

Section 1. For purposes of representation in Congress, election of the President and Vice President, and Article V of this Constitution, the District constituting the seat of government of the United States shall be treated as though it were a State.

Section 2. The exercise of the rights and powers conferred under this article shall be by the people of the District constituting the seat of government and shall be as provided by Congress.

Section 3. The twenty-third Amendment to the Constitution is hereby repealed.

Section 4. This article shall be inoperative, unless it shall have been ratified as an amendment to the Constitution by the legislatures of three-fourths of the several States within seven years from the date of its submission.

[a] The Equal Rights Amendment was proposed by Congress and submitted to the states in March, 1972. In July, 1978, Congress extended the deadline on ratification to June, 1982.

[b] Congress submitted this proposed amendment to the states for ratification in August, 1978.

TIME CHART OF THE UNITED STATES SUPREME COURT †

The following table is designed to aid the user in identifying the composition of the Court at any given time in American history. Each listing is headed by the Chief Justice, whose name is italicized. Associate Justices are listed following the Chief Justice in order of seniority. In addition to dates of appointment, the table provides information on political party affiliation. Following each Justice is a symbol representing his party affiliation at the time of appointment:

F = Federalist
DR = Democratic Republican
    (Jeffersonian)
D = Democrat

W = Whig
R = Republican
I = Independent

1789 *Jay* (F) J. Rutledge (F) Cushing (F) Wilson (F) Blair (F)	**1796–97** *Ellsworth* (F) Cushing (F) Wilson (F) Iredell (F) Paterson (F) S. Chase (F)	**1806** *J. Marshall* (F) Cushing (F) S. Chase (F) Washington (F) W. Johnson (DR) Livingston (DR)	**1826–28** *J. Marshall* (F) Washington (F) W. Johnson (DR) Duval (DR) Story (DR) Thompson (DR) Trimble (DR)
1790–91 *Jay* (F) J. Rutledge (F) Cushing (F) Wilson (F) Blair (F) Iredell (F)	**1798–99** *Ellsworth* (F) Cushing (F) Iredell (F) Paterson (F) S. Chase (F) Washington (F)	**1807–10** *J. Marshall* (F) Cushing (F) S. Chase (F) Washington (F) W. Johnson (DR) Livingston (DR) Todd (DR)	**1829** *J. Marshall* (F) Washington (F) W. Johnson (DR) Duval (DR) Story (DR) Thompson (DR) McLean (D)
1792 *Jay* (F) Cushing (F) Wilson (F) Blair (F) Iredell (F) T. Johnson (F)	**1800** *Ellsworth* (F) Cushing (F) Paterson (F) S. Chase (F) Washington (F) Moore (F)	**1811–22** *J. Marshall* (F) Washington (F) W. Johnson (DR) Livingston (DR) Todd (DR) Duval (DR) Story (DR)	**1830–34** *J. Marshall* (F) W. Johnson (DR) Duval (DR) Story (DR) Thompson (DR) McLean (D) Baldwin (D)
1793–94 *Jay* (F) Cushing (F) Wilson (F) Blair (F) Iredell (F) Paterson (F)	**1801–03** *J. Marshall* (F) Cushing (F) Paterson (F) S. Chase (F) Washington (F) Moore (F)	**1823–25** *J. Marshall* (F) Washington (F) W. Johnson (DR) Todd (DR) Duval (DR) Story (DR) Thompson (DR)	**1835** *J. Marshall* (F) Duval (DR) Story (DR) Thompson (DR) McLean (D) Baldwin (D) Wayne (D)
1795 *J. Rutledge* (F)* Cushing (F) Wilson (F) Blair (F) Iredell (F) Paterson (F)	**1804–05** *J. Marshall* (F) Cushing (F) Paterson (F) S. Chase (F) Washington (F) W. Johnson (DR)		

† Source: Chase and Ducat, Constitutional Interpretation, 2nd Edition, published in 1979 by West Publishing Co.

1836
Taney (D)
Story (DR)
Thompson (DR)
McLean (D)
Baldwin (D)
Wayne (D)
Barbour (D)

1837–40
Taney (D)
Story (DR)
Thompson (DR)
McLean (D)
Baldwin (D)
Wayne (D)
Barbour (D)
Catron (D)
McKinley (D)

1841–43
Taney (D)
Story (DR)
Thompson (DR)
McLean (D)
Baldwin (D)
Wayne (D)
Catron (D)
McKinley (D)
Daniel (D)

1844
Taney (D)
Story (DR)
McLean (D)
Baldwin (D)
Wayne (D)
Catron (D)
McKinley (D)
Daniel (D)

1845
Taney (D)
McLean (D)
Wayne (D)
Catron (D)
McKinley (D)
Daniel (D)
Nelson (D)
Woodbury (D)

1846–50
Taney (D)
McLean (D)
Wayne (D)
Catron (D)
McKinley (D)
Daniel (D)
Nelson (D)
Woodbury (D)
Grier (D)

1851–52
Taney (D)
McLean (D)
Wayne (D)
Catron (D)
McKinley (D)
Daniel (D)
Nelson (D)
Grier (D)
Curtis (W)

1853–57
Taney (D)
McLean (D)
Wayne (D)
Catron (D)
Daniel (D)
Nelson (D)
Grier (D)
Curtis (W)
Campbell (D)

1858–60
Taney (D)
McLean (D)
Wayne (D)
Catron (D)
Daniel (D)
Nelson (D)
Grier (D)
Campbell (D)
Clifford (D)

1861
Taney (D)
McLean (D)
Wayne (D)
Catron (D)
Nelson (D)
Grier (D)
Campbell (D)
Clifford (D)

1862
Taney (D)
Wayne (D)
Catron (D)
Nelson (D)
Grier (D)
Clifford (D)
Swayne (R)
Miller (R)
Davis (R)

1863
Taney (D)
Wayne (D)
Catron (D)
Nelson (D)
Grier (D)
Clifford (D)
Swayne (R)
Miller (R)
Davis (R)
Field (D)

1864–65
S. P. Chase (R)
Wayne (D)
Catron (D)* *
Nelson (D)
Grier (D)
Clifford (D)
Swayne (R)
Miller (R)
Davis (R)
Field (D)

1866
S. P. Chase (R)
Wayne (D)* *
Nelson (D)
Grier (D)
Clifford (D)
Swayne (R)
Miller (R)
Davis (R)
Field (D)

1867–69
S. P. Chase (R)
Nelson (D)
Grier (D)
Clifford (D)
Swayne (R)
Miller (R)
Davis (R)
Field (D)

1870–71
S. P. Chase (R)
Nelson (D)
Clifford (D)
Swayne (R)
Miller (R)
Davis (R)
Field (D)
Strong (R)
Bradley (R)

1872–73
S. P. Chase (R)
Clifford (D)
Swayne (R)
Miller (R)
Davis (R)
Field (D)
Strong (R)
Bradley (R)
Hunt (R)

1874–76
Waite (R)
Clifford D)
Swayne (R)
Miller (R)
Davis (R)
Field (D)
Strong (R)
Bradley (R)
Hunt (R)

1877–79
Waite (R)
Clifford (D)
Swayne (R)
Miller (R)
Field (D)
Strong (R)
Bradley (R)
Hunt (R)
Harlan (Ky.) (R)

1880
Waite (R)
Clifford (D)
Swayne (R)
Miller (R)
Field (D)
Bradley (R)
Hunt (R)
Harlan (Ky.) (R)
Woods (R)

1881
Waite (R)
Miller (R)
Field (D)
Bradley (R)
Hunt (R)
Harlan (Ky.) (R)
Woods (R)
Matthews (R)
Gray (R)

1882–87
Waite (R)
Miller (R)
Field (D)
Bradley (R)
Harlan (Ky.) (R)
Woods (R)
Matthews (R)
Gray (R)
Blatchford (R)

1888
Fuller (D)
Miller (R)
Field (D)
Bradley (R)
Harlan (Ky.) (R)
Matthews (R)
Gray (R)
Blatchford (R)
L. Lamar (D)

1889
Fuller (D)
Miller (R)
Field (D)
Bradley (R)
Harlan (Ky.) (R)
Gray (R)
Blatchford (R)
L. Lamar (D)
Brewer (R)

1890–91 *Fuller* (D) Field (D) Bradley (R) Harlan (Ky.) (R) Gray (R) Blatchford (R) L. Lamar (D) Brewer (R) Brown (R)	**1902** *Fuller* (D) Harlan (Ky.) (R) Brewer (R) Brown (R) Shiras (R) E. White (D) Peckham (D) McKenna (R) Holmes (R)	**1914–15** *E. White* (D) McKenna (R) Holmes (R) Day (R) Hughes (R) Van Devanter (R) J. Lamar (D) Pitney (R) McReynolds (D)	**1930–31** *Hughes* (R) Holmes (R) Van Devanter (R) McReynolds (D) Brandeis (R) Sutherland (R) Butler (D) Stone (R) Roberts (R)
1892 *Fuller* (D) Field (D) Harlan (Ky.) (R) Gray (R) Blatchford (R) L. Lamar (D) Brewer (R) Brown (R) Shiras (R)	**1903–05** *Fuller* (D) Harlan (Ky.) (R) Brewer (R) Brown (R) E. White (D) Peckham (D) McKenna (R) Holmes (R) Day (R)	**1916–20** *E. White* (D) McKenna (R) Holmes (R) Day (R) Van Devanter (R) Pitney (R) McReynolds (D) Brandeis (R)* * * Clarke (D)	**1932–36** *Hughes* (R) Van Devanter (R) McReynolds (D) Brandeis (R) Sutherland (R) Butler (D) Stone (R) Roberts (R) Cardozo (D)
1893 *Fuller* (D) Field (D) Harlan (Ky.) (R) Gray (R) Blatchford (R) Brewer R) Brown (R) Shiras (R) H. Jackson (D)	**1906–08** *Fuller* (D) Harlan (Ky.) (R) Brewer (R) E. White (D) Peckham (D) McKenna (R) Holmes (R) Day (R) Moody (R)	**1921** *Taft* (R) McKenna (R) Holmes (R) Day (R) Van Devanter (R) Pitney (R) McReynolds (D) Brandeis (R) Clarke (D)	**1937** *Hughes* (R) McReynolds (D) Brandeis (R) Sutherland (R) Butler (D) Stone (R) Roberts (R) Cardozo (D) Black (D)
1894 *Fuller* (D) Field (D) Harlan (Ky.) (R) Gray (R) Brewer (R) Brown (R) Shiras (R) H. Jackson (D) E. White (D)	**1909** *Fuller* (D) Harlan (Ky.) (R) Brewer (R) E. White (D) McKenna (R) Holmes (R) Day (R) Moody (R) Lurton (D)	**1922** *Taft* (R) McKenna (R) Holmes (R) Van Devanter (R) Pitney (R) McReynolds (D) Brandeis (R) Sutherland (R) Butler (D)	**1938** *Hughes* (R) McReynolds (D) Brandeis (R) Butler (D) Stone (R) Roberts (R) Cardozo (D) Black (D) Reed (D)
1895–97 *Fuller* (D) Field (D) Harlan (Ky.) (R) Gray (R) Brewer (R) Brown (R) Shiras (R) E. White (D) Peckham (D)	**1910–11** *E. White* (D) Harlan (Ky.) (R) McKenna (R) Holmes (R) Day (R) Lurton (D) Hughes (R) Van Devanter (R) J. Lamar (D)	**1923–24** *Taft* (R) McKenna (R) Holmes (R) Van Devanter (R) McReynolds (D) Brandeis (R) Sutherland (R) Butler (D) Sanford (R)	**1939** *Hughes* (R) McReynolds (D) Butler (D) Stone (R) Roberts (R) Black (D) Reed (D) Frankfurter (I) Douglas (D)
1898–1901 *Fuller* (D) Harlan (Ky.) (R) Gray (R) Brewer (R) Brown (R) Shiras (R) E. White (D) Peckham (D) McKenna (R)	**1912–13** *E. White* (D) McKenna (R) Holmes (R) Day (R) Lurton (D) Hughes (R) Van Devanter (R) J. Lamar (D) Pitney (R)	**1925–29** *Taft* (R) Holmes (R) Van Devanter (R) McReynolds (D) Brandeis (R) Sutherland (R) Butler (D) Sanford (R) Stone (R)	**1940** *Hughes* (R) McReynolds (D) Stone (R) Roberts (R) Black (D) Reed (D) Frankfurter (I) Douglas (D) Murphy (D)

1941–42	1953–54	1962–65	1970
Stone (R)	*Warren* (R)	*Warren* (R)	*Burger* (R)
Roberts (R)	Black (D)	Black (D)	Black (D)
Black (D)	Reed (D)	Douglas (D)	Douglas (D)
Reed (D)	Frankfurter (I)	Clark (D)	Harlan (N.Y.) (R)
Frankfurter (I)	Douglas (D)	Harlan (N.Y.) (R)	Brennan (D)
Douglas (D)	R. Jackson (D)	Brennan (D)	Stewart (R)
Murphy (D)	Burton (R)	Stewart (R)	B. White (D)
Byrnes (D)	Clark (D)	B. White (D)	T. Marshall (D)
R. Jackson (D)	Minton (D)	Goldberg (D)	Blackmun (R)
1943–44	**1955**	**1965–67**	**1971**
Stone (R)	*Warren* (R)	*Warren* (R)	*Burger* (R)
Roberts (R)	Black (D)	Black (D)	Douglas (D)
Black (D)	Reed (D)	Douglas (D)	Brennan (D)
Reed (D)	Frankfurter (I)	Clark (D)	Stewart (R)
Frankfurter (I)	Douglas (D)	Harlan (N.Y.) (R)	B. White (D)
Douglas (D)	Burton (R)	Brennan (D)	T. Marshall (D)
Murphy (D)	Clark (D)	Stewart (R)	Blackmun (R)
R. Jackson (D)	Minton (D)	B. White (D)	
W. Rutledge (D)	Harlan (N.Y.) (R)	Fortas (D)	**1972–75**
1945	**1956**	**1967–69**	*Burger* (R)
Stone (R)	*Warren* (R)	*Warren* (R)	Douglas (D)
Black (D)	Black (D)	Black (D)	Brennan (D)
Reed (D)	Reed (D)	Douglas (D)	Stewart (R)
Frankfurter (I)	Frankfurter (I)	Harlan (N.Y.) (R)	B. White (D)
Douglas (D)	Douglas (D)	Brennan (D)	T. Marshall (D)
Murphy (D)	Burton (R)	Stewart (R)	Blackmun (R)
R. Jackson (D)	Clark (D)	B. White (D)	Powell (D)
W. Rutledge (D)	Harlan (N.Y.) (R)	Fortas (D)	Rehnquist (R)
Burton (R)	Brennan (D)	T. Marshall (D)	
1946–48	**1957**		**1975–**
Vinson (D)	*Warren* (R)	**1969**	*Burger* (R)
Black (D)	Black (D)	*Burger* (R)	Brennan (D)
Reed (D)	Frankfurter (I)	Black (D)	Stewart (R)
Frankfurter (I)	Douglas (D)	Douglas (D)	B. White (D)
Douglas (D)	Burton (R)	Harlan (N.Y.) (R)	T. Marshall (D)
Murphy (D)	Clark (D)	Brennan (D)	Blackmun (R)
R. Jackson (D)	Harlan (N.Y.) (R)	Stewart (R)	Powell (D)
W. Rutledge (D)	Brennan (D)	B. White (D)	Rehnquist (R)
Burton (R)	Whittaker (R)	Fortas (D)	Stevens (R)
		T. Marshall (D)	
1949–52	**1958–61**		
Vinson (D)	*Warren* (R)	**1969–70**	
Black (D)	Black (D)	*Burger* (R)	
Reed (D)	Frankfurter (I)	Black (D)	
Frankfurter (I)	Douglas (D)	Douglas (D)	
Douglas (D)	Clark (D)	Harlan (N.Y.) (R)	
R. Jackson (D)	Harlan (N.Y.) (R)	Brennan (D)	
Burton (R)	Brennan (D)	Stewart (R)	
Clark (D)	Whittaker (R)	B. White (D)	
Minton (D)	Stewart (R)	T. Marshall (D)	

* Rutledge was a recess appointment whose confirmation was rejected by the Senate after the 1795 Term.

** Upon the death of Catron in 1865 and Wayne in 1867 their positions were abolished according to a congressional act of 1866. The Court's membership was reduced to eight until a new position was created by Congress in 1869. The new seat has generally been regarded as a re-creation of Wayne's seat.

*** According to Professor Henry Abraham, "Many—and with some justice—consider Brandeis a Democrat; however, he was in fact a registered Republican when nominated." *Freedom and the Court* 455 (3d ed., 1977).

ORGANIZATIONAL CHART OF UNITED STATES GOVERNMENT

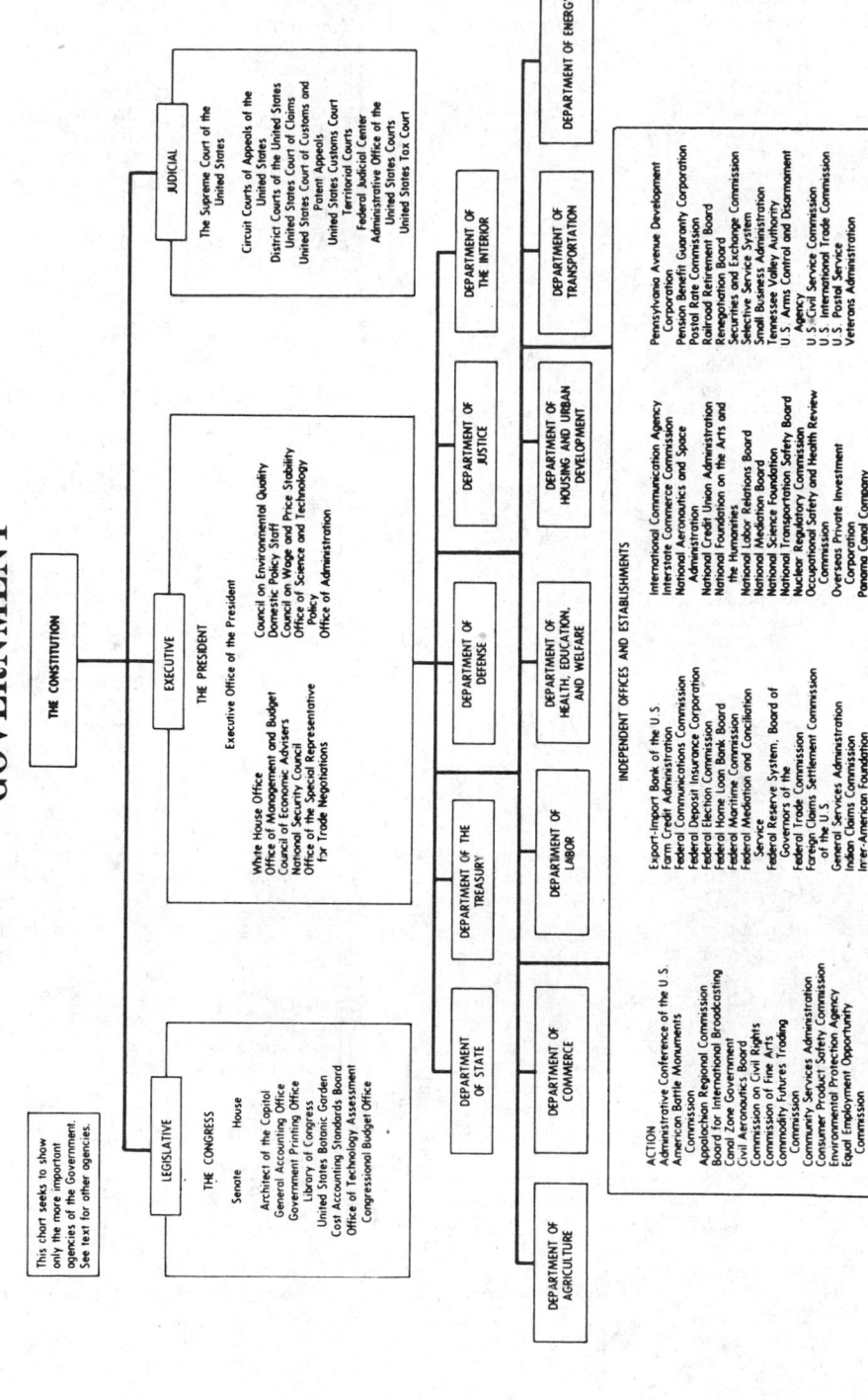

This chart seeks to show only the more important agencies of the Government. See text for other agencies.

THE CONSTITUTION

LEGISLATIVE

THE CONGRESS

Senate   House

Architect of the Capitol
General Accounting Office
Government Printing Office
Library of Congress
United States Botanic Garden
Cost Accounting Standards Board
Office of Technology Assessment
Congressional Budget Office

EXECUTIVE

THE PRESIDENT

Executive Office of the President

White House Office
Office of Management and Budget
Council of Economic Advisers
National Security Council
Office of the Special Representative For Trade Negotiations

Council on Environmental Quality
Domestic Policy Staff
Council on Wage and Price Stability
Office of Science and Technology Policy
Office of Administration

JUDICIAL

The Supreme Court of the United States

Circuit Courts of Appeals of the United States
District Courts of the United States
United States Court of Claims
United States Court of Customs and Patent Appeals
United States Customs Court
Territorial Courts
Federal Judicial Center
Administrative Office of the United States Courts
United States Tax Court

DEPARTMENT OF AGRICULTURE

DEPARTMENT OF COMMERCE

DEPARTMENT OF STATE

DEPARTMENT OF THE TREASURY

DEPARTMENT OF DEFENSE

DEPARTMENT OF JUSTICE

DEPARTMENT OF THE INTERIOR

DEPARTMENT OF ENERGY

DEPARTMENT OF LABOR

DEPARTMENT OF HEALTH, EDUCATION, AND WELFARE

DEPARTMENT OF HOUSING AND URBAN DEVELOPMENT

DEPARTMENT OF TRANSPORTATION

INDEPENDENT OFFICES AND ESTABLISHMENTS

ACTION
Administrative Conference of the U.S.
American Battle Monuments Commission
Appalachian Regional Commission
Board for International Broadcasting
Canal Zone Government
Civil Aeronautics Board
Commission on Civil Rights
Commission of Fine Arts
Commodity Futures Trading Commission
Community Services Administration
Consumer Product Safety Commission
Environmental Protection Agency
Equal Employment Opportunity Commission

Export-Import Bank of the U.S.
Farm Credit Administration
Federal Communications Commission
Federal Deposit Insurance Corporation
Federal Election Commission
Federal Home Loan Bank Board
Federal Maritime Commission
Federal Mediation and Conciliation Service
Federal Reserve System, Board of Governors of the
Federal Trade Commission
Foreign Claims Settlement Commission of the U.S.
General Services Administration
Indian Claims Commission
Inter-American Foundation

International Communication Agency
Interstate Commerce Commission
National Aeronautics and Space Administration
National Credit Union Administration
National Foundation on the Arts and the Humanities
National Labor Relations Board
National Mediation Board
National Science Foundation
National Transportation Safety Board
Nuclear Regulatory Commission
Occupational Safety and Health Review Commission
Overseas Private Investment Corporation
Panama Canal Company

Pennsylvania Avenue Development Corporation
Pension Benefit Guaranty Corporation
Postal Rate Commission
Railroad Retirement Board
Renegotiation Board
Securities and Exchange Commission
Selective Service System
Small Business Administration
Tennessee Valley Authority
U.S. Arms Control and Disarmament Agency
U.S. Civil Service Commission
U.S. International Trade Commission
U.S. Postal Service
Veterans Administration

[C319]

Source: United States Government Manual 1978/79.

*

TABLE OF BRITISH REGNAL YEARS

Sovereign	Accession	Length of reign
William I	Oct. 14, 1066	21
William II	Sept. 26, 1087	13
Henry I	Aug. 5, 1100	36
Stephen	Dec. 26, 1135	19
Henry II	Dec. 19, 1154	35
Richard I	Sept. 23, 1189	10
John	May 27, 1199	18
Henry III	Oct. 28, 1216	57
Edward I	Nov. 20, 1272	35
Edward II	July 8, 1307	20
Edward III	Jan. 25, 1326	51
Richard II	June 22, 1377	23
Henry IV	Sept. 30, 1399	14
Henry V	March 21, 1413	10
Henry VI	Sept. 1, 1422	39
Edward IV	March 4, 1461	23
Edward V	April 9, 1483	—
Richard III	June 26, 1483	3
Henry VII	Aug. 22, 1485	24
Henry VIII	April 22, 1509	38
Edward VI	Jan. 28, 1547	7
Mary	July 6, 1553	6
Elizabeth	Nov. 17, 1558	45
James I	March 24, 1603	23
Charles I	March 27, 1625	24
The Commonwealth	Jan. 30, 1649	11
Charles II	May 29, 1660	37
James II	Feb. 6, 1685	4
William and Mary	Feb. 13, 1689	14
Anne	March 8, 1702	13
George I	Aug. 1, 1714	13
George II	June 11, 1727	34
George III	Oct. 25, 1760	60
George IV	Jan. 29, 1820	11
William IV	June 26, 1830	7
Victoria	June 20, 1837	64
Edward VII	Jan. 22, 1901	9
George V	May 6, 1910	25
Edward VIII	Jan. 20, 1936	1
George VI	Dec. 11, 1936	15
Elizabeth II	Feb. 6, 1952	—

†